Microsoft®

ENCARTA®
COLLEGE
THESAURUS

Contents

THESAURUS DATABASE

General Editor
Susan Jellis

Thematic Section Editors
Diane Nicholls
David Hallworth

Quotations Editors
Stephen Adamson
James Randall

Project Manager
Katy McAdam

Production Editor
Nicky Thompson

COMPILERS AND EDITORS

Debra Bailey	Jennifer Goss Duby	Duncan Marshall
David Barnett	Stephen Handorf	Martha Mayou
Jane Bradbury	Orin Hargraves	Margaret Mullen
Patricia Bulhosen	Ruth Hein	Michael Munro
Rebecca Campbell	Anne-Marie Imbornoni	Susan Norton
Robert Clevenger	Margaret Jull Costa	Paula Parish
Dewayne Crawford	Barbara Kelly	Julie Plier
Huw Davies	Imogen Kerr	Karen Stern
Korey Egge	Stanley A. Kurzban	Fraser Sutherland
Gloria George	Laura Lawrie	Katharine Turok
Christina Gleeson	Jill Leatherbarrow	Donald Watt
Alice Grandison	Wendy Lee	Pamela White
Isabel Griffiths	Heloise McGuiness	Carol Zhong

Project Coordinators
David Barnett
Alasdair Maclean

Database Administrator
Peter Hosking

PROJECT ASSISTANTS

Heather Bateman   Katherine Hill   Charlotte Regan   Misty Shock

BLOOMSBURY REFERENCE

Publisher
Nigel Newton

Editor-in-Chief
Dr. Kathy Rooney

Dictionaries' Editor
Faye Carney

U.S. General Editor
Encarta® World English Dictionary
Anne H. Soukhanov

Production Director
Penny Edwards

Database Manager
Edmund Wright

Design Manager
Nathan Burton

ADVISORS FOR THE ENCARTA WORLD ENGLISH DATABASE

COLLEGE USAGE ADVISORY BOARD (UNITED STATES AND CANADA)

David Blair,
Senior Lecturer, Department
of Linguistics, Macquarie
University (Australia)

Nikolas Coupland,
Professor, Centre for Applied
English Language Studies,
University of Wales
(English in Wales)

Tony Deverson,
Senior Lecturer, Department
of English, University of
Canterbury, New Zealand
(New Zealand)

Scott Delancey, Ph.D.,
Department of Linguistics,
University of Oregon
(Native American English)

Margery Fee,
Professor, Department of
English, University of British
Columbia; author, *Oxford Guide
to Canadian Usage* (Canada)

Joshua Fishman,
Professor, City University
of New York (Yiddish)

Eva Hertel, Ph.D.,
English Language and Linguistics,
TU Chemnitz (East Africa)

Jacqueline Lam,
Senior Lecturer, Hong Kong
University of Science and
Technology (Hong Kong)

Naomi C. Losch,
Assistant Professor in
Hawaiian, Department
of Hawaiian and
Indo-Pacific Languages,
University of Hawaii at Manoa
(Hawaiian English)

Catherine Macafee, Ph.D.,
University of Aberdeen
(Scottish, Northern Irish)

Rajend Mesthrie,
Associate Professor, Department
of Linguistics, University of
Cape Town (South Africa)

Mark Newbrook, Ph.D.,
Senior Lecturer,
Department of Linguistics,
Monash University
(Malaysia and Singapore)

Mark Sebba, Ph.D.,
Department of Linguistics,
Lancaster University
(U.S. Black English)

Geneva Smitherman,
University Distinguished Professor;
Director, African American
Language and Literacy Program;
Director, "My Brother's Keeper"
Program, Department of English,
Michigan State University
(African American English)

Kamal Keskar Sridhar,
Associate Professor,
Department of Linguistics,
State University of New York,
Stony Brook (South Asia)

Loreto Todd, Ph.D.,
Professor of English,
Academy for Irish Cultural
Heritage, University of
Ulster at Coleraine,
Northern Ireland (Irish)

Don Winford,
Professor, Department
of Linguistics, Ohio State
University (Caribbean)

Foreword

THE *MICROSOFT® ENCARTA® COLLEGE THESAURUS* is unique among word finders in that it offers two quite different routes to choosing alternative and opposite words. One exploits the advantages of the alphabetical listing, while the other follows a more traditional system of organizing words according to concepts and themes, of the type pioneered by Roget. Why offer both in a single volume?

The virtues of the alphabetically organized thesaurus are well known—the A-Z structure makes the search for direct alternatives fast and efficient, and provides a very focused list of word choices. This is all the more true in the case of the present Thesaurus, whose editors have taken great care to ensure that the direct synonyms you are offered will substitute grammatically and stylistically for the entry word you are looking up.

But suppose you are a user who wants to search for alternatives in a less linear, more serendipitous way. You may, for example, wish to start your search from a broad area of meaning rather than a specific term. Or you may be less concerned with finding an alternative that belongs to the same grammatical category as the entry word. There are also many words that do not have true synonyms as such, but nonetheless belong to a network of associated terms that could provide exactly the word you are looking for.

In these situations what you need is a thesaurus that does some lateral thinking for you. So we decided the *Microsoft Encarta College Thesaurus* should offer the best of all possible worlds—the convenience of the A-Z format *and* the associative richness of the thematic approach. Imagine, for example, that you are trying to remember the name of the accent that goes under a letter and looks like a comma. If you look up **accent** in the A-Z list it sends you directly to the paragraph in the Thematic Section entitled ASPECTS OF LANGUAGE, where the various types of diacritics, including *cedilla*, are listed. Again, if you look up **clichéd** in the A-Z list, you are not only offered a dozen immediately usable alternatives but are also directed to the paragraph in the Thematic Section entitled BORING AND UNINTERESTING, where over 100 additional related terms can be found.

The *Microsoft Encarta College Thesaurus* has other features that enable you to narrow, or widen, the range of your search. Over 130 "Compare and Contrast" paragraphs refine the meaning distinctions between selected groups of closely related alternatives. Over 300 display panels list useful vocabulary sets, including names of constellations, figures of speech, and geologic time divisions. Finally, the Thesaurus offers up-to-date coverage of the latest technical terms and slang, such as *barista, ear candy, firewall, gray market, maquiladora, pointy-headed, private banking, spyware,* and *zero tolerance.* We recommend it as an invaluable companion volume to its sister publication, the *Microsoft Encarta College Dictionary.*

Introduction

A DICTIONARY IS AN ALPHABETICAL LIST of words and their meanings, but a thesaurus, or word finder, groups words of identical, closely similar, or related meanings together. Such is the case with the *Microsoft® Encarta® College Thesaurus*—a treasury of 350,000 words identical in meanings, sharing generally related meanings, or opposite in meaning.

This unique, 21st-century book is intended to help you answer these questions: I have one word in mind but I don't want to use that one—which word can I use instead? I have one word in mind, but I seek another one broader (or narrower) in meaning—which word can I use instead? I have one word in mind but I need its opposite—which word can I use as an antonym? I don't really know the word I'm looking for, but I know the general subject category it falls under—how on earth can I find the right word?

Here's how this book can help you. It has two sections. The first section provides a quick-access A-Z list of 300,000 words with identical or similar meanings (synonyms and closely related alternative words) arranged under 40,000 boldface headwords and senses. Over 18,000 opposite, or contrasted, words (antonyms) are also included. The second section is structured thematically. Five major themes contain 1,279 thematic categories. Within them you will find over 50,000 words related to or synonymous with one another. The five major themes and the numbered thematic categories are listed on pp. xvi-xxvi. Thus, it makes no difference how you begin your search for the right word. Look for it in section 1: the entries there give you lists of alternative words, and words with opposite or contrasting meaning. It then will send you by cross-references to section 2 for a broader overview of related alternative words. If you don't know what word you need, check the list of thematic categories and then go to the numbered paragraph in section 2 that is most likely to contain words that fall into the thematic category you have in mind.

SECTION 1: QUICK-REFERENCE A-Z LIST

Section 1 enables you to look up a word in alphabetical order and quickly find its most frequently used alternatives. The lists of alternatives reflect the ways words fit into the grammatical contexts of sentences. For instance, at **emancipation**, the first listed word—always given in boldface type—is the synonym **liberation**, substitutable with *emancipation*. **Liberation** establishes the meaning shared by it and the headword and approximated by the other related alternatives. In this entry, the related alternative words are *freedom, release, deliverance,* and *manumission*. As an assist in distinguishing how a word is used, the label *formal* is attached to *deliverance* and *manumission*, for they generally occur in formal contexts. A cross-reference then directs you to the numbered subject category in section 2, FREEDOM AND LIBERTY; 208. There you will find many words generally related to that topic, including *emancipation*. Thus the A-Z Quick-Reference Section also functions as an index for the Thematic Section.

Many English words function as multiple parts of speech. Entries for words with multiple parts of speech, such as *run*, contain multiple senses grouped by part of speech. Thus, the entry **run** contains eight verb senses and five noun senses. Verb phrases and idioms, such as *run a risk* and *run down,* are also alphabetically listed in section 1.

Many English words have multiple meanings. Thus, the lists of synonymous and related alternative words are divided into numbered senses reflecting their meanings in the *Microsoft Encarta College Thesaurus.* Sometimes the lists of alternative words with different meanings are totally distinct, as is the case with **virus.** At other times an alternative with more than one meaning itself will appear in more than one list of alternatives for the word being looked up. As an example, *reasonable* means "rational and sensible" and "fairly good." Thus, *reasonable* appears in the lists of alternatives for both these meanings at **fair.**

Care is required when choosing an alternative for any word. Only rarely can one word be exchanged for another in all possible contexts. For example, *sad* and *unhappy* are similar in meaning and are often interchangeable, but it would be unusual to speak of "an unhappy movie" or "a sad marriage." In this book, therefore, the lists of alternatives are broadly arranged such that the most general alternatives are near the beginnings of the lists, and those usable only in restrictive contexts appear near the ends of the lists, as at **government.** Here, the first alternative, **administration,** is set in boldface as the indicator of meaning, followed by other alternatives in this order: *rule, management, direction, regime, control, supervision, command, authority,* and *leadership.*

Over 130 "Compare and Contrast" notes discriminate the meanings of closely related, important, sets of words. For instance, at **secret** ("conveying a desire or a need for concealment") the note exposes the shades of meaning distinguishing *secret, clandestine, covert, furtive, stealthy,* and *surreptitious.*

This first section also contains notes in which parts and types of common entities or things are listed, as at **computer** and **video.** Entries like **guacamole,** which have no true synonyms or alternatives, are cross-referenced to categories in section 2 that cover broadly related words. Here, the cross-reference takes you from **guacamole** to the Thematic Section's SEASONINGS AND SAUCES; 1174.

SECTION 2: THEMATIC GROUPINGS

In the Thematic Section the words are organized in a much broader manner. Under five major themes, the words are grouped into 1,279 consecutively numbered thematic categories. The categories reflect general use of English in the 21st century. Each category is introduced by a quotation from the Bloomsbury Quotations Database. For instance, category 205 entitled **Extraordinary: Uncommon** opens with these words from George Washington Carver: "When you can do the common things of life in an uncommon way you'll command the attention of the world." Following the quotation is a list of broadly related words covering three parts of speech; any word not in italics can be looked up in section 1 for a narrower focus.

This list and all the others in the Thematic Section are generally more extensive than those in the A-Z Quick-Reference Section, for the goal of section 2 is to expose to you the rich network of semantic relationships characteristic of English.

Thus, the *Microsoft Encarta College Thesaurus* is a treasury of words for 21st-century users on the college and professional level, who, being computer-literate, need to find information quickly and easily. This book combines the commonly used A-Z word list with a totally new thematic section, thereby emerging as an uncommonly useful language resource.

How to Use the Thesaurus

This Thesaurus has two separate sections, a **Quick-Reference Section** and a **Thematic Section**. The Quick-Reference Section is organized alphabetically, while the Thematic Section groups words according to broad areas of meaning, or themes. The **Quick-Reference Section** is arranged like a dictionary: you look up an entry word and immediately find alternatives for its common meanings. Each meaning of a word is numbered and the first alternative, printed in **bold**, tells you exactly which

meaning is being illustrated. The lists of alternatives are arranged for ease of use, with the more general alternatives toward the beginning of the list. Alternatives that can be used only in more specific contexts are shown toward the end, often with a label, e.g., *informal* or *literary*, to indicate the type of language they belong to. You will sometimes also be offered words with opposite or contrasting meaning, introduced by the term *Opposite.*

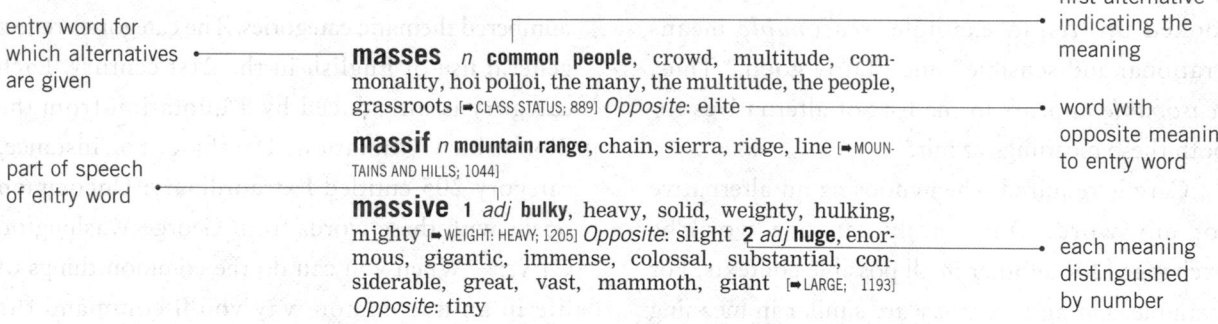

entry word for which alternatives are given

masses *n* **common people**, crowd, multitude, commonality, hoi polloi, the many, the multitude, the people, grassroots [➤ CLASS STATUS; 889] *Opposite:* elite

massif *n* **mountain range**, chain, sierra, ridge, line [➤ MOUNTAINS AND HILLS; 1044]

part of speech of entry word

massive **1** *adj* **bulky**, heavy, solid, weighty, hulking, mighty [➤ WEIGHT: HEAVY; 1205] *Opposite:* slight **2** *adj* **huge**, enormous, gigantic, immense, colossal, substantial, considerable, great, vast, mammoth, giant [➤ LARGE; 1193] *Opposite:* tiny

first alternative indicating the meaning

word with opposite meaning to entry word

each meaning distinguished by number

All entry words in the Quick-Reference Section, whether they have lists of alternatives or not, have a cross-reference to the Thematic Section. The Quick-Reference Section thus acts as an index to the Thematic Section.

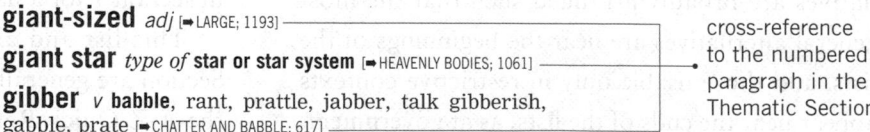

giant-sized *adj* [➤ LARGE; 1193]

giant star *type of* **star or star system** [➤ HEAVENLY BODIES; 1061]

gibber *v* **babble**, rant, prattle, jabber, talk gibberish, gabble, prate [➤ CHATTER AND BABBLE; 617]

cross-reference to the numbered paragraph in the Thematic Section

At some entries in the Quick-Reference Section there are also panels listing words that are not alternatives but *types of* the same thing, e.g., types of birds, or names for male or female animals. *Parts of* objects, e.g., parts of an aircraft or the human body, are shown in the same way.

digestive tract

◆ *parts of a digestive tract*
anus, appendix, bile duct, bladder, bowel, cecum, colon, duodenum, esophagus, gallbladder, gullet, gut, intestine, kidney, large intestine, liver, pancreas, rectum, small intestine, spleen, stomach, throat

gender

◆ *types of female animals*
bitch, cow, dam, doe, ewe, filly, heifer, hind, jenny, lioness, mare, nanny goat, sow, tigress, vixen

◆ *types of male animals*
billy goat, boar, buck, bull, bullock, colt, hart, jackass, ram, stag, stallion, steer, tom, tomcat, wether

◆ *types of male birds or female birds*
capon, cob, cock, cockerel, drake, duck, gander, goose, hen, pen, rooster

The *Compare and Contrast* notes shown after some entries help to discriminate between the meanings of closely related words by giving brief definitions that clarify their use.

> **Compare and Contrast:** *accomplish, achieve, attain, realize, carry out, pull off*
>
> CORE MEANING: to bring something to a successful conclusion
>
> *accomplish* to succeed in doing something; *achieve* to succeed in something, usually with effort; *attain* to reach a specific objective; *realize* to fulfill a specific vision or plan; *carry out* to perform or accomplish a task or activity; *pull off* (*informal*) to accomplish something, despite difficulties.

The **Thematic Section** is divided into 1,279 thematic paragraphs that are grouped under five main headings, e.g., *People and their Way of Life*, and over 40 subheadings, e.g., *Communication and Interaction*. A full list of these thematic paragraphs is given at the front of the book.

Each paragraph has a heading and a number and is introduced, where appropriate, by a lively quotation. Words relating to the theme of the paragraph are listed according to their part of speech, in alphabetical order. These lists include broadly related terms as well as direct alternatives. If a word has a list of alternatives in the Quick-Reference Section it is shown in roman type; otherwise it appears in *italic*.

paragraph number and heading →

1193 **Large**

← quotation illustrating the theme of the paragraph

Size is not a deterrent to success. I've never seen a small company that didn't want to be a big one. **Louis Gerstner, Jr.**

word that has no list of alternatives in A-Z section →

(*adj*) airy, almighty (*informal*), awkward, big, bulging, bulky, capacious, cavernous, colossal, commodious, considerable, cosmic, *cumbrous* (*archaic or literary*), elephantine, enormous, expansive, extensive, extra-large, fantastic, fat, full-size, galactic (*informal*), gargantuan, giant, *giant-sized*, gigantic, global, good-sized, grand, great, herculean, huge, hulking, humongous (*informal*), immeasurable, immense, inestimable, infinite, jumbo, king-size, large, life-size, mammoth, massive, maxi, measureless, *mega*, mighty, monolithic, monster, monstrous, monumental, mountainous, outsize, oversize, prodigious, queen-size, rambling, roomy, significant, sizable, spacious, spectacular, stupendous, substantial, substantive, terrific, thumping (*informal*), tidy, titanic, tremendous, unwieldy, vast, voluminous, walloping (*informal*), whopping (*informal*)

← word that is entered in A-Z section with lists of alternatives

each part of speech grouped separately →

(*n*) airiness, amplitude, bulkiness, *capaciousness*, *chunkiness*, cumbersomeness, enormity, expansiveness, extensiveness, *immenseness*, immensity, largeness, prodigiousness, roominess, *unwieldiness*, vastness, *voluminousness*

← label indicating word belongs to informal usage

Some paragraphs have additional cross-references to other paragraphs in the Thematic Section that deal with related topics.

1210 **Durable**

(*adj*) durable, imperishable, indestructible, rock-solid, rustproof, shatterproof, stable, strong, sturdy, toughened, unbreakable

(*n*) durability, imperishability, *indestructibility*, sturdiness

See also STRENGTH (201)

← cross-reference to related paragraph in Thematic Section

LIST OF
THEMATIC
CATEGORIES

People and their Way of Life

Qualities and Characteristics

Emotions and States of Mind

The Written Word

QUICK-REFERENCE SECTION

A

A1 (*informal*) *adj* **excellent**, first-rate, first-class, perfect, flawless, great, superb, topnotch (*informal*) [➡ EXTRAORDINARY: AMAZING; 204] *Opposite*: inferior

abalone *type of* **aquatic invertebrate** [➡ AQUATIC INVERTEBRATES; 1022]

abandon **1** *v* **dump**, discard, dispose of, throw out, throw away, ditch (*informal*) [➡ GET RID OF SOMETHING; 451] *Opposite*: keep **2** *v* **desert**, leave, forsake, leave behind, walk out on (*informal*) [➡ RUN AWAY AND AVOID; 10] **3** *v* **end**, call off, cancel, give up, stop, halt, abort [➡ CAUSE TO STOP; 266] *Opposite*: continue **4** *n* **recklessness**, wildness, license, intemperance, unrestraint, uninhibitedness [➡ FREEDOM AND LIBERTY; 208] *Opposite*: restraint

abandoned **1** *adj* **discarded**, forsaken, dumped, neglected, cast off [➡ UNPOPULAR AND UNWANTED; 258] **2** *adj* **empty**, deserted, derelict, vacant [➡ EMPTY; 1238] **3** *adj* **wild**, uncontrolled, unrestricted, uninhibited, unrestrained, out of control, reckless [➡ FREEDOM AND LIBERTY; 208] *Opposite*: restrained

abandonment *n* **desertion**, leaving behind, leaving, rejection, neglect, relinquishment [➡ EMPTY, 1238]

abandon ship *v* [➡ RUN AWAY AND AVOID; 10]

abase (*literary*) *v* **lower**, demean, degrade, belittle, humiliate, subjugate, denigrate [➡ UPSET, DISTRESS, AND HUMILIATE; 567] *Opposite*: respect

abasement (*literary*) *n* **degradation**, humiliation, effacement, belittlement, deprecation, denigration, subjugation, abnegation (*formal*) [➡ EMBARRASSMENT AND HUMILIATION; 542] *Opposite*: aggrandizement

abase yourself (*literary*) *v* **grovel**, humble yourself, demean yourself, debase yourself, degrade yourself, lower yourself, efface yourself [➡ FLATTER AND FAWN; 621]

abash *v* [➡ CONFUSE AND BEWILDER; 571]

abashed *adj* **embarrassed**, ashamed, mortified, disconcerted, dismayed, confused [➡ EMBARRASSMENT AND HUMILIATION; 542] *Opposite*: unabashed

abate (*formal or literary*) *v* **decrease**, subside, grow less, decline, fade away, fall, stop, halt, end, terminate, lessen [➡ CHANGE OF INTENSITY: LESS; 395] *Opposite*: rise

abatement **1** *n* **reduction**, cut, drop, fall, decline, diminution, lessening, decrease [➡ LESS; 126] *Opposite*: increase **2** *n* **deduction**, discount, cut, reduction, decrease, saving [➡ FUNDS, PAYMENTS, AND CHARGES; 800] *Opposite*: increment

abbey *n* **religious foundation**, religious house, cloister, monastery, convent, priory [➡ RELIGIOUS BUILDINGS; 1085]

abbot *n* [➡ RELIGIOUS PEOPLE; 778]

abbreviate *v* **shorten**, cut, cut short, condense, abridge, truncate, curtail, reduce [➡ CHANGE OF SIZE: SMALLER; 393] *Opposite*: lengthen

abbreviated *adj* **shortened**, condensed, abridged, truncated, curtailed, reduced [➡ CHANGE OF SIZE: SMALLER; 393] *Opposite*: full-length

abbreviation *n* **short form**, contraction, ellipsis, acronym, shortening, condensation, abridgment, truncation, curtailment, reduction [➡ ASPECTS OF LANGUAGE; 682]

ABCs **1** *n* **alphabet**, Roman alphabet, spelling system [➡ SYMBOLS, SIGNS, AND NUMBERS; 596] **2** *n* **basics**, fundamentals, essentials, rudiments, nitty-gritty (*informal*), nuts and bolts (*informal*) [➡ BASIC DETAILS; 688]

abdicate *v* **renounce**, relinquish, resign, step down, hand over, give up, abandon [➡ FORGO AND DENY ONESELF; 449] *Opposite*: accept

abdication *n* **resignation**, handing over, renunciation, abandonment, relinquishment [➡ FORGO AND DENY ONESELF; 449]

abdomen **1** *part of* **torso** [➡ PARTS OF THE BODY: TORSO, ETC.; 698] **2** *part of insect* [➡ PARTS OF AN INSECT; 1019]

abdominal *adj* **stomach**, belly, front, intestinal, gut [➡ THE DIGESTIVE TRACT; 709]

abdominals *type of* **muscle or tendon** [➡ THE MUSCLES; 718]

abduct *v* **kidnap**, make off with, seize, hold somebody against his or her will, capture, snatch (*informal*) [➡ STEAL AND ROB; 426]

abduction *n* **kidnap**, seizure, kidnapping, carrying off, capture, snatching (*informal*) [➡ CRIMES; 817]

abductor *n* **kidnapper**, hostage taker, captor, hijacker, snatcher (*informal*) [➡ CRIMINALS; 821]

abecedarian *n* [➡ STUDENTS AND PUPILS; 841]

aberrant *adj* **abnormal**, unusual, deviant, anomalous, peculiar, uncharacteristic, irregular, atypical, eccentric, odd [➡ DIFFERENCE; 149] *Opposite*: normal

aberration *n* **deviation**, abnormality, anomaly, irregularity, peculiarity, eccentricity, oddness, unusualness [➡ DIFFERENCE; 149]

abet **1** *v* **assist**, help, support, aid, back, back up [➡ HELP; 293] *Opposite*: hinder **2** *v* **encourage**, urge, connive, put up to, incite [➡ CAUSE OR COMPEL TO ACT; 271] *Opposite*: deter

abhor (*formal*) *v* **detest**, hate, loathe, dislike, despise, be repulsed, be revolted [➡ DISLIKE AND HATE; 577] *Opposite*: adore

abhorrence *n* **hatred**, loathing, detestation, disgust, repugnance, revulsion, abomination (*literary*), aversion (*formal*) [➡ DISLIKE AND HATE; 577] *Opposite*: adoration

See Compare and Contrast at **dislike**.

abhorrent (*formal*) *adj* **repugnant**, objectionable, repulsive, detestable, hateful, distasteful, disgusting [➥ DISGUSTING AND REPULSIVE; 230] *Opposite*: desirable

abide 1 *v* **put up with**, stand for, stand, bear, stomach, take, tolerate, accept [➥ TOLERATE AND ENDURE; 766] 2 *v* (*archaic*) **withstand**, endure, survive, resist, bear, weather, tolerate [➥ CONTINUE TO EXIST; 17] 3 *v* (*archaic*) **live**, have your home, stay, dwell (*literary*), lodge (*dated*) [➥ INHABIT; 20]

abide by *v* **obey**, follow, keep to, conform to, stick to, adhere to, accept [➥ OBEY AND ABIDE BY; 301] *Opposite*: defy

abiding *adj* **enduring**, remaining, surviving, long-lasting, unshakable, steadfast, permanent [➥ PERMANENCE: WITHOUT END; 94] *Opposite*: transient

ability *n* **aptitude**, skill, proficiency, competence, capacity, capability, talent, gift, knack [➥ SKILLS, TALENTS, AND ABILITIES; 526]

> **Compare and Contrast:** *ability, skill, competence, aptitude, talent, capacity, capability*
>
> CORE MEANING: the necessary skill, knowledge, or experience to do something
>
> *ability* natural and acquired skills or knowledge; *skill* proficiency gained through training or experience; *competence* ability measured against a standard; *aptitude* a natural tendency to do something well; *talent* an unusual natural ability to do something well; *capacity* mental or physical ability for something or to do something; *capability* the ability of a person or machine to do something.

a bit (*informal*) *adv* **slightly**, rather, somewhat, a little, a tad (*informal*) [➥ TO A CERTAIN EXTENT; 136] *Opposite*: very

abject 1 *adj* **hopeless**, miserable, wretched, dismal, extreme, utter [➥ ABSOLUTE AND ABSOLUTELY; 133] 2 *adj* **humble**, servile, meek, submissive, subservient, deferential, self-effacing [➥ EXPRESSING RESPECT AND APPROVAL; 637]

abjection 1 *n* **wretchedness**, misery, desolation, despair, despondence, distress, gloom, unhappiness, abjectness, hopelessness [➥ SADNESS, DISTRESS, AND DESPAIR; 539] *Opposite*: cheerfulness 2 *n* **humility**, humbleness, subservience, deference, servility, meekness, submissiveness [➥ LEVELS OF FORMALITY; 522] *Opposite*: confidence

abjectly 1 *adv* **wretchedly**, miserably, desolately, despairingly, despondently, gloomily, unhappily, hopelessly, dismally [➥ SADNESS, DISTRESS, AND DESPAIR; 539] *Opposite*: cheerfully 2 *adv* **humbly**, submissively, subserviently, deferentially, self-effacingly, meekly [➥ LEVELS OF FORMALITY; 522] *Opposite*: confidently

abjuration *n* **renunciation**, rejection, denial, repudiation, refrainment, avoidance, abstention, disavowal (*formal*), abnegation (*formal*) [➥ FORGO AND DENY ONESELF; 449] *Opposite*: affirmation

abjure 1 *v* **renounce**, reject, repudiate, deny, disavow, abnegate (*formal*) [➥ DENY AND REJECT; 644] 2 *v* (*literary*) **abstain**, refrain, reject, deny yourself, shun, give up, refuse, forswear (*archaic or literary*) [➥ FORGO AND DENY ONESELF; 449]

ablative *type of* **grammatical term** [➥ ASPECTS OF LANGUAGE; 682]

ablaze *adj* **on fire**, blazing, burning, in flames, alight, afire, aflame [➥ FIRE, FLAMMABILITY, AND BURNING; 1165]

able 1 *adj* **capable**, competent, proficient, adept, skilled [➥ TALENTED AND SKILLFUL; 527] *Opposite*: incompetent 2 *adj* **clever**, talented, intelligent, bright, gifted [➥ POSITIVE INTELLECTUAL CHARACTERISTICS; 524] *Opposite*: incapable

> *See Compare and Contrast at* **intelligent**.

able-bodied *adj* **healthy**, fit, well, active, strong, vigorous [➥ FIT AND STRONG; 736] *Opposite*: weak

ablutions (*formal or humorous*) *n* **washing**, bathing, cleansing, wash, cleanup, wash and brush up (*UK*) [➥ CLEAN AND POLISH; 403]

ably *adv* **capably**, well, skillfully, competently, with ease, proficiently, adeptly, easily [➥ TALENTED AND SKILLFUL; 527] *Opposite*: incompetently

abnegate (*formal*) *v* **renounce**, reject, deny, repudiate, abjure, give up, shun, refrain, abstain, disavow, forswear (*archaic or literary*) [➥ FORGO AND DENY ONESELF; 449] *Opposite*: accept

abnegation (*formal*) *n* **rejection**, renunciation, repudiation, denial, abstention, refrainment, avoidance, disavowal (*formal*) [➥ FORGO AND DENY ONESELF; 449] *Opposite*: acceptance

abnormal *adj* **irregular**, nonstandard, uncharacteristic, atypical, anomalous, unusual, strange, odd, peculiar, deviant, aberrant, malformed [➥ BIZARRE AND PECULIAR; 257] *Opposite*: normal

abnormality 1 *n* **irregularity**, aberration, anomaly, deviation, oddity, idiosyncrasy [➥ FAULTS, FLAWS, AND WEAKNESSES; 251] 2 *n* **defect**, deformity, irregularity, malformation, malfunction, fault [➥ FAULTS, FLAWS, AND WEAKNESSES; 251]

aboard 1 *adv* **on board**, on the ship, on the bus, on the train, on the plane [➥ LACK OF ACTIVITY OR MOTION; 342] 2 *adv* (*informal*) **involved**, participating, on the team, with us, on our side, on the books, with [➥ PRESENT AND AVAILABLE; 11] 3 *prep* **onto**, on, into, inside [➥ RELATIVE LOCATION; 161]

abode (*literary*) *n* **house**, home, residence, place, dwelling (*formal*), lodgings (*dated*) [➥ ACCOMMODATIONS; 855]

abolish *v* **put an end to**, eliminate, close down, bring to an end, stop, do away with, eradicate, get rid of, obliterate, end [➥ ABOLISH AND ANNUL; 452] *Opposite*: establish

abolition *n* **elimination**, ending, closing down, eradication, closure, obliteration [➥ ENDS AND DEPARTURES; 54] *Opposite*: establishment

abolitionist *n* **opponent**, objector, protester, eradicator, adversary, enemy, foe (*formal*) [➥ UNCOOPERATIVE OR REBELLIOUS PEOPLE; 566] *Opposite*: supporter

A-bomb *n* **neutron bomb**, nuclear missile, nuclear warhead, nuclear weapon, bomb, atomic bomb [➥ EXPLOSIVES; 1155]

abominable *adj* **dreadful**, repulsive, offensive, detestable, monstrous, terrible, awful, horrible, vile, horrendous, repugnant, atrocious, revulsive [➥ DISGUSTING AND REPULSIVE; 230]

Abominable Snowman n [➡ MYTHICAL BEINGS; 789]

abominate (*formal*) v **hate**, loathe, detest, despise, dislike, disapprove, abhor (*formal*) [➡ DISLIKE AND HATE; 577] *Opposite*: love

abomination 1 n **outrage**, disgrace, scandal, eyesore, atrocity, horror [➡ NUISANCES; 253] **2** n (*literary*) **hatred**, dislike, repugnance, loathing, revulsion, abhorrence, detestation, disgust [➡ DISLIKE AND HATE; 577] *Opposite*: love

aboriginal *adj* **indigenous**, original, native, autochthonous, local [➡ COUNTRIES AND REGIONS; 1067] *Opposite*: foreign

See Compare and Contrast at **native**.

abort v **end**, abandon, call off, call a halt, cancel, stop midstream, break off, halt, stop, quit, terminate (*formal*) [➡ CAUSE TO STOP; 266]

abortive *adj* **unsuccessful**, failed, fruitless, unproductive, futile, bungled (*informal*) [➡ UNSUCCESSFUL AND UNPROMISING; 76] *Opposite*: successful

abound 1 v **thrive**, flourish, prosper, proliferate, overflow, swarm, be plentiful, be abundant [➡ PROSPER AND ABOUND; 16] **2** v **brim**, overflow, throng, teem, be rich in, be abundant in [➡ PROSPER AND ABOUND; 16]

abounding *adj* **many**, varied, multifarious, plentiful, abundant, fruitful, plenteous (*literary*) [➡ MANY, MUCH, LARGE AMOUNT; 171] *Opposite*: scarce

about 1 *prep* **concerning**, regarding, in relation to, on the subject of, on, with reference to, as regards, vis-à-vis, re, apropos (*formal*) [➡ EXPRESSIONS OF REFERENCE; 63] **2** *adv* **approximately**, roughly, in the region of, around, almost, nearly, approaching, not far off, on the order of, nigh on to, roughly speaking, more or less, something like, just about, of the order of (*UK*), going on for (*UK*) [➡ APPROXIMATELY; 135] **3** *adv* **around**, close, nearby, near [➡ PRESENT AND AVAILABLE; 11]

about-face 1 n **turnaround**, reversal, shift, transformation, sea change, change of heart, change of tack, volte-face, about-turn (*UK*) [➡ DECISIVE MOMENTS; 44] **2** n **turn**, U-turn, 180° turn, revolution [➡ CHANGE DIRECTION OF MOTION; 344]

about to *prep* **ready to**, on the verge of, on the point of, just going to, set to, all set to, on the brink of [➡ FUTURE; 86]

about to happen *adv* [➡ ABOUT TO HAPPEN; 33]

above 1 *prep* **more than**, greater than, higher than, beyond, exceeding [➡ MORE AND EXCESS; 124] *Opposite*: below **2** *prep* **on top of**, over, higher than, atop (*literary*) [➡ RELATIVE LOCATION; 161] *Opposite*: below

above all *adv* **especially**, in particular, primarily, principally, most of all [➡ MAINLY AND PRIMARILY; 140]

above average *adj* [➡ GOOD, WELL, BETTER; 183]

aboveboard 1 *adj* **open**, fair, honest, forthright, straightforward, legal, lawful, correct, legitimate, regular, on the level (*informal*), kosher (*informal*) [➡ MORALLY GOOD; 774] *Opposite*: shady **2** *adv* **openly**, fairly, honestly, legally, lawfully [➡ LEGAL AND LEGITIMATE; 815] *Opposite*: illegally

above criticism *adj* [➡ MORALLY GOOD; 774]

abovementioned *adj* **said**, aforementioned (*formal*), aforesaid (*formal*) [➡ EXPRESSIONS OF REFERENCE; 63]

above reproach *adj* **blameless**, irreproachable, unimpeachable, honest, decent, virtuous, upright, honorable [➡ HONEST AND RELIABLE; 502] *Opposite*: dishonorable

above suspicion *adj* **honest**, decent, irreproachable, unimpeachable, innocent, reliable, trustworthy, dependable [➡ HONEST AND RELIABLE; 502] *Opposite*: dubious

abracadabra *interj* **hocus-pocus**, open sesame, voilà, hey presto (*informal*) [➡ THE SUPERNATURAL; 787]

abrade v **graze**, scrape, roughen, chafe, grind down, grind, scratch, scuff, rub, rasp [➡ WORSEN APPEARANCE; 382] *Opposite*: smooth

abrasion n **scrape**, scratch, scuff, graze [➡ CONDITIONS AFFECTING THE SKIN; 721]

abrasive 1 *adj* **rough**, coarse, harsh, rasping, scratchy, grainy [➡ PHYSICAL TEXTURE; 1222] *Opposite*: smooth **2** *adj* **rude**, sharp, harsh, brusque, argumentative, aggressive, unfriendly, gruff, severe [➡ RUDE AND HOSTILE; 625] *Opposite*: gentle

abrasively *adv* **harshly**, roughly, brusquely, aggressively, insensitively, unfeelingly [➡ RUDE AND HOSTILE; 625] *Opposite*: gently

abrasiveness n **harshness**, roughness, brusqueness, aggressiveness, insensitivity, unfeelingness [➡ BAD MANNERS AND SOCIAL SKILLS; 521] *Opposite*: gentleness

abreast 1 *adv* **side by side**, alongside, shoulder to shoulder, beside, level, next to [➡ RELATIVE LOCATION; 161] **2** *adj* **well-informed**, in touch, up-to-date, up on, up with, in on, au fait, au courant [➡ KNOWLEDGE AND WISDOM; 558]

abridge v **shorten**, edit, condense, abbreviate, reduce, curtail, slash [➡ CHANGE OF SIZE: SMALLER; 393] *Opposite*: expand

abridged *adj* **shortened**, edited, condensed, reduced, abbreviated [➡ CHANGE OF SIZE: SMALLER; 393] *Opposite*: complete

abridgement *see* **abridgment**

abridgment n **synopsis**, digest, condensation, précis, abstract, summary, brief [➡ SUMMARIES, OUTLINES, AND EXCERPTS; 588]

abroad *adv* **overseas**, away, out of the country [➡ COUNTRIES AND REGIONS; 1067]

abrogate (*formal*) v **repeal**, revoke, rescind, retract, annul, abolish, nullify, do away with [➡ ABOLISH AND ANNUL; 452]

See Compare and Contrast at **nullify**.

abrogation (*formal*) n **retraction**, repeal, annulment, abolition, rescindment, revocation, nullification [➡ ENDS AND DEPARTURES; 54]

abrupt 1 *adj* **sudden**, unexpected, unforeseen, rapid, hasty, immediate, quick, rushed [➡ HAPPENING QUICKLY; 104] *Opposite*: gradual **2** *adj* **curt**, short, brusque, terse, rude, gruff, snappy, snappish, sharp [➡ BAD-TEMPERED AND HUMORLESS; 626] *Opposite*: polite

abruptness 1 n **suddenness**, unexpectedness, rapidity, hastiness, quickness [➡ SPEED; 102] *Opposite*: slowness **2** n **brusqueness**, shortness, terseness, sharpness, rude-

ness, gruffness, snappiness [➡ BAD-TEMPERED AND HUMORLESS; 626]
Opposite: politeness

abscess *n* **boil**, pustule, swelling, eruption, blister, carbuncle, sore, inflammation [➡ CONDITIONS AFFECTING THE SKIN; 721]

abscond *v* **run away**, escape, break out, make off, elope, flee, run off [➡ RUN AWAY AND AVOID; 10]

absconder *n* **deserter**, runaway, escapee, fugitive, truant, absentee [➡ RUNAWAYS AND ABSENTEES; 9]

absence 1 *n* **nonappearance**, absenteeism, time off [➡ ABSENT AND UNAVAILABLE; 7] *Opposite*: presence 2 *n* **lack**, deficiency, want, dearth, privation, nonexistence [➡ ABSENT AND UNAVAILABLE; 7] *Opposite*: surplus

absent 1 *adj* **missing**, gone, out, away [➡ ABSENT AND UNAVAILABLE; 7] *Opposite*: present 2 *adj* **inattentive**, absent-minded, far away, preoccupied, vague [➡ NEUTRALITY AND INDIFFERENCE; 553] *Opposite*: alert 3 *adj* **lacking**, deficient, nonexistent, in short supply [➡ ABSENT AND UNAVAILABLE; 7] *Opposite*: present

absentee *n* **truant**, defaulter, runaway, absconder [➡ RUNAWAYS AND ABSENTEES; 9]

absenteeism *n* **absence**, nonattendance, nonappearance, truancy [➡ WORK-RELATED ACTIVITIES; 834]

absently *adv* **inattentively**, vaguely, dreamily, distractedly, abstractedly, absent-mindedly [➡ NEUTRALITY AND INDIFFERENCE; 553] *Opposite*: attentively

absent-minded *adj* **forgetful**, distracted, scatterbrained, preoccupied, vague, daydreaming, dreamy, inattentive, abstracted, idle [➡ NEGATIVE INTELLECTUAL CHARACTERISTICS; 525] *Opposite*: attentive

absent-mindedness *n* **forgetfulness**, vagueness, dreaminess, inattentiveness, distraction, abstraction, idleness [➡ NEGATIVE INTELLECTUAL CHARACTERISTICS; 525] *Opposite*: concentration

absent without leave *adj* **AWOL**, absent, missing, deserting, wanted, truant, absconding, disappeared, gone [➡ ABSENT AND UNAVAILABLE; 7] *Opposite*: present

absent yourself *v* **excuse yourself**, send your apologies, stay away [➡ LEAVE AND GO AWAY; 8] *Opposite*: attend

absolute 1 *adj* **total**, complete, utter, unqualified, out-and-out, outright, entire [➡ WHOLENESS AND COMPLETENESS; 198] 2 *adj* **unconditional**, unlimited, supreme, unmodified, unadulterated, pure, perfect, unquestionable, unequivocal, unbounded [➡ ABSOLUTE AND ABSOLUTELY; 133] *Opposite*: provisional 3 *adj* **conclusive**, resolved, firm, fixed, definite, unmovable, final, unchangeable, certain [➡ CERTAIN; 174] *Opposite*: unconfirmed 4 *n* **given**, rule, principle, truth, fundamental [➡ TRUE AND REAL; 171]

absolution *n* **forgiveness**, pardon, release, freedom, liberty [➡ RELIGIONS AND RELIGIOUS PRACTICES; 777]

absolutism *n* **totalitarianism**, despotism, dictatorship, tyranny, autocracy, authoritarianism [➡ STYLES AND SYSTEMS OF GOVERNMENT; 806]

absolve *v* **pardon**, forgive, clear, release, free, liberate, remit, excuse [➡ FORGET, FORGIVE, AND ACCEPT; 748] *Opposite*: punish

absorb 1 *v* **soak up**, attract, take in, take up, suck up,

sop up [➡ FILL; 406] *Opposite*: exude 2 *v* **understand**, learn, grasp, admit, take in, recognize, realize [➡ UNDERSTAND AND GRASP; 759] 3 *v* **engross**, fascinate, engage, captivate, grip, enthrall, rivet (*informal*) [➡ APPEAL TO AND AROUSE INTEREST; 575] *Opposite*: bore

absorbed *adj* **engrossed**, wrapped up, fascinated, captivated, immersed, rapt, engaged, enthralled, gripped, interested, riveted (*informal*) [➡ PENSIVENESS AND INTEREST; 538] *Opposite*: detached

absorbency *n* **porosity**, sponginess, permeability, penetrability, perviousness [➡ DENSITY AND CONSISTENCY; 1207]

absorbent *adj* **porous**, spongy, permeable, penetrable, pervious [➡ DENSITY AND CONSISTENCY; 1207]

absorbing *adj* **fascinating**, engrossing, captivating, gripping, enthralling, spellbinding, interesting, engaging, riveting (*informal*) [➡ INTERESTING AND MEANINGFUL; 190] *Opposite*: boring

absorption 1 *n* **preoccupation**, fascination, interest, captivation, engagement, immersion, raptness, concentration, enthrallment, engrossment [➡ ATTENTION AND ATTENTIVENESS; 763] 2 *n* **amalgamation**, incorporation, assimilation, combination, inclusion [➡ COMBINE AND MIX; 400] *Opposite*: rejection

absorptive *adj* [➡ DENSITY AND CONSISTENCY; 1207]

absorptivity *n* [➡ DENSITY AND CONSISTENCY; 1207]

abstain 1 *v* **desist**, refrain, withdraw, withhold, go without, give up, curb [➡ NOT DO AND REFUSE TO DO; 274] *Opposite*: indulge 2 *v* **sit on the fence**, stay neutral, not take sides, hedge [➡ ELECTIONS AND VOTING; 807] *Opposite*: vote

abstainer 1 *n* **refrainer**, avoider, shunner, teetotaler, withholder [➡ ASCETIC PEOPLE; 883] 2 *n* **nonvoter**, hedger, fence sitter [➡ ELECTIONS AND VOTING; 807]

abstemious *adj* **self-denying**, self-disciplined, moderate, ascetic, sober, temperate, teetotal [➡ SELF-DENIAL; 882] *Opposite*: unrestrained

abstemiousness *n* **sobriety**, self-denial, moderation, temperance, self-discipline, asceticism, judiciousness [➡ SELF-DENIAL; 882] *Opposite*: excess

abstention *n* **nonparticipation**, abstaining, refraining, holding back [➡ ELECTIONS AND VOTING; 807]

abstinence *n* **self-denial**, self-restraint, self-discipline, moderation, asceticism [➡ SELF-DENIAL; 882] *Opposite*: indulgence

abstinent *adj* **ascetic**, abstemious, sober, temperate, teetotal, dry [➡ SELF-DENIAL; 882] *Opposite*: indulgent

abstract 1 *adj* **nonconcrete**, intellectual, mental, immaterial, intangible, nonfigurative, nonrepresentational [➡ THE NATURE OF IDEAS; 771] *Opposite*: concrete 2 *adj* **theoretical**, conceptual, conjectural, hypothetical, speculative, academic [➡ FALSE AND UNREAL; 173] *Opposite*: practical 3 *n* **summary**, extract, précis, synopsis, abridgment, short version [➡ SUMMARIES, OUTLINES, AND EXCERPTS; 588] 4 *v* **conceptualize**, theorize, hypothesize, intellectualize [➡ DEVELOP THEORIES AND REASON; 744] 5 *v* **summarize**, condense, shorten, précis, abridge, synopsize [➡ CHANGE OF SIZE: SMALLER; 393] *Opposite*: expand 6 *v* **extract**, take out, select, remove, separate, isolate [➡EXTRACT AND SEVER; 341]

abstracted *adj* **inattentive**, preoccupied, vague, distant, distracted, absent-minded [➡NEUTRALITY AND INDIFFERENCE; 553] *Opposite*: alert

abstractedness *n* **preoccupation**, inattentiveness, inattention, pensiveness, distractedness, vagueness, dreaminess [➡NOT PAY ATTENTION; 764] *Opposite*: alertness

abstract expressionism *type of* **20th-century art movement** [➡ARTISTIC MOVEMENTS AND STYLES; 899]

abstraction 1 *n* **pensiveness**, preoccupation, dreaminess, vagueness, daydreaming, woolgathering [➡NOT PAY ATTENTION; 764] *Opposite*: concentration 2 *n* **concept**, idea, thought, notion, construct, generalization, perception, intellection (*formal*) [➡IDEAS AND THOUGHTS; 770] *Opposite*: fact 3 *n* **removal**, extraction, withdrawal, deduction [➡REMOVE SOMETHING; 338] *Opposite*: inclusion

abstractly *adv* **theoretically**, conceptually, hypothetically, in theory [➡UNCERTAIN; 175] *Opposite*: practically

abstruse *adj* **obscure**, perplexing, puzzling, complex, profound, mysterious, rarefied, technical, highbrow, recondite, difficult [➡DIFFICULTY AND COMPLEXITY; 242] *Opposite*: simple

See Compare and Contrast at **obscure**.

abstrusely *adv* **obscurely**, unclearly, unintelligibly, incomprehensibly, puzzlingly, perplexingly, mysteriously, profoundly [➡SECRET AND UNKNOWN; 179] *Opposite*: clearly

abstruseness *n* **complexity**, obscurity, difficulty, profundity, mysteriousness, perplexity [➡DIFFICULTY AND COMPLEXITY; 242] *Opposite*: simplicity

absurd 1 *adj* **ridiculous**, ludicrous, silly, strange, illogical, irrational, bizarre, incongruous, farcical [➡BIZARRE AND PECULIAR; 257] *Opposite*: reasonable 2 *adj* **meaningless**, pointless, futile, empty, purposeless, hollow [➡REDUNDANT AND USELESS; 240]

absurdity 1 *n* **illogicality**, irrationality, silliness, ludicrousness, ridiculousness, meaninglessness, incongruity, farcicality, preposterousness [➡BIZARRE AND PECULIAR; 257] *Opposite*: logic 2 *n* **farce**, joke, nonsense, incongruity [➡BIZARRE AND PECULIAR; 257]

absurdly *adv* **ridiculously**, farcically, nonsensically, ludicrously, incongruously, preposterously, oddly [➡BIZARRE AND PECULIAR; 257] *Opposite*: reasonably

absurdness 1 *n* **ludicrousness**, ridiculousness, preposterousness, irrationality, incongruity, illogicality, farcicality, silliness [➡BIZARRE AND PECULIAR; 257] *Opposite*: reasonableness 2 *n* **meaninglessness**, pointlessness, futility, emptiness, purposelessness, hollowness [➡REDUNDANT AND USELESS; 240]

abundance *n* **profusion**, plenty, richness, wealth, copiousness, lavishness [➡MANY, MUCH, LARGE AMOUNT; 117] *Opposite*: scarcity

abundant *adj* **plentiful**, copious, rich, profuse, ample, lavish [➡MANY, MUCH, LARGE AMOUNT; 117] *Opposite*: scarce

a bundle of laughs *n* **a barrel of laughs**, a lot of fun, a barrel of monkeys, laugh (*informal*), riot (*informal*), gas (*slang*), good fun (*UK*) [➡FUNNY AND AMUSING; 216]

abuse 1 *n* **mistreatment**, cruelty, ill-treatment, violence, maltreatment, neglect, exploitation [➡MALICIOUS ACTIONS OR BEHAVIOR; 296] 2 *n* **misuse**, exploitation, manipulation, taking advantage, mishandling, misapplication [➡MISUSE AND ABUSE; 471] 3 *n* **insults**, verbal abuse, swearing, name-calling, foul language, invective (*formal*) [➡INSULTS, ABUSE, AND SWEARING; 658] 4 *v* **exploit**, take advantage, misuse, manipulate [➡MISUSE AND ABUSE; 471] 5 *v* **treat badly**, ill-treat, mistreat, maltreat, molest, be violent toward, batter, hurt, harm, injure [➡WOUND A PERSON OR ANIMAL; 383] *Opposite*: look after 6 *v* **insult**, swear, shout abuse, hurl abuse, shout insults, call names, use foul language [➡INSULTS, ABUSE, AND SWEARING; 658] *Opposite*: compliment

See Compare and Contrast at **misuse**.

abused *adj* **ill-treated**, physically abused, battered, badly treated, injured, harmed, mistreated, maltreated, neglected, molested [➡IN TROUBLE AND DISADVANTAGED; 73] *Opposite*: looked after

abusive 1 *adj* **rude**, insulting, unmannerly, foul, offensive, obnoxious [➡RUDE AND HOSTILE; 625] *Opposite*: polite 2 *adj* **violent**, cruel, vicious, sadistic, rough [➡MORALLY BAD OR IMPROPER; 775] *Opposite*: gentle

abusiveness *n* **rudeness**, unpleasantness, impoliteness, nastiness, vulgarity, offensiveness [➡MALICIOUS ACTIONS OR BEHAVIOR; 296]

abut *v* **be next to**, adjoin, border, be adjacent to, touch, lie alongside, bound, neighbor [➡EXIST IN CLOSE PROXIMITY; 21]

abutment *n* **support**, buttress, prop, strut, brace, bulwark [➡SUPPORTS AND BASES; 1255]

abutting *adj* **adjoining**, next to, bordering, adjacent to, against, neighboring [➡CLOSENESS; 159]

abuzz *adj* **alive**, throbbing, humming, pulsating, busy, lively [➡ENERGY AND ENTHUSIASM; 496] *Opposite*: still

abysmal *adj* **terrible**, awful, dreadful, horrible, appalling, bad [➡BAD AND BADLY; 223] *Opposite*: superb

abyss *n* **gulf**, chasm, gorge, hole, void, depth [➡HOLES, GAPS, AND FORKS; 1252]

Abyssinian *type of* **cat** [➡FELINES; 983]

acacia *type of* **deciduous tree** [➡DECIDUOUS TREES; 1028]

academe (*formal*) *n* [➡EDUCATIONAL INSTITUTIONS; 813]

academia *n* **academic world**, academic circles, university, university circles, ivory tower, college circles, the academy, academe (*formal*), groves of academe (*literary*) [➡EDUCATIONAL INSTITUTIONS; 813]

academic 1 *adj* **educational**, school, college, university, scholastic [➡EDUCATION; 838] 2 *adj* **studious**, intellectual, scholarly, bookish, literary, learned [➡KNOWLEDGE AND WISDOM; 558] 3 *adj* **theoretical**, speculative, abstract, moot, hypothetical [➡FALSE AND UNREAL; 173] *Opposite*: practical 4 *n* **lecturer**, researcher, instructor, college lecturer, teacher, professor, scholar, tutor, don (*UK*) [➡EDUCATORS; 840]

academic circles *n* [➡EDUCATIONAL INSTITUTIONS; 813]

academic world n [➡ EDUCATIONAL INSTITUTIONS; 813]

academy n **school**, college, conservatory, conservatoire, arts school, private school, military institute [➡ EDUCATIONAL INSTITUTIONS; 813]

a cappella type of **musical term** [➡ MUSICAL TERMS; 912]

a case in point n **working example**, instance, case, paradigm, illustration, living proof, proof positive [➡ EVIDENCE AND PROOF; 69]

accede 1 v **agree**, assent, consent, comply, grant, allow [➡ AGREE; 645] Opposite: reject 2 v **come into**, inherit, succeed, take over, enter upon, attain, ascend [➡ GET; 420]

accelerate v **go faster**, speed up, increase speed, gather speed, pick up the pace, pick up speed, hurry, hasten, step up, quicken, rush, fast-track [➡ CHANGE OF SPEED: MORE; 396] Opposite: slow down

accelerated adj **speeded up**, faster, quicker, quickened up, hurried up, enhanced, augmented, fast-tracked, speeded, hastened [➡ MOVING QUICKLY; 103] Opposite: slowed down

acceleration 1 n **speeding up**, stepping up, hastening, hurrying, quickening, rushing [➡ CHANGE OF SPEED: MORE; 396] Opposite: deceleration 2 n **increase of rate**, increase of velocity, spurt, burst of speed [➡ SPEED; 102] Opposite: deceleration

accelerator type of **controls** [➡ INTERNAL PARTS OF A VEHICLE; 1146]

accelerator card type of **hardware** [➡ COMPUTERS AND COMPUTING; 1127]

accent 1 n **pronunciation**, inflection, intonation, tone of voice, enunciation, drawl, twang, brogue, burr [➡ THE SPOKEN WORD; 671] 2 n **emphasis**, stress, beat, accentuation, inflection, prominence [➡ MOST IMPORTANT THING; 197] 3 type of **diacritic** [➡ ASPECTS OF LANGUAGE; 682] 4 v **emphasize**, stress, accentuate, put stress on, give weight to, give prominence to, highlight, heighten, put the accent on, draw attention to [➡ CLAIM, INSIST, AND EMPHASIZE; 614]

accentuate v **emphasize**, highlight, put emphasis on, stress, draw attention to, bring out, put the accent on, heighten, make a feature of, give prominence to, give weight to [➡ CLAIM, INSIST, AND EMPHASIZE; 614] Opposite: play down

accentuation 1 n **prominence**, highlighting, attention, notice, emphasis, stress [➡ IMPORTANCE AND SIGNIFICANCE; 192] 2 n **accent**, rhythm, stress, inflection, beat, emphasis [➡ ASPECTS OF LANGUAGE; 682]

accept 1 v **receive**, take, agree to take, admit [➡ ACCEPT POSSESSION; 450] Opposite: refuse 2 v **consent**, agree, say yes, say you will, give a positive response, assent, accede [➡ APPROVE AND CONFIRM; 646] Opposite: turn down 3 v **take on**, undertake, acknowledge, assume, bear, shoulder [➡ AGREE; 645] Opposite: reject 4 v **believe**, recognize, agree, admit, acknowledge, understand, allow (formal) [➡ UNDERSTAND AND GRASP; 759] Opposite: deny 5 v **put up with**, endure, tolerate, bow, take, resign yourself [➡ TOLERATE AND ENDURE; 766]

acceptability n **suitability**, adequacy, appropriateness, tolerability [➡ ACCEPTABLE AND PASSABLE; 219]

acceptable 1 adj **satisfactory**, suitable, good enough, adequate, up to standard, tolerable, appropriate, all right, okay (informal) [➡ ACCEPTABLE AND PASSABLE; 219] Opposite: unacceptable 2 adj **welcome**, pleasing, gratifying, agreeable, enjoyable [➡ ACCEPTABLE AND PASSABLE; 219] Opposite: annoying

acceptably adv **well enough**, adequately, sufficiently well, suitably, tolerably, passably, reasonably [➡ ACCEPTABLE AND PASSABLE; 219] Opposite: unreasonably

acceptance 1 n **agreement**, assent, acquiescence, concurrence, accession, favorable reception [➡ AGREE; 645] Opposite: refusal 2 n **receipt**, taking, getting, reception, receiving [➡ ACCEPT POSSESSION; 450] Opposite: rejection 3 n **belief**, acknowledgment, credence, currency, agreement, approval [➡ AGREE; 645] 4 n **recognition**, approval, tolerance, acknowledgment, toleration [➡ FORGET, FORGIVE, AND ACCEPT; 748] Opposite: disapproval

accepted adj **conventional**, established, customary, acknowledged, usual, traditional, time-honored, received, expected, normal [➡ ORDINARINESS; 244] Opposite: unconventional

accepting adj **tolerant**, compliant, patient, long-suffering, uncomplaining, accommodating, acquiescent [➡ THE WILL AND WILLINGNESS; 563] Opposite: intolerant

access 1 n **way in**, entrance, entry, approach, gate, door [➡ DOORS AND ACCESS POINTS; 1101] Opposite: exit 2 n **right of entry**, admission, right to use, admittance, entrée, contact [➡ PERMIT AND ALLOW; 669] 3 v **get into**, gain access to, retrieve, call up, log on, read, open [➡ COMPUTERS AND COMPUTING; 1127]

accessibility n **convenience**, user-friendliness, openness, availability, approachability, ease of access, ease of understanding, ease of use [➡ USEFULNESS; 199]

accessible 1 adj **nearby**, available, reachable, easily reached, handy, to hand, at hand, within reach, open, manageable [➡ USEFULNESS; 199] Opposite: inaccessible 2 adj **comprehensible**, understandable, user-friendly, easy to use, clear, straightforward, simple [➡ EASE AND SIMPLICITY; 200] Opposite: obscure 3 adj **approachable**, affable, genial, friendly, welcoming [➡ FRIENDLINESS AND SOCIABILITY; 494] Opposite: unapproachable

accessibly 1 adv **conveniently**, handily, suitably, helpfully, usefully [➡ USEFULNESS; 199] Opposite: inconveniently 2 adv **clearly**, simply, understandably, comprehensibly, straightforwardly, helpfully [➡ EASE AND SIMPLICITY; 200] Opposite: obscurely

accession 1 n **attainment**, succession, taking over, taking office, appointment [➡ BEGINNINGS; 53] 2 n **agreement**, consent, concurrence, accord, assent, compliance [➡ AGREE; 645]

accessorize v **ornament**, decorate, beautify, trim, embellish, garnish, adorn [➡ DRESS, WEAR, AND UNDRESS; 868]

accessory 1 n [➡ ACCESSORIES, MILLINERY, AND LINGERIE; 867] 2 n **addition**, decoration, fixture, fitment, attachment, adjunct, auxiliary, add-on, extra, trimming, accompaniment, adornment, embellishment [➡ ORNAMENTS AND DECORATIONS; 1248] 3 n **accomplice**, partner, partner in crime, assistant, abettor, coconspirator, collaborator [➡ CRIMINALS; 821]

accessory

◆ *types of accessories*
ascot, bandanna, belt, bootlace, bow tie, corsage, cravat, cummerbund, earmuffs, glove, handkerchief, hat, jewelry, mitt, mitten, muff, muffler, neckerchief, necktie, pashmina, sash, scarf, shawl, stole, suspenders, tie, veil, wrap

access profile *n* [➡ E-COMMERCE; 1129]

access road *type of* **secondary road** [➡ ROADS; 1106]

access strip *type of* **secondary road** [➡ ROADS; 1106]

accident 1 *n* **chance**, coincidence, fortune, fate [➡ CHANCE, COINCIDENCE, AND ACCIDENT; 786] *Opposite*: design 2 *n* **crash**, collision, bump, smash, smashup, pileup (*informal*) [➡ TRAFFIC ACCIDENTS; 255] 3 *n* **mishap**, misfortune, calamity, catastrophe, disaster, industrial accident, upset, mistake [➡ DISASTERS; 252]

accidental *adj* **unintentional**, unintended, inadvertent, chance, unplanned, fortuitous [➡ CHANCE, COINCIDENCE, AND ACCIDENT; 786] *Opposite*: deliberate

accidentally *adv* **by chance**, by accident, by mistake, unintentionally, inadvertently, fortuitously, by coincidence, out of the blue [➡ UNPLANNED AND UNEXPECTED; 281] *Opposite*: on purpose

accident-prone *adj* **ill-fated**, unfortunate, unlucky, ill-starred, doomed, disaster-prone [➡ BAD LUCK AND UNLUCKY; 784]

acclaim 1 *v* **praise**, sing the praises of, give approval, hail, commend, applaud, cheer [➡ PRAISE AND ENCOURAGE; 647] *Opposite*: criticize 2 *n* **approval**, praise, commendation, acclamation, approbation, applause, compliments [➡ PRAISE AND ENCOURAGE; 647] *Opposite*: disapproval

acclaimed *adj* **praised**, admired, commended, celebrated, applauded [➡ EXTRAORDINARY: AMAZING, 204]

acclamation 1 *n* **acclaim**, praise, commendation, approbation, approval [➡ PRAISE AND ENCOURAGE; 647] 2 *n* **applause**, clapping, cheering, ovation, roar, cheers [➡ APPLAUSE; 652] *Opposite*: jeering

acclimate *v* **get used to**, become accustomed, accustom, adapt, adjust, familiarize, acclimatize [➡ CHANGE; 372]

acclimatization *n* **adaptation**, getting used to, becoming accustomed, adjustment, accommodation, familiarization [➡ CHANGE; 372]

acclimatize *v* **get used to**, become accustomed, accustom, adapt, adjust, familiarize [➡ CHANGE; 372]

acclimatize yourself *v* [➡ CHANGE OF MOOD AND COMPOSURE; 580]

accolade *n* **tribute**, honor, compliment, palm, award, praise, rave review (*informal*) [➡ REWARDS AND AWARDS; 439]

accommodate 1 *v* **contain**, have room for, hold, seat, have capacity for, be big enough for [➡ HOLD AND CONTAIN; 455] 2 *v* **house**, lodge, put up, billet, quarter, provide accommodations, provide lodgings (*UK*) [➡ TAKE CARE OF AND SPOIL; 300] 3 *v* **get used to**, adapt, adjust, become accustomed to, familiarize, acclimatize, acclimate [➡ CHANGE; 372] 4 *v* **assist**, help, oblige, be of service, find ways to help [➡ HELP; 293]

accommodating *adj* **helpful**, willing, obliging, compliant, cooperative, accepting, long-suffering [➡ THE WILL AND WILLINGNESS; 563] *Opposite*: uncooperative

accommodation 1 *n* **adjustment**, adaptation, alteration, change, modification [➡ CHANGE; 372] 2 *n* (*UK*) **accommodations**, housing, lodging, room, space, place [➡ ACCOMMODATIONS; 855]

accommodations *n* **housing**, lodging, room, space, place, accommodation (*UK*) [➡ ACCOMMODATIONS; 855]

accompanied by *adv* **along with**, together with, with, in the company of, in consort with (*archaic or formal*) [➡ RELATED; 142]

accompaniment *n* **supplement**, accessory, garnish, adjunct, complement, addition, auxiliary, trimming, side dish [➡ PHYSICAL OBJECTS; 1243]

accompanist *n* **pianist**, instrumentalist, musician, player [➡ MUSICIANS AND SINGERS; 908]

accompany 1 *v* **escort**, go with, go together with, go along with, attend, convoy [➡ ACCOMPANY AND FOLLOW; 337] 2 *v* **go together with**, come with, be an adjunct to, supplement, complement, be associated with, be tied in with [➡ RECIPROCITY AND INTERDEPENDENCE; 147]

accompanying *adj* **supplementary**, associated, complementary, additional, add-on [➡ MORE AND EXCESS; 124]

accomplice *n* **partner in crime**, assistant, accessory, collaborator, coconspirator, partner, abettor [➡ CRIMINALS; 821]

accomplish *v* **achieve**, complete, do, finish, get done, bring about, carry out, realize, attain, pull off (*informal*) [➡ CARRY OUT AN ACTION; 269]

Compare and Contrast: *accomplish, achieve, attain, realize, carry out, pull off*

CORE MEANING: to bring something to a successful conclusion

accomplish to succeed in doing something; *achieve* to succeed in something, usually with effort; *attain* to reach a specific objective; *realize* to fulfill a specific vision or plan; *carry out* to perform or accomplish a task or activity; *pull off* (*informal*) to accomplish something, despite difficulties.

See Compare and Contrast at **perform**.

accomplished *adj* **talented**, skillful, gifted, skilled, proficient, expert, consummate, able, adept, capable [➡ TALENTED AND SKILLFUL; 527]

accomplishment 1 *n* **completion**, execution, carrying out, finishing, realization, achievement, attainment [➡ CARRY OUT AN ACTION; 269] 2 *n* **feat**, achievement, triumph, success, deed, exploit [➡ SUCCESS; 82] 3 *n* **talent**, skill, ability, expertise, capability, endowment [➡ SKILLS, TALENTS, AND ABILITIES; 526]

accord 1 *v* **give**, allow, permit, render (*formal*), confer (*formal*), bestow (*formal*), afford (*formal*) [➡ GIVE AND PROVIDE; 430] 2 *v* **agree**, concur, fit, match, correspond, be in harmony with [➡ HARMONY; 155] *Opposite*: clash 3 *n* **agreement**, treaty, settlement, pact, deal [➡ OFFICIAL DOCUMENTS; 586] 4 *n* **con-**

sensus, harmony, concurrence, unity, agreement, solidarity [➡HARMONY; 155]

accordance *n* **consensus**, agreement, accord, harmony, concord, solidarity [➡HARMONY; 155] *Opposite*: disagreement

accordingly 1 *adv* **appropriately**, suitably, correspondingly, fittingly [➡APPROPRIATE, SUITABLE, AND ADVISABLE; 184] *Opposite*: inappropriately 2 *adv* **so**, for that reason, therefore, as a result, consequently, hence (*formal*), in consequence (*formal*), thus (*formal*) [➡CAUSATION; 168]

according to 1 *prep* **as said by**, as stated by, on the word of [➡EXPRESSIONS OF REFERENCE; 63] 2 *prep* **consistent with**, along with, in line with, in keeping with, in relation to, in proportion to, in accordance with, as per [➡HARMONY; 155] *Opposite*: counter to

according to plan *adv* **as intended**, as proposed, as organized, as arranged, as suggested, swimmingly, perfectly, flawlessly [➡CORRECT AND FAULTLESS; 182]

accordion *type of* **keyboard** [➡MUSICAL INSTRUMENTS; 910]

accost *v* **approach**, stop, confront, detain, hound, buttonhole (*informal*) [➡INITIATE AND ESTABLISH COMMUNICATION; 680]

account 1 *n* **report**, description, story, relation, narrative [➡EXPLAIN AND CLARIFY; 610] 2 *n* **explanation**, version, interpretation, justification, reason, excuse [➡EXPLAIN AND CLARIFY; 610] 3 *n* **bank account**, checking account, deposit account, savings account, current account (*UK*) [➡ACCOUNTING, BANKING, AND BUDGETING; 799] 4 *n* **arrangement**, credit, tally, balance, bill, tab (*informal*) [➡RECEIPTS AND INVOICES; 591]

accountability *n* **answerability**, responsibility, liability, culpability [➡RESPONSIBILITY; 170]

accountable *adj* **answerable**, responsible, liable, held responsible, blamed [➡RESPONSIBILITY; 170]

accountant *n* **bookkeeper**, auditor, certified public accountant, cost accountant [➡PEOPLE INVOLVED IN FINANCE; 804]

account for 1 *v* **explain**, justify, give an explanation for, give a reason for, answer for [➡EXPLAIN AND CLARIFY; 610] 2 *v* **comprise**, make up, total, represent, constitute, form [➡AMOUNT TO AND EQUAL; 70]

account holder *n* [➡ACCOUNTING, BANKING, AND BUDGETING; 799]

accounting *adj* [➡FINANCE AND ECONOMICS; 796]

accounts *n* **books**, balance sheet, financial statement [➡ACCOUNTING, BANKING, AND BUDGETING; 799]

accounts clerk *n* [➡PEOPLE INVOLVED IN FINANCE; 804]

accouterment *n* **accessory**, trapping, trimming, tool of the trade, equipment, appurtenance (*formal*) [➡PHYSICAL OBJECTS; 1243]

accouterments *n* [➡ORNAMENTS AND DECORATIONS; 1248]

accredit *v* **recognize**, sanction, endorse, authorize, certify, certificate, approve [➡APPROVE AND CONFIRM; 646]

accreditation *n* **authorization**, endorsement, approval, certification, sanction, recognition, qualification [➡APPROVE AND CONFIRM; 646]

accredited *adj* **credited**, attributed, qualified, endorsed,

official, recognized, certified, approved, ascribed (*formal*) [➡APPROPRIATE, SUITABLE, AND ADVISABLE; 184] *Opposite*: unofficial

accretion 1 *n* **accumulation**, buildup, increase, enlargement, addition, growth, amassment, agglomeration [➡CHANGE OF SIZE: BIGGER; 392] *Opposite*: erosion 2 *n* **deposit**, layer, mass, lump, bump, growth, addition, pile [➡MANY, MUCH, LARGE AMOUNT; 117]

accrual *n* **accumulation**, increase, buildup, accretion, addition, growth, enlargement [➡CHANGE OF SIZE: BIGGER; 392] *Opposite*: loss

accrue *v* **accumulate**, grow, mount up, build up, amass, increase, add, enlarge [➡CHANGE OF SIZE: BIGGER; 392] *Opposite*: dwindle

accumulate *v* **build up**, mount up, accrue, amass, collect, gather, hoard, add, store, pile up, assemble, stockpile [➡GET; 420] *Opposite*: disperse

See Compare and Contrast at **collect**.

accumulation 1 *n* **buildup**, accretion, accrual, gathering, growth, addition, increase, enlargement, amassing [➡CHANGE OF SIZE: BIGGER; 392] 2 *n* **collection**, stock, store, hoard, deposit, heap [➡COLLECTIONS AND MIXTURES OF THINGS; 1244]

accumulative 1 *adj* **acquisitive**, hoarding, materialistic, covetous, grasping, avaricious [➡GRASPING AND FINANCIALLY MEAN; 519] 2 *adj* **incremental**, increasing, rising, growing, mounting, amassing, piling up, progressive, gradual, cumulative [➡CHANGE OF SIZE: BIGGER; 392]

accumulator 1 *n* **collector**, saver, amasser, magpie (*informal*), squirrel (*informal*) [➡PEOPLE WHO COLLECT THINGS; 454] 2 *type of* **hardware** [➡COMPUTERS AND COMPUTING; 1127]

accuracy *n* **correctness**, accurateness, exactness, precision, truth, truthfulness, exactitude [➡EXACT; 203] *Opposite*: inaccuracy

accurate *adj* **precise**, correct, exact, true, truthful, perfect [➡EXACT; 203] *Opposite*: inaccurate

accursed (*archaic or literary*) 1 *adj* **doomed**, ill-fated, fated, ill-starred, damned, cursed, under a curse [➡BAD LUCK AND UNLUCKY; 784] *Opposite*: blessed 2 *adj* **awful**, horrible, terrible, appalling, hateful, detestable, vile, foul [➡EMOTIONALLY UNPLEASANT AND UPSETTING; 227]

accusation *n* **allegation**, indictment, claim, complaint, charge, denunciation [➡CRITICISMS AND ANGRY OUTBURSTS; 50]

accusative *type of* **grammatical term** [➡ASPECTS OF LANGUAGE; 682]

accusatorial (*formal*) 1 *adj* **critical**, judgmental, condemnatory, accusing, reproachful, reproving, fault-finding, harsh, severe, accusatory (*formal*) [➡ACCUSATORY AND DISAPPROVING; 634] 2 *adj* **adversarial**, confrontational, argumentative, combative, antagonistic [➡ACCUSATORY AND DISAPPROVING; 634] *Opposite*: amicable

accusatory (*formal*) *adj* [➡ACCUSATORY AND DISAPPROVING; 634]

accuse *v* **blame**, lay blame on, indict, point the finger, allege, fault, reproach, censure, charge, denunciate (*formal*), inculpate (*formal*) [➡ACCUSE, BLAME, AND CRITICIZE; 641]

accuser 1 *n* **challenger**, confronter, criticizer, opponent,

faultfinder, complainant [➡ ENEMIES AND TORMENTORS; 969] **2** *n* **indicter**, litigant, petitioner, appellant, complainant, prosecutor [➡ PEOPLE IN LAW COURTS; 820] **3** *n* **informer**, telltale, tattletale, talebearer, whistle-blower, sneak (*UK*) [➡ INTERFERING PEOPLE AND TATTLETALES; 950]

accusing *adj* **reproachful**, condemning, reproving, critical, condemnatory, accusatory (*formal*), accusatorial (*formal*) [➡ ACCUSATORY AND DISAPPROVING; 634]

accustom *v* **get to know**, get used to, acclimatize, acclimate, become accustomed to, familiarize, adjust, adapt, acquaint, inure [➡ LEARN AND DISCOVER; 762]

accustomed **1** *adj* **familiarized**, inured, adapted, comfortable, habituated (*formal*) [➡ COOL AND CALM; 536] *Opposite*: unaccustomed **2** *adj* **usual**, habitual, regular, familiar, customary, favorite, set [➡ ORDINARINESS; 244] *Opposite*: unusual

accustomed to *adj* **in the habit of**, given to, used to, at home, prone to, established [➡ KNOWLEDGE AND WISDOM; 558]

accustom yourself *v* [➡ CHANGE OF MOOD AND COMPOSURE; 580]

ace **1** *n* **champion**, star, expert, winner, victor, top player (*informal*) [➡ TALENTED OR INTELLIGENT PEOPLE; 528] **2** *v* (*slang*) **pass with flying colors**, do well, sail through, get an A on, max (*slang*) [➡ SUCCEED AND WIN; 79] *Opposite*: fail **3** *adj* (*informal*) **first-rate**, top, world-class, wonderful, excellent, brilliant, champion, star, leading, super (*informal*), topnotch (*informal*) [➡ EXTRAORDINARY: AMAZING; 204] *Opposite*: lousy (*informal*)

acerbic *adj* **cutting**, bitter, caustic, acid, sour, acrid, mordant, barbed, biting, critical, harsh, pointed, sarcastic [➡ RUDE AND HOSTILE; 625] *Opposite*: mild

acerbity *n* **sharpness**, bitterness, sourness, acidity, acrimony, mordancy, pointedness, causticity, causticness [➡ RUDE AND HOSTILE; 625]

acetate *type of* **plastic** [➡ PLASTICS; 1134]

acetylene *type of* **gas** [➡ GASES; 1275]

ache **1** *n* **pain**, throbbing, aching, twinge, headache, stomachache, backache [➡ PAIN AND OTHER PHYSICAL SENSATIONS; 733] **2** *v* **hurt**, throb, be painful, sting, smart, be killing [➡ PAIN AND OTHER PHYSICAL SENSATIONS; 733] **3** *v* (*formal*) **long**, desire, yearn, want, wish, burn, hanker, pine, crave, hunger [➡ DESIRE AND WANT; 579]

achene *n* [➡ PARTS OF TREES AND PLANTS; 1026]

achievable *adj* **attainable**, realizable, possible, reachable, doable, practicable, feasible, viable, realistic [➡ POSSIBLE AND PROBABLE; 177] *Opposite*: unrealistic

achieve *v* **attain**, realize, accomplish, reach, complete, do, carry out, succeed, triumph, pull off (*informal*) [➡ SUCCEED AND WIN; 79] *Opposite*: fail

> *See Compare and Contrast at* **accomplish**.

achievement *n* **attainment**, accomplishment, success, feat, triumph, realization [➡ SUCCESS; 82] *Opposite*: failure

achiever *n* **high-flier**, doer, self-starter, success, go-getter (*informal*) [➡ TALENTED OR INTELLIGENT PEOPLE; 528] *Opposite*: loser

Achilles heel *n* **weakness**, flaw, failing, weak point, chink in somebody's armor, weak spot [➡ FAULTS, FLAWS, AND WEAKNESSES; 251]

Achilles tendon *type of* **muscle or tendon** [➡ THE MUSCLES; 718]

aching **1** *adj* **painful**, achy, sore, tender, throbbing, sensitive, hurting [➡ PAIN AND OTHER PHYSICAL SENSATIONS; 733] **2** *n* **ache**, pain, painful feeling, throbbing, throb, twinge, sore spot, sting [➡ PAIN AND OTHER PHYSICAL SENSATIONS; 733] **3** *n* (*formal*) **longing**, desire, yearning, pining, itch, craving, hunger, hankering [➡ DESIRE AND WANT; 579]

achy *adj* **painful**, aching, sore, tender, throbbing, sensitive, hurting [➡ PAIN AND OTHER PHYSICAL SENSATIONS; 733]

acid **1** *adj* **acidic**, tart, sour, bitter, sharp [➡ TASTE; 703] *Opposite*: sweet **2** *adj* **cutting**, biting, caustic, acerbic, mordant, barbed, harsh, critical [➡ RUDE AND HOSTILE; 625] *Opposite*: mild

acid house *type of* **dance music** [➡ MUSIC, SONGS, AND SINGING; 907]

acidic *adj* **acid**, tart, sour, bitter, sharp [➡ TASTE; 703] *Opposite*: sweet

acidity *n* **sourness**, sharpness, tartness, bitterness [➡ TASTE; 703] *Opposite*: sweetness

acid jazz *type of* **dance music** [➡ MUSIC, SONGS, AND SINGING; 907]

acidly *adv* **sharply**, cuttingly, tartly, sourly, acerbically, bitterly, bitingly, caustically [➡ RUDE AND HOSTILE; 625] *Opposite*: sweetly

acid stomach *n* [➡ DISORDERS OF THE DIGESTIVE SYSTEM; 713]

acid test *n* **litmus test**, touchstone, trial, indicator, confirmation [➡ EVIDENCE AND PROOF; 69]

acknowledge **1** *v* **admit**, recognize, accept, concede, grant, confess, own up, fess up (*slang*), allow (*formal*) [➡ ADMIT AND CONFESS; 615] *Opposite*: deny **2** *v* **greet**, salute, wave, nod, hail [➡ GESTURES AND GESTICULATION; 653] *Opposite*: ignore **3** *v* **reply**, answer, respond, react, return, rejoin (*formal*) [➡ REPLY AND ANSWER; 668] *Opposite*: ignore

acknowledged *adj* **recognized**, approved, known, accredited, accepted, agreed [➡ KNOWN AND FAMOUS; 181] *Opposite*: denied

acknowledgment **1** *n* **greeting**, salutation, nod, wave, salute [➡ GREETINGS, FAREWELLS, AND SALUTATIONS; 659] **2** *n* **response**, reply, reaction, answer, retort, rejoinder (*formal*) [➡ REPLY AND ANSWER; 668] **3** *n* **recognition**, acceptance, admission, confession, appreciation, tribute [➡ AGREE; 645]

acme *n* **peak**, summit, top, zenith, pinnacle, culmination, apex, apogee [➡ INTERMEDIATE STAGES; 55] *Opposite*: nadir

acne *n* [➡ CONDITIONS AFFECTING THE SKIN; 721]

acned *adj* [➡ COMPLEXION; 480]

acolyte **1** *n* **attendant**, assistant, aide, helper [➡ SUBORDINATES AND ASSISTANTS; 966] **2** *n* **follower**, devotee, disciple, adherent, supporter, admirer, enthusiast [➡ DEVOTEES AND ADDICTED PEOPLE; 556]

acorn *type of* **nut** [➡ NUTS; 1185]

acoustic *adj* **audio**, aural, auditory, audile, sound [➡ ACOUSTICS; 1138]

acoustics *n* **audibility**, auditory range, sound quality [➡ ACOUSTICS; 1138]

acquaint *v* **make aware**, inform, let know, let in on, make familiar with, explain, notify, tell, run by, familiarize, apprise (*formal*) [➡ INFORM, ANNOUNCE, AND ISSUE; 611] *Opposite*: keep from

acquaintance 1 *n* **associate**, friend, contact, colleague, consociate (*formal*), confrère (*formal*) [➡ FRIENDS AND GUESTS; 963] *Opposite*: stranger 2 *n* **knowledge**, familiarity, understanding, awareness, conversance [➡ KNOWLEDGE AND WISDOM; 558] *Opposite*: ignorance 3 *n* **relationship**, contact, association, friendship, relations [➡ RELATIONSHIP TO ANOTHER; 973]

acquaintanceship 1 *n* **social circle**, circle, friendship group, company, acquaintance [➡ FRIENDS AND ACQUAINTANCES; 936] 2 *n* **knowledge**, familiarity, awareness, understanding, grasp, appreciation, acquaintance [➡ KNOWLEDGE AND WISDOM; 558] *Opposite*: unfamiliarity

acquainted *adj* [➡ RELATIONSHIP TO ANOTHER; 973]

acquiesce *v* **agree**, comply, accept, consent, assent, give in, submit, go along with, yield, concede, concur, accede [➡ AGREE; 645] *Opposite*: resist

See Compare and Contrast at **agree***.*

acquiescence *n* **agreement**, consent, compliance, submission, acceptance, assent [➡ AGREE; 645] *Opposite*: resistance

acquiescent *adj* **agreeable**, compliant, yielding, accepting, submissive, consenting, willing [➡ THE WILL AND WILLINGNESS; 563] *Opposite*: resistant

acquire 1 *v* **obtain**, get, get hold of, get your hands on, gain, attain, buy, purchase, come by, procure, secure, pick up [➡ GET; 420] *Opposite*: lose 2 *v* **develop**, learn, pick up, take up, assimilate [➡ LEARN AND DISCOVER; 762] *Opposite*: drop

See Compare and Contrast at **get***.*

acquisition 1 *n* **gaining**, attainment, achievement, getting hold of, purchase, procurement, acquirement [➡ FIND; 463] *Opposite*: loss 2 *n* **purchase**, possession, asset, gain [➡ PURCHASE; 422]

acquisitive *adj* **greedy**, covetous, grasping, avaricious, materialistic [➡ GRASPING AND FINANCIALLY MEAN; 519] *Opposite*: generous

acquisitiveness *n* **greed**, hoarding, avarice, covetousness, materialism [➡ GRASPING AND FINANCIALLY MEAN; 519] *Opposite*: generosity

acquit *v* **find not guilty**, clear, set free, free, release, exonerate [➡ TRIAL, PUNISHMENT, AND LEGAL OUTCOMES; 819] *Opposite*: convict

acquittal *n* **release**, discharge, freeing, clearing, exoneration [➡ TRIAL, PUNISHMENT, AND LEGAL OUTCOMES; 819] *Opposite*: conviction

acquit yourself (*formal*) *v* **conduct yourself**, act, behave, perform, work, comport yourself (*formal*) [➡ CARRY OUT AN ACTION; 269]

acre *type of* **nonmetric unit** [➡ SIZE AND DIMENSIONS; 1192]

acreage *n* **land**, estate, property, domain, acres [➡ SIZE AND DIMENSIONS; 1192]

acres 1 *n* **land**, estate, domain, property, acreage [➡ SIZE AND DIMENSIONS; 1192] 2 *n* (*informal*) **expanse**, stretch, tracts, swathes, lots [➡ MANY, MUCH, LARGE AMOUNT; 117]

acrid 1 *adj* **pungent**, harsh, unpleasant, choking, bitter, sour, tart [➡ TASTE; 703] *Opposite*: pleasant 2 *adj* **sharp**, cutting, caustic, bitter, vitriolic, mordant, trenchant, acerbic [➡ RUDE AND HOSTILE; 625] *Opposite*: mild

acridly *adv* **bitterly**, pungently, unpleasantly, sharply, sourly, acerbically, acidly [➡ TASTE; 703]

acrimonious *adj* **spiteful**, rancorous, discordant, hostile, unfriendly, harsh [➡ RUDE AND HOSTILE; 625] *Opposite*: amicable

acrimony *n* **bitterness**, spite, rancor, animosity, hostility, unfriendliness, ill will, bad blood, bad feeling [➡ ANTAGONISM; 552] *Opposite*: harmony

acrobat *n* **tumbler**, trapeze artist, circus performer, gymnast, funambulist, entertainer [➡ PEOPLE IN SPORTS AND LEISURE; 876]

acrobatic *adj* **gymnastic**, athletic, lithe, supple, flexible [➡ AGILITY OF THE BODY; 476]

acrobatics 1 *n* **gymnastics**, aerobics, calisthenics, physical exercises (*UK*) [➡ HOBBIES, GAMES, AND SPORTS; 875] 2 *n* **agility**, skill, dexterity, nimbleness, quickness, gymnastics, virtuosity [➡ SKILLS, TALENTS, AND ABILITIES; 526]

acronym *n* **abbreviation**, short form, shortening, contraction, condensation [➡ ASPECTS OF LANGUAGE; 682]

acrophobia *type of* **phobia** [➡ FEARS AND PHOBIAS; 554]

across *adv* **crossways**, crosswise, transversely, athwart, diagonally, from corner to corner [➡ ORIENTATION AND ALIGNMENT; 1223]

across-the-board *adj* **comprehensive**, sweeping, all-embracing, wide-ranging, far-reaching, universal, extensive, wholesale, root-and-branch [➡ ALL; 128]

acrostic *type of* **wordplay** [➡ JOKES AND TEASING; 674]

acrylic *type of* **synthetic fabric** [➡ FABRICS; 1132]

act 1 *n* **action**, deed, doing, undertaking, exploit, performance, achievement, accomplishment, feat [➡ ACTIONS OR UNDERTAKINGS; 259] 2 *n* **performance**, entertainment, turn, piece, item [➡ PERFORMANCES AND SHOWS; 42] 3 *n* **pretense**, show, sham, con, feint, ploy, play-acting, hamming, put-on (*informal*) [➡ DECEPTION AND LIES; 660] 4 *n* **law**, piece of legislation, statute, decree, enactment, measure, bill [➡ THE LAW AND LEGAL AUTHORITY; 814] 5 *v* **take action**, take steps, proceed, be active, perform, operate, work, get down to, get on, get going, do your stuff [➡ CARRY OUT AN ACTION; 269] 6 *v* **behave**, conduct yourself, perform, comport yourself (*formal*), acquit yourself (*formal*) [➡ CARRY OUT AN ACTION; 269] 7 *v* **pretend**, put on an act, put it on, play, fake, feign, ham it up, play-act (*informal*) [➡ PRETEND AND MIMIC; 60] 8 *v* **replace**, represent, act on behalf of, appear on behalf of, speak for [➡ REPRESENT SOMETHING OR

SOMEBODY; 59] **9** *v* **function**, work, take effect, produce a result, produce an effect, do its stuff [➡ FUNCTION SUCCESSFULLY; 469] **10** *v* **perform**, act out, be in, appear, play, represent, enact, portray [➡ THE PERFORMING ARTS; 904]

act for *v* [➡ REPRESENT SOMETHING OR SOMEBODY; 59]

acting 1 *n* **drama**, the theater, performing, the stage, performing arts, amateur dramatics (*UK*) [➡ THE PERFORMING ARTS; 904] **2** *adj* **temporary**, substitute, stand-in, interim [➡ FINITENESS, VARIABILITY, AND TRANSIENCE; 96] *Opposite*: permanent

action 1 *n* **act**, deed, exploit, achievement, accomplishment, feat, stroke [➡ ACTIONS OR UNDERTAKINGS; 259] *Opposite*: inaction **2** *n* **lawsuit**, suit, proceedings, charge, case [➡ TRIAL, PUNISHMENT, AND LEGAL OUTCOMES; 819] **3** *n* **battle**, fighting, combat, conflict, engagement, encounter, clash, skirmish, dogfight, raid, war, warfare [➡ AGGRESSIVE EVENTS; 39]

actionable *adj* **indictable**, litigious, suable, chargeable, imputable, litigable, prosecutable [➡ ILLEGAL; 816] *Opposite*: legal

actioner (*informal*) *n* [➡ FILM; 901]

action movie *n* [➡ FILM; 901]

action-packed *adj* **exciting**, thrilling, gripping, enthralling, suspenseful, dynamic, vigorous, fast-moving, energetic [➡ EMOTIONALLY PLEASANT; 187] *Opposite*: dull

action replay *n* [➡ REPETITION; 29]

activate *v* **make active**, set in motion, set off, turn on, trigger, start, get going, stimulate, galvanize, initiate, motivate, actuate (*formal*) [➡ CAUSE TO START; 266] *Opposite*: stop

activation *n* **start**, beginning, initiation, instigation, stimulation, motivation, galvanization, triggering [➡ BEGINNINGS; 53]

active 1 *adj* **lively**, vigorous, energetic, full of life, on the go, dynamic, full of zip (*informal*) [➡ ENERGY AND ENTHUSIASM; 496] *Opposite*: inactive **2** *adj* **in force**, functioning, effective, in action, operating, operational, functional, working [➡ HAPPENING AND IN PROGRESS; 32] **3** *adj* **working**, practicing, involved, committed, enthusiastic, keen [➡ EMPLOYMENT STATUS; 831] *Opposite*: half-hearted

actively *adv* **vigorously**, aggressively, energetically, enthusiastically, dynamically, keenly [➡ WITH ENTHUSIASM; 286] *Opposite*: half-heartedly

activeness *n* **activity**, liveliness, animation, energy, vigor, vitality [➡ ENERGY AND ENTHUSIASM; 496] *Opposite*: passiveness

activism *n* **direct action**, political action, social action, involvement, engagement, crusading, politicking, do-gooding (*informal*) [➡ GOVERNMENT POLICIES; 810]

activist *n* **campaigner**, protester, objector, militant, advocate [➡ UNCOOPERATIVE OR REBELLIOUS PEOPLE; 566]

activity 1 *n* **pursuit**, interest, hobby, occupation, leisure interest, endeavor, pastime [➡ LEISURE AND RECREATION; 874] **2** *n* **action**, movement, motion, bustle, commotion, goings-on (*informal*) [➡ EVENTS AND OCCURRENCES; 35] *Opposite*: inactivity

act of contrition *n* [➡ RELIGIOUS CONCEPTS; 776]

act on 1 *v* **follow up on**, tackle, start in on, take action

[➡ START AN ACTION; 260] **2** *v* **have an effect on**, work, affect, perform [➡ CHANGE; 372]

act on behalf of *v* [➡ REPRESENT SOMETHING OR SOMEBODY; 59]

actor 1 *n* **performer**, artist, thespian, artiste, player [➡ PERFORMERS; 905] **2** *type of* **entertainer** [➡ WORKERS IN ENTERTAINMENT AND MEDIA; 873]

act out 1 *v* **enact**, perform, portray, act, play, represent, dramatize [➡ THE PERFORMING ARTS; 904] **2** *v* **work out**, work through, exorcize, express, purge, expel [➡ GET RID OF SOMETHING; 451]

actress *n* **performer**, artist, thespian, artiste, player [➡ PERFORMERS; 905] **2** *type of* **entertainer** [➡ WORKERS IN ENTERTAINMENT AND MEDIA; 873]

actual *adj* **real**, genuine, authentic, concrete, tangible, definite [➡ TRUE AND REAL; 171]

actuality 1 *n* **fact**, certainty, reality, practicality, actual fact, real fact [➡ TRUE AND REAL; 171] **2** *n* **real life**, the real world, here and now, reality [➡ PRESENT; 85]

actualize *v* [➡ CAUSE TO HAPPEN; 31]

actually *adv* **in fact**, really, in point of fact, in reality, truly, essentially [➡ WORDS AND PHRASES EMPHASIZING THE TRUTH OF A MATTER; 172]

actuary *n* [➡ PEOPLE INVOLVED IN FINANCE; 804]

actuate (*formal*) *v* **activate**, put into action, set in motion, trigger, start, get going, stimulate [➡ CAUSE TO START; 265]

act up *v* **cause trouble**, be difficult, misbehave, malfunction, go wrong, be on the blink (*informal*), play up (*UK*) [➡ FAIL OR CEASE TO FUNCTION; 470] *Opposite*: behave

acuity *n* **keenness**, acuteness, sharpness, alertness, awareness [➡ POSITIVE INTELLECTUAL CHARACTERISTICS; 524]

acumen *n* **insight**, shrewdness, penetration, judgment, wisdom, expertise, intelligence, perspicacity, perspicuity [➡ SKILLS, TALENTS, AND ABILITIES; 526]

acupressure *type of* **complementary therapy** [➡ REMEDIES, TREATMENTS, AND OPERATIONS; 731]

acupuncture *type of* **complementary therapy** [➡ REMEDIES, TREATMENTS, AND OPERATIONS; 731]

a cut above *adj* **superior**, better, finer, first-class, first-rate, high class, outstanding [➡ SUPERIORITY; 152]

acute 1 *adj* **severe**, serious, critical, grave, important, desperate, dire [➡ IMPORTANT; 194] *Opposite*: moderate **2** *adj* **perceptive**, shrewd, intelligent, keen, sharp, astute, perspicacious [➡ POSITIVE INTELLECTUAL CHARACTERISTICS; 524] **3** *adj* **sharp**, sensitive, keen, heightened, finely tuned, discriminating, delicate [➡ STRENGTH; 201] *Opposite*: dull **4** *adj* **intense**, violent, strong, excruciating, piercing, stabbing [➡ STRENGTH; 201] *Opposite*: mild **5** *type of* **diacritic** [➡ ASPECTS OF LANGUAGE; 682]

acutely *adv* **very**, intensely, highly, deeply, extremely, terribly, severely [➡ TO A GREAT EXTENT; 132] *Opposite*: slightly

acuteness 1 *n* **intensity**, severity, gravity, seriousness [➡ DIFFICULTY AND COMPLEXITY; 242] **2** *n* **sharpness**, keenness, sensitivity, perceptiveness [➡ POSITIVE INTELLECTUAL CHARACTERISTICS; 524] *Opposite*: dullness

ad *n* **advertisement**, public notice, commercial, poster, flier, announcement, trailer, personal, classified ad, want ad (*informal*), hoarding (*UK*) [➡ ADVERTISING AND PUBLICITY; 604]

adage *n* **saying**, saw, proverb, maxim, axiom, motto [➡ THE ORAL TRADITION; 677]

adagio *type of* **musical term** [➡ MUSICAL TERMS; 912]

adamant *adj* **obstinate**, obdurate, unyielding, unbending, inflexible, unwavering, immovable, resolute, steadfast, stubborn, fixed, resistant [➡ COOL AND CALM; 536] *Opposite:* amenable

adapt 1 *v* **change**, alter, modify, adjust, vary, revise, amend, bend, fit, rework [➡ CHANGE; 372] *Opposite:* leave 2 *v* **become accustomed**, familiarize, get a feel for, get used to, acclimatize, acclimate, find your feet, settle in, adjust [➡ CHANGE OF MOOD AND COMPOSURE; 580]

adaptability *n* **flexibility**, adaptableness, malleability, compliance [➡ USEFULNESS; 199] *Opposite:* inflexibility

adaptable *adj* **flexible**, malleable, pliable, adjustable, compliant, easygoing [➡ USEFULNESS; 199] *Opposite:* inflexible

adaptation 1 *n* **alteration**, adjustment, acclimatization, modification, change [➡ CHANGE; 372] 2 *n* **version**, edition, revision, reworking, variation [➡ REPRESENTATIONS AND GENERAL EXAMPLES; 65]

adapter *n* **electric plug**, connector, converter, device [➡ PARTS OF MACHINES AND TOOLS; 1118]

add 1 *v* **put in**, insert, adjoin, append, affix, attach, include [➡ FASTEN, LINK, AND JOIN; 408] *Opposite:* delete 2 *v* **add up**, add together, total, combine, tally, tally up, count up, count, tot up [➡ ASSESS QUANTITY; 757] *Opposite:* subtract 3 *v* **enhance**, complement, improve, increase, supplement, swell, enlarge, intensify, augment (*formal*) [➡ IMPROVE SOMETHING; 374] *Opposite:* detract

added *adj* **additional**, extra, supplementary, further, other, auxiliary, new, more [➡ MORE AND EXCESS; 124]

added extras *n* [➡ MORE AND EXCESS; 124]

addendum *n* **addition**, supplement, appendix, postscript, P.S., add-on, rider, afterthought, codicil (*formal*) [➡ PARTS OF BOOKS AND DOCUMENTS; 593]

adder 1 *type of* **computer** [➡ COMPUTERS AND COMPUTING; 1127] 2 *type of* **poisonous snake** [➡ SNAKES; 995]

addict *n* **devotee**, fan, aficionado, aficionada, fanatic, buff, enthusiast, follower [➡ DEVOTEES AND ADDICTED PEOPLE; 556]

addicted *adj* [➡ UNDER THE INFLUENCE OF DRUGS OR ALCOHOL; 741]

addiction *n* **habit**, compulsion, dependence, need, obsession, craving [➡ FADS, FETISHES, AND IDOLATRY; 555]

addition 1 *n* **adding**, adding up, adding together, totaling, toting, calculation, count, accumulation, tallying, tally [➡ ASSESS QUANTITY; 757] 2 *n* **supplement**, add-on, appendage, addendum, adjunct, extra, additive, surcharge [➡ MORE AND EXCESS; 124]

additional *adj* **extra**, added, supplementary, other, further, bonus, surplus, superfluous [➡ MORE AND EXCESS; 124]

additionally *adv* **as well**, in addition, moreover, furthermore, also [➡ EXPRESSIONS INTRODUCING EXTRA INFORMATION; 139]

additive *n* **preservative**, stabilizer, improver, chemical, colorant [➡ ADDITIVES; 1172]

addle *v* **confuse**, befuddle, muddle, distract, bewilder, perplex, bemuse [➡ CONFUSE AND BEWILDER; 571]

addled 1 *adj* **confused**, muddled, bewildered, befuddled, perplexed, bemused, addlepated (*archaic*), addlebrained (*archaic*) [➡ CONFUSION, ANXIETY, AND WORRY; 540] *Opposite:* clear 2 *adj* **spoiled**, rotten, decayed, off, putrid, unwholesome, rancid, fetid [➡ IN BAD REPAIR; 1234] *Opposite:* fresh

addlepated (*archaic*) *adj* **confused**, muddled, bewildered, befuddled, perplexed, bemused, addled, addlebrained (*archaic*) [➡ CONFUSION, ANXIETY, AND WORRY; 540] *Opposite:* clear

add-on 1 *n* **attachment**, addendum, adjunct, appendage, supplement, frill, extra, addition [➡ MORE AND EXCESS; 124] 2 *adj* **supplementary**, accompanying, additional, extra, optional, auxiliary [➡ MORE AND EXCESS; 124] *Opposite:* essential

address 1 *n* **speech**, talk, discourse, lecture, report, statement [➡ ONE-WAY COMMUNICATION; 49] 2 *v* **direct**, deliver, dispatch, refer, forward [➡ DISPATCH AND SEND; 333] 3 *v* **speak**, lecture, talk, give a lecture, give a talk, make a speech [➡ INSTRUCT AND TEACH; 609] 4 *v* **tackle**, deal with, take in hand, attend, concentrate, focus, adopt [➡ ATTEMPT AN ACTION; 261] *Opposite:* ignore

adduce (*formal*) *v* **offer**, present, put forward, bring forward, give, cite [➡ SUGGEST, HINT, AND COMMENT; 612]

add up 1 *v* **add**, add together, total, combine, tally up, tally, count, count up, tot up, tote up (*informal*) [➡ ASSESS QUANTITY; 757] *Opposite:* subtract 2 *v* **make sense**, hang together, be consistent, ring true, come together [➡ MEAN SOMETHING; 61]

add up to *v* **come to**, number, total, amount to, mount up to, equal [➡ AMOUNT TO AND EQUAL; 70]

adenoidal *adj* **nasal**, thick, muffled, indistinct [➡ LOUD, HIGH, OR UNPLEASANT SOUNDS; 1266]

adenoids *part of* **mouth** [➡ THE MOUTH; 702]

adept *adj* **skillful**, skilled, expert, proficient, adroit, practiced, dexterous [➡ TALENTED AND SKILLFUL; 527] *Opposite:* inept

adeptness *n* **expertise**, proficiency, skill, adroitness, aptitude, dexterity [➡ SKILLS, TALENTS, AND ABILITIES; 526]

adequacy 1 *n* **sufficiency**, ampleness, abundance [➡ ENOUGH AND SUFFICIENT; 131] *Opposite:* insufficiency 2 *n* **competence**, capability, suitability, tolerability, appropriateness, acceptability [➡ ACCEPTABLE AND PASSABLE; 219] *Opposite:* inadequacy

adequate 1 *adj* **sufficient**, ample, enough, plenty [➡ ENOUGH AND SUFFICIENT; 131] *Opposite:* insufficient 2 *adj* **passable**, satisfactory, tolerable, acceptable, suitable [➡ ACCEPTABLE AND PASSABLE; 219] *Opposite:* inadequate

adequately *adv* **sufficiently**, passably, tolerably, effectively, satisfactorily, amply [➡ APPROPRIATE, SUITABLE, AND ADVISABLE; 184] *Opposite:* inadequately

adhere 1 *v* **stick to**, follow, keep to, stand by, abide by, obey, observe [➡ OBEY AND ABIDE BY; 301] *Opposite*: abandon **2** *v* **stick**, stick on, hold fast, hold, hold on, stay, remain, cling [➡ CONTACT: HOLD; 411]

adherence *n* **devotion**, obedience, observance, loyalty, faithfulness [➡ THE WILL AND WILLINGNESS; 563] *Opposite*: disobedience

adherent *n* **supporter**, believer, devotee, advocate, fanatic, enthusiast, aficionado, aficionada, member, zealot, follower, buff [➡ DEVOTEES AND ADDICTED PEOPLE; 556] *Opposite*: opponent

adhesion *n* **union**, sticking power, hold, grip, linkage, connection [➡ CONNECTIONS; 143] *Opposite*: separation

adhesive *n* **glue**, paste, gum, epoxy resin [➡ ADHESIVES; 1271]

ad hoc *adj* **unplanned**, informal, impromptu, improvised, off-the-cuff, unprepared, extemporized, makeshift [➡ UNPLANNED AND UNEXPECTED; 281] *Opposite*: planned

adieu **1** *interj* **goodbye**, au revoir, auf Wiedersehen, bye-bye (*informal*), so long (*informal*), see you later (*informal*), ciao (*informal*), adios (*informal*), farewell (*literary*) [➡ GREETINGS, FAREWELLS, AND SALUTATIONS; 659] *Opposite*: hello **2** *n* **farewell**, goodbye, sendoff, parting, commencement address, leave-taking (*literary*), valediction (*formal*) [➡ ENDS AND DEPARTURES; 54]

a dime a dozen *adj* **commonplace**, worthless, ordinary, run of the mill, two a penny (*UK*), ten a penny (*UK*) [➡ ORDINARINESS; 244] *Opposite*: unique

ad infinitum *adv* **endlessly**, for ever, ceaselessly, repeatedly, infinitely, without end, with no sign of stopping, with no end in sight, on and on [➡ PERMANENCE: WITHOUT END; 94]

adios (*informal*) *interj* **goodbye**, au revoir, auf Wiedersehen, adieu, bye-bye (*informal*), so long (*informal*), see you later (*informal*), ciao (*informal*), farewell (*literary*) [➡ GREETINGS, FAREWELLS, AND SALUTATIONS; 659]

Adirondack chair *type of* **seating** [➡ FURNITURE; 858]

adjacent *adj* **neighboring**, nearby, bordering, next, next door, flanking, close [➡ CLOSENESS; 159] *Opposite*: distant

adjective *type of* **word class** [➡ ASPECTS OF LANGUAGE; 682]

adjoin *v* **connect**, link up, attach, affix, be close to, be next to, border [➡ EXIST IN CLOSE PROXIMITY; 21]

adjoining *adj* **touching**, attached, connecting, contiguous (*formal*) [➡ CLOSENESS; 159] *Opposite*: detached

adjourn **1** *v* **suspend**, defer, delay, postpone, put off, shelve, hold back, interrupt, recess [➡ DELAY ACTION OR OCCURRENCE; 278] **2** *v* (*informal*) **stop**, end, finish, break off, call it a day, call a halt [➡ STOP ACTING; 264]

adjournment *n* **suspension**, postponement, deferment, recess, break, interruption, delay [➡ DELAY ACTION OR OCCURRENCE; 278]

adjudge **1** *v* **judge**, find, regard as, consider, decide, believe to be, deem (*formal*) [➡ ASSESS QUALITY; 755] **2** *v* **pronounce**, rule, announce, declare, adjudicate, sentence, charge, decide [➡ TRIAL, PUNISHMENT, AND LEGAL OUTCOMES; 819]

adjudicate *v* **arbitrate**, sit in judgment, pass judgment, referee, umpire, decide, judge, settle, resolve, adjudge [➡ ASSESS QUALITY; 755]

adjudication **1** *n* **judgment**, arbitration, mediation, negotiation, intercession [➡ TRIAL, PUNISHMENT, AND LEGAL OUTCOMES; 819] **2** *n* **settlement**, decision, judgment, decree, resolution, verdict [➡ TRIAL, PUNISHMENT, AND LEGAL OUTCOMES; 819]

adjudicator *n* **judge**, arbitrator, referee, umpire, mediator, negotiator [➡ ADVISERS, JUDGES, AND ARBITERS; 971]

adjunct **1** *n* **addition**, attachment, add-on, appendage, accessory, extra, optional extra [➡ PHYSICAL OBJECTS; 1243] **2** *n* **assistant**, aide, aide-de-camp, secretary, helper, personal assistant [➡ SUBORDINATES AND ASSISTANTS; 966] **3** *type of* **grammatical term** [➡ ASPECTS OF LANGUAGE; 682]

adjure **1** *v* **command**, order, instruct, charge, demand, insist, direct (*formal*) [➡ REQUEST AND DEMAND; 663] **2** *v* **appeal**, plead, beg, request, petition, call, entreat, importune (*formal*) [➡ REQUEST AND DEMAND; 663]

adjust *v* **regulate**, alter, fiddle with, correct, fine-tune, change, bend, amend, modify, adapt, vary, tweak (*informal*) [➡ CHANGE; 372]

adjustable *adj* **adaptable**, modifiable, changeable, variable, regulating, amendable, bendable, flexible, alterable [➡ USEFULNESS; 199] *Opposite*: fixed

adjustment *n* **change**, alteration, modification, tuning, fine-tuning, regulation, correction, amendment, variation [➡ CHANGE; 372]

adjutant *n* **assistant**, aide, aide-de-camp, secretary, personal assistant, helper [➡ MILITARY PERSONNEL; 828]

ad-lib **1** *v* **improvise**, do off the cuff, extemporize, make up on the spot, do cold, invent, make up, wing it (*informal*) [➡ UTTER AND PRONOUNCE; 608] **2** *adj* **off-the-cuff**, unplanned, informal, impromptu, improvised, makeshift, spontaneous, extemporized, ad hoc, unrehearsed, unprepared, made-up [➡ UNPLANNED AND UNEXPECTED; 281] *Opposite*: rehearsed

admin *n* [➡ WORK-RELATED ACTIVITIES; 834]

administer **1** *v* **manage**, direct, run, order, control, oversee, govern, be in charge of [➡ BE IN CHARGE; 270] **2** *v* **dispense**, give out, hand out, deal out, mete out, process, dole out (*informal*) [➡ DISPENSE, RATION, AND DISTRIBUTE; 434]

administrate *v* **control**, run, manage, direct, rule, govern, oversee, supervise, be in charge of [➡ BE IN CHARGE; 270]

administration **1** *n* **management**, direction, running, government, supervision, organization, admin, paperwork [➡ WORK-RELATED ACTIVITIES; 834] **2** *n* **government**, executive, management, organization, presidency [➡ LEGISLATIVE BODIES AND LEGISLATION; 809] **3** *n* **dispensation**, meting out, giving out, handing out, dealing out, processing, doling out (*informal*) [➡ DISPENSE, RATION, AND DISTRIBUTE; 434]

administrative *adj* **managerial**, directorial, organizational, clerical, secretarial, executive, governmental [➡ TYPES OF WORK; 835]

administrator *n* **manager**, superintendent, commissioner, overseer, officer, bureaucrat, supervisor, proprietor, governor, official, executive, director [➡ POLITICAL OFFICES AND POLITICIANS; 808]

admirable *adj* **estimable**, commendable, venerable,

good, splendid, worthy, marvelous, excellent [➡ ADMIRABLE AND COMMENDABLE; 185] *Opposite*: unworthy

admiration *n* **respect**, esteem, approbation, regard, approval, appreciation, veneration, wonder, awe [➡ LOVE, RESPECT, AND GOODWILL; 549] *Opposite*: disapproval

See Compare and Contrast at **regard**.

admire *v* **regard**, esteem, approve, think highly of, respect, venerate, like, be in awe of, appreciate, marvel at [➡ LIKE, LOVE, VALUE, AND ENJOY; 578] *Opposite*: disapprove

admired *adj* **respected**, venerated, esteemed, well-regarded, revered, well-liked, appreciated, prized [➡ POPULAR AND WANTED; 220] *Opposite*: despised

admirer *n* **fan**, devotee, follower, lover, aficionado, aficionada, enthusiast, fanatic [➡ DEVOTEES AND ADDICTED PEOPLE; 556]

admiring *adj* **appreciative**, approving, complimentary, flattering, favorable, deferential, positive, sympathetic, pleased [➡ APPRECIATION AND GRATITUDE; 535] *Opposite*: disapproving

admissibility *n* **acceptability**, tolerability, permissibility [➡ ACCEPTABLE AND PASSABLE; 219]

admissible *adj* **allowable**, permissible, acceptable, tolerable [➡ ACCEPTABLE AND PASSABLE; 219] *Opposite*: inadmissible

admission **1** *n* **admittance**, entrance, right of entry, access, permission, entry [➡ PERMIT AND ALLOW; 669] *Opposite*: exclusion **2** *n* **entrance fee**, entry fee, fee, charge, price, ticket price [➡ EXPENDITURE; 423] **3** *n* **confession**, declaration, profession, divulgence, disclosure, acknowledgment, statement [➡ ADMIT AND CONFESS; 615] *Opposite*: denial

admit **1** *v* **confess**, make a clean breast, acknowledge, own up, disclose, declare, state, concede, come clean (*informal*), fess up (*slang*) [➡ ADMIT AND CONFESS; 615] *Opposite*: deny **2** *v* **let in**, allow in, give access, permit, let pass, welcome [➡ PERMIT AND ALLOW; 669] *Opposite*: bar

admit defeat *v* **pull out**, withdraw, stop, call it a day, back out, back down, give in, cave in, backpedal, climb down, give way, surrender, submit, capitulate, lay down your arms, give up, throw in the towel (*informal*) [➡ FORGET, FORGIVE, AND ACCEPT; 748] *Opposite*: persevere

admittance *n* **admission**, entry, access, right of entry, entrance, permission [➡ PERMIT AND ALLOW; 669] *Opposite*: exclusion

admittedly *adv* **certainly**, definitely, indeed, undeniably, undoubtedly, really [➡ CERTAIN; 174]

admixture *n* [➡ COLLECTIONS AND MIXTURES OF THINGS; 1244]

admonish *v* **reprove**, caution, warn, reprimand, rebuke, reproach, scold, tell off (*informal*), chew out (*informal*), chide (*literary*) [➡ ACCUSE, BLAME, AND CRITICIZE; 641] *Opposite*: praise

admonishment *n* **reprimand**, rebuke, reproach, caution, dressing-down, reproof, scolding, admonition, talking-to (*informal*), telling-off (*informal*) [➡ CRITICISMS AND ANGRY OUTBURSTS; 50] *Opposite*: approval

admonition *n* **caution**, warning, reprimand, rebuke, reproach, scolding, dressing-down, admonishment,

talking-to (*informal*), telling-off (*informal*) [➡ CRITICISMS AND ANGRY OUTBURSTS; 50] *Opposite*: approval

admonitory **1** *adj* **reproving**, reproachful, rebuking, condemnatory, critical, disapproving [➡ ACCUSATORY AND DISAPPROVING; 634] *Opposite*: approving **2** *adj* **advisory**, cautionary, warning, deterrent, instructive, advice-giving, counseling [➡ ADVISE AND WARN; 613]

ad nauseam *adv* **on and on**, for ever, endlessly, interminably, ad infinitum [➡ PERMANENCE: WITHOUT END; 94]

ado *n* **bustle**, activity, commotion, bother, excitement, upheaval, trouble, ruckus, to-do (*informal*), hoo-hah (*slang*) [➡ CHAOS AND UPROAR; 51]

adobe *n* [➡ BUILDING MATERIALS; 1077]

adolescence *n* **teens**, youth, puberty, teenage years [➡ BABYHOOD, CHILDHOOD, AND ADOLESCENCE; 917]

adolescent **1** *n* **teenager**, youth, youngster, juvenile, minor [➡ CHILD OR YOUTH; 945] **2** *adj* **teenage**, young, youthful, juvenile, pubescent, pubertal, teen (*informal*) [➡ BABYHOOD, CHILDHOOD, AND ADOLESCENCE; 917]

adopt *v* **take on**, accept, assume, approve, take up, agree, espouse, implement, embrace [➡ ACCEPT POSSESSION; 450] *Opposite*: reject

adoption *n* **acceptance**, implementation, espousal, taking on, embracing, approval, agreement, taking up, assumption [➡ APPROVE AND CONFIRM; 646] *Opposite*: rejection

adoptive *adj* **legal**, step [➡ RELATIONSHIP TO ANOTHER; 973] *Opposite*: natural

adoptive parent *type of* **older relative** [➡ OLDER GENERATION RELATIVES; 959]

adorable *adj* **lovely**, gorgeous, delightful, lovable, delectable, endearing, charming, sweet, attractive, beautiful, wonderful [➡ BEAUTY AND ATTRACTIVENESS; 189] *Opposite*: detestable

adoration **1** *n* **esteem**, high regard, respect, admiration, adulation, worship, love [➡ LOVE, RESPECT, AND GOODWILL; 549] *Opposite*: hatred **2** *n* **worship**, reverence, idolization, glorification, veneration, honor, devotion, exaltation (*formal*) [➡ RELIGIONS AND RELIGIOUS PRACTICES; 777]

adore **1** *v* **love**, esteem, respect, admire, worship, adulate [➡ LIKE, LOVE, VALUE, AND ENJOY; 578] *Opposite*: hate **2** *v* **worship**, revere, idolize, glorify, venerate, honor, exalt (*formal*) [➡ RELIGIONS AND RELIGIOUS PRACTICES; 777] **3** *v* (*informal*) **like**, be crazy about (*informal*), be stuck on (*informal*), be mad about (*informal*), be keen on (*UK*) [➡ LIKE, LOVE, VALUE, AND ENJOY; 578]

adored *adj* **revered**, venerated, worshipped, idolized, cherished, much-loved, esteemed, admired [➡ POPULAR AND WANTED; 220] *Opposite*: hated

adoring *adj* **affectionate**, loving, doting, admiring, indulgent, tender, warm [➡ APPRECIATION AND GRATITUDE; 535] *Opposite*: cold

adorn *v* **decorate**, embellish, ornament, beautify, prettify, gild, titivate, garnish, enhance [➡ DECORATE, ADORN, AND APPLY COATINGS; 405] *Opposite*: strip

adornment *n* **decoration**, embellishment, ornamentation, beautification, prettification, gilding, trimming, titivation, enhancement, garnish [➡ IMPROVE APPEARANCE; 379]

adrenaline-charged *adj* [➡ INTERESTING AND MEANINGFUL; 190]

adrenaline-fueled *adj* [➡ INTERESTING AND MEANINGFUL; 190]

adrift 1 *adj* **drifting**, floating, loose, free [➡ AIMLESS AND ERRANT MOTION; 343] *Opposite*: stationary **2** *adv* **aimless**, wandering, drifting, at loose ends, lost, purposeless, floating, directionless, in limbo [➡ AIMLESS AND ERRANT MOTION; 343] *Opposite*: focused

adroit *adj* **skillful**, nimble, practiced, able, dexterous, adept, competent, accomplished, skilled [➡ TALENTED AND SKILLFUL; 527] *Opposite*: clumsy

adroitness *n* **skillfulness**, nimbleness, ability, dexterity, cleverness, competence, adeptness, capability [➡ SKILLS, TALENTS, AND ABILITIES; 526] *Opposite*: clumsiness

a drop in the bucket *n* [➡ FEW, LITTLE, SMALL AMOUNT; 120]

a drop in the ocean (*UK*) *n* [➡ FEW, LITTLE, SMALL AMOUNT; 120]

adulate *v* **flatter**, put on a pedestal, elevate, praise, adore, lionize, worship, revere [➡ PRAISE AND ENCOURAGE; 647] *Opposite*: disparage

adulation *n* **adoration**, praise, worship, hero worship, respect, admiration, reverence, idolization, glorification, exaltation (*formal*) [➡ LOVE, RESPECT, AND GOODWILL; 549] *Opposite*: disparagement

adulatory *adj* **praising**, flattering, fawning, sycophantic, obsequious, toadying [➡ INGRATIATING, 638] *Opposite*: disparaging

adult *adj* **mature**, fully developed, grown-up, grown, full-grown [➡ ADULTHOOD; 918] *Opposite*: immature

adulterate *v* **contaminate**, taint, make impure, spoil, pollute, infect, ruin [➡ DIRTY AND CONTAMINATE; 404] *Opposite*: purify

adulteration *n* **contamination**, debasement, pollution, tarnishing, corruption, infection, sullying (*literary*) [➡ DIRTY AND CONTAMINATE; 404] *Opposite*: purification

adulterer *n* [➡ VILLAINS AND THUGS; 947]

adulterous *adj* [➡ MORALLY BAD OR IMPROPER; 775]

adultery *n* [➡ MORALLY BAD OR IMPROPER; 775]

adulthood *n* **maturity**, parenthood, middle age, old age, later life, majority [➡ ADULTHOOD; 918] *Opposite*: childhood

advance 1 *v* **go forward**, move forward, move ahead, press forward, move on, proceed, progress, go ahead, press on [➡ PROCEED AND GO; 305] *Opposite*: retreat **2** *v* **improve**, enhance, take forward, increase, expand, progress, further, build up [➡ IMPROVE SOMETHING; 374] *Opposite*: regress **3** *n* **development**, improvement, spread, progress, expansion, encroachment, innovation, enhancement, increase [➡ PROGRESS AND ADVANCEMENT; 213] *Opposite*: decline **4** *n* **loan**, early payment, fee, money up front [➡ ACCOUNTING, BANKING, AND BUDGETING; 799]

advanced 1 *adj* **higher**, developed, sophisticated, complex, difficult [➡ POSITIVELY COMPLEX OR COMPLICATED; 217] *Opposite*: basic **2** *adj* **later**, far along, well along, far ahead, well ahead, future [➡ FUTURE; 86] *Opposite*: earlier **3** *adj* **pro-**

gressive, forward-thinking, unconventional, cutting-edge, innovative, forward-looking, radical [➡ POSITIVELY COMPLEX OR COMPLICATED; 217] *Opposite*: traditional

advancement *n* **progression**, progress, development, improvement, spread, expansion, encroachment, innovation, increase [➡ PROGRESS AND ADVANCEMENT; 213] *Opposite*: decline

advantage *n* **benefit**, gain, lead, pro, improvement, help, plus (*informal*) [➡ SOURCE OF HAPPINESS, PLEASURE, OR IMPROVEMENT; 209] *Opposite*: disadvantage

advantageous *adj* **beneficial**, helpful, useful, to your advantage, valuable, gainful, profitable, expedient, strategic [➡ USEFULNESS; 199] *Opposite*: disadvantageous

advent *n* **arrival**, start, beginning, coming on, dawn, initiation, introduction [➡ BEGINNINGS; 53] *Opposite*: departure

adventure *n* **escapade**, exploit, quest, venture, exploration, undertaking, voyage [➡ EVENTS AND OCCURRENCES; 35]

adventure movie *n* [➡ FILM; 901]

adventure playground *n* [➡ URBAN OUTDOOR SPACES; 1072]

adventurer 1 *n* **explorer**, traveler, voyager, buccaneer, swashbuckler, fortune hunter [➡ TRAVEL: TRAVELERS AND WALKERS; 319] **2** *n* **entrepreneur**, investor, speculator, trailblazer, pioneer, opportunist [➡ BUSINESS PEOPLE; 793]

adventuresome *adj* **risk-taking**, carefree, daring, thrill-seeking, adventurous, bold, audacious, brave, exploratory, courageous, venturesome (*formal*) [➡ COURAGE; 498] *Opposite*: unadventurous

adventurous *adj* **daring**, bold, audacious, brave, courageous, carefree, risk-taking, thrill-seeking, adventuresome, venturesome (*formal*) [➡ COURAGE; 498] *Opposite*: unadventurous

adverb *type of* **word class** [➡ ASPECTS OF LANGUAGE; 682]

adversarial *adj* **confrontational**, argumentative, combative, antagonistic, oppositional, accusatorial (*formal*) [➡ AGGRESSIVE AND BELLIGERENT; 518] *Opposite*: cooperative

adversary *n* **opponent**, challenger, rival, enemy, antagonist, opposition, foe (*formal*) [➡ ENEMIES AND TORMENTORS; 969] *Opposite*: supporter

adverse 1 *adj* **opposing**, contrary, hostile, adversative, antagonistic, adversarial, confrontational, argumentative, oppositional [➡ DISHARMONY; 156] *Opposite*: cooperative **2** *adj* **unfavorable**, unpleasant, poor, difficult, unhelpful, undesirable, unsympathetic, harmful [➡ DANGEROUS; 236] *Opposite*: favorable

adversely *adv* **unfavorably**, harmfully, badly, unpleasantly, poorly, unhelpfully, undesirably, unsympathetically, negatively [➡ DANGEROUS; 236] *Opposite*: favorably

adversity *n* **hardship**, difficulty, danger, misfortune, harsh conditions, hard times [➡ DIFFICULT SITUATIONS; 72] *Opposite*: privilege

advertise 1 *v* **promote**, publicize, market, present, push, puff [➡ ADVERTISING AND PUBLICITY; 604] **2** *v* **announce**, broadcast, make known, make public, shout from the rooftops, spread around, shout out, publicize, spread abroad (*UK*) [➡ INFORM, ANNOUNCE, AND ISSUE; 611] *Opposite*: keep under wraps

advertisement *n* **ad**, announcement, poster, billboard, commercial, classified ad, public notice, flier, trailer, want ad (*informal*), hoarding (*UK*), personal ad (*UK*) [➡ ADVERTISING AND PUBLICITY; 604]

advertiser *n* **publicist**, promoter, backer, supporter, advocate, seller [➡ BUSINESS PEOPLE; 793]

advertising *n* **publicity**, promotion, marketing, publicizing, public relations, P.R. [➡ ADVERTISING AND PUBLICITY; 604]

advice **1** *n* **recommendation**, suggestion, guidance, opinion, counsel (*formal or literary*) [➡ ADVICE; 689] *Opposite*: warning **2** *n* **information**, guidance, instruction, assistance, intelligence, news [➡ BASIC DETAILS; 688]

advisability *n* **wisdom**, prudence, sense, desirability, suitability [➡ APPROPRIATE, SUITABLE, AND ADVISABLE; 184] *Opposite*: foolishness

advisable *adj* **sensible**, wise, prudent, worthwhile, desirable, suitable, logical, sagacious, judicious [➡ APPROPRIATE, SUITABLE, AND ADVISABLE; 184] *Opposite*: unwise

advise **1** *v* **recommend**, direct, guide, instruct, warn, opine (*formal*), counsel (*formal or literary*) [➡ ADVISE AND WARN; 613] **2** *v* **inform**, let know, make aware, notify, instruct, tell [➡ INFORM, ANNOUNCE, AND ISSUE; 611]

See Compare and Contrast at **recommend**.

advisedly *adv* **deliberately**, carefully, purposefully, on purpose, with intent, intentionally, purposely [➡ INTENTIONAL AND DELIBERATE; 279] *Opposite*: carelessly

adviser *n* **consultant**, counselor, advice-giver, guru [➡ ADVISERS, JUDGES, AND ARBITERS; 971]

advisory *adj* **advice-giving**, consultative, counseling, review [➡ ADVISE AND WARN; 613]

advocacy *n* **support**, encouragement, backing, sponsorship, promotion, activism [➡ APPROVE AND CONFIRM; 646] *Opposite*: opposition

advocacy group *n* **alliance**, association, society, cartel, trade union, league, pressure group, lobby group, lobby, faction, group [➡ GROUPS WITH A COMMON INTEREST; 938]

advocate **1** *v* **support**, encourage, back, promote, be in favor of, sponsor [➡ APPROVE AND CONFIRM; 646] *Opposite*: discourage **2** *n* **supporter**, backer, promoter, believer, activist, campaigner, sponsor [➡ DEVOTEES AND ADDICTED PEOPLE; 556] *Opposite*: opponent

See Compare and Contrast at **recommend**.

aegis *n* **auspices**, sponsorship, guidance, protection, support, tutelage [➡ RESPONSIBILITY; 170]

aeons *n* [➡ LONG PERIODS OF TIME; 92]

aerate *v* **ventilate**, let breathe, expose, freshen [➡ CLEAN AND POLISH; 403] *Opposite*: close up

aeration *n* **ventilation**, airing, freshening [➡ HEATING, REFRIGERATION, AND VENTILATION; 1142]

aerial *adj* **midair**, airborne, above ground, in-flight, floating [➡ GENERAL LOCATIONS; 158] *Opposite*: terrestrial

aerie **1** *type of* **den or nest** [➡ ANIMAL OR BIRD ACCOMMODATIONS; 1079] **2** *n* **sanctuary**, hideaway, refuge, stronghold [➡ SAFE BUILDINGS OR PLACES; 1093]

aerobatics *n* **stunts**, maneuvers, aerial tricks [➡ HOBBIES, GAMES, AND SPORTS; 875]

aerobics *n* **exercises**, calisthenics, workout [➡ HOBBIES, GAMES, AND SPORTS; 875]

aerodrome (*UK*) *n* **airfield**, airport, landing strip, landing field, airstrip, air base, airdrome [➡ AIRWAYS; 1109]

aerodynamic *adj* **sleek**, smooth, slick, sweptback, clean, flowing [➡ ROUNDED SHAPE; 1218]

aerogram *n* **air letter**, airmail letter, aerogramme [➡ LETTERS AND WRITTEN MESSAGES; 584]

aerogramme *see* **aerogram**

aeronaut *n* [➡ DRIVERS; 1153]

aeroplane (*UK*) *n* **aircraft**, plane, airplane [➡ AIRCRAFT; 1148]

aerosol *n* **spray can**, spray, atomizer, mister [➡ CONTAINERS, RECEPTACLES, AND PACKAGING; 1245]

aerospace *n* **atmosphere**, upper atmosphere, space, troposphere, stratosphere, mesosphere, thermosphere, exosphere [➡ THE EARTH'S ATMOSPHERE; 1040]

aesthete *n* **art lover**, aesthetician, connoisseur, cognoscente [➡ PLEASURE-SEEKERS AND HEDONISTS; 886]

aesthetic *adj* **artistic**, visual, appealing, beautiful [➡ ARTISTIC MOVEMENTS AND STYLES; 899]

afar (*literary*) *adv* **far afield**, in the distance, far away, far and wide, far-off, far [➡ DISTANCE; 160] *Opposite*: nearby

a few *pron* **a small number**, some, one or two, not many, handful, hardly any [➡ FEW, LITTLE, SMALL AMOUNT; 120] *Opposite*: many

affability *n* **friendliness**, sociability, cordiality, joviality, gregariousness, pleasantness, warmth [➡ FRIENDLINESS AND SOCIABILITY; 494] *Opposite*: unfriendliness

affable *adj* **genial**, pleasant, friendly, sociable, jovial, gregarious, cordial, warm, easygoing [➡ FRIENDLINESS AND SOCIABILITY; 494] *Opposite*: unfriendly

affair *n* **matter**, issue, concern, business, situation, event, thing [➡ SITUATIONS; 71]

affairs *n* **business**, matters, dealings, activities, concerns, undertakings [➡ ACTIONS OR UNDERTAKINGS; 259]

affect **1** *v* **influence**, involve, shape, concern, change, modify, alter [➡ CHANGE; 372] **2** *v* **touch**, move, disturb, mark, distress, upset, shake [➡ UPSET, DISTRESS, AND HUMILIATE; 567] **3** *v* **assume**, put on, imitate, fake, adopt, pretend [➡ PRETEND AND MIMIC; 60]

affectation **1** *n* **showing off**, pretension, exaggeration, artificiality, affectedness, pretentiousness, artifice (*formal*) [➡ AFFECTATION, SELF-SATISFACTION, AND SNOBBISHNESS; 507] *Opposite*: naturalness **2** *n* **mannerism**, way, quirk, show, trait, habit, characteristic [➡ TEMPERAMENT AND BEHAVIOR; 492]

affected *adj* **pretentious**, artificial, exaggerated, unnatural, precious, la-di-da (*informal*) [➡ AFFECTATION, SELF-SATISFACTION, AND SNOBBISHNESS; 507] *Opposite*: natural

affectedness *n* **exaggeration**, pretension, artificiality, affectation, showing off, artifice (*formal*) [➡ AFFECTATION, SELF-SATISFACTION, AND SNOBBISHNESS; 507] *Opposite*: naturalness

affecting *adj* **moving**, touching, upsetting, distressing, disturbing, heartrending, heartwarming, affective [➡ EMOTIONALLY UNPLEASANT AND UPSETTING; 227]

affection *n* **liking**, fondness, warmth, friendliness, care, regard [➡ LOVE, RESPECT, AND GOODWILL; 549] *Opposite*: dislike

See Compare and Contrast at **love**.

affectionate *adj* **loving**, demonstrative, warm, friendly, kind, caring [➡ FRIENDLINESS AND SOCIABILITY; 494] *Opposite*: cold

affective *adj* **emotional**, sentimental, moving, touching, affecting, disturbing [➡ EMOTIONALLY UNPLEASANT AND UPSETTING; 227]

affenpinscher *type of* **small dog** [➡ DOGS; 980]

affianced (*formal*) *adj* **engaged**, attached, promised, spoken for, involved, betrothed (*formal*) [➡ MARITAL STATUS; 890] *Opposite*: unattached

affidavit *n* **sworn statement**, official declaration, affirmation, confirmation, proclamation, confession, document, legal instrument [➡ OFFICIAL DOCUMENTS; 586]

affiliate 1 *v* **link**, connect, join, associate, belong to, conglomerate [➡ CREATING CONNECTIONS; 144] 2 *n* **associate**, partner, colleague, member [➡ SUBORDINATES AND ASSISTANTS; 966]

affiliated *adj* [➡ RELATED; 142]

affiliation *n* **association**, relationship, connection, attachment, membership, link [➡ CONNECTIONS; 143]

affinity 1 *n* **empathy**, sympathy, fellow feeling, attraction, kinship, like-mindedness [➡ LOVE, RESPECT, AND GOODWILL; 549] *Opposite*: indifference 2 *n* **similarity**, resemblance, likeness, correspondence [➡ SIMILARITY; 148] *Opposite*: difference

affirm 1 *v* **assert**, insist, establish, state, verify, announce, pronounce, acknowledge, avow (*formal*) [➡ CLAIM, INSIST, AND EMPHASIZE; 614] 2 *v* **support**, confirm, encourage, sustain, uphold [➡ APPROVE AND CONFIRM; 646]

affirmation *n* **assertion**, confirmation, pronouncement, declaration, announcement, statement, verification, avowal (*formal*) [➡ INFORM, ANNOUNCE, AND ISSUE; 611] *Opposite*: denial

affirmative *adj* **assenting**, positive, confirmatory, agreeing, favorable [➡ EXPRESSING RESPECT AND APPROVAL; 637] *Opposite*: negative

affix 1 *v* **attach**, fix, fasten, stick, pin, glue [➡ FASTEN, LINK, AND JOIN; 408] *Opposite*: remove 2 *type of* **grammatical term** [➡ ASPECTS OF LANGUAGE; 682]

afflict *v* **trouble**, bother, affect, worry, distress, vex, upset [➡ UPSET, DISTRESS, AND HUMILIATE; 567]

afflicted *adj* **distressed**, aggrieved, stricken, plagued, tormented, hurt, suffering [➡ SADNESS, DISTRESS, AND DESPAIR; 539]

affliction 1 *n* **suffering**, difficulty, burden, problem, hardship, pain, trouble, misery, misfortune [➡ NUISANCES; 253] 2 *n* **illness**, sickness, disease, condition, disorder, complaint, infirmity, weakness [➡ ILLNESSES AND DISORDERS; 732]

affluence *n* **riches**, prosperity, material comfort, privileged circumstances, wealth, comfortable circumstances (*UK*) [➡ WEALTH AND WEALTHY; 891] *Opposite*: poverty

affluent *adj* **rich**, wealthy, well-off, well-to-do, prosperous, comfortable, born with a silver spoon in your mouth, well-heeled (*informal*) [➡ WEALTH AND WEALTHY; 891] *Opposite*: poor

afford 1 *v* **pay for**, have the funds for, manage to pay for, find the money for, come up with the money for, meet the expense of [➡ PURCHASE; 422] 2 *v* (*formal*) **give**, offer, present, allow, provide [➡ GIVE AND PROVIDE; 430]

affordable *adj* **reasonable**, within your means, inexpensive, cheap [➡ CHEAP AND INEXPENSIVE; 221] *Opposite*: expensive

afforest *v* **reforest**, tree-plant [➡ GROW AND CULTIVATE; 351] *Opposite*: deforest

affray *n* **scuffle**, fight, brawl, disturbance, commotion, tussle, donnybrook [➡ AGGRESSIVE EVENTS; 39] *Opposite*: agreement

affront 1 *n* **insult**, injury, slur, slight, outrage [➡ INSULTS, ABUSE, AND SWEARING; 658] *Opposite*: compliment 2 *v* **offend**, insult, upset, outrage, slight, disrespect [➡ INSULTS, ABUSE, AND SWEARING; 658] *Opposite*: compliment

affronted *adj* **insulted**, injured, slighted, disrespected, upset, outraged, in a huff (*informal*) [➡ SADNESS, DISTRESS, AND DESPAIR; 539] *Opposite*: pleased

Afghan hound *type of* **large dog** [➡ DOGS; 980]

afghani *type of* **currency** [➡ CURRENCIES; 798]

aficionada *n* **devotee**, enthusiast, adherent, fanatic, fan, addict, admirer, buff [➡ DEVOTEES AND ADDICTED PEOPLE; 556]

aficionado *n* **devotee**, enthusiast, adherent, fanatic, fan, addict, admirer, buff [➡ DEVOTEES AND ADDICTED PEOPLE; 556]

afire *see* **aflame**

aflame 1 *adj* **on fire**, burning, in flames, afire, ablaze [➡ FIRE, FLAMMABILITY, AND BURNING; 1165] *Opposite*: extinguished 2 *adj* **fired up**, enthusiastic, passionate, excited, fired, eager, avid, afire [➡ PLEASURE, EXCITEMENT, AND ELATION; 534] *Opposite*: apathetic

afloat *adj* **flooded**, awash, inundated, under water, submerged, swilling [➡ WET; 1240] *Opposite*: dry

aflutter *adv* **agitated**, excited, trembling, aquiver, nervous, keyed up (*informal*) [➡ PLEASURE, EXCITEMENT, AND ELATION; 534] *Opposite*: calm

afoot *adj* **happening**, going on, occurring, taking place, up, in the works, stirring, in the wind (*UK*) [➡ HAPPENING AND IN PROGRESS; 32]

aforementioned (*formal*) *adj* **above-mentioned**, said, aforesaid (*formal*) [➡ EXPRESSIONS OF REFERENCE; 63]

aforesaid (*formal*) *see* **aforementioned**

afraid *adj* **frightened**, fearful, terrified, petrified, scared, anxious [➡ FEAR AND PANIC; 543] *Opposite*: unafraid

afresh *adv* **anew**, again, once again, once more, over, another time [➡ AGAIN; 109]

African violet *type of* **perennial flower** [➡ FLOWERS; 1032]

Afro *type of* **hairstyle** [➡ HAIRSTYLES AND HAIRPIECES; 488]

afrobeat *type of* **world music** [➡ MUSIC, SONGS, AND SINGING; 907]

after **1** *prep* **later than**, past, gone [➡ AFTER, LAST, AND FOLLOWING; 165] *Opposite*: before **2** *prep* **behind**, following, to the rear of, next to [➡ RELATIVE LOCATION; 161] *Opposite*: ahead of **3** *prep* **in pursuit of**, in search of, in quest of, following, on the trail of, on the heels of [➡ DESIRE AND WANT; 579] **4** *prep* **regarding**, considering, taking into account, with, bearing in mind, taking into consideration [➡ RELATED; 142] **5** *prep* **following**, subsequent to [➡ AFTER, LAST, AND FOLLOWING; 165] *Opposite*: before **6** *prep* **in the manner of**, in imitation of, in the style of, similar to, like, in the same way as, à la [➡ SIMILARITY; 148] **7** *adv* **afterward**, subsequently, later, next [➡ AFTER, LAST, AND FOLLOWING; 165] *Opposite*: before **8** *conj* **when**, once, as soon as [➡ AFTER, LAST, AND FOLLOWING; 165] *Opposite*: before

after all *adv* **on balance**, finally, in the end, in spite of everything, nevertheless, in any case, all together, taken together [➡ ALTHOUGH, NEVERTHELESS, AND DESPITE; 169]

aftercare **1** *n* **post-operative care**, post-hospital care, home care, rehabilitation, rehab (*informal*) [➡ HEALING; 730] **2** *n* **support**, assistance, help, upkeep, maintenance, post sales service, aftersales service (*UK*) [➡ BUSINESS ACTIVITIES AND PHENOMENA; 794]

aftereffect *n* **repercussion**, reverberation, aftermath, aftershock, final outcome, end result, byproduct, side effect, consequence, effect, result, outcome [➡ RESULTS AND OUTCOMES; 83] *Opposite*: precursor

afterglow *n* **warmth**, glow, serenity, exhilaration, feel-good factor [➡ PLEASURE, EXCITEMENT, AND ELATION; 534]

afterlife *n* **afterworld**, next world, life after death, eternal life, spirit world, happy hunting ground, sweet hereafter (*formal*), hereafter (*formal*) [➡ RELIGIOUS CONCEPTS; 776]

aftermath *n* **result**, consequences, outcome, upshot, repercussion, aftereffects, aftershock, reverberation, end result [➡ RESULTS AND OUTCOMES; 83]

afternoon *n* **after lunch**, p.m., early afternoon, mid-afternoon, late afternoon, early evening [➡ TIMES OF DAY; 87] *Opposite*: morning

aftershave *n* [➡ PERSONAL HYGIENE; 491]

aftershock *n* [➡ RESULTS AND OUTCOMES; 83]

aftertaste *n* [➡ TASTE; 703]

after that *adv* **next**, afterward, later, subsequently, then [➡ AFTER, LAST, AND FOLLOWING; 165] *Opposite*: before

afterthought *n* **addition**, postscript, extra, addendum, reflection, second thought, reconsideration [➡ IDEAS AND THOUGHTS; 770]

afterward *adv* **next**, after that, later, subsequently, then [➡ AFTER, LAST, AND FOLLOWING; 165] *Opposite*: before

afterworld *n* **afterlife**, next world, life after death, eternal life, spirit world, happy hunting ground, here-

after (*formal*), sweet hereafter (*formal*) [➡ RELIGIOUS CONCEPTS; 776]

again *adv* **once more**, another time, yet again, over, over again, all over again, for a second time, once again [➡ AGAIN; 109]

again and again *adv* **repeatedly**, many times, over and over, time and again, persistently, over and over again, continually, continuously [➡ AGAIN; 109] *Opposite*: once

against **1** *prep* **in opposition to**, not in favor, hostile, critical, opposed, versus, anti (*informal*) [➡ UNWILLINGNESS AND STUBBORNNESS; 564] **2** *prep* **next to**, alongside, beside, touching, adjacent to, aligned with [➡ CLOSENESS; 159] **3** *prep* **in contradiction of**, contrary to, counter to, in contrast to, compared to [➡ OPPOSITE; 157]

against the law *adj* [➡ ILLEGAL; 816]

agape (*literary*) **1** *adj* **wide open**, open, ajar [➡ ORIENTATION AND ALIGNMENT; 1223] *Opposite*: closed **2** *adj* **astonished**, amazed, open-mouthed, agog, surprised, shocked [➡ PLEASURE, EXCITEMENT, AND ELATION; 534] *Opposite*: unaffected

agate *type of* **gemstone** [➡ PRECIOUS STONES; 1278]

age **1** *n* **era**, period, time, times, epoch [➡ EPOCHS AND ERAS; 89] **2** *n* **time of life**, stage, phase, stage of development, oldness [➡ THE STAGES OF LIFE; 916] **3** *v* **mature**, grow older, grow up, get on, advance in years [➡ CHANGE; 372]

aged *adj* **old**, elderly, matured, ripened, hoary, venerable, ancient [➡ OLD AGE; 919] *Opposite*: young

age group *n* **generation**, cohort, age range, age bracket, contemporaries [➡ GROUPS OF PEOPLE; 935]

ageless **1** *adj* **youthful**, fresh, unfading, unspoiled [➡ NEW, MODERN; 166] **2** *adj* **timeless**, endless, perpetual, everlasting, infinite, unending [➡ PERMANENCE: WITHOUT END; 94]

agency **1** *n* **organization**, bureau, society, charity, group, outfit (*informal*) [➡ INSTITUTIONS; 790] **2** *n* **activity**, action, work, intervention, help, support, assistance [➡ CAUSATION; 168]

agenda *n* **program**, schedule, plan, outline, memo, schema, itinerary [➡ LISTS AND SCHEDULES; 587]

agent **1** *n* **go-between**, manager, negotiator, mediator, representative, proxy [➡ REPRESENTATIVES AND PATRONS; 968] **2** *n* **cause**, means, driving force, instrument, vehicle, driver [➡ CAUSATION; 168]

agent provocateur *n* [➡ THE POLICE, ARREST, AND PRETRIAL PROCEEDINGS; 818]

age-old *adj* **ancient**, old, long-standing, venerable, hoary [➡ OLD, OLD-FASHIONED; 167] *Opposite*: recent

ages (*informal*) *n* **eternity**, days, eons, weeks, months, years, forever (*informal*), centuries (*informal*) [➡ LONG PERIODS OF TIME; 92] *Opposite*: moment

agglomeration *n* **accumulation**, mass, collection, cluster, group [➡ COLLECTIONS AND MIXTURES OF THINGS; 1244]

agglutinate *v* **adhere**, stick, clump, join, cling, cohere (*formal*) [➡ COMBINE AND MIX; 400] *Opposite*: separate

agglutination *n* **accretion**, cohesion, adhesion, clumping, joining [➡ COMBINE AND MIX; 400]

aide-de-camp *n* **assistant**, personal assistant, aide, secretary, helper, administrative assistant, staffer (*informal*), PA (*UK*) [➞ MILITARY PERSONNEL; 828]

aide-mémoire (*formal*) **1** *n* **summary**, outline, résumé, synopsis, digest, note [➞ SUMMARIES, OUTLINES, AND EXCERPTS; 588] **2** *n* **memory aid**, mnemonic, note, reminder, memorandum, outline, crib sheet, crib (*informal*) [➞ LETTERS AND WRITTEN MESSAGES; 584]

aid organization *n* [➞ CHARITY AND CHARITABLE INSTITUTIONS; 822]

aikido *type of* **combat sport** [➞ HOBBIES, GAMES, AND SPORTS; 875]

ail (*archaic or literary*) **1** *v* **trouble**, pain, distress, be wrong with, affect, afflict, be the matter with, bother, upset, worry [➞ UPSET, DISTRESS, AND HUMILIATE; 567] **2** *v* **be ill**, be sick, feel unwell, suffer, be in pain, feel pain, be weak, nauseate [➞ BECOME SICK, TREAT, AND RECOVER; 728]

aileron *part of* **aircraft** [➞ AIRCRAFT; 1148]

ailing 1 *adj* **underperforming**, failing, deteriorating, inadequate [➞ UNSUCCESSFUL AND UNPROMISING; 76] *Opposite*: thriving **2** *adj* (*dated*) **unwell**, ill, sick, unfit, laid up, under the weather, infirm, sickly, indisposed (*formal*) [➞ ILL AND SICK; 740] *Opposite*: well

ailment *n* **illness**, sickness, disease, disorder, complaint, weakness, condition, infirmity [➞ ILLNESSES AND DISORDERS; 732]

ailurophobia *type of* **phobia** [➞ FEARS AND PHOBIAS; 554]

aim 1 *v* **aspire**, plan, intend, try, mean, want, seek, set your sights on, have your sights on, strive for, endeavor (*formal*) [➞ ATTEMPT AN ACTION; 261] **2** *v* **point toward**, point, take aim, direct, mark, target, zero in, train, level [➞ MOVE SOMETHING INTO A NEW POSITION OR OVERTURN; 330] **3** *n* **goal**, purpose, intention, object, objective, target, ambition, wish, aspiration [➞ INTENTIONS AND PURPOSES; 772]

aimless *adj* **pointless**, meaningless, useless, worthless, purposeless, directionless [➞ LACK OF COMMITMENT AND UNRELIABILITY; 509] *Opposite*: purposeful

aimlessness *n* **pointlessness**, purposelessness, senselessness [➞ REDUNDANT AND USELESS; 240] *Opposite*: purposefulness

aioli *type of* **seasonings, sauces, and dips** [➞ SEASONINGS AND SAUCES; 1174]

air 1 *n* **atmosphere**, space, sky, heaven [➞ THE EARTH'S ATMOSPHERE; 1040] **2** *n* **appearance**, look, manner, tone, way of being, feeling, impression, aura, quality [➞ APPEARANCE AND ATMOSPHERE; 1237] **3** *n* **tune**, melody, song [➞ MUSIC, SONGS, AND SINGING; 907] **4** *v* **declare**, express, vent, make public, proclaim, reveal, publicize, spread, circulate, tell, announce, broadcast [➞ INFORM, ANNOUNCE, AND ISSUE; 611] *Opposite*: suppress **5** *v* **ventilate**, aerate, expose [➞ CLEAN AND POLISH; 403]

air bladder *part of* **fish** [➞ PARTS OF A FISH; 1011]

airborne *adj* **flying**, aerial, floating, midair, in-flight, above ground, on high, aloft [➞ GENERAL LOCATIONS; 158]

airborne army *n* [➞ THE ARMED FORCES; 827]

airborne operation *n* [➞ WARFARE AND WAR; 830]

air brake *part of* **aircraft** [➞ AIRCRAFT; 1148]

airbrush *v* **spraypaint**, color, blend, blend in, touch up, cover up, doctor, mask, conceal, paint, spray [➞ DECORATE, ADORN, AND APPLY COATINGS; 405]

air-circulation system *n* [➞ HEATING, REFRIGERATION, AND VENTILATION; 1142]

air conditioned *adj* **cooled**, ventilated, well-ventilated, cool, chilled [➞ HEATING, REFRIGERATION, AND VENTILATION; 1142] *Opposite*: heated

air conditioner *n* **air cooler**, air exchanger, ventilator, dehumidifier, extractor, AC [➞ HEATING, REFRIGERATION, AND VENTILATION; 1142] *Opposite*: heater

air conditioning *n* **air-cooling system**, ventilation system, air-circulation system, air exchange system, climate control [➞ HEATING, REFRIGERATION, AND VENTILATION; 1142] *Opposite*: heating

air cooler *type of* **cooling appliance** [➞ HEATING, REFRIGERATION, AND VENTILATION; 1142]

air-cooling system *n* [➞ HEATING, REFRIGERATION, AND VENTILATION; 1142]

aircraft *n* **airplane**, plane, flying machine, aeroplane (*UK*) [➞ AIRCRAFT; 1148]

---

aircraft

◆ *types of civil aircraft*
airliner, airship, autogiro, biplane, blimp, dirigible, executive jet, glider, hang glider, helicopter, jet, light plane, monoplane, paraglider, seaplane, skiplane, STOL, ultralight, zeppelin

◆ *types of military aircraft*
bomber, convertiplane, fighter, fighter-bomber, helicopter gunship, stealth bomber, transport, VTOL

◆ *parts of an aircraft*
aileron, air brake, autopilot, cabin, cockpit, ejection seat, fin, flight deck, flight recorder, fuselage, jet engine, joystick, landing gear, nose cone, nose wheel, propeller, rotor, rudder, tail, tailplane, tail rotor, turbofan, turbojet, turboprop, undercarriage, wing

---

aircraft carrier *type of* **military vessel** [➞ SHIPS AND BOATS; 1150]

airdrop *v* **parachute in**, airlift, send in, parachute, drop [➞ DISPATCH AND SEND; 333]

air duct *n* [➞ HEATING, REFRIGERATION, AND VENTILATION; 1142]

airedale *type of* **small dog** [➞ DOGS; 980]

air exchanger *type of* **cooling appliance** [➞ HEATING, REFRIGERATION, AND VENTILATION; 1142]

air exchange system *n* [➞ HEATING, REFRIGERATION, AND VENTILATION; 1142]

airfare *n* **fare**, tariff, charge, ticket price, seat rate [➞ FUNDS, PAYMENTS, AND CHARGES; 800]

airfield *n* **airstrip**, landing field, landing strip, airdrome, airport, air base, aerodrome (*UK*) [➞ AIRWAYS; 1109]

airfoil *part of* **external structure** [➞ EXTERNAL PARTS OF A VEHICLE; 1147]

air force *n* [➞ THE ARMED FORCES; 827]

airily *adv* **lightheartedly**, lightly, carelessly, casually, easily, brightly, cheerfully, gaily [➡ GOOD-TEMPERED AND HUMOROUS; 627] *Opposite*: seriously

airiness 1 *n* **lightheartedness**, buoyancy, animation, vivacity, cheerfulness, casualness, brightness, gaiety [➡ GOOD-TEMPERED AND HUMOROUS; 627] *Opposite*: seriousness 2 *n* **spaciousness**, openness, freshness, lightness [➡ LARGE; 1193] *Opposite*: closeness

airing 1 *n* **ventilation**, aeration, exposure to air, drying, freshening [➡ HEATING, REFRIGERATION, AND VENTILATION; 1142] 2 *n* **outing**, trip, excursion [➡ TRAVEL: JOURNEYS AND TRIPS; 318] 3 *n* **exposure**, expression, disclosure, divulgence, ventilation, discussion [➡ NEGOTIATION AND DEBATE; 46]

airless *adj* **stuffy**, close, muggy, unventilated, oppressive, heavy, stifling [➡ PHYSICALLY UNPLEASANT; 226] *Opposite*: airy

airlift *v* **fly**, transfer, winch, lift [➡ DISPATCH AND SEND; 333]

airline *n* **air company**, commercial airline, scheduled carrier, carrier [➡ AIRCRAFT; 1148]

airliner *type of* **civil aircraft** [➡ AIRCRAFT; 1148]

airlock 1 *n* **compartment**, cubicle, cell, chamber [➡ TYPES OF ROOMS; 1097] 2 *n* **blockage**, obstruction, air bubble, occlusion, block, obstacle [➡ PROBLEMS; 256]

airmail *v* **mail**, send, dispatch, post (*UK*) [➡ DISPATCH AND SEND; 333]

air offensive *n* [➡ WARFARE AND WAR; 830]

air pistol *type of* **gun** [➡ WEAPONS FOR SHOOTING; 1156]

airplane *n* **aircraft**, plane, aeroplane (*UK*) [➡ AIRCRAFT; 1148]

airplay *n* **airtime**, playing time, exposure, promotion, publicity, broadcast, plugging (*informal*) [➡ TELEVISION AND RADIO; 606]

airport *n* **airfield**, airdrome, airstrip, landing field, landing strip, aerodrome (*UK*) [➡ AIRWAYS; 1109]

airpower *n* **air strength**, airborne army, air defense, air force [➡ THE ARMED FORCES; 827]

air raid *n* **aerial attack**, aerial bombardment, air attack, bombing, air strike, air offensive, attack, raid, offensive [➡ AGGRESSIVE EVENTS; 39]

air rifle *type of* **gun** [➡ WEAPONS FOR SHOOTING; 1156]

air sac *part of* **respiratory system** [➡ RESPIRATORY ORGANS; 715]

airship *n* **dirigible**, zeppelin, blimp, aircraft [➡ AIRCRAFT; 1148]

airshow *n* **aerobatics**, flyover, stunts, show, exhibition [➡ PERFORMANCES AND SHOWS; 42]

airsick *adj* **nauseous**, queasy, sick, ill, motion sick [➡ ILL AND SICK; 740]

airsickness *n* **motion sickness**, nausea, queasiness, sickness [➡ ILL AND SICK; 740]

airspace *n* **territory**, skies, boundaries, limits, flight exclusion zone, no-fly-zone [➡ AIRWAYS; 1109]

air strike *n* **aerial attack**, aerial bombardment, bombing, air raid, air offensive, attack, raid, offensive [➡ AGGRESSIVE EVENTS; 39]

airstrip *n* **runway**, landing strip, strip, landing field, airfield [➡ AIRWAYS; 1109]

airtight 1 *adj* **sealed**, hermetically sealed, hermetic, impermeable [➡ IN GOOD REPAIR; 1232] 2 *adj* **sound**, strong, unquestionable, unassailable, watertight, flawless [➡ CERTAIN; 174] *Opposite*: vulnerable

airwaves *n* **radio waves**, frequencies, frequency bands, radio frequencies, broadcasting frequencies, radio signals [➡ TELEVISION AND RADIO; 606]

airway 1 *n* **airline**, air transport company, air network [➡ AIRWAYS; 1109] 2 *n* **air route**, air corridor, flight lane, air lane, route, flight path [➡ AIRWAYS; 1109] 3 *part of* **respiratory system** [➡ RESPIRATORY ORGANS; 715]

airworthiness *n* **safety**, soundness, reliability, working order [➡ SAFE AND SAFETY; 191]

airworthy *adj* **flyable**, flightworthy, in working order, in good order, safe, sound, reliable [➡ SAFE AND SAFETY; 191]

airy 1 *adj* **roomy**, ventilated, fresh, light, open, spacious [➡ LARGE; 1193] *Opposite*: stuffy 2 *adj* **unconcerned**, nonchalant, casual, light, carefree, lighthearted, buoyant, vivacious, cheerful, blithe (*literary*) [➡ GOOD-TEMPERED AND HUMOROUS; 627] *Opposite*: serious

aisle *n* **passageway**, gangway, walkway, passage, corridor, lane [➡ DOORS AND ACCESS POINTS; 1101]

ajar *adj* **half closed**, open, agape (*literary*) [➡ ORIENTATION AND ALIGNMENT; 1223]

a.k.a. *adj* **also known as**, better known as, otherwise known as, known to you and me as, alias, or [➡ NAME AND DESCRIBE; 665]

akin *adj* **similar**, of the same kind, parallel, like, analogous, alike, affiliated [➡ SIMILARITY; 148] *Opposite*: unlike

alabaster *type of* **stone** [➡ STONES, ROCKS, AND BOULDERS; 1057]

alacritous *adj* [➡ HAPPENING QUICKLY; 104]

alacrity *n* **promptness**, quickness, rapidity, speed, readiness, swiftness, keenness, zeal, eagerness [➡ SPEED; 102] *Opposite*: sluggishness

Aladdin's cave *n* [➡ STORES AND STORAGE BUILDINGS; 1088]

à la grecque *type of* **food presentation** [➡ COOKING AND FOOD PREPARATION; 353]

à la king *type of* **food presentation** [➡ COOKING AND FOOD PREPARATION; 353]

à la mode *type of* **food presentation** [➡ COOKING AND FOOD PREPARATION; 353]

alarm 1 *n* **fear**, apprehension, terror, fright, panic, unease, anxiety, distress, agitation, dread [➡ FEAR AND PANIC; 543] 2 *n* **alarm bell**, bell, warning, distress signal, siren, danger signal [➡ SIGNALING; 1140] 3 *type of* **clock** [➡ CLOCKS AND TIMERS; 1126] 4 *v* **frighten**, terrify, panic, distress, startle, scare, worry, upset, shock [➡ FRIGHTEN AND SHOCK; 568] *Opposite*: calm

alarm bell *n* [➡ SIGNALING; 1140]

alarm clock *type of* **clock** [➡ CLOCKS AND TIMERS; 1126]

alarmed *adj* **worried**, upset, distressed, shocked, frightened, startled, terrified, panicked, scared [➡CONFUSION, ANXIETY, AND WORRY; 540] *Opposite*: untroubled

alarming *adj* **disturbing**, upsetting, frightening, distressing, shocking, startling, disquieting, worrying, terrifying [➡FRIGHTENING; 231] *Opposite*: soothing

alarmist 1 *n* **pessimist**, doomsayer, doom merchant (*UK*) [➡GRUMPY AND NEGATIVE PEOPLE; 953] 2 *adj* **pessimistic**, gloomy, panicky, exaggerated, hysterical, over-the-top (*informal*), doom-laden (*UK*) [➡EMOTIONALLY UNPLEASANT AND UPSETTING; 227] *Opposite*: down-to-earth

alas *adv* **unfortunately**, sadly, regrettably, unhappily, unluckily, as luck would have it, more's the pity (*informal*) [➡EXPRESSIONS OF REGRET; 547]

Alaska *type of* **time zone** [➡TIMES OF DAY; 87]

albatross 1 *n* **millstone**, shackle, encumbrance, burden, impediment, hindrance [➡PROBLEMS; 256] 2 *type of* **sea bird** [➡SEA BIRDS; 1002]

albeit *conj* **although**, though, even though, even if, notwithstanding (*formal*) [➡ALTHOUGH, NEVERTHELESS, AND DESPITE; 169]

album 1 *n* **book**, folder, photograph album, photo album, autograph album, stamp album, sticker album, wedding album, baby book, scrapbook [➡BOOKS AND BOOKLETS; 590] 2 *n* **record**, LP, CD, tape, cassette, compilation, collection [➡RECORDINGS AND PLAYERS; 911]

albumen *n* **egg white**, white, white of egg [➡FOOD COMPONENTS; 1188]

alchemy *n* **pseudoscience**, experimentation, transformation [➡CHANGE; 372]

alcoholic *adj* **intoxicating**, inebriating, fermented, distilled, strong, hard, vinous, boozy (*slang*), spirituous (*formal*) [➡DRINKS; 1187] *Opposite*: nonalcoholic

alcove *n* **recess**, niche, bay, cubicle, nook [➡ALCOVES, CUBICLES, AND COMPARTMENTS; 1096]

al dente *adj* [➡STATE OF PREPARED FOOD; 1171]

alder *type of* **deciduous tree** [➡DECIDUOUS TREES; 1028]

alert 1 *adj* **attentive**, watchful, prepared, aware, vigilant, ready, observant, on the alert, on the ball (*informal*) [➡POSITIVE IMPATIENCE, ENTHUSIASM, AND ALERTNESS; 537] *Opposite*: unprepared 2 *n* **warning**, signal, alarm, siren, red alert, heads-up [➡SIGNPOSTS, SIGNALS, AND BILLBOARDS; 595] 3 *v* **warn**, forewarn, notify, draw somebody's attention to, tell, inform [➡ADVISE AND WARN; 613]

alertness *n* **attentiveness**, watchfulness, awareness, preparedness, vigilance, readiness [➡ENERGY AND ENTHUSIASM; 496] *Opposite*: inattentiveness

Alexander technique *type of* **complementary therapy** [➡REMEDIES, TREATMENTS, AND OPERATIONS; 731]

alfalfa *type of* **salad vegetable** [➡FRUIT AND VEGETABLES; 1176]

Alfredo *type of* **food presentation** [➡COOKING AND FOOD PREPARATION; 353]

alfresco 1 *adv* **out of doors**, outdoors, outside, in the open air, in the yard, on the lawn, on the patio [➡GENERAL LOCATIONS; 158] *Opposite*: indoors 2 *adj* **outdoor**, open-air, outside, yard, patio, picnic [➡GENERAL LOCATIONS; 158] *Opposite*: indoor

alga *n* [➡MICROORGANISMS, FUNGI, AND ALGAE; 1023]

alga

◆ *types of marine algae*
bladder wrack, brown alga, fucus, green alga, gulfweed, Irish moss, kelp, laminaria, phytoplankton, pond scum, red alga, rockweed, sea lettuce, seaweed, sea wrack, stonewort, tangle

algebra *n* [➡MATH; 597]

algorithm *n* **procedure**, process, system, set of rules [➡WAYS OF DOING THINGS; 294]

alias 1 *adj* **also known as**, also called, otherwise known as, under the name of, a.k.a. [➡NAME AND DESCRIBE; 665] 2 *n* **assumed name**, pseudonym, pen name, nom de plume, stage name [➡NAME AND DESCRIBE; 665]

alibi (*informal*) *n* **explanation**, excuse, defense, reason, account [➡EXPLAIN AND CLARIFY; 610]

alien 1 *n* **extraterrestrial**, creature from outer space, space invader, Martian, intelligent life form [➡SCIENCE FICTION; 1064] 2 *n* **foreigner**, stranger, immigrant, resident alien [➡STRANGERS; 972] 3 *adj* **unfamiliar**, unknown, strange, outlandish, unusual, weird, odd, peculiar [➡SECRET AND UNKNOWN; 179]

alienate *v* **estrange**, make unfriendly, disaffect, set against, distance, push away, separate, isolate, keep apart, turn away, turn your back on [➡REFUSING OR REJECTING RELATIONS; 975]

alienated *adj* **estranged**, disaffected, isolated, withdrawn, separate, indifferent [➡NEUTRALITY AND INDIFFERENCE; 553] *Opposite*: involved

alienation *n* **estrangement**, disaffection, unfriendliness, hostility, isolation, separation, dissension, division [➡SOLITARINESS; 941] *Opposite*: closeness

alien craft *n* [➡SCIENCE FICTION; 1064]

alight 1 *v* **get off**, get out, descend, dismount [➡ARRIVE BY TRANSPORT; 14] 2 *v* **land**, perch, rest, stop, settle [➡GO DOWNWARD; 307] 3 *adj* **burning**, on fire, in flames, blazing, ablaze, flaming [➡FIRE, FLAMMABILITY, AND BURNING; 1165]

align 1 *v* **bring into line**, line up, make straight, make parallel, make even [➡ARRANGE AND CREATE ORDER; 357] *Opposite*: disarrange 2 *v* **side with**, support, ally, affiliate, associate, line up with [➡ESTABLISHING RELATIONSHIPS WITH OTHERS; 974] *Opposite*: distance

aligned *adj* **allied**, united, associated, affiliated, ranged [➡RELATED; 142]

alignment 1 *n* **position**, arrangement, placement, configuration, orientation [➡ORIENTATION AND ALIGNMENT; 1223] *Opposite*: disorder 2 *n* **alliance**, association, coalition, grouping, affiliation, support [➡CONNECTIONS; 143]

alike *adj* **similar**, comparable, the same, identical, like [➡SIMILARITY; 148] *Opposite*: different

alikeness *n* [➡SIMILARITY; 148]

alimentary canal *see* **digestive tract**

alimony *n* **allowance**, maintenance, support, financial support, funding [➡ FUNDS, PAYMENTS, AND CHARGES; 800]

alive **1** *adj* **living**, animate, breathing [➡ LIVING THINGS AND LIVING; 976] *Opposite:* dead **2** *adj* **energetic**, busy, active, perky, vibrant, bustling, vivacious, animated, full of life [➡ ENERGY AND ENTHUSIASM; 496] *Opposite:* inactive **3** *adj* **animated**, thriving, active, flourishing, successful, blooming, buzzing [➡ SUCCESSFUL AND PROMISING; 81] *Opposite:* quiet **4** *adj* **full**, packed, teeming, awash, swarming, jumping (*informal*), hopping (*informal*) [➡ FULL; 1239] *Opposite:* dead **5** *adj* **aware**, sensitive, tuned in, alert, interested, homed in [➡ POSITIVE IMPATIENCE, ENTHUSIASM, AND ALERTNESS; 537] *Opposite:* unaware

See Compare and Contrast at **living**.

alive and kicking (*informal*) *adj* **going strong**, surviving, still with us, around, energetic, all right, hale and hearty, vigorous, alive and well [➡ FIT AND STRONG; 736] *Opposite:* dead

alive and well *adj* **safe**, all right, safe and sound, unharmed, uninjured, in good shape, okay (*informal*) [➡ SAFE AND SOUND; 737]

all **1** *adv* (*informal*) **altogether**, completely, entirely, very, wholly, totally [➡ WHOLENESS AND COMPLETENESS; 198] **2** *pron* **every one**, each and every one, every single one, each [➡ ALL; 128] *Opposite:* none **3** *pron* **every part**, the entire, the complete, the whole, every bit [➡ ALL; 128] *Opposite:* none

all alone *adj* [➡ SOLITARINESS; 941]

all along *adv* **from the start**, right from the start, from the very beginning, from the beginning, right from the outset, from the outset, all the time, the whole time, from the word go, from the get-go (*informal*) [➡ PERMANENCE: WITHOUT END; 94]

all and sundry *pron* **everyone**, everybody, one and all, every person, the whole world, every last one, each and every one [➡ ALL; 128] *Opposite:* nobody

all-around **1** *adj* **versatile**, exceptional, outstanding, talented, multitalented, multifaceted [➡ TALENTED AND SKILLFUL; 527] **2** *adj* **all-inclusive**, grand, inclusive, sweeping, large-scale, broad, comprehensive, all-embracing, wide-ranging, extensive, complete, across-the-board [➡ WHOLENESS AND COMPLETENESS; 198] *Opposite:* restricted **3** *adj* **on all sides**, in every direction, everywhere, in all directions [➡ GENERAL LOCATIONS; 158]

all at once **1** *adv* **at the same time**, all together, together, simultaneously, concurrently, in unison, as one [➡ CONCURRENT AND CONTEMPORANEOUS; 164] *Opposite:* independently **2** *adv* **suddenly**, all of a sudden, without warning, just like that, out of the blue, in a flash, in one fell swoop, unexpectedly, abruptly [➡ HAPPENING QUICKLY; 104] *Opposite:* gradually

all at sea *adj* [➡ INSECURITY AND LOSS OF COMPOSURE; 544]

allay *v* **dispel**, alleviate, calm, assuage, relieve, put to rest [➡ CHANGE OF INTENSITY: LESS; 395] *Opposite:* stimulate

all by yourself *adv* **without help**, on your own, by yourself, of your own accord, unaided, on your own account [➡ ACTING INDEPENDENTLY; 284] *Opposite:* jointly

all clear *n* **green light**, all-clear signal, nod, signal, clear coast, permission, approval, go-ahead (*informal*), okay (*informal*), thumbs up (*informal*) [➡ PERMIT AND ALLOW; 669]

all-clear signal *n* [➡ SIGNALING; 1140]

all-comers (*UK*) *n* **everyone**, everybody, one and all, all, the general public, the public [➡ ALL; 128]

all-consuming *adj* [➡ STRENGTH; 201]

all ears (*informal*) *adj* [➡ PENSIVENESS AND INTEREST; 538]

allegation *n* **claim**, accusation, assertion, contention, charge [➡ CLAIM, INSIST, AND EMPHASIZE; 614]

allege *v* **claim**, assert, contend, charge, declare [➡ CLAIM, INSIST, AND EMPHASIZE; 614]

alleged *adj* **supposed**, unproven, suspected, so-called, assumed, apparent, purported [➡ UNCERTAIN; 175] *Opposite:* confirmed

allegiance *n* **loyalty**, commitment, adherence, faithfulness, duty, fidelity [➡ CONNECTIONS; 143] *Opposite:* disloyalty

allegorical *adj* **metaphorical**, symbolic, emblematic, figurative, allegoric, metaphoric, fictional [➡ FALSE AND UNREAL; 173] *Opposite:* literal

allegory *n* **parable**, fable, metaphor, symbol, extended metaphor, tale, story [➡ THE ORAL TRADITION; 677]

allegro *type of* **musical term** [➡ MUSICAL TERMS; 912]

all-embracing *adj* **comprehensive**, complete, extensive, catholic, wide-ranging, across-the-board, broad, all-encompassing, all-inclusive, sweeping, large-scale, grand, inclusive, all-around [➡ WHOLENESS AND COMPLETENESS; 198] *Opposite:* narrow

all-encompassing *see* **all-embracing**

allergic *adj* **sensitive**, affected, sensitized, hypersensitive, averse (*formal*) [➡ SICKNESS; 729]

allergy **1** *n* **reaction**, allergic reaction, sensitivity, hypersensitivity [➡ ILLNESSES AND DISORDERS; 732] **2** *n* (*informal*) **dislike**, antipathy, distaste, hate, hatred, aversion (*formal*) [➡ DISLIKE AND HATE; 577]

alleviate *v* **ease**, lessen, assuage, improve, lighten, relieve [➡ CHANGE OF INTENSITY: LESS; 395] *Opposite:* aggravate

alleviation *n* **mitigation**, lessening, improvement, easing, assuagement, relief [➡ CHANGE OF INTENSITY: LESS; 395] *Opposite:* aggravation

alley *type of* **secondary road** [➡ ROADS; 1106]

alleyway *type of* **secondary road** [➡ ROADS; 1106]

all fingers and thumbs (*UK*) *adj* [➡ AGILITY OF THE BODY; 476]

all for *prep* **in favor of**, pro, for, in support of [➡ LIKE, LOVE, VALUE, AND ENJOY; 578] *Opposite:* against

alliance **1** *n* **coalition**, grouping, association, union, cooperation, agreement, treaty, pact, deal [➡ GROUPS WITH A COMMON INTEREST; 938] **2** *n* **relationship**, partnership, bond, link, tie [➡ CONNECTIONS; 143]

allied **1** *adj* **joined**, united, combined, amalgamated, aligned, partnered [➡ RELATED; 142] **2** *adj* **related**, associated, connected, akin, linked, similar [➡ RELATED; 142] *Opposite*: unrelated

alligator *type of* reptile [➡ REPTILES; 994]

all-important *adj* [➡ MOST IMPORTANT AND MAIN; 193]

all in 1 *adj* **exhausted**, weary, tired, tired out, worn out, bushed (*informal*) [➡ TIRED, ASLEEP, AND UNCONSCIOUS; 738] *Opposite*: fresh 2 *adj* (*UK*) **total**, inclusive, overall, global, all-inclusive [➡ WHOLENESS AND COMPLETENESS; 198]

all in all *adv* **all things considered**, on the whole, in general, generally speaking, when all is said and done, overall, taking everything into account [➡ SUMMARIZING EXPRESSIONS; 622]

all-inclusive *adj* **comprehensive**, grand, complete, broad, all-embracing, all-encompassing, wide-ranging, all in (*UK*) [➡ WHOLENESS AND COMPLETENESS; 198] *Opposite*: incomplete

all-in-one *type of* suit [➡ GARMENTS AND OUTFITS; 865]

all in the mind *adj* [➡ FALSE AND UNREAL; 173]

alliteration 1 *n* **assonance**, consonance, sound repetition, sound pattern, resonance, echo [➡ ASPECTS OF LANGUAGE; 682] 2 *type of* **figure of speech** [➡ FIGURES OF SPEECH; 673]

alliterative *adj* **repetitive**, echoing, assonant, poetic [➡ ASPECTS OF LANGUAGE; 682]

all-knowing *adj* [➡ KNOWLEDGE AND WISDOM; 558]

allocate *v* **assign**, allot, apportion, distribute, deal, share out, give, hand out, earmark, divide up, share [➡ DISPENSE, RATION, AND DISTRIBUTE; 434]

allocation 1 *n* **distribution**, provision, sharing out, apportionment, division, sharing [➡ DISPENSE, RATION, AND DISTRIBUTE; 434] 2 *n* **share**, portion, allotment, allowance [➡ AMOUNTS AND QUANTITIES; 112]

all of a flutter *adj* [➡ PLEASURE, EXCITEMENT, AND ELATION; 534]

all of a sudden *adv* **suddenly**, out of the blue, in a flash, in one fell swoop, on the spur of the moment, unexpectedly, abruptly, without warning, spontaneously, out of nowhere, all at once [➡ HAPPENING QUICKLY; 104] *Opposite*: gradually

all-or-nothing *adj* **win-or-lose**, uncompromising, winner-take-all, rigid, zero-sum, unyielding, high-stake, inflexible, unrelenting, tenacious, dogged [➡ ALL; 128] *Opposite*: flexible

allosaurus *type of* dinosaur [➡ DINOSAURS; 996]

allot *v* **assign**, designate, allocate, earmark, apportion, set aside, give, ration, allow [➡ DISPENSE, RATION, AND DISTRIBUTE; 434]

allotment 1 *n* **share**, portion, part, allocation, allowance, ration [➡ DISPENSE, RATION, AND DISTRIBUTE; 434] 2 *n* (*UK*) **vegetable garden**, vegetable patch, plot [➡ GARDENS; 1074]

all-out *adj* **maximum**, supreme, extreme, thoroughgoing, determined, concentrated [➡ WHOLENESS AND COMPLETENESS; 198] *Opposite*: half-hearted

all over *adj* **finished**, ended, concluded, over and done with, done, all up, done with (*UK*) [➡ PAST; 84]

all over again *adv* [➡ AGAIN; 109]

all over the place (*informal*) 1 *adj* **untidy**, in disorder, in disarray, in a mess, disorganized, topsy-turvy, in a state (*informal*) [➡ DISORDER AND CHAOS; 245] *Opposite*: tidy 2 *adv* **everywhere**, all over, here and there, high and low, far and wide, around, from one place to another, hither and thither, hither and yon (*UK*) [➡ GENERAL LOCATIONS; 158]

allow 1 *v* **let**, permit, agree, consent, tolerate, sanction, countenance (*formal*) [➡ PERMIT AND ALLOW; 669] *Opposite*: forbid 2 *v* **allocate**, set aside, make available, set a limit, allot, apportion [➡ DISPENSE, RATION, AND DISTRIBUTE; 434] 3 *v* (*formal*) **accept**, admit, acknowledge, admit as true, grant, concede [➡ ADMIT AND CONFESS; 615] *Opposite*: disallow

allowable *adj* **permissible**, acceptable, tolerable, admissible, suitable [➡ ACCEPTABLE AND PASSABLE; 219] *Opposite*: unacceptable

allowance *n* **payment**, grant, stipend, pocket money, pin money, budget [➡ INCOME; 460]

allowed *adj* **permitted**, allotted, authorized, approved, legitimate, accepted, recognized, sanctioned [➡ LEGAL AND LEGITIMATE; 815] *Opposite*: prohibited

allow for *v* **take into account**, take into consideration, make allowance for, make allowances for, bear in mind, keep in mind, consider [➡ PAY ATTENTION; 765]

alloy 1 *n* **blend**, amalgam, compound, mixture, composite [➡ COLLECTIONS AND MIXTURES OF THINGS; 1244] 2 *n* **additive**, contaminant, adulterant, pollutant, ingredient, component [➡ MORE AND EXCESS; 124]

See Compare and Contrast at **mixture**.

all-powerful *adj* **omnipotent**, invincible, supreme, almighty [➡ STRENGTH; 201] *Opposite*: weak

all-purpose *adj* **general purpose**, multipurpose, universal, overall, versatile, general, multiuse, flexible [➡ USEFULNESS; 199] *Opposite*: specialized

all right 1 *adj* **satisfactory**, good, pleasing, okay (*informal*) [➡ ACCEPTABLE AND PASSABLE; 219] *Opposite*: unsatisfactory 2 *adj* **acceptable**, fair to middling, good enough, reasonable, fair, passable, suitable, okay (*informal*), so-so (*informal*) [➡ ACCEPTABLE AND PASSABLE; 219] *Opposite*: unacceptable 3 *adj* **safe and sound**, uninjured, alive and well, safe, unharmed, okay (*informal*) [➡ SAFE AND SOUND; 737] *Opposite*: damaged 4 *interj* **yes**, sure, why not?, of course, agreed, by all means, fair enough (*informal*), okay (*informal*), no problem (*informal*) [➡ EXPRESSIONS OF AGREEMENT; 648] 5 *adv* **satisfactorily**, reasonably, acceptably, passably, okay (*informal*) [➡ ACCEPTABLE AND PASSABLE; 219] *Opposite*: unsatisfactorily 6 *adv* (*UK*) **certainly**, positively, obviously, without a doubt [➡ EXPRESSIONS OF AGREEMENT; 648]

all-round (*UK*) 1 *adj* **versatile**, exceptional, outstanding, talented, multitalented, multifaceted, all-around [➡ EXTRAORDINARY; UNCOMMON; 205] 2 *adj* **all-inclusive**, grand, inclusive, sweeping, large-scale, broad, comprehensive, all-embracing, wide-ranging, extensive, complete, across-the-board [➡ WHOLENESS AND COMPLETENESS; 198] *Opposite*: restricted 3 *adj* **on all sides**, in every direction, everywhere, in all directions [➡ GENERAL LOCATIONS; 158]

all-seeing *adj* [➡ KNOWLEDGE AND WISDOM; 558]

all set *adj* **ready**, ready to go, standing by, ready and waiting, at the ready, prepared [➡ COOL AND CALM; 536] *Opposite:* unprepared

all-singing, all-dancing *adj* [➡ EXTRAORDINARY: AMAZING; 204]

allspice *type of* **spice** [➡ HERBS AND SPICES; 1175]

all-star *adj* **star-studded**, celebrity, famous, prestigious, well-known, glittering, glamorous [➡ KNOWN AND FAMOUS; 181] *Opposite:* unknown

all-terrain vehicle *type of* **car** [➡ BIKES, CARS, AND CARRIAGES; 1149]

all the rage *adj* [➡ POPULAR AND WANTED; 220]

all the same *adv* **even so**, nevertheless, in spite of everything, despite everything, however, yet [➡ ALTHOUGH, NEVERTHELESS, AND DESPITE; 169]

all the time 1 *adv* **continually**, constantly, repeatedly, incessantly, permanently, endlessly [➡ PERMANENCE: WITHOUT END; 94] *Opposite:* occasionally 2 *adv* **all along**, from the start, from the outset, from the word go, from the get-go (*informal*) [➡ PERMANENCE: WITHOUT END; 94]

all things considered *adv* **all in all**, on the whole, when all's said and done, altogether, at the end of the day [➡ SUMMARIZING EXPRESSIONS; 622]

all thumbs *adj* [➡ AGILITY OF THE BODY; 476]

all-time *adj* **unsurpassed**, record, unprecedented, unparalleled, best, greatest [➡ EXTRAORDINARY: AMAZING; 204] *Opposite:* insignificant

all together 1 *adv* **together**, in agreement, united, as one, unanimous, in unison, in step, en masse, en bloc, jointly, as a unit, in partnership, in cooperation, in harmony, as a group, as a body, with one voice [➡ ACTING WITH OTHERS; 285] *Opposite:* independently 2 *adv* **simultaneously**, at the same time, all at once, together, concurrently [➡ CONCURRENT AND CONTEMPORANEOUS; 164] *Opposite:* separately

all told *adv* **altogether**, in total, all in all, in all, overall, all included [➡ ALL; 128] *Opposite:* in part

allude *v* **refer**, make reference, make allusion, mention, indicate, suggest, talk about, touch on, introduce, refer in passing, make a passing reference [➡ SUGGEST, HINT, AND COMMENT; 612]

allure *n* **attraction**, appeal, draw, magnetism, charm, glamour, fascination, charisma, pull (*informal*) [➡ INTERESTING AND MEANINGFUL; 190]

alluring *adj* **appealing**, attractive, tempting, interesting, fascinating, enthralling, charming, glamorous, captivating, charismatic, irresistible [➡ INTERESTING AND MEANINGFUL; 190] *Opposite:* repulsive

allusion *n* **reference**, mention, hint, suggestion, insinuation, quotation, citation [➡ SUGGEST, HINT, AND COMMENT; 612]

allusive *adj* **indirect**, oblique, hinting, referential, suggestive, indicative [➡ RETICENT AND UNFORTHCOMING; 631] *Opposite:* direct

alluvial *adj* **sedimentary**, silty, deposited, muddy, sandy, grainy [➡ EROSION PRODUCTS AND SOIL; 1058]

all-weather *adj* **year-round**, all-season, rain-or-shine, all-purpose, four-season [➡ PERMANENCE: WITHOUT END; 94]

ally 1 *v* **associate**, join, affiliate, align, connect, link [➡ ESTABLISHING RELATIONSHIPS WITH OTHERS; 974] 2 *n* **friend**, helper, supporter, assistant, partner, confederate, associate [➡ FRIENDS AND GUESTS; 963] *Opposite:* enemy

alma mater *n* **old school**, college, university, school, institution [➡ EDUCATIONAL INSTITUTIONS; 813]

almanac *n* **directory**, calendar, yearbook, handbook, manual, encyclopedia, reference book [➡ RECORDS; 585]

almighty 1 *adj* **omnipotent**, invincible, all-powerful, supreme, omnipresent [➡ STRENGTH; 201] 2 *adj* (*informal*) **enormous**, massive, huge, immense, gigantic, colossal, great, serious, terrible, terrific, frightful [➡ LARGE; 1193]

almond *type of* **nut** [➡ NUTS; 1185]

almost *adv* **nearly**, not quite, just about, virtually, practically, more or less [➡ TO A CERTAIN EXTENT; 136] *Opposite:* exactly

alms *n* **charity**, donation, contribution, gift, offering, handout, assistance, money [➡ GIFTS; 438]

aloft *adv* **in the air**, in flight, airborne, on the wing, high up, upward [➡ GENERAL LOCATIONS; 158] *Opposite:* below

alone 1 *adv* **unaccompanied**, by yourself, on your own, single-handedly, unaided, without help, solo [➡ ACTING INDEPENDENTLY; 284] 2 *adj* **lonely**, lonesome, abandoned, deserted, isolated, forlorn, solitary [➡ SOLITARINESS; 941]

along *prep* **next to**, beside, by the side of, alongside, by, adjacent to, near [➡ CLOSENESS; 159]

alongside *prep* **next to**, beside, at the side of, along, flanking, near [➡ CLOSENESS; 159]

along with *prep* **with**, together with, in company with, in conjunction with, as well as [➡ ALSO; 138]

aloof 1 *adj* **remote**, standoffish, proud, reserved, indifferent, distant, detached, unfriendly, cold, unapproachable, lofty, snooty (*informal*) [➡ UNFRIENDLINESS AND UNSOCIABILITY; 504] *Opposite:* friendly 2 *adj* **separate**, remote, distant, set apart, away, independent [➡ SOLITARINESS; 941] *Opposite:* close

aloofness 1 *n* **unfriendliness**, coldness, detachment, remoteness, reserve, standoffishness, indifference, distance, unapproachability, proudness, loftiness, snootiness (*informal*) [➡ UNFRIENDLINESS AND UNSOCIABILITY; 504] *Opposite:* friendliness 2 *n* **distance**, remoteness, separateness, independence [➡ SOLITARINESS; 941] *Opposite:* closeness

a lot 1 *adv* **a great deal**, lots, very much, a good deal, enormously, greatly, a whole heap (*informal*), whole bunches (*informal*) [➡ MANY, MUCH, LARGE AMOUNT; 117] 2 *pron* **plenty**, many, a large number, loads (*informal*), tons (*informal*), heaps (*informal*) [➡ MANY, MUCH, LARGE AMOUNT; 117] *Opposite:* a few

aloud 1 *adv* **audibly**, out loud, distinctly, noticeably, clearly, verbally [➡ PERCEPTIBLE; 25] *Opposite:* silently 2 *adv* **loudly**, noisily, riotously, blusteringly, boisterously, clamorously [➡ LOUD, HIGH, OR UNPLEASANT SOUNDS; 1266] *Opposite:* quietly

alp *n* [➡ MOUNTAINS AND HILLS; 1044]

alpaca 1 *type of* **large mammal** [➡ LARGE MAMMALS; 986] 2 *type of* **fabric from animals** [➡ FABRICS; 1132]

alpha *adj* **important**, dominant, chief, primary, leading, first [➡ FUNDAMENTAL; 195]

alphabet *n* **writing system**, script, character set, letters, symbols, ABCs [➡ SYMBOLS, SIGNS, AND NUMBERS; 596]

alphabet

♦ *types of alphabets*
Arabic, Braille, cuneiform, Cyrillic, Greek, Hebrew, hieroglyphics, hiragana, ideogram, kanji, katakana, phonetic alphabet, pictogram, Roman alphabet, runic

alphabetic *see* **alphabetical**

alphabetical *adj* **arranged**, in order, listed, in a list, sequential, consecutive, serial [➡ ORDER AND ORGANIZATION; 206]

alpine *adj* **mountainous**, mountain, high altitude, hilly, high [➡ MOUNTAINS AND HILLS; 1044]

alpine skiing *type of* **winter sport** [➡ HOBBIES, GAMES, AND SPORTS; 875]

alpinism *n* [➡ HOBBIES, GAMES, AND SPORTS; 875]

alpinist *n* [➡ PEOPLE IN SPORTS AND LEISURE; 876]

already *adv* **by now**, previously, before now, even now, by this time, now, at present [➡ PRESENT; 85]

alright *see* **all right**

also 1 *adv* **in addition**, and, what's more, moreover, furthermore, besides, additionally, plus (*informal*) [➡ ALSO; 138] 2 *adv* **too**, as well, likewise, similarly, correspondingly [➡ ALSO; 138]

also-ran *n* **loser**, failure, flop (*informal*), dud (*informal*) [➡ FAILURE; 77] *Opposite*: winner

altar *n* **table**, bench, slab, stand, platform, dais [➡ PARTS OF RELIGIOUS BUILDINGS; 1086]

alter *v* **change**, modify, adjust, vary, amend, revise, rework, correct, convert, shift [➡ CHANGE; 372] *Opposite*: maintain

See Compare and Contrast at **change**.

alteration *n* **modification**, adjustment, change, variation, amendment, revision, shift, adaptation, correction [➡ CHANGE; 372]

altercate *v* **argue**, quarrel, disagree, dispute, squabble, row [➡ ARGUE AND FIGHT; 643]

altercation *n* **argument**, quarrel, disagreement, dispute, exchange, squabble, clash, difference of opinion, confrontation, row, fight [➡ ARGUMENTS; 47]

alter ego *n* **double**, shadow, doppelgänger, twin, clone, stand-in [➡ SUBSTITUTES AND STAND-INS; 399]

alternate 1 *v* **interchange**, rotate, exchange, intersperse, substitute, swap (*informal*) [➡ CHANGE ONE THING FOR ANOTHER; 398] 2 *v* **fluctuate**, vary, swing, oscillate, vacillate, move between [➡ CHANGE; 372] 3 *adj* **every other**, alternating, every second [➡ FINITENESS, VARIABILITY, AND TRANSIENCE; 96] 4 *adj* **alternative**, substitute, different, another, other, replacement, backup [➡ DIFFERENCE; 149] *Opposite*: same 5 *n* **substitute**, stand-in, alternative, fill-in, replacement, surrogate, sub (*informal*) [➡ SUBSTITUTES AND STAND-INS; 399]

alternately *adv* **off and on**, in turn, by turns, one after the other, interchangeably [➡ FINITENESS, VARIABILITY, AND TRANSIENCE; 96] *Opposite*: consecutively

alternation *n* **change**, interchange, repetition, rotation, fluctuation, vacillation, oscillation, swing [➡ CHANGE; 372]

alternative 1 *n* **replacement**, substitute, substitution, change, another possibility, another course of action [➡ WAYS OF DOING THINGS; 294] 2 *n* **option**, choice, freedom of choice, discretion [➡ MAKE DECISIONS AND CHOICES; 752] 3 *adj* **other**, another, substitute, alternate, different [➡ DIFFERENCE; 149] 4 *adj* **unusual**, different, unconventional, out of the ordinary, marginal, unorthodox, complementary [➡ EXTRAORDINARY: UNCOMMON; 205] *Opposite*: conventional

alternatively *adv* **on the other hand**, otherwise, instead, then again [➡ EXPRESSIONS INTRODUCING EXTRA INFORMATION; 139]

alternative therapy *n* [➡ HEALING; 730]

alternator *part of* **engine** [➡ PARTS OF AN ENGINE; 1144]

although *conj* **though**, even though, even if, while, granting [➡ ALTHOUGH, NEVERTHELESS, AND DESPITE; 169]

altimeter *type of* **measuring device** [➡ MEASURING DEVICES; 1123]

altitude *n* **height**, elevation, height above sea level, loftiness, highness [➡ HEIGHT: HIGH; 1203]

alto *type of* **musical register** [➡ MUSICAL TERMS; 912]

altocumulus *type of* **cloud** [➡ CLOUDY AND RAINY WEATHER; 1052]

altogether 1 *adv* **in total**, all in all, all told, overall, in sum, in all [➡ ALL; 128] 2 *adv* **totally**, completely, wholly, thoroughly, entirely, fully [➡ TO A GREAT EXTENT; 132] 3 *adv* **on the whole**, when all's said and done, overall, in general, mostly, usually, generally, largely [➡ SUMMARIZING EXPRESSIONS; 622]

altostratus *type of* **cloud** [➡ CLOUDY AND RAINY WEATHER; 1052]

altruism *n* **unselfishness**, self-sacrifice, humanity, selflessness, philanthropy [➡ GENEROSITY AND KINDNESS; 495] *Opposite*: selfishness

altruist *n* [➡ PEOPLE WHO ARE APPROVED OF; 955]

altruistic *adj* **unselfish**, humane, selfless, philanthropic, noble, self-sacrificing [➡ GENEROSITY AND KINDNESS; 495] *Opposite*: selfish

alum (*informal*) *n* **graduate**, former student, ex-student, alumna, alumnus [➡ STUDENTS AND PUPILS; 841]

aluminum *type of* **metal** [➡ METALS; 1276]

alumna *n* **graduate**, former student, ex-student, alum (*informal*) [➡ STUDENTS AND PUPILS; 841]

alumnus *n* **graduate**, former student, ex-student, alum (*informal*) [➡ STUDENTS AND PUPILS; 841]

alveolus *part of* **respiratory system** [➡ RESPIRATORY ORGANS; 715]

always 1 *adv* **at all times**, continuously, all the time, continually, constantly, each time, every time [➡ PERMANENCE: WITHOUT END; 94] 2 *adv* **forever**, for all time, for eternity, until the end of time, for ever and a day, eternally, permanently [➡ PERMANENCE: WITHOUT END; 94]

a.m. *adj* **morning**, before noon, before lunch, pre-lunch [➡ TIMES OF DAY; 87] *Opposite:* p.m.

amalgam *n* **mixture**, mix, combination, blend, amalgamation, fusion [➡ COLLECTIONS AND MIXTURES OF THINGS; 1244]

See Compare and Contrast at **mixture**.

amalgamate *v* **merge**, join, combine, unite, integrate, mingle, fuse [➡ COMBINE AND MIX; 400] *Opposite:* separate

amalgamated *adj* **combined**, merged, joined, incorporated, united, integrated, fused, mingled [➡ RELATED; 142] *Opposite:* separated

amalgamation 1 *n* **merger**, union, incorporation, consolidation, unification [➡ CONNECTIONS; 143] **2** *n* **mixture**, combination, mix, blend, fusion, compound [➡ COLLECTIONS AND MIXTURES OF THINGS; 1244]

amanuensis *n* **secretary**, scribe, writer, copier, copyist, recorder, transcriber [➡ SUBORDINATES AND ASSISTANTS; 966]

amass *v* **accumulate**, collect, gather, stockpile, hoard, accrue, assemble, pile up, store up, build up [➡ GET; 420] *Opposite:* distribute

See Compare and Contrast at **collect**.

amateur 1 *adj* **unprofessional**, shoddy, slapdash, substandard, incompetent, inexpert, unskillful, amateurish, slipshod, clumsy, crude, inept, sloppy (*informal*) [➡ UNSKILLED; 529] *Opposite:* skillful **2** *adj* **part-time**, unpaid, nonprofessional, leisure, recreational [➡ EMPLOYMENT STATUS; 831] *Opposite:* full-time **3** *n* **layperson**, nonprofessional [➡ UNSKILLED PEOPLE; 530] *Opposite:* professional

amateur dramatics (*UK*) *n* [➡ HOBBIES, GAMES, AND SPORTS; 875]

amateurish *adj* **unprofessional**, shoddy, slapdash, clumsy, crude, substandard, slipshod, incompetent, inexpert, sloppy (*informal*) [➡ UNSKILLED; 529] *Opposite:* skillful

amateurishness *n* **unskillfulness**, clumsiness, ineptness, incompetence, unprofessionalism, shoddiness, sloppiness (*informal*) [➡ UNSKILLED; 529] *Opposite:* professionalism

amateur photographer *n* [➡ HOBBIES, GAMES, AND SPORTS; 875]

amaze *v* **astonish**, astound, shock, stun, startle, surprise, dumbfound, stagger, take aback, flabbergast (*informal*) [➡ SURPRISE AND IMPRESS; 574]

amazed *adj* **astonished**, astounded, shocked, stunned, startled, surprised, dumbfounded, staggered, taken aback, flabbergasted (*informal*) [➡ SURPRISE, SHOCK, AND AMAZEMENT; 545]

amazement *n* **astonishment**, wonder, admiration, shock, incredulity, surprise, bewilderment [➡ SURPRISE, SHOCK, AND AMAZEMENT; 545]

amazing *adj* **astonishing**, astounding, remarkable, wonderful, incredible, startling, marvelous, miraculous, surprising, staggering, mind-blowing (*informal*), mind-

boggling (*informal*) [➡ EXTRAORDINARY: AMAZING; 204] *Opposite:* unremarkable

ambassador *n* **diplomat**, envoy, representative, emissary, legate [➡ REPRESENTATIVES AND PATRONS; 968]

amber *type of* **orange** [➡ COLORS; 1224]

ambiance *n* **atmosphere**, feel, setting, environment, mood, character, air, quality, tone, vibe (*slang*) [➡ APPEARANCE AND ATMOSPHERE; 1237]

ambience *see* **ambiance**

ambient *type of* **electronic music** [➡ MUSIC, SONGS, AND SINGING; 907]

ambiguity *n* **vagueness**, uncertainty, haziness, doubt, indistinctness, obscurity, abstruseness, opacity, equivocality [➡ VAGUENESS; 243] *Opposite:* clarity

ambiguous *adj* **vague**, unclear, abstruse, equivocal, uncertain, indefinite, confusing, indistinct, hazy, woolly [➡ VAGUENESS; 243] *Opposite:* clear

ambiguousness *n* **abstruseness**, opacity, obscurity, vagueness, uncertainty, doubt, equivocality, dubiousness, confusion, indistinctness, indefiniteness [➡ VAGUENESS; 243] *Opposite:* clarity

ambit *n* **scope**, extent, range, realm, area, field, preserve, limit [➡ DEGREE AND EXTENT; 110]

ambition 1 *n* **drive**, determination, motivation, desire, spirit, get-up-and-go (*informal*) [➡ POSITIVE IMPATIENCE, ENTHUSIASM, AND ALERTNESS; 537] *Opposite:* apathy **2** *n* **goal**, aim, objective, aspiration, dream, hope, desire, purpose [➡ FEELINGS ABOUT THE FUTURE; 533]

ambitious 1 *adj* **determined**, ruthless, striving, motivated, aspiring, single-minded, go-getting (*informal*), pushy (*informal*) [➡ HARD-WORKING AND COMMITTED; 500] *Opposite:* unmotivated **2** *adj* **grand**, impressive, bold, large-scale, elaborate, magnificent [➡ EXTRAORDINARY: AMAZING; 204] *Opposite:* small-scale

ambitiously 1 *adv* **determinedly**, ruthlessly, single-mindedly, energetically, pushily (*informal*) [➡ HARD-WORKING AND COMMITTED; 500] *Opposite:* unambitiously **2** *adv* **optimistically**, overconfidently, unrealistically, idealistically, impractically, unworkably [➡ NEGATIVE INTELLECTUAL CHARACTERISTICS; 525] *Opposite:* realistically

ambivalence *n* **uncertainty**, contradiction, unsureness, doubt, inconsistency, indecision, fluctuation, incongruity, vacillation [➡ UNCERTAINTY; 559] *Opposite:* certainty

ambivalent *adj* **unsure**, undecided, hesitant, uncertain, indecisive, of two minds [➡ UNCERTAINTY; 559] *Opposite:* decisive

amble *v* **stroll**, saunter, wander, walk, mosey (*informal*), mooch (*slang*), promenade (*formal*) [➡ MOVE SLOWLY; 314]

ambulance *type of* **public service vehicle** [➡ VEHICLES; 1145]

ambush 1 *n* **trap**, surprise attack, ensnarement, ambuscade (*literary*) [➡ SUDDEN EVENTS; 52] **2** *v* **trap**, ensnare, lie in wait, take by surprise, waylay, ambuscade (*literary*) [➡ INITIATE AND ESTABLISH COMMUNICATION; 680]

ameliorate (*formal*) *v* **better**, perfect, amend, upgrade, enrich, improve, enhance [➡ IMPROVE SOMETHING; 374] *Opposite:* deteriorate

amelioration *n* **improvement**, enhancement, enrichment, upgrading, amendment, betterment (*formal*) [➡ IMPROVE SOMETHING; 374] *Opposite:* deterioration

amen (*informal*) *interj* **I agree**, you said it!, I'll say, yes, indeed, agreed [➡ EXPRESSIONS OF AGREEMENT; 648]

amenability *n* **acquiescence**, docility, willingness, responsiveness, pliability, cooperation, flexibility [➡ THE WILL AND WILLINGNESS; 563] *Opposite:* stubbornness

amenable *adj* **agreeable**, open, acquiescent, willing, docile, responsive, pliable, cooperative, flexible [➡ THE WILL AND WILLINGNESS; 563] *Opposite:* stubborn

amend *v* **alter**, adjust, modify, revise, change, improve, correct [➡ CORRECT AND PUT RIGHT; 377] *Opposite:* maintain

amendment *n* **alteration**, adjustment, modification, revision, change, improvement, correction [➡ CHANGE; 372]

amends *n* **compensation**, recompense, replacement, restitution, return, substitution [➡ TREATS; 210]

amenity 1 *n* **facility**, convenience, comfort, service, feature, nicety, creature comfort [➡ PHYSICAL OBJECTS; 1243] 2 *n* **pleasantness**, attractiveness, niceness, affability, goodness [➡ APPROPRIATE, SUITABLE, AND ADVISABLE; 184] *Opposite:* discomfort

americano *type of* **coffee** [➡ DRINKS; 1187]

American shorthair *type of* **cat** [➡ FELINES; 983]

amethyst 1 *type of* **gemstone** [➡ PRECIOUS STONES; 1278] 2 *type of* **purple** [➡ COLORS; 1224]

amiability *n* **friendliness**, amicability, sociability, cordiality, agreeableness, good nature, good humor, kindness, geniality, affability [➡ FRIENDLINESS AND SOCIABILITY; 494] *Opposite:* unfriendliness

amiable *adj* **friendly**, sociable, agreeable, affable, kind, likable, good-natured, good-humored, amicable, genial, cordial [➡ FRIENDLINESS AND SOCIABILITY; 494] *Opposite:* unfriendly

amicable *adj* **friendly**, good-natured, harmonious, agreeable, good-humored, kind, polite [➡ RELATIONSHIP TO ANOTHER; 973] *Opposite:* hostile

amicably *adv* **good-naturedly**, cordially, harmoniously, kindly, politely, good-humoredly, agreeably, affably [➡ RELATIONSHIP TO ANOTHER; 973] *Opposite:* acrimoniously

amid 1 *prep* **in the middle of**, among, in the midst of, within, in, amidst [➡ RELATIVE LOCATION; 161] 2 *prep* **accompanied by**, along with, in the course of, during, at the same time as, amidst [➡ CONCURRENT AND CONTEMPORANEOUS; 164]

amidst *see* **amid**

amigo *n* [➡ FRIENDS AND GUESTS; 963]

amino acid *type of* **nutrient** [➡ FOOD COMPONENTS; 1188]

amiss 1 *adv* **incorrectly**, inappropriately, mistakenly, wrongly, erroneously, awry [➡ INCORRECT AND ERRONEOUS; 222] *Opposite:* correctly 2 *adj* **incorrect**, inappropriate, mistaken, wrong, erroneous, awry [➡ INCORRECT AND ERRONEOUS; 222] *Opposite:* correct

amity (*formal*) *n* **friendship**, peace, good relations, goodwill, harmony, friendliness [➡ RELATIONSHIP TO ANOTHER; 973] *Opposite:* hostility

ammo (*informal*) *see* **ammunition**

ammunition *n* **bullets**, shells, missiles, bombs, grenades, ammo (*informal*) [➡ WEAPONS; 1154]

amnesia *n* **loss of memory**, memory loss, forgetfulness, obliviousness, oblivion, blankness, a total blank [➡ IGNORANCE; 557]

amnesty *n* **pardon**, reprieve, forgiveness, absolution, exoneration, remission [➡ TRIAL, PUNISHMENT, AND LEGAL OUTCOMES; 819]

amniocentesis *type of* **medical procedure** [➡ REMEDIES, TREATMENTS, AND OPERATIONS; 731]

amoeba *type of* **microorganism** [➡ MICROORGANISMS, FUNGI, AND ALGAE; 1023]

amoebic *adj* [➡ MICROORGANISMS, FUNGI, AND ALGAE; 1023]

among 1 *prep* **in the middle of**, in the midst of, amongst, amid, amidst, surrounded by, between, mid, midst [➡ RELATIVE LOCATION; 161] 2 *prep* **with**, along with, amongst, amid, together with, in the company of [➡ RELATIVE LOCATION; 161] 3 *prep* **as well as**, including, in addition to [➡ ALSO; 138]

amongst *see* **among**

amoral *adj* **unprincipled**, unethical, dishonorable, unscrupulous, immoral [➡ MORALLY BAD OR IMPROPER; 775] *Opposite:* principled

amorality *n* **wickedness**, sinfulness, unscrupulousness, immorality [➡ MORALLY BAD OR IMPROPER; 775] *Opposite:* morality

amorous *adj* **ardent**, passionate, affectionate, loving, romantic, sentimental, enamored, infatuated [➡ APPRECIATION AND GRATITUDE; 535] *Opposite:* dispassionate

amorphous *adj* **formless**, shapeless, nebulous, vague, unstructured, fluid [➡ SHAPELESSNESS; 1219] *Opposite:* defined

amorphousness *n* [➡ SHAPELESSNESS; 1219]

amortization *n* **repayment**, paying back, payback, paying off, remuneration [➡ OWE AND DESERVE; 465]

amortize *v* **pay back**, repay, pay off, remunerate [➡ GIVE MONEY; 433]

amount *n* **quantity**, sum, total, volume, expanse, extent, aggregate [➡ AMOUNTS AND QUANTITIES; 112]

amount to *v* **add up to**, total, come to, make, be equal to [➡ AMOUNT TO AND EQUAL; 70]

amour-propre (*formal*) *n* [➡ CONFIDENCE AND COMPOSURE; 499]

amp (*informal*) *type of* **audio equipment** [➡ AUDIO EQUIPMENT; 1139]

ampersand *n* **and sign**, and, symbol, character [➡ SYMBOLS, SIGNS, AND NUMBERS; 596]

amphibian 1 *n* [➡ LIVING THINGS AND LIVING; 976] 2 *type of* **military vehicle** [➡ VEHICLES; 1145]

amphibian

◆ *types of amphibians*
axolotl, bullfrog, cane toad, frog, horned toad, midwife toad, natterjack toad, newt, salamander, toad, tree frog, xenopus

amphitheater 1 *n* **stadium**, arena, bowl, ring, dome [➡ BUILDINGS FOR PUBLIC ENTERTAINMENT; 1084] 2 *n* **lecture theater**, theater, auditorium, lecture room [➡ BUILDINGS FOR PUBLIC ENTERTAINMENT; 1084]

ample *adj* **enough**, sufficient, adequate, plenty, plentiful, abundant, full, generous, liberal, copious, bounteous (*literary*), plenteous (*literary*) [➡ ENOUGH AND SUFFICIENT; 131] *Opposite*: insufficient

amplification 1 *n* **intensification**, strengthening, magnification, augmentation, extension, increase, enlargement [➡ CHANGE OF SIZE: BIGGER; 392] *Opposite*: reduction 2 *n* **elaboration**, clarification, development, expansion [➡ EXPLAIN AND CLARIFY; 610] *Opposite*: abbreviation

amplifier *type of* **audio equipment** [➡ AUDIO EQUIPMENT; 1139]

amplify 1 *v* **intensify**, increase, strengthen, magnify, enlarge, swell, augment (*formal*) [➡ CHANGE OF INTENSITY: MORE; 394] *Opposite*: reduce 2 *v* **enlarge on**, go into detail, elaborate, add to, expand, clarify, develop, augment (*formal*) [➡ EXPLAIN AND CLARIFY; 610] *Opposite*: abbreviate

See Compare and Contrast at **increase**.

amplitude *n* **largeness**, scale, plenty, fullness, breadth, generosity, bigness, profusion, bounty (*literary*) [➡ LARGE; 1193]

amply *adv* **sufficiently**, adequately, abundantly, thoroughly, fully, copiously, plentifully, liberally [➡ ENOUGH AND SUFFICIENT; 131] *Opposite*: insufficiently

ampoule *n* **container**, vessel, bottle, flask [➡ CONTAINERS, RECEPTACLES, AND PACKAGING; 1245]

ampule *see* ampoule

amputate *v* **cut off**, chop off, remove, sever, separate [➡ EXTRACT AND SEVER; 341]

amputation *type of* **medical procedure** [➡ REMEDIES, TREATMENTS, AND OPERATIONS; 731]

amulet *n* **charm**, good luck charm, talisman, lucky charm, juju [➡ LUCKY CHARMS; 785]

amuse 1 *v* **make laugh**, make smile, charm, please, divert, distract [➡ PLEASE AND AMUSE; 572] *Opposite*: depress 2 *v* **entertain**, keep busy, interest, absorb, engross, keep amused, fascinate [➡ APPEAL TO AND AROUSE INTEREST; 575] *Opposite*: bore

amused *adj* **smiling**, laughing, pleased, tickled, entertained [➡ PLEASURE, EXCITEMENT, AND ELATION; 534] *Opposite*: annoyed

amusement 1 *n* **laughter**, enjoyment, delight, fun, pleasure, glee, hilarity [➡ ENTERTAINMENT; 872] *Opposite*: sadness 2 *n* **entertainment**, pastime, hobby, distraction, diversion, recreation, pursuit [➡ LEISURE AND RECREATION; 874]

amusement arcade *n* [➡ BUILDINGS FOR PUBLIC ENTERTAINMENT; 1084]

amusement park *n* **fair**, theme park, amusements (*UK*), funfair (*UK*) [➡ URBAN OUTDOOR SPACES; 1072]

amusing *adj* **funny**, humorous, entertaining, comical, witty, droll, diverting, hilarious [➡ FUNNY AND AMUSING; 216]

anachronism *n* **relic**, survival, leftover, archaism, holdover [➡ OLD, OLD-FASHIONED; 167]

anachronistic *adj* **out-of-date**, dated, old-fashioned, old, obsolete, archaic, antiquated, outmoded, obsolescent, passé, outdated [➡ OLD, OLD-FASHIONED; 167] *Opposite*: contemporary

anaconda *type of* **nonpoisonous snake** [➡ SNAKES; 995]

anagram *type of* **wordplay** [➡ JOKES AND TEASING; 674]

anal fin *part of* **fish** [➡ PARTS OF A FISH; 1011]

analgesia 1 *n* **numbness**, painlessness, insensibility, insensitivity, unawareness [➡ TIRED, ASLEEP, AND UNCONSCIOUS; 738] *Opposite*: pain 2 *n* **pain control**, pain relief, pain management, pain killing, numbing, deadening [➡ REMEDIES, TREATMENTS, AND OPERATIONS; 731]

analgesic 1 *adj* **painkilling**, palliative, pain-relieving, deadening, anodyne, numbing [➡ REMEDIES, TREATMENTS, AND OPERATIONS; 731] 2 *n* **painkiller**, palliative, pain reliever, anodyne, anesthetic [➡ REMEDIES, TREATMENTS, AND OPERATIONS; 731]

analogous *adj* **similar**, equivalent, parallel, corresponding, comparable, like, related, akin, consonant (*formal*) [➡ SIMILARITY; 148] *Opposite*: different

analogue *n* **equivalent**, similarity, referent, correspondent (*formal*) [➡ SIMILARITY; 148]

analogy *n* **similarity**, likeness, equivalence, parallel, correspondence, correlation, comparison, resemblance, relation, consonance (*formal*) [➡ EQUALITY; 154] *Opposite*: contrast

analysis 1 *n* **examination**, study, investigation, scrutiny, breakdown, inquiry, exploration, evaluation, consideration, probe [➡ EXAMINE AND ASSESS; 753] 2 *n* **testing**, examination, assay, assessment [➡ EXAMINE AND ASSESS; 753] 3 *n* **psychoanalysis**, psychotherapy, psychiatry [➡ PSYCHOLOGY AND THE MIND; 769]

analyst 1 *n* **forecaster**, predictor, market analyst, expert, specialist, securities analyst, city analyst (*UK*) [➡ PEOPLE INVOLVED IN FINANCE; 804] 2 *n* **psychoanalyst**, psychotherapist, psychiatrist [➡ PEOPLE WHO WORK IN MEDICINE; 848]

analytic *adj* **logical**, investigative, diagnostic, systematic, critical, methodical, questioning, reasoned, rational [➡ THE NATURE OF IDEAS; 771] *Opposite*: illogical

analytical *see* analytic

analyze *v* **examine**, study, investigate, scrutinize, evaluate, consider, question, explore, probe, dissect, inspect [➡ EXAMINE AND ASSESS; 753]

anarchic 1 *adj* **revolutionary**, radical, anarchistic, rebellious, anarchical [➡ REBELLIOUSNESS AND DISOBEDIENCE; 565] 2 *adj* **lawless**, chaotic, disordered, disorderly, out of control, riotous [➡ DISORDER AND CHAOS; 245] *Opposite*: orderly

anarchical *see* **anarchic**

anarchist *n* **revolutionary**, rebel, nihilist, radical [➡PHILOSOPHICAL AND POLITICAL THINKERS; 781]

anarchistic *adj* **revolutionary**, antigovernment, anarchic, anarchical, rebellious [➡REBELLIOUSNESS AND DISOBEDIENCE; 565]

anarchy *n* **disorder**, chaos, lawlessness, anarchism, revolution, rebellion, ochlocracy, riot, mobocracy, mayhem (*informal*) [➡CHAOS AND UPROAR; 51] *Opposite*: order

an arm and a leg (*informal*) *n* **fortune**, a small fortune, king's ransom, pretty penny (*informal*) [➡LARGE AMOUNTS OF MONEY; 118] *Opposite*: pittance

anathema *n* **bane**, scourge, canker, thorn in somebody's side, irritant, abomination [➡NUISANCES; 253]

anathematize *v* [➡ACCUSE, BLAME, AND CRITICIZE; 641]

anatomical *adj* **functional**, structural, material, bodily, body [➡BIOLOGICAL SCIENCES; 1037]

anatomy 1 *n* **structure**, composition, makeup, framework, frame [➡QUALITIES AND CHARACTERISTICS; 1191] 2 *n* **analysis**, examination, investigation, review, study [➡EXAMINE AND ASSESS; 753] 3 *type of* **bioscience** [➡BIOLOGICAL SCIENCES; 1037]

ancestor 1 *n* **forebear**, antecedent, forefather, predecessor, progenitor [➡THE FAMILY; 956] *Opposite*: descendant 2 *n* **forerunner**, precursor, predecessor, progenitor, prototype, foregoer (*formal*) [➡OLDER GENERATION RELATIVES; 959] *Opposite*: successor

ancestral *adj* **family**, familial, inherited [➡THE FAMILY; 956]

ancestry *n* **lineage**, descent, origin, heritage, extraction, stock, pedigree, parentage, line [➡THE FAMILY; 956]

anchor 1 *n* **newscaster**, commentator, announcer, broadcaster, journalist, anchorperson, anchorman, anchorwoman, presenter (*UK*) [➡WORKERS IN ENTERTAINMENT AND MEDIA; 873] 2 *v* **fasten**, attach, fix, affix, secure, moor [➡FASTEN, LINK, AND JOIN; 408] *Opposite*: unfasten

anchorage *n* **port**, harbor, marina, dock, quay, wharf [➡WATERWAYS AND SEAWAYS; 1108]

anchorite *n* **hermit**, recluse, solitary [➡SOLITARY PEOPLE AND MISFITS; 942]

anchorman *see* **anchorperson**

anchorperson *n* **newscaster**, broadcaster, anchor, journalist, announcer, presenter (*UK*) [➡WORKERS IN ENTERTAINMENT AND MEDIA; 873]

anchorwoman *see* **anchorperson**

anchovy *type of* **ocean fish** [➡OCEAN FISH; 1009]

ancient 1 *adj* **antique**, early, earliest, prehistoric, primeval, primordial, primal, ageless, age-old, antediluvian (*informal*), olden (*archaic or literary*) [➡PAST; 84] *Opposite*: modern 2 *adj* **old-fashioned**, archaic, obsolete, outdated, antiquated, prehistoric, antediluvian (*informal*) [➡OLD, OLD-FASHIONED; 167] *Opposite*: up-to-date

ancient history *adj* [➡PAST; 84]

ancillary *adj* **auxiliary**, subsidiary, supplementary, additional, secondary, subordinate, adjuvant [➡INFERIORITY; 153] *Opposite*: main

ancillary building *n* [➡ANCILLARY BUILDINGS; 1080]

and 1 *conj* **then**, after that, next, as a consequence, afterward [➡CAUSATION; 168] 2 *conj* **in addition to**, as well as, with, along with, coupled with, combined with, plus (*informal*) [➡ALSO; 138] 3 *conj* **furthermore**, moreover, also, what is more, in addition, likewise [➡ALSO; 138]

andante *type of* **musical term** [➡MUSICAL TERMS; 912]

and/or *conj* **either/or**, one or both, either or both [➡ALSO; 138]

androecium *part of* **flower** [➡FLOWERS; 1032]

androgynous *adj* [➡GENDER IDENTITY AND SEXUALITY; 932]

android *n* **robot**, automaton, bionic person, machine, humanoid [➡SCIENCE FICTION; 1064]

Andromeda *type of* **constellation** [➡HEAVENLY BODIES; 1061]

anecdotal *adj* **subjective**, circumstantial, hearsay, unreliable, untrustworthy, undependable, sketchy [➡UNCERTAIN; 175] *Opposite*: objective

anecdote *n* **story**, tale, sketch, narrative, narration, yarn (*informal*) [➡THE ORAL TRADITION; 677]

anemia *n* [➡THE BLOOD AND CIRCULATION; 717]

anemic *adj* **weak**, feeble, lackluster, insipid, pale, colorless, bland, pallid, wishy-washy (*informal*), anodyne (*literary*) [➡WEAKNESS; 241] *Opposite*: strong

anemometer *type of* **measuring device** [➡MEASURING DEVICES; 1123]

anemone *type of* **flower grown from bulbs** [➡FLOWERS FROM BULBS; 1030]

aneroid barometer *type of* **measuring device** [➡MEASURING DEVICES; 1123]

anesthesia *type of* **medical procedure** [➡REMEDIES, TREATMENTS, AND OPERATIONS; 731]

anesthetic 1 *n* **painkiller**, local anesthetic, general anesthetic, sedative, analgesic [➡REMEDIES, TREATMENTS, AND OPERATIONS; 731] 2 *adj* **painkilling**, numbing, deadening, sedating [➡REMEDIES, TREATMENTS, AND OPERATIONS; 731]

anesthetize *v* **deaden**, numb, sedate, freeze, put under, put out, put to sleep [➡REMEDIES, TREATMENTS, AND OPERATIONS; 731]

anesthetized *adj* **knocked out**, out cold, under, asleep, sedated, deadened, numb, frozen [➡TIRED, ASLEEP, AND UNCONSCIOUS; 738]

anew *adv* **again**, afresh, once again, once more, over, new, de novo [➡AGAIN; 109]

angel 1 *n* **seraph**, archangel, cherub, messenger, spirit, guardian angel [➡RELIGIOUS CONCEPTS; 776] 2 *n* **backer**, sponsor, guarantor, patron, benefactor, financier [➡REPRESENTATIVES AND PATRONS; 968]

See Compare and Contrast at **backer**.

angelfish *type of* **flatfish** [➡OCEAN FISH; 1009]

angel food cake *type of* **cake** [➡CAKES, COOKIES, AND DESSERTS; 1181]

angelic *adj* **innocent**, good, saintly, adorable, virtuous, divine, caring, kind, appealing, pure (*literary*), beatific (*literary*) [➡MORALLY GOOD; 774] *Opposite:* wicked

angelica *type of* **herb** [➡HERBS AND SPICES; 1175]

anger 1 *n* **annoyance**, irritation, fury, rage, antagonism, resentment, wrath, dander, indignation, ire (*formal*) [➡IRRITATION AND ANGER; 541] *Opposite:* calm 2 *v* **annoy**, irritate, infuriate, incense, enrage, madden, exasperate, provoke, rile (*informal*), aggravate (*informal*) [➡ANGER AND ANNOY; 569] *Opposite:* pacify

Compare and Contrast: *anger, annoyance, irritation, resentment, indignation, fury, rage, ire, wrath*

CORE MEANING: a feeling of strong displeasure in response to an assumed injury

anger a strong feeling of grievance; *annoyance* mild anger and impatience; *irritation* impatience and exasperation; *resentment* aggrieved feelings caused by a sense of unfair treatment; *indignation* anger because something seems unfair or unreasonable; *fury* violent anger; *rage* sudden and extreme anger; *ire* (*literary*) strong anger; *wrath* strong anger, often with a desire for revenge.

angioplasty *type of* **medical procedure** [➡REMEDIES, TREATMENTS, AND OPERATIONS; 731]

angle 1 *n* **point of view**, viewpoint, approach, position, slant, perspective, outlook, direction [➡POINTS OF VIEW; 767] 2 *v* **slant**, tilt, turn, twist, slope, point, aim [➡MOVE SOMETHING INTO A NEW POSITION OR OVERTURN; 330] *Opposite:* level

angle for *v* **fish for**, seek, solicit, try for, try to get [➡OBTAIN POSSESSION BY PERSUASION; 457]

anglerfish *type of* **ocean fish** [➡OCEAN FISH; 1009]

angling *n* [➡HOBBIES, GAMES, AND SPORTS; 875]

angora *type of* **fabric from animals** [➡FABRICS; 1132]

angry *adj* **annoyed**, irritated, fuming, livid, irate, heated, gnashing your teeth, cross, furious, incensed, enraged, outraged, infuriated, wrathful, indignant, mad, choleric (*literary*), ireful (*literary*) [➡IRRITATION AND ANGER; 541] *Opposite:* calm

angst *n* **anguish**, torment, anxiety, trouble, sorrow, worry, fear [➡SADNESS, DISTRESS, AND DESPAIR; 539] *Opposite:* happiness

See Compare and Contrast at **worry**.

angst-ridden *adj* **anguished**, tormented, fearful, troubled, worried, anxious, sorrowful [➡SADNESS, DISTRESS, AND DESPAIR; 539] *Opposite:* content

anguish *n* **suffering**, torment, agony, torture, pain, distress, grief, sorrow, angst, affliction, anxiety [➡SADNESS, DISTRESS, AND DESPAIR; 539] *Opposite:* contentment

anguished *adj* **tormented**, suffering, agonized, tortured, painful, distressed, grief-stricken, sorrowful, angst-

ridden, anxious [➡SADNESS, DISTRESS, AND DESPAIR; 539] *Opposite:* content

angular *adj* **bony**, rawboned, rangy, lanky, gaunt, pointed, thin, gawky (*informal*) [➡BUILD; 477] *Opposite:* rounded

angularity *n* **boniness**, thinness, ranginess, lankiness, sharpness, gauntness, gawkiness (*informal*) [➡BUILD; 477] *Opposite:* roundness

animal 1 *n* **creature**, being, beast, mammal, organism [➡LIVING THINGS AND LIVING; 976] 2 *n* **monster**, beast, brute, swine [➡VILLAINS AND THUGS; 947] 3 *adj* **physical**, bodily, visceral, instinctive, innate, intuitive, inborn, instinctual, subconscious [➡LIVING THINGS AND LIVING; 976] *Opposite:* spiritual

animate 1 *v* **liven up**, enliven, rouse, bring to life, stir, stimulate [➡ENCOURAGE; 576] *Opposite:* put a damper on 2 *adj* **living**, alive, live, breathing, flesh and blood, conscious, sentient, moving [➡LIVING THINGS AND LIVING; 976] *Opposite:* inanimate

See Compare and Contrast at **living**.

animated *adj* **energetic**, active, vibrant, vivacious, dynamic, full of life, enthusiastic, excited, sparkling, spirited, lively, vigorous [➡POSITIVE IMPATIENCE, ENTHUSIASM, AND ALERTNESS; 537] *Opposite:* lifeless

animated film *n* [➡FILM; 901]

animation 1 *n* **liveliness**, energy, vibrancy, life, vigor, vivaciousness, dynamism, enthusiasm, excitement, activity, sparkle, spirit [➡ENERGY AND ENTHUSIASM; 496] *Opposite:* lifelessness 2 *n* **cartoon**, moving picture, animatronics, computer graphics, simulation [➡THE PICTORIAL ARTS; 897]

animatronics *n* [➡FILM; 901]

animosity *n* **hostility**, hatred, loathing, ill feeling, ill will, enmity, bitterness, acrimony, rancor, dislike, antagonism, no love lost, bad blood [➡ANTAGONISM; 552] *Opposite:* goodwill

See Compare and Contrast at **dislike**.

animus 1 *n* **hostility**, animosity, hatred, ill will, detestation, spitefulness [➡ANTAGONISM; 552] *Opposite:* friendliness 2 *n* **temperament**, personality, disposition, spirit, attitude [➡TEMPERAMENT AND BEHAVIOR; 492]

aniseed *type of* **spice** [➡HERBS AND SPICES; 1175]

ankle *part of* **leg or foot** [➡PARTS OF THE BODY: LEG AND FOOT; 694]

anklebone *type of* **bone** [➡THE BONES AND JOINTS; 719]

ankle-length *adj* [➡DESCRIBING CLOTHES; 869]

anklet *n* **bracelet**, chain, bangle, band [➡JEWELRY; 866]

ankylosaur *type of* **dinosaur** [➡DINOSAURS; 996]

annals *n* **records**, archives, chronicles, history, accounts, registers [➡RECORDS; 585]

anneal *v* **harden**, strengthen, toughen, galvanize, forge [➡HARDEN, CONGEAL, AND DRY; 387]

annex 1 *v* **take possession of**, seize, take over, capture, invade, take control of, appropriate, commandeer [➡ TAKE SOMETHING AWAY; 425] *Opposite*: surrender **2** *n* **extension**, new building, addition, ell, wing, supplementary building [➡ ANCILLARY BUILDINGS; 1080]

annexation *n* **capture**, seizure, takeover, occupation, invasion, appropriation [➡ TAKE SOMETHING AWAY; 425] *Opposite*: surrender

annihilate 1 *v* **destroy**, obliterate, extinguish, eradicate, exterminate, wipe out (*informal*) [➡ DESTRUCTION AND DEMOLITION; 359] *Opposite*: protect **2** *v* (*informal*) **defeat**, rout, thrash, overwhelm, crush, beat, conquer, overpower [➡ BEAT AND DEFEAT; 80] *Opposite*: lose

annihilation *n* **total destruction**, obliteration, extinction, eradication, extermination, wiping out (*informal*) [➡ BEAT AND DEFEAT; 80] *Opposite*: protection

anniversary *n* **birthday**, centennial, bicentennial, wedding anniversary, centenary (*UK*), bicentenary (*UK*) [➡ CEREMONIES AND ANNIVERSARIES; 38]

annotate *v* **gloss**, add footnotes, interpret, explain, make notes on, comment on, note, mark, mark up [➡ RECORD SOMETHING; 371]

annotated *adj* **glossed**, marked, marked up [➡ WRITING; 583]

annotation *n* **footnote**, gloss, marginal note, explanation, note, comment, mark [➡ PARTS OF BOOKS AND DOCUMENTS; 593]

announce *v* **proclaim**, make known, publicize, broadcast, declare, say, pronounce, state, herald, publish, read out, post, promulgate [➡ INFORM, ANNOUNCE, AND ISSUE; 611] *Opposite*: keep secret

announcement *n* **statement**, declaration, message, notice, proclamation, publication, broadcast, pronouncement, revelation [➡ INFORM, ANNOUNCE, AND ISSUE; 611]

announcer *n* **broadcaster**, telecaster, newscaster, anchor, reporter, presenter (*UK*) [➡ WORKERS IN ENTERTAINMENT AND MEDIA; 873]

annoy *v* **irritate**, infuriate, exasperate, get on your nerves, bother, madden, anger, frustrate, displease, provoke, irk, vex, put out, aggravate (*informal*), rile (*informal*), bug (*informal*), drive nuts (*informal*) [➡ ANGER AND ANNOY; 569] *Opposite*: please

Compare and Contrast: *annoy, irritate, exasperate, vex, irk*

CORE MEANING: to cause a mild degree of anger

annoy to cause anger or impatience; *irritate* to annoy slightly; *exasperate* to arouse anger or frustration; *vex* to annoy, especially causing upset or distress; *irk* to annoy by being tiresome or tedious.

See Compare and Contrast at **bother**.

annoyance *n* **irritation**, infuriation, exasperation, anger, frustration, displeasure, indignation [➡ IRRITATION AND ANGER; 541] *Opposite*: pleasure

See Compare and Contrast at **anger**.

annoyed *adj* **angry**, irritated, infuriated, exasperated, aggravated, upset, bothered, maddened, frustrated, displeased, provoked, incensed, put out, wound up (*informal*), riled (*informal*) [➡ IRRITATION AND ANGER; 541] *Opposite*: pleased

annoying *adj* **maddening**, irritating, infuriating, bothersome, exasperating, frustrating, trying, grating, aggravating (*informal*) [➡ IRRITATING; 228] *Opposite*: pleasing

annual *adj* **yearly**, twelve-monthly, once a year, once yearly, every twelve months [➡ TIMES OF YEAR; 88]

annual general meeting *n* [➡ MEETINGS AND ASSEMBLIES; 43]

annuity *n* **pension**, allowance, income, grant, stipend, endowment [➡ INCOME; 460]

annul *v* **cancel**, call off, withdraw, end, dissolve, rescind, invalidate, put an end to, terminate (*formal*) [➡ ABOLISH AND ANNUL; 452] *Opposite*: prolong

See Compare and Contrast at **nullify**.

annulment *n* **cancellation**, withdrawal, dissolution, invalidation, deletion, elimination, termination (*formal*) [➡ ENDS AND DEPARTURES; 54]

anode *n* **terminal**, connection, contact [➡ ELECTRONICS AND ELECTRICS; 1137]

anodyne 1 *adj* **painkilling**, palliative, pain-relieving, deadening, analgesic, numbing [➡ REMEDIES, TREATMENTS, AND OPERATIONS; 731] **2** *adj* (*literary*) **soothing**, comforting, relaxing, settling, calming, restful [➡ CALMING; 188] *Opposite*: stimulating **3** *adj* (*literary*) **insipid**, bland, tame, neutral, inoffensive, colorless, dull, antiseptic, unexciting, anemic [➡ BORING AND UNINTERESTING; 234] *Opposite*: exciting

anoint *v* **smear**, daub, rub, smooth, massage, oil [➡ DECORATE, ADORN, AND APPLY COATINGS; 405]

anomalous *adj* **irregular**, uncharacteristic, strange, abnormal, inconsistent, out of the ordinary, jarring, atypical, unusual [➡ BIZARRE AND PECULIAR; 257] *Opposite*: usual

anomaly *n* **irregularity**, incongruity, difference, variance, glitch, abnormality, inconsistency [➡ MISTAKES; 250]

anon (*archaic or literary*) *adv* **soon**, shortly, later, in a while, in a moment, in two shakes of a lamb's tail, presently (*formal or literary*) [➡ FUTURE; 86] *Opposite*: now

anonymity 1 *n* **secrecy**, obscurity, concealment, inconspicuousness, namelessness, facelessness, privacy, unrecognizability [➡ SECRET AND UNKNOWN; 179] **2** *n* **indistinctness**, blandness, insignificance, ordinariness, dullness [➡ UNIMPORTANT AND UNNECESSARY; 238] *Opposite*: distinctiveness

anonymous 1 *adj* **nameless**, unidentified, unnamed, unsigned, unspecified, unknown, secret, mysterious, shadowy [➡ SECRET AND UNKNOWN; 179] *Opposite*: named **2** *adj* **undistinguished**, indistinctive, ordinary, everyday, run of the mill, unexceptional, unmemorable, dull [➡ ORDINARINESS; 244] *Opposite*: distinctive

anonymously *adv* **incognito**, namelessly, in secret, secretly, in disguise [➡ SECRET AND UNKNOWN; 179]

anorak *type of* **jacket** [➡ GARMENTS AND OUTFITS; 865]

another *adj* **one more**, additional, a new, a different, a further, extra, added, any more, alternative [➡ MORE AND EXCESS; 124]

answer 1 *n* **response**, reply, reaction, riposte, retort, rejoinder (*formal*) [➡ REPLY AND ANSWER; 668] *Opposite*: question 2 *n* **solution**, key, way out, resolution, remedy [➡ SOLUTIONS; 215] *Opposite*: problem 3 *v* **reply**, respond, react, come back with, counter, retort, rejoin (*formal*) [➡ REPLY AND ANSWER; 668] *Opposite*: challenge 4 *v* **solve**, satisfy, resolve, lay to rest, meet, remedy, fulfill [➡ SOLVE AND INTERPRET; 760]

Compare and Contrast: *answer, reply, response, rejoinder, retort, riposte*

CORE MEANING: something said, written, or done in acknowledgment of a question or remark, or in reaction to a situation

answer an acknowledgment of a question, letter, or situation; *reply* a spoken or written answer, or a reaction to a situation; *response* a spoken or written answer, or a reaction to a situation; *rejoinder* (*formal*) a sharp, critical, angry, or clever reply, usually spoken; *retort* a sharp spoken reply, often to criticism; *riposte* a quick or witty spoken reply.

answerability *n* [➡ RESPONSIBILITY; 170]

answerable *adj* **responsible**, accountable, liable, chargeable, subject to blame, blamable, punishable [➡ RESPONSIBILITY; 170] *Opposite*: unaccountable

answer back *v* **retort**, argue, counter, respond, riposte, react, fight back, come back, be rude, talk back, contradict, cheek (*informal*) [➡ REPLY AND ANSWER; 668]

answer for 1 *v* **pay for**, suffer for, be punished for, make amends for, take the rap (*slang*), atone (*formal*) [➡ VENGEANCE AND REVENGE; 685] *Opposite*: get away with 2 *v* **be responsible for**, be accountable for, vouch for, take the responsibility for, be to blame for, be liable for [➡ APPROVE AND CONFIRM; 646]

answering machine *type of* **telecommunications equipment** [➡ TELECOMMUNICATIONS; 1130]

ant *n* [➡ INSECTS; 1012]

ant

◆ *types of ants*
army ant, carpenter ant, fire ant, flying ant, leafcutter ant, Pharaoh ant, red ant, slave ant, slave-making ant, soldier ant, white ant, worker ant

antagonism 1 *n* **resentment**, dislike, bitterness, hatred, antipathy, ill feeling, ill will, bad blood [➡ ANTAGONISM; 552] *Opposite*: friendliness 2 *n* **rivalry**, opposition, aggression, hostility, enmity, animosity [➡ RELATIONSHIP TO ANOTHER; 973] *Opposite*: cooperation

antagonist *n* **rival**, adversary, opponent, enemy, contender, competitor [➡ ENEMIES AND TORMENTORS; 969] *Opposite*: friend

antagonistic *adj* **aggressive**, hostile, opposed, unfriendly, incompatible, on the warpath (*informal*) [➡ IRRITATION AND ANGER; 541] *Opposite*: friendly

antagonize *v* **provoke**, irritate, annoy, upset, get your

back up, alienate, rile (*informal*) [➡ ANGER AND ANNOY; 569] *Opposite*: mollify

ante *n* **bet**, wager, stake, payment, raise [➡ GAMBLE AND TAKE RISKS; 466]

anteater *type of* **small mammal** [➡ SMALL MAMMALS; 990]

antebellum *adj* **early nineteenth-century**, eighteenth-century, colonial, historical, Federalist, prewar [➡ PAST; 84]

antecede *v* [➡ BEFORE, FIRST, AND PRECEDING; 163]

antecedence *n* [➡ BEFORE, FIRST, AND PRECEDING; 163]

antecedent *n* **precursor**, forerunner, ancestor, predecessor, forebear, originator [➡ BEFORE, FIRST, AND PRECEDING; 163]

antecedents *n* **past history**, background, previous circumstances, qualifications, experience, past [➡ PAST; 84]

antechamber *type of* **room in public buildings** [➡ TYPES OF ROOMS; 1097]

antedate *v* **predate**, go before, be earlier than, date from before, occur before [➡ BEFORE, FIRST, AND PRECEDING; 163]

antediluvian 1 *adj* **prehistoric**, ancient, old, primitive, primeval, primordial [➡ PAST; 84] *Opposite*: modern 2 *adj* (*informal*) **antiquated**, out-of-date, obsolete, old-fashioned, archaic, outmoded, outdated [➡ OLD, OLD-FASHIONED; 167] *Opposite*: up-to-date

See Compare and Contrast at **old-fashioned**.

antelope *type of* **deer or antelope** [➡ DEER AND ANTELOPES; 981]

antenatal (*UK*) *adj* **prenatal**, pregnancy, pre-birth [➡ REPRODUCTION AND HEREDITY; 725] *Opposite*: postnatal

antenna 1 *n* **feeler**, projection, tentacle, probe, protuberance, whisker [➡ PARTS OF AN INSECT; 1019] 2 *type of* **telecommunications equipment** [➡ TELECOMMUNICATIONS; 1130]

anterior (*formal*) *adj* [➡ BEFORE, FIRST, AND PRECEDING; 163]

anteroom *type of* **room in public buildings** [➡ TYPES OF ROOMS; 1097]

anthem *n* **song of praise**, national hymn, sacred song, psalm, hymn, chorale [➡ MUSIC, SONGS, AND SINGING; 907]

anther *part of* **flower** [➡ FLOWERS; 1032]

anthology *n* **collection**, compilation, album, omnibus, compendium, collected works [➡ COLLECTIONS AND MIXTURES OF THINGS; 1244]

anthropomorphize *v* **humanize**, personify, make human, give a human face to, sentimentalize, bring alive [➡ NAME AND DESCRIBE; 665]

anti (*informal*) *adj* **opposed**, against, antagonistic, ill-disposed, hostile, set against, averse (*formal*) [➡ UNWILLINGNESS AND STUBBORNNESS; 564] *Opposite*: pro

antiaircraft gun *type of* **gun** [➡ WEAPONS FOR SHOOTING; 1156]

antiballistic missile *type of* **explosive weapon** [➡ EXPLOSIVES; 1155]

anticipate 1 *v* **do in advance**, get ahead, forestall, do ahead, prepare for, antedate, beat somebody to it (*informal*) [→ BEFORE, FIRST, AND PRECEDING; 163] **2** *v* **expect**, foresee, look forward to, await, wait for, predict, be hopeful of, think likely [→ PREDICT AND ANTICIPATE; 750]

anticipated *adj* **expected**, predicted, projected, estimated, awaited, foreseen [→ FUTURE; 86] *Opposite*: unexpected

anticipation *n* **expectation**, expectancy, hope, eagerness, keenness, looking forward [→ FEELINGS ABOUT THE FUTURE; 533]

anticlimax *n* **letdown**, disappointment, deflation, comedown (*informal*) [→ FAILURE; 77] *Opposite*: climax

anticlockwise (*UK*) *adj* [→ DIRECTION OF MOTION; 345]

antics **1** *n* **clowning**, tricks, pranks, larks, frolics, capers, playfulness [→ JOKES AND TEASING; 674] **2** *n* **behavior**, actions, activities, tricks, conduct [→ TEMPERAMENT AND BEHAVIOR; 492]

antidote *n* **cure**, remedy, solution, answer, corrective, medicine [→ SOLUTIONS; 215] *Opposite*: poison

antihero *n* [→ VILLAINS AND THUGS; 947]

antineutron *type of* **elementary particle** [→ ELEMENTARY PARTICLES; 1279]

antipasto *part of* **meal** [→ MEALS AND PARTS OF MEALS; 1169]

antipathetic *adj* **opposed**, hostile, antagonistic, conflicting, anti (*informal*), averse (*formal*) [→ IRRITATION AND ANGER; 541] *Opposite*: sympathetic

antipathy *n* **opposition**, hostility, antagonism, hatred, dislike, ill feeling, ill will, aversion (*formal*) [→ ANTAGONISM; 552] *Opposite*: support

See Compare and Contrast at **dislike**.

antiproton *type of* **elementary particle** [→ ELEMENTARY PARTICLES; 1279]

antiquark *type of* **elementary particle** [→ ELEMENTARY PARTICLES; 1279]

antiquated *adj* **out-of-date**, old-fashioned, old, obsolete, archaic, outdated, outmoded, antediluvian (*informal*) [→ OLD, OLD-FASHIONED; 167] *Opposite*: modern

See Compare and Contrast at **old-fashioned**.

antique *adj* **old**, traditional, aged, historic, old-fashioned, vintage [→ OLD, OLD-FASHIONED; 167] *Opposite*: new

antiquity **1** *n* **ancient times**, the distant past, olden days, olden times, time immemorial, bygone days [→ PAST; 84] **2** *n* **relic**, remains, archaeological find, antique, artifact [→ PHYSICAL OBJECTS; 1243]

antiseptic **1** *adj* **sterile**, antibacterial, uncontaminated, clean, pure, disinfected, germ-killing [→ CLEAN AND HYGIENIC; 1233] *Opposite*: infected **2** *adj* **bland**, insipid, tame, uninteresting, colorless, dull, unexciting, anodyne (*literary*) [→ BORING AND UNINTERESTING; 234] *Opposite*: colorful

antisocial **1** *adj* **disruptive**, rebellious, harmful, inconsiderate, belligerent, disorderly [→ SELFISH AND UNKIND; 505] *Opposite*: constructive **2** *adj* **unsociable**, unfriendly, disagreeable, shy, reserved, withdrawn [→ UNFRIENDLINESS AND UNSOCIABILITY; 504] *Opposite*: sociable

antithesis *n* **opposite**, direct opposite, exact opposite, contrast, converse, contrary, reverse, opposition [→ OPPOSITE; 157]

antithetic *see* **antithetical**

antithetical (*formal*) *adj* **opposite**, differing, contradictory, opposed, contrary, contrasting [→ OPPOSITE; 157]

antitrade *type of* **wind** [→ WINDY AND STORMY WEATHER; 1053]

antonomasia *type of* **figure of speech** [→ FIGURES OF SPEECH; 673]

antonym *n* [→ OPPOSITE; 157]

antsy (*informal*) *adj* [→ IRRITATION AND ANGER; 541]

anus *part of* **digestive tract** [→ THE DIGESTIVE TRACT; 709]

anvil *part of* **ear** [→ THE EAR; 706]

anxiety *n* **nervousness**, worry, concern, unease, apprehension, disquiet, fretfulness, angst, fear [→ CONFUSION, ANXIETY, AND WORRY; 540] *Opposite*: calmness

See Compare and Contrast at **worry**.

anxious **1** *adj* **worried**, concerned, uneasy, apprehensive, restless, fretful, fearful, frightened, nervous [→ CONFUSION, ANXIETY, AND WORRY; 540] *Opposite*: calm **2** *adj* **eager**, keen, enthusiastic, concerned, impatient, itching, intent, yearning [→ POSITIVE IMPATIENCE, ENTHUSIASM, AND ALERTNESS; 537] *Opposite*: indifferent

anxiousness *n* [→ CONFUSION, ANXIETY, AND WORRY; 540]

any **1** *adj* **some**, one, several, a few [→ AMOUNTS AND QUANTITIES; 112] *Opposite*: none **2** *adj* **every**, each, whichever, whatever [→ ALL; 128] **3** *adv* **at all**, in the least, slightly, a little, somewhat, to some extent [→ TO A CERTAIN EXTENT; 136]

anybody *pron* **anyone**, any person, somebody, someone, everybody, everyone [→ PERSON; 931] *Opposite*: nobody

anyhow *adv* **anyway**, in any case, at any rate, nevertheless, nonetheless, besides, at least, well [→ ALTHOUGH, NEVERTHELESS, AND DESPITE; 169]

anyone *pron* **anybody**, any person, someone, somebody, everyone, everybody [→ PERSON; 931] *Opposite*: no one

anyplace (*informal*) *adv* **anywhere**, wherever, where, somewhere, everywhere, someplace (*informal*), everyplace (*informal*) [→ GENERAL LOCATIONS; 158]

anyway *adv* **anyhow**, at any rate, in any case, nevertheless, nonetheless, besides, at least, well [→ ALTHOUGH, NEVERTHELESS, AND DESPITE; 169]

anywhere *adv* **wherever**, where, somewhere, everywhere, someplace (*informal*), everyplace (*informal*), anyplace (*informal*) [→ GENERAL LOCATIONS; 158]

A-OK (*informal*) *adv* **excellent**, perfect, all right, just right, good, great (*informal*), fine (*informal*) [→ CORRECT AND FAULTLESS; 182]

aorta *type of* **blood vessel** [→ THE BLOOD AND CIRCULATION; 717]

apace *adv* **quickly**, rapidly, swiftly, briskly, like lightning, at a rate of knots (*UK*) [→ HAPPENING QUICKLY; 104] *Opposite*: slowly

apart *adv* **separately**, not together, at a distance, to one side, away from each other [➡ DISTANCE; 160] *Opposite*: together

apart from 1 *prep* **aside from**, except for, with the exception of, not counting, excluding, not including, except, besides, excepting (*formal*) [➡ NOT; 137] *Opposite*: including 2 *prep* **as well as**, in addition to, on top of, besides [➡ ALSO; 138]

apartment *n* [➡ RESIDENTIAL BUILDINGS; 1078]

apartment block (*UK*) *n* [➡ RESIDENTIAL BUILDINGS; 1078]

apartment building *n* [➡ RESIDENTIAL BUILDINGS; 1078]

apartment house *n* [➡ RESIDENTIAL BUILDINGS; 1078]

apathetic *adj* **indifferent**, uninterested, listless, dispirited, droopy, unconcerned, lethargic, lazy, bored [➡ NEUTRALITY AND INDIFFERENCE; 553] *Opposite*: enthusiastic

See Compare and Contrast at **impassive**.

apathy *n* **indifference**, unconcern, lethargy, laziness, boredom, ennui, droopiness, dispiritedness [➡ NEUTRALITY AND INDIFFERENCE; 553] *Opposite*: interest

apatosaur *type of* **dinosaur** [➡ DINOSAURS; 996]

ape 1 *type of* **primate** [➡ PRIMATES; 988] 2 *v* **imitate**, mimic, copy, reproduce, simulate, mirror, parrot [➡ PRETEND AND MIMIC; 60]

See Compare and Contrast at **imitate**.

aperitif 1 *n* [➡ DRINKS; 1187] 2 *part of* **meal** [➡ MEALS AND PARTS OF MEALS; 1169]

aperture *n* **opening**, hole, space, crack, slit, orifice (*literary*) [➡ HOLES, GAPS, AND FORKS; 1252]

apex *n* **top**, peak, summit, climax, zenith, head, high point [➡ EXTREMITIES OF PHYSICAL OBJECTS; 1250] *Opposite*: base

aphid *type of* **flying insect** [➡ FLYING INSECTS; 1013]

aphorism *n* **saying**, maxim, adage, cliché, saw, dictum (*formal*), precept (*formal*) [➡ FIGURES OF SPEECH; 673]

apiary *type of* **pen or cage** [➡ ANIMAL OR BIRD ACCOMMODATIONS; 1079]

apiece *adv* **each**, respectively, to each, for each, individually, separately [➡ APPORTIONMENT; 113] *Opposite*: collectively

aplenty *adj* [➡ MANY, MUCH, LARGE AMOUNT; 117]

aplomb *n* **assurance**, self-confidence, self-possession, composure, style, ease, poise [➡ CONFIDENCE AND COMPOSURE; 499] *Opposite*: awkwardness

apocalypse *n* **end of the world**, day of reckoning, Judgment Day, Armageddon, catastrophe, disaster, destruction [➡ RELIGIOUS CONCEPTS; 776]

apocryphal *adj* **mythical**, fictional, untrue, legendary, invented, made-up, dubious [➡ FALSE AND UNREAL; 173] *Opposite*: true

apogee *n* [➡ INTERMEDIATE STAGES; 55]

apologetic *adj* **sorry**, remorseful, contrite, repentant, rueful, diffident [➡ EMBARRASSMENT AND HUMILIATION; 542] *Opposite*: unrepentant

apologist *n* **defender**, supporter, ally, protector, champion, advocate [➡ SUPPORTERS, PROTECTORS, AND COMPATRIOTS; 970]

apologize *v* **make an apology**, ask for forgiveness, beg forgiveness, express regret, act contrite, say you're sorry [➡ APOLOGIZE AND RETRACT; 683]

apology 1 *n* **admission of guilt**, request for forgiveness, expression of regret, confession, act of contrition [➡ APOLOGIZE AND RETRACT; 683] 2 *n* (*humorous*) **poor substitute**, pathetic excuse, poor example, pretense, stopgap, imitation [➡ FAULTS, FLAWS, AND WEAKNESSES; 251] 3 *n* **defense**, excuse, explanation, justification [➡ APOLOGIZE AND RETRACT; 683]

apoplectic *adj* [➡ IRRITATION AND ANGER; 541]

apostate *n* **renouncer**, defector, deserter, renegade [➡ UNCOOPERATIVE OR REBELLIOUS PEOPLE; 566]

apostle 1 *n* **advocate**, supporter, promoter, champion, proponent, believer [➡ SUPPORTERS, PROTECTORS, AND COMPATRIOTS; 970] *Opposite*: detractor 2 *n* **disciple**, follower, missionary, messenger, devotee, adherent [➡ RELIGIOUS PEOPLE; 778] *Opposite*: leader

apostrophe *type of* **diacritic** [➡ ASPECTS OF LANGUAGE; 682]

apotheosis *n* **high point**, acme, apogee, climax, limit, zenith, pinnacle, peak [➡ INTERMEDIATE STAGES; 55] *Opposite*: nadir

appall *v* **horrify**, shock, disgust, dismay, upset, sicken, outrage, scandalize, distress [➡ UPSET, DISTRESS, AND HUMILIATE; 567] *Opposite*: please

appalled *adj* **horrified**, shocked, stunned, repelled, sickened, disgusted, revolted [➡ SURPRISE, SHOCK, AND AMAZEMENT; 545] *Opposite*: delighted

appalling 1 *adj* **horrifying**, shocking, disgusting, upsetting, sickening, outrageous, scandalous, distressing [➡ EMOTIONALLY UNPLEASANT AND UPSETTING; 227] *Opposite*: appealing 2 *adj* **awful**, terrible, dreadful, horrendous, inexcusable, unspeakable, atrocious, abysmal [➡ BAD AND BADLY; 223] *Opposite*: wonderful

appallingly *adv* **awfully**, terribly, dreadfully, horrendously, inexcusably, unspeakably, atrociously, abysmally [➡ DISGUSTING AND REPULSIVE; 230] *Opposite*: wonderfully

apparatus 1 *n* **device**, gadget, gear, tackle, kit, contraption, machine, tool [➡ DEVICES; 1115] 2 *n* **system**, method, mechanism, arrangement, operation, machine, machinery, organization [➡ WAYS OF DOING THINGS; 294]

apparel *n* **clothing**, clothes, garb, wear, kit, gear (*informal*), attire (*formal*) [➡ CLOTHES AND ACCESSORIES; 864]

apparent 1 *adj* **obvious**, clear, evident, plain, noticeable, perceptible, visible, plain as the nose on your face [➡ PERCEPTIBLE; 25] *Opposite*: unclear 2 *adj* **seeming**, ostensible, deceptive, superficial, specious, outward [➡ UNCERTAIN; 175] *Opposite*: actual

apparently 1 *adv* **it seems that**, it appears that, in fact, rumor has it that, it sounds as if, actually, evidently, obviously, according to the grapevine (*informal*) [➡ EXPRESSIONS OF UNCERTAINTY; 560] 2 *adv* **seemingly**, deceptively, spe-

ciously, ostensibly, outwardly, superficially [➡ UNCERTAIN; 175]
Opposite: actually

apparition *n* **ghost**, spirit, specter, phantom, ghoul, vision [➡ THE SUPERNATURAL; 787]

appassionato *type of* **musical term** [➡ MUSICAL TERMS; 912]

appeal 1 *n* **plea**, petition, application, request, call, entreaty [➡ REQUEST AND DEMAND; 663] 2 *n* **charm**, attractiveness, attraction, allure, influence, draw, interest, fascination, temptation, pull (*informal*) [➡ BEAUTY AND ATTRACTIVENESS; 189] *Opposite*: repulsion 3 *v* **request**, ask, plead, urge, petition, call, entreat [➡ REQUEST AND DEMAND; 663] 4 *v* **attract**, interest, fascinate, charm, tempt, entice, please, draw, pull (*informal*), grab (*informal*) [➡ APPEAL TO AND AROUSE INTEREST; 575] *Opposite*: repel

appealing *adj* **attractive**, tempting, interesting, pleasing, alluring, likable, engaging, charming, fascinating [➡ BEAUTY AND ATTRACTIVENESS; 189] *Opposite*: repulsive

appear 1 *v* **come into view**, come into sight, become visible, emerge, come out, show, materialize [➡ APPEAR AND EMERGE; 3] *Opposite*: disappear 2 *v* **happen**, occur, be found, exist, surface, emerge, arrive on the scene, grow, begin [➡ GRADUALLY COME INTO EXISTENCE; 1] 3 *v* **seem**, look, look as if, give the impression, give the idea, look like [➡ SEEM TO BE SOMETHING; 58] 4 *v* **perform**, be seen, act, play, take part in, play a part [➡ PARTICIPATE; 292] 5 *v* **turn up**, show, be seen, arrive, roll up, arrive on the scene, show up (*informal*) [➡ ARRIVE; 12]

appearance 1 *n* **emergence**, development, arrival, growth, beginning, advent [➡ BEGINNINGS; 53] *Opposite*: disappearance 2 *n* **look**, form, exterior, manifestation, outer shell, façade, outward show [➡ APPEARANCE AND ATMOSPHERE; 1237] 3 *n* **arrival**, entrance, advent, attendance, presence [➡ ARRIVAL; 13]

appease 1 *v* **mollify**, conciliate, pacify, placate, soothe, settle, quiet down, calm down, accede to somebody's demands [➡ SOOTHE AND CALM; 573] *Opposite*: provoke 2 *v* **satisfy**, assuage, attenuate, calm, soothe, ease [➡ SOOTHE AND CALM; 573] *Opposite*: intensify

appeasement *n* **conciliation**, pacification, accession, mollification, placation, concession [➡ APOLOGIZE AND RETRACT; 683] *Opposite*: provocation

appeaser *n* **conciliator**, pacifier, gratifier, mollifier [➡ ADVISERS, JUDGES, AND ARBITERS; 971]

appellant *n* [➡ TRIAL, PUNISHMENT, AND LEGAL OUTCOMES; 819]

appellation (*formal*) *n* **name**, designation, title, style, tag, nickname [➡ NAME AND DESCRIBE; 665]

append *v* **add**, add on, tag on, attach, affix, join [➡ FASTEN, LINK, AND JOIN; 408] *Opposite*: detach

appendage 1 *n* **addition**, attachment, adjunct, add-on, accessory, extra, supplement [➡ PHYSICAL OBJECTS; 1243] 2 *n* **extremity**, feeler, limb, member, projection, tentacle, flipper [➡ PARTS OF THE BODY: TORSO; 693]

appendectomy *type of* **medical procedure** [➡ REMEDIES, TREATMENTS, AND OPERATIONS; 731]

appendix 1 *part of* **digestive tract** [➡ THE DIGESTIVE TRACT; 709] 2 *n* **adjunct**, add-on, supplement, appendage, P.S., addition [➡ PARTS OF BOOKS AND DOCUMENTS; 593]

appertain (*formal*) *v* **relate**, belong, be associated with, be relevant to, have a bearing on, connect to [➡ BE ABOUT SOMETHING; 62]

appetite 1 *n* **hunger**, craving, taste, need to eat, desire for food, hungriness [➡ EAT AND NOT EAT; 710] 2 *n* **desire**, taste, enthusiasm, eagerness, keenness, inclination, hunger, passion, craving, wish [➡ DESIRE AND WANT; 579] *Opposite*: aversion (*formal*)

appetizer 1 *n* **sample**, introduction, sneak preview, taste, foretaste, example, taster (*UK*) [➡ INDICATIONS, SIGNS, AND WARNINGS; 68] 2 *part of* **meal** [➡ MEALS AND PARTS OF MEALS; 1169]

appetizing 1 *adj* **delicious**, tasty, mouthwatering, enticing, tempting, scrumptious (*informal*) [➡ TASTE; 703] *Opposite*: revolting 2 *adj* **tempting**, appealing, inviting, attractive, desirable, enticing [➡ INTERESTING AND MEANINGFUL; 190] *Opposite*: unappealing

applaud 1 *v* **clap**, give a round of applause, give a standing ovation, show your appreciation, congratulate, put your hands together [➡ APPLAUSE; 652] *Opposite*: boo 2 *v* **approve**, support, admire, celebrate, congratulate, praise [➡ PRAISE AND ENCOURAGE; 647] *Opposite*: condemn

applause 1 *n* **clapping**, round of applause, ovation, hand, handclapping, show of appreciation [➡ APPLAUSE; 652] *Opposite*: jeering 2 *n* **praise**, appreciation, approval, approbation, support, commendation [➡ PRAISE AND ENCOURAGE; 647] *Opposite*: condemnation

apple *type of* **fruit** [➡ FRUIT AND VEGETABLES; 1176]

apple green *type of* **green** [➡ COLORS; 1224]

applesauce *type of* **seasonings, sauces, and dips** [➡ SEASONINGS AND SAUCES; 1174]

appliance 1 *n* **domestic appliance**, labor-saving device, electrical equipment, machine, device [➡ HOUSEHOLD APPLIANCES; 1117] 2 *n* **application**, use, employment, utilization, purpose, usage [➡ USE; 467]

appliance

◆ *types of appliances*
blender, coffeemaker, dishwasher, food processor, garbage disposal, grill, iron, juicer, microwave, microwave oven, minibar, mixer, percolator, range, rotisserie, smoke alarm, smoke detector, spin-dryer, stove, television, toaster, tumble dryer, washing machine

applicable *adj* **appropriate**, valid, related, pertinent, relevant, germane [➡ APPROPRIATE, SUITABLE, AND ADVISABLE; 184] *Opposite*: unrelated

applicant *n* **candidate**, interviewee, claimant, hopeful, aspirant, contender, entrant [➡ WORKERS; 836]

See Compare and Contrast at **candidate**.

application 1 *n* **request**, claim, submission, bid, tender, presentation, solicitation [➡ REQUEST AND DEMAND; 663] 2 *n* **use**, function, purpose, relevance, appliance, usage [➡ USE; 467] 3 *n* **diligence**, concentration, hard work, effort, attention, single-mindedness, devotion [➡ HARD-WORKING AND COMMITTED; 500] *Opposite*: negligence 4 *type of* **software** [➡ COMPUTERS AND COMPUTING; 1127]

applied *adj* **practical**, functional, useful, everyday, pragmatic, realistic [➡ USEFULNESS; 199] *Opposite*: theoretical

appliqué *type of* **handicraft** [➡ CRAFTS AND CARVING; 355]

apply 1 *v* **submit an application**, request, ask, go in, put in, make a claim, sign up [➡ REQUEST AND DEMAND; 663] 2 *v* **use**, operate, put into operation, employ, utilize, direct, harness [➡ USE; 467] 3 *v* **be relevant**, relate, be appropriate, be valid, pertain, affect, concern [➡ BE ABOUT SOMETHING; 62] 4 *v* **put on**, rub on, spread over, smear, spread on, rub in [➡ DECORATE, ADORN, AND APPLY COATINGS; 405] *Opposite*: remove

apply yourself *v* **devote yourself**, work hard, concentrate, direct your efforts towards, attend to, apply your mind, pay attention to [➡ PAY ATTENTION; 765] *Opposite*: neglect

appoint 1 *v* **employ**, sign up, hire, assign, take on, engage, retain [➡ CONFER STATUS; 458] *Opposite*: dismiss 2 *v* (*formal*) **select**, choose, settle on, agree, pick, decide on, fix, arrange, allot [➡ MAKE DECISIONS AND CHOICES; 752] *Opposite*: reject

appointed *adj* **chosen**, selected, agreed, fixed, prearranged, allotted [➡ INTENTIONAL AND DELIBERATE; 279]

appointment 1 *n* **meeting**, date, scheduled time, engagement, rendezvous, prior arrangement, slot [➡ MEETINGS AND ASSEMBLIES; 43] 2 *n* **selection**, choice, employment, choosing, nomination, promotion [➡ WORK-RELATED ACTIVITIES; 834] 3 *n* **job**, position, opening, office, place, assignment, post [➡ JOB; 833]

apportion *v* **allocate**, allot, assign, divide up, distribute, dispense, dole out (*informal*), dish out (*informal*) [➡ DISPENSE, RATION, AND DISTRIBUTE; 434]

apposite *adj* **appropriate**, apt, pertinent, relevant, suitable, to the point [➡ APPROPRIATE, SUITABLE, AND ADVISABLE; 184] *Opposite*: inappropriate

appositeness *n* [➡ APPROPRIATE, SUITABLE, AND ADVISABLE; 184]

apposition *type of* **grammatical term** [➡ ASPECTS OF LANGUAGE; 682]

appraisal *n* **assessment**, evaluation, judgment, review, consideration [➡ SCORES AND EVALUATIONS; 598]

appraise *v* **assess**, evaluate, judge, review, consider, value, weigh up (*UK*) [➡ EXAMINE AND ASSESS; 753]

appreciable *adj* **considerable**, substantial, significant, noticeable, palpable, visible [➡ MANY, MUCH, LARGE AMOUNT; 117] *Opposite*: insignificant

appreciably *adv* **substantially**, significantly, noticeably, palpably, visibly, considerably [➡ MANY, MUCH, LARGE AMOUNT; 117] *Opposite*: insignificantly

appreciate 1 *v* **be grateful for**, be thankful for, be glad about, be pleased about, value, welcome [➡ LIKE, LOVE, VALUE, AND ENJOY; 578] 2 *v* **understand**, realize, be aware, recognize the value of, grasp, be conscious of [➡ UNDERSTAND AND GRASP; 759] 3 *v* **increase in value**, go up in price, rise, escalate, raise the value of, gain, grow [➡ ACCOUNTING, BANKING, AND BUDGETING; 799] *Opposite*: depreciate

appreciation 1 *n* **thanks**, gratitude, indebtedness, gratefulness, obligation, thankfulness [➡ APPRECIATION AND GRATITUDE; 535] 2 *n* **approval**, admiration, positive reception, enjoyment, pleasure [➡ LIKE, LOVE, VALUE, AND ENJOY; 578] *Opposite*:

disapproval 3 *n* **understanding**, grasp, comprehension, handle, awareness, judgment [➡ UNDERSTAND AND GRASP; 759] 4 *n* **rise**, increase, escalation, growth, inflation, gain [➡ CHANGE OF SIZE: BIGGER; 392] *Opposite*: depreciation

appreciative 1 *adj* **grateful**, thankful, indebted, obliged, beholden, in debt [➡ APPRECIATION AND GRATITUDE; 535] *Opposite*: ungrateful 2 *adj* **approving**, enthusiastic, admiring, positive, favorable, supportive [➡ ENTHUSIASTIC AND INQUISITIVE; 628] *Opposite*: disapproving

appreciatively *adv* **approvingly**, enthusiastically, admiringly, positively, favorably, supportively [➡ EXPRESSING RESPECT AND APPROVAL; 637] *Opposite*: disapprovingly

apprehend *v* **catch**, arrest, detain, take in for questioning, take into custody, capture, stop, seize, stop, pick up (*informal*), nab (*informal*) [➡ THE POLICE, ARREST, AND PRETRIAL PROCEEDINGS; 818] *Opposite*: release

apprehension 1 *n* **anxiety**, uneasiness, worry, trepidation, nervousness, fear, hesitation, dread, fearfulness, angst, misgiving, alarm, disquiet, foreboding, apprehensiveness [➡ FEELINGS ABOUT THE FUTURE; 533] *Opposite*: confidence 2 *n* **capture**, arrest, detention, seizure, taking, imprisonment [➡ TAKE SOMETHING AWAY; 425] *Opposite*: discharge

apprehensive *adj* **uneasy**, worried, nervous, fearful, hesitant, frightened, concerned, angst-ridden, anxious [➡ CONFUSION, ANXIETY, AND WORRY; 540] *Opposite*: confident

apprehensiveness *n* **fearfulness**, fear, anxiety, trepidation, apprehension, disquiet, foreboding, alarm, dread, hesitation, angst, misgiving [➡ INSECURITY AND LOSS OF COMPOSURE; 544] *Opposite*: confidence

apprentice *n* **trainee**, learner, beginner, novice, student, intern [➡ UNSKILLED PEOPLE; 530] *Opposite*: expert

See Compare and Contrast at **beginner**.

apprenticeship *n* **traineeship**, internship, training, education, preparation [➡ CLASSES, COURSEWORK, AND EXAMINATIONS; 842]

apprise (*formal*) *v* [➡ INFORM, ANNOUNCE, AND ISSUE; 611]

approach 1 *v* **move toward**, come up to, come near, draw near, come within reach of, come close to, loom, advance [➡ PROCEED AND GO; 305] *Opposite*: retreat 2 *v* **speak to**, talk to, get in touch with, contact, make contact with, sound out, waylay, accost, buttonhole (*informal*) [➡ INITIATE AND ESTABLISH COMMUNICATION; 680] 3 *v* **set about**, tackle, deal with, handle, manage, attempt, consider [➡ START AN ACTION; 260] 4 *v* **approximate**, come close to, be similar to, come near to, move toward, verge on [➡ SEEM TO BE SOMETHING; 58] 5 *n* **method**, line of attack, tactic, line, slant, style, attitude, methodology [➡ WAYS OF DOING THINGS; 294]

approachability 1 *n* **friendliness**, accessibility, openness, affability, cordiality, availability [➡ FRIENDLINESS AND SOCIABILITY; 494] *Opposite*: aloofness 2 *n* **user-friendliness**, accessibility, availability, ease of use, usability, usefulness, practicality, helpfulness [➡ USEFULNESS; 199] *Opposite*: inaccessibility

approachable 1 *adj* **friendly**, amicable, sociable, open, open-minded, amenable, welcoming, available, accessible [➡ FRIENDLINESS AND SOCIABILITY; 494] *Opposite*: forbidding 2 *adj*

user-friendly, accessible, usable, useful, helpful, practical [➡ USEFULNESS; 199] *Opposite:* inaccessible

approaching *adj* **imminent**, impending, pending, future, forthcoming, upcoming, oncoming, potential [➡ FUTURE; 86]

approbation *n* **approval**, consent, praise, admiration, esteem, commendation, regard [➡ PRAISE AND ENCOURAGE; 647] *Opposite:* disapproval

approbatory *adj* [➡ EXPRESSING RESPECT AND APPROVAL; 637]

appropriate 1 *adj* **suitable**, fitting, apt, apposite, right, correct, applicable [➡ APPROPRIATE, SUITABLE, AND ADVISABLE; 184] *Opposite:* inappropriate 2 *v* **take**, take over, misappropriate, seize, assume, usurp, adopt, arrogate (*formal*) [➡ TAKE SOMETHING AWAY; 425]

appropriateness *n* **suitability**, correctness, aptness, appositeness, relevance, pertinence, fitness [➡ APPROPRIATE, SUITABLE, AND ADVISABLE; 184]

appropriation *n* **seizure**, assumption, annexation, adoption, arrogation (*formal*) [➡ TAKE SOMETHING AWAY; 425]

approval 1 *n* **appreciation**, admiration, liking, praise, esteem, approbation [➡ LIKE, LOVE, VALUE, AND ENJOY; 578] 2 *n* **endorsement**, support, sanction, consent, agreement, authorization, say-so (*informal*) [➡ APPROVE AND CONFIRM; 646] *Opposite:* disdain

approve 1 *v* **favor**, like, support, agree, accept, commend, esteem, admire [➡ APPROVE AND CONFIRM; 646] *Opposite:* disapprove 2 *v* **grant**, consent, sanction, allow, pass, authorize, ratify, certify, endorse, okay (*informal*) [➡ PERMIT AND ALLOW; 669] *Opposite:* reject

approved *adj* **accepted**, permitted, official, agreed, appropriate, correct, sanctioned, ratified [➡ APPROPRIATE, SUITABLE, AND ADVISABLE; 184]

approving *adj* **positive**, favorable, appreciative, sympathetic, complimentary, admiring [➡ EXPRESSING RESPECT AND APPROVAL; 637] *Opposite:* disapproving

approvingly *adv* **positively**, favorably, appreciatively, sympathetically, admiringly [➡ EXPRESSING RESPECT AND APPROVAL; 637] *Opposite:* disapprovingly

approximate *adj* **estimated**, rough, loose, near, inexact, imprecise, ballpark (*informal*) [➡ APPROXIMATELY; 135] *Opposite:* exact

approximation *n* **estimate**, guess, calculation, guesstimate (*informal*) [➡ ASSESS QUANTITY; 757]

appurtenance (*formal*) *n* [➡ MORE AND EXCESS; 124]

apricot 1 *type of* **fruit** [➡ FRUIT AND VEGETABLES; 1176] 2 *type of* **orange** [➡ COLORS; 1224]

apron *n* **bib**, smock, pinafore, overall [➡ GARMENTS AND OUTFITS; 865]

apropos (*formal*) 1 *prep* **regarding**, concerning, about, on the subject of, in relation to, in connection with [➡ EXPRESSIONS OF REFERENCE; 63] 2 *adj* **appropriate**, suitable, fitting, apt, apposite, pertinent, right, correct, proper, seemly [➡ APPROPRIATE, SUITABLE, AND ADVISABLE; 184] *Opposite:* inappropriate

apse *n* [➡ PARTS OF RELIGIOUS BUILDINGS; 1086]

apt 1 *adj* **appropriate**, suitable, fitting, apposite, pertinent, right, correct, proper, seemly, apropos (*formal*) [➡ APPROPRIATE, SUITABLE, AND ADVISABLE; 184] *Opposite:* inappropriate 2 *adj* **quick**, capable, competent, able, skilled, ready [➡ TALENTED AND SKILLFUL; 527] *Opposite:* inept

aptitude *n* **ability**, skill, talent, gift, capacity, fitness, propensity [➡ SKILLS, TALENTS, AND ABILITIES; 526] *Opposite:* inability

See Compare and Contrast at **ability**, **talent**.

aptly *adv* **appropriately**, fittingly, suitably, rightly, pertinently, appositely, properly [➡ APPROPRIATE, SUITABLE, AND ADVISABLE; 184] *Opposite:* inappropriately

apt to *adj* **prone**, likely, given to, inclined, tending, disposed [➡ THE WILL AND WILLINGNESS; 563]

Apus *type of* **constellation** [➡ HEAVENLY BODIES; 1061]

aquamarine 1 *type of* **green** [➡ COLORS; 1224] 2 *type of* **gemstone** [➡ PRECIOUS STONES; 1278]

aquarium *type of* **pen or cage** [➡ ANIMAL OR BIRD ACCOMMODATIONS; 1079]

Aquarius 1 *type of* **astrological sign** [➡ FATE, DESTINY, AND ASTROLOGY; 782] 2 *type of* **constellation** [➡ HEAVENLY BODIES, 1061]

aquatic *adj* **water**, marine, sea, river [➡ THE SEAS, OCEANS, AND SHORES; 1041]

aqueduct 1 *n* **channel**, conduit, canal, watercourse, culvert, pipe [➡ WATERCOURSES; 1111] 2 *type of* **bridge** [➡ BRIDGES, TUNNELS, CROSSINGS, AND JUNCTIONS; 1112]

aqueous humor *part of* **eye** [➡ THE EYE; 698]

Aquila *type of* **constellation** [➡ HEAVENLY BODIES, 1061]

aquilline *adj* [➡ ANGULAR SHAPE; 1217]

aquiver *adj* [➡ INSECURITY AND LOSS OF COMPOSURE; 544]

Ara *type of* **constellation** [➡ HEAVENLY BODIES; 1061]

Arabian horse *type of* **horse** [➡ HORSES; 985]

Arabic *type of* **alphabet** [➡ SYMBOLS, SIGNS, AND NUMBERS; 596]

arachnid *n* [➡ LIVING THINGS AND LIVING; 976]

arachnid

◆ *types of arachnids*
black widow, brown recluse, daddy longlegs, funnel-web spider, harvestman, jumping spider, mite, money spider, redback, scorpion, spider, tarantula, trapdoor spider, water spider, wolf spider

arachnophobia *type of* **phobia** [➡ FEARS AND PHOBIAS; 554]

arbiter 1 *n* **arbitrator**, mediator, intermediary, negotiator, go-between, peacemaker, referee, conciliator, judge [➡ ADVISERS, JUDGES, AND ARBITERS; 971] 2 *n* **authority**, influence, role model, leader, example, trendsetter, style guru [➡ PEOPLE WHO ARE APPROVED OF; 955]

arbitrary *adj* **random**, chance, subjective, uninformed, illogical, capricious, indiscriminate, haphazard [➡ UNPLANNED AND UNEXPECTED; 281] *Opposite:* systematic

arbitrate *v* **judge**, adjudicate, pass judgment, decide, settle, sort out, mediate, referee, intercede, determine, adjudge, assess [➡ ASSESS QUALITY; 755]

arbitration *n* **adjudication**, negotiation, mediation, settlement, intercession [➡ NEGOTIATION AND DEBATE; 46]

arbitrator *n* **judge**, arbiter, mediator, go-between, intermediary, conciliator, negotiator, peacemaker, referee, umpire [➡ ADVISERS, JUDGES, AND ARBITERS; 971]

arbor *n* **bower**, retreat, nook, grove, dell (*literary*) [➡ GARDENS; 1074]

arboretum *part of* **garden** [➡ GARDENS; 1074]

arc *n* **curve**, arch, semicircle, sweep, bow, bend, curvature [➡ ROUNDED SHAPE; 1218]

arcade **1** *n* **walkway**, passageway, colonnade, cloister, loggia, gallery, portico, pergola [➡ ANCILLARY BUILDINGS; 1080] **2** *n* **shopping mall**, shopping arcade, precinct (*UK*) [➡ RETAIL OUTLETS; 1083] **3** *n* **video arcade**, game parlor, amusement arcade [➡ BUILDINGS FOR PUBLIC ENTERTAINMENT; 1084]

arcadia *n* [➡ NONEXISTENT PLACES; 1066]

arcane *adj* **mysterious**, secret, esoteric, deep, hidden, unfathomable, unknowable, obscure, impenetrable, inscrutable [➡ SECRET AND UNKNOWN; 179]

See Compare and Contrast at **obscure.**

arch **1** *n* **arc**, curve, semicircle, bend, bow, sweep, curvature [➡ ROUNDED SHAPE; 1218] **2** *n* **archway**, doorway, portico [➡ DOORS AND ACCESS POINTS; 1101] **3** *v* **curve**, bend, bow, arc [➡ CHANGE OF SHAPE; 385] *Opposite*: straighten **4** *adj* **playful**, mischievous, roguish, knowing, cunning, coy [➡ GOOD-TEMPERED AND HUMOROUS; 627]

archaic *adj* **old**, ancient, dated, outdated, out-of-date, antiquated, old-fashioned, outmoded, prehistoric, behind the times, antediluvian (*informal*) [➡ OLD, OLD-FASHIONED; 167] *Opposite*: modern

See Compare and Contrast at **old-fashioned.**

archangel *n* [➡ RELIGIOUS CONCEPTS; 776]

archbishop *n* [➡ RELIGIOUS PEOPLE; 778]

archbishopric *n* [➡ RELIGIOUS CONCEPTS; 776]

arch bridge *type of* **bridge** [➡ BRIDGES, TUNNELS, CROSSINGS, AND JUNCTIONS; 1112]

Archean *type of* **eon** [➡ EPOCHS AND ERAS; 89]

arched *adj* **curved**, rounded, round, high, bowed, bent, vaulted, domed, semicircular, hemispherical [➡ ROUNDED SHAPE; 1218]

archenemy *n* **opponent**, enemy, rival, challenger, foe (*formal*), nemesis (*literary*) [➡ ENEMIES AND TORMENTORS; 969] *Opposite*: ally

archetypal *adj* **typical**, model, representative, standard, archetypical, classic, exemplary, conventional, prototypical [➡ REPRESENTATIVE; 66] *Opposite*: unconventional

archetype *n* **model**, epitome, prototype, original, classic [➡ PERFECT EXAMPLES AND EMBODIMENTS; 67]

archetypical *adj* **typical**, model, representative, standard, archetypal, classic, exemplary, conventional, prototypical [➡ REPRESENTATIVE; 66] *Opposite*: unconventional

archipelago *n* [➡ THE CONTINENTS AND ISLANDS; 1048]

architect **1** *n* **designer**, draftsman, draftswoman, planner, engineer, builder, draftsperson [➡ DESIGNERS, CREATORS, AND INSTIGATORS; 347] **2** *n* **originator**, inventor, founder, creator, engineer, prime mover, builder [➡ DESIGNERS, CREATORS, AND INSTIGATORS; 347]

architectural *adj* [➡ BUILDING AND ARCHITECTURE; 1076]

architecture *n* **design**, planning, building, construction [➡ BUILDING AND ARCHITECTURE; 1076]

architecture

◆ *types of pre-20th-century architecture*
art nouveau, Baroque, Byzantine, cinquecento, classical, colonial, Corinthian, Decorated, Doric, Elizabethan, Empire, Georgian, Gothic, Gothic revival, Ionic, Mission, Moorish, neoclassical, Norman, Palladian, perpendicular, Renaissance, rococo, Romanesque, Tudor, Victorian

◆ *types of 20th-century architecture*
art deco, Bauhaus, brutalist, Federation, minimalist, moderne, modernist, postmodern

archive *n* **record**, file, documentation, document, library, collection, annal (*dated*) [➡ RECORDS; 585]

archly *adv* **playfully**, mischievously, roguishly, knowingly, cunningly, coyly [➡ GOOD-TEMPERED AND HUMOROUS; 627]

archness *n* **playfulness**, mischievousness, roguishness, cunning, coyness [➡ GOOD-TEMPERED AND HUMOROUS; 627]

archway *n* **arch**, arcade, pergola, portico, doorway, cloister [➡ DOORS AND ACCESS POINTS; 1101]

arc lamp *type of* **light** [➡ LIGHT; 1164]

arctic (*informal*) *adj* **freezing**, cold, chilly, wintry, frozen, icy, frosty, subzero, glacial, frigid [➡ COLD WEATHER; 1051] *Opposite*: tropical

ardent *adj* **passionate**, enthusiastic, keen, fervent, zealous, eager, devoted, dedicated, committed, fiery, fervid [➡ POSITIVE IMPATIENCE, ENTHUSIASM, AND ALERTNESS; 537] *Opposite*: dispassionate

ardor *n* **passion**, love, enthusiasm, zeal, fervor, eagerness, devotion, dedication, commitment [➡ LOVE, RESPECT, AND GOODWILL; 549] *Opposite*: indifference

arduous *adj* **difficult**, hard, laborious, grueling, demanding, strenuous, onerous, tiring, toilsome, taxing, operose (*formal*) [➡ PHYSICALLY UNPLEASANT; 226] *Opposite*: easy

See Compare and Contrast at **hard.**

arduousness *n* **difficulty**, laboriousness, strenuousness, onerousness, rigorousness [➡ DIFFICULTY AND COMPLEXITY; 242] *Opposite*: ease

area 1 *n* **part**, zone, extent, expanse, range, space, capacity, region, band, belt, stretch [➡ AREA AND RANGE; 111] **2** *n* **neighborhood**, locale, vicinity, part, quarter, spot, region, corner, district [➡ PLACE; 1065] **3** *n* **subject**, topic, field, question, matter, sphere, theme [➡ SUBJECT AREAS; 768]

area of expertise *n* [➡ SUBJECT AREAS; 768]

arena *n* **stadium**, grounds, showground, sports grounds, field, ring, amphitheater, dome, pitch (*UK*) [➡ URBAN OUTDOOR SPACES; 1072]

argon *type of* **gas** [➡ GASES; 1275]

argot *n* **jargon**, slang, idiom, speech, dialect, patois, vernacular [➡ THE SPOKEN WORD; 671]

arguable *adj* **debatable**, open to question, questionable, doubtful, dubious, uncertain, far from certain, disputable [➡ UNCERTAIN; 175] *Opposite*: certain

arguably *adv* **debatably**, questionably, perhaps, possibly, maybe, doubtfully, disputably [➡ POSSIBLE AND PROBABLE; 177] *Opposite*: certainly

argue 1 *v* **quarrel**, dispute, fight, disagree, bicker, squabble, fall out [➡ ARGUE AND FIGHT; 643] *Opposite*: agree **2** *v* **make a case**, contend, claim, say, maintain, reason [➡ CLAIM, INSIST, AND EMPHASIZE; 614] **3** *v* **debate**, dispute, discuss, go over, explore, hash out, thrash out [➡ TWO-WAY COMMUNICATION; 607]

See Compare and Contrast at **disagree**.

argument 1 *n* **quarrel**, fight, disagreement, dispute, row, spat, squabble [➡ ARGUMENTS; 47] **2** *n* **case**, line of reasoning, reason, contention, claim, position [➡ POINTS OF VIEW; 767]

argumentative *adj* **quarrelsome**, confrontational, contrary, belligerent, aggressive, challenging, awkward [➡ DIFFICULT TO PLEASE; 515] *Opposite*: peaceable

argumentativeness *n* [➡ DIFFICULT TO PLEASE; 515]

aria *type of* **musical form** [➡ MUSIC, SONGS, AND SINGING; 907]

arid 1 *adj* **dry**, parched, bone dry, baked, waterless, scorched, infertile, barren, sere (*archaic or literary*) [➡ DRY; 1242] *Opposite*: humid **2** *adj* **boring**, dull, uninteresting, dry, sterile, uninspired, unexciting, tepid, unimaginative [➡ BORING AND UNINTERESTING; 234] *Opposite*: exciting

See Compare and Contrast at **dry**.

aridity *n* **dryness**, waterlessness, drought, infertility, barrenness [➡ DRY; 1242] *Opposite*: humidity

aridness *n* **dryness**, parchedness, desiccation, dehydration, scorchedness [➡ DRY; 1242] *Opposite*: wetness

Aries 1 *type of* **astrological sign** [➡ FATE, DESTINY, AND ASTROLOGY; 782] **2** *type of* **constellation** [➡ HEAVENLY BODIES; 1061]

arise 1 *v* **happen**, occur, take place, come up, begin, start, appear, surface, commence, crop up (*informal*), come to pass (*archaic or literary*) [➡ HAPPEN; 27] **2** *v* **result from**, be the result of, arise from, arise out of, be caused by, stem from, come from, evolve [➡ GRADUALLY COME INTO EXISTENCE; 1] **3** *v* (*archaic or literary*) **get up**, stand up, rise, get to your feet, ascend [➡ GO UPWARD; 306] *Opposite*: sit down **4** *v* (*archaic*

or literary) **get out of bed**, get up, rise [➡ GO UPWARD; 306] *Opposite*: retire

aristocracy *n* **nobility**, upper classes, landed gentry, gentry, upper crust (*informal*), lords and ladies (*UK*), peers of the realm (*UK*) [➡ CLASS STATUS; 889] *Opposite*: lower class

aristocrat *n* **noble**, lord, lady, peer, grandee [➡ RULERS AND ARISTOCRACY; 823]

aristocrat

◆ *types of aristocrats*
baron, baroness, baronet, count, countess, crown prince, duchess, duke, earl, king, knight, maharajah, maharani, marchioness, marquess, prince, princess, queen, viscount, viscountess

aristocratic 1 *adj* **refined**, well-bred, patrician, noble [➡ CLASS STATUS; 889] *Opposite*: lowly **2** *adj* **noble**, titled, patrician, upper-class, blue blooded, highborn (*literary*) [➡ CLASS STATUS; 889] *Opposite*: lower-class

arithmetic *n* [➡ MATH; 597]

arithmetical *adj* [➡ MATH; 597]

arithmetic mean *n* [➡ MATH; 597]

arm 1 *n* **limb**, appendage, member [➡ PARTS OF THE BODY: ARM AND HAND; 695] **2** *n* **support**, armrest, rest [➡ FURNITURE; 858] **3** *n* **division**, wing, branch, subdivision, offshoot, limb [➡ SUBDIVISIONS AND OFFSHOOTS; 1253] **4** *v* **equip**, provide, supply, prepare, ready, furnish (*formal*) [➡ EQUIP AND SUPPLY; 435] *Opposite*: disarm

arm

◆ *parts of an arm or hand*
ball, cuticle, elbow, finger, fingernail, fingerprint, fingertip, fist, forearm, forefinger, funny bone (*informal*), hand, hangnail, heel, index finger, knuckle, little finger, middle finger, palm, pinkie (*informal*), ring finger, thumb, thumbnail, wrist

armada *n* **fleet**, flotilla, navy, squadron, task force [➡ GROUPS OF VEHICLES; 1152]

armadillo *type of* **small mammal** [➡ SMALL MAMMALS; 990]

Armageddon *n* **end of the world**, day of reckoning, Judgment Day, apocalypse, catastrophe, disaster, destruction [➡ RELIGIOUS CONCEPTS; 776]

armament *n* **arming**, mobilization, rearmament, deployment, buildup, preparation, disarmament [➡ WARFARE AND WAR; 830]

armaments *n* **arms**, weapons, weaponry, guns, missiles, artillery, munitions [➡ WEAPONS; 1154]

armature *n* [➡ PARTS OF MACHINES AND TOOLS; 1118]

armchair *type of* **seating** [➡ FURNITURE; 858]

armed *adj* **equipped**, fortified, prepared [➡ MILITARY; 829] *Opposite*: unarmed

armed forces *n* **military**, services, forces, defense force, army, militia, air force, navy [➡ THE ARMED FORCES; 827]

armed robbery *n* [➤CRIMES; 817]

armed services *n* [➤THE ARMED FORCES; 827]

armhole *n* **opening**, slit, hole [➤HOLES, GAPS, AND FORKS; 1252]

armistice *n* **truce**, peace agreement, settlement, cease-fire, resolution, treaty [➤HARMONY; 155]

armlet *type of* **jewelry** [➤JEWELRY; 866]

armoire *type of* **cabinet** [➤FURNITURE; 858]

armor **1** *n* **suit of armor**, chain mail, bulletproof vest, mail, breastplate, coat of mail, body armor, flak jacket, panoply [➤GARMENTS AND OUTFITS; 865] **2** *n* **protection**, reinforcement, defense, covering, cover, shell, shield [➤COVERS AND COATINGS; 1246]

armored *adj* **reinforced**, strengthened, steel-clad, bulletproof, protected, secure, covered [➤STRENGTH; 201] *Opposite*: unprotected

armored car *type of* **military vehicle** [➤VEHICLES; 1145]

armor-plated *adj* **reinforced**, steel-clad, armored, strengthened, bulletproof, protected, secure, covered [➤STRENGTH; 201] *Opposite*: unprotected

armory **1** *n* **arsenal**, arms depot, ordnance depot, munitions store, weapon store, gunroom, missile silo, magazine [➤STORES AND STORAGE BUILDINGS; 1088] **2** *n* **stock**, source, supply, array, range, set [➤COLLECTIONS AND MIXTURES OF THINGS; 1244]

armpit *part of* **torso** [➤PARTS OF THE BODY: TORSO; 693]

armrest *n* **support**, arm, rest [➤FURNITURE; 858]

arms *n* **weapons**, weaponry, armaments, guns, missiles, artillery, munitions [➤WEAPONS; 1154]

arms depot *type of* **storage space** [➤STORES AND STORAGE BUILDINGS; 1088]

arms reduction *n* [➤WARFARE AND WAR; 830]

army **1** *n* **military**, armed forces, defense force, militia, troops, soldiers, territorial army (*UK*) [➤THE ARMED FORCES; 827] **2** *n* **crowd**, throng, mass, host, multitude, legion, band [➤GROUPS OF PEOPLE; 935]

army ant *type of* **ant** [➤ANTS; 1014]

army cadet *n* [➤MILITARY PERSONNEL; 828]

army camp *n* [➤WARFARE AND WAR; 830]

army chaplain *n* [➤RELIGIOUS PEOPLE; 778]

aroma *n* **smell**, perfume, fragrance, scent, odor, bouquet, tang [➤SMELL AND SMELLING; 705]

See Compare and Contrast at **smell**.

aromatic *adj* **perfumed**, fragrant, sweet-smelling, scented, pungent, musky [➤SMELL AND SMELLING; 705] *Opposite*: odorless

around **1** *prep* **about**, all around, surrounding, covering, over [➤RELATIVE LOCATION; 161] **2** *prep* **close to**, near, in the vicinity, in the environs, round, in the neighborhood [➤CLOSENESS; 159] **3** *prep* **all over**, throughout, here and there, about, round, across [➤RELATIVE LOCATION; 161] **4** *prep* **approxi-**mately, about, in the region of, just about, roughly, more or less, give or take, almost, nearly, going on, roughly speaking, on the order of, going on for (*UK*) [➤APPROXIMATELY; 135] **5** *adv* **in**, here, round, about, present, available [➤PRESENT AND AVAILABLE; 11] **6** *adv* **from one place to another**, from place to place, about, everywhere, all over the place (*informal*) [➤GENERAL LOCATIONS; 158] **7** *adv* **roundabout**, near here, nearby, about, round, in the area, in the vicinity, roundabouts (*UK*), round here (*UK*) [➤CLOSENESS; 159]

around the bend (*slang*) *adj* [➤ECCENTRICITY AND IRRATIONALITY; 562]

around the clock *adv* **continuously**, nonstop, full-time, constantly, all day long, every hour in the day [➤PERMANENCE: WITHOUT END; 94] *Opposite*: sporadically

around-the-clock *adj* [➤PERMANENCE: WITHOUT END; 94]

arousal *n* **stimulation**, provocation, awakening, encouragement, excitement, urging [➤PLEASURE, EXCITEMENT, AND ELATION; 534]

arouse *v* **stimulate**, provoke, awaken, produce, stir, stir up, rouse [➤APPEAL TO AND AROUSE INTEREST; 575] *Opposite*: dampen

aroused *adj* [➤PLEASURE, EXCITEMENT, AND ELATION; 534]

arpeggio *type of* **musical term** [➤MUSICAL TERMS; 912]

arraign *v* **accuse**, impeach, prosecute, bring before the court [➤TRIAL, PUNISHMENT, AND LEGAL OUTCOMES; 819]

arraignment *n* **charge**, prosecution, legal process, legal action, indictment, impeachment, summons, citation, inculpation (*formal*) [➤TRIAL, PUNISHMENT, AND LEGAL OUTCOMES; 819] *Opposite*: exculpation (*formal*)

arrange **1** *v* **organize**, set up, coordinate, fix, fix up, make plans for, plan, settle, orchestrate, schedule [➤CAUSE TO HAPPEN; 31] *Opposite*: cancel **2** *v* **position**, put in order, place, assemble, put together, organize, display, lay out, pose, dispose (*formal*), array (*formal*) [➤POSITION SOMETHING; 325] *Opposite*: disarrange

arranged *adj* **decided**, agreed, set, settled, organized, prescribed, prepared, ready, planned, scheduled [➤CERTAIN; 174]

arranged marriage *n* [➤MARRIED STATE; 961]

arrangement **1** *n* **preparation**, plan, procedure, pre-arrangement, provision, settlement [➤WAYS OF DOING THINGS; 294] **2** *n* **agreement**, understanding, bargain, pact, deal [➤RECIPROCITY AND INTERDEPENDENCE; 147] **3** *n* **display**, array, composition, layout, assembly, collection, grouping [➤COLLECTIONS AND MIXTURES OF THINGS; 1244]

arrant *adj* **complete**, total, outright, unmitigated, utter, extreme, out-and-out, straight-out (*informal*) [➤ABSOLUTE AND ABSOLUTELY; 133]

arras *n* [➤FURNISHING AND HOUSEHOLD LINENS; 860]

array **1** *n* **collection**, selection, display, range, arrangement, assortment, grouping [➤COLLECTIONS AND MIXTURES OF THINGS; 1244] **2** *n* **dress**, clothing, regalia, finery, garb, apparel, attire (*formal*) [➤CLOTHES AND ACCESSORIES; 864] **3** *v* (*formal*) **arrange**, display, organize, set out, exhibit, group, put in order, order, range, lay out, dispose (*formal*) [➤ARRANGE AND CREATE ORDER; 357] **4** *v* (*literary*) **clothe**, dress, deck out, drape, attire (*formal*), bedeck (*literary*) [➡ DECORATE, ADORN, AND APPLY COATINGS; 405]

arrears *n* **amount overdue**, amount outstanding, debts, sum unpaid [➡ OWE AND DESERVE; 465] *Opposite*: credit

arrest 1 *v* **take into custody**, seize, capture, detain, catch, hold, apprehend, take in for questioning, stop [➡ THE POLICE, ARREST, AND PRETRIAL PROCEEDINGS; 818] *Opposite*: release 2 *v* (*formal*) **halt**, stop, block, prevent, obstruct, impede, bring to an end, hinder, stem, check [➡ CAUSE TO STOP; 266] *Opposite*: start 3 *v* (*formal*) **attract**, engage, catch, hold, fix, grab (*informal*) [➡ APPEAL TO AND AROUSE INTEREST; 575] 4 *n* **capture**, seizure, detention, apprehension, custody [➡ THE POLICE, ARREST, AND PRETRIAL PROCEEDINGS; 818] *Opposite*: release

arresting *adj* **impressive**, eye-catching, stunning, striking, interesting, fascinating, attractive, noticeable, attention grabbing [➡ BEAUTY AND ATTRACTIVENESS; 189] *Opposite*: uninteresting

arrière-pensée (*formal*) *n* [➡ IDEAS AND THOUGHTS; 770]

arrival 1 *n* **influx**, entrance, entry, coming, appearance [➡ ARRIVAL; 13] *Opposite*: departure 2 *n* **onset**, advent, occurrence, coming, appearance [➡ BEGINNINGS; 53] 3 *n* **newcomer**, visitor, guest, incomer, caller [➡ TRAVEL: TRAVELERS AND WALKERS; 319]

arrive 1 *v* **reach**, turn up, get there, land, disembark, pull in, appear, enter [➡ ARRIVE; 12] *Opposite*: depart 2 *v* **work out**, reach, come to, come up with, attain, decide on, hash out, thrash out [➡ MAKE DECISIONS AND CHOICES; 752] 3 *v* **succeed**, be successful, gain recognition, make your mark, make it (*informal*) [➡ SUCCEED AND WIN; 79]

arriviste *n* [➡ SELF-IMPORTANT AND SELF-SEEKING PEOPLE; 949]

arrogance *n* **conceit**, haughtiness, egotism, pride, overconfidence, superciliousness, self-importance, condescension [➡ MORALLY BAD OR IMPROPER; 775] *Opposite*: humility

arrogant *adj* **conceited**, haughty, egotistic, superior, proud, overconfident, supercilious, self-important, big-headed (*informal*) [➡ POMPOUS, LOUD, AND OVERCONFIDENT; 635] *Opposite*: humble

See Compare and Contrast at **proud**.

arrogate (*formal*) *v* **claim**, lay claim to, appropriate, misappropriate, assume, take over, demand, annex [➡ TAKE SOMETHING AWAY; 425] *Opposite*: cede (*formal*)

arrogation (*formal*) *n* **appropriation**, misappropriation, assumption, takeover, annexation, seizure [➡ TAKE SOMETHING AWAY; 425]

arrow 1 *n* **projectile**, missile, dart, barb, shaft, bolt [➡ PROJECTILES; 1159] 2 *n* **symbol**, sign, pointer, marker, indicator, cursor, signpost, road sign [➡ SYMBOLS, SIGNS, AND NUMBERS; 596]

arrowhead *n* **point**, tip, barb [➡ PROJECTILES; 1159]

arrowroot *n* **thickener**, starch, stiffener [➡ SEASONINGS AND SAUCES; 1174]

arsenal 1 *n* **weapon store**, munitions store, magazine, armory [➡ STORES AND STORAGE BUILDINGS; 1088] 2 *n* **store**, battery, fund, cache, collection, resource, stash (*informal*) [➡ COLLECTIONS AND MIXTURES OF THINGS; 1244]

arsenic *type of* **mineral** [➡ MINERALS; 1277]

arson *n* **pyromania**, burning, incineration, ignition, firebombing, torching (*slang*), incendiarism (*formal*), fire raising (*UK*) [➡ CRIMES; 817]

arsonist *n* **pyromaniac**, burner, firebomber, incendiary, firebug (*slang*), torcher (*slang*), fire raiser (*UK*) [➡ CRIMINALS; 821]

art 1 *n* **painting**, drawing, fine art, graphic arts, sculpture [➡ THE PICTORIAL ARTS; 897] 2 *n* **skill**, talent, knack, ability, virtuosity [➡ SKILLS, TALENTS, AND ABILITIES; 526]

art

◆ *types of pre-20th-century art movements*
art nouveau, Arts and Crafts, Baroque, classicism, impressionism, Mannerism, pointillism, post-impressionism, Pre-Raphaelitism, realism, Renaissance, Romanticism, symbolism

◆ *types of 20th-century art movements*
abstract expressionism, art deco, conceptual art, constructivism, cubism, Dada, expressionism, Fauvism, futurism, minimalism, modernism, op art, photorealism, pop art, postmodernism, socialist realism, surrealism, vorticism

art deco 1 *type of* **20th-century art movement** [➡ ARTISTIC MOVEMENTS AND STYLES; 899] 2 *type of* **20th-century architecture** [➡ BUILDING AND ARCHITECTURE; 1076]

artefact *see* **artifact**

arterial *adj* **major**, main, principal, through, trunk (*UK*) [➡ COMMUNICATION NETWORKS; 1105] *Opposite*: side

artery 1 *type of* **blood vessel** [➡ THE BLOOD AND CIRCULATION; 717] 2 *n* **route**, road, highway, line, channel, pathway, main line, conduit, major road, trunk road (*UK*) [➡ ROADS; 1106]

artful *adj* **crafty**, devious, sly, deceitful, cunning, wily, sneaky, foxy [➡ DECEITFUL; 513] *Opposite*: open

artfulness *n* **craftiness**, deviousness, slyness, cleverness, deceitfulness, cunning, wiles, sneakiness, artifice (*formal*) [➡ DECEITFUL; 513] *Opposite*: straightforwardness

art-house (*UK*) *adj* **highbrow**, intellectual, sophisticated, esoteric, specialist, avant-garde, trendy (*informal*) [➡ LEVELS OF EDUCATION AND SOPHISTICATION; 894] *Opposite*: lowbrow

arthritic *adj* **stiff**, swollen, aching, sore, painful, inflamed [➡ THE BONES AND JOINTS; 719]

arthritis *n* **stiffness**, swelling, ache, pain, soreness, inflammation [➡ THE BONES AND JOINTS; 719]

artichoke *type of* **vegetable** [➡ FRUIT AND VEGETABLES; 1176]

article 1 *n* **piece of writing**, editorial, piece, item, commentary, critique, exposé [➡ ANALYTICAL NONFICTION WRITING; 592] 2 *n* **object**, item, piece, thing, artifact [➡ PHYSICAL OBJECTS; 1243] 3 *n* **clause**, term, stipulation, condition, regulation, paragraph, section [➡ SUMMARIES, OUTLINES, AND EXCERPTS; 588] 4 *type of* **word class** [➡ ASPECTS OF LANGUAGE; 682]

articles (*UK*) *n* **training**, traineeship, apprenticeship, tutelage, course, qualifications, pupillage (*formal*) [➡ CLASSES, COURSEWORK, AND EXAMINATIONS; 842]

articulacy *n* **self-expression**, expressiveness, eloquence, fluency, articulateness, coherence, clarity, lucidity [➡ELOQUENT, TALKATIVE, AND LONG-WINDED; 632]

articulate 1 *adj* **eloquent**, clear, coherent, fluent, lucid, expressive, communicative, well-spoken [➡ELOQUENT, TALKATIVE, AND LONG-WINDED; 632] *Opposite*: inarticulate 2 *v* **enunciate**, pronounce, speak clearly, speak, say, utter [➡UTTER AND PRONOUNCE; 608] *Opposite*: mumble 3 *v* **speak about**, express, state, put into words, convey, verbalize, communicate, formulate [➡UTTER AND PRONOUNCE; 608] *Opposite*: keep secret

articulated 1 *adj* **modular**, jointed, coupled, linked, connected, interconnected [➡FASTEN, LINK, AND JOIN; 408] *Opposite*: rigid 2 *adj* **spoken**, voiced, uttered, expressed, pronounced, enunciated, said, verbalized, put into words, communicated [➡THE SPOKEN WORD; 671] *Opposite*: unspoken

articulateness *n* **eloquence**, expressiveness, fluency, self-expression, coherence, clarity, lucidity, articulacy [➡ELOQUENT, TALKATIVE, AND LONG-WINDED; 632]

articulation 1 *n* **enunciation**, pronunciation, speech, diction, delivery, voicing, vocalization [➡THE SPOKEN WORD; 671] 2 *n* **expression**, verbalization, communication, formulation [➡THE SPOKEN WORD; 671]

artifact *n* **object**, objet d'art, manufactured object, article, manufactured article, item, work of art, piece, thing, relic, product, archaeological find [➡PHYSICAL OBJECTS; 1243]

artifice (*formal*) 1 *n* **pretense**, ploy, trick, lie, sleight of hand, ruse [➡DECEPTION AND LIES; 660] 2 *n* **deception**, deceit, cunning, trickery, artfulness, wiles, craft [➡DECEPTION AND LIES; 660]

artificial 1 *adj* **false**, fake, mock, reproduction, synthetic, simulated, imitation, man-made [➡FALSE AND UNREAL; 173] *Opposite*: natural 2 *adj* **insincere**, false, put-on, pretend, fake, unnatural, contrived, feigned, hollow [➡FALSE AND UNREAL; 173] *Opposite*: sincere

artificial insemination *n* [➡REPRODUCTION AND HEREDITY; 725]

artificiality *n* **insincerity**, disingenuousness, affectedness, affectation, phoniness, inauthenticity, play-acting, pretentiousness, pretension [➡AFFECTATION, SELF-SATISFACTION, AND SNOBBISHNESS; 507] *Opposite*: sincerity

artillery *n* **weaponry**, arms, guns, armaments, weapons, missiles, cannons, howitzers [➡WEAPONS; 1154]

artilleryman *n* [➡MILITARY PERSONNEL; 828]

artisan *n* **craftsperson**, skilled worker, handicrafts worker, crafts worker, artist, artificer (*dated*) [➡ARTISTS; 900]

artist 1 *n* **painter**, illustrator, drawer, sketcher, cartoonist, sculptor [➡ARTISTS; 900] 2 *n* **performer**, artiste, singer, actor, musician, dancer, comedian, entertainer [➡MUSICIANS AND SINGERS; 908]

artiste *n* **performer**, entertainer, artist, singer, actor, musician, dancer, comedian [➡MUSICIANS AND SINGERS; 908]

artistic *adj* **creative**, imaginative, inventive, arty (*informal*) [➡ARTISTIC MOVEMENTS AND STYLES; 899]

artistry *n* **creativity**, originality, artistic ability, imagin-

ation, invention, ability, skill, skillfulness, talent, inventiveness [➡SKILLS, TALENTS, AND ABILITIES; 526]

artless *adj* **simple**, guileless, natural, unworldly, ingenuous, open, innocent, sincere, naive, unsophisticated, uncontrived, childlike, pure (*literary*) [➡NATURALNESS; 497] *Opposite*: disingenuous

artlessness *n* **guilelessness**, naturalness, innocence, unaffectedness, inexperience, unpretentiousness, ingenuousness, genuineness, candor, sincerity, unworldliness, openness, naiveté, spontaneity [➡NATURALNESS; 497] *Opposite*: disingenuousness

art nouveau 1 *type of* **pre-20th-century art movement** [➡ARTISTIC MOVEMENTS AND STYLES; 899] 2 *type of* **pre-20th-century architecture** [➡BUILDING AND ARCHITECTURE; 1076]

Arts and Crafts *type of* **pre-20th-century art movement** [➡ARTISTIC MOVEMENTS AND STYLES; 899]

artsy-craftsy (*informal*) *adj* **rustic**, artistic, creative, quaint, imaginative, homespun, inventive, homemade, overdecorative, traditional, fanciful, picturesque, pretentious, sentimental, kitschy [➡ARTISTIC MOVEMENTS AND STYLES; 899]

artwork 1 *n* **work of art**, creation, representation, reproduction, painting, drawing, sculpture, sketch, print, collage, mural, oeuvre (*formal*) [➡ARTWORKS; 898] 2 *n* **illustrations**, pictures, photographs, diagrams, plates, drawings, graphics [➡DRAWINGS, CHARTS, AND TABLES; 594]

arugula *type of* **salad vegetable** [➡FRUIT AND VEGETABLES; 1176]

as 1 *conj* **while**, when, during, whilst (*UK*) [➡CONCURRENT AND CONTEMPORANEOUS; 164] 2 *conj* **because**, since, seeing that, being as, considering that, inasmuch as [➡CAUSATION; 168]

as a matter of fact *adv* **actually**, in fact, really, in point of fact, to tell the truth, in consequence (*formal*) [➡WORDS AND PHRASES EMPHASIZING THE TRUTH OF A MATTER; 172]

ASAP *adv* [➡HAPPENING QUICKLY; 104]

as a result *adv* **consequently**, accordingly, so, therefore, thus (*formal*) [➡RESULTS AND OUTCOMES; 83]

as a result of *prep* **because of**, by, through, by means of, on account of, due to, thanks to, owing to, by dint of [➡CAUSATION; 168]

as a rule *adv* **usually**, in general, most of the time, generally, normally, as often as not, nine times out of ten [➡USUALLY; 108] *Opposite*: exceptionally

asbestos *type of* **mineral** [➡MINERALS; 1277]

ascend 1 *v* **rise**, climb, soar, go up, come up, arise (*archaic or literary*) [➡GO UPWARD; 306] *Opposite*: descend 2 *v* **climb**, go up, come up, mount, scale, get up, move upward [➡GO UPWARD; 306] *Opposite*: descend

ascendancy *n* **dominance**, domination, preeminence, predominance, power, upper hand, control, hegemony [➡SUPERIORITY; 152] *Opposite*: subordination

ascendant 1 *adj* (*literary*) **rising**, dominant, ascending, prevailing, mounting, overriding, climbing, upward, soaring, spiraling, moving up, uprising [➡DIRECTION OF MOTION; 345] *Opposite*: descendent 2 *adj* **dominant**, controlling, governing, ruling, influential, main, principal, leading, chief, foremost, major, superior, supreme [➡ MOST IMPORTANT AND MAIN; 193] *Opposite*: subordinate

ascendency *see* **ascendancy**

ascension (*formal*) *n* **rise**, ascent, climb, mounting, scaling, moving up, surmounting, traveling up [➡ GO UPWARD; 306] *Opposite*: descent

ascent 1 *n* **climb**, rise, mounting, scaling, ascension (*formal*) [➡ GO UPWARD; 306] *Opposite*: descent 2 *n* **gradient**, slope, incline, rake, angle, elevation [➡ MOUNTAINS AND HILLS; 1044]

ascertain *v* **determine**, discover, find out, learn, make certain [➡ LEARN AND DISCOVER; 762]

ascetic 1 *n* **abstainer**, celibate, puritan, penitent [➡ ASCETIC PEOPLE; 883] *Opposite*: hedonist 2 *adj* **austere**, abstinent, frugal, abstemious, Spartan, severe [➡ SELF-DENIAL; 882] *Opposite*: hedonistic

asceticism *n* **austerity**, self-discipline, abstemiousness, self-denial, self-restraint, abstinence, frugality, plainness, simplicity, severity, starkness, strictness, rigor [➡ SELF-DENIAL; 882] *Opposite*: hedonism

ascot *type of* **accessory** [➡ ACCESSORIES, MILLINERY, AND LINGERIE; 867]

ascribe (*formal*) 1 *v* **assign**, credit, attribute, accredit, chalk up, give credit [➡ GIVE AND PROVIDE; 430] 2 *v* **put down to**, attribute, blame on, lay at the door of, charge, impute [➡ CREATING CONNECTIONS; 144]

aseptic *adj* **clean**, sterile, pure, sterilized, uninfected, hygienic, uncontaminated, disinfected, germ-free, antiseptic, disease-free, purified, sanitized [➡ CLEAN AND HYGIENIC; 1233] *Opposite*: septic

asexual 1 *adj* **genderless**, androgynous, neutral, sexless [➡ GENDER IDENTITY AND SEXUALITY; 932] 2 *adj* **vegetative**, somatic, parthenogenetic, nonsexual [➡ REPRODUCTION AND HEREDITY; 725]

as far as *conj* **to the extent that**, to the degree that, insofar as, as much as, so far as, as concerns [➡ EXPRESSIONS OF REFERENCE; 63]

as far as I'm concerned *adv* [➡ EXPRESSIONS OF OPINION; 623]

as good as 1 *prep* **equal to**, equivalent to, the same as, on a par with, comparable with, tantamount to [➡ EQUALITY; 154] 2 *adv* **almost**, nearly, practically, virtually, effectively, more or less, to all intents and purposes [➡ TO A CERTAIN EXTENT; 136]

ash 1 *n* **residue**, cinders, slag, embers, powder, dust [➡ PRODUCTS OF FIRE; 1166] 2 *type of* **deciduous tree** [➡ DECIDUOUS TREES; 1028] 3 *type of* **gray** [➡ COLORS; 1224]

ashamed 1 *adj* **embarrassed**, mortified, humiliated, abashed, humbled, chagrined [➡ EMBARRASSMENT AND HUMILIATION; 542] *Opposite*: proud 2 *adj* **regretful**, reluctant, unwilling, uncomfortable, restrained, reserved, deterred [➡ EMBARRASSMENT AND HUMILIATION; 542] *Opposite*: bold

ashen *adj* **pallid**, wan, pasty, white as a sheet, drained of color, gray, grayish, pale, ashy [➡ COMPLEXION; 480] *Opposite*: rosy

ashes *n* **ruins**, remains, vestiges, remnants, fragments, debris [➡ REMAINDER AND REMAINDERS; 125]

ashore *adv* **aground**, onto land, onto dry land, on shore [➡ DIRECTION OF MOTION; 345]

ashy *see* **ashen**

aside 1 *adv* **sideways**, away, to the side, sidewise, to the left, on the side, to the right, to one side, apart, out of the way [➡ DIRECTION OF MOTION; 345] 2 *adv* **regardless**, however, anyway, anyhow, notwithstanding (*formal*) [➡ ALTHOUGH, NEVERTHELESS, AND DESPITE; 169] 3 *adv* **in reserve**, separately, away, to one side, up your sleeve [➡ UNRELATEDNESS AND SEPARATENESS; 146] 4 *n* **digression**, departure, tangent, interposition, parenthesis, excursion, excursus (*formal*) [➡ ONE WAY COMMUNICATION; 49] 5 *n* **whisper**, mumbled comment, remark, undertone, by-play, soliloquy [➡ THE SPOKEN WORD; 671]

aside from 1 *prep* **as well as**, in addition to, on top of, besides, over and beyond, above and beyond [➡ ALSO; 138] 2 *prep* **barring**, excluding, ignoring, except, except for, with the exception of, apart from, besides, other than, despite, outside of, excepting (*formal*), saving (*literary*) [➡ NOT; 137] *Opposite*: including

asinine *adj* **silly**, foolish, unintelligent [➡ NEGATIVE INTELLECTUAL CHARACTERISTICS; 525] *Opposite*: intelligent

as it were (*formal*) *adv* **so to speak**, in a manner of speaking, as you might say, so to say, as it seems, sort of (*informal*) [➡ SUMMARIZING EXPRESSIONS; 622]

ask 1 *v* **request**, inquire, solicit, question, query, probe, examine, test, catechize [➡ REQUEST AND DEMAND; 663] *Opposite*: answer 2 *v* **invite**, ask over, have over, summon, request, bid (*archaic*) [➡ ESTABLISHING RELATIONSHIPS WITH OTHERS; 974] 3 *v* **count on**, expect, demand, look for, require, call for, solicit [➡ REQUEST AND DEMAND; 663]

askance *adv* **doubtfully**, suspiciously, sideways, dubiously, distrustfully, skeptically, mistrustfully [➡ UNCERTAINTY; 559] *Opposite*: trustingly

askew *adv* **crookedly**, awry, out of kilter, off center, cockeyed, out of line (*informal*) [➡ ORIENTATION AND ALIGNMENT; 1223] *Opposite*: straight

ask for *v* **request**, provoke, solicit, inspire, demand, incite, petition for, induce, beg for, insist on, bring on, plead, bring to pass, sue (*formal*) [➡ REQUEST AND DEMAND; 663] *Opposite*: refuse

asking price *n* **price**, selling price, starting price, marked price [➡ EXPENDITURE; 423]

ask out *v* [➡ INITIATE AND ESTABLISH COMMUNICATION; 680]

aslant 1 *adv* **obliquely**, at an angle, on a slope, diagonally, slantingly, sideways, crookedly, crossways, crosswise [➡ ORIENTATION AND ALIGNMENT; 1223] *Opposite*: straight 2 *adj* **slanting**, slant, slantwise, oblique, diagonal, sloping, aslope, angled [➡ ORIENTATION AND ALIGNMENT; 1223]

asleep 1 *adj* **sleeping**, slumbering, dead to the world, napping, sound asleep, fast asleep, dozing, out like a light, snoozing (*informal*), having forty winks (*informal*) [➡ TIRED, ASLEEP, AND UNCONSCIOUS; 738] *Opposite*: awake 2 *adj* **numb**, dead, benumbed, without feeling, lifeless [➡ TIRED, ASLEEP, AND UNCONSCIOUS; 738]

as long as *conj* **providing**, on condition that, given that, provided that, if, with the proviso that, with the understanding that, on the assumption that, supposing that, since, because [➡ CAUSATION; 168]

as of (*formal*) *prep* **from**, after, on or after, beginning, starting, since, commencing (*formal*) [➡ AFTER, LAST, AND FOLLOWING; 165]

as one *adv* **simultaneously**, together, in concert, en masse, with one voice, in unison [➡ ACTING WITH OTHERS; 285] *Opposite*: separately

asp *type of* **poisonous snake** [➡ SNAKES; 995]

ASP *n* [➡ THE INTERNET; 1128]

asparagus *type of* **vegetable** [➡ FRUIT AND VEGETABLES; 1176]

aspect 1 *n* **feature**, facet, characteristic, part, piece, phase, side, trait, property, quality, attribute [➡ QUALITIES AND CHARACTERISTICS; 1191] 2 *n* **position**, outlook, side, standpoint, viewpoint, view [➡ POINTS OF VIEW; 767] 3 *n* **appearance**, look, quality, bearing, air, countenance, facial expression, expression, demeanor, mien (*formal*) [➡ APPEARANCE AND ATMOSPHERE; 1237]

aspen *type of* **deciduous tree** [➡ DECIDUOUS TREES; 1028]

as per *prep* **according to**, in accordance with, following, consistent with, in keeping with, in line with [➡ EXPRESSIONS OF REFERENCE; 63] *Opposite*: counter

asperity (*formal*) *n* **severity**, brusqueness, gruffness, harshness, sharpness, astringency, sternness, stringency [➡ BAD-TEMPERED AND HUMORLESS; 626] *Opposite*: affability

aspersion *n* **slander**, slur, slight, smear, accusation, criticism, disparagement, defamation, vilification, denunciation, calumny (*formal*) [➡ INSULTS, ABUSE, AND SWEARING; 658] *Opposite*: praise

asphalt 1 *n* **tar**, tarmac, bitumen, blacktop [➡ COVERS AND COATINGS; 1246] 2 *type of* **mineral** [➡ MINERALS; 1277]

asphyxia *n* **suffocation**, choking, lack of oxygen, oxygen deprivation, unconsciousness, blockage [➡ BREATHE AND NOT BREATHE; 716]

asphyxiate *v* **suffocate**, smother, choke, stifle, strangulate, throttle [➡ KILL; 923] *Opposite*: breathe

asphyxiation *n* **suffocation**, choking, smothering, stifling, throttling, strangling, gassing [➡ CAUSES OF DEATH; 921] *Opposite*: breathing

aspic *n* **jelly**, gel, mousseline [➡ SEASONINGS AND SAUCES; 1174]

aspidistra *type of* **foliage plant** [➡ FOLIAGE PLANTS; 1035]

aspirant *n* **candidate**, contender, applicant, job seeker, job hunter, office seeker, hopeful [➡ WORKERS; 836]

See Compare and Contrast at **candidate**.

aspirate 1 *v* **pronounce**, enunciate, articulate, sound, voice, say [➡ UTTER AND PRONOUNCE; 608] 2 *v* **remove**, extract, suck out, draw out, take out, suction [➡ EXTRACT AND SEVER; 341] *Opposite*: inject

aspiration *n* **ambition**, goal, objective, aim, end, target, hope, desire, want, wish [➡ FEELINGS ABOUT THE FUTURE; 533]

aspirational *adj* **ambitious**, self-improving, aspiring,

hopeful, eager, thrusting, motivated, materialistic, go-getting (*informal*) [➡ HARD-WORKING AND COMMITTED; 500] *Opposite*: unambitious

aspire *v* **seek**, aim, hope, desire, want, wish [➡ DESIRE AND WANT; 579]

aspiring *adj* **wishful**, hopeful, aspirant, would-be, ambitious, wannabe (*informal*) [➡ DESIRE AND WANT; 579]

as regards *prep* **with regard to**, regarding, concerning, with reference to, as to, vis-à-vis, re, in respect of [➡ EXPRESSIONS OF REFERENCE; 63]

ass *type of* **farm animal** [➡ FARM ANIMALS; 982]

assail 1 *v* **attack**, assault, set about, lay into, beset, raid, storm, charge, rush, blitz [➡ PHYSICAL ATTACK AND PUNISHMENT; 415] *Opposite*: defend 2 *v* **criticize**, attack, lay into, berate, revile, vituperate, abuse [➡ ACCUSE, BLAME, AND CRITICIZE; 641] *Opposite*: praise

assailant *n* **attacker**, mugger, accoster, goon, assaulter, aggressor [➡ ENEMIES AND TORMENTORS; 969]

assassin *n* **killer**, murderer, cutthroat, dispatcher, hired gun (*slang*), hit man (*slang*), slayer (*formal or literary*) [➡ CRIMINALS; 821]

assassinate *v* **kill**, murder, shoot, kill in cold blood, eliminate, liquidate, gun down (*informal*), snuff out (*informal*), wipe out (*slang*), slay (*formal or literary*) [➡ KILL; 923]

See Compare and Contrast at **kill**.

assassination *n* **foul play**, murder, killing, shooting, elimination, slaying, homicide, manslaughter [➡ CAUSES OF DEATH; 921]

assault 1 *n* **attack**, beating, stabbing, mugging, battering, pasting (*informal*) [➡ PHYSICAL ATTACK AND PUNISHMENT; 415] *Opposite*: defense 2 *n* **offensive**, attack, onslaught, incursion, storming, blitz, raid, charge [➡ AGGRESSIVE EVENTS; 39] *Opposite*: retreat 3 *v* **attack**, mug, set about, assail, lay into, strike, hit, batter, beat up (*informal*), jump (*informal*) [➡ PHYSICAL ATTACK AND PUNISHMENT; 415] *Opposite*: defend

assay 1 *v* **examine**, assess, analyze, evaluate, test, try, prove, inspect, scrutinize [➡ EXAMINE AND ASSESS; 753] 2 *v* (*literary*) **attempt**, try, take a shot at, undertake, take a stab at (*informal*), essay (*formal*), endeavor (*formal*) [➡ ATTEMPT AN ACTION; 261]

assegai *type of* **projectile** [➡ PROJECTILES; 1159]

assembler *n* [➡ COMPUTERS AND COMPUTING; 1127]

assemblage 1 *n* **accumulation**, grouping, assembly, collection, meeting, gathering, congregation [➡ COLLECTIONS AND MIXTURES OF THINGS; 1244] 2 *n* **crowd**, throng, assembly, group, mass, body, collection [➡ AUDIENCES AND ATTENDEES; 937]

assemble 1 *v* **bring together**, collect, pull together, draw together, accumulate, amass, gather, lump together [➡ COMBINE AND MIX; 400] *Opposite*: disband 2 *v* **muster**, collect, meet, come together, convene, congregate, rally, marshal, gather [➡ GET CLOSER TOGETHER; 310] 3 *v* **put together**, build, fit together, make, compile, connect, manufacture, construct, set up, throw together (*informal*) [➡ BUILD; 352] *Opposite*: take apart

See Compare and Contrast at **collect**.

assembly 1 *n* **gathering**, coming together, meeting, association, assemblage, congregation, congress [⮞ MEETINGS AND ASSEMBLIES; 43] 2 *n* **meeting**, congress, assemblage, gathering, muster, rally, get-together (*informal*) [⮞ MEETINGS AND ASSEMBLIES; 43] 3 *n* **legislative body**, legislature, council, government, representatives, community, congregation, conclave [⮞ LEGISLATIVE BODIES AND LEGISLATION; 809] 4 *n* **construction**, building, compilation, putting together, fabrication [⮞ BUILDING AND ARCHITECTURE; 1076] *Opposite*: destruction

assembly hall *n* [⮞ BUILDINGS FOR PUBLIC ENTERTAINMENT; 1084]

assembly plant *type of* **factory** [⮞ INDUSTRIAL BUILDINGS; 1087]

assembly point *n* **meeting point**, meeting place, rendezvous, rallying point, muster station (*UK*) [⮞ PUBLIC BUILDINGS AND MEETING PLACES; 1081]

assembly room *n* [⮞ BUILDINGS FOR PUBLIC ENTERTAINMENT; 1084]

assent 1 *v* **agree**, acquiesce, concur, go along with, subscribe to, approve, consent, grant, allow [⮞ AGREE; 645] *Opposite*: disagree 2 *n* **agreement**, acquiescence, concurrence, nod, acceptance, approval, approbation, sanction, consent [⮞ AGREE; 645] *Opposite*: disagreement

See Compare and Contrast at **agree**.

assert 1 *v* **declare**, state, insist on, proclaim, emphasize, stress, affirm, claim, allege, contend, avow (*formal*), aver (*formal*) [⮞ CLAIM, INSIST, AND EMPHASIZE; 614] *Opposite*: deny 2 *v* **stand up for**, profess, defend, maintain, uphold, support, champion, insist on [⮞ CLAIM, INSIST, AND EMPHASIZE; 614] *Opposite*: renounce

assertion *n* **declaration**, statement, proclamation, claim, allegation, contention, affirmation, avowal (*formal*) [⮞ CLAIM, INSIST, AND EMPHASIZE; 614] *Opposite*: denial

assertive *adj* **self-confident**, self-assured, confident, firm, forceful, emphatic, insistent, positive, decided, forward, aggressive, bold, pushy (*informal*) [⮞ CONFIDENCE AND COMPOSURE; 499] *Opposite*: shy

assertiveness *n* **confidence**, forcefulness, insistence, decisiveness, boldness, firmness, aggressiveness, pushiness [⮞ CONFIDENCE AND COMPOSURE; 499] *Opposite*: shyness

assess 1 *v* **measure**, calculate, evaluate, judge, weigh, consider, gauge, weigh up (*UK*) [⮞ EXAMINE AND ASSESS; 753] 2 *v* **tax**, review, charge, levy, evaluate, value, fine, rate [⮞ ASSESS QUANTITY; 757]

assessment 1 *n* **evaluation**, appraisal, estimation, measurement, judgment, review, consideration, opinion [⮞ POINTS OF VIEW; 767] 2 *n* **valuation**, calculation, taxation [⮞ ACCOUNTING, BANKING, AND BUDGETING; 799] 3 *n* **duty**, charge, impost, debt, bill [⮞ ACCOUNTING, BANKING, AND BUDGETING; 799]

assessor *n* **evaluator**, appraiser, judge, taxer, inspector, revenuer (*informal*) [⮞ ADVISERS, JUDGES, AND ARBITERS; 971]

asset 1 *n* **advantage**, strength, benefit, positive feature, quality, skill, talent, ability, qualification, power, endowment, boon, blessing, resource, plus (*informal*), plus point (*UK*) [⮞ SOURCE OF HAPPINESS, PLEASURE, OR IMPROVEMENT; 209] *Oppo-*

site: drawback 2 *n* **possession**, property, resource, holding [⮞ POSSESSIONS; 461]

assets *n* **possessions**, property, resources, material goods, worldly goods, wherewithal, belongings, wealth, chattels, money, estate, effects (*formal*) [⮞ FINANCIAL ASSETS; 462] *Opposite*: liabilities

asset-stripping *n* **profit taking**, profitmaking, selling off, buying and selling, trading, trafficking, profiteering, wheeling and dealing [⮞ BUSINESS ACTIVITIES AND PHENOMENA; 794]

assiduity *n* **diligence**, care, attention, application, industriousness, perseverance, conscientiousness, assiduousness, industry (*formal or literary*), sedulousness (*literary*), sedulity (*literary*) [⮞ HARD-WORKING AND COMMITTED; 500] *Opposite*: carelessness

assiduous *adj* **diligent**, persevering, industrious, tireless, painstaking, conscientious, thorough, meticulous, sedulous (*literary*) [⮞ HARD-WORKING AND COMMITTED; 500] *Opposite*: lazy

See Compare and Contrast at **careful**.

assiduousness *n* **diligence**, persistence, industriousness, attentiveness, tirelessness, indefatigability, sedulousness (*literary*) [⮞ HARD-WORKING AND COMMITTED; 500] *Opposite*: laziness

assign 1 *v* **allocate**, allot, give, dispense, disperse, consign, hand out, apportion, dole out (*informal*), ascribe (*formal*) [⮞ DISPENSE, RATION, AND DISTRIBUTE; 434] 2 *v* **appoint**, designate, delegate, send, transfer, detail [⮞ CONFER STATUS; 458]

assignation *n* **meeting**, tryst, rendezvous, appointment, date, get-together (*informal*) [⮞ MEETINGS AND ASSEMBLIES; 43]

assignment 1 *n* **task**, job, project, duty, obligation, mission [⮞ JOB; 833] 2 *n* **appointment**, duty, position, role, job, responsibilities [⮞ JOB; 833] 3 *n* **transfer**, handing out, consignment, allocation, delegation, designation [⮞ DISPENSE, RATION, AND DISTRIBUTE; 434]

See Compare and Contrast at **job**.

assimilate 1 *v* **integrate**, adapt, adjust, blend in, fit in, conform, espouse, embrace [⮞ COMBINE AND MIX; 400] 2 *v* **incorporate**, take in, digest, absorb, understand, learn [⮞ LEARN AND DISCOVER; 762] *Opposite*: reject

assimilation 1 *n* **integration**, adjustment, acclimatization, accommodation, adaptation [⮞ CHANGE; 372] 2 *n* **absorption**, incorporation, digestion, ingestion, inculcation [⮞ COMBINE AND MIX; 400]

assist 1 *v* **help**, aid, help out, lend a hand, give a hand, support, back, abet [⮞ HELP; 293] *Opposite*: hinder 2 *n* **a helping hand**, a hand, assistance, help, support, backing [⮞ KIND ACTIONS OR BEHAVIOR; 295] *Opposite*: hindrance

assistance *n* **help**, aid, support, backing, cooperation, collaboration, succor (*literary*) [⮞ KIND ACTIONS OR BEHAVIOR; 295] *Opposite*: hindrance

assistant 1 *n* **helper**, supporter, aide, subordinate, junior, executive assistant, intern, trainee, personal assistant, deputy, aide-de-camp, PA (*UK*) [⮞ SUBORDINATES

AND ASSISTANTS; 966] **2** *adj* **associate**, subordinate, secondary, junior, sub-, vice- [➥ RELATED; 142]

Compare and Contrast: *assistant, helper, deputy, aide*

CORE MEANING: somebody who helps another person in carrying out a task

assistant somebody who works to somebody else's instructions, often in a paid capacity; *helper* somebody who takes on an informal, often voluntary, role; *deputy* an officially designated chief assistant authorized to act on a superior's behalf; *aide* an assistant in military, political, or commercial contexts.

---

assisted *adj* **aided**, helped, abetted, supported, sponsored [➥ ACTING WITH OTHERS; 285] *Opposite:* unassisted

assize *n* **inquest**, court case, hearing, inquiry, examination [➥ TRIAL, PUNISHMENT, AND LEGAL OUTCOMES; 819]

assizes (*UK*) *n* **court session**, judicial proceedings, court sitting, circuit court [➥ TRIAL, PUNISHMENT, AND LEGAL OUTCOMES; 819]

associate **1** *v* **connect**, relate, link, correlate, bracket, combine, couple, think of [➥ CREATING CONNECTIONS; 144] *Opposite:* separate **2** *v* **mix**, socialize, spend time with, go around with (*informal*), see, be involved with, assort with [➥ ESTABLISHING RELATIONSHIPS WITH OTHERS; 974] *Opposite:* avoid **3** *v* **unite**, combine, join together, group together, join, yoke, amalgamate, conjoin (*formal*) [➥ CREATING CONNECTIONS; 144] *Opposite:* disband **4** *n* **partner**, colleague, business partner, fellow worker, coworker, confederate, accomplice, coconspirator [➥ COLLEAGUES AND EQUALS; 967] **5** *n* **companion**, comrade, acquaintance, friend, ally, crony, fellow (*dated*), confrère (*formal*) [➥ FRIENDS AND GUESTS; 963] **6** *adj* **subordinate**, secondary, junior, assistant, sub-, vice- [➥ RELATED; 142]

associated *adj* **related**, allied, linked, connected, accompanying, concomitant, supplementary, attendant [➥ RELATED; 142]

association **1** *n* **organization**, union, alliance, society, company, fraternity, group, sorority [➥ CLUBS AND SOCIETIES; 939] **2** *n* **friendship**, relationship, connection, fellowship, involvement [➥ RELATIONSHIP TO ANOTHER; 973] **3** *n* **connotation**, overtone, suggestion, memory, reminder, link, indication, hint [➥ MEANING; 690]

assonance **1** *n* **repetition**, recurrence, duplication, iteration, alliteration, echoing, rhyme, similarity [➥ ASPECTS OF LANGUAGE; 682] **2** *type of* **figure of speech** [➥ FIGURES OF SPEECH; 673]

assonant *adj* [➥ SOFT, LOW, OR PLEASANT SOUNDS; 1265]

as soon as *conj* **once**, the moment, the instant, the minute, immediately, when, after [➥ AFTER, LAST, AND FOLLOWING; 165]

assort *v* **classify**, separate, sort out, group, divide, categorize, class, arrange, methodize [➥ ARRANGE AND CREATE ORDER; 357] *Opposite:* disarrange

assorted *adj* **mixed**, various, miscellaneous, varied, multifarious [➥ DIFFERENCE; 149]

assortment *n* **variety**, collection, range, mixture, mixed bag, hodgepodge, group [➥ COLLECTIONS AND MIXTURES OF THINGS; 1244]

assort with *v* **associate**, mix with, socialize with, see,

spend time with, go around with (*informal*) [➥ ESTABLISHING RELATIONSHIPS WITH OTHERS; 974]

assuage *v* **moderate**, ease, soften, lessen, appease, satisfy, mitigate, alleviate, quiet, allay, temper, pacify, conciliate, placate [➥ CHANGE OF INTENSITY: LESS; 395] *Opposite:* inflame

assume **1** *v* **take for granted**, suppose, presume, presuppose, think, guess, imagine, believe [➥ DEVELOP THEORIES AND REASON; 744] **2** *v* **take up**, take responsibility, take on, take upon yourself, shoulder, undertake, accept, adopt, don [➥ ACCEPT POSSESSION; 450] **3** *v* **feign**, affect, fake, simulate, put on, act, pretend, sham, bluff [➥ PRETEND AND MIMIC; 60]

See Compare and Contrast at **deduce**.

---

assumed **1** *adj* **expected**, presumed, supposed, rumored, implicit, anticipated [➥ UNCERTAIN; 175] **2** *adj* **false**, artificial, fake, phony, bogus, feigned, untrue [➥ FALSE AND UNREAL; 173]

assumed name *n* **alias**, pseudonym, pen name, nom de plume, stage name, false identity [➥ NAME AND DESCRIBE; 665]

assuming *adj* **presumptuous**, pretentious, arrogant, haughty, high and mighty, supercilious [➥ POMPOUS, LOUD, AND OVERCONFIDENT; 635] *Opposite:* humble

assumption *n* **supposition**, statement, postulation, hypothesis, guess, theory, conjecture, notion, belief, idea [➥ IDEAS AND THOUGHTS; 770]

assurance **1** *n* **pledge**, declaration, word, guarantee, oath, promise, reassurance, assertion, warrant [➥ PROMISE AND ASSURE; 684] **2** *n* **self-confidence**, self-possession, self-reliance, confidence, poise, self-assurance, aplomb, composure [➥ CONFIDENCE AND COMPOSURE; 499] *Opposite:* timidity

assure **1** *v* **promise**, guarantee, give surety, pledge, swear, declare, reassure, convince [➥ PROMISE AND ASSURE; 684] **2** *v* **make certain**, ensure, guarantee, nail down, know for certain, substantiate, verify, secure [➥ MAKE POSSIBLE; 275]

assured **1** *adj* **certain**, guaranteed, sure, confident, solid [➥ CERTAIN; 174] *Opposite:* uncertain **2** *adj* **confident**, self-confident, self-assured, self-possessed, poised, cool [➥ CONFIDENCE AND COMPOSURE; 499] *Opposite:* diffident

aster *type of* **annual flower** [➥ FLOWERS; 1032]

asterisk **1** *type of* **punctuation mark** [➥ ASPECTS OF LANGUAGE; 682] **2** *n* **symbol**, sign, mark, character, star, reference mark [➥ SYMBOLS, SIGNS, AND NUMBERS; 596] **3** *v* **mark**, identify, label, indicate, specify, star [➥ NAME AND DESCRIBE; 665]

astern **1** *adv* **behind**, aft, at the back, in back of, at the rear, abaft, back of, forward [➥ RELATIVE LOCATION; 161] **2** *adv* **to the rear**, backward, in reverse [➥ DIRECTION OF MOTION; 345] *Opposite:* ahead

asteroid *type of* **heavenly body** [➥ HEAVENLY BODIES; 1061]

as the crow flies *adv* [➥ DIRECTION OF MOTION; 345]

astir **1** *adj* **awake**, out of bed, up, up and about, aroused, roused, awakened [➥ WIDE AWAKE AND CONSCIOUS; 735] *Opposite:* asleep **2** *adj* **active**, alive, moving, stirring, live, busy [➥ HAPPENING AND IN PROGRESS; 32] *Opposite:* inactive

as to *prep* **with regard to**, as regards, regarding, concerning, with respect to, with reference to, vis-à-vis, re [➡ EXPRESSIONS OF REFERENCE; 63]

astonish *v* **surprise**, amaze, astound, dumbfound, overwhelm, daze, render speechless, take your breath away, shock, flabbergast (*informal*) [➡ SURPRISE AND IMPRESS; 574]

astonished *adj* **surprised**, amazed, astounded, dumbfounded, incredulous, overwhelmed, dazed, speechless, bewildered, shocked, flabbergasted (*informal*) [➡ SURPRISE, SHOCK, AND AMAZEMENT; 545]

astonishing *adj* **amazing**, surprising, astounding, shocking, bewildering, beyond belief, mindblowing (*informal*) [➡ EXTRAORDINARY; AMAZING; 204] *Opposite*: predictable

astonishment *n* **surprise**, amazement, wonder, bewilderment, shock [➡ SURPRISE, SHOCK, AND AMAZEMENT; 545]

astound *v* **amaze**, astonish, surprise, shock, dumbfound, overwhelm, daze, render speechless, take your breath away, flabbergast (*informal*), blow away (*slang*) [➡ SURPRISE AND IMPRESS; 574]

astounded *adj* **astonished**, surprised, amazed, stunned, dazed, confused, speechless, thunderstruck, aghast, horrified, shocked, flabbergasted (*informal*), blown away (*slang*) [➡ SURPRISE, SHOCK, AND AMAZEMENT; 545]

astounding *adj* **amazing**, astonishing, surprising, shocking, beyond belief, mindblowing (*informal*) [➡ EXTRAORDINARY: AMAZING; 204] *Opposite*: unsurprising

astrakhan *type of* **fabric from animals** [➡ FABRICS; 1132]

astral **1** *adj* **stellar**, astronomical, astrophysical, cosmological, celestial, starry, stellular, sidereal [➡ THE SOLAR SYSTEM AND ASTRONOMY; 1060] **2** *adj* **immaterial**, spiritual, psychical, otherworldly, transcendent, ethereal, bodiless, metaphysical, incorporeal (*formal*) [➡ FATE, DESTINY, AND ASTROLOGY; 782] *Opposite*: material

astray *adv* **off course**, lost, off track, off target, off beam, amiss, afield, awry [➡ AIMLESS AND ERRANT MOTION; 343]

astride *prep* **on both sides of**, spanning, straddling, across [➡ RELATIVE LOCATION; 161]

astringency *n* **acerbity**, acidity, causticity, mordancy, sharpness, bite, sting, harshness, severity [➡ RUDE AND HOSTILE; 625] *Opposite*: blandness

astringent *adj* **harsh**, severe, biting, caustic, acerbic, mordant, cutting [➡ RUDE AND HOSTILE; 625] *Opposite*: bland

astrologer *n* **fortune-teller**, seer, soothsayer, prophet, forecaster, astrologist [➡ FATE, DESTINY, AND ASTROLOGY; 782]

astrological *adj* **zodiacal**, horoscopic, fortune-telling, prophetic, forecasting, soothsaying, stargazing [➡ FATE, DESTINY, AND ASTROLOGY; 782]

astrological sign *n* **sign of the zodiac**, birth sign, sun sign, constellation, house [➡ FATE, DESTINY, AND ASTROLOGY; 782]

astrological sign

◆ *types of astrological signs*
Aquarius, Aries, Cancer, Capricorn, Gemini, Leo, Libra, Pisces, Sagittarius, Scorpio, Taurus, Virgo

astrologist *n* [➡ FATE, DESTINY, AND ASTROLOGY; 782]

astrology *n* **fortune-telling**, clairvoyance, soothsaying, forecasting, prediction, prophecy [➡ FATE, DESTINY, AND ASTROLOGY; 782]

astronaut *n* **space traveler**, space pilot, cosmonaut, rocket pilot, spaceman, spacewoman, rocketeer [➡ SPACE TRAVEL AND EXPLORATION; 1062]

astronomer *n* **stargazer**, starwatcher, radio astronomer, astrophysicist, space scientist [➡ THE SOLAR SYSTEM AND ASTRONOMY; 1060]

astronomical **1** *adj* **astral**, planetary, cosmological, astrophysical, lunar, stellar, solar, cosmic [➡ THE SOLAR SYSTEM AND ASTRONOMY; 1060] **2** *adj* (*informal*) **exorbitant**, excessive, sky-high, through the ceiling, huge, enormous, vast, immense, prodigious, outrageous [➡ TOO MUCH; 119] *Opposite*: affordable

astronomically (*informal*) *adv* **exorbitantly**, exceedingly, excessively, inordinately, extremely, exceptionally, hugely, immensely, prodigiously, vastly [➡ TO A GREAT EXTENT; 132]

astronomical telescope *type of* **optical instrument** [➡ OPTICAL INSTRUMENTS; 1124]

astronomy *n* **stargazing**, starwatching, radio astronomy, astrophysics, space science [➡ THE SOLAR SYSTEM AND ASTRONOMY; 1060]

astute *adj* **shrewd**, smart, perceptive, judicious, incisive, wise, intelligent, clever, perspicacious [➡ POSITIVE INTELLECTUAL CHARACTERISTICS; 524] *Opposite*: credulous

astuteness *n* **shrewdness**, good judgment, smartness, intelligence, wisdom, sharpness, cleverness, perspicacity [➡ POSITIVE INTELLECTUAL CHARACTERISTICS; 524] *Opposite*: credulousness

asunder (*formal*) *adv* **apart**, open, in pieces, in bits, in halves, in two, in twain (*archaic or literary*) [➡ DIRECTION OF MOTION; 345] *Opposite*: together

as well *adv* **too**, also, additionally, in addition, on top [➡ ALSO; 138]

as well as *conj* **in addition to**, on top of, over and above, with, and, plus (*informal*) [➡ ALSO; 138]

as yet *adv* **at this time**, at present, up to now, so far, up to the present moment, yet [➡ BEFORE, FIRST, AND PRECEDING; 163]

asylum **1** *n* **refuge**, haven, safe haven, sanctuary, shelter, place of safety, safe house, retreat [➡ SAFE BUILDINGS OR PLACES; 1093] **2** *n* **protection**, refuge, sanctuary, shelter, safety [➡ SAFE AND SAFETY; 191]

asymmetric *adj* **unequal**, uneven, irregular, lopsided, disproportionate, distorted, unbalanced, asymmetrical [➡ ORIENTATION AND ALIGNMENT; 1223] *Opposite*: symmetrical

asymmetrical *see* **asymmetric**

asymmetry *n* **irregularity**, lopsidedness, unevenness, disproportionateness [➡ ORIENTATION AND ALIGNMENT; 1223] *Opposite*: symmetry

at a complete loss *adj* [➡ UNCERTAINTY; 559]

at a disadvantage *adj* **in a weak position**, disadvantaged, vulnerable, hampered, hindered, held back [➡ IN TROUBLE AND DISADVANTAGED; 73] *Opposite:* at an advantage

at a loss *adj* **stuck**, perplexed, stumped, confused, puzzled, beaten, defeated, uncertain, stymied [➡ UNCERTAINTY; 559]

at an advantage *adj* **in a strong position**, with the upper hand [➡ STRENGTH; 201] *Opposite:* at a disadvantage

at an angle *adv* [➡ ORIENTATION AND ALIGNMENT; 1223]

at any rate *adv* **in any case**, anyway, anyhow, in any event, regardless, at least, nonetheless, nevertheless [➡ SUMMARIZING EXPRESSIONS; 622]

at a rate of knots (*UK*) *adv* **at high speed**, fast, quickly, like lightning, like the wind, lickety-split (*informal*) [➡ MOVING QUICKLY; 103] *Opposite:* slowly

at a standstill *adv* **at a halt**, immobile, stationary, still, becalmed, motionless, stopped [➡ LACK OF ACTIVITY OR MOTION; 342] *Opposite:* on the move

atavistic *adj* **primitive**, primeval, primal, ancient, ancestral, archaic [➡ OLD, OLD-FASHIONED; 167] *Opposite:* modern

at death's door *adj* **ill**, dying, sinking, slipping away, fading, declining [➡ UNFIT AND WEAK; 739] *Opposite:* alive and kicking (*informal*)

at ease *adj* **comfortable**, relaxed, easy, calm, composed, unperturbed, happy [➡ COOL AND CALM; 536] *Opposite:* tense

atelier *type of* **room in the home** [➡ TYPES OF ROOMS; 1097]

at every turn *adv* **continually**, all the time, constantly, repeatedly [➡ PERMANENCE: WITHOUT END; 94] *Opposite:* occasionally

at fault *adj* **in the wrong**, to blame, guilty, wrong, responsible, mistaken, misguided, incorrect [➡ INCORRECT AND ERRONEOUS; 222] *Opposite:* in the right

at first *adv* **in the beginning**, at the start, originally, initially, at the outset, in the early days [➡ BEFORE, FIRST, AND PRECEDING; 163]

at first glance *see* **at first sight**

at first sight *adv* **on the face of it**, superficially, on the surface, ostensibly, apparently, at first glance [➡ UNCERTAIN; 175]

at hand 1 *adv* **nearby**, just around the corner, within reach, near, close by, handy, on hand, accessible, in sight [➡ CLOSENESS; 159] *Opposite:* distant 2 *adj* **imminent**, approaching, impending, on the way, coming, just around the corner, near, close, about to happen, in sight [➡ FUTURE; 86] *Opposite:* far-off

at heart *adv* **basically**, fundamentally, essentially, in fact, actually, truly, sincerely, really, in reality, in essence [➡ FUNDAMENTAL; 195] *Opposite:* superficially

atheism *n* **unbelief**, doubt, freethinking, skepticism, humanism, nonbelief, incredulity, agnosticism, disbelief, godlessness [➡ PHILOSOPHIES AND BELIEFS; 780] *Opposite:* belief

atheist *n* **unbeliever**, doubter, nonbeliever, skeptic, agnostic, freethinker, disbeliever, humanist [➡ PHILOSOPHICAL AND POLITICAL THINKERS; 781] *Opposite:* believer

atheistic *adj* **unbelieving**, nonbelieving, disbelieving, incredulous, irreligious, godless, ungodly, agnostic, skeptical, doubting, freethinking, humanistic [➡ PHILOSOPHIES AND BELIEFS; 780] *Opposite:* believing

athlete *n* **sportsperson**, contestant, participant, competitor, team member, player, jock (*informal*) [➡ PEOPLE IN SPORTS AND LEISURE; 876]

athletic *adj* **fit**, sporty, healthy, in good shape, physical, conditioned, agile, nimble, coordinated, lithe, muscular, toned, vigorous, energetic, strong, powerful, active [➡ AGILITY OF THE BODY; 476] *Opposite:* unfit

athleticism *n* **litheness**, suppleness, flexibility, power, activeness, muscularity, powerfulness, strength, vigor [➡ AGILITY OF THE BODY; 476] *Opposite:* clumsiness

athletics *n* [➡ HOBBIES, GAMES, AND SPORTS; 875]

at home 1 *adj* **comfortable**, at ease, relaxed, easy, comfy (*informal*) [➡ COOL AND CALM; 536] *Opposite:* uncomfortable 2 *adj* **accustomed**, adjusted, used to, familiar, confident, sure, competent, capable, proficient, skilled, experienced, knowledgeable, in control [➡ KNOWLEDGE AND WISDOM; 558] *Opposite:* ill at ease

athwart *adv* [➡ ORIENTATION AND ALIGNMENT; 1223]

at issue *adj* **under consideration**, under discussion, under debate, in question, in the balance, in doubt, to be decided, at stake [➡ IMPORTANT; 194]

Atlantic *type of* **time zone** [➡ TIMES OF DAY; 87]

at large 1 *adj* **in general**, on the whole, overall, as a whole, all together [➡ ALL; 128] 2 *adj* **free**, at liberty, unconfined, on the loose, escaped, out [➡ FREEDOM AND LIBERTY; 208] *Opposite:* confined

atlas *n* **book of maps**, diagrams, charts, plans, drawings, graphics [➡ BOOKS AND BOOKLETS; 590]

at last *adv* **eventually**, finally, ultimately, in the end, at length [➡ AFTER, LAST, AND FOLLOWING; 165] *Opposite:* immediately

at least 1 *adv* **as a minimum**, no less than [➡ ALTHOUGH, NEVERTHELESS, AND DESPITE; 169] *Opposite:* at best 2 *adv* **at any rate**, in any case, however, nonetheless, nevertheless [➡ SUMMARIZING EXPRESSIONS; 622]

at leisure *adj* **free**, at liberty, at ease, at rest, off, on your own, left to your own devices, unoccupied [➡ FREEDOM AND LIBERTY; 208] *Opposite:* busy

at length 1 *adv* (*formal*) **long-windedly**, in detail, in depth, verbosely, wordily, prolixly, ramblingly [➡ INARTICULATE, RAMBLING, AND AWKWARD; 633] *Opposite:* in brief 2 *adv* **eventually**, at last, at long last, finally, in the end [➡ AFTER, LAST, AND FOLLOWING; 165] *Opposite:* immediately

at liberty 1 *adj* **free**, at large, on the loose, released, unconfined, out, unrestricted, unconstrained [➡ FREEDOM AND LIBERTY; 208] *Opposite:* imprisoned 2 *adj* **at leisure**, free, permitted [➡ FREEDOM AND LIBERTY; 208]

at loggerheads *adj* **at odds**, at variance, fighting, quarreling, at each other's throats, in conflict, at daggers drawn [➡ DISHARMONY; 156]

at long last *adv* **finally**, in the end, ultimately, at last, at length, eventually [➡ AFTER, LAST, AND FOLLOWING; 165]

ATM *n* **cash machine**, automated teller machine, money machine, cashpoint (*UK*) [➡ ACCOUNTING, BANKING, AND BUDGETING; 799]

atmosphere 1 *n* **air**, sky, heaven, exosphere, ionosphere, mesosphere, ozonosphere, stratosphere, thermosphere, troposphere, ether (*literary*) [➡ THE EARTH'S ATMOSPHERE; 1040] **2** *n* **ambiance**, impression, feeling, feel, mood, tone, environment, surroundings, character, gestalt (*informal*) [➡ APPEARANCE AND ATMOSPHERE; 1237]

atmospheric *adj* **impressive**, distinctive, moody, special, full of character, full of atmospherc [➡ EMOTIONALLY PLEASANT; 107]

atmospherics *n* **interference**, disturbance, static, snow, hissing, crackling [➡ ACOUSTICS; 1138]

at no cost *adj* **free**, free of charge, gratis, for nothing, for free, on the house [➡ GIFTS; 438]

at odds 1 *adj* **in conflict**, at loggerheads, at variance, arguing, quarreling, in opposition, in contention [➡ DISHARMONY; 156] *Opposite*: in agreement **2** *adj* **contradictory**, incompatible, conflicting, inconsistent, in disagreement, at variance, in conflict, out of sync (*informal*) [➡ DISHARMONY; 156] *Opposite*: consistent

atoll *n* **island**, coral reef, coral island, isle, islet, coral isle, key, cay [➡ THE CONTINENTS AND ISLANDS; 1048]

atom *n* **particle**, bit, tiny part, iota, jot, molecule, fragment, grain, glimmer [➡ SMALL PIECES; 129]

atomic 1 *adj* **nuclear**, thermonuclear, fissionable [➡ ENERGY SOURCES; 1162] **2** *adj* **microscopic**, submicroscopic, minute, infinitesimal, minuscule, tiny, miniature [➡ SMALL; 1195] *Opposite*: gigantic

atomic bomb *type of* **explosive weapon** [➡ EXPLOSIVES; 1155]

atomizer *n* **spray**, spray can, vaporizer, aerosol [➡ CONTAINERS, RECEPTACLES, AND PACKAGING; 1245]

atonal *adj* **twelve-note**, twelve-tone, discordant, dissonant, inharmonious, unharmonious, cacophonous [➡ LOUD, HIGH, OR UNPLEASANT SOUNDS; 1266]

atonality *n* **twelve-note scale**, twelve-tone scale, serialism, discordance, dissonance, disharmony, lack of harmony, cacophony [➡ LOUD, HIGH, OR UNPLEASANT SOUNDS; 1266] *Opposite*: tonality

at once 1 *adv* **immediately**, straightaway, right away, right now, now, without further ado, without delay, promptly, in that instant, instantly, this instant [➡ PRESENT; 85] *Opposite*: later **2** *adv* **simultaneously**, at the same time, in unison, in chorus, together, all together, coincidentally, at one go (*UK*) [➡ CONCURRENT AND CONTEMPORANEOUS; 164] *Opposite*: separately

atone (*formal*) *v* **compensate**, make up, make amends, redress, apologize, do penance, say you're sorry, expiate, recompense [➡ APOLOGIZE AND RETRACT; 683]

at one fell swoop *adv* **at the same time**, at once, all together, simultaneously, at one go (*UK*), in unison, in chorus [➡ CONCURRENT AND CONTEMPORANEOUS; 164] *Opposite*: gradually

at one go (*UK*) *adv* **at the same time**, at once, all together,

at one fell swoop, simultaneously, in unison, in chorus [➡ CONCURRENT AND CONTEMPORANEOUS; 164] *Opposite*: gradually

atonement *n* **compensation**, amends, penitence, penance, punishment, expiation, apology, reparation, recompense [➡ APOLOGIZE AND RETRACT; 683]

at one time *adv* **in the past**, formerly, once, once upon a time, long ago, time was [➡ PAST; 84] *Opposite*: at present

at one with *adj* [➡ HARMONY; 155]

atop (*literary*) *prep* **on**, upon, on the top of, over, higher than, on the crest of, above [➡ RELATIVE LOCATION; 161] *Opposite*: beneath

at peace 1 *adj* **calm**, contented, relaxed, at ease, peaceful, comfortable, mellow [➡ COOL AND CALM; 536] *Opposite*: agitated **2** *adj* **dead**, at rest, no longer with us, passed away, deceased (*formal*), departed (*formal or literary*) [➡ DEAD AND DYING; 925]

at present *adv* **now**, right now, just now, presently, at the present time, at the moment, at this time, at this moment in time, at this point in time, currently, today, nowadays [➡ PRESENT; 85]

at random *adv* **haphazardly**, randomly, aimlessly, at the dictates of chance, unselectively [➡ DISORDER AND CHAOS; 245] *Opposite*: systematically

at rest 1 *adj* **stationary**, not working, inactive, immobile, still, not moving [➡ LACK OF ACTIVITY OR MOTION; 342] *Opposite*: active **2** *adj* **at ease**, at peace, free from worry, free from anxiety, reassured, comforted, relaxed [➡ COOL AND CALM; 536] *Opposite*: uneasy **3** *adj* **dead**, no longer with us, passed away, at peace, passed on, at peace, deceased (*formal*), departed (*formal or literary*) [➡ DEAD AND DYING; 925] *Opposite*: alive

at right angles *adv* [➡ ORIENTATION AND ALIGNMENT; 1223]

at risk 1 *adj* **endangered**, dying, vulnerable, threatened, imperiled (*formal*) [➡ IN DANGER; 237] *Opposite*: protected **2** *adj* **vulnerable**, susceptible, exposed, helpless, defenseless [➡ IN DANGER; 237] *Opposite*: safe **3** *adv* **at stake**, at issue, to be won or lost, riding on it, in the balance, up for grabs (*informal*) [➡ IN DANGER; 237]

atrium *n* **hall**, foyer, entrance hall, entrance, vestibule, reception area, porch, lobby, court, patio, concourse, narthex [➡ DOORS AND ACCESS POINTS; 1101]

atrocious 1 *adj* **bad**, terrible, dreadful, appalling, awful, frightful, dire, ghastly [➡ BAD AND BADLY; 223] **2** *adj* **brutal**, vicious, wicked, evil, cruel, vile, horrible, horrific, horrendous, hideous, unspeakable [➡ DISGUSTING AND REPULSIVE; 230]

atrociously 1 *adv* **badly**, terribly, appallingly, fearfully, dreadfully, awfully, frightfully [➡ BAD AND BADLY; 223] *Opposite*: wonderfully **2** *adv* **brutally**, viciously, wickedly, evilly, cruelly, horribly, horrifically, horrendously, hideously, unspeakably [➡ DISGUSTING AND REPULSIVE; 230]

atrociousness *n* **fearfulness**, dreadfulness, viciousness, wickedness, frightfulness, hideousness [➡ DISGUSTING AND REPULSIVE; 230]

atrocity 1 *n* **act of violence**, massacre, killing, outrage, brutality, barbarism, evil, murder, crime [➡ MALICIOUS ACTIONS OR BEHAVIOR; 296] **2** *n* **violence**, cruelty, viciousness, barbarity [➡ MALICIOUS ACTIONS OR BEHAVIOR; 296]

atrophy *v* **waste away**, waste, wither, weaken, shrivel, degenerate, deteriorate [➡ GET WORSE; 381]

at sea *adj* **lost**, bewildered, confused, puzzled, baffled, mystified, bemused, disoriented, not following [➡ CONFUSION, ANXIETY, AND WORRY; 540]

at somebody's expense *adv* [➡ JOKES AND TEASING; 674]

at speed *adv* **hurriedly**, hastily, in a hurry, rapidly, swiftly, speedily, quickly, in a rush [➡ HAPPENING QUICKLY; 104] *Opposite*: slowly

at stake *adj* **in the balance**, at risk, in danger, in jeopardy, at issue, to be won or lost, riding on it, up for grabs (*informal*) [➡ IN DANGER; 237]

attach 1 *v* **fasten**, join, connect, fix, put together, add, affix, append, stick, glue, screw, nail, clip [➡ FASTEN, LINK, AND JOIN; 408] *Opposite*: detach 2 *v* **assign**, award, attribute, accord, ascribe (*formal*), confer (*formal*), bestow (*formal*) [➡ GIVE AND PROVIDE; 430]

attaché *n* **diplomat**, public servant, civil servant, representative, envoy, ambassador, cultural attaché, military attaché [➡ POLITICAL OFFICES AND POLITICIANS; 808]

attaché case *type of* **baggage** [➡ CONTAINERS, RECEPTACLES, AND PACKAGING; 1245]

attached 1 *adj* **enclosed**, accompanying, supporting, supplementary [➡ PRESENT AND AVAILABLE; 11] 2 *adj* (*informal*) **emotionally involved**, devoted, fond of, close, friendly, involved, committed [➡ RELATIONSHIP TO ANOTHER; 973] *Opposite*: uninvolved

attachment 1 *n* **bond**, affection, connection, regard, friendship, liking, fondness, tenderness, warmth, love [➡ LOVE, RESPECT, AND GOODWILL; 549] 2 *n* **add-on**, accessory, extra, addition, supplement [➡ PARTS OF MACHINES AND TOOLS; 1118]

attack 1 *v* **harm**, assault, harass, bother, molest, assail, hit, strike, beat, hurt, damage [➡ PHYSICAL ATTACK AND PUNISHMENT; 415] *Opposite*: defend 2 *v* **criticize**, argue, confront, pounce on, disagree, lay into, take on, start in, start on (*informal*) [➡ ACCUSE, BLAME, AND CRITICIZE; 641] *Opposite*: support 3 *v* **infect**, occur, strike, hit, strike down, affect [➡ HAPPEN TO SOMEBODY; 30] 4 *v* **begin**, set to, deal with, tackle, pile in, turn to, start on (*informal*) [➡ START AN ACTION; 260] 5 *n* **violence**, assault, confrontation, act of violence, incident, strike, hit, raid, commencement of hostilities [➡ MALICIOUS ACTIONS OR BEHAVIOR; 296] *Opposite*: defense 6 *n* **bout**, dose, spell, occurrence, outbreak, spasm [➡ SUDDEN EVENTS; 52] 7 *n* **criticism**, condemnation, argument, disagreement [➡ CRITICISMS AND ANGRY OUTBURSTS; 50] *Opposite*: praise

attacker *n* **assailant**, aggressor, invader, enemy, foe (*formal*) [➡ UNCOOPERATIVE OR REBELLIOUS PEOPLE; 566] *Opposite*: defender

attack somebody's dignity *v* **insult**, call names, abuse, give offense, offend, hurl insults, taunt [➡ INSULTS, ABUSE, AND SWEARING; 658]

attain *v* **reach**, achieve, accomplish, conquer, manage, make, arrive at, realize [➡ SUCCEED AND WIN; 79] *Opposite*: fall short

See Compare and Contrast at **accomplish**.

attainable *adj* **within reach**, possible, achievable, realistic, reasonable, manageable [➡ POSSIBLE AND PROBABLE; 177] *Opposite*: unattainable

attainment 1 *n* **achievement**, accomplishment, realization, fulfillment, completion, execution [➡ SUCCESS; 82] *Opposite*: failure 2 *n* **skill**, ability, talent, achievement, accomplishment, success [➡ SKILLS, TALENTS, AND ABILITIES; 526]

attar *n* **essence**, extract, essential oil, distillate, perfume, scented oil [➡ PERSONAL HYGIENE; 491]

attempt 1 *v* **make an effort**, try, bid, make an attempt, have a shot, struggle, have a go (*informal*), take a stab (*informal*), have a crack (*informal*), endeavor (*formal*) [➡ ATTEMPT AN ACTION; 261] 2 *n* **effort**, try, go, shot, bid, endeavor, stab (*informal*), crack (*informal*) [➡ ATTEMPT AN ACTION; 261]

See Compare and Contrast at **try**.

attend 1 *v* **be present**, go to, be there, grace with your presence, join, appear, show up (*informal*) [➡ ARRIVE; 12] *Opposite*: miss 2 *v* **listen**, concentrate, focus, keep your mind on, pay attention, think about, apply your mind [➡ PAY ATTENTION; 765] *Opposite*: ignore

attendance 1 *n* **presence**, attending, appearance, being present [➡ PRESENT AND AVAILABLE; 11] 2 *n* **turnout**, audience, number present, gate, crowd [➡ AUDIENCES AND ATTENDEES; 937]

attendant 1 *adj* **associated**, linked, related, connected, consequent, resultant [➡ RELATED; 142] 2 *n* **assistant**, helper, aide, guide, employee, staff member [➡ SUBORDINATES AND ASSISTANTS; 966] 3 *n* **escort**, usher, bridesmaid, groomsman, pageboy, ring bearer, flower girl, best man, maid of honor, matron of honor [➡ SUBORDINATES AND ASSISTANTS; 966]

attend to *v* **deal with**, see to, tackle, turn your attention to, address, take care of, look after, pay attention to [➡ CARRY OUT AN ACTION; 269] *Opposite*: ignore

attention 1 *n* **notice**, concentration, thought, awareness, consideration, mind, interest [➡ ATTENTION AND ATTENTIVENESS; 763] *Opposite*: inattention 2 *n* **care**, courtesy, consideration, kindness, devotion, helpfulness, thoughtfulness, responsiveness, attentiveness [➡ KIND ACTIONS OR BEHAVIOR; 295] *Opposite*: neglect

attention-grabbing *adj* **eye-catching**, conspicuous, arresting, noticeable, striking, flamboyant [➡ PERCEPTIBLE; 25] *Opposite*: understated

attention seeker *n* [➡ SELF-IMPORTANT AND SELF-SEEKING PEOPLE; 949]

attention to detail *n* **meticulousness**, thoroughness, care, carefulness, exactness, assiduousness [➡ EXACT; 203]

attentive 1 *adj* **considerate**, responsive, helpful, caring, thoughtful, dutiful, conscientious, kind, courteous, assiduous [➡ GENEROSITY AND KINDNESS; 495] *Opposite*: inconsiderate 2 *adj* **paying attention**, listening carefully, concentrating, observant, focused, attending, alert, intent, rapt, all ears (*informal*) [➡ PENSIVENESS AND INTEREST; 538] *Opposite*: inattentive

attentiveness 1 *n* **care**, courtesy, thoughtfulness, consideration, kindness, devotion, helpfulness, responsiveness, attention [➡ GOOD MANNERS AND SOCIAL SKILLS; 520] *Opposite*: neglect 2 *n* **concentration**, attention, focus, alertness [➡ ATTENTION AND ATTENTIVENESS; 763] *Opposite*: inattention

attenuate *v* **reduce**, decrease, lessen, diminish, dilute, water down, take the edge off, temper, offset, mitigate, assuage, soothe, calm, lighten, thin, rarefy, weaken [➡CHANGE OF INTENSITY: LESS; 395] *Opposite*: intensify

attenuation *n* **reduction**, decrease, lessening, diminution, dilution, watering down, taking the edge off, tempering, offsetting, mitigation, lightening, thinning, rarefication, assuagement, weakening [➡CHANGE OF INTENSITY: LESS; 395] *Opposite*: intensification

attest *v* **show**, bear out, prove, confirm, corroborate, substantiate, verify [➡APPROVE AND CONFIRM; 646] *Opposite*: refute

attestation *n* **confirmation**, corroboration, substantiation, verification, testimony, proof [➡APOLOGIZE AND RETRACT; 683] *Opposite*: refutation

at that moment *adv* **just then**, then, at that point, at that time, at that point in time, at that juncture, at that moment in time [➡CONCURRENT AND CONTEMPORANEOUS; 164]

at the appointed time *adv* **promptly**, punctually, on time, at the right time, on the dot, at the appointed hour [➡PROMPTNESS: ON TIME; 99] *Opposite*: late

at the end of the day *adv* **when all's said and done**, basically, ultimately, in the end, all things considered, on balance, finally [➡SUMMARIZING EXPRESSIONS; 622]

at the heart of *adv* **central to**, integral to, fundamental to, at the core of, at the center of [➡FUNDAMENTAL; 195]

at the moment *adv* **now**, currently, at present, at the present time, at this point in time, at this moment in time, right now, just now, presently, today, nowadays [➡PRESENT; 85]

at the outset *adv* **at first**, initially, originally, in the beginning, to begin with, at the start [➡BEFORE, FIRST, AND PRECEDING; 163]

at the present time *adv* **now**, at present, at the moment, nowadays, currently, for the moment, just now, right now, at this moment in time [➡PRESENT; 85]

at the ready *adj* **prepared**, in readiness, ready, set, geared up, about to, to hand, at hand, open, out, up [➡PRESENT AND AVAILABLE; 11] *Opposite*: unprepared

at the rear *adv* **behind**, at the back, in back, to the rear, following, coming behind, coming after [➡RELATIVE LOCATION; 161] *Opposite*: in front

at the same time *adv* **together**, all at once, simultaneously, all together, in unison, in chorus, at one fell swoop, at one go (*UK*) [➡CONCURRENT AND CONTEMPORANEOUS; 164]

at the side of *prep* **beside**, next to, alongside, with, adjacent to, next door to, by [➡CLOSENESS; 159]

at the start *adv* **in the beginning**, at first, initially, originally, at the outset, to begin with, to start with [➡BEFORE, FIRST, AND PRECEDING; 163]

at this moment *adv* **now**, at present, at the moment, at this point in time, at this time, at the present time, currently, just now, right now [➡PRESENT; 85]

at this point *adv* [➡PRESENT; 85]

at this point in time *adv* [➡PRESENT; 85]

at this time *adv* **at the moment**, at present, now, at this moment in time, at this point in time, at the present time, currently, just now, right now [➡PRESENT; 85]

attic **1** *n* **loft**, garret, roof space, upper floor [➡TYPES OF ROOMS; 1097] **2** *type of* **storage space** [➡STORES AND STORAGE BUILDINGS; 1088]

at times *adv* **sometimes**, from time to time, on occasion, once in a while, now and then, now and again, every so often, every now and then, periodically, every now and again, occasionally [➡NEVER AND INFREQUENCY; 97] *Opposite*: rarely

attire (*formal*) *n* **clothing**, dress, clothes, outfit, garments, apparel, wear, garb, costume, wardrobe [➡CLOTHES AND ACCESSORIES; 864]

attired (*formal*) *adj* [➡DRESS, WEAR, AND UNDRESS; 868]

attitude **1** *n* **view**, opinion, viewpoint, point of view, feeling, thought, mind [➡POINTS OF VIEW; 767] **2** *n* **posture**, pose, position, bearing, stance, carriage (*formal*) [➡TEMPERAMENT AND BEHAVIOR; 492] **3** *n* (*informal*) **boldness**, brashness, arrogance, insolence, defiance, assertiveness [➡BAD MANNERS AND SOCIAL SKILLS; 521]

attorney *n* **lawyer**, advocate, counsel, legal representative, attorney at law, prosecutor, public defender, district attorney, criminal lawyer, counselor, barrister (*UK*), solicitor (*UK*) [➡PEOPLE IN LAW COURTS; 820]

attorney at law *n* [➡PEOPLE IN LAW COURTS; 820]

attract **1** *v* **draw**, bring together, pull, exert a pull on [➡GET; 420] *Opposite*: repel **2** *v* **entice**, appeal, fascinate, charm, interest, draw, invite [➡APPEAL TO AND AROUSE INTEREST; 575] *Opposite*: put off

attraction *n* **magnetism**, lure, desirability, hold, charm, fascination, allure, temptation, draw, attractiveness, pull (*informal*) [➡BEAUTY AND ATTRACTIVENESS; 189] *Opposite*: repulsion

attractive **1** *adj* **appealing**, alluring, charming, pleasing, inviting, eye-catching, lovely [➡BEAUTY AND ATTRACTIVENESS; 189] *Opposite*: unattractive **2** *adj* **good-looking**, beautiful, handsome, lovely, pretty, nice-looking, stunning [➡PEOPLE'S PHYSICAL APPEARANCE; 475] *Opposite*: ugly

See Compare and Contrast at **good-looking**.

attractively *adv* **nicely**, delightfully, charmingly, appealingly, prettily, beautifully, pleasantly [➡BEAUTY AND ATTRACTIVENESS; 189] *Opposite*: unattractively

attractiveness **1** *n* **good looks**, pleasant appearance, beauty, prettiness, charm [➡PEOPLE'S PHYSICAL APPEARANCE; 475] *Opposite*: ugliness **2** *n* **magnetism**, charisma, draw, appeal, lure, allure, charm, attraction, desirability, fascination, pull (*informal*) [➡BEAUTY AND ATTRACTIVENESS; 189] *Opposite*: repulsiveness

attribute *n* **quality**, characteristic, trait, property, feature, point, aspect, element [➡QUALITIES AND CHARACTERISTICS; 1191]

attribution *n* **credit**, acknowledgment, designation, ascription (*formal*) [➡CONNECTIONS; 143]

attributive 1 *adj* **prenominal**, preceding, modifying, qualifying [➡ ASPECTS OF LANGUAGE; 682] **2** *type of* **grammatical term** [➡ ASPECTS OF LANGUAGE; 682]

attrition 1 *n* **abrasion**, erosion, slow destruction [➡ EROSION AND WEATHERING; 1055] **2** *n* [➡ WORK-RELATED ACTIVITIES; 834]

attune *v* **adjust**, accustom, adapt, accommodate, acclimate, acclimatize, become used to, grow accustomed to [➡ CHANGE OF MOOD AND COMPOSURE; 580]

at variance *adj* **in conflict**, at odds, in disagreement, conflicting, contradictory, incompatible, inconsistent, out of sync (*informal*) [➡ DISHARMONY; 156] *Opposite:* consistent

at your leisure *adv* **at your convenience**, in your own time, at your own pace, when you feel like it, when it suits you [➡ HAPPENING SLOWLY; 106] *Opposite:* immediately

at your own pace *adv* **at your own speed**, at your convenience, at your leisure, unhurriedly, taking your time [➡ HAPPENING SLOWLY; 106] *Opposite:* immediately

atypical *adj* **different**, unusual, uncommon, strange, odd, abnormal, weird, peculiar [➡ BIZARRE AND PECULIAR; 257] *Opposite:* typical

aubergine *type of* **purple** [➡ COLORS; 1224]

auburn *type of* **brown** [➡ COLORS; 1224]

au courant *adj* [➡ KNOWLEDGE AND WISDOM; 558]

auction *n* **sale**, mart, Dutch auction, silent auction [➡ SALES AND SHOWS; 443]

audacious 1 *adj* **daring**, bold, brave, fearless, courageous, risky, foolhardy [➡ COURAGE; 498] *Opposite:* pusillanimous **2** *adj* **impudent**, bold, disrespectful, overconfident, cheeky (*informal*) [➡ RUDE AND HOSTILE; 625] *Opposite:* courteous

audaciousness *n* **daring**, boldness, courage, bravery, fearlessness, nerve, pluck, mettle, courageousness, guts (*slang*) [➡ COURAGE; 498] *Opposite:* pusillanimity

audacity 1 *n* **boldness**, daring, courage, bravery, fearlessness, courageousness, nerve, pluck, mettle, guts (*slang*) [➡ COURAGE; 498] *Opposite:* pusillanimity **2** *n* **impudence**, disrespect, boldness, rudeness, discourtesy, cheek (*informal*) [➡ BAD MANNERS AND SOCIAL SKILLS; 521] *Opposite:* courtesy

audibility *n* **loudness**, noise, distinctness, discernibility, perceptibility, decibel level, acoustics, clarity [➡ PERCEPTIBLE; 25] *Opposite:* inaudibility

audible *adj* **perceptible**, clear, distinct, noticeable, loud [➡ PERCEPTIBLE; 25] *Opposite:* inaudible

audience 1 *n* **spectators**, viewers, addressees, listeners, onlookers, watchers, hearers [➡ AUDIENCES AND ATTENDEES; 937] **2** *n* **meeting**, interview, consultation, appointment, hearing [➡ MEETINGS AND ASSEMBLIES; 43]

audio *adj* **acoustic**, auditory, aural, audial [➡ HEAR; 707]

audio equipment *n* [➡ RECORDINGS AND PLAYERS; 911]

---

audio equipment

◆ *types of audio equipment*
amp, amplifier, boom box, cassette recorder, CD player, compact disc player, gramophone (*dated*), hi-fi (*dated*), horn, jukebox, megaphone, PA, personal stereo, phonograph, preamplifier, radio, radio set, record player, sound system, stereo, stereo system, tape deck, tape player, tape recorder, transistor, tuner, wireless (*dated*)

◆ *parts of audio equipment*
audiotape, cartridge, cassette, CD, compact disc, DVD, earphone, earpiece, handset, headphones, headpiece, headset, loudspeaker, microphone, record, speaker, stylus, tone arm, turntable

audiotape *part of* **audio equipment** [➡ AUDIO EQUIPMENT; 1139]

audiovisual *adj* **video**, filmed, film, cinematic, movie, cinematographic [➡ THE PERFORMING ARTS; 904]

audit 1 *n* **review**, check, inspection, examination, assessment, appraisal, stocktaking, inventory [➡ EXAMINE AND ASSESS; 753] **2** *v* **review**, inspect, examine, assess, appraise, take stock [➡ EXAMINE AND ASSESS; 753]

audition 1 *n* **test**, tryout, trial, interview [➡ PREPARATORY EVENTS; 57] **2** *v* **try out**, test, hear, interview [➡ EXAMINE AND ASSESS; 753]

auditor 1 *n* **examiner**, accountant, assessor, checker [➡ PEOPLE INVOLVED IN FINANCE; 804] **2** *n* (*formal*) **listener**, hearer, eavesdropper [➡ LISTEN AND LISTENERS; 708]

auditorium *n* **hall**, lecture hall, theater, amphitheater [➡ BUILDINGS FOR PUBLIC ENTERTAINMENT; 1084]

auditory *adj* **aural**, hearing, audio, acoustic [➡ HEAR; 707]

au fait *adj* [➡ KNOWLEDGE AND WISDOM; 558]

auf Wiedersehen *interj* [➡ GREETINGS, FAREWELLS, AND SALUTATIONS; 659]

augment (*formal*) *v* **increase**, enlarge, expand, extend, amplify, strengthen, boost, intensify [➡ CHANGE OF INTENSITY: MORE; 394] *Opposite:* diminish

See Compare and Contrast at **increase**.

augmentation *n* **increase**, growth, rise, expansion, intensification, amplification, escalation, enlargement [➡ CHANGE OF INTENSITY: MORE; 394] *Opposite:* decrease

au gratin *type of* **food presentation** [➡ COOKING AND FOOD PREPARATION; 353]

augur *v* **foretell**, predict, portend, promise, prophesy, prognosticate, indicate, point to [➡ MEAN SOMETHING; 61]

augury 1 *n* **divination**, prediction, prophecy, forecasting, prognostication [➡ THE SUPERNATURAL; 787] **2** *n* **portent**, omen, auspice, indication, prediction, sign, prophecy, forewarning, forecast [➡ INDICATIONS, SIGNS, AND WARNINGS; 68]

august (*formal*) *adj* **imposing**, impressive, grand, majestic, dignified, stately, noble, eminent [➡ CLASS STATUS; 889] *Opposite:* humble

auk *type of* **sea bird** [➡ SEA BIRDS; 1002]

aunt *type of* **older relative** [➡ OLDER GENERATION RELATIVES; 959]

aura *n* **air**, atmosphere, force, appearance, quality, glow [➡ APPEARANCE AND ATMOSPHERE; 1237]

aural *adj* **auditory**, hearing, acoustic, audio [➡ HEAR; 707]

au revoir *interj* [➡ GREETINGS, FAREWELLS, AND SALUTATIONS; 659]

auricle *part of* **ear** [➡ THE EAR; 706]

Auriga *type of* **constellation** [➡ HEAVENLY BODIES; 1061]

auspice *n* **omen**, portent, augury, sign, indication, token, prediction [➡ INDICATIONS, SIGNS, AND WARNINGS; 681]

auspices *n* **sponsorship**, patronage, backing, support, help, umbrella [➡ RESPONSIBILITY; 170]

auspicious *adj* **favorable**, fortunate, promising, propitious, lucky, opportune, providential [➡ SUCCESSFUL AND PROMISING; 81] *Opposite*: inauspicious

austere 1 *adj* **serious**, grim, severe, unsmiling, harsh, ascetic, rigid, somber [➡ RUDE AND HOSTILE; 625] *Opposite*: gentle 2 *adj* **stark**, severe, simple, basic, sparse, Spartan, harsh [➡ PLAIN; 232] *Opposite*: comfortable 3 *adj* **plain**, bare, simple, clean, undecorated, unembellished, unadorned [➡ EASE AND SIMPLICITY; 200] *Opposite*: ornate

austerity 1 *n* **severity**, strictness, sternness, gravity, soberness, somberness, asceticism, seriousness, rigor [➡ UNFRIENDLINESS AND UNSOCIABILITY; 504] *Opposite*: levity 2 *n* **self-denial**, shortage, scarcity, economy [➡ TOO FEW, TOO LITTLE; 122] *Opposite*: plenty 3 *n* **plainness**, starkness, bareness, simplicity, cleanness [➡ PLAIN; 232] *Opposite*: opulence 4 *type of* **economic condition** [➡ FINANCE AND ECONOMICS; 796]

Australian Rules *type of* **ball game** [➡ HOBBIES, GAMES, AND SPORTS; 875]

autarchy *n* **autocracy**, absolute power, absolutism, despotism, tyranny, dictatorship [➡ STYLES AND SYSTEMS OF GOVERNMENT; 806] *Opposite*: democracy

authentic 1 *adj* **genuine**, original, authenticated, valid [➡ TRUE AND REAL; 171] *Opposite*: fake 2 *adj* **true**, reliable, dependable, trustworthy, faithful, accurate, genuine [➡ TRUE AND REAL; 171] *Opposite*: false

authenticate *v* **validate**, confirm, verify, substantiate, endorse, check [➡ APPROVE AND CONFIRM; 646]

authentication *n* **verification**, confirmation, substantiation, validation, certification, endorsement [➡ CERTAIN; 174]

authenticity *n* **genuineness**, legitimacy, validity, reality, truth, truthfulness [➡ TRUE AND REAL; 171]

author 1 *n* **writer**, novelist, playwright, dramatist, poet, journalist, essayist, biographer [➡ WRITERS AND STYLES; 914] 2 *n* **creator**, originator, inventor, source [➡ DESIGNERS, CREATORS, AND INSTIGATORS; 347]

authoritarian *adj* **strict**, demanding, totalitarian, despotic, absolute, dictatorial, tyrannical, autocratic [➡ BOSSY AND OVERBEARING; 516] *Opposite*: liberal

authoritarianism *n* **totalitarianism**, dictatorship, oppression, absolutism, tyranny, despotism, autocracy [➡ STYLES AND SYSTEMS OF GOVERNMENT; 806] *Opposite*: democracy

authoritative 1 *adj* **reliable**, trustworthy, dependable, respected, convincing, solid [➡ HONEST AND RELIABLE; 502] *Opposite*: unreliable 2 *adj* **commanding**, imposing, firm, confident, convincing, respected, influential [➡ STRENGTH; 201] *Opposite*: weak

authoritatively *adv* **with authority**, confidently, firmly, commandingly, convincingly [➡ STRENGTH; 201]

authoritativeness 1 *n* **reliability**, trustworthiness, dependability, validity, credibility, solidity [➡ STRENGTH; 201] *Opposite*: unreliability 2 *n* **authority**, command, standing, position, weight, influence, clout (*informal*) [➡ CONFIDENCE AND COMPOSURE; 499]

authority 1 *n* **power**, right, ability, influence, weight, clout (*informal*), say-so (*informal*) [➡ STRENGTH; 201] 2 *n* **citation**, source, evidence [➡ EVIDENCE AND PROOF; 69] 3 *n* **agency**, group, government department, board, corporation [➡ INSTITUTIONS; 790] 4 *n* **confidence**, conviction, knowledge, experience [➡ CERTAINTY; 561] 5 *n* **expert**, specialist, consultant, buff, expert witness [➡ TALENTED OR INTELLIGENT PEOPLE; 528]

authority figure *n* **mentor**, person of influence, leader, role model, example, guide, influence, idol, parent, boss [➡ IMPORTANT OR FAMOUS PEOPLE; 893]

authorization *n* **approval**, consent, endorsement, sanction, agreement, permission, leave (*formal*) [➡ PERMIT AND ALLOW; 669]

authorize *v* **approve**, allow, sanction, permit, give permission, consent, empower, okay (*informal*) [➡ PERMIT AND ALLOW; 669] *Opposite*: forbid

authorized *adj* **official**, lawful, legal, sanctioned, approved, ratified, accredited, certified [➡ LEGAL AND LEGITIMATE; 815] *Opposite*: unauthorized

authorship 1 *n* **writing**, composition, invention, production, output, generation [➡ CREATION; 346] 2 *n* **origin**, source, provenance, derivation, genesis, background [➡ BEGINNINGS; 53]

auto (*informal*) *n* [➡ BIKES, CARS, AND CARRIAGES; 1149]

autobiographer *n* [➡ WRITERS AND STYLES; 914]

autobiographical *adj* **nonfictional**, factual, first-person, real-life, true to life, narrative, historical, documentary [➡ TRUE AND REAL; 171] *Opposite*: biographical

autobiography *n* **memoirs**, life story, life history [➡ FICTION AND DRAMA; 913]

autochthonous *adj* [➡ COUNTRIES AND REGIONS; 1067]

See Compare and Contrast at **native**.

autocracy *n* **dictatorship**, monocracy, despotism, tyranny, absolutism, authoritarianism, totalitarianism [➡ STYLES AND SYSTEMS OF GOVERNMENT; 806] *Opposite*: democracy

autocrat *n* **dictator**, absolute ruler, tyrant, despot [➡ VILLAINS AND THUGS; 947]

autocratic 1 *adj* **despotic**, tyrannical, repressive, oppressive, monocratic [➡ STYLES AND SYSTEMS OF GOVERNMENT; 806] *Opposite*: democratic 2 *adj* **dictatorial**, domineering, bossy, overbearing, imperious, tyrannical [➞ BOSSY AND OVER-BEARING; 516]

autofocus *part of* **camera** [➞ PHOTOGRAPHY AND PHOTOGRAPHIC EQUIP-MENT; 1122]

autogamy *n* [➞ REPRODUCTION AND HEREDITY; 725]

autogiro *type of* **civil aircraft** [➞ AIRCRAFT; 1148]

autograph *n* **signature**, name, inscription, dedication [➞ NAME AND DESCRIBE; 665]

automated *adj* **automatic**, mechanical, programmed, preset, mechanized [➞ MACHINERY; 1114] *Opposite:* manual

automatic 1 *adj* **mechanized**, automated, mechanical, programmed, preset [➞ MACHINERY; 1114] *Opposite:* manual 2 *adj* **involuntary**, reflex, unconscious, instinctive, pro-grammed, unthinking, mindless, spontaneous, impulsive [➞ AUTOMATIC AND INSTINCTIVE; 280] *Opposite:* voluntary 3 *adj* **routine**, habitual, mechanical, regular, repeated, inevitable, usual, robotic, robot-like [➞ AUTOMATIC AND INSTINCTIVE; 280] *Oppo-site:* spontaneous 4 *type of* **gun** [➞ WEAPONS FOR SHOOTING; 1156]

automation *n* **mechanization**, computerization, robotics [➞ MACHINERY; 1114]

automaton *n* **robot**, android, mechanism, machine [➞ MACHINES AND MACHINE PARTS; 1116]

automobile *n* [➞ BIKES, CARS, AND CARRIAGES; 1149]

autonomous *adj* **self-governing**, sovereign, free, inde-pendent, separate [➞ STYLES AND SYSTEMS OF GOVERNMENT; 806] *Oppo-site:* dependent

autonomy *n* **independence**, self-government, self-rule, sovereignty [➞ STYLES AND SYSTEMS OF GOVERNMENT; 806] *Opposite:* dependence

autopilot *part of* **aircraft** [➞ AIRCRAFT; 1148]

autopsy *n* **postmortem**, dissection, analysis, debriefing, examination [➞ BURIAL AND PREPARATION FOR BURIAL; 929]

autosuggestion *n* **self-suggestion**, self-hypnosis, autohypnosis, power of suggestion, self-deception, self-delusion [➞ PSYCHOLOGY AND THE MIND; 769]

autumn 1 *n* (*UK*) **fall**, Indian summer, season, equinox, harvest time (*UK*) [➞ TIMES OF YEAR; 88] 2 *n* **end**, conclusion, close, culmination, decline [➞ ENDS AND DEPARTURES; 54] *Opposite:* beginning

autumnal *adj* **seasonal**, equinoctial [➞ TIMES OF YEAR; 88] *Oppo-site:* spring

auxiliary *adj* **supplementary**, secondary, support, sup-porting, assisting, ancillary, backup [➞ MORE AND EXCESS; 124] *Opposite:* main

avail *n* **benefit**, advantage, reward, gain, purpose, aim, profit [➞ RESULTS AND OUTCOMES; 83]

availability *n* **obtainability**, handiness, convenience, readiness, accessibility, disposal [➞ PRESENT AND AVAILABLE; 11] *Opposite:* unavailability

available *adj* **obtainable**, accessible, on hand, to be had, existing, offered, vacant [➞ PRESENT AND AVAILABLE; 11] *Opposite:* unavailable

avail yourself *v* **make use of**, use, benefit from, take, help yourself to [➞ MAKE GOOD USE OF SOMETHING; 473]

avalanche 1 *n* **snow slip**, fall, slide [➞ EROSION AND WEATHERING; 1055] 2 *n* **quantity**, increase, mass, flood, shower, storm, inundation (*formal*) [➞ MANY; MUCH, LARGE AMOUNT; 117]

avant-garde *adj* **new**, modern, experimental, uncon-ventional, innovative, advanced [➞ NEW, MODERN; 166] *Opposite:* traditional

avarice *n* **greed**, greediness, materialism, covetousness, acquisitiveness, avariciousness, desire, avidity, cupidity (*formal*) [➞ MORALLY BAD OR IMPROPER; 775] *Opposite:* generosity

avaricious *adj* **greedy**, rapacious, grasping, acquisitive, covetous, materialistic [➞ MORALLY BAD OR IMPROPER; 775] *Opposite:* generous

avariciousness *n* **greed**, greediness, materialism, cov-etousness, acquisitiveness, avarice, rapaciousness, desire [➞ MORALLY BAD OR IMPROPER; 775] *Opposite:* generosity

avenge *v* **retaliate**, punish, even the score, take ven-geance, get even, hit back, get back at, redress, revenge [➞ VENGEANCE AND REVENGE; 685]

avenger *n* **punisher**, retaliator, nemesis (*literary*) [➞ ENEMIES AND TORMENTORS; 969]

avenue 1 *n* **opportunity**, possibility, way, chance, opening [➞ WAYS OF DOING THINGS; 294] 2 *type of* **highway** [➞ ROADS; 1106]

aver (*formal*) *v* **affirm**, state, claim, declare, assert, main-tain, profess, swear, avow (*formal*) [➞ CLAIM, INSIST, AND EMPHASIZE; 614] *Opposite:* refute

average 1 *n* **mean**, arithmetic mean, mode, median, norm [➞ MATH; 597] 2 *adj* **regular**, normal, usual, typical, middling, mediocre, run-of-the-mill, common, ordinary [➞ ORDINARINESS; 244] *Opposite:* extraordinary 3 *v* **be around**, be in the region of, be more or less, be close to [➞ AMOUNT TO AND EQUAL; 70]

average down *v* **round down**, level down, bring down, lower, decrease [➞ CHANGE OF SIZE: SMALLER; 393]

averagely 1 *adv* **on average**, normally, typically, stand-ardly, commonly, usually [➞ USUALLY; 108] *Opposite:* excep-tionally 2 *adv* **passably**, tolerably, adequately, unspectacularly, indifferently, mediocrely, middlingly [➞ ACCEPTABLE AND PASSABLE; 219] *Opposite:* exceptionally

average out *v* **equalize**, level out, balance out, even out [➞ ARRANGE AND CREATE ORDER; 357]

average up *v* **round up**, level up, bring up, raise, increase [➞ CHANGE OF SIZE: BIGGER; 392]

averse (*formal*) *adj* **opposed**, antagonistic, loath, unen-thusiastic, ill-disposed, unfavorable, antipathetic, hostile, disinclined, unwilling, reluctant, hesitant, against, anti (*informal*) [➞ UNWILLINGNESS AND STUBBORNNESS; 564] *Opposite:* favorable

See Compare and Contrast at **unwilling**.

aversion (*formal*) *n* **dislike**, hatred, loathing, repug-nance, distaste, hate, antipathy, abhorrence, detestation, repulsion, disgust [➞ IRRITATION AND ANGER; 541] *Opposite:* liking

See Compare and Contrast at **dislike**.

avert 1 *v* **prevent**, stop, ward off, avoid, forestall, deter, forfend, obviate [➡ AVOID, PREVENT, LIMIT, AND CONTROL; 277] **2** *v* **turn away**, turn from, turn aside, divert, deflect, veer [➡ CHANGE DIRECTION OF MOTION; 344]

aviary *n* **birdcage**, coop, chicken coop, hen house, dovecote, chicken run (*UK*), pigeon loft (*UK*) [➡ ANIMAL OR BIRD ACCOMMODATIONS; 1079]

aviation *n* **flying**, flight, aeronautics, air travel [➡ TRAVEL: JOURNEYS AND TRIPS; 318]

aviator *n* **pilot**, flier, aeronaut, copilot [➡ DRIVERS; 1153]

avid *adj* **keen**, enthusiastic, passionate, eager, devoted, ardent, fervent [➡ DESIRE AND WANT; 579] *Opposite*: indifferent

avidity *n* **greed**, eagerness, voracity, covetousness, greediness, desire [➡ ENVY AND JEALOUSY; 548] *Opposite*: indifference

avidly *adv* **keenly**, enthusiastically, passionately, eagerly, devotedly, ardently, fervently [➡ WITH ENTHUSIASM; 286] *Opposite*: indifferently

avocado 1 *type of* **fruit** [➡ FRUIT AND VEGETABLES; 1176] **2** *type of* **green** [➡ COLORS; 1224]

avocation (*formal*) **1** *n* **occupation**, job, vocation, calling, profession, pursuit, employment, line, career [➡ PROFESSIONS; 845] **2** *n* **hobby**, pastime, diversion, amusement, sport, whimsy, distraction [➡ LEISURE AND RECREATION; 874]

avocet *type of* **sea bird** [➡ SEA BIRDS; 1002]

avoid 1 *v* **keep away**, stay away from, shun, steer clear, let alone, pass up [➡ AVOID OR ESCAPE CONTACT; 418] **2** *v* **evade**, circumvent, get around, get out of, dodge, duck, sidestep, elude, escape, shun, eschew [➡ NOT PAY ATTENTION; 764] *Opposite*: face **3** *v* **prevent**, forestall, avert, preclude (*formal*) [➡ AVOID, PREVENT, LIMIT, AND CONTROL; 277] *Opposite*: promote

avoidable *adj* **preventable**, unnecessary, needless, stoppable [➡ UNIMPORTANT AND UNNECESSARY; 238] *Opposite*: inevitable

avoidance **1** *n* **evasion**, escaping, evading, dodging, circumvention [➡ NOT PAY ATTENTION; 764] **2** *n* **prevention**, anticipation, averting, forestalling, annulment, stopping [➡ AVOID, PREVENT, LIMIT, AND CONTROL; 277] *Opposite*: promotion **3** *n* **abstention**, refraining, refrainment, holding off, eschewal [➡ FORGO AND DENY ONESELF; 449] *Opposite*: indulgence

avow (*formal*) *v* **affirm**, state, declare, acknowledge, admit, maintain, assert, depose, aver (*formal*) [➡ CLAIM, INSIST, AND EMPHASIZE; 614] *Opposite*: deny

avowal (*formal*) *n* **affirmation**, statement, confirmation, declaration, acknowledgment, admission, confession, profession [➡ ADMIT AND CONFESS; 615] *Opposite*: denial

avowed (*formal*) *adj* **affirmed**, stated, confirmed, declared, acknowledged, admitted, self-confessed, asserted [➡ KNOWN AND FAMOUS; 181] *Opposite*: unspoken

avowedly (*formal*) *adv* **admittedly**, by your own admission, openly, self-confessedly, frankly [➡ HONEST AND OPEN; 630]

avuncular *adj* **kindly**, kind, kindhearted, benign,

friendly, genial, good-humored, indulgent, helpful [➡ GOOD-TEMPERED AND HUMOROUS; 627] *Opposite*: unkindly

await 1 *v* **lie in wait for**, wait on, expect, look forward to, look out for, anticipate [➡ PREDICT AND ANTICIPATE; 750] **2** *v* **lie ahead**, be in store, be to come, loom, near, be approaching, draw near [➡ ABOUT TO HAPPEN; 33]

awaited *adj* **anticipated**, expected, presumed, waited for [➡ FUTURE; 86] *Opposite*: unexpected

awake *adj* **wide-awake**, conscious, wakeful, up, up and around, stirring, aware, alert, roused, aroused [➡ WIDE AWAKE AND CONSCIOUS; 735] *Opposite*: asleep

awaken 1 *v* **wake**, wake up, rouse, get up, stir [➡ WAKE AND REGAIN CONSCIOUSNESS; 724] **2** *v* **rouse**, arouse, set off, stir, promote, stimulate, initiate [➡ CAUSE TO START; 265] *Opposite*: suppress

awakening **1** *adj* **developing**, growing, emerging, emergent, new, arising (*archaic or literary*) [➡ ABOUT TO HAPPEN; 33] **2** *n* **arousal**, wakening, emergence, stirring [➡ BEGINNINGS; 53] **3** *n* **awareness**, attention, recognition, realization, revival [➡ KNOWLEDGE AND WISDOM; 558]

award **1** *n* **prize**, honor, reward, gift, grant, decoration, medal, accolade [➡ REWARDS AND AWARDS; 439] **2** *n* **verdict**, decision, determination, judgment, settlement [➡ TRIAL, PUNISHMENT, AND LEGAL OUTCOMES; 819] **3** *v* **give**, present, grant, endow, bestow (*formal*), confer (*formal*) [➡ REWARD; 436]

aware **1** *adj* **conscious**, alert, mindful, attentive, awake, responsive, sensible (*formal*), cognizant (*formal*) [➡ WIDE AWAKE AND CONSCIOUS; 735] *Opposite*: unaware **2** *adj* **knowledgeable**, interested, concerned, informed, experienced, discerning, perceptive [➡ KNOWLEDGE AND WISDOM; 558] *Opposite*: ignorant

Compare and Contrast: *aware, conscious, mindful, cognizant, sensible*

CORE MEANING: having knowledge of the existence of something

aware knowing something either intellectually or intuitively; *conscious* keenly aware of something and regarding it as important; *mindful* actively attentive, or deliberately keeping something in mind; *cognizant* (*formal*) having special knowledge about something; *sensible* (*formal*) keenly aware of something.

awareness **1** *n* **consciousness**, mindfulness, alertness, responsiveness, attentiveness, sentience, cognizance (*formal*) [➡ WIDE AWAKE AND CONSCIOUS; 735] *Opposite*: ignorance **2** *n* **knowledge**, understanding, grasp, appreciation, familiarity, recognition, perception, discernment [➡ KNOWLEDGE AND WISDOM; 558] *Opposite*: ignorance

awash **1** *adj* **soaked**, flooded, drenched, waterlogged, saturated, sopping, brimming [➡ WET; 1240] *Opposite*: dry **2** *adj* **oversupplied**, full of, overflowing, packed, crammed, inundated, overprovided, overstocked [➡ FULL; 1239] *Opposite*: lacking

away *adj* **absent**, gone, left, missing, not here [➡ ABSENT AND UNAVAILABLE; 7] *Opposite*: present

away day (*UK*) *n* [➡ TRAVEL: JOURNEYS AND TRIPS; 318]

awe **1** *n* **wonder**, admiration, respect, amazement, surprise, wonderment, astonishment, reverence, esteem, veneration, worship [➡ SURPRISE, SHOCK, AND AMAZEMENT; 545] **2** *n* **fear**, terror, dread, fright, trepidation, fearfulness [➡ FEAR AND PANIC; 543]

awe-inspiring *adj* **overwhelming**, grand, breathtaking, splendid, tremendous, remarkable, amazing, awesome, fearsome, astounding, humbling, impressive [➡ EXTRAORDINARY: AMAZING; 204]

awesome *adj* **overwhelming**, grand, breathtaking, splendid, tremendous, remarkable, amazing, awe-inspiring, fearsome, astounding, humbling [➡ EXTRAORDINARY: AMAZING; 204]

awesomely *adv* **impressively**, awe-inspiringly, overwhelmingly, fearsomely, formidably, strikingly, amazingly, astonishingly, tremendously, devastatingly, overpoweringly [➡ EXTRAORDINARY: AMAZING; 204]

awestricken *see* **awestruck**

awestruck *adj* **impressed**, overwhelmed, stunned, enthralled, rapt, captivated, mesmerized, fascinated, spellbound, awestricken [➡ SURPRISE, SHOCK, AND AMAZEMENT; 545] *Opposite*: unimpressed

awful *adj* **dreadful**, terrible, appalling, unpleasant, horrible, poor, horrific, shocking [➡ BAD AND BADLY; 223] *Opposite*: wonderful

awfully **1** *adv* **extremely**, very, really, terrifically, terribly, dreadfully [➡ TO A GREAT EXTENT; 132] **2** *adv* **badly**, unpleasantly, dreadfully, terribly, appallingly, horrifically, horribly, shockingly [➡ BAD AND BADLY; 223] *Opposite*: well

awfulness *n* **dreadfulness**, horror, misery, unpleasantness, terribleness, horridness, direness [➡ FAULTS, FLAWS, AND WEAKNESSES; 251]

awhile (*literary*) *adv* **a little**, for a moment, a moment or two, a short time, for a while, for a time, some time, for a bit, for a little bit [➡ FUTURE; 86]

a whole new ball game (*slang*) *n* **something else entirely**, another thing altogether, quite another matter, a different kettle of fish, a horse of a different color [➡ DIFFERENCE; 149]

awkward **1** *adj* **embarrassing**, tricky, problematic, difficult, thorny, complex [➡ DIFFICULTY AND COMPLEXITY; 242] *Opposite*: straightforward **2** *adj* **unwieldy**, cumbersome, bulky [➡ LARGE; 1193] *Opposite*: compact **3** *adj* **clumsy**, inelegant, graceless, uncoordinated, ungainly, gawky (*informal*) [➡ AGILITY OF THE BODY; 476] *Opposite*: graceful **4** *adj* **uncomfortable**, embarrassed, out of your depth, tongue-tied, self-conscious, gauche, inept, discomforted, ill at ease, uneasy, discomfited (*formal*) [➡ INSECURITY AND LOSS OF COMPOSURE; 544] *Opposite*: comfortable **5** *adj* (*UK*) **uncooperative**, difficult, stubborn, obstinate, obdurate [➡ REBELLIOUSNESS AND DISOBEDIENCE; 565] *Opposite*: cooperative

awkwardly **1** *adv* **clumsily**, inelegantly, gracelessly, cumbersomely, gawkily (*informal*) [➡ AGILITY OF THE BODY; 476] *Opposite*: easily **2** *adv* **uncomfortably**, uneasily, with embarrassment, self-consciously, gauchely, ineptly [➡ INSECURITY AND LOSS OF COMPOSURE; 544] *Opposite*: comfortably

awkwardness **1** *n* **clumsiness**, ineptness, inelegance, gracelessness, ungainliness, gawkiness (*informal*) [➡ AGILITY OF THE BODY; 476] *Opposite*: ease **2** *n* **discomfort**, unease, embarrassment, uneasiness, self-consciousness, gaucheness, discomfiture (*formal*) [➡ INSECURITY AND LOSS OF COMPOSURE; 544] *Opposite*: ease

awl *type of* **carpentry tool** [➡ HAND TOOLS; 1119]

awning *n* **canopy**, sunshade, sun shelter, blind [➡ COVERS AND COATINGS; 1246]

AWOL *adj* **absent without leave**, absent, missing, deserting, wanted, truant, absconding, disappeared, gone [➡ ABSENT AND UNAVAILABLE; 7] *Opposite*: present

awry **1** *adj* **crooked**, askew, skewed, off beam, out of kilter, twisted, out of true, off-center, cockeyed, aslant [➡ ORIENTATION AND ALIGNMENT; 1223] *Opposite*: straight **2** *adj* **amiss**, wrong, muddled, incorrect, astray, inappropriate, not as it should be [➡ INCORRECT AND ERRONEOUS; 222] *Opposite*: all right

ax **1** *type of* **cutting tool** [➡ CUTTING TOOLS; 1120] **2** *v* (*informal*) **dismiss**, lay off, let go, fire (*informal*), sack (*informal*), give the sack (*informal*), can (*slang*), discharge (*formal*) [➡ REVOKE STATUS; 459] *Opposite*: employ **3** *v* **reduce**, cut, cut back, scale down, slim down, downsize, decimate [➡ BUSINESS ACTIVITIES AND PHENOMENA; 794] *Opposite*: increase **4** *v* **sever**, cleave, cut, hack, chop (*informal*) [➡ TEAR, BREAK, AND CUT; 360]

axiom *n* **maxim**, adage, saying, saw, proverb, truism [➡ FIGURES OF SPEECH; 673]

axiomatic *adj* **self-evident**, goes without saying, obvious, manifest, clear, accepted [➡ CERTAIN; 174]

axis *n* **alliance**, partnership, bloc, league, federation, affiliation, alignment [➡ CONNECTIONS; 143]

axle *part of* **external structure** [➡ EXTERNAL PARTS OF A VEHICLE; 1147]

axolotl *type of* **amphibian** [➡ AMPHIBIANS; 1008]

aye *interj* **yes**, indeed, absolutely, yeah (*informal*), right (*informal*), yea (*archaic*) [➡ EXPRESSIONS OF AGREEMENT; 648] *Opposite*: no

aye-aye *type of* **primate** [➡ PRIMATES; 988]

Ayurvedic medicine *type of* **complementary therapy** [➡ REMEDIES, TREATMENTS, AND OPERATIONS; 731]

azalea *type of* **shrub or bush** [➡ BUSHES AND SHRUBS; 1027]

azure *type of* **blue** [➡ COLORS; 1224]

B

B2B *adj* [➡ E-COMMERCE; 1129]

B2C *adj* [➡ E-COMMERCE; 1129]

baa *type of* **animal sound** [➡ SOUNDS MADE BY ANIMALS; 1261]

babble (*UK*) *v* **gabble**, mutter, prattle, chatter, blather (*informal*), gab (*informal*) [➡ CHATTER AND BABBLE; 617]

babe 1 *n* (*slang*) **darling**, sweetheart, love, lover, sugar (*informal*), honey (*informal*), baby (*slang*) [➡ ENDEARMENTS; 656] 2 *n* (*literary or archaic*) **baby**, infant, little one, child, newborn, babe in arms, tot (*informal*), kid (*informal*) [➡ CHILD OR YOUTH; 945]

babe in arms *n* [➡ CHILD OR YOUTH; 945]

baboon *type of* **primate** [➡ PRIMATES; 988]

baby 1 *n* **infant**, child, newborn, babe in arms, tot (*informal*), little one, kid (*informal*), babe (*literary or archaic*) [➡ CHILD OR YOUTH; 945] 2 *n* (*slang*) **darling**, honey (*informal*), sugar (*informal*), sweetheart, love, lover, babe (*slang*) [➡ ENDEARMENTS; 656] 3 *v* **pamper**, coddle, mollycoddle, cosset, overprotect, spoil, indulge, make much of, fuss over [➡ TAKE CARE OF AND SPOIL; 300]

baby-faced *adj* **youthful**, boyish, girlish, childlike, wide-eyed, fresh-faced, cute [➡ FACIAL CHARACTERISTICS; 481] *Opposite*: wizened

baby grand *type of* **keyboard** [➡ MUSICAL INSTRUMENTS; 910]

babyhood *n* **infancy**, childhood, early years, youth [➡ BABYHOOD, CHILDHOOD, AND ADOLESCENCE; 917]

babyish *adj* **childish**, infantile, immature, puerile, adolescent, naive [➡ NEGATIVE INTELLECTUAL CHARACTERISTICS; 525] *Opposite*: mature

baby-sit *v* **look after**, watch, take care of, protect, tend to, mind [➡ TAKE CARE OF AND SPOIL; 300]

baby tooth *type of* **tooth** [➡ THE MOUTH; 702]

babywear *n* [➡ GARMENTS AND OUTFITS; 865]

bachelor *n* **unmarried man**, single man, unattached man, eligible male, confirmed bachelor [➡ MARITAL STATUS; 890]

Bach flower remedy *type of* **complementary therapy** [➡ REMEDIES, TREATMENTS, AND OPERATIONS; 731]

back 1 *n* **backbone**, spine, spinal column, vertebral column, vertebrae [➡ THE BONES AND JOINTS; 719] 2 *part of* **torso** [➡ PARTS OF THE BODY: TORSO; 693] 3 *adv* **behind**, to the rear, toward the back, backward, rearward [➡ DIRECTION OF MOTION; 345] *Opposite*: forward 4 *v* **go backward**, reverse, move backward, recede, back up [➡ GO BACKWARD; 309] *Opposite*: proceed

backache *n* **back pain**, back trouble, bad back, lumbago, sciatica, slipped disk [➡ PAIN AND OTHER PHYSICAL SENSATIONS; 733]

back and forth *adv* **backward and forward**, from side to side, to and fro, hither and thither, up and down [➡ DIRECTION OF MOTION; 345]

back-and-forth *adj* [➡ DIRECTION OF MOTION; 345]

back away *v* **recoil**, shrink, draw back, shy away, back off, withdraw, pull back, move away, retreat, backpedal [➡ GO BACKWARD; 309] *Opposite*: stay

backbiter *n* [➡ GRUMPY AND NEGATIVE PEOPLE; 953]

backbiting *n* **unkind remarks**, infighting, viciousness, spitefulness, backstabbing, badmouthing (*slang*) [➡ INSULTS, ABUSE, AND SWEARING; 658]

backbone 1 *n* **spine**, spinal column, vertebral column, back, vertebrae [➡ THE BONES AND JOINTS; 719] 2 *n* **mainstay**, support, prop, spine, pillar, strength [➡ CENTRAL PARTS OF PHYSICAL OBJECTS; 1251] 3 *n* **moral fiber**, strength of character, stamina, fortitude, courage, grit, determination, resilience, self-discipline, guts (*slang*) [➡ COURAGE; 498]

backbreaking *adj* **strenuous**, arduous, grueling, exhausting, taxing, wearisome, laborious, hard [➡ PHYSICALLY UNPLEASANT; 226] *Opposite*: easy

backcloth *n* **backdrop**, scenery, set, stage set, background, scene, reredos [➡ IN THE THEATER; 906]

backcomb (*UK*) *v* **tease**, brush, comb, style, coif (*formal*) [➡ CHANGE OF SHAPE; 385]

backcombed (*UK*) *adj* [➡ DESCRIBING HAIR; 486]

back country *n* **wilderness**, wilds, backwoods, rough country, sticks (*informal*) [➡ REMOTE PLACES; 1046]

backdate *v* **predate**, date, validate, sign, stamp [➡ NAME AND DESCRIBE; 665]

back down *v* **withdraw**, concede defeat, accept defeat, yield, admit defeat, admit you were wrong, backpedal, take back, back off, eat humble pie, give in, climb down, pull out, back out [➡ APOLOGIZE AND RETRACT; 683] *Opposite*: stand your ground

backdrop 1 *n* **backcloth**, scenery, set, stage set, background, scene [➡ IN THE THEATER; 906] 2 *n* **background**, setting, milieu, environment, framework, locale, conditions, surroundings, circumstances [➡ SITUATIONS; 71]

backer *n* **sponsor**, supporter, patron, promoter, benefactor, financier, champion, angel, guarantor [➡ REPRESENTATIVES AND PATRONS; 968]

backfire *v* **go wrong**, boomerang, miscarry, fail, not go as planned, rebound, flop (*informal*), bomb (*informal*) [➡ FAIL OR BE UNSUCCESSFUL; 75]

background **1** *n* **upbringing**, circumstances, personal history, family, experience, social class, education, training, credentials, qualifications [➡ STATUS; 888] **2** *n* **backdrop**, setting, milieu, environment, surroundings, conditions, locale, set [➡ SITUATIONS; 71]

backhanded *adj* **indirect**, doubtful, oblique, insincere, snide, sneaky [➡ RUDE AND HOSTILE; 625]

backing *n* **support**, help, assistance, sponsorship, patronage, aid, backup, funding, finance, money, grant, subsidy [➡ SOURCE OF HAPPINESS, PLEASURE, OR IMPROVEMENT; 209]

backlash *n* **reaction**, repercussion, counterattack, criticism, hostile response [➡ RESULTS AND OUTCOMES; 83]

backlog *n* **accumulation**, buildup, excess, surfeit, logjam, bottleneck [➡ MORE AND EXCESS; 124]

back off **1** *v* **retreat**, pull back, move away, go backward, recoil, shrink, draw back, shy away, withdraw, back away [➡ GO BACKWARD; 309] *Opposite*: advance **2** *v* **yield**, withdraw, admit you were wrong, backpedal, take back, back down, eat humble pie, give in, climb down [➡ APOLOGIZE AND RETRACT; 683] *Opposite*: insist

back out *v* **pull out**, withdraw, renege, go back on, cancel, change your mind, beg off, drop out, call off, cry off (*informal*), fink out (*slang*) [➡ NOT DO AND REFUSE TO DO; 274] *Opposite*: continue

backpack **1** *n* **rucksack**, knapsack, pack, bag, haversack [➡ CONTAINERS, RECEPTACLES, AND PACKAGING; 1245] **2** *v* [➡ TRAVEL: WAYS OF TRAVELING; 320]

backpacker *n* **traveler**, hiker, walker, hitchhiker, tourist [➡ TRAVEL: TRAVELERS AND WALKERS; 319]

back pain *n* **backache**, lumbago, back trouble, bad back, sciatica, slipped disk [➡ ILLNESSES AND DISORDERS; 732]

backpedal *v* **backtrack**, back down, shift ground, go back on your word, recant, retreat, do an about-face, back off [➡ APOLOGIZE AND RETRACT; 683]

backroom *adj* **unobtrusive**, clandestine, secret, private, secretive, hush-hush (*informal*) [➡ SECRET AND UNKNOWN; 179] *Opposite*: public

back seat *type of* **internal feature** [➡ INTERNAL PARTS OF A VEHICLE; 1146]

backside (*informal*) *n* **buttocks**, rump, behind, bottom, rear (*informal*), rear end (*informal*) [➡ PARTS OF THE BODY: TORSO; 693]

backslash *type of* **punctuation mark** [➡ ASPECTS OF LANGUAGE; 682]

backslide *v* **relapse**, go back to your old ways, lapse, revert, regress, slip back [➡ GET WORSE; 381]

backslider *n* **recidivist**, defaulter, transgressor, apostate, deserter, repeater [➡ LAZY OR UNSUCCESSFUL PEOPLE; 948]

backspace *type of* **hardware** [➡ COMPUTERS AND COMPUTING; 1127]

backstage *adv* **offstage**, behind the scenes, in the wings, in private, in secret [➡ SECRET AND UNKNOWN; 179]

backstreet *n* **alley**, back alley, lane, side street [➡ ROADS; 1106] *Opposite*: thoroughfare

back talk *n* **rudeness**, sassiness, cheekiness, impudence, impertinence, disrespect, sauciness, sauce (*informal*), mouth (*informal*), attitude (*informal*), lip (*slang*), cheek (*informal*) [➡ BAD MANNERS AND SOCIAL SKILLS; 521] *Opposite*: respect

back-to-back *adj* **consecutive**, end-to-end, nonstop, continuous, uninterrupted, following [➡ AFTER, LAST, AND FOLLOWING; 165]

back to front (*UK*) **1** *adv* **the wrong way around**, in reverse, inversely, contrariwise, inside out, backward [➡ ORIENTATION AND ALIGNMENT; 1223] **2** *adv* **thoroughly**, inside out, like the back of your hand, intimately, from A to Z [➡ WHOLENESS AND COMPLETENESS; 198]

backtrack **1** *v* **retrace your steps**, go back over the same ground, turn back, begin again [➡ GO BACKWARD; 309] **2** *v* **backpedal**, go into reverse, do a volte-face, do an about-face, do a U-turn, back down, back off, change your mind [➡ APOLOGIZE AND RETRACT; 683]

back up **1** *v* **corroborate**, substantiate, authenticate, vouch for, reinforce, second, support [➡ APPROVE AND CONFIRM; 646] *Opposite*: contradict **2** *v* **copy**, duplicate, make a backup, keep a backup, keep a copy [➡ COPY AND DUPLICATE; 402] **3** *v* **move backward**, reverse, go backward, recede [➡ GO BACKWARD; 309] *Opposite*: advance

backup **1** *n* **support**, encouragement, help, moral support, assistance, backing [➡ KIND ACTIONS OR BEHAVIOR; 295] **2** *n* **holdup**, stoppage, gridlock, snarl, tie-up, tailback (*UK*), snarl-up (*UK*) [➡ TRAVEL: TRAFFIC PROBLEMS AND TRAFFIC MANAGEMENT; 323] **3** *n* **standby**, reserve, substitute, reinforcement, help [➡ MORE AND EXCESS; 124] **4** *n* **copy**, duplicate, replica, substitute, alternate, fill-in, surrogate [➡ COPIES AND REPLICAS; 151]

backward **1** *adj* **rearward**, to the rear, toward the back [➡ DIRECTION OF MOTION; 345] *Opposite*: forward **2** *adj* **retrograde**, regressive, recessive [➡ DIRECTION OF MOTION; 345] *Opposite*: progressive **3** *adj* **shy**, diffident, hesitant, reluctant, timid, bashful, retiring [➡ RETICENT AND UNFORTHCOMING; 631] *Opposite*: confident **4** *adv* **toward the back**, back, rearward, behind, toward the rear [➡ DIRECTION OF MOTION; 345] *Opposite*: forward **5** *adv* **the wrong way**, in reverse, the wrong way around, back to front (*UK*) [➡ ORIENTATION AND ALIGNMENT; 1223]

backward and forward *adv* **back and forth**, to and fro, up and down, hither and thither, from side to side [➡ DIRECTION OF MOTION; 345]

backward-looking *adj* **retrospective**, nostalgic, retrograde, traditional, conservative [➡ THE NATURE OF IDEAS; 771] *Opposite*: forward-looking

backwater *n* **backwoods**, the middle of nowhere, the back of beyond (*UK*), boondocks (*informal*), sticks (*informal*) [➡ REMOTE PLACES; 1046]

backwoods **1** *n* **wilderness**, wilds, rough country, back country [➡ REMOTE PLACES; 1046] **2** *n* **the middle of nowhere**, backwater, boondocks (*informal*), sticks (*informal*), the back of beyond (*UK*) [➡ REMOTE PLACES; 1046]

backyard *n* **courtyard**, patio, deck, yard, terrace, porch, veranda [➡ GARDENS; 1074]

bacon *type of* **processed meat** [➡ TYPES AND CUTS OF MEAT; 1177]

bacterial *adj* **microbial**, bacteriological, infective, infectious, contagious, microscopic [➡ MICROORGANISMS, FUNGI, AND ALGAE; 1023]

bacteriological *adj* **microbiological**, biological, bacterial, pathological [➡ BIOLOGICAL SCIENCES; 1037]

bacteriology *type of* **bioscience** [➡ BIOLOGICAL SCIENCES; 1037]

bacteriophage *type of* **microorganism** [➡ MICROORGANISMS, FUNGI, AND ALGAE; 1023]

bacterium *type of* **microorganism** [➡ MICROORGANISMS, FUNGI, AND ALGAE; 1023]

bactrian camel *type of* **large mammal** [➡ LARGE MAMMALS; 986]

bad **1** *adj* **poor**, inferior, deficient, flawed, faulty, defective, substandard, imperfect, abysmal [➡ BAD AND BADLY; 223] *Opposite*: good **2** *adj* **awful**, terrible, dreadful, appalling, shocking, ghastly, horrific, unpleasant [➡ BAD AND BADLY; 223] *Opposite*: good **3** *adj* **evil**, wicked, corrupt, immoral, depraved, debauched, unscrupulous, ruthless, merciless, cruel, base, shameless [➡ MORALLY BAD OR IMPROPER; 775] *Opposite*: good **4** *adj* **naughty**, disobedient, troublesome, wayward, mischievous, unmanageable, unruly, willful, criminal, delinquent [➡ REBELLIOUSNESS AND DISOBEDIENCE; 565] *Opposite*: good **5** *adj* **unhealthy**, damaging, injurious, ruinous, dangerous, prejudicial, harmful [➡ DANGEROUS; 236] *Opposite*: good **6** *adj* **rotten**, off, decayed, decaying, decomposing, putrid, moldy, sour, stale, rancid [➡ DECAYING OR INFESTED; 1236] *Opposite*: fresh **7** *adj* **regretful**, penitent, remorseful, ashamed, apologetic, contrite, guilty, repentant, uneasy, sad [➡ SADNESS, DISTRESS, AND DESPAIR; 539] *Opposite*: good **8** *adj* **adverse**, difficult, unhappy, testing, unpleasant, distressing, harsh, austere [➡ BAD AND BADLY; 223] *Opposite*: good **9** *adj* **serious**, severe, grave, critical, life-threatening, acute [➡ DANGEROUS; 236] *Opposite*: slight

Compare and Contrast: *bad, criminal, delinquent, mischievous, naughty*

CORE MEANING: indicating wrongdoing

bad applies to a whole range of wrongdoing from the most trivial to the most immoral or evil; *criminal* punishable as a crime under the law; *delinquent* antisocial or unlawful, or (*formal*) neglecting a duty, commitment, or responsibility; *mischievous* playfully naughty or troublesome, or (*formal*) causing or meant to cause serious trouble, damage, or hurt; *naughty* badly behaved or disobedient, or (*humorous*) mildly indecent or sinful.

bad blood *n* **bad feeling**, ill feeling, bitterness, acrimony, antagonism, animosity, spite, spitefulness, rancor [➡ ANTAGONISM; 552] *Opposite*: affection

baddie (*informal*) *n* **bad character**, rogue, villain, scoundrel, outlaw, crook (*informal*), criminal, lawbreaker, evildoer, wrongdoer [➡ VILLAINS AND THUGS; 947] *Opposite*: hero

bad feeling *n* **spite**, rancor, spitefulness, bad blood, bitterness, acrimony, antagonism, animosity, ill feeling [➡ ANTAGONISM; 552] *Opposite*: affection

badge **1** *n* **brooch**, button, pin, clasp [➡ JEWELRY; 866] **2** *n* **insignia**, emblem, symbol, mark, device, coat of arms [➡ SYMBOLS, SIGNS, AND NUMBERS; 596]

badger **1** *type of* **small mammal** [➡ SMALL MAMMALS; 990] **2** *v* **pester**, press, harass, plague, harry, hassle (*informal*) [➡ COMPLAIN AND NAG; 686]

bad guy *n* [➡ VILLAINS AND THUGS; 947]

bad habit *n* **weakness**, failing, flaw, character defect, vice, foible [➡ FAULTS, FLAWS, AND WEAKNESSES; 251] *Opposite*: virtue

badinage *n* **banter**, repartee, teasing, joking, mockery, chitchat (*informal*) [➡ JOKES AND TEASING; 674]

badlands *n* [➡ REMOTE PLACES; 1046]

bad language *n* **swearing**, swearwords, vulgar language, profanities, coarse language, vulgarity, obscenities [➡ INSULTS, ABUSE, AND SWEARING; 658]

bad luck *n* **misfortune**, hard luck, ill luck, unluckiness, ill fortune [➡ BAD LUCK AND UNLUCKY; 784] *Opposite*: luck

badly **1** *adv* **poorly**, deficiently, faultily, defectively, imperfectly, shoddily, roughly, inadequately [➡ BAD AND BADLY; 223] *Opposite*: well **2** *adv* **seriously**, severely, gravely, critically, desperately, acutely [➡ CRITICALLY AND SERIOUSLY; 134] *Opposite*: slightly **3** *adv* **naughtily**, disobediently, troublesomely, waywardly, mischievously, unmanageably, willfully, rudely, improperly [➡ BAD MANNERS AND SOCIAL SKILLS; 521]

badly behaved *adj* **naughty**, disobedient, mischievous, unruly, unmanageable, wayward [➡ BAD MANNERS AND SOCIAL SKILLS; 521]

badly off *adj* **poor**, struggling, lacking, wanting, unfortunate, ill-supplied, ill-furnished, strapped (*informal*) [➡ POVERTY AND POOR; 892] *Opposite*: well-off

badly timed *adj* **ill-timed**, inopportune, mistimed, untimely, unseasonable, inconvenient [➡ PROMPTNESS: BADLY TIMED; 101] *Opposite*: well-timed

bad-mannered *adj* **rude**, ill-mannered, impolite, charmless, discourteous, unmannerly, ill-bred, coarse, uncouth, boorish [➥BAD MANNERS AND SOCIAL SKILLS; 521] *Opposite:* well-mannered

bad manners *n* **rudeness**, impoliteness, incivility, discourtesy, discourteousness, impertinence, insolence [➥BAD MANNERS AND SOCIAL SKILLS; 521] *Opposite:* courtesy

badminton *type of* **court game** [➥HOBBIES, GAMES, AND SPORTS; 875]

bad mood *n* **bad humor**, sulk, huff, bad temper, temper, mood [➥IRRITATION AND ANGER; 541]

badmouth (*slang*) *v* **criticize**, disparage, run down, belittle, defame, slur, slight, backstab [➥INSULTS, ABUSE, AND SWEARING; 658] *Opposite:* praise

badness *n* **evilness**, wickedness, immorality, evil, depravity, unscrupulousness, ruthlessness, mercilessness, cruelty [➥MORALLY BAD OR IMPROPER; 775] *Opposite:* goodness

bad taste *n* **tastelessness**, vulgarity, showiness, crassness, crudeness, cheapness, tackiness (*informal*) [➥IN POOR TASTE AND OVERSENTIMENTAL; 229] *Opposite:* good taste

bad temper *n* **spleen**, irritability, petulance, sulkiness, ill temper, bad mood, mood [➥IRRITATION AND ANGER; 541]

bad-tempered *adj* **cross**, ill-tempered, ill-humored, irascible, short-tempered, irritable, surly, crabby, grumpy, grouchy (*informal*), testy (*informal*), cranky (*informal*) [➥IRRITATION AND ANGER; 541] *Opposite:* good-tempered

bad-temperedness *n* [➥IRRITATION AND ANGER; 541]

baffle *v* **confuse**, perplex, puzzle, stump, nonplus, mystify, confound, bewilder, bemuse, befuddle, bamboozle (*informal*), flummox (*informal*) [➥CONFUSE AND BEWILDER; 571]

baffled *adj* **puzzled**, perplexed, mystified, lost, stumped, at sea, confounded, confused, bewildered, bemused, nonplussed, flummoxed (*informal*), bamboozled (*informal*) [➥CONFUSION, ANXIETY, AND WORRY; 540]

bafflement *n* **bewilderment**, perplexity, confusion, puzzlement, bemusement, befuddlement [➥CONFUSION, ANXIETY, AND WORRY; 540] *Opposite:* understanding

baffling *adj* **puzzling**, perplexing, mystifying, confusing, bewildering, mysterious, strange, unexplained, inexplicable [➥BIZARRE AND PECULIAR; 257] *Opposite:* obvious

bag 1 *n* **container**, receptacle, sack, paper bag, plastic bag [➥CONTAINERS, RECEPTACLES, AND PACKAGING; 1245] 2 *v* **take possession**, grab, occupy, reserve, keep, claim [➥GET; 420] 3 *v* **catch**, shoot, snare, take, capture, seize [➥GET; 420]

bag

◆ *types of bags*
clutch purse, fanny pack, handbag, mailbag, nosebag, pocketbook, pouch, purse, reticule, satchel, shopping bag, shoulder bag, sporran, tote bag

bag and baggage *adv* **lock, stock, and barrel**, entirely, completely, totally, in its entirety, root and branch [➥ALL; 128]

bagatelle 1 *n* (*formal*) **trifle**, trifling sum, nothing, a drop in the bucket, thing of no importance, detail, minor detail, a drop in the ocean (*UK*) [➥FEW, LITTLE, SMALL AMOUNT; 120] 2 *type of* **musical form** [➥MUSIC, SONGS, AND SINGING; 907]

bagel *type of* **roll or bun** [➥BREAD, FLOUR, AND BREAD PRODUCTS; 1179]

baggage *n* **luggage**, bags, suitcases, cases, belongings, personal belongings, gear (*informal*) [➥POSSESSIONS; 461]

baggage

◆ *types of baggage*
attaché case, backpack, briefcase, carryall, carrycase, case, duffel bag, haversack, kit bag, knapsack, luggage, overnight bag, pack, portmanteau, rucksack, suitcase, travel case, valise, vanity case, weekend bag

bagginess *n* **looseness**, formlessness, shapelessness, roominess, floppiness, droopiness, slackness [➥SHAPELESSNESS; 1219] *Opposite:* tightness

baggy *adj* **loose**, loose-fitting, slack, shapeless, saggy, flowing [➥SHAPELESSNESS; 1219] *Opposite:* tight

bagpipes *type of* **wind instrument** [➥MUSICAL INSTRUMENTS; 910]

bags *n* **luggage**, baggage, belongings, personal belongings, gear (*informal*) [➥POSSESSIONS; 461]

bag-snatcher *n* [➥CRIMINALS; 821]

baguette *type of* **bread** [➥BREAD, FLOUR, AND BREAD PRODUCTS; 1179]

baht *type of* **currency** [➥CURRENCIES; 798]

bail *n* **security**, surety, payment, financial guarantee, bond [➥TRIAL, PUNISHMENT, AND LEGAL OUTCOMES; 819]

Bailey bridge *type of* **bridge** [➥BRIDGES, TUNNELS, CROSSINGS, AND JUNCTIONS; 1112]

bailiff 1 *n* **sheriff's officer**, law officer, legal officer, dispossessor, evictor [➥PEOPLE IN LAW COURTS; 820] 2 *n* (*UK*) **steward**, agent, factor, estate manager, overseer, land agent [➥PEOPLE WHO GUARD AND PROTECT; 846]

bailiwick *n* [➥SUBJECT AREAS; 768]

bail out 1 *v* **post security**, obtain somebody's release, put up bail, stand surety (*UK*) [➥TRIAL, PUNISHMENT, AND LEGAL OUTCOMES; 819] 2 *v* **escape**, run away, desert, flee, evacuate, abandon, duck out, drop out [➥RUN AWAY AND AVOID; 10] *Opposite:* stick out 3 *v* **help**, rescue, save, assist, aid, come to somebody's aid [➥HELP; 293]

bait 1 *n* **lure**, attraction, enticement, temptation, inducement, draw, carrot, pull (*informal*) [➥TREATS; 210] 2 *v* **entice**, lure, tempt, attract, draw, pull (*informal*) [➥APPEAL TO AND AROUSE INTEREST; 575] 3 *v* **taunt**, tease, torment, harass, provoke, goad, razz (*informal*) [➥JOKES AND TEASING; 674]

baize *type of* **fabric from animals** [➥FABRICS; 1132]

bake 1 *v* **cook**, heat, harden, dry out [➥HARDEN, CONGEAL, AND DRY; 387] 2 *v* (*informal*) **swelter**, overheat, scorch, burn, roast, boil (*informal*) [➥CHANGE OF TEMPERATURE; 386] *Opposite:* freeze

bakery *type of* **food outlet** [➥RETAIL OUTLETS; 1083]

baking *adj* **sweltering**, boiling, blazing, burning, blistering, scorching (*informal*), roasting (*informal*) [➡ HOT WEATHER; 1050] *Opposite:* freezing

baking dish *n* [➡ TABLEWARE, FLATWARE, AND KITCHENWARE; 861]

baking sheet *n* [➡ TABLEWARE, FLATWARE, AND KITCHENWARE; 861]

baklava *type of* **dessert** [➡ CAKES, COOKIES, AND DESSERTS; 1181]

baksheesh *n* **bribe**, handout, tip, gift, token, kickback [➡ BRIBES; 440]

balaclava *type of* **headgear** [➡ ACCESSORIES, MILLINERY, AND LINGERIE; 867]

balalaika *type of* **stringed instrument** [➡ MUSICAL INSTRUMENTS; 910]

balance 1 *n* **equilibrium**, poise, sense of balance, stability, steadiness [➡ HARMONY; 155] *Opposite:* unsteadiness 2 *n* **weighing machine**, weighing scale, set of scales, weighing scales (*UK*) [➡ MEASURING DEVICES; 1123] 3 *n* **remainder**, surplus, rest, what's left, residue [➡ REMAINDER AND REMAINDERS; 125] 4 *v* **maintain equilibrium**, stay poised, keep upright, keep steady, poise, stabilize, steady, keep in place, hold steady [➡ POSITION SOMETHING; 325] *Opposite:* wobble 5 *v* **assess**, weigh, consider, compare, evaluate, calculate, weigh up (*UK*) [➡ EXAMINE AND ASSESS; 753] 6 *v* **equalize**, square, settle, even out, offset, even up, balance out [➡ ASSESS QUANTITY; 757] *Opposite:* weight

balanced 1 *adj* **fair**, impartial, unbiased, unprejudiced, disinterested, objective, reasonable, neutral, even-handed [➡ MORALLY GOOD; 774] *Opposite:* biased 2 *adj* **stable**, composed, well-adjusted, sensible, sane, poised, secure, together (*informal*) [➡ CONFIDENCE AND COMPOSURE; 499] *Opposite:* unbalanced

balance out *v* **even out**, offset, compensate, make up, redress the balance, even up, equalize [➡ EQUALITY; 154] *Opposite:* weight

balboa *type of* **currency** [➡ CURRENCIES; 798]

balcony 1 *n* **veranda**, terrace, loggia, lanai, gallery [➡ STAGES, PLATFORMS, AND RAISED AREAS; 1098] 2 *n* **circle**, upper circle, gallery, upper tier (*UK*) [➡ STAIRS AND STORIES; 1102] 3 *part of* **building** [➡ PARTS OF A BUILDING; 1095]

bald 1 *adj* **hairless**, balding, receding, thin on top, baldheaded [➡ BALDNESS AND BALDING; 487] *Opposite:* hirsute 2 *adj* **bare**, worn, threadbare, smooth, patchy, thin, worn out [➡ PHYSICAL TEXTURE; 1222] 3 *adj* **plain**, bold, blunt, frank, direct, straightforward, unadorned, simple [➡ HONEST AND OPEN; 630] *Opposite:* florid

bald as a coot *adj* [➡ BALDNESS AND BALDING; 487]

bald eagle *type of* **bird of prey** [➡ BIRDS OF PREY; 998]

balderdash *n* **rubbish**, nonsense, garbage, drivel, baloney (*informal*), claptrap (*informal*), tripe (*informal*), twaddle (*informal*), hogwash (*informal*), bunkum (*informal*) [➡ MEANINGLESS SPEECH OR WRITING; 676]

bald-faced *adj* **barefaced**, bold, brazen, shameless, unabashed, brash, blatant, sheer, outright, flagrant [➡ POMPOUS, LOUD, AND OVERCONFIDENT; 635] *Opposite:* meek

baldheaded *adj* **bald**, hairless, balding, receding, thin on top [➡ BALDNESS AND BALDING; 487] *Opposite:* hirsute

balding *adj* **bald**, baldheaded, hairless, receding, thin on top [➡ BALDNESS AND BALDING; 487] *Opposite:* hirsute

baldly *adv* **bluntly**, plainly, flatly, frankly, directly, straightforwardly, simply [➡ HONEST AND OPEN; 630]

baldness 1 *n* **hairlessness**, hair loss, baldheadedness, lack of hair [➡ BALDNESS AND BALDING; 487] *Opposite:* hairiness 2 *n* **bluntness**, plainness, frankness, directness, straightforwardness [➡ HONEST AND OPEN; 630] *Opposite:* deviousness

bale 1 *n* **bundle**, package, pack, roll, block, parcel [➡ COLLECTIONS AND MIXTURES OF THINGS; 1244] 2 *type of* **herd** [➡ GROUPS OF ANIMALS; 993]

baleful *adj* **threatening**, menacing, malevolent, sinister, malignant, vindictive, spiteful [➡ FRIGHTENING; 231] *Opposite:* benevolent

balk *v* **recoil**, draw back, hesitate, refuse, pull back, stop short, rein in [➡ HESITATE; 272] *Opposite:* leap at

ball 1 *n* **sphere**, orb, globe, globule, blob, droplet, pellet, spheroid, bead, marble [➡ ROUNDED SHAPE; 1218] 2 *type of* **sports equipment** [➡ SPORTS EQUIPMENT; 879] 3 *part of* **arm or hand** [➡ PARTS OF THE BODY: ARM AND HAND; 695]

ballad *n* **poem**, song, narrative, folk song, traditional song, epic poem [➡ MUSIC, SONGS, AND SINGING; 907]

ballast *n* **weight**, bulk, makeweight, stabilizer, balance, counterweight, counterbalance [➡ WEIGHT: HEAVY; 1205]

ball bearing *part of* **engine** [➡ PARTS OF AN ENGINE; 1144]

ball cock *n* **regulator**, controller, control, device [➡ FIXTURES; 859]

ballet *type of* **dance** [➡ DANCE; 903]

ballet shoe *type of* **shoe** [➡ FOOTWEAR; 871]

ball game *n* [➡ HOBBIES, GAMES, AND SPORTS; 875]

ball gown *type of* **dress** [➡ GARMENTS AND OUTFITS; 865]

ballistic *adj* **airborne**, air-to-air, surface-to-air, flying [➡ DIRECTION OF MOTION; 345]

ballistic missile *type of* **explosive weapon** [➡ EXPLOSIVES; 1155]

balloon 1 *n* **hot-air balloon**, helium balloon, inflatable, dirigible [➡ AIRCRAFT; 1148] 2 *v* **swell**, distend, inflate, expand, puff out, blow up, bloat [➡ CHANGE OF SIZE: BIGGER; 392] *Opposite:* deflate

ballot 1 *n* **vote**, secret ballot, poll, election, survey, opinion poll [➡ ELECTIONS AND VOTING; 807] 2 *v* **canvass**, consult, survey, poll, assess opinion, arrange a vote [➡ ASK PEOPLE QUESTIONS; 666]

ballpark 1 *n* **stadium**, playing field, field, ground, pitch (*UK*) [➡ URBAN OUTDOOR SPACES; 1072] 2 *adj* (*informal*) **approximate**, rough, estimated, inexact, imprecise, vague [➡ APPROXIMATELY; 135] *Opposite:* exact

ballpark figure (*informal*) *n* [➡ GUESS; 754]

ballpoint *type of* **pen** [➡ WRITING AND DRAWING IMPLEMENTS, AND MEDIA; 601]

ballroom *type of* **room in public buildings** [➡ TYPES OF ROOMS; 1097]

ballyhoo *n* **uproar**, racket, hullabaloo, commotion, ruckus, to-do (*informal*), shemozzle (*dated informal*) [➡CHAOS AND UPROAR; 51]

balm 1 *n* **ointment**, unguent, salve, oil, cream [➡LOTIONS, PASTES, AND GELS; 1272] **2** *n* **comfort**, relief, solace, consolation, palliative, tranquilizer [➡TREATS; 210]

balminess *n* [➡HOT WEATHER; 1050]

balmy *adj* **mild**, clement, pleasant, temperate, gentle, soft [➡HOT WEATHER; 1050] *Opposite*: wintry

baloney (*informal*) *n* **drivel**, balderdash, nonsense, garbage, tripe (*informal*), twaddle (*informal*), claptrap (*informal*), bunkum (*informal*), hogwash (*informal*), rubbish (*UK*) [➡MEANINGLESS SPEECH OR WRITING; 676]

baluster *n* **post**, support, leg, upright, pole, stick [➡STICKS, POLES, AND WEDGES; 1254]

balustrade *n* **railing**, handrail, guardrail, rail, banister, barrier, bar [➡STICKS, POLES, AND WEDGES; 1254]

bamboo *type of* **grass** [➡GRASS; 1031]

bamboozle (*informal*) 1 *v* **cheat**, deceive, con, trick, hoodwink, take in, swindle, dupe, fool [➡DECEPTION AND LIES; 660] **2** *v* **confuse**, bewilder, puzzle, bemuse, perplex, muddle, baffle, flummox (*informal*) [➡CONFUSE AND BEWILDER; 571]

bamboozled (*informal*) *adj* [➡CONFUSION, ANXIETY, AND WORRY; 540]

ban 1 *v* **forbid**, outlaw, prohibit, veto, bar, proscribe, disallow, interdict [➡REFUSE PERMISSION AND NOT ALLOW; 670] *Opposite*: allow **2** *n* **prohibition**, veto, bar, injunction, court order, embargo, sanction, interdict [➡THE LAW AND LEGAL AUTHORITY; 814]

banal *adj* **commonplace**, hackneyed, prosaic, predictable, ordinary, dull, boring, clichéd, trivial, facile [➡BORING AND UNINTERESTING; 234] *Opposite*: original

banality *n* **triteness**, predictability, ordinariness, dullness, triviality, facileness [➡ORDINARINESS; 244] *Opposite*: originality

banana *type of* **fruit** [➡FRUIT AND VEGETABLES; 1176]

band 1 *n* **group**, combo, ensemble [➡MUSICIANS AND SINGERS; 908] **2** *n* **gang**, crowd, mob, group, crew (*informal*), posse (*slang*) [➡GROUPS OF PEOPLE; 935] **3** *n* **stripe**, strip, belt, stretch, range [➡AREA AND RANGE; 111] **4** *type of* **herd** [➡GROUPS OF ANIMALS; 993]

band

♦ *types of bands*
big band, brass band, chamber orchestra, choir, chorale, chorus, dance band, duo, ensemble, jazz band, mariachi, octet, orchestra, pipe band, pop group, quartet, quintet, septet, sextet, sinfonietta, steel band, string band, string quartet, symphony orchestra, trio

bandage 1 *n* **dressing**, binding, strapping, compress [➡COVERS AND COATINGS; 1246] **2** *v* **dress**, bind, tie up, cover, bind up, strap up, swathe [➡DECORATE, ADORN, AND APPLY COATINGS; 405]

bandanna *n* **scarf**, neckerchief, headscarf, kerchief, headsquare (*UK*) [➡ACCESSORIES, MILLINERY, AND LINGERIE; 867]

B & B (*informal*) *type of* **hotel** [➡HOTELS, RESTAURANTS, AND CLUBS; 1082]

bandeau *type of* **headgear** [➡ACCESSORIES, MILLINERY, AND LINGERIE; 867]

bandicoot *type of* **marsupial** [➡MARSUPIALS; 992]

bandit *n* **outlaw**, robber, thief, thug, gangster, crook (*informal*), brigand (*literary*) [➡CRIMINALS; 821]

banditry *n* **lawlessness**, violence, crime, armed robbery, robbery, thieving [➡CRIMES; 817]

bandstand *n* **platform**, pavilion, stand, shelter, podium, dais, open-air stage [➡BUILDINGS FOR PUBLIC ENTERTAINMENT; 1084]

band together *v* **join up**, unite, associate, get together, combine, club together, amalgamate [➡GET CLOSER TOGETHER; 310]

bandwagon *n* **movement**, cause, trend, craze, fashion, lobby [➡FADS, FETISHES, AND IDOLATRY; 555]

bandwidth *n* [➡THE INTERNET; 1128]

bandy 1 *v* **exchange**, toss around, throw around, mention, debate, discuss, cite [➡TWO-WAY COMMUNICATION; 607] **2** *adj* **outward-curving**, bowed, bent, warped, convex, curvy [➡ROUNDED SHAPE; 1218] *Opposite*: straight

bandy-legged *adj* **bandy**, bent, bowlegged, bowed [➡BUILD; 477]

bandy words with *v* **argue**, dispute, bicker, wrangle, spar, have it out [➡ARGUE AND FIGHT; 643]

bane *n* **nuisance**, curse, blight, bother, irritation, annoyance, misery, pest (*informal*) [➡NUISANCES; 253] *Opposite*: blessing

bang 1 *n* **report**, explosion, boom, crash, knock, thud, thump, crack [➡IMPACT SOUNDS; 1260] **2** *n* **knock**, hit, bump, blow, thump, whack [➡PHYSICAL ATTACK AND PUNISHMENT; 415] **3** *v* **hit**, knock, thump, hammer, pound, batter, whack, thud, slam, smash, crash [➡CONTACT: IMPACT; 413] **4** *v* **bump**, knock, jolt, hit, collide, crash, bash (*informal*) [➡CONTACT: IMPACT; 413]

bang into *v* **bump into**, knock, hit, collide with, crash against, smash into, go slap into (*informal*) [➡CONTACT: IMPACT; 413]

bangle *type of* **jewelry** [➡JEWELRY; 866]

bangs *type of* **hairstyle** [➡HAIRSTYLES AND HAIRPIECES; 488]

banish 1 *v* **expel**, send away, exile, deport, evict, drive out, throw out, eject, cast out (*formal*) [➡EJECT AND EXCLUDE; 340] **2** *v* **get rid of**, remove, dismiss, eliminate, discard, do away with, drive out [➡GET RID OF SOMETHING; 451]

banishment *n* **expulsion**, exile, deportation, eviction, exclusion, transportation [➡EJECT AND EXCLUDE; 340]

banister *n* **handrail**, balustrade, guardrail, bar, rail, railing, barrier [➡STICKS, POLES, AND WEDGES; 1254]

banjo *type of* **stringed instrument** [➡MUSICAL INSTRUMENTS; 910]

bank 1 *n* **set**, row, tier, series, group, array, panel [➡COLLECTIONS AND MIXTURES OF THINGS; 1244] **2** *n* **store**, depository, reservoir, stock, collection, pool, cache, reserve, hoard [➡COLLECTIONS AND MIXTURES OF THINGS; 1244] **3** *n* **side**, edge, margin, embankment, border, shore [➡BARRIERS; 1113] **4** *n* **pile**, heap, mound, stack, mass [➡MANY, MUCH, LARGE AMOUNT; 117] **5** *v* **deposit**, pay in, cash in, put in [➡GIVE MONEY; 433]

Opposite: withdraw **6** *v* **have an account**, save, deposit, invest [➞ACCOUNTING, BANKING, AND BUDGETING; 799] **7** *v* **heap**, pile, mound, stack, mass, amass [➞STORE AND KEEP; 453] *Opposite*: disperse **8** *v* **tilt**, pitch, turn, lean, veer, incline, slope [➞TAKE UP A NEW POSITION; 312] *Opposite*: level off

bank account *n* **account**, deposit account, loan account, checking account, joint account, savings account, current account (*UK*) [➞ACCOUNTING, BANKING, AND BUDGETING; 799]

banker *n* **bank manager**, investment banker, banking executive, financier, merchant banker (*UK*) [➞PEOPLE INVOLVED IN FINANCE; 804]

banking *n* **investment**, lending, finance, funding, backing, financial transactions [➞ACCOUNTING, BANKING, AND BUDGETING; 799]

banknote *n* **bill**, dollar bill, Federal Reserve note, note (*UK*), paper money (*UK*) [➞CURRENCIES; 798] *Opposite*: coin

bank on *v* **count on**, depend on, rely on, trust, have confidence in, be sure of [➞LIKE, LOVE, VALUE, AND ENJOY; 578] *Opposite*: doubt

bankroll (*informal*) *v* **finance**, fund, back, pay, sponsor, invest, subsidize [➞GIVE MONEY; 433]

bankrupt **1** *adj* **insolvent**, penniless, ruined, broke (*informal*), bust (*informal*), cleaned out (*informal*) [➞POVERTY AND POOR; 892] *Opposite*: solvent **2** *v* **ruin**, destroy, liquidate, impoverish, make destitute, clean out (*informal*), bleed dry (*informal*) [➞TAKE SOMETHING AWAY; 425]

bankruptcy *n* **insolvency**, ruin, liquidation, economic failure, impoverishment, ruination [➞ACCOUNTING, BANKING, AND BUDGETING; 799]

banned **1** *adj* **barred**, disqualified, debarred, excluded, expelled [➞REFUSE PERMISSION AND NOT ALLOW; 670] *Opposite*: admitted **2** *adj* **forbidden**, proscribed, prohibited, illegal, illicit, controlled, restricted [➞ILLEGAL; 816] *Opposite*: permitted

banner **1** *n* **sign**, poster, flag, placard, streamer, hanging [➞SIGNPOSTS, SIGNALS, AND BILLBOARDS; 595] **2** *adj* **excellent**, exceptional, notable, outstanding, marvelous, tremendous, good [➞EXTRAORDINARY; UNCOMMON; 205]

banquet **1** *n* **feast**, dinner, meal, formal meal, ceremonial meal, blowout (*slang*) [➞PARTIES, DANCES, AND CELEBRATIONS; 37] **2** *type of* **meal** [➞MEALS AND PARTS OF MEALS; 1169]

banqueting hall *n type of* **room in public buildings** [➞TYPES OF ROOMS; 1097]

banshee *n* **spirit**, supernatural being, ghost, ghoul, specter, phantom [➞THE SUPERNATURAL; 787]

bantam *type of* **fowl** [➞FOOD BIRDS; 999]

banter **1** *n* **teasing**, mockery, joking, repartee, wit, badinage, chitchat (*informal*) [➞JOKES AND TEASING; 674] **2** *v* **tease**, mock, joke, poke fun at, make fun of, have a joke with, razz (*informal*) [➞JOKES AND TEASING; 674]

baobab *type of* **deciduous tree** [➞DECIDUOUS TREES; 1028]

baptism *n* **initiation**, introduction, debut, beginning, induction, rite, ceremony [➞BEGINNINGS; 53]

baptismal *adj* **christening**, naming, ceremonial, ritual, sacramental, initiatory, initiation, dedication [➞RELIGIOUS CONCEPTS; 776]

baptize *v* **christen**, bless, immerse, sprinkle, initiate, induct, receive [➞RELIGIONS AND RELIGIOUS PRACTICES; 777]

bar **1** *n* **rod**, pole, stick, staff, shaft, rail [➞STICKS, POLES, AND WEDGES; 1254] **2** *n* **block**, slab, piece, ingot [➞AMOUNTS OF SOLID OR SEMISOLID; 115] **3** *n* **obstruction**, hindrance, block, barrier, impediment, restriction [➞PROBLEMS; 256] **4** *n* **hostelry**, drinking place, watering hole (*informal*) [➞HOTELS, RESTAURANTS, AND CLUBS; 1082] **5** *v* **secure**, fasten, bolt, lock, barricade [➞BAR AND OBSTRUCT ACCESS; 410] **6** *v* **obstruct**, close off, hinder, get in the way, block, impede [➞MAKE IMPOSSIBLE; 276] **7** *v* **ban**, exclude, keep out, debar, prohibit, forbid, stop, restrain, prevent, restrict [➞REFUSE PERMISSION AND NOT ALLOW; 670] *Opposite*: admit **8** *prep* **excluding**, save, except, with the exception of, apart from, but [➞NOT; 137]

bar

◆ *types of bars or clubs*
bodega, casino, country club, joint (*slang*), nightclub, nightspot, roadhouse (*dated*), saloon, shebeen, speakeasy, tavern, wine bar

barb **1** *n* **point**, hook, tip, spur, spike, spine, prickle, thorn, sting [➞ANGULAR SHAPE; 1217] **2** *n* **gibe**, insult, dig, taunt, cutting remark [➞JOKES AND TEASING; 674]

barbaric *adj* **cruel**, brutal, vicious, ferocious, fierce, bloodthirsty, barbarous [➞MORALLY BAD OR IMPROPER; 775] *Opposite*: gentle

barbarism *n* **cruelty**, brutality, savagery, viciousness, ferociousness, bloodthirstiness, barbarousness [➞MORALLY BAD OR IMPROPER; 775] *Opposite*: gentleness

barbarity **1** *n* **cruelty**, brutality, savagery, viciousness, ferociousness, bloodthirstiness, barbarousness, barbarism [➞MORALLY BAD OR IMPROPER; 775] *Opposite*: gentleness **2** *n* **atrocity**, cruelty, outrage, assault, abuse, misdeed [➞MALICIOUS ACTIONS OR BEHAVIOR; 296]

barbarous *adj* **cruel**, brutal, vicious, ferocious, fierce, barbaric [➞MORALLY BAD OR IMPROPER; 775] *Opposite*: gentle

Barbary ape *type of* **primate** [➞PRIMATES; 988]

barbecue **1** *type of* **meal** [➞MEALS AND PARTS OF MEALS; 1169] **2** *v* **grill**, sear, flame, chargrill, cook on a spit, roast, broil [➞COOKING AND FOOD PREPARATION; 353]

barbecued *adj* [➞STATE OF PREPARED FOOD; 1171]

barbecue sauce *type of* **seasonings, sauces, and dips** [➞SEASONINGS AND SAUCES; 1174]

barbed **1** *adj* **pointed**, hooked, spiky, spiny, thorny, prickly [➞PHYSICAL TEXTURE; 1222] **2** *adj* **snide**, pointed, cutting, unkind, hurtful, acid, acerbic, taunting, cruel, sarcastic [➞RUDE AND HOSTILE; 625]

barber *n* **men's hair stylist**, hair stylist, stylist, coiffeur (*formal*) [➞HAIR STYLISTS; 851]

barbershop *n* [➞MUSIC, SONGS, AND SINGING; 907]

barbican *n* **tower**, keep, stronghold, turret, fortification [➞PARTS OF FORTRESSES; 1091]

bar code n [➡ NAME AND DESCRIBE; 665]

bard (*literary or humorous*) n **poet**, versifier, composer, wordsmith, songster, minstrel, writer [➡ WRITERS AND STYLES; 914]

bare 1 adj **naked**, nude, exposed, uncovered, undressed, unclothed, stripped [➡ DRESS, WEAR, AND UNDRESS; 868] *Opposite*: covered 2 adj **empty**, vacant, blank, clean, clear, cleared, unfurnished, unoccupied [➡ EMPTY; 1238] *Opposite*: full 3 adj **stark**, barren, austere, severe, hard, inhospitable, hostile [➡ PLAIN; 232] *Opposite*: lush 4 adj **simple**, unadorned, plain, basic, unembellished, undecorated [➡ EASE AND SIMPLICITY; 200] *Opposite*: ornate 5 adj **mere**, scant, meager, measly (*informal*) [➡ TOO FEW, TOO LITTLE; 122] 6 v **expose**, reveal, display, show, uncover, disclose [➡ CAUSE TO APPEAR; 5] *Opposite*: cover

See Compare and Contrast at **naked**.

barefaced adj **brazen**, blatant, unashamed, obvious, bald-faced, unabashed, outright, flagrant [➡ HONEST AND OPEN; 630]

barefaced lie n [➡ DECEPTION AND LIES; 660]

barefoot adj **unshod**, shoeless, barefooted [➡ DRESS, WEAR, AND UNDRESS; 868]

barefoot waterskiing *type of* **extreme sport** [➡ HOBBIES, GAMES, AND SPORTS; 875]

barely adv **hardly**, scarcely, only just, just about [➡ TO A CERTAIN EXTENT; 136] *Opposite*: easily

bareness n **emptiness**, nakedness, starkness, austerity, plainness, baldness [➡ PLAIN; 232]

barf (*informal*) 1 v **vomit**, spew, regurgitate, throw up (*informal*), bring up, hurl (*slang*) [➡ VOMIT AND BELCH; 712] 2 n [➡ VOMIT AND BELCH; 712]

barfly (*slang*) n [➡ LAZY OR UNSUCCESSFUL PEOPLE; 948]

bargain 1 n **good deal**, good buy, steal (*informal*) [➡ ECONOMICAL AND RESOURCEFUL; 207] 2 n **deal**, agreement, accord, arrangement, pact, covenant [➡ HARMONY; 155] 3 v **haggle**, barter, negotiate, make a deal, trade, wheel and deal, broker [➡ OBTAIN POSSESSION BY PERSUASION; 457] 4 adj **cheap**, low, reduced, inexpensive, rock-bottom, bargain-basement, giveaway (*informal*) [➡ CHEAP AND INEXPENSIVE; 221]

bargain-basement adj **cheap**, cut-rate, low-priced, reduced-price, bargain, rock-bottom, sale, cut-price (*UK*) [➡ CHEAP AND INEXPENSIVE; 221]

bargain for v **expect**, count on, take into account, depend on, reckon with, anticipate, make allowance for, make provision for, provide for, bargain on, allow (*formal*) [➡ PREDICT AND ANTICIPATE; 750]

bargain on v **expect**, count on, take into account, depend on, reckon with, anticipate, allow (*formal*), make allowance for, make provision for, provide for, bargain for [➡ PREDICT AND ANTICIPATE; 750]

barge 1 *type of* **motor vessel** [➡ SHIPS AND BOATS; 1150] 2 v **rush**, push, elbow, burst, surge, shove, charge [➡ CONTACT: IMPACT; 413]

barge in 1 v **walk in**, storm in, push in, rush in, breeze in, intrude [➡ ARRIVE; 12] 2 v **interrupt**, butt in, cut in, break in, interject [➡ INTERRUPT AND BUTT IN; 619]

barge into v **bump into**, collide with, clash with, smash into, knock into, bash into (*informal*), go slap into (*informal*) [➡ CONTACT: IMPACT; 413]

barista *type of* **person who works in restaurants** [➡ DOMESTIC AND KITCHEN WORKERS; 850]

baritone *type of* **musical register** [➡ MUSICAL TERMS; 912]

bark 1 *type of* **animal sound** [➡ SOUNDS MADE BY ANIMALS; 1261] 2 v **howl**, yap, growl, yowl, snarl [➡ SOUND EMISSION BY ANIMALS OR BIRDS; 364] 3 *type of* **sailing vessel** [➡ SHIPS AND BOATS; 1150]

barkeeper n [➡ DOMESTIC AND KITCHEN WORKERS; 850]

barley *type of* **cereal** [➡ CEREAL FOODS; 1178]

barn 1 n **outbuilding**, outhouse, shed, cowshed, store, storehouse [➡ ANCILLARY BUILDINGS; 1080] 2 *type of* **storage space** [➡ STORES AND STORAGE BUILDINGS; 1088]

barnacle *type of* **aquatic invertebrate** [➡ AQUATIC INVERTEBRATES; 1022]

barnacle goose *type of* **freshwater bird** [➡ FRESHWATER BIRDS; 1000]

barn dance *type of* **dance** [➡ DANCE; 903]

barn owl *type of* **owl** [➡ OWLS; 1001]

barnyard n **farmyard**, yard, court, forecourt [➡ THE COUNTRYSIDE AND OUTDOOR SPACES; 1071]

barograph *type of* **measuring device** [➡ MEASURING DEVICES; 1123]

barometer n **weatherglass**, indicator, gauge, aneroid barometer, barograph, statoscope [➡ MEASURING DEVICES; 1123]

barometric adj **atmospheric**, air, meteorological [➡ WEATHER AND CLIMATE; 1049]

baron 1 n **tycoon**, magnate, mogul, industrialist, captain of industry, boss, robber baron [➡ IMPORTANT OR FAMOUS PEOPLE; 893] 2 *type of* **aristocrat** [➡ RULERS AND ARISTOCRACY; 823]

baroness *type of* **aristocrat** [➡ RULERS AND ARISTOCRACY; 823]

baronet *type of* **aristocrat** [➡ RULERS AND ARISTOCRACY; 823]

baronial adj **grand**, impressive, opulent, stately, imposing, sumptuous [➡ EXPENSIVE AND LUXURIOUS; 218] *Opposite*: humble

baroque 1 adj **ornate**, ornamental, decorative, elaborate, exaggerated, rococo [➡ ARTISTIC MOVEMENTS AND STYLES; 899] *Opposite*: plain 2 adj **flamboyant**, exaggerated, overdone, over-the-top (*informal*) [➡ IN POOR TASTE AND OVERSENTIMENTAL; 229] *Opposite*: restrained

Baroque 1 *type of* **pre-20th-century architecture** [➡ BUILDING AND ARCHITECTURE; 1076] 2 *type of* **classical music** [➡ MUSIC, SONGS, AND SINGING; 907] 3 *type of* **pre-20th-century art movement** [➡ ARTISTIC MOVEMENTS AND STYLES; 899]

barouche *type of* **wagon or carriage** [➡ VEHICLES; 1145]

barque *see* **bark**

barracks n **quarters**, garrison, station, billet [➡ RESIDENTIAL BUILDINGS; 1078]

barracuda *type of* **tropical fish** [➡ OCEAN FISH; 1009]

barrage 1 n **bombardment**, salvo, volley, fusillade [➡ SUDDEN EVENTS; 52] 2 n **onslaught**, outpouring, hail, storm, flood, salvo

[➡SUDDEN EVENTS; 52] *Opposite*: trickle **3** *n* **dam**, dike, bank, embankment [➡BARRIERS; 1113]

barred **1** *adj* **striped**, banded, lined, stripy, streaked, streaky [➡DESCRIBING PATTERNS; 1227] **2** *adj* **grilled**, meshed, fenced, secure, solid, fastened [➡FASTEN, LINK, AND JOIN; 408] **3** *adj* **banned**, excluded, disqualified, debarred, not allowed, forbidden [➡REFUSE PERMISSION AND NOT ALLOW; 670] *Opposite*: admitted

barrel **1** *n* **tub**, cask, vat, butt, rain barrel, container, water butt (*UK*) [➡CONTAINERS, RECEPTACLES, AND PACKAGING; 1245] **2** *type of* **nonmetric unit** [➡SIZE AND DIMENSIONS; 1192]

barrel-chested *adj* [➡BUILD; 477]

barren **1** *adj* **infertile**, unproductive, sterile, unfruitful [➡REPRODUCTION AND HEREDITY; 725] *Opposite*: fertile **2** *adj* **desolate**, bleak, inhospitable, stark, harsh, austere, bare, empty, deserted, lonely, windswept [➡IN BAD REPAIR; 1234]

barrenness **1** *n* **emptiness**, bleakness, bareness, loneliness, inhospitableness, harshness, starkness, desolation, austereness [➡IN BAD REPAIR; 1234] **2** *n* **infertility**, sterility, unfruitfulness, unproductiveness [➡REPRODUCTION AND HEREDITY; 725] *Opposite*: fertility

barricade **1** *n* **blockade**, barrier, cordon, obstruction, fortification [➡BARRIERS; 1113] **2** *v* **secure**, obstruct, bar, fortify, block, blockade, lock up [➡IMPROVE STRENGTH AND DURABILITY; 378]

barrier **1** *n* **obstacle**, difficulty, stumbling block, sticking point, impediment, hindrance, obstruction [➡PROBLEMS; 256] **2** *n* **fence**, wall, barricade, blockade, block, obstacle, obstruction [➡BARRIERS; 1113]

barring *prep* **except for**, without, excluding, apart from [➡NOT; 137]

barrio *n* [➡COUNTRIES AND REGIONS; 1067]

barrister (*UK*) *n* **lawyer**, attorney, counselor, advocate, defender [➡PEOPLE IN LAW COURTS; 820]

barrow **1** *n* **wheelbarrow**, trolley, pushcart, transporter, trailer, truck, cart [➡BIKES, CARS, AND CARRIAGES; 1149] **2** *n* (*UK*) **cart**, handcart, pushcart, stall, fruit stall [➡BIKES, CARS, AND CARRIAGES; 1149] **3** *n* **burial mound**, mound, tumulus, long barrow, tomb, hill, swell, grave mound [➡BURIAL PLACES AND ACCESSORIES; 930]

bartender *type of* **person who works in restaurants** [➡DOMESTIC AND KITCHEN WORKERS; 850]

barter *v* **exchange**, trade, switch, negotiate, bargain, haggle, swap (*informal*) [➡PURCHASE; 422]

baryon *type of* **elementary particle** [➡ELEMENTARY PARTICLES; 1279]

basalt *type of* **stone** [➡STONES, ROCKS, AND BOULDERS; 1057]

bascule bridge *type of* **bridge** [➡BRIDGES, TUNNELS, CROSSINGS, AND JUNCTIONS; 1112]

base **1** *n* **foundation**, support, stand, pedestal, rest, pier [➡SUPPORTS AND BASES; 1255] **2** *n* **source**, origin, center, heart, starting point, root [➡BEGINNINGS; 53] **3** *n* **headquarters**, center, main office, seat, station [➡PLACE OF EMPLOYMENT; 832] **4** *v* **found**, ground, build, create, construct, center [➡INSTITUTE AND INAUGURATE; 348] **5** *adj* **dishonorable**, sordid, disreputable, squalid, immoral, ignoble [➡MORALLY BAD OR IMPROPER; 775]

See Compare and Contrast at **mean**.

baseball *type of* **ball game** [➡HOBBIES, GAMES, AND SPORTS; 875]

baseball cap *type of* **headgear** [➡ACCESSORIES, MILLINERY, AND LINGERIE; 867]

baseball player *n* [➡PEOPLE IN SPORTS AND LEISURE; 876]

baseboard *type of* **general fixtures** [➡FIXTURES; 859]

basejumping *type of* **extreme sport** [➡HOBBIES, GAMES, AND SPORTS; 875]

baseless *adj* **unfounded**, untrue, unjustified, unsubstantiated, groundless, unsupported, without foundation, without merit [➡UNCERTAIN; 175] *Opposite*: well-founded

baseline **1** *n* **starting point**, point of departure, reference point, reference line, starting position, zero [➡BEGINNINGS; 53] **2** *n* **standard**, model, criterion, starting point, quality check [➡PERFECT EXAMPLES AND EMBODIMENTS; 67] **3** *n* **reference**, control, check, set of data, set of values, set of results [➡BASIC DETAILS; 688] **4** *n* **boundary**, boundary line, line, periphery, white line, limit [➡EXTREMITIES OF PHYSICAL OBJECTS; 1250]

basement **1** *n* **cellar**, vault, crypt, lower ground floor [➡STAIRS AND STORIES; 1102] *Opposite*: attic **2** *type of* **storage space** [➡STORES AND STORAGE BUILDINGS; 1088]

baseness *n* **wickedness**, sordidness, vileness, immorality, ignobility, corruptness [➡MORALLY BAD OR IMPROPER; 775] *Opposite*: nobility

basenji *type of* **small dog** [➡DOGS; 980]

bash **1** *v* (*informal*) **thump**, punch, smash, whack, sock (*informal*), belt (*informal*), clobber (*informal*), knock around (*informal*), wallop (*informal*), cream (*slang*), clout (*UK*) [➡PHYSICAL ATTACK AND PUNISHMENT; 415] **2** *v* (*informal*) **criticize**, condemn, find fault with, attack, knock, abuse, put down (*informal*) [➡ACCUSE, BLAME, AND CRITICIZE; 641] **3** *n* (*informal*) **punch**, hit, blow, thump, knock, smash, whack, wallop (*informal*), belt (*informal*), clout, sock (*informal*) [➡PHYSICAL ATTACK AND PUNISHMENT; 415] **4** *n* (*informal*) **dent**, bump, smash, knock [➡CONTACT: IMPACT; 413] **5** *n* (*informal*) **party**, celebration, dance, ball, gala, shindig (*informal*), get-together (*informal*) [➡PARTIES, DANCES, AND CELEBRATIONS; 37]

bashful *adj* **shy**, timid, reserved, retiring, self-conscious, withdrawn, modest, blushing, reticent, diffident, timorous, coy [➡RETICENT AND UNFORTHCOMING; 631] *Opposite*: bold

bashfulness *n* **shyness**, modesty, self-consciousness, quietness, coyness, timidity, reserve, reticence, diffidence [➡RETICENT AND UNFORTHCOMING; 631] *Opposite*: boldness

basic **1** *adj* **essential**, central, key, principal, main, vital, critical, fundamental, important [➡FUNDAMENTAL; 195] **2** *adj* **rudimentary**, straightforward, elementary, undeveloped, uncomplicated, plain [➡EASE AND SIMPLICITY; 200]

basics *n* **fundamentals**, essentials, necessities, nitty-gritty (*informal*), nuts and bolts (*informal*) [➡BASIC DETAILS; 688]

basil *type of* **herb** [➡HERBS AND SPICES; 1175]

basilica *type of* **church** [➡RELIGIOUS BUILDINGS; 1085]

basilisk *type of* **reptile** [➧ REPTILES; 994]

basin 1 *n* **sink**, hand basin, washbasin, washbowl [➧ FIXTURES; 859] **2** *n* (*UK*) **bowl**, mixing bowl, dish [➧ CONTAINERS, RECEPTACLES, AND PACKAGING; 1245]

basis *n* **foundation**, base, root, source, starting point, beginning, core [➧ BEGINNINGS; 53]

bask 1 *v* **laze around**, lie, recline, lounge, stretch out, spread out [➧ LACK OF ACTIVITY OR MOTION; 342] **2** *v* **enjoy**, savor, relish, soak up, luxuriate, delight in, wallow [➧ LIKE, LOVE, VALUE, AND ENJOY; 578]

basket *n* **bag**, hamper, picnic basket, linen basket, wicker basket, shopping basket (*UK*) [➧ CONTAINERS, RECEPTACLES, AND PACKAGING; 1245]

basketball *type of* **ball game** [➧ HOBBIES, GAMES, AND SPORTS; 875]

basketry *n type of* **handicraft** [➧ CRAFTS AND CARVING; 355]

basque *type of* **upper body underwear** [➧ ACCESSORIES, MILLINERY, AND LINGERIE; 867]

bas-relief *n* **relief**, molding, basso-relievo, carving, paneling, decoration, sculpture [➧ SCULPTURE; 902]

bass 1 *adj* **deep**, deep-toned, low-voiced, low-pitched [➧ SOFT, LOW, OR PLEASANT SOUNDS; 1265] **2** *type of* **musical register** [➧ MUSIC, SONGS, AND SINGING; 907] **3** *type of* **freshwater fish** [➧ FRESHWATER FISH; 1010]

bass drum *type of* **percussion instrument** [➧ MUSICAL INSTRUMENTS; 910]

basset *type of* **small dog** [➧ DOGS; 980]

bass guitar *type of* **stringed instrument** [➧ MUSICAL INSTRUMENTS; 910]

bassinet *type of* **bed** [➧ FURNITURE; 858]

bassoon *type of* **wind instrument** [➧ MUSICAL INSTRUMENTS; 910]

baste 1 *v* **moisten**, drizzle, grease, cover, saturate, daub [➧ COOKING AND FOOD PREPARATION; 353] **2** *v* **thrash**, thump, clobber (*informal*), bash (*informal*), beat up (*informal*), wallop (*informal*) [➧ PHYSICAL ATTACK AND PUNISHMENT; 415] **3** *v* **sew**, stitch, tack, hem, seam [➧ CRAFTS AND CARVING; 355]

bastion 1 *n* **stronghold**, fortification, rampart, defense, bulwark [➧ FORTRESSES AND FORTIFICATIONS; 1090] **2** *n* **mainstay**, support, defender, upholder, supporter [➧ PERFECT EXAMPLES AND EMBODIMENTS; 67]

bat 1 *n* **racket**, paddle, willow, club [➧ SPORTS EQUIPMENT; 879] **2** *n* [➧ LIVING THINGS AND LIVING; 976] **3** *v* **flutter**, wink, flicker, flap, blink [➧ MOVE SOMETHING: ON THE SPOT; 336]

bat

◆ *types of flying mammals*
flying fox, flying squirrel, fruit bat, pipistrelle, vampire bat

batch *n* **lot**, consignment, group, set, bunch, collection [➧ COLLECTIONS AND MIXTURES OF THINGS; 1244]

bath 1 *n* **bathtub**, tub, hip bath (*UK*) [➧ FIXTURES; 859] **2** *n* **immersion**, soak, steam bath, bubble bath, sponge bath, mud bath, bed bath (*UK*) [➧ CLEAN AND POLISH; 403] **3** *n* **tank**, basin, reservoir, container [➧ CONTAINERS, RECEPTACLES, AND PACKAGING; 1245]

bathe 1 *v* **take a bath**, shower, wash, soak, immerse yourself [➧ CLEAN AND POLISH; 403] **2** *v* **immerse**, dip, soak, rinse, dunk, submerge, flood, inundate [➧ SOFTEN, LIQUEFY, AND DAMPEN; 388] **3** *v* **swim**, go for a dip, paddle [➧ HOBBIES, GAMES, AND SPORTS; 875]

bather *n* **swimmer**, diver, snorkeler, paddler, skinny-dipper (*informal*) [➧ PEOPLE IN SPORTS AND LEISURE; 876]

bathetic 1 *adj* **anticlimactic**, disappointing, unsatisfying [➧ EMOTIONALLY UNPLEASANT AND UPSETTING; 227] **2** *adj* **trite**, sentimental, unsatisfying, commonplace [➧ IN POOR TASTE AND OVERSENTIMENTAL; 229]

bathing suit *type of* **sportswear** [➧ GARMENTS AND OUTFITS; 865]

bathing trunks *type of* **sportswear** [➧ GARMENTS AND OUTFITS; 865]

bathos *n* **anticlimax**, letdown, comedown (*informal*) [➧ FAILURE; 77]

bathrobe *type of* **sleepwear** [➧ GARMENTS AND OUTFITS; 865]

bathroom *type of* **room in the home** [➧ TYPES OF ROOMS; 1097]

baths *n* **bathhouse**, Turkish bath, steam bath, sauna, Russian bath [➧ BUILDINGS FOR PUBLIC ENTERTAINMENT; 1084]

bathtub *type of* **plumbing fixtures** [➧ FIXTURES; 859]

baton 1 *n* **stick**, rod, wand, cane, pointer [➧ STICKS, POLES, AND WEDGES; 1254] **2** *type of* **club** [➧ BLUNT INSTRUMENTS AND WHIPS; 1158]

batsman *n* **batter**, hitter, cricketer (*UK*) [➧ PEOPLE IN SPORTS AND LEISURE; 876]

battalion *n* **throng**, crowd, mass, multitude, horde, host [➧ MANY, MUCH, LARGE AMOUNT; 117]

batten *v* **fasten**, fix, close, secure, batten down, lock up [➧ BAR AND OBSTRUCT ACCESS; 410] *Opposite:* open

batter 1 *v* **pound**, bang, thump, thrash, hit, hammer (*informal*) [➧ CONTACT: IMPACT; 413] **2** *v* **assault**, maim, brutalize, attack, abuse, injure, maltreat, beat [➧ WOUND A PERSON OR ANIMAL; 383]

battercake *type of* **pancake** [➧ CAKES, COOKIES, AND DESSERTS; 1181]

battered 1 *adj* **maltreated**, assaulted, abused, beaten, injured [➧ INJURED; 742] **2** *adj* **tattered**, decrepit, worn out, weather-beaten, damaged, beat-up (*informal*), knocked around (*informal*), tatty (*UK*) [➧ IN BAD REPAIR; 1234] *Opposite:* pristine

battering *n* **pounding**, buffeting, hammering, beating, pummeling, lashing [➧ PHYSICAL ATTACK AND PUNISHMENT; 415]

battery 1 *n* **series**, set, sequence, succession, run, string, array [➧ COLLECTIONS AND MIXTURES OF THINGS; 1244] **2** *n* [➧ ENERGY STORAGE AND GENERATION; 1163]

battle 1 *n* **fight**, clash, encounter, skirmish, engagement, combat, scuffle, melee, conflict, confrontation, fracas, fray, action [➧ AGGRESSIVE EVENTS; 39] **2** *n* **struggle**, crusade, fight, war, campaign, drive, wrangle [➧ AGGRESSIVE EVENTS; 39] **3** *v* **fight**, go to war, attack, come to blows, engage, join battle [➧ WARFARE AND WAR; 830] **4** *v* **struggle**, wrestle, contend, fight, strive, try [➧ COMPETE, CONTEND, AND COMBAT; 303]

See Compare and Contrast at **fight**.

battleax *n* **ax**, hatchet, tomahawk, halberd [➡ SWORDS AND KNIVES; 1157]

battle cruiser *type of* **military vessel** [➡ SHIPS AND BOATS; 1150]

battle cry *n* **whoop**, war cry, yell, shout, cry, rallying cry, cheer [➡ SOUNDS MADE BY PEOPLE; 1262]

battle dress *n* **soldier's uniform**, army uniform, uniform, fatigues, khakis, camouflage [➡ GARMENTS AND OUTFITS; 865]

battlefield *n* **battleground**, combat zone, arena, theater of war, front line, field, trenches [➡ WARFARE AND WAR; 830]

battleground *see* **battlefield**

battlements *n* **ramparts**, fortifications, walls, parapet, bulwark, stockade [➡ PARTS OF FORTRESSES; 1091]

battler *n* [➡ PEOPLE WHO ARE APPROVED OF; 955]

battleship *type of* **military vessel** [➡ SHIPS AND BOATS; 1150]

battleship gray *type of* **gray** [➡ COLORS; 1224]

batty (*informal*) *adj* **irrational**, eccentric, crazy (*informal*), around the bend (*slang*), nuts (*slang*), potty (*UK informal*) [➡ ECCENTRICITY AND IRRATIONALITY; 562] *Opposite*: rational

bauble *n* **trinket**, trifle, gewgaw, decoration, ornament [➡ ORNAMENTS AND DECORATIONS; 1248]

Bauhaus *type of* **20th-century architecture** [➡ BUILDING AND ARCHITECTURE; 1076]

baulk *see* **balk**

bauxite *type of* **mineral** [➡ MINERALS, 1277]

bawdy *adj* **ribald**, earthy, risqué, suggestive, indecent, off-color, rude [➡ MORALLY BAD OR IMPROPER; 775]

bawl 1 *v* **shout**, yell, roar, shriek, screech, holler (*informal*) [➡ SOUND EMISSION BY PEOPLE; 363] *Opposite*: whisper 2 *v* (*informal*) **cry**, howl, wail, sob, weep, blubber (*informal*) [➡ CRYING; 650] 3 *type of* **human sound** [➡ SOUNDS MADE BY PEOPLE; 1262]

bawl out (*informal*) *v* **tell off** (*informal*), chew out (*informal*), haul over the coals, read the riot act to, rap across the knuckles, take to task, rake over the coals, scold, tear off a strip (*UK*), give a talking-to (*informal*) [➡ ACCUSE, BLAME, AND CRITICIZE; 641]

bay 1 *n* **inlet**, cove, natural harbor, anchorage, haven (*literary*) [➡ THE SEAS, OCEANS, AND SHORES; 1041] 2 *n* **compartment**, alcove, cubicle, recess, loading bay [➡ ALCOVES, CUBICLES, AND COMPARTMENTS; 1096] 3 *type of* **brown** [➡ COLORS; 1224] 4 *n* **bark**, woof, yap, yelp, howl, cry, wail [➡ SOUNDS MADE BY ANIMALS; 1261] 5 *v* **woof**, bark, yap, yelp, howl, cry, wail [➡ SOUND EMISSION BY ANIMALS OR BIRDS; 364] 6 *type of* **evergreen tree** [➡ EVERGREEN AND CONIFEROUS TREES; 1029]

bay for *v* **demand**, insist on, be out for, cry for, shout for, yell for, howl for [➡ REQUEST AND DEMAND; 663]

bay leaf *type of* **herb** [➡ HERBS AND SPICES; 1175]

bayonet 1 *n* **blade**, knife, dagger, lance, spike [➡ SWORDS AND KNIVES; 1157] 2 *v* **stab**, spear, impale, spike, knife, run through (*literary*) [➡ STAB; 416]

bayou *n* **marsh**, marshland, everglade, wetlands, bog [➡ RIVERS, LAKES, AND STREAMS; 1042]

bay window *type of* **window** [➡ WINDOWS; 1100]

bazaar 1 *n* **market**, marketplace, souk, open market, flea market [➡ URBAN OUTDOOR SPACES; 1072] 2 *type of* **retail outlet** [➡ RETAIL OUTLETS; 1083]

bazooka *type of* **gun** [➡ WEAPONS FOR SHOOTING; 1156]

be 1 *v* **exist**, live, have being, be present, coexist, subsist [➡ EXIST; 15] 2 *v* **take place**, happen, occur, transpire, come about, ensue, befall (*archaic or literary*), come to pass (*archaic or literary*) [➡ HAPPEN; 27] 3 *v* **be situated**, be located, remain, be there, be present, stand, stay [➡ EXIST IN A PLACE; 19]

be a bundle of nerves (*informal*) *v* **be on edge**, be nervous, be like a cat on a hot tin roof, be high strung, be like a coiled spring, be uptight (*informal*) [➡ BE CONCERNED AND CARE; 581] *Opposite*: be relaxed

be accepted *v* **integrate**, assimilate, become one of, join, belong, pass muster, blend in, pass, get in [➡ ESTABLISHING RELATIONSHIPS WITH OTHERS; 974]

beach *n* **seashore**, seaside, coast, shore, coastline, shoreline, sand, strand [➡ THE SEAS, OCEANS, AND SHORES; 1041]

beach ball *type of* **toy** [➡ TOYS; 880]

beach chair *n type of* **seating** [➡ FURNITURE; 858]

beachcomber *n* **scavenger**, forager, explorer, collector, hoarder [➡ PEOPLE WHO COLLECT THINGS; 454]

beached *adj* **stranded**, aground, stuck, high and dry, run aground, shipwrecked, marooned [➡ LACK OF ACTIVITY OR MOTION; 342] *Opposite*: afloat

beachfront *n* [➡ THE SEAS, OCEANS, AND SHORES; 1041]

beach grass *type of* **grass** [➡ GRASS; 1031]

beachhead *n* **lodgment**, foothold, base, strategic position, position, foot in the door [➡ ADVANTAGES; 212]

beachwear *n* **swimwear**, leisurewear, summer clothes, bathing suit, swimsuit, bikini, swimming trunks, shorts [➡ GARMENTS AND OUTFITS; 865]

beacon 1 *n* **signal**, sign, alarm, warning, flare, warning light [➡ SIGNPOSTS, SIGNALS, AND BILLBOARDS; 595] 2 *n* **bonfire**, fire, flare [➡ FIRE, FLAMMABILITY, AND BURNING; 1165] 3 *n* (*literary*) **inspiration**, guiding light, encouragement, example, shining example, ideal, symbol of hope [➡ PERFECT EXAMPLES AND EMBODIMENTS; 67]

be acquainted with *v* **have knowledge of**, know about, be familiar with, be aware of, be informed of, be on familiar terms with [➡ KNOWLEDGE AND WISDOM; 558]

bead *n* **drop**, droplet, drip, blob, globule [➡ AMOUNTS OF LIQUID; 114]

beaded 1 *adj* **decorated**, ornate, bead-trimmed, encrusted, sequined, bejeweled (*literary*), bedizened (*literary*) [➡ DECORATE, ADORN, AND APPLY COATINGS; 405] 2 *adj* **covered**, dripping, sparkling, moist, soaked, drenched, wet [➡ MOIST; 1241]

beading *n* **edging**, border, trim, detail, molding, ornamentation [➡ ORNAMENTS AND DECORATIONS; 1248]

be adjoining *v* **abut**, border, border on, be alongside, be next door to, neighbor, adjoin [➡ EXIST IN CLOSE PROXIMITY; 21]

beads *type of* **necklace** [➡ JEWELRY; 866]

beady 1 *adj* **small**, round, shiny, bright, shining, twinkling [➡ SMALL; 1195] *Opposite*: wide 2 *adj* **beaded**, decorated, ornate, bead-trimmed, sequined, bejeweled (*literary*) [➡ DECORATE, ADORN, AND APPLY COATINGS; 405] 3 *adj* (*informal*) **watchful**, unblinking, piercing, attentive, bright, fixed [➡ FACIAL CHARACTERISTICS; 481]

be after *v* **want**, wish for, desire, try to get, look for, seek, need, aim for [➡ DESIRE AND WANT; 579]

be against *v* **oppose**, be opposed, object, disapprove, protest, be in opposition to, dislike, be an adversary of [➡ PROTEST AND EXPRESS DISAPPROVAL; 642]

beagle *type of* **small dog** [➡ DOGS; 980]

beak *part of* **bird** [➡ PARTS OF A BIRD; 1006]

beaked *adj* **hooked**, aquiline, Roman [➡ ANGULAR SHAPE; 1217]

beaker *n* **cup**, glass, mug, paper cup, plastic cup, tumbler [➡ CONTAINERS, RECEPTACLES, AND PACKAGING; 1245]

be alive *v* **live**, exist, be living, survive, be alive and kicking, be alive and well [➡ EXIST; 15]

be alive with *v* **be crawling with**, swarm with, seethe with, teem with, ooze, abound in [➡ PROSPER AND ABOUND; 16]

beam 1 *n* **girder**, rafter, joist, timber, shaft, plank, bar, RSJ (*UK*) [➡ BUILDING MATERIALS; 1077] 2 *n* **ray**, shaft of light, sunbeam, stream of light [➡ LIGHT; 1164] 3 *n* **smile**, grin, wide smile, big smile [➡ FACIAL EXPRESSIONS AND BLUSHING; 651] *Opposite*: scowl 4 *v* **smile**, grin, look happy [➡ FACIAL EXPRESSIONS AND BLUSHING; 651] *Opposite*: scowl 5 *v* **shine**, radiate, emit, send out, glow, gleam, flash, glimmer [➡ LIGHT EMISSION; 368]

beam bridge *type of* **bridge** [➡ BRIDGES, TUNNELS, CROSSINGS, AND JUNCTIONS; 1112]

beaming *adj* **smiling**, cheery, cheerful, sunny, genial, bright, warm, grinning [➡ FACIAL EXPRESSIONS AND BLUSHING; 651] *Opposite*: scowling

bean *type of* **pulse** [➡ PEAS AND BEANS; 1189]

beanbag *n* **cushion**, floor cushion, pouf, seat, sag bag (*UK*) [➡ FURNISHING AND HOUSEHOLD LINENS; 860]

be anchored in *v* **be based on**, be rooted in, be founded on, be grounded in [➡ BE ABOUT SOMETHING; 62]

bean counter (*slang*) *n* [➡ PEOPLE INVOLVED IN FINANCE; 804]

be angry *v* **seethe**, fume, boil, rage, go berserk, lose control, lose your temper, go off the deep end, hit the roof, gnash your teeth, see red (*informal*), go nuts (*slang*) [➡ GIVING VENT TO EMOTIONS; 679]

beanie *n type of* **hat** [➡ ACCESSORIES, MILLINERY, AND LINGERIE; 867]

beanpole *n* **support**, stick, pole, post, cane, trellis [➡ STICKS, POLES, AND WEDGES; 1254]

bean sprout *type of* **salad vegetable** [➡ FRUIT AND VEGETABLES; 1176]

bear 1 *type of* **large mammal** [➡ LARGE MAMMALS; 986] 2 *v* **tolerate**, stand, put up with, stomach, accept, allow, swallow,

abide, endure, suffer, go through [➡ TOLERATE AND ENDURE; 766] 3 *v* **support**, take, stand, sustain, hold, withstand [➡ HOLD AND CONTAIN; 455] 4 *v* **assume**, accept, shoulder, carry, take, take on, have [➡ ACCEPT POSSESSION; 450] *Opposite*: discard 5 *v* **show**, display, exhibit, present, evince, manifest [➡ POSSESS; 444] 6 *v* **carry**, convey, bring, take, transport, move [➡ MOVE SOMETHING TO ANOTHER LOCATION; 324] 7 *v* **produce**, develop, yield, give birth, bring forth, create, bring about, bring into being, generate [➡ ENGENDER; 350]

bearable *adj* **manageable**, tolerable, endurable, acceptable, sufferable, supportable (*literary*) [➡ ACCEPTABLE AND PASSABLE; 219] *Opposite*: unbearable

bear a grudge *v* **resent**, begrudge, feel bitter about, have hard feelings about, feel aggrieved, have a chip on your shoulder [➡ DISLIKE AND HATE; 577]

beard 1 *n* **facial hair**, whiskers, goatee, bush, stubble [➡ FACIAL HAIR; 489] 2 *v* **challenge**, confront, accost, stand up to, face up to, oppose [➡ ACCUSE, BLAME, AND CRITICIZE; 641]

bearded *adj* **unshaven**, hirsute, hairy, whiskery, bewhiskered, bristly [➡ FACIAL HAIR; 489] *Opposite*: clean-shaven

bearded dragon *type of* **reptile** [➡ REPTILES; 994]

beardless *adj* [➡ FACIAL HAIR; 489]

bear down on 1 *v* **advance on**, close in on, converge on, march on, charge, draw near, approach, accost [➡ GET CLOSER TOGETHER; 310] *Opposite*: retreat 2 *v* **push down**, press down, thrust, press, lean on, depress [➡ CONTACT: EXERT PRESSURE; 414]

bearer 1 *n* **carrier**, bringer, deliverer, conveyer, transporter, porter [➡ MESSENGERS AND COURIERS; 852] 2 *n* **holder**, possessor, owner, keeper, custodian, guardian [➡ OWNERS; 446]

bear false witness *v* **commit perjury**, lie, equivocate, stretch the truth [➡ DECEPTION AND LIES; 660]

bear fruit *v* **succeed**, be successful, show results, produce results, pay off, work out, turn out well [➡ SUCCEED AND WIN; 79] *Opposite*: fail

bear hug *n* **embrace**, cuddle, hug, clinch, squeeze [➡ PHYSICAL CONTACT AS COMMUNICATION; 655]

bearing 1 *n* **influence**, effect, impact, connection, relevance, sway [➡ IMPORTANCE AND SIGNIFICANCE; 192] 2 *n* **manner**, behavior, attitude, deportment, demeanor, posture, comportment (*formal*) [➡ TEMPERAMENT AND BEHAVIOR; 492] 3 *n* **compass reading**, direction, course, orientation, point of reference [➡ NAVIGATION; 1141]

bear in mind *v* **remember**, keep in mind, think of, consider, take into consideration, take into account, recall, recollect [➡ REMEMBER; 746] *Opposite*: forget

béarnaise *type of* **seasonings, sauces, and dips** [➡ SEASONINGS AND SAUCES; 1174]

bear out *v* **support**, verify, prove, substantiate, corroborate, uphold, validate, back up [➡ APPROVE AND CONFIRM; 646] *Opposite*: undermine

bearskin 1 *type of* **fabric from animals** [➡ FABRICS; 1132] 2 *type of* **headgear** [➡ ACCESSORIES, MILLINERY, AND LINGERIE; 867]

bear the brunt *v* **receive the impact**, take the strain, receive the full force, bear the burden, bear the responsibility, be in the front line, stand fast, endure, tolerate [➡ TOLERATE AND ENDURE; 766]

bear up v **hold up**, hold out, cope, manage, get along, get by, survive [➡ CONTINUE TO EXIST; 17] *Opposite*: give in

bear with v **be patient**, put up with, make allowance for, show forbearance, bear, stand, tolerate, accept, endure, forbear (*formal*) [➡ TOLERATE AND ENDURE; 766]

be a sign of v **indicate**, reflect, herald, mark, signify, symbolize, be indicative of, portend, anticipate [➡ MEAN SOMETHING; 61]

beast 1 n **creature**, animal, being, living thing, quadruped [➡ LIVING THINGS AND LIVING; 976]   **2** n **monster**, fiend, ogre, animal, brute (*literary*) [➡ VILLAINS AND THUGS; 947]

be a success v **succeed**, be successful, do well, arrive, work out, be a winner, be a smash hit, score high marks, make out, make it (*informal*) [➡ SUCCEED AND WIN; 79] *Opposite*: fail

be a symbol of v **symbolize**, represent, stand for, embody, personify, epitomize, be a figurehead [➡ REPRESENT SOMETHING OR SOMEBODY; 59]

beat 1 v **defeat**, overcome, overwhelm, thrash, trounce, outdo, outclass, get the better of, triumph over, wipe the floor with (*informal*), hammer (*informal*), slaughter (*slang*), cream (*slang*) [➡ BEAT AND DEFEAT; 80]   **2** v **hit**, strike, bang, hammer, thump, pound, punch, tap [➡ CONTACT: IMPACT; 413]   **3** v **throb**, palpitate, thump, pound, pulsate, drum, thud, knock [➡ EMIT SOUNDS THROUGH IMPACT AND ABRASION; 365]   **4** v **whisk**, whip, blend, mix, combine, stir, purée [➡ COOKING AND FOOD PREPARATION; 353]   **5** v **surpass**, break, smash, do better than, go one better than, better, best, top, outstrip, outdo, outshine, outdistance, outperform, outrun [➡ BEAT AND DEFEAT; 80]   **6** n **stroke**, blow, hit, bang, thump, knock, tap [➡ CONTACT: IMPACT; 413]   **7** n **rhythm**, pulse, pulsation, throb, thump, drumming, stress [➡ IMPACT SOUNDS; 1260]   **8** adj (*slang*) **tired**, exhausted, tired out, worn out, weary, ready to drop, dog-tired (*informal*), had it (*informal*) [➡ TIRED, ASLEEP, AND UNCONSCIOUS; 738] *Opposite*: fresh

See Compare and Contrast at **defeat**.

beat a hasty retreat v **depart**, leave, make off, run away, make a run for it, decamp, head off, flee, bolt [➡ RUN AWAY AND AVOID; 10]

beat around the bush v **digress**, ramble, waffle, rabbit, bumble, blather (*informal*), burble (*informal*) [➡ CHATTER AND BABBLE; 617]

beaten 1 adj **compressed**, packed down, trodden, flattened, crushed, trampled, compacted [➡ DENSITY AND CONSISTENCY; 1207]   **2** adj **defeated**, conquered, crushed, vanquished [➡ BEATEN AND DEFEATED; 78]

beaten-up adj **battered**, tattered, worn out, scruffy, tatty, old, dilapidated, decrepit, shabby, weather-beaten [➡ IN BAD REPAIR; 1234] *Opposite*: pristine

beater 1 n **whisk**, blade, attachment, paddle, stick [➡ TABLEWARE, FLATWARE, AND KITCHENWARE; 861]   **2** n (*informal*) **wreck**, rattletrap (*informal*), jalopy (*dated informal*), heap (*slang*), junker (*slang*) [➡ BIKES, CARS, AND CARRIAGES; 1149]

beatific (*literary*) adj **blissful**, radiant, sublime, heavenly, serene, saintly, ecstatic [➡ FACIAL EXPRESSIONS AND BLUSHING; 651]

beatification n **sanctification**, canonization, sainting, elevation, blessing, consecration [➡ RELIGIONS AND RELIGIOUS PRACTICES; 777]

beatify v **sanctify**, bless, consecrate, canonize, saint [➡ CONFER STATUS; 458]

beating 1 n **thrashing**, whipping, thumping, pounding, hiding (*informal*), walloping (*informal*) [➡ AGGRESSIVE EVENTS; 39]   **2** n **defeat**, setback, thrashing, trouncing, pasting (*informal*), hammering (*informal*) [➡ BEAT AND DEFEAT; 80]

beat it (*slang*) v **go away**, leave, depart, be off, head off, retreat, vamoose (*slang*) [➡ RUN AWAY AND AVOID; 10] *Opposite*: stay

be at odds v **disagree**, be at loggerheads, be in disagreement, be fighting, be quarreling, be at daggers drawn, be at each other's throats, be in conflict [➡ DISHARMONY; 156]

See Compare and Contrast at **disagree**.

be attracted v **fall for**, fall in love with, be infatuated with, take to, have a crush on (*informal*), be smitten (*literary or humorous*) [➡ LIKE, LOVE, VALUE, AND ENJOY; 578]

beat up (*informal*) v **attack**, assault, batter, mug, injure, hit, strike [➡ PHYSICAL ATTACK AND PUNISHMENT; 415]

beat-up (*informal*) adj **battered**, tattered, dilapidated, decrepit, shabby, scruffy, worn out, weather-beaten, old, seen better days, tatty, ratty (*informal*) [➡ IN BAD REPAIR; 1234] *Opposite*: pristine

be at variance v **contradict**, be at odds, disagree with, be in opposition to, be in conflict [➡ DISHARMONY; 156]

beau 1 n (*dated*) **boyfriend**, admirer, lover, steady (*informal*), suitor (*formal*), swain (*literary*), squire (*dated*), gallant (*archaic*) [➡ SEXUAL AND ROMANTIC RELATIONSHIPS; 964]   **2** n (*archaic*) **fop**, peacock, poseur, dandy (*informal*), swell (*dated informal*), popinjay (*dated*) [➡ MALE PERSON; 934]

beau monde n [➡ RICH PEOPLE; 895]

beaut (*informal*) n **beauty**, stunner (*informal*), peach (*informal*), knockout (*informal*), nice one (*UK*) [➡ AMAZING THINGS; 211]

beauteous (*literary*) adj **lovely**, beautiful, gorgeous, exquisite, elegant, attractive, handsome [➡ BEAUTY AND ATTRACTIVENESS; 189] *Opposite*: ugly

beautification n **enhancement**, sprucing up, remodeling, prettification, redecoration, embellishment, improvement, transformation, titivation, revamping [➡ IMPROVE APPEARANCE; 379]

beautiful 1 adj **good-looking**, lovely, gorgeous, stunning, striking, fine-looking, attractive, handsome, pretty [➡ PEOPLE'S PHYSICAL APPEARANCE; 475] *Opposite*: ugly   **2** adj **lovely**, picturesque, scenic, delightful, charming, wonderful, exquisite, pleasing, superb, magnificent [➡ BEAUTY AND ATTRACTIVENESS; 189] *Opposite*: unattractive

See Compare and Contrast at **good-looking**.

beautifully 1 *adv* **attractively**, gorgeously, stunningly, handsomely, prettily, charmingly, exquisitely, strikingly [➡ BEAUTY AND ATTRACTIVENESS; 189] *Opposite*: unattractively 2 *adv* **wonderfully**, delightfully, brilliantly, superbly, magnificently, excellently, marvelously, skillfully [➡ CORRECT AND FAULTLESS; 182] *Opposite*: poorly

beautiful people *n* [➡ RICH PEOPLE; 895]

beautify *v* **prettify**, smarten, enhance, remodel, spruce up, embellish, revamp, redecorate, titivate, doll up (*informal*) [➡ IMPROVE APPEARANCE; 379]

beauty 1 *n* **loveliness**, attractiveness, good looks, prettiness, exquisiteness, gorgeousness, splendor, magnificence [➡ BEAUTY AND ATTRACTIVENESS; 189] *Opposite*: unattractiveness 2 *n* **advantage**, attraction, benefit, upside, plus (*informal*) [➡ SOURCE OF HAPPINESS, PLEASURE, OR IMPROVEMENT; 209] *Opposite*: drawback

beauty parlor *n* **salon**, hair salon, beautician's (*UK*) [➡ RETAIL OUTLETS; 1083]

beauty product *n* [➡ MAKEUP AND BEAUTY PRODUCTS; 490]

beaver 1 *type of* **rodent** [➡ RODENTS; 989] 2 *v* (*informal*) **work**, labor, toil, exert yourself, keep at, persevere, persist, plug away (*informal*) [➡ CONTINUE AN ACTION; 262] *Opposite*: laze around

be aware of *v* **appreciate**, understand, be familiar with, be acquainted with, be informed about, have knowledge of, be up-to-date with, be abreast of, know, sense, feel, notice [➡ KNOWLEDGE AND WISDOM; 558]

be blunt *v* **speak plainly**, call a spade a spade, be to the point, be candid, be honest, be direct, be frank, be straightforward, lay it on the line (*informal*), be up-front (*informal*), shoot from the hip (*slang*) [➡ EXPLAIN AND CLARIFY; 610]

bebop *type of* **jazz music** [➡ MUSIC, SONGS, AND SINGING; 907]

be bothered *v* **be alarmed**, be anxious, worry, be apprehensive, be concerned, be nervous [➡ BE CONCERNED AND CARE; 581]

be burning to *v* **be dying to**, be desperate to, be yearning to, be eager to, be keen to, want madly to, be aching to [➡ DESIRE AND WANT; 579]

becalmed *adj* **stuck**, at a standstill, stationary, at a halt, marooned, stranded, in the doldrums [➡ LACK OF ACTIVITY OR MOTION; 342] *Opposite*: on the move

be carried away *v* **be overcome**, be moved, be overwhelmed, be transported, be over the moon, be swept off your feet, be caught up, be enraptured (*formal*) [➡ CHANGE OF MOOD AND COMPOSURE; 580]

because *conj* **since**, as, for [➡ CAUSATION; 168]

be caused by *v* **result from**, arise from, arise out of, be an effect of, follow from, stem from, develop out of [➡ CAUSATION; 168]

because of *prep* **owing to**, on account of, as a consequence of, due to, as a result of [➡ CAUSATION; 168] *Opposite*: despite

béchamel sauce *type of* **seasonings, sauces, and dips** [➡ SEASONINGS AND SAUCES; 1174]

beck (*UK*) *n* **stream**, rivulet, brook (*literary*), burn (*UK*) [➡ RIVERS, LAKES, AND STREAMS; 1042]

beckon *v* **signal**, sign, summon, gesture, indicate, motion [➡ GESTURES AND GESTICULATION; 653] *Opposite*: dismiss

be close to *v* **border on**, verge on, come close to, approach, be similar to, be almost, approximate [➡ SEEM TO BE SOMETHING; 58]

become 1 *v* **turn out to be**, turn into, develop, convert, grow into, come to be [➡ GRADUALLY COME INTO EXISTENCE; 1] 2 *v* **suit**, befit, flatter, enhance, show off, show to advantage [➡ IMPROVE SOMETHING; 374]

become acquainted *v* **meet**, meet for the first time, be introduced to, make somebody's acquaintance, get to know [➡ ESTABLISHING RELATIONSHIPS WITH OTHERS; 974]

become aware of *v* **notice**, detect, discern, make out, sense, perceive, observe [➡ LEARN AND DISCOVER; 762] *Opposite*: miss

become of *v* **happen to**, be the outcome of, befall (*archaic or literary*) [➡ HAPPEN TO SOMEBODY; 30]

becoming 1 *adj* **flattering**, attractive, fetching, charming, pretty, pleasant [➡ BEAUTY AND ATTRACTIVENESS; 189] *Opposite*: unattractive 2 *adj* **suitable**, appropriate, apt, fitting, befitting, in keeping, right, seemly [➡ APPROPRIATE, SUITABLE, AND ADVISABLE; 184] *Opposite*: inappropriate

be compatible 1 *v* **get along with**, be well-suited, be like-minded, be in harmony with, be attuned to, relate well to, have affinities with, get on with (*UK*) [➡ HARMONY; 155] *Opposite*: clash 2 *v* **be reconcilable**, be consistent with, be in keeping with, be in line with, match, coincide, corroborate, tally [➡ HARMONY; 155] *Opposite*: contradict

be concerned *v* **worry**, be anxious, be perturbed, be bothered, be troubled, agonize, brood, care, sweat (*informal*) [➡ BE CONCERNED AND CARE; 581]

be consistent with *v* **tally**, coincide with, match, bear out, corroborate, be in sync with (*informal*) [➡ HARMONY; 155] *Opposite*: contradict

becquerel *type of* **SI unit** [➡ SIZE AND DIMENSIONS; 1192]

be crazy about (*informal*) *v* **adore**, love, be besotted with, be passionate about, fall for, be all over, be mad about (*informal*), be nuts about (*slang*) [➡ LIKE, LOVE, VALUE, AND ENJOY; 578] *Opposite*: hate

bed 1 *n* [➡ FURNITURE; 858] 2 *n* **plot**, flowerbed, patch, border [➡ GARDENS; 1074] 3 *n* **layer**, band, base, strip, seam, stratum (*formal*) [➡ COVERS AND COATINGS; 1246] 4 *n* **bottom**, floor, base, seabed, riverbed [➡ EXTREMITIES OF PHYSICAL OBJECTS; 1250]

bed

◆ *types of beds*
bassinet, berth, bunk, bunk bed, cot, couchette, cradle, crib, day bed, divan, double bed, four-poster, futon, hammock, king-size bed, Murphy bed, queen-size bed, single bed, sofa bed, studio couch, trundle bed, twin bed, waterbed

bed and board *n* [➡ ACCOMMODATIONS; 855]

bed and breakfast *type of* **hotel** [➡ HOTELS, RESTAURANTS, AND CLUBS; 1082]

bedazzle *v* **amaze**, stun, impress, bewilder, daze, bemuse, stupefy, confuse [➡ CONFUSE AND BEWILDER; 571]

bedazzled (*literary*) *adj* **bewildered**, dazed, bemused, amazed, confused, stunned, stupefied, impressed [➡ CONFUSION, ANXIETY, AND WORRY; 540] *Opposite:* unimpressed

bedbug *type of* **parasitic insect** [➡ PARASITES; 1017]

bedchamber (*archaic or literary*) *type of* **room in the home** [➡ TYPES OF ROOMS; 1097]

bedding *n* **bedclothes**, bed linen, sheet, blanket, duvet, comforter, quilt, covers, eiderdown, bedcovers (*UK*) [➡ FURNISHING AND HOUSEHOLD LINENS; 860]

bedeck (*literary*) *v* **decorate**, festoon, adorn, ornament, deck out, garland, deck (*literary*), bejewel (*literary*), bedizen (*literary*) [➡ DECORATE, ADORN, AND APPLY COATINGS; 405] *Opposite:* strip

bedecked (*literary*) *adj* **decorated**, festooned, adorned, ornamented, decked out, garlanded, bejeweled (*literary*), decked (*literary*), bedizened (*literary*) [➡ DECORATE, ADORN, AND APPLY COATINGS; 405] *Opposite:* stripped

bedevil *v* **beset**, assail, torment, harass, trouble, pester, dog, gnaw, needle (*informal*) [➡ ANGER AND ANNOY; 569]

bedhead *n* **headboard**, rail, bedrail, bed end, bedpost [➡ FURNITURE; 858]

bedlam *n* **chaos**, pandemonium, confusion, anarchy, disorder, disarray, turmoil, commotion, uproar, mayhem (*informal*) [➡ CHAOS AND UPROAR; 51] *Opposite:* order

bed linen *n* **bedding**, bedclothes, sheet, blanket, pillowcase, covers, bedcovers (*UK*) [➡ FURNISHING AND HOUSEHOLD LINENS; 860]

bed of roses *n* [➡ PLEASANT SITUATIONS; 74]

bedpan *n* **chamber pot**, pot, potty, commode, receptacle [➡ CONTAINERS, RECEPTACLES, AND PACKAGING; 1245]

bedraggled *adj* **unkempt**, disheveled, untidy, messy, scruffy, grubby [➡ BADLY GROOMED; 483] *Opposite:* neat

bedridden *adj* **confined to bed**, flat on your back, laid up, incapacitated, disabled, out of action [➡ UNFIT AND WEAK; 739] *Opposite:* up and about

bedrock 1 *n* **rock layer**, substratum, solid rock, base, foundation [➡ SUPPORTS AND BASES; 1255] 2 *n* **basis**, base, core, heart, root, foundation, anchor [➡ MOST IMPORTANT THING; 197]

bedroom *n* **dormitory**, sleeping quarters, boudoir, room, dorm (*informal*), bedchamber (*archaic or literary*), chamber (*archaic or literary*) [➡ TYPES OF ROOMS; 1097]

bedroom community *n* [➡ HUMAN SETTLEMENTS; 1070]

bedside lamp *n* [➡ LIGHTING; 862]

bedside manner *n* **rapport**, style, approach, relationship, behavior, conduct, comportment (*formal*) [➡ TEMPERAMENT AND BEHAVIOR; 492]

bedsore *n* **ulcer**, pressure sore, ulceration, sore, bruise, decubitus ulcer [➡ CONDITIONS AFFECTING THE SKIN; 721]

bedspread *n* **coverlet**, cover, quilt, throw, eiderdown, spread, comforter, spread, counterpane (*dated*) [➡ FURNISHING AND HOUSEHOLD LINENS; 860]

bedstead *n* **bedframe**, frame, base, pallet, bed [➡ FURNITURE; 858]

bedtime *n* **time to retire**, time for bed, sleep time, time to turn in (*informal*), time to hit the hay (*informal*), time to hit the sack (*informal*) [➡ TIMES OF DAY; 87]

bee *type of* **flying insect** [➡ FLYING INSECTS; 1013]

beech *type of* **deciduous tree** [➡ DECIDUOUS TREES; 1028]

beef 1 *type of* **meat** [➡ TYPES AND CUTS OF MEAT; 1177] 2 *n* (*slang*) **complaint**, grumble, moan (*informal*), bellyache (*informal*), grouse (*informal*), gripe (*informal*) [➡ COMPLAIN AND NAG; 686] 3 *v* (*slang*) **complain**, grumble, carp, whine, moan (*informal*), bellyache (*informal*), grouse (*informal*), gripe (*informal*) [➡ COMPLAIN AND NAG; 686] *Opposite:* praise

beefburger *n type of* **processed meat** [➡ TYPES AND CUTS OF MEAT; 1177]

beefiness *n* **muscularity**, sturdiness, burliness, brawniness, stockiness, bulkiness [➡ MUSCLES AND MUSCULATURE; 479]

beefsteak fungus *type of* **fungus** [➡ MICROORGANISMS, FUNGI, AND ALGAE; 1023]

beef up (*informal*) *v* **strengthen**, improve, enhance, boost, reinforce, upgrade, build up [➡ IMPROVE STRENGTH AND DURABILITY; 378] *Opposite:* weaken

beefy *adj* **muscular**, brawny, heavy, hefty, burly, sturdy, well built, powerfully built, big, thickset, strapping (*informal*) [➡ MUSCLES AND MUSCULATURE; 479] *Opposite:* puny

beehive 1 *n* **apiary**, hive, skep (*UK*) [➡ ANIMAL OR BIRD ACCOMMODATIONS; 1079] 2 *type of* **hairstyle** [➡ HAIRSTYLES AND HAIRPIECES; 488]

beep 1 *n* **peep**, bleep, beep-beep, honk, hoot, parp (*UK*) [➡ CONTINUOUS SOUNDS; 1258] 2 *v* **peep**, bleep, beep-beep, honk, hoot, parp (*UK*) [➡ EMIT CONTINUOUS SOUNDS; 366]

beeper (*informal*) *n* **pager**, monitor, bleeper (*UK*) [➡ TELECOMMUNICATIONS; 1130]

beer belly (*slang*) *n* [➡ EXTRA WEIGHT; 478]

beer gut (*slang*) *n* [➡ EXTRA WEIGHT; 478]

beermat (*UK*) *n* **coaster**, mat, rest, bar cloth (*UK*) [➡ COVERS AND COATINGS; 1246]

beet *n* **sugar beet**, chard, Swiss chard, mangel-wurzel, mangel, beetroot (*UK*) [➡ FRUIT AND VEGETABLES; 1176]

beetle *n* [➡ INSECTS; 1012]

beetle

◆ *types of beetles*
cockroach, Colorado potato beetle, deathwatch beetle, dung beetle, flea beetle, Japanese beetle, ladybug, rhinoceros beetle, roach (*informal*), scarab, stag beetle, water beetle, weevil

befall (*archaic or literary*) *v* **happen**, occur, take place, come about, transpire, ensue, come somebody's way, come to pass (*archaic or literary*) [➡ HAPPEN TO SOMEBODY; 30]

befit v **suit**, become, be fitting, be suitable for, be appropriate, be right [➡ APPROPRIATE, SUITABLE, AND ADVISABLE; 184]

befitting adj **becoming**, suitable, appropriate, apt, fitting, in keeping, right, seemly [➡ APPROPRIATE, SUITABLE, AND ADVISABLE; 184] Opposite: unsuitable

before 1 prep **in front of**, facing, ahead of, afore [➡ RELATIVE LOCATION; 161] Opposite: behind 2 prep **previous to**, earlier than, sooner than, prior to, ahead of, by, afore [➡ BEFORE, FIRST, AND PRECEDING; 163] Opposite: after 3 adv **beforehand**, previously, earlier, in advance, in the past, already, formerly, afore [➡ BEFORE, FIRST, AND PRECEDING; 163] Opposite: afterward

beforehand adv **earlier**, in advance, before, early, ahead of time [➡ PROMPTNESS: EARLY; 98] Opposite: late

before long adv **soon**, in a short time, in a little while, shortly, after a short time, after a while, by and by (literary) [➡ FUTURE; 86]

before now adv **by now**, already, before this time, in the past, previously, before [➡ BEFORE, FIRST, AND PRECEDING; 163]

befriend v **make friends with**, take care of, look after, help, assist, support [➡ ESTABLISHING RELATIONSHIPS WITH OTHERS; 974] Opposite: shun

befuddle v **confuse**, muddle, mix up, bewilder, baffle, puzzle, stupefy, perplex, stump, nonplus, confound, flummox (informal) [➡ CONFUSE AND BEWILDER; 571] Opposite: enlighten

befuddled adj **confused**, muddled, baffled, puzzled, perplexed, stumped, nonplussed, flummoxed (informal) [➡ CONFUSION, ANXIETY, AND WORRY; 540] Opposite: clear-headed

befuddlement n **confusion**, perplexity, bewilderment, bafflement, puzzlement [➡ CONFUSION, ANXIETY, AND WORRY; 540] Opposite: clarity

beg v **ask for**, request, plead, solicit, entreat, implore (formal), supplicate (formal), beseech (literary) [➡ REQUEST AND DEMAND; 663]

beget v **cause**, bring about, precipitate, create, bring, produce, result in, lead to [➡ CAUSE TO HAPPEN; 31]

beg forgiveness v **apologize**, make an apology, express regret, say you're sorry [➡ APOLOGIZE AND RETRACT; 683]

beggar 1 n **mendicant**, homeless person, vagabond, vagrant, tramp, street dweller, panhandler, scrounger (informal), bum (informal) [➡ POOR PEOPLE; 896] 2 v **defy**, be beyond, confound, surpass, exceed, defeat [➡ BEAT AND DEFEAT; 80]

begin 1 v **start**, start on, commence, start in on, set in motion, embark on, set in train (UK) [➡ START AN ACTION; 260] Opposite: finish 2 v **bring into being**, instigate, initiate, inaugurate, activate, create, set off, set up, come into being, arise, start off, originate [➡ CAUSE TO START; 265] 3 v **start the ball rolling**, get down to, get to, get under way, set off, open, start, commence, launch, kick off (informal) [➡ START AN ACTION; 260] Opposite: end

beginner n **novice**, learner, trainee, apprentice, student, pupil, tyro, greenhorn [➡ UNSKILLED PEOPLE; 530] Opposite: old hand

Compare and Contrast: beginner, apprentice, greenhorn, novice, tyro

CORE MEANING: a person who has not acquired the necessary experience or skills to do something

beginner somebody who has just started to learn or do something; **apprentice** somebody who is being taught the skills of a trade over an agreed period of time by somebody fully trained; **greenhorn** somebody who lacks experience and may be naive or gullible; **novice** somebody with no previous experience or skill in the activity undertaken; **tyro** somebody who is raw and inexperienced.

beginning n **start**, opening, launch, establishment, creation, inauguration, initiation, activation, introduction, instigation, commencement (formal) [➡ BEGINNINGS; 53] Opposite: end

beg off v **back out**, bow out, duck out, cry off (informal), fink out (slang) [➡ NOT DO AND REFUSE TO DO; 274]

begonia type of **perennial flower** [➡ FLOWERS FROM BULBS; 1030]

begrime (literary) v [➡ DIRTY AND CONTAMINATE; 404]

begrimed (literary) adj [➡ DIRTY; 1235]

begrudge v **resent**, envy, be envious, be jealous, be resentful, grudge [➡ DISLIKE AND HATE; 577]

begrudging adj [➡ REBELLIOUSNESS AND DISOBEDIENCE; 565]

beg to differ v **disagree**, take issue with, demur, dissent, object, protest [➡ DENY AND REJECT; 644] Opposite: agree

beguile v **entice**, lure, charm, captivate, mesmerize, hypnotize, fascinate, enthrall, put under a spell, appeal to, attract [➡ APPEAL TO AND AROUSE INTEREST; 575]

beguiled adj [➡ PENSIVENESS AND INTEREST; 538]

beguilement n [➡ ATTENTION AND ATTENTIVENESS; 763]

beguiling adj **enticing**, charming, mesmeric, fascinating, captivating, enthralling, appealing, attractive, charismatic, mesmerizing [➡ BEAUTY AND ATTRACTIVENESS; 189]

behave 1 v **act**, perform, conduct yourself, deport yourself, work, run, comport yourself (formal) [➡ CARRY OUT AN ACTION; 269] 2 v **be good**, obey the rules, do the right thing, toe the line, keep out of mischief, mind your p's and q's [➡ OBEY AND ABIDE BY; 301] Opposite: misbehave

behavior n **actions**, deeds, activities, manners, conduct, performance, comportment (formal) [➡ TEMPERAMENT AND BEHAVIOR; 492]

behavioral adj **social**, interactive, behavior, communication, communicative, negotiating, developmental [➡ PSYCHOLOGY AND THE MIND; 769]

behead v **decapitate**, cut off somebody's head, guillotine, execute, put to death, kill [➡ KILL; 923]

behemoth n [➡ BIG THINGS; 1194]

behest (literary) n **request**, order, command, bidding, directive, call [➡ REQUEST AND DEMAND; 663]

behind 1 prep **following**, after, in the wake of, at the back of, at the rear of [➡ RELATIVE LOCATION; 161] 2 adv **at the**

back, at the rear, in the rear, after, following, last [→ RELATIVE LOCATION; 161] *Opposite*: in front **3** *adj* **behindhand**, late, overdue, behind schedule, in arrears [→ PROMPTNESS: LATE; 100] *Opposite*: ahead of time

behind closed doors *adv* **privately**, in private, in secret, secretly, confidentially, in secrecy [→ SECRET AND UNKNOWN; 179] *Opposite*: openly

behindhand *adj* **late**, behind, behind schedule, overdue, slow, in arrears [→ PROMPTNESS: LATE; 100] *Opposite*: early

behind schedule *adj* **behind**, late, slow, delayed, overdue, behindhand [→ PROMPTNESS: LATE; 100] *Opposite*: early

behind the scenes *adv* **out of sight**, surreptitiously, unobtrusively, unnoticed, in the background, quietly [→ SECRET AND UNKNOWN; 179] *Opposite*: openly

behind the times *adj* **old-fashioned**, dated, unfashionable, out-of-date, outmoded, old, outdated, old hat (*informal*) [→ OLD, OLD-FASHIONED; 167]

behind your back *adv* **without your knowledge**, furtively, surreptitiously, on the sly, slyly, secretively, sneakily [→ SECRET AND UNKNOWN; 179] *Opposite*: openly

behold (*archaic or literary*) *v* **look at**, look on, see, observe, witness, feast your eyes on [→ SEE; 699]

beholden *adj* **obliged**, grateful, in somebody's debt, indebted, obligated, bound [→ RELATIONSHIP TO ANOTHER; 973]

behoove (*formal*) *v* **be somebody's duty**, be somebody's bounden duty, fall to somebody, befit, be appropriate for, be fitting for, be incumbent upon somebody (*formal*) [→ APPROPRIATE, SUITABLE, AND ADVISABLE; 184]

beige *type of color* [→ COLORS; 1224]

beige

♦ *types of beige*
buff, butterscotch, café au lait, camel, coffee, dun, ecru, fawn, flesh color, honey, oatmeal

be in charge of *v* **control**, run, manage, head, lead, direct, operate, oversee, supervise, preside [→ BE IN CHARGE; 270]

be in contact with *v* **be in touch with**, communicate, have dealings with, correspond, interact with, touch base with [→ INITIATE AND ESTABLISH COMMUNICATION; 680] *Opposite*: ignore

being **1** *n* **existence**, life, actuality, presence, animation [→ THE STAGES OF LIFE; 916] *Opposite*: nothingness **2** *n* **self**, soul, mind, essence, spirit, core, heart, nature, personality, consciousness [→ PSYCHOLOGY AND THE MIND; 769] **3** *n* **life form**, organism, creature, living being, human being, person, individual, mortal [→ LIVING THINGS AND LIVING; 976]

belabor **1** *v* **overstate**, labor, stress, overemphasize, overdo, hammer home, harp on [→ CLAIM, INSIST, AND EMPHASIZE; 614] **2** *v* (*literary or humorous*) **beat**, hit, thrash, whip, cudgel, bludgeon [→ PHYSICAL ATTACK AND PUNISHMENT; 415]

belated *adj* **late**, delayed, postponed, deferred, tardy, overdue [→ PROMPTNESS: LATE; 100] *Opposite*: timely

belatedness *n* [→ PROMPTNESS: LATE; 100]

belch **1** *v* **bring up wind**, burp, hiccup, gulp, eruct, posset (*UK*) [→ VOMIT AND BELCH; 712] **2** *n* **burp**, hiccup, eructation [→ VOMIT AND BELCH; 712]

beleaguer **1** *v* **harass**, annoy, pester, plague, badger, hound, vex, worry, stress, hassle (*informal*) [→ UPSET, DISTRESS, AND HUMILIATE; 567] **2** *v* **besiege**, surround, lay siege to, threaten, menace [→ EXIST IN CLOSE PROXIMITY; 21]

beleaguered *adj* **stressed**, under pressure, harassed, fraught, careworn, struggling, besieged, under attack, long-suffering [→ SADNESS, DISTRESS, AND DESPAIR; 539] *Opposite*: carefree

belfry *n* **bell tower**, campanile, tower, spire, steeple [→ TOWERS; 1099]

belie *v* **contradict**, disprove, give the lie to, call into question, deny, oppose [→ DISHARMONY; 156] *Opposite*: confirm

belief **1** *n* **confidence**, trust, certainty, credence, acceptance [→ CERTAINTY; 561] *Opposite*: distrust **2** *n* **faith**, conviction, principle, creed, idea [→ POINTS OF VIEW; 767]

belief system *n* [→ POINTS OF VIEW; 767]

believability *n* **credibility**, plausibility, acceptability, trustworthiness, authenticity [→ TRUE AND REAL; 171]

believable *adj* **credible**, authentic, realistic, plausible, convincing, acceptable, true to life [→ POSSIBLE AND PROBABLE; 177] *Opposite*: unbelievable

believe **1** *v* **trust**, have faith in, be certain of, have confidence in, accept as true, rely on [→ CERTAINTY; 561] *Opposite*: disbelieve **2** *v* **consider**, think, suppose, judge, imagine, deem (*formal*) [→ HAVE AN OPINION OF SOMETHING; 756] *Opposite*: doubt

believer *n* **supporter**, advocate, fan, devotee, follower, disciple [→ RELIGIOUS PEOPLE; 778] *Opposite*: skeptic

belittle *v* **disparage**, demean, decry, deride, depreciate, put down (*informal*) [→ UPSET, DISTRESS, AND HUMILIATE; 567] *Opposite*: praise

belittlement *n* **depreciation**, disparagement, playing down, marginalization, disdain [→ INSULTS, ABUSE, AND SWEARING; 658] *Opposite*: praise

belittling *adj* **demeaning**, disparaging, depreciating, condescending, patronizing, sneering, derisive [→ MOCKING AND DISMISSIVE; 636] *Opposite*: supportive

bell **1** *n* **hand bell**, church bell, ship's bell, sleigh bell, school bell, alarm bell [→ SIGNALING; 1140] **2** *n* **buzzer**, doorbell, chime, alarm, alarm bell [→ SIGNALING; 1140]

bell-bottom pants *type of pants* [→ GARMENTS AND OUTFITS; 865]

bellicose *adj* **belligerent**, aggressive, warlike, pugnacious, combative, confrontational, argumentative, quarrelsome [→ AGGRESSIVE AND BELLIGERENT; 518] *Opposite*: compliant

bellicosity *n* [→ AGGRESSIVE AND BELLIGERENT; 518]

belligerence *n* **hostility**, pugnaciousness, bellicosity, warlike nature, aggression, ferociousness, violence, antagonism, argumentativeness, belligerency [→ AGGRESSIVE AND BELLIGERENT; 518]

belligerency *see* **belligerence**

belligerent *adj* **aggressive**, argumentative, quarrelsome, confrontational, pugnacious, spoiling for a fight [➡ AGGRESSIVE AND BELLIGERENT; 518] *Opposite:* cooperative

bellow 1 *n* **roar**, shout, yell, bawl, holler (*informal*) [➡ SOUNDS MADE BY PEOPLE; 1262] *Opposite:* whisper 2 *v* **shout**, roar, yell, bawl, thunder, holler (*informal*) [➡ GIVING VENT TO EMOTIONS; 679] *Opposite:* whisper

bellows *type of* **general tool** [➡ HAND TOOLS; 1119]

bell-shaped *adj* [➡ ROUNDED SHAPE; 1218]

bell tower *n* [➡ TOWERS; 1099]

belly *n* (*informal*) **stomach**, abdomen, middle, tummy (*informal*), gut (*slang*) [➡ PARTS OF THE BODY: TORSO; 693]

bellyache (*informal*) 1 *n* **upset stomach**, stomach ache, stomach pains, tummy ache (*informal*) [➡ DISORDERS OF THE DIGESTIVE SYSTEM; 713] 2 *n* **complaint**, grumble, moan (*informal*), grouse (*informal*), gripe (*informal*), beef (*slang*) [➡ COMPLAIN AND NAG; 686] 3 *v* **complain**, grumble, carp, whine, moan (*informal*), grouse (*informal*), gripe (*informal*), beef (*slang*) [➡ COMPLAIN AND NAG; 686]

bellybutton (*informal*) *n* **navel**, umbilicus [➡ PARTS OF THE BODY: TORSO; 693]

belly dance *type of* **dance** [➡ DANCE; 903]

belly flop *n* **fall**, flop, crash, dive [➡ FAILURE; 77]

belly laugh *n* **guffaw**, laugh, chortle, horselaugh, hoot, cry of mirth [➡ LAUGHTER; 649]

belong *v* **fit in**, fit, go, have its place, be in the right place, feel right, be appropriate [➡ HARMONY; 155]

belongings *n* **possessions**, property, things, stuff, luggage, baggage, personal effects, bits and pieces (*informal*), effects (*formal*) [➡ POSSESSIONS; 461]

beloved *adj* **much-loved**, dearly loved, adored, favorite, darling, treasured, dear, cherished [➡ POPULAR AND WANTED; 220] *Opposite:* despised

below 1 *prep* **less than**, under, beneath, not more than [➡ LESS; 126] 2 *adv* **underneath**, under, beneath, lower, inferior to [➡ INFERIORITY; 153] *Opposite:* above 3 *adv* **under**, underneath, beneath, lower than, further down [➡ RELATIVE LOCATION; 161] *Opposite:* above

below average *adj* [➡ INAPPROPRIATE AND UNSUITABLE; 224]

below par *adj* **unsatisfactory**, unacceptable, second-rate, poor, disappointing, inadequate, not up to scratch (*informal*) [➡ ORDINARINESS; 244] *Opposite:* satisfactory

below standard *adj* [➡ INAPPROPRIATE AND UNSUITABLE; 224]

belt 1 *type of* **accessory** [➡ ACCESSORIES, MILLINERY, AND LINGERIE; 867] 2 *n* **girdle**, tie, sash, cummerbund, strap, drawstring, binding, restraint [➡ FASTENERS, LINKS, AND NETWORKS; 1247] 3 *n* **band**, ring, strip, ribbon, line, stretch, stripe [➡ AMOUNTS OF SOLID OR SEMISOLID; 115] 4 *v* **fasten**, buckle, secure, attach, belt up [➡ FASTEN, LINK, AND JOIN; 408] *Opposite:* undo 5 *v* (*informal*) **hit**, thump, thrash, beat, strike, smash, smack, punch [➡ PHYSICAL ATTACK AND PUNISHMENT; 415] 6 *v* (*informal*) **dash**, rush, speed, hurry, race [➡ MOVE FAST; 313] *Opposite:* dawdle

belt up *v* **fasten your belt**, secure your belt, put on your belt, buckle up [➡ FASTEN, LINK, AND JOIN; 408]

beltway *type of* **highway** [➡ ROADS; 1106]

bemoan *v* **lament**, regret, mourn, complain, grumble, moan (*informal*), bewail (*formal*) [➡ COMPLAIN AND NAG; 686] *Opposite:* applaud

bemuse *v* **confuse**, daze, puzzle, perplex, stun, mystify, bewilder, baffle [➡ CONFUSE AND BEWILDER; 571]

bemused *adj* **confused**, dazed, puzzled, perplexed, mystified, bewildered, baffled [➡ CONFUSION, ANXIETY, AND WORRY; 540] *Opposite:* clear-headed

bemusement *n* [➡ CONFUSION, ANXIETY, AND WORRY; 540]

bemusing *adj* [➡ DIFFICULTY AND COMPLEXITY; 242]

bench 1 *n* **seat**, pew, stall, bleacher, form (*UK*) [➡ FURNITURE; 858] 2 *n* **worktable**, counter, work surface, worktop, workbench [➡ FURNITURE; 858]

benchmark *n* **standard**, yardstick, level, target, point of reference [➡ PERFECT EXAMPLES AND EMBODIMENTS; 67]

bend 1 *n* **curve**, turn, crook, twist, curvature, bow, corner [➡ ROUNDED SHAPE; 1218] 2 *v* **turn**, bow, twist, crook, change direction, bear [➡ CHANGE OF SHAPE; 385] *Opposite:* straighten 3 *v* **stoop**, bow, bend over, lean down, lean over, incline your body [➡ ASSUME A POSITION; 317] *Opposite:* straighten up

bendability *n* [➡ MALLEABLE AND ELASTIC; 1212]

bendable *adj* **flexible**, pliant, pliable, malleable, plastic, supple, bendy (*UK*) [➡ MALLEABLE AND ELASTIC; 1212] *Opposite:* inflexible

bendiness *n* [➡ MALLEABLE AND ELASTIC; 1212]

bend over backward *v* **do all you can**, put yourself out, pull out all the stops, do your utmost, go all out, make a supreme effort, give your all, try your best [➡ HARD WORK OR EFFORT; 298]

bendy (*UK*) *adj* **flexible**, malleable, plastic, supple, bendable [➡ MALLEABLE AND ELASTIC; 1212] *Opposite:* stiff

beneath 1 *prep* **under**, underneath, below, lower than, less than [➡ RELATIVE LOCATION; 161] *Opposite:* over 2 *adv* **underneath**, under, below, lower, less [➡ RELATIVE LOCATION; 161] *Opposite:* above

benediction *n* **approval**, sanction, blessing [➡ SOURCE OF HAPPINESS, PLEASURE, OR IMPROVEMENT; 209] *Opposite:* malediction (*formal*)

benefactor *n* **sponsor**, patron, supporter, backer [➡ REPRESENTATIVES AND PATRONS; 968]

beneficence *n* **generosity**, charity, benevolence, bigheartedness, magnanimity, kindness, goodness [➡ GENEROSITY AND KINDNESS; 495] *Opposite:* parsimony

beneficent 1 *adj* **charitable**, altruistic, generous, benevolent, humanitarian, philanthropic [➡ GENEROSITY AND KINDNESS; 495] *Opposite:* self-seeking 2 *adj* **beneficial**, helpful, useful, advantageous, favorable, valuable [➡ USEFULNESS; 199] *Opposite:* deleterious

beneficial *adj* **helpful**, useful, valuable, advantageous, positive, favorable, of assistance, of use, constructive, beneficent [➠USEFULNESS; 199] *Opposite*: detrimental

beneficiary *n* **recipient**, receiver, heir, payee, legatee [➠OWNERS; 446] *Opposite*: benefactor

benefit 1 *n* **advantage**, profit, help, assistance, use, value [➠SOURCE OF HAPPINESS, PLEASURE, OR IMPROVEMENT; 209] *Opposite*: detriment 2 *n* **subsidy**, allowance, payment, grant [➠SOCIAL WELFARE; 812] 3 *n* **fundraiser**, charity performance, charity event [➠PARTIES, DANCES, AND CELEBRATIONS; 37] 4 *v* **help**, promote, profit, do good to, advance, further, aid [➠IMPROVE SOMETHING; 374] *Opposite*: harm

benefit from *v* **profit from**, enjoy, use, gain from, take advantage of [➠GET; 420]

benevolence *n* **kindness**, compassion, generosity, munificence, goodwill, altruism, magnanimity [➠KIND ACTIONS OR BEHAVIOR; 295] *Opposite*: malevolence

benevolent *adj* **kind**, caring, compassionate, generous, giving, kindly, benign, munificent, altruistic [➠GENEROSITY AND KINDNESS; 495] *Opposite*: malevolent

benighted *adj* **ignorant**, unenlightened, unfortunate, disadvantaged [➠NEGATIVE INTELLECTUAL CHARACTERISTICS; 525] *Opposite*: enlightened

benign *adj* **kind**, benevolent, caring, kindly, gentle, nonthreatening, compassionate [➠GENEROSITY AND KINDNESS; 495] *Opposite*: malignant

benignity *n* **kindliness**, gentleness, benevolence, compassion, warm-heartedness [➠GENEROSITY AND KINDNESS; 495] *Opposite*: malice

be no more *v* **cease to exist**, disappear, die off, die out, peter out, vanish, become extinct, fade away [➠CEASE TO EXIST; 22] *Opposite*: come into being

bent 1 *adj* **twisted**, curved, bowed, crooked, turned [➠ROUNDED SHAPE; 1218] *Opposite*: straight 2 *adj* **determined**, set, fixed, resolved, decided, focused [➠DESIRE AND WANT; 579] 3 *n* **inclination**, gift, talent, flair [➠SKILLS, TALENTS, AND ABILITIES; 526]

See Compare and Contrast at **talent**.

be on course *v* **be set to**, be heading for, be on target for, be on track, be on the right track, be on route to, be headed for, be in line for [➠ABOUT TO HAPPEN; 33]

be partial to *v* **favor**, like, prefer, be biased toward, have a soft spot for [➠LIKE, LOVE, VALUE, AND ENJOY; 578] *Opposite*: disfavor (*formal*)

bequeath *v* **leave**, give, donate, hand down, will, hand on, bestow (*formal*), confer on (*formal*) [➠BEQUEATH AND BEQUESTS; 432]

bequest *n* **inheritance**, legacy, gift, donation, settlement, endowment [➠BEQUEATH AND BEQUESTS; 432]

berate *v* **rebuke**, shout at, harangue, criticize, scold, reprimand, tell off (*informal*) [➠ACCUSE, BLAME, AND CRITICIZE; 641] *Opposite*: praise

bereaved *adj* **mourning**, bereft, in mourning, grieving, orphaned, widowed [➠DEATH AND BEREAVEMENT; 927]

bereavement *n* **loss**, grief, sorrow, mourning [➠DEATH AND BEREAVEMENT; 927]

bereft 1 *adj* **bereaved**, mourning, in mourning, grieving, orphaned, widowed [➠DEATH AND BEREAVEMENT; 927] 2 *adj* **empty**, starved, devoid, deprived, stripped, without, lacking [➠LACK OF POSSESSION; 445]

beret *type of* **headgear** [➠ACCESSORIES, MILLINERY, AND LINGERIE; 867]

Bermuda shorts *type of* **pants** [➠GARMENTS AND OUTFITS; 865]

berry *n* [➠PARTS OF TREES AND PLANTS; 1026]

---

berry

◆ *types of berries*

bilberry, blackberry, black currant, blueberry, boysenberry, cranberry, currant, elderberry, gooseberry, huckleberry, juniper, loganberry, mulberry, raspberry, red currant, rowan, whortleberry

---

berserk *adj* **irrational**, mad, out of control, wild, off the deep end, bananas (*informal*), off your rocker (*informal*), crazy (*informal*), out to lunch (*slang*), around the bend (*slang*), nuts (*slang*) [➠ECCENTRICITY AND IRRATIONALITY; 562] *Opposite*: rational

berth 1 *type of* **bed** [➠FURNITURE; 858] 2 *n* **mooring**, dock, landing place, mooring place, wharf, quay [➠WATERWAYS AND SEAWAYS; 1108] 3 *v* **dock**, moor, tie up, come in, land, disembark [➠ARRIVE BY TRANSPORT; 14] *Opposite*: put out

beryl *type of* **gemstone** [➠PRECIOUS STONES; 1278]

beseech (*literary*) *v* **beg**, request, ask, entreat, plead, press, demand, implore (*formal*) [➠REQUEST AND DEMAND; 663]

beseeching (*literary*) *adj* **pleading**, begging, earnest, persuasive, imploring (*formal*), suppliant (*formal*), supplicatory (*formal*) [➠REQUEST AND DEMAND; 663] *Opposite*: diffident

beset 1 *adj* **plagued**, tormented, overwhelmed, overcome, harassed, surrounded, affected, full of [➠CONFUSION, ANXIETY, AND WORRY; 540] *Opposite*: free 2 *v* **harass**, annoy, hamper, trouble, overwhelm, affect, weigh down, assail [➠HAPPEN TO SOMEBODY; 30] *Opposite*: support 3 *v* (*formal*) **surround**, attack, overcome, overwhelm, assail, harass, hamper [➠UPSET, DISTRESS, AND HUMILIATE; 567]

beside *prep* **next to**, at the side of, alongside, by, near, nearby, close, adjacent, adjoining, contiguous (*formal*) [➠RELATIVE LOCATION; 161]

besides 1 *adv* **as well**, in addition, also, above and beyond, too [➠ALSO; 138] 2 *adv* **moreover**, what's more, further, more to the point, anyway, furthermore [➠EXPRESSIONS INTRODUCING EXTRA INFORMATION; 139]

beside the point *adj* **irrelevant**, unimportant, superfluous, immaterial, extraneous, inconsequential, insignificant, of no consequence [➠UNIMPORTANT AND UNNECESSARY; 238] *Opposite*: central

beside yourself 1 *adj* **upset**, distressed, frantic, worried sick, distraught, hysterical, excited, agitated, in a state (*informal*) [➠SADNESS, DISTRESS, AND DESPAIR; 539] *Opposite*: composed 2 *adj* **angry**, furious, enraged, wild, livid, ranting, raving [➠IRRITATION AND ANGER; 541] *Opposite*: calm

besiege *v* **surround**, siege, lay siege to, encircle, blockade, beleaguer, overwhelm [➡ EXIST IN CLOSE PROXIMITY; 21] *Opposite*: defend

besieged *adj* **overwhelmed**, inundated, beleaguered, weighed down, plagued, snowed under, beset [➡ SADNESS, DISTRESS, AND DESPAIR; 539]

besmear *v* [➡ DIRTY AND CONTAMINATE; 404]

besmirch *v* **sully**, defame, tarnish, damage, slander, drag in the mud [➡ ACCUSE, BLAME, AND CRITICIZE; 641] *Opposite*: praise

besmirched *adj* [➡ DIRTY; 1235]

besotted *adj* **infatuated**, love-struck, head over heels in love, fanatical, obsessed, smitten (*humorous or literary*) [➡ APPRECIATION AND GRATITUDE; 535] *Opposite*: repelled

bespatter *v* [➡ DIRTY AND CONTAMINATE; 404]

bespeak *v* **signify**, signal, indicate, convey, reveal, show, suggest, imply [➡ MEAN SOMETHING; 61]

be spoiling for *v* **look for**, expect, anticipate, itch for, be bent on, be out for [➡ DESIRE AND WANT; 579]

bespoke (*UK*) *adj* **custom-made**, tailor-made, made to measure, customized, custom-built, commissioned, tailored [➡ DESCRIBING CLOTHES; 869] *Opposite*: ready-to-wear

best 1 *adj* **top**, finest, greatest, unsurpassed, paramount, preeminent, superlative, Grade A, first class [➡ GOOD, WELL, BETTER; 183] *Opposite*: worst **2** *v* **outdo**, overcome, top, surpass, defeat [➡ BEAT AND DEFEAT; 80]

best bib and tucker (*informal*) *n* [➡ GARMENTS AND OUTFITS; 865]

best-case scenario *n* [➡ SITUATIONS; 71]

best clothes (*UK*) *n* [➡ GARMENTS AND OUTFITS; 865]

best friend *n* [➡ FRIENDS AND GUESTS; 963]

bestial *adj* **inhuman**, foul, degrading, cruel, brutish, base, boorish, sordid, repulsive [➡ MORALLY BAD OR IMPROPER; 775] *Opposite*: humane

bestiality *n* **cruelty**, inhumanity, savagery, brutality, depravity, wickedness [➡ MORALLY BAD OR IMPROPER; 775] *Opposite*: humanity

bestir yourself (*formal*) *v* **motivate yourself**, stir yourself, busy yourself, rouse yourself, get going, get off your backside (*informal*), be up and doing (*UK*) [➡ START AN ACTION; 260]

best man *n* **attendant**, groomsman, supporter [➡ SUPPORTERS, PROTECTORS, AND COMPATRIOTS; 970]

best mate (*UK*) *n* [➡ FRIENDS AND GUESTS; 963]

bestow (*formal*) *v* **give**, bequeath, donate, grant, present, impart, confer (*formal*) [➡ GIVE AND PROVIDE; 430] *Opposite*: withdraw

See Compare and Contrast at **give**.

bestride *v* **straddle**, span, sit astride, stand astride, be astride [➡ ASSUME A POSITION; 317]

bestseller *n* **record breaker**, hit, smash, success, winner,

moneymaker, runaway success, roaring success, big hit, smash hit, chart-topper, blockbuster (*informal*) [➡ ADVANTAGES; 212] *Opposite*: flop (*informal*)

bestselling *adj* **successful**, popular, blockbusting, hit, chart-topping, record-breaking, top [➡ SUCCESSFUL AND PROMISING; 81]

best togs (*informal*) *n* [➡ GARMENTS AND OUTFITS; 865]

be sure of *v* **count on**, depend on, rely on, depend upon, trust, rely upon, have confidence in, be certain about [➡ LIKE, LOVE, VALUE, AND ENJOY; 578] *Opposite*: doubt

bet 1 *v* **gamble**, stake, wager, put money on, lay a wager, ante, back, risk, play [➡ GAMBLE AND TAKE RISKS; 466] **2** *v* (*informal*) **think**, expect, anticipate, consider, believe, suppose [➡ PREDICT AND ANTICIPATE; 750] **3** *n* **wager**, ante, gamble, stake, play [➡ GAMBLE AND TAKE RISKS; 466] **4** *n* **option**, alternative, candidate, choice, plan [➡ MAKE DECISIONS AND CHOICES; 752]

bete noire (*literary*) *n* [➡ PROBLEMS; 256]

be that as it may *adv* **nevertheless**, nonetheless, despite that, even so, just the same, all the same, at the same time [➡ ALTHOUGH, NEVERTHELESS, AND DESPITE; 169]

be there *v* **be present**, be in attendance, go, turn up, stay, remain, attend [➡ EXIST IN A PLACE; 19]

be there for *v* **stand by**, support, help, care for, take care of, look after (*UK*) [➡ TAKE CARE OF AND SPOIL; 300] *Opposite*: abandon

be through with *v* **finish**, complete, conclude, do, finish off, wrap up, tie up, finish up [➡ COMPLETE AN ACTION; 263] *Opposite*: start

betoken (*literary*) *v* **represent**, indicate, signify, mean, connote, spell, suggest, presage [➡ REPRESENT SOMETHING OR SOMEBODY; 59]

betray 1 *v* **be disloyal**, give up, hand over, inform on, double cross, let down [➡ BETRAY CONFIDENCES AND GOSSIP; 618] *Opposite*: stand by **2** *v* **disclose**, leak, tell, give away, reveal, let slip, let drop, blab, let the cat out of the bag [➡ BETRAY CONFIDENCES AND GOSSIP; 618]

betrayal *n* **disloyalty**, unfaithfulness, bad faith, duplicity, infidelity, treachery, perfidy (*formal*) [➡ MALICIOUS ACTIONS OR BEHAVIOR; 296] *Opposite*: loyalty

betrothal (*formal*) *n* **engagement**, promise, pact, compact, troth (*archaic*) [➡ CEREMONIES AND ANNIVERSARIES; 38]

betrothed (*formal*) *n* **fiancé**, fiancée, husband-to-be, wife-to-be, girlfriend, boyfriend, intended (*dated or humorous*) [➡ RELATIVES BY MARRIAGE; 960]

better 1 *adj* **improved**, enhanced, superior [➡ GOOD, WELL, BETTER; 183] *Opposite*: worse **2** *adj* **healthier**, improved, well, recovering, in good health, restored, on the mend [➡ HEALING; 730] *Opposite*: worse **3** *v* (*formal*) **improve on**, top, outdo, outstrip, outshine, surpass, exceed [➡ BEAT AND DEFEAT; 80] **4** *v* (*formal*) **enhance**, improve, change for the better, advance, progress, ameliorate (*formal*) [➡ IMPROVE SOMETHING; 374] *Opposite*: worsen

better half *n* [➡ RELATIVES BY MARRIAGE; 960]

betterment (*formal*) *n* **furtherance**, improvement,

advancement, benefit, progress, upward mobility [➡PROGRESS AND ADVANCEMENT; 213] *Opposite*: deterioration

better-off *adj* **rich**, wealthy, affluent, comfortable, prosperous, well-heeled (*informal*) [➡WEALTH AND WEALTHY; 891] *Opposite*: poor

bettong *type of* **marsupial** [➡MARSUPIALS; 992]

between 1 *prep* **flanked by**, sandwiched between, stuck between, amid, among, in the middle of, betwixt (*literary*) [➡RELATIVE LOCATION; 161] 2 *prep* **connecting**, linking, joining, involving, concerning, relating [➡RELATIVE LOCATION; 161]

between a rock and a hard place *adj* [➡IN TROUBLE AND DISADVANTAGED; 73]

between ourselves 1 *adj* **private**, quiet, secret, discreet, hush-hush (*informal*), under wraps (*informal*) [➡SECRET AND UNKNOWN; 179] *Opposite*: public 2 *adv* **between you and me**, entre nous, off the record, confidentially, privately [➡EXPRESSIONS OF OPINION; 623]

between you and me *adv* [➡EXPRESSIONS OF OPINION; 623]

between you, me, and the bedpost *adv* [➡EXPRESSIONS OF OPINION; 623]

beveled *adj* **slanting**, oblique, chamfered, bias-cut, sloping, ground [➡ORIENTATION AND ALIGNMENT; 1223]

beverage (*formal*) *n* **drink**, hot drink, cold drink, liquid refreshment, brew (*informal*), pick-me-up (*informal*) [➡DRINKS; 1187]

bevy 1 *type of* **flock** [➡GROUPS OF BIRDS; 1007] 2 *type of* **herd** [➡GROUPS OF ANIMALS; 993]

bewail (*formal*) *v* **lament**, bemoan, complain, regret, grumble, grieve, deplore, moan (*informal*) [➡COMPLAIN AND NAG; 686] *Opposite*: applaud

beware *v* **be careful**, be cautious, be wary, look out, watch out, take heed, think twice [➡PAY ATTENTION; 765]

bewhiskered *adj* [➡FACIAL HAIR; 489]

bewilder *v* **confuse**, puzzle, baffle, perplex, confound, mystify, nonplus, stump, bemuse, daze, disconcert, disorient, bamboozle (*informal*), discombobulate (*informal*) [➡CONFUSE AND BEWILDER; 571]

bewildered *adj* **confused**, puzzled, dazed, bemused, befuddled, taken aback, disconcerted, panicky, baffled, disoriented [➡CONFUSION, ANXIETY, AND WORRY; 540] *Opposite*: clear-headed

bewildering *adj* **confusing**, puzzling, baffling, mystifying, incomprehensible, perplexing, disorienting, disconcerting [➡DIFFICULTY AND COMPLEXITY; 242] *Opposite*: clear

bewilderment *n* **confusion**, incomprehension, bafflement, puzzlement, perplexity, panic, disorientation, discombobulation (*informal*) [➡CONFUSION, ANXIETY, AND WORRY; 540] *Opposite*: clarity

bewitch *v* **enchant**, fascinate, captivate, charm, mesmerise, intrigue, appeal, interest [➡APPEAL TO AND AROUSE INTEREST; 575] *Opposite*: repel

bewitched *adj* [➡APPRECIATION AND GRATITUDE; 535]

bewitching *adj* [➡BEAUTY AND ATTRACTIVENESS; 189]

beyond *prep* **further than**, past, away from, clear of, ahead of, outside [➡RELATIVE LOCATION; 161]

beyond a doubt *adv* [➡CERTAIN; 174]

beyond a shadow of a doubt *adv* [➡CERTAIN; 174]

beyond doubt *adv* [➡CERTAIN; 174]

beyond question *adv* [➡CERTAIN; 174]

beyond repair *adj* [➡IN BAD REPAIR; 1234]

beyond the pale *adj* **unacceptable**, too much, inexcusable, indefensible, unjustifiable, intolerable, excessive, unreasonable, a bit much, over-the-top (*informal*) [➡UNACCEPTABLE AND UNFORGIVABLE; 225] *Opposite*: acceptable

bhangra *type of* **world music** [➡MUSIC, SONGS, AND SINGING; 907]

biannual 1 *adj* **twice-yearly**, twice-a-year, six-monthly, semiannual [➡TIMES OF YEAR; 88] 2 *adj* **every other year**, biennial, two-yearly, regular, periodic [➡TIMES OF YEAR; 88]

bias *n* **prejudice**, partiality, preference, unfairness, favoritism, predisposition, preconception [➡PREJUDICE; 550] *Opposite*: impartiality

bias-cut *adj* [➡DESCRIBING CLOTHES; 869]

biased *adj* **prejudiced**, unfair, partial, influenced, predisposed, subjective, jaundiced [➡THE NATURE OF IDEAS; 771] *Opposite*: unbiased

biathlon *type of* **winter sport** [➡HOBBIES, GAMES, AND SPORTS; 875]

biblical *adj* **scriptural**, holy, bible, sacred, theological, canonical [➡RELIGIOUS CONCEPTS; 776]

bibliography *n* **list**, index, appendix, checklist, catalog, directory, reading list, book list, list of references [➡LISTS AND SCHEDULES; 587]

bibliophile *n* [➡DEVOTEES AND ADDICTED PEOPLE; 556]

bicameral *adj* **two-tier**, two-house, dual, bilateral, bipartite, dualistic [➡STYLES AND SYSTEMS OF GOVERNMENT; 806]

bicentennial *n* **200th anniversary**, 200th birthday, anniversary, bicentenary (*UK*) [➡CEREMONIES AND ANNIVERSARIES; 38]

biceps *type of* **muscle or tendon** [➡THE MUSCLES; 718]

bicker *v* **argue**, dispute, quarrel, debate, squabble, wrangle [➡ARGUE AND FIGHT; 643] *Opposite*: agree

bicoastal *n* [➡TRAVEL: TRAVELERS AND WALKERS; 319]

bicycle *n* **bike** (*informal*), cycle, two-wheeler [➡BIKES, CARS, AND CARRIAGES; 1149]

bicycle lane *n* [➡TRAVEL: TRAFFIC PROBLEMS AND TRAFFIC MANAGEMENT; 323]

bid 1 *v* **tender**, offer, propose, submit, proffer [➡SUGGEST, HINT, AND COMMENT; 612] 2 *v* **try**, attempt, undertake, seek, strive, make a move, endeavor (*formal*) [➡ATTEMPT AN ACTION; 261] 3 *v* (*archaic*) **order**, call on, command, direct, tell, request, enjoin (*formal*) [➡REQUEST AND DEMAND; 663] 4 *n* **offer**, proposal, proposition, tender, submission [➡REQUEST AND DEMAND; 663] 5 *n* **attempt**, try, effort, undertaking, endeavor, move [➡ATTEMPT AN ACTION; 261]

biddable *adj* **compliant**, acquiescent, docile, obedient, amenable, pliant, pliable [➡ THE WILL AND WILLINGNESS; 563] *Opposite*: intractable (*formal*)

bidder *n* **buyer**, auction-goer, collector, dealer, purchaser, customer [➡ BUSINESS PEOPLE; 793]

bidding *n* **request**, command, order, will, call, behest (*literary*) [➡ REQUEST AND DEMAND; 663]

bidet *type of* **plumbing fixtures** [➡ FIXTURES; 859]

bide your time *v* **wait**, be patient, wait and see, play the waiting game, hold back, hold off, twiddle your thumbs, cool your heels (*informal*) [➡ SHIRK AND DELAY; 273]

biennial *adj* **two-yearly**, biannual, regular, periodic [➡ TIMES OF YEAR; 88]

bier *n* **stand**, rest, base, pedestal, table, platform [➡ SUPPORTS AND BASES; 1255]

biff (*informal*) *v* **hit**, punch, thump, knock, clout, wallop (*informal*), clobber (*informal*), belt (*informal*), clock (*slang*) [➡ PHYSICAL ATTACK AND PUNISHMENT; 415]

bifocals *type of* **glasses** [➡ GLASSES AND SPECTACLES; 1125]

bifurcate *v* **divide**, branch, split, fork, diverge, separate [➡ SEPARATE AND DIVIDE; 401] *Opposite*: converge

bifurcation *n* **fork**, junction, split, divergence, branching, division [➡ HOLES, GAPS, AND FORKS; 1252] *Opposite*: convergence

big 1 *adj* **large**, giant, immense, vast, great, gigantic, great big, huge, enormous, full-size, life-size, whopping (*informal*) [➡ LARGE; 1193] *Opposite*: small   2 *adj* **spacious**, capacious, roomy, large, deep [➡ LARGE; 1193] *Opposite*: cramped   3 *adj* **significant**, considerable, substantial, sizable, large, important, good [➡ IMPORTANT; 194] *Opposite*: insignificant   4 *adj* **extensive**, vast, immense, wide, great, broad [➡ WIDTH: WIDE; 1199] *Opposite*: narrow   5 *adj* **older**, elder, grown-up, adult, mature, of age [➡ ADULTHOOD; 918] *Opposite*: little   6 *adj* **bulky**, large, cumbersome, massive, outsize, beefy, brawny, heavy, hulking [➡ LARGE; 1193] *Opposite*: petite   7 *adj* **tall**, high, lofty, towering, soaring [➡ HEIGHT: HIGH; 1203] *Opposite*: short

bigamist *n* **polygamist**, adulterer, lawbreaker, criminal, two-timer (*informal*) [➡ CRIMINALS; 821]

bigamous *adj* **polygamous**, adulterous, criminal, illegal, two-timing (*informal*) [➡ ILLEGAL; 816] *Opposite*: monogamous

bigamy *n* **polygamy**, adultery, two-timing (*informal*) [➡ CRIMES; 817] *Opposite*: monogamy

big band *type of* **band** [➡ MUSICIANS AND SINGERS; 908]

big beat *type of* **dance music** [➡ MUSIC, SONGS, AND SINGING; 907]

big-box store *n type of* **retail outlet** [➡ RETAIL OUTLETS; 1083]

big business *n* **trade**, commerce, industry, business sector, business world, corporate world, private sector [➡ BUSINESS; 791]

big cat *type of* **cat** [➡ FELINES; 983]

big cheese (*slang*) *n* **key player**, VIP, major player, bigwig (*informal*), big shot (*informal*), big gun (*informal*),

---

biggie (*informal*), big wheel (*informal*), honcho (*slang*) [➡ IMPORTANT OR FAMOUS PEOPLE; 893] *Opposite*: nobody

big deal (*informal*) *n* **major concern**, federal case, matter of life and death, serious issue [➡ MOST IMPORTANT THING; 197]

big enchilada (*slang*) *n* [➡ IMPORTANT OR FAMOUS PEOPLE; 893]

Bigfoot *n* [➡ MYTHICAL BEINGS; 789]

biggie 1 *n* (*informal*) **big one**, giant, whopper (*informal*), colossus, monster [➡ BIG THINGS; 1194]   2 *n* (*slang*) **big name**, **big shot** (*informal*), bigwig (*informal*), big wheel (*informal*), big cheese (*slang*), VIP, star, celebrity [➡ IMPORTANT OR FAMOUS PEOPLE; 893] *Opposite*: nobody

big hair (*informal*) *type of* **hairstyle** [➡ HAIRSTYLES AND HAIRPIECES; 488]

bighead (*informal*) *n* **boaster**, bragger, show-off (*informal*), smart aleck (*informal*), know-it-all (*informal*) [➡ SELF-IMPORTANT AND SELF-SEEKING PEOPLE; 949]

bigheaded (*informal*) *adj* **conceited**, egotistical, arrogant, vain, self-centered, pompous, pretentious, immodest, full of yourself, swollen-headed, boastful, high and mighty, cocky (*informal*), too big for your britches (*informal*), too big for your boots (*informal*) [➡ POMPOUS, LOUD, AND OVERCONFIDENT; 635] *Opposite*: modest

big-hearted *adj* **kind**, good-natured, supportive, helpful, kindly, kindhearted, philanthropic, charitable, benevolent, beneficent [➡ GENEROSITY AND KINDNESS; 495] *Opposite*: mean-spirited

bight *n* [➡ THE SEAS, OCEANS, AND SHORES; 1041]

bigmouth (*informal*) 1 *n* **gossip**, gossipmonger, telltale, tattler, blabbermouth (*informal*), loudmouth (*informal*), tattletale (*informal*) [➡ INTERFERING PEOPLE AND TATTLETALES; 950]   2 *n* **boaster**, bragger, braggart, blowhard, know-it-all (*informal*) [➡ SELF-IMPORTANT AND SELF-SEEKING PEOPLE; 949]

big name *n* **famous name**, celebrity, star, superstar, VIP, public figure, somebody [➡ IMPORTANT OR FAMOUS PEOPLE; 893] *Opposite*: unknown

bigot *n* **extremist**, diehard, dogmatist, chauvinist, fanatic, racist [➡ GRUMPY AND NEGATIVE PEOPLE; 953]

bigoted *adj* **prejudiced**, dogmatic, opinionated, intolerant, narrow-minded, chauvinistic, fanatical, biased [➡ NEGATIVE INTELLECTUAL CHARACTERISTICS; 525] *Opposite*: open-minded

bigotry *n* **prejudice**, intolerance, bias, narrow-mindedness, chauvinism, fanaticism, racism [➡ MORALLY BAD OR IMPROPER; 775] *Opposite*: open-mindedness

big shot (*informal*) *n* **key player**, major player, VIP, bigwig (*informal*), big gun (*informal*), biggie (*informal*), big wheel (*informal*), big cheese (*slang*), honcho (*slang*) [➡ IMPORTANT OR FAMOUS PEOPLE; 893] *Opposite*: nobody

big time (*slang*) *adv* **greatly**, a great deal, on a grand scale, in a big way, to a great extent, massively (*informal*) [➡ TO A GREAT EXTENT; 132]

big toe *part of* **leg or foot** [➡ PARTS OF THE BODY: LEG AND FOOT; 694]

big top *n* [➡ BUILDINGS FOR PUBLIC ENTERTAINMENT; 1084]

bigwig (*informal*) *n* **key player**, major player, VIP, big shot (*informal*), big gun (*informal*), biggie (*informal*), big wheel (*informal*), big cheese (*slang*), honcho (*slang*) [➡ IMPORTANT OR FAMOUS PEOPLE; 893] *Opposite*: nobody

bike (*informal*) *n* **bicycle**, cycle, motorbike, motorcycle [➡ BIKES, CARS, AND CARRIAGES; 1149]

---

bike

◆ *types of bikes*
boneshaker, dirt bike, exercise bike, moped, motor scooter, mountain bike, racing bike, rickshaw, scooter, scrambler, tandem bicycle, ten-speed, three-wheeler, trail bike, tricycle, two-wheeler, unicycle

◆ *parts of a bike*
brake, chain, crossbar, derailleur, fender, fork, frame, handlebars, pedal, reflector, seat, spoke, tire, wheel

---

bike lane *n* [➡ TRAVEL: TRAFFIC PROBLEMS AND TRAFFIC MANAGEMENT; 323]

biker *n* **motorcyclist**, racer, rider [➡ TRAVEL: TRAVELERS AND WALKERS; 319]

bikini *n* **swimsuit**, two-piece, bathing suit [➡ GARMENTS AND OUTFITS; 865]

bilateral *adj* **two-sided**, two-pronged, joint, mutual, consensual [➡ ACTING WITH OTHERS; 285] *Opposite*: unilateral

bilberry *type of* **berry** [➡ FRUIT AND VEGETABLES; 1176]

bilby *type of* **marsupial** [➡ MARSUPIALS; 992]

bile (*literary*) *n* **bitterness**, irritability, vitriol, spleen, sourness, temper, wrath, anger, ire (*formal*) [➡ IRRITATION AND ANGER; 541] *Opposite*: sweetness

bile duct *part of* **digestive tract** [➡ THE DIGESTIVE TRACT; 709]

bilge 1 *n* **hull**, keel, base, bottom [➡ PARTS OF A SHIP OR BOAT; 1151] **2** *n* **hold**, interior, recesses, bowels, bottom [➡ PARTS OF A SHIP OR BOAT; 1151] **3** *n* **sludge**, mud, bilge water, silt, effluent, swill, sewage [➡ UNPLEASANT, DIRTY, AND TOXIC SUBSTANCES; 1268] **4** *n* (*informal*) **nonsense**, garbage, rubbish, trash, drivel, balderdash, twaddle (*informal*), bunkum (*informal*), claptrap (*informal*) [➡ MEANINGLESS SPEECH OR WRITING; 676]

bilingual *adj* **fluent**, multilingual, polyglot [➡ ASPECTS OF LANGUAGE; 682]

bilious *adj* **nauseous**, sickly, queasy, sick, ill, unwell, not a hundred percent, under the weather, green around the gills (*informal*), ailing (*dated*) [➡ ILL AND SICK; 740]

bilk (*informal*) *v* **cheat**, trick, deceive, con, swindle, defraud, take advantage of, dupe, bamboozle (*informal*) [➡ DECEPTION AND LIES; 660]

bill 1 *n* **invoice**, statement, demand, check, receipt, tab (*informal*), damage (*informal*) [➡ RECEIPTS AND INVOICES; 591] **2** *n* **amount**, total, sum, fee, price, debt [➡ EXPENDITURE; 423] **3** *n* **proposal**, measure, document, petition, proposition [➡ OFFICIAL DOCUMENTS; 586] **4** *n* **poster**, flyer, notice, advertisement, handbill, placard, leaflet [➡ ADVERTISING AND PUBLICITY; 604] **5** *n* **beak**, mouth, mandible [➡ PARTS OF A BIRD; 1006] **6** *v* **charge**, invoice, debit, send the bill to [➡ SELL; 441] **7** *v* **promote**, portray, publicize, hype, advertise, present, introduce, put forward [➡ ADVERTISING AND PUBLICITY; 604]

billboard *n* **sign**, poster, advertisement, panel, display, hoarding (*UK*) [➡ SIGNPOSTS, SIGNALS, AND BILLBOARDS; 595]

billet 1 *n* **accommodation**, quarters, boarding house, guest house, lodgings (*dated*) [➡ ACCOMMODATIONS; 855] **2** *v* **accommodate**, quarter, house, station, shelter, board, put up [➡ TAKE CARE OF AND SPOIL; 300]

billet-doux (*literary*) *n* **love letter**, letter, missive, note, valentine [➡ LETTERS AND WRITTEN MESSAGES; 584]

billfold *n* **wallet**, pocketbook, purse (*UK*) [➡ CONTAINERS, RECEPTACLES, AND PACKAGING; 1245]

billhook *type of* **cutting tool** [➡ CUTTING TOOLS; 1120]

billiards *type of* **target ball game** [➡ HOBBIES, GAMES, AND SPORTS; 875]

billionaire *n* **multimillionaire**, magnate, tycoon, moneybags (*informal*), fat cat (*slang*) [➡ RICH PEOPLE; 895]

billionth *n* **tiny part**, morsel, particle, modicum, touch, portion, fraction [➡ FEW, LITTLE, SMALL AMOUNT; 120]

billow 1 *v* **catch the wind**, swell, bulge, balloon, fill, mushroom, inflate [➡ CHANGE OF SIZE: BIGGER; 392] *Opposite*: sag **2** *v* **roll upward**, waft, rise, curl, flow [➡ GO UPWARD; 306] *Opposite*: fall **3** *n* **puff**, cloud, swell, swirl, rush, wave, surge [➡ AMOUNTS OF GAS; 116]

billy club *type of* **club** [➡ BLUNT INSTRUMENTS AND WHIPS; 1158]

billy goat *type of* **male animal** [➡ MALE OR FEMALE ANIMALS; 978]

bin 1 *n* **storage bin**, basket, container, silo, holder, box, tub, case, vat [➡ CONTAINERS, RECEPTACLES, AND PACKAGING; 1245] **2** *n* **wastebasket**, wastepaper basket, trash can, garbage can, dustbin, litter bin (*UK*), rubbish bin (*UK*), waste bin (*UK*) [➡ CONTAINERS, RECEPTACLES, AND PACKAGING; 1245] **3** *v* (*UK*) **throw away**, throw out, toss, discard, dispose of, jettison, chuck out (*informal*), ditch (*informal*) [➡ GET RID OF SOMETHING; 451] *Opposite*: keep

binary *adj* **two**, dual, twice, double, twin, twofold, dualistic [➡ MATH; 597]

binary star *n* *type of* **star or star system** [➡ HEAVENLY BODIES; 1061]

bind 1 *v* **attach**, connect, join, combine, unite, tie, fasten, fix, truss, rope [➡ FASTEN, LINK, AND JOIN; 408] *Opposite*: undo **2** *v* **oblige**, force, require, compel, coerce, constrain [➡ CAUSE OR COMPEL TO ACT; 271] **3** *n* **quandary**, tight situation, predicament, dilemma, muddle, impasse, fix (*informal*), hole (*informal*), jam (*informal*), pickle (*informal*) [➡ DIFFICULT SITUATIONS; 72] **4** *n* **nuisance**, drag, bore, annoyance, pain (*informal*), hassle (*informal*) [➡ NUISANCES; 253]

binder 1 *n* **folder**, file, ring binder, looseleaf folder, notebook [➡ CONTAINERS, RECEPTACLES, AND PACKAGING; 1245] **2** *n* **promise**, pledge, vow, obligation, assurance, guarantee, warrant, commitment [➡ PROMISE AND ASSURE; 684]

binding 1 *n* **tie**, band, attachment, fastening, truss [➡ FASTENERS, LINKS, AND NETWORKS; 1247] **2** *n* **edging**, cover, trim, stitching, strip [➡ FASTENERS, LINKS, AND NETWORKS; 1247] **3** *adj* **compulsory**, obligatory, required, necessary, mandatory, requisite (*formal*) [➡ NECESSARY AND ESSENTIAL; 196] *Opposite*: voluntary

bindweed *type of* **weed** [➡ WEEDS AND THISTLES; 1034]

binge 1 *n* **spree**, orgy, tear, rampage, splurge (*informal*), blast (*slang*), bender (*slang*) [➡ EVENTS AND OCCURRENCES; 35] **2** *v* **overdo**, indulge, overindulge, gorge, pig out (*informal*), splurge (*informal*), go on a bender (*slang*) [➡OVERDO SOMETHING; 290]

bingo *n* [➡HOBBIES, GAMES, AND SPORTS; 875]

binoculars *n* **opera glasses**, field glasses, eyeglasses (*formal*) [➡OPTICAL INSTRUMENTS; 1124]

biochemical *adj* **chemical**, biological, living, organic, natural [➡BIOLOGICAL SCIENCES; 1037]

biochemistry *type of* **bioscience** [➡BIOLOGICAL SCIENCES; 1037]

biodegradable *adj* **recyclable**, decomposable, ecological, environmental, green, ecofriendly [➡ECONOMICAL AND RESOURCEFUL; 207]

biogas *n* [➡GASES; 1275]

biographer *n* **writer**, author, autobiographer, historian, profiler, researcher [➡WRITERS AND STYLES; 914]

biographical *adj* **factual**, nonfiction, true, fact-based, realistic, authentic, historical, real [➡TRUE AND REAL; 171]

biography *n* **life story**, life history, profile, memoir, life, account, autobiography [➡ANALYTICAL NONFICTION WRITING; 592]

biological 1 *adj* **organic**, life, living, natural, biotic [➡BIOLOGICAL SCIENCES; 1037] 2 *adj* **natal**, birth, natural, genetic, true [➡THE FAMILY; 956] *Opposite:* adoptive

biological parent *n* [➡OLDER GENERATION RELATIVES; 959]

biologist [➡BIOLOGICAL SCIENCES; 1037]

biology *type of* **bioscience** [➡BIOLOGICAL SCIENCES; 1037]

biomedicine *n type of* **bioscience** [➡BIOLOGICAL SCIENCES; 1037]

bionic *adj* **electronic**, automatic, robotic, semirobotic, electromechanical [➡MACHINERY; 1114]

biophysics *n type of* **bioscience** [➡BIOLOGICAL SCIENCES; 1037]

biopic *n* **film**, movie, biography, documentary, life story, life history, life [➡FILM; 901]

biopsy *n* **cell removal**, operation, surgery, culture, tissue removal [➡REMEDIES, TREATMENTS, AND OPERATIONS; 731]

biorhythm *n* **cycle**, change, cyclical change, rhythm [➡CHANGE; 372]

biosatellite *type of* **spacecraft** [➡SPACE VEHICLES; 1063]

bioscience

◆ *types of biosciences*
anatomy, bacteriology, biochemistry, biology, biomedicine, biophysics, biotechnology, botany, ecology, genetics, microbiology, molecular biology, physiology, zoology

biosphere *n* **environment**, planet, earth, land, sea, atmosphere [➡NATURE AND THE ENVIRONMENT; 1038]

biotechnology *n type of* **bioscience** [➡BIOLOGICAL SCIENCES; 1037]

bipartisan *adj* **two-party**, dual-party, cross-party, joint, combined, bilateral, bipartite [➡ACTING WITH OTHERS; 285]

bipartite *adj* **two-part**, divided, split, mutual, shared, in common, common [➡APPORTIONMENT; 113]

biped *n* **two-legged animal**, human, primate, humanoid [➡LIVING THINGS AND LIVING; 976]

biplane *type of* **civil aircraft** [➡AIRCRAFT; 1148]

birch 1 *type of* **deciduous tree** [➡DECIDUOUS TREES; 1028] 2 *n* **cane**, rod, stick, switch, whip [➡BLUNT INSTRUMENTS AND WHIPS; 1158] 3 *v* **whip**, flog, punish, strike, thrash, lash, flay, beat, wallop (*informal*) [➡WHIP AND CLUB; 417]

bird *n* [➡LIVING THINGS AND LIVING; 976]

bird

◆ *types of common birds*
blue jay, bluebird, camp robber, cardinal, chickadee, finch, flycatcher, gorsbeak, grackle, hummingbird, mockingbird, mourning dove, nuthatch, pigeon, robin, sparrow, starling, swallow, swift, tanager, thrush, tufted titmouse, vireo, warbler, woodpecker, wren

◆ *types of flightless birds*
dodo, emu, kiwi, ostrich, peacock, penguin

◆ *types of freshwater birds*
barnacle goose, bittern, Canada goose, canvasback, coot, crane, duck, egret, flamingo, grebe, heron, ibis, kingfisher, loon, mallard, merganser, moorhen, snipe, spoonbill, stork, swan, teal

◆ *types of pet birds*
budgerigar, canary, cockatoo, homing pigeon, lovebird, macaw, mynah, parakeet, parrot

◆ *types of scavengers*
buzzard, condor, crow, jackdaw, lammergeier, magpie, marabou, raven, rook, vulture

◆ *types of sea birds*
albatross, auk, avocet, cormorant, flamingo, fulmar, gannet, guillemot, gull, kittiwake, osprey, oystercatcher, pelican, plover, puffin, seagull, shag, shearwater, skua, storm petrel, tern, wader

◆ *types of songbirds*
bluebird, flycatcher, hedge sparrow, lark, linnet, meadowlark, nightingale, nightjar, oriole, pied wagtail, pipit, skylark, thrush, titmouse, wagtail, warbler, weaverbird, woodlark, yellowhammer

◆ *parts of a bird*
beak, bill, breast, carina, cockscomb, comb, crest, crop, down, feather, gizzard, gorge, plumage, plume, quill, ruff, tail, talon, web, wing, wingtip, wishbone

birdbath *n* **basin**, bowl, receptacle [➡CONTAINERS, RECEPTACLES, AND PACKAGING; 1245]

birdbrained (*informal*) *adj* **silly**, foolish, stupid, dopey, asinine, witless, scatterbrained [➡NEGATIVE INTELLECTUAL CHARACTERISTICS; 525] *Opposite:* sensible

birdcage *n* **cage**, coop, pen, aviary, enclosure, henhouse, pigeon loft (*UK*) [➡ANIMAL OR BIRD ACCOMMODATIONS; 1079]

birdlike *adj* **dainty**, petite, small-boned, delicate, slight [➡BUILD; 477] *Opposite:* heavyset

bird of passage *n* [➡NOMADIC AND ROOTLESS LIFESTYLES; 884]

bird of prey *n* [➥ LIVING THINGS AND LIVING; 976]

bird of prey

◆ *types of birds of prey*
bald eagle, buteo, caracara, eagle, falcon, golden eagle, hawk, kestrel, kite, osprey, owl, peregrine falcon, sea eagle, sparrow hawk

birdseed *n* **seed**, grain, mixture, feed, chicken feed [➥ ANIMAL FEED; 1168]

birdsong *n* **call**, cry, song, trill, whistle, piping, tweet [➥ SOUNDS MADE BY BIRDS; 1263]

birdwatcher *n* **ornithologist**, bird lover, birder, twitcher (*UK*) [➥ PEOPLE IN SPORTS AND LEISURE; 876]

biretta *type of* **headgear** [➥ ACCESSORIES, MILLINERY, AND LINGERIE; 867]

Birman *type of* **cat** [➥ FELINES; 983]

birr *type of* **currency** [➥ CURRENCIES; 798]

birth **1** *n* **delivery**, labor, childbirth, nativity, parturition (*formal*), confinement (*dated*) [➥ REPRODUCTION AND HEREDITY; 725] *Opposite*: death **2** *n* **beginning**, origin, dawn, naissance, start, onset, outset, formation, commencement (*formal*), founding (*dated*) [➥ BEGINNINGS; 53] *Opposite*: end **3** *adj* **natal**, natural, true, biological, genetic [➥ REPRODUCTION AND HEREDITY; 725] *Opposite*: adoptive

birthdate *see* **birthday**

birthday *n* **date of birth**, birthdate, anniversary [➥ TIMES OF YEAR; 88]

birthday cake *type of* **cake** [➥ CAKES, COOKIES, AND DESSERTS; 1181]

birthmark *n* **mark**, stain, discoloration, blemish, strawberry mark, nevus, patch, mole [➥ CONDITIONS AFFECTING THE SKIN; 721]

birthplace *n* **origin**, source, home, hometown, place of birth, native land, homeland [➥ BEGINNINGS; 53]

birthright *n* **inheritance**, legacy, bequest, heritage, patrimony, due, entitlement [➥ BEQUEATH AND BEQUESTS; 432]

birth sign *n* **sign of the Zodiac**, astrological sign, star sign [➥ FATE, DESTINY, AND ASTROLOGY; 782]

biscuit *n* [➥ CAKES, COOKIES, AND DESSERTS; 1181]

bise *type of* **wind** [➥ WINDY AND STORMY WEATHER; 1053]

bisect *v* **cut in half**, intersect, divide, cut across, sever, cross, break in two, split, cleave, dissect, part, dichotomize (*formal*) [➥ TEAR, BREAK, AND CUT; 360] *Opposite*: join

bisection *n* **cutting in two**, halving, splitting, dissection, division, parting [➥ SEPARATE AND DIVIDE; 401] *Opposite*: union

bishop *n* [➥ RELIGIOUS PEOPLE; 778]

bishopric *n* [➥ RELIGIOUS CONCEPTS; 776]

bison *type of* **large mammal** [➥ LARGE MAMMALS; 986]

bisque *type of* **soup** [➥ SOUPS; 1186]

bistro *type of* **eating place** [➥ HOTELS, RESTAURANTS, AND CLUBS; 1082]

bit **1** *n* **small piece**, morsel, crumb, fragment, speck, spot,

trace, scrap, drop, tad (*informal*), smidgen (*informal*) [➥ SMALL PIECES; 129] **2** *n* **minute**, while, moment, second, a little while, jiffy (*informal*), jiff (*informal*) [➥ SHORT PERIODS OF TIME; 93] **3** *type of* **computer feature** [➥ COMPUTERS AND COMPUTING; 1127]

bit by bit *adv* **little by little**, a little at a time, slowly, by degrees, gradually, in stages, step by step [➥ HAPPENING SLOWLY; 106] *Opposite*: suddenly

bitch **1** *type of* **female animal** [➥ MALE OR FEMALE ANIMALS; 978] **2** *v* (*slang*) **be spiteful**, be malicious about, be nasty, slander, malign [➥ ACCUSE, BLAME, AND CRITICIZE; 641] **3** *v* (*slang*) **complain**, grumble, carp, gripe (*informal*), moan (*informal*), grouse (*informal*), beef (*slang*), bellyache (*informal*), whine, fuss, squawk (*informal*) [➥ COMPLAIN AND NAG; 686]

bitchily (*slang*) *adv* **maliciously**, unpleasantly, nastily, spitefully, cattily, venomously, shrewishly, cruelly, meanly, hatefully, viciously [➥ RUDE AND HOSTILE; 625] *Opposite*: kindly

bitchiness (*slang*) *n* **maliciousness**, unpleasantness, nastiness, spitefulness, cattiness, venom, shrewishness, hatefulness, meanness, viciousness [➥ AGGRESSIVE AND BELLIGERENT; 518] *Opposite*: kindness

bitchy (*slang*) *adj* **catty**, malicious, unpleasant, cruel, nasty, spiteful, venomous, shrewish, hateful, vicious, mean [➥ BEASTLY AND BRUTISH; 510] *Opposite*: kind

bite **1** *v* **sink your teeth into**, nibble, gnaw, bite off, bite into, masticate, chomp (*informal*) [➥ EAT AND NOT EAT; 710] **2** *v* **wound**, nip, snap, attack, maul, sink your teeth into [➥ PHYSICAL ATTACK AND PUNISHMENT; 415] **3** *v* **hurt**, sting, feel painful, nip, prick, smart [➥ PAIN AND OTHER PHYSICAL SENSATIONS; 733] **4** *n* **taste**, mouthful, nibble, chew, piece, morsel, bit, taster (*UK*) [➥ SMALL PIECES; 129] **5** *n* **wound**, sting, puncture, bite mark [➥ CONDITIONS AFFECTING THE SKIN; 721] **6** *n* **sharp taste**, spiciness, tartness, piquancy, tang, kick, smack [➥ TASTE; 703]

bite off more than you can chew *v* [➥ OVERDO SOMETHING; 290]

bite-sized *adj* **small**, little, minute, tiny, petite, diminutive [➥ SMALL; 1195] *Opposite*: big

bite the bullet *v* **take the bull by the horns**, do it, face up to, go for it (*slang*), grasp the nettle (*UK*) [➥ PREPARE FOR ACTION; 289] *Opposite*: avoid

bite the dust (*informal*) **1** *v* **fall down**, fall flat, take a fall, tumble, tumble down, come clattering down [➥ GO DOWNWARD; 307] **2** *v* **die**, pass away, kick the bucket (*informal*), croak (*informal*), expire (*formal or literary*), give up the ghost (*literary*), breathe your last (*literary*) [➥ DIE; 922] **3** *v* **fail**, go under, die a death, be unsuccessful, go bankrupt, go broke [➥ FAIL OR BE UNSUCCESSFUL; 75] *Opposite*: succeed

biting **1** *adj* **cold**, freezing, piercing, cutting, stinging, frigid, raw, icy, glacial, arctic (*informal*) [➥ COLD WEATHER; 1051] *Opposite*: hot **2** *adj* **sarcastic**, scathing, acerbic, mordant, satirical, cruel, scornful, derisive, mocking, wounding [➥ RUDE AND HOSTILE; 625] *Opposite*: sympathetic

bitingly *adv* **acidly**, acerbically, tartly, woundingly, cruelly, sarcastically, mordantly [➥ RUDE AND HOSTILE; 625] *Opposite*: sympathetically

bitmap *type of* **computer feature** [➥ COMPUTERS AND COMPUTING; 1127]

bit part *n* [→IN THE THEATER; 906]

bits and pieces (*informal*) **1** *n* **belongings**, things, odds and ends, stuff, personal possessions, gear (*informal*) [→POSSESSIONS; 461] **2** *n* **knickknacks**, leftovers, scraps, odds and ends, stuff, bric-a-brac [→COLLECTIONS AND MIXTURES OF THINGS; 1244]

bitter 1 *adj* **sour**, acid, acidic, tart, astringent, vinegary, pungent, harsh, acrid [→TASTE; 703] *Opposite*: sweet **2** *adj* **resentful**, embittered, sulky, cheated, angry, cynical, indignant, hard done by (*UK*) [→IRRITATION AND ANGER; 541] *Opposite*: glad **3** *adj* **unpleasant**, acrimonious, antagonistic, nasty, vicious, hostile, harsh [→RUDE AND HOSTILE; 625] *Opposite*: pleasant **4** *adj* **hostile**, nasty, vicious, rancorous, virulent, vehement [→IRRITATION AND ANGER; 541] **5** *adj* **cold**, freezing, icy, biting, raw, polar, sharp, piercing, cutting, stinging, glacial, arctic (*informal*) [→COLD WEATHER; 1051] *Opposite*: hot

bitterly 1 *adv* **resentfully**, acrimoniously, sulkily, sullenly, cynically, angrily, indignantly [→RUDE AND HOSTILE; 625] *Opposite*: gladly **2** *adv* **severely**, excessively, intensely, inordinately, desperately, terribly, penetratingly [→TO A GREAT EXTENT; 132] *Opposite*: slightly

bittern *type of* **freshwater bird** [→FRESHWATER BIRDS; 1000]

bitterness 1 *n* **resentment**, acrimony, unpleasantness, sullenness, anger, animosity, hostility, cynicism, indignation [→FEELINGS ABOUT THE PAST; 532] *Opposite*: pleasure **2** *n* **sourness**, acidity, sour taste, stringency, bitter taste, sharpness, tartness [→TASTE; 703] *Opposite*: sweetness

bittersweet *adj* **poignant**, nostalgic, affecting, touching, sentimental, with a sting in the tail [→EMOTIONALLY UNPLEASANT AND UPSETTING; 227]

bitty 1 *adj* (*informal*) **itsy-bitsy** (*informal*), tiny, minute, teeny (*informal*), teeny-weeny (*informal*), teensy-weensy (*informal*) [→SMALL; 1195] *Opposite*: large **2** *adj* (*UK*) **disjointed**, fragmented, scrappy, fragmentary, disconnected, sketchy [→UNFINISHEDNESS; 239] *Opposite*: cohesive

bitumen *n* **tar**, asphalt, tarmac, blacktop, paving [→BUILDING MATERIALS; 1077]

bivalve *type of* **aquatic invertebrate** [→AQUATIC INVERTEBRATES; 1022]

bivouac 1 *n* **camp**, encampment, temporary camp, mountaineering camp, military camp [→HUMAN SETTLEMENTS; 1070] **2** *n* **shelter**, awning, tent, pup tent, lean to [→RESIDENTIAL BUILDINGS; 1078] **3** *v* **camp**, set up camp, pitch a tent [→HOBBIES, GAMES, AND SPORTS; 875]

biweekly 1 *adv* **once every two weeks**, every other week, twice a month, once a fortnight (*UK*) [→TIMES OF YEAR; 88] **2** *adv* **twice a week**, semiweekly, every few days [→TIMES OF YEAR; 88]

bizarre *adj* **strange**, curious, inexplicable, out of the ordinary, unusual, weird, peculiar, odd, uncanny, fantastic, off the wall, out there (*informal*), wacky (*informal*) [→BIZARRE AND PECULIAR; 257] *Opposite*: ordinary

bizarreness *n* [→BIZARRE AND PECULIAR; 257]

blab (*informal*) *v* **tell tales**, gossip, spread rumors, tattle, leak, tell, tell on, talk out of turn, squeal (*informal*), spill the beans (*informal*), snitch (*slang*) [→BETRAY CONFIDENCES AND GOSSIP; 618]

blabber *v* **chatter**, babble, go on, drivel, jabber, blather (*informal*), yammer (*informal*), waffle (*UK informal*) [→CHATTER AND BABBLE; 617]

blabbermouth (*informal*) *n* **gossip**, chatterer, bigmouth (*informal*), chatterbox (*informal*), tattletale (*informal*), sneak (*UK*) [→INTERFERING PEOPLE AND TATTLETALES; 950]

black 1 *type of* **color** [→COLORS; 1224] **2** *adj* **dark**, gloomy, obscure, dusky, murky, dim, shadowy [→DESCRIBING LIGHT; 1228] *Opposite*: light

black

◆ *types of black*
blue-black, coal black, ebony, inky, jet black, pitch-black, raven, sable

black-and-blue *adj* **bruised**, aching, hurt, injured, battered, beaten [→INJURED; 742]

black-and-white *adj* **clear-cut**, straightforward, unambiguous, categorical, explicit, unequivocal, uncompromising [→EASE AND SIMPLICITY; 200] *Opposite*: ambiguous

black as night *adj* [→DESCRIBING LIGHT; 1228]

blackball *v* **exclude**, ban, keep out, reject, bar, debar, snub, shun, ostracize, boycott, blacklist [→REFUSING OR REJECTING RELATIONS; 975]

black bean *type of* **pulse** [→PEAS AND BEANS; 1189]

blackberry *type of* **berry** [→FRUIT AND VEGETABLES; 1176]

blackboard *n* **writing board**, board, chalkboard, slate, whiteboard [→WRITING AND DRAWING IMPLEMENTS, AND MEDIA; 601]

black bread *type of* **bread** [→BREAD, FLOUR, AND BREAD PRODUCTS; 1179]

black currant *type of* **berry** [→FRUIT AND VEGETABLES; 1176]

blacken 1 *v* **darken**, make black, dirty, turn black, besmirch, begrime (*literary*), sully (*literary*) [→CHANGE OF COLOR; 391] *Opposite*: lighten **2** *v* **slander**, libel, defame, vilify, malign, besmirch, denigrate, slur, speak ill of, asperse (*formal*), sully (*literary*) [→PROTEST AND EXPRESS DISAPPROVAL; 642] *Opposite*: praise

black-eyed pea *type of* **pulse** [→PEAS AND BEANS; 1189]

black fly *type of* **flying insect** [→FLYING INSECTS; 1013]

Black Forest cake *type of* **cake** [→CAKES, COOKIES, AND DESSERTS; 1181]

blackguard *n* **scoundrel**, rascal, rogue, villain, wretch (*formal*), rotter (*dated informal*), cad (*dated*) [→VILLAINS AND THUGS; 947]

blackhead *n* **blocked pore**, spot, pimple, blemish, zit (*slang*) [→CONDITIONS AFFECTING THE SKIN; 721]

black hole *type of* **star or star system** [→HEAVENLY BODIES; 1061]

blackjack *type of* **club** [→BLUNT INSTRUMENTS AND WHIPS; 1158]

black knight *n* [→BUSINESS PEOPLE; 793]

blacklist *v* **ban**, debar, bar, exclude, shut out, boycott, prohibit, outlaw, preclude (*formal*) [→REVOKE STATUS; 459]

black look n [→ FACIAL EXPRESSIONS AND BLUSHING; 651]

blackly 1 adv **angrily**, menacingly, threateningly, belligerently, aggressively, resentfully, furiously, sullenly [→ RUDE AND HOSTILE; 625] Opposite: optimistically 2 adv **hopelessly**, gloomily, lugubriously, dismally, dolefully, mournfully, sadly, somberly, depressingly [→ BAD-TEMPERED AND HUMORLESS; 626] Opposite: sunnily

black magic n [→ THE SUPERNATURAL; 787]

blackmail 1 n **extortion**, intimidation, bribery, corruption, extraction, protection, coercion, threat [→ CRIMES; 817] 2 v **extort**, extract, exact, hold to ransom, bribe, force, coerce, compel, threaten [→ CAUSE OR COMPEL TO ACT; 271]

blackmailer n **extortionist**, coercer, criminal, crook (informal) [→ CRIMINALS; 821]

blackness 1 n **darkness**, duskiness, dimness, shadow, gloom, dusk, murkiness, night [→ DESCRIBING LIGHT; 1228] Opposite: light 2 n **hopelessness**, despondency, gloominess, depression, dolefulness, gloom, mournfulness, lugubriousness, somberness, melancholy, pessimism [→ SADNESS, DISTRESS, AND DESPAIR; 539] Opposite: optimism 3 n **anger**, fury, temper, aggression, belligerence, resentment, menace, sullenness, hostility [→ IRRITATION AND ANGER; 541] Opposite: cheerfulness

black out v **faint**, pass out, lose consciousness, collapse, become unconscious, fall in a faint, swoon, keel over (informal), go out like a light (informal) [→ BECOME SICK, TREAT, AND RECOVER; 728] Opposite: come to

blackout 1 n **fainting fit**, seizure, loss of consciousness, collapse [→ ILLNESSES AND DISORDERS; 732] 2 n **power cut**, power outage, shutdown, power failure, brownout [→ SUDDEN EVENTS; 52] 3 n **embargo**, veto, clampdown, suppression, censorship, prohibition, curfew [→ REFUSE PERMISSION AND NOT ALLOW; 670]

black pepper type of **spice** [→ HERBS AND SPICES; 1175]

blacksnake type of **nonpoisonous snake** [→ SNAKES; 995]

black tie n [→ GARMENTS AND OUTFITS; 865]

black-tie adj **formal**, dressy, ceremonial, posh (informal) [→ DESCRIBING CLOTHES; 869] Opposite: casual

blacktop n **asphalt**, tar, bitumen, Tarmac [→ COVERS AND COATINGS; 1246]

black widow type of **arachnid** [→ ARACHNIDS; 1018]

bladder part of **digestive tract** [→ THE DIGESTIVE TRACT; 709]

bladder wrack type of **marine alga** [→ MICROORGANISMS, FUNGI, AND ALGAE; 1023]

blade 1 n **cutting edge**, knife-edge, edge, razor blade, knife blade [→ EXTREMITIES OF PHYSICAL OBJECTS; 1250] 2 n **vane**, fin, flat, propeller, sail, oar [→ PARTS OF A SHIP OR BOAT; 1151]

blame 1 v **hold responsible**, censure, accuse, point the finger at, hold accountable, attribute, impugn (formal), impute [→ CREATING CONNECTIONS; 144] Opposite: exculpate (formal) 2 v **criticize**, reproach, find fault with, condemn, think badly of, upbraid, reprimand, reprehend, denunciate (formal) [→ ACCUSE, BLAME, AND CRITICIZE; 641] Opposite: commend 3 n **responsibility**, guilt, culpability, fault, blameworthiness, liability, denunciation [→ MORALLY BAD OR IMPROPER; 775] Opposite: commendation

blameless adj **innocent**, virtuous, righteous, faultless, irreproachable, spotless, guiltless, in the clear, scrupulous, unblemished, untarnished, above suspicion, clean (slang), inculpable (formal) [→ MORALLY GOOD; 774] Opposite: guilty

blameworthy adj **responsible**, guilty, culpable, at fault, chargeable, to blame, blamable [→ MORALLY BAD OR IMPROPER; 775] Opposite: innocent

blanch v **go pale**, grow pale, turn white, lighten, blench, whiten, drain of color [→ CHANGE OF COLOR; 391] Opposite: redden

blancmange type of **dessert** [→ CAKES, COOKIES, AND DESSERTS; 1181]

bland 1 adj **insipid**, weak, tasteless, mild, plain, flat, flavorless, wishy-washy (informal) [→ TASTE; 703] Opposite: tasty 2 adj **featureless**, ordinary, dull, lackluster, humdrum, boring, flat, nondescript, unappealing, mediocre, unremarkable, vapid, banal [→ BORING AND UNINTERESTING; 234] Opposite: exciting

blandish (archaic) v [→ FLATTER AND FAWN; 621]

blandishment n **flattery**, cajolery, praise, fawning, soft words, smooth talk, sweet talk (informal), blarney (informal) [→ INGRATIATING; 638]

blandness 1 n **tastelessness**, weakness, insipidness, mildness, plainness, dullness, flatness [→ TASTE; 703] Opposite: tastiness 2 n **dullness**, banality, flatness, triteness, insipidness, vapidness [→ BORING AND UNINTERESTING; 234]

blank 1 adj **empty**, vacant, bare, clean, clear, plain, void [→ EMPTY; 1238] Opposite: full 2 adj **outright**, complete, total, absolute, unqualified, unmitigated, utter, downright, straight-out (informal) [→ ABSOLUTE AND ABSOLUTELY; 133] Opposite: partial 3 adj **uncomprehending**, impassive, vacant, empty, bemused, perplexed, unexpressive [→ FACIAL EXPRESSIONS AND BLUSHING; 651] Opposite: expressive 4 n **space**, void, gap, empty space, break [→ HOLES, GAPS, AND FORKS; 1252]

blanket 1 n **coverlet**, cover, covering, afghan, throw, spread, bedspread, electric blanket, over-blanket (UK) [→ COVERS AND COATINGS; 1246] 2 adj **comprehensive**, extensive, complete, total, wholesale, across-the-board, unlimited, absolute, unmitigated, straight-out (informal) [→ WHOLENESS AND COMPLETENESS; 198] Opposite: partial 3 v **cover**, obscure, encase, drape, carpet, swathe, overspread, overlay [→ CAUSE TO DISAPPEAR; 6] Opposite: uncover

blankness 1 n **emptiness**, void, vacancy, bareness, barrenness, vacuum, nothingness, vacuity (formal) [→ EMPTY; 1238] 2 n **expressionlessness**, vacancy, indifference, emotionlessness, vacuousness [→ UNINTERESTED AND DETACHED; 629] Opposite: animation 3 n **bewilderment**, confusion, obliviousness, incomprehension, lack of understanding [→ CONFUSION, ANXIETY, AND WORRY; 540] Opposite: acuity

blank out v **block out**, blot out, suppress, wipe out, erase, deny, refuse [→ NOT PAY ATTENTION; 764] Opposite: acknowledge

blank verse n [→ POETRY AND VERSE; 915]

blare v **ring out**, make a racket, boom, resound, shout, shriek, blast (informal) [→ EMIT CONTINUOUS SOUNDS; 366]

blare out v **ring out**, make a racket, blast out, resound, boom out [➡ EMIT CONTINUOUS SOUNDS; 366]

blaring adj **deafening**, earsplitting, cacophonous, raucous, booming, shrieking, rowdy [➡ LOUD, HIGH, OR UNPLEASANT SOUNDS; 1266] Opposite: quiet

blarney (informal) n **nonsense**, smooth talk, charm, drivel, flattery, garbage, claptrap (informal), bunk (slang) [➡ MEANINGLESS SPEECH OR WRITING; 676]

blasé adj **nonchalant**, laid back, cool, relaxed, unmoved, unconcerned, carefree, offhand [➡ NEUTRALITY AND INDIFFERENCE; 553] Opposite: concerned

blaspheme v **curse**, swear, issue oaths, use profanities, use foul language, cuss (informal) [➡ INSULTS, ABUSE, AND SWEARING; 658]

blasphemer n **swearer**, curser, profaner, foul mouth, cusser, profaner [➡ RELIGIOUS CONCEPTS; 776]

blasphemous adj **sacrilegious**, irreligious, offensive, improper, irreverent, impious, ungodly, profane (formal) [➡ RELIGIOUS CONCEPTS; 776] Opposite: pious

blasphemy 1 n **profanity**, sacrilege, wickedness, irreverence, violation, desecration [➡ RELIGIOUS CONCEPTS; 776] Opposite: piety 2 n **oath**, curse, profanity, swearword, cuss (informal), cussword (informal), imprecation (formal), execration (literary or formal) [➡ INSULTS, ABUSE, AND SWEARING; 658]

blast 1 n **explosion**, detonation, flash, flare, gust, boom, discharge (formal) [➡ SUDDEN EVENTS; 52] 2 v (informal) **blare**, resound, boom, make a racket, ring out [➡ EMIT CONTINUOUS SOUNDS; 366] 3 v **blow up**, explode, detonate, shoot, demolish, blow away (slang), discharge (formal) [➡ DESTRUCTION AND DEMOLITION; 359] 4 v (informal) **criticize**, attack, lambaste, vilify, castigate (formal), censure [➡ ACCUSE, BLAME, AND CRITICIZE; 641] 5 v **damage**, blight, disfigure, burn, blister, scar, sear, scorch [➡ WORSEN APPEARANCE; 382]

See Compare and Contrast at **criticize**.

blast off v **take off**, lift off, launch [➡ MOVE SOMETHING: THROUGH THE AIR; 334]

blastoff n **launch**, takeoff, liftoff [➡ BEGINNINGS; 53] Opposite: touchdown

blast out v **blare out**, ring out, make a racket, blare, boom, resound, thud [➡ EMIT CONTINUOUS SOUNDS; 366]

blatancy n **obviousness**, conspicuousness, ostentation, flagrancy, overtness, barefacedness, shamelessness, brazenness [➡ PERCEPTIBLE; 25] Opposite: subtlety

blatant adj **obvious**, unconcealed, barefaced, unashamed, deliberate, flagrant, transparent, patent, manifest, palpable, brazen [➡ INTENTIONAL AND DELIBERATE; 279] Opposite: furtive

blather (informal) 1 v **chatter**, go on, babble, blabber, jabber, ramble on, prate, prattle, drivel, yammer (informal), waffle (UK informal) [➡ CHATTER AND BABBLE; 617] 2 n **drivel**, prattle, chatter, babble, blabber, gossip, twaddle (informal) [➡ MEANINGLESS SPEECH OR WRITING; 676]

blaze 1 v **burn**, be on fire, burst into flames, rage, glow, shine, radiate, flash, flame, flare, illuminate [➡ FIRE, FLAMMABILITY, AND BURNING; 1165] 2 n **fire**, inferno, conflagration,

combustion [➡ FIRE, FLAMMABILITY, AND BURNING; 1165] 3 n **glare**, glow, flash, brightness, intensity, illumination, incandescence [➡ DESCRIBING LIGHT; 1228]

See Compare and Contrast at **fire**.

blaze a trail v [➡ START AN ACTION; 260]

blazer type of **jacket** [➡ GARMENTS AND OUTFITS; 865]

blazing 1 adj **intense**, raging, mighty, heated, furious, tremendous, violent, vehement, fierce [➡ STRENGTH; 201] 2 adj **burning**, glowing, shining, radiating, blistering, baking, roaring, searing, glaring, scorching (informal) [➡ FIRE, FLAMMABILITY, AND BURNING; 1165]

blazon v **splash**, embellish, emblazon, display, show [➡ DECORATE, ADORN, AND APPLY COATINGS; 405]

bleach v **lighten**, peroxide, blanch, blench, whiten, decolorize [➡ CHANGE OF COLOR; 391]

bleached adj **lightened**, faded, sun-bleached, washed-out, blanched, whitened [➡ DESCRIBING COLORS; 1226]

bleachers n **benches**, stands, risers, stand seats, seating, seats [➡ FURNITURE; 858]

bleak 1 adj **unwelcoming**, austere, miserable, bare, drab, dreary, depressing, desolate, uninviting, lonely, isolated, dismal [➡ PLAIN; 232] Opposite: welcoming 2 adj **hopeless**, unpromising, gloomy, doubtful, futile, grim [➡ DANGEROUS; 236] Opposite: promising 3 adj **cold**, harsh, wintry, cheerless, miserable, bitter, chilling, biting [➡ COLD WEATHER; 1051] Opposite: warm 4 adj **forlorn**, miserable, dejected, disheartened, downhearted, down, hopeless, sorrowful, sad, despairing, despondent, dour, depressing, funereal [➡ SADNESS, DISTRESS, AND DESPAIR; 539] Opposite: cheerful

bleakly adv **forlornly**, dismally, hopelessly, drearily, despondently, cheerlessly, miserably, austerely, dejectedly, drably, sorrowfully, desolately, sadly, despairingly [➡ SADNESS, DISTRESS, AND DESPAIR; 539] Opposite: cheerfully

bleakness 1 n **hopelessness**, despondency, sorrow, misery, sadness, dejection, despair [➡ FEELINGS ABOUT THE FUTURE; 533] Opposite: hopefulness 2 n **cheerlessness**, drabness, austerity, harshness, bareness, loneliness, isolation, desolation, dreariness [➡ PLAIN; 232] Opposite: comfort

blearily adv **fuzzily**, hazily, groggily, sleepily, drowsily, vaguely [➡ TIRED, ASLEEP, AND UNCONSCIOUS; 738] Opposite: clearly

bleary adj **hazy**, watery, unfocused, fuzzy, blurry, shadowy [➡ SEE; 699] Opposite: clear

bleary-eyed adj **sleepy**, tired, half-awake, dozy, groggy, heavy-lidded, drowsy, dopey, out of it, slumberous, torpid [➡ TIRED, ASLEEP, AND UNCONSCIOUS; 738] Opposite: alert

bleat 1 v **whine**, complain, nag, fuss, moan (informal), bellyache (informal), gripe (informal), squawk (informal), yammer (informal) [➡ COMPLAIN AND NAG; 686] 2 type of **animal sound** [➡ SOUNDS MADE BY ANIMALS; 1261]

bleed 1 v **lose blood**, hemorrhage, shed blood [➡ THE BLOOD AND CIRCULATION; 717] 2 v (informal) **extort**, exploit, drain, wring, deplete, suck the life out of, squeeze (informal), milk (informal), fleece (informal) [➡ USE UP AND WASTE; 474] 3 n **blood loss**, hemorrhage, nosebleed [➡ THE BLOOD AND CIRCULATION; 717]

bleed dry (*informal*) *v* drain, suck dry, deplete, bring to its knees, exploit, suck the life out of, squeeze (*informal*), fleece (*informal*) [➡ USE UP AND WASTE; 474] *Opposite*: replenish

bleeding *n* blood loss, hemorrhage, flow of blood, flow [➡ THE BLOOD AND CIRCULATION; 717]

bleep 1 *n* beep, tone, sound, noise [➡ CONTINUOUS SOUNDS; 1258] 2 *v* (*UK*) call, page, alert, signal, contact, summon, get (*informal*) [➡ TELEPHONE, PAGE, AND TEXT; 681]

bleeper (*UK*) *n* pager, monitor, beeper (*informal*) [➡ TELE-COMMUNICATIONS; 1130]

blemish 1 *n* mark, defect, imperfection, flaw, fault, stain, spot, blotch, discoloration, fleck, disfigurement, wart [➡ FAULTS, FLAWS, AND WEAKNESSES; 251] 2 *v* damage, tarnish, spoil, ruin, stain, injure, discolor, mar, vitiate [➡ WORSEN APPEARANCE; 382] *Opposite*: restore

See Compare and Contrast at **flaw***.*

blemished *adj* marked, stained, imperfect, flawed, tarnished, mottled, flecked, marred, discolored, scarred [➡ IN BAD REPAIR; 1234] *Opposite*: unblemished

blench 1 *v* go pale, grow pale, lighten, blanch, whiten, drain of color [➡ CHANGE OF COLOR; 391] *Opposite*: redden 2 *v* draw back, hesitate, falter, recoil, flinch, shrink back, quail [➡ HESITATE; 272]

blend 1 *v* mix, merge, combine, bring together, unify, intermingle, mingle, amalgamate, emulsify, meld [➡ COMBINE AND MIX; 400] *Opposite*: separate 2 *n* mixture, merger, combination, intermingling, balance, assortment, amalgam, composite, fusion [➡ COLLECTIONS AND MIXTURES OF THINGS; 1244]

See Compare and Contrast at **mixture***.*

blender *n* mixer, food processor, chopper, liquidizer (*UK*) [➡ HOUSEHOLD APPLIANCES; 1117]

bless 1 *v* sanctify, consecrate, hallow, extol, laud, exalt (*formal*) [➡ RELIGIONS AND RELIGIOUS PRACTICES; 777] *Opposite*: curse 2 *v* approve, sanction, support, endorse, back, commend [➡ APPROVE AND CONFIRM; 646] *Opposite*: decry

blessed 1 *adj* holy, sacred, sanctified, hallowed, consecrated, set apart [➡ RELIGIOUS CONCEPTS; 776] *Opposite*: profane (*formal*) 2 *adj* welcome, providential, lucky, fortunate, pleasant, happy [➡ EMOTIONALLY PLEASANT; 187] *Opposite*: unfortunate

blessing 1 *n* consecration, sanctification, benediction, dedication [➡ RELIGIONS AND RELIGIOUS PRACTICES; 777] 2 *n* approval, sanction, permission, consent, approbation, go-ahead (*informal*) [➡ APPROVE AND CONFIRM; 646] *Opposite*: veto 3 *n* lucky thing, good thing, miracle, piece of good fortune, stroke of luck, boon, godsend [➡ SOURCE OF HAPPINESS, PLEASURE, OR IMPROVEMENT; 209] *Opposite*: disaster

blight 1 *n* disfigurement, stain, scar, blot, affliction, disease, plague [➡ FAULTS, FLAWS, AND WEAKNESSES; 251] 2 *v* ruin, disfigure, stain, scar, impair, damage, blast, afflict [➡ WORSEN APPEARANCE; 382]

blimp *type of* civil aircraft [➡ AIRCRAFT; 1148]

blimpish (*UK*) *adj* bigoted, narrow-minded, prejudiced, intolerant, dogmatic, inflexible, rigid [➡ DIFFICULT TO PLEASE; 515] *Opposite*: tolerant

blind 1 *adj* sightless, unsighted, unseeing, eyeless, visionless, vision-impaired [➡ SEE; 699] *Opposite*: sighted 2 *n* screen, window shade, canopy, awning, visor, venetian blind, shade, roller blind (*UK*) [➡ COVERS AND COATINGS; 1246]

blind alley *n* dead end, cul-de-sac, impasse [➡ ROADS; 1106]

blind date *n* rendezvous, date, meeting, assignation, appointment [➡ MEETINGS AND ASSEMBLIES; 43]

blindfold *n* bandage, cloth, covering, scarf, band [➡ COVERS AND COATINGS; 1246]

blinding 1 *adj* glaring, dazzling, bright, bedazzling, strong [➡ DESCRIBING LIGHT; 1228] *Opposite*: soft 2 *adj* (*informal*) striking, extraordinary, outstanding, arresting, amazing, fantastic, superb [➡ EXTRAORDINARY: AMAZING; 204] *Opposite*: ordinary

blindness 1 *n* sightlessness, loss of sight, impaired vision [➡ SEE; 699] *Opposite*: sight 2 *n* thoughtlessness, carelessness, obliviousness, recklessness, rashness, impetuousness, heedlessness [➡ NEGATIVE INTELLECTUAL CHARACTERISTICS; 525] *Opposite*: thoughtfulness

blind spot *n* weakness, failing, failure, fault, flaw, block [➡ FAULTS, FLAWS, AND WEAKNESSES; 251] *Opposite*: strength

blini *type of* pancake [➡ CAKES, COOKIES, AND DESSERTS; 1181]

blink 1 *v* wink, bat an eyelid, flutter an eyelid, flicker an eyelid [➡ LOOKING AND LOOKS; 700] 2 *v* flash, wink, flicker, twinkle, signal, glisten, shine, shimmer, glimmer [➡ LIGHT EMISSION; 368]

blinker *type of* external feature [➡ EXTERNAL PARTS OF A VEHICLE; 1147]

blinkered *adj* inward-looking, insular, narrow-minded, narrow, limited [➡ NEGATIVE INTELLECTUAL CHARACTERISTICS; 525]

blinkeredness *n* insularity, narrow-mindedness, narrowness, limitation, restrictiveness [➡ NEGATIVE INTELLECTUAL CHARACTERISTICS; 525]

blink of an eye *n* [➡ SHORT PERIODS OF TIME; 93]

blintz *type of* pancake [➡ CAKES, COOKIES, AND DESSERTS; 1181]

blip *n* problem, glitch, error, failure, breakdown, malfunction, fault, bug (*informal*), gremlin (*informal*) [➡ FAULTS, FLAWS, AND WEAKNESSES; 251]

bliss *n* ecstasy, heaven, paradise, enjoyment, happiness, delight, pleasure, harmony, blessedness [➡ PLEASURE, EXCITEMENT, AND ELATION; 534] *Opposite*: misery

blissful *adj* heavenly, wonderful, delightful, idyllic, perfect, peaceful, pleasurable, enjoyable, harmonious, joyful, ecstatic, beatific (*literary*) [➡ EMOTIONALLY PLEASANT; 187] *Opposite*: miserable

blissfully *adv* supremely, wonderfully, ecstatically, delightfully, happily, blessedly, idyllically, joyfully, beatifically (*literary*) [➡ PLEASURE, EXCITEMENT, AND ELATION; 534] *Opposite*: miserably

blister 1 *n* sore, swelling, eruption, burn, blood blister [➡ CONDITIONS AFFECTING THE SKIN; 721] 2 *v* swell up, erupt, bubble, bulge, break out, suppurate [➡ EXCRETION AND EXCRETA; 722]

blistering *adj* **sweltering**, baking, blazing, burning, searing, intense, severe, roasting (*informal*), scorching (*informal*) [➡ HOT WEATHER; 1050] *Opposite:* freezing

blithe 1 *adj* (*literary*) **carefree**, cheerful, happy, merry, happy-go-lucky, easygoing, amiable, lighthearted [➡ CHEERFULNESS OF OUTLOOK; 503] *Opposite:* anxious 2 *adj* **casual**, unconcerned, indifferent, unthinking, uncaring, thoughtless, careless [➡ NEUTRALITY AND INDIFFERENCE; 553] *Opposite:* thoughtful

blithely 1 *adv* (*literary*) **merrily**, cheerfully, happily, gaily, amiably, lightheartedly, merrily, lightly, without a care in the world [➡ GOOD-TEMPERED AND HUMOROUS; 627] *Opposite:* anxiously 2 *adv* **casually**, carelessly, unthinkingly, indifferently, thoughtlessly, unconcernedly [➡ NEUTRALITY AND INDIFFERENCE; 553] *Opposite:* thoughtfully

blitheness (*literary*) *n* [➡ CHEERFULNESS OF OUTLOOK; 503]

blither (*informal*) *v* [➡ CHATTER AND BABBLE; 617]

blitz 1 *n* **bombardment**, blitzkrieg, saturation bombing, onslaught, offensive, barrage, salvo, cannonade, attack [➡ WARFARE AND WAR; 830] 2 *n* (*informal*) **onslaught**, attack, crackdown, concerted effort, cleanup, clear-out (*UK*), tidy-up (*UK*) [➡ SUDDEN EVENTS; 52] 3 *v* (*informal*) **crack down** (*informal*), concentrate on, focus on, come down on, lower the boom (*informal*), fall on, hit [➡ CARRY OUT AN ACTION; 269] 4 *v* **bombard**, bomb, blast, barrage, hit, target, strafe, saturate, overwhelm, attack, assault [➡ WARFARE AND WAR; 830] 5 *v* (*informal*) **clean**, clean up, tidy, clear away, clear up, whip round (*UK*) [➡ ARRANGE AND CREATE ORDER; 357]

blitzed (*informal*) *adj* [➡ UNDER THE INFLUENCE OF DRUGS OR ALCOHOL; 741]

blitzkrieg *n* [➡ WARFARE AND WAR; 830]

blizzard *n* **snowstorm**, whiteout, winter storm, storm [➡ COLD WEATHER; 1051]

bloat *v* **swell**, inflate, blow up, expand, distend, swell up, puff up, dilate, balloon [➡ CHANGE OF SIZE: BIGGER; 392] *Opposite:* contract

bloated *adj* **swollen**, distended, overstuffed, full, overfed, blown up, puffy, ballooned, dilated, stuffed (*informal*) [➡ ILL AND SICK; 740]

blob 1 *n* **splotch**, globule, spot, splash, dash, dribble, dollop, splash, drop, bead, dot, daub, splodge (*UK*) [➡ AMOUNTS OF SOLID OR SEMISOLID; 115] 2 *v* **splotch**, dot, dab, daub, smudge, splodge (*UK*) [➡ DECORATE, ADORN, AND APPLY COATINGS; 405]

bloc *n* **alliance**, coalition, union, federation, league, syndicate, confederacy, partnership [➡ TERRITORIES AND GROUPS OF NATIONS; 1068]

block 1 *n* **chunk**, hunk, lump, slab, wedge, tablet, mass, cake, brick [➡ LARGE PIECES; 130] 2 *n* **wing**, extension, addition, unit, module, part [➡ LARGE PIECES; 130] 3 *n* **expanse**, section, sector, zone, band, stretch, region [➡ LARGE PIECES; 130] 4 *n* (*UK*) **building**, apartment house, block of flats (*UK*) [➡ RESIDENTIAL BUILDINGS; 1078] 5 *v* **obstruct**, impede, hinder, jam, prevent, oppose, stop, blockade, bar, deter, frustrate, thwart, hamper, hold back [➡ MAKE IMPOSSIBLE; 276] *Opposite:* encourage

See Compare and Contrast at **hinder**.

blockade 1 *n* **barrier**, barricade, obstruction, line of defense, cordon [➡ BARRIERS; 1113] 2 *v* **deny access**, lay siege to, obstruct, defend, block, guard, shut in, impede, deter [➡ MAKE IMPOSSIBLE; 276]

blockage *n* **obstruction**, impasse, jam, bottleneck, snarl, logjam, obstacle, plug, snarl-up (*UK*) [➡ PROBLEMS; 256]

blockbuster (*informal*) *n* **runaway success**, hit, smash hit, epic, chartbuster, bestseller [➡ SUCCESS; 82] *Opposite:* flop (*informal*)

blockbusting *adj* **successful**, earthshattering, epic, outstanding, popular, chartbusting, record-breaking, sensational, earthshaking [➡ SUCCESSFUL AND PROMISING; 81]

blocked *adj* **congested**, impassable, choked up, plugged up, stopped up, jammed, gridlocked, choked, unnavigable, obstructed, clogged [➡ FULL; 1239] *Opposite:* clear

blocking *adj* **obstructive**, delaying, stalling, hindering, spoiling, filibustering [➡ REBELLIOUSNESS AND DISOBEDIENCE; 565] *Opposite:* cooperative

block off 1 *v* **close off**, block, close, cordon off, isolate, barricade, impede, dam, clog [➡ BAR AND OBSTRUCT ACCESS; 410] *Opposite:* free 2 *v* **obstruct**, obscure, hide, mask, cover, block out, screen, shroud [➡ CAUSE TO DISAPPEAR; 6] *Opposite:* reveal

block of flats (*UK*) *n* [➡ RESIDENTIAL BUILDINGS; 1078]

block out *v* **blank out**, blot out, suppress, wipe out, erase, deny, forget, repress, censor [➡ NOT PAY ATTENTION; 764] *Opposite:* acknowledge

block up *v* **jam**, fill, stop, obstruct, choke, clog up, plug up, dam, impede [➡ FILL; 406] *Opposite:* free

blond *adj* **fair-haired**, towheaded, flaxen, golden, straw-colored, pale, light-colored [➡ HAIR COLOR; 485] *Opposite:* dark

blonde *see* **blond**

blood 1 *n* **gore**, body fluid, plasma, lifeblood [➡ THE BLOOD AND CIRCULATION; 717] 2 *n* **family**, relations, kin, relatives, kindred, folk, clan, household [➡ THE FAMILY; 956] 3 *n* **lineage**, ancestry, extraction, heritage, stock, pedigree, genealogy, descent, origin, background, kinship [➡ STATUS; 888]

bloodbath *n* **massacre**, slaughter, atrocity, scene of carnage [➡ AGGRESSIVE EVENTS; 39]

blood blister *n* [➡ CONDITIONS AFFECTING THE SKIN; 721]

blood brother *n* **best friend**, friend, ally, supporter, amigo, buddy (*informal*), pal (*informal*), mate (*UK*) [➡ FRIENDS AND GUESTS; 963] *Opposite:* enemy

bloodcurdling *adj* **terrifying**, frightening, hair-raising, chilling, spine-tingling, spine-chilling, horrific, macabre, scary (*informal*) [➡ FRIGHTENING; 231] *Opposite:* comforting

bloodhound *n type of* **large dog** [➡ DOGS; 980]

bloodless 1 *adj* **nonviolent**, peaceful, nonaggressive, orderly, controlled, pacific [➡ PEACEFULNESS AND GENTLENESS; 214] *Opposite:* violent 2 *adj* **pale**, anemic, white, pallid, wan, ashen, sallow, peaked, pasty, sickly, white as a sheet, peaky (*UK*) [➡ COMPLEXION; 480] *Opposite:* ruddy

bloodletting *n* **quarrel**, fight, dispute, argument, fracas, disagreement, altercation, melee [➡ CHAOS AND UPROAR; 51]

bloodline *n* **descent**, heritage, lineage, ancestry, background, pedigree, family, history, origin, extraction, stock, genealogy [➡ STATUS; 888]

blood lust *n* **bloodthirstiness**, hatred, cruelty, inhumanity, revenge, passion, savagery [➡ MALICIOUS ACTIONS OR BEHAVIOR; 296]

blood money *n* **compensation**, money, recompense, retribution, atonement, reparation, redress, restitution [➡ FUNDS, PAYMENTS, AND CHARGES; 800]

blood orange *type of* **citrus fruit** [➡ FRUIT AND VEGETABLES; 1176]

blood red *type of* **red** [➡ COLORS; 1224]

blood relation *n* [➡ THE FAMILY; 956]

blood relative *n* [➡ THE FAMILY; 956]

bloodshed *n* **carnage**, killing, violence, slaughter, murder, massacre, butchery, mayhem (*informal*) [➡ CAUSES OF DEATH; 921]

bloodshot *adj* **red**, inflamed, sore, pink [➡ SEE; 699] *Opposite*: clear

bloodstone *type of* **gemstone** [➡ PRECIOUS STONES; 1278]

bloodstream *n* **flow**, circulation, blood, arteries, veins, capillaries [➡ THE BLOOD AND CIRCULATION; 717]

bloodsucker *n* **parasite**, leech, tick, mosquito, vampire [➡ PARASITES; 1017]

bloodsucking *adj* **parasitical**, leechlike, vampiric, vampirish [➡ SELFISH AND UNKIND; 505]

blood, sweat, and tears *n* [➡ HARD WORK OR EFFORT; 298]

bloodthirstiness *n* **ferociousness**, viciousness, cruelty, barbarism, brutality, barbarity, savagery [➡ MORALLY BAD OR IMPROPER; 775]

bloodthirsty *adj* **cruel**, gory, murderous, ferocious, vicious, horrible [➡ MORALLY BAD OR IMPROPER; 775]

blood vessel *n* [➡ THE BLOOD AND CIRCULATION; 717]

blood vessel

◆ *types of blood vessels*
aorta, artery, capillary, jugular vein, vein, venule

bloody *adj* **gory**, blood-spattered, bleeding, wounded, injured, bloodstained [➡ INJURED; 742]

bloom 1 *n* (*literary*) **flower**, flower head, blossom, posy, bud [➡ PARTS OF TREES AND PLANTS; 1026] 2 *n* **coloration**, tinge, tint, shadow, flush, blush [➡ DESCRIBING COLORS; 1226] *Opposite*: pallor 3 *v* **blossom**, flower, come into flower, come into bud [➡ GROW AND CULTIVATE; 351] *Opposite*: wither 4 *v* (*literary*) **thrive**, prosper, blossom, flourish, do well, mature, develop, grow [➡ PROSPER AND ABOUND; 16] *Opposite*: struggle 5 *v* (*literary*) **be a picture of health**, glow, be radiant, thrive, flourish, blossom [➡ PROSPER AND ABOUND; 16]

bloomers (*dated*) *type of* **lower body underwear** [➡ ACCESSORIES, MILLINERY, AND LINGERIE; 867]

blooming 1 *adj* **flourishing**, thriving, budding, up-and-coming, promising, prospering, doing well [➡ SUCCESSFUL AND PROMISING; 81] *Opposite*: struggling 2 *adj* **blossoming**, flowering, budding, in flower, in bloom [➡ VEGETATION; 1025]

blooper (*informal humorous*) *n* **mistake**, blunder, error, gaffe, misstep, faux pas (*literary*), clanger (*UK informal*), bloomer (*UK informal humorous*) [➡ MISTAKES; 250]

blossom 1 *n* **flower**, flower head, bloom, posy, bud [➡ PARTS OF TREES AND PLANTS; 1026] 2 *v* **bloom**, flower, bud, come into flower, come into bud [➡ GROW AND CULTIVATE; 351] *Opposite*: wither 3 *v* **flourish**, thrive, grow, bloom, prosper, do well [➡ SUCCEED AND WIN; 79] *Opposite*: struggle 4 *v* **develop**, grow, come out of your shell, mature, come out of yourself, blossom out, spread your wings [➡ PROSPER AND ABOUND; 16]

blossoming *adj* **developing**, growing, prospering, maturing, thriving, burgeoning, blooming [➡ SUCCESSFUL AND PROMISING; 81]

blossom out *v* **develop**, grow, come out of your shell, come out of yourself, blossom, spread your wings [➡ PROSPER AND ABOUND; 16]

blot 1 *n* **spot**, blemish, stain, mark, imperfection, discoloration, stigma, blotch, speck, fleck [➡ FAULTS, FLAWS, AND WEAKNESSES; 251] 2 *v* **stain**, tarnish, spoil, ruin, disfigure, mark, impair, discolor, fleck, speckle, drip [➡ WORSEN APPEARANCE; 382]

blotch *n* **blot**, mark, blemish, spot, stain, imperfection, splodge (*UK*) [➡ FAULTS, FLAWS, AND WEAKNESSES; 251]

blotchy *adj* **mottled**, blemished, marked, spotty, spotted, dappled, discolored, freckled, reddened, red [➡ COMPLEXION; 480] *Opposite*: plain

blot on the landscape *n* **eyesore**, scar, blemish, disfigurement, monstrosity, disgrace [➡ UGLINESS AND UNATTRACTIVENESS; 233]

blot out 1 *v* **conceal**, hide, cover, eclipse, block, shadow, obscure [➡ CAUSE TO DISAPPEAR; 6] *Opposite*: reveal 2 *v* **blank out**, block out, forget, erase, put out of your mind, wipe out, repress [➡ NOT PAY ATTENTION; 764] *Opposite*: recall

blotter *n* **logbook**, notebook, log, record, journal, diary [➡ WRITING AND DRAWING IMPLEMENTS, AND MEDIA; 601]

blouse *type of* **top** [➡ GARMENTS AND OUTFITS; 865]

blouson *type of* **jacket** [➡ GARMENTS AND OUTFITS; 865]

blow 1 *v* **whoosh**, gust, waft, puff, bluster, rage [➡ WINDY AND STORMY WEATHER; 1053] 2 *v* **move**, propel, drive, carry, waft, whoosh [➡ MOVE SOMETHING: THROUGH THE AIR; 334] 3 *v* (*slang*) **squander**, fritter away, waste, throw away, spend [➡ USE UP AND WASTE; 474] 4 *n* **knock**, crack, jolt, swipe, strike, hit, thump, whack, sideswipe, clout, bash (*informal*), wallop (*informal*) [➡ CONTACT: IMPACT; 413] 5 *n* **setback**, upset, disappointment, shock, kick in the teeth, misfortune, body blow [➡ DISASTERS; 252] *Opposite*: boost

blow a fuse (*informal*) *v* [➡ GIVING VENT TO EMOTIONS; 679]

blow a gasket (*informal*) *v* [➡ GIVING VENT TO EMOTIONS; 679]

blow away 1 *v* **distribute**, disperse, scatter, dispel, spread [➡ MOVE SOMETHING: THROUGH THE AIR; 334] 2 *v* (*slang*) **shoot**, kill, execute, murder, gun down (*informal*), waste (*slang*), knock off (*slang*) [➡ KILL; 923] 3 *v* (*slang*) **defeat**, beat, get the better of, trounce, thrash, hammer (*informal*), steamroller (*informal*), walk over (*informal*), cream (*slang*) [➡ BEAT AND DEFEAT; 80] 4 *v* (*slang*) **amaze**, overwhelm, overcome, affect, shake, psych, blow your mind (*informal*), knock out (*informal*) [➡ SURPRISE AND IMPRESS; 574]

blow-by-blow *adj* **thorough**, step by step, detailed, full, complete, in-depth, minute, precise [➡ WHOLENESS AND COMPLETENESS; 198] *Opposite*: sketchy

blower (*informal*) *n* **boaster**, egotist, show-off (*informal*), bigmouth (*informal*), loudmouth (*informal*) [➡ SELF-IMPORTANT AND SELF-SEEKING PEOPLE; 949]

blowhard *n* [➡ SELF-IMPORTANT AND SELF-SEEKING PEOPLE; 949]

blown-up 1 *adj* **air-filled**, inflated, hard, rigid, pumped-up [➡ RIGID AND HARD; 1211] *Opposite*: deflated 2 *adj* **distended**, swollen, bloated, enlarged, puffed-up, puffy [➡ FULL; 1239] *Opposite*: sagging 3 *adj* **overdone**, exaggerated, attention-grabbing, hyped, puffed-up, larger-than-life, over-the-top (*informal*) [➡ BIZARRE AND PECULIAR; 257] *Opposite*: understated 4 *adj* **bombed**, wrecked, burned-out, ruined, demolished [➡ IN BAD REPAIR; 1234]

blow off (*slang*) *v* **ignore**, dismiss, pay no attention to, make light of, neglect, avoid, shun, slough off [➡ NOT PAY ATTENTION; 764] *Opposite*: notice

blow out *v* **extinguish**, put out, snuff out, douse, dampen [➡ CAUSE TO STOP; 266] *Opposite*: ignite

blowout (*slang*) 1 *n* **puncture**, flat tire, flat (*informal*) [➡ TRAFFIC ACCIDENTS; 255] 2 *n* **certainty**, walkover (*informal*), cinch (*informal*), sure thing (*informal*), piece of cake (*informal*) [➡ EASY WORK; 299] 3 *n* **binge**, feast, pig out (*informal*) [➡ MEALS AND PARTS OF MEALS; 1169]

blow somebody's cover *v* **unmask**, expose, uncover, make known, bring to light [➡ BETRAY CONFIDENCES AND GOSSIP; 618]

blow the whistle *v* **inform**, report, turn in, expose, tell on, snitch (*slang*), squeal (*slang*), sneak (*UK*) [➡ BETRAY CONFIDENCES AND GOSSIP; 618]

blowtorch *type of* **general tool** [➡ HAND TOOLS; 1119]

blow up 1 *v* **destroy**, explode, detonate, blast, demolish, flatten [➡ DESTRUCTION AND DEMOLITION; 359] 2 *v* **inflate**, pump up, fill, puff up, swell, fill out, balloon, distend, expand [➡ CHANGE OF SIZE: BIGGER; 392] *Opposite*: deflate 3 *v* **enlarge**, magnify, expand, increase, make larger [➡ CHANGE OF SIZE: BIGGER; 392] *Opposite*: reduce 4 *v* (*informal*) **lose your temper**, explode, be furious, hit the roof, flare up, rage, storm, lose your cool, blow your top (*informal*), fly off the handle (*informal*), blow a fuse (*informal*), blow a gasket (*informal*), lose it (*informal*), go ballistic (*slang*), flip your lid (*slang*), go nuts (*slang*) [➡ GIVING VENT TO EMOTIONS; 679] 5 *v* (*informal*) **exaggerate**, overstress, embellish, embroider, make a mountain out of a molehill, inflate, lay on, amplify, overstate, dramatize [➡ CLAIM, INSIST, AND EMPHASIZE; 614] *Opposite*: play down

blowup *n* **enlargement**, magnification [➡ ARTWORKS; 898] *Opposite*: reduction

blowy (*informal*) *adj* **windy**, breezy, blustery, gusty, squally, turbulent, bracing [➡ WINDY AND STORMY WEATHER; 1053] *Opposite*: calm

blow your own horn *v* **brag**, boast, crow, show off, sing your own praises, fly your own kite (*UK*) [➡ BOAST; 616] *Opposite*: deprecate

blow your top (*informal*) *v* **flare up**, hit the roof, lose your temper, fly into a rage, explode, erupt, rage, storm, fly off the handle (*informal*), blow up (*informal*), lose it (*informal*), blow a fuse (*informal*), blow a gasket (*informal*), go ballistic (*slang*), go nuts (*slang*) [➡ GIVING VENT TO EMOTIONS; 679] *Opposite*: calm down

blowzy 1 *adj* **ruddy**, red-faced, rubicund, coarse complexioned [➡ COMPLEXION; 480] 2 *adj* **unkempt**, bedraggled, messy, tousled, disheveled [➡ BADLY GROOMED; 483] *Opposite*: smart

blubber (*informal*) *v* **sob**, weep, cry, snivel, whimper, burst into tears, break down, bawl (*informal*) [➡ CRYING; 650]

blubbering (*informal*) *n* [➡ CRYING; 650]

bludgeon 1 *v* **beat**, hit, slam, strike, batter, hammer, bash (*informal*) [➡ WHIP AND CLUB; 417] 2 *v* **cajole**, coerce, compel, bully, bulldoze, steamroller, intimidate [➡ CAUSE OR COMPEL TO ACT; 271] 3 *type of* **club** [➡ BLUNT INSTRUMENTS AND WHIPS; 1158]

blue 1 *adj* (*informal*) **depressed**, down, sad, fed up (*informal*), low, dejected, down in the dumps, melancholy, desolate, wretched, unhappy, downcast [➡ SADNESS, DISTRESS, AND DESPAIR; 539] *Opposite*: happy 2 *type of* **color** [➡ COLORS; 1224]

blue

◆ *types of blue*
azure, cobalt blue, cornflower blue, cyan, electric blue, ice blue, indigo, lapis lazuli, midnight blue, navy blue, peacock blue, powder blue, Prussian blue, royal blue, sapphire, saxe blue, sky blue, slate blue, steel blue, turquoise, ultramarine

bluebell *type of* **flower grown from bulbs** [➡ FLOWERS FROM BULBS; 1030]

blueberry *type of* **berry** [➡ FRUIT AND VEGETABLES; 1176]

bluebird 1 *type of* **songbird** [➡ SONGBIRDS; 1003] 2 *type of* **common bird** [➡ BIRDS; 997]

blue-black *type of* **black** [➡ COLORS; 1224]

blue-blooded *adj* **aristocratic**, noble, high-class, well-bred, refined, highborn (*literary*) [➡ CLASS STATUS; 889] *Opposite*: common

bluebottle *type of* **flying insect** [➡ FLYING INSECTS; 1013]

blue cheese *type of* **soft cheese** [➡ DAIRY PRODUCTS AND CHEESES; 1183]

blue-chip *adj* **top-class**, first-class, first-rate, top-grade, topnotch (*informal*), number one (*informal*) [➡ GOOD, WELL, BETTER; 183] *Opposite*: second-rate

blue-collar *adj* **manual**, proletarian, working class, laboring [➡ TYPES OF WORK; 835] *Opposite*: white-collar

blue-collar worker *n* [➡ WORKERS; 836]

bluegrass 1 *type of* **grass** [➡ GRASS; 1031] 2 *type of* **pop and vocal music** [➡ MUSIC, SONGS, AND SINGING; 907]

blue jay *type of* **common bird** [➡ BIRDS; 997]

blueprint *n* **plan**, drawing, design, proposal, outline, draft, scheme [➡ OFFICIAL DOCUMENTS; 586]

blues 1 *type of* **pop and vocal music** [➡ MUSIC, SONGS, AND SINGING; 907] **2** *n* (*informal*) **sadness**, melancholy, dejection, depression, despair, unhappiness, despondency, pessimism, doldrums [➡ SADNESS, DISTRESS, AND DESPAIR; 539] *Opposite:* happiness

blue whale *type of* **whale** [➡ WHALES; 991]

bluff 1 *v* **trick**, con, fake, lie, pretend, deceive, pass off, scam (*slang*) [➡ DECEPTION AND LIES; 660] **2** *n* **sham**, trick, con, pretense, fake, lie, deceit, ruse [➡ DECEPTION AND LIES; 660] **3** *n* **cliff**, headland, hillside, hill, mound, height [➡ MOUNTAINS AND HILLS; 1044] **4** *adj* **plain-spoken**, cheery, loud, hearty, forthright, no-nonsense, outspoken, direct, blunt [➡ HONEST AND OPEN; 630]

bluffness *n* **cheeriness**, heartiness, directness, bluntness, plain-spokenness, outspokenness, candidness [➡ HONEST AND OPEN; 630]

blunder 1 *n* **mistake**, gaffe, error, mix-up, misstep, slip-up (*informal*), bungle (*informal*), boo-boo (*informal*), blooper (*informal humorous*), howler (*slang*), faux pas (*literary*) [➡ MISTAKES; 250] **2** *v* **make a mistake**, get it wrong, err, slip up (*informal*), goof (*informal*), foul up (*informal*), mess up (*informal*) [➡ MESS UP AND MAKE MISTAKES; 472] **3** *v* **stumble**, stagger, lurch, flounder, trip, career [➡ AIMLESS AND ERRANT MOTION; 343]

See Compare and Contrast at **mistake**.

blunderbuss *type of* **gun** [➡ WEAPONS FOR SHOOTING; 1156]

blunder in *v* [➡ ARRIVE; 12]

blundering *adj* **clumsy**, careless, awkward, lumbering, ungainly, ham-handed (*informal*), ham-fisted (*informal*) [➡ DESCRIBING BODY MOVEMENTS; 288] *Opposite:* dexterous

blunt 1 *adj* **dull**, rounded, dulled, blunted, unsharpened [➡ ROUNDED SHAPE; 1218] *Opposite:* sharp **2** *adj* **uncompromising**, straightforward, direct, frank, honest, candid, straight-talking, no-nonsense, forthright, bluff [➡ HONEST AND OPEN; 630] *Opposite:* indirect **3** *v* **dampen**, dull, put a damper on, take the edge off, diminish, soothe, moderate, lessen [➡ CHANGE OF INTENSITY: LESS; 395] *Opposite:* heighten

bluntly *adv* **frankly**, straightforwardly, honestly, directly, candidly, openly, uncompromisingly [➡ HONEST AND OPEN; 630] *Opposite:* indirectly

bluntness *n* **candor**, frankness, directness, straightforwardness, honesty [➡ HONEST AND OPEN; 630] *Opposite:* mendacity

blur 1 *n* **distortion**, fuzziness, haze, impression, shape, shadow, haziness, cloudiness [➡ VAGUENESS; 243] **2** *v* **obscure**, cloud, make indistinct, hide, conceal, mist, fog [➡ CAUSE TO DISAPPEAR; 6] *Opposite:* clarify **3** *n* **blot**, blotch [➡ FAULTS, FLAWS, AND WEAKNESSES; 251] **4** *v* **distort**, confuse, shade [➡ CHANGE OF SHAPE; 385] *Opposite:* clear

blurb (*slang*) *n* **description**, write-up, summary, details, notes, gloss, info (*informal*) [➡ SUMMARIES, OUTLINES, AND EXCERPTS; 588]

blurred *adj* **blurry**, indistinct, unclear, hazy, distorted, fuzzy, imprecise, faint, vague [➡ VAGUENESS; 243] *Opposite:* distinct

blurry *adj* **fuzzy**, blurred, dim, shadowy, indistinct, unclear, hazy [➡ VAGUENESS; 243] *Opposite:* clear

blurt *v* **exclaim**, cry, utter, come out with, announce, burst out, let drop, let slip, ejaculate (*literary*) [➡ BETRAY CONFIDENCES AND GOSSIP; 618]

blush 1 *v* **go red**, flush, go red in the face, color, redden [➡ FACIAL EXPRESSIONS AND BLUSHING; 651] *Opposite:* blanch **2** *n* **rouge** (*dated*), makeup, cosmetic, blusher (*UK*) [➡ MAKEUP AND BEAUTY PRODUCTS; 490]

blusher (*UK*) *n* **makeup**, cosmetic, blush, rouge (*dated*) [➡ MAKEUP AND BEAUTY PRODUCTS; 490]

blushing *adj* **embarrassed**, self-conscious, red-faced, flushed, coy, shy, timid, modest [➡ RETICENT AND UNFORTHCOMING; 631] *Opposite:* bold

bluster 1 *v* **harangue**, threaten, bully, protest, rant, bristle, bridle, complain [➡ PROTEST AND EXPRESS DISAPPROVAL; 642] **2** *v* **blow**, gust, rage, puff, waft [➡ WINDY AND STORMY WEATHER; 1053]

blustery *adj* **windy**, gusty, stormy, squally, breezy, blowy (*informal*) [➡ WINDY AND STORMY WEATHER; 1053] *Opposite:* still

B movie *n* **supporting film**, short, supporting movie, B picture, trailer, support [➡ FILM; 901]

BO (*informal*) *n* **body odor**, smell, sweatiness, rankness, reek, perspiration, stench, stink [➡ SMELL AND SMELLING; 705]

boa *type of* **nonpoisonous snake** [➡ SNAKES; 995]

boa constrictor *type of* **nonpoisonous snake** [➡ SNAKES; 995]

boar 1 *type of* **male animal** [➡ MALE OR FEMALE ANIMALS; 978] **2** *type of* **large mammal** [➡ LARGE MAMMALS; 986]

board 1 *n* **plank**, slat, floorboard, timber, beam [➡ BUILDING MATERIALS; 1077] **2** *n* **panel**, sheet, boarding [➡ BUILDING MATERIALS; 1077] **3** *n* **committee**, panel, commission, management team, advisory group [➡ GROUPS WITH A COMMON INTEREST; 938] **4** *n* **food**, meal, sustenance, nourishment, rations, refreshment [➡ FOOD; 116] **5** *v* **embark**, enter, go on board, go aboard, go into, get on [➡ TRAVEL: WAYS OF TRAVELING; 320] *Opposite:* disembark **6** *v* **lodge** (*dated*), stay, live, room, be accommodated [➡ INHABIT; 20]

boarder *n* **lodger**, paying guest, resident, tenant, occupant, occupier [➡ INHABITANTS; 857]

boarding house *type of* **hotel** [➡ HOTELS, RESTAURANTS, AND CLUBS; 1082]

boarding school *type of* **school** [➡ EDUCATIONAL INSTITUTIONS; 813]

boardroom *type of* **room in public buildings** [➡ TYPES OF ROOMS; 1097]

board up *v* **close**, shutter, secure, cover up [➡ BAR AND OBSTRUCT ACCESS; 410]

boardwalk *n* **walkway**, footpath, path, causeway [➡ PATHWAYS; 1110]

boast 1 *v* **brag**, show off, crow, sing your own praises, blow your own horn, fly your own kite (*UK*) [➡ BOAST; 616] **2** *v* **have**, possess, pride yourself on, lay claim to, feature, display, enjoy [➡ POSSESS; 444] **3** *n* **claim**, assertion, brag, vaunt, pretension, avowal (*formal*) [➡ BOAST; 616]

boaster *n* [➡ SELF-IMPORTANT AND SELF-SEEKING PEOPLE; 949]

boastful *adj* **arrogant**, proud, conceited, full of yourself, bragging, immodest, vain, self-important, self-satisfied, overweening, complacent, bigheaded (*informal*) [➡ POMPOUS, LOUD, AND OVERCONFIDENT; 635] *Opposite*: modest

boastfulness *n* **immodesty**, arrogance, conceit, self-importance, showing off, bragging, boasting, self-aggrandizement [➡ POMPOUS, LOUD, AND OVERCONFIDENT; 635] *Opposite*: modesty

boasting 1 *n* **boastfulness**, bragging, showing off, arrogance, self-aggrandizement, conceit, immodesty, self-importance [➡ BOAST; 616] *Opposite*: modesty 2 *adj* **boastful**, swaggering, arrogant, self-important, conceited, cocky (*informal*) [➡ POMPOUS, LOUD, AND OVERCONFIDENT; 635] *Opposite*: modest

boat *n* **craft**, ship, vessel [➡ SHIPS AND BOATS; 1150]

boater *type of* **hat** [➡ ACCESSORIES, MILLINERY, AND LINGERIE; 867]

boat hook *n* [➡ PARTS OF A SHIP OR BOAT; 1151]

bob 1 *v* **move up and down**, nod, dip, bobble, jog [➡ BOUNCE, UNDULATE, AND VIBRATE; 308] 2 *v* **curtsy**, bow, nod, duck, genuflect [➡ GESTURES AND GESTICULATION; 653] 3 *type of* **hairstyle** [➡ HAIRSTYLES AND HAIRPIECES; 488]

bobbin *n* **reel**, spindle, spool, cylinder, roll, drum [➡ CONTAINERS, RECEPTACLES, AND PACKAGING; 1245]

bobble 1 *n* (*informal*) **mistake**, blunder, error, gaffe, slip, slip-up (*informal*), blooper (*informal*) [➡ MISTAKES; 250] 2 *n* (*UK*) **ball**, pom-pom, tassel [➡ ORNAMENTS AND DECORATIONS; 1248] 3 *v* **move up and down**, nod, bob, jog, dip [➡ BOUNCE, UNDULATE, AND VIBRATE; 308]

bobbly (*UK*) *adj* **bumpy**, lumpy, rough, knobby, textured, coarse [➡ PHYSICAL TEXTURE; 1222] *Opposite*: smooth

bobcat *type of* **cat** [➡ FELINES; 983]

bobsled 1 *n* **toboggan**, sled, sledge (*UK*), bobsleigh (*UK*) [➡ VEHICLES; 1145] 2 *type of* **winter sport** [➡ HOBBIES, GAMES, AND SPORTS; 875]

bod (*slang*) 1 *n* **body**, physique, build, figure, shape, form [➡ BODY; 691] 2 *n* **person**, character, individual, human being, man, woman [➡ PERSON; 931]

bode *v* **augur**, portend, promise, predict, divine, prefigure, betoken (*literary*) [➡ MEAN SOMETHING; 61]

bodega 1 *type of* **bar or club** [➡ HOTELS, RESTAURANTS, AND CLUBS; 1082] 2 *type of* **food outlet** [➡ RETAIL OUTLETS; 1083]

bodice *type of* **top** [➡ GARMENTS AND OUTFITS; 865]

bodily *adj* **physical**, corporal, corporeal, fleshly, material, human, biological [➡ LIVING THINGS AND LIVING; 976] *Opposite*: spiritual

body 1 *n* **form**, figure, frame, physique, build, bulk [➡ SHAPE; 1216] 2 *n* **corpse**, dead body, cadaver, remains, carcass, stiff (*slang*), deceased (*formal*) [➡ DEAD PERSON; 926] 3 *n* **organization**, group, association, federation, society, party [➡ INSTITUTIONS; 790] 4 *n* **quantity**, corpus, amount, mass, area, reservoir, supply [➡ COLLECTIONS AND MIXTURES OF THINGS; 1244] 5 *n* **bulk**, main part, essence, majority, mass, better part, lion's share [➡ BODY; 691]

body blow *n* **setback**, blow, disappointment, upset,

shock, letdown, kick in the teeth, trauma, upheaval [➡ DISASTERS; 252]

body builder *n* **athlete**, weightlifter, muscle builder [➡ PEOPLE IN SPORTS AND LEISURE; 876]

body fluid *n* **saliva**, blood, urine, sweat, semen, tears, lymph, mucus, gastric juice, synovia [➡ EXCRETION AND EXCRETA; 722]

bodyguard *n* **guard**, security officer, attendant, guardian, protection officer, muscle (*slang*), minder (*UK informal*) [➡ PEOPLE WHO GUARD AND PROTECT; 846]

body-hugging *adj* [➡ DESCRIBING CLOTHES; 869]

body language *n* **mannerisms**, stance, facial expression, movements, motion, physical response, gesture, bearing, behavior [➡ GESTURES AND GESTICULATION; 653]

body mist *n* [➡ PERSONAL HYGIENE; 491]

body odor *n* [➡ SMELL AND SMELLING; 705]

body spray *n* [➡ PERSONAL HYGIENE; 491]

body stocking *type of* **upper body underwear** [➡ ACCESSORIES, MILLINERY, AND LINGERIE; 867]

body suit *type of* **upper body underwear** [➡ ACCESSORIES, MILLINERY, AND LINGERIE; 867]

body warmer *type of* **top** [➡ GARMENTS AND OUTFITS; 865]

bodywork *part of* **external structure** [➡ EXTERNAL PARTS OF A VEHICLE; 1147]

bog *n* **swamp**, quagmire, mire, marsh, marshland, fen (*UK*), fenland (*UK*) [➡ WETLANDS; 1043]

bog down (*informal*) *v* [➡ GIVE TOO MUCH AND OVERBURDEN; 437]

bogey 1 *n* **worry**, problem, concern, bugaboo, bugbear, bother, annoyance, nuisance [➡ PROBLEMS; 256] 2 *n* **monster**, creature, beast, monstrosity, booger (*informal*) [➡ MYTHICAL BEINGS; 789]

bogeyman *see* **bogey**

bog garden *type of* **garden** [➡ GARDENS; 1074]

bogged down (*informal*) *adj* **caught up**, delayed, stalled, slowed down, held up, overinvolved, hindered, mired, stuck [➡ CONFUSION, ANXIETY, AND WORRY; 540] *Opposite*: freed up

boggle (*informal*) *v* **confuse**, baffle, perplex, astonish, overwhelm, throw, stun, disorient [➡ CONFUSE AND BEWILDER; 571]

boggy *adj* **marshy**, swampy, muddy, watery, wet, sloppy, soggy, sodden [➡ WET; 1240] *Opposite*: parched

bogus *adj* **false**, fake, counterfeit, phony, trick, hoax, sham, spurious, mock [➡ FALSE AND UNREAL; 173] *Opposite*: genuine

bohemian 1 *n* **free spirit**, freethinker, nonconformist, hippie, New Age traveler [➡ PLEASURE-SEEKERS AND HEDONISTS; 886] 2 *adj* **unconventional**, nonconformist, offbeat, alternative, carefree, relaxed, arty, avant-garde, laid-back (*informal*) [➡ PLEASURE-SEEKING AND EXCESS; 885] *Opposite*: conformist

boil 1 *v* **rage**, fume, seethe, be angry, be irate, be infuriated [➡ GIVING VENT TO EMOTIONS; 679] 2 *v* **simmer**, bubble, poach, cook, stew, heat [➡ COOKING AND FOOD PREPARATION; 353] 3 *n* **ulcer**, sore, spot, swelling, abscess, cyst [➡ CONDITIONS AFFECTING THE SKIN; 721] **4** v (*informal*) **overheat**, swelter, stew, bake, burn, roast (*informal*) [➡ PAIN AND OTHER PHYSICAL SENSATIONS; 733] *Opposite*: freeze

boil down to (*informal*) v **amount to**, come down to, end up as, add up to, wind up as [➡ AMOUNT TO AND EQUAL; 70]

boiler type of **heating appliance** [➡ HEATING, REFRIGERATION, AND VENTILATION; 1142]

boiler suit n **overalls**, coveralls, protective clothing, dungarees [➡ GARMENTS AND OUTFITS; 865]

boiling adj **hot**, sweltering, baking, steaming, torrid, blistering, searing, scalding, broiling, scorching (*informal*), roasting (*informal*) [➡ HOT WEATHER; 1050] *Opposite*: freezing

boiling hot adj [➡ HOT WEATHER; 1050]

boiling point n **crisis point**, danger level, flashpoint, high point, peak [➡ DECISIVE MOMENTS; 44]

boil over v **overflow**, bubble up, overheat, spill over, blow, erupt, explode [➡ CHANGE OF TEMPERATURE; 386]

boil with rage v [➡ GIVING VENT TO EMOTIONS; 679]

boisterous adj **energetic**, active, animated, rowdy, rambunctious, unruly, noisy, overexcited [➡ ENERGY AND ENTHUSIASM; 496] *Opposite*: placid

boisterousness **1** n **unruliness**, overexcitement, roughness, riotousness, rowdiness, rambunctiousness, disruptiveness, liveliness, noisiness, loudness, exuberance, rumbustiousness, animation [➡ ENERGY AND ENTHUSIASM; 496] *Opposite*: placidity **2** n **wildness**, turbulence, roughness, storminess [➡ WINDY AND STORMY WEATHER; 1053] *Opposite*: calmness **3** n **horseplay**, rough and tumble, high spirits, exuberance, roughhouse (*informal*), high jinks (*informal*) [➡ JOKES AND TEASING; 674]

bok choy type of **root vegetable** [➡ FRUIT AND VEGETABLES; 1176]

bold **1** adj **brave**, daring, courageous, audacious, valiant, unflinching, gallant (*literary*), intrepid (*literary or humorous*) [➡ COURAGE; 498] *Opposite*: cowardly **2** adj **confident**, forward, brash, brazen, self-assured, impudent, bold-faced, cheeky (*informal*), nervy (*informal*), not backwards in coming forwards (*UK*) [➡ CONFIDENCE AND COMPOSURE; 499] *Opposite*: timid **3** adj **conspicuous**, bright, vivid, flashy, showy, loud [➡ IN POOR TASTE AND OVERSENTIMENTAL; 229] *Opposite*: muted **4** adj **black**, heavy, boldface [➡ PRINTING; 600] *Opposite*: light

bold as brass (*UK*) adj [➡ CONFIDENCE AND COMPOSURE; 499]

boldface adj **black**, heavy, bold [➡ PRINTING; 600] *Opposite*: lightface

bold-faced adj **impudent**, brash, brazen, unconcerned, shameless, flagrant, barefaced, cheeky (*informal*), nervy (*informal*) [➡ POMPOUS, LOUD, AND OVERCONFIDENT; 635] *Opposite*: unassuming

boldly **1** adv **bravely**, courageously, daringly, audaciously, fearlessly, unflinchingly, valiantly, gallantly (*literary*), intrepidly (*literary or humorous*) [➡ COURAGE; 498] *Opposite*: cautiously **2** adv **confidently**, brashly, brazenly, shamelessly, impudently [➡ CONFIDENCE AND COMPOSURE; 499] *Opposite*: timidly

boldness **1** n **courage**, daring, audacity, bravery,

bravado, valor [➡ COURAGE; 498] *Opposite*: cowardice **2** n **confidence**, self-assurance, brashness, nerve, audaciousness, impudence, cheek (*informal*), chutzpah (*informal*) [➡ CONFIDENCE AND COMPOSURE; 499] *Opposite*: timidity

bole n **trunk**, stem, stalk [➡ PARTS OF TREES AND PLANTS; 1026]

bolero type of **top** [➡ GARMENTS AND OUTFITS; 865]

boletus type of **fungus** [➡ MICROORGANISMS, FUNGI, AND ALGAE; 1023]

bolide type of **heavenly body** [➡ HEAVENLY BODIES; 1061]

bolivar type of **currency** [➡ CURRENCIES; 798]

boliviano type of **currency** [➡ CURRENCIES; 798]

bollard n **post**, marker, pillar, stake, pole, cone [➡ STICKS, POLES, AND WEDGES; 1254]

bologna type of **processed meat** [➡ TYPES AND CUTS OF MEAT; 1177]

bolshevik (*informal*) n **communist**, leftie (*informal*), socialist, bolshie (*informal dated*), red (*informal*) [➡ PHILOSOPHICAL AND POLITICAL THINKERS; 781]

bolshie (*informal dated*) n **communist**, leftie (*informal*), socialist, bolshevik (*informal*), red (*informal*) [➡ PHILOSOPHICAL AND POLITICAL THINKERS; 781]

bolster v **boost**, strengthen, reinforce, encourage, shore up, buttress, support, sustain, augment (*formal*) [➡ CHANGE OF INTENSITY: MORE; 394] *Opposite*: undermine

bolt **1** n **bar**, pin, rod, catch, latch [➡ FASTENERS, LINKS, AND NETWORKS; 1247] **2** type of **projectile** [➡ PROJECTILES; 1159] **3** v **fasten**, secure, lock, lock up, attach, anchor [➡ FASTEN, LINK, AND JOIN; 408] *Opposite*: unlock **4** v **run off**, make a dash for it, run, make a run for it, disappear, escape, scram (*informal*), take off (*informal*) [➡ RUN AWAY AND AVOID; 10] **5** v **gulp**, wolf, gobble, guzzle (*informal*), devour, down, scarf (*informal*), scarf down (*informal*), scoff (*informal*) [➡ EAT AND NOT EAT; 710] *Opposite*: nibble

bolt from the blue n **surprise**, shock, upset, jolt, blow, bombshell (*informal*) [➡ SUDDEN EVENTS; 52]

bolthole n **hideaway**, refuge, sanctuary, den, place of safety, private space [➡ SAFE BUILDINGS OR PLACES; 1093]

bolt upright adv **erect**, upright, straight up, straight as a ramrod [➡ ORIENTATION AND ALIGNMENT; 1223] *Opposite*: bent

bomb **1** type of **explosive weapon** [➡ EXPLOSIVES; 1155] **2** n (*informal*) **failure**, letdown, catastrophe, fiasco, disaster, botch (*informal*), miscarriage (*formal*), flop (*informal*), washout (*informal*) [➡ DISASTERS; 252] *Opposite*: success **3** v **bombard**, shell, blast, barrage, blitz, explode, attack, assault [➡ WARFARE AND WAR; 830] **4** v (*informal*) **fail**, flop, fall flat, sink without trace, disappoint, flounder [➡ FAIL OR BE UNSUCCESSFUL; 75] *Opposite*: succeed

bombard **1** v **bomb**, shell, open fire on, blast, barrage, blitz, attack, assault, pound [➡ DESTRUCTION AND DEMOLITION; 359] **2** v **assail**, shower, flood, inundate, overrun, overwhelm [➡ GIVE TOO MUCH AND OVERBURDEN; 437]

bombardier n [➡ MILITARY PERSONNEL; 828]

bombardment **1** n **attack**, offensive, assault, salvo, bombing, shelling, pounding [➡ AGGRESSIVE EVENTS; 39] **2** n **barrage**, flood, onslaught, blitz, volley, hail, shower [➡ SUDDEN EVENTS; 52]

bombast *n* **pomposity**, pretentiousness, verboseness, affectation, grandiloquence, bluster, long-windedness [➡ MEANINGLESS SPEECH OR WRITING; 676] *Opposite*: directness

bombastic *adj* **pompous**, pretentious, verbose, long-winded, grandiloquent, blustering, affected [➡ POMPOUS, LOUD, AND OVERCONFIDENT; 635] *Opposite*: direct

bombe *type of* **dessert** [➡ CAKES, COOKIES, AND DESSERTS; 1181]

bombed (*slang*) *adj* [➡ UNDER THE INFLUENCE OF DRUGS OR ALCOHOL; 741]

bomber *type of* **military aircraft** [➡ AIRCRAFT; 1148]

bomber jacket *type of* **jacket** [➡ GARMENTS AND OUTFITS; 865]

bombshell (*informal*) *n* **shock**, surprise, bolt from the blue, blow, upset, disaster [➡ SUDDEN EVENTS; 52]

bomb site *n* **area of devastation**, crater, ruins, battlefield, wasteland [➡ URBAN OUTDOOR SPACES; 1072]

bona fide *adj* **genuine**, authentic, true, real, valid, aboveboard, legitimate, legal, authenticated, certified [➡ TRUE AND REAL; 171] *Opposite*: bogus

bonanza *n* **jackpot**, crock of gold, gold mine, stroke of luck, bonus, prize, wealth, windfall, pot of gold (*UK*) [➡ TREATS; 210]

bonbon *type of* **confectionery** [➡ CONFECTIONERY; 1182]

bond 1 *n* **tie**, link, connection, union, attachment, relationship, friendship, acquaintance [➡ CONNECTIONS; 143] **2** *n* **promise**, pledge, oath, word [➡ PROMISE AND ASSURE; 684] **3** *v* **adhere**, stick, glue, fix, join, bind, attach, cement, link, affix [➡ FASTEN, LINK, AND JOIN; 408] **4** *v* **connect**, get along, relate, become attached, hit it off (*informal*), get on (*UK*) [➡ ESTABLISHING RELATIONSHIPS WITH OTHERS; 974] *Opposite*: clash

bondage *n* **slavery**, enslavement, captivity, oppression, servitude, repression, suppression [➡ CAPTIVITY AND LOSS OF FREEDOM; 248] *Opposite*: freedom

bonded *adj* **fused together**, fused, stuck, glued, attached, merged, united, joined, welded [➡ CLOSENESS; 159] *Opposite*: split

bonding *n* **attachment**, closeness, tie, connection, love, affection, relationship [➡ CONNECTIONS; 143]

bone *n* [➡ THE BONES AND JOINTS; 719]

---

bone

◆ *types of bones*
anklebone, backbone, breastbone, carpal, cheekbone, clavicle, coccyx, collarbone, cranium, femur, fibula, humerus, ilium, jawbone, kneecap, long bone, mandible, maxilla, metacarpal, metatarsal, patella, pelvis, pubis, radius, rib, sacrum, shinbone, shoulder blade, skull, spinal column, spine, sternum, talus, tarsal, thighbone, tibia, ulna, vertebra, vertebral column, zygomatic bone

---

bone china *type of* **pottery** [➡ POTTERY; 1135]

bone dry *adj* **parched**, dry as a bone, arid, scorched, seared, baked [➡ DRY; 1242]

bone idle *adj* **lazy**, indolent, idle, slothful, lethargic, inactive [➡ LIFELESS, LAZY, AND UNENTHUSIASTIC; 506] *Opposite*: diligent

bone of contention *n* **disagreement**, sticking point, difficulty, problem, obstacle, hurdle, dispute, difference [➡ DISHARMONY; 156]

boner (*informal*) *n* **mistake**, blunder, error, gaffe, misstep, faux pas (*literary*), clanger (*UK informal*), bloomer (*UK informal humorous*) [➡ MISTAKES; 250]

boneshaker *type of* **bike** [➡ BIKES, CARS, AND CARRIAGES; 1149]

bone up (*informal*) *v* **find out about**, research, look into, read up on, study [➡ STUDYING; 844]

bonfire *n* **fire**, conflagration, blaze, beacon [➡ FIRE, FLAMMABILITY, AND BURNING; 1165]

bong *n* **bang**, blow, thud, crash, knock, clang, dong, bonk (*informal*) [➡ IMPACT SOUNDS; 1260]

bongo drums *type of* **percussion instrument** [➡ MUSICAL INSTRUMENTS; 910]

bonhomie *n* **friendliness**, sociability, affability, geniality, amenability, kindliness [➡ FRIENDLINESS AND SOCIABILITY; 494]

boniness *n* [➡ BUILD; 477]

bonk (*informal*) **1** *v* **hit**, bang, knock, tap, slap, thump, punch [➡ CONTACT: IMPACT; 413] **2** *n* **knock**, blow, slap, bang, tap, thud [➡ IMPACT SOUNDS; 1260]

bon mot *n* **witticism**, quip, joke, epigram, clever remark, pun [➡ JOKES AND TEASING; 674]

bonne bouche (*UK*) *n* [➡ MEALS AND PARTS OF MEALS; 1169]

bonnet *type of* **hat** [➡ ACCESSORIES, MILLINERY, AND LINGERIE; 867]

bonnet monkey *type of* **primate** [➡ PRIMATES; 988]

bonny *adj* **good-looking**, lovely, pretty, handsome, attractive, appealing, healthy [➡ PEOPLE'S PHYSICAL APPEARANCE; 475] *Opposite*: unattractive

bonsai *n* [➡ FOLIAGE PLANTS; 1035]

bonus **1** *n* **extra**, addition, advantage, windfall, benefit, dividend, plus (*informal*) [➡ MORE AND EXCESS; 124] **2** *n* **gratuity**, handout, pay supplement, reward [➡ REWARDS AND AWARDS; 439]

bon vivant *n* **pleasure-seeker**, lotus-eater, gourmet, epicure, gourmand, foodie (*informal*), bon viveur (*literary*) [➡ PLEASURE-SEEKERS AND HEDONISTS; 886] *Opposite*: ascetic

bon viveur (*literary*) *n* [➡ PLEASURE-SEEKERS AND HEDONISTS; 886]

bon voyage *interj* [➡ GREETINGS, FAREWELLS, AND SALUTATIONS; 659]

bony *adj* **skinny**, scrawny, lanky, lean, thin, emaciated, skeletal, gaunt, underweight, skin and bones [➡ BUILD; 477] *Opposite*: plump

boo **1** *n* **catcall**, jeer, hoot, raspberry [➡ UNFAVORABLE NONVERBAL RESPONSES; 654] *Opposite*: cheer **2** *type of* **human sound** [➡ SOUNDS MADE BY PEOPLE; 1262] **3** *v* **jeer**, hoot, catcall, hiss [➡ UNFAVORABLE NONVERBAL RESPONSES; 654] *Opposite*: applaud

boob (*informal*) *n* **fool**, dupe, chump (*informal*), sucker (*informal*), fall guy (*slang*) [➡ LAZY OR UNSUCCESSFUL PEOPLE; 948]

boo-boo (*informal*) *n* **blunder**, mistake, error, gaffe, slip-up (*informal*), snafu (*informal*), bungle (*informal*), faux pas (*literary*) [➡ MISTAKES; 250]

boob tube (*informal*) *n* television, TV (*informal*), tube (*informal*), small screen (*informal*), telly (*UK*), box (*UK slang*) [➡ TELEVISION AND RADIO; 606]

booby trap 1 *n* bomb, tripwire, mine, explosive device [➡ EXPLOSIVES; 1155] 2 *n* snare, trap, trick, ruse, con, ambush, setup (*informal*) [➡ DECEPTION AND LIES; 660]

boodle (*slang*) *n* [➡ LARGE AMOUNTS OF MONEY; 118]

boogie 1 *v* (*informal*) dance, jig, caper, jive, party (*informal*), bop (*informal*) [➡ FIDGET AND FROLIC; 311] 2 *n* jig, jive, party (*informal*) [➡ FIDGET AND FROLIC; 311] 3 *type of* dance music [➡ MUSIC, SONGS, AND SINGING; 907]

boogie-woogie *type of* jazz music [➡ MUSIC, SONGS, AND SINGING; 907]

book 1 *n* volume, tome, manuscript, paperback, hardback, hardcover [➡ BOOKS AND BOOKLETS; 590] 2 *v* reserve, order, engage, put your name down for, sign up [➡ PURCHASE; 422]

bookable 1 *adj* [➡ PRESENT AND AVAILABLE; 11] 2 *adj* [➡ ILLEGAL; 816]

bookcase *type of* cabinet [➡ FURNITURE; 858]

book in (*UK*) *v* check in, register, sign in, enlist, enroll [➡ ARRIVE; 12] *Opposite:* leave

booking *n* reservation, hold, option, deposit [➡ BUSINESS ACTIVITIES AND PHENOMENA; 794]

bookish *adj* studious, serious, academic, scholarly, brainy, well-read, well-informed, erudite, learned, pedantic [➡ KNOWLEDGE AND WISDOM; 558]

bookishness *n* studiousness, erudition, scholarliness, learning, learnedness [➡ LEVELS OF EDUCATION AND SOPHISTICATION; 894]

bookkeeper *n* [➡ PEOPLE INVOLVED IN FINANCE; 804]

booklet *n* brochure, pamphlet, leaflet, flier [➡ BOOKS AND BOOKLETS; 590]

book lover *n* [➡ DEVOTEES AND ADDICTED PEOPLE; 556]

books *n* records, accounts, financial statements, balance sheet, profit and loss, files, paperwork [➡ RECORDS; 585]

bookshelf *n* shelf, ledge, stand, rack, bookstand, bookrest [➡ FURNITURE; 858]

bookstore *type of* retail outlet [➡ RETAIL OUTLETS; 1083]

bookworm (*informal*) *n* avid reader, book lover, bibliophile [➡ PEOPLE IN SPORTS AND LEISURE; 876]

boom 1 *v* roar, rumble, thunder, bellow, resound, reverberate, sound [➡ EMIT CONTINUOUS SOUNDS; 366] 2 *v* grow, soar, rocket, increase, rise, expand, explode, surge, gain [➡ PROSPER AND ABOUND; 16] *Opposite:* collapse 3 *n* bang, roar, rumble, report, detonation, explosion, shot, blast [➡ CONTINUOUS SOUNDS; 1258] 4 *n* growth, increase, rise, upsurge, expansion, development, escalation, explosion, surge [➡ SUDDEN EVENTS; 52] *Opposite:* collapse 5 *n* pole, arm, bracket, beam [➡ STICKS, POLES, AND WEDGES; 1254] 6 *part of* sailing vessel [➡ PARTS OF A SHIP OR BOAT; 1151] 7 *type of* economic condition [➡ FINANCE AND ECONOMICS; 796] 8 *adj* prosperous, flourishing, affluent, successful, thriving [➡ SUCCESSFUL AND PROMISING; 81]

boom and bust *type of* economic condition [➡ FINANCE AND ECONOMICS; 796]

boom box *type of* audio equipment [➡ AUDIO EQUIPMENT; 1139]

boomerang 1 *type of* projectile [➡ PROJECTILES; 1159] 2 *v* rebound, bounce back, return, ricochet, come back [➡ CHANGE DIRECTION OF MOTION; 344]

booming 1 *adj* thriving, prosperous, wealthy, flourishing, successful, growing, on the up and up (*UK*) [➡ SUCCESSFUL AND PROMISING; 81] *Opposite:* failing 2 *adj* thunderous, roaring, resounding, resonant, sonorous, loud [➡ LOUD, HIGH, OR UNPLEASANT SOUNDS; 1266] *Opposite:* quiet

boon *n* advantage, benefit, bonus, help, godsend, windfall, gain [➡ SOURCE OF HAPPINESS, PLEASURE, OR IMPROVEMENT; 209] *Opposite:* disadvantage

boon companion *n* [➡ FRIENDS AND GUESTS; 963]

boondocks (*informal*) *n* backwater, middle of nowhere, country, provinces, sticks (*informal*), boonies (*informal*), Podunk (*informal*), back of beyond (*UK*) [➡ REMOTE PLACES; 1046]

boor *n* lout, oaf, churl, loudmouth (*informal*) [➡ VILLAINS AND THUGS; 947]

boorish *adj* rude, ill-mannered, impolite, coarse, rough, loutish, uncouth, crude, ignorant, churlish, base [➡ BAD MANNERS AND SOCIAL SKILLS; 521] *Opposite:* well-mannered

boorishness *n* crudeness, loutishness, uncouthness, incivility, rudeness, insensitivity, bad manners, crassness, vulgarity [➡ BAD MANNERS AND SOCIAL SKILLS; 521] *Opposite:* courteousness

boost 1 *v* increase, improve, enhance, make better, further, advance, heighten [➡ IMPROVE SOMETHING; 374] *Opposite:* reduce 2 *v* encourage, support, lift, uplift, give a boost to, give a lift, inspire, raise, build up, motivate [➡ IMPROVE STRENGTH AND DURABILITY; 378] *Opposite:* discourage 3 *n* improvement, increase, enhancement, lift, helping hand, shot in the arm, pep talk (*informal*) [➡ TREATS; 210] *Opposite:* blow

booster 1 *n* promoter, supporter, fan, advocate, admirer, idolizer, rooter, groupie (*informal*) [➡ DEVOTEES AND ADDICTED PEOPLE; 556] 2 *n* injection, inoculation, vaccination, immunization, shot (*informal*) [➡ REMEDIES, TREATMENTS, AND OPERATIONS; 731]

booster rocket *part of* spacecraft [➡ SPACE VEHICLES; 1063]

booster seat *type of* internal feature [➡ INTERNAL PARTS OF A VEHICLE; 1146]

boost up 1 *v* increase, improve, enhance, boost, add to, augment (*formal*) [➡ CHANGE OF SIZE: BIGGER; 392] *Opposite:* reduce 2 *v* encourage, support, lift, uplift, give a boost to, give a lift, inspire, rally, motivate, build up [➡ IMPROVE STRENGTH AND DURABILITY; 378] *Opposite:* discourage

boot *type of* boot [➡ FOOTWEAR; 871]

bootee *type of* boot [➡ FOOTWEAR; 871]

Boötes *type of* constellation [➡ HEAVENLY BODIES; 1061]

booth 1 *n* cubicle, stand, closet, compartment, sukkah, tabernacle [➡ ALCOVES, CUBICLES, AND COMPARTMENTS; 1096] 2 *type of* outbuilding [➡ ANCILLARY BUILDINGS; 1080]

bootlace n shoelace, cord, lace, strap, tie [➡ACCESSORIES, MILLINERY, AND LINGERIE; 867]

bootleg adj illegal, pirated, stolen, illicit, unlicensed, plagiarized [➡ILLEGAL; 816] Opposite: legal

bootless adj useless, scant, feeble, inadequate, unsuccessful, unprofitable [➡REDUNDANT AND USELESS; 240] Opposite: successful

bootlicker (informal) n [➡SUPERFICIAL OR INSINCERE PEOPLE; 951]

boot out (informal) v dismiss, get rid of, eject, evict, bounce, kick out (informal), give the boot (informal), give the heave-ho (informal), fire (informal), sack (informal), can (slang) [➡EJECT AND EXCLUDE; 340] Opposite: appoint

booty n loot, spoils, plunder, ill-gotten gains, valuables, pickings, proceeds, treasure, swag (slang) [➡PROCEEDS OF CRIME; 427]

bop (informal) 1 v dance, jig, caper, jive, boogie (informal), party (informal) [➡FIDGET AND FROLIC; 311] 2 v hit, bang, knock, tap, thump, punch, bash (informal), bonk (informal) [➡PHYSICAL ATTACK AND PUNISHMENT; 415] 3 n jig, dance, jive, boogie (informal) [➡DANCE; 903] 4 n disco, dance, party, ball, rave (slang) [➡PARTIES, DANCES, AND CELEBRATIONS; 37]

borage type of herb [➡HERBS AND SPICES; 1175]

border 1 n frontier, borderline, boundary, state line [➡GEOGRAPHIC BORDERS AND BOUNDARIES; 1069] 2 n edge, limit, boundary, margin, verge, rim, edging, frame, perimeter, periphery, circumference [➡EXTREMITIES OF PHYSICAL OBJECTS; 1250] Opposite: center 3 n flowerbed, bed, shrub border, herbaceous border [➡GARDENS; 1074] 4 v be next to, touch, be bounded by, border on, run alongside, be adjacent to, adjoin, abut, fringe, skirt, conjoin (formal) [➡EXIST IN CLOSE PROXIMITY; 21]

bordering adj adjoining, neighboring, adjacent, next door, nearby, contiguous (formal) [➡CLOSENESS; 159]

bordering on adj verging on, tantamount to, close to, on the brink of, on the verge of, approaching, on the threshold of [➡ABOUT TO HAPPEN; 33]

borderland n boundary, edge, frontier, outer fringe, limits, border, fringe, margin, outer limits, outer edge (UK) [➡GEOGRAPHIC BORDERS AND BOUNDARIES; 1069] Opposite: heartland

borderline 1 n frontier, boundary, state line, border [➡GEOGRAPHIC BORDERS AND BOUNDARIES; 1069] 2 adj marginal, disputed, uncertain, doubtful, unclear, dubious, undecided, in doubt, up in the air, up for grabs [➡UNCERTAIN; 175] Opposite: clear-cut

border on 1 v approach, be close to, resemble, be similar to [➡EXIST IN CLOSE PROXIMITY; 21] 2 v be next to, touch, be bounded by, border, adjoin, be adjacent to, fringe, skirt, abut, conjoin (formal) [➡EXIST IN CLOSE PROXIMITY; 21]

Border terrier type of small dog [➡DOGS; 980]

bore 1 v turn off (informal), weary, send to sleep, bore to death, bore to tears, bore stiff, bore rigid, tire [➡BORE AND FAIL TO INTEREST; 570] Opposite: interest 2 v drill, perforate, penetrate, pierce, tunnel, gouge, make a hole in [➡TEAR, BREAK, AND CUT; 360]

bored adj uninterested, tired, bored rigid, bored stiff, bored to death, bored to tears, jaded, fed up (informal) [➡NEUTRALITY AND INDIFFERENCE; 553] Opposite: fascinated

boredom n tedium, monotony, dullness, tediousness, ennui, world-weariness [➡BORING AND UNINTERESTING; 234] Opposite: interest

bored rigid adj [➡NEUTRALITY AND INDIFFERENCE; 553]

bored stiff adj [➡NEUTRALITY AND INDIFFERENCE; 553]

bored to death adj [➡NEUTRALITY AND INDIFFERENCE; 553]

bored to tears adj [➡NEUTRALITY AND INDIFFERENCE; 553]

borehole n well, hole, shaft [➡HOLES, GAPS, AND FORKS; 1252]

bore rigid v [➡BORE AND FAIL TO INTEREST; 570]

bore stiff v [➡BORE AND FAIL TO INTEREST; 570]

bore to death v [➡BORE AND FAIL TO INTEREST; 570]

bore to tears v [➡BORE AND FAIL TO INTEREST; 570]

boring adj uninteresting, tedious, dull, dreary, mind-numbing, tiresome, lackluster, unexciting, monotonous, repetitive, wearisome, humdrum, uninspiring [➡BORING AND UNINTERESTING; 234] Opposite: exciting

Compare and Contrast: boring, dull, monotonous, tedious, uninteresting

CORE MEANING: causing a state of impatience and weariness

boring lacking in interest, stimulation, or variety; dull uninteresting because of a lack of liveliness, humor, or variety; monotonous dull because of too much uniformity and a lack of variation; tedious wearying to the point of physical as well as mental discomfort; uninteresting failing to engage somebody's interest rather than arousing actual impatience or weariness.

born adj instinctive, congenital, innate, intuitive, natural, untaught, native [➡TALENTED AND SKILLFUL; 527] Opposite: trained

born-again adj reinvigorated, reborn, enthusiastic, avid, fervid, passionate, revitalized, zealous [➡POSITIVE IMPATIENCE, ENTHUSIASM, AND ALERTNESS; 537]

born with a silver spoon in your mouth adj [➡WEALTH AND WEALTHY; 891]

borough n area, district, municipality, division, township [➡HUMAN SETTLEMENTS; 1070]

borrow 1 v use, make use of, have access to, scrounge (informal), sponge [➡LEND, LEASE, AND BORROW; 428] Opposite: lend 2 v copy, plagiarize, derive, pirate, steal, appropriate [➡STEAL AND ROB; 426]

borscht type of soup [➡SOUPS; 1186]

borstal (UK) n reformatory, detention center, prison, jail, reform school, bail hostel (UK), youth custody centre (UK) [➡BUILDINGS FOR CONFINING PEOPLE; 1094]

borzoi type of large dog [➡DOGS; 980]

bosom 1 adj (informal) close, best, dearest, special, firm, dear, inseparable [➡RELATIONSHIP TO ANOTHER; 973] Opposite: distant 2 part of torso [➡PARTS OF THE BODY: TORSO; 693] 3 n (literary)

heart, center, midst, embrace, arms [➡ CENTRAL PARTS OF PHYSICAL OBJECTS; 1251]

bosom buddy n [➡ FRIENDS AND GUESTS; 963]

bosom friend (*UK*) n [➡ FRIENDS AND GUESTS; 963]

boson *type of* **elementary particle** [➡ ELEMENTARY PARTICLES; 1279]

boss 1 n **manager**, supervisor, chief, head, person in charge, superior, honcho (*informal*) [➡ BOSSES AND MANAGEMENT; 965] *Opposite*: subordinate 2 v **give orders**, tell what to do, boss around, order around, command, bully, domineer, push around, boss about (*UK*) [➡ CAUSE OR COMPEL TO ACT; 271] *Opposite*: obey

bossa nova *type of* **dance** [➡ DANCE; 903]

boss around v **give orders**, tell what to do, order around, boss, domineer, command, bully [➡ CAUSE OR COMPEL TO ACT; 271] *Opposite*: obey

bossily adv **imperiously**, dictatorially, domineeringly, officiously, authoritatively, high-handedly, persuasively, overbearingly [➡ BOSSY AND OVERBEARING; 516] *Opposite*: meekly

bossiness n **imperiousness**, officiousness, high-handedness, authoritarianism, overbearingness [➡ BOSSY AND OVERBEARING; 516] *Opposite*: meekness

bossy adj **domineering**, officious, dominant, high-handed, dictatorial, interfering, interventionist, overbearing, authoritarian, authoritative [➡ BOSSY AND OVERBEARING; 516] *Opposite*: meek

Boston rocker *type of* **seating** [➡ FURNITURE; 858]

bot n [➡ THE INTERNET; 1128]

botanic *see* **botanical**

botanical adj **botanic**, vegetal, plant [➡ BIOLOGICAL SCIENCES; 1037]

botanical garden n [➡ GARDENS; 1074]

botany *type of* **bioscience** [➡ BIOLOGICAL SCIENCES; 1037]

botch 1 n (*informal*) **fiasco**, failure, disaster, flop (*informal*) [➡ MISTAKES; 250] 2 v **spoil**, damage, bungle, ruin, do badly, make a mess of, fail, make a botch of (*informal*), foul up (*informal*), mess up (*informal*) [➡ MESS UP AND MAKE MISTAKES; 472]

botched adj **failed**, substandard, poor, ruined, inferior, slipshod, spoiled, messed up (*informal*), bungled (*informal*) [➡ UNSUCCESSFUL AND UNPROMISING; 76] *Opposite*: first-rate

botch up v [➡ MESS UP AND MAKE MISTAKES; 472]

botfly *type of* **parasitic insect** [➡ PARASITES; 1017]

bother 1 v **make an effort**, take the trouble, put yourself out, go to the trouble of, extend yourself [➡ ATTEMPT AN ACTION; 261] 2 v **worry**, trouble, disturb, upset, unsettle, annoy, perturb, fret, disconcert, irk, bug (*informal*) [➡ UPSET, DISTRESS, AND HUMILIATE; 567] 3 v **interrupt**, disturb, distract, trouble, pester, hassle (*informal*) [➡ ANGER AND ANNOY; 569] 4 n **trouble**, difficulty, problem, nuisance, inconvenience, worry, anxiety, vexation, thorny problem, hassle (*informal*) [➡ NUISANCES; 253]

Compare and Contrast: *bother, annoy, bug, disturb, trouble, worry*

CORE MEANING: to interfere with somebody's composure

bother to make somebody feel worried, anxious, or upset, or to disturb or interrupt somebody; ***annoy*** to irritate or harass somebody; ***bug*** (*informal*) to cause persistent trouble and annoyance; ***disturb*** to interrupt or distract somebody in the process of doing something, or to upset somebody's peace of mind; ***trouble*** to cause distress or inconvenience; ***worry*** to cause anxiety in somebody.

bothered adj **worried**, concerned, troubled, anxious, apprehensive, upset, hot and bothered, disturbed, alarmed, perturbed, nervous, tense [➡ CONFUSION, ANXIETY, AND WORRY; 540] *Opposite*: untroubled

bothersome adj **troublesome**, inconvenient, worrisome, niggling, difficult, vexing, annoying, incommodious (*formal*) [➡ IRRITATING; 228]

bo tree *type of* **evergreen tree** [➡ EVERGREEN AND CONIFEROUS TREES; 1029]

bottle n **flask**, jug, carafe, flagon, decanter, magnum, thermos, canteen [➡ CONTAINERS, RECEPTACLES, AND PACKAGING; 1245]

bottle green *type of* **green** [➡ COLORS; 1224]

bottleneck n **block**, blockage, restricted access, holdup, traffic jam, jam, logjam, chokepoint, pinchpoint [➡ TRAVEL: TRAFFIC PROBLEMS AND TRAFFIC MANAGEMENT; 323]

bottle opener *type of* **utensil** [➡ TABLEWARE, FLATWARE, AND KITCHENWARE; 861]

bottle up v **contain**, repress, suppress, keep in check, keep inside, restrain, control, curb [➡ WITHHOLD INFORMATION; 687]

bottom 1 n **base**, bed, foot, floor, substructure, foundation [➡ EXTREMITIES OF PHYSICAL OBJECTS; 1250] *Opposite*: top 2 n **end**, far end, foot, extremity, limit [➡ EXTREMITIES OF PHYSICAL OBJECTS; 1250] *Opposite*: top 3 n **underside**, underneath, bottom side, underbelly [➡ EXTREMITIES OF PHYSICAL OBJECTS; 1250] *Opposite*: top 4 *part of* **torso** [➡ PARTS OF THE BODY: TORSO; 693] 5 adj **lowest**, bottommost, lowermost, nethermost (*formal*) [➡ RELATIVE LOCATION; 161] *Opposite*: top

bottomless adj **unlimited**, unrestricted, endless, limitless, unending, infinite, inexhaustible, never-ending, boundless [➡ DEPTH: DEEP; 1201] *Opposite*: restricted

bottom line 1 n [➡ ACCOUNTING, BANKING, AND BUDGETING; 799] 2 n **fundamental issue**, key issue, fact of the matter, thing to bear in mind, crucial thing, what matters [➡ MOST IMPORTANT THING; 197] 3 n **lower limit**, threshold, floor, cutoff point, limit [➡ MAJORITY AND MAXIMUM; 141]

bottommost adj **lowest**, last, bottom, final [➡ RELATIVE LOCATION; 161] *Opposite*: topmost

botulinum *type of* **microorganism** [➡ MICROORGANISMS, FUNGI, AND ALGAE; 1023]

boudoir n **bedroom**, dressing room, chamber (*archaic or literary*), bedchamber (*archaic or literary*) [➡ TYPES OF ROOMS; 1097]

bouffant 1 adj **backcombed**, fluffy, full, puffed up, voluminous, teased [➡ DESCRIBING HAIR; 486] **2** *type of* **hairstyle** [➡ HAIRSTYLES AND HAIRPIECES; 488]

bougainvillea *type of* **climber** [➡ CLIMBERS; 1033]

bough *n* **branch**, limb, spur [➡ PARTS OF TREES AND PLANTS; 1026]

bouillabaisse *type of* **soup** [➡ SOUPS; 1186]

bouillon *type of* **soup** [➡ SOUPS; 1186]

boulder *n* **rock**, stone, sarsen [➡ STONES, ROCKS, AND BOULDERS; 1057]

boules *type of* **target ball game** [➡ HOBBIES, GAMES, AND SPORTS; 875]

boulevard *type of* **highway** [➡ ROADS; 1106]

bounce **1** *v* **rebound**, spring back, bound, spring up, recoil, ricochet [➡ BOUNCE, UNDULATE, AND VIBRATE; 308] **2** *v* **spring**, jump, bound, bob, bobble [➡ BOUNCE, UNDULATE, AND VIBRATE; 308] **3** *v* **eject**, evict, throw out, remove, expel, kick out (*informal*) [➡ GET RID OF SOMETHING; 451]

bounce back *v* **recover**, improve, get better, pull through, perk up, recuperate, pick up (*informal*) [➡ GET BETTER; 375]

bounciness **1** *n* **liveliness**, spirit, vivacity, friskiness, playfulness, verve, energy [➡ ENERGY AND ENTHUSIASM; 496] *Opposite*: lethargy **2** *n* **elasticity**, springiness, resistance, resilience, pliability, give [➡ MALLEABLE AND ELASTIC; 1212] *Opposite*: firmness

bouncy **1** *adj* **effervescent**, energetic, playful, lively, vivacious, animated, full of beans (*informal*) [➡ ENERGY AND ENTHUSIASM; 496] *Opposite*: lethargic **2** *adj* **springy**, elastic, pliable [➡ MALLEABLE AND ELASTIC; 1212] *Opposite*: firm

bound **1** *adj* **certain**, sure, guaranteed, destined, assured, inevitable, unavoidable [➡ CERTAIN; 174] *Opposite*: unlikely **2** *adj* **obliged**, compelled, forced, obligated, duty-bound, required, constrained [➡ RESPONSIBILITY; 170] *Opposite*: free **3** *v* **border**, border on, be next to, be contiguous to, touch, be adjacent to, be bounded by, adjoin, abut, fringe, skirt, conjoin (*formal*) [➡ EXIST IN CLOSE PROXIMITY; 21] **4** *n* **jump**, leap, spring, bounce, hop, vault, hurdle [➡ BOUNCE, UNDULATE, AND VIBRATE; 308]

boundary *n* **border**, frontier, borderline, state line, dividing line, limit, edge, margin, periphery [➡ GEOGRAPHIC BORDERS AND BOUNDARIES; 1069]

bounded **1** *adj* **surrounded**, bordered, enclosed, encircled, delimited (*formal*) [➡ CAPTIVITY AND LOSS OF FREEDOM; 248] **2** *adj* **restricted**, hemmed in, limited, constrained, confined, circumscribed (*formal*) [➡ CAPTIVITY AND LOSS OF FREEDOM; 248] *Opposite*: free

boundless *adj* **unlimited**, endless, limitless, infinite, ceaseless, never-ending, vast, without end, interminable, bottomless, illimitable (*formal*) [➡ PERMANENCE: WITHOUT END; 94] *Opposite*: restricted

bounds *n* **limits**, boundaries, confines, restrictions, constraints, restraints [➡ EXTREMITIES OF PHYSICAL OBJECTS; 1250]

bounteous (*literary*) **1** *adj* **generous**, giving, charitable, munificent, openhanded, magnanimous [➡ GENEROSITY AND KINDNESS; 495] *Opposite*: parsimonious **2** *adj* **abundant**, plentiful, ample, profuse, copious, plenteous (*literary*) [➡ MANY, MUCH, LARGE AMOUNT; 117] *Opposite*: scarce

bountiful (*literary*) **1** *adj* **generous**, giving, munificent, openhanded, magnanimous [➡ GENEROSITY AND KINDNESS; 495] *Opposite*: parsimonious **2** *adj* **plentiful**, generous, abundant, copious, profuse, ample, numerous, unstinting, plenteous (*literary*) [➡ MANY, MUCH, LARGE AMOUNT; 117] *Opposite*: scarce

See Compare and Contrast at **generous**.

bounty **1** *n* **reward**, price, prize, payment, gift [➡ REWARDS AND AWARDS; 439] **2** *n* (*literary*) **abundance**, plenty, plenteousness (*literary*) [➡ MANY, MUCH, LARGE AMOUNT; 117] *Opposite*: scarcity

bouquet **1** *n* **bunch**, spray, posy, arrangement, nosegay [➡ COLLECTIONS AND MIXTURES OF THINGS; 1244] **2** *n* **smell**, aroma, scent, fragrance, perfume, odor [➡ SMELL AND SMELLING; 705]

See Compare and Contrast at **smell**.

bourgeois **1** *adj* **middle-class**, conventional, conformist, unadventurous, staid, predictable [➡ CLASS STATUS; 889] **2** *n* **conservative**, traditionalist, conformist, reactionary, conventional person, stick-in-the-mud (*informal*) [➡ UNCOOPERATIVE OR REBELLIOUS PEOPLE; 566]

bout *n* **short period**, short time, session, spell, attack, fit, stretch, stint [➡ SHORT PERIODS OF TIME; 93]

boutique *type of* **retail outlet** [➡ RETAIL OUTLETS; 1083]

boutique hotel *n* [➡ HOTELS, RESTAURANTS, AND CLUBS; 1082]

bouzouki *type of* **stringed instrument** [➡ MUSICAL INSTRUMENTS; 910]

bovine (*literary*) *adj* **stupid**, slow, unintelligent, dim, dense, dull [➡ NEGATIVE INTELLECTUAL CHARACTERISTICS; 525]

bow **1** *n* **arc**, curve, arch, sweep, bend, kink [➡ ROUNDED SHAPE; 1218] **2** *n* **bob**, bend, curtsy, obeisance (*formal*) [➡ GESTURES AND GESTICULATION; 653] **3** *part of* **ship or boat** [➡ PARTS OF A SHIP OR BOAT; 1151] **4** *n* [➡ WEAPONS FOR SHOOTING; 1156] **5** *v* **bend**, bend over, lower, stoop, lean, curtsy, genuflect, bob, duck, nod [➡ GESTURES AND GESTICULATION; 653] *Opposite*: straighten up **6** *v* **distort**, deform, arch, droop, sag [➡ CHANGE OF SHAPE; 385] *Opposite*: straighten

bow

◆ *types of bows*
crossbow, Cupid's bow, longbow

bow and scrape *v* [➡ GESTURES AND GESTICULATION; 653]

bowdlerize *v* **censor**, edit, abridge, clean up, expurgate, amend [➡ WITHHOLD INFORMATION; 687]

bowed *adj* **curved**, bent, deformed, convex, hooked, arched, stooped, hunched [➡ ROUNDED SHAPE; 1218] *Opposite*: straight

bowel *part of* **digestive tract** [➡ THE DIGESTIVE TRACT; 709]

bowels *n* **guts**, entrails, viscera, innards (*informal*), insides (*informal*) [➡ THE DIGESTIVE TRACT; 709]

bower *n* **arbor**, retreat, grove, copse, den, hideaway, nook, dell (*literary*) [➡ GARDENS; 1074]

bowie knife *type of* **sword or knife** [➡ SWORDS AND KNIVES; 1157]

bowing and scraping n [➡GESTURES AND GESTICULATION; 653]

bowl 1 n **container**, vessel, dish, basin, mixing bowl, washbasin, pudding basin (UK) [➡TABLEWARE, FLATWARE, AND KITCHENWARE; 861] 2 n **hollow**, depression, crater, basin, valley, vale (literary) [➡GEOLOGIC FEATURES; 1056] 3 n **stadium**, arena, amphitheater, ballpark, venue [➡BUILDINGS FOR PUBLIC ENTERTAINMENT; 1084] 4 n **ball**, boule, wood (UK) [➡SPORTS EQUIPMENT; 879] 5 v **career**, career, roll along, travel, speed, traverse [➡MOVE FAST; 313] 6 v **roll**, pitch, throw, lob, hurl, cast, toss, fling, chuck (informal) [➡MOVE SOMETHING: THROUGH THE AIR; 334]

bowled over adj **astonished**, surprised, speechless, taken aback, thunderstruck, amazed, dumbfounded, staggered, stunned, flabbergasted (informal), floored (informal) [➡SURPRISE, SHOCK, AND AMAZEMENT; 545]

bowlegged adj **bandy-legged**, bandy, bent, bowed [➡BUILD; 477]

bowling type of **target ball game** [➡HOBBIES, GAMES, AND SPORTS; 875]

bowl over 1 v **astonish**, amaze, delight, overwhelm, take by surprise [➡SURPRISE AND IMPRESS; 574] 2 v **knock down**, knock over, scatter, upturn, overturn [➡MOVE SOMETHING: INTO A NEW POSITION OR OVERTURN; 330]

bow out v **back out**, beg off, duck out, cry off (informal), fink out (slang) [➡NOT DO AND REFUSE TO DO; 274]

bowsprit part of **sailing vessel** [➡PARTS OF A SHIP OR BOAT; 1151]

bow tie n **tie**, cravat, necktie [➡ACCESSORIES, MILLINERY, AND LINGERIE; 867]

bow to v **accept**, yield, resign yourself to, recognize, acknowledge, give in to, submit, succumb to, acquiesce, give way to [➡FORGET, FORGIVE, AND ACCEPT; 748] Opposite: reject

box 1 n **container**, case, chest, packet, carton, package, strongbox, punnet (UK) [➡CONTAINERS, RECEPTACLES, AND PACKAGING; 1245] 2 n **rectangle**, square, frame, check box, tick box (UK) [➡ANGULAR SHAPE; 1217] 3 n **cubicle**, stall, booth, compartment, enclosure [➡ALCOVES, CUBICLES, AND COMPARTMENTS; 1096] 4 n (slang) **television**, tube (informal), TV (informal), small screen (informal), boob tube (informal), telly (UK) [➡TELEVISION AND RADIO; 606] 5 v **fight**, spar, punch, hit, thump, land a punch [➡PHYSICAL ATTACK AND PUNISHMENT; 415]

box camera type of **photographic equipment** [➡PHOTOGRAPHY AND PHOTOGRAPHIC EQUIPMENT; 1122]

box car part of **train** [➡RAILROADS; 1107]

boxer 1 n [➡PEOPLE IN SPORTS AND LEISURE; 876] 2 type of **large dog** [➡DOGS; 980]

boxer shorts type of **lower body underwear** [➡ACCESSORIES, MILLINERY, AND LINGERIE; 867]

box in v **enclose**, surround, contain, shut in, trap, hem in [➡EXIST IN CLOSE PROXIMITY; 21]

boxing type of **combat sport** [➡HOBBIES, GAMES, AND SPORTS; 875]

boxwood type of **evergreen tree** [➡EVERGREEN AND CONIFEROUS TREES; 1029]

boy n **young man**, lad, schoolboy, son, youngster, child, teenager, youth [➡MALE PERSON; 934]

boycott v **refuse**, stay away from, impose sanctions, embargo, shun, proscribe, prohibit, reject [➡AVOID, PREVENT, LIMIT, AND CONTROL; 277]

boyfriend n **male friend**, date, escort, fiancé, mate, partner, steady (informal), suitor (formal), beau (dated) [➡SEXUAL AND ROMANTIC RELATIONSHIPS; 964]

boyhood n **childhood**, youth, early years [➡BABYHOOD, CHILDHOOD, AND ADOLESCENCE; 917]

boyish adj **youthful**, adolescent, childlike, gamine, young, fresh-faced [➡PEOPLE'S PHYSICAL APPEARANCE; 475]

boysenberry type of **berry** [➡FRUIT AND VEGETABLES; 1176]

boy wonder n [➡TALENTED OR INTELLIGENT PEOPLE; 528]

B picture n [➡FILM; 901]

bra type of **upper body underwear** [➡ACCESSORIES, MILLINERY, AND LINGERIE; 867]

brace n **support**, strut, prop, stay, bracket, buttress, reinforcement [➡SUPPORTS AND BASES; 1255]

bracelet type of **jewelry** [➡JEWELRY; 866]

brace yourself v **prepare yourself**, ready yourself, make preparations, get ready for, prime yourself, get ready, steel yourself [➡PREPARE FOR ACTION; 289]

brachiosaurus type of **dinosaur** [➡DINOSAURS; 996]

bracing adj **invigorating**, stimulating, brisk, healthy, cold, refreshing, revitalizing, restorative, fortifying [➡PHYSICALLY PLEASANT; 186] Opposite: soporific

bracket 1 n **support**, strut, prop, stay, brace [➡SUPPORTS AND BASES; 1255] 2 n **group**, set, range, cohort, band, collection, category, class, grade, sort, kind [➡VARIETIES, TYPES, AND KINDS; 145] 3 type of **punctuation mark** [➡ASPECTS OF LANGUAGE; 682] 4 v **connect**, link, join, relate, associate, group [➡CREATING CONNECTIONS; 144] Opposite: separate

bracket fungus type of **fungus** [➡MICROORGANISMS, FUNGI, AND ALGAE; 1023]

brackish adj **salty**, saline, salted, briny, salt [➡TASTE; 703] Opposite: fresh

bract part of **flower** [➡FLOWERS; 1032]

bradawl type of **carpentry tool** [➡HAND TOOLS; 1119]

brag v **boast**, blow your own horn, crow, show off, swagger, talk big [➡BOAST; 616] Opposite: underplay

braggadocio n [➡BOAST; 616]

braggart n **boaster**, egotist, show-off (informal), big-mouth (informal), loudmouth (informal) [➡SELF-IMPORTANT AND SELF-SEEKING PEOPLE; 949]

bragger n [➡SELF-IMPORTANT AND SELF-SEEKING PEOPLE; 949]

bragging 1 n **boasting**, boastfulness, showing off, arrogance, self-aggrandizement, hot air (informal) [➡BOAST; 616] Opposite: modesty 2 adj **boastful**, arrogant, self-important, conceited, swaggering, cocky (informal) [➡POMPOUS, LOUD, AND OVERCONFIDENT; 635] Opposite: modest

braid 1 v **plait**, interweave, interlace, intertwine, weave, thread, entwine [➡CRAFTS AND CARVING; 355] Opposite: unravel

2 *v* **decorate**, trim, edge, fringe, bind [➡ DECORATE, ADORN, AND APPLY COATINGS; 405] *Opposite*: strip

braids *type of* **hairstyle** [➡ HAIRSTYLES AND HAIRPIECES; 488]

Braille *type of* **alphabet** [➡ SYMBOLS, SIGNS, AND NUMBERS; 596]

brain 1 *n* **intelligence**, mind, intellect, head, wits, common sense, understanding [➡ DESCRIBING SOMEBODY'S INTELLECT; 523] **2** *n* (*informal*) **mastermind**, intellectual, genius, intellect, prodigy, egghead (*informal*), brainbox (*UK*) [➡ TALENTED OR INTELLIGENT PEOPLE; 528]

brainbox (*UK*) *n* [➡ TALENTED OR INTELLIGENT PEOPLE; 528]

brainchild *n* **idea**, invention, creation, innovation, breakthrough, discovery [➡ IDEAS AND THOUGHTS; 770]

brainless *adj* **foolish**, stupid, mindless, unintelligent, silly, senseless, obtuse [➡ NEGATIVE INTELLECTUAL CHARACTERISTICS; 525] *Opposite*: sensible

brainpower *n* **intellect**, brains, capacity, ability, intellectual capacity, mental ability, understanding, grasp, IQ, intelligence [➡ DESCRIBING SOMEBODY'S INTELLECT; 523]

brains *n* **intelligence**, common sense, wits, intellect, brainpower, mental ability [➡ DESCRIBING SOMEBODY'S INTELLECT; 523] *Opposite*: ignorance

brainstorm 1 *n* (*informal*) **bright idea**, inspiration, idea, breakthrough, innovation, brain wave [➡ IDEAS AND THOUGHTS; 770] **2** *n* **aberration**, fit, turn, disturbance, upset, attack [➡ SUDDEN EVENTS; 52] **3** *v* **think**, suggest, come up with, devise, dream up, free-associate [➡ THINK AND REFLECT; 743]

brainteaser *n* **problem**, puzzle, riddle, challenge, conundrum, mystery [➡ JOKES AND TEASING; 674]

brainwash *v* **persuade**, indoctrinate, condition, program, convince, mold, talk into [➡ INSTRUCT AND TEACH; 609]

brainy (*informal*) *adj* **intelligent**, clever, bright, quick, academic, intellectual, sharp, alert, brilliant, gifted, quick-witted, able [➡ POSITIVE INTELLECTUAL CHARACTERISTICS; 524] *Opposite*: unintelligent

braise *v* **cook**, stew, casserole, steam, simmer, poach, boil [➡ COOKING AND FOOD PREPARATION; 353]

braised *adj* [➡ STATE OF PREPARED FOOD; 1171]

brake 1 *v* **decelerate**, slow down, reduce speed, put on the brakes, lose speed, slam on the brakes, slow, slow up, ease up, let up [➡ CHANGE OF SPEED: LESS; 397] *Opposite*: accelerate **2** *n* **restraint**, constraint, curb, control, limitation, damper, deterrent, discouragement [➡ PROBLEMS; 256] *Opposite*: incentive **3** *type of* **controls** [➡ INTERNAL PARTS OF A VEHICLE; 1146] **4** *part of* **bike** [➡ BIKES, CARS, AND CARRIAGES; 1149]

brake light *type of* **external feature** [➡ EXTERNAL PARTS OF A VEHICLE; 1147]

bramble *type of* **shrub or bush** [➡ BUSHES AND SHRUBS; 1027]

bran *n* **fiber**, dietary fiber, cellulose, roughage, bulk [➡ FOOD COMPONENTS; 1188]

branch 1 *n* **bough**, limb, spur, twig [➡ PARTS OF TREES AND PLANTS; 1026] **2** *n* **local office**, division, area office, subdivision, outlet, office [➡ PLACE OF EMPLOYMENT; 832] *Opposite*: headquarters **3** *n* **division**, department, offshoot, wing, arm, subdivision [➡ SUBDIVISIONS AND OFFSHOOTS; 1253] **4** *n* **area**, field, topic, domain,

sphere, aspect, side [➡ SUBJECT AREAS; 768] **5** *n* **turnoff**, arm, tributary, fork, side road, turn, turning (*UK*) [➡ HOLES, GAPS, AND FORKS; 1252] **6** *v* **split**, fork, divide, diverge, separate, branch off, bifurcate [➡ SEPARATE AND DIVIDE; 401] *Opposite*: converge

branch off *v* **split**, fork, divide, turn off, leave, diverge, separate [➡ SEPARATE AND DIVIDE; 401] *Opposite*: merge

branch out *v* **diversify**, diverge, take a new direction, broaden, expand, separate from, split off [➡ SEPARATE AND DIVIDE; 401] *Opposite*: consolidate

brand 1 *n* **make**, product, brand name, variety, kind, sort, trade name, trademark, marque [➡ NAME AND DESCRIBE; 665] **2** *n* **type**, kind, sort, style, variety, class [➡ VARIETIES, TYPES, AND KINDS; 145] **3** *n* **identifying mark**, mark, marker, identification, label, stamp [➡ SYMBOLS, SIGNS, AND NUMBERS; 596] **4** *v* **mark**, imprint, stamp, label [➡ CREATE IMAGES; 356] **5** *v* **call**, classify, label, name, describe, class, categorize [➡ NAME AND DESCRIBE; 665]

brandish *v* **wield**, wave, flourish, handle, ply, flaunt, show off, display [➡ MOVE SOMETHING: ON THE SPOT; 336]

brand name *n* **trade name**, brand, label, make, trademark, registered trademark, marque, service mark [➡ NAME AND DESCRIBE; 665]

brand-new *adj* **new**, unused, pristine, fresh, mint, untouched, spanking new [➡ NEW, MODERN; 166] *Opposite*: old

brash 1 *adj* **aggressive**, arrogant, self-confident, brazen, presumptuous, bold, forceful, impudent, pushy (*informal*) [➡ POMPOUS, LOUD, AND OVERCONFIDENT; 635] *Opposite*: self-effacing **2** *adj* **hasty**, impetuous, rash, foolhardy, slapdash, hurried, impatient [➡ INCAUTIOUS AND CARELESS; 283] *Opposite*: measured **3** *adj* (*UK*) **loud**, garish, vulgar, gaudy, bright, tasteless, trashy [➡ IN POOR TASTE AND OVERSENTIMENTAL; 229] *Opposite*: muted

brashly *adv* **brazenly**, forcefully, insolently, assertively, rudely, obnoxiously, boldly, impudently [➡ POMPOUS, LOUD, AND OVERCONFIDENT; 635] *Opposite*: shyly

brashness *n* **boldness**, brazenness, forcefulness, insolence, assertiveness, rudeness, impudence, presumptuousness [➡ POMPOUS, LOUD, AND OVERCONFIDENT; 635] *Opposite*: shyness

brass 1 *type of* **metal** [➡ METALS; 1276] **2** *n* (*informal*) **nerve**, impudence, self-assurance, self-confidence, gall, boldness, assertiveness, chutzpah (*informal*), cheek (*informal*) [➡ BOSSY AND OVERBEARING; 516] *Opposite*: bashfulness

brass band *type of* **band** [➡ MUSICIANS AND SINGERS; 908]

brasserie *type of* **eating place** [➡ HOTELS, RESTAURANTS, AND CLUBS; 1082]

brassica *type of* **vegetable** [➡ FRUIT AND VEGETABLES; 1176]

brass tacks *n* **basics**, essentials, fundamentals, bare essentials, nuts and bolts (*informal*), nitty-gritty (*informal*) [➡ BASIC DETAILS; 688]

brassy 1 *adj* **harsh**, loud, metallic, strident, grating, high-pitched [➡ LOUD, HIGH, OR UNPLEASANT SOUNDS; 1266] *Opposite*: soft **2** *adj* **brazen**, strident, overbearing, brash, arrogant, forceful [➡ POMPOUS, LOUD, AND OVERCONFIDENT; 635] *Opposite*: self-effacing

brat *n* **little monster**, imp, spoiled brat, terror (*informal*), holy terror (*informal*) [➡ MISCHIEVOUS OR BADLY-BEHAVED CHILD; 946] *Opposite*: cherub

brattish *adj* [➡ AGGRESSIVE AND BELLIGERENT; 518]

bratty *adj* **obnoxious**, spoiled, demanding, overindulged, selfish, troublesome, ill-mannered [➡ AGGRESSIVE AND BELLIGERENT; 518] *Opposite*: well-behaved

bratwurst *type of* **processed meat** [➡ TYPES AND CUTS OF MEAT; 1177]

bravado *n* **audacity**, boldness, daring, bluster, boasting, show, swagger, braggadocio [➡ BOAST; 616] *Opposite*: cowardice

brave 1 *adj* **courageous**, valiant, heroic, bold, daring, fearless, plucky [➡ COURAGE; 498] *Opposite*: cowardly 2 *v* **defy**, face, stand up to, confront, take on, bear, endure, suffer [➡ TOLERATE AND ENDURE; 766] *Opposite*: shrink

brave out *v* **suffer**, face, bear, endure, stay the course, sit out, put up with, tough it out (*informal*), grin and bear it (*informal*) [➡ TOLERATE AND ENDURE; 766] *Opposite*: give up

bravery *n* **courage**, courageousness, valor, gallantry, daring, heroism, nerve, fearlessness, boldness, pluckiness, pluck, guts (*slang*) [➡ COURAGE; 498] *Opposite*: cowardice

See Compare and Contrast at **courage**.

bravo *interj* [➡ COMPLIMENTS; 657]

bravura 1 *n* **boldness**, daring, spirit, nerve, chutzpah (*informal*), guts (*slang*) [➡ COURAGE; 498] *Opposite*: timidity 2 *adj* **brilliant**, magnificent, exceptional, dazzling, outstanding, superlative, virtuoso [➡ EXTRAORDINARY: UNCOMMON; 205] *Opposite*: nondescript

brawl 1 *n* **scuffle**, fight, punch up, clash, affray, fracas, scrap (*informal*) [➡ AGGRESSIVE EVENTS; 39] 2 *v* **fight**, scuffle, tussle, wrestle, clash, scrap [➡ COMPETE, CONTEND, AND COMBAT; 303]

brawn 1 *n* **strength**, muscle, brute force, power, burliness, muscularity [➡ MUSCLES AND MUSCULATURE; 479] *Opposite*: weakness 2 *n* [➡ THE MUSCLES; 718]

brawniness *n* [➡ BUILD; 477]

brawny *adj* **muscular**, strong, powerfully built, hefty, burly, beefy, strapping (*informal*) [➡ MUSCLES AND MUSCULATURE; 479] *Opposite*: scrawny

bray 1 *v* **whinny**, neigh, cry, call [➡ SOUND EMISSION BY ANIMALS OR BIRDS; 364] 2 *v* **grate**, rasp, bark, bellow, snort, cackle, shriek, screech [➡ SOUND EMISSION BY PEOPLE; 363] *Opposite*: murmur 3 *n* **neigh**, whinny, cry, call, sound [➡ SOUNDS MADE BY ANIMALS; 1261]

braying *adj* **harsh**, loud, strident, jarring, grating, raucous [➡ LOUD, HIGH, OR UNPLEASANT SOUNDS; 1266] *Opposite*: soft

brazen *adj* **bold**, barefaced, shameless, brash, unabashed, unashamed, blatant, audacious, forward, bald-faced [➡ POMPOUS, LOUD, AND OVERCONFIDENT; 635] *Opposite*: discreet

brazenly *adv* **openly**, shamelessly, barefacedly, boldly, blatantly, audaciously, brashly, impudently, bald-facedly [➡ BAD MANNERS AND SOCIAL SKILLS; 521] *Opposite*: discreetly

brazenness *n* **shamelessness**, boldness, barefacedness, flagrancy, impudence, defiance, bald-facedness [➡ POMPOUS, LOUD, AND OVERCONFIDENT; 635] *Opposite*: discretion

brazen out *v* **face down**, stand your ground, face out, hold your own, stay the course, stick to your guns [➡ CONTINUE AN ACTION; 262] *Opposite*: cave in

brazier *n* **stove**, barbecue, grill, hibachi, fire, open fire [➡ FIRE, FLAMMABILITY, AND BURNING; 1165]

Brazil nut *type of* **nut** [➡ NUTS; 1185]

breach 1 *v* **get through**, break through, break, rupture, penetrate, open, crack open [➡ MOVE PAST, INTO, OR THROUGH SOMETHING; 331] *Opposite*: block 2 *v* **break**, violate, contravene, infringe, flout, disobey [➡ DISOBEY; 302] *Opposite*: honor 3 *n* **opening**, break, hole, crack, fissure, rupture [➡ HOLES, GAPS, AND FORKS; 1252] 4 *n* **violation**, contravention, infringement, defiance, betrayal, breaking [➡ BAD BEHAVIOR OR ACTIONS; 254] *Opposite*: compliance 5 *n* **rift**, separation, division, rupture, estrangement, drifting apart [➡ DISHARMONY; 156] *Opposite*: reconciliation

breach of the peace *n* **public disturbance**, public nuisance, nuisance, riot, fracas, commotion, ruckus, disorderly conduct, uproar [➡ CRIMES; 817] *Opposite*: order

bread 1 *n* **food**, daily bread, sustenance, nourishment, rations, diet, means of survival [➡ FOOD; 1167] 2 *n* (*dated slang*) **cash**, funds, finance, moola, bucks (*informal*), dough (*slang*) [➡ MONEY; 797]

bread

◆ *types of bread*
baguette, black bread, brioche, brown bread, challah, chapati, ciabatta, corn bread, crouton, flat bread, focaccia, matzo, nan, pita, poppadom, pumpernickel, puri, roti, rye bread, soda bread, sourdough, spoon bread, toast, tortilla, white bread

◆ *types of rolls or buns*
bagel, brioche, bun, croissant, crumpet, English muffin, roll

bread and butter 1 *n* **livelihood**, living, income, maintenance, upkeep, support, means of support, means [➡ INCOME; 460] 2 *n* **mainstay**, lifeblood, backbone, basis, core [➡ MOST IMPORTANT THING; 197]

bread-and-butter *adj* **basic**, primary, fundamental, essential, important, key, central, everyday, main [➡ FUNDAMENTAL; 195] *Opposite*: superfluous

bread knife *type of* **knife** [➡ CUTTING TOOLS; 1120]

breadth 1 *n* **width**, span, wideness, extent, size, girth [➡ WIDTH: WIDE; 1199] *Opposite*: depth 2 *n* **extensiveness**, extent, range, scope, span, coverage, scale [➡ DEGREE AND EXTENT; 110] *Opposite*: narrowness 3 *n* **latitude**, room, freedom, space, leeway, tolerance, broad-mindedness [➡ FREEDOM AND LIBERTY; 208] *Opposite*: restriction

breadthwise 1 *adj* **sideways**, side-to-side, widthways [➡ ORIENTATION AND ALIGNMENT; 1223] 2 *adv* **across**, from side to side, widthwise, breadthways (*UK*) [➡ ORIENTATION AND ALIGNMENT; 1223]

breadwinner *n* **wage earner**, worker, employee [➡ WORKERS; 836] *Opposite*: dependent

break 1 *v* **smash**, fracture, rupture, shatter, split, crack, sever [➡ TEAR, BREAK, AND CUT; 360] *Opposite*: mend **2** *v* **break down**, stop working, fail, collapse, crash, go down, go kaput (*informal*), bite the dust (*informal*) [➡ FAIL OR CEASE TO FUNCTION; 470] **3** *v* **infringe**, violate, contravene, breach, disobey, be in breach of, fall foul of, disregard [➡ DISOBEY; 302] *Opposite*: uphold **4** *v* **stop**, end, interrupt, disturb, break into, cut into [➡ CAUSE TO STOP; 266] **5** *v* **take a break**, break into, have a break, rest, stop, put your feet up, take it easy, relax, have time out, take five (*informal*), take a breather (*informal*) [➡ STOP ACTING; 264] **6** *v* **beat**, surpass, exceed, top, better, crack [➡ BEAT AND DEFEAT; 80] **7** *v* **destroy**, shatter, crush, overwhelm, defeat, rout [➡ BEAT AND DEFEAT; 80] **8** *v* **become known**, make public, become public, disclose, get around, get out, be revealed, leak out [➡ APPEAR AND EMERGE; 3] **9** *v* **decipher**, crack, decode, solve, unravel, unscramble [➡ SOLVE AND INTERPRET; 760] **10** *n* **disruption**, breakdown, discontinuity, interruption, pause, halt, cessation, opportunity, opening, occasion [➡ PAUSES AND PHASES; 56] **11** *n* (*informal*) **chance**, opportunity, opening, occasion, leg up, way in, start [➡ SOURCE OF HAPPINESS, PLEASURE, OR IMPROVEMENT; 209] **12** *n* **rest**, respite, coffee break, pause, lunch break, sit-down (*informal*), breather (*informal*), tea break (*UK*) [➡ PERIODS OF REST; 91] **13** *n* **time off**, trip, weekend trip, vacation, holiday (*UK*), weekend break (*UK*) [➡ PERIODS OF REST; 91] **14** *n* **interruption**, pause, space, disruption, halt, stop, getaway, intermission, recess [➡ PAUSES AND PHASES; 56]

breakable *adj* **fragile**, delicate, brittle, frail, flimsy [➡ FRAGILE; 1209] *Opposite*: sturdy

breakage *n* **breaking**, smashing, cracking, rupture, splintering, fracture, damage [➡ TEAR, BREAK, AND CUT; 360] *Opposite*: mending

break away *v* **secede**, separate, become independent, split, disaffiliate, gain autonomy, divide off [➡ SEPARATE AND DIVIDE; 401] *Opposite*: join

breakaway **1** *n* **separation**, rupture, severance, splitting up, breakup, parting [➡ ENDS AND DEPARTURES; 54] *Opposite*: fusion **2** *adj* **separate**, splinter, independent, autonomous, alternative, unconnected, nonaligned [➡ UNRELATEDNESS AND SEPARATENESS; 146] *Opposite*: mainstream

breakbeat *type of* **electronic music** [➡ MUSIC, SONGS, AND SINGING; 907]

break down **1** *v* **lose control**, cry, be overcome, collapse, burst into tears, lose it (*informal*) [➡ GIVING VENT TO EMOTIONS; 679] **2** *v* **stop working**, break, fail, go down, crash, go wrong, stop, go kaput (*informal*) [➡ FAIL OR CEASE TO FUNCTION; 470] **3** *v* **overcome**, defeat, destroy, knock down, smash down, wear down, work away at [➡ BEAT AND DEFEAT; 80] *Opposite*: build **4** *v* **analyze**, separate, dissect, break up, split, go through with a fine-tooth comb [➡ EXAMINE AND ASSESS; 753] **5** *v* **divide**, classify, categorize, split, separate, group [➡ SEPARATE AND DIVIDE; 401] *Opposite*: lump **6** *v* **decompose**, decay, putrefy, molder, disintegrate [➡ WORSEN SOMETHING; 380]

breakdown **1** *n* **failure**, collapse, cessation, halt, interruption, break [➡ FAILURE; 77] **2** *n* **analysis**, rundown, classification, dissection, summary, itemization [➡ EXAMINE AND ASSESS; 753]

break down and cry *v* [➡ GIVING VENT TO EMOTIONS; 679]

breaker *n* **wave**, roller, whitecap, white horse (*UK*) [➡ THE SEAS, OCEANS, AND SHORES; 1041]

breakfast *type of* **meal** [➡ MEALS AND PARTS OF MEALS; 1169]

breakfast cereal *n* [➡ CEREAL FOODS; 1178]

break free *v* **escape**, break away, break with, separate, get away, break out, disentangle yourself, cut loose (*informal*) [➡ AVOID OR ESCAPE CONTACT; 418]

breakfront *type of* **cabinet** [➡ FURNITURE; 858]

break in **1** *v* **tame**, train, discipline, domesticate, house-train, school, housebreak [➡ INSTRUCT AND TEACH; 609] **2** *v* **force an entry**, break into, burgle, break and enter, burglarize, force the lock, break down the door, get in [➡ STEAL AND ROB; 426] **3** *v* **interrupt**, butt in, interject, interpose, cut in, cut off [➡ INTERRUPT AND BUTT IN; 619]

break-in *n* **forced entry**, burglary, robbery, crime, felony, incident [➡ CRIMES; 817]

breaking *n* **contravention**, infringement, violation, breach, transgression, flouting [➡ CRIMES; 817] *Opposite*: observance

breaking and entering *n* [➡ CRIMES; 817]

breaking point *n* **verge of collapse**, limit, threshold, snapping point, crisis, breakpoint, edge, brink [➡ DECISIVE MOMENTS; 44]

break into **1** *v* **break in**, force an entry, burgle, break and enter, burglarize, break down the door, force the lock, get in [➡ MOVE PAST, INTO, OR THROUGH SOMETHING; 331] **2** *v* **begin**, burst into, launch into, embark on, burst out, start on (*informal*) [➡ START AN ACTION; 260] *Opposite*: break off

breakneck *adj* **quick**, speedy, hurried, hasty, rapid, swift, fast [➡ HAPPENING QUICKLY; 104] *Opposite*: slow

break new ground *v* **be the first**, blaze a trail, lead the way, be in the vanguard, set a trend, set an example [➡ START AN ACTION; 260]

break of day *n* **daybreak**, sunrise, daylight, first light, dawn, crack of dawn, sunup, morning, cockcrow (*archaic or literary*) [➡ TIMES OF DAY; 87] *Opposite*: sundown

break off **1** *v* **detach**, come off, snap off, come away, separate, break away [➡ SEPARATE AND DIVIDE; 401] *Opposite*: attach **2** *v* **end**, terminate, stop, cease, finish, halt, pause, falter [➡ STOP ACTING; 264] *Opposite*: begin

breakoff *n* **discontinuation**, ending, interruption, suspension, stopping, pause [➡ PAUSES AND PHASES; 56] *Opposite*: continuation

break open *v* **open**, divide, come apart, burst, shatter, part, crack, split, pry, prize [➡ SEPARATE AND DIVIDE; 401]

break out **1** *v* **begin**, start, erupt, burst into, embark on, burst out, explode [➡ SUDDENLY COME INTO EXISTENCE; 2] *Opposite*: end **2** *v* **escape**, break loose, burst out, break free, emerge, come out, get out, cut loose (*informal*) [➡ RUN AWAY AND AVOID; 10]

breakout *n* **escape**, getaway, flight, running away, running off, escaping, absconding [➡ ENDS AND DEPARTURES; 54]

breaks and beats *type of* **electronic music** [➡ MUSIC, SONGS, AND SINGING; 907]

break the ice *v* **get to know**, make friends, get acquainted, introduce yourself, set the ball rolling, make the first move [➡ INITIATE AND ESTABLISH COMMUNICATION; 680]

break through *v* **burst through**, penetrate, come

through, breach, wear down, break down, batter down, destroy, infiltrate [➡ MOVE PAST, INTO, OR THROUGH SOMETHING; 331]

breakthrough n advance, step forward, leap forward, new idea, innovation, revolution, invention, discovery, development [➡ PROGRESS AND ADVANCEMENT; 213]

break up 1 v divide, fragment, disintegrate, crumble, fall apart, fall to pieces [➡ TEAR, BREAK, AND CUT; 360] *Opposite:* fuse 2 v disperse, separate, split up, keep apart, divide up, tear apart, break down, cut up, section [➡ SEPARATE AND DIVIDE; 401] *Opposite:* unite 3 v separate, tell somebody it's over, split up, end, finish, ditch (*informal*), dump (*informal*) [➡ REFUSING OR REJECTING RELATIONS; 975]

breakup 1 n disintegration, fragmentation, division, crumbling, destruction, collapse [➡ TEAR, BREAK, AND CUT; 360] *Opposite:* merger 2 n ending, end, splitting up, finish, separation, divorce [➡ ENDS AND DEPARTURES; 54]

breakwater n offshore barrier, mole, sea wall, harbor wall, causeway, pier [➡ WATERWAYS AND SEAWAYS; 1108]

break with v separate, split, leave, part company, escape, pull away, secede [➡ REFUSING OR REJECTING RELATIONS; 975] *Opposite:* associate

bream type of freshwater fish [➡ FRESHWATER FISH; 1010]

breast 1 part of torso [➡ PARTS OF THE BODY: TORSO; 693] 2 type of cut [➡ TYPES AND CUTS OF MEAT; 1177] 3 part of bird [➡ PARTS OF A BIRD; 1006]

breastbone type of bone [➡ THE BONES AND JOINTS; 719]

breath 1 n gasp, sigh, pant, inhalation, exhalation [➡ BREATHE AND NOT BREATHE; 716] 2 n puff, waft, current, draft, gush, rush [➡ AMOUNTS OF GAS; 116]

breathe v respire, take breaths, inhale, exhale, suck in air, take in air, breathe in, breathe out, blow, puff [➡ BREATHE AND NOT BREATHE; 716]

breathe new life into v revitalize, reinvigorate, revive, resurrect, rejuvenate, boost [➡ IMPROVE STRENGTH AND DURABILITY; 378]

breather (*informal*) n rest, break, respite, time out, sit-down (*informal*) [➡ PERIODS OF REST; 91]

breathe your last (*literary*) v die, expire, go to meet your maker, pass away, pass on, depart this life (*formal*), give up the ghost (*literary*) [➡ DIE; 922]

breath freshener n [➡ PERSONAL HYGIENE; 491]

breathing 1 n inhalation, exhalation, panting, gasping, puffing, blowing [➡ BREATHE AND NOT BREATHE; 716] 2 adj living, alive, conscious, sentient, aware [➡ LIVING THINGS AND LIVING; 976]

breathing space n respite, relief, space, recovery time, time, rest, pause, breathing room, time off [➡ PAUSES AND PHASES; 56]

breathless adj out of breath, panting, gasping, puffing, winded, wheezing [➡ BREATHE AND NOT BREATHE; 716]

breathlessly adv eagerly, excitedly, with bated breath, on tenterhooks, anxiously, nervously [➡ POSITIVE IMPATIENCE, ENTHUSIASM, AND ALERTNESS; 537] *Opposite:* nonchalantly

breathlessness n panting, gasping, breathing difficulty, rapid breathing, shallow breathing [➡ BREATHE AND NOT BREATHE; 716]

breathtaking adj out of this world, wonderful, magnificent, spectacular, incredible, awesome, awe-inspiring, amazing, stunning, astounding, mind-blowing (*informal*) [➡ EXTRAORDINARY: AMAZING; 204] *Opposite:* banal

breathy adj wheezy, hissing, gasping, panting, husky [➡ BREATHE AND NOT BREATHE; 716]

breeches type of pants [➡ GARMENTS AND OUTFITS; 865]

breed 1 n type, strain, class, kind, variety, sort [➡ VARIETIES, TYPES, AND KINDS; 145] 2 v reproduce, have babies, propagate, procreate, multiply [➡ ENGENDER; 350] 3 v raise, rear, bring up, farm, produce, keep [➡ ENGENDER; 350] 4 v cause, create, generate, bring about, produce, give rise to, trigger [➡ CREATION; 346]

breeding n upbringing, education, background, social standing, refinement, good manners, manners [➡ STATUS; 888]

breeding ground n environment, conditions, source, medium, place, situation [➡ BEGINNINGS; 53]

breeze 1 n wind, gust, gentle wind, light wind, waft, zephyr, puff of air, draft [➡ WINDY AND STORMY WEATHER; 1053] 2 n (*informal*) child's play, cinch (*informal*), piece of cake (*informal*), walkaway (*informal*), walkover (*informal*), waltz (*informal*) [➡ EASY WORK; 299]

breeze block (*UK*) n [➡ BUILDING MATERIALS; 1077]

breeze in v [➡ ARRIVE; 12]

breezily adv brightly, cheerfully, cheerily, happily, merrily, easily, lightheartedly, flippantly [➡ GOOD-TEMPERED AND HUMOROUS; 627] *Opposite:* seriously

breeziness n lightheartedness, cheerfulness, brightness, cheeriness, flippancy [➡ CHEERFULNESS OF OUTLOOK; 503] *Opposite:* seriousness

breezy 1 adj blustery, gusty, windy, brisk, windswept, blowy (*informal*) [➡ WINDY AND STORMY WEATHER; 1053] *Opposite:* still 2 adj cheerful, cheery, jolly, lighthearted, flippant [➡ CHEERFULNESS OF OUTLOOK; 503] *Opposite:* serious

bresaola type of processed meat [➡ TYPES AND CUTS OF MEAT; 1177]

breviary n missal, prayer book, hymnal, book of psalms [➡ RELIGIOUS OBJECTS; 779]

brevity 1 n shortness, briefness, quickness, swiftness, transience [➡ FINITENESS, VARIABILITY, AND TRANSIENCE; 96] *Opposite:* length 2 n conciseness, succinctness, concision, pithiness, terseness, curtness [➡ SUCCINCT AND TO THE POINT; 640] *Opposite:* long-windedness

brew 1 n (*informal*) drink, potion, infusion, cocktail, swill, beverage (*formal*) [➡ DRINKS; 1187] 2 n mixture, mix, blend, combination, concoction, cocktail [➡ COLLECTIONS AND MIXTURES OF THINGS; 1244] 3 v prepare, make, infuse, steep, ferment, concoct, distill [➡ COOKING AND FOOD PREPARATION; 353] 4 v develop, loom, threaten, grow, blow up, gather force [➡ ABOUT TO HAPPEN; 33]

brewery type of factory [➡ INDUSTRIAL BUILDINGS; 1087]

briar see brier

bribe 1 n inducement, enticement, carrot, kickback, payola, baksheesh, slush fund, sweetener (*informal*), payoff (*informal*) [➡ BRIBES; 440] 2 v induce, corrupt, entice, suborn, persuade, win over, buy off, pay off (*informal*) [➡ CAUSE OR COMPEL TO ACT; 271]

bribery *n* **corruption**, inducement, enticement, subornation [➡ CRIMES; 817]

bric-a-brac *n* **knickknacks**, curios, ornaments, stuff, junk (*informal*), bits and pieces (*informal*), jumble (*UK*) [➡ JUNK AND USELESS OBJECTS; 1249]

brick 1 *n* [➡ BUILDING MATERIALS; 1077] 2 *n* **block**, slab, ingot, lump, piece, tablet, cake [➡ AMOUNTS OF SOLID OR SEMISOLID; 115]

brick-and-mortar *adj* [➡ E-COMMERCE; 1129]

brickbat 1 *n* **insult**, criticism, insinuation, suggestion, comment [➡ INSULTS, ABUSE, AND SWEARING; 658] 2 *type of* **projectile** [➡ PROJECTILES; 1159]

brick red *type of* **red** [➡ COLORS; 1224]

bricks and mortar *n* [➡ BUILDING MATERIALS; 1077]

brickwork *n* **fabric**, structure, bricks and mortar, masonry, stonework [➡ BUILDING MATERIALS; 1077]

bridal *adj* **wedding**, nuptial, marriage, ceremonial, honeymoon, celebratory [➡ CEREMONIES AND ANNIVERSARIES; 38]

bride *n* **wife**, wife-to-be, newlywed, spouse, partner, fiancée, intended (*dated or humorous*) [➡ RELATIVES BY MARRIAGE; 960]

bride and groom *n* [➡ RELATIVES BY MARRIAGE; 960]

bridegroom *n* **husband**, husband-to-be, newlywed, spouse, partner, fiancé, intended (*dated or humorous*) [➡ RELATIVES BY MARRIAGE; 960]

bridesmaid *n* **maid of honor**, attendant, matron of honor, flower girl [➡ SUPPORTERS, PROTECTORS, AND COMPATRIOTS; 970]

bridge 1 *n* [➡ BRIDGES, TUNNELS, CROSSINGS, AND JUNCTIONS; 1112] 2 *n* **bond**, tie, link, connection, conduit, association, channel, passage, join [➡ CONNECTIONS; 143] 3 *part of* **ship or boat** [➡ PARTS OF A SHIP OR BOAT; 1151] 4 *v* **link**, connect, join, span, tie together, associate [➡ FASTEN, LINK, AND JOIN; 408]

bridge

◆ *types of bridges*
aqueduct, arch bridge, Bailey bridge, bascule bridge, beam bridge, cable-stayed bridge, cantilever bridge, drawbridge, footbridge, gangplank, overpass, pontoon bridge, suspension bridge, swing bridge, viaduct, walkway

bridgehead *n* **foothold**, position, stepping stone, jumping-off point, vantage point, front line, foot in the door [➡ BEGINNINGS; 53]

bridle 1 *v* **bristle**, get angry, become annoyed, become indignant, prickle, get your hackles up [➡ GIVING VENT TO EMOTIONS; 679] 2 *v* **curb**, restrain, control, rein in, keep in check, arrest, contain [➡ AVOID, PREVENT, LIMIT, AND CONTROL; 277] *Opposite:* let loose

bridle path *n* **ride**, horse trail, path, track, trail, bridleway (*UK*) [➡ PATHWAYS; 1110]

bridleway (*UK*) *n* [➡ PATHWAYS; 1110]

Brie *type of* **soft cheese** [➡ DAIRY PRODUCTS AND CHEESES; 1183]

brief 1 *adj* **short-lived**, transitory, fleeting, ephemeral, short-term, momentary, passing [➡ HAPPENING QUICKLY; 104] *Opposite:* lasting 2 *adj* **short**, concise, succinct, to the point, pithy, epigrammatic [➡ SUCCINCT AND TO THE POINT; 640] *Opposite:* lengthy 3 *n* **synopsis**, summary, digest, abstract, outline [➡ SUMMARIES, OUTLINES, AND EXCERPTS; 588] 4 *n* **briefing**, instructions, guidelines, preparation, orders, ground rules [➡ BASIC DETAILS; 688] 5 *n* (*UK*) **task**, mission, mandate, assignment, duties, remit (*UK*) [➡ WORK IN GENERAL; 297] 6 *v* **inform**, tell, give instructions, prepare, instruct, direct, fill in, update [➡ INFORM, ANNOUNCE, AND ISSUE; 611]

briefcase *n* **document case**, attaché case, case, portfolio, music case, folder, bag, carrycase [➡ CONTAINERS, RECEPTACLES, AND PACKAGING; 1245]

briefing *n* **meeting**, conference, seminar, press conference, updating session, update, consultation [➡ MEETINGS AND ASSEMBLIES; 43]

briefs *type of* **lower body underwear** [➡ ACCESSORIES, MILLINERY, AND LINGERIE; 867]

brier *type of* **shrub or bush** [➡ BUSHES AND SHRUBS; 1027]

brig *type of* **sailing vessel** [➡ SHIPS AND BOATS; 1150]

brigade *n* **group**, team, crew, contingent, gang, unit [➡ GROUPS WITH A COMMON INTEREST; 938]

brigadier *n* [➡ MILITARY PERSONNEL; 828]

brigand (*literary*) *n* **lawbreaker**, bandit, thief, robber, thug, felon, gangster, outlaw [➡ CRIMINALS; 821]

brigantine *type of* **sailing vessel** [➡ SHIPS AND BOATS; 1150]

bright 1 *adj* **brilliant**, vivid, intense, dazzling, light, clear [➡ DESCRIBING LIGHT; 1228] *Opposite:* dark 2 *adj* **intelligent**, quick, sharp-witted, clever, smart, brainy (*informal*) [➡ POSITIVE INTELLECTUAL CHARACTERISTICS; 524] *Opposite:* unintelligent 3 *adj* **cheerful**, happy, lively, optimistic, positive, sunny, perky, upbeat (*informal*) [➡ CHEERFULNESS OF OUTLOOK; 503] *Opposite:* gloomy

See Compare and Contrast at **intelligent**.

brighten 1 *v* **feel better**, brighten up, look up, perk up, cheer up, snap out of it [➡ CHANGE OF MOOD AND COMPOSURE; 580] 2 *v* **make brighter**, lighten, make lighter, brighten up, illuminate, enhance [➡ CHANGE OF COLOR; 391] *Opposite:* darken 3 *v* **improve**, make better, enhance, animate, revivify, vivify, revitalize, add to, cheer up, liven up, jazz up (*informal*) [➡ IMPROVE SOMETHING; 374]

brighten up *v* **raise the spirits**, make brighter, brighten, lighten, make lighter, perk up, animate, come to life, revitalize, cheer up, jazz up (*informal*) [➡ ENCOURAGE; 576] *Opposite:* cast down

bright-eyed and bushy-tailed *adj* [➡ CHEERFULNESS OF OUTLOOK; 503]

brightly 1 *adv* **luminously**, lustrously, radiantly, glossily, glowingly, blazingly, brilliantly, intensely, vibrantly, fiercely, dazzlingly [➡ DESCRIBING LIGHT; 1228] *Opposite:* dully 2 *adv* **sunnily**, perkily, cheerfully, cheerily, optimistically, happily, enthusiastically [➡ GOOD-TEMPERED AND HUMOROUS; 627] *Opposite:* gloomily

brightness 1 *n* **illumination**, glare, intensity, brilliance, vividness, luster, clarity, glow [➡ DESCRIBING LIGHT; 1228] *Opposite*: dullness 2 *n* **sunniness**, high spirits, cheerfulness, optimism, cheeriness, enthusiasm, happiness, good humor [➡ PLEASURE, EXCITEMENT, AND ELATION; 534] *Opposite*: gloominess

brill *type of* **flatfish** [➡ OCEAN FISH; 1009]

brilliance 1 *n* **brightness**, intensity, vividness, luminosity, radiance, luster, shine, brilliancy [➡ DESCRIBING LIGHT; 1228] *Opposite*: dullness 2 *n* **cleverness**, wisdom, smartness, genius, talent, skill, virtuosity, ability, intelligence, braininess (*informal*), smarts (*informal*) [➡ POSITIVE INTELLECTUAL CHARACTERISTICS; 524] *Opposite*: stupidity

brilliancy *see* **brilliance**

brilliant 1 *adj* **luminous**, radiant, dazzling, sparkling, gleaming, shining, bright [➡ DESCRIBING LIGHT; 1228] *Opposite*: dull 2 *adj* **vivid**, bright, clear, intense, dazzling [➡ DESCRIBING COLORS; 1226] *Opposite*: faded 3 *adj* **talented**, virtuoso, inspired, skillful, gifted, exceptional, accomplished [➡ TALENTED AND SKILLFUL; 527] *Opposite*: mediocre 4 *adj* (*informal*) **wonderful**, superb, marvelous, excellent, magnificent, splendid, great [➡ EXTRAORDINARY: AMAZING; 204] *Opposite*: awful

brilliantly 1 *adv* **dazzlingly**, brightly, luminously, radiantly, intensely, vividly, fiercely [➡ DESCRIBING LIGHT; 1228] *Opposite*: dully 2 *adv* **ably**, giftedly, skillfully, exceptionally, consummately, adeptly [➡ TALENTED AND SKILLFUL; 527] *Opposite*: ineptly 3 *adv* **wonderfully**, marvelously, excellently, superbly, magnificently, splendidly [➡ EXTRAORDINARY: AMAZING; 204] *Opposite*: terribly

brim 1 *n* **ridge**, edge, top, rim, lip [➡ EXTREMITIES OF PHYSICAL OBJECTS; 1250] 2 *part of* **garment** [➡ PARTS OF A GARMENT; 870]

brimful *adj* **full to the top**, full, filled up, filled to the brim, overfull, overfilled, overflowing, spilling over [➡ FULL; 1239] *Opposite*: empty

brimming *adj* **bursting**, teeming, overflowing, packed, filled, crammed [➡ FULL; 1239]

brine *n* **saline**, salt water, sea water [➡ LIQUIDS; 1269]

bring 1 *v* **take along**, carry, fetch, convey, transport, take, get, pass [➡ MOVE SOMETHING TO ANOTHER LOCATION; 324] *Opposite*: take away 2 *v* **cause**, bring about, produce, lead to, result in, end in, make happen, create, beget, be the cause of, generate, effect (*formal*) [➡ CAUSE TO HAPPEN; 31] 3 *v* **command**, earn, produce, make, bring in, fetch, sell for, market for, give [➡ GET MONEY OR REWARD; 421]

bring about *v* **generate**, cause, produce, result in, end in, lead to, make happen, create, bring, beget, effect (*formal*) [➡ CAUSE TO HAPPEN; 31] *Opposite*: prevent

bring alive *v* **awaken**, bring to life, make real, animate, enliven, give life to, flesh out, breathe life into [➡ IMPROVE SOMETHING; 374]

bring around 1 *v* **sway**, reason, convince, persuade, win over, get around, cajole, get on your side, induce [➡ SOOTHE AND CALM; 573] *Opposite*: deter 2 *v* **rouse**, bring to, revive, awaken, wake up, resuscitate, get going [➡ WAKE AND REGAIN CONSCIOUSNESS; 724] *Opposite*: knock out

bring back 1 *v* **evoke**, recall, bring to mind, summon up, reawaken, stir up, rekindle, renew, revive [➡ REMIND;

747] 2 *v* **return**, replace, restore, reinstate, recapture, revive [➡ MOVE SOMETHING TO ANOTHER LOCATION; 324]

bring down 1 *v* **overthrow**, topple, depose, defeat, dethrone, seize power, humble [➡ BEAT AND DEFEAT; 80] *Opposite*: elect 2 *v* **fell**, floor, topple, demolish, knock over, knock down, knock the wind out of, deck (*informal*) [➡ MOVE SOMETHING INTO A NEW POSITION OR OVERTURN; 330] *Opposite*: raise

bring down a peg *v* **humble**, chasten, force to eat humble pie, cut somebody down to size, put somebody in their place, put somebody down (*informal*) [➡ UPSET, DISTRESS, AND HUMILIATE; 567]

bring down to earth *v* **disillusion**, disappoint, disenchant, enlighten, disabuse, set straight, open somebody's eyes, shatter somebody's illusions [➡ UPSET, DISTRESS, AND HUMILIATE; 567]

bring forth 1 *v* **deliver**, bear, give birth to, produce, yield, breed [➡ ENGENDER; 350] 2 *v* **yield**, bear, produce, give, generate, give rise to [➡ CREATION; 346]

bring forward 1 *v* **speed**, advance, reschedule, move forward, change [➡ CAUSE TO HAPPEN; 31] *Opposite*: delay 2 *v* **put on the table**, produce, present, offer, bring out, reveal, propose [➡ SUGGEST, HINT, AND COMMENT; 612] *Opposite*: withdraw

bring home *v* **make clear**, clarify, illustrate, illuminate, underline, emphasize [➡ EXPLAIN AND CLARIFY; 610]

bring home the bacon 1 *v* (*informal*) **provide**, keep a roof over your head, put food on the table, keep the wolf from the door, keep clothes on your back, make a living, earn your keep, feed your family [➡ GET MONEY OR REWARD; 421] 2 *v* (*UK informal*) **be successful**, bring off, come up with the goods, come through, keep your end of the bargain, see it through, make good your promise, deliver [➡ SUCCEED AND WIN; 79] *Opposite*: fail

bring in 1 *v* **introduce**, set up, establish, launch, start, phase in [➡ CAUSE TO START; 265] *Opposite*: end 2 *v* **recoup**, acquire, earn, make, take home, get paid [➡ GET MONEY OR REWARD; 421]

bring into being *v* **create**, establish, found, institute, set up, engender, start up, get underway [➡ INSTITUTE AND INAUGURATE; 348] *Opposite*: destroy

bring into disrepute *v* **discredit**, dishonor, disgrace, shame, smear, sully, tarnish [➡ UPSET, DISTRESS, AND HUMILIATE; 567] *Opposite*: bring credit to

bring into line *v* **standardize**, coordinate, synchronize, make uniform, harmonize, systematize, correct, discipline [➡ ARRANGE AND CREATE ORDER; 357]

bring off *v* **succeed**, carry off, achieve, accomplish, engineer, make work, pull off (*informal*) [➡ CARRY OUT AN ACTION; 269] *Opposite*: fail

bring on *v* **cause**, create, produce, make, start, set off [➡ CAUSE TO START; 265]

bring out 1 *v* **highlight**, spotlight, show up, reveal, bring to the surface, elicit, draw out [➡ CAUSE TO APPEAR; 5] *Opposite*: suppress 2 *v* **introduce**, produce, release, put on sale, launch, present, start, sell [➡ SELL; 441] *Opposite*: withdraw

bring shame on *v* **discredit**, sully, tarnish, smear, stain, stigmatize [➡UPSET, DISTRESS, AND HUMILIATE; 567] *Opposite:* bring credit to

bring to *v* **bring around**, rouse, awaken, wake up, revive, resuscitate [➡WAKE AND REGAIN CONSCIOUSNESS; 724] *Opposite:* knock out

bring to a close *v* **put a stop to**, end, halt, discontinue, run down, call a halt, bring to an end, finish, stop, conclude, complete, close, wind up, wrap up (*informal*) [➡CAUSE TO STOP; 266] *Opposite:* start

bring to a halt *v* [➡CAUSE TO STOP; 266]

bring to an end *v* **conclude**, bring to a close, put a stop to, end, stop, halt, complete, finish, call a halt, discontinue, run down, wind up, wrap up (*informal*) [➡CAUSE TO STOP; 266] *Opposite:* start

bring to a standstill *v* [➡CAUSE TO STOP; 266]

bring to completion *v* [➡COMPLETE AN ACTION; 263]

bring to fruition *v* [➡CAUSE TO HAPPEN; 31]

bring together 1 *v* **combine**, mix, mix together, blend, pool, concentrate, focus [➡COMBINE AND MIX; 400] *Opposite:* separate 2 *v* **gather**, amass, rally, compile, glean, round up, collate, collect, pull together, assemble [➡ARRANGE AND CREATE ORDER; 357] *Opposite:* distribute 3 *v* **reconcile**, integrate, unite, unify, link, join, connect, coordinate, organize [➡CREATING CONNECTIONS; 144]

bring to life *v* **make real**, animate, bring alive, anthropomorphize, give life to, awaken, breathe life into [➡CREATION; 346]

bring to light *v* **expose**, unearth, disclose, uncover, publicize, reveal [➡CAUSE TO APPEAR; 5] *Opposite:* hide

bring to mind *v* **summon up**, reawaken, rekindle, stir up, bring back, recall, think of, evoke, call to mind, recollect, think back to, conjure up [➡REMIND; 747]

bring to pass *v* [➡CAUSE TO HAPPEN; 31]

bring up 1 *v* **mention**, broach, raise, suggest, introduce, talk about, discuss [➡SUGGEST, HINT, AND COMMENT; 612] *Opposite:* gloss over 2 *v* **raise**, rear, care for, nurture, look after, educate [➡TAKE CARE OF AND SPOIL; 300] 3 *v* **vomit**, expel, spew, regurgitate, disgorge, discharge [➡VOMIT AND BELCH; 712]

bring up-to-date *v* **inform**, give the lowdown, look after, put in the picture, update, give the latest, fill in, keep posted, keep informed, let know [➡INFORM, ANNOUNCE, AND ISSUE; 611] *Opposite:* keep in the dark

brink 1 *n* **verge**, threshold, edge, point, precipice [➡BEGINNINGS; 53] 2 *n* **edge**, rim, lip, brim, border, periphery [➡EXTREMITIES OF PHYSICAL OBJECTS; 1250] *Opposite:* center

brinkmanship *n* **strategy**, tactics, politics, bluff, bluffing, bluster, politicking, maneuvering [➡DECEPTION AND LIES; 660]

briny 1 *adj* **salty**, salt, saline, salted, brackish [➡TASTE; 703] 2 *n* (*UK*) **sea**, ocean, deep, drink (*informal*) [➡THE SEAS, OCEANS, AND SHORES; 1041]

brio (*literary*) *n* **energy**, vigor, enthusiasm, go, gusto, sparkle, high spirits, oomph (*informal*) [➡ENERGY AND ENTHUSIASM; 496]

brioche *type of* **roll or bun** [➡BREAD, FLOUR, AND BREAD PRODUCTS; 1179]

briquette *n* **block**, lump, brick, piece, cake [➡AMOUNTS OF SOLID OR SEMISOLID; 115]

brisk 1 *adj* **energetic**, fast, quick, rapid, hurried, vigorous [➡MOVING QUICKLY; 103] *Opposite:* slow 2 *adj* **abrupt**, curt, impatient, brusque, hurried, no-nonsense, sharp [➡BAD-TEMPERED AND HUMORLESS; 626] *Opposite:* measured 3 *adj* **refreshing**, cool, cold, invigorating, stimulating, bracing, sharp, zesty, fresh, reviving [➡PHYSICALLY PLEASANT; 186] *Opposite:* warm

brisket *type of* **cut** [➡TYPES AND CUTS OF MEAT; 1177]

briskness 1 *n* **speed**, rapidity, vigor, efficiency, urgency, alacrity [➡SPEED; 102] *Opposite:* tardiness 2 *n* **abruptness**, coldness, reserve, brusqueness, curtness, sharpness, impatience [➡BAD-TEMPERED AND HUMORLESS; 626] *Opposite:* patience

bristle 1 *n* **stubble**, hackle, hair, spine, spike, quill [➡FACIAL HAIR; 489] 2 *v* **stiffen**, become erect, stand up, rise, prickle, stand on end, stick out, poke out [➡GO UPWARD; 306] 3 *v* **recoil**, resent, get your hackles up, object, bridle, get angry, become annoyed, become indignant, prickle, take umbrage [➡GIVING VENT TO EMOTIONS; 679] 4 *v* **brim**, be full, teem, overflow, be thick with, be packed with [➡PROSPER AND ABOUND; 16]

bristly *adj* **spiky**, coarse, wiry, stubbly, sharp, rough [➡PHYSICAL TEXTURE; 1222] *Opposite:* smooth

British shorthair *type of* **cat** [➡FELINES; 983]

brittle *adj* **hard**, stiff, inelastic, fragile, breakable, weak, frail, delicate [➡FRAGILE; 1209] *Opposite:* robust

brittleness *n* **hardness**, stiffness, fragility, weakness, frailty, delicacy, daintiness, delicate state [➡FRAGILE; 1209] *Opposite:* robustness

broach *v* **propose**, present, submit, mention, raise, bring up, introduce, approach, try out [➡SUGGEST, HINT, AND COMMENT; 612]

broad 1 *adj* **spacious**, wide, large, big, extensive, expansive, open [➡WIDTH: WIDE; 1199] *Opposite:* narrow 2 *adj* **comprehensive**, extensive, wide, far-reaching, wide-ranging, expansive, open, all-encompassing, general [➡WHOLENESS AND COMPLETENESS; 198] *Opposite:* restricted 3 *adj* **inexact**, rough, general, approximate, sketchy, hazy, imprecise [➡APPROXIMATELY; 135] *Opposite:* precise 4 *adj* **visible**, obvious, plain, clear, patent, transparent, unsubtle [➡PERCEPTIBLE; 25] *Opposite:* subtle 5 *adj* **distinctive**, distinct, thick, heavy, strong, marked, pronounced [➡THE SPOKEN WORD; 671] *Opposite:* slight 6 *n* (*UK*) **lake**, expanse of water, stretch of water, body of water, mere (*archaic or literary*) [➡RIVERS, LAKES, AND STREAMS; 1042]

broad bean *type of* **pulse** [➡PEAS AND BEANS; 1189]

broad-brush *adj* **inclusive**, comprehensive, broad, across-the-board, all-embracing, wide-ranging [➡WHOLENESS AND COMPLETENESS; 198] *Opposite:* narrow

broadcast 1 *v* **transmit**, air, show, televise, screen, put out, relay, rerun [➡TELEVISION AND RADIO; 606] 2 *v* **air**, spread, disseminate, publicize, make known, advertise, announce, shout [➡INFORM, ANNOUNCE, AND ISSUE; 611] 3 *v* **scatter**, sow, distribute, disseminate, strew, cast [➡SPREAD AND SCATTER; 332]

4 *n* **transmission**, program, show, airing, newscast, rerun, recording [➡ TELEVISION AND RADIO; 606]

broadcast

◆ *types of broadcasts*
call-in, commercial, concert, current affairs, distance learning, docudrama, documentary, drama, game show, infomercial, infotainment, makeover program, miniseries, news, newscast, news flash, newsreel, play, reality show, sitcom (*informal*), soap (*informal*), soap opera, sport, sportscast, talk show, telethon, travelogue

See Compare and Contrast at **scatter.**

broadcaster *n* **newscaster**, anchor, announcer, journalist, presenter (*UK*) [➡ WORKERS IN ENTERTAINMENT AND MEDIA; 873]

broaden *v* **widen**, extend, increase, make wider, become wider, thicken, expand, enlarge, stretch [➡ CHANGE OF SIZE: BIGGER; 392] *Opposite*: narrow

broadly *adv* **approximately**, sketchily, generally, largely, roughly, mostly [➡ USUALLY; 108]

broadly-based *adj* **wide**, broad, wide-ranging, extensive, sweeping, general, comprehensive [➡ WHOLENESS AND COMPLETENESS; 198]

broad-minded *adj* **tolerant**, progressive, liberal, permissive, open-minded, forward-thinking, nonjudgmental, freethinking, unprejudiced, open [➡ POSITIVE INTELLECTUAL CHARACTERISTICS; 524] *Opposite*: narrow-minded

broad-mindedness *n* **liberality**, open-mindedness, tolerance, progressiveness, permissiveness, openness, free thought [➡ POSITIVE INTELLECTUAL CHARACTERISTICS; 524] *Opposite*: narrow-mindedness

broadness **1** *n* **width**, breadth, wideness [➡ WIDTH: WIDE; 1199] **2** *n* **scope**, breadth, span, range, extensiveness, extent [➡ WHOLENESS AND COMPLETENESS; 198]

broadsheet *n* **paper**, newspaper, quality newspaper, serious newspaper, heavyweight (*slang*) [➡ NEWSPAPERS AND MAGAZINES; 605]

broadside *n* **attack**, diatribe, tirade, onslaught, volley, assault [➡ CRITICISMS AND ANGRY OUTBURSTS; 50]

broadsword *type of* **sword or knife** [➡ SWORDS AND KNIVES; 1157]

brocade *type of* **fabric from animals** [➡ FABRICS; 1132]

broccoli *type of* **vegetable** [➡ FRUIT AND VEGETABLES; 1176]

brochure *n* **booklet**, leaflet, pamphlet, catalog, information sheet, flier [➡ BOOKS AND BOOKLETS; 590]

brogue *n* **accent**, burr, drawl [➡ ASPECTS OF LANGUAGE; 682]

broil **1** *v* **grill**, barbecue, roast, cook [➡ COOKING AND FOOD PREPARATION; 353] **2** *v* **swelter**, burn, roast, bake, boil, cook [➡ PAIN AND OTHER PHYSICAL SENSATIONS; 733] *Opposite*: freeze **3** *v* (*archaic*) **fight**, brawl, clash, tussle, scuffle, scrap [➡ COMPETE, CONTEND, AND COMBAT; 303] **4** *n* (*archaic*) **brawl**, fight, riot, tussle, scuffle, clash, scrap, uproar, fracas, tumult [➡ AGGRESSIVE EVENTS; 39]

broiled *adj* [➡ STATE OF PREPARED FOOD; 1171]

broiler *type of* **fowl** [➡ FOOD BIRDS; 999]

broke (*informal*) *adj* **bankrupt**, penniless, poor, in the red, overdrawn, insolvent, in debt, poverty-stricken, destitute, ruined, bust (*informal*) [➡ POVERTY AND POOR; 892] *Opposite*: wealthy

broken **1** *adj* **wrecked**, fragmented, shattered, cracked, smashed, damaged, ruined, destroyed [➡ IN BAD REPAIR; 1234] *Opposite*: intact **2** *adj* **inoperative**, malfunctioning, faulty, defective, out of order, broken-down, worn-out, wrecked, had it (*informal*), busted (*informal*), bust (*informal*), kaput (*informal*), conked-out (*informal*) [➡ IN BAD REPAIR; 1234] *Opposite*: working **3** *adj* **beaten**, licked, defeated, dejected, crushed, dispirited, without hope [➡ SADNESS, DISTRESS, AND DESPAIR; 539] *Opposite*: triumphant

broken beat *type of* **dance music** [➡ MUSIC, SONGS, AND SINGING; 907]

broken-down **1** *adj* **inoperative**, malfunctioning, not working, broken, out of order, faulty, damaged, defective [➡ IN BAD REPAIR; 1234] *Opposite*: working **2** *adj* **in poor condition**, dilapidated, run-down, falling apart, ramshackle, worn-out [➡ IN BAD REPAIR; 1234]

brokenhearted *adj* **sad**, grief-stricken, disappointed, desolate, despairing, lovesick, upset, wretched, unhappy, miserable, depressed, crushed, despondent, melancholy, heartbroken, sorrowful, dejected [➡ SADNESS, DISTRESS, AND DESPAIR; 539] *Opposite*: overjoyed

broker *n* **trader**, agent, dealer, negotiator, stockbroker [➡ BUSINESS PEOPLE; 793]

bronchial *adj* [➡ RESPIRATORY ORGANS; 715]

bronchial tube *part of* **respiratory system** [➡ RESPIRATORY ORGANS; 715]

bronchiole *part of* **respiratory system** [➡ RESPIRATORY ORGANS; 715]

bronchus *part of* **respiratory system** [➡ RESPIRATORY ORGANS; 715]

bronco *type of* **horse** [➡ HORSES; 985]

brontosaurus *type of* **dinosaur** [➡ DINOSAURS; 996]

Bronx cheer (*informal*) *n* [➡ UNFAVORABLE NONVERBAL RESPONSES; 654]

bronze **1** *n* **sculpture**, figure, statue, statuette, effigy, bust, head, model, figurine [➡ SCULPTURE; 902] **2** *type of* **brown** [➡ COLORS; 1224]

bronzed *adj* **tanned**, brown, suntanned, golden-brown, coppery [➡ COMPLEXION; 480]

brooch *n* **pin**, badge, ornament, trinket, accessory [➡ JEWELRY; 866]

brood **1** *n* **young**, clutch, litter, issue, family, flock [➡ GROUPS OF ANIMALS; 993] **2** *type of* **flock** [➡ GROUPS OF BIRDS; 1007] **3** *n* **children**, offspring, family, progeny, kids (*informal*) [➡ YOUNGER GENERATION RELATIVES; 958] **4** *v* **ruminate**, worry, mope, dwell on, fret, agonize [➡ THINK AND REFLECT; 743]

broodily *adv* **thoughtfully**, pensively, meditatively, fretfully, sullenly, morosely, glumly, moodily [➡ SADNESS, DISTRESS, AND DESPAIR; 539] *Opposite*: cheerfully

broodiness *n* **pensiveness**, glumness, fretfulness, sullenness, moroseness, meditativeness, moodiness [➡ SADNESS, DISTRESS, AND DESPAIR; 539]

brooding *adj* **ominous**, menacing, threatening, gloomy, dark, heavy (*slang*) [➡ DANGEROUS; 236]

broodingly *adv* **glumly**, fretfully, sullenly, morosely, moodily, pensively, deep in thought, meditatively, musingly [➡ PENSIVENESS AND INTEREST; 538] *Opposite*: cheerfully

broodmare *type of* **horse** [➡ HORSES; 985]

broody **1** *adj* **sullen**, thoughtful, pensive, moody, glum, gloomy [➡ SADNESS, DISTRESS, AND DESPAIR; 539] *Opposite*: cheerful **2** *adj* **maternal**, motherly, tender, caring [➡ APPRECIATION AND GRATITUDE; 535]

brook **1** *n* **stream**, rivulet, river, creek, beck (*UK*), burn (*UK*) [➡ RIVERS, LAKES, AND STREAMS; 1042] **2** *v* (*literary*) **tolerate**, allow, accept, put up with, suffer, sanction, countenance (*formal*) [➡ TOLERATE AND ENDURE; 766]

broom **1** *n* **brush**, sweeper, besom [➡ HAND TOOLS; 1119] **2** *type of* **shrub or bush** [➡ BUSHES AND SHRUBS; 1027]

broomstick *n* **handle**, broom handle, pole, stick, stave, staff [➡ STICKS, POLES, AND WEDGES; 1254]

broth *type of* **soup** [➡ SOUPS; 1186]

brother **1** *type of* **same-generation relative** [➡ SAME-GENERATION RELATIVES; 957] **2** *n* **comrade**, member, colleague, associate [➡ FRIENDS AND GUESTS; 963]

brotherhood **1** *n* **association**, society, union, guild, organization, group [➡ INSTITUTIONS; 790] **2** *n* **comradeship**, friendship, companionship, unity, loyalty, camaraderie [➡ RELATIONSHIP TO ANOTHER; 973]

brother-in-law *type of* **in-law** [➡ RELATIVES BY MARRIAGE; 960]

brotherly *adj* **companionable**, fraternal, affectionate, kind, friendly, cordial, sympathetic [➡ FRIENDLINESS AND SOCIABILITY; 494]

brougham *type of* **wagon or carriage** [➡ VEHICLES; 1145]

brouhaha *n* **commotion**, ruckus, brawl, rumpus, melee, confusion, uproar, to-do (*informal*), free-for-all (*informal*) [➡ CHAOS AND UPROAR; 51]

brow **1** *n* **summit**, top, crest, ridge, peak, crown [➡ EXTREMITIES OF PHYSICAL OBJECTS; 1250] **2** *part of* **face** [➡ PARTS OF THE BODY: HEAD; 692]

browbeat *v* **intimidate**, badger, bully, dragoon, nag, push, pester, threaten, force, coerce, twist somebody's arm (*informal*) [➡ COMPLAIN AND NAG; 686] *Opposite*: persuade

browbeaten *adj* **downtrodden**, oppressed, intimidated, bullied, subjugated, cowed, broken, demoralized, frightened, scared [➡ CONFUSION, ANXIETY, AND WORRY; 540] *Opposite*: resistant

brown **1** *type of* **color** [➡ COLORS; 1224] **2** *adj* **tanned**, sunburned, bronzed [➡ COMPLEXION; 480] **3** *v* **fry**, grill, sear, toast, char, burn [➡ COOKING AND FOOD PREPARATION; 353]

brown

◆ *types of brown*
auburn, bay, bronze, burnt sienna, burnt umber, caramel, chestnut, chocolate, copper, hazel, henna, khaki, liver, mahogany, mocha, mousy, nut-brown, roan, russet, sorrel, tan, tawny, umber, walnut

brown alga *type of* **marine alga** [➡ MICROORGANISMS, FUNGI, AND ALGAE; 1023]

brown bread *type of* **bread** [➡ BREAD, FLOUR, AND BREAD PRODUCTS; 1179]

brown dwarf *type of* **star or star system** [➡ HEAVENLY BODIES; 1061]

brownfield site *n* [➡ URBAN OUTDOOR SPACES; 1072]

brownie *type of* **cake** [➡ CAKES, COOKIES, AND DESSERTS; 1181]

brownies *type of* **dessert** [➡ CAKES, COOKIES, AND DESSERTS; 1181]

brown recluse *type of* **arachnid** [➡ ARACHNIDS; 1018]

brownstone *type of* **house** [➡ RESIDENTIAL BUILDINGS; 1078]

browse **1** *v* **glance**, cruise, look, look through, leaf through, surf, peruse [➡ LOOKING AND LOOKS; 700] **2** *v* [➡ THE INTERNET; 1128]

browser **1** *n* [➡ THE INTERNET; 1128] **2** *type of* **software** [➡ COMPUTERS AND COMPUTING; 1127]

bruise **1** *n* **discoloration**, black eye, welt, bump, contusion, shiner (*informal*) [➡ CONDITIONS AFFECTING THE SKIN; 721] **2** *v* **hurt**, damage, mark, injure, discolor, bash (*informal*) [➡ WORSEN APPEARANCE; 382]

bruised **1** *adj* **injured**, hurt, sore, black-and-blue, damaged, aching, battered, painful, discolored [➡ INJURED; 742] *Opposite*: unhurt **2** *adj* **wounded**, upset, hurt, offended, affected, crushed [➡ SADNESS, DISTRESS, AND DESPAIR; 539] *Opposite*: unaffected

bruiser (*informal*) *n* **muscleman**, bodyguard, bouncer, tough, heavyweight, toughie (*informal*), heavy (*slang*) [➡ VILLAINS AND THUGS; 947]

brume (*literary*) *n* [➡ CLOUDY AND RAINY WEATHER; 1052]

brunch *type of* **meal** [➡ MEALS AND PARTS OF MEALS; 1169]

brunette *adj* **dark**, brown, chestnut, auburn [➡ HAIR COLOR; 485] *Opposite*: blond

brunt *n* **effect**, force, impact, burden, substance [➡ RESULTS AND OUTCOMES; 83]

bruschetta *type of* **cooked dish** [➡ PREPARED DISHES; 1170]

brush **1** *n* **broom**, sweeper, besom [➡ HAND TOOLS; 1119] **2** *n* **contact**, touch, stroke, graze, sweep, scrape [➡ CONTACT: TOUCH; 412] **3** *n* **encounter**, meeting, confrontation, skirmish, disagreement, argument, clash, run-in (*informal*) [➡ ARGUMENTS; 47] **4** *v* **scrub**, clear, coat, groom, sweep, clean, polish [➡ CLEAN AND POLISH; 403] **5** *v* **touch**, graze, scrape, sweep, stroke, skim, contact [➡ CONTACT: TOUCH; 412]

brush against *v* [➡ CONTACT: TOUCH; 412]

brushed *adj* **fleecy**, fluffy, downy, furry, soft, woolly [➡ PHYSICAL TEXTURE; 1222]

brushfire n [➡ FIRE, FLAMMABILITY, AND BURNING; 1165]

brush off v dismiss, rebuff, snub, reject, give the cold shoulder to, ignore [➡ REFUSING OR REJECTING RELATIONS; 975]

brushoff (informal) n **turndown**, rebuff, snub, rejection, cold shoulder [➡ MALICIOUS ACTIONS OR BEHAVIOR; 296]

brush up v reread, refresh, renew, revise, review, go over [➡ IMPROVE SOMETHING; 374]

brushwood n firewood, twigs, branches, undergrowth, kindling [➡ VEGETATION; 1025]

brusque adj abrupt, curt, offhand, rough, brisk, gruff, harsh, terse, short [➡ BAD-TEMPERED AND HUMORLESS; 626] Opposite: gentle

brusqueness n roughness, terseness, abruptness, offhandedness, lack of warmth, unfriendliness, asperity (formal) [➡ UNINTERESTED AND DETACHED; 629] Opposite: gentleness

Brussels sprout type of vegetable [➡ FRUIT AND VEGETABLES; 1176]

brutal 1 adj ruthless, cruel, vicious, fierce, pitiless, heartless, inhuman, inhumane, violent, ferocious [➡ MORALLY BAD OR IMPROPER; 775] Opposite: humane 2 adj harsh, severe, rough, callous, insensitive, unfeeling, unkind, terrible [➡ SELFISH AND UNKIND; 505] Opposite: kind

brutalist type of 20th-century architecture [➡ BUILDING AND ARCHITECTURE; 1076]

brutality n cruelty, viciousness, violence, rough treatment, harshness, ruthlessness, callousness, inhumanity [➡ MALICIOUS ACTIONS OR BEHAVIOR; 296] Opposite: gentleness

brutalize 1 v coarsen, harden, dehumanize, desensitize [➡ UPSET, DISTRESS, AND HUMILIATE; 567] Opposite: humanize 2 v abuse, assault, maltreat, ill-treat [➡ WOUND A PERSON OR ANIMAL; 383]

brute 1 n bully, thug, beast, swine, monster [➡ VILLAINS AND THUGS; 947] 2 n (literary) animal, beast, creature, monster [➡ LIVING THINGS AND LIVING; 976]

brutish 1 adj animal, wild, violent, bestial [➡ BEASTLY AND BRUTISH; 510] 2 adj cruel, ruthless, insensitive, pitiless, harsh, unfeeling, inhuman, inhumane [➡ SELFISH AND UNKIND; 505] Opposite: humane 3 adj loutish, boorish, rough, unrefined, uncivilized, coarse, crude [➡ RUDE AND HOSTILE; 625] Opposite: civilized

brutishly adv cruelly, harshly, unfeelingly, insensitively, callously, ruthlessly, inhumanly, inhumanely [➡ SELFISH AND UNKIND; 505] Opposite: humanely

brutishness n cruelty, harshness, unkindness, unfeelingness, insensitivity, callousness [➡ SELFISH AND UNKIND; 505] Opposite: humanity

bryony type of climber [➡ CLIMBERS; 1033]

BtoB adj [➡ E-COMMERCE; 1129]

bubble v fizz, effervesce, boil, simmer [➡ FROTH AND EFFERVESCE; 389]

bubble gum type of confectionery [➡ CONFECTIONERY; 1182]

bubbliness n [➡ CHEERFULNESS OF OUTLOOK; 503]

bubbly 1 adj effervescent, foamy, sparkling, fizzy, fizzing,

carbonated [➡ PHYSICAL TEXTURE; 1222] Opposite: still 2 adj cheerful, lively, sparkling, vivacious, bouncy, animated, full of life [➡ CHEERFULNESS OF OUTLOOK; 503] Opposite: sad

buccaneer n pirate, adventurer, swashbuckler [➡ VILLAINS AND THUGS; 947]

buck 1 type of male animal [➡ MALE OR FEMALE ANIMALS; 978] 2 n (informal) dollar, money, cash, dough (slang) [➡ CURRENCIES; 798] 3 n (informal) responsibility, blame, liability, culpability, fault, guilt [➡ RESPONSIBILITY; 170] 4 v jump, rear, kick, kick out, bound, spring [➡ BOUNCE, UNDULATE, AND VIBRATE; 308] 5 v resist, oppose, fly in the face of, go against, challenge, beat [➡ HESITATE; 272] 6 adj lowly, lowest, low-grade [➡ INFERIORITY; 153]

bucket n pail, container, vessel [➡ CONTAINERS, RECEPTACLES, AND PACKAGING; 1245]

buckets (informal) n lots, scores, loads (informal), tons (informal), heaps (informal), stacks (informal), piles (informal) [➡ MANY, MUCH, LARGE AMOUNT; 117]

bucket seat type of seating [➡ FURNITURE; 858]

buckle 1 n clasp, clip, fastener, catch, fastening, hasp [➡ FASTENERS, LINKS, AND NETWORKS; 1247] 2 part of garment [➡ PARTS OF A GARMENT; 870] 3 v fasten, clip, clasp, secure, close, do up [➡ FASTEN, LINK, AND JOIN; 408] Opposite: undo 4 v collapse, crumple, cave in, bulge, fold, warp, bend [➡ CHANGE OF SHAPE; 385] Opposite: straighten

buckle down (informal) v put your shoulder to the wheel, set to, get down to, knuckle down (informal), get on with (UK) [➡ START AN ACTION; 260]

buckshot type of projectile [➡ PROJECTILES; 1159]

buckskin type of leather [➡ FABRICS; 1132]

bucktooth (informal) type of tooth [➡ THE MOUTH; 702]

buck up 1 v (informal) cheer up, liven up, revive, cheer, raise your spirits, hearten [➡ CHANGE OF MOOD AND COMPOSURE; 580] 2 v improve, get better, look up, pick up (informal), take off (informal) [➡ GET BETTER; 375] 3 v (informal dated) hurry up, look lively, get going, get a move on (informal), get cracking (informal) [➡ START AN ACTION; 260]

bucolic adj rural, pastoral, rustic, country, countrified [➡ THE COUNTRYSIDE AND OUTDOOR SPACES; 1071] Opposite: urban

bud 1 n sprout, blossom, shoot, outgrowth [➡ PARTS OF TREES AND PLANTS; 1026] 2 v blossom, flower, grow, bloom, open out, flourish [➡ GROW AND CULTIVATE; 351]

budding adj promising, potential, up-and-coming, nascent, burgeoning [➡ SUCCESSFUL AND PROMISING; 81]

buddy (informal) n friend, playmate, soul mate, companion, partner, pal (informal), mate (UK) [➡ FRIENDS AND GUESTS; 963]

budge v move, shift, dislodge, nudge, push, shove [➡ MOVE SOMETHING TO ANOTHER LOCATION; 324]

budgerigar type of pet bird [➡ BIRDS; 997]

budget 1 n financial plan, financial statement, accounts, finances, funds, resources [➡ ACCOUNTING, BANKING, AND BUDGETING; 799] 2 adj cheap, economical, inexpensive, reasonable, low-priced, modest [➡ CHEAP AND INEXPENSIVE; 221] Opposite: expensive

3 *v* **plan**, account, make financial arrangements, make provisions, cost [➞ DISPENSE, RATION, AND DISTRIBUTE; 434]

budgetary *adj* **financial**, economic, fiscal, commercial, monetary [➞ FINANCE AND ECONOMICS; 796]

bud vase *n* [➞ CONTAINERS, RECEPTACLES, AND PACKAGING; 1245]

buff **1** *v* **polish**, rub, burnish, shine, clean, put a shine on, rub up (*UK*) [➞ CLEAN AND POLISH; 403] **2** *type of* **beige** [➞ COLORS; 1224] **3** *n* **fan**, enthusiast, admirer, expert, connoisseur, aficionado, aficionada [➞ TALENTED OR INTELLIGENT PEOPLE; 528] **4** *adj* (*informal*) **muscular**, fit, healthy, toned, hard [➞ FIT AND STRONG; 736]

buffalo **1** *type of* **large mammal** [➞ LARGE MAMMALS; 986] **2** *v* (*informal*) **confuse**, baffle, deceive, hoodwink, bewilder, dupe, bamboozle (*informal*) [➞ CONFUSE AND BEWILDER; 571] **3** *v* (*informal*) **intimidate**, coerce, threaten, inhibit, bully, browbeat, frighten, cow [➞ CAUSE OR COMPEL TO ACT; 271]

buffer **1** *n* **shock absorber**, bumper, cushion, barrier, shield, safeguard, defense, bulwark [➞ COVERS AND COATINGS; 1246] **2** *type of* **computer feature** [➞ COMPUTERS AND COMPUTING; 1127] **3** *v* **cushion**, shield, safeguard, defend, protect [➞ IMPROVE STRENGTH AND DURABILITY; 378]

buffet **1** *type of* **meal** [➞ MEALS AND PARTS OF MEALS; 1169] **2** *v* **rock**, pound, batter, bang, knock, strike, pummel [➞ CONTACT: IMPACT; 413]

buffeting *n* **battering**, pounding, knocking, beating, pummeling, bashing (*informal*) [➞ PHYSICAL ATTACK AND PUNISHMENT; 415]

buffoon *n* **clown**, joker, comedian, fool, wag (*informal*) [➞ LAZY OR UNSUCCESSFUL PEOPLE; 948]

buffoonery *n* **horseplay**, clowning, fooling around, frivolity, tomfoolery (*informal*) [➞ JOKES AND TEASING; 674]

bug **1** *n* **insect**, fly, pest, creature, creepy-crawly (*informal*) [➞ INSECTS; 1012] **2** *n* (*informal*) **germ**, microbe, virus, bacterium, infection, microorganism [➞ MICROORGANISMS, FUNGI, AND ALGAE; 1023] **3** *n* (*informal*) **fault**, error, mistake, problem, gremlin (*informal*) [➞ FAULTS, FLAWS, AND WEAKNESSES; 251] **4** *n* (*informal*) **listening device**, hidden microphone, surveillance device, wiretap [➞ TELECOMMUNICATIONS; 1130] **5** *v* (*informal*) **annoy**, irritate, infuriate, bother, madden, irk, get (*informal*) [➞ ANGER AND ANNOY; 569] **6** *v* **tap**, listen in on, keep under surveillance, spy on [➞ LISTEN AND LISTENERS; 708]

See Compare and Contrast at **bother**.

bugaboo *n* **worry**, problem, concern, bugbear, bogey, bother, annoyance, nuisance [➞ PROBLEMS; 256]

bugbear *n* **worry**, problem, concern, bugaboo, bogey, bother, annoyance, nuisance [➞ PROBLEMS; 256]

bug-eyed (*informal*) *adj* **popeyed**, staring, big-eyed, wide-eyed, agog, exophthalmic [➞ FACIAL EXPRESSIONS AND BLUSHING; 651]

buggy **1** *n* **cart**, vehicle, truck, transporter [➞ BIKES, CARS, AND CARRIAGES; 1149] **2** *n* **baby carriage**, stroller, perambulator (*formal*), pushchair (*UK*), pram (*UK*) [➞ BIKES, CARS, AND CARRIAGES; 1149] **3** *type of* **wagon or carriage** [➞ VEHICLES; 1145]

bugle **1** *v* **announce**, herald, trumpet, sound off [➞ INFORM,

ANNOUNCE, AND ISSUE; 611] **2** *type of* **brass instrument** [➞ MUSICAL INSTRUMENTS; 910]

build **1** *v* **construct**, put up, erect, make, put together, manufacture, assemble, fabricate [➞ BUILD; 352] **2** *v* **put together**, create, make, join, assemble, foster, encourage, build up [➞ CREATION; 346] **3** *n* **shape**, size, figure, body, physique, form, dimensions [➞ BODY; 691]

build in *v* **incorporate**, include, integrate, add in [➞ COMBINE AND MIX; 400] *Opposite:* exclude

building *n* **structure**, construction, edifice, erection (*formal*) [➞ BUILDING AND ARCHITECTURE; 1076]

building

◆ *parts of a building*
balcony, buttress, chimney, colonnade, doorway, elevation, elevator, escalator, exterior, façade, fire escape, frame, frontage, gable, guttering, landing, paternoster, porch, roof, smokestack, soffit, stairwell, veranda, vestibule, wall, window, wing

building blocks **1** *n* [➞ BASIC DETAILS; 688] **2** *type of* **toy** [➞ TOYS; 880]

building society (*UK*) *n* [➞ ACCOUNTING, BANKING, AND BUDGETING; 799]

build up **1** *v* **increase**, rise, develop, expand, enlarge, accumulate, amass, stock up [➞ CHANGE OF SIZE: BIGGER; 392] *Opposite:* fall off **2** *v* **boost**, bolster, pump up, inspire, encourage [➞ ENCOURAGE; 576] *Opposite:* discourage

buildup **1** *n* **accumulation**, backlog, accrual, collection, stockpile, logjam [➞ AMOUNTS AND QUANTITIES; 112] **2** *n* **hype**, publicity, puff, praise, flattery [➞ ADVERTISING AND PUBLICITY; 604]

built-in **1** *adj* **integral**, fitted, fixed, en suite, in-built, incorporated, integrated [➞ RELATIVE LOCATION; 161] **2** *adj* **natural**, inherent, innate, intrinsic, ingrained [➞ RELATED; 142] *Opposite:* acquired

built-up *adj* **urbanized**, urban, developed, residential, industrial [➞ HUMAN SETTLEMENTS; 1070]

bulb **1** *n* **corm**, rhizome, tuber, storage organ, underground part [➞ PARTS OF TREES AND PLANTS; 1026] **2** *type of* **rounded shape** [➞ ROUNDED SHAPE; 1218]

bulb

◆ *types of flowers grown from bulbs*
anemone, bluebell, crocus, cyclamen, daffodil, dahlia, freesia, gladiolus, hyacinth, iris, jonquil, lily, narcissus, snowdrop, tulip

bulbous *adj* **rounded**, spherical, bulging, globular, swollen [➞ ROUNDED SHAPE; 1218]

bulge **1** *v* **stick out**, protrude, expand, be full to bursting, swell, be swollen, puff out, puff up [➞ CHANGE OF SHAPE; 385] **2** *n* **protuberance**, swell, swelling, knot, lump, hump, knob, prominence, projection [➞ ROUNDED SHAPE; 1218]

bulging **1** *adj* **protruding**, protuberant, distended, swollen, swelling, bloated, expanded, extended, projecting [➞ LARGE; 1193] *Opposite:* concave **2** *adj* (*informal*) **full**, overfull, overfilled, overstuffed, crammed, full to bursting, stuffed (*informal*) [➡FULL; 1239] *Opposite*: flat

bulk 1 *n* size, mass, volume, immensity, vastness, bulkiness, massiveness, largeness [➡SIZE AND DIMENSIONS; 1192] **2** *n* form, body, weight, mass, hulk [➡SHAPE; 1216] **3** *n* greater part, main part, largest part, majority, substance, almost all, lion's share, chief part, best part [➡MAJORITY AND MAXIMUM; 141]

bulkhead *n* partition, wall, dividing wall, screen, divider [➡WALLS AND PARTITIONS; 1104]

bulkiness 1 *n* unwieldiness, awkwardness, ungainliness, cumbersomeness, ponderousness [➡LARGE; 1193] **2** *n* large size, largeness, weight, bulk, mass, thickness [➡LARGE; 1193] *Opposite*: compactness

bulk large *v* be prominent, figure prominently, loom large, dominate, be important, stand out [➡MOST IMPORTANT AND MAIN; 193]

bulk mail *n* [➡ADVERTISING AND PUBLICITY; 604]

bulk up (*informal*) *v* build up, increase, pad out, gain weight, gain muscle [➡CHANGE OF SIZE: BIGGER; 392]

bulky 1 *adj* unwieldy, cumbersome, awkward, ungainly, ponderous, unmanageable [➡LARGE; 1193] *Opposite*: manageable **2** *adj* large, huge, immense, massive, colossal, hulking [➡LARGE; 1193] *Opposite*: compact

bull 1 *type of* male animal [➡MALE OR FEMALE ANIMALS; 978] **2** *n* papal decree, decree, official statement, encyclical, instruction, edict, proclamation [➡RELIGIOUS CONCEPTS; 776]

bulldog *type of* large dog [➡DOGS; 980]

bulldoze 1 *v* flatten, raze, level, demolish, clear [➡DESTRUCTION AND DEMOLITION; 359] **2** *v* (*informal*) coerce, bully, bludgeon, browbeat, push, steamroller, railroad (*informal*) [➡CAUSE OR COMPEL TO ACT; 271]

bulldozer *type of* commercial or industrial vehicle [➡VEHICLES; 1145]

bullet *type of* projectile [➡PROJECTILES; 1159]

bulletin 1 *n* news report, update, news item, news summary, press release, news flash [➡TELEVISION AND RADIO; 606] **2** *n* official statement, communiqué, statement, announcement, press release, dispatch, notice, report [➡BASIC DETAILS; 688] **3** *n* periodical, journal, newsletter, newspaper, publication [➡NEWSPAPERS AND MAGAZINES; 605]

bulletin board *n* [➡THE INTERNET; 1128]

bulletproof 1 *adj* toughened, protective, armored, reinforced, shatterproof [➡RIGID AND HARD; 1211] **2** *adj* (*informal*) invulnerable, secure, invincible, unassailable, untouchable, above criticism [➡SAFE AND SAFETY; 191] *Opposite*: vulnerable

bulletproof glass *type of* glass [➡GLASS; 1136]

bullfrog *type of* amphibian [➡AMPHIBIANS; 1008]

bullheaded (*informal*) *adj* obstinate, headstrong, stubborn, intransigent, uncooperative, obdurate, willful, self-willed [➡UNWILLINGNESS AND STUBBORNNESS; 564]

bullheadedness (*informal*) *n* obstinacy, stubbornness,

willfulness, intransigence, self-will, obduracy [➡UNWILLINGNESS AND STUBBORNNESS; 564]

bullion *n* gold, gold bars, gold ingots [➡FINANCIAL ASSETS; 462]

bullish 1 *adj* (*informal*) optimistic, confident, buoyant, cheerful, enthusiastic, upbeat (*informal*), chipper (*informal*) [➡COOL AND CALM; 536] *Opposite*: pessimistic **2** *adj* muscular, strong, hulking, brawny [➡MUSCLES AND MUSCULATURE; 479]

bullishly (*informal*) *adv* confidently, optimistically, buoyantly, positively, cheerfully, hopefully, self-confidently, self-assuredly [➡COOL AND CALM; 536] *Opposite*: diffidently

bullishness (*informal*) *n* confidence, optimism, buoyancy, hopefulness, self-confidence, self-assuredness [➡FEELINGS ABOUT THE FUTURE; 533] *Opposite*: diffidence

bullnecked *adj* stocky, bullish, brawny, beefy, muscular, thickset [➡MUSCLES AND MUSCULATURE; 479]

bullock 1 *type of* male animal [➡MALE OR FEMALE ANIMALS; 978] **2** *type of* young animal [➡YOUNG ANIMALS; 977]

bullring *n* arena, ring, stadium, amphitheater, sports stadium [➡BUILDINGS FOR PUBLIC ENTERTAINMENT; 1084]

bull's eye *n* target, center, mark, middle, middle point [➡CENTRAL PARTS OF PHYSICAL OBJECTS; 1251]

bull terrier *type of* small dog [➡DOGS; 980]

bully 1 *n* tormentor, aggressor, persecutor, tyrant, oppressor, intimidator [➡VILLAINS AND THUGS; 947] **2** *v* intimidate, terrorize, persecute, torment, frighten, oppress, browbeat, harass [➡FRIGHTEN AND SHOCK; 568]

bullyboy 1 *n* thug, bully, oppressor, harasser, hooligan (*informal*), heavy (*slang*) [➡VILLAINS AND THUGS; 947] **2** *adj* aggressive, intimidating, bullying, rough, threatening, menacing, strong-arm (*informal*) [➡FRIGHTENING; 231]

bullying *n* intimidation, mistreatment, oppression, harassment, victimization, maltreatment, hounding [➡MALICIOUS ACTIONS OR BEHAVIOR; 296]

bully-off (*UK*) *n* start of play, start, kickoff, beginning, commencement (*formal*) [➡SPORTS TERMS; 877]

bulrush *type of* grass [➡GRASS; 1031]

bulwark 1 *n* fortification, embankment, earthwork, barricade, rampart, wall [➡BARRIERS; 1113] **2** *n* safeguard, protection, defense, buttress, buffer, barrier [➡SAFE AND SAFETY; 191]

bumble 1 *v* mumble, murmur, hesitate, mutter, stutter, burble (*informal*) [➡CHATTER AND BABBLE; 617] **2** *v* stumble, lumber, hesitate, blunder, stagger, lurch, shamble [➡WALK UNSTEADILY; 315]

bumblebee *type of* flying insect [➡FLYING INSECTS; 1013]

bumbler *n* [➡LAZY OR UNSUCCESSFUL PEOPLE; 948]

bumbling (*informal*) *adj* awkward, clumsy, blundering, lumbering, ungainly, inept, shambling [➡DESCRIBING BODY MOVEMENTS; 288] *Opposite*: graceful

bummer (*slang*) *n* annoyance, nuisance, disappointment, letdown, discouragement, pest (*informal*), downer (*informal*), comedown (*informal*) [➡NUISANCES; 253]

bump 1 *v* hit, knock, bang, strike, wallop (*informal*), bash (*informal*) [➡CONTACT: IMPACT; 413] 2 *v* jolt, bounce, jounce, jar, jerk, bound, spring [➡CONTACT: IMPACT; 413] 3 *v* collide, slam into, crash into, knock, smash into [➡CONTACT: IMPACT; 413] 4 *n* knock, collision, smash, accident, crash [➡CONTACT: IMPACT; 413] 5 *n* swelling, lump, bruise, bulge, contusion [➡CONDITIONS AFFECTING THE SKIN; 721] 6 *n* thud, thump, bang, crash, blow, smash [➡IMPACT SOUNDS; 1260]

bumper 1 *type of* external feature [➡EXTERNAL PARTS OF A VEHICLE; 1147] 2 *adj* plentiful, profuse, copious, extra-large, jumbo, mammoth, mega, super (*informal*), plenteous (*literary*) [➡MANY, MUCH, LARGE AMOUNT; 117] *Opposite*: meager

bumpiness *n* unevenness, roughness, lumpiness [➡PHYSICAL TEXTURE; 1222] *Opposite*: smoothness

bump into 1 *v* collide, slam into, crash into, knock into, smash into [➡CONTACT: IMPACT; 413] 2 *v* meet by chance, run into, happen upon, happen on, meet, come across [➡EXPERIENCE AND ENCOUNTER; 582]

bumpkin (*informal*) *n* [➡LEVELS OF EDUCATION AND SOPHISTICATION; 894]

bump off (*slang*) *v* kill, murder, get rid of, assassinate, do in (*informal*), do away with (*informal*), waste (*slang*) [➡KILL; 923]

bumptious *adj* full of yourself, pleased with yourself, self-satisfied, self-important, smug, conceited, arrogant, overbearing, brash, prideful [➡POMPOUS, LOUD, AND OVERCONFIDENT; 635] *Opposite*: modest

bumptiousness *n* self-importance, conceitedness, arrogance, pompousness, brashness, presumptuousness, pushiness (*informal*) [➡POMPOUS, LOUD, AND OVERCONFIDENT; 635] *Opposite*: modesty

bump up (*informal*) *v* increase, put up, boost, enhance, add to, inflate, augment (*formal*) [➡CHANGE OF SIZE: BIGGER; 392] *Opposite*: decrease

bumpy 1 *adj* uneven, rough, rutted, potholed [➡PHYSICAL TEXTURE; 1222] *Opposite*: smooth 2 *adj* uncomfortable, rough, bouncy, jarring, jerky [➡PHYSICALLY UNPLEASANT; 226] *Opposite*: smooth

bun 1 *type of* roll or bun [➡BREAD, FLOUR, AND BREAD PRODUCTS; 1179] 2 *type of* hairstyle [➡HAIRSTYLES AND HAIRPIECES; 488]

bunch 1 *n* group, set, lot, mixture, collection, assembly, cluster, clump [➡COLLECTIONS AND MIXTURES OF THINGS; 1244] 2 *n* (*informal*) gang, gathering, team, set, group, crew (*informal*) [➡GROUPS OF PEOPLE; 935] 3 *n* bouquet, posy, spray, corsage [➡COLLECTIONS AND MIXTURES OF THINGS; 1244] 4 *v* crowd together, huddle, form a group, gather, cluster [➡GET CLOSER TOGETHER; 310] *Opposite*: disperse

bundle 1 *n* package, pack, parcel, packet, bale, wad, roll [➡COLLECTIONS AND MIXTURES OF THINGS; 1244] 2 *n* (*slang*) fortune, big money, king's ransom, mint (*informal*) [➡LARGE AMOUNTS OF MONEY; 118] 3 *v* (*informal*) hustle, hurry, rush, push, shove [➡MOVE FAST; 313]

bundle up 1 *v* package, pack, wrap, parcel, tie up, parcel up (*UK*) [➡FASTEN, LINK, AND JOIN; 408] 2 *v* (*informal*) dress warmly, wrap up, wrap up warmly [➡DRESS, WEAR, AND UNDRESS; 868]

bung *n* stopper, plug, cork [➡COVERS AND COATINGS; 1246]

bungalow *type of* house [➡RESIDENTIAL BUILDINGS; 1078]

bungee jumping *type of* extreme sport [➡HOBBIES, GAMES, AND SPORTS; 875]

bungle (*informal*) *v* botch, mismanage, ruin, do badly, make a mess of, spoil, mess up (*informal*), make a hash of (*informal*), make a dog's dinner of (*UK*) [➡MESS UP AND MAKE MISTAKES; 472] *Opposite*: succeed

bungler (*informal*) *n* blunderer, incompetent, bumbler, botcher, muddler [➡UNSKILLED PEOPLE; 530]

bungling (*informal*) *adj* clumsy, unskillful, incompetent, inept, blundering, maladroit, useless, gauche, amateurish, ham-fisted (*informal*), ham-handed (*informal*) [➡UNSKILLED; 529] *Opposite*: competent

bunion *n* swelling, lump, enlargement, distension, bulge, bump, growth [➡CONDITIONS AFFECTING THE SKIN; 721]

bunk 1 *n* bed, single bed, berth, couchette, bunk bed [➡FURNITURE; 858] 2 *n* (*slang*) nonsense, humbug, rubbish, drivel, gibberish, garbage, bunkum (*informal*), claptrap (*informal*), twaddle (*informal*), hot air (*informal*), hogwash (*informal*), hooey (*informal*), hokum (*informal*) [➡MEANINGLESS SPEECH OR WRITING; 676]

bunk bed *type of* bed [➡FURNITURE; 858]

bunker 1 *n* underground shelter, shelter, dugout, foxhole, ditch, trench [➡SAFE BUILDINGS OR PLACES; 1093] 2 *n* bin, chest, container, box, store, coalbin [➡CONTAINERS, RECEPTACLES, AND PACKAGING; 1245] 3 *type of* storage space [➡STORES AND STORAGE BUILDINGS; 1088]

bunkhouse *type of* room in public buildings [➡TYPES OF ROOMS; 1097]

bunkum (*informal*) *n* nonsense, humbug, drivel, gibberish, garbage, claptrap (*informal*), twaddle (*informal*), hokum (*informal*), hot air (*informal*), hogwash (*informal*), hooey (*informal*), bunk (*slang*), rubbish (*UK*) [➡MEANINGLESS SPEECH OR WRITING; 676]

bunting *n* streamers, decorations, flags, paper chains, ticker tape, ribbons, garlands [➡ORNAMENTS AND DECORATIONS; 1248]

bunya *type of* evergreen tree [➡EVERGREEN AND CONIFEROUS TREES; 1029]

buoy 1 *n* marker, float, navigational aid [➡SIGNPOSTS, SIGNALS, AND BILLBOARDS; 595] 2 *v* keep afloat, hold up, sustain, maintain, prop up, keep up, buoy up [➡CAUSE TO CONTINUE; 267]

buoyancy 1 *n* lightness, weightlessness [➡WEIGHT: LIGHT; 1206] *Opposite*: heaviness 2 *n* resilience, resistance, flexibility, toughness [➡CHEERFULNESS OF OUTLOOK; 503] 3 *n* optimism, cheerfulness, good spirits, enthusiasm, jauntiness, lightheartedness [➡POSITIVE IMPATIENCE, ENTHUSIASM, AND ALERTNESS; 537] *Opposite*: moroseness

buoyant 1 *adj* floating, afloat, light [➡WEIGHT: LIGHT; 1206] 2 *adj* cheerful, optimistic, happy, jaunty, carefree, lighthearted, upbeat (*informal*) [➡PLEASURE, EXCITEMENT, AND ELATION; 534] *Opposite*: morose 3 *adj* resilient, resistant, flexible, tough [➡STRENGTH; 201]

buoyantly *adv* cheerfully, brightly, happily, optimistically, positively, confidently, hopefully [➡PLEASURE, EXCITEMENT, AND ELATION; 534] *Opposite*: morosely

buoy up v **cheer**, uplift, encourage, boost, lift, sustain [➡ ENCOURAGE; 576] *Opposite*: depress

bur n **seed husk**, husk, seedpod, pod, pericarp [➡ PARTS OF TREES AND PLANTS; 1026]

burb (*slang*) n [➡ HUMAN SETTLEMENTS; 1070]

burble 1 v **bubble**, ripple, babble, splash, murmur, plash (*literary*) [➡ EMIT CONTINUOUS SOUNDS; 366] **2** v (*informal*) **gush**, babble, ramble, go on about, prattle, waffle (*informal*) [➡ CHATTER AND BABBLE; 617] **3** *type of* **continuous sound** [➡ CONTINUOUS SOUNDS; 1258]

burden 1 n **load**, weight, cargo [➡ AMOUNTS AND QUANTITIES; 112] **2** n **problem**, drain, encumbrance, affliction, liability, weight, worry, tax, inconvenience, millstone, responsibility, duty, onus, obligation [➡ NUISANCES; 253] **3** n (*literary*) [➡ SUBJECT AREAS; 768] **4** v **weigh down**, saddle, encumber, trouble, yoke, inconvenience, load [➡ GIVE TOO MUCH AND OVER-BURDEN; 437]

See Compare and Contrast at **subject**.

burdened *adj* **loaded**, fraught, weighed down, laden, held back, troubled, hampered [➡ SADNESS, DISTRESS, AND DESPAIR; 539]

burdensome *adj* **onerous**, heavy, taxing, troublesome, arduous, oppressive, difficult, worrying [➡ IRRITATING; 228]

burdock *type of* **weed** [➡ WEEDS AND THISTLES; 1034]

bureau 1 n **government department**, agency, office, department, unit, section [➡ LEGISLATIVE BODIES AND LEGISLATION; 809] **2** n **chest of drawers**, dresser, chest [➡ FURNITURE; 858] **3** n **writing desk**, desk, writing table, escritoire [➡ FURNITURE; 858]

bureaucracy 1 n **system of government**, government, administration, civil service, establishment, organization, officialdom (*informal*) [➡ STYLES AND SYSTEMS OF GOVERNMENT; 806] **2** n **official procedure**, rules and regulations, formalities, paperwork, red tape (*informal*) [➡ WAYS OF DOING THINGS; 294]

bureaucrat n **official**, public servant, civil servant, administrator, office holder [➡ POLITICAL OFFICES AND POLITICIANS; 808]

bureaucratic 1 *adj* **administrative**, official, governmental, civil service, organizational [➡ STYLES AND SYSTEMS OF GOVERNMENT; 806] **2** *adj* **rigid**, inflexible, unbending, officious, involved, complex [➡ DIFFICULTY AND COMPLEXITY; 242]

burgeon (*literary*) 1 v **bud**, bloom, blossom, flower [➡ SUCCEED AND WIN; 79] **2** v **mushroom**, multiply, prosper, proliferate, flourish, grow rapidly [➡ PROSPER AND ABOUND; 16] *Opposite*: dwindle

burgeoning 1 *adj* **growing**, mushrooming, increasing, escalating, expanding, flourishing [➡ CHANGE OF SIZE: BIGGER; 392] *Opposite*: dwindling **2** *adj* **budding**, promising, up-and-coming, nascent [➡ SUCCESSFUL AND PROMISING; 81] *Opposite*: fading

burger *type of* **processed meat** [➡ TYPES AND CUTS OF MEAT; 1177]

burgher n **citizen**, resident, inhabitant, denizen, voter, taxpayer [➡ INHABITANTS; 857]

burglar n **thief**, robber, intruder, cat burglar, housebreaker, criminal [➡ CRIMINALS; 821]

burglarize v **rob**, steal, break into, break and enter, raid, burgle [➡ STEAL AND ROB; 426]

burglary 1 n **break-in**, theft, robbery, crime, housebreak [➡ CRIMES; 817] **2** n **breaking and entering**, **theft**, robbery, aggravated burglary, stealing, larceny [➡ CRIMES; 817]

burgle v **rob**, thieve, break in, burglarize, loot, steal from [➡ STEAL AND ROB; 426]

burgundy *type of* **red** [➡ COLORS; 1224]

burial n **interment**, committal, entombment, funeral [➡ BURIAL AND PREPARATION FOR BURIAL; 929]

burial chamber n **sepulcher**, tomb, mausoleum, vault, crypt [➡ BURIAL PLACES AND ACCESSORIES; 930]

burial ground n **cemetery**, graveyard, churchyard, necropolis, memorial park, God's Acre (*archaic*), garden of remembrance (*UK*) [➡ BURIAL PLACES AND ACCESSORIES; 930]

burial place n **last resting place**, grave, tomb, crypt, mausoleum [➡ BURIAL PLACES AND ACCESSORIES; 930]

buried 1 *adj* **underground**, concealed, hidden, covered, dug in, secreted [➡ ORIENTATION AND ALIGNMENT; 1223] *Opposite*: dug up **2** *adj* **suppressed**, hidden, covered up, repressed, forgotten, concealed, submerged, dormant [➡ SECRET AND UNKNOWN; 179] *Opposite*: exposed

burlap *type of* **fabric from plants** [➡ FABRICS; 1132]

burlesque 1 n **parody**, caricature, travesty, lampoon, skit, imitation, distortion, satire, mockery, sendup (*informal*) [➡ JOKES AND TEASING; 674] **2** n **variety show**, vaudeville, revue, extravaganza, spectacular, floor show, cabaret [➡ PERFORMANCES AND SHOWS; 42] **3** v **spoof**, mock, make fun of, lampoon, caricature, satirize, parody, send up (*informal*), take off (*informal*) [➡ JOKES AND TEASING; 674]

burliness n **brawniness**, heftiness, broad shoulders, muscularity, robustness, beefiness [➡ BUILD; 477] *Opposite*: slimness

burly *adj* **brawny**, hefty, broad-shouldered, husky, muscular, strong, robust, beefy [➡ BUILD; 477] *Opposite*: slim

Burmese cat *type of* **cat** [➡ FELINES; 983]

burn 1 v **blaze**, be ablaze, flame, smolder, glow [➡ FIRE, FLAMMABILITY, AND BURNING; 1165] **2** v **burn up**, burn down, gut, reduce to ashes, burn to a crisp, char, incinerate, burn away (*UK*) [➡ FIRE, FLAMMABILITY, AND BURNING; 1165] **3** v **scorch**, singe, sear, char, scald, blister [➡ FIRE, FLAMMABILITY, AND BURNING; 1165] **4** v **tingle**, sting, hurt, prickle, be on fire [➡ PAIN AND OTHER PHYSICAL SENSATIONS; 733] **5** v **go red**, flush, blush, redden, color, glow [➡ CHANGE OF COLOR; 391] **6** v **corrode**, eat away, eat into, etch [➡ DELETE AND ERASE; 339] **7** v **glow**, shine, twinkle, flare, glimmer [➡ LIGHT EMISSION; 368] **8** v **use up**, use, expend, consume [➡ USE UP AND WASTE; 474] **9** n **injury**, blister, scald, scorch [➡ CONDITIONS AFFECTING THE SKIN; 721] **10** n (*UK*) **stream**, rivulet, brook (*literary*), beck (*UK*) [➡ RIVERS, LAKES, AND STREAMS; 1042]

burn down v **incinerate**, go up in flames, burn to the ground, burn to a crisp, reduce to ashes, torch (*slang*) [➡ FIRE, FLAMMABILITY, AND BURNING; 1165]

burned-out 1 *adj* **exhausted**, worn out, tired out, drained, unwell, in poor health, stressed out (*informal*) [➡ TIRED, ASLEEP, AND UNCONSCIOUS; 738] **2** *adj* **gutted**, destroyed, reduced to ashes, incinerated, burned down, burned up, torched (*slang*) [➡ IN BAD REPAIR; 1234]

burner *n* **gas ring**, ring, heat, flame, gas jet, Bunsen burner, jet [➡ FIRE, FLAMMABILITY, AND BURNING; 1165]

burning 1 *adj* **red-hot**, piping hot, boiling hot, fiery hot, sweltering, fiery, boiling, hot, scorching (*informal*) [➡ TEMPERATURE: HOT; 1229] *Opposite*: cold 2 *adj* **on fire**, ablaze, blazing, flaming, smoldering, fiery [➡ FIRE, FLAMMABILITY, AND BURNING; 1165] *Opposite*: extinguished 3 *adj* **strong**, ardent, fervent, all-consuming, passionate, intense, fiery [➡ STRENGTH; 201] *Opposite*: weak 4 *adj* **important**, vital, crucial, urgent, significant, major [➡ IMPORTANT; 194] *Opposite*: routine 5 *adj* **smarting**, stinging, tingly, prickly, painful [➡ PAIN AND OTHER PHYSICAL SENSATIONS; 733] 6 *adj* **feverish**, febrile, flushed, hot, red, overheated, fevered [➡ ILL AND SICK; 740] *Opposite*: cool

burning hot *adj* [➡ TEMPERATURE: HOT; 1229]

burning up *adj* **hot**, overheated, feverish, burning hot, burning, fevered, sweltering, flushed [➡ ILL AND SICK; 740] *Opposite*: cold

burnish *v* **polish**, shine, buff, rub, clean, put a shine on, rub up (*UK*) [➡ CLEAN AND POLISH; 403]

burn out (*informal*) *v* **exhaust**, break down, wear out, tire, fatigue, flag, run down [➡ OVERDO SOMETHING; 290]

burnout *n* **exhaustion**, stress, tension, weariness, poor health, fatigue, breakdown [➡ ILL AND SICK; 740]

burn the candle at both ends *v* **overdo things**, wear yourself out, do too much, exhaust yourself, burn the midnight oil [➡ HARD WORK OR EFFORT; 298]

burn the midnight oil *v* **work late**, stay up, work day and night, work overtime, burn the candle at both ends, toil, keep your nose to the grindstone [➡ HARD WORK OR EFFORT; 298] *Opposite*: slack

burnt sienna *type of* **brown** [➡ COLORS; 1224]

burnt to a crisp *adj* [➡ STATE OF PREPARED FOOD; 1171]

burnt umber *type of* **brown** [➡ COLORS; 1224]

burn up 1 *v* **incinerate**, burn, burn down, reduce to ashes, burn to a crisp, go up in flames, burn to the ground [➡ FIRE, FLAMMABILITY, AND BURNING; 1165] 2 *v* (*informal*) **annoy**, irritate, vex, anger, obsess, consume, eat away at, eat up (*informal*) [➡ UPSET, DISTRESS, AND HUMILIATE; 567] *Opposite*: please

burn your bridges *v* **pass the point of no return**, cross the Rubicon, nail your colors to the mast [➡ MAKE DECISIONS AND CHOICES; 752]

burp 1 *n* [➡ VOMIT AND BELCH; 712] 2 *v* [➡ VOMIT AND BELCH; 712]

burr *n* **accent**, pronunciation, twang, drawl, brogue, enunciation, intonation, inflection, stress, accentuation, emphasis, tone of voice [➡ ASPECTS OF LANGUAGE; 682]

burritos *type of* **cooked dish** [➡ PREPARED DISHES; 1170]

burrow 1 *n* **hole**, warren, den, lair, hideaway, tunnel, earth, sett [➡ ANIMAL OR BIRD ACCOMMODATIONS; 1079] 2 *v* **dig**, tunnel, excavate, channel, dig out, grub, hollow out, delve (*archaic*) [➡ SEEK POSSESSION AND SEARCH; 456] 3 *v* **search**, dig, investigate, delve, scrabble, grope, ferret around, rummage,

forage [➡ SEEK POSSESSION AND SEARCH; 456] 4 *v* **nestle**, snuggle, cuddle, nuzzle, cozy up [➡ GET CLOSER TOGETHER; 310]

bursary *n* **scholarship**, grant, award, fund, exhibition (*UK*) [➡ INCOME; 460]

burst 1 *v* **rupture**, split open, disintegrate, break open, fracture, rip open, come apart, explode [➡ DESTRUCTION AND DEMOLITION; 359] 2 *v* **erupt**, spout, gush, rush, break out, surge, explode [➡ MOVE FAST; 313] *Opposite*: trickle 3 *n* **spurt**, eruption, gust, torrent, rupture, surge, rush [➡ SUDDEN EVENTS; 52] *Opposite*: trickle

bursting *adj* **full**, overflowing, teeming, bursting at the seams, full to bursting, packed, abounding, brimming with, full of, abounding in, loaded with, filled with, jam-packed (*informal*), stuffed (*informal*) [➡ FULL; 1239] *Opposite*: empty

bursting at the seams *adj* **crowded**, full, crammed, packed, seething, at full capacity, teeming, full to bursting, fit to bust, bulging, jam-packed (*informal*), stuffed (*informal*) [➡ FULL; 1239]

burst in on 1 *v* **interrupt**, intrude upon, intrude on, come upon, disturb, disrupt [➡ INTERRUPT AND BUTT IN; 619] 2 *v* **surprise**, take by surprise, catch unawares, take unawares, catch in the act, catch red-handed, catch in flagrante [➡ ARRIVE; 12]

burst into flames *v* [➡ FIRE, FLAMMABILITY, AND BURNING; 1165]

burst into tears *v* **break down**, dissolve in tears, break down and cry, burst out crying, lose control, be overcome, start sobbing, start weeping, lose it (*informal*) [➡ CRYING; 650] *Opposite*: laugh

burst out 1 *v* **start**, begin, commence, burst into, break into, break out [➡ SUDDENLY COME INTO EXISTENCE; 2] 2 *v* **exclaim**, shout, cry, call out, say, yell, blurt out [➡ BETRAY CONFIDENCES AND GOSSIP; 618] *Opposite*: whisper

burst out crying *v* [➡ GIVING VENT TO EMOTIONS; 679]

bury 1 *v* **inter**, put in the ground, lay to rest, entomb, put six feet under [➡ BURIAL AND PREPARATION FOR BURIAL; 929] *Opposite*: exhume 2 *v* **hide**, conceal, cover, put out of sight, submerge, secrete [➡ CAUSE TO DISAPPEAR; 6] *Opposite*: expose

bury the hatchet *v* **make up**, make peace, be reconciled, kiss and make up, resolve differences, fall upon each other's necks (*UK*) [➡ FORGET, FORGIVE, AND ACCEPT; 748] *Opposite*: fight

bus 1 *type of* **public service vehicle** [➡ VEHICLES; 1145] 2 *type of* **hardware** [➡ COMPUTERS AND COMPUTING; 1127] 3 *part of* **spacecraft** [➡ SPACE VEHICLES; 1063] 4 *v* **transport**, carry, take, convey, move, travel, journey [➡ TRAVEL: WAYS OF TRAVELING; 320]

busboy *type of* **person who works in restaurants** [➡ DOMESTIC AND KITCHEN WORKERS; 850]

busby *n* **bearskin**, helmet, headgear [➡ ACCESSORIES, MILLINERY, AND LINGERIE; 867]

bush 1 *n* **shrub**, plant, flowering shrub, hedging plant (*UK*) [➡ BUSHES AND SHRUBS; 1027] 2 *n* **scrubland**, wilds, outback, savanna, scrub [➡ DESERTS, PLAINS, AND MOORLAND; 1045]

bushed (*informal*) *adj* **exhausted**, tired, worn-out, dead on your feet, all in, done in (*informal*), dog-tired (*informal*), wiped out (*slang*) [➡ TIRED, ASLEEP, AND UNCONSCIOUS; 738] *Opposite*: refreshed

bushel *type of* **nonmetric unit** [➡ SIZE AND DIMENSIONS; 1192]

bushes *n* **undergrowth**, scrub, underbrush, shrubbery, greenery [➡ VEGETATION; 1025]

bushwhack (*informal*) *v* **ambush**, lie in wait for, hold up, surprise, attack [➡ COMPETE, CONTEND, AND COMBAT; 303]

bushy *adj* **luxuriant**, abundant, profuse, shaggy, thick, hairy, unkempt, wild [➡ DESCRIBING HAIR; 486] *Opposite*: sparse

busily *adv* **actively**, energetically, briskly, industriously, vigorously, enthusiastically, feverishly [➡ WITH ENTHUSIASM; 286] *Opposite*: lazily

business 1 *n* **commerce**, trade, industry, selling, production, big business, dealing [➡ BUSINESS; 791] 2 *n* **company**, corporation, conglomerate, establishment, partnership, firm, multinational, transnational, enterprise, venture, concern, organization [➡ BUSINESS ENTERPRISES AND RELATED BODIES; 792] 3 *n* **custom**, trade, dealings, transactions, sales [➡ BUSINESS ACTIVITIES AND PHENOMENA; 794] 4 *n* **concern**, affair, problem, responsibility, interest, sphere [➡ SUBJECT AREAS; 768] 5 *n* **matter**, affair, issue, situation, event, thing, to-do (*informal*) [➡ EVENTS AND OCCURRENCES; 35] 6 *adj* **commercial**, occupational, corporate, professional [➡ BUSINESS; 791] *Opposite*: private

businesslike 1 *adj* **efficient**, practical, professional, competent, systematic, methodical, organized, thorough, ordered, well-organized [➡ HARD-WORKING AND COMMITTED; 500] *Opposite*: unprofessional 2 *adj* **unemotional**, objective, professional, detached, uninvolved, impersonal [➡ NEUTRALITY AND INDIFFERENCE; 553] *Opposite*: emotional

business meeting *n* [➡ MEETINGS AND ASSEMBLIES; 43]

business park *type of* **industrial site** [➡ INDUSTRIAL BUILDINGS; 1087]

businessperson *n* **business executive**, executive, executive director, director, manager, entrepreneur [➡ BUSINESS PEOPLE; 793]

business suit *type of* **suit** [➡ GARMENTS AND OUTFITS; 865]

busk (*UK*) *v* **entertain**, perform, sing, play [➡ ENTERTAINMENT; 872]

bus lane *n* [➡ TRAVEL: TRAFFIC PROBLEMS AND TRAFFIC MANAGEMENT; 323]

busload *n* [➡ MANY, MUCH, LARGE AMOUNT; 117]

bust 1 *part of* **torso** [➡ PARTS OF THE BODY: TORSO; 693] 2 *n* **sculpture**, torso, statue, figure, model [➡ SCULPTURE; 902] 3 *n* (*slang*) **raid**, police raid, arrest, seizure, search [➡ THE POLICE, ARREST, AND PRETRIAL PROCEEDINGS; 818] 4 *v* (*informal*) **break**, smash, shatter, burst, fracture, rupture, damage [➡ TEAR, BREAK, AND CUT; 360] *Opposite*: mend 5 *v* (*slang*) **arrest**, capture, take prisoner, apprehend, take into custody, seize, detain, catch, stop, take downtown [➡ THE POLICE, ARREST, AND PRETRIAL PROCEEDINGS; 818]

busted (*informal*) *adj* **broken**, out of action, out of order, not working, smashed, kaput (*informal*), bust (*informal*) [➡ IN BAD REPAIR; 1234] *Opposite*: fixed

bustier *type of* **top** [➡ GARMENTS AND OUTFITS; 865]

bustle 1 *v* **busy yourself**, be on the go, be busy, hurry, rush around, rush, hustle [➡ MOVE FAST; 313] 2 *n* **activity**, movement, stir, hustle and bustle, commotion, flurry, hubbub [➡ CHAOS AND UPROAR; 51] *Opposite*: calm

bustling *adj* **busy**, active, full of go, full of life, hurried, full of commotion [➡ EMOTIONALLY PLEASANT; 187] *Opposite*: still

busy 1 *adj* **active**, on the go, hard-working, hard at it, diligent, industrious, in demand, occupied, harried [➡ HARD-WORKING AND COMMITTED; 500] *Opposite*: idle 2 *adj* **full**, full of activity, demanding, hard, tiring, hectic, eventful [➡ DIFFICULTY AND COMPLEXITY; 242] *Opposite*: empty 3 *adj* **engaged**, occupied, unavailable, taken [➡ ABSENT AND UNAVAILABLE; 7] *Opposite*: free

busybody (*informal*) *n* **interferer**, nosy person, chatterer, meddler, nuisance, gossip, bigmouth (*informal*), pest (*informal*) [➡ INTERFERING PEOPLE AND TATTLETALES; 950]

but 1 *prep* **however**, although, nevertheless, on the contrary [➡ NOT; 137] 2 *prep* **other than**, except, excluding, bar, save for [➡ NOT; 137] 3 *n* (*informal*) **objection**, proviso, provision, rider, condition, if [➡ PROBLEMS; 256]

butane *type of* **gas** [➡ GASES; 1275]

butch *adj* **masculine**, tough, strong, muscular, beefy, strapping (*informal*) [➡ BUILD; 477]

butcher 1 *n* **killer**, murderer, slaughterer, exterminator, slayer (*formal or literary*) [➡ PEOPLE WHO KILL; 924] 2 *v* **slaughter**, murder, kill, exterminate, massacre, assassinate, slay (*formal or literary*) [➡ KILL; 923] 3 *v* (*informal*) **botch**, ruin, make a mess of, spoil, make a hash of (*informal*), bungle (*informal*) [➡ MESS UP AND MAKE MISTAKES; 472]

butcher knife *type of* **knife** [➡ CUTTING TOOLS; 1120]

butcher's *type of* **food outlet** [➡ RETAIL OUTLETS; 1083]

butchery *n* **slaughter**, carnage, bloodshed, killing [➡ CAUSES OF DEATH; 921]

buteo *type of* **bird of prey** [➡ BIRDS OF PREY; 998]

butler *type of* **servant** [➡ DOMESTIC AND KITCHEN WORKERS; 850]

butt 1 *v* **ram**, hit, bump, strike, run into, push, knock against (*informal*) [➡ CONTACT: IMPACT; 413] 2 *n* **object**, target, victim, objective, mark, goal [➡ INTENTIONS AND PURPOSES; 772] 3 *n* **handle**, stock, grip [➡ EXTREMITIES OF PHYSICAL OBJECTS; 1250] 4 *n* **end**, stub, stump, base, nub end [➡ EXTREMITIES OF PHYSICAL OBJECTS; 1250] 5 *n* **barrel**, tub, drum, cask, container, keg [➡ CONTAINERS, RECEPTACLES, AND PACKAGING; 1245]

butte *n* **hill**, foothill, rise, mount, bluff, height [➡ MOUNTAINS AND HILLS; 1044]

butter *type of* **cooking fat and oil** [➡ FATS AND OILS; 1173]

butter bean *type of* **pulse** [➡ PEAS AND BEANS; 1189]

buttercup *type of* **perennial flower** [➡ FLOWERS; 1032]

butterfingered (*informal*) *adj* [➡ AGILITY OF THE BODY; 476]

butterflies (*informal*) *n* **nervousness**, excitement, anxiety, tenseness, apprehension, nerves (*informal*) [➡ FEELINGS ABOUT THE FUTURE; 533] *Opposite*: confidence

butterfly n [➡ INSECTS; 1012]

butterfly

◆ *types of butterflies*
cabbage butterfly, emperor butterfly, monarch butterfly, mourning cloak, painted lady, peacock butterfly, red admiral, swallowtail, tiger swallowtail, tortoiseshell

butter knife *type of* **flatware** [➡ TABLEWARE, FLATWARE, AND KITCHENWARE; 861]

butterscotch 1 *type of* **confectionery** [➡ CONFECTIONERY; 1182] 2 *type of* **beige** [➡ COLORS; 1224]

butter up (*informal*) v **flatter**, curry favor, get on the right side of, sweet-talk (*informal*), suck up (*informal*), soft-soap (*informal*) [➡ FLATTER AND FAWN; 621] *Opposite:* insult

but then again *adv* **but**, but then, then again, nonetheless, nevertheless, then, on the other hand [➡ ALTHOUGH, NEVERTHELESS, AND DESPITE; 169]

butt in 1 v **interrupt**, break in, cut in, interfere, interject, stick your nose in [➡ INTERRUPT AND BUTT IN; 619] *Opposite:* mind your own business 2 v **jump the line**, squeeze in, barge in, shove in, skip the line, jump the queue (*UK*), queue-jump (*UK*) [➡ ARRIVE; 12]

buttock *part of* **torso** [➡ PARTS OF THE BODY: TORSO; 693]

button 1 *part of* **garment** [➡ PARTS OF A GARMENT; 870] 2 n **push button**, switch, knob, key [➡ PARTS OF MACHINES AND TOOLS; 1118] 3 n **badge**, pin, brooch [➡ ORNAMENTS AND DECORATIONS; 1248] 4 v **fasten**, do up, close [➡ FASTEN, LINK, AND JOIN; 408] *Opposite:* undo

buttoned-down (*informal*) *adj* **conservative**, traditional, stuffy, formal, strait-laced, old-fashioned, conventional, strict, narrow-minded [➡ RETICENT AND UNFORTHCOMING; 631] *Opposite:* easygoing

buttonhole 1 *part of* **garment** [➡ PARTS OF A GARMENT; 870] 2 n (*UK*) flower, corsage, spray, **boutonniere** (*formal*) [➡ ORNAMENTS AND DECORATIONS; 1248] 3 v (*informal*) **accost**, waylay, corner, grab, confront, intercept, ambush [➡ INITIATE AND ESTABLISH COMMUNICATION; 680]

button-nosed *adj* [➡ FACIAL CHARACTERISTICS; 481]

button up (*informal*) v **be quiet**, keep quiet, be silent, say nothing, stop talking, shut up (*informal*), keep mum (*informal*) [➡ WITHHOLD INFORMATION; 687] *Opposite:* blather (*informal*)

buttress 1 n **support**, prop, reinforcement, flying buttress, structure [➡ PARTS OF A BUILDING; 1095] 2 v **strengthen**, support, prop, prop up, reinforce, shore up, hold up [➡ IMPROVE STRENGTH AND DURABILITY; 378]

buxom (*humorous*) *adj* **plump**, rounded, ample, curvaceous, curvy, shapely, well-rounded, well-padded [➡ BUILD; 477]

buy 1 v **pay for**, purchase, acquire, procure, obtain, get [➡ PURCHASE; 422] *Opposite:* sell 2 v (*informal*) **accept**, believe, fall for, credit, subscribe to, swallow (*informal*) [➡ FORGET, FORGIVE, AND ACCEPT; 748] *Opposite:* disbelieve 3 n **purchase**, acquisition, good buy, bad buy, good deal, bad deal, bargain [➡ PURCHASE; 422]

buyer n **purchaser**, consumer, shopper, bargain hunter, customer [➡ PURCHASER; 424] *Opposite:* seller

buy off v **bribe**, pay hush money to, induce, corrupt, suborn, pay off (*informal*) [➡ CAUSE OR COMPEL TO ACT; 271]

buy out v **acquire**, take over, purchase, take control [➡ PURCHASE; 422]

buyout n **takeover**, merger, acquisition, purchase [➡ BUSINESS ACTIVITIES AND PHENOMENA; 794]

buzz 1 n **noise**, hum, drone, murmur, hubbub [➡ CONTINUOUS SOUNDS; 1258] *Opposite:* silence 2 n (*informal*) **telephone call**, ring, phone call, call, tinkle (*UK*) [➡ TELEPHONE COMMUNICATION; 48] 3 n (*informal*) **thrill**, high, kick, lift, jolt [➡ AMAZING THINGS; 211] *Opposite:* downer (*informal*) 4 n (*informal*) **gossip**, talk, word, rumor, whisper, information, news, word of mouth [➡ GOSSIP; 678] 5 v **hum**, drone, murmur, whine, whir, hiss [➡ EMIT CONTINUOUS SOUNDS; 366]

buzzard *type of* **scavenger** [➡ BIRDS; 997]

buzz cut *type of* **hairstyle** [➡ HAIRSTYLES AND HAIRPIECES; 488]

buzzer n **signal**, bell, beeper (*informal*), bleeper (*UK*) [➡ SIGNALING; 1140]

buzzing *adj* **busy**, bustling, vibrant, full of life, lively, active, humming [➡ FULL; 1239] *Opposite:* still

buzz off (*informal*) v [➡ RUN AWAY AND AVOID; 10]

buzzword (*informal*) n **slogan**, catchword, saying, byword, catch phrase, axiom [➡ FIGURES OF SPEECH; 673]

by 1 *prep* **through**, via, in, by means of, as a result of [➡ RELATED; 142] 2 *prep* **with**, near, next to, beside [➡ RELATIVE LOCATION; 161] 3 *prep* **not later than**, before, sooner than [➡ BEFORE, FIRST, AND PRECEDING; 163]

by accident *adv* **unintentionally**, inadvertently, accidentally, fortuitously, coincidentally, by luck, by chance, by a quirk of fate [➡ UNPLANNED AND UNEXPECTED; 281] *Opposite:* on purpose

by a hairsbreadth *adv* **hardly**, by a fraction, by a whisker, by a nose, by the skin of your teeth, barely *Opposite:* easily [➡ TO A CERTAIN EXTENT; 136]

by all accounts *adv* **seemingly**, according to what is being said, apparently, it appears that, the word is that [➡ EXPRESSIONS OF UNCERTAINTY; 560]

by all means *adv* **certainly**, of course, please do [➡ EXPRESSIONS OF AGREEMENT; 648]

by and by (*literary*) *adv* **before long**, eventually, in a short time, in time, in a while, after a while, presently (*formal or literary*) [➡ FUTURE; 86] *Opposite:* immediately

by and large *adv* **generally**, as a rule, normally, usually, in general, on the whole [➡ USUALLY; 108] *Opposite:* specifically

by chance *adv* **accidentally**, by accident, unintentionally, inadvertently, coincidentally, unexpectedly, by luck, fortuitously, by coincidence, by a quirk of fate [➡ CHANCE, COINCIDENCE, AND ACCIDENT; 786] *Opposite:* on purpose

by choice *adv* **by preference**, voluntarily, willingly, of your own free will, eagerly, freely, readily [➡ THE WILL AND WILLINGNESS; 563] *Opposite:* unwillingly

by coincidence *adv* **by chance**, by a fluke, by a quirk of fate, as luck would have it, coincidentally, unintentionally, accidentally [➡ CHANCE, COINCIDENCE, AND ACCIDENT; 786] *Opposite*: by design

by degrees *adv* **little by little**, bit by bit, gradually, slowly, a little at a time, progressively, piecemeal [➡ HAPPENING SLOWLY; 106] *Opposite*: at once

by design *adv* **intentionally**, knowingly, on purpose, purposely, deliberately, purposefully, with intent [➡ INTENTIONAL AND DELIBERATE; 279] *Opposite*: by coincidence

by dint of *adv* **by means of**, by use of, using, as a result of, because of [➡ WAYS OF DOING THINGS; 294]

bye (*informal*) *interj* **goodbye**, au revoir, bye-bye (*informal*), ciao (*informal*), see you (*informal*), so long (*informal*), see you later (*informal*), adios (*informal*), ta-ta (*informal*) [➡ GREETINGS, FAREWELLS, AND SALUTATIONS; 659] *Opposite*: hello

bye-bye (*informal*) *see* **bye**

by-election *n* **election**, local election, poll, ballot *Opposite*: general election [➡ ELECTIONS AND VOTING; 807]

by far *adv* **considerably**, by a long way, much, easily, undoubtedly, certainly, without a doubt, beyond a doubt, by a long chalk (*UK*) [➡ TO A GREAT EXTENT; 132]

bygone *adj* **past**, former, previous, long-gone, departed (*formal or literary*), olden (*archaic or literary*) [➡ PAST; 84] *Opposite*: future

bygone days *n* [➡ PAST; 84]

by heart *adv* **by rote**, from memory, backward, off by heart (*UK*), off pat (*UK*) [➡ KNOWLEDGE AND WISDOM; 558]

by hook or by crook *adv* **one way or another**, somehow or other, no matter how, no matter what, no matter what it takes [➡ EXPRESSIONS OF AGREEMENT; 648]

by itself *adv* **of its own accord**, automatically, independently, without help [➡ AUTOMATIC AND INSTINCTIVE; 280]

bylaw *n* **regulation**, rule, ruling, statute, guideline, law [➡ THE LAW AND LEGAL AUTHORITY; 814]

byline *n* **acknowledgement**, credit, heading, strap line (*UK*) [➡ NEWSPAPERS AND MAGAZINES; 605]

by means of *adv* **by**, through, via, using, by way of, by dint of [➡ WAYS OF DOING THINGS; 294]

by mistake *adv* **accidentally**, mistakenly, inadvertently, wrongly, incorrectly, unintentionally, by accident, unexpectedly [➡ UNPLANNED AND UNEXPECTED; 281] *Opposite*: on purpose

by nature *adv* **characteristically**, naturally, innately, instinctively, normally, inherently [➡ TRUE AND REAL; 171]

by no means *adv* **not at all**, in no way, not the least bit, not in the slightest, absolutely not [➡ NOT; 137] *Opposite*: absolutely

bypass **1** *v* **go around**, avoid, get around, find a way around, sidestep, evade, circumvent, detour, skirt [➡ AVOID OR ESCAPE CONTACT; 418] **2** *type of* **highway** [➡ ROADS; 1106] **3** *type of* **medical procedure** [➡ REMEDIES, TREATMENTS, AND OPERATIONS; 731]

byproduct *n* **side effect**, spinoff, consequence, result, derivative, offshoot [➡ RESULTS AND OUTCOMES; 83]

by rights *adv* **in all fairness**, properly, to be fair, if justice were done, correctly, officially, legally [➡ LEGAL AND LEGITIMATE; 815]

byroad *type of* **secondary road** [➡ ROADS; 1106]

by rote *adv* **by heart**, from memory, off pat (*UK*), off by heart (*UK*) [➡ KNOWLEDGE AND WISDOM; 558]

bystander *n* **onlooker**, passer-by, witness, eyewitness, spectator, looker-on [➡ ONLOOKERS AND SPECTATORS; 701] *Opposite*: participant

byte *type of* **computer feature** [➡ COMPUTERS AND COMPUTING; 1127]

by the way *adv* **incidentally**, parenthetically, in passing, by the by, apropos (*formal*) [➡ EXPRESSIONS INTRODUCING EXTRA INFORMATION; 139]

byway *type of* **secondary road** [➡ ROADS; 1106]

by way of **1** *adv* **as**, by means of, in place of, as per [➡ REPRESENTATIVE; 66] **2** *adv* **via**, by, through, past [➡ DIRECTION OF MOTION; 345]

byword **1** *n* **embodiment**, perfect example, epitome, shining example [➡ PERFECT EXAMPLES AND EMBODIMENTS; 67] **2** *n* **catch phrase**, proverb, axiom, slogan, saying, buzzword (*informal*) [➡ FIGURES OF SPEECH; 673]

by yourself *adv* **on your own**, alone, without help, unaided, single-handed, all by yourself [➡ ACTING INDEPENDENTLY; 284]

byzantine **1** *adj* **complex**, intricate, tortuous, convoluted, complicated [➡ DIFFICULTY AND COMPLEXITY; 242] *Opposite*: straightforward **2** *adj* **devious**, scheming, underhand, deceitful, secretive, plotting, dishonest, calculating [➡ DECEITFUL; 513] *Opposite*: honest

Byzantine *type of* **pre-20th-century architecture** [➡ BUILDING AND ARCHITECTURE; 1076]

C

cab 1 *n* **taxi**, taxicab, yellow cab, hack, black cab (*UK*), minicab (*UK*) [➡VEHICLES; 1145] **2** *n* **cabin**, compartment, cockpit [➡INTERNAL PARTS OF A VEHICLE; 1146]

cabal 1 *n* **faction**, section, unit, group, sect, clique, cell, league, caucus, ring, gang, band [➡GROUPS WITH A COMMON INTEREST; 938] **2** *n* **plot**, scheme, conspiracy, connivance, collusion, artifice (*formal*) [➡DECEPTION AND LIES; 660]

cabana *n* **bathhouse**, shelter, change room, changing room (*UK*) [➡RESIDENTIAL BUILDINGS; 1078]

cabaret 1 *n* **show**, floor show, live entertainment, burlesque [➡PERFORMANCES AND SHOWS; 42] **2** *n* **nightclub**, club, bar, nightspot [➡BUILDINGS FOR PUBLIC ENTERTAINMENT; 1084]

cabbage *type of* **vegetable** [➡FRUIT AND VEGETABLES; 1176]

cabbage butterfly *type of* **butterfly** [➡MOTHS AND BUTTERFLIES; 1015]

caber *n* **log**, beam, pole, stick [➡STICKS, POLES, AND WEDGES; 1254]

cabin 1 *n* **hut**, log cabin, cottage, bungalow, chalet, lodge [➡RESIDENTIAL BUILDINGS; 1078] **2** *n* **compartment**, cubicle, stateroom, room, berth [➡ALCOVES, CUBICLES, AND COMPARTMENTS; 1096] **3** *part of* **aircraft** [➡AIRCRAFT; 1148] **4** *part of* **ship or boat** [➡PARTS OF A SHIP OR BOAT; 1151] **5** *part of* **spacecraft** [➡SPACE VEHICLES; 1063] **6** *part of* **train** [➡RAILROADS; 1107]

cabin cruiser *type of* **motor vessel** [➡SHIPS AND BOATS; 1150]

cabinet *n* [➡FURNITURE; 858]

cabinet

◆ *types of cabinets*
armoire, bookcase, breakfront, bureau, cassone, chest of drawers, china cabinet, closet, cocktail cabinet, commode, credenza, cupboard, display cabinet, display case, dresser, highboy, liquor cabinet, lowboy, press, secretary, sideboard, wardrobe, whatnot

cabinetmaking *n* [➡CRAFTS AND CARVING; 355]

cable *type of* **telecommunications equipment** [➡TELECOMMUNICATIONS; 1130]

cable car *type of* **rail vehicle** [➡RAILROADS; 1107]

cablegram *n* [➡LETTERS AND WRITTEN MESSAGES; 584]

cable railroad *type of* **railroad** [➡RAILROADS; 1107]

cable-stayed bridge *type of* **bridge** [➡BRIDGES, TUNNELS, CROSSINGS, AND JUNCTIONS; 1112]

caboodle (*informal*) *n* **lot**, whole lot, entirety, totality, integrality, ensemble, the whole kit and caboodle (*informal*), the whole enchilada (*slang*) [➡ALL; 128]

caboose *n* **car**, carriage, wagon, guard's van (*UK*) [➡RAILROADS; 1107]

cacciatore *type of* **food presentation** [➡COOKING AND FOOD PREPARATION; 353]

cache 1 *n* **hoard**, store, accumulation, reserve, collection [➡COLLECTIONS AND MIXTURES OF THINGS; 1244] **2** *type of* **computer feature** [➡COMPUTERS AND COMPUTING; 1127] **3** *v* **hide**, hoard, store, secrete, reserve, accumulate, collect [➡STORE AND KEEP; 453] *Opposite*: discard

cachet *n* **status**, prestige, distinction, respect, reputation, standing, importance, class, snob appeal [➡STATUS; 888]

cackle *v* **laugh**, hoot, screech, crow, guffaw, chortle [➡LAUGHTER; 649]

cacophonous *adj* **discordant**, unmusical, unmelodious, dissonant, inharmonious, jarring, harsh, strident, grating, loud, noisy [➡LOUD, HIGH, OR UNPLEASANT SOUNDS; 1266] *Opposite*: melodious

cacophony *n* **discord**, discordance, dissonance, disharmony, unmusicality, harshness, stridency, loudness, noise [➡CHAOS AND UPROAR; 51] *Opposite*: melodiousness

cad (*dated*) *n* **rogue**, scoundrel, rake, rascal, blackguard, scalawag (*dated informal*) [➡VILLAINS AND THUGS; 947] *Opposite*: gentleman

CAD *n* **computer-aided design**, computer graphics, graphics, product design, drafting [➡COMPUTERS AND COMPUTING; 1127]

cadaver *n* **corpse**, dead body, remains, body [➡DEAD PERSON; 926]

cadaverous 1 *adj* **bony**, skeletal, emaciated, wasted, gaunt, thin [➡BUILD; 477] *Opposite*: healthy **2** *adj* (*literary*) **pale**, pallid, wan, ashen, sallow, ghastly (*literary*) [➡COMPLEXION; 480] *Opposite*: rosy **3** *adj* (*formal or literary*) **corpse-like**, deathly, deathlike, skeletal, spectral, macabre [➡UNFIT AND WEAK; 739]

caddie 1 *n* **assistant**, porter, carrier, transporter [➡PEOPLE IN SPORTS AND LEISURE; 876] **2** *v* **transport**, assist, carry [➡PUSH, PULL, AND SLIDE; 335]

caddish *adj* **dishonorable**, ungallant, rascally, rakish, ungentlemanly [➡BAD MANNERS AND SOCIAL SKILLS; 521] *Opposite*: gallant

caddy *n* **container**, tin, box, receptacle, carton, casket, coffer, chest, tea caddy [➡CONTAINERS, RECEPTACLES, AND PACKAGING; 1245]

cadence 1 *n* **tempo**, rhythm, pace, pulse, stroke, beat [➡MUSICAL TERMS; 912] **2** *n* **lilt**, intonation, accent, modulation, inflection, tone [➡THE SPOKEN WORD; 671]

cadenza *n* **solo passage**, improvisation, solo, unaccompanied passage, showpiece, run of notes, roulade, riff [➡MUSICAL TERMS; 912]

cadet *n* **trainee**, plebe, police cadet, army cadet, sea cadet (*UK*) [➡ STUDENTS AND PUPILS; 841]

cadre 1 *n* **squad**, corps, unit, team, band, company, crew, force, troop, nucleus [➡ GROUPS OF PEOPLE; 935] 2 *n* **faction**, group, core, hard core, band, set, bloc, clique [➡ GROUPS WITH A COMMON INTEREST; 938]

café *type of* **eating place** [➡ HOTELS, RESTAURANTS, AND CLUBS; 1082]

café au lait 1 *type of* **coffee** [➡ DRINKS; 1187] 2 *type of* **beige** [➡ COLORS; 1224]

café noir *type of* **coffee** [➡ DRINKS; 1187]

café society *n* [➡ RICH PEOPLE; 895]

cafeteria *type of* **eating place** [➡ HOTELS, RESTAURANTS, AND CLUBS; 1082]

caffè latte *type of* **coffee** [➡ DRINKS; 1187]

caftan *type of* **dress** [➡ GARMENTS AND OUTFITS; 865]

cage 1 *n* **enclosure**, coop, pen, birdcage, crate [➡ ANIMAL OR BIRD ACCOMMODATIONS; 1079] 2 *v* **confine**, enclose, pen, coop up, impound, shut in, fence in, lock in, hem in [➡ CAPTIVITY AND LOSS OF FREEDOM; 248] *Opposite:* release

---

cage

◆ *types of pens or cages*
apiary, aquarium, aviary, beehive, birdcage, chicken coop, coop, corral, cowshed, doghouse, dovecote, henhouse, hutch, kennel, piggery, pig pen, pound, stable, stall, sty

---

caged *adj* **captive**, detained, confined, imprisoned, jailed, behind bars, in prison, locked up, interned, trapped, shut in, constricted, restrained, put away (*informal*), inside (*informal*), incarcerated (*formal*) [➡ CAPTIVITY AND LOSS OF FREEDOM; 248] *Opposite:* free

cagey (*informal*) *adj* **wary**, guarded, cautious, careful, reticent, evasive, secretive, chary [➡ INSECURITY AND LOSS OF COMPOSURE; 544] *Opposite:* reckless

---

See Compare and Contrast at **cautious**.

---

cagily (*informal*) *adv* **warily**, guardedly, cautiously, carefully, reticently, evasively, secretively [➡ INSECURITY AND LOSS OF COMPOSURE; 544] *Opposite:* recklessly

caginess (*informal*) *n* **wariness**, caution, reticence, evasiveness, chariness, shrewdness, cautiousness [➡ INSECURITY AND LOSS OF COMPOSURE; 544] *Opposite:* recklessness

cairn 1 *n* **landmark**, marker, waymark, signpost, direction post, milestone [➡ SIGNPOSTS, SIGNALS, AND BILLBOARDS; 595] 2 *n* **memorial**, monument, barrow, tomb, tombstone, gravestone, tablet, slab [➡ MONUMENTS; 1092]

cairn terrier *type of* **small dog** [➡ DOGS; 980]

cajole *v* **coax**, persuade, wheedle, entice, inveigle, flatter, sweet-talk (*informal*) [➡ CAUSE OR COMPEL TO ACT; 271] *Opposite:* compel

cajolery *n* [➡ INGRATIATING; 638]

cake 1 *n* **gateau**, pastry, fancy [➡ CAKES, COOKIES, AND DESSERTS;

1181] 2 *n* **bar**, block, slab, lump, tablet, cube, loaf [➡ AMOUNTS OF SOLID OR SEMISOLID; 115] 3 *v* **cover**, coat, encrust, congeal, coagulate [➡ DECORATE, ADORN, AND APPLY COATINGS; 405]

---

cake

◆ *types of cakes*
angel food cake, birthday cake, Black Forest cake, brownie, carrot cake, cheesecake, coffeecake, cruller, cupcake, Danish pastry, devil's food cake, doughnut, éclair, flapjack, fruitcake, gateau, gingerbread, jelly roll, key lime pie, macaroon, Madeira cake, madeleine, mince pie, muffin, pain au chocolat, petit four, seedcake, sponge cake, strudel, Swiss roll, torte, turnover, wedding cake

---

caked *adj* **covered**, coated, encrusted, layered [➡ FULL; 1239]

cakewalk (*informal*) *n* **child's play**, kid's stuff, easy victory, runaway victory, cinch (*informal*), piece of cake (*informal*), pushover (*informal*), walkover (*informal*) [➡ EASY WORK; 299]

calamitous *adj* **disastrous**, dreadful, catastrophic, ruinous, tragic, cataclysmic, devastating, appalling, shattering, earth-shattering, frightful, terrible, dire [➡ EMOTIONALLY UNPLEASANT AND UPSETTING; 227] *Opposite:* beneficial

calamity *n* **disaster**, catastrophe, mishap, misfortune, tragedy, blow [➡ DISASTERS; 252]

calcified *adj* [➡ RIGID AND HARD; 1211]

calcify *v* **harden**, set, solidify, fossilize, turn into stone, petrify [➡ HARDEN, CONGEAL, AND DRY; 387] *Opposite:* soften

calculable 1 *adj* **quantifiable**, countable, finite, assessable, reckonable, measurable [➡ ASSESS QUANTITY; 757] *Opposite:* incalculable 2 *adj* **predictable**, anticipated, expected, foreseeable, likely, knowable [➡ POSSIBLE AND PROBABLE; 177] *Opposite:* unpredictable

calculate *v* **work out**, compute, analyze, estimate, gauge, determine, reckon, evaluate, assess, weigh up (*UK*) [➡ ASSESS QUANTITY; 757]

calculated *adj* **intended**, designed, planned, considered, premeditated, deliberate [➡ INTENTIONAL AND DELIBERATE; 279] *Opposite:* spontaneous

calculating *adj* **scheming**, manipulative, devious, shrewd, conniving, cunning [➡ DECEITFUL; 513] *Opposite:* candid

calculatingly *adv* **intentionally**, deliberately, knowingly, shrewdly, purposefully, deviously, cunningly [➡ INTENTIONAL AND DELIBERATE; 279] *Opposite:* candidly

calculation 1 *n* **computation**, estimate, reckoning, sum, result, answer [➡ MATH; 597] 2 *n* **control**, cunning, scheming, intention, design, shrewdness, deviousness [➡ INTENTIONS AND PURPOSES; 772] *Opposite:* candidness

calculator *type of* **computer** [➡ COMPUTERS AND COMPUTING; 1127]

calculus *n* [➡ MATH; 597]

caldron *n* [➡ CONTAINERS, RECEPTACLES, AND PACKAGING; 1245]

calendar *n* **datebook**, appointment book, schedule, year planner, timetable, agenda, diary (*UK*) [➡ LISTS AND SCHEDULES; 587]

calendar month *type of* **time period** [➡ TIMES OF YEAR; 88]

calf 1 *type of* **young animal** [➡ YOUNG ANIMALS; 977] 2 *type of* **leather** [➡ FABRICS; 1132] 3 *part of* **leg or foot** [➡ PARTS OF THE BODY: LEG AND FOOT; 694]

calfskin *type of* **leather** [➡ FABRICS; 1132]

caliber 1 *n* **ability**, quality, capacity, talent, competence, capability, level, stature, standard [➡ SKILLS, TALENTS, AND ABILITIES; 526] 2 *n* **size**, bore, diameter, gauge, measure, magnitude, dimension [➡ SIZE AND DIMENSIONS; 1192]

calibrate *v* **standardize**, adjust, regulate, attune, bring into line, rectify [➡ CORRECT AND PUT RIGHT; 377]

calibration 1 *n* **standardization**, correction, adjustment, tuning, setting, regulation [➡ CHANGE; 372] 2 *n* **graduation**, gradation, mark, measurement, degree, point [➡ SCORES AND EVALUATIONS; 598]

calico *type of* **fabric from plants** [➡ FABRICS; 1132]

calico cat *type of* **cat** [➡ FELINES; 983]

calipers *type of* **measuring device** [➡ MEASURING DEVICES; 1123]

calisthenics *n* **exercises**, aerobics, isometrics, training, working out, gymnastics, exercise system, stretching [➡ HOBBIES, GAMES, AND SPORTS; 875]

call 1 *v* **shout**, cry out, scream, yell, call out, exclaim, cry [➡ UTTER AND PRONOUNCE; 608] 2 *v* **request**, summon, call on, invite, beckon, appeal, ask [➡ REQUEST AND DEMAND; 663] 3 *v* **phone**, telephone, give a call, call up, call in, phone up (*UK*), ring (*UK*) [➡ TELEPHONE, PAGE, AND TEXT; 681] 4 *v* **name**, describe, identify, entitle, label, term, dub, christen, baptize [➡ NAME AND DESCRIBE; 665] 5 *v* **visit**, call on, pay a visit, drop in, stop off, go to see, stop by, call by, come around, call in, look up, look in, pop in (*informal*) [➡ INITIATE AND ESTABLISH COMMUNICATION; 680] 6 *v* **arrange**, convene, set up, organize, assemble, gather, summon [➡ CAUSE TO HAPPEN; 31] 7 *n* **noise**, shout, cry, sound [➡ SOUNDS MADE BY PEOPLE; 1262] 8 *n* **song**, cry, birdsong [➡ SOUNDS MADE BY BIRDS; 1263] 9 *n* **phone call**, telephone call, buzz (*informal*), ring (*UK*) [➡ TELEPHONE COMMUNICATION; 48] 10 *n* **visit**, stop, call [➡ ARRIVAL; 13] 11 *n* **demand**, request, plea, appeal, bid, invitation [➡ REQUEST AND DEMAND; 663] 12 *n* **judgment**, verdict, decision, assessment, ruling, say [➡ TRIAL, PUNISHMENT, AND LEGAL OUTCOMES; 819]

call a halt *v* **end**, stop, halt, bring to an end, close, call it a day, finish, give up, break off, quit, call off, terminate (*formal*) [➡ CAUSE TO STOP; 266] *Opposite*: start up

call a spade a spade *v* **be direct**, speak plainly, be blunt, speak your mind, lay it on the line (*informal*) [➡ EXPLAIN AND CLARIFY; 610] *Opposite*: prevaricate

call attention to *v* **make known**, draw attention to, expose, publicize, highlight, point out [➡ CAUSE TO APPEAR; 5] *Opposite*: conceal

call by *v* **visit**, stop by, come around, drop in, call in, come by, stop off, look in, pop in (*informal*) [➡ INITIATE AND ESTABLISH COMMUNICATION; 680]

call down 1 *v* **invoke**, invite, request, appeal, pray, imprecate (*formal*) [➡ REQUEST AND DEMAND; 663] 2 *v* **reprimand**,

rebuke, reproach, admonish, scold, denounce, chide (*literary*) [➡ ACCUSE, BLAME, AND CRITICIZE; 641] *Opposite*: praise

caller *n* **visitor**, guest, friend [➡ FRIENDS AND GUESTS; 963]

call for 1 *v* **order**, demand, claim, clamor, request, ask [➡ REQUEST AND DEMAND; 663] 2 *v* **need**, require, justify, necessitate, cry out for, order, be in need of, demand, claim [➡ REQUEST AND DEMAND; 663]

call forth *v* **produce**, cause, inspire, provoke, stimulate, give rise to [➡ CAUSE TO HAPPEN; 31]

calligraphy *n* **handwriting**, hand, writing, script, print, lettering [➡ WRITING; 583]

call in 1 *v* **recall**, call back, pull in, take off the market [➡ REGAIN POSSESSION; 429] 2 *v* **summon**, invite in, call for, send for, bring in, have in [➡ CAUSE OR COMPEL TO ACT; 271] 3 *v* **phone**, call, telephone, give a call, call up, phone up (*UK*), ring (*UK*) [➡ TELEPHONE, PAGE, AND TEXT; 681] 4 *v* (*UK*) **visit**, drop in, drop by, come by, come around, stop by, call by, look in, stop off, pop in (*informal*) [➡ ARRIVE; 12]

call-in *type of* **broadcast** [➡ TELEVISION AND RADIO; 606]

calling *n* **vocation**, profession, occupation, business, work, mission [➡ PROFESSIONS; 845]

call into question *v* **query**, question, dispute, challenge, doubt, contest [➡ QUESTION THINGS; 751] *Opposite*: accept

call it a day *v* **stop**, finish, end, give up, break off, quit, call a halt, call off, bring to an end, halt [➡ STOP ACTING; 264] *Opposite*: start up

call it quits (*informal*) *v* [➡ STOP ACTING; 264]

call names *v* **insult**, abuse, hurl insults at, taunt, bait, laugh at, jeer at, mock, tease, rib (*informal*) [➡ INSULTS, ABUSE, AND SWEARING; 658] *Opposite*: compliment

call off *v* **cancel**, stop, abandon, suspend, shelve, break off, halt [➡ CAUSE TO STOP; 266]

call on 1 *v* **ask**, request, appeal to, urge, entreat, beg, invite, implore (*formal*), bid (*archaic*) [➡ REQUEST AND DEMAND; 663] 2 *v* **visit**, drop in on, go to see, look up, look in on, call in on (*UK*) [➡ INITIATE AND ESTABLISH COMMUNICATION; 680]

callous *adj* **heartless**, unfeeling, cold-hearted, hard-hearted, uncaring, insensitive, unsympathetic, cold, cruel, pitiless, hard, thick-skinned [➡ SELFISH AND UNKIND; 505] *Opposite*: warm-hearted

calloused *adj* **hard**, hardened, hard-skinned, rough, rough-skinned, tough-skinned, horny [➡ CONDITIONS AFFECTING THE SKIN; 721] *Opposite*: soft

callousness *n* **heartlessness**, insensitivity, cruelty, coldness, cold-heartedness, hardheartedness, pitilessness [➡ SELFISH AND UNKIND; 505] *Opposite*: warm-heartedness

call out 1 *v* **summon**, send for, call for, get, page [➡ INITIATE AND ESTABLISH COMMUNICATION; 680] 2 *v* **shout out**, exclaim, call, yell, make a noise, cry out, holler (*informal*) [➡ UTTER AND PRONOUNCE; 608]

call out for *v* **demand**, clamor, be in dire need of, require, request, beg, cry out for, need, necessitate, justify, claim [➡ REQUEST AND DEMAND; 663]

callow *adj* **inexperienced**, immature, naïve, adolescent, green, raw, youthful [➡ UNSKILLED; 529] *Opposite:* mature

callowness *n* [➡ NEGATIVE INTELLECTUAL CHARACTERISTICS; 525]

call together *v* **summon**, convene, hold, gather, collect, round up, muster, assemble [➡ COMBINE AND MIX; 400] *Opposite:* disperse

call to mind *v* **evoke**, recall, recollect, suggest, call up, stir up memories of, invoke, remind [➡ REMIND; 747] *Opposite:* forget

call up *v* **phone**, call, telephone, give a call, phone up (*UK*), ring (*UK*) [➡ TELEPHONE, PAGE, AND TEXT; 681]

call-up (*UK*) *n* **conscription**, mobilization, recruitment, enlistment, muster, call-to-arms, levy, national service, draft [➡ WARFARE AND WAR; 830] *Opposite:* demobilization

call upon 1 *v* **ask**, request, appeal to, urge, entreat, beg, invite, implore (*formal*), bid (*archaic*) [➡ REQUEST AND DEMAND; 663] 2 *v* **make demands on**, summon up, use, call for, demand, require [➡ REQUEST AND DEMAND; 663]

callus *n* **hard skin**, corn, bump, lump, nodule [➡ CONDITIONS AFFECTING THE SKIN; 721]

calm 1 *adj* **tranquil**, peaceful, still, cool, composed, unruffled, serene, relaxed, quiet [➡ COOL AND CALM; 536] *Opposite:* agitated 2 *n* **peace**, tranquillity, quietness, stillness, calmness, coolness, composure, serenity [➡ COOL AND CALM; 536] *Opposite:* turbulence 3 *v* **pacify**, calm down, quiet, quiet down, soothe, settle down, appease, subside [➡ SOOTHE AND CALM; 573] *Opposite:* excite

calmative *adj* **calming**, tranquilizing, soothing, pacifying, relaxing, quieting, sedative, palliative, comforting [➡ EMOTIONALLY PLEASANT; 187] *Opposite:* disturbing

calm down *v* **settle down**, relax, soothe, quiet down, quiet, pacify [➡ CHANGE OF MOOD AND COMPOSURE; 580] *Opposite:* agitate

calming *adj* **soothing**, reassuring, comforting, restful, sedative, relaxing, calmative, palliative, quieting [➡ CALMING; 188] *Opposite:* disturbing

calmness *n* **serenity**, tranquillity, quietness, stillness, peace, coolness, calm, composure [➡ COOL AND CALM; 536] *Opposite:* restlessness

calumny (*formal*) *n* **slander**, defamation, denigration, libel, lies, misrepresentation, lie, slur, smear [➡ INSULTS, ABUSE, AND SWEARING; 658]

calve *v* **give birth**, drop, reproduce, produce [➡ REPRODUCTION AND HEREDITY; 725]

calypso *type of* **world music** [➡ MUSIC, SONGS, AND SINGING; 907]

calyx *part of* **flower** [➡ FLOWERS; 1032]

cam *part of* **engine** [➡ PARTS OF AN ENGINE; 1144]

camaraderie *n* **friendship**, companionship, solidarity, company, comradeship, amity (*formal*) [➡ RELATIONSHIP TO ANOTHER; 973] *Opposite:* enmity

Cambrian *type of* **period** [➡ EPOCHS AND ERAS; 89]

camcorder *type of* **video equipment** [➡ PHOTOGRAPHY AND PHOTOGRAPHIC EQUIPMENT; 1122]

camel 1 *type of* **large mammal** [➡ LARGE MAMMALS; 986] 2 *type of* **beige** [➡ COLORS; 1224]

camelback *adj* **arched**, humped, curved, rounded [➡ ROUNDED SHAPE; 1218] *Opposite:* flat

camel hair *type of* **fabric from animals** [➡ FABRICS; 1132]

camellia *type of* **shrub or bush** [➡ BUSHES AND SHRUBS; 1027]

Camelopardalis *type of* **constellation** [➡ HEAVENLY BODIES; 1061]

Camembert *type of* **soft cheese** [➡ DAIRY PRODUCTS AND CHEESES; 1183]

cameo 1 *n* **character part**, cameo role, appearance, role, part, walk-on [➡ IN THE THEATER; 906] 2 *type of* **jewelry** [➡ JEWELRY; 866]

camera *type of* **photographic equipment** [➡ PHOTOGRAPHY AND PHOTOGRAPHIC EQUIPMENT; 1122]

camera-shy *adj* **reclusive**, retiring, reserved, private, aloof, shy [➡ RETICENT AND UNFORTHCOMING; 631] *Opposite:* extroverted

camisole *type of* **upper body underwear** [➡ ACCESSORIES, MILLINERY, AND LINGERIE; 867]

camouflage 1 *n* **concealment**, disguise, smoke screen, cover-up, façade [➡ COVERS AND COATINGS; 1246] 2 *v* **disguise**, mask, hide, conceal, obscure [➡ CAUSE TO DISAPPEAR; 6]

camp 1 *n* **site**, campground, encampment, base camp, campsite (*UK*), holiday camp (*UK*) [➡ HUMAN SETTLEMENTS; 1070] 2 *n* **group**, faction, followers, clique, supporters, cohorts [➡ GROUPS WITH A COMMON INTEREST; 938] 3 *v* **go camping**, camp out, sleep out [➡ HOBBIES, GAMES, AND SPORTS; 875]

campaign 1 *n* **movement**, crusade, operation, drive, fight, battle, war, promotion [➡ HARD WORK OR EFFORT; 298] 2 *v* **fight**, work, push, struggle, battle [➡ COMPETE, CONTEND, AND COMBAT; 303] 3 *v* **electioneer**, canvass, drum up support, solicit votes, stump, crusade, run [➡ ELECTIONS AND VOTING; 807]

campaigner *n* **activist**, crusader, fighter, supporter, champion, promoter [➡ DEVOTEES AND ADDICTED PEOPLE; 556]

campanile *n* [➡ TOWERS; 1099]

camper 1 *n* **vacationer**, vacationist, holidaymaker (*UK*) [➡ PEOPLE IN SPORTS AND LEISURE; 876] 2 *type of* **leisure vehicle** [➡ VEHICLES; 1145]

campground *n* **encampment**, camping area, campsite (*UK*) [➡ THE COUNTRYSIDE AND OUTDOOR SPACES; 1071]

camp robber *type of* **common bird** [➡ BIRDS; 997]

campsite 1 *n* **area**, pitch, site, place [➡ THE COUNTRYSIDE AND OUTDOOR SPACES; 1071] 2 *n* (*UK*), campground, encampment, camping area [➡ THE COUNTRYSIDE AND OUTDOOR SPACES; 1071]

campus *n* **grounds**, precincts, site, property, estate [➡ URBAN OUTDOOR SPACES; 1072]

camshaft *part of* **engine** [➡ PARTS OF AN ENGINE; 1144]

can 1 *type of* **container** [➡ CONTAINERS, RECEPTACLES, AND PACKAGING; 1245] 2 *v* (*slang*) **dismiss**, give notice, let go, lay off, terminate, fire (*informal*), sack (*informal*), discharge (*formal*) [➡ REVOKE STATUS; 459] *Opposite:* hire

Canada goose *type of* **freshwater bird** [➡ FRESHWATER BIRDS; 1000]

canal 1 *n* **waterway**, channel, seaway [➡ WATERWAYS AND SEAWAYS; 1108] 2 *n* **duct**, tube, passage, vessel [➡ WATERCOURSES; 1111]

canal boat *type of* **motor vessel** [➡ SHIPS AND BOATS; 1150]

canalize (*formal*) *v* **direct**, channel, funnel, guide, convey, conduct, lead, focus, concentrate [➡ MOVE SOMETHING TO ANOTHER LOCATION; 324] *Opposite*: diffuse

canapé *part of* **meal** [➡ MEALS AND PARTS OF MEALS; 1169]

canard (*literary*) *n* [➡ JOKES AND TEASING; 674]

canary *type of* **pet bird** [➡ BIRDS; 997]

canary yellow *type of* **yellow** [➡ COLORS; 1224]

cancan *type of* **dance** [➡ DANCE; 903]

cancel 1 *v* **call off**, stop, abandon, withdraw, scratch [➡ CAUSE TO STOP; 266] 2 *v* **annul**, revoke, stop, rescind, repeal, terminate (*formal*) [➡ ABOLISH AND ANNUL; 452]

canceled *adj* [➡ NOT HAPPENING; 34]

cancel out *v* **nullify**, efface, undo, contradict, neutralize, work against, **negate** (*formal*) [➡ MAKE IMPOSSIBLE; 276]

cancer 1 *n* **growth**, tumor, malignancy, disease, melanoma, sarcoma [➡ ILLNESSES AND DISORDERS; 732] 2 *n* **evil**, blight, scourge, canker, plague, menace, corruption, disease, bane, pest (*informal*) [➡ NUISANCES; 253]

Cancer 1 *type of* **astrological sign** [➡ FATE, DESTINY, AND ASTROLOGY; 782] 2 *type of* **constellation** [➡ HEAVENLY BODIES; 1061]

cancerous 1 *adj* **tumorous**, malignant, carcinomatous, carcinogenic, oncogenic, diseased [➡ SICKNESS; 729] *Opposite*: benign 2 *adj* **harmful**, pernicious, malign, malignant, noxious, damaging, deleterious, destructive, cankerous [➡ DANGEROUS; 236] *Opposite*: beneficent

candelabrum *n* **candleholder**, candlestick, chandelier, lamp holder, lamp, light fitting [➡ LIGHTING; 862]

candid *adj* **honest**, frank, open, truthful, sincere, blunt, straight, outspoken, forthright, straightforward, upfront [➡ HONEST AND OPEN; 630] *Opposite*: guarded

candida *type of* **microorganism** [➡ MICROORGANISMS, FUNGI, AND ALGAE; 1023]

candidacy *n* **application**, contention, entry, submission, candidature, standing [➡ ELECTIONS AND VOTING; 807]

candidate *n* **applicant**, contender, entrant, runner, aspirant, nominee, contestant [➡ COMPETITORS; 41]

Compare and Contrast: *candidate, contender, contestant, aspirant, applicant, entrant*

CORE MEANING: somebody who is seeking to be chosen for something or to win something

candidate somebody who is being considered for a job, grant, or prize, standing for election, or taking part in an examination; *contender* a competitor, especially somebody who has a good chance of winning; *contestant* somebody who takes part in a contest or competitive event; *aspirant* somebody aspiring to distinction or advancement; *applicant* somebody who has formally applied to be a candidate for something; *entrant* somebody who enters a competition or examination.

candidness *n* **honesty**, frankness, openness, truthfulness, bluntness, straightforwardness, outspokenness, candor [➡ HONEST AND OPEN; 630]

candied *adj* **crystallized**, glacé, preserved, sugar-coated, sugared, frosted, iced, glazed [➡ STATE OF PREPARED FOOD; 1171]

candle *n* **taper**, nightlight, rush light, rush candle, rush, wax light, torch, tallow candle, birthday candle, cake candle, votive candle [➡ LIGHTING; 862]

candlelight *n* **dim light**, soft light, low light, glow, glimmer, flicker, glim [➡ LIGHT; 1164]

candlelit *adj* [➡ DESCRIBING LIGHT; 1228]

candlestick *n* **candleholder**, candelabrum, chandelier, sconce [➡ LIGHTING; 862]

can-do (*informal*) *adj* **positive**, willing, confident, ambitious, eager, keen, go-getting (*informal*), upbeat (*informal*) [➡ CONFIDENCE AND COMPOSURE; 499] *Opposite*: diffident

candor *n* **frankness**, forthrightness, directness, candidness, outspokenness, bluntness, honesty [➡ HONEST AND OPEN; 630]

candy *n* [➡ CONFECTIONERY; 1182]

candy apple *type of* **confectionery on a stick** [➡ CONFECTIONERY; 1182]

candy store *type of* **food outlet** [➡ RETAIL OUTLETS; 1083]

candy-striped *adj* **striped**, pink-and-white striped, stripy (*UK*) [➡ DESCRIBING PATTERNS; 1227]

cane 1 *n* **bamboo**, wicker, rattan [➡ PLANT MATERIALS; 1133] 2 *n* **stick**, walking stick, staff [➡ STICKS, POLES, AND WEDGES; 1254] 3 *v* **beat**, thrash, strike, hit, punish [➡ PHYSICAL ATTACK AND PUNISHMENT; 415]

Canes Venatici *type of* **constellation** [➡ HEAVENLY BODIES; 1061]

cane toad *type of* **amphibian** [➡ AMPHIBIANS; 1008]

canine 1 *adj* **doggy**, doglike, doggish [➡ DOGS; 980] 2 *n* (*humorous*) **dog**, mongrel, cur, hound, pooch (*informal*), bow-wow (*babytalk*) [➡ DOGS; 980] 3 *type of* **tooth** [➡ THE MOUTH; 702]

canine

◆ *types of canines*
coyote, dingo, dog, fox, jackal, wolf

Canis Major *type of* **constellation** [➡ HEAVENLY BODIES; 1061]

Canis Minor *type of* **constellation** [➡ HEAVENLY BODIES; 1061]

canister *n* **container**, can, tin, flask, cylinder [➡ CONTAINERS, RECEPTACLES, AND PACKAGING; 1245]

canker *n* **evil**, cancer, scourge, blight, plague, menace, bane, corruption, disease, malignancy, pest (*informal*) [➡ NUISANCES; 253]

canned **1** *adj* **preserved**, conserved, tinned (*UK*) [➡ STATE OF PREPARED FOOD; 1171] *Opposite*: fresh **2** *adj* **prerecorded**, recorded, taped, reproduced, artificial, synthetic, non-spontaneous (*UK*) [➡ FALSE AND UNREAL; 173] *Opposite*: live

cannelloni *type of* **pasta** [➡ PASTA; 1180]

cannery *type of* **factory** [➡ INDUSTRIAL BUILDINGS; 1087]

canniness *n* **shrewdness**, astuteness, sharpness, smartness, cleverness, wiliness, craftiness [➡ POSITIVE INTELLECTUAL CHARACTERISTICS; 524]

cannon *type of* **gun** [➡ WEAPONS FOR SHOOTING; 1156]

cannonade *n* **barrage**, bombardment, hail, onslaught, pounding, volley [➡ SUDDEN EVENTS; 52]

cannonball *n* **projectile**, missile, ball, stone, grapeshot, shot, chain shot, shell [➡ PROJECTILES; 1159]

canny *adj* **shrewd**, astute, sharp, smart, clever, careful, cunning, sly, wily, crafty [➡ POSITIVE INTELLECTUAL CHARACTERISTICS; 524]

canoe *type of* **small vessel** [➡ SHIPS AND BOATS; 1150]

canola oil *type of* **cooking fat and oil** [➡ FATS AND OILS; 1173]

canonical *adj* **official**, recognized, acknowledged, established, undisputed, undoubted, unquestioned, uncontested, canonic [➡ TRUE AND REAL; 171] *Opposite*: apocryphal

canonization **1** *n* **making into a saint**, beatification, sanctification, consecration, hallowing, blessing [➡ RELIGIONS AND RELIGIOUS PRACTICES; 777] **2** *n* **idolization**, glorification, adoration, worship, adulation, veneration [➡ FADS, FETISHES, AND IDOLATRY; 555]

canonize **1** *v* **make into a saint**, beatify, sanctify, consecrate, hallow, bless [➡ CONFER STATUS; 458] **2** *v* **idolize**, glorify, adore, worship, venerate, revere [➡ LIKE, LOVE, VALUE, AND ENJOY; 578]

canoodle (*informal*) *v* **carry on**, kiss and cuddle, pet, smooch (*informal*), neck (*informal*), make out (*slang*) [➡ PHYSICAL CONTACT AS COMMUNICATION; 655]

can opener *type of* **utensil** [➡ TABLEWARE, FLATWARE, AND KITCHENWARE; 861]

canopy **1** *n* **awning**, cover, covering, shelter, blind, shade, sunshade [➡ COVERS AND COATINGS; 1246] **2** *n* **top**, crown, roof, covering, cover [➡ PARTS OF TREES AND PLANTS; 1026]

cant **1** *n* **clichés**, platitudes, banalities, commonplaces, triteness, corniness [➡ MEANINGLESS SPEECH OR WRITING; 676] **2** *n* **hypocrisy**, insincerity, false piety, humbug, lip service, tokenism [➡ DECEPTION AND LIES; 660] *Opposite*: sincerity **3** *n* **jargon**, slang, argot, patois, vernacular, lingo (*informal*), blather (*informal*) [➡ MEANINGLESS SPEECH OR WRITING; 676]

cantankerous *adj* **grumpy**, irascible, irritable, crusty, quarrelsome, ill-tempered, curmudgeonly, crabby, crotchety (*informal*), grouchy (*informal*), ornery (*informal*) [➡ DIFFICULT TO PLEASE; 515]

cantankerousness *n* [➡ DIFFICULT TO PLEASE; 515]

cantata *type of* **musical form** [➡ MUSIC, SONGS, AND SINGING; 907]

canteen *type of* **eating place** [➡ HOTELS, RESTAURANTS, AND CLUBS; 1082]

canter **1** *n* **trot**, run, gallop, jog, sprint [➡ PROCEED AND GO; 305] **2** *v* **run**, gallop, trot, jog, sprint [➡ MOVE FAST; 313]

canticle *type of* **musical form** [➡ MUSIC, SONGS, AND SINGING; 907]

cantilever *n* **beam**, plank, girder [➡ BUILDING MATERIALS; 1077]

cantilever bridge *type of* **bridge** [➡ BRIDGES, TUNNELS, CROSSINGS, AND JUNCTIONS; 1112]

canto *n* **stanza**, verse, strophe, section, division, segment, part [➡ POETRY AND VERSE; 915]

canton *n* **region**, district, area, borough, constituency, parish, province [➡ COUNTRIES AND REGIONS; 1067]

canvas **1** *type of* **fabric from plants** [➡ FABRICS; 1132] **2** *n* **painting**, oil painting, picture, old master, work of art, image, work, piece, opus [➡ ARTWORKS; 898] **3** *n* **background**, backdrop, setting, context, scene, panorama, overview [➡ SITUATIONS; 71]

canvasback *type of* **freshwater bird** [➡ FRESHWATER BIRDS; 1000]

canvass **1** *v* **campaign**, electioneer, drum up support, solicit votes, stump, crusade, appeal [➡ ELECTIONS AND VOTING; 807] **2** *v* **test**, research, investigate, survey, poll, ballot, circularize [➡ QUESTION THINGS; 751]

canvasser **1** *n* **campaigner**, supporter, party worker [➡ DEVOTEES AND ADDICTED PEOPLE; 556] **2** *n* **researcher**, investigator, examiner, pollster [➡ QUESTIONERS; 667]

canyon *n* **ravine**, gully, gorge, chasm, gulch, rift, coulee [➡ GEOLOGIC FEATURES; 1056]

cap **1** *type of* **headgear** [➡ ACCESSORIES, MILLINERY, AND LINGERIE; 867] **2** *n* **cover**, lid, top, stopper, plug [➡ COVERS AND COATINGS; 1246] **3** *n* **restraint**, limit, control, restriction, check, ceiling, threshold [➡ EXTREMITIES OF PHYSICAL OBJECTS; 1250] **4** *v* **cover**, top, stop, plug, overlay [➡ DECORATE, ADORN, AND APPLY COATINGS; 405] **5** *v* **surpass**, top, improve, better, outdo, outshine, excel [➡ BEAT AND DEFEAT; 80] **6** *v* **limit**, regulate, control, restrain, restrict, check [➡ CHANGE OF SIZE: SMALLER; 393]

capability *n* **ability**, capacity, competence, skill, resources, wherewithal [➡ SKILLS, TALENTS, AND ABILITIES; 526]

See Compare and Contrast at **ability**.

capable **1** *adj* **accomplished**, talented, skilled, gifted, clever, adept, efficient [➡ TALENTED AND SKILLFUL; 527] *Opposite*: inept **2** *adj* **able**, competent, proficient, efficient, qualified, adept [➡ TALENTED AND SKILLFUL; 527] *Opposite*: incapable

capably *adv* **competently**, proficiently, adeptly, ably, efficiently [➡ TALENTED AND SKILLFUL; 527] *Opposite*: ineptly

capacious *adj* **roomy**, spacious, large, ample, big, voluminous, commodious, extensive, vast, sizable [➡ LARGE; 1193] *Opposite*: cramped

capaciousness *n* [➡ LARGE; 1193]

capacity 1 *n* **ability**, capability, skill, talent, aptitude [➡ SKILLS, TALENTS, AND ABILITIES; 526] 2 *n* **volume**, space, room, size, dimensions [➡ SIZE AND DIMENSIONS; 1192] 3 *n* **role**, position, responsibility, function, office [➡ JOB; 833]

See Compare and Contrast at **ability.**

cape 1 *n* **promontory**, peninsula, headland, outcrop, point [➡ THE SEAS, OCEANS, AND SHORES; 1041] 2 *type of* **overcoat** [➡ GARMENTS AND OUTFITS; 865] 3 *type of* **house** [➡ RESIDENTIAL BUILDINGS; 1078]

Cape Cod *type of* **house** [➡ RESIDENTIAL BUILDINGS; 1078]

capellini *type of* **pasta** [➡ PASTA; 1180]

caper 1 *n* **escapade**, adventure, jaunt, lark, antics, jape (*archaic or literary*) [➡ EVENTS AND OCCURRENCES; 35] 2 *v* **frolic**, cavort, jump, leap, dance, prance, gambol, horse around [➡ FIDGET AND FROLIC; 311]

capillary *type of* **blood vessel** [➡ THE BLOOD AND CIRCULATION; 717]

cap in hand *adv* **humbly**, meekly, deferentially, submissively, subserviently, abjectly, on bended knee [➡ EXPRESSING RESPECT AND APPROVAL; 637] *Opposite:* **boldly**

capital 1 *n* **assets**, resources, funds, wealth, money, principal, investment [➡ FINANCIAL ASSETS; 462] 2 *n* **center**, headquarters, hub [➡ HUMAN SETTLEMENTS; 1070]

capitalist 1 *n* **entrepreneur**, financier, industrialist, businessperson, investor [➡ BUSINESS PEOPLE; 793] 2 *adj* **entrepreneurial**, industrial, consumerist, consumer, commercial [➡ STYLES AND SYSTEMS OF GOVERNMENT; 806]

capitalize *v* **fund**, finance, raise funding for, provide backing for [➡ GIVE MONEY; 433]

capitalize on *v* **make the most of**, maximize, take advantage of, use, utilize, build on, exploit [➡ MAKE GOOD USE OF SOMETHING; 473]

capital punishment *n* [➡ TRIAL, PUNISHMENT, AND LEGAL OUTCOMES; 819]

capitation 1 *n* **tax**, poll tax, levy, toll, duty [➡ TAX AND TAXATION; 802] 2 *n* **fee**, charge, payment, amount [➡ FUNDS, PAYMENTS, AND CHARGES; 800]

capitulate *v* **surrender**, submit, yield, succumb, give way, give in, give up [➡ NOT DO AND REFUSE TO DO; 274] *Opposite:* **resist**

See Compare and Contrast at **yield.**

capitulation *n* **surrender**, submission, defeat, retreat [➡ FAILURE; 77] *Opposite:* **resistance**

capon *type of* **male or female bird** [➡ MALE OR FEMALE BIRDS; 1005]

caponata *type of* **relish** [➡ SEASONINGS AND SAUCES; 1174]

cappelletti *type of* **pasta** [➡ PASTA; 1180]

cappuccino *type of* **coffee** [➡ DRINKS; 1187]

capriccio *type of* **musical form** [➡ MUSIC, SONGS, AND SINGING; 907]

capriccioso *type of* **musical term** [➡ MUSICAL TERMS; 912]

caprice *n* **whim**, impulse, quirk, fancy, fad, notion [➡ IDEAS AND THOUGHTS; 770]

capricious *adj* **unpredictable**, changeable, variable, impulsive, whimsical, unreliable, fickle, erratic, wayward, flighty [➡ LACK OF COMMITMENT AND UNRELIABILITY; 509] *Opposite:* predictable

capriciously *adv* **impulsively**, on impulse, unpredictably, changeably, on a whim, without rhyme or reason, quixotically, at your own sweet will, as the mood strikes you, as the fancy takes you (*UK*), as the spirit moves you (*UK*) [➡ UNPLANNED AND UNEXPECTED; 281] *Opposite:* predictably

capriciousness *n* **unpredictability**, changeability, variability, whimsicality, impulsiveness, unreliability, waywardness, fickleness [➡ LACK OF COMMITMENT AND UNRELIABILITY; 509] *Opposite:* predictability

Capricorn *type of* **astrological sign** [➡ FATE, DESTINY, AND ASTROLOGY; 782]

Capricornus *type of* **constellation** [➡ HEAVENLY BODIES; 1061]

capri pants *type of* **pants** [➡ GARMENTS AND OUTFITS; 865]

capsicum *type of* **salad vegetable** [➡ FRUIT AND VEGETABLES; 1176]

capsize *v* **overturn**, turn over, roll over, keel over, turn turtle [➡ MOVE SOMETHING: INTO A NEW POSITION OR OVERTURN; 330] *Opposite:* right

capstan *part of* **ship or boat** [➡ PARTS OF A SHIP OR BOAT; 1151]

capsule 1 *n* **pill**, tablet, lozenge [➡ REMEDIES, TREATMENTS, AND OPERATIONS; 731] 2 *n* **pod**, container, case, casing, shell [➡ CONTAINERS, RECEPTACLES, AND PACKAGING; 1245]

capsule collection *n* [➡ GARMENTS AND OUTFITS; 865]

capsule hotel *type of* **hotel** [➡ HOTELS, RESTAURANTS, AND CLUBS; 1082]

captain 1 *n* **head**, skipper, leader, chief, boss, commander, team leader [➡ IMPORTANT OR FAMOUS PEOPLE; 893] 2 *v* **lead**, skipper, manage, take charge, head, control [➡ BE IN CHARGE; 270]

captain of industry *n* [➡ BUSINESS PEOPLE; 793]

caption *n* **slogan**, subtitle, title, description, legend, heading, header, footer [➡ PARTS OF BOOKS AND DOCUMENTS; 593]

captious 1 *adj* **critical**, pedantic, trivial, petty, nitpicking, hairsplitting, pettifogging, negative, unfair, unjust [➡ DIFFICULT TO PLEASE; 515] *Opposite:* compliant 2 *adj* **confusing**, misleading, devious, bewildering, disingenuous, malicious, entrapping [➡ DECEITFUL; 513] *Opposite:* clear

captivate *v* **attract**, charm, enchant, fascinate, entrance, draw [➡ APPEAL TO AND AROUSE INTEREST; 575] *Opposite:* repel

captivated *adj* **enchanted**, fascinated, charmed, entranced, spellbound, enthralled, mesmerized, transfixed, stunned, impressed, riveted (*informal*) [➡ APPRECIATION AND GRATITUDE; 535] *Opposite:* repulsed

captivating *adj* **charming**, attractive, appealing, fascinating, charismatic, enchanting, entrancing [➡ BEAUTY AND ATTRACTIVENESS; 189]

captive 1 *n* **prisoner**, detainee, internee, prisoner of war, hostage [➡CAPTIVES AND PRISONERS; 249] *Opposite:* escapee 2 *adj* **imprisoned**, in prison, locked up, enslaved, confined, caged, incarcerated (*formal*) [➡CAPTIVITY AND LOSS OF FREEDOM; 248] *Opposite:* free 3 *adj* **attentive**, intent, fascinated, spellbound, rapt, ensnared, trapped [➡PENSIVENESS AND INTEREST; 538]

captivity *n* **imprisonment**, custody, detention, confinement, internment, incarceration (*formal*) [➡CAPTIVITY AND LOSS OF FREEDOM; 248] *Opposite:* freedom

captor *n* **abductor**, imprisoner, kidnapper, hostage taker, jailer, hijacker [➡CRIMINALS; 821] *Opposite:* liberator

capture 1 *v* **take**, seize, apprehend, arrest, pick up, catch, bag, net [➡TAKE SOMETHING AWAY; 425] *Opposite:* release 2 *v* **imprison**, detain, arrest, confine, take into custody, jail, incarcerate (*formal*) [➡CAPTIVITY AND LOSS OF FREEDOM; 248] *Opposite:* liberate 3 *v* **encapsulate**, summarize, sum up, portray, describe, depict, denote [➡REPRESENT SOMETHING OR SOMEBODY; 59] 4 *v* **secure**, attain, gain, acquire, obtain, gain control, win [➡GET; 420] *Opposite:* lose 5 *v* **catch**, seize, grab hold of, trap, ensnare, net, get (*informal*) [➡CONTACT: HOLD; 411] 6 *n* **imprisonment**, detention, arrest, seizure, apprehension, internment, incarceration (*formal*) [➡CAPTIVITY AND LOSS OF FREEDOM; 248] *Opposite:* release

capture your imagination *v* **fascinate**, excite, inspire, interest, enchant, entrance, enrapture (*formal*) [➡APPEAL TO AND AROUSE INTEREST; 575]

capuchin *type of* **primate** [➡PRIMATES; 988]

capybara *type of* **rodent** [➡RODENTS; 989]

car 1 *n* **automobile**, auto [➡BIKES, CARS, AND CARRIAGES; 1149] 2 *n* **cabin**, carriage, coach, compartment, wagon, sleeper, flatcar, Pullman, railway carriage (*UK*) [➡RAILROADS; 1107]

car

◆ *types of cars*
all-terrain vehicle, compact, convertible, coupe, dragster, four-by-four, hatchback, hot rod (*slang*), limo, limousine, minivan, off-roader (*informal*), racing car, roadster (*dated*), runabout, sedan, sport utility vehicle, sports car, station wagon, stock car, subcompact, SUV, three-wheeler, van

caracara *type of* **bird of prey** [➡BIRDS OF PREY; 998]

carafe *n* **flask**, decanter, bottle [➡TABLEWARE, FLATWARE, AND KITCHENWARE; 861]

caramel 1 *type of* **confectionery** [➡CONFECTIONERY; 1182] 2 *type of* **brown** [➡COLORS; 1224]

caramelize *v* **burn**, heat, scorch, brown, broil [➡COOKING AND FOOD PREPARATION; 353]

carapace *n* **case**, shell, covering, sheath, outside, exterior [➡COVERS AND COATINGS; 1246]

caravan *n* **convoy**, group, procession, parade, motorcade, column, line, cavalcade [➡GROUPS OF VEHICLES; 1152]

caraway *type of* **herb** [➡HERBS AND SPICES; 1175]

caraway seed *type of* **spice** [➡HERBS AND SPICES; 1175]

carbine *type of* **gun** [➡WEAPONS FOR SHOOTING; 1156]

carbohydrate *n* **biological compound**, simple carbohydrate, complex carbohydrate, starch, sugar, cellulose [➡FOOD COMPONENTS; 1188]

carbon *type of* **mineral** [➡MINERALS; 1277]

carbonara *type of* **food presentation** [➡COOKING AND FOOD PREPARATION; 353]

carbon copy *n* **replica**, duplicate, copy, facsimile, exact likeness, reproduction [➡COPIES AND REPLICAS; 151] *Opposite:* original

Carboniferous *type of* **period** [➡EPOCHS AND ERAS; 89]

car boot sale (*UK*) *n* [➡SALES AND SHOWS; 443]

carbuncle *n* **blemish**, boil, pustule, abscess, sore, spot (*UK*) [➡CONDITIONS AFFECTING THE SKIN; 721]

carcass *n* **corpse**, remains, cadaver, body, skeleton, shell [➡THE BONES AND JOINTS; 719]

carcinogenic *adj* **cancer-causing**, oncogenic, hazardous, toxic, poisonous, dangerous, noxious, unsafe [➡DANGEROUS; 236]

carcinomatous *adj* [➡SICKNESS; 729]

card 1 *n* **greeting card**, birthday card, anniversary card, postcard, picture postcard [➡LETTERS AND WRITTEN MESSAGES; 584] 2 *n* **pass**, identification card, membership card, business card, calling card [➡OFFICIAL DOCUMENTS; 586]

cardamom *type of* **spice** [➡HERBS AND SPICES; 1175]

cardboard 1 *n* **board**, paper, card, packaging, packing, wrapping [➡COVERS AND COATINGS; 1246] 2 *adj* **insubstantial**, unconvincing, phoney, plastic, wooden, flat, two-dimensional [➡FALSE AND UNREAL; 173] *Opposite:* substantial

cardboard box *type of* **container** [➡CONTAINERS, RECEPTACLES, AND PACKAGING; 1245]

card-carrying *adj* **official**, paid-up, bona fide, listed, genuine, authentic, committed, hundred percent [➡TRUE AND REAL; 171]

cardiac *adj* [➡THE BLOOD AND CIRCULATION; 717]

cardigan *type of* **sweater** [➡GARMENTS AND OUTFITS; 865]

cardinal 1 *adj* **basic**, fundamental, key, prime, serious, important, chief, principal, essential, central, core [➡IMPORTANT; 194] *Opposite:* secondary 2 *type of* **common bird** [➡BIRDS; 997]

cardiovascular *adj* **circulatory**, cardiac, vascular, heart, blood [➡THE BLOOD AND CIRCULATION; 717]

cardsharp *n* **cheat**, gambler, pro, hustler, swindler, con artist (*informal*), card shark (*slang*) [➡PEOPLE WHO DECEIVE; 661]

cardsharping *n* **cheating**, tricking, swindling, gambling, hustling [➡GAMBLE AND TAKE RISKS; 466]

card table *type of* **table** [➡FURNITURE; 858]

care 1 *v* **be concerned**, be interested, feel a concern, take an interest [➡BE CONCERNED AND CARE; 581] *Opposite:* disregard 2 *n* **upkeep**, maintenance, repair, overhaul, attention [➡REPAIR AND MEND; 376] 3 *n* **attention**, caution, precaution, carefulness, watchfulness, alertness [➡ATTENTION AND ATTENTIVENESS; 763] 4 *n* **worry**, concern, anxiety, trouble, unease, stress [➡CONFU-

SION, ANXIETY, AND WORRY; 540] **5** *n* **treatment**, provision, support, attention [➡ KIND ACTIONS OR BEHAVIOR; 295] **6** *n* **supervision**, guardianship, protection, custody, oversight (*formal*) [➡ RESPONSIBILITY; 170]

See Compare and Contrast at **worry**.

careen *v* **swerve**, sway, weave, lurch, swing, veer, blunder [➡ AIMLESS AND ERRANT MOTION; 343]

career **1** *n* **vocation**, job, occupation, profession, calling, livelihood, line of business [➡ PROFESSIONS; 845] **2** *v* **rush**, race, hurry, dash, speed, hurtle, tear [➡ MOVE FAST; 313]

career into *v* [➡ CONTACT: IMPACT; 413]

careerism *n* **determination**, single-mindedness, motivation, commitment, drive, professionalism [➡ HARD-WORKING AND COMMITTED; 500]

careerist **1** *n* **professional**, achiever, high flier, go-getter (*informal*) [➡ PEOPLE WHO ARE APPROVED OF; 955] **2** *adj* **single-minded**, determined, motivated, focused, professional [➡ HARD-WORKING AND COMMITTED; 500]

care for **1** *v* **take care of**, feel affection for, love, like, have a soft spot for, cherish, be fond of [➡ LIKE, LOVE, VALUE, AND ENJOY; 578] *Opposite:* dislike **2** *v* **look after**, tend, supervise, oversee, see to, attend to [➡ TAKE CARE OF AND SPOIL; 300] *Opposite:* ignore **3** *v* (*formal*) **want**, desire, wish for, like to have, appreciate [➡ LIKE, LOVE, VALUE, AND ENJOY; 578]

carefree *adj* **untroubled**, happy-go-lucky, cheery, relaxed, cheerful, lighthearted, blithe (*literary*) [➡ COOL AND CALM; 536] *Opposite:* troubled

carefreeness *n* **lightheartedness**, cheerfulness, cheeriness, happiness, jollity, buoyancy, breeziness, nonchalance, insouciance [➡ COOL AND CALM; 536] *Opposite:* anxiety

careful **1** *adj* **cautious**, wary, vigilant, watchful, alert, suspicious, chary, circumspect, cagey, guarded [➡ CAUTIOUS AND CAREFUL; 282] *Opposite:* reckless **2** *adj* **thorough**, meticulous, painstaking, particular, precise, conscientious, fastidious, assiduous, scrupulous, punctilious, finicky, fussy [➡ CAUTIOUS AND CAREFUL; 282] *Opposite:* careless **3** *adj* **prudent**, sensible, judicious, cautious, well thought-out, shrewd, wise [➡ THE NATURE OF IDEAS; 771] *Opposite:* foolish **4** *adj* **protective**, sympathetic, sensitive, gentle, tender, caring [➡ GENEROSITY AND KINDNESS; 495] *Opposite:* rough

---

Compare and Contrast: *careful, conscientious, scrupulous, thorough, meticulous, painstaking, assiduous, punctilious, finicky, fussy*

CORE MEANING: exercising care and attention in doing something

careful a wide-ranging term, suggesting attention to detail and implying cautiousness in avoiding errors or inaccuracies; *conscientious* showing great care, attention, and industriousness in carrying out a task; *scrupulous* having or showing careful regard for what is morally right; *thorough* extremely careful and accurate; *meticulous* extremely careful and precise; *painstaking* involving or showing great care and attention to detail; *assiduous* undeviating in effort and care; *punctilious* very careful about the conventions of correct behavior and etiquette; *finicky* concentrating too much on unimportant details; *fussy* tending to worry over details or trivial things.

See Compare and Contrast at **cautious**.

carefulness **1** *n* **caution**, care, suspicion, wariness, watchfulness, alertness, chariness, circumspection [➡ POSITIVE INTELLECTUAL CHARACTERISTICS; 524] *Opposite:* recklessness **2** *n* **attention to detail**, thoroughness, precision, care, meticulousness, conscientiousness, assiduousness [➡ HARD-WORKING AND COMMITTED; 500] *Opposite:* carelessness

caregiver *n* [➡ SUPPORTERS, PROTECTORS, AND COMPATRIOTS; 970]

careless **1** *adj* **slapdash**, happy-go-lucky, devil-may-care, casual, slipshod, sloppy, hasty, inaccurate, lackadaisical, lax [➡ INCAUTIOUS AND CARELESS; 283] *Opposite:* careful **2** *adj* **uncaring**, thoughtless, offhand, inconsiderate, unthinking, unconcerned, insensitive, unsympathetic, casual, cavalier, irresponsible, rash, reckless, negligent, heedless [➡ NEUTRALITY AND INDIFFERENCE; 553] *Opposite:* considerate

carelessly **1** *adv* **sloppily**, hastily, inaccurately, imprecisely, haphazardly, casually [➡ NEUTRALITY AND INDIFFERENCE; 553] *Opposite:* carefully **2** *adv* **uncaringly**, offhandedly, inconsiderately, unthinkingly, unsympathetically, insensitively, thoughtlessly, casually [➡ INCAUTIOUS AND CARELESS; 283] *Opposite:* considerately

carelessness *n* **sloppiness**, inattentiveness, inaccuracy, imprecision, negligence, inattention [➡ VAGUENESS; 243] *Opposite:* care

caress **1** *v* **stroke**, touch, pat, embrace, cuddle, hug, fondle [➡ CONTACT: TOUCH; 412] **2** *n* **touch**, stroke, pat, embrace, hug, cuddle [➡ PHYSICAL CONTACT AS COMMUNICATION; 655]

caretaker **1** *n* **caregiver**, attendant, nurse, minder (*UK*), carer (*UK*) [➡ ADOPTION, FOSTERING, AND EXTENDED FAMILY; 962] **2** *n* (*UK*) **concierge**, janitor, superintendent, porter, custodian, warden (*UK*) [➡ PEOPLE WHO GUARD AND PROTECT; 846]

careworn *adj* **haggard**, drawn, beleaguered, worried, burdened, weighed down, oppressed, exhausted, worn-out [➡ SADNESS, DISTRESS, AND DESPAIR; 539] *Opposite:* carefree

cargo *n* **load**, freight, consignment, shipment, goods, payload [➡ TRANSPORTATION, TRANSPORTERS, AND CARGOS; 322]

cargo pants *type of* **pants** [➡ GARMENTS AND OUTFITS; 865]

caribou *type of* **deer or antelope** [➡ DEER AND ANTELOPES; 981]

caricature **1** *n* **cartoon**, picture, drawing, sketch [➡ ARTWORKS; 898] **2** *n* **travesty**, misrepresentation, false impression, distortion, falsification, exaggeration, parody, satire, skit, sendup (*informal*) [➡ JOKES AND TEASING; 674]

caricaturist *n* **artist**, cartoonist, humorist, satirist [➡ ARTISTS; 900]

carina *part of* **bird** [➡ PARTS OF A BIRD; 1006]

Carina *type of* **constellation** [➡ HEAVENLY BODIES; 1061]

caring *adj* **kind**, thoughtful, gentle, helpful, considerate, compassionate, concerned, loving, affectionate, sensitive, attentive [➡ GENEROSITY AND KINDNESS; 495] *Opposite:* uncaring

carjack *v* [➡ STEAL AND ROB; 426]

carjacker *n* [➡ CRIMINALS; 821]

carjacking *n* [➡ CRIMES; 817]

carmine *type of* **red** [➡COLORS; 1224]

carnage *n* **killing**, bloodshed, slaughter, massacre, bloodbath, butchery [➡CAUSES OF DEATH; 921]

carnal (*formal*) *adj* **physical**, fleshy, sensual, sexual [➡MORALLY BAD OR IMPROPER; 775] *Opposite*: spiritual

carnality (*formal*) *n* [➡MORALLY BAD OR IMPROPER; 775]

carnation 1 *type of* **perennial flower** [➡FLOWERS; 1032] 2 *type of* **red** [➡COLORS; 1224]

carnelian *type of* **gemstone** [➡PRECIOUS STONES; 1278]

carnival 1 *n* **festival**, celebration, street party, fair, fete, parade, pageant, cavalcade, Mardi Gras [➡PARTIES, DANCES, AND CELEBRATIONS; 37] 2 *n* **fair**, fairground, sideshow, midway, amusement park, traveling fair, funfair (*UK*) [➡URBAN OUTDOOR SPACES; 1072]

carnivore *n* **flesh-eater**, meat-eater, predator, scavenger, omnivore, insectivore, fish-eater, raptor [➡EATERS, GOURMETS, AND DIETARY CHOICES; 714]

carnivorous *adj* **flesh-eating**, meat-eating, predatory, scavenging, insectivorous, fish-eating [➡EATERS, GOURMETS, AND DIETARY CHOICES; 714]

carob *type of* **evergreen tree** [➡EVERGREEN AND CONIFEROUS TREES; 1029]

carol *n* **song**, hymn, chant, chorus [➡MUSIC, SONGS, AND SINGING; 907]

carousal (*literary*) *n* **party**, celebration, binge, spree, bender (*informal*) [➡PARTIES, DANCES, AND CELEBRATIONS; 37]

carouse (*literary*) *v* **revel**, celebrate, drink, get drunk, raise the roof, go on the town, party (*informal*), paint the town red (*informal*) [➡LEISURE AND RECREATION; 874]

carousel 1 *n* **merry-go-round**, ride, roundabout (*UK*) [➡ENTERTAINMENT; 072] 2 *n* **container**, cassette, cartridge, drum, magazine, holder, rack, receptacle [➡CONTAINERS, RECEPTACLES, AND PACKAGING; 1245]

carouser (*literary*) *n* [➡PLEASURE-SEEKERS AND HEDONISTS; 886]

carousing (*literary*) *n* **festivities**, partying, revels, revelry, celebrations [➡PARTIES, DANCES, AND CELEBRATIONS; 37]

carp 1 *v* **complain**, grumble, find fault, nag, go on, criticize, crab, whine, object, moan (*informal*), grouse (*informal*), gripe (*informal*), knock (*slang*) [➡COMPLAIN AND NAG; 686] 2 *type of* **freshwater fish** [➡FRESHWATER FISH; 1010]

See Compare and Contrast at **complain**.

carpaccio *n* [➡PREPARED DISHES; 1170]

carpal *type of* **bone** [➡THE BONES AND JOINTS; 719]

car park (*UK*) *n* [➡URBAN OUTDOOR SPACES; 1072]

carpel *part of* **flower** [➡FLOWERS; 1032]

carpenter ant *type of* **ant** [➡ANTS; 1014]

carpentry *n* **joinery**, woodworking, turning, carving, cabinetmaking [➡CRAFTS AND CARVING; 355]

carper *n* [➡GRUMPY AND NEGATIVE PEOPLE; 953]

carpet 1 *n* **rug**, mat, runner, fitted carpet, carpet tiles, carpeting, floor covering, flooring [➡FURNISHING AND HOUSEHOLD LINENS; 860] 2 *n* **covering**, layer, blanket, mass, spread, cover [➡COVERS AND COATINGS; 1246] 3 *v* (*literary*) **cover**, swathe, coat, overlay, strew, spread [➡DECORATE, ADORN, AND APPLY COATINGS; 405]

carpeting *n* **floor covering**, flooring, matting, carpet tiles [➡FURNISHING AND HOUSEHOLD LINENS; 860]

carping 1 *adj* **critical**, nitpicking, complaining, dissatisfied, discontented, disapproving, disparaging [➡ACCUSATORY AND DISAPPROVING; 634] 2 *n* **complaining**, nitpicking, faultfinding, dissatisfaction, whining, criticism, moaning (*informal*), grousing (*informal*), griping (*informal*) [➡COMPLAIN AND NAG; 686]

carpool lane *n* [➡ROADS; 1106]

carport *n* **garage**, lean-to, shelter, porch, parking space [➡ANCILLARY BUILDINGS; 1080]

carriage 1 *n* **horse-drawn carriage**, coach, horse and carriage [➡BIKES, CARS, AND CARRIAGES; 1149] 2 *n* (*formal*) **bearing**, posture, deportment, air, presence, poise, pose, stance, attitude, gait, comportment (*formal*) [➡TEMPERAMENT AND BEHAVIOR; 492] 3 *n* **transportation**, delivery, carrying, haulage, conveyance, shipment [➡TRANSPORTATION, TRANSPORTERS, AND CARGOS; 322]

carriageway (*UK*) *n* **lane**, lane of traffic, roadway, road, thoroughfare, side of the road [➡ROADS; 1106]

carried *adj* **approved**, accepted, passed, agreed, supported, voted for [➡CERTAIN; 174] *Opposite*: rejected

carried away *adj* [➡PLEASURE, EXCITEMENT, AND ELATION; 534]

carrier *n* **transporter**, hauler, delivery service, carter, shipper, mover, exporter, importer, shipping agent, transferrer [➡TRANSPORTATION, TRANSPORTERS, AND CARGOS; 322]

carrion *n* **flesh**, meat, tissue, muscle, sinew, guts [➡ANIMAL FEED; 1168]

carrot 1 *type of* **root vegetable** [➡FRUIT AND VEGETABLES; 1176] 3 *n* **incentive**, inducement, bribe, bait, lure, sweetener (*informal*), sugared pill (*UK*) [➡BRIBES; 440]

carrot cake *type of* **cake** [➡CAKES, COOKIES, AND DESSERTS; 1181]

carroty *adj* **orange**, red, auburn, ginger [➡HAIR COLOR; 485]

carry 1 *v* **take**, bear, hold, support, clutch, sustain [➡MOVE SOMETHING TO ANOTHER LOCATION; 324] 2 *v* **transmit**, transport, convey, transfer, bring, lug, cart, move, pass on, conduct, pass, relay [➡MOVE SOMETHING TO ANOTHER LOCATION; 324] 3 *v* **contain**, include, involve, incorporate, hold, have [➡HOLD AND CONTAIN; 455] 4 *v* **have in stock**, stock, store, keep, supply, have available [➡STORE AND KEEP; 453] 5 *v* **approve**, accept, pass, agree, vote for, support [➡APPROVE AND CONFIRM; 646]

carryall *type of* **baggage** [➡CONTAINERS, RECEPTACLES, AND PACKAGING; 1245]

carrycase *type of* **baggage** [➡CONTAINERS, RECEPTACLES, AND PACKAGING; 1245]

carrying *adj* **loud**, resonant, resounding, booming, ringing, stentorian [➡LOUD, HIGH, OR UNPLEASANT SOUNDS; 1266] *Opposite*: quiet

carrying-on (*informal*) *n* **pranks**, goings-on (*informal*), doings (*informal*), high jinks (*informal*) [➠ BAD BEHAVIOR OR ACTIONS; 254]

carry off 1 *v* **take away**, take off, remove, steal, abduct, carry away, cart off [➠ REMOVE SOMETHING; 338] *Opposite*: bring back 2 *v* **succeed**, manage, accomplish, achieve, do, pull off (*informal*) [➠ SUCCEED AND WIN; 79] *Opposite*: fail

carry on 1 *v* **continue**, keep, keep on, keep at, go on, persist, keep going, be persistent, persevere [➠ CONTINUE AN ACTION; 262] *Opposite*: stop 2 *v* **complain**, grumble, carp, nag, go on, moan (*informal*) [➠ COMPLAIN AND NAG; 686]

carry out *v* **do**, perform, complete, achieve, succeed, accomplish, fulfill, execute, realize, pull off (*informal*), discharge (*formal*) [➠ CARRY OUT AN ACTION; 269] *Opposite*: neglect

See Compare and Contrast at **perform**.

carryout *n* **takeout**, fast food, takeaway (*UK*) [➠ MEALS AND PARTS OF MEALS; 1169]

carry over *v* **postpone**, defer, leave, reschedule, put back, adjourn [➠ DELAY ACTION OR OCCURRENCE; 278] *Opposite*: expedite (*formal*)

carryover *n* **leftover**, legacy, inheritance, residue, remnant, remainder, surplus [➠ REMAINDER AND REMAINDERS; 125]

car seat *type of* **internal feature** [➠ INTERNAL PARTS OF A VEHICLE; 1146]

carsick *adj* **sick**, nauseous, ill, unwell [➠ ILL AND SICK; 740]

cart 1 *n* **farm cart**, wagon, dray, tumbril, wain (*archaic or literary*) [➠ BIKES, CARS, AND CARRIAGES; 1149] 2 *n* **handcart**, pushcart, barrow, wheelbarrow, trolley [➠ BIKES, CARS, AND CARRIAGES; 1149] 3 *v* **carry**, lug, heave, haul, drag, draw [➠ MOVE SOMETHING TO ANOTHER LOCATION; 324]

carte blanche *n* **free rein**, blank check, complete freedom, full authority, complete discretion, free hand [➠ FREEDOM AND LIBERTY; 208]

cartel *n* **interest group**, lobby, alliance, association, union, league [➠ GROUPS WITH A COMMON INTEREST; 938]

car theft *n* [➠ CRIMES; 817]

car thief *n* [➠ CRIMINALS; 821]

carthorse *type of* **horse** [➠ HORSES; 985]

cartilage *n* [➠ THE BONES AND JOINTS; 719]

cart off *v* **remove**, drag off, take away, haul off, carry off, carry away [➠ REMOVE SOMETHING; 338]

carton *n* **box**, cardboard box, container, pack, sachet [➠ CONTAINERS, RECEPTACLES, AND PACKAGING; 1245]

cartoon 1 *n* **animation**, animated film, movie [➠ FILM; 901] 2 *n* **drawing**, caricature, picture, comic strip [➠ ARTWORKS; 898]

cartoonist *n* **artist**, animator, caricaturist, satirist, humorist [➠ ARTISTS; 900]

cartridge 1 *n* **container**, holder, casing, unit, cassette [➠ CONTAINERS, RECEPTACLES, AND PACKAGING; 1245] 2 *part of* **audio equipment** [➠ AUDIO EQUIPMENT; 1139]

cartwheel *v* **turn**, somersault, go head over heels, roll,

flip, flip over, turn over, tumble, flip-flop [➠ FIDGET AND FROLIC; 311]

carve 1 *v* **engrave**, inscribe, etch, cut, notch, score, scribe [➠ CRAFTS AND CARVING; 355] 2 *v* **slice**, pare, cut in slices, whittle, cut up, cut, shape, fashion, sculpt [➠ TEAR, BREAK, AND CUT; 360]

carve out *v* **create**, make, establish, build, set up, lay down, construct [➠ INSTITUTE AND INAUGURATE; 348]

carve up (*informal*) *v* **divide**, allocate, share out, apportion, distribute, allot, split up, partition [➠ DISPENSE, RATION, AND DISTRIBUTE; 434]

carve-up *n* **division**, allocation, distribution, partitioning, splitting up, share-out (*UK*) [➠ DISPENSE, RATION, AND DISTRIBUTE; 434]

carving 1 *n* **model**, statue, statuette, figure, figurine, bas-relief, frieze, artifact [➠ ARTWORKS; 898] 2 *n* **cutting**, engraving, etching, sculpting, fashioning, shaping, slicing [➠ CRAFTS AND CARVING; 355]

carving knife 1 *type of* **knife** [➠ CUTTING TOOLS; 1120] 2 *type of* **flatware** [➠ TABLEWARE, FLATWARE, AND KITCHENWARE; 861]

Casanova *n* **libertine**, Don Juan, gigolo, Romeo, ladies' man, lover, seducer, adulterer, satyr, stud (*informal*), Lothario (*literary*), philanderer (*dated*) [➠ PLEASURE-SEEKERS AND HEDONISTS; 886]

cascade 1 *n* **waterfall**, chute, cataract, falls, torrent, force (*UK*) [➠ RIVERS, LAKES, AND STREAMS; 1042] 2 *v* **flow**, pour, fall, drop, gush, spill, surge, tumble [➠ GO DOWNWARD; 307]

case 1 *n* **circumstance**, situation, instance, event, occasion, incident [➠ SITUATIONS; 71] 2 *n* **instance**, item, example, illustration, paradigm, a case in point [➠ PERFECT EXAMPLES AND EMBODIMENTS; 67] 3 *n* **job**, project, commission, assignment, task, problem, issue [➠ WORK IN GENERAL; 297] 4 *n* **court case**, legal action, lawsuit, suit, indictment, litigation [➠ TRIAL, PUNISHMENT, AND LEGAL OUTCOMES; 819] 5 *n* **argument**, reason, defense, justification, rationale, basis [➠ IDEAS AND THOUGHTS; 770] 6 *n* **container**, holder, box, casing, cover, folder, crate, pencil case, glasses case [➠ CONTAINERS, RECEPTACLES, AND PACKAGING; 1245] 7 *n* **suitcase**, overnight case, weekend case, briefcase, attaché case, travel case, carrycase [➠ CONTAINERS, RECEPTACLES, AND PACKAGING; 1245]

casebook *n* **record**, log, diary, journal, notebook [➠ BOOKS AND BOOKLETS; 590]

casehardened *adj* **unsympathetic**, unfeeling, hard, hardened, toughened, tough, hardhearted, hard-bitten, cynical, callous, insensitive, hard-boiled (*informal*), hard-nosed (*informal*) [➠ NEGATIVITY OF OUTLOOK; 514] *Opposite*: sensitive

case in point *n* [➠ PERFECT EXAMPLES AND EMBODIMENTS; 67]

casement *type of* **window** [➠ WINDOWS; 1100]

casern *n* [➠ RESIDENTIAL BUILDINGS; 1078]

cash *n* **money**, hard cash, ready money, coins, currency, notes, petty cash [➠ MONEY; 797]

cashew *type of* **nut** [➠ NUTS; 1185]

cashier 1 *n* **treasurer**, banker, bursar [➠ PEOPLE INVOLVED IN FINANCE; 804] 2 *n* **bank clerk**, clerk, teller, official, assistant

[➡ PEOPLE INVOLVED IN FINANCE; 804] **3** *v* **dismiss**, expel, drum out, court martial, boot out (*informal*), kick out (*informal*) [➡ REVOKE STATUS; 459]

cash in *v* **redeem**, trade in, sell, realize, bank [➡ SELL; 441]

cash-in-hand *adj* **in cash**, cash, no questions asked, unofficially, off the record [➡ TYPES OF WORK; 835]

cash in on *v* **take advantage**, benefit, do well from, exploit, make the most of, profit, ride on the coattails of [➡ MAKE GOOD USE OF SOMETHING; 473]

cashmere *type of* **fabric from animals** [➡ FABRICS; 1132]

cashpoint (*UK*) *n* **ATM**, cash machine, till, cash dispenser (*UK*) [➡ ACCOUNTING, BANKING, AND BUDGETING; 799]

casing *n* **covering**, case, outside, exterior, skin, sleeve, sheath, shell, carapace [➡ COVERS AND COATINGS; 1246]

casino **1** *n* **gaming club**, gambling den, nightclub, gaming house [➡ BUILDINGS FOR PUBLIC ENTERTAINMENT; 1084] **2** *type of* **bar or club** [➡ HOTELS, RESTAURANTS, AND CLUBS; 1082]

cask *n* **barrel**, tub, drum, butt, vat, container [➡ CONTAINERS, RECEPTACLES, AND PACKAGING; 1245]

casket **1** *n* **coffin**, sarcophagus, cist, box [➡ BURIAL PLACES AND ACCESSORIES; 930] **2** *type of* **container** [➡ CONTAINERS, RECEPTACLES, AND PACKAGING; 1245]

Cassandra *n* [➡ GRUMPY AND NEGATIVE PEOPLE; 953]

cassata *type of* **dessert** [➡ CAKES, COOKIES, AND DESSERTS; 1181]

cassava *type of* **root vegetable** [➡ FRUIT AND VEGETABLES; 1176]

casserole **1** *n* **cooking pot**, deep dish, covered dish, crockpot, oven dish (*UK*) [➡ TABLEWARE, FLATWARE, AND KITCHENWARE; 861] **2** *type of* **cooked dish** [➡ PREPARED DISHES, 1170] **3** *v* **braise**, stew, simmer, slow cook [➡ COOKING AND FOOD PREPARATION; 353]

cassette **1** *n* **cartridge**, tape, videotape [➡ RECORDINGS AND PLAYERS; 911] **2** *n* **case**, cartridge, holder, container, cover [➡ CONTAINERS, RECEPTACLES, AND PACKAGING; 1245] **3** *part of* **audio equipment** [➡ AUDIO EQUIPMENT; 1139]

cassette recorder *type of* **audio equipment** [➡ AUDIO EQUIPMENT; 1139]

Cassiopeia *type of* **constellation** [➡ HEAVENLY BODIES; 1061]

cassone *type of* **cabinet** [➡ FURNITURE; 858]

cassoulet *type of* **cooked dish** [➡ PREPARED DISHES; 1170]

cast **1** *v* **throw**, hurl, fling, toss, pitch, lob, chuck (*informal*) [➡ MOVE SOMETHING: THROUGH THE AIR; 334] **2** *v* **produce**, generate, create, give rise to, engender, breed [➡ CREATION; 346] **3** *v* **mold**, form, shape, model [➡ MANUFACTURE; 349] **4** *n* **company**, troupe, dramatis personae, actors, players, performers [➡ PERFORMERS; 905] **5** *type of* **flock** [➡ GROUPS OF BIRDS; 1007]

See Compare and Contrast at **throw**.

castanet *type of* **percussion instrument** [➡ MUSICAL INSTRUMENTS; 910]

cast an eye over *v* **scan**, skim, skim through, dip into, pick through, glance over, glance at [➡ LOOKING AND LOOKS; 700] *Opposite:* study

cast around *v* **scan**, skim, skim through, dip into, glance over, glance at [➡ SEEK POSSESSION AND SEARCH; 456] *Opposite:* study

cast a shadow over *v* **spoil**, hang over, darken, loom over, eclipse, chill, threaten, dampen [➡ WORSEN SOMETHING; 380] *Opposite:* brighten

cast aside *v* **get rid of**, put aside, throw away, toss aside, forget, ignore, dismiss, take no notice of, spurn, reject, abandon [➡ GET RID OF SOMETHING; 451] *Opposite:* keep

cast away *v* **give up**, throw away, cast off, discard, jettison, throw up (*informal*) [➡ GET RID OF SOMETHING; 451] *Opposite:* keep

castaway *n* **shipwrecked person**, survivor, exile [➡ SOLITARY PEOPLE AND MISFITS; 942]

cast down *v* **discourage**, dishearten, depress, demoralize, disparage, make unhappy [➡ UPSET, DISTRESS, AND HUMILIATE; 567] *Opposite:* cheer up

caste *n* **class**, social group, standing, background, social order, kind, status [➡ CLASS STATUS; 889]

castigate (*formal*) *v* **criticize**, reprimand, chastise, scold, rebuke, rake over the coals, censure, tell off (*informal*), blast (*informal*), haul over the coals (*UK*) [➡ ACCUSE, BLAME, AND CRITICIZE; 641] *Opposite:* praise

See Compare and Contrast at **criticize**.

castigation (*formal*) *n* **criticism**, rebuke, reprimand, scolding, telling-off (*informal*), chastisement (*formal*) [➡ CRITICISMS AND ANGRY OUTBURSTS; 50] *Opposite:* praise

castigatory (*formal*) *adj* [➡ ACCUSATORY AND DISAPPROVING; 634]

casting **1** *n* **molding**, forming, manufacture [➡ CREATION; 346] **2** *n* **object**, artifact, molding, cast [➡ REPRESENTATIONS AND GENERAL EXAMPLES; 65] **3** *n* **audition**, selection, screen test, interview, test, tryout [➡ PREPARATORY EVENTS; 57]

cast-iron *adj* **inflexible**, rigid, unchangeable, immutable, fixed, firm, ironclad [➡ UNWILLINGNESS AND STUBBORNNESS; 564] *Opposite:* flexible

castle *n* **fortress**, fort, citadel, stronghold, bastion, palace, chateau [➡ FORTRESSES AND FORTIFICATIONS; 1090]

castles in Spain *n* **flight of fancy**, castles in the air, castles in the sky, fancy, dream, fantasy, notion, pipe dream [➡ NONEXISTENT THINGS; 23] *Opposite:* reality

castles in the air *n* **flight of fancy**, castles in Spain, castles in the sky, fancy, dream, fantasy, notion, pipe dream [➡ NONEXISTENT THINGS; 23] *Opposite:* reality

castles in the sky *n* **flight of fancy**, castles in Spain, castles in the air, fancy, dream, fantasy, notion, pipe dream [➡ NONEXISTENT THINGS; 23] *Opposite:* reality

cast off *v* **discard**, get rid of, reject, dispose of, abandon, ditch (*informal*) [➡ GET RID OF SOMETHING; 451]

castoff **1** *n* **reject**, discard, hand-me-down, throwaway [➡ JUNK AND USELESS OBJECTS; 1249] *Opposite:* purchase **2** *adj* **discarded**, rejected, unwanted, old, secondhand, redundant, abandoned [➡ UNPOPULAR AND UNWANTED; 258] *Opposite:* new

castoffs *n* [➡ GARMENTS AND OUTFITS; 865]

cast out (*formal*) *v* **throw out**, evict, oust, eject, reject, remove, exile, banish, expel, exclude, boot out (*informal*), give somebody the boot (*informal*), sack (*informal*), dispossess (*archaic or formal*) [➡ GET RID OF SOMETHING; 451] *Opposite*: install

castrate *v* **neuter**, sterilize, geld, spay [➡ STERILIZE; 726]

castration *n* [➡ STERILIZE; 726]

casual 1 *adj* **unpremeditated**, unplanned, chance, unintentional, unintended, unexpected, off-the-cuff, spontaneous [➡ CHANCE, COINCIDENCE, AND ACCIDENT; 786] *Opposite*: premeditated 2 *adj* **seasonal**, informal, temporary, occasional, periodic [➡ NEVER AND INFREQUENCY; 97] *Opposite*: permanent 3 *adj* **informal**, nonchalant, relaxed, calm, cool, unconcerned, insouciant, laid-back (*informal*) [➡ UNINTERESTED AND DETACHED; 629] *Opposite*: formal 4 *adj* **indifferent**, careless, offhand, blasé, cavalier, slapdash, heedless [➡ NEUTRALITY AND INDIFFERENCE; 553] *Opposite*: careful

casual clothes *n* [➡ GARMENTS AND OUTFITS; 865]

casually 1 *adv* **informally**, nonchalantly, calmly, coolly, unconcernedly, insouciantly [➡ UNINTERESTED AND DETACHED; 629] *Opposite*: formally 2 *adv* **carelessly**, offhandedly, indifferently, unceremoniously, heedlessly, cavalierly [➡ NEUTRALITY AND INDIFFERENCE; 553] *Opposite*: carefully

casualness 1 *n* **informality**, nonchalance, calmness, coolness, insouciance, unconcern [➡ NEUTRALITY AND INDIFFERENCE; 553] *Opposite*: formality 2 *n* **indifference**, carelessness, negligence, disregard, heedlessness, inattention [➡ LACK OF COMMITMENT AND UNRELIABILITY; 509] *Opposite*: care

casuals *n* [➡ GARMENTS AND OUTFITS; 865]

casualty *n* **injured person**, wounded person, dead person, fatality, loss [➡ DEAD PERSON; 926]

casual wear *n* [➡ GARMENTS AND OUTFITS; 865]

casual work *n* [➡ TYPES OF WORK; 835]

casual worker *n* [➡ WORKERS; 836]

casuistry *n* **sophistry**, unsound reasoning, subtlety, twisting the facts, justification, vindication, excuse [➡ INTENTIONS AND PURPOSES; 772]

cat 1 *n* **feline**, kitten, kitty, mouser, tom, pussy cat, tabby, tom cat, puss (*dated*), moggy (*UK*) [➡ FELINES; 983] 2 *n* (*dated slang*) **man**, boy, fellow, guy (*informal*), fella (*informal*), kid (*informal*), dude (*slang*) [➡ MALE PERSON; 934]

cat

◆ *types of cats*

Abyssinian, American shorthair, big cat, Birman, bobcat, British shorthair, Burmese cat, calico cat, cheetah, Egyptian mau, jaguar, leopard, lion, lynx, Maine coon, Manx cat, mountain lion, Norwegian forest cat, ocelot, panther, Persian cat, Siamese cat, tabby, tiger, tortoiseshell, wildcat

cataclysm *n* **catastrophe**, disaster, upheaval, calamity, debacle, tragedy [➡ DISASTERS; 252]

cataclysmic *adj* **catastrophic**, disastrous, calamitous, dreadful, tragic, earth-shattering, devastating [➡ DANGEROUS; 236]

catacomb 1 *n* **underground cemetery**, crypt, vault, tomb, mausoleum, sepulcher, burial chamber, necropolis, burial ground [➡ BURIAL PLACES AND ACCESSORIES; 930] 2 *n* **tunnel network**, underground passage, labyrinth, warren, maze, tunnel, cave, cavern [➡ BRIDGES, TUNNELS, CROSSINGS, AND JUNCTIONS; 1112]

catalepsy *n* [➡ TIRED, ASLEEP, AND UNCONSCIOUS; 738]

cataleptic *adj* [➡ TIRED, ASLEEP, AND UNCONSCIOUS; 738]

catalog 1 *n* **list**, directory, file, index, register, log, record [➡ LISTS AND SCHEDULES; 587] 2 *n* **set**, collection, list, litany, series, string, sequence, succession, parade [➡ COLLECTIONS AND MIXTURES OF THINGS; 1244] 3 *v* **classify**, assemble, compile, arrange, categorize, record, sort, quantify, itemize [➡ ARRANGE AND CREATE ORDER; 357] 4 *v* **enter**, record, insert, include, document, register, log [➡ RECORD SOMETHING; 371] 5 *v* **itemize**, list, enumerate, document, detail, set out, record, make a list [➡ RECORD SOMETHING; 371]

cataloguing *n* **classification**, categorization, logging, sorting, taking down, arrangement [➡ ARRANGE AND CREATE ORDER; 357]

catalyst *n* **promoter**, facilitator, stimulus, spur, incentive, goad, spark [➡ BEGINNINGS; 53]

catamaran *type of* **sailing vessel** [➡ SHIPS AND BOATS; 1150]

cat-and-mouse *adj* **cruel**, sadistic, heartless, merciless, callous, exploitative [➡ MORALLY BAD OR IMPROPER; 775]

catapult *v* **hurtle**, shoot, throw, project, propel, toss, fling, sling, hurl [➡ DISPATCH AND SEND; 333]

cataract *n* **waterfall**, cascade, falls, chute, torrent, flume [➡ RIVERS, LAKES, AND STREAMS; 1042]

catarrh *n* **mucus**, phlegm, discharge [➡ EXCRETION AND EXCRETA; 722]

catastrophe *n* **disaster**, calamity, upheaval, devastation, ruin, misfortune, tragedy, cataclysm [➡ DISASTERS; 252] *Opposite*: good fortune

catastrophic *adj* **disastrous**, shattering, calamitous, appalling, terrible, ruinous, tragic, devastating, cataclysmic [➡ BAD AND BADLY; 223] *Opposite*: fortunate

catatonic 1 *adj* **inert**, rigid, unresponsive, withdrawn, impassive, introspective [➡ NEUTRALITY AND INDIFFERENCE; 553] 2 *adj* (*informal*) **unconscious**, asleep, comatose, inert, stupefied, incapable [➡ TIRED, ASLEEP, AND UNCONSCIOUS; 738]

catbird seat (*informal*) *n* [➡ SOURCE OF HAPPINESS, PLEASURE, OR IMPROVEMENT; 209]

catboat *type of* **sailing vessel** [➡ SHIPS AND BOATS; 1150]

cat burglar *n* [➡ CRIMINALS; 821]

catcall 1 *n* **jeer**, hiss, boo, whistle, shout, taunt, insult, mockery [➡ SOUNDS MADE BY PEOPLE; 1262] 2 *v* **taunt**, jeer, hiss, boo, shout, whistle [➡ UNFAVORABLE NONVERBAL RESPONSES; 654]

catch 1 *v* **grasp**, grab, hold, take, clutch, seize, grab hold of [➡ GET; 420] *Opposite*: drop 2 *v* **snare**, ensnare, entrap, hook, capture, net [➡ GET; 420] 3 *v* **capture**, arrest, apprehend, take prisoner, detain, seize, take captive, take hostage [➡ CAPTIVITY AND LOSS OF FREEDOM; 248] *Opposite*: release 4 *v* **contract**, become infected with, fall victim to, pick up, go down with, fall prey to [➡ BECOME SICK, TREAT, AND RECOVER; 728] **5** v **find**, discover, surprise, spot, notice, see [➡ FIND; 463] **6** v **hear**, perceive, notice, become aware of, grasp, understand [➡ HEAR; 707] **7** v **hit**, strike, knock, bump, bump into, crash into [➡ CONTACT: IMPACT; 413] **8** v **stick**, get trapped in, snag, cling, entangle, snarl, tangle [➡ FASTEN, LINK, AND JOIN; 408] *Opposite*: free **9** v **hold**, hold on to, gather, grasp, receive [➡ CONTACT: HOLD; 411] **10** n **fastening**, fastener, clasp, hook, latch, clip [➡ FASTENERS, LINKS, AND NETWORKS; 1247] **11** n (*informal*) **snag**, drawback, problem, difficulty, hitch, obstacle, impediment [➡ PROBLEMS; 256]

Catch-22 n **predicament**, no-win situation, dilemma [➡ DIFFICULT SITUATIONS; 72]

catch a glimpse of v **spot**, notice, spy, glimpse, catch sight of, get a view of, see [➡ SEE; 699]

catchall adj **general**, universal, all-encompassing, wide-ranging, blanket, comprehensive, complete [➡ WHOLENESS AND COMPLETENESS; 198]

catch fire v [➡ FIRE, FLAMMABILITY, AND BURNING; 1165]

catch hold of v **take**, grab, clutch, seize, grasp, snatch [➡ CONTACT: HOLD; 411]

catching adj **infectious**, contagious, communicable, transmittable, easily spread [➡ SICKNESS; 729]

catch light v [➡ FIRE, FLAMMABILITY, AND BURNING; 1165]

catch napping v **surprise**, catch on the hop, catch somebody with their pants down, take by surprise, catch in the act, catch red-handed, catch unawares, catch somebody off their guard, catch out (*informal*) [➡ SURPRISE AND IMPRESS; 574]

catch on (*informal*) **1** v **become popular**, rise in popularity, become fashionable, work, be in fashion, take off (*informal*) [➡ SUCCEED AND WIN; 791] *Opposite*: flop (*informal*) **2** v **understand**, be with you, follow you, comprehend, grasp, get your drift, get the message (*informal*), get the picture (*informal*) [➡ UNDERSTAND AND GRASP; 759] *Opposite*: misunderstand

catch out (*informal*) v **trip up**, wrong-foot, trick, discover, expose, trip, find out, catch [➡ SURPRISE AND IMPRESS; 574]

catch phrase n **catchword**, motto, slogan, tag [➡ THE SPOKEN WORD; 671]

catch sight of v **spot**, notice, spy, glimpse, catch a glimpse of, get a view of, see [➡ SEE; 699] *Opposite*: miss

catch some z's (*informal*) v [➡ SLEEP AND DREAM; 723]

catch unawares v **surprise**, startle, creep up on, give somebody a shock, ambush, pounce on, catch napping [➡ SURPRISE AND IMPRESS; 574]

catch up v **draw near**, draw level, get closer to, become equal, pull alongside, draw alongside, come up to, catch up with, overtake [➡ ACCOMPANY AND FOLLOW; 337] *Opposite*: fall behind

catchword n **catch phrase**, byword, motto, watchword, slogan, tag [➡ THE SPOKEN WORD; 671]

catchy adj **memorable**, attractive, likable, beguiling, haunting, appealing, popular, captivating [➡ INTERESTING AND MEANINGFUL; 190] *Opposite*: forgettable

catechesis *see* **catechism**

catechism 1 n **examination**, questioning, interrogation, dialectic [➡ ASK PEOPLE QUESTIONS; 666] **2** n **religious instruction**, religious education, religious teaching [➡ RELIGIOUS CONCEPTS; 776] **3** n **dogma**, party line, mantra, article of faith, tenet, propaganda, creed [➡ RELIGIONS AND RELIGIOUS PRACTICES; 777]

catechize v [➡ RELIGIONS AND RELIGIOUS PRACTICES; 777]

categorical adj **definite**, clear-cut, uncompromising, unconditional, unqualified, resounding, firm [➡ CERTAIN; 174] *Opposite*: tentative

categorization 1 n **classification**, cataloging, labeling, tagging, grouping, sorting [➡ ARRANGE AND CREATE ORDER; 357] **2** n **category**, class, group, set, grouping, division, classification [➡ COLLECTIONS AND MIXTURES OF THINGS; 1244]

categorize v **classify**, sort out, catalog, label, tag, group, pigeonhole, compartmentalize, organize [➡ ARRANGE AND CREATE ORDER; 357]

category n **class**, sort, grouping, type, kind, set, classification, group [➡ VARIETIES, TYPES, AND KINDS; 145]

See Compare and Contrast at **type**.

cater v **provide**, supply, outfit, accommodate, gratify, satisfy, make provision, tailor, serve, furnish (*formal*) [➡ EQUIP AND SUPPLY; 435]

cater-cornered adv **crossways**, sideways, catty-cornered, diagonally, across, corner to corner, crosswise, on the cross, obliquely, kitty-cornered [➡ ORIENTATION AND ALIGNMENT; 1223]

caterpillar *type of* **stage of insect development** [➡ INSECT STAGES; 1020]

caterwaul 1 v **howl**, yowl, wail, squall, squeal, shriek, cry [➡ SOUND EMISSION BY ANIMALS OR BIRDS; 364] **2** n **yowl**, howl, wail, squall, squeal, shriek, cry [➡ SOUNDS MADE BY ANIMALS; 1261]

catfish *type of* **freshwater fish** [➡ FRESHWATER FISH; 1010]

catgut n **cord**, line, thread, string, filament [➡ TEXTILES AND THREADS; 1131]

catharsis n **release**, liberation, freeing up, cleansing, purification, purging, purgation [➡ FREEDOM AND LIBERTY; 208]

cathartic 1 adj **therapeutic**, liberating, releasing, emotional, intense [➡ EMOTIONALLY PLEASANT; 187] **2** adj **purifying**, cleansing, excretory, expulsive, purgative (*formal*) [➡ EXCRETION AND EXCRETA; 722]

cathedral *type of* **church** [➡ RELIGIOUS BUILDINGS; 1085]

catheter n **tube**, line, drip, drain, feed, pipe [➡ WATERCOURSES; 1111]

catholic adj **wide-ranging**, broad, wide-reaching, all-embracing, extensive, varied [➡ DIFFERENCE; 149] *Opposite*: narrow

catkin n **flower**, tassel, ament [➡ PARTS OF TREES AND PLANTS; 1026]

catnap 1 n **nap**, doze, rest, siesta, power nap, sleep, snooze (*informal*), forty winks (*informal*) [➡ SLEEP AND DREAM; 723] **2** v **nap**, nod off, doze, sleep, catch some z's (*informal*), snooze (*informal*), catch forty winks (*informal*), drop off (*informal*) [➡ SLEEP AND DREAM; 723]

cat-o'-nine-tails *n* **whip**, scourge, lash, birch [➡ BLUNT INSTRUMENTS AND WHIPS; 1158]

CAT scan *type of* **medical procedure** [➡ REMEDIES, TREATMENTS, AND OPERATIONS; 731]

catsuit *type of* **suit** [➡ GARMENTS AND OUTFITS; 865]

cattiness *n* **spitefulness**, nastiness, meanness, maliciousness, malevolence, viciousness, unkindness [➡ BAD MANNERS AND SOCIAL SKILLS; 521] *Opposite*: kindness

cattle *n* **cows**, oxen, bulls, bullocks, steers, heifers, calves, beef, livestock [➡ FARM ANIMALS; 982]

cattle thief *n* [➡ CRIMINALS; 821]

catty *adj* **spiteful**, nasty, venomous, mean, malicious, malevolent, vicious, unkind [➡ RUDE AND HOSTILE; 625] *Opposite*: kind

catty-cornered *adv* [➡ ORIENTATION AND ALIGNMENT; 1223]

catwalk **1** *n* **stage**, walkway, runway, ramp, gangplank [➡ STAGES, PLATFORMS, AND RAISED AREAS; 1098] **2** *n* **bridge**, footbridge, walkway [➡ BRIDGES, TUNNELS, CROSSINGS, AND JUNCTIONS; 1112]

caucus **1** *n* **conclave**, assembly, committee, conference, convention, group [➡ MEETINGS AND ASSEMBLIES; 43] **2** *n* **faction**, bloc, alliance, league, union, interest group [➡ GROUPS WITH A COMMON INTEREST; 938]

caught up **1** *adj* **engrossed**, absorbed, captivated, enthralled, involved, occupied, abstracted, preoccupied [➡ PENSIVENESS AND INTEREST; 538] *Opposite*: indifferent **2** *adj* **involved**, embroiled, implicated, engaged, connected, mixed up, entangled, drawn in [➡ RELATED; 142] *Opposite*: uninvolved

cauldron *see* **caldron**

cauliflower *type of* **vegetable** [➡ FRUIT AND VEGETABLES; 1176]

caulk *v* **seal**, waterproof, fill, block, plug, line [➡ DECORATE, ADORN, AND APPLY COATINGS; 405]

causal *adj* **fundamental**, underlying, contributory, contributing, connecting, pivotal, instrumental, causative [➡ CAUSATION; 168]

causality *n* **cause and effect**, connection, interconnection, connectedness, causation, causativeness, fate, destiny, karma [➡ CONNECTIONS; 143]

causation *n* **action**, connection, interconnection, relationship, causality, causativeness [➡ CAUSATION; 168]

causative *adj* **causal**, instrumental, contributing, contributory, connective, relevant, two-way [➡ RELATED; 142]

cause **1** *n* **reason**, grounds, source, root, origin, basis, foundation [➡ CAUSATION; 168] *Opposite*: effect **2** *v* **make happen**, bring about, produce, set off, instigate, trigger, trigger off, begin, initiate, prompt, effect [➡ CAUSE TO HAPPEN; 31] *Opposite*: impede

cause offense *v* **be offensive**, shock, hurt somebody's feelings, offend, antagonize, irritate, put somebody's nose out of joint [➡ UPSET, DISTRESS, AND HUMILIATE; 567]

causeway *n* **walkway**, ramp, boardwalk, path, road, dike, land bridge [➡ BRIDGES, TUNNELS, CROSSINGS, AND JUNCTIONS; 1112]

caustic **1** *adj* **corrosive**, acid, acidic, corroding, burning [➡ PHYSICAL TEXTURE; 1222] **2** *adj* **sarcastic**, scathing, mordant, astringent, cutting, biting, acerbic, acid, razor-sharp, unkind [➡ RUDE AND HOSTILE; 625] *Opposite*: gentle

See Compare and Contrast at **sarcastic**.

cauterize *v* **seal**, close, burn, sear, treat [➡ FASTEN, LINK, AND JOIN; 408]

caution **1** *n* **carefulness**, thoughtfulness, attentiveness, attention, risk avoidance, care, restraint, cautiousness [➡ POSITIVE INTELLECTUAL CHARACTERISTICS; 524] **2** *n* **warning**, alert, notification, ultimatum, caveat [➡ ADVICE; 689] **3** *v* **warn**, alert, notify, signal, give notice, advise, admonish [➡ ADVISE AND WARN; 613]

cautionary *adj* **warning**, deterrent, admonitory, advisory, instructive [➡ ADVISE AND WARN; 613]

cautious *adj* **careful**, watchful, thoughtful, alert, vigilant, guarded, wary, restrained, precautious, circumspect, chary, prudent, cagey (*informal*) [➡ CAUTIOUS AND CAREFUL; 282] *Opposite*: reckless

Compare and Contrast: *cautious, careful, chary, circumspect, prudent, vigilant, wary, guarded, cagey*

CORE MEANING: attentive to risk or danger

cautious aware of potential risk and behaving accordingly; *careful* taking reasonable care to avoid risks; *chary* cautiously reluctant to act; *circumspect* taking into consideration all possible circumstances and consequences before acting; *prudent* showing good judgment or shrewdness; *vigilant* alert and conscious of possible dangers; *wary* showing watchfulness or suspicion; *guarded* reluctant to share information with others; *cagey* (*informal*) secretive and guarded.

cautiousness *n* **caution**, carefulness, thoughtfulness, attentiveness, wariness, care, restraint, prudence [➡ POSITIVE INTELLECTUAL CHARACTERISTICS; 524] *Opposite*: recklessness

cavalcade *n* **procession**, parade, column, line, convoy, caravan [➡ PERFORMANCES AND SHOWS; 42]

cavalier *adj* **careless**, offhand, inconsiderate, high-handed, arrogant, haughty, casual, rude [➡ LACK OF COMMITMENT AND UNRELIABILITY; 509] *Opposite*: polite

cavalry *n* **mounted troops**, horse regiment, horse soldiers [➡ THE ARMED FORCES; 827]

cave *n* **cavern**, grotto, hollow, pothole, fissure, cavity [➡ GEOLOGIC FEATURES; 1056]

caveat *n* **warning**, caution, admonition, qualification, stipulation, requirement, limitation, proviso [➡ ADVICE; 689]

cave in **1** *v* **collapse**, subside, fall in, fall down, topple, crash, tumble down [➡ CHANGE OF SHAPE; 385] **2** *v* **yield**, give in, give, admit defeat, concede [➡ FORGET, FORGIVE, AND ACCEPT; 748] *Opposite*: withstand

cave-in **1** *n* **collapse**, fall, drop, slide, demolition [➡ DISASTERS; 252] **2** *n* **capitulation**, yielding, collapse, surrender, concession, withdrawal, about-face, U-turn, about-turn (*UK*) [➡ DECISIVE MOMENTS; 44]

caver *n* [➡ PEOPLE IN SPORTS AND LEISURE; 876]

cavern *n* **cave**, grotto, pothole, hollow, cavity, fissure [➡ GEOLOGIC FEATURES; 1056]

cavernous 1 *adj* **vast**, spacious, deep, yawning, gaping, roomy, commodious [➡ LARGE; 1193] *Opposite*: cramped 2 *adj* **hollow**, echoing, resounding, sounding, resonant, reverberating, sonorous [➡ EMPTY; 1238]

caviar *n* **roe**, eggs, spawn [➡ SEAFOOD; 1190]

cavil *v* **quibble**, split hairs, be picky, complain, carp, object [➡ ARGUE AND FIGHT; 643] *Opposite*: accept

cavity *n* **hole**, space, hollow, crater, void, crack, opening, nook, fissure, cleft [➡ HOLES, GAPS, AND FORKS; 1252]

cavort *v* **frolic**, prance, caper, gambol, romp, dance, horse around [➡ FIDGET AND FROLIC; 311]

caw 1 *v* **call**, cry, croak, squawk [➡ SOUND EMISSION BY ANIMALS OR BIRDS; 364] 2 *n* **cry**, call, croak, croaking, squawk, squawking [➡ SOUNDS MADE BY BIRDS; 1263]

cayenne pepper *type of* **spice** [➡ HERBS AND SPICES; 1175]

cayman *type of* **reptile** [➡ REPTILES; 994]

CB *n* **radio**, shortwave radio, citizens' band, telecommunication, walkie-talkie [➡ TELEVISION AND RADIO; 606]

CD *part of* **audio equipment** [➡ AUDIO EQUIPMENT; 1139]

CD burner *type of* **hardware** [➡ COMPUTERS AND COMPUTING; 1127]

CD player 1 *n* **stereo**, personal stereo, hi-fi, CD, boom box, sound system, compact disc player [➡ RECORDINGS AND PLAYERS; 911] 2 *type of* **audio equipment** [➡ AUDIO EQUIPMENT; 1139]

CD-ROM *type of* **hardware** [➡ COMPUTERS AND COMPUTING; 1127]

CD writer *type of* **hardware** [➡ COMPUTERS AND COMPUTING; 1127]

cease *v* **stop**, finish, end, come to an end, come to a close, die away, die down, close down, conclude, terminate [➡ STOP ACTING; 264] *Opposite*: start

ceasefire *n* **truce**, armistice, cessation of hostilities, end of hostilities, break in fighting, negotiating period [➡ PAUSES AND PHASES; 56]

ceaseless *adj* **unending**, continual, constant, incessant, perpetual, never-ending, eternal, interminable, continuous, endless [➡ PERMANENCE: WITHOUT END; 94] *Opposite*: sporadic

ceaselessness *n* [➡ PERMANENCE: WITHOUT END; 94]

cease to exist *v* [➡ CEASE TO EXIST; 22]

cease trading *v* **go out of business**, shut down, go bankrupt, close, fold, go bust (*informal*) [➡ FAIL OR BE UNSUCCESSFUL; 75]

cecum *part of* **digestive tract** [➡ THE DIGESTIVE TRACT; 709]

cedar *type of* **evergreen tree** [➡ EVERGREEN AND CONIFEROUS TREES; 1029]

cede (*formal*) *v* **yield**, concede, give up, give way, let go, surrender, relinquish, abandon [➡ FORGET, FORGIVE, AND ACCEPT; 748] *Opposite*: resist

cedi *type of* **currency** [➡ CURRENCIES; 798]

cedilla *type of* **diacritic** [➡ ASPECTS OF LANGUAGE; 682]

ceilidh *n* **dance**, barn dance, party, celebration, singalong, singsong (*UK*) [➡ PARTIES, DANCES, AND CELEBRATIONS; 37]

ceiling 1 *n* [➡ ROOFS, ROOF PARTS, AND CEILINGS; 1103] 2 *n* **limit**, threshold, cutoff point, cap, check, constraint, control [➡ MAJORITY AND MAXIMUM; 141]

celeb (*informal*) *n* [➡ IMPORTANT OR FAMOUS PEOPLE; 893]

celebrate 1 *v* **enjoy yourself**, have fun, have a good time, make merry, revel, party (*informal*), rejoice (*literary*) [➡ LEISURE AND RECREATION; 874] *Opposite*: lament 2 *v* **commemorate**, observe, mark, keep, remember, honor [➡ REMEMBER; 746] 3 *v* **praise**, acclaim, commend, applaud, hail, sing the praises [➡ PRAISE AND ENCOURAGE; 647]

celebrated *adj* **famous**, renowned, eminent, distinguished, illustrious, notable, great, feted, admired [➡ KNOWN AND FAMOUS; 181] *Opposite*: unknown

celebration 1 *n* **festivity**, party, festival, gala, fete, jamboree, revel [➡ PARTIES, DANCES, AND CELEBRATIONS; 37] 2 *n* **commemoration**, remembrance, observance, salutation, memorial, salute [➡ CEREMONIES AND ANNIVERSARIES; 38]

celebratory *adj* **festive**, triumphant, special, congratulatory, commemorative [➡ PARTIES, DANCES, AND CELEBRATIONS; 37]

celebrity 1 *n* **superstar**, star, personality, name, figure, household name, public figure, luminary, icon, celeb (*informal*), big shot (*informal*), personage (*formal*) [➡ IMPORTANT OR FAMOUS PEOPLE; 893] *Opposite*: nobody 2 *n* **fame**, renown, notoriety, superstardom, prominence, stardom, recognition, acclaim, popularity [➡ KNOWN AND FAMOUS; 181] *Opposite*: obscurity

celerity (*literary*) *n* **speed**, rapidity, swiftness, alacrity, haste, briskness, hurry, speediness [➡ SPEED; 102] *Opposite*: slowness

celery *type of* **salad vegetable** [➡ FRUIT AND VEGETABLES; 1176]

celesta *type of* **keyboard** [➡ MUSICAL INSTRUMENTS; 910]

celestial 1 *adj* **heavenly**, holy, spiritual, godly, otherworldly, saintly [➡ RELIGIOUS CONCEPTS; 776] 2 *adj* **cosmic**, astronomic, planetary, galactic, solar, lunar, extraterrestrial, space [➡ THE SOLAR SYSTEM AND ASTRONOMY; 1060]

celibacy *n* [➡ SELF-DENIAL; 882]

celibate 1 *adj* **chaste**, abstinent, self-restrained [➡ SELF-DENIAL; 882] 2 *n* [➡ ASCETIC PEOPLE; 883]

cell 1 *n* **lockup**, prison cell, jail cell [➡ BUILDINGS FOR CONFINING PEOPLE; 1094] 2 *n* **group**, sect, faction, cabal, caucus, offshoot [➡ GROUPS WITH A COMMON INTEREST; 938] 3 *type of* **room in public buildings** [➡ TYPES OF ROOMS; 1097]

cellar *type of* **storage space** [➡ STORES AND STORAGE BUILDINGS; 1088]

cello *type of* **stringed instrument** [➡ MUSICAL INSTRUMENTS; 910]

cellphone *type of* **telecommunications equipment** [➡ TELECOMMUNICATIONS; 1130]

cellular phone *type of* **telecommunications equipment** [➡ TELECOMMUNICATIONS; 1130]

cellulite *n* fat, fatty deposits, lumpiness, dimpling, orange-peel skin (*UK*) [➡CONDITIONS AFFECTING THE SKIN; 721]

celluloid *type of* plastic [➡PLASTICS; 1134]

cement 1 *n* [➡BUILDING MATERIALS; 1077] 2 *n* glue, adhesive, paste, epoxy resin [➡ADHESIVES; 1271] 3 *v* join, stick, fix, glue, fasten together [➡FASTEN, LINK, AND JOIN; 408] *Opposite*: separate 4 *v* strengthen, reinforce, make stronger, prop up, fortify, buttress [➡IMPROVE STRENGTH AND DURABILITY; 378] *Opposite*: undermine

cemetery *n* graveyard, burial ground, churchyard, garden of remembrance, mausoleum, memorial park, boneyard (*informal*) [➡BURIAL AND PREPARATION FOR BURIAL; 929]

cenotaph *n* war memorial, monument, memorial [➡MONUMENTS; 1092]

Cenozoic *type of* era [➡EPOCHS AND ERAS; 89]

censor 1 *v* edit, cut, remove, expurgate, bowdlerize, amend, blue-pencil [➡WITHHOLD INFORMATION; 687] 2 *v* stifle, gag, repress, suppress, control [➡WITHHOLD INFORMATION; 687]

censored *adj* cut, expurgated, bowdlerized, blue-penciled, changed, amended [➡SECRET AND UNKNOWN; 179] *Opposite*: complete

censorious *adj* disapproving, critical, severe, stern, hypercritical, overcritical, contemptuous [➡ACCUSATORY AND DISAPPROVING; 634] *Opposite*: approving

censoriousness *n* [➡ANTAGONISM; 552]

censorship *n* restriction, control, cutting, editing, bowdlerization, expurgation, suppression [➡WITHHOLD INFORMATION; 687]

censure 1 *n* criticism, disapproval, condemnation, denunciation, deprecation, scorn, contempt [➡ANTAGONISM; 552] *Opposite*: approval 2 *v* criticize, fault, reprimand, condemn, reproach, scorn, denounce, knock (*slang*), slate (*UK*) [➡PROTEST AND EXPRESS DISAPPROVAL; 642] *Opposite*: praise

See Compare and Contrast at **criticize, disapprove**.

census 1 *n* population count, survey, poll, registration [➡ELECTIONS AND VOTING; 807] 2 *n* survey, count, poll, tally, register, information gathering, fact finding [➡ELECTIONS AND VOTING; 807]

cent *n* [➡CURRENCIES; 798]

centaur *type of* mythological creature [➡MYTHICAL CREATURES; 1036]

Centaurus *type of* constellation [➡HEAVENLY BODIES; 1061]

centenary (*UK*) *n* anniversary, birthday, centennial [➡CEREMONIES AND ANNIVERSARIES; 38]

centennial *n* anniversary, birthday, centenary (*UK*) [➡CEREMONIES AND ANNIVERSARIES; 38]

center 1 *n* midpoint, middle, halfway point, focal point, focus, bull's eye, epicenter [➡CENTRAL PARTS OF PHYSICAL OBJECTS; 1251] *Opposite*: edge 2 *n* filling, inside, middle, core, layer, kernel, heart, interior [➡CENTRAL PARTS OF PHYSICAL OBJECTS; 1251] *Opposite*: coating 3 *n* downtown, inner city, heart [➡HUMAN SETTLEMENTS; 1070] 4 *n* complex, facility, development, building [➡PUBLIC BUILDINGS AND MEETING PLACES; 1081] 5 *n* cluster, concentration, focus, magnet, hotbed, breeding ground,

birthplace [➡PLACE; 1065] 6 *n* middle ground, consensus, majority, middle course, happy medium, middle America, center ground, middle England (*UK*) [➡COUNTRIES AND REGIONS; 1067] *Opposite*: extreme 7 *n* axis, pivot, pivotal point, fulcrum [➡CENTRAL PARTS OF PHYSICAL OBJECTS; 1251] 8 *n* focus, heart, core, nub, bottom, root [➡CENTRAL PARTS OF PHYSICAL OBJECTS; 1251] *Opposite*: periphery 9 *v* place, position, arrange, balance, adjust, align [➡POSITION SOMETHING; 325] 10 *v* focus on, turn on, concentrate on, home in on, revolve around, come to grips with, relate to, address, involve, target, examine, deal with [➡BE ABOUT SOMETHING; 62] *Opposite*: ignore

center island *n* [➡BRIDGES, TUNNELS, CROSSINGS, AND JUNCTIONS; 1112]

centerpiece *n* center of attention, focus, flagship, key feature, heart, core, linchpin, cornerstone, foundation, pride and joy, jewel in the crown [➡MOST IMPORTANT THING; 197]

center stage *adv* in the limelight, into the limelight, to the fore, at the fore, to the front, at the front, at the center of attention [➡FUNDAMENTAL; 195]

centigram *type of* metric unit [➡SIZE AND DIMENSIONS; 1192]

centiliter *type of* metric unit [➡SIZE AND DIMENSIONS; 1192]

centimeter *type of* metric unit [➡SIZE AND DIMENSIONS; 1192]

centipede *type of* land invertebrate [➡LAND INVERTEBRATES; 1021]

central 1 *adj* middle, mid, inner, innermost [➡CENTRAL PARTS OF PHYSICAL OBJECTS; 1251] *Opposite*: outer 2 *adj* vital, dominant, essential, fundamental, chief, most important, crucial, principal, significant, main, predominant, key, pivotal, focal [➡IMPORTANT; 194] *Opposite*: unimportant

Central *type of* time zone [➡TIMES OF DAY; 87]

central heating *n* [➡HEATING, REFRIGERATION, AND VENTILATION; 1142]

centralism *n* control, concentration, monopolism, authoritarianism, centralization [➡STYLES AND SYSTEMS OF GOVERNMENT; 806]

centrality *n* importance, significance, criticality, supremacy, uniqueness, import, consequence (*formal*) [➡IMPORTANCE AND SIGNIFICANCE; 192] *Opposite*: irrelevance

centralization *n* unification, integration, concentration, control, domination, monopolization, centralism [➡GOVERNMENT POLICIES; 810] *Opposite*: decentralization

centralize *v* unify, consolidate, integrate, compact, concentrate, collect, merge [➡COMBINE AND MIX; 400] *Opposite*: decentralize

central processing unit *type of* hardware [➡COMPUTERS AND COMPUTING; 1127]

central reservation (*UK*) *n* [➡BARRIERS; 1113]

centrist *adj* middle-of-the-road, moderate, mainstream, reasonable, uncontroversial, safe [➡STYLES AND SYSTEMS OF GOVERNMENT; 806] *Opposite*: extreme

centuries old *adj* [➡OLD, OLD-FASHIONED; 167]

century *n* period, era, time, span, epoch [➡EPOCHS AND ERAS; 89]

C.E.O. *n* chief executive officer, boss, head, manager, chief executive, supervisor, chief, number one (*informal*), managing director (*UK*), MD (*UK*) [➡ BUSINESS PEOPLE; 793]

cep *type of* **fungus** [➡ MICROORGANISMS, FUNGI, AND ALGAE; 1023]

Cepheus *type of* **constellation** [➡ HEAVENLY BODIES; 1061]

ceramic 1 *adj* **earthenware**, clay, pottery, terra cotta, ironstone china, ironstone, stoneware, porcelain [➡ POTTERY; 1135] 2 *type of* **pottery** [➡ POTTERY; 1135]

cereal *n* **breakfast cereal**, porridge, grits, mush (*dated*) [➡ CEREAL FOODS; 1178]

cereal

◆ *types of cereals*
barley, corn, millet, oat, rice, rye, sorghum, wheat

cerebral *adj* **intellectual**, rational, highbrow, logical, analytical, brainy (*informal*) [➡ THE NATURE OF IDEAS; 771] *Opposite*: intuitive

ceremonial 1 *adj* **ritual**, traditional, ritualistic, formal, official, grand, state [➡ CEREMONIES AND ANNIVERSARIES; 38] *Opposite*: informal 2 *n* **rite**, ritual, ceremony, pomp, pageantry, formality [➡ CEREMONIES AND ANNIVERSARIES; 38]

ceremonial dress *n* [➡ GARMENTS AND OUTFITS; 865]

ceremonious *adj* **formal**, solemn, dignified, grand, majestic, regal, imperious, pompous [➡ LEVELS OF FORMALITY; 522] *Opposite*: informal

ceremony *n* **rite**, ritual, formality, formal procedure, service, observance, ceremonial [➡ CEREMONIES AND ANNIVERSARIES; 38]

cerise *type of* **pink** [➡ COLORS; 1224]

certain 1 *adj* **sure**, convinced, positive, confident, firm, definite, assured [➡ CERTAINTY; 561] *Opposite*: unsure 2 *adj* **particular**, specific, individual, precise, specified, one [➡ EXACT; 203] 3 *adj* **reliable**, dependable, undeniable, guaranteed, clear, certified, assured, accurate [➡ CERTAIN; 174] *Opposite*: uncertain 4 *adj* **some**, a number of, a few, several, selected, a selection of, a variety of [➡ AMOUNTS AND QUANTITIES; 112] *Opposite*: all

certainly 1 *adv* **surely**, positively, definitely, without doubt, undoubtedly, unquestionably [➡ CERTAINTY; 561] *Opposite*: possibly 2 *adv* **indeed**, absolutely, definitely, of course, sure, emphatically, indubitably (*formal*) [➡ CERTAIN; 174]

certainty 1 *n* **foregone conclusion**, safe bet, inevitability, cast-iron certainty (*UK*) [➡ CERTAIN; 174] 2 *n* **confidence**, conviction, faith, belief, assurance, firmness, sureness, certitude [➡ CERTAINTY; 561] *Opposite*: uncertainty

certifiable *adj* [➡ TRUE AND REAL; 171]

certificate *n* **document**, license, diploma, credential, documentation, record, permit [➡ OFFICIAL DOCUMENTS; 586]

certification *n* **guarantee**, warranty, documentation, authorization, accreditation, endorsement [➡ OFFICIAL DOCUMENTS; 586]

certified *adj* **official**, licensed, approved, authorized, accredited, credentialed, professional, expert, qualified [➡ QUALIFICATIONS; 843]

certify *v* **confirm**, state, verify, endorse, attest, declare [➡ APPROVE AND CONFIRM; 646]

certitude *n* **conviction**, certainty, sureness, assurance, confidence, belief, faith [➡ CERTAINTY; 561]

Cesarean section *type of* **medical procedure** [➡ REMEDIES, TREATMENTS, AND OPERATIONS; 731]

cessation *n* **end**, termination, close, stop, ending, pause, interruption [➡ ENDS AND DEPARTURES; 54] *Opposite*: start

cesspit *n* **tank**, pit, sewer, drain, gutter, cesspool [➡ WATERCOURSES; 1111]

Cetus *type of* **constellation** [➡ HEAVENLY BODIES; 1061]

ceviche *type of* **cooked dish** [➡ PREPARED DISHES; 1170]

CFA franc *type of* **currency** [➡ CURRENCIES; 798]

CFO *n* [➡ PEOPLE INVOLVED IN FINANCE; 804]

cha-cha *type of* **dance** [➡ DANCE; 903]

chafe 1 *v* **rub**, scrape, irritate, scratch, abrade, wear down [➡ WORSEN APPEARANCE; 382] 2 *v* **annoy**, bother, provoke, vex, irritate, aggravate (*informal*) [➡ ANGER AND ANNOY; 569]

chaff 1 *v* **tease**, mock, make fun of, josh (*informal*), pull somebody's leg (*informal*) [➡ JOKES AND TEASING; 674] 2 *n* **joking**, banter, repartee, teasing [➡ JOKES AND TEASING; 674]

chagrin *n* **humiliation**, mortification, vexation, irritation, disappointment, embarrassment, sorrow, annoyance [➡ EMBARRASSMENT AND HUMILIATION; 542]

chagrined *adj* [➡ EMBARRASSMENT AND HUMILIATION; 542]

chain 1 *n* **cable**, hawser, restraint, shackle, manacle [➡ FASTENERS, LINKS, AND NETWORKS; 1247] 2 *n* **group**, string, franchise, series [➡ BUSINESS ENTERPRISES AND RELATED BODIES; 792] 3 *n* **sequence**, series, string, succession, procession [➡ CHAIN OF EVENTS; 162] 4 *type of* **necklace** [➡ JEWELRY; 866] 5 *part of* **bike** [➡ BIKES, CARS, AND CARRIAGES; 1149] 6 *v* **bind**, manacle, shackle, lock up, restrain, immobilize, chain up [➡ FASTEN, LINK, AND JOIN; 408]

chain reaction *n* **series of events**, train of events, domino effect, knock-on effect (*UK*) [➡ EVENTS AND OCCURRENCES; 35]

chain store *type of* **retail outlet** [➡ RETAIL OUTLETS; 1083]

chair 1 *type of* **seating** [➡ FURNITURE; 858] 2 *n* **chairperson**, presiding officer, president, head, leader [➡ BUSINESS PEOPLE; 793] 3 *v* **preside**, take the chair, lead, direct, oversee, manage [➡ BE IN CHARGE; 270]

chair lift *type of* **leisure vehicle** [➡ VEHICLES; 1145]

chairperson *n* **presiding officer**, president, chair, head, leader [➡ BUSINESS PEOPLE; 793]

chaise longue *type of* **seating** [➡ FURNITURE; 858]

chalcedony *type of* **gemstone** [➡ PRECIOUS STONES; 1278]

chalet *type of* **house** [➡ RESIDENTIAL BUILDINGS; 1078]

chalice (*literary*) *n* **cup**, goblet, vessel [➡ CONTAINERS, RECEPTACLES, AND PACKAGING; 1245]

chalk 1 *type of* **stone** [➡ STONES, ROCKS, AND BOULDERS; 1057] 2 *v* **write**, draw, mark, doodle, scribble, sketch [➡ CREATE IMAGES; 356]

chalkboard n [➡ WRITING AND DRAWING IMPLEMENTS, AND MEDIA; 601]

chalk up v **score**, mark up, gain, win, obtain, get, collect, accumulate, rack up (*informal*) [➡ GET MONEY OR REWARD; 421]

chalky 1 *adj* **crumbly**, dry, powdery, fine, dusty, soft [➡ PHYSICAL TEXTURE; 1222] **2** *adj* **white**, pale, pallid, anemic, ghostly, deathly, ashen [➡ COMPLEXION; 480]

challah *type of* **bread** [➡ BREAD, FLOUR, AND BREAD PRODUCTS; 1179]

challenge 1 *v* **confront**, defy, brave, face up to [➡ ACCUSE, BLAME, AND CRITICIZE; 641] **2** *v* **dare**, defy, throw down the gauntlet to, test [➡ GAMBLE AND TAKE RISKS; 466] **3** *v* **dispute**, contest, object to, question, argue, oppose [➡ DENY AND REJECT; 644] **4** *n* **test**, trial, task, contest, encounter [➡ NON-AGGRESSIVE/SPORTING EVENTS; 40]

challenger n **contestant**, contender, competitor, opponent, pretender, rival [➡ COMPETITORS; 41]

challenging 1 *adj* **demanding**, taxing, testing, difficult, tough, trying, tricky, exigent (*formal*) [➡ POSITIVELY COMPLEX OR COMPLICATED; 217] *Opposite:* easy **2** *adj* **stimulating**, thought-provoking, interesting, inspiring, exciting, puzzling, perplexing [➡ INTERESTING AND MEANINGFUL; 190] *Opposite:* routine **3** *adj* **defiant**, disobedient, rebellious, insolent, impudent, bold [➡ REBELLIOUSNESS AND DISOBEDIENCE; 565] *Opposite:* compliant

Chamaeleon *type of* **constellation** [➡ HEAVENLY BODIES; 1061]

chamber 1 *n* **cavity**, hollow, compartment, space, slot [➡ HOLES, GAPS, AND FORKS; 1252] **2** *n* **hall**, assembly room, meeting room, boardroom, legislative chamber, judicial chamber [➡ TYPES OF ROOMS; 1097]

chamberlain n **official**, attendant, courtier, servant, manager, supervisor, administrator [➡ ADMINISTRATIVE OFFICERS; 811]

chambermaid *type of* **servant** [➡ DOMESTIC AND KITCHEN WORKERS; 850]

chamber music *type of* **classical music** [➡ MUSIC, SONGS, AND SINGING; 907]

chamber orchestra *type of* **band** [➡ MUSICIANS AND SINGERS; 908]

chamber pot n [➡ CONTAINERS, RECEPTACLES, AND PACKAGING; 1245]

chambray *type of* **fabric from plants** [➡ FABRICS; 1132]

chameleon 1 *type of* **reptile** [➡ REPTILES; 994] **2** *n* **changeable person**, butterfly, trimmer, dilettante [➡ SUPERFICIAL OR INSINCERE PEOPLE; 951]

chamois 1 *type of* **deer or antelope** [➡ DEER AND ANTELOPES; 981] **2** *type of* **leather** [➡ FABRICS; 1132]

chamomile *type of* **herb** [➡ HERBS AND SPICES; 1175]

champ 1 *v* **chew**, munch, grind, masticate, chomp (*informal*) [➡ EAT AND NOT EAT; 710] **2** *n* (*informal*) **champion**, winner, victor, title holder [➡ COMPETITORS; 41]

champion 1 *n* **winner**, victor, title holder, champ (*informal*) [➡ COMPETITORS; 41] **2** *n* **defender**, supporter, backer, campaigner, advocate, guardian [➡ DEVOTEES AND ADDICTED PEOPLE; 556] **3** *v* **defend**, support, back, campaign, fight for, advocate, side with, stand up for [➡ APPROVE AND CONFIRM; 646]

championship n **finals**, contest, challenge, title fight, battle, competition, tournament [➡ NON-AGGRESSIVE/SPORTING EVENTS; 40]

chance 1 *n* **possibility**, probability, likelihood, opening, opportunity, option, prospect, occasion [➡ POSSIBLE AND PROBABLE; 177] **2** *n* **luck**, fate, fortune, destiny, good fortune [➡ CHANCE, COINCIDENCE, AND ACCIDENT; 786] **3** *n* **gamble**, risk, hazard, venture, stake [➡ GAMBLE AND TAKE RISKS; 466] **4** *v* **risk**, hazard, gamble, try, attempt, venture [➡ GAMBLE AND TAKE RISKS; 466] **5** *adj* **accidental**, coincidental, casual, fortuitous, unintended, unplanned [➡ CHANCE, COINCIDENCE, AND ACCIDENT; 786] *Opposite:* planned

chancel n [➡ PARTS OF RELIGIOUS BUILDINGS; 1086]

chancellor n **president**, leader, head of state, premier, prime minister, head of government [➡ POLITICAL OFFICES AND POLITICIANS; 808]

chance meeting n [➡ CHANCE EVENTS; 36]

chance occurrence n **coincidence**, accident, twist of fate, quirk, happenstance, fluke (*informal*) [➡ CHANCE EVENTS; 36]

chance on v **stumble on**, happen on, strike on, hit on, come across, run into, find [➡ FIND; 463]

chancy *adj* **risky**, hazardous, dangerous, perilous, uncertain, precarious, unreliable, dicey (*informal*) [➡ DANGEROUS; 236] *Opposite:* safe

chandelier *type of* **light** [➡ LIGHT; 1164]

change 1 *n* **alteration**, modification, variation, transformation, revolution, conversion, adjustment, amendment, difference [➡ CHANGE; 372] **2** *n* **coins**, cash, loose change [➡ MONEY; 797] **3** *v* **alter**, modify, vary, shift, revolutionize, transform, adjust, amend [➡ CHANGE; 372] **4** *v* **exchange**, replace, substitute, change over, trade, switch, convert, transmute, swap (*informal*) [➡ EXCHANGE AND INTERCHANGE; 448]

Compare and Contrast: *change, alter, modify, convert, vary, shift, transform, transmute*

CORE MEANING: to make or become different

change to make or become different in any way; *alter* to change, especially to change an aspect of something; *modify* to make minor changes or alterations, especially in order to improve something; *convert* to change something from one form or function to another; *vary* to change within a range of possibilities, or in connection with something else, with a suggestion of instability; *shift* to change from one position or direction to another; *transform* to make a radical change into a different form; *transmute* to change into another form.

changeability 1 *n* **unpredictability**, unsettledness, variableness, variability, irregularity, instability [➡ FINITENESS, VARIABILITY, AND TRANSIENCE; 96] *Opposite:* constancy **2** *n* **indecisiveness**, fickleness, unpredictability, flightiness, volatility, instability, untrustworthiness, unreliability, changeableness [➡ LACK OF COMMITMENT AND UNRELIABILITY; 509] *Opposite:* constancy

changeable *adj* **variable**, unsettled, unpredictable, unreliable, unstable, unfixed, irregular, undependable, erratic, inconsistent, inconstant [➡ FINITENESS, VARIABILITY, AND TRANSIENCE; 96] *Opposite:* constant

change around 1 v alter, modify, amend, adjust, jiggle around, juggle, play around with [➡CHANGE; 372] Opposite: leave alone 2 v reorganize, move around, rethink, alter, change, juggle around, tamper with [➡POSITION SOMETHING; 325] Opposite: leave alone 3 v swap (informal), exchange, substitute, change, change over, reverse, replace, switch [➡EXCHANGE AND INTERCHANGE; 448]

change course v [➡CHANGE DIRECTION OF MOTION; 344]

changed adj altered, different, transformed, reformed, rehabilitated, improved, new [➡CHANGE; 372] Opposite: unchanged

change direction 1 v veer off, swerve, turn, bend, curve around [➡CHANGE DIRECTION OF MOTION; 344] 2 v start afresh, change course, change tack, have a rethink, turn over a new leaf, have second thoughts [➡MAKE DECISIONS AND CHOICES; 752]

change for the better 1 v improve, get better, look up, progress, pick up (informal) [➡IMPROVE SOMETHING; 374] Opposite: deteriorate 2 n improvement, progress, development, upswing, upturn [➡SOURCE OF HAPPINESS, PLEASURE, OR IMPROVEMENT; 209] Opposite: deterioration

changeless adj unchanging, consistent, fixed, immutable, permanent, everlasting, eternal, unalterable [➡PERMANENCE: WITHOUT CHANGE; 95] Opposite: changing

changelessness n immutability [➡PERMANENCE: WITHOUT CHANGE; 95]

change of heart n volte-face, second thoughts, rethink, change of attitude, change of opinion, U-turn, about-face, about-turn (UK) [➡DECISIVE MOMENTS; 44]

change over v switch, substitute, convert, transfer, change around, exchange, swap (informal) [➡CHANGE ONE THING FOR ANOTHER; 398]

changeover n move, reversal, conversion, alteration, substitution, swap (informal) [➡CHANGE ONE THING FOR ANOTHER; 398]

change your mind v have second thoughts, come around, relent, back out, pull out, go back on, do an about-face, do a U-turn, do an about-turn (UK), come round (UK) [➡MAKE DECISIONS AND CHOICES; 752]

changing adj altering, varying, shifting, moving, fluctuating, mutable [➡FINITENESS, VARIABILITY, AND TRANSIENCE; 96] Opposite: changeless

channel 1 n station, network, frequency [➡TELEVISION AND RADIO; 606] 2 n canal, conduit, waterway, strait, passage [➡WATERWAYS AND SEAWAYS; 1108] 3 n means, outlet, conduit, path, way, avenue, route [➡WAYS OF DOING THINGS; 294] 4 n ditch, dike, groove, drain, trench, duct [➡WATERCOURSES; 1111] 5 v direct, control, feed, conduct, route [➡MOVE SOMETHING TO ANOTHER LOCATION; 324]

chant 1 n song, hymn, mantra, tune, carol, psalm [➡MUSIC, SONGS, AND SINGING; 907] 2 v sing, recite, repeat, vocalize, intone (formal) [➡MUSIC, SONGS, AND SINGING; 907]

chanterelle type of fungus [➡MICROORGANISMS, FUNGI, AND ALGAE; 1023]

chanteuse n [➡MUSICIANS AND SINGERS; 908]

chanting n [➡MUSIC, SONGS, AND SINGING; 907]

chantry n [➡PARTS OF RELIGIOUS BUILDINGS; 1086]

chaos n disorder, confusion, bedlam, anarchy, pandemonium, commotion, disarray, turmoil, madness, unruliness [➡DISORDER AND CHAOS; 245] Opposite: order

chaotic adj disordered, muddled, confused, messy, untidy, hectic, frenzied, unruly, anarchic, tumultuous [➡DISORDER AND CHAOS; 245] Opposite: orderly

chapati type of bread [➡BREAD, FLOUR, AND BREAD PRODUCTS; 1179]

chapel n sanctuary, oratory, chantry, side chapel, side altar [➡RELIGIOUS BUILDINGS; 1085]

chaperon 1 n supervisor, attendant, overseer, governess, escort, guardian, companion, duenna, warden (UK) [➡SUPPORTERS, PROTECTORS, AND COMPATRIOTS; 970] 2 v supervise, oversee, escort, watch, look after, conduct, attend, guard, safeguard, accompany, shepherd [➡TAKE CARE OF AND SPOIL; 300]

chaperone see chaperon

chaplain n minister, vicar, priest, pastor, school chaplain, rabbi, prison chaplain, army chaplain, air force chaplain [➡RELIGIOUS PEOPLE; 778]

chaplet type of headgear [➡ACCESSORIES, MILLINERY, AND LINGERIE; 867]

chaps type of pants [➡GARMENTS AND OUTFITS; 865]

chapter 1 n section, part, subdivision, division, segment, unit [➡PARTS OF BOOKS AND DOCUMENTS; 593] 2 n period, episode, stage, phase, interval, era, clause [➡PERIODS OF TIME; 90]

Chapter 11 n [➡ACCOUNTING, BANKING, AND BUDGETING; 799]

char 1 v burn, singe, scorch, carbonize, sear, cauterize [➡FIRE, FLAMMABILITY, AND BURNING; 1165] 2 n (UK) domestic, help, cleaner [➡DOMESTIC AND KITCHEN WORKERS; 850]

character 1 n nature, quality, temperament, personality, disposition, spirit, makeup [➡TEMPERAMENT AND BEHAVIOR; 492] 2 n charm, appeal, atmosphere, attractiveness, charisma [➡BEAUTY AND ATTRACTIVENESS; 189] 3 n honor, integrity, strength, uprightness, rectitude, moral fiber [➡MORALLY GOOD; 774] 4 n eccentric, personality, oddity, original [➡ECCENTRICITY AND IRRATIONALITY; 562] 5 n person, individual, creature, sort, type, fellow [➡PERSON; 931]

character assassination n defamation, slander, libel, affront, verbal abuse, verbal assault, public humiliation, attack, hatchet job (UK) [➡INSULTS, ABUSE, AND SWEARING; 658]

character-building adj challenging, demanding, instructive, educative, empowering, trying [➡USEFULNESS; 199]

characterful adj individual, distinctive, strong, upright, inspiring, honorable [➡MORALLY GOOD; 774]

characteristic 1 n trait, feature, quality, attribute, point, property [➡QUALITIES AND CHARACTERISTICS; 1191] 2 adj typical, distinguishing, distinctive, individual, representative, specific, normal [➡REPRESENTATIVE; 66] Opposite: uncharacteristic

characteristically adv typically, usually, normally, naturally, routinely, symptomatically, habitually [➡USUALLY; 108] Opposite: unusually

characterization n description, classification,

account, portrayal, depiction, report, representation [➡ REPRESENTATIONS AND GENERAL EXAMPLES; 65]

characterize 1 *v* **describe**, portray, illustrate, depict, brand, stamp [➡ NAME AND DESCRIBE; 665] 2 *v* **typify**, set apart, distinguish, differentiate, exemplify, indicate [➡ REPRESENT SOMETHING OR SOMEBODY; 59]

characterless *adj* **bland**, dull, soulless, uninteresting, insipid, nondescript, uninspired, tepid [➡ BORING AND UNINTERESTING; 234] *Opposite*: interesting

characterlessness *n* **dullness**, soullessness, insipidness [➡ BORING AND UNINTERESTING; 234]

charade *n* **pretense**, farce, sham, fake, travesty, imitation, simulation, make-believe [➡ DECEPTION AND LIES; 660]

charbroiled *adj* [➡ STATE OF PREPARED FOOD; 1171]

charcoal gray *type of* **gray** [➡ COLORS; 1224]

charge 1 *v* **accuse**, indict, allege, arraign, incriminate, lay the blame on, blame [➡ ACCUSE, BLAME, AND CRITICIZE; 641] *Opposite*: absolve 2 *v* **attack**, rush, storm, assault, assail, launch an attack on [➡ MOVE FAST; 313] *Opposite*: retreat 3 *v* **rush**, dash, hurtle, stampede, hurry, race [➡ MOVE FAST; 313] 4 *n* **cost**, price, expense, rate, amount, fee, payment [➡ EXPENDITURE; 423] 5 *n* **custody**, care, responsibility, control, trust, safekeeping, burden, duty, concern [➡ RESPONSIBILITY; 170] 6 *n* **accusation**, indictment, allegation, arraignment, imputation [➡ THE POLICE, ARREST, AND PRETRIAL PROCEEDINGS; 818] 7 *n* **assault**, attack, advance, offensive, onslaught, push [➡ WARFARE AND WAR; 830] 8 *n* **order**, command, direction, instruction, injunction, exhortation (*formal*) [➡ REQUEST AND DEMAND; 663]

chargeable 1 *adj* **punishable**, criminal, indictable, imputable, actionable, serious [➡ ILLEGAL; 816] 2 *adj* **taxable**, liable to tax, declarable, dutiable [➡ TAX AND TAXATION; 802]

charged *adj* **emotional**, exciting, electric, thrilling, stimulating [➡ INTERESTING AND MEANINGFUL; 190] *Opposite*: calm

charger *type of* **horse** [➡ HORSES; 985]

chargrill *v* [➡ COOKING AND FOOD PREPARATION; 353]

chariness *n* **wariness**, caution, circumspection [➡ INSECURITY AND LOSS OF COMPOSURE; 544]

chariot *type of* **wagon or carriage** [➡ VEHICLES; 1145]

charisma *n* **charm**, personality, appeal, magnetism, allure, captivation, attractiveness [➡ INTERESTING AND MEANINGFUL; 190]

charismatic *adj* **magnetic**, compelling, alluring, fascinating, captivating, charming, appealing [➡ INTERESTING AND MEANINGFUL; 190]

charitable 1 *adj* **generous**, giving, benevolent, altruistic, helpful, liberal, openhanded, bountiful (*literary*) [➡ GENEROSITY AND KINDNESS; 495] *Opposite*: uncharitable 2 *adj* **considerate**, understanding, accepting, sympathetic, tolerant, gracious, lenient, indulgent [➡ FRIENDLINESS AND SOCIABILITY; 494] *Opposite*: unforgiving

charitable foundation *n* [➡ CHARITY AND CHARITABLE INSTITUTIONS; 822]

charitable organization *n* [➡ CHARITY AND CHARITABLE INSTITUTIONS; 822]

charitable trust *n* [➡ CHARITY AND CHARITABLE INSTITUTIONS; 822]

charity 1 *n* **aid**, contributions, gifts, donations, help, assistance, offerings, handouts, alms [➡ KIND ACTIONS OR BEHAVIOR; 295] 2 *n* **aid organization**, charitable trust, charitable foundation, aid agency [➡ CHARITY AND CHARITABLE INSTITUTIONS; 822] 3 *n* **kindness**, tolerance, humanity, compassion, generosity, altruism, goodwill, benevolence, sympathy, understanding, consideration [➡ KIND ACTIONS OR BEHAVIOR; 295] *Opposite*: unkindness

charity appeal *n* [➡ PERFORMANCES AND SHOWS; 42]

charity event *n* [➡ PERFORMANCES AND SHOWS; 42]

charity performance *n* [➡ PERFORMANCES AND SHOWS; 42]

charlatan *n* **fake**, fraud, swindler, quack, counterfeit, pretender, sham, impostor, con artist (*slang*) [➡ PEOPLE WHO DECEIVE; 661]

charlatanism *n* **quackery**, trickery, pretense [➡ DECEPTION AND LIES; 660]

Charleston *type of* **dance** [➡ DANCE; 903]

charm 1 *n* **attraction**, appeal, allure, charisma, magic, fascination, magnetism, lure [➡ BEAUTY AND ATTRACTIVENESS; 189] 2 *n* **ornament**, keepsake, trinket, talisman, amulet, memento, accessory, lucky piece [➡ ORNAMENTS AND DECORATIONS; 1248] 3 *type of* **jewelry** [➡ JEWELRY; 866] 4 *type of* **flock** [➡ GROUPS OF BIRDS; 1007] 5 *v* **captivate**, enchant, beguile, hypnotize, mesmerize, enthrall, win over, fascinate, entrance, enrapture (*formal*) [➡ APPEAL TO AND AROUSE INTEREST; 575]

charmed 1 *adj* **lucky**, fortunate, enchanted, magical, fairy-tale, protected [➡ LUCK; 783] *Opposite*: unlucky 2 *adj* **delighted**, pleased, enchanted, thrilled, glad, happy [➡ APPRECIATION AND GRATITUDE; 535]

charmer *n* **smooth talker**, enchanter, fascinator, smooth operator, ladies' man, Romeo, Casanova, flirt, seducer, siren, smoothie (*informal*), Lothario (*literary*), coquette (*literary*) [➡ SUPERFICIAL OR INSINCERE PEOPLE; 951]

charming *adj* **delightful**, amiable, attractive, appealing, charismatic, fascinating, enchanting, persuasive, captivating, alluring, enthralling, entrancing [➡ BEAUTY AND ATTRACTIVENESS; 189] *Opposite*: unattractive

charmless *adj* **unattractive**, unappealing, uninteresting, unsympathetic, unprepossessing, ugly, unpleasant [➡ SELFISH AND UNKIND; 505] *Opposite*: charming

charnel house *n* [➡ BURIAL PLACES AND ACCESSORIES; 930]

chart 1 *n* **diagram**, plan, graph, table, graphic representation, visual aid, map [➡ DRAWINGS, CHARTS, AND TABLES; 594] 2 *v* **register**, record, project, plot, chronicle, log, follow, map, outline [➡ RECORD SOMETHING; 371]

charter 1 *n* **contract**, deed, agreement, license, grant, approval, commission [➡ OFFICIAL DOCUMENTS; 586] 2 *v* **rent**, lease, hire, take on, commission, let [➡ PURCHASE; 422]

chary *adj* **wary**, cautious, suspicious, guarded, cagey, careful, circumspect [➡ INSECURITY AND LOSS OF COMPOSURE; 544] *Opposite*: reckless

See Compare and Contrast at **cautious**.

chase 1 *v* **pursue**, run after, hunt, hound, follow, trail, track, look for, search for, go after, go in pursuit of, tail [➡ ACCOMPANY AND FOLLOW; 337] **2** *v* **race**, dash, rush, career, hurtle, hurry [➡ MOVE FAST; 313] **3** *n* **pursuit**, hunt, hunting [➡ SEEK POSSESSION AND SEARCH; 456]

See Compare and Contrast at **follow.**

chaser 1 *n* **pursuer**, follower, hunter, shadow, tail, tracker [➡ ENEMIES AND TORMENTORS; 969] **2** *n* [➡ DRINKS; 1187]

chasm *n* **crater**, gulf, gap, abyss, gorge, rift, crevasse, arroyo, break, gulch, cleft, ravine, split, void [➡ HOLES, GAPS, AND FORKS; 1252]

chasseur *type of* **food presentation** [➡ COOKING AND FOOD PREPARATION; 353]

chassis *part of* **external structure** [➡ EXTERNAL PARTS OF A VEHICLE; 1147]

chaste *adj* **innocent**, uncorrupted, virtuous, unblemished, unsullied, spotless, faithful, pure (*literary*) [➡ MORALLY GOOD; 774] *Opposite*: impure

chasten 1 *v* **punish**, reprimand, discipline, censure, chastise, correct, castigate (*formal*) [➡ ACCUSE, BLAME, AND CRITICIZE; 641] **2** *v* **subdue**, suppress, restrain, tame, humble, subjugate [➡ UPSET, DISTRESS, AND HUMILIATE; 567]

chasteness *n* **pureness**, innocence, purity, virtuousness, faithfulness [➡ MORALLY GOOD; 774] *Opposite*: immorality

chastise *v* **reprimand**, discipline, censure, punish, rebuke, reprove, penalize, correct, scold, chasten, upbraid, tell off (*informal*), castigate (*formal*) [➡ ACCUSE, BLAME, AND CRITICIZE; 641] *Opposite*: praise

chastisement (*formal*) *n* **reprimand**, discipline, punishment, rebuke, scolding, correction, censure, penalty, telling off (*informal*) [➡ CRITICISMS AND ANGRY OUTBURSTS; 50] *Opposite*: praise

chastity *n* **purity**, innocence, virtue [➡ MORALLY GOOD; 774]

chat 1 *v* **talk**, converse, gossip, dialogue, gab (*informal*), chitchat (*informal*), yak (*informal*), shoot the breeze (*slang*), jaw (*slang*), chew the fat (*slang*) [➡ TWO-WAY COMMUNICATION; 607] **2** *v* [➡ THE INTERNET; 1128] **3** *n* **conversation**, one-on-one, heart-to-heart, tête-à-tête, talk, dialogue, exchange, discussion, back-and-forth [➡ INFORMAL COMMUNICATION; 45]

chateau *type of* **house** [➡ RESIDENTIAL BUILDINGS; 1078]

Chateaubriand *type of* **steak** [➡ TYPES AND CUTS OF MEAT; 1177]

chat room *n* [➡ THE INTERNET; 1128]

chattels *n* **possessions**, belongings, things, stuff, personal property, material, holdings, gear (*informal*) [➡ POSSESSIONS; 461]

chatter 1 *v* **babble**, prattle, rant, gossip, go on, rattle on, talk a blue streak (*informal*) [➡ CHATTER AND BABBLE; 617] **2** *n* **talk**, gossip, chat, conversation [➡ INFORMAL COMMUNICATION; 45] **3** *type of* **human sound** [➡ SOUNDS MADE BY PEOPLE; 1262]

chatterbox (*informal*) *n* **talker**, gossip, chatterer, tattler, blabbermouth (*informal*), gabber (*informal*) [➡ INTERFERING PEOPLE AND TATTLETALES; 950]

chatterer *n* **talker**, gossip, tattler, chatterbox (*informal*), blabbermouth (*informal*), gabber (*informal*) [➡ INTERFERING PEOPLE AND TATTLETALES; 950]

chattering classes (*UK*) *n* [➡ CLASS STATUS; 889]

chattily *adv* **conversationally**, informally [➡ ELOQUENT, TALKATIVE, AND LONG-WINDED; 632]

chattiness *n* **garrulity**, loquacity, communicativeness, informality [➡ ELOQUENT, TALKATIVE, AND LONG-WINDED; 632]

chatty 1 *adj* **talkative**, garrulous, loquacious, forthcoming, gossipy, friendly [➡ ELOQUENT, TALKATIVE, AND LONG-WINDED; 632] *Opposite*: quiet **2** *adj* **informal**, friendly, personal, casual, relaxed [➡ LEVELS OF FORMALITY; 522] *Opposite*: formal

See Compare and Contrast at **talkative.**

chauffeur *n* **driver**, motorist, valet [➡ DRIVERS; 1153]

chauvinism *n* **bigotry**, sexism, prejudice, narrow-mindedness, dogmatism, machismo, jingoism, xenophobia [➡ PREJUDICE; 550]

chauvinist *n* **bigot**, sexist, racist, homophobe, jingoist, xenophobe [➡ SELF-IMPORTANT AND SELF-SEEKING PEOPLE; 949]

chauvinistic *adj* **bigoted**, prejudiced, opinionated, dogmatic, narrow-minded, homophobic, xenophobic, jingoistic, racist, nationalistic [➡ NEGATIVE INTELLECTUAL CHARACTERISTICS; 525]

cheap 1 *adj* **inexpensive**, economy, low-priced, economical, discounted, low-cost, on sale, cut-rate, reduced, bargain, bargain-basement, for a song, cut-price (*UK*) [➡ CHEAP AND INEXPENSIVE; 221] *Opposite*: expensive **2** *adj* **shoddy**, inferior, second-rate, substandard, common, tawdry, cheapo (*informal*), chintzy (*informal*) [➡ ORDINARINESS; 244] *Opposite*: superior **3** *adj* **contemptible**, despicable, shameful, low, base, scurvy [➡ IN POOR TASTE AND OVERSENTIMENTAL; 229] *Opposite*: admirable **4** *adj* **stingy**, tightfisted, miserly, parsimonious, close-fisted (*informal*), penny-pinching (*informal*), mean (*UK*) [➡ GRASPING AND FINANCIALLY MEAN; 519] *Opposite*: generous

cheapen *v* **denigrate**, demean, belittle, lower, degrade, devalue, depreciate, undervalue [➡ WORSEN SOMETHING; 380] *Opposite*: elevate

cheaply *adv* **inexpensively**, economically, reasonably, modestly, competitively, on the cheap (*informal*) [➡ CHEAP AND INEXPENSIVE; 221] *Opposite*: expensively

cheapness 1 *n* **tawdriness**, inferiority, shoddiness, tackiness (*informal*) [➡ IN POOR TASTE AND OVERSENTIMENTAL; 229] *Opposite*: tastefulness **2** *n* **stinginess**, tightfistedness, miserliness, parsimony, close-fistedness (*informal*), meanness (*UK*) [➡ GRASPING AND FINANCIALLY MEAN; 519] *Opposite*: generosity

cheapo (*informal*) *adj* [➡ CHEAP AND INEXPENSIVE; 221]

cheapskate (*informal*) *n* **miser**, skinflint, killjoy, scrooge (*informal*), tightwad (*informal*) [➡ FINANCIALLY MEAN PEOPLE; 952]

cheat 1 *v* **deceive**, trick, con, swindle, defraud, dupe, bamboozle (*informal*), bilk (*informal*) [➡ FALSIFY AND CHEAT; 176] **2** *n* **double-dealer**, rogue, cheater, charlatan, double-crosser, trickster, shyster (*informal*), con man (*slang*), con artist (*slang*) [➡ PEOPLE WHO DECEIVE; 661]

cheating 1 *adj* **duplicitous**, double-dealing, dishonest, unprincipled, deceitful, underhand, false [➡ DECEITFUL; 513] *Opposite*: honest 2 *n* **dishonesty**, deceit, deception, duplicity, chicanery, double-dealing, misappropriation, fraud, embezzlement, fiddling (*informal*) [➡ DECEPTION AND LIES; 660]

check 1 *v* **test**, test out, prove, try, try out, examine [➡ EXAMINE AND ASSESS; 753] 2 *v* **make sure**, ensure, verify, confirm, certify, establish [➡ APPROVE AND CONFIRM; 646] 3 *v* **limit**, hold in, stop, impede, hold up, hold back, delay, restrain, inhibit, repress, constrain, withhold, curb [➡ AVOID, PREVENT, LIMIT, AND CONTROL; 277] *Opposite*: expedite (*formal*) 4 *n* **inspection**, examination, test, assessment, trial, safety test, safety check, safety inspection, investigation [➡ EXAMINE AND ASSESS; 753] 5 *n* **safeguard**, curb, restraint, buttress, catch, rein [➡ AVOID, PREVENT, LIMIT, AND CONTROL; 277] 6 *n* **payment**, form, order, draft, instruction, authorization [➡ MANUALS AND INSTRUCTIONS; 589] 7 *n* **bill**, invoice, score, tab (*informal*), damage (*informal*) [➡ RECEIPTS AND INVOICES; 591]

checked *adj* **check**, checkered, patterned, crisscross, plaid, squared [➡ DESCRIBING PATTERNS; 1227]

checker 1 *n* **inspector**, examiner, assessor, regulator, overseer, supervisor [➡ SURVEYORS, EXAMINERS, AND JUDGES; 853] 2 *type of* **game piece** [➡ GAME PIECES; 878]

checkered 1 *adj* **uneven**, inconsistent, variable, changeable, volatile, unpredictable, up-and-down, irregular, patchy [➡ FINITENESS, VARIABILITY, AND TRANSIENCE; 96] *Opposite*: even 2 *adj* **check**, checked, squared, patterned, crisscross, plaid [➡ DESCRIBING PATTERNS; 1227]

check in *v* **register**, sign in, sign up, sign on, enroll [➡ ARRIVE; 12]

check-in *n* **registration desk**, registration, reception desk, reception area, desk [➡ DOORS AND ACCESS POINTS; 1101]

checklist *n* **list**, specification, spec, agenda, worksheet [➡ LISTS AND SCHEDULES; 587]

checkmate *n* **check**, mate, end, ending, victory, defeat [➡ SUCCESS; 82] *Opposite*: stalemate

check out 1 *v* **inspect**, investigate, look into, explore, examine, scrutinize, research, take a look at, have a look at [➡ EXAMINE AND ASSESS; 753] 2 *v* **leave**, depart, vacate, sign out, exit [➡ LEAVE AND GO AWAY; 8]

check over *v* **look over**, reread, go through, go over, examine, edit, give the once-over (*informal*) [➡ EXAMINE AND ASSESS; 753]

checkpoint *n* **barrier**, turnpike, frontier, border, spot check, frontier post [➡ BARRIERS; 1113]

checkup *n* **examination**, looking over, physical, medical, inspection, health check, survey, doctor's visit, review, scan, lookover (*informal*), once-over (*informal*) [➡ REMEDIES, TREATMENTS, AND OPERATIONS; 731]

check up on *v* **keep an eye on**, check on, spy on, watch, monitor [➡ EXAMINE AND ASSESS; 753] *Opposite*: ignore

cheddar *type of* **hard cheese** [➡ DAIRY PRODUCTS AND CHEESES; 1183]

cheek *part of* **face** [➡ PARTS OF THE BODY: HEAD; 692]

cheekbone 1 *type of* **bone** [➡ THE BONES AND JOINTS; 719] 2 *part of* **face** [➡ PARTS OF THE BODY: HEAD; 692]

cheek by jowl *adv* **side by side**, on top of one another, close together, together, close, in each other's pocket [➡ CLOSENESS; 159]

cheekily (*informal*) *adv* **audaciously**, boldly, defiantly, irreverently, insolently, brazenly, disrespectfully, impudently, sassily, impertinently (*formal*) [➡ RUDE AND HOSTILE; 625] *Opposite*: respectfully

cheekiness (*informal*) *n* **impudence**, disrespect, effrontery, insolence, irreverence, brazenness, audacity, sassiness [➡ BAD MANNERS AND SOCIAL SKILLS; 521] *Opposite*: respect

cheek-to-cheek *adv* **close**, close up, close together, together, intimately [➡ CLOSENESS; 159]

cheeky (*informal*) *adj* **rude**, bold, sassy, mischievous, disrespectful, pert, naughty, defiant, insolent, brazen, impudent, impertinent (*formal*) [➡ BAD MANNERS AND SOCIAL SKILLS; 521] *Opposite*: respectful

cheep 1 *v* **chirp**, peep, tweet, twitter, sing, warble [➡ SOUND EMISSION BY ANIMALS OR BIRDS; 364] 2 *type of* **bird sound** [➡ SOUNDS MADE BY BIRDS; 1263]

cheeping *n* **chirping**, tweeting, peeping, twittering, singing, warbling [➡ SOUNDS MADE BY BIRDS; 1263]

cheer 1 *n* **cheerfulness**, optimism, merriment, joyfulness, liveliness, good spirits [➡ PLEASURE, EXCITEMENT, AND ELATION; 534] *Opposite*: gloom 2 *v* **applaud**, shout, root for, hail, praise [➡ PRAISE AND ENCOURAGE; 647] *Opposite*: boo

cheerful *adj* **happy**, cheery, bright, smiling, joyful, merry, jovial, sunny, in good spirits, jaunty, vivacious, gleeful, optimistic, chirpy (*informal*), chipper (*informal*) [➡ PLEASURE, EXCITEMENT, AND ELATION; 534] *Opposite*: sad

cheerfully 1 *adv* **happily**, optimistically, merrily, joyfully, gleefully, with good cheer, sunnily, vivaciously, jauntily, chirpily (*informal*) [➡ PLEASURE, EXCITEMENT, AND ELATION; 534] *Opposite*: sadly 2 *adv* **gladly**, willingly, readily, with pleasure [➡ THE WILL AND WILLINGNESS; 563] *Opposite*: grudgingly

cheerfulness *n* **happiness**, joyfulness, cheer, cheeriness, merriment, exuberance, optimism, joviality, jollity, vivaciousness, jauntiness, chirpiness (*informal*) [➡ PLEASURE, EXCITEMENT, AND ELATION; 534] *Opposite*: sadness

cheeriness *n* **cheerfulness**, happiness, joyfulness, liveliness, joviality, jauntiness, chirpiness (*informal*) [➡ PLEASURE, EXCITEMENT, AND ELATION; 534] *Opposite*: gloominess

cheering *adj* **heartening**, encouraging, positive, uplifting, promising, hopeful [➡ EMOTIONALLY PLEASANT; 187] *Opposite*: discouraging

cheerleader *n* **performer**, supporter, cheerer [➡ PEOPLE IN SPORTS AND LEISURE; 876]

cheerless *adj* **gloomy**, depressing, dismal, miserable, sad, unhappy, somber, sullen, dour, morose, drab [➡ EMOTIONALLY UNPLEASANT AND UPSETTING; 227] *Opposite*: bright

cheerlessness *n* **bleakness**, dreariness, gloominess, soullessness, wintriness, dinginess, somberness, dismalness, sullenness, dourness, moroseness, drabness [➡ EMOTIONALLY UNPLEASANT AND UPSETTING; 227] *Opposite*: brightness

cheer on *v* **encourage**, root for, support, plump for, laud, egg on [➡ PRAISE AND ENCOURAGE; 647] *Opposite*: discourage

cheers (*UK*) 1 *interj* **thanks**, thank you, thanks a lot [➡GREETINGS, FAREWELLS, AND SALUTATIONS; 659] 2 *interj* **goodbye**, be seeing you, au revoir, bye (*informal*), bye-bye (*informal*) [➡GREETINGS, FAREWELLS, AND SALUTATIONS; 659]

cheer up *v* **perk up**, brighten, brighten up, liven, enliven [➡PLEASE AND AMUSE; 572] *Opposite*: depress

cheery *adj* **happy**, joyful, smiling, cheerful, merry, jovial, jolly, jaunty, radiant, chirpy (*informal*), bright and breezy (*UK*) [➡PLEASURE, EXCITEMENT, AND ELATION; 534] *Opposite*: gloomy

cheese *n* [➡DAIRY PRODUCTS AND CHEESES; 1183]

cheese

◆ *types of hard cheeses*
cheddar, Edam, Emmenthaler, Gouda, Gruyère, Monterey Jack, Parmesan, pecorino, Provolone, Stilton, Swiss

◆ *types of soft cheeses*
blue cheese, Brie, Camembert, chèvre, cottage cheese, cream cheese, feta, Gorgonzola, mascarpone, mozzarella, ricotta, Roquefort, Taleggio

cheesecake *type of* **cake** [➡CAKES, COOKIES, AND DESSERTS; 1181]

cheesecloth *type of* **fabric from plants** [➡FABRICS; 1132]

cheeseparing 1 *adj* **stingy**, miserly, mean-spirited, avaricious, miserable, tightfisted, cheap, close-fisted (*informal*) [➡GRASPING AND FINANCIALLY MEAN; 519] *Opposite*: generous 2 *n* **stinginess**, miserliness, mean-spiritedness, avarice, cheapness, tightfistedness, close-fistedness (*informal*) [➡GRASPING AND FINANCIALLY MEAN; 519] *Opposite*: generosity

cheesy 1 *adj* [➡SMELL AND SMELLING; 705] 2 *adj* (*informal*) **tasteless**, cheap, tawdry, unpleasant, tacky (*informal*) [➡IN POOR TASTE AND OVERSENTIMENTAL; 229] *Opposite*: stylish

cheetah *type of* **cat** [➡FELINES; 983]

chef *type of* **person who works in restaurants** [➡DOMESTIC AND KITCHEN WORKERS; 850]

chemical *n* **substance**, element, compound [➡SUBSTANCES; 1267]

chemise *type of* **upper body underwear** [➡ACCESSORIES, MILLINERY, AND LINGERIE; 867]

chemistry *n* **interaction**, attraction, understanding, empathy, sympathy, rapport, harmony, nonverbal communication, vibes (*slang*) [➡COMMUNICATION; 602]

chemotherapy *type of* **medical procedure** [➡REMEDIES, TREATMENTS, AND OPERATIONS; 731]

chenille *type of* **fabric from animals** [➡FABRICS; 1132]

cheongsam *type of* **dress** [➡GARMENTS AND OUTFITS; 865]

cherish *v* **treasure**, appreciate, relish, take pleasure in, esteem, revere, value, prize, apprize (*formal*) [➡LIKE, LOVE, VALUE, AND ENJOY; 578] *Opposite*: neglect

cherished *adj* **valued**, precious, beloved, esteemed, appreciated, treasured, prized, unforgettable, memorable [➡POPULAR AND WANTED; 220] *Opposite*: neglected

cherry *type of* **fruit** [➡FRUIT AND VEGETABLES; 1176]

cherry bomb *type of* **firework** [➡EXPLOSIVES; 1155]

cherry-pick *v* **select**, choose, pick, handpick, pick and choose, help yourself, opt, pick out, single out [➡MAKE DECISIONS AND CHOICES; 752]

cherry red *type of* **red** [➡COLORS; 1224]

cherry tomato *type of* **salad vegetable** [➡FRUIT AND VEGETABLES; 1176]

cherub *n* **angel**, cupid, amoretto, putto [➡RELIGIOUS CONCEPTS; 776]

cherubic 1 *adj* **angelic**, cute, innocent, attractive, lovable, adorable [➡PEOPLE'S PHYSICAL APPEARANCE; 475] 2 *adj* **holy**, divine, spiritual, saintly, blessed, godly, supernatural, ethereal, seraphic [➡RELIGIOUS CONCEPTS; 776]

chervil *type of* **herb** [➡HERBS AND SPICES; 1175]

chessman *type of* **game piece** [➡GAME PIECES; 878]

chest 1 *n* **upper body**, torso, rib cage, ribs, trunk [➡PARTS OF THE BODY: TORSO; 693] 2 *type of* **container** [➡CONTAINERS, RECEPTACLES, AND PACKAGING; 1245]

chesterfield *n* [➡FURNITURE; 858]

chestnut 1 *type of* **deciduous tree** [➡DECIDUOUS TREES; 1028] 2 *type of* **nut** [➡NUTS; 1185] 3 *type of* **brown** [➡COLORS; 1224] 4 *n* (*informal*) **joke**, tired joke, anecdote, cliché, old favorite (*informal*) [➡JOKES AND TEASING; 674]

chestnut-haired *adj* [➡HAIR COLOR; 485]

chest of drawers *type of* **cabinet** [➡FURNITURE; 858]

chesty (*UK*) *adj* **wheezy**, rasping, phlegmy, congested [➡LOUD, HIGH, OR UNPLEASANT SOUNDS; 1266]

chèvre *type of* **soft cheese** [➡DAIRY PRODUCTS AND CHEESES; 1183]

chevron *n* **V-shape**, V, stripe, badge, insignia, rank [➡SYMBOLS, SIGNS, AND NUMBERS; 596]

chevrotain *type of* **deer or antelope** [➡DEER AND ANTELOPES; 981]

chew 1 *v* **masticate**, chew up, gnaw, grind, crush, squash, champ, munch, chomp (*informal*) [➡EAT AND NOT EAT; 710] 2 *n* **portion**, plug, wad [➡AMOUNTS OF SOLID OR SEMISOLID; 115]

chewing gum *type of* **confectionery** [➡CONFECTIONERY; 1182]

chew on *v* [➡THINK AND REFLECT; 743]

chew out (*informal*) *v* **scold**, reproach, reprimand, take to task, bawl out (*informal*), tell off (*informal*) [➡ACCUSE, BLAME, AND CRITICIZE; 641]

chew over *v* **meditate**, ponder, think about, ruminate on, consider, mull over, deliberate, contemplate, weigh, muse on, reflect on, perpend (*archaic*) [➡THINK AND REFLECT; 743]

chew the cud *v* [➡THINK AND REFLECT; 743]

chew the fat (*slang*) *v* **chat**, converse, chatter, gossip, natter (*informal*) [➡TWO-WAY COMMUNICATION; 607]

chew up 1 *v* **damage**, crush, rip up, injure, destroy, mangle [➡DESTRUCTION AND DEMOLITION; 359] 2 *v* **chew**, grind, masticate, champ, munch, consume, chomp (*informal*) [➡EAT AND NOT EAT; 710]

chewy *adj* **rubbery**, stringy, fibrous, gristly, leathery [➡ STATE OF PREPARED FOOD; 1171] *Opposite*: tender

chiasmus *type of* **figure of speech** [➡ FIGURES OF SPEECH; 673]

chic 1 *adj* **stylish**, fashionable, well-dressed, attractive, smart, elegant, well-groomed, well put together, modish, dashing, hip, classy (*informal*), tony (*informal*), swanky (*informal*), well turned-out (*UK*) [➡ WELL-GROOMED; 482] *Opposite*: unfashionable 2 *n* **style**, elegance, panache, stylishness, modishness, classiness (*informal*) [➡ WELL-GROOMED; 482]

chicanery *n* **deception**, trickery, verbiage, smoke and mirrors, talk, nonsense, underhandedness, double-dealing, waffle (*informal*), hot air (*informal*), flimflam (*slang*) [➡ MEANINGLESS SPEECH OR WRITING; 676]

chicanes *n* [➡ TRAVEL: TRAFFIC PROBLEMS AND TRAFFIC MANAGEMENT; 323]

chichi *adj* **contrived**, recherché, self-conscious, pretentious, affected, too much, over-the-top (*informal*), uncool (*slang*) [➡ AFFECTATION, SELF-SATISFACTION, AND SNOBBISHNESS; 507]

chick *type of* **young bird** [➡ YOUNG BIRDS; 1004]

chickadee *type of* **common bird** [➡ BIRDS; 997]

chicken 1 *type of* **fowl** [➡ FOOD BIRDS; 999] 2 *type of* **meat** [➡ TYPES AND CUTS OF MEAT; 1177] 3 *adj* (*informal*) **cowardly**, frightened, scared, reluctant, fearful, apprehensive, jumpy, afraid, hesitant, craven, faint-hearted, gutless, lily-livered (*dated*) [➡ COWARDICE AND WEAKNESS OF WILL; 508] *Opposite*: brave

See Compare and Contrast at **cowardly**.

chicken coop *type of* **pen or cage** [➡ ANIMAL OR BIRD ACCOMMODATIONS; 1079]

chicken feed (*informal*) *n* **small change**, next to nothing, small potatoes (*informal*), small beer (*informal*), chump change (*slang*) [➡ SMALL AMOUNTS OF MONEY; 121]

chicken out (*slang*) *v* **back out**, drop out, think better of something, give up, withdraw, renege, lose your nerve, cop out (*slang*) [➡ NOT DO AND REFUSE TO DO; 274]

chickpea *type of* **pulse** [➡ PEAS AND BEANS; 1189]

chickweed *type of* **weed** [➡ WEEDS AND THISTLES; 1034]

chide (*literary*) *v* **reproach**, scold, reprimand, rebuke, blame, take to task, nag, reprove, tell off (*informal*) [➡ ACCUSE, BLAME, AND CRITICIZE; 641] *Opposite*: praise

chief 1 *n* **ruler**, head, boss, captain, commander, leader, superior, supremo (*informal*) [➡ BOSSES AND MANAGEMENT; 965] 2 *adj* **principal**, main, topmost, leading, foremost, paramount, primary, dominant, first, highest [➡ MOST IMPORTANT AND MAIN; 193]

chief executive *n* **C.E.O.**, boss, leader, president [➡ BUSINESS PEOPLE; 793]

chiefly *adv* **primarily**, mainly, essentially, mostly, predominantly, in the main, largely, for the most part, principally, above all, first and foremost [➡ MAINLY AND PRIMARILY; 140]

chieftain *n* **tribal chief**, ruler, chief, overlord, lord [➡ BOSSES AND MANAGEMENT; 965]

chieftainship *n* **leadership**, command, authority, rank, status, position [➡ STATUS; 888]

chiffon *type of* **synthetic fabric** [➡ FABRICS; 1132]

chigger *type of* **parasitic insect** [➡ PARASITES; 1017]

chignon *type of* **hairstyle** [➡ HAIRSTYLES AND HAIRPIECES; 488]

chigoe *type of* **parasitic insect** [➡ PARASITES; 1017]

chihuahua *type of* **small dog** [➡ DOGS; 980]

chilblain *n* **swelling**, inflammation, blister [➡ CONDITIONS AFFECTING THE SKIN; 721]

child 1 *n* **youngster**, young person, teenager, adolescent, youth, juvenile, kid (*informal*), teen (*informal*) [➡ CHILD OR YOUTH; 945] 2 *n* **offspring**, descendant, spawn, scion, son, daughter [➡ YOUNGER GENERATION RELATIVES; 958] 3 *n* **baby**, infant, newborn, toddler, preschooler, nursling, suckling, neonate [➡ CHILD OR YOUTH; 945] 4 *n* **result**, product, outcome, creation [➡ RESULTS AND OUTCOMES; 83]

See Compare and Contrast at **youth**.

childbearing *n* **reproduction**, pregnancy, gestation, childbirth, motherhood [➡ REPRODUCTION AND HEREDITY; 725]

childbirth *n* **giving birth**, delivery, labor, contractions, childbearing, labor pains, parturition [➡ REPRODUCTION AND HEREDITY; 725]

childhood *n* **babyhood**, infancy, youth, upbringing, infanthood, nonage, early years [➡ BABYHOOD, CHILDHOOD, AND ADOLESCENCE; 917] *Opposite*: adulthood

childish 1 *adj* **immature**, irresponsible, silly, self-indulgent, foolish, babyish, infantile, juvenile [➡ BAD MANNERS AND SOCIAL SKILLS; 521] *Opposite*: mature 2 *adj* **childlike**, juvenile, innocent, ingenuous [➡ NEGATIVE INTELLECTUAL CHARACTERISTICS; 525]

childishness *n* **immaturity**, silliness, irresponsibility, pettiness [➡ BAD MANNERS AND SOCIAL SKILLS; 521] *Opposite*: maturity

childlike *adj* **innocent**, naive, candid, uncomplicated, unsophisticated, trusting, simple, guileless, ingenuous, pure (*literary*) [➡ NEGATIVE INTELLECTUAL CHARACTERISTICS; 525] *Opposite*: jaded

childproof *adj* **safe**, tamper-proof, secure [➡ SAFE AND SAFETY; 191]

child seat *type of* **internal feature** [➡ INTERNAL PARTS OF A VEHICLE; 1146]

child's play *n* **piece of cake** (*informal*), picnic (*informal*), walkover (*informal*), pushover (*informal*), cinch (*informal*), breeze (*informal*), walk in the park (*informal*) [➡ EASY WORK; 299]

chili *type of* **spice** [➡ HERBS AND SPICES; 1175]

chili sauce *type of* **seasonings, sauces, and dips** [➡ SEASONINGS AND SAUCES; 1174]

chill 1 *n* **coldness**, coolness, low temperature, chilliness, nippiness, frostiness, nip [➡ COLD WEATHER; 1051] *Opposite*: warmth 2 *n* **sudden fear**, anxiety, apprehension, wariness, shudder [➡ FEAR AND PANIC; 543] 3 *n* **gloom**, depression, pall, shadow [➡ NUISANCES; 253] 4 *n* **unfriendliness**, aloofness, detachment, coolness, coldness, remoteness, indifference, chilliness [➡ ANTAGONISM; 552] *Opposite:* warmth   **5** *adj* **biting**, freezing, wintry, nippy, chilly [➡ COLD WEATHER; 1051]   **6** *adj* **remote**, uninvolved, aloof, indifferent, chilly, cold, icy [➡ NEUTRALITY AND INDIFFERENCE; 553] *Opposite:* warm **7** *v* **cool**, freeze, make colder, put on ice, refrigerate [➡ CHANGE OF TEMPERATURE; 386] *Opposite:* warm **8** *v* **discourage**, depress, deter, dispirit, cast a shadow over, frighten [➡ UPSET, DISTRESS, AND HUMILIATE; 567] *Opposite:* encourage **9** *v* (*slang*) **relax**, loosen up, rest, take it easy, have a break, put your feet up, lie down, calm down, be calm, chill out (*slang*) [➡ STOP ACTING; 264]

chilled **1** *adj* **ice-cold**, freezing, frozen, refrigerated, cooled, iced [➡ TEMPERATURE: COLD; 1231] *Opposite:* hot **2** *adj* (*slang*) **cool**, relaxed, unflustered, calm, laid-back (*informal*) [➡ COOL AND CALM; 536] *Opposite:* agitated

chilled out (*slang*) *adj* [➡ COOL AND CALM; 536]

chilliness **1** *n* **coolness**, coldness, frostiness, nippiness, low temperature, chill, nip [➡ COLD WEATHER; 1051] *Opposite:* warmth **2** *n* **unfriendliness**, aloofness, stiffness, detachment, formality, coldness, reserve, chill [➡ ANTAGONISM; 552] *Opposite:* friendliness

chilling *adj* **frightening**, alarming, unsettling, distressing, terrifying, disturbing, unnerving, nerve-racking, scary (*informal*) [➡ FRIGHTENING; 231] *Opposite:* reassuring

chill out (*slang*) **1** *v* **calm down**, take it easy, stop worrying, lighten up (*informal*) [➡ CHANGE OF MOOD AND COMPOSURE; 580] **2** *v* **relax**, loosen up, rest, unwind, kick back (*informal*), chill (*slang*) [➡ CHANGE OF MOOD AND COMPOSURE; 580]

chillout *type of* **electronic music** [➡ MUSIC, SONGS, AND SINGING; 907]

chilly **1** *adj* **cold**, cool, nippy, chill, frosty, icy [➡ COLD WEATHER; 1051] *Opposite:* warm **2** *adj* **frigid**, formal, supercilious, aloof, detached, frosty, icy, reserved, cold, unfriendly [➡ UNFRIENDLINESS AND UNSOCIABILITY; 504] *Opposite:* warm

chime **1** *n* **clang**, ding, ding dong, sound, peal [➡ RINGING AND HOOTING SOUNDS; 1259] **2** *v* **strike**, peal, ring, sound, ring out, toll [➡ EMIT RINGING AND HOOTING SOUNDS; 367]

chime in **1** *v* **butt in**, interrupt, interject, voice your opinion, speak up, have your say, put your two cents in, pipe up, chip in (*informal*) [➡ INTERRUPT AND BUTT IN; 619] **2** *v* **agree**, be compatible, be consistent, be in line, be in agreement, be in accord [➡ HARMONY; 155] *Opposite:* contradict

chimera *n* **fantasy**, fancy, whimsy, illusion, mirage, figment, daydream [➡ NONEXISTENT THINGS; 23]

Chimera *type of* **mythological creature** [➡ MYTHICAL CREATURES; 1036]

chimerical *adj* **imaginary**, fantastical, illusory, unreal [➡ FALSE AND UNREAL; 173]

chimes *n* **bells**, glockenspiel, carillon [➡ MUSICAL INSTRUMENTS; 910]

chiminea *n* [➡ HOUSEHOLD APPLIANCES; 1117]

chimney *part of* **building** [➡ PARTS OF A BUILDING; 1095]

chimp *type of* **primate** [➡ PRIMATES; 988]

chimpanzee *type of* **primate** [➡ PRIMATES; 988]

chin *part of* **face** [➡ PARTS OF THE BODY: HEAD; 692]

china **1** *n* **tableware**, dishes, plates, cups, saucers, serving plates, platters [➡ TABLEWARE, FLATWARE, AND KITCHENWARE; 861] **2** *n* **figurines**, collectibles, porcelain, breakables, china doll [➡ POTTERY; 1135]

china cabinet *type of* **cabinet** [➡ FURNITURE; 858]

chinchilla *type of* **rodent** [➡ RODENTS; 989]

Chinese walls (*UK*) *n* [➡ SAFE AND SAFETY; 191]

chink **1** *n* **narrow opening**, crack, crevice, slit, opening, fissure [➡ HOLES, GAPS, AND FORKS; 1252] **2** *type of* **ringing sound** [➡ RINGING AND HOOTING SOUNDS; 1259]

chink in somebody's armor *n* **weak spot**, weakness, Achilles heel, flaw, failing, defect [➡ FAULTS, FLAWS, AND WEAKNESSES; 251]

chinless *adj* **weak**, ineffectual, irresolute, inept, spineless, timid [➡ COWARDICE AND WEAKNESS OF WILL; 508] *Opposite:* bold

chinook *type of* **wind** [➡ WINDY AND STORMY WEATHER; 1053]

chinos *type of* **pants** [➡ GARMENTS AND OUTFITS; 865]

chintz *type of* **fabric from plants** [➡ FABRICS; 1132]

chintzy **1** *adj* **tightfisted**, cheap, miserly, stingy, parsimonious, ungenerous, penny-pinching (*informal*) [➡ GRASPING AND FINANCIALLY MEAN; 519] *Opposite:* generous **2** *adj* **trashy**, cheap, inferior, shoddy, gaudy, showy, tawdry, tacky (*informal*), cheesy (*informal*) [➡ IN POOR TASTE AND OVERSENTIMENTAL; 229] *Opposite:* superior

chip **1** *n* **piece**, bit, crumb, flake, chunk, morsel [➡ SMALL PIECES; 129] **2** *n* **mark**, damage, imperfection, flaw, blemish [➡ FAULTS, FLAWS, AND WEAKNESSES; 251] **3** *n* **token**, counter, marker, playing piece, poker chip [➡ GAME PIECES; 870] **4** *type of* **processed potato** [➡ FRUIT AND VEGETABLES; 1176] **5** *type of* **hardware** [➡ COMPUTERS AND COMPUTING; 1127] **6** *v* **break off**, fragment, hew, flake, pare, whittle, chisel [➡ TEAR, BREAK, AND CUT; 360] **7** *v* **damage**, disfigure, mark, blemish, notch [➡ WORSEN APPEARANCE; 382]

chip away at *v* **weaken**, wear away, eat into, erode, diminish [➡ WORSEN SOMETHING; 380]

chipboard *n* [➡ BUILDING MATERIALS; 1077]

chip in (*informal*) **1** *v* **contribute**, help, participate, collaborate, take part, partake, share the expense, go shares in [➡ GIVE MONEY; 433] **2** *v* **chime in**, butt in, interject, voice your opinion, say what you think, speak up, put in your two cents' worth, pipe up, have your say [➡ INTERRUPT AND BUTT IN; 619]

chipmunk *type of* **rodent** [➡ RODENTS; 989]

chip off the old block (*informal*) *n* **younger version**, mirror image, clone, living image, replica, spitting image (*informal*) [➡ COPIES AND REPLICAS; 151]

chipped *adj* [➡ IN BAD REPAIR; 1234]

chipper (*informal*) *adj* **cheerful**, high-spirited, lively, good-humored, exuberant, bright, sprightly, energetic, frisky, animated, perky, chirpy (*informal*), upbeat (*informal*) [➡ PLEASURE, EXCITEMENT, AND ELATION; 534] *Opposite:* glum

chipping *n* **chip**, piece, fragment, bit, shaving, shard [➡ SMALL PIECES; 129]

chippings (*UK*) *n* **stones**, pebbles, gravel, shingle [➡SMALL PIECES; 129]

chiropractic *n* [➡REMEDIES, TREATMENTS, AND OPERATIONS; 731]

chirp *type of* **bird sound** [➡SOUNDS MADE BY BIRDS; 1263]

chirpiness (*informal*) *n* [➡CHEERFULNESS OF OUTLOOK; 503]

chirpy (*informal*) *adj* **lively**, vivacious, alert, bright, effervescent, cheery, cheerful, happy, high-spirited, in good spirits, chipper (*informal*) [➡PLEASURE, EXCITEMENT, AND ELATION; 534] *Opposite*: gloomy

chirrup *type of* **bird sound** [➡SOUNDS MADE BY BIRDS; 1263]

chisel *type of* **cutting tool** [➡CUTTING TOOLS; 1120]

chiseled *adj* **regular**, clean-cut, strong, delicate, fine-boned [➡FACIAL CHARACTERISTICS; 481]

chit (*dated*) *n* **receipt**, bill, check, tally, account, tab (*informal*) [➡RECEIPTS AND INVOICES; 591]

chitchat (*informal*) **1** *v* **talk**, discuss, have a tête-à-tête, gossip, babble, chatter, have a chat, natter (*informal*) [➡TWO-WAY COMMUNICATION; 607] **2** *n* **chatter**, gossip, chat, conversation, talk, natter (*informal*), gab (*informal*) [➡INFORMAL COMMUNICATION; 45]

chivalrous **1** *adj* **gallant**, courtly, brave, valiant, loyal, magnanimous, noble [➡GOOD MANNERS AND SOCIAL SKILLS; 520] *Opposite*: cowardly **2** *adj* **courteous**, mannerly, gracious, polite, civil, well-mannered, attentive, considerate [➡GOOD MANNERS AND SOCIAL SKILLS; 520] *Opposite*: discourteous

chivalry **1** *n* **gallantry**, courtliness, loyalty, valor, courage, bravery, magnanimity, nobility [➡GOOD MANNERS AND SOCIAL SKILLS; 520] *Opposite*: cowardice **2** *n* **courtesy**, courteousness, politeness, attentiveness, gentility, good manners, kindness, consideration, civility [➡GOOD MANNERS AND SOCIAL SKILLS; 520] *Opposite*: discourteousness

chive *type of* **herb** [➡HERBS AND SPICES; 1175]

chivvy *v* **urge**, pester, harass, badger, pressure, push, hassle (*informal*) [➡CAUSE OR COMPEL TO ACT; 271] *Opposite*: discourage

chlorine *type of* **gas** [➡GASES; 1275]

chock **1** *n* **wedge**, block, doorstop, chuck [➡STICKS, POLES, AND WEDGES; 1254] **2** *v* **brace**, steady, fix, block, stop [➡FASTEN, LINK, AND JOIN; 408] *Opposite*: release

chock-a-block (*informal*) *adj* **packed**, jammed, crammed, full, crowded, bursting, filled, teeming, brimful, full up, jam-packed (*informal*), chock-full (*informal*), wall-to-wall (*informal*), packed out (*informal*), heaving (*UK*) [➡FULL; 1239] *Opposite*: empty

chock-full (*informal*) *adj* **packed**, jammed, crammed, full, crowded, bursting, filled, teeming, brimful, full up, jam-packed (*informal*), chock-a-block (*informal*), wall-to-wall (*informal*), packed out (*informal*), heaving (*UK*) [➡FULL; 1239] *Opposite*: empty

chocolate **1** *type of* **confectionery** [➡CONFECTIONERY; 1182] **2** *type of* **brown** [➡COLORS; 1224]

chocolate-box *adj* **pretty**, romanticized, picturesque, soft-focus, attractive, sentimental, twee (*UK*) [➡IN POOR TASTE AND OVERSENTIMENTAL; 229]

choice **1** *n* **selection**, choosing, pick, election, adoption [➡MAKE DECISIONS AND CHOICES; 752] **2** *n* **range**, selection, variety, set, group [➡COLLECTIONS AND MIXTURES OF THINGS; 1244] **3** *adj* **excellent**, high-quality, superior, special, prime, best, select [➡SUPERIORITY; 152]

choir *type of* **band** [➡MUSICIANS AND SINGERS; 908]

choke **1** *v* **strangle**, throttle, stifle, suffocate, asphyxiate, garrote [➡KILL; 923] **2** *v* **obstruct**, clog, block, stop up, congest, plug, dam, fill, fill up, gag, halt [➡FILL; 406] *Opposite*: free up (*informal*) **3** *v* **fill with emotion**, freeze up, weep, well up, become teary-eyed [➡GIVING VENT TO EMOTIONS; 679] **4** *type of* **controls** [➡INTERNAL PARTS OF A VEHICLE; 1146]

choke back *v* **suppress**, hold back, fight back, stifle, repress, stop [➡WITHHOLD INFORMATION; 687] *Opposite*: let out

choked *adj* [➡FULL; 1239]

choked up **1** *adj* (*informal*) **emotional**, weepy, tearful [➡SADNESS, DISTRESS, AND DESPAIR; 539] **2** *adj* **congested**, clogged, blocked [➡FULL; 1239]

choker *type of* **necklace** [➡JEWELRY; 866]

choler (*literary or archaic*) *n* [➡IRRITATION AND ANGER; 541]

choleric (*literary*) *adj* [➡IRRITATION AND ANGER; 541]

cholesterol *n* **fat**, saturated fat, saturated fatty acid, fatty acid, lipid, dietary fat [➡FOOD COMPONENTS; 1188]

chomp (*informal*) *v* **chew**, munch, crunch, eat, masticate, gnaw, bite on, grind [➡EAT AND NOT EAT; 710]

chomping at the bit *adj* [➡DESIRE AND WANT; 579]

choose **1** *v* **select**, pick, take, pick out, point out, indicate, elect, vote for, decide on, plump for, cherry-pick, go for (*informal*) [➡MAKE DECISIONS AND CHOICES; 752] *Opposite*: reject **2** *v* **decide**, want, prefer, desire, wish, opt [➡MAKE DECISIONS AND CHOICES; 752]

choose up *v* **select team members**, choose sides, pick sides [➡MAKE DECISIONS AND CHOICES; 752]

choosiness (*informal*) *n* [➡DIFFICULT TO PLEASE; 515]

choosy (*informal*) *adj* **particular**, hard to please, fussy, picky, fastidious, demanding, selective, finicky, persnickety (*informal*), faddy (*UK*) [➡DIFFICULT TO PLEASE; 515] *Opposite*: indifferent

chop **1** *v* **cut up**, chop up, slice, hack, ax, lop, hew, sever, slash, split, fell [➡TEAR, BREAK, AND CUT; 360] **2** *type of* **cut** [➡TYPES AND CUTS OF MEAT; 1177]

chop-chop (*informal*) *interj* **quickly**, immediately, right away, fast, right now, at once, without delay, with no delay, on the double [➡HAPPENING QUICKLY; 104]

chop down *v* **shorten**, decrease, cut back, cut down, deliver a blow to, dispense with, lop off [➡CHANGE OF SIZE: SMALLER; 393]

chophouse *type of* **eating place** [➡HOTELS, RESTAURANTS, AND CLUBS; 1082]

chopper **1** *type of* **cutting tool** [➡CUTTING TOOLS; 1120] **2** *n* (*slang*) *type of* **tooth** [➡THE MOUTH; 702]

choppy *adj* **uneven**, broken up, variable, shifting, changing, irregular, jerky, rough [➡WINDY AND STORMY WEATHER; 1053] *Opposite:* smooth

chops (*informal*) *n* **jaw**, mouth [➡PARTS OF THE BODY: HEAD; 692]

chopstick *type of* **flatware** [➡TABLEWARE, FLATWARE, AND KITCHENWARE; 861]

chop suey *type of* **cooked dish** [➡PREPARED DISHES; 1170]

chop up *v* **cut up**, chop, cut into pieces, mill, slice, cube, dice, mince, grind [➡TEAR, BREAK, AND CUT; 360]

choral *adj* **vocal**, harmonic, sung [➡MUSICAL TERMS; 912]

chorale 1 *type of* **band** [➡MUSICIANS AND SINGERS; 908] 2 *type of* **musical form** [➡MUSIC, SONGS, AND SINGING; 907]

chord *n* **harmony**, triad, arpeggio, major chord, minor chord [➡NOTES AND CHORDS; 909]

chore 1 *n* **routine**, bore, hard work, imposition, inconvenience [➡NUISANCES; 253] 2 *n* **task**, job, errand, odd job, assignment, responsibility, duty [➡WORK IN GENERAL; 297]

See Compare and Contrast at **job**.

choreograph 1 *v* **create**, compose, design, arrange, put together, devise [➡ARRANGE AND CREATE ORDER; 357] 2 *v* **plan**, maneuver, direct, strategize, manage, manipulate, stage-manage, organize [➡MAKE POSSIBLE; 275]

choreography 1 *n* **composition**, dance routine, step design, step sequence, step arrangement, dance composition [➡DANCE; 903] 2 *n* **maneuvering**, direction, management, manipulation, strategy, planning, stage management [➡WAYS OF DOING THINGS; 294]

chorister *n* **singer**, musician, treble [➡MUSICIANS AND SINGERS; 908]

chorizo *type of* **processed meat** [➡TYPES AND CUTS OF MEAT; 1177]

chortle 1 *n* **laugh**, chuckle, gurgle, giggle, snicker, cackle, snigger [➡LAUGHTER; 649] 2 *type of* **human sound** [➡SOUNDS MADE BY PEOPLE; 1262] 3 *v* **chuckle**, laugh, gurgle, giggle, snicker, cackle, snigger [➡LAUGHTER; 649]

chorus 1 *n* **refrain**, chorus line, response, repeat, repetition, reprise [➡MUSIC, SONGS, AND SINGING; 907] 2 *type of* **band** [➡MUSICIANS AND SINGERS; 908] 3 *v* **speak at once**, speak together, speak in unison [➡UTTER AND PRONOUNCE; 608]

chosen *adj* **selected**, select, elect, preferred, special [➡SUPERIORITY; 152]

choux pastry *n* [➡BREAD, FLOUR, AND BREAD PRODUCTS; 1179]

chow 1 *n* (*slang*) **food**, grub (*informal*), nosh (*informal*), eats (*slang*), chuck, victuals, vittles (*archaic*) [➡FOOD; 1167] 2 *type of* **small dog** [➡DOGS; 980]

chow-chow *type of* **relish** [➡SEASONINGS AND SAUCES; 1174]

chowder *type of* **soup** [➡SOUPS; 1186]

chow down (*informal*) *v* **eat**, dine, eat heartily, gulp, gobble, wolf, nosh (*informal*) [➡EAT AND NOT EAT; 710]

chow mein *type of* **cooked dish** [➡PREPARED DISHES; 1170]

christen 1 *v* **baptize**, name, bless, sanctify [➡RELIGIONS AND RELIGIOUS PRACTICES; 777] 2 *v* **name**, nickname, call, dub, label,

style (*formal*) [➡NAME AND DESCRIBE; 665] 3 *v* (*informal*) **launch**, inaugurate, debut [➡CAUSE TO START; 265]

christening 1 *n* **baptism**, ceremony, rite, naming [➡RELIGIONS AND RELIGIOUS PRACTICES; 777] 2 *n* (*informal*) **launch**, first use, inauguration, debut [➡BEGINNINGS; 53]

Christian name *n* **first name**, given name, forename, personal name, praenomen, name, middle name [➡NAME AND DESCRIBE; 665]

chrome yellow *type of* **yellow** [➡COLORS; 1224]

chromium *type of* **metal** [➡METALS; 1276]

chromosome *n* **genetic material**, DNA, RNA [➡REPRODUCTION AND HEREDITY; 725]

chronic 1 *adj* **long-lasting**, lingering, persistent, continuing, enduring, lasting, prolonged, protracted [➡PERMANENCE: WITHOUT END; 94] *Opposite:* fleeting 2 *adj* **habitual**, persistent, ingrained, inveterate, established, confirmed, long-standing [➡PERMANENCE: WITHOUT END; 94] *Opposite:* occasional

chronicle 1 *n* **record**, history, account, annals, journal, narrative, story [➡RECORDS; 585] 2 *v* **report**, record, recount, relate, narrate, keep track of, make note of, set down, register, write down [➡RECORD SOMETHING; 371]

chronological *adj* **sequential**, consecutive, linear [➡CHAIN OF EVENTS; 162]

chronology 1 *n* **sequence of events**, order of events, time line, timetable, train of events, things as they happened [➡CHAIN OF EVENTS; 162] 2 *n* **account**, record, chronicle, narrative, history, annals, list [➡LISTS AND SCHEDULES; 587]

chronometer *n* [➡CLOCKS AND TIMERS; 1126]

chrysalis *type of* **stage of insect development** [➡INSECT STAGES; 1020]

chrysanthemum *type of* **perennial flower** [➡FLOWERS; 1032]

chrysoprase *type of* **gemstone** [➡PRECIOUS STONES; 1278]

chubbiness *n* **plumpness**, roundness, fleshiness, stoutness, fatness, obesity [➡BUILD; 477] *Opposite:* slenderness

chubby *adj* **plump**, rotund, round, fleshy, stout, fat, overweight, obese [➡BUILD; 477] *Opposite:* slender

chuck 1 *v* (*informal*) **throw**, hurl, toss, fling, pitch, lob [➡MOVE SOMETHING: THROUGH THE AIR; 334] 2 *v* (*informal*) **get rid of**, throw out, throw away, dispose of, discard [➡GET RID OF SOMETHING; 451] *Opposite:* keep 3 *v* (*informal*) **quit**, resign, walk off, leave, walk out, give up, throw in the towel (*informal*) [➡STOP ACTING; 264] 4 *v* **tap**, pat lightly, pat, tickle [➡PHYSICAL CONTACT AS COMMUNICATION; 655] 5 *n* **chock**, wedge, block, clamp [➡AMOUNTS OF SOLID OR SEMISOLID; 115] 6 *n* **food**, provisions, grub (*informal*), provender (*literary or humorous*) [➡FOOD; 1167] 7 *type of* **cut** [➡TYPES AND CUTS OF MEAT; 1177]

See Compare and Contrast at **throw**.

chuckle 1 *v* **laugh**, laugh to yourself, chortle, laugh inwardly, giggle, gurgle, snicker, snigger [➡LAUGHTER; 649] 2 *n* **laughter**, chortle, inward laughter, giggle, snicker, gurgle, snigger [➡LAUGHTER; 649] 3 *type of* **human sound** [➡SOUNDS MADE BY PEOPLE; 1262]

chuck out (*informal*) *v* **get rid of**, throw out, dispose of, discard [➞ GET RID OF SOMETHING; 451]

chug 1 *v* (*informal*) **continue**, keep going, keep at it, persist, plug away (*informal*) [➞ CONTINUE AN ACTION; 262] *Opposite*: stop 2 *v* (*slang*) **gulp**, gulp down, guzzle (*informal*), swig (*informal*) [➞ EAT AND NOT EAT; 710] 3 *type of* **continuous sound** [➞ CONTINUOUS SOUNDS; 1258]

chugalug (*informal*) *v* [➞ DRINK; 711]

chum (*informal*) *n* **friend**, associate, acquaintance, companion, pal (*informal*), buddy (*informal*), mate (*UK*) [➞ FRIENDS AND GUESTS; 963] *Opposite*: stranger

chumminess (*informal*) *n* **friendliness**, sociability, closeness, intimacy, friendship, matiness (*UK*) [➞ RELATIONSHIP TO ANOTHER; 973]

chummy (*informal*) *adj* **friendly**, sociable, congenial, close, intimate, inseparable, matey (*UK*) [➞ FRIENDLINESS AND SOCIABILITY; 494]

chunk *n* **piece**, hunk, mass, lump, portion, amount [➞ LARGE PIECES; 130]

chunkiness 1 *n* [➞ LARGE; 1193] 2 *n* (*informal*) [➞ BUILD; 477]

chunky 1 *adj* **lumpy**, bumpy, coarse, rough [➞ PHYSICAL TEXTURE; 1222] *Opposite*: smooth 2 *adj* **solid**, heavy, hefty, weighty, substantial, strong [➞ WEIGHT: HEAVY; 1205] *Opposite*: lightweight 3 *adj* (*informal*) **stocky**, stout, fat, chubby, plump, hefty, thickset, heavy [➞ BUILD; 477] *Opposite*: slender

church *type of* **place of worship** [➞ RELIGIOUS BUILDINGS; 1085]

church

◆ *types of churches*
abbey, basilica, cathedral, chapel, meeting house, minster, tabernacle, temple

churchgoer *n* **worshiper**, congregant, communicant [➞ RELIGIOUS PEOPLE; 778]

churchyard *n* **graveyard**, burial ground, cemetery, necropolis, boneyard (*informal*) [➞ BURIAL PLACES AND ACCESSORIES; 930]

churlish 1 *adj* **rude**, boorish, coarse, truculent, crass, ill-bred, bad-mannered, impolite [➞ BAD MANNERS AND SOCIAL SKILLS; 521] *Opposite*: polite 2 *adj* **ill-natured**, irritable, unpleasant, grumpy, sullen, surly [➞ BAD-TEMPERED AND HUMORLESS; 626] *Opposite*: pleasant

churlishly *adv* [➞ BAD MANNERS AND SOCIAL SKILLS; 521]

churlishness *n* [➞ BAD MANNERS AND SOCIAL SKILLS; 521]

churn *v* **mix**, roil, agitate, shake, whip, toss, stir up, stir, blend [➞ COMBINE AND MIX; 400]

churn out *v* **mass-produce**, manufacture, turn out, roll out, issue [➞ MANUFACTURE; 349]

chute 1 *n* **shaft**, tube, channel, sluice, raceway, spillway, slide, trough [➞ WATERCOURSES; 1111] 2 *n* **waterfall**, cascade, cataract, descent, drop, rapids [➞ RIVERS, LAKES, AND STREAMS; 1042]

chutney *type of* **relish** [➞ SEASONINGS AND SAUCES; 1174]

chutzpah (*informal*) 1 *n* **boldness**, self-confidence, self-assurance, assertiveness, bravado, forcefulness [➞ CONFIDENCE AND COMPOSURE; 499] 2 *n* **gall**, boldness, nerve, impudence, effrontery, audacity, cheek (*informal*) [➞ BAD MANNERS AND SOCIAL SKILLS; 521]

CIA *n* **security service**, intelligence service, federal bureau, counterintelligence service, spy organization, intelligence-gathering organization [➞ LEGISLATIVE BODIES AND LEGISLATION; 809]

ciabatta *type of* **bread** [➞ BREAD, FLOUR, AND BREAD PRODUCTS; 1179]

ciao (*informal*) *interj* **hello**, goodbye, hi (*informal*), so long (*informal*), see you later (*informal*) [➞ GREETINGS, FAREWELLS, AND SALUTATIONS; 659]

cicada *type of* **flying insect** [➞ FLYING INSECTS; 1013]

cilantro *type of* **herb** [➞ HERBS AND SPICES; 1175]

ciliate *type of* **microorganism** [➞ MICROORGANISMS, FUNGI, AND ALGAE; 1023]

C in C *n* **commander in chief**, five-star general, generalissimo, commander, leader, chief of staff, field marshal, president [➞ BUSINESS PEOPLE; 793]

cinch 1 *n* (*informal*) **snap**, child's play, piece of cake (*informal*), breeze (*informal*), walk in the park (*informal*), gift (*informal*), no-brainer (*slang*) [➞ EASY WORK; 299] 2 *n* (*informal*) **sure bet**, certainty, dead certainty, sure thing (*informal*) [➞ CERTAIN; 174] 3 *n* **girth**, restraint, belt, strap [➞ FASTENERS, LINKS, AND NETWORKS; 1247] 4 *v* **bind**, restrain, fix, tighten, gird (*literary*) [➞ FASTEN, LINK, AND JOIN; 408] 5 *v* (*dated informal*) **guarantee**, assure, insure, settle, make certain [➞ APPROVE AND CONFIRM; 646]

cinder block *n* [➞ BUILDING MATERIALS; 1077]

cinders *n* **embers**, ashes, residue, coals [➞ PRODUCTS OF FIRE; 1166]

cinema 1 *n* **movies**, motion pictures, film, pictures (*informal dated*) [➞ FILM; 901] 2 *n* (*UK*) [➞ BUILDINGS FOR PUBLIC ENTERTAINMENT; 1084]

cinematic *adj* **filmic**, photographic, movielike, filmmaking, moviemaking [➞ THE PERFORMING ARTS; 904]

cinematography *n* **photography**, shooting, film making, picture making, movie making, camera work [➞ FILM; 901]

cinnabar moth *type of* **moth** [➞ MOTHS AND BUTTERFLIES; 1015]

cinnamon *type of* **spice** [➞ HERBS AND SPICES; 1175]

cinquecento *type of* **pre-20th-century architecture** [➞ BUILDING AND ARCHITECTURE; 1076]

cipher 1 *n* **code**, secret message, symbols, cryptograph, encryption, cryptogram [➞ SYMBOLS, SIGNS, AND NUMBERS; 596] 2 *n* **nobody**, nonentity, nothing, zero [➞ NONE; 123]

circa *prep* **approximately**, about, around, roughly, round about, on or about [➞ APPROXIMATELY; 135] *Opposite*: exactly

circadian *adj* **daily**, 24-hour, 24-hourly, diurnal, day by day, day-to-day, everyday, quotidian (*formal*) [➞ TIMES OF DAY; 87]

circle 1 *n* **ring**, loop, round, sphere, disk, ball [➞ ROUNDED SHAPE; 1218] 2 *n* **group**, gang, set, clique, crowd [➞ FRIENDS AND

ACQUAINTANCES; 936] **3** *v* **go around**, orbit, fly around, fly in a circle, circumnavigate, revolve [➡ PROCEED AND GO; 305] **4** *v* **encircle**, surround, ring, enclose, bound, contain [➡ EXIST IN CLOSE PROXIMITY; 21]

circlet *n* **band**, coronet, tiara, diadem, crown, wreath [➡ ROUNDED SHAPE; 1218]

circuit 1 *n* **route**, track, trail, path [➡ ROADS; 1106] **2** *n* **tour**, trip, journey, route [➡ TRAVEL: JOURNEYS AND TRIPS; 318]

circuitous 1 *adj* **indirect**, winding, meandering, roundabout, twisting, tortuous, devious [➡ DIRECTION OF MOTION; 345] *Opposite*: direct **2** *adj* **complicated**, convoluted, discursive, tangential, long-winded [➡ INARTICULATE, RAMBLING, AND AWKWARD; 633] *Opposite*: straightforward

circuitously 1 *adv* **indirectly**, tortuously, in a roundabout way, obliquely, meanderingly, windingly, twistingly [➡ DIRECTION OF MOTION; 345] *Opposite*: directly **2** *adv* **complicatedly**, convolutedly, discursively, tangentially, long-windedly [➡ INARTICULATE, RAMBLING, AND AWKWARD; 633] *Opposite*: straightforwardly

circuitry *n* **electrical system**, electrical structure, electric circuit, circuit board, motherboard, printed circuit, integrated circuit [➡ PARTS OF MACHINES AND TOOLS; 1118]

circular 1 *adj* **spherical**, rounded, globular, round [➡ ROUNDED SHAPE; 1218] **2** *n* **leaflet**, flier, pamphlet, advertisement, handbill, handout, tract, brochure [➡ ADVERTISING AND PUBLICITY; 604]

circularity *n* **indirectness**, circuitousness, obliqueness, roundaboutness, convolutedness, tortuousness, complexity [➡ INARTICULATE, RAMBLING, AND AWKWARD; 633] *Opposite*: directness

circulate 1 *v* **pass around**, distribute, hand out, give out, send out, spread, issue, disseminate, make known [➡ INFORM, ANNOUNCE, AND ISSUE; 611] *Opposite*: conceal **2** *v* **flow**, move, travel, pass [➡ PROCEED AND GO; 305] **3** *v* (*informal*) **mingle**, socialize, mix, meet people, be sociable, network, party (*informal*) [➡ ESTABLISHING RELATIONSHIPS WITH OTHERS; 974]

circulation 1 *n* **flow**, movement, passage, motion, rotation [➡ SELF-PROPULSION; 304] **2** *n* **exchange**, flow, transmission, spread, dissemination [➡ SELF-PROPULSION; 304] **3** *n* **distribution**, readership, sales [➡ NEWSPAPERS AND MAGAZINES; 605]

circumference *n* **perimeter**, boundary, bounds, limits, edge, border, fringe [➡ EXTREMITIES OF PHYSICAL OBJECTS; 1250] *Opposite*: middle

circumflex *type of* **diacritic** [➡ ASPECTS OF LANGUAGE; 682]

circumlocution *n* **periphrasis**, indirectness, roundaboutness, long-windedness, convolutedness, obliqueness, circuitousness [➡ INARTICULATE, RAMBLING, AND AWKWARD; 633] *Opposite*: directness

circumlocutory *adj* **periphrastic**, indirect, meandering, roundabout, long-winded, circuitous, convoluted, oblique, tortuous [➡ INARTICULATE, RAMBLING, AND AWKWARD; 633] *Opposite*: direct

circumnavigate *v* **orbit**, circle, travel around, fly around, go around, fly round, sail around [➡ TRAVEL: WAYS OF TRAVELING; 320]

circumscribe (*formal*) *v* **limit**, restrict, define, demar-

cate, mark out, confine, delineate (*formal*) [➡ AVOID, PREVENT, LIMIT, AND CONTROL; 277]

circumscription (*formal*) *n* **restriction**, limit, limitation, constraint, restraint, curb [➡ REFUSE PERMISSION AND NOT ALLOW; 670] *Opposite*: freedom

circumspect *adj* **cautious**, prudent, careful, guarded, wary, judicious, chary, cagey (*informal*) [➡ INSECURITY AND LOSS OF COMPOSURE; 544] *Opposite*: reckless

See Compare and Contrast at **cautious**.

circumspection *n* **care**, carefulness, caution, cautiousness, judiciousness, guardedness, wariness, chariness, prudence, caginess (*informal*) [➡ INSECURITY AND LOSS OF COMPOSURE; 544] *Opposite*: recklessness

circumstance 1 *n* **condition**, situation, state of affairs, status quo, context [➡ SITUATIONS; 71] **2** *n* (*formal*) **event**, occurrence, incident, instance, happening, episode, case [➡ EVENTS AND OCCURRENCES; 35]

circumstantial *adj* **incidental**, contingent, indirect, inferred, conditional, anecdotal, secondary [➡ UNCERTAIN; 175] *Opposite*: concrete

circumvent *v* **avoid**, get around, evade, skirt, dodge, sidestep, bypass, get out of, elude [➡ NOT PAY ATTENTION; 764]

circumvention *n* **avoidance**, evasion, escape, sidestepping, dodging, bypassing, eluding [➡ NOT PAY ATTENTION; 764]

circus 1 *n* [➡ BUILDINGS FOR PUBLIC ENTERTAINMENT; 1084] **2** *n* (*informal*) **show**, festival, spectacle, extravaganza, event, revel [➡ PERFORMANCES AND SHOWS; 42]

cirque *n* **combe**, hollow, valley, glaciated valley, cwm (*UK*), corrie (*UK*) [➡ GEOLOGIC FEATURES; 1056]

cirrocumulus *type of* **cloud** [➡ CLOUDY AND RAINY WEATHER; 1052]

cirrus *type of* **cloud** [➡ CLOUDY AND RAINY WEATHER; 1052]

cistern *n* **water tank**, storage tank, tank, reservoir, container, boiler, underground tank, hot water tank [➡ CONTAINERS, RECEPTACLES, AND PACKAGING; 1245]

citadel *n* **fortress**, stronghold, bastion, fort, castle, refuge, sanctuary [➡ FORTRESSES AND FORTIFICATIONS; 1090]

citation *n* **quotation**, quote, mention, reference, excerpt, extract, illustration [➡ SUMMARIES, OUTLINES, AND EXCERPTS; 588]

cite (*formal*) *v* **quote**, mention, refer to, allude to [➡ RECITE, REPEAT, AND NARRATE; 620]

citified *adj* **oversophisticated**, sophisticated, cosmopolitan, slick, suave, urbane [➡ LEVELS OF EDUCATION AND SOPHISTICATION; 894] *Opposite*: countrified

citizen *n* **inhabitant**, national, resident, legal resident, voter, naturalized citizen, native [➡ INHABITANTS; 857]

citizenry *n* **people**, community, public, electorate, voters, population, populace, general public [➡ GROUPS IN SOCIETY; 940]

citizenship 1 *n* **nationality**, residency, right of abode (*UK*) [➡ STATUS; 888] **2** *n* **social responsibility**, public spirit, social conscience, civic duty [➡ MORALLY GOOD; 774]

citrine *type of* **yellow** [➡COLORS; 1224]

citron 1 *type of* **citrus fruit** [➡FRUIT AND VEGETABLES; 1176] **2** *type of* **yellow** [➡COLORS; 1224]

citrus *type of* **fruit** [➡FRUIT AND VEGETABLES; 1176]

citrus

◆ *types of citrus fruit*
blood orange, citron, clementine, grapefruit, lemon, lime, mandarin, orange, ortanique, pomelo, satsuma, tangerine

city 1 *n* **metropolis**, municipality, conurbation, capital, town [➡HUMAN SETTLEMENTS; 1070] **2** *adj* **urban**, metropolitan, town, municipal [➡HUMAN SETTLEMENTS; 1070]

Compare and Contrast: *city, conurbation, metropolis, town, municipality*

CORE MEANING: an urban area where a large number of people live

city a large municipal center governed under a charter granted by the state; in the United Kingdom, a town having a cathedral or having such a status conferred on it by the Crown; in Canada, a large municipal unit incorporated by the provincial government, but now used generally for any large urban area; *conurbation* an urban region formed or enlarged by the merging of adjacent cities and towns through expansion or development; *metropolis* a large or important city, sometimes the capital of a country, state, or region; *town* a populated area smaller than a city and larger than a village; *municipality* a city, town, or area with some degree of self-government.

city dweller *n* **urbanite**, townie (*informal*) [➡INHABITANTS; 857]

city-state *n* [➡COUNTRIES AND REGIONS; 1067]

civic *adj* **public**, municipal, local, community, town, city, civil [➡HUMAN SETTLEMENTS; 1070] *Opposite*: private

civil 1 *adj* **public**, political, municipal, civic, civilian, domestic, interior [➡BELONGING OR RELATING TO PEOPLE; 943] **2** *adj* **courteous**, polite, respectful, well-mannered, accommodating, obliging, gracious, considerate, amicable [➡GOOD MANNERS AND SOCIAL SKILLS; 520] *Opposite*: rude

civilian *n* **noncombatant**, private citizen, citizen, member of the public, neutral [➡PERSON; 931]

civilian clothes *n* [➡GARMENTS AND OUTFITS; 865]

civility *n* **politeness**, courtesy, good manners, courteousness, respect, graciousness, consideration [➡GOOD MANNERS AND SOCIAL SKILLS; 520] *Opposite*: rudeness

civilization 1 *n* **society**, nation, culture, empire, polity [➡GROUPS IN SOCIETY; 940] **2** *n* **development**, evolution, progress, cultivation, refinement, sophistication, advancement [➡LEVELS OF EDUCATION AND SOPHISTICATION; 894]

civilize *v* **enlighten**, educate, cultivate, improve, advance, develop, refine, humanize [➡IMPROVE SOMETHING; 374]

civilized *adj* **cultured**, educated, refined, enlightened, polite, elegant, urbane [➡GOOD MANNERS AND SOCIAL SKILLS; 520] *Opposite*: barbarous

civilizing *adj* **humanizing**, taming, educating, cultivating, refining, enlightening [➡MORALLY GOOD; 774]

civil liberties *n* **privileges**, freedoms, rights, human rights, civil rights, constitutional rights [➡THE LAW AND LEGAL AUTHORITY; 814]

civilly *adv* **politely**, respectfully, courteously, amicably, considerately, graciously [➡GOOD MANNERS AND SOCIAL SKILLS; 520] *Opposite*: rudely

civil rights *n* **human rights**, rights, constitutional rights, civil liberties, privileges, freedoms [➡THE LAW AND LEGAL AUTHORITY; 814]

civil servant *n* **public servant**, government employee, bureaucrat, official, administrator [➡ADMINISTRATIVE OFFICERS; 811]

civvies (*informal*) *n* [➡GARMENTS AND OUTFITS; 865]

clack *v* **snap**, click, clap, bang, rap, smack, clatter [➡EMIT SOUNDS THROUGH IMPACT AND ABRASION; 365]

clad *adj* **dressed**, clothed, covered, attired (*formal*), arrayed (*literary*) [➡DRESS, WEAR, AND UNDRESS; 868]

cladding *n* **covering**, layer, facing, casing, shell, shield [➡COVERS AND COATINGS; 1246]

clafoutis *type of* **dessert** [➡CAKES, COOKIES, AND DESSERTS; 1181]

claim 1 *v* **maintain**, assert, say, state, declare, argue, allege, profess, aver (*formal*) [➡CLAIM, INSIST, AND EMPHASIZE; 614] **2** *v* **ask for**, call for, demand, apply for, request, appeal, sue [➡REQUEST AND DEMAND; 663] *Opposite*: deny **3** *v* **receive**, obtain, take, pick up, retrieve, collect [➡GET MONEY OR REWARD; 421] **4** *n* **assertion**, statement, accusation, declaration, allegation, contention [➡CLAIM, INSIST, AND EMPHASIZE; 614] **5** *n* **demand**, request, application, petition, call [➡REQUEST AND DEMAND; 663] **6** *n* **right**, entitlement, prerogative, privilege, due, title [➡POSSESS; 444]

claimant *n* **applicant**, plaintiff, pretender, petitioner, appellant, suitor, supplicant (*formal*) [➡PEOPLE WHO MAKE REQUESTS; 664]

clairvoyance *n* **psychic power**, telepathy, prophecy, fortune telling, palm reading, astrology, soothsaying, augury, second sight, extrasensory perception, ESP, sixth sense, divining [➡THE SUPERNATURAL; 787]

clairvoyant 1 *n* **psychic**, mystic, spiritualist, telepathist, diviner, seer, mind reader, medium [➡PEOPLE WITH SUPERNATURAL POWERS; 788] **2** *adj* **intuitive**, psychic, telepathic, second-sighted, perceptive, farsighted [➡THE SUPERNATURAL; 787]

clam *type of* **aquatic invertebrate** [➡AQUATIC INVERTEBRATES; 1022]

clambake *type of* **meal** [➡MEALS AND PARTS OF MEALS; 1169]

clamber *v* **climb**, scramble, crawl, scale [➡GO UPWARD; 306]

clam diggers *type of* **pants** [➡GARMENTS AND OUTFITS; 865]

clamminess 1 *n* **dampness**, wetness, moistness, dankness, sliminess [➡PHYSICAL TEXTURE; 1222] *Opposite*: dryness **2** *n* **humidity**, mugginess, closeness, heat, airlessness, stuffiness, dampness, stickiness, moistness [➡HOT WEATHER; 1050] *Opposite*: dryness

clammy 1 *adj* **damp**, wet, moist, dank, slimy [➠MOIST; 1241] *Opposite*: dry 2 *adj* **humid**, muggy, close, sticky, sweaty [➠HOT WEATHER; 1050] *Opposite*: dry

clamor 1 *v* **shout**, scream, yell, cry, screech, bellow, bawl, holler (*informal*) [➠SOUND EMISSION BY PEOPLE; 363] *Opposite*: whisper 2 *v* **demand**, insist, appeal, cry out, bay, call out [➠REQUEST AND DEMAND; 663] 3 *n* **appeal**, demand, call, request, cry, outcry [➠REQUEST AND DEMAND; 663] 4 *n* **uproar**, din, commotion, racket, noise, shouting, outcry, agitation, hubbub, hullabaloo [➠CHAOS AND UPROAR; 51] *Opposite*: quiet

clamorous *adj* **noisy**, vociferous, loud, rowdy, boisterous, deafening, riotous, raucous [➠LOUD, HIGH, OR UNPLEASANT SOUNDS; 1266] *Opposite*: tranquil

clamp *v* **fasten**, hold, compress, fix, brace, clinch, close, make fast [➠FASTEN, LINK, AND JOIN; 408]

clamp down *v* **shut down**, take tough action, come down hard, restrict, limit, curb, crack down (*informal*) [➠AVOID, PREVENT, LIMIT, AND CONTROL; 277] *Opposite*: relent

clampdown *n* **crackdown**, restriction, curb, suppression, embargo, shutdown, squelching (*slang*) [➠ENDS AND DEPARTURES; 54]

clam up (*informal*) *v* **stop talking**, choke, refuse to speak, remain silent, be unforthcoming, be unwilling to talk, withhold information, dry up (*informal*), shut up (*informal*) [➠WITHHOLD INFORMATION; 687]

clan 1 *n* **tribe**, family, relations, relatives, kinfolk, kin [➠THE FAMILY; 956] 2 *n* (*informal*) **clique**, fraternity, band, coterie, set, circle, in-group [➠FRIENDS AND ACQUAINTANCES; 936]

clandestine *adj* **secret**, underground, covert, concealed, stealthy, furtive, undercover, surreptitious, illegal [➠SECRET AND UNKNOWN; 179] *Opposite*: open

See Compare and Contrast at **secret**.

clang 1 *v* **clank**, sound, toll, ring, reverberate, resound, clink, chime, jangle, jingle [➠EMIT SOUNDS THROUGH IMPACT AND ABRASION; 365] 2 *n* **clank**, ring, bang, clink, jangle, ding-dong, knell, clangor [➠IMPACT SOUNDS; 1260]

clanging *adj* [➠LOUD, HIGH, OR UNPLEASANT SOUNDS; 1266]

clank *n* **clang**, clink, clatter, clash, bang, crash, jangle, clangor [➠IMPACT SOUNDS; 1260]

clannish *adj* **cliquey**, cliquish, unfriendly, unsociable, aloof, exclusive, exclusionary, insular, narrow, parochial [➠UNFRIENDLINESS AND UNSOCIABILITY; 504] *Opposite*: open

clap 1 *v* **applaud**, give a standing ovation, put your hands together, give a round of applause, acclaim, cheer [➠APPLAUSE; 652] *Opposite*: boo 2 *n* **slap**, pat, tap, thrust, thwack, wallop (*informal*) [➠IMPACT SOUNDS; 1260]

clapboard *n* [➠BUILDING MATERIALS; 1077]

clapping *n* **applause**, appreciation, ovation, acclamation, acclaim, support [➠APPLAUSE; 652] *Opposite*: jeering

claptrap (*informal*) *n* **nonsense**, humbug, drivel, hogwash (*informal*), twaddle (*informal*), rot (*informal*), bunkum (*informal*), rubbish (*UK*) [➠MEANINGLESS SPEECH OR WRITING; 676] *Opposite*: sense

claret *type of* **red** [➠COLORS; 1224]

clarification *n* **explanation**, amplification, illumination, clearing up, explaining, interpretation, elucidation (*formal*) [➠EXPLAIN AND CLARIFY; 610] *Opposite*: obfuscation

clarify 1 *v* **elucidate**, make clear, explain, clear up, illuminate, interpret, spell out, amplify on, simplify, shed light on [➠EXPLAIN AND CLARIFY; 610] *Opposite*: confuse 2 *v* **refine**, purify, cleanse, filter, process [➠CLEAN AND POLISH; 403] *Opposite*: cloud

clarinet *type of* **wind instrument** [➠MUSICAL INSTRUMENTS; 910]

clarity *n* **clearness**, lucidity, simplicity, precision, intelligibility, transparency [➠CONCISE AND CLEAR; 202] *Opposite*: ambiguity

clash 1 *v* **fight**, conflict, disagree, quarrel, collide, come to blows, be at odds, spar, argue, row, skirmish [➠ARGUE AND FIGHT; 643] *Opposite*: agree 2 *v* **clatter**, clank, clang, crash, bang, jar [➠EMIT SOUNDS THROUGH IMPACT AND ABRASION; 365] 3 *v* **conflict**, mismatch, jar, contravene [➠DISHARMONY; 156] *Opposite*: match 4 *n* **clank**, clatter, clang, crash, bang, smash [➠IMPACT SOUNDS; 1260] 5 *n* **battle**, conflict, disagreement, collision, quarrel, argument, row, brush, fight, skirmish [➠ARGUMENTS; 47] *Opposite*: agreement

See Compare and Contrast at **fight**.

clashing *adj* **inharmonious**, conflicting, jarring, incompatible, nonmatching, mismatched [➠DIFFERENCE; 149] *Opposite*: compatible

clasp 1 *v* **grasp**, hold, clutch, embrace, hug, clinch, grip, fasten [➠CONTACT: HOLD; 411] *Opposite*: release 2 *n* **fastener**, hook, catch, hook and eye, snap, fastening, clip, popper (*UK*), press stud (*UK*) [➠FASTENERS, LINKS, AND NETWORKS; 1247]

clasp knife *type of* **knife** [➠CUTTING TOOLS; 1120]

class 1 *n* **group**, set, tutorial group, course group, tutor group (*UK*) [➠STUDENTS AND PUPILS; 841] 2 *n* **lesson**, period, session, lecture, seminar, course, tutorial, discussion [➠CLASSES, COURSEWORK, AND EXAMINATIONS; 842] 3 *n* **division**, category, rank, order, group, grade, caste, status, genre, classification [➠VARIETIES, TYPES, AND KINDS; 145] 4 *n* **refinement**, sophistication, elegance, style, flair, panache, taste, chic [➠GOOD MANNERS AND SOCIAL SKILLS; 520] *Opposite*: tackiness (*informal*) 5 *v* **categorize**, classify, rank, assign, group, grade, brand, arrange, pigeonhole [➠ARRANGE AND CREATE ORDER; 357]

See Compare and Contrast at **type**.

class-conscious *adj* **snobbish**, classist, elitist, stuck-up (*informal*) [➠NEGATIVE INTELLECTUAL CHARACTERISTICS; 525] *Opposite*: egalitarian

classic 1 *adj* **timeless**, immortal, unforgettable, memorable, abiding, lasting, ageless [➠PERMANENCE: WITHOUT END; 94] 2 *adj* **definitive**, typical, characteristic, standard, model, usual, common, archetypal, traditional [➠REPRESENTATIVE; 66] *Opposite*: atypical 3 *adj* **simple**, stylish, elegant, chic, understated, restrained [➠EASE AND SIMPLICITY; 200] 4 *n* **masterpiece**, landmark, benchmark, model, masterwork, prototype [➠PERFECT EXAMPLES AND EMBODIMENTS; 67]

classical 1 *adj* **traditional**, conventional, orthodox, usual, typical, established, old [➠REPRESENTATIVE; 66] *Opposite*:

modern **2** *type of* **pre-20th-century architecture** [➠ BUILDING AND ARCHITECTURE; 1076]

classicism *type of* **pre-20th-century art movement** [➠ ARTISTIC MOVEMENTS AND STYLES; 899]

classification **1** *n* **organization**, cataloging, arrangement, sorting, ordering, triage, grouping, taxonomy, categorization [➠ VARIETIES, TYPES, AND KINDS; 145] **2** *n* **category**, class, group, grouping, set, ranking, division [➠ COLLECTIONS AND MIXTURES OF THINGS; 1244]

classified *adj* **secret**, confidential, top secret, off the record, hush-hush (*informal*) [➠ SECRET AND UNKNOWN; 179] *Opposite*: open

classify *v* **categorize**, order, organize, pigeonhole, catalog, grade, class, arrange, sort, group, rank, brand [➠ ARRANGE AND CREATE ORDER; 357]

classiness (*informal*) *n* **refinement**, sophistication, elegance, stylishness, class, exclusiveness, exclusivity, urbanity, chic [➠ GOOD MANNERS AND SOCIAL SKILLS; 520] *Opposite*: tackiness (*informal*)

classless *adj* **egalitarian**, meritocratic, equal, open, free, unrestricted [➠ FREEDOM AND LIBERTY; 208] *Opposite*: class-conscious

classmate *n* **fellow student**, fellow pupil, contemporary, peer [➠ STUDENTS AND PUPILS; 841]

classroom *n* **schoolroom**, teaching space, seminar room, tutorial room, lecture theater, lecture hall, laboratory, language laboratory [➠ TYPES OF ROOMS; 1097]

classy (*informal*) *adj* **refined**, sophisticated, elegant, stylish, chic, fashionable, tasteful, exclusive, upmarket, upscale [➠ LEVELS OF EDUCATION AND SOPHISTICATION; 894] *Opposite*: tacky (*informal*)

clatter **1** *v* **rattle**, bang, clang, smash, clank, jangle, clash [➠ EMIT SOUNDS THROUGH IMPACT AND ABRASION; 365] **2** *n* **clang**, rattle, bang, jangle, clank, clash, racket [➠ IMPACT SOUNDS; 1260]

clause **1** *n* **section**, article, part, division, passage, item [➠ SUMMARIES, OUTLINES, AND EXCERPTS; 588] **2** *type of* **grammatical term** [➠ ASPECTS OF LANGUAGE; 682]

claustrophobia *type of* **phobia** [➠ FEARS AND PHOBIAS; 554]

claustrophobic *adj* **enclosed**, confining, oppressive, suffocating, stifling, restricting, restricted, shut in [➠ PHYSICALLY UNPLEASANT; 226]

clavichord *type of* **keyboard** [➠ MUSICAL INSTRUMENTS; 910]

clavicle *type of* **bone** [➠ THE BONES AND JOINTS; 719]

claw **1** *v* **scrape**, scratch, scrabble, tear, graze, pierce [➠ CONTACT: TOUCH; 412] **2** *n* **talon**, nail, hook [➠ PARTS OF THE BODY: ARM AND HAND; 695]

claw back *v* **recover**, regain, recoup, retrieve [➠ REGAIN POSSESSION; 429] *Opposite*: lose

clay **1** *n* **soil**, earth, dirt, mud [➠ EROSION PRODUCTS AND SOIL; 1058] **2** *type of* **mineral** [➠ MINERALS; 1277]

claymore *type of* **sword or knife** [➠ SWORDS AND KNIVES; 1157]

clean **1** *adj* **spotless**, dirt-free, unsoiled, fresh, sparkling, squeaky-clean, hygienic, sanitary, uncontaminated,

unpolluted, sterile [➠ CLEAN AND HYGIENIC; 1233] *Opposite*: dirty **2** *adj* **pure**, wholesome, untainted, unadulterated, unpolluted [➠ MORALLY GOOD; 774] *Opposite*: impure **3** *adj* **neat**, tidy, orderly, shipshape, immaculate, spick-and-span [➠ ORDER AND ORGANIZATION; 206] *Opposite*: slovenly **4** *v* **scrub**, scour, wipe, cleanse, dust, vacuum, launder, mop, polish [➠ CLEAN AND POLISH; 403] *Opposite*: soil

clean as a new pin *adj* [➠ CLEAN AND HYGIENIC; 1233]

clean-cut *adj* **neat**, well-groomed, tidy, smart, presentable, sharp, well turned-out (*UK*) [➠ WELL-GROOMED; 482] *Opposite*: untidy

cleaned out (*informal*) *adj* **ruined**, penniless, out of cash, bankrupt, finished [➠ POVERTY AND POOR; 892]

cleaner **1** *n* **domestic**, domestic worker, help, home help (*UK*), char (*UK*) [➠ DOMESTIC AND KITCHEN WORKERS; 850] **2** *n* **cleaning product**, detergent, stain remover, cleanser, soap, disinfectant, antiseptic, bleach, antibacterial cleaner, laundry detergent, washing-up liquid (*UK*) [➠ CLEANING AGENTS; 863]

cleaning *n* **housework**, spring-cleaning, scrubbing, dusting, washing, vacuuming [➠ CLEAN AND POLISH; 403]

cleanliness *n* **hygiene**, sanitation, purity, spotlessness [➠ CLEAN AND HYGIENIC; 1233] *Opposite*: uncleanliness

clean-living *adj* **abstemious**, teetotal, moderate, wholesome [➠ SELF-DENIAL; 882]

cleanly *adv* **easily**, efficiently, effectively, neatly, simply, quickly [➠ MOVING QUICKLY; 103]

cleanness *n* **purity**, freshness, simplicity, clearness, neatness, order [➠ CLEAN AND HYGIENIC; 1233] *Opposite*: impurity

clean out **1** *v* (*informal*) **bankrupt**, impoverish, reduce, drain, bleed dry (*informal*) [➠ TAKE SOMETHING AWAY; 425] **2** *v* **unclog**, flush, clear, clean, wash out, clean off, sluice down, unblock [➠ EMPTY AND UNLOAD; 407] *Opposite*: block up

cleanse *v* **rinse**, clean, rinse out, bathe, purify [➠ CLEAN AND POLISH; 403] *Opposite*: soil

cleanser **1** *n* **cleaner**, cleaning product, detergent, stain remover, soap, disinfectant, antiseptic [➠ CLEANING AGENTS; 863] **2** *n* **makeup remover**, cleansing cream, lotion, cream, cold cream, face wash [➠ MAKEUP AND BEAUTY PRODUCTS; 490]

clean-shaven *adj* **shaved**, smooth, smooth-shaven, hairless [➠ FACIAL HAIR; 489] *Opposite*: bearded

cleansing *n* **cleaning**, washing, scrubbing, bathing, rinsing, flushing, disinfection, sanitization, purification [➠ CLEAN AND POLISH; 403]

clean up **1** *v* **smarten**, spruce up, tidy up, sanitize, clear up, mop up, blitz (*informal*) [➠ CLEAN AND POLISH; 403] **2** *v* **wipe out**, eradicate, eliminate, get rid of, do away with [➠ GET RID OF SOMETHING; 451] **3** *v* (*slang*) **make a fortune**, hit the jackpot, strike it rich, be laughing all the way to the bank, make a mint (*informal*), make a pile (*informal*) [➠ GET MONEY OR REWARD; 421]

cleanup *n* **crackdown**, clampdown, elimination, onslaught, attack, offensive [➠ ENDS AND DEPARTURES; 54]

clear **1** *adj* **transparent**, translucent, see-through, sheer, filmy, limpid, pellucid (*literary*) [➠ VISUAL TEXTURE; 1221] *Oppo-*

site: opaque **2** *adj* **strong**, rich, pure, vibrant [➡ STRENGTH; 201] *Opposite*: indistinct **3** *adj* **unblemished**, perfect, pure, flawless, faultless [➡ COMPLEXION; 480] **4** *adj* **well-defined**, sharp, distinct, clear-cut [➡ PERCEPTIBLE; 25] *Opposite*: indistinct **5** *adj* **ringing**, pure, bell-like, resounding [➡ SOFT, LOW, OR PLEASANT SOUNDS; 1265] *Opposite*: muffled **6** *adj* **sure**, positive, obvious, evident, certain [➡ CERTAIN; 174] *Opposite*: unclear **7** *adj* **obvious**, apparent, understandable, comprehensible, lucid, patent, plain, unambiguous, unmistakable, evident, apprehensible (*formal*) [➡ CONCISE AND CLEAR; 202] *Opposite*: unclear **8** *adj* **unobstructed**, empty, free, free-flowing, open, unencumbered, uncluttered, unhampered [➡ EMPTY; 1238] *Opposite*: blocked **9** *adj* **cloudless**, bright, sunny, fine, fair, sunshiny, unclouded [➡ HOT WEATHER; 1050] *Opposite*: cloudy **10** *v* **tidy**, clear out, empty, straighten, clean up [➡ ARRANGE AND CREATE ORDER; 357] **11** *v* **free**, vindicate, exonerate, absolve, acquit, release, discharge, exculpate (*formal*) [➡ FREEDOM AND LIBERTY; 208] **12** *v* **evaporate**, dissipate, disperse, disappear, settle [➡ DISAPPEAR; 4] *Opposite*: form **13** *v* **unblock**, free, unclutter, unclog, empty [➡ EMPTY AND UNLOAD; 407] *Opposite*: block **14** *v* (*informal*) **net**, earn, gain, take home, make, bring in [➡ GET MONEY OR REWARD; 421] *Opposite*: lose

clearance *n* **permission**, authorization, consent, approval, green light, sanction, go-ahead (*informal*), okay (*informal*) [➡ PERMIT AND ALLOW; 669] *Opposite*: prohibition

clear-cut *adj* **precise**, unambiguous, definite, clear, straightforward, specific, black-and-white [➡ CONCISE AND CLEAR; 202] *Opposite*: ambiguous

clear-headed *adj* **lucid**, alert, coherent, perceptive, decisive, logical, realistic, sensible [➡ POSITIVE INTELLECTUAL CHARACTERISTICS; 524] *Opposite*: muddled

clearing *n* **glade**, clearance, clear-cut, dell (*literary*) [➡ THE COUNTRYSIDE AND OUTDOOR SPACES; 1071]

clearly *adv* **obviously**, evidently, undoubtedly, plainly, visibly, unmistakably, noticeably, openly, distinctly, patently, unambiguously, without a doubt [➡ CERTAIN; 174] *Opposite*: ambiguously

clearness **1** *n* **translucency**, transparency, flawlessness, luminousness, limpidity [➡ VISUAL TEXTURE; 1221] *Opposite*: opacity **2** *n* **directness**, unambiguousness, clarity, lucidity, comprehensibility, plainness [➡ CONCISE AND CLEAR; 202] *Opposite*: vagueness **3** *n* **emptiness**, cleanness, unclutteredness, uncrowdedness [➡ EMPTY; 1238] *Opposite*: clutter

clear out **1** *v* **leave**, depart, get going, head off, be off, push off (*informal*) [➡ LEAVE AND GO AWAY; 8] **2** *v* **empty**, clear, clean up, turn out, throw out, clean out (*informal*), chuck out (*informal*) [➡ EMPTY AND UNLOAD; 407]

clear-sighted *adj* **perceptive**, insightful, percipient, realistic, sensible, practical, wise, clear-eyed, discerning [➡ POSITIVE INTELLECTUAL CHARACTERISTICS; 524] *Opposite*: confused

clear-thinking *adj* [➡ POSITIVE INTELLECTUAL CHARACTERISTICS; 524]

clear up **1** *v* **straighten**, clear, clean up, tidy, put away, arrange [➡ ARRANGE AND CREATE ORDER; 357] **2** *v* **resolve**, solve, clarify, explain, settle, sort out, get to the bottom of, illuminate, decipher [➡ EXPLAIN AND CLARIFY; 610] *Opposite*: complicate

clearwing *type of* **moth** [➡ MOTHS AND BUTTERFLIES; 1015]

cleave **1** *v* **slice**, cut, slash, hew, chop, sever, split,

sunder (*literary*), smite (*archaic or literary*) [➡ TEAR, BREAK, AND CUT; 360] *Opposite*: join **2** *v* (*literary*) **stick**, hold on, stick to like glue, cling, link, embrace, conjoin (*formal*) [➡ CONTACT: HOLD; 411] *Opposite*: separate

cleaver *type of* **knife** [➡ CUTTING TOOLS; 1120]

cleft *n* **fissure**, crevice, crack, gap, split, break, chimney [➡ HOLES, GAPS, AND FORKS; 1252]

clematis *type of* **climber** [➡ CLIMBERS; 1033]

clemency *n* **mercy**, leniency, forgiveness, pity, compassion, kindness, moderation [➡ MORALLY GOOD; 774] *Opposite*: heartlessness

clement *adj* **mild**, moderate, temperate, balmy, pleasant, warm, gentle [➡ HOT WEATHER; 1050] *Opposite*: inclement

clementine *type of* **citrus fruit** [➡ FRUIT AND VEGETABLES; 1176]

clench *v* **compress**, grit, tighten, clasp, scrunch, clamp [➡ CONTACT: EXERT PRESSURE; 414] *Opposite*: relax

clerestory *n* [➡ PARTS OF RELIGIOUS BUILDINGS; 1086]

clergy *n* **priesthood**, ministry, ordained priests, clerics [➡ RELIGIOUS PEOPLE; 778] *Opposite*: laity

clergyman *n* [➡ RELIGIOUS PEOPLE; 778]

clergywoman *n* [➡ RELIGIOUS PEOPLE; 778]

cleric *n* **priest**, minister, ecclesiastic [➡ RELIGIOUS PEOPLE; 778]

clerical **1** *adj* **secretarial**, office, bookkeeping, accounting [➡ TYPES OF WORK; 835] **2** *adj* **priestly**, religious, ecclesiastical, church [➡ RELIGIOUS CONCEPTS; 776]

clerical worker *n* [➡ OFFICE WORKERS; 847]

clerk **1** *n* **office worker**, counter clerk, bank clerk, accounts clerk, worker, assistant, salesclerk, deskclerk, receptionist [➡ OFFICE WORKERS; 847] **2** *n* **administrator**, official, recorder, clerk to the council, clerk to the governors [➡ OFFICE WORKERS; 847]

clever **1** *adj* **ingenious**, shrewd, astute, adroit, crafty, wily, cunning, knowing [➡ POSITIVE INTELLECTUAL CHARACTERISTICS; 524] *Opposite*: inept **2** *adj* **skillful**, quick, adroit, gifted, dexterous, adept, able [➡ TALENTED AND SKILLFUL; 527] *Opposite*: clumsy **3** *adj* **bright**, intelligent, smart, knowledgeable, intellectual, quick, alert, brainy (*informal*), on the ball (*informal*) [➡ POSITIVE INTELLECTUAL CHARACTERISTICS; 524] *Opposite*: foolish **4** *adj* **glib**, smart, slick, pert, flippant, superficial, pat [➡ UNINTERESTED AND DETACHED; 629] **5** *adj* (*UK*) **useful**, handy, convenient, ingenious, effective, neat, nifty (*informal*) [➡ USEFULNESS; 199] *Opposite*: useless

See Compare and Contrast at **intelligent**.

cleverly *adv* **ingeniously**, shrewdly, smartly, skillfully, expertly [➡ POSITIVE INTELLECTUAL CHARACTERISTICS; 524] *Opposite*: ineptly

cleverness *n* **skill**, ingenuity, quickness, shrewdness, talent, expertise, adeptness, dexterity, smartness, intelligence [➡ POSITIVE INTELLECTUAL CHARACTERISTICS; 524] *Opposite*: ineptness

cliché *n* **truism**, formula, line, platitude, prosaism, saying, saw, adage, chestnut (*informal*) [➡ FIGURES OF SPEECH; 673]

clichéd *adj* **corny**, hackneyed, trite, passé, old, stereotypical, unoriginal, timeworn, dull, overused, lifeless, unimaginative [➡ BORING AND UNINTERESTING; 234] *Opposite:* original

cliché-ridden *adj* [➡ BORING AND UNINTERESTING; 234]

click 1 *n* **clack**, tick, snap, clunk [➡ IMPACT SOUNDS; 1260] 2 *v* **snap**, tick, clack, clunk [➡ EMIT SOUNDS THROUGH IMPACT AND ABRASION; 365] 3 *v* (*informal*) **make sense**, sink in, become clear, fall into place [➡ UNDERSTAND AND GRASP; 759] 4 *v* (*informal*) **connect**, relate to, be on the same wavelength, hit it off (*informal*), get on (*UK*) [➡ ESTABLISHING RELATIONSHIPS WITH OTHERS; 974] *Opposite:* clash

click rate *n* [➡ THE INTERNET; 1128]

clicks-and-mortar *adj* [➡ E-COMMERCE; 1129]

client *n* **customer**, shopper, consumer, user, end user, buyer, purchaser, patron, regular [➡ BUSINESS ACTIVITIES AND PHENOMENA; 794]

clientele *n* **customers**, clients, regulars, patrons, custom, consumers, trade, business, footfall, following [➡ BUSINESS ACTIVITIES AND PHENOMENA; 794]

cliff *n* **precipice**, rock face, face, crag, overhang, bluff, escarpment [➡ MOUNTAINS AND HILLS; 1044]

cliffhanger *n* **crisis**, tiebreaker, knife-edge, nailbiter (*informal*) [➡ DECISIVE MOMENTS; 44]

climate 1 *n* **weather**, temperature, environment, microclimate, macroclimate, climatic zone [➡ WEATHER AND CLIMATE; 1049] 2 *n* **atmosphere**, situation, ambiance, surroundings, environment, conditions, feeling, mood, sense [➡ SITUATIONS; 71]

climate change *n* [➡ WEATHER AND CLIMATE; 1049]

climatic *adj* [➡ WEATHER AND CLIMATE; 1049]

climatology *n* [➡ WEATHER AND CLIMATE; 1049]

climax *n* **peak**, high point, pinnacle, culmination, height, highlight, apex, acme, summit, apogee [➡ DECISIVE MOMENTS; 44]

climb 1 *v* **scale**, go up, move up, mount, ascend, clamber, scramble, scrabble [➡ GO UPWARD; 306] *Opposite:* descend 2 *v* **rise**, soar, go up, rocket, escalate, shoot up, increase, sky-rocket (*informal*) [➡ CHANGE OF SIZE: BIGGER; 392] *Opposite:* descend 3 *n* **ascent**, scramble [➡ GO UPWARD; 306] *Opposite:* descent 4 *n* **increase**, rise, upswing, hike [➡ CHANGE OF INTENSITY: MORE; 394] *Opposite:* fall

climb down 1 *v* **back down**, retreat, make concessions, give way, backpedal, eat humble pie, eat your words (*informal*), eat crow (*informal*) [➡ APOLOGIZE AND RETRACT; 683] *Opposite:* stand your ground 2 *v* **descend**, go down, get down, come down, dismount [➡ GO DOWNWARD; 307] *Opposite:* ascend

climbdown *n* **change of mind**, concession, U-turn, shift, retreat, change of heart [➡ DECISIVE MOMENTS; 44]

climber 1 *n* **mountaineer**, rock climber, alpinist, hiker,

walker, rambler, backpacker [➡ PEOPLE IN SPORTS AND LEISURE; 876] 2 *n* **climbing plant**, trailer, creeper, vine [➡ CLIMBERS; 1033]

climber

◆ *types of climbers*

bougainvillea, bryony, clematis, convolvulus, grapevine, honeysuckle, ivy, jasmine, kudzu, liana, morning glory, passionflower, rattan, sarsaparilla, Virginia creeper, wisteria, woodbine

climbing *n* **mountaineering**, hiking, alpinism, rock climbing, artificial climbing, free climbing, bouldering, mountain climbing, hillwalking (*UK*) [➡ HOBBIES, GAMES, AND SPORTS; 875]

clime (*literary*) *n* **climate**, weather, zone, region, place, country [➡ WEATHER AND CLIMATE; 1049]

clinch 1 *v* **settle**, seal, close, tie up, decide, finalize, determine, resolve, wrap up (*informal*) [➡ APPROVE AND CONFIRM; 646] 2 *n* **embrace**, hug, hold, bear hug, cuddle, squeeze [➡ CONTACT: HOLD; 411]

cling 1 *v* **clutch**, grasp, hug, hang on to, hold, embrace [➡ CONTACT: HOLD; 411] *Opposite:* let go 2 *v* **adhere**, grip, stick, hug, fit tightly, hang, cohere (*formal*), cleave (*literary*) [➡ EXIST IN A PLACE; 19] 3 *v* **retain**, maintain, hold to, keep to [➡ STORE AND KEEP; 453] *Opposite:* give up 4 *v* **be dependent on**, depend on, hang on, attach, latch onto (*informal*) [➡ DESIRE AND WANT; 579]

clingy 1 *adj* **dependent**, insecure, anxious, clinging [➡ UNCERTAINTY; 559] *Opposite:* independent 2 *adj* (*informal*) **clinging**, figure-hugging, tight-fitting, snug, close-fitting [➡ DESCRIBING CLOTHES; 869] *Opposite:* baggy

clinic 1 *n* **hospital**, health center, consulting room, private clinic, treatment center, doctor's office, surgery (*UK*) [➡ HOSPITALS AND CLINICS; 826] 2 *n* **workshop**, seminar, class, practicum, meeting [➡ MEETINGS AND ASSEMBLIES; 43]

clinical 1 *adj* **scientific**, medical, experimental, quantifiable, proven [➡ THE NATURE OF IDEAS; 771] 2 *adj* **detached**, disinterested, dispassionate, scientific, cold, analytical, distant, uninvolved, objective, unemotional [➡ NEUTRALITY AND INDIFFERENCE; 553] *Opposite:* personal

clinical psychologist *n* [➡ PEOPLE WHO WORK IN MEDICINE; 848]

clinician *n* [➡ PEOPLE WHO WORK IN MEDICINE; 848]

clink 1 *v* **clank**, jingle, tinkle, chink, jangle [➡ EMIT SOUNDS THROUGH IMPACT AND ABRASION; 365] 2 *n* **clank**, chink, jingle, jangle, tinkle [➡ IMPACT SOUNDS; 1260] 3 *type of* **ringing sound** [➡ RINGING AND HOOTING SOUNDS; 1259] 4 *n* (*dated slang*) [➡ BUILDINGS FOR CONFINING PEOPLE; 1094]

clinker *n* [➡ PRODUCTS OF FIRE; 1166]

clip 1 *v* **cut**, trim, shorten, shear, cut off, prune, crop, pare, shave [➡ TEAR, BREAK, AND CUT; 360] 2 *v* **fasten**, attach, pin, staple, secure, fix [➡ FASTEN, LINK, AND JOIN; 408] *Opposite:* undo 3 *n* **excerpt**, passage, extract, quotation, quote, piece, sound bite [➡ SUMMARIES, OUTLINES, AND EXCERPTS; 588] 4 *n* **fastener**, pin, staple, paperclip, clasp, barrette [➡ FASTENERS, LINKS, AND NETWORKS; 1247]

clip-clop *type of* **impact sound** [➡ IMPACT SOUNDS; 1260]

clip-on *adj* **attachable**, fasten-on, hook-on, separable, removable, separate [➡ FASTEN, LINK, AND JOIN; 408]

clipped 1 *adj* **trimmed**, neat, cut back, tidy, cut, pared, sheared, cropped, shaved [➡ DESCRIBING HAIR; 486] **2** *adj* **distinct**, short, brusque, concise, curt, abrupt, terse [➡ SUCCINCT AND TO THE POINT; 640]

clipper *type of* **historical vessel** [➡ SHIPS AND BOATS; 1150]

clippers *type of* **cutting tool** [➡ CUTTING TOOLS; 1120]

clipping *n* **extract**, excerpt, article, feature, piece, cutting (*UK*) [➡ SUMMARIES, OUTLINES, AND EXCERPTS; 588]

clippings *n* **trimmings**, parings, ends, pieces [➡ REMAINDER AND REMAINDERS; 125]

clique *n* **group**, in-group, faction, set, gang, elite, coterie, circle, fraternity, clan (*informal*) [➡ FRIENDS AND ACQUAINTANCES; 936]

cliquey *adj* **cliquish**, exclusive, clannish, unfriendly, unsociable, aloof, insular, selective, superior, limited, restricted, privileged, elite, exclusionary [➡ UNFRIENDLINESS AND UNSOCIABILITY; 504] *Opposite*: open

cloak 1 *type of* **overcoat** [➡ GARMENTS AND OUTFITS; 865] **2** *n* (*literary*) **screen**, cover, shroud, veil, façade, pretense [➡ COVERS AND COATINGS; 1246] **3** *v* **cover**, hide, conceal, shroud, veil, envelop, wrap, swathe, mask, camouflage [➡ CAUSE TO DISAPPEAR; 6] *Opposite*: reveal

cloak-and-dagger *adj* **secret**, clandestine, undercover, covert, mysterious, hush-hush (*informal*) [➡ SECRET AND UNKNOWN; 179] *Opposite*: aboveboard

cloaked *adj* [➡ IMPERCEPTIBLE; 26]

clobber (*informal*) *v* **hit**, thump, beat, strike, drub, punch, bash (*informal*), belt (*informal*), clock (*slang*) [➡ PHYSICAL ATTACK AND PUNISHMENT; 415]

cloche 1 *n* **cover**, cold frame, protection [➡ COVERS AND COATINGS; 1246] **2** *type of* **hat** [➡ ACCESSORIES, MILLINERY, AND LINGERIE; 867]

clock 1 *n* **timepiece**, timer, chronometer [➡ CLOCKS AND TIMERS; 1126] **2** *type of* **measuring device** [➡ MEASURING DEVICES; 1123] **3** *n* **regulator**, timer, device, control, meter, dial [➡ PARTS OF MACHINES AND TOOLS; 1118] **4** *v* (*slang*) **hit**, wallop (*informal*), bash (*informal*), biff (*informal*), belt (*informal*), clobber (*informal*) [➡ PHYSICAL ATTACK AND PUNISHMENT; 415]

clock

◆ *types of clocks*
alarm, alarm clock, clock radio, cuckoo clock, digital clock, grandfather clock, hourglass, pocket watch, quartz clock, stopwatch, sundial, watch, wristwatch

clock radio *type of* **clock** [➡ CLOCKS AND TIMERS; 1126]

clock up *v* **achieve**, reach, score, attain, accomplish, record, total, chalk up, rack up (*informal*) [➡ GET; 420]

clockwise *adj* [➡ DIRECTION OF MOTION; 345]

clockwork 1 *n* **mechanism**, device, machinery [➡ PARTS OF MACHINES AND TOOLS; 1118] **2** *n* **regularity**, preciseness, accuracy, flawlessness, smoothness, efficiency [➡ EXACT; 203]

clod *n* **lump**, clump, chunk, wad, hunk, glob (*informal*) [➡ AMOUNTS OF SOLID OR SEMISOLID; 115]

clog 1 *v* **block**, clog up, stop up, choke, obstruct, congest, jam, gridlock, fill up, clutter up [➡ FILL; 406] *Opposite*: unblock **2** *type of* **shoe** [➡ FOOTWEAR; 871]

clogged *adj* **blocked**, obstructed, choked, congested [➡ FULL; 1239]

clogged up *adj* [➡ FULL; 1239]

clog up *v* **block**, jam, obstruct, congest, stop up, choke, fill up, clutter up, clog [➡ FILL; 406] *Opposite*: unblock

cloister 1 *n* **quadrangle**, colonnade, arcade, portico, walkway, gallery [➡ PARTS OF RELIGIOUS BUILDINGS; 1086] **2** *n* **monastery**, abbey, friary, convent, nunnery [➡ RELIGIOUS BUILDINGS; 1085] **3** *v* **seclude**, shelter, retreat, withdraw, closet, withdraw from the world, confine, shut away, sequester (*formal*) [➡ CAUSE TO DISAPPEAR; 6]

cloistered *adj* **secluded**, sheltered, confined, protected, insulated, isolated, sequestered (*formal*) [➡ SOLITARINESS; 941] *Opposite*: accessible

clomp *v* **clump**, stomp, stamp, thump, bang, clunk, plod, galumph (*informal*) [➡ PROCEED AND GO; 305] *Opposite*: tiptoe

clone 1 *n* **replica**, duplicate, genetic copy, twin, double, copy, carbon copy, emulation [➡ COPIES AND REPLICAS; 151] **2** *v* **duplicate**, copy, make a replica of, replicate, emulate, reproduce, re-create [➡ COPY AND DUPLICATE; 402]

See Compare and Contrast at **copy**.

clonk *v* **knock**, bump, crash into, thump, bang, clunk, clink, thud [➡ EMIT SOUNDS THROUGH IMPACT AND ABRASION; 365]

clop *type of* **impact sound** [➡ IMPACT SOUNDS; 1260]

close 1 *adj* **near**, nearby, close by, adjacent, handy, local, on your doorstep, within walking distance, close at hand, neighboring [➡ CLOSENESS; 159] *Opposite*: distant **2** *adj* **intimate**, familiar, dear, devoted, loving, attached, friendly, warm, chummy (*informal*) [➡ FRIENDLINESS AND SOCIABILITY; 494] *Opposite*: distant **3** *adj* **careful**, rigorous, particular, keen, meticulous, minute, tight, firm, secure [➡ EXACT; 203] *Opposite*: lax **4** *adj* **compact**, tight, concentrated, dense, packed, solid, cramped, confined, compressed [➡ DENSITY AND CONSISTENCY; 1207] *Opposite*: loose **5** *adj* **similar**, faithful, precise, exact, literal, strict, accurate, near, strong, pronounced, marked, definite, firm [➡ SIMILARITY; 148] **6** *adj* **silent**, secretive, taciturn, uncommunicative, quiet, mum (*informal*) [➡ RETICENT AND UNFORTHCOMING; 631] *Opposite*: open **7** *adj* **oppressive**, muggy, airless, sultry, heavy, sticky, sweltering, uncomfortable, humid [➡ HOT WEATHER; 1050] *Opposite*: fresh **8** *adj* **stingy**, miserly, tight, tightfisted, grudging, ungenerous, niggardly, penny-pinching (*informal*), close-fisted (*informal*), parsimonious (*formal*) [➡ GRASPING AND FINANCIALLY MEAN; 519] *Opposite*: generous **9** *v* **shut**, lock, seal, close up, slam, put up the shutters, secure, bolt [➡ FASTEN, LINK, AND JOIN; 408] *Opposite*: open **10** *v* **come together**, meet, join, unite, gather, fuse, link, connect, couple [➡ GET CLOSER TOGETHER; 310] **11** *v* **shut down**, close down, close up shop, go out of business, stop trading, go into liquidation, discontinue, fold, collapse, go bust (*informal*) [➡ STOP ACTING; 264] *Opposite*: open **12** *v* **block**, bar, plug, obstruct, seal off, blockade [➡ FASTEN, LINK, AND JOIN; 408] *Opposite*: unblock **13** *v* **con-**

clude, end, finish, complete, be over, bring to a close, draw to a close, culminate, terminate, wind up, discontinue, wrap, wrap up (*informal*) [➡ COMPLETE AN ACTION; 263] *Opposite:* start **14** *n* **end**, conclusion, finale, completion, finish, ending, cessation, denouement, windup, wrap [➡ ENDS AND DEPARTURES; 54] *Opposite:* start

close at hand *adj* **nearby**, near, on hand, around, close by, just a stone's throw away, adjacent, handy, convenient, local, within spitting distance (*informal*) [➡ CLOSENESS; 159]

close by *adj* **nearby**, near, round the corner, on hand, close at hand, around, just a stone's throw away, adjacent, handy, convenient, local, within spitting distance (*informal*) [➡ CLOSENESS; 159]

close call *n* **close thing**, close shave, near miss, narrow escape, lucky escape, narrow squeak [➡ RESULTS AND OUTCOMES; 83]

close-cropped *adj* **short**, close-cut, trimmed, close-trimmed [➡ DESCRIBING HAIR; 486]

closed **1** *adj* **shut**, locked, bolted, padlocked, fastened, barred, sealed, secure [➡ FASTEN, LINK, AND JOIN; 408] *Opposite:* open **2** *adj* **impassable**, inaccessible, blocked, obstructed, impenetrable, unnavigable [➡ FASTEN, LINK, AND JOIN; 408] *Opposite:* open **3** *adj* **settled**, concluded, terminated, decided, ended, over [➡ FINITENESS, VARIABILITY, AND TRANSIENCE; 96] *Opposite:* unfinished **4** *adj* **narrow-minded**, closed-minded, prejudiced, bigoted, intolerant [➡ NEGATIVE INTELLECTUAL CHARACTERISTICS; 525] *Opposite:* open **5** *adj* **exclusive**, restricted, private, limited, cliquish, cliquey, clannish, elite [➡ UNFRIENDLINESS AND UNSOCIABILITY; 504] *Opposite:* open

closed book *n* **mystery**, puzzle, enigma, conundrum, riddle [➡ SECRETS AND MYSTERIES; 180]

closed-minded *adj* **narrow-minded**, intolerant, prejudiced, bigoted, closed [➡ NEGATIVE INTELLECTUAL CHARACTERISTICS; 525] *Opposite:* open-minded

closed-mindedness *n* [➡ NEGATIVE INTELLECTUAL CHARACTERISTICS; 525]

close down **1** *v* **end**, shut down, pull the plug on, close, conclude, finish, wind down, bring to an end, complete, terminate, wrap up (*informal*) [➡ CAUSE TO STOP; 266] *Opposite:* start **2** *v* **shut**, go out of business, cease trading, come to an end, wind down, shut up [➡ STOP ACTING; 264] *Opposite:* open

closedown *n* **closure**, closing down, shutting, shutting down, closing, winding up [➡ ENDS AND DEPARTURES; 54]

close-fisted (*informal*) *adj* **stingy**, miserly, tight, niggardly, parsimonious, grudging, ungenerous, tightfisted, penny-pinching (*informal*) [➡ GRASPING AND FINANCIALLY MEAN; 519] *Opposite:* generous

close-fitting *adj* **body-hugging**, tight-fitting, figure-hugging, clinging, well-fitting, tight, fitted, skintight, snug, constricting, clingy (*informal*) [➡ DESCRIBING CLOTHES; 869] *Opposite:* baggy

close friend *n* [➡ FRIENDS AND GUESTS; 963]

close in *v* **draw near**, bear down, move in, approach, creep up, converge [➡ ARRIVE; 12] *Opposite:* move away

close-knit *adj* **close**, supportive, strong, caring, cohe-

sive, interdependent [➡ RELATIONSHIP TO ANOTHER; 973] *Opposite:* loose

close-lipped *adj* **reticent**, closemouthed, tight-lipped, silent, reserved, buttoned up (*informal*) [➡ RETICENT AND UNFORTHCOMING; 631] *Opposite:* forthcoming

closely **1** *adv* **carefully**, thoroughly, faithfully, meticulously, to the letter, strictly, watchfully, narrowly, diligently, attentively, intently [➡ EXACT; 203] *Opposite:* casually **2** *adv* **intimately**, personally, directly, strongly, very much [➡ CLOSENESS; 159] *Opposite:* distantly **3** *adv* **densely**, compactly, tightly, thickly [➡ CLOSENESS; 159] *Opposite:* loosely

closemouthed *adj* **reticent**, tight-lipped, close-lipped, silent, reserved, buttoned up (*informal*) [➡ RETICENT AND UNFORTHCOMING; 631] *Opposite:* forthcoming

closeness **1** *n* **nearness**, proximity, contact, convenience, imminence [➡ CLOSENESS; 159] *Opposite:* distance **2** *n* **intimacy**, familiarity, friendship, nearness, understanding, empathy, confidence, lovingness, attachment, chumminess (*informal*) [➡ RELATIONSHIP TO ANOTHER; 973] *Opposite:* distance **3** *n* **airlessness**, stuffiness, mugginess, sultriness, oppressiveness, heaviness [➡ HOT WEATHER; 1050] *Opposite:* freshness

close on (*UK*) *adv* **nearly**, close to, almost, near enough, not far off [➡ TO A CERTAIN EXTENT; 136]

close relative *n* [➡ THE FAMILY; 956]

close-run *adj* **near**, close, closely contested, neck and neck, hard-fought, nip and tuck (*informal*) [➡ CLOSENESS; 159]

close shave *see* **close call**

closet **1** *v* **cloister**, seclude, confine, shut up, lock up, sequester (*formal*) [➡ CAUSE TO DISAPPEAR; 6] **2** *adj* **secret**, private, clandestine, undeclared, unprofessed, unrevealed [➡ SECRET AND UNKNOWN; 179] *Opposite:* open **3** *type of* **cabinet** [➡ FURNITURE; 858] **4** *type of* **room in the home** [➡ TYPES OF ROOMS; 1097]

close thing *see* **close call**

close to **1** *prep* **on the brink of**, on the point of, near to, about to, considering, getting ready to [➡ FUTURE; 86] **2** *prep* **like**, similar to, resembling, akin to, bordering on, not unlike [➡ SIMILARITY; 148] **3** *adv* **nearly**, almost, near enough, not far off, close on (*UK*) [➡ TO A CERTAIN EXTENT; 136]

close to tears *adj* [➡ SADNESS, DISTRESS, AND DESPAIR; 539]

close up **1** *v* **shut**, close, lock, lock up, secure, bolt, seal [➡ FASTEN, LINK, AND JOIN; 408] *Opposite:* open **2** *v* **huddle together**, squeeze up, squash up, bunch up, move up, move together [➡ GET CLOSER TOGETHER; 310]

close-up *n* **detail**, zoom, camera shot, shot, photo, photograph, picture [➡ PHOTOGRAPHY AND PHOTOGRAPHIC EQUIPMENT; 1122]

close your eyes to *v* **ignore**, overlook, disregard, turn a blind eye to, pay no attention to, take no heed of, pay no heed to, let pass, take no notice of, condone [➡ NOT PAY ATTENTION; 764] *Opposite:* notice

closing *adj* **final**, concluding, last, finishing, ultimate, dying, terminating, departing [➡ AFTER, LAST, AND FOLLOWING; 165] *Opposite:* opening

closing stages *n* **last part**, final stages, conclusion, end, finale, endgame, closure [➡ ENDS AND DEPARTURES; 54]

closure 1 *n* **end**, conclusion, finish, closing, shutting, shutting down, termination, ending, cessation [➥ENDS AND DEPARTURES; 54] *Opposite*: opening 2 *n* **finality**, resolution, conclusiveness, definiteness, stoppage, stop, cloture [➥ENDS AND DEPARTURES; 54]

clot 1 *n* **mass**, lump, accumulation, globule, blob, glob (*informal*), gob (*slang*) [➥AMOUNTS OF SOLID OR SEMISOLID; 115] 2 *v* **coagulate**, coalesce, thicken, congeal, set, form clots, solidify [➥HARDEN, CONGEAL, AND DRY; 387]

cloth 1 *n* **material**, fabric, textile, stuff, dry goods, yard goods [➥TEXTILES AND THREADS; 1131] 2 *n* **rag**, duster, tablecloth, handkerchief, napkin [➥FURNISHING AND HOUSEHOLD LINENS; 860]

clothe *v* **dress**, fit out, cover, garb, cloak, don, attire (*formal*), array (*literary*) [➥DRESS, WEAR, AND UNDRESS; 868] *Opposite*: undress

clothes *n* **clothing**, garments, dress, outfit, apparel, wardrobe, wear, attire (*formal*) [➥CLOTHES AND ACCESSORIES; 864]

clothes moth *type of* **moth** [➥MOTHS AND BUTTERFLIES; 1015]

clothing *n* **clothes**, garments, apparel, dress, wardrobe, wear, outfit, attire (*formal*) [➥CLOTHES AND ACCESSORIES; 864]

cloud 1 *n* **mist**, fog, haze, bank of cloud, cloud cover [➥CLOUDY AND RAINY WEATHER; 1052] 2 *v* **veil**, blur, obscure, shadow, make unclear, overshadow, confuse, darken, dim [➥CAUSE TO DISAPPEAR; 6] *Opposite*: clarify

cloud

◆ *types of clouds*
altocumulus, altostratus, cirrocumulus, cirrus, cumulonimbus, cumulus, funnel cloud, mare's-tail, nimbus, rain cloud, storm cloud, stratocumulus, stratus, thundercloud, thunderhead

cloudburst *n* **rainstorm**, downpour, deluge, flood, shower [➥CLOUDY AND RAINY WEATHER; 1052]

cloud-cuckoo-land *n* **dream world**, fantasy world, land of make-believe, dreamland, la-la land, pipe dream, fantasy [➥NONEXISTENT PLACES; 1066]

clouded 1 *adj* **troubled**, anxious, concerned, worried, apprehensive, disquieted (*archaic or literary*) [➥CONFUSION, ANXIETY, AND WORRY; 540] *Opposite*: untroubled 2 *adj* **opaque**, cloudy, murky, misty, hazy, fogged up, muddy [➥VISUAL TEXTURE; 1221] *Opposite*: clear

cloudiness 1 *n* **muddiness**, murkiness, dirtiness, mistiness, opacity, muckiness (*informal*) [➥VISUAL TEXTURE; 1221] *Opposite*: transparency 2 *n* **vagueness**, confusion, ambiguousness, uncertainness, imprecision, obfuscation [➥VAGUENESS; 243] *Opposite*: clarity 3 *n* **darkness**, gloominess, dullness, grayness [➥CLOUDY AND RAINY WEATHER; 1052] *Opposite*: brightness

cloudless *adj* **clear**, blue, sunny, bright, brilliant, sunshiny [➥HOT WEATHER; 1050] *Opposite*: cloudy

cloud nine *n* **seventh heaven**, raptures [➥PLEASURE, EXCITEMENT, AND ELATION; 534]

cloud over *v* [➥CLOUDY AND RAINY WEATHER; 1052]

cloudy 1 *adj* **overcast**, gray, gloomy, dull, hazy, leaden [➥CLOUDY AND RAINY WEATHER; 1052] *Opposite*: bright 2 *adj* **murky**, muddy, opaque, milky, churned up, unstrained [➥VISUAL TEXTURE; 1221] *Opposite*: transparent 3 *adj* **uncertain**, unclear, vague, confused, imprecise, indistinct, ambiguous, hazy [➥VAGUENESS; 243] *Opposite*: clear

clout 1 *n* (*informal*) **influence**, power, authority, weight, sway, effectiveness, pull (*informal*) [➥SKILLS, TALENTS, AND ABILITIES; 526] 2 *n* **thump**, whack, smack, blow, cuff, wallop (*informal*) [➥PHYSICAL ATTACK AND PUNISHMENT; 415] 3 *v* **hit**, strike, thump, smack, slap, whack, bash (*informal*), wallop (*informal*) [➥PHYSICAL ATTACK AND PUNISHMENT; 415]

clove 1 *n* **piece**, segment, section, portion, fragment, wedge [➥AMOUNTS OF SOLID OR SEMISOLID; 115] 2 *type of* **spice** [➥HERBS AND SPICES; 1175]

clover *n* **ease**, good life, high life [➥PLEASANT SITUATIONS; 74]

cloverleaf *n* **highway interchange**, junction, intersection, crossroads, traffic circle, crossing, rotary [➥BRIDGES, TUNNELS, CROSSINGS, AND JUNCTIONS; 1112]

clown 1 *type of* **entertainer** [➥WORKERS IN ENTERTAINMENT AND MEDIA; 873] 2 *n* (*informal*) [➥JOKERS AND TEASES; 675] 3 *v* **clown around**, fool around, horse around, play the fool, be silly, play for laughs, joke, jest (*literary*), lark about (*UK*) [➥JOKES AND TEASING; 674]

clown around *v* [➥JOKES AND TEASING; 674]

clowning *n* **joking**, buffoonery, horseplay, playing around, fooling around, comedy, tomfoolery (*informal*), jesting (*literary*) [➥JOKES AND TEASING; 674] *Opposite*: seriousness

cloy *v* **nauseate**, sicken, be too much, satiate, pall, glut, sate [➥GIVE TOO MUCH AND OVERBURDEN; 437]

cloying 1 *adj* **syrupy**, sticky, sickly, sugary, saccharine [➥TASTE; 703] 2 *adj* **sentimental**, nauseating, sickly-sweet, sickening, heavy, mawkish [➥EMOTIONALLY UNPLEASANT AND UPSETTING; 227]

club 1 *n* **association**, society, guild, organization, union, alliance, fellowship, group, league [➥CLUBS AND SOCIETIES; 939] 2 *n* **weapon**, blunt instrument, stick, cudgel [➥BLUNT INSTRUMENTS AND WHIPS; 1158] 3 *n* **nightclub**, disco, discotheque, casino, private club, country club [➥HOTELS, RESTAURANTS, AND CLUBS; 1082] 4 *type of* **sports equipment** [➥SPORTS EQUIPMENT; 879] 5 *v* **batter**, hit, bludgeon, bang, strike, smash, beat, slug, cudgel, bash (*informal*) [➥WHIP AND CLUB; 417]

club

◆ *types of clubs*
baton, billy club, blackjack, bludgeon, cudgel, mace, nightstick, shillelagh, truncheon

club sandwich *n* [➥PREPARED DISHES; 1170]

cluck 1 *v* **cackle**, squawk, clack, make a commotion [➥SOUND EMISSION BY ANIMALS OR BIRDS; 364] 2 *v* **fuss**, coo, chuckle, tut [➥GIVING VENT TO EMOTIONS; 679] 3 *type of* **bird sound** [➥SOUNDS MADE BY BIRDS; 1263]

clue *n* **sign**, hint, evidence, inkling, suspicion, trace, indication, intimation, pointer, cue [➥ADVICE; 689]

clued-in *adj* **knowledgeable**, well-informed, up to speed, au fait, on the ball (*informal*) [➥KNOWLEDGE AND WISDOM; 558] *Opposite*: clueless (*informal*)

clueless (*informal*) *adj* **naive**, inexperienced, impractical, incompetent, ignorant, ill-informed, green, oblivious [➡ IGNORANCE; 557] *Opposite*: well-informed

cluelessness (*informal*) *n* [➡ IGNORANCE; 557]

clump 1 *n* **bunch**, cluster, mass, tuft, thicket, batch, bundle [➡ COLLECTIONS AND MIXTURES OF THINGS; 1244] 2 *v* **clomp**, plod, stomp, clatter, tramp, stamp, clunk [➡ EMIT SOUNDS THROUGH IMPACT AND ABRASION; 365]

clumpy *adj* **ungainly**, awkward, cumbersome, unwieldy, chunky, bulky, inelegant, heavy [➡ WEIGHT: HEAVY; 1205] *Opposite*: dainty

clumsiness *n* **awkwardness**, ungainliness, ineptness, gaucheness, gaucherie, inelegance [➡ AGILITY OF THE BODY; 476] *Opposite*: gracefulness

clumsy *adj* **awkward**, inept, ungainly, maladroit, gauche, all thumbs, lumbering, inelegant, blundering, heavy-handed, ham-fisted (*informal*), gawky (*informal*), bungling (*informal*) [➡ DESCRIBING BODY MOVEMENTS; 288] *Opposite*: graceful

clunk *n* **clang**, clank, clink, thud [➡ IMPACT SOUNDS; 1260]

clunker (*informal*) *n* [➡ BIKES, CARS, AND CARRIAGES; 1149]

clunky *adj* **chunky**, heavy, solid, bulky, awkward, unwieldy, clumpy [➡ WEIGHT: HEAVY; 1205]

cluster 1 *n* **bunch**, group, collection, band, gathering, constellation, knot, mass, bundle [➡ COLLECTIONS AND MIXTURES OF THINGS; 1244] 2 *v* **gather**, come together, bunch, group, collect, huddle, crowd, assemble, round up, bundle (*informal*) [➡ GET CLOSER TOGETHER; 310] *Opposite*: disperse

clutch 1 *v* **grasp**, hold, grab, grip, hang on to, clasp, seize, catch, grapple, clench [➡ CONTACT: HOLD; 411] 2 *n* [➡ CONTACT: HOLD; 411] 3 *type of* **controls** [➡ INTERNAL PARTS OF A VEHICLE; 1146] 4 *type of* **flock** [➡ GROUPS OF BIRDS; 1007]

clutch purse *type of* **bag** [➡ CONTAINERS, RECEPTACLES, AND PACKAGING; 1245]

clutter 1 *n* **mess**, litter, disorder, confusion, untidiness, muddle, chaos [➡ DISORDER AND CHAOS; 245] *Opposite*: order 2 *v* **encumber**, litter, strew, fill, cover, muddle, disarrange, mess up (*informal*) [➡ CREATE DISORDER AND CAUSE CHAOS; 358] *Opposite*: free

cluttered *adj* **untidy**, messy, disordered, muddled, jumbled, disarranged, mixed-up (*informal*) [➡ DISORDER AND CHAOS; 245] *Opposite*: orderly

clutter up *v* [➡ CREATE DISORDER AND CAUSE CHAOS; 358]

coach 1 *n* **trainer**, teacher, instructor, tutor [➡ EDUCATORS; 840] 2 *type of* **wagon or carriage** [➡ VEHICLES; 1145] 3 *part of* **train** [➡ RAILROADS; 1107] 4 *v* **teach**, train, prepare, instruct, tutor, drill, educate, school [➡ INSTRUCT AND TEACH; 609]

See Compare and Contrast at **teach**.

coaching *n* **training**, education, schooling, teaching, tutoring, instruction, preparation, drilling [➡ TEACHING; 839]

coachwork *n* **bodywork**, exterior, outside, paintwork [➡ EXTERNAL PARTS OF A VEHICLE; 1147]

coagulate *v* **clot**, congeal, thicken, coalesce, set, gel, jell, cake, curdle [➡ HARDEN, CONGEAL, AND DRY; 387] *Opposite*: thin

coagulated *adj* [➡ DENSITY AND CONSISTENCY; 1207]

coagulation 1 *n* **clotting**, thickening, setting, congealing, gelling, jelling, caking, coalescence [➡ HARDEN, CONGEAL, AND DRY; 387] 2 *n* **clot**, lump, ball, mass, cake, glob (*informal*), gob (*slang*) [➡ AMOUNTS OF SOLID OR SEMISOLID; 115]

coal *type of* **mineral** [➡ MINERALS; 1277]

coal black *type of* **black** [➡ COLORS; 1224]

coalesce *v* **merge**, unite, combine, amalgamate, come together, band together, join, blend, mingle, fuse, meld, conjoin (*formal*), cleave (*literary*) [➡ COMBINE AND MIX; 400] *Opposite*: separate

coalescence *n* **union**, combination, amalgamation, meld, merger, merging, coming together, banding together, joining, mingling, blending, fusing, melding, conjoining (*formal*), cleaving (*literary*) [➡ COMBINE AND MIX; 400] *Opposite*: separation

coalfield *n* **coalmine**, seam, mine, pit, colliery, mine workings, excavation [➡ INDUSTRIAL BUILDINGS; 1087]

coal gas *type of* **gas** [➡ GASES; 1275]

coalition *n* **alliance**, union, partnership, combination, league, association, federation, merger, confederacy, confederation [➡ GROUPS WITH A COMMON INTEREST; 938]

coalmine *n* **colliery**, mine, pit, coalface, quarry, coalfield, mine workings, excavation [➡ INDUSTRIAL BUILDINGS; 1087]

coarse 1 *adj* **rough**, uneven, abrasive, stiff, bristly, grainy, granular, harsh, thick, crude [➡ PHYSICAL TEXTURE; 1222] *Opposite*: smooth 2 *adj* **indelicate**, tasteless, vulgar, uncouth, crude, rude, uncivil, foul-mouthed, loutish, boorish, bad-mannered, crass, gross, obscene, smutty (*informal*) [➡ BAD MANNERS AND SOCIAL SKILLS; 521] *Opposite*: polite 3 *adj* **unrefined**, crude, untreated, organic, unprocessed, raw [➡ RAW AND NATURAL; 1214] *Opposite*: refined

coarsely 1 *adv* **roughly**, thickly, crudely, unevenly, harshly [➡ PHYSICAL TEXTURE; 1222] *Opposite*: finely 2 *adv* **indelicately**, tastelessly, vulgarly, crudely, rudely, loutishly, uncivilly, boorishly, brashly, uncouthly, crassly, grossly, obscenely, smuttily (*informal*) [➡ BAD MANNERS AND SOCIAL SKILLS; 521] *Opposite*: politely

coarsen *v* **roughen**, harden, toughen, season, stiffen, thicken [➡ HARDEN, CONGEAL, AND DRY; 387] *Opposite*: soften

coarseness 1 *n* **roughness**, thickness, unevenness, stiffness, crudeness, abrasiveness, graininess, granularity, harshness [➡ PHYSICAL TEXTURE; 1222] *Opposite*: smoothness 2 *n* **indelicateness**, tastelessness, vulgarity, uncouthness, crassness, grossness, obscenity, rudeness, incivility, crudeness, bad manners, boorishness, loutishness, smuttiness (*informal*) [➡ BAD MANNERS AND SOCIAL SKILLS; 521] *Opposite*: politeness

coast 1 *n* **shore**, shoreline, coastline, beach, seashore, seaside, bank, strand, seaboard [➡ THE SEAS, OCEANS, AND SHORES; 1041] *Opposite*: interior 2 *v* **glide**, cruise, drift, sail, freewheel, breeze, slide [➡ PROCEED AND GO; 305] *Opposite*: struggle

coastal *adj* **seaside**, littoral, sea, ocean, beach, shore, shoreline, coastline [➡ THE SEAS, OCEANS, AND SHORES; 1041]

coaster *type of* **motor vessel** [➡ SHIPS AND BOATS; 1150]

coastline n shoreline, seashore, coast, shore, seaboard, seaside, beach, strand [➡ THE SEAS, OCEANS, AND SHORES; 1041] *Opposite*: interior

coast-to-coast adj comprehensive, extensive, complete, umbrella, blanket, nationwide, countrywide [➡ WHOLENESS AND COMPLETENESS; 198]

coat 1 n [➡ GARMENTS AND OUTFITS; 865] 2 n fur, wool, fleece, hide, skin, hair, pelt [➡ COVERS AND COATINGS; 1246] 3 n covering, coating, layer, veneer, glaze, undercoat, crust, cake, overlay, varnish [➡ COVERS AND COATINGS; 1246] 4 v cover, paint, smother, dip, smear, spread, conceal, hide, spread over, varnish [➡ DECORATE, ADORN, AND APPLY COATINGS; 405]

coat

◆ *types of jackets*
anorak, blazer, blouson, bomber jacket, double-breasted jacket, flak jacket, fleece, jacket, Nehru jacket, reefer, safari jacket, single-breasted jacket, smoking jacket, sports jacket, tailcoat, tails, tux (*informal*), tuxedo, waterproof jacket, windbreaker

◆ *types of overcoats*
cape, cloak, duffle coat, frock coat, greatcoat, overcoat, parka, pea coat, poncho, raincoat, slicker, topcoat, trench coat

coated adj covered, caked, frosted, glazed, treated, layered, dusted, smeared, crusted, plastered, painted, overlaid, encrusted [➡ DECORATE, ADORN, AND APPLY COATINGS; 405]

coating n covering, veneer, varnish, glaze, layer, coat, undercoat, crust, cake, overlay [➡ COVERS AND COATINGS; 1246]

coat of arms n crest, emblem, badge, logo, design, shield [➡ SYMBOLS, SIGNS, AND NUMBERS; 596]

coat rack n rack, hooks, coat tree [➡ FURNITURE; 858]

coattail part of garment [➡ PARTS OF A GARMENT; 870]

coat tree n coat rack, hat stand, coat hanger [➡ FURNITURE; 858]

coauthor n [➡ SUPPORTERS, PROTECTORS, AND COMPATRIOTS; 970]

coax v wheedle, persuade, cajole, win over, charm, entice, inveigle, lure, tempt, sweet-talk (*informal*), twist somebody's arm (*informal*) [➡ CAUSE OR COMPEL TO ACT; 271]

cob 1 type of male or female bird [➡ MALE OR FEMALE BIRDS; 1005] 2 type of horse [➡ HORSES; 985] 3 n [➡ AMOUNTS OF SOLID OR SEMISOLID; 115]

cobalt blue type of blue [➡ COLORS; 1224]

cobble 1 n cobblestone, paving stone, paver, sett, stone, flagstone, flag [➡ STONES, ROCKS, AND BOULDERS; 1057] 2 v mend, repair, patch, patch up, stitch, put back together [➡ REPAIR AND MEND; 376]

cobbled adj paved, cobblestoned, flagged [➡ PHYSICAL TEXTURE; 1222]

cobbler type of dessert [➡ CAKES, COOKIES, AND DESSERTS; 1181]

cobblestone n cobble, paving stone, paver, sett, stone, flagstone, flag [➡ STONES, ROCKS, AND BOULDERS; 1057]

cobble together v improvise, rig, concoct, contrive, devise, invent, fix up, knock together (*informal*), whip up (*informal*) [➡ CREATION; 346]

cobnut type of nut [➡ NUTS; 1185]

cobra type of poisonous snake [➡ SNAKES; 995]

cobwebs n sluggishness, tiredness, torpor, lethargy, listlessness [➡ UNPLEASANT, DIRTY, AND TOXIC SUBSTANCES; 1268] *Opposite*: liveliness

coccus type of microorganism [➡ MICROORGANISMS, FUNGI, AND ALGAE; 1023]

coccyx type of bone [➡ THE BONES AND JOINTS; 719]

cochineal n coloring, food dye, dye, food additive, additive [➡ DYES AND COLORANTS; 1270]

cochlea part of ear [➡ THE EAR; 706]

cock 1 v tilt, lift, slant, angle, incline, elevate [➡ MOVE SOMETHING INTO A NEW POSITION OR OVERTURN; 330] *Opposite*: lower 2 type of male or female bird [➡ MALE OR FEMALE BIRDS; 1005]

cock-a-doodle-doo n crowing, crow, cry, call [➡ SOUNDS MADE BY BIRDS; 1263]

cock-a-hoop adj elated, delighted, thrilled, overjoyed, jubilant, ecstatic, excited, pleased, happy, exhilarated, euphoric, exultant, over the moon (*UK informal*) [➡ PLEASURE, EXCITEMENT, AND ELATION; 534] *Opposite*: dejected

cock-a-leekie type of soup [➡ SOUPS; 1186]

cock-and-bull story n [➡ DECEPTION AND LIES; 660]

cockatoo type of pet bird [➡ BIRDS; 997]

cockcrow (*archaic or literary*) n dawn, sunrise, sunup, daybreak, the crack of dawn, morning, first light, morn (*literary*) [➡ TIMES OF DAY; 87] *Opposite*: sunset

cockerel type of male or female bird [➡ MALE OR FEMALE BIRDS; 1005]

cockeyed 1 adj (*informal*) foolish, absurd, madcap, ridiculous, silly, outlandish, crazy (*informal*), wacky (*informal*) [➡ BIZARRE AND PECULIAR; 257] *Opposite*: sensible 2 adj misaligned, crooked, askew, awry, uneven, out of kilter, off-center, off the beam [➡ ORIENTATION AND ALIGNMENT; 1223] *Opposite*: straight

cockiness n [➡ POMPOUS, LOUD, AND OVERCONFIDENT; 635]

cockle type of aquatic invertebrate [➡ AQUATIC INVERTEBRATES; 1022]

cockpit 1 n arena, battleground, fight arena, boxing ring, floor, ring, theater, field [➡ ALCOVES, CUBICLES, AND COMPARTMENTS; 1096] 2 part of aircraft [➡ AIRCRAFT; 1148]

cockroach type of beetle [➡ BEETLES AND WEEVILS; 1016]

cockscomb part of bird [➡ PARTS OF A BIRD; 1006]

cocksure adj smug, arrogant, conceited, confident, overconfident, self-assured, self-confident, cavalier, supercilious, showy, pompous, cocky (*informal*) [➡ POMPOUS, LOUD, AND OVERCONFIDENT; 635] *Opposite*: modest

cocksureness n [➡ POMPOUS, LOUD, AND OVERCONFIDENT; 635]

cocktail n concoction, mixture, brew, blend, combination, mix, mélange (*literary or formal*) [➡ COLLECTIONS AND MIXTURES OF THINGS; 1244]

cocktail cabinet *type of* **cabinet** [➡ FURNITURE; 858]

cocktail dress *type of* **dress** [➡ GARMENTS AND OUTFITS; 865]

cocktail party *n* [➡ PARTIES, DANCES, AND CELEBRATIONS; 37]

cocktail snacks *n* [➡ PREPARED DISHES; 1170]

cocky (*informal*) *adj* **smug**, arrogant, boastful, brash, self-assured, self-confident, swaggering, conceited, self-satisfied, overconfident [➡ POMPOUS, LOUD, AND OVERCONFIDENT; 635] *Opposite*: modest

coconspirator *n* **collaborator**, partner in crime, accomplice, partner, associate, abettor, accessory [➡ SUPPORTERS, PROTECTORS, AND COMPATRIOTS; 970]

coconut *type of* **nut** [➡ NUTS; 1185]

coconut matting *type of* **fiber** [➡ PLANT MATERIALS; 1133]

cocoon 1 *n* **sheath**, covering, shell, case, bubble, layer, nest, coat [➡ COVERS AND COATINGS; 1246] 2 *v* **wrap**, cover, envelop, insulate, protect, cushion, isolate, shelter, cosset [➡ TAKE CARE OF AND SPOIL; 300] *Opposite*: expose

cocotte *n* [➡ TABLEWARE, FLATWARE, AND KITCHENWARE; 861]

cod *type of* **ocean fish** [➡ OCEAN FISH; 1009]

coda 1 *n* **conclusion**, ending, end, close, finale, finish, tail end [➡ ENDS AND DEPARTURES; 54] *Opposite*: introduction 2 *n* **addendum**, postscript, addition, afterthought, adjunct, appendix [➡ PARTS OF BOOKS AND DOCUMENTS; 593]

coddle *v* **pamper**, mollycoddle, indulge, baby, overprotect, cosset, fuss, spoil, cocoon [➡ TAKE CARE OF AND SPOIL; 300]

code 1 *n* **cipher**, cryptogram, encryption, cryptograph, enigma, puzzle [➡ SYMBOLS, SIGNS, AND NUMBERS; 596] 2 *n* **program**, programming, data, instructions, machine code, language, information [➡ SYMBOLS, SIGNS, AND NUMBERS; 596] 3 *n* **system**, policy, convention, regulations, rules, laws, protocol, canon, procedure [➡ WAYS OF DOING THINGS; 294]

codec *type of* **software** [➡ COMPUTERS AND COMPUTING; 1127]

code-named *adj* **alias**, known as, dubbed, identified, named, called, designated, a.k.a. [➡ NAME AND DESCRIBE; 665]

code of behavior *n* [➡ WAYS OF DOING THINGS; 294]

code of conduct *n* **agreement**, rules, guidelines, regulations, protocol, procedure, convention, principle [➡ WAYS OF DOING THINGS; 294]

code of practice *n* **regulations**, rules, guidelines, principles, protocol, procedure, convention [➡ WAYS OF DOING THINGS; 294]

codependent *adj* [➡ RELATIONSHIP TO ANOTHER; 973]

codex *n* **manuscript**, scroll, papyrus, palimpsest, parchment, text, book, volume, collection [➡ BOOKS AND BOOKLETS; 590]

codger (*informal*) *n* **man**, fellow, guy (*informal*), geezer (*slang*) [➡ MALE PERSON; 934]

codicil (*formal*) *n* **appendix**, supplement, addition, rider, add-on, adjunct, extra [➡ PARTS OF BOOKS AND DOCUMENTS; 593]

codification *n* **systematization**, organization, categorization, classification, collation, arrangement, methodization [➡ ARRANGE AND CREATE ORDER; 357]

codify *v* **organize**, collect, collate, gather together, arrange, order, classify, categorize, methodize, systemize, array (*formal*) [➡ ARRANGE AND CREATE ORDER; 357]

coefficient *n* **number**, constant, factor, amount, quantity, measurement, figure [➡ MATH; 597]

coerce *v* **force**, press, pressure, force somebody's hand, compel, bully, intimidate, drive, strong-arm (*informal*), twist somebody's arm (*informal*), put the arm on (*informal*) [➡ CAUSE OR COMPEL TO ACT; 271]

coercion *n* **pressure**, compulsion, force, intimidation, bullying, duress, strong-arm tactics, strong-arming (*informal*) [➡ MORALLY BAD OR IMPROPER; 775]

coercive *adj* **forced**, forcible, intimidating, bullying, strong, powerful, tough, strong-arm (*informal*) [➡ PHYSICALLY UNPLEASANT; 226] *Opposite*: gentle

coexist 1 *v* **live**, exist, cohabit, live together, coincide, co-occur, concur [➡ EXIST WITH OTHERS; 18] 2 *v* **harmonize**, synchronize, collaborate, cooperate, reconcile, cohabit, live and let live, coevolve [➡ HARMONY; 155]

coexistence 1 *n* **cohabitation**, living together, co-occurrence, symbiosis, concomitance, simultaneity, synchronicity, concurrence, coincidence, contemporaneity, synchronism [➡ CONCURRENT AND CONTEMPORANEOUS; 164] 2 *n* **harmony**, accord, cohabitation, coevolution, synchronization, reconciliation, cooperation, collaboration [➡ HARMONY; 155]

coexistent *adj* **concurrent**, simultaneous, contemporaneous, coincident, concomitant, synchronous [➡ CONCURRENT AND CONTEMPORANEOUS; 164]

coextensive *adj* **coincident**, equivalent, equal, parallel, corresponding, comparable, conterminous (*formal*), coterminous (*formal*) [➡ CONCURRENT AND CONTEMPORANEOUS; 164]

coffee 1 *n* [➡ DRINKS; 1187] 2 *type of* **beige** [➡ COLORS; 1224]

coffee

◆ *types of coffee*
americano, café au lait, café noir, caffè latte, cappuccino, decaf, espresso, Greek coffee, iced coffee, Irish coffee, latte, mocha, mochaccino, Turkish coffee

coffee bar *type of* **eating place** [➡ HOTELS, RESTAURANTS, AND CLUBS; 1082]

coffee break *n* **time off**, break, rest, time out, breather (*informal*) [➡ PERIODS OF REST; 91]

coffeecake *type of* **cake** [➡ CAKES, COOKIES, AND DESSERTS; 1181]

coffeemaker *n* **percolator**, espresso machine, drip pot, coffeepot, filter, French press pot [➡ HOUSEHOLD APPLIANCES; 1117]

coffee shop *type of* **eating place** [➡ HOTELS, RESTAURANTS, AND CLUBS; 1082]

coffee table *type of* **table** [➡ FURNITURE; 858]

coffer *n* **strongbox**, chest, casket, treasure chest, safe, treasury [➡ CONTAINERS, RECEPTACLES, AND PACKAGING; 1245]

coffers *n* **funds**, reserves, assets, capital, resources, money, treasury [➡ FINANCIAL ASSETS; 462]

coffin *n* **box**, casket, sarcophagus, cist [➡ BURIAL PLACES AND ACCESSORIES; 930]

cog 1 *n* **component**, part, gear, mechanism, cogwheel, wheel, gearwheel, flywheel, sprocket-wheel [➡ PARTS OF MACHINES AND TOOLS; 1118] 2 *part of* **engine** [➡ PARTS OF AN ENGINE; 1144]

cogency *n* **power**, strength, intensity, vigor, coherence, clarity, lucidity, force, weight, persuasiveness [➡ THE NATURE OF IDEAS; 771]

cogent *adj* **forceful**, convincing, persuasive, clear, lucid, strong, logical, rational, coherent, sound [➡ THE NATURE OF IDEAS; 771] *Opposite*: unconvincing

See Compare and Contrast at **valid**.

cogitate (*formal*) *v* **think**, consider, reflect, deliberate, ponder, ruminate, muse, meditate [➡ THINK AND REFLECT; 743]

cogitation (*formal*) *n* **thought**, consideration, rumination, musing, reflection, meditation, pondering, deliberation [➡ THINK AND REFLECT; 743]

cognate *adj* **similar**, alike, related, kindred, equivalent, associated [➡ RELATED; 142] *Opposite*: different

cognition *n* **thought**, reasoning, understanding, perception, reason, intellect, awareness, intuition, cognizance (*formal*) [➡ PSYCHOLOGY AND THE MIND; 769]

cognitive *adj* **reasoning**, mental, intellectual, cerebral, perceptive, rational, thinking, thought [➡ PSYCHOLOGY AND THE MIND; 769]

cognizance (*formal*) *n* **knowledge**, awareness, grasp, perception, understanding, acquaintance, appreciation [➡ KNOWLEDGE AND WISDOM; 558] *Opposite*: ignorance

cognizant (*formal*) *adj* **knowing**, aware, conscious, acquainted, familiar, mindful, sensible (*formal*) [➡ KNOWLEDGE AND WISDOM; 558] *Opposite*: ignorant

See Compare and Contrast at **aware**.

cognomen (*formal*) *n* [➡ NAME AND DESCRIBE; 665]

cognoscente *n* [➡ LEVELS OF EDUCATION AND SOPHISTICATION; 894]

cognoscenti *n* **connoisseurs**, experts, specialists, authorities, pundits, literati (*formal*) [➡ LEVELS OF EDUCATION AND SOPHISTICATION; 894]

cogwheel 1 *n* **cog**, wheel, gearwheel, gear, flywheel [➡ PARTS OF MACHINES AND TOOLS; 1118] 2 *part of* **engine** [➡ PARTS OF AN ENGINE; 1144]

cohabit *v* **live together**, shack up (*informal*), live in sin (*dated or humorous*) [➡ EXIST WITH OTHERS; 18]

cohabitation *n* **living together**, sharing, living in sin (*dated or humorous*) [➡ MARITAL STATUS; 890]

cohabitee *n* **partner**, domestic partner, spousal equivalent, significant other [➡ SEXUAL AND ROMANTIC RELATIONSHIPS; 964]

cohere (*formal*) 1 *v* **adhere**, bind, stick, join together, stick together, gel (*informal*) [➡ COMBINE AND MIX; 400]

2 *v* **conform**, match, tally, correspond, hang together, follow [➡ HARMONY; 155] *Opposite*: disagree

coherence *n* **consistency**, unity, rationality, logic, lucidity, reason, soundness [➡ ORDER AND ORGANIZATION; 206] *Opposite*: inconsistency

coherent 1 *adj* **consistent**, logical, sound, reasoned, reasonable, rational [➡ THE NATURE OF IDEAS; 771] *Opposite*: inconsistent 2 *adj* **intelligible**, clear, comprehensible, articulate, lucid, rational [➡ THE NATURE OF IDEAS; 771] *Opposite*: unintelligible

cohesion *n* **sticking together**, unity, consistency, solidity, organization, pulling together, interconnection, interrelatedness [➡ HARMONY; 155] *Opposite*: disintegration

cohesive *adj* **unified**, consistent, solid, interconnected, organized, interrelated [➡ HARMONY; 155] *Opposite*: fragmented

cohort 1 *n* **unit**, troop, regiment, legion, army, group [➡ GROUPS OF PEOPLE; 935] 2 *n* **supporter**, accomplice, associate, partner, ally, follower, crony [➡ FRIENDS AND GUESTS; 963]

coiffeur (*formal*) *n* [➡ HAIR STYLISTS; 851]

coiffeuse (*formal*) *n* [➡ HAIR STYLISTS; 851]

coiffure (*formal*) 1 *n* **hairstyle**, haircut, hairdo (*informal*) [➡ HAIRSTYLES AND HAIRPIECES; 488] 2 *v* **style**, arrange, dress, cut, coif (*formal*) [➡ IMPROVE APPEARANCE; 379]

coil 1 *n* **loop**, curl, spiral, twist, twirl, helix [➡ ROUNDED SHAPE; 1218] 2 *part of* **engine** [➡ PARTS OF AN ENGINE; 1144] 3 *v* **wind**, convolute, twine, curl, loop, spiral, twist, twirl [➡ POSITION SOMETHING AROUND SOMETHING; 327]

coiled *adj* **wound**, looped, twisted, helical, spiral, convoluted, twisting, curled [➡ ROUNDED SHAPE; 1218] *Opposite*: straight

coin 1 *n* **currency**, money, coinage, denomination, change [➡ MONEY; 797] 2 *v* **invent**, think up, make up, create, devise [➡ INSTITUTE AND INAUGURATE; 348]

coinage 1 *n* [➡ CURRENCIES; 798] 2 *n* [➡ ASPECTS OF LANGUAGE; 682]

coincide *v* **accord**, agree, match, correspond, concur, tally, overlap [➡ HARMONY; 155] *Opposite*: differ

coincidence 1 *n* **accident**, chance, luck, twist of fate, quirk, happenstance, synchronicity, fluke (*informal*) [➡ CHANCE EVENTS; 36] 2 *n* (*formal*) **concurrence**, correspondence, correlation, agreement, relationship, link [➡ CONNECTIONS; 143]

coincidental 1 *adj* **accidental**, chance, unplanned, spontaneous, unexpected, unpredicted, uncalculated, unintentional, fluky (*informal*) [➡ CHANCE, COINCIDENCE, AND ACCIDENT; 786] *Opposite*: intentional 2 *adj* **concurrent**, corresponding, simultaneous, synchronous, correlated, related, linked [➡ RELATED; 142] *Opposite*: separate

coincidentally *adv* **accidentally**, by accident, by chance, unpredictably, unexpectedly, out of the blue, spontaneously, unintentionally, luckily, fortunately [➡ CHANCE, COINCIDENCE, AND ACCIDENT; 786] *Opposite*: intentionally

coir *type of* **fiber** [➡ PLANT MATERIALS; 1133]

coke *type of* **mineral** [➡ MINERALS; 1277]

col *n* **pass**, saddle, gap, dip, passage, defile [➡ GEOLOGIC FEATURES; 1056]

cola *type of* **evergreen tree** [➡ EVERGREEN AND CONIFEROUS TREES; 1029]

cola nut *type of* **nut** [➡ NUTS; 1185]

cold 1 *adj* **chilly**, freezing, icy, frosty, bitter, wintry, frozen, subzero, arctic (*informal*) [➡ TEMPERATURE: COLD; 1231] *Opposite*: hot 2 *adj* **emotionless**, unfriendly, unemotional, unsympathetic, unkind, callous, uncaring, impersonal, hardhearted, aloof, distant, unfeeling, indifferent, formal, cool, remote, detached, icy, stony, frosty [➡ UNFRIENDLINESS AND UNSOCIABILITY; 504] *Opposite*: friendly 3 *n* **coldness**, chill, chilliness, frost, iciness, wintriness, winter [➡ TEMPERATURE: COLD; 1231] *Opposite*: heat 4 *n* **common cold**, head cold, flu, influenza, chill [➡ ILLNESSES AND DISORDERS; 732]

cold-blooded *adj* **pitiless**, hardhearted, cold, coldhearted, callous, cruel, premeditated, ruthless, heartless, uncaring, unemotional, unfeeling, merciless, remorseless [➡ SELFISH AND UNKIND; 505] *Opposite*: compassionate

cold-bloodedness *n* **pitilessness**, coldness, hardheartedness, cold-heartedness, callousness, cruelty, emotionlessness, unfeelingness, ruthlessness, heartlessness, mercilessness, remorselessness [➡ BAD MANNERS AND SOCIAL SKILLS; 521] *Opposite*: compassion

cold front *n* [➡ COLD WEATHER; 1051]

cold-hearted *adj* **cold-blooded**, cruel, callous, ruthless, unfeeling, uncaring, hardhearted, hard, remorseless, unsympathetic, cold [➡ SELFISH AND UNKIND; 505] *Opposite*: compassionate

cold-heartedness *n* **cold-bloodedness**, cruelty, callousness, ruthlessness, unfeelingness, hardheartedness, hardness, remorselessness [➡ BAD MANNERS AND SOCIAL SKILLS; 521] *Opposite*: compassion

coldness 1 *n* **cold**, chilliness, frostiness, iciness, wintriness [➡ TEMPERATURE: COLD; 1231] *Opposite*: warmness 2 *n* **emotionlessness**, unkindness, unfriendliness, aloofness, distantness, unfeelingness, indifference, coolness, remoteness, frostiness, iciness, stoniness, callousness, impersonality, hardheartedness, cold-heartedness, formality [➡ NEUTRALITY AND INDIFFERENCE; 553] *Opposite*: friendliness

cold shoulder *n* **rebuff**, rejection, snub, slight, brushoff (*informal*), slap in the face (*informal*), putdown (*informal*) [➡ MALICIOUS ACTIONS OR BEHAVIOR; 296] *Opposite*: welcome

cold snap *n* **freeze**, frost, iciness, wintriness, cold spell [➡ COLD WEATHER; 1051]

cold spell *n* [➡ COLD WEATHER; 1051]

coleslaw *n* [➡ PREPARED DISHES; 1170]

coleus *type of* **foliage plant** [➡ FOLIAGE PLANTS; 1035]

colic *n* **stomachache**, cramp, indigestion, irritable bowel syndrome, stitch, pain, bellyache (*informal*), tummy ache (*informal*) [➡ DISORDERS OF THE DIGESTIVE SYSTEM; 713]

collaborate *v* **work together**, join forces, team up, work in partnership, pool resources, act as a team, cooperate [➡ HELP; 293]

collaboration *n* **cooperation**, teamwork, partnership, association, alliance, relationship [➡ RECIPROCITY AND INTERDEPENDENCE; 147]

collaborative *adj* **cooperative**, concerted, collective, joint, combined, shared, two-way, common, united, mutual [➡ ACTING WITH OTHERS; 285]

collaborator 1 *n* **colleague**, coworker, partner, teammate, associate, ally [➡ COLLEAGUES AND EQUALS; 967] 2 *n* **traitor**, turncoat, spy, agent, double agent [➡ PEOPLE WHO DECEIVE; 661]

collage *n* **collection**, combination, assortment, hodgepodge, medley, montage, mixture [➡ COLLECTIONS AND MIXTURES OF THINGS; 1244]

collapse 1 *v* **fall down**, cave in, give way, crumple, subside, disintegrate [➡ CEASE TO EXIST; 22] 2 *v* **fail**, end, fold, break down, dissolve, flop, bomb (*informal*) [➡ FAIL OR BE UNSUCCESSFUL; 75] 3 *v* **fold**, disassemble, fold up, put away, minimize, shut down [➡ CHANGE OF SHAPE; 385] 4 *n* **failure**, ruin, downfall, breakdown, flop, fall, end, folding, bankruptcy [➡ FAILURE; 77] 5 *n* **illness**, breakdown, attack, crisis, crack-up (*informal*) [➡ ILLNESSES AND DISORDERS; 732]

collapsible *adj* **folding**, foldup, stacking, foldaway, portable, inflatable, knockdown [➡ CHANGE OF SHAPE; 385]

collar 1 *part of* **garment** [➡ PARTS OF A GARMENT; 870] 2 *type of* **necklace** [➡ JEWELRY; 866] 3 *v* (*slang*) **catch**, corner, grab, seize, arrest, get ahold of (*informal*), nab (*informal*) [➡ GET; 420]

collarbone *type of* **bone** [➡ THE BONES AND JOINTS; 719]

collard greens *type of* **vegetable** [➡ FRUIT AND VEGETABLES; 1176]

collate *v* **order**, organize, collect, gather, assemble, check, compare, arrange, classify, codify, systematize [➡ ARRANGE AND CREATE ORDER; 357]

collateral *n* **security**, surety, warranty, guarantee, insurance, indemnity [➡ INSURANCE; 801]

collation 1 *n* **ordering**, organization, collection, gathering, assembling, checking, comparison, arrangement, classification, codification, systematization [➡ ARRANGE AND CREATE ORDER; 357] 2 *n* **meal**, snack, buffet, spread (*informal*), repast (*literary*) [➡ MEALS AND PARTS OF MEALS; 1169]

colleague *n* **coworker**, associate, assistant, partner, collaborator, teammate [➡ COLLEAGUES AND EQUALS; 967]

collect 1 *v* **gather**, amass, assemble, accumulate, garner, bring together, pull together [➡ COMBINE AND MIX; 400] *Opposite*: disperse 2 *v* **store**, hoard, amass, stockpile, accumulate, treasure, save, squirrel [➡ STORE AND KEEP; 453]

Compare and Contrast: *collect, accumulate, gather, amass, assemble, stockpile, hoard*

CORE MEANING: to bring dispersed things together

collect to bring things together, or to make a collection of similar things as a hobby; *accumulate* to obtain things over a period of time; *gather* to bring together things from various locations; *amass* to obtain a large number of things over an extended period; *assemble* to bring things together in an orderly way; *stockpile* to collect and store things in large amounts for future use; *hoard* to collect and store things in large amounts, often secretly.

collected *adj* **calm**, composed, poised, placid, serene, unruffled, imperturbable, cool, together (*informal*) [➡ COOL AND CALM; 536] *Opposite*: flustered

collection 1 *n* **group**, gathering, assortment, assembly, assemblage, pool, throng [➡COLLECTIONS AND MIXTURES OF THINGS; 1244] **2** *n* **compendium**, compilation, set, corpus, anthology, collectanea, album [➡COLLECTIONS AND MIXTURES OF THINGS; 1244]

collective 1 *adj* **shared**, cooperative, communal, joint, united, combined, mutual, collegial, group [➡BELONGING OR RELATING TO PEOPLE; 943] *Opposite*: individual **2** *n* **cooperative**, colony, kibbutz, commune, farm, enclave, co-op (*informal*) [➡GROUPS WITH A COMMON INTEREST; 938]

collectively *adv* **en masse**, cooperatively, communally, jointly, together, mutually [➡ACTING WITH OTHERS; 285] *Opposite*: individually

collective noun *type of* **word class** [➡ASPECTS OF LANGUAGE; 682]

collectivism 1 *n* **communism**, socialism, syndicalism, anarcho-syndicalism, Marxism, Leninism, Maoism, communalism, communitarianism, power-sharing, Stalinism [➡STYLES AND SYSTEMS OF GOVERNMENT; 806] **2** *type of* **economic system** [➡FINANCE AND ECONOMICS; 796]

collectivist *adj* **communist**, socialist, syndicalist, anarcho-syndicalist, Marxist, Leninist, Maoist, communalist, communitarian, Stalinist [➡STYLES AND SYSTEMS OF GOVERNMENT; 806]

collector *n* **gatherer**, amasser, gleaner, hoarder, accumulator [➡PEOPLE WHO COLLECT THINGS; 454]

college *n* **school**, university, academy, seminary, institution [➡EDUCATIONAL INSTITUTIONS; 813]

collegial 1 *adj* **shared**, reciprocal, mutual, interconnected, community, uncompetitive [➡BELONGING OR RELATING TO PEOPLE; 943] **2** *adj* **collegiate**, scholastic, academic, educational, institutional [➡EDUCATION; 838]

collegiate *adj* **academic**, university, scholastic, educational, institutional, collegial [➡EDUCATION; 838]

collide *v* **hit**, strike, crash, bump, bump into, run into, run over, ram, go into, plow into, rear-end [➡CONTACT: IMPACT; 413]

collie *type of* **large dog** [➡DOGS; 980]

colliery *n* **coalmine**, shaft, seam, pit, mine, coalface, excavation, quarry [➡INDUSTRIAL BUILDINGS; 1087]

collision 1 *n* **crash**, smash, accident, impact, rear-ender, fender-bender (*informal*), pileup (*informal*) [➡TRAFFIC ACCIDENTS; 255] **2** *n* **clash**, conflict, confrontation, disagreement, difficulty, overlap [➡ARGUMENTS; 47]

collocation *n* [➡ASPECTS OF LANGUAGE; 682]

colloquial *adj* **informal**, idiomatic, conversational, everyday, spoken, slang [➡COMMUNICATIVE STYLE; 624] *Opposite*: formal

colloquialism *n* **idiom**, popular expression, common term, vulgarism [➡FIGURES OF SPEECH; 673]

colloquium *n* **seminar**, symposium, discussion, roundtable, conference, debate, workshop, class, meeting [➡MEETINGS AND ASSEMBLIES; 43]

colloquy (*formal*) *n* **discussion**, meeting, conference, seminar, conversation, debate [➡MEETINGS AND ASSEMBLIES; 43]

collude *v* **conspire**, plot, scheme, plan, get together, join

together, connive, machinate, be in cahoots (*informal*) [➡DEVELOP THEORIES AND REASON; 744]

collusion *n* **conspiracy**, complicity, involvement, agreement, knowledge, consent, approval [➡RELATIONSHIP TO ANOTHER; 973]

colobus *type of* **primate** [➡PRIMATES; 988]

cologne *n* **fragrance**, perfume, toilet water, scent, aftershave, eau de toilette [➡PERSONAL HYGIENE; 491]

colon 1 *part of* **digestive tract** [➡THE DIGESTIVE TRACT; 709] **2** *type of* **punctuation mark** [➡ASPECTS OF LANGUAGE; 682]

colón *type of* **currency** [➡CURRENCIES; 798]

colonel *n* [➡MILITARY PERSONNEL; 828]

colonia *n* [➡UNDESIRABLE ACCOMMODATIONS; 856]

colonial 1 *adj* **foreign**, overseas, expatriate [➡STYLES AND SYSTEMS OF GOVERNMENT; 806] **2** *n* **expatriate**, settler, emigrant, émigré, migrant, colonist, colonialist, colonizer, expat (*informal*) [➡PEOPLE LIVING AWAY FROM HOME; 887] **3** *type of* **pre-20th-century architecture** [➡BUILDING AND ARCHITECTURE; 1076] **4** *type of* **house** [➡RESIDENTIAL BUILDINGS; 1078]

colonialism *n* **expansionism**, colonization, imperialism, interventionism [➡STYLES AND SYSTEMS OF GOVERNMENT; 806]

colonialist *adj* **expansionist**, imperialist, interventionist, colonial [➡STYLES AND SYSTEMS OF GOVERNMENT; 806]

colonist *n* **settler**, immigrant, pioneer, migrant, explorer, colonial, colonizer, conqueror, invader, planter (*archaic*) [➡PEOPLE LIVING AWAY FROM HOME; 887] *Opposite*: native

colonization *n* **settlement**, establishment, foundation, occupation, annexation [➡STYLES AND SYSTEMS OF GOVERNMENT; 806]

colonize *v* **settle**, people, inhabit, take over, take possession of, lay claim to, annex [➡EXIST WITH OTHERS; 18]

colonizer *n* **settler**, immigrant, colonist, explorer, conqueror, invader, pioneer, colonialist, colonial, migrant, planter (*archaic*) [➡PEOPLE LIVING AWAY FROM HOME; 887]

colonnade 1 *n* **arcade**, walkway, portico, porch, loggia, galleria [➡ANCILLARY BUILDINGS; 1080] **2** *part of* **building** [➡PARTS OF A BUILDING; 1095]

colony 1 *n* **settlement**, outpost, dependency, protectorate, satellite [➡TERRITORIES AND GROUPS OF NATIONS; 1068] **2** *n* **gathering**, group, collection, cluster, association, society [➡GROUPS OF PEOPLE; 935] **3** *type of* **flock** [➡GROUPS OF BIRDS; 1007] **4** *type of* **herd** [➡GROUPS OF ANIMALS; 993]

color 1 *n* [➡DESCRIBING COLORS; 1226] **2** *n* **hue**, tint, shade, dye, wash, glaze, paint, pigment, coloration, saturation [➡DYES AND COLORANTS; 1270] **3** *v* **tint**, dye, paint, shade, wash [➡CHANGE OF COLOR; 391] *Opposite*: bleach **4** *v* **blush**, go red, flush, redden [➡FACIAL EXPRESSIONS AND BLUSHING; 651] *Opposite*: blanch **5** *v* **affect**, influence, incline, shade, modify, tint, alter, slant, bias [➡CHANGE; 372]

color

♦ *types of colors*
beige, black, blue, brown, gray, green, orange, pink, purple, red, white, yellow

Colorado potato beetle *type of* **beetle** [➡ BEETLES AND WEEVILS; 1016]

colorant *n* **dye**, hair dye, hair color, pigment, stain, tint, color, rinse, bleach, henna, peroxide [➡ DYES AND COLORANTS; 1270]

coloration *n* **pattern**, coloring, color, pigmentation, shade, tint, tinge, flush [➡ DESCRIBING COLORS; 1226]

coloratura *type of* **musical form** [➡ MUSIC, SONGS, AND SINGING; 907]

colored *adj* **tinted**, dyed, painted, highlighted, stained, bleached [➡ DESCRIBING COLORS; 1226]

colorful **1** *adj* **bright**, multicolored, multihued, polychrome, rich, vivid, vibrant, gaudy, lively [➡ DESCRIBING COLORS; 1226] *Opposite:* dull **2** *adj* **interesting**, full of character, flamboyant, intriguing, lively, imaginative, vibrant, exciting, unusual [➡ INTERESTING AND MEANINGFUL; 190] *Opposite:* uninteresting

coloring *n* **complexion**, skin tone, skin color, ruddiness, pallor, tan [➡ COMPLEXION; 480]

colorless **1** *adj* **neutral**, monochrome, pale, pallid, dull, drab [➡ DESCRIBING COLORS; 1226] *Opposite:* colorful **2** *adj* **dull**, drab, dreary, nondescript, monotonous, uninteresting, prosaic, uneventful [➡ BORING AND UNINTERESTING; 234] *Opposite:* interesting

colors *n* **insignia**, flag, ensign, standard [➡ SYMBOLS, SIGNS, AND NUMBERS; 596]

color therapy *type of* **complementary therapy** [➡ REMEDIES, TREATMENTS, AND OPERATIONS; 731]

colossal *adj* **huge**, massive, immense, gigantic, enormous, vast, titanic, oversize [➡ LARGE; 1193] *Opposite:* tiny

colossus *n* **giant**, titan, leviathan, behemoth, juggernaut, goliath, hulk [➡ BIG THINGS; 1194]

colt **1** *type of* **young animal** [➡ YOUNG ANIMALS; 977] **2** *type of* **male animal** [➡ MALE OR FEMALE ANIMALS; 978]

Columba *type of* **constellation** [➡ HEAVENLY BODIES; 1061]

columbine *type of* **perennial flower** [➡ FLOWERS; 1032]

column **1** *n* **pillar**, post, support, pilaster, stake, pole, pier, buttress, underpinning [➡ STICKS, POLES, AND WEDGES; 1254] **2** *n* **line**, file, string, procession, cavalcade, convoy, queue (*UK*) [➡ AREA AND RANGE; 111] **3** *n* **article**, feature, editorial, piece, contribution, paragraph [➡ NEWSPAPERS AND MAGAZINES; 605]

columnist *n* **writer**, journalist, newspaper columnist, magazine columnist, correspondent, contributor, essayist [➡ WORKERS IN ENTERTAINMENT AND MEDIA; 873]

coma *n* **unconsciousness**, blackout, stupor, oblivion, persistent vegetative state [➡ TIRED, ASLEEP, AND UNCONSCIOUS; 738]

Coma Berenices *type of* **constellation** [➡ HEAVENLY BODIES; 1061]

comatose **1** *adj* **unconscious**, passed out, blacked out, out for the count (*informal*) [➡ TIRED, ASLEEP, AND UNCONSCIOUS; 738] **2** *adj* (*informal*) **exhausted**, tired, spent, used up, all in, beat (*slang*) [➡ TIRED, ASLEEP, AND UNCONSCIOUS; 738] *Opposite:* energetic

comb **1** *v* **untangle**, unsnarl, disentangle, get knots out of, run through [➡ ARRANGE AND CREATE ORDER; 357] **2** *v* **search**, examine, scrutinize, explore, rake, go over, scour [➡ SEEK

POSSESSION AND SEARCH; 456] **3** *type of* **cosmetic tool** [➡ HAND TOOLS; 1119] **4** *part of* **bird** [➡ PARTS OF A BIRD; 1006]

combat **1** *n* **battle**, fight, war, contest, struggle, fighting, warfare, active service, engagement, conflict [➡ AGGRESSIVE EVENTS; 39] **2** *v* **fight**, battle, oppose, contest, contend, struggle [➡ COMPETE, CONTEND, AND COMBAT; 303] **3** *v* **resist**, prevent, check, reduce, stop, tackle, fight back [➡ MAKE IMPOSSIBLE; 276]

combatant *n* **fighter**, soldier, enemy, warrior, participant, opponent, competitor [➡ UNCOOPERATIVE OR REBELLIOUS PEOPLE; 566]

combative *adj* **argumentative**, antagonistic, aggressive, belligerent, confrontational, bellicose, contentious, truculent, feisty (*informal*) [➡ IRRITATION AND ANGER; 541] *Opposite:* peaceable

combat officer *n* [➡ MILITARY PERSONNEL; 828]

combat sports *n* [➡ HOBBIES, GAMES, AND SPORTS; 875]

combat zone *n* **battleground**, battlefield, front line, theater of war, war zone, trench [➡ WARFARE AND WAR; 830]

combination **1** *n* **mixture**, grouping, blend, amalgamation, recipe, mishmash [➡ COLLECTIONS AND MIXTURES OF THINGS; 1244] **2** *n* **arrangement**, permutation, code, pattern, order, sequence [➡ SYMBOLS, SIGNS, AND NUMBERS; 596]

See Compare and Contrast at **mixture**.

combine **1** *v* **unite**, join, merge, coalesce, mingle, come together, link, relate, conjoin (*formal*) [➡ COMBINE AND MIX; 400] *Opposite:* divide **2** *v* **mix**, blend, intermix, amalgamate, bring together, mingle, fuse, commingle (*literary*) [➡ COMBINE AND MIX; 400] *Opposite:* separate **3** *n* **syndicate**, cartel, bloc, trust, association, chain, conglomerate [➡ BUSINESS ENTERPRISES AND RELATED BODIES; 792] **4** *n* **harvester**, thresher, reaper [➡ VEHICLES; 1145]

combined *adj* **joint**, mutual, shared, collective, united, pooled [➡ ACTING WITH OTHERS; 285] *Opposite:* individual

combine harvester *type of* **commercial or industrial vehicle** [➡ VEHICLES; 1145]

combining form *type of* **grammatical term** [➡ ASPECTS OF LANGUAGE; 682]

combustible *adj* **flammable**, inflammable, explosive, burnable, ignitable [➡ FIRE, FLAMMABILITY, AND BURNING; 1165]

combustion *n* **ignition**, fire, burning, incineration [➡ ENERGY; 1161]

come **1** *v* **arrive**, appear, turn up, get here, roll up, show your face [➡ ARRIVE; 12] *Opposite:* go **2** *v* **happen**, occur, take place, fall, befall (*archaic or literary*) [➡ HAPPEN; 27] **3** *v* **approach**, move toward, draw closer to, get nearer to, come up to [➡ PROCEED AND GO; 305] *Opposite:* leave **4** *v* **originate**, hail from, derive, come from, stem from, arise, emanate [➡ GRADUALLY COME INTO EXISTENCE; 1] **5** *v* **reach**, extend, stretch, go, touch [➡ EXIST IN A PLACE; 19]

come about *v* **happen**, occur, take place, transpire, fall out, come to pass (*archaic or literary*) [➡ HAPPEN; 27]

come across **1** *v* **come by**, stumble across, meet, find, stumble upon, encounter, happen upon, come upon, fall upon, strike, get, obtain, acquire, luck into (*informal*)

[➡FIND; 463] *Opposite*: lose **2** *v* **look**, appear, seem, strike, impress, give an impression [➡SEEM TO BE SOMETHING; 58]

come alive *v* **bloom**, thrive, blossom, take off, enliven, brighten up, cheer up, liven [➡GET BETTER; 375]

come along **1** *v* **appear**, arrive, turn up, occur, materialize, show up (*informal*) [➡ARRIVE; 12] *Opposite*: disappear **2** *v* **progress**, make headway, proceed, advance, unfold, open up [➡GET BETTER; 375] **3** *v* **accompany**, chaperone, escort, tag along, follow, attend, keep company [➡ACCOMPANY AND FOLLOW; 337]

come apart *v* **tear**, fall apart, break, shatter, collapse, disintegrate [➡TEAR, BREAK, AND CUT; 360]

come around **1** *v* **consent**, acquiesce, comply, yield, compromise, agree, see eye to eye, change your mind [➡FORGET, FORGIVE, AND ACCEPT; 748] **2** *v* **revive**, come to, wake up, awaken, regain consciousness [➡WAKE AND REGAIN CONSCIOUSNESS; 724] **3** *v* **visit**, call, stop by, come by, call by, drop in, swing by, pop in (*informal*) [➡ARRIVE; 12]

come at *v* **rush**, pounce on, attack, threaten, fly at, leap at, jump (*informal*) [➡MOVE FAST; 313]

come back **1** *v* **return**, reappear, flood back, rush back, revive [➡ARRIVE; 12] *Opposite*: go away **2** *v* **reply**, answer, retort, respond, talk back, answer back, riposte, react, reciprocate [➡REPLY AND ANSWER; 668]

comeback **1** *n* **retaliation**, reply, retort, response, riposte, answer, witticism, rejoinder (*formal*) [➡REPLY AND ANSWER; 668] **2** *n* **return**, revival, reappearance, recovery, reinstatement, relaunch, rebirth, regeneration, renewal, remergence [➡REPETITION; 29]

come between *v* **interfere**, set against, meddle, alienate, disaffect, separate, divide, estrange, pull apart [➡SEPARATE AND DIVIDE; 401] *Opposite*: unite

come by *v* **happen upon**, come upon, fall upon, stumble upon, come across, obtain, acquire, get, find, encounter, luck into (*informal*) [➡GET; 420] *Opposite*: lose

come clean (*informal*) *v* **bare**, reveal, confess, own up, tell the truth, make a clean breast of it, tell all, put your hand up to something (*UK*) [➡ADMIT AND CONFESS; 615] *Opposite*: keep secret

comedian *n* **humorist**, comic, standup, clown, wit, joker, jester, funnyman [➡WORKERS IN ENTERTAINMENT AND MEDIA; 873]

come down **1** *v* **decrease**, drop, go down, dip, plunge, plummet [➡GO DOWNWARD; 307] *Opposite*: go up **2** *v* (*UK*) **lose status**, suffer reverses, know misfortune, have a run of bad luck, have a change of fortune [➡FAIL OR BE UNSUCCESSFUL; 75]

comedown (*informal*) *n* **disillusionment**, blow, disappointment, letdown, reality check (*informal*), downer (*slang*) [➡FAILURE; 77] *Opposite*: boost

come down in favor of *v* **approve**, back, support, get behind, come down on the side of, endorse [➡APPROVE AND CONFIRM; 646]

come down in sheets (*informal*) *v* **pour**, sheet down, pelt down, come down in torrents [➡CLOUDY AND RAINY WEATHER; 1052]

come down in torrents *see* **come down in sheets**

come down on *v* **take to task**, pick on, be hard on, scold, punish, chastise, criticize, yell at, rebuke, reprimand, chew out (*informal*), tell off (*informal*), come down on like a ton of bricks (*informal*) [➡ACCUSE, BLAME, AND CRITICIZE; 641]

come down on like a ton of bricks (*informal*) *v* [➡ACCUSE, BLAME, AND CRITICIZE; 641]

come down on the side of *v* **support**, come down in favor of, favor, back, endorse, side with, get behind [➡MAKE DECISIONS AND CHOICES; 752] *Opposite*: oppose

come down to *v* **signify**, amount to, mean, hinge on, boil down to (*informal*) [➡AMOUNT TO AND EQUAL; 70]

come down with *v* **contract**, sicken, incubate, take to your bed, catch, get, succumb [➡BECOME SICK, TREAT, AND RECOVER; 728] *Opposite*: fight off

comedy *n* **funniness**, joking, amusement, entertainment, humor, wit, pleasantry, slapstick, farce, clowning, jesting (*literary*) [➡ENTERTAINMENT; 872] *Opposite*: tragedy

come first **1** *v* **head**, top, be at the top, be at the head, be in the lead, win, triumph [➡SUCCEED AND WIN; 79] *Opposite*: lose **2** *v* **be your priority**, be your main concern, be the most important thing, be paramount, be the only thing that matters [➡MOST IMPORTANT AND MAIN; 193]

come forward *v* **volunteer**, offer, put up your hand, step forward, step up to the plate, reveal yourself, present yourself, emerge, materialize, surface, appear [➡ARRIVE; 12] *Opposite*: hold back

come from **1** *v* **originate from**, be from, hail from, live in, grow up in, have your roots in [➡EXIST IN A PLACE; 19] **2** *v* **descend**, derive, issue, emanate, originate, emerge [➡CAUSATION; 168]

come in **1** *v* **finish**, cross the line, be placed, finish up, end up [➡COMPLETE AN ACTION; 263] **2** *v* **land**, berth, enter, arrive, pull in, touch down, dock [➡ARRIVE BY TRANSPORT; 14] *Opposite*: depart

come into *v* **inherit**, receive, be left, be bequeathed [➡GET MONEY OR REWARD; 421]

come into being *v* **come about**, begin life, develop, take form, take shape, materialize [➡GRADUALLY COME INTO EXISTENCE; 1]

come into bud *v* **blossom**, flower, bud, come to life, burgeon (*literary*) [➡GROW AND CULTIVATE; 351]

come into contact with **1** *v* **meet**, encounter, experience, come across, have dealings with [➡EXPERIENCE AND ENCOUNTER; 582] **2** *v* **touch**, brush against, press against, rub up against, meet, strike, be contaminated by, be affected by [➡CONTACT; TOUCH; 412]

come into flower *v* **blossom**, bloom, come into bloom, flower, come to life [➡GROW AND CULTIVATE; 351]

come into sight *v* **appear**, emerge, come into view, become visible, heave into view (*literary*) [➡APPEAR AND EMERGE; 3] *Opposite*: disappear

comeliness (*archaic or literary*) *n* **attractiveness**, beauty, good looks [➡PEOPLE'S PHYSICAL APPEARANCE; 475]

comely (*archaic or literary*) *adj* **attractive**, beautiful, good-looking [➡ PEOPLE'S PHYSICAL APPEARANCE; 475]

come off (*informal*) *v* **happen**, occur, take place, come about, succeed, work [➡ SUCCEED AND WIN; 79] *Opposite*: fail

come on *v* **start**, begin, go on, occur, kick in (*informal*) [➡ SUDDENLY COME INTO EXISTENCE; 2] *Opposite*: stop

come out *v* **emerge**, materialize, appear, surface, come to light, leak out [➡ APPEAR AND EMERGE; 3]

come out of 1 *v* **originate**, grow, develop, arise, have roots in, be rooted in, come from [➡ GRADUALLY COME INTO EXISTENCE; 1] 2 *v* **survive**, live through, escape, endure, come through, get through [➡ TOLERATE AND ENDURE; 766]

come out on top *v* **succeed**, triumph, win, emerge triumphant [➡ SUCCEED AND WIN; 79]

come out with *v* **utter**, confess, admit, make known, blurt, broadcast [➡ ADMIT AND CONFESS; 615] *Opposite*: conceal

come over 1 *v* **affect**, engulf, flow over, sweep over [➡ HAPPEN TO SOMEBODY; 30] 2 *v* (*UK*) **visit**, stop by, drop in, swing by, call, call by, pop in (*informal*) [➡ INITIATE AND ESTABLISH COMMUNICATION; 680]

comestible (*formal*) *adj* **edible**, eatable, digestible [➡ FOOD; 1167]

comestibles (*formal*) *n* **food**, provisions, fare, groceries [➡ FOOD; 1167]

comet *type of* **heavenly body** [➡ HEAVENLY BODIES; 1061]

come through *v* **survive**, endure, last, prevail, get through, make it (*informal*) [➡ CONTINUE TO EXIST; 17]

come to 1 *v* **regain consciousness**, awaken, wake up, revive, come around, come to life [➡ WAKE AND REGAIN CONSCIOUSNESS; 724] *Opposite*: black out 2 *v* **amount to**, total, add up to, equal, make [➡ AMOUNT TO AND EQUAL; 70]

come to a close *v* **end**, finish, conclude, come to an end, stop, terminate, draw to a close, wind down [➡ STOP ACTING; 264] *Opposite*: begin

come to a decision *v* **make up your mind**, reach a verdict, decide, make a choice, reach an agreement [➡ MAKE DECISIONS AND CHOICES; 752] *Opposite*: prevaricate

come to a halt *v* **stop**, come to rest, come to a stop, shut down, stop in your tracks, stop dead, cease [➡ STOP ACTING; 264] *Opposite*: continue

come to an end *v* **finish**, end, conclude, stop, cease, run out, run your term, dry up, fizzle out [➡ STOP ACTING; 264] *Opposite*: continue

come to a standstill *v* **come to a halt**, stop dead, shut down, come to a stop, come to rest, stop in your tracks, cease [➡ STOP ACTING; 264] *Opposite*: continue

come to blows *v* **fight**, exchange blows, start fighting, raise your fists, go for each other, have a fight [➡ COMPETE, CONTEND, AND COMBAT; 303]

come together 1 *v* **meet**, rendezvous, converge, gather together, congregate, assemble, group, rally, huddle, crowd together, get together [➡ GET CLOSER TOGETHER; 310] *Opposite*: disperse 2 *v* **combine**, mingle, meld, unite, take shape,

crystallize, cohere (*formal*), gel (*informal*) [➡ GET CLOSER TOGETHER; 310] *Opposite*: separate

come to grief *v* **fall flat**, go up in smoke, come to a bad end, collapse, fizzle, fail, fall short, founder, go on the rocks (*informal*), come to a sticky end (*informal*) [➡ FAIL OR BE UNSUCCESSFUL; 75] *Opposite*: succeed

come to grips with *v* **cope with**, deal with, manage, handle, tackle, come to terms with, accept, face up to, face, bite the bullet, confront [➡ CARRY OUT AN ACTION; 269]

come to life *v* **awaken**, come to, revive, regenerate, breathe, bloom, blossom, bud, regain consciousness, come alive, perk up, come around [➡ WAKE AND REGAIN CONSCIOUSNESS; 724] *Opposite*: flag

come to light *v* **leak out**, surface, emerge, come out, arise, be revealed, become public knowledge [➡ APPEAR AND EMERGE; 3]

come to naught 1 *v* (*archaic or literary*) *see* **come to nothing**

come to nothing *v* **end in failure**, fail, end in tears, fall apart, fall through, founder, collapse, go wrong, go down the tube (*informal*), come to naught (*archaic or literary*) [➡ FAIL OR BE UNSUCCESSFUL; 75] *Opposite*: succeed

come to pass (*archaic or literary*) *v* **happen**, occur, come about, take place, transpire [➡ HAPPEN; 27]

come to rest *v* **pause**, stop, come to a halt, come to a standstill, halt, land, settle [➡ STOP ACTING; 264]

come to terms with *v* **accept**, deal with, cope with, put behind you, get over, resign yourself to [➡ FORGET, FORGIVE, AND ACCEPT; 748]

come up *v* **arise**, turn up, happen, occur, come about, crop up (*informal*) [➡ SUDDENLY COME INTO EXISTENCE; 2]

come up against *v* **experience**, encounter, meet, run into, hit [➡ EXPERIENCE AND ENCOUNTER; 582]

come up for air *v* **take a break**, relax, break off, rest, take a breather (*informal*), take five (*informal*) [➡ STOP ACTING; 264] *Opposite*: continue

come upon *v* **happen upon**, fall upon, come across, encounter, meet, stumble upon, find, bump into, chance upon, turn up [➡ FIND; 463]

comeuppance (*informal*) *n* **due**, punishment, just deserts, poetic justice, nemesis, what you deserve, what's coming to you [➡ RESULTS AND OUTCOMES; 83]

come up to *v* **match**, meet, equal, satisfy, reach, fulfill [➡ EQUALITY; 154]

come up with *v* **create**, produce, provide, supply, find, get hold of, procure, get your hands on, furnish (*formal*) [➡ GIVE AND PROVIDE; 430]

come what may *adv* **anyhow**, no matter what, regardless, anyway, whatever happens, whatever it takes [➡ ALTHOUGH, NEVERTHELESS, AND DESPITE; 169]

comfort 1 *n* **well-being**, ease, relief, security, relaxation, contentment, luxury, coziness [➡ TREATS; 210] *Opposite*: discomfort 2 *n* **consolation**, reassurance, relief, cheer, solace, a sight for sore eyes, succor (*literary*) [➡ TREATS; 210] *Opposite*:

distress 3 v **cheer**, cheer up, encourage, gladden, hearten, bolster [➧SOOTHE AND CALM; 573] *Opposite*: depress **4** v **pacify**, soothe, console, reassure, calm, relieve, ease, placate [➧SOOTHE AND CALM; 573] *Opposite*: upset

comfortable 1 adj **snug**, relaxing, restful, secure, cozy, comfy (*informal*) [➧PHYSICALLY PLEASANT; 186] *Opposite*: uncomfortable **2** adj **relaxed**, at ease, contented, happy, easy, calm [➧COOL AND CALM; 536] *Opposite*: on edge **3** adj **well-to-do**, rich, wealthy, affluent, comfortably off, well-off, well-heeled (*informal*) [➧WEALTH AND WEALTHY; 891] *Opposite*: poor

comfortably adv **at ease**, restfully, contentedly, happily, securely, easily [➧COOL AND CALM; 536] *Opposite*: uncomfortably

comforted adj **consoled**, supported, reassured, cheered, heartened, soothed, gladdened [➧COOL AND CALM; 536] *Opposite*: distressed

comforter 1 n **consoler**, reliever, comfort, support, ray of sunshine [➧TREATS; 210] **2** n **quilt**, eiderdown, duvet [➧FURNISHING AND HOUSEHOLD LINENS; 860]

comforting adj **heartening**, bolstering, uplifting, reassuring, cheering, encouraging, calming, consoling, soothing, kindly, kind [➧EMOTIONALLY PLEASANT; 187] *Opposite*: upsetting

comfy (*informal*) adj **comfortable**, secure, snug, cozy, relaxing, restful [➧PHYSICALLY PLEASANT; 186] *Opposite*: uncomfortable

comic 1 adj **amusing**, funny, humorous, droll, side-splitting, hilarious, farcical, comical, rib-tickling (*informal*) [➧FUNNY AND AMUSING; 216] *Opposite*: tragic **2** n **joker**, jester, comedian, standup, clown, wit, funnyman, humorist [➧WORKERS IN ENTERTAINMENT AND MEDIA; 873] **3** n **comic book**, magazine, funny book, funny paper, comic strip, graphic novel [➧NEWSPAPERS AND MAGAZINES; 605]

See Compare and Contrast at **funny.**

comical adj **amusing**, funny, humorous, droll, hilarious, sidesplitting, farcical, comic, rib-tickling (*informal*) [➧FUNNY AND AMUSING; 216] *Opposite*: tragic

See Compare and Contrast at **funny.**

comicality n **funniness**, drollness, hilariousness, humor, comicalness [➧FUNNY AND AMUSING; 216]

comicalness see **comicality**

comic opera type of **classical music** [➧MUSIC, SONGS, AND SINGING; 907]

comics n **funnies**, comic books, comic strips, cartoons, cartoon strips, caricatures [➧NEWSPAPERS AND MAGAZINES; 605]

coming 1 adj **forthcoming**, pending, impending, approaching, imminent, near-term, upcoming, future, next [➧FUTURE; 86] *Opposite*: past **2** n **emergence**, launch, arrival, appearance, approach, entrance, advent [➧ARRIVAL; 13] *Opposite*: departure

comings and goings n **activity**, movements, to-ing and fro-ing, goings-on (*informal*) [➧EVENTS AND OCCURRENCES; 35]

coming up adj **imminent**, impending, forthcoming, upcoming, about to happen, pending, in the offing, on the agenda, on the horizon, in the cards (*informal*) [➧FUTURE; 86]

comma type of **punctuation mark** [➧ASPECTS OF LANGUAGE; 682]

command 1 n **order**, directive, commandment, demand, charge, instruction, mandate, decree [➧REQUEST AND DEMAND; 663] **2** n **knowledge**, facility, knack, grasp, expertise, understanding, appreciation [➧KNOWLEDGE AND WISDOM; 558] **3** n **authority**, control, rule, domination, power, sway, dominion [➧STRENGTH; 201] **4** v **order**, direct, demand, charge, instruct, decree [➧REQUEST AND DEMAND; 663] *Opposite*: obey **5** v **control**, dominate, rule, lead, be in charge, direct [➧CAUSE OR COMPEL TO ACT; 271]

commandant n **superior**, chief, commander, chief officer, commanding officer, commander in chief [➧MILITARY PERSONNEL; 828]

command economy type of **economic system** [➧FINANCE AND ECONOMICS; 796]

commandeer v **seize**, requisition, hijack, take, grab, appropriate, confiscate, sequester, capture, annex [➧TAKE SOMETHING AWAY; 425] *Opposite*: request

commandeering n **appropriation**, acquisition, confiscation, seizure, sequestration, takeover, capture, hijacking, annexing, taking [➧TAKE SOMETHING AWAY; 425]

commander n **superior**, chief, commandant, chief officer, commanding officer, commander in chief [➧MILITARY PERSONNEL; 828]

commanding adj **impressive**, forceful, strong, powerful, imposing, authoritative, unassailable, imperious, masterful [➧STRENGTH; 201] *Opposite*: weak

commandingly adv **authoritatively**, impressively, imperiously, masterfully, majestically, regally, grandly, strikingly [➧ELOQUENT, TALKATIVE, AND LONG-WINDED; 632] *Opposite*: timidly

command module part of **spacecraft** [➧SPACE VEHICLES; 1063]

commando n **SWAT team**, trooper, paratrooper, SAS (*UK*) [➧MILITARY PERSONNEL; 828]

commemorate v **honor**, remember, celebrate, observe, venerate, memorialize [➧REMEMBER; 746] *Opposite*: ignore

commemoration n **memorial**, tribute, honor, remembrance, commemorative [➧CEREMONIES AND ANNIVERSARIES; 38]

commemorative 1 adj **memorial**, in memory, honoring, dedicatory, celebratory [➧CEREMONIES AND ANNIVERSARIES; 38] **2** n **remembrance**, memorial, tribute, commemoration [➧CEREMONIES AND ANNIVERSARIES; 38]

commence v **begin**, start, originate, inaugurate, instigate, initiate, launch, embark on [➧START AN ACTION; 260] *Opposite*: terminate

commencement (*formal*) **1** n **beginning**, start, origination, inauguration, instigation, initiation, dawn, dawning, onset, opening, startup, commencing (*formal*) [➧BEGINNINGS; 53] *Opposite*: end **2** n **graduation**, graduation day, graduation ceremony [➧CLASSES, COURSEWORK, AND EXAMINATIONS; 842]

commend 1 v **praise**, speak well of, acclaim, extol, laud, mention, applaud [➧PRAISE AND ENCOURAGE; 647] *Opposite*:

denigrate **2** v **entrust**, convey, hand over, consign, commit, give [➡ GIVE AND PROVIDE; 430] *Opposite*: keep

commendable *adj* **praiseworthy**, admirable, worthy, creditable, laudable, estimable [➡ ADMIRABLE AND COMMENDABLE; 185] *Opposite*: lamentable

commendation **1** n **praise**, approval, recommendation, acclamation, approbation [➡ APPROVE AND CONFIRM; 646] *Opposite*: criticism **2** n **award**, citation, certificate, honor, honorable mention, medal, prize, special mention (*UK*) [➡ REWARDS AND AWARDS; 439]

commensurate (*formal*) *adj* **equal**, proportionate, corresponding, appropriate, adequate, matching [➡ EQUALITY; 154] *Opposite*: disproportionate

comment **1** n **remark**, observation, statement, aside, reference, mention, note, good word, dictum (*formal*) [➡ SUGGEST, HINT, AND COMMENT; 612] **2** n **judgment**, observation, criticism, analysis, critique [➡ SUGGEST, HINT, AND COMMENT; 612] **3** n **explanation**, interpretation, clarification, expansion, commentary, interpolation, note, annotation [➡ SUGGEST, HINT, AND COMMENT; 612] **4** v **observe**, remark, mention, state, note, point out [➡ SUGGEST, HINT, AND COMMENT; 612]

commentary **1** n **comment**, explanation, observation, note, annotation, clarification, interpretation [➡ SUGGEST, HINT, AND COMMENT; 612] **2** n **review**, essay, report, treatise, thesis, analysis [➡ ANALYTICAL NONFICTION WRITING; 592]

commentate v **describe**, explain, report, review, expound, pontificate, discuss, interpret, analyze [➡ SUGGEST, HINT, AND COMMENT; 612]

commentator n **critic**, observer, reporter, analyst, reviewer, pundit, interpreter [➡ WORKERS IN ENTERTAINMENT AND MEDIA; 873]

commerce n **trade**, business, market, export, import, buying, selling, exchange, retail, wholesale [➡ BUSINESS; 791]

commercial **1** *adj* **business**, business-related, trade, industrial, mercantile, for-profit, nonprofit [➡ BUSINESS; 791] **2** *adj* **profitable**, salable, marketable, viable, money-making, profitmaking, unprofitable [➡ BUSINESS; 791] **3** n **advertisement**, ad, infomercial, trailer, proms (*informal*) [➡ ADVERTISING AND PUBLICITY; 604] **4** *type of* **broadcast** [➡ TELEVISION AND RADIO; 606]

commingle (*literary*) v **combine**, mix, mingle [➡ COMBINE AND MIX; 400]

commiserate v **sympathize**, pity, empathize, show compassion, offer condolences, console [➡ GIVING VENT TO EMOTIONS; 679]

commiseration n **sympathy**, condolences, compassion [➡ COMPASSION AND FORGIVENESS; 551]

commiserations *interj* **bad luck**, never mind, better luck next time, hard luck, sorry, too bad [➡ EXPRESSIONS OF REGRET; 547] *Opposite*: congratulations

commission **1** n **payment**, costs, percentage, cut (*informal*) [➡ INCOME; 460] **2** n **task**, assignment, duty, job, charge, mission [➡ JOB; 833] **3** n **committee**, authority, agency, administration, board, group, working group [➡ GROUPS WITH A COMMON INTEREST; 938] **4** n **formal order**, command, directive, instruction, charge, contract, assignment, warrant [➡ REQUEST AND DEMAND; 663] **5** n **authority**, power, responsibility,

position, appointment [➡ WORK IN GENERAL; 297] **6** v **assign**, appoint, authorize, contract, order, hire [➡ CONFER STATUS; 458]

commissioner n **official**, officer, representative, administrator [➡ POLITICAL OFFICES AND POLITICIANS; 808]

commit **1** v **obligate**, pledge, bind, promise, oblige, require, constrain, compel [➡ PROMISE AND ASSURE; 684] **2** v **earmark**, designate, dedicate, reserve, devote, pledge [➡ PROMISE AND ASSURE; 684] **3** v **do**, perform, execute, carry out, perpetrate, cause [➡ CARRY OUT AN ACTION; 269] **4** v **entrust**, give, consign, place, hand over, assign, commend, confide, turn over [➡ GIVE AND PROVIDE; 430]

commit hara-kiri v *see* **commit suicide**

commitment **1** n **promise**, pledge, vow, obligation, assurance, binder, word, guarantee, warrant [➡ PROMISE AND ASSURE; 684] **2** n **dedication**, loyalty, devotion, steadfastness, allegiance, faithfulness, staunchness [➡ HARD-WORKING AND COMMITTED; 500] *Opposite*: indifference **3** n **obligation**, duty, responsibility, liability, charge [➡ WORK IN GENERAL; 297]

commit suicide v **kill yourself**, take your own life, end it all, fall on your sword, commit hara-kiri [➡ DIE; 922]

committed *adj* **devoted**, dedicated, loyal, staunch, steadfast, unswerving, faithful, dyed-in-the-wool [➡ HARD-WORKING AND COMMITTED; 500] *Opposite*: uncommitted

committee n **group**, board, team, commission, working group, agency [➡ GROUPS WITH A COMMON INTEREST; 938]

commit to memory v **learn**, memorize, learn by heart [➡ REMEMBER; 746]

commode *type of* **cabinet** [➡ FURNITURE; 858]

commodious *adj* **spacious**, roomy, capacious, sizable, ample [➡ LARGE; 1193] *Opposite*: cramped

commodity n **product**, service, goods, article of trade [➡ BUSINESS PRODUCTS; 795]

common **1** *adj* **shared**, mutual, joint, public, for all, communal, collective, conjoint, corporate [➡ BELONGING OR RELATING TO PEOPLE; 943] *Opposite*: individual **2** *adj* **everyday**, usual, customary, familiar, normal, nothing special, ordinary, commonplace, conventional, unexceptional, regular, garden-variety [➡ ORDINARINESS; 244] *Opposite*: extraordinary **3** *adj* **widespread**, frequent, general, universal, familiar, regular, generic, ubiquitous, commonplace [➡ ORDINARINESS; 244] *Opposite*: rare **4** *adj* **vulgar**, coarse, ill-mannered, rough, low-class, unrefined [➡ LEVELS OF EDUCATION AND SOPHISTICATION; 894] *Opposite*: refined **5** n **green**, park, open space, playing field, playground, recreational area, recreation ground [➡ THE COUNTRYSIDE AND OUTDOOR SPACES; 1071]

common denominator n **shared quality**, shared belief, commonality, common ground, unifying factor [➡ CONNECTIONS; 143]

commoner n [➡ CLASS STATUS; 889]

commonly *adv* **usually**, normally, frequently, generally, regularly, universally, ordinarily, routinely [➡ USUALLY; 108] *Opposite*: unusually

commonness n **ordinariness**, normalness, frequency, prevalence, regularity [➡ ORDINARINESS; 244]

common noun *type of* **word class** [➡ ASPECTS OF LANGUAGE; 682]

commonplace 1 *adj* **ordinary**, everyday, usual, routine, common, conventional, normal, familiar, unexceptional [➡ ORDINARINESS; 244] *Opposite*: extraordinary 2 *adj* **dull**, pedestrian, hackneyed, obvious, stale, unoriginal, trite, tired, uninteresting, humdrum [➡ BORING AND UNINTERESTING; 234] *Opposite*: original

commons *type of* **eating place** [➡ HOTELS, RESTAURANTS, AND CLUBS; 1082]

common sense *n* **good judgment**, good sense, practicality, realism, knowledge, judgment, reasonableness, horse sense (*informal*) [➡ POSITIVE INTELLECTUAL CHARACTERISTICS; 524]

commonsense *adj* **sensible**, practical, down-to-earth, realistic, commonsensical [➡ THE NATURE OF IDEAS; 771]

commonsensical *see* **commonsense**

commonwealth *n* **nation**, people, nationality, state, country, kingdom, republic [➡ TERRITORIES AND GROUPS OF NATIONS; 1068]

commotion *n* **ruckus**, tumult, uproar, turmoil, hubbub, disorder, upheaval, hullabaloo, racket, fuss, din, stir, disturbance, furor, to-do (*informal*) [➡ CHAOS AND UPROAR; 51] *Opposite*: peace

communal *adj* **shared**, public, collective, joint, mutual [➡ BELONGING OR RELATING TO PEOPLE; 943] *Opposite*: individual

communally *adv* **mutually**, jointly, collectively, together, publicly [➡ RECIPROCITY AND INTERDEPENDENCE; 147] *Opposite*: individually

commune 1 *n* **community**, collective, collective farm, kibbutz, cooperative [➡ HUMAN SETTLEMENTS; 1070] 2 *v* **communicate**, converse, empathize, feel, connect, be in touch with [➡ INITIATE AND ESTABLISH COMMUNICATION; 680]

communicable *adj* **infectious**, catching, transmissible, contagious, transmittable [➡ SICKNESS; 729]

communicant *n* **church member**, churchgoer, worshiper [➡ RELIGIOUS PEOPLE; 778]

communicate 1 *v* **converse**, talk, speak, commune, be in touch, correspond, write, be in contact [➡ TWO-WAY COMMUNICATION; 607] 2 *v* **convey**, share, impart, transmit, reveal, put out, publicize [➡ INFORM, ANNOUNCE, AND ISSUE; 611] 3 *v* **connect**, interconnect, lead into, link, join, transfer [➡ EXIST IN CLOSE PROXIMITY; 21]

communication 1 *n* **contact**, interaction, consultation, transfer, exchange, transmission [➡ COMMUNICATION; 602] 2 *n* **message**, communiqué, announcement, statement, letter, e-mail, phone call, videoconference, teleconference, conference call, fax [➡ COMMUNICATION; 602]

communications 1 *n* **infrastructure**, public services, transportation, transport network, links [➡ COMMUNICATION NETWORKS; 1105] 2 *n* **telecommunications**, broadcasting, postal system, data lines, network [➡ COMMUNICATION; 602]

communicative *adj* **talkative**, open, forthcoming, outgoing, unrestrained, chatty, expansive [➡ ELOQUENT, TALKATIVE, AND LONG-WINDED; 632] *Opposite*: reticent

communion *n* **unity**, spiritual union, empathy, closeness, relationship, intimacy [➡ CONNECTIONS; 143]

communiqué *n* **announcement**, statement, communication, press release, bulletin, report, dispatch, message [➡ LETTERS AND WRITTEN MESSAGES; 584]

communism *n* **collectivism**, socialism, communalism, Marxism, Leninism, Trotskyism, Maoism [➡ PHILOSOPHIES AND BELIEFS; 780]

communist *n* **socialist**, collectivist, communalist, Marxist, Trotskyist, Maoist, red (*informal*) [➡ PHILOSOPHICAL AND POLITICAL THINKERS; 781] *Opposite*: capitalist

community 1 *n* **neighborhood**, area, village, hamlet, commune [➡ HUMAN SETTLEMENTS; 1070] 2 *n* **kinship**, unity, identity, cooperation, convergence, similarity [➡ SIMILARITY; 148] *Opposite*: isolation 3 *n* **society**, public, people, population, group [➡ GROUPS IN SOCIETY; 940]

community garden *type of* **garden** [➡ GARDENS; 1074]

commute 1 *v* **travel**, go back and forth, shuttle, car-pool [➡ TRAVEL: WAYS OF TRAVELING; 320] 2 *v* **convert**, alter, exchange, transform, substitute, change, transmute, metamorphose [➡ CHANGE ONE THING FOR ANOTHER; 398]

commuter *n* [➡ WORKERS; 836]

commuter belt (*UK*) *n* [➡ HUMAN SETTLEMENTS; 1070]

compact 1 *adj* **dense**, solid, packed in, packed together, compressed, compacted, condensed, squashed, squeezed, close [➡ DENSITY AND CONSISTENCY; 1207] *Opposite*: loose 2 *adj* **small**, neat, trim, tiny, miniature, pocket-sized, reduced, efficient [➡ SMALL; 1195] *Opposite*: large 3 *v* **compress**, pack, squeeze, squash, tamp, press, condense [➡ CHANGE OF SIZE: SMALLER; 393] *Opposite*: loosen 4 *type of* **car** [➡ BIKES, CARS, AND CARRIAGES; 1149] 5 *n* **contract**, pact, agreement, deal, treaty [➡ PROMISE AND ASSURE; 684]

compact disc *type of* **audio equipment** [➡ AUDIO EQUIPMENT; 1139]

compact disc player 1 *n* **stereo**, personal stereo, hi-fi, CD, boom box, sound system, CD player [➡ RECORDINGS AND PLAYERS; 911] 2 *type of* **audio equipment** [➡ AUDIO EQUIPMENT; 1139]

compactness 1 *n* **density**, solidity, compression, firmness [➡ DENSITY AND CONSISTENCY; 1207] *Opposite*: looseness 2 *n* **smallness**, neatness, trimness, tininess, miniaturization [➡ ORDER AND ORGANIZATION; 206] *Opposite*: largeness

companion 1 *n* **friend**, acquaintance, confidant, colleague, buddy (*informal*), chum (*informal*), mate (*UK*) [➡ FRIENDS AND GUESTS; 963] 2 *n* **escort**, attendant, chaperon, fellow traveler, arm candy (*slang*) [➡ FRIENDS AND GUESTS; 963]

companionability *n* **friendliness**, bonhomie, camaraderie, affability [➡ FRIENDLINESS AND SOCIABILITY; 494]

companionable *adj* **friendly**, sociable, close, intimate, chummy (*informal*), pally (*informal*) [➡ FRIENDLINESS AND SOCIABILITY; 494] *Opposite*: frosty

companionship *n* **company**, friendship, camaraderie, comradeship, esprit de corps [➡ RELATIONSHIP TO ANOTHER; 973] *Opposite*: enmity

company 1 *n* **business**, corporation, firm, concern, enterprise, establishment, house, syndicate [➡ BUSINESS ENTERPRISES AND RELATED BODIES; 792] 2 *n* **companionship**, friendship, camaraderie, comradeship, esprit de corps [➡RELATIONSHIP TO ANOTHER; 973] *Opposite*: isolation **3** *n* **group**, crowd, circle, set, party, coterie, gathering, band, assembly, congregation [➡FRIENDS AND ACQUAINTANCES; 936] *Opposite*: individual **4** *n* **visitors**, guests, friends, companions, invitees [➡FRIENDS AND GUESTS; 963] **5** *n* **theater company**, troupe, theater group, ballet, touring company, concert party, band, corps, troop [➡PERFORMERS; 905]

comparable *adj* **similar**, analogous, akin, equal, equivalent, as good as, like [➡SIMILARITY; 148] *Opposite*: dissimilar

comparative *adj* **relative**, reasonable, fair [➡TO A CERTAIN EXTENT; 136] *Opposite*: absolute

compare **1** *v* **evaluate**, contrast, assess, measure up, match up to, weigh against, put side by side, balance, judge, comparison-shop [➡EXAMINE AND ASSESS; 753] **2** *v* **liken**, associate, link, relate, equate [➡CREATING CONNECTIONS; 144] **3** *v* **equal**, match, measure up, parallel, compete, rival, stand the test, stand the pace [➡SUCCEED AND WIN; 79]

compare notes *v* **exchange information**, tell, relate, share, pass on, swap opinions, pool, trade [➡TWO-WAY COMMUNICATION; 607]

comparison **1** *n* **contrast**, judgment, assessment, evaluation, appraisal [➡EXAMINE AND ASSESS; 753] **2** *n* **association**, link, relationship, similarity, likeness, resemblance, difference, divergence, contrast, affinity, analogy, semblance, parallel [➡CONNECTIONS; 143]

compartment **1** *n* **cubicle**, booth, partition, box, stall [➡ALCOVES, CUBICLES, AND COMPARTMENTS; 1096] **2** *part of* **train** [➡RAILROADS; 1107]

compartmentalize *v* [➡SEPARATE AND DIVIDE; 401]

compass **1** *n* **scope**, range, area, extent, breadth, ambit, remit (*UK*) [➡SIZE AND DIMENSIONS; 1192] **2** *type of* **measuring device** [➡MEASURING DEVICES; 1123]

compassion *n* **sympathy**, empathy, concern, kindness, consideration, care, kindheartedness, benevolence [➡COMPASSION AND FORGIVENESS; 551] *Opposite*: coldness

compassionate *adj* **sympathetic**, empathetic, feeling, concerned, kind, kindly, kindhearted, considerate, caring, gentle, benevolent [➡GENEROSITY AND KINDNESS; 495] *Opposite*: unfeeling

compassionless *adj* **unsympathetic**, unkind, unfeeling, uncaring, cold [➡UNFRIENDLINESS AND UNSOCIABILITY; 504]

compatible **1** *adj* **well-matched**, like-minded, well-suited, companionable, friendly, attuned, harmonious [➡HARMONY; 155] *Opposite*: incompatible **2** *adj* **matching**, fitting, consistent, corresponding, harmonizing, conformant, congruent (*formal*) [➡HARMONY; 155] *Opposite*: incompatible

compatriot *n* **national**, fellow citizen, countryman, countrywoman [➡SUPPORTERS, PROTECTORS, AND COMPATRIOTS; 970] *Opposite*: foreigner

compel *v* **force**, induce, require, coerce, oblige, make, pressurize, constrain, twist somebody's arm (*informal*), lean on (*informal*) [➡CAUSE OR COMPEL TO ACT; 271]

compelling **1** *adj* **convincing**, persuasive, gripping, captivating, fascinating, enthralling, absorbing, exciting [➡INTERESTING AND MEANINGFUL; 190] *Opposite*: unconvincing **2** *adj*

forceful, powerful, urgent, undeniable, insistent, involuntary, compulsive [➡STRENGTH; 201]

compendium *n* **collection**, anthology, digest [➡COLLECTIONS AND MIXTURES OF THINGS; 1244]

compensate **1** *v* **recompense**, reimburse, pay off, pay compensation, pay damages, pay costs, give back, pay, reward [➡REWARD; 436] **2** *v* **balance**, counterweigh, counteract, counterbalance, offset, make up for, even up [➡CORRECT AND PUT RIGHT; 377]

compensation **1** *n* **recompense**, return, reward, reimbursement, payment, damages, costs, reparation, blood money [➡REWARDS AND AWARDS; 439] **2** *n* **advantage**, reward, recompense, return, benefit, plus (*informal*) [➡TREATS; 210]

compete **1** *v* **contest**, contend, vie, strive, participate, take part, enter, play [➡COMPETE, CONTEND, AND COMBAT; 303] **2** *v* **compare**, equal, measure up, rival, match, parallel, stand the test, stand the pace [➡SUCCEED AND WIN; 79]

competence *n* **ability**, capability, skill, fitness, aptitude, proficiency, competency, experience, expertise, know-how (*informal*) [➡SKILLS, TALENTS, AND ABILITIES; 526] *Opposite*: ineptitude

See Compare and Contrast at **ability**.

competent *adj* **able**, capable, skilled, proficient, adept, expert, fit, knowledgeable, experienced [➡TALENTED AND SKILLFUL; 527] *Opposite*: inept

competition **1** *n* **rivalry**, opposition, antagonism, war, struggle [➡NON-AGGRESSIVE/SPORTING EVENTS; 40] *Opposite*: cooperation **2** *n* **contest**, match, race, struggle, battle, mano a mano [➡NON-AGGRESSIVE/SPORTING EVENTS; 40]

competitive **1** *adj* **spirited**, aggressive, rivalrous, adversarial, ready for action, driven, cutthroat, bloodthirsty, gung ho (*informal*) [➡BOSSY AND OVERBEARING; 516] *Opposite*: passive **2** *adj* **reasonable**, modest, good, inexpensive, cheap, viable, economical, low-cost [➡CHEAP AND INEXPENSIVE; 221] *Opposite*: expensive

competitor *n* **contestant**, participant, entrant, player, opponent, challenger, contender, rival, sportsperson [➡COMPETITORS; 41]

compilation **1** *n* **gathering**, compiling, collecting, assembling, composing, collation, drawing together, bringing together, accumulation [➡ARRANGE AND CREATE ORDER; 357] *Opposite*: dispersal **2** *n* **collection**, set, anthology, assemblage, edition, compendium [➡COLLECTIONS AND MIXTURES OF THINGS; 1244]

compile **1** *v* **amass**, accumulate, collect, bring together, assemble, gather, pile up, hoard [➡STORE AND KEEP; 453] *Opposite*: disperse **2** *v* **list**, draw up, compose, set down, register, record, put together [➡RECORD SOMETHING; 371]

complacency *n* **satisfaction**, smugness, self-satisfaction, contentment, gratification, self-righteousness [➡COOL AND CALM; 536] *Opposite*: anxiety

complacent *adj* **satisfied**, self-satisfied, smug, gratified, content, contented, self-righteous [➡NEUTRALITY AND INDIFFERENCE; 553] *Opposite*: anxious

complain *v* **protest**, criticize, grumble, whine, carp, find fault, nitpick, nag, murmur, object, grouse, moan (*informal*), gripe (*informal*), knock (*slang*) [➡ COMPLAIN AND NAG; 686] *Opposite*: praise

Compare and Contrast: *complain, object, protest, grumble, grouse, carp, gripe, whine, nag*

CORE MEANING: to indicate dissatisfaction with something

complain to express discontent or unhappiness about a situation; *object* to be opposed to something, or express opposition to it; *protest* to express strong disapproval or disagreement; *grumble* to disagree in a discontented way, possibly repeatedly or continually; *grouse* to complain regularly and continually, often in a way that is not constructive; *carp* to keep complaining or finding fault, especially about unimportant things; *gripe* (*informal*) to complain continually and irritatingly; *whine* to complain in an unreasonable, repeated, or irritating way; *nag* to find fault with somebody regularly and repeatedly.

complainer *n* **whiner**, objector, protester, grumbler, faultfinder, nitpicker, carper, knocker (*informal*), moaner (*informal*) [➡ GRUMPY AND NEGATIVE PEOPLE; 953]

complaint 1 *n* **grievance**, criticism, protest, grumble, objection, moan (*informal*) [➡ COMPLAIN AND NAG; 686] *Opposite*: praise 2 *n* **illness**, condition, ailment, disorder [➡ SICKNESS; 729]

complaisant *adj* **acquiescent**, amenable, tractable, willing [➡ THE WILL AND WILLINGNESS; 563]

complement 1 *n* **accompaniment**, foil, match, balance, counterpart, supplement, pair [➡ HARMONY; 155] 2 *n* **quota**, set, allowance, quantity, number, amount [➡ AMOUNTS AND QUANTITIES; 112] 3 *v* **complete**, add, supplement, round out, make up for, perfect, accompany [➡ CHANGE OF SIZE: BIGGER; 392] *Opposite*: detract 4 *v* **balance**, set off, harmonize, match, be a foil for [➡ HARMONY; 155] *Opposite*: clash

complementary *adj* **balancing**, opposite, matching, corresponding [➡ HARMONY; 155] *Opposite*: clashing

complementary therapy *n* [➡ REMEDIES, TREATMENTS, AND OPERATIONS; 731]

complete 1 *adj* **finished**, completed, concluded, accomplished, fulfilled, done [➡ WHOLENESS AND COMPLETENESS; 198] *Opposite*: unfinished 2 *adj* **whole**, comprehensive, wide-ranging, broad, ample, widespread, far-reaching, thorough, wholesale, all-embracing, all-inclusive, overall, extensive, full [➡ WHOLENESS AND COMPLETENESS; 198] *Opposite*: partial 3 *adj* **absolute**, extreme, utter, great, downright, perfect, total, entire [➡ ABSOLUTE AND ABSOLUTELY; 133] 4 *v* **finish**, finalize, conclude, end, bring to an end, put the finishing touches on, put the last touches on [➡ COMPLETE AN ACTION; 263] *Opposite*: start 5 *v* **accomplish**, achieve, fulfill, carry out, realize, perfect [➡ COMPLETE AN ACTION; 263]

completed *adj* **finished**, accomplished, finalized, done, complete, concluded, over, over and done with, ended [➡ WHOLENESS AND COMPLETENESS; 198] *Opposite*: unfinished

completely *adv* **totally**, wholly, entirely, fully, extensively, finally, utterly, absolutely, downright, thor-

oughly, from top to bottom, from tip to toe [➡ WHOLENESS AND COMPLETENESS; 198] *Opposite*: partially

completeness *n* **wholeness**, fullness, extensiveness, comprehensiveness, inclusiveness, broadness [➡ WHOLENESS AND COMPLETENESS; 198] *Opposite*: partiality

completion *n* **conclusion**, close, achievement, accomplishment, end, finishing point [➡ ENDS AND DEPARTURES; 54] *Opposite*: start

complex 1 *adj* **complicated**, difficult, convoluted, involved, dense, byzantine, labyrinthine, thorny [➡ DIFFICULTY AND COMPLEXITY; 242] *Opposite*: simple 2 *adj* **multifaceted**, compound, composite, multipart, intricate, multifarious [➡ POSITIVELY COMPLEX OR COMPLICATED; 217] *Opposite*: simple 3 *n* **development**, center, campus, facility, multiuse building, multiplex [➡ BUILDING AND ARCHITECTURE; 1076] 4 *n* (*informal*) **fixation**, psychosis, phobia, obsession, hang-up (*informal*), neurosis (*dated*) [➡ PSYCHOLOGY AND THE MIND; 769]

complexion 1 *n* **skin**, face, coloring, appearance, features [➡ COMPLEXION; 480] 2 *n* **nature**, character, cast, tone, aspect [➡ APPEARANCE AND ATMOSPHERE; 1237]

complexity *n* **difficulty**, intricacy, complication, involvedness, density, convolution [➡ DIFFICULTY AND COMPLEXITY; 242] *Opposite*: simplicity

compliance 1 *n* **obedience**, acquiescence, agreement, submission, amenability, amenableness, docility, passivity [➡ THE WILL AND WILLINGNESS; 563] *Opposite*: defiance 2 *n* **conformity**, fulfillment, observance, accordance [➡ HARMONY; 155] *Opposite*: noncompliance

compliant 1 *adj* **acquiescent**, obedient, biddable, yielding, amenable, accommodating, submissive, docile [➡ THE WILL AND WILLINGNESS; 563] *Opposite*: defiant 2 *adj* **conforming**, in compliance, compatible, conformant [➡ HARMONY; 155] *Opposite*: noncompliant

compliantly *adv* **acquiescently**, passively, amenably, submissively, obediently, accommodatingly [➡ THE WILL AND WILLINGNESS; 563] *Opposite*: defiantly

complicate *v* **make difficulties**, set hurdles, thwart, confound, confuse, muddle, muddy, obscure, obfuscate [➡ CREATE DISORDER AND CAUSE CHAOS; 358] *Opposite*: simplify

complicated *adj* **complex**, difficult, intricate, byzantine, thorny, dense, convoluted, problematical, full of twists and turns, labyrinthine [➡ DIFFICULTY AND COMPLEXITY; 242] *Opposite*: simple

complication *n* **difficulty**, snag, problem, impediment, obstacle, hurdle, barrier [➡ PROBLEMS; 256] *Opposite*: solution

complicity *n* **involvement**, collusion, collaboration, connivance, participation, support [➡ RECIPROCITY AND INTERDEPENDENCE; 147] *Opposite*: detachment

compliment 1 *n* **praise**, commendation, tribute, accolade, approval, kudos, encomium (*formal*) [➡ PRAISE AND ENCOURAGE; 647] *Opposite*: criticism 2 *v* **flatter**, praise, admire, congratulate, approve, pay tribute to, butter up (*informal*) [➡ PRAISE AND ENCOURAGE; 647] *Opposite*: criticize

complimentary 1 *adj* **flattering**, admiring, kind, gracious, civil, approving [➡ EXPRESSING RESPECT AND APPROVAL; 637] *Opposite*: critical 2 *adj* **free**, gratis, courtesy, on the house, free of charge [➡ GIFTS; 438]

comply with *v* **obey**, fulfill, observe, conform, abide by, submit to [➡ OBEY AND ABIDE BY; 301] *Opposite*: disobey

component *n* **constituent**, module, section, factor, element, piece, part, cog [➡ QUALITIES AND CHARACTERISTICS; 1191] *Opposite*: whole

comportment (*formal*) *n* **conduct**, bearing, deportment, carriage (*formal*), demeanor, manner, style, manners, attitude, behavior [➡ TEMPERAMENT AND BEHAVIOR; 492]

compose 1 *v* **make up**, comprise, constitute, combine, unite [➡ COMBINE AND MIX; 400]   2 *v* **arrange**, order, set out, marshal, organize, put together, dispose (*formal*) [➡ ARRANGE AND CREATE ORDER; 357] *Opposite*: disturb   3 *v* **create**, invent, make up, make, compile, write [➡ INSTITUTE AND INAUGURATE; 348]

composed *adj* **calm**, collected, self-possessed, serene, unruffled, poised, tranquil [➡ COOL AND CALM; 536] *Opposite*: flustered

composer *n* **creator**, originator, musician, writer, author [➡ MUSICIANS AND SINGERS; 908]

compose yourself *v* **calm yourself**, control yourself, calm down, get a hold of yourself, settle down, relax, unwind, pull yourself together, get a grip on yourself (*informal*), chill out (*slang*) [➡ CHANGE OF MOOD AND COMPOSURE; 580] *Opposite*: panic

composite 1 *adj* **compound**, complex, multiple, multipart, multifactorial, multifarious [➡ DIFFERENCE; 149] *Opposite*: simple   2 *n* **amalgam**, mixture, complex, compound, fusion, synthesis, combination, aggregate, amalgamation [➡ COLLECTIONS AND MIXTURES OF THINGS; 1244]

composition 1 *n* **constitution**, makeup, structure, components, constituents, parts [➡ APPEARANCE AND ATMOSPHERE; 1237]   2 *n* **work of art**, creation, work, opus, masterpiece, piece [➡ ARTWORKS; 898]   3 *n* **arrangement**, configuration, conformation, structure, alignment [➡ QUALITIES AND CHARACTERISTICS; 1191]

compos mentis *adj* **sane**, clear-headed, clear-thinking, rational [➡ POSITIVE INTELLECTUAL CHARACTERISTICS; 524]

composure *n* **calm**, serenity, self-possession, tranquility, self-control, poise, calmness, equanimity (*formal*) [➡ COOL AND CALM; 536] *Opposite*: agitation

compote *type of* **preserve** [➡ SUGAR AND PRESERVES; 1184]

compound 1 *n* **mix**, mixture, complex, amalgam, composite, combination [➡ COLLECTIONS AND MIXTURES OF THINGS; 1244]   2 *adj* **multiple**, complex, composite, multifaceted, multifarious, multipart, multifactorial [➡ POSITIVELY COMPLEX OR COMPLICATED; 217] *Opposite*: simple

See Compare and Contrast at **mixture**.

comprehend 1 *v* **understand**, know, realize, grasp, figure out, have a handle on, follow, take in, get (*informal*) [➡ UNDERSTAND AND GRASP; 759]   2 *v* (*formal*) **include**, incorporate, bring in, add in, involve [➡ HOLD AND CONTAIN; 455]

comprehensible *adj* **understandable**, clear, logical, plain, coherent, intelligible, lucid, graspable [➡ CONCISE AND CLEAR; 202] *Opposite*: unintelligible

comprehensibly *adv* **intelligibly**, understandably, coherently, clearly, plainly, lucidly, logically, articu-

lately, distinctly [➡ THE NATURE OF IDEAS; 771] *Opposite*: unintelligibly

comprehension *n* **understanding**, grasp, knowledge, command, conception, ability [➡ KNOWLEDGE AND WISDOM; 558]

comprehensive *adj* **complete**, inclusive, full, all-inclusive, wide-ranging, broad, ample, widespread, far-reaching, across-the-board, thorough, all-embracing [➡ WHOLENESS AND COMPLETENESS; 198] *Opposite*: incomplete

comprehensiveness *n* **inclusiveness**, completeness, all-inclusiveness, exhaustiveness, generality, extensiveness, fullness, breadth, depth [➡ WHOLENESS AND COMPLETENESS; 198]

compress 1 *v* **squeeze**, condense, pack together, squash, constrict, compact, tamp [➡ CHANGE OF SIZE: SMALLER; 393] *Opposite*: expand   2 *n* **pad**, wad, cold compress, ice pack, wrapping, poultice [➡ COVERS AND COATINGS; 1246]

comprise *v* **include**, encompass, contain, cover, consist of, embrace [➡ POSSESS; 444] *Opposite*: exclude

compromise 1 *n* **agreement**, settlement, arrangement, bargain, concession, deal [➡ SOLUTIONS; 215]   2 *v* **cooperate**, bargain, negotiate, meet halfway, find the middle ground, give in, concede [➡ HARMONY; 155] *Opposite*: confront

compulsion 1 *n* **coercion**, force, pressure, obligation, duress [➡ CAPTIVITY AND LOSS OF FREEDOM; 248]   2 *n* **urge**, impulse, desire, craving, force, need [➡ FEELINGS ABOUT THE FUTURE; 533]

compulsive 1 *adj* **obsessive**, neurotic, habitual, uncontrollable, irrational, driven [➡ PSYCHOLOGY AND THE MIND; 769] *Opposite*: rational   2 *adj* **gripping**, compelling, mesmerizing, attention-grabbing, exciting, thrilling, interesting [➡ INTERESTING AND MEANINGFUL; 190] *Opposite*: boring

compulsory *adj* **required**, obligatory, necessary, enforced, essential, unavoidable [➡ NECESSARY AND ESSENTIAL; 196] *Opposite*: optional

compunction *n* **regret**, scruple, reluctance, qualm, second thoughts, guilt, remorse, shame [➡ FEELINGS ABOUT THE PAST; 532]

computation *n* **calculation**, reckoning, totaling, addition, subtraction, multiplication, division [➡ MATH; 597] *Opposite*: estimation

compute *v* **calculate**, work out, total, add, subtract, multiply, divide [➡ ASSESS QUANTITY; 757] *Opposite*: estimate

computer *n* [➡ COMPUTERS AND COMPUTING; 1127]

computer

◆ *types of computers*
adder, calculator, handheld computer, laptop, mainframe, microcomputer, minicomputer, notebook, palmtop, PC, PDA, personal computer, personal digital assistant, personal organizer, supercomputer, tablet computer, workstation

◆ *types of computer features*
bit, bitmap, buffer, byte, cache, cursor, desktop, directory, emoticon, folder, pixel, platform, smiley, subdirectory, wallpaper, window, word

◆ *types of hardware*
accelerator card, accumulator, backspace, bus, CD

burner, CD writer, CD-ROM, central processing unit, chip, console, CPU, disk, disk drive, diskette, DVD, firmware, floppy disk, FPU, hard disk, integrated circuit, interface, joystick, keyboard, memory, microchip, microprocessor, modem, monitor, motherboard, mouse, network, numeric keypad, parallel, platform, port, printed circuit, printer, processor, RAM, readout, ROM, scanner, screen, serial, server, simulator, sound card, space bar, terminal, touch screen, trackball, VDT, video display terminal, visual display unit

◆ *types of software*
application, browser, CAD, codec, computer-aided design, cookie, database, emulator, firmware, freeware, GUI, interface, macro, OCR, operating system, OS, patch, program, screensaver, search engine, shareware, simulator, spell checker, spreadsheet, virus, word processor, worm

computer-aided design *n* **CAD**, computer graphics, graphics, product design, drafting [➡ COMPUTERS AND COMPUTING; 1127]

computer graphics *n* [➡ COMPUTERS AND COMPUTING; 1127]

computer modeling *n* [➡ COMPUTERS AND COMPUTING; 1127]

computer processing *n* [➡ COMPUTERS AND COMPUTING; 1127]

computer program *n* [➡ COMPUTERS AND COMPUTING; 1127]

computer programmer *n* [➡ COMPUTERS AND COMPUTING; 1127]

computer science *n* [➡ COMPUTERS AND COMPUTING; 1127]

computer scientist *n* [➡ COMPUTERS AND COMPUTING; 1127]

computer technology *n* [➡ COMPUTERS AND COMPUTING; 1127]

comrade *n* **friend**, companion, buddy (*informal*), pal (*informal*), chum (*informal*), mate (*UK*) [➡ FRIENDS AND GUESTS; 963] *Opposite*: enemy

comradely *adj* **friendly**, companionable, brotherly [➡ FRIENDLINESS AND SOCIABILITY; 494]

comradeship *n* **camaraderie**, brotherhood, friendship [➡ RELATIONSHIP TO ANOTHER; 973]

con 1 *v* **swindle**, defraud, cheat, trick, do (*informal*), rip off (*informal*) [➡ STEAL AND ROB; 426] 2 *v* (*informal*) **deceive**, hoodwink, trick, mislead, dupe, inveigle, entrap, take in, lure, sweet-talk (*informal*), pull a fast one (*slang*), hustle (*slang*) [➡ DECEPTION AND LIES; 660] 3 *n* **negative**, disadvantage, minus, objection, downside [➡ PROBLEMS; 256] *Opposite*: pro 4 *n* (*slang*) **convict**, prisoner, jailbird (*slang*) [➡ CAPTIVES AND PRISONERS; 249] 5 *n* **confidence game**, fraud, ploy, rip-off (*informal*), scam (*slang*), confidence trick (*UK*) [➡ DECEPTION AND LIES; 660]

con artist (*slang*) *n* **trickster**, cheat, swindler, fraud, shark (*informal*), con man (*slang*) [➡ PEOPLE WHO DECEIVE; 661]

con brio *type of* **musical term** [➡ MUSICAL TERMS; 912]

concave *adj* **curved in**, dished, hollow, sunken [➡ ROUNDED SHAPE; 1218] *Opposite*: convex

conceal 1 *v* **hide**, cover, cover up, secrete, screen, obscure, mask, disguise, camouflage [➡ CAUSE TO DISAPPEAR; 6] *Opposite*: reveal 2 *v* **suppress**, keep quiet, keep under

wraps, sit on, censor, cover up, hold back, disguise [➡ WITHHOLD INFORMATION; 687] *Opposite*: divulge

concealed 1 *adj* **hidden**, covered, buried, obscured, masked [➡ IMPERCEPTIBLE; 26] *Opposite*: visible 2 *adj* **secret**, cloaked, masked, veiled, disguised, camouflaged, hidden away [➡ SECRET AND UNKNOWN; 179] *Opposite*: open

concealer *n* [➡ MAKEUP AND BEAUTY PRODUCTS; 490]

concealment *n* **cover-up**, disguise, camouflage, suppression [➡ SECRET AND UNKNOWN; 179] *Opposite*: revelation

concede 1 *v* **acknowledge**, grant, admit, accept, allow (*formal*), own (*formal*) [➡ FORGET, FORGIVE, AND ACCEPT; 748] *Opposite*: deny 2 *v* **yield**, give in, give up, admit defeat, compromise, forfeit [➡ FORGET, FORGIVE, AND ACCEPT; 748] *Opposite*: stand firm

conceit *n* **self-importance**, pride, vanity, arrogance, superiority, self-satisfaction, narcissism, bigheadedness (*informal*) [➡ AFFECTATION, SELF-SATISFACTION, AND SNOBBISHNESS; 507] *Opposite*: modesty

conceited *adj* **self-important**, proud, vain, arrogant, high and mighty, superior, self-satisfied, narcissistic, stuck-up (*informal*), bigheaded (*informal*) [➡ POMPOUS, LOUD, AND OVERCONFIDENT; 635] *Opposite*: modest

See Compare and Contrast at **proud**.

conceitedness *n* **self-importance**, arrogance, narcissism, bigheadedness [➡ AFFECTATION, SELF-SATISFACTION, AND SNOBBISHNESS; 507]

conceivable *adj* **imaginable**, believable, possible, plausible, likely, feasible, credible [➡ POSSIBLE AND PROBABLE; 177] *Opposite*: implausible

conceive 1 *v* **imagine**, visualize, envision, envisage, think up, picture [➡ DREAM, IMAGINE, AND FANTASIZE; 749] 2 *v* **create**, think up, dream up, make up, elaborate, form, invent, formulate, devise [➡ INSTITUTE AND INAUGURATE; 348] 3 *v* **consider**, regard, think of, look on, perceive, apprehend, comprehend [➡ DEVELOP THEORIES AND REASON; 744]

concentrate 1 *v* **think**, focus, ponder, muse, deliberate, contemplate, give attention to [➡ THINK AND REFLECT; 743] *Opposite*: daydream 2 *v* **converge**, come together, assemble, collect, cluster, mass [➡ GET CLOSER TOGETHER; 310] *Opposite*: disperse 3 *v* **thicken**, strengthen, reduce, purify, distill [➡ HARDEN, CONGEAL, AND DRY; 387] *Opposite*: dilute 4 *n* **distillate**, essence, quintessence, reduction [➡ SOLIDS; 1274]

concentrated 1 *adj* **focused**, intense, concerted, rigorous, strenuous, determined, resolute [➡ STRENGTH; 201] *Opposite*: half-hearted 2 *adj* **strong**, thick, condensed, reduced [➡ NOT IN A NATURAL STATE; 1215] *Opposite*: diluted

concentration 1 *n* **attentiveness**, attention, absorption, awareness, focus, application [➡ ATTENTION AND ATTENTIVENESS; 763] *Opposite*: distraction 2 *n* **strength**, intensity, potency [➡ DENSITY AND CONSISTENCY; 1207] *Opposite*: dilution

concept *n* **idea**, notion, thought, impression, perception, conception, theory, model, hypothesis, view, belief [➡ IDEAS AND THOUGHTS; 770]

conception 1 *n* **comprehension**, understanding, grasp, command [➡ UNDERSTAND AND GRASP; 759] 2 *n* **idea**, notion, concept, thought, impression, perception, theory, model, hypothesis, view, belief [➞ IDEAS AND THOUGHTS; 770] **3** *n* **beginning**, start, outset, origin, formation, commencement (*formal*) [➞ BEGINNINGS; 53]

conceptual art *type of* **20th-century art movement** [➞ ARTISTIC MOVEMENTS AND STYLES; 899]

concern 1 *v* **worry**, trouble, disturb, bother, upset, alarm, disquiet (*archaic or literary*) [➞ UPSET, DISTRESS, AND HUMILIATE; 567] *Opposite*: reassure **2** *v* **relate**, affect, be about, have to do with, be connected with [➞ BE ABOUT SOMETHING; 62] **3** *n* **anxiety**, worry, apprehension, distress, alarm, unease, disquiet, fear, trepidation, fretfulness, nervousness, uneasiness [➞ CONFUSION, ANXIETY, AND WORRY; 540] *Opposite*: reassurance **4** *n* **interest**, business, point, item, affair, matter, involvement [➞ SUBJECT AREAS; 768] **5** *n* **company**, firm, business, enterprise, establishment, house, outfit (*informal*) [➞ BUSINESS ENTERPRISES AND RELATED BODIES; 792]

concerned *adj* **worried**, anxious, disturbed, alarmed, fretful, apprehensive, uneasy, upset, nervous, afraid [➞ CONFUSION, ANXIETY, AND WORRY; 540] *Opposite*: carefree

concerning *prep* **about**, relating to, regarding, with reference to, as to, in relation to, pertaining to, re, with regard to, as regards, in connection with, apropos, vis-à-vis [➞ EXPRESSIONS OF REFERENCE; 63]

concert 1 *n* **recital**, performance, show, gig (*informal*) [➞ PERFORMANCES AND SHOWS; 42] **2** *type of* **broadcast** [➞ TELEVISION AND RADIO; 606]

concerted 1 *adj* **concentrated**, intensive, rigorous, strenuous, determined, resolute [➞ STRENGTH; 201] *Opposite*: half-hearted **2** *adj* **combined**, collaborative, joint, mutual [➞ ACTING WITH OTHERS; 285] *Opposite*: solitary

concerted effort *n* [➞ HARD WORK OR EFFORT; 298]

concert hall *n* [➞ BUILDINGS FOR PUBLIC ENTERTAINMENT; 1084]

concertina *type of* **keyboard** [➞ MUSICAL INSTRUMENTS; 910]

concerto *type of* **musical form** [➞ MUSIC, SONGS, AND SINGING; 907]

concession 1 *n* **privilege**, allowance, dispensation, indulgence, acknowledgment, recognition, consideration [➞ KIND ACTIONS OR BEHAVIOR; 295] **2** *n* **yielding**, surrendering, granting, giving way, conceding, compromise [➞ GIFTS; 438] **3** *n* **concession stand**, franchise, outlet, sublicense, business, enterprise, concern [➞ BUSINESS ENTERPRISES AND RELATED BODIES; 792] **4** *n* (*UK*) **reduction**, discount, allowance, markdown, decrease [➞ EXPENDITURE; 423]

conch *type of* **aquatic invertebrate** [➞ AQUATIC INVERTEBRATES; 1022]

conchiglie *type of* **pasta** [➞ PASTA; 1180]

concierge 1 *n* **helper**, porter, agent, intermediary, booker, assistant [➞ SUBORDINATES AND ASSISTANTS; 966] **2** *n* **caretaker**, janitor, doorman, superintendent, doorkeeper, gatekeeper, porter, custodian, bouncer, security guard, warden, super (*informal*) [➞ PEOPLE WHO GUARD AND PROTECT; 846]

conciliate *v* **reconcile**, appease, placate, pacify, make peace, mollify, soothe, resolve [➞ APOLOGIZE AND RETRACT; 683] *Opposite*: provoke

conciliation *n* **reconciliation**, appeasement, pacification, reunion, mollification, mediation, resolution [➞ HARMONY; 155] *Opposite*: provocation

conciliator *n* **peacemaker**, mediator, intermediary, arbitrator, arbiter, go-between, negotiator, referee, appeaser [➞ ADVISERS, JUDGES, AND ARBITERS; 971] *Opposite*: troublemaker

conciliatory *adj* **appeasing**, peacemaking, placatory, pacifying, assuaging, mollifying [➞ CALMING; 188] *Opposite*: provocative

concise *adj* **brief**, short, to the point, succinct, summarizing, terse, short and sweet, crisp, curt, abridged [➞ SUCCINCT AND TO THE POINT; 640] *Opposite*: verbose

conciseness *n* **succinctness**, concision, terseness, brevity, shortness, curtness [➞ SUCCINCT AND TO THE POINT; 640] *Opposite*: wordiness

concision *n* **succinctness**, conciseness, terseness, brevity, shortness, curtness [➞ SUCCINCT AND TO THE POINT; 640] *Opposite*: wordiness

conclave *n* **meeting**, assembly, council, congress, gathering, caucus [➞ MEETINGS AND ASSEMBLIES; 43]

conclude 1 *v* **end**, close, finish, terminate, finish off, halt, call a halt, wrap up (*informal*) [➞ COMPLETE AN ACTION; 263] *Opposite*: start **2** *v* **deduce**, assume, presume, decide, reckon, construe, suppose, infer, work out, figure out [➞ MAKE DECISIONS AND CHOICES; 752] *Opposite*: speculate **3** *v* **settle**, complete, close, clinch, arrange, achieve, accomplish, bring about, determine, resolve [➞ APPROVE AND CONFIRM; 646]

See Compare and Contrast at **deduce**.

concluded *adj* **decided**, settled, determined, resolved, clinched, established [➞ WHOLENESS AND COMPLETENESS; 198] *Opposite*: unresolved

concluding *adj* **closing**, final, last, ultimate, ending [➞ AFTER, LAST, AND FOLLOWING; 165] *Opposite*: opening

conclusion 1 *n* **deduction**, assumption, inference, supposition, decision [➞ IDEAS AND THOUGHTS; 770] **2** *n* **end**, close, finish, termination, wrap-up, finale, windup, ending, closing [➞ ENDS AND DEPARTURES; 54] *Opposite*: start

conclusive *adj* **decisive**, beyond question, definite, convincing, irrefutable, incontrovertible, sure, certain, final, categorical [➞ CERTAIN; 174] *Opposite*: unconvincing

concoct 1 *v* **prepare**, cook, make, put together, mix up, stir up, create, produce, fix, rustle up (*informal*) [➞ MEAL PREPARATION; 354] **2** *v* **make up**, create, devise, invent, dream up, fabricate, think up, put together, formulate, conceive, cook up (*informal*) [➞ DREAM, IMAGINE, AND FANTASIZE; 749]

concoction 1 *n* **mixture**, brew, blend, potion, drink [➞ COLLECTIONS AND MIXTURES OF THINGS; 1244] **2** *n* **invention**, creation, fabrication, fantasy, fiction [➞ NONEXISTENT THINGS; 23]

concomitance *n* **accompaniment**, coexistence, conjunction, combination, association, connection [➞ CONNECTIONS; 143] *Opposite*: independence

concomitant 1 *adj* **attendant**, associated, accompanying, connected, affiliated, related [➞ RELATED; 142] *Opposite*: unrelated **2** *adj* **simultaneous**, parallel, concurrent, coexistent, contemporaneous [➞ CONCURRENT AND CONTEMPORANEOUS; 164] *Opposite*: independent

concord 1 *n* **agreement**, harmony, unity, accord, peace, accordance, friendship [➠ HARMONY; 155] *Opposite*: conflict **2** *n* **treaty**, pact, agreement, settlement, compact [➠ OFFICIAL DOCUMENTS; 586]

concourse 1 *n* **open space**, public space, forecourt, courtyard, square, mall, hall, space [➠ URBAN OUTDOOR SPACES; 1072] **2** *n* **crowd**, throng, horde, multitude, mass [➠ AUDIENCES AND ATTENDEES; 937] **3** *n* **gathering**, assembly, meeting, rally, muster [➠ MEETINGS AND ASSEMBLIES; 43]

concrete 1 *n* [➠ BUILDING MATERIALS; 1077] **2** *adj* **tangible**, existing, actual, material, solid, physical, real [➠ TRUE AND REAL; 171] *Opposite*: insubstantial **3** *adj* **specific**, particular, distinct, certain, definite [➠ CONCISE AND CLEAR; 202] *Opposite*: indeterminate

concubine *n* **mistress**, kept woman, hetaera, odalisque [➠ SEXUAL AND ROMANTIC RELATIONSHIPS; 964]

concur 1 *v* **agree**, harmonize, be in accord, correspond, coincide, see eye to eye, be together [➠ AGREE; 645] *Opposite*: conflict **2** *v* **coincide**, synchronize, fall together, coexist [➠ EXIST WITH OTHERS; 18] *Opposite*: diverge **3** *v* **assent**, go along with, agree to, acquiesce, accept, consent [➠ PERMIT AND ALLOW; 669] *Opposite*: resist

See Compare and Contrast at **agree**.

concurrence 1 *n* **agreement**, accord, harmony, consensus, correspondence, coincidence, togetherness [➠ HARMONY; 155] *Opposite*: conflict **2** *n* **simultaneity**, coexistence, concomitance, coincidence, synchronism, accompaniment [➠ CONCURRENT AND CONTEMPORANEOUS; 164]

concurrent *adj* **simultaneous**, synchronous, parallel, coexisting, contemporaneous, concomitant, contemporary [➠ CONCURRENT AND CONTEMPORANEOUS; 164] *Opposite*: separate

condemn 1 *v* **censure**, denounce, deprecate, criticize, attack, revile, disparage, slam (*informal*), pan (*informal*) [➠ PROTEST AND EXPRESS DISAPPROVAL; 642] *Opposite*: commend **2** *v* **rebuke**, reprove, reprimand, reproach, blame, criticize [➠ ACCUSE, BLAME, AND CRITICIZE; 641] *Opposite*: commend **3** *v* **convict**, sentence, find guilty, doom, judge [➠ TRIAL, PUNISHMENT, AND LEGAL OUTCOMES; 819] *Opposite*: absolve

See Compare and Contrast at **criticize**.

condemnation 1 *n* **censure**, disapproval, blame, denunciation, criticism, reproof, attack [➠ CRITICISMS AND ANGRY OUTBURSTS; 50] *Opposite*: commendation **2** *n* **conviction**, sentence, judgment [➠ TRIAL, PUNISHMENT, AND LEGAL OUTCOMES; 819] *Opposite*: absolution

condemnatory *adj* **disapproving**, critical, disparaging, reproving, denouncing, judgmental [➠ ACCUSATORY AND DISAPPROVING; 634] *Opposite*: approving

condensation 1 *n* **wetness**, dampness, damp, humidity, water, mist, droplets [➠ MOIST; 1241] **2** *n* **concentration**, compression, reduction [➠ DENSITY AND CONSISTENCY; 1207] **3** *n* **abbreviation**, shortening, abridgment, summarization, cutting [➠ SUMMARIES, OUTLINES, AND EXCERPTS; 588] *Opposite*: expansion

condense 1 *v* **concentrate**, compress, compact, squeeze, pack into, consolidate [➠ CHANGE OF SIZE: SMALLER; 393] *Opposite*: expand **2** *v* **abbreviate**, shorten, abridge, shrink, summarize, reduce, cut down, précis, edit, contract [➠ CHANGE OF SIZE: SMALLER; 393] *Opposite*: expand

condensed 1 *adj* **shortened**, reduced, summarized, edited, abbreviated, cut, abridged, compressed, précised, abstracted [➠ CHANGE OF SIZE: SMALLER; 393] *Opposite*: expanded **2** *adj* **concentrated**, thickened, reduced, evaporated, thick, dense [➠ NOT IN A NATURAL STATE; 1215] *Opposite*: diluted

condescend 1 *v* **patronize**, humiliate, talk down, look down on, disdain [➠ INSULTS, ABUSE, AND SWEARING; 658] *Opposite*: respect **2** *v* **deign**, lower yourself, stoop, humble, demean, lower [➠ PERMIT AND ALLOW; 669]

condescending *adj* **patronizing**, disdainful, superior, haughty, pompous, arrogant, lofty, supercilious, snobbish, contemptuous, snooty (*informal*) [➠ POMPOUS, LOUD, AND OVERCONFIDENT; 635] *Opposite*: deferential

condescendingly *adv* **patronizingly**, pompously, superciliously, loftily, disdainfully, haughtily, arrogantly, snobbishly, contemptuously, snootily (*informal*) [➠ RUDE AND HOSTILE; 625] *Opposite*: deferentially

condescension *n* **disdain**, superciliousness, aloofness, haughtiness, arrogance, snobbery, pomposity, contempt, snootiness (*informal*) [➠ ANTAGONISM; 552] *Opposite*: deference

condiment *n* [➠ SEASONINGS AND SAUCES; 1174]

condition 1 *n* **state**, form, order, repair, fitness [➠ STATE; 1208] **2** *n* **stipulation**, clause, proviso, provision, requirement, prerequisite, specification, term, restriction, precondition, rider [➠ NECESSARY AND ESSENTIAL; 196] **3** *n* **disorder**, illness, complaint, ailment [➠ SICKNESS; 729] **4** *v* **acclimatize**, get used to, prepare, train, get ready, shape up [➠ CHANGE; 372]

conditional 1 *adj* **provisional**, restricted, restrictive, qualified, uncertain, unconfirmed [➠ RECIPROCITY AND INTERDEPENDENCE; 147] *Opposite*: unrestricted **2** *type of* **grammatical term** [➠ ASPECTS OF LANGUAGE; 682]

conditioned *adj* **trained**, broken in, inured, hardened, accustomed, habituated (*formal*) [➠ CHANGE; 372] *Opposite*: untrained

conditioning *n* **training**, breaking in, taming, habituation (*formal*) [➠ CHANGE; 372]

conditions *n* **circumstances**, situation, surroundings, setting, environment, state of affairs [➠ SITUATIONS; 71]

condo (*informal*) *n* [➠ RESIDENTIAL BUILDINGS; 1078]

condolence *n* **sympathy**, commiseration, pity, comfort, concern [➠ COMPASSION AND FORGIVENESS; 551]

condolences *n* **commiserations**, words of comfort, deepest sympathy [➠ GREETINGS, FAREWELLS, AND SALUTATIONS; 659]

condominium *n* **apartment building**, house, cooperative, condo (*informal*), co-op (*informal*), apartment block (*UK*) [➠ RESIDENTIAL BUILDINGS; 1078]

condone *v* **overlook**, excuse, disregard, forgive, ignore, pardon, tolerate, make allowances for, turn a blind eye to [➠ FORGET, FORGIVE, AND ACCEPT; 748] *Opposite*: oppose

condor *type of* **scavenger** [➠ BIRDS; 997]

conducive *adj* **favorable**, helpful, contributing to, encouraging, advantageous, beneficial [➡ EMOTIONALLY PLEASANT; 187]

conduct 1 *v* **lead**, show, direct, steer, accompany, pilot, shepherd, guide, usher [➡ ACCOMPANY AND FOLLOW; 337] **2** *v* **manage**, run, control, direct, organize, handle, operate, oversee, supervise [➡ BE IN CHARGE; 270] **3** *n* **behavior**, demeanor, ways, manner, deportment, bearing, mien (*formal*), comportment (*formal*) [➡ TEMPERAMENT AND BEHAVIOR; 492] **4** *n* **management**, handling, organization, administration, running, controlling, oversight, care, charge, supervision, superintendence [➡ WAYS OF DOING THINGS; 294]

See Compare and Contrast at **guide**.

conduction *n* **transmission**, transference, transfer, conveyance, passage [➡ MOVE SOMETHING TO ANOTHER LOCATION; 324]

conduct yourself *v* **behave**, act, behave yourself, carry yourself, comport yourself (*formal*), acquit yourself (*formal*) [➡ CARRY OUT AN ACTION; 269]

conduit *n* **channel**, canal, duct, tube, pipe, ditch, drain, outlet, watercourse [➡ WATERCOURSES; 1111]

cone 1 *type of* **rounded shape** [➡ ROUNDED SHAPE; 1218] **2** *part of* **eye** [➡ THE EYE; 698]

Conestoga wagon *type of* **wagon or carriage** [➡ VEHICLES; 1145]

confab (*informal*) *n* **chat**, tête à tête, heart to heart [➡ INFORMAL COMMUNICATION; 45]

confectioners' sugar *n* [➡ SUGAR AND PRESERVES; 1184]

confectionery *n* [➡ CONFECTIONERY; 1182]

confectionery

◆ *types of confectionery*
bonbon, bubble gum, butterscotch, candy, caramel, chewing gum, chocolate, fondant, fudge, gum, gumdrop, hard candy, humbug, jawbreaker, jellybean, licorice, marshmallow, marzipan, nougat, peppermint, praline, rock candy, sweetmeat (*archaic*), taffy, toffee, truffle

◆ *types of confectionery on a stick*
candy apple, cotton candy, lollipop, sucker

confederacy *n* **union**, league, association, alliance, grouping, confederation, coalition, federation, partnership [➡ GROUPS WITH A COMMON INTEREST; 938]

confederate 1 *n* **partner**, associate, ally, colleague, accomplice, coconspirator, sidekick (*informal*) [➡ SUPPORTERS, PROTECTORS, AND COMPATRIOTS; 970] *Opposite*: rival **2** *adj* **allied**, united, joined, associated, affiliated [➡ RELATED; 142] *Opposite*: rival **3** *v* **ally**, unite, join, affiliate, associate, link [➡ CREATING CONNECTIONS; 144] *Opposite*: disconnect

confederation *n* **association**, league, union, coalition, confederacy, federation, alliance, partnership, grouping [➡ GROUPS WITH A COMMON INTEREST; 938]

confer 1 *v* **discuss**, consider, talk over, go over, hash over, put your heads together, thrash out (*UK*) [➡ TWO-WAY COMMUNICATION; 607] **2** *v* (*formal*) **award**, present, grant, give,

bestow (*formal*) [➡ REWARD; 436] *Opposite*: withhold

See Compare and Contrast at **give**.

conference 1 *n* **session**, meeting, consultation, discussion, talks, colloquium [➡ MEETINGS AND ASSEMBLIES; 43] **2** *n* **symposium**, seminar, convention, forum, meeting, congress, summit [➡ MEETINGS AND ASSEMBLIES; 43] **3** *n* **league**, association, alliance, union, federation [➡ AUDIENCES AND ATTENDEES; 937]

confess 1 *v* **admit**, own up, acknowledge, make a clean breast, come clean (*informal*) [➡ ADMIT AND CONFESS; 615] *Opposite*: deny **2** *v* **declare**, profess, affirm, assert, make known, acknowledge [➡ ADMIT AND CONFESS; 615] *Opposite*: repress

confession 1 *n* **admission**, concession, revelation, acknowledgment [➡ ADMIT AND CONFESS; 615] *Opposite*: denial **2** *n* **declaration**, affirmation, profession, assertion, statement, acknowledgment [➡ ADMIT AND CONFESS; 615]

confidant *n* **friend**, soul mate, alter ego, sister, brother, amigo, intimate, sounding board, best friend [➡ FRIENDS AND GUESTS; 963]

confidante *n* **friend**, intimate, sister, soul mate [➡ FRIENDS AND GUESTS; 963]

confide *v* **unburden**, disclose, reveal, divulge, tell, pass on, make known, confess, open your heart [➡ BETRAY CONFIDENCES AND GOSSIP; 618] *Opposite*: withhold

confidence 1 *n* **self-assurance**, sureness, self-confidence, poise, assurance, self-reliance, buoyancy, coolness [➡ CONFIDENCE AND COMPOSURE; 499] *Opposite*: timidity **2** *n* **assurance**, certainty, conviction, belief, faith, trust, support, loyalty [➡ COOL AND CALM; 536] *Opposite*: doubt **3** *n* **secret**, intimacy, classified information [➡ SECRETS AND MYSTERIES; 180]

confidence game *see* **con game**

confidence trick *see* **con game**

confident 1 *adj* **self-assured**, poised, self-confident, self-possessed, cool, assured, assertive, self-reliant, buoyant, upbeat [➡ CONFIDENCE AND COMPOSURE; 499] *Opposite*: timid **2** *adj* **definite**, sure, certain, positive, convinced, secure [➡ CERTAINTY; 561] *Opposite*: unsure

confidential 1 *adj* **private**, secret, classified, censored, off the record, restricted, hush-hush (*informal*) [➡ SECRET AND UNKNOWN; 179] *Opposite*: unrestricted **2** *adj* **intimate**, private, close, personal [➡ RELATIONSHIP TO ANOTHER; 973] **3** *adj* **sound**, stable, trusted, trustworthy, reliable, dependable, faithful [➡ HONEST AND RELIABLE; 502] *Opposite*: untrustworthy

confidentially *adv* **behind the scenes**, privately, in secret, just between you and me, one on one, behind closed doors, sub rosa, in confidence, off the record, in camera [➡ SECRET AND UNKNOWN; 179] *Opposite*: openly

configuration *n* **shape**, outline, formation, conformation, arrangement, alignment, structure [➡ SHAPE; 1216]

configure *v* **arrange**, design, set up, construct, align, shape [➡ ARRANGE AND CREATE ORDER; 357]

confine 1 *v* **restrain**, restrict, limit, narrow, keep, curb [➡ REFUSE PERMISSION AND NOT ALLOW; 670] *Opposite*: unleash **2** *v* **detain**, quarantine, imprison, jail, lock up, impound, shut in, keep, incarcerate (*formal*), sequester (*formal*) [➡CAPTIVITY AND LOSS OF FREEDOM; 248] *Opposite*: release

confined 1 *adj* **limited**, narrowed, kept, restricted, cramped, curbed, restrained [➡CAPTIVITY AND LOSS OF FREEDOM; 248] *Opposite*: open 2 *adj* **constricted**, small, cramped, enclosed [➡SMALL; 1195] *Opposite*: open

confinement 1 *n* (*dated*) **childbirth**, giving birth, labor [➡REPRODUCTION AND HEREDITY; 725] 2 *n* **imprisonment**, quarantine, internment, detention, captivity, incarceration (*formal*) [➡CAPTIVITY AND LOSS OF FREEDOM; 248] *Opposite*: freedom 3 *n* **limitation**, scope, restriction, restraint, limit, bounds, boundary [➡CAPTIVITY AND LOSS OF FREEDOM; 248]

confines *n* **limits**, boundaries, borders, limitations, margins, precincts, restrictions [➡EXTREMITIES OF PHYSICAL OBJECTS; 1250]

confirm 1 *v* **corroborate**, verify, substantiate, bear out, prove, authenticate, validate, back up [➡APPROVE AND CONFIRM; 646] *Opposite*: refute 2 *v* **settle**, check, authorize, approve, sanction, endorse, ratify [➡APPROVE AND CONFIRM; 646] 3 *v* (*formal*) **strengthen**, firm up, fortify, reinforce, deepen, enhance [➡IMPROVE STRENGTH AND DURABILITY; 378] *Opposite*: undermine

confirmation 1 *n* **corroboration**, verification, substantiation, authentication, evidence, affirmation [➡EVIDENCE AND PROOF; 69] 2 *n* **validation**, authorization, approval, sanction, endorsement, ratification [➡PERMIT AND ALLOW; 669]

confirmed *adj* **long-established**, established, dyed-in-the-wool, inveterate, deep-rooted, complete, definite, incorrigible, set, fixed, longtime [➡UNWILLINGNESS AND STUBBORNNESS; 564]

confiscate *v* **take away**, remove, sequester, seize, impound, appropriate, commandeer, repossess [➡TAKE SOMETHING AWAY; 425] *Opposite*: restore

confiscation *n* **seizure**, repossession, appropriation, removal, sequestration, impounding [➡TAKE SOMETHING AWAY; 425] *Opposite*: return

conflagration *n* **fire**, blaze, inferno, forest fire, brushfire, bushfire [➡FIRE, FLAMMABILITY, AND BURNING; 1165]

See Compare and Contrast at **fire**.

conflate *v* **combine**, amalgamate, consolidate, merge [➡COMBINE AND MIX; 400]

conflation *n* **combination**, amalgamation, consolidation, merger [➡COMBINE AND MIX; 400]

conflict 1 *n* **battle**, fight, war, struggle, encounter, skirmish, clash, engagement [➡AGGRESSIVE EVENTS; 39] *Opposite*: peace 2 *n* **opposition**, disagreement, clash, divergence, difference, argument, variance, quarrel, inconsistency, discord, contradiction, dispute, tension, fracas [➡ARGUMENTS; 47] *Opposite*: concord 3 *v* **disagree**, oppose, clash, dispute, be at odds, be incompatible, differ, diverge [➡DISHARMONY; 156] *Opposite*: concur 4 *v* **fight**, quarrel, struggle, argue, scrap, skirmish, tussle [➡ACCUSE, BLAME, AND CRITICIZE; 641] *Opposite*: agree

See Compare and Contrast at **fight**.

conflicting *adj* **contradictory**, incompatible, at odds,

inconsistent, differing, contrary [➡DISHARMONY; 156] *Opposite*: consistent

confluence *n* **meeting**, convergence, union, joining together, coming together, flowing together [➡CONNECTIONS; 143] *Opposite*: divergence

conform 1 *v* **fit in**, imitate, follow, toe the line, obey, adapt, comply, follow the crowd, play the game, kowtow [➡OBEY AND ABIDE BY; 301] *Opposite*: rebel 2 *v* **agree**, match, correspond, fit, coincide, match up, measure up [➡HARMONY; 155] *Opposite*: contradict

conformism *n* **conventionality**, toeing the line, conformity, orthodoxy, traditionalism, compliance [➡THE WILL AND WILLINGNESS; 563] *Opposite*: dissidence

conformist 1 *n* **yes man**, traditionalist, follower, sheep [➡LAZY OR UNSUCCESSFUL PEOPLE; 948] *Opposite*: rebel 2 *adj* **conventional**, traditional, orthodox, obedient, unadventurous, unquestioning [➡UNADVENTUROUS AND DULL; 517] *Opposite*: rebellious

conformity 1 *n* **toeing the line**, playing the game, conformism, conventionality, traditionalism, orthodoxy [➡ORDINARINESS; 244] *Opposite*: rebellion 2 *n* **agreement**, compliance, consistency, correspondence, accord, obedience, submission [➡HARMONY; 155] *Opposite*: divergence

confound 1 *v* **confuse**, muddle, mix up, mistake, misperceive [➡CONFUSE AND BEWILDER; 571] *Opposite*: distinguish 2 *v* **stun**, amaze, puzzle, mystify, confuse, bewilder, baffle, perplex, floor [➡CONFUSE AND BEWILDER; 571]

confounded 1 *adj* (*informal*) **annoying**, irritating, wretched, blasted (*informal*), darned (*informal*), pesky (*informal*) [➡BAD AND BADLY; 223] 2 *adj* **confused**, perplexed, mystified, baffled, puzzled, bewildered [➡CONFUSION, ANXIETY, AND WORRY; 540]

confrère (*formal*) *n* **colleague**, associate, collaborator, coworker [➡COLLEAGUES AND EQUALS; 967]

confront 1 *v* **challenge**, oppose, antagonize, provoke, meet, threaten, defy [➡ACCUSE, BLAME, AND CRITICIZE; 641] 2 *v* **encounter**, handle, tackle, face up to, meet, face, deal with, brazen out [➡COMPETE, CONTEND, AND COMBAT; 303]

confrontation 1 *n* **hostility**, war, battle, fight, clash, skirmish, conflict [➡AGGRESSIVE EVENTS; 39] 2 *n* **opposition**, argument, disagreement, quarrel, altercation, war of words, conflict, row, face-off, mano a mano [➡ARGUMENTS; 47] *Opposite*: consensus

confrontational *adj* **argumentative**, quarrelsome, hostile, challenging, aggressive, provocative, militant, combative, truculent, belligerent, in-your-face (*informal*) [➡AGGRESSIVE AND BELLIGERENT; 518] *Opposite*: amicable

confuse 1 *v* **puzzle**, perplex, baffle, mystify, bewilder, confound, bamboozle (*informal*) [➡CONFUSE AND BEWILDER; 571] *Opposite*: enlighten 2 *v* **cloud**, muddy the waters, complicate, blur, muddy, obscure [➡CREATE DISORDER AND CAUSE CHAOS; 358] *Opposite*: clarify 3 *v* **muddle**, misperceive, mix up, mistake, confound [➡COMBINE AND MIX; 400] *Opposite*: distinguish

confused 1 *adj* **puzzled**, perplexed, baffled, mystified, bewildered, bemused, befuddled [➡CONFUSION, ANXIETY, AND WORRY; 540] *Opposite*: enlightened 2 *adj* **disordered**, disorderly, muddled, mixed up, in disarray, jumbled, disorganized, chaotic, tangled [➡DISORDER AND CHAOS; 245] *Opposite*: orderly

confusing *adj* **unclear**, puzzling, perplexing, baffling, mystifying, bewildering, befuddling [➡ DIFFICULTY AND COMPLEXITY; 242] *Opposite:* clear

confusion **1** *n* **bewilderment**, perplexity, puzzlement, mystification, uncertainty, misunderstanding [➡ CONFUSION, ANXIETY, AND WORRY; 540] *Opposite:* understanding **2** *n* **misperception**, misunderstanding, mix-up, muddle, mistake, slip-up (*informal*) [➡ MISTAKES; 250] *Opposite:* clarity **3** *n* **disorder**, chaos, turmoil, upheaval, commotion, muddle, mayhem (*informal*) [➡ DISORDER AND CHAOS; 245] *Opposite:* order **4** *n* **embarrassment**, awkwardness, disorientation, uncertainty, self-consciousness [➡ EMBARRASSMENT AND HUMILIATION; 542] *Opposite:* confidence

conga drum *type of* **percussion instrument** [➡ MUSICAL INSTRUMENTS; 910]

con game (*informal*) *n* **swindle**, confidence game, confidence trick, rip-off (*informal*), snow job (*slang*) [➡ DECEPTION AND LIES; 660]

congeal *v* **set**, clot, coagulate, thicken, solidify, harden, gel [➡ HARDEN, CONGEAL, AND DRY; 387] *Opposite:* liquefy

congealed *adj* **set**, dried, coagulated, clotted [➡ DENSITY AND CONSISTENCY; 1207]

congenial *adj* **agreeable**, friendly, affable, amiable, pleasant, genial, good-natured, hospitable [➡ FRIENDLINESS AND SOCIABILITY; 494] *Opposite:* hostile

congeniality *n* **affability**, bonhomie, geniality [➡ HARMONY; 155]

congenital **1** *adj* **inherited**, hereditary, inborn, inbred, genetic, natural, organic, innate [➡ REPRODUCTION AND HEREDITY; 725] *Opposite:* acquired **2** *adj* **ingrained**, established, long-established, habitual, inveterate, incorrigible [➡ FREQUENT AND OFTEN; 107]

congest *v* **clog**, overfill, overcrowd, block, jam, crowd, pack, choke, obstruct [➡ FILL; 406] *Opposite:* clear

congested **1** *adj* **overfilled**, jammed, choked, clogged, blocked, crowded, overcrowded, packed, crammed, jam-packed (*informal*) [➡ FULL; 1239] *Opposite:* empty **2** *adj* **obstructed**, clogged, mucous, stuffy, filled, blocked [➡ FULL; 1239] *Opposite:* clear

congestion **1** *n* **overcrowding**, bottleneck, cramming, jamming, blocking, crowding, mobbing [➡ FULL; 1239] *Opposite:* emptiness **2** *n* **blockage**, clogging, obstruction [➡ PROBLEMS; 256]

conglomerate **1** *n* **corporation**, multinational, company, firm, business [➡ BUSINESS ENTERPRISES AND RELATED BODIES; 792] **2** *type of* **stone** [➡ STONES, ROCKS, AND BOULDERS; 1057]

conglomeration **1** *n* **assortment**, hodgepodge, potpourri, collection, accumulation, miscellany [➡ COLLECTIONS AND MIXTURES OF THINGS; 1244] **2** *n* **composite**, accumulation, mass, collection, assembly, gathering [➡ COLLECTIONS AND MIXTURES OF THINGS; 1244]

Congo franc *type of* **currency** [➡ CURRENCIES; 798]

congratulate *v* **commend**, toast, pat on the back, cheer, applaud, praise, acknowledge [➡ PRAISE AND ENCOURAGE; 647] *Opposite:* denigrate

congratulations *interj* **compliments**, greetings, hats off, well done, cheers (*informal*), way to go (*slang*), felicitations (*formal*) [➡ COMPLIMENTS; 657] *Opposite:* commiserations

congregate *v* **gather**, assemble, collect, meet, mass, flock, come together [➡ GET CLOSER TOGETHER; 310] *Opposite:* disperse

congregation **1** *n* **worshipers**, churchgoers, parishioners, flock [➡ RELIGIOUS PEOPLE; 778] **2** *n* **gathering**, crowd, throng, host, mass, assembly, audience [➡ AUDIENCES AND ATTENDEES; 937]

congress *n* **assembly**, council, conference, meeting, convention [➡ MEETINGS AND ASSEMBLIES; 43]

congressperson *n* **Representative**, senator, legislator, lawmaker, deputy [➡ POLITICAL OFFICES AND POLITICIANS; 808]

congruent (*formal*) *adj* **corresponding**, consistent, matching, compatible, similar, harmonious, harmonizing [➡ HARMONY; 155] *Opposite:* disparate

conifer *n* [➡ PLANTS AND TREES; 1024]

conjectural *adj* **speculative**, tentative, unsubstantial, unsupported [➡ UNCERTAIN; 175]

conjecture **1** *n* **guesswork**, estimation, guess, surmise, inference, speculation, assumption, supposition [➡ GUESS; 754] **2** *v* **estimate**, imagine, guess, speculate, infer, assume, suppose [➡ GUESS; 754]

conjoin (*formal*) *v* **link**, join, connect, couple [➡ FASTEN, LINK, AND JOIN; 408]

conjugal *adj* **marital**, matrimonial, married, wedded, spousal, connubial (*literary*) [➡ MARRIED STATE; 961] *Opposite:* unmarried

conjugation *type of* **grammatical term** [➡ ASPECTS OF LANGUAGE; 682]

conjunction **1** *n* **combination**, aggregation, unification, coincidence, concurrence, juxtaposition, union, combining [➡ CONNECTIONS; 143] **2** *type of* **word class** [➡ ASPECTS OF LANGUAGE; 682]

conjunctiva *part of* **eye** [➡ THE EYE; 698]

conjure **1** *v* **raise**, summon, call up, invoke, conjure up [➡ CAUSE TO APPEAR; 5] **2** *v* **mesmerize**, charm, trick, voodoo, spellbind [➡ HOBBIES, GAMES, AND SPORTS; 875]

conjurer *type of* **entertainer** [➡ WORKERS IN ENTERTAINMENT AND MEDIA; 873]

conjure up **1** *v* **evoke**, create, recall, call up, bring to mind [➡ REMIND; 747] **2** *v* **raise**, conjure, summon, call up, invoke [➡ CAUSE TO APPEAR; 5]

conjuror *see* **conjurer**

conked-out (*informal*) *adj* **asleep**, dead to the world, crashed-out (*slang*) [➡ TIRED, ASLEEP, AND UNCONSCIOUS; 738]

conk out (*informal*) **1** *v* **fail**, break, wear out, malfunction, stall, break down, die, fade [➡ FAIL OR CEASE TO FUNCTION; 470] *Opposite:* kick in (*informal*) **2** *v* **collapse**, pass out, doze off, nod off, fall asleep, drop off (*informal*), crash out (*slang*) [➡ SLEEP AND DREAM; 723] *Opposite:* wake up

con man (*slang*) *n* **cheat**, fraud, swindler, huckster, hustler, con artist (*slang*) [➡ PEOPLE WHO DECEIVE; 661]

con moto *type of* **musical term** [➡ MUSICAL TERMS; 912]

connect 1 *v* **attach**, join, link, fix, tie, unite, bond, link up, network, hook up (*informal*) [➡ FASTEN, LINK, AND JOIN; 408] *Opposite*: disconnect 2 *v* **associate**, relate, link, tie, link up [➡ CREATING CONNECTIONS; 144] *Opposite*: separate 3 *v* **get along**, bond, click (*informal*), hook up (*informal*), hit it off (*informal*), get on (*UK*) [➡ ESTABLISHING RELATIONSHIPS WITH OTHERS; 974]

connected 1 *adj* **joined**, attached, fixed, united, tied, coupled, correlative, together [➡ CLOSENESS; 159] *Opposite*: separate 2 *adj* **linked**, associated, related, allied, coupled [➡ RELATED; 142] *Opposite*: unrelated

connection 1 *n* **joining**, fitting together, assembly, linking, piecing together, construction [➡ FASTEN, LINK, AND JOIN; 408] 2 *n* **context**, association, relationship, correlation, relation, link [➡ CONNECTIONS; 143] 3 *n* **bond**, tie, union, link, join, fixture, joint, coupling [➡ CONNECTIONS; 143]

connections 1 *n* **influence**, network, associates, acquaintances, links, friends, contacts, friends in high places [➡ SUPPORTERS, PROTECTORS, AND COMPATRIOTS; 970] 2 *n* **relations**, relatives, associations, links, family [➡ THE FAMILY; 956]

connive *v* **plot**, scheme, conspire, coconspire, collude, plan, hatch, cook up (*informal*) [➡ CAUSE TO HAPPEN; 31]

conniver *n* **maneuverer**, manipulator, schemer, plotter, intriguer, planner, conspirator, deceiver [➡ PEOPLE WHO DECEIVE; 661]

conniving *adj* **devious**, scheming, conspiratorial, sly, crafty, deceitful [➡ DECEITFUL; 513] *Opposite*: ingenuous

connoisseur *n* **specialist**, authority, expert, enthusiast, aficionado, aficionada, buff, cognoscente [➡ TALENTED OR INTELLIGENT PEOPLE; 528]

connotation *n* **implication**, association, suggestion, meaning, undertone, subtext, overtone, inference, reference, nuance [➡ MEANING; 690]

connote *v* **mean**, signify, suggest, intimate, imply, indicate, signal, purport (*formal*), betoken (*literary*) [➡ MEAN SOMETHING; 61]

connubial (*literary*) *adj* **nuptial**, marital, matrimonial, wedded, conjugal, connubial, married [➡ MARRIED STATE; 961] *Opposite*: unmarried

conquer 1 *v* **seize**, take, take over, take control of, capture, dominate [➡ BEAT AND DEFEAT; 80] *Opposite*: surrender 2 *v* **defeat**, beat, overpower, overthrow, subjugate, vanquish, confound [➡ BEAT AND DEFEAT; 80] *Opposite*: lose 3 *v* **overcome**, surmount, get the better of, triumph over, master, defeat [➡ BEAT AND DEFEAT; 80] *Opposite*: give in

See Compare and Contrast at **defeat**.

conquered *adj* **defeated**, beaten, vanquished, overpowered [➡ BEATEN AND DEFEATED; 78]

conqueror *n* **defeater**, vanquisher, subjugator, captor, victor, conquistador [➡ ENEMIES AND TORMENTORS; 969] *Opposite*: vanquished

conquest 1 *n* **defeat**, subjugation, downfall, beating, overthrow, takeover, rout, invasion, occupation, capture, acquisition, annexation [➡ BEAT AND DEFEAT; 80] *Oppo-*

site: surrender 2 *n* **victory**, success, triumph, win [➡ SUCCESS; 82] *Opposite*: defeat

conscience *n* **scruples**, principles, ethics, integrity, sense of right and wrong, morality [➡ MORAL CONCEPTS; 773]

conscience-stricken *adj* **guilty**, sorry, remorseful, guilt-ridden, contrite [➡ EMBARRASSMENT AND HUMILIATION; 542]

conscientious 1 *adj* **careful**, thorough, meticulous, painstaking, punctilious, scrupulous, reliable, diligent, hard-working, assiduous, industrious, attentive, dependable [➡ HARD-WORKING AND COMMITTED; 500] *Opposite*: careless 2 *adj* **dutiful**, responsible, honorable, upright, upstanding, honest [➡ HONEST AND RELIABLE; 502] *Opposite*: dishonest

See Compare and Contrast at **careful**.

conscientiousness *n* **scrupulousness**, thoroughness, assiduousness, meticulousness, carefulness, care, industriousness, diligence, reliability, attentiveness, dependability, punctiliousness [➡ HONEST AND RELIABLE; 502] *Opposite*: carelessness

conscious 1 *adj* **awake**, wide awake, sleepless, insomniac [➡ WIDE AWAKE AND CONSCIOUS; 735] *Opposite*: unconscious 2 *adj* **aware**, mindful, sentient, sensible, cognizant (*formal*) [➡ KNOWLEDGE AND WISDOM; 558] *Opposite*: unaware 3 *adj* **deliberate**, intentional, premeditated, willful, determined, considered [➡ INTENTIONAL AND DELIBERATE; 279] *Opposite*: unintentional

See Compare and Contrast at **aware**.

consciously *adv* **deliberately**, intentionally, knowingly, determinedly, willfully, on purpose [➡ INTENTIONAL AND DELIBERATE; 279] *Opposite*: unintentionally

consciousness *n* **awareness**, realization, perception, mindfulness, notice, cognizance (*formal*) [➡ KNOWLEDGE AND WISDOM; 558] *Opposite*: unconsciousness

conscript 1 *v* **call up**, recruit, draft, enlist, enroll [➡ WARFARE AND WAR; 830] 2 *n* **recruit**, draftee, novice, rookie (*informal*) [➡ MILITARY PERSONNEL; 828]

conscription *n* **recruitment**, draft, mobilization, enlistment, enrollment, call to arms, call-up (*UK*) [➡ WARFARE AND WAR; 830]

consecrate *v* **sanctify**, bless, set apart, hallow, dedicate, devote [➡ RELIGIONS AND RELIGIOUS PRACTICES; 777] *Opposite*: desecrate

consecrated *adj* **hallowed**, sanctified, sacred, holy, blessed, sacrosanct [➡ RELIGIOUS CONCEPTS; 776] *Opposite*: desecrated

consecration *n* **sanctification**, dedication, blessing, hallowing [➡ RELIGIOUS CONCEPTS; 776] *Opposite*: desecration

consecutive *adj* **successive**, uninterrupted, following, repeated, serial, sequential, succeeding, next [➡ AFTER, LAST, AND FOLLOWING; 165] *Opposite*: alternate

consensus *n* **agreement**, accord, harmony, compromise, consent, unanimity [➡ HARMONY; 155] *Opposite*: disagreement

consent 1 *v* **permit**, allow, approve, accept, sanction, endorse, okay (*informal*) [➡ PERMIT AND ALLOW; 669] *Opposite*: forbid 2 *v* **agree**, comply, assent, acquiesce, accede, concur, subscribe [➡ AGREE; 645] *Opposite*: refuse **3** *n* **agreement**, accord, consensus, harmony [➡ PERMIT AND ALLOW; 669] **4** *n* **permission**, approval, assent, blessing, sanction, authority, agreement, green light, acquiescence, concurrence, allowance, sufferance, compliance, say-so (*informal*), okay (*informal*), go-ahead (*informal*) [➡ PERMIT AND ALLOW; 669] *Opposite*: refusal

See Compare and Contrast at **agree.**

consequence **1** *n* (*formal*) **importance**, significance, value, concern, import, magnitude, moment (*formal*) [➡ IMPORTANCE AND SIGNIFICANCE; 192] **2** *n* **result**, effect, outcome, end result, corollary, aftereffect, aftermath, upshot [➡ RESULTS AND OUTCOMES; 83]

consequent *adj* **resulting**, resultant, consequential, following, subsequent, ensuing [➡ AFTER, LAST, AND FOLLOWING; 165]

consequential **1** *adj* **important**, significant, momentous, far-reaching, substantial, major [➡ IMPORTANT; 194] *Opposite*: inconsequential **2** *adj* **resulting**, resultant, consequent, following, subsequent, ensuing [➡ AFTER, LAST, AND FOLLOWING; 165]

consequently *adv* **as a result**, so, therefore, subsequently, accordingly, thus (*formal*) [➡ CAUSATION; 168]

conservation *n* **preservation**, upkeep, maintenance, protection, management, safeguarding, saving [➡ PREVENT CONTACT OR ATTACK; 419] *Opposite*: destruction

conservative **1** *adj* **traditional**, middle-of-the-road, conventional, conformist, unadventurous, old-fashioned, traditionalist, old-school [➡ UNADVENTUROUS AND DULL; 517] *Opposite*: avant-garde **2** *adj* **cautious**, moderate, careful [➡ ECONOMICAL AND RESOURCEFUL; 207] *Opposite*: speculative **3** *n* **traditionalist**, conformist, fundamentalist, purist, diehard [➡ UNCOOPERATIVE OR REBELLIOUS PEOPLE; 566] *Opposite*: progressive

conservatory **1** *n* **school of the arts**, music school, art school, school of dance, conservatoire [➡ EDUCATIONAL INSTITUTIONS; 813] **2** *n* **greenhouse**, hothouse, garden room, porch, glasshouse (*UK*) [➡ ANCILLARY BUILDINGS; 1080]

conserve **1** *v* **preserve**, save, keep, protect, safeguard, take care of, support, maintain, manage, sustain [➡ STORE AND KEEP; 453] *Opposite*: destroy **2** *v* **store**, save, keep, eke out, be careful with, go easy on (*informal*) [➡ STORE AND KEEP; 453] *Opposite*: expend **3** *n* **jam**, marmalade, preserve [➡ SUGAR AND PRESERVES; 1184]

consider **1** *v* **think through**, mull over, chew over, reflect, deliberate, contemplate, take into account, ponder, study, ruminate, cogitate (*formal*), weigh up (*UK*) [➡ THINK AND REFLECT; 743] **2** *v* **judge**, believe, think, regard as, deem (*formal*) [➡ HAVE AN OPINION OF SOMETHING; 756] **3** *v* **respect**, bear in mind, care about, take into consideration, count [➡ PAY ATTENTION; 765] *Opposite*: disregard

considerable *adj* **substantial**, significant, large, extensive, sizable, great, huge [➡ LARGE; 1193] *Opposite*: insignificant

considerably *adv* **significantly**, much, noticeably, by far, greatly, substantially, extensively, sizably, largely [➡ TO A GREAT EXTENT; 132] *Opposite*: slightly

considerate *adj* **thoughtful**, kind, understanding, caring, sensitive, attentive, sympathetic, respectful, solicitous, mindful [➡ GENEROSITY AND KINDNESS; 495] *Opposite*: inconsiderate

consideration **1** *n* **thought**, reflection, contemplation, attention, deliberation (*formal*) [➡ IDEAS AND THOUGHTS; 770] **2** *n* **respect**, concern, thoughtfulness, kindness, selflessness, sympathy, sensitivity, understanding, care, courtesy, considerateness [➡ GENEROSITY AND KINDNESS; 495] *Opposite*: thoughtlessness **3** *n* **matter**, factor, point, issue, fact, item [➡ SUBJECT AREAS; 768] **4** *n* **regard**, esteem, importance, significance, weight, substance, consequence (*formal*) [➡ IMPORTANCE AND SIGNIFICANCE; 192]

considered *adj* **careful**, measured, well-thought-out, painstaking [➡ THE NATURE OF IDEAS; 771] *Opposite*: rash

considering *prep* **bearing in mind**, allowing for, in view of, given, taking into account [➡ EXPRESSIONS OF REFERENCE; 63] *Opposite*: excluding

consign **1** *v* **entrust**, commit, hand over, give [➡ DISPENSE, RATION, AND DISTRIBUTE; 434] **2** *v* **relegate**, dispatch, condemn, banish, get rid of, dispose of, pack off (*informal*) [➡ GET RID OF SOMETHING; 451] **3** *v* **deliver**, transfer, send, send off, dispatch, remit, hand over, ship [➡ DISPATCH AND SEND; 333]

consignment *n* **batch**, delivery, shipment, load, package, quantity [➡ TRANSPORTATION, TRANSPORTERS, AND CARGOS; 322]

consist **1** *v* **contain**, be made up of, be made of, entail, involve, comprise [➡ POSSESS; 444] **2** *v* **reside**, lie, be based on, depend on, be defined by [➡ AMOUNT TO AND EQUAL; 70]

consistency **1** *n* **constancy**, steadiness, reliability, uniformity, evenness, stability, regularity, dependability [➡ PERMANENCE: WITHOUT CHANGE; 95] *Opposite*: inconsistency **2** *n* **texture**, thickness, runniness, feel, makeup [➡ DENSITY AND CONSISTENCY; 1207]

consistent **1** *adj* **reliable**, steady, dependable, constant, unswerving, unfailing, regular, stable [➡ PERMANENCE: WITHOUT CHANGE; 95] *Opposite*: inconsistent **2** *adj* **coherent**, uniform, harmonious, even [➡ HARMONY; 155] *Opposite*: contradictory

consistently **1** *adv* **time after time**, time and again, again and again, repeatedly, every time, constantly, without fail, over and over, always [➡ PERMANENCE: WITHOUT CHANGE; 95] *Opposite*: erratically **2** *adv* **reliably**, steadily, dependably, constantly, unswervingly, unfailingly, regularly [➡ PERMANENCE: WITHOUT END; 94] *Opposite*: inconsistently

consolation *n* **comfort**, solace, relief, support, succor (*literary*) [➡ TREATS; 210] *Opposite*: grief

consolatory *adj* **comforting**, consoling, cheering, soothing [➡ CALMING; 188]

console **1** *v* **comfort**, cheer up, soothe, calm, relieve, support, solace [➡ SOOTHE AND CALM; 573] *Opposite*: depress **2** *type of* **hardware** [➡ COMPUTERS AND COMPUTING; 1127] **3** *type of* **table** [➡ FURNITURE; 858]

consolidate **1** *v* **combine**, unite, join, fuse, merge, associate, amalgamate [➡ COMBINE AND MIX; 400] *Opposite*: split up **2** *v* **strengthen**, firm up, establish, confirm, enhance [➡ IMPROVE STRENGTH AND DURABILITY; 378] *Opposite*: weaken

consolidation **1** *n* **alliance**, merging, union, link, association, amalgamation, partnership, joining [➡ CONNECTIONS; 143] *Opposite*: split **2** *n* **strengthening**, firming, establishment, solidification, firming up [⟶ IMPROVE STRENGTH AND DURABILITY; 378] *Opposite*: weakening

consoling *adj* **comforting**, soothing, cheering, calming [⟶ GENEROSITY AND KINDNESS; 495]

consommé *type of* **soup** [⟶ SOUPS; 1186]

consonant with (*formal*) *adj* **in agreement with**, at one with, consistent with, compatible with, in harmony with [⟶ HARMONY; 155] *Opposite*: incompatible

consort 1 *n* (*formal*) **companion**, partner, associate, spouse, wife, husband [⟶ RELATIVES BY MARRIAGE; 960] 2 *n* **ensemble**, group, orchestra, band [⟶ MUSICIANS AND SINGERS; 908]

consortium *n* **group**, grouping, association, conglomerate, syndicate, confederation [⟶ BUSINESS ENTERPRISES AND RELATED BODIES; 792]

consort with (*formal*) *v* **associate with**, accompany, mix, mingle, hang around, hang out (*informal*) [⟶ ESTABLISHING RELATIONSHIPS WITH OTHERS; 974]

conspicuous 1 *adj* **visible**, noticeable, obvious, exposed, on show, in the limelight [⟶ PERCEPTIBLE; 25] *Opposite*: inconspicuous 2 *adj* **eye-catching**, striking, prominent, outstanding, notable, marked, noticeable, obvious, evident, patent, overt, blatant, plain, clear [⟶ PERCEPTIBLE; 25] *Opposite*: unremarkable

conspicuously *adv* **noticeably**, obviously, clearly, evidently, blatantly, visibly [⟶ PERCEPTIBLE; 25] *Opposite*: inconspicuously

conspicuousness *n* **obviousness**, plainness, prominence, overtness [⟶ PERCEPTIBLE; 25]

conspiracy *n* **plot**, scheme, plan, intrigue, collusion, machination, sedition, treachery [⟶ BAD BEHAVIOR OR ACTIONS; 254]

conspirator *n* **schemer**, plotter, conniver, collaborator, accomplice [⟶ PEOPLE WHO DECEIVE; 661]

conspiratorial *adj* **private**, shared, confidential, complicit, collusive, thick as thieves [⟶ RELATIONSHIP TO ANOTHER; 973]

conspire 1 *v* **plot**, connive, plan, work against [⟶ PREDICT AND ANTICIPATE; 750] 2 *v* **combine**, work together, unite, collaborate, collude, contrive, devise, machinate [⟶ DEVELOP THEORIES AND REASON; 744]

constable *n* [⟶ THE POLICE, ARREST, AND PRETRIAL PROCEEDINGS; 818]

constabulary *n* [⟶ THE POLICE, ARREST, AND PRETRIAL PROCEEDINGS; 818]

constancy 1 *n* **faithfulness**, loyalty, fidelity, dependability, reliability, devotion [⟶ HARD-WORKING AND COMMITTED; 500] *Opposite*: unfaithfulness 2 *n* **steadiness**, firmness, consistency, steadfastness, endurance, single-mindedness [⟶ PERMANENCE: WITHOUT CHANGE; 95] *Opposite*: inconsistency

constant 1 *adj* **continuous**, endless, relentless, continual, persistent, perpetual, unbroken, unceasing, ceaseless, unremitting, incessant [⟶ PERMANENCE: WITHOUT END; 94] *Opposite*: intermittent 2 *adj* **frequent**, persistent, recurrent, incessant, recurring, continual [⟶ FREQUENT AND OFTEN; 107] *Opposite*: occasional 3 *adj* **steady**, stable, even, invariable, unvarying, regular, uniform, unchanging [⟶ PERMANENCE: WITHOUT CHANGE; 95] *Opposite*: irregular 4 *adj* **faithful**, loyal, trustworthy, devoted, bosom, staunch, steadfast [⟶ HARD-WORKING AND COMMITTED; 500] *Opposite*: disloyal

constantly *adv* **continually**, continuously, always, regularly, frequently, persistently, relentlessly, incessantly, remorselessly, endlessly, ceaselessly, perpetually, forever, repetitively [⟶ PERMANENCE: WITHOUT END; 94] *Opposite*: intermittently

constellation 1 *n* **group**, gathering, collection, assemblage, pattern, arrangement, cluster, galaxy [⟶ COLLECTIONS AND MIXTURES OF THINGS; 1244] 2 *n* [⟶ THE SOLAR SYSTEM AND ASTRONOMY; 1060]

constellation

◆ *types of constellations (of the northern hemisphere)*
Andromeda, Aquila, Aries, Auriga, Boötes, Camelopardalis, Cancer, Canes Venatici, Canis Minor, Cassiopeia, Cepheus, Coma Berenices, Corona Borealis, Cygnus, Delphinus, Draco, Equuleus, Gemini, Hercules, Hydra, Lacerta, Leo, Leo Minor, Lyra, Mynx, Ophiuchus, Orion, Pegasus, Perseus, Pisces, Polaris (Northern Star), Sagitta, Serpens, Taurus, Triangulum, Ursa Major, Ursa Minor, Virgo

◆ *types of constellations (of the southern hemisphere)*
Apus, Aquarius, Aquila, Ara, Canis Major, Capricornus, Carina, Centaurus, Cetus, Chamaeleon, Columba, Corona Australis, Corvus, Crater, Crux, Dorado, Eridanus, Fornax, Grus, Hydra, Hydrus, Indus, Lepus, Libra, Lupus, Monoceros, Musca, Octans, Ophiuchus, Orion, Pavo, Phoenix, Pictor, Piscis Austrinus, Puppis, Pyxis, Sagittarius, Scorpius, Sculptor, Serpens, Sextans, Triangulum Australe, Tuscana, Vela, Virgo, Volans

consternation *n* **dismay**, disquiet, alarm, anxiety, worry, concern, dread, trepidation, bewilderment [⟶ SADNESS, DISTRESS, AND DESPAIR; 539] *Opposite*: composure

constituency 1 *n* **area**, borough, ward, region [⟶ HUMAN SETTLEMENTS; 1070] 2 *n* **electorate**, voters, population, public, community, citizenry [⟶ GROUPS IN SOCIETY; 940]

constituent 1 *n* **voter**, citizen, resident [⟶ INHABITANTS; 857] 2 *n* **ingredient**, element, component, part [⟶ PHYSICAL OBJECTS; 1243] 3 *adj* **basic**, essential, integral, component, fundamental, principal [⟶ FUNDAMENTAL; 195]

constitute 1 *v* **make up**, form, compose, represent [⟶ POSSESS; 444] 2 *v* **amount to**, represent, add up to, signify, total, equal [⟶ AMOUNT TO AND EQUAL; 70] *Opposite*: fall short of 3 *v* (*formal*) **set up**, establish, found, create, institute, start, organize [⟶ INSTITUTE AND INAUGURATE; 348] *Opposite*: disband

constitution 1 *n* **charter**, bill, statute, instrument of government (*UK*) [⟶ LEGISLATIVE BODIES AND LEGISLATION; 809] 2 *n* **health**, makeup, disposition, nature, condition [⟶ PHYSICAL STATES; 734] 3 *n* **establishment**, creation, formation, organization, foundation [⟶ BEGINNINGS; 53] 4 *n* **composition**, structure, makeup, components, constituents, parts [⟶ QUALITIES AND CHARACTERISTICS; 1191]

constitutional *adj* **legitimate**, legal, lawful, statutory [⟶ LEGAL AND LEGITIMATE; 815] *Opposite*: unconstitutional

constrain 1 *v* **oblige**, compel, pressure, make, coerce, force [⟶ CAUSE OR COMPEL TO ACT; 271] 2 *v* **limit**, restrain, hold back, confine, restrict, constrict, hamper, hinder, inhibit, check [⟶ AVOID, PREVENT, LIMIT, AND CONTROL; 277]

constrained *adj* **forced**, unnatural, inhibited, controlled, unspontaneous, embarrassed, guarded, self-conscious, reserved [➥CAPTIVITY AND LOSS OF FREEDOM; 248] *Opposite*: natural

constraint *n* **restriction**, limitation, restraint, constriction, limit, control [➥CAPTIVITY AND LOSS OF FREEDOM; 248] *Opposite*: freedom

constrict 1 *v* **tighten**, narrow, contract, compress, shrink, squeeze [➥CONTACT: EXERT PRESSURE; 414] *Opposite*: loosen 2 *v* **limit**, restrict, constrain, narrow, control, restrain, inhibit [➥CAPTIVITY AND LOSS OF FREEDOM; 248] *Opposite*: extend

constricted *adj* **limited**, restricted, restrained, bound, confined, held, trapped, straitened [➥CAPTIVITY AND LOSS OF FREEDOM; 248] *Opposite*: free

constriction 1 *n* **restriction**, constraint, limitation, limit, condition, check [➥CAPTIVITY AND LOSS OF FREEDOM; 248] 2 *n* **tightening**, contraction, narrowing, compression, shrinking [➥CHANGE OF SIZE: SMALLER; 393] *Opposite*: loosening

construct 1 *v* **build**, make, create, put up, erect, raise, assemble, fabricate, fashion, form [➥BUILD; 352] *Opposite*: knock down 2 *v* **compose**, put together, create, structure, piece together [➥CREATION; 346] *Opposite*: take apart 3 *n* **concept**, hypothesis, theory, paradigm, idea [➥IDEAS AND THOUGHTS; 770]

construction 1 *n* **creation**, assembly, manufacture, production, erection, formation, composition [➥CREATION; 346] *Opposite*: destruction 2 *n* **building**, edifice, structure, creation, erection [➥BUILDING AND ARCHITECTURE; 1076] 3 *n* **interpretation**, understanding, comprehension, meaning, explanation, reading, take (*informal*), spin (*slang*) [➥IDEAS AND THOUGHTS; 770]

constructive *adj* **positive**, helpful, productive, useful, beneficial, practical, fruitful, profitable [➥CHEERFULNESS OF OUTLOOK; 503] *Opposite*: unhelpful

constructively *adv* **usefully**, beneficially, helpfully, fruitfully, positively, profitably, practically, productively [➥USEFULNESS; 199] *Opposite*: unhelpfully

constructivism *type of* **20th-century art movement** [➥ARTISTIC MOVEMENTS AND STYLES; 899]

construe *v* **interpret**, take, read, see, understand [➥UNDERSTAND AND GRASP; 759]

consul *n* **diplomat**, ambassador, representative, emissary, envoy [➥POLITICAL OFFICES AND POLITICIANS; 808]

consult 1 *v* **ask**, check, discuss, talk to, confer, see, sound out, turn to, call on [➥ASK PEOPLE QUESTIONS; 666] 2 *v* **refer**, look up, turn to, check, access, visit [➥EXAMINE AND ASSESS; 753]

consultant *n* **adviser**, expert, specialist, professional, authority, mentor, counselor [➥BOSSES AND MANAGEMENT; 965]

consultation *n* **discussion**, dialogue, talk, session, meeting, conference, soundings [➥NEGOTIATION AND DEBATE; 46]

consume 1 *v* **eat**, drink, devour, munch, feed on, ingest, put away (*informal*), chomp (*informal*), guzzle (*informal*) [➥EAT AND NOT EAT; 710] 2 *v* **use**, use up, expend, spend, utilize, exhaust, get through [➥USE UP AND WASTE; 474] *Opposite*: conserve 3 *v* **destroy**, annihilate, burn up, incinerate, burn down, raze, devour [➥DESTRUCTION AND DEMOLITION; 359]

consumer *n* **buyer**, purchaser, shopper, customer, user, end user [➥PURCHASER; 424]

consummate 1 *v* **complete**, carry out, achieve, accomplish, conclude, effectuate [➥COMPLETE AN ACTION; 263] 2 *adj* **skilled**, skillful, expert, accomplished, talented, competent [➥TALENTED AND SKILLFUL; 527] *Opposite*: inept 3 *adj* **perfect**, excellent, complete, ideal, flawless, supreme [➥EXTRAORDINARY: AMAZING; 204] *Opposite*: imperfect 4 *adj* **utter**, out-and-out, total, complete, absolute, unmitigated, chronic, errant, unredeemed [➥ABSOLUTE AND ABSOLUTELY; 133]

consumption 1 *n* **ingesting**, feasting, feeding, eating, drinking, intake, ingestion [➥EAT AND NOT EAT; 710] 2 *n* **depletion**, use, expenditure, utilization, spending, using up, burning up [➥USE UP AND WASTE; 474] *Opposite*: conservation

contact 1 *n* **interaction**, communication, touching base, dealings, connection, exchange, commerce [➥COMMUNICATION; 602] 2 *n* **advocate**, reference, acquaintance, connection, friend, link, associate [➥SUPPORTERS, PROTECTORS, AND COMPATRIOTS; 970] 3 *v* **get in touch**, make contact, drop a line, communicate, write, telephone, call, phone, cold-call, e-mail, touch base, ring up (*UK*) [➥INITIATE AND ESTABLISH COMMUNICATION; 680]

contagious *adj* **transmissible**, transmittable, spreadable, infectious, catching, communicable [➥SICKNESS; 729]

contain 1 *v* **cover**, take in, comprise, encompass, hold, have, enclose, surround, include, harbor, comprehend (*formal*) [➥HOLD AND CONTAIN; 455] *Opposite*: exclude 2 *v* **check**, control, restrain, hold back, inhibit, suppress, repress [➥AVOID, PREVENT, LIMIT, AND CONTROL; 277] *Opposite*: unleash 3 *v* **limit**, control, keep in check, delimit, restrict, confine [➥AVOID, PREVENT, LIMIT, AND CONTROL; 277]

contained *adj* **limited**, controlled, checked, confined, restricted, kept in check, delimited (*formal*) [➥CAPTIVITY AND LOSS OF FREEDOM; 248] *Opposite*: unbounded

container 1 *n* [➥CONTAINERS, RECEPTACLES, AND PACKAGING; 1245] 2 *part of* **garden** [➥GARDENS; 1074]

container

◆ *types of containers*
barrel, box, caddy, can, cardboard box, carton, cartridge, case, cask, casket, chest, cover, crate, creel, cylinder, drawer, drum, hamper, holder, jar, jerry can, jewel case, keg, pencil case, pigeonhole, pillbox, pot, storage bin, storage tank, tea caddy, trunk

container garden *type of* **garden** [➥GARDENS; 1074]

container ship *type of* **motor vessel** [➥SHIPS AND BOATS; 1150]

contaminate *v* **soil**, pollute, foul, taint, infect, sully, dirty [➥DIRTY AND CONTAMINATE; 404] *Opposite*: purify

contaminated *adj* **dirty**, dirtied, filthy, soiled, polluted, unclean, adulterated, diseased, spoiled, ruined, tainted, stained, infected, infested, fouled, corrupted, unhealthy, unsanitary, unhygienic, noxious, poisonous, poisoned, impure [➥DIRTY; 1235] *Opposite*: pure

contamination *n* **pollution**, adulteration, corruption, infection, uncleanness, impurity [➥DIRTY AND CONTAMINATE; 404] *Opposite*: decontamination

contemplate 1 *v* **look**, gaze, stare, watch, examine, observe, survey, scrutinize [➥LOOKING AND LOOKS; 700] 2 *v* **weigh**, muse, deliberate, consider, think, mull over, turn over in your mind, reflect, study, ponder [➥THINK AND REFLECT; 743]

3 *v* **anticipate**, expect, plan, think of, consider, intend, envisage, envision [➡ PREDICT AND ANTICIPATE; 750] **4** *v* **meditate**, muse, imagine, envisage, envision, think, picture [➡ DREAM, IMAGINE, AND FANTASIZE; 749]

contemplation 1 *n* **inspection**, observation, survey, review, scrutiny, examination [➡ LOOKING AND LOOKS; 700] **2** *n* **thought**, meditation, consideration, study, reflection, deliberation (*formal*), navel-gazing (*humorous*) [➡ THINK AND REFLECT; 743]

contemplative *adj* **thoughtful**, meditative, deep in thought, lost in thought, absorbed, pensive, reflective, introspective, musing, brooding [➡ PENSIVENESS AND INTEREST; 538] *Opposite*: unthinking

contemporaneity *n* **concurrence**, simultaneity, coexistence [➡ CONCURRENT AND CONTEMPORANEOUS; 164]

contemporaneous *adj* **concurrent**, coexistent, concomitant, contemporary, simultaneous, synchronous [➡ CONCURRENT AND CONTEMPORANEOUS; 164]

contemporaneousness *see* **contemporaneity**

contemporaries *n* **age group**, generation, peers, coeval (*formal*) [➡ CONCURRENT AND CONTEMPORANEOUS; 164]

contemporarily *adv* [➡ CONCURRENT AND CONTEMPORANEOUS; 164]

contemporary 1 *adj* **current**, modern, up-to-date, latest, present-day, existing, present, ongoing [➡ PRESENT; 85] *Opposite*: old **2** *n* **peer**, colleague, classmate, coeval (*formal*) [➡ COLLEAGUES AND EQUALS; 967] **3** *type of* **house** [➡ RESIDENTIAL BUILDINGS; 1078]

contempt *n* **disdain**, dislike, disrespect, disapproval, scorn, hatred, derision, condescension [➡ ANTAGONISM; 552] *Opposite*: admiration

contemptibility *n* **shamefulness**, reprehensibility, vileness, contemptibleness [➡ UNACCEPTABLE AND UNFORGIVABLE; 225]

contemptible *adj* **despicable**, disgraceful, shameful, detestable, distasteful, disreputable, shabby, unworthy [➡ UNACCEPTABLE AND UNFORGIVABLE; 225] *Opposite*: laudable

contemptibleness *see* **contemptibility**

contemptibly *adv* **despicably**, shamefully, disgracefully, dishonorably, detestably, shabbily, unworthily, meanly, loathsomely, vilely, badly, dreadfully, shockingly, appallingly [➡ MORALLY BAD OR IMPROPER; 775] *Opposite*: laudably

contemptuous *adj* **scornful**, derisive, disdainful, disapproving, sneering, disrespectful, condescending, supercilious [➡ MOCKING AND DISMISSIVE; 636] *Opposite*: admiring

contemptuousness *n* **scornfulness**, disrespect, scorn, disdain, derision, contempt, condescension, disdainfulness [➡ MOCKING AND DISMISSIVE; 636] *Opposite*: admiration

contend 1 *v* **argue**, assert, allege, insist, maintain, state, declare [➡ CLAIM, INSIST, AND EMPHASIZE; 614] **2** *v* **compete**, vie, challenge, run, put yourself forward, enter, nominate yourself [➡ COMPETE, CONTEND, AND COMBAT; 303] **3** *v* **struggle**, resist, oppose, deal with, put up with, cope [➡ COMPETE, CONTEND, AND COMBAT; 303]

contender *n* **candidate**, nominee, competitor, contestant, challenger, entrant, runner (*UK*) [➡ COMPETITORS; 41]

See Compare and Contrast at **candidate**.

contend with *v* **deal with**, cope with, face, experience [➡ EXPERIENCE AND ENCOUNTER; 582]

content 1 *n* **substance**, matter, subject matter, theme, gist, contents, subject [➡ BASIC DETAILS; 688] **2** *adj* **gratified**, happy, satisfied, contented, pleased, comfortable, at ease, relaxed [➡ PLEASURE, EXCITEMENT, AND ELATION; 534] *Opposite*: unhappy **3** *v* **gladden**, soothe, satisfy, please, make happy, gratify, comfort [➡ PLEASE AND AMUSE; 572] *Opposite*: dissatisfy

contented *adj* **happy**, satisfied, pleased, content, comfortable, at ease, relaxed, gratified [➡ PLEASURE, EXCITEMENT, AND ELATION; 534] *Opposite*: unhappy

contention 1 *n* **assertion**, position, argument, opinion, belief, claim [➡ POINTS OF VIEW; 767] **2** *n* **argument**, disagreement, dispute, debate, conflict, controversy, strife, disputation (*formal*) [➡ CRITICISMS AND ANGRY OUTBURSTS; 50] *Opposite*: harmony

contentious 1 *adj* **controversial**, polemical, provocative, divisive, debatable, critical, disputatious (*formal*) [➡ UNCERTAIN; 175] *Opposite*: uncontroversial **2** *adj* **argumentative**, combative, quarrelsome, antagonistic, touchy, naysaying, belligerent, litigious, hot-blooded, prickly (*informal*) [➡ AGGRESSIVE AND BELLIGERENT; 518] *Opposite*: easygoing

contentment *n* **serenity**, gladness, satisfaction, happiness, pleasure, gratification, ease [➡ APPRECIATION AND GRATITUDE; 535] *Opposite*: discontent

contest 1 *n* **competition**, tournament, challenge, race, match, fight, gala (*UK*), game [➡ NON-AGGRESSIVE/SPORTING EVENTS; 40] **2** *v* **challenge**, dispute, question, oppose, query, argue [➡ DENY AND REJECT; 644] *Opposite*: accept

contestant *n* **competitor**, contender, participant, participator, challenger, entrant, opponent, rival, runner (*UK*) [➡ COMPETITORS; 41]

See Compare and Contrast at **candidate**.

context *n* **setting**, background, circumstances, situation, framework, frame of reference, milieu, perspective, environment [➡ SITUATIONS; 71]

contextual *adj* **background**, related, circumstantial, framing [➡ RELATED; 142]

contiguity (*formal*) *n* **proximity**, nearness, closeness [➡ CLOSENESS; 159]

contiguous (*formal*) *adj* **adjoining**, bordering, next to, adjacent, side by side, cross-border [➡ CLOSENESS; 159]

continent *n* **landmass**, mainland, land [➡ THE CONTINENTS AND ISLANDS; 1048]

continental quilt *n* [➡ FURNISHING AND HOUSEHOLD LINENS; 860]

contingency *n* **eventuality**, possibility, likelihood, exigency, emergency, incident [➡ CHANCE EVENTS; 36]

contingent 1 *adj* **depending**, liable, dependent, reliant, conditional, subject, provisional [➡ RECIPROCITY AND INTERDEPENDENCE; 147] **2** *n* **commission**, legation, committee, party, group, deputation, delegation [➡ GROUPS OF PEOPLE; 935]

continual *adj* **repeated**, frequent, recurrent, incessant, constant, persistent, repetitive [➡PERMANENCE: WITHOUT END; 94] *Opposite*: intermittent

continuance *n* **extension**, protraction, extending, protracting, perpetuation, endurance, continuation, persistence, maintenance, prolongation [➡PERMANENCE: WITHOUT END; 94] *Opposite*: halting

continuation 1 *n* **continuance**, extension, drawing out, persistence, maintenance, furtherance, prolongation, perpetuation, protraction [➡PERMANENCE: WITHOUT END; 94] *Opposite*: halting 2 *n* **addition**, sequel, installment, extension, carryover, follow-up, follow-on, spinoff [➡PERMANENCE: WITHOUT END; 94]

continue 1 *v* **prolong**, maintain, carry on, keep going [➡CAUSE TO CONTINUE; 267] *Opposite*: stop 2 *v* **last**, endure, linger, remain, stay, persist [➡CONTINUE TO EXIST; 17] *Opposite*: end 3 *v* **renew**, restart, resume, reprise, revive, regenerate, proceed, pick up where you left off [➡CONTINUE AN ACTION; 262]

continuing *adj* **ongoing**, current, enduring, remaining, unending, lasting, permanent, persistent, steady, constant, perpetual [➡PERMANENCE: WITHOUT END; 94] *Opposite*: finished

continuity *n* **steadiness**, endurance, continuousness, permanence, stability [➡PERMANENCE: WITHOUT CHANGE; 95] *Opposite*: interruption

continuous *adj* **incessant**, unceasing, nonstop, unremitting, constant, unbroken, uninterrupted, endless [➡PERMANENCE: WITHOUT END; 94] *Opposite*: intermittent

continuousness *n* **continuity**, constancy, permanence [➡PERMANENCE: WITHOUT END; 94]

continuum *n* [➡PERMANENCE: WITHOUT END; 94]

contort *v* **grimace**, distort, twist, screw, warp, deform [➡CHANGE OF SHAPE; 385]

contortionist *type of* **entertainer** [➡WORKERS IN ENTERTAINMENT AND MEDIA; 873]

contour *n* **outline**, delineation, silhouette, relief, curve, line, shape [➡SHAPE; 1216]

contra *prep* [➡FOREIGN WORDS AND PHRASES; 672]

contraband *n* [➡PROCEEDS OF CRIME; 427]

contract 1 *n* **agreement**, bond, indenture, pact, convention, deal, treaty [➡OFFICIAL DOCUMENTS; 586] 2 *v* **diminish**, grow smaller, shrink, tighten, narrow, shrivel, wither [➡CHANGE OF SIZE: SMALLER; 393] *Opposite*: expand 3 *v* **sign**, commission, sign up, commit, engage, hire, employ [➡CONFER STATUS; 458] 4 *v* **incubate**, catch, become infected with, get, develop, come down with, go down (*UK*) [➡BECOME SICK, TREAT, AND RECOVER; 728] *Opposite*: fight off

contraction 1 *n* **reduction**, shrinkage, tightening, narrowing, retrenchment, shriveling, withering [➡CHANGE OF SIZE: SMALLER; 393] *Opposite*: expansion 2 *n* **tightening**, jerking, cramp, spasm, tic, convulsion [➡PAIN AND OTHER PHYSICAL SENSATIONS; 733] 3 *n* **shortening**, merging, combining, abbreviation, ellipsis, reduction [➡ASPECTS OF LANGUAGE; 682]

contractor *n* **servicer**, worker, independent, freelancer, subcontractor, supplier, outworker (*UK*) [➡BUSINESS PEOPLE; 793]

contract out *v* **delegate**, offer, subcontract, outsource, farm, farm out, lease [➡DISPENSE, RATION, AND DISTRIBUTE; 434]

contradict 1 *v* **deny**, oppose, challenge, dispute, refute, reverse, gainsay (*formal*), controvert (*formal*), negate (*formal*) [➡DENY AND REJECT; 644] *Opposite*: confirm 2 *v* **disprove**, cancel, refute, dispute, undermine, cancel out, run counter to [➡DISHARMONY; 156] *Opposite*: support

See Compare and Contrast at **disagree**.

contradiction 1 *n* **illogicality**, flaw, inconsistency, incongruity, ambiguity, paradox, dichotomy, conflict [➡DISHARMONY; 156] 2 *n* **denial**, disagreement, challenge, negation, opposition, refutation, disputation (*formal*) [➡DENY AND REJECT; 644] *Opposite*: confirmation

contradictory *adj* **inconsistent**, self-contradictory, contrary, opposing, clashing, conflicting, at odds, differing, incongruous, ambiguous, paradoxical [➡DISHARMONY; 156] *Opposite*: consistent

contraption *n* **gadget**, machine, device, apparatus, contrivance, mechanism, thingamajig (*informal*), doodad (*informal*), gizmo (*informal*) [➡DEVICES; 1115]

contrarily *adv* **disobediently**, rebelliously, stubbornly, willfully, defiantly, obstinately, uncooperatively, perversely [➡WITHOUT ENTHUSIASM; 287] *Opposite*: cooperatively

contrariness *n* **disobedience**, uncooperativeness, perversity, rebelliousness, willfulness, defiance, obstinacy, stubbornness [➡UNWILLINGNESS AND STUBBORNNESS; 564] *Opposite*: cooperation

contrary 1 *adj* **conflicting**, opposing, different, differing, divergent, dissimilar, antagonistic, disagreeing [➡DISHARMONY; 156] *Opposite*: similar 2 *adj* **disobedient**, rebellious, obstinate, uncooperative, defiant, difficult, perverse, stubborn, willful [➡UNWILLINGNESS AND STUBBORNNESS; 564] *Opposite*: cooperative 3 *n* **opposite**, inverse, other side of the coin, converse, reverse, antithesis [➡OPPOSITE; 157]

contrast 1 *n* **difference**, dissimilarity, distinction, disparity, gap, divergence [➡DIFFERENCE; 149] *Opposite*: similarity 2 *v* **compare**, juxtapose, analogize, weigh, distinguish, differentiate, discriminate [➡EXAMINE AND ASSESS; 753] 3 *v* **stand out**, stick out like a sore thumb, differ, diverge, conflict, disagree [➡DIFFERENCE; 149] *Opposite*: agree

contrasting *adj* **conflicting**, opposing, complementary, different, distinct, divergent, dissimilar, antagonistic [➡DIFFERENCE; 149] *Opposite*: similar

contravene *v* **break**, flout, breach, disobey, disregard, infringe, violate [➡DISOBEY; 302] *Opposite*: observe

contravention *n* **breaking**, flouting, breach, infringement, disobeying, violation [➡BAD BEHAVIOR OR ACTIONS; 254] *Opposite*: observance

contribute 1 *v* **donate**, pay, underwrite, subsidize, back, fund, add, give, supply, provide, sponsor, endow [➡GIVE AND PROVIDE; 430] 2 *v* **weigh in**, have a say, add, throw in, say, interject, interpose, chip in (*informal*) [➡INTERRUPT AND BUTT IN; 619] 3 *v* **cause**, further, influence, impact, participate, promote, aid, support, enhance [➡PARTICIPATE; 292]

contribution 1 *n* **influence**, input, role, involvement, say, impact, aid, support [➡ ACTIONS OR UNDERTAKINGS; 259] **2** *n* **donation**, gift, giving, payment, subsidy, backing, endowment, supply, provision [➡ GIFTS; 438]

contributor *n* **donor**, funder, sponsor, giver, supplier, provider, backer, underwriter, benefactor [➡ SUPPORTERS, PROTECTORS, AND COMPATRIOTS; 970]

contributory *adj* **related**, influential, causal, causative, contributing, instrumental, responsible [➡ CAUSATION; 168]

contrite *adj* **sorry**, repentant, remorseful, regretful, apologetic, penitent, ashamed [➡ EMBARRASSMENT AND HUMILIATION; 542] *Opposite*: impenitent

contriteness *see* contrition

contrition *n* **remorse**, repentance, penitence, regret, sorrow, apology, shame, contriteness [➡ FEELINGS ABOUT THE PAST; 532] *Opposite*: impenitence

contrivance **1** *n* **gadget**, device, apparatus, machine, contraption, thingamajig (*informal*), gizmo (*informal*) [➡ DEVICES; 1115] **2** *n* **plot**, plan, plot, ruse, scheme, machination, means, device, setup (*informal*) [➡ WAYS OF DOING THINGS; 294]

contrive *v* **design**, lay out, engineer, arrange, plan, manufacture, plot, machinate, scheme, cook up (*informal*) [➡ CAUSE TO HAPPEN; 31]

contrived *adj* **forced**, artificial, unnatural, manufactured, fixed, false, affected, unspontaneous [➡ FALSE AND UNREAL; 173] *Opposite*: genuine

control **1** *v* **restrain**, limit, restrict, hold back, rein in, contain [➡ AVOID, PREVENT, LIMIT, AND CONTROL; 277] **2** *v* **operate**, work, run, use, utilize, manipulate, maneuver [➡ USE; 467] **3** *v* **manage**, command, supervise, run, direct, organize [➡ BE IN CHARGE; 270] **4** *v* **rule**, manipulate, influence, dominate, oppress, have a hold over, hold sway over, dictate [➡ BE IN CHARGE; 270] **5** *v* **oversee**, monitor, regulate, inspect, limit, restrict [➡ EXAMINE AND ASSESS; 753] **6** *n* **switch**, regulator, controller, governor, circuit breaker, rheostat, resistor, mechanism, device [➡ ELECTRONICS AND ELECTRICS; 1137] **7** *n* **power**, jurisdiction, rule, domination, hegemony, management, direction, running [➡ RESPONSIBILITY; 170] **8** *n* **skill**, manipulation, influence, handling, expertise, skillfulness [➡ SKILLS, TALENTS, AND ABILITIES; 526] **9** *n* **limit**, limitation, constraint, restriction, restraint, regulation, check, curb [➡ CAPTIVITY AND LOSS OF FREEDOM; 248]

controllable *adj* **manageable**, governable, untroublesome, tractable, easy to deal with, well-behaved, well-disciplined, well-regulated [➡ THE WILL AND WILLINGNESS; 563] *Opposite*: uncontrollable

controlled **1** *adj* **contained**, unflappable, under control, self-controlled, self-possessed, composed, calm, cool, unemotional, reserved, restrained, limited, restricted, in check, tamed, deliberate, disciplined, moderate, guarded, inhibited [➡ CONFIDENCE AND COMPOSURE; 499] *Opposite*: unconstrained **2** *adj* **accurate**, measured, precise, meticulous, exact, well-ordered, organized, orderly, ordered, coordinated, structured, restrained, disciplined [➡ INTENTIONAL AND DELIBERATE; 279] *Opposite*: unplanned **3** *adj* **regulated**, structured, planned, measured, delimited (*formal*) [➡ ORDER AND ORGANIZATION; 206] *Opposite*: free

controller **1** *n* **supervisor**, manager, organizer, regulator, director, checker, overseer [➡ BOSSES AND MANAGEMENT; 965] **2** *n* **regulator**, switch, control, device, governor, rheostat [➡ ELECTRONICS AND ELECTRICS; 1137]

control panel *n* **instrument panel**, console, dashboard, dash, instrumentation [➡ PARTS OF MACHINES AND TOOLS; 1118]

controls *n* **instrument panel**, wheel, helm [➡ PARTS OF MACHINES AND TOOLS; 1118]

controversial *adj* **contentious**, provocative, hotly debated, debatable, divisive, hot, notorious, scandalous, heated, polemic [➡ UNCERTAIN; 175]

controversy *n* **disagreement**, argument, debate, storm, hullabaloo, dispute, polemic [➡ ARGUMENTS; 47] *Opposite*: agreement

contumacious (*formal*) *adj* **insubordinate**, rebellious, disobedient, defiant, noncompliant, recalcitrant [➡ REBELLIOUSNESS AND DISOBEDIENCE; 565] *Opposite*: conformist

contumely (*archaic or literary*) *n* **criticism**, disparagement, vilification [➡ CRITICISMS AND ANGRY OUTBURSTS; 50]

conundrum *n* **puzzle**, mystery, challenge, problem, riddle, enigma [➡ SECRETS AND MYSTERIES; 180]

See *Compare and Contrast* at **problem**.

conurbation *n* **urban area**, built-up area, urban sprawl, city, metropolis, megalopolis, municipality [➡ HUMAN SETTLEMENTS; 1070]

See *Compare and Contrast* at **city**.

convalesce *v* **improve**, recover, recuperate, get better, rally, pull through, rest [➡ BECOME SICK, TREAT, AND RECOVER; 728] *Opposite*: deteriorate

convalescence *n* **recuperation**, recovery, restoration, rehabilitation, R and R, improvement, getting better [➡ HEALING; 730] *Opposite*: deterioration

convalescent *adj* **convalescing**, recovering, recuperating, improving, getting better, mending, on the mend [➡ HEALING; 730] *Opposite*: deteriorating

convene *v* **call together**, assemble, summon, set up, organize, arrange, call up, convoke [➡ COMBINE AND MIX; 400] *Opposite*: disband

convenience *n* **suitability**, expediency, ease, handiness, opportuneness, accessibility, closeness, nearness [➡ USEFULNESS; 199] *Opposite*: inconvenience

convenience store *type of* **retail outlet** [➡ RETAIL OUTLETS; 1083]

convenient **1** *adj* **suitable**, expedient, opportune, fitting, appropriate, useful [➡ APPROPRIATE, SUITABLE, AND ADVISABLE; 184] *Opposite*: inconvenient **2** *adj* **handy**, close at hand, adjacent, near, close, nearby, accessible [➡ USEFULNESS; 199] *Opposite*: out-of-the-way

conveniently *adv* **suitably**, expediently, handily, opportunely, accessibly, fittingly, appropriately, usefully [➡ USEFULNESS; 199] *Opposite*: inconveniently

convent *n* **nunnery**, religious foundation, religious community [➡ RELIGIOUS BUILDINGS; 1085]

convention 1 *n* **gathering**, meeting, conference, congress, assembly, reunion, caucus, get-together (*informal*) [➡MEETINGS AND ASSEMBLIES; 43] **2** *n* **agreement**, pact, resolution, contract, settlement, treaty, concord, bond, covenant [➡OFFICIAL DOCUMENTS; 586] **3** *n* **rule**, principle, custom, practice, habit, precept (*formal*) [➡WAYS OF DOING THINGS; 294]

conventional 1 *adj* **conservative**, conformist, predictable, unadventurous, middle-of-the-road, orthodox, unoriginal, straight (*slang*) [➡UNADVENTUROUS AND DULL; 517] *Opposite*: adventurous **2** *adj* **usual**, established, standard, normal, regular, typical, traditional, common [➡ORDINARINESS; 244] *Opposite*: unusual

conventionality *n* **conformism**, conservatism, orthodoxy, predictability [➡APPROPRIATE, SUITABLE, AND ADVISABLE; 184] *Opposite*: unconventionality

converge *v* **meet**, join, touch, unite, congregate, come together [➡FASTEN, LINK, AND JOIN; 408] *Opposite*: diverge

convergence *n* **meeting**, junction, union, coming together, conjunction, merging [➡CONNECTIONS; 143] *Opposite*: divergence

conversance *n* **familiarity**, acquaintance, awareness, knowledge [➡KNOWLEDGE AND WISDOM; 558]

conversant *adj* **familiar**, up-to-date, au fait, acquainted, aware, au courant, knowledgeable, up to speed, up on (*informal*) [➡KNOWLEDGE AND WISDOM; 558] *Opposite*: unfamiliar

conversation *n* **talk**, chat, discussion, tête-à-tête, dialogue, exchange, colloquy (*formal*) [➡INFORMAL COMMUNICATION; 45]

conversational 1 *adj* **informal**, chatty, relaxed, casual, familiar, intimate [➡ELOQUENT, TALKATIVE, AND LONG-WINDED; 632] *Opposite*: formal **2** *adj* **colloquial**, spoken, everyday, vernacular, informal, ordinary [➡COMMUNICATIVE STYLE; 624]

conversationalist *n* **talker**, communicator, gossip, raconteur, anecdotalist, speaker, chatterbox (*informal*) [➡SPEAKERS AND ORATORS; 603]

converse 1 *v* **talk**, speak, communicate, chat, discuss, natter (*informal*) [➡TWO-WAY COMMUNICATION; 607] **2** *n* **contrary**, opposite, reverse, inverse, antithesis, other side of the coin [➡OPPOSITE; 157] *Opposite*: same **3** *adj* **opposite**, contrary, opposing, reverse, inverse, adverse, counter, antithetical (*formal*) [➡OPPOSITE; 157] *Opposite*: same

conversely *adv* **on the other hand**, equally, by the same token, on the contrary, in opposition, contrariwise [➡OPPOSITE; 157]

conversion 1 *n* **change**, adaptation, alteration, translation, renovation, transformation, transfiguration [➡CHANGE; 372] **2** *n* **switch**, change, changeover, transfer, move, transition, substitution, exchange [➡CHANGE ONE THING FOR ANOTHER; 398]

convert 1 *v* **change**, adapt, alter, renovate, remodel, transform, transfigure, transmute [➡CHANGE; 372] **2** *v* **switch**, change, change over, transfer, go over, exchange, substitute [➡CHANGE ONE THING FOR ANOTHER; 398] **3** *v* **win over**, convince, induce, talk into, persuade, bring around, talk round (*UK*) [➡INSTRUCT AND TEACH; 609]

See Compare and Contrast at **change**.

convertible 1 *adj* **adaptable**, exchangeable, alterable, translatable, changeable, transformable [➡USEFULNESS; 199] **2** **type of car** [➡BIKES, CARS, AND CARRIAGES; 1149]

convertiplane *type of* **military aircraft** [➡AIRCRAFT; 1148]

convex *adj* **curved**, curving, arched, rounded, bowed, U-shaped [➡ROUNDED SHAPE; 1218] *Opposite*: concave

convey 1 *v* **take**, carry, transport, bear, send, ship, transfer, deliver [➡DISPATCH AND SEND; 333] **2** *v* **communicate**, express, suggest, put across, get across, mean [➡MEAN SOMETHING; 61]

conveyance *n* **transportation**, transport, carriage, transference, transmission, passage, consignment, shipment, delivery [➡TRANSPORTATION, TRANSPORTERS, AND CARGOS; 322]

convict 1 *v* **find guilty**, sentence, imprison, condemn, detain, put away (*informal*) [➡TRIAL, PUNISHMENT, AND LEGAL OUTCOMES; 819] *Opposite*: acquit **2** *n* **criminal**, offender, prisoner, felon, lawbreaker [➡CAPTIVES AND PRISONERS; 249]

conviction 1 *n* **belief**, opinion, principle, faith, persuasion, view [➡POINTS OF VIEW; 767] **2** *n* **certainty**, certitude, confidence, assurance, sincerity, passion, fervor [➡CERTAINTY; 561] *Opposite*: doubt **3** *n* **sentence**, verdict, condemnation, imprisonment [➡TRIAL, PUNISHMENT, AND LEGAL OUTCOMES; 819] *Opposite*: acquittal

convince *v* **persuade**, prove, sway, influence, convert, win over, satisfy, assure, induce, talk into [➡INSTRUCT AND TEACH; 609]

convinced 1 *adj* **persuaded**, influenced, swayed, won over, converted, induced [➡CERTAINTY; 561] *Opposite*: doubtful **2** *adj* **certain**, sure, positive, persuaded, confident, satisfied [➡CERTAINTY; 561] *Opposite*: unsure **3** *adj* **committed**, strong, firm, staunch, wholehearted, earnest [➡COOL AND CALM; 536]

convincing 1 *adj* **persuasive**, believable, credible, valid, realistic, true-to-life, compelling, forceful, influential, strong [➡TRUE AND REAL; 171] *Opposite*: unconvincing **2** *adj* **undoubted**, substantial, resounding, considerable, conclusive, definite [➡WHOLENESS AND COMPLETENESS; 198] *Opposite*: doubtful

See Compare and Contrast at **valid**.

convincingly *adv* **persuasively**, credibly, believably, realistically, influentially, forcefully, compellingly, strongly [➡TRUE AND REAL; 171] *Opposite*: unconvincingly

convivial *adj* **pleasant**, welcoming, warm, friendly, hospitable, genial, sociable, cordial, companionable [➡FRIENDLINESS AND SOCIABILITY; 494] *Opposite*: unfriendly

conviviality *n* **pleasantness**, welcome, warmth, friendliness, hospitality, geniality, cordiality, companionableness [➡FRIENDLINESS AND SOCIABILITY; 494] *Opposite*: unfriendliness

convivially *adv* **affably**, sociably, genially, cordially [➡GOOD-TEMPERED AND HUMOROUS; 627]

convoluted *adj* **intricate**, complex, complicated, long-winded, elaborate, difficult, tortuous, drawn-out, long-drawn-out [➡DIFFICULTY AND COMPLEXITY; 242] *Opposite*: straightforward

convolvulus *type of* **climber** [➡CLIMBERS; 1033]

convoy 1 n **group**, band, party, fleet, line, file, procession [➡ GROUPS OF PEOPLE; 935] 2 n **motorcade**, cavalcade, cortege, caravan, flotilla, fleet [➡ GROUPS OF VEHICLES; 1152]

convulse v **shake**, jerk, tremble, shudder, quiver, agitate, judder, go into spasm [➡ PHYSICAL REACTIONS; 316]

convulsion n **seizure**, fit, spasm, paroxysm, tremor, shaking [➡ PAIN AND OTHER PHYSICAL SENSATIONS; 733]

convulsive adj **jerky**, sudden, abrupt, violent, uncontrollable, irregular [➡ DESCRIBING BODY MOVEMENTS; 288]

coo type of **bird sound** [➡ SOUNDS MADE BY BIRDS; 1263]

COO n [➡ BUSINESS PEOPLE; 793]

co-occur v **coexist**, coincide, concur [➡ EXIST WITH OTHERS; 18]

cook 1 v **heat**, boil, prepare, fry, roast, bake, grill, steam, barbecue, flambé, scramble, broil, braise, poach, microwave, sauté, stir-fry, casserole [➡ COOKING AND FOOD PREPARATION; 353] 2 n **chef**, cordon bleu, sous-chef, short-order cook, commis chef (UK) [➡ DOMESTIC AND KITCHEN WORKERS; 850]

cooked adj **heated**, baked, prepared, broiled, roasted, microwaved, boiled, grilled, stewed, steamed, fried, sautéed, flambéed, stir-fried, barbecued, braised, casseroled, scrambled, poached [➡ STATE OF PREPARED FOOD; 1171] Opposite: raw

cookery see **cooking**

cookie 1 n [➡ CAKES, COOKIES, AND DESSERTS; 1181] 2 n (informal) **person**, character, individual, sort (informal), type (informal), dude (slang) [➡ PERSON; 931] 3 n [➡ THE INTERNET; 1128] 4 type of **software** [➡ COMPUTERS AND COMPUTING; 1127]

cooking n **cookery**, cuisine, catering, food service, home economics [➡ COOKING AND FOOD PREPARATION; 353]

---

cooking

◆ types of food presentations
à la grecque, à la king, à la mode, Alfredo, au gratin, cacciatore, carbonara, chasseur, en brochette, en croûte, en papillote, florentine, julienne, lyonnaise, marinière, meunière, mornay, Newburg, ripieno, stroganoff, Thermidor

---

cookout type of **meal** [➡ MEALS AND PARTS OF MEALS; 1169]

cook the books (slang) v **embezzle**, cheat, misappropriate, peculate (formal) [➡ FALSIFY AND CHEAT; 176]

cook up 1 v **prepare**, concoct, make, throw together (informal), rustle up (informal), fix (informal) [➡ MEAL PREPARATION; 354] 2 v (informal) **invent**, think up, concoct, devise, plan, plot, contrive [➡ DEVELOP THEORIES AND REASON; 744]

cool 1 adj **cold**, chilly, chill, nippy, fresh, frigid, subzero, frosty, arctic (informal) [➡ COLD WEATHER; 1051] Opposite: warm 2 adj (slang) **wonderful**, fantastic, magnificent, excellent, terrific, good, groovy (dated slang) [➡ EXTRAORDINARY: AMAZING; 204] Opposite: awful 3 adj **calm**, unruffled, nonchalant, casual, imperturbable, unflappable, level-headed, equable, dispassionate, unemotional, tranquil, serene, composed, collected, placid [➡ COOL AND CALM; 536] Opposite: excited 4 adj **unfriendly**, unenthusiastic, offhand, icy, distant, detached, cold, chilly, glacial, frosty, frigid, muted, aloof, unsociable, impersonal, inhospitable [➡ RUDE AND HOSTILE; 625] Oppo-

site: friendly 5 adj (informal) **fashionable**, sophisticated, stylish, trendy (informal), nifty (informal), hip (slang), with-it (dated informal), groovy (dated slang) [➡ NEW, MODERN; 166] Opposite: unfashionable 6 v **make cold**, freshen, refrigerate, chill, cool off, cool down [➡ CHANGE OF TEMPERATURE; 386] Opposite: warm 7 v **wane**, dampen down, dampen, cool off, decrease, abate (formal or literary) [➡ CHANGE OF INTENSITY: LESS; 395] Opposite: increase

cool bag (UK) see **cool box**

cool box (UK) n **cooler**, chiller, cool bag (UK) [➡ CONTAINERS, RECEPTACLES, AND PACKAGING; 1245]

cool down 1 v **turn cold**, cool, cool off, freshen [➡ CHANGE OF TEMPERATURE; 386] Opposite: warm up 2 v **calm down**, compose yourself, settle down, simmer down, back off, cool off (informal), chill (slang) [➡ CHANGE OF MOOD AND COMPOSURE; 580] Opposite: flare up

cooler 1 n **chiller**, cool box (UK), cool bag (UK) [➡ HEATING, REFRIGERATION, AND VENTILATION; 1142] 2 n (slang) [➡ BUILDINGS FOR CONFINING PEOPLE; 1094]

---

cooler

◆ types of cooling appliances
air conditioner, air cooler, air exchanger, deepfreeze, freezer, fridge, icebox, refrigerator

---

cooling tower n [➡ INDUSTRIAL BUILDINGS; 1087]

cool jazz type of **jazz music** [➡ MUSIC, SONGS, AND SINGING; 907]

coolly 1 adv **calmly**, casually, nonchalantly, equably, imperturbably, dispassionately, unflappably, unemotionally, collectedly, evenly, placidly, serenely, tranquilly, sedately [➡ COOL AND CALM; 536] Opposite: excitedly 2 adv **coldly**, unenthusiastically, impersonally, distantly, unsociably, inhospitably, frostily, icily, frigidly, aloofly [➡ UNINTERESTED AND DETACHED; 629] Opposite: enthusiastically

coolness 1 n **cold**, coldness, chill, chilliness, freshness, rawness, nippiness, nip, iciness, frostiness [➡ COLD WEATHER; 1051] Opposite: warmth 2 n **calmness**, level-headedness, detachment, aloofness, distance, tranquility, calm, peace, serenity, composure, poise, assurance, self-assurance, self-possession, imperturbability, unflappability, equanimity (formal) [➡ COOL AND CALM; 536] 3 n **unfriendliness**, chill, chilliness, reserve, hostility, inhospitality, unsociability, coldness, iciness [➡ BAD MANNERS AND SOCIAL SKILLS; 521] Opposite: friendliness

cool off 1 v **turn cold**, cool, freshen, grow chilly [➡ CHANGE OF TEMPERATURE; 386] Opposite: warm up 2 v (informal) **calm down**, compose yourself, settle down, simmer down, cool down, chill (slang) [➡ CHANGE OF MOOD AND COMPOSURE; 580] Opposite: flare up

coop n **pen**, cage, run, enclosure, hutch, hut, house [➡ ANIMAL OR BIRD ACCOMMODATIONS; 1079]

co-op (informal) 1 n **cooperative**, collective, mutual society, friendly society (UK) [➡ BUSINESS ENTERPRISES AND RELATED BODIES; 792] 2 n **condominium**, apartment house, apartment building, apartment block (UK), block of flats (UK) [➡ RESIDENTIAL BUILDINGS; 1078]

cooperate 1 v **collaborate**, work together, unite, liaise, band, join forces, conjoin (formal) [➡ ESTABLISHING RELATIONSHIPS

WITH OTHERS; 974] *Opposite*: compete **2** *v* **oblige**, accommodate, help, aid, assist, play the game, play ball (*informal*) [➡HELP; 293] *Opposite*: hinder

cooperation *n* **collaboration**, assistance, help, support, teamwork, aid [➡RECIPROCITY AND INTERDEPENDENCE; 147] *Opposite*: hindrance

cooperative 1 *adj* **obliging**, helpful, supportive, accommodating, willing, compliant, complaisant [➡THE WILL AND WILLINGNESS; 563] *Opposite*: difficult **2** *adj* **joint**, two-way, mutual, shared, collaborative, common, communal, united [➡BELONGING OR RELATING TO PEOPLE; 943] **3** *n* **collective**, company, organization, association, enterprise, co-op (*informal*) [➡PLACE OF EMPLOYMENT; 832]

cooperatively 1 *adv* **helpfully**, obligingly, accommodatingly, supportively, willingly, compliantly, complaisantly [➡THE WILL AND WILLINGNESS; 563] *Opposite*: unhelpfully **2** *adv* **together**, jointly, communally, in common, unitedly, in unison, in concert [➡ACTING WITH OTHERS; 285] *Opposite*: alone

cooperativeness *n* [➡THE WILL AND WILLINGNESS; 563]

co-opt *v* **appoint**, designate, choose, bring on board, draft, invite, nominate [➡CONFER STATUS; 458] *Opposite*: exclude

coop up *v* **cage**, enclose, pen, house, imprison, shut up, confine [➡CAPTIVITY AND LOSS OF FREEDOM; 248] *Opposite*: let out

coordinate *v* **organize**, direct, manage, synchronize, harmonize, integrate, bring together, match, color-coordinate [➡ARRANGE AND CREATE ORDER; 357]

coordinates *n* [➡GARMENTS AND OUTFITS; 865]

coordination 1 *n* **organization**, direction, management, logistics, harmonization, synchronization, bringing together, matching, color-coordination [➡ARRANGE AND CREATE ORDER; 357] *Opposite*: disorganization **2** *n* **dexterity**, skill, adroitness, grace, proficiency, expertise, facility [➡SKILLS, TALENTS, AND ABILITIES; 526] *Opposite*: clumsiness

coot *type of* **freshwater bird** [➡FRESHWATER BIRDS; 1000]

cope *v* **manage**, handle, deal with, survive, get through, get by, muddle through, hack it (*informal*) [➡CONTINUE TO EXIST; 17] *Opposite*: fail

copied *adj* **imitated**, imitative, counterfeit, mock, imitation, phony, sham, ersatz, derivative, fake, artificial, bogus, derived, unoriginal, plagiarized, pirated, plagiaristic, forged, me-too (*informal*) [➡FALSE AND UNREAL; 173] *Opposite*: original

copious *adj* **abundant**, plentiful, profuse, many, numerous, ample, liberal, bountiful (*literary*), bounteous (*literary*) [➡MANY, MUCH, LARGE AMOUNT; 117] *Opposite*: scant

cop out (*slang*) *v* **back out**, get out, evade, avoid, withdraw, shirk, dodge [➡NOT PAY ATTENTION; 764]

cop-out (*slang*) *n* **excuse**, way around, dodge, evasion, escape, subterfuge [➡NOT PAY ATTENTION; 764]

copper 1 *type of* **metal** [➡METALS; 1276] **2** *type of* **brown** [➡COLORS; 1224]

copperhead *type of* **poisonous snake** [➡SNAKES; 995]

coppice *n* **wood**, copse, thicket, grove, covert [➡WOODS, FORESTS, AND JUNGLES; 1047]

copse *n* **wood**, coppice, thicket, grove, covert [➡WOODS, FORESTS, AND JUNGLES; 1047]

copy 1 *n* **reproduction**, duplicate, replica, facsimile, print, carbon copy, photocopy, backup copy, cover version, fake, counterfeit, imitation, model, clone, knockoff (*informal*) [➡REPRESENTATIONS AND GENERAL EXAMPLES; 65] *Opposite*: original **2** *n* **item**, book, disk, version, publication [➡COPIES AND REPLICAS; 151] **3** *n* **text**, words, manuscript, typescript, file, hard copy [➡WRITING; 583] **4** *v* **reproduce**, duplicate, clone, fake, counterfeit, replicate, photocopy, recreate [➡COPY AND DUPLICATE; 402] **5** *v* **imitate**, mimic, emulate, ape, simulate, impersonate, mime, mock [➡PRETEND AND MIMIC; 60] *Opposite*: originate

Compare and Contrast: *copy, reproduce, duplicate, clone, replicate, re-create*

CORE MEANING: to make something that resembles something else to a greater or lesser degree

copy to make an identical version of something; *reproduce* to make a copy by technical means; *duplicate* to create an identical version of something two or more times; *clone* to make a near or exact reproduction, especially of a piece of equipment or an organism; *replicate* to create an identical version of something repeatedly and exactly; *re-create* to make something that appears to be the same as something that no longer exists, or that exists in a different place.

See Compare and Contrast at **imitate**.

coquettish (*literary*) *adj* **flirtatious**, flirty, teasing, coy [➡FLIRTATIOUS; 639]

coral 1 *type of* **aquatic invertebrate** [➡AQUATIC INVERTEBRATES; 1022] **2** *type of* **pink** [➡COLORS; 1224]

coral snake *type of* **poisonous snake** [➡SNAKES; 995]

cord *n* **string**, twine, rope, cable, flex, thread, lead [➡FASTENERS, LINKS, AND NETWORKS; 1247]

cordial 1 *adj* **pleasant**, affable, genial, friendly, affectionate, warm, amiable, jovial, convivial [➡FRIENDLINESS AND SOCIABILITY; 494] *Opposite*: unfriendly **2** *n* [➡DRINKS; 1187]

cordiality *n* **pleasantness**, geniality, affability, friendliness, affection, warmth, conviviality, joviality, amiability [➡FRIENDLINESS AND SOCIABILITY; 494] *Opposite*: unfriendliness

cordless *adj* **battery**, battery-operated, freestyle, handheld, mobile, remote, wireless [➡DESCRIBING TECHNOLOGY; 1160]

córdoba *type of* **currency** [➡CURRENCIES; 798]

cordon *n* **barrier**, barricade, obstruction, obstacle, line, chain [➡BARRIERS; 1113]

cordon off *v* **close**, bar, isolate, block off, barricade, rope [➡SEPARATE AND DIVIDE; 401] *Opposite*: open

cords *type of* **pants** [➡GARMENTS AND OUTFITS; 865]

corduroy *type of* **fabric from plants** [➡FABRICS; 1132]

core 1 *n* **center**, heart, hub, nucleus, middle, interior, mainstay, focal point, basis, crux, meat, substance, midpoint [➡MOST IMPORTANT THING; 197] **2** *n* **essence**, spirit, soul, heart, gist, center [➡CENTRAL PARTS OF PHYSICAL OBJECTS; 1251] **3** *n* **sample**, plug, extract [➡REPRESENTATIONS AND GENERAL EXAMPLES; 65] **4** *adj*

essential, central, fundamental, main, principal, basic, primary, staple, underlying [➡ MOST IMPORTANT AND MAIN; 193] *Opposite*: peripheral

corgi *type of* small dog [➡ DOGS; 980]

coriander *type of* spice [➡ HERBS AND SPICES; 1175]

Corinthian *type of* pre-20th-century architecture [➡ BUILDING AND ARCHITECTURE; 1076]

corker (*dated informal*) *n* [➡ AMAZING THINGS; 211]

corkscrew *type of* utensil [➡ TABLEWARE, FLATWARE, AND KITCHENWARE; 861]

cormorant *type of* sea bird [➡ SEA BIRDS; 1002]

corn *type of* cereal [➡ CEREAL FOODS; 1178]

corn bread *type of* bread [➡ BREAD, FLOUR, AND BREAD PRODUCTS; 1179]

cornea *part of* eye [➡ THE EYE; 698]

corner **1** *n* **angle**, crook, bend [➡ ANGULAR SHAPE; 1217] **2** *n* **bend**, turn, curve, junction, intersection, turning (*UK*) [➡ BRIDGES, TUNNELS, CROSSINGS, AND JUNCTIONS; 1112] *Opposite*: straight **3** *n* **place**, spot, area, location, locality, region, district, section, position [➡ PLACE; 1065] **4** *v* **pin down**, surround, trap, restrict, confront, detain, waylay, accost [➡ ACCUSE, BLAME, AND CRITICIZE; 641]

cornerstone *n* **foundation stone**, keystone, foundation, basis [➡ BUILDING MATERIALS; 1077]

corner store *type of* retail outlet [➡ RETAIL OUTLETS; 1083]

corner the market *v* **dominate**, monopolize, control, command, predominate, prevail [➡ POSSESS; 444]

cornet *type of* brass instrument [➡ MUSICAL INSTRUMENTS; 910]

cornflower blue *type of* blue [➡ COLORS; 1224]

cornice *n* [➡ ROOFS, ROOF PARTS, AND CEILINGS; 1103]

corniche *type of* secondary road [➡ ROADS; 1106]

cornichon *type of* relish [➡ SEASONINGS AND SAUCES; 1174]

Cornish pasty (*UK*) *n* [➡ BREAD, FLOUR, AND BREAD PRODUCTS; 1179]

cornmeal *type of* flour [➡ BREAD, FLOUR, AND BREAD PRODUCTS; 1179]

corn oil *type of* cooking fat and oil [➡ FATS AND OILS; 1173]

cornrow *type of* hairstyle [➡ HAIRSTYLES AND HAIRPIECES; 488]

cornstarch *type of* flour [➡ BREAD, FLOUR, AND BREAD PRODUCTS; 1179]

corn syrup *n* [➡ SUGAR AND PRESERVES; 1184]

cornucopia *n* **abundance**, profusion, wealth, copiousness, plethora, excess, bounty (*literary*) [➡ MANY, MUCH, LARGE AMOUNT; 117] *Opposite*: dearth

corny *adj* **unsophisticated**, trite, banal, clichéd, hackneyed, unoriginal, old, well-worn, overworked, homespun, folksy, downhome (*informal*), cornpone (*informal*) [➡ BORING AND UNINTERESTING; 234] *Opposite*: original

corolla *part of* flower [➡ FLOWERS; 1032]

corollary *n* **consequence**, result, effect, outcome, upshot, repercussion [➡ RESULTS AND OUTCOMES; 83]

Corona Australis *type of* constellation [➡ HEAVENLY BODIES; 1061]

Corona Borealis *type of* constellation [➡ HEAVENLY BODIES; 1061]

coronet *n* **crown**, tiara, diadem, circlet, wreath [➡ JEWELRY; 866]

corporate **1** *adj* **business**, company, commercial, trade [➡ BUSINESS; 791] **2** *adj* **communal**, shared, group, community, mutual, joint [➡ BELONGING OR RELATING TO PEOPLE; 943] *Opposite*: individual

corporate raider *n* [➡ BUSINESS PEOPLE; 793]

corporation *n* **company**, business, firm, establishment, concern, organization, house, conglomerate, group, multinational, transnational [➡ BUSINESS ENTERPRISES AND RELATED BODIES; 792]

corps **1** *n* **force**, troop, group, company, cadre, band, outfit (*informal*) [➡ GROUPS OF PEOPLE; 935] **2** *n* **group**, body, company, organization, league, service [➡ THE ARMED FORCES; 827]

corpse *n* **dead body**, cadaver, carcass, stiff (*slang*) [➡ DEAD PERSON; 926]

corpulence *n* **obeseness**, plumpness, fleshiness, middle-age spread, spare tire, beer belly (*slang*), beer gut (*slang*), embonpoint (*humorous*) [➡ BUILD; 477]

corpulent *adj* **obese**, fat, fleshy, rotund, plump, overweight, pudgy (*informal*), podgy (*UK*) [➡ BUILD; 477] *Opposite*: slim

corral *type of* pen or cage [➡ ANIMAL OR BIRD ACCOMMODATIONS; 1079]

correct **1** *v* **rectify**, fix, put right, sort out, mark, amend, emend [➡ CORRECT AND PUT RIGHT; 377] **2** *v* **modify**, amend, alter, adjust, revise, improve, tweak, polish [➡ IMPROVE SOMETHING; 374] **3** *adj* **precise**, right, accurate, exact, truthful, true [➡ EXACT; 203] *Opposite*: inaccurate **4** *adj* **appropriate**, suitable, proper, acceptable, approved, accepted, standard, comme il faut [➡ CORRECT AND FAULTLESS; 182] *Opposite*: incorrect

correction *n* **alteration**, improvement, rectification, modification, amendment, adjustment, tweak [➡ IMPROVE SOMETHING; 374]

correctional facility *n* [➡ BUILDINGS FOR CONFINING PEOPLE; 1094]

correctly **1** *adv* **precisely**, right, accurately, rightly, perfectly, exactly [➡ CORRECT AND FAULTLESS; 182] *Opposite*: inaccurately **2** *adv* **appropriately**, suitably, properly, acceptably, fittingly, decorously [➡ APPROPRIATE, SUITABLE, AND ADVISABLE; 184] *Opposite*: incorrectly

correctness **1** *n* **precision**, rightness, truth, accuracy, exactness, perfection [➡ EXACT; 203] *Opposite*: inaccuracy **2** *n* **appropriateness**, suitability, acceptability, fittingness, uprightness, rectitude, conventionality [➡ APPROPRIATE, SUITABLE, AND ADVISABLE; 184] *Opposite*: incorrectness

correlate *v* **relate**, associate, compare, link, draw a parallel, connect [➡ CREATING CONNECTIONS; 144] *Opposite*: dissociate

correlation *n* **association**, connection, relationship, link, parallel, correspondence [➡ CONNECTIONS; 143]

correspond 1 *v* agree, resemble, parallel, match, match up, marry, relate, tally [➡ CREATING CONNECTIONS; 144] *Opposite*: conflict 2 *v* **communicate**, keep in touch, write, drop a line, fax, e-mail [➡ INITIATE AND ESTABLISH COMMUNICATION; 680]

correspondence 1 *n* **letters**, mail, communication, messages, memos, faxes, e-mail, notes [➡ COMMUNICATION; 602] 2 *n* **agreement**, similarity, resemblance, association, connection, match, equivalence, correlation, conformity [➡ CONNECTIONS; 143] *Opposite*: clash

correspondent 1 *n* **communicator**, letter-writer, writer, pen pal, pen friend (*UK*) [➡ SUPPORTERS, PROTECTORS, AND COMPATRIOTS; 970] 2 *n* **foreign correspondent**, newspaperman, newspaperwoman, columnist, reporter, journalist, stringer, contributor, author, writer [➡ WORKERS IN ENTERTAINMENT AND MEDIA; 873]

corresponding *adj* **consistent**, conforming, agreeing, matching, equivalent, parallel, analogous [➡ HARMONY; 155]

corridor 1 *n* **passage**, passageway, hall, hallway, walkway [➡ DOORS AND ACCESS POINTS; 1101] 2 *n* **strip**, access strip, air corridor, flight path [➡ AREA AND RANGE; 111]

corrie (*UK*) *n* [➡ GEOLOGIC FEATURES; 1056]

corroborate *v* **verify**, validate, document, support, agree, substantiate, back up, uphold [➡ APPROVE AND CONFIRM; 646] *Opposite*: contradict

corrode *v* **rust**, disintegrate, destroy, decompose, decay, crumble, flake, wear away, oxidize, eat away [➡ GO BAD AND CORRODE; 390]

corroded *adj* **rusty**, discolored, rusted, tarnished, blemished, oxidized, weathered, stained, marked [➡ DECAYING OR INFESTED; 1236] *Opposite*: pristine

corrosion *n* **erosion**, weathering, decay, rust, deterioration, decomposition, oxidization [➡ GO BAD AND CORRODE; 390]

corrosive 1 *adj* **harsh**, scarring, eroding, destructive, acidic, caustic, acid [➡ PHYSICAL TEXTURE; 1222] *Opposite*: gentle 2 *adj* **sarcastic**, undermining, harsh, bitter, biting, caustic, mordant, acerbic, cutting [➡ RUDE AND HOSTILE; 625] *Opposite*: kind

corrugated *adj* **ridged**, crenelated, ribbed, grooved, wavy, uneven [➡ PHYSICAL TEXTURE; 1222] *Opposite*: smooth

corrupt 1 *adj* **immoral**, unethical, dishonest, shady, fraudulent, sleazy, on the take (*informal*), crooked (*informal*) [➡ MORALLY BAD OR IMPROPER; 775] *Opposite*: honest 2 *v* **debase**, degrade, taint, pervert, warp, spoil, contaminate, alter, damage, distort, harm, abuse [➡ MISUSE AND ABUSE; 471]

corrupted *adj* **debased**, degraded, sullied, despoiled, spoiled, besmirched, soiled, stained, contaminated, tainted, fouled, polluted, tarnished, ruined, infected, dirtied [➡ IN BAD REPAIR; 1234] *Opposite*: pure (*literary*)

corruption 1 *n* **dishonesty**, exploitation, bribery, sleaze, fraud, gerrymandering, venality, cronyism, Tammany Hall [➡ MORALLY BAD OR IMPROPER; 775] *Opposite*: honesty 2 *n* **depravity**, perversion, immorality, harm, debasement, degeneracy, abuse, vice [➡ CRIMES; 817] *Opposite*: purity (*literary*)

corruptness *n* **dishonesty**, immorality, sleaziness, degenerateness [➡ MORALLY BAD OR IMPROPER; 775]

corsage 1 *n* **bouquet**, spray, posy, flowers, arrangement, boutonniere (*formal*), buttonhole (*UK*) [➡ ORNAMENTS AND DECORATIONS; 1248] 2 *type of* **accessory** [➡ ACCESSORIES, MILLINERY, AND LINGERIE; 867]

corset *type of* **lower body underwear** [➡ ACCESSORIES, MILLINERY, AND LINGERIE; 867]

Corvus *type of* **constellation** [➡ HEAVENLY BODIES; 1061]

cosh *v* **hit**, bludgeon, club, strike [➡ WHIP AND CLUB; 417]

cosmetic 1 *adj* **ornamental**, decorative, aesthetic [➡ DECORATE, ADORN, AND APPLY COATINGS; 405] 2 *adj* **superficial**, skin-deep, surface, token, outer, outward [➡ UNIMPORTANT AND UNNECESSARY; 238] *Opposite*: in-depth

cosmetic

◆ *types of cosmetics*
beauty product, blush, concealer, eyeliner, eye shadow, face powder, foundation, greasepaint, kohl, lip pencil, lipstick, makeup, maquillage, mascara, nail polish, powder, rouge (*dated*)

cosmic 1 *adj* **intergalactic**, interplanetary, interstellar, galactic, planetary, space, extraterrestrial, celestial [➡ THE SOLAR SYSTEM AND ASTRONOMY; 1060] *Opposite*: terrestrial 2 *adj* **universal**, vast, enormous, huge, immense, colossal, global [➡ LARGE; 1193] *Opposite*: tiny

cosmonaut *n* [➡ SPACE TRAVEL AND EXPLORATION; 1062]

cosmopolitan *adj* **multicultural**, multiethnic, pluralistic, diverse, international, multinational, broad-based [➡ POSITIVELY COMPLEX OR COMPLICATED; 217] *Opposite*: provincial

cosmos *n* **universe**, space, outer space, ether, heaven [➡ THE SOLAR SYSTEM AND ASTRONOMY; 1060]

cosset *v* **shelter**, protect, spoil, mollycoddle, coddle, indulge, pamper [➡ TAKE CARE OF AND SPOIL; 300] *Opposite*: neglect

cost 1 *n* **price**, charge, rate, fee, price tag, asking price, total [➡ EXPENDITURE; 423] 2 *n* **budget**, amount, outlay, expenditure, expense, outgoings (*UK*) [➡ EXPENDITURE; 423] 3 *n* **effort**, suffering, detriment, loss, expense, sacrifice, damage (*informal*) [➡ NUISANCES; 253]

costar 1 *n* **star**, movie star, actor, lead, film star (*UK*) [➡ PERFORMERS; 905] 2 *type of* **entertainer** [➡ WORKERS IN ENTERTAINMENT AND MEDIA; 873] 3 *v* **perform**, collaborate, entertain, star, appear, act [➡ THE PERFORMING ARTS; 904] 4 *v* **feature**, showcase, spotlight, star [➡ THE PERFORMING ARTS; 904]

cost-cutting *n* **saving**, cutbacks, economizing, cutting back, belt-tightening, thrift, thriftiness, frugality, downsizing, downshifting [➡ ACCOUNTING, BANKING, AND BUDGETING; 799]

cost-effective *adj* **lucrative**, moneymaking, profitable, bankable, gainful, economical, commercial, worthwhile [➡ ECONOMICAL AND RESOURCEFUL; 207] *Opposite*: uneconomical

cost-effectiveness *n* [➡ ECONOMICAL AND RESOURCEFUL; 207]

costly 1 *adj* **expensive**, overpriced, inflated, high, exorbitant, pricey (*informal*) [➡ EXPENSIVE AND OVERPRICED; 247] *Opposite*: inexpensive 2 *adj* **luxurious**, precious, valuable, lavish, rich, sumptuous [➡ EXPENSIVE AND LUXURIOUS; 218] *Opposite*: basic 3 *adj* **damaging**, harmful, detrimental, hurtful [➡ DANGEROUS; 236]

costs *n* **price**, charges, budget, expenses, outlay, expenditure, overheads [➡ EXPENDITURE; 423]

costume *n* **clothes**, clothing, regalia, dress, outfit, uniform, getup (*informal*), gear (*informal*), attire (*formal*) [➡ CLOTHES AND ACCESSORIES; 864]

costume drama *n* **play**, spectacle, drama, historical drama, period piece [➡ THE PERFORMING ARTS; 904]

cot *type of* **bed** [➡ FURNITURE; 858]

coterie *n* **clique**, circle, band [➡ FRIENDS AND ACQUAINTANCES; 936]

cottage *type of* **house** [➡ RESIDENTIAL BUILDINGS; 1078]

cottage cheese *type of* **soft cheese** [➡ DAIRY PRODUCTS AND CHEESES; 1183]

cottage garden *type of* **garden** [➡ GARDENS; 1074]

cotton *type of* **fabric from plants** [➡ FABRICS; 1132]

cotton candy *type of* **confectionery on a stick** [➡ CONFECTIONERY; 1182]

cotton on (*informal*) *v* **comprehend**, understand, follow, grasp, realize, catch on (*informal*), get (*informal*) [➡ UNDERSTAND AND GRASP; 759]

cotylosaur *type of* **dinosaur** [➡ DINOSAURS; 996]

couch 1 *n* **sofa**, settee, divan, chaise longue, chesterfield, love seat [➡ FURNITURE; 858] 2 *v* **express**, phrase, put, dress up, word, formulate [➡ NAME AND DESCRIBE; 665]

couchette *type of* **bed** [➡ FURNITURE; 858]

couch grass *type of* **grass** [➡ GRASS; 1031]

cough up (*informal*) *v* **pay up**, pay, give, fork out (*informal*), fork up (*informal*), shell out (*informal*), fork over (*informal*) [➡ GIVE MONEY; 433]

coulis *type of* **seasonings, sauces, and dips** [➡ SEASONINGS AND SAUCES; 1174]

coulomb *type of* **SI unit** [➡ SIZE AND DIMENSIONS; 1192]

council *n* **assembly**, meeting, board, congress, body, convention, association [➡ LEGISLATIVE BODIES AND LEGISLATION; 809]

counsel 1 *n* (*formal or literary*) **advice**, guidance, direction, warning, guidelines, suggestions [➡ ADVICE; 689] 2 *v* **support**, advise, help, guide, aid [➡ ADVISE AND WARN; 613] 3 *v* (*formal or literary*) **advise**, recommend, advocate, encourage, direct, suggest, instruct, warn [➡ ADVISE AND WARN; 613]

See Compare and Contrast at **recommend**.

counseling *n* **therapy**, psychotherapy, psychoanalysis, analysis, treatment, couple counseling, personal therapy, behavior therapy, cocounseling [➡ PSYCHOLOGY AND THE MIND; 769]

counselor *n* **therapist**, psychotherapist, psychoanalyst, analyst, social worker, guidance counselor [➡ ADVISERS, JUDGES, AND ARBITERS; 971]

count 1 *v* **add up**, total, calculate, tot up, tote up, tally, reckon, count up, number-crunch (*slang*) [➡ ASSESS QUANTITY; 757] 2 *v* **consider**, regard, view, hold, esteem, deem (*formal*)

[➡ DEVELOP THEORIES AND REASON; 744] 3 *v* **make your mark**, weigh, amount to something, matter, be important, make a difference, signify [➡ MEAN SOMETHING; 61] 4 *n* **calculation**, computation, reckoning, head count, bottom line, number crunching (*slang*) [➡ SCORES AND EVALUATIONS; 598] 5 *n* **total**, sum total, sum, amount, tally [➡ AMOUNTS AND QUANTITIES; 112] 6 *type of* **aristocrat** [➡ RULERS AND ARISTOCRACY; 823]

countable *adj* **calculable**, measurable, assessable, finite, reckonable, quantifiable [➡ ASSESS QUANTITY; 757] *Opposite*: incalculable

count against *v* **weigh against**, detract, diminish, hurt, backfire, reverse, militate against, counter, oppose [➡ MAKE IMPOSSIBLE; 276] *Opposite*: help

countenance 1 *n* **expression**, face, features, physiognomy, mien (*formal*), visage (*literary*) [➡ PARTS OF THE BODY: HEAD; 692] 2 *v* (*formal*) **tolerate**, stand for, put up with, allow, approve, condone, stomach [➡ TOLERATE AND ENDURE; 766]

counter 1 *type of* **game piece** [➡ GAME PIECES; 878] 2 *n* [➡ MEASURING DEVICES; 1123] 3 *v* **contradict**, dispute, refute, oppose, answer, defy [➡ DENY AND REJECT; 644] 4 *v* **counteract**, offset, foil, frustrate, thwart, neutralize [➡ MAKE IMPOSSIBLE; 276]

counteract *v* **counter**, offset, respond, frustrate, thwart, neutralize, stabilize, lessen, reduce [➡ MAKE IMPOSSIBLE; 276]

counterattack *n* **attack**, revenge, counteroffensive, defense, retaliation, response, reaction [➡ AGGRESSIVE EVENTS; 39]

counterbalance 1 *v* **tip the scales**, offset, balance, correct, compensate [➡ ARRANGE AND CREATE ORDER; 357] 2 *n* **counterweight**, makeweight, ballast [➡ ARRANGE AND CREATE ORDER; 357]

counterclockwise *adj* [➡ DIRECTION OF MOTION; 345]

counterfeit 1 *adj* **fake**, forged, bootleg, phony, bogus, sham, feigned, ersatz, faux [➡ FALSE AND UNREAL; 173] *Opposite*: genuine 2 *v* **forge**, fake, copy, fabricate, imitate, simulate, bootleg [➡ FALSIFY AND CHEAT; 176] 3 *n* **forgery**, copy, fake, imitation, reproduction, pirated edition [➡ REPRESENTATIONS AND GENERAL EXAMPLES; 65] *Opposite*: original

counterfeited *adj* [➡ FALSE AND UNREAL; 173]

counterfeiter *n* **forger**, criminal, fraudster, imitator, faker, bootlegger, pirate [➡ CRIMINALS; 821]

countermand *v* **cancel**, revoke, stop, reverse, annul, retract, go against [➡ APOLOGIZE AND RETRACT; 683]

counterpart *n* **opposite number**, equal, equivalent, colleague [➡ COLLEAGUES AND EQUALS; 967]

counterrevolutionary 1 *n* **rebel**, insurgent, insurrectionist, anarchist, radical [➡ UNCOOPERATIVE OR REBELLIOUS PEOPLE; 566] 2 *adj* **anti-revolutionary**, counterinsurgent, moderate, democratic, pacifist [➡ STYLES AND SYSTEMS OF GOVERNMENT; 806] *Opposite*: revolutionary

countertenor *type of* **musical register** [➡ MUSICAL TERMS; 912]

counter to *prep* **against the grain**, against, contrary to, in opposition to, at odds with [➡ OPPOSITE; 157]

countess *type of* **aristocrat** [➡ RULERS AND ARISTOCRACY; 823]

countless *adj* **uncountable**, innumerable, myriad,

limitless, immeasurable, incalculable, numerous [➡MANY, MUCH, LARGE AMOUNT; 117] *Opposite*: few

count on *v* **depend on**, be sure of, rely on, trust, bank on, lean on, count upon [➡LIKE, LOVE, VALUE, AND ENJOY; 578]

count out *v* **exclude**, weed out, leave out, omit, disregard [➡EJECT AND EXCLUDE; 340] *Opposite*: include

countrified 1 *adj* **rustic**, rural, unspoiled [➡THE COUNTRY-SIDE AND OUTDOOR SPACES; 1071] *Opposite*: urban 2 *adj* **unsophisticated**, unpolished, unfashionable, simple, rough, ordinary, homespun [➡LEVELS OF EDUCATION AND SOPHISTICATION; 894] *Opposite*: urbane

country 1 *n* **republic**, state, nation, realm, kingdom, principality, fatherland, motherland, nation state [➡COUNTRIES AND REGIONS; 1067] 2 *n* **farmland**, woodland, grazing, pastures, wilderness, countryside, prairie [➡THE COUNTRYSIDE AND OUTDOOR SPACES; 1071] *Opposite*: town 3 *n* **people**, inhabitants, residents, nation, population, voters, populace, citizenry [➡GROUPS IN SOCIETY; 940]

country and western *type of* **pop and vocal music** [➡MUSIC, SONGS, AND SINGING; 907]

country club *type of* **bar or club** [➡HOTELS, RESTAURANTS, AND CLUBS; 1082]

country cousin *n* [➡LEVELS OF EDUCATION AND SOPHISTICATION; 894]

country house *type of* **house** [➡RESIDENTIAL BUILDINGS; 1078]

countryman *n* **compatriot**, national, fellow citizen, inhabitant, native [➡SUPPORTERS, PROTECTORS, AND COMPATRIOTS; 970]

countryside *n* [➡THE COUNTRYSIDE AND OUTDOOR SPACES; 1071]

countrywoman *n* **compatriot**, national, fellow citizen, inhabitant, native [➡SUPPORTERS, PROTECTORS, AND COMPATRIOTS; 970]

count up *v* **total**, add up, count, calculate, tot up, tally, reckon [➡ASSESS QUANTITY; 757]

county *n* **region**, section, province, district, canton [➡COUNTRIES AND REGIONS; 1067]

county fair *n* [➡PERFORMANCES AND SHOWS; 42]

coup 1 *n* **coup d'état**, overthrow, revolution, rebellion, putsch, takeover, upheaval [➡AGGRESSIVE EVENTS; 39] 2 *n* **feather in somebody's cap**, achievement, accomplishment, triumph, feat, success [➡SUCCESS; 82]

coup de grâce *n* **deathblow**, last nail in the coffin, knockout punch, killer punch [➡ENDS AND DEPARTURES; 54]

coup d'état *n* **overthrow**, coup, revolution, rebellion, putsch, takeover, upheaval [➡AGGRESSIVE EVENTS; 39]

coupe *type of* **car** [➡BIKES, CARS, AND CARRIAGES; 1149]

couple 1 *n* **twosome**, pair, duo, dyad [➡GROUPS OF PEOPLE; 935] 2 *v* **combine**, link, join, connect, pair, team, fasten [➡FASTEN, LINK, AND JOIN; 408] *Opposite*: separate

coupled with *prep* **together with**, in addition to, on top of, as well as, besides [➡ALSO; 138]

couplet *n* **verse**, distich, stanza, unit, rhyme [➡POETRY AND VERSE; 915]

coupling 1 *n* **link**, join, connection, connector, coupler

[➡FASTENERS, LINKS, AND NETWORKS; 1247] 2 *n* **combination**, juxtaposition, pairing, blend, mixture [➡CONNECTIONS; 143]

coupon *n* **voucher**, ticket, token, slip, form [➡RECEIPTS AND INVOICES; 591]

courage *n* **bravery**, nerve, pluck, valor, daring, audacity, mettle, spirit, resolution, fearlessness, guts (*slang*) [➡COOL AND CALM; 536] *Opposite*: cowardice

Compare and Contrast: *courage, bravery, fearlessness, nerve, guts, pluck, mettle*

CORE MEANING: personal resoluteness in the face of danger or difficulties

courage the ability to show resoluteness and determination, whether physical, mental, or moral, against a wide range of difficulties or dangers; *bravery* extreme lack of fear; *fearlessness* resoluteness in the face of dangers or challenges; *nerve* coolness, steadiness, and self-assurance; *guts* (*slang*) strength of character and boldness; *pluck* resolution and willingness to continue struggling against the odds; *mettle* spirited determination.

courageous *adj* **brave**, daring, bold, spirited, plucky, audacious, fearless, gutsy (*informal*), dauntless (*literary*), intrepid (*literary or humorous*) [➡COURAGE; 498] *Opposite*: cowardly

courageousness *see* **courage**

courier 1 *n* **messenger**, carrier, biker, dispatch rider [➡MESSENGERS AND COURIERS; 852] 2 *n* (*UK*) **vacation rep**, rep, agent, guide [➡TRAVEL: SIGHTSEEING AND TOURISM; 321]

course 1 *n* **sequence**, progression, development, passage, path, way, progress [➡DIRECTION OF MOTION; 345] 2 *n* **direction**, route, path, track, road, way [➡DIRECTION OF MOTION; 345] 3 *n* **option**, choice, possibility, route, avenue, strategy, alternative, plan, procedure, policy, enterprise [➡WAYS OF DOING THINGS; 294] 4 *n* **lesson**, class, program, module, curriculum, lecture series [➡CLASSES, COURSEWORK, AND EXAMINATIONS; 842] 5 *v* **flow**, pour, run, gush, stream, surge [➡PROCEED AND GO; 305] *Opposite*: trickle

course of action *n* **strategy**, course, policy, plan, method, procedure, system, formula, route, mission, enterprise, undertaking, choice, option, alternative, modus operandi, avenue [➡WAYS OF DOING THINGS; 294]

coursework *n* **assignments**, homework, reading, project [➡CLASSES, COURSEWORK, AND EXAMINATIONS; 842]

court 1 *n* **law court**, court of law, district court, juvenile court, small-claims court, appellate court, high court, Federal Court, Supreme Court, Court of Appeals, magistrate's court (*UK*) [➡TRIAL, PUNISHMENT, AND LEGAL OUTCOMES; 819] 2 *n* **courtyard**, square, yard, patio, piazza, close, enclosure, quad (*informal*) [➡URBAN OUTDOOR SPACES; 1072] 3 *v* (*dated*) **date**, go out, see, pay court to (*dated*) [➡ESTABLISHING RELATIONSHIPS WITH OTHERS; 974] 4 *v* **woo**, cozy up to, curry favor with, pander to, flatter, ingratiate [➡FLATTER AND FAWN; 621] *Opposite*: shun 5 *v* **risk**, invite, encourage, incite, attract, ask for, tempt [➡INITIATE AND ESTABLISH COMMUNICATION; 680] *Opposite*: avoid

court case *n* **lawsuit**, suit, case, hearing, indictment, prosecution, complaint, litigation, action, class action, proceedings, appeal [➡TRIAL, PUNISHMENT, AND LEGAL OUTCOMES; 819]

courteous *adj* **polite**, well-mannered, considerate, chivalrous, civil, genteel, gallant [➡ GOOD MANNERS AND SOCIAL SKILLS; 520] *Opposite:* rude

courteousness *n* **politeness**, good manners, courtesy, consideration, civility, manners, gallantry, gentility [➡ GOOD MANNERS AND SOCIAL SKILLS; 520] *Opposite:* rudeness

courtesy *n* **politeness**, good manners, courteousness, consideration, civility, manners, gallantry, gentility [➡ GOOD MANNERS AND SOCIAL SKILLS; 520] *Opposite:* rudeness

courthouse *n* **court**, courtroom, law court, court of law [➡ TRIAL, PUNISHMENT, AND LEGAL OUTCOMES; 819]

courtier *n* **flatterer**, sycophant, self-seeker, creature, toady, climber, hanger-on, leech [➡ SUPERFICIAL OR INSINCERE PEOPLE; 951]

courtly *adj* **courteous**, chivalrous, polite, civil, refined, genteel [➡ GOOD MANNERS AND SOCIAL SKILLS; 520] *Opposite:* rude

court order *n* **legal ruling**, order, sanction, interdict, veto, ban, bar, prohibition, injunction, restriction, embargo, summons, restraining order, exclusion order, ruling, proscription (*formal*), gagging order (*UK*) [➡ TRIAL, PUNISHMENT, AND LEGAL OUTCOMES; 819]

courtship *n* **wooing**, dating, engagement [➡ SEXUAL AND ROMANTIC RELATIONSHIPS; 964]

courtyard *n* **patio**, yard, square, court, enclosure, piazza, quad (*informal*) [➡ URBAN OUTDOOR SPACES; 1072]

couscous *type of* **cooked dish** [➡ PREPARED DISHES; 1170]

cousin 1 *type of* **same-generation relative** [➡ SAME-GENERATION RELATIVES; 957] **2** *n* **friend**, companion, colleague, partner, counterpart [➡ SUPPORTERS, PROTECTORS, AND COMPATRIOTS; 970]

cove *n* **bay**, inlet, harbor [➡ THE SEAS, OCEANS, AND SHORES; 1041]

covenant *n* **agreement**, contract, treaty, promise, pledge, bond, pact [➡ OFFICIAL DOCUMENTS; 586]

cover 1 *v* **conceal**, hide, cover up, obscure, disguise, mask, bury, ensconce [➡ CAUSE TO DISAPPEAR; 6] *Opposite:* expose **2** *v* **protect**, shield, guard, shelter, defend, safeguard, screen, fend [➡ PREVENT CONTACT OR ATTACK; 419] **3** *v* **wrap**, coat, cover up, envelop, swathe, overlay, enfold, shroud [➡ DECORATE, ADORN, AND APPLY COATINGS; 405] *Opposite:* reveal **4** *v* **deal with**, include, comprise, embrace, take in, contain, report on [➡ BE ABOUT SOMETHING; 62] **5** *v* **travel**, cross, traverse, pass through, go through [➡ TRAVEL: WAYS OF TRAVELING; 320] **6** *n* **covering**, wrapping, jacket, shell, case, top, lid [➡ COVERS AND COATINGS; 1246] **7** *n* **shelter**, concealment, protection, hiding place, refuge, asylum [➡ COVERS AND COATINGS; 1246] **8** *type of* **container** [➡ CONTAINERS, RECEPTACLES, AND PACKAGING; 1245]

coverage *n* **attention**, treatment, reporting, exposure, handling, analysis, reportage [➡ NEWSPAPERS AND MAGAZINES; 605]

coveralls *n* [➡ GARMENTS AND OUTFITS; 865]

covered *adj* **enclosed**, roofed, sheltered, protected, shielded [➡ SAFE AND SAFETY; 191] *Opposite:* exposed

covered market *type of* **retail outlet** [➡ RETAIL OUTLETS; 1083]

covered wagon *type of* **wagon or carriage** [➡ VEHICLES; 1145]

covering *n* **cover**, casing, top, lid, layer, wrapper, shell, jacket [➡ COVERS AND COATINGS; 1246]

coverlet *n* **bedspread**, cover, throw, counterpane (*dated*), bedcover (*UK*) [➡ FURNISHING AND HOUSEHOLD LINENS; 860]

covert 1 *adj* **secret**, clandestine, underground, concealed, hidden, furtive, undercover, surreptitious, veiled, hush-hush (*informal*) [➡ SECRET AND UNKNOWN; 179] *Opposite:* open **2** *n* **copse**, wood, thicket, coppice, undergrowth [➡ WOODS, FORESTS, AND JUNGLES; 1047]

See Compare and Contrast at **secret**.

covertness *n* **secrecy**, stealth, concealment, surreptitiousness, underhandedness, furtiveness [➡ SECRET AND UNKNOWN; 179] *Opposite:* openness

cover up 1 *v* **conceal**, hide, obscure, mask, disguise, bury [➡ CAUSE TO DISAPPEAR; 6] *Opposite:* expose **2** *v* **suppress**, keep under wraps, keep secret, paper over, hide, conceal, hush up (*informal*) [➡ WITHHOLD INFORMATION; 687] *Opposite:* divulge

cover-up *n* **conspiracy**, plot, scheme, smoke screen, figleaf, whitewash (*informal*) [➡ WITHHOLD INFORMATION; 687]

covet *v* **want**, long for, yearn for, crave, hanker after, desire, wish for [➡ DESIRE AND WANT; 579]

See Compare and Contrast at **want**.

coveted *adj* **sought-after**, longed for, wanted, fashionable, desired, desirable, popular, in demand [➡ POPULAR AND WANTED; 220] *Opposite:* scorned

covetous *adj* **envious**, jealous, greedy, avaricious, acquisitive, desirous (*formal*) [➡ ENVY AND JEALOUSY; 548] *Opposite:* generous

covetousness *n* **envy**, enviousness, jealousy, avarice, avariciousness, greed, greediness, acquisitiveness, cupidity (*formal*) [➡ MORALLY BAD OR IMPROPER; 775]. *Opposite:* generosity

covey *type of* **flock** [➡ GROUPS OF BIRDS; 1007]

coving *n* [➡ ROOFS, ROOF PARTS, AND CEILINGS; 1103]

cow 1 *type of* **female animal** [➡ MALE OR FEMALE ANIMALS; 978] **2** *type of* **farm animal** [➡ FARM ANIMALS; 982] **3** *v* **intimidate**, scare, frighten, bully, overawe, browbeat [➡ FRIGHTEN AND SHOCK; 568]

coward *n* **sissy**, deserter, runaway, weakling, chicken (*informal*), quitter (*informal*), scaredy-cat (*informal*), fraidy-cat (*informal*), yellowbelly (*slang*), milksop (*dated*) [➡ LAZY OR UNSUCCESSFUL PEOPLE; 948]

cowardice *n* **weakness**, fearfulness, spinelessness, fear, timidity, faint-heartedness, pusillanimity (*formal*), cravenness (*literary*) [➡ COWARDICE AND WEAKNESS OF WILL; 508] *Opposite:* courage

cowardliness *n* [➡ COWARDICE AND WEAKNESS OF WILL; 508]

cowardly *adj* **gutless**, spineless, weak, craven, faint-hearted, chinless, pusillanimous, chicken (*informal*), lily-livered (*dated*) [➡ COWARDICE AND WEAKNESS OF WILL; 508] *Opposite:* brave

cowboy *n* **cowhand**, cowman, herdsman, stockman, rancher, ranchero, gaucho, cowpuncher (*informal*) [➡FARMERS, GARDENERS, AND MANUAL WORKERS; 849]

cowboy boot *type of* **boot** [➡FOOTWEAR; 871]

cowboy hat *type of* **hat** [➡ACCESSORIES, MILLINERY, AND LINGERIE; 867]

cowboy movie *n* **western**, horse opera, oater (*slang*) [➡FILM; 901]

cowed *adj* **intimidated**, browbeaten, scared, frightened, submissive [➡FEAR AND PANIC; 543] *Opposite*: defiant

cower *v* **shrink**, cringe, tremble, recoil, shy away [➡PHYSICAL REACTIONS; 316] *Opposite*: stand your ground

cowl *n* **hood**, cover, cloak, top [➡ACCESSORIES, MILLINERY, AND LINGERIE; 867]

cowlick *type of* **hairstyle** [➡HAIRSTYLES AND HAIRPIECES; 488]

coworker *n* **colleague**, fellow worker, collaborator, associate, workmate, workfellow [➡COLLEAGUES AND EQUALS; 967]

cowshed 1 *n* **barn**, stable, corral, pen, stockyard [➡ANCILLARY BUILDINGS; 1080] 2 *type of* **pen or cage** [➡ANIMAL OR BIRD ACCOMMODATIONS; 1079]

cowslip *type of* **perennial flower** [➡FLOWERS; 1032]

cox *v* **steer**, direct, pilot, navigate [➡TRAVEL: WAYS OF TRAVELING; 320]

coxswain *v* **steer**, direct, pilot, navigate [➡TRAVEL: WAYS OF TRAVELING; 320]

coy 1 *adj* **teasing**, playful, engaging, coquettish (*literary*) [➡FLIRTATIOUS; 639] 2 *adj* **shy**, bashful, timid, modest, reserved, demure [➡RETICENT AND UNFORTHCOMING; 631] *Opposite*: brazen

coyote *type of* **canine** [➡CANINES; 979]

coypu *type of* **rodent** [➡RODENTS; 989]

cozy 1 *adj* **snug**, warm, pleasant, comfortable, appealing, inviting, welcoming, comfy (*informal*) [➡PHYSICALLY PLEASANT; 186] *Opposite*: inhospitable 2 *adj* **familiar**, friendly, intimate, close, warm, loving, gemütlich [➡EMOTIONALLY PLEASANT; 187] *Opposite*: cold 3 *adj* **expedient**, convenient, self-serving, cliquey, clannish, cushy (*informal*) [➡UNFRIENDLINESS AND UNSOCIABILITY; 504]

cozy up *v* **ingratiate yourself**, curry favor, make overtures, pander, insinuate, worm your way in, apple-polish (*informal*) [➡ESTABLISHING RELATIONSHIPS WITH OTHERS; 974] *Opposite*: distance yourself

crab *type of* **crustacean** [➡AQUATIC INVERTEBRATES; 1022]

crabbed *adj* **bad-tempered**, crabby, grumpy, irritable, out of sorts, touchy, short-tempered, surly, cantankerous, snappy, sullen, petulant, cross, grouchy (*informal*), testy (*informal*), tetchy (*informal*), cranky (*informal*) [➡IRRITATION AND ANGER; 541] *Opposite*: easygoing

crabbiness *n* **bad-temperedness**, bad temper, irritability, grumpiness, cantankerousness, snappiness, touchiness, petulance, crossness, sullenness, grouchiness (*informal*), testiness (*informal*), tetchiness (*informal*), crankiness (*informal*) [➡IRRITATION AND ANGER; 541] *Opposite*: equanimity (*formal*)

crabby *adj* **grumpy**, bad-tempered, short-tempered, irritable, snappy, surly, cross, sullen, sulky, touchy, cantankerous, crabbed, tetchy (*informal*), grouchy (*informal*), testy (*informal*), cranky (*informal*) [➡IRRITATION AND ANGER; 541] *Opposite*: easygoing

crabgrass *type of* **grass** [➡GRASS; 1031]

crab louse *type of* **parasitic insect** [➡PARASITES; 1017]

crack 1 *v* **break**, fracture, split, splinter, snap, rupture, chink, fissure, cleave, disintegrate [➡TEAR, BREAK, AND CUT; 360] 2 *v* **break down**, go to pieces, lose control, collapse, crack up (*informal*), lose it (*informal*) [➡FAIL OR CEASE TO FUNCTION; 470] 3 *v* **bang**, bump, hit, whack, bash (*informal*), wallop (*informal*) [➡CONTACT: IMPACT; 413] 4 *v* (*informal*) **solve**, work out, figure out, fathom, decipher, decode, decrypt, break [➡SOLVE AND INTERPRET; 760] 5 *n* **fissure**, flaw, break, fracture, chink, fault, crevice, gap, rift, cleft, crevasse [➡HOLES, GAPS, AND FORKS; 1252] 6 *n* (*informal*) **blow**, crash, bang, snap, pop, clap [➡IMPACT SOUNDS; 1260] 7 *n* **weakness**, flaw, fault, imperfection, defect [➡FAULTS, FLAWS, AND WEAKNESSES; 251] 8 *n* (*informal*) **gibe**, quip, dig, joke, aside, remark, wisecrack (*informal*), gag (*informal*), jape (*archaic or literary*), jest (*literary*) [➡JOKES AND TEASING; 674] 9 *adj* **expert**, topflight, crackerjack, ace (*informal*) [➡SUPERIORITY; 152]

crack a joke *v* **make a joke**, quip, joke, jest (*literary*) [➡JOKES AND TEASING; 674]

crackbrained *adj* **eccentric**, irrational, foolish, stupid, crazed, crazy (*informal*) [➡BIZARRE AND PECULIAR; 257] *Opposite*: rational

crack down (*informal*) *v* **clamp down**, tighten up, come down hard, get tough [➡REFUSE PERMISSION AND NOT ALLOW; 670]

cracked 1 *adj* **fractured**, broken, split, splintered, cleft, fissured [➡IN BAD REPAIR; 1234] *Opposite*: intact 2 *adj* (*informal*) **irrational**, eccentric, crazed, crackbrained, foolish, stupid, crazy (*informal*) [➡ECCENTRICITY AND IRRATIONALITY; 562] *Opposite*: rational

cracker-barrel *adj* **straightforward**, unsophisticated, folksy, uncultivated, simple [➡LEVELS OF EDUCATION AND SOPHISTICATION; 894] *Opposite*: sophisticated

crackle 1 *v* **crunch**, snap, pop, sizzle, crack, scrunch, rat-a-tat-tat [➡EMIT SOUNDS THROUGH IMPACT AND ABRASION; 365] 2 *n* **crack**, snap, pop, sizzle, crunch, scrunch [➡CONTINUOUS SOUNDS; 1258]

crack of dawn *n* **daybreak**, dawn, daylight, sunrise, first light, morning, sunup, cockcrow (*archaic or literary*) [➡TIMES OF DAY; 87] *Opposite*: dusk

crackpot (*informal*) *adj* **impractical**, unrealistic, eccentric, wild, outlandish, crazy (*informal*) [➨ THE NATURE OF IDEAS; 771] *Opposite*: realistic

crack up (*informal*) **1** *v* **break down**, go to pieces, lose control, collapse, crack (*informal*), lose it (*informal*) [➨ FAIL OR CEASE TO FUNCTION; 470] **2** *v* **break up**, laugh, guffaw, giggle, titter [➨ PLEASE AND AMUSE; 572]

crack-up (*informal*) **1** *n* **breakdown**, collapse, crisis, meltdown, burnout [➨ ENDS AND DEPARTURES; 54] **2** *n* **crash**, accident, wreck, smash, collision [➨ TRAFFIC ACCIDENTS; 255]

cradle 1 *type of* **bed** [➨ FURNITURE; 858] **2** *n* **support**, frame, structure, framework, underpinning, foundation [➨ CONTAINERS, RECEPTACLES, AND PACKAGING; 1245] **3** *v* **hold**, embrace, support, cuddle, clasp, rock [➨ CONTACT: HOLD; 411] *Opposite*: drop

craft 1 *n* **skill**, dexterity, expertise, ability, craftsmanship, technique, artistry [➨ SKILLS, TALENTS, AND ABILITIES; 526] **2** *n* **trade**, profession, art, job, calling, métier [➨ PROFESSIONS; 845] **3** *n* **vehicle**, vessel, boat, aircraft, spacecraft [➨ SHIPS AND BOATS; 1150] **4** *n* **cunning**, deceit, slyness, wiliness, shrewdness, guile, sneakiness, deviousness, underhandedness [➨ DECEITFUL; 513] *Opposite*: forthrightness **5** *v* **make**, fashion, create, manufacture, construct, shape, hew, produce [➨ MANUFACTURE; 349]

craftiness *n* **cunning**, slyness, shrewdness, wiliness, guile, underhandedness, deceit, deviousness, sneakiness [➨ DECEITFUL; 513] *Opposite*: forthrightness

craftsmanship *n* **skill**, artistry, workmanship, expertise, technique, ability, dexterity, craft [➨ SKILLS, TALENTS, AND ABILITIES; 526]

craftsperson *n* **craftsworker**, artisan, artist [➨ ARTISTS; 900]

crafty *adj* **cunning**, sneaky, sly, shrewd, devious, manipulative, astute, wily, deceitful, underhand [➨ DECEITFUL; 513] *Opposite*: forthright

crag *n* **cliff**, rock face, precipice, peak, scarp, mountain, escarpment, bluff [➨ MOUNTAINS AND HILLS; 1044]

craggy 1 *adj* **rocky**, stony, rough, rugged, uneven, steep [➨ ORIENTATION AND ALIGNMENT; 1223] *Opposite*: even **2** *adj* **lined**, rugged, wrinkled, wrinkly, weathered, weather-beaten, rough-hewn [➨ FACIAL CHARACTERISTICS; 481] *Opposite*: smooth

cram 1 *v* **stuff**, pack, fill up, ram, shove, force [➨ FILL; 406] *Opposite*: remove **2** *v* (*informal*) **study**, review, go over, memorize, peruse, learn, revise (*UK*) [➨ STUDYING; 844] *Opposite*: forget

crammed *adj* **full**, packed, filled, crowded, cramped, full up, stuffed (*informal*), jam-packed (*informal*) [➨ FULL; 1239] *Opposite*: empty

cramp 1 *n* **spasm**, pain, contraction, shooting pain, twinge, convulsion [➨ PAIN AND OTHER PHYSICAL SENSATIONS; 733] **2** *v* **restrict**, hamper, limit, constrict, constrain, hold back [➨ AVOID, PREVENT, LIMIT, AND CONTROL; 277]

cramped *adj* **overcrowded**, confined, restricted, close, small [➨ SMALL; 1195] *Opposite*: spacious

cranberry *type of* **berry** [➨ FRUIT AND VEGETABLES; 1176]

crane 1 *n* **hoist**, derrick, winch, gantry [➨ MACHINES AND MACHINE PARTS; 1116] **2** *type of* **freshwater bird** [➨ FRESHWATER BIRDS; 1000]

crane fly *type of* **flying insect** [➨ FLYING INSECTS; 1013]

cranial osteopathy *type of* **complementary therapy** [➨ REMEDIES, TREATMENTS, AND OPERATIONS; 731]

cranium *type of* **bone** [➨ THE BONES AND JOINTS; 719]

crank 1 *part of* **engine** [➨ PARTS OF AN ENGINE; 1144] **2** *v* **turn**, reel, wind, activate, move [➨ MOVE SOMETHING: ON THE SPOT; 336]

crankiness 1 *n* (*informal*) **crabbiness**, irritability, bad temper, touchiness, crossness, peevishness, cantankerousness, grouchiness (*informal*) [➨ IRRITATION AND ANGER; 541] *Opposite*: affability **2** *n* (*UK informal*) **eccentricity**, nonconformity, originality, idiosyncrasy, quirkiness, bizarreness [➨ BIZARRE AND PECULIAR; 257]

crankshaft *part of* **engine** [➨ PARTS OF AN ENGINE; 1144]

crank up *v* **start**, turn on, wind up, activate, get going [➨ CAUSE TO START; 265] *Opposite*: turn off

cranky 1 *adj* (*informal*) **irritable**, crabby, cantankerous, bad-tempered, touchy, cross, peevish, grouchy (*informal*), ornery (*informal*) [➨ IRRITATION AND ANGER; 541] *Opposite*: good-humored **2** *adj* (*UK informal*) **eccentric**, quirky, idiosyncratic, bizarre, strange, weird, original [➨ BIZARRE AND PECULIAR; 257] *Opposite*: ordinary

cranny *n* **crevice**, crack, fissure, chink, cleft, split, hole, opening [➨ HOLES, GAPS, AND FORKS; 1252]

crappie *type of* **freshwater fish** [➨ FRESHWATER FISH; 1010]

crash 1 *n* **collision**, accident, smash, smashup, pileup (*informal*) [➨ TRAFFIC ACCIDENTS; 255] **2** *n* **failure**, breakdown, collapse, shutdown [➨ FAILURE; 77] **3** *n* **bang**, smash, din, clatter, clang, boom, crack, thump, thud, crunch, racket, wallop (*informal*) [➨ IMPACT SOUNDS; 1260] **4** *n* **bankruptcy**, failure, collapse, liquidation [➨ ACCOUNTING, BANKING, AND BUDGETING; 799] **5** *n* [➨ COMPUTERS AND COMPUTING; 1127] **6** *v* **collide**, run into, smash into, bump into, hurtle, hit [➨ CONTACT: IMPACT; 413] **7** *v* **break down**, collapse, fizzle, fail [➨ FAIL OR CEASE TO FUNCTION; 470] **8** *v* **boom**, bang, thunder, clash, clatter, roar, rumble, resound [➨ EMIT SOUNDS THROUGH IMPACT AND ABRASION; 365] **9** *v* **go under**, go bankrupt, fold, collapse, fail, go belly up, go broke (*informal*) [➨ ACCOUNTING, BANKING, AND BUDGETING; 799] *Opposite*: thrive **10** *v* [➨ COMPUTERS AND COMPUTING; 1127]

crash course *n* **training**, orientation, workshop, immersion, induction (*UK*) [➨ CLASSES, COURSEWORK, AND EXAMINATIONS; 842]

crash helmet *type of* **headgear** [➨ ACCESSORIES, MILLINERY, AND LINGERIE; 867]

crash-land *v* **collide**, crash, fall, smash, come down, land, ditch (*informal*) [➨ GO DOWNWARD; 307]

crass *adj* **insensitive**, tactless, thoughtless, vulgar, obnoxious, gross, asinine [➨ BAD MANNERS AND SOCIAL SKILLS; 521] *Opposite*: sensitive

crassness *n* **insensitivity**, vulgarity, tactlessness, obnoxiousness, grossness, asininity, thoughtlessness [➨ BAD MANNERS AND SOCIAL SKILLS; 521] *Opposite*: sensitivity

crate *type of* **container** [➨ CONTAINERS, RECEPTACLES, AND PACKAGING; 1245]

crater *n* **pit**, depression, hole, cavity, hollow [➨ GEOLOGIC FEATURES; 1056] *Opposite*: mound

Crater *type of* **constellation** [➡ HEAVENLY BODIES; 1061]

cravat *type of* **accessory** [➡ ACCESSORIES, MILLINERY, AND LINGERIE; 867]

crave 1 *v* **desire**, long for, need, want, yearn for, require, hanker after, hunger after, thirst for, pine for, be dying for [➡ DESIRE AND WANT; 579] *Opposite*: dislike 2 *v* (*archaic*) **ask**, beg, pray, request, entreat, sue (*formal*), implore (*formal*), beseech (*literary*) [➡ REQUEST AND DEMAND; 663] *Opposite*: reject

See Compare and Contrast at **want**.

craven *adj* **cowardly**, gutless, spineless, weak, timorous, fearful, faint-hearted, spiritless, pusillanimous (*formal*), lily-livered (*dated*) [➡ COWARDICE AND WEAKNESS OF WILL; 508] *Opposite*: bold

See Compare and Contrast at **cowardly**.

cravenness (*literary*) *n* [➡ COWARDICE AND WEAKNESS OF WILL; 508]

craving *n* **longing**, desire, passion, hunger, thirst, yearning, hankering, yen, appetite [➡ DESIRE AND WANT; 579] *Opposite*: dislike

crawl 1 *v* **creep**, edge, inch, wriggle, slither, snake, grovel [➡ MOVE SLOWLY; 314] 2 *v* **skulk**, scuttle, creep, sneak, slink, move at a snail's pace [➡ MOVE SLOWLY; 314] 3 *v* (*informal*) **grovel**, ingratiate yourself, flatter, fawn, suck up (*informal*), butter up (*informal*), apple-polish (*slang*) [➡ FLATTER AND FAWN; 621] *Opposite*: alienate 4 *v* **apologize**, eat humble pie, grovel, humiliate yourself, prostrate yourself, eat your words, eat crow (*informal*) [➡ APOLOGIZE AND RETRACT; 683]

crayfish *type of* **crustacean** [➡ AQUATIC INVERTEBRATES; 1022]

craze *n* **fad**, trend, fashion, enthusiasm, rage, obsession, vogue, thing (*informal*) [➡ FADS, FETISHES, AND IDOLATRY; 555]

crazed *adj* **irrational**, distraught, overwrought, wild, inflamed, excited, fevered, demented (*informal*), crazy (*informal*), cracked (*informal*) [➡ IRRITATION AND ANGER; 541] *Opposite*: rational

craziness (*informal*) *n* **foolishness**, stupidity, folly, idiocy, madness [➡ ECCENTRICITY AND IRRATIONALITY; 562] *Opposite*: reasonableness

crazy (*informal*) 1 *adj* **foolish**, unwise, silly, senseless, irrational, wild, stupid, outrageous, outlandish, ridiculous, bizarre, peculiar, weird, eccentric, odd, zany, cracked (*informal*) [➡ ECCENTRICITY AND IRRATIONALITY; 562] *Opposite*: sensible 2 *adj* **fond**, keen, passionate, enthusiastic, devoted, avid [➡ APPRECIATION AND GRATITUDE; 535] *Opposite*: lukewarm

creak 1 *v* **squeak**, screech, scrape, grate, groan, rasp [➡ EMIT SOUNDS THROUGH IMPACT AND ABRASION; 365] 2 *n* **screech**, squeak, scrape, grate, groan, rasp [➡ CONTINUOUS SOUNDS; 1258]

creaky 1 *adj* **squeaky**, rusty, grating, rasping [➡ LOUD, HIGH, OR UNPLEASANT SOUNDS; 1266] 2 *adj* (*informal*) **stiff**, rigid, inflexible, firm [➡ IN BAD REPAIR; 1234] *Opposite*: supple

cream 1 *n* [➡ DAIRY PRODUCTS AND CHEESES; 1183] 2 *n* **ointment**, salve, balm, unguent, emulsion [➡ LOTIONS, PASTES, AND GELS; 1272] 3 *n* **best**, elite, finest, cream of the crop, pick of the bunch [➡ SUPERIORITY; 152] *Opposite*: dregs 4 *type of* **white** [➡ COLORS; 1224] 5 *v* (*slang*) **defeat**, thrash, hammer (*informal*), clobber

(*informal*), demolish (*informal*) [➡ BEAT AND DEFEAT; 80] 6 *v* **blend**, soften, mash, emulsify, combine [➡ COOKING AND FOOD PREPARATION; 353]

cream cheese *type of* **soft cheese** [➡ DAIRY PRODUCTS AND CHEESES; 1183]

cream off *v* **skim off**, handpick, select, choose, pick out, cherry-pick, single out [➡ MAKE DECISIONS AND CHOICES; 752] *Opposite*: reject

crease 1 *n* **pleat**, fold, tuck, gather [➡ CHANGE OF SHAPE; 385] 2 *n* **crinkle**, crumple, wrinkle, rumple, pucker [➡ CHANGE OF SHAPE; 385] 3 *n* **furrow**, wrinkle, line, groove, crow's foot, laugh line [➡ FACIAL CHARACTERISTICS; 481] 4 *v* **fold**, pleat, tuck, gather [➡ CHANGE OF SHAPE; 385] 5 *v* **crumple**, wrinkle, scrunch, crinkle, rumple, pucker [➡ CHANGE OF SHAPE; 385] *Opposite*: smooth

creased *adj* **wrinkled**, wrinkly, crinkled, crinkly, lined, crumpled, rumpled, puckered, furrowed, rutted, wizened [➡ IN BAD REPAIR; 1234] *Opposite*: smooth

create 1 *v* **make**, produce, generate, fashion, form, craft, build, construct [➡ MANUFACTURE; 349] *Opposite*: destroy 2 *v* **invent**, design, originate, initiate, give rise to, coin, conceive [➡ CREATION; 346] 3 *v* **establish**, set up, found, start, get going [➡ INSTITUTE AND INAUGURATE; 348]

See Compare and Contrast at **make**.

creation 1 *n* **formation**, making, conception, construction, manufacture, design, establishment [➡ CREATION; 346] *Opposite*: destruction 2 *n* **nature**, cosmos, universe, life, world [➡ NATURE AND THE ENVIRONMENT; 1038] 3 *n* **invention**, handiwork, fabrication, innovation, concept, conception [➡ BEGINNINGS; 53]

creative 1 *adj* **original**, imaginative, inspired, artistic, inventive, resourceful, ingenious, innovative, productive [➡ POSITIVE INTELLECTUAL CHARACTERISTICS; 524] *Opposite*: unimaginative 2 *n* (*informal*) [➡ BUSINESS PEOPLE; 793]

creativeness *n* *see* **creativity**

creativity *n* **originality**, imagination, inspiration, ingenuity, inventiveness, resourcefulness, creativeness, vision, innovation [➡ POSITIVE INTELLECTUAL CHARACTERISTICS; 524]

creator *n* **maker**, inventor, originator, architect, designer, author, initiator [➡ DESIGNERS, CREATORS, AND INSTIGATORS; 347] *Opposite*: destroyer

creature 1 *n* **being**, living being, person, man, woman, human being, individual, mortal, soul [➡ PERSON; 931] 2 *n* **animal**, beast, organism, insect, critter (*slang*) [➡ LIVING THINGS AND LIVING; 976]

crèche 1 *n* **Nativity**, display, scene, tableau, spectacle, exhibit, crib (*UK*) [➡ RELIGIOUS OBJECTS; 779] 2 *n* (*UK*) **playgroup**, kindergarten, playschool, nursery [➡ EDUCATIONAL INSTITUTIONS; 813]

credence *n* **credibility**, authority, weight, belief, confidence, acceptance [➡ TRUE AND REAL; 171]

credential *n* **qualification**, diploma, recommendation, testimonial, certificate [➡ QUALIFICATIONS; 843]

credentialed *adj* **qualified**, certified, licensed, accredited [➡ QUALIFICATIONS; 843]

credentials *n* **identification**, authorization, ID, permit, pass, badge [➞ OFFICIAL DOCUMENTS; 586]

credenza *type of* **cabinet** [➞ FURNITURE; 858]

credibility *n* **trustworthiness**, reliability, authority, standing, sincerity, integrity, believability [➞ TRUE AND REAL; 171]

credible 1 *adj* **believable**, convincing, plausible, likely, probable, realistic [➞ POSSIBLE AND PROBABLE; 177] *Opposite*: unbelievable 2 *adj* **trustworthy**, reliable, sincere, dependable, sound, tried [➞ TRUE AND REAL; 171] *Opposite*: unreliable

credibly *adv* **believably**, realistically, convincingly, plausibly, reliably [➞ POSSIBLE AND PROBABLE; 177] *Opposite*: unconvincingly

credit 1 *n* **praise**, recognition, thanks, acclaim, glory, acknowledgment, tribute, brownie points (*informal*) [➞ PRAISE AND ENCOURAGE; 647] *Opposite*: blame 2 *n* **standing**, position, status, esteem, prestige, honor, character, repute (*formal*) [➞ STATUS; 888] 3 *n* **belief**, confidence, trust, faith [➞ COOL AND CALM; 536] *Opposite*: disbelief 4 *v* **believe**, accept, trust, have faith in, have confidence in, rely on [➞ APPROVE AND CONFIRM; 646] *Opposite*: disbelieve 5 *v* **acknowledge**, recognize, acclaim, pay tribute, praise, attribute [➞ PRAISE AND ENCOURAGE; 647]

creditable *adj* **admirable**, praiseworthy, good, worthy, laudable, commendable, honorable, respectable [➞ ADMIRABLE AND COMMENDABLE; 185] *Opposite*: poor

credit control *n* [➞ BUSINESS ACTIVITIES AND PHENOMENA; 794]

credit union *n* [➞ ACCOUNTING, BANKING, AND BUDGETING; 799]

credo *n* **creed**, doctrine, ideology, principle, view, belief, stand, stance, philosophy, dogma [➞ RELIGIOUS CONCEPTS; 776]

credulity *n* **gullibility**, naiveté, innocence, trust, imprudence, credulousness [➞ NEGATIVE INTELLECTUAL CHARACTERISTICS; 525] *Opposite*: astuteness

credulous *adj* **gullible**, naive, trusting, imprudent, unsuspecting, innocent, uncritical [➞ NEGATIVE INTELLECTUAL CHARACTERISTICS; 525] *Opposite*: astute

credulousness *see* **credulity**

creed *n* **faith**, dogma, doctrine, credo, belief, article of faith, principle [➞ RELIGIONS AND RELIGIOUS PRACTICES; 777]

creek 1 *n* **stream**, rivulet, arroyo, brook, channel, crick (*slang*) [➞ RIVERS, LAKES, AND STREAMS; 1042] 2 *n* **cove**, bay, inlet, gulf [➞ THE SEAS, OCEANS, AND SHORES; 1041]

creel *type of* **container** [➞ CONTAINERS, RECEPTACLES, AND PACKAGING; 1245]

creep 1 *v* **tiptoe**, skulk, steal, sneak, slink, sidle [➞ MOVE SLOWLY; 314] 2 *v* **crawl**, slither, inch, edge, worm, snake [➞ MOVE SLOWLY; 314]

creeper *n* **climber**, trailer, vine, liana [➞ CLIMBERS; 1033]

creepiness (*informal*) *n* **eeriness**, scariness, weirdness, uncanniness, strangeness, spookiness (*informal*) [➞ FRIGHTENING; 231]

creep up on *v* **sneak up on**, surprise, stalk, take by surprise [➞ ACCOMPANY AND FOLLOW; 337]

creepy (*informal*) *adj* **eerie**, disturbing, spine-chilling, uncanny, weird, strange, hair-raising, unnerving, unsettling, scary (*informal*), spooky (*informal*) [➞ FRIGHTENING; 231]

creepy-crawly (*informal*) *n* **insect**, bug, beetle, centipede, millipede, caterpillar [➞ INSECTS; 1012]

cremate *v* **incinerate**, burn, consume, immolate (*literary*) [➞ FIRE, FLAMMABILITY, AND BURNING; 1165]

cremation *n* **burning**, incineration, immolation (*formal*) [➞ BURIAL AND PREPARATION FOR BURIAL; 929]

crème brûlée *type of* **dessert** [➞ CAKES, COOKIES, AND DESSERTS; 1181]

crème caramel *type of* **dessert** [➞ CAKES, COOKIES, AND DESSERTS; 1181]

crème de la crème *n* **best**, cream, pick, flower, elite [➞ SUPERIORITY; 152]

crème fraîche *n* [➞ DAIRY PRODUCTS AND CHEESES; 1183]

crepe 1 *type of* **pancake** [➞ CAKES, COOKIES, AND DESSERTS; 1181] 2 *type of* **synthetic fabric** [➞ FABRICS; 1132]

crepe de Chine *type of* **fabric from animals** [➞ FABRICS; 1132]

crepuscular (*literary*) *adj* [➞ DESCRIBING LIGHT; 1228]

crescendo 1 *n* **increase**, upsurge, swelling, buildup, climax, loudening [➞ CHANGE OF INTENSITY: MORE; 394] 2 *type of* **musical term** [➞ MUSICAL TERMS; 912]

crescent 1 *adj* **semicircular**, hemispherical, curved, arced, falcate [➞ ROUNDED SHAPE; 1218] 2 *type of* **rounded shape** [➞ ROUNDED SHAPE; 1218]

cress *type of* **salad vegetable** [➞ FRUIT AND VEGETABLES; 1176]

crest 1 *n* **top**, peak, summit, crown, apex, pinnacle, roof, ridge [➞ EXTREMITIES OF PHYSICAL OBJECTS; 1250] *Opposite*: base 2 *n* **tuft**, topknot, growth, cockscomb, comb [➞ PARTS OF A BIRD; 1006] 3 *n* **coat of arms**, blazon, emblem, symbol, heraldry [➞ SYMBOLS, SIGNS, AND NUMBERS; 596]

crestfallen *adj* **downcast**, dejected, disappointed, deflated, subdued, down, depressed, sad, disconsolate, discouraged [➞ SADNESS, DISTRESS, AND DESPAIR; 539] *Opposite*: confident

Cretaceous *type of* **period** [➞ EPOCHS AND ERAS; 89]

cretonne *type of* **fabric from plants** [➞ FABRICS; 1132]

crevasse *n* **fissure**, cleft, crack, split, fracture, chimney, bergschrund [➞ GEOLOGIC FEATURES; 1056]

crevice *n* **crack**, fissure, chink, split, cleft, fracture, cranny, opening, interstice [➞ HOLES, GAPS, AND FORKS; 1252]

crew 1 *n* **team**, squad, staff, troop, company, corps, party [➞ THE WORK FORCE; 837] 2 *n* (*informal*) **group**, gang, party, circle, crowd, band, assembly, bunch (*informal*) [➞ GROUPS OF PEOPLE; 935]

crew cut *type of* **hairstyle** [➞ HAIRSTYLES AND HAIRPIECES; 488]

crew neck *type of* **sweater** [➞ GARMENTS AND OUTFITS; 865]

crib 1 v (*informal*) **cheat**, copy, plagiarize, steal, borrow, pilfer [➡ FALSIFY AND CHEAT; 176] 2 *type of* **bed** [➡ FURNITURE; 858]

crick 1 n **pain**, strain, discomfort, cramp, spasm [➡ PAIN AND OTHER PHYSICAL SENSATIONS; 733] 2 v **strain**, hurt, pull, cramp, wrench, kink, rick (*UK*) [➡ PAIN AND OTHER PHYSICAL SENSATIONS; 733]

cricket *type of* **ball game** [➡ HOBBIES, GAMES, AND SPORTS; 875]

cricketer n [➡ PEOPLE IN SPORTS AND LEISURE; 876]

crime 1 n **offense**, misdeed, felony, misdemeanor, transgression, violation, illegality, infringement [➡ CRIMES; 817] 2 n **corruption**, wrongdoing, misconduct, lawbreaking, delinquency, criminality, organized crime, black market, gray market, insider trading [➡ CRIMES; 817] 3 n **wrong**, sin, fault, transgression [➡ MORALLY BAD OR IMPROPER; 775]

crime novel n **detective story**, police procedural, whodunit [➡ FICTION AND DRAMA; 913]

criminal 1 n **offender**, convict, prisoner, felon, lawbreaker, delinquent, perpetrator, gangster, outlaw, crook (*informal*), lowlife (*informal*), hood (*slang*) [➡ CRIMINALS; 821] 2 adj **illegal**, wrong, against the law, illicit, unlawful, felonious, lawless, illegitimate, crooked (*informal*) [➡ ILLEGAL; 816] *Opposite*: legal 3 adj **scandalous**, excessive, iniquitous, senseless, outrageous, wicked, disgraceful, shameful, sinful, immoral [➡ MORALLY BAD OR IMPROPER; 775]

See Compare and Contrast at **bad**.

criminality n **delinquency**, misconduct, wrongdoing, corruption, lawbreaking, malfeasance (*formal*) [➡ CRIMES; 817] *Opposite*: honesty

criminalization 1 n **outlawing**, illegalization, banning, interdiction, proscription (*formal*) [➡ THE LAW AND LEGAL AUTHORITY; 814] *Opposite*: legalization 2 n **corruption**, delinquency, marginalization, alienation, deterioration [➡ TRIAL, PUNISHMENT, AND LEGAL OUTCOMES; 819] *Opposite*: rehabilitation

criminalize 1 v **outlaw**, ban, forbid, proscribe, interdict [➡ REFUSE PERMISSION AND NOT ALLOW; 670] *Opposite*: legalize 2 v **corrupt**, marginalize, deprave, pervert [➡ TRIAL, PUNISHMENT, AND LEGAL OUTCOMES; 819] *Opposite*: rehabilitate

criminal lawyer n [➡ PEOPLE IN LAW COURTS; 820]

criminally adv **illegally**, unlawfully, lawlessly, illegitimately, feloniously [➡ ILLEGAL; 816] *Opposite*: legally

criminal world n **underworld**, gangland, lowlife [➡ CRIMINALS; 821]

crimp 1 v **fold**, crumple, crinkle, press, rumple, scrunch [➡ CHANGE OF SHAPE; 385] 2 v **pleat**, gather, fold, concertina, ruche, goffer [➡ CHANGE OF SHAPE; 385] *Opposite*: smooth 3 v **interfere**, hamper, hinder, constrain, curb, keep in check [➡ AVOID, PREVENT, LIMIT, AND CONTROL; 277]

crimped adj [➡ DESCRIBING HAIR; 486]

crimson *type of* **red** [➡ COLORS; 1224]

cringe 1 v **recoil**, wince, flinch, shrink, shy away, cower, quail [➡ PHYSICAL REACTIONS; 316] 2 v **squirm**, blush, wince, suffer embarrassment [➡ PHYSICAL REACTIONS; 316]

crinkle 1 v **crumple**, crease, rumple, wrinkle, ruffle, pucker, scrunch [➡ CHANGE OF SHAPE; 385] *Opposite*: straighten

out 2 n **wrinkle**, fold, crease, line, pucker, wave, corrugation [➡ CHANGE OF SHAPE; 385]

crinkled adj **creased**, lined, wrinkled, crumpled, rumpled, puckered, corrugated [➡ PHYSICAL TEXTURE; 1222] *Opposite*: straight

crinkly adj **wrinkled**, creased, furrowed, wavy, puckered [➡ IN BAD REPAIR; 1234] *Opposite*: smooth

crinoline *type of* **lower body underwear** [➡ ACCESSORIES, MILLINERY, AND LINGERIE; 867]

crippling adj **damaging**, debilitating, incapacitating, destabilizing, swingeing [➡ DANGEROUS; 236]

crisis 1 n **disaster**, catastrophe, emergency, calamity, predicament, crunch [➡ DISASTERS; 252] 2 n **turning point**, head, watershed, crossroads, defining moment [➡ DECISIVE MOMENTS; 44]

crisis point n **critical stage**, flashpoint, breaking point, crunch time [➡ DECISIVE MOMENTS; 44]

crisp 1 adj **crunchy**, brittle, hard, crusty, crispy, crumbly, al dente [➡ PHYSICAL TEXTURE; 1222] *Opposite*: soggy 2 adj **snappy**, brusque, terse, curt, sharp, blunt, gruff, short, brief, snappish [➡ UNINTERESTED AND DETACHED; 629] 3 adj **cold**, cool, fresh, frosty, chilly, bracing, invigorating, brisk [➡ COLD WEATHER; 1051] *Opposite*: warm 4 adj **incisive**, decisive, confident, businesslike, efficient, competent [➡ CONFIDENCE AND COMPOSURE; 499] *Opposite*: hesitant 5 *type of* **dessert** [➡ CAKES, COOKIES, AND DESSERTS; 1181]

crispy adj **crunchy**, brittle, hard, crusty, crisp [➡ PHYSICAL TEXTURE; 1222] *Opposite*: soggy

crisscross 1 n **lattice**, network, grid [➡ FASTENERS, LINKS, AND NETWORKS; 1247] 2 v **cross**, traverse, intersect, overlap, cross over, go across, cut across [➡ MOVE PAST, INTO, OR THROUGH SOMETHING; 331]

criterion n **standard**, principle, measure, norm, condition, benchmark, gauge, yardstick [➡ WAYS OF DOING THINGS; 294]

critic 1 n **reviewer**, columnist, commentator, reporter, journalist [➡ WORKERS IN ENTERTAINMENT AND MEDIA; 873] 2 n **evaluator**, appraiser, judge, commentator [➡ SURVEYORS, EXAMINERS, AND JUDGES; 853] 3 n **detractor**, opponent, enemy, censor, criticizer, faultfinder, denigrator, knocker (*informal*), decrier (*formal*) [➡ ENEMIES AND TORMENTORS; 969] *Opposite*: supporter

critical 1 adj **unfavorable**, disparaging, disapproving, nitpicking, judgmental, unsympathetic, derogatory, faultfinding, censorious [➡ ACCUSATORY AND DISAPPROVING; 634] *Opposite*: favorable 2 adj **analytical**, judicious, diagnostic, serious, detailed, searching [➡ THE NATURE OF IDEAS; 771] 3 adj **significant**, decisive, vital, important, essential, crucial, key, indispensable [➡ IMPORTANT; 194] *Opposite*: insignificant 4 adj **dangerous**, serious, grave, life-threatening, perilous, precarious, acute, dire, desperate [➡ DANGEROUS; 236]

critically adv **seriously**, gravely, dangerously, perilously, precariously, acutely, desperately [➡ CRITICALLY AND SERIOUSLY; 134] *Opposite*: mildly

criticism 1 n **censure**, disapproval, reproach, disparagement, condemnation, denigration, blame, denunciation, brickbat (*informal*) [➡ CRITICISMS AND ANGRY OUTBURSTS; 50] *Opposite*: praise 2 n **analysis**, appreciation, assessment, evaluation, critique, comment, review, peer review, report [➡ EXAMINE AND ASSESS; 753]

criticize 1 *v* **disapprove**, censure, disparage, carp, complain, pass judgment on, find fault with, pick holes in, condemn, maul, decry, lash, nitpick, knock (*informal*), pan (*informal*), blast (*informal*), castigate (*formal*), slate (*UK*) [➡ ACCUSE, BLAME, AND CRITICIZE; 641] *Opposite*: praise 2 *v* **assess**, analyze, dissect, evaluate, appraise, critique, review [➡ EXAMINE AND ASSESS; 753]

> **Compare and Contrast:** *criticize, censure, castigate, blast, condemn, find fault with, pick holes in, nitpick*
>
> CORE MEANING: to express disapproval or dissatisfaction with somebody or something
>
> *criticize* to point out faults; *censure* to make a formal, often public or official, statement of disapproval; *castigate* (*formal*) to criticize or rebuke severely; *blast* (*informal*) to criticize severely; *condemn* to give an unfavorable judgment on somebody or something; *find fault with* to criticize, often unfairly; *pick holes in* to look for and find mistakes, particularly in an argument; *nitpick* to find fault, often unjustifiably, with insignificant details.

> *See Compare and Contrast at* **disapprove**.

critique 1 *n* **analysis**, assessment, evaluation, account, review, criticism, appraisal [➡ ANALYTICAL NONFICTION WRITING; 592] 2 *v* **assess**, evaluate, criticize, comment, review, peer-review, appraise [➡ EXAMINE AND ASSESS; 753]

croak 1 *n* **cry**, caw, rasp, squawk [➡ SOUNDS MADE BY ANIMALS; 1261] 2 *v* **call**, cry, squawk, caw, rasp [➡ SOUND EMISSION BY ANIMALS OR BIRDS; 364] 3 *v* **rasp**, grate, gutturalize, growl [➡ SOUND EMISSION BY PEOPLE; 363] 4 *v* (*slang*) [➡ DIE; 922] 5 *v* (*informal*) **grumble**, mutter, complain, moan, grouse (*informal*) [➡ COMPLAIN AND NAG; 686]

croaky *adj* **hoarse**, rasping, guttural [➡ LOUD, HIGH, OR UNPLEASANT SOUNDS; 1266]

crochet *type of* **handicraft** [➡ CRAFTS AND CARVING; 355]

crockery *n* **tableware**, china, earthenware, plates, dishes [➡ TABLEWARE, FLATWARE, AND KITCHENWARE; 861]

crocodile *type of* **reptile** [➡ REPTILES; 994]

crocus *type of* **flower grown from bulbs** [➡ FLOWERS FROM BULBS; 1030]

croissant *type of* **roll or bun** [➡ BREAD, FLOUR, AND BREAD PRODUCTS; 1179]

crony *n* **friend**, acquaintance, colleague, companion, comrade, confederate, pal (*informal*), buddy (*informal*), chum (*informal*) [➡ FRIENDS AND GUESTS; 963] *Opposite*: enemy

cronyism *n* **favoritism**, nepotism, patronage [➡ PREJUDICE; 550]

crook 1 *n* (*informal*) **criminal**, offender, felon, robber, lawbreaker, outlaw, convict, perpetrator, jailbird (*slang*), malefactor (*formal*) [➡ CRIMINALS; 821] 2 *n* **staff**, rod, stick, crosier [➡ STICKS, POLES, AND WEDGES; 1254]

crooked 1 *adj* **bent**, curved, warped, twisted, kinked, circuitous, indirect, roundabout, meandering, ser-

pentine, winding [➡ ORIENTATION AND ALIGNMENT; 1223] *Opposite*: straight 2 *adj* (*informal*) **dishonest**, criminal, corrupt, fraudulent, illegal, shady, questionable, underhand, unlawful, devious, unscrupulous, deceitful [➡ DECEITFUL; 513] *Opposite*: honest 3 *adj* **uneven**, jagged, zigzag, oblique, askew [➡ ORIENTATION AND ALIGNMENT; 1223] *Opposite*: straight

crookedly 1 *adv* **indirectly**, askance, aslant, obliquely [➡ ORIENTATION AND ALIGNMENT; 1223] 2 *adv* (*informal*) **illegally**, dishonestly, corruptly, fraudulently, shadily, underhandedly, deceitfully, deviously, unscrupulously [➡ DECEITFUL; 513] *Opposite*: honestly

crookedness *n* **dishonesty**, shadiness, corruption, illegality, fraudulence, deviousness, deceitfulness, unscrupulousness [➡ DECEITFUL; 513] *Opposite*: honesty

croon *v* **sing**, serenade, murmur, hum, warble [➡ SOUND EMISSION BY PEOPLE; 363]

crop 1 *n* **harvest**, yield, produce, cash crop, catch crop [➡ COLLECTIONS AND MIXTURES OF THINGS; 1244] 2 *type of* **hairstyle** [➡ HAIRSTYLES AND HAIRPIECES; 488] 3 *part of* **bird** [➡ PARTS OF A BIRD; 1006] 4 *v* **collect**, harvest, gather, pick, bring in, reap, garner, ingather [➡ GROW AND CULTIVATE; 351] 5 *v* **cut**, shorten, clip, trim, shear, curtail, pare, shave [➡ EXTRACT AND SEVER; 341]

cropped *adj* **short-haired**, close-cropped, clipped [➡ DESCRIBING HAIR; 486]

crop up (*informal*) *v* **appear**, happen, turn up, arise, emerge, occur [➡ SUDDENLY COME INTO EXISTENCE; 2]

croquet *type of* **target ball game** [➡ HOBBIES, GAMES, AND SPORTS; 875]

croquette *type of* **processed potato** [➡ FRUIT AND VEGETABLES; 1176]

crosier *n* **staff**, rod, stick, crook [➡ STICKS, POLES, AND WEDGES; 1254]

cross 1 *n* **symbol**, mark, sign [➡ SYMBOLS, SIGNS, AND NUMBERS; 596] 2 *n* **Celtic cross**, Greek cross, Latin cross, Maltese cross, St. Andrew's cross, St. George's cross, cross of Lorraine, St. Anthony's cross, tau cross [➡ RELIGIOUS OBJECTS; 779] 3 *type of* **angular shape** [➡ ANGULAR SHAPE; 1217] 4 *v* **traverse**, go across, crisscross, cut across, span, intersect, overlap, cross over [➡ MOVE PAST, INTO, OR THROUGH SOMETHING; 331] 5 *v* **thwart**, frustrate, impede, oppose, obstruct, resist, annoy, foil, vie, circumvent [➡ ANGER AND ANNOY; 569] *Opposite*: assist 6 *adj* **irritated**, angry, irritable, annoyed, snappy, fractious, out of sorts, cantankerous, bad-tempered, cranky (*informal*) [➡ IRRITATION AND ANGER; 541]

crossbar *part of* **bike** [➡ BIKES, CARS, AND CARRIAGES; 1149]

cross-border *adj* [➡ CLOSENESS; 159]

crossbow *type of* **bow** [➡ WEAPONS FOR SHOOTING; 1156]

crossbreed *v* **hybridize**, cross, interbreed, mongrelize [➡ COMBINE AND MIX; 400]

crosscheck 1 *v* **validate**, substantiate, double-check, document, verify [➡ EXAMINE AND ASSESS; 753] 2 *n* **validation**, substantiation, double-checking, documentation, verification [➡ EXAMINE AND ASSESS; 753]

cross-country 1 *adj* **off-road**, rough, outdoor, all-terrain [➡ THE COUNTRYSIDE AND OUTDOOR SPACES; 1071] 2 *type of* **track and field** [➡ HOBBIES, GAMES, AND SPORTS; 875]

cross-country skiing *type of* **winter sport** [➡ HOBBIES, GAMES, AND SPORTS; 875]

cross-cultural *adj* **multicultural**, multiracial, multiethnic, diverse, cosmopolitan [➡ LEVELS OF EDUCATION AND SOPHISTICATION; 894]

crosscurrent *n* [➡ DIFFERENCE; 149]

cross-examination *n* **questioning**, re-examination, interrogation, cross-questioning, probe, review, double-checking, investigation, grilling (*informal*), third degree (*informal*) [➡ TRIAL, PUNISHMENT, AND LEGAL OUTCOMES; 819]

cross-examine *v* **question**, cross-question, interrogate, quiz, probe, review, investigate, double-check, re-examine, bombard, give the third degree (*informal*), grill (*informal*) [➡ ASK PEOPLE QUESTIONS; 666]

cross-fertilization 1 *n* **pollination**, fertilization, cross-pollination [➡ COMBINE AND MIX; 400] 2 *n* **exchange**, interchange, interaction, synthesis, synergy, sharing [➡ EXCHANGE AND INTERCHANGE; 448]

cross-fertilize 1 *v* **fertilize**, pollinate, cross-pollinate [➡ EXCHANGE AND INTERCHANGE; 448] 2 *v* **exchange**, interchange, interact, synthesize, share, exchange ideas [➡ TWO-WAY COMMUNICATION; 607]

crossfire *n* **clash**, disagreement, conflict, antagonism, flak, barrage, clash of opinions, fireworks (*informal*) [➡ ARGUMENTS; 47]

crossing 1 *n* **journey**, adventure, trip, voyage, passage [➡ TRAVEL: JOURNEYS AND TRIPS; 318] 2 *n* **intersection**, junction, overpass, grade crossing, crosswalk, crossroads, ford, border point, level crossing (*UK*), flyover (*UK*) [➡ BRIDGES, TUNNELS, CROSSINGS, AND JUNCTIONS; 1112]

crossly *adv* **grumpily**, angrily, snappily, impatiently, irately, irritably, furiously [➡ BAD-TEMPERED AND HUMORLESS; 626] *Opposite*: good-naturedly

cross out *v* **score out**, score through, strike out, strike through, rub out, wipe out, edit out, delete, erase, obliterate, scrap, remove, cut, cross off, cancel, cancel out, scrub (*informal*), scrub out (*informal*) [➡ DELETE AND ERASE; 339]

crossover 1 *n* **switch**, change, sea change, conversion, move, transmutation [➡ CHANGE; 372] 2 *n* **overlap**, common ground, commonality [➡ CONNECTIONS; 143]

crosspatch (*dated informal*) *n* **curmudgeon**, malcontent, grouch (*informal*), grump (*informal*), pain (*informal*) [➡ GRUMPY AND NEGATIVE PEOPLE; 953]

cross-purposes *n* **disagreement**, disparity, variance, contrast, frustration, misunderstanding, crossed wires (*informal*) [➡ MISUNDERSTAND AND FAIL TO GRASP; 761]

cross-question *v* **cross-examine**, re-examine, interrogate, question, review, probe, investigate, double-check, quiz, bombard, grill (*informal*), give the third degree (*informal*) [➡ TRIAL, PUNISHMENT, AND LEGAL OUTCOMES; 819]

cross-questioning *n* **cross-examination**, re-examination, interrogation, review, double-checking, investigation, probing, questioning, third degree (*informal*) [➡ TRIAL, PUNISHMENT, AND LEGAL OUTCOMES; 819]

cross-reference *n* **citation**, reference, documentation, source, note [➡ PARTS OF BOOKS AND DOCUMENTS; 593]

crossroads 1 *n* **junction**, intersection, crossing, crossway, traffic circle, rotary, roundabout (*UK*) [➡ BRIDGES, TUNNELS, CROSSINGS, AND JUNCTIONS; 1112] 2 *n* **turning point**, landmark, decision, moment of truth, crisis, crunch, juncture (*formal*) [➡ DECISIVE MOMENTS; 44]

cross section 1 *n* **view**, section, slice, layer, plane, stratum (*formal*) [➡ AREA AND RANGE; 111] 2 *n* **sample**, example, range, representation [➡ REPRESENTATIONS AND GENERAL EXAMPLES; 65]

cross swords *v* **clash**, argue, disagree, do battle, fight, butt heads, lock horns, conflict [➡ ARGUE AND FIGHT; 643] *Opposite*: agree

crosswalk *n* [➡ BRIDGES, TUNNELS, CROSSINGS, AND JUNCTIONS; 1112]

crossways *see* **crosswise**

crosswise *adv* **crossways**, sideways, diagonally, cattycornered, across, corner to corner, cater-cornered, on the cross, obliquely, kitty-cornered [➡ ORIENTATION AND ALIGNMENT; 1223]

crossword *n* **acrostic**, mind-bender, game, puzzle, cryptic crossword [➡ HOBBIES, GAMES, AND SPORTS; 875]

crotchetiness (*informal*) *n* **grumpiness**, grouchiness, tetchiness [➡ DIFFICULT TO PLEASE; 515]

crotchety (*informal*) *adj* **grumpy**, bad-tempered, irritable, difficult, cantankerous, crusty, crabby, touchy, tetchy, peevish, surly, short-tempered, cranky (*informal*) [➡ IRRITATION AND ANGER; 541] *Opposite*: good-humored

crouch *v* **squat**, bend, hunker, stoop, duck, bow [➡ ASSUME A POSITION; 317]

croup *part of* **horse** [➡ HORSES; 985]

crouton *type of* **bread** [➡ BREAD, FLOUR, AND BREAD PRODUCTS; 1179]

crow 1 *type of* **scavenger** [➡ BIRDS; 997] 2 *v* **caw**, cry, call, squawk, screech [➡ SOUND EMISSION BY ANIMALS OR BIRDS; 364] 3 *v* **gloat**, boast, brag, show off, swagger, blow your own horn [➡ BOAST; 616]

crowbar *type of* **general tool** [➡ HAND TOOLS; 1119]

crowd 1 *n* **troop**, throng, mass, multitude, swarm, horde, mob, host, pack, assembly, gathering, press, crush [➡ GROUPS OF PEOPLE; 935] 2 *n* **group**, set, gang, circle, clique [➡ GROUPS WITH A COMMON INTEREST; 938] 3 *v* **throng**, flock, herd, assemble, gather, mass, congregate, swarm [➡ GET CLOSER TOGETHER; 310] 4 *v* **overcrowd**, pack, cram, squeeze, squash, jam, jampack (*informal*), pile (*informal*) [➡ FILL; 406]

crowded *adj* **overcrowded**, packed, full, teeming, swarming, busy, congested, jammed, jam-packed (*informal*), mobbed (*informal*) [➡ FULL; 1239] *Opposite*: deserted

crown 1 *n* **circlet**, coronet, tiara, diadem [➡ JEWELRY; 866] 2 *n* **trophy**, prize, garland, honor, laurels, award [➡ REWARDS AND AWARDS; 439] 3 *n* **top**, peak, summit, pinnacle, head, crest, brow [➡ EXTREMITIES OF PHYSICAL OBJECTS; 1250] 4 *v* **cap**, top, round off, complete, finish off, put the finishing touch to [➡ COMPLETE AN ACTION; 263]

crown prince *type of* **aristocrat** [➡ RULERS AND ARISTOCRACY; 823]

crow's foot *n* **wrinkle**, line, laughter line [➡ FACIAL CHARACTERISTICS; 481]

crow's nest *part of* **ship or boat** [➡ PARTS OF A SHIP OR BOAT; 1151]

crucial *adj* **vital**, critical, central, decisive, key, essential, fundamental, important, necessary, imperative [➡ IMPORTANT; 194] *Opposite*: trivial

crucible 1 *n* **container**, pot, receptacle, vat, kettle, vessel, cauldron [➡ CONTAINERS, RECEPTACLES, AND PACKAGING; 1245] 2 *n* **ordeal**, trial, test, baptism of fire [➡ DIFFICULT SITUATIONS; 72] 3 *n* **hotbed**, hothouse, forcing ground, melting pot, ground zero, breeding ground [➡ BEGINNINGS; 53]

crucifixion 1 *n* **execution**, killing, punishment [➡ CAUSES OF DEATH; 921] 2 *n* **ordeal**, victimization, torment, agony, suffering, misery, torture, persecution [➡ DIFFICULT SITUATIONS; 72]

crucify 1 *v* **execute**, kill, hang, punish [➡ KILL; 923] 2 *v* **torment**, victimize, attack, savage, maul [➡ ACCUSE, BLAME, AND CRITICIZE; 641]

crud 1 *n* (*slang*) **filth**, scum, grime, slime, sludge, dirt, muck (*informal*) [➡ UNPLEASANT, DIRTY, AND TOXIC SUBSTANCES; 1268] 2 *n* (*informal*) **nonsense**, gibberish, malarkey (*informal*), twaddle (*informal*), bunkum (*informal*) [➡ MEANINGLESS SPEECH OR WRITING; 676]

cruddy (*slang*) *adj* **filthy**, scummy, grimy, slimy, sludgy, mucky (*informal*), scuzzy (*slang*) [➡ DIRTY; 1235] *Opposite*: spotless

crude 1 *adj* **raw**, unrefined, unprocessed [➡ RAW AND NATURAL; 1214] *Opposite*: refined 2 *adj* **approximate**, rough, inaccurate, inexact, loose, sketchy, broad-brush [➡ APPROXIMATELY; 135] *Opposite*: accurate 3 *adj* **unpolished**, basic, simple, rudimentary, makeshift, unsophisticated, rough, unfinished, unskillful, rough-hewn [➡ UNFINISHEDNESS; 239] *Opposite*: sophisticated 4 *adj* **vulgar**, indecent, rude, coarse, obscene, offensive, foul-mouthed, uncouth, indelicate, boorish, unrefined, earthy, smutty (*informal*) [➡ BAD MANNERS AND SOCIAL SKILLS; 521] *Opposite*: delicate

crudeness 1 *n* **primitiveness**, roughness, rawness, coarseness, simplicity, rusticity [➡ UNFINISHEDNESS; 239] *Opposite*: sophistication 2 *n* **vulgarity**, crudity, coarseness, rudeness, offensiveness, uncouthness, indelicacy, earthiness, smuttiness (*informal*) [➡ BAD MANNERS AND SOCIAL SKILLS; 521] *Opposite*: delicacy

crudity 1 *n* **rudeness**, crudeness, coarseness, vulgarity, offensiveness, smuttiness (*informal*) [➡ BAD MANNERS AND SOCIAL SKILLS; 521] *Opposite*: delicacy 2 *n* **roughness**, coarseness, rawness, simplicity, rusticity, primitiveness [➡ LEVELS OF EDUCATION AND SOPHISTICATION; 894] *Opposite*: sophistication

cruel 1 *adj* **unkind**, merciless, nasty, pitiless, brutal, malicious, wounding, spiteful, vindictive, heartless, ruthless, harsh, vicious, callous, mean [➡ SELFISH AND UNKIND; 505] *Opposite*: kind 2 *adj* **painful**, punishing, devastating, harsh, hard, forbidding, unpleasant [➡ EMOTIONALLY UNPLEASANT AND UPSETTING; 227] *Opposite*: pleasant

cruelly *adv* **unkindly**, nastily, brutally, maliciously, viciously, harshly, callously, heartlessly, pitilessly, ruthlessly, meanly, mercilessly [➡ SELFISH AND UNKIND; 505] *Opposite*: kindly

cruelty *n* **unkindness**, nastiness, brutality, malice, spite, spitefulness, vindictiveness, mercilessness, viciousness, ruthlessness, callousness, heartlessness, harshness, meanness [➡ MALICIOUS ACTIONS OR BEHAVIOR; 296] *Opposite*: kindness

cruise 1 *v* **voyage**, sail, journey, travel, boat, set sail, tour, island-hop [➡ TRAVEL: WAYS OF TRAVELING; 320] 2 *v* **coast**, skim, spin, travel, glide, drift, freewheel, float, proceed [➡ PROCEED AND GO; 305] 3 *n* **voyage**, vacation, trip, journey, tour [➡ TRAVEL: JOURNEYS AND TRIPS; 318]

cruise missile *type of* **explosive weapon** [➡ EXPLOSIVES; 1155]

cruiser *type of* **military vessel** [➡ SHIPS AND BOATS; 1150]

cruller *type of* **cake** [➡ CAKES, COOKIES, AND DESSERTS; 1181]

crumb *n* **morsel**, scrap, tidbit, bit, speck, spot, fragment, iota, atom, smidgen [➡ SMALL PIECES; 129]

crumble 1 *v* **smash**, beat, crush, grind, powder, pound, pulverize [➡ TEAR, BREAK, AND CUT; 360] 2 *v* **disintegrate**, dissolve, deteriorate, fall apart, fall down, collapse, cave in, implode [➡ TEAR, BREAK, AND CUT; 360]

crumbling *adj* **disintegrating**, decomposing, decaying, putrefying, caving in, peeling, collapsing, breaking up, falling in, falling apart, on its last legs, in bad condition, falling to pieces, in ruins, rundown, rickety, crumbly, dilapidated, rotting, rotten, ramshackle, fragile, subsiding, derelict, moldering [➡ DECAYING OR INFESTED; 1236] *Opposite*: solid

crumbly *adj* **brittle**, powdery, flaky, friable, crumbling, fragile [➡ FRAGILE; 1209] *Opposite*: solid

crumhorn *type of* **wind instrument** [➡ MUSICAL INSTRUMENTS; 910]

crummy (*informal*) 1 *adj* **inferior**, shoddy, shabby, worthless, poor-quality, cheap, trashy, chintzy, rubbishy, terrible, tacky (*informal*), lousy (*informal*) [➡ IN BAD REPAIR; 1234] *Opposite*: superior 2 *adj* **unwell**, sick, ill, sickly, miserable, under the weather, terrible, lousy (*informal*) [➡ UNFIT AND WEAK; 739] *Opposite*: healthy

crumpet *type of* **roll or bun** [➡ BREAD, FLOUR, AND BREAD PRODUCTS; 1179]

crumple *v* **crease**, crinkle, rumple, crush, screw, wrinkle, scrunch, pucker [➡ CHANGE OF SHAPE; 385] *Opposite*: smooth

crumpled *adj* **creased**, wrinkled, wrinkly, crinkly, lined, puckered, crinkled, rumpled, crushed [➡ IN BAD REPAIR; 1234] *Opposite*: smooth

crunch 1 *v* **munch**, chew, champ, chomp (*informal*) [➡ EAT AND NOT EAT; 710] 2 *n* **crisis**, moment of truth, crunch time, critical situation, crux, critical point, decisive moment, head [➡ DECISIVE MOMENTS; 44]

crunchy *adj* **crispy**, crisp, brittle, crusty [➡ PHYSICAL TEXTURE; 1222] *Opposite*: soggy

crusade 1 *n* **cause**, campaign, movement, battle, fight, war, struggle, action [➡ NON-AGGRESSIVE/SPORTING EVENTS; 40] 2 *v* **campaign**, lobby, struggle, battle, apply yourself, exert yourself, put your back into [➡ COMPETE, CONTEND, AND COMBAT; 303]

crusader *n* **campaigner**, supporter, advocate, champion, activist, lobbyist [➡ DEVOTEES AND ADDICTED PEOPLE; 556]

crush 1 *v* **squash**, squeeze, compress, press, mash, pound, purée [➡ CHANGE OF SHAPE; 385] 2 *v* **quell**, suppress, put down, quash, subdue, overcome, conquer, subjugate [➡ BEAT AND DEFEAT; 80] *Opposite*: resist 3 *v* **defeat**, rout, massacre, trounce, overwhelm, slaughter (*slang*), cream (*slang*)

[➥BEAT AND DEFEAT; 80] **4** v **humiliate**, devastate, mortify, put down, abash, chagrin [➥UPSET, DISTRESS, AND HUMILIATE; 567] **5** n (informal) **infatuation**, passion, affection, fondness, liking, love [➥LOVE, RESPECT, AND GOODWILL; 549] Opposite: dislike **6** n **press**, squash, squeeze, crowd, throng [➥GROUPS OF PEOPLE; 935]

See Compare and Contrast at **love**.

crushed adj **crumpled**, creased, wrinkled, crinkly, crinkled, rumpled, wrinkly [➥IN BAD REPAIR; 1234] Opposite: smooth

crushing adj **devastating**, overwhelming, swingeing, severe, draconian, humiliating, serious, grave [➥EMOTIONALLY UNPLEASANT AND UPSETTING; 227] Opposite: mild

crushingly adv **triumphantly**, exultantly, superciliously, haughtily, contemptuously, disdainfully [➥TO A GREAT EXTENT; 132]

crust n **coating**, outside, outer layer, shell, top, skin, scab, covering, casing, layer, film [➥COVERS AND COATINGS; 1246]

crustacean type of **aquatic invertebrate** [➥AQUATIC INVERTEBRATES; 1022]

crusted adj **encrusted**, caked, coated, covered, thick, encased [➥DECORATE, ADORN, AND APPLY COATINGS; 405]

crusty 1 adj **crispy**, crisp, hard, brittle, crunchy [➥PHYSICAL TEXTURE; 1222] Opposite: soft **2** adj **grumpy**, bad-tempered, irritable, testy, cantankerous, peevish, crabby, surly, tetchy, crotchety (informal), grouchy (informal), cranky (informal) [➥BAD-TEMPERED AND HUMORLESS; 626] Opposite: good-humored

crutch 1 n **stick**, support, prop, walking aid, walker, staff, rest, baby walker (UK), walking frame (UK) [➥STICKS, POLES, AND WEDGES; 1254] **2** n **prop**, support, aid, help, buttress, support system [➥TREATS; 210]

crux n **root**, bottom, heart, core, nub, bottom line, nitty-gritty (informal) [➥MOST IMPORTANT THING; 197]

Crux type of **constellation** [➥HEAVENLY BODIES; 1061]

cry 1 v **weep**, sob, snivel, whimper, shed tears, howl, wail, cry your eyes out, whine, blubber (informal), bawl (informal) [➥CRYING; 650] Opposite: laugh **2** v **shout**, exclaim, shout out, call, call out, yell, scream, shriek, yelp, roar, bellow, holler (informal) [➥SOUND EMISSION BY PEOPLE; 363] Opposite: whisper **3** n **call**, shout, exclamation, yell, scream, shriek, yelp, bellow, holler (informal) [➥SOUNDS MADE BY PEOPLE; 1262] Opposite: whisper

crying 1 adj **desperate**, deplorable, awful, horrible, terrible, dreadful, lousy (informal) [➥EMOTIONALLY UNPLEASANT AND UPSETTING; 227] **2** adj **in tears**, tearful, teary, sobbing, weeping, howling, wailing, sniveling, whining, whimpering, weepy (informal), bawling (informal), blubbering (informal), lachrymose (literary) [➥SADNESS, DISTRESS, AND DESPAIR; 539]

cry out 1 v **shout out**, shout, cry, call, call out, yell, roar, scream, howl, exclaim, holler (informal) [➥GIVING VENT TO EMOTIONS; 679] Opposite: whisper **2** v **need**, be in need of, require, demand, call for, ask for, lack [➥REQUEST AND DEMAND; 663]

crypt n **vault**, tomb, catacomb, sepulcher, burial chamber, cellar, basement, undercroft [➥PARTS OF RELIGIOUS BUILDINGS; 1086]

cryptic adj **mysterious**, enigmatic, puzzling, obscure, ambiguous, hidden, secret [➥SECRET AND UNKNOWN; 179] Opposite: straightforward

See Compare and Contrast at **obscure**.

crystal 1 n **mineral**, rock crystal, quartz [➥PRECIOUS STONES; 1278] **2** type of **glass** [➥GLASS; 1136]

crystal clear 1 adj **clean**, sparkling, limpid, transparent, crystalline, translucent [➥CLEAN AND HYGIENIC; 1233] Opposite: muddy **2** adj **obvious**, clear, clear as day, clear-cut, distinct, sharp, intelligible, explicit, well-defined, unambiguous, lucid, plain, understood, understandable, comprehensible [➥CONCISE AND CLEAR; 202] Opposite: opaque

crystalline 1 adj **crystal-like**, glassy, sparkling [➥VISUAL TEXTURE; 1221] **2** adj **clear**, transparent, crystal clear, limpid, translucent [➥VISUAL TEXTURE; 1221] Opposite: opaque

crystallization n **manifestation**, representation, outward expression, illustration, summation, final product, mature expression [➥PERFECT EXAMPLES AND EMBODIMENTS; 67]

crystallize v **form**, take shape, fall into place, come together, shape up, set, grow, mature, resolve itself, sort itself out, develop, manifest, gel (informal) [➥GRADUALLY COME INTO EXISTENCE; 1] Opposite: disintegrate

cry your eyes out v **weep**, sob, blubber (informal) [➥CRYING; 650]

cub 1 n **novice**, beginner, learner, apprentice, trainee, fledgling, stripling, rookie (informal), tenderfoot (informal) [➥UNSKILLED PEOPLE; 530] Opposite: old hand **2** type of **young animal** [➥YOUNG ANIMALS; 977]

cubbyhole n **compartment**, cubby (informal), nook, cranny, pigeonhole, cupboard, closet, storeroom, niche, cubicle [➥ALCOVES, CUBICLES, AND COMPARTMENTS; 1096]

cube type of **angular shape** [➥ANGULAR SHAPE; 1217]

cubicle n **compartment**, booth, partition, stall, workspace [➥ALCOVES, CUBICLES, AND COMPARTMENTS; 1096]

cubism type of **20th-century art movement** [➥ARTISTIC MOVEMENTS AND STYLES; 899]

cubist adj **abstract**, geometric, modern [➥ARTISTIC MOVEMENTS AND STYLES; 899]

cuckoo (informal) adj **eccentric**, strange, weird, unusual, bizarre, unconventional [➥BIZARRE AND PECULIAR; 257] Opposite: ordinary

cuckoo clock type of **clock** [➥CLOCKS AND TIMERS; 1126]

cucumber type of **salad vegetable** [➥FRUIT AND VEGETABLES; 1176]

cuddle 1 v **hug**, embrace, clasp, hold, nuzzle, cling, fondle, snuggle, nestle, huddle, curl up, draw close, cozy up [➥PHYSICAL CONTACT AS COMMUNICATION; 655] **2** n **embrace**, hug, clasp, hold, clinch [➥PHYSICAL CONTACT AS COMMUNICATION; 655]

cuddle up v **snuggle up**, curl up, cozy up [➥GET CLOSER TOGETHER; 310]

cuddly *adj* **soft**, lovable, fluffy, warm, endearing, appealing, huggable, embraceable [➡ PHYSICAL TEXTURE; 1222]

cudgel 1 *type of* **club** [➡ BLUNT INSTRUMENTS AND WHIPS; 1158] 2 *v* **hit**, bludgeon, whack, pound, batter, club, thrash, beat, bash (*informal*) [➡ WHIP AND CLUB; 417]

cue 1 *n* **signal**, prompt, sign, indication, reminder, nod, hint, clue, key [➡ INDICATIONS, SIGNS, AND WARNINGS; 68] 2 *v* **prompt**, signal, show, indicate, remind, nod [➡ GESTURES AND GESTICULATION; 653]

cuff 1 *n* (*slang*) **handcuff**, manacle, shackle, restraint, fetter, irons, bracelet (*slang*) [➡ FASTENERS, LINKS, AND NETWORKS; 1247] 2 *part of* **garment** [➡ PARTS OF A GARMENT; 870] 3 *v* **buffet**, slap, strike, hit, rap, box somebody's ears (*dated*) [➡ PHYSICAL ATTACK AND PUNISHMENT; 415]

cuff link *type of* **jewelry** [➡ JEWELRY; 866]

cuisine *n* **food**, fare, cooking, gastronomy, cookery [➡ FOOD; 1167]

cul-de-sac *n* **dead end**, impasse, blind alley, no through road (*UK*) [➡ ROADS; 1106]

culinary *adj* **cooking**, gastronomic, cookery, food [➡ FOOD; 1167]

cull 1 *v* **discard**, reject, remove, scrap, get rid of, cast off, weed out [➡ GET RID OF SOMETHING; 451] *Opposite*: retain 2 *v* **pick**, select, choose, gather, harvest, collect, amass, garner, glean, sift, winnow [➡ GET; 420] 3 *n* **reject**, scrap, discard, castoff, second [➡ JUNK AND USELESS OBJECTS; 1249]

culminate *v* **end**, conclude, finish, terminate, climax, close, cap, crown [➡ STOP ACTING; 264] *Opposite*: start

culmination *n* **conclusion**, finale, peak, height, zenith, result, end, termination, climax, apex, apogee, consummation [➡ ENDS AND DEPARTURES; 54]

culottes *type of* **pants** [➡ GARMENTS AND OUTFITS; 865]

culpability *n* **blameworthiness**, liability, blame, guilt, fault, accountability, responsibility, answerability [➡ MORALLY BAD OR IMPROPER; 775] *Opposite*: innocence

culpable *adj* **guilty**, in the wrong, to blame, blameworthy, responsible, liable, at fault [➡ MORALLY BAD OR IMPROPER; 775] *Opposite*: innocent

culprit *n* **offender**, criminal, guilty party, perpetrator, wrongdoer, felon, lawbreaker, malefactor (*formal*) [➡ CRIMINALS; 821]

cult 1 *n* **sect**, religious group, religious persuasion, movement [➡ RELIGIOUS PEOPLE; 778] 2 *n* **fad**, craze, trend, adoration, veneration, worship [➡ FADS, FETISHES, AND IDOLATRY; 555] 3 *adj* **alternative**, offbeat, out of the ordinary, unusual, trendy (*informal*) [➡ BIZARRE AND PECULIAR; 257] *Opposite*: mainstream

cultivate 1 *v* **farm**, grow, plow, plant, tend [➡ GROW AND CULTIVATE; 351] 2 *v* **promote**, encourage, nurture, work on, foster, support, help, develop, improve, enrich [➡ MAKE POSSIBLE; 275] *Opposite*: neglect

cultivated *adj* **refined**, educated, cultured, sophisticated, urbane, polished, civilized [➡ LEVELS OF EDUCATION AND SOPHISTICATION; 894] *Opposite*: uncouth

cultivation 1 *n* **farming**, agriculture, husbandry, crop growing, agronomy, gardening, tilling [➡ GROW AND CULTIVATE; 351] 2 *n* **development**, promotion, encouragement, nurturing, fostering [➡ PROGRESS AND ADVANCEMENT; 213] *Opposite*: neglect 3 *n* **refinement**, education, culture, sophistication, urbanity, civilization [➡ LEVELS OF EDUCATION AND SOPHISTICATION; 894] *Opposite*: uncouthness

cultivator *n* **grower**, farmer, gardener, planter, agronomist, tiller [➡ FARMERS, GARDENERS, AND MANUAL WORKERS; 849]

cultural 1 *adj* **national**, social, ethnic, folk, traditional, racial [➡ BELONGING OR RELATING TO PEOPLE; 943] 2 *adj* **artistic**, literary, intellectual, educational, edifying, enlightening, enriching, civilizing [➡ INTERESTING AND MEANINGFUL; 190]

culture 1 *n* **sophistication**, refinement, urbanity, civilization, cultivation, polish, taste, discernment, discrimination [➡ LEVELS OF EDUCATION AND SOPHISTICATION; 894] *Opposite*: uncouthness 2 *n* **civilization**, society, mores, traditions, customs, way of life, lifestyle, background, ethnicity [➡ GROUPS IN SOCIETY; 940] 3 *n* **ethos**, philosophy, values, principles, beliefs [➡ PHILOSOPHIES AND BELIEFS; 780] 4 *n* **art, music, and literature**, arts, humanities, fine arts, performing arts, visual arts [➡ LEVELS OF EDUCATION AND SOPHISTICATION; 894]

cultured *adj* **refined**, well-educated, learned, educated, erudite, cultivated, urbane, civilized, highbrow [➡ LEVELS OF EDUCATION AND SOPHISTICATION; 894] *Opposite*: uncouth

culvert *n* **duct**, channel, conduit, tunnel, main, sewer, drain, watercourse, ditch, gutter [➡ WATERCOURSES; 1111]

cum (*informal*) *prep* **with**, together with, along with, in combination with, also used as, functioning as [➡ ALSO; 138]

cumbersome *adj* **unwieldy**, awkward, weighty, bulky, clumsy, burdensome, ungainly, heavy, cumbrous (*archaic or literary*) [➡ WEIGHT: HEAVY; 1205] *Opposite*: manageable

cumbersomeness *n* **unwieldiness**, awkwardness, weightiness, hulkiness [➡ LARGE; 1193]

cumbrous (*archaic or literary*) *adj* [➡ LARGE, 1193]

cumin *type of* **spice** [➡ HERBS AND SPICES; 1175]

cummerbund *type of* **accessory** [➡ ACCESSORIES, MILLINERY, AND LINGERIE; 867]

cumulative *adj* **increasing**, snowballing, swelling, accumulative, growing, aggregate, compound, collective, amassed [➡ RELATED; 142] *Opposite*: diminishing

cumulonimbus *type of* **cloud** [➡ CLOUDY AND RAINY WEATHER; 1052]

cumulus *type of* **cloud** [➡ CLOUDY AND RAINY WEATHER; 1052]

cuneiform *type of* **alphabet** [➡ SYMBOLS, SIGNS, AND NUMBERS; 596]

cunning 1 *adj* **sly**, wily, crafty, sneaky, shrewd, canny, guileful, scheming, foxy, astute, Machiavellian, calculating [➡ DECEITFUL; 513] *Opposite*: guileless 2 *adj* **ingenious**, inventive, resourceful, creative, innovative, clever, artful [➡ POSITIVE INTELLECTUAL CHARACTERISTICS; 524] 3 *n* **slyness**, wiliness, craftiness, sneakiness, shrewdness, astuteness, canniness, guile, foxiness, artifice (*formal*) [➡ DECEITFUL; 513] *Opposite*: guilelessness 4 *n* **skill**, cleverness, ingenuity, creativity, dexterity, adroitness, ability, inventiveness, resourcefulness, expertise, art, craft, deftness [➡ SKILLS, TALENTS, AND ABILITIES; 526]

cup 1 *n* **mug**, beaker, demitasse, teacup [➡ TABLEWARE, FLATWARE,

AND KITCHENWARE; 861] **2** *n* **trophy**, chalice, goblet, prize [➥REWARDS AND AWARDS; 439]

cupboard *type of* **cabinet** [➥FURNITURE; 858]

cupcake *type of* **cake** [➥CAKES, COOKIES, AND DESSERTS; 1181]

cupidity (*formal*) *n* **greed**, avarice, covetousness, materialism, conspicuous consumption, rapacity, acquisitiveness, greediness, avariciousness, avidity [➥MORALLY BAD OR IMPROPER; 775] *Opposite*: generosity

Cupid's bow *type of* **bow** [➥WEAPONS FOR SHOOTING; 1156]

cupola *n* **dome**, vault, roof, ceiling [➥ROOFS, ROOF PARTS, AND CEILINGS; 1103]

cur *n* **mongrel**, dog, hound, mutt (*slang*) [➥DOGS; 980] *Opposite*: purebred

curable *adj* **treatable**, remediable, correctable, mendable, repairable, fixable, improvable [➥HEALING; 730] *Opposite*: incurable

curate **1** *n* **priest**, minister, cleric, ecclesiastic [➥RELIGIOUS PEOPLE; 778] **2** *v* **create**, mount, install, stage [➥INSTITUTE AND INAUGURATE; 348]

curative *adj* **healing**, remedial, restorative, therapeutic, palliative, medicinal, health-giving, healthful, beneficial, salutary [➥HEALING; 730] *Opposite*: injurious

curator *n* **custodian**, keeper, steward, guardian, overseer, superintendent, supervisor, warden (*UK*) [➥PEOPLE WHO GUARD AND PROTECT; 846]

curb **1** *n* **control**, limit, restriction, restraint, check [➥CAPTIVITY AND LOSS OF FREEDOM; 248] **2** *v* **restrain**, control, limit, hold back, rein in, curtail, cut back [➥AVOID, PREVENT, LIMIT, AND CONTROL; 277] *Opposite*: promote

curd *n* [➥DAIRY PRODUCTS AND CHEESES; 1183]

curdle **1** *v* **coagulate**, clot, thicken, congeal, gel [➥HARDEN, CONGEAL, AND DRY; 387] *Opposite*: separate **2** *v* (*informal*) **go sour**, go bad, turn, sour, spoil, ferment, go off (*UK*) [➥GO BAD AND CORRODE; 390]

cure **1** *v* **heal**, treat, make well, restore to health, alleviate, doctor [➥BECOME SICK, TREAT, AND RECOVER; 728] *Opposite*: exacerbate **2** *n* **treatment**, therapy, medicine, medication, remedy, antidote [➥HEALING; 730] **3** *v* **preserve**, smoke, dry, salt, pickle [➥COOKING AND FOOD PREPARATION; 353]

cure-all *n* **panacea**, universal remedy, magic potion, magic bullet, antidote, elixir, remedy, cure, answer, solution, nostrum [➥SOLUTIONS; 215]

curfew *n* **restriction**, time limit, deadline, limitation, regulation, control [➥ENDS AND DEPARTURES; 54]

curio *n* **trinket**, antique, curiosity, souvenir, knick-knack, bric-a-brac, novelty, gewgaw, novelty item [➥ORNAMENTS AND DECORATIONS; 1248]

curiosity **1** *n* **inquisitiveness**, interest, prying, nosiness (*informal*), snooping (*informal*) [➥ATTENTION AND ATTENTIVENESS; 763] *Opposite*: disinterest **2** *n* **oddity**, rarity, novelty, curio, strange thing, marvel, wonder, phenomenon [➥EXTRAORDINARY: UNCOMMON; 205]

curious **1** *adj* **inquisitive**, inquiring, interested, questioning, probing, prying, nosy (*informal*), snooping

(*informal*) [➥PENSIVENESS AND INTEREST; 538] *Opposite*: uninterested **2** *adj* **peculiar**, odd, strange, unusual, intriguing, remarkable, bizarre, weird [➥BIZARRE AND PECULIAR; 257] *Opposite*: ordinary

curiousness *n* **strangeness**, peculiarity, oddness, bizarreness [➥BIZARRE AND PECULIAR; 257]

curl **1** *v* **swirl**, spiral, twirl, twist, curve, coil, corkscrew, eddy [➥POSITION SOMETHING: AROUND SOMETHING; 327] **2** *v* **twist**, coil, bend, wind, wave, crimp [➥POSITION SOMETHING: AROUND SOMETHING; 327] **3** *n* **coil**, twist, whorl, spiral, eddy, corkscrew [➥ROUNDED SHAPE; 1218] **4** *n* **ringlet**, wave, lock, spit curl, kiss curl (*UK*) [➥HAIR; 484]

curling *type of* **winter sport** [➥HOBBIES, GAMES, AND SPORTS; 875]

curl up *v* **double up**, crouch, hug your knees, roll into a ball, go into a fetal position, coil, bend [➥ASSUME A POSITION; 317] *Opposite*: straighten

curly *adj* **wavy**, coiled, twisted, frizzy, crimped, curling, kinky, corkscrew [➥ROUNDED SHAPE; 1218] *Opposite*: straight

curmudgeon *n* **malcontent**, grouch (*informal*), grump (*informal*), pain (*informal*), crosspatch (*dated informal*) [➥GRUMPY AND NEGATIVE PEOPLE; 953]

curmudgeonly *adj* **bad-tempered**, crabby, cantankerous, grumpy, grumbly, testy, tetchy, irascible, peevish, moody, irritable, grouchy (*informal*), cranky (*informal*) [➥NEGATIVITY OF OUTLOOK; 514] *Opposite*: pleasant

currant *type of* **berry** [➥FRUIT AND VEGETABLES; 1176]

currency **1** *n* **money**, legal tender, coinage, coins, exchange, notes, cash, bills, paper money [➥CURRENCIES; 798] **2** *n* **prevalence**, frequency, vogue, commonness, popularity, circulation, acceptance, predominance [➥PRESENT AND AVAILABLE; 11]

currency

◆ *types of currencies*
afghani (Afghanistan), baht (Thailand), balboa (Panama), birr (Ethiopia), bolivar (Venezuela), boliviano (Bolivia), cedi (Ghana), CFA franc (Benin, Burkina Faso, Cameroon, Central African Republic, Chad, Rep. of Congo, Côte d'Ivoire, Equatorial Guinea, Gabon, Guinea-Bissau, Mali, Niger, Senegal, Togo), colón (Costa Rica, El Salvador), Congo franc (Dem. Rep. of Congo), córdoba (Nicaragua), dalasi (Gambia), denar (Former Yugoslav Rep. of Macedonia), deutsche mark (Germany), dinar (Algeria, Bahrain, Iraq, Jordan, Kuwait, Libya, Sudan, Tunisia, Yugoslavia), dirham (Morocco, United Arab Emirates), dobra (São Tomé and Príncipe), dollar (Antigua and Barbuda, Australia, Bahamas, Barbados, Belize, Canada, Dominica, Ecuador, Fiji, Grenada, Guyana, Hong Kong, Jamaica, Kiribati, Liberia, Marshall Islands, Micronesia, Namibia, Nauru, New Zealand, Palau, St. Kitts and Nevis, St. Lucia, St. Vincent and the Grenadines, Singapore, Solomon Islands, Taiwan, Trinidad and Tobago, Tuvalu, United States, Zimbabwe), dong (Vietnam), drachma (Greece), dram (Armenia), escudo (Cape Verde, Portugal), euro (Austria, Belgium, Finland, France, Germany, Greece, Ireland, Italy, Luxembourg, Netherlands, Portugal, Spain), forint (Hungary), franc (Belgium, Burundi, Comoros, Djibouti, France, Guinea, Liech-

tenstein, Luxembourg, Madagascar, Monaco, Rwanda, Switzerland), gourde (Haiti), guarani (Paraguay), guilder (Netherlands, Suriname), hryvnia (Ukraine), kina (Papua New Guinea), kip (Laos), koruna (Czech Republic, Slovakia), krona (Iceland, Sweden), krone (Denmark, Norway), kroon (Estonia), kuna (Croatia), kwacha (Malawi, Zambia), kwanza (Angola), kyat (Myanmar), lari (Georgia), lat (Latvia), lek (Albania), lempira (Honduras), leone (Sierra Leone), leu (Moldova, Romania), lev (Bulgaria), lilangeni (Swaziland), lira (Italy, Malta, Turkey), litas (Lithuania), loti (Lesotho), manat (Azerbaijan, Turkmenistan), marka (Bosnia and Herzegovina), markka (Finland), metical (Mozambique), naira (Nigeria), nakfa (Eritrea), ngultrum (Bhutan), ouguiya (Mauritania), pa'anga (Tonga), pataca (Macau), peseta (Andorra, Spain), peso (Argentina, Chile, Columbia, Cuba, Dominican Republic, Mexico, Philippines, Uruguay), pound (Cyprus, Egypt, Lebanon, Syria, United Kingdom), pula (Botswana), punt (Ireland), quetzal (Guatemala), rand (South Africa), real (Brazil), rial (Iran, Oman, Yemen), riel (Cambodia), ringgit (Malaysia), riyal (Qatar, Saudi Arabia), rubel (Belarus), ruble (Russia, Tajikistan), rufiyaa (Maldives), rupee (India, Mauritius, Nepal, Pakistan, Seychelles, Sri Lanka), rupiah (Indonesia), santim (Latvia), schilling (Austria), shekel (Israel), shilling (Kenya, Somalia, Tanzania, Uganda), sol (Peru), som (Kyrgyzstan, Uzbekistan), taka (Bangladesh), tala (Samoa), tenge (Kazakhstan), tolar (Slovenia), tughrik (Mongolia), vatu (Vanuatu), won (North Korea, South Korea), yen (Japan), yuan (China), zloty (Poland)

current 1 *adj* **present**, existing, actual, in progress, recent, up-to-date, contemporary, present-day, modern [➡ PRESENT; 85] *Opposite*: dated 2 *n* **flow**, stream, undercurrent, tide, flux, undertow, bore [➡ RIVERS, LAKES, AND STREAMS; 1042]

curriculum *n* **course**, prospectus, program, syllabus, core curriculum [➡ CLASSES, COURSEWORK, AND EXAMINATIONS; 842]

curriculum vitae *n* [➡ SUMMARIES, OUTLINES, AND EXCERPTS; 588]

curried *adj* [➡ STATE OF PREPARED FOOD; 1171]

curry *type of* **cooked dish** [➡ PREPARED DISHES; 1170]

curry favor *v* **ingratiate yourself**, cozy up, get in good with, play up to, grovel, crawl (*informal*), suck up (*slang*), apple-polish (*slang*), get in with (*UK*) [➡ ESTABLISHING RELATIONSHIPS WITH OTHERS; 974]

curse 1 *n* **swearword**, oath, expletive, epithet, blasphemy, profanity, obscenity [➡ INSULTS, ABUSE, AND SWEARING; 658] 2 *n* **jinx**, spell, magic, setback, blow, anathema, whammy (*informal*), execration (*literary or formal*) [➡ NUISANCES; 253] *Opposite*: blessing 3 *n* **scourge**, plague, blight, bane, misfortune, trouble, torment, ordeal, affliction, trial, tribulation [➡ NUISANCES; 253] 4 *v* **swear**, blaspheme, damn, use bad language, cuss (*informal*) [➡ INSULTS, ABUSE, AND SWEARING; 658] 5 *v* **plague**, afflict, trouble, blight, torment, scourge, burden, beset [➡ HAPPEN TO SOMEBODY; 30]

cursed 1 *adj* **damned**, afflicted, banned, anathematized, blighted [➡ IRRITATING; 228] *Opposite*: blessed 2 *adj* (*informal*) **annoying**, irritating, bothersome, vexatious, perturbing, trying, damnable, abominable, cussed (*informal*), execrable (*formal*) [➡ UNACCEPTABLE AND UNFORGIVABLE; 225]

cursor *n* **pointer**, arrow, marker, indicator [➡ COMPUTERS AND COMPUTING; 1127]

cursory *adj* **superficial**, hasty, brief, passing, quick, rapid, perfunctory, hurried, fleeting, desultory [➡ HAPPENING QUICKLY; 104] *Opposite*: thorough

curt *adj* **abrupt**, brisk, brusque, rude, brief, terse, offhand, snappy, blunt, summary, peremptory, short, snippy (*informal*) [➡ BAD-TEMPERED AND HUMORLESS; 626] *Opposite*: civil

curtail *v* **limit**, restrain, restrict, hold back, cut back, curb, rein in, shorten, inhibit, decrease, clip, pare down, trim, cut short [➡ AVOID, PREVENT, LIMIT, AND CONTROL; 277] *Opposite*: extend

curtailment *n* **limitation**, restriction, curb, shortening, reduction, decrease, cut [➡ AVOID, PREVENT, LIMIT, AND CONTROL; 277] *Opposite*: extension

curtain *n* **drape**, blind, screen, shutter, shade [➡ FURNISHING AND HOUSEHOLD LINENS; 860]

curtain raiser *n* **prelude**, overture, prologue, preamble, lead-in [➡ BEGINNINGS; 53]

curtness *n* **brusqueness**, abruptness, shortness, briskness, snappiness, peremptoriness, rudeness, terseness, bluntness, snippiness (*informal*) [➡ SUCCINCT AND TO THE POINT; 640] *Opposite*: civility

curtsy 1 *v* **genuflect**, bow, bob, kneel, stoop, greet [➡ GESTURES AND GESTICULATION; 653] 2 *n* **bow**, genuflection, bob, obeisance (*formal*) [➡ GESTURES AND GESTICULATION; 653]

curvaceous *adj* **curvy**, rounded, curved, shapely, voluptuous [➡ BUILD; 477]

curvature *n* **curving**, bend, twist, warp, arc, curve, arch [➡ ROUNDED SHAPE; 1218]

curve 1 *n* **arc**, bend, bow, arch, camber, curvature, turn [➡ ROUNDED SHAPE; 1218] 2 *v* **bend**, bow, curl, coil, twist, turn, hook, arch [➡ CHANGE OF SHAPE; 385] *Opposite*: straighten

curved *adj* **bent**, bowed, curled, coiled, rounded, arched, warped, hooked, curvilinear [➡ ROUNDED SHAPE; 1218] *Opposite*: straight

curvilinear *see* **curved**

curviness *n* **roundedness**, sinuousness, shapeliness, curvaceousness [➡ ROUNDED SHAPE; 1218]

curving 1 *adj* **bent**, warped, twisted, bowed, crooked, distorted, hooked, coiled, arched [➡ ROUNDED SHAPE; 1218] *Opposite*: straight 2 *adj* **curved**, curvy, bending, sinuous, snaking, winding, meandering, curvilinear, undulating [➡ ROUNDED SHAPE; 1218] *Opposite*: straight

curvy *adj* **undulating**, wavy, rounded, curved, curvilinear, curvaceous [➡ ROUNDED SHAPE; 1218] *Opposite*: straight

cushion 1 *n* **pillow**, bolster, pad, headrest, beanbag, hassock [➡ FURNISHING AND HOUSEHOLD LINENS; 860] 2 *v* **protect**, shield, guard, support, bolster, pad [➡ PREVENT CONTACT OR ATTACK; 419] *Opposite*: expose 3 *v* **mitigate**, moderate, lessen, stifle, soften, suppress, dampen, muffle [➡ CHANGE OF INTENSITY: LESS; 395] *Opposite*: exacerbate

cushy (*informal*) *adj* **easy**, comfortable, undemanding, cozy, agreeable, pleasant [➡ EASE AND SIMPLICITY; 200] *Opposite*: difficult

cushy number (*UK*) *n* [➡ EASY WORK; 299]

cusp 1 *n* **point**, tip, nib, end [➡ EXTREMITIES OF PHYSICAL OBJECTS; 1250] 2 *n* **crossover**, border, limit, edge, verge, boundary, watershed [➡ EXTREMITIES OF PHYSICAL OBJECTS; 1250]

cuspid *type of* **tooth** [➡ THE MOUTH; 702]

cuss (*informal*) *v* **swear**, curse, blaspheme, profane, use bad language, damn [➡ INSULTS, ABUSE, AND SWEARING; 658]

cussed (*informal*) *adj* **annoying**, irritating, uncooperative, obstinate, stubborn, pigheaded, perverse [➡ UNWILLINGNESS AND STUBBORNNESS; 564] *Opposite*: cooperative

cussedness (*informal*) *n* **pigheadedness**, stubbornness, obstinacy, willfulness, perversity [➡ UNWILLINGNESS AND STUBBORNNESS; 564] *Opposite*: cooperation

custard *type of* **dessert** [➡ CAKES, COOKIES, AND DESSERTS; 1181]

custodial 1 *adj* **protective**, safeguarding, safekeeping, sheltered, supervisory [➡ SAFE AND SAFETY; 191] 2 *adj* **prison**, jail, secure, penal, residential [➡ CAPTIVITY AND LOSS OF FREEDOM; 248]

custodian 1 *n* **guardian**, curator, keeper, defender, upholder, protector, overseer, warden (*UK*) [➡ SUPPORTERS, PROTECTORS, AND COMPATRIOTS; 970] 2 *n* **caretaker**, janitor, concierge, night watchman, superintendent, super (*informal*), warden (*UK*) [➡ PEOPLE WHO GUARD AND PROTECT; 846]

custody 1 *n* **protection**, keeping, safekeeping, care, charge, guardianship, supervision, trusteeship, watch [➡ RESPONSIBILITY; 170] 2 *n* **detention**, arrest, confinement, imprisonment, incarceration (*formal*) [➡ CAPTIVITY AND LOSS OF FREEDOM; 248] *Opposite*: liberty

custom 1 *n* **tradition**, practice, convention, institution, ritual, habit, norm, routine [➡ WAYS OF DOING THINGS; 294] *Opposite*: novelty 2 *n* **habit**, practice, routine, pattern, way, wont [➡ WAYS OF DOING THINGS; 294] 3 *n* **trade**, business, patronage, clientele, market, client base, goodwill [➡ BUSINESS ACTIVITIES AND PHENOMENA; 794]

See Compare and Contrast at **habit**.

customarily *adv* **usually**, normally, habitually, regularly, routinely, as a matter of course, as a rule, typically, ordinarily [➡ USUALLY; 108] *Opposite*: unusually

customary 1 *adj* **usual**, normal, habitual, expected, routine, regular, accustomed, ordinary, everyday [➡ ORDINARINESS; 244] *Opposite*: exceptional 2 *adj* **traditional**, conventional, time-honored, established, long-established, general [➡ PERMANENCE: WITHOUT END; 94] *Opposite*: unconventional 3 *adj* **typical**, characteristic, usual, habitual, normal, wonted (*literary*) [➡ ORDINARINESS; 244] *Opposite*: uncharacteristic

See Compare and Contrast at **usual**.

custom-built *adj* **specially made**, commissioned, made-to-order, custom-made, customized, personalized, bespoke (*UK*) [➡ EXTRAORDINARY: UNCOMMON; 205] *Opposite*: off-the-rack

customer *n* **client**, buyer, purchaser, patron, shopper, consumer, habitué [➡ PURCHASER; 424]

customize *v* **modify**, tailor, adapt, alter, make to order, make specially, convert [➡ CHANGE; 372]

customized *adj* **modified**, tailored, adapted, made-to-order, personalized, custom-made, specially made, commissioned, custom-built [➡ EXTRAORDINARY: UNCOMMON; 205] *Opposite*: mass-produced

custom-made *adj* **specially made**, commissioned, made-to-order, custom-built, customized, personalized, bespoke (*UK*) [➡ EXTRAORDINARY: UNCOMMON; 205] *Opposite*: mass-produced

customs *n* **tax**, duty, levy, impost, toll, payment [➡ ADMINISTRATIVE OFFICERS; 811]

cut 1 *v* **chop**, slice, carve, saw, hack, slash, sever, cube, dice, mince [➡ TEAR, BREAK, AND CUT; 360] *Opposite*: join 2 *v* **pierce**, score, nick, incise, engrave, scratch, carve, lacerate, gash, slit [➡ TEAR, BREAK, AND CUT; 360] *Opposite*: seal 3 *v* **reduce**, decrease, limit, curtail, cut down, cut back, restrict, diminish [➡ CHANGE OF SIZE: SMALLER; 393] *Opposite*: increase 4 *v* **edit**, shorten, censor, condense, chop, prune, slash, remove, expurgate, excise, abridge, abbreviate, reduce [➡ DELETE AND ERASE; 339] *Opposite*: restore 5 *v* **stop**, discontinue, bring to an end, bring to a halt, finish, cut off, choke off, disconnect, withdraw, withhold [➡ CAUSE TO STOP; 266] *Opposite*: continue 6 *n* **scratch**, wound, slash, graze, incision, nick, puncture [➡ HOLES, GAPS, AND FORKS; 1252] 7 *n* **reduction**, decrease, cutback, decline, drop, fall [➡ CHANGE OF SIZE: SMALLER; 393] *Opposite*: increase 8 *n* **share**, commission, percentage, kickback, rake-off (*informal*) [➡ MEASURABLE PORTIONS; 127]

cut-and-dried 1 *adj* **decided**, finished, settled, fixed, agreed, sorted out, done and dusted (*UK*) [➡ WHOLENESS AND COMPLETENESS; 198] *Opposite*: undecided 2 *adj* **predictable**, obvious, open-and-shut, anticipated, expected, foreseen, plain, plain as the nose on your face, clear, plodding, trite, hackneyed, plain as a pikestaff (*UK*) [➡ PERCEPTIBLE; 25] *Opposite*: unexpected

cut back *v* **reduce**, curtail, curb, decrease, restrain, hold back, rein in, cut down, contract, retrench, downsize [➡ CHANGE OF SIZE: SMALLER; 393] *Opposite*: develop

cutback *n* **reduction**, cut, decrease, decline, drop, falloff, phasedown, downturn, retrenchment [➡ LESS; 126]

cut corners *v* [➡ UNDERDO SOMETHING; 291]

cut dead *v* **snub**, coldshoulder, rebuff [➡ REFUSING OR REJECTING RELATIONS; 975]

cut down 1 *v* **reduce**, decrease, cut back, ease up on, rein back, contract, shorten, abate (*formal or literary*) [➡ CHANGE OF SIZE: SMALLER; 393] *Opposite*: increase 2 *v* **fell**, chop down, bring down, hack down, lop, clear [➡ TEAR, BREAK, AND CUT; 360] 3 *v* (*informal*) **kill**, strike down, slaughter, mow down, assassinate, slay (*formal or literary*) [➡ KILL; 923]

cute 1 *adj* **attractive**, pretty, delightful, charming, appealing, endearing, adorable, sweet, darling, lovable [➡ PEOPLE'S PHYSICAL APPEARANCE; 475] *Opposite*: ugly 2 *adj* **shrewd**, cunning, smart, sharp, quick, quick-witted [➡ POSITIVE INTELLECTUAL CHARACTERISTICS; 524]

cuteness 1 *n* **adorability**, lovability, attractiveness, appeal, charm, delightfulness, beauty, prettiness, loveliness, handsomeness, looks, comeliness (*archaic or literary*) [➡ BEAUTY AND ATTRACTIVENESS; 189] *Opposite*: ugliness **2** *n* **shrewdness**, cunning, smartness, sharpness, quick-wittedness, wiliness [➡ POSITIVE INTELLECTUAL CHARACTERISTICS; 524]

cutesy *adj* **mawkish**, saccharine, sugary, chocolate-box, kitsch, precious, tacky (*informal*), twee (*UK*) [➡ IN POOR TASTE AND OVERSENTIMENTAL; 229] *Opposite*: austere

cut glass *type of* **glass** [➡ GLASS; 1136]

cut-glass (*UK*) *adj* **upper-class**, plummy, posh (*informal*), public-school (*UK*) [➡ CLASS STATUS; 889] *Opposite*: broad

cuticle *part of* **arm or hand** [➡ PARTS OF THE BODY: ARM AND HAND; 695]

cut in *v* **interrupt**, break in, butt in, interject, move in, interpose, interpolate [➡ INTERRUPT AND BUTT IN; 619]

cut it (*informal*) *v* [➡ SUCCEED AND WIN; 79]

cut it close *v* [➡ GAMBLE AND TAKE RISKS; 466]

cutlass *type of* **sword or knife** [➡ SWORDS AND KNIVES; 1157]

cutlet *type of* **cut** [➡ TYPES AND CUTS OF MEAT; 1177]

cut loose (*informal*) *v* **get free**, get away, escape, make a break, break away, break free, break loose, burst out, get out, disentangle yourself [➡ RUN AWAY AND AVOID; 10]

cut no ice *v* [➡ FAIL OR BE UNSUCCESSFUL; 75]

cut off **1** *v* **remove**, sever, amputate, excise, detach, take off [➡ EXTRACT AND SEVER; 341] *Opposite*: reconnect **2** *v* **interrupt**, stop, cut short, cut in, butt in, break in [➡ INTERRUPT AND BUTT IN; 619] **3** *v* **stop**, disconnect, discontinue, bring to an end, halt, bring to a halt, withdraw, finish, withhold [➡ CAUSE TO STOP; 266] *Opposite*: restore **4** *v* **isolate**, separate, keep apart, strand, detach, maroon, island [➡ UNFASTEN AND UNDO; 409] *Opposite*: connect

cutoff **1** *n* **limit**, end point, end date, deadline, expiry, finish, point of no return [➡ ENDS AND DEPARTURES; 54] *Opposite*: start **2** *n* **stoppage**, end, finish, halt, freeze, break, termination, severance, breakdown, failure [➡ ENDS AND DEPARTURES; 54] *Opposite*: continuation

cutoffs *type of* **pants** [➡ GARMENTS AND OUTFITS; 865]

cut out **1** *v* **remove**, take away, excise, extract, take out, delete [➡ EXTRACT AND SEVER; 341] *Opposite*: put in **2** *v* **give up**, stop, renounce, forgo, do without, quit [➡ FORGO AND DENY ONESELF; 449] **3** *v* **exclude**, ignore, overlook, isolate, marginalize, freeze out, eliminate, snub, cut dead [➡ NOT PAY ATTENTION; 764] *Opposite*: include

cutout **1** *n* **shape**, template, stencil, outline, silhouette [➡ SHAPE; 1216] **2** *n* **safety device**, kill switch, circuit breaker, safety switch, trip switch [➡ PARTS OF MACHINES AND TOOLS; 1118]

cut out for *adj* **suited**, suitable, designed, destined, right, appropriate, qualified [➡ APPROPRIATE, SUITABLE, AND ADVISABLE; 184]

cut-rate *adj* **reduced**, cheap, economy, budget, bargain, discount, sale, inexpensive [➡ CHEAP AND INEXPENSIVE; 221]

cut short *v* **break off**, discontinue, call a halt, suspend, stop in full flow, stop, interrupt, terminate (*formal*) [➡ CAUSE TO STOP; 266]

cutter **1** *n* [➡ CUTTING TOOLS; 1120] **2** *type of* **military vessel** [➡ SHIPS AND BOATS; 1150] **3** *type of* **motor vessel** [➡ SHIPS AND BOATS; 1150]

cutter

◆ *types of cutting tools*
ax, billhook, chisel, chopper, clippers, hatchet, hoe, knife, machete, pickax, plow, razor blade, scissors, scythe, shears, sickle

cut the mustard (*informal*) *v* [➡ SUCCEED AND WIN; 79]

cutthroat *adj* **merciless**, pitiless, ruthless, unsparing, fierce, aggressive, cruel, callous, competitive [➡ SELFISH AND UNKIND; 505] *Opposite*: merciful

cutting **1** *adj* **hurtful**, wounding, unkind, acerbic, critical, spiteful, harsh, callous, heartless, sharp, caustic, stinging, abrasive [➡ RUDE AND HOSTILE; 625] *Opposite*: kind **2** *adj* **cold**, biting, icy, sharp, keen, penetrating, piercing, harsh [➡ COLD WEATHER; 1051] *Opposite*: mild **3** *n* **sprig**, offshoot, scion [➡ PARTS OF TREES AND PLANTS; 1026]

cutting edge **1** *n* **vanguard**, van, forefront, edge, leading edge, lead, sharp end, frontier, top, limit, uncharted territory, front line, front, avant-garde, fore (*literary*) [➡ NEW, MODERN; 166] *Opposite*: rearguard **2** *n* **sharp edge**, razor edge, knife edge, serrated edge, blade, razor blade, knife blade [➡ EXTREMITIES OF PHYSICAL OBJECTS; 1250]

cutting-edge *adj* **leading-edge**, front-line, pioneering, trailblazing, radical, innovative, brand-new, forward-looking, progressive, revolutionary, unconventional, avant-garde, edgy [➡ NEW, MODERN; 166] *Opposite*: old-fashioned

cutting garden *type of* **garden** [➡ GARDENS; 1074]

cuttingly *adv* **harshly**, abrasively, hurtfully, sharply, severely, caustically, tartly, acerbically, acidly, mordantly, bitingly [➡ RUDE AND HOSTILE; 625] *Opposite*: kindly

cuttlefish *type of* **aquatic invertebrate** [➡ AQUATIC INVERTEBRATES; 1022]

cut to the chase (*informal*) *v* [➡ EXPLAIN AND CLARIFY; 610]

cut up **1** *v* **chop**, mince, slice, chop up, dice, shred, cube [➡ TEAR, BREAK, AND CUT; 360] **2** *adj* (*informal*) **distressed**, upset, affected, distraught, heartbroken, miserable [➡ SADNESS, DISTRESS, AND DESPAIR; 539] *Opposite*: happy

cutup (*informal*) *n* **joker**, clown, prankster, comic, comedian, wisecracker (*informal*), wise guy (*informal*), smart aleck (*informal*) [➡ JOKERS AND TEASES; 675]

cut your losses *v* [➡ LEAVE AND GO AWAY; 8]

cut your teeth on *v* [➡ START AN ACTION; 260]

CV *n* **curriculum vitae**, résumé, qualifications, employment record, vita [➡ SUMMARIES, OUTLINES, AND EXCERPTS; 588]

cyan *type of* **blue** [➡ COLORS; 1224]

cybercafé *type of* **eating place** [➡ HOTELS, RESTAURANTS, AND CLUBS; 1082]

cybermall *n* [➡ E-COMMERCE; 1129]

cybermarketing *n* [➡ E-COMMERCE; 1129]

cybermediary *n* [➡ E-COMMERCE; 1129]

cybernetics *n* **artificial intelligence**, information technology, AI, IT [➡ COMPUTERS AND COMPUTING; 1127]

cyberspace *n* **virtual reality**, Internet, World Wide Web, information superhighway, data superhighway, infobahn [➡ THE INTERNET; 1128]

cyber warfare *n* [➡ THE INTERNET; 1128]

cyclamen *type of* **flower grown from bulbs** [➡ FLOWERS FROM BULBS; 1030]

cycle *n* **series**, sequence, set, round, rotation, succession, phase, progression, run [➡ CHAIN OF EVENTS; 162]

cycle lane (*UK*) *n* [➡ TRAVEL: TRAFFIC PROBLEMS AND TRAFFIC MANAGEMENT; 323]

cycle track (*UK*) *n* [➡ TRAVEL: TRAFFIC PROBLEMS AND TRAFFIC MANAGEMENT; 323]

cyclic *see* **cyclical**

cyclical *adj* **recurring**, returning, repeated, cyclical, recurrent [➡ FREQUENT AND OFTEN; 107] *Opposite*: unique

cyclone *n* **storm**, windstorm, hurricane, typhoon, tornado, tempest, whirlwind, tropical storm [➡ WINDY AND STORMY WEATHER; 1053]

cygnet *type of* **young bird** [➡ YOUNG BIRDS; 1004]

Cygnus *type of* **constellation** [➡ HEAVENLY BODIES; 1061]

cylinder 1 *n* **tube**, roll, pipe, chamber, piston [➡ ROUNDED SHAPE; 1218] 2 *n* **container**, drum, canister, tank, bottle [➡ CONTAINERS, RECEPTACLES, AND PACKAGING; 1245] 3 *part of* **engine** [➡ PARTS OF AN ENGINE; 1144]

cylindrical *adj* **tubular**, tube-shaped, cylinder-shaped, rod-shaped, rodlike [➡ ROUNDED SHAPE; 1218]

cymbal *type of* **percussion instrument** [➡ MUSICAL INSTRUMENTS; 910]

cynic *n* **skeptic**, doubter, detractor, disparager, misanthropist, pessimist, scoffer [➡ GRUMPY AND NEGATIVE PEOPLE; 953]

cynical 1 *adj* **distrustful**, skeptical, suspicious, disparaging, negative, detracting, pessimistic, misanthropic, scoffing [➡ NEGATIVITY OF OUTLOOK; 514] *Opposite*: naive 2 *adj* **sarcastic**, mocking, scornful, sardonic, sneering, derisive, contemptuous, scathing [➡ MOCKING AND DISMISSIVE; 636] *Opposite*: respectful

cynicism *n* **skepticism**, sarcasm, distrust, doubt, scorn, suspicion, pessimism, disparagement [➡ UNCERTAINTY; 559] *Opposite*: naiveté

cypress *type of* **evergreen tree** [➡ EVERGREEN AND CONIFEROUS TREES; 1029]

Cyrillic *type of* **alphabet** [➡ SYMBOLS, SIGNS, AND NUMBERS; 596]

cyst *n* **swelling**, lump, polyp, nodule, growth, tumor, ganglion, sac, blister, wen [➡ ILLNESSES AND DISORDERS; 732]

czar *see* **tsar**

D

dab 1 *v* pat, wipe, apply, touch, tap [➡ DECORATE, ADORN, AND APPLY COATINGS; 405] **2** *n* **bit**, blob, spot, dash, drop, pat, daub, smidgeon (*informal*) [➡ AMOUNTS OF LIQUID; 114]

dabble 1 *v* experiment, try your hand, dip into, play at, putter, fiddle, toy with [➡ PARTICIPATE; 292] **2** *v* **dip**, paddle, splash, immerse [➡ FIDGET AND FROLIC; 311]

dachshund *type of* small dog [➡ DOGS; 980]

dad (*informal*) *n* father, pop (*informal*), pa (*informal*), daddy (*informal*), papa (*dated*) [➡ OLDER GENERATION RELATIVES; 959]

Dada *type of* 20th-century art movement [➡ ARTISTIC MOVEMENTS AND STYLES; 899]

daddy (*informal*) *see* dad

daddy longlegs *type of* arachnid [➡ ARACHNIDS; 1018]

dado 1 *n* panel, molding, frieze, feature [➡ ROOFS, ROOF PARTS, AND CEILINGS; 1103] **2** *type of* general fixtures [➡ FIXTURES; 859]

dado rail *n* [➡ ROOFS, ROOF PARTS, AND CEILINGS; 1103]

daemon 1 *n* demigod, supernatural being, spirit [➡ MYTHICAL BEINGS; 789] **2** *n* guardian spirit, inspiration, guiding force, inner spirit, muse [➡ PSYCHOLOGY AND THE MIND; 769]

daffodil *type of* flower grown from bulbs [➡ FLOWERS FROM BULBS; 1030]

daffy (*informal*) *adj* silly, wacky (*informal*), goofy (*informal*), ditzy (*informal*), giddy (*dated*), dippy (*UK*) [➡ NEGATIVE INTELLECTUAL CHARACTERISTICS; 525] *Opposite*: sensible

dagger *type of* sword or knife [➡ SWORDS AND KNIVES; 1157]

dahlia *type of* flower grown from bulbs [➡ FLOWERS FROM BULBS; 1030]

daily 1 *adv* every day, each day, on a daily basis, day by day, day after day [➡ FREQUENT AND OFTEN; 107] **2** *adj* everyday, day-to-day, regular, diurnal, circadian, per diem, quotidian (*formal*) [➡ TIMES OF DAY; 87]

daintiness *n* delicacy, elegance, gracefulness, refinement, prettiness, neatness, exquisiteness, deftness [➡ WELL-GROOMED; 482] *Opposite*: clumsiness

dainty *adj* pretty, delicate, graceful, refined, exquisite, elegant, petite, neat, deft [➡ DESCRIBING BODY MOVEMENTS; 288] *Opposite*: clumsy

dais *n* platform, podium, pulpit, stage, stand [➡ STAGES, PLATFORMS, AND RAISED AREAS; 1098]

daisy *type of* perennial flower [➡ FLOWERS; 1032]

dalasi *type of* currency [➡ CURRENCIES; 798]

dale *n* valley, glen, vale (*literary*), dene (*UK*) [➡ GEOLOGIC FEATURES; 1056] *Opposite*: hill

dalliance (*literary*) *n* flirtation, romance, relationship, liaison, involvement, coquetry (*literary*) [➡ SEXUAL AND ROMANTIC RELATIONSHIPS; 964]

dally *v* linger, dawdle, loiter, hang around, waste time, dilly-dally, fritter away [➡ SHIRK AND DELAY; 273] *Opposite*: hurry

dalmatian *type of* large dog [➡ DOGS; 980]

dam 1 *n* barrier, barrage, weir, wall, boom, block, obstruction [➡ BARRIERS; 1113] **2** *type of* female animal [➡ MALE OR FEMALE ANIMALS; 978] **3** *v* block, block up, stem, hold back, control, inhibit, blockade, hinder, obstruct, impede, restrict [➡ AVOID, PREVENT, LIMIT, AND CONTROL; 277]

damage 1 *n* injury, harm, hurt, impairment, destruction, mutilation, loss [➡ FAULTS, FLAWS, AND WEAKNESSES; 251] *Opposite*: reparation **2** *n* (*informal*) cost, price, bill, total, amount [➡ EXPENDITURE; 423] **3** *v* injure, harm, spoil, hurt, smash up, break, scratch, dent, wound, mar, ravage [➡ DESTRUCTION AND DEMOLITION; 359] *Opposite*: repair

See Compare and Contrast at **harm**.

damaged *adj* injured, hurt, spoiled, dented, scratched, smashed, broken, impaired, marred, beat-up (*informal*) [➡ IN BAD REPAIR; 1234] *Opposite*: pristine

damages *n* compensation, costs, reparation, reimbursement, recompense [➡ FUNDS, PAYMENTS, AND CHARGES; 800]

damaging *adj* harmful, destructive, negative, detrimental, hurtful, injurious [➡ DANGEROUS; 236] *Opposite*: harmless

damask 1 *type of* red [➡ COLORS; 1224] **2** *type of* fabric from plants [➡ FABRICS; 1132]

damning *adj* critical, negative, disapproving, unfavorable, condemning, incriminatory, pejorative (*formal*) [➡ ACCUSATORY AND DISAPPROVING; 634] *Opposite*: complimentary

damp 1 *adj* dank, moist, humid, soggy, clammy, wet, wettish [➡ MOIST; 1241] *Opposite*: dry **2** *adj* half-hearted, indifferent, insipid, unenthusiastic, weak [➡ NEUTRALITY AND INDIFFERENCE; 553] *Opposite*: enthusiastic **3** *n* moisture, dampness, humidity, clamminess, wetness, dankness [➡ MOIST; 1241] *Opposite*: dryness **4** *v* dampen, moisten, humidify, wet [➡ SOFTEN, LIQUEFY, AND DAMPEN; 388] *Opposite*: dry out **5** *v* check, curb, restrain, hinder, hamper, inhibit, stifle [➡ MAKE IMPOSSIBLE; 276] *Opposite*: encourage

See Compare and Contrast at **wet**.

damp down *v* dampen, diminish, check, dull, curb, reduce, stifle, restrain, inhibit [➡ CHANGE OF INTENSITY: LESS; 395] *Opposite*: increase

dampen 1 *v* damp, moisten, humidify, wet [➡ SOFTEN, LIQUEFY, AND DAMPEN; 388] *Opposite*: dry out **2** *v* damp down, reduce, diminish, check, dull, inhibit, stifle [➡ CHANGE OF INTENSITY: LESS; 395] *Opposite*: increase

damper 1 *n* **discouragement**, inhibition, hindrance, impediment, obstruction, curb, obstacle, check, restraint [➡ PROBLEMS; 256] *Opposite:* spur 2 *n* **regulator**, stopper, control, controller [➡ PARTS OF MACHINES AND TOOLS; 1118] 3 *n* **mute**, muffler, softener, silencer (*UK*) [➡ ACOUSTICS; 1138]

damply *adv* **indifferently**, half-heartedly, insipidly, wetly, unenthusiastically, weakly [➡ NEUTRALITY AND INDIFFERENCE; 553] *Opposite:* enthusiastically

dampness *n* **humidity**, moisture, moistness, clamminess, wetness, damp, sogginess [➡ MOIST; 1241] *Opposite:* dryness

damsel (*archaic or literary*) *n* [➡ FEMALE PERSON; 933]

damson *type of* **fruit** [➡ FRUIT AND VEGETABLES; 1176]

dance 1 *v* **twirl**, pirouette, sway, turn, bop (*informal*), boogie (*informal*) [➡ FIDGET AND FROLIC; 311] 2 *v* **gambol**, prance, skip, caper, frolic, hop, jump, leap, cavort, wiggle [➡ FIDGET AND FROLIC; 311] 3 *n* **ball**, disco, prom, hop (*dated informal*), rave (*slang*) [➡ PARTIES, DANCES, AND CELEBRATIONS; 37]

dance

◆ *types of dances*
ballet, barn dance, belly dance, bop (*informal*), bossa nova, cancan, cha-cha, Charleston, fandango, flamenco, foxtrot, jig, jitterbug, jive, lambada, limbo, lindy hop, line dancing, macarena, mambo, merengue, minuet, morris dancing, polka, quadrille, quickstep, rumba, salsa, samba, square dance, step dancing, strathspey, tango, tap dance, waltz

dance band *type of* **band** [➡ MUSICIANS AND SINGERS; 908]

dancer *type of* **entertainer** [➡ WORKERS IN ENTERTAINMENT AND MEDIA; 873]

dandelion *type of* **weed** [➡ WEEDS AND THISTLES; 1034]

dandified *adj* **dressed up**, dressed to kill, overdressed, fashionable, natty, dapper, modish, foppish [➡ WELL-GROOMED; 482] *Opposite:* scruffy

dandle 1 *v* **jiggle**, jog, bounce, dance, rock, shake [➡ MOVE SOMETHING: ON THE SPOT; 336] 2 *v* **pet**, stroke, caress, fondle, pamper, rub, cuddle, nuzzle [➡ PHYSICAL CONTACT AS COMMUNICATION; 655]

dandruff *n* **scurf**, scale, skin flake [➡ CONDITIONS AFFECTING THE SKIN; 721]

dandy 1 *adj* (*informal dated*) **excellent**, fine, superb, great (*informal*), swell (*dated informal*), cool (*slang*), groovy (*dated slang*) [➡ GOOD, WELL, BETTER; 183] *Opposite:* bad 2 *n* (*dated*) **fop**, fashion plate, clotheshorse (*informal*), dude (*slang*), beau (*archaic*), coxcomb (*archaic*) [➡ MALE PERSON; 934]

dandyish (*dated*) *adj* [➡ WELL-GROOMED; 482]

danger 1 *n* **hazard**, risk, peril, threat, menace, jeopardy, endangerment, vulnerability [➡ DANGER; 235] *Opposite:* safety 2 *n* **chance**, possibility, likelihood, risk [➡ POSSIBLE AND PROBABLE; 177]

dangerous 1 *adj* **unsafe**, hazardous, risky, treacherous, perilous, precarious, chancy, daring, threatening [➡ DANGEROUS; 236] *Opposite:* safe 2 *adj* **grave**, serious, critical, grievous, alarming [➡ DANGEROUS; 236] *Opposite:* safe

dangerously 1 *adv* **hazardously**, treacherously, perilously, precariously, riskily, uncertainly [➡ DANGEROUS; 236] *Opposite:* safely 2 *adv* **seriously**, severely, gravely, critically, grievously, alarmingly [➡ CRITICALLY AND SERIOUSLY; 134] *Opposite:* slightly

dangerousness *n* [➡ DANGER; 235]

dangle *v* **hang**, hang down, swing, sway, suspend, droop, sag, draggle [➡ GO DOWNWARD; 307] *Opposite:* stick up

dangling *adj* [➡ ORIENTATION AND ALIGNMENT; 1223]

Danish pastry *type of* **cake** [➡ CAKES, COOKIES, AND DESSERTS; 1181]

dank *adj* **damp**, moist, chilly, clammy, humid, soggy, wet, fusty [➡ MOIST; 1241] *Opposite:* warm

See Compare and Contrast at **wet**.

dankness *n* **wetness**, dampness, moistness, humidity, clamminess, chilliness, fustiness, sogginess [➡ MOIST; 1241] *Opposite:* warmth

dapper *adj* **neat**, elegant, smart, trim, well-dressed, tidy, spruce, well-groomed, debonair, modish, sporty, stylish, well turned-out (*UK*) [➡ WELL-GROOMED; 482] *Opposite:* scruffy

dappled *adj* **speckled**, spotted, mottled, stippled, piebald, flecked, variegated [➡ DESCRIBING PATTERNS; 1227]

dare 1 *v* **venture**, risk, gamble, face up to, have the courage, have the guts, have the nerve, have the cheek (*UK*) [➡ ATTEMPT AN ACTION; 261] 2 *v* **challenge**, defy, taunt, provoke, goad, urge [➡ GAMBLE AND TAKE RISKS; 466] 3 *v* **presume**, venture, have the audacity, be so bold, take the liberty, have the nerve, have the cheek (*UK*) [➡ CARRY OUT AN ACTION; 269] 4 *n* **taunt**, challenge, provocation, ultimatum, goad, spur, stimulus [➡ NON-AGGRESSIVE/SPORTING EVENTS; 40]

daredevil 1 *n* **risk-taker**, madcap, hothead, show-off (*informal*) [➡ SELF-IMPORTANT AND SELF-SEEKING PEOPLE; 949] *Opposite:* stick-in-the-mud (*informal*) 2 *adj* **reckless**, rash, madcap, hotheaded, bold, foolhardy, fearless, adventurous, wild, risk-taking, intrepid (*literary or humorous*) [➡ COURAGE; 498] *Opposite:* staid

daresay *v* **guess**, suppose, expect, assume, admit, acknowledge [➡ QUESTION THINGS; 751] *Opposite:* deny

daring 1 *adj* **bold**, brave, audacious, courageous, enterprising, heroic, adventurous, valiant, plucky, intrepid (*literary or humorous*), gallant (*literary*), dauntless (*literary*) [➡ COURAGE; 498] *Opposite:* cowardly 2 *adj* **dangerous**, risky, unsafe, hazardous, treacherous, perilous [➡ DANGEROUS; 236] *Opposite:* safe 3 *n* **bravery**, nerve, boldness, audacity, courage, heroism, adventurousness, valor, intrepidity [➡ COURAGE; 498] *Opposite:* cowardice

daringly *adv* **boldly**, bravely, audaciously, courageously, heroically, valiantly, adventurously [➡ COURAGE; 498] *Opposite:* timidly

dark 1 *adj* **dim**, shady, shadowy, murky, gloomy, dusky, black, obscure, opaque [➡ DESCRIBING LIGHT; 1228] *Opposite:* bright 2 *adj* **black**, brunette, brown, chestnut, sable [➡ HAIR COLOR; 485] *Opposite:* fair 3 *adj* **gloomy**, depressing, bleak, sad, unhappy, cheerless, dreary, dismal, joyless, somber [➡ EMOTIONALLY UNPLEASANT AND UPSETTING; 227] *Opposite:* cheery 4 *adj* **sinister**, mysterious, threatening, evil, nefarious, wicked, nasty, spooky (*informal*) [➡ DANGEROUS; 236] *Opposite*: good **5** n **darkness**, dusk, gloom, dimness, shadows, obscurity, blackness, night, nighttime [➡ DESCRIBING LIGHT; 1228] *Opposite*: light

darken v **blacken**, dim, deepen, cast a shadow, grow dim, grow dark, cloud over, obscure [➡ CHANGE OF COLOR; 391] *Opposite*: brighten

dark glasses n **sunglasses**, shades (*informal*) [➡ GLASSES AND SPECTACLES; 1125]

darkly 1 adv **threateningly**, sinisterly, forebodingly, menacingly, warningly, ominously, enigmatically, with intent [➡ RETICENT AND UNFORTHCOMING; 631] *Opposite*: cheerily **2** adv **gloomily**, bleakly, dismally, forbiddingly, depressingly, cheerlessly, joylessly, somberly [➡ BAD-TEMPERED AND HUMORLESS; 626] *Opposite*: brightly

darkness n **dark**, night, dusk, gloom, dimness, shadows, obscurity, blackness, nightfall, nighttime [➡ TIMES OF DAY; 87] *Opposite*: light

darkroom type of **photographic equipment** [➡ PHOTOGRAPHY AND PHOTOGRAPHIC EQUIPMENT; 1122]

dark star type of **star or star system** [➡ HEAVENLY BODIES; 1061]

darling 1 n **sweetheart**, dear, love, dearest, pet, beloved, sweetie (*informal*), honey (*informal*) [➡ ENDEARMENTS; 656] **2** n **favorite**, firm favorite, pet, the apple of somebody's eye, fair-haired boy [➡ PEOPLE WHO ARE APPROVED OF; 955] **3** adj **wonderful**, gorgeous, lovely, adorable, dear, cute, charming, precious, sweet [➡ BEAUTY AND ATTRACTIVENESS; 189] *Opposite*: horrible

darn v **sew**, stitch, repair, mend, sew up [➡ CRAFTS AND CARVING; 355] *Opposite*: tear

dart 1 n **arrow**, barb, shaft, missile, projectile [➡ PROJECTILES; 1159] **2** v **dash**, scurry, whiz, rush, run, tear, sprint, zoom (*informal*), zip (*informal*), scoot (*informal*), shoot (*informal*) [➡ MOVE FAST; 313] *Opposite*: saunter

dash 1 type of **punctuation mark** [➡ ASPECTS OF LANGUAGE; 682] **2** n **sprint**, rush, run, race, surge [➡ PROCEED AND GO; 305] **3** n **trace**, splash, drop, pinch, soupçon, touch, bit, smidgen (*informal*) [➡ AMOUNTS OF LIQUID; 114] *Opposite*: dollop (*informal*) **4** n **verve**, vigor, spirit, flair, panache, élan (*literary*) [➡ ENERGY AND ENTHUSIASM; 496] **5** v **rush**, hurry, hasten, tear, race, run, dart, scurry, sprint, bolt, zip (*informal*) [➡ MOVE FAST; 313] *Opposite*: amble **6** v (*formal*) **knock**, throw, hurl, slam, fling, sling [➡ MOVE SOMETHING: THROUGH THE AIR; 334] **7** v (*formal*) **smash**, break, shatter, crash, splinter [➡ TEAR, BREAK, AND CUT; 360] **8** v **frustrate**, confound, foil, shatter, discourage, disappoint, crush, thwart, destroy [➡ MAKE IMPOSSIBLE; 276] *Opposite*: encourage **9** v **shatter**, ruin, crush, blight, destroy, spoil [➡ MAKE IMPOSSIBLE; 276] *Opposite*: bolster

dashboard type of **internal feature** [➡ INTERNAL PARTS OF A VEHICLE; 1146]

dashing 1 adj (*dated*) **spirited**, confident, jaunty, flamboyant, bold, dynamic, adventurous, daring, swashbuckling, gallant (*literary*) [➡ COURAGE; 498] *Opposite*: staid **2** adj **elegant**, stylish, chic, debonair, fashionable, smart, showy, striking [➡ WELL-GROOMED; 482] *Opposite*: dowdy

dashingly adv **adventurously**, dynamically, confidently, boldly, spiritedly, jauntily, self-confidently, flamboyantly, gallantly (*literary*) [➡ COURAGE; 498]

dastardly adj **low**, shameful, dishonorable, mean, reprehensible, ignoble, immoral, sneaky, cowardly, base, despicable [➡ MORALLY BAD OR IMPROPER; 775] *Opposite*: honorable

data n **information**, statistics, facts, figures, numbers, records, documents, files [➡ BASIC DETAILS; 688]

database n **data bank**, store, folder, list, archive, catalog, record [➡ COMPUTERS AND COMPUTING; 1127]

data processing n **information retrieval**, data handling, number-crunching (*slang*) [➡ COMPUTERS AND COMPUTING; 1127]

date 1 n **day**, day of the week, year, time [➡ TIMES OF YEAR; 88] **2** n **time**, point in time, period, era, day, epoch, age [➡ EPOCHS AND ERAS; 89] **3** n **meeting**, rendezvous, appointment, blind date, engagement, assignation, tryst, get-together (*informal*) [➡ MEETINGS AND ASSEMBLIES; 43] **4** type of **fruit** [➡ FRUIT AND VEGETABLES; 1176]

dated adj **old-fashioned**, old, behind the times, unfashionable, passé, outmoded, out, out-of-date, old hat (*informal*), square (*dated slang*) [➡ OLD, OLD-FASHIONED; 167] *Opposite*: up-to-date

dateline n **heading**, subheading, subhead, identification [➡ PARTS OF BOOKS AND DOCUMENTS; 593]

dative n type of **grammatical term** [➡ ASPECTS OF LANGUAGE; 682]

datum n [➡ BASIC DETAILS; 688]

daub 1 v **smear**, spread, slap, spatter, slop, splatter, apply, cover, paint [➡ DECORATE, ADORN, AND APPLY COATINGS; 405] **2** n **blot**, blotch, spot, splotch, stain [➡ AMOUNTS OF SOLID OR SEMI-SOLID; 115]

daughter type of **younger relative** [➡ YOUNGER GENERATION RELATIVES; 958]

daughter-in-law type of **in-law** [➡ RELATIVES BY MARRIAGE; 960]

daunt v **put off**, deter, discourage, intimidate, scare, frighten, overwhelm, dishearten, overawe, unnerve, unman, dismay, faze, subdue [➡ FRIGHTEN AND SHOCK; 568] *Opposite*: encourage

daunted adj [➡ INSECURITY AND LOSS OF COMPOSURE; 544]

daunting adj **intimidating**, unnerving, discouraging, frightening, overwhelming, formidable, disheartening, dismaying, demoralizing, scary (*informal*), fazing (*UK*) [➡ FRIGHTENING; 231] *Opposite*: heartening

dauntless (*literary*) adj **resolute**, determined, confident, fearless, bold, undaunted, valiant, indomitable, heroic, daring, stouthearted, intrepid (*literary or humorous*) [➡ COURAGE; 498] *Opposite*: timid

dauntlessness (*literary*) n [➡ COURAGE; 498]

davenport 1 type of **seating** [➡ FURNITURE; 858] **2** type of **table** [➡ FURNITURE; 858]

dawdle 1 v **loiter**, delay, linger, plod, lag, fall behind, dally, tarry [➡ MOVE SLOWLY; 314] *Opposite*: hurry **2** v **waste time**, hang around, dally, linger, delay, dilly-dally, loiter, shilly-shally, plod, lag behind, kill time, fritter away, procrastinate [➡ DELAY ACTION OR OCCURRENCE; 278] *Opposite*: hurry

dawdler 1 n **straggler**, stroller, wanderer, laggard, dallier, dilly-dallier, foot-dragger (*informal*), slowpoke (*informal*), moocher (*UK slang*) [➡ LAZY OR UNSUCCESSFUL PEOPLE; 948]

Opposite: leader **2** *n* **idler**, slacker, shirker, timewaster, shilly-shallier, lazybones (*informal*), goldbrick (*informal*), lollygagger (*dated*) [➡ LAZY OR UNSUCCESSFUL PEOPLE; 948]

dawdling **1** *n* **dilly-dallying**, shilly-shallying, delaying, tarrying, loitering, dragging your feet, lagging behind, lingering, stalling [➡ DELAY ACTION OR OCCURRENCE; 278] *Opposite*: haste **2** *adj* **slow**, sluggish, measured, leisurely, casual, deliberate, unhurried [➡ MOVING SLOWLY; 105] *Opposite*: hasty

dawn **1** *n* **sunrise**, crack of dawn, daybreak, first light, daylight, morning, sunup, cockcrow (*archaic or literary*) [➡ TIMES OF DAY; 87] *Opposite*: dusk **2** *n* **beginning**, start, birth, emergence, dawning, origin, genesis, advent, commencement (*formal*), inception (*formal*) [➡ BEGINNINGS; 53] *Opposite*: end **3** *v* **begin**, start, be born, emerge, originate, commence, appear [➡ SUDDENLY COME INTO EXISTENCE; 2] *Opposite*: end **4** *v* **occur**, cross your mind, register with, strike, become clear to, become apparent to [➡ UNDERSTAND AND GRASP; 759]

day **1** *n* **daylight hours**, daylight, daytime, sunlight hours [➡ TIMES OF DAY; 87] *Opposite*: night **2** *n* **date**, day of the week, calendar day [➡ TIMES OF YEAR; 88] **3** *n* **time**, era, period, generation, epoch, date, age [➡ TIMES OF YEAR; 88]

day after day *adv* **day in day out**, relentlessly, continually, constantly, without respite, persistently, ceaselessly, regularly [➡ PERMANENCE: WITHOUT END; 94] *Opposite*: intermittently

day bed *type of* **bed** [➡ FURNITURE; 858]

daybreak *n* **dawn**, crack of dawn, first light, daylight, morning, sunrise, sunup [➡ TIMES OF DAY; 87] *Opposite*: dusk

day by day *adv* **gradually**, slowly, little by little, bit by bit, step by step, progressively, steadily [➡ HAPPENING SLOWLY; 106] *Opposite*: all at once

daydream **1** *n* **reverie**, fantasy, musing, contemplation, dream, fancy, pipe dream [➡ DREAM, IMAGINE, AND FANTASIZE; 749] **2** *v* **dream**, have your head in the clouds, be miles away, be inattentive, fantasize, muse, be lost in thought, stare into space, contemplate, stargaze, imagine, zone out (*slang*), woolgather (*UK*) [➡ DREAM, IMAGINE, AND FANTASIZE; 749] *Opposite*: concentrate

daydreamer *n* **idealist**, dreamer, fantasist, visionary, woolgatherer [➡ LAZY OR UNSUCCESSFUL PEOPLE; 948]

daydreaming **1** *n* **reverie**, woolgathering, pensiveness, dreaminess, inattention, inattentiveness, negligence, preoccupation, distraction [➡ DREAM, IMAGINE, AND FANTASIZE; 749] *Opposite*: concentration **2** *adj* **fantasizing**, imagining, dreaming, dreamy, pensive, inattentive, negligent, preoccupied, distracted, in a world of your own, wandering, lost in thought, distant, unmindful, zoning out (*slang*), woolgathering (*UK*) [➡ PENSIVENESS AND INTEREST; 538] *Opposite*: concentrating

day in day out *adv* [➡ PERMANENCE: WITHOUT END; 94]

daylight **1** *n* **day**, daytime, sunshine, light of day, hours of daylight [➡ LIGHT; 1164] *Opposite*: nighttime **2** *n* **dawn**, crack of dawn, sunrise, daybreak, first light, morning, sunup, cockcrow (*archaic or literary*) [➡ TIMES OF DAY; 87] *Opposite*: dusk

day off *n* [➡ PERIODS OF REST; 91]

Day of Judgment *n* [➡ RELIGIOUS CONCEPTS; 776]

day out *n* **outing**, trip, spree, jaunt, tour, visit, day trip, break, excursion, journey, day away, field trip, away day (*UK*) [➡ TRAVEL: JOURNEYS AND TRIPS; 318]

day room *n* **lounge**, den, recreation room, seating area, reception room, sitting room [➡ TYPES OF ROOMS; 1097]

days gone by *n* **former times**, earlier times, previous times, days of old, olden days, yesteryear, past [➡ PAST; 84] *Opposite*: future

daytime *n* **day**, daylight, hours of daylight, morning, afternoon [➡ TIMES OF DAY; 87] *Opposite*: nighttime

day-to-day *adj* **everyday**, commonplace, daily, routine, usual, habitual, regular, customary [➡ ORDINARINESS; 244] *Opposite*: unusual

day trip *n* **excursion**, outing, day out, trip, field trip, visit, jaunt, tour [➡ TRAVEL: JOURNEYS AND TRIPS; 318]

day tripper *n* **tourist**, traveler, vacationer, sightseer, holidaymaker (*UK*) [➡ TRAVEL: TRAVELERS AND WALKERS; 319]

daze **1** *n* **confusion**, stupor, shock, bewilderment, bemusement, bafflement, astonishment, surprise [➡ CONFUSION, ANXIETY, AND WORRY; 540] **2** *v* **stun**, shock, astonish, astound, surprise, bemuse, confound, bewilder, baffle, stupefy, stagger, confuse [➡ CONFUSE AND BEWILDER; 571]

dazed *adj* **confused**, stunned, shocked, astonished, astounded, surprised, bemused, overcome, bewildered, stupefied, confounded, baffled [➡ CONFUSION, ANXIETY, AND WORRY; 540] *Opposite*: alert

dazzle **1** *v* **amaze**, astonish, astound, impress, overwhelm, stun, awe, dumbfound, hypnotize, take somebody's breath away, bowl over, overpower [➡ SURPRISE AND IMPRESS; 574] *Opposite*: bore **2** *v* **bedazzle**, blind, daze, confuse, overwhelm [➡ CONFUSE AND BEWILDER; 571] **3** *n* **glare**, brightness, reflection, blaze, brilliance [➡ DESCRIBING LIGHT; 1228]

dazzling **1** *adj* **stunning**, amazing, astounding, incredible, alluring, glittering, glittery, impressive, awing, overpowering [➡ EXTRAORDINARY: AMAZING; 204] *Opposite*: unimpressive **2** *adj* **bright**, glaring, glittering, blazing, luminous, fierce, intense [➡ DESCRIBING LIGHT; 1228] *Opposite*: dull

deactivate *v* **neutralize**, disable, switch off, turn off, disengage [➡ CAUSE TO STOP; 266] *Opposite*: activate

dead **1** *adj* **lifeless**, passed on, late, defunct, gone (*informal*), departed (*formal or literary*), deceased (*formal*) [➡ DEAD AND DYING; 925] *Opposite*: alive **2** *adj* **numb**, benumbed, stiff, insensitive, frozen, unresponsive [➡ TIRED, ASLEEP, AND UNCONSCIOUS; 738] *Opposite*: sensitive **3** *adj* **boring**, quiet, dull, uninteresting, deadly, flat [➡ BORING AND UNINTERESTING; 234] *Opposite*: exciting **4** *adj* **finished**, obsolete, over, ended, empty, exhausted, extinct, done with (*UK*) [➡ REDUNDANT AND USELESS; 240] *Opposite*: current **5** *adj* **silent**, blank, quiet, down, inactive, inert, extinct [➡ LACK OF ACTIVITY OR MOTION; 342] *Opposite*: live

dead as a dodo *adj* [➡ DEAD AND DYING; 925]

dead as a doornail *adj* [➡ DEAD AND DYING; 925]

deadbeat (*slang*) *n* **loafer**, idler, waster, ne'er-do-well, layabout, bum (*informal*) [➡ LAZY OR UNSUCCESSFUL PEOPLE; 948]

deaden *v* **soften**, dull, muffle, dampen, mute, stifle [➡ CHANGE OF INTENSITY: LESS; 395] *Opposite*: amplify

dead end 1 *n* **cul-de-sac**, blind alley, impasse, roadblock, no through road (*UK*) [➡ EXTREMITIES OF PHYSICAL OBJECTS; 1250] 2 *n* **block**, stalemate, standstill, impasse, deadlock, end of the road [➡ PROBLEMS; 256] 3 *type of* **secondary road** [➡ ROADS; 1106]

deadened *adj* **desensitized**, unfeeling, insensitive, insensible, numb, anesthetized, frozen [➡ TIRED, ASLEEP, AND UNCONSCIOUS; 738] *Opposite*: sensitive

deadhead *v* **take away**, cut off, remove [➡ EXTRACT AND SEVER; 341]

dead heat *n* **draw**, tie, photo finish, drawn game, stalemate, deuce [➡ RESULTS AND OUTCOMES; 83]

deadline *n* **time limit**, limit, goal, aim, target, cutoff date, closing date [➡ ENDS AND DEPARTURES; 54] *Opposite*: extension

deadlock *n* **impasse**, stalemate, gridlock, standstill, logjam, block, end of the road [➡ DIFFICULT SITUATIONS; 72]

deadly 1 *adv* **completely**, absolutely, extremely, very, perfectly, wholly, terribly [➡ CRITICALLY AND SERIOUSLY; 134] *Opposite*: slightly 2 *adj* **lethal**, fatal, terminal, mortal, poisonous, noxious, toxic [➡ DEADLY; 928] *Opposite*: harmless 3 *adj* (*informal*) **boring**, tedious, tiresome, dull, dead, uninteresting [➡ BORING AND UNINTERESTING; 234] *Opposite*: interesting 4 *adj* **extreme**, implacable, mortal, sworn, absolute, irreconcilable [➡ DANGEROUS; 236]

deadpan *adj* **unsmiling**, straight-faced, poker-faced, expressionless, blank, po-faced [➡ FACIAL EXPRESSIONS AND BLUSHING; 651] *Opposite*: expressive

dead ringer (*informal*) *n* **double**, doppelgänger, image, spitting image (*informal*), look-alike (*informal*) [➡ COPIES AND REPLICAS; 151] *Opposite*: opposite

dead to the world *adj* **asleep**, fast asleep, sound asleep, sleeping, sleeping like a baby, slumbering, napping, snoozing (*informal*) [➡ TIRED, ASLEEP, AND UNCONSCIOUS; 738] *Opposite*: awake

deaf 1 *adj* **hearing-impaired**, deafened, tone-deaf [➡ HEAR; 707] *Opposite*: hearing 2 *adj* **unresponsive**, indifferent, oblivious, heedless, unmoved, unaffected [➡ NEUTRALITY AND INDIFFERENCE; 553] *Opposite*: mindful

deafening *adj* **loud**, earsplitting, ear-piercing, booming, thunderous, resounding [➡ LOUD, HIGH, OR UNPLEASANT SOUNDS; 1266] *Opposite*: quiet

deal 1 *n* **transaction**, contract, agreement, arrangement, pact, treaty, covenant, compact [➡ EXCHANGE AND INTERCHANGE; 448] 2 *v* **distribute**, share out, give out, allocate, apportion, dispense, dole out (*informal*) [➡ DISPENSE, RATION, AND DISTRIBUTE; 434] *Opposite*: receive 3 *v* **trade**, do business, exchange, sell, transact business, hawk [➡ SELL; 441] *Opposite*: buy

dealer *n* **trader**, merchant, seller, broker, supplier, wholesaler [➡ PEOPLE INVOLVED IN FINANCE; 804]

dealership 1 *n* **charter**, authorization, agreement, right, license, franchise [➡ BUSINESS ENTERPRISES AND RELATED BODIES; 792] 2 *n* **premises**, showroom, offices, workplace, workshop, site, place of business [➡ PLACE OF EMPLOYMENT; 832]

dealings *n* **transactions**, contact, communication, business, connections, relations [➡ COMMUNICATION; 602]

deal out *v* **give out**, issue, distribute, mete out, administer, dispense, allocate, assign, dish out (*informal*), dole out (*informal*) [➡ DISPENSE, RATION, AND DISTRIBUTE; 434] *Opposite*: collect

deal with *v* **cope**, manage, handle, see to, take care of, sort out, take in hand, contend [➡ CARRY OUT AN ACTION; 269]

dear 1 *adj* **beloved**, cherished, prized, valued, precious, loved [➡ POPULAR AND WANTED; 220] *Opposite*: hated 2 *n* **darling**, sweetheart, dearest, beloved, pet, love [➡ ENDEARMENTS; 656] 3 *adj* **expensive**, costly, extortionate, valuable, exorbitant, pricey (*informal*) [➡ EXPENSIVE AND OVERPRICED; 247] *Opposite*: cheap

dearest *n* **love**, sweetheart, pet, precious, sugar (*informal*), honey (*informal*), sweetie (*informal*) [➡ ENDEARMENTS; 656]

dearly *adv* **greatly**, extremely, exceedingly, profoundly, sincerely, deeply [➡ TO A GREAT EXTENT; 132]

dearth *n* **lack**, shortage, scarcity, drought, famine, want, deficiency, absence, need [➡ TOO FEW, TOO LITTLE; 122] *Opposite*: glut

See Compare and Contrast at **lack**.

death 1 *n* **passing**, bereavement, loss, demise (*formal*), decease (*formal*), expiry (*formal or literary*) [➡ DEATH AND BEREAVEMENT; 927] *Opposite*: birth 2 *n* **end**, fall, downfall, ruin, collapse, overthrow, demise (*formal*) [➡ ENDS AND DEPARTURES; 54] *Opposite*: beginning 3 *n* **fatality**, casualty, loss of life, killing, murder, mortality (*archaic*) [➡ DEAD PERSON; 926] *Opposite*: birth

deathblow *n* **body blow**, final blow, last straw, last nail in the coffin, end, destruction [➡ ENDS AND DEPARTURES; 54]

death cap *type of* **fungus** [➡ MICROORGANISMS, FUNGI, AND ALGAE; 1023]

death knell *n* **finish**, end point, end of the road, point of no return, last straw, last nail in the coffin, death warrant [➡ ENDS AND DEPARTURES; 54]

deathless *adj* **eternal**, timeless, immortal, everlasting, undying, perpetual, ceaseless [➡ PERMANENCE: WITHOUT END; 94] *Opposite*: mortal

deathlike *adj* **skeletal**, gaunt, ashen, spectral, pallid, corpselike, deathly, cadaverous (*formal or literary*), ghastly (*literary*) [➡ COMPLEXION; 480]

deathly 1 *adj* **deadly**, deathlike, tomblike, deep, stony, ghastly (*literary*) [➡ EMOTIONALLY UNPLEASANT AND UPSETTING; 227] 2 *adv* **extremely**, intensely, deadly, intensively, absolutely, totally [➡ CRITICALLY AND SERIOUSLY; 134] *Opposite*: slightly

death mask *n* **effigy**, cast, head, model, sculpture, mold [➡ SCULPTURE; 902]

death rattle *n* **gurgle**, rattle, rasp, wheeze, croak, gasp [➡ SOUNDS MADE BY PEOPLE; 1262]

death's head moth *type of* **moth** [➡ MOTHS AND BUTTERFLIES; 1015]

death toll *n* **fatalities**, death rate, mortality rate, fatality rate, loss of life, mortality [➡ DEAD PERSON; 926]

deathtrap (*informal*) *n* **safety risk**, hazard, minefield, pitfall, health hazard, firetrap, threat to life and limb [➡ PROBLEMS; 256]

death warrant *n* **death knell**, end, finish, end point, end of the road, point of no return, final blow, last straw, last nail in the coffin [➡ ENDS AND DEPARTURES; 54]

deathwatch beetle *type of* **beetle** [➡ BEETLES AND WEEVILS; 1016]

debacle *n* **disaster**, catastrophe, fiasco, shambles, tragedy, calamity, misfortune, farce [➡ DISASTERS; 252] *Opposite*: success

debar *v* **exclude**, expel, bar, ban, prohibit, veto, refuse, disqualify, disallow [➡ REFUSE PERMISSION AND NOT ALLOW; 670] *Opposite*: admit

debark *v* **disembark**, alight, go ashore, land, get off, arrive [➡ ARRIVE BY TRANSPORT; 14] *Opposite*: embark

debarkation *n* **disembarkation**, alighting, going ashore, landing, getting off, arrival [➡ ARRIVAL; 13]

debase 1 *v* **degrade**, impair, adulterate, sully, corrupt, taint, tarnish, soil, defile (*formal*) [➡ WORSEN SOMETHING; 380] *Opposite*: purify 2 *v* **humiliate**, demean, degrade, shame, humble, disgrace, dishonor, lower [➡ UPSET, DISTRESS, AND HUMILIATE; 567] *Opposite*: glorify

debasement 1 *n* **humiliation**, degradation, disgrace, shame, disparagement, ignominy, dishonor [➡ EMBARRASSMENT AND HUMILIATION; 542] *Opposite*: glorification 2 *n* **ruination**, adulteration, corruption, defilement, tarnishing,

sullying, spoilage [➡ WORSEN SOMETHING; 380] *Opposite*: purification

debatable *adj* **arguable**, dubious, controversial, doubtful, contentious, unsettled, undecided, questionable, disputable, open to question, undetermined [➡ UNCERTAIN; 175] *Opposite*: settled

debatably *adv* **arguably**, disputably, questionably, dubiously, doubtfully, maybe, uncertainly, possibly, perhaps [➡ POSSIBLE AND PROBABLE; 177] *Opposite*: indisputably

debate 1 *v* **discuss**, argue, dispute, deliberate, contest, question [➡ TWO-WAY COMMUNICATION; 607] *Opposite*: conclude 2 *n* **discussion**, argument, dispute, examination, consideration, deliberation (*formal*) [➡ NEGOTIATION AND DEBATE; 46] *Opposite*: conclusion 3 *v* **ponder**, wonder, deliberate, consider, contemplate, meditate, think over, weigh up (*UK*) [➡ QUESTION THINGS; 751] *Opposite*: decide

debater *n* **speaker**, orator, public speaker, disputant, arguer [➡ SPEAKERS AND ORATORS; 603]

debauched *adj* **decadent**, dissolute, degenerate, dissipated, immoral, self-indulgent [➡ MORALLY BAD OR IMPROPER; 775] *Opposite*: moral

debauchee *n* [➡ PLEASURE-SEEKERS AND HEDONISTS; 886]

debauchery *n* **decadence**, dissoluteness, immorality, self-indulgence [➡ MORALLY BAD OR IMPROPER; 775] *Opposite*: morality

debilitate *v* **weaken**, incapacitate, enervate, drain, hamper, encumber, hinder [➡ AVOID, PREVENT, LIMIT, AND CONTROL; 277] *Opposite*: fortify

debilitated *adj* **weakened**, incapacitated, enervated, drained, hampered, encumbered, hindered [➡ UNFIT AND WEAK; 739] *Opposite*: fortified

See Compare and Contrast at **weak**.

debilitating *adj* **weakening**, incapacitating, enervating, draining, devastating, sapping [➡ PHYSICALLY UNPLEASANT; 226] *Opposite*: refreshing

debility *n* **weakness**, incapacity, frailty, encumbrance, ineffectiveness, enfeeblement, enervation [➡ FAULTS, FLAWS, AND WEAKNESSES; 251] *Opposite*: strength

debit 1 *v* **deduct**, take out, withdraw, subtract, charge, record [➡ GET MONEY OR REWARD; 421] *Opposite*: credit 2 *n* **withdrawal**, subtraction, deduction, debt, charge, record, bill [➡ ACCOUNTING, BANKING, AND BUDGETING; 799] *Opposite*: credit

debonair *adj* **suave**, elegant, refined, charming, well-groomed, urbane, cultured, dashing, cultivated [➡ WELL-GROOMED; 482] *Opposite*: graceless

debouch *v* **emerge**, move out, spread out, exit, come out, issue [➡ EMIT AND EMANATE; 361] *Opposite*: confine

debrief *v* **question**, interrogate, interview, examine, quiz, probe [➡ ASK PEOPLE QUESTIONS; 666]

debriefing *n* **interrogation**, questioning, interview, examination, probing, quizzing, sounding out [➡ ASK PEOPLE QUESTIONS; 666] *Opposite*: briefing

debris *n* **wreckage**, remains, fragments, rubble, waste, garbage, trash, flotsam and jetsam [➡ JUNK AND USELESS OBJECTS; 1249]

debt 1 *n* **arrears**, liability, debit, balance, balance due, bill [➡ OWE AND DESERVE; 465] *Opposite*: credit 2 *n* **obligation**, duty, responsibility, dues, liability, commitment [➡ RESPONSIBILITY; 170]

debtor *n* **borrower**, mortgagor, insolvent, defaulter, pledger, nonpayer [➡ PEOPLE INVOLVED IN FINANCE; 804]

debug *v* **clear up**, correct, sort out, repair, fix, restore, service, mend [➡ REPAIR AND MEND; 376] *Opposite*: corrupt

debunk *v* **expose**, show up, deflate, demystify, discredit, set straight, throw light on, lay bare [➡ DENY AND REJECT; 644] *Opposite*: perpetuate

debut *n* **entrance**, introduction, unveiling, presentation, inauguration, coming out [➡ BEGINNINGS; 53] *Opposite*: retirement

decade *n* **period**, era, time, epoch [➡ EPOCHS AND ERAS; 89]

decadence *n* **corruption**, debauchery, depravity, dissolution, self-indulgence, profligacy, dissipation, excess [➡ MORALLY BAD OR IMPROPER; 775] *Opposite*: decency

decadent *adj* **debauched**, corrupt, depraved, dissolute, degenerate, immoral, licentious, profligate, self-indulgent [➡ PLEASURE-SEEKING AND EXCESS; 885] *Opposite*: innocent

decadently *adv* **dissolutely**, degenerately, immorally, profligately, self-indulgently, licentiously (*formal*) [➡ PLEASURE-SEEKING AND EXCESS; 885] *Opposite*: innocently

decaf *type of* **coffee** [➡ DRINKS; 1187]

decagram *type of* **metric unit** [➡ SIZE AND DIMENSIONS; 1192]

decaliter *type of* **metric unit** [➡ SIZE AND DIMENSIONS; 1192]

decameter *type of* **metric unit** [➡ SIZE AND DIMENSIONS; 1192]

decamp *v* **run away**, run off, escape, flee, abscond, leave, retreat, desert, flit (*UK*) [➡ RUN AWAY AND AVOID; 10] *Opposite*: stay

decant *v* **pour**, pour out, transfer, empty, empty out, draw off [➡ EMPTY AND UNLOAD; 407] *Opposite*: fill

decanter *n* **carafe**, flask, vessel, bottle, pitcher, container [➡ TABLEWARE, FLATWARE, AND KITCHENWARE; 861]

decapitate *v* **behead**, guillotine, execute, amputate, truncate, kill [➡ KILL; 923]

decapitation *n* **beheading**, amputation, killing, guillotining, execution [➡ CAUSES OF DEATH; 921]

decathlon *type of* **track and field** [➡ HOBBIES, GAMES, AND SPORTS; 875]

decay 1 *v* **decompose**, rot, fester, grow moldy, molder, crumble, putrefy, corrode, waste away, perish (*UK*) [➡ GO BAD AND CORRODE; 390] 2 *v* **decline**, degenerate, deteriorate, fall off, dwindle, wane [➡ CEASE TO EXIST; 22] *Opposite*: flourish 3 *n* **deterioration**, decline, degeneration, falling-off, falloff, dwindling, waning [➡ ENDS AND DEPARTURES; 54] *Opposite*: growth 4 *n* **decomposition**, rot, mold, rotting, putrefaction, corrosion [➡ WORSEN SOMETHING; 380]

decayed *adj* **decomposed**, rotten, rotting, putrefied,

moldy, corroded, perished (*UK*) [➡ DECAYING OR INFESTED; 1236] *Opposite*: fresh

decaying *adj* **decomposing**, rotting, rotten, putrefying, moldy, crumbling, moldering [➡ DECAYING OR INFESTED; 1236] *Opposite*: fresh

decease (*formal*) *n* **death**, passing, departure, release, demise (*formal*), expiry (*formal or literary*) [➡ DEATH AND BEREAVEMENT; 927] *Opposite*: birth

deceased (*formal*) 1 *n* **corpse**, cadaver, body, decedent (*formal*), departed (*formal or literary*) [➡ DEAD PERSON; 926] 2 *adj* **dead**, late, lifeless, defunct, extinct, departed (*formal or literary*) [➡ DEAD AND DYING; 925] *Opposite*: alive

See Compare and Contrast at **dead**.

deceit *n* **dishonesty**, treachery, deceitfulness, deception, trickery, sham, pretense, cheating, duplicity, falseness, guile, fraud [➡ DECEPTION AND LIES; 660] *Opposite*: honesty

deceitful *adj* **dishonest**, deceiving, fraudulent, untrustworthy, cunning, lying, devious, cheating, faithless [➡ DECEITFUL; 513] *Opposite*: honest

deceitfully *adv* **dishonestly**, cunningly, fraudulently, deviously, treacherously, craftily, by deceit, faithlessly [➡ FALSE AND UNREAL; 173] *Opposite*: honestly

deceitfulness *n* **dishonesty**, deceit, treachery, lies, falseness, fraudulence, untrustworthiness, faithlessness [➡ DECEITFUL; 513] *Opposite*: honesty

deceive 1 *v* **mislead**, betray, trick, take in, lie to, swindle, double-cross, con, misinform, cheat, hoodwink, defraud, dupe, delude [➡ DECEPTION AND LIES; 660] 2 *v* **cheat**, two-time, betray, step out (*informal*), cuckold (*literary*) [➡ DECEPTION AND LIES; 660]

deceiver *n* **liar**, fraud, swindler, cheat, quack, huckster, con artist (*informal*), fraudster (*UK*) [➡ PEOPLE WHO DECEIVE; 661]

deceiving *adj* **misleading**, lying, cheating, devious, deceptive, unreliable, dishonest, illusory, fraudulent, fallacious, faithless, specious, cunning, plausible, glib, false, pretending, insincere, untrustworthy [➡ DECEITFUL; 513] *Opposite*: honest

decelerate *v* **slow down**, slow, slow up, brake, lose speed, reduce speed, lose pace [➡ CHANGE OF SPEED: LESS; 397] *Opposite*: accelerate

deceleration *n* **slowing down**, slowing up, slowing, braking, checking, retardation [➡ CHANGE OF SPEED: LESS; 397] *Opposite*: acceleration

decency 1 *n* **politeness**, decorum, decorousness, civility, courtesy, politesse, correctness, dignity [➡ GOOD MANNERS AND SOCIAL SKILLS; 520] *Opposite*: incivility 2 *n* **modesty**, respectability, uprightness, integrity, wholesomeness, propriety, righteousness, morality, honesty [➡ MORALLY GOOD; 774] *Opposite*: decadence

decent 1 *adj* **moral**, honest, virtuous, wholesome, demure, modest, honorable, pure (*literary*) [➡ MORALLY GOOD; 774] *Opposite*: decadent 2 *adj* **good**, right, proper, correct, suitable, appropriate, fitting [➡ APPROPRIATE, SUITABLE, AND ADVISABLE; 184] *Opposite*: inappropriate 3 *adj* **reasonable**, respectable, adequate, sizable, generous, ample, moderate, passable, sufficient [➡ACCEPTABLE AND PASSABLE; 219] *Opposite*: inadequate **4** *adj* (*informal*) **dressed**, clothed, clad, garbed, covered, attired (*formal*) [➡DRESS, WEAR, AND UNDRESS; 868] *Opposite*: undressed **5** *adj* **respectable**, upright, polite, civilized, well-mannered, well-brought-up, courteous, considerate [➡GOOD MANNERS AND SOCIAL SKILLS; 520]

decently **1** *adv* **morally**, respectably, demurely, properly, virtuously, righteously [➡MORALLY GOOD; 774] *Opposite*: improperly **2** *adv* **politely**, decorously, graciously, civilly, affably, courteously, correctly [➡GOOD MANNERS AND SOCIAL SKILLS; 520] *Opposite*: rudely

decentralization *n* **devolution**, subsidiarity, regionalization, delegation, reorganization [➡STYLES AND SYSTEMS OF GOVERNMENT; 806] *Opposite*: centralization

decentralize *v* **devolve**, regionalize, reorganize, disperse, distribute, spread out [➡SEPARATE AND DIVIDE; 401] *Opposite*: centralize

deception **1** *n* **dishonesty**, duplicity, deceptiveness, deceit, cheating, trickery [➡DECEPTION AND LIES; 660] *Opposite*: truthfulness **2** *n* **trick**, ruse, sham, fraud, con, pretext [➡DECEPTION AND LIES; 660]

deceptive *adj* **misleading**, illusory, deceiving, dishonest, false, unreliable, illusive, pretended, disingenuous, devious, deceitful, fraudulent, phony, spurious, specious [➡FALSE AND UNREAL; 173] *Opposite*: reliable

deceptiveness *n* **falseness**, falsity, disingenuousness, deviousness, spuriousness, speciousness, deceitfulness, fraudulence, phoniness, unreliableness, unreliability, inaccurateness, inaccuracy, illusoriness, unrepresentativeness [➡FALSE AND UNREAL; 173] *Opposite*: reliability

decide **1** *v* **make a decision**, choose, come to a decision, make your mind up, settle on, fix on, agree, resolve, adopt, elect, select, plump for, pick, take, opt, go for (*informal*) [➡MAKE DECISIONS AND CHOICES; 752] *Opposite*: equivocate **2** *v* **settle**, determine, conclude, resolve, decree, rule [➡MAKE DECISIONS AND CHOICES; 752] *Opposite*: put off

decided **1** *adj* **obvious**, definite, absolute, categorical, unquestionable, unambiguous, unequivocal, certain, distinct, particular, clear-cut, unmistakable, indisputable [➡CERTAIN; 174] *Opposite*: unclear **2** *adj* **determined**, resolute, decisive, firm, sure, certain, unfaltering, unwavering, definite, unhesitating, emphatic [➡CERTAINTY; 561] *Opposite*: hesitant

decidedly *adv* **categorically**, definitely, absolutely, distinctly, particularly, unquestionably, unambiguously, unequivocally, emphatically, undoubtedly, obviously, unmistakably [➡ABSOLUTE AND ABSOLUTELY; 133] *Opposite*: possibly

deciding *adj* **determining**, decisive, conclusive, key, pivotal, significant, critical, crucial [➡MOST IMPORTANT AND MAIN; 193] *Opposite*: insignificant

deciduous tree *n* [➡PLANTS AND TREES; 1024]

---

deciduous tree

◆ *types of deciduous trees*
acacia, alder, ash, aspen, baobab, beech, birch, chestnut, dogwood, elder, elm, ginkgo, gleditsia, hawthorn, hickory, hornbeam, horse chestnut, Judas tree, laburnum, lime, magnolia, maple, mesquite, mimosa, mulberry, oak, plane tree, poplar, rowan, sassafras, silver birch, sumac, sycamore, teak, tulip tree, willow

decigram *type of* **metric unit** [➡SIZE AND DIMENSIONS; 1192]

deciliter *type of* **metric unit** [➡SIZE AND DIMENSIONS; 1192]

decimal *n* **number**, fraction, unit [➡SYMBOLS, SIGNS, AND NUMBERS; 596]

decimate *v* **devastate**, destroy, annihilate, ruin, cut a swath through, slaughter, lay waste, demolish, cut down [➡DESTRUCTION AND DEMOLITION; 359]

decimation *n* **devastation**, destruction, slaughter, annihilation, ruin, demolition, obliteration [➡CAUSES OF DEATH; 921]

decimeter *type of* **metric unit** [➡SIZE AND DIMENSIONS; 1192]

decipher *v* **decode**, decrypt, interpret, translate, make out, work out, read, crack, make sense of, figure out, puzzle out, untangle [➡SOLVE AND INTERPRET; 760] *Opposite*: encode

decipherable *adj* **readable**, legible, intelligible, comprehensible, understandable, fathomable, identifiable, soluble, solvable, resolvable, clear [➡CONCISE AND CLEAR; 202] *Opposite*: unintelligible

decision **1** *n* **choice**, result, conclusion, verdict, pronouncement, judgment, resolution, assessment, evaluation, ruling, finding, outcome, decree [➡MAKE DECISIONS AND CHOICES; 752] **2** *n* **determination**, resolve, firmness, willpower, strength of mind, strength of will, certitude, surety, resolution, decisiveness [➡CERTAINTY; 561] *Opposite*: indecision

decisive **1** *adj* **conclusive**, pivotal, key, critical, significant, crucial, vital, influential, important, convincing, final, definitive, authoritative [➡IMPORTANT; 194] *Opposite*: insignificant **2** *adj* **strong-minded**, resolute, determined, certain, clear-sighted, focused, positive, earnest, purposeful, definite, firm [➡CERTAINTY; 561] *Opposite*: uncertain

decisively **1** *adv* **conclusively**, authoritatively, once and for all, finally, definitively [➡IMPORTANT; 194] **2** *adv* **resolutely**, determinedly, assertively, unfalteringly, unwaveringly, positively, definitely, firmly [➡INTENTIONAL AND DELIBERATE; 279] *Opposite*: uncertainly

decisiveness *n* **resoluteness**, determination, conclusiveness, authoritativeness, positiveness, purposefulness, firmness, certainty, definiteness [➡CERTAINTY; 561] *Opposite*: indecisiveness

deck **1** *part of* **ship or boat** [➡PARTS OF A SHIP OR BOAT; 1151] **2** *n* **level**, floor, surface, area, sun deck, car deck, top deck [➡PARTS OF A SHIP OR BOAT; 1151] **3** *v* (*informal*) **hit**, knock down, knock over, floor, thump, punch, strike [➡PHYSICAL ATTACK AND PUNISHMENT; 415] **4** *v* (*literary*) **adorn**, decorate, hang, cover, wreathe, dress, clothe, garb, bedeck (*literary*) [➡DECORATE, ADORN, AND APPLY COATINGS; 405] *Opposite*: strip

deck chair *type of* **seating** [➡FURNITURE; 858]

deck hand *n* **sailor**, seaman, rating (*UK*) [➡ TRAVEL: TRAVELERS AND WALKERS; 319]

declaim *v* **hold forth**, pronounce, proclaim, declare, utter, sermonize, pontificate, trumpet, state, assert, deliver, orate (*formal*) [➡ INSTRUCT AND TEACH; 609] *Opposite*: mutter

declamatory *adj* **dramatic**, formal, oratorical, rhetorical, theatrical, pompous, melodramatic, booming, arresting [➡ ELOQUENT, TALKATIVE, AND LONG-WINDED; 632] *Opposite*: low-key

declaration *n* **statement**, announcement, assertion, speech, pronouncement, affirmation, testimony, deposition, avowal (*formal*) [➡ ONE-WAY COMMUNICATION; 49]

declare *v* **announce**, state, speak out, assert, affirm, pronounce, proclaim [➡ INFORM, ANNOUNCE, AND ISSUE; 611]

déclassé *adj* [➡ CLASS STATUS; 889]

declassification *n* **release**, publication, open access, derestriction, decontrol, delimitation (*formal*) [➡ INFORM, ANNOUNCE, AND ISSUE; 611] *Opposite*: restriction

declassify *v* **release**, publish, derestrict, open up, bring out, make public [➡ INFORM, ANNOUNCE, AND ISSUE; 611] *Opposite*: classify

decline **1** *v* **refuse**, turn down, reject, pass up, beg off, eschew, spurn, take a rain check (*informal*) [➡ FORGO AND DENY ONESELF; 449] *Opposite*: accept **2** *v* **weaken**, fail, deteriorate, degenerate, fall off, decay, wane, drop, wilt, go to seed, flag, sink, worsen [➡ DISAPPEAR; 4] *Opposite*: improve **3** *n* **deterioration**, falling-off, falloff, decay, fall, degeneration, regression, decrease [➡ FAILURE; 77] *Opposite*: improvement

declining *adj* **deteriorating**, decreasing, lessening, falling, diminishing, weakening, waning, failing, fading, flagging, dwindling, disappearing, vanishing, worsening, sinking, abating (*formal or literary*) [➡ CEASE TO EXIST; 22] *Opposite*: improving

decode *v* **decipher**, make out, make sense of, interpret, translate, decrypt, work out, crack, puzzle out [➡ SOLVE AND INTERPRET; 760] *Opposite*: encode

decoder *n* **cryptographer**, decipherer, interpreter, translator [➡ PEOPLE WHO WORK WITH LANGUAGE AND CODE; 854]

décolletage *part of* **garment** [➡ PARTS OF A GARMENT; 870]

décolleté *adj* **low-necked**, low-cut, plunging, low, revealing [➡ DESCRIBING CLOTHES; 869]

decommission *v* **retire**, mothball, withdraw, take out, neutralize, discharge [➡ REVOKE STATUS; 459] *Opposite*: introduce

decompose *v* **rot**, decay, crumble, get moldy, fester, molder, putrefy, spoil, go off (*UK*) [➡ GO BAD AND CORRODE; 390]

decomposed *adj* **rotten**, disintegrated, decayed, putrid, putrefied, fetid, spoiled, moldy, perished (*UK*) [➡ DECAYING OR INFESTED; 1236] *Opposite*: fresh

decomposing *adj* **rotting**, disintegrating, decaying, putrid, putrefying, fetid, crumbling, spoiling, festering, moldering, moldy, sour, stale, going bad, rancid, infected, diseased, bad, rank (*literary*), off (*UK*), going off (*UK*), perishing (*UK*) [➡ DECAYING OR INFESTED; 1236] *Opposite*: fresh

decomposition *n* **decay**, rottenness, putrefaction, breakdown, disintegration, corrosion, fetidness, putridness, moldiness, rot [➡ GO BAD AND CORRODE; 390] *Opposite*: soundness

deconstruct *v* **analyze**, critique, criticize, decompose, review, take apart (*informal*) [➡ EXAMINE AND ASSESS; 753]

decontaminate *v* **cleanse**, clean up, clean, purify, disinfect, fumigate, neutralize [➡ CLEAN AND POLISH; 403] *Opposite*: contaminate

decontrol *v* **deregulate**, delimit, free, set free, loosen [➡ FREEDOM AND LIBERTY; 208] *Opposite*: control

decor *n* **decoration**, furnishings, interior decoration, scheme, design, style, ornamentation, color scheme [➡ ORNAMENTS AND DECORATIONS; 1248]

decorate **1** *v* **beautify**, adorn, ornament, embellish, trim, garnish, wreathe, garland, enhance, festoon, deck (*literary*), bedeck (*literary*), array (*literary*) [➡ DECORATE, ADORN, AND APPLY COATINGS; 405] *Opposite*: strip **2** *v* **paint**, smarten up, do up, spruce, fix up [➡ IMPROVE APPEARANCE; 379] **3** *v* **honor**, award, garland, recognize, acknowledge [➡ CONFER STATUS; 458]

decorated *adj* **ornamented**, ornate, adorned, festooned, draped, wreathed, encircled, edged, inset, picked out, sequined, veneered, carved, beaded, etched, framed, tinted, painted, dyed, enameled, swathed, garlanded, trimmed, encrusted, sewn, bead-trimmed, inscribed, bordered, patterned, incised, stitched, bedecked (*literary*), decked (*literary*), bejeweled (*literary*) [➡ DECORATE, ADORN, AND APPLY COATINGS; 405] *Opposite*: plain

Decorated *type of* **pre-20th-century architecture** [➡ BUILDING AND ARCHITECTURE; 1076]

decoration **1** *n* **beautification**, adornment, ornament, ornamentation, embellishment, trimming [➡ IMPROVE APPEARANCE; 379] **2** *n* **feature**, festoon, beading, border, carving, garland, sequin, wreath [➡ ORNAMENTS AND DECORATIONS; 1248] **3** *n* **honor**, medal, award, sash, ribbon, emblem [➡ REWARDS AND AWARDS; 439]

decorative *adj* **ornamental**, pretty, attractive, pleasing to the eye, enhancing, ornate, embellished [➡ BEAUTY AND ATTRACTIVENESS; 189] *Opposite*: ugly

decorous *adj* **well-mannered**, well-behaved, good, correct, modest, demure, sedate, seemly, proper, appropriate, respectable, restrained, suitable [➡ GOOD MANNERS AND SOCIAL SKILLS; 520] *Opposite*: improper

decorousness *n* [➡ GOOD MANNERS AND SOCIAL SKILLS; 520]

decorum *n* **dignity**, good behavior, propriety, sedateness, modesty, appropriateness, correctness, demureness, politesse, restraint, politeness, tact, gentility [➡ GOOD MANNERS AND SOCIAL SKILLS; 520] *Opposite*: abandon

decoy **1** *n* **lure**, trap, snare, trick, distraction, bait, red herring, inducement, smoke screen [➡ REPRESENTATIONS AND GENERAL EXAMPLES; 65] **2** *v* **entice**, lure, lead astray, distract, entrap, ensnare, bait, allure [➡ DECEPTION AND LIES; 660]

decrease **1** *v* **reduce**, cut, diminish, cut down, contract, shrink [➡ CHANGE OF SIZE: SMALLER; 393] *Opposite*: increase **2** *v* **diminish**, decline, dwindle, subside, lessen, fall, drop off (*informal*) [➡ DISAPPEAR; 4] **3** *n* **reduction**, cut, diminution, lessening, decline, shrinkage, drop, fall, loss, cutback [➞CHANGE OF SIZE: SMALLER; 393] *Opposite*: increase

decreasing *adj* diminishing, declining, reducing, dwindling, shrinking, lessening, falling, subsiding [➞CHANGE OF SIZE: SMALLER; 393] *Opposite*: increasing

decree 1 *n* ruling, verdict, announcement, pronouncement, declaration, judgment, diktat, order, law, command, proclamation, statute [➞REQUEST AND DEMAND; 663] *Opposite*: request 2 *v* command, rule, pronounce, announce, dictate, declare, order, lay down the law, authorize, proclaim, direct (*formal*) [➞REQUEST AND DEMAND; 663]

decrepit 1 *adj* dilapidated, crumbling, decaying, falling to pieces, falling apart, on its last legs, broken-down, battered, rickety [➞IN BAD REPAIR; 1234] *Opposite*: pristine 2 *adj* (*archaic or humorous*) old, feeble, frail, weak, infirm [➞UNFIT AND WEAK; 739] *Opposite*: vigorous

See Compare and Contrast at **weak**.

decrepitude 1 *n* decay, dilapidation, ruin, shabbiness [➞IN BAD REPAIR; 1234] *Opposite*: soundness 2 *n* infirmity, frailty, feebleness, weakness, debility, decline [➞UNFIT AND WEAK; 739]

decrescendo *type of* musical term [➞MUSICAL TERMS; 912]

decriminalization *n* legalization, acceptance, allowance, toleration, sanction [➞TRIAL, PUNISHMENT, AND LEGAL OUTCOMES; 819] *Opposite*: criminalization

decriminalize *v* make legal, legalize, authorize, sanction, permit, accept, allow, tolerate [➞PERMIT AND ALLOW; 669] *Opposite*: outlaw

decriminalized *adj* [➞LEGAL AND LEGITIMATE; 815]

See Compare and Contrast at **legal**.

decry *v* criticize, complain, belittle, disparage, deprecate, run down, denounce, rail, condemn [➞PROTEST AND EXPRESS DISAPPROVAL; 642] *Opposite*: praise

decrypt *v* [➞THE INTERNET; 1128]

dedicate 1 *v* reserve, devote, set aside, earmark, give over to [➞GIVE AND PROVIDE; 430] 2 *v* give, commit, devote, consecrate, pledge, donate, offer, bestow (*formal*) [➞GIVE AND PROVIDE; 430]

dedicated *adj* committed, devoted, steadfast, loyal, faithful, enthusiastic, keen, staunch, stalwart, out-and-out [➞HARD-WORKING AND COMMITTED; 500] *Opposite*: uncommitted

dedicatedly *adv* wholeheartedly, loyally, steadfastly, devotedly, enthusiastically, unreservedly, faithfully, stalwartly, staunchly [➞HARD-WORKING AND COMMITTED; 500] *Opposite*: half-heartedly

dedication *n* devotion, commitment, enthusiasm, keenness, perseverance, allegiance, loyalty, ardor, staunchness, devotedness [➞ENERGY AND ENTHUSIASM; 496]

deduce 1 *v* conclude, judge, suppose, reckon, gather, deem (*formal*) [➞HAVE AN OPINION OF SOMETHING; 756] 2 *v* infer, assume, presume, reason, construe, figure out, work out, realize, comprehend, understand [➞DEVELOP THEORIES AND REASON; 744]

Compare and Contrast: *deduce, infer, assume, reason, conclude, work out, figure out*

CORE MEANING: to reach a logical conclusion on the basis of information

deduce to reach a conclusion using available knowledge; *infer* to draw a conclusion from specific circumstances or evidence; *assume* to take a premise or information as true without checking or confirming it; *reason* to consider information and use it to reach a conclusion in a logical way; *conclude* to form an opinion or make a judgment after much consideration; *work out* to find a solution or explanation by careful thought or reasoning; *figure out* to find a solution or reach a conclusion by careful thought or reasoning.

deduct *v* subtract, take away, take, remove, abstract, withhold, decrease by [➞REMOVE SOMETHING; 338] *Opposite*: add

deduction 1 *n* subtraction, removal, withdrawal, abstraction, contribution, payment [➞REMOVE SOMETHING; 338] *Opposite*: addition 2 *n* inference, assumption, conclusion, presumption, judgment, reasoning, supposition, interpretation, analysis [➞IDEAS AND THOUGHTS; 770]

deductive *adj* logical, inferential, reasonable, empirical, rational [➞THE NATURE OF IDEAS; 771] *Opposite*: illogical

deed 1 *n* action, feat, act, endeavor, exploit, accomplishment, achievement, effort [➞ACTIONS OR UNDERTAKINGS; 259] 2 *n* document, title deed, title, charter, record, certificate, lease, voucher [➞OFFICIAL DOCUMENTS; 586]

deem (*formal*) *v* think, believe, consider, estimate, suppose, reason, judge, reckon, regard, hold, view [➞HAVE AN OPINION OF SOMETHING; 756]

deep 1 *adj* bottomless, profound, unfathomable, subterranean, cavernous, yawning, abysmal [➞DEPTH: DEEP; 1201] *Opposite*: shallow 2 *adj* low, rumbling, booming, sonorous, resonant, rich [➞SOFT, LOW, OR PLEASANT SOUNDS; 1265] *Opposite*: shrill 3 *adj* profound, unfathomable, multifaceted, multilayered, mysterious, meaningful [➞INTERESTING AND MEANINGFUL; 190] *Opposite*: facile 4 *adj* deep-seated, innate, inherent, entrenched, subconscious, deep-rooted, hidden [➞THE NATURE OF IDEAS; 771] *Opposite*: superficial 5 *adj* intense, profound, concentrated, immersed, absorbed [➞STRENGTH; 201] *Opposite*: superficial 6 *adj* hidden, secret, arcane, mysterious, silent, untold, inscrutable [➞SECRET AND UNKNOWN; 179] *Opposite*: open

deepen 1 *v* intensify, extend, expand, concentrate, accumulate, increase, develop, grow, heighten, strengthen, reinforce [➞CHANGE OF INTENSITY: LESS; 395] *Opposite*: weaken 2 *v* dig out, excavate, hollow out, scoop out, extend, expand [➞CHANGE OF INTENSITY: MORE; 394] *Opposite*: fill in

deepfreeze *type of* cooling appliance [➞HEATING, REFRIGERATION, AND VENTILATION; 1142]

deep in thought *adj* contemplative, thoughtful, pensive, lost in thought, mulling things over, miles away (*UK*) [➞PENSIVENESS AND INTEREST; 538]

deeply *adv* intensely, extremely, profoundly, severely, acutely, genuinely, totally, sincerely, truly, greatly, entirely [➞TO A GREAT EXTENT; 132] *Opposite*: mildly

deepness 1 *n* depth, profundity, profoundness, bottomlessness, fathomlessness [➡ DEPTH: DEEP; 1201] **2** n **lowness**, resonance, sonority, low pitch [➡ SOFT, LOW, OR PLEASANT SOUNDS; 1265]

deep-rooted adj **innate**, deep-seated, inherent, entrenched, established, core, subconscious [➡ STRENGTH; 201] Opposite: superficial

deep-sea adj **marine**, oceanic, ocean [➡ THE SEAS, OCEANS, AND SHORES; 1041]

deep-seated adj **innate**, deep-rooted, inherent, entrenched, subconscious, ingrained [➡ THE NATURE OF IDEAS; 771] Opposite: superficial

deer n [➡ LIVING THINGS AND LIVING; 976]

deer

◆ types of deer or antelope
antelope, caribou, chamois, chevrotain, dik-dik, elk, fallow deer, gazelle, gnu, impala, moose, okapi, reindeer, springbok, Thomson's gazelle, wapiti, white-tailed deer

deer fly type of **flying insect** [➡ FLYING INSECTS; 1013]

deerstalker type of **hat** [➡ ACCESSORIES, MILLINERY, AND LINGERIE; 867]

deer tick type of **parasitic insect** [➡ PARASITES; 1017]

de-escalate v **scale down**, scale back, cut back, reduce, decrease, slow, damp down, check, diminish, curb, step down, pull back [➡ CHANGE OF INTENSITY: LESS; 395] Opposite: escalate

de-escalation n **reduction**, stepping down, scaling down, cutback, decrease, phasedown [➡ CHANGE OF INTENSITY: LESS; 395] Opposite: escalation

deface v **spoil**, ruin, mar, disfigure, mutilate, vandalize, impair, damage, injure [➡ WORSEN APPEARANCE; 382] Opposite: renovate

defacement n **disfigurement**, mutilation, vandalism, destruction, damage, injury [➡ BAD BEHAVIOR OR ACTIONS; 254] Opposite: restoration

de facto **1** adv **in effect**, to all intents and purposes, in reality, actually, effectively, in fact [➡ FOREIGN WORDS AND PHRASES; 672] **2** adj **actual**, genuine, effective, existing, real [➡ TRUE AND REAL; 171]

defamation n **insult**, offense, slander, libel, slur, smear, denigration, vilification, character assassination, calumny (formal) [➡ INSULTS, ABUSE, AND SWEARING; 658] Opposite: praise

defamatory adj **insulting**, offensive, slanderous, libellous, derogatory, disparaging, deprecating [➡ ACCUSATORY AND DISAPPROVING; 634] Opposite: complimentary

defame v **insult**, slander, libel, denigrate, cast aspersion on, deprecate, disparage, offend, vilify, bad-mouth [➡ INSULTS, ABUSE, AND SWEARING; 658] Opposite: praise

See Compare and Contrast at **malign**.

default **1** v **fail to pay**, evade, dodge, shirk, duck, duck out, let lapse [➡ OWE AND DESERVE; 465] Opposite: pay **2** n **evasion**,

avoidance, nonpayment, defaulting, nonattendance, nonappearance [➡ OWE AND DESERVE; 465]

defaulter n **nonpayer**, debtor, cheat, shirker, absentee [➡ PEOPLE INVOLVED IN FINANCE; 804]

defeat **1** n **overthrow**, conquest, downfall, rout [➡ BEAT AND DEFEAT; 80] Opposite: victory **2** n **loss**, reverse, setback, thrashing, beating, rout, trouncing, whitewash (informal), hiding (informal) [➡ BEAT AND DEFEAT; 80] Opposite: victory **3** v **beat**, overcome, overpower, overwhelm, conquer, crush, rout, trounce, whitewash, thrash, vanquish, triumph over, cream (slang) [➡ BEAT AND DEFEAT; 80] Opposite: lose **4** v **baffle**, confound, foil, frustrate, thwart, stump, bamboozle (informal) [➡ CONFUSE AND BEWILDER; 571]

Compare and Contrast: defeat, beat, conquer, vanquish, overcome, triumph over, thrash, trounce

CORE MEANING: to win a victory

defeat to win a victory over an enemy or competitor, or to cause failure; **beat** to defeat in a contest, or to overcome a difficulty; **conquer** to defeat decisively in battle, or to overcome a difficulty; **vanquish** to defeat decisively in battle or competition; **overcome** to win or succeed after a struggle; **triumph over** to succeed against an adversary or against difficult odds; **thrash** to gain an easy decisive victory in a sporting contest; **trounce** to defeat an opponent convincingly.

defeated adj **beaten**, overcome, overpowered, overwhelmed, conquered, crushed, routed, whitewashed, trounced, vanquished, subjugated [➡ BEATEN AND DEFEATED; 78] Opposite: victorious

defeatism n **pessimism**, resignation, despondency, despair, negativity, spinelessness, fatalism [➡ FEELINGS ABOUT THE FUTURE; 533] Opposite: optimism

defeatist **1** adj **pessimistic**, negative, fatalistic, resigned, despondent, despairing, spineless [➡ NEGATIVITY OF OUTLOOK; 514] Opposite: optimistic **2** n **pessimist**, loser, fatalist, doomsayer, doom-monger, Cassandra, quitter (informal) [➡ LAZY OR UNSUCCESSFUL PEOPLE; 948] Opposite: optimist

defecate (formal) v **excrete**, eliminate waste, empty the bowels, have a bowel movement, evacuate, expel [➡ EXCRETION AND EXCRETA; 722]

defecation n **excretion**, evacuation, elimination [➡ EXCRETION AND EXCRETA; 722]

defect **1** n **flaw**, fault, imperfection, blemish, shortcoming, failing, deficiency, weakness [➡ FAULTS, FLAWS, AND WEAKNESSES; 251] **2** v **desert**, change sides, abscond, go over, turn traitor, decamp [➡ RUN AWAY AND AVOID; 10]

See Compare and Contrast at **flaw**.

defective adj **faulty**, imperfect, flawed, substandard, malfunctioning, out of order, not working, unreliable, on the blink (informal) [➡ IN BAD REPAIR; 1234] Opposite: perfect

defectiveness n **faultiness**, failure, inadequacy, unreliability, imperfection, malfunction [➡ REDUNDANT AND USELESS; 240]

defector n traitor, turncoat, renegade, convert, rebel, apostate [➡ UNCOOPERATIVE OR REBELLIOUS PEOPLE; 566] *Opposite*: loyalist

defend 1 v **protect**, guard, shield, look after, preserve, secure [➡ PREVENT CONTACT OR ATTACK; 419] *Opposite*: attack 2 v **support**, stand up for, stick up for, stand for, represent, uphold, endorse, back, champion [➡ APPROVE AND CONFIRM; 646] *Opposite*: oppose

> See Compare and Contrast at **safeguard**.

defendant n **perpetrator**, offender, respondent, suspect, culprit [➡ PEOPLE IN LAW COURTS; 820] *Opposite*: accuser

defender 1 n **supporter**, champion, advocate, sponsor, upholder, backer [➡ DEVOTEES AND ADDICTED PEOPLE; 556] *Opposite*: opponent 2 n **protector**, guard, guardian, escort, bodyguard, warden (*UK*) [➡ PEOPLE WHO GUARD AND PROTECT; 846] *Opposite*: attacker

defense 1 n **protection**, resistance, guard, security, cover, shield, firewall, Chinese walls (*UK*) [➡ SAFE AND SAFETY; 191] *Opposite*: attack 2 n **justification**, argument, vindication, plea, apology, excuse, alibi (*informal*) [➡ TRIAL, PUNISHMENT, AND LEGAL OUTCOMES; 819] *Opposite*: accusation

defense force n **army**, armed forces, armed services, military, fighters, national guard, task force [➡ THE ARMED FORCES; 827]

defenseless adj **unprotected**, unarmed, exposed, unguarded, vulnerable, helpless, wide open, weak, frail, powerless [➡ IN DANGER; 237] *Opposite*: protected

defenselessness n **vulnerability**, helplessness, powerlessness, weakness, frailty [➡ DANGER; 235] *Opposite*: strength

defenses 1 n **fortifications**, battlements, earthworks, ramparts, barricades, emplacements, lines [➡ FORTRESSES AND FORTIFICATIONS; 1090] 2 n **resistance**, immunity, protection, shield, safeguard, resilience [➡ STRENGTH; 201]

defensible 1 adj **defendable**, impregnable, unassailable, invulnerable, secure, strong [➡ STRENGTH; 201] *Opposite*: vulnerable 2 adj **justifiable**, valid, cast-iron, secure, rock-solid, sound [➡ ACCEPTABLE AND PASSABLE; 219] *Opposite*: indefensible

defensibly adv **excusably**, justifiably, explicably, forgivably, understandably, pardonably [➡ ACCEPTABLE AND PASSABLE; 219] *Opposite*: unjustifiably

defensive 1 adj **self-justifying**, self-protective, apologetic, distrustful, wary, cautious [➡ INSECURITY AND LOSS OF COMPOSURE; 544] *Opposite*: aggressive 2 adj **protective**, protecting, defending, shielding, fortified, armored [➡ STRENGTH; 201]

defensively adv **sensitively**, oversensitively, protectively, warily, cautiously, apologetically [➡ INSECURITY AND LOSS OF COMPOSURE; 544] *Opposite*: aggressively

defer 1 v **put off**, reschedule, put back, postpone, delay, adjourn, suspend [➡ DELAY ACTION OR OCCURRENCE; 278] *Opposite*: bring forward 2 v **bow to**, submit, be deferential, accede, comply, accept, concede, give way [➡ AGREE; 645]

deference n **respect**, esteem, regard, reverence, admiration, awe, obsequiousness, submissiveness [➡ LOVE, RESPECT, AND GOODWILL; 549] *Opposite*: disrespect

deferential adj **respectful**, admiring, reverent, polite, obsequious, courteous, submissive [➡ EXPRESSING RESPECT AND APPROVAL; 637] *Opposite*: disrespectful

deferment n **adjournment**, suspension, postponement, delay, stay, deferral, rain check (*informal*) [➡ DELAY ACTION OR OCCURRENCE; 278]

deferral n **postponement**, adjournment, delay, stay, deferment, rain check (*informal*) [➡ PAUSES AND PHASES; 56]

defiance n **insubordination**, disobedience, insolence, rebelliousness, boldness, cheekiness, noncooperation, cheek (*informal*) [➡ REBELLIOUSNESS AND DISOBEDIENCE; 565] *Opposite*: compliance

defiant adj **disobedient**, insolent, insubordinate, rebellious, bold, cheeky (*informal*) [➡ REBELLIOUSNESS AND DISOBEDIENCE; 565] *Opposite*: compliant

deficiency 1 n **lack**, shortage, absence, deficit, dearth, insufficiency, paucity, scarcity [➡ TOO FEW, TOO LITTLE; 122] *Opposite*: excess 2 n **inadequacy**, defect, flaw, fault, imperfection, shortcoming, failing, weakness [➡ FAULTS, FLAWS, AND WEAKNESSES; 251]

> See Compare and Contrast at **lack**.

deficient 1 adj **lacking**, poor, underprovided, undersupplied, short, incomplete, wanting, scarce [➡ LACK OF POSSESSION; 445] *Opposite*: abundant 2 adj **inadequate**, flawed, faulty, unsatisfactory, defective, poor, shoddy, imperfect, not up to scratch (*informal*) [➡ INAPPROPRIATE AND UNSUITABLE; 224] *Opposite*: perfect

deficiently adv **inadequately**, defectively, faultily, incorrectly, wrongly, imperfectly, weakly, poorly, shoddily [➡ INAPPROPRIATE AND UNSUITABLE; 224] *Opposite*: perfectly

deficit n **shortfall**, shortage, arrears, discrepancy, debit, scarcity, insufficiency, dearth [➡ TOO FEW, TOO LITTLE; 122] *Opposite*: surplus

> See Compare and Contrast at **lack**.

defile 1 v (*formal*) **corrupt**, taint, besmirch, sully, spoil, tarnish, pollute, ruin, degrade, contaminate [➡ WORSEN SOMETHING; 380] *Opposite*: purify 2 v (*formal*) **dishonor**, desecrate, sully, violate, debase [➡ RELIGIONS AND RELIGIOUS PRACTICES; 777] *Opposite*: respect 3 n **pass**, valley, gorge, gap [➡ GEOLOGIC FEATURES; 1056]

defiled (*formal*) 1 adj **corrupted**, tainted, besmirched, sullied, tarnished, spoiled, polluted, ruined, degraded, contaminated [➡ DIRTY; 1235] *Opposite*: untarnished 2 adj **dishonored**, desecrated, sullied, violated, debased [➡ MORALLY BAD OR IMPROPER; 775] *Opposite*: respected

define 1 v **describe**, outline, express, state, explain, term [➡ NAME AND DESCRIBE; 665] 2 v **characterize**, classify, identify, distinguish, specify, label [➡ NAME AND DESCRIBE; 665] 3 v **mark out**, outline, delimit, demarcate, mark, delineate (*formal*), circumscribe (*formal*) [➡ NAME AND DESCRIBE; 665]

defined adj **clear**, distinct, definite, well-defined, sharp, demarcated [➡ CONCISE AND CLEAR; 202] *Opposite*: indistinct

defining moment *n* **turning point**, landmark, watershed, crossroads, moment of truth, crisis, crunch [➡ DECISIVE MOMENTS; 44]

definite 1 *adj* **fixed**, settled, positive, assured, known, stated [➡ CERTAIN; 174] *Opposite*: indefinite 2 *adj* **sure**, certain, positive, fixed, final, confident [➡ CERTAINTY; 561] *Opposite*: uncertain 3 *adj* **exact**, specific, explicit, clear-cut, unambiguous, distinct, crystal clear [➡ EXACT; 203] *Opposite*: vague 4 *adj* **obvious**, recognized, significant, unquestionable, unmistakable, important, well-defined, noteworthy [➡ IMPORTANT; 194] *Opposite*: dubious

definite article *type of* **word class** [➡ ASPECTS OF LANGUAGE; 682]

definitely *adv* **certainly**, absolutely, positively, unquestionably, without doubt, beyond doubt, undeniably, categorically [➡ CERTAIN; 174] *Opposite*: perhaps

definiteness *n* **certainty**, assurance, assuredness, conviction, finality, confidence, determination [➡ CERTAIN; 174] *Opposite*: uncertainty

definition 1 *n* **meaning**, description, explanation, classification, characterization, designation, demarcation, delineation (*formal*) [➡ NAME AND DESCRIBE; 665] 2 *n* **clarity**, sharpness, distinctness, focus, clearness, exactness [➡ EXACT; 203] *Opposite*: haziness

definitive 1 *adj* **conclusive**, final, decisive, ultimate, absolute, complete [➡ ABSOLUTE AND ABSOLUTELY; 133] *Opposite*: tentative 2 *adj* **authoritative**, conclusive, perfect, best, classic, state-of-the-art, standard [➡ EXTRAORDINARY: AMAZING; 204]

definitively *adv* **finally**, ultimately, once and for all, conclusively, absolutely [➡ ABSOLUTE AND ABSOLUTELY; 133] *Opposite*: temporarily

deflate 1 *v* **let the air out**, go down, let down, collapse, shrink, puncture [➡ EMPTY AND UNLOAD; 407] *Opposite*: inflate 2 *v* **belittle**, disappoint, flatten, squash, quash, snub, humiliate, destroy, take the wind out of somebody's sails, put down (*informal*) [➡ UPSET, DISTRESS, AND HUMILIATE; 567] *Opposite*: boost 3 *v* **devalue**, depress, decrease, reduce, lower [➡ CHANGE OF SIZE: SMALLER; 393]

deflated 1 *adj* **emptied**, flattened, shrunk, collapsed, let down, punctured, squashed [➡ IN BAD REPAIR; 1234] *Opposite*: inflated 2 *adj* **subdued**, humiliated, flattened, humbled, dispirited, disappointed, put down (*informal*) [➡ SADNESS, DISTRESS, AND DESPAIR; 539] *Opposite*: exhilarated

deflation 1 *n* **depression**, devaluation, depreciation, reduction, decrease, lowering [➡ MARKET FORCES; 803] *Opposite*: inflation 2 *type of* **economic condition** [➡ FINANCE AND ECONOMICS; 796]

deflect 1 *v* **bounce**, glance, ricochet, rebound, bend, swerve, refract [➡ CHANGE DIRECTION OF MOTION; 344] 2 *v* **turn aside**, ward off, repel, redirect, sidetrack, avert, prevent, draw away [➡ PREVENT CONTACT OR ATTACK; 419] *Opposite*: attract

deflection *n* **refraction**, ricochet, rebound, glance, bend, swerve [➡ CHANGE DIRECTION OF MOTION; 344]

deforest *v* **log**, denude, strip, clear-cut, desolate, devastate, lay waste [➡ DESTRUCTION AND DEMOLITION; 359]

deform *v* **distort**, bend, warp, buckle, bow, twist [➡ CHANGE OF SHAPE; 385]

deformation *n* **distortion**, twist, buckle, bend, warp [➡ CHANGE OF SHAPE; 385]

deformed 1 *adj* **misshapen**, distorted, bent, warped, malformed, mutilated, buckled, bowed, twisted, shrunken, contorted, crooked [➡ ORIENTATION AND ALIGNMENT; 1223] 2 *adj* **abnormal**, corrupted, perverted, spoiled, ruined, damaged, spoilt (*UK*) [➡ IN BAD REPAIR; 1234]

deformity *n* **disfigurement**, malformation, distortion, abnormality, misshapenness, irregularity [➡ ORIENTATION AND ALIGNMENT; 1223]

defraud *v* **deceive**, swindle, cheat, trick, take advantage of, con, dupe, bilk (*informal*), fleece (*informal*), rip off (*informal*) [➡ STEAL AND ROB; 426]

defray *v* **pay**, cover, meet, contribute, finance, bear the cost of [➡ GIVE MONEY; 433]

defrock *v* **unfrock**, excommunicate, disqualify, drum out, expel, demote, dismiss [➡ REVOKE STATUS; 459]

defrost *v* **melt**, thaw, thaw out, deice, unfreeze [➡ SOFTEN, LIQUEFY, AND DAMPEN; 388] *Opposite*: freeze

deft *adj* **skillful**, adroit, neat, nimble, dexterous, handy, precise, adept, nifty (*informal*) [➡ TALENTED AND SKILLFUL; 527] *Opposite*: clumsy

deftness *n* **skill**, dexterity, precision, handiness, swiftness, neatness, adroitness, niftiness (*informal*) [➡ SKILLS, TALENTS, AND ABILITIES; 526] *Opposite*: clumsiness

defunct 1 *adj* **obsolete**, invalid, redundant, outdated, out-of-date [➡ PAST; 84] *Opposite*: current 2 *adj* **dead**, expired, extinct, gone (*informal*), deceased (*formal*), departed (*formal or literary*) [➡ DEAD AND DYING; 925] *Opposite*: alive

See Compare and Contrast at **dead**.

defuse *v* **resolve**, calm, soothe, smooth out, neutralize, rescue, save, recover, mollify, cool, placate [➡ IMPROVE SOMETHING; 374] *Opposite*: aggravate

defy *v* **challenge**, confront, disobey, rebel, resist, dare, flout, disregard, treat with contempt [➡ DISOBEY; 302] *Opposite*: obey

degeneracy *n* **depravity**, wickedness, corruption, dissoluteness, decadence, wantonness, immorality [➡ MORALLY BAD OR IMPROPER; 775] *Opposite*: morality

degenerate 1 *v* **deteriorate**, collapse, relapse, worsen, reduce, sink, slip, fall [➡ GET WORSE; 381] *Opposite*: improve 2 *adj* **debased**, decadent, immoral, debauched, corrupt, perverted, wicked [➡ MORALLY BAD OR IMPROPER; 775] *Opposite*: moral

degeneration *n* **deterioration**, collapse, disintegration, falling apart, worsening, relapse [➡ WORSEN SOMETHING; 380] *Opposite*: regeneration

degenerative *adj* **wasting**, worsening, deteriorating, progressive [➡ WORSEN SOMETHING; 380]

degradation 1 *n* **humiliation**, disgrace, shame, mortification, misery, infamy, obloquy (*formal or literary*) [➡ EMBARRASSMENT AND HUMILIATION; 542] 2 *n* **squalor**, filth, dilapidation, deprivation, poverty, ruin [➡ IN BAD REPAIR; 1234]

degrade 1 v **humiliate**, shame, disgrace, mortify, demean, debase, corrupt, vitiate [➡ UPSET, DISTRESS, AND HUMILIATE; 567] *Opposite*: exalt (*formal*) 2 v **damage**, destroy, reduce, cut down, worsen, lower, vitiate [➡ DESTRUCTION AND DEMOLITION; 359] *Opposite*: upgrade 3 v **decay**, decompose, disintegrate, break down, rot, perish (*UK*) [➡ GO BAD AND CORRODE; 390]

degrading adj **humiliating**, debasing, demeaning, undignified, corrupting, mortifying, shameful, unbecoming [➡ EMOTIONALLY UNPLEASANT AND UPSETTING; 227] *Opposite*: dignified

degree 1 n **extent**, quantity, intensity, magnitude, level, amount [➡ DEGREE AND EXTENT; 110] 2 n **grade**, gradation, mark, notch, step, unit, point [➡ DEGREE AND EXTENT; 110]

degree Celsius *type of* **SI unit** [➡ SIZE AND DIMENSIONS; 1192]

degree Fahrenheit *type of* **nonmetric unit** [➡ SIZE AND DIMENSIONS; 1192]

dehumanize v **desensitize**, brutalize, degrade, debase [➡ WOUND A PERSON OR ANIMAL; 383] *Opposite*: humanize

dehydrate v **dry out**, dry up, become dry, desiccate, parch [➡ HARDEN, CONGEAL, AND DRY; 387]

dehydrated adj **dry**, dried out, arid, parched, desiccated, shriveled, dried up, thirsty [➡ DRY; 1242]

See Compare and Contrast at **dry**.

dehydration n **dryness**, drying out, drying up, desiccation, thirst [➡ ILL AND SICK; 740]

deice v **unfreeze**, melt, thaw, thaw out [➡ SOFTEN, LIQUEFY, AND DAMPEN; 388] *Opposite*: ice up

deification n **elevation**, veneration, adoration, beatification, exaltation (*formal*) [➡ PRAISE AND ENCOURAGE; 647]

deify v **idolize**, worship, glorify, adore, venerate, beatify, exalt (*formal*) [➡ LIKE, LOVE, VALUE, AND ENJOY; 578]

deign v **condescend**, lower yourself, stoop, consent, agree, force yourself, demean yourself [➡ AGREE; 645]

deity n **divinity**, god, goddess, divine being, immortal [➡ RELIGIOUS CONCEPTS; 776]

dejected adj **sad**, disappointed, unhappy, miserable, depressed, disconsolate, gloomy, crestfallen, dismal, doleful, glum, down in the mouth (*informal*), blue (*informal*) [➡ SADNESS, DISTRESS, AND DESPAIR; 539] *Opposite*: cheerful

dejection n **sadness**, unhappiness, misery, gloom, depression, glumness, gloominess [➡ SADNESS, DISTRESS, AND DESPAIR; 539] *Opposite*: cheerfulness

delay 1 n **postponement**, interruption, stay, suspension, adjournment, deferral, deferment [➡ DELAY ACTION OR OCCURRENCE; 278] 2 n **interval**, wait, pause, break, lull, lag, holdup, stoppage, setback [➡ PROBLEMS; 256] 3 v **postpone**, put off, suspend, adjourn, defer, reschedule, shelve, put back, table, put on the back burner [➡ DELAY ACTION OR OCCURRENCE; 278] *Opposite*: bring forward 4 v **procrastinate**, hesitate, linger, dawdle, pause, prolong, lag, wait, loiter [➡ MOVE SLOWLY; 314] *Opposite*: hurry up 5 v **slow down**, slow up, hold up, set back, obstruct,

impede, hinder [➡ DELAY ACTION OR OCCURRENCE; 278] *Opposite*: speed up

delayed adj **late**, behind, behind schedule, overdue, tardy, deferred, put off, put back, pushed back, held up, hindered, caught up, stuck, postponed [➡ PROMPTNESS: LATE; 100] *Opposite*: early

delayering n [➡ BUSINESS ACTIVITIES AND PHENOMENA; 794]

delectable 1 adj **delicious**, tasty, mouthwatering, appetizing, luscious, enjoyable, palatable, scrumptious (*informal*) [➡ TASTE; 703] *Opposite*: tasteless 2 adj **delightful**, charming, adorable, appealing, heavenly, lovely, attractive [➡ BEAUTY AND ATTRACTIVENESS; 189] *Opposite*: unappealing

delectably 1 adv **deliciously**, appetizingly, mouthwateringly, tastily, scrumptiously (*informal*) [➡ TASTE; 703] 2 adv **delightfully**, attractively, beautifully, adorably, charmingly, gorgeously [➡ BEAUTY AND ATTRACTIVENESS; 189]

delectation (*formal*) n **enjoyment**, delight, pleasure, appreciation, entertainment, amusement [➡ PLEASURE, EXCITEMENT, AND ELATION; 534]

delegate 1 v **hand over**, farm out, pass on, give, assign, allocate, allot, entrust [➡ DISPENSE, RATION, AND DISTRIBUTE; 434] *Opposite*: retain 2 v **designate**, assign, appoint, allocate, deputize, order, depute (*formal*) [➡ DISPENSE, RATION, AND DISTRIBUTE; 434] 3 n **representative**, agent, envoy, ambassador, deputy, emissary [➡ REPRESENTATIVES AND PATRONS; 968]

delegation 1 n **commission**, deputation, mission, lobby [➡ GROUPS WITH A COMMON INTEREST; 938] 2 n **allocation**, handing over, assignment, giving out, passing on, entrustment [➡ DISPENSE, RATION, AND DISTRIBUTE; 434] *Opposite*: retention

delete v **erase**, remove, strike out, cross out, obliterate, cancel, score, scrap, scratch, rub out, scrub (*informal*), expunge (*formal*) [➡ DELETE AND ERASE; 339] *Opposite*: insert

deleterious adj **damaging**, harmful, injurious, destructive, adverse, detrimental, negative [➡ DANGEROUS; 236] *Opposite*: beneficial

deletion n **removal**, obliteration, erasure, loss, omission, crossing out, scoring, cutting [➡ REMOVE SOMETHING; 338] *Opposite*: addition

delft *type of* **pottery** [➡ POTTERY; 1135]

deli *type of* **food outlet** [➡ RETAIL OUTLETS; 1083]

deliberate 1 adj **intentional**, purposeful, premeditated, conscious, calculated, planned [➡ INTENTIONAL AND DELIBERATE; 279] *Opposite*: accidental 2 adj **careful**, thoughtful, slow, cautious, unhurried, measured, considered, methodical, wary, meditative [➡ CAUTIOUS AND CAREFUL; 282] *Opposite*: hasty 3 v **think**, reflect, consider, mull over, ponder, think about, weigh up (*UK*) [➡ THINK AND REFLECT; 743]

deliberately 1 adv **intentionally**, on purpose, purposely, with intent, consciously, calculatingly, by design, knowingly, purposefully [➡ INTENTIONAL AND DELIBERATE; 279] *Opposite*: accidentally 2 adv **thoughtfully**, carefully, slowly, cautiously, methodically, unhurriedly, warily [➡ CAUTIOUS AND CAREFUL; 282] *Opposite*: hastily

deliberation 1 n (*formal*) **reflection**, thought, consideration, care, forethought, premeditation, calculation [➡ THINK AND REFLECT; 743] *Opposite*: impulsiveness 2 n **discussion**, debate, negotiation, planning, pondering, thought, consideration [➡ NEGOTIATION AND DEBATE; 46]

deliberations (formal) n [➡ MEETINGS AND ASSEMBLIES; 43]

deliberative (formal) adj **considered**, premeditated, planned, calculated, thought through, purposeful, intentional [➡ THE NATURE OF IDEAS; 771] Opposite: casual

delicacy 1 n **tidbit**, treat, luxury, dainty, fancy [➡ MEALS AND PARTS OF MEALS; 1169] 2 n **sensitivity**, tact, diplomacy, consideration, care, thoughtfulness, feeling, sympathy [➡ GOOD MANNERS AND SOCIAL SKILLS; 520] Opposite: insensitivity 3 n **refinement**, fastidiousness, subtlety, elegance, fineness, polish [➡ GOOD MANNERS AND SOCIAL SKILLS; 520] Opposite: vulgarity 4 n **gracefulness**, attractiveness, elegance, charm, grace, fluidity, smoothness [➡ BEAUTY AND ATTRACTIVENESS; 189] Opposite: awkwardness 5 n **fragility**, flimsiness, slenderness, frailty, weakness, daintiness [➡ WEAKNESS; 241] Opposite: sturdiness 6 n **precision**, skill, care, deftness, adroitness, dexterity, fineness, accuracy, sensitivity [➡ EXACT; 203] Opposite: inaccuracy

delicate 1 adj **fragile**, frail, weak, slight, flimsy, insubstantial [➡ WEAKNESS; 241] Opposite: robust 2 adj **subtle**, faint, slight, gentle, mild, pale, soft, elusive, tantalizing [➡ IMPERCEPTIBLE; 26] Opposite: overpowering 3 adj **sensitive**, refined, thoughtful, considerate, sympathetic, tactful, diplomatic [➡ GOOD MANNERS AND SOCIAL SKILLS; 520] Opposite: tactless 4 adj **fine**, precise, detailed, accurate, skilled [➡ EXACT; 203] Opposite: rough 5 adj **refined**, graceful, elegant, dainty, nice, attractive [➡ BEAUTY AND ATTRACTIVENESS; 189] Opposite: inelegant 6 adj **difficult**, tricky, complicated, sensitive, awkward, sticky, uncomfortable [➡ DIFFICULTY AND COMPLEXITY; 242] Opposite: straightforward

See Compare and Contrast at **fragile**.

delicately 1 adv **finely**, carefully, precisely, skillfully, dexterously, deftly, adroitly [➡ EXACT; 203] Opposite: clumsily 2 adv **faintly**, subtly, slightly, elusively, softly, mildly [➡ IMPERCEPTIBLE; 26] Opposite: intensely 3 adv **gracefully**, elegantly, daintily, nicely, attractively, with refinement, pleasantly [➡ BEAUTY AND ATTRACTIVENESS; 189] Opposite: inelegantly 4 adv **tactfully**, diplomatically, sensitively, carefully, thoughtfully, sympathetically [➡ GOOD MANNERS AND SOCIAL SKILLS; 520] Opposite: tactlessly

delicateness n **fragility**, fragileness, frailty, vulnerability, feebleness, weakness, thinness, delicacy, frailness [➡ WEAKNESS; 241] Opposite: robustness

delicatessen type of **food outlet** [➡ RETAIL OUTLETS; 1083]

delicious 1 adj **tasty**, appetizing, yummy, luscious, delectable, mouthwatering, scrumptious (informal), delish (slang) [➡ TASTE; 703] Opposite: tasteless 2 adj **delightful**, lovely, wonderful, pleasant, enjoyable, appealing, enchanting, charming, delectable [➡ EMOTIONALLY PLEASANT; 187] Opposite: unpleasant

deliciousness 1 n **delectableness**, palatability, lusciousness, sweetness, tastiness, scrumptiousness (informal) [➡ TASTE; 703] Opposite: tastelessness 2 n **delightfulness**, charm, sweetness, attractiveness, pleasantness, appeal [➡ EMOTIONALLY PLEASANT; 187] Opposite: unpleasantness

delight 1 n **joy**, enjoyment, pleasure, happiness, glee, gladness, enchantment, amusement, satisfaction [➡ PLEAS-

URE, EXCITEMENT, AND ELATION; 534] Opposite: displeasure 2 v **please**, charm, amuse, thrill, gratify, make happy, enchant [➡ PLEASE AND AMUSE; 572] Opposite: disappoint 3 v **take pleasure in**, appreciate, revel in, relish, enjoy, savor, bask in [➡ LIKE, LOVE, VALUE, AND ENJOY; 578] Opposite: dislike

delighted adj **pleased**, happy, charmed, enchanted, thrilled, elated, overjoyed, over the moon (UK informal) [➡ PLEASURE, EXCITEMENT, AND ELATION; 534] Opposite: unhappy

delightful adj **pleasant**, charming, lovely, wonderful, enjoyable, amusing, agreeable, enchanting, pleasing [➡ EMOTIONALLY PLEASANT; 187] Opposite: unpleasant

delightfulness n [➡ EMOTIONALLY PLEASANT; 187]

delimit (formal) v **set the limits**, demarcate, define, restrict, mark out, bound, delineate (formal) [➡ SEPARATE AND DIVIDE; 401]

delimitation (formal) n **demarcation**, definition, marking out, limitation, restriction, allocation, delineation (formal) [➡ AVOID, PREVENT, LIMIT, AND CONTROL; 277]

delineate 1 v (formal) **define**, describe, explain, portray, present, set out [➡ NAME AND DESCRIBE; 665] 2 v **outline**, delimit, mark out, demarcate, define, allocate, set [➡ NAME AND DESCRIBE; 665]

delineation 1 n (formal) **description**, definition, explanation, setting down [➡ EXPLAIN AND CLARIFY; 610] 2 n **demarcation**, definition, allocation, marking out, outlining, delimitation (formal) [➡ NAME AND DESCRIBE; 665]

delinquency 1 n **criminal behavior**, crime, felony, lawbreaking, misbehavior, wrongdoing [➡ BAD BEHAVIOR OR ACTIONS; 254] Opposite: uprightness 2 n (formal) **negligence**, carelessness, recklessness, failure, irresponsibility, dereliction [➡ MORALLY BAD OR IMPROPER; 775] Opposite: carefulness

delinquent 1 adj **criminal**, aberrant, antisocial, offending, felonious, wrong, bad [➡ MORALLY BAD OR IMPROPER; 775] Opposite: law-abiding 2 adj (formal) **negligent**, careless, reckless, irresponsible, neglectful, failing [➡ LACK OF COMMITMENT AND UNRELIABILITY; 509] Opposite: dutiful 3 n **criminal**, guilty party, felon, lawbreaker, wrongdoer, crook (informal) [➡ CRIMINALS; 821]

See Compare and Contrast at **bad**.

deliquesce v [➡ SOFTEN, LIQUEFY, AND DAMPEN; 388]

delirious 1 adj **feverish**, fevered, hot, hallucinating, rambling, restless, confused [➡ ILL AND SICK; 740] Opposite: rational 2 adj **elated**, ecstatic, transported, in seventh heaven, beside yourself, excited, emotional, high, on cloud nine (informal), over the moon (UK informal) [➡ PLEASURE, EXCITEMENT, AND ELATION; 534] Opposite: dejected

delirium 1 n **fever**, hallucination, restlessness, confusion, frenzy, disorientation [➡ ILL AND SICK; 740] Opposite: clarity 2 n **ecstasy**, elation, fervor, euphoria, excitement, happiness [➡ PLEASURE, EXCITEMENT, AND ELATION; 534] Opposite: dejection

delish (slang) adj [➡ TASTE; 703]

deliver 1 v **carry**, bring, transport, distribute, send, convey, supply, provide [➡ MOVE SOMETHING TO ANOTHER LOCATION;

324] *Opposite*: take away **2** v **produce**, provide, supply, dispense, serve, give, present, furnish (*formal*) [➡EQUIP AND SUPPLY; 435] **3** v (*literary*) **set free**, release, rescue, save, liberate, free [➡FREEDOM AND LIBERTY; 208] *Opposite*: capture **4** v **hand over**, give up, surrender, transfer, relinquish, consign, cede (*formal*) [➡GIVE AND PROVIDE; 430] *Opposite*: keep

deliverance (*formal*) n **rescue**, release, liberation, relief, escape, freedom, delivery [➡FREEDOM AND LIBERTY; 208] *Opposite*: capture

delivery 1 n **distribution**, transfer, transport, sending, conveyance, carriage, provision, supply [➡TRANSPORTATION, TRANSPORTERS, AND CARGOS; 322] **2** n **manner of speaking**, presentation, approach, manner, technique [➡TEMPERAMENT AND BEHAVIOR; 492] **3** n **rescue**, release, liberation, relief, escape, freedom, deliverance (*formal*) [➡FREEDOM AND LIBERTY; 208] *Opposite*: capture

dell (*literary*) n **small valley**, glade, hollow, clearing, basin, dip, dene (*UK*) [➡THE COUNTRYSIDE AND OUTDOOR SPACES; 1071]

delphinium *type of* **perennial flower** [➡FLOWERS; 1032]

Delphinus *type of* **constellation** [➡HEAVENLY BODIES; 1061]

delta n **estuary**, outlet, mouth, channel [➡THE SEAS, OCEANS, AND SHORES; 1041]

deltoid *adj* [➡ANGULAR SHAPE; 1217]

delude v **deceive**, take in, cheat, mislead, con, fool, trick, dupe, hoodwink, pull the wool over somebody's eyes [➡DECEPTION AND LIES; 660]

deluded *adj* **mistaken**, deceived, misled, duped, conned, tricked, fooled, gullible [➡NEGATIVE INTELLECTUAL CHARACTERISTICS; 525]

deluge 1 n **torrent**, downpour, cloudburst, rainstorm, monsoon [➡CLOUDY AND RAINY WEATHER; 1052] **2** n **flood**, torrent, overflow, surge, cascade, inundation (*formal*) [➡MANY, MUCH, LARGE AMOUNT; 117] *Opposite*: drought **3** v **overwhelm**, overload, overrun, swamp, bury, shower, bombard, engulf, snow under, saturate, inundate [➡GIVE TOO MUCH AND OVERBURDEN; 437] **4** v **inundate**, flood, swamp, drown, soak, drench, saturate [➡SOFTEN, LIQUEFY, AND DAMPEN; 388] *Opposite*: dry up

delusion 1 n **illusion**, hallucination, vision, mirage, figment of the imagination, fantasy, apparition, image [➡NONEXISTENT THINGS; 23] *Opposite*: reality **2** n **misunderstanding**, misapprehension, misbelief, false impression, misconception, mistake, aberration [➡MISUNDERSTAND AND FAIL TO GRASP; 761]

delusive *adj* **deceptive**, chimerical, misleading, specious, illusory, imaginary, vain [➡FALSE AND UNREAL; 173] *Opposite*: genuine

deluxe *adj* **sumptuous**, luxurious, luxury, exclusive, select, expensive, plush (*informal*) [➡EXPENSIVE AND LUXURIOUS; 218] *Opposite*: cheap

delve 1 v **look into**, investigate, research, probe, dig, explore, examine, inquire [➡EXAMINE AND ASSESS; 753] **2** v (*archaic*) **dig**, burrow, tunnel, scrabble, scratch, root, rootle (*UK*) [➡SEEK POSSESSION AND SEARCH; 456] **3** n **rummage**, hunt, dig, search, dive, plunge, dip into, reach [➡SEEK POSSESSION AND SEARCH; 456]

demagogic *adj* **rabble-rousing**, inflammatory, manipu-

lative, declamatory, stirring, emotional, demagogical [➡ELOQUENT, TALKATIVE, AND LONG-WINDED; 632]

demagogical *see* **demagogic**

demagogue n **firebrand**, agitator, manipulator, crowd pleaser, haranguer, orator, tub-thumper (*informal*) [➡UNCOOPERATIVE OR REBELLIOUS PEOPLE; 566]

demand 1 v **insist**, command, order, require, stipulate, exact, claim [➡REQUEST AND DEMAND; 663] *Opposite*: request **2** v **ask**, inquire, question, query, want, challenge, plead [➡REQUEST AND DEMAND; 663] *Opposite*: answer **3** v **require**, need, want, call for, necessitate, command, claim, press for [➡NEED AND REQUIRE; 464] **4** n **request**, call, claim, petition, mandate, ultimatum, plea [➡REQUEST AND DEMAND; 663] *Opposite*: response **5** n **requirement**, need, pressure, exigency, claim, necessity [➡NECESSARY AND ESSENTIAL; 196]

demanding 1 *adj* **difficult**, hard, challenging, tough, severe, serious, trying, arduous, stressful, taxing, exacting, time-consuming [➡DIFFICULTY AND COMPLEXITY; 242] *Opposite*: easy **2** *adj* **insistent**, self-centered, persistent, dissatisfied, discontented, needy [➡DIFFICULT TO PLEASE; 515] *Opposite*: satisfied

demarcate 1 v **define**, mark out, delineate, draw, fix, establish, determine, delimit [➡SEPARATE AND DIVIDE; 401] **2** v **separate**, distinguish, differentiate, isolate, discriminate, segregate [➡SEPARATE AND DIVIDE; 401] *Opposite*: unite

demarcation n **separation**, differentiation, distinction, discrimination, segregation, isolation [➡SEPARATE AND DIVIDE; 401]

dematerialize v [➡CEASE TO EXIST; 22]

demean v **degrade**, debase, humiliate, disgrace, humble, lower, put down (*informal*) [➡UPSET, DISTRESS, AND HUMILIATE; 567] *Opposite*: uplift

demeanor n **manner**, conduct, behavior, character, deportment, performance, appearance, bearing, attitude, image, expression, air, mien (*formal*) [➡TEMPERAMENT AND BEHAVIOR; 492]

demean yourself v **lower yourself**, swallow your pride, stoop low, go down on your knees, abase yourself (*literary*) [➡CHANGE OF MOOD AND COMPOSURE; 580]

demented (*informal*) *adj* **irrational**, unreasonable, wild, frenzied, frantic, uncontrolled, crazy (*informal*), manic (*informal*) [➡ECCENTRICITY AND IRRATIONALITY; 562] *Opposite*: rational

demerger (*UK*) n **separation**, split, break, breakup, divergence, dissolution, division, partition [➡ENDS AND DEPARTURES; 54] *Opposite*: merger

demerit n **disadvantage**, failing, shortcoming, drawback, fault, imperfection [➡FAULTS, FLAWS, AND WEAKNESSES; 251] *Opposite*: merit

demesne (*formal*) n [➡REALMS AND RULES; 824]

demijohn n **bottle**, flagon, magnum, jeroboam, rehoboam, Methuselah [➡CONTAINERS, RECEPTACLES, AND PACKAGING; 1245]

demise (*formal*) **1** n **death**, passing, departure, decease (*formal*), expiry (*formal or literary*), expiration (*archaic*) [➡DEATH AND BEREAVEMENT; 927] *Opposite*: birth **2** n **end**, termination, finish, failure, ruin, downfall [➡ENDS AND DEPARTURES; 54] *Opposite*: creation

demo 1 *n* (*informal*) **sample**, showpiece, example, specimen, demonstrator, demo tape [➡ REPRESENTATIONS AND GENERAL EXAMPLES; 65] **2** *n* (*informal*) **demonstration**, presentation, display, show, exhibition, exposition [➡ SALES AND SHOWS; 443] **3** *n* (*UK*) **protest**, demonstration, protest march, march, protest rally, rally, parade, sit-in, sit-down [➡ MEETINGS AND ASSEMBLIES; 43]

demobilization *n* **discharge**, release, disbandment, dismissal, retirement [➡ FREEDOM AND LIBERTY; 208] *Opposite*: mobilization

demobilize *v* **discharge**, dismiss, disband, release, retire [➡ FREEDOM AND LIBERTY; 208] *Opposite*: mobilize

democracy 1 *n* **social equality**, equality, egalitarianism, classlessness, consensus, fairness [➡ STYLES AND SYSTEMS OF GOVERNMENT; 806] *Opposite*: inequality **2** *n* **democratic system**, democratic state, democratic organization, representative form of government, republic, parliamentary government [➡ STYLES AND SYSTEMS OF GOVERNMENT; 806] *Opposite*: dictatorship

democrat *n* **egalitarian**, populist, republican, social democrat, constitutionalist, moderate [➡ POLITICAL OFFICES AND POLITICIANS; 808] *Opposite*: totalitarian

democratic 1 *adj* **self-governing**, self-ruled, independent, autonomous, elected, representative [➡ STYLES AND SYSTEMS OF GOVERNMENT; 806] *Opposite*: autocratic **2** *adj* **egalitarian**, free, classless, equal, open, unrestricted, uncensored [➡ EQUALITY; 154] *Opposite*: repressive

demolish 1 *v* **knock down**, tear down, pull down, bulldoze, blow up, flatten, destroy, raze [➡ DESTRUCTION AND DEMOLITION; 359] *Opposite*: build **2** *v* **destroy**, ruin, flatten, smash, wreck, ravage, trash (*informal*) [➡ DESTRUCTION AND DEMOLITION; 359] *Opposite*: preserve **3** *v* (*informal*) **beat**, annihilate, defeat, rout, thrash, trounce [➡ BEAT AND DEFEAT; 80] **4** *v* (*informal*) **disprove**, tear to pieces, dismantle, undermine, take apart (*informal*) [➡ GET RID OF SOMETHING; 451] *Opposite*: support **5** *v* (*informal*) **devour**, wolf, gobble, eat, consume, eat up (*informal*), scarf (*informal*), scarf down (*informal*), scoff (*informal*) [➡ EAT AND NOT EAT; 710] *Opposite*: nibble

demolished *adj* [➡ IN BAD REPAIR; 1234]

demolition *n* **destruction**, pulling down, knocking down, annihilation, devastation, flattening [➡ DESTRUCTION AND DEMOLITION; 359] *Opposite*: construction

demon 1 *n* **fiend**, evil spirit, devil, monster [➡ THE SUPERNATURAL; 787] *Opposite*: angel **2** *n* **fear**, anxiety, terror, torment, trouble, worry [➡ PROBLEMS; 256] **3** *n* (*informal*) **expert**, genius, fiend, whiz (*informal*), wizard (*informal*), ace (*informal*) [➡ TALENTED OR INTELLIGENT PEOPLE; 528]

demonstrable 1 *adj* **obvious**, palpable, patent, evident, noticeable, perceptible, discernible, apparent, clear [➡ PERCEPTIBLE; 25] *Opposite*: imperceptible **2** *adj* **provable**, verifiable, self-evident, confirmable, comprehensible, certain, sure, definite [➡ CERTAIN; 174] *Opposite*: doubtful

demonstrably *adv* **obviously**, palpably, patently, evidently, noticeably, perceptibly, discernibly, apparently, clearly [➡ PERCEPTIBLE; 25] *Opposite*: imperceptibly

demonstrate 1 *v* **explain**, expound, display, operate, instruct, show, show off, put something through its paces [➡ EXPLAIN AND CLARIFY; 610] **2** *v* **prove**, validate, establish, reveal, make evident, make plain, determine, exhibit, show [➡ CAUSE TO APPEAR; 5] **3** *v* **protest**, march, rally, lobby, support, parade [➡ PROTEST AND EXPRESS DISAPPROVAL; 642]

demonstration 1 *n* **presentation**, display, illustration, explanation, exposition, show [➡ PERFORMANCES AND SHOWS; 42] **2** *n* **proof**, evidence, validation, establishment, revelation, determination [➡ EVIDENCE AND PROOF; 69]

demonstrative *adj* **affectionate**, warm, loving, friendly, emotional, effusive, open, expressive [➡ FRIENDLINESS AND SOCIABILITY; 494] *Opposite*: reserved

demonstratively *adv* **affectionately**, warmly, lovingly, emotionally, effusively, openly, expressively [➡ HONEST AND OPEN; 630] *Opposite*: reservedly

demonstrator 1 *n* **protester**, supporter, activist, campaigner, lobbyist, marcher [➡ UNCOOPERATIVE OR REBELLIOUS PEOPLE; 566] **2** *n* **presenter**, instructor, tutor, teacher, trainer, expounder [➡ EDUCATORS; 840]

demoralization *n* **discouragement**, deflation, undermining, depression, dejection, disheartenment [➡ SADNESS, DISTRESS, AND DESPAIR; 539] *Opposite*: encouragement

demoralize *v* **dishearten**, undermine, dispirit, deflate, discourage, depress [➡ UPSET, DISTRESS, AND HUMILIATE; 567] *Opposite*: encourage

demoralized *adj* **disheartened**, dispirited, downhearted, discouraged, deflated, depressed, dejected [➡ SADNESS, DISTRESS, AND DESPAIR; 539] *Opposite*: optimistic

demoralizing *adj* **disheartening**, discouraging, depressing, dispiriting, crushing, disturbing, distressing, upsetting, off-putting, unsettling, intimidating [➡ EMOTIONALLY UNPLEASANT AND UPSETTING; 227] *Opposite*: encouraging

demote *v* **downgrade**, relegate, move down, devalue, reduce, reduce to the ranks, lower, humble [➡ REVOKE STATUS; 459] *Opposite*: promote

demotion *n* **relegation**, downgrading, devaluation, reduction, lowering [➡ REVOKE STATUS; 459] *Opposite*: promotion

demotivate *v* **discourage**, demoralize, dishearten, dispirit, deter, put off, daunt, dissuade [➡ UPSET, DISTRESS, AND HUMILIATE; 567] *Opposite*: motivate

demotivation *n* **demoralization**, discouragement, disheartenment, deterrence, putting off, dissuasion [➡ NEUTRALITY AND INDIFFERENCE; 553] *Opposite*: motivation

demur *v* **object**, protest, raise objections, balk, express doubts, doubt, be reluctant, jib [➡ PROTEST AND EXPRESS DISAPPROVAL; 642] *Opposite*: agree

See Compare and Contrast at **object***.*

demure 1 *adj* **modest**, sedate, decorous, reserved, shy, retiring, diffident, bashful [➡ GOOD MANNERS AND SOCIAL SKILLS; 520] *Opposite*: bold **2** *adj* **prim**, coy, prudish, strait-laced [➡ EXCESSIVE SENSITIVITY; 511] *Opposite*: pert

demurely 1 *adv* **modestly**, sedately, decorously, reservedly, shyly, retiringly, diffidently, bashfully [➡ GOOD MANNERS AND SOCIAL SKILLS; 520] *Opposite*: boldly **2** *adv* **primly**, coyly, prudishly [➡ EXCESSIVE SENSITIVITY; 511] *Opposite*: pertly

demureness *n* [➡ GOOD MANNERS AND SOCIAL SKILLS; 520]

demutualize *v* [➡ BUSINESS ACTIVITIES AND PHENOMENA; 794]

demystification *n* **clarification**, explanation, interpretation, revelation, decipherment, translation, elucidation (*formal*) [➡ EXPLAIN AND CLARIFY; 610] *Opposite*: obfuscation

demystify *v* **clarify**, explain, elucidate, interpret, reveal, decipher, translate [➡ EXPLAIN AND CLARIFY; 610] *Opposite*: obscure

den 1 *n* [➡ ANIMAL OR BIRD ACCOMMODATIONS; 1079] 2 *type of* **room in the home** [➡ TYPES OF ROOMS; 1097]

den

◆ *types of den or nests*
aerie, burrow, drey, earth, form, hole, lair, lodge, nest, sett, tunnel, warren

denar *type of* **currency** [➡ CURRENCIES; 798]

denationalization *n* [➡ SOCIAL, POLITICAL, AND ECONOMIC CHANGE; 373]

denationalize *v* [➡ SOCIAL, POLITICAL, AND ECONOMIC CHANGE; 373]

denial 1 *n* **disavowal** (*formal*), refutation, rejection, rebuttal, contradiction, defiance, denunciation, dissent, repudiation [➡ DENY AND REJECT; 644] *Opposite*: confirmation 2 *n* **refusal**, deprivation, withholding, begrudging, turning down, rejection [➡ REFUSE PERMISSION AND NOT ALLOW; 670]

denigrate 1 *v* **disparage**, vilify, pour scorn on, degrade, belittle, malign, depreciate, put down (*informal*) [➡ ACCUSE, BLAME, AND CRITICIZE; 641] *Opposite*: glorify 2 *v* **defame**, slander, libel, abuse, stigmatize, insult [➡ INSULTS, ABUSE, AND SWEARING; 658] *Opposite*: praise

denigration 1 *n* **disparagement**, vilification, scorn, depreciation, belittling, belittlement [➡ CRITICISMS AND ANGRY OUTBURSTS; 50] *Opposite*: glorification 2 *n* **defamation**, slander, libel, abuse, stigmatization [➡ INSULTS, ABUSE, AND SWEARING; 658] *Opposite*: commendation

denim *type of* **fabric from plants** [➡ FABRICS; 1132]

denizen *n* **inhabitant**, resident, citizen, occupant, native, tenant, dweller (*literary*) [➡ INHABITANTS; 857]

denotation *n* **meaning**, import, sense, signification, significance, substance [➡ MEANING; 690] *Opposite*: connotation

denote 1 *v* **mean**, signify, stand for, represent, symbolize, designate [➡ MEAN SOMETHING; 61] *Opposite*: connote 2 *v* **refer to**, allude to, imply, convey, express, designate [➡ MEAN SOMETHING; 61]

denouement *n* **ending**, end, finale, conclusion, termination, finish [➡ ENDS AND DEPARTURES; 54] *Opposite*: opening

denounce 1 *v* **criticize**, censure, deplore, deprecate, condemn, decry [➡ PROTEST AND EXPRESS DISAPPROVAL; 642] *Opposite*: support 2 *v* **accuse**, point the finger at, blame, charge, inform, betray [➡ ACCUSE, BLAME, AND CRITICIZE; 641]

See Compare and Contrast at **disapprove**.

de novo *adv* [➡ AGAIN; 109]

dense 1 *adj* **crowded**, packed, packed in, full, jam-packed (*informal*) [➡ FULL; 1239] *Opposite*: sparse 2 *adj* **thick**, solid, impenetrable, compressed, condensed, compact, opaque, dark, deep, intense, even [➡ DENSITY AND CONSISTENCY; 1207] *Opposite*: transparent 3 *adj* **complicated**, complex, difficult, obscure, deep, opaque, involved, impenetrable, heavy-going [➡ DIFFICULTY AND COMPLEXITY; 242] *Opposite*: clear

denseness 1 *n* **crowdedness**, crowding, tightness, impenetrability, closeness, density [➡ DENSITY AND CONSISTENCY; 1207] *Opposite*: roominess 2 *n* **thickness**, opacity, solidity, impenetrability, darkness, compression, depth, intensity, heaviness, evenness [➡ DENSITY AND CONSISTENCY; 1207] *Opposite*: transparency 3 *n* **complexity**, difficulty, complication, obscurity, opacity, impenetrability [➡ DIFFICULTY AND COMPLEXITY; 242] *Opposite*: clarity

density *n* **thickness**, compactness, mass, concentration, bulk, solidity, concreteness [➡ DENSITY AND CONSISTENCY; 1207]

dent 1 *n* **hollow**, indentation, depression, dimple, cavity, impression, dip, indent [➡ HOLES, GAPS, AND FORKS; 1252] *Opposite*: lump 2 *n* (*informal*) **blow**, knock, shock, setback, reversal [➡ PROBLEMS; 256] *Opposite*: boost 3 *n* (*informal*) **reduction**, hole, cut, dip, decrease, dint [➡ CHANGE OF SIZE: SMALLER; 393] 4 *v* **knock**, hit, bump, bang, indent, damage, dint [➡ WORSEN APPEARANCE; 382] 5 *v* **damage**, hurt, undermine, diminish, lessen, reduce [➡ CHANGE OF SIZE: SMALLER; 393]

denture 1 *part of* **mouth** [➡ THE MOUTH; 702] 2 *type of* **tooth** [➡ THE MOUTH; 702]

denude *v* **strip**, uncover, bare, remove, shed, discard [➡ REMOVE SOMETHING; 338] *Opposite*: cover

denunciate (*formal*) *v* **condemn**, criticize, accuse, censure, reprove, admonish, rebuke [➡ PROTEST AND EXPRESS DISAPPROVAL; 642] *Opposite*: commend

denunciation *n* **condemnation**, criticism, accusation, censure, reproof, admonition, scolding, rebuke [➡ CRITICISMS AND ANGRY OUTBURSTS; 50] *Opposite*: commendation

Denver boot *n* [➡ FASTENERS, LINKS, AND NETWORKS; 1247]

deny 1 *v* **repudiate**, refute, reject, contradict, disagree, negate (*formal*) [➡ DENY AND REJECT; 644] *Opposite*: agree 2 *v* **refuse**, disallow, block, forbid, prevent, stand in the way [➡ REFUSE PERMISSION AND NOT ALLOW; 670] *Opposite*: permit 3 *v* **forgo**, renounce, disavow, reject, disown, give up, turn down, decline, repudiate, abjure (*literary*), forswear (*archaic or literary*) [➡ FORGO AND DENY ONESELF; 449]

deodorant *n* **roll-on**, deodorizer, spray, cream, lotion [➡ PERSONAL HYGIENE; 491]

deodorize *v* **freshen**, scent, refresh, perfume, aromatize, fragrance [➡ CLEAN AND POLISH; 403]

depart 1 *v* **start out**, set out, move off, set off, leave, proceed, advance, go forward, sally, set forth (*literary*) [➡ LEAVE AND GO AWAY; 8] *Opposite*: return 2 *v* **pull out**, leave, go away, disappear, be off, head off, make tracks (*informal*), quit (*archaic*) [➡ LEAVE AND GO AWAY; 8] *Opposite*: arrive 3 *v* **deviate**, diverge, differ, vary, change, digress, meander, stray [➡ CHANGE DIRECTION OF MOTION; 344] *Opposite*: stick to 4 *v* (*formal*) **die**, pass on, pass away, expire, succumb, depart this life (*formal*), decease (*formal*), perish (*literary*) [➡ DIE; 922]

departed (*formal or literary*) *adj* **dead**, late, defunct, lamented, lifeless, deceased (*formal*) [➡ DEAD AND DYING; 925] *Opposite*: living

See Compare and Contrast at **dead**.

departing *n* **leaving**, going away, withdrawal, departure, retreat, parting, leave-taking (*literary*) [➡ ENDS AND DEPARTURES; 54] *Opposite*: arriving

department 1 *n* **subdivision**, division, branch, sector, section, constituent part [➡ SUBDIVISIONS AND OFFSHOOTS; 1253] 2 *n* (*informal*) **responsibility**, area, specialty, realm, sphere, field [➡ SUBJECT AREAS; 768]

department store *type of* **retail outlet** [➡ RETAIL OUTLETS; 1083]

depart this life (*formal*) *v* [➡ DIE; 922]

departure 1 *n* **leaving**, going away, parting, exit, exodus, withdrawal, retreat, leave-taking (*literary*) [➡ ENDS AND DEPARTURES; 54] *Opposite*: arrival 2 *n* **change**, deviation, divergence, digression, variation, difference, novelty [➡ CHANGE; 372] 3 *n* **venture**, project, enterprise, endeavor, undertaking, course of action [➡ ACTIONS OR UNDERTAKINGS; 259]

depend *v* **be contingent**, hinge on, rest on, be subject to, hang on, be governed by, be determined by, be influenced by [➡ RECIPROCITY AND INTERDEPENDENCE; 147]

dependability *n* **reliability**, steadiness, trustworthiness, loyalty, fidelity, steadfastness, constancy, soundness, staunchness [➡ HONEST AND RELIABLE; 502] *Opposite*: unreliability

dependable *adj* **reliable**, trustworthy, loyal, faithful, steady, responsible, steadfast, trusty, staunch [➡ HONEST AND RELIABLE; 502] *Opposite*: unreliable

dependence 1 *n* **reliance**, trust, confidence, belief, hope, faith [➡ RECIPROCITY AND INTERDEPENDENCE; 147] *Opposite*: independence 2 *n* **need**, requirement, necessity, want [➡ DESIRE AND WANT; 579] 3 *n* **addiction**, dependency, reliance, need, craving, habit, enslavement [➡ UNDER THE INFLUENCE OF DRUGS OR ALCOHOL; 741]

dependency 1 *n* **territory**, colony, dependent state, dependent territory, adjunct [➡ COUNTRIES AND REGIONS; 1067] 2 *n* **dependence**, need, reliance, addiction, habit, craving, enslavement [➡ RELATIONSHIP TO ANOTHER; 973]

dependent 1 *adj* **reliant on**, in need of, at the mercy of, hooked on (*slang*) [➡ DESIRE AND WANT; 579] 2 *adj* **needy**, reliant, helpless, supported [➡ POVERTY AND POOR; 892] *Opposite*: independent 3 *adj* **contingent**, conditional, determined, subject, related [➡ RECIPROCITY AND INTERDEPENDENCE; 147] *Opposite*: independent 4 *type of* **younger relative** [➡ YOUNGER GENERATION RELATIVES; 958]

depend on 1 *v* **need**, require, rely on, be dependent on, lean on, look to [➡ RECIPROCITY AND INTERDEPENDENCE; 147] 2 *v* **rely on**, count on, trust, be sure of, be certain of [➡ LIKE, LOVE, VALUE, AND ENJOY; 578] *Opposite*: mistrust

depict *v* **portray**, show, represent, describe, illustrate, paint, give a picture of [➡ REPRESENT SOMETHING OR SOMEBODY; 59]

depiction *n* **representation**, portrayal, description, illustration, delineation, drawing, picture [➡ REPRESENTATIONS AND GENERAL EXAMPLES; 65]

deplete *v* **use up**, drain, exhaust, diminish, lessen,

run down, eat up (*informal*) [➡ USE UP AND WASTE; 474] *Opposite*: increase

depletion *n* **reduction**, exhaustion, diminution, lessening, running down, weakening [➡ CHANGE OF SIZE: SMALLER; 393] *Opposite*: restoration

deplorable 1 *adj* **disgraceful**, terrible, awful, appalling, unacceptable, dreadful, shocking, unpardonable, unforgivable, shameful [➡ BAD AND BADLY; 223] *Opposite*: praiseworthy 2 *adj* **pitiful**, lamentable, woeful, appalling, shameful, pathetic, wretched, execrable (*formal*) [➡ EMOTIONALLY UNPLEASANT AND UPSETTING; 227]

deplorably *adv* **disgracefully**, appallingly, unpardonably, unforgivably, shockingly, shamefully, unacceptably, execrably (*formal*) [➡ BAD AND BADLY; 223] *Opposite*: excellently

deplore 1 *v* **censure**, condemn, criticize, deprecate, disapprove, abhor (*formal*) [➡ PROTEST AND EXPRESS DISAPPROVAL; 642] *Opposite*: praise 2 *v* **lament**, bemoan, regret, be sorry, rue, bewail (*formal*) [➡ COMPLAIN AND NAG; 686]

See Compare and Contrast at **disapprove**.

deploy 1 *v* **position**, arrange, set up, set out, install, organize, array (*literary*) [➡ POSITION SOMETHING; 325] 2 *v* **use**, employ, implement, utilize, adopt [➡ USE; 467]

deployment 1 *n* **placement**, disposition, positioning, distribution, arrangement, organization, setting out [➡ MOVE SOMETHING TO ANOTHER LOCATION; 324] 2 *n* **utilization**, employment, implementation [➡ USE; 467]

depoliticize *v* **humanize**, personalize, socialize, neutralize [➡ SOCIAL, POLITICAL, AND ECONOMIC CHANGE; 373] *Opposite*: politicize

depopulate *v* **clear**, relocate, remove, clear out, evacuate [➡ EMPTY AND UNLOAD; 407] *Opposite*: populate

depopulation *n* **clearance**, relocation, removal, evacuation, abandonment [➡ SOCIAL, POLITICAL, AND ECONOMIC CHANGE; 373] *Opposite*: settlement

deport *v* **expel**, extradite, banish, exile, transport, expatriate, send back [➡ EJECT AND EXCLUDE; 340]

deportation *n* **exile**, banishment, extradition, expatriation, expulsion, transportation [➡ EJECT AND EXCLUDE; 340]

deportee *n* **exile**, outcast, expatriate, expat (*informal*) [➡ PEOPLE LIVING AWAY FROM HOME; 887]

deportment *n* **manner**, gait, attitude, posture, bearing, demeanor, behavior, carriage (*formal*) [➡ TEMPERAMENT AND BEHAVIOR; 492]

depose *v* **overthrow**, oust, topple, throw out, remove, unseat [➡ REVOKE STATUS; 459] *Opposite*: install

deposit 1 *v* **pay in**, credit, put in, bank, consign, add [➡ GIVE MONEY; 433] *Opposite*: withdraw 2 *v* **put**, put down, set down, leave, place, drop, dump [➡ POSITION SOMETHING; 325] *Opposite*: remove 3 *v* **accumulate**, lay down, leave behind, build up, pile up, add to [➡ POSITION SOMETHING; 325] 4 *n* **credit**, payment, sum [➡ FUNDS, PAYMENTS, AND CHARGES; 800] *Opposite*: withdrawal 5 *n* **security**, guarantee, pledge, surety [➡ INSURANCE; 801] 6 *n* **sediment**, residue, accretion, layer, accumulation, buildup [➡ SOLIDS; 1274]

deposition 1 *n* **statement**, testimony, admission, sworn testimony, confession [➞ TRIAL, PUNISHMENT, AND LEGAL OUTCOMES; 819] **2** *n* **removal**, unseating, installation, overthrow, ousting [➞ REVOKE STATUS; 459] **3** *n* **accumulation**, accretion, sedimentation, silting, buildup [➞ REMAINDER AND REMAINDERS; 125]

depositor *n* **saver**, investor, account holder, creditor [➞ PEOPLE INVOLVED IN FINANCE; 804]

depository *type of* **storage space** [➞ STORES AND STORAGE BUILDINGS; 1088]

depot 1 *n* **railroad station**, bus station, terminus [➞ PUBLIC BUILDINGS AND MEETING PLACES; 1081] **2** *n* **yard**, maintenance yard, goods yard, garage, workshop, siding [➞ INDUSTRIAL BUILDINGS; 1087] **3** *type of* **storage space** [➞ STORES AND STORAGE BUILDINGS; 1088]

deprave *v* **lead astray**, corrupt, degrade, ruin, debase, debauch (*formal*) [➞ WORSEN SOMETHING; 380]

depraved *adj* **debauched**, immoral, corrupt, evil, wicked, degenerate, decadent, dissolute, wanton [➞ MORALLY BAD OR IMPROPER; 775] *Opposite*: righteous

depravity *n* **debauchery**, immorality, corruption, wickedness, evil, decadence, dissoluteness, degeneracy, wantonness, vice [➞ MORALLY BAD OR IMPROPER; 775] *Opposite*: righteousness

deprecate *v* **condemn**, censure, denigrate, denounce, deplore, criticize, disapprove, decry, belittle [➞ PROTEST AND EXPRESS DISAPPROVAL; 642] *Opposite*: approve

deprecating *adj* **condemnatory**, disapproving, derogatory, deprecatory, pejorative (*formal*) [➞ ACCUSATORY AND DISAPPROVING; 634] *Opposite*: approving

deprecation *n* **disapproval**, denigration, condemnation, censure, criticism [➞ CRITICISMS AND ANGRY OUTBURSTS; 50] *Opposite*: praise

deprecatory 1 *adj* **disapproving**, derogatory, critical, denigrating, condemnatory, pejorative (*formal*) [➞ ACCUSATORY AND DISAPPROVING; 634] *Opposite*: approving **2** *adj* **apologetic**, sorry, repentant, contrite, remorseful [➞ EMBARRASSMENT AND HUMILIATION; 542] *Opposite*: unrepentant

depreciate 1 *v* **lessen**, devalue, deflate, decline, downgrade [➞ CHANGE OF INTENSITY: LESS; 395] *Opposite*: appreciate **2** *v* **denigrate**, belittle, disparage, run down, criticize, dis (*slang*) [➞ ACCUSE, BLAME, AND CRITICIZE; 641] *Opposite*: commend

depreciation *n* **devaluation**, reduction, decrease, decline, downgrading, fall, drop [➞ CHANGE OF INTENSITY: LESS; 395] *Opposite*: rise

depreciatory *adj* **belittling**, deprecatory, critical, denigrating, derogatory, disapproving, pejorative (*formal*) [➞ ACCUSATORY AND DISAPPROVING; 634] *Opposite*: complimentary

depredation *n* **plunder**, destruction, pillage, despoliation, attack, sack [➞ DESTRUCTION AND DEMOLITION; 359]

depress 1 *v* **sadden**, dishearten, discourage, dispirit, demoralize, bum out (*slang*) [➞ UPSET, DISTRESS, AND HUMILIATE; 567] *Opposite*: cheer up **2** *v* **press down**, push down, press, push, lower, move downward [➞ MOVE SOMETHING: DOWNWARD; 329] *Opposite*: release

depressant 1 *n* **sedative**, drug, narcotic, tranquilizer, downer (*slang*) [➞ REMEDIES, TREATMENTS, AND OPERATIONS; 731] **2** *adj*

sedative, tranquilizing, sedating, calming, narcotic [➞ REMEDIES, TREATMENTS, AND OPERATIONS; 731]

depressed 1 *adj* **unhappy**, miserable, dejected, low, disheartened, sad, down, glum, despondent, blue (*informal*), down in the dumps (*informal*) [➞ SADNESS, DISTRESS, AND DESPAIR; 539] *Opposite*: happy **2** *adj* **rundown**, deprived, poor, underprivileged, neglected, derelict [➞ POVERTY AND POOR; 892] *Opposite*: affluent

depressing *adj* **sad**, miserable, disheartening, discouraging, gloomy, dismal, disappointing [➞ EMOTIONALLY UNPLEASANT AND UPSETTING; 227] *Opposite*: cheering

depression 1 *n* **downheartedness**, unhappiness, despair, sadness, gloominess, misery, hopelessness, melancholy, dejection [➞ SADNESS, DISTRESS, AND DESPAIR; 539] *Opposite*: happiness **2** *n* **slump**, recession, decline, downturn, slide, poverty [➞ MARKET FORCES; 803] *Opposite*: recovery **3** *n* **hollow**, dip, dent, impression, dimple, indent [➞ HOLES, GAPS, AND FORKS; 1252] *Opposite*: hump **4** *type of* **economic condition** [➞ FINANCE AND ECONOMICS; 796]

depressive *adj* **gloomy**, depressing, cheerless, miserable, bleak, grim [➞ EMOTIONALLY UNPLEASANT AND UPSETTING; 227] *Opposite*: cheerful

deprivation *n* **lack**, deficiency, scarcity, denial, withdrawal, removal, dispossession, deficit, poverty [➞ POVERTY AND POOR; 892] *Opposite*: plenty

deprive *v* **divest**, rob, deny, take away, remove, withdraw, dispossess (*archaic or formal*) [➞ TAKE SOMETHING AWAY; 425] *Opposite*: provide

deprived *adj* **disadvantaged**, underprivileged, poor, destitute, depressed, rundown, dispossessed [➞ POVERTY AND POOR; 892] *Opposite*: privileged

deprived of *adj* **without**, lacking, wanting, short of, starved of, shorn of [➞ LACK OF POSSESSION; 445]

depth 1 *n* **deepness**, profundity, distance [➞ DEPTH: DEEP; 1201] **2** *n* **intensity**, vigor, strength, power, concentration, extent [➞ STRENGTH; 201] *Opposite*: weakness **3** *n* **complexity**, profundity, seriousness, gravity, wisdom, penetration, deepness [➞ DIFFICULTY AND COMPLEXITY; 242] *Opposite*: flippancy

depth charge *type of* **explosive weapon** [➞ EXPLOSIVES; 1155]

deputation *n* **delegation**, commission, mission, lobby group (*UK*) [➞ GROUPS WITH A COMMON INTEREST; 938]

depute *v* **delegate**, hand over, relinquish, allot, transfer, pass on [➞ CHANGE ONE THING FOR ANOTHER; 398]

deputize *v* **stand in**, represent, fill in, act, replace, substitute, sub (*informal*) [➞ REPRESENT SOMETHING OR SOMEBODY; 59]

deputy *n* **second-in-command**, assistant, agent, delegate, representative [➞ SUBORDINATES AND ASSISTANTS; 966]

See Compare and Contrast at **assistant**.

derail *v* **disrupt**, upset, wreck, ruin, spoil, overturn, unsettle, disorganize, interfere, dislocate, disturb, derange, disorder [➞ MAKE IMPOSSIBLE; 276]

derailleur *part of* **bike** [➞ BIKES, CARS, AND CARRIAGES; 1149]

derange 1 *v* **distress**, unsettle, upset, disorder, shake,

shock [→ UPSET, DISTRESS, AND HUMILIATE; 567] **2** *v* **upset**, disrupt, wreck, disturb, spoil, unsettle, disorganize, dislocate, interfere, derail, disorder [→ CREATE DISORDER AND CAUSE CHAOS; 358]

deranged *adj* [→ ECCENTRICITY AND IRRATIONALITY; 562]

derangement **1** *n* **imbalance**, irrationality, madness, insanity, instability [→ ECCENTRICITY AND IRRATIONALITY; 562] *Opposite*: sanity **2** *n* **disorder**, confusion, muddle, upset, disorganization, mess [→ DISORDER AND CHAOS; 245] *Opposite*: order

derby **1** *n* **contest**, race, match, clash, sporting event [→ NON-AGGRESSIVE/SPORTING EVENTS; 40] **2** *type of* **hat** [→ ACCESSORIES, MILLINERY, AND LINGERIE; 867]

deregulate *v* **free**, relax, liberalize, decontrol, derestrict, release [→ FREEDOM AND LIBERTY; 208] *Opposite*: regulate

derelict *adj* **dilapidated**, in ruins, rundown, ruined, neglected, abandoned, deserted [→ IN BAD REPAIR; 1234]

dereliction **1** *n* **neglect**, negligence, disregard, recklessness, carelessness, delinquency [→ BAD BEHAVIOR OR ACTIONS; 254] *Opposite*: regard **2** *n* **abandonment**, desertion, neglect, dilapidation, default, relinquishment [→ IN BAD REPAIR; 1234]

deride *v* **ridicule**, scoff, disparage, mock, scorn, disdain, put down (*informal*), knock (*slang*) [→ PROTEST AND EXPRESS DISAPPROVAL; 642] *Opposite*: admire

See Compare and Contrast at **ridicule**.

de rigueur *adj* [→ NECESSARY AND ESSENTIAL; 196]

derision *n* **disparagement**, scorn, disdain, mockery, ridicule, contempt, disrespect, contumely (*archaic or literary*) [→ JOKES AND TEASING; 674] *Opposite*: admiration

derisive *adj* **mocking**, scathing, sarcastic, irreverent, contemptuous, scornful, disdainful, cynical, sardonic [→ MOCKING AND DISMISSIVE; 636] *Opposite*: admiring

derisively *adv* **mockingly**, scathingly, sarcastically, irreverently, contemptuously, scornfully, disdainfully, cynically, sardonically [→ RUDE AND HOSTILE; 625] *Opposite*: admiringly

derisory *adj* **pitiful**, laughable, insulting, ridiculous, contemptible, mean, inadequate, pathetic (*informal*) [→ UNIMPORTANT AND UNNECESSARY; 238] *Opposite*: generous

derivation *n* **origin**, root, source, beginning, seed, cradle, descent [→ BEGINNINGS; 53]

See Compare and Contrast at **origin**.

derivative **1** *adj* **unoriginal**, imitative, plagiaristic, copied, derived [→ SIMILARITY; 148] *Opposite*: original **2** *n* **offshoot**, byproduct, spinoff, result, end product [→ RESULTS AND OUTCOMES; 83]

derive **1** *v* **originate**, stem, spring, arise, descend, come from, grow, draw on [→ GRADUALLY COME INTO EXISTENCE; 1] **2** *v* **get**, gain, obtain, draw, receive, take [→ GET; 420]

dermal *adj* [→ THE SKIN; 720]

dermatological *adj* [→ THE SKIN; 720]

dermis *n* [→ THE SKIN; 720]

derogatory *adj* **disparaging**, critical, insulting, offensive, deprecating, belittling, pejorative (*formal*) [→ ACCUSATORY AND DISAPPROVING; 634] *Opposite*: complimentary

derrick **1** *n* **crane**, hoist, winch, elevator, lift (*UK*) [→ MACHINES AND MACHINE PARTS; 1116] **2** *n* **wellhead**, rig, gantry, oil platform, frame, support [→ SUPPORTS AND BASES; 1255]

derring-do (*dated*) *n* **boldness**, bravery, courage, daring, bravado, guts (*slang*) [→ COURAGE; 498] *Opposite*: cowardice

desalinate *v* **purify**, desalt, detoxify, distill, refine, sweeten [→ CLEAN AND POLISH; 403]

desalination *n* **purification**, detoxification, distillation, salt removal [→ CLEAN AND POLISH; 403]

descale *v* **clean out** (*informal*), scrape, scour, flush, clean [→ CLEAN AND POLISH; 403]

descant *n* **harmony**, part, line, tune, air, melody [→ MUSIC, SONGS, AND SINGING; 907]

descend **1** *v* **go down**, move down, come down, slide down, fall down, tumble down [→ GO DOWNWARD; 307] *Opposite*: ascend **2** *v* **slope**, incline, fall away, go downhill, drop away, run down [→ GO DOWNWARD; 307] *Opposite*: ascend **3** *v* **derive**, originate, come from, stem, spring [→ GRADUALLY COME INTO EXISTENCE; 1] **4** *v* **lower yourself**, stoop, sink, resort, fall, decline [→ GET WORSE; 381] *Opposite*: rise **5** *v* **arrive**, drop in, appear, turn up, show up [→ ARRIVE; 12] *Opposite*: leave **6** *v* **fall**, fall on, affect, come over, come upon, hit, pervade, prevail [→ HAPPEN TO SOMEBODY; 30]

descendant *n* **successor**, offspring, progeny, child, heir, inheritor [→ THE FAMILY; 956] *Opposite*: ancestor

descendent *adj* **descending**, down, downward, plunging, sinking, sliding, downhill [→ DIRECTION OF MOTION; 345] *Opposite*: ascendant (*literary*)

descent **1** *n* **fall**, drop, dive, tumble, plunge, crash [→ GO DOWNWARD; 307] *Opposite*: ascent **2** *n* **decline**, deterioration, depreciation, degeneration, drop, plunge, tumble, downward spiral [→ FAILURE; 77] *Opposite*: improvement **3** *n* **ancestry**, parentage, lineage, origin, succession, pedigree, background [→ THE FAMILY; 956]

describe **1** *v* **explain**, portray, depict, illustrate, express, communicate [→ EXPLAIN AND CLARIFY; 610] **2** *v* **label**, refer to, define, designate, pronounce, call, term, style (*formal*) [→ NAME AND DESCRIBE; 665]

description **1** *n* **account**, report, explanation, portrayal, picture, narrative, depiction [→ NAME AND DESCRIBE; 665] **2** *n* **type**, sort, kind, class, variety, category [→ VARIETIES, TYPES, AND KINDS; 145]

descriptive **1** *adj* **explanatory**, illustrative, narrative, informative, factual [→ EXPLAIN AND CLARIFY; 610] *Opposite*: imaginative **2** *adj* **evocative**, expressive, vivid, graphic, eloquent, colorful, imaginative [→ ELOQUENT, TALKATIVE, AND LONG-WINDED; 632]

descry (*literary*) *v* [→ SEE; 699]

desecrate *v* **defile**, vandalize, insult, violate, outrage, lay waste to, commit sacrilege against, damage, blaspheme [→ WORSEN SOMETHING; 380] *Opposite*: consecrate

desecration *n* **violation**, defilement, vandalism, sacrilege, despoliation, ruin, damage [➡ BAD BEHAVIOR OR ACTIONS; 254] *Opposite*: consecration

deseed *v* pit, stone, core [➡ COOKING AND FOOD PREPARATION; 353]

desegregate *v* integrate, unify, unite, bring together, merge, reconcile, reunite [➡ COMBINE AND MIX; 400] *Opposite*: segregate

desegregation *n* integration, unification, reunion, reconciliation, merging [➡ COMBINE AND MIX; 400] *Opposite*: segregation

deselect *v* reject, abandon, discard, cast off, remove, dump (*informal*), ditch (*informal*) [➡ GET RID OF SOMETHING; 451] *Opposite*: select

desensitize *v* numb, deaden, dull, soothe, pacify, lull [➡ SOOTHE AND CALM; 573] *Opposite*: sensitize

desert 1 *n* wasteland, wilderness, barren region, arid region, waste [➡ DESERTS, PLAINS, AND MOORLAND; 1045] 2 *n* reward, return, recompense, wages, just reward, punishment, comeuppance (*informal*) [➡ REWARDS AND AWARDS; 439] 3 *v* abandon, leave high and dry, leave, forsake, discard, walk out on (*informal*), dump (*informal*), ditch (*informal*) [➡ REFUSING OR REJECTING RELATIONS; 975] *Opposite*: support 4 *v* abscond, leave, go AWOL, jump ship, go missing, take off (*informal*) [➡ RUN AWAY AND AVOID; 10] *Opposite*: stay

deserted 1 *adj* empty, abandoned, isolated, uninhabited, forsaken, desolate, derelict [➡ EMPTY; 1238] *Opposite*: inhabited 2 *adj* abandoned, discarded, forsaken, solitary, cast off, ditched (*informal*) [➡ SOLITARINESS; 941]

deserter *n* absconder, runaway, fugitive, defector, traitor, renegade, apostate, AWOL [➡ RUNAWAYS AND ABSENTEES; 9]

desertion *n* absconding, abandonment, running away, disappearance, departure, leaving [➡ ENDS AND DEPARTURES; 54]

deserve *v* merit, be worthy, earn, warrant, justify, rate, ask for [➡ OWE AND DESERVE; 465]

deservedly *adv* justly, rightly, justifiably, reasonably, properly, with good reason [➡ MORALLY GOOD; 774] *Opposite*: unreasonably

deserving *adj* worthy, commendable, admirable, praiseworthy, justified, justifiable, eligible [➡ ADMIRABLE AND COMMENDABLE; 185] *Opposite*: unworthy

desiccate *v* dry up, wither, dry out, dehydrate, parch, dry, shrivel, shrink [➡ HARDEN, CONGEAL, AND DRY; 387]

desiccated *adj* dry, dried, dried out, shriveled, dehydrated, shrunken [➡ DRY; 1242] *Opposite*: moist

See Compare and Contrast at **dry**.

desiccation *n* dryness, dehydration, withering, shriveling, drying [➡ DRY; 1242]

design 1 *v* create, invent, conceive, originate, fabricate, draw up, construct [➡ CREATION; 346] 2 *v* plan, intend, aim, devise, propose, suggest [➡ PREDICT AND ANTICIPATE; 750] 3 *n* project, scheme, enterprise, plan, strategy, proposal, policy [➡ WAYS OF DOING THINGS; 294] 4 *n* drawing, blueprint, plan, sketch, outline, model, layout [➡ DRAWINGS, CHARTS, AND TABLES; 594] 5 *n* pattern, motif, figure, shape, device, outline [➡ PATTERNS;

1225] 6 *n* intention, purpose, scheme, plan, object, aim, end, point, target, goal, will [➡ INTENTIONS AND PURPOSES; 772]

designate 1 *v* call, label, title, entitle, term, describe, define, refer to, style (*formal*) [➡ NAME AND DESCRIBE; 665] 2 *v* specify, point out, indicate, choose, select, allocate [➡ MAKE DECISIONS AND CHOICES; 752] 3 *v* assign, select, choose, delegate, allocate, elect, appoint, authorize [➡ CONFER STATUS; 458] 4 *adj* in waiting, elect, to be [➡ FUTURE; 86]

designation *n* title, name, description, term, label, alias, nickname [➡ NAME AND DESCRIBE; 665]

designedly *adv* intentionally, on purpose, purposely, deliberately, purposefully, by design, willfully [➡ INTENTIONAL AND DELIBERATE; 279] *Opposite*: accidentally

designer 1 *n* creator, inventor, originator, engineer, stylist, artist, graphic designer [➡ DESIGNERS, CREATORS, AND INSTIGATORS; 347] 2 *adj* fashionable, stylish, chic, expensive, exclusive, upscale, trendy (*informal*), chi-chi (*informal*), upmarket (*UK*) [➡ DESCRIBING CLOTHES; 869] *Opposite*: mass-produced

designing *adj* scheming, conniving, deceitful, wily, manipulative, crafty [➡ DECEITFUL; 513] *Opposite*: ingenuous

desirability 1 *n* appropriateness, aptness, rightness, suitability, advantage [➡ APPROPRIATE, SUITABLE, AND ADVISABLE; 184] 2 *n* appeal, attractiveness, attraction, allure, prestige, cachet, popularity [➡ BEAUTY AND ATTRACTIVENESS; 189]

desirable 1 *adj* wanted, needed, necessary, required, looked-for, desired, anticipated, appropriate, suitable, right, advantageous [➡ POPULAR AND WANTED; 220] *Opposite*: undesirable 2 *adj* attractive, pleasing, enviable, pleasant, popular, sought after [➡ POPULAR AND WANTED; 220] *Opposite*: undesirable

desire 1 *v* want, wish for, long for, covet, crave, yearn for, be dying for (*informal*) [➡ DESIRE AND WANT; 579] 2 *v* (*formal*) request, ask, require, appeal, entreat, beg, implore (*formal*) [➡ REQUEST AND DEMAND; 663] 3 *n* wish, want, longing, craving, yearning, need, aspiration, plea, request, appeal, entreaty, petition [➡ DESIRE AND WANT; 579]

See Compare and Contrast at **want**.

desired *adj* wanted, anticipated, sought after, looked-for, favorite, chosen, preferred [➡ POPULAR AND WANTED; 220] *Opposite*: unwanted

desirous (*formal*) *adj* eager, hopeful, wishing for, longing for, hoping for, wanting [➡ POSITIVE IMPATIENCE, ENTHUSIASM, AND ALERTNESS; 537]

desirously (*formal*) *adv* [➡ POSITIVE IMPATIENCE, ENTHUSIASM, AND ALERTNESS; 537]

desirousness (*formal*) *n* [➡ DESIRE AND WANT; 579]

desist *v* cease, stop, discontinue, give up, end, abstain [➡ STOP ACTING; 264] *Opposite*: continue

desk *type of* table [➡ FURNITURE; 858]

desk lamp *n* [➡ LIGHTING; 862]

desktop *type of* computer feature [➡ COMPUTERS AND COMPUTING; 1127]

desolate 1 *adj* **deserted**, isolated, bleak, abandoned, forsaken, uninhabited, wild, barren [➡ IN BAD REPAIR; 1234] *Opposite*: populous 2 *adj* **unhappy**, forlorn, miserable, depressed, inconsolable, wretched, dejected, despondent, mournful, sad [➡ SADNESS, DISTRESS, AND DESPAIR; 539] *Opposite*: happy 3 *adj* **depressing**, gloomy, dismal, austere, forbidding, unwelcoming, grim, bleak [➡ EMOTIONALLY UNPLEASANT AND UPSETTING; 227] *Opposite*: cheerful

desolately *adv* **unhappily**, sadly, mournfully, miserably, inconsolably, wretchedly, dejectedly, despondently [➡ SADNESS, DISTRESS, AND DESPAIR; 539] *Opposite*: happily

desolation 1 *n* **unhappiness**, misery, despair, anguish, sadness, wretchedness, despondency [➡ SADNESS, DISTRESS, AND DESPAIR; 539] *Opposite*: happiness 2 *n* **barrenness**, isolation, bleakness, emptiness, dereliction, devastation [➡ EMPTY; 1238]

despair 1 *n* **misery**, desolation, hopelessness, anguish, gloom, depression, despondency, dejection [➡ SADNESS, DISTRESS, AND DESPAIR; 539] *Opposite*: joy 2 *v* **lose hope**, give up hope, have no hope, see no light at the end of the tunnel, lose heart, give up on, sink, plumb the depths [➡ CHANGE OF MOOD AND COMPOSURE; 580] *Opposite*: hope

despairing *adj* **hopeless**, desolate, miserable, pained, despondent, desperate, weary, depressed, long-suffering, inconsolable, bleak [➡ SADNESS, DISTRESS, AND DESPAIR; 539] *Opposite*: hopeful

desperado *n* **criminal**, outlaw, gangster, bandit, villain, renegade, bad guy, baddie (*informal*) [➡ VILLAINS AND THUGS; 947]

desperate 1 *adj* **frantic**, anxious, worried, distressed, distracted, despairing, at the end of your rope, fraught, frantic [➡ CONFUSION, ANXIETY, AND WORRY; 540] *Opposite*: calm 2 *adj* **eager**, dying, raring, bursting, impatient, determined, in urgent need [➡ POSITIVE IMPATIENCE, ENTHUSIASM, AND ALERTNESS; 537] *Opposite*: loath 3 *adj* **reckless**, careless, rash, impulsive, dangerous, violent, risky, drastic [➡ INCAUTIOUS AND CARELESS; 283] *Opposite*: safe 4 *adj* **hopeless**, wretched, irredeemable, deplorable, dreadful [➡ SADNESS, DISTRESS, AND DESPAIR; 539] *Opposite*: hopeful 5 *adj* **serious**, grave, extreme, critical, threatening, acute [➡ DANGEROUS; 236] *Opposite*: harmless

desperately 1 *adv* **frantically**, anxiously, frenziedly, hastily, distractedly, distraughtly, worriedly [➡ SADNESS, DISTRESS, AND DESPAIR; 539] *Opposite*: calmly 2 *adv* **very much**, badly, to a great extent, dreadfully, urgently [➡ TO A GREAT EXTENT; 132] *Opposite*: hardly

desperation 1 *n* **anxiety**, worry, fear, distraction, nervousness, harassment [➡ CONFUSION, ANXIETY, AND WORRY; 540] *Opposite*: calmness 2 *n* **hopelessness**, despair, despondency, misery, anguish, desolation [➡ SADNESS, DISTRESS, AND DESPAIR; 539] *Opposite*: hopefulness

despicable *adj* **appalling**, dreadful, contemptible, wicked, shameful, disgraceful, vile, loathsome [➡ BAD AND BADLY; 223] *Opposite*: admirable

despise *v* **loathe**, scorn, look down on, hate, spurn, deride, feel contempt [➡ DISLIKE AND HATE; 577] *Opposite*: admire

despised *adj* **hated**, reviled, loathed, shunned, scorned, derided [➡ UNPOPULAR AND UNWANTED; 258] *Opposite*: beloved

despite *prep* **in spite of**, regardless of, in the face of, even with, even though, although, notwithstanding (*formal*) [➡ ALTHOUGH, NEVERTHELESS, AND DESPITE; 169]

despoil *v* **rob**, plunder, sack, pillage, loot, rifle, ransack [➡ STEAL AND ROB; 426]

despoilment *n* **despoliation**, vandalism, defacement, destruction, desecration, defilement [➡ DESTRUCTION AND DEMOLITION; 359]

despoliation *n* **plundering**, pillage, sack, theft, robbery, appropriation [➡ CRIMES; 817]

despondency *n* **hopelessness**, sadness, misery, dejection, depression, unhappiness, gloom, cheerlessness, joylessness, discouragement [➡ SADNESS, DISTRESS, AND DESPAIR; 539] *Opposite*: cheerfulness

despondent *adj* **hopeless**, low, dejected, despairing, downhearted, downcast, unhappy, sad, pessimistic, miserable, glum, discouraged [➡ SADNESS, DISTRESS, AND DESPAIR; 539] *Opposite*: cheerful

despot *n* **dictator**, tyrant, autocrat, oppressor, authoritarian, disciplinarian, martinet [➡ VILLAINS AND THUGS; 947]

despotic *adj* **tyrannical**, dictatorial, autocratic, authoritarian, repressive, absolute, high-handed, domineering [➡ BOSSY AND OVERBEARING; 516] *Opposite*: democratic

despotism *n* **tyranny**, dictatorship, absolutism, autocracy, authoritarianism, repression [➡ MORALLY BAD OR IMPROPER; 775] *Opposite*: democracy

dessert *n* **sweet** (*UK*), pudding (*UK*) [➡ MEALS AND PARTS OF MEALS; 1169]

dessert

◆ *types of desserts*
baklava, blancmange, bombe, brownies, cake, cassatta, clafoutis, cobbler, crème brûlée, crème caramel, crisp, custard, flan, fruit salad, granita, ice cream, junket, meringue, mousse, pannacotta, pavlova, peach Melba, pie, profiteroles, pudding, sorbet, soufflé, sundae, syllabub, tart, tiramisu, zabaglione

dessertspoon *type of* **flatware** [➡ TABLEWARE, FLATWARE, AND KITCHENWARE; 861]

dessertspoonful *n* [➡ AMOUNTS AND QUANTITIES; 112]

destabilization *n* **weakening**, subversion, undermining, disruption, dislocation [➡ WORSEN SOMETHING; 380]

destabilize *v* **undermine**, subvert, weaken, threaten, disrupt, dislocate, strike at the foundations, knock off balance [➡ WORSEN SOMETHING; 380] *Opposite*: strengthen

destination 1 *n* **journey's end**, terminus, last stop, end point [➡ ENDS AND DEPARTURES; 54] *Opposite*: starting point 2 *n* **end**, purpose, target, aim, goal, objective, intention [➡ INTENTIONS AND PURPOSES; 772]

destined *adj* **intended**, meant, fated, designed, certain, predestined, preordained, ordained (*formal*) [➡ FATE, DESTINY, AND ASTROLOGY; 782]

destiny 1 *n* **fate**, fortune, lot, luck, providence, future [➡ FATE, DESTINY, AND ASTROLOGY; 782] 2 *n* **purpose**, vocation, intention, call, calling [➡ INTENTIONS AND PURPOSES; 772]

destitute *adj* **poor**, penniless, impoverished, insolvent,

needy, deprived, indigent (*formal*) [➡ POVERTY AND POOR; 892]
Opposite: solvent

destitution *n* **poverty**, penury, hardship, need, insolvency, deprivation, impoverishment, want, privation, misery, indigence (*formal*) [➡ POVERTY AND POOR; 892] *Opposite*: prosperity

destroy 1 *v* **obliterate**, annihilate, demolish, devastate, tear down, raze, wipe out (*informal*) [➡ DESTRUCTION AND DEMOLITION; 359] *Opposite*: build 2 *v* **ruin**, damage, break, break up, spoil, wreck, trash (*slang*) [➡ DESTRUCTION AND DEMOLITION; 359] *Opposite*: conserve 3 *v* **abolish**, put an end to, get rid of, end, extinguish, do away with, rescind, finish (*informal*), terminate (*formal*) [➡ CAUSE TO STOP; 266] *Opposite*: sustain 4 *v* **defeat**, crush, subdue, demolish, overcome, overthrow, wipe out (*informal*), annihilate (*informal*) [➡ BEAT AND DEFEAT; 80]

destroyed *adj* **demolished**, devastated, ruined, wrecked, smashed, damaged, shattered, in shreds, in pieces, wiped out (*slang*) [➡ IN BAD REPAIR; 1234] *Opposite*: intact

destroyer 1 *n* **destructive force**, natural disaster, cause of death, killer, demolisher, slayer (*formal or literary*) [➡ DISASTERS; 252] *Opposite*: creator 2 *type of* **military vessel** [➡ SHIPS AND BOATS; 1150]

destroying angel *type of* **fungus** [➡ MICROORGANISMS, FUNGI, AND ALGAE; 1023]

destruction *n* **obliteration**, annihilation, devastation, demolition, ruin, damage [➡ DESTRUCTION AND DEMOLITION; 359] *Opposite*: construction

destructive 1 *adj* **damaging**, devastating, harmful, detrimental, injurious [➡ DANGEROUS; 236] 2 *adj* **unhelpful**, critical, negative, damaging, disparaging, harsh, caustic, vicious, hurtful [➡ RUDE AND HOSTILE; 625] *Opposite*: constructive

destructiveness 1 *n* **harmfulness**, power, force, violence, ferocity, roughness [➡ DANGER; 235] 2 *n* **criticism**, negativity, harshness, viciousness, hurtfulness, unhelpfulness [➡ AGGRESSIVE AND BELLIGERENT; 518] *Opposite*: helpfulness

desultorily *adv* **casually**, haphazardly, randomly, erratically, aimlessly, indiscriminately [➡ DISORDER AND CHAOS; 245] *Opposite*: methodically

desultory *adj* **aimless**, casual, random, unfocused, haphazard, erratic, indiscriminate [➡ DISORDER AND CHAOS; 245] *Opposite*: methodical

detach *v* **separate**, remove, disengage, disconnect, isolate, cut off, unfasten [➡ UNFASTEN AND UNDO; 409] *Opposite*: attach

detachable *adj* **removable**, separable, clip-on, hook-on, attachable, separate [➡ UNRELATEDNESS AND SEPARATENESS; 146] *Opposite*: fixed

detached 1 *adj* **separate**, disconnected, standing apart, apart, removed, separated, isolated [➡ UNRELATEDNESS AND SEPARATENESS; 146] *Opposite*: connected 2 *adj* **aloof**, indifferent, unemotional, unbiased, uninvolved, disinterested, distant, impassive, impersonal [➡ NEUTRALITY AND INDIFFERENCE; 553] *Opposite*: involved

detached house *type of* **house** [➡ RESIDENTIAL BUILDINGS; 1078]

detachment 1 *n* **aloofness**, remoteness, indifference, impassiveness, distance, coldness [➡ NEUTRALITY AND INDIFFERENCE; 553] *Opposite*: involvement 2 *n* **objectivity**, disinterest, disinterestedness, impartiality, fairness, unbiasedness, dispassion [➡ POSITIVE INTELLECTUAL CHARACTERISTICS; 524] 3 *n* **disconnection**, separation, disengagement, disentanglement, extrication, uncoupling, severance [➡ SEPARATE AND DIVIDE; 401] *Opposite*: connection 4 *n* **group**, unit, task force, detail, party, posse (*informal*) [➡ MILITARY PERSONNEL; 828]

detail 1 *n* **part**, feature, aspect, point, element, fact, factor, facet [➡ QUALITIES AND CHARACTERISTICS; 1191] 2 *n* **group**, unit, task force, detachment, party, posse (*informal*) [➡ MILITARY PERSONNEL; 828] 3 *v* **list**, specify, describe, itemize, particularize, note, notify [➡ EXPLAIN AND CLARIFY; 610] 4 *v* **assign**, delegate, allocate, conscript, designate, order [➡ CAUSE OR COMPEL TO ACT; 271]

detailed *adj* **full**, thorough, comprehensive, complete, exhaustive, meticulous, in depth [➡ WHOLENESS AND COMPLETENESS; 198] *Opposite*: sketchy

details *n* **particulars**, facts, information, minutiae, niceties, fine points, specifics [➡ BASIC DETAILS; 688]

detain 1 *v* **delay**, hold up, keep, keep back, impede, slow up, hinder [➡ DELAY ACTION OR OCCURRENCE; 278] *Opposite*: let go 2 *v* **arrest**, hold, keep in custody, capture, confine, control, restrain [➡ THE POLICE, ARREST, AND PRETRIAL PROCEEDINGS; 818] *Opposite*: release

detained *adj* **in custody**, in detention, under arrest, behind bars, in prison, imprisoned, locked up, held, interned, apprehended, captive, arrested, seized, caged, trapped, shut in, constricted, restrained, confined, jailed, inside (*informal*), put away (*informal*), incarcerated (*formal*) [➡ CAPTIVITY AND LOSS OF FREEDOM; 248] *Opposite*: at liberty

detainee *n* **prisoner**, captive, internee, hostage, convict [➡ CAPTIVES AND PRISONERS; 249]

detect *v* **notice**, sense, become aware of, perceive, spot, distinguish, identify, discover [➡ USING THE SENSES; 697]

detectable *adj* **obvious**, visible, noticeable, measurable, demonstrable, evident [➡ PERCEPTIBLE; 25] *Opposite*: undetectable

detection *n* **discovery**, uncovering, finding, recognition, exposure, revealing [➡ FIND; 463] *Opposite*: concealment

detective *n* **investigator**, private detective, plainclothes officer, private eye (*informal*), gumshoe (*dated informal*), dick (*dated slang*) [➡ THE POLICE, ARREST, AND PRETRIAL PROCEEDINGS; 818]

detective novel *n* [➡ FICTION AND DRAMA; 913]

detective story *n* [➡ FICTION AND DRAMA; 913]

detector *n* **sensor**, indicator, gauge, finder [➡ PARTS OF MACHINES AND TOOLS; 1118]

detente *see* **détente**

détente *n* **rapprochement**, agreement, cooperation, compromise, accommodation, truce [➡ HARMONY; 155] *Opposite*: hostility

detention *n* **custody**, imprisonment, confinement, arrest, locking up, incarceration (*formal*) [➡ CAPTIVITY AND LOSS OF FREEDOM; 248] *Opposite*: release

detention center n [➡ BUILDINGS FOR CONFINING PEOPLE; 1094]

detention facility n [➡ BUILDINGS FOR CONFINING PEOPLE; 1094]

deter v discourage, put off, daunt, dissuade, prevent, frighten [➡ UPSET, DISTRESS, AND HUMILIATE; 567] Opposite: encourage

detergent n cleaner, cleansing agent, cleanser, shampoo, laundry detergent, dishwashing liquid, soap, washing-up liquid (UK) [➡ CLEANING AGENTS; 863]

deteriorate v get worse, worsen, decline, depreciate, go downhill, weaken, wane, fail, fade [➡ GET WORSE; 381] Opposite: improve

deteriorated adj [➡ DECAYING OR INFESTED; 1230]

deteriorating adj worsening, getting worse, falling, fading, waning, failing [➡ WORSEN SOMETHING; 380] Opposite: improving

deterioration n worsening, decline, weakening, drop, descent, depreciation [➡ WORSEN SOMETHING; 380] Opposite: improvement

determinant n cause, determining factor, factor, element, basis, contributing factor [➡ MOST IMPORTANT THING; 197]

determination n strength of mind, willpower, resolve, purpose, fortitude, grit, strength of character [➡ STRENGTH OF WILL; 501] Opposite: weakness

determine 1 v find out, verify, clarify, uncover, establish, ascertain (formal) [➡ LEARN AND DISCOVER; 762] 2 v decide, settle, conclude, resolve, agree, finalize [➡ MAKE DECISIONS AND CHOICES; 752] 3 v influence, affect, shape, form, mold [➡ CREATION; 346] 4 v control, regulate, govern, fix, limit, define [➡ CAUSE TO HAPPEN; 31]

determined adj strong-minded, resolute, gritty, single-minded, unwavering, firm, dogged, indomitable, untiring, heroic [➡ STRENGTH OF WILL; 501] Opposite: irresolute

determiner type of word class [➡ ASPECTS OF LANGUAGE; 682]

determining adj decisive, causal, defining, influential, shaping, responsible [➡ MOST IMPORTANT AND MAIN; 193] Opposite: irrelevant

deterrence n discouragement, dissuasion, preemption, prevention, restriction, limitation [➡ PROBLEMS; 256] Opposite: encouragement

deterrent 1 adj warning, preventive, restrictive, restraining, limiting, constraining [➡ AVOID, PREVENT, LIMIT, AND CONTROL; 277] Opposite: encouraging 2 n restraint, disincentive, rein, curb, limit, constraint, limitation [➡ AVOID, PREVENT, LIMIT, AND CONTROL; 277] Opposite: incitement

detest v hate, loathe, despise, dislike, abhor (formal), abominate (formal) [➡ DISLIKE AND HATE; 577] Opposite: love

detestable adj hateful, despicable, repugnant, vile, revolting, abominable, loathsome, abhorrent (formal) [➡ EMOTIONALLY UNPLEASANT AND UPSETTING; 227] Opposite: lovable

detestation n hatred, hate, abhorrence, loathing, dislike, abomination (literary) [➡ IRRITATION AND ANGER; 541] Opposite: adoration

detested adj [➡ UNPOPULAR AND UNWANTED; 258]

dethrone v depose, oust, unseat, overthrow, over-whelm, triumph, defeat, remove [➡ REVOKE STATUS; 459] Opposite: install

detonate v explode, blow up, set off, ignite, spark off, discharge (formal) [➡ CAUSE TO START; 265]

detonation n explosion, blast, ignition, report, bang, discharge (formal) [➡ SUDDEN EVENTS; 52]

detour n deviation, diversion, roundabout route, alternative route, long way around, indirect route, bypass, long way round (UK) [➡ TRAVEL: JOURNEYS AND TRIPS; 318]

detox (informal) n [➡ REMEDIES, TREATMENTS, AND OPERATIONS; 731]

detoxication see **detoxification**

detoxification 1 n cleansing, decontamination, depollution, purification, reclamation, cleaning, clearing [➡ CLEAN AND POLISH; 403] Opposite: contamination 2 n [➡ HEALING; 730]

detoxify v cleanse, purify, clear, clean, depollute, decontaminate, reclaim [➡ CLEAN AND POLISH; 403] Opposite: contaminate

detract v take away from, diminish, lessen, reduce, weaken, undermine [➡ WORSEN SOMETHING; 380] Opposite: bolster

detraction 1 n lessening, reduction, subtraction, taking away, deduction, diminution [➡ CHANGE OF SIZE: SMALLER; 393] Opposite: addition 2 n (formal) slander, abuse, disparagement, aspersion, denigration, calumny (formal) [➡ INSULTS, ABUSE, AND SWEARING; 658] Opposite: praise

detractor n critic, disparager, cynic, heckler, attacker, decrier (formal), knocker (UK informal) [➡ GRUMPY AND NEGATIVE PEOPLE; 953] Opposite: supporter

detriment n disadvantage, loss, harm, damage, injury, impairment [➡ PROBLEMS; 256] Opposite: advantage

detrimental adj harmful, damaging, disadvantageous, unfavorable, negative, injurious [➡ DANGEROUS; 236] Opposite: beneficial

detritus n debris, litter, waste, trash, rubbish, flotsam and jetsam, leftovers, scraps, garbage [➡ JUNK AND USELESS OBJECTS; 1249]

de trop adj [➡ TOO MUCH; 119]

deuce n tie, draw, even-steven (informal), level pegging (UK) [➡ SPORTS TERMS; 877]

deutsche mark type of currency [➡ CURRENCIES; 798]

devaluation n deflation, depreciation, reduction, depression, devaluing, weakening [➡ MARKET FORCES; 803] Opposite: appreciation

devalue v diminish, lessen, undervalue, bring down, cheapen, revalue, devaluate, degrade, debase, reduce [➡ CHANGE OF INTENSITY: LESS; 395] Opposite: overvalue

devastate 1 v destroy, demolish, ravage, wreck, ruin, spoil [➡ DESTRUCTION AND DEMOLITION; 359] Opposite: preserve 2 v overwhelm, overcome, shock, distress, upset, shatter, confound, destroy [➡ UPSET, DISTRESS, AND HUMILIATE; 567] Opposite: comfort

devastated adj overwhelmed, overcome, shattered, confounded, shocked, distressed, upset, distraught [➡ SADNESS, DISTRESS, AND DESPAIR; 539] *Opposite*: comforted

devastating 1 *adj* **destructive**, harmful, damaging, ruinous, injurious, dreadful [➡ DANGEROUS; 236] **2** *adj* **overwhelming**, shocking, upsetting, disturbing, distressing, shattering, demoralizing [➡ EMOTIONALLY UNPLEASANT AND UPSETTING; 227] *Opposite*: comforting

devastatingly *adv* **terribly**, dreadfully, overwhelmingly, extraordinarily, hugely, extremely, very [➡ EXTRAORDINARY: AMAZING; 204]

devastation *n* **destruction**, damage, ruin, desolation, waste, wreckage [➡ DESTRUCTION AND DEMOLITION; 359] *Opposite*: preservation

develop 1 *v* **grow**, mature, progress, advance, change, improve, ripen [➡ CHANGE; 372] **2** *v* **arise**, result, happen, stem, come, come into being [➡ GRADUALLY COME INTO EXISTENCE; 1] **3** *v* **acquire**, pick up, foster, create, breed, get, obtain [➡ GET; 420] **4** *v* **expand**, enlarge, extend, increase, widen, build up, work up [➡ CHANGE OF SIZE: BIGGER; 392] *Opposite*: contract **5** *v* **work out**, flesh out, expound, fill in, explain, elaborate, enlarge, amplify [➡ EXPLAIN AND CLARIFY; 610] *Opposite*: outline **6** *v* **build on**, exploit, utilize, build [➡ MAKE GOOD USE OF SOMETHING; 473] **7** *v* **improve**, do up, renovate, refurbish, remodel, upgrade [➡ MANUFACTURE; 349]

developed *adj* **technologically advanced**, industrialized, advanced, established, settled [➡ WEALTH AND WEALTHY; 891] *Opposite*: developing

developer 1 *n* **designer**, creator, inventor, brains, maker, originator [➡ DESIGNERS, CREATORS, AND INSTIGATORS; 347] **2** *n* **buyer**, property developer, land developer, contractor, speculator [➡ BUSINESS PEOPLE; 793] **3** *type of* **photographic equipment** [➡ PHOTOGRAPHY AND PHOTOGRAPHIC EQUIPMENT; 1122]

developing *adj* **emerging**, emergent, evolving [➡ ABOUT TO HAPPEN; 33] *Opposite*: developed

development 1 *n* **event**, happening, occurrence, change, incident, stage [➡ EVENTS AND OCCURRENCES; 35] **2** *n* **growth**, expansion, progress, advance, change, increase, enlargement, improvement, elaboration [➡ PROGRESS AND ADVANCEMENT; 213] *Opposite*: stasis **3** *n* **enhancement**, expansion, advancement, training, education, extension [➡ TEACHING; 839]

developmental 1 *adj* **developing**, growing, evolving, changing, progressive [➡ HAPPENING AND IN PROGRESS; 32] *Opposite*: static **2** *adj* **age-related**, age-linked, growth-related, hormonal, child-development [➡ REPRODUCTION AND HEREDITY; 725]

deviance *n* **nonconformity**, unconventionality, eccentricity, unorthodoxy, aberration, abnormality, deviation, deviancy [➡ DIFFERENCE; 149] *Opposite*: conformity

deviant *adj* **different**, divergent, nonstandard, aberrant, irregular, out of the ordinary, unusual, unexpected [➡ DIFFERENCE; 149] *Opposite*: standard

deviate 1 *v* **differ**, depart, diverge, stray, digress [➡ CHANGE DIRECTION OF MOTION; 344] *Opposite*: conform **2** *v* **diverge**, move away, stray, depart, swerve, turn aside, turn from, turn off [➡ CHANGE DIRECTION OF MOTION; 344] *Opposite*: keep to

deviation 1 *n* **difference**, departure, change, divergence, variation, digression [➡ CHANGE DIRECTION OF MOTION; 344] **2** *n* **nonconformity**, unconventionality, eccentricity, unorthodoxy,

aberration, abnormality, deviance, deviancy [➡ DIFFERENCE; 149]

device 1 *n* **machine**, tool, piece of equipment, mechanism, apparatus, appliance, gadget, contrivance, contraption [➡ DEVICES; 1115] **2** *n* **expedient**, maneuver, stratagem, ruse, dodge, trick, means, ploy, scheme, method, way, plan [➡ WAYS OF DOING THINGS; 294] **3** *n* **design**, emblem, logo, badge, crest, symbol [➡ SYMBOLS, SIGNS, AND NUMBERS; 596]

devil *n* [➡ VILLAINS AND THUGS; 947]

devil's food cake *type of* **cake** [➡ CAKES, COOKIES, AND DESSERTS; 1181]

devious 1 *adj* **deceitful**, tricky, scheming, designing, wily, underhand, conniving, Machiavellian, sneaky, cunning, crafty, shifty, sly [➡ DECEITFUL; 513] *Opposite*: straightforward **2** *adj* **circuitous**, oblique, meandering, tortuous, winding, roundabout [➡ DIRECTION OF MOTION; 345] *Opposite*: direct

deviously *adv* **deceitfully**, sneakily, cunningly, artfully, subtly, cleverly [➡ DECEITFUL; 513] *Opposite*: straightforwardly

deviousness *n* **guile**, cunning, artfulness, deceitfulness, untrustworthiness, shadiness, underhandedness [➡ DECEITFUL; 513] *Opposite*: straightforwardness

devise *v* **think up**, plan, figure out, work out, invent, create, formulate, set up, concoct, conceive, contrive [➡ INSTITUTE AND INAUGURATE; 348]

devoid *adj* **empty**, barren, without, bereft, lacking, wanting [➡ LACK OF POSSESSION; 445] *Opposite*: full

devolution *n* **decentralization**, delegation, transference, transfer [➡ STYLES AND SYSTEMS OF GOVERNMENT; 806] *Opposite*: centralization

devolve *v* **transfer**, decentralize, give to, hand to, pass to, delegate, entrust [➡ GIVE AND PROVIDE; 430] *Opposite*: centralize

Devonian *type of* **period** [➡ EPOCHS AND ERAS; 89]

devote *v* **dedicate**, give, offer, apply, assign, allocate, allot, bestow (*formal*) [➡ GIVE AND PROVIDE; 430]

devoted 1 *adj* **committed**, loving, caring, affectionate, kind, fond, attentive, supportive, dedicated, dutiful [➡ GENEROSITY AND KINDNESS; 495] *Opposite*: uncaring **2** *adj* **dedicated**, loyal, dutiful, faithful, staunch, constant, committed [➡ HARD-WORKING AND COMMITTED; 500] *Opposite*: uncommitted **3** *adj* **keen**, enthusiastic, dedicated, ardent, fervent, zealous, fanatical [➡ ENERGY AND ENTHUSIASM; 496] *Opposite*: unenthusiastic

devotedly 1 *adv* **lovingly**, caringly, affectionately, kindly, fondly, attentively, supportively [➡ GENEROSITY AND KINDNESS; 495] *Opposite*: uncaringly **2** *adv* **loyally**, faithfully, dutifully, staunchly, consistently, unfailingly [➡ HARD-WORKING AND COMMITTED; 500] *Opposite*: unreliably **3** *adv* **keenly**, enthusiastically, ardently, fervently, fanatically, zealously [➡ APPRECIATION AND GRATITUDE; 535] *Opposite*: unenthusiastically

devotee 1 *n* **fan**, follower, supporter, aficionado, aficionada, enthusiast [➡ DEVOTEES AND ADDICTED PEOPLE; 556] **2** *n* **disciple**, follower, believer, votary [➡ SUPPORTERS, PROTECTORS, AND COMPATRIOTS; 970]

devotion 1 *n* **commitment**, attachment, love, fondness, affection, adoration [➡ APPRECIATION AND GRATITUDE; 535] *Opposite*:

dislike **2** *n* **dedication**, care, attentiveness, support, loyalty, fidelity, constancy, commitment, steadfastness [➡ LOVE, RESPECT, AND GOODWILL; 549] *Opposite*: neglect **3** *n* **enthusiasm**, admiration, zeal, keenness, fervor [➡ ENERGY AND ENTHUSIASM; 496] *Opposite*: apathy **4** *n* (*formal*) **piety**, devoutness, religious zeal, religious fervor, religious observance, dedication, consecration, commitment [➡ MORALLY GOOD; 774] *Opposite*: impiety

devotional *adj* **religious**, worshipful, worshiping, prayerful, holy, sacred, ceremonial, ritual [➡ RELIGIONS AND RELIGIOUS PRACTICES; 777]

devotions *n* **prayers**, holy rites, observances, supplications (*formal*) [➡ RELIGIONS AND RELIGIOUS PRACTICES, 777]

devour **1** *v* **consume**, demolish, dispose of, gulp, wolf, gobble, scarf (*informal*), scarf down (*informal*), scoff (*informal*) [➡ EAT AND NOT EAT; 710] **2** *v* (*literary*) **overwhelm**, overcome, engulf, consume, destroy, use up, obsess [➡ UPSET, DISTRESS, AND HUMILIATE; 567]

devout **1** *adj* **religious**, pious, spiritual, devoted, dedicated, committed, staunch [➡ RELIGIOUS CONCEPTS; 776] *Opposite*: uncommitted **2** *adj* (*formal*) **sincere**, heartfelt, deep, earnest, fervent, serious [➡ TRUE AND REAL; 171] *Opposite*: insincere

devoutly (*formal*) *adv* **sincerely**, earnestly, fervently, deeply, seriously [➡ TO A GREAT EXTENT; 132] *Opposite*: insincerely

devoutness *n* **piety**, spirituality, religious fervor, religious zeal, piousness [➡ RELIGIOUS CONCEPTS; 776] *Opposite*: impiety

dew *n* **droplets**, precipitation, condensation, dewdrops [➡ MOIST; 1241]

dewdrop *n* **bead of moisture**, droplet, drop, drip [➡ AMOUNTS OF LIQUID; 114]

dewy *adj* **wet**, dew-covered, heavy with dew, damp, moist [➡ MOIST; 1241] *Opposite*: dry

dewy-eyed *adj* **innocent**, naive, trusting, inexperienced, unrealistic, idealistic, sentimental, soppy (*informal*) [➡ NEGATIVE INTELLECTUAL CHARACTERISTICS; 525] *Opposite*: down-to-earth

dexterity **1** *n* **deftness**, skill, adroitness, handiness, legerdemain, agility, nimbleness, dexterousness [➡ SKILLS, TALENTS, AND ABILITIES; 526] *Opposite*: clumsiness **2** *n* **ingenuity**, acuity, sharpness, quickness, resourcefulness, quick-wittedness, ability [➡ POSITIVE INTELLECTUAL CHARACTERISTICS; 524] *Opposite*: ineptitude

dexterous **1** *adj* **deft**, adroit, handy, nimble-fingered, nimble, agile, expert [➡ TALENTED AND SKILLFUL; 527] *Opposite*: clumsy **2** *adj* **quick-witted**, sharp, acute, resourceful, clever, skillful, ingenious, able, adept, efficient [➡ POSITIVE INTELLECTUAL CHARACTERISTICS; 524] *Opposite*: inept

dexterousness *n* [➡ SKILLS, TALENTS, AND ABILITIES; 526]

dextrose *type of* **nutrient** [➡ FOOD COMPONENTS; 1188]

dextrous *see* **dexterous**

dhow *type of* **sailing vessel** [➡ SHIPS AND BOATS; 1150]

diacritic *n* [➡ ASPECTS OF LANGUAGE; 682]

---

diacritic

◆ *types of diacritics*
accent, acute, apostrophe, cedilla, circumflex, dieresis, grave, háček, krouzek, ogonek, tilde, umlaut

diadem *n* **crown**, tiara, circlet, coronet, wreath, headband, headdress [➡ JEWELRY; 866]

diagnose *v* **make a diagnosis**, identify, analyze, spot, detect, make out, establish [➡ MAKE DECISIONS AND CHOICES; 752]

diagnosis **1** *n* **identification**, analysis, judgment, finding, verdict, opinion, conclusion [➡ POINTS OF VIEW; 767] **2** *type of* **medical procedure** [➡ REMEDIES, TREATMENTS, AND OPERATIONS; 731]

diagnostic *adj* **analytic**, analytical, indicative, investigative, problem-solving, pinpointing [➡ EXAMINE AND ASSESS; 753]

diagonal *adj* **slanting**, oblique, sloping, crossways, crosswise, transverse, kitty-cornered, cater-cornered [➡ ORIENTATION AND ALIGNMENT; 1223]

diagram *n* **drawing**, figure, illustration, plan, map, chart, table, graph, scheme, schema [➡ DRAWINGS, CHARTS, AND TABLES; 594]

diagrammatic *adj* **graphic**, illustrative, pictorial, visual, drawn [➡ REPRESENTATIVE; 66] *Opposite*: verbal

dial **1** *n* **knob**, handle, control, button [➡ PARTS OF MACHINES AND TOOLS; 1118] **2** *n* **face**, gauge, indicator, disk, control panel, clock face [➡ PARTS OF MACHINES AND TOOLS; 1118] **3** *v* **call**, telephone, phone, call up, ring up (*UK*), phone up (*UK*), ring (*UK*) [➡ TELEPHONE, PAGE, AND TEXT; 681]

dialect *n* **vernacular**, language, parlance, tongue, idiom, talk [➡ ASPECTS OF LANGUAGE; 682]

See Compare and Contrast at **language**.

dialectic **1** *n* **tension**, conflict, interaction, clash, opposition, contention [➡ ARGUMENTS; 47] *Opposite*: harmony **2** *n* **discussion**, debate, investigation, examination, analysis, disputation (*formal*) [➡ EXAMINE AND ASSESS; 753]

dialogue **1** *n* **discussion**, exchange of ideas, channel of communication, discourse, interchange, information flow, negotiation [➡ NEGOTIATION AND DEBATE; 46] **2** *n* (*formal*) **conversation**, interview, chat, discussion, discourse, talk [➡ INFORMAL COMMUNICATION; 45]

dialysis *type of* **medical procedure** [➡ REMEDIES, TREATMENTS, AND OPERATIONS; 731]

diamanté **1** *adj* **glittery**, sparkly, glittering, sparkling, diamantine, rhinestone [➡ BEAUTY AND ATTRACTIVENESS; 189] *Opposite*: dull **2** *n* **rhinestones**, paste, strass [➡ PRECIOUS STONES; 1278]

diameter *n* **width**, thickness, breadth, length, distance, span [➡ WIDTH: WIDE; 1199]

diametrically *adv* **absolutely**, completely, utterly, totally, entirely, wholly [➡ ABSOLUTE AND ABSOLUTELY; 133] *Opposite*: partially

diamond **1** *n* **rhombus**, parallelogram, lozenge, equilateral [➡ ANGULAR SHAPE; 1217] **2** *type of* **gemstone** [➡ PRECIOUS STONES; 1278]

diamondback *type of* **poisonous snake** [➡SNAKES; 995]

diaphanous *adj* **transparent**, delicate, gauzy, see-through, sheer, gossamer, filmy, thin [➡VISUAL TEXTURE; 1221] *Opposite*: opaque

diaphragm 1 *type of* **muscle or tendon** [➡THE MUSCLES; 718] 2 *part of* **camera** [➡PHOTOGRAPHY AND PHOTOGRAPHIC EQUIPMENT; 1122]

diarist *n* **memoirist**, writer, autobiographer, author, chronicler, memoir writer [➡WRITERS AND STYLES; 914]

diary 1 *n* **journal**, record, log, chronicle, memoir, account [➡RECORDS; 585] 2 *n* (*UK*) **appointment book**, personal organizer, year planner, calendar, schedule [➡LISTS AND SCHEDULES; 587]

diaspora *n* **dispersion**, scattering, movement, displacement, migration, spread [➡SEPARATE AND DIVIDE; 401] *Opposite*: concentration

diatribe *n* **criticism**, attack, tirade, denunciation, harangue, rant, discourse, invective (*formal*) [➡CRITICISMS AND ANGRY OUTBURSTS; 50]

dice 1 *v* **cube**, cut up, chop, cut into cubes [➡TEAR, BREAK, AND CUT; 360] 2 *v* **gamble**, risk, stake, bet, wager, venture, hazard, chance [➡GAMBLE AND TAKE RISKS; 466]

dice with death *v* **face danger**, sail close to the wind, play a dangerous game, cut it fine, play Russian roulette, court disaster, run a risk, take a risk [➡GAMBLE AND TAKE RISKS; 466]

dicey (*informal*) *adj* **risky**, dangerous, hazardous, chancy, uncertain, unpredictable, dubious [➡DANGEROUS; 236] *Opposite*: safe

dichotomy *n* **contrast**, opposition, irreconcilable difference, contradiction, gulf, separation, clash [➡DIFFERENCE; 149] *Opposite*: harmony

dicker (*informal*) *v* **bargain**, haggle, argue, trade, wrangle, exchange [➡ARGUE AND FIGHT; 643]

dictate 1 *v* **speak**, say, say aloud, read out, read aloud, utter, verbalize [➡RECITE, REPEAT, AND NARRATE; 620] 2 *v* **order**, state, command, decree, lay down, prescribe, impose, ordain (*formal*) [➡REQUEST AND DEMAND; 663] 3 *v* **control**, determine, have a bearing on, influence, shape, affect, direct (*formal*) [➡CAUSE TO HAPPEN; 31] 4 *n* **principle**, rule, standard, tenet, precept (*formal*) [➡IDEAS AND THOUGHTS; 770] 5 *n* **command**, order, decree, prescription, injunction, directive, diktat, edict, pronouncement [➡REQUEST AND DEMAND; 663]

dictation *n* **transcription**, notation, transcript [➡WRITING; 583]

dictator *n* **tyrant**, ruler, despot, autocrat, authoritarian, totalitarian [➡VILLAINS AND THUGS; 947] *Opposite*: democrat

dictatorial *adj* **tyrannical**, despotic, autocratic, authoritarian, overbearing, domineering, arrogant, imperious, officious, high-handed, heavy-handed, bossy, dogmatic [➡BOSSY AND OVERBEARING; 516] *Opposite*: democratic

dictatorship 1 *n* **despotism**, autocracy, totalitarianism, authoritarianism, tyranny, repression, absolute rule, single party rule [➡STYLES AND SYSTEMS OF GOVERNMENT; 806] *Opposite*: democracy 2 *n* **regime**, government, rule, era, reign, leadership, junta, reign of terror [➡STYLES AND SYSTEMS OF GOVERNMENT; 806]

diction 1 *n* **pronunciation**, enunciation, articulation, delivery, elocution, projection, speech, accent [➡ASPECTS OF LANGUAGE; 682] 2 *n* **wording**, language, expression, phraseology, phrasing, style, choice of words [➡ASPECTS OF LANGUAGE; 682]

dictionary *n* **lexicon**, vocabulary, glossary, phrase book, word list, thesaurus [➡LISTS AND SCHEDULES; 587]

dictum (*formal*) *n* **pronouncement**, dictate, saying, statement, maxim, motto, aphorism, truism [➡THE ORAL TRADITION; 677]

dicynodont *type of* **dinosaur** [➡DINOSAURS; 996]

didactic *adj* **educational**, instructive, informative, edifying, teaching, improving, moralizing, moralistic, moral [➡INTERESTING AND MEANINGFUL; 190]

didgeridoo *type of* **wind instrument** [➡MUSICAL INSTRUMENTS; 910]

die 1 *v* **expire**, pass away, pass on, kick the bucket (*slang*), croak (*slang*), depart this life (*formal*), decease (*formal*), perish (*literary*), give up the ghost (*literary*) [➡DIE; 922] *Opposite*: live 2 *v* **stop**, give out, go dead, break down, fail, go down, crash, pack in (*informal*), conk out (*informal*) [➡FAIL OR CEASE TO FUNCTION; 470] *Opposite*: start

die a death (*UK*) *v* [➡CEASE TO EXIST; 22]

die away *v* **fade**, fade away, dwindle, fizzle, ebb, wane, diminish, dip, drop, decline, recede, peter out [➡CEASE TO EXIST; 22] *Opposite*: revive

die down *v* **subside**, decrease, lessen, diminish, decline, recede, abate (*formal or literary*) [➡CHANGE OF INTENSITY: LESS; 395] *Opposite*: revive

diehard 1 *adj* **intransigent**, reactionary, conservative, traditionalist, dyed-in-the-wool, fogyish, conformist, stick-in-the-mud (*informal*) [➡UNWILLINGNESS AND STUBBORNNESS; 564] *Opposite*: progressive 2 *n* **reactionary**, conservative, traditionalist, fogy, conformist, member of the old guard, member of the old school, stick-in-the-mud (*informal*), intransigent (*formal*) [➡UNCOOPERATIVE OR REBELLIOUS PEOPLE; 566] *Opposite*: progressive

die of *v* **succumb**, fall victim to, surrender, yield, submit, capitulate [➡DIE; 922] *Opposite*: survive

die off *v* **die out**, become extinct, expire, pass away, pass on, disappear, vanish, perish (*literary*) [➡CEASE TO EXIST; 22] *Opposite*: survive

die out *v* **become extinct**, disappear, vanish, die off, pass away, pass on, expire, perish (*literary*) [➡CEASE TO EXIST; 22] *Opposite*: survive

dieresis *type of* **diacritic** [➡ASPECTS OF LANGUAGE; 682]

diet 1 *n* **food**, fare, nourishment, nutrition, regime, regimen [➡FOOD; 1167] 2 *n* **regime**, intake, supply, regimen, stock, quantity [➡AMOUNTS AND QUANTITIES; 112] 3 *n* **parliament**, legislature, assembly, council, congress, senate [➡LEGISLATIVE BODIES AND LEGISLATION; 809] 4 *v* **slim**, starve, fast, cut back, cut down, abstain, reduce, slenderize (*dated*) [➡EAT AND NOT EAT; 710] *Opposite*: binge

dietary *adj* **nutritional**, dietetic, eating, alimentary, alimental, nutritive [➡FOOD; 1167]

dieter *n* **weightwatcher**, faster, starver, abstainer, slimmer (*UK*) [→ EATERS, GOURMETS, AND DIETARY CHOICES; 714]

differ 1 *v* **be different**, be unlike, be at variance, vary, fluctuate, change, diverge, contrast [→ DIFFERENCE; 149] *Opposite*: match 2 *v* **disagree**, argue, quarrel, fall out, wrangle, be at odds, be at variance, clash [→ ARGUE AND FIGHT; 643] *Opposite*: agree

See Compare and Contrast at **disagree**.

difference 1 *n* **change**, alteration, variance, modification, transformation, metamorphosis [→ DIFFERENCE; 149] *Opposite*: consistency 2 *n* **dissimilarity**, disparity, distinction, differentiation, divergence, variation, variance, contrast, diversity, discrepancy [→ DIFFERENCE; 149] *Opposite*: similarity 3 *n* **argument**, dispute, disagreement, quarrel, tiff, spat [→ ARGUMENTS; 47]

difference of opinion *n* [→ ARGUMENTS; 47]

different 1 *adj* **dissimilar**, diverse, unlike, unalike, poles apart, changed, altered, not the same, worlds apart, like night and day, like oil and water, as like as chalk and cheese (*UK*) [→ DIFFERENCE; 149] *Opposite*: similar 2 *adj* **distinct**, separate, discrete, another [→ DIFFERENCE; 149] *Opposite*: same 3 *adj* **unusual**, special, singular, distinctive, atypical, out of the ordinary, uncommon, unique [→ EXTRAORDINARY: UNCOMMON; 205] *Opposite*: run-of-the-mill

differential *n* **difference**, discrepancy, disparity, gap, variance, distinction [→ SPEED; 102]

differentiate *v* **distinguish**, discriminate, tell apart, set apart, discern, separate, segregate, single out [→ EXAMINE AND ASSESS; 753] *Opposite*: confuse

differentiation 1 *n* **distinction**, discrimination, delineation, demarcation, separation [→ DIFFERENCE; 149] *Opposite*: assimilation 2 *n* **difference**, diversity, variation, distinction, discrepancy, disparity [→ DIFFERENCE; 149] *Opposite*: similarity

differently *adv* **in a different way**, another way, in your own way, otherwise, inversely, contrarily [→ DIFFERENCE; 149] *Opposite*: similarly

differing *adj* **opposing**, contradictory, contrary, divergent, different, opposite, conflicting, clashing [→ DISHARMONY; 156] *Opposite*: similar

difficult 1 *adj* **hard**, tricky, complicated, thorny, complex, intricate, knotty (*UK*) [→ DIFFICULTY AND COMPLEXITY; 242] *Opposite*: easy 2 *adj* **problematic**, hard, tough, trying, grim, challenging, demanding, testing, easier said than done, arduous, tiring, strenuous, grueling [→ PHYSICALLY UNPLEASANT; 226] *Opposite*: simple 3 *adj* **incomprehensible**, unintelligible, impenetrable, involved, complicated, complex, intricate, abstruse, obscure [→ DIFFICULTY AND COMPLEXITY; 242] *Opposite*: simple 4 *adj* **obstinate**, stubborn, recalcitrant, intractable, fractious, unmanageable, awkward [→ UNWILLINGNESS AND STUBBORNNESS; 564] *Opposite*: amenable

See Compare and Contrast at **hard**.

difficulty 1 *n* **complexity**, complicatedness, intricacy, adversity, complication, trickiness [→ DIFFICULTY AND COMPLEXITY; 242] 2 *n* **problem**, snag, obstacle, impediment, stumbling block, hurdle [→ PROBLEMS; 256] 3 *n* **trouble**, effort, struggle,

exertion, strain, sweat, striving, toil [→ HARD WORK OR EFFORT; 298] *Opposite*: ease

diffidence *n* **shyness**, hesitancy, reserve, timidity, reticence, quietness [→ RETICENT AND UNFORTHCOMING; 631] *Opposite*: brashness

diffident *adj* **shy**, hesitant, insecure, timid, reticent, reserved, retiring, unobtrusive, self-effacing, quiet [→ RETICENT AND UNFORTHCOMING; 631] *Opposite*: brash

diffract *v* **bend**, deflect, curve, divert, spread, diffuse [→ SPREAD AND SCATTER; 332]

diffraction *n* **deflection**, bending, curving, diversion, spreading, diffusion [→ CHANGE DIRECTION OF MOTION; 344]

diffuse 1 *v* **disperse**, spread, disseminate, distribute, circulate, scatter, strew [→ DISPENSE, RATION, AND DISTRIBUTE; 434] *Opposite*: concentrate 2 *adj* **dispersed**, spread, disseminated, distributed, circulated, scattered, strewn [→ ORIENTATION AND ALIGNMENT; 1223] *Opposite*: concentrated 3 *adj* **wordy**, verbose, prolix, long-winded, drawn-out, rambling, long-drawn-out (*UK*) [→ INARTICULATE, RAMBLING, AND AWKWARD; 633] *Opposite*: concise

See Compare and Contrast at **wordy**.

diffusely *adv* **wordily**, verbosely, prolixly, long-windedly, turgidly, ramblingly [→ INARTICULATE, RAMBLING, AND AWKWARD; 633] *Opposite*: concisely

diffusion *n* **dispersal**, dispersion, dissemination, distribution, circulation, transmission, flow [→ DISPENSE, RATION, AND DISTRIBUTE; 434] *Opposite*: concentration

dig 1 *v* **break up**, plow, turn, hoe, till, rake [→ TEAR, BREAK, AND CUT; 360] 2 *v* **excavate**, tunnel, hollow out, burrow, mine, quarry [→ USE TOOLS AND MACHINERY; 468] 3 *v* **prod**, nudge, push, shove, jab, poke [→ CONTACT: TOUCH; 412] 4 *n* **poke**, prod, nudge, push, shove, jab [→ CONTACT: TOUCH; 412] 5 *n* **gibe**, taunt, jeer, crack, insult, slur, remark [→ JOKES AND TEASING; 674] *Opposite*: compliment

digest 1 *v* **process**, assimilate, absorb, break down, consume, eat [→ EAT AND NOT EAT; 710] 2 *v* **assimilate**, absorb, take in, take on board, grasp, process [→ UNDERSTAND AND GRASP; 759] *Opposite*: ignore 3 *n* **abridgment**, résumé, summary, condensation, abstract, précis [→ SUMMARIES, OUTLINES, AND EXCERPTS; 588] 4 *n* **publication**, journal, magazine, periodical, book, tome, volume [→ BOOKS AND BOOKLETS; 590]

digestible *adj* **edible**, palatable, eatable, consumable, comestible (*formal*), esculent (*formal*) [→ FOOD; 1167] *Opposite*: indigestible

digestif *n* [→ DRINKS; 1187]

digestion *n* **assimilation**, ingestion, absorption, incorporation, breakdown, consumption [→ EAT AND NOT EAT; 710]

digestive *adj* **peptic**, gastric, intestinal, gastrointestinal, duodenal, excretory [→ EAT AND NOT EAT; 710]

digestive tract *n* **bowels**, guts, intestines, viscera, innards (*informal*), insides (*informal*) [→ THE DIGESTIVE TRACT; 709]

digestive tract

◆ *parts of a digestive tract*
anus, appendix, bile duct, bladder, bowel, cecum, colon, duodenum, esophagus, gallbladder, gullet, gut, intestine, kidney, large intestine, liver, pancreas, rectum, small intestine, spleen, stomach, throat

digger 1 *n* **miner**, excavator, gravedigger, gold digger, prospector, archaeologist [➡ FARMERS, GARDENERS, AND MANUAL WORKERS; 849] **2** *n* **excavator**, bulldozer, earthmover, crawler, backhoe, shovel [➡ VEHICLES; 1145]

diggings *n* **excavation**, mine, quarry, pit, dig [➡ HOLES, GAPS, AND FORKS; 1252]

dig into 1 *v* **stick into**, push into, sink into, stab, prod, jab [➡ CONTACT: TOUCH; 412] **2** *v* **examine**, look at, delve into, investigate, go into, probe, research [➡ EXAMINE AND ASSESS; 753] *Opposite*: ignore

dig in your heels *v* **stand firm**, hold your ground, stand your ground, hold out, resist, persist, stick it out, be stubborn [➡ NOT DO AND REFUSE TO DO; 274] *Opposite*: give in

digit *n* **number**, numeral, figure, cipher, character, symbol [➡ SYMBOLS, SIGNS, AND NUMBERS; 596]

digital *adj* **numerical**, numerary, numeral, alphanumeric, cardinal, ordinal, arithmetical [➡ MATH; 597]

digital cash *n* [➡ E-COMMERCE; 1129]

digital clock *type of* **clock** [➡ CLOCKS AND TIMERS; 1126]

digital signature *n* [➡ E-COMMERCE; 1129]

dignified *adj* **distinguished**, honorable, decorous, stately, noble, gracious, imposing, grand, venerable, regal, majestic, self-respecting, proper, respectable, exalted (*formal*) [➡ CONFIDENCE AND COMPOSURE; 499] *Opposite*: undignified

dignify *v* **distinguish**, grace, glorify, venerate, honor, exalt (*formal*) [➡ CONFER STATUS; 458] *Opposite*: degrade

dignitary *n* **notable**, VIP, worthy, celebrity, luminary, public figure, bigwig (*informal*), personage (*formal*) [➡ IMPORTANT OR FAMOUS PEOPLE; 893] *Opposite*: nobody

dignity 1 *n* **self-respect**, self-esteem, pride, self-possession, self-worth [➡ CONFIDENCE AND COMPOSURE; 499] *Opposite*: ignominy **2** *n* **formality**, gravity, solemnity, grandeur, decorum, stateliness, majesty, poise, composure [➡ GOOD MANNERS AND SOCIAL SKILLS; 520] *Opposite*: informality **3** *n* **worthiness**, worth, nobility, nobleness, goodness, excellence, respectability, propriety, seemliness [➡ MORALLY GOOD; 774] *Opposite*: unworthiness

dig out 1 *v* **uncover**, excavate, dig up, unearth, expose, extricate, remove [➡ FIND; 463] *Opposite*: bury **2** *v* (*informal*) **retrieve**, find, discover, locate, reveal, bring to light, dredge up [➡ FIND; 463]

digress *v* **deviate**, depart, wander, go off on a tangent, stray, ramble, divagate (*literary*) [➡ CHATTER AND BABBLE; 617] *Opposite*: focus

digression *n* **deviation**, departure, aside, parenthesis, detour, excursion, foray [➡ DIFFERENCE; 149] *Opposite*: focus

dig up 1 *v* **unearth**, excavate, disinter, exhume, expose,

uncover [➡ CAUSE TO APPEAR; 5] *Opposite*: bury **2** *v* (*informal*) **bring to light**, dredge up, expose, reveal, find, discover [➡ FIND; 463] *Opposite*: hide

dik-dik *type of* **deer or antelope** [➡ DEER AND ANTELOPES; 981]

dike 1 *n* **embankment**, dam, barrier, bank, wall, fortification, sea wall, barrage [➡ BARRIERS; 1113] **2** *n* **ditch**, watercourse, channel, drain, conduit, gutter, trench [➡ WATERCOURSES; 1111]

diktat *n* **command**, decree, edict, dictate, order, instruction [➡ REQUEST AND DEMAND; 663]

dilapidated *adj* **decrepit**, rundown, derelict, ramshackle, on its last legs, the worse for wear, tumbledown, broken-down, ruined, destroyed, wrecked, shabby, beat-up (*informal*) [➡ IN BAD REPAIR; 1234] *Opposite*: pristine

dilapidation *n* **disrepair**, dereliction, decrepitude, decay, ruin, destruction, collapse, shabbiness [➡ IN BAD REPAIR; 1234]

dilate 1 *v* **expand**, widen, open, enlarge, increase, stretch, distend, amplify [➡ CHANGE OF SIZE: BIGGER; 392] *Opposite*: contract **2** *v* **amplify**, expatiate, expand, dwell on, expound, elucidate, elaborate [➡ EXPLAIN AND CLARIFY; 610] *Opposite*: abbreviate

dilation *n* **expansion**, opening, enlargement, increase, distension, stretching [➡ CHANGE OF SIZE: BIGGER; 392] *Opposite*: contraction

dilatory *adj* **slow**, tardy, remiss, behindhand, slack, problem, negligent, lazy, lagging, dragging, flagging, laggard, slow-paced, slow-going [➡ MOVING SLOWLY; 105] *Opposite*: prompt

dilemma *n* **quandary**, tight spot, Catch-22, predicament, impasse, problem, catch [➡ PROBLEMS; 256]

dilettante *n* **amateur**, dabbler, abecedarian, neophyte, novice [➡ UNSKILLED PEOPLE; 530] *Opposite*: expert

diligence *n* **assiduousness**, meticulousness, conscientiousness, thoroughness, attentiveness, carefulness, persistence, industry (*formal or literary*) [➡ HARD-WORKING AND COMMITTED; 500] *Opposite*: carelessness

diligent *adj* **industrious**, assiduous, painstaking, meticulous, conscientious, thorough, attentive, careful, persistent [➡ HARD-WORKING AND COMMITTED; 500] *Opposite*: lazy

dill *type of* **herb** [➡ HERBS AND SPICES; 1175]

dilly (*slang*) *n* [➡ AMAZING THINGS; 211]

dilly-dally *v* **dawdle**, dally, delay, shilly-shally, drag your heels, waste time [➡ SHIRK AND DELAY; 273] *Opposite*: hurry

dilly-dallying *n* [➡ DELAY ACTION OR OCCURRENCE; 278]

dilute 1 *v* **thin**, weaken, water down, adulterate [➡ CHANGE OF INTENSITY: LESS; 395] *Opposite*: concentrate **2** *v* **reduce**, attenuate, temper, mitigate, water down, take the edge off, offset [➡ CHANGE OF INTENSITY: LESS; 395] *Opposite*: increase **3** *adj* **weak**, watered down, thinned, watery, insipid, diluted [➡ FLUID AND NONSOLID; 1213] *Opposite*: concentrated

diluted *adj* **weak**, watered down, thinned, watery, dilute [➡ FLUID AND NONSOLID; 1213] *Opposite*: concentrated

dilution 1 *n* **thinning**, weakening, watering down, watering [➡CHANGE OF INTENSITY: LESS; 395] **2** *n* **reduction**, attenuation, enfeeblement, erosion, weakening [➡CHANGE OF INTENSITY: LESS; 395] *Opposite:* strengthening **3** *n* **concentration**, strength, intensity, potency [➡DEGREE AND EXTENT; 110]

dim 1 *adj* **badly lit**, murky, gloomy, shadowy, dusky, dark [➡DESCRIBING LIGHT; 1228] *Opposite:* bright **2** *adj* **soft**, faint, muted, weak, diffuse, dull [➡DESCRIBING LIGHT; 1228] *Opposite:* strong **3** *adj* **indistinct**, vague, blurred, blurry, hazy, faint, unclear, shadowy, subdued [➡VAGUENESS; 243] *Opposite:* clear **4** *v* **turn down**, lower, darken, reduce [➡CHANGE OF INTENSITY: LESS; 395] *Opposite:* turn up

dime *n* [➡CURRENCIES; 798]

dimension 1 *n* **measurement**, length, height, width, breadth [➡SIZE AND DIMENSIONS; 1192] **2** *n* **aspect**, element, facet, feature, factor, component [➡QUALITIES AND CHARACTERISTICS; 1191]

dimensions *n* **size**, scope, extent, magnitude, proportions [➡SIZE AND DIMENSIONS; 1192]

dime store *type of* **retail outlet** [➡RETAIL OUTLETS; 1083]

diminish 1 *v* **reduce**, lessen, make smaller, weaken, moderate, contract [➡CHANGE OF INTENSITY: LESS; 395] *Opposite:* increase **2** *v* **shrink**, ebb, fade, fade away, fade out, peter out, taper [➡CEASE TO EXIST; 22] *Opposite:* grow

diminishing *adj* **lessening**, fading, waning, weakening, falling, shrinking [➡CEASE TO EXIST; 22] *Opposite:* increasing

diminuendo *type of* **musical term** [➡MUSIC, SONGS, AND SINGING; 907]

diminution *n* **decrease**, reduction, lessening, attenuation, shrinking, dwindling, contraction [➡CHANGE OF INTENSITY: LESS; 395] *Opposite:* growth

diminutive *adj* **small**, little, tiny, minuscule, miniature, minute, pocket-size, pint-size (*informal*) [➡SMALL; 1195] *Opposite:* huge

dimly 1 *adv* **softly**, faintly, mutedly, weakly, diffusely [➡DESCRIBING LIGHT; 1228] *Opposite:* brightly **2** *adv* **indistinctly**, vaguely, hazily, faintly, obscurely, blurrily, unclearly [➡VAGUENESS; 243] *Opposite:* clearly

dimmer *n* **light switch**, dimmer switch, brightness control, regulator, rheostat [➡PARTS OF MACHINES AND TOOLS; 1118]

dimness 1 *n* **murkiness**, gloom, gloominess, shadowiness, duskiness, darkness [➡DESCRIBING LIGHT; 1228] *Opposite:* brightness **2** *n* **softness**, faintness, weakness, diffuseness, dullness [➡DESCRIBING LIGHT; 1228] *Opposite:* brightness **3** *n* **indistinctness**, vagueness, blurriness, haziness, faintness, shadowiness [➡VAGUENESS; 243] *Opposite:* clearness

dimple *n* **hollow**, depression, pit, indentation, dent, dint [➡FACIAL CHARACTERISTICS; 481] *Opposite:* bump

dimpled 1 *adj* **dimply**, cleft, indented, dented, chubby, plump [➡FACIAL CHARACTERISTICS; 481] *Opposite:* smooth **2** *adj* **textured**, indented, dented, pocked, pockmarked, pitted, orange-peel, uneven [➡FACIAL CHARACTERISTICS; 481] *Opposite:* smooth

din 1 *n* **noise**, hubbub, rumpus, racket, hullabaloo, commotion, disturbance, pandemonium, tumult [➡CHAOS AND UPROAR; 51] **2** *v* **drum into**, hammer, inculcate, instill, impress [➡CLAIM, INSIST, AND EMPHASIZE; 614]

dinar *type of* **currency** [➡CURRENCIES; 798]

dine *v* **eat**, feast, banquet, consume, ingest, partake [➡EAT AND NOT EAT; 710]

diner 1 *n* **patron**, customer, guest [➡EATERS, GOURMETS, AND DIETARY CHOICES; 714] **2** *type of* **eating place** [➡RETAIL OUTLETS; 1083]

ding 1 *n* **ringing**, ring, dong, ding-dong, ding-a-ling, ting-a-ling, tinkle [➡RINGING AND HOOTING SOUNDS; 1259] **2** *n* (*informal*) **dent**, indentation, dint, hollow, dimple, pit, mark [➡HOLES, GAPS, AND FORKS; 1252] **3** *v* **ring**, tinkle, dong, ding-dong [➡EMIT RINGING AND HOOTING SOUNDS; 367]

ding-a-ling *type of* **ringing sound** [➡RINGING AND HOOTING SOUNDS; 1259]

ding-dong *type of* **ringing sound** [➡RINGING AND HOOTING SOUNDS; 1259]

dinge *n* **filth**, grime, mess, dirt, muck (*informal*), grunge (*informal*) [➡UNPLEASANT, DIRTY, AND TOXIC SUBSTANCES; 1268] *Opposite:* cleanliness

dinghy *type of* **small vessel** [➡SHIPS AND BOATS; 1150]

dinginess 1 *n* **dirtiness**, discoloration, griminess, dullness, dreariness, grubbiness [➡DIRTY; 1235] *Opposite:* brightness **2** *n* **shabbiness**, drabness, squalidness, cheerlessness, seediness [➡IN BAD REPAIR; 1234] *Opposite:* neatness

dingo *type of* **canine** [➡CANINES; 979]

dingy 1 *adj* **dirty**, grimy, soiled, grubby, dull, begrimed (*literary*), besmirched (*literary*) [➡DIRTY; 1235] *Opposite:* clean **2** *adj* **shabby**, drab, squalid, tatty, worn, cheerless, seedy, poor [➡IN BAD REPAIR; 1234] *Opposite:* bright

dining car *part of* **train** [➡RAILROADS; 1107]

dining hall *type of* **room in public buildings** [➡TYPES OF ROOMS; 1097]

dining room *type of* **room in the home** [➡TYPES OF ROOMS; 1097]

dining table *type of* **table** [➡FURNITURE; 858]

dinky (*informal*) **1** *adj* **small**, compact, neat, natty, cute [➡SMALL; 1195] *Opposite:* hefty **2** *adj* **small**, little, tiny, minute, insignificant, paltry, limited, cramped [➡SMALL; 1195] *Opposite:* substantial

dinner *type of* **meal** [➡MEALS AND PARTS OF MEALS; 1169]

dinner service *n* [➡TABLEWARE, FLATWARE, AND KITCHENWARE; 861]

dinnertime *n* **mealtime**, suppertime, lunchtime, teatime [➡TIMES OF DAY; 87]

dinosaur *n* **relic**, fossil, vestige, leftover, hangover, has-been (*informal*) [➡REMAINDER AND REMAINDERS; 125]

dinosaur

◆ *types of dinosaurs*

allosaurus, ankylosaur, apatosaur, brachiosaurus, brontosaurus, cotylosaur, dicynodont, diplodocus, hadrosaur, ichthyosaur, iguanodon, megalosaur, mosasaur, oviraptor, pelycosaur, plesiosaur, pteranodon, pterodactyl, pterosaur, stegosaur, titanosaur, triceratops, tyrannosaur, velociraptor

dint 1 *n* **indent**, dent, indentation, depression, hollow, pit, mark [➡ HOLES, GAPS, AND FORKS; 1252] **2** v **dent**, damage, mark, spoil, blemish [➡ TEAR, BREAK, AND CUT; 360]

dip **1** v **plunge**, immerse, dunk, douse, bathe, wet, wash, rinse, submerge, duck, submerge [➡ SOFTEN, LIQUEFY, AND DAMPEN; 388] **2** v **drop**, drop down, descend, decline, sink, fall, fall away, drop away, plummet [➡ GO DOWNWARD; 307] *Opposite*: rise **3** v **slope**, incline, slant, descend, fall away, drop away, recede, veer [➡ GO DOWNWARD; 307] *Opposite*: level **4** n **fall**, decline, drop, depression, falling off, slump, downturn, plunge [➡ LESS; 126] *Opposite*: rise **5** n **swim**, plunge, bathe [➡ HOBBIES, GAMES, AND SPORTS; 875] **6** n **hollow**, depression, incline, slope, rise and fall, concavity, sinkage [➡ HOLES, GAPS, AND FORKS; 1252] **7** n [➡ SEASONINGS AND SAUCES; 1174]

diphthong *type of* **grammatical term** [➡ ASPECTS OF LANGUAGE; 682]

dip into v **skim**, flick through, flip through, glance, browse, look through, cast an eye over [➡ READ; 758] *Opposite*: study

diplodocus *type of* **dinosaur** [➡ DINOSAURS; 996]

diploma n **certificate**, qualification, credential [➡ QUALIFICATIONS; 843]

diplomacy **1** n **international relations**, mediation, negotiation, peacekeeping [➡ GOVERNMENT POLICIES; 810] **2** n **tact**, skill, subtlety, discretion, savoir-faire, address [➡ GOOD MANNERS AND SOCIAL SKILLS; 520] *Opposite*: tactlessness

diplomat **1** n **civil servant**, envoy, representative, attaché, ambassador, consul, legate, cultural attaché, military attaché, public servant [➡ ADMINISTRATIVE OFFICERS; 811] **2** n **tactician**, peacekeeper, negotiator, mediator, go-between, PR expert, moderator [➡ POLITICAL OFFICES AND POLITICIANS; 808]

diplomatic **1** adj **political**, ambassadorial, consular, embassy [➡ STYLES AND SYSTEMS OF GOVERNMENT; 806] **2** adj **tactful**, subtle, suave, discreet, sensitive, cautious, politic, wily [➡ GOOD MANNERS AND SOCIAL SKILLS; 520] *Opposite*: tactless

dipper n **ladle**, scoop, spoon [➡ SPOONS, SCOOPS, AND SHOVELS; 1121]

dippy (*UK*) adj [➡ ECCENTRICITY AND IRRATIONALITY; 562]

dipstick *type of* **measuring device** [➡ MEASURING DEVICES; 1123]

dire adj **terrible**, awful, dreadful, calamitous, horrible, ominous, dismal, grim, disastrous, appalling, frightful (*UK*) [➡ UNACCEPTABLE AND UNFORGIVABLE; 225] *Opposite*: wonderful

direct **1** v **manage**, control, regulate, rule, oversee, supervise, preside, produce [➡ BE IN CHARGE; 270] **2** v (*formal*) **order**, give orders, instruct, give instructions, command, charge, dictate, tell [➡ REQUEST AND DEMAND; 663] *Opposite*: request **3** v **show the way**, guide, lead, put on the right track, point in the right direction, point, give directions, steer [➡ ACCOMPANY AND FOLLOW; 337] **4** v **aim**, point, turn, target, train, level, focus, address [➡ POSITION SOMETHING; 325] **5** adj **straight**, shortest, through, unswerving, undeviating, nonstop, uninterrupted, express [➡ DIRECTION OF MOTION; 345] *Opposite*: circuitous **6** adj **precise**, exact, absolute, complete, unequivocal, immediate, close [➡ EXACT; 203] *Opposite*: vague **7** adj **straightforward**, honest, open, candid, frank, sincere, plain-spoken, outspoken, blunt, up-front (*informal*) [➡ HONEST AND OPEN; 630] *Opposite*: devious **8** adv **directly**, straight, nonstop, right, in a straight line, as the crow flies [➡ DIRECTION OF MOTION; 345] *Opposite*: indirectly

See Compare and Contrast at **guide**.

direction **1** n **management**, control, government, guidance, leadership, administration, command, supervision [➡ BUSINESS; 791] **2** n **way**, course, track, route, path, bearing, road [➡ DIRECTION OF MOTION; 345] **3** n **trend**, course, route, focus, aim, target, objective, tendency [➡ INTENTIONS AND PURPOSES; 772]

directional adj **maneuvering**, steering, turning, reversing, guiding, indicator [➡ DIRECTION OF MOTION; 345]

directions n **instructions**, information, orders, guidelines, commands, tips [➡ ADVICE; 689]

directive n **order**, command, instruction, direction, edict, demand [➡ REQUEST AND DEMAND; 663]

directly **1** adv **in a straight line**, straight, right, unswervingly, nonstop, as the crow flies [➡ DIRECTION OF MOTION; 345] *Opposite*: indirectly **2** adv **completely**, diametrically, absolutely, wholly, unequivocally, in every respect [➡ ABSOLUTE AND ABSOLUTELY; 133] **3** adv **openly**, honestly, frankly, straightforwardly, truthfully, candidly, sincerely, bluntly, clearly, exactly, precisely, unambiguously [➡ HONEST AND OPEN; 630] *Opposite*: ambiguously **4** adv (*formal*) **immediately**, quickly, at once, promptly, without delay, speedily, soon, right away [➡ HAPPENING QUICKLY; 104]

direct mail n **promotional mailing**, circular, junk mail, unsolicited mail, mailing, advertising, mail shot (*UK*) [➡ ADVERTISING AND PUBLICITY; 604]

directness n **honesty**, openness, straightforwardness, truthfulness, sincerity, frankness, bluntness [➡ HONEST AND OPEN; 630] *Opposite*: deviousness

director n **manager**, leader, executive, boss, administrator, principal, chief [➡ BOSSES AND MANAGEMENT; 965]

directorate n **board of directors**, executive, executive board, executive committee, board, board of controllers, board of executives [➡ BOSSES AND MANAGEMENT; 965]

director-general n **president**, head, director, chairperson, chief executive, chief administrator, executive director [➡ BOSSES AND MANAGEMENT; 965]

directorship n **director's post**, management post, executive post, managerial position, presidency [➡ BOSSES AND MANAGEMENT; 965]

directory *type of* **computer feature** [➡ COMPUTERS AND COMPUTING; 1127]

dirge n **elegy**, requiem, funeral hymn, lament, chant, song [➡ RELIGIONS AND RELIGIOUS PRACTICES; 777]

dirham *type of* **currency** [➡ CURRENCIES; 798]

dirigible *type of* **civil aircraft** [➡ AIRCRAFT; 1148]

dirk *type of* **sword or knife** [➡ SWORDS AND KNIVES; 1157]

dirndl *type of* **skirt** [➡ GARMENTS AND OUTFITS; 865]

dirt **1** n **grime**, filth, mud, dust, muck (*informal*) [➡ UNPLEASANT, DIRTY, AND TOXIC SUBSTANCES; 1268] **2** n **soil**, earth, clay, loam, mud [➡ EROSION PRODUCTS AND SOIL; 1058] **3** n **gossip**, scandal, filth, smut, lowdown (*informal*), scuttlebutt (*slang*) [➡ GOSSIP; 678]

dirt bike *type of* **bike** [➡ BIKES, CARS, AND CARRIAGES; 1149]

dirt-cheap (*informal*) **1** *adj* **cheap**, reduced, cut-rate, bargain, inexpensive, discounted, cut-price (*UK*) [➡ CHEAP AND INEXPENSIVE; 221] *Opposite*: dear **2** *adv* **cheaply**, at a knockdown price, at bargain-basement prices, for a song, for next to nothing, on sale, on the cheap (*informal*) [➡ CHEAP AND INEXPENSIVE; 221]

dirt-free *adj* [➡ CLEAN AND HYGIENIC; 1233]

dirtied *adj* [➡ DIRTY; 1235]

dirtiness *n* griminess, filthiness, messiness, muddiness, grubbiness, pollution [➡ DIRTY; 1235] *Opposite*: cleanliness

dirt track *type of* **secondary road** [➡ ROADS, 1106]

dirty **1** *adj* **unclean**, filthy, grimy, soiled, grubby, muddy, polluted, foul, squalid, sullied (*literary*) [➡ DIRTY; 1235] *Opposite*: clean **2** *adj* **dishonest**, illegal, corrupt, unfair, immoral, fraudulent, unscrupulous, crooked (*informal*) [➡ MORALLY BAD OR IMPROPER; 775] *Opposite*: honest **3** *adj* **dull**, muted, muddy, cloudy, murky [➡ DESCRIBING COLORS; 1226] *Opposite*: clear **4** *v* **soil**, stain, pollute, foul, defile (*formal*), sully (*literary*) [➡ DIRTY AND CONTAMINATE; 404] *Opposite*: clean

> **Compare and Contrast:** *dirty, filthy, grubby, grimy, soiled, squalid, unclean*
>
> CORE MEANING: not clean
>
> *dirty* stained or marked with dirt; *filthy* extremely or disgustingly dirty; *grubby* slightly dirty; *grimy* heavily ingrained with accumulated dirt; *soiled* stained or marked, especially during normal use; *squalid* insanitary and unpleasant; *unclean* dirty or impure, especially in moral or religious contexts.

dirty look *n* [➡ FACIAL EXPRESSIONS AND BLUSHING; 651]

dirty tricks *n* **unfair tactics**, foul play, deviousness, dishonesty, trickery [➡ DECEPTION AND LIES; 660]

dirty word *n* **swear word**, expletive, four-letter word, cussword (*informal*) [➡ INSULTS, ABUSE, AND SWEARING; 658]

dis (*slang*) **1** *v* **insult**, affront, disrespect, belittle, disparage, denigrate, lessen, put down (*informal*) [➡ INSULTS, ABUSE, AND SWEARING; 658] *Opposite*: compliment **2** *v* **criticize**, attack, denigrate, maul, savage, find fault with, trash (*informal*) [➡ ACCUSE, BLAME, AND CRITICIZE; 641] *Opposite*: support

disability *n* **incapacity**, infirmity, frailty, debility, ill health [➡ ILLNESSES AND DISORDERS; 732]

disable *v* **incapacitate**, restrict, inactivate, deactivate, put out of action, knock out, spike (*informal*) [➡ CAUSE TO STOP; 266]

disablement *n* **impairment**, incapacitation, deactivation, spiking (*informal*) [➡ ILLNESSES AND DISORDERS; 732]

disabuse *v* **persuade out of**, disillusion, enlighten, set straight, shatter somebody's illusions, correct, deprive [➡ INFORM, ANNOUNCE, AND ISSUE; 611]

disadvantage *n* **difficulty**, drawback, shortcoming, weakness, hindrance, handicap, detriment, minus, demerit, inconvenience [➡ FAULTS, FLAWS, AND WEAKNESSES; 251] *Opposite*: advantage

disadvantaged *adj* **deprived**, underprivileged, needy, destitute, poor, in need, lacking, badly off [➡ POVERTY AND POOR; 892] *Opposite*: privileged

disadvantageous *adj* **detrimental**, damaging, hurtful, harmful, injurious, prejudicial, inconvenient, troublesome, unhelpful [➡ DANGEROUS; 236] *Opposite*: advantageous

disadvantageously *adv* **detrimentally**, harmfully, hurtfully, inconveniently, injuriously, prejudicially, unhelpfully [➡ DANGEROUS; 236] *Opposite*: desirably

disaffect *v* **estrange**, disillusion, disenchant, dissatisfy, alienate, disgruntle, turn off (*informal*) [➡ UPSET, DISTRESS, AND HUMILIATE; 567]

disaffected *adj* **disillusioned**, dissatisfied, disgruntled, cynical, alienated, estranged, apathetic [➡ NEUTRALITY AND INDIFFERENCE; 553] *Opposite*: enthusiastic

disaffection *n* **disillusionment**, alienation, estrangement, dissatisfaction, cynicism, apathy [➡ NEUTRALITY AND INDIFFERENCE; 553] *Opposite*: enthusiasm

disagree **1** *v* **demur**, differ, take issue with, agree to differ, be at odds [➡ PROTEST AND EXPRESS DISAPPROVAL; 642] *Opposite*: agree **2** *v* **differ**, vary, diverge, conflict, oppose, deviate, be dissimilar, contradict [➡ DIFFERENCE; 149] *Opposite*: agree **3** *v* **argue**, quarrel, wrangle, dispute, bicker, clash, fall out, row, fight [➡ ARGUE AND FIGHT; 643] *Opposite*: agree

> **Compare and Contrast:** *disagree, differ, argue, dispute, take issue with, contradict, agree to differ, be at odds*
>
> CORE MEANING: to have or express a difference of opinion with somebody
>
> *disagree* to have or put forward a different view or opinion from somebody; *differ* to have different opinions about something; *argue* to express disagreement with somebody, especially continuously or angrily; *dispute* to have a heated argument; *take issue with* to disagree strongly with somebody or something; *contradict* to argue against the truth or correctness of somebody's statement or claim; *agree to differ* to stop arguing and accept that the opposing viewpoints are irreconcilable; *be at odds* to be in disagreement, especially over a period of time or about a particular issue.

disagreeable **1** *adj* **displeasing**, distasteful, offensive, nasty, unpleasant, dislikable, horrible [➡ EMOTIONALLY UNPLEASANT AND UPSETTING; 227] *Opposite*: agreeable **2** *adj* **bad-tempered**, unfriendly, unhelpful, difficult, contrary, ornery, rude, surly, brusque, crabby, quarrelsome [➡ AGGRESSIVE AND BELLIGERENT; 518] *Opposite*: pleasant

disagreement **1** *n* **dispute**, difference of opinion, quarrel, argument, misunderstanding, discord, conflict, wrangle, dissent, clash, falling-out [➡ ARGUMENTS; 47] *Opposite*: agreement **2** *n* **difference**, divergence, incongruity, discrepancy, dissimilarity, disparity, variance, deviation [➡ DIFFERENCE; 149] *Opposite*: agreement

disallow **1** *v* (*formal*) **reject**, refuse, deny, throw, disapprove, turn down, negate (*formal*) [➡ REFUSE PERMISSION AND NOT ALLOW; 670] *Opposite*: pass **2** *v* **cancel**, prohibit, forbid, veto, bar, ban, outlaw, overrule, exclude, preclude (*formal*) [➡ REFUSE PERMISSION AND NOT ALLOW; 670] *Opposite*: allow

disallowed *adj* **rejected**, forbidden, banned, excluded, vetoed, prohibited, overruled, precluded (*formal*) [➡ REFUSE PERMISSION AND NOT ALLOW; 670] *Opposite*: allowed

disappear 1 *v* **vanish**, fade, fade away, go, evaporate, dissolve, melt, wane, withdraw, ebb, depart, flee, recede, dematerialize, dissipate [➡ DISAPPEAR; 4] *Opposite*: appear 2 *v* **cease to exist**, die out, die off, expire, pass away, vanish, perish (*formal*) [➡ CEASE TO EXIST; 22] *Opposite*: appear

disappearance *n* **vanishing**, evaporation, fading, loss, desertion, withdrawal, departure [➡ ENDS AND DEPARTURES; 54] *Opposite*: appearance

disappearing *adj* **vanishing**, waning, endangered, threatened, dying [➡ IN DANGER; 237]

disappoint *v* **let down**, disillusion, fail, dissatisfy, dishearten, upset, thwart, frustrate, sadden, disenchant [➡ UPSET, DISTRESS, AND HUMILIATE; 567] *Opposite*: please

disappointed *adj* **let down**, dissatisfied, disillusioned, upset, saddened, thwarted, disenchanted, frustrated [➡ SADNESS, DISTRESS, AND DESPAIR; 539] *Opposite*: satisfied

disappointing *adj* **unsatisfactory**, unacceptable, second-rate, poor, below par, inadequate, not up to scratch (*informal*) [➡ BAD AND BADLY; 223] *Opposite*: satisfactory

disappointment 1 *n* **dissatisfaction**, displeasure, distress, discontent, disenchantment, disillusionment, frustration, regret [➡ SADNESS, DISTRESS, AND DESPAIR; 539] *Opposite*: satisfaction 2 *n* **setback**, failure, frustration, defeat, drawback, hindrance, inconvenience [➡ NUISANCES; 253]

disapprobation (*formal*) *n* **disfavor**, condemnation, disapproval, dislike, displeasure, censure, discontentment, dissatisfaction [➡ ANTAGONISM; 552] *Opposite*: approval

disapproval *n* **condemnation**, displeasure, dissatisfaction, censure, discontentment, disapprobation (*formal*) [➡ IRRITATION AND ANGER; 541] *Opposite*: approval

disapprove 1 *v* **condemn**, censure, criticize, dislike, object, frown on, reject, not hold with, have a problem with, deplore, denounce [➡ DISLIKE AND HATE; 577] *Opposite*: approve 2 *v* (*formal*) **reject**, refuse, veto, turn down, deny, throw out, negate (*formal*) [➡ PROTEST AND EXPRESS DISAPPROVAL; 642] *Opposite*: approve

Compare and Contrast: *disapprove, frown on, object, criticize, condemn, deplore, denounce, censure*

CORE MEANING: to have an unfavorable opinion of something or somebody

disapprove to judge somebody or something negatively based on personal standards; *frown on* to dislike or disapprove of something; *object* to be opposed to something, or express opposition; *criticize* to point out flaws or faults; *condemn* to give an unfavorable judgment on somebody or something; *deplore* to disapprove of something strongly; *denounce* to criticize or condemn publicly and harshly; *censure* to make a formal, often public or official, statement of disapproval.

disapproving *adj* **critical**, judgmental, negative, censorious, stern, harsh [➡ ACCUSATORY AND DISAPPROVING; 634] *Opposite*: approving

disarm 1 *v* **deactivate**, defuse, make safe, neutralize [➡ MAKE IMPOSSIBLE; 276] *Opposite*: arm 2 *v* **win over**, charm, enchant, beguile, win the affection of, put off guard, captivate [➡ PLEASE AND AMUSE; 572] *Opposite*: annoy

disarmament *n* **arms reduction**, nuclear disarmament, unilateral disarmament, decommissioning, demilitarization, demobilization [➡ WARFARE AND WAR; 830]

disarming *adj* **charming**, enchanting, attractive, appealing, captivating, winning, beguiling [➡ EMOTIONALLY PLEASANT; 187] *Opposite*: cold

disarrange *v* **disorder**, disturb, jumble, dishevel, mix up, mess up (*informal*) [➡ CREATE DISORDER AND CAUSE CHAOS; 358] *Opposite*: order

disarranged *adj* **disordered**, untidy, rumpled, messy, jumbled, disheveled, mixed up, messed up [➡ DISORDER AND CHAOS; 245]

disarray 1 *n* **confusion**, dismay, panic, alarm, hysteria, frenzy, disorder [➡ DISORDER AND CHAOS; 245] *Opposite*: order 2 *n* **mess**, disorder, chaos, confusion, untidiness, shambles, clutter, jumble, tangle [➡ DISORDER AND CHAOS; 245] *Opposite*: order

disassemble *v* **take apart**, take to bits, undo, take down, take to pieces, strip [➡ UNFASTEN AND UNDO; 409] *Opposite*: assemble

disassociate 1 *v* **dissociate**, separate, split, set apart, disentangle, isolate, withdraw [➡ SEPARATE AND DIVIDE; 401] *Opposite*: associate 2 *v* **distance**, detach, set apart, dissociate, draw back, disconnect, extricate [➡ SEPARATE AND DIVIDE; 401] *Opposite*: implicate

disaster 1 *n* **tragedy**, ruin, adversity, catastrophe, calamity, cataclysm, misadventure, mischance, misfortune [➡ DISASTERS; 252] 2 *n* (*informal*) **failure**, debacle, fiasco, shambles, farce, mess, catastrophe, calamity, blow [➡ FAILURE; 77] *Opposite*: success

disastrous 1 *adj* **calamitous**, catastrophic, tragic, terrible, devastating, dreadful [➡ UNSUCCESSFUL AND UNPROMISING; 76] 2 *adj* **unsuccessful**, unfortunate, luckless, doomed, unlucky, grievous, ill-starred [➡ UNSUCCESSFUL AND UNPROMISING; 76] *Opposite*: successful

disavow *v* **disown**, deny, renounce, reject, recant, refute, give up, forswear (*archaic or literary*) [➡ DENY AND REJECT; 644]

disavowal (*formal*) *n* **repudiation**, denial, negation, renunciation, abjuration, refutation, recantation, rejection, forswearing (*archaic or literary*) [➡ DENY AND REJECT; 644] *Opposite*: avowal (*formal*)

disband *v* **break up**, split up, scatter, separate, part, disperse, split [➡ SEPARATE AND DIVIDE; 401]

disbar *v* **expel**, throw out, dismiss, banish, exclude, remove, discharge (*formal*) [➡ REFUSE PERMISSION AND NOT ALLOW; 670]

disbarment *n* **expulsion**, dismissal, banishment, exclusion, removal, discharge (*formal*) [➡ REFUSE PERMISSION AND NOT ALLOW; 670]

disbelief *n* **incredulity**, doubt, distrust, mistrust, suspicion [➡ UNCERTAINTY; 559]

disbelieve *v* **distrust**, doubt, mistrust, suspect, be suspicious of, question, have no faith in [➡ UNCERTAINTY; 559] *Opposite*: believe

disbeliever n **doubter**, agnostic, atheist, nonbeliever, skeptic [➡ PHILOSOPHICAL AND POLITICAL THINKERS; 781] *Opposite*: believer

disbelieving adj **unconvinced**, incredulous, suspicious, doubtful, distrustful, skeptical [➡ UNCERTAINTY; 559] *Opposite*: believing

disburden (archaic) v [➡ ADMIT AND CONFESS; 615]

disburse v **pay out**, pay, spend, expend, lay out, give out, distribute [➡ DISPENSE, RATION, AND DISTRIBUTE; 434]

disbursement n **payment**, expenditure, expense, costs, distribution, pay out [➡ EXPENDITURE; 423]

discard v **throw away**, abandon, dispose of, remove, get rid of, reject, thrust aside, cast off, shed, dispense with [➡ GET RID OF SOMETHING; 451] *Opposite*: keep

discarded adj **cast off**, thrown away, thrown out, rejected, dispensed with, tossed out, waste, superfluous, unwanted [➡ UNPOPULAR AND UNWANTED; 258] *Opposite*: kept

disc camera type of **photographic equipment** [➡ PHOTOGRAPHY AND PHOTOGRAPHIC EQUIPMENT; 1122]

discern 1 v **make out**, notice, see, perceive, discover, observe, catch sight of, glimpse, detect, spot [➡ LOOKING AND LOOKS; 700] *Opposite*: miss 2 v **understand**, perceive, distinguish, fathom, be aware of, detect [➡ UNDERSTAND AND GRASP; 759] *Opposite*: miss 3 v **distinguish**, tell the difference, separate, discriminate, differentiate, determine, detect, recognize, know by sight [➡ KNOWLEDGE AND WISDOM; 558]

discernible adj **visible**, apparent, obvious, perceptible, noticeable, distinct, palpable, evident, marked [➡ PERCEPTIBLE; 25]

discerning adj **discriminating**, sharp, astute, judicious, sensitive, shrewd, selective [➡ POSITIVE INTELLECTUAL CHARACTERISTICS; 524] *Opposite*: indiscriminate

discernment n **judgment**, acumen, discrimination, perspicacity, taste, shrewdness, sensitivity, selectivity [➡ POSITIVE INTELLECTUAL CHARACTERISTICS; 524]

discharge 1 v **emit**, send out, excrete, expel, ooze, leak, exude [➡ LIQUID EMISSION; 370] 2 v **dismiss**, relieve of duty, send away, fire, bounce, terminate, sack (informal), can (slang) [➡ REVOKE STATUS; 459] 3 v **free**, release, set free, emancipate, liberate, loose [➡ FREEDOM AND LIBERTY; 208] 4 v (formal) **pay off**, clear, settle, satisfy, liquidate, square, quit (archaic) [➡ FUNDS, PAYMENTS, AND CHARGES; 800] 5 n **emission**, flow, secretion, excretion, seepage, pus [➡ EMIT AND EMANATE; 361] 6 n **release**, liberation, emancipation, expulsion, ejection [➡ FREEDOM AND LIBERTY; 208]

See Compare and Contrast at **perform**.

disciple n **follower**, believer, supporter, devotee, partisan, adherent, student, pupil, scholar, learner [➡ SUPPORTERS, PROTECTORS, AND COMPATRIOTS; 970]

disciplinarian n **tyrant**, martinet, despot, authoritarian, stickler [➡ VILLAINS AND THUGS; 947]

disciplinary adj **punitive**, corrective, penal, penalizing [➡ TRIAL, PUNISHMENT, AND LEGAL OUTCOMES; 819]

discipline 1 n **punishment**, correction, chastisement (formal), castigation (formal) [➡ TRIAL, PUNISHMENT, AND LEGAL OUTCOMES; 819] *Opposite*: persuasion 2 n **regulation**, order, control, restraint, authority, obedience [➡ ORDER AND ORGANIZATION; 206] *Opposite*: chaos 3 n **self-control**, self-restraint, restraint, control, regulation, strictness, mastery, continence [➡ STRENGTH OF WILL; 501] 4 n **subject**, branch of learning, field [➡ CLASSES, COURSEWORK, AND EXAMINATIONS; 842] 5 v **punish**, chastise, correct, chasten, castigate (formal) [➡ TRIAL, PUNISHMENT, AND LEGAL OUTCOMES; 819] 6 v **instruct**, educate, exercise, drill, prepare, train, regulate, teach, school [➡ INSTRUCT AND TEACH; 609]

disciplined adj **controlled**, self-controlled, orderly, well-ordered, methodical, meticulous, restrained, systematic, well-organized, ordered [➡ ORDER AND ORGANIZATION; 206] *Opposite*: undisciplined

disclaim v **deny**, disown, renounce, reject, repudiate, refute, turn your back on [➡ DENY AND REJECT; 644]

disclaimer 1 n **rider**, proviso, qualification, provision, condition, stipulation, requirement, criterion, clause, specification, prerequisite [➡ NECESSARY AND ESSENTIAL; 196] 2 n **repudiation**, denial, renunciation, negation, disassociation [➡ DENY AND REJECT; 644]

disclose v **reveal**, unveil, divulge, make known, relate, release [➡ INFORM, ANNOUNCE, AND ISSUE; 611] *Opposite*: conceal

disclosure n **revelation**, exposé, discovery, leak, confession, admission, release [➡ ADMIT AND CONFESS; 615]

disco type of **dance music** [➡ MUSIC, SONGS, AND SINGING; 907]

discolor v **fade**, stain, color, darken, tarnish, dull, dye, bruise, scorch [➡ CHANGE OF COLOR; 391]

discoloration n **staining**, stain, tint, mark, streak, bloom, yellowing, bruising [➡ DESCRIBING COLORS; 1226]

discolored adj **stained**, dirty, tarnished, faded, streaked, yellowed, bruised [➡ DESCRIBING COLORS; 1226]

discombobulate (informal) v [➡ CONFUSE AND BEWILDER; 571]

discomfit (formal) v **embarrass**, unsettle, disconcert, distress, rattle, fluster, unnerve, make uncomfortable, make self-conscious, perturb, take aback, put off his or her stride, throw (informal), discombobulate (informal), discompose (formal) [➡ CONFUSE AND BEWILDER; 571] *Opposite*: relax

discomfited (formal) adj [➡ INSECURITY AND LOSS OF COMPOSURE; 544]

discomfiting (formal) adj **disconcerting**, embarrassing, unsettling, disturbing, distressing, upsetting, nerve-racking, off-putting [➡ EMOTIONALLY UNPLEASANT AND UPSETTING; 227] *Opposite*: reassuring

discomfiture (formal) n **embarrassment**, awkwardness, confusion, unease, disconcertment, discomposure, uneasiness [➡ EMBARRASSMENT AND HUMILIATION; 542]

discomfort 1 n **ache**, pain, soreness, tenderness, irritation [➡ PAIN AND OTHER PHYSICAL SENSATIONS; 733] 2 n **uneasiness**, worry, distress, anxiety, embarrassment, awkwardness [➡ EMBARRASSMENT AND HUMILIATION; 542]

discomposure n **agitation**, upset, uneasiness, embarrassment, discomfort, dismay, confusion [➡ EMBARRASSMENT AND HUMILIATION; 542]

disconcert v **unsettle**, perturb, rattle, fluster, unnerve, take aback, discombobulate (informal), throw (informal), discompose (*formal*), discomfit (*formal*) [➡CONFUSE AND BEWILDER; 571] *Opposite*: relax

disconcerted *adj* **unsettled**, thrown off balance, confused, flustered, taken aback, perturbed, thrown (*informal*) [➡CONFUSION, ANXIETY, AND WORRY; 540] *Opposite*: calm

disconcerting *adj* **disturbing**, alarming, confusing, perplexing, bewildering, upsetting, distressing, perturbing, unnerving [➡EMOTIONALLY UNPLEASANT AND UPSETTING; 227] *Opposite*: soothing

disconnect *v* **cut off**, detach, separate, divide, disengage, sever [➡UNFASTEN AND UNDO; 409] *Opposite*: connect

disconnected *adj* **detached**, severed, disengaged, separated, divided [➡UNFASTEN AND UNDO; 409] *Opposite*: attached

disconnection 1 *n* **stoppage**, interruption, cessation, cutting off, discontinuation, withdrawal, suspension [➡ENDS AND DEPARTURES; 54] *Opposite*: connection 2 *n* **separation**, severance, decoupling, disengagement, break, detachment [➡SEPARATE AND DIVIDE; 401] *Opposite*: connection

disconsolate *adj* **unhappy**, dejected, gloomy, melancholy, sad, discontent, unsatisfied, miserable [➡SADNESS, DISTRESS, AND DESPAIR; 539] *Opposite*: content

discontent *n* **dissatisfaction**, unhappiness, displeasure, disgruntlement, sadness, gloominess [➡SADNESS, DISTRESS, AND DESPAIR; 539] *Opposite*: contentment

discontented *adj* **dissatisfied**, unhappy, disgruntled, malcontent, displeased, grumbling, grumpy, sullen, resentful [➡SADNESS, DISTRESS, AND DESPAIR; 539] *Opposite*: contented

discontentment *n* **dissatisfaction**, discontent, displeasure, unhappiness, irritation, annoyance [➡SADNESS, DISTRESS, AND DESPAIR; 539] *Opposite*: contentment

discontinuation *n* **cessation**, termination, suspension, withdrawal, stoppage, interruption [➡ENDS AND DEPARTURES; 54] *Opposite*: continuation

discontinue *v* **stop**, cease, halt, end, suspend, break off, withdraw, terminate (*formal*) [➡CAUSE TO STOP; 266] *Opposite*: continue

discontinued *adj* **obsolete**, finished, superseded, out-of-date, withdrawn, dropped, unobtainable [➡ABSENT AND UNAVAILABLE; 7]

discontinuity *n* **break**, gap, cutoff, cutout, disjointedness, incoherence [➡FINITENESS, VARIABILITY, AND TRANSIENCE; 96] *Opposite*: continuity

discontinuous *adj* **intermittent**, sporadic, broken, irregular, disjointed, spasmodic, uneven [➡FINITENESS, VARIABILITY, AND TRANSIENCE; 96] *Opposite*: continuous

discord 1 *n* **disagreement**, conflict, dispute, argument, friction, dissension [➡DISHARMONY; 156] *Opposite*: accord 2 *n* **dissonance**, cacophony, disharmony, inharmoniousness, discordance [➡LOUD, HIGH, OR UNPLEASANT SOUNDS; 1266] *Opposite*: harmony

discordant 1 *adj* **disagreeing**, conflicting, frictional, dissenting, acrimonious, disputatious (*formal*) [➡DISHARMONY; 156] 2 *adj* **dissonant**, jarring, harsh, inharmonious, cacophonous, shrill, unmusical [➡LOUD, HIGH, OR UNPLEASANT SOUNDS; 1266] *Opposite*: harmonious

discount 1 *n* **reduction**, money off, markdown, price cut, cut rate, concession, deduction, rebate [➡FUNDS, PAYMENTS, AND CHARGES; 800] 2 *v* **disregard**, overlook, ignore, disbelieve, pass over, omit, slight, write off (*informal*) [➡NOT PAY ATTENTION; 764] *Opposite*: accept 3 *v* **reduce**, mark down, lower, take off, deduct, subtract [➡FUNDS, PAYMENTS, AND CHARGES; 800] *Opposite*: put up

discounted *adj* **reduced**, cut-rate, sale, cheap, promotional, bargain-basement, on special, on sale, on offer (*UK*), cut-price (*UK*), on special offer (*UK*) [➡CHEAP AND INEXPENSIVE; 221]

discourage 1 *v* **dissuade**, oppose, hinder, inhibit, prevent, stop, suppress [➡MAKE IMPOSSIBLE; 276] *Opposite*: encourage 2 *v* **dispirit**, dishearten, cast down, depress, dismay, disappoint, deject (*archaic*) [➡UPSET, DISTRESS, AND HUMILIATE; 567] *Opposite*: cheer

discouraged *adj* **disheartened**, dispirited, downcast, depressed, dejected, low, melancholy, hopeless, gloomy, unenthusiastic [➡SADNESS, DISTRESS, AND DESPAIR; 539] *Opposite*: positive

discouragement 1 *n* **disappointment**, dismay, despair, depression, low spirits, melancholy, pessimism, gloominess, worry [➡SADNESS, DISTRESS, AND DESPAIR; 539] *Opposite*: hopefulness 2 *n* **dissuasion**, caution, warning, opposition, deterrence [➡ADVICE; 689] *Opposite*: encouragement 3 *n* **deterrent**, hindrance, obstacle, impediment, damper, restraint [➡PROBLEMS; 256] *Opposite*: incentive

discouraging *adj* **disheartening**, depressing, dispiriting, gloomy, unpromising, inauspicious, ominous, unfavorable [➡EMOTIONALLY UNPLEASANT AND UPSETTING; 227] *Opposite*: encouraging

discourse 1 *n* **dissertation**, treatise, homily, sermon, address, speech [➡ONE-WAY COMMUNICATION; 49] 2 *n* **dialogue**, conversation, discussion, communication, speech, talk, chat [➡INFORMAL COMMUNICATION; 45] 3 *v* (*formal*) **converse**, debate, compare notes, have a discussion, discuss, negotiate, confer, reason, deliberate, consult, parley, have a word (*UK*) [➡TWO-WAY COMMUNICATION; 607]

discourteous *adj* **rude**, ill-mannered, impolite, insolent, uncivil, unmannerly, disrespectful [➡BAD MANNERS AND SOCIAL SKILLS; 521] *Opposite*: polite

discourteousness *n* **impoliteness**, rudeness, disrespect, unmannerliness, incivility, uncouthness, impertinence, impudence, insolence [➡BAD MANNERS AND SOCIAL SKILLS; 521] *Opposite*: politeness

discourtesy *n* **rudeness**, impoliteness, disrespect, incivility, insolence [➡BAD MANNERS AND SOCIAL SKILLS; 521] *Opposite*: politeness

discover 1 *v* **find out**, learn, determine, notice, realize, see, discern, ascertain (*formal*) [➡LEARN AND DISCOVER; 762] 2 *v* **come across**, find, turn up, uncover, unearth, dig up, locate, detect, encounter [➡FIND; 463]

discoverer *n* **inventor**, originator, pioneer, innovator, creator, architect [➡DESIGNERS, CREATORS, AND INSTIGATORS; 347]

discovery 1 *n* **find**, innovation, breakthrough, invention, finding [➡CREATION; 346] 2 *n* **detection**, finding, unearthing, sighting, encounter, location [➡FIND; 463]

discredit 1 *v* **slur**, demean, smear, insult, humiliate,

disgrace [→INSULTS, ABUSE, AND SWEARING; 658] **2** v **question**, doubt, disbelieve, query, suspect, dispute [→QUESTION THINGS; 751]

discreditable adj **shameful**, disreputable, ignominious, disgraceful, reprehensible, appalling, wrong [→UNACCEPTABLE AND UNFORGIVABLE; 225]

discreditably adv **disreputably**, shamefully, disgracefully, ignominiously, reprehensibly, appallingly [→MORALLY BAD OR IMPROPER; 775]

discreet **1** adj **tactful**, prudent, circumspect, cautious, careful, diplomatic, judicious [→GOOD MANNERS AND SOCIAL SKILLS; 520] Opposite: tactless **2** adj **inconspicuous**, subtle, unnoticeable, unobtrusive, understated, tasteful, restrained, modest [→IMPERCEPTIBLE; 26] Opposite: obvious

discrepancy n **inconsistency**, difference, incongruity, divergence, disagreement [→DIFFERENCE; 149] Opposite: correspondence

discrete adj **separate**, distinct, disconnected, detached, isolated, unconnected [→UNRELATEDNESS AND SEPARATENESS; 146]

discretion **1** n **freedom of choice**, will, pleasure, option, choice, decision [→MAKE DECISIONS AND CHOICES; 752] **2** n **carefulness**, prudence, caution, canniness, maturity, responsibility, moderation, foresight, judgment, diplomacy, tact, acumen, discrimination [→CONFIDENCE AND COMPOSURE; 499]

discretionary adj **optional**, flexible, open, unrestricted [→POSSIBLE AND PROBABLE; 177] Opposite: mandatory

discriminate v **distinguish**, tell apart, differentiate, separate, categorize, classify [→EXAMINE AND ASSESS; 753]

discriminating adj **discerning**, sharp, astute, selective, judicious, tasteful, cultivated, refined [→POSITIVE INTELLECTUAL CHARACTERISTICS; 524]

discrimination **1** n **bias**, prejudice, unfairness, inequity, bigotry, intolerance [→PREJUDICE; 550] **2** n **taste**, judgment, good taste, discernment, insight, acumen, perception, refinement, percipience [→POSITIVE INTELLECTUAL CHARACTERISTICS; 524] **3** n **distinction**, difference, differential, contrast [→DIFFERENCE; 149]

discriminatory adj **biased**, prejudiced, unfair, bigoted, inequitable, intolerant [→MORALLY BAD OR IMPROPER; 775]

discursive adj **broad**, lengthy, conversational, expansive, informal, free, loose, rambling, musing, roundabout [→ELOQUENT, TALKATIVE, AND LONG-WINDED; 632] Opposite: concise

discursiveness n **informality**, breadth, expansiveness, freeness, roundaboutness [→ELOQUENT, TALKATIVE, AND LONG-WINDED; 632] Opposite: concision

discus **1** type of **sports equipment** [→SPORTS EQUIPMENT; 879] **2** type of **track and field** [→HOBBIES, GAMES, AND SPORTS; 875]

discuss v **talk over**, deliberate, debate, converse, confer, chew over, hash out, chat, kick around (informal), discourse (formal), thrash out (UK) [→TWO-WAY COMMUNICATION; 607]

discussion n **conversation**, debate, argument, dialogue, chat, talk, confab (informal) [→INFORMAL COMMUNICATION; 45]

discussion group n **class**, seminar, tutorial, roundtable, committee, working party (UK) [→CLASSES, COURSEWORK, AND EXAMINATIONS; 842]

disdain **1** n **scorn**, contempt, derision, condescension, disparagement, disregard, aloofness [→DISLIKE AND HATE; 577] Opposite: respect **2** v **despise**, scorn, spurn, hold in contempt, disparage, turn your nose up at [→DISLIKE AND HATE; 577] Opposite: respect

disdainful adj **sneering**, scornful, derisive, condescending, aloof, contemptuous, mocking [→MOCKING AND DISMISSIVE; 636] Opposite: respectful

disease n **illness**, sickness, ailment, infection, syndrome, malady, virus, disorder, complaint, bug (informal) [→SICKNESS; 729] Opposite: health

diseased adj **unhealthy**, unwell, sickly, ill, sick, ailing (dated) [→ILL AND SICK; 740] Opposite: healthy

disease-ridden adj [→ILL AND SICK; 740]

disembark v **come ashore**, go ashore, land, get off, arrive in port, debark [→ARRIVE BY TRANSPORT; 14] Opposite: embark

disembarkation n **arrival**, alighting, debarkation, landing, getting off [→ARRIVAL; 13]

disembodied adj **ghostly**, spiritual, intangible, ethereal, immaterial, incorporeal (formal) [→IMPERCEPTIBLE; 26] Opposite: tangible

disembowel v **eviscerate**, gut, fillet, exenterate [→WOUND A PERSON OR ANIMAL; 383]

disenchant v [→UPSET, DISTRESS, AND HUMILIATE; 567]

disenchanted adj **disillusioned**, disappointed, dissatisfied, crestfallen, embittered, let down, unhappy [→SADNESS, DISTRESS, AND DESPAIR; 539] Opposite: idealistic

disenchantment n **disillusionment**, disappointment, dissatisfaction, embitterment, bitterness, world-weariness, unhappiness [→SADNESS, DISTRESS, AND DESPAIR; 539] Opposite: idealism

disenfranchise v **marginalize**, exclude, alienate, subjugate, disqualify [→REVOKE STATUS; 459] Opposite: enfranchise

disenfranchisement n **marginalization**, exclusion, alienation, subjugation, disqualification [→REVOKE STATUS; 459] Opposite: enfranchisement

disengage v **undo**, unfasten, unlock, untie, uncouple, free, extricate, separate [→UNFASTEN AND UNDO; 409] Opposite: fasten

disengagement **1** n **withdrawal**, disentanglement, detachment, disconnection, extrication, breaking away, break [→ENDS AND DEPARTURES; 54] Opposite: engagement **2** n **release**, uncoupling, separation, extrication, withdrawal, disentanglement [→ENDS AND DEPARTURES; 54] Opposite: attachment

disentangle v **unravel**, unscramble, untie, separate, straighten out, sort out, extricate, untangle [→ARRANGE AND CREATE ORDER; 357] Opposite: entangle

disequilibrium n **imbalance**, instability, uncertainty, flux, volatility [→UNCERTAIN; 175] Opposite: equilibrium

disestablish v **reform**, repudiate, renounce, reevaluate, disclaim [→SOCIAL, POLITICAL, AND ECONOMIC CHANGE; 373] Opposite: establish

disfavor 1 *n* **disrepute**, unpopularity, discredit, disgrace, obscurity, disapproval [➡DIFFICULT SITUATIONS; 72] *Opposite*: favor **2** *n* **distaste**, disdain, disapproval, displeasure, scorn, disapprobation (*formal*) [➡DISLIKE AND HATE; 577] *Opposite*: favor

disfigure *v* **mutilate**, scar, deface, mar, spoil, harm, damage, blemish [➡WOUND A PERSON OR ANIMAL; 383] *Opposite*: enhance

disfigured *adj* [➡IN BAD REPAIR; 1234]

disfigurement *n* **scar**, mutilation, defacement, deformity, blemish, defect, mark, blotch [➡WOUND A PERSON OR ANIMAL; 383] *Opposite*: enhancement

disgorge *v* **expel**, eject, empty, pour out, spew, erupt [➡LIQUID EMISSION; 370] *Opposite*: retain

disgrace 1 *n* **shame**, discredit, scandal, ignominy, humiliation, degradation, dishonor [➡DIFFICULT SITUATIONS; 72] **2** *v* **bring shame on**, discredit, bring into disrepute, shame, degrade, tarnish, stain, humiliate [➡UPSET, DISTRESS, AND HUMILIATE; 567]

disgraced *adj* **discredited**, shamed, condemned, humiliated, fallen, shunned [➡UNPOPULAR AND UNWANTED; 258] *Opposite*: popular

disgraceful *adj* **shameful**, shocking, outrageous, scandalous, discreditable, reprehensible, appalling, dreadful [➡UNACCEPTABLE AND UNFORGIVABLE; 225]

disgruntle *v* **displease**, irritate, anger, annoy, dissatisfy, peeve (*informal*) [➡ANGER AND ANNOY; 569] *Opposite*: satisfy

disgruntled *adj* **discontented**, dissatisfied, resentful, displeased, unhappy, irritated, angry, sullen, annoyed, put out, peeved (*informal*) [➡IRRITATION AND ANGER; 541] *Opposite*: contented

disguise 1 *v* **cover up**, hide, conceal, mask, masquerade, veil, camouflage, cloak [➡CAUSE TO DISAPPEAR; 6] *Opposite*: reveal **2** *n* **mask**, costume, camouflage, masquerade, cover, cloak, front, veneer, concealment [➡GARMENTS AND OUTFITS; 865]

disguised *adj* **camouflaged**, masked, masquerading, cloaked, veiled, hidden, concealed [➡IMPERCEPTIBLE; 26] *Opposite*: overt

disgust 1 *n* **revulsion**, repugnance, abhorrence, repulsion, antipathy, loathing, hatred, aversion (*formal*) [➡DISLIKE AND HATE; 577] *Opposite*: attraction **2** *v* **sicken**, repulse, revolt, repel, shock, turn your stomach, nauseate [➡FRIGHTEN AND SHOCK; 568] *Opposite*: please

See Compare and Contrast at **dislike**.

disgusted *adj* **sickened**, revolted, repulsed, repelled, offended, appalled [➡SADNESS, DISTRESS, AND DESPAIR; 539] *Opposite*: charmed

disgusting *adj* **revolting**, repulsive, sickening, ghastly, filthy, sordid, horrible, nauseating, repellent [➡DISGUSTING AND REPULSIVE; 230] *Opposite*: attractive

dish 1 *n* **plate**, bowl, saucer [➡TABLEWARE, FLATWARE, AND KITCHENWARE; 861] **2** *n* **food item**, course, recipe [➡PREPARED DISHES; 1170]

---

dish

◆ *types of cooked dishes*

bruschetta, burritos, casserole, cassoulet, ceviche, chop suey, chow mein, couscous, curry, fajitas, falafel, fish cake, fondue, fricassee, frijoles, frittata, goulash, gruel, Irish stew, kedgeree, lasagne, meat loaf, miso, moussaka, nachos, nasi goreng, paella, pilaf, pirozkhi, pizza, quiche, ragout, ratatouille, risotto, sambal, satay, sauerkraut, stew, stir-fry, surf 'n' turf, tacos, tagine, tamale, tempura, teriyaki, tofu, yakitori

disharmonious *adj* **conflicting**, discordant, tense, uneasy, bitter, resentful, at odds [➡DISHARMONY; 156] *Opposite*: harmonious

disharmony *n* **conflict**, disagreement, discord, tension, unrest, bitterness, resentment [➡DISHARMONY; 156] *Opposite*: harmony

dishcloth *n* **dishrag**, dish towel, kitchen cloth, towel, washing-up cloth (*UK*), drying-up cloth (*UK*) [➡FURNISHING AND HOUSEHOLD LINENS; 860]

dishearten *v* **discourage**, depress, sadden, cast down, dismay, bring down, dampen, disappoint, deject (*archaic*) [➡UPSET, DISTRESS, AND HUMILIATE; 567] *Opposite*: buoy up

disheartened *adj* **discouraged**, depressed, saddened, dismayed, dejected, disconsolate, downcast, dispirited, crestfallen, low [➡SADNESS, DISTRESS, AND DESPAIR; 539] *Opposite*: encouraged

disheartening *adj* **intimidating**, off-putting, daunting, dispiriting, depressing, demoralizing, discouraging, dismaying [➡EMOTIONALLY UNPLEASANT AND UPSETTING; 227] *Opposite*: encouraging

disheveled *adj* **unkempt**, wild, tousled, ruffled, untidy, scruffy, unruly [➡BADLY GROOMED; 483] *Opposite*: well-groomed

dishonest *adj* **lying**, deceitful, false, untruthful, fraudulent, corrupt, unfair, insincere, mendacious, underhand, misleading [➡DECEITFUL; 513] *Opposite*: honest

dishonesty *n* **deceit**, deceitfulness, fraudulence, lying, untruthfulness, corruption, treachery, duplicity, cheating, trickery [➡DECEPTION AND LIES; 660] *Opposite*: honesty

dishonor 1 *n* **disgrace**, shame, discredit, ignominy, disrepute, infamy [➡DIFFICULT SITUATIONS; 72] *Opposite*: honor **2** *v* **shame**, disgrace, discredit, defame, bring into disrepute, bring shame on [➡UPSET, DISTRESS, AND HUMILIATE; 567] *Opposite*: honor

dishonorable *adj* **disgraceful**, disreputable, discreditable, shameful, ignominious, ignoble [➡MORALLY BAD OR IMPROPER; 775] *Opposite*: honorable

dish out (*informal*) *v* **distribute**, parcel out, allot, hand out, deal out, mete out, dole out (*informal*) [➡DISPENSE, RATION, AND DISTRIBUTE; 434]

dish the dirt (*informal*) *v* [➡BETRAY CONFIDENCES AND GOSSIP; 618]

dishwasher *type of* **appliance** [➡HOUSEHOLD APPLIANCES; 1117]

dishy (*informal*) *adj* **good-looking**, nice-looking, cute, attractive, handsome, gorgeous, pretty, sexy, hunky (*informal*), buff (*slang*) [➡PEOPLE'S PHYSICAL APPEARANCE; 475] *Opposite*: ugly

disillusion *v* **disenchant**, bring down to earth, disappoint, let down, dishearten, dissatisfy [➡ UPSET, DISTRESS, AND HUMILIATE; 567] *Opposite:* inspire

disillusioned *adj* **disenchanted**, disappointed, disheartened, cynical [➡ SADNESS, DISTRESS, AND DESPAIR; 539] *Opposite:* starry-eyed

disillusionment *n* **disenchantment**, disappointment, cynicism, letdown, discouragement [➡ SADNESS, DISTRESS, AND DESPAIR; 539] *Opposite:* gratification

disincentive *n* **deterrent**, discouragement, hindrance, impediment, encumbrance [➡ PROBLEMS; 256] *Opposite:* incentive

disinclination *n* **reluctance**, unwillingness, opposition, hesitation, aversion (*formal*) [➡ UNWILLINGNESS AND STUBBORNNESS; 564] *Opposite:* inclination

disincline *v* **put off**, deter, discourage, dissuade, prevent [➡ BORE AND FAIL TO INTEREST; 570] *Opposite:* encourage

disinclined *adj* **reluctant**, unwilling, opposed, unenthusiastic, loath, hesitant, averse (*formal*) [➡ UNWILLINGNESS AND STUBBORNNESS; 564] *Opposite:* inclined

See Compare and Contrast at **unwilling**.

disinfect *v* **sterilize**, sanitize, purify, fumigate, cleanse, clean thoroughly, clean, decontaminate [➡ CLEAN AND POLISH; 403] *Opposite:* contaminate

disinfectant *n* **antiseptic**, sanitizer, sterilizer, purifier [➡ CLEANING AGENTS; 863]

disinfected *adj* [➡ CLEAN AND HYGIENIC; 1233]

disinformation *n* **deception**, falsehood, propaganda, half-truth, misinformation, untruth [➡ DECEPTION AND LIES; 660] *Opposite:* truth

disingenuous *adj* **dishonest**, insincere, untruthful, deceitful, hypocritical, misleading, duplicitous [➡ DECEITFUL; 513] *Opposite:* honest

disingenuousness *n* **dishonesty**, insincerity, untruthfulness, deceit, hypocrisy, duplicity, duplicitousness [➡ DECEITFUL; 513] *Opposite:* honesty

disinherit *v* **cut off**, disown, leave penniless, cut out, divest, deprive, dispossess (*archaic or formal*) [➡ REVOKE STATUS; 459] *Opposite:* bequeath

disintegrate *v* **crumble**, fragment, break, collapse, split, breakdown, degenerate [➡ CEASE TO EXIST; 22] *Opposite:* combine

disintegration *n* **breakdown**, breakup, collapse, fragmentation, crumbling, dissolution, degeneration [➡ ENDS AND DEPARTURES; 54]

disinter 1 *v* **exhume**, dig up, unearth [➡ BURIAL AND PREPARATION FOR BURIAL; 929] *Opposite:* bury 2 *v* (*formal*) **uncover**, unearth, bring to light, expose, reveal, disclose, divulge, unveil [➡ CAUSE TO APPEAR; 5] *Opposite:* cover up

disinterest *n* **indifference**, unconcern, apathy, disregard, heedlessness, listlessness, insouciance [➡ NEUTRALITY AND INDIFFERENCE; 553] *Opposite:* interest

disinterested *adj* **fair-minded**, unbiased, impartial, without prejudice, neutral, objective [➡ POSITIVE INTELLECTUAL CHARACTERISTICS; 524] *Opposite:* biased

disinterestedness *n* **impartiality**, objectivity, fair-mindedness, neutrality, distance [➡ POSITIVE INTELLECTUAL CHARACTERISTICS; 524] *Opposite:* bias

disinterment 1 *n* **exhumation**, digging up, unearthing, exposure [➡ BURIAL AND PREPARATION FOR BURIAL; 929] *Opposite:* interment 2 *n* (*formal*) **exposure**, unearthing, discovery, revelation, uncovering, disclosure [➡ INFORM, ANNOUNCE, AND ISSUE; 611] *Opposite:* concealment

disjoint 1 *v* **split**, separate, come apart, sever, divide, disconnect, dismember [➡ UNFASTEN AND UNDO; 409] *Opposite:* join 2 *v* **dislocate**, dislodge, move, relocate, separate [➡ SEPARATE AND DIVIDE; 401] *Opposite:* retain

disjointed *adj* **rambling**, fragmented, incoherent, disorganized, disorderly, jumpy, jerky, unconnected [➡ INARTICULATE, RAMBLING, AND AWKWARD; 633] *Opposite:* coherent

disjointedness *n* **disjunction**, disjuncture, incoherence, dislocation, disconnection, disconnectedness [➡ UNRELATEDNESS AND SEPARATENESS; 146] *Opposite:* coherence

disk *type of* **hardware** [➡ COMPUTERS AND COMPUTING; 1127]

disk drive *type of* **hardware** [➡ COMPUTERS AND COMPUTING; 1127]

diskette *type of* **hardware** [➡ COMPUTERS AND COMPUTING; 1127]

dislikable *adj* **disagreeable**, unpleasant, offensive, repugnant, horrible, obnoxious [➡ DISGUSTING AND REPULSIVE; 230] *Opposite:* likable

dislike 1 *v* **hate**, detest, loathe, frown on, disapprove, abhor (*formal*) [➡ DISLIKE AND HATE; 577] *Opposite:* like 2 *n* **hatred**, hate, loathing, abhorrence, pet peeve, displeasure, disinclination, distaste, disgust, repugnance, antipathy, animosity, revulsion, aversion (*formal*), bete noire (*literary*), pet hate (*UK*) [➡ DISLIKE AND HATE; 577] *Opposite:* liking

Compare and Contrast: *dislike, distaste, hatred, hate, disgust, loathing, repugnance, abhorrence, animosity, antipathy, aversion, revulsion*

CORE MEANING: not liking somebody or something

dislike a feeling or attitude of disapproval; ***distaste*** mild dislike, mainly of behavior and activities; ***hatred*** **or** ***hate*** intense dislike or hostility; ***disgust*** a feeling of horrified and sickened disapproval; ***loathing*** intense dislike; ***repugnance*** strong disgust, mainly of behavior and activities; ***abhorrence*** a feeling of aversion or intense disapproval, mainly of behavior and activities; ***animosity*** a feeling of hostility and resentment; ***antipathy*** a deep-seated dislike or hostility; ***aversion*** (*formal*) a strong feeling of dislike; ***revulsion*** a sudden violent feeling of disgust.

dislocate 1 *v* **put out of place**, displace, put out of joint, disjoint, dislodge, disarticulate [➡ UNFASTEN AND UNDO; 409] *Opposite:* replace 2 *v* **disrupt**, interrupt, disturb, upset, disorder, perturb [➡ CREATE DISORDER AND CAUSE CHAOS; 358] *Opposite:* restore

dislocation 1 *n* **displacement**, disarticulation, dislodgment [➡ MOVE SOMETHING TO ANOTHER LOCATION; 324] 2 *n* **disruption**, interruption, disturbance, disorder, upset, confusion [➡ DISORDER AND CHAOS; 245]

dislodge v **remove**, get out, extricate, free, displace, dislocate [➡ FREEDOM AND LIBERTY; 208] *Opposite*: wedge

disloyal adj **unfaithful**, treacherous, untrue, false, fickle, untrustworthy, faithless, perfidious (*formal*) [➡ LACK OF COMMITMENT AND UNRELIABILITY; 509] *Opposite*: loyal

disloyalty n **unfaithfulness**, treachery, falseness, infidelity, betrayal, fickleness, untrustworthiness, perfidy (*formal*) [➡ LACK OF COMMITMENT AND UNRELIABILITY; 509] *Opposite*: loyalty

dismal adj **miserable**, gloomy, depressing, dreary, dull, murky, bleak, drab, grim, cheerless [➡ EMOTIONALLY UNPLEASANT AND UPSETTING; 227] *Opposite*: bright

dismantle v [➡ UNFASTEN AND UNDO; 409]

dismay 1 v **disappoint**, shock, sadden, depress, perturb, discourage [➡ UPSET, DISTRESS, AND HUMILIATE; 567] *Opposite*: comfort 2 n **disappointment**, shock, consternation, apprehension, panic, alarm, sadness, depression [➡ SADNESS, DISTRESS, AND DESPAIR; 539] *Opposite*: comfort

dismayed adj **discouraged**, disheartened, demoralized, downcast, depressed, intimidated, perturbed, distressed, fed up (*informal*) [➡ SADNESS, DISTRESS, AND DESPAIR; 539] *Opposite*: heartened

dismember v **tear limb from limb**, cut into pieces, cut up, dissect, tear apart, mutilate, disarticulate, disjoint [➡ WOUND A PERSON OR ANIMAL; 383]

dismemberment n **taking apart**, mutilation, division, maiming, splitting off, disintegration [➡ WOUND A PERSON OR ANIMAL; 383]

dismiss 1 v **give notice**, discharge, let go, lay off, terminate, fire (*informal*), can (*slang*), sack (*UK*) [➡ REVOKE STATUS; 459] *Opposite*: detain 2 v **send away**, allow to go, release, send home [➡ REVOKE STATUS; 459] 3 v **reject**, set aside, think no more of, put out of your mind, shelve, disdain, scorn, write off (*informal*) [➡ NOT PAY ATTENTION; 764] *Opposite*: dwell on

dismissal n **removal**, notice, discharge, release, firing (*informal*), sack (*UK*) [➡ REVOKE STATUS; 459] *Opposite*: appointment

dismissive adj **flippant**, indifferent, unconcerned, trivializing, contemptuous, glib, facetious, airy, frivolous [➡ MOCKING AND DISMISSIVE; 636] *Opposite*: attentive

dismount v **get down**, get off, alight, descend [➡ GO DOWNWARD; 307] *Opposite*: mount

disobedience n **defiance**, noncompliance, breaking the rules, insubordination, waywardness, brattiness, naughtiness, rebellion [➡ REBELLIOUSNESS AND DISOBEDIENCE; 565] *Opposite*: obedience

disobedient adj **defiant**, noncompliant, rebellious, insubordinate, badly behaved, bratty, naughty, wayward [➡ REBELLIOUSNESS AND DISOBEDIENCE; 565] *Opposite*: obedient

disobey v **defy**, refuse to comply, break the rules, contravene, violate, go against, flout, challenge [➡ DISOBEY; 302]

disobliging adj **unhelpful**, uncooperative, unaccommodating, rude, unfriendly, discourteous [➡ REBELLIOUSNESS AND DISOBEDIENCE; 565] *Opposite*: obliging

disorder 1 n **chaos**, disarray, confusion, mess, muddle, turmoil, anarchy, bedlam, unrest, mayhem (*informal*) [➡ DISORDER AND CHAOS; 245] *Opposite*: order 2 n **complaint**, illness, sickness, ailment, syndrome, malady, condition [➡ SICKNESS; 729]

disordered adj **chaotic**, messy, muddled, topsy-turvy, higgledy-piggledy, anarchic, tangled, disorderly, jumbled [➡ DISORDER AND CHAOS; 245] *Opposite*: well-ordered

disorderliness n **confusion**, messiness, muddle, chaos, disarray, disarrangement, disorder, disruption [➡ DISORDER AND CHAOS; 245] *Opposite*: orderliness

disorderly 1 adj **muddled**, jumbled, confused, messy, unsystematic, disorganized, higgledy-piggledy, topsy-turvy, anarchic, disordered, chaotic [➡ DISORDER AND CHAOS; 245] 2 adj **unruly**, riotous, uncontrollable, rebellious, wild, unmanageable, rowdy, boisterous, undisciplined [➡ REBELLIOUSNESS AND DISOBEDIENCE; 565] *Opposite*: orderly

disorderly conduct n [➡ CRIMES; 817]

disorganization n **inefficiency**, ineptitude, ineffectiveness, incompetence, disorder, inadequacy [➡ UNSKILLED; 529] *Opposite*: organization

disorganize v **muddle**, mix up, confuse, jumble, dislocate, disorder, upset, mess up (*informal*) [➡ CREATE DISORDER AND CAUSE CHAOS; 358] *Opposite*: organize

disorganized adj **muddled**, jumbled, confused, messy, unsystematic, higgledy-piggledy, topsy-turvy, disordered, chaotic, incoherent, disjointed, anarchic, disorderly [➡ DISORDER AND CHAOS; 245] *Opposite*: organized

disorient v **confuse**, perplex, fox, befuddle, fuddle, puzzle, mystify, baffle, bewilder, stupefy, nonplus, confound, disorientate, throw (*informal*), flummox (*informal*), bamboozle (*informal*) [➡ CONFUSE AND BEWILDER; 571] *Opposite*: orient

disorientate see **disorient**

disorientation n **puzzlement**, bafflement, stupefaction, bewilderment, confusion, uncertainty, incomprehension, perplexity, panic [➡ CONFUSION, ANXIETY, AND WORRY; 540]

disoriented adj **confused**, unsettled, bewildered, perplexed, at a loss, at sea, mixed-up (*informal*), thrown (*informal*) [➡ INSECURITY AND LOSS OF COMPOSURE; 544] *Opposite*: clear-headed

disown v **renounce**, reject, wash your hands of, turn your back on, disclaim, deny, repudiate [➡ FORGO AND DENY ONESELF; 449] *Opposite*: acknowledge

disparage v **belittle**, laugh at, mock, ridicule, pour scorn on, sneer, criticize, vilify, denigrate, run down, deride, scorn [➡ ACCUSE, BLAME, AND CRITICIZE; 641] *Opposite*: praise

disparagement n **belittling**, mocking, ridicule, criticism, derision, scorn, vilification, denigration [➡ CRITICISMS AND ANGRY OUTBURSTS; 50] *Opposite*: praise

disparaging adj **critical**, unfavorable, disapproving, censorious, unsympathetic, judgmental, scornful [➡ ACCUSATORY AND DISAPPROVING; 634] *Opposite*: approving

disparate adj **dissimilar**, unlike, unequal, different, incongruent, unrelated, contrasting, distinct [➡ DIFFERENCE; 149] *Opposite*: similar

disparity *n* **difference**, inequality, discrepancy, disproportion, gap, inconsistency, incongruence [➡DIFFERENCE; 149] *Opposite:* parity

dispassion *n* **aloofness**, coolness, calmness, impassivity, serenity, detachment, objectivity [➡NEUTRALITY AND INDIFFERENCE; 553] *Opposite:* enthusiasm

dispassionate *adj* **calm**, composed, unflustered, unemotional, detached, cool, aloof, objective, impassive, serene [➡NEUTRALITY AND INDIFFERENCE; 553] *Opposite:* fiery

dispassionately *adv* **impassively**, objectively, disinterestedly, without bias, serenely, unflappably, unemotionally, undemonstratively, imperturbably, evenly, calmly, coolly, equably, neutrally, remotely, distantly, aloofly [➡UNINTERESTED AND DETACHED; 629] *Opposite:* emotionally

dispatch 1 *v* **send off**, send out, post, mail, ship, transmit, forward, remit [➡DISPATCH AND SEND; 333] *Opposite:* keep 2 *v* **kill**, murder, assassinate, put to death, slaughter, destroy, slay (*formal or literary*) [➡KILL; 923] 3 *n* **message**, communication, notice, letter, report [➡LETTERS AND WRITTEN MESSAGES; 584]

dispatch rider *n* **courier**, messenger, deliverer [➡MESSENGERS AND COURIERS; 852]

dispel *v* **dismiss**, chase away, drive out, disperse, scatter, dissipate, oust [➡GET RID OF SOMETHING; 451] *Opposite:* attract

dispensable *adj* **expendable**, superfluous, unessential, unnecessary, replaceable, surplus to requirements [➡REDUNDANT AND USELESS; 240] *Opposite:* indispensable

dispensary *n* **drugstore**, pharmacy, chemist's (*UK*) [➡RETAIL OUTLETS; 1083]

dispensation *n* **indulgence**, allowance, special consideration, privilege, exemption, release [➡FREEDOM AND LIBERTY; 208]

dispense *v* **give out**, hand out, distribute, allot, mete out, dole out (*informal*), dish out (*informal*), bestow (*formal*) [➡DISPENSE, RATION, AND DISTRIBUTE; 434] *Opposite:* withhold

dispenser *n* **distributor**, slot machine, machine, vending machine [➡MACHINES AND MACHINE PARTS; 1116]

dispense with *v* [➡GET RID OF SOMETHING; 451]

dispersal *n* **dispersion**, spreading, scattering, diffusion, distribution, thinning out, diaspora [➡MOVE SOMETHING TO ANOTHER LOCATION; 324] *Opposite:* concentration

disperse *v* **scatter**, go away, disband, break up, dissolve, separate, diffuse, melt away, disappear [➡SPREAD AND SCATTER; 332] *Opposite:* concentrate

dispersion *n* **dispersal**, spreading, scattering, diffusion, distribution, thinning out [➡MOVE SOMETHING TO ANOTHER LOCATION; 324] *Opposite:* concentration

dispirit *v* **dishearten**, discourage, dampen, depress, dismay, cast down, deject (*archaic*) [➡UPSET, DISTRESS, AND HUMILIATE; 567] *Opposite:* rouse

dispirited *adj* **disheartened**, discouraged, dejected, depressed, downhearted, low, disconsolate, dismayed, crestfallen, demoralized [➡SADNESS, DISTRESS, AND DESPAIR; 539] *Opposite:* cheerful

dispiriting *adj* **disheartening**, depressing, demoralizing, upsetting, saddening [➡EMOTIONALLY UNPLEASANT AND UPSETTING; 227] *Opposite:* uplifting

displace 1 *v* **move**, relocate, shift, transfer, put out of place, dislocate, dislodge [➡MOVE SOMETHING TO ANOTHER LOCATION; 324] *Opposite:* restore 2 *v* **oust**, supplant, replace, supersede, succeed, depose [➡REVOKE STATUS; 459] *Opposite:* restore

displacement *n* **movement**, dislocation, dislodgment, shift, supplanting, translation, transposition [➡MOVE SOMETHING TO ANOTHER LOCATION; 324]

display 1 *v* **show**, exhibit, put on show, present, put on view, demonstrate, expose, reveal [➡CAUSE TO APPEAR; 5] *Opposite:* conceal 2 *v* **flaunt**, parade, show off, strut, pose, brandish, flash (*informal*) [➡CAUSE TO APPEAR; 5] *Opposite:* conceal 3 *n* **show**, exhibition, presentation, demonstration, parade, spectacle, ceremony, pageant [➡PERFORMANCES AND SHOWS; 42]

display cabinet *type of* **cabinet** [➡FURNITURE; 858]

display case *type of* **cabinet** [➡FURNITURE; 858]

displease *v* **anger**, annoy, irritate, upset, put out, offend, dissatisfy, irk, peeve (*informal*) [➡ANGER AND ANNOY; 569] *Opposite:* please

displeased *adj* **annoyed**, dissatisfied, put out, irked, unhappy, irritated, upset, peeved (*informal*) [➡IRRITATION AND ANGER; 541] *Opposite:* pleased

displeasing *adj* [➡INAPPROPRIATE AND UNSUITABLE; 224]

displeasure *n* **anger**, annoyance, irritation, disapproval, discontentment, discontent, unhappiness [➡IRRITATION AND ANGER; 541] *Opposite:* pleasure

disport (*archaic or humorous*) *v* **show off**, pose, swagger, strut, flaunt, display [➡CAUSE TO APPEAR; 5]

disposable *adj* **throwaway**, one-use, nonrefundable [➡FINITENESS, VARIABILITY, AND TRANSIENCE; 96] *Opposite:* reusable

disposal *n* **removal**, discarding, clearance, dumping, throwing away [➡REMOVE SOMETHING; 338] *Opposite:* retention

dispose 1 *v* **incline**, influence, persuade, prompt, encourage, predispose (*formal*) [➡ENCOURAGE; 576] 2 *v* (*formal*) **position**, place, set out, arrange, set, marshal, array (*formal*) [➡POSITION SOMETHING; 325] 3 *v* **settle**, resolve, fix, decide, determine, rule [➡MAKE DECISIONS AND CHOICES; 752]

disposed *adj* **willing**, likely, liable, inclined, of a mind, feeling like, predisposed, ready, prepared [➡THE WILL AND WILLINGNESS; 563] *Opposite:* unwilling

dispose of 1 *v* **throw away**, throw out, dispense with, discard, get rid of, jettison, scrap, dump, ax (*informal*), ditch (*informal*), chuck (*informal*), bin (*UK*) [➡GET RID OF SOMETHING; 451] *Opposite:* keep 2 *v* **transfer**, pass on, divest yourself of, relieve yourself of, sell [➡GET RID OF SOMETHING; 451] *Opposite:* keep 3 *v* **kill**, murder, execute, assassinate, dispatch, do away with (*informal*) [➡KILL; 923] 4 *v* (*formal*) **attend to**, determine, settle, sort out, sort, eliminate, mop up [➡CARRY OUT AN ACTION; 269] 5 *v* (*formal*) **consume**, demolish, get through, devour, use up, finish off, finish up [➡USE UP AND WASTE; 474]

disposition *n* **nature**, character, temperament, temper, outlook, mood, personality [➡TEMPERAMENT AND BEHAVIOR; 492]

dispossess (*archaic or formal*) *v* **deprive**, divest, strip, rob, disinherit, take away [➡ TAKE SOMETHING AWAY; 425]

dispossessed *adj* **evicted**, expelled, ejected, turned out, driven out, homeless, cast out (*formal*) [➡ NOMADIC AND ROOTLESS LIFESTYLES; 884]

dispossession *n* **deprivation**, denial, withdrawal, removal [➡ TOO FEW, TOO LITTLE; 122]

disproportion *n* **imbalance**, discrepancy, disparity, inequality, inconsistency, inequity [➡ DIFFERENCE; 149] *Opposite*: equality

disproportionate *adj* **uneven**, unequal, lopsided, inconsistent, top-heavy, unbalanced, disparate [➡ DIFFERENCE; 149] *Opposite*: corresponding

disproportionately *adv* **excessively**, unduly, unreasonably, extremely, too, overly [➡ TOO MUCH; 119] *Opposite*: slightly

disprove *v* **refute**, invalidate, contradict, challenge, negate (*formal*), controvert (*formal*) [➡ DENY AND REJECT; 644] *Opposite*: prove

disputable *adj* **arguable**, debatable, moot, questionable, uncertain, doubtful [➡ UNCERTAIN; 175] *Opposite*: incontrovertible

disputation (*formal*) *n* **argument**, strife, conflict, debate, disagreement, contention, controversy [➡ ARGUMENTS; 47] *Opposite*: agreement

disputatious (*formal*) *adj* **argumentative**, quarrelsome, awkward, difficult, contrary, perverse, fractious, troublesome, hostile, disputative (*formal*) [➡ DIFFICULT TO PLEASE; 515] *Opposite*: conciliatory

disputatiously (*formal*) *adv* **argumentatively**, quarrelsomely, awkwardly, contrarily, perversely, fractiously, troublesomely, hostilely [➡ RUDE AND HOSTILE; 625] *Opposite*: agreeably

disputatiousness (*formal*) *n* **argumentativeness**, quarrelsomeness, awkwardness, contrariness, fractiousness, troublesomeness [➡ DIFFICULT TO PLEASE; 515]

disputative (*formal*) *adj* **argumentative**, quarrelsome, awkward, difficult, contrary, perverse, fractious, troublesome, hostile, disputatious (*formal*) [➡ DIFFICULT TO PLEASE; 515] *Opposite*: conciliatory

dispute 1 *v* **challenge**, question, contest, query, doubt, impugn (*formal*) [➡ QUESTION THINGS; 751] *Opposite*: accept 2 *v* **argue**, debate, discuss, quarrel, wrangle, disagree [➡ ARGUE AND FIGHT; 643] *Opposite*: agree 3 *n* **argument**, disagreement, quarrel, difference, clash, row [➡ ARGUMENTS; 47] *Opposite*: agreement

See Compare and Contrast at **disagree**.

disqualification *n* **ineligibility**, banning, barring, disentitlement, debarment, exclusion, prohibition [➡ REFUSE PERMISSION AND NOT ALLOW; 670] *Opposite*: entitlement

disqualified *adj* **ineligible**, banned, barred, debarred, prohibited, excluded [➡ REFUSE PERMISSION AND NOT ALLOW; 670] *Opposite*: eligible

disqualify *v* **ban**, bar, debar, prohibit, exclude, elim-

inate, rule out, except (*formal*) [➡ REFUSE PERMISSION AND NOT ALLOW; 670] *Opposite*: allow

disquiet 1 *n* **unrest**, uneasiness, concern, worry, anxiety, foreboding, alarm [➡ INSECURITY AND LOSS OF COMPOSURE; 544] *Opposite*: calmness 2 *v* (*archaic or literary*) **worry**, disturb, upset, disconcert, perturb, unsettle, bother, fluster [➡ UPSET, DISTRESS, AND HUMILIATE; 567]

disquieted (*archaic or literary*) *adj* [➡ INSECURITY AND LOSS OF COMPOSURE; 544]

disquieting *adj* **worrying**, disturbing, alarming, unsettling, troubling, distressing [➡ EMOTIONALLY UNPLEASANT AND UPSETTING; 227] *Opposite*: reassuring

disquisition (*formal*) *n* **essay**, tract, discussion, address, speech, debate [➡ ONE-WAY COMMUNICATION; 49]

disquisitional (*formal*) *adj* **verbose**, wordy, long-winded, rambling, digressive [➡ INARTICULATE, RAMBLING, AND AWKWARD; 633] *Opposite*: concise

disregard 1 *v* **ignore**, take no notice of, turn a blind eye to, discount, pay no attention to, forget [➡ NOT PAY ATTENTION; 764] *Opposite*: heed 2 *n* **disrespect**, indifference, contempt, disdain, neglect [➡ NEUTRALITY AND INDIFFERENCE; 553] *Opposite*: regard

disregarded 1 *adj* **ignored**, omitted, overlooked, unheeded, unnoticed, marginalized, unsung [➡ UNPOPULAR AND UNWANTED; 258] *Opposite*: noticed 2 *adj* **snubbed**, slighted, disparaged, dishonored, ridiculed [➡ IN TROUBLE AND DISADVANTAGED; 73] *Opposite*: respected

disrepair *n* **poor shape**, bad shape, bad condition, poor order, disorder, shabbiness [➡ IN BAD REPAIR; 1234]

disreputable *adj* **notorious**, infamous, scandalous, disgraceful, seedy [➡ MORALLY BAD OR IMPROPER; 775] *Opposite*: reputable

disrepute *n* **disgrace**, ill repute, disrespect, disregard, discredit, opprobrium, shame, dishonor [➡ DIFFICULT SITUATIONS; 72]

disrespect 1 *n* **disregard**, contempt, insolence, impertinence, impudence [➡ ANTAGONISM; 552] *Opposite*: respect 2 *v* **insult**, affront, belittle, disparage, denigrate, put down (*informal*), dis (*slang*) [➡ PROTEST AND EXPRESS DISAPPROVAL; 642] *Opposite*: respect

disrespectable *adj* **dishonorable**, frowned on, disreputable, unpopular, infamous, notorious [➡ MORALLY BAD OR IMPROPER; 775] *Opposite*: respectable

disrespectful *adj* **rude**, impolite, bad-mannered, discourteous, insolent, ill-mannered, impertinent (*formal*) [➡ BAD MANNERS AND SOCIAL SKILLS; 521] *Opposite*: respectful

disrobe (*formal*) *v* **strip**, undress, unclothe, uncover, divest (*formal or humorous*) [➡ DRESS, WEAR, AND UNDRESS; 868] *Opposite*: dress

disrupt *v* **disturb**, upset, interrupt, dislocate, disorder, unsettle, mess up (*informal*) [➡ CREATE DISORDER AND CAUSE CHAOS; 358]

disruption *n* **disturbance**, commotion, trouble, interruption, distraction, interference, disorder [➡ PROBLEMS; 256]

disruptive *adj* **troublesome**, troublemaking, unruly, disorderly, unsettling, upsetting, disrupting, disturbing, distracting [➡ IRRITATING; 228]

disruptively *adv* noisily, rudely, raucously, wildly, boisterously, rowdily, obtrusively [➡ POMPOUS, LOUD, AND OVER-CONFIDENT; 635] *Opposite:* unobtrusively

disruptiveness *n* unruliness, rowdiness, disorderliness, indiscipline, naughtiness [➡ REBELLIOUSNESS AND DISOBEDIENCE; 565]

diss (*slang*) *see* dis

dissatisfaction *n* displeasure, discontent, disappointment, unhappiness, frustration [➡ IRRITATION AND ANGER; 541] *Opposite:* satisfaction

dissatisfied *adj* disgruntled, displeased, discontented, disappointed, unhappy, frustrated, fed up (*informal*) [➡ IRRITATION AND ANGER; 541] *Opposite:* satisfied

dissatisfy *v* disgruntle, displease, disappoint, put out, frustrate, peeve (*informal*) [➡ ANGER AND ANNOY; 569] *Opposite:* satisfy

dissect 1 *v* cut up, cut apart, divide, dismember, slice up, separate, dichotomize (*formal*), dissever (*formal*) [➡ TEAR, BREAK, AND CUT; 360] 2 *v* scrutinize, break down, examine, study, explore, analyze, anatomize [➡ EXAMINE AND ASSESS; 753]

dissection 1 *n* cutting up, partition, division, separation, segmentation, splitting up, dismemberment [➡ TEAR, BREAK, AND CUT; 360] 2 *n* examination, analysis, investigation, scrutiny, observation, going-over (*informal*) [➡ EXAMINE AND ASSESS; 753]

dissemble 1 *v* pretend, mislead, act, put on an act, dissimulate, feign, play-act (*informal*) [➡ DECEPTION AND LIES; 660] 2 *v* (*formal*) disguise, conceal, hide, suppress, mask, cloak, veil, camouflage, obscure, dissimulate [➡ WITHHOLD INFORMATION; 687] *Opposite:* disclose

dissembler (*formal*) *n* [➡ PEOPLE WHO DECEIVE; 661]

disseminate *v* distribute, broadcast, circulate, spread, publicize, publish, propagate [➡ INFORM, ANNOUNCE, AND ISSUE; 611]

See Compare and Contrast at **scatter**.

dissemination *n* distribution, broadcasting, diffusion, propagation, spreading, giving out [➡ INFORM, ANNOUNCE, AND ISSUE; 611]

dissension *n* opposition, disagreement, dissent, discord, rebellion, conflict [➡ DISHARMONY; 156] *Opposite:* consent

dissent 1 *v* disagree, oppose, rebel, dispute, differ, divide, vary [➡ PROTEST AND EXPRESS DISAPPROVAL; 642] *Opposite:* agree 2 *n* opposition, disagreement, dissension, discord, rebellion, conflict, difference [➡ DISHARMONY; 156] *Opposite:* consent

dissenter *n* rebel, dissident, nonconformist, insurgent, mutineer, malcontent, revolutionist [➡ UNCOOPERATIVE OR REBELLIOUS PEOPLE; 566]

dissertation *n* thesis, paper, study, critique, essay, exposition, tract [➡ ANALYTICAL NONFICTION WRITING; 592]

disservice *n* damage, harm, wrong, injury, difficulty [➡ NUISANCES; 253] *Opposite:* service

dissever (*formal*) *v* [➡ SEPARATE AND DIVIDE; 401]

dissidence *n* disagreement, unorthodoxy, nonconformity, independence, rebellion, resistance [➡ REBELLIOUSNESS AND DISOBEDIENCE; 565] *Opposite:* conformism

dissident 1 *n* dissenter, rebel, nonconformist, protester, insurgent, mutineer, revolutionist, malcontent [➡ UNCOOPERATIVE OR REBELLIOUS PEOPLE; 566] *Opposite:* conformist 2 *adj* rebel, rebellious, dissenting, unorthodox, nonconforming, nonconformist [➡ REBELLIOUSNESS AND DISOBEDIENCE; 565] *Opposite:* conformist

dissimilar *adj* unlike, different, far from, unrelated, disparate, divergent, unalike, contradictory [➡ DIFFERENCE; 149] *Opposite:* similar

dissimilarity *n* difference, variation, distinction, contrast, divergence, unlikeness [➡ DIFFERENCE; 149] *Opposite:* similarity

dissimulate *v* disguise, conceal, hide, suppress, mask, cloak, veil, camouflage, obscure, dissemble (*formal*) [➡ WITHHOLD INFORMATION; 687] *Opposite:* disclose

dissimulation (*formal*) *n* concealment, suppression, disguise, camouflage, dishonesty, subterfuge [➡ DECEPTION AND LIES; 660] *Opposite:* disclosure

dissipate 1 *v* dispel, disperse, dissolve, scatter, drive away, disintegrate [➡ SPREAD AND SCATTER; 332] 2 *v* squander, waste, fritter away, throw away, blow (*slang*) [➡ GIVE MONEY; 433]

dissipated *adj* dissolute, degenerate, debauched, self-indulgent, immoral, intemperate [➡ PLEASURE-SEEKING AND EXCESS; 885] *Opposite:* upright

dissipation *n* debauchery, indulgence, rakishness, overindulgence, degeneracy, intemperance [➡ PLEASURE-SEEKING AND EXCESS; 885] *Opposite:* uprightness

dissociate *v* distance, detach, divorce, separate, disconnect, disassociate [➡ SEPARATE AND DIVIDE; 401] *Opposite:* associate

dissociation *n* detachment, separation, disconnection, severance, alienation, division, disassociation [➡ SEPARATE AND DIVIDE; 401] *Opposite:* association

dissolute *adj* degenerate, depraved, immoral, debauched, self-indulgent, dissipated [➡ PLEASURE-SEEKING AND EXCESS; 885] *Opposite:* upright

dissoluteness *n* decadence, overindulgence, extravagance, self-indulgence, degeneracy, recklessness, wastefulness, profligacy, dissipation, depravity, licentiousness (*formal*) [➡ PLEASURE-SEEKING AND EXCESS; 885] *Opposite:* temperance

dissolution *n* closure, disbanding, termination, ending, suspension, conclusion [➡ ENDS AND DEPARTURES; 54] *Opposite:* inauguration

dissolve 1 *v* melt, soften, liquefy, thaw, run [➡ SOFTEN, LIQUEFY, AND DAMPEN; 388] *Opposite:* solidify 2 *v* disappear, dissipate, dispel, disperse, melt away, evaporate, vanish [➡ CEASE TO EXIST; 22] *Opposite:* appear 3 *v* disband, close, break up, suspend, end, disperse, adjourn [➡ CAUSE TO STOP; 266] *Opposite:* inaugurate

dissonance *n* discord, disagreement, dissension, conflict, difference, difference of opinion [➡DISHARMONY; 156] *Opposite*: harmony

dissonant *adj* **discordant**, unmusical, harsh, inharmonious, cacophonous, jarring [➡LOUD, HIGH, OR UNPLEASANT SOUNDS; 1266] *Opposite*: harmonious

dissuade *v* **deter**, put off, discourage, advise against, persuade against, talk out of [➡ADVISE AND WARN; 613] *Opposite*: persuade

dissuasion *n* **discouragement**, deterrence, persuasion, opposition, warning [➡ADVICE; 689] *Opposite*: encouragement

dissuasive *adj* **discouraging**, opposing, inhibitive, hindering [➡ADVISE AND WARN; 613] *Opposite*: encouraging

distance 1 *n* **space**, expanse, void, vastness, gap [➡DISTANCE; 160] *Opposite*: closeness 2 *n* **coldness**, aloofness, detachment, reserve, remoteness [➡UNINTERESTED AND DETACHED; 629] *Opposite*: warmth 3 *v* **dissociate**, move away, detach, separate, avoid [➡NOT PAY ATTENTION; 764] *Opposite*: associate

distance learning *type of* **broadcast** [➡TELEVISION AND RADIO; 606]

distant 1 *adj* **faraway**, remote, far-off, far-flung, outlying, far, isolated, secluded [➡DISTANCE; 160] *Opposite*: near 2 *adj* **aloof**, cold, unfriendly, detached, reserved, unsociable, cool, withdrawn [➡UNINTERESTED AND DETACHED; 629] *Opposite*: warm 3 *adj* **vague**, faint, indistinct, hazy, obscure [➡VAGUENESS; 243] *Opposite*: clear

distantly 1 *adv* **vaguely**, faintly, indistinctly, abstractedly, far, remotely [➡VAGUENESS; 243] *Opposite*: clearly 2 *adv* **coldly**, coolly, aloofly, reservedly, unsociably [➡UNINTERESTED AND DETACHED; 629] *Opposite*: warmly

distaste *n* **dislike**, revulsion, disgust, disfavor, aversion (*formal*) [➡DISLIKE AND HATE; 577] *Opposite*: love

See Compare and Contrast at **dislike**.

distasteful *adj* **repugnant**, offensive, disgusting, repulsive, objectionable, revolting, obnoxious, odious [➡DISGUSTING AND REPULSIVE; 230] *Opposite*: pleasant

distastefulness *n* **unpleasantness**, offensiveness, nastiness, unattractiveness, hideousness, repulsiveness [➡DISGUSTING AND REPULSIVE; 230] *Opposite*: pleasantness

distend *v* **swell**, bloat, balloon, inflate, swell up, expand, increase, enlarge [➡CHANGE OF SIZE: BIGGER; 392] *Opposite*: deflate

distended *adj* **swollen**, bloated, inflated, enlarged, expanded [➡CHANGE OF SIZE: BIGGER; 392]

distension *n* **swelling**, swollenness, tightness, expansion, enlargement, dilation [➡CHANGE OF SIZE: BIGGER; 392]

distill 1 *v* **purify**, refine, condense, concentrate, extract, disinfect, sanitize, clean, decontaminate, cleanse [➡CLEAN AND POLISH; 403] *Opposite*: pollute 2 *v* **extract**, glean, cull, garner, collect, gather, obtain [➡GET; 420]

distillate *n* **essence**, tincture, concentrate, extract, distillation [➡LIQUIDS; 1269]

distillation 1 *n* **concentration**, condensation, refinement, purification, extraction, decontamination [➡CLEAN AND POLISH; 403] *Opposite*: dilution 2 *n* **essence**, epitome,

embodiment, summation, condensation, image, concentration, concentrate [➡PERFECT EXAMPLES AND EMBODIMENTS; 67] 3 *n* **distillate**, tincture, extract, concentrate [➡LIQUIDS; 1269] *Opposite*: solution

distillery *type of* **factory** [➡INDUSTRIAL BUILDINGS; 1087]

distinct 1 *adj* **separate**, different, dissimilar, discrete, diverse, divergent, distinctive, individual [➡DIFFERENCE; 149] *Opposite*: same 2 *adj* **clear**, definite, well-defined, noticeable, marked, apparent, conspicuous, manifest, patent, plain, evident [➡PERCEPTIBLE; 25] *Opposite*: unclear

distinction 1 *n* **difference**, division, dissimilarity, discrepancy, otherness [➡DIFFERENCE; 149] *Opposite*: similarity 2 *n* **merit**, excellence, note, worth, accolade, award, decoration, honor [➡REWARDS AND AWARDS; 439] *Opposite*: disgrace 3 *n* **feature**, characteristic, idiosyncrasy, peculiarity, trait, particularity, individualism [➡PERSONAL ECCENTRICITIES; 493]

distinctive *adj* **characteristic**, idiosyncratic, distinguishing, individual, typical, unique, distinct [➡EXTRAORDINARY: UNCOMMON; 205] *Opposite*: common

distinctively *adv* **characteristically**, idiosyncratically, peculiarly, individually, typically, uniquely, particularly, specifically [➡UNRELATEDNESS AND SEPARATENESS; 146]

distinctiveness *n* **uniqueness**, individuality, particularity, individualism, singularity [➡UNRELATEDNESS AND SEPARATENESS; 146] *Opposite*: sameness

distinctly *adv* **definitely**, clearly, noticeably, markedly, particularly, specifically, conspicuously, manifestly, patently, plainly [➡PERCEPTIBLE; 25] *Opposite*: vaguely

distinctness *n* [➡PERCEPTIBLE; 25]

distinguish 1 *v* **differentiate**, tell apart, tell between, discriminate, decide, extricate, separate [➡EXAMINE AND ASSESS; 753] 2 *v* **set apart**, single out, characterize, mark, classify, individualize, singularize (*formal*) [➡SEPARATE AND DIVIDE; 401] 3 *v* **make out**, discern, see, recognize, perceive, pick out, notice, observe [➡LOOKING AND LOOKS; 700]

distinguishability *n* [➡PERCEPTIBLE; 25]

distinguishable 1 *adj* **different**, unique, distinct, special, divergent, discrete [➡DIFFERENCE; 149] 2 *adj* **discernible**, obvious, noticeable, clear, evident, apparent [➡PERCEPTIBLE; 25] *Opposite*: indistinguishable

distinguished *adj* **illustrious**, eminent, famous, famed, well-known, renowned, great, prominent, celebrated, notable [➡LEVELS OF EDUCATION AND SOPHISTICATION; 894] *Opposite*: undistinguished

distinguishing *adj* **unique**, individual, personal, distinctive, characteristic, peculiar [➡EXTRAORDINARY: UNCOMMON; 205] *Opposite*: typical

distort 1 *v* **misrepresent**, interfere with, twist, alter, garble, change, falsify, mislead [➡CHANGE; 372] 2 *v* **deform**, disfigure, twist, warp, alter, bend [➡CHANGE OF SHAPE; 385] *Opposite*: straighten

distorted 1 *adj* **one-sided**, slanted, partial, inaccurate, partisan, misleading, biased, unfair [➡FALSE AND UNREAL; 173] *Opposite*: accurate 2 *adj* **twisted**, malformed, warped, bent, contorted, deformed, misshapen [➡IN BAD REPAIR; 1234]

Opposite: straight **3** *adj* **unrecognizable**, grotesque, unnatural, monstrous, bizarre [➡ UGLINESS AND UNATTRACTIVENESS; 233]

distortion **1** *n* **misrepresentation**, alteration, lie, falsehood, falsification, bias, spin (*slang*) [➡ DECEPTION AND LIES; 660] **2** *n* **bend**, buckle, twist, deformation, warp, disfigurement [➡ CHANGE OF SHAPE; 385]

distract **1** *v* **sidetrack**, divert, confuse, addle, befuddle, disturb [➡ CONFUSE AND BEWILDER; 571] **2** *v* **entertain**, amuse, divert, absorb, engross, engage [➡ PLEASE AND AMUSE; 572]

distracted **1** *adj* **unfocused**, abstracted, preoccupied, sidetracked, diverted, confused, dreamy, inattentive, vague, absent-minded, distrait (*literary*) [➡ NEUTRALITY AND INDIFFERENCE; 553] *Opposite*: attentive **2** *adj* **troubled**, agitated, anxious, perplexed, confused, upset, twitchy (*UK*) [➡ CONFUSION, ANXIETY, AND WORRY; 540] *Opposite*: assured

distracting *adj* **off-putting**, disturbing, diverting, disrupting [➡ IRRITATING; 228]

distraction **1** *n* **interruption**, disruption, commotion, disturbance, interference [➡ DISORDER AND CHAOS; 245] **2** *n* **diversion**, entertainment, hobby, pastime, leisure activity, amusement, recreation [➡ LEISURE AND RECREATION; 874] **3** *n* **agitation**, anxiety, bewilderment, confusion, desperation, trouble, upset [➡ CONFUSION, ANXIETY, AND WORRY; 540]

distrait (*literary*) *adj* **inattentive**, distracted, unmindful, dreamy, vague, preoccupied, absent-minded, woolgathering [➡ NEUTRALITY AND INDIFFERENCE; 553] *Opposite*: alert

distraught *adj* **distressed**, beside yourself, out of your mind, hysterical, upset, troubled, worried, flustered, agitated, disturbed, panic-stricken, distrait (*archaic*) [➡ CONFUSION, ANXIETY, AND WORRY; 540] *Opposite*: calm

distress **1** *n* **suffering**, pain, sorrow, anguish, agony, grief, misery, ache, pang, concern, worry, angst [➡ SADNESS, DISTRESS, AND DESPAIR; 539] *Opposite*: peace **2** *n* **trouble**, danger, difficulty, misfortune, rigor, hardship, trial [➡ DIFFICULT SITUATIONS; 72] **3** *v* **upset**, disturb, trouble, bother, afflict, torment, stress, worry [➡ UPSET, DISTRESS, AND HUMILIATE; 567] *Opposite*: soothe

distressed **1** *adj* **upset**, distraught, troubled, concerned, worried, anxious, unhappy, bothered, distrait (*archaic*) [➡ SADNESS, DISTRESS, AND DESPAIR; 539] *Opposite*: content **2** *adj* **in pain**, suffering, anguished, tormented, miserable, aching [➡ SADNESS, DISTRESS, AND DESPAIR; 539] **3** *adj* [➡ DESCRIBING CLOTHES; 869]

distressing *adj* **upsetting**, worrying, difficult, stressful, painful, sad [➡ EMOTIONALLY UNPLEASANT AND UPSETTING; 227]

distress signal *n* **call for help**, cry for help, alarm bell, alarm, call, cry, alert, SOS [➡ SOUNDS MADE BY PEOPLE; 1262]

distribute **1** *v* **deal out**, hand out, share out, allocate, give out, issue, dispense, allot, mete out, dole out (*informal*), dish out (*informal*) [➡ DISPENSE, RATION, AND DISTRIBUTE; 434] **2** *v* **deliver**, supply, circulate, spread out, spread, disperse, disseminate, scatter [➡ SPREAD AND SCATTER; 332]

See Compare and Contrast at **scatter**.

distributer *see* **distributor**

distribution **1** *n* **sharing**, allocation, giving out, division, allotment [➡ DISPENSE, RATION, AND DISTRIBUTE; 434] **2** *n* **delivery**, supply, circulation, spreading, dispersal, dissemination,

scattering [➡ DISPENSE, RATION, AND DISTRIBUTE; 434] **3** *n* **spreading**, dispersal, dissemination, scattering [➡ MOVE SOMETHING TO ANOTHER LOCATION; 324]

distributor **1** *n* **supplier**, provider, wholesaler, broker, trader, merchant, distributer, purveyor (*formal*) [➡ BUSINESS PEOPLE; 793] **2** *part of* **engine** [➡ PARTS OF AN ENGINE; 1144]

district *n* **locality**, area, barrio, neighborhood, quarter, borough, ward, constituency [➡ COUNTRIES AND REGIONS; 1067]

district attorney *n* [➡ PEOPLE IN LAW COURTS; 820]

distrust **1** *n* **suspicion**, disbelief, doubt, misgiving, cynicism, mistrust, wariness, chariness [➡ UNCERTAINTY; 559] *Opposite*: trust **2** *v* **disbelieve**, doubt, be suspicious of, mistrust, suspect [➡ QUESTION THINGS; 751] *Opposite*: trust

distrustful *adj* **suspicious**, doubting, wary, nervous, disbelieving, cynical, mistrustful, chary [➡ UNCERTAINTY; 559] *Opposite*: trusting

disturb **1** *v* **interrupt**, distract, bother, disrupt, annoy, get in the way, intrude [➡ ANGER AND ANNOY; 569] **2** *v* **upset**, worry, bother, concern, perturb, agitate, scare, alarm, frighten, trouble [➡ UPSET, DISTRESS, AND HUMILIATE; 567] **3** *v* **move**, transfer, shift, dislocate, remove [➡ MOVE SOMETHING TO ANOTHER LOCATION; 324] **4** *v* **spoil**, unsettle, upset, meddle, tamper, jumble, muddle, mess up (*informal*) [➡ CREATE DISORDER AND CAUSE CHAOS; 358]

See Compare and Contrast at **bother**.

disturbance **1** *n* **trouble**, commotion, riot, uproar, fracas, disorder, disruption, ruckus [➡ CHAOS AND UPROAR; 51] **2** *n* **annoyance**, interruption, intrusion, bother, disruption, irritation, distraction [➡ NUISANCES; 253]

disturbed **1** *adj* **troubled**, bothered, concerned, worried, distressed, anxious, uneasy, upset, agitated, distraught [➡ CONFUSION, ANXIETY, AND WORRY; 540] *Opposite*: unconcerned **2** *adj* **unstable**, troubled, traumatized, unbalanced, unhinged, messed up (*informal*) [➡ ECCENTRICITY AND IRRATIONALITY; 562] *Opposite*: stable

disturbing *adj* **worrying**, troubling, alarming, upsetting, distressing, disquieting, disconcerting, unsettling, ominous, unnerving [➡ EMOTIONALLY UNPLEASANT AND UPSETTING; 227] *Opposite*: reassuring

disunite *v* **split**, divide, separate, undo, dissolve, break, sever [➡ UNFASTEN AND UNDO; 409] *Opposite*: unite

disunity *n* **disagreement**, discord, divergence, dissent, conflict, dispute, division [➡ DISHARMONY; 156] *Opposite*: unity

disuse *n* **neglect**, abandonment, unemployment, dereliction [➡ IN BAD REPAIR; 1234] *Opposite*: use

disused *adj* **empty**, abandoned, neglected, derelict, deserted [➡ IN BAD REPAIR; 1234] *Opposite*: occupied

ditch **1** *n* **channel**, trench, dike, drain, waterway, conduit, gully, trough [➡ WATERCOURSES; 1111] **2** *v* (*informal*) **scrap**, get rid of, drop, split up with, discard, throw out, leave, dump (*informal*), chuck (*informal*), give somebody the boot (*informal*) [➡ REFUSING OR REJECTING RELATIONS; 975]

dither *v* **hesitate**, dally, dawdle, waste time, vacillate, waver, shilly-shally [➡ HESITATE; 272]

ditherer n **vacillator**, dawdler, waverer, hesitater [➤LAZY OR UNSUCCESSFUL PEOPLE; 948]

dithering n **indecisiveness**, indecision, hesitation, irresolution, wavering, hesitancy, shilly-shallying, uncertainty, faltering, vacillation [➤UNCERTAINTY; 559] *Opposite*: decisiveness

ditsy (*informal*) adj **empty-headed**, forgetful, absentminded, scatterbrained, vague, woolly-headed, unreliable, eccentric, frivolous, dizzy (*informal*) [➤LACK OF COMMITMENT AND UNRELIABILITY; 509]

ditty n **song**, poem, rhyme, limerick, nursery rhyme, ode [➤MUSIC, SONGS, AND SINGING; 907]

diurnal 1 adj **day**, daytime, daylight [➤TIMES OF DAY; 87] *Opposite*: nocturnal 2 adj **daily**, 24-hour, 24-hourly, circadian, quotidian (*formal*) [➤TIMES OF DAY; 87]

diva n **prima donna**, singer, chanteuse, soprano [➤MUSICIANS AND SINGERS; 908]

divan n **settee**, couch, sofa [➤FURNITURE; 858]

dive 1 v **jump**, leap, drop, lunge, submerge [➤GO DOWNWARD; 307] *Opposite*: surface 2 v **plummet**, plunge, fall, nose-dive, crash, free-fall, go down, decrease [➤CHANGE OF INTENSITY: LESS; 395] *Opposite*: shoot up 3 n **lunge**, leap, drop, jump [➤GO DOWNWARD; 307] 4 n **plunge**, fall, nosedive, crash, free-fall, descent, plummet, decrease [➤CHANGE OF INTENSITY: LESS; 395] 5 n (*informal*) **bar**, saloon, hangout (*informal*), dump (*informal*), joint (*slang*), honky-tonk (*slang*) [➤BUILDINGS FOR PUBLIC ENTERTAINMENT; 1084]

diver n **swimmer**, deep-sea diver, snorkeler, frogman, scuba diver, aquanaut [➤PEOPLE IN SPORTS AND LEISURE; 876]

diverge 1 v **deviate**, move away, wander, depart, swerve, separate [➤SEPARATE AND DIVIDE; 401] *Opposite*: converge 2 v **differ**, disagree, vary, conflict [➤PROTEST AND EXPRESS DISAPPROVAL; 642] *Opposite*: concur 3 v **digress**, ramble, stray, deviate [➤CHATTER AND BABBLE; 617]

divergence 1 n **deviation**, departure, discrepancy, disagreement, separation, crosscurrent [➤DIFFERENCE; 149] *Opposite*: convergence 2 n **difference**, difference of opinion, disagreement, variance, conflict, nonconformity [➤DISHARMONY; 156] *Opposite*: agreement

divergent adj **different**, differing, deviating, conflicting, contradictory, opposing, opposite, contrary [➤DIFFERENCE; 149] *Opposite*: similar

divers (*literary*) adj **various**, miscellaneous, assorted, sundry, several, distinct, disparate, different [➤DIFFERENCE; 149] *Opposite*: similar

diverse 1 adj **varied**, miscellaneous, assorted, sundry [➤DIFFERENCE; 149] 2 adj **different**, dissimilar, unlike, distinct, separate, opposite, disparate [➤DIFFERENCE; 149] *Opposite*: similar

diversely adv **varyingly**, variously, distinctly, separately, dissimilarly, differently, peculiarly, inconsistently, disparately [➤DIFFERENCE; 149] *Opposite*: similarly

diversification n **change**, divergence, variation, modification, broadening, branching out, expansion [➤CHANGE; 372] *Opposite*: specialization

diversify v **branch out**, expand, spread, broaden your horizons, vary, differentiate [➤CHANGE; 372] *Opposite*: specialize

diversion 1 n **distraction**, entertainment, pastime, hobby, leisure activity, amusement, recreation [➤LEISURE AND RECREATION; 874] 2 n **change**, alteration, departure, digression, deviation [➤CHANGE; 372]

diversionary adj **distracting**, diverting, misleading, deflecting, deceptive [➤FALSE AND UNREAL; 173]

diversity n **variety**, assortment, multiplicity, range, mixture [➤COLLECTIONS AND MIXTURES OF THINGS; 1244] *Opposite*: uniformity

divert 1 v **redirect**, deflect, reroute, switch [➤CHANGE DIRECTION OF MOTION; 344] 2 v **distract**, sidetrack, turn away, avert, deter, dissuade [➤APPEAL TO AND AROUSE INTEREST; 575] *Opposite*: focus 3 v **entertain**, amuse, please, delight, gladden, regale, recreate [➤PLEASE AND AMUSE; 572]

divest 1 v **strip**, rid, dissociate, separate, part from, deny, deprive, rob [➤TAKE SOMETHING AWAY; 425] *Opposite*: give 2 v [➤BUSINESS ACTIVITIES AND PHENOMENA; 794]

divide 1 v **split**, separate, partition, segregate, break up, part, carve up (*informal*) [➤SEPARATE AND DIVIDE; 401] *Opposite*: join 2 v **share**, share out, divide up, deal out, distribute, allocate, apportion, allot, split, divvy (*informal*), dole out (*informal*) [➤DISPENSE, RATION, AND DISTRIBUTE; 434] 3 v **cause a rift**, split up, break up, split, come between, differ, dissent [➤UNFASTEN AND UNDO; 409] *Opposite*: unite 4 n **gulf**, rift, division, split, gap, boundary [➤HOLES, GAPS, AND FORKS; 1252]

divided highway *type of* **highway** [➤ROADS; 1106]

dividend n **bonus**, extra, payment, share, surplus, disbursement [➤FUNDS, PAYMENTS, AND CHARGES; 800]

divider n **partition**, separator, screen [➤WALLS AND PARTITIONS; 1104]

dividers *type of* **measuring device** [➤MEASURING DEVICES; 1123]

dividing line n **distinction**, margin, borderline, border, watershed, divider [➤GEOGRAPHIC BORDERS AND BOUNDARIES; 1069]

divination n **prophecy**, prediction, forecast, foretelling, insight, premonition, second sight [➤PREDICT AND ANTICIPATE; 750]

divine 1 adj **heavenly**, celestial, godly, godlike, deific (*formal*) [➤RELIGIOUS CONCEPTS; 776] *Opposite*: earthly 2 adj (*informal or humorous*) **great**, exquisite, delightful, lovely, pleasing, heavenly, cool (*slang*) [➤EMOTIONALLY PLEASANT; 187] 3 v **discover**, guess, presume, deduce, discern, perceive [➤UNDERSTAND AND GRASP; 759]

divine intervention n [➤RELIGIOUS CONCEPTS; 776]

divinely (*informal*) adv **exquisitely**, beautifully, delightfully, well, pleasingly, attractively [➤EMOTIONALLY PLEASANT; 187]

divinity n **religion**, theology, religious studies, spirituality, mysticism [➤CLASSES, COURSEWORK, AND EXAMINATIONS; 842]

divisible adj **isolatable**, detachable, separable, dividable [➤UNRELATEDNESS AND SEPARATENESS; 146] *Opposite*: inseparable

division 1 n **separation**, splitting up, partition, dissection, detachment, disunion [➤SEPARATE AND DIVIDE; 401] *Opposite*: union 2 n **sharing out**, distribution, allotment, allocation, apportionment, sharing [➤DISPENSE, RATION, AND DIS-

TRIBUTE; 434] **3** *n* **split**, rift, disagreement, discord, break, schism, rupture, gulf, divide, disharmony, dissonance [➡DISHARMONY; 156] *Opposite*: unity **4** *n* **boundary**, partition, border, dividing line, demarcation [➡GEOGRAPHIC BORDERS AND BOUNDARIES; 1069] **5** *n* **category**, classification, type, class, grouping, group [➡VARIETIES, TYPES, AND KINDS; 145] **6** *n* **department**, section, group, branch, sector [➡SUBDIVISIONS AND OFFSHOOTS; 1253]

divisive *adj* **discordant**, troublesome, disruptive, conflict-ridden, contentious, acrimonious [➡DISHARMONY; 156]

divisiveness *n* **disruptiveness**, dissension, disagreement, discord, disunity, acrimony, schism [➡DISHARMONY; 156]

divorce **1** *n* **separation**, split, breakup, split-up, annulment [➡ENDS AND DEPARTURES; 54] *Opposite*: marriage **2** *v* **dissociate**, disconnect, separate, distance, detach, break up, split up, break apart [➡SEPARATE AND DIVIDE; 401] *Opposite*: associate

divorced *adj* **separated**, removed, unconnected, split, detached, broken up [➡MARITAL STATUS; 890] *Opposite*: together

divot *n* **turf**, sod, clump, clod, piece, lump [➡AMOUNTS OF SOLID OR SEMISOLID; 115]

divulge *v* **reveal**, tell, make known, disclose, let drop, give away, let slip [➡BETRAY CONFIDENCES AND GOSSIP; 618]

divvy (*informal*) *v* **divide up**, divide, share out, deal out, distribute, allocate, split, apportion, allot, dole out (*informal*) [➡DISPENSE, RATION, AND DISTRIBUTE; 434]

divvy up (*informal*) *v* [➡SEPARATE AND DIVIDE; 401]

Dixieland *type of* **jazz music** [➡MUSIC, SONGS, AND SINGING; 907]

dizzily *adv* **dazedly**, woozily, lightheadedly, shakily, unsteadily, groggily, giddily (*dated*) [➡ILL AND SICK; 740] *Opposite*: steadily

dizziness *n* **faintness**, giddiness, wooziness, vertigo, shakiness, lightheadedness, unsteadiness [➡UNFIT AND WEAK; 739]

dizzy **1** *adj* (*informal*) **frivolous**, flippant, silly, lighthearted, perky, frolicsome, playful, giddy (*dated*) [➡LACK OF COMMITMENT AND UNRELIABILITY; 509] **2** *adj* **faint**, giddy, woozy, shaky, lightheaded, dazed, vertiginous, unsteady, wobbly (*informal*) [➡UNFIT AND WEAK; 739]

DJ **1** *n* **disc jockey**, MC, broadcaster, deejay (*informal*), jock (*informal*), radio presenter (*UK*) [➡WORKERS IN ENTERTAINMENT AND MEDIA; 873] **2** *n* **dinner jacket**, tuxedo, black tie, tux (*informal*) [➡GARMENTS AND OUTFITS; 865]

DNS *n* [➡THE INTERNET; 1128]

do **1** *v* (*informal*) **cheat**, trick, con, swindle, defraud, bamboozle (*informal*) [➡DECEPTION AND LIES; 660] **2** *v* **perform**, accomplish, act, carry out, complete, achieve, make, execute, get something done [➡CARRY OUT AN ACTION; 269] **3** *v* **see to**, fix, prepare, sort out, look after, make sure of, organize, ensure [➡ATTEMPT AN ACTION; 261] **4** *v* **solve**, work out, resolve, figure out, puzzle out [➡DEVELOP THEORIES AND REASON; 744]

See Compare and Contrast at **perform**.

doable *adj* **achievable**, possible, workable, feasible, attainable [➡POSSIBLE AND PROBABLE; 177] *Opposite*: impossible

do a U-turn *v* [➡CHANGE DIRECTION OF MOTION; 344]

do away with **1** *v* **abolish**, dispense with, remove, dispose of, get rid of, eradicate [➡ABOLISH AND ANNUL; 452] *Opposite*: retain **2** *v* (*informal*) **kill**, murder, assassinate, finish off (*informal*), do in (*informal*), blow away (*slang*) [➡KILL; 923]

do battle *v* [➡COMPETE, CONTEND, AND COMBAT; 303]

Doberman pinscher *type of* **large dog** [➡DOGS; 980]

dobra *type of* **currency** [➡CURRENCIES; 798]

docile *adj* **quiet**, passive, unassuming, compliant, submissive, tame, meek, obedient, biddable, pliable [➡THE WILL AND WILLINGNESS; 563] *Opposite*: wild

docility *n* **quietness**, submissiveness, meekness, tameness, gentleness, obedience, compliance [➡THE WILL AND WILLINGNESS; 563] *Opposite*: fierceness

dock **1** *n* **berth**, mooring, anchorage, wharf, quay, marina, waterfront, port [➡WATERWAYS AND SEAWAYS; 1108] **2** *type of* **industrial site** [➡INDUSTRIAL BUILDINGS; 1087] **3** *type of* **weed** [➡WEEDS AND THISTLES; 1034] **4** *v* **come in**, tie up, land, berth, moor [➡ARRIVE BY TRANSPORT; 14] **5** *v* **cut**, cut off, crop, stop, reduce, curtail, deduct [➡TAKE SOMETHING AWAY; 425] *Opposite*: increase

docket **1** *n* **tag**, sticker, label, marker, ticket, receipt, invoice, note, tab (*informal*), chit (*dated*) [➡RECEIPTS AND INVOICES; 591] **2** *n* **agenda**, program, schedule, calendar, timetable, card, bill, slate, roster [➡RECORDS; 585] **3** *v* **label**, tag, identify, disclose, declare [➡NAME AND DESCRIBE; 665]

dockominium *type of* **apartment** [➡RESIDENTIAL BUILDINGS; 1078]

dockside *n* **wharf**, jetty, dock, quayside, quay, landing stage, harbor, pier, waterfront, wharfage, port [➡WATERWAYS AND SEAWAYS; 1108]

dockyard *n* **shipyard**, boatyard, dry dock [➡WATERWAYS AND SEAWAYS; 1108]

doctor **1** *v* **treat**, care for, look after, cure, heal, minister to [➡TAKE CARE OF AND SPOIL; 300] **2** *v* **amend**, modify, adjust, meddle with, rework, tamper with, falsify, change, alter, fix [➡CHANGE; 372] **3** *n* **consultant**, registrar, clinician, medical practitioner, specialist, surgeon, GP, general practitioner, family doctor, physician, medic (*informal*) [➡PEOPLE WHO WORK IN MEDICINE; 848] **4** *n* **academic**, scholar, expert, specialist, Doctor of Philosophy, Ph.D. [➡QUALIFICATIONS; 843]

doctorate *n* **higher degree**, research degree, university degree, Ph.D., Doctor of Philosophy [➡QUALIFICATIONS; 843]

doctrinaire *adj* **rigid**, inflexible, stern, strict, unbending, dogmatic [➡NEGATIVE INTELLECTUAL CHARACTERISTICS; 525] *Opposite*: liberal

doctrine *n* **policy**, principle, set of guidelines, canon, dogma, rule, guideline, creed, code [➡WAYS OF DOING THINGS; 294]

docudrama *type of* **broadcast** [➡TELEVISION AND RADIO; 606]

document **1** *n* **text**, file, article, essay, paper, manuscript, deed, certificate, record [➡WRITING; 583] **2** *v* **record**, keep a record, detail, write down, provide evidence, give proof, verify, authenticate, support [➡RECORD SOMETHING; 371]

documentary *type of* **broadcast** [➡TELEVISION AND RADIO; 606]

documentation *n* **certification**, papers, credentials, documents, citations, records [➡ OFFICIAL DOCUMENTS; 586]

dodder 1 *v* **tremble**, shake, waver, quake, quiver, judder, shudder [➡ PHYSICAL REACTIONS; 316] **2** *v* **totter**, reel, teeter, stagger, wobble, sway, waver, lurch, weave [➡ WALK UNSTEADILY; 315] *Opposite*: stride

doddering *adj* **tottering**, reeling, teetering, staggering, wobbling, shaking, swaying, wavering, rocking, lurching, weaving [➡ DESCRIBING BODY MOVEMENTS; 288]

doddery *adj* **shaky**, unsteady, tottery, feeble, frail, weak [➡ UNFIT AND WEAK; 739] *Opposite*: steady

dodecahedron *type of* **angular shape** [➡ ANGULAR SHAPE; 1217]

dodge 1 *v* **move**, cut, duck, move away, avoid, sidestep [➡ AVOID OR ESCAPE CONTACT; 418] **2** *v* **avoid**, evade, shirk, elude, get out of [➡ NOT PAY ATTENTION; 764]

dodo *type of* **flightless bird** [➡ BIRDS; 997]

doe *type of* **female animal** [➡ MALE OR FEMALE ANIMALS; 978]

doer *n* **achiever**, dynamo, go-getter (*informal*), live wire (*informal*) [➡ PEOPLE WHO ARE APPROVED OF; 955]

doff *v* **take off**, lift, tip, tilt, remove, peel off, shed, discard [➡ DRESS, WEAR, AND UNDRESS; 868] *Opposite*: don

dog 1 *n* **canine**, mongrel, hound, bitch, pup, puppy, pooch (*informal*), mutt (*slang*) [➡ DOGS; 980] **2** *type of* **canine** [➡ CANINES; 979] **3** *v* **follow**, pursue, chase, trail, track, stalk, hunt [➡ ACCOMPANY AND FOLLOW; 337] **4** *v* **bother**, beleaguer, harass, vex, plague, afflict, pester, badger, hound, trouble, hassle (*informal*) [➡ COMPLAIN AND NAG; 686]

dog

◆ *types of large dogs*
Afghan hound, Alsatian, bloodhound, borzoi, boxer, bulldog, collie, dalmatian, Doberman pinscher, German shepherd, Great Dane, greyhound, guide dog, husky, Labrador, mastiff, Newfoundland, Old English sheepdog, Pyrenean mountain dog, retriever, rottweiler, Saint Bernard, setter, sheepdog, wolfhound

◆ *types of small dogs*
affenpinscher, airedale, basenji, basset, beagle, Border terrier, bull terrier, cairn terrier, chihuahua, chow, corgi, dachshund, fox terrier, foxhound, Jack Russell, Pekingese, pomeranian, poodle, pug, Scottie, sealyham, shar-pei, shih tzu, spaniel, terrier, whippet, Yorkshire terrier

dog days *n* [➡ TIMES OF YEAR; 88]

dog-eared *adj* **damaged**, tattered, battered, well-read, worn, well-thumbed [➡ IN BAD REPAIR; 1234]

dogfight *n* **fight**, conflict, combat, encounter, raid, clash, engagement, battle, fracas, fray, skirmish, scrap (*informal*) [➡ AGGRESSIVE EVENTS; 39]

dogfish *type of* **ocean fish** [➡ OCEAN FISH; 1009]

dogged *adj* **determined**, single-minded, unwavering, indefatigable, steadfast, resolute, stubborn, persistent, relentless [➡ UNWILLINGNESS AND STUBBORNNESS; 564] *Opposite*: half-hearted

doggedness *n* **perseverance**, persistence, single-mindedness, tenacity, resolve, steadfastness, staying power, determination, indefatigability [➡ UNWILLINGNESS AND STUBBORNNESS; 564] *Opposite*: apathy

doggerel 1 *n* **verse**, poetry, rhyme, limerick, ditty [➡ FICTION AND DRAMA; 913] **2** *n* **gibberish**, nonsense, prattle, rubbish, garbage, twaddle (*informal*), baloney (*informal*) [➡ MEANINGLESS SPEECH OR WRITING; 676]

doggy *adj* [➡ DOGS; 980]

doghouse *type of* **pen or cage** [➡ ANIMAL OR BIRD ACCOMMODATIONS; 1079]

dog in the manger (*UK*) *n* [➡ GRUMPY AND NEGATIVE PEOPLE; 953]

dogleg 1 *n* **sharp bend**, angle, corner, curve, bend, turn, hairpin bend (*UK*) [➡ ANGULAR SHAPE; 1217] **2** *v* **bend**, turn, curve, swerve [➡ CHANGE DIRECTION OF MOTION; 344]

dogma *n* **creed**, doctrine, philosophy, canon, belief, view, code, tenets (*formal*) [➡ IDEAS AND THOUGHTS; 770]

dogmatic *adj* **rigid**, inflexible, unbending, strict, intransigent, narrow, doctrinaire, fixed [➡ NEGATIVE INTELLECTUAL CHARACTERISTICS; 525] *Opposite*: flexible

dogmatism *n* **intransigence**, inflexibility, strictness, presumption, arrogance, rigidity, firmness [➡ NEGATIVE INTELLECTUAL CHARACTERISTICS; 525] *Opposite*: openness

dog of war (*UK*) *n* [➡ MILITARY PERSONNEL; 828]

do-gooder (*informal*) *n* [➡ INTERFERING PEOPLE AND TATTLETALES; 950]

dogsled *type of* **leisure vehicle** [➡ VEHICLES; 1145]

dog-tired (*informal*) *adj* **exhausted**, worn out, shattered, tired, all in, tired out, fatigued, done in (*informal*) [➡ TIRED, ASLEEP, AND UNCONSCIOUS; 738] *Opposite*: fresh

dogwood *type of* **deciduous tree** [➡ DECIDUOUS TREES; 1028]

doily *n* [➡ ORNAMENTS AND DECORATIONS; 1248]

do in (*informal*) *v* **kill**, murder, assassinate, finish off (*informal*), do away with (*informal*), blow away (*slang*) [➡ KILL; 923]

doings (*informal*) *n* **activities**, actions, events, happenings, deeds, comings and goings, accomplishments, undertakings, goings-on (*informal*) [➡ ACTIONS OR UNDERTAKINGS; 259]

doldrums 1 *n* **stagnation**, sluggishness, boredom, lethargy, lassitude [➡ SADNESS, DISTRESS, AND DESPAIR; 539] *Opposite*: energy **2** *n* **gloominess**, melancholy, dejection, despondency, pessimism, misery, gloom, glumness, sadness, unhappiness, blues (*informal*) [➡ SADNESS, DISTRESS, AND DESPAIR; 539] *Opposite*: cheerfulness

doleful *adj* **unhappy**, miserable, sad, woeful, dejected, mournful, down, downcast, forlorn, gloomy, glum, despondent, down in the dumps (*informal*) [➡ SADNESS, DISTRESS, AND DESPAIR; 539] *Opposite*: cheerful

dolefulness *n* **sadness**, unhappiness, misery, mournfulness, woefulness, dejectedness, gloom, despondency, cheerlessness [➡ SADNESS, DISTRESS, AND DESPAIR; 539] *Opposite*: cheerfulness

dole out (*informal*) *v* **share out**, dispense, distribute,

allocate, allot, deal out, divide up, apportion, serve, give out, issue, deal, dish out (*informal*) [➡ DISPENSE, RATION, AND DISTRIBUTE; 434] *Opposite*: hoard

doll *n* **toy**, figurine, figure, model, puppet, dolly (*informal*) [➡ TOYS; 880]

dollar *n* **dollar bill**, big one, buck (*informal*), greenback (*slang*) [➡ CURRENCIES; 798]

dollhouse *type of* **toy** [➡ TOYS; 880]

dollop (*informal*) *n* **blob**, spoonful, spoon, squirt, drop [➡ AMOUNTS OF SOLID OR SEMISOLID; 115]

doll up (*informal*) *v* **dress up**, smarten up, spruce up, titivate, smarten, glam up [➡ DRESS, WEAR, AND UNDRESS; 868] *Opposite*: tone down

dolly (*informal*) *n* **figurine**, toy, model, figure, puppet, plaything [➡ TOYS; 880]

dolmen *n* **megalith**, obelisk, trilithon, monument, standing stone [➡ ANCIENT MANMADE STRUCTURES; 1089]

dolphin *type of* **marine mammal** [➡ MARINE MAMMALS; 987]

domain 1 *n* **area**, field, sphere, sphere of influence, province, realm, dominion, territory, purview [➡ PLACE; 1065] 2 *n* [➡ THE INTERNET; 1128]

dome 1 *n* **vault**, cupola, roof, ceiling [➡ ROOFS, ROOF PARTS, AND CEILINGS; 1103] 2 *type of* **rounded shape** [➡ ROUNDED SHAPE; 1218]

domed *adj* **vaulted**, hemispherical, rounded, round [➡ ROUNDED SHAPE; 1218]

domestic 1 *adj* **home**, family, house, household, familial, marital, conjugal, married, matrimonial [➡ ACCOMMODATIONS; 855] *Opposite*: public 2 *adj* **national**, local, internal, inland, native, home [➡ COUNTRIES AND REGIONS; 1067] *Opposite*: international

domesticate *v* **tame**, break, bring under control, control, housebreak, housetrain, train [➡ INSTRUCT AND TEACH; 609]

domesticated *adj* **tame**, pet, trained, tamed, housetrained, farm, housebroken [➡ GOOD MANNERS AND SOCIAL SKILLS; 520] *Opposite*: wild

domestication *n* **taming**, training, housetraining, housebreaking, subjugation [➡ TEACHING; 839]

domesticity *n* **home life**, family life, home comforts, married life, creature comforts [➡ PLEASANT SITUATIONS; 74]

domestic partner *n* **cohabitee**, partner, spousal equivalent, significant other [➡ SEXUAL AND ROMANTIC RELATIONSHIPS; 964]

domicile (*formal*) *n* **home**, residence, house, apartment, quarters, dwelling (*formal*), abode (*literary*), flat (*UK*) [➡ ACCOMMODATIONS; 855]

domiciliary *adj* [➡ ACCOMMODATIONS; 855]

dominance *n* **supremacy**, ascendancy, domination, power, authority, control, governance (*formal*) [➡ STRENGTH; 201] *Opposite*: weakness

dominant 1 *adj* **domineering**, bossy, overbearing, officious, authoritarian, assertive, forceful [➡ BOSSY AND OVER-

BEARING; 516] *Opposite*: weak 2 *adj* **leading**, main, central, foremost, prevailing, governing, principal, major, chief, ascendant, influential [➡ MOST IMPORTANT AND MAIN; 193] *Opposite*: minor

dominate 1 *v* **control**, rule, lead, govern, direct, dictate, take over [➡ CAUSE OR COMPEL TO ACT; 271] 2 *v* **overlook**, overshadow, tower above, tower over, dwarf [➡ EXIST IN CLOSE PROXIMITY; 21]

domination *n* **power**, control, command, authority, dominion, dominance, supremacy, ascendancy, government, rule [➡ STRENGTH; 201]

domineering *adj* **bossy**, dominant, overbearing, officious, authoritarian, forceful, dictatorial, assertive [➡ BOSSY AND OVERBEARING; 516] *Opposite*: meek

dominion 1 *n* **power**, authority, control, command, domination, dominance, say-so (*informal*) [➡ STRENGTH; 201] 2 *n* **territory**, colony, province, region, protectorate, state, domain [➡ PLACE; 1065]

domino *type of* **game piece** [➡ GAME PIECES; 878]

don 1 *v* **put on**, throw on, get into, pull on, dress in, slip on [➡ DRESS, WEAR, AND UNDRESS; 868] *Opposite*: take off 2 *n* (*UK*) **university teacher**, lecturer, tutor, academic, fellow (*UK*) [➡ EDUCATORS; 840]

donate *v* **give**, contribute, bequeath, provide, offer, bestow (*formal*) [➡ GIVE AND PROVIDE; 430]

See Compare and Contrast at **give**.

donation *n* **gift**, contribution, payment, bequest, endowment, bestowment (*formal*) [➡ GIFTS; 438]

done *adj* **complete**, completed, ended, finished, through, ready, prepared, made [➡ WHOLENESS AND COMPLETENESS; 198]

done and dusted (*UK*) *adj* [➡ WHOLENESS AND COMPLETENESS; 198]

done for (*informal*) 1 *adj* **finished**, in serious trouble, in deep trouble, in hot water, in dire straits [➡ IN TROUBLE AND DISADVANTAGED; 73] 2 *adj* **exhausted**, tired, worn out, shattered, tired out, fatigued, dog-tired (*informal*) [➡ TIRED, ASLEEP, AND UNCONSCIOUS; 738] *Opposite*: fresh

done in (*informal*) *adj* [➡ TIRED, ASLEEP, AND UNCONSCIOUS; 738]

dong *type of* **currency** [➡ CURRENCIES; 798]

Don Juan *n* [➡ PLEASURE-SEEKERS AND HEDONISTS; 886]

donkey *type of* **farm animal** [➡ FARM ANIMALS; 982]

donkeywork (*informal*) *n* **hard work**, heavy labor, hard graft (*UK*) [➡ HARD WORK OR EFFORT; 298]

donnish (*UK*) *adj* **academic**, bookish, learned, dry, serious, intellectual, scholarly, erudite, pedantic [➡ LEVELS OF EDUCATION AND SOPHISTICATION; 894]

donnybrook *n* [➡ CHAOS AND UPROAR; 51]

donor *n* **giver**, contributor, benefactor, patron, supporter, subscriber [➡ REPRESENTATIVES AND PATRONS; 968]

Don Quixote *n* [➡ PLEASURE-SEEKERS AND HEDONISTS; 886]

doodad (*informal*) *n* [➡ PHYSICAL OBJECTS; 1243]

doodle 1 *v* **draw**, sketch, scribble, squiggle [➡ CREATE IMAGES; 356] **2** *n* **drawing**, sketch, scribble, picture, squiggle [➡ ARTWORKS; 898]

doofer (*slang*) *n* [➡ PHYSICAL OBJECTS; 1243]

doohickey (*informal*) *n* **gadget**, whatchamacallit, thingamajig (*informal*), thingummy (*informal*), whatsit (*informal*), doodad (*informal*), widget (*humorous*), doofer (*slang*) [➡ PHYSICAL OBJECTS; 1243]

doom 1 *n* **fate**, destiny, lot, kismet, portion (*literary*) [➡ FATE, DESTINY, AND ASTROLOGY; 782] **2** *n* **disaster**, trouble, end, death, tragedy, ruin, catastrophe, misfortune, calamity [➡ DISASTERS; 252]

doomed 1 *adj* **fated**, destined, damned, condemned, predestined [➡ FATE, DESTINY, AND ASTROLOGY; 782] **2** *adj* **hopeless**, disaster-prone, ruined, lost, damned, ill-fated, unlucky, done for (*informal*) [➡ IN TROUBLE AND DISADVANTAGED; 73]

doom-laden (*UK*) *adj* **gloomy**, pessimistic, dismal, depressing, despairing, hopeless, full of despair [➡ SADNESS, DISTRESS, AND DESPAIR; 539] *Opposite*: upbeat (*informal*)

doomsday *n* **end of the world**, end of time, Last Judgment, Judgment Day, Day of Judgment, day of reckoning, Armageddon [➡ RELIGIOUS CONCEPTS; 776]

door *n* **entrance**, gate, entry, exit, access, flap, ingress (*formal*), egress (*formal*) [➡ DOORS AND ACCESS POINTS; 1101]

doorplate *n* **name plate**, sign, plaque, house sign, plate [➡ DOORS AND ACCESS POINTS; 1101]

doorstep *n* **entrance**, threshold, access, doorway, front doorstep, step [➡ DOORS AND ACCESS POINTS; 1101]

doorway 1 *n* **entrance**, door, front entrance, entry, entryway, front door, entranceway [➡ DOORS AND ACCESS POINTS; 1101] **2** *part of* **building** [➡ PARTS OF A BUILDING; 1095]

do out of (*informal*) *v* [➡ TAKE SOMETHING AWAY; 425]

doowop *type of* **pop and vocal music** [➡ MUSIC, SONGS, AND SINGING; 907]

doozy (*slang*) *n* [➡ AMAZING THINGS; 211]

dopey *adj* [➡ NEGATIVE INTELLECTUAL CHARACTERISTICS; 525]

doppelgänger *n* **double**, mirror image, shadow, twin, clone, alter ego, look-alike (*informal*), spitting image (*informal*) [➡ COPIES AND REPLICAS; 151]

Dorado *type of* **constellation** [➡ HEAVENLY BODIES; 1061]

Doric *type of* **pre-20th-century architecture** [➡ BUILDING AND ARCHITECTURE; 1076]

dorm (*informal*) *n* **student house**, frat house, dormitory, hall, residence, hall of residence (*UK*) [➡ RESIDENTIAL BUILDINGS; 1078]

dormant 1 *adj* **inactive**, asleep, sleeping, quiescent, quiet [➡ LACK OF ACTIVITY OR MOTION; 342] *Opposite*: active **2** *adj* **latent**, undeveloped, hidden, unexpressed [➡ TIRED, ASLEEP, AND UNCONSCIOUS; 738]

dormer window *type of* **window** [➡ WINDOWS; 1100]

dormitory 1 *n* **student house**, hall, frat house, residence,

dorm (*informal*), hall of residence (*UK*) [➡ RESIDENTIAL BUILDINGS; 1078] **2** *type of* **room in public buildings** [➡ TYPES OF ROOMS; 1097]

dormouse *type of* **rodent** [➡ RODENTS; 989]

dorsal fin *part of* **fish** [➡ PARTS OF A FISH; 1011]

dory *type of* **small vessel** [➡ SHIPS AND BOATS; 1150]

DOS *n* [➡ THE INTERNET; 1128]

dosage *n* **amount**, quantity, dose, measure, prescription [➡ AMOUNTS AND QUANTITIES; 112]

dose 1 *n* **amount**, quantity, dosage, measure, prescription [➡ AMOUNTS AND QUANTITIES; 112] **2** *n* (*informal*) **bout**, spell, period, attack, experience [➡ SHORT PERIODS OF TIME; 93] **3** *v* **treat**, give medicine to, dose up, medicate [➡ TAKE CARE OF AND SPOIL; 300]

doss (*UK*) *n* **sleep**, nap, catnap, siesta, snooze (*informal*), forty winks (*informal*) [➡ SLEEP AND DREAM; 723]

dossier *n* **file**, record, report, folder, profile, database [➡ RECORDS; 585]

dot 1 *n* **spot**, point, mark, blotch, speck, particle [➡ AMOUNTS OF LIQUID; 114] **2** *v* **speckle**, sprinkle, pepper, fleck, spot, mark [➡ DISPENSE, RATION, AND DISTRIBUTE; 434]

dot-com *n* [➡ BUSINESS ENTERPRISES AND RELATED BODIES; 792]

doting *adj* **fond**, loving, devoted, affectionate, adoring, caring [➡ APPRECIATION AND GRATITUDE; 535]

dotted *adj* **scattered**, sprinkled, spotted, speckled, spread, strewn [➡ GENERAL LOCATIONS; 158]

dotty 1 *adj* **unconventional**, odd, eccentric, idiosyncratic, strange, bizarre [➡ BIZARRE AND PECULIAR; 257] *Opposite*: normal **2** *adj* **absurd**, impractical, illogical, foolish, nonsensical [➡ NEGATIVE INTELLECTUAL CHARACTERISTICS; 525] *Opposite*: practical **3** *adj* (*informal*) **mad**, fond, besotted, doting, infatuated, smitten (*humorous or literary*), crazy (*informal*) [➡ APPRECIATION AND GRATITUDE; 535]

double 1 *adj* **dual**, binary, twofold, duple, twin, paired [➡ APPORTIONMENT; 113] **2** *adv* **twice**, twofold, twice over, two times [➡ APPORTIONMENT; 113] **3** *n* **duo**, pair, duet, couple [➡ GROUPS OF PEOPLE; 935] **4** *n* **doppelgänger**, clone, alter ego, twin, stand-in, duplicate, match, look-alike (*informal*), spitting image (*informal*) [➡ COPIES AND REPLICAS; 151] **5** *v* **increase twofold**, double up, amplify, magnify, expand, multiply, augment (*formal*) [➡ CHANGE OF INTENSITY: MORE; 394] *Opposite*: lessen **6** *v* **bend**, fold, double up, bend over, fold up [➡ CHANGE OF SHAPE; 385]

double act *n* **pair**, twosome, duo, couple, two-hander (*UK*) [➡ WORKERS IN ENTERTAINMENT AND MEDIA; 873]

double agent *n* **spy**, mole, infiltrator, inside agent, secret agent, plant (*informal*) [➡ INTERFERING PEOPLE AND TATTLETALES; 950]

double back *v* [➡ CHANGE DIRECTION OF MOTION; 344]

double bass *type of* **stringed instrument** [➡ MUSICAL INSTRUMENTS; 910]

double bed *type of* **bed** [➡ FURNITURE; 858]

double-book (*UK*) *v* **overbook**, overfill, overextend, overstretch [➡ OVERDO SOMETHING; 290]

double-breasted jacket *type of* **jacket** [➡ GARMENTS AND OUTFITS; 865]

double check *n* **second check**, reassessment, check, verification [➡ EXAMINE AND ASSESS; 753]

double-check *v* **make sure**, ensure, reassure yourself, check, verify, insure [➡ EXAMINE AND ASSESS; 753]

double-cross 1 *v* **betray**, con, let down, cheat, sell out, swindle, deceive, dupe, stab in the back (*informal*) [➡ DECEPTION AND LIES; 660] 2 *n* **betrayal**, deception, swindle, trick, con, stab in the back (*informal*) [➡ DECEPTION AND LIES; 660]

double-crosser *n* **swindler**, cheat, trickster, liar, fraudster, double-dealer, rat (*slang*) [➡ PEOPLE WHO DECEIVE; 661]

double-dealer *n* **swindler**, liar, cheat, fraudster, trickster, double-crosser, rat (*slang*) [➡ PEOPLE WHO DECEIVE; 661]

double-dealing 1 *n* **duplicity**, betrayal, deceit, cheating, treachery, deception [➡ DECEPTION AND LIES; 660] *Opposite*: honesty 2 *adj* **duplicitous**, deceitful, double-faced, cheating, swindling, two-faced, dishonest, false, treacherous, double-crossing [➡ DECEITFUL; 513] *Opposite*: honest

double-edged *adj* **ambiguous**, two-edged, disingenuous, ironic, sly [➡ VAGUENESS; 243] *Opposite*: ingenuous

double-faced *adj* **insincere**, deceitful, dishonest, two-faced, false, double-crossing, double-dealing, duplicitous, treacherous [➡ DECEITFUL; 513] *Opposite*: honest

double-jointed *adj* **flexible**, supple, agile, lithe [➡ AGILITY OF THE BODY; 476]

double-quick (*informal*) *adv* **rapidly**, swiftly, speedily, promptly, quickly, instantly, fast [➡ HAPPENING QUICKLY; 104] *Opposite*: slowly

doublespeak *n* [➡ DECEPTION AND LIES; 660]

double talk 1 *n* **gibberish**, nonsense, trash, garbage, hogwash (*informal*), malarkey (*informal*), twaddle (*informal*), rubbish (*UK*) [➡ MEANINGLESS SPEECH OR WRITING; 676] 2 *n* **sophistry**, doublespeak, deceit, jargon, smoke and mirrors [➡ DECEPTION AND LIES; 660]

double up *v* **bend**, fold, double, bend over, fold up [➡ CHANGE OF SHAPE; 385]

double whammy (*slang*) *n* [➡ DISASTERS; 252]

doubt 1 *v* **disbelieve**, mistrust, suspect, have reservations, have doubts, distrust, question, query [➡ UNCERTAINTY; 559] *Opposite*: believe 2 *n* **hesitation**, uncertainty, reservation, misgiving, distrust, disbelief, qualm, suspicion [➡ UNCERTAINTY; 559] *Opposite*: certainty

doubter *n* **nonbeliever**, cynic, doubting Thomas, agnostic, pessimist, skeptic [➡ UNCERTAINTY; 559] *Opposite*: believer

doubtful 1 *adj* **unsure**, uncertain, hesitant, undecided, disbelieving, cynical, unconvinced, distrustful, skeptical, in doubt [➡ UNCERTAINTY; 559] *Opposite*: certain 2 *adj* **unlikely**, unpromising, uncertain, insecure, shaky, in doubt, improbable [➡ IMPOSSIBLE AND IMPROBABLE; 178] *Opposite*: probable 3 *adj* **unreliable**, dubious, suspect, questionable, untrustworthy, shady, suspicious, fishy (*informal*) [➡ UNCERTAIN; 175] *Opposite*: reliable

Compare and Contrast: *doubtful, uncertain, unsure, in doubt, dubious, skeptical*

CORE MEANING: feeling doubt or uncertainty

doubtful undecided or feeling hesitant; *uncertain* or *unsure* lacking certainty or confidence; *in doubt* still undecided and liable to change; *dubious* doubtful and, often, suspicious; *skeptical* questioning the truth or likelihood of something.

doubtfully *adv* **uncertainly**, hesitantly, distrustfully, doubtingly, suspiciously, apprehensively [➡ UNCERTAINTY; 559] *Opposite*: confidently

doubtfulness 1 *n* **uncertainty**, hesitancy, indecision, doubt, distrust, suspicion, apprehension [➡ UNCERTAINTY; 559] *Opposite*: certainty 2 *n* **unlikelihood**, improbability, chance in a million, slim chance [➡ IMPOSSIBLE AND IMPROBABLE; 178] *Opposite*: likelihood

doubting *adj* **hesitant**, doubtful, distrustful, suspicious, unbelieving [➡ UNCERTAINTY; 559] *Opposite*: trusting

doubtless *adv* **no doubt**, without a doubt, probably, almost certainly, without question, beyond question, beyond a shadow of a doubt, undoubtedly [➡ CERTAIN; 174] *Opposite*: possibly

dough (*slang*) *n* **cash**, currency, money, chips, greenbacks (*slang*), bread (*dated slang*) [➡ MONEY; 797]

doughnut *type of* **cake** [➡ CAKES, COOKIES, AND DESSERTS; 1181]

doughty (*archaic*) *adj* **brave**, determined, tough, spirited, indomitable, hardy, formidable, feisty (*informal*), intrepid (*literary or humorous*) [➡ COURAGE; 498] *Opposite*: feeble

dour 1 *adj* **severe**, unfriendly, sour, stern, hard-faced, grim, harsh [➡ FACIAL EXPRESSIONS AND BLUSHING; 651] *Opposite*: kindly 2 *adj* (*UK*) **determined**, stubborn, set, purposeful, resolute, resolved [➡ UNWILLINGNESS AND STUBBORNNESS; 564] *Opposite*: indecisive

dourly 1 *adv* **severely**, sourly, sternly, dryly, grimly, harshly [➡ BAD-TEMPERED AND HUMORLESS; 626] *Opposite*: kindly 2 *adv* (*UK*) **determinedly**, stubbornly, purposefully, resolutely [➡ WITHOUT ENTHUSIASM; 287] *Opposite*: indecisively

dourness 1 *n* **severity**, unfriendliness, sourness, sternness, grimness [➡ UNFRIENDLINESS AND UNSOCIABILITY; 504] *Opposite*: kindness 2 *n* (*UK*) **determination**, stubbornness, purpose, drive, resoluteness, resolve [➡ UNWILLINGNESS AND STUBBORNNESS; 564] *Opposite*: indecision

douse 1 *v* **drench**, soak, wet, souse, cover, saturate, sop, drown, immerse [➡ SOFTEN, LIQUEFY, AND DAMPEN; 388] 2 *v* **quench**, extinguish, put out, smother, snuff [➡ CHANGE OF INTENSITY: LESS; 395]

dovecote *type of* **pen or cage** [➡ ANIMAL OR BIRD ACCOMMODATIONS; 1079]

dove gray *type of* **gray** [➡ COLORS; 1224]

dovetail *v* **fit together**, slot in, join together, come together, unite [➡ FASTEN, LINK, AND JOIN; 408] *Opposite*: separate

dowdily *adv* **plainly**, frumpily, drably, unfashionably, drearily [➡ BADLY GROOMED; 483] *Opposite*: fashionably

dowdiness *n* **drabness**, plainness, dullness, dreariness, frumpiness [→ BADLY GROOMED; 483]

dowdy *adj* **plain**, frumpy, drab, unfashionable, dreary [→ BADLY GROOMED; 483] *Opposite:* fashionable

dowel *n* **rod**, pin, peg [→ FASTENERS, LINKS, AND NETWORKS; 1247]

do without *v* **abstain**, deny yourself, go without, keep off, forgo [→ FORGO AND DENY ONESELF; 449]

down **1** *prep* **along**, through, the length of [→ DIRECTION OF MOTION; 345] **2** *adj* **depressed**, unhappy, miserable, dejected, downhearted, downcast, despondent, sad, low, down in the dumps (*informal*), blue (*informal*) [→ SADNESS, DISTRESS, AND DESPAIR; 539] *Opposite:* happy **3** *adj* **listed**, nominated, scheduled, timetabled, tabled [→ PRESENT AND AVAILABLE; 11] **4** *adj* **out of action**, inoperative, not working, out of order [→ IN BAD REPAIR; 1234] *Opposite:* working **5** *adj* **behind**, losing, short [→ IN TROUBLE AND DISADVANTAGED; 73] *Opposite:* winning **6** *v* **consume**, eat, drink, gulp down, swallow, knock back (*informal*), put away (*informal*), guzzle (*informal*) [→ EAT AND NOT EAT; 710] **7** *v* **knock down**, floor, overpower, overcome, defeat, bring down [→ BEAT AND DEFEAT; 80] **8** *v* **put down**, lay down, throw down, set down, lay aside, put aside [→ MOVE SOMETHING: DOWNWARD; 329] *Opposite:* pick up **9** *part of* **bird** [→ PARTS OF A BIRD; 1006]

down-and-out *adj* **destitute**, penniless, homeless, on the streets, broke (*informal*), on the skids (*slang*) [→ POVERTY AND POOR; 892] *Opposite:* well-heeled (*informal*)

down-at-heel *adj* [→ POVERTY AND POOR; 892]

downbeat **1** *adj* **pessimistic**, gloomy, dark, bleak, negative, depressing [→ INSECURITY AND LOSS OF COMPOSURE; 544] *Opposite:* upbeat (*informal*) **2** *type of* **electronic music** [→ MUSIC, SONGS, AND SINGING; 907]

downcast *adj* **sad**, pessimistic, dejected, depressed, down, disappointed, discouraged, disheartened, unhappy, downhearted, dismayed [→ SADNESS, DISTRESS, AND DESPAIR; 539] *Opposite:* cheerful

downer (*informal*) *n* **disappointment**, shame, pity, letdown, discouragement, comedown (*informal*), bummer (*slang*) [→ NUISANCES; 253]

downfall *n* **failure**, ruin, fall, end, demise (*formal*) [→ FAILURE; 77] *Opposite:* success

downgrade *v* **demote**, reduce, lower, relegate [→ REVOKE STATUS; 459] *Opposite:* upgrade

downhearted *adj* **sad**, pessimistic, dejected, disappointed, depressed, down, upset, in low spirits, unhappy, disheartened, downcast, discouraged, dismayed [→ SADNESS, DISTRESS, AND DESPAIR; 539] *Opposite:* cheerful

downhill **1** *adj* **easy**, simple, effortless, plain sailing, straightforward [→ EASE AND SIMPLICITY; 200] *Opposite:* uphill **2** *type of* **winter sport** [→ HOBBIES, GAMES, AND SPORTS; 875]

downhome (*informal*) *adj* [→ ORDINARINESS; 244]

downiness *n* **softness**, fluffiness, fleeciness [→ PHYSICAL TEXTURE; 1222]

down in the dumps *adj* **miserable**, unhappy, gloomy, depressed, low, dejected, downhearted, downcast, sad, despondent, down in the mouth (*informal*), blue (*informal*) [→ SADNESS, DISTRESS, AND DESPAIR; 539] *Opposite:* happy

down in the mouth (*informal*) *adj* [→ SADNESS, DISTRESS, AND DESPAIR; 539]

download *v* **transfer**, copy, move, take [→ THE INTERNET; 1128]

downmarket *adj* **low quality**, inferior, cheap, low cost, second-rate, mediocre, shoddy, shabby, tacky (*informal*) [→ ORDINARINESS; 244] *Opposite:* upmarket

down payment *n* **installment**, payment, deposit, disbursement [→ FUNDS, PAYMENTS, AND CHARGES; 800]

downplay *v* **tone down**, moderate, restrain, soften, modulate, give a lower profile, talk down [→ CHANGE OF INTENSITY: LESS; 395] *Opposite:* highlight

downpour *n* **heavy shower**, deluge, rainstorm, cloudburst, torrent, monsoon, inundation (*formal*) [→ CLOUDY AND RAINY WEATHER; 1052]

downright *adv* **positively**, undeniably, unquestionably, undoubtedly, totally [→ ABSOLUTE AND ABSOLUTELY; 133] *Opposite:* questionably

downriver *adv* [→ DIRECTION OF MOTION; 345]

downscale *adj* **inferior**, cheap, low quality, shoddy, shabby, second-rate. *Opposite:* superiortacky (*informal*) [→ ORDINARINESS; 244]

downside *n* **negative aspect**, shortcoming, weakness, snag, stumbling block, pitfall, problem [→ NUISANCES; 253] *Opposite:* advantage

downsize *v* **slim down**, cut back, economize, rationalize, trim, reduce [→ BUSINESS ACTIVITIES AND PHENOMENA; 794] *Opposite:* expand

downstairs *adv* **below**, down the stairs, down, down below [→ GENERAL LOCATIONS; 158]

downswing **1** *n* **fall**, slump, decline, dip, downturn, recession [→ MARKET FORCES; 803] *Opposite:* upswing **2** *type of* **economic condition** [→ FINANCE AND ECONOMICS; 796]

downtime *n* **stoppage**, lost time, idle time, interruption [→ PERIODS OF REST; 91]

down-to-earth *adj* **practical**, realistic, sensible, matter-of-fact, pragmatic, no-nonsense [→ POSITIVE INTELLECTUAL CHARACTERISTICS; 524] *Opposite:* fanciful

down to the wire *adj* [→ PROMPTNESS: LATE; 100]

downtrodden *adj* **browbeaten**, subjugated, broken, oppressed, demoralized, beaten, defeated [→ SADNESS, DISTRESS, AND DESPAIR; 539]

downturn **1** *n* **slump**, recession, dip, decline, depression, downward spiral [→ MARKET FORCES; 803] *Opposite:* upturn **2** *type of* **economic condition** [→ FINANCE AND ECONOMICS; 796]

downward **1** *adj* **descending**, down, downhill, sliding, descendent, plunging, sinking [→ DIRECTION OF MOTION; 345] *Opposite:* upward **2** *adv* [→ DIRECTION OF MOTION; 345]

downy *adj* **silky**, soft, velvety, furry, feathery, fluffy [→ PHYSICAL TEXTURE; 1222] *Opposite:* rough

dowry *n* **wedding gift**, present, grant, settlement, portion, payment, money [→ GIFTS; 438]

doyen *n* **leading figure**, senior member, leading light, notable, leader [➡ IMPORTANT OR FAMOUS PEOPLE; 893]

doyenne *n* **leading figure**, senior member, leading light, notable, leader [➡ IMPORTANT OR FAMOUS PEOPLE; 893]

do your homework (*informal*) *v* **prepare**, research, plan, find out [➡ EXAMINE AND ASSESS; 753]

doze 1 *v* **nap**, sleep, slumber, snooze (*informal*) [➡ SLEEP AND DREAM; 723] **2** *n* **nap**, slumber, sleep, snooze (*informal*) [➡ SLEEP AND DREAM; 723]

dozens (*informal*) *n* **lots**, loads (*informal*), tons (*informal*), oodles (*informal*), heaps (*informal*) [➡ MANY, MUCH, LARGE AMOUNT; 117]

doze off *v* **fall asleep**, go to sleep, nod off, nod, drift off, drop off (*informal*) [➡ SLEEP AND DREAM; 723] *Opposite:* wake up

dozily *adv* **sleepily**, tiredly, lethargically, sluggishly, drowsily [➡ TIRED, ASLEEP, AND UNCONSCIOUS; 738] *Opposite:* alertly

doziness *n* **sleepiness**, tiredness, lethargy, sluggishness, drowsiness [➡ TIRED, ASLEEP, AND UNCONSCIOUS; 738] *Opposite:* alertness

dozy 1 *adj* **sleepy**, drowsy, tired, dozing, nodding, lethargic [➡ TIRED, ASLEEP, AND UNCONSCIOUS; 738] *Opposite:* alert **2** *adj* (*UK*) **silly**, foolish, dreamy, scatterbrained, daffy (*informal*), ditsy (*informal*) [➡ NEGATIVE INTELLECTUAL CHARACTERISTICS; 525]

drab 1 *adj* **gloomy**, dull, dingy, dowdy, dreary, cheerless, plain, somber, gray [➡ PLAIN; 232] *Opposite:* bright **2** *adj* **uninteresting**, unexciting, monotonous, boring, dreary, dull [➡ BORING AND UNINTERESTING; 234] *Opposite:* interesting

drably *adv* **somberly**, gloomily, grayly, drearily, dingily, cheerlessly [➡ BORING AND UNINTERESTING; 234] *Opposite:* brightly

drabness *n* **dullness**, plainness, dowdiness, dreariness, dinginess, cheerlessness, gloominess [➡ BORING AND UNINTERESTING; 234]

drachma *type of* **currency** [➡ CURRENCIES; 798]

Draco *type of* **constellation** [➡ HEAVENLY BODIES; 1061]

Draconian *n* **harsh**, severe, strict, strong, austere, ruthless [➡ STRENGTH; 201] *Opposite:* mild

draft 1 *n* **current**, flow, waft, breeze, breath [➡ WINDY AND STORMY WEATHER; 1053] **2** *n* **recruitment**, mobilization, enlistment, enrollment, call-up (*UK*) [➡ WARFARE AND WAR; 830] **3** *n* (*dated*) **medicine**, concoction, tonic, mixture, brew [➡ DRINK; 711] **4** *n* **outline**, sketch, summary, plan, rough copy, version [➡ REPRESENTATIONS AND GENERAL EXAMPLES; 65] **5** *v* **recruit**, conscript, sign up, enlist, enroll, call up [➡ WARFARE AND WAR; 830] *Opposite:* discharge **6** *v* **draw up**, prepare, sketch out, outline, write, plan, design, compose, rough out [➡ CREATE IMAGES; 356]

drag 1 *v* **pull**, haul, draw, heave, lug, tug, tow, trail, draggle [➡ PUSH, PULL, AND SLIDE; 335] **2** *v* **dawdle**, lag, crawl, creep, loiter, linger [➡ MOVE SLOWLY; 314] *Opposite:* fly **3** *n* (*informal*) [➡ NUISANCES; 253]

See Compare and Contrast at **pull**.

dragging *adj* **slow**, tedious, tiresome, wearisome,

uninteresting, boring
interesting

draggy (*informal*) 1
snail-paced, logy, sl
(*informal*) [➡ HAPPENING SLO
some, tedious, dragg
boring [➡ BORING AND UNINTER

drag in *v* **bring in**, invol
suck in [➡ SUGGEST, HINT, AND C

dragnet 1 *n* **search**, hu
quest [➡ SEEK POSSESSION AND SE
game net, trap, snare [➡ CO

dragon *type of* **mythologic**

dragonfly *type of* **flying i**

dragoon *v* **coerce**, press,
harass, force, compel [➡ CAUS

drag out *v* **extend**, prolong
protract, spin out [➡ CONTINUE A

dragster *type of* **car** [➡ BIKES,

drag up *v* **return to**, bring up,
rake up (*informal*) [➡ SUGGEST, HI

drag your feet *v* **hold back**,
take your time, stall, lag, pr
[➡ SHIRK AND DELAY; 273]

drain 1 *v* **use up**, exhaust, co
(*informal*) [➡ USE UP AND WASTE;
2 *n* **sewer**, ditch, channel, culv
1111]

drained *adj* **exhausted**, weak,
shattered, sapped, all in [➡ TIRE
Opposite: energetic

drainer *type of* **utensil** [➡ TABLEWARE,

draining *adj* **exhausting**, trying,
ing, taxing, enervating, fatiguing

drake *type of* **male or female bird**

dram 1 *n* [➡ DRINKS; 1187] **2** *type of*
DIMENSIONS; 1192] **3** *type of* **currency** [➡ CU

drama 1 *n* **play**, stage show, perfo
spectacle, tragedy, comedy [➡ FICTION A
ment, commotion, fuss, performance
(*informal*) [➡ DISASTERS; 252] **3** *type of* br
RADIO; 606]

dramatic *adj* **affected**, melodrama
trionic, studied, intense, vivid [➡ AFFE
AND SNOBBISHNESS; 507] *Opposite:* natural

dramatically 1 *adv* **melodramatically**,
histrionically, theatrically, affectedly
ISFACTION, AND SNOBBISHNESS; 507] *Opposite:* nat
ically, noticeably, severely, considerab
significantly, markedly [➡ ABSOLUTE AND ABSOL
modestly

dramatics *n* **histrionics**, hysterics, e

motion, fu
BISHNESS; 507]

dramatis

dramatis

[➡ WRITERS AND

dramatiz
adaptation

dramati
lish, lay o
290] *Oppos*

dramatu

drape *v*
orate, arr
NGS; 405]

drapery
AND HOUSEH

drastic
reaching
133] *Opp*

draw
represe
2 *v* **pull**
AND SLIDE]
gain, ta
take ou
5 *v* **attr**
charm
equal,
induce
crowd
deadl

See

draw
forge
[➡ WITH

draw
reco
appr

dra
wea
stur

dra
JUNC

dr
1245

dr
AND

dr
[➡

d
t
o

ss, drama [➡AFFECTATION, SELF-SATISFACTION, AND SNOB-

personae n [➡PERFORMERS; 905]

t n **playwright**, writer, author, scriptwriter
STYLES; 914]

ation n **staging**, performance, production,
[➡FICTION AND DRAMA; 913]

ze v **exaggerate**, sensationalize, play up, embel-
n, overstate, blow up (*informal*) [➡OVERDO SOMETHING;
te: play down

rgy n [➡THE PERFORMING ARTS; 904]

swathe, dress, wrap, cover, clothe, adorn, dec-
ange, array (*literary*) [➡DECORATE, ADORN, AND APPLY COATI-

n **curtains**, hangings, drapes, swags [➡FURNISHING
LD LINENS; 860]

adj radical, severe, extreme, dire, sweeping, far-
, harsh, strong, desperate [➡ABSOLUTE AND ABSOLUTELY;
site: modest

1 v **sketch**, illustrate, copy, depict, describe,
nt, portray, pencil, crayon [➡CREATE IMAGES; 356]
drag, haul, move, tow, tug, lug, heave [➡PUSH, PULL,
335] *Opposite*: shove **3** v **get**, obtain, extract, derive,
ke, elicit [➡GET; 420] **4** v **pull out**, extract, withdraw,
t, unsheathe [➡CAUSE TO APPEAR; 5] *Opposite*: put away
act, pull, lure, appeal, entice, bring in, captivate,
[➡APPEAL TO AND AROUSE INTEREST; 575] **6** v **finish equal**, tie,
square, even [➡EQUALITY; 154] **7** n **attraction**, magnet,
ment, lure, enticement, pull, allurement, appeal,
puller (*UK*) [➡TREATS; 210] **8** n **dead heat**, tie, stalemate,
ck, standoff, photo finish [➡RESULTS AND OUTCOMES; 83]

Compare and Contrast at **pull**.

a veil over v **conceal**, keep quiet about, ignore,
, hush up (*informal*), keep mum about (*informal*)
HOLD INFORMATION; 687] *Opposite*: expose

back v **move away**, draw away, withdraw, retreat,
, fall back, drop out [➡GO BACKWARD; 309] *Opposite*:
oach

wback n **disadvantage**, problem, downside, negative,
kness, shortcoming, hitch, snag, obstacle, minus,
bling block [➡NUISANCES; 253] *Opposite*: advantage

wbridge type of **bridge** [➡BRIDGES, TUNNELS, CROSSINGS, AND
IONS; 1112]

wer type of **container** [➡CONTAINERS, RECEPTACLES, AND PACKAGING;

awers type of **lower body underwear** [➡ACCESSORIES, MILLINERY,
LINGERIE; 867]

aw in v **involve**, implicate, engage, ensnare, hook
PPEAL TO AND AROUSE INTEREST; 575]

rawing n **sketch**, picture, illustration, diagram, por-
ayal, depiction, cartoon, representation, doodle,
tline [➡DRAWINGS, CHARTS, AND TABLES; 594]

drawing room type of **room in the home** [➡TYPES OF ROOMS;
1097]

drawl n **pronunciation**, intonation, inflection, enunciation, twang, brogue, burr [➡ASPECTS OF LANGUAGE; 682]

drawn adj **haggard**, strained, pinched, tired, wan,
drained, careworn, tense, fraught [➡FACIAL EXPRESSIONS AND BLU-
SHING; 651] *Opposite*: relaxed

draw near v **approach**, get closer, come nearer, come
up, creep up, move in on, converge [➡ARRIVE; 12] *Opposite*:
move away

drawn-out adj **protracted**, lengthy, long, convoluted,
interminable, dragging, lingering [➡HAPPENING SLOWLY; 106]
Opposite: swift

draw off v **pour**, siphon off, pull, drain off, suck up,
abstract, pump, tap [➡EJECT AND EXCLUDE; 340]

draw on v **use**, employ, be inspired by, resort to, fall
back on, bring into play, utilize, exploit, make use of,
rely on [➡USE; 467]

draw out v **prolong**, extend, make last, lengthen, stretch,
protract, drag out, spin out [➡CAUSE TO CONTINUE; 267] *Opposite*:
cut short

drawstring 1 n **tie**, string, lace, belt [➡FASTENERS, LINKS, AND
NETWORKS; 1247] **2** part of **garment** [➡PARTS OF A GARMENT; 870]

draw the short straw v **get a raw deal**, do badly, be
unlucky, come off worst, lose out, get the worst of it,
miss out, be hard done by [➡FAIL OR BE UNSUCCESSFUL; 75]

draw up v **draft**, put together, assemble, prepare, write,
set down, sketch out, outline [➡CREATE IMAGES; 356]

dray n **wagon**, cart, low-loader, transporter, truck, lorry
(*UK*) [➡BIKES, CARS, AND CARRIAGES; 1149]

dread 1 v **fear**, be afraid of, be terrified of, be frightened
of, be worried about, be anxious about, shrink from
[➡FEARS AND PHOBIAS; 554] *Opposite*: look forward to **2** n **terror**,
fear, trepidation, anxiety, dismay, alarm, fright, horror
[➡FEAR AND PANIC; 543] *Opposite*: confidence

dreadful adj **terrible**, awful, horrible, frightful, alarming, shocking, appalling, outrageous, vile, ghastly [➡DIS-
GUSTING AND REPULSIVE; 230] *Opposite*: lovely

dreadfully adv **terribly**, awfully, really, extremely, very,
truly, appallingly, outrageously [➡TO A GREAT EXTENT; 132]

dreadfulness n **awfulness**, horror, misery, ghastliness,
gruesomeness, atrociousness, vileness, hideousness [➡DIS-
GUSTING AND REPULSIVE; 230]

dreadlocks type of **hairstyle** [➡HAIRSTYLES AND HAIRPIECES; 488]

dream 1 n **vision**, daydream, reverie, nightmare, hal-
lucination, delusion, trance, fantasy [➡NONEXISTENT THINGS; 23]
Opposite: reality **2** n **aspiration**, wish, goal, hope, ambition,
desire, pipe dream, castle in Spain, castle in the air
[➡DESIRE AND WANT; 579] **3** n **delight**, joy, pleasure, marvel, ideal
[➡AMAZING THINGS; 211] *Opposite*: nightmare **4** v **fantasize**, visu-
alize, imagine, fancy, daydream, envisage, think [➡DREAM,
IMAGINE, AND FANTASIZE; 749]

dreamer n **visionary**, idealist, romantic, fantasist [➡LAZY
OR UNSUCCESSFUL PEOPLE; 948] *Opposite*: realist

dreamily *adv* **vaguely**, distantly, distractedly, languorously, abstractedly, pensively, absent-mindedly [➡ NEUTRALITY AND INDIFFERENCE; 553]

dreaminess 1 *n* **pensiveness**, abstraction, vagueness, wistfulness, languor, absent-mindedness [➡ NOT PAY ATTENTION; 764] 2 *n* **perfection**, beauty, exquisiteness, loveliness, gorgeousness [➡ BEAUTY AND ATTRACTIVENESS; 189]

dreamland *n* **paradise**, heaven, nirvana, fairyland, fantasy world, never-never land, cloud-cuckoo-land, land of make-believe, dream world, la-la land [➡ NONEXISTENT PLACES; 1066] *Opposite*: real world

dreamlike *adj* **unreal**, fantastic, surreal, weird, bizarre, otherworldly, illusory, trancelike [➡ FALSE AND UNREAL; 173] *Opposite*: real

dream up *v* **concoct**, think up, invent, imagine, come up with, devise, cook up (*informal*) [➡ DREAM, IMAGINE, AND FANTASIZE; 749]

dream world *n* **fantasy world**, land of make-believe, storyland, fairyland, never-never land, cloud-cuckoo-land, dreamland [➡ NONEXISTENT PLACES; 1066] *Opposite*: real world

dreamy 1 *adj* **pensive**, vague, faraway, wistful, preoccupied, distracted, inattentive, distrait (*literary*) [➡ NEUTRALITY AND INDIFFERENCE; 553] *Opposite*: alert 2 *adj* **wonderful**, beautiful, superb, out of this world, fantastic, terrific (*informal*) [➡ EXTRAORDINARY: AMAZING; 204] *Opposite*: ordinary

drearily *adv* **dully**, monotonously, boringly, tediously, uninterestingly, routinely [➡ BORING AND UNINTERESTING; 234] *Opposite*: interestingly

dreariness 1 *n* **dullness**, monotony, tedium, boredom, routine [➡ BORING AND UNINTERESTING; 234] *Opposite*: excitement 2 *n* **bleakness**, misery, cheerlessness, grimness, gloominess, drabness [➡ EMOTIONALLY UNPLEASANT AND UPSETTING; 227] *Opposite*: cheerfulness

dreary 1 *adj* **dull**, boring, monotonous, tedious, lifeless, unexciting, routine [➡ BORING AND UNINTERESTING; 234] *Opposite*: interesting 2 *adj* **bleak**, cheerless, dismal, miserable, grim, desolate, depressing, drab, gloomy [➡ SADNESS, DISTRESS, AND DESPAIR; 539] *Opposite*: cheerful

dredge *v* **search**, scour, comb, ransack, rummage, dig up [➡ SEEK POSSESSION AND SEARCH; 456]

dredger *type of* **motor vessel** [➡ SHIPS AND BOATS; 1150]

dredge up *v* **unearth**, dig up, drag up, bring up, uncover, rake up (*informal*) [➡ CAUSE TO APPEAR; 5] *Opposite*: bury

dregs 1 *n* (*literary*) **relics**, remains, vestiges, remainder, remnants, residue, leftovers [➡ REMAINDER AND REMAINDERS; 125] 2 *n* **remains**, residue, sediment, silt, lees, deposit, waste, grounds [➡ UNPLEASANT, DIRTY, AND TOXIC SUBSTANCES; 1268]

drench *v* **soak**, wet, saturate, douse, steep, flood, inundate [➡ SOFTEN, LIQUEFY, AND DAMPEN; 388] *Opposite*: dry out

drenched *adj* **soaked**, sodden, wet, inundated, saturated, soaked to the skin, dripping wet, sopping, sopping wet [➡ WET; 1240] *Opposite*: dry

dress 1 *v* **wear**, put on, dress up, clothe, slip into, don, attire (*formal*), array (*literary*) [➡ DRESS, WEAR, AND UNDRESS; 868] *Opposite*: undress 2 *v* **adorn**, decorate, deck out, ornament, trim, bedeck (*literary*) [➡ DECORATE, ADORN, AND APPLY COATINGS; 405]

3 *n* **clothing**, clothes, costume, garb, wear, outfit, gear (*informal*) [➡ CLOTHES AND ACCESSORIES; 864]

dress

◆ *types of dresses*
ball gown, caftan, cheongsam, cocktail dress, evening gown, frock, gown, jumper, kimono, muumuu, robe, sari, shalwar-kameez, sheath, shift, shirtdress, sundress, wedding dress

dress circle *n* [➡ IN THE THEATER; 906]

dress code *n* [➡ CLOTHES AND ACCESSORIES; 864]

dress down *v* **scold**, reprimand, lecture, rebuke, censure, tell off (*informal*), chew out (*informal*) [➡ ACCUSE, BLAME, AND CRITICIZE; 641] *Opposite*: praise

dressed *adj* **turned out**, robed, garbed, outfitted, kitted out (*UK*) [➡ DRESS, WEAR, AND UNDRESS; 868] *Opposite*: undressed

dresser *type of* **cabinet** [➡ FURNITURE; 858]

dressing 1 *n* **bandage**, covering, gauze [➡ COVERS AND COATINGS; 1246] 2 *type of* **seasonings, sauces, and dips** [➡ SEASONINGS AND SAUCES; 1174]

dressing room *type of* **room in public buildings** [➡ TYPES OF ROOMS; 1097]

dressing table *type of* **table** [➡ FURNITURE; 858]

dressmaking *n* **couture**, tailoring, sewing [➡ CRAFTS AND CARVING; 355]

dress rehearsal *n* **practice**, run through, trial, rehearsal, preparation, dry run, tryout, dummy run (*UK*) [➡ PREPARATORY EVENTS; 57]

dress sense *n* **flair**, stylishness, fashion sense, panache, chic, elegance [➡ WELL-GROOMED; 482]

dress suit *type of* **suit** [➡ GARMENTS AND OUTFITS; 865]

dress uniform *n* [➡ GARMENTS AND OUTFITS; 865]

dress up *v* **disguise**, revamp, embellish, decorate, titivate, do up, doll up (*informal*) [➡ DECORATE, ADORN, AND APPLY COATINGS; 405]

dressy *adj* **elegant**, fashionable, stylish, chic, classy (*informal*) [➡ DESCRIBING CLOTHES; 869] *Opposite*: sloppy

drey *type of* **den or nest** [➡ ANIMAL OR BIRD ACCOMMODATIONS; 1079]

dribble 1 *v* **drool**, salivate, slobber, slaver, drivel [➡ EXCRETION AND EXCRETA; 722] 2 *v* **trickle**, ooze, drip, seep, leak, drop [➡ LIQUID EMISSION; 370] *Opposite*: gush

dried *adj* **dehydrated**, dried out, dried up, desiccated, dry [➡ DRY; 1242]

drift 1 *v* **float**, flow, glide, coast, waft, wander, go with the flow [➡ MOVE SLOWLY; 314] 2 *n* **gist**, meaning, point, sense, idea, implication, theme [➡ MEANING; 690]

drifter *n* **wanderer**, tramp, vagabond, rolling stone, vagrant, bird of passage [➡ NOMADIC AND ROOTLESS LIFESTYLES; 884]

drifting *adj* **wandering**, nomadic, homeless, itinerant, traveling, migratory, rootless, migrant, peripatetic [➡ NOMADIC AND ROOTLESS LIFESTYLES; 884] *Opposite*: settled

driftwood *n* flotsam, jetsam, wreckage, refuse, waste, trash [➤ JUNK AND USELESS OBJECTS; 1249]

drill 1 *n* practice, exercise, discipline, training, instruction, preparation [➤ PREPARATORY EVENTS; 57] 2 *type of* carpentry tool [➤ HAND TOOLS; 1119] 3 *type of* fabric from plants [➤ FABRICS; 1132] 4 *v* bore, make a hole, pierce, puncture, penetrate [➤ TEAR, BREAK, AND CUT; 360] 5 *v* train, coach, school, discipline, instruct, teach [➤ INSTRUCT AND TEACH; 609]

See Compare and Contrast at **teach**.

drily *adv* ironically, humorously, wittily, subtly, wryly [➤ GOOD-TEMPERED AND HUMOROUS; 627]

drink 1 *v* swallow, down, sip, gulp, slurp, lap up, swig (*informal*), knock back (*informal*), imbibe (*formal or humorous*) [➤ DRINK; 711] 2 *n* thirst-quencher, liquid refreshment, soft drink, cold drink, hot drink, beverage (*formal*) [➤ DRINKS; 1187] 3 *n* mouthful, taste, gulp, swallow, sip, swill, swig (*informal*), slurp (*informal*) [➤ DRINK; 711] 4 *n* alcoholic drink, nip, pick-me-up, cocktail, aperitif, chaser, digestif, liqueur, nightcap, intoxicating liquor, liquor, shot (*informal*), tipple (*informal*), snifter (*informal*), hard stuff (*informal*), booze (*slang*), hooch (*slang*) [➤ DRINKS; 1187]

drinkable *adj* fit to drink, safe to drink, filtered, potable [➤ CLEAN AND HYGIENIC; 1233]

drinking fountain *n* water spout, jet, faucet, tap (*UK*) [➤ FIXTURES; 859]

drinks party (*UK*) *n* [➤ PARTIES, DANCES, AND CELEBRATIONS; 37]

drip 1 *v* dribble, trickle, drop, leak, seep, ooze [➤ LIQUID EMISSION; 370] *Opposite:* gush 2 *n* drop, trickle, dribble, leak [➤ AMOUNTS OF LIQUID; 114] *Opposite:* stream

drip-dry *adj* wash-and-wear, crease-resistant, noniron (*UK*) [➤ DESCRIBING CLOTHES; 869]

dripping 1 *adj* wet, soaked, drenched, sodden, saturated, sopping, sopping wet, soaked to the skin, wet through [➤ WET; 1240] *Opposite:* dry 2 *type of* cooking fat and oil [➤ FATS AND OILS; 1173]

dripping wet *adj* [➤ WET; 1240]

drive 1 *v* steer, handle, guide, direct, operate, pilot, lead [➤ TRAVEL: WAYS OF TRAVELING; 320] 2 *v* take, run, chauffeur, transport [➤ ACCOMPANY AND FOLLOW; 337] 3 *v* power, run, cause to move, set in motion [➤ USE TOOLS AND MACHINERY; 468] 4 *v* force, make, coerce, constrain, impel, compel, oblige [➤ CAUSE OR COMPEL TO ACT; 271] 5 *v* push, propel, urge, goad, send, hurl, shove, thrust [➤ PUSH, PULL, AND SLIDE; 335] 6 *v* hammer, push, force, plunge, sink, thrust, pound [➤ MOVE PAST, INTO, OR THROUGH SOMETHING; 331] 7 *n* energy, determination, ambition, initiative, motivation, effort, enterprise, push, vitality, get-up-and-go (*informal*) [➤ ENERGY AND ENTHUSIASM; 496] *Opposite:* lethargy 8 *n* urge, desire, need, instinct, passion [➤ POSITIVE IMPATIENCE, ENTHUSIASM, AND ALERTNESS; 537] 9 *n* campaign, crusade, push, fundraiser, appeal [➤ NON-AGGRESSIVE/SPORTING EVENTS; 40]

drive-in *type of* eating place [➤ HOTELS, RESTAURANTS, AND CLUBS; 1082]

drive insane *v* [➤ CONFUSE AND BEWILDER; 571]

drivel *n* nonsense, balderdash, gibberish, bunkum (*informal*), hokum (*informal*), hogwash (*informal*), malar-

key (*informal*), twaddle (*informal*), bunk (*slang*) [➤ MEANINGLESS SPEECH OR WRITING; 676]

drive mad (*informal*) *v* [➤ CONFUSE AND BEWILDER; 571]

driven *adj* ambitious, determined, obsessed, motivated, compelled, energetic [➤ HARD-WORKING AND COMMITTED; 500] *Opposite:* apathetic

drive nuts (*informal*) *v* [➤ CONFUSE AND BEWILDER; 571]

driver *n* chauffeur, motorist, valet, teamster [➤ DRIVERS; 1153]

drive round the bend (*UK*) *v* [➤ CONFUSE AND BEWILDER; 571]

driver's seat *type of* internal feature [➤ INTERNAL PARTS OF A VEHICLE; 1146]

drive-through *type of* food outlet [➤ RETAIL OUTLETS; 1083]

drive up the wall (*informal*) *v* exasperate, infuriate, make your blood boil, enrage, irritate, irk, annoy, drive mad (*informal*) [➤ ANGER AND ANNOY; 569]

driveway *type of* secondary road [➤ ROADS; 1106]

driving 1 *adj* heavy, pouring, lashing [➤ CLOUDY AND RAINY WEATHER; 1052] *Opposite:* light 2 *adj* powerful, dynamic, energetic, motivating, forceful, compelling, influential, major [➤ STRENGTH; 201]

driving rain *n* [➤ CLOUDY AND RAINY WEATHER; 1052]

drizzle 1 *n* light rain, trickle, shower, sprinkle [➤ CLOUDY AND RAINY WEATHER; 1052] *Opposite:* downpour 2 *v* rain, spot, shower, sprinkle, trickle, dribble, drip, drop, spit (*UK*) [➤ CLOUDY AND RAINY WEATHER; 1052] *Opposite:* pour

drizzling *adj* [➤ CLOUDY AND RAINY WEATHER; 1052]

drizzly *adj* damp, wet, rainy, misty [➤ CLOUDY AND RAINY WEATHER; 1052]

drogue parachute *part of* spacecraft [➤ SPACE VEHICLES; 1063]

droll *adj* amusing, funny, comic, witty, humorous, comical, entertaining, quaint, absurd [➤ FUNNY AND AMUSING; 216] *Opposite:* dull

See Compare and Contrast at **funny**.

drollness *n* [➤ FUNNY AND AMUSING; 216]

drolly *adv* amusingly, comically, humorously, wittily, absurdly, entertainingly [➤ FUNNY AND AMUSING; 216]

dromedary *type of* large mammal [➤ LARGE MAMMALS; 986]

drone 1 *v* hum, buzz, whine, murmur, whir [➤ EMIT CONTINUOUS SOUNDS; 366] 2 *n* buzz, hum, whine, murmur, whir [➤ CONTINUOUS SOUNDS; 1258]

drone on *v* [➤ CHATTER AND BABBLE; 617]

drool *v* dribble, salivate, slobber, slaver, drivel [➤ EXCRETION AND EXCRETA; 722]

droop 1 *v* sag, wilt, bow, hang down, flop, sink, slouch [➤ TAKE UP A NEW POSITION; 312] 2 *v* tire, tire out, wear out, flag, wilt, fade, slump, subside [➤ GET WORSE; 381] *Opposite:* perk up

droopiness 1 *n* tiredness, fatigue, weariness, exhaustion, apathy [➤ TIRED, ASLEEP, AND UNCONSCIOUS; 738] *Opposite:* freshness 2 *n* floppiness, limpness, lifelessness, slackness, bagginess, flaccidity [➡ MALLEABLE AND ELASTIC; 1212] *Opposite*: stiffness

droopy 1 *adj* **tired**, tired out, worn out, fatigued, weary, exhausted [➡ TIRED, ASLEEP, AND UNCONSCIOUS; 738] *Opposite*: fresh 2 *adj* **hanging**, floppy, limp, dangling, sagging, lifeless, flaccid, slack, baggy [➡ MALLEABLE AND ELASTIC; 1212] *Opposite*: upright

drop 1 *v* **let fall**, let go, release, throw down [➡ MOVE SOMETHING: DOWNWARD; 329] 2 *v* **fall**, go down, plunge, plummet, crash, jump down, dive, slump, decline [➡ GO DOWNWARD; 307] *Opposite*: rise 3 *v* **drip**, trickle, ooze, seep, dribble [➡ LIQUID EMISSION; 370] *Opposite*: pour 4 *v* **abandon**, stop, shelve, give up, discontinue, cut, leave out, dump, cut out, ditch (*informal*) [➡ STOP ACTING; 264] *Opposite*: maintain 5 *n* **droplet**, drip, bead, globule, dewdrop, drib [➡ AMOUNTS OF LIQUID; 114] 6 *n* **descent**, fall, plunge, decline, dip, declivity [➡ GO DOWNWARD; 307] *Opposite*: ascent 7 *n* **reduction**, decrease, decline, fall, cut, deterioration, falling off, slump, sag, downswing [➡ LESS; 126] *Opposite*: increase

drop a line *v* **write**, get in touch, correspond, contact, send a letter, send a note [➡ INITIATE AND ESTABLISH COMMUNICATION; 680]

drop back *v* **fall behind**, fall back, drop behind, slow down, lag behind, straggle [➡ MOVE SLOWLY; 314]

drop behind *v* **fall back**, fall behind, drop back, slow down, lag behind, straggle [➡ MOVE SLOWLY; 314]

drop in *v* **call**, call by, call in, come around, drop by, drop over, look in, stop by, visit, come round (*UK*) [➡ ARRIVE; 12]

droplet *n* **drop**, drip, bead, dewdrop, globule, drib [➡ AMOUNTS OF LIQUID; 114]

drop off (*informal*) 1 *v* **go to sleep**, nod off, fall asleep, doze off, drift off, drowse, snooze (*informal*) [➡ SLEEP AND DREAM; 723] 2 *v* **deliver**, unload, deposit, leave [➡ DISPENSE, RATION, AND DISTRIBUTE; 434] *Opposite*: pick up

drop out *v* **leave**, give up, quit, withdraw, stop, abandon [➡ STOP ACTING; 264] *Opposite*: carry on

dropper *n* **dispenser**, measurer, tube, glass dropper, eye dropper, ear dropper [➡ MEASURING DEVICES; 1123]

droppings *n* **dung**, muck, stools, feces, manure, excreta [➡ EXCRETION AND EXCRETA; 722]

dross *n* **rubbish**, trash, garbage, scum, waste, junk (*informal*) [➡ JUNK AND USELESS OBJECTS; 1249]

drought *n* **lack**, dearth, deficiency, scarcity, famine [➡ TOO FEW, TOO LITTLE; 122] *Opposite*: abundance

drove 1 *n* **throng**, horde, crowd, gaggle, multitude, group [➡ GROUPS OF PEOPLE; 935] *Opposite*: trickle 2 *type of* **herd** [➡ GROUPS OF ANIMALS; 993]

droves *n* **multitudes**, hordes, crowds, scores, flocks [➡ MANY, MUCH, LARGE AMOUNT; 117]

drown 1 *v* **go down**, go under, sink, die [➡ DIE; 922] *Opposite*: float 2 *v* **drench**, soak, swamp, saturate, flood, submerge, engulf, inundate, overwater (*UK*) [➡ SOFTEN, LIQUEFY, AND DAMPEN; 388] *Opposite*: dry 3 *v* **cover**, mask, obscure, hide, overlie, overwhelm, drown out [➡ CAUSE TO DISAPPEAR; 6] *Opposite*: amplify

drowse *v* **doze**, be sleepy, nap, have a nap, catnap, sleep, nod off, slumber, snooze (*informal*), have forty winks (*informal*) [➡ SLEEP AND DREAM; 723] *Opposite*: wake

drowsiness *n* **sleepiness**, lethargy, stupor, tiredness [➡ TIRED, ASLEEP, AND UNCONSCIOUS; 738] *Opposite*: wakefulness

drowsy *adj* **sleepy**, tired, dozy, lethargic, somnolent, nodding, snoozing (*informal*) [➡ TIRED, ASLEEP, AND UNCONSCIOUS; 738] *Opposite*: awake

drub *v* **beat**, pound, thrash, defeat, hammer (*informal*), whip (*informal*), lick (*informal*) [➡ BEAT AND DEFEAT; 80]

drubbing *n* **beating**, thrashing, hammering (*informal*), pasting (*informal*), licking (*informal*) [➡ BEAT AND DEFEAT; 80]

drudge 1 *n* **worker**, menial (*formal*) [➡ WORKERS; 836] *Opposite*: drone 2 *v* **work**, toil, labor, grind, plod, slog [➡ HARD WORK OR EFFORT; 298]

drudgery *n* **labor**, toil, work, chore, grind, slog [➡ HARD WORK OR EFFORT; 298]

See Compare and Contrast at **work**.

drug *n* **medication**, medicine, painkiller [➡ REMEDIES, TREATMENTS, AND OPERATIONS; 731]

drug-dealer *n* [➡ CRIMINALS; 821]

druggist 1 *n* **pharmacist**, apothecary (*archaic*), chemist (*UK*) [➡ PEOPLE WHO WORK IN MEDICINE; 848] 2 *type of* **retail outlet** [➡ RETAIL OUTLETS; 1083]

drug-runner *n* [➡ CRIMINALS; 821]

drug squad *n* [➡ THE POLICE, ARREST, AND PRETRIAL PROCEEDINGS; 818]

drugstore *type of* **retail outlet** [➡ RETAIL OUTLETS; 1083]

druid *n* [➡ RELIGIOUS PEOPLE; 778]

drum 1 *type of* **percussion instrument** [➡ MUSICAL INSTRUMENTS; 910] 2 *n* **barrel**, cask, cylinder, container [➡ CONTAINERS, RECEPTACLES, AND PACKAGING; 1245] 3 *v* **play the drums**, pulsate, throb, tap, thump [➡ EMIT SOUNDS THROUGH IMPACT AND ABRASION; 365]

drum into *v* **impress**, instill, drive into, teach, din in, inculcate, repeat [➡ INSTRUCT AND TEACH; 609]

drumming *n* **thudding**, pounding, beating, hammering, tapping, throbbing [➡ IMPACT SOUNDS; 1260]

drum 'n' bass *type of* **dance music** [➡ MUSIC, SONGS, AND SINGING; 907]

drumroll *n* **roll of drums**, tattoo, rattle, rumble, crescendo, buildup, paradiddle (*UK*) [➡ IMPACT SOUNDS; 1260]

drumstick 1 *n* **stick**, wire brush, mallet, beater, baton [➡ STICKS, POLES, AND WEDGES; 1254] 2 *type of* **cut** [➡ TYPES AND CUTS OF MEAT; 1177]

drum up *v* **gather**, stimulate, rally, foster, encourage, whip up, arouse, mobilize, stir up, create [➡ GET; 420] *Opposite*: suppress

drunk *adj* **inebriated**, intoxicated, plastered (*informal*), liquored up (*informal*), under the influence (*informal*), smashed (*informal*), bombed (*slang*), stewed (*slang*), tanked (*slang*), loaded (*slang*), tanked-up (*slang*), sloshed (*slang*), soused (*slang*), crocked (*slang*) [➡ UNDER THE INFLUENCE OF DRUGS OR ALCOHOL; 741] *Opposite*: sober,

drunkard *n* [➡ PLEASURE-SEEKERS AND HEDONISTS; 886]

druthers (*informal*) *n* **preference**, free choice, first choice, fancy, cup of tea [➡ APPRECIATION AND GRATITUDE; 535]

dry 1 *adj* **dehydrated**, dried out, dried up, arid, waterless, desiccated, dry as a bone, parched, shriveled, sere (*literary*) [➡ DRY; 1242] *Opposite*: wet 2 *adj* **thirsty**, dehydrated, parched, in need of a drink, gasping (*UK*) [➡ DRINK; 711] 3 *adj* **deadpan**, wry, ironic, understated, laconic, deprecating, matter-of-fact, sarcastic, sardonic, emotionless [➡ MOCKING AND DISMISSIVE; 636] 4 *adj* **uninteresting**, dull, tedious, boring, monotonous, dreary, unexciting, uninspired [➡ BORING AND UNINTERESTING; 234] *Opposite*: interesting 5 *adj* **teetotal**, abstinent, abstemious, temperate, antialcohol, alcohol-free [➡ SELF-DENIAL; 882] 6 *v* **make dry**, rub, rub down, towel, wipe, soak up, mop up [➡ HARDEN, CONGEAL, AND DRY; 387] *Opposite*: wet 7 *v* **desiccate**, become dry, dry out, dry up, dehydrate, parch, wither [➡ HARDEN, CONGEAL, AND DRY; 387] *Opposite*: swell

Compare and Contrast: *dry, dehydrated, desiccated, arid, parched, shriveled, sere*

CORE MEANING: lacking moisture

dry having little or no moisture; *dehydrated* experiencing fluid loss, or preserved by drying; *desiccated* (used of products, especially food) free from moisture, or preserved by drying; *arid* (used of land) dry from lack of rain; *parched* dry from excessive heat or lack of rain; *shriveled* dry, shrunken, and wrinkled; *sere* (*literary*) dry and withered.

dryad *n* **wood nymph**, fairy, naiad, pixie, nymph, elf, sprite [➡ MYTHICAL BEINGS; 789]

dry as a bone *adj* [➡ DRY; 1242]

dry-clean *v* **clean**, launder, wash, valet [➡ CLEAN AND POLISH; 403]

dry-eyed *adj* **unemotional**, impassive, expressionless, unmoved, stoical, stoic [➡ NEUTRALITY AND INDIFFERENCE; 553] *Opposite*: tearful

dry land *n* **solid ground**, shore, beach, terra firma [➡ THE SEAS, OCEANS, AND SHORES; 1041] *Opposite*: sea

dryness 1 *n* **aridness**, aridity, waterlessness, dehydration, drought, desiccation, parchedness [➡ DRY; 1242] *Opposite*: wetness 2 *n* **wryness**, irony, understatement, matter-of-factness, sarcasm [➡ MOCKING AND DISMISSIVE; 636]

dry out 1 *v* **air**, dry, dry off, tumble dry, tumble, hang out to dry [➡ HARDEN, CONGEAL, AND DRY; 387] 2 *v* **shrivel up**, curl up, dry up, wither, become dehydrated [➡ HARDEN, CONGEAL, AND DRY; 387]

dry run *n* **rehearsal**, run-through, tryout, trial run, trial, practice, dummy run (*UK*) [➡ PREPARATORY EVENTS; 57]

dry up 1 *v* **desiccate**, become dry, dry out, dry, dehydrate, parch, wither, shrink [➡ HARDEN, CONGEAL, AND DRY; 387] *Opposite*: swell 2 *v* (*informal*) **falter**, lose the thread, stop midstream, forget your lines, come to a halt, finish, stop dead, shut up, stop talking, hesitate [➡ HESITATE; 272] *Opposite*: continue 3 *v* **fail**, run out, be used up, come to an end, disappear, stop [➡ DISAPPEAR; 4] *Opposite*: continue

dual *adj* **double**, twin, twofold [➡ APPORTIONMENT; 113]

dualism *n* **symmetry**, contrast, dichotomy, opposition, polarity, differentiation, duality [➡ DIFFERENCE; 149]

duality *n* **dichotomy**, division, dyad, contrast, opposition, complement, dualism [➡ DIFFERENCE; 149]

dub 1 *v* **call**, nickname, christen, hail as, label, style (*formal*) [➡ NAME AND DESCRIBE; 665] 2 *type of* **electronic music** [➡ MUSIC, SONGS, AND SINGING; 907]

dubbin (*UK*) *n* **polish**, wax, blacking, dressing, waterproofing, weatherproofing [➡ COVERS AND COATINGS; 1246]

dubiety (*formal*) *n* **doubtfulness**, doubt, dubiousness, uncertainty, hesitancy, suspicion [➡ UNCERTAIN; 175] *Opposite*: certitude

dubious 1 *adj* **doubtful**, uncertain, unsure, undecided, unconvinced, in doubt, questioning, hesitant, suspicious, skeptical [➡ UNCERTAINTY; 559] *Opposite*: certain 2 *adj* **suspect**, untrustworthy, questionable, shady, unsavory, fishy (*informal*) [➡ MORALLY BAD OR IMPROPER; 775] *Opposite*: trustworthy 3 *adj* **ambiguous**, doubtful, debatable, uncertain, questionable, imprecise, vague [➡ UNCERTAIN; 175] *Opposite*: unambiguous

See Compare and Contrast at **doubtful**.

dubiously *adv* **doubtfully**, uncertainly, unsurely, questioningly, hesitantly, suspiciously [➡ UNCERTAINTY; 559] *Opposite*: certainly

dubiousness 1 *n* **doubt**, doubtfulness, uncertainty, hesitancy, suspicion, incertitude [➡ UNCERTAINTY; 559] *Opposite*: certainty 2 *n* **fallibility**, unreliability, improbability, ambiguity, vagueness, flimsiness, shakiness [➡ UNCERTAIN; 175] *Opposite*: reliability

duchess *type of* **aristocrat** [➡ RULERS AND ARISTOCRACY; 823]

duchy *n* **dukedom**, estate, territory, barony, principality, region [➡ REALMS AND RULES; 824]

duck 1 *n* **water bird**, waterfowl, diver [➡ FRESHWATER BIRDS; 1000] 2 *type of* **fowl** [➡ FOOD BIRDS; 999] 3 *type of* **meat** [➡ TYPES AND CUTS OF MEAT; 1177] 4 *type of* **male or female bird** [➡ MALE OR FEMALE BIRDS; 1005] 5 *v* **stoop**, bend, bow, bob, nod, dip, lower, drop [➡ ASSUME A POSITION; 317] *Opposite*: straighten 6 *v* **avoid**, evade, dodge, sidestep, circumvent, elude, escape [➡ NOT DO AND REFUSE TO DO; 274] *Opposite*: confront

duckboard *n* **walkway**, boardwalk, path, planking, catwalk, gangplank [➡ PATHWAYS; 1110]

duckling *type of* **young bird** [➡ YOUNG BIRDS; 1004]

duck out *v* **back out**, pull out, drop out, withdraw, get out, renege, avoid [➡ NOT DO AND REFUSE TO DO; 274]

duct *n* **channel**, canal, pipe, tube, vessel, conduit [➡ WATERCOURSES; 1111]

ductile *adj* **pliable**, malleable, elastic, pliant, plastic, flexible [➡ MALLEABLE AND ELASTIC; 1212]

See Compare and Contrast at **pliable**.

dud (*informal*) 1 *n* **failure**, fiasco, letdown, disappointment, flop (*informal*), washout (*informal*) [➡ FAILURE;

77] *Opposite*: success **2** *adj* **useless**, worthless, ineffective, broken, no good [➡ REDUNDANT AND USELESS; 240] *Opposite*: usable

dude (*slang*) **1** *n* **man**, boy, gentleman, fellow, guy (*informal*), fella (*informal*) [➡ MALE PERSON; 934] **2** *n* **fop**, fashion victim, dandy (*informal*), swell (*dated informal*), hipster (*slang*) [➡ MALE PERSON; 934]

duds (*informal*) *n* [➡ CLOTHES AND ACCESSORIES; 864]

due 1 *adj* **expected**, scheduled, appointed, anticipated, looked-for, awaited [➡ FUTURE; 86] **2** *adj* **appropriate**, fitting, suitable, proper, right and proper, correct [➡ APPROPRIATE, SUITABLE, AND ADVISABLE; 184] *Opposite*: undue **3** *adj* **owing**, unpaid, outstanding, payable, owed, in arrears [➡ OWE AND DESERVE; 465] *Opposite*: paid **4** *adv* **directly**, exactly, direct, dead, straight, precisely [➡ DIRECTION OF MOTION, 345] *Opposite*: indirectly

due diligence *n* [➡ BUSINESS ACTIVITIES AND PHENOMENA; 794]

duel 1 *n* **contest**, fight, battle, gunfight, combat, clash [➡ AGGRESSIVE EVENTS; 39] **2** *v* **fight**, clash, battle, contest, struggle, conflict [➡ COMPETE, CONTEND, AND COMBAT; 303]

duelist *n* **fighter**, combatant, opponent, gunfighter, contender, dueler [➡ COMPETITORS; 41]

dues *n* **fees**, subscription, payment, charge, levy, toll [➡ TAX AND TAXATION; 802]

duet *n* **duo**, double act, twosome, couple, pair, double [➡ GROUPS OF PEOPLE; 935]

due to *prep* **because of**, owing to, by reason of, as a result of, attributable to, thanks to, down to [➡ EXPRESSIONS OF REFERENCE; 63]

duffel bag *type of* **baggage** [➡ CONTAINERS, RECEPTACLES, AND PACKAGING; 1245]

duffle coat *type of* **overcoat** [➡ GARMENTS AND OUTFITS; 865]

dugong *type of* **marine mammal** [➡ MARINE MAMMALS; 987]

dugout 1 *n* **bunker**, trench, foxhole, ditch, hollow, pit [➡ HOLES, GAPS, AND FORKS; 1252] **2** *type of* **small vessel** [➡ SHIPS AND BOATS; 1150]

duke *type of* **aristocrat** [➡ RULERS AND ARISTOCRACY; 823]

dulcet *adj* **melodious**, melodic, honeyed, soothing, pleasant, soft [➡ SOFT, LOW, OR PLEASANT SOUNDS; 1265] *Opposite*: harsh

dull 1 *adj* **boring**, uninteresting, tedious, monotonous, dreary, dry, unexciting, lackluster, mind-numbing, lifeless, deadly (*informal*) [➡ BORING AND UNINTERESTING; 234] *Opposite*: interesting **2** *adj* **cloudy**, overcast, gloomy, gray, leaden, dismal [➡ CLOUDY AND RAINY WEATHER; 1052] *Opposite*: bright **3** *adj* **dark**, dim, muted, faded, lackluster, insipid [➡ DESCRIBING COLORS; 1226] *Opposite*: bright **4** *adj* **stupid**, obtuse, plodding, sluggish, unintelligent [➡ NEGATIVE INTELLECTUAL CHARACTERISTICS; 525] *Opposite*: bright **5** *v* **deaden**, dampen, stultify, cloud, blunt, reduce, blur, muffle, allay, assuage [➡ CHANGE OF INTENSITY: LESS; 395] *Opposite*: accentuate

See Compare and Contrast at **boring**.

dullness 1 *n* **tediousness**, tedium, monotony, dreariness, dryness, lifelessness, flatness, insipidness, unimaginativeness [➡ BORING AND UNINTERESTING; 234] *Opposite*: liveliness

2 *n* **cloudiness**, gloom, half-light, gloominess, grayness, leadenness [➡ CLOUDY AND RAINY WEATHER; 1052] *Opposite*: brightness **3** *n* **darkness**, dimness, drabness, dowdiness, dinginess, murkiness [➡ DESCRIBING COLORS; 1226] *Opposite*: brightness

dull-witted *adj* [➡ NEGATIVE INTELLECTUAL CHARACTERISTICS; 525]

dully 1 *adv* **boringly**, uninterestingly, drearily, tediously, monotonously, mind-numbingly [➡ BORING AND UNINTERESTING; 234] *Opposite*: interestingly **2** *adv* **dimly**, faintly, weakly, feebly, insipidly, wanly [➡ DESCRIBING COLORS; 1226] *Opposite*: brightly **3** *adv* **bleakly**, monotonously, drearily, dismally, listlessly, lifelessly [➡ UNINTERESTED AND DETACHED; 629] *Opposite*: brightly **4** *adv* **unintelligently**, stupidly, dimly, obtusely, sluggishly [➡ NEGATIVE INTELLECTUAL CHARACTERISTICS; 525] *Opposite*: intelligently

duly *adv* **accordingly**, suitably, fittingly, appropriately, properly, correctly [➡ RESULTS AND OUTCOMES; 83] *Opposite*: unduly

dumb *adj* [➡ ABSENCE OF SOUND; 1257]

dumbfound *v* **astonish**, amaze, astound, surprise, stagger, confound, stun, flabbergast (*informal*) [➡ CONFUSE AND BEWILDER; 571]

dumbfounded *adj* **astonished**, amazed, astounded, thunderstruck, staggered, surprised, stunned, flabbergasted (*informal*) [➡ SURPRISE, SHOCK, AND AMAZEMENT; 545] *Opposite*: nonplussed

dumbstruck *adj* [➡ SURPRISE, SHOCK, AND AMAZEMENT; 545]

dumdum bullet *type of* **projectile** [➡ PROJECTILES; 1159]

dummy 1 *n* **mannequin**, model, lay figure, figure, form [➡ REPRESENTATIONS AND GENERAL EXAMPLES; 65] **2** *n* **copy**, replica, imitation, fake, mock-up, duplicate [➡ COPIES AND REPLICAS; 151] *Opposite*: original **3** *adj* **imitation**, fake, mock, pretend, replica, false, bogus [➡ FALSE AND UNREAL; 173] *Opposite*: original

dummy run *n* **rehearsal**, run-through, dry run, trial run, trial, practice, tryout [➡ PREPARATORY EVENTS; 57]

dump 1 *v* (*informal*) **abandon**, discard, leave, desert, walk out on (*informal*), chuck (*informal*), finish with (*informal*) [➡ REFUSING OR REJECTING RELATIONS; 975] *Opposite*: stay **2** *v* **put**, leave, abandon, tip, throw, unload, deposit, plunk, plonk, chuck (*informal*) [➡ GET RID OF SOMETHING; 451] **3** *v* **get rid of**, abandon, leave, dispose of, discard, ditch (*informal*) [➡ GET RID OF SOMETHING; 451] *Opposite*: keep **4** *n* (*informal*) **pigpen**, eyesore, mess, monstrosity, hovel, hole (*informal*), tip (*UK*), pigsty (*UK*) [➡ UNDESIRABLE ACCOMMODATIONS; 856] **5** *n* **landfill**, garbage dump, junkyard, scrapheap, scrapyard (*UK*), tip (*UK*), rubbish dump (*UK*) [➡ STORES AND STORAGE BUILDINGS; 1088]

dumper *n* **litterer**, litterbug (*informal*), fly-tipper (*UK*), tipper (*UK*) [➡ DIRTY AND SLOVENLY PEOPLE; 954]

dumpiness *n* [➡ BUILD; 477]

dump on *v* [➡ GIVE TOO MUCH AND OVERBURDEN; 437]

dump truck *type of* **commercial or industrial vehicle** [➡ VEHICLES; 1145]

dun *type of* **beige** [➡ COLORS; 1224]

dune *n* **bank**, sandbank, hill, mound, ridge, hump [➡ THE SEAS, OCEANS, AND SHORES; 1041]

dune buggy *type of* **leisure vehicle** [➡ VEHICLES; 1145]

dung *n* **manure**, droppings, slurry, muck, fertilizer, excrement [➡ UNPLEASANT, DIRTY, AND TOXIC SUBSTANCES; 1268]

dung beetle *type of* **beetle** [➡ BEETLES AND WEEVILS; 1016]

dungeon *n* **prison**, cell, jail, vault, oubliette, chamber [➡ BUILDINGS FOR CONFINING PEOPLE; 1094]

dunk *v* **dip**, submerge, immerse, soak, steep, plunge, put in [➡ MOVE SOMETHING: DOWNWARD; 329]

duo 1 *n* **pair**, twosome, couple, double act, two of a kind, duet [➡ GROUPS OF PEOPLE; 935] 2 *type of* **band** [➡ MUSICIANS AND SINGERS; 908]

duodenum *part of* **digestive tract** [➡ THE DIGESTIVE TRACT; 709]

dupe 1 *v* **fool**, trick, deceive, con, take in, cheat, hoodwink, swindle, pull the wool over somebody's eyes [➡ DECEPTION AND LIES; 660] 2 *n* **victim**, target, fool, sucker (*informal*), fall guy (*slang*), cuckold (*literary*) [➡ VICTIMS OF DECEIT; 662]

duple *adj* [➡ APPORTIONMENT; 113]

duplex *type of* **apartment** [➡ RESIDENTIAL BUILDINGS; 1078]

duplicate 1 *v* **copy**, replicate, photocopy, reproduce, make two of, clone [➡ COPY AND DUPLICATE; 402] 2 *v* **repeat**, replicate, reproduce, copy, do again, redo, double [➡ COPY AND DUPLICATE; 402] 3 *n* **copy**, replacement, photocopy, spare, carbon copy, reproduction, replica, facsimile [➡ COPIES AND REPLICAS; 151] *Opposite*: original 4 *adj* **identical**, matching, replica, replacement, spare [➡ SAMENESS; 150] *Opposite*: original

See Compare and Contrast at **copy**.

duplication 1 *n* **repetition**, replication, doubling, copying, photocopying, reduplication [➡ SAMENESS; 150] 2 *n* **replica**, duplicate, copy, print, facsimile, carbon copy, photocopy [➡ COPIES AND REPLICAS; 151] *Opposite*: original

duplicitous *adj* **double-dealing**, two-faced, tricky, deceitful, dishonest, disloyal, unfaithful, treacherous, fraudulent, misleading, deceptive [➡ DECEITFUL; 513] *Opposite*: honest

duplicitousness *n* [➡ DECEITFUL; 513]

duplicity *n* **deceit**, deception, dishonesty, disloyalty, unfaithfulness, treachery, fraudulence, betrayal, deceitfulness [➡ DECEPTION AND LIES; 660] *Opposite*: honesty

durability *n* **toughness**, sturdiness, strength, robustness, resilience, stability, permanence, hardiness, endurance, indestructibility [➡ DURABLE; 1210] *Opposite*: flimsiness

durable *adj* **tough**, sturdy, strong, robust, long-lasting, resilient, heavy-duty, stable, enduring, permanent, hardy, indestructible, hard-wearing [➡ DURABLE; 1210] *Opposite*: flimsy

duration *n* **length**, extent, period, time, interval, spell [➡ PERIODS OF TIME; 90]

duress *n* **pressure**, force, threat, coercion, compulsion, constraint [➡ CAPTIVITY AND LOSS OF FREEDOM; 248] *Opposite*: persuasion

during *prep* **throughout**, through, in, in the course of [➡ CONCURRENT AND CONTEMPORANEOUS; 164]

dusk *n* **twilight**, sunset, nightfall, sundown, evening, even (*literary*), eventide (*literary*) [➡ TIMES OF DAY; 87] *Opposite*: dawn

dusky *adj* **shadowy**, dark, darkish, gray, dim, grayish, hazy [➡ DESCRIBING COLORS; 1226] *Opposite*: bright

dust 1 *n* **powder**, dirt, sand, earth, soil, filth, grime [➡ UNPLEASANT, DIRTY, AND TOXIC SUBSTANCES; 1268] 2 *v* **clean**, clean up, wipe, wipe down, wipe up, brush [➡ CLEAN AND POLISH; 403] 3 *v* **sprinkle**, brush, cover, scatter, sift, dredge [➡ DECORATE, ADORN, AND APPLY COATINGS; 405]

dustbin (*UK*) *n* **garbage can**, trash can, wastebasket, bin (*UK*), litter bin (*UK*), rubbish bin (*UK*), wastepaper bin (*UK*), wheelie bin (*UK*) [➡ CONTAINERS, RECEPTACLES, AND PACKAGING; 1245]

dust bowl *n* **desert**, waste, wasteland, wilderness [➡ DESERTS, PLAINS, AND MOORLAND; 1045]

dust cloth *n* **cloth**, rag, duster (*UK*) [➡ FURNISHING AND HOUSEHOLD LINENS; 860]

duster (*UK*) *n* **rag**, feather duster, dust cloth, cloth [➡ FURNISHING AND HOUSEHOLD LINENS; 860]

dust jacket *n* **cover**, jacket, outer, dust cover, paper cover, outer cover, wrapper [➡ COVERS AND COATINGS; 1246]

dustpan *n* **pan**, scoop, shovel, receptacle, container, collector, box [➡ CONTAINERS, RECEPTACLES, AND PACKAGING; 1245]

dustsheet (*UK*) *n* **dust cover**, cover, sheet, drop cloth, throw, cloth [➡ COVERS AND COATINGS; 1246]

dusty *adj* **dirty**, grimy, filthy, sandy, grubby, sooty [➡ DIRTY; 1235] *Opposite*: clean

Dutch colonial *type of* **house** [➡ RESIDENTIAL BUILDINGS; 1078]

dutiful *adj* **obedient**, well-behaved, compliant, loyal, devoted, respectful [➡ HARD-WORKING AND COMMITTED; 500] *Opposite*: disobedient

duty 1 *n* **responsibility**, obligation, onus, burden, calling, liability [➡ RESPONSIBILITY; 170] 2 *n* **job**, task, function, responsibility, obligation, undertaking [➡ JOB; 833] 3 *n* **tax**, payment, levy, due, impost, toll [➡ TAX AND TAXATION; 802]

See Compare and Contrast at **job**.

duty-bound *adj* **constrained**, compelled, obliged, forced, obligated, required [➡ RESPONSIBILITY; 170]

duty-free 1 *adj* (*informal*) **tax-free**, tax-exempt, untaxed, nontaxable, nontaxed [➡ TAX AND TAXATION; 802] 2 *type of* **retail outlet** [➡ RETAIL OUTLETS; 1083]

duvet *n* **comforter**, quilt, eiderdown, coverlet [➡ FURNISHING AND HOUSEHOLD LINENS; 860]

DVD 1 *type of* **video equipment** [➡ PHOTOGRAPHY AND PHOTOGRAPHIC EQUIPMENT; 1122] 2 *type of* **hardware** [➡ COMPUTERS AND COMPUTING; 1127] 3 *part of* **audio equipment** [➡ AUDIO EQUIPMENT; 1139]

dwarf star *type of* **star or star system** [➡ HEAVENLY BODIES; 1061]

dwell (*literary*) *v* **reside**, live, have your home, stay, inhabit, lodge (*dated*), abide (*archaic*) [➡ INHABIT; 20] *Opposite*: leave

dweller *n* **inhabitant**, resident, occupant, occupier, tenant [➞INHABITANTS; 857]

dwelling (*formal*) *n* **house**, home, residence, place of abode, lodging, abode (*literary*) [➞ACCOMMODATIONS; 855]

dwell on *v* **think about**, ponder, brood over, mull over, go on about, turn over, keep talking about, linger on, keep thinking about, wallow in, linger upon, spend too much time thinking about [➞THINK AND REFLECT; 743] *Opposite*: forget

dwindle *v* **decrease**, decline, diminish, fall off, drop, lessen, shrink, fade, fade away, disappear, drop off (*informal*) [➞DISAPPEAR; 4] *Opposite*: increase

dwindling *adj* **declining**, decreasing, diminishing, deteriorating, falling [➞CEASE TO EXIST; 22] *Opposite*: burgeoning

dye 1 *v* **color**, stain, tint, change the color of [➞CHANGE OF COLOR; 391] 2 *n* **coloring**, color, colorant, stain, pigment [➞DESCRIBING COLORS; 1226] 3 *n* **hair dye**, color, colorant, tint, rinse, peroxide, bleach, henna [➞DYES AND COLORANTS; 1270]

dyed-in-the-wool *adj* **long-established**, confirmed, committed, dedicated, incorrigible, diehard [➞UNADVENTUROUS AND DULL; 517]

dying 1 *adj* **last**, final, ultimate, closing, ending [➞AFTER, LAST, AND FOLLOWING; 165] 2 *adj* **disappearing**, failing, fading, vanishing, becoming extinct, on its last legs [➞CEASE TO EXIST; 22] *Opposite*: thriving

dying to *adj* **desperate to**, eager to, longing to, bursting to, impatient to, raring to, keen to [➞DESIRE AND WANT; 579]

dynamic *adj* **active**, self-motivated, energetic, vibrant, forceful, full of life, vigorous, go-ahead (*informal*) [➞ENERGY AND ENTHUSIASM; 496] *Opposite*: lethargic

dynamics 1 *n* **changing aspects**, subtleties, forces at work, dynamic forces, underlying forces, undercurrents [➞BASIC DETAILS; 688] 2 *n* **louds and softs**, dynamic range, changes in volume, crescendos, diminuendos, dynamic contrast [➞CHANGE; 372]

dynamism *n* **vitality**, vigor, energy, drive, enthusiasm, zing (*informal*), zip (*informal*) [➞ENERGY AND ENTHUSIASM; 496] *Opposite*: lethargy

dynamite 1 *v* **blow up**, blast, explode, detonate, wreck, destroy [➞DESTRUCTION AND DEMOLITION; 359] 2 *type of* **explosive material** [➞EXPLOSIVES; 1155]

dynamo 1 *n* **electric generator**, generator, motor, turbine [➞ENERGY STORAGE AND GENERATION; 1163] 2 *n* (*informal*) **extrovert**, live wire (*informal*), go getter (*informal*), live one (*informal*) [➞PEOPLE WHO ARE APPROVED OF; 955]

dynastic *adj* **hereditary**, successional, imperial, sovereign, ruling [➞THE FAMILY; 956]

dynasty 1 *n* **reign**, rule, empire, period, era [➞REALMS AND RULES; 824] 2 *n* **family**, house, line [➞THE FAMILY; 956]

dyspepsia *n* **indigestion**, heartburn, acid stomach, upset stomach, unsettled stomach, digestive disorder, stomachache [➞DISORDERS OF THE DIGESTIVE SYSTEM; 713]

dyspeptic *adj* [➞PAIN AND OTHER PHYSICAL SENSATIONS; 733]

dysphemism 1 *n* **offensiveness**, rudeness, vulgarity, obscenity, ribaldry, indecency [➞INSULTS, ABUSE, AND SWEARING; 658] *Opposite*: euphemism 2 *n* **obscenity**, swear word, expletive, oath, profanity, four-letter word [➞INSULTS, ABUSE, AND SWEARING; 658] *Opposite*: euphemism

dysphemistic *adj* **vulgar**, lewd, offensive, obscene, rude, ribald [➞INSULTS, ABUSE, AND SWEARING; 658] *Opposite*: euphemistic

E

each 1 *pron* **every one**, each one, all, both [➡ ALL; 128] **2** *adj* **every**, all, both, every single [➡ ALL; 128]

eager *adj* **keen**, enthusiastic, excited, raring to go, ready, willing, impatient, fervent, zealous, bright-eyed and bushy-tailed (*informal*) [➡ DESIRE AND WANT; 579] *Opposite*: unenthusiastic

eagerly *adv* **keenly**, enthusiastically, excitedly, readily, willingly, impatiently, fervently, zealously [➡ WITH ENTHUSIASM; 286] *Opposite*: unenthusiastically

eagerness *n* **keenness**, enthusiasm, excitement, readiness, willingness, zeal, impatience, fervor [➡ POSITIVE IMPATIENCE, ENTHUSIASM, AND ALERTNESS; 537] *Opposite*: apathy

eagle *type of* **bird of prey** [➡ BIRDS OF PREY; 998]

eagle-eyed *adj* **observant**, hawk-eyed, sharp-sighted, sharp-eyed, alert, not missing much, attentive, quick, on the ball (*informal*) [➡ POSITIVE INTELLECTUAL CHARACTERISTICS; 524] *Opposite*: unobservant

eaglet *type of* **young bird** [➡ YOUNG BIRDS; 1004]

ear 1 *n* **external ear**, outer ear, earlobe, lobe [➡ THE EAR; 706] **2** *n* **ability**, sensitivity, talent, knack, facility, feel [➡ SKILLS, TALENTS, AND ABILITIES; 526] **3** *n* **attention**, hearing, heed, regard [➡ THE SENSES; 696]

ear

◆ *parts of an ear*
anvil, auricle, cochlea, eardrum, hammer, incus, internal ear, malleus, middle ear, stapes, stirrup, tympanic membrane, tympanum, vestibule

ear candy (*slang*) *n* [➡ SOFT, LOW, OR PLEASANT SOUNDS; 1265]

eardrop *type of* **jewelry** [➡ JEWELRY; 866]

eardrum *part of* **ear** [➡ THE EAR; 706]

earful (*informal*) *n* **scolding**, lecture, piece of your mind, reprimand, talking-to (*informal*), telling-off (*informal*) [➡ CRITICISMS AND ANGRY OUTBURSTS; 50]

earl *type of* **aristocrat** [➡ RULERS AND ARISTOCRACY; 823]

earlier 1 *adv* **before**, in advance, previously, formerly, beforehand, ahead, at an earlier time [➡ BEFORE, FIRST, AND PRECEDING; 163] *Opposite*: later **2** *adj* **previous**, former, past, prior [➡ BEFORE, FIRST, AND PRECEDING; 163] *Opposite*: later

earliest *adj* **first**, initial, original [➡ BEFORE, FIRST, AND PRECEDING; 163] *Opposite*: latest

earlobe *n* [➡ THE EAR; 706]

early 1 *adv* **early on**, at the beginning, before time, in advance, ahead of schedule, beforehand, prematurely, untimely [➡ PROMPTNESS: EARLY; 98] *Opposite*: late **2** *adv* **soon**, promptly, without delay, now, as soon as possible [➡ PRO-MPTNESS: EARLY; 98] *Opposite*: later **3** *adj* **initial**, first, primary, premature [➡ PROMPTNESS: EARLY; 98] *Opposite*: later **4** *adj* **timely**, prompt, quick, speedy, immediate, hasty [➡ BEFORE, FIRST, AND PRECEDING; 163] *Opposite*: tardy

early music *type of* **classical music** [➡ MUSIC, SONGS, AND SINGING; 907]

early years *n* **babyhood**, infancy, childhood, youth, formative years [➡ BABYHOOD, CHILDHOOD, AND ADOLESCENCE; 917] *Opposite*: adulthood

earmark *v* **allocate**, assign, allot, set aside, put aside, put by, put to one side, mark down, tag, save, reserve, keep [➡ DISPENSE, RATION, AND DISTRIBUTE; 434]

earmuffs *type of* **accessory** [➡ ACCESSORIES, MILLINERY, AND LINGERIE; 867]

earn 1 *v* **make**, be paid, take home, receive, get, bring in, produce, gross, net, clear (*informal*) [➡ GET MONEY OR REWARD; 421] **2** *v* **deserve**, work for, win, warrant, merit, be worthy of, rate, secure, gain [➡ OWE AND DESERVE; 465]

earnest 1 *adj* **serious**, solemn, grave, sober, intense, deep [➡ BAD-TEMPERED AND HUMORLESS; 626] *Opposite*: frivolous **2** *adj* **sincere**, heartfelt, deep, intense, strong [➡ TRUE AND REAL; 171] *Opposite*: superficial

earnestly *adv* **sincerely**, seriously, solemnly, intensely, deeply, strongly [➡ BAD-TEMPERED AND HUMORLESS; 626]

earnestness *n* **sincerity**, seriousness, solemnity, intensity, feeling, depth [➡ BAD-TEMPERED AND HUMORLESS; 626]

earnings 1 *n* **pay**, salary, wage, wages, income, take-home pay, paycheck, pay envelope, pay packet (*UK*) [➡ INCOME; 460] **2** *n* **profit**, revenue, gain, return, dividend, interest, yield [➡ INCOME; 460]

earphone *n* **earpiece**, phone, receiver, stereo phone, stereo headphone, headphones [➡ AUDIO EQUIPMENT; 1139]

earpiece *n* **earphone**, headset, headphones [➡ AUDIO EQUIPMENT; 1139]

earring *n* *type of* **jewelry** [➡ JEWELRY; 866]

earshot *n* **hearing range**, range, hearing distance, hearing [➡ CLOSENESS; 159]

earsplitting *adj* **loud**, piercing, shrill, deafening, noisy, thunderous [➡ LOUD, HIGH, OR UNPLEASANT SOUNDS; 1266] *Opposite*: quiet

earth 1 *n* **soil**, ground, dirt, mud, terrain, gravel, loam, topsoil [➡ THE EARTH; 1039] **2** *type of* **den or nest** [➡ ANIMAL OR BIRD ACCOMMODATIONS; 1079]

Earth *n* **world**, globe, planet [➡ HEAVENLY BODIES; 1061]

earthenware *type of* **pottery** [➡ POTTERY; 1135]

earthling *n* **human being**, human, earthly being, intelligent life-form, human life-form, homo sapiens [➡ SCIENCE FICTION; 1064] *Opposite*: extraterrestrial

earthly 1 *adj* **worldly**, material, mortal, secular, everyday, human [➡ THE EARTH; 1039] *Opposite*: heavenly 2 *adj* **possible**, imaginable, conceivable [➡ POSSIBLE AND PROBABLE; 177]

earthmover *n* **bulldozer**, power shovel, excavator, steam shovel, front-end loader [➡ VEHICLES; 1145]

earthquake *n* **tremor**, trembling, shaking, upheaval, volcanic activity, seismic activity, quake (*informal*) [➡ VOLCANOES AND EARTHQUAKES; 1054]

earth science

◆ *types of earth sciences*
geochemistry, geology, hydrogeology, mineralogy, orology, pedology, petrology, soil science, stratigraphy

earthshaking *adj* **momentous**, earthshattering, tremendous, remarkable, stunning, devastating [➡ IMPORTANT; 194] *Opposite*: trivial

earthshattering *adj* **earthshaking**, momentous, tremendous, remarkable, stunning, devastating [➡ IMPORTANT, 194] *Opposite*: trivial

earthward *adv* **toward the earth**, toward the ground, downward, down, in a nose-dive, earthbound [➡ DIRECTION OF MOTION; 345] *Opposite*: skyward

earthwork *n* **fortification**, rampart, bulwark, barrier [➡ FORTRESSES AND FORTIFICATIONS; 1090]

earthworm *type of* **land invertebrate** [➡ LAND INVERTEBRATES; 1021]

earthy 1 *adj* **unpretentious**, down-to-earth, no-nonsense, simple, unsophisticated, basic, practical [➡ LEVELS OF EDUCATION AND SOPHISTICATION; 894] *Opposite*: refined 2 *adj* **vulgar**, crude, gross, bawdy, rude, dirty, coarse, rough, raunchy (*informal*) [➡ MORALLY BAD OR IMPROPER; 775]

ease 1 *n* **effortlessness**, easiness, simplicity, straightforwardness, facility [➡ EASE AND SIMPLICITY; 200] *Opposite*: difficulty 2 *n* **comfort**, luxury, affluence, wealth [➡ PLEASANT SITUATIONS; 74] *Opposite*: hardship 3 *v* **relieve**, alleviate, reduce, lessen, mitigate, improve, make better, take pressure off [➡ CORRECT AND PUT RIGHT; 377] *Opposite*: worsen 4 *v* **slide**, slip, edge, push gently, draw out, maneuver, guide, work [➡ PUSH, PULL, AND SLIDE; 335] 5 *v* **make easier**, facilitate, help, aid, assist, smooth, improve, relieve [➡ MAKE POSSIBLE; 275] *Opposite*: hinder

easel *n* **stand**, frame, tripod, support, mount [➡ WRITING AND DRAWING IMPLEMENTS, AND MEDIA; 601]

ease up *v* **relax**, slow down, slacken off, calm down, ease off, lighten up, take five (*informal*) [➡ CHANGE OF MOOD AND COMPOSURE; 580]

easily 1 *adv* **with no trouble**, without difficulty, without problems, effortlessly, simply, straightforwardly [➡ EASE AND SIMPLICITY; 200] 2 *adv* **without doubt**, by far, by a long shot, by a long way, definitely, certainly, undoubtedly, clearly, by a long chalk (*UK*) [➡ CERTAIN; 174]

Eastern *type of* **time zone** [➡ TIMES OF DAY; 87]

Eastertide (*literary*) *n* [➡ TIMES OF YEAR; 88]

Eastertime *n* [➡ TIMES OF YEAR; 88]

easy 1 *adj* **simple**, trouble-free, straightforward, effortless, uncomplicated, undemanding, unproblematic, painless [➡ EASE AND SIMPLICITY; 200] *Opposite*: difficult 2 *adj* **informal**, relaxed, calm, cool, tranquil, stress-free, at ease, easygoing, laid-back (*informal*) [➡ EMOTIONALLY PLEASANT; 187] *Opposite*: tense 3 *adj* **comfortable**, affluent, luxurious, undemanding, leisurely [➡ PHYSICALLY PLEASANT; 186] *Opposite*: hard

Compare and Contrast: *easy, simple, straightforward, uncomplicated*

CORE MEANING: not difficult to do or achieve

easy a general word indicating the lack of effort required to do, achieve, or understand something; ***simple*** not at all complicated and so able to be done or understood quickly or with very little effort; ***straightforward*** describes a process or action that is easy to carry out; ***uncomplicated*** not especially difficult, but requiring some degree of effort or thought.

easy chair *type of* **seating** [➡ FURNITURE; 858]

easygoing *adj* **relaxed**, casual, tolerant, even-tempered, calm, blasé, unconcerned, carefree, mellow, laid-back (*informal*) [➡ FRIENDLINESS AND SOCIABILITY; 494] *Opposite*: anxious

easy listening *type of* **pop and vocal music** [➡ MUSIC, SONGS, AND SINGING; 907]

easy on the ear *adj* [➡ SOFT, LOW, OR PLEASANT SOUNDS; 1265]

easy ride *n* [➡ EASY WORK; 299]

easy street *n* [➡ PLEASANT SITUATIONS; 74]

eat 1 *v* **consume**, have, gobble, wolf, munch, devour, bolt, gorge, swallow, scoff (*informal*), chomp (*informal*), scarf (*informal*), scarf down (*informal*) [➡ EAT AND NOT EAT; 710] 2 *v* **have a meal**, dine, lunch, breakfast, snack [➡ EAT AND NOT EAT; 710] 3 *v* (*slang*) **bother**, annoy, trouble, worry, plague, vex [➡ UPSET, DISTRESS, AND HUMILIATE; 567]

eat away *v* **erode**, corrode, eat into, wear away, wear down, grind down, rot, whittle away [➡ CHANGE OF INTENSITY: LESS; 395]

eat crow (*informal*) *v* **apologize**, retract, say you're sorry, take it all back, eat your words (*informal*) [➡ APOLOGIZE AND RETRACT; 683] *Opposite*: stand firm

eater *n* **guzzler** (*informal*), consumer, feeder, diner, devourer [➡ EATERS, GOURMETS, AND DIETARY CHOICES; 714]

eatery (*informal*) *n* **restaurant**, diner, cafeteria, bistro, eating place, roadhouse, café, brasserie, self-service restaurant (*UK*), wine bar (*UK*) [➡ HOTELS, RESTAURANTS, AND CLUBS; 1082]

eat humble pie *v* [➡ APOLOGIZE AND RETRACT; 683]

eat into 1 *v* **use up**, eat up, gobble up, reduce, consume, make inroads into, guzzle (*informal*) [➡ USE UP AND WASTE; 474] 2 *v* **corrode**, rust, pockmark, attack, destroy, eat away, wear away [➡ WORSEN SOMETHING; 380]

eats (*slang*) *n* **food**, provisions, grub (*informal*), nosh (*informal*), chow (*informal*), chuck, tucker (*UK informal*) [➡ FOOD; 1167]

eat up 1 *v* **consume**, down, gobble, scarf (*informal*), scarf down (*informal*), scoff (*informal*), guzzle (*informal*) [➡ USE UP AND WASTE; 474] **2** *v* **absorb**, obsess, take over, consume, dominate, possess [➡ APPEAL TO AND AROUSE INTEREST; 575] **3** *v* (*informal*) **lap up**, love, applaud, rave about, enthuse about [➡ PRAISE AND ENCOURAGE; 647] *Opposite:* hate

eat your heart out (*informal*) *v* **brood**, dwell on, grieve, pine [➡ BE CONCERNED AND CARE; 581]

eat your words (*informal*) *v* **apologize**, retract, say you're sorry, eat humble pie, take it all back, eat crow (*informal*) [➡ APOLOGIZE AND RETRACT; 683] *Opposite:* stand firm

eau de cologne *n* **perfume**, cologne, fragrance, scent, toilet water, eau de toilette [➡ PERSONAL HYGIENE; 491]

eau de toilette *n* [➡ PERSONAL HYGIENE; 491]

eaves *n* [➡ ROOFS, ROOF PARTS, AND CEILINGS; 1103]

eavesdrop *v* **listen in**, overhear, tap, spy, pry, nose around, snoop (*informal*) [➡ LISTEN AND LISTENERS; 708]

eavesdropper *n* **listener**, spy, observer [➡ LISTEN AND LISTENERS; 708]

ebb 1 *v* **recede**, go out, flow away, retreat, fall away, subside [➡ GO BACKWARD; 309] *Opposite:* come in **2** *v* **fade**, diminish, recede, fail, disappear, decline, abate (*formal or literary*) [➡ DISAPPEAR; 4] *Opposite:* surge **3** *n* **receding tide**, ebb tide, outgoing tide, falling tide [➡ THE SEAS, OCEANS, AND SHORES; 1041] *Opposite:* flow

ebb and flow 1 *v* **fluctuate**, vacillate, vary [➡ CHANGE; 372] **2** *n* **shift**, fluctuation, vacillation, variation, flux, variability [➡ CHANGE; 372]

ebony *type of* **black** [➡ COLORS; 1224]

ebullience *n* **joviality**, enthusiasm, liveliness, happiness, cheerfulness, bounciness, jolliness, brightness [➡ ENERGY AND ENTHUSIASM; 496] *Opposite:* lugubriousness

ebullient *adj* **jovial**, enthusiastic, lively, happy, bouncy, cheerful, bright, jolly [➡ ENERGY AND ENTHUSIASM; 496] *Opposite:* lugubrious

e-business 1 *n* [➡ E-COMMERCE; 1129] **2** *n* [➡ BUSINESS ENTERPRISES AND RELATED BODIES; 792]

eccentric 1 *adj* **odd**, unconventional, unorthodox, unusual, peculiar, strange, weird, bizarre [➡ BIZARRE AND PECULIAR; 257] *Opposite:* conventional **2** *n* **oddity**, character, original, case (*informal*) [➡ SOLITARY PEOPLE AND MISFITS; 942]

eccentricity 1 *n* **oddness**, unconventionality, peculiarity, strangeness, weirdness, bizarreness [➡ TEMPERAMENT AND BEHAVIOR; 492] *Opposite:* conventionality **2** *n* **quirk**, peculiarity, foible, idiosyncrasy, oddity, irregularity [➡ PERSONAL ECCENTRICITIES; 493]

ecclesiastic *n* **clergyman**, clergywoman, priest, cleric, minister [➡ RELIGIOUS PEOPLE; 778]

ecclesiastical *adj* **church**, clerical, religious, priestly, apostolic, papal [➡ RELIGIONS AND RELIGIOUS PRACTICES; 777] *Opposite:* secular

echelon *n* **level**, rank, grade, tier, class, stratum (*formal*) [➡ STATUS; 888]

echo 1 *n* **reverberation**, resonance, repeat, boom, ricochet

[➡ SOUNDS; 1256] **2** *v* **reverberate**, resonate, resound, boom, rebound, ricochet, come back, bounce back [➡ EMIT CONTINUOUS SOUNDS; 366] **3** *v* **repeat**, reiterate, copy, parrot, confirm, endorse, reaffirm [➡ RECITE, REPEAT, AND NARRATE; 620]

echoing *adj* **resounding**, reverberating, reflecting, ringing, resonant, resonating [➡ LOUD, HIGH, OR UNPLEASANT SOUNDS; 1266]

éclair *type of* **cake** [➡ CAKES, COOKIES, AND DESSERTS; 1181]

eclectic *adj* **heterogeneous**, varied, wide-ranging, extensive, diverse, catholic [➡ DIFFERENCE; 149] *Opposite:* narrow

eclecticism *n* **extensiveness**, range, diversity, scope, variety, heterogeneity [➡ DIFFERENCE; 149]

eclipse 1 *v* **hide**, conceal, obscure, cover, darken [➡ CAUSE TO DISAPPEAR; 6] **2** *v* **outdo**, overshadow, outshine, surpass, overwhelm, overpower [➡ BEAT AND DEFEAT; 80]

ecofriendly *adj* **biodegradable**, green, environmentally friendly, sustainable [➡ ECONOMICAL AND RESOURCEFUL; 207]

E. coli *type of* **microorganism** [➡ MICROORGANISMS, FUNGI, AND ALGAE; 1023]

ecological *adj* **environmental**, environmentally friendly, natural, biological, organic [➡ BIOLOGICAL SCIENCES; 1037]

ecologist *n* **environmentalist**, biologist, natural scientist, naturalist, conservationist [➡ PHILOSOPHICAL AND POLITICAL THINKERS; 781]

ecology *type of* **bioscience** [➡ BIOLOGICAL SCIENCES; 1037]

e-commerce *n* [➡ E-COMMERCE; 1129]

economic 1 *adj* **financial**, monetary, fiscal, pecuniary, commercial [➡ FINANCE AND ECONOMICS; 796] **2** *adj* **profitable**, cost-effective, moneymaking, lucrative, efficient [➡ ECONOMICAL AND RESOURCEFUL; 207] *Opposite:* uneconomic

economical 1 *adj* **frugal**, parsimonious, thrifty, careful, sparing, cautious, stingy [➡ GRASPING AND FINANCIALLY MEAN; 519] *Opposite:* wasteful **2** *adj* **inexpensive**, cheap, cost-effective, low-cost, budget, reasonable, efficient [➡ ECONOMICAL AND RESOURCEFUL; 207] *Opposite:* expensive

economize *v* **cut back**, cut down, retrench, save, scrimp and save, tighten your belt, be careful, rein in, pinch pennies [➡ FORGO AND DENY ONESELF; 449] *Opposite:* spend

economy 1 *n* **frugality**, thrift, cost-cutting, saving, parsimony, stinginess, financial prudence [➡ GRASPING AND FINANCIALLY MEAN; 519] *Opposite:* extravagance **2** *n* **saving**, cutback, retrenchment, reduction, scaling-down, penny-pinching [➡ ECONOMICAL AND RESOURCEFUL; 207] **3** *adj* **cheap**, budget, reduced, family, low-cost, bargain [➡ CHEAP AND INEXPENSIVE; 221] *Opposite:* expensive

economy

◆ *types of economic conditions*
austerity, boom, boom and bust, deflation, depression, downswing, downturn, hyperinflation, inflation, inflationary spiral, recession, recovery, reflation, slump, stagflation, upswing, upturn

◆ *types of economic systems*
collectivism, command economy, free enterprise economy, free market economy, market economy, mixed economy, new economy, planned economy, private economy, service economy

ecosystem *n* **bionetwork**, biome, biota, ecology, environment, flora and fauna [➡ NATURE AND THE ENVIRONMENT; 1038]

ecru *type of* **beige** [➡ COLORS; 1224]

ecstasy 1 *n* **joy**, delight, elation, bliss, rapture, euphoria, happiness, seventh heaven, thrill, excitement, pleasure [➡ PLEASURE, EXCITEMENT, AND ELATION; 534] *Opposite*: misery **2** *n* **trance**, high, frenzy, state (*informal*) [➡ PLEASURE, EXCITEMENT, AND ELATION; 534] *Opposite*: stupor

ecstatic 1 *adj* **overjoyed**, delighted, thrilled, elated, blissful, rapturous, in raptures, euphoric, in seventh heaven, jubilant, joyful, joyous, gleeful, happy, on cloud nine (*informal*), over the moon (*UK informal*) [➡ PLEASURE, EXCITEMENT, AND ELATION; 534] *Opposite*: miserable **2** *adj* **elated**, high, over-excited, frenzied, in a frenzy, excited [➡ PLEASURE, EXCITEMENT, AND ELATION; 534] *Opposite*: calm

Edam *type of* **hard cheese** [➡ DAIRY PRODUCTS AND CHEESES; 1183]

eddy *n* **whirlpool**, swirl, vortex, whirl, maelstrom, current [➡ RIVERS, LAKES, AND STREAMS; 1042]

edema *n* [➡ CONDITIONS AFFECTING THE SKIN; 721]

edge 1 *n* **border**, rim, boundary, perimeter, periphery, side, limit, verge, edging, frame, circumference, lip, bank [➡ EXTREMITIES OF PHYSICAL OBJECTS; 1250] **2** *n* **advantage**, upper hand, superiority, control, authority, power [➡ SUPERIORITY; 152] **3** *n* **brink**, verge, threshold, point [➡ EXTREMITIES OF PHYSICAL OBJECTS; 1250] **4** *n* **sharpness**, bitterness, acidity, harshness, venom [➡ LOUD, HIGH, OR UNPLEASANT SOUNDS; 1266] **5** *v* **approach**, skirt, sidle, pick your way, creep, tiptoe, edge [➡ MOVE SLOWLY; 314] **6** *v* **border**, frame, trim, fringe, enclose, decorate, flank, encircle, girdle [➡ EXIST IN CLOSE PROXIMITY; 21]

edge city (*informal*) *n* [➡ HUMAN SETTLEMENTS; 1070]

edgewise *adv* **sideways**, side-on, crossways, across, obliquely, laterally, on its side, edgeways (*UK*) [➡ ORIENTATION AND ALIGNMENT; 1223]

edgily *adv* **tensely**, uneasily, nervously, agitatedly, anxiously, twitchily, jumpily, impatiently, restlessly, irritably [➡ POSITIVE IMPATIENCE, ENTHUSIASM, AND ALERTNESS; 537] *Opposite*: calmly

edginess *n* [➡ POSITIVE IMPATIENCE, ENTHUSIASM, AND ALERTNESS; 537]

edging *n* **border**, trim, fringe, hem, frill, decoration, margin, surround, edge [➡ EXTREMITIES OF PHYSICAL OBJECTS; 1250]

edgy *adj* **nervous**, on edge, anxious, jumpy, jittery, oversensitive, tense, stressed, uneasy, like a cat on a hot tin roof, touchy, irritable, moody, agitated, restless, prickly (*informal*), tetchy (*informal*), uptight (*informal*), wired (*slang*), like a cat on hot bricks (*UK*) [➡ POSITIVE IMPATIENCE, ENTHUSIASM, AND ALERTNESS; 537] *Opposite*: relaxed

edible *adj* **eatable**, fit for human consumption, palatable, appetizing, comestible (*formal*) [➡ FOOD; 1167] *Opposite*: poisonous

edict *n* **proclamation**, announcement, pronouncement, decree, statute, act, diktat, order, command, ruling, statement, declaration, law [➡ OFFICIAL DOCUMENTS; 586]

edification *n* **improvement**, education, enlightenment, instruction, elevation [➡ TEACHING; 839] *Opposite*: obfuscation

edifice 1 *n* **building**, construction, pile, structure, mansion [➡ BUILDING AND ARCHITECTURE; 1076] **2** *n* **organization**, network, structure, association, group, society, order [➡ GROUPS IN SOCIETY; 940]

edify *v* **enlighten**, inform, educate, instruct, improve, teach [➡ INSTRUCT AND TEACH; 609] *Opposite*: obfuscate

edifying *adj* **educational**, informative, illuminating, instructive, scholastic, enlightening [➡ INTERESTING AND MEANINGFUL; 190]

edit 1 *v* **rewrite**, revise, amend, rework, correct, check over, alter, tidy up, rearrange, rehash, improve, change [➡ CORRECT AND PUT RIGHT; 371] **2** *v* **oversee**, run, manage, be in charge of, direct, control [➡ BE IN CHARGE; 270]

edited 1 *adj* **amended**, corrected, revised, rewritten, redrafted, modified [➡ CHANGE; 372] *Opposite*: unedited **2** *adj* **abridged**, concise, shortened, summarized, truncated [➡ CHANGE OF SIZE: SMALLER; 393] *Opposite*: complete

edition *n* **version**, publication, copy, issue, impression, printing, imprint [➡ BOOKS AND BOOKLETS; 590]

editor 1 *n* **publishing supervisor**, publishing manager, editor in chief, managing editor, executive editor [➡ WORKERS IN ENTERTAINMENT AND MEDIA; 873] **2** *n* **line editor**, copy editor, copyreader, corrector, checker, cutter, subeditor (*UK*) [➡ WORKERS IN ENTERTAINMENT AND MEDIA; 873]

editorial *n* **editorial column**, viewpoint, perspective, essay, commentary, exposition, article, leader (*UK*) [➡ NEWSPAPERS AND MAGAZINES; 605]

editorialize *v* **expound**, pontificate, spout, preach, sermonize, opine (*formal*) [➡ INFORM, ANNOUNCE, AND ISSUE; 611]

edit out *v* **delete**, remove, cut, omit, abridge, cut back, leave out, chop, miss out (*UK*) [➡ DELETE AND ERASE; 339]

educate *v* **teach**, instruct, edify, tutor, train, coach, inform, school [➡ INSTRUCT AND TEACH; 609]

See Compare and Contrast at **teach**.

educated 1 *adj* **well-informed**, well-read, learned, erudite, knowledgeable, scholarly [➡ LEVELS OF EDUCATION AND SOPHISTICATION; 894] *Opposite*: uneducated **2** *adj* **cultured**, cultivated, tasteful, sophisticated, refined, accomplished, polished, highbrow [➡ LEVELS OF EDUCATION AND SOPHISTICATION; 894] *Opposite*: boorish

educated guess *n* **guess**, estimation, estimate, approximation, postulate, opinion, guesstimate (*informal*) [➡ GUESS; 754]

education *n* **teaching**, learning, schooling, tutoring, instruction, edification, training, tutelage [➡ TEACHING; 839]

educational *adj* **instructive**, enlightening, didactic, edifying, informative, scholastic [➡ INTERESTING AND MEANINGFUL; 190]

educationalist *n* [➡ EDUCATORS; 840]

educator *n* **teacher**, instructor, lecturer, professor, educationalist, mentor, tutor, coach, guru [➡ EDUCATORS; 840]

eel *type of* **ocean fish** [➡ OCEAN FISH; 1009]

eerie *adj* **unnerving**, uncanny, weird, strange, peculiar, unnatural, supernatural, ghostly, ghostlike, paranormal, spine-chilling, disconcerting, sinister, scary (*informal*), spooky (*informal*), creepy (*informal*) [➡ BIZARRE AND PECULIAR; 257]

eerily *adv* **disconcertingly**, unnervingly, strangely, weirdly, uncannily, creepily (*informal*), spookily (*informal*) [➡ BIZARRE AND PECULIAR; 257]

eeriness *n* [➡ BIZARRE AND PECULIAR; 257]

efface *v* **obliterate**, eradicate, destroy, wear away, rub out, rub away, smooth away, erode, delete, cancel out, wipe out (*informal*) [➡ DELETE AND ERASE; 339]

effect **1** *n* **result**, consequence, outcome, upshot, end product, conclusion, fruit [➡ RESULTS AND OUTCOMES; 83] **2** *n* **influence**, weight, force, power, validity, clout (*informal*) [➡ APPEARANCE AND ATMOSPHERE; 1237] **3** *n* **impression**, meaning, sense, impact, purpose, drift [➡ MEANING; 690] **4** *v* (*formal*) **achieve**, carry out, produce, bring about, realize, perform, accomplish, create, make [➡ CAUSE TO HAPPEN; 31]

effective **1** *adj* **successful**, efficient, productive, useful, helpful, valuable, fruitful, effectual (*formal*), efficacious (*formal*) [➡ USEFULNESS; 199] *Opposite:* ineffective **2** *adj* **real**, actual, in effect, active, operative, current [➡ TRUE AND REAL; 171] *Opposite:* nominal **3** *adj* **operational**, operative, in force, in operation, in effect, with effect, applicable [➡ HAPPENING AND IN PROGRESS; 32] *Opposite:* inoperative

Compare and Contrast: *effective, efficient, effectual, efficacious*

CORE MEANING: producing a result

effective causing the desired or intended result; *efficient* capable of achieving the desired result with the minimum use of resources, time, and effort; *effectual* (*formal*) potentially successful in producing a desired or intended result; *efficacious* (*formal*) having the power to achieve the desired result, especially an improvement in somebody's physical condition.

effectively **1** *adv* **efficiently**, successfully, productively, well, excellently, commendably, effectually (*formal*), meritoriously (*formal*) [➡ USEFULNESS; 199] *Opposite:* ineffectively **2** *adv* **in effect**, in fact, actually, really, essentially, to all intents and purposes, realistically [➡ TRUE AND REAL; 171] *Opposite:* nominally

effectiveness *n* **efficiency**, productiveness, efficacy, success, use, usefulness, helpfulness, value [➡ USEFULNESS; 199] *Opposite:* ineffectiveness

effects (*formal*) *n* **belongings**, property, personal property, possessions, things, paraphernalia [➡ POSSESSIONS; 461]

effectual (*formal*) *adj* **effective**, worthwhile, successful, productive, helpful, fruitful, useful, efficacious (*formal*) [➡ USEFULNESS; 199] *Opposite:* ineffectual

See Compare and Contrast at **effective.**

effervesce *v* **hiss**, fizz, bubble, sparkle, froth, foam [➡ FROTH AND EFFERVESCE; 389]

effervescence **1** *n* **fizz**, bubbles, sparkle, froth, foam, fizziness, frothiness, foaminess, bubbliness [➡ FOAM; 1273] **2** *n* **vivacity**, vibrancy, vitality, animation, sparkle, liveliness, joie de vivre, enthusiasm, bubbliness [➡ ENERGY AND ENTHUSIASM; 496] *Opposite:* languor

effervescent **1** *adj* **fizzy**, sparkling, bubbly, aerated, bubbling, gassy (*informal*) [➡ VISUAL TEXTURE; 1221] *Opposite:* still **2** *adj* **lively**, vibrant, bubbly, bouncy, sparkling, vivacious, animated [➡ ENERGY AND ENTHUSIASM; 496] *Opposite:* dull

efficacious (*formal*) *adj* **effective**, efficient, successful, productive, useful, worthwhile, valuable, effectual (*formal*) [➡ USEFULNESS; 199] *Opposite:* ineffective

See Compare and Contrast at **effective.**

efficacy *n* **effectiveness**, efficiency, usefulness, productiveness, worth, value, ability [➡ USEFULNESS; 199] *Opposite:* ineffectiveness

efficiency *n* **competence**, efficacy, effectiveness, productivity, proficiency, adeptness [➡ HARD-WORKING AND COMMITTED; 500] *Opposite:* inefficiency

efficiency apartment *type of* **apartment** [➡ RESIDENTIAL BUILDINGS; 1078]

efficient **1** *adj* **well-organized**, effective, competent, capable, able, professional, proficient, resourceful, effectual (*formal*) [➡ HARD-WORKING AND COMMITTED; 500] *Opposite:* ineffective **2** *adj* **inexpensive**, timesaving, laborsaving, economical, cost-effective, productive [➡ ECONOMICAL AND RESOURCEFUL; 207] *Opposite:* wasteful

See Compare and Contrast at **effective.**

effigy *n* **image**, statue, icon, figure, figurine, dummy, carving, representation, likeness [➡ REPRESENTATIONS AND GENERAL EXAMPLES; 65]

effluence *n* [➡ UNPLEASANT, DIRTY, AND TOXIC SUBSTANCES; 1268]

effluent *n* **waste**, sewage, bilge water, seepage, runoff, overflow, emission, discharge [➡ UNPLEASANT, DIRTY, AND TOXIC SUBSTANCES; 1268]

effort **1** *n* **exertion**, energy, determination, force, strength, labor, power, sweat, struggle, work, muscle (*informal*), elbow grease (*informal*), industry (*formal or literary*) [➡ HARD WORK OR EFFORT; 298] *Opposite:* ease **2** *n* **attempt**, try, endeavor, go, shot, stab (*informal*), crack (*informal*) [➡ ATTEMPT AN ACTION; 261]

effortless *adj* **easy**, natural, unforced, graceful, unproblematic, uncomplicated, painless, undemanding [➡ EASE AND SIMPLICITY; 200] *Opposite:* strenuous

effortlessness *n* **ease**, naturalness, smoothness, simplicity, facility, confidence, grace [➡ EASE AND SIMPLICITY; 200] *Opposite*: difficulty

effrontery *n* **impudence**, nerve, boldness, gall, arrogance, brashness, shamelessness, cheekiness, cheek (*informal*), chutzpah (*informal*) [➡ BAD MANNERS AND SOCIAL SKILLS; 521]

effusion *n* **outpouring**, gush, rush, expression, declaration, proclamation, pouring, outflow, discharge [➡ THE SPOKEN WORD; 671]

effusive *adj* **gushing**, demonstrative, fulsome, vociferous, extravagant, unreserved, ebullient, gushy, lavish, unrestrained, profuse, expansive [➡ ELOQUENT, TALKATIVE, AND LONG WINDED; 632] *Opposite*: reserved

effusively *adv* **fulsomely**, vociferously, unrestrainedly, demonstratively, profusely, lavishly, gushingly, extravagantly, ebulliently, gushily, expansively [➡ ENTHUSIASTIC AND INQUISITIVE; 628] *Opposite*: reservedly

e.g. *adv* **for example**, for instance, say, let's say, perhaps, maybe [➡ WRITTEN CONVENTIONS; 599]

egalitarian *adj* **equal**, classless, free, democratic, equal opportunity [➡ EQUALITY; 154]

egg **1** *n* **reproductive cell**, ovum, egg cell, ovule [➡ EGGS, SPERM, AND SPAWN; 727] **2** *v* **urge**, incite, spur, encourage, push, egg on, pressure, drive [➡ CAUSE OR COMPEL TO ACT; 271] *Opposite*: dissuade

egghead (*informal*) *n* **intellectual**, brain (*informal*), bookworm (*informal*), rocket scientist (*informal*), brainbox (*UK*) [➡ LEVELS OF EDUCATION AND SOPHISTICATION; 894]

egg on *v* **encourage**, urge, push, incite, spur, egg, pressure, drive [➡ CAUSE OR COMPEL TO ACT; 271] *Opposite*: dissuade

eggplant *type of* **vegetable** [➡ FRUIT AND VEGETABLES; 1176]

eggshell **1** *n* **protective covering**, shell, case, casing, covering [➡ COVERS AND COATINGS; 1246] **2** *type of* **white** [➡ COLORS; 1224]

ego *n* **personality**, character, self, self-image, self-worth, self-esteem, individuality [➡ PSYCHOLOGY AND THE MIND; 769]

egocentric *adj* **selfish**, egoistical, conceited, vain, self-centered, self-important, egotistic, egoistic, insensitive, inconsiderate, self-absorbed, self-obsessed, narcissistic [➡ SELFISH AND UNKIND; 505]

egocentricity *n* [➡ SELFISH AND UNKIND; 505]

egocentrism *n* [➡ SELFISH AND UNKIND; 505]

egoism *n* **conceit**, vanity, self-importance, selfishness, self-centeredness, egotism, arrogance, self-absorption, narcissism [➡ SELFISH AND UNKIND; 505]

egoist *n* **egotist**, egomaniac, narcissist, individualist, self-seeker, self-publicist, self-aggrandizer, boaster, show-off (*informal*) [➡ SELF-IMPORTANT AND SELF-SEEKING PEOPLE; 949]

egoistic *adj* **selfish**, egotistic, conceited, self-centered, vain, egocentric, self-seeking, insensitive, inconsiderate, self-absorbed, self-obsessed [➡ SELFISH AND UNKIND; 505] *Opposite*: altruistic

egoistical *adj* [➡ SELFISH AND UNKIND; 505]

egomaniac *n* **egotist**, egoist, narcissist, self-publicist,

self-aggrandizer, individualist, boaster, show-off (*informal*) [➡ SELF-IMPORTANT AND SELF-SEEKING PEOPLE; 949]

egotism *n* **egoism**, self-centeredness, selfishness, conceit, vanity, arrogance, self-importance, self-absorption, narcissism [➡ SELFISH AND UNKIND; 505] *Opposite*: altruism

egotist *n* **egoist**, egomaniac, narcissist, self-seeker, individualist, self-publicist, self-aggrandizer, boaster, show-off (*informal*) [➡ SELF-IMPORTANT AND SELF-SEEKING PEOPLE; 949]

egotistic *adj* [➡ SELFISH AND UNKIND; 505]

See Compare and Contrast at **proud**.

egotistical *adj* [➡ SELFISH AND UNKIND; 505]

egret *type of* **freshwater bird** [➡ FRESHWATER BIRDS; 1000]

Egyptian mau *type of* **cat** [➡ FELINES; 983]

eiderdown *n* **quilt**, comforter, continental quilt, duvet, bedspread, bedcover (*UK*) [➡ FURNISHING AND HOUSEHOLD LINENS; 860]

either **1** *adj* **whichever**, any, both, each [➡ ALSO; 138] **2** *adj* **each**, both, one or the other, either one [➡ ALSO; 138]

ejaculate (*literary*) *v* **exclaim**, cry, cry out, shout, utter, voice [➡ UTTER AND PRONOUNCE; 608]

eject **1** *v* **expel**, emit, get rid of, spew, spout, disgorge, discharge (*formal*), cast out (*formal*) [➡ EJECT AND EXCLUDE; 340] **2** *v* **expel**, banish, drive out, throw out, remove, oust, evict, force out, bounce (*informal*), kick out (*informal*) [➡ GET RID OF SOMETHING; 451]

ejection seat *part of* **aircraft** [➡ AIRCRAFT; 1148]

eke out **1** *v* **make something last**, spin out, make a little go a long way, draw out, use sparingly, drag out, make something go further, stretch [➡ CAUSE TO CONTINUE; 267] *Opposite*: squander **2** *v* **supplement**, complement, add to, pad out, make up, increase, extend, stretch out [➡ CHANGE OF INTENSITY: MORE; 394] *Opposite*: diminish **3** *v* **scrape**, scratch, scrape together, scratch out, make, earn, scrimp, manage, get by [➡ CAUSE TO CONTINUE; 267]

elaborate **1** *adj* **complex**, complicated, intricate, detailed, involved, convoluted, sophisticated [➡ DIFFICULTY AND COMPLEXITY; 242] *Opposite*: straightforward **2** *adj* **sumptuous**, extravagant, ornate, decorative, rich, elegant, ostentatious, baroque, intricate [➡ POSITIVELY COMPLEX OR COMPLICATED; 217] *Opposite*: simple **3** *v* **expound**, expand, enlarge, go into detail, explain, go on, particularize, amplify, flesh out [➡ EXPLAIN AND CLARIFY; 610] *Opposite*: condense **4** *v* **complicate**, work up, build on, develop, detail [➡ CHANGE; 372] *Opposite*: simplify

elaborately *adv* **decoratively**, sumptuously, intricately, ornately, richly, extravagantly, fussily, ostentatiously [➡ EXPENSIVE AND LUXURIOUS; 218] *Opposite*: simply

elaborateness *n* [➡ DIFFICULTY AND COMPLEXITY; 242]

elaboration *n* **amplification**, embellishment, explanation, expansion, development [➡ EXPLAIN AND CLARIFY; 610]

élan (*literary*) *n* **panache**, verve, vivacity, flair, dash, style, brio (*literary*) [➡ ENERGY AND ENTHUSIASM; 496]

elapse *v* **pass**, pass by, intervene, slip away, go by, lapse [➡ HAPPEN; 27]

elastic 1 *adj* **stretchy**, expandable, flexible, supple, resilient, springy [➡ MALLEABLE AND ELASTIC; 1212] *Opposite*: rigid 2 *adj* **flexible**, adaptable, changeable, variable, mutable, supple, pliant, pliable [➡ USEFULNESS; 199] *Opposite*: inflexible

See Compare and Contrast at **pliable**.

elasticized *adj* **stretchy**, elastic, expanding, expandable, stretchable, elasticated (*UK*) [➡ MALLEABLE AND ELASTIC; 1212] *Opposite*: rigid

elate *v* **exhilarate**, thrill, excite, lift, uplift, exalt (*formal*) [➡ PLEASE AND AMUSE; 572] *Opposite*: dishearten

elated *adj* **ecstatic**, overjoyed, thrilled, delighted, euphoric, jubilant, excited, in seventh heaven, high, on cloud nine (*informal*) [➡ PLEASURE, EXCITEMENT, AND ELATION; 534] *Opposite*: disheartened

elation *n* **ecstasy**, delight, euphoria, jubilation, excitement, exultation, joy, rapture, glee [➡ PLEASURE, EXCITEMENT, AND ELATION; 534] *Opposite*: despair

elbow 1 *part of* **arm or hand** [➡ PARTS OF THE BODY: ARM AND HAND; 695] 2 *v* **prod**, jostle, nudge, shove, dig, poke, bump, push [➡ CONTACT: IMPACT; 413]

elbowroom 1 *n* **space**, room, room to spare, room to maneuver [➡ AREA AND RANGE; 111] 2 *n* **scope**, freedom, room to maneuver, leeway, choice, free rein [➡ FREEDOM AND LIBERTY; 208]

elder 1 *n* **leader**, head, chief [➡ BOSSES AND MANAGEMENT; 965] 2 *type of* **shrub or bush** [➡ BUSHES AND SHRUBS; 1027] 3 *type of* **deciduous tree** [➡ DECIDUOUS TREES; 1028] 4 *see* **elderberry**

elderberry *type of* **berry** [➡ FRUIT AND VEGETABLES; 1176]

elderly *adj* **aging**, old, aged, mature, of advanced years, senior [➡ OLD AGE; 919] *Opposite*: young

eldest *adj* **oldest**, first-born, first [➡ BEFORE, FIRST, AND PRECEDING; 163]

El Dorado *n* [➡ NONEXISTENT PLACES; 1066]

elect 1 *v* **vote for**, return, vote into office, pick, select, choose [➡ CONFER STATUS; 458] 2 *v* **choose**, opt for, decide on, select, designate, nominate, pick out [➡ MAKE DECISIONS AND CHOICES; 752] 3 *adj* **designated**, future, chosen, selected [➡ FUTURE; 86]

elected *adj* **chosen**, designated, selected, voted, nominated, adopted, picked out [➡ ELECTIONS AND VOTING; 807]

election 1 *n* **vote**, voting, poll, balloting [➡ ELECTIONS AND VOTING; 807] 2 *n* **selection**, choice, appointment, designation, nomination [➡ ELECTIONS AND VOTING; 807]

electioneer *v* **campaign**, whistle-stop, canvass, run, stump (*informal*) [➡ ELECTIONS AND VOTING; 807]

elective 1 *adj* **voting**, chosen by election, filled by election, passed by vote [➡ ELECTIONS AND VOTING; 807] *Opposite*: appointed 2 *adj* **optional**, voluntary, noncompulsory, free, selective, discretionary [➡ FREEDOM AND LIBERTY; 208] *Opposite*: compulsory

elector *n* **voter**, member of the electorate, voting member, constituent [➡ ELECTIONS AND VOTING; 807]

electoral *adj* **democratic**, voting, election, polling, balloting [➡ ELECTIONS AND VOTING; 807]

electorate *n* **people**, voters, registered voters, voting public, constituency [➡ ELECTIONS AND VOTING; 807]

electric 1 *adj* **electrical**, electronic, electrically powered, battery-operated, plug-in, rechargeable, power-driven, mains powered (*UK*) [➡ ENERGY SOURCES; 1162] 2 *adj* **absorbing**, charged, exciting, thrilling, emotional, stimulating, electrifying, captivating, stirring [➡ INTERESTING AND MEANINGFUL; 190] *Opposite*: boring

electrical *see* **electric**

electric blanket *n* [➡ FURNISHING AND HOUSEHOLD LINENS; 860]

electric blue *type of* **blue** [➡ COLORS; 1224]

electric guitar *type of* **stringed instrument** [➡ MUSICAL INSTRUMENTS; 910]

electricity *n* **current**, voltage, power, energy, electrical energy, juice (*slang*) [➡ ENERGY SOURCES; 1162]

electrified 1 *adj* **excited**, captivated, thrilled, transfixed, awestruck, amazed, astounded, charged, stimulated [➡ SURPRISE, SHOCK, AND AMAZEMENT; 545] *Opposite*: bored 2 *adj* **electric**, electrically powered, wired-up, connected [➡ ELECTRONICS AND ELECTRICS; 1137]

electrify *v* **captivate**, transfix, thrill, excite, exhilarate, astonish, amaze, surprise, shock, stun, stimulate, charge [➡ APPEAL TO AND AROUSE INTEREST; 575] *Opposite*: bore

electrifying *adj* **exciting**, stirring, thrilling, captivating, stimulating, emotional, moving [➡ INTERESTING AND MEANINGFUL; 190] *Opposite*: boring

electro *type of* **electronic music** [➡ MUSIC, SONGS, AND SINGING; 907]

electrode *n* **conductor**, rod, anode, cathode, probe [➡ ELECTRONICS AND ELECTRICS; 1137]

electron *type of* **elementary particle** [➡ ELEMENTARY PARTICLES; 1279]

electronic 1 *adj* **electric**, microelectronic, electrical, automated, automatic, synthesized, transistorized [➡ ELECTRONICS AND ELECTRICS; 1137] 2 *adj* **computerized**, high-tech, on-screen, online, computer, automatic [➡ COMPUTERS AND COMPUTING; 1127]

electronica *type of* **electronic music** [➡ MUSIC, SONGS, AND SINGING; 907]

electronic cash *n* [➡ E-COMMERCE; 1129]

electronics *n* **microchip technology**, microelectronics, computer electronics, integrated circuit technology, semiconductor technology, electronic engineering [➡ ELECTRONICS AND ELECTRICS; 1137]

electronic signature *n* [➡ E-COMMERCE; 1129]

electron microscope *type of* **optical instrument** [➡ OPTICAL INSTRUMENTS; 1124]

elegance *n* **grace**, style, sophistication, chic, taste, refinement, stylishness, modishness, smartness, class (*informal*), classiness (*informal*) [➡ WELL-GROOMED; 482] *Opposite*: inelegance

elegant *adj* **sophisticated**, stylish, graceful, chic, well-designed, well-dressed, smart, neat, tasteful, refined, classy (*informal*) [➡ WELL-GROOMED; 482] *Opposite*: inelegant

elegiac (*formal*) *adj* **mournful**, sad, melancholic, funereal, plaintive, nostalgic, bittersweet [➡ EMOTIONALLY PLEASANT; 187] *Opposite*: cheerful

elegy *n* **funeral song**, dirge, requiem, poem, speech, composition [➡ MUSIC, SONGS, AND SINGING; 907]

element 1 *n* **component**, part, section, division, portion, group, constituent [➡ AMOUNTS AND QUANTITIES; 112] 2 *n* **hint**, amount, quantity, touch, bit, degree [➡ FEW, LITTLE, SMALL AMOUNT; 120] 3 *n* **factor**, cause, feature, component, ingredient, aspect [➡ QUALITIES AND CHARACTERISTICS; 1191] 4 *n* **habitat**, environment, milieu, medium, domain, sphere [➡ PLACE; 1065]

elemental *adj* **rudimentary**, basic, fundamental, essential, primary [➡ FUNDAMENTAL; 195]

elementary *adj* **basic**, simple, straightforward, uncomplicated, plain, fundamental, rudimentary, easy, introductory [➡ EASE AND SIMPLICITY; 200]

elementary particle *n* [➡ SMALL PIECES; 129]

elementary particle

◆ *types of elementary particles*
antineutron, antiproton, antiquark, baryon, boson, electron, fermion, hadron, kaon, lepton, meson, muon, neutrino, neutron, photon, pion, positron, proton, quark, tauon

elementary school *type of* **school** [➡ EDUCATIONAL INSTITUTIONS; 813]

elements *n* **rudiments**, basics, fundamentals, essentials, foundations, origins, features [➡ BASIC DETAILS; 688]

elephant *type of* **large mammal** [➡ LARGE MAMMALS; 986]

elephantine 1 *adj* **ponderous**, lumbering, clumsy, slow, heavy, ungainly, awkward [➡ AGILITY OF THE BODY; 476] *Opposite*: dainty 2 *adj* **huge**, enormous, colossal, gigantic, massive, great [➡ LARGE; 1193] *Opposite*: minute

elevate 1 *v* **lift**, lift up, raise, uplift, hoist, upraise [➡ MOVE SOMETHING: UPWARD; 328] *Opposite*: lower 2 *v* **promote**, raise, advance, move up, further, exalt, improve [➡ CONFER STATUS; 458] *Opposite*: demote

See Compare and Contrast at **raise**.

elevated 1 *adj* **raised**, raised up, lifted, high, higher [➡ HEIGHT: HIGH; 1203] 2 *adj* **preeminent**, eminent, important, prominent, high, grand, superior, lofty [➡ IMPORTANT; 194] *Opposite*: lowly

elevation 1 *n* **height**, altitude, rise [➡ HEIGHT: HIGH; 1203] *Opposite*: depth 2 *n* **raise**, promotion, advancement, boost [➡ CONFER STATUS; 458] *Opposite*: demotion 3 *part of* **building** [➡ PARTS OF A BUILDING; 1095]

elevator 1 *n* [➡ STAIRS AND STORIES; 1102] 2 *part of* **building** [➡ PARTS OF A BUILDING; 1095] 3 *n* **storage plant**, silo, grain elevator [➡ STORES AND STORAGE BUILDINGS; 1088]

elevenses (*UK*) *n* **morning snack**, mid-morning snack, snack, nibble, bite [➡ MEALS AND PARTS OF MEALS; 1169]

eleventh hour *n* [➡ PROMPTNESS: LATE; 100]

eleventh-hour *adj* **ultimate**, last-minute, last-ditch, final [➡ PROMPTNESS: LATE; 100]

elf *n* **pixie**, imp, sprite, fairy, gnome, goblin, brownie, Puck, leprechaun [➡ MYTHICAL BEINGS; 789]

elfin *adj* **sylphlike**, petite, dainty, tiny, waiflike, fragile [➡ BUILD; 477]

elicit 1 *v* **provoke**, cause, produce, bring about, occasion, prompt, stimulate [➡ CAUSE TO HAPPEN; 31] 2 *v* **draw out**, draw, bring out, extract, obtain, bring forth, educe (*formal*) [➡ OBTAIN POSSESSION BY PERSUASION; 457] *Opposite*: repress

eligibility *n* **suitability**, aptness, entitlement, appropriateness, fitness, worthiness, admissibility [➡ APPROPRIATE, SUITABLE, AND ADVISABLE; 184] *Opposite*: unsuitability

eligible 1 *adj* **qualified**, entitled, suitable, fit, appropriate, adequate, worthy, authorized [➡ APPROPRIATE, SUITABLE, AND ADVISABLE; 184] *Opposite*: ineligible 2 *adj* **single**, unmarried, unattached, available [➡ MARITAL STATUS; 890]

eliminate 1 *v* **remove**, eradicate, abolish, get rid of, do away with, reject, disregard, throw out, exclude, jettison [➡ GET RID OF SOMETHING; 451] 2 *v* **destroy**, kill, exterminate, liquidate, wipe out (*informal*), waste (*slang*) [➡ KILL; 923] *Opposite*: preserve 3 *v* **defecate**, urinate, excrete, expel, pass, purge [➡ EXCRETION AND EXCRETA; 722]

elimination *n* **removal**, abolition, exclusion, rejection, eradication, dismissal [➡ REMOVE SOMETHING; 338] *Opposite*: preservation

elision *n* [➡ ASPECTS OF LANGUAGE; 682]

elite 1 *n* **best**, cream, cream of the crop, elect, crème de la crème, chosen, select few [➡ LEVELS OF EDUCATION AND SOPHISTICATION; 894] 2 *adj* **choice**, best, select, selective, leading, top, exclusive [➡ EXTRAORDINARY: AMAZING; 204] *Opposite*: run-of-the-mill

elitism *n* **exclusiveness**, exclusivity, superiority, selectivity, selectiveness, snobbery [➡ PREJUDICE; 550]

elitist *adj* **exclusive**, discriminatory, selective, superior, snobbish, highbrow, snooty (*informal*) [➡ UNFRIENDLINESS AND UNSOCIABILITY; 504] *Opposite*: egalitarian

elixir 1 *n* **medicine**, tincture, solution, tonic, preparation, mixture [➡ REMEDIES, TREATMENTS, AND OPERATIONS; 731] 2 *n* **potion**, restorative, tonic, cure-all, snake oil, pick-me-up (*informal*), draft (*dated*) [➡ DRINKS; 1187]

Elizabethan *type of* **pre-20th-century architecture** [➡ BUILDING AND ARCHITECTURE; 1076]

elk *type of* **deer or antelope** [➡ DEER AND ANTELOPES; 981]

ellipsis *n* **abbreviation**, contraction, elision, truncation, abridgment, compression [➡ ASPECTS OF LANGUAGE; 682]

elliptical 1 *adj* **oval**, ovoid, ovate, egg-shaped, elongated [➡ ROUNDED SHAPE; 1218] 2 *adj* **concise**, succinct, cryptic, indirect, oblique, ambiguous, obscure [➡ INARTICULATE, RAMBLING, AND AWKWARD; 633] *Opposite*: verbose

elm *type of* **deciduous tree** [➡ DECIDUOUS TREES; 1028]

elocution n **diction**, articulation, pronunciation, enunciation, delivery, vocalization [➡ASPECTS OF LANGUAGE; 682]

elongate v **lengthen**, draw out, extend, stretch [➡CHANGE OF SIZE: BIGGER; 392] *Opposite:* shorten

elongated adj **lengthened**, stretched out, extended, drawn-out [➡LENGTH: LONG; 1197] *Opposite:* shortened

elope v **run away**, run off, escape, decamp, abscond, flee, desert, bolt [➡RUN AWAY AND AVOID; 10] *Opposite:* return

elopement n **flight**, escape, desertion, decampment, truancy, departure [➡ENDS AND DEPARTURES; 54] *Opposite:* return

eloquence n **expressiveness**, articulateness, articulacy, persuasiveness, expression, fluency [➡ELOQUENT, TALKATIVE, AND LONG-WINDED; 632] *Opposite:* inarticulacy

eloquent adj **expressive**, fluent, articulate, well-spoken, persuasive, stirring, powerful, moving [➡ELOQUENT, TALKATIVE, AND LONG-WINDED; 632] *Opposite:* inarticulate

else 1 adj **different**, new, other, experimental [➡DIFFERENCE; 149] 2 adv **as well**, besides, in addition, other, more, further [➡MORE AND EXCESS; 124] 3 adv **other**, otherwise, differently, different, new [➡DIFFERENCE; 149]

elucidate v **explain**, clarify, explicate, expound, illuminate, interpret, spell out [➡EXPLAIN AND CLARIFY; 610] *Opposite:* confuse

elucidation n **clarification**, illumination, exposition, explanation, explication, interpretation [➡EXPLAIN AND CLARIFY; 610] *Opposite:* obfuscation

elude 1 v **escape**, flee, evade, get away, dodge, avoid, give somebody the slip, slip through the net [➡AVOID OR ESCAPE CONTACT; 418] 2 v **baffle**, confound, foil, puzzle, stump, thwart [➡CONFUSE AND BEWILDER; 571]

elusive adj **indefinable**, subtle, intangible, vague, indescribable, abstract, mysterious, obscure, tenuous [➡VAGUENESS; 243] *Opposite:* obvious

elusiveness n **indefinability**, subtlety, intangibility, vagueness, tenuousness, obscurity [➡VAGUENESS; 243] *Opposite:* accessibility

emaciated adj **thin**, wasted, skeletal, withered, shrunken, gaunt, pinched, skinny, scrawny, lean, scraggy [➡BUILD; 477] *Opposite:* plump

See Compare and Contrast at **thin**.

emaciation n **thinness**, skinniness, gauntness, scrawniness, scragginess, leanness [➡BUILD; 477] *Opposite:* plumpness

e-mail 1 n **electronic mail**, electronic message, communication, correspondence [➡THE INTERNET; 1128] 2 *type of* **telecommunications equipment** [➡TELECOMMUNICATIONS; 1130] 3 v **send**, send by e-mail, dispatch, forward, transmit, mail [➡DISPATCH AND SEND; 333]

emanate 1 v **originate**, come, stem, spring, derive, start, arise, proceed [➡GRADUALLY COME INTO EXISTENCE; 1] 2 v (*formal*) **radiate**, emit, give off, give out, send out, ooze [➡EMIT AND EMANATE; 361] *Opposite:* absorb

emancipate v **liberate**, set free, free, release, unshackle, unfetter, let go, untie [➡FREEDOM AND LIBERTY; 208] *Opposite:* enslave

emancipated adj [➡FREEDOM AND LIBERTY; 208]

emancipation n **liberation**, freedom, release, deliverance (*formal*), manumission (*formal*) [➡FREEDOM AND LIBERTY; 208]

emasculate (*formal*) v **weaken**, enfeeble, undermine, enervate, unnerve [➡UPSET, DISTRESS, AND HUMILIATE; 567] *Opposite:* empower

emasculated adj **ineffectual**, powerless, helpless, impotent, weak [➡COWARDICE AND WEAKNESS OF WILL; 508] *Opposite:* strong

embalm v **mummify**, conserve, preserve, fix, keep, protect [➡BURIAL AND PREPARATION FOR BURIAL; 929]

embankment n **ridge**, bank, mound, defenses, dam, levee [➡BARRIERS; 1113]

embargo 1 n **ban**, restriction, prohibition, restraint, stoppage, impediment, bar, block (*UK*) [➡LEGISLATIVE BODIES AND LEGISLATION; 809] *Opposite:* permission 2 v **forbid**, prohibit, ban, stop, restrict, block, impede, bar [➡MAKE IMPOSSIBLE; 276] *Opposite:* permit 3 v **confiscate**, seize, take away, expropriate, snatch, sequestrate (*UK*) [➡TAKE SOMETHING AWAY; 425]

embark v **board**, get on, go aboard [➡TRAVEL: WAYS OF TRAVELING; 320] *Opposite:* disembark

embark on v **begin**, start, engage in, attempt, tackle, initiate, enter into, undertake, set about [➡START AN ACTION; 260] *Opposite:* complete

embarrass v **humiliate**, mortify, shame, disconcert, show up, discomfit (*formal*) [➡UPSET, DISTRESS, AND HUMILIATE; 567] *Opposite:* honor

embarrassed adj **uncomfortable**, self-conscious, ill at ease, nervous, ashamed, mortified, humiliated [➡EMBARRASSMENT AND HUMILIATION; 542] *Opposite:* proud

embarrassing adj **awkward**, uncomfortable, uneasy, disconcerting, trying, excruciating, humiliating, distressing [➡EMOTIONALLY UNPLEASANT AND UPSETTING; 227]

embarrassment n **awkwardness**, blushing, humiliation, mortification, shame, discomfiture (*formal*) [➡EMBARRASSMENT AND HUMILIATION; 542] *Opposite:* pride

embassy n **consulate**, legation, mission, delegation, deputation [➡ADMINISTRATIVE OFFICES; 811]

embed v **implant**, set in, insert, drive in, push in, surround, entrench [➡POSITION SOMETHING: BETWEEN, BESIDE, OR INSIDE SOMETHING; 326]

embellish 1 v **decorate**, adorn, embroider, beautify, ornament, trim [➡IMPROVE APPEARANCE; 379] *Opposite:* simplify 2 v **exaggerate**, elaborate, overdo, aggrandize, enhance, enlarge, embroider [➡BOAST; 616] *Opposite:* understate

embellishment 1 n **decoration**, adornment, ornamentation, embroidery, beautification, trimming [➡ORNAMENTS AND DECORATIONS; 1248] 2 n **exaggeration**, elaboration, aggrandizement, enhancement, enlargement, embroidery [➡BOAST; 616] *Opposite:* understatement

ember n **cinder**, ash, coal [➡PRODUCTS OF FIRE; 1166]

embezzle v **misappropriate**, misuse, appropriate, steal, cheat, pilfer, filch, skim (*informal*), rip off (*informal*) [➡ STEAL AND ROB; 426]

See Compare and Contrast at **steal***.*

embezzlement *n* **misappropriation**, misuse, appropriation, theft, larceny, pilfering, fraud [➡ CRIMES; 817]

embezzler *n* **swindler**, fraud, thief, larcenist, pilferer, con man (*slang*), fraudster (*UK*) [➡ CRIMINALS; 821]

embitter *v* **disillusion**, poison, sour, estrange, alienate [➡ UPSET, DISTRESS, AND HUMILIATE; 567]

embittered *adj* **disillusioned**, bitter, resentful, sour, disaffected, cynical, estranged [➡ IRRITATION AND ANGER; 541] *Opposite*: mellow

emblazon 1 *v* **decorate**, adorn, embellish, ornament, illustrate, inscribe, embroider [➡ DECORATE, ADORN, AND APPLY COATINGS; 405] 2 *v* (*literary*) **extol**, celebrate, glorify, praise, honor, publicize [➡ PRAISE AND ENCOURAGE; 647]

emblem *n* **symbol**, crest, logo, sign, badge, motif, device, insignia [➡ SYMBOLS, SIGNS, AND NUMBERS; 596]

emblematic *adj* **symbolic**, representative, characteristic, illustrative, exemplary, emblematical [➡ REPRESENTATIVE; 66]

emblematical *adj* **symbolic**, representative, characteristic, illustrative, exemplary, emblematic [➡ REPRESENTATIVE; 66]

embodiment *n* **personification**, example, quintessence, incarnation, epitome, expression, symbol, representation [➡ PERFECT EXAMPLES AND EMBODIMENTS; 67]

embody *v* **exemplify**, symbolize, represent, personify, epitomize, express, stand for [➡ REPRESENT SOMETHING OR SOMEBODY; 59]

embolden *v* **encourage**, hearten, buoy up, bolster, reassure, inspire, support [➡ ENCOURAGE; 576] *Opposite*: discourage

emboss *v* **stamp**, chase, tool, engrave, mark, decorate [➡ CREATE IMAGES; 356]

embrace 1 *v* **hug**, hold, enfold, cuddle, clasp, squeeze [➡ PHYSICAL CONTACT AS COMMUNICATION; 655] 2 *v* **accept**, welcome, adopt, take up, support, take on [➡ ACCEPT POSSESSION; 450] *Opposite*: reject 3 *v* **comprise**, contain, include, incorporate, involve, encompass [➡ HOLD AND CONTAIN; 455] *Opposite*: exclude 4 *n* **hold**, hug, cuddle, clinch, clasp, squeeze, encirclement [➡ PHYSICAL CONTACT AS COMMUNICATION; 655]

embroider 1 *v* **sew**, stitch, cross-stitch, trim, decorate, adorn [➡ CRAFTS AND CARVING; 355] 2 *v* **elaborate**, embellish, exaggerate, overstate, inflate, blow up [➡ CLAIM, INSIST, AND EMPHASIZE; 614] *Opposite*: understate

embroidery *type of* **handicraft** [➡ CRAFTS AND CARVING; 355]

embroil *v* **involve**, entangle, enmesh, ensnare, entrap, catch [➡ COMBINE AND MIX; 400]

embryo *n* **beginning**, rudiment, germ, kernel, seed, nucleus, basis [➡ BEGINNINGS; 53]

embryonic *adj* **developing**, emergent, nascent, primary, early, budding [➡ FUTURE; 86] *Opposite*: advanced

emcee (*informal*) 1 *n* **MC**, master of ceremonies, host, compere (*UK*), presenter (*UK*) [➡ WORKERS IN ENTERTAINMENT AND MEDIA; 873] 2 *v* **host**, present, introduce, compere (*UK*) [➡ MAKE POSSIBLE; 275]

emend *v* **alter**, correct, amend, revise, rewrite, edit, polish [➡ CORRECT AND PUT RIGHT; 377]

emerald *type of* **gemstone** [➡ PRECIOUS STONES; 1278]

emerald green *type of* **green** [➡ COLORS; 1224]

emerge 1 *v* **come out**, appear, materialize, come into view, come into sight, surface, crop up (*informal*) [➡ APPEAR AND EMERGE; 3] *Opposite*: disappear 2 *v* **come to light**, transpire, leak out [➡ APPEAR AND EMERGE; 3] 3 *v* **arise**, appear, occur, develop, begin [➡ GRADUALLY COME INTO EXISTENCE; 1]

emergence *n* **appearance**, rise, advent, arrival, development, occurrence, beginning [➡ BEGINNINGS; 53] *Opposite*: decline

emergency 1 *n* **crisis**, disaster, tragedy, accident, danger, trauma, predicament, difficulty [➡ DIFFICULT SITUATIONS; 72] 2 *adj* **spare**, extra, backup, alternative, reserve, substitute [➡ MORE AND EXCESS; 124]

emergent *adj* **developing**, up-and-coming, embryonic, growing, nascent, budding, promising [➡ FUTURE; 86] *Opposite*: obsolescent

emery board *type of* **cosmetic tool** [➡ HAND TOOLS; 1119]

emigrant *n* **expatriate**, migrant, immigrant, settler, exile, refugee, defector, displaced person [➡ PEOPLE LIVING AWAY FROM HOME; 887] *Opposite*: native

emigrate *v* **trek**, migrate, travel, move away, leave, relocate, evacuate, defect [➡ LEAVE AND GO AWAY; 8] *Opposite*: return

emigration *n* **migration**, expatriation, exile, relocation, exodus, flight, evacuation, defection [➡ TRAVEL: JOURNEYS AND TRIPS; 318] *Opposite*: return

émigré *n* [➡ PEOPLE LIVING AWAY FROM HOME; 887]

eminence *n* **distinction**, renown, reputation, fame, importance, prominence, prestige [➡ CLASS STATUS; 889] *Opposite*: anonymity

eminent *adj* **well-known**, renowned, important, distinguished, famous, celebrated, prominent, outstanding [➡ KNOWN AND FAMOUS; 181] *Opposite*: unknown

eminently *adv* **very**, highly, extremely, exceedingly, exceptionally, signally [➡ TO A GREAT EXTENT; 132]

emir *n* **ruler**, commander, prince, leader, governor [➡ RULERS AND ARISTOCRACY; 823]

emirate *n* **principality**, country, state, nation, land, territory, region [➡ COUNTRIES AND REGIONS; 1067]

emissary *n* **representative**, envoy, ambassador, messenger, agent, delegate [➡ REPRESENTATIVES AND PATRONS; 968]

emission *n* **release**, production, discharge, emanation, secretion, radiation [➡ EMIT AND EMANATE; 361] *Opposite*: absorption

emit *v* **produce**, release, give off, give out, send out, discharge, secrete, radiate, emanate (*formal*) [➡EMIT AND EMANATE; 361] *Opposite*: absorb

Emmenthaler *type of* **hard cheese** [➡DAIRY PRODUCTS AND CHEESES; 1183]

emollient 1 *adj* **soothing**, palliative, placatory, calmative, calming [➡CALMING; 188] *Opposite*: disruptive 2 *n* **balm**, lotion, moisturizer, ointment, salve, cream [➡REMEDIES, TREATMENTS, AND OPERATIONS; 731] *Opposite*: irritant

emolument (*formal or humorous*) *n* **payment**, remuneration, reward, fee, compensation, benefit [➡INCOME; 460]

See Compare and Contrast at **wage**.

emoticon 1 *n* [➡SYMBOLS, SIGNS, AND NUMBERS; 596] 2 *type of* **computer feature** [➡COMPUTERS AND COMPUTING; 1127]

emotion *n* **feeling**, sentiment, reaction, passion, excitement, sensation [➡FEELINGS; 531]

emotional 1 *adj* **moving**, touching, poignant, affecting, bittersweet, exciting, heart-rending, weepy (*informal*) [➡EMOTIONALLY PLEASANT; 187] 2 *adj* **expressive**, open, demonstrative, emotive, sensitive, sentimental, responsive, passionate [➡ELOQUENT, TALKATIVE, AND LONG-WINDED; 632] *Opposite*: impassive

emotionally *adv* **expressively**, passionately, fervently, ardently, warmly, enthusiastically [➡ENTHUSIASTIC AND INQUISITIVE; 628] *Opposite*: coldly

emotionless *adj* **impassive**, blank, unemotional, detached, cold, unaffected [➡NEUTRALITY AND INDIFFERENCE; 553] *Opposite*: emotional

emotive *adj* **sensitive**, emotional, poignant, affecting, moving, impassioned, touching [➡EMOTIONALLY PLEASANT; 187]

empathize *v* **identify with**, understand, sympathize, commiserate, relate to, feel for, feel someone's pain (*informal*) [➡BE CONCERNED AND CARE; 581] *Opposite*: dismiss

empathy *n* **understanding**, sympathy, compassion, responsiveness, identification, fellow feeling [➡COMPASSION AND FORGIVENESS; 551] *Opposite*: indifference

emperor *n* **ruler**, tsar, sovereign, king, head of state, monarch [➡RULERS AND ARISTOCRACY; 823] *Opposite*: subject

emperor butterfly *type of* **butterfly** [➡MOTHS AND BUTTERFLIES; 1015]

emperor moth *type of* **moth** [➡MOTHS AND BUTTERFLIES; 1015]

emphasis *n* **stress**, importance, weight, accent, prominence, significance [➡IMPORTANCE AND SIGNIFICANCE; 192]

emphasize *v* **highlight**, stress, accentuate, call attention to, underline, underscore, point up, point out [➡CLAIM, INSIST, AND EMPHASIZE; 614] *Opposite*: understate

emphatic 1 *adj* **forceful**, categorical, vigorous, definite, unequivocal, insistent [➡ENTHUSIASTIC AND INQUISITIVE; 628] *Opposite*: hesitant 2 *adj* **resounding**, absolute, ringing, clear, evident, obvious, glaring [➡STRENGTH; 201] *Opposite*: ambiguous

empire *n* **territory**, realm, kingdom, domain [➡TERRITORIES AND GROUPS OF NATIONS; 1068]

Empire *type of* **pre-20th-century architecture** [➡BUILDING AND ARCHITECTURE; 1076]

empirical *adj* **experiential**, experimental, observed, pragmatic, practical, realistic, firsthand [➡TRUE AND REAL; 171] *Opposite*: theoretical

empiricism *n* **pragmatism**, experimentation, observation, practicality [➡PHILOSOPHIES AND BELIEFS; 780]

empiricist *n* **pragmatist**, observer, experimenter, realist, researcher, scientist [➡PHILOSOPHICAL AND POLITICAL THINKERS; 781] *Opposite*: theorist

employ 1 *v* **pay**, retain, use, hire, take on, engage, commission [➡WORK-RELATED ACTIVITIES; 834] *Opposite*: dismiss 2 *v* **use**, utilize, make use of, occupy, spend, put to use, devote, keep busy, exercise [➡USE; 467] *Opposite*: waste 3 *n* **employment**, service, pay, hire, engagement, occupation, work [➡WORK-RELATED ACTIVITIES; 834] *Opposite*: unemployment

See Compare and Contrast at **use**.

employed *adj* **working**, in a job, in employment, engaged, active, busy, hired, on duty, laboring, at work, in work (*UK*) [➡EMPLOYMENT STATUS; 831] *Opposite*: unemployed

employee *n* **worker**, operative, servant, wage earner, member, underling, hand, hired hand [➡SUBORDINATES AND ASSISTANTS; 966] *Opposite*: employer

employer *n* **boss**, company, manager, owner, proprietor, firm, business, establishment, organization, outfit (*informal*) [➡BOSSES AND MANAGEMENT; 965] *Opposite*: employee

employment 1 *n* **service**, pay, hire, engagement, occupation, work, employ (*archaic*) [➡WORK-RELATED ACTIVITIES; 834] *Opposite*: unemployment 2 *n* **occupation**, job, profession, trade, work [➡JOB; 833]

emporium *n* **retail store**, department store, warehouse, bazaar, corner store, market, general store, store, Aladdin's cave [➡RETAIL OUTLETS; 1083]

empower 1 *v* **authorize**, allow, sanction, permit, vest, invest, endow, enable [➡PERMIT AND ALLOW; 669] *Opposite*: forbid 2 *v* **inspire**, embolden, encourage, galvanize, rouse, energize [➡IMPROVE STRENGTH AND DURABILITY; 378] *Opposite*: discourage

empowerment 1 *n* **authorization**, enablement, enabling, permission, consent, leave (*formal*) [➡PERMIT AND ALLOW; 669] *Opposite*: embargo 2 *n* **liberation**, enfranchisement, emancipation, inspiration, encouragement, confidence-building, equality [➡FREEDOM AND LIBERTY; 208]

empress *n* **ruler**, tsarina, sovereign, queen, head of state, monarch [➡RULERS AND ARISTOCRACY; 823] *Opposite*: subject

emptiness 1 *n* **bareness**, barrenness, blankness, desolation, hollowness, sparseness, vacuum, vacancy, void, vacuity (*formal*) [➡EMPTY; 1238] *Opposite*: fullness 2 *n* **meaninglessness**, worthlessness, purposelessness, hollowness, futility, aimlessness, pointlessness [➡REDUNDANT AND USELESS; 240] *Opposite*: purpose

empty 1 *adj* **unfilled**, bare, blank, vacant, hollow, void, unoccupied, uninhabited [➡EMPTY; 1238] *Opposite*: full 2 *adj* **idle**, futile, ineffectual, unproductive, insincere [➡WASTEFUL

AND UNECONOMICAL; 246] **3** *adj* **meaningless**, purposeless, pointless, barren, hollow, futile, aimless, worthless [➡ REDUNDANT AND USELESS; 240] *Opposite*: meaningful **4** *v* **drain**, clear, pour out, discharge, clear out, evacuate, exhaust, void [➡ EMPTY AND UNLOAD; 407] *Opposite*: fill

See Compare and Contrast at **vacant, vain**.

empty-handed *adj* **unsuccessful**, frustrated, thwarted, unrewarded, defeated, lacking, wanting [➡ LACK OF POSSESSION; 445] *Opposite*: successful

empty-headed *adj* **stupid**, silly, vacuous, frivolous, inane, foolish [➡ NEGATIVE INTELLECTUAL CHARACTERISTICS; 525] *Opposite*: intelligent

emu *type of* **flightless bird** [➡ BIRDS; 997]

emulate **1** *v* **imitate**, follow, copy, mimic, ape, model yourself on, pattern yourself after [➡ PRETEND AND MIMIC; 60] **2** *v* **compete with**, vie with, contend with, rival, outdo, match [➡ COMPETE, CONTEND, AND COMBAT; 303]

See Compare and Contrast at **imitate**.

emulation *n* **imitation**, competition, rivalry, mimicry, simulation, impersonation, aping, copying, echoing [➡ REPRESENTATIONS AND GENERAL EXAMPLES; 65] *Opposite*: originality

emulator *type of* **software** [➡ COMPUTERS AND COMPUTING; 1127]

emulsify *v* **blend**, combine, beat together, stir together, mix, shake up, cream [➡ COMBINE AND MIX; 400] *Opposite*: separate

emulsion *n* **suspension**, blend, mixture, cream, mix, combination [➡ COLLECTIONS AND MIXTURES OF THINGS; 1244]

enable *v* **allow**, permit, make possible, empower, qualify, aid, assist, support, facilitate, authorize [➡ MAKE POSSIBLE; 275] *Opposite*: prevent

enact **1** *v* **pass**, ratify, endorse, decree, sanction, legislate, authorize, proclaim, ordain (*formal*) [➡ APPROVE AND CONFIRM; 646] *Opposite*: reject **2** *v* **perform**, act out, play, portray, represent, present [➡ THE PERFORMING ARTS; 904]

enactment **1** *n* **performance**, performing, acting out, portrayal, representation, presentation, acting, depiction, play-acting [➡ PERFORMANCES AND SHOWS; 42] **2** *n* **passing**, ratification, ratifying, endorsement, sanctioning, authorization, legislation [➡ APPROVE AND CONFIRM; 646]

enamel **1** *n* **coating**, varnish, veneer, glaze, lacquer, surface, top layer, gloss [➡ COVERS AND COATINGS; 1246] **2** *type of* **pottery** [➡ POTTERY; 1135] **3** *v* **coat**, paint, varnish, lacquer, cover, protect, dip, glaze [➡ DECORATE, ADORN, AND APPLY COATINGS; 405]

enamored *adj* **in love**, charmed, captivated, taken with, besotted, infatuated, sold on, loving, bewitched, amorous, entranced, attracted, fond, hooked (*slang*), smitten (*humorous or literary*), keen on (*UK*), mad on (*UK*) [➡ APPRECIATION AND GRATITUDE; 535] *Opposite*: repelled

en bloc *adv* **all together**, all at once, en masse, as one, collectively, as a whole, as a group [➡ ALL; 128] *Opposite*: separately

en brochette *type of* **food presentation** [➡ COOKING AND FOOD PREPARATION; 353]

encamp *v* **set up camp**, set up, install, base, settle, position, place [➡ INHABIT; 20]

encampment *n* **camp**, military camp, campground, base camp, army camp, bivouac, advance camp, campsite [➡ HUMAN SETTLEMENTS; 1070]

encapsulate *v* **sum up**, summarize, put in a nutshell, epitomize, condense, capture, compress [➡ EXPLAIN AND CLARIFY; 610] *Opposite*: expand

encase *v* **cover**, enclose, sheathe, coat, wrap, swathe [➡ CAUSE TO DISAPPEAR; 6] *Opposite*: uncover

encased *adj* **covered**, enclosed, sheathed, coated, wrapped, swathed [➡ CAPTIVITY AND LOSS OF FREEDOM; 248] *Opposite*: uncovered

enchant *v* **charm**, captivate, fascinate, enthrall, entrance, bewitch, hypnotize, mesmerize, beguile, enrapture (*formal*) [➡ APPEAL TO AND AROUSE INTEREST; 575] *Opposite*: disgust

enchanted *adj* **charmed**, enthralled, captivated, delighted, entranced, bewitched, hypnotized, mesmerized, beguiled, enraptured (*formal*) [➡ APPRECIATION AND GRATITUDE; 535] *Opposite*: disgusted

enchanting *adj* **charming**, captivating, enthralling, alluring, delightful, entrancing, fascinating, bewitching, hypnotizing, mesmerizing, beguiling [➡ BEAUTY AND ATTRACTIVENESS; 189] *Opposite*: disgusting

enchantingly *adv* **charmingly**, captivatingly, appealingly, mesmerizingly, beguilingly, enthrallingly, fascinatingly, beautifully, delightfully, entrancingly, bewitchingly [➡ EMOTIONALLY PLEASANT; 187] *Opposite*: disgustingly

enchantment *n* **charm**, attraction, delight, fascination, allure, magic [➡ PLEASURE, EXCITEMENT, AND ELATION; 534]

encircle *v* **surround**, enclose, ring, circle, enfold, hem in, circumscribe, encompass, girdle (*literary*) [➡ EXIST IN CLOSE PROXIMITY; 21]

enclave **1** *n* **region**, reserve, territory, commune, area, district, ghetto [➡ TERRITORIES AND GROUPS OF NATIONS; 1068] **2** *n* **group**, community, class, clique, clan (*informal*) [➡ GROUPS WITH A COMMON INTEREST; 938]

enclose **1** *v* **surround**, hem in, encircle, enfold, ring, circle, encompass [➡ EXIST IN CLOSE PROXIMITY; 21] **2** *v* **wall**, fence, hedge, pen, seal off, cordon off, confine [➡ BAR AND OBSTRUCT ACCESS; 410] **3** *v* **include**, put in, attach, insert, add, append [➡ HOLD AND CONTAIN; 455] *Opposite*: leave out

enclosed *adj* **surrounded**, bounded, hemmed in, fenced, walled, encircled, sealed off, cordoned off [➡ CAPTIVITY AND LOSS OF FREEDOM; 248] *Opposite*: open

enclosure **1** *n* **inclusion**, attachment, insertion, addition, insert, appendix [➡ PARTS OF BOOKS AND DOCUMENTS; 593] **2** *n* **field**, arena, stockade, pen, corral, paddock, compound [➡ THE COUNTRYSIDE AND OUTDOOR SPACES; 1071]

encode *v* **encrypt**, code, put into code, scramble, convert, translate, express in code [➡ CAUSE TO DISAPPEAR; 6] *Opposite*: decode

encomium (*formal*) *n* [➡ PRAISE AND ENCOURAGE; 647]

encompass *v* **include**, cover, take in, incorporate,

involve, embrace, contain, comprise, embody, hold, comprehend (*formal*) [➡ POSSESS; 444] *Opposite:* exclude

encore *n* **repeat**, extra, impromptu item, curtain call, reprise, return, repetition [➡ REPETITION; 29]

encounter 1 *v* **meet**, come across, bump into, run into, come upon, stumble upon, chance upon [➡ INITIATE AND ESTABLISH COMMUNICATION; 680] 2 *v* **face**, confront, contend with, grapple with, combat, do battle with, clash with [➡ EXPERIENCE AND ENCOUNTER; 582] *Opposite:* avoid 3 *n* **meeting**, chance meeting, happenstance [➡ CHANCE EVENTS; 36] 4 *n* **confrontation**, engagement, contest, argument, skirmish, run-in (*informal*) [➡ AGGRESSIVE EVENTS; 39]

encourage 1 *v* **inspire**, hearten, cheer, raise your spirits, buoy up, reassure, boost, embolden [➡ ENCOURAGE; 576] *Opposite:* discourage 2 *v* **support**, egg on, urge, animate, incite, inspire, motivate, spur, prompt [➡ PRAISE AND ENCOURAGE; 647] *Opposite:* discourage 3 *v* **foster**, assist, help, aid, nurture [➡ MAKE POSSIBLE; 275] *Opposite:* stifle

encouragement *n* **support**, backup, help, reassurance, inspiration, praise, cheer, backing, reinforcement, boost, lift [➡ SOURCE OF HAPPINESS, PLEASURE, OR IMPROVEMENT; 209] *Opposite:* discouragement

encouraging *adj* **hopeful**, heartening, cheering, reassuring, promising, inspiring, positive, boosting, uplifting [➡ EMOTIONALLY PLEASANT; 187] *Opposite:* discouraging

encroach *v* **intrude**, infringe, invade, trespass, make inroads into, eat into, violate, impinge (*formal*) [➡ PARTICIPATE; 292] *Opposite:* respect

encroachment *n* **infringement**, violation, advance, intrusion, invasion, impingement (*formal*) [➡ BAD BEHAVIOR OR ACTIONS; 254]

en croûte *type of* **food presentation** [➡ COOKING AND FOOD PREPARATION; 353]

encrusted *adj* **covered**, coated, thick, crusted, caked, enveloped [➡ DECORATE, ADORN, AND APPLY COATINGS; 405] *Opposite:* bare

encrypt *v* **encode**, code, put into code, scramble, translate, express in code, convert [➡ THE INTERNET; 1128] *Opposite:* decode

encryption *n* [➡ THE INTERNET; 1128]

encumber *v* **burden**, hinder, hamper, impede, get in the way, weigh down, load, saddle with, tax, inconvenience, handicap [➡ AVOID, PREVENT, LIMIT, AND CONTROL; 277] *Opposite:* facilitate

encumbrance *n* **burden**, hindrance, nuisance, impediment, handicap, tax, strain, inconvenience [➡ NUISANCES; 253] *Opposite:* help

encyclopedia *n* **reference work**, compendium, compilation, fact file, information database, data bank, almanac [➡ BOOKS AND BOOKLETS; 590]

encyclopedic *adj* **comprehensive**, full, complete, indepth, thorough, wide-ranging, all-encompassing, exhaustive, universal, broad [➡ WHOLENESS AND COMPLETENESS; 198] *Opposite:* narrow

end 1 *n* **finish**, conclusion, ending, closing stages, last part, culmination, termination, close, expiration, completion, finale, windup [➡ ENDS AND DEPARTURES; 54] *Opposite:*

beginning 2 *n* **extremity**, edge, side, tip, top, point, bottom, boundary, base, border, limit [➡ EXTREMITIES OF PHYSICAL OBJECTS; 1250] *Opposite:* middle 3 *n* **purpose**, aim, reason, objective, goal, object, intention, design [➡ INTENTIONS AND PURPOSES; 772] 4 *n* **remnant**, leftover, stub, scrap, remainder [➡ REMAINDER AND REMAINDERS; 125] *Opposite:* whole 5 *n* **death**, downfall, decline, ruin, dissolution, extinction, annihilation, demise (*formal*) [➡ DEATH AND BEREAVEMENT; 927] *Opposite:* birth 6 *n* **consequence**, outcome, upshot, result [➡ RESULTS AND OUTCOMES; 83] 7 *v* **stop**, finish, conclude, close, terminate, halt, wind down, bring to an end, put an end to, put a stop to, come to an end, end up, finish off, leave off [➡ CAUSE TO STOP; 266] *Opposite:* begin 8 *v* **result**, finish, conclude, culminate, end up, wrap up (*informal*), wind up (*informal*) [➡ CEASE TO EXIST; 22]

endanger *v* **put in danger**, jeopardize, risk, compromise, threaten, expose, imperil (*formal*) [➡ PUT AT RISK; 384] *Opposite:* protect

endangered *adj* **rare**, in danger of extinction, dying out, scarce, threatened, vanishing [➡ FEW, LITTLE, SMALL AMOUNT; 120] *Opposite:* common

endear *v* **commend**, recommend, ingratiate, make appealing, insinuate [➡ ESTABLISHING RELATIONSHIPS WITH OTHERS; 974] *Opposite:* alienate

endearing *adj* **appealing**, attractive, charming, engaging, winning, lovable [➡ EMOTIONALLY PLEASANT; 187] *Opposite:* unappealing

endearingly *adv* **charmingly**, appealingly, ingenuously, fetchingly, sweetly, adorably [➡ EMOTIONALLY PLEASANT; 187] *Opposite:* unappealingly

endearment *n* **kind word**, sweet nothing, blandishment, loving word, flattery, compliment, sweet talk (*informal*) [➡ ENDEARMENTS; 656] *Opposite:* insult

endeavor 1 *v* (*formal*) **try**, strive, attempt, make every effort, do your utmost, do your best, undertake, struggle, work hard to, labor [➡ ATTEMPT AN ACTION; 261] *Opposite:* neglect 2 *n* **attempt**, effort, try, exertion, best shot, work, hard work, industry, striving, struggle [➡ ATTEMPT AN ACTION; 261] 3 *n* **enterprise**, undertaking, bid, venture, foray, effort, exercise, work, preoccupation, vocation, job, career [➡ ACTIONS OR UNDERTAKINGS; 259]

See Compare and Contrast at **try**.

endemic *adj* **widespread**, prevalent, common, rife, rampant, pervasive [➡ PRESENT AND AVAILABLE; 11] *Opposite:* rare

ending *n* **end**, finish, finale, conclusion, culmination, windup, closing stages, epilogue, termination, completion, consummation [➡ ENDS AND DEPARTURES; 54] *Opposite:* beginning

end it all *v* **commit suicide**, kill yourself, take your own life, do away with yourself, die by your own hand, commit hara-kiri, commit suttee [➡ DIE; 922]

endive *type of* **salad vegetable** [➡ FRUIT AND VEGETABLES; 1176]

endless 1 *adj* **boundless**, infinite, limitless, without end, interminable, never-ending, ceaseless, unending, uninterrupted, unbroken, unceasing [➡ PERMANENCE: WITHOUT END; 94] *Opposite:* finite 2 *adj* **eternal**, continual, continuous, nonstop, perpetual, everlasting, constant, persistent [➡PERMANENCE: WITHOUT END; 94] *Opposite*: temporary

end on (*UK*) *adj* **end-to-end**, endwise, endways [➡ORIENTATION AND ALIGNMENT; 1223]

endorse 1 *v* **sanction**, approve, ratify, recommend, countersign, authorize, validate, certify, OK (*informal*) [➡APPROVE AND CONFIRM; 646] *Opposite*: reject **2** *v* **support**, back, advocate, subscribe to, favor, vouch for, approve, sanction, ratify [➡APPROVE AND CONFIRM; 646] *Opposite*: denounce

endorsed *adj* **permitted**, recognized, sanctioned, recommended, authorized, validated, certified, OK'ed (*informal*) [➡LEGAL AND LEGITIMATE; 815] *Opposite*: disallowed

endorsement 1 *n* **authorization**, commendation, confirmation, countersignature, ratification, seal of approval, testimonial, certification, validation, OK (*informal*) [➡APPROVE AND CONFIRM; 646] **2** *n* **backing**, support, advocacy, sanction, encouragement, approval, affirmation, ratification [➡APPROVE AND CONFIRM; 646]

endoscopy *type of* **medical procedure** [➡REMEDIES, TREATMENTS, AND OPERATIONS; 731]

endow *v* **award**, donate, give, bequeath, provide, grant, bestow (*formal*) [➡REWARD; 436]

endowment 1 *n* **donation**, gift, bequest, legacy, award, grant, benefaction [➡BEQUEATH AND REQUESTS; 432] **2** *n* **natural gift**, talent, ability, capability, aptitude, faculty, attribute [➡SKILLS, TALENTS, AND ABILITIES; 526]

end product *n* **outcome**, end result, result, upshot, product, consequence [➡RESULTS AND OUTCOMES; 83]

end result *n* **outcome**, end product, result, upshot, product, consequence [➡RESULTS AND OUTCOMES; 83]

end table *type of* **table** [➡FURNITURE; 858]

end up *v* **finish up**, finish off, transpire, turn out, result in, culminate in, wind up (*informal*), come to pass (*archaic or literary*) [➡COMPLETE AN ACTION; 263] *Opposite*: start out

endurable *adj* **tolerable**, manageable, bearable, passable, sufferable [➡ACCEPTABLE AND PASSABLE; 219] *Opposite*: intolerable

endurance 1 *n* **staying power**, strength, stamina, fortitude, resolution, durability, survival [➡STRENGTH OF WILL; 501] *Opposite*: weakness **2** *n* **stamina**, fortitude, tolerance, grit, guts (*slang*) [➡HARD-WORKING AND COMMITTED; 500] **3** *n* **persistence**, perseverance, tenacity, continuance, survival, duration [➡PERMANENCE: WITHOUT END; 94]

endure 1 *v* **bear**, tolerate, undergo, put up with, go through, stomach, withstand, sustain, stand, experience, brave, suffer [➡TOLERATE AND ENDURE; 766] *Opposite*: succumb **2** *v* **last**, continue, go on, persist, survive, persevere, prevail, live, live on, remain [➡CONTINUE TO EXIST; 17] *Opposite*: perish (*literary*)

enduring *adj* **lasting**, continuing, durable, stable, long-term, persistent, permanent [➡PERMANENCE: WITHOUT END; 94] *Opposite*: short-lived

end user *n* **user**, purchaser, shopper, consumer, client, buyer [➡BUSINESS ACTIVITIES AND PHENOMENA; 794] *Opposite*: producer

endways *adv* **endways on**, jutting out, end foremost, end

uppermost, endwise, end on (*UK*) [➡ORIENTATION AND ALIGNMENT; 1223]

endwise *adv* **endways on**, jutting out, end foremost, end uppermost, endways, end on (*UK*) [➡ORIENTATION AND ALIGNMENT; 1223]

enemy *n* **opponent**, adversary, rival, opposition, competitor, antagonist, foe (*formal*), nemesis (*literary*) [➡ENEMIES AND TORMENTORS; 969] *Opposite*: friend

energetic 1 *adj* **lively**, active, vigorous, brisk, animated, spirited, bouncy, robust, bouncing, enthusiastic, peppy (*informal*), full of beans (*informal*) [➡ENERGY AND ENTHUSIASM; 496] *Opposite*: lethargic **2** *adj* **strenuous**, vigorous, brisk, dynamic, challenging, arduous [➡PHYSICALLY UNPLEASANT; 226] *Opposite*: easy

energetically *adv* **vigorously**, actively, briskly, forcefully, dynamically, powerfully, enthusiastically [➡WITH ENTHUSIASM; 286] *Opposite*: lethargically

energize *v* **invigorate**, strengthen, boost, galvanize, electrify, motivate, animate, empower, revitalize, pep up (*informal*) [➡IMPROVE STRENGTH AND DURABILITY; 378] *Opposite*: enervate

energizing *adj* **invigorating**, stimulating, enlivening, revitalizing, reviving, vitalizing, motivating, activating, animating, galvanizing, enabling [➡PHYSICALLY PLEASANT; 186] *Opposite*: draining

energy 1 *n* **vigor**, liveliness, dynamism, vitality, drive, verve, vivacity, oomph (*informal*), get-up-and-go (*informal*), vim (*informal*), go (*informal*), élan (*literary*) [➡ENERGY AND ENTHUSIASM; 496] *Opposite*: lethargy **2** *n* **power**, force, strength, momentum, resources [➡ENERGY; 1161]

enervate *v* **weaken**, debilitate, sap your strength, drain, fatigue, exhaust, undermine, weary, wear out, deplete, enfeeble, tire, wipe out, devitalize (*formal*) [➡TIRED, ASLEEP, AND UNCONSCIOUS; 738] *Opposite*: invigorate

enervated *adj* [➡TIRED, ASLEEP, AND UNCONSCIOUS; 738]

See Compare and Contrast at **weak**.

enervating *adj* **exhausting**, weakening, enfeebling, fatiguing, draining, wearying, tiring, depleting, sapping [➡PHYSICALLY UNPLEASANT; 226] *Opposite*: invigorating

enervation *n* [➡TIRED, ASLEEP, AND UNCONSCIOUS; 738]

enfeeble *v* **weaken**, debilitate, enervate, deplete, exhaust, wear out, fatigue, sap, undermine, devitalize (*formal*), emasculate (*formal*) [➡WOUND A PERSON OR ANIMAL; 383] *Opposite*: strengthen

enfold *v* **enclose**, surround, wrap, wrap up, envelop, enwrap, clasp, hug, swathe, embrace [➡EXIST IN CLOSE PROXIMITY; 21]

enforce 1 *v* **apply**, carry out, impose, implement, make compulsory, administer [➡CARRY OUT AN ACTION; 269] **2** *v* **coerce**, oblige, compel, require, insist on, urge [➡CAUSE OR COMPEL TO ACT; 271]

enforced *adj* **compulsory**, obligatory, forced, imposed, required, prescribed [➡CAPTIVITY AND LOSS OF FREEDOM; 248] *Opposite*: optional

enforcement *n* implementation, application, execution, putting into practice, administration, prosecution [➡ CARRY OUT AN ACTION; 269]

enfranchise *v* give somebody the vote, empower, emancipate, liberate, naturalize [➡ ELECTIONS AND VOTING; 807] *Opposite*: disenfranchise

enfranchisement *n* empowerment, naturalization, suffrage, manumission (*formal*) [➡ ELECTIONS AND VOTING; 807] *Opposite*: disenfranchisement

engage 1 *v* involve, occupy, engross, absorb, take part, participate [➡ APPEAL TO AND AROUSE INTEREST; 575] 2 *v* appoint, take on, employ, hire, contract, secure, retain [➡ WORK-RELATED ACTIVITIES; 834] *Opposite*: dismiss 3 *v* battle, fight, combat, contest, encounter [➡ COMPETE, CONTEND, AND COMBAT; 303] 4 *v* hold, keep, absorb, charm, attract, draw [➡ PAY ATTENTION; 765] *Opposite*: repel 5 *v* connect, slot in, fit into place, interlock, join, mesh, hook up (*informal*) [➡ FASTEN, LINK, AND JOIN; 408] *Opposite*: disengage

engaged 1 *adj* spoken for, involved, promised, tied up, betrothed (*formal*), affianced (*formal*) [➡ MARITAL STATUS; 890] *Opposite*: unattached 2 *adj* busy, occupied, unavailable, in use, being used, employed, reserved, booked [➡ ABSENT AND UNAVAILABLE; 7] *Opposite*: free

engagement 1 *n* appointment, meeting, rendezvous, assignation, visit, date, commitment, arrangement, tryst [➡ MEETINGS AND ASSEMBLIES; 43] 2 *n* employment, job, position, situation, post, gig (*informal*) [➡ JOB; 833] 3 *n* battle, fight, encounter, conflict, action, skirmish, clash [➡ WARFARE AND WAR; 830]

See Compare and Contrast at **fight.**

engaging *adj* attractive, appealing, charming, winning, fetching, pleasing, likable, enchanting, disarming [➡ BEAUTY AND ATTRACTIVENESS; 189] *Opposite*: unattractive

engender 1 *v* produce, cause, create, bring about, stimulate, provoke, prompt [➡ ENGENDER; 350] 2 *v* (*formal*) beget, give birth to, generate, propagate, spawn [➡ REPRODUCTION AND HEREDITY; 725]

engine *n* machine, motor, turbine, piston engine, steam engine, internal combustion engine [➡ ENGINES AND HYDRAULICS; 1143]

engine

◆ *parts of an engine*
alternator, ball bearing, cam, camshaft, cog, cogwheel, coil, crank, crankshaft, cylinder, distributor, gasket, gear, gearbox, gearing, lever, manifold, oil pan, piston, pump, radiator, seal, shaft, solenoid, spark plug, starter, tappet, valve

engineer *v* bring about, cause, contrive, concoct, plot, fix up, plan, orchestrate, wangle (*informal*) [➡ CAUSE TO HAPPEN; 31]

engine room *part of* ship or boat [➡ PARTS OF A SHIP OR BOAT; 1151]

English breakfast *type of* meal [➡ MEALS AND PARTS OF MEALS; 1169]

English horn *type of* wind instrument [➡ MUSICAL INSTRUMENTS; 910]

English muffin *type of* roll or bun [➡ BREAD, FLOUR, AND BREAD PRODUCTS; 1179]

engorge *v* swell up, swell, puff up, expand, blow up [➡ CHANGE OF SIZE: BIGGER; 392] *Opposite*: deflate

engorged *adj* [➡ FULL; 1239]

engorgement *n* [➡ FULL; 1239]

engrave *v* etch, score, scratch, carve, incise, cut in, inscribe [➡ CREATE IMAGES; 356]

engraving 1 *n* etching, lithograph, print, reproduction, woodcut, picture [➡ ARTWORKS; 898] 2 *n* engraved design, carving, etching, linocut, inscription, image, design [➡ ARTWORKS; 898]

engross *v* absorb, captivate, hold your attention, hold, engage, occupy, involve, enthrall, mesmerize [➡ APPEAL TO AND AROUSE INTEREST; 575] *Opposite*: bore

engrossed *adj* absorbed, captivated, enthralled, gripped, held, immersed, occupied, engaged, riveted (*informal*) [➡ PENSIVENESS AND INTEREST; 538] *Opposite*: bored

engrossing *adj* absorbing, captivating, enthralling, gripping, interesting, fascinating, mesmerizing, riveting (*informal*) [➡ INTERESTING AND MEANINGFUL; 190] *Opposite*: uninteresting

engulf *v* swallow up, overcome, overwhelm, immerse, submerge, swamp, surround, consume, whelm (*literary*) [➡ EXIST IN CLOSE PROXIMITY; 21]

enhance *v* improve, add to, increase, boost, develop, enrich, strengthen, heighten, augment (*formal*) [➡ IMPROVE SOMETHING; 374] *Opposite*: impair

enhanced *adj* improved, greater, strengthened, heightened, boosted, higher, superior, enriched [➡ GOOD, WELL, BETTER; 183] *Opposite*: diminished

enhancement *n* improvement, augmentation, development, enrichment, heightening, boost [➡ PROGRESS AND ADVANCEMENT; 213] *Opposite*: detraction

enigma *n* paradox, conundrum, problem, mystery, puzzle, riddle, question, perplexity [➡ SECRETS AND MYSTERIES; 180]

See Compare and Contrast at **problem.**

enigmatic *adj* mysterious, inscrutable, puzzling, perplexing, unfathomable, unknowable, inexplicable [➡ SECRET AND UNKNOWN; 179] *Opposite*: straightforward

See Compare and Contrast at **obscure.**

enjoin (*formal*) *v* order, command, instruct, direct, tell, charge, bid (*archaic*) [➡ CAUSE OR COMPEL TO ACT; 271] *Opposite*: forbid

enjoy 1 *v* like, delight in, appreciate, revel in, relish, love, adore [➡ LIKE, LOVE, VALUE, AND ENJOY; 578] *Opposite*: dislike 2 *v* benefit from, have, experience, be blessed with, possess, own [➡ POSSESS; 444] *Opposite*: lack

enjoyable *adj* pleasant, agreeable, pleasing, entertaining, amusing, pleasurable, gratifying, fun [➡ EMOTIONALLY PLEASANT; 187] *Opposite*: boring

enjoyment *n* **pleasure**, delight, satisfaction, gratification, fun, amusement [➡ PLEASURE, EXCITEMENT, AND ELATION; 534] *Opposite*: boredom

enjoy yourself *v* **be amused**, be delighted, let yourself go, play, party (*informal*), whoop it up (*informal*) [➡ LEISURE AND RECREATION; 874]

enlarge **1** *v* **increase**, expand, broaden, widen, lengthen, extend, add to, amplify [➡ CHANGE OF SIZE: BIGGER; 392] *Opposite*: decrease **2** *v* **detail**, elaborate, expand, amplify, flesh out, develop [➡ CHANGE OF INTENSITY: MORE; 394] *Opposite*: compress

See Compare and Contrast at **increase**.

enlargement *n* **expansion**, extension, amplification, increase, widening, broadening, elongation, development, elaboration [➡ CHANGE OF SIZE: BIGGER; 392] *Opposite*: decrease

enlarger *type of* **photographic equipment** [➡ PHOTOGRAPHY AND PHOTOGRAPHIC EQUIPMENT; 1122]

enlighten *v* **tell**, inform, explain to, instruct, edify, educate, clarify [➡ EXPLAIN AND CLARIFY; 610]

enlightened **1** *adj* **rational**, unprejudiced, reasonable, logical, open-minded, tolerant [➡ POSITIVE INTELLECTUAL CHARACTERISTICS; 524] *Opposite*: irrational **2** *adj* **educated**, aware, informed, knowledgeable, wise [➡ KNOWLEDGE AND WISDOM; 558] *Opposite*: unaware

enlightening *adj* **informative**, instructive, edifying, helpful, educational, educative, illuminating, clarifying [➡ INTERESTING AND MEANINGFUL; 190] *Opposite*: uninformative

enlightenment *n* **explanation**, illumination, clarification, insight, information, instruction, education [➡ KNOWLEDGE AND WISDOM; 558] *Opposite*: ignorance

enlist **1** *v* **join**, join up, sign on, sign up, enroll, volunteer [➡ PARTICIPATE; 292] **2** *v* **recruit**, conscript, procure, solicit, count on, register, sign up, muster, commission [➡ GET; 420] *Opposite*: reject

enliven *v* **liven up**, cheer up, invigorate, wake up, cheer, brighten, pep up (*informal*) [➡ IMPROVE SOMETHING; 374]

en masse *adv* **all together**, as one, all at once, as a whole, as a group, en bloc, collectively [➡ ALL; 128] *Opposite*: singly

enmesh *v* **entangle**, tangle, trap, catch, catch up, ensnare, embroil, involve [➡ CAPTIVITY AND LOSS OF FREEDOM; 248] *Opposite*: disentangle

enmity *n* **hostility**, hate, hatred, ill will, animosity, antagonism, antipathy, rancor [➡ ANTAGONISM; 552] *Opposite*: goodwill

ennui *n* **boredom**, languor, world-weariness, tedium, weariness, dissatisfaction [➡ NEUTRALITY AND INDIFFERENCE; 553] *Opposite*: excitement

enormity **1** *n* **atrociousness**, horror, monstrousness, wickedness, heinousness, nefariousness, flagrancy [➡ BAD BEHAVIOR OR ACTIONS; 254] *Opposite*: goodness **2** *n* **atrocity**, abomination, outrage, evil, horror, crime [➡ BAD BEHAVIOR OR ACTIONS;

254] *Opposite*: kindness **3** *n* **size**, extent, vastness, scale, immensity, hugeness, magnitude [➡ LARGE; 1193]

enormous *adj* **huge**, vast, massive, giant, mammoth, gigantic, colossal, astronomic, gargantuan, titanic, immense [➡ LARGE; 1193] *Opposite*: tiny

enormously *adv* **extremely**, very, a lot, a great deal, hugely, immensely, vastly, colossally, massively (*informal*) [➡ TO A GREAT EXTENT; 132] *Opposite*: slightly

enough *adj* **sufficient**, adequate, ample, plenty, abundant, plentiful [➡ ENOUGH AND SUFFICIENT; 131] *Opposite*: insufficient

en papillote *type of* **food presentation** [➡ COOKING AND FOOD PREPARATION; 353]

enquire *v* **ask**, find out, query, investigate, probe, search, question [➡ ASK PEOPLE QUESTIONS; 666] *Opposite*: reply

enrage *v* **infuriate**, anger, make your blood boil, madden, incense [➡ ANGER AND ANNOY; 569] *Opposite*: calm

enraged *adj* **furious**, infuriated, angry, beside yourself, fuming, incensed, hopping mad (*informal*) [➡ IRRITATION AND ANGER; 541] *Opposite*: calm

enrapture (*formal*) *v* **entrance**, delight, captivate, enchant, mesmerize, thrill, enthrall, transport [➡ SURPRISE AND IMPRESS; 574] *Opposite*: bore

enraptured (*formal*) *adj* [➡ PLEASURE, EXCITEMENT, AND ELATION; 534]

enrich *v* **augment** (*formal*), supplement, improve, enhance, deepen, develop [➡ IMPROVE SOMETHING; 374] *Opposite*: diminish

enrichment *n* **enhancement**, improvement, augmentation, amelioration, upgrading, development, supplementation [➡ IMPROVE SOMETHING; 374] *Opposite*: diminution

enroll *v* **register**, sign up, put your name down, join, join up, sign on, volunteer [➡ PARTICIPATE; 292]

enrollment *n* **registration**, matriculation, signing up, admission, acceptance, membership [➡ TEACHING; 839] *Opposite*: resignation

en route *adv* **on the way**, while traveling, on the journey, on the road, heading for, in transit [➡ TRAVEL: WAYS OF TRAVELING; 320]

ensconce (*archaic or literary*) *v* **entrench**, hide, hide away, conceal, screen, shield [➡ POSITION SOMETHING; 325] *Opposite*: expose

ensemble **1** *n* **band**, company, troupe, group, corps, assemblage, outfit (*informal*) [➡ MUSICIANS AND SINGERS; 908] **2** *n* **suit**, costume, coordinates, outfit (*informal*), getup (*informal*), rigout (*UK*) [➡ CLOTHES AND ACCESSORIES; 864] **3** *n* **collection**, assembly, aggregate, set, combination, composite, amalgamation [➡ COLLECTIONS AND MIXTURES OF THINGS; 1244] **4** *adj* **collaborative**, collective, joint, group, cooperative, communal [➡ RECIPROCITY AND INTERDEPENDENCE; 147] *Opposite*: solo

enshrine *v* **protect**, treasure, hallow, preserve, cherish [➡ LIKE, LOVE, VALUE, AND ENJOY; 578]

enshroud *v* **obscure**, hide, mask, shield, cover, shroud [➡ CAUSE TO DISAPPEAR; 6] *Opposite*: expose

ensign *n* **flag**, pennant, colors, banner, standard, emblem, badge [➡ SYMBOLS, SIGNS, AND NUMBERS; 596]

enslave *v* **subjugate**, dominate, subject, bind, yoke, enchain (*formal or literary*), enthrall (*literary*) [➡ CAPTIVITY AND LOSS OF FREEDOM; 248] *Opposite:* liberate

ensnare *v* **entangle**, tangle, enmesh, catch up, catch, trap, snare, entrap [➡ CAPTIVITY AND LOSS OF FREEDOM; 248] *Opposite:* set free

ensue 1 *v* **follow**, succeed, follow on, result, arise, supervene (*formal*) [➡ HAPPEN; 27] *Opposite:* precede 2 *v* **result**, follow, proceed, arise, derive, develop, stem [➡ GRADUALLY COME INTO EXISTENCE; 1] *Opposite:* precede

ensuing *adj* **resultant**, subsequent, succeeding, resulting, following, later [➡ AFTER, LAST, AND FOLLOWING; 165] *Opposite:* preceding

ensure *v* **make sure**, make certain, safeguard, guarantee, confirm, certify, warrant [➡ CAUSE TO HAPPEN; 31]

entail *v* **involve**, require, demand, need, necessitate [➡ CAUSE TO HAPPEN; 31]

entangle *v* **tangle**, snare, ensnare, catch up, enmesh, entrap, trap, catch, interweave [➡ CAPTIVITY AND LOSS OF FREEDOM; 248] *Opposite:* free

entanglement *n* **predicament**, tangle, muddle, morass, mess, imbroglio [➡ DIFFICULT SITUATIONS; 72]

entente *n* [➡ HARMONY; 155]

enter 1 *v* **go in**, go into, come in, come into, cross the threshold, pass into, pass in, move into, move in, arrive in, arrive, flow into [➡ ARRIVE; 12] *Opposite:* leave 2 *v* **input**, insert, put in, record, register, note, put down, type, write down, write, key in, key [➡ RECORD SOMETHING; 371] *Opposite:* delete 3 *v* **submit**, put in, propose, hand in, state, put forward, announce [➡ SUGGEST, HINT, AND COMMENT; 612] 4 *v* **compete**, participate, take part, take up, try, contest, play [➡ COMPETE, CONTEND, AND COMBAT; 303] 5 *v* **join**, sign up, agree to, enlist, enroll, register [➡ PARTICIPATE; 292] 6 *v* **walk on**, come on, appear, make an entrance [➡ ARRIVE; 12] *Opposite:* exit

enter into *v* **become involved in**, take part in, join in, throw yourself into, participate in, take up, undertake [➡ PARTICIPATE; 292] *Opposite:* withdraw

enter on *v* **start**, begin, enter upon, move into, start out on, embark upon, commence, undertake [➡ START AN ACTION; 260] *Opposite:* finish

enterprise 1 *n* **initiative**, innovativeness, creativity, inventiveness, originality, readiness, boldness, willingness, get-up-and-go (*informal*) [➡ POSITIVE INTELLECTUAL CHARACTERISTICS; 524] *Opposite:* apathy 2 *n* **venture**, project, activity, endeavor, undertaking, scheme [➡ ACTIONS OR UNDERTAKINGS; 259] 3 *n* **business**, company, firm, corporation, organization, operation, establishment [➡ BUSINESS ENTERPRISES AND RELATED BODIES; 792]

enterprise zone *type of* **industrial site** [➡ INDUSTRIAL BUILDINGS; 1087]

enterprising *adj* **innovative**, inventive, imaginative, resourceful, adventurous, ingenious, creative, entrepreneurial, original, bold, go-ahead (*informal*), intrepid

(*literary or humorous*) [➡ POSITIVE INTELLECTUAL CHARACTERISTICS; 524] *Opposite:* unadventurous

entertain 1 *v* **amuse**, divert, distract, regale, interest, tickle [➡ PLEASE AND AMUSE; 572] *Opposite:* bore 2 *v* **accommodate**, wine and dine, feed, invite, regale, treat [➡ ENTERTAINMENT; 872] *Opposite:* visit 3 *v* **consider**, think about, give thought to, contemplate, think over, ponder [➡ THINK AND REFLECT; 743] *Opposite:* reject

entertainer *n* **performer**, artiste, artist [➡ WORKERS IN ENTERTAINMENT AND MEDIA; 873]

entertainer

◆ *types of entertainers*
actor, actress, clown, comedian, comic, conjurer, contortionist, costar, dancer, DJ, double act, impressionist, juggler, magician, mime, movie star, musician, rapper, singer, stand-up comedian, stooge, straight man, street entertainer, street musician, street performer, trapeze artist, ventriloquist

entertaining *adj* **amusing**, enjoyable, diverting, pleasurable, charming, hilarious, humorous, engaging, compelling [➡ EMOTIONALLY PLEASANT; 187] *Opposite:* dull

entertainingly *adv* **amusingly**, interestingly, humorously, engagingly, enjoyably, compellingly [➡ EMOTIONALLY PLEASANT; 187] *Opposite:* boringly

entertainment 1 *n* **entertaining**, performing, acting, show business, theater, show biz (*informal*) [➡ ENTERTAINMENT; 872] 2 *n* **amusement**, fun, diversion, distraction, enjoyment, recreation [➡ ENTERTAINMENT; 872] *Opposite:* boredom 3 *n* **show**, production, concert, attraction, performance, cabaret [➡ PERFORMANCES AND SHOWS; 42]

enter upon *v* **start**, begin, enter on, move into, start out on, embark upon, undertake [➡ START AN ACTION; 260] *Opposite:* finish

enthrall *v* **captivate**, charm, mesmerize, beguile, fascinate, enchant, engross, grip, entrance, rivet (*informal*) [➡ APPEAL TO AND AROUSE INTEREST; 575] *Opposite:* bored

enthralled *adj* **fascinated**, engrossed, gripped, captivated, absorbed, charmed, entranced, enchanted, beguiled [➡ PENSIVENESS AND INTEREST; 538] *Opposite:* bored

enthralling *adj* **fascinating**, beguiling, engrossing, gripping, captivating, absorbing, enchanting, alluring, riveting (*informal*) [➡ INTERESTING AND MEANINGFUL; 190] *Opposite:* boring

enthrone (*formal*) *v* **crown**, instate, ordain, swear in, consecrate, install, inaugurate [➡ CONFER STATUS; 458] *Opposite:* dethrone

enthuse 1 *v* **stimulate**, galvanize, excite, spur to action, impassion, stir up, whip up, fire [➡ APPEAL TO AND AROUSE INTEREST; 575] *Opposite:* bore 2 *v* **be enthusiastic**, be passionate, talk excitedly, show enthusiasm, rave, be effusive, gush, effuse (*formal*), wax lyrical (*literary*) [➡ PRAISE AND ENCOURAGE; 647]

enthused *adj* [➡ PLEASURE, EXCITEMENT, AND ELATION; 534]

enthusiasm 1 *n* **eagerness**, interest, passion, fervor, gusto, zeal, zest, keenness, excitement, fire [➡ POSITIVE IMPATIENCE, ENTHUSIASM, AND ALERTNESS; 537] *Opposite:* apathy **2** *n* **craze**, interest, hobby, passion, mania, pastime, pursuit, fad, fashion, leisure pursuit [➡ FADS, FETISHES, AND IDOLATRY; 555]

enthusiast *n* **fan**, fanatic, buff, aficionado, aficionada, devotee, supporter, nut (*informal*), wonk (*informal*), freak (*informal*) [➡ DEVOTEES AND ADDICTED PEOPLE; 556]

enthusiastic *adj* **eager**, keen, passionate, fervent, excited, wholehearted, animated, aflame, afire [➡ APPRECIATION AND GRATITUDE; 535] *Opposite:* apathetic

enthusiastically *adv* **keenly**, eagerly, passionately, fervently, excitedly, wholeheartedly [➡ WITH ENTHUSIASM; 286] *Opposite:* apathetically

entice *v* **lure**, tempt, induce, seduce, bribe, cajole, invite, attract [➡ APPEAL TO AND AROUSE INTEREST; 575] *Opposite:* put off

enticement *n* **lure**, temptation, incentive, inducement, bribery, bribe, draw, attraction, invitation, bait [➡ CAUSATION; 168] *Opposite:* deterrent

enticing *adj* **tempting**, alluring, inviting, attractive, appealing, tantalizing, desirable [➡ BEAUTY AND ATTRACTIVENESS; 189] *Opposite:* uninviting

enticingly *adv* **temptingly**, invitingly, alluringly, appealingly, tantalizingly, desirably, mouthwateringly, attractively [➡ BEAUTY AND ATTRACTIVENESS; 189] *Opposite:* uninvitingly

entire **1** *adj* **whole**, complete, full, total, perfect, all-inclusive [➡ WHOLENESS AND COMPLETENESS; 198] *Opposite:* part **2** *adj* **absolute**, complete, total, thorough, unqualified, unmitigated [➡ ABSOLUTE AND ABSOLUTELY; 133] *Opposite:* partial

entirety *n* **sum**, whole, wholeness, totality, entireness, total, completeness, fullness [➡ WHOLENESS AND COMPLETENESS; 198] *Opposite:* part

entitle **1** *v* **enable**, allow, permit, sanction, authorize, warrant [➡ PERMIT AND ALLOW; 669] *Opposite:* debar **2** *v* **title**, call, name, dub, label, designate [➡ NAME AND DESCRIBE; 665]

entitled **1** *adj* **permitted**, in your own right, eligible, allowed, enabled, authorized [➡ PERMIT AND ALLOW; 669] *Opposite:* barred **2** *adj* **titled**, called, named, dubbed, labeled, designated [➡ NAME AND DESCRIBE; 665]

entitlement *n* **right**, power, prerogative, privilege, claim, title [➡ POSSESS; 444]

entity *n* **object**, thing, article, being, unit, individual [➡ PHYSICAL OBJECTS; 1243] *Opposite:* nonentity

entourage *n* **staff**, associates, following, followers, train, backup, support, retinue, hangers-on, groupies (*informal*) [➡ FRIENDS AND ACQUAINTANCES; 936]

entrails *n* **guts**, intestines, bowels, viscera, innards (*informal*), insides (*informal*) [➡ CENTRAL PARTS OF PHYSICAL OBJECTS; 1251]

entrance **1** *n* **entry**, way in, doorway, door, opening, entrance hall, foyer, lobby, access [➡ DOORS AND ACCESS POINTS; 1101] *Opposite:* exit **2** *n* **arrival**, entry, appearance, entering, ingress (*formal*) [➡ ARRIVAL; 13] *Opposite:* departure **3** *n* **admission**, entry, ticket, pass, admittance, access [➡ PERMIT AND ALLOW; 669] **4** *v* **captivate**, engross, fascinate, charm, delight, spellbind, enthrall, mesmerize, enchant, rivet (*informal*) [➡ SURPRISE AND IMPRESS; 574] *Opposite:* bore

entranced *adj* [➡ PENSIVENESS AND INTEREST; 538]

entrance hall **1** *n* **lobby**, foyer, reception area, hallway, vestibule, reception [➡ DOORS AND ACCESS POINTS; 1101] **2** *type of room in public buildings* [➡ TYPES OF ROOMS; 1097]

entrancing *adj* **captivating**, enchanting, enthralling, spellbinding, fascinating, delightful, mesmerizing, riveting (*informal*) [➡ INTERESTING AND MEANINGFUL; 190] *Opposite:* boring

entrant *n* **applicant**, contestant, candidate, participant, competitor, player, runner, contender [➡ COMPETITORS; 41]

See Compare and Contrast at **candidate.**

entrap *v* **trick**, deceive, ensnare, trap, lure, catch, capture, entangle, decoy, inveigle [➡ DECEPTION AND LIES; 660]

entrapment *n* **trap**, frame, snare, trick, setup (*informal*), sting (*slang*), frame-up (*slang*) [➡ CAPTIVITY AND LOSS OF FREEDOM; 248]

entreat *v* **plead**, beg, pray, ask, request, implore (*formal*), beseech (*literary*) [➡ REQUEST AND DEMAND; 663] *Opposite:* demand

entreaty *n* **appeal**, plea, petition, request, supplication (*formal*), suit (*formal*) [➡ REQUEST AND DEMAND; 663] *Opposite:* demand

entrée **1** *n* **appetizer**, starter, hors d'oeuvre, first course, antipasto [➡ MEALS AND PARTS OF MEALS; 1169] **2** *n* **introduction**, induction, entrance, access, admittance [➡ BEGINNINGS; 53] *Opposite:* exclusion

entrench *v* **embed**, ensconce, ingrain, root, establish, cement [➡ MOVE PAST, INTO, OR THROUGH SOMETHING; 331]

entre nous (*formal*) *adv* **between ourselves**, between you and me, in confidence, between you, me, and the bedpost, confidentially, privately, between you, me, and the gatepost (*UK*) [➡ FOREIGN WORDS AND PHRASES; 672] *Opposite:* publicly

entrepreneur *n* **businessperson**, trader, organizer, impresario, financier [➡ BUSINESS PEOPLE; 793]

entrepreneurial *adj* **business**, small-business, commercial, risk-taking, empire-building, tactical, innovative, groundbreaking [➡ BUSINESS; 791]

entresol *n* [➡ STAIRS AND STORIES; 1102]

entrust *v* **trust**, commend, delegate, assign, deliver, hand over [➡ GIVE AND PROVIDE; 430] *Opposite:* deprive

entry **1** *n* **admission**, entrance, access, pass, ticket, admittance [➡ ARRIVAL; 13] **2** *n* **record**, item, note, account, statement, minute [➡ RECORDS; 585] **3** *n* **entrance**, doorway, door, opening, access, ingress (*formal*) [➡ DOORS AND ACCESS POINTS; 1101] *Opposite:* exit **4** *n* **application**, submission, attempt, effort, go, try [➡ REQUEST AND DEMAND; 663] *Opposite:* withdrawal

entwine *v* **tangle**, entangle, twist, interweave, interlace, interlink, enmesh [➡ FASTEN, LINK, AND JOIN; 408] *Opposite:* undo

enumerate **1** *v* **detail**, list, spell out, itemize, catalog, name, specify [➡ NAME AND DESCRIBE; 665] **2** *v* **count**, number, tally, compute, reckon, total [➡ ASSESS QUANTITY; 757] *Opposite:* estimate

enunciate **1** *v* **pronounce**, articulate, voice, utter, speak, say, vocalize [➡ UTTER AND PRONOUNCE; 608] *Opposite*: mumble **2** *v* **express**, spell out, detail, state, put forward, voice, clarify [➡ EXPLAIN AND CLARIFY; 610] *Opposite*: suppress

enunciation **1** *n* **pronunciation**, articulation, diction, speech [➡ ASPECTS OF LANGUAGE; 682] **2** *n* **expression**, assertion, declaration, proclamation, clarification [➡ INFORM, ANNOUNCE, AND ISSUE; 611] *Opposite*: suppression

envelop *v* **enclose**, encircle, encase, engulf, swathe, shroud, cloak, wrap, cover, surround [➡ EXIST IN CLOSE PROXIMITY; 21] *Opposite*: unwrap

envelope *n* **cover**, wrapper, covering, wrapping, casing, packet [➡ COVERS AND COATINGS; 1246]

enviable *adj* **desirable**, fortunate, lucky, privileged, to die for, happy [➡ POPULAR AND WANTED; 220] *Opposite*: unenviable

envious *adj* **jealous**, green with envy, resentful, spiteful, covetous, green, grudging, begrudging [➡ ENVY AND JEALOUSY; 548]

enviousness *n* [➡ ENVY AND JEALOUSY; 548]

environment **1** *n* **nature**, ecosystem, earth, world, natural world, habitat [➡ NATURE AND THE ENVIRONMENT; 1038] **2** *n* **surroundings**, setting, situation, atmosphere, scene, ambiance, milieu, environs, location [➡ PLACE; 1065] **3** *n* **background**, upbringing, circumstances, conditions, situation, milieu [➡ SITUATIONS; 71]

environmental *adj* **ecological**, conservation, conservational, environmentally friendly, ecofriendly, green [➡ ECONOMICAL AND RESOURCEFUL; 207]

environmentalist *n* **ecologist**, conservationist, preservationist, green [➡ PHILOSOPHICAL AND POLITICAL THINKERS; 781]

environs *n* **vicinity**, neighborhood, surroundings, locality, environment [➡ PLACE; 1065]

envisage (*formal*) *v* **imagine**, visualize, envision, foresee, predict, see, picture [➡ PREDICT AND ANTICIPATE; 750]

envision *v* **imagine**, envisage, foresee, predict, visualize, see, picture [➡ PREDICT AND ANTICIPATE; 750]

envoy *n* **representative**, diplomat, attaché, emissary, herald, messenger, ambassador, consul, legate [➡ REPRESENTATIVES AND PATRONS; 968]

envy **1** *n* **jealousy**, greed, bitterness, resentment, spite [➡ ENVY AND JEALOUSY; 548] *Opposite*: goodwill **2** *v* **covet**, desire, resent, begrudge, grudge [➡ DESIRE AND WANT; 579]

Eocene *type of* **epoch** [➡ EPOCHS AND ERAS; 89]

eon *n* **long time**, eternity, years, ages (*informal*), forever (*informal*) [➡ LONG PERIODS OF TIME; 92] *Opposite*: moment

epaulet *n* **decoration**, insignia, strap, chevron [➡ ORNAMENTS AND DECORATIONS; 1248]

ephemeral *adj* **short-lived**, passing, fleeting, brief, momentary, temporary, transitory, transient, evanescent [➡ FINITENESS, VARIABILITY, AND TRANSIENCE; 96] *Opposite*: lasting

See Compare and Contrast at **temporary**.

ephemeralness *n* **brevity**, transitoriness, transience, fleetingness, temporariness, evanescence, moment-

ariness [➡ FINITENESS, VARIABILITY, AND TRANSIENCE; 96] *Opposite*: timelessness

epic **1** *n* **classic**, historical fiction, costume drama, period piece, extravaganza, blockbuster (*informal*) [➡ FICTION AND DRAMA; 913] **2** *adj* **marathon**, heroic, classic, larger-than-life, impressive, ambitious, grand [➡ EXTRAORDINARY: AMAZING; 204] *Opposite*: minuscule

epicene *adj* [➡ GENDER IDENTITY AND SEXUALITY; 932]

epicenter *n* [➡ CENTRAL PARTS OF PHYSICAL OBJECTS; 1251]

epicure *n* **gourmet**, gastronome, connoisseur, epicurean, bon vivant, foodie (*informal*) [➡ EATERS, GOURMETS, AND DIETARY CHOICES; 714]

epicurean **1** *adj* **hedonistic**, decadent, pleasure-seeking, pleasure-loving, sensualist [➡ PLEASURE-SEEKING AND EXCESS; 885] *Opposite*: spartan **2** *adj* **gastronomic**, gourmet, connoisseur, gourmand, decadent, foodie (*informal*) [➡ PLEASURE-SEEKING AND EXCESS; 885] *Opposite*: ascetic **3** *see* **epicure**

epicureanism *n* [➡ PLEASURE-SEEKING AND EXCESS; 885]

epidemic **1** *n* **plague**, outbreak, endemic, scourge, contagion, pandemic [➡ SICKNESS; 729] **2** *n* **spate**, wave, rash, craze, increase, rise [➡ SUDDEN EVENTS; 52] *Opposite*: decrease **3** *adj* **widespread**, wide-ranging, prevalent, rampant, sweeping, rife, endemic [➡ PRESENT AND AVAILABLE; 11] *Opposite*: restricted

See Compare and Contrast at **widespread**.

epidermis *n* **skin**, hide, flesh, cuticle, integument, layer [➡ THE SKIN; 720]

epigram *n* **witticism**, saying, axiom, ditty, rhyme, quip [➡ FIGURES OF SPEECH; 673]

epilogue *n* **conclusion**, coda, speech, monologue [➡ PARTS OF BOOKS AND DOCUMENTS; 593] *Opposite*: prologue

episode **1** *n* **incident**, affair, chapter, event, occurrence, occasion, scene, experience, period [➡ EVENTS AND OCCURRENCES; 35] **2** *n* **installment**, chapter, part, section, scene [➡ PARTS OF BOOKS AND DOCUMENTS; 593] **3** *n* **occurrence**, incidence, attack, outbreak, bout, spell [➡ EVENTS AND OCCURRENCES; 35]

episodic **1** *adj* **sporadic**, intermittent, periodic, discontinuous, intervallic, occasional, irregular [➡ FINITENESS, VARIABILITY, AND TRANSIENCE; 96] *Opposite*: regular **2** *adj* **serialized**, discontinuous, divided [➡ NEVER AND INFREQUENCY; 97]

epistle (*formal*) *n* **letter**, missive, communication, message, communiqué, dispatch [➡ LETTERS AND WRITTEN MESSAGES; 584]

epitaph *n* **inscription**, legend, caption, epigraph [➡ BURIAL AND PREPARATION FOR BURIAL; 929]

epithet *n* **nickname**, description, label, sobriquet, appellation (*formal*), handle (*slang*), moniker (*slang*) [➡ NAME AND DESCRIBE; 665]

epitome *n* **essence**, personification, embodiment, model, quintessence, archetype, height [➡ PERFECT EXAMPLES AND EMBODIMENTS; 67] *Opposite*: antithesis

epitomize *v* **typify**, characterize, exemplify, personify, embody, symbolize [➡ REPRESENT SOMETHING OR SOMEBODY; 59]

epoch *n* **era**, age, time, period, eon, date [➡ EPOCHS AND ERAS; 89]

epoch-making *adj* **historic**, crucial, important, momentous, earthshattering, pivotal, key, consequential [➡ IMPORTANT; 194] *Opposite*: insignificant

epoxide *type of* **plastic** [➡ PLASTICS; 1134]

equable *adj* **composed**, calm, easygoing, unflappable, placid, level-headed, phlegmatic, serene, tranquil, dispassionate, easy [➡ CONFIDENCE AND COMPOSURE; 499] *Opposite*: jumpy

equably *adv* **calmly**, evenly, serenely, tranquilly, coolly, composedly, dispassionately, placidly, level-headedly, steadily [➡ CONFIDENCE AND COMPOSURE; 499] *Opposite*: jumpily

equal 1 *adj* **identical**, equivalent, like, alike, the same, one and the same [➡ SAMENESS; 150] *Opposite*: unequal **2** *adj* **on a par**, even, uniform, level, on a plane, on level pegging (*UK*) [➡ EQUALITY; 154] *Opposite*: unequal **3** *n* **match**, equivalent, counterpart, parallel, peer, compeer (*formal*) [➡ EQUALITY; 154] **4** *v* **come to**, amount to, equate, make, correspond, total [➡ AMOUNT TO AND EQUAL; 70] **5** *v* **match**, rival, keep pace with, copy, meet, approximate [➡ EQUALITY; 154]

equality *n* **parity**, fairness, equivalence, likeness, equal opportunity, impartiality, egalitarianism [➡ EQUALITY; 154] *Opposite*: inequality

equalize *v* **match**, level, even out, align, line up, balance [➡ EQUALITY; 154] *Opposite*: differentiate

equally 1 *adv* **similarly**, likewise, in the same way, by the same token, alike, correspondingly, so [➡ ALSO; 138] *Opposite*: conversely **2** *adv* **evenly**, uniformly, regularly, equivalently, alike, proportionately, correspondingly [➡ EQUALITY; 154] *Opposite*: unequally

equal to *adj* **up to**, able to, capable of, fit for, ready for [➡ TALENTED AND SKILLFUL; 527]

equanimity *n* **composure**, calmness, level-headedness, equability, self-control, poise [➡ COOL AND CALM; 536] *Opposite*: volatility

equate *v* **associate**, liken, link, connect, parallel, compare [➡ CREATING CONNECTIONS; 144] *Opposite*: contrast

equation *n* **reckoning**, calculation, comparison, equivalence, equality, balance [➡ MATH; 597]

equestrian *adj* **riding**, equine, show jumping, horsy, horseracing, horse-riding (*UK*) [➡ HORSES; 985]

equidistant *adj* **halfway between**, midway between, between, in between, intermediate, middle [➡ RELATIVE LOCATION; 161]

equilateral *adj* **symmetrical**, regular, square, rectangular, triangular [➡ ANGULAR SHAPE; 1217]

equilibrium *n* **balance**, symmetry, steadiness, stability, evenness, equipoise (*formal*) [➡ HARMONY; 155] *Opposite*: imbalance

equine *adj* [➡ HORSES; 985]

equinox *n* [➡ TIMES OF YEAR; 88]

equip 1 *v* **provide**, endow, fit out, outfit, arm, set up, supply, stock, furnish (*formal*), kit out (*UK*) [➡ EQUIP AND SUPPLY; 435] **2** *v* **prepare**, train, school, qualify, ground [➡ INSTRUCT AND TEACH; 609]

equipment *n* **tools**, apparatus, tackle, utensils, paraphernalia, kit, gear (*informal*) [➡ DEVICES; 1115]

equitable (*formal*) *adj* **fair**, evenhanded, reasonable, justifiable, rightful, impartial, just, unbiased [➡ EQUALITY; 154] *Opposite*: unfair

equity *n* **fairness**, impartiality, justice, evenhandedness, fair play, justness, parity [➡ EQUALITY; 154] *Opposite*: injustice

equivalence *n* **correspondence**, sameness, likeness, similarity, equality, uniformity [➡ EQUALITY; 154] *Opposite*: difference

equivalent 1 *adj* **equal**, corresponding, correspondent, alike, same, comparable, similar, like [➡ EQUALITY; 154] *Opposite*: different **2** *n* **counterpart**, equal, opposite number, parallel, twin, peer [➡ EQUALITY; 154]

equivocal *adj* **vague**, ambiguous, confusing, ambivalent, misleading, oblique, unclear, shifty, evasive [➡ RETICENT AND UNFORTHCOMING; 631] *Opposite*: unambiguous

equivocate *v* **prevaricate**, beat around the bush, vacillate, be evasive, quibble, fudge (*informal*) [➡ WITHHOLD INFORMATION; 687] *Opposite*: speak your mind

equivocation *n* **vagueness**, indirectness, ambiguity, prevarication, weasel words (*informal*) [➡ WITHHOLD INFORMATION; 687] *Opposite*: directness

Equuleus *type of* **constellation** [➡ HEAVENLY BODIES; 1061]

era *n* **age**, epoch, eon, time, period, years, date [➡ EPOCHS AND ERAS; 89]

eradicate *v* **eliminate**, get rid of, destroy, exterminate, do away with, stamp out, remove, wipe out (*informal*) [➡ GET RID OF SOMETHING; 451] *Opposite*: introduce

eradication *n* **abolition**, purge, annihilation, extermination, obliteration, extinction [➡ ENDS AND DEPARTURES; 54] *Opposite*: introduction

erase *v* **rub out**, remove, delete, expunge, obliterate, wipe out (*informal*) [➡ DELETE AND ERASE; 339]

erasure *n* **removal**, destruction, eradication, elimination, deletion, obliteration [➡ REMOVE SOMETHING; 338]

erect 1 *v* **build**, construct, assemble, set up, raise, put up [➡ BUILD; 352] *Opposite*: demolish **2** *v* **create**, set up, found, initiate, establish, institute [➡ INSTITUTE AND INAUGURATE; 348] **3** *adj* **straight**, upright, vertical, rigid, stiff, perpendicular [➡ ORIENTATION AND ALIGNMENT; 1223] *Opposite*: prone

erection 1 *n* (*formal*) **building**, structure, construction [➡ BUILDING AND ARCHITECTURE; 1076] **2** *n* **building**, construction, assembly, creation, formation [➡ CREATION; 346]

eremite (*literary*) *n* [➡ SOLITARY PEOPLE AND MISFITS; 942]

Eridanus *type of* **constellation** [➡ HEAVENLY BODIES; 1061]

erode *v* **wear away**, wear down, corrode, eat away, eat into, grind down [➡ CHANGE OF SIZE: SMALLER; 393]

eroded *adj* **weathered**, worn, weather-beaten, corroded [➡ IN BAD REPAIR; 1234]

erosion *n* **corrosion**, attrition, destruction, loss [➡ EROSION AND WEATHERING; 1055]

erotic *adj* **sexy**, sensual, stimulating, suggestive, amatory, erogenous, hot (*slang*) [➡ PHYSICALLY PLEASANT; 186] *Opposite*: off-putting

err *v* **go wrong**, blunder, slip up (*informal*), go astray, stumble, get something wrong [➡ MESS UP AND MAKE MISTAKES; 472]

errand *n* **task**, duty, run, chore, job, mission [➡ WORK IN GENERAL; 297]

errant *adj* **wayward**, sinful, naughty, misbehaving, delinquent, rowdy [➡ MORALLY BAD OR IMPROPER; 775] *Opposite*: well-behaved

erratic *adj* **unpredictable**, unreliable, inconsistent, irregular, changeable, intermittent, uneven, fitful, variable, off and on, on-again off-again (*informal*) [➡ FINITENESS, VARIABILITY, AND TRANSIENCE; 96] *Opposite*: consistent

erroneous *adj* **mistaken**, flawed, wrong, specious, inaccurate, incorrect, invalid, untrue [➡ INCORRECT AND ERRONEOUS; 222] *Opposite*: correct

error *n* **mistake**, fault, blunder, inaccuracy, miscalculation, slip, oversight, slip-up (*informal*), boo-boo (*informal*) [➡ MISTAKES; 250]

See Compare and Contrast at **mistake**.

ersatz *adj* **faux**, artificial, substitute, reproduction, imitation, simulated, false, mock, synthetic [➡ FALSE AND UNREAL; 173] *Opposite*: genuine

erstwhile *adj* **former**, previous, past, old, earlier, ex, sometime, onetime [➡ PAST; 84] *Opposite*: current

erudite *adj* **scholarly**, knowledgeable, well-educated, well-read, cultured, learned, intellectual, bookish, literary, academic, studious [➡ LEVELS OF EDUCATION AND SOPHISTICATION; 894] *Opposite*: uneducated

erudition *n* **knowledge**, learnedness, education, learning, culture, sophistication, scholarship [➡ KNOWLEDGE AND WISDOM; 558] *Opposite*: ignorance

See Compare and Contrast at **knowledge**.

erupt 1 *v* **explode**, blow up, break out, flare up, go off, go bang, burst forth, vent [➡ SUDDENLY COME INTO EXISTENCE; 2] *Opposite*: subside 2 *v* **blow your top** (*informal*), explode, lose your temper, hit the roof, blow a fuse (*informal*), fly off the handle (*informal*) [➡ GIVING VENT TO EMOTIONS; 679] *Opposite*: hold back

eruption *n* **outbreak**, outburst, explosion, upsurge, epidemic, wave, discharge, emission [➡ SUDDEN EVENTS; 52]

escalate *v* **intensify**, worsen, heighten, go from bad to worse, deteriorate, spiral, increase, rocket, accelerate, grow rapidly [➡ CHANGE OF INTENSITY: MORE; 394]

escalating *adj* **mounting**, rising, intensifying, ever-increasing, swelling, increasing, growing, accelerating [➡ CHANGE OF INTENSITY: MORE; 394] *Opposite*: diminishing

escalation *n* **rise**, growth, boom, increase, climb, acceleration, appreciation, intensification [➡ CHANGE OF INTENSITY: MORE; 394] *Opposite*: reduction

escalator 1 *n* **moving staircase**, staircase, stairway, stairs [➡ STAIRS AND STORIES; 1102] 2 *part of* **building** [➡ PARTS OF A BUILDING; 1095]

escapade *n* **adventure**, jaunt, antic, caper, spree, exploit, stunt [➡ EVENTS AND OCCURRENCES; 35]

escape 1 *v* **flee**, run away, get away, break out, run off, get out, break away from, bolt, cut and run, abscond [➡ RUN AWAY AND AVOID; 10] 2 *v* **avoid**, evade, dodge, elude, shake off [➡ AVOID OR ESCAPE CONTACT; 418] *Opposite*: face 3 *v* **leak out**, leak, drip, seep, flow, drain, discharge, issue [➡ EMIT AND EMANATE; 361] 4 *n* **seepage**, leakage, leak, outflow, discharge, drip, spurt, emission [➡ PROCEED AND GO; 305] 5 *n* **flight**, getaway, break, breakout, escaping, running away, running off, exodus [➡ ENDS AND DEPARTURES; 54] 6 *n* **diversion**, distraction, pastime, leisure activity, escapism [➡ LEISURE AND RECREATION; 874]

escapee *n* **runaway**, fugitive, absconder, deserter, fleer [➡ RUNAWAYS AND ABSENTEES; 9]

escapism *n* **diversion**, distraction, entertainment, relaxation, daydreaming, avoidance, escape [➡ ENTERTAINMENT; 872]

escapist *adj* **diverting**, distracting, entertaining, relaxing, fantasy [➡ CALMING; 188] *Opposite*: realistic

escarpment *n* **cliff**, bluff, scarp, ridge, incline, slope [➡ GEOLOGIC FEATURES; 1056]

eschew *v* **avoid**, shun, have nothing to do with, steer clear of, give a wide berth to, fight shy of, turn your back on, disdain, abstain from, abjure (*literary*) [➡ NOT DO AND REFUSE TO DO; 274] *Opposite*: embrace

escort 1 *n* **guide**, attendant, bodyguard, chaperon, aide, companion, minder (*UK*) [➡ SUPPORTERS, PROTECTORS, AND COMPATRIOTS; 970] 2 *v* **accompany**, guide, usher, lead, attend, shepherd, chaperon, conduct [➡ ACCOMPANY AND FOLLOW; 337]

escritoire *type of* **table** [➡ FURNITURE; 858]

escudo *type of* **currency** [➡ CURRENCIES; 798]

esophagus *part of* **digestive tract** [➡ THE DIGESTIVE TRACT; 709]

esoteric *adj* **obscure**, mysterious, abstruse, impenetrable, cryptic, arcane, secret, mystical, occult [➡ POSITIVELY COMPLEX OR COMPLICATED; 217] *Opposite*: straightforward

ESP *n* **extra-sensory perception**, psychic powers, clairvoyance, second sight, telepathy, fortune telling, palm reading, prophecy, soothsaying, divining [➡ PREDICT AND ANTICIPATE; 750]

espadrille *type of* **shoe** [➡ FOOTWEAR; 871]

esparto *type of* **grass** [➡ GRASS; 1031]

especial *adj* **special**, unusual, exceptional, extraordinary, outstanding, remarkable, notable, marked, striking, signal [➡ EXTRAORDINARY: AMAZING; 204] *Opposite*: ordinary

especially 1 *adv* **exceptionally**, remarkably, notably, markedly, outstandingly, unusually, uniquely [➡ TO A GREAT EXTENT; 132] 2 *adv* **particularly**, in particular, specially, above all, more than ever, expressly, specifically, exclusively, mainly, chiefly, principally [➡ MAINLY AND PRIMARILY; 140]

esplanade *type of* **secondary road** [➡ROADS; 1106]

espousal *n* **adoption**, backing, support, championship, promotion, advocacy, taking up, siding with [➡AGREE; 645] *Opposite*: opposition

espouse 1 *v* **take up**, adopt, support, back, advocate, promote, embrace, champion [➡APPROVE AND CONFIRM; 646] *Opposite*: oppose 2 *v* (*archaic*) **marry**, wed, take your vows, walk down the aisle, get hitched (*informal*), tie the knot (*informal*) [➡ESTABLISHING RELATIONSHIPS WITH OTHERS; 974]

espresso *type of* **coffee** [➡DRINKS; 1187]

espy (*literary*) *v* **notice**, spy, catch sight of, spot, sight, see, observe, discern, discover, make out, descry (*literary*) [➡SEE; 699]

essay 1 *n* **paper**, thesis, dissertation, composition, article, treatise, theme [➡ANALYTICAL NONFICTION WRITING; 592] 2 *v* (*formal*) **try**, endeavor, strive, have a shot, attempt, have a go (*informal*), have a crack (*informal*) [➡ATTEMPT AN ACTION; 261]

essence 1 *n* **spirit**, core, heart, quintessence, crux, kernel, soul, principle, substance, lifeblood [➡MOST IMPORTANT THING; 197] 2 *n* **concentrate**, extract, tincture, distillate, concentration, distillation [➡LIQUIDS; 1269]

essential 1 *adj* **necessary**, vital, indispensable, important, crucial, critical, needed [➡NECESSARY AND ESSENTIAL; 196] *Opposite*: unnecessary 2 *adj* **fundamental**, basic, elemental, key, central, chief, main, principal, cardinal [➡FUNDAMENTAL; 195] *Opposite*: secondary 3 *adj* **necessity**, requisite, prerequisite, sine qua non, requirement, must [➡NECESSARY AND ESSENTIAL; 196]

See Compare and Contrast at **necessary**.

essentially 1 *adv* **fundamentally**, basically, in essence, in effect, really, in actual fact, to all intents and purposes, principally [➡SUMMARIZING EXPRESSIONS; 622] 2 *adv* **effectively**, more or less, broadly, in the main, for the most part, largely, to a large extent [➡MAINLY AND PRIMARILY; 140]

essentials *n* **basics**, fundamentals, prerequisites, rudiments, necessities, requisites, nuts and bolts (*informal*), nitty-gritty (*informal*) [➡MOST IMPORTANT THING; 197] *Opposite*: frills

establish 1 *v* **set up**, found, institute, start, create, begin, launch, bring about, form, inaugurate, organize [➡INSTITUTE AND INAUGURATE; 348] *Opposite*: close down 2 *v* **ascertain** (*formal*), determine, find out, prove, confirm, verify, show, corroborate, authenticate [➡LEARN AND DISCOVER; 762] *Opposite*: disprove

established *adj* **recognized**, well-known, traditional, conventional, customary, time-honored, proven, reputable [➡KNOWN AND FAMOUS; 181] *Opposite*: new

establishment 1 *n* **founding**, formation, creation, setting up, institution, launch, establishing, instituting, bringing about, organization [➡BEGINNINGS; 53] *Opposite*: dissolution 2 *n* **institution**, business, firm, company, concern, enterprise, corporation, organization, outfit (*informal*) [➡INSTITUTIONS; 790] 3 *n* **authorities**, powers that be, the ruling classes, the established order, the system [➡GOVERNMENT AND POLITICS; 805]

estate 1 *n* **plantation**, land, park, lands, parkland, domain, manor, country estate [➡THE COUNTRYSIDE AND OUTDOOR SPACES; 1071] 2 *n* **area**, zone, business park, development, housing development, industrial estate (*UK*) [➡HUMAN SETTLEMENTS; 1070] 3 *n* **assets**, property, holdings, worth, fortune, wealth [➡FINANCIAL ASSETS; 462]

esteem 1 *v* **appreciate**, cherish, hold dear, venerate, value, respect, admire, approve, honor, prize [➡LIKE, LOVE, VALUE, AND ENJOY; 578] *Opposite*: scorn 2 *n* **regard**, respect, admiration, high regard, honor, reverence, approval, good opinion, appreciation [➡LOVE, RESPECT, AND GOODWILL; 549] *Opposite*: contempt

See Compare and Contrast at **regard**.

esteemed *adj* **respected**, valued, honored, revered, admired, well-regarded, venerated [➡POPULAR AND WANTED; 220] *Opposite*: scorned

estimable *adj* **admirable**, worthy, deserving, laudable, venerable, good, reputable, prized, praiseworthy [➡ADMIRABLE AND COMMENDABLE; 185] *Opposite*: unimpressive

estimate 1 *v* **approximate**, guess, assess, reckon, value, appraise, guesstimate (*informal*) [➡ASSESS QUANTITY; 757] *Opposite*: calculate 2 *n* **approximation**, estimation, guess, educated guess, evaluation, assessment, appraisal, guesstimate (*informal*), ballpark figure (*informal*) [➡EXAMINE AND ASSESS; 753] 3 *n* **quote**, price, estimation, valuation, costing, assessment [➡SCORES AND EVALUATIONS; 598] *Opposite*: cost

estimated *adj* **projected**, assessed, valued, appraised, approximate [➡EXAMINE AND ASSESS; 753]

estimation 1 *n* **educated guess**, approximation, estimate, assessment, valuation, appraisal, guesstimate (*informal*), ballpark figure (*informal*) [➡EXAMINE AND ASSESS; 753] 2 *n* **opinion**, assessment, inference, evaluation, view, belief, judgment [➡POINTS OF VIEW; 767] *Opposite*: fact

estop (*archaic*) *v* **prevent**, stop, thwart, prohibit, halt, forbid, ward off [➡REFUSE PERMISSION AND NOT ALLOW; 670]

estranged *adj* **alienated**, separated, apart, at odds, on bad terms [➡RELATIONSHIP TO ANOTHER; 973]

estrangement *n* **separation**, hostility, rupture, distancing, disaffection, falling-out, discord, breakup, split, division, unfriendliness, schism, breach, alienation, disagreement, divorce, parting of the ways [➡RELATIONSHIP TO ANOTHER; 973] *Opposite*: reconciliation

estuary *n* **river mouth**, bay, inlet, sound, creek [➡RIVERS, LAKES, AND STREAMS; 1042] *Opposite*: source

e-tailing *n* [➡E-COMMERCE; 1129]

et al. *adv* **and company**, and co., and others, et cetera, and the rest [➡WRITTEN CONVENTIONS; 599]

etc. *adv* **et cetera**, and so on, and so forth, and the like, and the rest, and that (*informal*), and all that (*informal*) [➡WRITTEN CONVENTIONS; 599]

et cetera *adv* [➡FOREIGN WORDS AND PHRASES; 672]

etch *v* **engrave**, scratch, scrape, cut, incise, score, carve [➡CREATE IMAGES; 356]

etching *n* **engraving**, drawing, print, design, impression, imprint, inscription [➡ ARTWORKS; 898]

eternal *adj* **everlasting**, undying, unending, never-ending, perpetual, endless, ceaseless, timeless, interminable, infinite, immortal [➡ PERMANENCE: WITHOUT END; 94] *Opposite*: transient

eternal life *n* [➡ RELIGIOUS CONCEPTS; 776]

eternity *n* **time without end**, perpetuity, infinity, all time, ever and a day [➡ LONG PERIODS OF TIME; 92]

ether (*literary*) *n* **air**, atmosphere, heaven, sky [➡ THE EARTH'S ATMOSPHERE; 1040]

ethereal 1 *adj* **ghostly**, otherworldly, unearthly, wraith-like, eerie [➡ VAGUENESS; 243] *Opposite*: earthly **2** *adj* **waiflike**, frail, delicate, airy, insubstantial, light, fragile [➡ FRAGILE; 1209] *Opposite*: substantial

ethic *n* **moral belief**, ethos, idea, principle, code, tenet [➡ IDEAS AND THOUGHTS; 770]

ethical *adj* **moral**, principled, right, fair, decent, proper, fitting, virtuous, just, honorable, upright [➡ MORALLY GOOD; 774] *Opposite*: unethical

ethics *n* **principles**, morals, beliefs, moral code, moral principles, moral values, integrity, conscience [➡ MORAL CONCEPTS; 773]

ethnic *adj* **cultural**, traditional, folkloric, racial, indigenous, national [➡ BELONGING OR RELATING TO PEOPLE; 943]

ethnicity *n* **culture**, way of life, origin, background, traditions, customs [➡ LIFESTYLE; 881]

ethos *n* **philosophy**, beliefs, principles, code, character, tenet, attitude, spirit, moral belief [➡ MORAL CONCEPTS; 773]

etiquette *n* **manners**, good manners, protocol, custom, propriety, decorum, politeness [➡ GOOD MANNERS AND SOCIAL SKILLS; 520] *Opposite*: bad manners

étude *type of* **musical form** [➡ MUSIC, SONGS, AND SINGING; 907]

etymology *n* [➡ ASPECTS OF LANGUAGE; 682]

eucalyptus *type of* **evergreen tree** [➡ EVERGREEN AND CONIFEROUS TREES; 1029]

eulogize *v* **praise**, extol, laud, sing the praises of, praise to the skies, rave about, glorify, acclaim, hail, exalt (*formal*), wax lyrical (*literary*) [➡ PRAISE AND ENCOURAGE; 647] *Opposite*: criticize

eulogy *n* **tribute**, acclamation, acclaim, praise, homage, panegyric, exaltation (*formal*), encomium (*formal*) [➡ PRAISE AND ENCOURAGE; 647] *Opposite*: criticism

euphemism *n* **neutral term**, understatement, rewording, bowdlerization, code word, synonym, weasel word (*informal*) [➡ FIGURES OF SPEECH; 673] *Opposite*: dysphemism

euphemistic *adj* **inoffensive**, polite, bowdlerized, cleaned up, neutral, understated, indirect, oblique, softened, innocuous [➡ VAGUENESS; 243] *Opposite*: dysphemistic

euphonious *adj* [➡ SOFT, LOW, OR PLEASANT SOUNDS; 1265]

euphoniousness *n* [➡ SOFT, LOW, OR PLEASANT SOUNDS; 1265]

euphonium *type of* **brass instrument** [➡ MUSICAL INSTRUMENTS; 910]

euphony *n* [➡ SOFT, LOW, OR PLEASANT SOUNDS; 1265]

euphoria *n* **elation**, ecstasy, jubilation, rapture, excitement, exhilaration, bliss, exultation, joy [➡ PLEASURE, EXCITEMENT, AND ELATION; 534] *Opposite*: despair

euphoric *adj* **overjoyed**, elated, ecstatic, joyful, joyous, excited, exhilarated, blissful, exultant, enraptured (*formal*), over the moon (*UK informal*) [➡ PLEASURE, EXCITEMENT, AND ELATION; 534] *Opposite*: despairing

euro *type of* **currency** [➡ CURRENCIES; 798]

evacuate 1 *v* **empty**, abandon, withdraw from, leave, vacate, relinquish, clear, clear out [➡ RUN AWAY AND AVOID; 10] *Opposite*: fill **2** *v* **send away**, remove from, move out of, clear from [➡ EJECT AND EXCLUDE; 340] *Opposite*: bring in

evacuation *n* **removal**, clearing, emptying, withdrawal, flight, emigration, migration, departure, retreat, exodus [➡ EJECT AND EXCLUDE; 340] *Opposite*: influx

evacuee *n* **refugee**, émigré, emigrant, migrant [➡ PEOPLE LIVING AWAY FROM HOME; 887]

evade 1 *v* **avoid**, dodge, escape, elude, shirk, skirt, duck, sidestep [➡ NOT PAY ATTENTION; 764] **2** *v* **equivocate**, prevaricate, hedge, stonewall (*informal*), fudge (*informal*) [➡ WITHHOLD INFORMATION; 687]

evaluate *v* **assess**, appraise, gauge, estimate, calculate, weigh, value, price, weigh up (*UK*) [➡ ASSESS QUALITY; 755]

evaluation *n* **assessment**, appraisal, estimation, calculation, valuation, estimate, costing [➡ SCORES AND EVALUATIONS; 598]

evaluator *n* **assessor**, surveyor, inspector, judge [➡ ADVISERS, JUDGES, AND ARBITERS; 971]

evanescence *n* [➡ FINITENESS, VARIABILITY, AND TRANSIENCE; 96]

evanescent *adj* **short-lived**, fleeting, momentary, ephemeral, passing, brief, transient [➡ FINITENESS, VARIABILITY, AND TRANSIENCE; 96] *Opposite*: permanent

See Compare and Contrast at **temporary**.

evangelical *adj* **enthusiastic**, fervent, eager, zealous, keen, intense, proselytizing [➡ RELIGIONS AND RELIGIOUS PRACTICES; 777] *Opposite*: apathetic

evangelist *n* [➡ RELIGIOUS PEOPLE; 778]

evangelize *v* [➡ RELIGIONS AND RELIGIOUS PRACTICES; 777]

evaporate *v* **vanish**, fade away, fade, disappear, melt away, disperse, dissolve, vaporize [➡ DISAPPEAR; 4] *Opposite*: solidify

evaporation *n* **vaporization**, drying up, loss, vanishing, disappearance, dehydration [➡ ENDS AND DEPARTURES; 54]

evasion 1 *n* **avoidance**, dodging, elusion, circumvention, skirting, shirking, ducking, fudging (*informal*) [➡ NOT PAY ATTENTION; 764] **2** *n* **prevarication**, equivocation, hedging, stonewalling (*informal*) [➡ WITHHOLD INFORMATION; 687]

evasive *adj* **elusive**, slippery, shifty, indirect, oblique,

equivocal, ambiguous, vague, misleading, cagey (*informal*) [➡ RETICENT AND UNFORTHCOMING; 631] *Opposite*: direct

evasiveness *n* **indirectness**, equivocation, shiftiness, elusiveness, ambiguousness, vagueness, slipperiness, caginess (*informal*) [➡ RETICENT AND UNFORTHCOMING; 631] *Opposite*: directness

eve *n* **day before**, evening before, night before [➡ TIMES OF YEAR; 88]

even 1 *adj* **smooth**, flat, level, straight, unfluctuating, uniform [➡ PHYSICAL TEXTURE; 1222] *Opposite*: uneven **2** *adj* **equal**, similar, level, on a par, just as, drawn, at the same time, tied, even-steven (*informal*), on level pegging (*UK*) [➡ EQUALITY; 154] *Opposite*: unequal **3** *adj* **constant**, steady, uniform, unvarying, unchanging, regular [➡ PERMANENCE: WITHOUT CHANGE; 95] *Opposite*: fluctuating **4** *n* (*literary*) **evening**, twilight, dusk, nightfall, sunset, sundown [➡ TIMES OF DAY; 87]

evenhanded *adj* **fair**, impartial, unbiased, just, equal, balanced, dispassionate, nonpartisan, fair-minded, equitable (*formal*) [➡ EQUALITY; 154] *Opposite*: biased

evenhandedly *adv* **fairly**, impartially, justly, equally, dispassionately, equitably (*formal*) [➡ EQUALITY; 154] *Opposite*: unfairly

evenhandedness *n* **fairness**, impartiality, equity, justice, neutrality, fair-mindedness, equality [➡ EQUALITY; 154] *Opposite*: partiality

even if *conj* **though**, albeit, although, even though [➡ ALTHOUGH, NEVERTHELESS, AND DESPITE; 169]

evening *n* **twilight**, sunset, dusk, nightfall, late afternoon, sundown, even (*literary*) [➡ TIMES OF DAY; 87] *Opposite*: morning

evening dress *n* [➡ GARMENTS AND OUTFITS; 865]

evening gown *type of* **dress** [➡ GARMENTS AND OUTFITS; 865]

even less *adv* **still less**, much less, let alone [➡ NOT; 137] *Opposite*: even more

evenly *adv* **consistently**, equally, uniformly, steadily, equably, regularly [➡ PHYSICAL TEXTURE; 1222] *Opposite*: irregularly

even more *adv* **still more**, all the more, yet more [➡ MAINLY AND PRIMARILY; 140] *Opposite*: even less

evenness *n* **consistency**, sameness, symmetry, uniformity, flatness, steadiness, constancy, levelness [➡ PHYSICAL TEXTURE; 1222] *Opposite*: irregularity

even out 1 *v* **flatten**, level, smooth, square, align [➡ ARRANGE AND CREATE ORDER; 357] **2** *v* **balance out**, balance, level out, balance up, equalize, make the same, even up, offset [➡ EQUALITY; 154] *Opposite*: unbalance

even so *adv* **all the same**, nonetheless, be that as it may, nevertheless, yet, despite that, even if, even supposing, still [➡ ALTHOUGH, NEVERTHELESS, AND DESPITE; 169]

event *n* **occasion**, happening, occurrence, incident, affair, episode, experience [➡ EVENTS AND OCCURRENCES; 35]

even-tempered *adj* **calm**, unflappable, equable, placid, imperturbable, serene, steady [➡ CONFIDENCE AND COMPOSURE; 499] *Opposite*: temperamental

eventful *adj* **exciting**, action-packed, lively, busy, hectic, important, momentous [➡ EMOTIONALLY PLEASANT; 187] *Opposite*: dull

eventide (*literary*) *n* [➡ TIMES OF DAY; 87]

eventual *adj* **ultimate**, final, last, ensuing, subsequent, concluding [➡ AFTER, LAST, AND FOLLOWING; 165] *Opposite*: immediate

eventuality (*formal*) *n* **possibility**, prospect, case, contingency, outcome, result, consequence, upshot [➡ CHANCE EVENTS; 36]

eventually *adv* **finally**, ultimately, sooner or later, in the end, in due course, in time, at the end of the day, in the long run [➡ AFTER, LAST, AND FOLLOWING; 165] *Opposite*: immediately

even up *v* **equalize**, stabilize, even out, redress the balance, balance up, square, redress [➡ ARRANGE AND CREATE ORDER; 357] *Opposite*: unbalance

ever *adv* **always**, forever, eternally, all the time, constantly, continually, perpetually, endlessly, interminably, continuously [➡ PERMANENCE: WITHOUT END; 94] *Opposite*: never

everglade *n* [➡ WETLANDS; 1043]

evergreen 1 *n* [➡ PLANTS AND TREES; 1024] **2** *adj* **immortal**, perennial, ever popular, classic, timeless, ageless, favorite [➡ PERMANENCE: WITHOUT END; 94] *Opposite*: stale

---

evergreen

◆ *types of evergreen trees*
bay, bo tree, boxwood, bunya, carob, cedar, cola, cypress, eucalyptus, fir, fir tree, gum tree, holly, juniper, kahikatea, kauri, larch, laurel, mahogany, mangrove, monkey puzzle, pine, redwood, sandalwood, sequoia, spruce, yew

---

everlasting *adj* **eternal**, endless, ceaseless, never-ending, perpetual, undying, unending, interminable, forever, continuous, permanent [➡ PERMANENCE: WITHOUT END; 94] *Opposite*: transient

evermore (*literary*) *adv* **forever**, for all time, always, eternally [➡ PERMANENCE: WITHOUT END; 94]

ever-present *adj* **ubiquitous**, chronic, pervasive, omnipresent [➡ PRESENT AND AVAILABLE; 11]

ever so *adv* **extremely**, fantastically, very much so, exceptionally, really, incredibly, awfully, terribly, real (*informal*) [➡ TO A GREAT EXTENT; 132] *Opposite*: not at all

every *adj* **each**, all, every single, every one [➡ ALL; 128]

everybody *n* **everyone**, all, all and sundry, one and all, each one, each person, every person, every last one, every Tom, Dick, and Harry, every man jack (*UK*) [➡ ALL; 128] *Opposite*: nobody

everyday *adj* **ordinary**, average, normal, unremarkable, common, commonplace, daily, run-of-the-mill, routine, usual [➡ ORDINARINESS; 244] *Opposite*: extraordinary

every now and again *adv* [➡ NEVER AND INFREQUENCY; 97]

every now and then *adv* **occasionally**, now and then, now and again, once in a while, on occasion, from time to time, every so often, off and on, on and off [➡ NEVER AND INFREQUENCY; 97] *Opposite:* constantly

everyone *n* **everybody**, all, all and sundry, one and all, each person, each one, every person, every last one, every Tom, Dick, and Harry, every man jack (*UK*) [➡ ALL; 128] *Opposite:* no one

every so often *adv* [➡ NEVER AND INFREQUENCY; 97]

everything *n* **all**, the whole thing, the lot, the whole lot, entirety, the whole shebang (*informal*), the whole kit and caboodle (*informal*), the whole ball of wax (*informal*), the whole enchilada (*slang*) [➡ ALL; 128] *Opposite:* nothing

everywhere *adv* **all over**, ubiquitously, far and wide, the world over, universally, all over the place (*informal*) [➡ GENERAL LOCATIONS; 158]

evict *v* **throw out**, expel, turn out, eject, remove, force out, dislodge, put out, kick out (*informal*) [➡ EJECT AND EXCLUDE; 340] *Opposite:* install

eviction *n* **removal**, expulsion, ejection, throwing out, exclusion, dislodgment, kicking out (*informal*) [➡ EJECT AND EXCLUDE; 340]

evidence 1 *n* **indication**, sign, signal, mark, suggestion, proof [➡ EVIDENCE AND PROOF; 69] 2 *n* **proof**, confirmation, facts, data, substantiation, verification, support, testimony, grounds [➡ EVIDENCE AND PROOF; 69] 3 *v* **show**, demonstrate, evince, make clear, prove, verify, substantiate, corroborate, support [➡ CAUSE TO APPEAR; 5]

evident *adj* **obvious**, plain, apparent, clear, manifest, palpable, unmistakable, marked, patent, distinct [➡ CERTAIN; 174] *Opposite:* obscure

evidently 1 *adv* **obviously**, clearly, plainly, manifestly, palpably, unmistakably, patently, markedly, distinctly [➡ PERCEPTIBLE; 25] 2 *adv* **apparently**, seemingly, as far as we know, it would seem, as far as one can tell [➡ UNCERTAIN; 175]

evil 1 *adj* **wicked**, malevolent, sinful, malicious, criminal, immoral [➡ MORALLY BAD OR IMPROPER; 775] *Opposite:* good 2 *adj* **foul**, vile, nasty, horrible, unpleasant, revolting, disgusting, obnoxious [➡ DISGUSTING AND REPULSIVE; 230] *Opposite:* pleasant 3 *n* **wickedness**, malevolence, sin, iniquity, vice, immorality [➡ MORALLY BAD OR IMPROPER; 775] *Opposite:* good

evildoer *n* **wrongdoer**, sinner, criminal, offender, delinquent, villain, malefactor (*formal*) [➡ VILLAINS AND THUGS; 947] *Opposite:* benefactor

evilness *n* **wickedness**, badness, evil, immorality, sinfulness, vice [➡ MORALLY BAD OR IMPROPER; 775] *Opposite:* goodness

evil spirit *n* [➡ RELIGIOUS CONCEPTS; 776]

evince *v* **show**, display, reveal, exhibit, manifest, demonstrate, make clear [➡ CAUSE TO APPEAR; 5] *Opposite:* conceal

eviscerate *v* [➡ WOUND A PERSON OR ANIMAL; 383]

evocation *n* **recreation**, elicitation, recall, air, hint, trace, suggestion [➡ SUGGEST, HINT, AND COMMENT; 612]

evocative *adj* **reminiscent**, suggestive, redolent, haunting [➡ INTERESTING AND MEANINGFUL; 190]

evocatively *adv* **reminiscently**, hauntingly, sug-

gestively, redolently, emotively [➡ ELOQUENT, TALKATIVE, AND LONG-WINDED; 632]

evoke *v* **call to mind**, bring to mind, suggest, call up, induce, arouse, remind, stir up, conjure, draw out, educe (*formal*) [➡ REMIND; 747] *Opposite:* suppress

evolution *n* **development**, fruition, growth, progress, progression, advancement [➡ PROGRESS AND ADVANCEMENT; 213] *Opposite:* regression

evolve *v* **develop**, grow, progress, advance, go forward, change, unfold [➡ GRADUALLY COME INTO EXISTENCE; 1] *Opposite:* regress

ewe *type of* **female animal** [➡ MALE OR FEMALE ANIMALS; 978]

ewer *n* **jug**, pitcher, vessel, bottle, container, pot [➡ TABLEWARE, FLATWARE, AND KITCHENWARE; 861]

ex 1 *n* (*informal*) [➡ SEXUAL AND ROMANTIC RELATIONSHIPS; 964] 2 *adj* **former**, sometime, onetime, erstwhile, lapsed [➡ PAST; 84] *Opposite:* future

exacerbate *v* **make worse**, worsen, aggravate, impair, intensify [➡ WORSEN SOMETHING; 380] *Opposite:* soothe

exact 1 *adj* **correct**, precise, accurate, strict, faithful, literal [➡ EXACT; 203] *Opposite:* approximate 2 *adj* **careful**, meticulous, precise, particular, thorough, rigorous, strict, scrupulous [➡ POSITIVE INTELLECTUAL CHARACTERISTICS; 524] *Opposite:* careless 3 *v* **demand**, obtain, extort, extract, wrest, pinch, take [➡ REQUEST AND DEMAND; 663]

exacting *adj* **demanding**, testing, challenging, rigorous, tough, thorough, onerous [➡ DIFFICULTY AND COMPLEXITY; 242] *Opposite:* easy

exactitude *n* **precision**, correctness, accuracy, meticulousness, exactness, faithfulness, scrupulousness, thoroughness, closeness, literalness, rigor [➡ EXACT; 203] *Opposite:* carelessness

exactly *adv* **precisely**, just, accurately, closely, faithfully, correctly, unerringly [➡ EXACT; 203] *Opposite:* approximately

exactness *n* **precision**, accuracy, exactitude, correctness, meticulousness, strictness, faithfulness, thoroughness, scrupulousness [➡ EXACT; 203] *Opposite:* vagueness

exaggerate *v* **overstress**, embellish, embroider, make a mountain out of a molehill, inflate, lay on, amplify, overstate [➡ CLAIM, INSIST, AND EMPHASIZE; 614] *Opposite:* understate

exaggerated *adj* **overstated**, inflated, embroidered, embellished, blown up, larger-than-life, extravagant, hyperbolic [➡ BIZARRE AND PECULIAR; 257] *Opposite:* understated

exaggeration *n* **overstatement**, hyperbole, embellishment, embroidery, overemphasis, overestimation, amplification [➡ CLAIM, INSIST, AND EMPHASIZE; 614] *Opposite:* understatement

exalt (*formal*) 1 *v* **promote**, raise, elevate, intensify, boost, lift [➡ CHANGE OF INTENSITY: MORE; 394] 2 *v* **praise**, laud, acclaim, applaud, pay tribute to, extol, lionize, revere, sing the praises of [➡ PRAISE AND ENCOURAGE; 647] *Opposite:* disparage

exaltation 1 *n* (*formal*) **adulation**, adoration, acclaim, acclamation, praise, applause [➡ PRAISE AND ENCOURAGE; 647] *Opposite:* condemnation 2 *n* (*formal*) **excitement**, rapture, exhilaration, happiness, joy [➡PLEASURE, EXCITEMENT, AND ELATION; 534] *Opposite*: despair **3** (*literary*) *type of* **flock** [➡GROUPS OF BIRDS; 1007]

exalted (*formal*) *adj* **high**, lofty, glorious, dignified, illustrious, high-ranking, noble, grand [➡SUPERIORITY; 152] *Opposite*: lowly

exam *n* **examination**, test, final, blue book, quiz, assessment, paper, question paper, oral exam [➡CLASSES, COURSEWORK, AND EXAMINATIONS; 842]

examination 1 *n* **inspection**, scrutiny, checkup, investigation, analysis, consideration, study, check, going-over (*informal*) [➡EXAMINE AND ASSESS; 753] **2** *n* **test**, assessment, exam, final, blue book, quiz, paper, question paper, oral exam [➡CLASSES, COURSEWORK, AND EXAMINATIONS; 842]

examine 1 *v* **look at**, inspect, scrutinize, observe, study, survey, scan [➡LOOKING AND LOOKS; 700] **2** *v* **consider**, think about, look into, investigate, research, analyze, appraise, sift, weigh, weigh up (*UK*) [➡EXAMINE AND ASSESS; 753] **3** *v* **test**, assess, grade, judge, question, survey, audit [➡ASSESS QUALITY; 755]

examiner *n* **inspector**, auditor, surveyor, superintendent, assessor, judge, grader [➡SURVEYORS, EXAMINERS, AND JUDGES; 853]

example 1 *n* **sample**, instance, case, case in point, specimen, illustration [➡REPRESENTATIONS AND GENERAL EXAMPLES; 65] **2** *n* **model**, pattern, paradigm, standard, paragon, exemplar (*literary*) [➡PERFECT EXAMPLES AND EMBODIMENTS; 67]

exasperate *v* **infuriate**, madden, frustrate, annoy, irritate, incense, enrage, vex, irk, drive mad (*informal*), rile (*informal*), wind up (*informal*), bug (*informal*), drive round the bend (*UK*) [➡ANGER AND ANNOY; 569] *Opposite*: placate

See Compare and Contrast at **annoy**.

exasperated *adj* **infuriated**, maddened, frustrated, annoyed, incensed, irritated, enraged, wound up (*informal*), riled (*informal*) [➡IRRITATION AND ANGER; 541] *Opposite*: placated

exasperating *adj* **infuriating**, maddening, frustrating, vexing, annoying, irksome, galling, tiresome, tedious [➡IRRITATING; 228] *Opposite*: calming

exasperation *n* **frustration**, irritation, enragement, annoyance, vexation, anger, fury, madness [➡IRRITATION AND ANGER; 541]

excavate *v* **dig**, mine, quarry, dig out, exhume, unearth, hollow out, scoop out, dig up [➡FIND; 463] *Opposite*: bury

exceed *v* **go beyond**, surpass, go above, go over, top, outdo, overdo, outstrip, beat [➡OVERDO SOMETHING; 290] *Opposite*: fall short

exceedingly *adv* **very**, exceptionally, remarkably, extremely, extraordinarily, outstandingly, especially, highly [➡EXTRAORDINARY: AMAZING; 204] *Opposite*: slightly

excel *v* **shine**, stand out, outshine, outclass, surpass, outrival, top, best, outdo, outstrip [➡SUCCEED AND WIN; 79] *Opposite*: fall behind

excellence *n* **fineness**, brilliance, superiority, distinction, quality, merit [➡EXTRAORDINARY: AMAZING; 204] *Opposite*: mediocrity

excellent *adj* **outstanding**, brilliant, exceptional, admirable, superb, tremendous, first-rate [➡EXTRAORDINARY: AMAZING; 204] *Opposite*: poor

except *prep* **apart from**, except for, but, excluding, with the exception of, aside from, bar, excepting (*formal*) [➡NOT; 137] *Opposite*: including

except for *prep* [➡NOT; 137]

excepting (*formal*) *prep* **except**, apart from, except for, but, excluding, with the exception of, aside from, bar [➡NOT; 137] *Opposite*: including

exception *n* **exclusion**, omission, exemption, concession, allowance [➡ABSENT AND UNAVAILABLE; 7]

exceptionable (*formal*) *adj* **offensive**, obnoxious, rude, objectionable, repugnant, unpleasant, reprehensible, insufferable, intolerable, unacceptable [➡UNACCEPTABLE AND UNFORGIVABLE; 225] *Opposite*: inoffensive

exceptional *adj* **excellent**, brilliant, special, extraordinary, incomparable, unique, outstanding, remarkable, phenomenal [➡EXTRAORDINARY: AMAZING; 204] *Opposite*: ordinary

exceptionality *n* **rarity**, infrequency, extraordinariness, uniqueness, remarkableness [➡NEVER AND INFREQUENCY; 97] *Opposite*: normality

excerpt *n* **extract**, passage, quote, quotation, selection, piece, citation [➡SUMMARIES, OUTLINES, AND EXCERPTS; 588]

excess 1 *n* **surplus**, glut, overload, surfeit, over-abundance, superfluity, oversufficiency, overkill, overflow [➡TOO MUCH; 119] *Opposite*: shortage **2** *n* **over-indulgence**, intemperance, dissipation, inordinateness, prodigality, extravagance, immoderation (*formal*) [➡MORALLY BAD OR IMPROPER; 775] *Opposite*: moderation **3** *adj* **extra**, additional, surplus, spare, superfluous, leftover [➡MORE AND EXCESS; 124]

excesses *n* **extremes**, dissipation, intemperance, over-indulgence, prodigality, extravagance, immoderation (*formal*) [➡MORALLY BAD OR IMPROPER; 775]

excessive *adj* **extreme**, too much, unnecessary, unwarranted, undue, disproportionate, over the top [➡TOO MUCH; 119] *Opposite*: moderate

excessively *adv* **very**, extremely, overly, exceptionally, markedly, greatly, terribly [➡TO A GREAT EXTENT; 132] *Opposite*: moderately

excessiveness *n* **extremeness**, exorbitance, extravagance, immoderateness (*formal*), immoderation (*formal*) [➡TOO MUCH; 119] *Opposite*: moderation

exchange 1 *v* **switch**, replace, trade, barter, substitute, swap (*informal*), swap over (*informal*) [➡EXCHANGE AND INTERCHANGE; 448] *Opposite*: keep **2** *n* **conversation**, argument, talk, chat, discussion, altercation, interchange, negotiation, give-and-take (*informal*) [➡INFORMAL COMMUNICATION; 45] **3** *n* **trade**, switch, barter, replacement, substitute, swap (*informal*) [➡EXCHANGE AND INTERCHANGE; 448]

exchangeable *adj* **redeemable**, transferable, negotiable, commutable, interchangeable, replaceable, returnable [➤ SAMENESS; 150]

exchange blows v **fight**, scuffle, go for each other, trade punches, brawl, scrap, clash, spar, scrap [➤ PHYSICAL ATTACK AND PUNISHMENT; 415]

excise v **delete**, remove, edit, cut out, expunge, erase, expurgate, eliminate [➤ EXTRACT AND SEVER; 341] *Opposite*: insert

excision n **editing**, deletion, removal, cutting out, erasure, expurgation, elimination [➤ REMOVE SOMETHING; 338] *Opposite*: insertion

excitability n **nervousness**, edginess, moodiness, fieriness, quick-temperedness, emotionality, impulsiveness, volatility [➤ EXCESSIVE SENSITIVITY; 511] *Opposite*: coolness

excitable adj **nervous**, emotional, edgy, impulsive, volatile, passionate, hasty, high-strung [➤ EXCESSIVE SENSITIVITY; 511] *Opposite*: unflappable

excite 1 v **stimulate**, enthuse, animate, motivate, enliven, electrify, thrill, rouse, arouse, energize [➤ APPEAL TO AND AROUSE INTEREST; 575] *Opposite*: bore 2 v **incite**, agitate, provoke, instigate, stir up, awaken, wind up (*informal*), psych (*informal*) [➤ CAUSE TO HAPPEN; 31] *Opposite*: soothe

excited 1 adj **happy**, enthusiastic, eager, animated, motivated, thrilled [➤ PLEASURE, EXCITEMENT, AND ELATION; 534] *Opposite*: indifferent 2 adj **agitated**, nervous, provoked, overwrought, hot and bothered, upset, stirred up, fraught, distracted, anxious, wound up (*informal*), psyched (*informal*) [➤ CONFUSION, ANXIETY, AND WORRY; 540] *Opposite*: calm

excitedly adv **happily**, enthusiastically, eagerly, hungrily, impatiently, animatedly, breathlessly, elatedly [➤ PLEASURE, EXCITEMENT, AND ELATION; 534] *Opposite*: indifferently

excitement 1 n **enthusiasm**, eagerness, anticipation, pleasure, exhilaration, enjoyment, delight, interest, elation [➤ POSITIVE IMPATIENCE, ENTHUSIASM, AND ALERTNESS; 537] *Opposite*: indifference 2 n **agitation**, tension, unrest, ferment, restlessness, turmoil, flurry, flutter [➤ INSECURITY AND LOSS OF COMPOSURE; 544] *Opposite*: calm

exciting adj **thrilling**, exhilarating, stirring, stimulating, electrifying, moving, rousing, sensational, breathtaking [➤ EMOTIONALLY PLEASANT; 187] *Opposite*: boring

exclaim v **cry out**, cry, shout, call out, call, yell, scream, bellow [➤ SOUND EMISSION BY PEOPLE; 363] *Opposite*: whisper

exclamation n **shout**, cry, yell, scream, howl, shriek, expletive, interjection, outcry [➤ SOUNDS MADE BY PEOPLE; 1262] *Opposite*: whisper

exclamation mark type of **punctuation mark** [➤ ASPECTS OF LANGUAGE; 682]

exclude 1 v **keep out**, bar, reject, leave out, prevent, prohibit, leave out in the cold, stop, ban, blackball [➤ MAKE IMPOSSIBLE; 276] *Opposite*: welcome 2 v **reject**, rule out, eliminate, discount, ignore, dismiss, disregard, omit, leave out, except (*formal*) [➤ NOT PAY ATTENTION; 764] *Opposite*: include

excluding prep **exclusive of**, not including, without, apart from [➤ NOT; 137] *Opposite*: including

exclusion 1 n **keeping out**, barring, rejection, leaving out, prohibiting, segregation, omission [➤ EJECT AND EXCLUDE; 340] *Opposite*: welcome 2 n **rejection**, elimination, mar-

ginalization, prohibition, veto, barring [➤ REFUSE PERMISSION AND NOT ALLOW; 670] *Opposite*: inclusion 3 n **ban**, refusal, sanction, embargo, prohibition, bar, veto [➤ REFUSE PERMISSION AND NOT ALLOW; 670]

exclusive 1 adj **high-class**, elite, select, restricted, limited, private, fashionable, special [➤ EXPENSIVE AND LUXURIOUS; 218] *Opposite*: inclusive 2 adj **sole**, complete, undivided, full, whole, absolute, total [➤ UNRELATEDNESS AND SEPARATENESS; 146] *Opposite*: partial

exclusively adv **solely**, wholly, completely, entirely, fully, totally, utterly, absolutely, singularly, alone [➤ ABSOLUTE AND ABSOLUTELY; 133] *Opposite*: partially

exclusiveness 1 n **luxury**, sophistication, refinement, superiority, stylishness, elegance, classiness (*informal*) [➤ EXPENSIVE AND LUXURIOUS; 218] 2 n **selectiveness**, restrictedness, exclusivity, elitism, snobbery [➤ PREJUDICE; 550]

exclusive of adj **not including**, excluding, leaving out, without, except for, excepting (*formal*) [➤ NOT; 137] *Opposite*: including

excommunicate v **exclude**, bar, debar, expel, eject, throw out, remove, anathematize [➤ RELIGIONS AND RELIGIOUS PRACTICES; 777] *Opposite*: admit

excommunication n **exclusion**, barring, debarring, expulsion, ejection, throwing out, removal [➤ RELIGIONS AND RELIGIOUS PRACTICES; 777] *Opposite*: admission

excoriate 1 v (*formal*) **criticize**, denounce, attack, berate, upbraid, rebuke, condemn, haul over the coals, take to task, censure, castigate (*formal*) [➤ ACCUSE, BLAME, AND CRITICIZE; 641] *Opposite*: commend 2 v **skin**, peel, pare, strip, flay [➤ WOUND A PERSON OR ANIMAL; 383]

excoriation (*formal*) n [➤ IRRITATION AND ANGER; 541]

excrement n [➤ EXCRETION AND EXCRETA; 722]

excrescence n **monstrosity**, eyesore, blot, growth, outgrowth [➤ NUISANCES; 253]

excreta n [➤ EXCRETION AND EXCRETA; 722]

excrete v [➤ EXCRETION AND EXCRETA; 722]

excretion n [➤ EXCRETION AND EXCRETA; 722]

excretory adj [➤ EXCRETION AND EXCRETA; 722]

excruciating 1 adj **agonizing**, painful, unbearable, awful, terrible, severe, sharp, piercing, insufferable, racking, tormenting [➤ PHYSICALLY UNPLEASANT; 226] *Opposite*: pleasant 2 adj **embarrassing**, tedious, stultifying, irritating, infuriating, painful, insufferable, cringe-making (*informal*), toe-curling (*informal*) [➤ EMOTIONALLY UNPLEASANT AND UPSETTING; 227] *Opposite*: enthralling

exculpate (*formal*) v **free**, let off, excuse, clear, release, acquit, exonerate [➤ FORGET, FORGIVE, AND ACCEPT; 748] *Opposite*: arraign

exculpation (*formal*) n **acquittal**, exoneration, discharge, pardon, clearing [➤ FORGET, FORGIVE, AND ACCEPT; 748] *Opposite*: arraignment

excursion 1 n **trip**, jaunt, outing, junket, tour, day trip, pleasure trip [➤ TRAVEL: JOURNEYS AND TRIPS; 318] 2 n (*formal*) **digression**, departure, detour, deviation, tangent, red herring [➤ ONE-WAY COMMUNICATION; 49] **3** *n* **group**, team, party, expedition [➤ GROUPS WITH A COMMON INTEREST; 938]

excusable *adj* **understandable**, forgivable, justifiable, explicable, pardonable, defensible, allowable, permissible [➤ ACCEPTABLE AND PASSABLE; 219] *Opposite*: inexcusable

excuse **1** *v* **forgive**, pardon, let off, acquit, absolve, let go, let off the hook, exonerate, exculpate (*formal*) [➤ FORGET, FORGIVE, AND ACCEPT; 748] *Opposite*: blame **2** *v* **overlook**, make allowances for, pass over, tolerate, justify, explain, bear with, defend [➤ APPROVE AND CONFIRM; 646] **3** *v* **exempt**, release, let off, free, relieve, discharge, spare, except (*formal*) [➤ FREEDOM AND LIBERTY; 208] *Opposite*: oblige **4** *n* **justification**, reason, explanation, pretext, defense, apology, plea, vindication, alibi (*informal*) [➤ CAUSATION; 168]

excused *adj* **exempted**, released, exempt, let off, relieved, discharged [➤ FREEDOM AND LIBERTY; 208] *Opposite*: required

excuse yourself *v* [➤ LEAVE AND GO AWAY; 8]

exec (*informal*) *n* [➤ BUSINESS PEOPLE; 793]

execrable (*formal*) *adj* **terrible**, awful, appalling, disgusting, repulsive, deplorable, revolting, abominable, atrocious [➤ BAD AND BADLY; 223] *Opposite*: excellent

execrate (*literary or formal*) *v* [➤ INSULTS, ABUSE, AND SWEARING; 658]

execration (*literary or formal*) *n* [➤ INSULTS, ABUSE, AND SWEARING; 658]

execute **1** *v* **carry out**, perform, implement, complete, accomplish, achieve, fulfill, finish (*informal*), effect (*formal*) [➤ CARRY OUT AN ACTION; 269] **2** *v* **put to death**, kill, murder, hang, electrocute, guillotine, slay (*formal or literary*) [➤ KILL; 923]

See Compare and Contrast at **kill, perform**.

execution **1** *n* **implementation**, performance, accomplishment, carrying out, completing, finishing, effecting [➤ CARRY OUT AN ACTION; 269] **2** *n* **putting to death**, capital punishment, the death sentence, killing, hanging, slaying [➤ CAUSES OF DEATH; 921]

executive **1** *n* **manager**, senior manager, director, administrator, official [➤ BUSINESS PEOPLE; 793] **2** *adj* **decision-making**, policymaking, managerial, management, administrative, supervisory [➤ TYPES OF WORK; 835] **3** *adj* **expensive**, exclusive, high class, superior, select, fashionable, high-status, luxurious [➤ EXPENSIVE AND LUXURIOUS; 218]

executive jet *type of* **civil aircraft** [➤ AIRCRAFT; 1148]

executor *n* **doer**, prime mover, initiator, originator, architect, facilitator, organizer [➤ DESIGNERS, CREATORS, AND INSTIGATORS; 347]

exemplar (*literary*) *n* **ideal**, model, paradigm, example, archetype, epitome [➤ PERFECT EXAMPLES AND EMBODIMENTS; 67]

exemplary **1** *adj* **admirable**, praiseworthy, excellent, perfect, ideal, commendable [➤ ADMIRABLE AND COMMENDABLE; 185] **2** *adj* (*formal*) **model**, archetypal, textbook, typical, classic, prototypical [➤ REPRESENTATIVE; 66]

exemplification *n* [➤ REPRESENTATIONS AND GENERAL EXAMPLES; 65]

exemplify *v* **demonstrate**, typify, represent, illustrate, show, epitomize, embody, characterize, personify [➤ REPRESENT SOMETHING OR SOMEBODY; 59]

exempt **1** *adj* **excused**, exempted, released, relieved, discharged, let off, excepted, not liable, immune, freed, off the hook (*informal*) [➤ FREEDOM AND LIBERTY; 208] *Opposite*: required **2** *v* **excuse**, free, let off, let go, release, relieve, spare, discharge, pardon, except (*formal*) [➤ FORGET, FORGIVE, AND ACCEPT; 748] *Opposite*: oblige

exemption *n* **exception**, immunity, release, indemnity, exclusion, freedom, discharge, absolution [➤ FREEDOM AND LIBERTY; 208] *Opposite*: obligation

exercise **1** *n* **physical movements**, aerobics, workout, calisthenics, cardiovascular exercise, training, drills [➤ HOBBIES, GAMES, AND SPORTS; 875] **2** *n* **physical activity**, working out, training, drill [➤ HOBBIES, GAMES, AND SPORTS; 875] *Opposite*: inactivity **3** *n* (*formal*) **implementation**, carrying out, use, application, employment, practice [➤ USE; 467] *Opposite*: avoidance **4** *v* **work out**, train, do exercises, drill [➤ FIDGET AND FROLIC; 311] **5** *v* **use**, put into effect, implement, apply, employ, bring to bear, exert, carry out, effect (*formal*) [➤ USE; 467] *Opposite*: avoid

exercise bike *type of* **bike** [➤ BIKES, CARS, AND CARRIAGES; 1149]

exercises *n* **military exercises**, maneuvers, drills, war games [➤ WARFARE AND WAR; 830]

exert *v* **bring to bear**, use, apply, exercise, make use of, employ, wield, utilize [➤ USE; 467]

exertion *n* **effort**, action, application, physical exertion, energy, hard work, force, toil, pains, labor [➤ HARD WORK OR EFFORT; 298] *Opposite*: ease

exert yourself *v* **make an effort**, try hard, push yourself, strive, labor, strain, work hard, put your all into something, work flat out, work up a sweat [➤ HARD WORK OR EFFORT; 298]

exhale *v* **breathe out**, blow out, puff out, let your breath out, respire [➤ BREATHE AND NOT BREATHE; 716] *Opposite*: inhale

exhaust **1** *v* **tire out**, wear out, drain, fatigue, weaken, tire, do in (*informal*) [➤ TIRED, ASLEEP, AND UNCONSCIOUS; 738] *Opposite*: refresh **2** *v* **use up**, use, wear out, consume, drain, deplete, sap, run through, expend, dissipate, finish (*informal*) [➤ USE UP AND WASTE; 474] *Opposite*: renew

exhausted *adj* **tired**, worn out, fatigued, drained, wearied, spent, all in, pooped (*informal*), done in (*informal*), bushed (*informal*), dog-tired (*informal*), beat (*slang*), shattered (*UK*) [➤ TIRED, ASLEEP, AND UNCONSCIOUS; 738] *Opposite*: refreshed

exhausting *adj* **tiring**, wearing, fatiguing, killing, grueling, arduous, strenuous, wearying, draining, shattering (*UK*) [➤ PHYSICALLY UNPLEASANT; 226] *Opposite*: refreshing

exhaustion *n* **tiredness**, fatigue, collapse, overtiredness, enervation [➤ TIRED, ASLEEP, AND UNCONSCIOUS; 738] *Opposite*: energy

exhaustive *adj* **thorough**, complete, comprehensive, in-depth, full, extensive, far-reaching, meticulous, all-inclusive, intensive, sweeping [➤ WHOLENESS AND COMPLETENESS; 198] *Opposite*: superficial

exhaust pipe *type of* **external feature** [➤ EXTERNAL PARTS OF A VEHICLE; 1147]

exhibit 1 *v* **display**, show, unveil, put on a display, put on view, reveal, demonstrate [➤ CAUSE TO APPEAR; 5] *Opposite*: hide 2 *v* **show off**, parade, flaunt, expose, display, demonstrate [➤ CAUSE TO APPEAR; 5] 3 *n* **exhibition**, display, show, showcase, showing, exposition, parade, revelation, demonstration [➤ PERFORMANCES AND SHOWS; 42]

exhibition 1 *n* **display**, show, showing, demonstration, exposition, trade fair, presentation, fair, retrospective, showcase [➤ PERFORMANCES AND SHOWS; 42] 2 *n* (*UK*) **grant**, scholarship, bursary, award, fund [➤ INCOME; 460]

exhibition hall *n* [➤ BUILDINGS FOR PUBLIC ENTERTAINMENT; 1084]

exhibitionist *n* **attention seeker**, grandstander, braggart, show-off (*informal*), play-actor (*informal*) [➤ SELF-IMPORTANT AND SELF-SEEKING PEOPLE; 949]

exhilarate *v* **excite**, elate, thrill, enliven, invigorate, lift, stimulate, hearten, psych (*informal*) [➤ SURPRISE AND IMPRESS; 574] *Opposite*: bore

exhilarated *adj* **elated**, ecstatic, euphoric, overjoyed, delighted, inspired, energized, excited, psyched (*informal*), exalted (*formal*), over the moon (*UK informal*) [➤ PLEASURE, EXCITEMENT, AND ELATION; 534] *Opposite*: indifferent

exhilarating *adj* [➤ PHYSICALLY PLEASANT; 186]

exhilaration *n* **excitement**, elation, high spirits, animation, happiness, delight, joy [➤ PLEASURE, EXCITEMENT, AND ELATION; 534]

exhort *v* **urge**, press, push, pressure, insist, encourage, spur, goad, prod [➤ CAUSE OR COMPEL TO ACT; 271] *Opposite*: forbid

exhortation (*formal*) *n* **appeal**, call, encouragement, urging, incitement, advice, counsel (*formal or literary*) [➤ ADVICE; 689]

exhume *v* **dig up**, disinter, unearth, disentomb, disclose [➤ BURIAL AND PREPARATION FOR BURIAL; 929] *Opposite*: bury

exigency (*formal*) *n* **need**, demand, requirement, emergency, necessity, pressure, constraint [➤ NECESSARY AND ESSENTIAL; 196]

exigent (*formal*) 1 *adj* **urgent**, pressing, crucial, vital, important, necessary, needful, insistent [➤ IMPORTANT; 194] *Opposite*: unimportant 2 *adj* **demanding**, tough, testing, challenging, taxing, tricky, exacting, burdensome, difficult, arduous [➤ PHYSICALLY UNPLEASANT; 226] *Opposite*: easy

exile 1 *n* **émigré**, tax exile, expatriate, deportee, refugee, outcast, D.P. [➤ PEOPLE LIVING AWAY FROM HOME; 887] 2 *n* **banishment**, deportation, expulsion, separation, ostracism, expatriation [➤ ABSENT AND UNAVAILABLE; 7] 3 *v* **banish**, send away, deport, expel, separate, eject, oust, drive out, cast out (*formal*) [➤ EJECT AND EXCLUDE; 340]

exist 1 *v* **be**, be real, be present, be existent, happen, occur [➤ EXIST; 15] 2 *v* **live**, be, survive, continue living, stay alive, subsist, endure, last [➤ CONTINUE TO EXIST; 17]

existence *n* **being**, life, reality, presence, survival, actuality, animation [➤ THE STAGES OF LIFE; 916]

existent (*formal*) *adj* **existing**, current, present, extant, ongoing, in existence, surviving [➤ PRESENT AND AVAILABLE; 11]

existentialist *n* [➤ PHILOSOPHICAL AND POLITICAL THINKERS; 781]

existing *adj* **present**, current, in effect, prevailing, standing, remaining, surviving [➤ PRESENT; 85]

exit 1 *n* **way out**, door, outlet, egress (*formal*) [➤ DOORS AND ACCESS POINTS; 1101] *Opposite*: entrance 2 *n* **departure**, exodus, walking out, leaving, going away, withdrawal, leave-taking (*literary*) [➤ ENDS AND DEPARTURES; 54] *Opposite*: arrival 3 *v* **go out**, leave, depart, go, walk out, withdraw, escape, take off (*informal*) [➤ LEAVE AND GO AWAY; 8] *Opposite*: enter

exodus *n* **mass departure**, departure, migration, emigration, flight, evacuation, exit, hegira [➤ ENDS AND DEPARTURES; 54] *Opposite*: arrival

exonerate *v* **clear**, absolve, acquit, vindicate, forgive, pardon, free, exculpate (*formal*) [➤ FORGET, FORGIVE, AND ACCEPT; 748] *Opposite*: blame

exoneration 1 *n* **pardon**, absolution, acquittal, vindication, exculpation (*formal*) [➤ FORGET, FORGIVE, AND ACCEPT; 748] *Opposite*: blame 2 *n* **release**, freeing, liberation, exemption, discharge [➤ FREEDOM AND LIBERTY; 208]

exorbitance *n* [➤ TOO MUCH; 119]

exorbitant *adj* **excessive**, inflated, ridiculous, dear, overpriced, unreasonable, extortionate, outrageous, inordinate, steep (*informal*) [➤ EXPENSIVE AND OVERPRICED; 247] *Opposite*: reasonable

exorcize *v* **get rid of**, get free of, banish, drive out, force out, expel [➤ GET RID OF SOMETHING; 451]

exosphere *n* [➤ THE EARTH'S ATMOSPHERE; 1040]

exotic 1 *adj* **unusual**, out of the ordinary, novel, striking, interesting, bizarre, mysterious, glamorous, colorful, outlandish, strange, different, exceptional [➤ EXTRAORDINARY: UNCOMMON; 205] *Opposite*: ordinary 2 *adj* **foreign**, from abroad, tropical, alien, nonnative [➤ EXTRAORDINARY: UNCOMMON; 205] *Opposite*: familiar

expand *v* **make bigger**, get bigger, enlarge, increase, develop, swell, inflate, spread out, open out, grow, magnify, multiply [➤ CHANGE OF SIZE: BIGGER; 392] *Opposite*: contract

See Compare and Contrast at **increase**.

expandable *adj* **stretchy**, elastic, foldup, foldout, pullout, inflatable, pliant, foldaway [➤ MALLEABLE AND ELASTIC; 1212]

expand upon *v* **enlarge on**, elaborate on, give details, embellish, amplify, develop [➤ EXPLAIN AND CLARIFY; 610]

expanse *n* **area**, breadth, stretch, span, region, spread, vastness [➤ SIZE AND DIMENSIONS; 1192]

expansion *n* **growth**, development, increase, extension, spreading out, opening out, enlargement [➤ CHANGE OF SIZE: BIGGER; 392] *Opposite*: contraction

expansionism *n* [➤ STYLES AND SYSTEMS OF GOVERNMENT; 806]

expansionist *adj* [➤ STYLES AND SYSTEMS OF GOVERNMENT; 806]

expansive 1 *adj* **communicative**, generous, magnanimous, friendly, open, unreserved, unrestrained, outgoing, extroverted [➤ ELOQUENT, TALKATIVE, AND LONG-WINDED; 632]

Opposite: reserved   **2** *adj* **extensive**, spread-out, spacious, roomy, sizable, wide, sprawling, vast, capacious [➠ LARGE; 1193] *Opposite*: cramped

expansively   **1** *adv* **at length**, extensively, widely, comprehensively, broadly, lengthily, thoroughly [➠ ELOQUENT, TALKATIVE, AND LONG-WINDED; 632] *Opposite*: briefly   **2** *adv* **effusively**, lavishly, openly, generously, jovially, enthusiastically [➠ ENTHUSIASTIC AND INQUISITIVE; 628]

expansiveness   **1** *n* **size**, large size, mass, extent, reach, scale, largeness, vastness [➠ LARGE; 1193]   **2** *n* **effusiveness**, lavishness, openness, generousness, enthusiasm, extravagance, magnanimity [➠ ENERGY AND ENTHUSIASM; 496] *Opposite*: reserve

expat (*informal*) *n* **expatriate**, emigrant, colonial, émigré, tax exile, deportee, refugee, exile [➠ PEOPLE LIVING AWAY FROM HOME; 887] *Opposite*: native

expatiate   *v* [➠ INSTRUCT AND TEACH; 609]

expatriate   *n* **émigré**, tax exile, emigrant, deportee, refugee, colonial, exile, expat (*informal*) [➠ PEOPLE LIVING AWAY FROM HOME; 887] *Opposite*: native

expect   **1** *v* **imagine**, suppose, guess, think, believe, assume, presume, reckon [➠ UNCERTAINTY; 559]   **2** *v* **wait for**, anticipate, look forward to, await, look ahead, hope for, envisage [➠ PREDICT AND ANTICIPATE; 750]   **3** *v* **demand**, require, insist on, count on, anticipate [➠ REQUEST AND DEMAND; 663]

expectancy   *n* **anticipation**, expectation, hope, suspense, bated breath, belief, prospect, probability [➠ FEELINGS ABOUT THE FUTURE; 533]

expectant   **1** *adj* **eager**, hopeful, in suspense, hoping, on tenterhooks, excited, anxious, keen [➠ PLEASURE, EXCITEMENT, AND ELATION; 534]   **2** *adj* **pregnant**, expecting, in the family way (*dated informal*) [➠ REPRODUCTION AND HEREDITY; 725]

expectantly   *adv* **hopefully**, eagerly, excitedly, keenly, anxiously, with interest, with bated breath [➠ PLEASURE, EXCITEMENT, AND ELATION; 534]

expectation   *n* **hope**, anticipation, expectancy, belief, prospect, probability, suspense, bated breath [➠ FEELINGS ABOUT THE FUTURE; 533]

expected   *adj* **likely**, probable, foreseeable, predictable, awaited, anticipated [➠ POSSIBLE AND PROBABLE; 177] *Opposite*: surprising

expecting   *adj* **pregnant**, expectant, in the family way (*dated informal*) [➠ REPRODUCTION AND HEREDITY; 725]

expectorant   *n* **cough medicine**, linctus, cough syrup, medicine, cough mixture (*UK*) [➠ REMEDIES, TREATMENTS, AND OPERATIONS; 731]

expediency   **1** *n* **convenience**, practicality, pragmatism, usefulness, feasibility [➠ USEFULNESS; 199]   **2** *n* **appropriateness**, suitability, fitness, advisability, convenience [➠ APPROPRIATE, SUITABLE, AND ADVISABLE; 184] *Opposite*: unsuitability

expedient   **1** *adj* **appropriate**, fitting, suitable, advisable, necessary, opportune [➠ APPROPRIATE, SUITABLE, AND ADVISABLE; 184] *Opposite*: inappropriate   **2** *adj* **advantageous**, convenient, practical, useful, beneficial, self-serving, politic, pragmatic [➠ USEFULNESS; 199] *Opposite*: altruistic   **3** *n* **measure**,

means, method, maneuver, device, way [➠ WAYS OF DOING THINGS; 294]

expediently   **1** *adv* **appropriately**, suitably, fittingly, correctly, necessarily, opportunely, advisably [➠ APPROPRIATE, SUITABLE, AND ADVISABLE; 184] *Opposite*: inappropriately   **2** *adv* **advantageously**, conveniently, practically, beneficially, pragmatically [➠ USEFULNESS; 199] *Opposite*: altruistically

expedite   (*formal*) *v* **speed up**, accelerate, hurry up, advance, further, facilitate, rush [➠ MAKE POSSIBLE; 275] *Opposite*: impede

expedition   **1** *n* **journey**, excursion, voyage, trip, outing, mission, tour, trek, jaunt [➠ TRAVEL: JOURNEYS AND TRIPS; 318]   **2** *n* **team**, party, crew, group, company, troop [➠ GROUPS WITH A COMMON INTEREST; 938]

expeditious   *adj* **speedy**, prompt, quick, swift, hasty, efficient [➠ HAPPENING QUICKLY; 104] *Opposite*: slow

expel   **1** *v* **dismiss**, fire, eject, oust, throw out, banish, sack (*informal*) [➠ REVOKE STATUS; 459]   **2** *v* **drive out**, force out, push out, eject, flush out [➠ EJECT AND EXCLUDE; 340]

expend   **1** *v* **use up**, use, consume, spend, burn up, apply, utilize [➠ USE UP AND WASTE; 474] *Opposite*: conserve   **2** *v* (*formal*) **spend**, disburse, pay out, lay out, pay [➠ GIVE MONEY; 433] *Opposite*: save

expendable   **1** *adj* **dispensable**, disposable, superfluous, unessential, nonessential, inessential, unneeded [➠ UNIMPORTANT AND UNNECESSARY; 238] *Opposite*: indispensable   **2** *adj* **consumable**, replaceable, throwaway, disposable, usable [➠ FINITENESS, VARIABILITY, AND TRANSIENCE; 96] *Opposite*: durable

expenditure   *n* **spending**, expenses, payments, outflow, costs, overheads, disbursement, outlay, outgoings (*UK*) [➠ EXPENDITURE; 423] *Opposite*: income

expense   **1** *n* **cost**, expenditure, outlay, disbursement, outflow, payment, overhead [➠ EXPENDITURE; 423] *Opposite*: income   **2** *n* **price**, rate, figure, amount, price tag, fee, toll, premium, tariff [➠ EXPENDITURE; 423]   **3** *n* **sacrifice**, cost, detriment, disadvantage, loss [➠ NUISANCES; 253]

expenses   **1** *n* **expenditure**, outlay, incidentals, costs, overheads, outgoings (*UK*) [➠ EXPENDITURE; 423] *Opposite*: income   **2** *n* [➠ FUNDS, PAYMENTS, AND CHARGES; 800]

expensive   **1** *adj* **luxurious**, exclusive, affluent, lavish, classy (*informal*), posh (*informal*) [➠ EXPENSIVE AND LUXURIOUS; 218] *Opposite*: cheap   **2** *adj* **costly**, dear, high-priced, big-ticket, steep (*informal*), pricey (*informal*) [➠ EXPENSIVE AND OVERPRICED; 247] *Opposite*: cheap

expensively   *adv* **luxuriously**, extravagantly, affluently, lavishly [➠ EXPENSIVE AND LUXURIOUS; 218] *Opposite*: cheaply

experience   **1** *n* **involvement**, knowledge, skill, practice, understanding, familiarity, capability, proficiency, know-how (*informal*) [➠ KNOWLEDGE AND WISDOM; 558]   **2** *n* **occurrence**, incident, episode, encounter, event, happening [➠ EVENTS AND OCCURRENCES; 35]   **3** *v* **feel**, go through, face, live through, undergo, come across, suffer [➠ EXPERIENCE AND ENCOUNTER; 582]

experienced   *adj* **knowledgeable**, skilled, practiced, qualified, veteran, expert, proficient, skillful [➠ KNOWLEDGE AND WISDOM; 558] *Opposite*: inexperienced

experiment 1 *n* trial, test, tryout, research, experimentation [➡ EXAMINE AND ASSESS; 753] **2** *v* test, try out, investigate, try, trial (*UK*) [➡ EXAMINE AND ASSESS; 753]

experimental *adj* new, tentative, investigational, untried, trial [➡ EXTRAORDINARY: UNCOMMON; 205]

experimentation *n* testing, research, investigation, trialing (*UK*) [➡ EXAMINE AND ASSESS; 753]

expert 1 *n* specialist, authority, professional, connoisseur, maven, doyen, whiz (*informal*) [➡ TALENTED OR INTELLIGENT PEOPLE; 528] *Opposite*: amateur **2** *adj* skilled, skillful, practiced, proficient, professional, knowledgeable, adept [➡ TALENTED AND SKILLFUL; 527] *Opposite*: inexperienced

expertise *n* skill, knowledge, proficiency, capability, know-how (*informal*) [➡ KNOWLEDGE AND WISDOM; 558]

expertness *n* skillfulness, dexterity, knowledge, expertise, proficiency, capability, ability, skill, experience [➡ SKILLS, TALENTS, AND ABILITIES; 526] *Opposite*: inexperience

expiate *v* make amends, compensate, make up for, recompense, redress, do penance, amend, correct, put right, atone (*formal*) [➡ APOLOGIZE AND RETRACT; 683]

expiation *n* [➡ APOLOGIZE AND RETRACT; 683]

expiration *n* [➡ ENDS AND DEPARTURES; 54]

expire 1 *v* end, run out, finish, terminate, conclude, elapse, lapse, invalidate [➡ CEASE TO EXIST; 22] **2** *v* (*formal or literary*) die, pass away, pass on, perish (*literary*), breathe your last (*literary*), decease (*formal*) [➡ DIE; 922]

expiry 1 *n* end, ending, running out, finish, finishing, expiration, termination [➡ ENDS AND DEPARTURES; 54] *Opposite*: beginning **2** *n* (*formal or literary*) death, passing, dying, decease (*formal*), demise (*formal*) [➡ DEATH AND BEREAVEMENT; 927]

explain 1 *v* make clear, describe, put in plain words, elucidate, clarify, explicate, illuminate, enlighten, expound [➡ EXPLAIN AND CLARIFY; 610] **2** *v* justify, account for, defend, rationalize, vindicate, support [➡ APPROVE AND CONFIRM; 646]

explanation 1 *n* description, account, clarification, enlightenment, details, elucidation (*formal*) [➡ EXPLAIN AND CLARIFY; 610] **2** *n* reason, justification, rationalization, vindication, account, excuse [➡ CAUSATION; 168]

explanatory *adj* descriptive, instructive, illustrative, illuminating, clarifying, expounding, advisory, helpful, explicatory, elucidatory (*formal*) [➡ EXPLAIN AND CLARIFY; 610]

expletive *n* swearword, curse, oath, exclamation, obscenity, four-letter word, cussword (*informal*), invective (*formal*) [➡ INSULTS, ABUSE, AND SWEARING; 658]

explicable *adj* explainable, understandable, reasonable, justifiable, rational [➡ CORRECT AND FAULTLESS; 182] *Opposite*: inexplicable

explicate *v* explain, elucidate, spell out, clarify, expound, illuminate, make clear, make plain [➡ EXPLAIN AND CLARIFY; 610]

explication *n* [➡ EXPLAIN AND CLARIFY; 610]

explicit 1 *adj* clear, obvious, open, overt, plain, unambiguous, unequivocal, categorical, perspicuous [➡ CONCISE AND CLEAR; 202] *Opposite*: implicit **2** *adj* definite, precise, exact, specific, unequivocal [➡ EXACT; 203] *Opposite*: vague **3** *adj* frank, uninhibited, candid, open, graphic, raw [➡ HONEST AND OPEN; 630]

explicitly *adv* clearly, openly, obviously, overtly, plainly, unambiguously, unequivocally [➡ HONEST AND OPEN; 630] *Opposite*: implicitly

explode 1 *v* blow up, go off, burst, erupt, burst out, blast, detonate, shatter [➡ DESTRUCTION AND DEMOLITION; 359] **2** *v* get angry, fly into a rage, hit the ceiling, hit the roof, blow up (*informal*), fly off the handle (*informal*), go ballistic (*slang*) [➡ GIVING VENT TO EMOTIONS; 679] **3** *v* disprove, prove wrong, discredit, invalidate, nullify, challenge, negate (*formal*) [➡ DENY AND REJECT; 644]

exploit 1 *v* use, develop, make use of, take advantage of, utilize, make the most of [➡ MAKE GOOD USE OF SOMETHING; 473] *Opposite*: waste **2** *v* take advantage of, abuse, misuse, ill-use, manipulate, play on [➡ MISUSE AND ABUSE; 471] **3** *n* feat, deed, adventure, activity, heroic act, daring act, achievement [➡ ACTIONS OR UNDERTAKINGS; 259]

exploitable 1 *adj* usable, utilizable, consumable, available [➡ USEFULNESS; 199] **2** *adj* gullible, credulous, innocent, vulnerable [➡ NEGATIVE INTELLECTUAL CHARACTERISTICS; 525] *Opposite*: shrewd

exploitation 1 *n* misuse, abuse, mistreatment, taking advantage, manipulation, corruption [➡ MISUSE AND ABUSE; 471] **2** *n* use, utilization, development, management, operation [➡ USE; 467]

exploitative *adj* unfair, unequal, abusive, manipulative [➡ MORALLY BAD OR IMPROPER; 775] *Opposite*: fair

exploration 1 *n* traveling, discovery, journeying, adventure, voyaging [➡ TRAVEL: JOURNEYS AND TRIPS; 318] **2** *n* examination, investigation, survey, study, consideration, probe, search, assessment, evaluation [➡ EXAMINE AND ASSESS; 753]

exploratory *adj* investigative, examining, probing, tentative, experimental, fact-finding, empirical, trial [➡ EXAMINE AND ASSESS; 753]

explore 1 *v* travel, discover, reconnoiter, see the sights, sightsee, survey, tour, scout [➡ TRAVEL: WAYS OF TRAVELING; 320] **2** *v* investigate, study, search, look at, survey, open up, go into, delve into, deal with [➡ EXAMINE AND ASSESS; 753]

explorer *n* traveler, voyager, surveyor, pioneer, pathfinder [➡ TRAVEL: TRAVELERS AND WALKERS; 319]

explosion 1 *n* bang, blast, detonation, eruption, burst [➡ SUDDEN EVENTS; 52] **2** *n* outburst, fit, eruption, paroxysm, burst, release, flare-up (*informal*) [➡ CRITICISMS AND ANGRY OUTBURSTS; 50] **3** *n* upsurge, leap, flood, outbreak, eruption, increase [➡ CHANGE OF SIZE: BIGGER; 392] *Opposite*: slump

explosive 1 *adj* volatile, unstable, unpredictable, dangerous [➡ DANGEROUS; 236] *Opposite*: stable **2** *adj* short-tempered, quick-tempered, hotheaded, volatile, fiery, touchy [➡ EXCESSIVE SENSITIVITY; 511] *Opposite*: placid

explosive

◆ *types of explosive material*
dynamite, gelignite, gunpowder, napalm, nitroglycerin, plastic explosive, propellant, TNT

◆ *types of explosive weapons*
A-bomb, antiballistic missile, atomic bomb, ballistic missile, bomb, booby trap, cruise missile, depth charge, firebomb, guided missile, hand grenade, hydrogen bomb, mine, missile, Molotov cocktail, nail bomb, neutron bomb, nuclear missile, nuclear warhead, nuclear weapon, pipe bomb, smart bomb, smoke bomb, time bomb, torpedo, warhead

exponent 1 *n* **advocate**, proponent, promoter, fan, champion, backer, booster, supporter [➡ DEVOTEES AND ADDICTED PEOPLE; 556] 2 *n* **interpreter**, explainer, performer, practitioner [➡ WRITERS AND STYLES; 914]

export 1 *v* **sell abroad**, sell overseas, send abroad, send overseas, ship, trade, distribute, freight [➡ SELL; 441] *Opposite*: import 2 *v* **spread**, transfer, carry across, pass on, disseminate, distribute [➡ DISPENSE, RATION, AND DISTRIBUTE; 434]

expose 1 *v* **open up**, reveal, uncover, bare, display, show [➡ CAUSE TO APPEAR; 5] *Opposite*: cover 2 *v* **subject**, lay open to, put in danger, endanger, imperil (*formal*) [➡ PUT AT RISK; 384] 3 *v* **blow the whistle on**, unmask, reveal, lay bare, bring to light, take the wraps off, catch out [➡ BETRAY CONFIDENCES AND GOSSIP; 618] *Opposite*: cover up

exposé *n* **disclosure**, revelation, leak, exposure, discovery, uncovering, mudraking [➡ NEWSPAPERS AND MAGAZINES; 605]

exposed *adj* **unprotected**, visible, uncovered, bare, showing, out in the open, out, open, wide-open [➡ PERCEPTIBLE; 25] *Opposite*: covered

exposition 1 *n* **description**, discussion, explanation, account, clarification, elucidation (*formal*) [➡ ONE-WAY COMMUNICATION; 49] 2 *n* **exhibition**, fair, show, trade fair, display, demonstration, showcase [➡ PERFORMANCES AND SHOWS; 42]

expostulate *v* **disagree**, protest, object, reprove, remonstrate, admonish, complain, argue [➡ PROTEST AND EXPRESS DISAPPROVAL; 642]

See Compare and Contrast at **object**.

exposure 1 *n* **contact**, experience, introduction, acquaintance [➡ KNOWLEDGE AND WISDOM; 558] 2 *n* **revelation**, disclosure, revealing, unveiling, publicity, coverage [➡ NEWSPAPERS AND MAGAZINES; 605]

exposure meter *part of* **camera** [➡ PHOTOGRAPHY AND PHOTOGRAPHIC EQUIPMENT; 1122]

expound *v* **explain**, expand on, talk about, develop, illustrate, expand, spell out, explicate [➡ EXPLAIN AND CLARIFY; 610]

express 1 *v* **state**, articulate, utter, voice, communicate, put across, convey, say, vent, broach, air [➡ UTTER AND PRONOUNCE; 608] 2 *v* **squeeze out**, extract, press out, force out [➡ REMOVE SOMETHING; 338] 3 *adj* **fast**, rapid, direct, nonstop, prompt [➡ HAPPENING QUICKLY; 104] *Opposite*: slow 4 *adj* **precise**, explicit, definite, exact, specific, unambiguous [➡ EXACT; 203] *Opposite*: vague

expression 1 *n* **look**, face, air, appearance, countenance, mien (*formal*) [➡ FACIAL EXPRESSIONS AND BLUSHING; 651] 2 *n* **phrase**, idiom, turn of phrase, term, saying, set phrase [➡ THE SPOKEN WORD; 671] 3 *n* **communication**, manifestation, illustration, example, demonstration, representation, articulation, utterance, statement [➡ REPRESENTATIONS AND GENERAL EXAMPLES; 65] 4 *n* **extraction**, squeezing out, pressing out, forcing out [➡ REMOVE SOMETHING; 338]

expressionism *type of* **20th-century art movement** [➡ ARTISTIC MOVEMENTS AND STYLES; 899]

expressionless *adj* **straight-faced**, unresponsive, impassive, poker-faced, inexpressive, vacant, unreadable, deadpan, blank, lifeless, vacuous, unemotional [➡ FACIAL EXPRESSIONS AND BLUSHING; 651] *Opposite*: expressive

expressive 1 *adj* **communicative**, sensitive, open, easy-to-read, animated, mobile, dramatic [➡ HONEST AND OPEN; 630] *Opposite*: impassive 2 *adj* **representative**, representing, demonstrating, signifying, indicative, indicating [➡ REPRESENTATIVE; 66]

expressively *adv* **meaningfully**, dramatically, emotionally, sensitively, vividly [➡ INTERESTING AND MEANINGFUL; 190] *Opposite*: blandly

expressivity *n* **articulacy**, eloquence, self-expression, fluency, clarity, lucidity, perspicuity, articulateness [➡ ELOQUENT, TALKATIVE, AND LONG-WINDED; 632] *Opposite*: inarticulacy

expressly *adv* **specifically**, particularly, explicitly, clearly, definitely, deliberately, unambiguously [➡ INTENTIONAL AND DELIBERATE; 279]

expressway *type of* **highway** [➡ ROADS; 1106]

expropriate *v* **steal**, confiscate, seize, commandeer, appropriate, sequester, impound, take, annex [➡ TAKE SOMETHING AWAY; 425]

expulsion *n* **dismissal**, exclusion, throwing out, eviction, removal, ejection, discharge, kicking out (*informal*) [➡ EJECT AND EXCLUDE; 340] *Opposite*: admittance

expunge *v* **obliterate**, purge, erase, delete, rub out, cross out, edit out, remove, cut, censor, wipe out (*informal*) [➡ DELETE AND ERASE; 339] *Opposite*: insert

expurgate *v* [➡ CORRECT AND PUT RIGHT; 377]

expurgated *adj* **cut down**, abridged, censored, edited, bowdlerized, cut [➡ LESS; 126]

expurgation *n* [➡ CHANGE; 372]

exquisite 1 *adj* **beautiful**, gorgeous, delicate, attractive, superb, wonderful, pretty, good-looking, lovely, fine [➡ BEAUTY AND ATTRACTIVENESS; 189] *Opposite*: ugly 2 *adj* **excellent**, perfect, delightful, flawless, wonderful, admirable [➡ EXTRAORDINARY: AMAZING; 204] *Opposite*: flawed 3 *adj* **discriminating**, discerning, sensitive, fastidious, refined, delicate, exacting, tasteful, perfect, elegant, impeccable [➡ POSITIVE INTELLECTUAL CHARACTERISTICS; 524] 4 *adj* **intense**, touching, moving, excruciating, poignant, acute, stabbing, piercing, sharp [➡ STRENGTH; 201] *Opposite*: dull

exquisitely 1 *adv* **beautifully**, finely, delicately, intricately, superbly, skillfully, wonderfully, divinely (*informal*) [➡ EXTRAORDINARY: AMAZING; 204] *Opposite*: clumsily 2 *adv* **tastefully**, perfectly, discerningly, sensitively, delicately, impeccably, elegantly, discriminatingly, fastidiously [➡ BEAUTY AND ATTRACTIVENESS; 189]

exquisiteness *n* **beauty**, delicacy, daintiness, perfection, attractiveness, elegance, loveliness [➡ BEAUTY AND ATTRACTIVENESS; 189] *Opposite:* ugliness

extant *adj* **existing**, in existence, present, living, surviving, existent (*formal*) [➡ PRESENT; 85] *Opposite:* lost

See Compare and Contrast at **living**.

extemporaneous *adj* **extempory**, extemporal, unrehearsed, impromptu, ad-lib, spontaneous, off-the-cuff [➡ HAPPENING QUICKLY; 104] *Opposite:* rehearsed

extempore 1 *adj* **extemporaneous**, ad-lib, off-the-cuff, impromptu, unrehearsed, spontaneous [➡ HAPPENING QUICKLY; 104] *Opposite:* rehearsed 2 *adv* **extemporaneously**, ad lib, off the cuff, impromptu, spontaneously, offhand [➡ HAPPENING QUICKLY; 104] *Opposite:* rehearsed

extemporize *v* **ad-lib**, improvise, speak off the cuff, play it by ear, make it up as you go along, do on the fly, wing it (*informal*) [➡ UTTER AND PRONOUNCE; 608] *Opposite:* prepare

extend 1 *v* **spread**, spread out, range, cover, encompass, outspread [➡ EXIST IN A PLACE; 19] 2 *v* **continue**, reach, stretch, go on, run, run on, go, carry on [➡ CONTINUE TO EXIST; 17] 3 *v* **make bigger**, expand, enlarge, make longer, lengthen, widen, broaden, pull out [➡ CHANGE OF SIZE: BIGGER; 392] *Opposite:* curtail 4 *v* **prolong**, stretch out, drag out, lengthen, postpone, delay, put off, spin out [➡ CAUSE TO CONTINUE; 267] *Opposite:* cut short 5 *v* **increase**, expand, widen, broaden, add to, develop [➡ CHANGE OF SIZE: BIGGER; 392] *Opposite:* decrease 6 *v* **offer**, give, hold out, proffer, tender, present [➡ PROFFER AND HAND OVER; 431] *Opposite:* withdraw

See Compare and Contrast at **increase**.

extended *adj* **lengthy**, protracted, long, prolonged, stretched, long-drawn-out, drawn-out [➡ HAPPENING SLOWLY; 106] *Opposite:* cut short

extension 1 *n* **additional room**, addition, lean-to, conservatory, annex, porch, wing [➡ ANCILLARY BUILDINGS; 1080] 2 *n* **expansion**, enlargement, lengthening, broadening, increase, augmentation [➡ CHANGE OF SIZE: BIGGER; 392] *Opposite:* contraction 3 *n* **delay**, postponement, leeway, allowance, extra time [➡ PERIODS OF TIME; 90]

extensive 1 *adj* **big**, large, huge, vast, massive, wide, broad [➡ LARGE; 1193] *Opposite:* restricted 2 *adj* **wide**, widespread, wide-ranging, general, all-embracing, far-reaching, all-encompassing, broad [➡ GENERAL LOCATIONS; 158] *Opposite:* narrow

extensively 1 *adv* **at length**, lengthily, widely, far, broadly, expansively, comprehensively [➡ WHOLENESS AND COMPLETENESS; 198] *Opposite:* briefly 2 *adv* **significantly**, considerably, greatly, to a great extent, to a large extent, much, highly [➡ TO A GREAT EXTENT; 132] *Opposite:* insignificantly

extensiveness *n* **breadth**, comprehensiveness, fullness, richness, vastness, range, broadness [➡ LARGE; 1193] *Opposite:* narrowness

extent 1 *n* **degree**, amount, level, range, scope, magnitude [➡ DEGREE AND EXTENT; 110] 2 *n* **size**, area, coverage, limit, boundary [➡ SIZE AND DIMENSIONS; 1192]

extenuating *adj* **mitigating**, explanatory, justifying, moderating, palliative, qualifying [➡ CAUSATION; 168]

exterior 1 *adj* **external**, outside, outdoor, peripheral, outward, outer [➡ EXTREMITIES OF PHYSICAL OBJECTS; 1250] *Opposite:* interior 2 *n* **outside**, façade, elevation, surface, shell [➡ PARTS OF A BUILDING; 1095] *Opposite:* interior 3 *n* **appearance**, look, aura, veneer, front, mien (*formal*) [➡ APPEARANCE AND ATMOSPHERE; 1237]

exterminate *v* **kill**, eliminate, annihilate, massacre, destroy, murder, eradicate, assassinate, decimate, liquidate, wipe out (*informal*), take out (*slang*), terminate (*formal*) [➡ KILL; 923]

extermination *n* **extinction**, annihilation, execution, killing, slaughter, massacre, butchery, termination [➡ CAUSES OF DEATH; 921] *Opposite:* preservation

external *adj* **outside**, exterior, outdoor, peripheral, outward, outer [➡ EXTREMITIES OF PHYSICAL OBJECTS; 1250] *Opposite:* internal

externalize *v* **express**, give voice to, utter, get off your chest, voice, convey [➡ UTTER AND PRONOUNCE; 608] *Opposite:* internalize

externally *adv* **outwardly**, on the outside, on the exterior, on the surface, superficially, outside, visibly [➡ PERCEPTIBLE; 25] *Opposite:* inwardly

extinct *adj* **nonexistent**, inexistent, died out, destroyed, vanished, lost, defunct, dead, wiped out (*slang*) [➡ DEAD AND DYING; 925] *Opposite:* living

See Compare and Contrast at **dead**.

extinction *n* **death**, extermination, destruction, loss, annihilation, disappearance, elimination [➡ ENDS AND DEPARTURES; 54] *Opposite:* survival

extinguish 1 *v* **douse**, quench, snuff, stub out, smother, switch off, put out, turn off (*informal*) [➡ CAUSE TO STOP; 266] *Opposite:* light 2 *v* **end**, take away, destroy, snuff out, do away with, terminate (*formal*) [➡ DESTRUCTION AND DEMOLITION; 359] 3 *v* **eclipse**, overshadow, outshine, obscure, show up, surpass [➡ CAUSE TO DISAPPEAR; 6]

extol (*formal or literary*) *v* **praise**, commend, eulogize, admire, worship, exalt (*formal*) [➡ PRAISE AND ENCOURAGE; 647] *Opposite:* deprecate

extort *v* **extract**, obtain under duress, obtain by threat, wrest, wring, force, squeeze, blackmail, shake down, screw (*slang*) [➡ STEAL AND ROB; 426]

extortion *n* **coercion**, threats, blackmail, squeezing, force, pressure, shakedown (*slang*), exaction (*formal*) [➡ CRIMES; 817]

extortionate *adj* **expensive**, exorbitant, inflated, high, overpriced, extravagant, usurious [➡ EXPENSIVE AND OVERPRICED; 247] *Opposite:* reasonable

extra 1 *adj* **additional**, further, added, spare, second, superfluous [➡ MORE AND EXCESS; 124] 2 *adv* **more**, in addition, further, on top, spare, beyond, above [➡ MORE AND EXCESS; 124] 3 *adv* **especially**, particularly, ultra, exceptionally, more

[➡ TO A GREAT EXTENT; 132] **4** *n* **optional extra**, addition, add-on, supplement, bonus, luxury, trimming, extravagance, treat (*UK*) [➡ MORE AND EXCESS; 124]

extract 1 *v* **take out**, remove, haul out, pull out, dig out, mine, dig up [➡ EXTRACT AND SEVER; 341] *Opposite*: put in **2** *v* **obtain**, unearth, extricate, root out, dig out, separate, isolate, get, winkle out (*UK*) [➡ EXTRACT AND SEVER; 341] **3** *v* **extort**, force, wrest, wring, drag, winkle out (*UK*), wheedle out (*UK*) [➡ TAKE SOMETHING AWAY; 425] **4** *n* **excerpt**, cutting, quotation, citation, abstract [➡ SUMMARIES, OUTLINES, AND EXCERPTS; 588]

extraction 1 *n* **removal**, taking out, withdrawal, pulling out, drawing out, abstraction, mining [➡ REMOVE SOMETHING; 338] *Opposite*: insertion **2** *n* **origin**, birth, descent, ancestry, family, lineage, line, heritage [➡ THE FAMILY; 956]

extracurricular 1 *adj* **additional**, supplementary, optional, secondary, extramural, subsidiary [➡ CLASSES, COURSEWORK, AND EXAMINATIONS; 842] *Opposite*: regular **2** *adj* (*informal*) **extramarital**, adulterous, clandestine, illicit, improper [➡ MORALLY BAD OR IMPROPER; 775]

extradite *v* **deport**, expel, banish, transfer, repatriate, hand over, send back, return [➡ EJECT AND EXCLUDE; 340]

extradition *n* **repatriation**, handing over, deportation, expulsion, return, arrest [➡ EJECT AND EXCLUDE; 340]

extra-large *adj* **outsize**, outsized, giant, jumbo, oversized, mammoth, mega, super, gigantic, oversize, large size, economy size [➡ LARGE; 1193] *Opposite*: undersized

extramarital *adj* **adulterous**, extracurricular, illicit, clandestine, improper, unlawful [➡ MORALLY BAD OR IMPROPER; 775]

extramural *adj* **external**, extracurricular, additional, optional, vocational [➡ EDUCATION; 838]

extraneous 1 *adj* **irrelevant**, unrelated, unconnected, inappropriate, beside the point, inapplicable [➡ REDUNDANT AND USELESS; 240] *Opposite*: pertinent **2** *adj* **inessential**, unimportant, unnecessary, superfluous, peripheral, minor [➡ UNIMPORTANT AND UNNECESSARY; 238] *Opposite*: essential

extraordinaire 1 *adj* **excellent**, extraordinary, superb, exceptional, remarkable [➡ EXTRAORDINARY: AMAZING; 204] *Opposite*: ordinary **2** *adj* **extemporary**, extemporal, unrehearsed, impromptu, ad lib, spontaneous [➡ HAPPENING QUICKLY; 104] *Opposite*: rehearsed

extraordinarily 1 *adv* **extremely**, very, unusually, particularly, amazingly, surprisingly, astonishingly [➡ TO A GREAT EXTENT; 132] **2** *adv* **strangely**, oddly, unusually, bizarrely, abnormally, unexpectedly [➡ EXTRAORDINARY: UNCOMMON; 205] *Opposite*: normally

extraordinary 1 *adj* **strange**, odd, unusual, unexpected, astonishing, surprising, amazing, bizarre, weird, peculiar, uncommon [➡ EXTRAORDINARY: UNCOMMON; 205] *Opposite*: ordinary **2** *adj* **special**, particular, exceptional, remarkable, great, wonderful [➡ EXTRAORDINARY: AMAZING; 204] *Opposite*: normal

extrapolate *v* **infer**, generalize, induce, deduce, conclude, reason, draw conclusions [➡ SOLVE AND INTERPRET; 760]

extrasensory *adj* **telepathic**, psychic, clairvoyant, mystic, mystical, paranormal [➡ THE SUPERNATURAL; 787]

extrasensory perception *n* [➡ THE SUPERNATURAL; 787]

extraterrestrial 1 *adj* **celestial**, interplanetary, Martian, alien, interstellar, otherworldly [➡ THE SOLAR SYSTEM AND ASTRONOMY; 1060] *Opposite*: terrestrial **2** *n* **alien**, creature, creature from outer space, space invader, ET, Martian, little green man (*humorous*) [➡ SCIENCE FICTION; 1064] *Opposite*: earthling

extravagance 1 *n* **profligacy**, overspending, wastefulness, excessiveness, lavishness, prodigality [➡ WASTEFUL AND UNECONOMICAL; 246] *Opposite*: prudence **2** *n* **luxury**, indulgence, folly, nonessential, overindulgence, extra, treat (*UK*) [➡ TREATS; 210] *Opposite*: essential

extravagant 1 *adj* **profligate**, wasteful, excessive, spendthrift, overgenerous, prodigal [➡ WASTEFUL AND UNECONOMICAL; 246] *Opposite*: thrifty **2** *adj* **exaggerated**, overstated, profuse, excessive, elaborate, overdone, ornate, gaudy, showy [➡ IN POOR TASTE AND OVERSENTIMENTAL; 229] *Opposite*: restrained

extravaganza *n* **show**, musical, variety performance, burlesque, gala, festival, spectacular, pageant [➡ PERFORMANCES AND SHOWS; 42]

extreme 1 *adj* **great**, tremendous, severe, intense, acute, excessive [➡ DIFFICULTY AND COMPLEXITY; 242] *Opposite*: insignificant **2** *adj* **radical**, fanatical, immoderate, zealous, excessive, intemperate [➡ NEGATIVE INTELLECTUAL CHARACTERISTICS; 525] *Opposite*: moderate **3** *adj* **farthest**, furthest, outermost, ultimate, maximum, utmost [➡ DISTANCE; 160] **4** *adj* **dangerous**, life-threatening, thrilling, risky, exciting, punishing [➡ DANGEROUS; 236] *Opposite*: safe **5** *n* **limit**, boundary, edge, end, pole, extremity, margin [➡ EXTREMITIES OF PHYSICAL OBJECTS; 1250]

extremely *adv* **very**, tremendously, enormously, awfully, really, particularly, exceptionally, exceedingly [➡ TO A GREAT EXTENT; 132] *Opposite*: somewhat

extreme sport *n* **adrenaline sport**, alternative sport, Xtreme sport [➡ HOBBIES, GAMES, AND SPORTS; 875]

extremism *n* **radicalism**, fanaticism, zealotry, activism, intemperance, immoderation (*formal*) [➡ FADS, FETISHES, AND IDOLATRY; 555] *Opposite*: moderation

extremist 1 *n* **radical**, fanatic, activist, revolutionary, rebel, terrorist [➡ PHILOSOPHICAL AND POLITICAL THINKERS; 781] *Opposite*: moderate **2** *adj* **radical**, fanatical, revolutionary, rebel, terrorist, extreme, intemperate, immoderate [➡ REBELLIOUSNESS AND DISOBEDIENCE; 565] *Opposite*: moderate

extremity 1 *n* **edge**, limit, boundary, margin, extreme, end, fringe [➡ EXTREMITIES OF PHYSICAL OBJECTS; 1250] *Opposite*: center **2** *n* **limb**, hand, foot, arm, leg, appendage [➡ PARTS OF THE BODY: TORSO; 693]

extricate *v* **get out**, extract, remove, disentangle, detach, disengage, disconnect, free, rescue [➡ REMOVE SOMETHING; 338] *Opposite*: engage

extrication *n* **disconnection**, detachment, disentanglement, disengagement, release, rescue, freeing [➡ REMOVE SOMETHING; 338] *Opposite*: engagement

extroversion *n* **sociability**, friendliness, self-confidence, socialness, outgoingness, gregariousness [➡ FRIENDLINESS AND SOCIABILITY; 494] *Opposite*: introversion

extrovert 1 *n* **outgoing person**, gregarious person, assertive person, socializer, befriender, live wire (*informal*), live one (*informal*) [➡ PLEASURE-SEEKERS AND HEDONISTS; 886] *Opposite*: introvert **2** *adj* **sociable**, outgoing, gregarious, extroverted, friendly, social [➡FRIENDLINESS AND SOCIABILITY; 494] *Opposite*: introverted

exuberance *n* **enthusiasm**, excitement, liveliness, energy, high spirits, cheerfulness [➡CHEERFULNESS OF OUTLOOK; 503] *Opposite*: apathy

exuberant *adj* **enthusiastic**, excited, lively, energetic, high-spirited, cheerful, boisterous, animated, vigorous, buoyant, vivacious [➡ENERGY AND ENTHUSIASM; 496] *Opposite*: lethargic

exude 1 *v* **radiate**, give out, give off, display, show, project, convey, ooze, emanate (*formal*) [➡EMIT AND EMANATE; 361] *Opposite*: absorb **2** *v* **secrete**, release, ooze, leak, discharge, weep, emit [➡LIQUID EMISSION; 370]

exult *v* **revel**, take pride, gloat, glory, triumph, wallow, rejoice (*literary*) [➡GIVING VENT TO EMOTIONS; 679] *Opposite*: lament

exultant *adj* **jubilant**, overjoyed, triumphant, joyful, thrilled, happy, elated, proud, gleeful, victorious, triumphalist, over the moon (*UK informal*) [➡PLEASURE, EXCITEMENT, AND ELATION; 534] *Opposite*: miserable

exultation *n* **happiness**, triumph, joy, rejoicing, jubilation, celebration [➡PLEASURE, EXCITEMENT, AND ELATION; 534] *Opposite*: misery

eyas *type of* **young bird** [➡YOUNG BIRDS; 1004]

eye 1 *part of* **face** [➡PARTS OF THE BODY: HEAD; 692] **2** *n* **appreciation**, sense, taste, discrimination, discernment, perceptiveness, judgment [➡SKILLS, TALENTS, AND ABILITIES; 526] **3** *v* **look at**, stare at, gaze at, watch, observe, ogle, eyeball (*informal*), eye up (*UK*) [➡LOOKING AND LOOKS; 700]

eye

♦ *parts of an eye*
aqueous humor, cone, conjunctiva, cornea, eyeball, iris, lens, macula, optic nerve, pupil, retina, rod, vitreous humor

eyeball 1 *v* (*informal*) **stare at**, glare at, have a good look at, look at, gaze at, watch, eye, ogle, eye up (*UK*) [➡LOOKING AND LOOKS; 700] **2** *n* [➡THE EYE; 698]

eyebrow 1 *n* [➡THE EYE; 698] **2** *part of* **face** [➡PARTS OF THE BODY: HEAD; 692]

eye-catching *adj* **striking**, noticeable, attention-grabbing, startling, arresting, conspicuous, stunning, dazzling, astonishing [➡BEAUTY AND ATTRACTIVENESS; 189] *Opposite*: unremarkable

eyeful (*informal*) *n* **look**, view, glance, squint, gander (*informal*) [➡LOOKING AND LOOKS; 700]

eyeglasses (*formal*) *type of* **glasses** [➡GLASSES AND SPECTACLES; 1125]

eyelash *n* [➡THE EYE; 698]

eyelet *n* **hole**, grommet, eyehole, perforation, loophole, orifice (*literary*) [➡HOLES, GAPS, AND FORKS; 1252]

eyelid *n* [➡THE EYE; 698]

eyeliner *n* [➡MAKEUP AND BEAUTY PRODUCTS; 490]

eye opener *n* **revelation**, discovery, realization, surprise, shock, shocker (*informal*) [➡DECISIVE MOMENTS; 44]

eye pencil *n* [➡MAKEUP AND BEAUTY PRODUCTS; 490]

eye shadow *n* [➡MAKEUP AND BEAUTY PRODUCTS; 490]

eyesight *n* **vision**, sight, sightedness, eye, view, perception, range of vision [➡SEE; 699]

eyesore *n* **blot on the landscape**, blot, monstrosity, blemish, fright, horror (*informal*) [➡NUISANCES; 253]

eyetooth *type of* **tooth** [➡THE MOUTH; 702]

eye up (*UK*) *v* [➡LOOKING AND LOOKS; 700]

eyewitness *n* **witness**, observer, bystander, onlooker, looker-on, watcher, spectator [➡ONLOOKERS AND SPECTATORS; 701]

e-zine *n* [➡THE INTERNET; 1128]

F

fable *n* **tale**, legend, parable, myth, story, allegory [➡ THE ORAL TRADITION; 677]

fabled 1 *adj* **legendary**, wonderful, remarkable, extraordinary, famous, impressive, renowned, outstanding, important, epic [➡ KNOWN AND FAMOUS; 181] *Opposite*: unknown 2 *adj* **fictitious**, mythical, imaginary, legendary, fairy-tale, fabulous, mythological, enchanted, magic, magical, storybook, make-believe [➡ FALSE AND UNREAL; 173] *Opposite*: factual

fabric 1 *n* **cloth**, material, textile, stuff, yard goods, dry goods, piece goods, drapery (*UK*) [➡ TEXTILES AND THREADS; 1131] 2 *n* **structure**, foundation, framework, basics, makeup, composition, constitution, frame, organization [➡ QUALITIES AND CHARACTERISTICS; 1191] 3 *n* **brickwork**, stonework, masonry, structure, superstructure, material, facing, cladding, tiling, roofing [➡ BUILDING AND ARCHITECTURE; 1076]

fabric

◆ *types of fabrics from animals*
alpaca, angora, astrakhan, baize, bearskin, brocade, camel hair, cashmere, chenille, crepe de Chine, felt, flannel, fur, gabardine, horsehair, jersey, lambswool, leather, loden, mohair, shahtoosh, silk, snakeskin, taffeta, tweed, twill, vicuna, wool, worsted

◆ *types of fabrics from plants*
burlap, calico, canvas, chambray, cheesecloth, chintz, corduroy, cotton, cretonne, damask, denim, drill, flannelette, gauze, gingham, grosgrain, hessian, lawn, linen, madras, moleskin, muslin, organdy, poplin, sacking, sailcloth, seersucker, tarpaulin, terry, terry cloth, ticking, velour, velvet, voile

◆ *types of synthetic fabrics*
acrylic, chiffon, crepe, fishnet, fleece, lamé, moquette, nylon, percale, polyester, PVC, rayon, sateen, satin, spandex, tulle, viscose

fabricate 1 *v* **construct**, make, manufacture, produce, engineer, put together, formulate, assemble, devise, build, form [➡ MANUFACTURE; 349] *Opposite*: destroy 2 *v* **invent**, make up, concoct, dream up, trump up, contrive, counterfeit, fake, feign, cook up (*informal*) [➡ DECEPTION AND LIES; 660]

fabricated *adj* **invented**, made-up, untrue, fictitious, fictional, false, fake, contrived, counterfeited, feigned [➡ FALSE AND UNREAL; 173] *Opposite*: genuine

fabrication 1 *n* **construction**, manufacture, production, assembly, creation, building [➡ CREATION; 346] 2 *n* **untruth**, lie, invention, falsehood, cock-and-bull story, fiction, fib (*informal*) [➡ DECEPTION AND LIES; 660] *Opposite*: truth 3 *n* **counterfeit**, forgery, fake, imitation [➡ REPRESENTATIONS AND GENERAL EXAMPLES; 65]

See Compare and Contrast at **lie.**

fabulous *adj* **excellent**, wonderful, tremendous, magnificent, marvelous, great, remarkable, extraordinary, amazing, fantastic, outstanding [➡ EXTRAORDINARY: AMAZING; 204] *Opposite*: awful

façade 1 *n* **frontage**, portico, fascia, front [➡ PARTS OF A BUILDING; 1095] 2 *n* **pretense**, veneer, impression, front, face, public image, mask [➡ APPEARANCE AND ATMOSPHERE; 1237]

face 1 *n* **countenance**, features, mug (*slang*), visage (*literary*) [➡ PARTS OF THE BODY: HEAD; 692] 2 *n* (*informal*) **nerve**, gall, boldness, audacity, pluck, impudence, effrontery, insolence, cheek (*informal*) [➡ BAD MANNERS AND SOCIAL SKILLS; 521] 3 *n* **expression**, look, appearance, air, aspect [➡ FACIAL EXPRESSIONS AND BLUSHING; 651] 4 *n* **outside**, surface, aspect, façade, wall, frontage [➡ EXTREMITIES OF PHYSICAL OBJECTS; 1250] *Opposite*: back 5 *v* **be opposite**, be in front of, stand in front of, stand facing, look toward, look [➡ EXIST IN CLOSE PROXIMITY; 21] 6 *v* **confront**, tackle, meet, cope with, challenge, deal with, handle, play, play against, be drawn against, encounter [➡ INITIATE AND ESTABLISH COMMUNICATION; 680] *Opposite*: avoid 7 *v* **accept**, admit, be realistic, realize, bite the bullet, come to terms with [➡ FORGET, FORGIVE, AND ACCEPT; 748] *Opposite*: deny

face

◆ *parts of a face*
brow, cheek, cheekbone, chin, chops (*informal*), eye, eyebrow, hairline, jaw, jawline, jowl, lips, mandible, mouth, nose, temple

faceless *adj* **impersonal**, featureless, unidentified, anonymous, nameless, unnamed, unidentifiable, unknown, undisclosed, mysterious, unrevealed, characterless [➡ SECRET AND UNKNOWN; 179]

face-lift *n* **renovation**, modernization, refurbishment, redecoration, restoration, makeover, rehab (*informal*) [➡ IMPROVE APPEARANCE; 379]

face-off *n* **confrontation**, conflict, argument, showdown, challenge, run-in (*informal*), set-to (*informal*) [➡ ARGUMENTS; 47]

face pack *n* **face mask**, facial, beauty treatment, mudpack [➡ MAKEUP AND BEAUTY PRODUCTS; 490]

face powder *n* [➡ MAKEUP AND BEAUTY PRODUCTS; 490]

face-saving *adj* **dignified**, diplomatic, tactical, tactful, restorative [➡ INTENTIONAL AND DELIBERATE; 279] *Opposite*: humiliating

facet 1 *n* **aspect**, feature, part, component, factor, issue, quality, side [➡ QUALITIES AND CHARACTERISTICS; 1191] 2 *n* **surface**, face, side, plane, façade [➡ EXTREMITIES OF PHYSICAL OBJECTS; 1250]

face the music *v* **accept responsibility**, face the storm, face up to your actions, take the flak, bite the bullet, take the heat, take the rap (*slang*), grasp the nettle (*UK*) [➡ FORGET, FORGIVE, AND ACCEPT; 748]

facetious 1 *adj* **flippant**, silly, ill-timed, ill-judged, inappropriate, inane, glib, frivolous, foolish [➡ MOCKING AND DISMISSIVE; 636] *Opposite*: earnest **2** *adj* **lighthearted**, playful, humorous, witty, droll, amusing, funny, comical, jokey, waggish (*informal*) [➡ JOKES AND TEASING; 674] *Opposite*: serious

See Compare and Contrast at **funny**.

facetiousness 1 *n* **flippancy**, frivolousness, inappropriateness, silliness, inanity, glibness, frivolity, foolishness [➡ NEGATIVE INTELLECTUAL CHARACTERISTICS; 525] *Opposite*: earnestness **2** *n* **lightheartedness**, wittiness, wit, drollness, humorousness, funniness, comicalness, humor, playfulness, jokiness, waggishness (*informal*) [➡ JOKES AND TEASING; 674] *Opposite*: seriousness

face to face 1 *adv* **in person**, in the flesh, personally, head-on, man to man, woman to woman, person to person [➡ HONEST AND OPEN; 630] **2** *adv* **head on**, opposite, in confrontation, nose to nose, head to head [➡ CLOSENESS; 159]

face-to-face *adj* [➡ CLOSENESS; 159]

face up to *v* **accept**, admit, come to terms with, realize, confront, tackle head on, bite the bullet, deal with, grasp the nettle (*UK*) [➡ FORGET, FORGIVE, AND ACCEPT; 748] *Opposite*: deny

facial *n* **beauty treatment**, face mask, face pack, makeover, massage, facial scrub, mudpack [➡ MAKEUP AND BEAUTY PRODUCTS; 490]

facial expression *n* [➡ FACIAL EXPRESSIONS AND BLUSHING; 651]

facial hair *n* [➡ FACIAL HAIR; 489]

facile *adj* **superficial**, simplistic, flippant, trite, inane, glib, facetious, shallow, casual, slick, cursory [➡ BORING AND UNINTERESTING; 234] *Opposite*: profound

facilitate *v* **make easy**, ease, make possible, enable, smooth, simplify, help, aid, assist, expedite, accelerate [➡ MAKE POSSIBLE; 275] *Opposite*: impede

facilitation *n* **easing**, simplification, enablement, enabling, assistance, help, expedition, acceleration [➡ KIND ACTIONS OR BEHAVIOR; 295] *Opposite*: obstruction

facilitator *n* **organizer**, architect, originator, prime mover, initiator, helper, spur, expediter, catalyst, mediator, implementer, enabler, driving force [➡ DESIGNERS, CREATORS, AND INSTIGATORS; 347]

facilities *n* **amenities**, services, conveniences, toilet, accommodations, lavatory, bathroom [➡ TYPES OF ROOMS; 1097]

facility 1 *n* **skill**, capability, capacity, talent, flair, competence, ability, gift, aptitude, knack, proficiency, efficiency [➡ SKILLS, TALENTS, AND ABILITIES; 526] *Opposite*: inability **2** *n* **service**, provision, resource, feature, advantage, means [➡ PHYSICAL OBJECTS; 1243]

facing *prep* **opposite**, in front of, fronting [➡ RELATIVE LOCATION; 161]

facsimile *n* **copy**, duplicate, reproduction, replica, likeness, double [➡ COPIES AND REPLICAS; 151]

fact 1 *n* **truth**, reality, actuality, verity (*formal*) [➡ TRUE AND REAL; 171] *Opposite*: fiction **2** *n* **piece of information**, detail, point, circumstance, datum, statistic, element [➡ BASIC DETAILS; 688] **3** *n* **happening**, deed, occurrence, event, act, circumstance [➡ EVENTS AND OCCURRENCES; 35]

fact-based *adj* [➡ TRUE AND REAL; 171]

faction 1 *n* **section**, party, splinter group, bloc, division, group, offshoot, side, clique, circle [➡ GROUPS WITH A COMMON INTEREST; 938] **2** *n* **conflict**, division, disunity, schism, disharmony, discord, strife, sectarianism, dissension, disagreement, contention [➡ DISHARMONY; 156] *Opposite*: agreement

factional 1 *adj* **sectarian**, dissenting, disaffected, separatist, schismatic, discordant, divisive [➡ DISHARMONY; 156] *Opposite*: united **2** *adj* **dramatized**, semirealistic, docudramatic, historical, pseudohistorical, documentary [➡ TRUE AND REAL; 171]

factious *adj* **divisive**, sectarian, schismatic, discordant, contentious, controversial [➡ DISHARMONY; 156] *Opposite*: unifying

factitious *adj* **contrived**, artificial, simulated, affected, unnatural, insincere [➡ FALSE AND UNREAL; 173] *Opposite*: genuine

fact of life *n* **reality**, practicality, fact, truth, actuality [➡ TRUE AND REAL; 171]

factor *n* **influence**, thing, feature, aspect, reason, cause, part, dynamic, issue, element, consideration, circumstance, component [➡ CAUSATION; 168]

factory *n* **plant**, works, installation, industrial unit, manufacturing plant, shop floor (*UK*) [➡ INDUSTRIAL BUILDINGS; 1087]

factory

◆ *types of factories*
assembly plant, brewery, cannery, distillery, forge, foundry, machine shop, maquiladora, mill, mint, pottery, sawmill, smithy, steelworks, sweatshop, water mill, workshop

factory ship *type of* **motor vessel** [➡ SHIPS AND BOATS; 1150]

factory worker *n* [➡ WORKERS; 836]

factotum *type of* **servant** [➡ DOMESTIC AND KITCHEN WORKERS; 850]

facts 1 *n* **particulars**, details, specifics, essentials, data, statistics, figures [➡ BASIC DETAILS; 688] **2** *n* **truth**, evidence, reality, actuality, proof [➡ EVIDENCE AND PROOF; 69]

fact sheet *n* **information sheet**, information leaflet, booklet, brochure, handout, sheet, leaflet, document [➡ MANUALS AND INSTRUCTIONS; 589]

factual 1 *adj* **truthful**, accurate, realistic, honest, true-life, genuine, real, actual, faithful [➡ TRUE AND REAL; 171] *Opposite*: fictional **2** *adj* **objective**, hard, verifiable, bona fide, authentic, genuine, scientific, accurate, exact [➡ TRUE AND REAL; 171] *Opposite*: subjective

factually *adv* **truthfully**, accurately, exactly, really, precisely, objectively, literally, concretely, empirically, realistically [➡ TRUE AND REAL; 171]

faculty 1 *n* **sense**, power, endowment, capability, function [➡ THE SENSES; 696] **2** *n* **ability**, facility, gift, talent, knack, aptitude, capacity, capability, genius [➡ SKILLS, TALENTS, AND ABILITIES; 526] *Opposite*: inability **3** *n* **staff**, teaching body, teaching staff, teachers, professors [➡ EDUCATORS; 840]

fad *n* **fashion**, craze, trend, whim, vogue, cult, rage, mania [➥ FADS, FETISHES, AND IDOLATRY; 555]

faddiness (*UK*) *n* **fussiness**, fastidiousness, pickiness, faddishness, choosiness (*informal*), persnicketiness (*informal*) [➥ DIFFICULT TO PLEASE; 515]

faddishness *n* **fussiness**, fastidiousness, pickiness, choosiness (*informal*), persnicketiness (*informal*), faddiness (*UK*) [➥ DIFFICULT TO PLEASE; 515]

faddy (*UK*) *adj* **fussy**, finicky, picky, particular, faddish, choosy (*informal*), persnickety (*informal*) [➥ DIFFICULT TO PLEASE; 515]

fade 1 *v* **disappear**, weaken, die away, diminish, fade away, fade out, tail off, decline, dwindle, fail [➥ DISAPPEAR; 4] *Opposite*: grow 2 *v* **become paler**, lighten, become lighter, lose color, bleach [➥ CHANGE OF INTENSITY: LESS; 395] *Opposite*: darken 3 *v* **wane**, wither, die, waste away, wilt, dwindle, evaporate, recede, droop, shrivel, languish [➥ CEASE TO EXIST; 22] *Opposite*: flourish

fade away 1 *v* **disappear**, vanish, fade, evaporate, dwindle, diminish, fade out, peter out [➥ DISAPPEAR; 4] 2 *v* **waste away**, shrivel, wane, wither, atrophy, shrink [➥ DISAPPEAR; 4] *Opposite*: thrive

fading *adj* **disappearing**, declining, dying, vanishing, diminishing, waning, failing, dwindling [➥ CEASE TO EXIST; 22] *Opposite*: growing

faience *type of* **pottery** [➥ POTTERY; 1135]

fail 1 *v* **be unsuccessful**, nose-dive, miss the mark, go belly up, fall flat, come to nothing, miscarry, bomb (*informal*), flop (*informal*) [➥ FAIL OR BE UNSUCCESSFUL; 75] *Opposite*: succeed 2 *v* **fall short**, not make the grade, not be up to scratch, flunk (*informal*), fluff (*informal*) [➥ FAIL OR BE UNSUCCESSFUL; 75] *Opposite*: pass 3 *v* **stop working**, break down, crash, go down, stop, seize up, grind to a halt, die, give up, collapse, go on the blink (*informal*) [➥ FAIL OR CEASE TO FUNCTION; 470] 4 *v* **let down**, disappoint, neglect, forsake, desert, betray [➥ UPSET, DISTRESS, AND HUMILIATE; 567] *Opposite*: satisfy 5 *v* **go out of business**, go bankrupt, crash, fold, go under, collapse, flop (*informal*), bomb (*informal*) [➥ FAIL OR BE UNSUCCESSFUL; 75] *Opposite*: thrive 6 *v* **weaken**, fade, diminish, dwindle, decline, wane, disappear [➥ DISAPPEAR; 4] *Opposite*: rally

failed *adj* **unsuccessful**, botched, disastrous, futile, abortive, miscarried [➥ UNSUCCESSFUL AND UNPROMISING; 76] *Opposite*: successful

failing 1 *n* **shortcoming**, flaw, weakness, weak point, fault, imperfection, deficiency, defect, weak spot [➥ FAULTS, FLAWS, AND WEAKNESSES; 251] 2 *prep* **without**, in the absence of, lacking [➥ LACK OF POSSESSION; 445] 3 *adj* **deteriorating**, worsening, weakening, fading, waning, dwindling, dying, inadequate, declining [➥ UNSUCCESSFUL AND UNPROMISING; 76] *Opposite*: strengthening

See Compare and Contrast at **flaw**.

fail-safe *adj* **foolproof**, guaranteed, dependable, reliable, goofproof (*informal*) [➥ SAFE AND SAFETY; 191] *Opposite*: unreliable

failure 1 *n* **disappointment**, letdown, catastrophe, fiasco, disaster, miscarriage, bomb (*informal*), botch (*informal*),

flop (*informal*) [➥ FAILURE; 77] *Opposite*: success 2 *n* **breakdown**, stoppage, malfunction, crash, collapse, seizure [➥ FAILURE; 77] 3 *n* **bankruptcy**, closure, crash, collapse, insolvency, ruin [➥ FAILURE; 77]

faint 1 *adj* **dim**, weak, faded, indistinct, feeble, unclear, shadowy, hazy, distant, muffled, soft, pale [➥ DESCRIBING COLORS; 1226] *Opposite*: bright 2 *adj* **slight**, diminished, muffled, soft, low, quiet [➥ SOFT, LOW, OR PLEASANT SOUNDS; 1265] *Opposite*: loud 3 *adj* **dizzy**, giddy, woozy, unsteady, vertiginous, lightheaded, wobbly (*informal*) [➥ ILL AND SICK; 740] 4 *v* **pass out**, collapse, black out, fall down, lose consciousness [➥ BECOME SICK, TREAT, AND RECOVER; 728] *Opposite*: come to

faint-hearted *adj* **fearful**, apprehensive, hesitant, cowardly, shy, timorous, retiring, tentative, coy, pusillanimous, nervous, diffident [➥ COWARDICE AND WEAKNESS OF WILL; 508] *Opposite*: bold

See Compare and Contrast at **cowardly**.

faint-heartedness *n* [➥ COWARDICE AND WEAKNESS OF WILL; 508]

faintly 1 *adv* **dimly**, weakly, slightly, indistinctly, feebly, unclearly, hazily, distantly, softly, palely, quietly [➥ DESCRIBING COLORS; 1226] *Opposite*: brightly 2 *adv* **slightly**, softly, barely, indistinctly, imperceptibly, quietly [➥ SOFT, LOW, OR PLEASANT SOUNDS; 1265] *Opposite*: loudly

faintness 1 *n* **dimness**, weakness, feebleness, indistinctness, haziness, paleness [➥ WEAKNESS; 241] *Opposite*: brightness 2 *n* **slightness**, quietness, weakness, feebleness, softness [➥ SOFT, LOW, OR PLEASANT SOUNDS; 1265] *Opposite*: loudness 3 *n* **dizziness**, giddiness, wooziness, vertigo, lightheadedness, unsteadiness [➥ ILL AND SICK; 740]

fair 1 *adj* **reasonable**, just, fair-minded, open-minded, impartial, rational, evenhanded, nondiscriminatory, unbiased, objective, dispassionate, honest [➥ EQUALITY; 154] *Opposite*: biased 2 *adj* **light**, blond, fair-haired, flaxen, tow-headed, pale [➥ HAIR COLOR; 485] *Opposite*: dark 3 *adj* **adequate**, passable, average, reasonable, decent, moderate, mediocre, fair to middling, ordinary, run-of-the-mill, acceptable [➥ ACCEPTABLE AND PASSABLE; 219] 4 *adj* **good**, bright, sunny, clear, cloudless, pleasant, fine (*informal*) [➥ HOT WEATHER; 1050] *Opposite*: inclement 5 *adj* **pleasing**, attractive, good-looking, lovely, pretty, beautiful [➥ PEOPLE'S PHYSICAL APPEARANCE; 475] *Opposite*: unattractive 6 *n* **festival**, sale, exposition, bazaar, trade fair, trade event, show, exhibition, gala [➥ SALES AND SHOWS; 443] 7 *n* **carnival**, fairground, midway, amusement park, theme park, traveling fair, funfair (*UK*) [➥ PERFORMANCES AND SHOWS; 42]

fair enough 1 *adj* **acceptable**, understandable, reasonable, justified, warranted, okay (*informal*) [➥ ACCEPTABLE AND PASSABLE; 219] *Opposite*: unfair 2 *interj* (*informal*) **all right**, that's fine, fine, okay (*informal*), no problem (*informal*) [➥ EXPRESSIONS OF AGREEMENT; 648]

fairground *n* **theme park**, amusement park, playground, park, midway, carnival, fair, funfair (*UK*) [➥ URBAN OUTDOOR SPACES; 1072]

fair-haired *adj* **fair**, blond, flaxen, tow-headed [➥ HAIR COLOR; 485] *Opposite*: dark

fairly 1 *adv* **moderately**, rather, reasonably, somewhat, comparatively, relatively, tolerably, passably, quite [➥ TO A CERTAIN EXTENT; 136] 2 *adv* **honestly**, justly, properly, without favoritism, legitimately, impartially, equally, objectively, fair and square, equitably (*formal*) [➡ EQUALITY; 154] *Opposite*: unfairly **3** *adv* **completely**, positively, literally, practically, absolutely, really, accurately, fully, utterly [➡ TO A GREAT EXTENT; 132]

fair-minded *adj* **fair**, open-minded, evenhanded, non-discriminatory, impartial, reasonable, disinterested, dispassionate, just, objective, honest [➡ POSITIVE INTELLECTUAL CHARACTERISTICS; 524] *Opposite*: prejudiced

fairness *n* **justice**, equality, evenhandedness, impartiality, fair-mindedness, objectivity [➡ EQUALITY; 154] *Opposite*: unfairness

fair to middling *adj* [➡ ACCEPTABLE AND PASSABLE; 219]

fairy *n* **pixie**, brownie, sprite, elf, leprechaun, imp, genie, jinni, gremlin (*informal*), fay (*literary*) [➡ MYTHICAL BEINGS; 789]

fairyland *n* **wonderland**, dreamland, dream world, seventh heaven, heaven, paradise, cloud nine [➡ NONEXISTENT PLACES; 1066]

fairy lights (*UK*) *n* [➡ LIGHTING; 862]

fairy ring champignon *type of* **fungus** [➡ MICROORGANISMS, FUNGI, AND ALGAE; 1023]

fairy story (*UK*) **1** *n* **invention**, fabrication, lie, untruth, falsehood, fairy tale, fantasy, excuse, tall tale, tall story, fiction, cock-and-bull story, fib (*informal*), canard (*literary*) [➡ DECEPTION AND LIES; 660] **2** *n* **myth**, fairy tale, folk tale, folk story, legend, fable, tale, story [➡ THE ORAL TRADITION; 677]

fairy tale **1** *n* **folk tale**, folk story, myth, legend, fable, tale, story, fairy story (*UK*) [➡ FICTION AND DRAMA; 913] **2** *n* **invention**, fabrication, lie, untruth, falsehood, fantasy, excuse, tall tale, tall story, fiction, cock-and-bull story, fib (*informal*), canard (*literary*), fairy story (*UK*) [➡ DECEPTION AND LIES; 660]

fairy-tale **1** *adj* **mythical**, enchanted, magic, magical, imaginary, legendary, fabled, fabulous, make-believe [➡ FALSE AND UNREAL; 173] *Opposite*: real **2** *adj* **fortunate**, happy, storybook, perfect, romantic, traditional, enchanting, wonderful, beautiful, magical, glamorous, fascinating, dazzling [➡ EXTRAORDINARY; AMAZING; 204] *Opposite*: unhappy **3** *adj* **fabricated**, unbelievable, make-believe, made-up, highly colored, incredible, mythical [➡ IMPOSSIBLE AND IMPROBABLE; 178] *Opposite*: truthful

fait accompli *n* [➡ TRUE AND REAL; 171]

faith **1** *n* **trust**, confidence, reliance, conviction, belief, assurance [➡ COOL AND CALM; 536] *Opposite*: disbelief **2** *n* **loyalty**, devotion, faithfulness, commitment, dedication, fidelity, constancy, allegiance, fealty (*archaic or literary*) [➡ RELIGIOUS CONCEPTS; 776] *Opposite*: disloyalty

faithful **1** *adj* **correct**, true, realistic, authentic, close, accurate, exact, true to life, truthful, believable [➡ TRUE AND REAL; 171] *Opposite*: unrealistic **2** *adj* **loyal**, devoted, trusty, trustworthy, staunch, dependable, reliable, dedicated, committed, true, constant [➡ HARD-WORKING AND COMMITTED; 500] *Opposite*: faithless

faithfully *adv* **loyally**, devotedly, trustworthily, staunchly, dependably [➡ HARD-WORKING AND COMMITTED; 500] *Opposite*: faithlessly

faithfulness **1** *n* **correctness**, closeness, realism, authenticity, accuracy, truthfulness, truth, exactness, believability, fidelity [➡ TRUE AND REAL; 171] *Opposite*: unreality **2** *n* **loyalty**, devotion, staunchness, dependability, reliability, fidelity, constancy [➡ HONEST AND RELIABLE; 502] *Opposite*: faithlessness

faith healer *n* [➡ PEOPLE WITH SUPERNATURAL POWERS; 788]

faithless *adj* **dishonest**, disloyal, untrustworthy, unfaithful, fickle, untrue, inconstant [➡ LACK OF COMMITMENT AND UNRELIABILITY; 509] *Opposite*: faithful

faithlessly *adv* **dishonestly**, unfaithfully, deceitfully, disloyally, treacherously, untrustworthily [➡ LACK OF COMMITMENT AND UNRELIABILITY; 509] *Opposite*: faithfully

faithlessness *n* **dishonesty**, infidelity, inconstancy, fickleness, disloyalty, unfaithfulness [➡ LACK OF COMMITMENT AND UNRELIABILITY; 509] *Opposite*: faithfulness

fajitas *type of* **cooked dish** [➡ PREPARED DISHES; 1170]

fake **1** *n* **imitation**, copy, replica, simulation, mock-up, facsimile, counterfeit, phony, forgery, fraud, sham [➡ DECEPTION AND LIES; 660] *Opposite*: original **2** *adj* **false**, bogus, sham, counterfeit, phony, forged, replica, imitation, simulated, mock, faux, pretend, ersatz [➡ FALSE AND UNREAL; 173] *Opposite*: genuine **3** *v* **falsify**, copy, counterfeit, forge, replicate, reproduce [➡ FALSIFY AND CHEAT; 176] **4** *v* **simulate**, feign, pretend, act, dissemble, dissimulate [➡ PRETEND AND MIMIC; 60]

faked *adj* [➡ FALSE AND UNREAL; 173]

faker *n* **fraud**, fake, liar, pretender, impostor, hypocrite, phony [➡ PEOPLE WHO DECEIVE; 661]

falafel *type of* **cooked dish** [➡ PREPARED DISHES; 1170]

falcon *type of* **bird of prey** [➡ BIRDS OF PREY; 998]

fall **1** *v* **drop**, go down, descend, plunge, plummet [➡ GO DOWNWARD; 307] *Opposite*: ascend **2** *v* **tumble**, fall over, fall down, drop, trip over, go head over heels, collapse [➡ GO DOWNWARD; 307] **3** *v* **decrease**, reduce, sink, come down [➡ CHANGE OF SIZE: SMALLER; 393] *Opposite*: increase **4** *n* **season**, equinox, Indian summer, autumn, harvest time (*UK*) [➡ TIMES OF YEAR; 88] **5** *n* **reduction**, decrease, drop, tumble, descent, plummet, plunge, collapse [➡ CHANGE OF SIZE: SMALLER; 393] *Opposite*: increase **6** *n* **waterfall**, rapids, cataract, cascade, white water [➡ RIVERS, LAKES, AND STREAMS; 1042] **7** *part of* **flower** [➡ FLOWERS; 1032]

fallacious *adj* **mistaken**, erroneous, misleading, deceptive, false, wrong [➡ FALSE AND UNREAL; 173] *Opposite*: correct

fallaciousness *n* [➡ FALSE AND UNREAL; 173]

fallacy *n* **misconception**, myth, error, mistake, delusion, misjudgment [➡ MISTAKES; 250]

fall apart *v* **disintegrate**, crumble, collapse, fall to pieces, break up, fail, fall to bits (*UK*) [➡ TEAR, BREAK, AND CUT; 360] *Opposite*: come together

fall asleep *v* **nod off**, doze off, go to sleep, drop off (*informal*) [➡ SLEEP AND DREAM; 723] *Opposite*: wake up

fall away *v* [➡ DISAPPEAR; 4]

fall back **1** *v* **retreat**, withdraw, draw back, run away, regroup [➡ GO BACKWARD; 309] *Opposite*: advance **2** *v* **drop behind**,

fall behind, drop back, lag, lag behind, lose ground, hang back [➧ GO BACKWARD; 309] *Opposite*: catch up

fallback *n* **replacement**, contingency, alternative, stand-in, substitute, reserve, backup [➧ SOLUTIONS; 215]

fall back on *v* **resort to**, rely on, turn to, depend on, have recourse to [➧ MAKE DECISIONS AND CHOICES; 752]

fall behind 1 *v* **be delayed**, be late, be in arrears, default [➧ OWE AND DESERVE; 465] 2 *v* **drop back**, drop behind, fall back, lag, lag behind, lose ground [➧ GO BACKWARD; 309] *Opposite*: keep up

fall by the wayside *v* **come to nothing**, fold, collapse, fail, abandon, drop out [➧ FAIL OR BE UNSUCCESSFUL; 75]

fall down 1 *v* **collapse**, fall over, tumble, trip over, trip, fall [➧ GO DOWNWARD; 307] 2 *v* **fail**, be unsuccessful, disappoint, go wrong, flop (*informal*) [➧ FAIL OR BE UNSUCCESSFUL; 75] *Opposite*: succeed

fall flat *v* **fail**, miss the target, flop (*informal*), bomb (*informal*) [➧ FAIL OR BE UNSUCCESSFUL; 75] *Opposite*: succeed

fall for 1 *v* **fall in love with**, be attracted to, be taken with, be stuck on (*informal*), take a shine to (*informal*), be crazy about (*informal*), be smitten (*literary or humorous*) [➧ LIKE, LOVE, VALUE, AND ENJOY; 578] *Opposite*: go off 2 *v* **be duped by**, be deceived by, be tricked by, be taken in by, believe, accept, swallow (*informal*) [➧ FORGET, FORGIVE, AND ACCEPT; 748] *Opposite*: see through

fall foul of *v* **come into conflict with**, tangle with, have a brush with, come up against [➧ DISHARMONY; 156]

fall guy (*slang*) 1 *n* **dupe**, stooge, fool, gull, sucker (*informal*), chump (*informal*) [➧ VICTIMS OF DECEIT; 662] 2 *n* **scapegoat**, whipping boy, victim, butt, sucker (*informal*) [➧ VICTIMS OF DECEIT; 662]

fallibility *n* **imperfection**, frailty, weakness, shortcoming, failure, failing [➧ NEGATIVE INTELLECTUAL CHARACTERISTICS; 525] *Opposite*: infallibility

fallible *adj* **imperfect**, mortal, weak, frail, human [➧ COWARDICE AND WEAKNESS OF WILL; 508] *Opposite*: infallible

falling *adj* **dwindling**, dropping, deteriorating, tumbling, sinking, dipping, decreasing, subsiding, diminishing, declining, lessening, plummeting [➧ CEASE TO EXIST; 22] *Opposite*: rising

falling apart *adj* [➧ IN BAD REPAIR; 1234]

falling down *adj* [➧ IN BAD REPAIR; 1234]

falling-out *n* **quarrel**, fight, disagreement, misunderstanding, rift, split, dispute, row [➧ ARGUMENTS; 47] *Opposite*: reconciliation

falling star *type of* **heavenly body** [➧ HEAVENLY BODIES; 1061]

falling to pieces *adj* **dilapidated**, shabby, falling down, tumbledown, rundown, tatty [➧ IN BAD REPAIR; 1234] *Opposite*: pristine

fall into place *v* **work out**, shape up, make sense, come together, sort itself out, take shape, become clear [➧ APPEAR AND EMERGE; 3]

fall in with 1 *v* **meet**, join, come across, bump into, run into, get to know, make the acquaintance of [➧ ESTABLISHING

RELATIONSHIPS WITH OTHERS; 974] *Opposite*: avoid 2 *v* **agree with**, accept, support, go along with, comply with [➧ AGREE; 645] *Opposite*: reject

fall off *v* **decline**, go down, decrease, plunge, reduce, drop [➧ CHANGE OF SIZE: SMALLER; 393] *Opposite*: increase

falloff *n* **decrease**, decline, falling off, reduction, drop, cut [➧ LESS; 126] *Opposite*: increase

fall out *v* **quarrel**, argue, disagree, come to blows, row, have words, fight, have a fight, have a row [➧ ARGUE AND FIGHT; 643] *Opposite*: make up

fallout *n* **consequence**, result, outcome, effect, upshot, knock-on effect (*UK*) [➧ RESULTS AND OUTCOMES; 83]

fall over *v* **tumble**, fall down, collapse, trip, trip over, go head over heels [➧ GO DOWNWARD; 307]

fallow 1 *adj* **uncultivated**, unplanted, unseeded, unused, untilled [➧ EMPTY; 1238] *Opposite*: cultivated 2 *adj* **inactive**, unproductive, idle, sterile, infertile, barren, uncreative [➧ REDUNDANT AND USELESS; 240] *Opposite*: creative

fallow deer *type of* **deer or antelope** [➧ DEER AND ANTELOPES; 981]

fall prey to *v* [➧ EXPERIENCE AND ENCOUNTER; 582]

fall short *v* **be deficient**, be wanting, be lacking, prove inadequate, not make the grade, not be up to snuff, not be up to scratch, fail [➧ FAIL OR BE UNSUCCESSFUL; 75] *Opposite*: succeed

fall through *v* **fail**, go wrong, come to nothing, miscarry, misfire, not come off [➧ FAIL OR BE UNSUCCESSFUL; 75] *Opposite*: succeed

fall to pieces *v* **disintegrate**, come apart, crumble, fall apart, break up, fall to bits (*UK*) [➧ TEAR, BREAK, AND CUT; 360]

fall victim to *v* [➧ EXPERIENCE AND ENCOUNTER; 582]

false 1 *adj* **incorrect**, untruthful, untrue, wrong, dishonest, fabricated, deceitful, made-up, insincere, deceptive [➧ FALSE AND UNREAL; 173] *Opposite*: true 2 *adj* **mistaken**, erroneous, fallacious, misleading, deceiving [➧ INCORRECT AND ERRONEOUS; 222] *Opposite*: correct 3 *adj* **artificial**, bogus, sham, phony, counterfeit, forged, copied, fake, fictitious, pretend, put-on, made-up, insincere [➧ FALSE AND UNREAL; 173] *Opposite*: real

falsehood 1 *n* **lie**, untruth, tale, fiction, invention, misrepresentation, cock-and-bull story, tall tale, fairy tale, myth, fabrication, false report, story (*informal*), fib (*informal*), canard (*literary*), fairy story (*UK*) [➧ DECEPTION AND LIES; 660] 2 *n* **deception**, dishonesty, mendacity, deceit, fabrication, deceitfulness, lying [➧ DECEPTION AND LIES; 660]

See Compare and Contrast at **lie**.

false impression *n* **mistaken belief**, misconception, misreading, wrong idea, misapprehension, erroneous belief [➧ MISTAKES; 250]

falsely 1 *adv* **mistakenly**, wrongly, fallaciously, erroneously, deceivingly [➧ INCORRECT AND ERRONEOUS; 222] *Opposite*: rightly 2 *adv* **incorrectly**, misleadingly, deceptively, dishonestly, deceitfully, untruthfully, insincerely [➧ FALSE AND UNREAL; 173] *Opposite*: honestly

falseness 1 *n* **incorrectness**, dishonesty, deceit, deceitfulness, speciousness, insincerity [➡DECEPTION AND LIES; 660] *Opposite*: honesty 2 *n* **mistakenness**, erroneousness, wrongness, fallaciousness, deceptiveness, deception [➡INCORRECT AND ERRONEOUS; 222] *Opposite*: rightness

falsetto *type of* **musical register** [➡MUSICAL TERMS; 912]

falsification *n* **fabrication**, distortion, forgery, misrepresentation, deception, alteration, fiddling (*informal*) [➡DECEPTION AND LIES; 660] *Opposite*: correction

falsified *adj* **fabricated**, forged, untrue, counterfeit, false, fake, made-up, phony, doctored [➡FALSE AND UNREAL; 173] *Opposite*: true

falsify *v* **fabricate**, fake, forge, rig, misrepresent, alter, change, doctor, fix (*informal*), fiddle (*informal*) [➡FALSIFY AND CHEAT; 176]

falsity *n* **falseness**, spuriousness, hollowness, inaccuracy, deceptiveness, fallaciousness, incorrectness, speciousness, untruth [➡DECEPTION AND LIES; 660] *Opposite*: correctness

falter 1 *v* **hesitate**, pause, waver, stammer, stutter, vacillate, fumble, tail off [➡HESITATE; 272] *Opposite*: continue 2 *v* **fail**, weaken, fade, wane, abate (*formal or literary*) [➡CEASE TO EXIST; 22] *Opposite*: rally 3 *v* **stumble**, trip up, stagger, totter, sway, lurch, trip [➡WALK UNSTEADILY; 315]

See Compare and Contrast at **hesitate**.

faltering *adj* **hesitant**, tentative, halting, timid, uncertain, broken [➡UNCERTAINTY; 559]

falteringly *adv* **hesitantly**, timidly, insecurely, uncertainly, gingerly, haltingly [➡UNCERTAINTY; 559] *Opposite*: confidently

fame *n* **renown**, celebrity, reputation, distinction, recognition, eminence, prominence, notoriety, illustriousness, infamy, legend, myth [➡KNOWN AND FAMOUS; 181] *Opposite*: obscurity

famed *adj* **well-known**, famous, celebrated, renowned, eminent, prominent, illustrious, legendary, recognized, infamous, notorious (*archaic*) [➡KNOWN AND FAMOUS; 181] *Opposite*: unknown

familial *adj* **family**, ancestral, household, domestic, matrimonial, marital, hereditary [➡THE FAMILY; 956]

familiar 1 *adj* **well-known**, recognizable, common, customary, accustomed, habitual, usual, recurring, everyday, frequent, regular, wonted (*literary*) [➡KNOWN AND FAMOUS; 181] *Opposite*: unfamiliar 2 *adj* **accustomed**, habitual, usual, recurring, everyday, typical, frequent, traditional, time-honored, established, regular, wonted (*literary*) [➡ORDINARINESS; 244] *Opposite*: unusual 3 *adj* **acquainted**, conversant, accustomed, used to, at home with, at ease with, au fait, aware, cognizant of (*formal*) [➡KNOWLEDGE AND WISDOM; 558] 4 *adj* **friendly**, intimate, easy, informal, personal, cozy, relaxed, close [➡EMOTIONALLY PLEASANT; 187] *Opposite*: formal

familiarity 1 *n* **knowledge**, understanding, acquaintance, awareness, ease, expertise, fluency, skill, experience, know-how (*informal*) [➡KNOWLEDGE AND WISDOM; 558] *Opposite*: unfamiliarity 2 *n* **intimacy**, informality, friend-

ship, ease, closeness, friendliness, relaxedness, casualness [➡FRIENDLINESS AND SOCIABILITY; 494] *Opposite*: formality

familiarization *n* **acquaintance**, getting used to, adjustment, adaptation, becoming accustomed, accommodation, habituation (*formal*) [➡KNOWLEDGE AND WISDOM; 558]

familiarize *v* **acquaint**, tell, explain, make clear, train, drill [➡INSTRUCT AND TEACH; 609]

familiarize yourself *v* **get to know**, adapt, get used to, acclimatize yourself, acquaint yourself, accustom yourself, adjust, pick up, become au fait, catch on (*informal*) [➡LEARN AND DISCOVER; 762]

familiarly *adv* **intimately**, closely, informally, cozily, casually [➡FRIENDLINESS AND SOCIABILITY; 494] *Opposite*: distantly

family 1 *n* **relations**, relatives, folks, children, family unit, extended family, nuclear family, nearest and dearest, loved ones, kinfolk, kin, people (*informal*), clan (*informal*) [➡THE FAMILY; 956] 2 *n* **lineage**, descendants, dynasty, ancestors, line, family tree, blood [➡THE FAMILY; 956] 3 *n* **category**, genus, species, type, kind, line, breed, strain, variety, group [➡VARIETIES, TYPES, AND KINDS; 145] 4 *adj* **domestic**, household, everyday, intimate, private [➡THE FAMILY; 956]

family circle *n* **household**, family, family unit, home, house, ménage (*formal*) [➡THE FAMILY; 956]

family member *n* [➡THE FAMILY; 956]

family name *n* **surname**, last name, maternal name, paternal name, name, second name, patronymic, matronymic [➡NAME AND DESCRIBE; 665]

family room *type of* **room in the home** [➡TYPES OF ROOMS; 1097]

family tree *n* **ancestry**, pedigree, genealogy, ancestors, descendants, lineage [➡THE FAMILY; 956]

family unit *n* **family**, family circle, household, ménage (*formal*) [➡THE FAMILY; 956]

famine *n* **food shortage**, shortage, scarcity, dearth, want, starvation, deprivation [➡EAT AND NOT EAT; 710] *Opposite*: abundance

famish *v* [➡EAT AND NOT EAT; 710]

famished *adj* **hungry**, ravenous, underfed, unfed, starving (*informal*), starved (*informal*) [➡EAT AND NOT EAT; 710] *Opposite*: sated

famous *adj* **well-known**, famed, celebrated, renowned, eminent, prominent, illustrious, legendary, recognized, notorious (*archaic*) [➡KNOWN AND FAMOUS; 181] *Opposite*: unknown

famously 1 *adv* **notably**, memorably, eminently, prominently, distinctively, notoriously (*archaic*) [➡SUCCESSFUL AND PROMISING; 81] 2 *adv* **well**, excellently, superbly, like a house on fire, like nobody's business [➡TO A GREAT EXTENT; 132]

fan 1 *n* **admirer**, enthusiast, aficionado, aficionada, follower, devotee, buff, addict, fanatic, supporter, groupie (*informal*) [➡DEVOTEES AND ADDICTED PEOPLE; 556] 2 *v* **waft**, blow, cool, wave, percolate, circulate [➡MOVE SOMETHING: ON THE SPOT; 336] 3 *v* **stir up**, stimulate, provoke, increase, fuel, encourage, generate, incite, foment, agitate [➡CHANGE OF INTENSITY: MORE; 394] *Opposite*: defuse

fanatic 1 *n* **extremist**, zealot, radical, fundamentalist, crusader, partisan [➡ DEVOTEES AND ADDICTED PEOPLE; 556] **2** *n* **fan**, enthusiast, devotee, buff, follower, supporter, addict, admirer, obsessive, maniac, aficionado, aficionada, nut (*informal*), groupie (*informal*) [➡ DEVOTEES AND ADDICTED PEOPLE; 556] **3** *adj* **fanatical**, obsessive, passionate, addicted, extreme, enthusiastic, frenzied, devoted, dedicated, fervent, fixated, zealous, keen [➡ ENERGY AND ENTHUSIASM; 496] *Opposite:* indifferent

fanatical *adj* **fanatic**, obsessive, dedicated, fervent, fixated, zealous, enthusiastic, keen, passionate, devoted, extreme, addicted, frenzied [➡ ENERGY AND ENTHUSIASM; 496] *Opposite:* indifferent

fanaticism *n* **extremism**, radicalism, zeal, keenness, dedication, passion, fervor, devotion [➡ FADS, FETISHES, AND IDOLATRY; 555] *Opposite:* indifference

fanciful *adj* **imaginary**, fantastic, whimsical, unbelievable, out of this world, far-fetched, unlikely, bizarre, curious, invented [➡ IMPOSSIBLE AND IMPROBABLE; 178] *Opposite:* prosaic

fancy 1 *adj* **elaborate**, ornate, decorative, ornamental, intricate, showy, rococo [➡ POSITIVELY COMPLEX OR COMPLICATED; 217] **2** *adj* **expensive**, upmarket, lavish, extravagant, upscale, posh (*informal*), swanky (*informal*) [➡ EXPENSIVE AND LUXURIOUS; 218] *Opposite:* plain **3** *v* **imagine**, picture, think, conjure, believe, consider, visualize, interpret, assume, suppose, conceive [➡ DREAM, IMAGINE, AND FANTASIZE; 749] **4** *n* **notion**, dream, hope, desire, fantasy, daydream, castle in the air, castle in Spain, whim, illusion, reverie, vagary [➡ NONEXISTENT THINGS; 23]

fancy-free *adj* **free**, at liberty, unfettered, unconstrained, at leisure, footloose, carefree, liberated [➡ PLEASURE-SEEKING AND EXCESS; 885] *Opposite:* tied

fandango *type of* **dance** [➡ DANCE; 903]

fanfare *n* **display**, trumpet blast, salute, elaboration, flourish, ballyhoo, pomp [➡ NOTES AND CHORDS; 909]

fang *type of* **tooth** [➡ THE MOUTH; 702]

fanlight *type of* **window** [➡ WINDOWS; 1100]

fanny pack *type of* **bag** [➡ CONTAINERS, RECEPTACLES, AND PACKAGING; 1245]

fan out *v* **spread out**, separate, expand, broaden, disperse, scatter, split up [➡ SEPARATE AND DIVIDE; 401] *Opposite:* assemble

fantasia *type of* **musical form** [➡ MUSIC, SONGS, AND SINGING; 907]

fantasize *v* **daydream**, imagine, dream, picture, visualize, invent, romanticize, conjure up, contrive [➡ DREAM, IMAGINE, AND FANTASIZE; 749]

fantastic 1 *adj* **excellent**, terrific (*informal*), superb, great, marvelous, fabulous, wonderful, tremendous, brilliant [➡ EXTRAORDINARY; AMAZING; 204] *Opposite:* awful **2** *adj* **bizarre**, eccentric, imaginary, strange, fanciful, weird, whimsical, grotesque, odd, wild, crazy (*informal*) [➡ IMPOSSIBLE AND IMPROBABLE; 178] *Opposite:* normal **3** *adj* **incredible**, unbelievable, implausible, improbable, unlikely, far-fetched, out of this world, extraordinary, preposterous, absurd, bizarre, amazing, fanciful, illusory [➡ IMPOSSIBLE AND IMPROBABLE; 178] *Opposite:* plausible **4** *adj* **enormous**, huge, great, tremendous, big, large, prodigious, extensive, extended, extravagant, extreme [➡ LARGE; 1193] *Opposite:* tiny

fantastical *adj* [➡ FALSE AND UNREAL; 173]

fantasy 1 *n* **dream**, daydream, image, fancy, hope, desire, vision, whimsy, pipe dream, illusion [➡ NONEXISTENT THINGS; 23] **2** *n* **imagination**, unreality, fancy, caprice, power of invention, imaginativeness, illusion, dream, fiction [➡ NONEXISTENT THINGS; 23] *Opposite:* reality

fantasy world *n* [➡ NONEXISTENT PLACES; 1066]

fan the flames *v* **exacerbate**, aggravate, inflame, make worse, worsen, intensify [➡ WORSEN SOMETHING; 380] *Opposite:* calm

far 1 *adv* **far off**, far away, far afield, far and wide, distantly, remotely, afar (*literary*), yonder [➡ DISTANCE; 160] *Opposite:* close **2** *adv* **much**, greatly, considerably, a lot, significantly, widely, extensively, extremely, immeasurably [➡ TO A GREAT EXTENT; 132] *Opposite:* barely **3** *adj* **distant**, remote, far-off, faraway, far-flung, outlying, far-removed [➡ DISTANCE; 160] *Opposite:* near

farad *type of* **SI unit** [➡ SIZE AND DIMENSIONS; 1192]

far afield *adv* **far away**, far off, far, far and wide, distantly, remotely, afar (*literary*), yonder [➡ DISTANCE; 160] *Opposite:* close

far and away *adv* **easily**, by far, much, considerably, greatly, significantly, extremely [➡ TO A GREAT EXTENT; 132] *Opposite:* barely

far and wide *adv* **everywhere**, all over, far afield, afar (*literary*), throughout, all around, high and low, generally, universally [➡ GENERAL LOCATIONS; 158]

far away *adj* [➡ DISTANCE; 160]

faraway 1 *adj* **remote**, far-off, far-flung, outlying, distant, far [➡ DISTANCE; 160] *Opposite:* nearby **2** *adj* **dreamy**, preoccupied, bemused, distant, in a world of your own, daydreaming, engrossed, rapt, absorbed, absent-minded [➡ NEUTRALITY AND INDIFFERENCE; 553] *Opposite:* alert

farce *n* **shambles**, travesty, absurdity, circus, sham, mockery, charade, embarrassment, disgrace [➡ DISORDER AND CHAOS; 245]

farcical *adj* **absurd**, ridiculous, ludicrous, silly, nonsensical, preposterous, embarrassing, foolish, incompetent, risible, laughable, derisory [➡ FUNNY AND AMUSING; 216] *Opposite:* solemn

fare 1 *n* **price**, tariff, ticket, cost, fee, entrance fee, toll, charge, tab (*informal*) [➡ EXPENDITURE; 423] **2** *n* **passenger**, customer, client, payer, rider [➡ TRAVEL: TRAVELERS AND WALKERS; 319] **3** *n* **food**, menu, meal, dishes, provisions, cuisine, victuals, food and drink, regimen, board, comestibles (*formal*) [➡ FOOD; 1167] **4** *v* **do**, get on, manage, cope, get by, proceed, progress, advance, perform, turn out, get along [➡ CONTINUE TO EXIST; 17]

farewell 1 *n* **goodbye**, sendoff, departure, exit, leaving, parting, leave-taking (*literary*), valediction (*formal*) [➡ ENDS AND DEPARTURES; 54] *Opposite:* greeting **2** *n* (*literary*) **goodbye**, au revoir, adieu, auf Wiedersehen, bye-bye (*informal*), so long (*informal*), ciao (*informal*), adios (*informal*), see you later (*informal*) [➡GREETINGS, FAREWELLS, AND SALUTATIONS; 659] *Opposite*: hello

far-fetched *adj* **unbelievable**, fantastic, implausible, incredible, fanciful, unlikely, improbable, exaggerated, unconvincing, mind-boggling (*informal*) [➡IMPOSSIBLE AND IMPROBABLE; 178] *Opposite*: believable

far-flung 1 *adj* **widespread**, extensive, sweeping, diffuse, wide-ranging [➡GENERAL LOCATIONS; 158] *Opposite*: restricted 2 *adj* **distant**, remote, far-off, faraway, outlying, extreme, far [➡DISTANCE; 160] *Opposite*: nearby

far from *prep* **anything but**, unlike, different from, poles apart from [➡DIFFERENCE; 149] *Opposite*: near

farm 1 *n* **cattle farm**, dairy farm, sheep farm, fish farm, plantation, ranch, smallholding (*UK*) [➡AGRICULTURE AND FARMING; 1075] 2 *n* **farmhouse**, farmstead, homestead, ranch, grange (*UK*) [➡AGRICULTURE AND FARMING; 1075] 3 *v* **cultivate**, work, till, plow, grow, plant, raise [➡GROW AND CULTIVATE; 351]

farm animal *n* [➡LIVING THINGS AND LIVING; 976]

farm animal

◆ *types of farm animals*
ass, cow, donkey, goat, hog, horse, mule, ox, pig, sheep

farmer *n* **agriculturalist**, grower, rancher, crofter, tenant farmer, sharecropper, truck farmer, dairy farmer, agronomist, market gardener, planter, agrarian, smallholder (*UK*) [➡FARMERS, GARDENERS, AND MANUAL WORKERS; 849]

farmers' market *type of* **food outlet** [➡RETAIL OUTLETS; 1083]

farm hand *n* **farmworker**, laborer, seasonal worker, harvester, ranch hand, hired hand [➡FARMERS, GARDENERS, AND MANUAL WORKERS; 849]

farmhouse *type of* **house** [➡RESIDENTIAL BUILDINGS; 1078]

farming *n* **agribusiness**, agriculture, husbandry, cultivation, market gardening, agronomy, crop raising, ranching [➡AGRICULTURE AND FARMING; 1075]

farmland *n* [➡AGRICULTURE AND FARMING; 1075]

farm out *v* **delegate**, subcontract, contract out, send out, hand out, assign, allocate, turn over, pass on [➡DISPENSE, RATION, AND DISTRIBUTE; 434]

farmstead *n* **homestead**, farm, ranch, grange (*UK*) [➡AGRICULTURE AND FARMING; 1075]

farmyard *n* **yard**, barnyard, cattle yard, stable yard [➡THE COUNTRYSIDE AND OUTDOOR SPACES; 1071]

far off *adv* [➡DISTANCE; 160]

far-off *adj* **distant**, remote, far, faraway, far-flung, outlying, extreme [➡DISTANCE; 160] *Opposite*: nearby

far-out (*slang*) *adj* **unusual**, avant-garde, bizarre, offbeat, unconventional, ultramodern, outlandish, kinky (*informal*) [➡EXTRAORDINARY: AMAZING; 204] *Opposite*: ordinary

farrago *n* **hodgepodge**, potpourri, mishmash, medley, mixture, mix, blend, jumble, miscellany [➡COLLECTIONS AND MIXTURES OF THINGS; 1244]

far-reaching *adj* **extensive**, sweeping, broad, across-

the-board, comprehensive, influential, important, in-depth, widespread, wide-ranging [➡WHOLENESS AND COMPLETENESS; 198] *Opposite*: limited

farsighted 1 *adj* [➡SEE; 699] 2 *adj* **wise**, visionary, far-seeing, provident, prophetic, judicious, perceptive, astute, cautious, sensible, prudent, discerning, sagacious [➡THE NATURE OF IDEAS; 771] *Opposite*: short-sighted

farsightedness 1 *n* [➡SEE; 699] 2 *n* **foresight**, providence, prescience, forethought, wisdom, sagacity, perceptiveness, judiciousness, perception, cautiousness, caution, prudence, vision [➡POSITIVE INTELLECTUAL CHARACTERISTICS; 524] *Opposite*: short-sightedness

farthermost *adj* [➡DISTANCE; 160]

farthest *adj* **furthest**, utmost, uttermost, outermost, furthermost, farthest away, furthest away, extreme, far-thermost [➡DISTANCE; 160]

fascinate *v* **captivate**, charm, enthrall, attract, mesmerize, interest, absorb, intrigue, appeal, beguile, allure, entice, put under a spell, bewitch, enchant, spellbind, transfix, rivet (*informal*) [➡APPEAL TO AND AROUSE INTEREST; 575] *Opposite*: repel

fascinated *adj* **captivated**, rapt, spellbound, charmed, involved, intent, absorbed, engrossed, enthralled, gripped, immersed, mesmerized, entranced, enchanted, transfixed, riveted (*informal*) [➡PENSIVENESS AND INTEREST; 538] *Opposite*: uninterested

fascinating *adj* **captivating**, charming, attractive, enthralling, mesmerizing, interesting, absorbing, intriguing, appealing, beguiling, alluring, enticing, spellbinding, enchanting, riveting (*informal*) [➡INTERESTING AND MEANINGFUL; 190] *Opposite*: repellent

fascination *n* **captivation**, charm, attraction, appeal, allure, lure, interest, enthrallment, enchantment, beguilement, charisma, glamour [➡PLEASURE, EXCITEMENT, AND ELATION; 534]

fashion 1 *n* **style**, way, manner, mode, method, approach, technique, custom, usage [➡WAYS OF DOING THINGS; 294] 2 *n* **trend**, craze, fad, vogue, mode, taste, in thing, rage [➡FADS, FETISHES, AND IDOLATRY; 555] 3 *v* **shape**, mold, form, make, fit, alter, transform, create, frame, devise, adapt, pattern, fabricate [➡CREATION; 346]

See Compare and Contrast at **make**.

fashionable *adj* **chic**, stylish, designer, up-to-the-minute, in, cool, in vogue, modish, up-to-date, modern, voguish, trendy (*informal*), happening (*informal*), swanky (*informal*), hip (*slang*) [➡NEW, MODERN; 166] *Opposite*: dated

fashionably *adv* **stylishly**, modishly, chicly, elegantly, trendily (*informal*) [➡WELL-GROOMED; 482]

fashion-conscious *adj* **chic**, stylish, fashionable, elegant, modish, voguish, up-to-the-minute, trendy (*informal*), tony (*informal*), swanky (*informal*), hip (*slang*) [➡WELL-GROOMED; 482] *Opposite*: outmoded

fashionista (*informal*) *n* [➡SELF-IMPORTANT AND SELF-SEEKING PEOPLE; 949]

[→...RMANCES AND SHOWS; 42]

[→...SELF-IMPORTANT AND SELF-SEEKING PEOPLE; 949]

...n [→... quick, speedy, rapid, swift, express, hasty, speed, prompt, immediate, expeditious, fleet, ...ged, brisk, flying [→MOVING QUICKLY; 103] Opposite: slow **2** adj ...ad, gaining, in advance [→BEFORE, FIRST, AND PRECEDING; 163] ...oposite: slow **3** adj **sudden**, sharp, fleeting, momentary, ...hort-lived, brief, abrupt, hurried, precipitous [→HAPPENING QUICKLY; 104] Opposite: long-lasting **4** adj **debauched**, wild, reckless, dissolute, profligate, wanton, loose [→MORALLY BAD OR IMPROPER; 775] **5** adj **firm**, steadfast, constant, unwavering, faithful, staunch [→HONEST AND RELIABLE; 502] Opposite: fickle **6** adv **quickly**, speedily, rapidly, swiftly, promptly, without delay, at once, immediately, in a flash, like lightning, in no time, on the double, hastily, expeditiously, briskly [→MOVING QUICKLY; 103] Opposite: slowly **7** adv **firmly**, firm, tightly, tight, stable, securely, fixed, steadily, tenaciously, fixedly, solidly, steady [→RIGID AND HARD; 1211] Opposite: loosely **8** v **abstain**, starve yourself, go without [→EAT AND NOT EAT; 710] Opposite: feast **9** n **diet**, abstention, starvation, cleansing, hunger strike, abstinence [→EAT AND NOT EAT; 738]

fast asleep adj [→TIRED, ASLEEP, AND UNCONSCIOUS; 738]

fasten 1 v **secure**, attach, fix, clip, clasp, affix, join, chain, tie, hook, hitch, pin, nail, connect, close [→FASTEN, LINK, AND JOIN; 408] Opposite: detach **2** v **shut**, close, tie, tie up, do up, button, zip, zip up, lock, secure [→FASTEN, LINK, AND JOIN; 408] Opposite: undo

fastener n **clasp**, fastening, tie, closure, snap, pin, clip, toggle, hook and eye, buckle, button, zipper, catch, press stud (UK), popper (UK) [→FASTENERS, LINKS, AND NETWORKS; 1247]

fastening n **clasp**, tie, closure, fastener, clip, buckle, catch, button, zipper, snap, hook and eye, pin, gripper snap, hook, latch, lock, press stud (UK), popper (UK) [→FASTENERS, LINKS, AND NETWORKS; 1247]

fast food n [→PREPARED DISHES; 1170]

fastidious 1 adj **demanding**, fussy, finicky, picky, particular, difficult, careful, painstaking, exacting, precise, meticulous, exact, thorough, assiduous, persnickety (informal), choosy (informal), faddy (UK) [→DIFFICULT TO PLEASE; 515] Opposite: easygoing **2** adj **delicate**, refined, particular, dainty, squeamish [→GOOD MANNERS AND SOCIAL SKILLS; 520] Opposite: slovenly

fastidiousness 1 n **fussiness**, meticulousness, care, carefulness, neatness, preciseness, precision, assiduousness, conscientiousness, thoroughness, exactness [→HARD-WORKING AND COMMITTED; 500] Opposite: carelessness **2** n **delicacy**, delicateness, daintiness, refinedness, squeamishness [→GOOD MANNERS AND SOCIAL SKILLS; 520] Opposite: crudeness

fast lane n [→ROADS; 1106]

fastness 1 n (archaic or literary) **stronghold**, fortress, castle, citadel, refuge, retreat, fort, fortification, redoubt [→FORTRESSES AND FORTIFICATIONS; 1090] **2** n **speediness**, swiftness, alacrity, speed, haste, pace, rapidity, rapidness, fleetness (literary) [→SPEED; 102]

fast talker n [→PEOPLE WHO DECEIVE; 661]

fast track n **push**, boost, way forward, advancement, furthering, progress, promotion [→PROGRESS AND ADVANCEMENT; 213]

fast-track v **advance**, accelerate, forge ahead, progress, develop, go forward, further, promote, boost, move along, push forward, speed up [→MAKE POSSIBLE; 275]

fat 1 n **oil**, lard, grease, shortening [→FATS AND OILS; 1173] **2** type of nutrient [→FOOD COMPONENTS; 1188] **3** n **flab**, adipose tissue, padding, insulation, blubber (informal) [→UNPLEASANT, DIRTY, AND TOXIC SUBSTANCES; 1268] **4** adj **overweight**, plump, chubby, stout, portly, obese, heavy, corpulent, tubby (informal), pudgy (informal), podgy (UK) [→BUILD; 477] Opposite: thin **5** adj **fatty**, greasy, oily, oleaginous [→PHYSICAL TEXTURE; 1222] Opposite: lean **6** adj **thick**, hefty, sizable, big, large, huge, enormous, wide, chunky [→LARGE; 1193] Opposite: slim **7** adj **rich**, wealthy, affluent, well-off, prosperous, well-to-do [→WEALTH AND WEALTHY; 891] Opposite: poor

fatal 1 adj **deadly**, lethal, incurable, terminal, mortal, final [→DEADLY; 928] **2** adj **ruinous**, disastrous, destructive, serious, grave, critical [→DANGEROUS; 236] Opposite: beneficial **3** adj **decisive**, critical, crucial, fateful, pivotal, momentous, important, significant [→IMPORTANT; 194] Opposite: unimportant

See Compare and Contrast at **deadly**.

fatalism n **resignation**, passivity, acceptance, stoicism, pessimism, defeatism, despondency, despair [→FEELINGS ABOUT THE FUTURE; 533]

fatalistic adj **philosophical**, defeatist, resigned, stoic... stoical, passive [→COOL AND CALM; 536]

fatality 1 n **death**, accident, casualty, loss, de... (formal) [→DEATH AND BEREAVEMENT; 927] **2** n **deadliness**, fat... deathliness, lethalness, noxiousness, mortall... [→DANGER; 235]

fatally 1 adv **lethally**, terminally, mortall... seriously [→CRITICALLY AND SERIOUSLY; 134] **2** adv s... ously, hopelessly, critically, disastrousl... ICALLY AND SERIOUSLY; 134]

fata morgana (literary) n [→NONEXIST...

fat cat (slang) **1** n [→RICH PEOPLE; 89...

fate 1 n **destiny**, fortune, provi... lot [→FATE, DESTINY, AND ASTROLOGY; 782] result, upshot, end [→RESULTS ...

fated adj **predetermine**... ordained, meant, in... doomed [→FATE, DESTINY, A...

fateful 1 adj **critic**... crucial, historic... **2** adj **ominous**,... fated, tragic [→...

father 1 ... (informal) ... **2** n **ance**... progen... desc... archi... **4** n **priest**,... **5** v **beget**, sire,... [→REPRODUCTION AND HE... after, nurture, take c...

fa...
fat...
por...
(info...
[→BUIL...
fatten...
(UK) [→...
fatteni...
fatten u...
[→CHANGE OF S...
fatty adj g...
TEXTURE; 1222] O...
fatuity (form...
stupidity, chi...
lessness, point...
CHARACTERISTICS; 525]...
fatuous adj uni...
stupid, childish, ...
[→NEGATIVE INTELLECTUAL C...
fatuously adv uni...
stupidly, inanely, m...

fatherhood *n* **paternity**, parenthood, kinship [➞ RELATIONSHIP TO ANOTHER; 973] *Opposite:* motherhood

father-in-law *type of* **in-law** [➞ RELATIVES BY MARRIAGE; 960]

fatherland *n* **homeland**, native land, home, motherland, mother country, old country [➞ COUNTRIES AND REGIONS; 1067]

fatherliness *n* **protectiveness**, benevolence, affection, supportiveness, kindness [➞ GENEROSITY AND KINDNESS; 495]

fatherly *adj* **paternal**, protective, concerned, caring, loving, supportive, kind [➞ GENEROSITY AND KINDNESS; 495]

fathom **1** *v* **comprehend**, understand, work out, figure out, grasp, think through, make out, divine [➞ UNDERSTAND AND GRASP; 759] **2** *v* **sound**, measure, plumb, gauge, probe [➞ ASSESS QUANTITY; 757]

fathomable *adj* **comprehensible**, understandable, penetrable, graspable, intelligible, apprehensible [➞ EASE AND SIMPLICITY; 200] *Opposite:* unfathomable

fathomless **1** *adj* **incomprehensible**, immeasurable, unfathomable, obscure, incalculable, mysterious, impenetrable, profound, cryptic, deep, recondite [➞ DIFFICULTY AND COMPLEXITY; 242] *Opposite:* fathomable **2** *adj* **deep**, immeasurable, unfathomable, bottomless, inestimable [➞ DEPTH: DEEP; 1201] *Opposite:* shallow

fathomlessness *n* [➞ DEPTH: DEEP; 1201]

fatigue *n* **exhaustion**, tiredness, weariness, weakness, lethargy, lassitude [➞ TIRED, ASLEEP, AND UNCONSCIOUS; 738] *Opposite:* energy

fatigued *adj* **exhausted**, weary, tired, drained, worn-out, done in (*informal*), done for (*informal*), pooped (*informal*), beat (*slang*), wiped out (*slang*) [➞ TIRED, ASLEEP, AND UNCONSCIOUS; 738] *Opposite:* fresh

fatigues *type of* **pants** [➞ GARMENTS AND OUTFITS; 865]

fatiguing *adj* [➞ PHYSICALLY UNPLEASANT; 226]

ness *n* **obesity**, plumpness, chubbiness, stoutness, ...liness, heaviness, size, corpulence, tubbiness ...mal), flabbiness (*informal*), pudginess (*informal*) ... 477] *Opposite:* thinness

... *v* **stuff**, plump, build up, feed, fatten up, feed up ...CHANGE OF SIZE: BIGGER; 392] *Opposite:* starve

...**g** *adj* **calorific**, fatty, rich, greasy, oily [➞ FOOD; 1167]

... *v* **stuff**, build up, feed, fatten, feed up (*UK*) ...E: BIGGER; 392] *Opposite:* starve

...easy, fat, oily, blubbery (*informal*) [➞ PHYSICAL ...posite: lean

...*l*) *n* **unintelligence**, complacency, silliness, ...ldishness, foolishness, inanity, mind... ...essness, senselessness [➞ NEGATIVE INTELLECTUAL ...Opposite: sensibleness

...ntelligent, complacent, unaware, silly, ...ointless, meaningless, foolish, inane ...ARACTERISTICS; 525] *Opposite:* sensible

...ntelligently, complacently, foolishly, ...indlessly, pointlessly, senselessly,

childishly, meaninglessly [➞ NEGATIVE INTELLECTUAL CH... 525] *Opposite:* sensibly

fatuousness *n* **unintelligence**, complac... foolishness, stupidity, inanity, mind... lessness, senselessness [➞ NEGATIVE INTELLECT... *Opposite:* sensibleness

faucet *n* **spout**, spigot, nozzle, outlet... tap [➞ FIXTURES; 859]

fault **1** *n* **responsibility**, liability, bur... accountability [➞ RESPONSIBILITY; 170] **2** *n* ... blunder, slip, omission, lapse, overs... (*informal*) [➞ MISTAKES; 250] **3** *n* **shortcoming**, failin... defect, flaw, deficiency, drawback, foible [➞ FAUL... WEAKNESSES; 251] *Opposite:* strength **4** *n* **defect**, flaw... fection, blemish, weakness [➞ FAULTS, FLAWS, AND WEAKNESS... *Opposite:* asset **5** *v* **blame**, criticize, condemn, find f... with, question, censure [➞ ACCUSE, BLAME, AND CRITICIZE; 641] *Oppo...* site: praise

See Compare and Contrast at **flaw**.

faultfinder *n* **critic**, carper, complainer, grumbler, nitpicker, moaner (*informal*), grouser (*informal*) [➞ GRUMPY AND NEGATIVE PEOPLE; 953]

faultfinding **1** *n* **criticism**, grumbling, nitpicking [➞ COMPLAIN AND NAG; 686] **2** *adj* **critical**, reproachful, carping, damning, unfavorable, nitpicky [➞ DIFFICULT TO PLEASE; 515] *Opposite:* uncritical

faultily *adv* **imperfectly**, incorrectly, wrongly, defectively, deficiently, mistakenly, inadequately [➞ INCORRECT AND ERRONEOUS; 222] *Opposite:* properly

faultless *adj* **flawless**, perfect, impeccable, immaculate, blameless, spotless, irreproachable, correct, ideal [➞ CORRECT AND FAULTLESS; 182] *Opposite:* imperfect

faultlessness *n* **flawlessness**, perfection, purity, impeccability, immaculateness, irreproachability, blamelessness, spotlessness, correctness [➞ CORRECT AND FAULTLESS; 182] *Opposite:* imperfection

fault line *n* **crack**, rift, split, fissure, fault, fracture [➞ VOLCANOES AND EARTHQUAKES; 1054]

faulty **1** *adj* **out of order**, defective, broken-down, broken, on the blink (*informal*) [➞ IN BAD REPAIR; 1234] *Opposite:* perfect **2** *adj* **flawed**, imperfect, incorrect, incoherent, contradictory, defective, deficient, confused [➞ INCORRECT AND ERRONEOUS; 222] *Opposite:* sound

fauna *n* **animals**, creatures, wildlife, beasts [➞ LIVING THINGS AND LIVING; 976]

Fauvism *type of* **20th-century art movement** [➞ ARTISTIC MOVEMENTS AND STYLES; 899]

faux *adj* **fake**, artificial, unreal, reproduction, false, ersatz [➞ FALSE AND UNREAL; 173] *Opposite:* genuine

faux pas (*literary*) *n* **gaffe**, blunder, mistake, indiscretion, misstep, blooper (*informal humorous*), howler (*slang*) [➞ MISTAKES; 250]

See Compare and Contrast at **mistake**.

fava bean *type of* **pulse** [➡ PEAS AND BEANS; 1189]

favela *n* [➡ UNDESIRABLE ACCOMMODATIONS; 856]

favor 1 *n* **good turn**, errand, kindness, courtesy, service, indulgence [➡ KIND ACTIONS OR BEHAVIOR; 295] *Opposite:* disservice 2 *n* **approval**, support, kindness, esteem, sympathy, partiality, preference [➡ SOURCE OF HAPPINESS, PLEASURE, OR IMPROVEMENT; 209] *Opposite:* disfavor 3 *n* **gift**, trinket, token, present, keepsake, memento [➡ GIFTS; 438] 4 *v* **prefer**, choose, support, back, approve, esteem [➡ APPROVE AND CONFIRM; 646] *Opposite:* reject 5 *v* **assist**, help, aid, advance, promote, benefit, further, increase, encourage, facilitate, improve [➡ MAKE POSSIBLE; 275] *Opposite:* hinder

See Compare and Contrast at **regard**.

favorable 1 *adj* **advantageous**, auspicious, propitious, helpful, beneficial [➡ GOOD, WELL, BETTER; 183] *Opposite:* inauspicious 2 *adj* **promising**, auspicious, satisfactory, fortunate, advantageous, encouraging [➡ APPROPRIATE, SUITABLE, AND ADVISABLE; 184] *Opposite:* unfavorable 3 *adj* **approving**, positive, constructive, good, sympathetic, encouraging, complimentary, flattering, kind [➡ EXPRESSING RESPECT AND APPROVAL; 637] *Opposite:* negative

favorite 1 *adj* **chosen**, beloved, pet, favored [➡ POPULAR AND WANTED; 220] 2 *n* **pet**, darling, beloved [➡ PEOPLE WHO ARE APPROVED OF; 955] 3 *n* **choice**, preference, pick [➡ SOURCE OF HAPPINESS, PLEASURE, OR IMPROVEMENT; 209]

favoritism *n* **preferentialism**, preference, partiality, nepotism, bias, discrimination, prejudice [➡ PREJUDICE; 550] *Opposite:* impartiality

fawn 1 *v* **flatter**, grovel, toady, kowtow, crawl (*informal*), butter up (*informal*) [➡ FLATTER AND FAWN; 621] 2 *type of* **young animal** [➡ YOUNG ANIMALS; 977] 3 *type of* **beige** [➡ COLORS; 1224]

fawning *adj* **flattering**, obsequious, smarmy, sycophantic, servile [➡ INGRATIATING; 638]

fax 1 *n* **facsimile**, message, document, transmission, copy [➡ LETTERS AND WRITTEN MESSAGES; 584] 2 *type of* **telecommunications equipment** [➡ TELECOMMUNICATIONS; 1130] 3 *v* **send**, transmit, convey, communicate, telex, deliver [➡ DISPATCH AND SEND; 333]

fay (*literary*) *n* [➡ MYTHICAL BEINGS; 789]

faze *v* **fluster**, disconcert, disturb, put off, deter, daunt, intimidate, upset, discourage, confuse, throw (*informal*) [➡ CONFUSE AND BEWILDER; 571] *Opposite:* encourage

fear 1 *n* **anxiety**, apprehension, distress, terror, dread, horror, fright, panic, alarm, trepidation [➡ FEAR AND PANIC; 543] *Opposite:* assurance 2 *n* **worry**, concern, anxiety, terror, nightmare, phobia [➡ CONFUSION, ANXIETY, AND WORRY; 540] 3 *v* **dread**, be afraid, be scared, be apprehensive, be frightened, be anxious [➡ FEARS AND PHOBIAS; 554]

fearful 1 *adj* **worried**, afraid, scared, apprehensive, frightened, anxious, timid, nervous [➡ CONFUSION, ANXIETY, AND WORRY; 540] *Opposite:* fearless 2 *adj* (*informal*) **terrible**, dreadful, appalling, awful, horrible, frightful, atrocious, dire, horrendous, abysmal, bad [➡ BAD AND BADLY; 223] *Opposite:* wonderful 3 *adj* **frightening**, terrifying, terrible, frightful, horrific, fearsome, scary (*informal*) [➡ FRIGHTENING; 231]

fearfully 1 *adv* (*informal*) **terribly**, dreadfully, awfully, horribly, frightfully, horrendously, extremely, very,

intensely [➡ TO A GREAT EXTENT; 132] 2 *adv* **worriedly**, nervously, timidly, uneasily, apprehensively, anxiously [➡ FEAR AND PANIC; 543] *Opposite:* fearlessly 3 *adv* **frighteningly**, terrifyingly, terribly, frightfully, horrifically, scarily (*informal*) [➡ FRIGHTENING; 231]

fearfulness 1 *n* **worriedness**, anxiety, apprehension, awe, fear, dread, trepidation, alarm, terror, horror [➡ FEELINGS ABOUT THE FUTURE; 533] *Opposite:* bravery 2 *n* **scariness**, terribleness, frightfulness, horror, terror [➡ FRIGHTENING; 231] 3 *n* (*informal*) **terribleness**, atrociousness, dreadfulness, awfulness, horror, frightfulness, hatefulness, horridness, severity [➡ DISGUSTING AND REPULSIVE; 230]

fearless *adj* **courageous**, brave, bold, unafraid, daring, plucky, valiant, heroic, confident, audacious, intrepid (*literary or humorous*) [➡ COURAGE; 498] *Opposite:* cowardly

fearlessness *n* **courage**, bravery, boldness, heroism, valor, audacity, daring, pluckiness, valiantness, confidence, pluck [➡ COURAGE; 498] *Opposite:* cowardice

See Compare and Contrast at **courage**.

fearsome 1 *adj* **frightening**, formidable, terrifying, alarming, awesome, fearful, terrible [➡ FRIGHTENING; 231] 2 *adj* **impressive**, awesome, formidable, awe-inspiring, tremendous, striking [➡ EXTRAORDINARY: AMAZING; 204]

feasibility *n* **viability**, possibility, probability, likelihood, practicability, practicality, achievability [➡ POSSIBLE AND PROBABLE; 171] *Opposite:* impossibility

feasible *adj* **viable**, possible, practicable, achievable, reasonable, realistic, practical, likely [➡ POSSIBLE AND PROBABLE; 171] *Opposite:* impossible

feast 1 *n* **banquet**, dinner, meal, buffet, spread (*informal*), repast (*literary*) [➡ MEALS AND PARTS OF MEALS; 1169] 2 *n* **celebration**, festival, holiday, feast day, holy day, saint's day [➡ PARTIES, DANCES, AND CELEBRATIONS; 37] 3 *n* **delight**, treat, indulgence, pleasure, joy, enjoyment [➡ TREATS; 210] 4 *v* **eat**, dine, indulge, partake, gobble, pig out (*informal*) [➡ EAT AND NOT EAT; 710] *Opposite:* fast

feat *n* **achievement**, accomplishment, deed, exploit, act, coup [➡ ACTIONS OR UNDERTAKINGS; 259]

feather *part of* **bird** [➡ PARTS OF A BIRD; 1006]

feathery *adj* **downy**, fluffy, soft, light, plumy, plumose [➡ PHYSICAL TEXTURE; 1222]

feature 1 *n* **characteristic**, trait, mark, attribute, quality, facet, aspect, element, highlight [➡ QUALITIES AND CHARACTERISTICS; 1191] 2 *n* **facial feature**, contour, lineament (*literary*) [➡ FACIAL CHARACTERISTICS; 481] 3 *n* **article**, piece, report, item, story, column [➡ NEWSPAPERS AND MAGAZINES; 605] 4 *v* **contain**, include, present, introduce, bring out, highlight, bring forward [➡ CAUSE TO APPEAR; 5] 5 *v* **perform**, star, appear, act, turn up, costar [➡ THE PERFORMING ARTS; 904] 6 *v* **highlight**, star, include, showcase, show, costar [➡ CAUSE TO APPEAR; 5] 7 *v* **figure**, appear, participate, take part, play a part [➡ PARTICIPATE; 292]

feature film *n* [➡ FILM; 901]

featureless *adj* **dull**, drab, bland, uninspired, unremarkable, undistinguished, unimaginative [➡ PLAIN; 232] *Opposite:* distinctive

febrile *adj* **feverish**, fevered, flushed, hot, delirious, pyretic [➡ILL AND SICK; 740]

feces *n* [➡EXCRETION AND EXCRETA; 722]

feckless *adj* **good-for-nothing**, useless, hopeless, spineless, feeble, weak, ineffectual, worthless, incompetent, ineffective, unreliable, irresponsible, aimless [➡LACK OF COMMITMENT AND UNRELIABILITY; 509] *Opposite*: dynamic

fecklessness *n* **uselessness**, hopelessness, spinelessness, feebleness, irresponsibility, aimlessness, unreliability [➡LACK OF COMMITMENT AND UNRELIABILITY; 509] *Opposite*: dynamism

fecund **1** *adj* **productive**, creative, prolific, industrious, fruitful, dynamic [➡USEFULNESS; 199] **2** *adj* (*formal*) **fertile**, prolific, productive, fruitful, rich [➡REPRODUCTION AND HEREDITY; 725] *Opposite*: infertile

fecundity *n* **fertility**, prolificness, productiveness, fruitfulness, richness [➡REPRODUCTION AND HEREDITY; 725] *Opposite*: infertility

federal *adj* **central**, centralized, national, state, civic [➡STYLES AND SYSTEMS OF GOVERNMENT; 806] *Opposite*: regional

federate **1** *v* **unite**, join, amalgamate, come together, merge, coalesce, associate [➡CREATING CONNECTIONS; 144] *Opposite*: devolve **2** *v* **associate**, unite, combine, join, confederate, amalgamate [➡COMBINE AND MIX; 400] *Opposite*: disassociate

federation **1** *n* **alliance**, coalition, confederation, grouping, partnership, association, amalgamation, confederacy, group [➡INSTITUTIONS; 790] **2** *n* **combination**, union, association, confederation, amalgamation [➡INSTITUTIONS; 790]

Federation *type of* **20th-century architecture** [➡BUILDING AND ARCHITECTURE; 1076]

fedora *type of* **hat** [➡ACCESSORIES, MILLINERY, AND LINGERIE; 867]

fed up (*informal*) *adj* **bored**, miserable, jaded, discontented, tired, sick and tired, annoyed, disgruntled, dissatisfied [➡SADNESS, DISTRESS, AND DESPAIR; 539] *Opposite*: happy

fee **1** *n* **payment**, remuneration, salary, pay, stipend, emolument (*formal or humorous*) [➡INCOME; 460] **2** *n* **charge**, subscription, toll, tariff, cost, fare, rate [➡FUNDS, PAYMENTS, AND CHARGES; 800]

See Compare and Contrast at **wage**.

feeble **1** *adj* **weak**, frail, delicate, shaky, thin, meager [➡UNFIT AND WEAK; 739] *Opposite*: robust **2** *adj* **unconvincing**, ineffectual, poor, half-hearted, ineffective, weak, pathetic (*informal*) [➡WEAKNESS; 241] *Opposite*: convincing

See Compare and Contrast at **weak**.

feeble-minded *adj* **ill-considered**, incoherent, ill-defined, ineffectual, weak, half-baked (*informal*) [➡NEGATIVE INTELLECTUAL CHARACTERISTICS; 525] *Opposite*: well-thought-out

feeble-mindedness *n* **irresolution**, indecision, ineffectuality, indecisiveness, half-heartedness, irresoluteness, hesitancy, weakness [➡NEGATIVE INTELLECTUAL CHARACTERISTICS; 525] *Opposite*: resoluteness

feebleness **1** *n* **weakness**, fragility, delicateness, frailty, shakiness, thinness, meagerness [➡WEAKNESS; 241] *Opposite*: robustness **2** *n* **ineffectuality**, weakness, half-heartedness, ineffectiveness [➡COWARDICE AND WEAKNESS OF WILL; 508] *Opposite*: effectiveness

feebly **1** *adv* **weakly**, frailly, delicately, shakily, thinly, meagerly [➡WEAKNESS; 241] *Opposite*: robustly **2** *adv* **unconvincingly**, half-heartedly, pathetically, ineffectively, ineffectually, weakly, softly [➡ILL AND SICK; 740] *Opposite*: convincingly

feed **1** *v* **nourish**, nurse, suckle, breast-feed, serve, provide for, nurture [➡TAKE CARE OF AND SPOIL; 300] *Opposite*: starve **2** *v* **eat**, consume, partake, devour, swallow [➡EAT AND NOT EAT; 710] **3** *v* **support**, sustain, nourish, nurture, encourage, maintain, strengthen, bolster [➡IMPROVE STRENGTH AND DURABILITY; 378] **4** *n* **food**, feedstuff, fodder, provender, forage [➡ANIMAL FEED; 1168]

feedback *n* **response**, reaction, comment, criticism, advice, pointer, opinion, view, reply [➡REPLY AND ANSWER ; 668]

feed into *v* **contribute**, provide, deliver, flow into, lead into, kick in (*informal*) [➡EQUIP AND SUPPLY; 435] *Opposite*: draw on

feedstuff *n* [➡ANIMAL FEED; 1168]

feel **1** *v* **touch**, finger, handle, sense, fondle, manipulate, stroke, caress [➡USING THE SENSES; 697] **2** *v* **sense**, experience, undergo, be aware of, bear, suffer [➡USING THE SENSES; 697] **3** *v* **think**, believe, consider, comprehend, understand, be of the opinion, know, suspect, deem (*formal*) [➡HAVE AN OPINION OF SOMETHING; 756] **4** *n* **sensation**, touch, texture, finish, sense, composition [➡TEXTURE; 1220] **5** *n* **impression**, atmosphere, air, feeling, ambiance, quality, aura, mood, character [➡APPEARANCE AND ATMOSPHERE; 1237]

feeler *n* **sensor**, antenna, whisker [➡PARTS OF AN INSECT; 1019]

feel for *v* **sympathize**, feel sorry for, pity, commiserate, empathize, be moved by, understand [➡BE CONCERNED AND CARE; 581]

feel-good *adj* **upbeat** (*informal*), optimistic, positive, happy, cheerful, satisfying, cheering, sanguine, contented [➡EMOTIONALLY PLEASANT; 187] *Opposite*: downbeat

feeling **1** *n* **sensation**, sense, sensitivity, touch [➡THE SENSES; 696] *Opposite*: numbness **2** *n* **emotion**, sentiment, mood, reaction, sense, impression, response [➡FEELINGS; 531] **3** *n* **opinion**, view, point of view, belief, impression, consideration, attitude, sentiment [➡POINTS OF VIEW; 767] **4** *n* **affection**, concern, regard, love, sympathy, attachment, sensitivity, compassion, pity, empathy [➡COMPASSION AND FORGIVENESS; 551] *Opposite*: antipathy **5** *n* **hunch**, instinct, suspicion, intuition, idea, gut reaction, notion, presentiment [➡IDEAS AND THOUGHTS; 770] **6** *n* **air**, atmosphere, ambiance, feel, mood, impression, quality, aura, character [➡APPEARANCE AND ATMOSPHERE; 1237]

feelingly *adv* **expressively**, passionately, emotionally, sensitively, with feeling, moodily, sympathetically, powerfully, fervently [➡ELOQUENT, TALKATIVE, AND LONG-WINDED; 632] *Opposite*: impassively

feel like **1** *v* **want**, desire, crave, wish, long for [➡DESIRE AND WANT; 579] **2** *v* **seem**, appear, resemble, look like [➡SEEM TO BE SOMETHING; 58]

feel sorry for *v* **pity**, empathize, feel for, commiserate

felonious adj [→ILLEGAL; 816]

felony n crime, offense, misdemeanor, wrongdoing, law-breaking, delinquency [→CRIMES; 817]

felt type of fabric from animals [→FABRICS; 1132]

felt-tipped pen type of pen [→WRITING AND DRAWING IMPLEMENTS, AND MEDIA; 601]

felucca type of sailing vessel [→SHIPS AND BOATS; 1150]

female 1 adj feminine, womanly, womanlike, ladylike, girlish [→GENDER IDENTITY AND SEXUALITY; 932] Opposite: masculine 2 n woman, lady, girl [→FEMALE PERSON; 933] Opposite: male

feminine adj female, womanly, womanlike, ladylike, girlish [→GENDER IDENTITY AND SEXUALITY; 932] Opposite: masculine

femininity n femaleness, feminineness, womanliness, girlishness [→GENDER IDENTITY AND SEXUALITY; 932] Opposite: masculinity

feminism n women's movement, women's liberation, women's rights, women's studies, radicalism, women's lib (informal) [→PHILOSOPHIES AND BELIEFS; 780]

feminist n suffragette, activist, radical, campaigner, women's libber (informal) [→PHILOSOPHICAL AND POLITICAL THINKERS; 781]

femur type of bone [→THE BONES AND JOINTS; 719]

fen n marsh, wetland, fenland, bog, lowland [→ 1043] Opposite: desert

fence 1 n barrier, boundary, hurdle, he... enclosure, screen, paling, trellis, palisade, ... [→BARRIERS; 1113] 2 v enclose, hedge, shut in, ... surround, encompass, pen, gird (litera... [→ ACCESS; 410] Opposite: open up 3 v evade, ... fight off, contest [→COMPETE, CONTEND, AND ...

fencer n [→PEOPLE IN SPORTS AND LEISUR...

fencing 1 n fence, railing, pa... link fencing, palisade, rail... banter, wordplay, raillery... combat sport [→HOBBIES, GAMES...

fender 1 n fireguard, ... 859] 2 part of extern... 3 part of bike [→BIKE...

fender-bend...

fend for v ... support [→...

fend f... yours... your... yo... w...

...CONCERNED AND CARE; ...te, make believe, with, sympathize ...O AND MIMIC; 60] 581]

...sincere, pretend, fake,

feign v preten... [→ ...E AND UNREAL; 173] Opposite: invent, affect, a...

feigned adj ..., maneuver, ruse, gambit, sham, affect..., wile, artifice (formal) [→DECEPTION genuine

feint n tri... sham, do... [→ AND LIES; 660] adv [→WITH ENTHUSIASM; 286] AND ENERGY AND ENTHUSIASM; 496]

feisti... (...rmal) adj lively, spirited, energetic, aggres-

feisti... ...mal) ..., full-blooded, go-getting (informal), gutsy [→ ... AND ENTHUSIASM; 496] Opposite: feeble

feis... sive [→ENERGY AND ENTHUSIASM; 496]

...(inf... type of mineral [→MINERALS; 1277]

fe...dar ...(formal) n congratulations, compliments,

...citations ...les, blessings, greetings, salutations (formal) best ...es, [→GREE...NGS, FAREWELLS, AND SALUTATIONS; 659]

felicitous ... adj appropriate, apt, suitable, apposite, well-chosen, ...tting, relevant, pertinent, germane [→APPROPRIATE, SUITA..., AND ADVISABLE; 184] Opposite: inapposite 2 adj fortunate, lucky, fortuitous, timely, happy, blessed, joyous, pro-pitious [→LUCK; 783] Opposite: unfortunate

felicity 1 n happiness, contentment, joy, pleasure, luck, blessedness, timeliness, fortunateness, bliss, delight, ecstasy [→PLEASURE, EXCITEMENT, AND ELATION; 534] Opposite: unhap-piness 2 n appropriateness, aptness, suitability, appo-siteness, fittingness, choiceness, relevance [→APPROPRIATE, SUITABLE, AND ADVISABLE; 184] Opposite: inappropriateness

feline adj graceful, slinky, subtle, elegant, stealthy [→AGILITY OF THE BODY; 476]

fell 1 v cut down, chop down, chop, clear-fell, clear-cut [→MOVE SOMETHING INTO A NEW POSITION OR OVERTURN; 330] 2 v knock down, knock out, floor, demolish (informal), deck (informal), take out (slang) [→MOVE SOMETHING INTO A NEW POSITION OR OVERTURN; 330] Opposite: set up

fella (informal) n [→MALE PERSON; 934]

fellow 1 n member, associate, researcher, academic [→COL-LEAGUES AND EQUALS; 967] 2 n man, boy, guy (informal) [→MALE PERSON; 934] 3 n (dated) companion, colleague, associate, partner, comrade, coworker [→COLLEAGUES AND EQUALS; 967]

fellow feeling n sympathy, empathy, support, affinity, mutuality, sensitivity, awareness [→COMPASSION AND FORGIVENESS; 551] Opposite: hostility

fellowship 1 n communion, companionship, cama-raderie, comradeship, friendship, friendliness, part-nership, mutuality, cooperativeness, solidarity, sociability [→RELATIONSHIP TO ANOTHER; 973] Opposite: enmity 2 n society, association, college, affiliation, cooperative, community, group, club, fraternity, brotherhood [→INSTI-TUTIONS; 790]

felon n criminal, murderer, offender, thief, killer, robber, outlaw, lawbreaker, delinquent [→CRIMINALS; 821]

---

w... cr... st... mi...

ferr... searc... [→SEEK ...

ferret around, ... POSSESSION ...

ferret ou... discern [→ ... out, uncove... SEARCH; 456] Op...

ferry 1 type of ... carry, ship, co... send [→MOVE SOMET...

ferryboat type ...

fertile 1 adj lush... luxuriant, bounti... Opposite: barren ... erative, fecund (for...

fertility n fruitfu... ductiveness, fecundity... [→USEFULNESS; 199] Oppos...

fertilization 1 n in...

on..., at ba..., welcome

fenland n ma... [→ 1043] Opposite: deser...

fennel 1 *type of* **herb** [➡HERBS AND SPICES; 1175] **2** *type of* **vegetable** [➡FRUIT AND VEGETABLES; 1176]

fenugreek *type of* **spice** [➡HERBS AND SPICES; 1175]

feral *adj* **wild**, untamed, undomesticated, savage, uncontrollable, uncontrolled, regressive [➡DANGEROUS; 236] *Opposite*: domesticated

fer-de-lance *type of* **poisonous snake** [➡SNAKES; 995]

ferment 1 *v* **agitate**, inflame, stir up, incite, provoke, cause [➡CAUSE TO HAPPEN; 31] **2** *n* **uproar**, tumult, confusion, excitement, commotion, upheaval, agitation, turmoil, turbulence, unrest, disquiet, mayhem (*informal*) [➡CHAOS AND UPROAR; 51] *Opposite*: peace

fermion *type of* **elementary particle** [➡ELEMENTARY PARTICLES; 1279]

fern *type of* **foliage plant** [➡FOLIAGE PLANTS; 1035]

ferocious 1 *adj* **fierce**, vicious, violent, cruel, brutal, aggressive, unruly, wild, savage, merciless, barbarous [➡DANGEROUS; 236] *Opposite*: gentle **2** *adj* **intense**, strong, heated, raging, extreme, unstoppable [➡STRENGTH; 201] *Opposite*: mild

ferociously 1 *adv* **fiercely**, viciously, cruelly, violently, brutally, wildly, savagely, mercilessly, barbarously [➡DANGEROUS; 236] *Opposite*: gently **2** *adv* **intensely**, heatedly, strongly, extremely, overwhelmingly, uncontrollably [➡STRENGTH; 201] *Opposite*: mildly

ferociousness *n* **fierceness**, ferocity, viciousness, violence, brutality, aggressiveness, wildness, savagery, mercilessness, cruelty [➡STRENGTH; 201] *Opposite*: gentleness

ferocity 1 *n* **fierceness**, ferociousness, cruelty, wildness, viciousness, violence, aggressiveness, savagery, mercilessness [➡STRENGTH; 201] *Opposite*: gentleness **2** *n* **intensity**, strength, extremeness, severity [➡STRENGTH; 201] *Opposite*: mildness

ferret 1 *type of* **small mammal** [➡SMALL MAMMALS; 990] **2** *v* **hunt**, search, search out, rummage, dig out, flush out, delve [➡SEEK POSSESSION AND SEARCH; 456]

ferret around *v* **look for**, search out, delve, search, hunt around, rummage, ferret about (*UK*) [➡SEEK POSSESSION AND SEARCH; 456]

ferret 1 *v* **discover**, uncover, find, reveal, unveil, [➡FIND; 463] *Opposite*: conceal **2** *v* **track down**, flush out, hunt down, catch, locate [➡SEEK POSSESSION AND SEARCH; 456] *Opposite*: hide

ferry 1 *type of* **motor vessel** [➡SHIPS AND BOATS; 1150] **2** *v* **transport**, convey, transmit, pass, take, bring, bear, lug, [➡MOVING TO ANOTHER LOCATION; 324]

ferryboat *type of* **motor vessel** [➡SHIPS AND BOATS; 1150]

fertile productive, abundant, rich, fruitful, bountiful (*literary*) [➡MANY, MUCH, LARGE AMOUNT; 117] *adj* **productive**, fruitful, prolific, generative (*literary*) [➡USEFULNESS; 199] *Opposite*: infertile

fertility *n* fruitfulness, richness, lushness, productiveness, abundance, luxuriance, potency [...] *Opposite*: barrenness

fertilization *n* insemination, impregnation, pol-

fertilize insemination, conception, in vitro fertilization, insemination, [REPRODUCTION AND HEREDITY; 725] **2** *n* **fertilizer** and top dressing, feeding enrich, nourish [➡GROW AND CULTIVATE; 351] *Opposite*: exhaust

fertilize pollinate, fertilize, top-dress, compost, [REPRODUCTION... GROW AND CULTIVATE; 351]

fertilizer *n* **manure**, top-dress, top dressing, peat [➡GROW AND CULTIVATE; 351]

fervent *adj* **enthusiastic**, ardent, passionate, zealous, fanatical, enricher, intense, vehement, heated [➡SUBSTANCES; 1268] [APPRECIATION... keen, passionate] *Opposite*: indifferent burning, [GRATITUDE; 535]

fervid *adj* [➡APPRECIATION AND GRATITUDE; 535]

fervor *n* **passion**, dedication, enthusiasm, zeal, commitment, feeling, vehemence, intenseness, ardor [➡PLEASURE, EXCITEMENT, AND ELATION; 534] *Opposite*: indifference

fescue *type of* **grass** [➡GRASS; 1031]

fess up (*slang*) *v* [➡ADMIT AND CONFESS; 615]

fester *v* **rankle**, irritate, gall, embitter, annoy, gnaw, chafe, fret, aggravate (*informal*), rile (*informal*) [➡GET WORSE; 381]

festival *n* **feast day**, holiday, celebration, anniversary, birthday, jubilee, commemoration, fiesta, carnival, event, party, gala, fete, fair [➡PARTIES, DANCES, AND CELEBRATIONS; 37]

festive *adj* **celebratory**, cheerful, joyful, merry, happy, jolly, jovial, festal, gala [➡PARTIES, DANCES, AND CELEBRATIONS; 37] *Opposite*: sad

festiveness *n* **merriness**, joyfulness, cheerfulness, happiness, jolliness, joviality [➡PLEASURE, EXCITEMENT, AND ELATION; 534] *Opposite*: lugubriousness

festivities *n* **revels**, revelry, celebrations, merriment, partying, carousing (*literary*) [➡PARTIES, DANCES, AND CELEBRATIONS; 37]

festivity 1 *n* **party**, event, gala, carnival, fete, fiesta, entertainment, celebration, revelry [➡PARTIES, DANCES, AND CELEBRATIONS; 37] **2** *n* **good cheer**, rejoicing, merriment, pleasure, enjoyment, happiness, cheeriness, gaiety, joy [➡TREATS; 210] *Opposite*: sadness

festoon 1 *n* **garland**, decoration, swag, ornament, chain, drape, streamer [➡ORNAMENTS AND DECORATIONS; 1248] **2** *v* **decorate**, adorn, swathe, hang, drape, embellish, do up [➡DECORATE, ADORN, AND APPLY COATINGS; 405] *Opposite*: strip

festooned *adj* **garlanded**, wreathed, hung, decorated, draped, swathed, bedecked (*literary*), decked (*literary*) [➡DECORATE, ADORN, AND APPLY COATINGS; 405] *Opposite*: unadorned

feta *type of* **soft cheese** [➡DAIRY PRODUCTS AND CHEESES; 1183]

fetch 1 *v* **get**, obtain, bring, carry, bring back, retrieve, take, get ahold of (*informal*) [➡GET; 420] **2** *v* **sell for**, make, raise, get, draw, realize, procure, bring, bring in [➡GET MONEY OR REWARD; 421]

fetching *adj* **attractive**, eye-catching, handsome, good-

looking, stylish, appealing, becoming, captivating, enticing, alluring, beautiful, cute, dishy (*informal*) [➥ PEOPLE'S PHYSICAL APPEARANCE; 475] *Opposite*: unattractive

fete 1 *n* holiday, anniversary, jubilee, centennial, feast day, commemoration, centenary (*UK*) [➥ PARTIES, DANCES, AND CELEBRATIONS; 37] 2 *v* honor, commemorate, lionize, entertain, praise, welcome, celebrate, congratulate [➥ PRAISE AND ENCOURAGE; 647]

fête *see* fete

fetid *adj* rotten, putrid, foul, squalid, fusty, stinking, smelly, decaying, malodorous, noisome, rank (*literary*) [➥ DECAYING OR INFESTED; 1236] *Opposite*: fresh

fetish 1 *n* talisman, charm, idol, image, totem, amulet [➥ LUCKY CHARMS; 785] 2 *n* obsession, fixation, mania, craze, engrossment, preoccupation, passion, thing (*informal*) [➥ FADS, FETISHES, AND IDOLATRY; 555] *Opposite*: aversion (*formal*)

fetishize *v* [➥ LIKE, LOVE, VALUE, AND ENJOY; 578]

fetlock *part of* horse [➥ HORSES; 985]

fetter 1 *n* shackle, bond, chain, yoke, handcuff, irons, restraint [➥ FASTENERS, LINKS, AND NETWORKS; 1247] 2 *v* tie, bind, chain, restrain, hamper, restrict, confine, impede, shackle [➥ CAPTIVITY AND LOSS OF FREEDOM; 248]

fettuccine *type of* pasta [➥ PASTA; 1180]

feud 1 *n* dispute, argument, row, quarrel, bad blood, grudge, disagreement, hostility, vendetta, strife [➥ ARGUMENTS; 47] *Opposite*: friendship 2 *v* fight, argue, dispute, quarrel, disagree, battle, clash, bicker, row [➥ COMPETE, CONTEND, AND COMBAT; 303]

feudal *adj* out-of-date, outdated, old-fashioned, medieval, primitive [➥ STYLES AND SYSTEMS OF GOVERNMENT; 806] *Opposite*: modern

fever 1 *n* temperature, infection, disease, illness, malaise [➥ ILLNESSES AND DISORDERS; 732] 2 *n* passion, fervor, excitement, agitation, vehemence, enthusiasm, zeal, eagerness, fanaticism, impatience [➥ POSITIVE IMPATIENCE, ENTHUSIASM, AND ALERTNESS; 537]

fevered *adj* feverish, agitated, restless, frenzied, excited, heated, enthusiastic, zealous, nervous, fanatical, impatient, passionate, intense [➥ POSITIVE IMPATIENCE, ENTHUSIASM, AND ALERTNESS; 537] *Opposite*: calm

feverish *adj* excited, agitated, nervous, heated, intense, busy, exciting, vehement, enthusiastic, zealous, fevered, fanatical, impatient, passionate [➥ POSITIVE IMPATIENCE, ENTHUSIASM, AND ALERTNESS; 537] *Opposite*: tranquil

few *adj* insufficient, a small number of, hardly any, not many, only some, a small amount of, scarce, rare, uncommon, limited, in short supply, thin on the ground, few and far between (*informal*) [➥ FEW, LITTLE, SMALL AMOUNT; 120] *Opposite*: many

few and far between (*informal*) *adj* scarce, infrequent, rare, sporadic, uncommon, in short supply, unusual, thin on the ground [➥ NEVER AND INFREQUENCY; 97] *Opposite*: commonplace

fewer *adj* less, rarer, scarcer [➥ LESS; 126] *Opposite*: more

fey *adj* whimsical, fanciful, otherworldly, unworldly, fan-

tastical, capricious, irrational [➥ LACK OF COMMITMENT AND UNRELIABILITY; 509]

fez *type of* headgear [➥ ACCESSORIES, MILLINERY, AND LINGERIE; 867]

fiancé *n* husband-to-be, boyfriend, future husband, groom, intended (*dated or humorous*), betrothed (*formal*) [➥ RELATIVES BY MARRIAGE; 960]

fiancée *n* wife-to-be, girlfriend, future wife, bride, betrothed (*formal*), intended (*dated or humorous*) [➥ RELATIVES BY MARRIAGE; 960]

fiasco *n* debacle, disaster, mess, shambles, failure, flop (*informal*) [➥ FAILURE; 77] *Opposite*: success

fiat 1 *n* official sanction, sanction, authorization, permission, agreement, approval [➥ PERMIT AND ALLOW; 669] 2 *n* order, command, decree, edict, instruction, directive [➥ REQUEST AND DEMAND; 663]

fib (*informal*) 1 *n* untruth, white lie, lie, tall tale, falsification, fabrication, story (*informal*), whopper (*informal*) [➥ DECEPTION AND LIES; 660] *Opposite*: truth 2 *v* lie, not tell the truth, misrepresent, tell stories, prevaricate, feign, dissemble, pull the wool over somebody's eyes, deceive, fake, pretend [➥ DECEPTION AND LIES; 660] *Opposite*: come clean (*informal*)

See Compare and Contrast at lie.

fibber (*informal*) *n* liar, deceiver, fabricator, prevaricator, perjurer, falsifier, storyteller (*informal*), dissembler (*formal*) [➥ PEOPLE WHO DECEIVE; 661]

fibbing (*informal*) *n* [➥ DECEPTION AND LIES; 660]

fiber 1 *n* thread, yarn, string, filament, twine, strand [➥ TEXTILES AND THREADS; 1131] 2 *n* makeup, composition, structure, character, stuff, grain [➥ QUALITIES AND CHARACTERISTICS; 1191] 3 *n* grit, strength, fortitude, backbone, character, integrity [➥ COURAGE; 498] *Opposite*: weakness 4 *type of* nutrient [➥ FOOD COMPONENTS; 1188]

fiber

◆ *types of fibers*
cane, coconut matting, coir, jute, kapok, matting, raffia, ramie, rattan, seagrass, sisal, straw, wicker

fiberboard *n* [➥ BUILDING MATERIALS; 1077]

fibrous *adj* tough, leathery, stringy, rubbery, chewy [➥ PHYSICAL TEXTURE; 1222] *Opposite*: tender

fibula *type of* bone [➥ THE BONES AND JOINTS; 719]

fickle *adj* inconsistent, changeable, capricious, inconstant, indecisive, vacillating, unfaithful, faithless, frivolous, unpredictable, unreliable, erratic [➥ LACK OF COMMITMENT AND UNRELIABILITY; 509] *Opposite*: constant

fickleness *n* inconsistency, changeability, capriciousness, inconstancy, indecisiveness, vacillation, unfaithfulness, uncertainty, faithlessness, frivolity, unpredictability, unreliability [➥ LACK OF COMMITMENT AND UNRELIABILITY; 509] *Opposite*: constancy

fiction 1 *n* creative writing, works of fiction, literature, narrative, novels, short stories [➥ FICTION AND DRAMA; 913] *Oppo-

site: nonfiction **2** *n* **work of fiction**, novel, fantasy, story, short story, tale [➡ FICTION AND DRAMA; 913] **3** *n* **invention**, fantasy, imagination, nonsense, illusion, fancy, unrealism [➡ FALSE AND UNREAL; 173] *Opposite*: reality **4** *n* **falsehood**, fabrication, lie, untruth, misrepresentation, deceit, fib (*informal*) [➡ DECEPTION AND LIES; 660] *Opposite*: fact

fictional *adj* **imaginary**, imagined, illusory, unreal, false, fantastic, fictitious, untrue [➡ FALSE AND UNREAL; 173] *Opposite*: real

fictionalization *n* **fictional account**, fictional version, account, narrative, story, version, dramatization [➡ FICTION AND DRAMA; 913]

fictionalize *v* **dramatize**, novelize, recount, adapt [➡ RECORD SOMETHING; 371]

fictitious *adj* **untrue**, fabricated, invented, made-up, false, pretend, fictional [➡ FALSE AND UNREAL; 173] *Opposite*: factual

fiddle **1** *type of* **stringed instrument** [➡ MUSICAL INSTRUMENTS; 910] **2** *n* (*informal*) **swindle**, fraud, cheat, hoax, con, contrivance, scam (*slang*) [➡ CRIMES; 817] **3** *v* (*informal*) **defraud**, swindle, cheat, con, hoax, deceive, diddle (*slang*) [➡ STEAL AND ROB; 426] **4** *v* (*informal*) **falsify**, doctor, tamper with, manipulate, fix, cook the books (*slang*) [➡ FALSIFY AND CHEAT; 176] **5** *v* **fidget**, play, play around, toy, pick at, jiggle, twiddle [➡ CONTACT: TOUCH; 412] **6** *v* **meddle**, tamper, interfere, mess, play, play around, mess around (*informal*) [➡ CHANGE; 372] **7** *v* **tinker**, manipulate, adjust, jiggle, play with, retune [➡ CHANGE; 372] *Opposite*: leave alone

fiddling **1** *adj* **petty**, unimportant, trifling, trivial, insignificant, piddling (*informal*) [➡ UNIMPORTANT AND UNNECESSARY; 238] *Opposite*: significant **2** *n* (*informal*) **fraud**, deception, cheating, fixing, swindling, falsification [➡ CRIMES; 817]

fidelity *n* **loyalty**, faithfulness, reliability, trustworthiness, dependability, devotion, conformity, commitment [➡ RELATIONSHIP TO ANOTHER; 973] *Opposite*: infidelity

fidget **1** *v* **twitch**, squirm, fret, shuffle, jiggle, joggle, wriggle, move around [➡ FIDGET AND FROLIC; 311] *Opposite*: freeze **2** *v* **fiddle**, play, play around, toy, jiggle, twiddle [➡ CONTACT: TOUCH; 412] *Opposite*: leave alone

fidgetiness *n* **twitchiness**, fretfulness, restlessness, squirminess, uneasiness, nervousness, jumpiness, agitation [➡ INSECURITY AND LOSS OF COMPOSURE; 544] *Opposite*: stillness

fidgety *adj* **twitchy**, fretful, restless, squirmy, uneasy, nervous, jumpy, jittery, agitated [➡ INSECURITY AND LOSS OF COMPOSURE; 544] *Opposite*: still

field **1** *n* **meadow**, pasture, grassland, grazing, lea (*literary*) [➡ THE COUNTRYSIDE AND OUTDOOR SPACES; 1071] **2** *n* **sports grounds**, playing field, turf, arena, ground, park, pitch (*UK*) [➡ URBAN OUTDOOR SPACES; 1072] **3** *n* **subject**, area, topic, discipline, theme, province, domain, line of work, sphere [➡ SUBJECT AREAS; 768] **4** *v* **catch**, retrieve, pick up, go after, fetch, return [➡ GET; 420] **5** *v* **deal with**, handle, tackle, take care of, see to, look after, take [➡ CARRY OUT AN ACTION; 269] *Opposite*: ignore

fielder *n* **player**, baseball player, sportsperson, outfielder, infielder, cricketer [➡ PEOPLE IN SPORTS AND LEISURE; 876] *Opposite*: batter

field hockey *type of* **ball game** [➡ HOBBIES, GAMES, AND SPORTS; 875]

field marshal *n* [➡ MILITARY PERSONNEL; 828]

field mushroom *type of* **fungus** [➡ MICROORGANISMS, FUNGI, AND ALGAE; 1023]

field test *n* **field trial**, test, trial, experiment, assay, controlled test [➡ PREPARATORY EVENTS; 57]

field-test *v* **test**, try out, study, put through its paces, trial (*UK*) [➡ ATTEMPT AN ACTION; 261]

fieldwork *n* **research**, information-gathering, investigation, fact-finding, exploration, examination, observation [➡ CLASSES, COURSEWORK, AND EXAMINATIONS; 842]

fiend *n* **villain**, evil person, brute, beast, monster, terror, ogre [➡ VILLAINS AND THUGS; 947] *Opposite*: angel

fiendish **1** *adj* **cruel**, evil, brutal, monstrous, villainous, malicious, malevolent, wicked, wretched, inhuman, barbarous [➡ MORALLY BAD OR IMPROPER; 775] *Opposite*: pleasant **2** *adj* **cunning**, ingenious, clever, crafty, devilish, brilliant [➡ POSITIVE INTELLECTUAL CHARACTERISTICS; 524] **3** *adj* **impossible**, tricky, difficult, hard, perplexing, trying [➡ DIFFICULTY AND COMPLEXITY; 242] *Opposite*: straightforward

fiendishly **1** *adv* **cruelly**, brutally, wickedly, inhumanly, maliciously, villainously, barbarously, malevolently, monstrously [➡ MORALLY BAD OR IMPROPER; 775] *Opposite*: pleasantly **2** *adv* **extremely**, excessively, extraordinarily, incredibly, impossibly, horribly [➡ TO A GREAT EXTENT; 132]

fierce **1** *adj* **violent**, ferocious, aggressive, brutal, severe, stern, angry, vicious, furious [➡ AGGRESSIVE AND BELLIGERENT; 518] *Opposite*: gentle **2** *adj* **intense**, violent, extreme, savage, ferocious, wild, raging, almighty (*informal*) [➡ STRENGTH; 201] *Opposite*: mild **3** *adj* **strong**, powerful, profound, deep, turbulent, passionate, defiant, ardent, intense, violent [➡ STRENGTH; 201] *Opposite*: mild

fiercely **1** *adv* **violently**, ferociously, aggressively, brutally, severely, sternly, angrily, viciously, furiously [➡ AGGRESSIVE AND BELLIGERENT; 518] *Opposite*: gently **2** *adv* **extremely**, exceedingly, very, passionately, resolutely, intensely [➡ TO A GREAT EXTENT; 132] *Opposite*: mildly **3** *adv* **ferociously**, intensely, strongly, brightly, hotly, with a will [➡ STRENGTH; 201] *Opposite*: feebly

fierceness **1** *n* **ferocity**, brutality, violence, aggressiveness, severity, sternness, anger, viciousness [➡ MALICIOUS ACTIONS OR BEHAVIOR; 296] *Opposite*: gentleness **2** *n* **intensity**, violence, strength, power, turbulence, aggressiveness, ferocity, savageness, wildness [➡ STRENGTH; 201] *Opposite*: mildness

fiery **1** *adj* **burning**, blistering, sweltering, blazing, flaming, hot, baking, scorching (*informal*), sizzling (*informal*) [➡ TEMPERATURE: HOT; 1229] *Opposite*: icy **2** *adj* **fierce**, passionate, heated, angry, furious, intense, powerful, ardent, turbulent, forceful [➡ STRENGTH; 201] *Opposite*: mild

fiesta *n* **feast**, holiday, festival, carnival, celebration, gala, fete, event [➡ PARTIES, DANCES, AND CELEBRATIONS; 37]

fife *type of* **wind instrument** [➡ MUSICAL INSTRUMENTS; 910]

fifth wheel *n* **supernumerary**, third wheel, ghost at t⸱

to end, to close, as a final point [➡ SUMMARIZING EXPRESSIONS; 622] *Opposite*: firstly **2** *adv* **at last**, at length, at long last, ultimately, after all, in the end, at the end of the day [➡ AFTER, LAST, AND FOLLOWING; 165] *Opposite*: initially **3** *adv* **conclusively**, completely, decisively, irrevocably, definitively, irreversibly, beyond doubt [➡ CERTAIN; 174] *Opposite*: tentatively

finance 1 *n* **money**, economics, business, investment, backing, sponsorship, funding [➡ FUNDS, PAYMENTS, AND CHARGES; 800] **2** *v* **back**, invest in, pay for, fund, support, sponsor, put money into, bankroll (*informal*) [➡ GIVE MONEY; 433]

finances *n* **money**, funds, assets, cash, capital, savings, investments, value, stock, shares [➡ FINANCIAL ASSETS; 462]

financial *adj* **monetary**, fiscal, economic, pecuniary, monetarist, commercial, business [➡ FINANCE AND ECONOMICS; 796]

financier *n* **banker**, investor, backer, sponsor, supporter, investment banker, merchant banker (*UK*) [➡ PEOPLE INVOLVED IN FINANCE, 804]

finch *type of* **common bird** [➡ BIRDS; 997]

find 1 *v* **discover**, locate, come across, hit upon, unearth, uncover, stumble on, light on [➡ FIND; 463] **2** *v* **recover**, regain, get back, retrieve, discover, locate [➡ FIND; 463] *Opposite*: lose **3** *v* **realize**, understand, get, obtain, attain, acquire, achieve, get ahold of (*informal*) [➡ GET; 420] **4** *n* **discovery**, bargain, treasure trove, treasure, novelty, invention [➡ FIND; 463]

find fault *v* **criticize**, nag, nitpick, carp, get at, pick holes in, complain about [➡ COMPLAIN AND NAG; 686] *Opposite*: praise

find fault with *v* [➡ ACCUSE, BLAME, AND CRITICIZE; 641]

See Compare and Contrast at **criticize**.

finding 1 *n* **verdict**, ruling, result, sentence, decision, pronouncement, judgment [➡ TRIAL, PUNISHMENT, AND LEGAL OUTCOMES; 819] **2** *n* **discovery**, conclusion, result, verdict, outcome, definition [➡ RESULTS AND OUTCOMES; 83]

find out 1 *v* **discover**, learn, realize, observe, note, notice, detect, hear about, get wind of, catch on (*informal*) [➡ LEARN AND DISCOVER; 762] **2** *v* **catch**, expose, uncover, reveal, unmask [➡ FIND; 463]

fine 1 *adj* **tiny**, minute, light, delicate, small, thin, wafer-thin, slight [➡ WIDTH: NARROW AND THIN; 1200] **2** *adj* **bright**, sunny, warm, beautiful, fair, pleasant, clear [➡ HOT WEATHER; 1050] *Opposite*: dull **3** *adj* (*informal*) **acceptable**, satisfactory, well, all right, okay (*informal*), good, reasonable, adequate, sufficient [➡ ACCEPTABLE AND PASSABLE; 219] *Opposite*: unsatisfactory **4** *adj* **outstanding**, superb, excellent, superior, exceptional, select, first-rate [➡ GOOD, WELL, BETTER; 183] *Opposite*: poor **5** *adj* **light**, slight, faint, thin, tenuous, insubstantial, flimsy, gauzy, diaphanous, translucent, subtle [➡ IMPERCEPTIBLE; 26] *Opposite*: heavy **6** *adj* **delicate**, dainty, slender, refined, thin, slight, sharp, chiseled, well-honed [➡ FRAGILE; 1209] *Opposite*: coarse **7** *adj* **subtle**, keen, sharp, skilled, refined, discerning, discriminating, perceptive, fastidious [➡ CONCISE AND CLEAR; 202] *Opposite*: dull **8** *n* **penalty**, punishment, payment, forfeit, levy, charge [➡ TRIAL, PUNISHMENT, AND LEGAL OUTCOMES; 819] **9** *v* **penalize**, punish, levy, charge [➡ TRIAL, PUNISHMENT, AND LEGAL OUTCOMES; 819]

fine art *n* [➡ THE PICTORIAL ARTS; 897]

finely 1 *adv* **delicately**, lightly, thinly, closely, intricately, sharply, daintily [➡ CONCISE AND CLEAR; 202] *Opposite*: coarsely **2** *adv* **excellently**, outstandingly, exceptionally, superbly, magnificently, wonderfully, stupendously, marvelously [➡ GOOD, WELL, BETTER; 183] *Opposite*: poorly **3** *adv* **subtly**, keenly, sharply, discerningly, discriminatingly, perceptively, fastidiously [➡ CONCISE AND CLEAR; 202]

fineness 1 *n* **excellence**, greatness, superiority, quality, distinction, caliber, superbness, refinement [➡ EXTRAORDINARY: AMAZING; 204] *Opposite*: poorness **2** *n* **delicacy**, sheerness, thinness, narrowness, slenderness, daintiness, lightness, minuteness, flimsiness [➡ WIDTH: NARROW AND THIN; 1200] *Opposite*: coarseness

fine points *n* [➡ BASIC DETAILS; 688]

finery *n* **regalia**, jewelry, evening dress, morning dress, dress uniform, ceremonial dress, glad rags (*informal*), attire (*formal*) [➡ CLOTHES AND ACCESSORIES; 864]

finesse 1 *n* **skill**, flair, grace, poise, assurance, refinement, elegance [➡ SKILLS, TALENTS, AND ABILITIES; 526] *Opposite*: clumsiness **2** *n* **subtlety**, delicacy, diplomacy, tact, discretion, sensitivity [➡ GOOD MANNERS AND SOCIAL SKILLS; 520] *Opposite*: tactlessness

finest *adj* **premium**, handpicked, optimum, best, supreme, deluxe, luxury [➡ SUPERIORITY; 152] *Opposite*: worst

fine-tune *v* **modify**, adjust, tune, polish up, perfect, hone, tweak (*informal*) [➡ CORRECT AND PUT RIGHT; 377]

fine-tuning *n* **adjustment**, refinement, modification, perfection, tuning [➡ IMPROVE SOMETHING; 374]

finger 1 *n* **digit**, limb, member, extremity [➡ PARTS OF THE BODY: ARM AND HAND; 695] **2** *n* **portion**, slither, slice, bit, helping, smidgen (*informal*) [➡ AMOUNTS AND QUANTITIES; 112] *Opposite*: hunk **3** *v* **handle**, touch, feel, manipulate, toy with, fiddle with, pick up [➡ CONTACT: TOUCH; 412] **4** *v* (*slang*) **pick out**, inform on, identify, single out, point out, name, point to [➡ ACCUSE, BLAME, AND CRITICIZE; 641]

finger food *n* [➡ PREPARED DISHES; 1170]

fingernail *part of* **arm or hand** [➡ PARTS OF THE BODY: ARM AND HAND; 695]

fingerprint 1 *n* **impression**, print, mark, pattern, thumbprint, whorl [➡ PARTS OF THE BODY: ARM AND HAND; 695] **2** *n* **characteristic**, identification, evidence, pattern, diagnostic, sign [➡ EVIDENCE AND PROOF; 69]

fingertip 1 *adj* **sensitive**, delicate, fine, sensitized, accurate, probing [➡ EXACT; 203] **2** *part of* **arm or hand** [➡ PARTS OF THE BODY: ARM AND HAND; 695]

finicky *adj* **fastidious**, fussy, picky, particular, choosy (*informal*), persnickety (*informal*) [➡ DIFFICULT TO PLEASE; 515] *Opposite*: sloppy

See Compare and Contrast at **careful**.

finish 1 *v* **end**, stop, terminate, close, cease, conclude, complete, wrap up (*informal*) [➡ COMPLETE AN ACTION; 263] *Opposite*: start **2** *v* (*informal*) **destroy**, ruin, annihilate, defeat, exhaust, deplete, overwhelm, devastate [➡ BEAT AND DEFEAT; 80] **3** *v* **use up**, drain, exhaust, polish off, empty, finish off, demolish (*informal*), clean out (*informal*) [➡ USE UP AND WASTE; 474] *Opposite*: stock up **4** *v* **polish**, buff, rub, varnish, lacquer, gild [➡ CLEAN AND POLISH; 403] **5** *n* **end**, ending, close, conclusion, completion, cessation, finale, termination [➡ ENDS AND DEPARTURES; 54] *Opposite*: start **6** *n* **surface**, texture, appearance, quality, varnish, gloss, gilt, polish [➡ TEXTURE; 1220]

finished 1 *adj* **over**, ended, at an end, broken down, broken up, broken off, over and done with, done [➡ WHOLENESS AND COMPLETENESS; 198] **2** *adj* **refined**, perfect, polished, elegant, professional [➡ TALENTED AND SKILLFUL; 527] *Opposite*: rough **3** *adj* **polished**, buffed, varnished, glossed, gilded, planed [➡ IN GOOD REPAIR; 1232] *Opposite*: unfinished **4** *adj* **ruined**, wrecked, lost, destroyed, devastated, washed-up (*informal*), done for (*informal*) [➡ BEATEN AND DEFEATED; 78]

finish off 1 *v* **complete**, bring to an end, wind up, fulfill, conclude, finalize, close, wrap up (*informal*) [➡ COMPLETE AN ACTION; 263] *Opposite*: start up **2** *v* **use up**, eat up, exhaust, polish off, demolish (*informal*), clean out (*informal*) [➡ USE UP AND WASTE; 474] *Opposite*: stock up **3** *v* (*informal*) **eliminate**, kill, exterminate, dispatch, dispose of, polish off, put an end to, put somebody out of (his or her) misery (*humorous*) [➡ KILL; 923]

finish up *v* **eat up**, consume, wolf, finish off, scarf (*informal*), scarf down (*informal*), scoff (*informal*), demolish (*informal*), knock back (*informal*) [➡ EAT AND NOT EAT; 710] *Opposite*: leave

finite *adj* **limited**, restricted, determinate, fixed, set, predetermined, predictable [➡ FINITENESS, VARIABILITY, AND TRANSIENCE; 96] *Opposite*: infinite

fink out (*slang*) *v* [➡ NOT DO AND REFUSE TO DO; 274]

fipple flute *type of* **wind instrument** [➡ MUSICAL INSTRUMENTS; 910]

fir *type of* **evergreen tree** [➡ EVERGREEN AND CONIFEROUS TREES; 1029]

fir cone *n* [➡ PARTS OF TREES AND PLANTS; 1026]

fire 1 *n* **blaze**, flames, bonfire, conflagration, inferno [➡ FIRE, FLAMMABILITY, AND BURNING; 1165] **2** *n* **combustion**, conflagration, ignition [➡ FIRE, FLAMMABILITY, AND BURNING; 1165] **3** *n* **passion**, ardor, fervor, excitement, enthusiasm, vigor, spirit, intensity, energy [➡ POSITIVE IMPATIENCE, ENTHUSIASM, AND ALERTNESS; 537] *Opposite*: apathy **4** *v* **shoot**, set off, detonate, trigger, launch, discharge (*formal*) [➡ USE TOOLS AND MACHINERY; 468] **5** *v* **excite**, arouse, inspire, enthuse, enliven, animate [➡ ENCOURAGE; 576] **6** *v* (*informal*) **dismiss**, let go, get rid of, lay off, throw out, give somebody the pink slip, sack (*informal*), can (*slang*) [➡ EJECT AND EXCLUDE; 340] *Opposite*: take on

---

Compare and Contrast: *fire*, *blaze*, *conflagration*, *inferno*

CORE MEANING: indicates burning and flames

fire a general word describing flames that were started deliberately and are under control, for example, a bonfire, or uncontrolled flames, whether caused accidentally or on purpose; *blaze* suggests a greater degree of intensity and brightness and more rapid burning than *fire*; *conflagration* a fairly formal word suggesting a fierce, destructive fire, especially one that affects a large building or area; *inferno* a mainly journalistic term for a fierce, destructive fire.

---

fire alarm *n* **bell**, siren, buzzer, Klaxon, warning, alarm, signal [➡ SIGNALING; 1140]

fire and brimstone *n* [➡ RELIGIOUS CONCEPTS; 776]

fire ant *type of* **ant** [➡ ANTS; 1014]

firearm *n* **gun**, weapon, handgun, pistol, rifle, shotgun [➡ WEAPONS FOR SHOOTING; 1156]

fireball 1 *n* **ball lightning**, ball of fire, flash, lightning [➡ FIRE, FLAMMABILITY, AND BURNING; 1165] **2** *type of* **heavenly body** [➡ HEAVENLY BODIES; 1061]

firebomb *type of* **explosive weapon** [➡ EXPLOSIVES; 1155]

firebrand *n* **troublemaker**, agitator, hothead, revolutionary, demagogue [➡ UNCOOPERATIVE OR REBELLIOUS PEOPLE; 566]

firebreak *n* **clearing**, opening, strip, break, barrier, glade, fireguard [➡ THE COUNTRYSIDE AND OUTDOOR SPACES; 1071]

firecracker *type of* **firework** [➡ EXPLOSIVES; 1155]

fire drill *n* **fire practice**, drill, rehearsal, evacuation, exercise, practice [➡ PREPARATORY EVENTS; 57]

fired up *adj* **enthused**, motivated, eager, passionate, on fire, enthusiastic [➡ PLEASURE, EXCITEMENT, AND ELATION; 534] *Opposite*: apathetic

fire escape 1 *n* **stairway**, ladder, escape hatch, staircase, emergency exit, exit, way out, fire door, steps [➡ STAIRS AND STORIES; 1102] **2** *part of* **building** [➡ PARTS OF A BUILDING; 1095]

firefly *type of* **flying insect** [➡ FLYING INSECTS; 1013]

fireguard 1 *n* **fire screen**, screen, guard, fender, frame [➡ COVERS AND COATINGS; 1246] **2** *n* **firebreak**, clearing, strip, glade, opening [➡ THE COUNTRYSIDE AND OUTDOOR SPACES; 1071]

firelight *n* **glow**, glimmer, flame, flare, blaze [➡ LIGHT; 1164]

fireplace 1 *n* **hearth**, inglenook, fire, fireside, chimney corner (*UK*) [➡ ALCOVES, CUBICLES, AND COMPARTMENTS; 1096] **2** *type of* **general fixture** [➡ FIXTURES; 859]

firepower *n* **weapons**, arms, guns, armaments, munitions [➡ WEAPONS; 1154]

fire practice *n* **fire drill**, drill, practice, rehearsal, evacuation, exercise [➡ PREPARATORY EVENTS; 57]

fireproof *adj* **incombustible**, nonflammable, flame-retardant, fire-retardant, fire-resistant, flame-resistant [➡ FIRE, FLAMMABILITY, AND BURNING; 1165] *Opposite*: combustible

fireside *n* **hearth**, inglenook, fireplace, chimney corner (*UK*) [➡ ALCOVES, CUBICLES, AND COMPARTMENTS; 1096]

firetrap *n* **fire hazard**, danger, deathtrap (*informal*) [➡ DANGER; 235]

firetruck *type of* **public service vehicle** [➡ VEHICLES; 1145]

fire up 1 *v* **get going**, initiate, start off, set off, launch, trigger [➡ USE TOOLS AND MACHINERY; 468] **2** *v* **ignite**, fire, light, kindle, set alight, spark [➡ FIRE, FLAMMABILITY, AND BURNING; 1165] **3** *v* **enthuse**, motivate, incite, stimulate, excite, arouse, stir up, work up, set off [➡ ENCOURAGE; 576]

firewall *n* [➡ SAFE AND SAFETY; 191]

firewood *n* **logs**, kindling, wood, fuel [➡ ENERGY SOURCES; 1162]

firework

◆ *types of fireworks*
cherry bomb, firecracker, girandole, pinwheel, rocket, Roman candle, sparkler, squib, torpedo

firing *n* **gunfire**, fire, shooting, shots [➡ IMPACT SOUNDS; 1260]

firing line 1 *n* **front line**, front, battlefront, vanguard [➡ WARFARE AND WAR; 830] 2 *n* **forefront**, vanguard, lead, cutting edge, leading edge [➡ DIFFICULT SITUATIONS; 72]

firkin *n* [➡ CONTAINERS, RECEPTACLES, AND PACKAGING; 1245]

firm 1 *adj* **solid**, compact, hard, rigid, dense, stiff, unyielding [➡ RIGID AND HARD; 1211] *Opposite:* soft 2 *adj* **secure**, stable, fixed, strong, safe, steady, well-founded [➡ SAFE AND SAFETY; 191] *Opposite:* unstable 3 *adj* **determined**, certain, definite, fixed, resolved, unchangeable, resolute, positive, concrete [➡ CERTAINTY; 561] *Opposite:* uncertain 4 *v* **harden**, stiffen, solidify, set, press down, compress, tamp, compact [➡ HARDEN, CONGEAL, AND DRY; 387] *Opposite:* soften 5 *n* **company**, business, partnership, multinational, corporation, organization, practice [➡ BUSINESS ENTERPRISES AND RELATED BODIES; 792]

firmament (*literary*) *n* **sky**, heaven, vault, azure, space, ether, expanse [➡ THE EARTH'S ATMOSPHERE; 1040]

firmly 1 *adv* **resolutely**, inflexibly, determinedly, decisively, definitely, steadfastly, confidently [➡ CERTAINTY; 561] *Opposite:* irresolutely 2 *adv* **tightly**, securely, steadily, powerfully, strongly, safely, densely [➡ STRENGTH, 201] *Opposite:* loosely

firmness 1 *n* **hardness**, rigidity, compactness, density, stiffness, solidity [➡ RIGID AND HARD; 1211] *Opposite:* softness 2 *n* **stability**, steadiness, strength, safety [➡ SAFE AND SAFETY; 191] *Opposite:* instability 3 *n* **determination**, steadfastness, resolve, resolution, decisiveness, insistence, control, rigidity [➡ HARD-WORKING AND COMMITTED; 500] *Opposite:* uncertainty

firm up 1 *v* **settle**, conclude, tie up, confirm, establish, decide [➡ MAKE DECISIONS AND CHOICES; 752] 2 *v* **stabilize**, balance, steady, settle [➡ IMPROVE STRENGTH AND DURABILITY; 378] *Opposite:* destabilize

firmware 1 *type of* **software** [➡ COMPUTERS AND COMPUTING; 1127] 2 *type of* **hardware** [➡ COMPUTERS AND COMPUTING; 1127]

first 1 *adj* **primary**, initial, original, opening, earliest, foremost, former [➡ BEFORE, FIRST, AND PRECEDING; 163] *Opposite:* last 2 *adj* **chief**, head, principal, leading, major, main, paramount [➡ MOST IMPORTANT AND MAIN; 193] *Opposite:* minor 3 *adj* **fundamental**, basic, key, elementary, primary, essential [➡ FUNDAMENTAL; 195] *Opposite:* advanced 4 *adv* **firstly**, initially, at the outset, in the beginning, to begin with, to start with, primarily, formerly, originally [➡ BEFORE, FIRST, AND PRECEDING; 163] *Opposite:* lastly

first aid *n* **emergency treatment**, medical treatment, medical care, resuscitation, mouth-to-mouth, CPR, emergency medicine [➡ HEALING; 730]

first and foremost *adv* **most importantly**, primarily, above all, predominantly, firstly, in the first place [➡ MAINLY AND PRIMARILY; 140] *Opposite:* lastly

first-born *n* [➡ YOUNGER GENERATION RELATIVES; 958]

first-class *adj* **best**, superb, unrivaled, first-rate, excellent, outstanding, exceptional, topnotch (*informal*) [➡ EXTRAORDINARY: AMAZING; 204] *Opposite:* poor

firsthand 1 *adj* **direct**, actual, immediate, personal [➡ PRESENT; 85] *Opposite:* secondhand 2 *adv* **directly**, personally, from the horse's mouth, straight [➡ BELONGING OR RELATING TO INDIVIDUALS; 944] *Opposite:* indirectly

first light *n* **dawn**, daybreak, sunrise, daylight, sunup, morning, the crack of dawn, break of day, cockcrow (*archaic or literary*) [➡ TIMES OF DAY; 87] *Opposite:* dusk

firstly *adv* **to start with**, initially, first of all, at the outset, first, to begin with, primarily, originally [➡ BEFORE, FIRST, AND PRECEDING; 163] *Opposite:* lastly

first name *n* **name**, Christian name, given name, moniker (*slang*) [➡ NAME AND DESCRIBE; 665] *Opposite:* surname

first principles *n* [➡ BASIC DETAILS; 688]

first-rate *adj* **best**, superb, first-class, unrivaled, excellent, outstanding, exceptional, topnotch (*informal*) [➡ EXTRAORDINARY: AMAZING; 204] *Opposite:* poor

firth (*UK*) *n* **estuary**, inlet, fjord, sound, river mouth, creek [➡ THE SEAS, OCEANS, AND SHORES; 1041]

fir tree *type of* **evergreen tree** [➡ EVERGREEN AND CONIFEROUS TREES; 1029]

fish 1 *n* [➡ LIVING THINGS AND LIVING; 976] 2 *v* **catch fish**, angle, go fishing, trawl, cast a line, fly-fish [➡ HOBBIES, GAMES, AND SPORTS; 875] 3 *v* **search**, seek, trawl, probe, dig around, scout, nose around (*Informal*) [➡ SEEK POSSESSION AND SEARCH; 456]

fish

◆ *types of flatfish*
angelfish, brill, flounder, halibut, lemon sole, manta, plaice, pompano, ray, skate, sole, stingray, turbot

◆ *types of freshwater fish*
bass, bream, carp, catfish, crappie, goldfish, grayling, guppy, loach, minnow, mullet, Nile perch, perch, pike, piranha, roach, stickleback, tench, tilapia, trout

◆ *types of ocean fish*
anchovy, anglerfish, cod, dogfish, eel, haddock, hake, herring, John Dory, ling, mackerel, monkfish, pilchard, salmon, sardine, sea bream, shark, sprat, sturgeon, whitebait, whiting

◆ *types of tropical fish*
barracuda, flying fish, kingfish, mahi-mahi, marlin, pomfret, sailfish, sawfish, snapper, swordfish, tuna

◆ *parts of a fish*
air bladder, anal fin, dorsal fin, fin, gill, pectoral fin, pelvic fin, roe, scale, tail

fish cake *type of* **cooked dish** [➡ PREPARED DISHES; 1170]

fisheye lens *part of* **camera** [➡ PHOTOGRAPHY AND PHOTOGRAPHIC EQUIPMENT; 1122]

fish for *v* **search for**, angle for, be after, invite, hope for, look for, encourage [➡ OBTAIN POSSESSION BY PERSUASION; 457]

fishing *n* **angling**, casting, trawling, harpooning, whaling, spinning, fly-fishing [➡ HOBBIES, GAMES, AND SPORTS; 875]

fish knife *type of* **flatware** [➡ TABLEWARE, FLATWARE, AND KITCHENWARE; 861]

fishnet *n* **mesh**, netting, net, tulle, gauze, lace [➡ FABRICS; 1132]

fish out (*informal*) *v* **pull out**, take out, haul out, drag out, dig out, extract [➡ EXTRACT AND SEVER; 341] *Opposite*: put in

fish owl *type of* **owl** [➡ OWLS; 1001]

fishy (*informal*) *adj* **dubious**, suspicious, irregular, underhand, shady, shifty, devious, strange, odd, doubtful, questionable [➡ BIZARRE AND PECULIAR; 257] *Opposite*: aboveboard

fission *n* **breaking up**, separation, splitting, division, schism, scission [➡ SEPARATE AND DIVIDE; 401] *Opposite*: fusion

fissure *n* **crack**, split, crevice, fracture, cleft, opening, slit, break, gap [➡ HOLES, GAPS, AND FORKS; 1252]

fist 1 *n* (*informal*) **hand**, knuckle, paw (*informal*), duke (*slang*) [➡ PARTS OF THE BODY: ARM AND HAND; 695] 2 *n* **fistful**, handful, bunch, wad [➡ AMOUNTS OF SOLID OR SEMISOLID; 115]

fist fight *n* [➡ AGGRESSIVE EVENTS; 39]

fistful *n* **handful**, bunch, fist, wad [➡ AMOUNTS OF SOLID OR SEMISOLID; 115]

fit 1 *v* **measure**, tailor, size, take in, take up, let out [➡ CHANGE; 372] 2 *v* **match**, suit, correspond, tally [➡ EQUALITY; 154] 3 *v* **install**, put in, mount, fix, provide with, add, equip, supply [➡ EQUIP AND SUPPLY; 435] 4 *adj* **appropriate**, fitting, right, proper, acceptable, adequate, suitable, apt [➡ APPROPRIATE, SUITABLE, AND ADVISABLE; 184] *Opposite*: unfit 5 *adj* **healthy**, well, fine, in fine fettle, hale and hearty, strong, robust, in shape, on top form, athletic, vigorous, buff (*informal*) [➡ FIT AND STRONG; 736] *Opposite*: unfit 6 *n* **convulsion**, spasm, petit mal, grand mal, epileptic fit, turn, paroxysm, outburst [➡ ILLNESSES AND DISORDERS; 732]

fitful *adj* **disturbed**, sporadic, broken, restless, irregular, intermittent, erratic [➡ FINITENESS, VARIABILITY, AND TRANSIENCE; 96] *Opposite*: undisturbed

fit in 1 *v* **conform**, blend in, integrate, go well with, assimilate, get on, settle down [➡ COMBINE AND MIX; 400] 2 *v* **find time for**, squeeze in, manage, cope with, take on, incorporate [➡ CARRY OUT AN ACTION; 269]

fitness 1 *n* **health**, strength, robustness, vigor [➡ PHYSICAL STATES; 734] *Opposite*: weakness 2 *n* **suitability**, appropriateness, aptness, qualification, capability, ability [➡ APPROPRIATE, SUITABLE, AND ADVISABLE; 184] *Opposite*: inappropriateness

fit out *v* **equip**, supply, set up, kit out, fit up, refit, furnish (*formal*) [➡ EQUIP AND SUPPLY; 435]

fitted 1 *adj* **tailored**, close-fitting, formfitting, trim, snug [➡ DESCRIBING CLOTHES; 869] *Opposite*: baggy 2 *adj* **built-in**, fixed, permanent, attached, incorporated [➡ RELATIVE LOCATION; 161] *Opposite*: freestanding

fitted carpet *n* [➡ FURNISHING AND HOUSEHOLD LINENS; 860]

fitting *adj* **suitable**, appropriate, right, correct, proper, apt, decent, fit, timely, relevant [➡ APPROPRIATE, SUITABLE, AND ADVISABLE; 184] *Opposite*: inappropriate

fittingness *n* **suitability**, appropriateness, rightness, correctness, properness, aptness, timeliness, relevance [➡ APPROPRIATE, SUITABLE, AND ADVISABLE; 184] *Opposite*: inappropriateness

fit up *v* **equip**, supply, set up, kit out, fit out, refit, furnish (*formal*) [➡ EQUIP AND SUPPLY; 435]

five o'clock shadow *n* **beard**, stubble, bristles [➡ FACIAL HAIR; 489]

fiver *n* [➡ CURRENCIES; 798]

fix 1 *v* **mend**, repair, correct, put to rights, patch up, renovate, sort out, resolve, renew, refurbish, overhaul, restore [➡ REPAIR AND MEND; 376] *Opposite*: break 2 *v* **agree**, arrange, establish, organize, set up, schedule, set a date for, settle [➡ CAUSE TO HAPPEN; 31] *Opposite*: cancel 3 *v* (*informal*) **prepare**, make ready, get ready, cook, rustle up (*informal*), scare up (*informal*) [➡ MEAL PREPARATION; 354] 4 *v* **fasten**, attach, glue, stick, secure, install, fit, position, locate, join, affix [➡ FASTEN, LINK, AND JOIN; 408] *Opposite*: detach 5 *v* (*informal*) **rig**, manipulate, massage, arrange, fiddle (*informal*), hustle (*slang*) [➡ FALSIFY AND CHEAT; 176] 6 *n* (*informal*) **dilemma**, predicament, tight spot, quandary, corner, mess, hole (*informal*) [➡ DIFFICULT SITUATIONS; 72] 7 *n* (*informal*) **solution**, answer, resolution, remedy [➡ SOLUTIONS; 215] 8 *n* (*informal*) **con**, fraud, swindle, trick, setup (*informal*), hustle (*slang*) [➡ DECEPTION AND LIES; 660] 9 *n* (*humorous*) **dose**, injection, shot (*informal*), hit (*slang*) [➡ AMOUNTS AND QUANTITIES; 112]

fixated *adj* **obsessed**, absorbed, fanatical, engrossed, paranoid, neurotic, passionate, single-minded, intense, stuck on (*informal*), hooked (*slang*) [➡ PENSIVENESS AND INTEREST; 538] *Opposite*: indifferent

fixatedly *adv* **obsessively**, fanatically, intensely, single-mindedly, keenly, fervently, overenthusiastically, passionately, neurotically (*informal*) [➡ PENSIVENESS AND INTEREST; 538] *Opposite*: indifferently

fixation *n* **obsession**, fascination, mania, passion, addiction, paranoia, preoccupation, fixed idea, idée fixe, thing (*informal*), complex (*informal*), neurosis (*dated*) [➡ FADS, FETISHES, AND IDOLATRY; 555]

fixative 1 *n* **preservative**, preserver, spray, varnish, coating [➡ COVERS AND COATINGS; 1246] 2 *n* **glue**, adhesive, cement, paste, gum, bonder [➡ ADHESIVES; 1271]

fixed 1 *adj* **secure**, immovable, immobile, static, motionless, stationary, stable, permanent [➡ PERMANENCE: WITHOUT CHANGE; 95] *Opposite*: fluid 2 *adj* **set**, unchanging, flat, preset, predetermined, permanent [➡ PERMANENCE: WITHOUT CHANGE; 95] *Opposite*: variable 3 *adj* **rigid**, inflexible, hard-and-fast, cast-iron [➡ PERMANENCE: WITHOUT CHANGE; 95] *Opposite*: flexible

fixed idea *n* [➡ IDEAS AND THOUGHTS; 770]

fixedness *n* **secureness**, immovability, immobility, motionlessness, stability, permanence [➡ PERMANENCE: WITHOUT CHANGE; 95] *Opposite*: fluidity

fixings 1 *n* **ingredients**, elements, constituents, components, parts, makings [➡ PREPARED DISHES; 1170] 2 *n* (*informal*) **trimmings**, accompaniments, accessories, dressing, extras [➡ ORNAMENTS AND DECORATIONS; 1248]

fixture (*UK*) *n* **match**, game, meeting, contest, clash, event [➡ NON-AGGRESSIVE/SPORTING EVENTS; 40]

fixtures *n* **accessories**, decorations, equipment, furniture [➤FIXTURES; 859]

fixtures

◆ *types of general fixtures*
baseboard, ceiling rose, dado, fender, fireplace, looking glass, mantel, mantelpiece, mirror, picture molding, radiator, socket, wainscot

◆ *types of plumbing fixtures*
ball cock, basin, bathtub, bidet, drinking fountain, faucet, hand basin, hot tub, nozzle, plumbing, rose, sauna, shower, sink, sitz bath, spa, spigot, spout, sprinkler, tank, toilet, towel rail, tub, vanity, washbasin, washbowl, wash-hand basin, whirlpool

fix up 1 *v* **arrange**, schedule, plan, make plans for, organize, set up, settle, agree [➤ARRANGE AND CREATE ORDER; 357] 2 *v* **repair**, renew, refurbish, renovate, redecorate, overhaul, restore, mend, correct, patch up, sort out [➤REPAIR AND MEND; 376]

fizz 1 *v* **effervesce**, sparkle, bubble, froth, foam, fizzle, hiss [➤FROTH AND EFFERVESCE; 389] 2 *n* **effervescence**, sparkle, bubbles, froth, foam, fizzle [➤FOAM; 1273]

fizzle 1 *v* **fizz**, hiss, sizzle, spit, sputter, buzz, bubble, effervesce [➤FROTH AND EFFERVESCE; 389] 2 *v* **fail**, fade away, peter out, disappear, come to an end, vanish, dissolve, die out, end [➤DISAPPEAR; 4] *Opposite*: flourish

fizzy *adj* **effervescent**, sparkling, bubbly, carbonated, foamy, frothy [➤VISUAL TEXTURE; 1221] *Opposite*: still

fjord *n* **inlet**, sound, creek, firth (*UK*) [➤THE SEAS, OCEANS, AND SHORES; 1041]

flab *n* **fat**, chubbiness, plumpness, corpulence, pudginess (*informal*) [➤EXTRA WEIGHT; 478]

flabbergast (*informal*) *v* **amaze**, astonish, astound, dumbfound, stun, surprise, shock, stagger, bowl over, flummox (*informal*) [➤CONFUSE AND BEWILDER; 571]

flabbergasted (*informal*) *adj* **amazed**, astonished, astounded, dumbfounded, stunned, surprised, shocked, staggered, bowled over, flummoxed (*informal*) [➤SURPRISE, SHOCK, AND AMAZEMENT; 545]

flabbiness (*informal*) *n* **flaccidity**, looseness, softness, slackness, floppiness, limpness [➤MUSCLES AND MUSCULATURE; 479] *Opposite*: firmness

flabby (*informal*) *adj* **flaccid**, loose, soft, slack, saggy, floppy, limp [➤MUSCLES AND MUSCULATURE; 479] *Opposite*: firm

flaccid *adj* **limp**, soft, loose, drooping, sagging, lax, slack, flabby (*informal*) [➤MALLEABLE AND ELASTIC; 1212] *Opposite*: firm

flag 1 *n* **standard**, ensign, pennant, colors, pennon, banner, emblem, streamer [➤SYMBOLS, SIGNS, AND NUMBERS; 596] 2 *v* **weaken**, tire, weary, wane, fade, wilt, slump, droop, fail, pall, sag, dwindle, languish, diminish, decline, ebb, abate (*formal or literary*) [➤CEASE TO EXIST; 22] *Opposite*: rally 3 *v* **mark**, highlight, identify, label, signal, warn, select, indicate, signpost [➤NAME AND DESCRIBE; 665]

flagellate 1 *v* **whip**, flog, scourge, lash, beat, thrash,

punish [➤WHIP AND CLUB; 417] 2 *type of* **microorganism** [➤MICROORGANISMS, FUNGI, AND ALGAE; 1023]

flagellation *n* **whipping**, flogging, scourging, lashing, beating, thrashing, punishment [➤PHYSICAL ATTACK AND PUNISHMENT; 415]

flagging *adj* **weakening**, tiring, wearied, waning, fading, wilting, slumping, drooping, failing, dwindling, diminishing, declining, ebbing, palling, sagging, languishing, abating (*formal or literary*) [➤CEASE TO EXIST; 22] *Opposite*: rallying

flagon *n* **bottle**, carafe, flask, canteen, carboy, demijohn, container [➤TABLEWARE, FLATWARE, AND KITCHENWARE; 861]

flagpole *n* **flagstaff**, staff, pole, mast, post [➤STICKS, POLES, AND WEDGES; 1254]

flagrant *adj* **blatant**, scandalous, obvious, deliberate, brazen, unashamed, open, overt, patent, manifest, barefaced, bald-faced, shameless, immodest, glaring [➤INTENTIONAL AND DELIBERATE; 279] *Opposite*: covert

flagship 1 *n* **warship**, man-of-war, ship of the line, capital ship, battleship, dreadnought [➤SHIPS AND BOATS; 1150] 2 *n* **star**, leader, jewel, pearl, pièce de résistance, ne plus ultra [➤MOST IMPORTANT THING; 197] 3 *adj* **prize**, star, lead, top, leading [➤MOST IMPORTANT AND MAIN; 193]

flagstaff *n* **flagpole**, staff, pole, mast, post [➤STICKS, POLES, AND WEDGES; 1254]

flagstone *n* **paving stone**, slab, block, cobblestone, cobble, curbstone [➤BUILDING MATERIALS; 1077]

flag-waving *n* **patriotism**, chauvinism, jingoism, nationalism, loyalism, triumphalism [➤PREJUDICE; 550]

flail 1 *v* **thrash**, wave, whirl, flap, flounder, swing [➤MOVE SOMETHING; ON THE SPOT; 336] 2 *v* **flog**, beat, batter, hit, strike, bash

flail around *v* **flounder**, writhe, struggle, squirm, stagger, stumble [➤FIDGET AND FROLIC; 311]

flair 1 *n* **talent**, skill, aptitude, feel, gift, ability, knack, bent, genius [➤SKILLS, TALENTS, AND ABILITIES; 526] *Opposite*: ineptitude 2 *n* **elegance**, stylishness, style, chic, panache, dash, verve, taste, glamour [➤CONFIDENCE AND COMPOSURE; 499] *Opposite*: inelegance

See Compare and Contrast at **talent**.

flak (*informal*) *n* **criticism**, condemnation, censure, disapproval, hostility, hassle (*informal*) [➤CRITICISMS AND ANGRY OUTBURSTS; 50] *Opposite*: support

flake 1 *n* **shaving**, fleck, sliver, chip, scale, fragment, snowflake, bit, patch [➤SMALL PIECES; 129] 2 *v* **peel**, crumble, chip, come off, scale, blister, chip off [➤TEAR, BREAK, AND CUT; 360]

flake out (*slang*) *v* **collapse**, fall asleep, doze off, faint, pass out, drop off (*informal*) [➤SLEEP AND DREAM; 723]

flak jacket *type of* **jacket** [➤GARMENTS AND OUTFITS; 865]

flaky *adj* **peeling**, crumbling, crumbly, chipped, scaly, blistering, blistered [➤IN BAD REPAIR; 1234]

flaky pastry *n* [➤BREAD, FLOUR, AND BREAD PRODUCTS; 1179]

flamboyance *n* **showiness**, ostentation, flashiness,

gaudiness, splendor, luridness, glitziness, loudness, grandiosity, colorfulness [➡ EXTRAORDINARY: AMAZING; 204] *Opposite*: modesty

flamboyant *adj* **showy**, ostentatious, colorful, flashy, gaudy, lurid, glitzy, loud, outrageous, extravagant [➡ EXTRAORDINARY: AMAZING; 204] *Opposite*: understated

flame 1 *n* **fire**, blaze, flare, spark, flicker, conflagration, flash [➡ FIRE, FLAMMABILITY, AND BURNING; 1165] 2 *type of* **orange** [➡ COLORS; 1224] 3 *v* **burn**, blaze, light up, glow, flare, flicker, spark, burst into flames, kindle [➡ FIRE, FLAMMABILITY, AND BURNING; 1165] 4 *v* [➡ THE INTERNET; 1128]

flamenco 1 *type of* **dance** [➡ DANCE; 903] 2 *type of* **world music** [➡ MUSIC, SONGS, AND SINGING; 907]

flameproof *adj* **nonflammable**, noninflammable, incombustible, fireproof, fire-retardant, fire-resistant [➡ FIRE, FLAMMABILITY, AND BURNING; 1165] *Opposite*: inflammable

flame-retardant *see* **flameproof**

flamethrower *type of* **gun** [➡ WEAPONS FOR SHOOTING; 1156]

flaming 1 *adj* **blazing**, burning, flaring, flickering, sparking, on fire, fiery, glowing, afire, ablaze, alight [➡ FIRE, FLAMMABILITY, AND BURNING; 1165] *Opposite*: doused 2 *adj* **intense**, angry, passionate, blazing, heated, fierce, furious, violent, stormy, ardent [➡ STRENGTH; 201] *Opposite*: calm

flamingo 1 *type of* **freshwater bird** [➡ FRESHWATER BIRDS; 1000] 2 *type of* **sea bird** [➡ SEA BIRDS; 1002]

flammable *adj* **inflammable**, combustible, incendiary, igneous [➡ FIRE, FLAMMABILITY, AND BURNING; 1165] *Opposite*: fireproof

flan 1 *n* **quiche**, pie, tart, tartlet, pastry [➡ BREAD, FLOUR, AND BREAD PRODUCTS; 1179] 2 *type of* **dessert** [➡ CAKES, COOKIES, AND DESSERTS; 1181]

flange *n* [➡ FASTENERS, LINKS, AND NETWORKS; 1247]

flank 1 *n* **side**, edge, verge, margin, border, rim, wing [➡ EXTREMITIES OF PHYSICAL OBJECTS; 1250] 2 *type of* **cut** [➡ TYPES AND CUTS OF MEAT; 1177] 3 *part of* **horse** [➡ HORSES; 985] 4 *v* **border**, edge, line, skirt, fringe, verge [➡ EXIST IN CLOSE PROXIMITY; 21]

flannel *type of* **fabric from animals** [➡ FABRICS; 1132]

flannelette *type of* **fabric from plants** [➡ FABRICS; 1132]

flap 1 *n* **tab**, fold, lappet, lap, tail, tailpiece, fly, skirt, apron [➡ EXTREMITIES OF PHYSICAL OBJECTS; 1250] 2 *n* **flutter**, wave, flail, shake, wag, beat [➡ MOVE SOMETHING: ON THE SPOT; 336]

flapjack *type of* **pancake** [➡ CAKES, COOKIES, AND DESSERTS; 1181]

flare 1 *v* **burn**, blaze, flame, flicker, flash, flare up, sparkle [➡ FIRE, FLAMMABILITY, AND BURNING; 1165] 2 *n* **flash**, blaze, flicker, flame, burst, sparkle [➡ LIGHT; 1164]

flared *adj* **widening**, wide, spreading, broadening, flaring, full, splayed [➡ DESCRIBING CLOTHES; 869] *Opposite*: tapered

flare up *v* **erupt**, break out, explode, heat up, blaze, boil over, burst out [➡ SUDDENLY COME INTO EXISTENCE; 2] *Opposite*: die down

flare-up (*informal*) *n* **outbreak**, eruption, flash, outburst, explosion [➡ SUDDEN EVENTS; 52]

flaring *adj* **widening**, bell-shaped, broadening, spreading, splaying [➡ CHANGE OF SIZE: BIGGER; 392] *Opposite*: tapering

flash 1 *v* **glint**, sparkle, twinkle, flare, flicker, glisten, gleam, glimmer [➡ LIGHT EMISSION; 368] 2 *v* **pass quickly**, rush, speed, race, zoom, fly, dash, zip (*informal*) [➡ MOVE FAST; 313] *Opposite*: crawl 3 *v* (*informal*) **flaunt**, show, show off, display, exhibit, flourish [➡ CAUSE TO APPEAR; 5] 4 *n* **blaze**, spark, flare, flicker, sparkle, twinkle, burst, explosion, streak, flame [➡ LIGHT; 1164] 5 *n* **moment**, instant, second, twinkling, minute, trice, wink, jiffy (*informal*) [➡ SHORT PERIODS OF TIME; 93] 6 *n* **news flash**, update, bulletin, announcement, report, communication [➡ TELEVISION AND RADIO; 606] 7 *part of* **camera** [➡ PHOTOGRAPHY AND PHOTOGRAPHIC EQUIPMENT; 1122]

flashback *n* **memory**, recurrence, remembrance, recollection, hallucination, evocation, recovered memory [➡ MEMORY; 745]

flash flood *n* **deluge**, downpour, cloudburst, spate, surge, inundation (*formal*) [➡ CLOUDY AND RAINY WEATHER; 1052]

flashiness *n* **showiness**, ostentatiousness, ostentation, glitziness, glitter, gaudiness, loudness, flamboyance, tawdriness, tastelessness, tackiness (*informal*) [➡ IN POOR TASTE AND OVERSENTIMENTAL; 229] *Opposite*: drabness

flashlight *n* **penlight**, light, lamp, lantern, flash (*informal*), torch (*UK*) [➡ LIGHT; 1164]

flashpoint 1 *n* **crisis**, breaking point, climax, turning point, crossroads [➡ DECISIVE MOMENTS; 44] 2 *n* **trouble spot**, hot spot, minefield, inferno, hornet's nest [➡ DIFFICULT SITUATIONS; 72]

flashy *adj* **showy**, ostentatious, glitzy, gaudy, loud, flamboyant, tawdry, tasteless, tacky (*informal*) [➡ IN POOR TASTE AND OVERSENTIMENTAL; 229] *Opposite*: understated

flask *n* **bottle**, flagon, carafe, hip flask, decanter, canteen, container [➡ TABLEWARE, FLATWARE, AND KITCHENWARE; 861]

flat 1 *adj* **level**, even, smooth, plane, horizontal, flush, uniform, regular [➡ ORIENTATION AND ALIGNMENT; 1223] *Opposite*: uneven 2 *adj* **unexciting**, dull, monotonous, tedious, boring, dreary, lifeless, uninteresting, stale, insipid [➡ BORING AND UNINTERESTING; 234] *Opposite*: exciting 3 *adj* **categorical**, downright, absolute, out-and-out, emphatic, unequivocal, point-blank, total, complete, utter, unqualified, thorough, definite [➡ ABSOLUTE AND ABSOLUTELY; 133] *Opposite*: equivocal 4 *adj* **fixed**, set, preset, invariable, non-negotiable, predetermined [➡ PERMANENCE: WITHOUT CHANGE; 95] *Opposite*: variable 5 *n* **surface**, plane, level, face, blade [➡ EXTREMITIES OF PHYSICAL OBJECTS; 1250]

flat bread *type of* **bread** [➡ BREAD, FLOUR, AND BREAD PRODUCTS; 1179]

flat broke (*informal*) *adj* [➡ POVERTY AND POOR; 892]

flatly 1 *adv* **categorically**, flat, absolutely, unequivocally, emphatically, point-blank, totally, completely, utterly, thoroughly, definitely [➡ HONEST AND OPEN; 630] *Opposite*: equivocally 2 *adv* **dully**, monotonously, lifelessly, blandly, tediously, impassively, unenthusiastically [➡ UNINTERESTED AND DETACHED; 629] *Opposite*: animatedly

flatmate (*UK*) *n* **cohabitee**, cohabitant, housemate, friend, roommate, roomie (*informal*) [➡ SUPPORTERS, PROTECTORS, AND COMPATRIOTS; 970]

flatness 1 *n* **levelness**, evenness, smoothness, horizontalness, horizontality, flushness, uniformity, regularity [➡PHYSICAL TEXTURE; 1222] *Opposite*: unevenness **2** *n* **dullness**, monotony, monotonousness, tedium, boringness, dreariness, staleness, insipidness [➡BORING AND UNINTERESTING; 234] *Opposite*: excitement

flatten 1 *v* **squash**, crush, level, even out, compress, roll out, smooth [➡CHANGE OF SHAPE; 385] **2** *v* **knock over**, knock down, poleax, fell, crush, floor, deck (*informal*), KO (*informal*) [➡MOVE SOMETHING: INTO A NEW POSITION OR OVERTURN; 330]

flatter *v* **compliment**, praise, cajole, sweet-talk (*informal*), butter up (*informal*), soft-soap (*informal*), blarney (*informal*), blandish (*archaic*) [➡FLATTER AND FAWN; 621] *Opposite*: insult

flatterer *n* **toady**, sycophant, fawner, yes man, bootlicker (*informal*) [➡PEOPLE WHO DECEIVE; 661] *Opposite*: critic

flattering 1 *adj* **gratifying**, pleasing, satisfying, satisfactory, cheering, pleasurable [➡EMOTIONALLY PLEASANT; 187] *Opposite*: galling **2** *adj* **obsequious**, smooth, toadyish, sycophantic [➡INGRATIATING; 638] *Opposite*: uncomplimentary **3** *adj* **becoming**, complimentary, kind, sympathetic, suitable, favorable [➡BEAUTY AND ATTRACTIVENESS; 189] *Opposite*: unbecoming

flattery *n* **sycophancy**, obsequiousness, toadyism, adulation, fawning, sweet talk (*informal*), soft soap (*informal*), snow job (*slang*), blandishment (*formal*) [➡INGRATIATING; 638] *Opposite*: insult

flat top *type of* **hairstyle** [➡HAIRSTYLES AND HAIRPIECES; 488]

flatulence *n* **pomposity**, pretentiousness, bombast, verbosity, grandiloquence, turgidity, gassiness [➡POMPOUS, LOUD, AND OVERCONFIDENT; 635] *Opposite*: simplicity

flatulent *adj* **pompous**, pretentious, bombastic, verbose, grandiloquent, turgid, gassy (*informal*) [➡POMPOUS, LOUD, AND OVERCONFIDENT; 635] *Opposite*: unpretentious

flatware *n* **knives and forks**, tableware, silverware, silver, silver plate, flat silver, fighting irons (*UK*) [➡TABLEWARE, FLATWARE, AND KITCHENWARE; 861]

flatware

◆ *types of flatware*
butter knife, carving knife, chopstick, dessertspoon, fish knife, fork, knife, pastry fork, pastry slice, serving spoon, soupspoon, spoon, steak knife, tablespoon, teaspoon

flaunt *v* **show off**, exhibit, display, parade, flourish, brandish, vaunt, boast, sport (*informal*) [➡CAUSE TO APPEAR; 5] *Opposite*: hide

flavor 1 *n* **taste**, savor, zest, tang, essence, aroma, relish, piquancy, smack [➡TASTE; 703] *Opposite*: tastelessness **2** *n* **additive**, seasoning, extract, spice, essence, condiment, herb, flavoring [➡ADDITIVES; 1172] **3** *n* **hint**, sense, feeling, feel, suggestion, touch, idea, aspect, air [➡FEW, LITTLE, SMALL AMOUNT; 120] **4** *v* **season**, spice, lace, salt, ginger [➡COOKING AND FOOD PREPARATION; 353] **5** *v* **characterize**, distinguish, mark, pervade, run through, enhance, season, imbue, color [➡CHANGE; 372]

flavorful *adj* **tasty**, tangy, appetizing, palatable, toothsome, savory [➡TASTE; 703] *Opposite*: unappetizing

flavoring *n* **flavor**, additive, seasoning, extract, spice, herb, essence, condiment [➡ADDITIVES; 1172]

flavorless *adj* **tasteless**, bland, insipid, flat, watery, weak, boring, anodyne (*literary*) [➡TASTE; 703] *Opposite*: tasty

flavorlessness *n* [➡TASTE; 703]

flavorsome *adj* [➡TASTE; 703]

flaw *n* **fault**, error, defect, mistake, failing, blemish, imperfection, weakness, weak spot, shortcoming [➡FAULTS, FLAWS, AND WEAKNESSES; 251]

Compare and Contrast: *flaw, imperfection, fault, defect, failing, blemish*

CORE MEANING: something that detracts from perfection

flaw an unintended mark or crack that prevents something from being totally perfect and detracts from its value, or a weakness in somebody's character or in a plan, theory, or system; *imperfection* a fault that makes a person or thing less than perfect; *fault* something that detracts from the integrity, functioning, or perfection of a thing, or a weakness in somebody's character, usually more serious than a flaw; *defect* a fault in a machine, system, or plan, especially one that prevents it from functioning correctly, or a personal weakness; *failing* something that mars somebody or something in some way, especially an unfortunate feature of somebody's character; *blemish* a mark of some kind that detracts from something's appearance, especially the complexion or skin, or a feature that detracts from somebody's otherwise undamaged reputation or record.

flawed *adj* **faulty**, defective, damaged, blemished, imperfect, inconsistent, unsound, weak [➡IN BAD REPAIR; 1234] *Opposite*: perfect

flawless *adj* **perfect**, faultless, immaculate, impeccable, unblemished, unspoiled, spotless, pure, sound [➡CORRECT AND FAULTLESS; 182] *Opposite*: imperfect

flawlessly *adv* **perfectly**, faultlessly, immaculately, impeccably, spotlessly, soundly, purely [➡CORRECT AND FAULTLESS; 182] *Opposite*: imperfectly

flawlessness *n* **perfection**, faultlessness, immaculateness, impeccability, spotlessness, soundness, purity [➡CORRECT AND FAULTLESS; 182] *Opposite*: imperfection

flaxen 1 *adj* **fair-haired**, fair, blond, blonde, golden-haired, tow-colored [➡HAIR COLOR; 485] **2** *type of* **yellow** [➡COLORS; 1224]

flay 1 *v* **whip**, lash, thrash, flog, beat, scourge [➡WHIP AND CLUB; 417] **2** *v* **criticize**, censure, condemn, pillory, lambaste, blast (*informal*), slate (*UK*) [➡ACCUSE, BLAME, AND CRITICIZE; 641] *Opposite*: endorse

flea *type of* **parasitic insect** [➡PARASITES; 1017]

fleabag (*informal*) *n* [➡UNDESIRABLE ACCOMMODATIONS; 856]

flea beetle *type of* **beetle** [➡BEETLES AND WEEVILS; 1016]

flea market *type of* **retail outlet** [➡RETAIL OUTLETS; 1083]

fleapit (*UK*) *n* **cinema**, theater, venue [➡BUILDINGS FOR PUBLIC ENTERTAINMENT; 1084]

fleck *n* **speck**, spot, speckle, dot, flyspeck, splash, streak, mark, freckle [➡ SMALL PIECES; 129]

flecked *adj* **marked**, speckled, dotted, streaked, stippled, splashed, freckled, spotted [➡ DESCRIBING PATTERNS; 1227]

fledgling 1 *type of* **young bird** [➡ YOUNG BIRDS; 1004] 2 *n* **novice**, beginner, learner, tyro, neophyte, amateur, newcomer, recruit, freshman, rookie (*informal*) [➡ UNSKILLED PEOPLE; 530] *Opposite*: expert 3 *adj* **inexperienced**, new, untried, young, inexpert, unqualified, green, raw, unseasoned [➡ UNSKILLED; 529] *Opposite*: experienced

flee *v* **run away**, escape, fly, take flight, run off, abscond, bolt, make off, take off (*informal*) [➡ RUN AWAY AND AVOID; 10]

fleece 1 *v* (*informal*) **swindle**, con, cheat, take for a ride, defraud, rip off (*informal*), hustle (*slang*) [➡ STEAL AND ROB; 426] 2 *type of* **jacket** [➡ GARMENTS AND OUTFITS; 865] 3 *type of* **synthetic fabric** [➡ FABRICS; 1132]

fleeciness *n* **woolliness**, downiness, fluffiness, furriness, fuzziness, flocculence, softness, shagginess [➡ PHYSICAL TEXTURE; 1222]

fleecy *adj* **woolly**, fluffy, flocculent, soft, shaggy, downy, furry [➡ PHYSICAL TEXTURE; 1222]

fleet *n* **navy**, flotilla, armada, convoy, task force, marine (*formal*) [➡ GROUPS OF VEHICLES; 1152]

fleeting *adj* **brief**, transitory, short-lived, momentary, passing, ephemeral, evanescent, transient [➡ FINITENESS, VARIABILITY, AND TRANSIENCE; 96] *Opposite*: permanent

See Compare and Contrast at **temporary**.

fleetness (*literary*) *n* [➡ SPEED; 102]

flesh 1 *n* **tissue**, soft tissue, muscle [➡ THE SKIN; 720] 2 *n* **skin**, surface, epithelium, epidermis, dermis, complexion [➡ THE SKIN; 720] 3 *n* **meat**, beef, lamb, pork, ham, chicken, turkey, fish [➡ TYPES AND CUTS OF MEAT; 1177] 4 *n* **pulp**, pulpiness, meat [➡ CENTRAL PARTS OF PHYSICAL OBJECTS; 1251] 5 *n* **relatives**, family, relations, blood relatives, kin, kinsfolk, flesh and blood, folk, lineage [➡ THE FAMILY; 956] 6 *n* **body**, flesh and blood, physicality, corporeality, corpus, soma, matter [➡ BODY; 691] 7 *n* **substance**, details, information, reality, solidness, meat, weight, matter [➡ BASIC DETAILS; 688] 8 *part of* **fruit** [➡ FRUIT AND VEGETABLES; 1176]

flesh and blood *n* [➡ THE FAMILY; 956]

flesh-and-blood *adj* [➡ LIVING THINGS AND LIVING; 976]

flesh color *type of* **beige** [➡ COLORS; 1224]

fleshiness *n* **beefiness**, stoutness, portliness, heftiness, corpulence, fatness, plumpness, chubbiness [➡ BUILD; 477]

fleshly 1 *adj* **bodily**, corporeal, physical, corporal, human, material, somatic [➡ LIVING THINGS AND LIVING; 976] *Opposite*: psychological 2 *adj* **carnal**, bodily, erotic, animal, voluptuous, sensual, sensuous, lascivious, wanton [➡ MORALLY BAD OR IMPROPER; 775] *Opposite*: ascetic 3 *adj* **worldly**, secular, material, human, mundane, earthly [➡ RELIGIOUS CONCEPTS; 776] *Opposite*: spiritual

flesh out *v* **amplify**, elaborate, pad, pad out, expand, give substance to, embellish, add to, fill out, bring alive,

make real, explain, expound, augment (*formal*) [➡ CHANGE OF SIZE: BIGGER; 392] *Opposite*: condense

fleshy *adj* **plump**, ample, overweight, fat, corpulent, chubby, heavy [➡ BUILD; 477] *Opposite*: slender

flex 1 *v* **bend**, loosen up, activate, move, warm up, stretch, arch [➡ CHANGE OF SHAPE; 385] *Opposite*: straighten 2 *v* **contract**, tense, tighten, control [➡ CHANGE OF SIZE: SMALLER; 393] *Opposite*: relax

flexibility *n* **suppleness**, litheness, elasticity, give, plasticity, springiness [➡ MALLEABLE AND ELASTIC; 1212] *Opposite*: rigidity

flexible 1 *adj* **supple**, lithe, elastic, plastic, stretchy, bendable, malleable, springy, bendy (*UK*) [➡ MALLEABLE AND ELASTIC; 1212] *Opposite*: rigid 2 *adj* **adaptable**, accommodating, variable, compliant, open, acquiescent, tractable, amenable, malleable, docile [➡ THE WILL AND WILLINGNESS; 563] *Opposite*: intractable

flexibly 1 *adv* **compliantly**, amenably, malleably, biddably, docilely, submissively, openly, adaptably, accommodatingly [➡ THE WILL AND WILLINGNESS; 563] *Opposite*: uncooperatively 2 *adv* **lithely**, elastically, stretchily, tractably, malleably, springily [➡ MALLEABLE AND ELASTIC; 1212] *Opposite*: rigidly

flextime *n* [➡ WORK-RELATED ACTIVITIES; 834]

flick 1 *n* (*informal*) **movie**, motion picture, film, picture, big screen, silver screen [➡ FILM; 901] 2 *v* **brush**, tap, glance, flip, graze, skim, strike, ping, touch [➡ MOVE SOMETHING: THROUGH THE AIR; 334]

flicker 1 *v* **sparkle**, glimmer, flash, waver, sputter, gutter, shimmer, blink, twinkle, glint [➡ LIGHT EMISSION; 368] 2 *n* **glimmer**, spark, sparkle, twinkle, glint, flash, glance [➡ FEW, LITTLE, SMALL AMOUNT; 120] *Opposite*: beam 3 *n* **trace**, ghost, impression, flash, glimmer, suggestion [➡ FEW, LITTLE, SMALL AMOUNT; 120]

flickering *adj* [➡ DESCRIBING LIGHT; 1228]

flick through *v* **look through**, dip into, leaf through, flip through, riffle, skim, scan, browse [➡ READ; 758] *Opposite*: scrutinize

flier 1 *n* (*informal*) **venture**, undertaking, endeavor, risk, attempt, try, effort [➡ ACTIONS OR UNDERTAKINGS; 259] 2 *n* **leaflet**, handout, advertisement, notice, insert, handbill, flysheet [➡ ADVERTISING AND PUBLICITY; 604]

flight 1 *n* **trip**, journey, airlift, voyage, tour, expedition, hop (*informal*) [➡ TRAVEL: JOURNEYS AND TRIPS; 318] 2 *n* **escape**, departure, getaway, breakout, evasion, breakaway [➡ ENDS AND DEPARTURES; 54] 3 *type of* **flock** [➡ GROUPS OF BIRDS; 1007]

flight deck *part of* **aircraft** [➡ AIRCRAFT; 1148]

flightiness *n* **capriciousness**, changeability, frivolity, volatility, erraticism, waywardness, inconsistency, unreliability, irresponsibility, fickleness, whimsicality, giddiness (*dated*) [➡ LACK OF COMMITMENT AND UNRELIABILITY; 509] *Opposite*: reliability

flight of fancy *n* **fantasy**, pipe dream, fancy, dream, daydream, castle in the air, castle in Spain [➡ NONEXISTENT THINGS; 23]

flight recorder *part of* **aircraft** [➡ AIRCRAFT; 1148]

flighty *adj* **unreliable**, capricious, changeable, erratic, undependable, variable, inconsistent, whimsical, fickle, impulsive, wayward [➡ LACK OF COMMITMENT AND UNRELIABILITY; 509] *Opposite*: dependable

flimflam (*slang*) *n* [➡ DECEPTION AND LIES; 660]

flimsily 1 *adv* **lightly**, weakly, delicately, insubstantially, fragilely, feebly, airily [➡ WEAKNESS; 241] *Opposite*: sturdily 2 *adv* **weakly**, unconvincingly, implausibly, inadequately, poorly, unsoundly [➡ UNCERTAIN; 175] *Opposite*: strongly

flimsiness *n* **fragility**, weakness, delicacy, frailty, feebleness, insubstantiality, ricketiness [➡ WEAKNESS; 241] *Opposite*: sturdiness

flimsy 1 *adj* **fragile**, weak, delicate, insubstantial, slight, light, rickety, thin [➡ WEAKNESS; 241] *Opposite*: sturdy 2 *adj* **poor**, feeble, unconvincing, inadequate, weak, unsound, implausible, tenuous [➡ UNCERTAIN; 175] *Opposite*: sound

See Compare and Contrast at **fragile**.

flinch *v* **recoil**, start, cringe, shy away, balk, draw back, quail, wince [➡ PHYSICAL REACTIONS; 316] *Opposite*: stand your ground

See Compare and Contrast at **recoil**.

fling 1 *v* **throw**, toss, hurl, pitch, lob, let fly, cast, sling, chuck (*informal*) [➡ MOVE SOMETHING: THROUGH THE AIR; 334] 2 *n* (*informal*) **romance**, love affair, affair, involvement, relationship [➡ SEXUAL AND ROMANTIC RELATIONSHIPS; 964]

See Compare and Contrast at **throw**.

flint *type of* **stone** [➡ STONES, ROCKS, AND BOULDERS; 1057]

flinty *adj* **stern**, unemotional, hard, inflexible, pitiless, stony, obdurate, cruel, unbending, steely, unyielding, merciless, relentless, callous, unfeeling [➡ SELFISH AND UNKIND; 505] *Opposite*: soft

flip 1 *v* **turn over**, toss, flick, spin, overturn, reverse [➡ MOVE SOMETHING: INTO A NEW POSITION OR OVERTURN; 330] 2 *v* (*slang*) **lose your temper**, explode, go off the deep end, go berserk, hit the roof, see red (*informal*), blow a fuse (*informal*), blow up (*informal*), lose it (*informal*), go ballistic (*slang*), flip your lid (*slang*), go nuts (*slang*) [➡ GIVING VENT TO EMOTIONS; 679] 3 *adj* (*informal*) **flippant**, casual, joking, jokey, dismissive, offhand, carefree, cheeky (*informal*), jesting (*literary*) [➡ MOCKING AND DISMISSIVE; 636] *Opposite*: serious

flip-flop 1 *n* **backward somersault**, backflip, tumble, flip, somersault, backward flip, backward handspring [➡ FIDGET AND FROLIC; 311] 2 (*informal*) *type of* **shoe** [➡ FOOTWEAR; 871]

flip over *v* **tip**, upset, upturn, flip, overturn, tumble, turn over, capsize, turn turtle, topple, cartwheel, tip over, tip up (*UK*) [➡ MOVE SOMETHING: INTO A NEW POSITION OR OVERTURN; 330]

flippancy *n* **levity**, facetiousness, glibness, offhandedness, impertinence, frivolity, lightness, jokiness, jesting (*literary*) [➡ MOCKING AND DISMISSIVE; 636] *Opposite*: seriousness

flippant *adj* **facetious**, offhand, glib, dismissive, frivo-

lous, superficial, jokey, insouciant, flip (*informal*) [➡ MOCKING AND DISMISSIVE; 636] *Opposite*: serious

flip through *v* **leaf through**, browse, flick through, skim through, scan, glance at, riffle, dip into [➡ READ; 758]

flip your lid (*slang*) *v* **lose your temper**, explode, go off the deep end, go berserk, hit the roof, see red (*informal*), blow a fuse (*informal*), blow up (*informal*), lose it (*informal*), go nuts (*slang*), flip (*slang*), go ballistic (*slang*) [➡ GIVING VENT TO EMOTIONS; 679]

flirt 1 *v* **trifle**, toy, play, seduce, lead on, dally, philander [➡ DECEPTION AND LIES; 660] 2 *v* **flick**, jerk, toss, flip, propel, tip [➡ MOVE SOMETHING: THROUGH THE AIR; 334]

flirtation *n* **romance**, fling, love affair, entanglement, liaison, intimacy, amour (*dated*) [➡ RELATIONSHIP TO ANOTHER; 973]

flirtatious *adj* [➡ FLIRTATIOUS; 639]

flirt with *v* **consider**, toy with, entertain, think about, trifle with, mess with, dabble [➡ THINK AND REFLECT; 743]

flit *v* **fly**, flutter, dart, skim, flash, dip, swoop [➡ MOVE FAST; 313]

float 1 *v* **hover**, soar, drift, glide, hang, lift [➡ PROCEED AND GO; 305] *Opposite*: drop 2 *v* **sail**, swim, drift, glide, tread water [➡ MOVE SLOWLY; 314] *Opposite*: sink 3 *v* **propose**, suggest, put forward, promote, offer, present [➡ SUGGEST, HINT, AND COMMENT; 612] *Opposite*: reject

floating *adj* **fluctuating**, detached, variable, moving, free, uncontrolled [➡ FINITENESS, VARIABILITY, AND TRANSIENCE; 96] *Opposite*: fixed

flock 1 *v* **gather**, collect, congregate, assemble, cluster, herd, group [➡ GET CLOSER TOGETHER; 310] *Opposite*: disperse 2 *type of* **herd** [➡ GROUPS OF ANIMALS; 993]

flock

◆ *types of flocks*
bevy (of quail/larks), brood (of chickens), cast (of hawks), charm (of finches), clutch (of chickens), colony (of gulls), covey (of partridges), exaltation (of larks) (*literary*), flight (of doves/swallows), gaggle (of geese), herd (of swans), kettle (of hawks), mob (of emus), murmuration (of starlings) (*literary*), muster (of peacocks), nye (of pheasants) (*literary*), rookery (of penguins), siege (of herons), skein (of geese), watch (of nightingales) (*literary*), wedge (of swans in flight), wisp (of snipe)

floe *n* **ice floe**, iceberg, ice field, icecap, ice sheet, glacier [➡ GEOLOGIC FEATURES; 1056]

flog *v* **whip**, lash, beat, thrash, scourge, whale, flay [➡ WHIP AND CLUB; 417]

flood 1 *n* **deluge**, overflow, downpour, torrent, tidal wave, inundation (*formal*) [➡ CLOUDY AND RAINY WEATHER; 1052] *Opposite*: drought 2 *n* **abundance**, glut, excess, stream, rush, surplus, outpouring, wave, surge [➡ MANY, MUCH, LARGE AMOUNT; 117] *Opposite*: shortage 3 *v* **inundate**, submerge, overflow, swamp, saturate, drown, engulf, deluge [➡ GIVE TOO MUCH AND OVERBURDEN; 437] *Opposite*: ebb

flooded *adj* **underwater**, swamped, waterlogged, inundated, drowned, submerged, engulfed, deluged [➡ WET; 1240]

floodgate n **head gate**, sluicegate, water gate, lock, weir, penstock, sluice [➡ WATERWAYS AND SEAWAYS; 1108]

floodlight 1 n **illumination**, lighting, stream, flood, searchlight, spotlight, beacon, beam [➡ LIGHT; 1164] 2 v **light up**, illuminate, light, irradiate, spotlight, beam, shine a light on, illumine (*formal*) [➡ LIGHT EMISSION; 368]

floodlit adj **illuminated**, lit up, well-lit, irradiated, illumined (*literary*), lit [➡ DESCRIBING LIGHT; 1228]

floodplain n **plain**, valley, delta, water meadow, fen, mudflat, marsh [➡ WETLANDS; 1043]

flood tide 1 n **inflow**, high tide, current [➡ THE SEAS, OCEANS, AND SHORES; 1041] 2 n **groundswell**, swell, surge, wave, upsurge, barrage, bombardment [➡ MANY, MUCH, LARGE AMOUNT; 117]

floor 1 n **story**, level, deck [➡ STAIRS AND STORIES; 1102] 2 n **bottom**, base, level, surface, flat, ground [➡ EXTREMITIES OF PHYSICAL OBJECTS; 1250] 3 v **astonish**, stupefy, astound, stagger, confound, amaze, stun, stump, baffle, bewilder, flabbergast (*informal*), flummox (*informal*) [➡ CONFUSE AND BEWILDER; 571]

floorboards n [➡ BUILDING MATERIALS; 1077]

floorcovering n [➡ FURNISHING AND HOUSEHOLD LINENS; 860]

floor cushion n [➡ FURNISHING AND HOUSEHOLD LINENS; 860]

flooring n **parquet**, floorboards, terrazzo, woodblocks, floor tiles, floor covering, carpeting [➡ BUILDING MATERIALS; 1077]

floor it (*slang*) v [➡ MOVE FAST; 313]

floor lamp n [➡ LIGHTING; 862]

floor manager n **supervisor**, overseer, manager, duty officer, line manager [➡ BOSSES AND MANAGEMENT; 965]

floor plan n **layout**, plan, design, arrangement, allocation, disposition [➡ DRAWINGS, CHARTS, AND TABLES; 594]

floor tiles n [➡ BUILDING MATERIALS; 1077]

flop 1 v **collapse**, slump, fall down, slacken, sag, droop, wilt, flag [➡ CHANGE OF SHAPE; 385] *Opposite*: stand up 2 v (*informal*) **fail**, fold, close, crash, nose-dive, bomb (*informal*) [➡ FAIL OR BE UNSUCCESSFUL; 75] *Opposite*: succeed 3 n (*informal*) **failure**, fiasco, dead loss, loser, dud (*informal*), washout (*informal*), lemon (*informal*), bomb (*informal*), turkey (*slang*), dead duck (*slang*) [➡ FAILURE; 77] *Opposite*: hit

flop about (*UK*) v [➡ LACK OF ACTIVITY OR MOTION; 342]

flop around v [➡ LACK OF ACTIVITY OR MOTION; 342]

flophouse (*informal*) n [➡ UNDESIRABLE ACCOMMODATIONS; 856]

floppiness n **limpness**, droopiness, looseness, slackness, softness, sagginess, flabbiness (*informal*) [➡ MALLEABLE AND ELASTIC; 1212] *Opposite*: firmness

floppy adj **limp**, droopy, lank, loose, flappy, soft, flaccid, saggy, flabby (*informal*), bendy (*UK*) [➡ MALLEABLE AND ELASTIC; 1212] *Opposite*: firm

floppy disk *type of* **hardware** [➡ COMPUTERS AND COMPUTING; 1127]

flora n **plants**, flowers, vegetation, plant life [➡ VEGETATION; 1025]

flora and fauna n [➡ LIVING THINGS AND LIVING; 976]

floral adj **flowery**, flowered, bloomy, floriated, wreathed, flower-patterned, florescent (*formal*) [➡ DESCRIBING PATTERNS; 1227]

floral-patterned adj [➡ DESCRIBING PATTERNS; 1227]

florentine *type of* **food presentation** [➡ COOKING AND FOOD PREPARATION; 353]

floret 1 n **floweret**, bud, blossom, bloom, flower [➡ PARTS OF TREES AND PLANTS; 1026] 2 *part of* **flower** [➡ FLOWERS; 1032]

florid 1 adj **ornate**, baroque, elaborate, fancy, flowery, flamboyant, ostentatious, showy, rococo, extravagant [➡ IN POOR TASTE AND OVERSENTIMENTAL; 229] *Opposite*: plain 2 adj **ruddy**, red, sanguine, rosy, heightened, blowzy [➡ COMPLEXION; 480] *Opposite*: pallid

flotation 1 n **launch**, initiation, debut, inauguration, introduction, commencement (*formal*) [➡ BUSINESS ACTIVITIES AND PHENOMENA; 794] 2 *type of* **complementary therapy** [➡ REMEDIES, TREATMENTS, AND OPERATIONS; 731]

flotilla n **fleet**, armada, convoy, task force, navy [➡ GROUPS OF VEHICLES; 1152]

flotsam n **debris**, refuse, driftwood, jetsam, wreckage, waste, junk (*informal*) [➡ JUNK AND USELESS OBJECTS; 1249]

flotsam and jetsam n [➡ JUNK AND USELESS OBJECTS; 1249]

flounce v **prance**, storm, stomp, strut, swagger, bounce [➡ MOVE FAST; 313]

flounce out v [➡ LEAVE AND GO AWAY; 8]

flounder 1 v **splash**, struggle, thrash, wallow, stumble, flap, flail [➡ FIDGET AND FROLIC; 311] 2 v **dither**, hesitate, falter, get into difficulties, waver, dawdle, delay, struggle, get nowhere, have difficulty [➡ HESITATE; 272] 3 *type of* **flatfish** [➡ OCEAN FISH; 1009]

flour v **dust**, cover, coat, sprinkle, dredge [➡ COOKING AND FOOD PREPARATION; 353]

flour

◆ *types of flour*
cornmeal, cornstarch, meal, plain flour, self-rising flour, wheatmeal, whole-wheat

flourish 1 v **be successful**, succeed, thrive, grow, do well, prosper, increase, boom, fare well, blossom, burgeon (*literary*) [➡ PROSPER AND ABOUND; 16] *Opposite*: decline 2 v **shake**, show, flaunt, display, wave, brandish, wield, swing [➡ MOVE SOMETHING: ON THE SPOT; 336] 3 n **embellishment**, curl, curlicue, decoration, ornament [➡ ORNAMENTS AND DECORATIONS; 1248] 4 n **grand gesture**, display, fanfare, show, bravado, swagger [➡ GESTURES AND GESTICULATION; 653]

flourishing adj **doing well**, thriving, successful, booming, healthy, prosperous, in the ascendant, faring well, burgeoning, blossoming [➡ SUCCESSFUL AND PROMISING; 81] *Opposite*: declining

floury adj **starchy**, crumbly, crumbling, farinaceous, floured, powdery [➡ PHYSICAL TEXTURE; 1222]

flout v **disobey**, break, ignore, defy, contravene, be in breach of, scorn, spurn, scoff [➡ DISOBEY; 302] *Opposite*: obey

flow 1 v **run**, pour, flood, stream, gush, surge, roll [➡ PROCEED

AND GO; 305] **2** *v* **spring**, arise, emerge, emanate, issue, well up [➡GRADUALLY COME INTO EXISTENCE; 1] **3** *n* **movement**, current, stream, course, drift, tide [➡RIVERS, LAKES, AND STREAMS; 1042]

flower **1** *n* **floret**, flower head, bud, blossom, bloom [➡PARTS OF TREES AND PLANTS; 1026] **2** *n* **best**, pick, height, choicest, elite, cream [➡SUPERIORITY; 152] *Opposite*: worst **3** *v* **bloom**, bud, blossom, open, come into bloom [➡GROW AND CULTIVATE; 351] *Opposite*: fade **4** *v* **develop**, come to fruition, flourish, peak, blossom, thrive, mature [➡PROSPER AND ABOUND; 16] *Opposite*: wane

flower

♦ *types of annual flowers*
aster, forget-me-not, lobelia, marigold, nasturtium, pansy, petunia, poppy, stock, sunflower, sweet pea

♦ *types of perennial flowers*
African violet, begonia, buttercup, carnation, chrysanthemum, columbine, cowslip, daisy, delphinium, foxglove, fuchsia, geranium, lily of the valley, lotus, lupine, orchid, pelargonium, peony, pink, primrose, rose, snapdragon, sweet william, violet, wallflower

♦ *parts of a flower*
androecium, anther, bract, calyx, carpel, corolla, fall, filament, floret, glume, gynoecium, involucre, lemma, lip, nectary, ovary, ovule, palea, pedicel, peduncle, perianth, petal, pistil, receptacle, sepal, spur, stamen, stigma, style, tepal

flowerbed *n* **plot**, garden plot, patch, border, herbaceous border, bed [➡GARDENS; 1074]

flowered *adj* **floral**, flowery, flower-patterned, floral-patterned [➡DESCRIBING PATTERNS; 1227]

flower garden *type of* **garden** [➡GARDENS; 1074]

flowering *n* **peak**, high point, acme, blossoming, pinnacle, zenith [➡INTERMEDIATE STAGES; 55] *Opposite*: nadir

flower-patterned *adj* [➡DESCRIBING PATTERNS; 1227]

flowerpot *n* **plant pot**, planter, tub, jardinière, urn, window box, container [➡CONTAINERS, RECEPTACLES, AND PACKAGING; 1245]

flower show *n* [➡PERFORMANCES AND SHOWS; 42]

flowery **1** *adj* **ornate**, ornamental, baroque, embellished, florid, fancy, elaborate, extravagant [➡POSITIVELY COMPLEX OR COMPLICATED; 217] *Opposite*: plain **2** *adj* **floral**, flowered, flower-patterned, floriated [➡DESCRIBING PATTERNS; 1227]

flowing *adj* **graceful**, smooth, curving, sinuous, elegant, fluid, unbroken, rolling, fluent [➡ROUNDED SHAPE; 1218] *Opposite*: jerky

flu *n* [➡ILLNESSES AND DISORDERS; 732]

flub (*slang*) *v* [➡MESS UP AND MAKE MISTAKES; 472]

fluctuate *v* **vary**, alter, ebb and flow, rise and fall, come and go, swing, oscillate, vacillate, waver, sway, change [➡CHANGE; 372]

fluctuating *adj* **changing**, changeable, shifting, mutable, unstable, inconsistent, unsettled, alterable, variable, inconstant, oscillating, varying, vacillating, wavering,

swaying [➡FINITENESS, VARIABILITY, AND TRANSIENCE; 96] *Opposite*: constant

fluctuation *n* **variation**, vacillation, rise and fall, oscillation, flux, ebb and flow, instability, changeability, variability, wavering [➡FINITENESS, VARIABILITY, AND TRANSIENCE; 96] *Opposite*: steadiness

flue *n* **vent**, chimney, outlet, shaft, duct, tube, pipe, ventilation shaft [➡ROOFS, ROOF PARTS, AND CEILINGS; 1103]

fluency *n* **effortlessness**, eloquence, articulacy, ease, facility, confidence, smoothness, glibness [➡EASE AND SIMPLICITY; 200] *Opposite*: hesitancy

fluent **1** *adj* **easy**, flowing, confident, assured, smooth, effortless, glib, self-assured [➡COOL AND CALM; 536] *Opposite*: halting **2** *adj* **articulate**, eloquent, voluble, smooth-spoken, smooth-tongued, silver-tongued [➡ELOQUENT, TALKATIVE, AND LONG-WINDED; 632] *Opposite*: tongue-tied

fluently *adv* **assuredly**, easily, confidently, smoothly, effortlessly, glibly [➡COOL AND CALM; 536] *Opposite*: awkwardly

fluff **1** *v* (*informal*) **do badly**, make a mess of, botch, ruin, spoil, mess up (*informal*), bungle (*informal*), flub (*slang*) [➡MESS UP AND MAKE MISTAKES; 472] **2** *n* **fuzz**, lint, hair [➡UNPLEASANT, DIRTY, AND TOXIC SUBSTANCES; 1268] **3** *v* **fluff up**, plump up, ruffle, shake, pat [➡CHANGE OF SHAPE; 385]

fluffiness **1** *n* **furriness**, fuzziness, hairiness, woolliness, fleeciness, downiness [➡PHYSICAL TEXTURE; 1222] **2** *n* **lightness**, airiness, softness, flimsiness, frothiness, insubstantiality [➡PHYSICAL TEXTURE; 1222] *Opposite*: heaviness

fluff up *v* [➡MESS UP AND MAKE MISTAKES; 472]

fluffy **1** *adj* **fleecy**, cottony, feathery, downy, furry, fuzzy, soft [➡PHYSICAL TEXTURE; 1222] **2** *adj* **frothy**, foamy, bubbly, soft, light [➡PHYSICAL TEXTURE; 1222]

flugelhorn *type of* **brass instrument** [➡MUSICAL INSTRUMENTS; 910]

fluid **1** *n* **liquid**, solution, water [➡LIQUIDS; 1269] *Opposite*: solid **2** *adj* **unsolidified**, runny, liquid, liquefied, molten, melted, watery [➡FLUID AND NONSOLID; 1213] *Opposite*: solid **3** *adj* **effortless**, flowing, smooth, graceful, elegant, sinuous [➡COOL AND CALM; 536] *Opposite*: jerky **4** *adj* **changeable**, fluctuating, unstable, adaptable, flexible, unpredictable, adjustable, shifting, indefinite [➡FINITENESS, VARIABILITY, AND TRANSIENCE; 96] *Opposite*: constant

fluid dram *type of* **nonmetric unit** [➡SIZE AND DIMENSIONS; 1192]

fluidity **1** *n* **variability**, changeableness, changeability, flexibility, mutability, volatility, uncertainty, indefiniteness [➡FINITENESS, VARIABILITY, AND TRANSIENCE; 96] *Opposite*: fixedness **2** *n* **smoothness**, gracefulness, grace, agility, flexibility, plasticity [➡EASE AND SIMPLICITY; 200] *Opposite*: jerkiness

fluid ounce *type of* **nonmetric unit** [➡SIZE AND DIMENSIONS; 1192]

fluke (*informal*) *n* **stroke of luck**, accident, coincidence, lucky break, chance occurrence, chance, freak [➡CHANCE EVENTS; 36] *Opposite*: mischance

fluky (*informal*) *adj* [➡LUCK; 783]

flummox (*informal*) *v* **confuse**, perplex, baffle, stump, bewilder, confound, stagger, stun, floor, bemuse, fox, disconcert, nonplus, throw (*informal*), flabbergast (*informal*) [➡ CONFUSE AND BEWILDER; 571]

flummoxed (*informal*) *adj* **confused**, perplexed, confounded, baffled, stumped, bemused, bewildered, at sea, mystified, at a loss, puzzled, foxed, disconcerted, nonplussed, thrown (*informal*), flabbergasted (*informal*) [➡ CONFUSION, ANXIETY, AND WORRY; 540]

flunk (*informal*) *v* **fail**, be unsuccessful, not pass, do badly, bomb (*informal*) [➡ FAIL OR BE UNSUCCESSFUL; 75] *Opposite:* ace (*informal*)

flunkey (*informal*) *see* **flunky**

flunky 1 *n* (*informal*) **minion**, sidekick, assistant, helper, subordinate [➡ SUBORDINATES AND ASSISTANTS; 966] **2** *type of* **servant** [➡ DOMESTIC AND KITCHEN WORKERS; 850]

fluoresce *v* [➡ LIGHT EMISSION; 368]

fluorescence *n* [➡ DESCRIBING LIGHT; 1228]

fluorescent *adj* **glowing**, bright, shining, luminous, flaming, incandescent [➡ DESCRIBING LIGHT; 1228]

fluorescent lamp *type of* **light** [➡ LIGHT; 1164]

fluorite *type of* **mineral** [➡ MINERALS; 1277]

flurry 1 *n* **burst**, spell, outbreak, bout, flood, bustle, commotion, fuss [➡ SUDDEN EVENTS; 52] **2** *n* **wind**, gust, puff, squall, shower [➡ WINDY AND STORMY WEATHER; 1053] **3** *v* **fluster**, agitate, disturb, disconcert, perturb, rattle, disquiet (*archaic or literary*) [➡ UPSET, DISTRESS, AND HUMILIATE; 567] *Opposite:* soothe

flush 1 *v* **redden**, blush, go red, color, glow, bloom, tint [➡ CHANGE OF COLOR; 391] *Opposite:* pale **2** *v* **clear**, wash out, cleanse, rinse, swill, flood, clean out (*informal*) [➡ CLEAN AND POLISH; 403] **3** *n* **blush**, high color, redness, rosiness, ruddiness, bloom, tint [➡ PAIN AND OTHER PHYSICAL SENSATIONS; 733] *Opposite:* pallor **4** *adj* **even**, level, flat, true [➡ ORIENTATION AND ALIGNMENT; 1223] *Opposite:* uneven **5** *adj* (*informal*) [➡ WEALTH AND WEALTHY; 891]

flushed *adj* **red-faced**, rosy, red, blushing, glowing, reddened [➡ COMPLEXION; 480] *Opposite:* pale

fluster *v* **disconcert**, agitate, confuse, upset, bother, perturb, disturb, disquiet (*archaic or literary*) [➡ CONFUSE AND BEWILDER; 571] *Opposite:* soothe

flustered *adj* **harassed**, agitated, nervous, disconcerted, rattled, confused, ruffled, disturbed, perturbed, in a tizzy (*informal*), in a flap (*informal*), het up (*UK*) [➡ CONFUSION, ANXIETY, AND WORRY; 540] *Opposite:* calm

flute 1 *n* **groove**, channel, indentation, line, furrow, corrugation, pleat [➡ HOLES, GAPS, AND FORKS; 1252] *Opposite:* ridge **2** *type of* **wind instrument** [➡ MUSICAL INSTRUMENTS; 910]

fluted *adj* **grooved**, corrugated, furrowed, lined, indented, pleated, channeled [➡ PHYSICAL TEXTURE; 1222] *Opposite:* flat

flutter 1 *v* **beat**, flap, wave, tremble, quiver, waver, flicker, pulsate [➡ MOVE SOMETHING: ON THE SPOT; 336] **2** *n* **fluster**, excitement, flurry, agitation, confusion, perturbation, commotion, flap (*informal*), tizzy (*informal*), state (*informal*) [➡ INSECURITY AND LOSS OF COMPOSURE; 544] *Opposite:* composure

flux *n* **fluidity**, mutability, fluctuation, instability, unrest, change [➡ CHANGE; 372] *Opposite:* stability

fly 1 *v* **hover**, soar, wing, take wing, take off, glide, flutter, sail, take to the air, coast [➡ PROCEED AND GO; 305] **2** *v* **zoom**, tear, dash, hurry, race, rush, get a move on (*informal*) [➡ MOVE FAST; 313] *Opposite:* dawdle **3** *v* **bolt**, run away, escape, flee, take flight, take off, run off, fly the coop, split (*slang*) [➡ RUN AWAY AND AVOID; 10] *Opposite:* stand your ground **4** *n* [➡ INSECTS; 1012]

fly

◆ *types of flying insects*
aphid, bee, black fly, bluebottle, bumblebee, cicada, crane fly, deer fly, dragonfly, firefly, fruit fly, gnat, grasshopper, greenfly, hornet, horsefly, locust, mayfly, midge, mosquito, no-see-um, punkie, tsetse fly, wasp, whitefly

fly agaric *type of* **fungus** [➡ MICROORGANISMS, FUNGI, AND ALGAE; 1023]

flyaway *adj* **unmanageable**, unruly, uncontrollable, hard to handle, awkward, difficult [➡ DESCRIBING HAIR; 486] *Opposite:* manageable

flyblown 1 *adj* **maggoty**, wormy, infested, worm-eaten, festering [➡ DECAYING OR INFESTED; 1236] **2** *adj* **dirty**, filthy, contaminated, tainted, unclean, unhealthy [➡ DIRTY; 1235] *Opposite:* clean

fly-by-night *adj* **unscrupulous**, dubious, unreliable, shifty, questionable, shady, untrustworthy, undependable, crooked (*informal*) [➡ LACK OF COMMITMENT AND UNRELIABILITY; 509] *Opposite:* reputable

flycatcher 1 *type of* **songbird** [➡ SONGBIRDS; 1003] **2** *type of* **common bird** [➡ BIRDS; 997]

flying 1 *adj* **hovering**, airborne, soaring, in the air, on the wing, winged [➡ GENERAL LOCATIONS; 158] **2** *adj* **rapid**, brief, speedy, hurried, short, hasty, snatched, fleeting [➡ HAPPENING QUICKLY; 104]

flying ant *type of* **ant** [➡ ANTS; 1014]

flying fish *type of* **tropical fish** [➡ OCEAN FISH; 1009]

flying fox *type of* **flying mammal** [➡ FLYING MAMMALS; 984]

flying saucer *n* **UFO**, spaceship, spacecraft [➡ SCIENCE FICTION; 1064]

flying squirrel *type of* **flying mammal** [➡ FLYING MAMMALS; 984]

fly in the face of *v* **challenge**, disagree with, go against, contradict, oppose, defy [➡ DISOBEY; 302] *Opposite:* conform

fly in the ointment *n* **drawback**, complaint, impediment, snag, hitch, sticking point, obstacle [➡ PROBLEMS; 256]

fly into a rage *v* **erupt**, explode, lose your temper, hit the roof, go wild, hit the ceiling, lose your head, blow your top (*informal*), fly off the handle (*informal*), see red (*informal*), blow up (*informal*), lose it (*informal*), go ballistic (*slang*), flip your lid (*slang*), go nuts (*slang*) [➡ GIVING VENT TO EMOTIONS; 679] *Opposite:* calm down

flyleaf *n* **front page**, first page, frontispiece, page, leaf [➡ PARTS OF BOOKS AND DOCUMENTS; 593]

fly off the handle (*informal*) *v* **erupt**, explode, lose your temper, fly into a rage, hit the roof, go wild, hit the ceiling, lose your head, blow your top (*informal*), see red (*informal*), blow up (*informal*), lose it (*informal*), go ballistic (*slang*), flip your lid (*slang*), go nuts (*slang*) [➡ GIVING VENT TO EMOTIONS; 679] *Opposite*: calm down

flysheet *n* flier, handbill, handout, sheet, notice [➡ ADVERTISING AND PUBLICITY; 604]

fly the coop (*informal*) *v* escape, leave, run away, flee, bolt, run off, take off (*informal*) [➡ RUN AWAY AND AVOID; 10] *Opposite*: remain

foal 1 *type of* young animal [➡ YOUNG ANIMALS; 977] 2 *v* produce young, produce offspring, breed, give birth, reproduce, drop a foal [➡ REPRODUCTION AND HEREDITY; 725]

foam 1 *n* bubbles, froth, fizz, lather, suds [➡ FOAM; 1273] 2 *v* froth up, effervesce, froth, bubble, fizz, lather, boil [➡ FROTH AND EFFERVESCE; 389]

foam at the mouth *v* rage, seethe, fume, boil, splutter [➡ GIVING VENT TO EMOTIONS; 679]

fob off 1 *v* foist, palm off, dump, pass on, offload, sell a pig in a poke [➡ GIVE TOO MUCH AND OVERBURDEN; 437] 2 *v* mislead, misinform, deceive, stall, pull the wool over somebody's eyes, trick [➡ DECEPTION AND LIES; 660] 3 *v* cheat, con, palm off, rip off (*informal*), do (*informal*) [➡ DECEPTION AND LIES; 660]

focaccia *type of* bread [➡ BREAD, FLOUR, AND BREAD PRODUCTS; 1179]

focal *adj* principal, pivotal, central, crucial, important, main [➡ FUNDAMENTAL; 195] *Opposite*: peripheral

focal point *n* central point, pivot, core, center, focus, heart, hub [➡ CENTRAL PARTS OF PHYSICAL OBJECTS; 1251] *Opposite*: periphery

fo'c's'le *part of* ship or boat [➡ PARTS OF A SHIP OR BOAT; 1151]

focus 1 *n* nub, central point, core, spotlight, center, center of attention [➡ CENTRAL PARTS OF PHYSICAL OBJECTS; 1251] 2 *n* emphasis, attention, effort, concentration, motivation, single-mindedness, application [➡ ATTENTION AND ATTENTIVENESS; 763] 3 *n* focal point, heart, hub, nucleus, meeting point, rallying point [➡ CENTRAL PARTS OF PHYSICAL OBJECTS; 1251] 4 *v* concentrate, direct, converge, meet, come together, bring together, fix, center, aim [➡ COMBINE AND MIX; 400]

focused *adj* motivated, concentrated, fixated, attentive, absorbed, engrossed, intensive, dedicated, single-minded, determined, driven, resolute, firm, persistent, strong-minded, dogged [➡ POSITIVE INTELLECTUAL CHARACTERISTICS; 524]

fodder *n* food, silage, hay, feed, feedstuff, provender, forage, rations [➡ ANIMAL FEED; 1168]

foe (*formal*) *n* adversary, enemy, antagonist, rival, opponent [➡ ENEMIES AND TORMENTORS; 969] *Opposite*: friend

foehn *type of* wind [➡ WINDY AND STORMY WEATHER; 1053]

foetid *see* fetid

fog 1 *n* mist, vapor, smog, haze, miasma, murkiness, condensation, precipitation, peasouper (*UK*) [➡ CLOUDY AND RAINY WEATHER; 1052] 2 *n* muddle, stupor, confusion, daze, haze, trance, bewilderment [➡ PAIN AND OTHER PHYSICAL SENSATIONS; 733] *Opposite*: clarity 3 *v* obscure, cloud, bewilder, confuse, stupefy, muddle, fuddle, dim, perplex [➡ CONFUSE AND BEWILDER; 571] *Opposite*: sharpen

fogginess 1 *n* mistiness, murkiness, haziness, cloudiness, gloom, murk, haze, darkness, precipitation, condensation [➡ CLOUDY AND RAINY WEATHER; 1052] *Opposite*: brightness 2 *n* obscurity, confusion, unclearness, doubtfulness, bewilderment, perplexity [➡ CONFUSION, ANXIETY, AND WORRY; 540] *Opposite*: clarity

foggy 1 *adj* hazy, misty, cloudy, murky, smoggy, dim, vaporous [➡ CLOUDY AND RAINY WEATHER; 1052] *Opposite*: clear 2 *adj* unclear, vague, confused, muddled, bewildered, stupefied, fuddled [➡ VAGUENESS; 243] *Opposite*: precise

foghorn *n* horn, siren, hooter, Klaxon [➡ SIGNALING; 1140]

fog light *type of* external feature [➡ EXTERNAL PARTS OF A VEHICLE; 1147]

fogy *n* [➡ UNCOOPERATIVE OR REBELLIOUS PEOPLE; 566]

fogyish *adj* [➡ REBELLIOUSNESS AND DISOBEDIENCE; 565]

foible *n* weakness, fault, shortcoming, quirk, idiosyncrasy, eccentricity, bad habit, imperfection [➡ PERSONAL ECCENTRICITIES; 493] *Opposite*: strength

foie gras *type of* processed meat [➡ TYPES AND CUTS OF MEAT; 1177]

foil 1 *v* stop, frustrate, thwart, outwit, halt, halt in its tracks, balk, hinder, throw a monkey wrench in the works (*informal*), throw a spanner in the works (*UK*) [➡ MAKE IMPOSSIBLE; 276] 2 *type of* sword or knife [➡ SWORDS AND KNIVES; 1157]

foist *v* force upon, inflict upon, thrust upon, impose, palm off, pass off, finagle (*informal*) [➡ GIVE TOO MUCH AND OVERBURDEN; 437]

fold 1 *v* double over, bend, fold up, fold over, double, pleat, crease, crinkle, corrugate [➡ CHANGE OF SHAPE; 385] *Opposite*: straighten 2 *v* go out of business, close, shut down, go bankrupt, collapse, go under, go bust (*informal*), go to the wall (*UK*) [➡ FAIL OR BE UNSUCCESSFUL; 75] 3 *n* crinkle, crease, wrinkle, pleat, doubling, folding, bend [➡ CHANGE OF SHAPE; 385]

foldaway *see* folding

folded *adj* doubled, doubled over, doubled up, bent over, turned under, turned up, creased, gathered, pleated, crumpled, bent [➡ ORIENTATION AND ALIGNMENT; 1223] *Opposite*: outspread

folder *type of* computer feature [➡ COMPUTERS AND COMPUTING; 1127]

folding *adj* portable, foldup, traveling, foldaway, collapsible, hinged, compact, camping [➡ CHANGE OF SHAPE; 385]

fold up *v* bend flat, bend, collapse, double, fold over, fold down [➡ CHANGE OF SHAPE; 385]

foldup *see* folding

foliage *n* leaves, greenery, vegetation, undergrowth, shrubbery, plants, verdure [➡ PARTS OF TREES AND PLANTS; 1026]

foliage plant *n* houseplant, potted plant, indoor plant [➡ FOLIAGE PLANTS; 1035]

foliage plant

◆ *types of foliage plants*
aspidistra, coleus, fern, moss, poinsettia, rubber plant, sansevieria, spider plant, yucca

folk 1 *adj* **traditional**, popular, common, widespread, vernacular, general, conventional, informal, unofficial [➡ OLD, OLD-FASHIONED; 167] **2** *n* **people**, folks, the people, the population, everyone, most people, the silent majority, society [➡ GROUPS IN SOCIETY; 940] **3** *type of* **pop and vocal music** [➡ MUSIC, SONGS, AND SINGING; 907]

folklore 1 *n* **legends**, traditional stories, urban myths, folk tales, received wisdom [➡ THE ORAL TRADITION; 677] **2** *n* **myth**, legend, oral tradition, mythology, tradition, traditional beliefs, custom [➡ THE ORAL TRADITION; 677]

folks 1 *n* (*informal*) **people**, folk, the people, the population, everyone, most people, the silent majority, society [➡ GROUPS IN SOCIETY; 940] **2** *n* (*informal*) **everyone**, everybody, ladies and gentlemen, boys and girls, girls and boys, you guys, friends, comrades, dearly beloved, guys (*informal*), you lot (*UK*) [➡ GROUPS IN SOCIETY; 940] **3** *n* **relatives**, relations, nearest and dearest, family, kinfolk, kith and kin, people (*informal*) [➡ THE FAMILY; 956]

folk singer *n* **singer**, folkie, balladeer, troubadour [➡ MUSICIANS AND SINGERS; 908]

folk story *n* [➡ THE ORAL TRADITION; 677]

folksy 1 *adj* **simple**, unsophisticated, unpretentious, wholesome, traditional, downhome (*informal*) [➡ LEVELS OF EDUCATION AND SOPHISTICATION; 894] **2** *adj* **friendly**, informal, relaxed, congenial, easygoing [➡ NATURALNESS; 497] *Opposite*: restrained

folk tale *n* **tale**, story, legend, myth, ballad, fable, allegory [➡ THE ORAL TRADITION; 677]

follicle *n* **sac**, cavity, gland, hair follicle [➡ THE SKIN; 720]

follow 1 *v* **stalk**, pursue, chase, trail, track, tag on, tag along, hunt, tail (*informal*) [➡ ACCOMPANY AND FOLLOW; 337] *Opposite*: precede **2** *v* **monitor**, shadow, check on, trail, keep an eye on, track, chart, survey, tail (*informal*) [➡ LOOKING AND LOOKS; 700] **3** *v* **keep on**, go along, stay on, keep to, stick to [➡ ACCOMPANY AND FOLLOW; 337] **4** *v* **obey**, abide by, keep to, respect, adhere to, stick to, go by, go along with [➡ OBEY AND ABIDE BY; 301] *Opposite*: break **5** *v* **understand**, see, comprehend, grasp, get the gist, get the idea, catch on (*informal*), cotton on (*informal*) [➡ UNDERSTAND AND GRASP; 759] **6** *v* **enjoy**, admire, support, keep up with, be keen on (*UK*) [➡ LIKE, LOVE, VALUE, AND ENJOY; 578] **7** *v* **come out of**, ensue, result, develop, arise [➡ HAPPEN; 27]

Compare and Contrast: *follow, chase, pursue, tail, shadow, stalk, trail*

CORE MEANING: to go after

follow to take the same route behind another person, for example by walking down the street or driving along the same road, deliberately or by chance, and not necessarily with the intention of closing the gap; *chase* to try to reach, catch, or overtake another person who is in front; *pursue* to make an effort to catch up with the person being followed; *tail* (*informal*) to follow secretly for purposes of surveillance; *shadow* to follow secretly, used especially to talk about the activities of spies and detectives; *stalk* to follow or try to get close to a person or hunted animal unobtrusively, especially obsessively to follow and criminally harass a person; *trail* to follow tracks or traces left by a person or animal no longer in sight.

follower *n* **supporter**, fan, admirer, hanger-on, devotee, disciple, adherent [➡ SUPPORTERS, PROTECTORS, AND COMPATRIOTS; 970]

following *adj* **next**, subsequent, succeeding, ensuing, resulting [➡ AFTER, LAST, AND FOLLOWING; 165] *Opposite*: previous

follow-on 1 *adj* **resulting**, consequent, resultant, ensuing, secondary, subsequent [➡ AFTER, LAST, AND FOLLOWING; 165] **2** *n* **side effect**, continuation, consequence, result, repercussion, carryover, spinoff, knock-on (*UK*), knock-on effect (*UK*) [➡ RESULTS AND OUTCOMES; 83]

follow through *v* **complete**, see through, bring to completion, bring to the end, finish off, finish [➡ COMPLETE AN ACTION; 263] *Opposite*: drop

follow-up *n* **continuation**, addition, supplement, complement, development, sequel [➡ AFTER, LAST, AND FOLLOWING; 165]

folly *n* **irrationality**, foolishness, madness, stupidity, idiocy, silliness, recklessness, foolhardiness, imprudence, craziness (*informal*) [➡ NEGATIVE INTELLECTUAL CHARACTERISTICS; 525] *Opposite*: prudence

foment *v* **foster**, stir up, stimulate, incite, generate, provoke, drum up, increase, encourage, whip up, fan [➡ CAUSE TO HAPPEN; 31] *Opposite*: dampen

fond *adj* **loving**, tender, affectionate, caring, warm, warm-hearted, doting [➡ GENEROSITY AND KINDNESS; 495] *Opposite*: uncaring

fondant *type of* **confectionery** [➡ CONFECTIONERY; 1182]

fondle *v* **massage**, touch, stroke, caress, pet, pat, feel, rub [➡ CONTACT: TOUCH; 412]

fondness *n* **liking**, affection, weakness, soft spot, partiality, keenness, love, attachment [➡ LOVE, RESPECT, AND GOODWILL; 549] *Opposite*: dislike

See Compare and Contrast at **love**.

fond of *adj* **devoted to**, taken with, attached to, partial to, soft on, keen on (*UK*) [➡ APPRECIATION AND GRATITUDE; 535] *Opposite*: indifferent

fondue *type of* **cooked dish** [➡ PREPARED DISHES; 1170]

font 1 *n* (*literary*) **source**, supply, wellspring, fount, basis, origin, well [➡ BEGINNINGS; 53] **2** *n* (*literary*) **fountain**, spring, water source, well, source [➡ RIVERS, LAKES, AND STREAMS; 1042] **3** *n* **typeface**, lettering, type style, type [➡ PRINTING; 600]

food 1 *n* **nourishment**, nutrition, nutriment, diet, sustenance, nutrients [➡ FOOD; 1167] **2** *n* **staple**, foodstuff, fare, provisions, groceries, victuals, rations, cuisine, fodder, grub (*informal*), chow (*slang*) [➡ FOOD; 1167]

foodie (*informal*) *n* **gourmet**, bon vivant, epicure, connoisseur, epicurean, glutton, gastronome, gourmand, bon viveur (*literary*), food lover (*UK*) [➡ EATERS, GOURMETS, AND DIETARY CHOICES; 714]

food lover (*UK*) *n* **gourmet**, epicure, connoisseur, epicurean, glutton, gastronome, gourmand, bon vivant, foodie (*informal*), bon viveur (*literary*) [➡ EATERS, GOURMETS, AND DIETARY CHOICES; 714]

food processor *type of* **appliance** [➡ HOUSEHOLD APPLIANCES; 1117]

foodstuff *n* food, staple, essential, ingredient, provisions, groceries, rations, fodder [➡ FOOD; 1167]

foofaraw *n* [➡ CHAOS AND UPROAR; 51]

fool 1 *n* dolt (*informal*), dope (*informal*), boob (*informal*), sucker (*informal*), ding-dong (*informal*), dingbat (*slang*), mug (*UK slang*), twit (*UK dated*) [➡ LAZY OR UNSUCCESSFUL PEOPLE; 948] 2 *v* mislead, trick, deceive, take in, con, dupe, pull the wool over somebody's eyes, hoodwink, bamboozle (*informal*) [➡ DECEPTION AND LIES; 660]

fool around 1 *v* clown, act the fool, play around, horse around, mess around (*informal*) [➡ LEISURE AND RECREATION; 874] 2 *v* putter, idle, mess around (*informal*), fiddle around (*informal*), footle (*informal*), futz (*informal*), lollygag (*dated*) [➡ LACK OF ACTIVITY OR MOTION; 342]

foolhardiness *n* recklessness, imprudence, stupidity, idiocy, foolishness, folly, silliness, madness, craziness (*informal*) [➡ NEGATIVE INTELLECTUAL CHARACTERISTICS; 525] *Opposite*: prudence

foolhardy *adj* reckless, rash, imprudent, foolish, unwise, irresponsible, risky, unsafe, mad, silly, stupid [➡ NEGATIVE INTELLECTUAL CHARACTERISTICS; 525] *Opposite*: sensible

foolish 1 *adj* stupid, silly, unwise, imprudent, thoughtless, irrational, rash, reckless. *Opposite*: wise [➡ NEGATIVE INTELLECTUAL CHARACTERISTICS; 525] 2 *adj* ridiculous, laughable, silly, ludicrous, absurd, risible (*formal*) [➡ FUNNY AND AMUSING; 216]

foolishness *n* irrationality, stupidity, idiocy, silliness, imprudence, thoughtlessness, folly, foolhardiness, recklessness, madness [➡ NEGATIVE INTELLECTUAL CHARACTERISTICS; 525] *Opposite*: wisdom

foolproof *adj* secure, safe, infallible, fail-safe, perfect, guaranteed, sure-fire (*informal*) [➡ SAFE AND SAFETY; 191] *Opposite*: risky

foot 1 *n* base, bottom, end [➡ EXTREMITIES OF PHYSICAL OBJECTS; 1250] *Opposite*: top 2 *n* [➡ PARTS OF THE BODY: LEG AND FOOT; 694] 3 *type of* nonmetric unit [➡ SIZE AND DIMENSIONS; 1192]

footage *n* film, shots, tape, videotape, material [➡ TELEVISION AND RADIO; 606]

football 1 *type of* ball game [➡ HOBBIES, GAMES, AND SPORTS; 875] 2 *type of* sports equipment [➡ SPORTS EQUIPMENT; 879] 3 *n* problem, matter, point, issue, hot potato, bone of contention [➡ PROBLEMS; 256]

footbridge *type of* bridge [➡ BRIDGES, TUNNELS, CROSSINGS, AND JUNCTIONS; 1112]

footer *n* addendum, title, footnote, note, text, gloss [➡ PARTS OF BOOKS AND DOCUMENTS; 593] *Opposite*: header

footfall *n* footstep, step, tread, pace, sound [➡ IMPACT SOUNDS; 1260]

foothill *n* hill, slope, base, foot, bottom, lower reach [➡ MOUNTAINS AND HILLS; 1044] *Opposite*: summit

foothold *n* position, base, purchase, grip, toehold, footing [➡ ADVANTAGES; 212]

footing 1 *n* stability, equilibrium, purchase, foothold, grip, balance [➡ ADVANTAGES; 212] 2 *n* basis, position, foundation, base, support, structure [➡ SUPPORTS AND BASES; 1255]

footle (*informal*) 1 *v* fool around, idle, putter, dawdle, fiddle around (*informal*), mess around (*informal*), futz (*informal*) [➡ LACK OF ACTIVITY OR MOTION; 342] 2 *v* chatter, prattle, blabber, blather (*informal*), blab (*informal*), gab (*informal*), gas (*informal*), natter (*informal*) [➡ CHATTER AND BABBLE; 617] 3 *n* nonsense, rubbish, prattle, balderdash, bunkum (*informal*), claptrap (*informal*), blather (*informal*), bunk (*slang*), poppycock (*dated informal*) [➡ MEANINGLESS SPEECH OR WRITING; 676]

footlights 1 *n* acting, the stage, the theater, the limelight [➡ IN THE THEATER; 906] 2 *type of* light [➡ LIGHT; 1164]

footling (*informal*) *adj* trivial, unimportant, insignificant, trifling, inconsequential, piddling (*informal*), piffling (*informal*) [➡ UNIMPORTANT AND UNNECESSARY; 238] *Opposite*: important

footloose *adj* free, unattached, uncommitted, unrestricted, single, unmarried [➡ PLEASURE-SEEKING AND EXCESS; 885]

footloose and fancy free *adj* [➡ MARITAL STATUS; 890]

footman *type of* servant [➡ DOMESTIC AND KITCHEN WORKERS; 850]

footnote *n* note, annotation, cross-reference, appendix, addendum, postscript, footer [➡ PARTS OF BOOKS AND DOCUMENTS; 593]

footpad *part of* spacecraft [➡ SPACE VEHICLES; 1063]

footpath *n* path, trail, track, causeway, towpath, walkway, boardwalk, bridle path, footway, bridleway (*UK*) [➡ PATHWAYS; 1110]

footprint *n* footmark, print, imprint, impression, outline, mark, trail, track, spoor [➡ EVIDENCE AND PROOF; 69]

footrest *n* rail, bar, stool, footstool, foot rail, support, ottoman [➡ FURNITURE; 858]

footsore *adj* tired, weary, exhausted, aching, sore [➡ TIRED, ASLEEP, AND UNCONSCIOUS; 738]

footstep *n* sound, step, tread, pace, footfall [➡ IMPACT SOUNDS; 1260]

footstool *n* footrest, stool, support, ottoman [➡ FURNITURE; 858]

footway *n* footpath, path, trail, track, causeway, boardwalk, bridle path, walkway, towpath, bridleway (*UK*) [➡ PATHWAYS; 1110]

footwear *n* [➡ GARMENTS AND OUTFITS; 865]

footwear

◆ *types of boots*
boot, bootee, cowboy boot, galoshes, gum boot, hiking boot, jackboot, mukluk, rubber, waders, walking boot

◆ *types of shoes*
ballet shoe, clog, espadrille, flip-flop (*informal*), moccasin, mule, oxford, platform, plimsoll, pump, sandal, shoe, slingback, slipper, sneaker, snowshoe, stiletto heel, thong, wedge heel, wingtip, zori

footwork *n* cunning, skill, negotiation, horse-trading, deviousness, maneuvering, politicking [➡ MALICIOUS ACTIONS OR BEHAVIOR; 296]

fop *n* peacock, narcissus, poseur, poser (*informal*), dandy (*dated*), popinjay (*dated*), beau (*archaic*) [➡ MALE PERSON; 934]

foppish *adj* **vain**, affected, preening, narcissistic, self-obsessed, decadent, dandyish (*dated*) [➡ WELL-GROOMED; 482]

for 1 *prep* **aimed at**, intended for, designed for, meant for, used for [➡ INTENTIONS AND PURPOSES; 772] **2** *prep* **in favor of**, in support of, pro [➡ LIKE, LOVE, VALUE, AND ENJOY; 578] *Opposite*: against

forage 1 *n* **food**, feed, fodder, silage [➡ ANIMAL FEED; 1168] **2** *n* **quest**, search, hunt, exploration, foray, sortie [➡ SEEK POSSESSION AND SEARCH; 456] **3** *v* **look for**, search, seek, scavenge, rummage, hunt [➡ SEEK POSSESSION AND SEARCH; 456]

for all *prep* **despite**, in spite of, for all that, notwithstanding (*formal*) [➡ ALTHOUGH, NEVERTHELESS, AND DESPITE; 169]

forasmuch as (*formal*) *conj* **since**, inasmuch as, in view of the fact that, because, on account of, whereas (*formal*) [➡ CAUSATION; 168]

for a start *adv* [➡ EXPRESSIONS INTRODUCING EXAMPLES; 64]

foray *n* **raid**, incursion, venture, sortie, expedition, attack, assault [➡ AGGRESSIVE EVENTS; 39]

forbear (*formal*) *v* **refrain**, restrain yourself, abstain, hold back, withhold [➡ NOT DO AND REFUSE TO DO; 274]

forbearance (*formal*) *n* **patience**, self-control, restraint, tolerance, moderation, leniency, mercy [➡ GENEROSITY AND KINDNESS; 495] *Opposite*: impatience

forbearing (*formal*) *adj* **patient**, long-suffering, forgiving, tolerant, lenient, merciful, moderate [➡ STRENGTH OF WILL; 501] *Opposite*: impatient

forbid *v* **prohibit**, ban, bar, prevent, outlaw, stop, hinder, inhibit [➡ REFUSE PERMISSION AND NOT ALLOW; 670] *Opposite*: allow

forbidden *adj* **prohibited**, banned, outlawed, illegal, illicit [➡ UNACCEPTABLE AND UNFORGIVABLE; 225] *Opposite*: permissible

forbidding 1 *adj* **hostile**, unfriendly, dark, grim, bleak, dismal, stern, gloomy, harsh, severe [➡ RUDE AND HOSTILE; 625] *Opposite*: welcoming **2** *adj* **uninviting**, unpleasant, dismal, depressing, bleak, grim, off-putting, inhospitable, unwelcoming [➡ EMOTIONALLY UNPLEASANT AND UPSETTING; 227] *Opposite*: hospitable **3** *adj* **threatening**, ominous, menacing, sinister, dangerous, alarming, frightening, ferocious, fierce, perilous, life-threatening, disturbing [➡ DANGEROUS; 236]

force 1 *n* **power**, strength, energy, might, vigor, potency, dynamism [➡ ENERGY; 1161] *Opposite*: weakness **2** *n* **influence**, weight, power, strength, intensity, cogency [➡ STRENGTH; 201] **3** *v* **compel**, oblige, make, impose, coerce, constrain, drive [➡ CAUSE OR COMPEL TO ACT; 271] **4** *v* **push**, shove, break down, break open, press, prize, pry [➡ CONTACT: EXERT PRESSURE; 414]

forced 1 *adj* **strained**, unnatural, affected, put on, artificial [➡ INARTICULATE, RAMBLING, AND AWKWARD; 633] *Opposite*: natural **2** *adj* **involuntary**, compulsory, required, obligatory, enforced, mandatory [➡ CAPTIVITY AND LOSS OF FREEDOM; 248] *Opposite*: voluntary

force-feed 1 *v* **fatten**, fatten up, feed, nourish, sustain, keep alive, feed up (*UK*) [➡ GIVE TOO MUCH AND OVERBURDEN; 437] **2** *v* **teach**, brainwash, program, ram down somebody's throat, cram [➡ INSTRUCT AND TEACH; 609]

forceful 1 *adj* **powerful**, vigorous, strong, dynamic, potent, influential, energetic, mighty [➡ STRENGTH; 201] *Oppo-*

site: **weak 2** *adj* **persuasive**, convincing, compelling, valid, powerful, influential, weighty, cogent, vehement [➡ STRENGTH; 201] *Opposite*: unconvincing

forcefulness 1 *n* **strength**, power, vigor, dynamism, influence, weight, powerfulness, potency [➡ STRENGTH; 201] *Opposite*: weakness **2** *n* **persuasiveness**, validity, cogency, powerfulness, power, weightiness, weight [➡ STRENGTH; 201]

force out *v* **drive out**, expel, turn out, oust, evict, throw out [➡ EJECT AND EXCLUDE; 340]

forceps *type of* **medical instrument** [➡ HAND TOOLS; 1119]

forces *n* **armed forces**, military, services, army, navy, air force, marines (*formal*) [➡ THE ARMED FORCES; 827]

forcible 1 *adj* **compulsory**, violent, aggressive, armed [➡ PHYSICALLY UNPLEASANT; 226] *Opposite*: peaceful **2** *adj* **effective**, forceful, powerful, convincing, persuasive, influential, weighty [➡ STRENGTH; 201] *Opposite*: weak

forcibly 1 *adv* **by force**, compulsorily, under duress, against your will, under protest [➡ WITHOUT ENTHUSIASM; 287] *Opposite*: peacefully **2** *adv* **powerfully**, effectively, convincingly, persuasively, influentially [➡ STRENGTH; 201] *Opposite*: weakly

ford 1 *n* **shallows**, crossing, passage, stepping stone [➡ BRIDGES, TUNNELS, CROSSINGS, AND JUNCTIONS; 1112] **2** *v* **cross**, traverse, negotiate, cross over, wade [➡ MOVE PAST, INTO, OR THROUGH SOMETHING; 331]

fore (*literary*) *n* **front**, forefront, forepart, bow, face, frontage, façade [➡ EXTREMITIES OF PHYSICAL OBJECTS; 1250] *Opposite*: back

fore-and-aft sail *part of* **sailing vessel** [➡ PARTS OF A SHIP OR BOAT; 1151]

forearm 1 *v* **prepare**, forewarn, tip off, prime, alert, give advance notice, give advance warning, warn [➡ ADVISE AND WARN; 613] **2** *part of* **arm or hand** [➡ PARTS OF THE BODY: ARM AND HAND; 695]

forebear 1 *n* [➡ OLDER GENERATION RELATIVES; 959] **2** *n* **ancestor**, forerunner, antecedent, predecessor, grandparent, forefather, precursor [➡ THE FAMILY; 956] *Opposite*: descendant

foreboding 1 *n* **premonition**, presentiment, feeling, fear, intuition, feeling in the bones [➡ FEELINGS ABOUT THE FUTURE; 533] **2** *adj* **ominous**, menacing, threatening, sinister, forbidding, dark [➡ DANGEROUS; 236] *Opposite*: encouraging

forecast 1 *v* **predict**, estimate, calculate, project, anticipate, foretell, guess, conjecture [➡ PREDICT AND ANTICIPATE; 750] **2** *n* **prediction**, estimate, guess, calculation, conjecture, projection, prognostication, prognosis, best guess [➡ PREDICT AND ANTICIPATE; 750]

forecaster *n* **forward planner**, interpreter, analyst, prophet [➡ PEOPLE INVOLVED IN FINANCE; 804]

foreclose (*formal*) *v* **exclude**, shut out, close out, ban, exile, bar [➡ MAKE IMPOSSIBLE; 276]

forecourt *n* **space**, area, courtyard, concourse, square, piazza, atrium [➡ URBAN OUTDOOR SPACES; 1072]

forefather *n* [➡ OLDER GENERATION RELATIVES; 959]

forefinger *part of* **arm or hand** [➡ PARTS OF THE BODY: ARM AND HAND; 695]

forefront 1 *n* **front**, head, vanguard, lead, van, leading edge, pole position [➡ BEGINNINGS; 53] *Opposite*: back 2 *n* **foreground**, forepart, front, frontage, face, façade, fore (*literary*) [➡ EXTREMITIES OF PHYSICAL OBJECTS; 1250] *Opposite*: background

forego 1 *v* (*formal*) **precede**, come first, go before, herald, pave the way, anticipate [➡ BEFORE, FIRST, AND PRECEDING; 163] 2 *see* **forgo**

foregoing *adj* **previous**, prior, preceding, earlier, former, above-mentioned, above [➡ BEFORE, FIRST, AND PRECEDING; 163]

foregone *adj* **inevitable**, predetermined, inescapable, unavoidable, fated, predictable, ordained (*formal*) [➡ CERTAIN; 174] *Opposite*: uncertain

foreground *n* **forefront**, front, center, center stage, focus, focal point, fore (*literary*) [➡ CENTRAL PARTS OF PHYSICAL OBJECTS; 1251] *Opposite*: background

foreign 1 *adj* **alien**, external, extraneous, imported, overseas, extraterritorial, transcontinental, distant, far-off, remote [➡ DISTANCE; 160] *Opposite*: indigenous 2 *adj* **strange**, unfamiliar, unknown, alien, exotic, outlandish [➡ EXTRAORDINARY: UNCOMMON; 205] *Opposite*: familiar 3 *adj* **unrelated**, extraneous, irrelevant, external, unconnected, irrelative [➡ UNRELATEDNESS AND SEPARATENESS; 146] *Opposite*: relevant

foreigner *n* **stranger**, foreign person, alien, immigrant, newcomer, outsider, refugee, nonnational [➡ STRANGERS; 912] *Opposite*: national

foreknowledge *n* **premonition**, prescience, feeling, foresight, intuition, intelligence [➡ FEELINGS ABOUT THE FUTURE; 533] *Opposite*: hindsight

foreleg 1 *n* **front leg**, forelimb, limb, leg, appendage [➡ PARTS OF THE BODY: LEG AND FOOT; 694] 2 *part of* **horse** [➡ HORSES; 985]

foremost *adj* **chief**, leading, primary, prime, notable, principal, main, top, important [➡ SUPERIORITY; 152]

forename *n* **first name**, given name, Christian name, nickname, pet name, middle name, moniker (*slang*) [➡ NAME AND DESCRIBE; 665] *Opposite*: surname

forerunner 1 *n* **portent**, indication, omen, sign, harbinger, foreshadowing, augury, precursor [➡ INDICATIONS, SIGNS, AND WARNINGS; 68] 2 *n* **forebear**, ancestor, antecedent, precursor, predecessor, forefather, grandparent [➡ OLDER GENERATION RELATIVES; 959]

foresee *v* **expect**, foretell, prophesy, divine, predict, forecast, anticipate, foreknow (*formal*) [➡ PREDICT AND ANTICIPATE; 750] *Opposite*: look back

foreseeable 1 *adj* **predictable**, probable, likely, imaginable, conceivable, calculable, estimative, anticipatable [➡ POSSIBLE AND PROBABLE; 177] *Opposite*: unforeseeable 2 *adj* **near**, immediate, imminent, prospective, impending, short-term [➡ FUTURE; 86] *Opposite*: far-off

foreshadow *v* **presage**, indicate, suggest, warn of, augur, prefigure, foretell, predict [➡ MEAN SOMETHING; 61]

foreshank *type of* **cut** [➡ TYPES AND CUTS OF MEAT; 1177]

foreshore *n* **shore**, beach, mudflat, sand, shingle, rocks, tidemark, high-water mark, low-water mark [➡ THE SEAS, OCEANS, AND SHORES; 1041]

foresight 1 *n* **forethought**, prudence, farsightedness, anticipation, sagacity, precaution [➡ PREDICT AND ANTICIPATE; 750] 2 *n* **premonition**, insight, prescience, intuition, foreknowledge, hindsight, prevision (*formal or literary*) [➡ POSITIVE INTELLECTUAL CHARACTERISTICS; 524]

forest *n* **woods**, woodland, forestry, plantation, jungle, timberland [➡ WOODS, FORESTS, AND JUNGLES; 1047]

forestall 1 *v* **prevent**, avert, preempt, obviate, hinder, thwart, block, preclude (*formal*) [➡ MAKE IMPOSSIBLE; 276]

forest fire *n* [➡ FIRE, FLAMMABILITY, AND BURNING; 1165]

forest green *type of* **green** [➡ COLORS; 1224]

foretaste *n* **sample**, token, indication, example, taste, preview, insight, taster (*UK*) [➡ INDICATIONS, SIGNS, AND WARNINGS; 68] *Opposite*: recollection

foretell (*literary*) *v* **predict**, prophesy, presage, portend, forecast, prognosticate, divine [➡ PREDICT AND ANTICIPATE; 750] *Opposite*: review

forethought *n* **anticipation**, consideration, foresight, prudence, planning, precaution, farsightedness, prevision (*formal or literary*) [➡ PREDICT AND ANTICIPATE; 750] *Opposite*: afterthought

forever 1 *adv* **eternally**, for all time, in perpetuity, indefinitely, ad infinitum, evermore (*literary*), forevermore (*literary*) [➡ PERMANENCE: WITHOUT END; 94] *Opposite*: momentarily 2 *adv* (*informal*) **incessantly**, persistently, repeatedly, continually, endlessly, constantly, always, at all times, ever [➡ PERMANENCE: WITHOUT END; 94] *Opposite*: never

forevermore (*literary*) *adv* **forever**, until the end of time, eternally, for all time, in perpetuity, indefinitely, ad infinitum, forever and ever, evermore (*literary*) [➡ PERMANENCE: WITHOUT END; 94]

forewarn *v* **warn**, caution, alert, tip off, put on the alert, prepare, prime [➡ ADVISE AND WARN; 613]

forewarning *n* **warning**, notice, notification, word of warning, signal, tip-off (*informal*) [➡ ADVICE; 689]

foreword *n* **preface**, introduction, prelude, preamble, prologue, overture [➡ PARTS OF BOOKS AND DOCUMENTS; 593] *Opposite*: conclusion

for example *adv* [➡ EXPRESSIONS INTRODUCING EXAMPLES; 64]

forfeit 1 *n* **penalty**, forfeiture, loss, penalization, punishment, fine [➡ NUISANCES; 253] 2 *v* **lose**, pay for, be deprived of, pay with, be stripped of [➡ LOSE AND FORFEIT; 447] 3 *v* **surrender**, sacrifice, give up, part with, go without, forgo [➡ FORGO AND DENY ONESELF; 449]

forfeiture *n* **penalty**, forfeit, loss, penalization, punishment, fine [➡ TRIAL, PUNISHMENT, AND LEGAL OUTCOMES; 819]

forge 1 *n* **furnace**, hearth, oven [➡ FIRE, FLAMMABILITY, AND BURNING; 1165] 2 *type of* **factory** [➡ INDUSTRIAL BUILDINGS; 1087] 3 *v* **shape**, form, build, create, fashion, construct, establish, make [➡ MANUFACTURE; 349] 4 *v* **counterfeit**, fake, falsify, copy, imitate, duplicate [➡ FALSIFY AND CHEAT; 176]

forge ahead *v* **take the lead**, come to the fore, make progress, make headway, move forward, plow on [➡ SUCCEED AND WIN; 79] *Opposite:* lag

forged *adj* **fake**, counterfeit, false, spurious, phony, specious, inauthentic, bogus [➡ FALSE AND UNREAL; 173] *Opposite:* genuine

forger *n* **counterfeiter**, falsifier, faker, coiner, imitator, copier, criminal, crook (*informal*) [➡ CRIMINALS; 821]

forgery *n* **fake**, counterfeit, sham, phony, imitation, falsification, copy [➡ CRIMES; 817] *Opposite:* original

forget 1 *v* **overlook**, disremember, fail to recall, be unable to remember, be unable to call to mind, be unable to summon up, be unable to picture [➡ FORGET, FORGIVE, AND ACCEPT; 748] *Opposite:* remember   2 *v* **stop thinking about**, put out of your mind, disregard, put behind you, turn your back on, erase from your mind, ignore, neglect, blank over [➡ NOT PAY ATTENTION; 764] *Opposite:* attend to

See Compare and Contrast at **neglect**.

forgetful 1 *adj* **absent-minded**, inclined to forget, vague, absent, oblivious, insensible, preoccupied, dreamy, scatterbrained [➡ NEGATIVE INTELLECTUAL CHARACTERISTICS; 525] *Opposite:* mindful   2 *adj* **inattentive**, neglectful, negligent, wandering, careless, unfocused [➡ NEGATIVE INTELLECTUAL CHARACTERISTICS; 525] *Opposite:* attentive

forgetfulness *n* **absent-mindedness**, amnesia, obliviousness, insensibleness, vagueness [➡ NEGATIVE INTELLECTUAL CHARACTERISTICS; 525]

forget-me-not *type of* **annual flower** [➡ FLOWERS; 1032]

forgettable *adj* **unmemorable**, unremarkable, undistinguished, mediocre, ordinary, uninteresting, boring [➡ ORDINARINESS; 244] *Opposite:* unforgettable

forgivable *adj* **pardonable**, excusable, allowable, defensible, justifiable, understandable [➡ ACCEPTABLE AND PASSABLE; 219] *Opposite:* unforgivable

forgive *v* **pardon**, excuse, forgive and forget, let off, absolve, exonerate [➡ FORGET, FORGIVE, AND ACCEPT; 748] *Opposite:* blame

forgiveness 1 *n* **pardon**, absolution, amnesty, exoneration, reconciliation, exculpation (*formal*) [➡ COMPASSION AND FORGIVENESS; 551] *Opposite:* blame   2 *n* **clemency**, pity, mercy, compassion, understanding, tolerance [➡ COMPASSION AND FORGIVENESS; 551] *Opposite:* ruthlessness

forgiving *adj* **merciful**, pardoning, lenient, magnanimous, sympathetic, compassionate, understanding, tolerant, forbearing (*formal*) [➡ GENEROSITY AND KINDNESS; 495] *Opposite:* unforgiving

forgo *v* **do without**, sacrifice, pass by, waive, relinquish, give up, abstain from, go without, decline, skip [➡ FORGO AND DENY ONESELF; 449] *Opposite:* take up

forgotten *adj* **lost**, gone, neglected, disregarded, buried, unremembered [➡ ABSENT AND UNAVAILABLE; 7] *Opposite:* immortal

for instance *adv* [➡ EXPRESSIONS INTRODUCING EXAMPLES; 64]

forint *type of* **currency** [➡ CURRENCIES; 798]

fork 1 *n* **divide**, split, divergence, junction, branch, cleft,

division, bifurcation [➡ HOLES, GAPS, AND FORKS; 1252]   2 *part of* **bike** [➡ BIKES, CARS, AND CARRIAGES; 1149]   3 *type of* **flatware** [➡ TABLEWARE, FLATWARE, AND KITCHENWARE; 861]

forked *adj* **split**, cleft, divided, branched, pronged, bifurcated [➡ ANGULAR SHAPE; 1217] *Opposite:* undivided

forked lightning (*UK*) *n* [➡ WINDY AND STORMY WEATHER; 1053]

fork out (*informal*) *v* [➡ GIVE MONEY; 433]

fork over (*informal*) *v* [➡ GIVE MONEY; 433]

fork up (*informal*) *v* [➡ GIVE MONEY; 433]

for life *adv* **for good**, forever, always, for keeps, permanently [➡ PERMANENCE: WITHOUT END; 94]

forlorn 1 *adj* **miserable**, sad, dejected, despondent, unhappy, hopeless, desperate [➡ SADNESS, DISTRESS, AND DESPAIR; 539] *Opposite:* cheerful   2 *adj* **desolate**, neglected, abandoned, lonely, lost, forsaken, deserted, pitiful [➡ SOLITARINESS; 941] *Opposite:* cherished

forlornly *adv* **miserably**, sadly, dejectedly, despondently, unhappily, hopelessly, desperately, desolately, pitifully [➡ SADNESS, DISTRESS, AND DESPAIR; 539] *Opposite:* cheerfully

form 1 *n* **structure**, state, condition, nature, status [➡ STATE; 1208]   2 *n* **procedure**, method, system, arrangement, formula, custom, usage, practice, ritual [➡ WAYS OF DOING THINGS; 294]   3 *n* **type**, variety, kind, mode, manner, style, way [➡ VARIETIES, TYPES, AND KINDS; 145]   4 *n* **shape**, configuration, appearance, outline, look [➡ SHAPE; 1216]   5 *n* **document**, paper, questionnaire, pro forma, blank, table, sheet [➡ OFFICIAL DOCUMENTS; 586]   6 *type of* **den or nest** [➡ ANIMAL OR BIRD ACCOMMODATIONS; 1079]   7 *v* **develop**, take shape, materialize, come into being, arise, grow [➡ GRADUALLY COME INTO EXISTENCE; 1]   8 *v* **fashion**, shape, mold, model, create, construct, develop, produce [➡ CREATION; 346]   9 *v* **start**, found, create, bring into being, establish, make, develop [➡ INSTITUTE AND INAUGURATE; 348]

formal 1 *adj* **conventional**, reserved, stiff, prim, starched, decorous, correct, smart [➡ LEVELS OF FORMALITY; 522] *Opposite:* relaxed   2 *adj* **official**, proper, prescribed, recognized, strict, ceremonial, correct [➡ LEVELS OF FORMALITY; 522] *Opposite:* informal

formal attire *n* [➡ GARMENTS AND OUTFITS; 865]

formality 1 *n* **conventionalism**, correctness, stiffness, primness, reserve, decorum, smartness [➡ LEVELS OF FORMALITY; 522] *Opposite:* informality   2 *n* **procedure**, requirement, regulation, custom, ritual, ceremony, form, rule [➡ WAYS OF DOING THINGS; 294]

formalization *n* **validation**, ratification, solemnization, reinforcement, celebration, enactment, sanctification [➡ APPROVE AND CONFIRM; 646]

formalize *v* **validate**, ratify, solemnize, reinforce, celebrate, enact, sanctify, honor [➡ APPROVE AND CONFIRM; 646]

formally *adv* **officially**, properly, lawfully, correctly, strictly, ceremoniously, legally [➡ LEVELS OF FORMALITY; 522] *Opposite:* informally

formal wear *n* [➡ GARMENTS AND OUTFITS; 865]

format 1 *n* **structure**, presentation, organization, arrangement, setup, plan, layout, design, system [➡ QUALITIES AND CHARACTERISTICS; 1191]   2 *v* **arrange**, lay out, organize, configure, set up, plan, structure, construct [➞ARRANGE AND CREATE ORDER; 357]

formation 1 *n* **creation**, development, construction, establishment, foundation, realization, materialization, growth, founding (*dated*) [➞CREATION; 346] **2** *n* **arrangement**, configuration, shape, structure, pattern, disposition, setup, organization [➞QUALITIES AND CHARACTERISTICS; 1191]

formative *adj* **influential**, determinative, seminal, decisive, developmental, creative, foundational, constructive [➞FUNDAMENTAL; 195]

formative years *n* **childhood**, early life, early years, early childhood, infancy, babyhood, immaturity, adolescence, youth [➞BABYHOOD, CHILDHOOD, AND ADOLESCENCE; 917] *Opposite*: maturity

former *adj* **previous**, past, ex-, earlier, prior, first, last, anterior [➞PAST; 84]

formerly *adv* **previously**, before, in the past, once, earlier, once upon a time, in earlier times [➞PAST; 84]

former times *n* [➞PAST; 84]

formidable 1 *adj* **difficult**, tough, daunting, arduous, challenging, forbidding, terrible [➞DIFFICULTY AND COMPLEXITY; 242] *Opposite*: easy **2** *adj* **awe-inspiring**, impressive, remarkable, astounding, awesome, amazing, admirable [➞EXTRAORDINARY: AMAZING; 204] *Opposite*: uninspiring **3** *adj* **alarming**, frightening, dreadful, fearsome, redoubtable, terrifying, intimidating [➞FRIGHTENING; 231] *Opposite*: encouraging

formidably 1 *adv* **dauntingly**, forbiddingly, horrendously, worryingly, disturbingly, fearfully, terribly, dreadfully [➞DIFFICULTY AND COMPLEXITY; 242] *Opposite*: wonderfully **2** *adv* **awesomely**, impressively, compellingly, overwhelmingly, wonderfully, admirably, inspiringly, convincingly [➞EXTRAORDINARY: AMAZING; 204] **3** *adv* **frighteningly**, redoubtably, terrifyingly, viciously, alarmingly, dauntingly, intimidatingly, fearsomely, dreadfully [➞FRIGHTENING; 231] *Opposite*: encouragingly

formless *adj* **shapeless**, amorphous, unformed, unshaped, unstructured, indistinct, unshapen, unrecognizable [➞SHAPELESSNESS; 1219] *Opposite*: distinct

formlessness *n* [➞SHAPELESSNESS; 1219]

formula 1 *n* **method**, plan, modus operandi, recipe, prescription, procedure, rule, blueprint, formulation, principle, formulary (*archaic*) [➞WAYS OF DOING THINGS; 294] **2** *n* **cliché**, stock phrase, expression, phrase, formulation [➞FIGURES OF SPEECH; 673]

formulaic 1 *adj* **prescribed**, standard, rigid, fixed, set, methodic, systematic [➞BORING AND UNINTERESTING; 234] **2** *adj* **unoriginal**, imitative, clichéd, overused, cookie-cutter, mechanical, automatic [➞ORDINARINESS; 244] *Opposite*: original

formulate 1 *v* **devise**, invent, prepare, put together, make, come up with, plan, create, originate [➞INSTITUTE AND INAUGURATE; 348] **2** *v* **express**, frame, put into words, verbalize, voice, articulate, communicate, convey, put across [➞UTTER AND PRONOUNCE; 608]

formulation 1 *n* **preparation**, design, construction, creation, invention, origination, interpretation, devising, drawing up, making [➞CREATION; 346] **2** *n* **expression**, articu-

lation, verbalization, communication, presentation, conveyance, utterance [➞EXPLAIN AND CLARIFY; 610]

Fornax *type of* **constellation** [➞HEAVENLY BODIES; 1061]

for nothing *adj* **free of charge**, for free, gratis, at no expense, toll-free, cost-free (*UK*) [➞GIFTS; 438]

for now *adv* **for the time being**, for the moment, in the interim, pro tem [➞PRESENT; 85] *Opposite*: always

forsake 1 *v* **abandon**, leave, disown, quit, desert, cast off, reject, ditch (*informal*) [➞RUN AWAY AND AVOID; 10] *Opposite*: support **2** *v* **renounce**, relinquish, give up, turn your back on, sacrifice, abstain from [➞FORGO AND DENY ONESELF; 449]

forsaken *adj* **abandoned**, cast off, discarded, deserted, jilted, left in the lurch, rejected, disowned, ditched (*informal*) [➞SOLITARINESS; 941] *Opposite*: supported

for sale *adj* **available**, on the market, on sale, purchasable [➞PRESENT AND AVAILABLE; 11]

for sure 1 *adv* (*informal*) **certainly**, of course, naturally, definitely, okay (*informal*) [➞CERTAIN; 174] **2** *adv* **definitely**, securely, positively, confidently, with certainty, with confidence, with assurance [➞EXPRESSIONS OF AGREEMENT; 648] *Opposite*: tentatively

forswear (*archaic or literary*) 1 *v* **reject**, renounce, abjure, give up, disown, dissociate from [➞FORGO AND DENY ONESELF; 449] *Opposite*: resort to **2** *v* **deny**, disavow, contradict, disclaim, swear, reject, gainsay (*formal*) [➞DENY AND REJECT; 644] *Opposite*: admit

forsythia *type of* **shrub or bush** [➞BUSHES AND SHRUBS; 1027]

fort *n* **fortification**, fortress, stronghold, citadel, castle, garrison, fastness [➞FORTRESSES AND FORTIFICATIONS; 1090]

forte 1 *n* **strong point**, specialty, strong suit, gift, strength, talent [➞SKILLS, TALENTS, AND ABILITIES; 526] *Opposite*: failing **2** *type of* **musical term** [➞MUSICAL TERMS; 912]

forth (*formal*) 1 *adv* **forward**, ahead, onward [➞DIRECTION OF MOTION; 345] *Opposite*: back **2** *adv* **out**, into view, into the open, into the world [➞DIRECTION OF MOTION; 345] *Opposite*: back

forthcoming 1 *adj* **approaching**, impending, imminent, upcoming, future, coming [➞FUTURE; 86] *Opposite*: distant **2** *adj* **available**, ready, offered, supplied, in the offing, there [➞PRESENT AND AVAILABLE; 11] *Opposite*: unavailable **3** *adj* **helpful**, open, obliging, cooperative, informative, communicative [➞THE WILL AND WILLINGNESS; 563] *Opposite*: reticent

for the meantime *adv* **meanwhile**, in the meantime, in the interim, in the intervening time, for now, for the time being, temporarily, for the moment [➞PRESENT; 85]

for the time being *adv* **for now**, for the moment, in the interim, pro tem [➞PRESENT; 85]

forthright *adj* **straightforward**, direct, frank, outspoken, plain-spoken, blunt, candid, honest, up-front (*informal*) [➞HONEST AND OPEN; 630] *Opposite*: timid

forthrightness *n* **frankness**, candor, directness, candidness, outspokenness, bluntness, honesty [➞HONEST AND OPEN; 630] *Opposite*: timidity

forthwith *adv* **immediately**, without delay, at once, directly, straightaway, instantly [➞PRESENT; 85] *Opposite*: later

fortification 1 *n* **strengthening**, reinforcement, defense, buttressing, building up [➡IMPROVE STRENGTH AND DURABILITY; 378] *Opposite*: erosion 2 *n* **ramparts**, defenses, buttresses, walls, ditches, protection [➡FORTRESSES AND FORTIFICATIONS; 1090]

fortified 1 *adj* **encouraged**, heartened, invigorated, reinvigorated, stimulated, refreshed, exhilarated, cheered, revived [➡COOL AND CALM; 536] *Opposite*: drained 2 *adj* **defended**, protected, walled, garrisoned, secured, safeguarded, armored [➡SAFE AND SAFETY; 191] *Opposite*: exposed 3 *adj* **reinforced**, strengthened, hardened, buttressed, toughened, supported, braced [➡STRENGTH; 201] *Opposite*: unsupported

fortify 1 *v* **make stronger**, strengthen, reinforce, brace, support, buttress, toughen, harden [➡IMPROVE STRENGTH AND DURABILITY; 378] *Opposite*: weaken 2 *v* **defend**, protect, wall, garrison, secure, safeguard [➡PREVENT CONTACT OR ATTACK; 419] *Opposite*: expose 3 *v* **give a boost to**, revive, refresh, reinvigorate, invigorate, exhilarate, hearten, cheer, encourage, pep up (*informal*) [➡ENCOURAGE; 576] *Opposite*: drain 4 *v* **build up**, boost, bolster, support, sustain, strengthen, augment (*formal*) [➡IMPROVE STRENGTH AND DURABILITY; 378] *Opposite*: weaken 5 *v* **enrich**, boost, enhance, improve, mix, lace [➡CHANGE OF INTENSITY: MORE; 394] *Opposite*: deplete

fortissimo *type of* **musical term** [➡MUSICAL TERMS; 912]

fortitude *n* **strength**, courage, resilience, staying power, grit, stamina, determination, endurance, guts (*slang*) [➡COURAGE; 498] *Opposite*: weakness

fortnightly *adv* [➡TIMES OF YEAR; 88]

fortress *n* **stronghold**, fort, citadel, fortification, bastion, castle [➡FORTRESSES AND FORTIFICATIONS; 1090]

fortuitous *adj* **accidental**, chance, casual, unexpected, unplanned, incidental [➡CHANCE, COINCIDENCE, AND ACCIDENT; 786] *Opposite*: planned

fortunate 1 *adj* **lucky**, providential, happy, opportune, auspicious, fortuitous [➡LUCK; 783] *Opposite*: unfortunate 2 *adj* **privileged**, lucky, blessed, well-off, prosperous [➡WEALTH AND WEALTHY; 891] *Opposite*: unfortunate

fortunately 1 *adv* **as luck would have it**, by chance, luckily, providentially, opportunely, auspiciously, fortuitously [➡LUCK; 783] *Opposite*: unfortunately 2 *adv* **happily**, luckily, mercifully, thank goodness, thank heavens [➡EXPRESSIONS OF SURPRISE AND PLEASURE; 546] *Opposite*: unfortunately

fortune 1 *n* **wealth**, riches, affluence, opulence, prosperity, treasure [➡FINANCIAL ASSETS; 462] *Opposite*: poverty 2 *n* **luck**, chance, providence, accident, fate [➡LUCK; 783] *Opposite*: design 3 *n* **destiny**, fate, kismet, karma, future, lot [➡FATE, DESTINY, AND ASTROLOGY; 782] *Opposite*: past 4 *n* **mint** (*informal*), pile (*informal*), tidy sum (*informal*), an arm and a leg (*informal*) [➡LARGE AMOUNTS OF MONEY; 118] *Opposite*: pittance

fortune-teller *n* **clairvoyant**, seer, soothsayer, psychic, medium, astrologer, mystic [➡PEOPLE WITH SUPERNATURAL POWERS; 788]

fortune-telling *n* [➡THE SUPERNATURAL; 787]

forty winks (*informal*) *n* **nap**, doze, sleep, siesta, catnap, power nap, snooze (*informal*) [➡SLEEP AND DREAM; 723]

forum 1 *n* **opportunity**, medium, environment, setting, scene, aid [➡SITUATIONS; 71] 2 *n* **meeting**, debate, discussion, conference, assembly, roundtable, council [➡MEETINGS AND ASSEMBLIES; 43]

forward 1 *adv* **onward**, ahead, frontward, up, to the fore [➡DIRECTION OF MOTION; 345] *Opposite*: backward 2 *adv* **to the fore**, into view, into the open, up [➡DIRECTION OF MOTION; 345] *Opposite*: back 3 *adj* **onward**, advancing, frontward, headlong, headfirst, accelerative [➡DIRECTION OF MOTION; 345] *Opposite*: backward 4 *adj* **presumptuous**, self-assured, bold, familiar, brazen, uninhibited, forthright, direct, overfriendly, cheeky (*informal*) [➡POMPOUS, LOUD, AND OVERCONFIDENT; 635] *Opposite*: reticent 5 *v* **advance**, promote, further, accelerate, progress [➡CAUSE TO HAPPEN; 31] *Opposite*: hold back 6 *v* **send**, dispatch, mail, pass on, redirect, post (*UK*), send on (*UK*) [➡DISPATCH AND SEND; 333]

forward-looking *adj* **progressive**, modern, forward-thinking, avant-garde, open-minded, revolutionary [➡THE NATURE OF IDEAS; 771] *Opposite*: backward-looking

forwardness *n* **boldness**, directness, brazenness, forthrightness, self-assurance, presumptuousness, overfriendliness, informality, cheek (*informal*) [➡POMPOUS, LOUD, AND OVERCONFIDENT; 635] *Opposite*: reticence

forward-thinking *adj* **progressive**, advanced, modern, forward-looking, radical, avant-garde, revolutionary, cutting-edge [➡POSITIVE INTELLECTUAL CHARACTERISTICS; 524] *Opposite*: old-fashioned

fosse *n* [➡WATERCOURSES; 1111]

fossil *n* **relic**, remnant, vestige, remains [➡REMAINDER AND REMAINDERS; 125]

fossilization *n* **petrification**, preservation, calcification, hardening, solidification, ossification, turning into stone [➡HARDEN, CONGEAL, AND DRY; 387]

fossilize *v* **turn into stone**, petrify, solidify, harden, calcify, ossify [➡HARDEN, CONGEAL, AND DRY; 387]

foster 1 *v* **look after**, care for, take in, bring up, nurture, raise, adopt [➡TAKE CARE OF AND SPOIL; 300] 2 *v* **promote**, further, advance, cultivate, forward, encourage [➡MAKE POSSIBLE; 275] *Opposite*: discourage 3 *adj* **stand-in**, substitute, adoptive, temporary, short-term [➡RELATIONSHIP TO ANOTHER; 973] *Opposite*: natural

foster child *n* **child**, dependant, adoptee, ward [➡ADOPTION, FOSTERING, AND EXTENDED FAMILY; 962] *Opposite*: foster parent

foster father *n* [➡ADOPTION, FOSTERING, AND EXTENDED FAMILY; 962]

foster mother *n* [➡ADOPTION, FOSTERING, AND EXTENDED FAMILY; 962]

foster parent *n* **guardian**, substitute parent, foster father, foster mother, carer (*UK*) [➡ADOPTION, FOSTERING, AND EXTENDED FAMILY; 962] *Opposite*: foster child

foul 1 *adj* **unpleasant**, disgusting, offensive, distasteful, filthy, indecent, dirty [➡DISGUSTING AND REPULSIVE; 230] *Opposite*: pleasant 2 *adj* (*informal*) **horrible**, rotten, unpleasant, nasty, dreadful, frightful, abominable [➡EMOTIONALLY UNPLEASANT AND UPSETTING; 227] *Opposite*: charming 3 *adj* **vulgar**, obscene, lewd, uncouth, unwholesome, coarse, filthy, indecent, profane (*formal*) [➡MORALLY BAD OR IMPROPER; 775] *Opposite*: decent 4 *adj* **inclement**, stormy, wet, unpleasant, rotten, dreadful, frightful [➡CLOUDY AND RAINY WEATHER; 1052] *Opposite*: fair 5 *adj* **unclean**, stinking, polluted, tainted, soiled, fetid, rank (*literary*) [➡ DIRTY; 1235] *Opposite*: clean **6** *adj* **dishonest**, shady, criminal, treacherous, dishonorable, crooked (*informal*) [➡ MORALLY BAD OR IMPROPER; 775] *Opposite*: legitimate **7** *v* **entangle**, tangle up, catch, ensnarl, snarl, ensnare [➡ CAPTIVITY AND LOSS OF FREEDOM; 248] *Opposite*: free **8** *v* **pollute**, soil, make dirty, contaminate, taint, mess up (*informal*), defile (*formal*), sully (*literary*) [➡ DIRTY AND CONTAMINATE; 404]

foully *adv* **offensively**, obscenely, disgustingly, repugnantly, revoltingly, unpleasantly, grossly, abhorrently (*formal*) [➡ DISGUSTING AND REPULSIVE; 230] *Opposite*: delightfully

foul-mouthed *adj* **blasphemous**, crude, rude, dirty, vulgar, coarse [➡ BAD MANNERS AND SOCIAL SKILLS; 521] *Opposite*: polite

foulness **1** *n* **filth**, filthiness, squalor, pollution, dirt, mire, uncleanness, vileness, murkiness, dirtiness, muckiness (*informal*), muck (*informal*) [➡ DIRTY; 1235] *Opposite*: cleanness **2** *n* **vulgarity**, obscenity, lewdness, profanity, uncouthness, unwholesomeness, coarseness, filth, indecency [➡ MORALLY BAD OR IMPROPER; 775] *Opposite*: decency

foul play **1** *n* **criminal action**, treachery, dishonesty, villainy, violence, crime, treacherousness [➡ MORALLY BAD OR IMPROPER; 775] *Opposite*: honesty **2** *n* **deviousness**, unfairness, cheating, trickery, monkey business (*informal*), shenanigans (*informal*) [➡ MALICIOUS ACTIONS OR BEHAVIOR; 296]

foul-smelling *adj* **smelly**, reeking, malodorous, fetid, rotten, putrid, nauseating, sour, rancid, rank (*literary*) [➡ SMELL AND SMELLING; 705] *Opposite*: sweet-smelling

foul-tasting *adj* **nasty**, disgusting, unpleasant, indigestible, revolting, nauseating, unpalatable, rancid, bitter, sour [➡ TASTE; 703]

foul up (*informal*) *v* [➡ MESS UP AND MAKE MISTAKES; 472]

foul-up (*informal*) *n* **blunder**, slip, mix-up, error, mistake, mishap, bungle (*informal*), slip-up (*informal*) [➡ MISTAKES; 250] *Opposite*: success

found *v* **originate**, set up, create, start, bring into being, initiate, institute, establish [➡ INSTITUTE AND INAUGURATE; 348] *Opposite*: close

foundation **1** *n* **basis**, grounds, substance, groundwork, underpinning, footing [➡ SUPPORTS AND BASES; 1255] **2** *n* **establishment**, institution, charity, institute, society, organization [➡ INSTITUTIONS; 790]

foundation garment *type of* **lower body underwear** [➡ ACCESSORIES, MILLINERY, AND LINGERIE; 867]

founder **1** *n* **creator**, originator, initiator, organizer, forefather, author [➡ DESIGNERS, CREATORS, AND INSTIGATORS; 347] **2** *v* **sink**, go down, plunge, wallow, submerge, wreck [➡ TAKE UP A NEW POSITION; 312] *Opposite*: float **3** *v* **fail**, break down, come to nothing, fall through, miscarry, misfire, come to grief [➡ FAIL OR BE UNSUCCESSFUL; 75] *Opposite*: succeed

foundling (*dated*) *n* **orphan**, waif, stray, urchin, outcast, ragamuffin (*dated*) [➡ SOLITARY PEOPLE AND MISFITS; 942]

foundry *type of* **factory** [➡ INDUSTRIAL BUILDINGS; 1087]

fount (*literary*) *n* **source**, fountain, well, spring, wellspring, fountainhead, origin [➡ RIVERS, LAKES, AND STREAMS; 1042]

fountain **1** *n* **cascade**, water feature, spout, jet, spring,

source, spray [➡ RIVERS, LAKES, AND STREAMS; 1042] **2** *n* **source**, origin, cause, beginning, fountainhead, fount [➡ BEGINNINGS; 53]

fountainhead **1** *n* **source**, origin, fount, seed, nucleus [➡ BEGINNINGS; 53] **2** *n* **spring**, source, wellspring, wellhead, fount, fountain [➡ RIVERS, LAKES, AND STREAMS; 1042]

fountain pen *type of* **pen** [➡ WRITING AND DRAWING IMPLEMENTS, AND MEDIA; 601]

four-by-four *type of* **car** [➡ BIKES, CARS, AND CARRIAGES; 1149]

four-letter word *n* **swearword**, vulgarity, vulgarism, obscenity, expletive, oath, curse, cussword (*informal*) [➡ INSULTS, ABUSE, AND SWEARING; 658] *Opposite*: euphemism

four-poster *type of* **bed** [➡ FURNITURE; 858]

foursome *n* **group of four**, quartet, group, ensemble [➡ GROUPS OF PEOPLE; 935]

fourth *n* **quarter**, twenty-five percent, fourth part [➡ MEASURABLE PORTIONS; 127]

fowl *n* [➡ LIVING THINGS AND LIVING; 976]

fowl

◆ *types of fowl*
bantam, broiler, chicken, duck, goose, grouse, guinea fowl, partridge, pheasant, pigeon, quail, turkey, waterfowl, wildfowl, woodcock

fox **1** *type of* **canine** [➡ CANINES; 979] **2** *v* **deceive**, trick, outwit, fool, con, hoodwink, bamboozle (*informal*) [➡ DECEPTION AND LIES; 660] **3** *v* **confuse**, baffle, muddle, puzzle, perplex, stump, flummox (*informal*) [➡ CONFUSE AND BEWILDER; 571] *Opposite*: enlighten

foxglove *type of* **perennial flower** [➡ FLOWERS; 1032]

foxhound *type of* **small dog** [➡ DOGS; 980]

fox terrier *type of* **small dog** [➡ DOGS; 980]

foxtrot *type of* **dance** [➡ DANCE; 903]

foxy **1** *adj* **sly**, cunning, crafty, sharp, wily, astute, shrewd, tricky [➡ DECEITFUL; 513] *Opposite*: naive **2** *adj* **foxlike**, vulpine, canine, pungent, strong, sharp [➡ SMELL AND SMELLING; 705]

foyer **1** *n* **lobby**, vestibule, reception area, hall, entrance hall, hallway [➡ DOORS AND ACCESS POINTS; 1101] **2** *type of* **room in public buildings** [➡ TYPES OF ROOMS; 1097]

FPU *type of* **hardware** [➡ COMPUTERS AND COMPUTING; 1127]

fracas *n* **quarrel**, row, fight, brawl, melee, argument, disturbance, scuffle [➡ CHAOS AND UPROAR; 51] *Opposite*: calm

fraction **1** *n* **little bit**, little, small part, tiny proportion, small percentage [➡ SMALL PIECES; 129] **2** *n* **part**, portion, segment, section, division, element [➡ MEASURABLE PORTIONS; 127] *Opposite*: whole

fractional *adj* **slight**, small, tiny, minuscule, insignificant, paltry [➡ SMALL; 1195] *Opposite*: great

fractionally *adv* **slightly**, marginally, just, a little, a fraction [➡ TO A CERTAIN EXTENT; 136] *Opposite*: greatly

fractious *adj* **irritable**, peevish, restless, complaining, grumpy, touchy, testy (*informal*) [➡ IRRITATION AND ANGER; 541] *Opposite*: even-tempered

fracture 1 *n* **break**, breakage, crack, rupture, fissure, hairline fracture, splintering [➡ HOLES, GAPS, AND FORKS; 1252] *Opposite*: repair 2 *v* **crack**, break, rupture, splinter, split, shatter [➡ TEAR, BREAK, AND CUT; 360] *Opposite*: mend

fractured *adj* [➡ IN BAD REPAIR; 1234]

fragile 1 *adj* **delicate**, brittle, flimsy, breakable, frail, insubstantial, frangible, friable [➡ FRAGILE; 1209] *Opposite*: sturdy 2 *adj* **tenuous**, unstable, delicate, precarious, shaky, slight [➡ WEAKNESS; 241] *Opposite*: stable 3 *adj* **frail**, weak, delicate, infirm, feeble, in poor health [➡ UNFIT AND WEAK; 739] *Opposite*: strong

---

Compare and Contrast: *fragile, delicate, frail, flimsy, frangible, friable*

CORE MEANING: easily broken or damaged

fragile not having a strong structure or not made of robust materials, and therefore easily broken or damaged; *delicate* similar to *fragile*, used especially to talk about things that are beautiful or remarkable because of their fragility; *frail* easily broken or damaged, or physically weak and vulnerable to injury; *flimsy* too easily broken, torn, or damaged, especially used of badly or cheaply made goods, or of light and insubstantial clothing; *frangible* capable of being broken or easily damaged; *friable* easily reduced to tiny particles.

---

fragility 1 *n* **brittleness**, flimsiness, delicateness, delicacy, breakability, friability, crumbliness, insubstantiality [➡ FRAGILE; 1209] *Opposite*: solidity 2 *n* **tenuousness**, instability, delicacy, delicateness, precariousness, shakiness [➡ UNCERTAIN; 175] *Opposite*: stability 3 *n* **frailty**, weakness, feebleness, ill health, infirmity [➡ UNFIT AND WEAK; 739] *Opposite*: strength

fragment 1 *n* **piece**, portion, bit, splinter, sliver, section, part, chip, scrap [➡ SMALL PIECES; 129] *Opposite*: whole 2 *v* **break**, divide, break up, disintegrate, crumble, shatter, fall to pieces, split, fall apart, destroy [➡ TEAR, BREAK, AND CUT; 360] *Opposite*: fuse

fragmentary *adj* **incomplete**, disconnected, scrappy, patchy, fragmented, bitty (*UK*) [➡ UNFINISHEDNESS; 239] *Opposite*: entire

fragmentation *n* **disintegration**, destruction, shattering, breaking up, crumbling, division [➡ TEAR, BREAK, AND CUT; 360] *Opposite*: fusion

fragmented *adj* **disjointed**, uneven, scrappy, patchy, bitty (*UK*) [➡ UNFINISHEDNESS; 239] *Opposite*: continuous

fragrance 1 *n* **smell**, scent, perfume, bouquet, aroma, odor [➡ SMELL AND SMELLING; 705] 2 *n* **cologne**, scent, perfume, toilet water, eau de toilette, attar [➡ PERSONAL HYGIENE; 491]

See Compare and Contrast at **smell**.

---

fragranced *adj* **perfumed**, scented, sweet-smelling, fragrant [➡ SMELL AND SMELLING; 705]

fragrant *adj* **perfumed**, aromatic, scented, sweet-

smelling, fragranced, odorous [➡ SMELL AND SMELLING; 705] *Opposite*: smelly

fraidy-cat (*informal*) *n* [➡ LAZY OR UNSUCCESSFUL PEOPLE; 948]

frail 1 *adj* **weak**, infirm, delicate, feeble, puny, in poor health, fragile [➡ UNFIT AND WEAK; 739] *Opposite*: robust 2 *adj* **flimsy**, insubstantial, fragile, delicate, spindly, brittle [➡ WEAKNESS; 241] *Opposite*: sturdy

---

See Compare and Contrast at **fragile, weak**.

---

frailness *see* **frailty**

frailty 1 *n* **infirmity**, weakness, feebleness, fragility, ill health, frailness [➡ UNFIT AND WEAK; 739] *Opposite*: robustness 2 *n* **shortcoming**, weakness, imperfection, failing, defect, flaw, vice [➡ FAULTS, FLAWS, AND WEAKNESSES; 251] *Opposite*: strength

frame 1 *n* **structure**, framework, scaffold, skeleton, support, construction [➡ PARTS OF A BUILDING; 1095] 2 *n* **edge**, surround, border, mount, setting, edging [➡ EXTREMITIES OF PHYSICAL OBJECTS; 1250] 3 *n* **body**, form, build, physique, skeleton, structure [➡ THE BONES AND JOINTS; 719] 4 *part of* **bike** [➡ BIKES, CARS, AND CARRIAGES; 1149] 5 *v* **enclose**, mount, border, edge, outline, surround [➡ EXIST IN CLOSE PROXIMITY; 21] *Opposite*: inset 6 *v* (*slang*) **trap**, entrap, trick, entice, set up (*informal*) [➡ FALSIFY AND CHEAT; 176]

frame of mind *n* **mood**, mental state, mental condition, humor, temper, disposition [➡ PSYCHOLOGY AND THE MIND; 769]

frame of reference *n* **context**, situation, standpoint, background, setting, belief system [➡ POINTS OF VIEW; 767]

frame-up (*slang*) *n* **trap**, entrapment, snare, setup (*informal*), sting (*slang*) [➡ DECEPTION AND LIES; 660]

framework 1 *n* **structure**, frame, scaffold, skeleton, support, construction [➡ QUALITIES AND CHARACTERISTICS; 1191] 2 *n* **outline**, agenda, basis, context, background, charter, structure [➡ WAYS OF DOING THINGS; 294]

franc *type of* **currency** [➡ CURRENCIES; 798]

franchise 1 *n* **permit**, contract, authorization, charter, agreement, license [➡ PERMIT AND ALLOW; 669] 2 *v* **license**, permit, contract, contract out, grant, authorize [➡ PERMIT AND ALLOW; 669]

frangible *adj* **breakable**, fragile, brittle, easily broken [➡ FRAGILE; 1209]

See Compare and Contrast at **fragile**.

---

frank *adj* **forthright**, free, honest, guileless, open, blunt, truthful, candid, aboveboard, outspoken [➡ HONEST AND OPEN; 630] *Opposite*: insincere

frankfurter *n* **hot dog**, sausage, wiener, wienerwurst, frank (*informal*) [➡ TYPES AND CUTS OF MEAT; 1177]

frankness *n* **honesty**, forthrightness, openness, bluntness, truthfulness, guilelessness, outspokenness, candor [➡ HONEST AND RELIABLE; 502] *Opposite*: insincerity

frantic 1 *adj* **panicky**, hysterical, beside yourself, desperate, agitated, wild, worried, anxious, uptight (*informal*) [➡ CONFUSION, ANXIETY, AND WORRY; 540] *Opposite*: calm 2 *adj* **frenzied**, frenetic, hectic, feverish, wild, last-minute [➡ DISORDER AND CHAOS; 245] *Opposite*: calm

frappe n [➡DRINKS; 1187]

frappé n [➡DRINKS; 1187]

fraternal 1 adj **sibling**, brotherly, brother's, familial, genealogical [➡THE FAMILY; 956] 2 adj **comradely**, brotherly, friendly, amicable, communal, amiable [➡FRIENDLINESS AND SOCIABILITY; 494] Opposite: hostile

fraternity 1 n **society**, frat, group, guild, association, gang, clan (informal) [➡STUDENTS AND PUPILS; 841] 2 n **community**, network, group, world, clan (informal) [➡GROUPS WITH A COMMON INTEREST; 938] 3 n **brotherliness**, brotherhood, comradeship, mutual support, friendship, friendliness [➡FRIENDLINESS AND SOCIABILITY; 494] Opposite: hostility

fraternization n **mixing**, socializing, intercourse, mingling, partying, collaborating, involvement, relations [➡COMMUNICATION; 602] Opposite: avoidance

fraternize v **associate**, socialize, mix, hobnob, hang out (informal), go around with (informal), consort (formal) [➡ESTABLISHING RELATIONSHIPS WITH OTHERS; 974] Opposite: avoid

fraud 1 n **deception**, con, scheme, swindle, deceit, fake, racket, counterfeit, imitation, sham, wooden nickel, scam (slang) [➡CRIMES; 817] 2 n **dishonesty**, deceit, deception, double-dealing, trickery, cheating, snake oil, smoke and mirrors [➡DECEPTION AND LIES; 660] Opposite: honesty 3 n **impostor**, charlatan, hoaxer, swindler, cheat, fake, sham, phony, fraudster [➡PEOPLE WHO DECEIVE; 661]

fraud squad n [➡THE POLICE, ARREST, AND PRETRIAL PROCEEDINGS; 818]

fraudster (UK) n **swindler**, cheat, hoaxer, charlatan, impostor, fraud, fake, sham, phony, confidence trickster (UK) [➡PEOPLE WHO DECEIVE; 661]

fraudulence n **deceit**, duplicity, deceitfulness, illegitimacy, dishonesty, deception, illegality, imposture (formal) [➡DECEPTION AND LIES; 660] Opposite: honesty

fraudulent adj **fake**, deceitful, untrue, duplicitous, dishonest, sham, false, falsified, counterfeit, imitation, illegal [➡FALSE AND UNREAL; 173] Opposite: genuine

fraught 1 adj **full**, charged, filled, weighed down, laden, beset (formal) [➡FULL; 1239] Opposite: free 2 adj **tense**, anxious, nervous, troubled, apprehensive, uptight (informal) [➡CONFUSION, ANXIETY, AND WORRY; 540] Opposite: calm

fray 1 v **unravel**, ravel, wear, wear out, tatter, distress [➡TEAR, BREAK, AND CUT; 360] Opposite: mend 2 n **fight**, argument, quarrel, fracas, dispute, disagreement, affray [➡AGGRESSIVE EVENTS; 39]

frayed adj **threadbare**, worn, tattered, ragged, unraveled, distressed [➡IN BAD REPAIR; 1234]

frazzled (informal) adj **exhausted**, weary, tired out, drained, fatigued, stressed out (informal) [➡TIRED, ASLEEP, AND UNCONSCIOUS; 738] Opposite: lively

freak 1 n **curiosity**, rarity, oddity, aberration, anomaly, one-off (UK) [➡MISTAKES; 250] 2 n **chance**, surprise, happenstance, accident, fluke (informal), one-off (UK) [➡CHANCE EVENTS; 36] 3 n (informal) **enthusiast**, fanatic, fiend, buff, lover, nut (informal) [➡DEVOTEES AND ADDICTED PEOPLE; 556]

freakish adj **variable**, volatile, changeable, unpredictable, inexplicable, mercurial [➡FINITENESS, VARIABILITY, AND TRANSIENCE; 96] Opposite: stable

freaky adj **weird**, strange, amazing, grotesque, unexpected, unusual, odd, unnatural, abnormal, bizarre, chance [➡BIZARRE AND PECULIAR; 257] Opposite: commonplace

freckle n **spot**, mark, patch, speckle, speck, blotch, mole [➡COMPLEXION; 480]

freckled adj **speckled**, freckly, dappled, spotted, stippled, dotted, flecked [➡COMPLEXION; 480]

freckly adj [➡COMPLEXION; 480]

free 1 adj **liberated**, unbound, released, emancipated, freed, set free [➡FREEDOM AND LIBERTY; 208] Opposite: imprisoned 2 adj **allowed**, at liberty, permitted, able, welcome, unrestricted [➡FREEDOM AND LIBERTY; 208] Opposite: restricted 3 adj **open**, uninhibited, uncontrolled, spontaneous, honest, expansive [➡HONEST AND OPEN; 630] Opposite: inhibited 4 adj **unrestricted**, unregimented, unconventional, loose, unstructured, open [➡FREEDOM AND LIBERTY; 208] Opposite: conventional 5 adj **relaxing**, off, available, unoccupied, on vacation, on holiday (UK) [➡FREEDOM AND LIBERTY; 208] Opposite: working 6 adj **gratis**, free of charge, without charge, at no cost, complimentary, on the house [➡GIFTS; 438] Opposite: expensive 7 v **release**, let go, set free, liberate, emancipate, deliver (literary) [➡FREEDOM AND LIBERTY; 208] Opposite: imprison 8 v **exempt**, rid, unburden, excuse, pardon, let off [➡FREEDOM AND LIBERTY; 208] Opposite: hamper

free-and-easy adj **indulgent**, overindulgent, lax, overfamiliar, relaxed, laid-back (informal) [➡COOL AND CALM; 536] Opposite: uptight (informal)

freebie (informal) n **free sample**, handout, perk, free gift, free offer, free go, giveaway (informal) [➡GIFTS; 438]

freedom 1 n **liberty**, autonomy, lack of restrictions, self-determination, independence, choice, free will, sovereignty [➡FREEDOM AND LIBERTY; 208] Opposite: restriction 2 n **frankness**, openness, abandon, free expression, ease, candor [➡HONEST AND OPEN; 630] Opposite: inhibition 3 n **looseness**, inventiveness, nonconformity [➡REBELLIOUSNESS AND DISOBEDIENCE; 565] Opposite: conformity

free enterprise economy type of **economic system** [➡FINANCE AND ECONOMICS; 796]

free fall 1 n **skydive**, jump, descent, drop, fall, dive [➡GO DOWNWARD; 307] 2 n **decline**, descent, collapse, confusion, turmoil, chaos [➡FAILURE; 77] Opposite: upturn

free-fall 1 v **skydive**, drop, plummet, fall, descend, jump, parachute, dive [➡GO DOWNWARD; 307] Opposite: soar 2 v **drop**, plummet, collapse, decline, fall apart, self-destruct, bomb (informal) [➡FAIL OR BE UNSUCCESSFUL; 75]

free-for-all (informal) n **brawl**, fight, brouhaha, riot, scuffle, fracas, commotion, set-to (informal) [➡CHAOS AND UPROAR; 51]

free gift n **free sample**, free offer, giveaway (informal), freebie (informal) [➡GIFTS; 438]

freehand adj **without a pattern**, by eye, by hand, untraced, sketchy, free [➡ARTISTIC MOVEMENTS AND STYLES; 899]

freehanded adj **generous**, openhanded, unstinting, giving, liberal, bountiful (literary) [➡GENEROSITY AND KINDNESS; 495] Opposite: stingy

freehold 1 n **tenure**, ownership, right, occupancy [➡ACCOM-

MODATIONS; 855] **2** *n* **property**, estate, land, building, holding [➡ POSSESSIONS; 461]

freeholder *n* **property owner**, landowner, owner, holder, landlord, landholder [➡ OWNERS; 446]

freeing *n* **release**, liberation, acquittal, emancipation, freedom, deliverance (*formal*) [➡ FREEDOM AND LIBERTY; 208] *Opposite*: capture

freelance *adj* **self-employed**, temporary, irregular, casual, ad hoc [➡ EMPLOYMENT STATUS; 831] *Opposite*: permanent

freelancer *n* [➡ WORKERS; 836]

freelancing *n* [➡ TYPES OF WORK; 835]

freeload (*informal*) *v* **sponge**, live off others, parasitize, take advantage, use others, scrounge (*informal*) [➡ TAKE SOMETHING AWAY; 425]

freeloader (*informal*) *n* **slacker**, sponge, parasite, idler, hanger-on, user, sponger (*informal*), scrounger (*informal*) [➡ LAZY OR UNSUCCESSFUL PEOPLE; 948]

freely **1** *adv* **liberally**, generously, unreservedly, without restraint, without stinting, to all comers [➡ FREEDOM AND LIBERTY; 208] *Opposite*: parsimoniously **2** *adv* **without restrictions**, at will, at liberty, easily, spontaneously, without obstruction [➡ FREEDOM AND LIBERTY; 208]

free market economy *type of* **economic system** [➡ FINANCE AND ECONOMICS; 796]

free of charge *adj* **gratis**, free, without charge, at no cost, complimentary, on the house, toll-free, cost-free (*UK*) [➡ GIFTS; 438]

free-range *adj* **unconfined**, happy, free, loose, at large, uncaged, unrestricted, at liberty [➡ FREEDOM AND LIBERTY; 208] *Opposite*: battery

freesia *type of* **flower grown from bulbs** [➡ FLOWERS FROM BULBS; 1030]

free spirit *n* **individualist**, nonconformist, maverick, freethinker, rebel [➡ UNCOOPERATIVE OR REBELLIOUS PEOPLE; 566] *Opposite*: conformist

freestanding *adj* **self-supporting**, unconnected, separate, detached, unattached, isolated [➡ UNRELATEDNESS AND SEPARATENESS; 146] *Opposite*: attached

freethinker *n* **individualist**, free spirit, nonconformist, nonbeliever, skeptic, rationalist [➡ UNCOOPERATIVE OR REBELLIOUS PEOPLE; 566] *Opposite*: conformist

freethinking *adj* **independent**, open-minded, enlightened, nonconformist, liberal, unconventional, radical, individualistic, rational, tolerant [➡ POSITIVE INTELLECTUAL CHARACTERISTICS; 524] *Opposite*: conformist

free time *n* **leisure**, leisure time, spare time, time off, recreation, rest time [➡ PERIODS OF REST; 91]

free up **1** *v* **make available**, empty, make space for, clear, liberate [➡ EMPTY AND UNLOAD; 407] *Opposite*: occupy **2** *v* (*informal*) **loosen**, unjam, unblock, unsnarl, unclog, clear [➡ UNFASTEN AND UNDO; 409] *Opposite*: snarl

free verse *n* [➡ POETRY AND VERSE; 915]

freeware *type of* **software** [➡ COMPUTERS AND COMPUTING; 1127]

freeway *type of* **highway** [➡ ROADS; 1106]

freewheel **1** *v* **take it easy**, drift, go with the flow, cruise [➡ LACK OF ACTIVITY OR MOTION; 342] *Opposite*: struggle **2** *v* **coast**, sail, glide, cruise, roll along [➡ PROCEED AND GO; 305]

freewheeling **1** *adj* **carefree**, free and easy, easygoing, unrestricted, self-indulgent, permissive, laissez faire, laid-back (*informal*) [➡ CHEERFULNESS OF OUTLOOK; 503] **2** *adj* **wide-ranging**, open-ended, unstructured, unrestricted, no-holds-barred, open, undefined [➡ FREEDOM AND LIBERTY; 208] *Opposite*: methodical

free will *n* **autonomy**, self-determination, choice, liberty, freedom, independence [➡ FREEDOM AND LIBERTY; 208] *Opposite*: dependence

freeze **1** *v* **turn to ice**, solidify, congeal, harden, ice up, ice over [➡ HARDEN, CONGEAL, AND DRY; 387] *Opposite*: thaw **2** *v* **hold**, fix, restrict, stop, control, halt, immobilize, check, arrest [➡ CAUSE TO STOP; 266] **3** *v* **halt**, stop, stop in your tracks, stop dead, stiffen, immobilize [➡ STOP ACTING; 264] *Opposite*: relax **4** *v* **refrigerate**, chill, cool, preserve [➡ CHANGE OF TEMPERATURE; 386] *Opposite*: thaw **5** *v* **suspend**, stop, halt, hold, break off, mothball, shelve [➡ CAUSE TO STOP; 266] *Opposite*: resume **6** *n* **restriction**, halt, embargo, check, stoppage, suspension, interruption, stay [➡ ENDS AND DEPARTURES; 54] *Opposite*: resumption

freeze out *v* **exclude**, ostracize, give the cold shoulder, ignore, neglect, reject, drive away, send to Coventry (*UK*) [➡ REFUSING OR REJECTING RELATIONS; 975] *Opposite*: welcome

freezer *type of* **cooling appliance** [➡ HEATING, REFRIGERATION, AND VENTILATION; 1142]

freeze up *v* **ice over**, ice up, harden, solidify, freeze [➡ HARDEN, CONGEAL, AND DRY; 387] *Opposite*: thaw

freezing *adj* **cold**, subzero, icy, chilly, bitter, glacial [➡ COLD WEATHER; 1051] *Opposite*: hot

freight **1** *n* **cargo**, goods, merchandise, consignment, load, goods in transit [➡ TRANSPORTATION, TRANSPORTERS, AND CARGOS; 322] **2** *n* **carriage**, shipping, conveyance, transport, transportation, shipment [➡ TRANSPORTATION, TRANSPORTERS, AND CARGOS; 322]

freight car *part of* **train** [➡ RAILROADS; 1107]

freighter *type of* **motor vessel** [➡ SHIPS AND BOATS; 1150]

French bean *type of* **pulse** [➡ PEAS AND BEANS; 1189]

French dressing *type of* **seasonings, sauces, and dips** [➡ SEASONINGS AND SAUCES; 1174]

French fries *type of* **processed potato** [➡ FRUIT AND VEGETABLES; 1176]

French horn *type of* **brass instrument** [➡ MUSICAL INSTRUMENTS; 910]

French kiss *v* [➡ PHYSICAL CONTACT AS COMMUNICATION; 655]

French twist *type of* **hairstyle** [➡ HAIRSTYLES AND HAIRPIECES; 488]

French window *type of* **window** [➡ WINDOWS; 1100]

frenetic *adj* **frantic**, frenzied, hectic, distracted, feverish, chaotic, wild, uncontrolled, furious, intense [➡ DISORDER AND CHAOS; 245] *Opposite*: calm

frenzied *adj* **frantic**, hyperactive, hysterical, feverish, hectic, overexcited, wild, furious, chaotic, violent [➡ DISORDER AND CHAOS; 245] *Opposite*: calm

frenziedly *adv* **uncontrollably**, wildly, excitedly, hysterically, frantically, feverishly, chaotically, violently, hectically [➡ DISORDER AND CHAOS; 245] *Opposite*: calmly

frenzy 1 *n* **fury**, turmoil, fever, rage, passion, anger, agitation, state (*informal*) [➡ INSECURITY AND LOSS OF COMPOSURE; 544] *Opposite*: calmness **2** *n* **whirl**, fit, tumult, rush, flurry, turmoil [➡ DISORDER AND CHAOS; 245]

frequency *n* **incidence**, occurrence, regularity, rate of recurrence, rate [➡ FREQUENT AND OFTEN; 107]

frequent 1 *adj* **recurrent**, common, everyday, normal, numerous, many, repeated, regular [➡ FREQUENT AND OFTEN; 107] *Opposite*: infrequent **2** *v* **visit**, haunt, patronize, hang around, spend time at, go to regularly [➡ EXIST IN A PLACE; 19] *Opposite*: avoid

fresco *n* **wall painting**, mural, frieze, wall, painting [➡ ARTWORKS; 898]

fresh 1 *adj* **new**, renewed, additional, replacement, other, different [➡ NEW, MODERN; 166] *Opposite*: old **2** *adj* **clean**, bright, unmarked, unsullied, immaculate, spanking new, brand-new, pristine, spotless [➡ CLEAN AND HYGIENIC; 1233] *Opposite*: soiled **3** *adj* **wholesome**, crisp, pleasant, airy, refreshing, clean, breezy, unpolluted [➡ IN GOOD REPAIR; 1232] *Opposite*: musty **4** *adj* **at its best**, garden-fresh, crisp, moist, juicy [➡ TASTE; 703] *Opposite*: rotting **5** *adj* **novel**, original, new, inventive, innovative, creative [➡ EXTRAORDINARY; UNCOMMON; 205] *Opposite*: hackneyed **6** *adj* **alert**, energetic, lively, vigorous, active, full of beans (*informal*) [➡ WIDE AWAKE AND CONSCIOUS; 735] *Opposite*: tired

See Compare and Contrast at **now**.

freshen *v* **tidy**, neaten, dust, clean, air, air out, ventilate, refresh, revive, clean up [➡ CLEAN AND POLISH; 403]

freshen up *v* **wash**, shower, change, wash up, clean up, powder your nose (*informal*) [➡ CLEAN AND POLISH; 403]

fresh-faced *adj* **youthful**, young-looking, baby-faced, boyish, girlish [➡ FACIAL CHARACTERISTICS; 481]

freshly *adv* **newly**, recently, just now, a moment ago, just this minute, not long [➡ PAST; 84]

freshness 1 *n* **cleanness**, cleanliness, brightness, sparkle, brilliance [➡ CLEAN AND HYGIENIC; 1233] *Opposite*: grubbiness **2** *n* **crispness**, juiciness, flavor, moistness [➡ TASTE; 703] *Opposite*: staleness **3** *n* **novelty**, originality, newness, inventiveness, innovation, creativity [➡ EXTRAORDINARY; UNCOMMON; 205] *Opposite*: tiredness

fret *v* **worry**, fuss, agonize, vex, trouble, bother, upset, hassle (*informal*) [➡ BE CONCERNED AND CARE; 581] *Opposite*: calm down

fretful *adj* **worried**, restless, agitated, unsettled, distressed, irritable, upset, touchy, nervous, anxious [➡ CONFUSION, ANXIETY, AND WORRY; 540] *Opposite*: calm

fretfulness *n* **anxiety**, restlessness, agitation, distress, unease, worry, upset, disquiet, irritation, nervousness, apprehension [➡ CONFUSION, ANXIETY, AND WORRY; 540] *Opposite*: calmness

friability *n* [➡ FRAGILE; 1209]

friable *adj* **crumbly**, powdery, workable, light [➡ FRAGILE; 1209] *Opposite*: heavy

See Compare and Contrast at **fragile**.

friar *n* [➡ RELIGIOUS PEOPLE; 778]

friary *n* **religious community**, monastery, religious foundation, fraternity, brotherhood, house [➡ RELIGIOUS BUILDINGS; 1085]

fricassee *type of* **cooked dish** [➡ PREPARED DISHES; 1170]

friction 1 *n* **rubbing**, abrasion, contact, chafing, rasping, brushing [➡ ENERGY; 1161] **2** *n* **hostility**, conflict, tension, antagonism, disagreement, discord, strife [➡ DISHARMONY; 156] *Opposite*: accord

fridge *type of* **cooling appliance** [➡ HEATING, REFRIGERATION, AND VENTILATION; 1142]

fried 1 *adj* [➡ STATE OF PREPARED FOOD; 1171] **2** *adj* (*slang*) **tired**, exhausted, run-down, weary, spent, bushed (*informal*), done for (*informal*), wiped out (*slang*), beat (*slang*) [➡ TIRED, ASLEEP, AND UNCONSCIOUS; 738] *Opposite*: fresh

friend 1 *n* **comrade**, companion, pal (*informal*), chum (*informal*), buddy (*informal*), mate (*UK*) [➡ FRIENDS AND GUESTS; 963] *Opposite*: foe (*formal*) **2** *n* **acquaintance**, contact, colleague, associate, partner, comrade, workmate [➡ FRIENDS AND GUESTS; 963] *Opposite*: stranger **3** *n* **ally**, helper, supporter, well-wisher, collaborator [➡ FRIENDS AND GUESTS; 963] *Opposite*: rival

friendless *adj* [➡ SOLITARINESS; 941]

friendliness *n* **openness**, sociability, pleasantness, approachability, outgoingness, responsiveness, affability, kindliness [➡ FRIENDLINESS AND SOCIABILITY; 494] *Opposite*: reserve

friendly *adj* **welcoming**, approachable, outgoing, open, pleasant, affable, kindly, responsive, sociable [➡ FRIENDLINESS AND SOCIABILITY; 494] *Opposite*: unfriendly

friendship 1 *n* **companionship**, comradeship, camaraderie, closeness, familiarity, amity (*formal*) [➡ RELATIONSHIP TO ANOTHER; 973] *Opposite*: animosity **2** *n* **bond**, relationship, alliance, attachment, acquaintance, rapport [➡ RELATIONSHIP TO ANOTHER; 973]

fries *type of* **processed potato** [➡ FRUIT AND VEGETABLES; 1176]

frieze *n* **decoration**, band, strip, panel, mural, fresco, wall painting [➡ ARTWORKS; 898]

frigate *type of* **military vessel** [➡ SHIPS AND BOATS; 1150]

fright 1 *n* **fear**, terror, anxiety, foreboding, dread, panic [➡ FEAR AND PANIC; 543] *Opposite*: composure **2** *n* **scare**, shock, start, turn, seizure, heart attack (*informal*) [➡ SUDDEN EVENTS; 52]

frighten *v* **scare**, terrify, alarm, startle, upset, worry, panic [➡ FRIGHTEN AND SHOCK; 568] *Opposite*: soothe

frightened *adj* **scared**, afraid, terrified, alarmed, startled, anxious, upset, worried, panicky [➡ FEAR AND PANIC; 543] *Opposite*: calm

frightening *adj* **terrifying**, alarming, startling, fearsome, fearful, redoubtable, upsetting, scary (*informal*) [➡ FRIGHTENING; 231] *Opposite*: soothing

frightful *adj* **appalling**, horrible, unpleasant, dreadful, awful, terrible [➡ BAD AND BADLY; 223] *Opposite*: pleasant

frightfully *adv* **terribly**, extremely, awfully, dreadfully, excessively, very, fearfully, horribly, tremendously, monstrously [➡ TO A GREAT EXTENT; 132]

frightfulness *n* **awfulness**, atrociousness, severity, badness, hideousness, horror, horridness, hatefulness, dreadfulness [➡ DISGUSTING AND REPULSIVE; 230] *Opposite*: pleasantness

frigid 1 *adj* **unfriendly**, standoffish, cold, distant, frosty, forbidding, icy, aloof [➡ UNFRIENDLINESS AND UNSOCIABILITY; 504] *Opposite*: warm 2 *adj* **cold**, frosty, chilly, icy, freezing, glacial [➡ TEMPERATURE: COLD; 1231] *Opposite*: torrid

frigidity *n* **coldness**, frostiness, iciness, cold-heartedness, aloofness, formality, reserve, standoffishness [➡ UNFRIENDLINESS AND UNSOCIABILITY; 504] *Opposite*: warmth

frigidly *adv* **coldly**, icily, frostily, unemotionally, unfeelingly, distantly, coolly, cold-heartedly, uncaringly, impersonally [➡ RUDE AND HOSTILE; 625] *Opposite*: warmly

frijoles *type of* **cooked dish** [➡ PREPARED DISHES; 1170]

frill 1 *n* **decoration**, flounce, trimming, ruffle, ruche, edging, lace [➡ ORNAMENTS AND DECORATIONS; 1248] 2 *n* **extra**, add-on, luxury, decoration, accompaniment, embellishment, gimmick, addition, superfluity [➡ MORE AND EXCESS; 124]

frills *n* **accompaniments**, trappings, added extras, embellishments, add-ons, additions, superfluities, trimmings, flourishes [➡ MORE AND EXCESS; 124]

frilly *adj* **lacy**, ruched, gathered, pleated, fancy, delicate, decorated [➡ BEAUTY AND ATTRACTIVENESS; 189] *Opposite*: plain

fringe 1 *n* **tassel**, edging, edge, border, trimming, trim [➡ ORNAMENTS AND DECORATIONS; 1248] 2 *n* **periphery**, edge, extreme, perimeter, border, limit, margin [➡ EXTREMITIES OF PHYSICAL OBJECTS; 1250] *Opposite*: center 3 *adj* **peripheral**, outlying, marginal, far-flung, frontier, border [➡ EXTREMITIES OF PHYSICAL OBJECTS; 1250] *Opposite*: central 4 *adj* **unconventional**, extreme, radical, marginal, extremist, alternative [➡ EXTRAORDINARY: UNCOMMON; 205] *Opposite*: mainstream

fringe benefit *n* **extra**, compensation, perk, privilege, reward, perquisite (*formal*) [➡ GIFTS; 438]

frippery *n* [➡ JUNK AND USELESS OBJECTS; 1249]

frisk 1 *v* **play**, frolic, gambol, cavort, kick up your heels, leap, romp, dance [➡ FIDGET AND FROLIC; 311] *Opposite*: plod 2 *v* **search**, pat down, body search, examine, inspect, check [➡ SEEK POSSESSION AND SEARCH; 456]

friskily *adv* **playfully**, energetically, excitably, excitedly, enthusiastically, bouncily [➡ WITH ENTHUSIASM; 286] *Opposite*: lethargically

friskiness *n* **playfulness**, excitability, excitement, liveliness, enthusiasm, bounciness [➡ ENERGY AND ENTHUSIASM; 496] *Opposite*: lethargy

frisky *adj* **playful**, frolicsome, excitable, excited, light-

hearted, energetic, lively, bouncy, spirited [➡ ENERGY AND ENTHUSIASM; 496] *Opposite*: lethargic

frittata *type of* **cooked dish** [➡ PREPARED DISHES; 1170]

fritter away *v* **dissipate**, waste, squander, misspend, gamble away, idle away, use up [➡ USE UP AND WASTE; 474] *Opposite*: conserve

frivolity 1 *n* **playfulness**, perkiness, lightheartedness, merriment, gaiety, dizziness, silliness, giddiness (*dated*) [➡ CHEERFULNESS OF OUTLOOK; 503] *Opposite*: seriousness 2 *n* **triviality**, frivolousness, unimportance, inconsequentiality, superficiality, silliness, foolishness [➡ UNIMPORTANT AND UNNECESSARY; 238] *Opposite*: seriousness

frivolous 1 *adj* **playful**, frolicsome, perky, lighthearted, silly, flippant, dizzy (*informal*), giddy (*dated*) [➡ CHEERFULNESS OF OUTLOOK; 503] *Opposite*: serious 2 *adj* **trivial**, silly, inconsequential, idle, shallow, vain [➡ UNIMPORTANT AND UNNECESSARY; 238] *Opposite*: serious

frivolously 1 *adv* **playfully**, lightheartedly, perkily, dizzily, flippantly, lightly, giddily (*dated*) [➡ CHEERFULNESS OF OUTLOOK; 503] *Opposite*: seriously 2 *adv* **thoughtlessly**, idly, inconsequentially, trivially, foolishly, vainly [➡ UNIMPORTANT AND UNNECESSARY; 238] *Opposite*: responsibly

frizz *v* **curl**, crimp, frizzle, perm, kink [➡ CHANGE OF SHAPE; 385] *Opposite*: straighten

frizzed *adj* [➡ DESCRIBING HAIR; 486]

frizzle 1 *v* **burn**, shrivel, scorch, sear, dry up, wrinkle, char [➡ FIRE, FLAMMABILITY, AND BURNING; 1165] 2 *v* **frizz**, curl, perm, crimp, kink [➡ CHANGE OF SHAPE; 385] *Opposite*: straighten 3 *v* **sizzle**, fry, pan-fry, sauté, grill, barbecue, heat [➡ COOKING AND FOOD PREPARATION; 353]

frizzy *adj* **curled**, wiry, curly, kinky, frizzed [➡ DESCRIBING HAIR; 486] *Opposite*: straight

frock (*dated*) *type of* **dress** [➡ GARMENTS AND OUTFITS; 865]

frock coat *type of* **overcoat** [➡ GARMENTS AND OUTFITS; 865]

frog *type of* **amphibian** [➡ AMPHIBIANS; 1008]

frogmarch *v* **propel**, march, accompany, take, carry, bundle (*informal*) [➡ ACCOMPANY AND FOLLOW; 337]

frogspawn (*UK*) *n* **eggs**, spawn, tadpoles [➡ EGGS, SPERM, AND SPAWN; 727]

frolic *v* **play**, skip, cavort, frisk, gambol, leap, romp, dance, kick up your heels [➡ FIDGET AND FROLIC; 311] *Opposite*: plod

frolicsome *adj* **playful**, frisky, frivolous, lighthearted, spirited, lively [➡ ENERGY AND ENTHUSIASM; 496] *Opposite*: solemn

from hand to mouth *adv* **from payday to payday**, on a strict budget, from day to day, from paycheck to paycheck, near the poverty line, on the breadline (*UK*) [➡ POVERTY AND POOR; 892]

from the bottom of your heart *adv* **sincerely**, wholeheartedly, truly, honestly, unequivocally [➡ HONEST AND OPEN; 630] *Opposite*: insincerely

from the horse's mouth *adv* **from a reliable source**, on good authority, reliably, authoritatively, directly, at first hand [➡ WORDS AND PHRASES EMPHASIZING THE TRUTH OF A MATTER; 172] *Opposite*: indirectly

from time to time *adv* **occasionally**, now and then, now and again, once in a while, infrequently, periodically [➡ NEVER AND INFREQUENCY; 97] *Opposite*: frequently

frond *n* **leaf**, branch, palm leaf, fern leaf [➡ PARTS OF TREES AND PLANTS; 1026]

front 1 *n* **façade**, face, frontage, obverse, head, fore (*literary*) [➡ EXTREMITIES OF PHYSICAL OBJECTS; 1250] *Opposite*: back 2 *n* (*UK*) **impertinence**, cockiness, nerve, gall, audacity, impudence, chutzpah (*informal*), cheek (*informal*) [➡ BAD MANNERS AND SOCIAL SKILLS; 521]

frontage *n* **front**, façade, face, outlook, front part [➡ PARTS OF A BUILDING; 1095] *Opposite*: rear

frontal *adj* **forward**, anterior, front, fore (*literary*) [➡ RELATIVE LOCATION; 161] *Opposite*: posterior (*formal*)

frontbencher (*UK*) *n* [➡ POLITICAL OFFICES AND POLITICIANS; 808]

front door *n* **main entrance**, main door, door, entrance, entry [➡ DOORS AND ACCESS POINTS; 1101] *Opposite*: exit

frontier *n* **border**, boundary, limit, edge, border line, front line [➡ GEOGRAPHIC BORDERS AND BOUNDARIES; 1069]

frontispiece *n* **illustration**, print, picture, photograph, drawing, image, sketch, reproduction, plate [➡ PARTS OF BOOKS AND DOCUMENTS; 593]

front line 1 *n* **front**, war zone, battle zone, combat zone, ground zero [➡ GEOGRAPHIC BORDERS AND BOUNDARIES; 1069] 2 *n* **forefront**, cutting edge, leading edge, sharp end, vanguard, uncharted territory, firing line, fore (*literary*) [➡ DIFFICULT SITUATIONS; 72]

front of house *n* [➡ IN THE THEATER; 906]

front-page *adj* **headline**, important, significant, momentous, attention-grabbing, eye-catching, far-reaching [➡ IMPORTANT; 194]

frontrunner (*informal*) *n* **leader**, head, favorite, prime candidate, number one (*informal*), top dog (*informal*) [➡ IMPORTANT OR FAMOUS PEOPLE; 893] *Opposite*: straggler

frontward *adv* **ahead**, to the fore, forward [➡ DIRECTION OF MOTION; 345] *Opposite*: backward

frost 1 *n* **ice**, rime, hoar frost [➡ COLD WEATHER; 1051] 2 *n* **cold**, frostiness, iciness, coolness, frigidity, chill [➡ COLD WEATHER; 1051] *Opposite*: warmth

frosted *adj* **ice-covered**, frosty, iced, icy, snowy, white, frozen [➡ COLD WEATHER; 1051] *Opposite*: thawed

frostily *adv* **coldly**, icily, coolly, frigidly, angrily, bitterly [➡ RUDE AND HOSTILE; 625] *Opposite*: warmly

frostiness 1 *n* **iciness**, coldness, cold, chill, rawness, wintriness [➡ COLD WEATHER; 1051] *Opposite*: warmth 2 *n* **coldness**, aloofness, frigidity, coolness, iciness, standoffishness, reserve [➡ UNFRIENDLINESS AND UNSOCIABILITY; 504] *Opposite*: warmth

frosting 1 *n* **icing**, cake coating, decoration, topping, ganache, royal icing (*UK*) [➡ SUGAR AND PRESERVES; 1184] 2 *n* **dullness**, opaqueness, opacity, matt surface, matt finish, texturing [➡ VISUAL TEXTURE; 1221]

frosty 1 *adj* **icy**, cold, chilly, freezing, frigid, cool, glacial [➡ COLD WEATHER; 1051] *Opposite*: warm 2 *adj* **cold**, unfriendly, cool, icy, frigid, standoffish, aloof, reserved, chilling, cold-hearted [➡ UNFRIENDLINESS AND UNSOCIABILITY; 504] *Opposite*: warm

froth 1 *n* **foam**, bubbles, lather, head, fizz, spume (*literary*) [➡ FOAM; 1273] 2 *n* **triviality**, trivia, frivolity, superficiality, shallowness, lightheartedness, inconsequentiality, nonsense [➡ MEANINGLESS SPEECH OR WRITING; 676] *Opposite*: substance 3 *v* **to become foamy**, foam, bubble, lather, lather up, produce a head, fizz, ferment [➡ FROTH AND EFFERVESCE; 389]

frothiness 1 *n* **foaminess**, bubbliness, fizziness, fizz, soapiness, sudsiness [➡ VISUAL TEXTURE; 1221] 2 *n* **triviality**, insubstantiality, lightness, frivolity, pettiness, superficiality, shallowness, lightheartedness, inconsequentiality [➡ UNIMPORTANT AND UNNECESSARY; 238] *Opposite*: seriousness

frothy 1 *adj* **foamy**, foam-covered, lathered, lathered up, bubbly, soapy, fizzing, sudsy [➡ VISUAL TEXTURE; 1221] 2 *adj* **light**, inconsequential, superficial, trivial, shallow, frivolous, lighthearted [➡ UNIMPORTANT AND UNNECESSARY; 238] *Opposite*: serious

frown 1 *v* **knit your brow**, scowl, glare, glower, lower, pull a face [➡ FACIAL EXPRESSIONS AND BLUSHING; 651] *Opposite*: smile 2 *n* **scowl**, glare, glower, grimace, puckered brow [➡ FACIAL EXPRESSIONS AND BLUSHING; 651] *Opposite*: smile

frown on *v* **disapprove**, take a dim view of, frown upon, condemn, disfavor, dislike, object to, oppose, be against, deplore [➡ DISLIKE AND HATE; 577] *Opposite*: favor

See Compare and Contrast at **disapprove**.

frown upon *see* **frown on**

frowzy *adj* **unkempt**, disheveled, frayed, messy, shabby, untidy, slovenly, rumpled, disorganized, frazzled (*informal*) [➡ BADLY GROOMED; 483] *Opposite*: neat

frozen 1 *adj* **ice-covered**, cold, solid, freezing, iced up, icy [➡ COLD WEATHER; 1051] 2 *adj* **immobile**, stationary, unmoving, still, motionless, petrified [➡ LACK OF ACTIVITY OR MOTION; 342] *Opposite*: mobile

fructose *type of* **nutrient** [➡ FOOD COMPONENTS; 1188]

frugal *adj* **thrifty**, prudent, economical, sparing, penny-wise, careful, parsimonious, stingy, meager, penny-pinching (*informal*), tight [➡ GRASPING AND FINANCIALLY MEAN; 519] *Opposite*: profligate

frugality *n* **thrift**, stinginess, parsimony, prudence, economy, thriftiness, penny-pinching (*informal*) [➡ GRASPING AND FINANCIALLY MEAN; 519] *Opposite*: profligacy

fruit 1 *n* [➡ FRUIT AND VEGETABLES; 1176] 2 *n* **ovary**, berry, pod, capsule, achene, drupe, fruitlet [➡ PARTS OF TREES AND PLANTS; 1026] 3 *n* **produce**, bounty, harvest, crop, yield [➡ RESULTS AND OUTCOMES; 83] 4 *n* **product**, result, consequence, reward, fruition, maturing, outcome, end result [➡ RESULTS AND OUTCOMES; 83] 5 *v* **produce fruit**, bear fruit, ripen, mature [➡ GROW AND CULTIVATE; 351]

fruit

◆ *types of fruit*

apple, apricot, avocado, banana, blackcurrant, cherry, citrus, damson, date, fig, grape, guava, kiwi fruit, kumquat, lychee, mango, melon, nectarine, olive, papaya, passion fruit, peach, pear, pineapple, plum, pomegranate, quince, raspberry, redcurrant, strawberry, watermelon

◆ *parts of a fruit*

flesh, juice, kernel, peel, pip, pit, pith, pulp, rind, seed, skin, stone

fruit bat *type of* **flying mammal** [➡FLYING MAMMALS; 984]

fruitcake *type of* **cake** [➡CAKES, COOKIES, AND DESSERTS; 1181]

fruit fly *type of* **flying insect** [➡FLYING INSECTS; 1013]

fruitful *adj* **productive**, fertile, rich, prolific, abundant, successful, profitable, rewarding, effective, prosperous [➡SUCCESSFUL AND PROMISING; 81] *Opposite:* fruitless

fruitfulness *n* **productivity**, abundance, profitability, prosperity, fertility, effectiveness, success, richness, prosperousness [➡SUCCESS; 82] *Opposite:* fruitlessness

fruition *n* **completion**, maturity, readiness, realization, culmination, fulfillment [➡ENDS AND DEPARTURES; 54]

fruit juice *n* [➡DRINKS; 1187]

fruitless *adj* **unsuccessful**, futile, useless, unproductive, wasted, unrewarding, ineffective [➡UNSUCCESSFUL AND UNPROMISING; 76] *Opposite:* fruitful

fruitlessness *n* **uselessness**, futility, unproductiveness, failure, inadequacy, ineffectiveness [➡REDUNDANT AND USELESS; 240] *Opposite:* fruitfulness

fruit salad *type of* **dessert** [➡CAKES, COOKIES, AND DESSERTS; 1181]

fruity 1 *adj* **rich**, sweet, tangy, zesty, lemony, plummy, grapey [➡TASTE; 703] 2 *adj* **mellow**, deep, rich, plummy, harmonious, mellifluous, resonant [➡SOFT, LOW, OR PLEASANT SOUNDS; 1265] *Opposite:* shrill

frumpiness *n* [➡BADLY GROOMED; 483]

frumpy *adj* [➡BADLY GROOMED; 483]

frustrate 1 *v* **thwart**, prevent, foil, stop, block, hinder, obstruct, stymie [➡MAKE IMPOSSIBLE; 276] *Opposite:* promote 2 *v* **discourage**, exasperate, irritate, upset, disturb, annoy, bother, vex, try, infuriate, aggravate (*informal*) [➡ANGER AND ANNOY; 569] *Opposite:* encourage

frustrated 1 *adj* **unfulfilled**, unsatisfied, irritated, upset, angry, exasperated, discouraged [➡IRRITATION AND ANGER; 541] *Opposite:* satisfied 2 *adj* **foiled**, blocked, stymied, obstructed, hindered, thwarted [➡UNSUCCESSFUL AND UNPROMISING; 76] *Opposite:* successful

frustrating *adj* **annoying**, unsatisfying, exasperating, infuriating, maddening, provoking, vexing, challenging, wearisome, trying, galling, irritating, upsetting, disturbing, discouraging, disappointing, aggravating (*informal*) [➡IRRITATING; 228] *Opposite:* satisfying

frustration 1 *n* **prevention**, hindrance, blocking, foiling, defeat, obstruction, thwarting [➡PROBLEMS; 256] *Opposite:*

success 2 *n* **dissatisfaction**, irritation, disturbance, annoyance, nuisance, vexation, disappointment, exasperation, weariness, infuriation [➡IRRITATION AND ANGER; 541] *Opposite:* satisfaction

fry *v* **cook**, sauté, stir-fry, fry up, deep-fry, brown [➡COOKING AND FOOD PREPARATION; 353]

frying pan *n* **pan**, skillet, spider (*dated*), omelette pan (*UK*) [➡TABLEWARE, FLATWARE, AND KITCHENWARE; 861]

fuchsia 1 *type of* **perennial flower** [➡FLOWERS; 1032] 2 *type of* **pink** [➡COLORS; 1224]

fucus *type of* **marine alga** [➡MICROORGANISMS, FUNGI, AND ALGAE; 1023]

fuddle 1 *v* **confuse**, bewilder, stupefy, muddle, dull, cloud, befuddle, bemuse, puzzle, befog (*literary*) [➡CONFUSE AND BEWILDER; 571] *Opposite:* clarify 2 *n* **muddle**, dither, mess, state (*informal*) [➡CONFUSION, ANXIETY, AND WORRY; 540]

fuddled *adj* [➡CONFUSION, ANXIETY, AND WORRY; 540]

fuddy-duddy (*informal*) *n* **fogy**, reactionary, stick-in-the-mud (*informal*), stuffed shirt (*informal*) [➡UNCOOPERATIVE OR REBELLIOUS PEOPLE; 566]

fudge 1 *type of* **confectionery** [➡CONFECTIONERY; 1182] 2 *n* (*informal*) **nonsense**, rubbish, garbage, verbiage, waffle (*informal*), gobbledygook (*informal*) [➡MEANINGLESS SPEECH OR WRITING; 676] 3 *v* (*informal*) **falsify**, doctor, alter, massage, fabricate, exaggerate, misrepresent, distort, fiddle (*informal*), fix (*informal*) [➡FALSIFY AND CHEAT; 176] 4 *v* (*informal*) **prevaricate**, beat around the bush, evade the issue, waffle (*informal*) [➡SHIRK AND DELAY; 273]

fuel 1 *n* **petroleum**, firewood, oil, coal, gas, fossil fuel, energy, gasoline, petrol (*UK*) [➡ENERGY SOURCES; 1162] 2 *v* **power**, fire, run, drive, operate, work [➡USE TOOLS AND MACHINERY; 468] 3 *v* **stimulate**, increase, promote, fire, energize, encourage, invigorate, add to, feed [➡CHANGE OF INTENSITY: MORE; 394] *Opposite:* quell

fug *n* **fog**, smog, haze, smoke, miasma [➡HOT WEATHER; 1050]

fuggy (*UK*) *adj* **stuffy**, smoky, stale, airless, suffocating, foggy, hazy, smoke-filled [➡HOT WEATHER; 1050] *Opposite:* bracing

fugitive 1 *n* **escapee**, deserter, absconder, outlaw, runaway [➡RUNAWAYS AND ABSENTEES; 9] 2 *adj* **brief**, fleeting, elusive, short, quick [➡HAPPENING QUICKLY; 104]

fugue 1 *n* **fugue state**, blackout, amnesia, memory loss [➡TIRED, ASLEEP, AND UNCONSCIOUS; 738] 2 *type of* **musical form** [➡MUSIC, SONGS, AND SINGING; 907]

fulcrum *n* **pivot**, hinge, swivel, support, point [➡PARTS OF MACHINES AND TOOLS; 1118]

fulfill 1 *v* **achieve**, accomplish, bear out, realize, live up to, bring about, make happen, satisfy, bring to fruition, justify, follow through [➡COMPLETE AN ACTION; 263] 2 *v* **carry out**, execute, follow, obey, complete, comply with, accomplish, perform, implement, discharge (*formal*) [➡OBEY AND ABIDE BY; 301] *Opposite:* neglect 3 *v* **satisfy**, meet, conform to, be in conformity with, accord with, be in accordance with, agree with, be in agreement with, match [➡HARMONY; 155] *Opposite:* fall short 4 *v* **complete**, finish, see through, go through with, make it through, survive, get through [➡COMPLETE AN ACTION; 263] *Opposite:* abandon 5 *v* **supply**, fill, deliver, provide, furnish (*formal*) [➡ GIVE AND PROVIDE; 430] *Opposite*: renege **6** *v* **succeed**, do proud, gain fulfillment, make good, fulfill your potential, make it (*informal*) [➡ SUCCEED AND WIN; 79]

See Compare and Contrast at **perform**.

fulfilled *adj* **satisfied**, content, happy, pleased, rewarded, contented [➡ APPRECIATION AND GRATITUDE; 535] *Opposite*: frustrated

fulfilling *adj* **satisfying**, rewarding, pleasing, gratifying, enjoyable [➡ EMOTIONALLY PLEASANT; 187] *Opposite*: frustrating

fulfillment 1 *n* **achievement**, realization, execution, completion, accomplishment, implementation, discharge (*formal*) [➡ SUCCESS; 82] *Opposite*: neglect **2** *n* **contentment**, serenity, inner peace, self-actualization, nirvana, satisfaction, joy, success, gratification, self-realization [➡ COOL AND CALM; 536] *Opposite*: dissatisfaction

fulguration (*formal*) *n* [➡ WINDY AND STORMY WEATHER; 1053]

full 1 *adj* **occupied**, complete, bursting, packed, filled, crowded, crammed, full up, jam-packed (*informal*), chock-full (*informal*), chock-a-block (*informal*) [➡ FULL; 1239] *Opposite*: empty **2** *adj* **complete**, broad, extensive, comprehensive, detailed, inclusive, thorough [➡ WHOLENESS AND COMPLETENESS; 198] *Opposite*: sketchy **3** *adj* **satiated**, satisfied, bursting, sated, replete, gorged, full up, stuffed (*informal*) [➡ EAT AND NOT EAT; 710] *Opposite*: hungry **4** *adj* **plump**, round, chubby, ample, broad, rounded, rotund, pudgy (*informal*) [➡ BUILD; 477] *Opposite*: thin **5** *adj* **sonorous**, resonant, rich, deep, plummy, mellow, mellifluous, harmonious [➡ SOFT, LOW, OR PLEASANT SOUNDS; 1265] *Opposite*: shrill

full-blooded *adj* **vigorous**, hearty, thoroughgoing, forceful, robust, out-and-out [➡ FIT AND STRONG; 736] *Opposite*: feeble

full-blown *adj* **complete**, full, full-scale, full-size, developed, advanced, mature, total, out-and-out, all-out [➡ WHOLENESS AND COMPLETENESS; 198] *Opposite*: incomplete

full-bodied *adj* **flavorful**, rich, intense, powerful, strong, tasty, aromatic [➡ TASTE; 703] *Opposite*: insipid

full dress *n* **formal attire**, dress uniform, jacket and tie, evening dress, black tie, formal wear [➡ GARMENTS AND OUTFITS; 865]

full-fashioned *adj* **shaped**, close-fitting, tailored, well-fitting, figure-hugging, tight [➡ DESCRIBING CLOTHES; 869] *Opposite*: loose-fitting

full-fledged 1 *adj* **complete**, developed, mature, full-size, full-grown, grown, total, adult, full-term [➡ ADULTHOOD; 918] **2** *adj* **qualified**, seasoned, genuine, real, actual, bona fide, out-and-out, experienced [➡ TRUE AND REAL; 171]

full-frontal (*informal*) *adj* **all-out**, unrestrained, wholehearted, uninhibited, concerted, committed, unambiguous, direct, full-on, total, full, complete, full-scale [➡ WHOLENESS AND COMPLETENESS; 198] *Opposite*: half-hearted

full-grown *adj* **developed**, grown, matured, adult, full-size, experienced, seasoned, grown-up, full-term, full-fledged, ripe [➡ ADULTHOOD; 918] *Opposite*: immature

full-length 1 *adj* **ankle-length**, floor-length, long [➡ DESCRIBING CLOTHES; 869] *Opposite*: short **2** *adj* **head-to-toe**, whole-body,

full, long, tall [➡ LENGTH: LONG; 1197] **3** *adj* **unabridged**, complete, uncut, unedited, unexpurgated, uncensored, standard-length, whole [➡ WHOLENESS AND COMPLETENESS; 198] *Opposite*: abridged

fullness 1 *n* **completeness**, richness, abundance [➡ WHOLENESS AND COMPLETENESS; 198] *Opposite*: emptiness **2** *n* **roundness**, plumpness, chubbiness, ampleness, pudginess (*informal*) [➡ BUILD; 477] *Opposite*: thinness

full of *adj* **alive with**, awash with, thick with, resplendent with, crammed with, replete with, beset with (*formal*) [➡ FULL; 1239]

full of beans (*informal*) *adj* **lively**, animated, bouncy, perky, energetic, active, happy, vigorous, spirited, bubbly [➡ ENERGY AND ENTHUSIASM; 496] *Opposite*: morose

full of life *adj* **vivacious**, lively, perky, spirited, energetic, dynamic, animated, active, bubbly, vigorous [➡ ENERGY AND ENTHUSIASM; 496] *Opposite*: lethargic

full of yourself *adj* **conceited**, vain, self-satisfied, self-centered, self-absorbed, egocentric, pompous, self-important, arrogant [➡ POMPOUS, LOUD, AND OVERCONFIDENT; 635] *Opposite*: modest

full-scale 1 *adj* **life-size**, full-size, complete, full [➡ WHOLENESS AND COMPLETENESS; 198] **2** *adj* **total**, full-blown, unrestrained, all-out, unlimited, complete, full, out-and-out [➡ WHOLENESS AND COMPLETENESS; 198] *Opposite*: partial

full-size *adj* **normal**, standard, regular, ordinary [➡ LARGE; 1193]

full speed ahead *adv* [➡ MOVING QUICKLY; 103]

full steam ahead *adv* [➡ MOVING QUICKLY; 103]

full-time *adj* **around the clock**, permanent, round-the-clock, twenty-four-hour, day and night, twenty-four-hour-a-day [➡ PERMANENCE: WITHOUT END; 94] *Opposite*: part-time

full-timer *n* **full-time employee**, full-time worker, full-time member of staff [➡ WORKERS; 836] *Opposite*: part-timer

full to bursting *adj* [➡ FULL; 1239]

full to capacity *adj* [➡ FULL; 1239]

full to overflowing *adj* [➡ FULL; 1239]

full up 1 *adj* **full**, bursting, satisfied, satiated, replete, stuffed (*informal*) [➡ EAT AND NOT EAT; 710] *Opposite*: hungry **2** *adj* **filled**, complete, bursting, packed, jam-packed (*informal*), chock-full (*informal*), chock-a-block (*informal*) [➡ FULL; 1239] *Opposite*: empty

fully *adv* **completely**, entirely, wholly, totally, altogether, quite, absolutely [➡ WHOLENESS AND COMPLETENESS; 198] *Opposite*: partially

fulmar *type of* **sea bird** [➡ SEA BIRDS; 1002]

fulminate *v* **rail**, rant and rave, rage, rant, thunder, criticize [➡ PROTEST AND EXPRESS DISAPPROVAL; 642] *Opposite*: praise

fulsome *adj* **flattering**, excessive, immoderate, effusive, overgenerous, lavish, fawning [➡ INGRATIATING; 638]

fumble 1 *v* **grope**, scrabble, rummage, root, search, feel, dig [➡ SEEK POSSESSION AND SEARCH; 456] **2** *v* **mishandle**, botch, botch up, blunder, muddle, muddle up, bungle (*informal*), mess up (*informal*) [➡ MESS UP AND MAKE MISTAKES; 472] **3** *n* **mistake**, error, blunder, botched job, mess, misstep, mess-up (*informal*), slip-up (*informal*) [➡ MISTAKES; 250]

fume **1** *v* **seethe**, rage, bristle, be angry, be furious, simmer, smolder [➡ GIVING VENT TO EMOTIONS; 679] **2** *n* **emission**, vapor, miasma, smog, smoke, haze, gas [➡ GASES; 1275] **3** *n* **stench**, odor, smell, stink, reek [➡ SMELL AND SMELLING; 705]

fumes *n* [➡ GASES; 1275]

fumigate *v* **sterilize**, disinfect, decontaminate, delouse, smoke, cleanse, clean [➡ CLEAN AND POLISH; 403]

fumigation *n* **disinfection**, decontamination, smoking, delousing, cleansing, sterilization, cleaning [➡ CLEAN AND POLISH; 403]

fuming *adj* **furious**, irate, incensed, enraged, seething, livid, angry, cross, beside yourself, mad, teed off (*informal*) [➡ IRRITATION AND ANGER; 541]

fun **1** *n* **amusement**, excitement, enjoyment, entertainment, merriment, pleasure, diversion [➡ LEISURE AND RECREATION; 874] *Opposite*: boredom **2** *adj* (*informal*) **amusing**, entertaining, enjoyable, exciting, pleasurable, great (*informal*), cool (*slang*) [➡ EMOTIONALLY PLEASANT; 187] *Opposite*: boring

funambulist *n* [➡ PEOPLE IN SPORTS AND LEISURE; 876]

fun and games *n* [➡ JOKES AND TEASING; 674]

function **1** *n* **purpose**, meaning, role, job, occupation, task, utility [➡ INTENTIONS AND PURPOSES; 772] **2** *n* **event**, gathering, meeting, affair, party, occasion, soiree [➡ PARTIES, DANCES, AND CELEBRATIONS; 37] **3** *v* **work**, perform, operate, run, go, behave, act, serve [➡ FUNCTION SUCCESSFULLY; 469] *Opposite*: malfunction

functional **1** *adj* **practical**, useful, handy, purposeful, efficient, serviceable [➡ USEFULNESS; 199] *Opposite*: worthless **2** *adj* **operational**, operative, running, going, working [➡ HAPPENING AND IN PROGRESS; 32] *Opposite*: inoperative

functionary *n* **official**, representative, bureaucrat, lackey, employee, minion (*archaic or literary*) [➡ SUBORDINATES AND ASSISTANTS; 966]

functionless *adj* [➡ REDUNDANT AND USELESS; 240]

fund **1** *n* **reserve**, account, supply, endowment, stock, trust, nest egg, deposit [➡ ACCOUNTING, BANKING, AND BUDGETING; 799] **2** *n* **supply**, stock, store, source, collection, bank [➡ AMOUNTS AND QUANTITIES; 112] **3** *v* **finance**, support, back, sponsor, subsidize, underwrite, pay for [➡ GIVE MONEY; 433]

fundamental **1** *adj* **basic**, primary, original, essential, elementary, elemental, deep, deep-seated, underlying, structural [➡ FUNDAMENTAL; 195] *Opposite*: secondary **2** *adj* **central**, essential, vital, ultimate, major, necessary, important [➡ IMPORTANT; 194] *Opposite*: superfluous

fundamentalism *n* [➡ RELIGIOUS CONCEPTS; 776]

fundamentalist *n* [➡ RELIGIOUS PEOPLE; 778]

fundamentally *adv* **basically**, essentially, primarily, deeply, necessarily, profoundly [➡ FUNDAMENTAL; 195] *Opposite*: superficially

fundamentals *n* **basics**, rudiments, essentials, ground rules, brass tacks, first principles, details, nitty-gritty (*informal*) [➡ BASIC DETAILS; 688]

funding *n* **backing**, support, finance, subsidy, money, cash, capital, currency, aid, resources, income [➡ ACCOUNTING, BANKING, AND BUDGETING; 799]

fundraiser **1** *n* **campaigner**, crusader, supporter, representative, moneymaker [➡ CHARITY AND CHARITABLE INSTITUTIONS; 822] **2** *n* **appeal**, campaign, crusade, push, drive, telethon, fun run, tag day, flag day (*UK*) [➡ CHARITY AND CHARITABLE INSTITUTIONS; 822] **3** *n* [➡ PERFORMANCES AND SHOWS; 42]

funeral *n* **service**, memorial, interment, burial, cremation, rites, wake, procession [➡ BURIAL AND PREPARATION FOR BURIAL; 929]

funeral director *n* [➡ BURIAL AND PREPARATION FOR BURIAL; 929]

funeral home *n* [➡ BURIAL AND PREPARATION FOR BURIAL; 929]

funeral mass *n* [➡ BURIAL AND PREPARATION FOR BURIAL; 929]

funeral parlor *n* [➡ BURIAL AND PREPARATION FOR BURIAL; 929]

funeral rites *n* [➡ BURIAL AND PREPARATION FOR BURIAL; 929]

funerary *adj* [➡ BURIAL AND PREPARATION FOR BURIAL; 929]

funereal *adj* **gloomy**, melancholy, sorrowful, mournful, sad, depressing, solemn, dismal, lugubrious, elegiac (*formal*) [➡ EMOTIONALLY UNPLEASANT AND UPSETTING; 227] *Opposite*: cheerful

funfair (*UK*) *n* **fair**, fairground, theme park, amusement park, carnival [➡ URBAN OUTDOOR SPACES; 1072]

fungal *adj* **fungiform**, mycological, fungoid, fungous [➡ MICROORGANISMS, FUNGI, AND ALGAE; 1023]

fungus *n* [➡ MICROORGANISMS, FUNGI, AND ALGAE; 1023]

fungus
◆ *types of fungi* beefsteak fungus, boletus, bracket fungus, cep, chanterelle, death cap, destroying angel, fairy ring champignon, field mushroom, fly agaric, horn of plenty, inky cap, lichen, mildew, mold, morel, mushroom, orange-peel fungus, oyster mushroom, puffball, stinkhorn, toadstool, truffle, yeast

funicular *type of* **rail vehicle** [➡ RAILROADS; 1107]

funk **1** *n* (*slang*) **stench**, smell, odor, stink [➡ SMELL AND SMELLING; 705] **2** *type of* **dance music** [➡ MUSIC, SONGS, AND SINGING; 907]

funky **1** *adj* (*slang*) **rhythmic**, driving, jazzy (*slang*) [➡ MUSICAL TERMS; 912] **2** *adj* (*informal*) **up-to-date**, fashionable, trendy (*informal*), cool (*informal*), happening (*informal*), fab (*dated informal*), hip (*slang*), groovy (*dated slang*), unconventional (*UK*) [➡ NEW, MODERN; 166] **3** *adj* (*slang*) **smelly**, fetid, malodorous, putrid, stinky (*informal*), rank (*literary*) [➡ SMELL AND SMELLING; 705]

fun-loving *adj* **playful**, joyful, high-spirited, frivolous, exuberant, outgoing, extrovert, gregarious, boisterous [➡ CHEERFULNESS OF OUTLOOK; 503] *Opposite*: staid

funnel **1** *n* **chimney**, pipe, flue, smokestack, conduit [➡ ROOFS, ROOF PARTS, AND CEILINGS; 1103] **2** *v* **channel**, direct, focus, guide, concentrate, siphon [➡ MOVE SOMETHING TO ANOTHER LOCATION; 324]

funnel cloud *type of* **cloud** [➡ CLOUDY AND RAINY WEATHER; 1052]

funnel-web spider *type of* **arachnid** [➡ ARACHNIDS; 1018]

funnily 1 *adv* **strangely**, curiously, surprisingly, oddly, unusually, remarkably, bizarrely [➡ BIZARRE AND PECULIAR; 257] 2 *adv* **comically**, humorously, amusingly, hilariously, wittily, sidesplittingly, uproariously, drolly [➡ FUNNY AND AMUSING; 216]

funniness *n* **humor**, comedy, comicalness, wit, wittiness, absurdity [➡ FUNNY AND AMUSING; 216] *Opposite*: solemnity

funny 1 *adj* **comical**, hilarious, amusing, comic, droll, witty, humorous, facetious, sidesplitting, uproarious, waggish (*informal*) [➡ FUNNY AND AMUSING; 216] *Opposite*: serious 2 *adj* **strange**, odd, weird, curious, peculiar, unusual, perplexing [➡ BIZARRE AND PECULIAR; 257] *Opposite*: normal 3 *adj* **quaint**, unconventional, eccentric, quirky, odd, offbeat, peculiar, off-the-wall (*informal*) [➡ BIZARRE AND PECULIAR; 257] 4 *adj* **unwell**, sick, nauseous, faint, giddy (*dated*), peculiar (*UK*) [➡ UNFIT AND WEAK; 739] 5 *n* (*informal*) **joke**, pun, witticism, bon mot, gag (*informal*), jest (*literary*) [➡ JOKES AND TEASING; 674]

> **Compare and Contrast:** *funny, comic, comical, droll, facetious, humorous, witty, hilarious, sidesplitting*
>
> CORE MEANING: causing or intended to cause amusement
>
> *funny* causing amusement or laughter, whether intentionally or not; *comic* used in the same way as *funny*, especially to describe books, poems, or plays; *comical* funny to the extent of being absurd, especially if this is unintentional; *droll* funny because it is whimsical or odd, or drily humorous; *facetious* supposed to be funny but ill-timed, inappropriate, or silly; *humorous* giving rise to amusement, smiles, or laughter, but more genial, sympathetic, or light-hearted than is necessarily the case with *funny*; *witty* using words in a clever, inventive, humorous way; *hilarious* extremely funny; *sidesplitting* very funny indeed, especially causing a great deal of uncontrollable laughter

funny bone *part of* **arm or hand** (*informal*) [➡ PARTS OF THE BODY: ARM AND HAND; 695]

fur 1 *n* **hair**, pelt, fleece, coat, fuzz, down [➡ THE SKIN; 720] 2 *type of* **fabric from animals** [➡ FABRICS; 1132]

furious 1 *adj* **angry**, livid, fuming, irate, infuriated, upset, beside yourself, mad, hopping mad (*informal*) [➡ IRRITATION AND ANGER; 541] *Opposite*: calm 2 *adj* **energetic**, concerted, all-out, breakneck, violent, uncompromising, frantic, feverish, desperate, ferocious, vehement, manic (*informal*), full-on [➡ HAPPENING QUICKLY; 104]

furiously 1 *adv* **angrily**, irately, wrathfully, heatedly, crossly [➡ IRRITATION AND ANGER; 541] 2 *adv* **energetically**, feverishly, frantically, desperately, violently, ferociously, vehemently [➡ HAPPENING QUICKLY; 104] *Opposite*: sluggishly

furiousness 1 *n* **anger**, rage, fury, wrath, crossness, ire (*formal*) [➡ IRRITATION AND ANGER; 541] 2 *n* **violence**, energy, vigor, ferocity, passion, vehemence, desperation [➡ DISORDER AND CHAOS; 245]

furl *v* **roll up**, wrap up, curl, curl up, tie up, wind up, fold up [➡ POSITION SOMETHING: AROUND SOMETHING; 327] *Opposite*: unfurl

furlough 1 *n* **leave of absence**, leave, absence, vacation, R & R, holiday (*UK*) [➡ PERIODS OF REST; 91] 2 *n* **layoff**, shutdown, unemployment [➡ WORK-RELATED ACTIVITIES; 834]

furnace 1 *n* **heater**, oven, kiln, boiler, blast furnace, incinerator [➡ FIRE, FLAMMABILITY, AND BURNING; 1165] 2 *type of* **heating appliance** [➡ HEATING, REFRIGERATION, AND VENTILATION; 1142]

furnish (*formal*) *v* **supply**, provide, equip, give, deliver, hand over, endow, yield [➡ EQUIP AND SUPPLY; 435]

furnished *adj* **equipped**, fitted out, well-appointed, well-found [➡ FULL; 1239] *Opposite*: unfurnished

furnishings *n* **furniture**, fixtures, tables, chairs, cabinets, beds [➡ FURNITURE; 858]

furniture *n* **fixtures**, tables, chairs, cabinets, beds, furnishings [➡ FURNITURE; 858]

furor 1 *n* **uproar**, outcry, commotion, controversy, protest, tumult, rumpus, disturbance, indignation, ruckus [➡ CHAOS AND UPROAR; 51] 2 *n* **excitement**, hysteria, hype, frenzy, commotion, ballyhoo, hubbub, fuss, to-do (*informal*), hoo-hah (*slang*) [➡ CHAOS AND UPROAR; 51]

furore *see* furor

furred *adj* **hairy**, furry, fuzzy, downy, fleecy, woolly [➡ PHYSICAL TEXTURE; 1222]

furriness *n* **hairiness**, fuzziness, woolliness, fleeciness, fluffiness, downiness [➡ PHYSICAL TEXTURE; 1222] *Opposite*: baldness

furrow 1 *n* **channel**, groove, rut, undulation, gully, crease, line, trough [➡ WATERCOURSES; 1111] 2 *v* **wrinkle**, crease, gather, draw, contract [➡ CHANGE OF SHAPE; 385]

furrowed *adj* **wrinkled**, crumply, creasy, wrinkly, crinkly [➡ IN BAD REPAIR; 1234] *Opposite*: smooth

furry *adj* **hairy**, fuzzy, woolly, furred, downy, fleecy [➡ PHYSICAL TEXTURE; 1222]

further 1 *adj* **additional**, more, extra, added, supplementary, auxiliary [➡ MORE AND EXCESS; 124] 2 *v* **advance**, promote, foster, broaden, expand, spread, extend, help, boost [➡ CAUSE TO CONTINUE; 267] *Opposite*: prevent

furthermore *adv* **also**, in addition, besides, additionally, moreover, what's more [➡ EXPRESSIONS INTRODUCING EXTRA INFORMATION; 139]

furthermost *adj* **farthest**, furthest, greatest, remotest, nethermost (*formal*) [➡ DISTANCE; 160]

furthest *adj* **farthest**, utmost, uttermost, outermost, furthermost, extreme [➡ DISTANCE; 160]

furtive *adj* **secretive**, stealthy, secret, sly, sneaky, surreptitious, clandestine, shifty [➡ SECRET AND UNKNOWN; 179] *Opposite*: open

> *See Compare and Contrast at* **secret**.

furtiveness 1 *n* **secrecy**, stealth, covertness, surreptitiousness, discreetness, discretion, shiftiness, sneakiness [➡ SECRET AND UNKNOWN; 179] 2 *n* **sneakiness**, suspiciousness, guiltiness, slyness, craftiness [➡ DECEITFUL; 513]

furuncle *n* [➡ CONDITIONS AFFECTING THE SKIN; 721]

fury *n* **anger**, rage, wrath, ferocity, ire (*formal*) [➡ IRRITATION AND ANGER; 541]

See Compare and Contrast at **anger**.

fuse *v* **combine**, blend, mingle, meld, coalesce, unite, merge [➡ COMBINE AND MIX; 400]

fuselage *part of* **aircraft** [➡ AIRCRAFT; 1148]

fusilier *n* [➡ MILITARY PERSONNEL; 828]

fusilli *type of* **pasta** [➡ PASTA; 1180]

fusion *n* **synthesis**, union, combination, mixture, blend, merging, meld [➡ COLLECTIONS AND MIXTURES OF THINGS; 1244]

fuss 1 *n* **commotion**, excitement, bother, bustle, activity, to-do (*informal*) [➡ CHAOS AND UPROAR; 51] **2** *n* **worry**, concern, bother, trouble, hassle (*informal*) [➡ PROBLEMS; 256] **3** *n* **protest**, controversy, argument, complaint, reaction, noise, row, storm [➡ CHAOS AND UPROAR; 51] **4** *v* **worry**, fret, stew, bother, niggle [➡ BE CONCERNED AND CARE; 581]

fussbudget (*informal*) *n* **worrier**, worrywart (*informal*), worryguts (*informal*) [➡ GRUMPY AND NEGATIVE PEOPLE; 953]

fussiness 1 *n* **trivialness**, pedantry, obsessiveness, prissiness, hairsplitting, preciseness, assiduousness, scrupulousness, niceness [➡ DIFFICULT TO PLEASE; 515] **2** *n* **meticulousness**, dogmatism, inflexibility, fastidiousness, exactness, choosiness (*informal*) [➡ DIFFICULT TO PLEASE; 515] **3** *n* **elaborateness**, frilliness, ornateness, overstatement [➡ IN POOR TASTE AND OVERSENTIMENTAL; 229]

fuss over *v* [➡ TAKE CARE OF AND SPOIL; 300]

fussy 1 *adj* **picky**, particular, finicky, fastidious, selective, inflexible, exacting, choosy (*informal*), persnickety (*informal*) [➡ DIFFICULT TO PLEASE; 515] *Opposite*: laid-back (*informal*) **2** *adj* **elaborate**, busy, frilly, ornate, over-elaborate, precious [➡ IN POOR TASTE AND OVERSENTIMENTAL; 229] **3** *adj* **trivial**, pedantic, obsessive, prissy, assiduous, scrupulous, painstaking [➡ DIFFICULT TO PLEASE; 515]

See Compare and Contrast at **careful**.

fusty 1 *adj* **stale**, moldy, damp, fetid, musty, mildewy, rotten [➡ DIRTY; 1235] **2** *adj* **stuffy**, antiquated, dull, boring, old-fashioned, outdated, conservative [➡ BORING AND UNINTERESTING; 234] *Opposite*: trendy (*informal*)

futile *adj* **useless**, pointless, fruitless, unsuccessful, vain, ineffectual, wasted, ineffective [➡ REDUNDANT AND USELESS; 240] *Opposite*: useful

futility *n* **uselessness**, pointlessness, ineffectiveness, ineffectuality, vainness, senselessness [➡ REDUNDANT AND USELESS; 240] *Opposite*: usefulness

futon *type of* **bed** [➡ FURNITURE; 858]

future 1 *n* **prospect**, outlook, potential, time ahead, time to come, what's in store [➡ FUTURE; 86] *Opposite*: past **2** *adj* **upcoming**, forthcoming, coming, imminent, yet to come, impending [➡ FUTURE; 86] *Opposite*: past

futures *n* **stocks**, commodities, contracts, investments [➡ ACCOUNTING, BANKING, AND BUDGETING; 799]

futurism *type of* **20th-century art movement** [➡ ARTISTIC MOVEMENTS AND STYLES; 899]

futuristic *adj* **innovative**, revolutionary, ahead of its time, advanced, ultramodern, space-age, high-tech, science fiction [➡ NEW, MODERN; 166] *Opposite*: antiquated

fuzz *n* **down**, hair, fur, lint, fluff, nap [➡ HAIR; 484]

fuzziness 1 *n* **hairiness**, fluffiness, woolliness, down, wool, hair, fur, fuzz [➡ PHYSICAL TEXTURE; 1222] **2** *n* **uncertainty**, vagueness, unsureness, incoherence, ambiguity, indistinctness, unclearness [➡ VAGUENESS; 243] *Opposite*: clarity **3** *n* **blurriness**, unclearness, nebulousness, haziness, vagueness, mistiness, shadowiness, bleariness, indistinctness [➡ VISUAL TEXTURE; 1221]

fuzzy 1 *adj* **hairy**, furry, fluffy, downy, woolly [➡ DESCRIBING HAIR; 486] **2** *adj* **blurry**, unclear, nebulous, hazy, vague, misty, shadowy, bleary, indistinct [➡ VISUAL TEXTURE; 1221] *Opposite*: clear **3** *adj* **unsure**, ambiguous, vague, unclear, indistinct, incoherent, uncertain, ill-defined, woolly [➡ VAGUENESS; 243] *Opposite*: clear

G

gab (*informal*) **1** *v* **chatter**, chat, prattle, rattle on, jabber, gossip, gush, go on, talk a mile a minute, spout, talk ten to the dozen, talk nineteen to the dozen, natter (*informal*), gas (*informal*), talk the hind legs off a donkey (*UK*) [➡ CHATTER AND BABBLE; 617] **2** *n* **chat**, chatter, talk, conversation, gossip, chitchat (*informal*) [➡ INFORMAL COMMUNICATION; 45]

gabardine *type of* **fabric from animals** [➡ FABRICS; 1132]

gabbing (*informal*) *n* [➡ INFORMAL COMMUNICATION; 45]

gabble **1** *v* **chat**, chatter, swap gossip, prattle, blabber, gab (*informal*), natter (*informal*), blather (*informal*), blab (*informal*), footle (*informal*) [➡ CHATTER AND BABBLE; 617] **2** *n* **gibberish**, chatter, prattle, rubbish, nonsense, blabber, gab (*informal*), twaddle (*informal*), blather (*informal*) [➡ MEANINGLESS SPEECH OR WRITING; 676]

gabby (*informal*) *adj* **talkative**, chatty, garrulous, voluble, gushing, loquacious [➡ ELOQUENT, TALKATIVE, AND LONG-WINDED; 632] *Opposite:* taciturn

gable *part of* **building** [➡ PARTS OF A BUILDING; 1095]

gad (*humorous*) *v* **socialize**, go partying, go clubbing, have a night on the town, gallivant (*informal*), party (*informal*), paint the town red (*informal*), live it up (*slang*) [➡ LEISURE AND RECREATION; 874]

gadabout (*humorous*) *n* **pleasure-seeker**, fun lover, social butterfly, partygoer, raver (*informal*), gadder (*dated*) [➡ PLEASURE-SEEKERS AND HEDONISTS; 886]

gadfly **1** *n* (*dated*) **nuisance**, pest, irritator, tormentor, meddler, pesterer, busybody (*informal*) [➡ INTERFERING PEOPLE AND TATTLETALES; 950] **2** *type of* **parasitic insect** [➡ PARASITES; 1017]

gadget **1** *n* **device**, tool, appliance, implement, contraption, utensil, apparatus [➡ DEVICES; 1115] **2** *n* **thingamajig** (*informal*), thingamabob (*informal*), gizmo (*informal*), doohickey (*informal*), jigger (*informal*), doodad (*informal*), widget (*humorous*) [➡ PHYSICAL OBJECTS; 1243]

gaff *part of* **sailing vessel** [➡ PARTS OF A SHIP OR BOAT; 1151]

gaffe *n* **blunder**, solecism, mistake, error, boo-boo (*informal*), blooper (*informal humorous*), howler (*slang*), faux pas (*literary*) [➡ MISTAKES; 250]

gag **1** *n* **restraint**, curb, muzzle, tape, binding [➡ FASTENERS, LINKS, AND NETWORKS; 1247] **2** *n* (*informal*) **joke**, one-liner, funny, shaggy-dog story, quip, witticism, practical joke, crack (*informal*) [➡ JOKES AND TEASING; 674] **3** *n* **ban**, gag order, injunction, restriction, interdiction, prohibition, court order, gagging order (*UK*) [➡ TRIAL, PUNISHMENT, AND LEGAL OUTCOMES; 819] **4** *v* **muzzle**, stifle, muffle, restrain, curb, bind up, seal somebody's lips [➡ CAPTIVITY AND LOSS OF FREEDOM; 248] **5** *v* **suppress**, silence, interdict, prohibit, ban, muzzle, restrict, bind over [➡ MAKE IMPOSSIBLE; 276] **6** *v* **choke**, retch, suffocate, stifle, hyperventilate, heave (*informal*) [➡ VOMIT AND BELCH; 712]

gaggle **1** *n* **crowd**, group, horde, throng, multitude, pack, mob, drove [➡ GROUPS OF PEOPLE; 935] **2** *type of* **flock** [➡ GROUPS OF BIRDS; 1007]

gag order *n* **restraining order**, injunction, gag, interdiction, prohibition, curb, court order, ban, restriction [➡ TRIAL, PUNISHMENT, AND LEGAL OUTCOMES; 819]

gaiety *n* **joyfulness**, lightheartedness, happiness, liveliness, merriment, cheerfulness, vivacity, high spirits, vivaciousness [➡ PLEASURE, EXCITEMENT, AND ELATION; 534] *Opposite:* misery

gaily *adv* **happily**, joyfully, cheerily, merrily, brightly, lightheartedly, vivaciously [➡ PLEASURE, EXCITEMENT, AND ELATION; 534] *Opposite:* sadly

gain **1** *v* **get**, achieve, acquire, obtain, secure, collect, earn, reap [➡ GET; 420] *Opposite:* lose **2** *v* **increase**, add, put on, grow, expand, enlarge, extend, multiply [➡ CHANGE OF SIZE: BIGGER; 392] *Opposite:* decrease **3** *n* **achievement**, improvement, advantage, advance, increase, expansion, addition [➡ SOURCE OF HAPPINESS, PLEASURE, OR IMPROVEMENT; 209] *Opposite:* setback **4** *n* **advantage**, profit, reward, benefit, return, acquisition, payback [➡ INCOME; 460] *Opposite:* loss

See Compare and Contrast at **get**.

gain access *v* **get into**, enter, infiltrate, access, get permission, get ahold of (*informal*) [➡ ARRIVE; 12]

gainful *adj* **profitable**, advantageous, lucrative, rewarding, useful, paid, productive, beneficial, remunerative [➡ USEFULNESS; 199] *Opposite:* unprofitable

gain ground *v* **progress**, advance, improve, expand, spread, develop [➡ SUCCEED AND WIN; 79] *Opposite:* fall back

gain on *v* **near**, close in on, approach, catch up on, close the gap, get closer to, get nearer to [➡ ACCOMPANY AND FOLLOW; 337]

gainsay (*formal*) *v* **oppose**, contradict, argue, refute, deny, contravene, dispute, naysay, negate (*formal*), disaffirm (*formal*) [➡ DENY AND REJECT; 644] *Opposite:* agree

gait *n* **walk**, step, pace, bearing, manner, style, posture [➡ TEMPERAMENT AND BEHAVIOR; 492]

gala *n* **festival**, celebration, party, ball, festivity, social event, concert, entertainment, special occasion [➡ PARTIES, DANCES, AND CELEBRATIONS; 37]

galactic **1** *adj* (*informal*) **huge**, enormous, immense, vast, extensive, colossal, gargantuan, gigantic [➡ LARGE; 1193] *Opposite:* infinitesimal **2** *adj* **celestial**, cosmic, planetary, astronomic, space [➡ THE SOLAR SYSTEM AND ASTRONOMY; 1060] *Opposite:* terrestrial

galaxy **1** *n* **gathering**, assembly, meeting, cluster, collection, congregation [➡ COLLECTIONS AND MIXTURES OF THINGS; 1244] **2** *type of* **star or star system** [➡ HEAVENLY BODIES; 1061]

gale n **wind**, windstorm, storm, tempest, hurricane, howling wind, gust, blow (*informal*) [➡ WINDY AND STORMY WEATHER; 1053] *Opposite*: breeze

gale-force adj [➡ WINDY AND STORMY WEATHER; 1053]

gall 1 n **audacity**, impudence, boldness, nerve, effrontery, insolence, cheek (*informal*), face (*informal*), moxie (*slang*) [➡ BAD MANNERS AND SOCIAL SKILLS; 521] 2 n **sore**, rub, irritation, lesion, wound, blister [➡ ILLNESSES AND DISORDERS; 732] 3 v **irritate**, annoy, infuriate, anger, vex, madden, provoke, incense, outrage, aggravate (*informal*) [➡ ANGER AND ANNOY; 569] *Opposite*: please

gallant 1 adj (*literary*) **brave**, courageous, heroic, valiant, fearless, noble, spirited, bold, dauntless (*literary*), intrepid (*literary or humorous*) [➡ COURAGE; 498] *Opposite*: cowardly 2 adj **courteous**, chivalrous, polite, gentlemanly, thoughtful, magnanimous, gracious [➡ GOOD MANNERS AND SOCIAL SKILLS; 520] *Opposite*: rude

gallantry 1 n (*literary*) **courage**, bravery, heroism, valor, daring, nerve, fearlessness, boldness [➡ COURAGE; 498] *Opposite*: cowardice 2 n **courtesy**, thoughtfulness, chivalry, politeness, attentiveness, gentility, graciousness [➡ GOOD MANNERS AND SOCIAL SKILLS; 520] *Opposite*: boorishness

gallbladder part of **digestive tract** [➡ THE DIGESTIVE TRACT; 709]

galleon type of **historical vessel** [➡ SHIPS AND BOATS; 1150]

gallery 1 n **colonnade**, portico, arcade, galleria, corridor, walkway, passageway [➡ ANCILLARY BUILDINGS; 1080] 2 n **balcony**, veranda, porch [➡ STAIRS AND STORIES; 1102] 3 type of **room in public buildings** [➡ TYPES OF ROOMS; 1097]

galley 1 part of **ship or boat** [➡ PARTS OF A SHIP OR BOAT; 1151] 2 type of **historical vessel** [➡ SHIPS AND BOATS; 1150]

galling adj **frustrating**, annoying, irritating, infuriating, exasperating, maddening, vexing [➡ IRRITATING; 228] *Opposite*: soothing

gallivant (*informal*) v **globetrot**, tour, travel around, gad (*humorous*), wander, rove, meander, ramble [➡ TRAVEL: WAYS OF TRAVELING; 320] *Opposite*: stay put

gallon type of **nonmetric unit** [➡ SIZE AND DIMENSIONS; 1192]

gallons (*UK*) n **lots**, loads (*informal*), tons (*informal*), heaps (*informal*), oodles (*informal*) [➡ MANY, MUCH, LARGE AMOUNT; 117] *Opposite*: few

gallop 1 n **sprint**, dash, charge, bolt, mad dash, run [➡ SUDDEN EVENTS; 52] 2 v **dash**, career, hurtle, run, fly, bolt, sprint, charge, race [➡ MOVE FAST; 313]

gallows n **scaffold**, gibbet, gallows tree, crossbeam, arm, beam [➡ ANCIENT MANMADE STRUCTURES; 1089]

galore adj **abundant**, plentiful, copious, aplenty, plenteous (*literary*) [➡ MANY, MUCH, LARGE AMOUNT; 117] *Opposite*: scant

galoshes type of **boot** [➡ FOOTWEAR; 871]

galumph (*informal*) v [➡ MOVE SLOWLY; 314]

galvanize v **stimulate**, spur, rouse, electrify, fire up, stir up, animate, incite [➡ CAUSE TO START; 265] *Opposite*: dampen

gam type of **herd** [➡ GROUPS OF ANIMALS; 993]

gambit n **stratagem**, maneuver, ploy, scheme, strategy, ruse [➡ WAYS OF DOING THINGS; 294]

gamble 1 v **bet**, wager, back, game, risk, stake, put money on, lay bets [➡ GAMBLE AND TAKE RISKS; 466] 2 v **risk**, stake, venture, hazard, chance, speculate, bet [➡ GAMBLE AND TAKE RISKS; 466] *Opposite*: play safe 3 n **wager**, bet, stake [➡ GAMBLE AND TAKE RISKS; 466] 4 n **chance**, risk, hazard, venture, speculation [➡ GAMBLE AND TAKE RISKS; 466]

gamble away v **squander**, lose, fritter away, waste, throw away, pour down the drain [➡ USE UP AND WASTE; 474]

gambler 1 n **bettor**, risker, wagerer, speculator, plunger (*informal*), high roller (*slang*), gamester (*archaic*) [➡ PEOPLE IN SPORTS AND LEISURE; 876] 2 n **risk-taker**, adventurer, speculator, risker [➡ PEOPLE IN SPORTS AND LEISURE; 876]

gambling n **betting**, gaming, bookmaking [➡ GAMBLE AND TAKE RISKS; 466]

gambol v **frolic**, skip, hop, spring, leap, bound, caper, frisk, romp [➡ FIDGET AND FROLIC; 311]

game 1 n **pastime**, sport, diversion, amusement, entertainment, recreation [➡ LEISURE AND RECREATION; 874] 2 n **match**, fixture, competition, contest, derby, event [➡ NON-AGGRESSIVE/SPORTING EVENTS; 40] 3 n **wild animals**, big game, game birds, game fish [➡ TYPES AND CUTS OF MEAT; 1177] 4 adj **willing**, ready, up for, disposed, inclined, on for [➡ THE WILL AND WILLINGNESS; 563] *Opposite*: unwilling 5 adj **brave**, spirited, plucky, resolute, determined, tough, gutsy (*informal*), spunky (*informal*), feisty (*informal*) [➡ COURAGE; 498] *Opposite*: spiritless

gamekeeper n **warden**, game warden, breeder, keeper, handler, steward [➡ FARMERS, GARDENERS, AND MANUAL WORKERS; 849]

gamelan type of **percussion instrument** [➡ MUSICAL INSTRUMENTS; 910]

gamely adv **bravely**, sportingly, spiritedly, stoically, determinedly, resolutely, gutsily (*informal*), spunkily (*informal*), feistily (*informal*) [➡ COURAGE; 498] *Opposite*: weakly

game piece n [➡ TOYS; 880]

---

game piece

◆ *types of game pieces*
checker, chessman, chip, counter, domino, jack, tiddlywink

---

game plan n **plan**, strategy, scheme, stratagem, ploy, maneuver [➡ WAYS OF DOING THINGS; 294]

games n **sports**, competition, tournament, cup, sports event, meet, knockout (*UK*) [➡ NON-AGGRESSIVE/SPORTING EVENTS; 40]

game show type of **broadcast** [➡ TELEVISION AND RADIO; 606]

gamine adj [➡ PEOPLE'S PHYSICAL APPEARANCE; 475]

gammon type of **meat** [➡ TYPES AND CUTS OF MEAT; 1177]

gamut n **range**, scale, length, scope, extent, breadth, array [➡ DEGREE AND EXTENT; 110]

gander 1 n (*informal*) **look**, peek, glimpse, glance [➡ LOOKING AND LOOKS; 700] 2 type of **male or female bird** [➡ MALE OR FEMALE BIRDS; 1005]

gang 1 n mob, band, ring, clique, posse (*slang*) [➡FRIENDS AND ACQUAINTANCES; 936] 2 n team, squad, group, lineup, crew (*informal*), posse (*slang*) [➡GROUPS OF PEOPLE; 935] 3 *type of* herd [➡GROUPS OF ANIMALS; 993]

gangland n underworld, criminal world, organized crime, vice, racketeering [➡CRIMES; 817]

gangling *adj* lanky, gangly, tall, rangy, awkward, gawky (*informal*) [➡BUILD; 477] *Opposite:* elegant

ganglion n swelling, tumor, lump, knot, concentration, cyst [➡ILLNESSES AND DISORDERS; 732]

gangly *adj* lanky, gangling, tall, rangy, awkward, gawky (*informal*) [➡BUILD; 477] *Opposite:* elegant

gangplank n bridge, walkway, footway, footbridge, gangway, passage [➡BRIDGES, TUNNELS, CROSSINGS, AND JUNCTIONS; 1112]

gangrene 1 n infection, decay, rot, decomposition, putrefaction, disease [➡ILLNESSES AND DISORDERS; 732] *Opposite:* health 2 v fester, putrefy, decompose, decay, molder, rot [➡GO BAD AND CORRODE; 390] *Opposite:* recover

gangrenous *adj* infected, festering, diseased, decaying, rotting, decomposing, putrescent, putrid [➡SICKNESS; 729] *Opposite:* healthy

gangsta rap *type of* pop and vocal music [➡MUSIC, SONGS, AND SINGING; 907]

gangster n criminal, thug, goon, hoodlum, racketeer, Mafioso, hooligan (*informal*), mobster (*informal*), gorilla (*informal*) [➡CRIMINALS; 821]

gang up on v unite against, join forces against, combine against, pick on, mob, surround, target, put pressure on [➡ACCUSE, BLAME, AND CRITICIZE; 641]

gangway n walkway, footway, aisle, passage, passageway, corridor [➡PATHWAYS; 1110]

gannet *type of* sea bird [➡SEA BIRDS; 1002]

gantry n scaffold, framework, support [➡SUPPORTS AND BASES; 1255]

gap 1 n break, opening, breach, slit, fissure, crack, aperture, cavity, hole [➡HOLES, GAPS, AND FORKS; 1252] 2 n interval, hiatus, pause, break, interruption, lull, interlude, space [➡PAUSES AND PHASES; 56] *Opposite:* continuity 3 n disparity, difference, divergence, mismatch, inequality, disproportion, imparity, variance [➡DIFFERENCE; 149] *Opposite:* parity 4 n chasm, gorge, ravine, canyon, rift, gully, gulch [➡GEOLOGIC FEATURES; 1056]

gape 1 v stare, gaze, ogle, look hard, gawk (*informal*), rubberneck (*informal*), gawp (*UK informal*) [➡LOOKING AND LOOKS; 700] 2 v part, separate, divide, yawn, break open, fall open [➡SEPARATE AND DIVIDE; 401]

See Compare and Contrast at **gaze.**

gaping *adj* wide, wide open, huge, yawning, cavernous, deep, abysmal [➡WIDTH: WIDE; 1199]

garage 1 n carport, cover, shed, car stall, outbuilding, parking garage, lockup (*UK*) [➡STORES AND STORAGE BUILDINGS; 1088] 2 n service station, gas station, petrol station (*UK*) [➡RETAIL OUTLETS; 1083] 3 *type of* dance music [➡MUSIC, SONGS, AND SINGING; 907]

4 *type of* outbuilding [➡ANCILLARY BUILDINGS; 1080] 5 *type of* industrial site [➡INDUSTRIAL BUILDINGS; 1087]

garage sale n [➡SALES AND SHOWS; 443]

garb 1 n clothing, dress, costume, apparel, outfit, kit, duds (*informal*), gear (*informal*), threads (*slang*), attire (*formal*), weeds (*archaic or literary*) [➡CLOTHES AND ACCESSORIES; 864] 2 v clothe, dress, do up, dress up, attire (*formal*), array (*literary*) [➡DRESS, WEAR, AND UNDRESS; 868]

garbage 1 n trash, refuse, compost, debris, litter, waste, junk (*informal*), rubbish (*UK*) [➡JUNK AND USELESS OBJECTS; 1249] 2 n nonsense, trivia, drivel, rubbish, hogwash (*informal*), baloney (*informal*), gobbledygook (*informal*) [➡MEANINGLESS SPEECH OR WRITING; 676] *Opposite:* sense

garbage can n wastebasket, trash can, ash can, rubbish bin (*UK*), waste bin (*UK*), litter bin (*UK*) [➡CONTAINERS, RECEPTACLES, AND PACKAGING; 1245]

garbage disposal *type of* appliance [➡HOUSEHOLD APPLIANCES; 1117]

garbage dump n junkyard, landfill, scrapheap, tip (*UK*), scrapyard (*UK*) [➡STORES AND STORAGE BUILDINGS; 1088]

garbage truck *type of* public service vehicle [➡VEHICLES; 1145]

garbagy *adj* [➡REDUNDANT AND USELESS; 240]

garbanzo *type of* pulse [➡PEAS AND BEANS; 1189]

garbanzo bean *see* **garbanzo**

garbed *adj* arrayed, clothed, dressed, robed, wearing, kitted out, turned out [➡DRESS, WEAR, AND UNDRESS; 868]

garble v jumble, confuse, muddle, mangle, distort, corrupt, pervert, twist [➡CREATE DISORDER AND CAUSE CHAOS; 358]

garbled *adj* jumbled, confused, muddled, distorted, mangled, corrupted, twisted, misconstrued [➡INARTICULATE, RAMBLING, AND AWKWARD; 633] *Opposite:* clear

garden 1 n yard, back yard, plot, patch, bower, allotment (*UK*) [➡GARDENS; 1074] 2 n park, gardens, public park, green, common, botanical garden, parkland [➡URBAN OUTDOOR SPACES; 1072] 3 v plant, cultivate, tend, work, grow, weed, sow, raise [➡GROW AND CULTIVATE; 351]

garden

◆ *types of gardens*
bog garden, community garden, container garden, cottage garden, cutting garden, flower garden, herb garden, Japanese garden, kitchen garden, knot garden, orchard, raised bed garden, rock garden, rose garden, vegetable garden, vegetable plot, water garden

◆ *parts of a garden*
arbor, arboretum, bed, border, container, flowerbed, lawn, patio, pergola, planter, rockery, shrubbery, water feature, window box

garden apartment *type of* apartment [➡RESIDENTIAL BUILDINGS; 1078]

garden center *type of* retail outlet [➡RETAIL OUTLETS; 1083]

gardener n horticulturist, landscape gardener, grower,

planter, landscaper, weeder, landscape architect [➡ FARMERS, GARDENERS, AND MANUAL WORKERS; 849]

gardenia *type of* **shrub or bush** [➡ BUSHES AND SHRUBS; 1027]

garden party *n* [➡ PARTIES, DANCES, AND CELEBRATIONS; 37]

garden shed *type of* **outbuilding** [➡ ANCILLARY BUILDINGS; 1080]

garden-variety *adj* [➡ ORDINARINESS; 244]

gargantuan *adj* **huge**, large, gigantic, enormous, vast, massive, colossal, immense [➡ LARGE; 1193] *Opposite:* tiny

gargle 1 *v* **rinse your mouth**, rinse, wash out, disinfect, freshen, cleanse, swill [➡ CLEAN AND POLISH; 403] 2 *v* **gurgle**, bubble, burble [➡ EMIT CONTINUOUS SOUNDS; 366]

gargoyle *n* **ornament**, decoration, carving, figurehead, effigy [➡ SCULPTURE; 902]

garish *adj* **gaudy**, showy, lurid, vulgar, brash, loud, tasteless, tawdry, bright [➡ IN POOR TASTE AND OVERSENTIMENTAL; 229] *Opposite:* tasteful

garishness *n* **gaudiness**, tawdriness, vulgarity, brashness, loudness, tastelessness, showiness, luridness, brightness [➡ IN POOR TASTE AND OVERSENTIMENTAL; 229] *Opposite:* subtlety

garland 1 *n* **wreath**, chaplet, coronet, circlet, crown [➡ ORNAMENTS AND DECORATIONS; 1248] 2 *n* **festoon**, swag, drape, chain, lei [➡ ORNAMENTS AND DECORATIONS; 1248]

garlic *type of* **vegetable** [➡ FRUIT AND VEGETABLES; 1176]

garment *n* **clothing**, vestment, costume, dress, coat, skirt, apparel, attire (*formal*), frock (*dated*), raiment (*archaic or literary*) [➡ CLOTHES AND ACCESSORIES; 864]

garment

◆ *parts of a garment*
brim, buckle, button, buttonhole, coattail, collar, cuff, décolletage, drawstring, gusset, hem, lace, lapel, leg, lining, neck, neckband, neckline, pocket, sash, sleeve, strap, waistband, zipper

garner 1 *v* **gather**, bring in, save, lay down, store, put away, harvest, reap [➡ GET; 420] *Opposite:* scatter 2 *v* **acquire**, get, gain, collect, bring together, search out, earn, accumulate [➡ GET; 420] *Opposite:* squander

garnet 1 *type of* **red** [➡ COLORS; 1224] 2 *type of* **gemstone** [➡ PRECIOUS STONES; 1278]

garnish 1 *v* **enhance**, improve, set off, embellish, decorate, glaze, dress up, pretty up, prettify, deck (*literary*) [➡ COOKING AND FOOD PREPARATION; 353] 2 *n* **enhancer**, sauce, accompaniment, relish, side dish, gravy, trimmings, fixings (*informal*) [➡ SEASONINGS AND SAUCES; 1174] 3 *n* **embellishment**, decoration, adornment, ornament, trimming, enhancement [➡ ORNAMENTS AND DECORATIONS; 1248]

garret *n* **attic**, loft, gable, penthouse, top story, upper floor, roof space [➡ TYPES OF ROOMS; 1097]

garrison *n* **barracks**, quarters, military base, casern [➡ RESIDENTIAL BUILDINGS; 1078]

garrote *v* [➡ KILL; 923]

garrulous *adj* **talkative**, voluble, chatty, effusive, loquacious, verbose, long-winded, gushing, chattering, gassy (*informal*), gaseous (*informal*) [➡ ELOQUENT, TALKATIVE, AND LONG-WINDED; 632] *Opposite:* taciturn

See Compare and Contrast at **talkative**.

garrulousness *n* **verbosity**, volubility, chattiness, prattling, long-windedness, talkativeness, effusiveness, gift of the gab (*informal*), loquacity (*formal*) [➡ ELOQUENT, TALKATIVE, AND LONG-WINDED; 632] *Opposite:* taciturnity

garter *type of* **lower body underwear** [➡ ACCESSORIES, MILLINERY, AND LINGERIE; 867]

garter snake *type of* **nonpoisonous snake** [➡ SNAKES; 995]

gas 1 *n* **air**, vapor, fume, smoke [➡ GASES; 1275] 2 *n* (*slang*) **experience**, thrill, blast (*slang*), trip (*slang*) [➡ TREATS; 210] *Opposite:* drag 3 *n* (*slang*) **chatter**, prattle, nonsense, rubbish, bombast, balderdash, chitchat (*informal*), gab (*informal*), blather (*informal*), footle (*informal*), bunkum (*informal*), claptrap (*informal*), bunk (*slang*), poppycock (*dated informal*) [➡ MEANINGLESS SPEECH OR WRITING; 676] 4 *v* (*informal*) **chat**, gossip, chitchat (*informal*), natter (*informal*), yak (*informal*), jaw (*slang*), chew the fat (*slang*) [➡ GOSSIP; 678]

gas

◆ *types of gases*
acetylene, argon, butane, chlorine, coal gas, greenhouse gas, helium, hydrogen, inert gas, marsh gas, methane, mustard gas, natural gas, neon, nerve gas, nitrogen, nitrous oxide, noble gas, oxygen, poison gas, propellant, tear gas

gaseous 1 *adj* **vaporous**, gassy, steamy, smoky, fumy, gasiform [➡ FLUID AND NONSOLID; 1213] 2 *adj* **carbonated**, fizzy, bubbly, sparkling, effervescent, gassy [➡ FLUID AND NONSOLID; 1213] *Opposite:* still 3 *adj* (*informal*) **talkative**, verbose, long-winded, chatty, chattering, loquacious, voluble, effusive, garrulous, gushing, prattling, gassy (*informal*) [➡ ELOQUENT, TALKATIVE, AND LONG-WINDED; 632] *Opposite:* tight-lipped

gash 1 *n* **wound**, slash, cut, tear, laceration, incision [➡ HOLES, GAPS, AND FORKS; 1252] 2 *v* **cut**, slash, wound, tear, lacerate, gouge [➡ TEAR, BREAK, AND CUT; 360]

gasket 1 *n* **seal**, washer, ring, liner, lining [➡ PARTS OF MACHINES AND TOOLS; 1118] 2 *part of* **engine** [➡ PARTS OF AN ENGINE; 1144]

gasoline *n* [➡ ENERGY SOURCES; 1162]

gasometer *type of* **storage space** [➡ STORES AND STORAGE BUILDINGS; 1088]

gasp 1 *n* **wheeze**, pant, huff, puff, breath [➡ BREATHE AND NOT BREATHE; 716] 2 *type of* **human sound** [➡ SOUNDS MADE BY PEOPLE; 1262]

gasping 1 *adj* **out of breath**, winded, breathless, panting, wheezing, puffing, puffed (*UK*) [➡ BREATHE AND NOT BREATHE; 716] 2 *adj* (*UK*) **thirsty**, parched, dry, dehydrated, thirsting [➡ DRINK; 711] 3 *adj* (*UK*) **desperate**, dying, longing, craving, yearning, burning [➡ DESIRE AND WANT; 579]

gas station *n* **service station**, service area, garage, gas pumps, filling station, petrol station (*UK*), petrol pumps (*UK*) [➡ RETAIL OUTLETS; 1083]

gassy 1 *adj* **carbonated**, fizzy, bubbly, sparkling, effervescent, gaseous [➡ FLUID AND NONSOLID; 1213] *Opposite*: still 2 *adj* **vaporous**, gaseous, steamy, smoky, fumy, gasiform [➡ FLUID AND NONSOLID; 1213] 3 *adj* (*informal*) **talkative**, verbose, long-winded, chatty, gossipy, garrulous, chattering, loquacious, voluble, gushing, prattling, gaseous (*informal*) [➡ ELOQUENT, TALKATIVE, AND LONG-WINDED; 632] *Opposite*: tight-lipped

gastric *adj* **stomach**, abdominal, intestinal, digestive, gastrointestinal, tummy (*informal*) [➡ THE DIGESTIVE TRACT; 709]

gastrodome *type of* **eating place** [➡ HOTELS, RESTAURANTS, AND CLUBS; 1082]

gastrointestinal *adj* **stomach**, abdominal, intestinal, digestive, gastric, tummy (*informal*) [➡ THE DIGESTIVE TRACT; 709]

gastronome *n* **gourmet**, epicure, food lover, connoisseur, bon vivant, gourmand, foodie (*informal*), bon viveur (*literary*) [➡ EATERS, GOURMETS, AND DIETARY CHOICES; 714] *Opposite*: glutton

gastronomic *adj* **culinary**, cooking, food, gourmet, epicurean [➡ FOOD; 1167]

gastronomy *n* **cookery**, cooking, cuisine, food, gourmet food, gourmandise, epicureanism [➡ FOOD; 1167]

gasworks *n* **gas plant**, power station, installation, power plant [➡ INDUSTRIAL BUILDINGS; 1087]

gate 1 *n* **entrance**, entry, door, gateway, opening, postern, doorway, access [➡ DOORS AND ACCESS POINTS; 1101] 2 *n* **attendance**, crowd, turnout, audience [➡ AUDIENCES AND ATTENDEES; 937] 3 *n* **receipts**, proceeds, revenue, take, takings [➡ INCOME; 460]

gateau *type of* **cake** [➡ CAKES, COOKIES, AND DESSERTS; 1181]

gatecrash *v* **crash** (*informal*), sneak in, barge in, invade, intrude, trespass [➡ ARRIVE; 12]

gatecrasher (*UK*) *n* **partycrasher**, intruder, interloper, trespasser, invader [➡ STRANGERS; 972] *Opposite*: guest

gatehouse *type of* **outbuilding** [➡ ANCILLARY BUILDINGS; 1080]

gateleg table *type of* **table** [➡ FURNITURE; 858]

gatepost *n* **support**, upright, post, frame, doorpost, door jamb [➡ STICKS, POLES, AND WEDGES; 1254]

gateway 1 *n* **entry**, doorway, entryway, entrance, opening, access, postern, door [➡ DOORS AND ACCESS POINTS; 1101] 2 *n* **opening**, first step, opportunity, access, way in, chance [➡ ADVANTAGES; 212]

gather 1 *v* **meet**, get together, collect, congregate, assemble, join together, gather round, gather together [➡ GET CLOSER TOGETHER; 310] *Opposite*: disperse 2 *v* **collect**, bring together, draw together, amass, pull together, pile up, gather together, muster, marshal, round up, mobilize [➡ COMBINE AND MIX; 400] *Opposite*: distribute 3 *v* **harvest**, pick, collect, garner, pluck, reap [➡ GET; 420] *Opposite*: scatter 4 *v* **understand**, infer, conclude, hear, assume, deduce, surmise [➡ UNDERSTAND AND GRASP; 759] *Opposite*: misunderstand 5 *v* **pleat**, fold, pucker, ruche, shirr, crimp, ruck, bunch

[➡ CHANGE OF SHAPE; 385] *Opposite*: smooth 6 *n* **fold**, pleat, pucker, wrinkle, ruck, crease [➡ ORNAMENTS AND DECORATIONS; 1248]

See Compare and Contrast at **collect**.

gathering *n* **meeting**, assembly, congregation, crowd, jamboree, rally, get-together (*informal*) [➡ MEETINGS AND ASSEMBLIES; 43]

gathering place *n* **meeting place**, center, assembly point, forum [➡ PUBLIC BUILDINGS AND MEETING PLACES; 1081]

gather together *v* [➡ GET CLOSER TOGETHER; 310]

gather up *v* **pick up**, take up, draw up, scoop up, dredge up, haul up [➡ CONTACT: HOLD; 411] *Opposite*: put down

gauche *adj* **awkward**, uncouth, tactless, callow, graceless, clumsy [➡ BAD MANNERS AND SOCIAL SKILLS; 521] *Opposite*: poised

gaucheness *n* **uncouthness**, awkwardness, tactlessness, gracelessness, clumsiness, callowness [➡ BAD MANNERS AND SOCIAL SKILLS; 521] *Opposite*: poise

gaucherie *n* [➡ AGILITY OF THE BODY; 476]

gaudiness *n* **showiness**, luridness, flamboyance, garishness, tawdriness, loudness, cheapness, vividness, extravagance, colorfulness, tackiness (*informal*) [➡ IN POOR TASTE AND OVERSENTIMENTAL; 229] *Opposite*: tastefulness

gaudy *adj* **garish**, flashy, kitschy, loud, showy, colorful, lurid, extravagant, cheap, flamboyant, tawdry, tacky (*informal*) [➡ IN POOR TASTE AND OVERSENTIMENTAL; 229] *Opposite*: tasteful

gauge 1 *v* **evaluate**, judge, assess, determine, measure, appraise, estimate, test, calculate, guess, weigh [➡ EXAMINE AND ASSESS; 753] 2 *n* **measurement**, estimate, assessment, measure, test, yardstick, indication, criterion, standard, benchmark, indicator [➡ MEASURING DEVICES; 1123]

gaunt *adj* **thin**, skinny, lean, bony, emaciated, scrawny, skeletal, haggard [➡ BUILD; 477] *Opposite*: plump

gauntness *n* **thinness**, skinniness, leanness, boniness, scrawniness, scragginess [➡ BUILD; 477] *Opposite*: plumpness

gauze *type of* **fabric from plants** [➡ FABRICS; 1132]

gauzy *adj* **thin**, delicate, filmy, see-through, gossamer, light, diaphanous, transparent [➡ VISUAL TEXTURES; 1221] *Opposite*: heavy

gawk (*informal*) *v* **gape**, stare, gaze, goggle, watch, ogle, rubberneck (*informal*) [➡ LOOKING AND LOOKS; 700] *Opposite*: ignore

See Compare and Contrast at **gaze**.

gawkiness (*informal*) *n* **awkwardness**, clumsiness, inelegance, gracelessness, ungainliness [➡ AGILITY OF THE BODY; 476] *Opposite*: gracefulness

gawky (*informal*) *adj* **awkward**, clumsy, gangling, gangly, ungainly, inelegant, graceless [➡ AGILITY OF THE BODY; 476] *Opposite*: graceful

gaze 1 *v* **look**, stare, watch, contemplate, gape, eye, scrutinize, observe, goggle, ogle, gawk (*informal*), rubberneck (*informal*) [➡ LOOKING AND LOOKS; 700] *Opposite*: ignore 2 *n* **stare**, look, contemplation, observation, scrutiny, regard (*formal*) [➡ LOOKING AND LOOKS; 700]

Compare and Contrast: *gaze, gape, gawk, ogle, rubberneck, stare*

CORE MEANING: to look at somebody or something steadily or at length

gaze to look for a long time with unwavering attention; *gape* to look at somebody or something in surprise or wonder, usually with an open mouth; *gawk* to stare stupidly or rudely; *ogle* to look steadily at somebody for sexual enjoyment or to show sexual interest; *rubberneck* (*informal*) to stare at somebody or something in an over-inquisitive or insensitive way; *stare* to look at somebody or something directly and intently without moving the eyes away, as a result of curiosity or surprise, or to express rudeness or defiance.

---

gazebo *type of* **outbuilding** [➡ ANCILLARY BUILDINGS; 1080]

gazelle *type of* **deer or antelope** [➡ DEER AND ANTELOPES; 981]

gazette *n* **newspaper**, paper, journal, periodical, newsletter, publication, newssheet (*UK*) [➡ NEWSPAPERS AND MAGAZINES; 605]

gazillion (*slang*) *n* [➡ MANY, MUCH, LARGE AMOUNT; 117]

gazpacho *type of* **soup** [➡ SOUPS; 1186]

gear 1 *n* (*informal*) **kit**, stuff, things, paraphernalia, tackle, trappings, equipment, apparatus [➡ POSSESSIONS; 461] 2 *n* (*informal*) **clothes**, clothing, kit, outfit, togs (*informal*) [➡ CLOTHES AND ACCESSORIES; 864] 3 *part of* **engine** [➡ PARTS OF AN ENGINE; 1144]

gearbox *part of* **engine** [➡ PARTS OF AN ENGINE; 1144]

geared up *adj* **ready**, prepared, set, equipped, operational, outfitted, fitted out (*UK*) [➡ ORDER AND ORGANIZATION; 206] *Opposite*: unprepared

gearing 1 *part of* **engine** [➡ PARTS OF AN ENGINE; 1144] 2 *n* (*UK*) [➡ OWE AND DESERVE; 465]

gearshift *type of* **controls** [➡ INTERNAL PARTS OF A VEHICLE; 1146]

gear to *v* **adjust to**, align with, adapt to, tailor, modify, customize [➡ CHANGE; 372]

gear up *v* **get ready**, prepare yourself, ready yourself, prepare, mobilize [➡ PREPARE FOR ACTION; 289] *Opposite*: wind down

gearwheel *n* [➡ PARTS OF MACHINES AND TOOLS; 1118]

gecko *type of* **reptile** [➡ REPTILES; 994]

gee (*informal*) *interj* [➡ EXPRESSIONS OF SURPRISE AND PLEASURE; 546]

gee whiz (*informal*) *interj* [➡ EXPRESSIONS OF SURPRISE AND PLEASURE; 546]

geezer (*informal*) *n* [➡ MALE PERSON; 934]

Geiger counter *type of* **measuring device** [➡ MEASURING DEVICES; 1123]

gel 1 *n* **cream**, lotion, balm, ointment, salve, emollient, unguent, liniment [➡ LOTIONS, PASTES, AND GELS; 1272] 2 *v* (*informal*) **come together**, take shape, crystallize, develop, form, hang together, materialize [➡ GRADUALLY COME INTO EXISTENCE; 1] 3 *v* (*informal*) **see eye to eye**, relate, get along, get along like a house on fire, hit it off (*informal*), click (*informal*), get on (*UK*), get on like a house on fire (*UK*) [➡ ESTABLISHING RELATIONSHIPS WITH OTHERS; 974] 4 *v* **congeal**, thicken, coagulate, clot, harden, set, solidify [➡ HARDEN, CONGEAL, AND DRY; 387] *Opposite*: liquefy

gelatinous *adj* **jellylike**, gummy, gooey, sticky, viscous, glutinous [➡ PHYSICAL TEXTURE; 1222]

geld *v* **castrate**, neuter, spay, sterilize, emasculate (*formal or literary*), vasectomize [➡ STERILIZE; 726]

gelignite *type of* **explosive material** [➡ EXPLOSIVES; 1155]

gem 1 *n* **jewel**, stone, precious stone, cut stone, gemstone, rock (*informal*) [➡ PRECIOUS STONES; 1278] 2 *n* (*informal*) **treasure**, pearl, star, godsend, paragon, nugget, prize, peach (*informal*) [➡ AMAZING THINGS; 211]

Gemini 1 *type of* **astrological sign** [➡ FATE, DESTINY, AND ASTROLOGY; 782] 2 *type of* **constellation** [➡ HEAVENLY BODIES; 1061]

gemstone *n* **jewel**, stone, gem, precious stone, cut stone, rock (*informal*) [➡ PRECIOUS STONES; 1278]

---

gemstone

◆ *types of gemstones*
agate, amethyst, aquamarine, beryl, bloodstone, carnelian, chalcedony, chrysoprase, diamond, emerald, garnet, jade, lapis lazuli, moonstone, mother-of-pearl, onyx, opal, pearl, ruby, sapphire, sard, topaz, tourmaline, turquoise

---

gender *n* **sex**, sexual category, sexual characteristics, masculinity, femininity, sexual role [➡ GENDER IDENTITY AND SEXUALITY; 932]

---

gender

◆ *types of female animals*
bitch, cow, dam, doe, ewe, filly, heifer, hind, jenny, lioness, mare, nanny goat, sow, tigress, vixen

◆ *types of male animals*
billy goat, boar, buck, bull, bullock, colt, hart, jackass, ram, stag, stallion, steer, tom, tomcat, wether

◆ *types of male birds or female birds*
capon, cob, cock, cockerel, drake, duck, gander, goose, hen, pen, rooster

---

genderless *adj* [➡ GENDER IDENTITY AND SEXUALITY; 932]

gene *n* **genetic factor**, inheritable factor, protein sequence, DNA segment, RNA component, genetic material [➡ REPRODUCTION AND HEREDITY; 725]

genealogical *adj* **hereditary**, ancestral, family, pedigree [➡ THE FAMILY; 956]

genealogy *n* **family tree**, descent, lineage, pedigree, family, ancestors, forebears, descendants [➡ THE FAMILY; 956]

general 1 *adj* **overall**, universal, all-purpose, wide-ranging, broad, common, broad-spectrum [➡ WHOLENESS AND

COMPLETENESS; 198] *Opposite*: specific **2** *adj* **usual**, typical, conventional, customary, accustomed [➡ORDINARINESS; 244] *Opposite*: unusual **3** *adj* **widespread**, common, universal, wide-ranging, broad [➡GENERAL LOCATIONS; 158] *Opposite*: unique **4** *adj* **unspecific**, undefined, unclear, vague [➡VAGUENESS; 243] *Opposite*: specific

general election *n* [➡ELECTIONS AND VOTING; 807]

generalities *n* [➡BASIC DETAILS; 688]

generality 1 *n* **generalization**, sweeping statement, simplification, oversimplification, overview, broad view [➡SUMMARIES, OUTLINES, AND EXCERPTS; 588] *Opposite*: detail **2** *n* **platitude**, cliché, banality, truism, axiom, chestnut (*informal*), bromide (*dated*) [➡FIGURES OF SPEECH; 673]

generalization *n* **sweeping statement**, simplification, oversimplification, overview, generality, broad view [➡SUMMARIES, OUTLINES, AND EXCERPTS; 588] *Opposite*: detail

generalize *v* **simplify**, oversimplify, take a broad view, make a sweeping statement [➡EXPLAIN AND CLARIFY; 610] *Opposite*: specify

generalized *adj* **widespread**, sweeping, comprehensive, general, global, universal, indiscriminate [➡WHOLENESS AND COMPLETENESS; 198] *Opposite*: isolated

generally *adv* **usually**, normally, in general, in the main, by and large, commonly, mostly, largely, as a rule, all in all [➡USUALLY; 108] *Opposite*: rarely

generally speaking *adv* **in the main**, on the whole, in general, by and large, mostly, largely, as a rule, all in all, usually, normally [➡SUMMARIZING EXPRESSIONS; 622] *Opposite*: exceptionally

general public *n* **population**, populace, ordinary people, hoi polloi, rank and file [➡GROUPS IN SOCIETY; 940] *Opposite*: elite

general store *type of* **retail outlet** [➡RETAIL OUTLETS; 1083]

generate *v* **make**, produce, create, cause, engender, spawn, breed [➡INSTITUTE AND INAUGURATE; 348] *Opposite*: prevent

generation 1 *n* **age group**, peer group, peers, cohort, compeers (*formal*), group [➡GROUPS OF PEOPLE; 935] **2** *n* **age**, era, epoch, period, eon, phase [➡EPOCHS AND ERAS; 89] **3** *n* **production**, making, creation, invention, initiation, origination [➡CREATION; 346] *Opposite*: prevention

generator 1 *n* **producer**, maker, creator, originator, initiator, author [➡DESIGNERS, CREATORS, AND INSTIGATORS; 347] **2** *n* [➡ENERGY STORAGE AND GENERATION; 1163]

generic *adj* **general**, broad, common, basic, nonspecific, standard, universal, all-purpose [➡ORDINARINESS; 244] *Opposite*: specific

generically *adv* **generally**, broadly, commonly, basically, widely, loosely, universally [➡USUALLY; 108] *Opposite*: specifically

generosity *n* **kindness**, big-heartedness, openhandedness, liberality, munificence, charity, bounty (*literary*), bounteousness (*literary*) [➡GENEROSITY AND KINDNESS; 495] *Opposite*: stinginess

generous 1 *adj* **kind**, liberal, big-hearted, openhanded, munificent, giving, charitable, magnanimous, bountiful

(*literary*) [➡GENEROSITY AND KINDNESS; 495] *Opposite*: stingy **2** *adj* **substantial**, large, lavish, liberal, plentiful, princely, unstinting [➡MANY, MUCH, LARGE AMOUNT; 117] *Opposite*: meager

Compare and Contrast: *generous, magnanimous, munificent, bountiful, liberal*

CORE MEANING: giving readily to others

generous willing to give money, help, or time freely; *magnanimous* very generous, kind, or forgiving; *munificent* very generous, especially on a grand scale; *bountiful* (*literary*) generous, particularly to less fortunate people; *liberal* free with money, time, or other assets.

generously *adv* **kindly**, big-heartedly, openhandedly, liberally, munificently, charitably [➡GENEROSITY AND KINDNESS; 495] *Opposite*: stingily

genesis *n* **origin**, origins, beginning, start, birth, dawn, creation [➡BEGINNINGS; 53]

genetic *adj* **hereditary**, inherited, heritable, inherent, genomic, chromosomal, innate, inborn, native, natural [➡REPRODUCTION AND HEREDITY; 725] *Opposite*: learned

genetics *type of* **bioscience** [➡BIOLOGICAL SCIENCES; 1037]

genial *adj* **friendly**, amiable, warm, welcoming, hospitable, gracious, pleasant, kindly, cordial, convivial, sociable [➡FRIENDLINESS AND SOCIABILITY; 494] *Opposite*: unfriendly

geniality *n* **friendliness**, warmth, cordiality, amiability, conviviality, sociability, hospitableness, kindness, graciousness, pleasantness [➡FRIENDLINESS AND SOCIABILITY; 494] *Opposite*: hostility

genie *n* **sprite**, spirit, apparition, jinni, imp [➡MYTHICAL BEINGS; 789]

genitive *n* *type of* **grammatical term** [➡ASPECTS OF LANGUAGE; 682]

genius 1 *n* **mastermind**, prodigy, intellect, virtuoso, whiz kid (*informal*), brain (*informal*) [➡TALENTED OR INTELLIGENT PEOPLE; 528] **2** *n* **brilliance**, intellect, brains, virtuosity, intelligence, gift, talent, knack, aptitude, capacity, ability, flair, smarts (*informal*) [➡POSITIVE INTELLECTUAL CHARACTERISTICS; 524] *Opposite*: stupidity

See Compare and Contrast at **talent**.

genocide *n* **killing**, slaughter, massacre, ethnic cleansing, liquidation, extermination, annihilation [➡CAUSES OF DEATH; 921]

genre *n* **type**, sort, kind, category, field, variety, genus [➡VARIETIES, TYPES, AND KINDS; 145]

See Compare and Contrast at **type**.

gent (*informal*) *n* **gentleman**, man, fellow, guy (*informal*) [➡MALE PERSON; 934]

genteel 1 *adj* **refined**, proper, polite, courteous, discreet, well-mannered, mannerly, civil, decorous [➡GOOD MANNERS AND SOCIAL SKILLS; 520] *Opposite*: vulgar **2** *adj* **pretentious**, snobbish, condescending, patronizing, affected, snooty (*informal*) [➡AFFECTATION, SELF-SATISFACTION, AND SNOBBISHNESS; 507] *Opposite*: modest

genteelness n [➡GOOD MANNERS AND SOCIAL SKILLS; 520]

gentility n **refinement**, propriety, manners, breeding, decorum, courtesy, discretion, politeness, courteousness, urbanity, elegance, civility [➡GOOD MANNERS AND SOCIAL SKILLS; 520] *Opposite:* vulgarity

gentle 1 adj **mild**, calm, kind, tender, moderate, placid, temperate [➡GENEROSITY AND KINDNESS; 495] 2 adj **soft**, light, soothing, mellow, restful, peaceful, quiet [➡PEACEFULNESS AND GENTLENESS; 214] *Opposite:* rough

gentleman 1 n **man**, male, guy (*informal*), fellow (*dated*) [➡MALE PERSON; 934] 2 n **nobleman**, aristocrat, squire, grandee [➡CLASS STATUS; 889]

gentlemanly adj **chivalrous**, gallant, courteous, polite, civil, gracious, correct [➡GOOD MANNERS AND SOCIAL SKILLS; 520] *Opposite:* rude

gentleness 1 n **mildness**, calmness, kindness, tenderness, placidity [➡GENEROSITY AND KINDNESS; 495] *Opposite:* harshness 2 n **quietness**, softness, lightness, smoothness, mellowness, restfulness, peacefulness [➡PEACEFULNESS AND GENTLENESS; 214] *Opposite:* harshness

gentrification n **redevelopment**, refurbishment, urban renewal, renovation, restoration, improvement, transformation [➡SOCIAL, POLITICAL, AND ECONOMIC CHANGE; 373] *Opposite:* neglect

gentrify v **redevelop**, refurbish, renovate, restore, improve, smarten up, spruce up, transform, do up, raise standards, move up the scale [➡SOCIAL, POLITICAL, AND ECONOMIC CHANGE; 373]

gentry n **upper class**, nobility, aristocracy, elite, ruling class, landed gentry [➡CLASS STATUS; 889] *Opposite:* working class

genuflect 1 v **kneel**, bow, curtsy, bend the knee, bob [➡GESTURES AND GESTICULATION; 653] 2 v **bow to**, defer to, kowtow, show respect for, grovel, prostrate, respect, crawl (*informal*) [➡FLATTER AND FAWN; 621] *Opposite:* disrespect

genuflection n **kneeling**, curtsy, bow, bob, dip [➡GESTURES AND GESTICULATION; 653]

genuine 1 adj **real**, authentic, indisputable, true, unadulterated, actual, legitimate, valid [➡TRUE AND REAL; 171] *Opposite:* fake 2 adj **sincere**, honest, frank, open, unaffected, candid, unpretentious [➡HONEST AND RELIABLE; 502] *Opposite:* false

genuineness n **authenticity**, realness, substance, legitimacy, validity, truth, candidness, indisputability [➡TRUE AND REAL; 171]

genus n **type**, kind, sort, species, class, group, category, genre [➡VARIETIES, TYPES, AND KINDS; 145]

geochemistry type of **earth science** [➡EARTH SCIENCES; 1059]

geographic adj **physical**, topographical, terrestrial, earthly, environmental [➡THE EARTH; 1039]

geographical see **geographic**

geography n **topography**, natural features, characteristics, layout [➡THE COUNTRYSIDE AND OUTDOOR SPACES; 1071]

geologic division n **eon**, era, epoch, period [➡EPOCHS AND ERAS; 89]

geologic division

◆ *types of eons (from oldest to most recent)*
pre-Archean, Archean, Proterozoic, Phanerozoic

◆ *types of eras (from oldest to most recent)*
Paleozoic, Mesozoic, Cenozoic

◆ *types of periods (from oldest to most recent)*
Cambrian, Ordovician, Silurian, Devonian, Carboniferous, Permian, Triassic, Jurassic, Cretaceous, Tertiary, Quaternary

◆ *types of epochs (from oldest to most recent)*
Paleocene, Eocene, Oligocene, Miocene, Pliocene, Pleistocene, Holocene

geology type of **earth science** [➡EARTH SCIENCES; 1059]

geometric adj **regular**, symmetrical, ordered, orderly, linear, formal [➡ORDER AND ORGANIZATION; 206] *Opposite:* random

geometry n [➡MATH; 597]

Georgian type of **pre-20th-century architecture** [➡BUILDING AND ARCHITECTURE; 1076]

geranium type of **perennial flower** [➡FLOWERS; 1032]

gerbil type of **rodent** [➡RODENTS; 989]

geriatric adj **elderly**, aged, old, senior [➡OLD AGE; 919] *Opposite:* young

germ 1 n **bug** (*informal*), microbe, microorganism, bacteria, virus [➡MICROORGANISMS, FUNGI, AND ALGAE; 1023] 2 n **origin**, seed, embryo, rudiment, kernel, spark, beginning, bud, nucleus [➡BEGINNINGS; 53]

germane adj **relevant**, useful, connected, to the point, of interest, suitable, appropriate, apropos (*formal*) [➡FUNDAMENTAL; 195] *Opposite:* irrelevant

German shepherd type of **large dog** [➡DOGS; 980]

germ-free adj **sterile**, antiseptic, hygienic, sanitary, uninfected, sterilized, sanitized [➡CLEAN AND HYGIENIC; 1233] *Opposite:* contaminated

germinate v **sprout**, grow, develop, take root, evolve, propagate, incubate [➡GROW AND CULTIVATE; 351]

germination n **sprouting**, propagation, incubation, growth, development [➡BEGINNINGS; 53]

gestation n **development**, growth, incubation, maturation, pregnancy [➡REPRODUCTION AND HEREDITY; 725]

gesticulate v **gesture**, wave, signal, motion, sign, indicate, point [➡GESTURES AND GESTICULATION; 653]

gesticulation n **sign**, signal, gesture, wave, motion, movement [➡GESTURES AND GESTICULATION; 653]

gesture 1 n **sign**, signal, gesticulation, motion, wave, shrug, nod, movement [➡GESTURES AND GESTICULATION; 653] 2 n **act**, action, deed, token, intimation, indication, sign [➡KIND ACTIONS OR BEHAVIOR; 295] 3 v **gesticulate**, signal, shrug, nod, wave, motion, indicate, point [➡GESTURES AND GESTICULATION; 653]

get 1 v **become**, grow, begin, have, attain [➡GET; 420]

2 *v* **cause**, make, induce, persuade, urge, prevail on [➧ CAUSE OR COMPEL TO ACT; 271]   **3** *v* **catch**, contract, acquire, develop, be infected with, pick up, come down with [➧ BECOME SICK, TREAT, AND RECOVER; 728]   **4** *v* **move**, step, progress, walk, climb [➧ PROCEED AND GO; 305]   **5** *v* **obtain**, acquire, find, search out, procure, annex, secure, gain, dig up (*informal*), get ahold of (*informal*) [➧ GET; 420]   **6** *v* (*informal*) **understand**, comprehend, grasp, follow, perceive, learn [➧ UNDERSTAND AND GRASP; 759]

Compare and Contrast: *get, acquire, obtain, gain, procure, secure*

CORE MEANING: to come into possession of something

get to become the owner of something or to succeed in finding and possessing it; ***acquire*** to get possession of something, sometimes suggesting that time or effort was involved; ***obtain*** to get something, especially by making an effort or having the necessary qualifications; ***gain*** to get something through effort, skill, or merit; ***procure*** to get something, especially with effort or special care; ***secure*** to get something, especially after using considerable effort to persuade somebody to grant or allow it.

---

get acquainted *v* [➧ ESTABLISHING RELATIONSHIPS WITH OTHERS; 974]

get across *v* **put across**, put over, convey, impart, communicate, get over, pass on [➧ EXPLAIN AND CLARIFY; 610]

get a grip (*informal*) *v* **calm down**, get hold of yourself, compose yourself, control yourself, chill out (*slang*) [➧ CHANGE OF MOOD AND COMPOSURE; 580]

get ahead *v* **advance**, climb the ladder, progress, make progress, prosper, be successful [➧ SUCCEED AND WIN; 79] *Opposite:* fail

get ahead of *v* **pass**, pass by, be in front of, overtake [➧ MOVE PAST, INTO, OR THROUGH SOMETHING; 331] *Opposite:* hold back

get ahold of *v* **grasp**, secure, grip, clutch, snare, lay hands on, collar (*slang*), catch, trap [➧ CONTACT: HOLD; 411]

get along **1** *v* **like**, be compatible with, work well with, relate to, gel with (*informal*), get on (*UK*) [➧ ESTABLISHING RELATIONSHIPS WITH OTHERS; 974] *Opposite:* dislike **2** *v* **survive**, get by, manage, cope, live, progress, fare, make out, muddle through [➧ CONTINUE TO EXIST; 17]

get a move on (*informal*) *v* **speed up**, hurry up, get going, get moving, accelerate, hurry, make tracks (*informal*), get cracking (*informal*), step on it (*slang*), step on the gas (*slang*), get the lead out (*slang*) [➧ CHANGE OF SPEED: MORE; 396] *Opposite:* slow down

get angry *v* **bristle**, bridle, explode, lose your cool, hit the roof, lose your temper, blow up (*informal*) [➧ GIVING VENT TO EMOTIONS; 679]

get a raw deal *v* **suffer**, draw the short straw, be hard done by, be put upon, come off badly, be badly done by (*UK*) [➧ FAIL OR BE UNSUCCESSFUL; 75]

get around **1** *v* **become known**, break out, circulate, get out, be revealed, spread, leak [➧ APPEAR AND EMERGE; 3] **2** *v* **avoid**, go around, bypass, sidestep, evade, circumvent [➧ NOT DO AND REFUSE TO DO; 274] *Opposite:* comply

get at **1** *v* **reach**, find, contact, speak to, write to, call [➧ INITIATE AND ESTABLISH COMMUNICATION; 680] **2** *v* **annoy**, tease, irritate,

---

get to, rub the wrong way, get under your skin (*informal*) [➧ ANGER AND ANNOY; 569]

get away *v* **leave**, go away, escape, flee, depart, absent yourself [➧ RUN AWAY AND AVOID; 10]

getaway *n* **escape**, exit, retreat, breakout, flight, departure [➧ ENDS AND DEPARTURES; 54]

get away from *v* **elude**, shake off, lose, escape from, outrun, evade [➧ AVOID OR ESCAPE CONTACT; 418]

get away with *v* **get off**, get off scot-free, escape, evade, elude, pull off (*informal*) [➧ SUCCEED AND WIN; 79] *Opposite:* answer for

get a word in edgewise *v* **get a word in**, have your say, voice your opinion, say anything, speak [➧ INTERRUPT AND BUTT IN; 619]

get back *v* **retrieve**, recoup, repossess, regain, recuperate, reclaim, recover [➧ REGAIN POSSESSION; 429] *Opposite:* lose

get back at *v* **get even**, turn the tables on, take revenge, even the score, fight back, pay back, get your own back (*UK*) [➧ VENGEANCE AND REVENGE; 685]

get behind *v* **support**, endorse, back, join forces, put in a good word for [➧ APPROVE AND CONFIRM; 646] *Opposite:* oppose

get better *v* **recover**, recuperate, improve, turn the corner, bounce back, convalesce, mend, pull through, get well, buck up (*informal*), ameliorate (*formal*) [➧ BECOME SICK, TREAT, AND RECOVER; 728] *Opposite:* deteriorate

get bigger *v* **swell**, grow, inflate, mount, expand, increase, balloon, mushroom, swell up, distend, wax (*literary*) [➧ CHANGE OF SIZE: BIGGER; 392] *Opposite:* shrink

get by *v* **survive**, manage, cope, scrape by, fare, make out, muddle through, get along, get on (*UK*) [➧ CONTINUE TO EXIST; 17]

get carried away *v* [➧ OVERDO SOMETHING; 290]

get cracking (*informal*) *v* **get going**, make a start, get moving, get a move on (*informal*), get on (*UK*) [➧ START AN ACTION; 260]

get done *v* **accomplish**, achieve, complete, finish, do, effect (*formal*) [➧ COMPLETE AN ACTION; 263]

get down *v* **descend**, get off, dismount, come down, climb down [➧ GO DOWNWARD; 307]

get down to *v* **get to work**, begin, start, concentrate, focus, knuckle down (*informal*), get on (*UK*) [➧ START AN ACTION; 260] *Opposite:* put off

get down to business *v* **get on with it**, get down to it, get down to brass tacks, get down to the nitty-gritty, stop beating about the bush, make a start, get to work [➧ START AN ACTION; 260]

get down to it *v* [➧ START AN ACTION; 260]

get even *v* **get back at**, take revenge, turn the tables, get you back, even the score, pay back, fight back, get your own back (*UK*) [➧ VENGEANCE AND REVENGE; 685]

get free of *v* **get rid of**, exorcize, escape, jettison, eliminate, purge [➧ GET RID OF SOMETHING; 451]

get-go (*informal*) *n* **beginning**, start, outset, genesis, commencement (*formal*), inception (*formal*) [➡ BEGINNINGS; 53] *Opposite*: finish

get going 1 *v* **start**, make a start, hurry up, stir, push off, get a move on (*informal*), get cracking (*informal*), buck up (*informal dated*), get on (*UK*) [➡ START AN ACTION; 260] 2 *v* **start up**, turn on, activate, operate, power, actuate (*formal*) [➡ CAUSE TO START; 265] *Opposite*: turn off

get hitched (*informal*) *v* **get married**, marry, walk down the aisle, tie the knot (*informal*), wed (*formal or literary*) [➡ ESTABLISHING RELATIONSHIPS WITH OTHERS; 974]

get hold of 1 *v* **obtain**, find, acquire, search out, lay hands on, locate, scare up (*informal*) [➡ GET; 420] 2 *v* **contact**, reach, find, get in touch with, talk to, run to ground, get through to, locate [➡ TELEPHONE, PAGE, AND TEXT; 681]

get hold of the wrong end of the stick *v* [➡ MIS-UNDERSTAND AND FAIL TO GRASP; 761]

get in 1 *v* **arrive**, enter, appear, show up (*informal*) [➡ ARRIVE; 12] *Opposite*: depart 2 *v* **join**, be accepted, be included, make the cut, make the grade, make the team [➡ SUCCEED AND WIN; 79]

get in a lather (*informal*) *v* [➡ GIVING VENT TO EMOTIONS; 679]

get in a state *v* [➡ GIVING VENT TO EMOTIONS; 679]

get in good with *v* [➡ ESTABLISHING RELATIONSHIPS WITH OTHERS; 974]

get in on the act (*informal*) *v* **take part**, join in, be included, be involved, jump on the bandwagon, interfere, participate [➡ PARTICIPATE; 292]

get in the way *v* **obstruct**, hinder, impede, interfere, encumber, hamper [➡ AVOID, PREVENT, LIMIT, AND CONTROL; 277]

get into 1 *v* **gain entry**, enter, open, access, hack into, penetrate [➡ COMPUTERS AND COMPUTING; 1127] *Opposite*: get out of 2 *v* **put on**, slip into, don, change into, dress in [➡ DRESS, WEAR, AND UNDRESS; 868] *Opposite*: take off

get in touch with *v* **call**, contact, reach, speak to, write to, write, get ahold of (*informal*), ring up (*UK*) [➡ TELEPHONE, PAGE, AND TEXT; 681]

get into your stride *v* **get going**, get up to speed, get the hang of something, get off the ground [➡ CARRY OUT AN ACTION; 269]

get involved *v* **interfere**, intervene, join in, be drawn in, step in, muscle in (*informal*), put your oar in (*UK*) [➡ PARTICIPATE; 292] *Opposite*: hold back

get in with *v* **ingratiate yourself**, make friends with, curry favor, gain the favor of, associate with [➡ ESTABLISHING RELATIONSHIPS WITH OTHERS; 974]

get it (*informal*) *v* **understand**, see, get the drift, follow, comprehend, cotton on (*informal*), get the message (*informal*), get the picture (*informal*) [➡ UNDERSTAND AND GRASP; 759] *Opposite*: misunderstand

get it in the neck (*informal*) *v* **take the blame**, take the rap (*slang*) [➡ TOLERATE AND ENDURE; 766]

get it off your chest *v* **bare your soul**, tell somebody, let it out, unburden yourself, share [➡ ADMIT AND CONFESS; 615] *Opposite*: bottle up

get it wrong *v* **misunderstand**, blunder, err, get the wrong idea, get the wrong end of the stick, make a mistake, misinterpret, misconstrue [➡ MISUNDERSTAND AND FAIL TO GRASP; 761]

get less *v* **subside**, die down, lessen, reduce, fall, decrease [➡ CHANGE OF SIZE: SMALLER; 393] *Opposite*: grow

get longer *v* **lengthen**, elongate, grow, extend, spread out, draw out [➡ CHANGE OF SIZE: BIGGER; 392] *Opposite*: shorten

get lost *v* **lose your way**, lose your bearings, go astray, go wrong, take a wrong turn [➡ AIMLESS AND ERRANT MOTION; 343]

get married *v* **marry**, walk down the aisle, get hitched (*informal*), tie the knot (*informal*), wed (*formal or literary*) [➡ ESTABLISHING RELATIONSHIPS WITH OTHERS; 974]

get moving *v* **hurry up**, speed up, get going, make a move, get a move on (*informal*), get your skates on (*informal*), get the lead out (*slang*), step on the gas (*slang*) [➡ CHANGE OF SPEED: MORE; 396]

get off 1 *v* **leave**, depart, exit, go, embark, quit, go away [➡ LEAVE AND GO AWAY; 8] *Opposite*: arrive 2 *v* **dismount**, get down, descend, come down, climb off, disembark [➡ GO DOWNWARD; 307] *Opposite*: get on

get on 1 *v* **deal with**, handle, manage, accept, progress [➡ CONTINUE AN ACTION; 262] *Opposite*: mismanage 2 *v* **board**, climb on, mount, get on board, embark [➡ TRAVEL: WAYS OF TRAVELING; 320] *Opposite*: get off 3 *v* (*UK*) **like**, be compatible, work well with, relate, get along, gel (*informal*) [➡ ESTABLISHING RELATIONSHIPS WITH OTHERS; 974] *Opposite*: dislike 4 *v* (*UK*) **make a start**, get going, begin, start, get down to, get a move on (*informal*) [➡ START AN ACTION; 260] *Opposite*: defer

get on your high horse *v* **give yourself airs**, put on airs, act haughtily, lord it [➡ GIVING VENT TO EMOTIONS; 679]

get on your nerves *v* **annoy**, irritate, bother, put your back up, irk, aggravate (*informal*), bug (*informal*), drive up the wall (*informal*) [➡ ANGER AND ANNOY; 569]

get out *v* **leave**, depart, quit, evacuate, retreat, go away, clear out, exit, buzz off (*informal*) [➡ LEAVE AND GO AWAY; 8] *Opposite*: enter

get-out (*UK*) *n* [➡ CLOTHES AND ACCESSORIES; 864]

get out of *v* **evade**, avoid, dodge, duck, get around, wriggle out of, sidestep, circumvent, escape, renege [➡ NOT DO AND REFUSE TO DO; 274] *Opposite*: participate

get over 1 *v* **recover**, live through, endure, survive, get beyond, pass though, recuperate [➡ CONTINUE TO EXIST; 17] *Opposite*: succumb 2 *v* **come to terms with**, accept, surmount, overcome, conquer, rise above, face up to [➡ FORGET, FORGIVE, AND ACCEPT; 748] 3 *v* **convey**, communicate, impart, pass on, get across, put over, put across [➡ INFORM, ANNOUNCE, AND ISSUE; 611]

get ready *v* **prepare**, steel, prime, brace, organize, make ready, gear up [➡ PREPARE FOR ACTION; 289]

get rid of *v* **dispose of**, discard, throw away, throw out, jettison, dispense with, offload, dump, chuck out (*informal*) [➡ GET RID OF SOMETHING; 451] *Opposite*: keep

get smaller *v* **shrink**, shrivel up, narrow, deflate, recede, wane, decrease [➡ CHANGE OF SIZE: SMALLER; 393] *Opposite*: swell

get somewhere *v* **make headway**, make progress, make inroads, achieve, make a breakthrough, progress [➡ SUCCEED AND WIN; 79] *Opposite*: fall behind

get stirred up *v* [➡ GIVING VENT TO EMOTIONS; 679]

get stuck in (*UK*) *v* [➡ START AN ACTION; 260]

get the better of *v* **defeat**, beat, trounce, triumph over, get the upper hand [➡ BEAT AND DEFEAT; 80]

get the drift *v* **understand**, see, follow, get it (*informal*), get the message (*informal*), cotton on (*informal*), get the picture (*informal*) [➡ UNDERSTAND AND GRASP; 759]

get the hang of *v* **learn**, pick up, understand, master [➡ UNDERSTAND AND GRASP; 759]

get the message (*informal*) *v* **understand**, get the drift, take the hint, grasp, follow, see, get it (*informal*) [➡ UNDERSTAND AND GRASP; 759]

get the most out of *v* **maximize**, make the most of, get the full benefit, exploit, milk (*informal*) [➡ MAKE GOOD USE OF SOMETHING; 473]

get the picture (*informal*) *v* **understand**, follow, see, grasp, get it (*informal*), catch on (*informal*), cotton on (*informal*), get the message (*informal*) [➡ UNDERSTAND AND GRASP; 759]

get the wrong end of the stick *v* **misconstrue**, misinterpret, make a mistake, misunderstand, misread, get it wrong, err, take amiss [➡ MISUNDERSTAND AND FAIL TO GRASP; 761]

get the wrong idea *v* **misunderstand**, misread, misinterpret, misconstrue, misjudge, err, take amiss, get it wrong [➡ MISUNDERSTAND AND FAIL TO GRASP; 761]

get the wrong impression *v* [➡ MISUNDERSTAND AND FAIL TO GRASP; 761]

get thinner *v* **narrow**, taper, slim down, lose weight, slenderize (*dated*) [➡ CHANGE OF SIZE: SMALLER; 393]

get through 1 *v* **survive**, come through, endure, weather, ride out, overcome [➡ CONTINUE TO EXIST; 17] 2 *v* **use**, consume, wear out, go through, expend, devour, eat, use up, finish [➡ USE UP AND WASTE; 474] 3 *v* **breach**, break through, penetrate, cross, pass, traverse, negotiate [➡ MOVE PAST, INTO, OR THROUGH SOMETHING; 331]

get to 1 *v* **annoy**, irritate, bother, irk, affect, distract, disturb, aggravate (*informal*), bug (*informal*) [➡ ANGER AND ANNOY; 569] 2 *v* **reach**, make, arrive at, attain [➡ ARRIVE; 12]

get-together (*informal*) *n* **meeting**, gathering, social, assembly, rendezvous, powwow (*informal*) [➡ MEETINGS AND ASSEMBLIES; 43]

get to grips with *v* [➡ UNDERSTAND AND GRASP; 759]

get to know *v* **become acquainted with**, be introduced to, meet, become familiar with [➡ ESTABLISHING RELATIONSHIPS WITH OTHERS; 974]

get to the point *v* [➡ EXPLAIN AND CLARIFY; 610]

get to work *v* [➡ START AN ACTION; 260]

get to your feet *v* **stand up**, rise, stand, get up, arise (*archaic or literary*) [➡ GO UPWARD; 306]

get under way *v* **begin**, start, proceed, launch, commence, kick off (*informal*) [➡ START AN ACTION; 260] *Opposite*: come to a halt

getup (*informal*) *n* **outfit**, clothes, costume, suit, dress, garb, gear (*informal*), rig (*informal*), attire (*formal*) [➡ CLOTHES AND ACCESSORIES; 864]

get-up-and-go (*informal*) *n* **energy**, vitality, verve, life, drive, ambition, push, enthusiasm, vigor [➡ ENERGY AND ENTHUSIASM; 496]

get up to speed *v* [➡ UNDERSTAND AND GRASP; 759]

get used to *v* **become accustomed to**, get into the habit, adjust, adapt, acclimatize, grow used to [➡ CHANGE; 372]

get wind of *v* [➡ LEARN AND DISCOVER; 762]

get worse *v* [➡ GET WORSE; 381]

get your bearings *v* **orient yourself**, find your way, find your feet, adjust, adapt, acquaint yourself with, get oriented, familiarize yourself with [➡ CHANGE; 372]

get your own back (*UK*) *v* **take revenge**, get even, retaliate, avenge yourself, even the score, get back at, turn the tables, fight back [➡ VENGEANCE AND REVENGE; 685]

gewgaw *n* [➡ ORNAMENTS AND DECORATIONS; 1248]

geyser *n* **hot spring**, spring, natural spring, fountain, jet, spout [➡ RIVERS, LAKES, AND STREAMS; 1042]

ghastly 1 *adj* **horrifying**, shocking, upsetting, distressing, grisly, grim, horrific, gruesome, frightening, hair raising [➡ FRIGHTENING; 231] *Opposite*: pleasant 2 *adj* **terrible**, horrible, appalling, dreadful, nasty, rotten, foul, vile, horrid, disgusting, unbearable, unpleasant [➡ DISGUSTING AND REPULSIVE; 230] *Opposite*: pleasant 3 *adj* (*informal*) **ill**, sick, unwell, dreadful, bad, under the weather [➡ ILL AND SICK; 740] *Opposite*: well 4 *adj* (*literary*) **pale**, pallid, ashen, wan, deathly, cadaverous (*literary*) [➡ COMPLEXION; 480] *Opposite*: rosy

ghee *type of* **cooking fat and oil** [➡ FATS AND OILS; 1173]

gherkin *n* **pickled cucumber**, dill pickle, pickle, cornichon [➡ SEASONINGS AND SAUCES; 1174]

ghetto *n* [➡ UNDESIRABLE ACCOMMODATIONS; 856]

ghost *n* [➡ THE SUPERNATURAL; 787]

ghostlike *adj* **eerie**, wraithlike, spectral, ghostly, supernatural, ethereal, otherworldly, indistinct, insubstantial, creepy (*informal*), spooky (*informal*) [➡ VAGUENESS; 243]

ghostly *adj* **ethereal**, wraithlike, spectral, indistinct, supernatural, eerie, ghostlike, insubstantial, otherworldly, creepy (*informal*), spooky (*informal*) [➡ VAGUENESS; 243]

ghostwrite *v* **cowrite**, write, compose, author, coauthor, draft [➡ RECORD SOMETHING; 371]

ghostwriter *n* **cowriter**, writer, composer, author, coauthor, drafter [➡ WRITERS AND STYLES; 914]

ghoul *n* [➡ THE SUPERNATURAL; 787]

ghoulish 1 *adj* **morbid**, macabre, dark, chilling, ghastly, twisted, gloomy, unhealthy [➡ FRIGHTENING; 231] **2** *adj* **cruel**, savage, brutal, fiendish, bloodthirsty, grim, grisly, gruesome, hideous [➡ SELFISH AND UNKIND; 505] *Opposite:* gentle

ghoulishly 1 *adv* **morbidly**, darkly, chillingly, twistedly, gloomily, unhealthily [➡ BAD-TEMPERED AND HUMORLESS; 626] **2** *adv* **cruelly**, savagely, brutally, fiendishly, bloodthirstily, grimly, gruesomely, hideously [➡ RUDE AND HOSTILE; 625] *Opposite:* gently

ghoulishness *n* [➡ THE SUPERNATURAL; 787]

GI *n* **soldier**, private, enlisted person, draftee, volunteer, conscript, recruit, veteran [➡ MILITARY PERSONNEL; 828]

giant 1 *n* [➡ BIG THINGS; 1194] **2** *n* [➡ MYTHICAL BEINGS; 789] **3** *adj* **huge**, enormous, vast, large, massive, great [➡ LARGE; 1193] *Opposite:* tiny

giant-sized *adj* [➡ LARGE; 1193]

giant star *type of* **star or star system** [➡ HEAVENLY BODIES; 1061]

gibber *v* **babble**, rant, prattle, jabber, talk gibberish, gabble, prate [➡ CHATTER AND BABBLE; 617]

gibbering *adj* [➡ INARTICULATE, RAMBLING, AND AWKWARD; 633]

gibberingly *adv* [➡ INARTICULATE, RAMBLING, AND AWKWARD; 633]

gibberish *n* **nonsense**, prattle, babble, gabble, rubbish, drivel, rot (*informal*), twaddle (*informal*) [➡ MEANINGLESS SPEECH OR WRITING; 676] *Opposite:* sense

gibbon *type of* **primate** [➡ PRIMATES; 988]

gibe 1 *n* **jeer**, taunt, sneer, remark, joke, scoff, quip, jest (*literary*) [➡ JOKES AND TEASING; 674] **2** *v* **taunt**, mock, tease, jeer, ridicule, scoff, sneer, ride (*informal*), razz (*informal*), rag (*dated*) [➡ JOKES AND TEASING; 674]

giblets *n* **guts**, offal, innards (*informal*) [➡ TYPES AND CUTS OF MEAT; 1177]

giddily 1 *adv* **dizzily**, unsteadily, lightheadedly, woozily, shakily, unstably [➡ ILL AND SICK; 740] *Opposite:* steadily **2** *adv* (*dated*) **frivolously**, capriciously, volatilely, excitedly, flightily, foolishly, impulsively [➡ LACK OF COMMITMENT AND UNRELIABILITY; 509] *Opposite:* sensibly

giddiness 1 *n* **dizziness**, unsteadiness, lightheadedness, wooziness, shakiness, instability [➡ ILL AND SICK; 740] *Opposite:* steadiness **2** *n* (*dated*) **frivolity**, capriciousness, volatility, overexcitement, flightiness, silliness, foolishness, impulsiveness [➡ LACK OF COMMITMENT AND UNRELIABILITY; 509] *Opposite:* seriousness

giddy 1 *adj* **dizzy**, unsteady, off-balance, lightheaded, woozy, shaky, unstable [➡ ILL AND SICK; 740] *Opposite:* steady **2** *adj* (*dated*) **frivolous**, scatterbrained, capricious, volatile, excited, flighty, silly, foolish, impulsive [➡ LACK OF COMMITMENT AND UNRELIABILITY; 509] *Opposite:* serious

gift 1 *n* **present**, donation, contribution, reward, bequest, award, endowment, grant, offering [➡ GIFTS; 438] **2** *n* **talent**, skill, ability, flair, knack, genius, aptitude, bent [➡ SKILLS, TALENTS, AND ABILITIES; 526]

See Compare and Contrast at **talent**.

gifted *adj* **talented**, skilled, able, exceptional, skillful,

out of the ordinary, extraordinary, remarkable [➡ TALENTED AND SKILLFUL; 527] *Opposite:* ordinary

See Compare and Contrast at **intelligent**.

gift of gab (*informal*) *n* [➡ ELOQUENT, TALKATIVE, AND LONG-WINDED; 632]

giftwrap *v* **wrap**, wrap up, package, envelop, enclose, encase, decorate, adorn [➡ DECORATE, ADORN, AND APPLY COATINGS; 405]

gig (*informal*) *n* [➡ PERFORMANCES AND SHOWS; 42]

gigantic *adj* **huge**, enormous, massive, vast, gargantuan, colossal, titanic, oversize, large, great [➡ LARGE; 1193] *Opposite:* tiny

gigantically *adv* **hugely**, colossally, vastly, enormously, greatly, massively (*informal*) [➡ TO A GREAT EXTENT; 132]

giggle 1 *v* **titter**, snicker, chuckle, laugh, chortle, twitter, snicker, cackle, snigger [➡ LAUGHTER; 649] **2** *n* **titter**, chuckle, laugh, chortle, twitter, snicker, cackle, snigger [➡ LAUGHTER; 649] **3** *type of* **human sound** [➡ SOUNDS MADE BY PEOPLE; 1262]

giggly *adj* **silly**, hysterical, immature, tittering, sniggering, chuckling, laughing, chortling, twittering, snickering [➡ CHEERFULNESS OF OUTLOOK; 503] *Opposite:* serious

gigolo *n* [➡ PLEASURE-SEEKERS AND HEDONISTS; 886]

gila monster *type of* **reptile** [➡ REPTILES; 994]

gild *v* [➡ DECORATE, ADORN, AND APPLY COATINGS; 405]

gilded *adj* **golden**, gold-plated, gilt, gold [➡ METALS; 1276]

gild the lily *v* **overdo it**, get carried away, go too far, lay it on thick, go over the top (*informal*), over-egg the pudding (*UK*) [➡ OVERDO SOMETHING; 290]

gilet *type of* **top** [➡ GARMENTS AND OUTFITS; 865]

gill 1 *part of* **fish** [➡ PARTS OF A FISH; 1011] **2** *type of* **nonmetric unit** [➡ SIZE AND DIMENSIONS; 1192]

gilt 1 *n* **gold**, gold leaf, gold plate [➡ COVERS AND COATINGS; 1246] **2** *adj* **golden**, gold-plated, gilded, gold [➡ METALS; 1276]

gimmick *n* **trick**, ploy, stunt, device, promotion, tactic [➡ WAYS OF DOING THINGS; 294]

ginger 1 *type of* **orange** [➡ COLORS; 1224] **2** *type of* **spice** [➡ HERBS AND SPICES; 1175]

gingerbread *type of* **cake** [➡ CAKES, COOKIES, AND DESSERTS; 1181]

ginger group *n* [➡ GROUPS WITH A COMMON INTEREST; 938]

gingerly *adv* **cautiously**, tentatively, warily, delicately, carefully, gently [➡ CAUTIOUS AND CAREFUL; 282] *Opposite:* boldly

gingham *type of* **fabric from plants** [➡ FABRICS; 1132]

ginkgo *type of* **deciduous tree** [➡ DECIDUOUS TREES; 1028]

ginseng *type of* **spice** [➡ HERBS AND SPICES; 1175]

giraffe *type of* **large mammal** [➡ LARGE MAMMALS; 986]

girandole *type of* **firework** [➡ EXPLOSIVES; 1155]

gird (*literary*) *v* [➡ DECORATE, ADORN, AND APPLY COATINGS; 405]

girder *n* **beam**, joist, bar, rafter, crossbeam, support [➡ BUILDING MATERIALS; 1077]

girdle *n* **belt**, sash, cummerbund, tie, drawstring, cord, band [➡ ACCESSORIES, MILLINERY, AND LINGERIE; 867]

gird your loins *v* **brace yourself**, get ready, grit your teeth, prepare yourself, steel yourself [➡ PREPARE FOR ACTION; 289]

girl *n* [➡ FEMALE PERSON; 933]

girlfriend *n* **partner**, lover, sweetheart, fiancée, lady friend (*informal*), inamorata (*literary*) [➡ SEXUAL AND ROMANTIC RELATIONSHIPS; 964] *Opposite*: boyfriend

girlhood *n* **childhood**, youth, infancy, early years, adolescence, teens, formative years, salad days (*literary*) [➡ BABYHOOD, CHILDHOOD, AND ADOLESCENCE; 917] *Opposite*: boyhood

girlish *adj* **youthful**, adolescent, childlike, young [➡ PEOPLE'S PHYSICAL APPEARANCE; 475]

girlishness *n* [➡ PEOPLE'S PHYSICAL APPEARANCE; 475]

girth *n* **circumference**, breadth, width, span, thickness, wideness, size, bulk [➡ WIDTH: WIDE; 1199] *Opposite*: height

gist *n* **idea**, essence, substance, general picture, point, meaning, sense, nucleus, kernel, nub [➡ MEANING; 690]

give **1** *v* **provide**, offer, contribute, present, donate, bequeath, pass, hand, hand over, lend, deliver, give away, furnish (*formal*) [➡ GIVE AND PROVIDE; 430] *Opposite*: take **2** *v* **grant**, award, assign, allot, accord, bestow (*formal*), confer (*formal*) [➡ GIVE AND PROVIDE; 430] *Opposite*: withhold **3** *v* **impart**, convey, communicate, pass on, share, lend, afford (*formal*) [➡ DISPENSE, RATION, AND DISTRIBUTE; 434] *Opposite*: withhold **4** *v* **perform**, put on, stage, produce, organize, deliver, carry out [➡ CARRY OUT AN ACTION; 269] **5** *v* **devote**, dedicate, give up, sacrifice, spend, surrender, allocate [➡ DISPENSE, RATION, AND DISTRIBUTE; 434] *Opposite*: withhold **6** *v* **yield**, collapse, break, go, split, crack, fracture, shatter, crumble, give way [➡ TEAR, BREAK, AND CUT; 360] *Opposite*: hold up

Compare and Contrast: *give, present, confer, bestow, donate, grant*

CORE MEANING: to hand over something to somebody

give to hand over a possession to somebody else to keep or use; *present* to give something in a formal or ceremonial way; *confer* (*formal*) to give somebody an honor, privilege, or award, often at a formal ceremony; *bestow* (*formal*) to present somebody with something, especially something unexpected or undeserved; *donate* to give a contribution to a charitable organization or another good cause, or, in a medical context, to give blood for blood transfusions or organs for transplant; *grant* to agree to allow a request, favor, or privilege, especially at the discretion of a person in authority, or formally or officially to give money.

give a beating (*UK*) *v* **attack**, assault, batter, hit, smack, beat up (*informal*) [➡ PHYSICAL ATTACK AND PUNISHMENT; 415]

give a boost *v* **strengthen**, boost, lift, encourage, boost up, give a lift, uplift, fortify, support, improve [➡ ENCOURAGE; 576] *Opposite*: deflate

give a call *v* [➡ TELEPHONE, PAGE, AND TEXT; 681]

give a hand *v* [➡ HELP; 293]

give a lift *v* **encourage**, boost, boost up, strengthen, fortify, give a boost, lift, uplift, support, improve [➡ ENCOURAGE; 576] *Opposite*: deflate

give-and-take (*informal*) *n* **cooperation**, compromise, reciprocity, collaboration, teamwork, helpfulness, understanding [➡ RECIPROCITY AND INTERDEPENDENCE; 147] *Opposite*: selfishness

give a new lease on life *v* [➡ IMPROVE STRENGTH AND DURABILITY; 378]

give a ring (*UK*) *v* [➡ TELEPHONE, PAGE, AND TEXT; 681]

give a rough idea *v* [➡ EXPLAIN AND CLARIFY; 610]

give a shot (*informal*) *v* [➡ ATTEMPT AN ACTION; 261]

give a tinkle *v* [➡ TELEPHONE, PAGE, AND TEXT; 681]

give away **1** *v* **get rid of**, donate, offer, give, pass on, give out, hand out, distribute, provide, bestow (*formal*) [➡ DISPENSE, RATION, AND DISTRIBUTE; 434] *Opposite*: keep **2** *v* **disclose**, reveal, let slip, betray, divulge, tell [➡ BETRAY CONFIDENCES AND GOSSIP; 618] *Opposite*: keep secret

giveaway **1** *n* **telltale sign**, clue, hint, indication, symptom, betrayal [➡ EVIDENCE AND PROOF; 69] **2** *n* (*informal*) **gift**, special offer, free sample, trial offer, promotion, gimmick, freebie (*informal*) [➡ GIFTS; 438] **3** *adj* (*informal*) **bargain**, rock-bottom, low, introductory, special, exceptional, bargain-basement [➡ CHEAP AND INEXPENSIVE; 221] *Opposite*: exorbitant

give a wide berth *v* **steer clear**, avoid, avoid like the plague, shun, keep at arm's length, keep well away, keep your distance [➡ AVOID OR ESCAPE CONTACT; 418] *Opposite*: seek out

give back *v* **return**, restore, hand back, repay, refund, reimburse [➡ GIVE AND PROVIDE; 430] *Opposite*: keep

give chase (*formal*) *v* **pursue**, follow in hot pursuit, follow, go after, chase, run down [➡ ACCOMPANY AND FOLLOW; 337]

give heed *v* [➡ PAY ATTENTION; 765]

give in **1** *v* **lose**, admit defeat, surrender, concede, submit, give up, quit, capitulate, defer, throw in the towel (*informal*) [➡ FORGET, FORGIVE, AND ACCEPT; 748] *Opposite*: stand your ground **2** *v* (*UK*) **hand over**, hand in, deliver, submit, present, tender, proffer [➡ PROFFER AND HAND OVER; 431] *Opposite*: withhold

give instructions *v* **direct**, inform, brief, instruct, tell, guide, give orders [➡ EXPLAIN AND CLARIFY; 610]

give it a try *v* [➡ ATTEMPT AN ACTION; 261]

give leave (*formal*) *v* [➡ PERMIT AND ALLOW; 669]

given **1** *adj* **known**, assumed, agreed, specified, prearranged, set, certain, particular, fixed [➡ KNOWN AND FAMOUS; 181] **2** *prep* **because of**, in view of, as a result of, taking into consideration, taking into account [➡ CAUSATION; 168]

given name *n* **first name**, Christian name, forename, name, moniker (*slang*) [➡ NAME AND DESCRIBE; 665]

give notice *v* [➡ REVOKE STATUS; 459]

given that *conj* **providing**, provided that, as long as, only if, assuming that, allowing that [➡CAUSATION; 168]

give off *v* **emit**, radiate, send out, discharge, exude, spew, give out [➡EMIT AND EMANATE; 361]

give or take *adv* [➡APPROXIMATELY; 135]

give out 1 *v* **hand out**, distribute, provide, offer, allot, assign, hand over, give away, award [➡DISPENSE, RATION, AND DISTRIBUTE; 434] *Opposite*: keep 2 *v* **declare**, announce, proclaim, pronounce, reveal, publish, make known, name [➡INFORM, ANNOUNCE, AND ISSUE; 611] *Opposite*: withhold 3 *v* **emit**, send out, transmit, give off, radiate, discharge, exude [➡EMIT AND EMANATE; 361] 4 *v* **run out**, dry up, fail, come to an end, end, finish, disappear [➡DISAPPEAR; 4] *Opposite*: hold out 5 *v* **fail**, collapse, break, yield, go, give, snap, pack in (*informal*) [➡FAIL OR CEASE TO FUNCTION; 470] *Opposite*: hold

give over to 1 *v* **dedicate**, devote, allocate, reserve, allot, use [➡GIVE AND PROVIDE; 430] 2 *v* (*literary*) **give up**, relinquish, hand over, surrender, abandon, turn over to [➡PROFFER AND HAND OVER; 431]

give permission *v* **consent**, agree, allow, let, authorize, sanction, permit, give leave (*formal*) [➡PERMIT AND ALLOW; 669] *Opposite*: forbid

give refuge *v* [➡TAKE CARE OF AND SPOIL; 300]

give rise to *v* [➡CAUSE TO HAPPEN; 31]

give shelter to *v* [➡TAKE CARE OF AND SPOIL; 300]

give somebody their cards (*UK*) *v* [➡REVOKE STATUS; 459]

give somebody the slip *v* **lose**, shake off, get away from, escape from, avoid, slip through somebody's fingers [➡AVOID OR ESCAPE CONTACT; 418]

give the boot (*informal*) *v* [➡REVOKE STATUS; 459]

give the brushoff *v* [➡REFUSING OR REJECTING RELATIONS; 975]

give the bum's rush (*slang*) *v* [➡REFUSING OR REJECTING RELATIONS; 975]

give the cold shoulder to *v* **ignore**, rebuff, exclude, look straight through, freeze out, ostracize, snub, cold-shoulder, send to Coventry (*UK*) [➡REFUSING OR REJECTING RELATIONS; 975]

give the go-ahead *v* [➡PERMIT AND ALLOW; 669]

give the heave-ho (*informal*) *v* [➡REVOKE STATUS; 459]

give the lie to *v* **contradict**, belie, rebut, refute, conflict with, run counter to, negate (*formal*) [➡DENY AND REJECT; 644]

give the once-over (*informal*) *v* **examine**, inspect, check out, scrutinize, look at, check over, vet [➡EXAMINE AND ASSESS; 753]

give the sack (*informal*) *v* [➡REVOKE STATUS; 459]

give the third degree (*informal*) *v* [➡ASK PEOPLE QUESTIONS; 666]

See Compare and Contrast at **question**.

give up 1 *v* **admit defeat**, give in, surrender, concede, submit, quit, capitulate, defer, throw in the towel (*informal*) [➡STOP ACTING; 264] *Opposite*: stand your ground

2 *v* **hand over**, part with, surrender, relinquish, give away, deliver, convey, transfer, give in [➡PROFFER AND HAND OVER; 431] *Opposite*: keep 3 *v* **despair**, abandon, lose hope, give up on [➡CHANGE OF MOOD AND COMPOSURE; 580] 4 *v* **stop**, quit, leave off, renounce, abstain from, abandon, pack in (*informal*) [➡FORGO AND DENY ONESELF; 449] *Opposite*: stick with 5 *v* **devote**, dedicate, give, surrender, sacrifice, allocate, spend [➡GIVE AND PROVIDE; 430] *Opposite*: withhold 6 *v* **reveal**, disclose, divulge, tell, let slip, betray [➡BETRAY CONFIDENCES AND GOSSIP; 618] *Opposite*: keep secret

give up on 1 *v* **stop**, give up, quit, abandon, leave off, chuck (*informal*) [➡STOP ACTING; 264] 2 *v* **despair**, abandon, lose hope, give up [➡CHANGE OF MOOD AND COMPOSURE; 580]

give up the ghost (*literary*) *v* [➡DIE; 922]

give your word *v* **promise**, vow, swear, assure, give your assurance [➡PROMISE AND ASSURE; 684]

gizmo (*informal*) *n* **gadget**, device, contraption, appliance, thing, thingamabob (*informal*), thingamajig (*informal*), doodad (*informal*), doohickey (*informal*), jigger (*informal*), widget (*humorous*) [➡DEVICES; 1115]

gizzard *part of* **bird** [➡PARTS OF A BIRD; 1006]

glacé *adj* [➡STATE OF PREPARED FOOD; 1171]

glacial 1 *adj* **icy**, ice-cold, freezing, biting, bitter, cold, polar [➡COLD WEATHER; 1051] *Opposite*: tropical 2 *adj* **hostile**, unfriendly, icy, cold, cool, withering, contemptuous [➡RUDE AND HOSTILE; 625] *Opposite*: warm

glacial deposit *n* [➡EROSION PRODUCTS AND SOIL; 1058]

glaciated valley *n* [➡GEOLOGIC FEATURES; 1056]

glacier *n* **ice field**, icecap, ice floe, iceberg, floe [➡MOUNTAINS AND HILLS; 1044]

glad 1 *adj* **delighted**, happy, pleased, content, grateful, thankful, appreciative [➡PLEASURE, EXCITEMENT, AND ELATION; 534] *Opposite*: sad 2 *adj* **willing**, ready, prepared, happy, eager, set [➡THE WILL AND WILLINGNESS; 563] *Opposite*: unwilling

gladden *v* **delight**, please, cheer, bring joy to, hearten, cheer up, elate [➡PLEASE AND AMUSE; 572] *Opposite*: sadden

gladdened *adj* [➡PLEASURE, EXCITEMENT, AND ELATION; 534]

glade *n* **clearing**, opening, gap, open space, dell (*literary*) [➡THE COUNTRYSIDE AND OUTDOOR SPACES; 1071]

gladiator 1 *n* **fighter**, fencer, sword fighter, warrior, battler [➡COMPETITORS; 41] 2 *n* **campaigner**, lobbyist, supporter, advocate, champion, fighter, battler [➡DEVOTEES AND ADDICTED PEOPLE; 556]

gladiolus *type of* **flower grown from bulbs** [➡FLOWERS FROM BULBS; 1030]

gladness *n* **happiness**, cheerfulness, delight, joy, pleasure, contentment [➡PLEASURE, EXCITEMENT, AND ELATION; 534] *Opposite*: sadness

glad rags (*informal*) *n* **best clothes**, finery, black tie, Sunday best, best bib and tucker (*informal*), best togs (*informal*) [➡CLOTHES AND ACCESSORIES; 864]

glamor *see* **glamour**

glamorize 1 *v* **romanticize**, idealize, exaggerate, embellish, dress up, giftwrap, varnish [➡BOAST; 616] *Opposite:* understate **2** *v* **beautify**, decorate, adorn, do up, dress up, doll up (*informal*) [➡IMPROVE APPEARANCE; 379]

glamorous *adj* **stylish**, fashionable, glitzy, dazzling, ...lendid, beautiful, desirable, exciting, opulent, trendy ...ormal) [➡WELL-GROOMED; 482] *Opposite:* drab

...our **1** *n* **allure**, charm, appeal, fascination, attrac-...itement, desirability, opulence, pull (*informal*) ...ATTRACTIVENESS; 189] *Opposite:* dullness **2** *n* **good** ...y, glitz, glitziness, style, stylishness, trendi-.../) [➡WELL-GROOMED; 482] *Opposite:* drabness

...) *v* [➡IMPROVE APPEARANCE; 379]

...ep, peek, glimpse, squint, scan, skim, ...gh [➡LOOKING AND LOOKS; 700] *Opposite:* gaze ...r, gleam, glitter, flash, reflect [➡LIGHT ...ook, peek, glimpse, squint, scan ...te: gaze

...ricochet, reflect, deflect, ...; 344]

...lateral, slanting, tan-...AND ALIGNMENT; 1223]

...look daggers [➡FACIAL ...glimmer, glitter, ...LIGHT EMISSION; 368] ...he eye, show ...ower, scowl, ...rightness, ...glitter,

...dent, PER-...t,

(torn diagonal section — fragmentary text)

...globe, glob

...CAL INSTRU-

...shadow, obscurity ...pessimism, ...misery, des-...choly [➡FEELINGS]

...despondently, unhap-...pefully, unhap-...Opposite: ...PAIR; 539]

...murkiness, shade, ...DESCRIBING LIGHT; 1228] ...pessimism, gloom, ...unhappiness

...dim, overcast, dull, ...Opposite: bright **2** *adj* ...misery, miserable, dis-...happiness

...ncholy, miserable, blue ...melancholy, pessimistic, blue ...woeful, pessimistic [➡SADNESS, DISTRESS, ...(*informal*) ...s (*informal*)

...NEGATIVE PEOPLE; 953]

...ANT, DIRTY, AND TOXIC SUBSTANCES; 1268]

...on, veneration, elevation, dei-...extolment, exaltation (*formal*)

...lionize, deify, elevate, venerate, ...PRAISE AND ENCOURAGE; 647] ...formal) Oppo-

...ificent, wonderful, splendid, cele-...EXTRAORDINARY; AMAZING; 204] Oppo-...standing [➡EXTRAORDINARY; AMAZING; 204]

...ence, splendor, beauty, wonder, grand-

glass snake *type of* **reptile** [➡REPTILES; 994]

glassware *n* [➡TABLEWARE, FLATWARE, AND KITCHENWARE; 861]

glassy 1 *adj* **smooth**, slippery, shiny, glossy, slick, polished, gleaming, reflective, transparent, lustrous, glazed, varnished [➡VISUAL TEXTURE; 1221] *Opposite:* dull **2** *adj* **expressionless**, glazed, dazed, blank, vacant, distant, faraway, empty [➡FACIAL EXPRESSIONS AND BLUSHING; 651] *Opposite:* alert

glaze 1 *v* **varnish**, finish, seal, coat, cover, veneer, paint [➡DECORATE, ADORN, AND APPLY COATINGS; 405] **2** *n* **coating**, varnish, finish, seal, cover, coat, veneer, paint [➡COVERS AND COATINGS; 1246]

glazed 1 *adj* **glassy**, blank, fixed, expressionless, dull, faraway, vacant, distant, unfocused [➡FACIAL EXPRESSIONS AND BLUSHING; 651] *Opposite:* alert **2** *adj* **glossy**, shiny, smooth, lustrous, varnished, gleaming, polished, glassy [➡VISUAL TEXTURE; 1221] *Opposite:* dull

gleam 1 *v* **shine**, glow, beam, burn, blaze, glare [➡LIGHT EMISSION; 368] **2** *v* **flash**, flicker, twinkle, shimmer, sparkle, glitter, glimmer, glisten, glint, flare [➡LIGHT EMISSION; 368] **3** *n* **glow**, shine, beam, ray, blaze, glare [➡DESCRIBING LIGHT; 1228] **4** *n* **flicker**, flash, twinkle, shimmer, sparkle, glitter, glimmer, glisten, glint, flare [➡DESCRIBING LIGHT; 1228]

gleaming *adj* **shiny**, polished, luminous, lustrous, glossy, shining, glowing, glistening, glimmering [➡VISUAL TEXTURE; 1221] *Opposite:* dull

glean *v* [➡GET; 420]

gleditsia *type of* **deciduous tree** [➡DECIDUOUS TREES; 1028]

glee 1 *n* **delight**, happiness, pleasure, joy, elation, excitement, cheerfulness, hilarity, merriment, laughter, amusement, gaiety, jollity [➡PLEASURE, EXCITEMENT, AND ELATION; 534] *Opposite:* sadness **2** *n* **triumph**, jubilation, smugness, exultance [➡PLEASURE, EXCITEMENT, AND ELATION; 534] *Opposite:* despondency

gleeful 1 *adj* **delighted**, happy, pleased, joyful, elated, thrilled, excited, cheerful, merry, jolly, gay (*dated*), over the moon (*UK informal*) [➡PLEASURE, EXCITEMENT, AND ELATION; 534] *Opposite:* sad **2** *adj* **triumphant**, jubilant, smug, gloating, ...ultant [➡PLEASURE, EXCITEMENT, AND ELATION; 534] *Opposite:* des-...dent

...fulness *n* [➡PLEASURE, EXCITEMENT, AND ELATION; 534]

...alley, gorge, ravine, dale, cleft, hollow, defile, ...y), dell (*literary*), chine (*UK*), dene (*UK*) [➡GEO-...056]

...e of **headgear** [➡ACCESSORIES, MILLINERY, AND LINGERIE;

...e, fluent, smooth, convincing, slick, ...AND LONG-WINDED; 632] *Opposite:* hesitant ...ow, facile, casual, simplistic [➡UNINTER-...] *Opposite:* profound

...n **persuasiveness**, fluency, slickness, smooth-...LOQUENT, TALKATIVE, AND LONG-WINDED; 632] *Opposite:* hesitation **superficiality**, shallowness, facileness, casualness [➡NEUTRALITY AND INDIFFERENCE; 553] *Opposite:* profoundness

glide 1 *v* **slither**, slide, slide along, slip, skate, float, sashay (*humorous*) [➡PROCEED AND GO; 305] **2** *v* **fly**, soar, wheel, drift, coast, hover, float [➡PROCEED AND GO; 305]

glider *type of* **civil aircraft** [➡ AIRCRAFT; 1148]

glimmer 1 *v* **twinkle**, shine, gleam, flicker, glow, reflect, sparkle, spark, glisten, shimmer [➡ LIGHT EMISSION; 368] 2 *n* **shine**, twinkle, gleam, flicker, glow, spark [➡ DESCRIBING LIGHT; 1228]

glimmering *adj* [➡ DESCRIBING LIGHT; 1228]

glimpse 1 *n* **look**, glance, peek, peep, sight [➡ LOOKING AND LOOKS; 700] 2 *n* **hint**, sight, foretaste, indication, pointer, sign, preview [➡ FEW, LITTLE, SMALL AMOUNT; 120] 3 *v* **see**, catch sight of, glance at, peek at, peep at, look at [➡ SEE; 699]

glint 1 *v* **sparkle**, flash, wink, shine, twinkle, spark, gleam, shimmer, glimmer [➡ LIGHT EMISSION; 368] 2 *n* **flash**, sparkle, shine, twinkle, spark, gleam, shimmer, glimmer [➡ DESCRIBING LIGHT; 1228]

glinting *adj* [➡ DESCRIBING LIGHT; 1228]

glisten 1 *v* **gleam**, sparkle, glint, flash, reflect, shine, shimmer, glow [➡ LIGHT EMISSION; 368] 2 *n* **sparkle**, gleam, glint, flash, shine, shimmer, sheen, glow [➡ DESCRIBING LIGHT; 1228]

glistening *adj* **gleaming**, shining, sparkly, shiny, glittering, sparkling, glimmering, flashing, shimmering, glowing [➡ DESCRIBING LIGHT; 1228]

glitch *n* **hitch**, problem, malfunction, fault, anomaly, bug (*informal*), hiccup (*informal*) [➡ PROBLEMS; 256]

glitter 1 *v* **gleam**, sparkle, shine, dazzle, shimmer, glisten, flash, twinkle, glint [➡ LIGHT EMISSION; 368] 2 *n* **sparkle**, gleam, shimmer, flash, twinkle, glisten, glimmer [➡ LIGHT; 1164] 3 *n* **tinsel**, sequins, spangles [➡ ORNAMENTS AND DECORATIONS; 1248] 4 *n* **dazzle**, splendor, flashiness, glamour, showiness, glitziness, attraction, allure, charisma [➡ BEAUTY AND ATTRACTIVENESS; 189]

glitterati *n* [➡ IMPORTANT OR FAMOUS PEOPLE; 893]

glittering *adj* **impressive**, sparkling, dazzling, splendid, scintillating, glitzy, gleaming, magnificent, showy, flashing, shimmering, star-studded, starry [➡ EXTRAORDINARY: AMAZING; 204]

glittery *adj* **shiny**, sparkly, shimmering, brilliant, dazzling, reflecting [➡ DESCRIBING LIGHT; 1228]

glitz *n* **glamour**, style, stylishness, glitziness, showiness, ostentation, pizzazz (*informal*) [➡ WELL-GROOMED; 482]

glitziness 1 *n* **glamour**, glitter, style, glitz, stylishness, pizzazz (*informal*) [➡ WELL-GROOMED; 482] 2 *n* **showiness**, tawdriness, flashiness, extravagance, tastelessness, ostentation, snazziness (*informal*), swankiness (*informal*) [➡ IN POOR TASTE AND OVERSENTIMENTAL; 229]

glitzy *adj* **showy**, ostentatious, flashy, extravagant, swanky (*informal*), plush (*informal*), ritzy (*informal*) [➡ IN POOR TASTE AND OVERSENTIMENTAL; 229]

gloat *v* **revel**, wallow, exult, smirk, delight, rejoice (*literary*) [➡ BOAST; 616]

gloating *adj* [➡ PLEASURE, EXCITEMENT, AND ELATION; 534]

glob (*informal*) *n* **blob**, gobbet, drop, globule, lump, splotch, dollop (*informal*), gob (*slang*), splodge (*UK*) [➡ AMOUNTS OF SOLID OR SEMISOLID; 115]

global 1 *adj* **worldwide**, international [➡ WHOLENESS AND COM-

PLETENESS; 198] *Opposite*: local 2 *adj* **universal**, comprehensive, total, inclusive, overall, large-scale [➡ LARGE; 1193]

globalization *n* [➡ BUSINESS ACTIVITIES AND PHENOMENA; 794]

globally 1 *adv* **internationally**, worldwide, universally [➡ WHOLENESS AND COMPLETENESS; 198] *Opposite*: locally 2 *adv* **altogether**, as a whole, generally, universally, totally, comprehensively [➡ ALL; 128]

globe 1 *n* **sphere**, ball, orb, world, earth, rondure (*archaic*) [➡ ROUNDED SHAPE; 1218] 2 *n* **earth**, world, planet [➡ THE EARTH; 1039]

globetrot *v* **travel**, journey, tour, shuttle, backpack [➡ TRAVEL: WAYS OF TRAVELING; 320]

globetrotter *n* **tourist**, backpacker, journeyer, adventurer, explorer, voyager, vacationer, traveler, jetsetter (*informal*), excursionist (*dated*), holidaymaker (*U*[➡ TRAVEL: TRAVELERS AND WALKERS; 319]

globular *adj* **spherical**, round, circular, bulbous, rotund, rounded, orbicular (*formal*) [➡ ROUNDED SHAPE; 1218]

globule *n* **drop**, blob, bead, gobbet, ball, bubble (*informal*) [➡ AMOUNTS OF SOLID OR SEMISOLID; 115]

glockenspiel *type of* **percussion instrument** [➡ MU... MENTS; 910]

gloom 1 *n* **darkness**, shade, murkiness, dimness, murk, gloominess, dreariness [➡ DESCRIBING LIGHT; 1228] *Opposite*: brightness 2 despair, sadness, dejection, unhappiness, pondency, gloominess, depression, melan... ABOUT THE FUTURE; 533] *Opposite*: happiness

gloomily *adv* **miserably**, disconsolately, pessimistically, sullenly, glumly, unh... pily, dolefully [➡ SADNESS, DISTRESS, AND DES... cheerfully

gloominess 1 *n* **dimness**, darkness, shadow, murk, gloom, dreariness... *Opposite*: brightness 2 *n* **despondenc**... depression, despair, dejection, ... [➡ FEELINGS ABOUT THE FUTURE; 533] *Opposite...*

gloomy 1 *adj* **dark**, depressin... dismal, murky [➡ DESCRIBING LIGHT; 12... **depressed**, low, low-spirited, m... consolate, unhappy, sad, glum... (*informal*), down in the dump... AND DESPAIR; 539] *Opposite*: cheerf...

gloomy Gus *n* [➡ GRUMPY AND...

glop (*informal*) *n* [➡ UNPLEAS...

glorification *n* **adorat...** fication, praise, worshi... [➡ PRAISE AND ENCOURAGE; 647]

glorify *v* **worship**, ado... praise, extol, exalt (*f...*

glorious *adj* **mag...** brated, superb, out... site: shameful

glory 1 *n* **magnifi...**

eur, brilliance, exaltation (*formal*) [➡ TREATS; 210] **2** *n* **credit**, fame, praise, laurels, triumph, success, admiration, stardom [➡ SUCCESS; 82] *Opposite*: criticism

glory days *n* [➡ PLEASANT SITUATIONS; 74]

glory in *v* **enjoy**, lap up, wallow in, make the most of, revel in, exult in, take pride in, delight, jubilate (*archaic*) [➡ LIKE, LOVE, VALUE, AND ENJOY; 578] *Opposite*: despise

gloss **1** *n* **luster**, polish, shine, brightness, sheen [➡ COVERS AND COATINGS; 1246] **2** *n* **annotation**, commentary, footnote, explanation, comment, definition [➡ PARTS OF BOOKS AND DOCUMENTS; 593] **3** *n* **interpretation**, explanation, spin (*slang*) [➡ POINTS OF VIEW; 767]

glossary *n* **lexicon**, dictionary, word list, vocabulary, thesaurus, appendix, supplement [➡ LISTS AND SCHEDULES; 587]

glossiness **1** *n* **shininess**, smoothness, sheen, patina, luster, sleekness, finish, silkiness [➡ VISUAL TEXTURE; 1221] **2** *n* (*informal*) **veneer**, surface, façade [➡ COVERS AND COATINGS; 1246]

gloss over *v* **skim over**, pass over, dismiss, evade, dodge [➡ NOT PAY ATTENTION; 764] *Opposite*: dwell on

glossy *adj* **sleek**, silky, silken, lustrous, shiny, polished, smooth, burnished, slick [➡ VISUAL TEXTURE; 1221] *Opposite*: dull

glossy magazine (*UK*) *n* [➡ NEWSPAPERS AND MAGAZINES; 605]

glove **1** *type of* **sports equipment** [➡ SPORTS EQUIPMENT; 879] **2** *type of* **accessory** [➡ ACCESSORIES, MILLINERY, AND LINGERIE; 867]

glove compartment *type of* **internal feature** [➡ INTERNAL PARTS OF A VEHICLE; 1146]

glow **1** *n* **radiance**, ruddiness, light, luminosity, glimmering, afterglow [➡ LIGHT; 1164] **2** *v* **burn**, blaze, flame, shine, smolder, flush, blush [➡ FACIAL EXPRESSIONS AND BLUSHING; 651]

glower *v* **glare**, frown, scowl, look daggers, look hard, stare [➡ FACIAL EXPRESSIONS AND BLUSHING; 651]

glowering *adj* **angry**, dark, scowling, sullen, surly [➡ FACIAL EXPRESSIONS AND BLUSHING; 651]

glowing **1** *adj* **bright**, shimmering, radiant, lustrous, shining, gleaming [➡ DESCRIBING LIGHT; 1228] *Opposite*: dull **2** *adj* **fulsome**, complimentary, flattering, appreciative, congratulatory [➡ EXPRESSING RESPECT AND APPROVAL; 637] *Opposite*: derogatory **3** *adj* **healthy-looking**, tanned, rosy, shining, radiant, blooming, blushing [➡ COMPLEXION; 480] *Opposite*: pale

glowworm *type of* **stage of insect development** [➡ INSECT STAGES; 1020]

glucose *type of* **nutrient** [➡ FOOD COMPONENTS; 1188]

glue **1** *n* **adhesive**, paste, superglue, cement, gum [➡ ADHESIVES; 1271] **2** *v* **paste**, stick, fasten, attach, join, cement, bond [➡ FASTEN, LINK, AND JOIN; 408]

gluey *adj* **sticky**, gummy, tacky, glutinous, thick, viscous, gooey [➡ PHYSICAL TEXTURE; 1222]

gluiness *n* [➡ FLUID AND NONSOLID; 1213]

glum *adj* **gloomy**, down, morose, sad, low, negative, depressed, sullen, sulky, miserable, dreary, saturnine, blue (*informal*) [➡ SADNESS, DISTRESS, AND DESPAIR; 539] *Opposite*: cheerful

glume *part of* **flower** [➡ FLOWERS; 1032]

glumness *n* **pessimism**, unhappiness, misery, depression, dejection, moodiness, sullenness, dreariness, gloominess [➡ SADNESS, DISTRESS, AND DESPAIR; 539] *Opposite*: cheerfulness

glut *n* **excess**, surplus, superfluity, flood, overabundance, accumulation, surfeit, oversupply [➡ TOO MUCH; 119] *Opposite*: shortage

glutinous *adj* **sticky**, gluey, gooey, tacky, gummy, viscous, gelatinous [➡ PHYSICAL TEXTURE; 1222]

glutton *n* **overeater**, gourmand, gorger, epicure, epicurean, foodie (*informal*) [➡ PLEASURE-SEEKERS AND HEDONISTS; 886]

gluttonous *adj* **greedy**, voracious, insatiable, excessive, desirous (*formal*) [➡ GRASPING AND FINANCIALLY MEAN; 519]

gluttony *n* **greed**, greediness, excess, piggishness, rapaciousness, gourmandising, voraciousness [➡ MORALLY BAD OR IMPROPER; 775]

glyph *n* [➡ SYMBOLS, SIGNS, AND NUMBERS; 596]

gnarled *adj* **knotted**, twisted, bent, knotty, crooked, knobby, contorted, distorted [➡ IN BAD REPAIR; 1234] *Opposite*: straight

gnash *v* **grind**, clench, grit, grate, rasp, gnaw [➡ FACIAL EXPRESSIONS AND BLUSHING; 651]

gnash your teeth *v* **be fuming**, be upset, grind your teeth, be frustrated [➡ GIVING VENT TO EMOTIONS; 679]

gnat **1** *n* **midge**, mosquito, fly, firefly, insect, bug, no-see-um, punkie [➡ INSECTS; 1012] **2** *type of* **flying insect** [➡ FLYING INSECTS; 1013]

gnaw *v* **worry**, trouble, bother, cause anxiety, concern, distress, bedevil, fret, aggravate (*informal*) [➡ UPSET, DISTRESS, AND HUMILIATE; 567] *Opposite*: comfort

gneiss *type of* **stone** [➡ STONES, ROCKS, AND BOULDERS; 1057]

gnome *n* **elf**, sprite, goblin, troll, leprechaun, fairy, brownie, pixie, fay (*literary*) [➡ MYTHICAL BEINGS; 789]

gnu *type of* **deer or antelope** [➡ DEER AND ANTELOPES; 981]

go **1** *v* **leave**, go away, go off, depart, set off, set out, exit, walk off, move out, move, be off, take off (*informal*), quit (*archaic*) [➡ LEAVE AND GO AWAY; 8] *Opposite*: come **2** *v* **move**, move on, proceed, progress, make for, travel [➡ TRAVEL: WAYS OF TRAVELING; 320] **3** *v* **work**, run, function, operate, move, perform [➡ FUNCTION SUCCESSFULLY; 469] *Opposite*: stop **4** *v* **reach**, extend, stretch, spread [➡ PROCEED AND GO; 305] **5** *v* **become**, get, grow, come to be [➡ CHANGE; 372] **6** *v* **die**, pass away, expire, pass on, depart (*formal*) [➡ DIE; 922] *Opposite*: live **7** *n* **try**, attempt, turn, chance, shot, stab (*informal*) [➡ ATTEMPT AN ACTION; 261] **8** *n* **energy**, liveliness, enthusiasm, spirit, verve, vigor, drive [➡ ENERGY AND ENTHUSIASM; 496] *Opposite*: lethargy **9** *n* (*informal*) **energy**, life, zest, zip (*informal*), oomph (*informal*), pizzazz (*informal*) [➡ POSITIVE IMPATIENCE, ENTHUSIASM, AND ALERTNESS; 537]

go about *v* **perform**, carry out, accomplish, transact, set about, approach, tackle, attempt, undertake, do, effect (*formal*), get on with (*UK*) [➡ CARRY OUT AN ACTION; 269]

goad **1** *v* **provoke**, prod, push, stir, stimulate, spur, incite, annoy, hound, badger, drive, aggravate (*informal*), hassle (*informal*) [➡CAUSE OR COMPEL TO ACT; 271] *Opposite*: calm **2** *n* **stick**, prod, poker, rod, whip, crop, spur [➡STICKS, POLES, AND WEDGES; 1254] **3** *n* **stimulus**, impetus, driving force, spur, stimulation, incitement, provocation [➡BEGINNINGS; 53]

See Compare and Contrast at **motive**.

go adrift *v* **wander**, drift, stray, go astray, deviate, err [➡AIMLESS AND ERRANT MOTION; 343]

go after *v* **try for**, aim for, target, go all-out for, do your utmost, bend over backward, go for (*informal*), pull out all the stops (*UK*) [➡ATTEMPT AN ACTION; 261]

go against *v* **violate**, disobey, infringe, buck (*informal*), fly in the face of [➡DISOBEY; 302]

go-ahead (*informal*) *n* **permission**, consent, approval, green light, support, acceptance [➡PERMIT AND ALLOW; 669]

goal 1 *n* **objective**, aim, end, ambition, purpose, target, object, aspiration [➡INTENTIONS AND PURPOSES; 772] **2** *n* **goalmouth**, penalty area, box, area, goal line [➡SPORTS TERMS; 877]

goalmouth *n* **penalty area**, box, area, goal line, line, goal [➡SPORTS TERMS; 877]

go along with *v* **acquiesce**, concur, agree, grant, accept, accede, consent [➡FORGET, FORGIVE, AND ACCEPT; 748] *Opposite*: refuse

goanna *type of* **reptile** [➡REPTILES; 994]

go around 1 *v* **circulate**, spread, pass on, hand on, disseminate, transmit [➡INFORM, ANNOUNCE, AND ISSUE; 611] **2** *v* **travel**, go from place to place, ride, walk, move [➡TRAVEL: WAYS OF TRAVELING; 320] **3** *v* **revolve**, rotate, twirl, spin, twist, circle, gyrate, turn [➡MOVE SOMETHING: ON THE SPOT; 336]

go-around (*informal*) *n* **argument**, disagreement, fight, tiff, quarrel, row, dispute, go-round (*informal*) [➡ARGUMENTS; 47] *Opposite*: agreement

go around with (*informal*) *v* **accompany**, escort, tag along, spend time with, be together [➡ACCOMPANY AND FOLLOW; 337]

go astray *v* **stray**, get lost, transgress, go off the rails, deviate, err, wander [➡AIMLESS AND ERRANT MOTION; 343]

goat 1 *type of* **farm animal** [➡FARM ANIMALS; 982] **2** *type of* **meat** [➡TYPES AND CUTS OF MEAT; 1177]

goatee *n* [➡FACIAL HAIR; 489]

goat moth *type of* **moth** [➡MOTHS AND BUTTERFLIES; 1015]

go away 1 *v* **leave**, get away, move, depart, be off, head off [➡LEAVE AND GO AWAY; 8] *Opposite*: stay **2** *v* **disappear**, vanish, fade, fade away, recede, depart, leave [➡DISAPPEAR; 4] *Opposite*: stay

go AWOL *v* [➡RUN AWAY AND AVOID; 10]

go awry *v* [➡FAIL OR CEASE TO FUNCTION; 470]

gob (*slang*) *n* **lump**, clot, blob, drop, spot, glob (*informal*) [➡AMOUNTS OF SOLID OR SEMISOLID; 115]

go back *v* **return**, turn back, revert, revisit, retrace your steps, backtrack, double back, retreat [➡GO BACKWARD; 309] *Opposite*: advance

go back on *v* **change your mind**, backtrack, break your promise, have second thoughts, retract, renege, reconsider, betray [➡APOLOGIZE AND RETRACT; 683] *Opposite*: keep your word

go back over *v* **reconsider**, reexamine, repeat, revise, return to, go back to, revisit, rethink [➡THINK AND REFLECT; 743]

go backward *v* **reverse**, retreat, regress, lose ground, fall back [➡GO BACKWARD; 309] *Opposite*: advance

go bad *v* **decay**, rot, go moldy, decompose, putrefy, go sour, go rancid, sour, spoil, molder, go off (*UK*) [➡GO BAD AND CORRODE; 390]

go ballistic (*slang*) *v* [➡GIVING VENT TO EMOTIONS; 679]

go bananas (*informal*) *v* [➡GIVING VENT TO EMOTIONS; 679]

go bankrupt *v* **fail**, collapse, fold, go to the wall, go bust (*informal*), go out of business (*UK*) [➡FAIL OR BE UNSUCCESSFUL; 75]

gobbet *n* [➡AMOUNTS OF SOLID OR SEMISOLID; 115]

gobble 1 *v* **gobble up**, gobble down, bolt, wolf, gorge, gulp, eat up, guzzle (*informal*), scarf down (*slang*) [➡EAT AND NOT EAT; 710] *Opposite*: nibble **2** *v* (*informal humorous*) **use up**, go through, run through, consume, eat into, use, spend [➡USE UP AND WASTE; 474] *Opposite*: conserve

gobble down *v* **gobble**, gobble up, bolt, wolf, gorge, gulp, eat up, guzzle (*informal*), scarf down (*slang*) [➡EAT AND NOT EAT; 710] *Opposite*: nibble

gobbledygook (*informal*) *n* **nonsense**, jargon, gibberish, drivel, rubbish, balderdash, waffle (*informal*), mumbo jumbo (*informal*), bunkum (*informal*), claptrap (*informal*), footle (*informal*), bunk (*slang*), poppycock (*dated informal*) [➡MEANINGLESS SPEECH OR WRITING; 676]

gobble up *v* **eat up**, gobble, bolt, wolf, gorge, gulp, guzzle (*informal*), scarf down (*slang*) [➡EAT AND NOT EAT; 710] *Opposite*: nibble

go belly up *v* [➡FAIL OR BE UNSUCCESSFUL; 75]

go berserk *v* **lose control**, lose your temper, lose your cool, be beside yourself, hit the roof, be furious, be angry, throw a fit (*informal*), go bananas (*informal*), lose it (*informal*), go mad (*UK*) [➡GIVING VENT TO EMOTIONS; 679]

go-between *n* **mediator**, intermediary, broker, arbitrator, messenger, agent, negotiator [➡ADVISERS, JUDGES, AND ARBITERS; 971]

go beyond *v* **surpass**, outdo, rise above, overtake, pass, outrun, overdo, transcend, overshoot, overhaul [➡OVERDO SOMETHING; 290]

goblet *n* **glass**, cup, chalice, wine glass [➡TABLEWARE, FLATWARE, AND KITCHENWARE; 861]

goblin *n* **elf**, sprite, imp, gnome, troll, hobgoblin, brownie [➡MYTHICAL BEINGS; 789]

go bust (*informal*) *v* **go bankrupt**, go under, shut down, fail, go to the wall, close down, cease trading, stop trading, go out of business, bust (*informal*) [➡BUSINESS ACTIVITIES AND PHENOMENA; 794]

go by *v* **pass**, pass by, elapse, lapse [➡HAPPEN; 27]

go-cart *type of* **leisure vehicle** [➡VEHICLES; 1145]

god *n* **deity**, divinity, idol, spirit, supernatural being [➡RELIGIOUS CONCEPTS; 776]

goddess *n* **deity**, divinity, idol, spirit, supernatural being [➡RELIGIOUS CONCEPTS; 776]

go dead *v* [➡FAIL OR CEASE TO FUNCTION; 470]

godless *adj* [➡RELIGIOUS CONCEPTS; 776]

godlessness *n* [➡RELIGIOUS CONCEPTS; 776]

godlike *adj* **divine**, superhuman, transcendent, heavenly, holy, godly [➡RELIGIOUS CONCEPTS; 776]

godliness 1 *n* **religiousness**, holiness, devoutness, goodness, saintliness, righteousness, piousness [➡RELIGIOUS CONCEPTS; 776] *Opposite*: wickedness 2 *n* **divinity**, holiness, heavenliness, transcendence, sacredness [➡RELIGIOUS CONCEPTS; 776]

godly (*formal*) 1 *adj* **religious**, devout, holy, pious, saintly, good, righteous [➡RELIGIOUS CONCEPTS; 776] *Opposite*: wicked 2 *adj* **divine**, holy, heavenly, transcendent, godlike, superhuman [➡RELIGIOUS CONCEPTS; 776]

go down 1 *v* **descend**, drop, sink, dive, plunge, plummet, lower, fall, crash [➡GO DOWNWARD; 307] *Opposite*: go up 2 *v* **deteriorate**, decline, slip, go downhill, get worse, worsen, weaken [➡GET WORSE; 381] *Opposite*: improve 3 *v* (*slang*) **happen**, occur, take place, go on, come about, transpire [➡HAPPEN; 27]

go downhill *v* **deteriorate**, worsen, fail, get worse, go down, degenerate, flounder, decline, weaken, go from bad to worse, go to the dogs (*informal*) [➡GET WORSE; 381] *Opposite*: improve

go down the drain *v* [➡FAIL OR BE UNSUCCESSFUL; 75]

go down the tube (*informal*) *v* [➡FAIL OR BE UNSUCCESSFUL; 75]

go down with (*informal*) *v* **catch**, become ill with, contract, pick up, come down with [➡BECOME SICK, TREAT, AND RECOVER; 728]

godparent *n* [➡ADOPTION, FOSTERING, AND EXTENDED FAMILY; 962]

God's Acre (*archaic*) *n* [➡BURIAL PLACES AND ACCESSORIES; 930]

godsend *n* **blessing**, boon, stroke of luck, bonus, benefit [➡SOURCE OF HAPPINESS, PLEASURE, OR IMPROVEMENT; 209] *Opposite*: disaster

go easy on (*informal*) 1 *v* **treat gently**, indulge, give somebody a break, sympathize, oblige, please, humor, cosset, coddle, pamper [➡TAKE CARE OF AND SPOIL; 300] *Opposite*: punish 2 *v* **take it easy**, slow down, avoid, stint, temper, take it steady (*UK*) [➡UNDERDO SOMETHING; 291] *Opposite*: overdo

gofer (*informal*) *n* **runner**, messenger, minion, assistant, lackey (*archaic*) [➡WORKERS; 836]

go for 1 *v* (*informal*) **try for**, go after, target, aim for, set your sights on [➡ATTEMPT AN ACTION; 261] 2 *v* (*informal*) **like**, enjoy, prefer, follow, love, go in for [➡LIKE, LOVE, VALUE, AND ENJOY; 578] *Opposite*: dislike 3 *v* (*informal*) **choose**, pick, select, prefer, opt for, settle on [➡MAKE DECISIONS AND CHOICES; 752] *Opposite*: refuse 4 *v* **attack**, lay into, set upon, assault, tear into, turn on [➡PHYSICAL ATTACK AND PUNISHMENT; 415]

go for it (*slang*) *v* [➡ATTEMPT AN ACTION; 261]

go forward *v* **advance**, progress, go on, move along, proceed, move on, move ahead, move forward [➡PROCEED AND GO; 305] *Opposite*: go back

go from bad to worse *v* **worsen**, take a turn for the worse, deteriorate, degenerate, go downhill, fall apart, decline, disintegrate, go to pot (*informal*), go to the dogs (*informal*), go to rack and ruin (*informal*) [➡GET WORSE; 381] *Opposite*: improve

go full tilt *v* [➡MOVE FAST; 313]

go-getter (*informal*) *n* **achiever**, doer, self-starter, high-flier, live wire (*informal*), live one (*informal*) [➡PEOPLE WHO ARE APPROVED OF; 955] *Opposite*: layabout

go-getting (*informal*) *adj* **ambitious**, high-powered, determined, positive, single-minded, proactive, can-do (*informal*) [➡ENERGY AND ENTHUSIASM; 496]

goggle *v* **stare**, gaze, gape, ogle, look, scrutinize, watch, gawk (*informal*) [➡LOOKING AND LOOKS; 700]

goggle-eyed *adj* [➡FACIAL EXPRESSIONS AND BLUSHING; 651]

goggles *n* **glasses**, spectacles, specs (*informal*) [➡GLASSES AND SPECTACLES; 1125]

go hard (*UK*) *v* **solidify**, set hard, harden, stiffen, go rigid, coagulate, congeal, set [➡HARDEN, CONGEAL, AND DRY; 387] *Opposite*: soften

go haywire (*informal*) *v* [➡FAIL OR CEASE TO FUNCTION; 470]

go in *v* **enter**, set foot in, gain admittance, step in, access [➡ARRIVE; 12] *Opposite*: leave

go in for 1 *v* **like**, prefer, follow, love, practice, enjoy [➡LIKE, LOVE, VALUE, AND ENJOY; 578] *Opposite*: dislike 2 *v* (*UK*) **enter**, compete in, take part in, take up [➡PARTICIPATE; 292]

going 1 *n* **departure**, exit, disappearance [➡ENDS AND DEPARTURES; 54] *Opposite*: arrival 2 *n* **conditions**, circumstances, situation, case, setup, state of things [➡WAYS OF DOING THINGS; 294] 3 *adj* **successful**, profitable, moneymaking, working [➡SUCCESSFUL AND PROMISING; 81] *Opposite*: bankrupt 4 *adj* **accepted**, standard, valid, current, present [➡PRESENT AND AVAILABLE; 11] 5 *adj* **available**, obtainable, ready, free, open, on offer, untaken, existing, up for grabs (*informal*) [➡PRESENT AND AVAILABLE; 11] *Opposite*: taken

going begging *adj* [➡PRESENT AND AVAILABLE; 11]

going on *adj* [➡HAPPENING AND IN PROGRESS; 32]

going on for (*UK*) *adv* **approximately**, around, about, close to, in the region of, nearly, not far off [➡APPROXIMATELY; 135]

going-over (*informal*) 1 *n* **examination**, inspection, check, investigation, analysis, review, consideration, perusal [➡EXAMINE AND ASSESS; 753] 2 *n* **overhaul**, service, restoration, checkup, improvement, wash, renovation, scrub, dust, makeover [➡CLEAN AND POLISH; 403] 3 *n* **rebuke**, reprimand, scolding, talking-to (*informal*), telling-off (*informal*), roasting (*informal*) [➡CRITICISMS AND ANGRY OUTBURSTS; 50]

going rate *n* **market price**, standard price, usual price, average price, price, rate [➡FUNDS, PAYMENTS, AND CHARGES; 800]

goings-on (*informal*) *n* **activity**, comings and goings, affairs, toing and froing, hustle and bustle, hugger-mugger, carryings-on (*informal*), high jinks (*informal*), palaver (*humorous*) [➡ EVENTS AND OCCURRENCES; 35]

going strong *adj* [➡ SUCCESSFUL AND PROMISING; 81]

go in search of *v* [➡ SEEK POSSESSION AND SEARCH; 456]

go into 1 *v* discuss, go over, talk about, look into, examine, consider, assess [➡ EXAMINE AND ASSESS; 753] *Opposite:* ignore 2 *v* enter, go in, set foot in, gain admittance, step in, access [➡ ARRIVE; 12] *Opposite:* leave

go into detail *v* elaborate, enlarge on, amplify, expand, explain, specify [➡ EXPLAIN AND CLARIFY; 610]

go into liquidation *v* [➡ FAIL OR BE UNSUCCESSFUL; 75]

go in with *v* partner, join, cooperate, merge, combine, associate [➡ ESTABLISHING RELATIONSHIPS WITH OTHERS; 974]

gold 1 *type of* metal [➡ METALS; 1276] 2 *n* treasure, bullion, ingots, gold plate, sovereigns, doubloons, jewelry, pieces of eight, nuggets, bars [➡ FINANCIAL ASSETS; 462] 3 *n* wealth, money, assets, resources, riches, affluence, prosperity [➡ FINANCIAL ASSETS; 462] 4 *n* (*informal*) first place, first prize, title, medal, trophy [➡ REWARDS AND AWARDS; 439] 5 *type of* orange [➡ COLORS; 1224] 6 *adj* gilded, gilt, gold-leaf, gold-plated, golden [➡ METALS; 1276] 7 *type of* yellow [➡ COLORS; 1224]

gold brick *n* fake, fraud, fool's gold, counterfeit, swindle, forgery [➡ DECEPTION AND LIES; 660]

goldbrick (*informal*) 1 *v* shirk, loaf, idle, slack, laze around, malinger [➡ LACK OF ACTIVITY OR MOTION; 342] 2 *n* shirker, loafer, idler, slacker, malingerer, layabout [➡ LAZY OR UNSUCCESSFUL PEOPLE; 948]

gold digger *n* [➡ SUPERFICIAL OR INSINCERE PEOPLE; 951]

golden 1 *adj* excellent, unique, first-rate, wonderful, superb, first-class, ideal, terrific (*informal*), one-off (*UK*) [➡ EXTRAORDINARY: AMAZING; 204] 2 *adj* gold, gold-plated, gold-leaf, gilt, gilded [➡ METALS; 1276] 3 *adj* idyllic, best, peak, utopian, paradisiac, ideal [➡ GOOD, WELL, BETTER; 183] 4 *adj* superior, special, elite, select, favored, esteemed, favorite, privileged, promising [➡ ADMIRABLE AND COMMENDABLE; 185] 5 *type of* orange [➡ COLORS; 1224]

golden age *n* peak, pinnacle, apex, summit, zenith, best of times [➡ INTERMEDIATE STAGES; 55]

golden ager *n* [➡ OLD PEOPLE; 920]

golden eagle *type of* bird of prey [➡ BIRDS OF PREY; 998]

golden-haired *adj* [➡ HAIR COLOR; 485]

golden handshake (*informal*) *n* [➡ FUNDS, PAYMENTS, AND CHARGES; 800]

golden mean *n* middle, midway, mean [➡ MEASURABLE PORTIONS; 127] *Opposite:* extreme

golden opportunity *n* opportunity, advantage, chance, chance of a lifetime, good fortune, break (*informal*) [➡ SOURCE OF HAPPINESS, PLEASURE, OR IMPROVEMENT; 209]

golden parachute (*informal*) *n* [➡ FUNDS, PAYMENTS, AND CHARGES; 800]

goldenrod *type of* weed [➡ WEEDS AND THISTLES; 1034]

golden rule *n* standard, belief, tenet, code, guide, guideline, principle [➡ WAYS OF DOING THINGS; 294]

golden syrup (*UK*) *n* [➡ SUGAR AND PRESERVES; 1184]

goldfish *type of* freshwater fish [➡ FRESHWATER FISH; 1010]

gold mine *n* moneymaker, treasure-trove, treasure house [➡ TREATS; 210]

gold-plated *adj* gilded, gilt, gold-leaf, golden, gold [➡ METALS; 1276]

gold standard *n* benchmark, system, yardstick, touchstone, criterion, paradigm [➡ PERFECT EXAMPLES AND EMBODIMENTS; 67]

golf *type of* target ball game [➡ HOBBIES, GAMES, AND SPORTS; 875]

golly (*dated informal*) *interj* goodness, my, gosh (*informal*), heavens (*informal*), wow (*informal*), gee (*informal*), oh my (*informal*), gee whiz (*informal*), heavens to Betsy (*informal*), my word (*dated*) [➡ EXPRESSIONS OF SURPRISE AND PLEASURE; 546]

go missing *v* disappear, vanish, abscond, escape, go AWOL [➡ RUN AWAY AND AVOID; 10]

go moldy *v* [➡ GO BAD AND CORRODE; 390]

gondola *type of* small vessel [➡ SHIPS AND BOATS; 1150]

gone 1 *adj* (*informal*) dead, passed away, passed on, no more, deceased (*formal*), departed (*formal or literary*) [➡ DEAD AND DYING; 925] *Opposite:* alive 2 *adj* absent, away, left, disappeared, moved out, vanished [➡ ABSENT AND UNAVAILABLE; 7] *Opposite:* present 3 *adj* used up, spent, finished, consumed, depleted, drained, exhausted [➡ ABSENT AND UNAVAILABLE; 7] *Opposite:* remaining

goner (*slang*) *n* corpse, dead body, cadaver, stiff (*slang*) [➡ DEAD PERSON; 926]

gonfalon *n* pennant, banner, flag, standard, ensign [➡ SYMBOLS, SIGNS, AND NUMBERS; 596]

go nuts (*slang*) *v* lose your temper, go off the deep end, blow up (*informal*), go haywire (*informal*), blow your top (*informal*) [➡ GIVING VENT TO EMOTIONS; 679]

gonzo (*slang*) *adj* exaggerated, idiosyncratic, subjective, personalized, biased, partial [➡ BIZARRE AND PECULIAR; 257] *Opposite:* objective

goo (*informal*) 1 *n* sludge, slush, slop, sticky stuff, gook (*informal*), gunk (*informal*), goop (*informal*) [➡ UNPLEASANT, DIRTY, AND TOXIC SUBSTANCES; 1268] 2 *n* slush, sentimentality, emotionalism, mush, corn (*informal*), schmaltz (*informal*), slop (*informal*) [➡ IN POOR TASTE AND OVERSENTIMENTAL; 229]

good 1 *adj* high-quality, first-class, superior, excellent, first-rate, fine (*informal*) [➡ GOOD, WELL, BETTER; 183] *Opposite:* poor 2 *adj* skillful, skilled, able, proficient, accomplished, talented, capable, clever, competent, expert [➡ TALENTED AND SKILLFUL; 527] *Opposite:* bad 3 *adj* virtuous, decent, respectable, moral, upright, noble, worthy, blameless, wholesome [➡ MORALLY GOOD; 774] *Opposite:* bad 4 *adj* enjoyable, pleasant, nice, lovely, satisfactory, agreeable, delightful [➡ EMOTIONALLY PLEASANT; 187] *Opposite:* bad 5 *adj* suitable, helpful, beneficial, sound, safe, advantageous, reliable, trustworthy, useful [➡ USEFULNESS; 199] *Opposite:* useless 6 *adj* nice, lovely, clear, mild, pleasant, fair, sunny, fine (*informal*) [➡ HOT WEATHER; 1050]

Opposite: unpleasant **7** *adj* **obedient**, well-behaved, well-mannered, polite, courteous, well-brought-up (*UK*) [➡ GOOD MANNERS AND SOCIAL SKILLS; 520] *Opposite*: naughty **8** *adj* **effective**, useful, valuable, right, appropriate, beneficial [➡ USEFULNESS; 199] *Opposite*: unsuitable **9** *n* **benefit**, help, advantage, usefulness, profit, gain [➡ SOURCE OF HAPPINESS, PLEASURE, OR IMPROVEMENT; 209]

good afternoon *interj* [➡ GREETINGS, FAREWELLS, AND SALUTATIONS; 659]

goodbye 1 *interj* see you (*informal*), bye (*informal*), see you later (*informal*), ta-ta (*informal*), ciao (*informal*), hasta la vista (*informal*), so long (*informal*), later (*informal*), farewell (*literary*) [➡ GREETINGS, FAREWELLS, AND SALUTATIONS; 659] *Opposite*: hello **2** *n* **departure**, farewell, sendoff, going, parting, valediction (*formal*), leave-taking (*literary*) [➡ ENDS AND DEPARTURES; 54] *Opposite*: greeting

good cause *n* **charitable organization**, voluntary organization, deserving cause, charity, benefit [➡ CHARITY AND CHARITABLE INSTITUTIONS; 822]

good day *interj* [➡ GREETINGS, FAREWELLS, AND SALUTATIONS; 659]

good deed *n* **good turn**, favor, kindness, service [➡ KIND ACTIONS OR BEHAVIOR; 295]

good enough *adj* **all right**, presentable, passable, satisfactory, sufficient, adequate [➡ ACCEPTABLE AND PASSABLE; 219] *Opposite*: inadequate

good faith *n* **honesty**, lawfulness, sincerity, probity, integrity, virtue [➡ MORALLY GOOD; 774]

good-for-nothing *adj* [➡ REDUNDANT AND USELESS; 240]

good fortune *n* **luck**, fortuity, good luck, chance, a stroke of luck, lucky break [➡ LUCK; 783] *Opposite*: misfortune

good guy (*informal*) *n* **hero**, winner, goody (*UK*) [➡ PEOPLE WHO ARE APPROVED OF; 955] *Opposite*: baddie (*informal*)

good health *n* **fitness**, strength, vigor, healthiness, robustness [➡ FIT AND STRONG; 736] *Opposite*: illness

goodhearted *adj* **kindhearted**, kind, caring, generous, giving, decent, well-meaning [➡ GENEROSITY AND KINDNESS; 495]

good humor *n* [➡ PLEASURE, EXCITEMENT, AND ELATION; 534]

good-humored *adj* **friendly**, good-natured, good-tempered, easygoing, genial, affable, humorous, pleasant, happy, cheerful, amiable [➡ GOOD-TEMPERED AND HUMOROUS; 627] *Opposite*: ill-tempered

good judgment *n* **judiciousness**, acumen, astuteness, wisdom, perspicacity, good sense [➡ POSITIVE INTELLECTUAL CHARACTERISTICS; 524]

good life *n* **luxury**, comfort, ease, life of ease, life of Riley, lap of luxury, a place in the sun [➡ PLEASANT SITUATIONS; 74]

good-looking *adj* **attractive**, handsome, beautiful, lovely, pretty, gorgeous, stunning, nice-looking [➡ PEOPLE'S PHYSICAL APPEARANCE; 475] *Opposite*: unattractive

Compare and Contrast: *good-looking, attractive, beautiful, handsome, lovely, pretty*

CORE MEANING: having a pleasing facial appearance

good-looking used of either men or women to indicate pleasing looks; *attractive* pleasing in appearance or manner, or sexually desirable; *beautiful* pleasing to the senses, especially pleasing to look at, and often used to describe women whose appearance is generally considered ideal or perfect; *handsome* with good facial features or a pleasing general appearance, generally used of men, but also of women who have strong but attractive features; *lovely* pleasing to look at, most often used of women; *pretty* with an attractive, pleasant face that is appealing, rather than outstandingly beautiful, most often used of women.

good looks *n* **beauty**, attractiveness, prettiness, handsomeness, loveliness, comeliness (*archaic or literary*) [➡ PEOPLE'S PHYSICAL APPEARANCE; 475]

good luck *interj* [➡ GREETINGS, FAREWELLS, AND SALUTATIONS; 659]

good luck charm *n* [➡ LUCKY CHARMS; 785]

goodly *adj* **large**, substantial, fair, considerable, reasonable, sizable [➡ MANY, MUCH, LARGE AMOUNT; 117]

good-mannered *adj* [➡ GOOD MANNERS AND SOCIAL SKILLS; 520]

good manners *n* **propriety**, manners courtesy, decorum, etiquette, civility, courteousness [➡ GOOD MANNERS AND SOCIAL SKILLS; 520] *Opposite*: bad manners

good morning *interj* [➡ GREETINGS, FAREWELLS, A SALUTATIONS; 659]

good name *n* **reputation**, credit, standing, status, prestige, popularity, renown, repute (*formal*) [SUCCESS; 82]

good-natured *adj* **pleasant**, cheerful, friendly, kind, happy, helpful, agreeable, genial, affable, amiable [➡ FRIENDLINESS AND SOCIABILITY; 494] *Opposite*: disagreeable

good-naturedness *n* [➡ FRIENDLINESS AND SOCIABILITY; 494]

goodness *n* **virtuousness**, decency, kindness, honesty, integrity, good, righteousness [➡ MORALLY; 774] *Opposite*: badness

goodness gracious *interj* [➡ EXPRESSING SURPRISE AND PLEASURE; 546]

good night *interj* **sleep well**, sleep tight (*informal*) [➡ GREETINGS, FAREWELLS, AND SALUTATIONS; 659]

good offices *n* **intervention**, intrusion, support, mediation, help, aid [➡ KIND ACTIONS OR BEHAVIOR; 295]

good on you (*UK*) *interj* [➡ COMPLIMENT]

goods 1 *n* **wares**, stock, articles, produce, supplies, commodities, merchandise [➡ BUSINESS; 795] **2** *n* **property**, personal property, belongings and chattels, things, possessions [➡ POSSESSIONS; 46] *n* **merchandise**, imports, exports, cargo, freight, commodities, wares, produce [➡ BUSINESS PRODUCTS; 795]

goods and chattels *n* [➡ POSSESSIONS]

good sense *n* **prudence**, reason, practicality, intelligence, gumption (*informal*) [➡ INTELLECTUAL CHARACTERISTICS; 524]

good-sized *adj* **sizable**, generous, big, substantial, large, considerable [➡ LARGE; 1193] *Opposite*: small

goods yard *n* [➡ URBAN OUTDOOR SPACES; 1072]

good taste *n* **discernment**, style, elegance, judgment, refinement, tastefulness, discrimination [➡ LEVELS OF EDUCATION AND SOPHISTICATION; 894] *Opposite*: bad taste

good-tempered *adj* **placid**, good-natured, good-humored, easygoing, amicable, genial, affable, friendly, sociable [➡ GOOD-TEMPERED AND HUMOROUS; 627] *Opposite*: bad-tempered

good-temperedly *adv* **placidly**, amicably, genially, affably, sociably, good-humoredly, good-naturedly [➡ GOOD-TEMPERED AND HUMOROUS; 627]

good thing *n* **advantage**, blessing, boon, benefit, plus (*informal*) [➡ SOURCE OF HAPPINESS, PLEASURE, OR IMPROVEMENT; 209]

good turn *n* **favor**, kindness, good deed, service [➡ KIND ACTIONS OR BEHAVIOR; 295]

goodwill *n* **kindness**, friendliness, favor, helpfulness, benevolence, generosity, concern, willingness, care [➡ LOVE, RESPECT, AND GOODWILL; 549] *Opposite*: malice

good word *n* **recommendation**, defense, testimonial, reference, character [➡ SOURCE OF HAPPINESS, PLEASURE, OR IMPROVEMENT; 209]

goody **1** *n* **treat**, perk, bonus, reward, extravagance, luxury [➡ AMUSING THINGS; 211] **2** *n* **tidbit**, candy, snack, sweet (*UK*) [➡ CONFECTIONERY; 1182] **3** *n* (*UK*) **hero**, good guy, winner [➡ PEOPLE WHO ARE APPROVED OF; 955] *Opposite*: baddie (*informal*) **4** *interj* (*informal*) **good**, splendid, wonderful, great (*informal*), super (*informal*), terrific (*informal*), smashing (*UK*) [➡ EXPRESSIONS OF SURPRISE AND PLEASURE; 546]

goody-goody (*informal*) **1** *n* **teacher's pet**, goody two-shoes (*informal*), bluenose (*dated informal*) [➡ SUPERFICIAL OR INSINCERE PEOPLE;] **2** *adj* **sanctimonious**, smug, self-satisfied, self-righteous, prudish, holier-than-thou (*informal*) [➡ AFFECTATION, SATISFACTION, AND SNOBBISHNESS; 507]

goody two-shoes (*informal*) *n* [➡ SUPERFICIAL OR INSINCERE PEOPLE; 951]

gooey **1** **tacky**, viscous, thick, glutinous, gummy, mushy, liquescent, latinous, runny, gluey [➡ PHYSICAL TEXTURE; 1222] **2** *adj* (*halshy*) **slushy**, corny, cloying, sentimental, mushy, soppy (*informal*), schmaltzy (*informal*) [➡ IN POOR TASTE AND OVERSENTIMENTAL;]

gooeyness [➡ FLUID AND NONSOLID; 1213]

goof (*informal*) *n* **error**, blunder, slip, gaffe, mistake, misstep, slip (*informal*), faux pas (*literary*) [➡ MISTAKES; 250] **2** *v* **mistake** **it wrong**, make a blunder, blunder, go wrong, slip (*informal*), miscue (*informal*), err (*formal*) [➡ MESS UP AND MAKE MISTAKES; 472] **3** *v* **botch**, mix up, muddle, mess up (*informal*), screw up (*informal*), bungle (*informal*) [➡ MESS UP AND MAKE MISTAKES;]

goof around (*informal*) *v* [➡ JOKES AND TEASING; 674]

go off **1** *v* **blow up**, go up, detonate [➡ DESTRUCTION AND DEMOLITION;] **leave**, go away, go, depart, set off, take off (*informal*) [➡ LEAVE AND GO AWAY; 8] *Opposite*: stay **3** *v* (*UK*) **decay**, decompose, putrefy, molder, go bad, rot [➡ GO BAD AND CORRODE; 390]

go off in a huff *v* [➡ LEAVE AND GO AWAY; 8]

go off the deep end *v* **lose your temper**, lose your cool, hit the roof, go berserk, lose control, be beside yourself, go bananas (*informal*), throw a fit (*informal*), go nuts (*slang*) [➡ GIVING VENT TO EMOTIONS; 679] *Opposite*: calm down

go off the rails *v* [➡ FAIL OR BE UNSUCCESSFUL; 75]

goof off (*informal*) *v* [➡ JOKES AND TEASING; 674]

goofproof (*informal*) *adj* [➡ SAFE AND SAFETY; 191]

gook (*informal*) *n* [➡ UNPLEASANT, DIRTY, AND TOXIC SUBSTANCES; 1268]

go on **1** *v* **continue**, last, keep on, keep up, persist, carry on, keep going, endure, persevere [➡ CONTINUE AN ACTION; 262] *Opposite*: stop **2** *v* **occur**, happen, take place, come about [➡ HAPPEN; 27] **3** *v* **blabber**, chatter, prattle, blather (*informal*), blab (*informal*), natter (*informal*), gab (*informal*), gas (*informal*), footle (*informal*) [➡ CHATTER AND BABBLE; 617]

goon *n* **thug**, gangster, attacker, assailant, hoodlum, criminal, gorilla (*informal*), hood (*slang*) [➡ VILLAINS AND THUGS; 947]

go one better *v* **surpass**, outdo, top, crown, better, beat [➡ BEAT AND DEFEAT; 80]

go on the blink (*informal*) *v* [➡ FAIL OR CEASE TO FUNCTION; 470]

go on the rampage *v* [➡ GIVING VENT TO EMOTIONS; 679]

goop (*informal*) *n* **slime**, mess, goo (*informal*), gunk (*informal*), gook (*informal*), crud (*slang*) [➡ UNPLEASANT, DIRTY, AND TOXIC SUBSTANCES; 1268]

goopy (*informal*) *adj* [➡ FLUID AND NONSOLID; 1213]

goose **1** *type of* **fowl** [➡ FOOD BIRDS; 999] **2** *type of* **male or female bird** [➡ MALE OR FEMALE BIRDS; 1005] **3** *type of* **meat** [➡ TYPES AND CUTS OF MEAT; 1177]

gooseberry *type of* **berry** [➡ FRUIT AND VEGETABLES; 1176]

goose bumps *n* [➡ CONDITIONS AFFECTING THE SKIN; 721]

goose egg (*slang*) *n* [➡ NONE; 123]

goose step *v* **strut**, stride, tramp, pace, walk, march [➡ PROCEED AND GO; 305]

go out **1** *v* **socialize**, meet friends, party (*informal*), go out on the town (*informal*), paint the town red (*informal*) [➡ LEISURE AND RECREATION; 874] **2** *v* **ebb**, recede, flow out [➡ EMIT AND EMANATE; 361]

go out of business *v* **go bankrupt**, fold, close down, shut down, go belly up, go under, fail, go bust (*informal*), bust (*informal*), go to the wall (*UK*) [➡ BUSINESS ACTIVITIES AND PHENOMENA; 794]

go over *v* **discuss**, go into, examine, look at, study, read, peruse, revise, look into, consider, review, revisit [➡ EXAMINE AND ASSESS; 753] *Opposite*: ignore

go over like a lead balloon (*slang*) *v* **fail**, crash, fizzle, sink without trace, bomb (*informal*) [➡ FAIL OR BE UNSUCCESSFUL; 75]

go over the top *v* **overdo it**, get carried away, gild the lily, go to town (*informal*), go mad (*slang*), over-egg the pudding (*UK*) [➡ OVERDO SOMETHING; 290]

go pale *v* [➡ FACIAL EXPRESSIONS AND BLUSHING; 651]

gopher *type of* **rodent** [➡ RODENTS; 989]

go postal (*informal*) *v* [➡ GIVING VENT TO EMOTIONS; 679]

go rancid *v* [➡ GO BAD AND CORRODE; 390]

gore 1 *v* **wound**, pierce, stab, spear, stick, gouge, run through (*literary*) [➡ STAB; 416]   2 *n* **blood**, violence, bloodletting, slaughter, killing, carnage, bloodshed [➡ CAUSES OF DEATH; 921]

go red *v* [➡ FACIAL EXPRESSIONS AND BLUSHING; 651]

gorge 1 *n* **valley**, ravine, canyon, defile, gap, chasm, arroyo, gulch [➡ GEOLOGIC FEATURES; 1056]   2 *part of* **bird** [➡ PARTS OF A BIRD; 1006]   3 *v* **devour**, wolf, bolt, gobble, consume, eat, guzzle (*informal*), scarf down (*slang*) [➡ EAT AND NOT EAT; 710] *Opposite*: nibble   4 *v* **overeat**, stuff, binge, glut, sate, satiate [➡ EAT AND NOT EAT; 710]

gorgeous *adj* **beautiful**, magnificent, stunning, elegant, attractive, striking, good-looking, dazzling, lovely, exquisite, adorable [➡ BEAUTY AND ATTRACTIVENESS; 189] *Opposite*: unattractive

gorgeousness *n* **elegance**, magnificence, beauty, splendor, exquisiteness, good looks, prettiness, attractiveness, loveliness [➡ BEAUTY AND ATTRACTIVENESS; 189]

Gorgonzola *type of* **soft cheese** [➡ DAIRY PRODUCTS AND CHEESES; 1183]

gorilla 1 *type of* **primate** [➡ PRIMATES; 988]   2 *n* (*informal*) **thug**, brute, bully, hoodlum, goon, heavy (*slang*), hood (*slang*) [➡ VILLAINS AND THUGS; 947]

go rotten *v* [➡ GO BAD AND CORRODE; 390]

go-round *see* **go-around**

gorsbeak *type of* **common bird** [➡ BIRDS; 997]

gorse *type of* **shrub or bush** [➡ BUSHES AND SHRUBS; 1027]

gory 1 *adj* **bloody**, bloodstained, blood-soaked [➡ IN BAD REPAIR, 1234]   2 *adj* **violent**, gruesome, brutal, bloodthirsty, fierce, horrific [➡ PHYSICALLY UNPLEASANT; 226] *Opposite*: pleasant   3 *adj* **disgusting**, gruesome, grisly, unpleasant, ghastly, horrible [➡ DISGUSTING AND REPULSIVE; 230] *Opposite*: delightful

go separate ways *v* [➡ REFUSING OR REJECTING RELATIONS; 975]

gosh (*informal*) *interj* **goodness**, my goodness, goodness gracious, gracious, my, heavens (*informal*), gee (*informal*), oh my (*informal*), wow (*informal*), golly (*dated informal*) [➡ EXPRESSIONS OF SURPRISE AND PLEASURE; 546]

go sky-high *v* [➡ CHANGE OF INTENSITY: MORE; 394]

gosling *type of* **young bird** [➡ YOUNG BIRDS; 1004]

go-slow (*UK*) *n* **slowdown**, stoppage, strike [➡ WORK-RELATED ACTIVITIES; 834]

go sour *v* [➡ GO BAD AND CORRODE; 390]

gospel *type of* **pop and vocal music** [➡ MUSIC, SONGS, AND SINGING; 907]

gossamer 1 *n* **threads**, filaments, spider's web, cobwebs [➡ FASTENERS, LINKS, AND NETWORKS; 1247]   2 *adj* **delicate**, flimsy, sheer, filmy, ethereal, transparent, diaphanous, gauzy [➡ VISUAL TEXTURE; 1221] *Opposite*: robust

gossip 1 *n* **chatter**, chat, talk, conversation, blather (*informal*) [➡ INFORMAL COMMUNICATION; 45]   2 *n* **rumor**, hearsay, tittle-tattle, scandal, chitchat (*informal*) [➡ GOSSIP; 678]   3 *n* **tattler**, telltale, rumormonger, gossipmonger, scandalmonger, blabbermouth (*informal*), tattletale (*informal*), bigmouth (*informal*) [➡ INTERFERING PEOPLE AND TATTLE-TALES; 950]   4 *v* **chatter**, talk, converse, chat, natter (*informal*) [➡ BETRAY CONFIDENCES AND GOSSIP; 618]

gossipy *adj* [➡ ELOQUENT, TALKATIVE, AND LONG-WINDED; 632]

See Compare and Contrast at **talkative**.

gossipmonger *n* **telltale**, gossip, rumormonger, scandalmonger, tattler, bigmouth (*informal*), blabbermouth (*informal*), tattletale (*informal*) [➡ INTERFERING PEOPLE AND TATTLE-TALES; 950]

go stale *v* [➡ GO BAD AND CORRODE; 390]

go the distance *v* **complete**, finish, achieve, accomplish, carry out, fulfill, realize [➡ COMPLETE AN ACTION; 263] *Opposite*: give up

Gothic 1 *adj* **supernatural**, melodramatic, eerie, grotesque, gloomy, creepy (*informal*), spooky (*informal*) [➡ FRIGHTENING; 231]   2 *type of* **pre-20th-century architecture** [➡ BUILDING AND ARCHITECTURE; 1076]

Gothic revival *type of* **pre-20th-century architecture** [➡ BUILDING AND ARCHITECTURE; 1076]

go through 1 *v* **experience**, endure, undergo, bear, suffer [➡ EXPERIENCE AND ENCOUNTER; 582]   2 *v* **examine**, look through, look over, go over, study, inspect, check [➡ EXAMINE AND ASSESS; 753]   3 *v* **use**, get through, run through, consume, utilize, make use of, use up, spend [➡ USE UP AND WASTE; 474] *Opposite*: keep

go through the roof *v* **soar**, rocket, rise, shoot up, spiral upward, surge, spiral [➡ CHANGE OF SIZE: BIGGER; 392] *Opposite*: plummet

go to bed *v* **retire**, turn in (*informal*), hit the hay (*informal*), hit the sack (*informal*) [➡ SLEEP AND DREAM; 723]

go to meet your maker *v* [➡ DIE; 922]

go too far *v* [➡ OVERDO SOMETHING; 290]

go to pieces *v* **break down**, crack, lose control, collapse, crumple, fall apart, crack up (*informal*) [➡ GIVING VENT TO EMOTIONS; 679]

go to pot (*informal*) *v* **deteriorate**, disintegrate, fall apart, go downhill, go from bad to worse, worsen, take a turn for the worse, degenerate, decline, go to the dogs (*informal*), go to rack and ruin (*informal*) [➡ GET WORSE; 381] *Opposite*: improve

go to rack and ruin (*informal*) *v* **deteriorate**, disintegrate, fall apart, go downhill, go from bad to worse, worsen, take a turn for the worse, degenerate, decline, go to the dogs (*informal*), go to pot (*informal*) [➡ GET WORSE; 381] *Opposite*: improve

go to seed *v* [➡ FAIL OR BE UNSUCCESSFUL; 75]

go to sleep *v* **fall asleep**, nod off, doze off, drift off, drop off (*informal*) [➡ SLEEP AND DREAM; 723] *Opposite:* wake up

go to the dogs (*informal*) *v* **go downhill**, deteriorate, degenerate, decline, worsen, take a turn for the worse, fall apart, go from bad to worse, go to pot (*informal*), go to rack and ruin (*informal*) [➡ GET WORSE; 381] *Opposite:* improve

go to the wall *v* **go bankrupt**, fold, go under, fail, close down, shut down, go bust (*informal*) [➡ FAIL OR BE UNSUCCESSFUL; 75]

go to waste *v* **be wasted**, go down the drain, fall by the wayside, go to seed, go down the tube (*informal*) [➡ FAIL OR BE UNSUCCESSFUL; 75]

got up (*informal*) *adj* [➡ DRESS, WEAR, AND UNDRESS; 868]

gouache *n* [➡ WRITING AND DRAWING IMPLEMENTS, AND MEDIA; 601]

Gouda *type of* **hard cheese** [➡ DAIRY PRODUCTS AND CHEESES; 1183]

gouge 1 *v* **scratch**, score, scrape, mark, cut into, gash, chisel [➡ EXTRACT AND SEVER; 341] 2 *v* **extort**, extract, wring, wrest, squeeze, overcharge [➡ TAKE SOMETHING AWAY; 425] 3 *n* **score**, scratch, gash, groove, hollow, scrape, cavity [➡ HOLES, GAPS, AND FORKS; 1252]

gouge out *v* **dig out**, hollow out, press out, squeeze out, force out, chisel out, scoop, hollow [➡ EXTRACT AND SEVER; 341]

goulash *type of* **cooked dish** [➡ PREPARED DISHES; 1170]

go under 1 *v* **collapse**, go to the wall, fold, fail, go bust (*informal*), bite the dust (*informal*) [➡ FAIL OR BE UNSUCCESSFUL; 75] 2 *v* **lose consciousness**, pass out, black out, faint [➡ BECOME SICK, TREAT, AND RECOVER; 728]

go underground *v* [➡ RUN AWAY AND AVOID; 10]

go up *v* **explode**, go off, detonate, blow up, ignite, go up in smoke [➡ FIRE, FLAMMABILITY, AND BURNING; 1165]

go up in smoke 1 *v* **burn**, catch fire, burst into flames, burn to a crisp, burn to the ground, catch light [➡ FIRE, FLAMMABILITY, AND BURNING; 1165] 2 *v* **fail**, fold, collapse, go wrong, go awry, bomb (*informal*) [➡ FAIL OR BE UNSUCCESSFUL; 75]

gourde *type of* **currency** [➡ CURRENCIES; 798]

gourmand *n* **food lover**, glutton, gastronome, gourmet, epicure, foodie (*informal*) [➡ PLEASURE-SEEKERS AND HEDONISTS; 886]

gourmandise *n* [➡ EAT AND NOT EAT; 710]

gourmandising *n* [➡ EAT AND NOT EAT; 710]

gourmet *n* **gastronome**, food lover, epicure, epicurean, connoisseur, gourmand, foodie (*informal*) [➡ EATERS, GOURMETS, AND DIETARY CHOICES; 714]

govern *v* **rule**, preside over, oversee, administer, administrate, direct, run, manage, head, reign, control, dominate, regulate, preside [➡ BE IN CHARGE; 270]

governess *n* **tutor**, teacher, instructor, schoolteacher, educator, coach [➡ EDUCATORS; 840]

government *n* **administration**, rule, management, direction, regime, control, supervision, command, authority, leadership [➡ GOVERNMENT AND POLITICS; 805]

governmental *adj* **administrative**, parliamentary, legis-lative, executive, constitutional, organizational, managerial, lawmaking [➡ GOVERNMENT AND POLITICS; 805]

governor *n* **director**, ruler, manager, administrator, chief, head, superintendent, regulator, controller [➡ BOSSES AND MANAGEMENT; 965]

governorship *n* **administration**, leadership, stewardship, directorship, captaincy, office, tenure [➡ POLITICAL OFFICES AND POLITICIANS; 808]

go well *v* [➡ SUCCEED AND WIN; 79]

go white *v* [➡ FACIAL EXPRESSIONS AND BLUSHING; 651]

go wild *v* **run riot**, rampage, run amok, go on the rampage, run wild, go nuts (*slang*) [➡ GIVING VENT TO EMOTIONS; 679]

go with 1 *v* (*informal*) **date**, go out with, see, socialize, go steady [➡ ESTABLISHING RELATIONSHIPS WITH OTHERS; 974] 2 *v* **adopt**, accept, follow, run with, support, go along with, concur [➡ APPROVE AND CONFIRM; 646]

go without *v* **not have**, do without, be without, lack, want, be deprived, forgo [➡ FORGO AND DENY ONESELF; 449] *Opposite:* have

gown *n* **dress**, robe, evening dress, wedding dress, ball gown [➡ GARMENTS AND OUTFITS; 865]

go wrong 1 *v* **fail**, break down, not work, not succeed, go awry, be unsuccessful, be a failure [➡ FAIL OR BE UNSUCCESSFUL; 75] *Opposite:* succeed 2 *v* **make a mistake**, misjudge, blunder, err, slip up (*informal*), goof (*informal*) [➡ MESS UP AND MAKE MISTAKES; 472]

GP *n* **family doctor**, doctor, clinician, practitioner, medic (*informal*), general practitioner (*dated*) [➡ PEOPLE WHO WORK IN MEDICINE; 848]

grab 1 *v* **grasp**, clutch, grip, take hold of, seize, snatch, take [➡ CONTACT: HOLD; 411] *Opposite:* let go 2 *v* **snatch**, seize, remove, steal, take, lift (*informal*), heist (*slang*) [➡ TAKE SOMETHING AWAY; 425] 3 *v* (*informal*) **affect**, appeal, impress, attract, please, influence [➡ APPEAL TO AND AROUSE INTEREST; 575]

grab bag *n* [➡ COLLECTIONS AND MIXTURES OF THINGS; 1244]

grab hold of *v* **grab**, grasp, grip, snatch, clutch, clench, take [➡ CONTACT: HOLD; 411]

grace 1 *n* **elegance**, refinement, loveliness, beauty, polish, style, poise, charm [➡ WELL-GROOMED; 482] *Opposite:* awkwardness 2 *n* **kindness**, kindliness, decency, favor, mercy, mercifulness, charity, benevolence, clemency, leniency [➡ MORALLY GOOD; 774] *Opposite:* unkindness 3 *n* **blessing**, prayer, thanks, thanksgiving [➡ RELIGIOUS CONCEPTS; 776] 4 *v* **adorn**, embellish, enhance, decorate, ornament, beautify [➡ DECORATE, ADORN, AND APPLY COATINGS; 405] *Opposite:* deface 5 *v* **dignify**, honor, favor, distinguish [➡ IMPROVE SOMETHING; 374] *Opposite:* demean

graceful 1 *adj* **elegant**, beautiful, supple, agile, nimble, lithe, flowing, smooth, attractive, fluid [➡ AGILITY OF THE BODY; 476] *Opposite:* graceless 2 *adj* **poised**, dignified, polished, refined, stylish, polite, charming, gracious [➡ GOOD MANNERS AND SOCIAL SKILLS; 520] *Opposite:* awkward 3 *adj* **flowing**, fluid, smooth, easy on the eyes, attractive, elegant [➡ BEAUTY AND ATTRACTIVENESS; 189] *Opposite:* ugly

gracefully *adv* **stylishly**, with poise, charmingly, elegantly, graciously [➡WELL-GROOMED; 482] *Opposite*: awkwardly

gracefulness 1 *n* **elegance**, grace, smoothness, fluidity, subtlety, delicacy, cleanness [➡BEAUTY AND ATTRACTIVENESS; 189] *Opposite*: inelegance 2 *n* **poise**, dignity, refinement, grace, restraint, politeness, delicacy, tact, diplomacy, graciousness [➡GOOD MANNERS AND SOCIAL SKILLS; 520] *Opposite*: awkwardness

graceless 1 *adj* **clumsy**, ungainly, inelegant, awkward, maladroit, gawky (*informal*), bumbling (*informal*), ham-fisted (*informal*), ham-handed (*informal*) [➡AGILITY OF THE BODY; 476] *Opposite*: graceful 2 *adj* **rude**, impolite, ill-mannered, boorish, offensive, crude, uncouth [➡BAD MANNERS AND SOCIAL SKILLS; 521] *Opposite*: polite

gracelessness 1 *n* **inelegance**, awkwardness, clumsiness, ungainliness, unskillfulness, maladroitness (*formal*) [➡AGILITY OF THE BODY; 476] *Opposite*: gracefulness 2 *n* **rudeness**, impoliteness, mannerlessness, bad manners, boorishness, offensiveness, crudeness, uncouthness [➡BAD MANNERS AND SOCIAL SKILLS; 521] *Opposite*: politeness

grace period *n* **extension**, overtime, overrun, extra time (*UK*) [➡PAUSES AND PHASES; 56]

gracious 1 *adj* **kind**, polite, tactful, courteous, civil, diplomatic, amiable, cordial, affable [➡GOOD MANNERS AND SOCIAL SKILLS; 520] *Opposite*: rude 2 *adj* **condescending**, haughty, superior, patronizing, high and mighty, snooty (*informal*) [➡AFFECTATION, SELF-SATISFACTION, AND SNOBBISHNESS; 507] *Opposite*: genuine 3 *adj* **luxurious**, elegant, comfortable, well-off, plush (*informal*), classy (*informal*) [➡EXPENSIVE AND LUXURIOUS; 218] 4 *adj* **merciful**, compassionate, lenient, humane, charitable, understanding [➡MORALLY GOOD; 774] *Opposite*: harsh

graciously 1 *adv* **kindly**, politely, tactfully, courteously, civilly, diplomatically, amiably, cordially, affably [➡GOOD MANNERS AND SOCIAL SKILLS; 520] *Opposite*: rudely 2 *adv* **luxuriously**, elegantly, comfortably [➡EXPENSIVE AND LUXURIOUS; 218]

graciousness *n* **kindness**, courteousness, politeness, civility, affability, diplomacy, cordiality [➡GOOD MANNERS AND SOCIAL SKILLS; 520] *Opposite*: rudeness

grackle *type of* **common bird** [➡BIRDS; 997]

gradation *n* **nuance**, degree, stage, progression, shift, shade [➡DEGREE AND EXTENT; 110]

grade 1 *n* **score**, mark, rating, ranking, evaluation [➡SCORES AND EVALUATIONS; 598] 2 *n* **hill**, gradient, incline, slope, ascent, descent, pitch, rise [➡MOUNTAINS AND HILLS; 1044] 3 *n* **rank**, position, status, standing, class, category, condition, quality, caliber, degree [➡VARIETIES, TYPES, AND KINDS; 145] 4 *v* **classify**, categorize, sort, arrange, order, rate, rank, mark, score, group [➡ARRANGE AND CREATE ORDER; 357]

Grade A *adj* [➡GOOD, WELL, BETTER; 183]

grade school *type of* **school** [➡EDUCATIONAL INSTITUTIONS; 813]

gradient *n* **slope**, incline, ramp, hill, rise, pitch, ascent, grade, descent [➡MOUNTAINS AND HILLS; 1044]

gradual *adj* **slow**, measured, slow but sure, plodding, continuing, steady, regular, ongoing [➡HAPPENING SLOWLY; 106] *Opposite*: rapid

graduate 1 *v* **progress**, move up, advance, go forward, move on, proceed, go on, step up [➡PROCEED AND GO; 305] *Oppo-*

site: fall back 2 *v* **mark off**, measure off, divide up, regulate [➡SEPARATE AND DIVIDE; 401] 3 *v* **arrange**, order, categorize, classify, rank, rate, group [➡ARRANGE AND CREATE ORDER; 357]

graduate school *n* [➡EDUCATIONAL INSTITUTIONS; 813]

graduate student *n* [➡STUDENTS AND PUPILS; 841]

graduation 1 *n* **matriculation**, qualification, completion, validation, attainment, promotion, advancement, valediction (*formal*) [➡CLASSES, COURSEWORK, AND EXAMINATIONS; 842] 2 *n* **award ceremony**, graduation day, ceremony, commencement, passing out (*UK*) [➡CEREMONIES AND ANNIVERSARIES; 38] 3 *n* **mark**, division, line, unit, step, scale, point, scale point, calibration [➡CHANGE; 372] 4 *n* **calibration**, division, measurement, marking up, marking out, verification, ranking, classification [➡ARRANGE AND CREATE ORDER; 357]

graffiti *n* **drawing**, doodle, scrawl, scribble, writing, lettering [➡WRITING; 583]

graft 1 *n* **implant**, insert, transplant, scion, slip, implantation [➡COMBINE AND MIX; 400] 2 *type of* **medical procedure** [➡REMEDIES, TREATMENTS, AND OPERATIONS; 731] 3 *v* **splice**, attach, join, embed, implant, insert, transplant [➡FASTEN, LINK, AND JOIN; 408]

grain 1 *n* **cereal**, wheat, corn, barley, maize, oat, rice, millet, rye, sorghum [➡CEREAL FOODS; 1178] 2 *n* **seed**, kernel, germ [➡CEREAL FOODS; 1178] 3 *n* **particle**, speck, fragment, crumb, bit, piece [➡SMALL PIECES; 129] 4 *n* **pattern**, direction, configuration, arrangement, texture, weave [➡PATTERNS; 1225]

grain elevator *type of* **storage space** [➡STORES AND STORAGE BUILDINGS; 1088]

graininess *n* [➡VISUAL TEXTURE; 1221]

grainy *adj* [➡VISUAL TEXTURE; 1221]

gram *type of* **metric unit** [➡SIZE AND DIMENSIONS; 1192]

grammar *n* **syntax**, sentence structure, language rules, parsing [➡ASPECTS OF LANGUAGE; 682]

grammar

◆ *types of grammatical terms*
ablative, accusative, adjunct, affix, apposition, attributive, clause, combining form, conditional, conjugation, dative, diphthong, genitive, indicative, infinitive, inflection, intransitive, modal, nominative, object, participle, plural, predicate, prefix, prenominal, preterit, sentence, subject, subjunctive, suffix, transitive, vocative

◆ *types of word classes*
adjective, adverb, article, collective noun, common noun, conjunction, definite article, determiner, indefinite article, interjection, modifier, noun, particle, phrasal verb, preposition, pronoun, proper noun, qualifier, quantifier, substantive, verb

grammar school *type of* **school** [➡EDUCATIONAL INSTITUTIONS; 813]

grammatical 1 *adj* **linguistic**, syntactic, structural [➡ASPECTS OF LANGUAGE; 682] 2 *adj* **correct**, well-formed, right, proper, standard, acceptable [➡ASPECTS OF LANGUAGE; 682]

gramophone (*dated*) *type of* **audio equipment** [➡AUDIO EQUIPMENT; 1139]

gramps (*informal*) *type of* **older relative** [➡ OLDER GENERATION RELATIVES; 959]

grampus *type of* **marine mammal** [➡ MARINE MAMMALS; 987]

gran (*informal*) *n* **grandmother**, grandma (*informal*), nana (*informal*), granny (*informal*) [➡ OLDER GENERATION RELATIVES; 959]

granary *n* **warehouse**, barn, grain elevator, silo, storeroom, hayloft [➡ STORES AND STORAGE BUILDINGS; 1088]

grand 1 *adj* **outstanding**, impressive, imposing, majestic, magnificent, splendid, striking, ostentatious, luxurious [➡ EXTRAORDINARY: AMAZING; 204] *Opposite:* humble 2 *adj* **ambitious**, impressive, far-reaching, major, substantial, extensive, comprehensive, all-encompassing, all-inclusive [➡ LARGE; 1193] *Opposite:* limited 3 *adj* **distinguished**, illustrious, celebrated, well-known, famous, revered, respected [➡ KNOWN AND FAMOUS; 181] *Opposite:* ordinary 4 *adj* **wonderful**, fantastic, excellent, memorable, great, fine, good [➡ GOOD, WELL, BETTER; 183] *Opposite:* poor

grandchild *type of* **younger relative** [➡ YOUNGER GENERATION RELATIVES; 958]

granddad (*informal*) *n* **grandfather**, grandpa (*informal*), gramps (*informal*) [➡ OLDER GENERATION RELATIVES; 959]

granddaughter *type of* **younger relative** [➡ YOUNGER GENERATION RELATIVES; 958]

grandee *n* **dignitary**, notable, public figure, VIP, personage (*formal*) [➡ IMPORTANT OR FAMOUS PEOPLE; 893]

grandeur *n* **splendor**, magnificence, sumptuousness, opulence, majesty, dignity, stateliness, greatness, grandness [➡ EXTRAORDINARY: AMAZING; 204] *Opposite:* austerity

grandfather *n* **granddad** (*informal*), grandpa (*informal*), gramps (*informal*) [➡ OLDER GENERATION RELATIVES; 959]

grandfather clock *type of* **clock** [➡ CLOCKS AND TIMERS; 1126]

grandiloquence *n* **pomposity**, bombast, loftiness, fustian, rhetoric, magniloquence (*formal*), orotundity (*formal*) [➡ BOAST; 616]

grandiloquent *adj* **pompous**, lofty, haughty, bombastic, high-flown, high-sounding, magniloquent (*formal*), orotund (*formal*) [➡ POMPOUS, LOUD, AND OVERCONFIDENT; 635] *Opposite:* plain

grandiose 1 *adj* **pretentious**, pompous, flamboyant, ostentatious, extravagant, high-flying [➡ POMPOUS, LOUD, AND OVERCONFIDENT; 635] *Opposite:* modest 2 *adj* **magnificent**, lavish, splendid, impressive, stately, imposing, grand [➡ EXTRAORDINARY: AMAZING; 204] *Opposite:* modest 3 *adj* **elaborate**, ambitious, complex, impenetrable, unfathomable [➡ DIFFICULTY AND COMPLEXITY; 242] *Opposite:* simple

grandiosity 1 *n* **pretentiousness**, pompousness, self-importance, affectedness, pomposity, bombast [➡ BOAST; 616] *Opposite:* unpretentiousness 2 *n* **magnificence**, lavishness, impressiveness, stateliness, imposingness, grandness, splendor [➡ EXTRAORDINARY: AMAZING; 204] *Opposite:* modesty 3 *n* **elaborateness**, ambitiousness, complexity, impenetrability, unfathomability [➡ DIFFICULTY AND COMPLEXITY; 242] *Opposite:* simplicity

grandly 1 *adv* **majestically**, magnificently, splendidly, luxuriously, impressively, imposingly [➡ EXTRAORDINARY: AMAZING; 204] *Opposite:* simply 2 *adv* **ostentatiously**, flam-

boyantly, pompously, extravagantly, pretentiously, loftily, haughtily [➡ POMPOUS, LOUD, AND OVERCONFIDENT; 635] *Opposite:* humbly

grandma (*informal*) *n* **grandmother**, granny (*informal*), gran (*informal*), nana (*informal*) [➡ OLDER GENERATION RELATIVES; 959]

grandmother *n* **grandma** (*informal*), nana (*informal*), gran (*informal*), granny (*informal*) [➡ OLDER GENERATION RELATIVES; 959]

grandness *n* **magnificence**, splendor, majesty, dignity, stateliness, greatness, grandeur, grandiosity [➡ EXTRAORDINARY: AMAZING; 204] *Opposite:* simplicity

grandpa (*informal*) *n* **grandfather**, granddad (*informal*), gramps (*informal*) [➡ OLDER GENERATION RELATIVES; 959]

grandparent *type of* **older relative** [➡ OLDER GENERATION RELATIVES; 959]

grand piano *type of* **keyboard** [➡ MUSICAL INSTRUMENTS; 910]

grandson *type of* **younger relative** [➡ YOUNGER GENERATION RELATIVES; 958]

grandstand *v* **show off**, play to the gallery, ham up, attract attention, impress, showboat (*informal*) [➡ BOAST; 616]

grand total *n* [➡ ALL; 128]

granita *type of* **dessert** [➡ CAKES, COOKIES, AND DESSERTS; 1181]

granite *type of* **stone** [➡ STONES, ROCKS, AND BOULDERS; 1057]

granny (*informal*) *n* **grandmother**, nana (*informal*), grandma (*informal*), gran (*informal*) [➡ OLDER GENERATION RELATIVES; 959]

grant 1 *v* **allow**, permit, agree to, consent to, approve of, go along with, concede, admit [➡ AGREE; 645] *Opposite:* prohibit 2 *v* **give**, accord, award, sign over, present, confer (*formal*), cede (*formal*), bestow (*formal*) [➡ GIVE AND PROVIDE; 430] 3 *n* **funding**, scholarship, endowment, contribution, donation, award, gift, bequest, allowance [➡ GIFTS; 438]

See Compare and Contrast at **give**.

granular *adj* **gritty**, grainy, rough, coarse, granulated, granulose [➡ PHYSICAL TEXTURE; 1222] *Opposite:* smooth

granulated *adj* **ground**, coarse, grainy, gritty, rough [➡ PHYSICAL TEXTURE; 1222]

granule *n* **grain**, pellet, particle, morsel, crumb, piece [➡ SMALL PIECES; 129]

grape *type of* **fruit** [➡ FRUIT AND VEGETABLES; 1176]

grapefruit *type of* **citrus fruit** [➡ FRUIT AND VEGETABLES; 1176]

grapevine 1 *n* **rumor mill**, gossip, word of mouth, viral marketing, bush telegraph (*informal*), scuttlebutt (*slang*) [➡ GOSSIP; 678] 2 *type of* **climber** [➡ CLIMBERS; 1033]

graph *n* **chart**, diagram, grid, display [➡ DRAWINGS, CHARTS, AND TABLES; 594]

graphic 1 *adj* **explicit**, realistic, vivid, striking, detailed, leaving nothing to the imagination, full, clear, lifelike [➡ CONCISE AND CLEAR; 202] *Opposite:* sketchy 2 *adj* **illustrative**, pictorial, drawn, diagrammatic, decorative, visual [➡ ARTISTIC MOVEMENTS AND STYLES; 899]

graphic arts n [➡ THE PICTORIAL ARTS; 897]

graphic designer n [➡ DESIGNERS, CREATORS, AND INSTIGATORS; 347]

graphic novel n [➡ FICTION AND DRAMA; 913]

graphite type of **mineral** [➡ MINERALS; 1277]

grapple 1 v **struggle**, wrestle, seize, grab, grasp, tackle, fight [➡ CONTACT: HOLD; 411] 2 v **contend**, deal with, cope, face, handle, tackle, struggle, wrestle, do battle [➡ COMPETE, CONTEND, AND COMBAT; 303]

grapple with v [➡ ATTEMPT AN ACTION; 261]

grasp 1 v **take hold of**, clutch, grab, seize, grip, clasp, snatch, grapple, clench [➡ CONTACT: HOLD; 411] Opposite: let go 2 v **understand**, comprehend, see the point of, follow, get, get the picture (informal), get the message (informal) [➡ UNDERSTAND AND GRASP; 759] 3 n **grip**, hold, clutch, clasp, clench [➡ CONTACT: HOLD; 411] 4 n **understanding**, comprehension, knowledge, awareness, perception, sense [➡ KNOWLEDGE AND WISDOM; 558] 5 n **reach**, scope, extent, range, capacity, control [➡ DEGREE AND EXTENT; 110]

grasping adj **greedy**, avaricious, covetous, selfish, acquisitive, miserly [➡ GRASPING AND FINANCIALLY MEAN; 519] Opposite: generous

graspingness n [➡ GRASPING AND FINANCIALLY MEAN; 519]

grasp the nettle (UK) v [➡ ATTEMPT AN ACTION; 261]

grass 1 n [➡ VEGETATION; 1025] 2 n **grassland**, meadow, pasture, prairie, sward, greensward (archaic or literary) [➡ THE COUNTRYSIDE AND OUTDOOR SPACES; 1071]

grass

♦ types of grasses
bamboo, beach grass, bluegrass, bulrush, couch grass, crabgrass, esparto, fescue, Kentucky bluegrass, lyme grass, marram, meadow fescue, pampas grass, reed, rye grass, spinifex, sugar cane, sword grass, timothy

grass green type of **green** [➡ COLORS; 1224]

grasshopper type of **flying insect** [➡ FLYING INSECTS; 1013]

grassland n **plains**, prairie, savanna, steppe, heath, pampas, downland, moor, parkland, lea (literary), heathland (UK), downs (UK) [➡ DESERTS, PLAINS, AND MOORLAND; 1045]

grassroots 1 n **masses**, hoi polloi, rank and file, ranks, also-rans, little men [➡ CLASS STATUS; 889] 2 n **basis**, origin, foundation, base, root, bedrock [➡ SUPPORTS AND BASES; 1255] 3 adj **popular**, proletarian, public, common, ordinary, mass [➡ BELONGING OR RELATING TO PEOPLE; 943]

grass snake type of **nonpoisonous snake** [➡ SNAKES; 995]

grassy adj **green**, verdant, lush [➡ VEGETATION; 1025]

grate 1 n **grill**, lattice, grille, trellis, grid, pierced screen, screen, vent [➡ COVERS AND COATINGS; 1246] 2 v **shred**, scrape, rasp, file, grind, rub [➡ COOKING AND FOOD PREPARATION; 353] 3 v **irritate**, annoy, exasperate, vex, chafe, gravel, aggravate (informal), peeve (informal), nettle (informal) [➡ ANGER AND ANNOY; 569] Opposite: please

grateful 1 adj **thankful**, appreciative, obliged, indebted, glad [➡ APPRECIATION AND GRATITUDE; 535] Opposite: ungrateful 2 adj (archaic or literary) **comforting**, gratifying, satisfying, pleasing, pleasant, refreshing [➡ EMOTIONALLY PLEASANT; 187] Opposite: unwelcome

gratefully adv **appreciatively**, thankfully, gladly [➡ APPRECIATION AND GRATITUDE; 535] Opposite: ungratefully

gratefulness n **thankfulness**, appreciativeness, appreciation, gratitude, thanks [➡ APPRECIATION AND GRATITUDE; 535] Opposite: ingratitude

grater type of **utensil** [➡ TABLEWARE, FLATWARE, AND KITCHENWARE; 861]

gratification n **satisfaction**, fulfillment, indulgence, enjoyment, delight, pleasure [➡ PLEASURE, EXCITEMENT, AND ELATION; 534] Opposite: displeasure

gratified adj [➡ PLEASURE, EXCITEMENT, AND ELATION; 534]

gratify v **please**, satisfy, indulge, fulfill, oblige, humor, delight, enchant [➡ PLEASE AND AMUSE; 572] Opposite: displease

gratifying adj **rewarding**, satisfying, agreeable, heartwarming, acceptable, pleasing, enjoyable [➡ EMOTIONALLY PLEASANT; 187]

grating 1 n **grille**, grate, lattice, grid, screen, vent [➡ COVERS AND COATINGS; 1246] 2 adj **rough**, harsh, raucous, strident, discordant, gruff, hoarse [➡ LOUD, HIGH, OR UNPLEASANT SOUNDS; 1266] Opposite: mellifluous 3 adj **irritating**, annoying, infuriating, insensitive, vexing, aggravating (informal) [➡ IRRITATING; 228] Opposite: pleasant

gratis adj **free**, free of charge, on the house, complimentary, for nothing, gratuitous, costless, toll-free, cost-free (UK) [➡ GIFTS; 438]

gratitude n **thanks**, thankfulness, appreciation, gratefulness, appreciativeness [➡ APPRECIATION AND GRATITUDE; 535] Opposite: ingratitude

gratuitous 1 adj **unwarranted**, uncalled-for, wanton, unjustified, unnecessary, unreasonable, needless, superfluous [➡ REDUNDANT AND USELESS; 240] Opposite: necessary 2 adj **free**, gratis, complimentary, at no charge, costless, toll-free, for nothing, free of charge, on the house, cost-free (UK) [➡ GIFTS; 438]

gratuitously adv **unnecessarily**, irrelevantly, pointlessly, without cause, unreasonably, needlessly, wantonly, superfluously [➡ REDUNDANT AND USELESS; 240] Opposite: necessarily

gratuitousness n **pointlessness**, needlessness, futility, unhelpfulness, unwarrantedness, wantonness, superfluousness [➡ REDUNDANT AND USELESS; 240]

gratuity n **tip**, perquisite, perk, token, donation [➡ GIFTS; 438]

grave 1 n **tomb**, crypt, vault, burial chamber, sepulcher, mausoleum [➡ BURIAL PLACES AND ACCESSORIES; 930] 2 type of **diacritic** [➡ ASPECTS OF LANGUAGE; 682] 3 type of **musical term** [➡ MUSICAL TERMS; 912] 4 adj **serious**, severe, weighty, momentous, crucial, critical, vital, important [➡ IMPORTANT; 194] Opposite: minor 5 adj **solemn**, serious, somber, grim, earnest, thoughtful, unsmiling, sober [➡ CONFUSION, ANXIETY, AND WORRY; 540] Opposite: cheerful 6 adj **ominous**, foreboding, forbidding, fateful, dire, dangerous [➡ DANGEROUS; 236] Opposite: favorable

gravedigger *n* [➡ BURIAL AND PREPARATION FOR BURIAL; 929]

gravel 1 *n* **stones**, pebbles, shingle, chippings (*UK*) [➡ STONES, ROCKS, AND BOULDERS; 1057] 2 *v* (*informal*) **annoy**, irritate, grate, vex, chafe, exasperate, peeve (*informal*), nettle (*informal*) [➡ ANGER AND ANNOY; 569] 3 *v* (*informal*) **bewilder**, puzzle, confuse, perplex, baffle, buffalo (*informal*) [➡ CONFUSE AND BEWILDER; 571]

gravelly 1 *adj* **croaky**, gruff, hoarse, rough, harsh, rasping, raspy [➡ LOUD, HIGH, OR UNPLEASANT SOUNDS; 1266] *Opposite*: velvety 2 *adj* **pebbly**, shingly, stony, rocky, gritty [➡ PHYSICAL TEXTURE; 1222]

gravely 1 *adv* **grimly**, sternly, austerely, seriously, solemnly, thoughtfully, somberly [➡ PENSIVENESS AND INTEREST; 538] *Opposite*: cheerfully 2 *adv* **fatally**, dangerously, critically, incurably, mortally, grievously, badly [➡ CRITICALLY AND SERIOUSLY; 134]

grave mound *n* [➡ BURIAL AND PREPARATION FOR BURIAL; 929]

graven image *n* [➡ REPRESENTATIONS AND GENERAL EXAMPLES; 65]

gravestone *n* **headstone**, marker, cenotaph, tombstone, memorial, monument [➡ BURIAL PLACES AND ACCESSORIES; 930]

graveyard *n* **cemetery**, churchyard, necropolis, burial ground, boneyard (*informal*) [➡ BURIAL PLACES AND ACCESSORIES; 930]

graveyard shift *n* [➡ WORK-RELATED ACTIVITIES; 834]

gravid *adj* [➡ REPRODUCTION AND HEREDITY; 725]

gravidity *n* [➡ REPRODUCTION AND HEREDITY; 725]

gravidness *n* [➡ REPRODUCTION AND HEREDITY; 725]

gravitas *n* **seriousness**, gravity, sobriety, solemnness, somberness [➡ IMPORTANCE AND SIGNIFICANCE; 192]

gravitate 1 *v* **sink**, settle, drop, fall, descend, drift down [➡ GO DOWNWARD; 307] *Opposite*: rise 2 *v* **incline**, lean, move, drift, be attracted, be drawn, be pulled [➡ PROCEED AND GO; 305] *Opposite*: repel

gravitation *n* **movement**, attraction, gravity [➡ ENERGY; 1161]

gravity 1 *n* **gravitation**, gravitational force, pull, draw [➡ ENERGY; 1161] 2 *n* **seriousness**, importance, significance, severity, enormity, magnitude [➡ IMPORTANCE AND SIGNIFICANCE; 192] *Opposite*: insignificance 3 *n* **solemnity**, grimness, sedateness, dignity, earnestness, thoughtfulness, somberness [➡ POSITIVE INTELLECTUAL CHARACTERISTICS; 524] *Opposite*: cheerfulness

gravy *type of* **seasonings, sauces, and dips** [➡ SEASONINGS AND SAUCES; 1174]

gravy train *n* [➡ EASY WORK; 299]

gray 1 *type of* **color** [➡ COLORS; 1224] 2 *type of* **SI unit** [➡ SIZE AND DIMENSIONS; 1192]

gray

◆ *types of gray*
ash, battleship gray, charcoal gray, dove gray, grizzled, gunmetal, pearl gray, pewter, putty, silver gray, slate, steel gray, taupe

grayling *type of* **freshwater fish** [➡ FRESHWATER FISH; 1010]

gray whale *type of* **whale** [➡ WHALES; 991]

graze 1 *v* **browse**, crop, nibble, forage, eat, feed [➡ EAT AND NOT EAT; 710] 2 *v* **glance**, brush, skim, sweep, touch [➡ CONTACT: TOUCH; 412] 3 *v* **scrape**, scratch, scuff, rub, skin, abrade, break [➡ WOUND A PERSON OR ANIMAL; 383] 4 *n* **scratch**, scrape, abrasion, lesion, scuff mark, scuff [➡ CONDITIONS AFFECTING THE SKIN; 721]

grease 1 *n* **fat**, lard, oil [➡ FATS AND OILS; 1173] 2 *v* **lubricate**, oil, smear [➡ DECORATE, ADORN, AND APPLY COATINGS; 405]

grease gun *type of* **general tool** [➡ HAND TOOLS; 1119]

greasepaint *type of* **cosmetic** [➡ MAKEUP AND BEAUTY PRODUCTS; 490]

greasiness *n* **fattiness**, griminess, sliminess, oiliness, oleaginousness, unctuousness [➡ PHYSICAL TEXTURE; 1222]

greasy *adj* **oily**, fatty, slippery, slimy, oleaginous, unctuous, lubricious (*literary*) [➡ PHYSICAL TEXTURE; 1222]

greasy spoon (*informal*) *type of* **eating place** [➡ HOTELS, RESTAURANTS, AND CLUBS; 1082]

great 1 *adj* **huge**, immense, enormous, vast, large, big, grand [➡ LARGE; 1193] *Opposite*: tiny 2 *adj* **countless**, inordinate, prodigious, excessive, boundless, pronounced, abundant, numerous, unlimited [➡ MANY, MUCH, LARGE AMOUNT; 117] *Opposite*: limited 3 *adj* **important**, significant, momentous, critical, major, weighty, serious [➡ IMPORTANT; 194] *Opposite*: unimportant 4 *adj* **absolute**, utter, complete, downright, intense, profound, extreme [➡ ABSOLUTE AND ABSOLUTELY; 133] *Opposite*: slight 5 *adj* **famous**, illustrious, eminent, distinguished, celebrated, impressive, remarkable, talented, skillful, notable [➡ KNOWN AND FAMOUS; 181] *Opposite*: ordinary 6 *adj* **noble**, elevated, lofty, imposing, stately, grand, impressive, heroic, splendid, majestic, exalted (*formal*) [➡ EXTRAORDINARY: AMAZING; 204] *Opposite*: lowly 7 *adj* (*informal*) **wonderful**, fantastic, magnificent, excellent, terrific, good, incredible, ace (*informal*), awesome (*slang*), cool (*slang*), groovy (*dated slang*) [➡ EXTRAORDINARY: AMAZING; 204] *Opposite*: awful

great-aunt *type of* **older relative** [➡ OLDER GENERATION RELATIVES; 959]

greatcoat *type of* **overcoat** [➡ GARMENTS AND OUTFITS; 865]

Great Dane *type of* **large dog** [➡ DOGS; 980]

greater *adj* **better**, superior, larger, bigger, more, grander [➡ SUPERIORITY; 152]

greatest *n* **most**, maximum, record, furthermost, utmost, supreme, best, peak [➡ MAJORITY AND MAXIMUM; 141]

great-grandchild *type of* **younger relative** [➡ YOUNGER GENERATION RELATIVES; 958]

great-granddaughter *type of* **younger relative** [➡ YOUNGER GENERATION RELATIVES; 958]

great-grandfather *type of* **older relative** [➡ OLDER GENERATION RELATIVES; 959]

great-grandmother *type of* **older relative** [➡ OLDER GENERATION RELATIVES; 959]

great-grandparent *type of* **older relative** [➡ OLDER GENERATION RELATIVES; 959]

great-grandson *type of* **younger relative** [➞ YOUNGER GENERATION RELATIVES; 958]

greatly 1 *adv* **very much**, really, to a great extent, to the highest degree, deeply, seriously, considerably, wholly, completely, exceedingly, terribly, awfully [➞ TO A GREAT EXTENT; 132] *Opposite*: hardly 2 *adv* **importantly**, significantly, momentously, critically, seriously, prominently, impressively [➞ EXTRAORDINARY: AMAZING; 204]

great-nephew *type of* **younger relative** [➞ YOUNGER GENERATION RELATIVES; 958]

greatness 1 *n* **magnitude**, enormity, immensity, vastness, size, largeness [➞ SIZE AND DIMENSIONS; 1192] 2 *n* **importance**, prominence, seriousness, significance, weightiness, magnitude [➞ IMPORTANCE AND SIGNIFICANCE; 192] *Opposite*: insignificance 3 *n* **fame**, eminence, distinction, impressiveness, prominence, preeminence, renown, merit, excellence [➞ EXTRAORDINARY: AMAZING; 204] *Opposite*: commonness

great-niece *type of* **younger relative** [➞ YOUNGER GENERATION RELATIVES; 958]

great-uncle *type of* **older relative** [➞ OLDER GENERATION RELATIVES; 959]

grebe *type of* **freshwater bird** [➞ FRESHWATER BIRDS; 1000]

greed 1 *n* **gluttony**, voracity, ravenousness, greediness, insatiability, hunger, self-indulgence, appetite, craving [➞ MORALLY BAD OR IMPROPER; 775] *Opposite*: moderation 2 *n* **avarice**, covetousness, greediness, materialism, acquisitiveness, passion, longing, desire [➞ GRASPING AND FINANCIALLY MEAN; 519] *Opposite*: generosity

greedily 1 *adv* **voraciously**, ravenously, insatiably, hungrily, avidly, gluttonously [➞ WITH ENTHUSIASM; 286] *Opposite*: sparingly 2 *adv* **covetously**, avariciously, acquisitively, materialistically, passionately, desirously (*formal*) [➞ GRASPING AND FINANCIALLY MEAN; 519] *Opposite*: generously

greediness 1 *n* **gluttony**, voracity, ravenousness, insatiability, greed, hunger, self-indulgence, appetite, craving [➞ MORALLY BAD OR IMPROPER; 775] *Opposite*: moderation 2 *n* **greed**, avarice, covetousness, acquisitiveness, materialism, passion, longing, desire [➞ GRASPING AND FINANCIALLY MEAN; 519] *Opposite*: generosity

greedy 1 *adj* **gluttonous**, voracious, ravenous, insatiable, hungry [➞ MORALLY BAD OR IMPROPER; 775] *Opposite*: moderate 2 *adj* **avaricious**, covetous, grasping, materialistic, acquisitive [➞ GRASPING AND FINANCIALLY MEAN; 519] *Opposite*: generous

Greek *type of* **alphabet** [➞ SYMBOLS, SIGNS, AND NUMBERS; 596]

Greek coffee *type of* **coffee** [➞ DRINKS; 1187]

green *type of* **color** [➞ COLORS; 1224]

green

◆ *types of green*
apple green, aquamarine, avocado, bottle green, emerald green, forest green, grass green, jade, jade green, lime green, Lincoln green, lovat, Nile green, olive green, pea green, sage green, sea green, viridian

green alga *type of* **marine alga** [➞ MICROORGANISMS, FUNGI, AND ALGAE; 1023]

green around the gills (*informal*) *adj* [➞ ILL AND SICK; 740]

greenbelt *n* [➞ THE COUNTRYSIDE AND OUTDOOR SPACES; 1071]

greenery *n* **foliage**, vegetation, greens, plants, leaves [➞ VEGETATION; 1025]

green-eyed *adj* [➞ ENVY AND JEALOUSY; 548]

greenfield (*UK*) *adj* **undeveloped**, out-of-town, rural, country [➞ THE COUNTRYSIDE AND OUTDOOR SPACES; 1071] *Opposite*: urban

greenfield site *n* [➞ THE COUNTRYSIDE AND OUTDOOR SPACES; 1071]

greenfly *type of* **flying insect** [➞ FLYING INSECTS; 1013]

greenhorn *n* **novice**, recruit, initiate, beginner, neophyte, newcomer, apprentice, tenderfoot (*informal*) [➞ UNSKILLED PEOPLE; 530]

See Compare and Contrast at **beginner**.

greenhouse *n* **orangery**, hothouse, conservatory, glasshouse (*UK*) [➞ ANCILLARY BUILDINGS; 1080]

greenhouse gas *type of* **gas** [➞ GASES; 1275]

green light *n* **permission**, clearance, consent, approval, stamp of approval, go-ahead (*informal*), OK (*informal*), thumbs up (*informal*) [➞ AGREE; 645] *Opposite*: red light

green onion *type of* **salad vegetable** [➞ FRUIT AND VEGETABLES; 1176]

greens 1 *n* **greenery**, foliage, vegetation, plants, leaves [➞ VEGETATION; 1025] 2 *type of* **vegetable** [➞ FRUIT AND VEGETABLES; 1176]

green with envy *adj* [➞ ENVY AND JEALOUSY; 548]

greet 1 *v* **welcome**, meet, make the acquaintance of, receive [➞ ESTABLISHING RELATIONSHIPS WITH OTHERS; 974] 2 *v* **address**, speak to, acknowledge, hail, salute, accost [➞ GESTURES AND GESTICULATION; 653] *Opposite*: ignore 3 *v* **respond to**, react to, receive, meet, hail, reply [➞ REPLY AND ANSWER; 668]

greeter *type of* **person who works in restaurants** [➞ DOMESTIC AND KITCHEN WORKERS; 850]

greeting *n* **salutation**, welcome, welcoming, reception, acknowledgment, address [➞ GREETINGS, FAREWELLS, AND SALUTATIONS; 659]

gregarious *adj* **outgoing**, sociable, social, extrovert, extroverted, expressive, expansive, unreserved, companionable, convivial [➞ FRIENDLINESS AND SOCIABILITY; 494] *Opposite*: shy

gregariousness *n* **sociability**, friendliness, openness, unreservedness, conviviality, companionability [➞ FRIENDLINESS AND SOCIABILITY; 494] *Opposite*: shyness

gremlin (*informal*) 1 *n* **jinx**, malfunction, blip, glitch, bug (*informal*) [➞ PROBLEMS; 256] 2 *n* [➞ MYTHICAL BEINGS; 789]

grenade *type of* **projectile** [➞ PROJECTILES; 1159]

greyhound *type of* **large dog** [➞ DOGS; 980]

grid *n* **network**, lattice, net, web, gridiron, grating, trellis, framework, crisscross [➞ FASTENERS, LINKS, AND NETWORKS; 1247]

griddle *v* **grill**, sear, barbecue, cook, broil [➞ COOKING AND FOOD PREPARATION; 353]

griddlecake *type of* **pancake** [➡CAKES, COOKIES, AND DESSERTS; 1181]

gridiron *n* **grid**, lattice, grating, framework, network [➡FASTENERS, LINKS, AND NETWORKS; 1247]

gridlock **1** *n* **traffic jam**, jam, congestion, sig alert, backup, holdup, snarl, snarl-up (*UK*), tailback (*UK*) [➡TRAVEL: TRAFFIC PROBLEMS AND TRAFFIC MANAGEMENT; 323] **2** *n* **deadlock**, stalemate, standstill, logjam, impasse, standoff [➡LACK OF ACTIVITY OR MOTION; 342]

grief *n* **sorrow**, heartache, anguish, misery, unhappiness, angst, woe, pain [➡SADNESS, DISTRESS, AND DESPAIR; 539] *Opposite*: joy

grief-stricken *adj* **grieving**, distraught, traumatized, inconsolable, heartbroken, devastated, anguished, desolate, despairing, brokenhearted, agonized, distressed, wretched, weeping, tearful [➡SADNESS, DISTRESS, AND DESPAIR; 539] *Opposite*: happy

grievance **1** *n* **complaint**, protest, criticism, objection, grumble, gripe (*informal*), moan (*informal*) [➡COMPLAIN AND NAG; 686] **2** *n* **injustice**, wrong, cause of distress, ill-treatment, unfairness, infringement, injury, trial, tribulation [➡NUISANCES; 253]

grieve **1** *v* **mourn**, feel sad, be sad, lament, be distressed, be upset, be unhappy, suffer, sorrow (*literary*) [➡GIVING VENT TO EMOTIONS; 679] *Opposite*: rejoice (*literary*) **2** *v* **hurt**, afflict, pain, distress, upset, sadden, depress, aggrieve (*formal*) [➡UPSET, DISTRESS, AND HUMILIATE; 567] *Opposite*: cheer

grieving *n* [➡DEATH AND BEREAVEMENT; 927]

grievous **1** *adj* **serious**, significant, critical, dangerous, grave, mortal [➡BAD AND BADLY; 223] *Opposite*: slight **2** *adj* **dreadful**, awful, terrible, shameful, painful, severe, grave [➡EMOTIONALLY UNPLEASANT AND UPSETTING; 227]

grievously **1** *adv* **seriously**, significantly, critically, dangerously, gravely, mortally [➡CRITICALLY AND SERIOUSLY; 134] *Opposite*: slightly **2** *adv* **dreadfully**, awfully, terribly, shamefully, painfully, severely, gravely [➡EMOTIONALLY UNPLEASANT AND UPSETTING; 227]

griffin *type of* **mythological creature** [➡MYTHICAL CREATURES; 1036]

grill **1** *v* (*informal*) **question**, interrogate, examine, press, probe, quiz, cross-examine, put somebody through the mill (*informal*), give somebody the third degree (*informal*) [➡ASK PEOPLE QUESTIONS; 666] **2** *v* **cook**, barbecue, toast, brown, frizzle [➡COOKING AND FOOD PREPARATION; 353] **3** *n* **griddle**, grate, barbecue, rotisserie [➡HOUSEHOLD APPLIANCES; 1117]

See Compare and Contrast at **question**.

grille **1** *n* **grating**, lattice, framework, grid, trellis, grate, network [➡FASTENERS, LINKS, AND NETWORKS; 1247] **2** *part of* **external structure** [➡EXTERNAL PARTS OF A VEHICLE; 1147]

grim **1** *adj* **forbidding**, ugly, unattractive, uninviting, gray, dingy [➡UGLINESS AND UNATTRACTIVENESS; 233] *Opposite*: attractive **2** *adj* **depressing**, bleak, dismal, gloomy, cheerless, ominous, hopeless [➡EMOTIONALLY UNPLEASANT AND UPSETTING; 227] *Opposite*: hopeful **3** *adj* **stern**, serious, dour, severe, morose, surly, unkind [➡BAD-TEMPERED AND HUMORLESS; 626] *Opposite*: kind **4** *adj* **shocking**, ghastly, horrible, horrific, grue-

some, grisly, macabre, repugnant, distasteful, hideous, unpleasant [➡FRIGHTENING; 231] *Opposite*: pleasant

grimace **1** *n* **scowl**, frown, smirk, sneer, pout, long face [➡FACIAL EXPRESSIONS AND BLUSHING; 651] *Opposite*: smile **2** *v* **frown**, scowl, smirk, sneer, pout, pull a face, make a face [➡FACIAL EXPRESSIONS AND BLUSHING; 651] *Opposite*: smile

grime *n* **filth**, dirt, stain, soot, dust, grunge (*informal*), muck (*informal*) [➡UNPLEASANT, DIRTY, AND TOXIC SUBSTANCES; 1268]

grim-faced *adj* [➡FACIAL EXPRESSIONS AND BLUSHING; 651]

griminess *n* **dirtiness**, dinginess, filthiness, grubbiness, dustiness, squalidness, muckiness (*informal*) [➡DIRTY; 1235] *Opposite*: cleanliness

grimly **1** *adv* **depressingly**, bleakly, gloomily, dismally, cheerlessly, ominously [➡BAD-TEMPERED AND HUMORLESS; 626] *Opposite*: cheerily **2** *adv* **forbiddingly**, uninvitingly, unattractively, dingily, dismally, gloomily [➡EMOTIONALLY UNPLEASANT AND UPSETTING; 227] *Opposite*: warmly **3** *adv* **sternly**, seriously, dourly, severely, morosely, unkindly [➡BAD-TEMPERED AND HUMORLESS; 626] *Opposite*: kindly **4** *adv* **shockingly**, horribly, horrifically, hideously, gruesomely, repugnantly, distastefully [➡FRIGHTENING; 231] *Opposite*: pleasantly

grimness **1** *n* **bleakness**, cheerlessness, dismalness, ominousness, gloominess, hopelessness [➡EMOTIONALLY UNPLEASANT AND UPSETTING; 227] *Opposite*: brightness **2** *n* **forbiddingness**, ugliness, unattractiveness, grayness, dinginess, gloominess [➡UGLINESS AND UNATTRACTIVENESS; 233] *Opposite*: attractiveness **3** *n* **sternness**, seriousness, dourness, severity, moroseness, unkindness [➡BAD-TEMPERED AND HUMORLESS; 626] *Opposite*: kindness **4** *n* **gruesomeness**, horror, hideousness, grisliness, dreadfulness, unpleasantness [➡FRIGHTENING; 231] *Opposite*: pleasantness

grimy *adj* **dirty**, grubby, smudged, soiled, filthy, dusty, mucky (*informal*), grungy (*informal*) [➡DIRTY; 1235] *Opposite*: clean

See Compare and Contrast at **dirty**.

grin **1** *v* **smile**, beam, smirk, laugh, chortle, chuckle [➡FACIAL EXPRESSIONS AND BLUSHING; 651] *Opposite*: frown **2** *n* **beam**, smile, smirk, laugh, chortle, chuckle [➡FACIAL EXPRESSIONS AND BLUSHING; 651] *Opposite*: frown

grin and bear it (*informal*) *v* **put up with**, take the bad with the good, weather, ride out, lump (*informal*), take the rough with the smooth (*UK*) [➡TOLERATE AND ENDURE; 766] *Opposite*: welcome

grind **1** *v* **crush**, break up, mill, pound, mince, pulverize [➡TEAR, BREAK, AND CUT; 360] **2** *v* **grate**, rasp, gnash, scrape [➡EMIT SOUNDS THROUGH IMPACT AND ABRASION; 365] *Opposite*: glide **3** *v* **sharpen**, file, whet, abrade, polish, smooth [➡CLEAN AND POLISH; 403] *Opposite*: blunt **4** *n* (*informal*) **toil**, chore, slog, tedium, routine, drudgery [➡HARD WORK OR EFFORT; 298]

grind down **1** *v* **wear**, erode, eat away, abrade, rub, pound [➡TEAR, BREAK, AND CUT; 360] **2** *v* **oppress**, tyrannize, persecute, harass, weaken, destroy [➡UPSET, DISTRESS, AND HUMILIATE; 567] *Opposite*: nurture

grinder *n* **mill**, mincer, crusher, pounder, pulverizer, mortar [➡TABLEWARE, FLATWARE, AND KITCHENWARE; 861]

grinding **1** *adj* **crushing**, oppressive, relentless, unending, never-ending, eternal [➧PHYSICALLY UNPLEASANT; 226] **2** *adj* **grating**, crunching, earsplitting, screeching, squealing, noisy, cacophonous [➧LOUD, HIGH, OR UNPLEASANT SOUNDS; 1266] *Opposite*: pleasant

grindingly **1** *adv* **crushingly**, oppressively, relentlessly, unendingly, eternally, never-endingly [➧PHYSICALLY UNPLEASANT; 226] **2** *adv* **gratingly**, shrilly, noisily, stridently, cacophonously [➧LOUD, HIGH, OR UNPLEASANT SOUNDS; 1266] *Opposite*: pleasantly

grind to a halt *v* [➧FAIL OR CEASE TO FUNCTION; 470]

grinning *adj* [➧FACIAL EXPRESSIONS AND BLUSHING; 651]

grip **1** *n* **grasp**, hold, clasp, clutch [➧CONTACT: HOLD; 411] *Opposite*: release **2** *n* **control**, rule, command, authority, clutches, charge, power, sway [➧STRENGTH; 201] **3** *n* **understanding**, comprehension, grasp, command, appreciation, awareness, mastery [➧UNDERSTAND AND GRASP; 759] *Opposite*: ignorance **4** *v* **grasp**, clasp, clutch, catch, seize, hold [➧CONTACT: HOLD; 411] *Opposite*: release **5** *v* **stick**, adhere, cling, hang on, cleave to (*literary*) [➧CONTACT: HOLD; 411] **6** *v* **overwhelm**, fill, pervade, suffuse, swamp, drown [➧HAPPEN TO SOMEBODY; 30] **7** *v* **fascinate**, enthrall, spellbind, transfix, mesmerize, rivet (*informal*) [➧APPEAL TO AND AROUSE INTEREST; 575] *Opposite*: bore

gripe (*informal*) **1** *v* **complain**, grumble, protest, object, moan (*informal*) [➧COMPLAIN AND NAG; 686] **2** *n* **complaint**, grumble, grievance, protest, objection, moan (*informal*) [➧COMPLAIN AND NAG; 686] *Opposite*: compliment

See Compare and Contrast at **complain**.

gripped *adj* **absorbed**, engrossed, rapt, obsessed, enthralled, spellbound, riveted (*informal*) [➧PENSIVENESS AND INTEREST; 538] *Opposite*: bored

gripping *adj* **fascinating**, spellbinding, enthralling, mesmerizing, transfixing, absorbing, engrossing, riveting (*informal*) [➧INTERESTING AND MEANINGFUL; 190] *Opposite*: boring

grisliness *n* **gruesomeness**, ghastliness, grimness, hideousness, dreadfulness, horror [➧FRIGHTENING; 231] *Opposite*: pleasantness

grisly *adj* **gruesome**, ghastly, horrible, horrific, horrid, grim, dreadful, shocking, macabre, hideous, repugnant [➧FRIGHTENING; 231] *Opposite*: pleasant

gristle *n* **cartilage**, tendon, sinew [➧THE BONES AND JOINTS; 719]

gristly *adj* **tough**, chewy, sinewy, stringy, leathery, rubbery, fibrous [➧STATE OF PREPARED FOOD; 1171] *Opposite*: tender

grit **1** *n* **gravel**, stones, pebbles, sand, shingle [➧EROSION PRODUCTS AND SOIL; 1058] **2** *n* **determination**, perseverance, tenacity, bravery, fortitude, courage [➧COURAGE; 498] *Opposite*: cowardice **3** *v* **clench**, grind, gnash, grate [➧CONTACT: EXERT PRESSURE; 414]

grits *n* [➧CEREAL FOODS; 1178]

gritty **1** *adj* **determined**, persistent, resolute, courageous, persevering, tenacious, brave [➧COURAGE; 498] *Opposite*: cowardly **2** *adj* **realistic**, graphic, harsh, stark, uncompromising, unflinching [➧EMOTIONALLY UNPLEASANT AND UPSETTING; 227] *Opposite*: romantic **3** *adj* **grainy**, coarse, rough, granular, sandy, gravelly [➧PHYSICAL TEXTURE; 1222] *Opposite*: smooth

grit your teeth *v* **steel yourself**, nerve yourself, brace

yourself, persevere, hold on tight [➧PREPARE FOR ACTION; 289] *Opposite*: knuckle under

grizzled *type of* **gray** [➧COLORS; 1224]

grizzly (*UK*) *adj* **fractious**, irritable, crying, whiny, whining [➧IRRITATION AND ANGER; 541]

groan **1** *v* **creak**, squeak, squeal, screech, grind, grate [➧EMIT SOUNDS THROUGH IMPACT AND ABRASION; 365] **2** *v* **moan**, cry out, whimper, grunt, growl, sigh [➧SOUND EMISSION BY PEOPLE; 363] *Opposite*: laugh **3** *v* (*informal*) **grumble**, complain, carp, moan, gripe (*informal*) [➧COMPLAIN AND NAG; 686] **4** *type of* **human sound** [➧SOUNDS MADE BY PEOPLE; 1262]

groceries *n* **food**, shopping, provisions, rations, victuals, fare, provender (*literary or humorous*) [➧FOOD; 1167]

grocery store *type of* **food outlet** [➧RETAIL OUTLETS; 1083]

groggily *adv* **weakly**, sleepily, unsteadily, dazedly, blearily, woozily, slowly, muzzily, shakily [➧TIRED, ASLEEP, AND UNCONSCIOUS; 738] *Opposite*: alertly

grogginess *n* **tiredness**, fatigue, sleepiness, unsteadiness, bleariness, wooziness, dizziness, faintness [➧TIRED, ASLEEP, AND UNCONSCIOUS; 738] *Opposite*: alertness

groggy *adj* **tired**, sleepy, slow, unsteady, bleary, muzzy, shaky, dazed, weak, woozy, faint, dizzy, wobbly (*informal*) [➧TIRED, ASLEEP, AND UNCONSCIOUS; 738] *Opposite*: alert

groin **1** *part of* **torso** [➧PARTS OF THE BODY: TORSO; 693] **2** *n* **breakwater**, mole, barrier, bulwark, jetty, projection [➧BARRIERS; 1113]

groom **1** *v* **clean**, clean up, brush, comb, tidy, spruce [➧CLEAN AND POLISH; 403] **2** *v* **prime**, train, coach, prepare, tutor, mentor [➧INSTRUCT AND TEACH; 609] *Opposite*: hinder

groomsman *n* [➧RELATIVES BY MARRIAGE; 960]

groove **1** *n* **channel**, furrow, rut, trench, indentation, hollow [➧HOLES, GAPS, AND FORKS; 1252] *Opposite*: ridge **2** *v* (*slang*) **listen**, harmonize, enjoy, dance, chill (*slang*), chill out (*slang*) [➧CHANGE OF MOOD AND COMPOSURE; 580]

grope **1** *v* **fumble**, feel, cast about, scrabble, flounder, finger [➧SEEK POSSESSION AND SEARCH; 456] **2** *v* (*informal*) **fondle**, touch, molest, caress, feel up (*informal*) [➧CONTACT: TOUCH; 412]

grosgrain *type of* **fabric from plants** [➧FABRICS; 1132]

gross **1** *adj* **aggregate**, combined, whole, overall, total [➧ALL; 128] *Opposite*: net **2** *adj* **flagrant**, blatant, glaring, arrant, serious, obvious, major, significant [➧INTENTIONAL AND DELIBERATE; 279] *Opposite*: minor **3** *adj* **coarse**, vulgar, crass, rude, crude, uncouth [➧BAD MANNERS AND SOCIAL SKILLS; 521] *Opposite*: polite **4** *adj* **uncultured**, uncivilized, uncultivated, unsophisticated, unpolished, unrefined [➧LEVELS OF EDUCATION AND SOPHISTICATION; 894] *Opposite*: cultured **5** *adj* (*slang*) **disgusting**, unpleasant, sickening, foul, nasty, awful, dreadful, repugnant, repellent, revolting, nauseating, vile, hideous, abhorrent (*formal*) [➧DISGUSTING AND REPULSIVE; 230] *Opposite*: pleasant **6** *adj* **overweight**, obese, fat, heavy, stout, flabby (*informal*) [➧BUILD; 477] *Opposite*: slim **7** *v* **earn**, make, get, receive, bring in, clear (*informal*) [➧GET MONEY OR REWARD; 421] *Opposite*: lose

grossly **1** *adv* **wholly**, totally, completely, utterly, unacceptably, obviously, clearly, exceptionally [➧TO A GREAT EXTENT; 132] *Opposite*: slightly **2** *adv* **rudely**, coarsely, uncouthly, crassly, crudely, vulgarly [➡ MORALLY BAD OR IMPROPER; 775] *Opposite*: politely

grossness *n* [➡ DISGUSTING AND REPULSIVE; 230]

gross out (*slang*) *v* **disgust**, sicken, nauseate, offend, repel, revolt [➡ UPSET, DISTRESS, AND HUMILIATE; 567] *Opposite*: delight

gross revenue *n* [➡ INCOME; 460]

grotesque 1 *adj* **distorted**, bizarre, misshapen, monstrous, gross (*slang*) *Opposite*: attractive [➡ UGLINESS AND UNATTRACTIVENESS; 233] **2** *adj* **incongruous**, ridiculous, ludicrous, laughable, outrageous, outlandish, surreal, weird, fantastic [➡ BIZARRE AND PECULIAR; 257] *Opposite*: fitting

grotto *n* **cavern**, pothole, hollow, cave [➡ GEOLOGIC FEATURES; 1056]

grouch (*informal*) **1** *n* **complaint**, grumble, whine, grouse (*informal*), moan (*informal*), gripe (*informal*) [➡ COMPLAIN AND NAG; 686] *Opposite*: praise **2** *n* **grumbler**, complainer, malcontent, moaner (*informal*), grouser (*informal*), crank (*informal*), grump (*informal*) [➡ GRUMPY AND NEGATIVE PEOPLE; 953] **3** *v* **complain**, grumble, sulk, gripe (*informal*), moan (*informal*), bellyache (*informal*) [➡ COMPLAIN AND NAG; 686]

grouchily (*informal*) *adv* [➡ BAD-TEMPERED AND HUMORLESS; 626]

grouchiness (*informal*) *n* **peevishness**, irritability, cantankerousness, crabbiness, bad temper, grumpiness, petulance, testiness (*informal*), tetchiness (*informal*), crankiness (*informal*) [➡ BAD-TEMPERED AND HUMORLESS; 626] *Opposite*: equanimity (*formal*)

grouchy (*informal*) *adj* **bad-tempered**, complaining, touchy, grumpy, crabby, peevish, cantankerous, irritable, petulant, snappy, ill-tempered, snappish, testy (*informal*), cranky (*informal*) [➡ BAD-TEMPERED AND HUMORLESS; 626] *Opposite*: even-tempered

ground **1** *n* **earth**, soil, land, field, dry land, terra firma, terrain [➡ THE COUNTRYSIDE AND OUTDOOR SPACES; 1071] **2** *n* **playing field**, field, arena, ballpark, stadium, pitch (*UK*) [➡ URBAN OUTDOOR SPACES; 1072] **3** *adj* **crushed**, pulverized, broken up, milled, minced, pounded, powdered [➡ NOT IN A NATURAL STATE; 1215] **4** *v* **punish**, deal with, chastise [➡ REFUSE PERMISSION AND NOT ALLOW; 670] **5** *v* **base**, substantiate, support, build, justify, found [➡ INSTITUTE AND INAUGURATE; 348] **6** *v* **initiate**, prepare, coach, instruct, tutor, train [➡ INSTRUCT AND TEACH; 609]

ground beef *type of* **processed meat** [➡ TYPES AND CUTS OF MEAT; 1177]

groundbreaking *adj* **innovative**, pioneering, revolutionary, radical, trailblazing, brand-new, cutting-edge, leading-edge [➡ EXTRAORDINARY: AMAZING; 204] *Opposite*: old hat (*informal*)

ground cloth *n* **tarpaulin**, sheeting, cover, throw, rug, tarp (*informal*) [➡ COVERS AND COATINGS; 1246]

ground forces *n* [➡ THE ARMED FORCES; 827]

ground glass *type of* **glass** [➡ GLASS; 1136]

groundhog *type of* **rodent** [➡ RODENTS; 989]

grounding *n* **foundation**, basis, preparation, training, instruction, education [➡ TEACHING; 839]

groundless *adj* **baseless**, unsupported, unjustified,

unwarranted, unfounded, unsubstantiated [➡ REDUNDANT AND USELESS; 240] *Opposite*: sound

ground meat *type of* **processed meat** [➡ TYPES AND CUTS OF MEAT; 1177]

groundnut *type of* **nut** [➡ NUTS; 1185]

ground plan **1** *n* **outline**, sketch, blueprint, draft, preliminary design, plan [➡ DRAWINGS, CHARTS, AND TABLES; 594] **2** *n* **floor plan**, plan, scale drawing, blueprint, diagram, drawing [➡ DRAWINGS, CHARTS, AND TABLES; 594]

ground rule *n* **fundamental**, axiom, stipulation, point of departure, modus operandi, tenet (*formal*) [➡ WAYS OF DOING THINGS; 294]

grounds **1** *n* **basis**, foundation, reason, justification, argument, proof [➡ CAUSATION; 168] **2** *n* **estate**, land, park, parkland, gardens, surroundings [➡ THE COUNTRYSIDE AND OUTDOOR SPACES; 1071] **3** *n* **dregs**, lees, sediment, residue, deposit, sludge [➡ UNPLEASANT, DIRTY, AND TOXIC SUBSTANCES; 1268]

groundswell **1** *n* **upsurge**, wave, outpouring, rise, swell [➡ CHANGE OF SIZE: BIGGER; 392] **2** *n* **swell**, wave, storm, squall, heavy sea, tempest [➡ THE SEAS, OCEANS, AND SHORES; 1041]

groundwork *n* **foundation**, basis, base, footing, underpinning, preliminaries [➡ WORK IN GENERAL; 297]

group **1** *n* **collection**, cluster, set, assemblage, assembly, clutch [➡ COLLECTIONS AND MIXTURES OF THINGS; 1244] *Opposite*: individual **2** *n* **grouping**, set, faction, crowd, company, troop, troupe, party, band, knot, unit, clique [➡ GROUPS OF PEOPLE; 935] *Opposite*: individual **3** *n* **musical group**, band, trio, duo, quartet, quintet, sextet, septet, octet, orchestra, ensemble [➡ MUSICIANS AND SINGERS; 908] *Opposite*: soloist **4** *n* **alliance**, federation, consortium, amalgamation, confederation, confederacy [➡ GROUPS WITH A COMMON INTEREST; 938] **5** *v* **gather**, assemble, congregate, convene, cluster, collect [➡ GET CLOSER TOGETHER; 310] *Opposite*: disperse **6** *v* **classify**, categorize, arrange, sort, bracket, class [➡ ARRANGE AND CREATE ORDER; 357]

groupie (*informal*) *n* **follower**, fan, enthusiast, supporter, aficionado, aficionada, booster, junkie (*informal*) [➡ DEVOTEES AND ADDICTED PEOPLE; 556] *Opposite*: detractor

grouping **1** *n* **alliance**, federation, consortium, assemblage, alignment, combination, group, confederacy [➡ GROUPS OF PEOPLE; 935] **2** *n* **category**, class, set, type, group, grade [➡ VARIETIES, TYPES, AND KINDS; 145]

group together *v* [➡ GET CLOSER TOGETHER; 310]

grouse **1** *v* (*informal*) **complain**, grumble, moan, gripe (*informal*), bellyache (*informal*) [➡ COMPLAIN AND NAG; 686] **2** *n* (*informal*) **complaint**, grumble, objection, protest, moan (*informal*), gripe (*informal*) [➡ COMPLAIN AND NAG; 686] **3** *type of* **fowl** [➡ FOOD BIRDS; 999] **4** *type of* **meat** [➡ TYPES AND CUTS OF MEAT; 1177]

See Compare and Contrast at **complain**.

grout **1** *n* **mortar**, filling, plaster, cement, putty, sealant [➡ BUILDING MATERIALS; 1077] **2** *v* **fill**, mortar, plaster, cement, render, face [➡ DECORATE, ADORN, AND APPLY COATINGS; 405]

grouts (*UK*) *n* **dregs**, lees, residue, sediment, deposit, sludge [➡ UNPLEASANT, DIRTY, AND TOXIC SUBSTANCES; 1268]

grove *n* **copse**, coppice, orchard, wood, stand, plantation [➡ WOODS, FORESTS, AND JUNGLES; 1047]

grovel 1 v **plead**, beg, cringe, fawn, bow and scrape, humble yourself, demean yourself, kowtow, crawl (*informal*) [➡ FLATTER AND FAWN; 621] *Opposite*: alienate 2 v **crawl**, crouch, stoop, kneel [➡ ASSUME A POSITION; 317] *Opposite*: stand up

grow 1 v **produce**, cultivate, nurture, breed, raise, propagate [➡ GROW AND CULTIVATE; 351] 2 v **develop**, grow up, mature, shoot up, sprout, flourish [➡ CHANGE OF SIZE: BIGGER; 392] 3 v **expand**, enlarge, swell, extend, spread, increase [➡ CHANGE OF SIZE: BIGGER; 392] *Opposite*: shrink 4 v **increase**, multiply, intensify, escalate, strengthen, develop [➡ CHANGE OF SIZE: BIGGER; 392] *Opposite*: decrease

growing adj **rising**, mounting, upward, budding, emergent, increasing [➡ CHANGE OF SIZE: BIGGER; 392] *Opposite*: decreasing

growl 1 v **roar**, snarl, bark, howl, rumble, yap [➡ SOUND EMISSION BY ANIMALS OR BIRDS; 364] 2 n **snarl**, bark, howl, rumble, roar, yap [➡ SOUNDS MADE BY ANIMALS; 1261]

grow less v **weaken**, wear off, fade, subside, decrease, abate (*formal or literary*) [➡ CHANGE OF INTENSITY: LESS; 395] *Opposite*: increase

grown adj **grown-up**, full-fledged, adult, full-grown, developed, mature [➡ ADULTHOOD; 918] *Opposite*: immature

grown-up adj **adult**, mature, developed, grown, responsible, sensible, full-fledged, full-size, full-grown [➡ ADULTHOOD; 918] *Opposite*: immature

growth 1 n **growing**, development, evolution, progress, advance, progression [➡ PROGRESS AND ADVANCEMENT; 213] *Opposite*: decay 2 n **increase**, enlargement, expansion, augmentation, development, intensification, escalation [➡ CHANGE OF SIZE: BIGGER; 392] *Opposite*: reduction 3 n **tumor**, cyst, lump, swelling, outgrowth, carcinoma [➡ ILLNESSES AND DISORDERS; 732]

grow up 1 v **grow**, develop, mature, evolve, flourish, come of age [➡ CHANGE; 372] 2 v **take shape**, arise, be born, develop, come about, evolve [➡ GRADUALLY COME INTO EXISTENCE; 1]

grub 1 v **dig**, burrow, root out, excavate, pull up, uproot, dredge up, unearth, dig up [➡ MOVE SOMETHING: UPWARD; 328] 2 v **search**, hunt, rummage, forage, scour, ferret (*UK*) [➡ SEEK POSSESSION AND SEARCH; 456] 3 n **larva**, maggot, caterpillar, bug, creepy-crawly (*informal*) [➡ INSECT STAGES; 1020] 4 n (*informal*) **food**, victuals, sustenance, feed, nourishment, nosh (*informal*) [➡ FOOD; 1167]

grubbiness 1 n **dirtiness**, griminess, filthiness, muddiness, sloppiness, dinginess, squalidness, muckiness (*informal*) [➡ DIRTY; 1235] *Opposite*: cleanness 2 n **sordidness**, squalidness, seediness, contemptibleness, despicableness, dishonorableness [➡ MORALLY BAD OR IMPROPER; 775] *Opposite*: purity

grubby 1 adj **dirty**, grimy, soiled, filthy, muddy, sloppy, dingy, squalid, mucky (*informal*) [➡ DIRTY; 1235] *Opposite*: clean 2 adj **sordid**, squalid, seedy, contemptible, despicable, despised, dishonorable [➡ MORALLY BAD OR IMPROPER; 775] *Opposite*: honorable

See Compare and Contrast at **dirty**.

grudge 1 n **complaint**, rancor, bitterness, resentment, dislike, hatred, antipathy, chip on your shoulder (*informal*) [➡ ANTAGONISM; 552] 2 v **resent**, hold against, begrudge, loathe, mind, envy [➡ DISLIKE AND HATE; 577]

grudging adj **reluctant**, unwilling, complaining, resentful, rancorous, disinclined, loath [➡ UNWILLINGNESS AND STUBBORNNESS; 564] *Opposite*: willing

gruel type of **cooked dish** [➡ PREPARED DISHES; 1170]

grueling adj **arduous**, demanding, exhausting, taxing, tough, harsh, harrowing, hard, punishing, nerve-racking [➡ EMOTIONALLY UNPLEASANT AND UPSETTING; 227] *Opposite*: easy

gruesome adj **grisly**, ghastly, horrible, horrific, horrid, dreadful, shocking, frightening, macabre, hideous, repugnant, ferocious [➡ FRIGHTENING; 231] *Opposite*: pleasant

gruesomeness n **grisliness**, ghastliness, horror, dreadfulness, hideousness, repugnance, horridness [➡ FRIGHTENING; 231] *Opposite*: pleasantness

gruff 1 adj **bad-tempered**, grumpy, angry, impatient, brusque, curt, stern, crusty, abrupt, surly, crotchety (*informal*), snippy (*informal*) [➡ BAD-TEMPERED AND HUMORLESS; 626] *Opposite*: friendly 2 adj **hoarse**, husky, gravelly, rasping, harsh, throaty, deep, thick, croaky [➡ LOUD, HIGH, OR UNPLEASANT SOUNDS; 1266] *Opposite*: soft

gruffness 1 n **grumpiness**, crustiness, abruptness, curtness, sternness, crotchetiness (*informal*), snippiness (*informal*) [➡ BAD-TEMPERED AND HUMORLESS; 626] *Opposite*: pleasantness 2 n **hoarseness**, huskiness, thickness, throatiness, harshness, deepness [➡ LOUD, HIGH, OR UNPLEASANT SOUNDS; 1266] *Opposite*: softness

grumble 1 v **complain**, protest, mutter, object, moan (*informal*), grouse (*informal*), gripe (*informal*), bellyache (*informal*) [➡ COMPLAIN AND NAG; 686] 2 n **complaint**, protest, objection, moan (*informal*), grouse (*informal*), gripe (*informal*) [➡ COMPLAIN AND NAG; 686]

See Compare and Contrast at **complain**.

grumbler n **complainer**, malcontent, whiner, groaner, grouch (*informal*), moaner (*informal*) [➡ GRUMPY AND NEGATIVE PEOPLE; 953]

grumpiness n **bad-temperedness**, irritability, cantankerousness, petulance, crabbiness, snappiness, crankiness (*informal*), grouchiness (*informal*), testiness (*informal*) [➡ IRRITATION AND ANGER; 541] *Opposite*: cheerfulness

grumpy adj **bad-tempered**, irritable, sullen, cantankerous, ill-tempered, complaining, cross, petulant, crabby, sulky, snappy, cranky (*informal*), grouchy (*informal*), testy (*informal*) [➡ IRRITATION AND ANGER; 541] *Opposite*: cheerful

grunge 1 n (*informal*) **filth**, grime, dirt, mess, muck (*informal*), rubbish (*UK*) [➡ UNPLEASANT, DIRTY, AND TOXIC SUBSTANCES; 1268] *Opposite*: cleanliness 2 type of **rock music** [➡ MUSIC, SONGS, AND SINGING; 907]

grunginess (*informal*) n [➡ IN BAD REPAIR; 1234]

grungy (*informal*) adj **shabby**, dirty, scruffy, unkempt, dilapidated, threadbare, tattered, ragged, untidy, worn-out, mucky (*informal*) [➡ IN BAD REPAIR; 1234] *Opposite*: clean

grunt 1 v **mumble**, murmur, rumble, grumble, groan, snort [➡ SOUND EMISSION BY ANIMALS OR BIRDS; 364] 2 n **mumble**,

murmur, rumble, grumble, groan [➡ SOUNDS MADE BY PEOPLE; 1262]
3 *type of* **animal sound** [➡ SOUNDS MADE BY ANIMALS; 1261]

Grus *type of* **constellation** [➡ HEAVENLY BODIES; 1061]

Gruyère *type of* **hard cheese** [➡ DAIRY PRODUCTS AND CHEESES; 1183]

G-string *type of* **lower body underwear** [➡ ACCESSORIES, MILLINERY, AND LINGERIE; 867]

guacamole *type of* **seasonings, sauces, and dips** [➡ SEASONINGS AND SAUCES; 1174]

guano *n* [➡ UNPLEASANT, DIRTY, AND TOXIC SUBSTANCES; 1268]

guarani *type of* **currency** [➡ CURRENCIES; 798]

guarantee **1** *n* **assurance**, promise, pledge, agreement, security, surety, word [➡ PROMISE AND ASSURE; 684] **2** *n* **warranty**, certification, undertaking, contract, agreement, pledge [➡ OFFICIAL DOCUMENTS; 586] **3** *v* **assure**, ensure, promise, pledge, warrant, certify, secure [➡ PROMISE AND ASSURE; 684]

guaranteed *adj* **certain**, definite, sure, cast-iron, failsafe, assured, sure-fire (*informal*), in the bag (*informal*) [➡ CERTAIN; 174] *Opposite:* uncertain

guarantor *n* **backer**, sponsor, underwriter, supporter, patron, angel [➡ PEOPLE INVOLVED IN FINANCE; 804]

See Compare and Contrast at **backer**.

guard **1** *v* **protect**, defend, safeguard, shield, watch over, secure, watch [➡ PREVENT CONTACT OR ATTACK; 419] **2** *n* **protector**, sentinel, sentry, picket, lookout, watch, bouncer [➡ PEOPLE WHO GUARD AND PROTECT; 846] **3** *n* **safeguard**, security, protection, shield, fortification, defense [➡ COVERS AND COATINGS; 1246]

See Compare and Contrast at **safeguard**.

guarded **1** *adj* **protected**, secured, watched over, defended, safeguarded, shielded, fortified [➡ SAFE AND SAFETY; 191] *Opposite:* unprotected **2** *adj* **wary**, cautious, careful, circumspect, hesitant, restrained, noncommittal, cagey (*informal*) [➡ RETICENT AND UNFORTHCOMING; 631] *Opposite:* open

See Compare and Contrast at **cautious**.

guardedly *adv* **carefully**, cautiously, warily, suspiciously, circumspectly, cagily (*informal*) [➡ RETICENT AND UNFORTHCOMING; 631] *Opposite:* openly

guardhouse **1** *n* **prison**, jail, lockup, cells, detention center, penitentiary [➡ BUILDINGS FOR CONFINING PEOPLE; 1094] **2** *type of* **outbuilding** [➡ ANCILLARY BUILDINGS; 1080]

guardian **1** *n* **protector**, guard, sentinel, keeper, custodian, warden (*UK*) [➡ SUPPORTERS, PROTECTORS, AND COMPATRIOTS; 970] **2** *n* **protector**, godparent, custodian, caretaker, keeper, warden (*UK*), carer (*UK*) [➡ ADOPTION, FOSTERING, AND EXTENDED FAMILY; 962]

guardian angel (*informal*) *n* [➡ PEOPLE WHO ARE APPROVED OF; 955]

guardianship *n* **protection**, custody, care, responsibility, supervision, charge, guard, keeping [➡ ADOPTION, FOSTERING, AND EXTENDED FAMILY; 962]

guardrail *n* **handrail**, rail, banister, railing, paling, balustrade [➡ STICKS, POLES, AND WEDGES; 1254]

guava *type of* **fruit** [➡ FRUIT AND VEGETABLES; 1176]

guerrilla *n* **freedom fighter**, rebel, insurgent, irregular, paramilitary, revolutionary [➡ UNCOOPERATIVE OR REBELLIOUS PEOPLE; 566]

guess **1** *v* **deduce**, presume, speculate, suppose, estimate, conjecture [➡ GUESS; 754] **2** *v* **predict**, solve, fathom, work out, conjecture, estimate, guesstimate (*informal*) [➡ PREDICT AND ANTICIPATE; 750] **3** *n* **deduction**, conjecture, supposition, presumption, speculation, estimate, guesstimate (*informal*) [➡ GUESS; 754]

guesstimate (*informal*) **1** *n* **guess**, estimate, conjecture, projection, reckoning, theory [➡ GUESS; 754] **2** *v* **estimate**, guess, reckon, conjecture, project, speculate [➡ GUESS; 754]

guesswork *n* **conjecture**, deduction, presumption, speculation, estimation, reasoning [➡ GUESS; 754]

guest *n* **visitor**, caller, invitee, boarder, lodger, visitant (*archaic*) [➡ FRIENDS AND GUESTS; 963] *Opposite:* host

guestroom *n* **room**, bedroom, spare room [➡ TYPES OF ROOMS; 1097]

guest worker *n* [➡ WORKERS; 836]

guff (*informal*) *n* **nonsense**, rubbish, rigmarole, stuff, stuff and nonsense, verbiage, drivel, talk, gobbledygook (*informal*), waffle (*informal*), blather (*informal*), flimflam (*slang*), jive (*slang*) [➡ MEANINGLESS SPEECH OR WRITING; 676] *Opposite:* sense

guffaw **1** *v* **laugh**, chuckle, chortle, roar, crack up (*informal*), howl (*slang*) [➡ LAUGHTER; 649] **2** *n* **chuckle**, laugh, chortle, roar, belly laugh, horselaugh [➡ LAUGHTER; 649]

GUI *type of* **software** [➡ COMPUTERS AND COMPUTING; 1127]

guidance **1** *n* **leadership**, direction, supervision, management, control, regulation [➡ RELATIONSHIP TO ANOTHER; 973] **2** *n* **help**, assistance, advice, support, counseling, direction [➡ ADVICE; 689]

guidance counselor *n* **adviser**, therapist, mediator, counselor [➡ ADVISERS, JUDGES, AND ARBITERS; 971]

guide **1** *v* **direct**, show, steer, lead, conduct, channel, funnel, point, pilot, escort, shepherd, usher [➡ ACCOMPANY AND FOLLOW; 337] **2** *v* **steer**, drive, pilot, direct, handle, manage [➡ TRAVEL: WAYS OF TRAVELING; 320] **3** *n* **leader**, director, attendant, chaperon, controller, monitor [➡ ADVISERS, JUDGES, AND ARBITERS; 971] **4** *n* **tour guide**, leader, escort, conductor, director, pilot, courier (*UK*) [➡ TRAVEL: SIGHTSEEING AND TOURISM; 321] **5** *n* **influence**, standard, model, ideal, guiding light, example, benchmark [➡ PERFECT EXAMPLES AND EMBODIMENTS; 67] **6** *n* **guidebook**, handbook, manual, instructions, vade mecum, compendium [➡ MANUALS AND INSTRUCTIONS; 589]

guidebook *n* handbook, instructions, travel guide, vade mecum, manual, compendium [➡ MANUALS AND INSTRUCTIONS; 589]

guided missile *type of* explosive weapon [➡ EXPLOSIVES; 1155]

guide dog *type of* large dog [➡ DOGS; 980]

guideline *n* advice, recommendation, standard, guide, parameter, instruction, policy, rule, regulation, directions [➡ ADVICE; 689]

guidelines *n* [➡ WAYS OF DOING THINGS; 294]

guiding principle *n* [➡ WAYS OF DOING THINGS; 294]

guild *n* club, union, society, association, league, federation, company, organization [➡ INSTITUTIONS; 790]

guilder *type of* currency [➡ CURRENCIES; 798]

guile *n* cunning, treachery, astuteness, slyness, wiliness, craftiness, cleverness, deviousness, deceit, duplicity, trickiness, deceitfulness [➡ DECEITFUL; 513] *Opposite:* frankness

guileful *adj* cunning, treacherous, sly, astute, wily, crafty, clever, devious, shifty, sneaky, deceitful, underhand [➡ DECEITFUL; 513] *Opposite:* naive

guileless *adj* naive, frank, candid, ingenuous, straightforward, open, honest, truthful, transparent [➡ NATURALNESS; 497] *Opposite:* guileful

guilelessness *n* [➡ NATURALNESS; 497]

guillemot *type of* sea bird [➡ SEA BIRDS; 1002]

guillotine *v* behead, decapitate, execute, kill [➡ KILL; 923]

guilt 1 *n* fault, responsibility, blame, culpability, guiltiness [➡ MORALLY BAD OR IMPROPER; 775] *Opposite:* innocence 2 *n* remorse, shame, self-reproach, conscience, contriteness, compunction, contrition [➡ FEELINGS ABOUT THE PAST; 532]

guilt complex *n* [➡ PSYCHOLOGY AND THE MIND; 769]

guiltiness 1 *n* culpability, guilt, responsibility, fault, sin, wrongdoing [➡ MORALLY BAD OR IMPROPER; 775] *Opposite:* innocence 2 *n* shame, remorse, guilt, guilty conscience, self-reproach, regret, contrition [➡ FEELINGS ABOUT THE PAST; 532] *Opposite:* shamelessness

guiltless *adj* innocent, blameless, faultless, unimpeachable, irreproachable, impeccable [➡ MORALLY GOOD; 774] *Opposite:* guilty

guiltlessness *n* [➡ MORALLY GOOD; 774]

guilt-ridden *adj* guilty, fearful, anguished, tormented, haunted, remorseful, mortified, awkward, uncomfortable [➡ EMBARRASSMENT AND HUMILIATION; 542] *Opposite:* unashamed

guilty 1 *adj* culpable, responsible, at fault, blameworthy, in the wrong, to blame [➡ MORALLY BAD OR IMPROPER; 775] *Opposite:* innocent 2 *adj* shamefaced, remorseful, embarrassed, mortified, guilt-ridden, uncomfortable, awkward [➡ EMBARRASSMENT AND HUMILIATION; 542] *Opposite:* unashamed

guilty conscience *n* guilt complex, conscience, twinge, pang, guilt trip (*slang*) [➡ FEELINGS ABOUT THE PAST; 532]

guilty party *n* [➡ CRIMINALS; 821]

guinea fowl *type of* fowl [➡ FOOD BIRDS; 999]

guinea pig *type of* rodent [➡ RODENTS; 989]

guise 1 *n* appearance, semblance, show, pretext, excuse, façade, pretense [➡ REPRESENTATIONS AND GENERAL EXAMPLES; 65] 2 *n* form, appearance, shape, light, phase, manifestation [➡ APPEARANCE AND ATMOSPHERE; 1237] 3 *n* costume, disguise, dress, outfit, mask, rig (*informal*), getup (*informal*) [➡ CLOTHES AND ACCESSORIES; 864]

guitar *type of* stringed instrument [➡ MUSICAL INSTRUMENTS; 910]

gulch *n* ravine, gorge, gully, valley, gap, chasm, arroyo [➡ GEOLOGIC FEATURES; 1056]

gulf 1 *n* bight, bay, inlet, sound, cove, harbor [➡ THE SEAS, OCEANS, AND SHORES; 1041] 2 *n* hole, abyss, chasm, gap, hollow, vacuum [➡ HOLES, GAPS, AND FORKS; 1252]

gulfweed *type of* marine alga [➡ MICROORGANISMS, FUNGI, AND ALGAE; 1023]

gull *type of* sea bird [➡ SEA BIRDS; 1002]

gullet *n* crop, maw, throat, craw, esophagus, gorge [➡ THE DIGESTIVE TRACT; 709]

gullibility *n* trustfulness, innocence, credulity, unwariness, acceptance, naiveté [➡ NEGATIVE INTELLECTUAL CHARACTERISTICS; 525] *Opposite:* shrewdness

gullible *adj* naive, susceptible, innocent, trusting, accepting, credulous [➡ NEGATIVE INTELLECTUAL CHARACTERISTICS; 525] *Opposite:* discerning

gully 1 *n* ravine, gorge, valley, gap, chasm, gulch, crevasse, arroyo, channel [➡ GEOLOGIC FEATURES; 1056] 2 *n* channel, ditch, furrow, rut, culvert, drain [➡ HOLES, GAPS, AND FORKS; 1252]

gulp 1 *v* swallow, drink, toss down, guzzle (*informal*), swig (*informal*), knock back (*informal*), slug (*informal*), quaff (*literary or humorous*) [➡ DRINK; 711] *Opposite:* sip 2 *n* swallow, drink, guzzle (*informal*), swig (*informal*), slug (*informal*), quaff (*literary or humorous*) [➡ DRINK; 711] *Opposite:* sip 3 *n* mouthful, drink, swallow, draft, swig (*informal*), slug (*informal*) [➡ DRINK; 711] *Opposite:* sip

gulp back *v* stifle, suppress, restrain, hold back, fight back, choke back [➡ WITHHOLD INFORMATION; 687]

gulp down *v* wolf, swill, swallow, down, gobble, stuff, chugalug (*informal*), chug (*slang*) [➡ DRINK; 711] *Opposite:* sip

gum 1 *n* secretion, exudate, resin, latex, juice, sap [➡ PARTS OF TREES AND PLANTS; 1026] 2 *n* glue, adhesive, paste, cement, epoxy resin, superglue [➡ ADHESIVES; 1271] 3 *type of* con-

fectionery [➡CONFECTIONERY; 1182] **4** *part of* **mouth** [➡THE MOUTH; 702]
5 *v* **stick**, glue, paste, bond, cement, affix [➡FASTEN, LINK, AND JOIN; 408] *Opposite:* unstick

gumbo *type of* **soup** [➡SOUPS; 1186]

gum boot *type of* **boot** [➡FOOTWEAR; 871]

gumdrop *type of* **confectionery** [➡CONFECTIONERY; 1182]

gumminess *n* [➡FLUID AND NONSOLID; 1213]

gummy *adj* **sticky**, gooey, gluey, tacky, adhesive, viscid [➡PHYSICAL TEXTURE; 1222]

gumption (*informal*) **1** *n* **common sense**, sense, shrewdness, practicality, presence of mind, initiative, resourcefulness, horse sense (*informal*) [➡POSITIVE INTELLECTUAL CHARACTERISTICS; 524] *Opposite:* stupidity **2** *n* **courage**, nerve, bravery, mettle, pluck, guts (*slang*), moxie (*slang*) [➡COURAGE; 498]

gumshoe (*dated informal*) *n* **sleuth**, detective, private detective, private eye, private investigator [➡THE POLICE, ARREST, AND PRETRIAL PROCEEDINGS; 818]

gum tree *type of* **evergreen tree** [➡EVERGREEN AND CONIFEROUS TREES; 1029]

gun *n* **firearm**, handgun, shooter (*informal*), piece (*slang*) [➡WEAPONS FOR SHOOTING; 1156]

gun

◆ *types of guns*
air pistol, air rifle, antiaircraft gun, automatic, bazooka, blunderbuss, cannon, carbine, flamethrower, handgun, howitzer, machine gun, magnum, mortar, musket, pistol, revolver, rifle, sawed-off shotgun, semiautomatic, shotgun, submachine gun, Tommy gun (*informal*)

gunboat *type of* **military vessel** [➡SHIPS AND BOATS; 1150]

gun down (*informal*) *v* **kill**, assassinate, shoot, shoot down, mow down, murder, blow away (*slang*) [➡KILL; 923]

gunfight *n* **gun battle**, shootout, firefight, fight, duel, shooting [➡AGGRESSIVE EVENTS; 39]

gunfire *n* **firing**, shooting, barrage of bullets, volley, salvo, barrage [➡IMPACT SOUNDS; 1260]

gung ho (*informal*) **1** *adj* **enthusiastic**, eager, keen, zealous, ardent, bullish (*informal*) [➡ENERGY AND ENTHUSIASM; 496] *Opposite:* reluctant **2** *adj* **combative**, belligerent, militaristic, bellicose, aggressive, trigger-happy (*informal*) [➡MILITARY; 829] *Opposite:* peaceable

gunk (*informal*) *n* **grease**, mess, filth, dirt, slime, muck (*informal*) [➡UNPLEASANT, DIRTY, AND TOXIC SUBSTANCES; 1268]

gunky (*informal*) *adj* **greasy**, slimy, messy, filthy, dirty, mucky (*informal*) [➡DIRTY; 1235] *Opposite:* clean

gunman **1** *n* **sniper**, murderer, assassin, killer, gangster, gunslinger (*informal*), hit man (*slang*) [➡PEOPLE WHO KILL; 924] **2** *n* **marksman**, markswoman, shot, crack shot, good shot, deadeye (*informal*) [➡PEOPLE WHO KILL; 924]

gunmetal *type of* **gray** [➡COLORS; 1224]

gunner *n* **soldier**, shooter, artilleryman, fusilier, rifleman, bombardier [➡MILITARY PERSONNEL; 828]

gunpowder *type of* **explosive material** [➡EXPLOSIVES; 1155]

guns *n* **weapons**, ordnance, firepower, artillery, arms, armaments, weaponry [➡WEAPONS; 1154]

gunshot *n* **firing**, shooting, gunfire, volley, barrage, salvo [➡IMPACT SOUNDS; 1260]

gunwale *part of* **ship or boat** [➡PARTS OF A SHIP OR BOAT; 1151]

guppy *type of* **freshwater fish** [➡FRESHWATER FISH; 1010]

gurdwara *type of* **place of worship** [➡RELIGIOUS BUILDINGS; 1085]

gurgle **1** *v* **bubble**, slosh, splash, ripple, murmur, gush, babble, burble [➡EMIT CONTINUOUS SOUNDS; 366] **2** *v* **babble**, burble, coo, warble, crow, croon [➡SOUND EMISSION BY PEOPLE; 363] **3** *n* **burble**, babble, coo, murmur, warble [➡CONTINUOUS SOUNDS; 1258] **4** *n* **slosh**, bubble, splash, ripple, murmur, babble, burble [➡CONTINUOUS SOUNDS; 1258]

guru **1** *n* **spiritual leader**, religious teacher, maharishi, spiritual guide, spiritual advisor, counselor, sage (*literary*) [➡RELIGIOUS PEOPLE; 778] **2** *n* **leader**, authority, leading light, expert, pundit, specialist [➡TALENTED OR INTELLIGENT PEOPLE; 528]

gush **1** *v* **pour**, flood, stream, surge, spurt, jet, flow [➡LIQUID EMISSION; 370] *Opposite:* trickle **2** *v* **be effusive**, prattle, flatter, ooze, admire, enthuse, babble [➡CHATTER AND BABBLE; 617] *Opposite:* criticize **3** *n* **flood**, flow, spurt, jet, stream, surge, rush [➡AMOUNTS OF LIQUID; 114] *Opposite:* trickle

gushing **1** *adj* **pouring**, flowing, overflowing, spouting, torrential, spurting [➡MOVING QUICKLY; 103] *Opposite:* trickling **2** *adj* **effusive**, voluble, enthusiastic, emotional, sentimental, glib, hammy (*informal*) [➡ENTHUSIASTIC AND INQUISITIVE; 628] *Opposite:* reserved

gushingly *adv* **effusively**, volubly, enthusiastically, emotionally, sentimentally, glibly, hammily (*informal*) [➡ENTHUSIASTIC AND INQUISITIVE; 628] *Opposite:* reservedly

gusset *n* **patch**, insert, inset, reinforcement, support, enlargement, extension [➡PARTS OF A GARMENT; 870]

gussy up (*informal*) *v* [➡IMPROVE APPEARANCE; 379]

gust **1** *n* **squall**, draft, flurry, breeze, blast, puff [➡WINDY AND STORMY WEATHER; 1053] *Opposite:* calm **2** *n* **burst**, explosion, expulsion, eruption, outburst, rush [➡SUDDEN EVENTS; 52] **3** *v* **blow**, bluster, squall [➡WINDY AND STORMY WEATHER; 1053]

gusto *n* **enjoyment**, delight, enthusiasm, passion, zest, pleasure [➡PLEASURE, EXCITEMENT, AND ELATION; 534] *Opposite:* apathy

gusty *adj* **windy**, breezy, squally, stormy, blustery, blowy (*informal*) [➡WINDY AND STORMY WEATHER; 1053] *Opposite:* calm

gut **1** *part of* **digestive tract** [➡THE DIGESTIVE TRACT; 709] **2** *n* (*slang*) **belly**, stomach, paunch, bay window (*slang*), beer gut (*slang*), beer belly (*slang*) [➡THE DIGESTIVE TRACT; 709] **3** *v* **strip**, clear out, empty, empty out, plunder, ransack [➡EMPTY AND UNLOAD; 407] **4** *v* **disembowel**, eviscerate, clean, prepare, dress [➡COOKING AND FOOD PREPARATION; 353] **5** *v* **ruin**, damage, destroy, burn, raze, burn out (*informal*) [➡FIRE, FLAMMABILITY, AND BURNING; 1165] *Opposite:* build up **6** *adj* **instinctive**, intuitive, emotional, automatic, unconscious, instant, knee-jerk (*informal*) [➡THE NATURE OF IDEAS; 771] *Opposite:* considered

gut feeling *n* **guess**, hunch, instinct, impression, intuition, gut reaction [➡ FEELINGS; 531] *Opposite:* fact

gutless *adj* **cowardly**, spineless, spiritless, weak, timid, craven [➡ COWARDICE AND WEAKNESS OF WILL; 508] *Opposite:* plucky

See Compare and Contrast at **cowardly**.

gutlessness *n* [➡ COWARDICE AND WEAKNESS OF WILL; 508]

gut reaction *n* **guess**, hunch, instinct, impression, intuition, gut feeling [➡ FEELINGS; 531]

guts **1** *n* **intestines**, bowels, stomach, viscera, entrails, insides (*informal*), innards (*informal*) [➡ THE DIGESTIVE TRACT; 709] **2** *n* **interior**, recesses, bowels, inner workings, heart, core, center [➡ CENTRAL PARTS OF PHYSICAL OBJECTS; 1251] **3** *n* (*slang*) **courage**, bravery, strength of character, pluck, resolve, willpower, daring, mettle, nerve [➡ COURAGE; 498] *Opposite:* cowardice

See Compare and Contrast at **courage**.

gutsy (*informal*) **1** *adj* **brave**, plucky, courageous, fearless, determined, indomitable, daring, intrepid (*literary or humorous*) [➡ COURAGE; 498] *Opposite:* cowardly **2** *adj* **passionate**, impassioned, emotional, intense, fiery, heartfelt [➡ ENTHUSIASTIC AND INQUISITIVE; 628] *Opposite:* insipid

gutted *adj* **cleaned**, disemboweled, eviscerated, prepared, dressed [➡ STATE OF PREPARED FOOD; 1171]

gutter **1** *n* **drain**, sewer, channel, trench, groove, trough, ditch [➡ WATERCOURSES; 1111] **2** *v* **flicker**, sputter, waver, drip, fade, fade out [➡ CEASE TO EXIST; 22] *Opposite:* flare

guttering **1** *n* **gutters**, channels, trenches, grooves, sewers, troughs, ditching, drainage [➡ WATERCOURSES; 1111] **2** *part of* **building** [➡ PARTS OF A BUILDING; 1095]

guttural *adj* **harsh**, rough, rasping, throaty, deep, low, gruff, grating, raucous [➡ LOUD, HIGH, OR UNPLEASANT SOUNDS; 1266] *Opposite:* melodious

guy **1** *n* (*informal*) **man**, fellow, gentleman, boy, fella (*informal*), gent (*informal*), type (*informal*), lad (*informal*), dude (*slang*), brother (*slang*), bod (*slang*) [➡ MALE PERSON; 934] **2** *n* (*UK*) **effigy**, figure, model, manikin, scarecrow, image [➡ REPRESENTATIONS AND GENERAL EXAMPLES; 65]

guys (*informal*) *n* **people**, folks, gang, everybody [➡ FRIENDS AND ACQUAINTANCES; 936]

guywire *n* **rope**, lashing, string, halyard, hawser, guy (*informal*) [➡ FASTENERS, LINKS, AND NETWORKS; 1247]

guzzle (*informal*) **1** *v* **gulp**, gobble, wolf, stuff, consume, eat, drink, devour, swallow, toss down, swig (*informal*), scoff (*informal*), knock back (*informal*), scarf (*slang*), scarf down (*slang*) [➡ EAT AND NOT EAT; 710] *Opposite:* nibble **2** *v* **consume**, use, devour, burn up, use up, get through [➡ USE UP AND WASTE; 474] *Opposite:* conserve

gym (*informal*) *n* **exercise room**, sports club, health club, sports hall, aerobics studio, gymnasium, fitness centre (*UK*), sports centre (*UK*), leisure centre (*UK*) [➡ BUILDINGS FOR PUBLIC ENTERTAINMENT; 1084]

gymkhana (*UK*) *n* **horse show**, riding show, equestrian show, showjumping competition, riding competition, horse-riding show [➡ NON-AGGRESSIVE/SPORTING EVENTS; 40]

gymnasium *n* **exercise room**, sports club, health club, sports hall, aerobics studio, gym (*informal*), fitness centre (*UK*), sports centre (*UK*), leisure centre (*UK*) [➡ BUILDINGS FOR PUBLIC ENTERTAINMENT; 1084]

gymnast *n* [➡ PEOPLE IN SPORTS AND LEISURE; 876]

gymnastic **1** *adj* **athletic**, acrobatic, sporty, sporting [➡ AGILITY OF THE BODY; 476] **2** *adj* **energetic**, athletic, acrobatic, lithe, supple, agile, active [➡ AGILITY OF THE BODY; 476] *Opposite:* stiff

gymnastics *n* **aerobics**, calisthenics, exercises, physical training, physical exercises (*UK*) [➡ HOBBIES, GAMES, AND SPORTS; 875]

gynoecium *part of* **flower** [➡ FLOWERS; 1032]

gypsum *type of* **mineral** [➡ MINERALS; 1277]

gypsy *n* **nomad**, traveler, drifter, wanderer [➡ NOMADIC AND ROOTLESS LIFESTYLES; 884]

gypsy moth *type of* **moth** [➡ MOTHS AND BUTTERFLIES; 1015]

gyrate *v* **rotate**, whirl, spin, revolve, twirl, spiral, turn, twist, twizzle [➡ MOVE SOMETHING: ON THE SPOT; 336]

gyration *n* **whirling**, twirling, spinning, turning, revolving, rotation, revolution, twisting [➡ MOVE SOMETHING: ON THE SPOT; 336]

gyratory *adj* **spiral**, rotating, revolving, spinning, whirling, turning, spiraling [➡ DIRECTION OF MOTION; 345] *Opposite:* still

H

haberdashery *n* [➡ GARMENTS AND OUTFITS; 865]

habit **1** *n* **custom**, routine, tradition, convention, pattern, practice, wont (*formal*) [➡ WAYS OF DOING THINGS; 294] *Opposite:* deviation **2** *n* **tendency**, inclination, leaning, preference, fondness, bent, thing (*informal*) [➡ TEMPERAMENT AND BEHAVIOR; 492] **3** *n* **addiction**, problem, dependency, weakness, fixation, obsession [➡ FADS, FETISHES, AND IDOLATRY; 555] **4** *n* **uniform**, garb, apparel, outfit, garment, attire (*formal*) [➡ CLOTHES AND ACCESSORIES; 864]

Compare and Contrast: *habit, custom, tradition, practice, routine, wont*

CORE MEANING: established pattern of behavior

habit an action or behavior pattern that is regular, repetitive, often unconscious, and sometimes compulsive; *custom* the way somebody normally or routinely behaves in a situation, or a traditional practice in a particular community or group of people; *tradition* a long-established action or pattern of behavior in a particular community or group of people, especially one that has been handed down from generation to generation; *practice* an established way of doing something, especially one that has developed through experience and knowledge; *routine* a typical pattern of behavior that is regularly followed on a day-to-day basis, sometimes with the suggestion that this is monotonous and tedious; *wont* (*formal*) something that somebody does regularly or habitually.

---

habitable *adj* **inhabitable**, livable, fit for human habitation, comfortable, fit to live in [➡ IN GOOD REPAIR; 1232] *Opposite:* uninhabitable

habitat *n* **home**, locale, environment, surroundings, territory, haunt, habitation [➡ PLACE; 1065]

habitation **1** *n* **occupancy**, occupation, tenancy, inhabitance, residence, inhabitation (*archaic*) [➡ ACCOMMODATIONS; 855] **2** *n* **house**, home, lodging, residence, place, crib (*slang*), pad (*slang dated*), dwelling (*formal*), abode (*literary*) [➡ ACCOMMODATIONS; 855] **3** *n* **building**, structure, housing, construction, architecture, houses [➡ BUILDING AND ARCHITECTURE; 1076]

habitual **1** *adj* **regular**, usual, routine, customary, normal, consistent, ordinary [➡ ORDINARINESS; 244] *Opposite:* unusual **2** *adj* **persistent**, frequent, chronic, long-term, ongoing, regular [➡ PERMANENCE: WITHOUT END; 94] *Opposite:* occasional **3** *adj* **characteristic**, usual, customary, typical, expected, wonted (*literary*) [➡ ORDINARINESS; 244] *Opposite:* uncharacteristic

See Compare and Contrast at **usual**.

habitually *adv* **usually**, routinely, customarily, consistently, normally, regularly, often, typically [➡ USUALLY; 108] *Opposite:* unusually

habituate *v* **familiarize**, adjust, accustom, inure, acclimatize, orientate [➡ CHANGE OF MOOD AND COMPOSURE; 580] *Opposite:* disorientate

habituation (*formal*) *n* **familiarization**, adjustment, acclimatization, orientation, adaptation, conditioning [➡ CHANGE; 372] *Opposite:* disorientation

háček *type of* **diacritic** [➡ ASPECTS OF LANGUAGE; 682]

hacienda *type of* **house** [➡ RESIDENTIAL BUILDINGS; 1078]

hack **1** *v* **cut**, chop, slash, lacerate, scythe, hew, slice [➡ TEAR, BREAK, AND CUT; 360] *Opposite:* splice **2** *v* (*informal*) **cope**, manage, handle, deal with, succeed, make do, survive, get by [➡ TOLERATE AND ENDURE; 766] **3** *v* [➡ THE INTERNET; 1128] **4** *type of* **horse** [➡ HORSES; 985] **5** *n* (*informal*) **drudge**, slave, factotum, flunky (*informal*), menial (*formal*) [➡ WORKERS; 836] *Opposite:* specialist **6** *n* (*informal*) **journalist**, scribbler, writer, stringer, reporter [➡ WORKERS IN ENTERTAINMENT AND MEDIA; 873]

hackneyed *adj* **trite**, clichéd, tired, stale, everyday, commonplace, unimaginative, worn-out [➡ BORING AND UNINTERESTING; 234] *Opposite:* original

haddock *type of* **ocean fish** [➡ OCEAN FISH; 1009]

had it (*informal*) **1** *adj* **out of order**, broken, finished, no good, useless, kaput (*informal*), past its best (*UK*) [➡ IN BAD REPAIR; 1234] *Opposite:* brand-new **2** *adj* **exhausted**, worn out, tired, weary, spent, done for (*informal*), beat (*slang*), shattered (*UK*) [➡ TIRED, ASLEEP, AND UNCONSCIOUS; 738] *Opposite:* fresh

hadron *type of* **elementary particle** [➡ ELEMENTARY PARTICLES; 1279]

hadrosaur *type of* **dinosaur** [➡ DINOSAURS; 996]

haggard *adj* **worn**, fatigued, tired, faded, exhausted, worn-down, gaunt, drawn, worn-out [➡ FACIAL CHARACTERISTICS; 481] *Opposite:* fresh

haggle *v* **bargain**, barter, quibble, negotiate, wrangle, beat down (*informal*), dicker (*informal*) [➡ ARGUE AND FIGHT; 643]

hail **1** *n* **storm**, volley, burst, flood, barrage, shower, rain [➡ SUDDEN EVENTS; 52] **2** *v* **greet**, welcome, address, speak to, call to, wave to [➡ GESTURES AND GESTICULATION; 653] *Opposite:* ignore **3** *v* **acclaim**, acknowledge, salute, uphold, confirm, affirm, rave about [➡ APPROVE AND CONFIRM; 646] *Opposite:* reject **4** *v* **summon**, call, call over, flag down, wave, signal, beckon [➡ GESTURES AND GESTICULATION; 653] *Opposite:* dismiss

hair **1** *n* **tresses**, curls, mop, shock, locks (*literary*), mane (*literary or informal*) [➡ HAIR; 484] **2** *n* **coat**, fur, wool, pelt, fleece, beard, whiskers, fuzz, mustache, mane (*literary or informal*) [➡ THE SKIN; 720]

hairband *type of* **headgear** [➡ ACCESSORIES, MILLINERY, AND LINGERIE; 867]

hairbrush *type of* **cosmetic tool** [➡ HAND TOOLS; 1119]

haircut **1** *n* **trim**, cut, restyling, clip, restyle [➡ HAIRSTYLES AND

HAIRPIECES; 488] **2** *n* **hairstyle**, style, hairdo (*informal*), coiffure (*formal*) [➡ HAIRSTYLES AND HAIRPIECES; 488]

hairdo (*informal*) *n* **haircut**, hairstyle, style, do (*slang*), coiffure (*formal*) [➡ HAIRSTYLES AND HAIRPIECES; 488]

hairdresser *n* **stylist**, barber, hair stylist, cutter, coiffeur (*formal*), coiffeuse (*formal*) [➡ HAIR STYLISTS; 851]

hairdressing *n* **hair gel**, styling gel, mousse, hair cream, styling spray, hair spray [➡ HAIRSTYLES AND HAIRPIECES; 488]

hairiness *n* **furriness**, shagginess, fuzziness, hirsuteness, fluffiness, downiness [➡ HAIR; 484] *Opposite*: baldness

hairless *adj* **bald**, receding, thin on top, bald as a coot, shaved, shaven, baldheaded, beardless, clean-shaven, tonsured [➡ BALDNESS AND BALDING; 487] *Opposite*: hairy

hairline *part of* **face** [➡ PARTS OF THE BODY: HEAD; 692]

hairpiece *n* [➡ HAIRSTYLES AND HAIRPIECES; 488]

hair-raising *adj* **terrifying**, horrifying, extraordinary, spine-tingling, frightening, alarming, thrilling, scary (*informal*) [➡ FRIGHTENING; 231] *Opposite*: calming

hair salon *type of* **retail outlet** [➡ RETAIL OUTLETS; 1083]

hairsplitting *n* **quibbling**, nitpicking, cavilling, pettifoggery, equivocation, pedantry [➡ DIFFICULT TO PLEASE; 515]

hairstyle *n* **haircut**, style, cut, hairdo (*informal*), coiffure (*formal*) [➡ HAIRSTYLES AND HAIRPIECES; 488]

hairstyle

◆ *types of hairstyles*
Afro, bangs, beehive, big hair (*informal*), bob, bouffant, braids, bun, buzz cut, chignon, cornrow, cowlick, crew cut, crop, dreadlocks, flat top, French twist, mohawk, mullet, pageboy, pigtail, plait, pompadour, ponytail, ringlet, topknot

hair stylist *n* [➡ HAIR STYLISTS; 851]

hairy **1** *adj* **hirsute**, bearded, bushy, furry, shaggy, long-haired, stubbly [➡ DESCRIBING HAIR; 486] *Opposite*: hairless **2** *adj* (*informal*) **dangerous**, hazardous, treacherous, risky, perilous, scary (*informal*) [➡ DANGEROUS; 236] *Opposite*: safe

hajj *n* [➡ TRAVEL: JOURNEYS AND TRIPS; 318]

hajji *n* [➡ TRAVEL: TRAVELERS AND WALKERS; 319]

hake *type of* **ocean fish** [➡ OCEAN FISH; 1009]

halal *adj* [➡ FOOD; 1167]

halcyon (*literary*) *adj* **untroubled**, calm, peaceful, still, tranquil, heavenly, quiet, idyllic, serene [➡ CALMING; 188] *Opposite*: turbulent

halcyon days (*literary*) *n* [➡ PLEASANT SITUATIONS; 74]

hale *adj* **healthy**, well, fit, robust, in good shape, in peak condition, lusty, vigorous, hearty [➡ FIT AND STRONG; 736] *Opposite*: unhealthy

hale and hearty *adj* [➡ FIT AND STRONG; 736]

half *n* [➡ MEASURABLE PORTIONS; 127]

half-baked (*informal*) **1** *adj* **unplanned**, ill-considered, impulsive, ill-conceived [➡ THE NATURE OF IDEAS; 771] *Opposite*: considered **2** *adj* **impractical**, silly, unrealistic, idealistic, starry-eyed, romantic [➡ THE NATURE OF IDEAS; 771] *Opposite*: sensible

half-hearted *adj* **unenthusiastic**, perfunctory, lukewarm, indifferent, lackadaisical, reluctant, unwilling, feeble, weak, spiritless, uninterested [➡ NEUTRALITY AND INDIFFERENCE; 551] *Opposite*: wholehearted

half-heartedly *adv* **unenthusiastically**, perfunctorily, lukewarmly, indifferently, lackadaisically, reluctantly, unwillingly, feebly, weakly, spiritlessly, unintcrestedly [➡ WITHOUT ENTHUSIASM; 287] *Opposite*: wholeheartedly

half-light *n* **twilight**, semi-darkness, dusk, gloom, gloominess, penumbra [➡ DESCRIBING LIGHT; 1228]

half-truth *n* [➡ DECEPTION AND LIES; 660]

halfway **1** *adv* **midway**, centrally, in the middle, between, in-between, medially, partway [➡ RELATIVE LOCATION; 161] **2** *adv* **almost**, nearly, mostly, partially, partly, substantially [➡ TO A CERTAIN EXTENT; 136] *Opposite*: completely **3** *adj* **middle**, central, intermediate, mid, midway, median, medial [➡ RELATIVE LOCATION; 161]

halibut *type of* **flatfish** [➡ OCEAN FISH; 1009]

hall **1** *n* **gallery**, great hall, room, public room, ballroom [➡ TYPES OF ROOMS; 1097] **2** *n* **mansion**, dormitory, manor, tower, castle, lodge, country seat, grange (*UK*) [➡ RESIDENTIAL BUILDINGS; 1078]

hallmark **1** *n* **seal**, stamp, trademark, symbol, logo, mark, guarantee, assurance, promise, brand [➡ SYMBOLS, SIGNS, AND NUMBERS; 596] **2** *n* **characteristic**, feature, trait, property, quality, token, sign, indication [➡ QUALITIES AND CHARACTERISTICS; 1191]

hall of residence (*UK*) *n* **residence**, frat house, dormitory, residence hall, student house, hall, dorm (*informal*), lodgings (*dated*) [➡ RESIDENTIAL BUILDINGS; 1078]

hallow *v* **consecrate**, sanctify, bless, deify, revere, respect, honor [➡ RELIGIONS AND RELIGIOUS PRACTICES; 777] *Opposite*: desecrate

hallowed *adj* **sacred**, holy, sanctified, blessed, consecrated, deified, revered, respected, honored [➡ RELIGIOUS CONCEPTS; 776] *Opposite*: profane (*formal*)

hallucinate *v* **see things**, have delusions, have visions, fantasize, be delirious, imagine, have nightmares [➡ DREAM, IMAGINE, AND FANTASIZE; 749]

hallucination *n* **vision**, illusion, figment of the imagination, phantasm, mirage, delusion, delirium, fantasy, nightmare [➡ NONEXISTENT THINGS; 23]

hallway *n* **hall**, entry, lobby, antechamber, vestibule, entrance, foyer, passage, corridor, passageway [➡ DOORS AND ACCESS POINTS; 1101]

halo *n* **corona**, aureole, nimbus, aura, radiance, crown [➡ ROUNDED SHAPE; 1218]

halt **1** *n* **standstill**, stop, close, break, pause, cessation, termination, end [➡ ENDS AND DEPARTURES; 54] *Opposite*: start **2** *v* **stop**, pause, cease, freeze, come to an end, come to a close, come to a standstill, finish, bring to an end, bring to a close, arrest, cut short, close down, bring to a standstill, immobilize, terminate (*formal*) [➥ CAUSE TO STOP; 266] *Opposite:* begin

halter 1 *n* **bridle**, rein, strap, lead, noose, collar, tether [➥ FASTENERS, LINKS, AND NETWORKS; 1247] **2** *type of* **top** [➥ GARMENTS AND OUTFITS; 865]

halting *adj* **hesitant**, uncertain, tentative, stumbling, faltering, awkward, ham-fisted (*informal*), ham-handed (*informal*) [➥ DESCRIBING BODY MOVEMENTS; 288] *Opposite:* firm

halve 1 *v* **bisect**, divide, cut in two, cut in half [➥ SEPARATE AND DIVIDE; 401] *Opposite:* double **2** *v* **split**, split fifty-fifty, go halves on, share, share out, cut up, divide up, divvy up (*informal*), carve up (*informal*) [➥ DISPENSE, RATION, AND DISTRIBUTE; 434] **3** *v* **decrease**, reduce, cut, slash, cut down, cut back, pare down, downsize [➥ CHANGE OF SIZE: SMALLER; 393] *Opposite:* double

ham 1 *v* **overact**, lay it on thick, overplay, overdo it, mug, exaggerate [➥ OVERDO SOMETHING; 290] **2** *type of* **processed meat** [➥ TYPES AND CUTS OF MEAT; 1177]

hamburger *type of* **processed meat** [➥ TYPES AND CUTS OF MEAT; 1177]

ham-fisted (*informal*) *see* **ham-handed**

ham-fistedness (*informal*) *see* **ham-handedness**

ham-handed (*informal*) *adj* **clumsy**, inelegant, inept, blundering, awkward, all thumbs, heavy-handed, ham-fisted (*informal*), all fingers and thumbs (*UK*) [➥ UNSKILLED; 529] *Opposite:* dexterous

ham-handedness (*informal*) *n* [➥ UNSKILLED; 529]

ham it up *v* [➥ OVERDO SOMETHING; 290]

hamlet *n* **village**, settlement, homestead, community, colony [➥ HUMAN SETTLEMENTS; 1070] *Opposite:* city

hammer 1 *type of* **carpentry tool** [➥ HAND TOOLS; 1119] **2** *part of* **ear** [➥ THE EAR; 706] **3** *v* **strike**, pound, hit, knock, beat, nail, batter, drum, drive [➥ USE TOOLS AND MACHINERY; 468] **4** *v* (*informal*) **batter**, beat, assault, attack, brutalize [➥ PHYSICAL ATTACK AND PUNISHMENT; 415] **5** *v* (*informal*) **defeat**, beat, thrash, trounce, walk over (*informal*), whip (*informal*), paste (*slang*), slaughter (*slang*), cream (*slang*) [➥ BEAT AND DEFEAT; 80] **6** *v* (*informal*) **criticize**, disparage, condemn, censure, put down (*informal*), slam (*informal*) [➥ ACCUSE, BLAME, AND CRITICIZE; 641] *Opposite:* praise

hammering 1 *n* (*informal*) **defeat**, beating, thrashing, trouncing, hiding (*informal*), slaughter (*slang*) [➥ BEAT AND DEFEAT; 80] *Opposite:* victory **2** *n* **pounding**, buffeting, battering, beating, lashing, pummeling [➥ PHYSICAL ATTACK AND PUNISHMENT; 415]

hammer out 1 *v* **beat**, pound, forge, shape, craft, reshape [➥ CHANGE OF SHAPE; 385] **2** *v* **accomplish**, establish, arrive at, reach, produce, settle, work out, agree, agree on, decide on, hash out, thrash out (*UK*) [➥ TWO-WAY COMMUNICATION; 607]

hammer throw *type of* **track and field** [➥ HOBBIES, GAMES, AND SPORTS; 875]

hammock *type of* **bed** [➥ FURNITURE; 858]

hammy (*informal*) *adj* [➥ AFFECTATION, SELF-SATISFACTION, AND SNOBBISHNESS; 507]

hamper 1 *n* **basket**, picnic basket, pannier [➥ CONTAINERS, RECEPTACLES, AND PACKAGING; 1245] **2** *v* **hinder**, obstruct, get in the way of, impede, slow down, weigh down, hold back, fetter, shackle, encumber, debilitate [➥ AVOID, PREVENT, LIMIT, AND CONTROL; 277] *Opposite:* facilitate

See Compare and Contrast at **hinder**.

hamster *type of* **rodent** [➥ RODENTS; 989]

hamstring *type of* **muscle or tendon** [➥ THE MUSCLES; 718]

hamstrung *adj* **constrained**, restricted, thwarted, confined, cramped, stymied [➥ IN TROUBLE AND DISADVANTAGED; 73] *Opposite:* liberated

hand 1 *part of* **arm or hand** [➥ PARTS OF THE BODY: ARM AND HAND; 695] **2** *n* **pointer**, needle, indicator, arrow, finger, big hand, small hand [➥ PARTS OF MACHINES AND TOOLS; 1118] **3** *n* **influence**, part, share, role, involvement, participation [➥ KIND ACTIONS OR BEHAVIOR; 295] **4** *n* **clap**, ovation, standing ovation, round of applause, burst of applause, handclap [➥ APPLAUSE; 652] *Opposite:* boo **5** *n* **handwriting**, writing, script, scrawl, scribble, calligraphy [➥ WRITING; 583] **6** *v* **give**, hand over, offer, pass, tender, dispense, administer, distribute, provide, furnish (*formal*) [➥ PROFFER AND HAND OVER; 431] *Opposite:* take

hand around *v* [➥ DISPENSE, RATION, AND DISTRIBUTE; 434]

handbag *n* **bag**, shoulder bag, clutch bag, backpack, purse, pocketbook [➥ CONTAINERS, RECEPTACLES, AND PACKAGING; 1245]

hand basin *type of* **plumbing fixtures** [➥ FIXTURES; 859]

handbill *n* **leaflet**, flier, pamphlet, advertisement, circular, handout, tract, brochure [➥ ADVERTISING AND PUBLICITY; 604]

handbook *n* **manual**, instruction manual, guide, guidebook, instruction book, user's guide, owner's manual, reference book, reference, source book, almanac, booklet, brochure, encyclopedia [➥ MANUALS AND INSTRUCTIONS; 589]

handcuff 1 *n* **manacles**, chains, shackles, fetters, irons, restraints, cuffs (*slang*), bracelets (*slang*) [➥ FASTENERS, LINKS, AND NETWORKS; 1247] **2** *v* **chain**, manacle, shackle, fasten, tie up, secure, restrain, cuff (*slang*) [➥ CAPTIVITY AND LOSS OF FREEDOM; 248] *Opposite:* release

hand down *v* **leave**, bequeath, pass down, transmit, will, hand on, pass on [➥ BEQUEATH AND BEQUESTS; 432]

handful 1 *n* **some**, a few, one or two, not many, hardly any, a minority, a trickle, a bit (*informal*) [➥ FEW, LITTLE, SMALL AMOUNT; 120] *Opposite:* many **2** *n* (*informal*) **test**, trial, problem, nuisance, hard work, tall order (*informal*) [➥ PROBLEMS; 256]

hand grenade *type of* **explosive weapon** [➥ EXPLOSIVES; 1155]

handgun *type of* **gun** [➥ WEAPONS FOR SHOOTING; 1156]

handheld computer *type of* **computer** [➥ COMPUTERS AND COMPUTING; 1127]

hand-hot *adj* [➥ TEMPERATURE: MEDIUM; 1230]

handicap *n* [➥ FAULTS, FLAWS, AND WEAKNESSES; 251]

handicraft *n* **craft**, handcraft, handiwork, skill, art, ability [➡ CRAFTS AND CARVING; 355]

handicraft

◆ *types of handicrafts*
appliqué, basketry, crochet, dressmaking, embroidery, knitting, lacemaking, macramé, needlepoint, needlework, sewing, smocking, stitching, tapestry, tatting, weaving

handily **1** *adv* **conveniently**, closely, accessibly, nearby, in easy reach, within reach, at hand [➡ CLOSENESS; 159] *Opposite*: inconveniently **2** *adv* **skillfully**, dexterously, cleverly, neatly, ably, proficiently, competently, usefully, practically [➡ USEFULNESS; 199] *Opposite*: awkwardly

hand in **1** *v* **submit**, give, give in, tender, offer, proffer, present [➡ PROFFER AND HAND OVER; 431] *Opposite*: withhold **2** *v* **surrender**, return, give up, give back, hand over, relinquish [➡ PROFFER AND HAND OVER; 431] *Opposite*: withhold

handiness **1** *n* **convenience**, proximity, closeness, accessibility [➡ CLOSENESS; 159] *Opposite*: inconvenience **2** *n* **usefulness**, utility, efficacy, helpfulness, practicality, usability, versatility [➡ USEFULNESS; 199] *Opposite*: uselessness **3** *n* **skillfulness**, skill, dexterity, practicality, cleverness, ingenuity, ability, competence, proficiency [➡ SKILLS, TALENTS, AND ABILITIES; 526] *Opposite*: awkwardness

handiwork **1** *n* **deed**, action, achievement, work, creation, accomplishment [➡ ACTIONS OR UNDERTAKINGS; 259] **2** *n* **handicraft**, craft, skill, talent, art, dexterity, ability, proficiency [➡ SKILLS, TALENTS, AND ABILITIES; 526]

handkerchief *n* **tissue**, paper handkerchief, facial tissue, hankie (*informal*) [➡ ACCESSORIES, MILLINERY, AND LINGERIE; 867]

handle **1** *n* **grip**, holder, handgrip [➡ PARTS OF MACHINES AND TOOLS; 1118] **2** *n* (*slang*) **name**, title, nickname, sobriquet, pet name, moniker (*slang*) [➡ NAME AND DESCRIBE; 665] **3** *v* **touch**, finger, feel, move, hold, pick up [➡ CONTACT: TOUCH; 412] **4** *v* **control**, deal with, run, cope with, conduct, carry out, see to, treat, get a grip on, come to grips with, get to grips with (*UK*) [➡ CARRY OUT AN ACTION; 269] **5** *v* **manage**, operate, conduct, supervise, take charge of, run, carry out [➡ USE; 467] **6** *v* **trade in**, sell, buy, deal in, import, export, market [➡ SELL; 441]

handlebar mustache *n* [➡ FACIAL HAIR; 489]

handlebars *part of* **bike** [➡ BIKES, CARS, AND CARRIAGES; 1149]

handler *n* **trainer**, coach, manager, supervisor [➡ EDUCATORS; 840]

handling *n* **treatment**, management, conduct, supervision, control, hold, usage, use [➡ USE; 467]

hand-me-down *adj* **secondhand**, castoff, recycled, used, worn [➡ OLD, OLD-FASHIONED; 167] *Opposite*: brand-new

hand on *v* [➡ BEQUEATH AND BEQUESTS; 432]

hand out *v* **dispense**, distribute, administer, give away, give out, pass out, donate, award [➡ DISPENSE, RATION, AND DISTRIBUTE; 434] *Opposite*: take in

handout **1** *n* **windfall**, bonus, gift, donation, charity, contribution, gratuity, free sample, giveaway (*informal*), freebie (*informal*) [➡ GIFTS; 438] **2** *n* **document**, leaflet, brochure, pamphlet, booklet, flier, handbill, press release, press kit, advertisement, fact sheet (*UK*) [➡ ADVERTISING AND PUBLICITY; 604]

hand over *v* **give up**, tender, surrender, entrust, relinquish, cede, give away, renounce, devolve, extradite, deliver, abdicate, assign, transfer, convey, confer (*formal*), bestow (*formal*) [➡ PROFFER AND HAND OVER; 431] *Opposite*: withhold

handover *n* **delivery**, abdication, assignment, conferral, bestowal, transfer, transference, conveyance, surrender, devolution, extradition [➡ EXCHANGE AND INTERCHANGE; 448]

hand over fist *adv* **in large amounts**, copiously, prolifically, profusely, generously, freely, rapidly, quickly, easily [➡ MANY, MUCH, LARGE AMOUNT; 117] *Opposite*: gradually

handpicked *adj* **select**, elite, exclusive, finest, top-quality, crack, chosen [➡ POPULAR AND WANTED; 220] *Opposite*: run-of-the-mill

hand puppet *type of* **toy** [➡ TOYS; 880]

handrail *n* **banister**, rail, railing, guardrail, balustrade, guide rail [➡ STICKS, POLES, AND WEDGES; 1254]

hand round (*UK*) *v* [➡ DISPENSE, RATION, AND DISTRIBUTE; 434]

hands down *adv* **easily**, decisively, unquestionably, safely, clearly, unmistakably, incontrovertibly, indubitably (*formal*) [➡ CERTAIN; 174] *Opposite*: questionably

handset *n* **receiver**, earpiece, mouthpiece, phone, telephone [➡ AUDIO EQUIPMENT; 1139]

handshake *n* **handclasp**, grasp, greeting, grip, shake [➡ PHYSICAL CONTACT AS COMMUNICATION; 655]

hands-off *adj* **detached**, remote, distant, non-interventionist, laissez-faire, uninvolved, laid-back (*informal*) [➡ NEUTRALITY AND INDIFFERENCE; 553] *Opposite*: hands-on

handsome **1** *adj* **good-looking**, fine, attractive, striking, beautiful, gorgeous, fetching [➡ PEOPLE'S PHYSICAL APPEARANCE; 475] *Opposite*: ugly **2** *adj* **generous**, substantial, sizable, attractive, liberal, considerable, abundant, ample, princely [➡ MANY, MUCH, LARGE AMOUNT; 117] *Opposite*: ungenerous

See Compare and Contrast at **good-looking**.

handsomely *adv* **generously**, substantially, sizably, attractively, well, liberally, considerably, abundantly, amply [➡ MANY, MUCH, LARGE AMOUNT; 117] *Opposite*: ungenerously

hands-on *adj* **practical**, active, applied, proactive, energetic, direct [➡ ENERGY AND ENTHUSIASM; 496] *Opposite*: hands-off

handspring *n* **somersault**, cartwheel, flip, flip-flop, vault [➡ FIDGET AND FROLIC; 311]

hand-to-hand *adj* **unarmed**, close-range, face-to-face, direct, bareknuckle, head-on [➡ CLOSENESS; 159]

handwork *n* **handiwork**, handicraft, skill, art, craft [➡ CRAFTS AND CARVING; 355]

handwriting *n* **script**, writing, calligraphy, penmanship, scrawl, scribble, hand [➡ WRITING; 583]

handy **1** *adj* **convenient**, near, nearby, within reach, in easy reach, close, accessible, manageable, at hand

[➡ CLOSENESS; 159] *Opposite*: inconvenient **2** *adj* **useful**, helpful, practical, usable, well-designed, versatile, multipurpose, natty, neat, clever, nifty (*informal*) [➡ USEFULNESS; 199] *Opposite*: useless **3** *adj* **skillful**, dexterous, practical, clever, skilled, able, competent, proficient [➡ TALENTED AND SKILLFUL; 527] *Opposite*: awkward

hang **1** *v* **suspend**, dangle, droop, drape, hang down, swing, hang up, sling, hang out (*informal*), hook up (*informal*) [➡ POSITION SOMETHING; 325] *Opposite*: take down **2** *v* **lynch**, suspend by the neck, execute, put to death, swing (*informal*) [➡ KILL; 923] **3** *v* **droop**, flop, drape, sag, trail, nod, fold [➡ TAKE UP A NEW POSITION; 312] *Opposite*: stick up **4** *v* (*informal*) **relax**, chill out, hang around, hang loose, hang out [➡ LACK OF ACTIVITY OR MOTION; 342]

hangar *type of* **storage space** [➡ STORES AND STORAGE BUILDINGS; 1088]

hang around **1** *v* **wait**, linger, loiter, dawdle, remain, dally, stay, hover, pass time, haunt, frequent, bide, lie around (*informal*), hang out (*informal*) [➡ LACK OF ACTIVITY OR MOTION; 342] **2** *v* **associate**, mix, go out, keep company, spend time with, mess around (*informal*), hang out with (*informal*), consort (*formal*) [➡ ESTABLISHING RELATIONSHIPS WITH OTHERS; 974]

hang back *v* **hesitate**, drag your feet, drag your heels, linger, drop behind, drop back, lag behind, fall back, lag [➡ MOVE SLOWLY; 314] *Opposite*: forge ahead

hangdog *adj* **guilty**, dejected, furtive, intimidated, sheepish, humiliated, defeated, shamefaced, wretched, downcast, miserable [➡ EMBARRASSMENT AND HUMILIATION; 542] *Opposite*: chirpy (*informal*)

hang down *v* **sag**, dangle, droop, swing, hang, flop, nod, trail, drape [➡ TAKE UP A NEW POSITION; 312] *Opposite*: stick up

hanger *n* **coat hanger**, hook, peg, support, nail, knob [➡ SUPPORTS AND BASES; 1255]

hanger-on *n* **follower**, sycophant, disciple, proselyte, associate, worshiper, groupie (*informal*) [➡ DEVOTEES AND ADDICTED PEOPLE; 556]

hang fire *v* [➡ SHIRK AND DELAY; 273]

hang glider *type of* **civil aircraft** [➡ AIRCRAFT; 1148]

hanging **1** *n* **execution**, lynching, killing [➡ CAUSES OF DEATH; 921] **2** *n* **wall hanging**, tapestry, carpet, drape, drapery, swag, curtain [➡ FURNISHING AND HOUSEHOLD LINENS; 860]

hang loose (*informal*) *v* [➡ LACK OF ACTIVITY OR MOTION; 342]

hangnail *part of* **arm or hand** [➡ PARTS OF THE BODY: ARM AND HAND; 695]

hang on **1** *v* **grip**, grasp, clutch, cling, hold on, keep a hold on, latch on [➡ CONTACT: HOLD; 411] *Opposite*: let go **2** *v* **persevere**, keep it up, stick with it, stick it out, hold on, cling on, persist, see it through, hang in (*informal*) [➡ CONTINUE AN ACTION; 262] *Opposite*: give up **3** *v* **depend on**, hinge on, follow from, turn on, rely on [➡ RECIPROCITY AND INTERDEPENDENCE; 147] **4** *v* **wait**, linger, stay, hold on, remain, persevere, hang around, loiter, stick around (*informal*) [➡ LACK OF ACTIVITY OR MOTION; 342] *Opposite*: leave

hang out **1** *v* **suspend**, dangle, drape, swing, hang up, display, hang, sling, hook up (*informal*) [➡ POSITION SOMETHING;

325] *Opposite*: take down **2** *v* (*informal*) **spend time**, loiter, hang around, frequent, haunt, stay [➡ LACK OF ACTIVITY OR MOTION; 342] **3** *v* (*informal*) **relax**, hang around, loll around, mess around (*informal*), chill out (*slang*) [➡ LACK OF ACTIVITY OR MOTION; 342] **4** *v* (*informal*) **associate**, mix, be friendly, hang around, interact, keep company, go around, mess around (*informal*), consort (*formal*) [➡ ESTABLISHING RELATIONSHIPS WITH OTHERS; 974]

hangout (*informal*) *n* **haunt**, den, retreat, meeting place, lair (*informal*), hidey-hole (*informal*), stamping ground (*informal*) [➡ PUBLIC BUILDINGS AND MEETING PLACES; 1081]

hangover *n* **relic**, leftover, remnant, aftermath, aftereffect, inheritance, legacy [➡ RESULTS AND OUTCOMES; 83]

hang together *v* **make sense**, add up, hold up, tell the complete story, give the full picture, wash (*informal*), cohere (*formal*) [➡ MEAN SOMETHING; 61] *Opposite*: fall apart

hang up **1** *v* **suspend**, dangle, droop, drape, swing, sling, hang out (*informal*), hook up (*informal*) [➡ POSITION SOMETHING; 325] *Opposite*: take down **2** *v* **put the phone down**, disconnect, get off the phone, replace the receiver, end the conversation, ring off (*UK*) [➡ TELEPHONE, PAGE, AND TEXT; 681] *Opposite*: pick up

hang-up (*informal*) *n* **anxiety**, worry, complex, inhibition, fixation, obsession, phobia, fear, problem, neurosis (*dated*) [➡ PSYCHOLOGY AND THE MIND; 769]

hank *n* **coil**, length, reel, skein, ball, bundle [➡ AMOUNTS OF SOLID OR SEMISOLID; 115]

hanker *v* **yearn**, crave, desire, long, ache, hunger, thirst, have a yen, obsess [➡ DESIRE AND WANT; 579]

hanker after *v* [➡ DESIRE AND WANT; 579]

hankering *n* **yearning**, craving, longing, desire, ache, hunger, thirst, yen, urge [➡ DESIRE AND WANT; 579] *Opposite*: dislike

haphazard *adj* **random**, chaotic, hit-or-miss, slapdash, disorganized, messy, jumbled, arbitrary, indiscriminate, unsystematic, irregular, unselective, unplanned, careless, all over the place (*informal*) [➡ DISORDER AND CHAOS; 245] *Opposite*: systematic

haphazardness *n* [➡ DISORDER AND CHAOS; 245]

hapless *adj* **unfortunate**, unlucky, luckless, ill-fated, wretched, miserable, ill-starred, star-crossed, doomed [➡ BAD LUCK AND UNLUCKY; 784] *Opposite*: fortunate

haplessness *n* **misfortune**, bad luck, ill fortune, wretchedness, misery, doom [➡ BAD LUCK AND UNLUCKY; 784] *Opposite*: luck

happen *v* **occur**, take place, go on, come about, ensue, turn out, transpire, materialize, chance, crop up (*informal*), go down (*slang*), come to pass (*archaic or literary*) [➡ HAPPEN; 27]

happenchance *n* [➡ CHANCE EVENTS; 36]

happening **1** *n* **occurrence**, event, incident, episode, phenomenon, experience [➡ EVENTS AND OCCURRENCES; 35] **2** *adj* (*informal*) **fashionable**, stylish, in, up-to-the-minute, edgy, bang up-to-date, trendy (*informal*) [➡ NEW, MODERN; 166] *Opposite*: old-fashioned

happen on v [➡ FIND; 463]

happenstance n **accident**, coincidence, chance, happenchance, fluke (*informal*) [➡ CHANCE EVENTS; 36]

happen upon v [➡ FIND; 463]

happily 1 adv **luckily**, fortunately, thankfully, as good luck would have it, opportunely, well, favorably [➡ LUCK; 783] *Opposite*: sadly 2 adv **gladly**, willingly, cheerfully, freely, voluntarily, unreservedly, enthusiastically, eagerly [➡ WITH ENTHUSIASM; 286] *Opposite*: unwillingly 3 adv **cheerfully**, contentedly, joyfully, gleefully, blissfully, merrily, gladly [➡ PLEASURE, EXCITEMENT, AND ELATION; 534] *Opposite*: sadly

happiness n **contentment**, pleasure, gladness, cheerfulness, joy, glee, bliss, delight, exhilaration, ecstasy [➡ PLEASURE, EXCITEMENT, AND ELATION; 534] *Opposite*: sadness

happy 1 adj **content**, contented, pleased, glad, joyful, cheerful, excited, blissful, exultant, ecstatic, delighted, cheery, jovial, in high spirits, on top of the world, pleased, pleased as punch, on cloud nine (*informal*), over the moon (*UK informal*) [➡ PLEASURE, EXCITEMENT, AND ELATION; 534] *Opposite*: sad 2 adj **lucky**, fortunate, favorable, opportune [➡ LUCK; 783] *Opposite*: unlucky 3 adj (*informal*) [➡ UNDER THE INFLUENCE OF DRUGS OR ALCOHOL; 741]

happy-go-lucky adj **carefree**, optimistic, easygoing, lighthearted, nonchalant, unconcerned, blithe (*literary*) [➡ CHEERFULNESS OF OUTLOOK; 503] *Opposite*: anxious

hara-kiri n [➡ CAUSES OF DEATH; 921]

harangue 1 v **berate**, lecture, criticize, rant, address, sermonize, scold, perorate (*formal*) [➡ ACCUSE, BLAME, AND CRITICIZE; 641] 2 n **tirade**, diatribe, criticism, lecture, rant, address, scolding, jeremiad (*formal*) [➡ CRITICISMS AND ANGRY OUTBURSTS; 50]

harass v **annoy**, pester, bother, pursue, worry, badger, hound, nag, bully, trouble, stress, harry, hassle (*informal*) [➡ ANGER AND ANNOY; 569]

harassed 1 adj **stressed**, under pressure, distraught, beleaguered, worried, strained, harried, agitated, hassled (*informal*) [➡ SADNESS, DISTRESS, AND DESPAIR; 539] *Opposite*: relaxed 2 adj **put upon**, pressured, persecuted, singled out, discriminated against, teased [➡ IN TROUBLE AND DISADVANTAGED; 73]

harassment n **pestering**, nuisance, annoyance, irritation, persecution, provocation, bother, agitation [➡ MALICIOUS ACTIONS OR BEHAVIOR; 296]

harbinger n **forerunner**, herald, portent, omen, indication [➡ INDICATIONS, SIGNS, AND WARNINGS; 68]

harbor 1 n **port**, dock, anchorage, waterfront, wharf, quay, marina, haven (*literary*) [➡ THE SEAS, OCEANS, AND SHORES; 1041] 2 v **believe**, embrace, entertain, hold, cherish [➡ THINK AND REFLECT; 743] 3 v **protect**, shelter, conceal, hide, give refuge to [➡ PREVENT CONTACT OR ATTACK; 419]

hard 1 adj **firm**, stiff, rigid, solid, tough, unbreakable, durable [➡ RIGID AND HARD; 1211] *Opposite*: soft 2 adj **awkward**, difficult, problematical, tricky, thorny, tough, demanding, grueling, testing, challenging, complex, arduous, troublesome, laborious, strenuous [➡ DIFFICULTY AND COMPLEXITY; 242] *Opposite*: easy 3 adj **cruel**, callous, harsh, severe, unkind, tough, brutal, thick-skinned, strict, remorseless,

pitiless [➡ SELFISH AND UNKIND; 505] *Opposite*: kind 4 adj **intense**, fast, violent, brutal, fierce, powerful, relentless, remorseless [➡ DIFFICULTY AND COMPLEXITY; 242] *Opposite*: gentle 5 adv **intensely**, fast, violently, fiercely, powerfully, rigorously, relentlessly, remorselessly [➡ DIFFICULTY AND COMPLEXITY; 242] *Opposite*: gently

Compare and Contrast: *hard, difficult, strenuous, tough, arduous, laborious*

CORE MEANING: requiring effort or exertion

hard requiring mental or physical effort or exertion to do or achieve; *difficult* requiring considerable planning or effort to accomplish; *strenuous* requiring physical effort, energy, stamina, or strength; *tough* needing great effort to deal with; *arduous* requiring hard work or continuous physical effort; *laborious* requiring unwelcome, often tedious, effort and exertion.

hard as nails adj [➡ SELFISH AND UNKIND; 505]

hard-bitten adj **tough**, hardened, cynical, stubborn, uncompromising, casehardened, hard-edged, hard-boiled (*informal*), hard-nosed (*informal*) [➡ SELFISH AND UNKIND; 505]

hard-boiled (*informal*) adj **unsentimental**, hardened, tough, cynical, unfeeling, hard-edged, casehardened [➡ SELFISH AND UNKIND; 505] *Opposite*: soft-boiled

hard candy type of **confectionery** [➡ CONFECTIONERY; 1182]

hardcore type of **dance music** [➡ MUSIC, SONGS, AND SINGING; 907]

hard-core adj **uncompromising**, committed, dedicated, firm, staunch, faithful, unshakable, intransigent, diehard, obstinate [➡ UNWILLINGNESS AND STUBBORNNESS; 564]

hard disk type of **hardware** [➡ COMPUTERS AND COMPUTING; 1127]

harden 1 v **solidify**, set, freeze, consolidate, settle, coagulate, congeal [➡ HARDEN, CONGEAL, AND DRY; 387] *Opposite*: soften 2 v **toughen**, strengthen, reinforce, fortify, stabilize [➡ IMPROVE STRENGTH AND DURABILITY; 378] *Opposite*: weaken

hardened adj **hard-bitten**, toughened, tough, cynical, unsentimental, casehardened, hard-edged, hard-boiled (*informal*) [➡ SELFISH AND UNKIND; 505]

hardened criminal n [➡ CRIMINALS; 821]

hard feelings n [➡ ANTAGONISM; 552]

hard graft (*UK*) n [➡ HARD WORK OR EFFORT; 298]

hardhat type of **headgear** [➡ ACCESSORIES, MILLINERY, AND LINGERIE; 867]

hardheaded adj **shrewd**, sharp, practical, no-nonsense, tough, businesslike, logical, pragmatic [➡ POSITIVE INTELLECTUAL CHARACTERISTICS; 524] *Opposite*: soft

hardhearted adj **callous**, cold, hard, insensitive, unfeeling, unsympathetic, unemotional, uncaring, pitiless, stony [➡ SELFISH AND UNKIND; 505] *Opposite*: kind

hardheartedness n **callousness**, coldness, insensitivity, pitilessness, stoniness, hardness, heartlessness [➡ SELFISH AND UNKIND; 505] *Opposite*: kindness

hard-hitting adj [➡ STRENGTH; 201]

hardiness *n* **toughness**, hardihood, stamina, durability, robustness, resilience, endurance [➡STRENGTH; 201] *Opposite*: frailty

hard labor *n* [➡HARD WORK OR EFFORT; 298]

hardline *adj* **uncompromising**, inflexible, rigid, extreme, radical, fanatical, strong, hard-nosed (*informal*) [➡UNWILL-INGNESS AND STUBBORNNESS; 564]

hardliner *n* [➡GRUMPY AND NEGATIVE PEOPLE; 953]

hardly *adv* **barely**, only just, scarcely, by a hair's breadth, by the skin of your teeth, by a whisker [➡TO A CERTAIN EXTENT; 136]

hardly any *pron* [➡FEW, LITTLE, SMALL AMOUNT; 120]

hardly ever *adv* [➡NEVER AND INFREQUENCY; 97]

hardness *n* **rigidity**, stiffness, firmness, inflexibility, solidity, resistance, toughness [➡RIGID AND HARD; 1211] *Opposite*: softness

hard-nosed (*informal*) *adj* [➡SELFISH AND UNKIND; 505]

hard-pressed *adj* [➡IN TROUBLE AND DISADVANTAGED; 73]

hardship *n* **adversity**, privation, lack, poverty, destitution, need, want, suffering, difficulty [➡POVERTY AND POOR; 892] *Opposite*: comfort

hard taskmaster *n* [➡GRUMPY AND NEGATIVE PEOPLE; 953]

hard times *n* [➡DIFFICULT SITUATIONS; 72]

hard to follow *adj* [➡DIFFICULTY AND COMPLEXITY; 242]

hard to please *adj* [➡DIFFICULT TO PLEASE; 515]

hard up (*informal*) *adj* **short of money**, poor, impoverished, in a bad way, impecunious, badly off, strapped for cash (*informal*), broke (*informal*), strapped (*informal*) [➡POVERTY AND POOR; 892] *Opposite*: well-off

hardware *n* **equipment**, apparatus, tackle, gear, kit [➡DEVICES; 1115]

hardware store *type of* **retail outlet** [➡RETAIL OUTLETS; 1083]

hard-wearing *adj* **durable**, strong, resilient, indestructible, heavy-duty, weatherproof, long-lasting, tough [➡STRENGTH; 201]

hard work *n* [➡HARD WORK OR EFFORT; 298]

hard-working *adj* [➡HARD-WORKING AND COMMITTED; 500]

hardy *adj* **robust**, resilient, enduring, tough, strong, resistant [➡STRENGTH; 201] *Opposite*: frail

hare 1 *type of* **small mammal** [➡SMALL MAMMALS; 990] 2 *type of* **meat** [➡TYPES AND CUTS OF MEAT; 1177]

harem pants *type of* **pants** [➡GARMENTS AND OUTFITS; 865]

haricot *type of* **pulse** [➡PEAS AND BEANS; 1189]

hark (*literary or humorous*) *v* **listen to**, hear, pay attention to, heed [➡PAY ATTENTION; 765]

hark back *v* **go back to**, revisit, recall, relive, revive, return to [➡REMIND; 747]

harm 1 *n* **damage**, hurt, injury, destruction, mal-

treatment, detriment, impairment [➡DESTRUCTION AND DEMO-LITION; 359] *Opposite*: help 2 *v* **hurt**, damage, spoil, injure, impair, cause detriment, wound [➡WOUND A PERSON OR ANIMAL; 383] *Opposite*: help

Compare and Contrast: *harm, damage, **hurt**, injure, wound*

CORE MEANING: to weaken or impair something or somebody

harm to cause physical or mental impairment or deterioration; *damage* to cause physical deterioration that makes an object less useful, valuable, or able to function, or to impair something abstract such as a chance or somebody's reputation; *hurt* to cause physical or mental pain or harm to people and animals; *injure* to cause physical harm to a person or animal, usually causing at least a temporary loss of function or use, or to impair something abstract such as somebody's reputation or pride; *wound* to inflict physical harm on somebody, especially as a result of the use of a weapon, a violent incident, or a serious accident, or to upset or offend somebody.

harmattan *type of* **wind** [➡WINDY AND STORMY WEATHER; 1053]

harmed *adj* **injured**, damaged, hurt, wounded, impaired, abused, affected, maltreated [➡INJURED; 742] *Opposite*: untouched

harmful *adj* **damaging**, injurious, destructive, detrimental, dangerous, unsafe, risky, toxic, poisonous [➡DANGEROUS; 236] *Opposite*: harmless

harmless 1 *adj* **inoffensive**, innocuous, innocent, meaningless, bland, mild, anodyne (*literary*) [➡MORALLY GOOD; 774] *Opposite*: offensive 2 *adj* **safe**, risk-free, undamaging, nontoxic, unhazardous, undisruptive, sound [➡SAFE AND SAFETY; 191] *Opposite*: harmful

harmlessness 1 *n* **inoffensiveness**, naiveté, innocence, wholesomeness, blandness [➡MORALLY GOOD; 774] *Opposite*: offensiveness 2 *n* **innocuousness**, safety, mildness, nontoxicity [➡SAFE AND SAFETY; 191]

harmonic *adj* [➡SOFT, LOW, OR PLEASANT SOUNDS; 1265]

harmonica *type of* **wind instrument** [➡MUSICAL INSTRUMENTS; 910]

harmonious 1 *adj* **musical**, melodious, tuneful, pleasant-sounding, sweet, pleasant, symphonic [➡SOFT, LOW, OR PLEASANT SOUNDS; 1265] *Opposite*: discordant 2 *adj* **agreeable**, congruous, balanced, matching, corresponding, concordant, consonant (*formal*), congruent (*formal*) [➡HARMONY; 155] *Opposite*: discordant 3 *adj* **friendly**, cordial, affable, congenial, agreeable, amicable, congenial [➡RELATIONSHIP TO ANOTHER; 973] *Opposite*: hostile

harmoniously 1 *adv* **musically**, tunefully, melodiously, sweetly, pleasantly, symphonically [➡SOFT, LOW, OR PLEASANT SOUNDS; 1265] *Opposite*: discordantly 2 *adv* **amicably**, cordially, agreeably, pleasantly, affably, congenially [➡RELATIONSHIP TO ANOTHER; 973] *Opposite*: acrimoniously

harmoniousness *n* [➡SOFT, LOW, OR PLEASANT SOUNDS; 1265]

harmonize 1 *v* **go with**, match, blend, complement, tone, correspond [➡HARMONY; 155] *Opposite*: jar 2 *v* **bring into line**, synchronize, standardize, make uniform, make conform, regularize, make proportionate, balance [➡ARRANGE AND CREATE ORDER; 357]

harmonized *adj* in line, consistent, coordinated, matched, in step, coherent, in time, in agreement [➡HARMONY; 155] *Opposite:* uncoordinated

harmonizing *adj* consistent, toning, matching, agreeing, coordinating, harmonious, complementary, congruent (*formal*) [➡HARMONY; 155] *Opposite:* inconsistent

harmony *n* agreement, accord, concord, synchronization, congruence, coordination, coherence [➡HARMONY; 155] *Opposite:* discord

harness 1 *v* tie together, strap up, yoke, bind, attach, connect, join, hitch, couple [➡FASTEN, LINK, AND JOIN; 408] *Opposite:* separate 2 *v* control, exploit, employ, channel, utilize, use [➡USE; 467]

harp *type of* stringed instrument [➡MUSICAL INSTRUMENTS; 910]

harp on *v* complain, go on, keep on, whine, grumble, dwell on, repeat, nag, moan (*informal*), rag (*dated*) [➡COMPLAIN AND NAG; 686]

harpoon *type of* projectile [➡PROJECTILES; 1159]

harpsichord *type of* keyboard [➡MUSICAL INSTRUMENTS; 910]

harried *adj* harassed, put upon, bothered, agitated, stressed, distraught, under pressure, beleaguered, pressured, hassled (*informal*) [➡SADNESS, DISTRESS, AND DESPAIR; 539] *Opposite:* calm

harrowing *adj* disturbing, upsetting, traumatic, distressing, frightening, tormenting, vexing, dreadful, worrying, stressful, scary (*informal*) [➡EMOTIONALLY UNPLEASANT AND UPSETTING; 227] *Opposite:* relaxing

harry *v* harass, bother, pester, badger, annoy, irritate, worry, distress, stress, agitate, hound, bully, pursue, hassle (*informal*), aggravate (*informal*) [➡ANGER AND ANNOY; 569]

harsh 1 *adj* severe, bleak, austere, inhospitable, stark, bitter [➡PHYSICALLY UNPLEASANT; 226] *Opposite:* mild 2 *adj* cruel, unkind, unsympathetic, insensitive, callous, bitter, critical [➡SELFISH AND UNKIND; 505] *Opposite:* kind 3 *adj* punitive, exacting, strict, stern, severe, unforgiving, tough [➡PHYSICALLY UNPLEASANT; 226] *Opposite:* lenient 4 *adj* discordant, loud, blaring, raucous, jangly, strident, piercing, penetrating [➡LOUD, HIGH, OR UNPLEASANT SOUNDS; 1266] *Opposite:* pleasant

harsh conditions *n* [➡DIFFICULT SITUATIONS; 72]

harshness 1 *n* severity, austerity, ruggedness, bleakness, starkness, roughness [➡PHYSICALLY UNPLEASANT; 226] *Opposite:* gentleness 2 *n* callousness, cruelty, ruthlessness, strictness, severity, unkindness, insensitivity [➡SELFISH AND UNKIND; 505] *Opposite:* gentleness

hart *type of* male animal [➡MALE OR FEMALE ANIMALS; 978]

harvest 1 *n* crop, yield, produce, return, fruitage, ingathering [➡INCOME; 460] 2 *v* reap, gather, collect, bring in, pick, garner, mow, ingather [➡GET; 420]

harvestman *type of* arachnid [➡ARACHNIDS; 1018]

harvest mite *type of* parasitic insect [➡PARASITES; 1017]

hash *v* chop, cut up, grind, shred, mince, dice [➡COOKING AND FOOD PREPARATION; 353]

hash browns *type of* processed potato [➡FRUIT AND VEGETABLES; 1176]

hasp *n* [➡FASTENERS, LINKS, AND NETWORKS; 1247]

hassle (*informal*) 1 *n* bother, annoyance, irritation, disturbance, stress, trouble, difficulty, agitation, pain (*informal*) [➡NUISANCES; 253] 2 *v* harass, irritate, annoy, bother, get on your nerves, pester, disturb, stress, agitate, badger, worry, trouble, aggravate (*informal*) [➡ANGER AND ANNOY; 569] *Opposite:* leave alone

hassled (*informal*) *adj* [➡CONFUSION, ANXIETY, AND WORRY; 540]

hassle-free (*informal*) *adj* [➡EASE AND SIMPLICITY; 200]

hassock *n* [➡FURNITURE; 858]

hasta la vista (*informal*) *interj* [➡GREETINGS, FAREWELLS, AND SALUTATIONS; 659]

haste *n* speed, swiftness, rapidity, alacrity, rush, hurriedness, quickness [➡SPEED; 102] *Opposite:* slowness

hasten *v* hurry, make haste, rush, speed up, speed, accelerate, move along, race [➡MOVE FAST; 313]

hastily *adv* hurriedly, quickly, fast, at speed, speedily, in a hurry, at a fast pace, rapidly [➡HAPPENING QUICKLY; 104] *Opposite:* slowly

hastiness *n* impulsiveness, impetuosity, rashness, thoughtlessness, carelessness [➡LACK OF COMMITMENT AND UNRELIABILITY; 509] *Opposite:* carefulness

hasty *adj* quick, speedy, hurried, swift, rapid, rushed, fast [➡MOVING QUICKLY; 103] *Opposite:* slow

hat 1 *type of* headgear [➡ACCESSORIES, MILLINERY, AND LINGERIE; 867] 2 *type of* accessory [➡ACCESSORIES, MILLINERY, AND LINGERIE; 867]

hatch 1 *v* give forth, emerge, produce, break open, come out [➡ENGENDER; 350] 2 *v* devise, come up with, originate, formulate, plan, scheme [➡DEVELOP THEORIES AND REASON; 744] 3 *v* shade, mark, crisscross, crosshatch, highlight [➡CREATE IMAGES; 356]

hatchback *type of* car [➡BIKES, CARS, AND CARRIAGES; 1149]

hatchet *type of* cutting tool [➡CUTTING TOOLS; 1120]

hatchet man (*slang*) *n* [➡VILLAINS AND THUGS; 947]

hate 1 *v* detest, loathe, dislike, despise, abhor (*formal*) [➡DISLIKE AND HATE; 577] *Opposite:* love 2 *n* hatred, abhorrence, detestation, odium, revulsion, disgust, dislike, animosity, distaste, loathing, aversion (*formal*) [➡DISLIKE AND HATE; 577] *Opposite:* love

See Compare and Contrast at **dislike**.

hated *adj* loathed, detested, despicable, despised, unloved, unpopular, abhorrent (*formal*) [➡UNPOPULAR AND UNWANTED; 258] *Opposite:* loved

hateful *adj* horrible, detestable, vile, odious, unbearable, intolerable, insufferable, revolting, repulsive, disgusting, terrible [➡DISGUSTING AND REPULSIVE; 230] *Opposite:* lovable

hatred *n* hate, abhorrence, detestation, loathing, odium, revulsion, disgust, animosity, dislike, aversion (*formal*) [➡DISLIKE AND HATE; 577] *Opposite:* love

See Compare and Contrast at **dislike**.

hat stand *n* [➡FURNITURE; 858]

haughtily *adv* **proudly**, arrogantly, conceitedly, self-importantly, condescendingly, snootily (*informal*) [➡AFFECTATION, SELF-SATISFACTION, AND SNOBBISHNESS; 507] *Opposite*: modestly

haughtiness *n* **arrogance**, conceit, pride, self-importance, overconfidence, superiority, hauteur, snootiness (*informal*) [➡AFFECTATION, SELF-SATISFACTION, AND SNOBBISHNESS; 507] *Opposite*: modesty

haughty *adj* **supercilious**, proud, self-important, superior, high and mighty, self-aggrandizing, arrogant, conceited, condescending, snooty (*informal*), stuck-up (*informal*) [➡AFFECTATION, SELF-SATISFACTION, AND SNOBBISHNESS; 507] *Opposite*: humble

haul *v* **tow**, drag, pull, lug, tug, heave [➡PUSH, PULL, AND SLIDE; 335] *Opposite*: shove

See Compare and Contrast at **pull**.

haul over the coals *v* **rebuke**, scold, reprimand, take to task, tell off (*informal*), bawl out (*informal*), chew out (*informal*), excoriate (*formal*), castigate (*formal*) [➡ACCUSE, BLAME, AND CRITICIZE; 641]

haunch 1 *n* **upper leg**, hip, buttock, thigh, loin, hunkers (*dated informal*) [➡PARTS OF THE BODY: LEG AND FOOT; 694] 2 *n* **loin**, side, flank, hindquarter, thigh, rump [➡PARTS OF THE BODY: TORSO; 693]

haunt 1 *v* **trouble**, disturb, worry, bother, preoccupy, plague, discomfit (*formal*) [➡ANGER AND ANNOY; 569] *Opposite*: soothe 2 *v* **walk**, roam, frequent, prowl, inhabit, skulk in, lurk in, visit [➡EXIST IN A PLACE; 19] *Opposite*: leave 3 *n* **meeting place**, stomping ground, rendezvous, stamping ground (*informal*), hangout (*informal*) [➡PUBLIC BUILDINGS AND MEETING PLACES; 1081]

haunted 1 *adj* **eerie**, ghostly, weird, sinister, spooky (*informal*), creepy (*informal*) [➡FRIGHTENING; 231] 2 *adj* **troubled**, preoccupied, worried, disturbed, anxious, obsessed, terrified, frightened, unnerved [➡CONFUSION, ANXIETY, AND WORRY; 540] *Opposite*: relaxed

haunting *adj* **lingering**, melancholy, poignant, evocative, moving, unforgettable, memorable, lasting, recurring [➡PERMANENCE: WITHOUT END; 94] *Opposite*: forgettable

hauteur *n* **haughtiness**, arrogance, superiority, loftiness, snobbishness, self-importance, pride, superciliousness [➡AFFECTATION, SELF-SATISFACTION, AND SNOBBISHNESS; 507] *Opposite*: humility

haut monde *n* **elite**, crème de la crème, high society, rich and famous, aristocracy, upper class, upper crust (*informal*), top brass (*informal*), jet set (*informal*), in-crowd (*informal*) [➡IMPORTANT OR FAMOUS PEOPLE; 893] *Opposite*: masses

have 1 *v* **possess**, own, boast, exhibit, enjoy [➡POSSESS; 444] *Opposite*: lack 2 *v* **must**, need, ought to, should, require, be necessary [➡NEED AND REQUIRE; 464] 3 *v* **receive**, obtain, grasp, get, gain, come up with, take [➡GET; 420] *Opposite*: lose 4 *v* **consume**, take, partake, eat, drink, devour [➡EAT AND NOT EAT; 710] *Opposite*: abstain 5 *v* **think of**, come up with, devise, develop, entertain, nurse [➡DEVELOP THEORIES AND REASON; 744] 6 *v* **experience**, undergo, partake, engage in, take part in, enjoy [➡EXPERIENCE AND ENCOUNTER; 582] 7 *v* **be affected by**, suffer from, suffer with, be afflicted with, be sick with, be laid up with [➡BECOME SICK, TREAT, AND RECOVER; 728] 8 *v* **organize**, carry out, arrange, hold, give, put together, plan [➡CAUSE TO HAPPEN; 31] 9 *v* **tolerate**, put up with, allow, permit, endure, suffer [➡TOLERATE AND ENDURE; 766] 10 *v* **produce**, bear, give birth to, bring forth [➡ENGENDER; 350]

have a brush with *v* [➡EXPERIENCE AND ENCOUNTER; 582]

have a conniption (*informal*) *v* [➡GIVING VENT TO EMOTIONS; 679]

have a crack (*informal*) *v* [➡ATTEMPT AN ACTION; 261]

have a crush on (*informal*) *v* [➡LIKE, LOVE, VALUE, AND ENJOY; 578]

have a fit (*informal*) *v* [➡GIVING VENT TO EMOTIONS; 679]

have a go (*informal*) *v* [➡ATTEMPT AN ACTION; 261]

have a hand in *v* **partake in**, play a part in, play a role in, participate, be part of, contribute to, be involved in, make a contribution to, have a share in [➡PARTICIPATE; 292]

have a high opinion of *v* [➡LIKE, LOVE, VALUE, AND ENJOY; 578]

have a high regard for *v* [➡LIKE, LOVE, VALUE, AND ENJOY; 578]

have a horror of *v* **fear**, dread, be frightened of, be afraid of, be scared of, be terrified of [➡FEARS AND PHOBIAS; 554]

have a joke with *v* [➡JOKES AND TEASING; 674]

have a lark (*UK*) *v* [➡JOKES AND TEASING; 674]

have a laugh *v* [➡JOKES AND TEASING; 674]

have a look at *v* [➡LOOKING AND LOOKS; 700]

have a look-see *v* [➡LOOKING AND LOOKS; 700]

have a shot *v* [➡ATTEMPT AN ACTION; 261]

have a soft spot for *v* [➡LIKE, LOVE, VALUE, AND ENJOY; 578]

have a stab (*informal*) *v* [➡ATTEMPT AN ACTION; 261]

have a weakness for *v* [➡LIKE, LOVE, VALUE, AND ENJOY; 578]

have a yen for *v* [➡DESIRE AND WANT; 579]

have down pat *v* [➡KNOWLEDGE AND WISDOM; 558]

have forty winks (*informal*) *v* [➡SLEEP AND DREAM; 723]

have hysterics (*informal*) *v* [➡LAUGHTER; 649]

have in mind *v* **propose**, suggest, be thinking of, come up with, intend, mean [➡DREAM, IMAGINE, AND FANTASIZE; 749]

have it in for *v* **persecute**, harass, bully, victimize, target, pick on [➡DISLIKE AND HATE; 577] *Opposite*: favor

have kittens (*informal*) *v* [➡GIVING VENT TO EMOTIONS; 679]

have knowledge of *v* [➡KNOWLEDGE AND WISDOM; 558]

haven 1 *n* **refuge**, safe place, place of safety, sanctuary, shelter, asylum, retreat [➡SAFE BUILDINGS OR PLACES; 1093] 2 *n* (*literary*) **harbor**, port, anchorage, dock, port of call [➡THE SEAS, OCEANS, AND SHORES; 1041]

have need of *v* [➡ NEED AND REQUIRE; 464]

have-nots *n* **disadvantaged**, poor, deprived, underprivileged, underclass, unfortunates [➡ POOR PEOPLE; 896] *Opposite*: privileged

have off pat (*UK*) *v* [➡ KNOWLEDGE AND WISDOM; 558]

have on *v* **wear**, be dressed in, be clothed in, show off, flaunt, display, adorn, put on, cover, sport (*formal*) [➡ DRESS, WEAR, AND UNDRESS; 868]

have possession of *v* [➡ POSSESS; 444]

haversack *n* **rucksack**, backpack, pack, knapsack, shoulder bag, carryall, bag, duffel bag, tote bag, holdall (*UK*) [➡ CONTAINERS, RECEPTACLES, AND PACKAGING; 1245]

have second thoughts *v* **change your mind**, go back on, reconsider, think better of it, get cold feet, renege [➡ MAKE DECISIONS AND CHOICES; 752]

have to do with *v* **relate to**, concern, involve, be regarding, be in connection with, affect, deal with, touch on [➡ BE ABOUT SOMETHING; 62]

have your eye on *v* **want**, desire, aim for, be after, hanker, covet [➡ DESIRE AND WANT; 579]

havoc *n* **chaos**, destruction, disorder, turmoil, disaster, confusion, devastation, mayhem (*informal*) [➡ DISORDER AND CHAOS; 245] *Opposite*: order

Hawaii-Aleutian *type of* **time zone** [➡ TIMES OF DAY; 87]

Hawaiian guitar *type of* **stringed instrument** [➡ MUSICAL INSTRUMENTS; 910]

hawk 1 *type of* **bird of prey** [➡ BIRDS OF PREY; 998] **2** *v* **sell**, peddle, vend, deal, market, push (*slang*) [➡ SELL; 441] *Opposite*: buy

hawker *n* **dealer**, vendor, seller, marketer, salesperson, pusher (*slang*) [➡ SELLERS; 442] *Opposite*: client

hawk-eyed *adj* **eagle-eyed**, sharp-eyed, sharp-sighted, observant, perceptive, quick, alert [➡ SEE; 699] *Opposite*: unobservant

hawkish *adj* **aggressive**, belligerent, warmongering, warlike, militant, combative, pugnacious [➡ AGGRESSIVE AND BELLIGERENT; 518] *Opposite*: peaceable

hawk moth *type of* **moth** [➡ MOTHS AND BUTTERFLIES; 1015]

hawser *n* **cable**, rope, chain, towline, tow [➡ FASTENERS, LINKS, AND NETWORKS; 1247]

hawthorn 1 *type of* **shrub or bush** [➡ BUSHES AND SHRUBS; 1027] **2** *type of* **deciduous tree** [➡ DECIDUOUS TREES; 1028]

hay *n* **straw**, feed, fodder, dry feed, winter feed, silage, grass [➡ ANIMAL FEED; 1168]

hayloft *type of* **storage space** [➡ STORES AND STORAGE BUILDINGS; 1088]

hayrack *n* **rack**, trough, manger, feeder [➡ CONTAINERS, RECEPTACLES, AND PACKAGING; 1245]

haywire (*informal*) *adj* **wild**, out of order, erratic, nonfunctional, confused, fuddled, irrational, on the blink (*informal*) [➡ DISORDER AND CHAOS; 245] *Opposite*: functional

hazard 1 *n* **danger**, threat, risk, peril, menace, deathtrap (*informal*) [➡ DANGER; 235] *Opposite*: safeguard **2** *v* **suggest**, proffer, put forward, propose [➡ SUGGEST, HINT, AND COMMENT; 612] **3** *v* **risk**, take a chance, chance, gamble, venture, endanger, jeopardize, put at risk, imperil (*formal*) [➡ GAMBLE AND TAKE RISKS; 466] *Opposite*: protect

hazardous *adj* **dangerous**, unsafe, harmful, risky, lethal, perilous, menacing, precarious, threatening [➡ DANGEROUS; 236] *Opposite*: safe

hazardousness *n* [➡ DANGER; 235]

haze 1 *n* **mist**, fog, miasma, cloud, vapor, smog, smoke [➡ CLOUDY AND RAINY WEATHER; 1052] **2** *v* **become cloudy**, mist over, cloud over, darken [➡ CLOUDY AND RAINY WEATHER; 1052] *Opposite*: clear

hazel *type of* **brown** [➡ COLORS; 1224]

hazelnut *type of* **nut** [➡ NUTS; 1185]

hazily *adv* **indistinctly**, vaguely, dimly, fuzzily, imprecisely, unclearly, obscurely [➡ VAGUENESS; 243] *Opposite*: clearly

haziness 1 *n* **mistiness**, fogginess, cloudiness, obscurity, smokiness, dimness, fuzziness [➡ CLOUDY AND RAINY WEATHER; 1052] *Opposite*: clarity **2** *n* **confusion**, muddle, uncertainty, indistinctness, vagueness, obscurity [➡ VAGUENESS; 243] *Opposite*: clarity

hazy 1 *adj* **misty**, foggy, cloudy, obscure, blurred, out-of-focus, dim, smoky, fuzzy [➡ CLOUDY AND RAINY WEATHER; 1052] *Opposite*: clear **2** *adj* **unclear**, indistinct, muddled, confused, obscure, imprecise, vague [➡ VAGUENESS; 243] *Opposite*: distinct

head 1 *n* **skull**, cranium, dome, crown, nut (*informal*), bean (*slang*), noodle (*slang*), pate (*archaic or humorous*) [➡ PARTS OF THE BODY: HEAD; 692] **2** *n* **mind**, intelligence, intellect, sense, brain, brains, wit, gray matter (*informal*) [➡ POSITIVE INTELLECTUAL CHARACTERISTICS; 524] **3** *n* **boss**, leader, chief, president, controller, supervisor, master [➡ BOSSES AND MANAGEMENT; 965] **4** *n* **top**, peak, crown, promontory, apex, height, summit [➡ EXTREMITIES OF PHYSICAL OBJECTS; 1250] *Opposite*: base **5** *n* **introduction**, beginning, start, opening, heading, header [➡ BEGINNINGS; 53] *Opposite*: end **6** *n* (*UK*) [➡ EDUCATORS; 840] **7** *v* **come first**, lead, be first, precede, be foremost [➡ ACCOMPANY AND FOLLOW; 337] *Opposite*: follow **8** *v* **control**, rule, regulate, have control over, lead, supervise, command, be in charge, direct [➡ BE IN CHARGE; 270] *Opposite*: support **9** *v* **go**, move, journey, advance, proceed, commence, set out, travel [➡ PROCEED AND GO; 305]

headache 1 *n* [➡ PAIN AND OTHER PHYSICAL SENSATIONS; 733] **2** (*informal*) *n* **annoyance**, pain, bother, bore, nuisance, problem, worry, difficulty [➡ NUISANCES; 253] *Opposite*: relief

headband *n* **hairband**, sweatband, bandeau, circlet, headdress, Alice band (*UK*) [➡ ACCESSORIES, MILLINERY, AND LINGERIE; 867]

headboard *n* [➡ FURNITURE; 858]

head-butt 1 *v* **hit**, strike, butt, jab, whack, thump [➡ PHYSICAL ATTACK AND PUNISHMENT; 415] **2** *n* **blow**, hit, butt, jab, whack, thump [➡ PHYSICAL ATTACK AND PUNISHMENT; 415]

headdress *type of* **headgear** [➡ ACCESSORIES, MILLINERY, AND LINGERIE; 867]

header 1 *n* **shot**, pass, goal [➡ SPORTS TERMS; 877] **2** *n* **heading**, title, caption, slogan, legend, banner, running head, running title, headpiece [➡ PARTS OF BOOKS AND DOCUMENTS; 593] *Opposite:* footer

headfirst *adv* **headlong**, head over heels, diving, pitching, plunging, somersaulting [➡ DIRECTION OF MOTION; 345]

headgear *n* [➡ GARMENTS AND OUTFITS; 865]

headgear

◆ *types of hats*

beanie, boater, bonnet, cloche, cowboy hat, deerstalker, derby, fedora, homburg, Panama hat, picture hat, pillbox, porkpie hat, rain hat, sailor hat, sombrero, sou'wester, stovepipe hat, sunhat, ten-gallon hat, top hat, topper, toque, trilby

◆ *types of headgear*

balaclava, bandeau, baseball cap, bearskin, beret, biretta, busby, cap, chaplet, cloth cap, cowl, crash helmet, fez, glengarry, hairband, hardhat, hat, headband, headdress, headscarf, helmet, hood, mantilla, mobcap, skullcap, tam-o'-shanter, tippet, topee, turban, yarmulke, yashmak

head honcho (*slang*) *n* [➡ IMPORTANT OR FAMOUS PEOPLE; 893]

headhunter *n* [➡ BUSINESS PEOPLE; 793]

headily 1 *adv* **exhilaratingly**, thrillingly, invigoratingly, excitingly, stimulatingly, giddily [➡ EMOTIONALLY PLEASANT; 187] *Opposite:* dully **2** *adv* **pungently**, aromatically, strongly, richly, spicily, piquantly, potently, intoxicatingly (*formal*) [➡ STRENGTH; 201] *Opposite:* mildly **3** *adv* **impetuously**, impulsively, recklessly, rashly, hastily, imprudently (*formal*) [➡ INCAUTIOUS AND CARELESS; 283] *Opposite:* cautiously

heading 1 *n* **title**, caption, headline, banner, header, slogan, legend [➡ PARTS OF BOOKS AND DOCUMENTS; 593] **2** *n* **direction**, bearing, course, route, trajectory [➡ DIRECTION OF MOTION; 345]

headland *n* **promontory**, cape, peninsula, point, bluff, cliff [➡ THE SEAS, OCEANS, AND SHORES; 1041]

headlight 1 *type of* **external feature** [➡ EXTERNAL PARTS OF A VEHICLE; 1147] **2** *type of* **light** [➡ LIGHT; 1164]

headline 1 *n* **caption**, banner, title, heading, header, legend [➡ NEWSPAPERS AND MAGAZINES; 605] **2** *v* **feature**, present, top, introduce, advertise, publicize, promote [➡ ENTERTAINMENT; 872] **3** *v* **top the bill**, feature, star, head, top, lead [➡ THE PERFORMING ARTS; 904]

headlong 1 *adv* **headfirst**, head over heels, diving, pitching, plunging, tumbling, somersaulting [➡ DIRECTION OF MOTION; 345] **2** *adv* **impetuously**, rashly, recklessly, hastily, hurriedly, impulsively, abruptly, precipitously [➡ HAPPENING QUICKLY; 104] *Opposite:* carefully **3** *adj* **impetuous**, rash, reckless, hasty, hurried, impulsive, abrupt, precipitous [➡ HAPPENING QUICKLY; 104] *Opposite:* considered

head louse *type of* **parasitic insect** [➡ PARASITES; 1017]

headmaster *n* [➡ EDUCATORS; 840]

headmistress *n* [➡ EDUCATORS; 840]

head off 1 *v* **divert**, reroute, redirect, turn back, intercept, turn aside [➡ CHANGE DIRECTION OF MOTION; 344] **2** *v* **forestall**, block, prevent, stop, avert, fend off [➡ AVOID OR ESCAPE CONTACT; 418] *Opposite:* encourage **3** *v* **leave**, go away, depart, take off, commence, set off, go forward, get going (*informal*) [➡ LEAVE AND GO AWAY; 8] *Opposite:* remain

head office *n* **headquarters**, HQ, control center, command center, center of operations, nerve center, main center [➡ PLACE OF EMPLOYMENT; 832]

head of government *n* **leader**, ruler, prime minister, president, premier, head of state [➡ POLITICAL OFFICES AND POLITICIANS; 808]

head of state *n* **premier**, president, leader, ruler, sovereign, monarch, chancellor, head of government [➡ POLITICAL OFFICES AND POLITICIANS; 808]

head-on 1 *adv* **straight on**, straight ahead, frontally, directly, full steam ahead, full speed ahead [➡ DIRECTION OF MOTION; 345] **2** *adv* **unflinchingly**, uncompromisingly, with guns blazing, confrontationally, bluntly, aggressively [➡ RUDE AND HOSTILE; 625] *Opposite:* indirectly **3** *adj* **face-to-face**, frontal, uncompromising, direct, confrontational, blunt, aggressive [➡ RUDE AND HOSTILE; 625] *Opposite:* indirect

head over heels 1 *adv* **headfirst**, headlong, diving, plunging, pitching, somersaulting [➡ DIRECTION OF MOTION; 345] **2** *adv* **deeply**, passionately, rapturously, madly, desperately, wildly, completely [➡ APPRECIATION AND GRATITUDE; 535]

head over heels in love *adj* [➡ APPRECIATION AND GRATITUDE; 535]

headphones *n* **earphones**, earpiece, headset, receiver, phones (*informal*) [➡ AUDIO EQUIPMENT; 1139]

headpiece 1 *n* **header**, heading, design, ornament, decoration, pattern [➡ ORNAMENTS AND DECORATIONS; 1248] **2** *part of* **audio equipment** [➡ AUDIO EQUIPMENT; 1139]

headquarters *n* **head office**, HQ, control center, command center, center of operations, nerve center [➡ PLACE OF EMPLOYMENT; 832]

headrest *type of* **internal feature** [➡ INTERNAL PARTS OF A VEHICLE; 1146]

headscarf *type of* **headgear** [➡ ACCESSORIES, MILLINERY, AND LINGERIE; 867]

headset *n* **headphones**, receiver, earpiece, earphones [➡ AUDIO EQUIPMENT; 1139]

headship *n* **leadership**, direction, management, control, regime, guidance, authority [➡ QUALIFICATIONS; 843]

head start *n* **advantage**, edge, lead, helping hand, help, boost, flying start [➡ ADVANTAGES; 212] *Opposite:* disadvantage

headstone *n* **tombstone**, gravestone, stone, slab, memorial, memorial stone [➡ BURIAL PLACES AND ACCESSORIES; 930]

headstrong *adj* **impetuous**, impulsive, reckless, rash, willful, determined, stubborn, obstinate, pigheaded, intractable (*formal*) [➡ UNWILLINGNESS AND STUBBORNNESS; 564] *Opposite:* docile

head teacher (*UK*) *n* **principal**, headmaster, headmistress, rector, head (*UK*) [➡ EDUCATORS; 840]

head-to-head 1 *adv* **adjacent**, next to, end-to-end, in line, together [➡ CLOSENESS; 159] **2** *adj* **one-on-one**, face-to-

face, direct, intimate, personal, individual [➡CLOSENESS; 159]
3 *n* **encounter**, meeting, discussion, dialogue, confrontation, showdown [➡NEGOTIATION AND DEBATE; 46]

headwaiter *type of* **person who works in restaurants** [➡DOMESTIC AND KITCHEN WORKERS; 850]

headway *n* **progress**, movement, advance, progression, improvement, inroads, advancement [➡SUCCESS; 82]

headwind *n* **breeze**, wind, gale, gust [➡WINDY AND STORMY WEATHER; 1053]

heady 1 *adj* **exhilarating**, thrilling, invigorating, exciting, stimulating, giddy [➡EMOTIONALLY PLEASANT; 187] *Opposite*: dull **2** *adj* **pungent**, aromatic, strong, rich, spicy, piquant, potent, intoxicating (*formal*) [➡SMELL AND SMELLING; 705] *Opposite*: mild **3** *adj* **impetuous**, imprudent, impulsive, reckless, rash, hasty [➡LACK OF COMMITMENT AND UNRELIABILITY; 509] *Opposite*: cautious

heal 1 *v* **cure**, restore to health, make well, nurse, mend, repair [➡TAKE CARE OF AND SPOIL; 300] *Opposite*: worsen **2** *v* **make good**, settle, patch up, reconcile, set right, restore, rebuild, rectify [➡IMPROVE SOMETHING; 374] *Opposite*: damage

healer *n* **doctor**, faith healer, naturopath, homeopath, therapist, shaman, witch doctor [➡PEOPLE WHO WORK IN MEDICINE; 848]

healing 1 *n* **recovery**, restoration, recuperation, therapy, treatment, reinvigoration, cure [➡HEALING; 730] **2** *adj* **curative**, remedial, therapeutic, medicinal, curing, restorative, soothing, health-giving [➡HEALING; 730]

health *n* **fitness**, condition, healthiness, well-being, strength, vigor, shape, physical condition [➡PHYSICAL STATES; 734]

healthful *adj* **healthy**, good for your health, good for you, beneficial, wholesome, nourishing, nutritious, health-giving, advantageous, salubrious (*formal*) [➡CLEAN AND HYGIENIC; 1233] *Opposite*: unhealthy

healthiness *n* **health**, good condition, robustness, well-being, fitness, vigor [➡PHYSICAL STATES; 734]

healthy 1 *adj* **fit**, well, strong, vigorous, in good physical shape, hale and hearty, in fine fettle, in the pink (*dated*) [➡FIT AND STRONG; 736] *Opposite*: sick **2** *adj* **healthful**, good for your health, good for you, beneficial, nourishing, wholesome, nutritious, health-giving, advantageous, salubrious (*formal*) [➡CLEAN AND HYGIENIC; 1233] *Opposite*: unhealthy

heap 1 *n* **mound**, pile, stack, mountain, bundle, mass, load, lot, oodles (*informal*) [➡MANY, MUCH, LARGE AMOUNT; 117] **2** *v* **pile up**, pile, layer, mound, mass, build up, stack, collect, accumulate, arrange, gather [➡COMBINE AND MIX; 400]

heaps (*informal*) *n* **lots**, loads (*informal*), tons (*informal*), piles (*informal*), oodles (*informal*) [➡MANY, MUCH, LARGE AMOUNT; 117]

heap up 1 *v* **pile up**, pile, mound, mass, stack, build up [➡COMBINE AND MIX; 400] **2** *v* **collect**, amass, gather, accumulate, stockpile, hoard [➡STORE AND KEEP; 453]

hear 1 *v* **make out**, catch, get, overhear, pick up, perceive [➡HEAR; 707] **2** *v* **gather**, learn, find out, understand, pick up, get to know, get wind of [➡LEARN AND DISCOVER; 762] **3** *v* **understand**, pay attention to, attend to, heed, take notice of,

listen to, get, hearken (*archaic*) [➡LISTEN AND LISTENERS; 708] *Opposite*: miss **4** *v* **listen to**, catch, get, pick up, receive [➡LISTEN AND LISTENERS; 708] **5** *v* **sit in judgment**, try, judge, preside over, examine, consider [➡TRIAL, PUNISHMENT, AND LEGAL OUTCOMES; 819]

hear from *v* **have news of**, have contact with, be in touch with, be contacted by, have a call from, have a letter from [➡INITIATE AND ESTABLISH COMMUNICATION; 680]

hearing 1 *n* **earshot**, range, hearing distance, reach [➡CLOSENESS; 159] **2** *n* **trial**, inquiry, investigation, examination, consideration [➡TRIAL, PUNISHMENT, AND LEGAL OUTCOMES; 819]

hearing-impaired *adj* [➡HEAR; 707]

hearken (*archaic*) *v* [➡LISTEN AND LISTENERS; 708]

hear of *v* **consider**, conceive, tolerate, permit, admit, allow (*formal*), countenance (*formal*) [➡TOLERATE AND ENDURE; 766]

hearsay *n* **rumor**, gossip, tittle-tattle, idle talk, word of mouth, scuttlebutt (*slang*) [➡GOSSIP; 678] *Opposite*: fact

hearse *type of* **commercial or industrial vehicle** [➡VEHICLES; 1145]

heart 1 *n* **core**, heart of hearts, mind, sentiment, soul, nature, temperament, mood, emotion, spirit [➡TEMPERAMENT AND BEHAVIOR; 492] **2** *n* **compassion**, sympathy, empathy, feeling, sensitivity, kindness, tenderness, affection, concern [➡COMPASSION AND FORGIVENESS; 551] *Opposite*: cruelty **3** *n* **spirit**, courage, bravery, fortitude, pluck, resolution [➡COURAGE; 498] **4** *type of* **rounded shape** [➡ROUNDED SHAPE; 1218]

heartache *n* **sorrow**, sadness, distress, anguish, despair, despondency, misery [➡SADNESS, DISTRESS, AND DESPAIR; 539] *Opposite*: joy

heart attack 1 **cardiac arrest**, coronary, seizure [➡ILLNESSES AND DISORDERS; 732] **2** (*informal*) *n* **shock**, fit, stroke, nervous breakdown, breakdown, apoplexy [➡SUDDEN EVENTS; 52]

heartbreak *n* **grief**, despair, anguish, sorrow, pain, misery, suffering [➡SADNESS, DISTRESS, AND DESPAIR; 539] *Opposite*: joy

heartbreaking *adj* **tragic**, distressing, upsetting, sad, heartrending, moving, poignant, pitiful, pathetic, painful [➡EMOTIONALLY UNPLEASANT AND UPSETTING; 227] *Opposite*: uplifting

heartbroken *adj* **inconsolable**, forlorn, despairing, dejected, disconsolate, distraught, brokenhearted [➡SADNESS, DISTRESS, AND DESPAIR; 539] *Opposite*: thrilled

heartburn *n* **stomach pain**, acid stomach, indigestion, colic, dyspepsia [➡DISORDERS OF THE DIGESTIVE SYSTEM; 713]

hearten *v* **encourage**, inspire, raise your spirits, uplift, buoy, cheer up, cheer, gladden [➡ENCOURAGE; 576] *Opposite*: dishearten

heartened *adj* [➡COOL AND CALM; 536]

heartening *adj* **encouraging**, promising, cheering, optimistic, reassuring, hopeful, positive, comforting [➡CALMING; 188] *Opposite*: disheartening

heartfelt *adj* **sincere**, genuine, earnest, warm, cordial,

heedful *adj* **mindful**, vigilant, watchful, thoughtful, careful, attentive [➡ PENSIVENESS AND INTEREST; 538] *Opposite*: heedless

heedless *adj* **neglectful**, oblivious, without regard, rash, reckless, careless, unmindful, thoughtless [➡ NEUTRALITY AND INDIFFERENCE; 553] *Opposite*: careful

heedlessness *n* **thoughtlessness**, recklessness, carelessness, neglectfulness, rashness, obliviousness [➡ NEUTRALITY AND INDIFFERENCE; 553] *Opposite*: carefulness

heel 1 *v* **repair**, resole, mend, fix, reinforce, patch up [➡ REPAIR AND MEND; 376] 2 *part of* **leg or foot** [➡ PARTS OF THE BODY: LEG AND FOOT; 694] 3 *part of* **arm or hand** [➡ PARTS OF THE BODY: ARM AND HAND; 695]

heel in *v* **dig in**, put in, bury, cover [➡ CAUSE TO DISAPPEAR; 6]

heft 1 *v* **lift**, hoist, heave, raise, raise up, swing [➡ MOVE SOMETHING: UPWARD; 328] 2 *n* **weight**, bulk, size, mass, immensity, heaviness [➡ WEIGHT: HEAVY; 1205] *Opposite*: lightness

heftiness *n* **robustness**, burliness, stoutness, heaviness, stockiness, bulkiness, sturdiness, beefiness [➡ WEIGHT: HEAVY; 1205]

hefty 1 *adj* **bulky**, large, robust, sturdy, stocky, stout, beefy, brawny, thickset, heavy [➡ BUILD; 477] *Opposite*: slight 2 *adj* **heavy**, weighty, substantial, cumbersome, awkward [➡ WEIGHT: HEAVY; 1205]

hegemony *n* **domination**, control, supremacy, dominion, power, authority [➡ STRENGTH; 201]

heifer 1 *type of* **female animal** [➡ MALE OR FEMALE ANIMALS; 978] 2 *type of* **young animal** [➡ YOUNG ANIMALS; 977]

height 1 *n* **tallness**, stature, altitude, loftiness, elevation [➡ HEIGHT: HIGH; 1203] *Opposite*: depth 2 *n* **pinnacle**, summit, peak, top, apex, acme, zenith [➡ EXTREMITIES OF PHYSICAL OBJECTS; 1250] *Opposite*: nadir

heighten *v* **intensify**, amplify, increase, enhance, add to, reinforce, crank up [➡ CHANGE OF INTENSITY: MORE; 394]

heinous *adj* **monstrous**, atrocious, odious, dreadful, shocking, scandalous, wicked, evil, terrible [➡ MORALLY BAD OR IMPROPER; 775]

heir *n* **successor**, inheritor, beneficiary, legatee, recipient, heritor (*archaic*) [➡ YOUNGER GENERATION RELATIVES; 958]

heirloom *n* **family treasure**, inheritance, valuable, gift, bequest, treasure [➡ BEQUEATH AND BEQUESTS; 432]

heist (*slang*) *n* **robbery**, theft, raid, swoop, attack, lift (*informal*) [➡ CRIMES; 817]

helical *adj* [➡ ROUNDED SHAPE; 1218]

helicopter *type of* **civil aircraft** [➡ AIRCRAFT; 1148]

helicopter gunship *type of* **military aircraft** [➡ AIRCRAFT; 1148]

helideck *n* **landing pad**, helipad, heliport, helistop, landing strip, platform, runway [➡ AIRWAYS; 1109]

heliotrope *type of* **purple** [➡ COLORS; 1224]

helipad *n* **landing pad**, helideck, heliport, helistop, landing strip, platform, runway [➡ AIRWAYS; 1109]

heliport *see* **helipad**

helistop *see* **helipad**

helium *type of* **gas** [➡ GASES; 1275]

helix *n* **spiral**, coil, corkscrew, spring, ringlet [➡ ROUNDED SHAPE; 1218]

hell 1 *n* **hades**, underworld, perdition, inferno, abyss, netherworld (*formal*) [➡ RELIGIOUS CONCEPTS; 776] *Opposite*: heaven 2 *n* **torture**, misery, torment, agony, anguish, nightmare, suffering, pain, purgatory [➡ DIFFICULT SITUATIONS; 72]

hello *interj* **greetings**, good morning, good day, morning, good afternoon, hi (*informal*), ciao (*informal*), howdy (*informal*) [➡ GREETINGS, FAREWELLS, AND SALUTATIONS; 659] *Opposite*: goodbye

helm *part of* **ship or boat** [➡ PARTS OF A SHIP OR BOAT; 1151]

helmet 1 *type of* **sports equipment** [➡ SPORTS EQUIPMENT; 879] 2 *type of* **headgear** [➡ ACCESSORIES, MILLINERY, AND LINGERIE; 867]

help 1 *v* **aid**, assist, help out, lend a hand, be of assistance, facilitate, rally round, abet [➡ HELP; 293] *Opposite*: hinder 2 *v* **relieve**, improve, ease, alleviate, amend, better, ameliorate (*formal*) [➡ IMPROVE SOMETHING; 374] *Opposite*: worsen 3 *v* **avoid**, evade, dodge, stop, refrain from, prevent [➡ AVOID, PREVENT, LIMIT, AND CONTROL; 277] 4 *n* **assistance**, aid, benefit, support, service, relief, comfort, advantage, succor (*literary*) [➡ KIND ACTIONS OR BEHAVIOR; 295] *Opposite*: hindrance

helper *n* **assistant**, aid, aide, collaborator, coworker, colleague, partner [➡ SUBORDINATES AND ASSISTANTS; 966]

See Compare and Contrast at **assistant**.

helpful 1 *adj* **useful**, beneficial, advantageous, of use, effective, valuable [➡ USEFULNESS; 199] *Opposite*: useless 2 *adj* **obliging**, accommodating, supportive, caring, cooperative [➡ THE WILL AND WILLINGNESS; 563] *Opposite*: unhelpful

helpfully *adv* **carefully**, attentively, beneficially, favorably, obligingly, cooperatively, accommodatingly, supportively [➡ THE WILL AND WILLINGNESS; 563] *Opposite*: unhelpfully

helpfulness 1 *n* **usefulness**, effectiveness, utility, benefit, advantageousness, value [➡ USEFULNESS; 199] *Opposite*: uselessness 2 *n* **kindness**, neighborliness, goodwill, concern, care, attentiveness, cooperation, support [➡ GENEROSITY AND KINDNESS; 495] *Opposite*: unhelpfulness

helping *n* **serving**, plateful, portion, ration, selection [➡ AMOUNTS AND QUANTITIES; 112]

helping hand *n* **help**, assistance, support, aid, boost, push [➡ KIND ACTIONS OR BEHAVIOR; 295]

helpless *adj* **powerless**, weak, feeble, dependent, vulnerable, unaided, defenseless [➡ COWARDICE AND WEAKNESS OF WILL; 508] *Opposite*: self-reliant

helplessness *n* **powerlessness**, weakness, feebleness, vulnerability, dependence, defenselessness [➡ COWARDICE AND WEAKNESS OF WILL; 508] *Opposite*: confidence

helpmate *n* **assistant**, associate, spouse, teammate, partner, coworker, helper, companion [➡ SUBORDINATES AND ASSISTANTS; 966]

helpmeet (*archaic*) *n* [➡ SUBORDINATES AND ASSISTANTS; 966]

help out v **help**, lend a hand, abet, aid, assist [➡HELP; 293]

help yourself v **use**, make use of, appropriate, take, have [➡GET; 420]

helter-skelter 1 adv **hurriedly**, in confusion, carelessly, haphazardly, pell-mell [➡DISORDER AND CHAOS; 245] Opposite: calmly 2 adj **chaotic**, disorganized, confused, haphazard [➡DISORDER AND CHAOS; 245] Opposite: ordered

hem 1 v **edge**, turn up, shorten, lengthen, sew up, stitch, tailor [➡CRAFTS AND CARVING; 355] Opposite: let down 2 part of **garment** [➡PARTS OF A GARMENT; 870]

hem and haw v [➡HESITATE; 272]

hem in v **enclose**, close in, encircle, confine, restrict, surround, circumscribe (formal) [➡CAPTIVITY AND LOSS OF FREEDOM; 248] Opposite: release

hemisphere type of **rounded shape** [➡ROUNDED SHAPE, 1218]

hemispherical adj [➡ROUNDED SHAPE; 1218]

hemmed in adj [➡CAPTIVITY AND LOSS OF FREEDOM; 248]

hemorrhage 1 n **loss**, outflow, outpouring, seeping away, depletion, drop, seepage, flow [➡EMIT AND EMANATE; 361] 2 v **lose**, flow away, seep away, pour out, drain away, gush, bleed [➡LIQUID EMISSION; 370]

hen type of **male or female bird** [➡MALE OR FEMALE BIRDS; 1005]

hence (formal) 1 adv **therefore**, for this reason, consequently, that's why, and so, so, thus (formal) [➡CAUSATION; 168] 2 adv **from now**, from this time, henceforth, later, in future, hereafter (formal), henceforward (formal) [➡FUTURE; 86]

henceforth adv **from now on**, from this time, in future, hereafter (formal), henceforward (formal) [➡FUTURE; 86]

henceforward (formal) adv [➡FUTURE; 86]

hendiadys type of **figure of speech** [➡FIGURES OF SPEECH; 673]

henhouse n **coop**, pen, barn, shelter, shed, hutch [➡ANIMAL OR BIRD ACCOMMODATIONS; 1079]

henna type of **brown** [➡COLORS; 1224]

henry type of **SI unit** [➡SIZE AND DIMENSIONS; 1192]

heptathlon type of **track and field** [➡HOBBIES, GAMES, AND SPORTS; 875]

herald 1 n **messenger**, crier, announcer, proclaimer, courier, representative [➡MESSENGERS AND COURIERS; 852] 2 n (literary) **sign**, harbinger, indication, omen, portent, precursor, forerunner [➡INDICATIONS, SIGNS, AND WARNINGS; 68] 3 v **signal**, prefigure, foreshadow, presage, indicate, foreshow (archaic) [➡REPRESENT SOMETHING OR SOMEBODY; 59] 4 v **proclaim**, announce, give out, publish, tout, publicize, make public [➡INFORM, ANNOUNCE, AND ISSUE; 611]

herb n [➡HERBS AND SPICES; 1175]

herb

♦ types of herbs
angelica, basil, bay leaf, borage, caraway, chamomile, chervil, chive, cilantro, coriander, dill, fennel, hyssop, lemongrass, lovage, marjoram, mint, oregano, parsley, rosemary, sage, savory, spearmint, tarragon, thyme

herbal medicine type of **complementary therapy** [➡REMEDIES, TREATMENTS, AND OPERATIONS; 731]

herb garden type of **garden** [➡GARDENS; 1074]

herculean adj **superhuman**, colossal, enormous, phenomenal, extraordinary, huge, titanic [➡LARGE; 1193] Opposite: small

Hercules type of **constellation** [➡HEAVENLY BODIES; 1061]

herd 1 n **people**, masses, mob, hoi polloi, crowd, sheep [➡GROUPS OF PEOPLE; 935] 2 n [➡GROUPS OF ANIMALS; 993] 3 type of **flock** [➡GROUPS OF BIRDS; 1007] 4 v **round up**, steer, gather together, collect, drove, drive [➡COMBINE AND MIX; 400] 5 v **shepherd**, usher, direct, guide, funnel, channel, steer [➡ACCOMPANY AND FOLLOW; 337]

herd

♦ types of herds
bale (of turtles), band (of gorillas), bevy (of roe deer), colony (of ants/sea lions), drove (of sheep), flock (of sheep), gam (of whales), gang (of elk), kennel (of dogs), leash (of foxes), litter (of cubs/kittens), mob (of kangaroos), pack (of wolves), pod (of porpoises/seals/walrus/whales), pride (of lions), rookery (of seals), school (of porpoises/whales), skulk (of foxes), troop (of kangaroos/monkeys)

here adv **at this time**, at this point, now, at this juncture [➡PRESENT; 85]

hereabout adj **nearby**, near, around here, close [➡CLOSENESS; 159]

hereafter (formal) adv **after this**, in future, henceforth, from now on, from this time, henceforward (formal) [➡FUTURE; 86]

hereditary 1 adj **genetic**, transmissible, inborn, inbred, inherited, innate [➡REPRODUCTION AND HEREDITY; 725] 2 adj **inherited**, heritable, traditional, family [➡THE FAMILY; 956]

heresy n **dissent**, deviation, unorthodoxy, sacrilege, profanation (formal), heterodoxy (formal) [➡MORALLY BAD OR IMPROPER; 775]

heretic n [➡RELIGIOUS CONCEPTS; 776]

heretical adj **unorthodox**, sacrilegious, dissenting, unconventional, deviating, heterodox (formal), profane (formal) [➡MORALLY BAD OR IMPROPER; 775]

here today and gone tomorrow adj **short-lived**, temporary, brief, short, fleeting, transitory, transient, ephemeral [➡FINITENESS, VARIABILITY, AND TRANSIENCE; 96] Opposite: lasting

heretofore (formal) adv [➡PAST; 84]

herewith *adv* **with this**, together with this, enclosed, with, attached [➡ GENERAL LOCATIONS; 158]

heritable *adj* **inheritable**, transferable, transmissible, hereditary [➡ REPRODUCTION AND HEREDITY; 725]

heritage *n* **inheritance**, legacy, tradition, birthright, custom, culture [➡ BEQUEATH AND BEQUESTS; 432]

hermaphrodite *adj* **androgynous**, epicene, intersexual [➡ GENDER IDENTITY AND SEXUALITY; 932]

hermaphroditism *n* [➡ GENDER IDENTITY AND SEXUALITY; 932]

hermetic *adj* **airtight**, enclosed, closed [➡ IN GOOD REPAIR; 1232]

hermit *n* **recluse**, loner, solitary, eremite (*literary*) [➡ SOLITARY PEOPLE AND MISFITS; 942]

hermitage *n* [➡ RELIGIOUS BUILDINGS; 1085]

hermit crab *type of* **crustacean** [➡ AQUATIC INVERTEBRATES; 1022]

hero 1 *n* **superman**, champion, conqueror, idol [➡ PEOPLE WHO ARE APPROVED OF; 955] 2 *n* **male lead**, leading actor, leading man, star, protagonist, lead [➡ IMPORTANT OR FAMOUS PEOPLE; 893]

heroic *adj* **daring**, stout, valiant, brave, epic, superhuman, courageous, fearless, intrepid (*literary or humorous*), gallant (*literary*) [➡ COURAGE; 498]

heroics *n* **recklessness**, rashness, irresponsibility, going over the top, overdoing it, derring-do (*dated*) [➡ COURAGE; 498] *Opposite*: timidity

heroine 1 *n* **superwoman**, champion, conqueror, idol [➡ PEOPLE WHO ARE APPROVED OF; 955] 2 *n* **female lead**, leading actress, leading lady, star, protagonist, lead [➡ IMPORTANT OR FAMOUS PEOPLE; 893]

heroism *n* **valor**, bravery, courageousness, fearlessness, boldness, pluckiness, pluck, gallantry, daring, intrepidness [➡ COURAGE; 498]

heron *type of* **freshwater bird** [➡ FRESHWATER BIRDS; 1000]

hero worship *n* **adulation**, idolization, idealization, admiration, glorification, veneration, worship [➡ FADS, FETISHES, AND IDOLATRY; 555]

hero-worship *v* [➡ LIKE, LOVE, VALUE, AND ENJOY; 578]

hero-worshiper *n* [➡ DEVOTEES AND ADDICTED PEOPLE; 556]

herring *type of* **ocean fish** [➡ OCEAN FISH; 1009]

hertz *type of* **SI unit** [➡ SIZE AND DIMENSIONS; 1192]

hesitancy *n* **indecision**, caution, uncertainty, tentativeness, timidity, doubtfulness, reluctance, hesitation, disinclination, diffidence [➡ INSECURITY AND LOSS OF COMPOSURE; 544] *Opposite*: decisiveness

hesitant *adj* **cautious**, tentative, timid, shy, undecided, doubtful, uncertain, diffident [➡ INSECURITY AND LOSS OF COMPOSURE; 544] *Opposite*: decisive

See Compare and Contrast at **unwilling**.

hesitate 1 *v* **be uncertain**, be indecisive, vacillate, waver, falter, dither, shilly-shally, pause, dilly-dally, dawdle, delay, stumble [➡ HESITATE; 272] 2 *v* **be unwilling**, think twice, scruple, have qualms, be reluctant, hang back [➡ SHIRK AND DELAY; 273]

Compare and Contrast: *hesitate, pause, falter, stumble, waver, vacillate*

CORE MEANING: to show uncertainty or indecision

hesitate to be slow in doing something, or take a short break in an activity, as a result of uncertainty or reluctance; *pause* to stop doing something briefly before continuing, or to wait intentionally for a short period before doing something; *falter* to show a loss of confidence, especially to speak or say something with a series of short stoppages, for example, because of nervousness, fear, awkwardness, or incompetence; *stumble* to speak or act hesitatingly, confusedly, or incompetently; *waver* to become unsure or begin to change from a previous opinion; *vacillate* to be indecisive or irresolute, changing between one opinion and another.

hesitation 1 *n* **uncertainty**, indecision, vacillation, wavering, faltering, dithering, shilly-shallying, pause, delay, dilly-dallying, dawdling [➡ UNCERTAINTY; 559] *Opposite*: decisiveness 2 *n* **unwillingness**, qualms, reluctance, disinclination, hesitancy, indecision [➡ UNWILLINGNESS AND STUBBORNNESS; 564] *Opposite*: willingness

hessian *type of* **fabric from plants** [➡ FABRICS; 1132]

heterogeneity *n* [➡ DIFFERENCE; 149]

heterogeneous *adj* **varied**, mixed, assorted, diverse, various, dissimilar, unrelated [➡ UNRELATEDNESS AND SEPARATENESS; 146] *Opposite*: homogeneous

het up *adj* **on edge**, agitated, jittery, jumpy, excited, anxious, all of a flutter, keyed up (*informal*), wound up (*informal*), in a state (*informal*) [➡ CONFUSION, ANXIETY, AND WORRY; 540]

heuristic *adj* **experiential**, empirical, experimental, investigative, exploratory [➡ THE NATURE OF IDEAS; 771]

hew 1 *v* **cut**, chop, fell, cleave, ax, slash, hack [➡ TEAR, BREAK, AND CUT; 360] 2 *v* **carve**, fashion, sculpt, shape, model [➡ CRAFTS AND CARVING; 355]

hex *n* **curse**, spell, jinx, voodoo [➡ BAD LUCK AND UNLUCKY; 784]

hexagonal *adj* [➡ ANGULAR SHAPE; 1217]

heyday *n* **prime**, zenith, glory days, peak, halcyon days (*literary*) [➡ PLEASANT SITUATIONS; 74]

hey presto (*informal*) *interj* [➡ EXPRESSIONS OF SURPRISE AND PLEASURE; 546]

hi (*informal*) *interj* [➡ GREETINGS, FAREWELLS, AND SALUTATIONS; 659]

hiatus *n* **pause**, break, interruption, space, lull, interval, time away, gap [➡ PAUSES AND PHASES; 56]

hibernate *v* **lie dormant**, take cover, overwinter, hide, hide away, sleep, keep cover, hole up (*slang*) [➡ SLEEP AND DREAM; 723]

hiccup 1 *n* (*informal*) **hitch**, glitch, interruption, delay, setback [➡ PROBLEMS; 256] 2 *v* [➡ VOMIT AND BELCH; 712]

hickory *type of* **deciduous tree** [➡ DECIDUOUS TREES; 1028]

hickory nut *type of* nut [➡ NUTS; 1185]

hidden 1 *adj* **concealed**, out of sight, unseen, secreted, veiled, buried [➡ IMPERCEPTIBLE; 26] 2 *adj* **unknown**, secret, mysterious, clandestine, covert, obscure, cryptic, mystifying [➡ SECRET AND UNKNOWN; 179]

hidden agenda *n* **ulterior motive**, secret plan, motivation, driving force, impetus, incentive [➡ CAUSATION; 168]

hide 1 *v* **conceal**, put out of sight, hide from view, secrete, veil, bury, cover, screen, shroud, inter [➡ CAUSE TO DISAPPEAR; 6] *Opposite:* flaunt 2 *v* **go underground**, take cover, disappear, keep cover, hole up (*slang*) [➡ RUN AWAY AND AVOID; 10] 3 *v* **keep secret**, withhold, hold back, keep back, suppress, obscure, keep quiet, hush up (*informal*), keep mum (*informal*) [➡ WITHHOLD INFORMATION; 687] *Opposite:* disclose 4 *type of* leather [➡ FABRICS; 1132]

hideaway *n* **hiding place**, refuge, sanctuary, asylum, retreat, safe place, shelter, hideout, den, safe house, place of escape, lair (*informal*), hidey-hole (*informal*) [➡ SAFE BUILDINGS OR PLACES; 1093]

hidebound *adj* **narrow-minded**, prejudiced, conservative, conventional, parochial, reactionary [➡ UNADVENTUROUS AND DULL; 517] *Opposite:* broad-minded

hideous *adj* **ugly**, revolting, repugnant, repulsive, unsightly, gruesome, shocking, dreadful [➡ UGLINESS AND UNATTRACTIVENESS; 233]

hideousness *n* **ugliness**, repulsiveness, unsightliness, gruesomeness, dreadfulness, repugnance, horribleness [➡ UGLINESS AND UNATTRACTIVENESS; 233]

hideout *n* **hideaway**, safe house, refuge, sanctuary, retreat, den, shelter, hiding place, place of escape, safe place, asylum, lair (*informal*), hidey-hole (*informal*) [➡ SAFE BUILDINGS OR PLACES; 1093]

hidey-hole (*informal*) *n* **hiding place**, hideaway, safe house, safe place, shelter, hideout, nook, refuge, sanctuary, retreat, den, stash (*informal*), lair (*informal*) [➡ SAFE BUILDINGS OR PLACES; 1093]

hiding (*informal*) *n* **beating**, whacking, thumping, smacking, spanking, whack, thump, smack, spank, wallop (*informal*), walloping (*informal*) [➡ PHYSICAL ATTACK AND PUNISHMENT; 415]

hiding place *n* **hideaway**, hole, place of escape, den, safe house, safe place, hideout, sanctuary, retreat, refuge, asylum, recess, nook, stash (*informal*), hidey-hole (*informal*), lair (*informal*) [➡ SAFE BUILDINGS OR PLACES; 1093]

hierarchical *adj* **ranked**, graded, tiered, ordered, classified, categorized [➡ ORDER AND ORGANIZATION; 206]

hierarchy *n* **chain of command**, ladder, pecking order, grading, order, pyramid [➡ CONNECTIONS; 143]

hieroglyph *n* **symbol**, pictograph, picture, ideogram, cipher, glyph, pictogram, hieroglyphic [➡ SYMBOLS, SIGNS, AND NUMBERS; 596]

hieroglyphics *type of* **alphabet** [➡ SYMBOLS, SIGNS, AND NUMBERS; 596]

hifalutin (*informal*) *adj* **pretentious**, affected, grandiose, grandiloquent, high-flown, pompous, snobbish, la-di-da

(*informal*), highfalutin (*informal*) [➡ AFFECTATION, SELF-SATISFACTION, AND SNOBBISHNESS; 507] *Opposite:* down-to-earth

hi-fi (*dated*) 1 *n* **sound system**, stereo system, stereo, CD player, cassette recorder, personal stereo [➡ RECORDINGS AND PLAYERS; 911] 2 *type of* **audio equipment** [➡ AUDIO EQUIPMENT; 1139]

higgledy-piggledy *adj* **untidy**, topsy-turvy, in a mess, jumbled, confused, random, disordered, disorderly, mixed-up (*informal*) [➡ DISORDER AND CHAOS; 245] *Opposite:* ordered

high 1 *adj* **tall**, lofty, elevated, towering, soaring, skyscraping [➡ HEIGHT: HIGH; 1203] *Opposite:* low 2 *adj* **in height**, from top to bottom, from head to foot, from top to toe, tall, in elevation [➡ HEIGHT: HIGH; 1203] 3 *adj* **above average**, great, extraordinary, elevated, extreme, astronomical, prohibitive, abnormal [➡ EXPENSIVE AND OVERPRICED; 247] *Opposite:* normal 4 *adj* **high-pitched**, shrill, piercing, penetrating, sharp, soprano, falsetto [➡ LOUD, HIGH, OR UNPLEASANT SOUNDS; 1266] *Opposite:* low-pitched 5 *adj* **important**, eminent, prominent, high-ranking, superior, distinguished, lofty, high-level, exalted (*formal*) [➡ IMPORTANT; 194] *Opposite:* low 6 *n* **high point**, peak, climax, summit, high spot (*UK*) [➡ INTERMEDIATE STAGES; 55] *Opposite:* low point 7 *n* (*informal*) **lift**, kick, boost, thrill, tonic, pleasure, excitement, buzz (*informal*) [➡ TREATS; 210]

high achiever *n* **high flier**, success, star, winner, success story, go-getter (*informal*) [➡ IMPORTANT OR FAMOUS PEOPLE; 893]

high and dry *adj* **helpless**, in the lurch, washed up, stranded, abandoned, destitute, deserted, up the creek (*informal*), swinging in the wind (*informal*) [➡ IN TROUBLE AND DISADVANTAGED; 73]

high and low *adv* **everywhere**, all over, here, there, and everywhere, in every nook and cranny, all over the place (*informal*), everyplace (*informal*) [➡ GENERAL LOCATIONS; 158]

high and mighty *adj* **arrogant**, disdainful, overbearing, conceited, proud, haughty, self-important, full of yourself, condescending, stuck-up (*informal*) [➡ AFFECTATION, SELF-SATISFACTION, AND SNOBBISHNESS; 507]

highborn (*literary*) *adj* [➡ CLASS STATUS; 889]

highboy *type of* **cabinet** [➡ FURNITURE; 858]

highbrow 1 *adj* **intellectual**, cultured, academic, scholarly, exclusive, elitist, serious [➡ THE NATURE OF IDEAS; 771] *Opposite:* lowbrow 2 *n* **intellectual**, academic, scholar, philosopher, sage (*literary*) [➡ TALENTED OR INTELLIGENT PEOPLE; 528]

highchair *type of* **seating** [➡ FURNITURE; 858]

high-class *adj* **high-quality**, fancy, formal, elegant, superior, glitzy, posh (*informal*), ritzy (*informal*), swanky (*informal*) [➡ EXPENSIVE AND LUXURIOUS; 218] *Opposite:* cheap

high court *n* **court**, supreme court, principal court [➡ TRIAL, PUNISHMENT, AND LEGAL OUTCOMES; 819]

highest *adj* **top**, topmost, utmost, ultimate, premier, record, supreme [➡ SUPERIORITY; 152]

highfalutin (*informal*) *adj* **pretentious**, pompous, affected, grandiose, snobbish, high-flown, grandiloquent, la-di-da (*informal*), hifalutin (*informal*) [➡ AFFECTATION, SELF-SATISFACTION, AND SNOBBISHNESS; 507] *Opposite:* down-to-earth

high-fidelity *adj* [➡ ACOUSTICS; 1138]

high-flier *n* **high achiever**, success, winner, success story, star, go-getter (*informal*) [➡ IMPORTANT OR FAMOUS PEOPLE; 893]

high-flown *adj* **affected**, pretentious, grandiose, high-sounding, grandiloquent, pompous, snobbish, high-falutin (*informal*), la-di-da (*informal*), exalted (*formal*) [➡ POMPOUS, LOUD, AND OVERCONFIDENT; 635] *Opposite*: down-to-earth

high-flyer *see* **high-flier**

high-grade *adj* **high-quality**, quality, finest, superior, prime, select, best, first-class, choice, luxury, premium, first-rate, super (*informal*) [➡ SUPERIORITY; 152] *Opposite*: low-grade

high ground **1** *n* **upland**, highland, plateau, hillside, hilltop, fell (*UK*) [➡ MOUNTAINS AND HILLS; 1044] *Opposite*: lowland **2** *n* **refuge**, shelter, cover, protection, sanctuary, haven [➡ SAFE BUILDINGS OR PLACES; 1093] **3** *n* **principled stance**, moral stand, high road [➡ MORAL CONCEPTS; 773]

high-handed *adj* **bossy**, autocratic, dominant, undemocratic, domineering, overbearing, imperious, cavalier, arrogant, inconsiderate, dictatorial [➡ BOSSY AND OVERBEARING; 516]

high-handedness *n* **bossiness**, arrogance, imperiousness, inconsiderateness, overbearingness, inconsideration [➡ BOSSY AND OVERBEARING; 516]

high jinks (*informal*) *n* **mischief**, mischievousness, trouble, no good, nonsense, antics, monkey business (*informal*), carryings-on (*informal*), shenanigans (*informal*) [➡ CHAOS AND UPROAR; 51]

high jump *type of* **track and field** [➡ HOBBIES, GAMES, AND SPORTS; 875]

highland *n* **upland**, plateau, high ground, hilltop, moorland, fell (*UK*) [➡ MOUNTAINS AND HILLS; 1044] *Opposite*: lowland

high-level *adj* **sophisticated**, elevated, advanced, complex, top, elite [➡ POSITIVELY COMPLEX OR COMPLICATED; 217] *Opposite*: unsophisticated

high life *n* **good life**, life of Riley, life of ease, lap of luxury, easy street, clover, bed of roses, primrose path (*literary*) [➡ PLEASANT SITUATIONS; 74]

highlight **1** *n* **high point**, climax, best part, icing on the cake, acme, high spot (*UK*), best bit (*UK*) [➡ DECISIVE MOMENTS; 44] **2** *v* **emphasize**, draw attention to, underline, stress, focus on, show up, underscore, bring to light, showcase [➡ CLAIM, INSIST, AND EMPHASIZE; 614]

highlighter *type of* **pen** [➡ WRITING AND DRAWING IMPLEMENTS, AND MEDIA; 601]

highly **1** *adv* **extremely**, very, exceedingly, very much, greatly, decidedly, vastly [➡ TO A GREAT EXTENT; 132] *Opposite*: modestly **2** *adv* **favorably**, approvingly, kindly, warmly, graciously, well, very well [➡ ENTHUSIASTIC AND INQUISITIVE; 628] *Opposite*: unfavorably

highly unlikely *adj* [➡ IMPOSSIBLE AND IMPROBABLE; 178]

high-minded *adj* **principled**, worthy, moral, noble, upright, fair, ethical, righteous [➡ HONEST AND RELIABLE; 502] *Opposite*: base

high-occupancy vehicle lane *n* [➡ TRAVEL: TRAFFIC PROBLEMS AND TRAFFIC MANAGEMENT; 323]

high-pitched *adj* **shrill**, high, piercing, penetrating, sharp, falsetto, soprano [➡ LOUD, HIGH, OR UNPLEASANT SOUNDS; 1266]

high point *n* **best moment**, climax, icing on the cake, acme, highlight, best part, best bit (*UK*), high spot (*UK*) [➡ DECISIVE MOMENTS; 44]

high-powered *adj* **successful**, dynamic, driven, ambitious, energetic, efficient, influential, hard-driving, Type A, go-getting (*informal*) [➡ TALENTED AND SKILLFUL; 527]

high-pressure *adj* **stressful**, difficult, relentless, pressured, intense, strenuous, demanding [➡ PHYSICALLY UNPLEASANT; 226] *Opposite*: easy

high profile *n* **prominence**, conspicuousness, eminence, celebrity, notoriety, prestige, fame [➡ KNOWN AND FAMOUS; 181] *Opposite*: anonymity

high-profile *adj* **prominent**, prestigious, conspicuous, famous, eminent, notorious (*archaic*) [➡ KNOWN AND FAMOUS; 181] *Opposite*: discreet

high-quality *adj* [➡ GOOD, WELL, BETTER; 183]

high-ranking *adj* [➡ CLASS STATUS; 889]

high-rise **1** *adj* **multistory**, high, tall, big, lofty, soaring, towering [➡ HEIGHT: HIGH; 1203] **2** *n* **skyscraper**, apartment building, apartment house, office tower, office block, block of flats (*UK*), apartment block (*UK*), tower block (*UK*) [➡ RESIDENTIAL BUILDINGS; 1078]

high roller (*slang*) *n* [➡ RICH PEOPLE; 895]

high school *type of* **school** [➡ EDUCATIONAL INSTITUTIONS; 813]

high society *n* **upper classes**, elite, Four Hundred, polite society, beautiful people, upper crust (*informal*), jet set (*informal*) [➡ CLASS STATUS; 889]

high-sounding *adj* **imposing**, high-flown, grandiloquent, grandiose, lofty, pompous, pretentious, extravagant [➡ POMPOUS, LOUD, AND OVERCONFIDENT; 635]

high-spirited *adj* **lively**, exuberant, merry, cheerful, vivacious, excited, boisterous [➡ ENERGY AND ENTHUSIASM; 496] *Opposite*: lethargic

high spirits *n* **liveliness**, exuberance, merriness, cheerfulness, vivacity, excitement, joie de vivre, happiness, brio (*literary*) [➡ PLEASURE, EXCITEMENT, AND ELATION; 534] *Opposite*: depression

high spot (*UK*) *n* **best moment**, high point, climax, best part, icing on the cake, acme, highlight, best bit (*UK*) [➡ DECISIVE MOMENTS; 44]

high-strung *adj* **excitable**, nervous, edgy, tense, jittery, easily upset, skittish, volatile, anxious [➡ EXCESSIVE SENSITIVITY; 511] *Opposite*: laid-back (*informal*)

hightail it (*slang*) *v* [➡ RUN AWAY AND AVOID; 10]

high-tech *adj* **advanced**, technological, computerized, digital, modern, futuristic, sophisticated, multimedia, state-of-the-art [➡ DESCRIBING TECHNOLOGY; 1160]

highway *type of* **highway** [➡ ROADS; 1106]

highway robbery (*informal*) *n* [➡ CRIMES; 817]

hijack 1 *v* **take over**, seize, commandeer, capture, skyjack [➡ TAKE SOMETHING AWAY; 425] **2** *v* (*informal*) **steal**, appropriate, take over, commandeer, borrow [➡ STEAL AND ROB; 426] **3** *n* **takeover**, skyjacking, capture, seizure [➡ CRIMES; 817]

hijinks (*informal*) *see* **high jinks**

hike 1 *v* **ramble**, trek, walk, climb, scramble, trudge, tramp, slog [➡ PROCEED AND GO; 305] **2** *n* **trek**, ramble, walk, climb, scramble, trudge, slog, tramp (*UK*) [➡ TRAVEL: JOURNEYS AND TRIPS; 318]

hiker *n* **walker**, rambler, backpacker, trekker, climber [➡ PEOPLE IN SPORTS AND LEISURE; 876]

hiking boot *type of* **boot** [➡ FOOTWEAR; 871]

hilarious *adj* **funny**, sidesplitting, comic, comical, humorous, entertaining, uproarious, riotous, mirthful, rib-tickling, hysterical (*informal*) [➡ FUNNY AND AMUSING; 216]

> See Compare and Contrast at **funny**.

hilariousness *n* **humorousness**, uproariousness, comicalness, mirthfulness, funniness, amusingness, humor [➡ FUNNY AND AMUSING; 216]

hilarity *n* **amusement**, laughter, merriment, mirth, glee, joviality, cheerfulness, comedy, hysterics (*informal*) [➡ ENTERTAINMENT; 872] *Opposite:* sadness

hill 1 *n* **mountain**, peak, knoll, mount, mound, hummock, tor [➡ MOUNTAINS AND HILLS; 1044] *Opposite:* valley **2** *n* **gradient**, slope, incline, rise [➡ MOUNTAINS AND HILLS; 1044] *Opposite:* drop

hillock *n* **mound**, hummock, knoll, hill [➡ MOUNTAINS AND HILLS; 1044]

hilltop *n* **top**, summit, peak, pinnacle, brow, crown, crest [➡ MOUNTAINS AND HILLS; 1044] *Opposite:* base

hilly *adj* **mountainous**, undulating, bumpy, alpine, craggy, rolling [➡ MOUNTAINS AND HILLS; 1044] *Opposite:* flat

hind 1 *adj* **back**, rear, rearmost, posterior (*formal*), hindmost (*literary*) [➡ RELATIVE LOCATION; 161] *Opposite:* fore (*literary*) **2** *type of* **female animal** [➡ MALE OR FEMALE ANIMALS; 978]

hinder *v* **hold back**, delay, deter, hamper, encumber, obstruct, get in the way, thwart, impede, block [➡ AVOID, PREVENT, LIMIT, AND CONTROL; 277] *Opposite:* facilitate

---

Compare and Contrast: *hinder, block, hamper, hold back, impede, obstruct*

CORE MEANING: to put difficulties in the way of progress

hinder to delay or restrict the development or progress of something, either accidentally or by deliberate interference; *block* to prevent movement through, into, or out of something, or prevent something from taking place; *hamper* to restrict the free movement or action of somebody or something; *hold back* to keep something from happening or to restrain somebody from doing something; *impede* to interfere with the movement, progress, or development of somebody or something; *obstruct* to cause a serious delay in action or progress, or to cause a major physical blockage in a road or passageway.

---

hindleg *n* [➡ PARTS OF THE BODY: LEG AND FOOT; 694]

hindmost (*literary*) *adj* **last**, rear, final, back, rearmost [➡ RELATIVE LOCATION; 161] *Opposite:* foremost

hindquarters *n* **back**, rear, rear legs, hind legs [➡ HORSES; 985] *Opposite:* front

hindrance 1 *n* **obstruction**, impediment, barrier, obstacle, encumbrance, difficulty, burden, deterrent [➡ PROBLEMS; 256] **2** *n* **interference**, interruption, limitation, prevention, sabotage, obstruction, hampering [➡ PROBLEMS; 256] *Opposite:* assistance

hindsight *n* **reflection**, retrospection, perception, observation, remembrance, recall [➡ MEMORY; 745] *Opposite:* foresight

hinge *n* **pivot**, axis, fulcrum, joint, crux, center [➡ CENTRAL PARTS OF PHYSICAL OBJECTS; 1251]

hinge on *v* **depend on**, hang on, turn on, be dependent on, rest on, rely on, pivot on [➡ RECIPROCITY AND INTERDEPENDENCE; 147]

hint 1 *v* **suggest**, intimate, insinuate, imply, mention, indicate, signal [➡ SUGGEST, HINT, AND COMMENT; 612] **2** *n* **suggestion**, clue, intimation, mention, indication, insinuation, warning, telltale sign, tip-off (*informal*) [➡ SUGGEST, HINT, AND COMMENT; 612] **3** *n* **tip**, advice, pointer, suggestion, clue, help [➡ ADVICE; 689] **4** *n* **trace**, tinge, suggestion, dash, taste, breath, whisper, whiff, touch, element [➡ FEW, LITTLE, SMALL AMOUNT; 120]

hinterland *n* **vicinity**, environs, surroundings, neighborhood [➡ PLACE; 1065] *Opposite:* heartland

hip 1 *part of* **torso** [➡ PARTS OF THE BODY: TORSO; 693] **2** *adj* (*slang*) **fashionable**, current, all the rage, in vogue, cool, modish, stylish, trendy (*informal*), à la mode (*dated*), with-it (*dated informal*) [➡ NEW, MODERN; 166]

hip flask *n* [➡ CONTAINERS, RECEPTACLES, AND PACKAGING; 1245]

hip hop *type of* **dance music** [➡ MUSIC, SONGS, AND SINGING; 907]

hip-huggers *type of* **pants** [➡ GARMENTS AND OUTFITS; 865]

hipness (*slang*) *n* [➡ NEW, MODERN; 166]

hippopotamus *type of* **large mammal** [➡ LARGE MAMMALS; 986]

hipster (*slang*) *n* [➡ MALE PERSON; 934]

hiragana *type of* **alphabet** [➡ SYMBOLS, SIGNS, AND NUMBERS; 596]

hire 1 *v* **employ**, appoint, take on, contract, sign up, take into service, engage [➡ CONFER STATUS; 458] **2** *v* **rent**, lease, let, charter, engage, book [➡ LEND, LEASE, AND BORROW; 428]

hired gun (*slang*) *n* [➡ PEOPLE WHO KILL; 924]

hire out *v* **rent out**, rent, lend, lend out, lease, let [➡ LEND, LEASE, AND BORROW; 428]

hirsute *adj* **hairy**, long-haired, unshorn, unshaven, shaggy [➡ DESCRIBING HAIR; 486] *Opposite:* bald

hirsuteness *n* [➡ HAIR; 484]

hiss 1 *v* **jeer**, boo, hoot, mock, ridicule [➡ UNFAVORABLE NONVERBAL RESPONSES; 654] *Opposite:* cheer **2** *v* **whisper**, murmur, rustle, whistle, susurrate [➡ EMIT CONTINUOUS SOUNDS; 366] **3** *n* [➡ UNFAVORABLE NONVERBAL RESPONSES; 654] **4** *type of* **continuous sound** [➡ CONTINUOUS SOUNDS; 1258]

historic 1 *adj* **significant**, momentous, notable, famous, remarkable, extraordinary, celebrated, important [➡ IMPORTANT; 194] *Opposite*: insignificant **2** *adj* **historical**, old, ancient, antique, past, bygone [➡ OLD, OLD-FASHIONED; 167] *Opposite*: modern

historical *adj* **past**, old, ancient, antique, historic, bygone [➡ OLD, OLD-FASHIONED; 167] *Opposite*: modern

historically 1 *adv* **in history**, over all, factually, archaeologically [➡ PAST; 84] **2** *adv* **traditionally**, generally, usually, as a rule, in the main, by and large, in general [➡ USUALLY; 108]

history 1 *n* **past**, times gone by, times past, olden times, antiquity [➡ PAST; 84] *Opposite*: present **2** *n* **account**, record, chronicle, narration, memoir, saga, description, story, annal (*dated*) [➡ FICTION AND DRAMA; 913]

histrionic *adj* **theatrical**, dramatic, exaggerated, melodramatic, unrestrained, over-the-top (*informal*) [➡ AFFECTATION, SELF-SATISFACTION, AND SNOBBISHNESS; 507] *Opposite*: restrained

histrionics *n* **dramatics**, tantrums, hysterics, scene, melodrama, drama [➡ CHAOS AND UPROAR; 51]

hit 1 *v* **strike**, punch, thump, slap, beat, smack, batter, knock, whack, bang, cuff, rap, slug, sock (*informal*) [➡ PHYSICAL ATTACK AND PUNISHMENT; 415] **2** *v* **crash into**, strike, bang into, bump into, collide with, run into, smash into, ram, bash into (*informal*) [➡ CONTACT: IMPACT; 413] **3** *v* **affect**, afflict, damage, hurt, disadvantage [➡ HAPPEN TO SOMEBODY; 30] **4** *v* (*slang*) **reach**, attain, gain, win, achieve, arrive at, come to, sink to, fall to, rise to (*informal*) [➡ ARRIVE; 12] **5** *n* **blow**, knock, smack, slap, bump, cuff, rap, thump, stroke, shot, punch, lick (*informal*) [➡ CONTACT: IMPACT; 413] **6** *n* **success**, winner, triumph, sensation, market leader, knockout, smash, bestseller [➡ SUCCESS; 82] *Opposite*: flop (*informal*)

hit back *v* **retaliate**, get even, strike back, react, even the score, counterattack, get back, respond, get your own back (*UK*) [➡ COMPETE, CONTEND, AND COMBAT; 303]

hitch 1 *v* **hitchhike**, get a ride, be given a ride, put your thumb out, get a lift, be given a lift, thumb a lift [➡ TRAVEL: WAYS OF TRAVELING; 320] **2** *v* **fasten**, hook, harness, join, tether, attach, connect, tie, couple, lash, make fast, yoke [➡ FASTEN, LINK, AND JOIN; 408] *Opposite*: undo **3** *n* **snag**, catch, drawback, glitch, delay, hindrance, problem, trouble, difficulty, holdup, hang-up, fly in the ointment [➡ PROBLEMS; 256]

hitchhike *v* **hitch**, get a ride, be given a ride, hitch, put your thumb out, thumb a lift, get a lift, be given a lift [➡ TRAVEL: WAYS OF TRAVELING; 320]

hitchhiker *n* [➡ TRAVEL: TRAVELERS AND WALKERS; 319]

hi-tech *adj* [➡ DESCRIBING TECHNOLOGY; 1160]

hither and thither *adv* **here and there**, backward and forward, back and forth, everywhere, all over the place (*informal*) [➡ DIRECTION OF MOTION; 345]

hither and yon (*UK*) *adv* [➡ DIRECTION OF MOTION; 345]

hitherto *adv* **up till now**, up till then, until now, until then, till now, till then, previously, thus far, so far, yet, before, until this time, until that time [➡ PAST; 84]

hit it off (*informal*) *v* **get on well**, connect, get on, make friends, take to each other, get along like a house on

fire, bond, click (*informal*) [➡ ESTABLISHING RELATIONSHIPS WITH OTHERS; 974] *Opposite*: clash

hit man (*slang*) *n* **assassin**, murderer, killer, contract killer, hired gun (*slang*) [➡ PEOPLE WHO KILL; 924]

hit on 1 *v* **think of**, chance upon, discover, realize, arrive at, find, stumble on, come up with, find out, uncover, detect, turn up [➡ LEARN AND DISCOVER; 762] **2** *v* (*slang*) **chat up**, flirt, lead on, make eyes at, pick up (*informal*) [➡ ESTABLISHING RELATIONSHIPS WITH OTHERS; 974]

hit-or-miss *adj* **haphazard**, random, unplanned, unpredictable, careless, slapdash, casual, cursory, aimless, indiscriminate [➡ DISORDER AND CHAOS; 245] *Opposite*: planned

hit out 1 *v* **strike out**, lash out, lunge, go for, attack [➡ PHYSICAL ATTACK AND PUNISHMENT; 415] **2** *v* **criticize**, attack, assail, condemn, lambaste, lay into (*informal*), castigate (*formal*), excoriate (*formal*) [➡ PROTEST AND EXPRESS DISAPPROVAL; 642]

hit squad (*slang*) *n* **task force**, team, squad, unit, commando, working party (*UK*) [➡ GROUPS WITH A COMMON INTEREST; 938]

hit the big time (*slang*) *v* [➡ SUCCEED AND WIN; 79]

hit the gas *v* [➡ MOVE FAST; 313]

hit the hay (*informal*) *v* **go to bed**, retire, say goodnight, get to sleep, get some rest, turn in (*informal*), hit the sack (*informal*), get some shuteye (*informal*) [➡ SLEEP AND DREAM; 723]

hit the jackpot *v* [➡ SUCCEED AND WIN; 79]

hit the road *v* [➡ LEAVE AND GO AWAY; 8]

hit the roof *v* **lose your temper**, be angry, fly into a rage, go berserk, see red (*informal*), fly off the handle (*informal*), lose it (*informal*), blow your top (*informal*), go nuts (*slang*), go ballistic (*slang*) [➡ GIVING VENT TO EMOTIONS; 679] *Opposite*: calm down

hit the sack (*informal*) *see* **hit the hay**

hit upon *v* **stumble on**, chance upon, discover, realize, arrive at, uncover, come up with, think of, detect [➡ LEARN AND DISCOVER; 762]

hive *v* **store**, put away, save, put aside, hoard, squirrel, accumulate, amass, garner, stockpile, keep [➡ STORE AND KEEP; 453] *Opposite*: discard

hive off *v* **cream off**, skim off, transfer, separate, split off, divide off, farm out, subdivide [➡ SEPARATE AND DIVIDE; 401] *Opposite*: merge

hives *n* [➡ CONDITIONS AFFECTING THE SKIN; 721]

hoagie *n* [➡ PREPARED DISHES; 1170]

hoard 1 *v* **save**, store, amass, stockpile, accumulate, collect, gather, put aside, hide away, squirrel, stash (*informal*) [➡ STORE AND KEEP; 453] *Opposite*: throw away **2** *n* **store**, pile, mass, reserve, supply, stockpile, heap, cache, collection, stash (*informal*) [➡ COLLECTIONS AND MIXTURES OF THINGS; 1244]

See Compare and Contrast at **collect**.

hoarder *n* **collector**, saver, accumulator, miser, squirrel (*informal*), magpie (*informal*), pack rat (*informal*) [→ PEOPLE WHO COLLECT THINGS; 454]

hoarding (*UK*) *n* **billboard**, advertisement, placard, poster, bulletin board, notice board (*UK*) [→ SIGNPOSTS, SIGNALS, AND BILLBOARDS; 595]

hoar frost *n* **frost**, ice, rime [→ COLD WEATHER; 1051]

hoarse *adj* **croaky**, gruff, gravelly, husky, rough, throaty, raucous, guttural, rasping, grating [→ LOUD, HIGH, OR UNPLEASANT SOUNDS; 1266] *Opposite*: smooth

hoarseness *n* **croakiness**, gruffness, huskiness, roughness, harshness, throatiness, raucousness, gutturalness [→ LOUD, HIGH, OR UNPLEASANT SOUNDS; 1266] *Opposite*: smoothness

hoary 1 *adj* **overused**, old, ancient, age-old, stale, worn, worn-out, tired, antediluvian (*informal*) [→ OLD, OLD-FASHIONED; 167] *Opposite*: fresh 2 *adj* **white**, snow-white, whitened, snowy, silvery, silver, silvered, gray, grayed [→ HAIR COLOR; 485]

hoax 1 *n* **trick**, deception, practical joke, joke, swindle, ruse, prank, fraud, con, confidence game, con game (*informal*), put-up job (*informal*), scam (*slang*), confidence trick (*UK*) [→ DECEPTION AND LIES; 660] 2 *v* **deceive**, trick, con, swindle, mislead, dupe, pull the wool over somebody's eyes, defraud [→ DECEPTION AND LIES; 660]

hoaxer *n* **trickster**, practical joker, joker, swindler, deceiver, con artist (*slang*), fraudster (*UK*) [→ PEOPLE WHO DECEIVE; 661]

hobble 1 *v* **limp**, hop, shuffle, shamble, totter, stagger, stumble [→ WALK UNSTEADILY; 315] 2 *n* **limp**, shuffle, stagger, shamble, stumble, totter [→ PROCEED AND GO; 305]

hobble skirt *type of* **skirt** [→ GARMENTS AND OUTFITS; 865]

hobby *n* **pastime**, leisure pursuit, diversion, relaxation, sideline, interest, thing (*informal*) [→ LEISURE AND RECREATION; 874] *Opposite*: job

hobbyhorse *n* **favorite subject**, pet topic, idée fixe, bee in your bonnet, obsession, preoccupation, thing (*informal*) [→ FADS, FETISHES, AND IDOLATRY; 555]

hobgoblin *n* **goblin**, imp, elf, pixie, sprite, fairy, brownie, gremlin (*informal*), fay (*literary*) [→ MYTHICAL BEINGS; 789]

hobnob *v* **socialize**, mix, fraternize, associate, go around, be in, mingle, hang out (*informal*) [→ ESTABLISHING RELATIONSHIPS WITH OTHERS; 974] *Opposite*: shun

hobo *n* **traveler**, itinerant, vagrant, tramp, drifter [→ NOMADIC AND ROOTLESS LIFESTYLES; 884]

hock 1 *part of* **horse** [→ HORSES; 985] 2 *type of* **cut** [→ TYPES AND CUTS OF MEAT; 1177] 3 *v* (*slang*) **pawn**, deposit, exchange, pledge [→ EXCHANGE AND INTERCHANGE; 448] *Opposite*: redeem

hockey *n* [→ HOBBIES, GAMES, AND SPORTS; 875]

hockey stick *type of* **sports equipment** [→ SPORTS EQUIPMENT; 879]

hodgepodge *n* **jumble**, medley, mass, assortment, mishmash, potpourri, mixture, miscellany, mixed bag, melange (*literary or formal*), hotchpotch (*UK*) [→ COLLECTIONS AND MIXTURES OF THINGS; 1244]

hoe 1 *v* **turn over**, weed, dig, dig out, loosen [→ USE TOOLS AND MACHINERY; 468] 2 *type of* **cutting tool** [→ CUTTING TOOLS; 1120]

hoedown *n* [→ PARTIES, DANCES, AND CELEBRATIONS; 37]

hog 1 *v* (*informal*) **monopolize**, take over, help yourself, take the lion's share of, hang onto, keep, corner [→ TAKE SOMETHING AWAY; 425] 2 *type of* **farm animal** [→ FARM ANIMALS; 982]

hoggish *adj* [→ BEASTLY AND BRUTISH; 510]

hoglike *adj* [→ BEASTLY AND BRUTISH; 510]

hogwash (*informal*) *n* **nonsense**, gibberish, humbug, garbage, baloney (*informal*), claptrap (*informal*), hooey (*informal*), bunkum (*informal*), twaddle (*informal*), rubbish (*UK*) [→ MEANINGLESS SPEECH OR WRITING; 676]

ho hum (*informal*) *interj* **oh no**, oh well, here we go again, whatever (*informal*), OK (*informal*), right (*informal*) [→ EXPRESSIONS OF SURPRISE AND PLEASURE; 546]

hoi polloi *n* **common herd**, general public, masses, ordinary people, proletariat, populace, plebs, lower classes, public, commoners, lumpenproletariat, underclass [→ CLASS STATUS; 889] *Opposite*: aristocracy

hoist 1 *v* **lift**, raise, pull, heave, erect, elevate, upraise, uplift, winch, heft [→ MOVE SOMETHING UPWARD; 328] 2 *n* **winch**, crane, elevator, pulley, lift (*UK*) [→ MACHINES AND MACHINE PARTS; 1116]

See Compare and Contrast at **raise.**

---

hoity-toity (*informal*) *adj* **haughty**, arrogant, snobbish, proud, disdainful, self-important, conceited, stuck-up, snooty (*informal*), posh (*informal*) [→ AFFECTATION, SELF-SATISFACTION, AND SNOBBISHNESS; 507] *Opposite*: down-to-earth

hokum (*informal*) *n* **nonsense**, humbug, garbage, claptrap (*informal*), hooey (*informal*), bunkum (*informal*), hogwash (*informal*), twaddle (*informal*), rubbish (*UK*) [→ MEANINGLESS SPEECH OR WRITING; 676]

hold 1 *v* **grasp**, clutch, grip, clasp, seize, grab, cling to, embrace, cleave to (*literary*) [→ CONTACT: HOLD; 411] *Opposite*: release 2 *v* **fix**, secure, fasten, bind, attach, keep, wedge [→ FASTEN, LINK, AND JOIN; 408] 3 *v* **embrace**, hug, cuddle, enfold, squeeze, grasp, hold tight, hold close, clasp [→ CONTACT: HOLD; 411] 4 *v* **contain**, accommodate, stow, carry, take in, have space for, comprise, seat, store, take [→ HOLD AND CONTAIN; 455] 5 *v* **detain**, restrain, confine, shut in, imprison, keep, remand, lock up, incarcerate (*formal*) [→ TRIAL, PUNISHMENT, AND LEGAL OUTCOMES; 819] *Opposite*: let go 6 *v* **arrange**, convene, call, conduct, have, run, call together, assemble, organize [→ CAUSE TO HAPPEN; 31] 7 *v* **possess**, have, keep, retain, own, maintain, enjoy, occupy [→ POSSESS; 444] 8 *v* **believe**, think, maintain, presume, consider, regard, view, reckon, feel, opine (*formal*), deem (*formal*) [→ DEVELOP THEORIES AND REASON; 744] 9 *v* **sustain**, maintain, continue, keep up, carry on, extend, draw out, stretch out [→ CONTINUE TO EXIST; 17] 10 *v* **wait**, hold on, hang on, stay on the line [→ TELEPHONE, PAGE, AND TEXT; 681] *Opposite*: hang up 11 *n* **grip**, grasp, clasp, clutch, embrace, clamp, clench [→ CONTACT: HOLD; 411] 12 *n* **control**, power, influence, claim, sway, grasp, command, spell [→ IMPORTANCE AND SIGNIFICANCE; 192] 13 *n* **storage space**, storeroom, cargo bay, compartment, storage [→ STORES AND STORAGE BUILDINGS; 1088] 14 *part of* **ship or boat** [→ PARTS OF A SHIP OR BOAT; 1151]

hold accountable *v* [→ ACCUSE, BLAME, AND CRITICIZE; 641]

hold back 1 v **restrain**, inhibit, suppress, repress, contain, control, check, limit, hamper, obstruct, hinder, impede [➡ AVOID, PREVENT, LIMIT, AND CONTROL; 277] *Opposite:* let go 2 v **keep back**, retain, keep, reserve, keep hold of, save, withhold, hide, conceal, delay, stifle [➡ STORE AND KEEP; 453] *Opposite:* release

See Compare and Contrast at **hinder.**

hold captive v [➡ CAPTIVITY AND LOSS OF FREEDOM; 248]

hold close v **hug**, embrace, hold tight, cuddle, enfold, squeeze, grasp, clasp [➡ CONTACT: HOLD; 411] *Opposite:* release

hold dear v [➡ LIKE, LOVE, VALUE, AND ENJOY; 578]

hold down (*informal*) v **keep**, retain, maintain, manage, hang onto, look after, keep hold of [➡ STORE AND KEEP; 453] *Opposite:* lose

holder 1 n **container**, pouch, receptacle, vessel, box, frame, pocket, caddy [➡ CONTAINERS, RECEPTACLES, AND PACKAGING; 1245] 2 n **owner**, possessor, proprietor, controller, bearer, defender [➡ OWNERS; 446]

hold forth v **speak out**, harangue, preach, lecture, discourse, go on, rant, orate (*formal*), opine (*formal*) [➡ UTTER AND PRONOUNCE; 608] *Opposite:* bottle up

hold in 1 v **keep in check**, restrain, keep back, hold back, control, bridle, constrain, inhibit [➡ CAPTIVITY AND LOSS OF FREEDOM; 248] *Opposite:* release 2 v **restrain**, keep the lid on, control, bridle, suppress, repress, inhibit [➡ AVOID, PREVENT, LIMIT, AND CONTROL; 277] *Opposite:* let out

hold in contempt v [➡ DISLIKE AND HATE; 577]

holding 1 n **land**, field, property, farm, croft, plot, allotment, acreage [➡ THE COUNTRYSIDE AND OUTDOOR SPACES; 1071] 2 n **stock**, investment, share, property, interest, bond, asset [➡ POSSESSIONS; 461]

hold in high regard v **revere**, respect, venerate, idolize, esteem, admire, think highly of, have a high opinion of [➡ LIKE, LOVE, VALUE, AND ENJOY; 578] *Opposite:* despise

hold in the highest regard v [➡ LIKE, LOVE, VALUE, AND ENJOY; 578]

hold off 1 v **refrain**, postpone, delay, put off, avoid, keep from, defer, adjourn, remit [➡ SHIRK AND DELAY; 273] *Opposite:* speed up 2 v **resist**, fend off, keep away, keep off, repel, repulse, keep at bay, rebuff, rebut [➡ AVOID OR ESCAPE CONTACT; 418] *Opposite:* yield

hold on 1 v **wait**, hang on, be patient, wait a minute, hold your horses (*informal*), wait up (*informal*), chill out (*slang*) [➡ SHIRK AND DELAY; 273] 2 v **persist**, persevere, keep on, stand your ground, stand firm, stick at it, last out, stick it out, hold out, hang in there (*informal*) [➡ TOLERATE AND ENDURE; 766] *Opposite:* give up 3 v **grasp**, grip, keep hold of, hold fast, stick, clasp, clutch, hang on [➡ CONTACT: HOLD; 411] *Opposite:* let go

hold onto 1 v **retain**, keep, hang onto, save, hoard, store, set aside [➡ STORE AND KEEP; 453] *Opposite:* give up 2 v **grasp**, clasp, clutch, grip, stick, keep hold of, hold fast, hang onto, cling to [➡ CONTACT: HOLD; 411] *Opposite:* release

hold out 1 v **extend**, give, present, offer, proffer, stretch out [➡ PROFFER AND HAND OVER; 431] *Opposite:* withdraw 2 v **endure**,

stand your ground, persist, stand firm, withstand, persevere, stand fast, last, resist [➡ TOLERATE AND ENDURE; 766] *Opposite:* give in

hold out on v **not tell**, keep something from, hide something from, withhold something from [➡ WITHHOLD INFORMATION; 687] *Opposite:* tell

hold over v **defer**, delay, postpone, put off, suspend, adjourn, keep, hold up, shelve [➡ DELAY ACTION OR OCCURRENCE; 278] *Opposite:* bring forward

hold prisoner v [➡ CAPTIVITY AND LOSS OF FREEDOM; 248]

hold responsible v [➡ ACCUSE, BLAME, AND CRITICIZE; 641]

hold sway v **have authority**, have influence, have power, be in power, be in control, reign, govern, rule, rule the roost [➡ BE IN CHARGE; 270]

hold the fort v **look after things**, take care of things, take over, take charge, mind things, attend to things [➡ BE IN CHARGE; 270]

hold up 1 v **delay**, slow down, slow up, impede, hinder, set back, detain, hold back, remit, suspend, postpone, defer [➡ DELAY ACTION OR OCCURRENCE; 278] *Opposite:* speed up 2 v **rob**, raid, mug, stick up (*informal*), do (*slang*) [➡ STEAL AND ROB; 426] 3 v **survive**, bear up, keep up, endure, keep going, hold out, last [➡ CONTINUE TO EXIST; 17] *Opposite:* give up 4 v **support**, shore up, keep up, prop, sustain, buttress [➡ IMPROVE STRENGTH AND DURABILITY; 378] *Opposite:* bring down

holdup 1 n **theft**, raid, robbery, assault, mugging, stickup (*informal*), heist (*slang*) [➡ CRIMES; 817] 2 n **delay**, hitch, glitch, snag, stoppage, obstruction, difficulty, bottleneck, hindrance, snafu (*informal*) [➡ PROBLEMS; 256]

hold with v **approve of**, endorse, support, subscribe to, agree with, like, accept, countenance (*formal*) [➡ APPROVE AND CONFIRM; 646] *Opposite:* disapprove

hold your own 1 v **bear up**, persevere, be stable, be comfortable, persist, endure, hang on [➡ TOLERATE AND ENDURE; 766] *Opposite:* succumb 2 v **match up**, stand your ground, stand firm, look after yourself, take care of yourself, give a good account of yourself, compete, acquit yourself well (*formal*) [➡ CONTINUE AN ACTION; 262]

hole 1 n **cavity**, hollow, void, chasm, gulf, abyss, pit, dip [➡ HOLES, GAPS, AND FORKS; 1252] 2 n **aperture**, gap, opening, crack, break, outlet, puncture, fissure, tear, perforation [➡ HOLES, GAPS, AND FORKS; 1252] 3 n **burrow**, lair, retreat, run, sett, warren, den, earth (*UK*) [➡ ANIMAL OR BIRD ACCOMMODATIONS; 1079] 4 n **flaw**, weakness, fault, error, defect, inconsistency [➡ FAULTS, FLAWS, AND WEAKNESSES; 251] *Opposite:* strength 5 n (*informal*) **hovel**, slum, shack, pigpen, dump (*informal*), fleabag (*informal*), pigsty (*UK*), fleapit (*UK*) [➡ UNDESIRABLE ACCOMMODATIONS; 856]

hole-and-corner (*UK*) adj **secret**, hidden, clandestine, private, undercover, secretive [➡ SECRET AND UNKNOWN; 179] *Opposite:* public

hole-in-the-wall (*informal*) n **restaurant**, bar, bistro, café, dive (*informal*), joint (*slang*) [➡ HOTELS, RESTAURANTS, AND CLUBS; 1082]

hole up (*slang*) v **hide**, shut up, hibernate, seclude, closet, retreat [➡ LEAVE AND GO AWAY; 8] *Opposite:* emerge

holey *adj* **leaky**, porous, perforated, worn, torn, punctured [➡ IN BAD REPAIR; 1234]

holiday 1 *n* **day off**, break, long weekend, personal day, trip, outing, leave, R & R [➡ PERIODS OF REST; 91] 2 *n* **leave**, time off, break, vacation, sabbatical, leave of absence [➡ PERIODS OF REST; 91] *Opposite*: work 3 *n* **legal holiday**, federal holiday, anniversary, feast, saint's day, carnival, festival, public holiday (*UK*), bank holiday (*UK*) [➡ PARTIES, DANCES, AND CELEBRATIONS; 37] 4 *v* (*UK*) **be on holiday**, stay, relax, vacation, be on vacation, sojourn (*literary*) [➡ LACK OF ACTIVITY OR MOTION; 342] *Opposite*: work

holidaymaker (*UK*) *n* **traveler**, sightseer, vacationer, visitor, tourist, day tripper [➡ TRAVEL: TRAVELERS AND WALKERS; 319] *Opposite*: resident

holier-than-thou (*informal*) *adj* **self-righteous**, pious, smug, superior, sanctimonious, pompous [➡ AFFECTATION, SELF-SATISFACTION, AND SNOBBISHNESS; 507] *Opposite*: self-effacing

holiness *n* **sanctity**, sacredness, piety, godliness, religiousness, saintliness, consecration, devoutness, devotion, purity [➡ RELIGIOUS CONCEPTS; 776]

holistic *adj* **all-inclusive**, rounded, full, complete, general, universal, whole [➡ WHOLENESS AND COMPLETENESS; 198]

hollandaise *type of* **seasonings, sauces, and dips** [➡ SEASONINGS AND SAUCES; 1174]

holler (*informal*) 1 *v* **shout**, yell, scream, shriek, howl, bawl, bellow, call [➡ SOUND EMISSION BY PEOPLE; 363] *Opposite*: whisper 2 *n* **yell**, shout, scream, shriek, howl, bellow, call [➡ SOUNDS MADE BY PEOPLE; 1262] *Opposite*: whisper

hollow 1 *adj* **empty**, void, unfilled, vacant, unoccupied [➡ EMPTY; 1238] *Opposite*: solid 2 *adj* **concave**, depressed, sunken, indented, cavernous [➡ ROUNDED SHAPE; 1218] *Opposite*: convex 3 *adj* **resonating**, echoing, deep, low, dull, muffled, muted, dead, heavy, reverberating, reverberant, resounding [➡ SOFT, LOW, OR PLEASANT SOUNDS; 1265] *Opposite*: high-pitched 4 *adj* **insincere**, empty, worthless, futile, vain, false, insignificant, unconvincing, cynical, meaningless [➡ FALSE AND UNREAL; 173] *Opposite*: sincere 5 *n* **cavity**, recess, indentation, cup, nook, curve, hole, cave, cavern [➡ HOLES, GAPS, AND FORKS; 1252] *Opposite*: bulge 6 *n* **valley**, crater, dip, depression, basin, trough, bowl, dell (*literary*) [➡ GEOLOGIC FEATURES; 1056] *Opposite*: hill 7 *v* **excavate**, scoop, dig out, gouge, tunnel, burrow, scrape, carve out [➡ EMPTY AND UNLOAD; 407] *Opposite*: fill

See Compare and Contrast at **vain**.

hollowly 1 *adv* **dully**, deeply, flatly, heavily, resoundingly, reverberantly [➡ SOFT, LOW, OR PLEASANT SOUNDS; 1265] *Opposite*: shrilly 2 *adv* **insincerely**, emptily, worthlessly, futilely, vainly, falsely, unconvincingly, cynically, meaninglessly [➡ FALSE AND UNREAL; 173] *Opposite*: sincerely

hollowness 1 *n* **void**, empty space, cavity, emptiness, concavity, openness [➡ HOLES, GAPS, AND FORKS; 1252] *Opposite*: solidity 2 *n* **insincerity**, emptiness, worthlessness, futility, vainness, falseness, unconvincingness, meaninglessness [➡ FALSE AND UNREAL; 173] *Opposite*: sincerity

holly *type of* **evergreen tree** [➡ EVERGREEN AND CONIFEROUS TREES; 1029]

holocaust *n* [➡ AGGRESSIVE EVENTS; 39]

Holocene *type of* **epoch** [➡ EPOCHS AND ERAS; 89]

holy 1 *adj* **sacred**, consecrated, hallowed, sanctified, blessed, divine [➡ RELIGIOUS CONCEPTS; 776] 2 *adj* **saintly**, righteous, devout, religious, godly, pious, pure, virtuous, faithful [➡ RELIGIOUS CONCEPTS; 776] *Opposite*: irreligious

holy day *n* [➡ RELIGIOUS CONCEPTS; 776]

Holy Father *n* [➡ RELIGIOUS PEOPLE; 778]

holy man *n* [➡ RELIGIOUS PEOPLE; 778]

holy of holies *n* [➡ RELIGIOUS CONCEPTS, 776]

holy rites *n* [➡ RELIGIOUS CONCEPTS; 776]

holy sister *n* [➡ RELIGIOUS PEOPLE; 778]

homage *n* **deference**, reverence, respect, service, duty, worship, honor, praise, tribute [➡ LOVE, RESPECT, AND GOODWILL; 549] *Opposite*: disrespect

homburg *type of* **hat** [➡ ACCESSORIES, MILLINERY, AND LINGERIE; 867]

home 1 *n* **residence**, house, habitat, quarters, address, dwelling (*formal*), domicile (*formal*), abode (*literary*) [➡ ACCOMMODATIONS; 855] 2 *n* **family**, household, family circle, family unit, background, home environment [➡ THE FAMILY; 956] 3 *n* **birthplace**, place of birth, homeland, home town, native land, fatherland, motherland, native soil [➡ COUNTRIES AND REGIONS; 1067] 4 *n* **institution**, residence, residential home, children's home, assisted living, rest home, eldercare, nursing home, establishment, hospice [➡ PUBLIC BUILDINGS AND MEETING PLACES; 1081] 5 *adj* **internal**, domestic, inland, interior, local, national [➡ GOVERNMENT AND POLITICS; 805] *Opposite*: foreign 6 *adj* **home-based**, household, homegrown, family, domestic, homespun, homemade, home-produced [➡ ACCOMMODATIONS; 855] *Opposite*: industrial 7 *adv* **homeward**, back home, in, home sweet home, back at the ranch (*informal*) [➡ DIRECTION OF MOTION; 345]

homebrew *n* [➡ DRINKS; 1187]

homecoming *n* **return**, arrival, repatriation, visit, revisiting [➡ ARRIVAL; 13] *Opposite*: emigration

home fries *type of* **processed potato** [➡ FRUIT AND VEGETABLES; 1176]

home help (*UK*) *n* **domestic**, cleaner, maid, au pair, housekeeper, carer (*UK*) [➡ DOMESTIC AND KITCHEN WORKERS; 850]

home in *v* **focus**, zoom in, move in, aim, take aim, point, zero in, concentrate on, pinpoint [➡ FIND; 463] *Opposite*: draw back

homeland *n* **native country**, mother country, native land, fatherland, motherland, home, birthplace, land of birth, land of origin [➡ COUNTRIES AND REGIONS; 1067]

homeless *adj* **on the streets**, living rough, dispossessed, destitute, vagrant, displaced, itinerant, poor, adrift [➡ POVERTY AND POOR; 892] *Opposite*: housed

homelessness *n* [➡ POVERTY AND POOR; 892]

homely 1 *adj* **unattractive**, plain, unappealing, ugly, mousy, unlovely [➡ PLAIN; 232] *Opposite*: attractive 2 *adj* **simple**, plain, ordinary, unpretentious, cozy, informal, comfortable [➡ PLAIN; 232] *Opposite*: fancy

homeopathy *type of* **complementary therapy** [➤ REMEDIES, TREATMENTS, AND OPERATIONS; 731]

home page *n* [➤ THE INTERNET; 1128]

home rule *n* **self-government**, autonomy, self-rule, independence, separatism, nationalism [➤ STYLES AND SYSTEMS OF GOVERNMENT; 806]

homesick *adj* **nostalgic**, sad, melancholy, pining, unsettled, upset, wistful, unhappy [➤ SADNESS, DISTRESS, AND DESPAIR; 539] *Opposite*: content

homesickness *n* [➤ SADNESS, DISTRESS, AND DESPAIR; 539]

homespun *adj* **plain**, simple, ordinary, unsophisticated, down-to-earth, uncomplicated, straightforward, unpretentious [➤ PLAIN; 232] *Opposite*: sophisticated

homestead 1 *n* **farm**, farmstead, ranch, croft, estate, smallholding (*UK*) [➤ HUMAN SETTLEMENTS; 1070] 2 *type of* **house** [➤ RESIDENTIAL BUILDINGS; 1078]

home town *n* **birthplace**, home, home base, back yard, home ground, turf (*informal*) [➤ HUMAN SETTLEMENTS; 1070]

home truth *n* **fact**, truth, bitter pill, criticism [➤ ADVICE; 689] *Opposite*: lie

homework 1 *n* **schoolwork**, exercise, lesson, study, assignment, coursework, project, task [➤ CLASSES, COURSEWORK, AND EXAMINATIONS; 842] 2 *n* (*informal*) **preparation**, reading, research, groundwork, reading up, fact-finding, legwork (*informal*) [➤ CLASSES, COURSEWORK, AND EXAMINATIONS; 842]

homeworker (*UK*) *n* [➤ WORKERS; 836]

homeworking (*UK*) *n* [➤ TYPES OF WORK; 835]

homicidal *adj* **murderous**, destructive, killer, killing, bloodthirsty, dangerous, violent, vindictive [➤ AGGRESSIVE AND BELLIGERENT; 518] *Opposite*: harmless

homicide *n* **killing**, murder, slaughter, manslaughter, assassination [➤ CAUSES OF DEATH; 921]

homily *n* **lecture**, sermon, talk, speech, discourse, oration [➤ ONE-WAY COMMUNICATION; 49]

homing pigeon *type of* **pet bird** [➤ BIRDS; 997]

hominid *n* **primate**, hominoid, anthropoid [➤ PERSON; 931]

hominoid *see* **hominid**

homochromatic *adj* [➤ DESCRIBING COLORS; 1226]

homochromous *adj* [➤ DESCRIBING COLORS; 1226]

homogeneity 1 *n* **sameness**, similarity, equality, homogeneousness, consistency, regularity [➤ SAMENESS; 150] 2 *n* **uniformity**, consistency, evenness, regularity, smoothness, harmony [➤ SAMENESS; 150] *Opposite*: unevenness

homogeneous 1 *adj* **same**, similar, standardized, consistent, equal, regular, identical [➤ SAMENESS; 150] *Opposite*: heterogeneous 2 *adj* **uniform**, consistent, even, regular, smooth, harmonized [➤ SAMENESS; 150] *Opposite*: uneven

homogeneousness 1 *n* **sameness**, similarity, equality, homogeneity, consistency, regularity [➤ SAMENESS; 150] 2 *n* **uniformity**, regularity, consistency, evenness, smoothness, harmony [➤ SAMENESS; 150] *Opposite*: unevenness

homogenize 1 *v* **standardize**, normalize, even out, regulate, make the same, make uniform [➤ ARRANGE AND CREATE ORDER; 357] *Opposite*: distinguish 2 *v* **smooth**, emulsify, mix, beat, whip, combine, treat [➤ COOKING AND FOOD PREPARATION; 353] *Opposite*: separate out

homophobic *adj* [➤ NEGATIVE INTELLECTUAL CHARACTERISTICS; 525]

homo sapiens *n* [➤ PERSON; 931]

honcho (*slang*) *n* [➤ IMPORTANT OR FAMOUS PEOPLE; 893]

hone 1 *v* **improve**, refine, enhance, polish, sharpen, perfect, work on, practice, groom, prepare [➤ IMPROVE SOMETHING; 374] *Opposite*: impair 2 *v* **sharpen**, whet, file, grind, polish, point [➤ CLEAN AND POLISH; 403] *Opposite*: blunt

honest 1 *adj* **upright**, trustworthy, moral, good, decent, law-abiding, reliable, responsible, scrupulous, honorable [➤ MORALLY GOOD; 774] *Opposite*: immoral 2 *adj* **truthful**, authentic, true, sincere, frank, candid, straightforward, direct, open [➤ HONEST AND OPEN; 630] *Opposite*: untruthful

honestly 1 *adv* **fairly**, justly, in all conscience, decently, reliably, scrupulously, in good conscience, honorably [➤ HONEST AND OPEN; 630] *Opposite*: immorally 2 *adv* **really**, truly, truthfully, candidly, openly, in all honesty, genuinely, sincerely [➤ TRUE AND REAL; 171] *Opposite*: untruthfully

honesty 1 *n* **uprightness**, morality, trustworthiness, goodness, scrupulousness, decency, rectitude, righteousness, fairness, honor, reliability [➤ MORALLY GOOD; 774] *Opposite*: immorality 2 *n* **sincerity**, truthfulness, integrity, frankness, candor, openness, authenticity, straightforwardness, directness [➤ HONEST AND RELIABLE; 502] *Opposite*: dishonesty

honey 1 *n* (*informal*) **darling**, dear, dearest, sweetheart, sugar (*informal*), sweetie (*informal*), honeybunch (*informal*), honeybun (*informal*), sweetie pie (*informal*) [➤ ENDEARMENTS; 656] 2 *type of* **preserve** [➤ SUGAR AND PRESERVES; 1184] 3 *type of* **beige** [➤ COLORS; 1224]

honeybun (*informal*) *n* [➤ ENDEARMENTS; 656]

honeybunch (*informal*) *n* [➤ ENDEARMENTS; 656]

honeyed 1 *adj* **ingratiating**, sugarcoated, cloying, flattering, fawning, persuasive [➤ INGRATIATING; 638] *Opposite*: sharp 2 *adj* **melodious**, soft, dulcet, sweet, pleasing, soothing, melodic, mellifluous [➤ SOFT, LOW, OR PLEASANT SOUNDS; 1265] *Opposite*: harsh

honeymoon period *n* [➤ PLEASANT SITUATIONS; 74]

honey-pie (*informal*) *n* [➤ ENDEARMENTS; 656]

honeysuckle *type of* **climber** [➤ CLIMBERS; 1033]

honk 1 *n* **hoot**, beep, blare, blast, blow, tootle (*informal*) [➤ RINGING AND HOOTING SOUNDS; 1259] 2 *type of* **continuous sound** [➤ CONTINUOUS SOUNDS; 1258] 3 *v* **beep**, hoot, blare, blast, blow, tootle (*informal*) [➤ EMIT RINGING AND HOOTING SOUNDS; 367]

honky-tonk (*slang*) 1 *n* [➤ BUILDINGS FOR PUBLIC ENTERTAINMENT; 1084] 2 *type of* **jazz music** [➤ MUSIC, SONGS, AND SINGING; 907]

honor 1 *n* **integrity**, decency, righteousness, principle, uprightness, scrupulousness, rectitude, morality, character [➤ MORALLY GOOD; 774] *Opposite*: baseness 2 *n* **respect**, admiration, esteem, regard, reverence, devotion [➤ LOVE, RESPECT, AND GOODWILL; 549] *Opposite*: scorn 3 *n* **dignity**, distinction, nobility, pride, decorum, graciousness [➡GOOD MANNERS AND SOCIAL SKILLS; 520] **4** *n* **reputation**, image, good name, name, renown, repute (*formal*) [➡NAME AND DESCRIBE; 665] *Opposite*: disgrace **5** *n* **award**, distinction, tribute, credit, accolade, compliment, commendation, commemoration, remembrance, recognition, medal, badge, certificate, medallion, degree, blue ribbon, gold medal [➡REWARDS AND AWARDS; 439] *Opposite*: blot **6** *n* **privilege**, occasion, opportunity, milestone, high-water mark, peak [➡TREATS; 210] *Opposite*: disgrace **7** *v* **esteem**, respect, admire, revere, reverence, venerate, pay tribute to, pay homage to, toast, exalt (*formal*) [➡LIKE, LOVE, VALUE, AND ENJOY; 578] *Opposite*: disparage **8** *v* **keep**, stick to, carry out, fulfill [➡OBEY AND ABIDE BY; 301] *Opposite*: break

honorable **1** *adj* **moral**, decent, worthy, proper, upright, noble, good, fair, righteous, right, ethical, principled [➡MORALLY GOOD; 774] *Opposite*: immoral **2** *adj* **respectable**, decent, admirable, praiseworthy, worthy, laudable [➡MORALLY GOOD; 774] *Opposite*: shameful

honorarium *n* **payment**, fee, grant, scholarship, stipend, allowance, exhibition (*UK*) [➡GIFTS; 438]

See Compare and Contrast at **wage**.

honorary **1** *adj* **nominal**, token, symbolic, titular [➡REPRESENTATIVE; 66] **2** *adj* **unpaid**, voluntary, unsalaried, amateur, volunteer, complimentary, pro bono, unwaged (*UK*) [➡EMPLOYMENT STATUS; 831] *Opposite*: salaried

honored *adj* **privileged**, pleased, flattered, grateful, thrilled [➡PLEASURE, EXCITEMENT, AND ELATION; 534] *Opposite*: insulted

hooch (*slang*) *n* [➡DRINKS; 1187]

hood **1** *type of* **headgear** [➡ACCESSORIES, MILLINERY, AND LINGERIE; 867] **2** *part of* **external structure** [➡EXTERNAL PARTS OF A VEHICLE; 1147] **3** *n* (*slang*) **hoodlum**, gangster, criminal, lawbreaker, thug, hooligan (*informal*), mobster (*informal*), ruffian (*dated*) [➡VILLAINS AND THUGS; 947] **4** *n* (*slang*) **neighborhood**, area, district, region, quarter, turf (*informal*) [➡PLACE; 1065]

hoodlum *n* **gangster**, criminal, lawbreaker, thug, vandal, delinquent, mobster (*informal*), hooligan (*informal*), hood (*slang*), ruffian (*dated*) [➡VILLAINS AND THUGS; 947]

hoodwink *v* **trick**, deceive, dupe, delude, take in, con, fool, pull the wool over somebody's eyes [➡DECEPTION AND LIES; 660]

hooey (*informal*) *n* **nonsense**, humbug, gibberish, garbage, baloney (*informal*), hogwash (*informal*), bunkum (*informal*), twaddle (*informal*), claptrap (*informal*), bunk (*slang*), rubbish (*UK*) [➡MEANINGLESS SPEECH OR WRITING; 676] *Opposite*: fact

hoof *part of* **horse** [➡HORSES; 985]

hoo-hah (*slang*) *n* **scene**, row, fuss, commotion, hubbub, disturbance, hullabaloo, stir, flap (*informal*), to-do (*informal*) [➡CHAOS AND UPROAR; 51]

hook **1** *n* **peg**, hanger, nail, knob, catch, fishhook, meat hook, boat hook [➡FASTENERS, LINKS, AND NETWORKS; 1247] **2** *v* **fasten**, attach, secure, join, tie, couple, button, fix [➡FASTEN, LINK, AND JOIN; 408]

hook and eye *n* **fastener**, fastening, clasp, catch, clip [➡FASTENERS, LINKS, AND NETWORKS; 1247]

hooked **1** *adj* (*slang*) **obsessed**, infatuated, enthusiastic, keen, captivated, passionate, smitten (*humorous or literary*) [➡PENSIVENESS AND INTEREST; 538] *Opposite*: unenthusiastic **2** *adj* **bent**, curved, bowed, curving, angular, aquiline [➡ROUNDED SHAPE; 1218] *Opposite*: straight

hook up **1** *v* **connect**, link up, plug in, wire up, electrify [➡FASTEN, LINK, AND JOIN; 408] *Opposite*: disconnect **2** *v* (*informal*) **get together**, take up with, meet up, meet, pair off, make friends [➡INITIATE AND ESTABLISH COMMUNICATION; 680] *Opposite*: part

hooligan (*informal*) *n* **criminal**, gangster, lawbreaker, thug, hoodlum, vandal, delinquent, mobster (*informal*), ruffian (*dated*) [➡VILLAINS AND THUGS; 947]

hoop *n* **ring**, loop, band, circle, round, girdle [➡ROUNDED SHAPE; 1218]

hoopla (*informal*) *n* [➡MEANINGLESS SPEECH OR WRITING; 676]

hooray *interj* [➡EXPRESSIONS OF SURPRISE AND PLEASURE; 546]

hoot **1** *n* **beep**, honk, blare, blast, tootle (*informal*) [➡RINGING AND HOOTING SOUNDS; 1259] **2** *n* **whoop**, howl, shout, roar, cry, yell [➡SOUNDS MADE BY BIRDS; 1263] **3** *n* (*slang*) **laughingstock**, laugh (*informal*), riot (*informal*), scream (*informal*), gas (*slang*) [➡FUNNY AND AMUSING; 216] **4** *type of* **continuous sound** [➡CONTINUOUS SOUNDS; 1258] **5** *v* **beep**, honk, blare, blow, tootle (*informal*) [➡EMIT RINGING AND HOOTING SOUNDS; 367] **6** *v* **shout**, howl, whoop, roar, cry out, yell [➡SOUND EMISSION BY ANIMALS OR BIRDS; 364]

hoot owl *type of* **owl** [➡OWLS; 1001]

hop **1** *v* **jump**, skip, leap, bounce, dance, pogo (*UK*) [➡BOUNCE, UNDULATE, AND VIBRATE; 308] **2** *v* **spring**, bound, leap, bounce, jump, vault [➡BOUNCE, UNDULATE, AND VIBRATE; 308] **3** *n* **leap**, jump, skip, bound, step, spring [➡PROCEED AND GO; 305] **4** *n* (*informal*) **flight**, journey, trip, stage, leg, step [➡TRAVEL, JOURNEYS AND TRIPS; 318] **5** *n* (*dated informal*) **dance**, party, disco, hoedown, barn dance, social, shindig (*informal*), bop (*informal*) [➡PARTIES, DANCES, AND CELEBRATIONS; 37]

hope **1** *v* **want**, expect, trust, anticipate, wish, yearn, long, look forward to [➡DESIRE AND WANT; 579] *Opposite*: despair **2** *n* **confidence**, expectation, optimism, anticipation, faith, courage, hopefulness [➡FEELINGS ABOUT THE FUTURE; 533] *Opposite*: despair **3** *n* **likelihood**, prospect, possibility, promise, potential, chance [➡POSSIBLE AND PROBABLE; 177] *Opposite*: impossibility **4** *n* **desire**, aspiration, dream, expectation, plan, wish, goal [➡DESIRE AND WANT; 579]

hopeful **1** *adj* **confident**, expectant, optimistic, positive, encouraged, buoyant, anticipative [➡COOL AND CALM; 536] *Opposite*: pessimistic **2** *adj* **promising**, encouraging, positive, rosy, propitious, likely [➡EMOTIONALLY PLEASANT; 187] *Opposite*: discouraging **3** *adj* **aspiring**, prospective, would-be, potential, budding, embryonic, possible [➡POSSIBLE AND PROBABLE; 177] **4** *n* **aspirant**, candidate, applicant, contender, seeker [➡COMPETITORS; 41]

hopefully **1** *adv* **with any luck**, with a bit of luck, all being well [➡POSSIBLE AND PROBABLE; 177] **2** *adv* **confidently**, expectantly, optimistically, positively, buoyantly [➡COOL AND CALM; 536] *Opposite*: despairingly

hopefulness **1** *n* **confidence**, hope, optimism, expectation, anticipation, positiveness, positivity [➡FEELINGS ABOUT THE FUTURE; 533] *Opposite*: despair **2** *n* **promise**, encouragement, positiveness, positivity, rosiness, propitiousness [➡ EMOTIONALLY PLEASANT; 187]

hopeless 1 *adj* **impossible**, desperate, unpromising, fruitless, bleak, doomed, bad [➡ EMOTIONALLY UNPLEASANT AND UPSETTING; 227] *Opposite*: promising 2 *adj* **despairing**, desperate, in despair, despondent, disheartened, downhearted, forlorn, depressed, miserable, morose, bummed out (*informal*) [➡ SADNESS, DISTRESS, AND DESPAIR; 539] *Opposite*: positive 3 *adj* **useless**, bad, pathetic, inept, incompetent, terrible, clueless (*informal*) [➡ UNSKILLED; 529] *Opposite*: excellent

hopelessly 1 *adv* **terribly**, desperately, badly, completely, totally, utterly, awfully, very [➡ TO A GREAT EXTENT; 132] *Opposite*: slightly 2 *adv* **despairingly**, in despair, desperately, despondently, downheartedly, forlornly, miserably, bleakly [➡ SADNESS, DISTRESS, AND DESPAIR; 539] *Opposite*: positively

hopelessness 1 *n* **despair**, desperation, despondency, bleakness, depression, misery [➡ FEELINGS ABOUT THE FUTURE; 533] *Opposite*: hope 2 *n* **impossibility**, desperateness, fruitlessness, bleakness, futility [➡ IMPOSSIBLE AND IMPROBABLE; 178] *Opposite*: promise 3 *n* **uselessness**, ineptness, ineptitude, incompetence, inability, cluelessness (*informal*) [➡ UNSKILLED; 529] *Opposite*: excellence

hopping mad (*informal*) *adj* **enraged**, furious, irate, apoplectic, beside yourself, seething, angry, annoyed [➡ IRRITATION AND ANGER; 541] *Opposite*: calm

horde *n* **throng**, crowd, mass, gang, group, multitude, host, flock, pack [➡ GROUPS OF PEOPLE; 935]

hordes *n* [➡ MANY, MUCH, LARGE AMOUNT; 117]

horizon *n* **skyline**, distance, vanishing point, vista, prospect, limit [➡ VIEWS AND OUTLOOKS; 1073]

horizontal *adj* **level**, flat, straight, plane [➡ ORIENTATION AND ALIGNMENT; 1223] *Opposite*: vertical

horn 1 *n* **siren**, hooter, alarm, buzzer, bleeper, alert [➡ AUDIO EQUIPMENT; 1139] 2 *n* **antler**, spine, barb, projection, tusk, point, spike [➡ EXTREMITIES OF PHYSICAL OBJECTS; 1250] 3 *type of* **controls** [➡ INTERNAL PARTS OF A VEHICLE; 1146] 4 *type of* **brass instrument** [➡ MUSICAL INSTRUMENTS; 910]

hornbeam *type of* **deciduous tree** [➡ DECIDUOUS TREES; 1028]

hornblende *type of* **stone** [➡ STONES, ROCKS, AND BOULDERS; 1057]

horned lizard *type of* **reptile** [➡ REPTILES; 994]

horned toad *type of* **amphibian** [➡ AMPHIBIANS; 1008]

horned viper *type of* **poisonous snake** [➡ SNAKES; 995]

hornet *type of* **flying insect** [➡ FLYING INSECTS; 1013]

hornet's nest *n* [➡ DIFFICULT SITUATIONS; 72]

horn in (*informal*) *v* [➡ INTERRUPT AND BUTT IN; 619]

horn of plenty 1 *n* **cornucopia**, abundance, treasure chest, ready supply, never-ending supply, treasure house, treasury, Aladdin's cave [➡ MANY, MUCH, LARGE AMOUNT; 117] *Opposite*: famine 2 *type of* **fungus** [➡ MICROORGANISMS, FUNGI, AND ALGAE; 1023]

horny *adj* [➡ DIFFICULTY AND COMPLEXITY; 242]

horrendous 1 *adj* **dreadful**, awful, terrible, dire, unbear-

able, atrocious, unspeakable, horrific, ghastly, hideous, horrible, appalling, upsetting, shocking, staggering [➡ EMOTIONALLY UNPLEASANT AND UPSETTING; 227] *Opposite*: wonderful 2 *adj* (*informal*) **outrageous**, exorbitant, sky-high, shocking, dreadful, terrible [➡ EXPENSIVE AND OVERPRICED; 247]

horrible *adj* **unpleasant**, bad, awful, vile, nasty, dreadful, disgusting, horrid, hideous, horrendous, horrific, horrifying, terrible, atrocious, repulsive, unspeakable, ghastly, appalling [➡ EMOTIONALLY UNPLEASANT AND UPSETTING; 227] *Opposite*: pleasant

horribly 1 *adv* **unpleasantly**, dreadfully, badly, terribly, unbearably, disgustingly, hideously, awfully, atrociously, unspeakably, horrifically, horrendously, appallingly [➡ EMOTIONALLY UNPLEASANT AND UPSETTING; 227] *Opposite*: pleasantly 2 *adv* **extremely**, greatly, very, totally, utterly, absolutely, unbearably, outrageously [➡ TO A GREAT EXTENT; 132]

horrid 1 *adj* **disgusting**, awful, dreadful, nasty, vile, horrible, unspeakable, loathsome, repellent, despicable, beastly [➡ DISGUSTING AND REPULSIVE; 230] *Opposite*: pleasant 2 *adj* **dreadful**, shocking, appalling, horrific, frightful, hideous [➡ FRIGHTENING; 231]

horridly *adv* **nastily**, unkindly, callously, meanly, despicably, vilely, awfully, hatefully, horribly, unspeakably, appallingly, rottenly (*informal*) [➡ EMOTIONALLY UNPLEASANT AND UPSETTING; 227] *Opposite*: pleasantly

horridness 1 *n* **nastiness**, beastliness, unpleasantness, hatefulness, meanness, unkindness [➡ MALICIOUS ACTIONS OR BEHAVIOR; 296] *Opposite*: pleasantness 2 *n* **disgustingness**, loathsomeness, vileness, dreadfulness, unpleasantness [➡ DISGUSTING AND REPULSIVE; 230] *Opposite*: attractiveness 3 *n* **dreadfulness**, frightfulness, terribleness, awfulness, horror, shockingness [➡ FRIGHTENING; 231]

horrific *adj* **appalling**, dreadful, awful, horrendous, horrifying, shocking, ghastly, sickening, gruesome, horrible, terrible [➡ DISGUSTING AND REPULSIVE; 230] *Opposite*: wonderful

horrified 1 *adj* **appalled**, shocked, aghast, sickened, disgusted, revolted, dismayed, horror-struck [➡ SURPRISE, SHOCK, AND AMAZEMENT; 545] *Opposite*: delighted 2 *adj* **dismayed**, depressed, shocked, perplexed, disturbed, perturbed, confounded, upset, alarmed [➡ SADNESS, DISTRESS, AND DESPAIR; 539]

horrify 1 *v* **appall**, disgust, revolt, shock, sicken, repel [➡ FRIGHTEN AND SHOCK; 568] *Opposite*: delight 2 *v* **dismay**, depress, shock, perplex, disturb, perturb, confound, upset, alarm [➡ UPSET, DISTRESS, AND HUMILIATE; 567]

horrifying 1 *adj* **horrific**, horrible, horrendous, terrible, sickening, appalling, shocking, gruesome, dreadful, awful, ghastly [➡ DISGUSTING AND REPULSIVE; 230] *Opposite*: delightful 2 *adj* **shocking**, upsetting, disturbing, perplexing, perturbing, alarming, dismaying, depressing [➡ EMOTIONALLY UNPLEASANT AND UPSETTING; 227]

horror *n* **fear**, shock, revulsion, dismay, disgust, repulsion, terror, dread, distress, alarm, panic [➡ FEAR AND PANIC; 543] *Opposite*: delight

horror-stricken *see* **horror-struck**

horror-struck *adj* **horror-stricken**, petrified, scared stiff, terrified, horrified, stunned, shocked, aghast, frightened, appalled, dismayed, paralyzed [➡ SURPRISE, SHOCK, AND AMAZEMENT; 545]

hors de combat *adj* **wounded**, out of action, incapacitated, injured, disabled, in the hospital [➡ INJURED; 742] *Opposite*: able

hors d'oeuvre *n* **appetizer**, starter, entrée, crudités, first course, snack, munchies (*slang*), nibbles (*UK*) [➡ MEALS AND PARTS OF MEALS; 1169]

horse 1 *n* **mount**, pony, charger, steed (*literary*) [➡ HORSES; 985] 2 *type of* **farm animal** [➡ FARM ANIMALS; 982]

---

horse

◆ *types of horses*
Arabian horse, bronco, broodmare, carthorse, charger, cob, hack, hunter, mustang, pacer, packhorse, pony, racehorse, saddle horse, Shetland pony, shire horse, thoroughbred, trotter, warhorse, workhorse

◆ *parts of a horse*
croup, fetlock, flank, foreleg, hindquarters, hock, hoof, mane, pastern, shank, withers

---

horse around *v* **fool around**, play around, clown, act the fool, cavort, romp [➡ FIDGET AND FROLIC; 311]

horseback riding *n* [➡ HOBBIES, GAMES, AND SPORTS; 875]

horse chestnut 1 *type of* **deciduous tree** [➡ DECIDUOUS TREES; 1028] 2 *type of* **nut** [➡ NUTS; 1185]

horsefly *type of* **flying insect** [➡ FLYING INSECTS; 1013]

horsehair *type of* **fabric from animals** [➡ FABRICS; 1132]

horseman *n* **rider**, jockey, equestrian, huntsman, knight, cavalier [➡ PEOPLE IN SPORTS AND LEISURE; 876]

horseplay *n* **rough-and-tumble**, boisterousness, play, fun, horsing around, exuberance, clowning around, roughhouse (*informal*) [➡ LEISURE AND RECREATION; 874]

horse sense (*informal*) *n* **common sense**, good sense, sense, wit, judgment, wisdom [➡ POSITIVE INTELLECTUAL CHARACTERISTICS; 524]

horseshoe 1 *n* **lucky charm**, talisman, mascot, amulet, token [➡ LUCKY CHARMS; 785] 2 *n* **crescent**, curve, arc, loop, bend [➡ ROUNDED SHAPE; 1218]

horseshoe crab *type of* **crustacean** [➡ AQUATIC INVERTEBRATES; 1022]

horse show *n* [➡ PERFORMANCES AND SHOWS; 42]

horse thief *n* [➡ CRIMINALS; 821]

horsewoman *n* **rider**, jockey, equestrian, huntswoman [➡ PEOPLE IN SPORTS AND LEISURE; 876]

horsy *adj* **equestrian**, equine [➡ HORSES; 985]

horticultural *adj* **gardening**, garden, agricultural, viticultural, vinicultural, nursery, market garden (*UK*) [➡ AGRICULTURE AND FARMING; 1075]

horticulture *n* **gardening**, cultivation, propagation, agriculture, viticulture, viniculture, truck farming, market gardening (*UK*) [➡ AGRICULTURE AND FARMING; 1075]

hose 1 *n* **tube**, pipe, line, hosepipe, garden hose [➡ WATERCOURSES; 1111] 2 *v* **rinse**, water, spray, sluice, wash, soak, wash down, hose down [➡ CLEAN AND POLISH; 403]

hose down *v* **wash**, clean, sluice, rinse, hose, wash down [➡ CLEAN AND POLISH; 403] *Opposite*: dry

hosepipe *n* **hose**, tube, pipe, garden hose [➡ WATERCOURSES; 1111]

hosiery *n* [➡ ACCESSORIES, MILLINERY, AND LINGERIE; 867]

hospice *n* **nursing home**, hospital, rest home, sanatorium, clinic [➡ HOSPITALS AND CLINICS; 826]

hospitable *adj* **welcoming**, friendly, warm, open, generous, kind, cordial, sociable [➡ FRIENDLINESS AND SOCIABILITY; 494] *Opposite*: unfriendly

hospital *n* **infirmary**, sanatorium, rest home, hospice, sickbay, clinic, medical center, healthcare center [➡ HOSPITALS AND CLINICS; 826]

hospitality *n* **welcome**, friendliness, warmth, kindness, generosity, cordiality, sociableness, openness [➡ FRIENDLINESS AND SOCIABILITY; 494] *Opposite*: unfriendliness

host 1 *n* **entertainer**, master of ceremonies, MC, emcee (*informal*), presenter (*UK*), compere (*UK*) [➡ WORKERS IN ENTERTAINMENT AND MEDIA; 873] 2 *n* **crowd**, swarm, cloud, congregation, mass, multitude, horde, army [➡ MANY, MUCH, LARGE AMOUNT; 117] 3 *v* **accommodate**, lay on, hold, present, introduce, put on, emcee (*informal*), compere (*UK*) [➡ ENTERTAINMENT; 872]

hostage *n* **captive**, prisoner, detainee, victim [➡ CAPTIVES AND PRISONERS; 249]

hostel 1 *n* **shelter**, refuge, boarding house, single room occupancy, flophouse (*informal*) [➡ SAFE BUILDINGS OR PLACES; 1093] 2 *n* **inn**, hotel, bed and breakfast, guesthouse, motel, pension, lodgings (*dated*) [➡ HOTELS, RESTAURANTS, AND CLUBS; 1082]

hostess *n* **entertainer**, MC, emcee (*informal*), presenter (*UK*), compere (*UK*) [➡ WORKERS IN ENTERTAINMENT AND MEDIA; 873]

hostile 1 *adj* **unfriendly**, aggressive, intimidating, antagonistic, unreceptive, unsympathetic, argumentative, inimical [➡ AGGRESSIVE AND BELLIGERENT; 518] *Opposite*: friendly 2 *adj* **adverse**, harsh, unfavorable, unwelcoming, unpleasant, tough, inimical [➡ PHYSICALLY UNPLEASANT; 226] *Opposite*: pleasant

hostilities *n* **fighting**, warfare, conflict, battle, aggression [➡ AGGRESSIVE EVENTS; 39]

hostility *n* **aggression**, anger, unfriendliness, resentment, antagonism, opposition, enmity, argumentativeness, intimidation, inimicalness [➡ ANTAGONISM; 552] *Opposite*: friendliness

hot 1 *adj* **warm**, burning, boiling, blistering, searing, fiery, heated, scalding, sizzling (*informal*) [➡ TEMPERATURE: HOT; 1229] *Opposite*: cold 2 *adj* **sweltering**, stifling, muggy, sultry, boiling, oppressive, broiling, scorching (*informal*) [➡ HOT WEATHER; 1050] *Opposite*: mild 3 *adj* **spicy**, peppery, piquant, pungent, fiery, strong, red-hot [➡ TASTE; 703] *Opposite*: mild 4 *adj* **passionate**, fierce, angry, emotional, strong, intense, excitable, vehement, ardent, fervent, stormy, torrid [➡ EXCESSIVE SENSITIVITY; 511] *Opposite*: dispassionate

hot air (*informal*) *n* **nonsense**, drivel, stuff and nonsense, lies, bravado, bragging, boasting, baloney (*informal*), twaddle (*informal*), malarkey (*informal*), blather (*informal*), rubbish (*UK*) [➡ MEANINGLESS SPEECH OR WRITING; 676]

hot and bothered *adj* **worried**, anxious, edgy, flustered, in a panic, out of joint, worked up (*informal*), uptight (*informal*), in a flap (*informal*), in a tizzy (*informal*) [➡ CONFUSION, ANXIETY, AND WORRY; 540] *Opposite*: composed

hotbed *n* **breeding ground**, source, focus, hothouse, center [➡ BEGINNINGS; 53]

hot-blooded *adj* **passionate**, volatile, hot-tempered, ardent, fierce, temperamental, excitable, mercurial, fiery, impassioned, fervent [➡ EXCESSIVE SENSITIVITY; 511] *Opposite*: cold-blooded

hotcake *type of* **pancake** [➡ CAKES, COOKIES, AND DESSERTS; 1181]

hotel *n* [➡ HOTELS, RESTAURANTS, AND CLUBS; 1082]

hotel

◆ *types of hotels*
B & B (*informal*), bed and breakfast, boarding house, capsule hotel, hostel, inn, lodge, motel, pension, rooming house, youth hostel

hotelier *n* **innkeeper**, landlord, landlady, proprietor, manager, licensee [➡ BUSINESS PEOPLE; 793]

hotfoot *adv* **immediately**, at once, without delay, instantly, urgently, quickly, rapidly, fast, hastily, directly, straight, straightaway [➡ MOVING QUICKLY; 103] *Opposite*: slowly

hothead *n* **firebrand**, tearaway, madcap, loose cannon (*slang*) [➡ UNCOOPERATIVE OR REBELLIOUS PEOPLE; 566]

hotheaded *adj* **impetuous**, volatile, rash, irascible, on a short fuse, reckless, impulsive, hasty, madcap, impatient, incautious, excitable, fiery [➡ EXCESSIVE SENSITIVITY; 511] *Opposite*: prudent

hotheadedness *n* [➡ EXCESSIVE SENSITIVITY; 511]

hothouse *n* **greenhouse**, orangery, conservatory, winter garden, glasshouse (*UK*) [➡ ANCILLARY BUILDINGS; 1080]

hotly *adv* **passionately**, fiercely, ardently, fervently, vehemently, stormily, angrily, emotionally, strongly, intensely, excitably [➡ EXCESSIVE SENSITIVITY; 511] *Opposite*: dispassionately

hotness 1 *n* **heat**, high temperature, temperature, warmness, warmth [➡ TEMPERATURE: HOT; 1229] *Opposite*: coldness 2 *n* **overheating**, sweatiness, stickiness, warmness, warmth, heat, feverishness, high temperature [➡ ILL AND SICK; 740] 3 *n* **spiciness**, heat, fieriness, piquancy, pepperiness, strength [➡ TASTE; 703] *Opposite*: mildness

hot pants *type of* **pants** [➡ GARMENTS AND OUTFITS; 865]

hot potato *n* **difficulty**, controversy, tricky problem, knotty problem, sensitive issue, live issue, bone of contention, problem, issue [➡ PROBLEMS; 256]

hot rod (*slang*) *type of* **car** [➡ BIKES, CARS, AND CARRIAGES; 1149]

hotshot (*informal*) *n* **high-flier**, achiever, star, expert, top gun (*informal*), go-getter (*informal*), bigwig (*informal*), whiz (*informal*), big shot (*informal*) [➡ IMPORTANT OR FAMOUS PEOPLE; 893]

hot-tempered *adj* **excitable**, fiery, hot-blooded, volatile, quick-tempered, impatient, irascible, irritable, bad-tempered, ill-tempered, dyspeptic, prickly (*informal*) [➡ EXCESSIVE SENSITIVITY; 511] *Opposite*: relaxed

hot toddy *n* [➡ DRINKS; 1187]

hot tub *type of* **plumbing fixtures** [➡ FIXTURES; 859]

hot under the collar (*informal*) *adj* **indignant**, agitated, excited, angry, flustered, anxious, worked up (*informal*) [➡ IRRITATION AND ANGER; 541] *Opposite*: cool

hot water (*informal*) *n* **trouble**, bother, difficulty, controversy, conflict [➡ DIFFICULT SITUATIONS; 72]

hound 1 *n* **dog**, wolfhound, deerhound, basset hound, foxhound, greyhound [➡ DOGS; 980] 2 *v* **pursue**, chase, harass, pester, persecute, hunt, badger, dog [➡ ACCOMPANY AND FOLLOW; 337]

hour 1 *n* **60 minutes**, time, period, o'clock [➡ TIMES OF DAY; 87] 2 *n* **time**, period, era, age, day, epoch [➡ PERIODS OF TIME; 90]

hourglass *type of* **clock** [➡ CLOCKS AND TIMERS; 1126]

house 1 *n* **residence**, home, address, building, crib (*slang*), pad (*dated slang*), dwelling (*formal*), domicile (*formal*), abode (*literary*) [➡ RESIDENTIAL BUILDINGS; 1078] 2 *n* **household**, family, dynasty, community, line, stock, clan [➡ THE FAMILY; 956] 3 *n* **company**, firm, organization, business, establishment, corporation, business, partnership, outfit (*informal*) [➡ BUSINESS ENTERPRISES AND RELATED BODIES; 792] 4 *type of* **dance music** [➡ MUSIC, SONGS, AND SINGING; 907] 5 *v* **accommodate**, lodge, shelter, give shelter to, take in, put up [➡ TAKE CARE OF AND SPOIL; 300] 6 *v* **contain**, keep, store, hold, retain, accommodate [➡ HOLD AND CONTAIN; 455]

house

◆ *types of apartments*
apartment, bed-sitter, condominium, dockominium, duplex, efficiency apartment, garden apartment, loft, penthouse, split-level, studio

◆ *types of houses*
brownstone, bungalow, cabana, cabin, cape, Cape Cod, chalet, chateau, colonial, contemporary, cottage, country house, detached house, Dutch colonial, farmhouse, hacienda, homestead, igloo, lodge, manor, manor house, mansion, mobile home, palace, pied-à-terre, raised ranch, ranch, ranch house, row house, semidetached, shack, starter home, timeshare, town house, villa, walk-up

houseboat *type of* **motor vessel** [➡ SHIPS AND BOATS; 1150]

housebreaker *n* [➡ CRIMINALS; 821]

housecoat *n* **robe**, wrap, bathrobe, kimono, gown, dressing gown (*UK*) [➡ GARMENTS AND OUTFITS; 865]

house guest *n* **visitor**, guest, lodger, boarder [➡ FRIENDS AND GUESTS; 963]

household 1 *n* **family**, home, family circle, family unit, house, ménage (*formal*) [➡ THE FAMILY; 956] 2 *adj* **domestic**, home, family, everyday, domiciliary [➡ ACCOMMODATIONS; 855] *Opposite*: industrial

household name *n* **celebrity**, star, superstar, megastar, luminary, public figure, icon, celeb (*informal*) [➡ IMPORTANT OR FAMOUS PEOPLE; 893] *Opposite*: unknown

housekeeper *n* [➡ DOMESTIC AND KITCHEN WORKERS; 850]

housekeeping 1 *n* **organization**, maintenance, upkeep, management, running [➡ WORK IN GENERAL; 297] 2 *n* **housework**, chores, cleaning, housecleaning, tidying, tidying up [➡ WORK IN GENERAL; 297]

house of correction *n* [➡ BUILDINGS FOR CONFINING PEOPLE; 1094]

house of God *n* [➡ RELIGIOUS BUILDINGS; 1085]

house of worship *n* **house of God**, church, cathedral, synagogue, mosque, temple, chapel, meetinghouse, minster [➡ RELIGIOUS BUILDINGS; 1085]

houseplant *n* **plant**, bonsai, indoor plant, potted plant, pot plant (*UK*) [➡ FOLIAGE PLANTS; 1035]

housing 1 *n* **lodging**, shelter, board, accommodations, home, accommodation (*UK*) [➡ ACCOMMODATIONS; 855] 2 *n* **cover**, covering, case, casing, frame, guard [➡ COVERS AND COATINGS; 1246]

housing development *n* [➡ HUMAN SETTLEMENTS; 1070]

housing estate *n* **estate**, development, urban development, residential area, housing development, housing project, public housing, council estate (*UK*) [➡ HUMAN SETTLEMENTS; 1070]

housing project *n* [➡ HUMAN SETTLEMENTS; 1070]

hovel *n* **slum**, shack, squat, dump (*informal*), hole (*informal*), fleapit (*UK*) [➡ UNDESIRABLE ACCOMMODATIONS; 856]

hover 1 *v* **float**, hang, drift, soar, fly [➡ PROCEED AND GO; 305] *Opposite*: descend 2 *v* **linger**, stay close, hang around, wait, remain, loiter [➡ EXIST IN A PLACE; 19] *Opposite*: leave

hovercraft *type of* **motor vessel** [➡ SHIPS AND BOATS; 1150]

HOV lane *n* [➡ TRAVEL: TRAFFIC PROBLEMS AND TRAFFIC MANAGEMENT; 323]

how *adv* **in what way**, by what means, by what method, in what manner, just how, exactly how [➡ WAYS OF DOING THINGS; 294]

howdy (*informal*) *interj* [➡ GREETINGS, FAREWELLS, AND SALUTATIONS; 659]

however *adv* **though**, but, on the other hand, yet, still, nevertheless, nonetheless, conversely, then again, in spite of this [➡ ALTHOUGH, NEVERTHELESS, AND DESPITE; 169] *Opposite*: also

howitzer *type of* **gun** [➡ WEAPONS FOR SHOOTING; 1156]

howl 1 *v* **yowl**, bay, cry, wail, scream, shriek, whine, moan, holler (*informal*) [➡ SOUND EMISSION BY ANIMALS OR BIRDS; 364] *Opposite*: murmur 2 *n* **wail**, yowl, cry, scream, shriek, whine, moan, holler (*informal*) [➡ SOUNDS MADE BY PEOPLE; 1262] *Opposite*: murmur 3 *type of* **animal sound** [➡ SOUNDS MADE BY ANIMALS; 1261]

howl down *v* **drown out**, shout down, boo, jeer, mock, taunt, heckle [➡ UNFAVORABLE NONVERBAL RESPONSES; 654] *Opposite*: cheer

howler (*slang*) *n* **blunder**, gaffe, error, mistake, mala-

propism, boner (*informal*), blooper (*informal humorous*) [➡ MISTAKES; 250]

howling *adj* **violent**, whistling, gale-force, hurricane-force, breathtaking, wailing, loud [➡ WINDY AND STORMY WEATHER; 1053] *Opposite*: gentle

how the land lies *n* [➡ SITUATIONS; 71]

how things stand *n* [➡ SITUATIONS; 71]

hryvnia *type of* **currency** [➡ CURRENCIES; 798]

HTML *n* [➡ THE INTERNET; 1128]

hub 1 *n* **center**, core, heart, focus, focal point, nucleus, nerve center, boss (*informal*) [➡ CENTRAL PARTS OF PHYSICAL OBJECTS; 1251] *Opposite*: periphery 2 *n* **center**, middle, boss, pivot [➡ CENTRAL PARTS OF PHYSICAL OBJECTS; 1251] *Opposite*: spoke

hubbub *n* **noise**, racket, hullabaloo, din, uproar, clamor, tumult [➡ CHAOS AND UPROAR; 51] *Opposite*: silence

hubby (*informal*) *n* [➡ RELATIVES BY MARRIAGE; 960]

hubcap *type of* **external feature** [➡ EXTERNAL PARTS OF A VEHICLE; 1147]

huckleberry *type of* **berry** [➡ FRUIT AND VEGETABLES; 1176]

huckster *n* [➡ SELLERS; 442]

huddle 1 *n* **group**, cluster, knot, crowd, clump, mass, jumble [➡ GROUPS OF PEOPLE; 935] *Opposite*: scattering 2 *v* **gather together**, crowd together, throng together, cluster, come together, bunch (*informal*) [➡ GET CLOSER TOGETHER; 310] *Opposite*: scatter 3 *v* **crouch**, bend, cower, nestle, hunch, curl up, snuggle up, huddle up [➡ ASSUME A POSITION; 317]

huddle together *v* [➡ GET CLOSER TOGETHER; 310]

huddle up *v* [➡ GET CLOSER TOGETHER; 310]

hue 1 *n* **color**, tint, tinge, tone, shade [➡ DESCRIBING COLORS; 1226] 2 *n* **type**, kind, sort, description, manner, variety [➡ VARIETIES, TYPES, AND KINDS; 145]

hue and cry *n* **uproar**, furor, commotion, protest, public outcry, public outrage [➡ CHAOS AND UPROAR; 51] *Opposite*: acceptance

huff 1 *n* **sulk**, mood, bad mood, fit of pique, temper, snit, grumps (*informal*) [➡ IRRITATION AND ANGER; 541] 2 *v* **puff**, pant, wheeze, gasp, blow, breathe, snort, huff and puff [➡ BREATHE AND NOT BREATHE; 716] 3 *v* **bluster**, grumble, complain, rant, gripe (*informal*) [➡ COMPLAIN AND NAG; 686] *Opposite*: calm down

huffily *adv* **sulkily**, grumpily, indignantly, moodily, touchily, resentfully [➡ BAD-TEMPERED AND HUMORLESS; 626] *Opposite*: good-naturedly

huffiness *n* [➡ DIFFICULT TO PLEASE; 515]

huffy *adj* **touchy**, sensitive, moody, grumpy, sulky, bad-tempered, piqued, offended [➡ BAD-TEMPERED AND HUMORLESS; 626] *Opposite*: good-natured

hug 1 *v* **embrace**, hold close, enfold, cuddle, clasp, squeeze [➡ PHYSICAL CONTACT AS COMMUNICATION; 655] 2 *n* **cuddle**, clinch, clasp, bear hug, embrace, squeeze [➡ PHYSICAL CONTACT AS COMMUNICATION; 655]

huge 1 *adj* **enormous**, vast, gigantic, massive, giant, mammoth, colossal, titanic, humongous (*informal*)

[➡ LARGE; 1193] *Opposite*: tiny **2** *adj* (*informal*) [➡ EXTRAORDINARY: AMAZING; 204]

hugely *adv* **enormously**, immensely, overwhelmingly, vastly, tremendously, incredibly, extremely, massively (*informal*) [➡ TO A GREAT EXTENT; 132] *Opposite*: slightly

huggermugger *n* [➡ DISORDER AND CHAOS; 245]

hulk **1** *n* **giant**, goliath, colossus, titan, ogre, monster [➡ BIG THINGS; 1194] **2** *n* **shell**, skeleton, frame, carcass, wreck, remains, ruins [➡ EXTREMITIES OF PHYSICAL OBJECTS; 1250]

hulking *adj* **bulky**, vast, massive, colossal, enormous, large, husky [➡ LARGE; 1193] *Opposite*: dainty

hull **1** *n* **body**, exterior, underside, keel, casing, structure [➡ EXTERNAL PARTS OF A VEHICLE; 1147] *Opposite*: interior **2** *part of* **ship or boat** [➡ PARTS OF A SHIP OR BOAT; 1151]

hullaballoo *see* **hullabaloo**

hullabaloo *n* **noise**, racket, hubbub, din, uproar, clamor, tumult [➡ CHAOS AND UPROAR; 51] *Opposite*: silence

hum **1** *v* **drone**, whine, purr, buzz, whir, vibrate [➡ EMIT CONTINUOUS SOUNDS; 366] **2** *n* **whine**, drone, purr, buzz, vibration, whir [➡ CONTINUOUS SOUNDS; 1258] **3** *type of* **human sound** [➡ SOUNDS MADE BY PEOPLE; 1262]

human **1** *n* **person**, being, human being, individual, creature, homo sapiens, hominid [➡ PERSON; 931] **2** *type of* **primate** [➡ PRIMATES; 988] **3** *adj* **humanoid**, hominid, hominoid, anthropological, anthropoid, social, mortal [➡ LIVING THINGS AND LIVING; 976] *Opposite*: animal

human being *n* **person**, human, being, individual, creature, homo sapiens, hominid [➡ PERSON; 931]

hum and haw (*UK*) *v* [➡ HESITATE; 272]

humane *adj* **compassionate**, caring, kind, gentle, humanitarian, kindly, benevolent, charitable [➡ GENEROSITY AND KINDNESS; 495] *Opposite*: cruel

humanitarian *adj* **caring**, charitable, benevolent, philanthropic, public-spirited, altruistic [➡ MORALLY GOOD; 774] *Opposite*: uncaring

humanities *n* [➡ CLASSES, COURSEWORK, AND EXAMINATIONS; 842]

humanity **1** *n* **humankind**, people, human race, mortality, homo sapiens [➡ PERSON; 931] **2** *n* **kindness**, charity, compassion, sympathy, mercy, benevolence [➡ GENEROSITY AND KINDNESS; 495] *Opposite*: cruelty

humanize **1** *v* **civilize**, cultivate, improve, soften, refine, tame [➡ IMPROVE SOMETHING; 374] *Opposite*: brutalize **2** *v* **anthropomorphize**, personify, personalize [➡ NAME AND DESCRIBE; 665]

humanizing *adj* **civilizing**, improving, progressive, refining, softening, taming [➡ MORALLY GOOD; 774] *Opposite*: brutalizing

humankind *n* **human race**, humanity, people, mortality, homo sapiens [➡ PERSON; 931]

humanly *adv* **at all**, feasibly, physically, realistically, in any way, by any means [➡ POSSIBLE AND PROBABLE; 177]

humanoid *n* [➡ PERSON; 931]

human race *n* **humankind**, humanity, people, mortality, homo sapiens [➡ PERSON; 931]

human rights *n* **basic rights**, civil liberties, civil rights, citizens' rights, inalienable rights, rights [➡ THE LAW AND LEGAL AUTHORITY; 814]

humble **1** *adj* **modest**, unassuming, retiring, meek, self-effacing, unpretentious, shy [➡ RETICENT AND UNFORTHCOMING; 631] *Opposite*: arrogant **2** *adj* **lowly**, poor, modest, simple, underprivileged, disadvantaged, mean (*archaic*) [➡ CLASS STATUS; 889] *Opposite*: privileged **3** *adj* **respectful**, subservient, servile, deferential, obliging, obsequious, meek [➡ LEVELS OF FORMALITY; 522] *Opposite*: brazen **4** *v* **humiliate**, chasten, shame, bring down a peg, force to eat humble pie, put somebody in their place, cut somebody down to size, put somebody down (*informal*) [➡ UPSET, DISTRESS, AND HUMILIATE; 567] *Opposite*: glorify **5** *v* **degrade**, debase, demean, lower, reduce, abase (*literary*) [➡ INSULTS, ABUSE, AND SWEARING; 658] *Opposite*: exalt (*formal*)

humbled *adj* **shamed**, chastened, crestfallen, mortified, sheepish, humiliated [➡ EMBARRASSMENT AND HUMILIATION; 542] *Opposite*: proud

humbleness *n* **humility**, modesty, meekness, self-effacement, shyness, unpretentiousness [➡ RETICENT AND UNFORTHCOMING; 631] *Opposite*: arrogance

humbling **1** *adj* **chastening**, awe-inspiring, awesome, overwhelming [➡ EXTRAORDINARY: AMAZING; 204] *Opposite*: uplifting (*formal*) **2** *adj* **mortifying**, embarrassing, shaming, sobering, crushing, discomfiting (*formal*) [➡ EMOTIONALLY UNPLEASANT AND UPSETTING; 227] *Opposite*: heartening

humbly **1** *adv* **modestly**, unassumingly, meekly, simply, unpretentiously [➡ RETICENT AND UNFORTHCOMING; 631] *Opposite*: arrogantly **2** *adv* **respectfully**, deferentially, obsequiously, subserviently, meekly, obligingly [➡ LEVELS OF FORMALITY; 522] *Opposite*: brazenly

humbug **1** *n* **nonsense**, gibberish, garbage, claptrap (*informal*), twaddle (*informal*), bunkum (*informal*), hogwash (*informal*), hooey (*informal*), baloney (*informal*), bunk (*slang*), rubbish (*UK*) [➡ MEANINGLESS SPEECH OR WRITING; 676] *Opposite*: fact **2** *n* **deception**, hypocrisy, lies, deceit, propaganda, sham, pretense, insincerity, hokum (*informal*) [➡ DECEPTION AND LIES; 660] *Opposite*: sincerity **3** *type of* **confectionery** [➡ CONFECTIONERY; 1182]

humdinger (*slang*) *n* [➡ AMAZING THINGS; 211]

humdrum *adj* **dull**, boring, routine, unexciting, everyday, tedious, monotonous [➡ BORING AND UNINTERESTING; 234] *Opposite*: exciting

humerus *type of* **bone** [➡ THE BONES AND JOINTS; 719]

humid *adj* **moist**, damp, steamy, tropical, sticky, clammy, muggy, sultry [➡ MOIST; 1241] *Opposite*: arid

See Compare and Contrast at **wet**.

humidify *v* **moisten**, dampen, saturate, impregnate [➡ SOFTEN, LIQUEFY, AND DAMPEN; 388] *Opposite*: dry out

humidity *n* **moisture**, moistness, dampness, clamminess, stickiness, damp, mugginess, wetness [➡ MOIST; 1241] *Opposite*: aridity

humiliate *v* **chasten**, embarrass, demean, degrade, disgrace, shame, show up, humble, debase, dishonor, put down (*informal*) [➡ UPSET, DISTRESS, AND HUMILIATE; 567] *Opposite*: dignify

humiliated *adj* **chastened**, humbled, shamed, mortified, disgraced, demeaned, degraded, shown up, embarrassed, dishonored [➡ EMBARRASSMENT AND HUMILIATION; 542] *Opposite*: proud

humiliating *adj* **chastening**, humbling, embarrassing, mortifying, shameful, demeaning, degrading, crushing, dishonoring [➡ EMOTIONALLY UNPLEASANT AND UPSETTING; 227] *Opposite*: gratifying

humiliation *n* **disgrace**, shame, mortification, embarrassment, dishonor, degradation [➡ EMBARRASSMENT AND HUMILIATION; 542] *Opposite*: dignity

humility *n* **self-effacement**, unpretentiousness, humbleness, modesty, meekness, shyness [➡ RETICENT AND UNFORTHCOMING; 631] *Opposite*: arrogance

humming *adj* **droning**, whining, purring, buzzing, whirring, vibrating [➡ SOFT, LOW, OR PLEASANT SOUNDS; 1265] *Opposite*: silent

hummingbird *type of* **common bird** [➡ BIRDS; 997]

hummock *n* **hillock**, mound, knoll, hill, rise [➡ MOUNTAINS AND HILLS; 1044] *Opposite*: dip

hummus *type of* **seasonings, sauces, and dips** [➡ SEASONINGS AND SAUCES; 1174]

humongous (*informal*) *adj* **enormous**, gigantic, colossal, massive, vast, huge [➡ LARGE; 1193] *Opposite*: tiny

humor 1 *n* **funniness**, wit, comedy, comicality, comicalness, the funny side, hilarity, absurdity [➡ FUNNY AND AMUSING; 216] *Opposite*: seriousness 2 *n* **wit**, wittiness, sense of humor, sparkle, drollness, sense of fun [➡ CHEERFULNESS OF OUTLOOK; 503] *Opposite*: dourness 3 *n* **comedy**, satire, black humor, spoof, slapstick, joking, jesting (*literary*) [➡ JOKES AND TEASING; 674] 4 *v* **go along with**, indulge, accommodate, please, pacify, string along (*informal*) [➡ TAKE CARE OF AND SPOIL; 300] *Opposite*: oppose

humorist 1 *n* **comedian**, comic, standup comedian, impressionist, entertainer, satirist, standup [➡ WORKERS IN ENTERTAINMENT AND MEDIA; 873] 2 *n* **joker**, wit, satirist, punster, clown, wag (*informal*) [➡ JOKERS AND TEASES; 675]

humorless 1 *adj* **sullen**, serious, sour, dour, dull, po-faced (*UK*) [➡ NEGATIVITY OF OUTLOOK; 514] *Opposite*: merry 2 *adj* **unfunny**, unamusing, dull, unwitty, serious, straight [➡ BORING AND UNINTERESTING; 234] *Opposite*: funny

humorous *adj* **funny**, amusing, entertaining, hilarious, comical, comic, tongue-in-cheek, jokey, droll, witty [➡ FUNNY AND AMUSING; 216] *Opposite*: serious

See Compare and Contrast at **funny.**

humorously *adv* **funnily**, amusingly, entertainingly, hilariously, jokily, wittily, comically, drolly [➡ GOOD-TEMPERED AND HUMOROUS; 627] *Opposite*: seriously

hump *n* **bulge**, bump, lump, swelling, protuberance, mound [➡ ROUNDED SHAPE; 1218] *Opposite*: dip

humpback whale *type of* **whale** [➡ WHALES; 991]

humungous *see* **humongous**

hunch 1 *n* **feeling**, gut feeling, sixth sense, premonition, intuition, instinct, idea [➡ FEELINGS; 531] 2 *v* **bend**, huddle, stoop, crouch, lean forward, bend forward [➡ ASSUME A POSITION; 317] *Opposite*: straighten

hundred percent *adj* [➡ ALL; 128]

hunger 1 *n* **starvation**, food shortage, lack of food, malnutrition, famine, deprivation [➡ EAT AND NOT EAT; 710] *Opposite*: surfeit 2 *n* **appetite**, emptiness, craving, hungriness, ravenousness, famishment [➡ EAT AND NOT EAT; 710] 3 *n* **craving**, desire, need, wish, passion, yearning, longing, thirst, hankering, aversion [➡ DESIRE AND WANT; 579] 4 *v* **crave**, yearn, long for, desire, hanker, thirst for [➡ DESIRE AND WANT; 579] *Opposite*: spurn

hunger after *v* [➡ DESIRE AND WANT; 579]

hungrily 1 *adv* **eagerly**, impatiently, keenly, enthusiastically, excitedly, avidly [➡ WITH ENTHUSIASM; 286] *Opposite*: nonchalantly 2 *adv* **ravenously**, greedily, appreciatively, eagerly, enthusiastically, raveningly, voraciously [➡ WITH ENTHUSIASM; 286] *Opposite*: unenthusiastically

hungry 1 *adj* **famished**, ravenous, empty, ravening, voracious, starving (*informal*), starved (*informal*), peckish (*informal*) [➡ EAT AND NOT EAT; 710] *Opposite*: full 2 *adj* (*informal*) **ambitious**, driven, thrusting, power-hungry, aggressive, keen [➡ DESIRE AND WANT; 579] *Opposite*: content 3 *adj* **avid**, eager, keen, greedy, thirsty, desirous (*formal*) [➡ POSITIVE IMPATIENCE, ENTHUSIASM, AND ALERTNESS; 537] *Opposite*: nonchalant

hung up (*informal*) 1 *adj* **obsessed**, fixated, preoccupied, infatuated, possessed, captivated, into (*informal*) [➡ APPRECIATION AND GRATITUDE; 535] *Opposite*: repelled 2 *adj* **anxious**, worried, caught up, bothered, concerned, nervous [➡ CONFUSION, ANXIETY, AND WORRY; 540] *Opposite*: relaxed

hunk *n* **chunk**, piece, lump, slab, wedge [➡ LARGE PIECES; 130]

hunker *v* **squat**, crouch, cower, get on all fours, crawl, stoop, kneel [➡ ASSUME A POSITION; 317] *Opposite*: stand

hunker down *v* **squat down**, squat, crouch, crouch down, kneel, kneel down [➡ ASSUME A POSITION; 317] *Opposite*: stand up

hunky (*informal*) *adj* **muscular**, well-built, masculine, stocky, solid, brawny, handsome [➡ PEOPLE'S PHYSICAL APPEARANCE; 475] *Opposite*: puny

hunky-dory (*informal*) *adj* [➡ APPROPRIATE, SUITABLE, AND ADVISABLE; 184]

hunt 1 *v* **chase**, pursue, stalk, follow, track, prey on, trail [➡ ACCOMPANY AND FOLLOW; 337] *Opposite*: flee 2 *v* **seek out**, hunt down, track down, chase, pursue, hound [➡ SEEK POSSESSION AND SEARCH; 456] *Opposite*: evade 3 *v* **search**, seek, rummage, look, ferret around, ferret about (*UK*), rootle (*UK*) [➡ SEEK POSSESSION AND SEARCH; 456] *Opposite*: find 4 *n* **search**, quest, chase, pursuit, expedition, rummage [➡ SEEK POSSESSION AND SEARCH; 456]

hunt down *v* **find**, catch, track down, capture, get hold of, seek out [➡ SEEK POSSESSION AND SEARCH; 456] *Opposite*: flee

hunted *adj* **panic-stricken**, alarmed, startled, frightened, unsettled, disturbed [➡ FEAR AND PANIC; 543] *Opposite*: relaxed

hunter 1 *n* **seeker**, pursuer, searcher, chaser [➡ PEOPLE IN

SPORTS AND LEISURE; 876] *Opposite*: prey **2** *n* **stalker**, predator, tracker, killer, pursuer, chaser [➡ PEOPLE WHO KILL; 924] *Opposite*: prey **3** *type of* **horse** [➡ HORSES; 985]

hunting *n* **blood sport**, fox hunting, deer stalking, hare coursing, shooting, stalking [➡ HOBBIES, GAMES, AND SPORTS; 875]

hurdle **1** *n* **obstacle**, difficulty, problem, stumbling block, snag, impediment [➡ PROBLEMS; 256] *Opposite*: aid **2** *v* **jump**, leap, jump over, leap over, fly over, clear, vault, vault over [➡ BOUNCE, UNDULATE, AND VIBRATE; 308]

hurl **1** *v* **fling**, throw, launch, toss, heave, chuck (*informal*) [➡ MOVE SOMETHING: THROUGH THE AIR; 334] **2** *v* (*slang*) **vomit**, be sick, gag, retch, spew, barf (*informal*), throw up (*informal*), heave (*informal*), puke (*slang*) [➡ VOMIT AND BELCH; 712]

> *See Compare and Contrast at* **throw**.

hurl abuse *v* [➡ ACCUSE, BLAME, AND CRITICIZE; 641]

hurling *type of* **ball game** [➡ HOBBIES, GAMES, AND SPORTS; 875]

hurl insults *v* [➡ ACCUSE, BLAME, AND CRITICIZE; 641]

hurly-burly *n* **commotion**, chaos, turmoil, confusion, bustle, hustle and bustle, turbulence [➡ CHAOS AND UPROAR; 51] *Opposite*: peace

hurrah *interj* [➡ EXPRESSIONS OF SURPRISE AND PLEASURE; 546]

hurricane *n* **storm**, gale, tempest, tropical storm, tornado, cyclone, typhoon, whirlwind, twister (*informal*) [➡ WINDY AND STORMY WEATHER; 1053]

hurricane lamp *type of* **light** [➡ LIGHT; 1164]

hurried **1** *adj* **quick**, rushed, speedy, swift, sudden, hasty, spur-of-the-moment, snatched [➡ HAPPENING QUICKLY; 104] *Opposite*: leisurely **2** *adj* **rushed**, pressurized, under pressure, harried, hassled (*informal*) [➡ SADNESS, DISTRESS, AND DESPAIR; 539] *Opposite*: relaxed

hurriedly *adv* **quickly**, speedily, swiftly, suddenly, hastily, on the spur of the moment, impulsively [➡ HAPPENING QUICKLY; 104] *Opposite*: slowly

hurry **1** *v* **rush**, speed, hasten, run, dash, scurry, make haste [➡ MOVE FAST; 313] *Opposite*: delay **2** *v* **speed up**, accelerate, quicken, hasten, hustle [➡ CHANGE OF SPEED: MORE; 396] *Opposite*: slow down **3** *n* **haste**, rush, dash, flurry, frenzy, panic [➡ DISORDER AND CHAOS; 245] **4** *n* **urgency**, time pressure, panic, rush, haste, imperativeness, emergency [➡ DIFFICULT SITUATIONS; 72]

hurry up *v* **speed up**, accelerate, quicken, hasten, hustle [➡ CHANGE OF SPEED: MORE; 396] *Opposite*: slow down

hurt **1** *v* **injure**, harm, wound, damage, mar, maim, bruise, impair, burn, cut, spoil, break [➡ WOUND A PERSON OR ANIMAL; 383] *Opposite*: benefit **2** *v* **impair**, damage, mar, spoil, ruin [➡ WORSEN SOMETHING; 380] *Opposite*: improve **3** *v* **ache**, be sore, be painful, throb, trouble, sting, smart, kill (*informal*) [➡ PAIN AND OTHER PHYSICAL SENSATIONS; 733] *Opposite*: soothe **4** *v* **offend**, upset, insult, injure, wound, cause offense [➡ UPSET, DISTRESS, AND HUMILIATE; 567] *Opposite*: comfort **5** *n* **injury**, damage, harm, pain, soreness, ache, suffering, tenderness, discomfort [➡ PAIN AND OTHER PHYSICAL SENSATIONS; 733] *Opposite*: benefit **6** *n* **upset**, pain, distress, sadness, damage, injury, suffering, offense [➡ SADNESS, DISTRESS, AND DESPAIR; 539] *Opposite*: gratification **7** *adj* **upset**, offended,

wounded, unhappy, indignant, injured, miffed (*informal*) [➡ SADNESS, DISTRESS, AND DESPAIR; 539] *Opposite*: gratified

> *See Compare and Contrast at* **harm**.

hurtful *adj* **upsetting**, unkind, cruel, spiteful, cutting, wounding, insensitive, tactless, inappropriate [➡ EMOTIONALLY UNPLEASANT AND UPSETTING; 227] *Opposite*: kind

hurting *adj* **sad**, aching, heartbroken, brokenhearted, down, low, blue (*informal*) [➡ SADNESS, DISTRESS, AND DESPAIR; 539] *Opposite*: happy

hurtle *v* **dash**, career, tear, race, plunge, crash, fly [➡ MOVE FAST; 313] *Opposite*: plod

hurtling *adj* [➡ MOVING QUICKLY; 103]

husband *n* **spouse**, partner, other half, significant other, mate, hubby (*informal*), man (*slang*) [➡ RELATIVES BY MARRIAGE; 960] *Opposite*: wife

husband-to-be *n* [➡ RELATIVES BY MARRIAGE; 960]

hush **1** *v* **silence**, quiet, quiet down, mute, shut up (*informal*), shush (*informal*) [➡ CAUSE TO STOP; 266] **2** *interj* **be quiet**, quiet, shush, silence, not a word, shut up (*informal*) [➡ UNFAVORABLE NONVERBAL RESPONSES; 654] **3** *n* **stillness**, silence, quiet, quietness, tranquillity, peace, peacefulness [➡ ABSENCE OF SOUND; 1257] *Opposite*: noise

hushed *adj* **quiet**, silent, muted, soft, whispered, low [➡ SOFT, LOW, OR PLEASANT SOUNDS; 1265] *Opposite*: loud

hush-hush (*informal*) *adj* **secret**, confidential, top-secret, cloak-and-dagger, clandestine, undercover, classified, on the q.t., under wraps (*informal*) [➡ SECRET AND UNKNOWN; 179] *Opposite*: public

hush money (*informal*) *n* **bribe**, pacifier, incentive, payoff (*informal*), sweetener (*informal*) [➡ PROCEEDS OF CRIME; 427]

hush up (*informal*) *v* **cover up**, suppress, conceal, keep quiet, keep secret, sit on, whitewash [➡ WITHHOLD INFORMATION; 687] *Opposite*: reveal

husk *n* **shell**, casing, pod, covering, skin, outside, case [➡ PARTS OF TREES AND PLANTS; 1026] *Opposite*: kernel

huskily *adv* **throatily**, hoarsely, roughly, gruffly, drily, croakily, gutturally, raspingly, gratingly [➡ LOUD, HIGH, OR UNPLEASANT SOUNDS; 1266] *Opposite*: clearly

huskiness *n* **throatiness**, hoarseness, dryness, roughness, gruffness, croakiness, gutturalness, rasp [➡ LOUD, HIGH, OR UNPLEASANT SOUNDS; 1266] *Opposite*: clearness

husky **1** *adj* **burly**, strong, solid, broad, hulking, big, bulky [➡ BUILD; 477] **2** *adj* **throaty**, hoarse, dry, rough, gruff, croaky, grating, rasping, raspy, gravelly, guttural [➡ LOUD, HIGH, OR UNPLEASANT SOUNDS; 1266] *Opposite*: clear **3** *type of* **large dog** [➡ DOGS; 980]

hustle **1** *v* **propel**, jostle, manhandle, push, shove, bundle (*informal*) [➡ MOVE SOMETHING TO ANOTHER LOCATION; 324] **2** *v* (*slang*) **solicit**, tout, push, peddle, hawk [➡ SELL; 441] **3** *v* (*informal*) **hurry**, hurry up, get going, get cracking, get a move on (*informal*), buck up (*informal dated*) [➡ MOVE FAST; 313] *Opposite*: slow down

hustle and bustle *n* **commotion**, chaos, turmoil, confusion, hurly-burly, fuss, hubbub, bustle [➠CHAOS AND UPROAR; 511] *Opposite*: calm

hustler *n* [➠PEOPLE WHO DECEIVE; 661]

hut *n* **shed**, lean-to, cabin, shelter, shack, shanty, outbuilding [➠ANCILLARY BUILDINGS; 1080]

hutch *type of* **pen or cage** [➠ANIMAL OR BIRD ACCOMMODATIONS; 1079]

hutzpah *see* **chutzpah**

hyacinth *type of* **flower grown from bulbs** [➠FLOWERS FROM BULBS; 1030]

hyaena *see* **hyena**

hybrid *n* **cross**, crossbreed, mix, amalgam, mixture, fusion [➠COMBINE AND MIX; 400]

hybridize *v* [➠COMBINE AND MIX; 400]

Hydra *type of* **constellation** [➠HEAVENLY BODIES; 1061]

hydrangea *type of* **shrub or bush** [➠BUSHES AND SHRUBS; 1027]

hydrofoil *type of* **motor vessel** [➠SHIPS AND BOATS; 1150]

hydrogen *type of* **gas** [➠GASES; 1275]

hydrogen bomb *type of* **explosive weapon** [➠EXPLOSIVES; 1155]

hydrogeology *type of* **earth science** [➠EARTH SCIENCES; 1059]

hydrophobia *type of* **phobia** [➠FEARS AND PHOBIAS; 554]

hydroplane *v* **skid**, slide, swerve, slew, veer, aquaplane (*UK*) [➠PUSH, PULL, AND SLIDE; 335]

hydrotherapy *type of* **complementary therapy** [➠REMEDIES, TREATMENTS, AND OPERATIONS; 731]

Hydrus *type of* **constellation** [➠HEAVENLY BODIES; 1061]

hygiene *n* **cleanliness**, sanitation, sanitariness, cleanness, sterility, sanitization, asepsis, asepticism, disinfection [➠CLEAN AND HYGIENIC; 1233]

hygienic *adj* **clean**, sterile, disinfected, sanitary, germfree, sanitized, aseptic [➠CLEAN AND HYGIENIC; 1233] *Opposite*: unhygienic

hymn **1** *n* **song**, chant, carol, chorus, anthem, canticle, psalm [➠MUSIC, SONGS, AND SINGING; 907] **2** *v* **praise**, celebrate, eulogize, extol, laud, acclaim, panegyrize (*archaic*) [➠PRAISE AND ENCOURAGE; 647] *Opposite*: criticize

hypallage *type of* **figure of speech** [➠FIGURES OF SPEECH; 673]

hype **1** *n* **publicity**, propaganda, buildup, excitement, puff, hard sell, hysteria, hot air (*informal*), flimflam (*slang*) [➠ADVERTISING AND PUBLICITY; 604] **2** *v* **publicize**, advertise, build up, tout, push, plug (*informal*) [➠ADVERTISING AND PUBLICITY; 604]

hyper (*informal*) **1** *adj* **hyperactive**, restless, frenzied, agitated, overactive, manic (*informal*), keyed up (*informal*), wired (*slang*) [➠INSECURITY AND LOSS OF COMPOSURE; 544] *Opposite*: placid **2** *adj* **excitable**, hotheaded, on the edge, volatile, high-strung, erratic, unstable [➠EXCESSIVE SENSITIVITY; 511] *Opposite*: calm

hyperactive *adj* **restless**, agitated, frenzied, overactive,

manic (*informal*), hyper (*informal*), keyed up (*informal*), wired (*slang*) [➠INSECURITY AND LOSS OF COMPOSURE; 544] *Opposite*: placid

hyperbaton *type of* **figure of speech** [➠FIGURES OF SPEECH; 673]

hyperbole *n* **exaggeration**, overstatement, overemphasis, magnification, inflation, embellishment [➠FIGURES OF SPEECH; 673] *Opposite*: understatement

hypercritical *adj* **overcritical**, censorious, nitpicking, finicky, negative, pedantic, fussy [➠DIFFICULT TO PLEASE; 515] *Opposite*: lenient

hyperinflation *type of* **economic condition** [➠FINANCE AND ECONOMICS; 796]

hypermarket *type of* **retail outlet** [➠RETAIL OUTLETS; 1083]

hypersensitive *adj* **touchy**, oversensitive, thinskinned, easily offended, easily hurt, quick to take offense, delicate [➠EXCESSIVE SENSITIVITY; 511] *Opposite*: thickskinned

hypersensitivity *n* [➠EXCESSIVE SENSITIVITY; 511]

hyperventilate *v* [➠BREATHE AND NOT BREATHE; 716]

hyphen *type of* **punctuation mark** [➠ASPECTS OF LANGUAGE; 682]

hypnotherapy *type of* **complementary therapy** [➠REMEDIES, TREATMENTS, AND OPERATIONS; 731]

hypnotic (*informal*) *adj* **fascinating**, mesmerizing, entrancing, spellbinding, compelling, enthralling, magnetic, absorbing [➠INTERESTING AND MEANINGFUL; 190] *Opposite*: uninteresting

hypnotize *v* **fascinate**, mesmerize, spellbind, entrance, enthrall, compel, absorb [➠APPEAL TO AND AROUSE INTEREST; 575] *Opposite*: bore

hypnotizing *adj* [➠INTERESTING AND MEANINGFUL; 190]

hypochondriac *n* [➠GRUMPY AND NEGATIVE PEOPLE; 953]

hypocrisy *n* **insincerity**, double standard, pretense, duplicity, two-facedness, falseness [➠DECEITFUL; 513] *Opposite*: sincerity

hypocrite *n* **charlatan**, fraud, phoney, double-dealer, pretender, dissembler (*formal*) [➠PEOPLE WHO DECEIVE; 661]

hypocritical *adj* **insincere**, two-faced, duplicitous, deceitful, phony, false, dishonest [➠DECEITFUL; 513] *Opposite*: genuine

hypothesis *n* **theory**, premise, suggestion, supposition, proposition, guess, assumption, postulate, postulation [➠IDEAS AND THOUGHTS; 770]

hypothesize *v* **imagine**, conjecture, put forward, assume, offer, theorize, postulate, posit (*formal*) [➠DEVELOP THEORIES AND REASON; 744]

hypothetical *adj* **theoretical**, imaginary, supposed, conjectural, proposed, assumed, putative, suppositional, suppositious (*formal*) [➠FALSE AND UNREAL; 173] *Opposite*: real

hyrax *type of* **small mammal** [➠SMALL MAMMALS; 990]

hyssop *type of* **herb** [➠HERBS AND SPICES; 1175]

hysterectomy 1 *type of* **medical procedure** [➡REMEDIES, TREATMENTS, AND OPERATIONS; 731] **2** *n* [➡STERILIZE; 726]

hysteria *n* **panic**, hysterics, frenzy, madness, emotion, excitement, mania [➡INSECURITY AND LOSS OF COMPOSURE; 544] *Opposite*: calm

hysteric *adj* [➡FEAR AND PANIC; 543]

hysterical 1 *adj* **panic-stricken**, out of control, agitated, overexcited, feverish, frenetic, frenzied, frantic, beside yourself, distraught, distracted, hysteric, hyper (*informal*), manic (*informal*) [➡FEAR AND PANIC; 543] *Opposite*: composed **2** *adj* **uncontrollable**, frenzied, intense, violent, unrestrained, wild, furious [➡NEGATIVE INTELLECTUAL CHARACTERISTICS; 525] *Opposite*: controlled **3** *adj* (*informal*) **hilarious**,

uproarious, highly amusing, sidesplitting, comical, funny [➡FUNNY AND AMUSING; 216] *Opposite*: sad

hysterically 1 *adv* **frantically**, feverishly, frenziedly, frenetically, agitatedly, distractedly, overexcitedly [➡FEAR AND PANIC; 543] *Opposite*: calmly **2** *adv* **uncontrollably**, violently, wildly, frenziedly, unrestrainedly, intensely, loudly, openly [➡NEGATIVE INTELLECTUAL CHARACTERISTICS; 525] *Opposite*: quietly **3** *adv* (*informal*) **uproariously**, hilariously, sidesplittingly, riotously, screamingly, extraordinarily, unbelievably [➡FUNNY AND AMUSING; 216] *Opposite*: mildly

hysterics 1 *n* **hysteria**, panic, frenzy, agitation, distraction, mania, overexcitement [➡FEAR AND PANIC; 543] *Opposite*: calmness **2** *n* (*informal*) **fits**, fits of laughter, stitches, laughter [➡LAUGHTER; 649]

I

ibis *type of* **freshwater bird** [➡ FRESHWATER BIRDS; 1000]

ice 1 *n* **frost**, snow, hoar frost, rime, slush [➡ COLD WEATHER; 1051] 2 *v* **freeze up**, freeze, freeze solid, freeze over, ice over, ice up [➡ HARDEN, CONGEAL, AND DRY; 387] *Opposite*: thaw 3 *v* **decorate**, finish off, frost, embellish, adorn [➡ DECORATE, ADORN, AND APPLY COATINGS; 405] 4 *v* **chill**, cool, cool down [➡ CHANGE OF TEMPERATURE; 386] *Opposite*: heat

iceberg *n* [➡ GEOLOGIC FEATURES; 1056]

ice blue *type of* **blue** [➡ COLORS; 1224]

icebox *n* **refrigerator**, fridge, freezer, fridge-freezer (*UK*) [➡ HEATING, REFRIGERATION, AND VENTILATION; 1142]

icebreaker 1 *n* **opener**, starter, opening, introduction [➡ ONE-WAY COMMUNICATION; 49] 2 *type of* **motor vessel** [➡ SHIPS AND BOATS; 1150]

icecap *n* [➡ GEOLOGIC FEATURES; 1056]

ice-cold *adj* **freezing**, frozen, icy, subzero, chilled, chilly, chill, bitter [➡ COLD WEATHER; 1051] *Opposite*: boiling

ice cream *n* **cone**, ice-cream cone, sherbet, sorbet, ice, gelato, ninety-nine (*UK*), cornet (*UK*) [➡ CAKES, COOKIES, AND DESSERTS; 1181]

iced *adj* **chilled**, cool, refrigerated, frozen, cold, on the rocks (*informal*) [➡ TEMPERATURE: COLD; 1231] *Opposite*: hot

ice dancing *type of* **winter sport** [➡ HOBBIES, GAMES, AND SPORTS; 875]

iced coffee *type of* **coffee** [➡ DRINKS; 1187]

ice over *v* **freeze**, freeze over, freeze up, harden, solidify, ice up, ice [➡ HARDEN, CONGEAL, AND DRY; 387] *Opposite*: thaw

ice pack *n* **compress**, cold compress, wrapping, poultice [➡ REMEDIES, TREATMENTS, AND OPERATIONS; 731]

ice up *v* **freeze**, freeze over, freeze up, ice over, frost up, ice [➡ HARDEN, CONGEAL, AND DRY; 387]

ichthyosaur *type of* **dinosaur** [➡ DINOSAURS; 996]

iciness *n* **coldness**, coolness, frostiness, unfriendliness, hostility, disdain, remoteness, aloofness [➡ UNFRIENDLINESS AND UNSOCIABILITY; 504] *Opposite*: warmth

icing 1 *n* **frosting**, decoration, glaze, glazing, ganache [➡ COVERS AND COATINGS; 1246] 2 *n* **freezing**, freezing over, freezing up [➡ HARDEN, CONGEAL, AND DRY; 387]

icing on the cake *n* [➡ AMAZING THINGS; 211]

icky (*informal*) 1 *adj* **sticky**, gooey, tacky, messy, disgusting, horrid, nasty [➡ PHYSICAL TEXTURE; 1222] 2 *adj* **nasty**, unpleasant, horrid, funny, uncomfortable, horrible, yucky (*informal*) [➡ DISGUSTING AND REPULSIVE; 230] 3 *adj* **sentimental**, too much, saccharine, over-the-top (*informal*), sloppy (*informal*), schmaltzy (*informal*), tacky (*informal*) [➡ IN POOR TASTE AND OVERSENTIMENTAL; 229]

icon 1 *n* **image**, likeness, representation, sign, picture, photograph, drawing, portrait [➡ ARTWORKS; 898] 2 *n* **idol**, star, model, symbol, embodiment, personification, incarnation, ideal, exemplar (*literary*) [➡ FADS, FETISHES, AND IDOLATRY; 555]

iconoclast *n* **revolutionary**, radical, free thinker, subversive, individualist, reformer, rebel [➡ UNCOOPERATIVE OR REBELLIOUS PEOPLE; 566] *Opposite*: conservative

iconoclastic *adj* **radical**, revolutionary, subversive, individualistic, free-thinking [➡ EXTRAORDINARY: UNCOMMON; 205] *Opposite*: conservative

icy 1 *adj* **freezing**, frozen, frosty, ice-cold, subzero, cold, chilly, polar, glacial, wintry, bitter, arctic (*informal*) [➡ COLD WEATHER; 1051] 2 *adj* **unfriendly**, frosty, hostile, distant, aloof, cold, cool, disdainful [➡ UNFRIENDLINESS AND UNSOCIABILITY; 504] *Opposite*: warm

ID *n* **identification**, identity card, passport, papers, documents, ID card (*informal*) [➡ OFFICIAL DOCUMENTS; 586]

idea 1 *n* **opinion**, belief, view, viewpoint, outlook, judgment [➡ IDEAS AND THOUGHTS; 770] 2 *n* **suggestion**, design, plan, scheme, proposal, initiative, recommendation [➡ IDEAS AND THOUGHTS; 770] 3 *n* **concept**, impression, notion, understanding, perception, thought, sense, knowledge [➡ IDEAS AND THOUGHTS; 770] 4 *n* **plan**, inspiration, solution, brainchild, notion, brainstorm (*informal*) [➡ IDEAS AND THOUGHTS; 770] 5 *n* **aim**, objective, plan, object, goal, intention, purpose, point, intent (*formal*) [➡ INTENTIONS AND PURPOSES; 772] 6 *n* **gist**, précis, outline, sketch, snapshot, overview, summary [➡ INDICATIONS, SIGNS, AND WARNINGS; 68]

ideal 1 *n* **principle**, standard, belief, value [➡ MORAL CONCEPTS; 773] 2 *n* **epitome**, height, model, archetype, essence, stereotype, paradigm, icon, exemplar (*literary*) [➡ PERFECT EXAMPLES AND EMBODIMENTS; 67] 3 *adj* **best**, model, ultimate, idyllic, superlative, supreme, perfect [➡ GOOD, WELL, BETTER; 183]

idealism 1 *n* **naiveté**, romanticism, impracticality, optimism [➡ NEGATIVE INTELLECTUAL CHARACTERISTICS; 525] *Opposite*: realism 2 *n* **perfectionism**, fundamentalism, commitment, principle, morality, fanaticism, zeal, fervor [➡ HARD-WORKING AND COMMITTED; 500]

idealist 1 *n* **romantic**, optimist, dreamer [➡ LAZY OR UNSUCCESSFUL PEOPLE; 948] *Opposite*: realist 2 *n* **perfectionist**, fundamentalist, crusader, zealot, fanatic [➡ DEVOTEES AND ADDICTED PEOPLE; 556]

idealistic 1 *adj* **naive**, unrealistic, romantic, impractical, optimistic [➡ NEGATIVE INTELLECTUAL CHARACTERISTICS; 525] *Opposite*: realistic 2 *adj* **uncompromising**, principled, committed, unswerving, unwavering, perfectionist, fervent, ardent [➡ HARD-WORKING AND COMMITTED; 500]

idealize *v* **romanticize**, put on a pedestal, view through rose-tinted glasses, venerate, overemphasize, fetishize [➡ LIKE, LOVE, VALUE, AND ENJOY; 578]

idealized *adj* **perfect**, flawless, faultless, ideal, unrealistic, fanciful [➡ EXTRAORDINARY: UNCOMMON; 205]

ideally 1 *adv* **in an ideal world**, preferably, if possible, if at all possible [➡ POSSIBLE AND PROBABLE; 177] 2 *adv* **perfectly**, supremely, superlatively, well [➡ USEFULNESS; 199]

idée fixe *n* **obsession**, pet topic, hobbyhorse, fixation, bee in your bonnet, thing (*informal*) [➡ FADS, FETISHES, AND IDOLATRY; 555]

idem *adv* **the same**, the same thing, the same as before [➡ WRITTEN CONVENTIONS; 599]

identical *adj* **same**, indistinguishable, equal, matching, alike, like, duplicate, impossible to tell apart, one and the same, like peas in a pod [➡ SAMENESS; 150] *Opposite*: different

identicalness *n* [➡ SAMENESS; 150]

identifiable *adj* **recognizable**, distinguishable, perceptible, discernible, detectable, classifiable [➡ PERCEPTIBLE; 25]

identification 1 *n* **recognition**, classification, naming, detection, discovery [➡ NAME AND DESCRIBE; 665] 2 *n* **ID**, documentation, proof of identity, papers, credentials, documents [➡ OFFICIAL DOCUMENTS; 586] 3 *n* **empathy**, sympathy, affinity, rapport, bonding, association, connection, relationship, link [➡ COMPASSION AND FORGIVENESS; 551]

identify 1 *v* **recognize**, classify, name, find, categorize, detect, isolate, pinpoint, label, distinguish, characterize, ascertain (*formal*) [➡ NAME AND DESCRIBE; 665] 2 *v* **equate**, connect, relate, link, associate [➡ CREATING CONNECTIONS; 144]

identify with *v* **empathize with**, sympathize with, relate to, feel for, have sympathy for, feel empathy with [➡ BE CONCERNED AND CARE; 581]

identity *n* **individuality**, uniqueness, distinctiveness, self, character, personality [➡ TEMPERAMENT AND BEHAVIOR; 492]

identity card *n* **pass**, card, passport, ID card (*informal*) [➡ OFFICIAL DOCUMENTS; 586]

ideogram *n* [➡ SYMBOLS, SIGNS, AND NUMBERS; 596]

ideological *adj* **conceptual**, philosophical, moral, political, ethical, sociopolitical, religious [➡ PHILOSOPHIES AND BELIEFS; 780]

ideology *n* **philosophy**, belief, creed, dogma, line, system [➡ PHILOSOPHIES AND BELIEFS; 780]

idiocy *n* [➡ NEGATIVE INTELLECTUAL CHARACTERISTICS; 525]

idiolect *n* **speech pattern**, turn of phrase, style, dialect, idiom, vocabulary, lexis, syntax, language [➡ ASPECTS OF LANGUAGE; 682]

See Compare and Contrast at **language**.

idiom 1 *n* **expression**, phrase, set phrase, turn of phrase, saying, figure of speech [➡ FIGURES OF SPEECH; 673] 2 *n* **language**, dialect, speech, style, vernacular, syntax, lexicon, lexis [➡ ASPECTS OF LANGUAGE; 682]

idiomatic *adj* **natural**, fluent, colloquial, vernacular, native [➡ COMMUNICATIVE STYLE; 624] *Opposite*: stilted

idiosyncrasy *n* **quirk**, peculiarity, eccentricity, foible, habit, characteristic, feature [➡ PERSONAL ECCENTRICITIES; 493]

idiosyncratic *adj* **characteristic**, personal, individual, distinctive, eccentric, peculiar, quirky, particular, unique, all your own [➡ EXTRAORDINARY: UNCOMMON; 205]

idiotic *adj* [➡ BIZARRE AND PECULIAR; 257]

idle 1 *adj* **inactive**, inoperative, unoccupied, at rest, still, immobile, off, down [➡ LACK OF ACTIVITY OR MOTION; 342] *Opposite*: working 2 *adj* **lazy**, indolent, shiftless, slothful, sluggish, workshy (*UK*) [➡ LIFELESS, LAZY, AND UNENTHUSIASTIC; 506] *Opposite*: diligent 3 *adj* **frivolous**, futile, pointless, worthless, useless, vain [➡ REDUNDANT AND USELESS; 240] 4 *adj* **unfounded**, baseless, groundless, frivolous, meaningless, speculative, casual [➡ THE NATURE OF IDEAS; 771] 5 *adj* **empty**, hollow, ineffectual, impotent, meaningless [➡ UNIMPORTANT AND UNNECESSARY; 238] 6 *v* **laze**, laze around, hang around, sit around, loaf around, waste, while away, fritter away, goof off (*informal*) [➡ LACK OF ACTIVITY OR MOTION; 342] 7 *v* **turn over**, run, tick over (*informal*) [➡ FUNCTION SUCCESSFULLY; 469] 8 *v* **dismiss**, fire, lay off (*informal*), can (*slang*), make redundant (*UK*) [➡ REVOKE STATUS; 459]

See Compare and Contrast at **vain**.

idle away *v* **while away**, fritter away, waste, pass, spend, occupy [➡ USE UP AND WASTE; 474]

idleness *n* **laziness**, sloth, inertia, indolence, apathy, lethargy, sluggishness, slothfulness (*formal*) [➡ LACK OF ACTIVITY OR MOTION; 342] *Opposite*: activity

idler *n* **loafer**, sloth, malingerer, timewaster, shirker, slacker, lazybones (*informal*), slouch (*informal*) [➡ LAZY OR UNSUCCESSFUL PEOPLE; 948] *Opposite*: workaholic

idle rich *n* [➡ RICH PEOPLE; 895]

idly 1 *adv* **lazily**, indolently, shiftlessly, slothfully (*formal*) [➡ LIFELESS, LAZY, AND UNENTHUSIASTIC; 506] 2 *adv* **frivolously**, futilely, pointlessly, worthlessly, uselessly, vainly [➡ REDUNDANT AND USELESS; 240]

idol 1 *n* **hero**, star, pinup, obsession, ideal, favorite [➡ PEOPLE WHO ARE APPROVED OF; 955] 2 *n* **icon**, graven image, statue, carving, sculpture, symbol, god, deity [➡ RELIGIOUS OBJECTS; 779]

idolater *n* **fan**, admirer, fanatic, devotee, aficionado, aficionada, follower, hero-worshiper, worshiper [➡ DEVOTEES AND ADDICTED PEOPLE; 556]

idolatry *n* **worship**, hero worship, adoration, admiration, veneration, idolization, adulation, reverence, fanaticism, devotion, obsession [➡ FADS, FETISHES, AND IDOLATRY; 555]

idolization *n* **worship**, hero worship, adoration, admiration, veneration, idolatry, adulation, reverence, fanaticism, devotion, obsession [➡ FADS, FETISHES, AND IDOLATRY; 555] *Opposite*: denigration

idolize *v* **worship**, hero-worship, adore, look up to, admire, venerate, revere, put on a pedestal, exalt (*formal*) [➡ LIKE, LOVE, VALUE, AND ENJOY; 578] *Opposite*: denigrate

idyll *n* **nirvana**, honeymoon, honeymoon period, heaven, paradise, utopia, arcadia [➡ PLEASANT SITUATIONS; 74] *Opposite*: nightmare

idyllic 1 *adj* **peaceful**, calm, tranquil, restful, relaxing, serene, heavenly, sublime, perfect, blissful, ideal, pleasant [➡ CALMING; 188] *Opposite*: nightmarish **2** *adj* **picturesque**, scenic, unspoiled, serene, tranquil, calm, peaceful, beautiful, glorious, charming, delightful [➡ BEAUTY AND ATTRACTIVENESS; 189]

i.e. *adv* **that is to say**, that is, namely, viz., to be precise, to be exact, specifically, in so many words, in other words [➡ WRITTEN CONVENTIONS; 599]

if **1** *n* **doubt**, uncertainty, question mark, unknown, unknown quantity, gamble [➡ UNCERTAIN; 175] **2** *n* **stipulation**, condition, rider, proviso, qualification, provision, reservation, but (*informal*) [➡ NECESSARY AND ESSENTIAL; 196]

iffy (*informal*) **1** *adj* **risky**, chancy, shaky, suspicious, dubious, unreliable, dicey (*informal*) [➡ DANGEROUS; 236] *Opposite*: reliable **2** *adj* **unsure**, undecided, doubtful, hesitant, up in the air, tentative, in doubt, touch and go, uncertain [➡ UNCERTAIN; 175] *Opposite*: certain

if need be *adv* **if necessary**, if required, if essential, if needs must, if it comes to it, if it comes to the crunch, if push comes to shove, should it be necessary [➡ NECESSARY AND ESSENTIAL; 196]

if truth be told *adv* **to be honest**, to tell the truth, to be frank, frankly, in fact, as a matter of fact, in actual fact, actually [➡ WORDS AND PHRASES EMPHASIZING THE TRUTH OF A MATTER; 172]

if you ask me *adv* [➡ EXPRESSIONS OF OPINION; 623]

igloo *type of* **house** [➡ RESIDENTIAL BUILDINGS; 1078]

ignite **1** *v* **catch fire**, catch light, go up in flames, burst into flames, flare up, kindle, burn, explode, go off [➡ FIRE, FLAMMABILITY, AND BURNING; 1165] *Opposite*: go out **2** *v* **set fire to**, light, put a match to, set alight, kindle, burn, detonate, blow up, set light to (*UK*) [➡ FIRE, FLAMMABILITY, AND BURNING; 1165] *Opposite*: put out **3** *v* **stir up**, stir, inflame, fan the flames of, kindle, awaken, provoke, incite, fire, fire up [➡ CAUSE TO HAPPEN; 31] *Opposite*: dampen

ignition *n* **explosion**, detonation, eruption, burst, blast-off, start [➡ BEGINNINGS; 53]

ignoble *adj* **dishonorable**, shameful, despicable, immoral, dastardly, base, low, reprehensible, contemptible, shabby, disgraceful [➡ MORALLY BAD OR IMPROPER; 775] *Opposite*: honorable

See Compare and Contrast at **mean**.

ignominious *adj* **humiliating**, embarrassing, shameful, disgraceful, reprehensible, dishonorable, disreputable, despicable, discreditable, discomfiting (*formal*) [➡ EMOTIONALLY UNPLEASANT AND UPSETTING; 227] *Opposite*: honorable

ignominy *n* **humiliation**, embarrassment, shame, disgrace, dishonor, infamy, disrepute, discredit, discomfiture (*formal*) [➡ EMBARRASSMENT AND HUMILIATION; 542] *Opposite*: honor

ignorance *n* **unawareness**, unfamiliarity, obliviousness, inexperience, witlessness [➡ IGNORANCE; 557] *Opposite*: knowledge

ignorant *adj* **unaware**, uninformed, ill-informed, unfamiliar, oblivious, unconscious, unknowing, unwit-

ting, unenlightened, in the dark, inexperienced [➡ IGNORANCE; 557] *Opposite*: aware

ignore *v* **pay no attention to**, take no notice of, close your eyes to, pay no heed to, disregard, not take into account, overlook, discount, dispense with, turn your back on, flout, snub, pass over, look through [➡ NOT PAY ATTENTION; 764] *Opposite*: notice

ignored *adj* **overlooked**, unnoticed, disregarded, discounted, unheeded, passed over, flouted, snubbed [➡ IMPERCEPTIBLE; 26] *Opposite*: noted

iguana *type of* **reptile** [➡ REPTILES; 994]

iguanodon *type of* **dinosaur** [➡ DINOSAURS; 996]

ilium *type of* **bone** [➡ THE BONES AND JOINTS; 719]

ilk *n* **type**, like, sort, kind, class, breed, manner, character, stripe, variety [➡ VARIETIES, TYPES, AND KINDS; 145]

ill **1** *adj* **unwell**, sick, under the weather, laid up, in poor health, nauseous, ailing (*dated*) [➡ ILL AND SICK; 740] *Opposite*: well **2** *adj* **unkind**, unfriendly, hostile, harsh, mean, cruel, hard, unpleasant, bad [➡ BAD AND BADLY; 223] *Opposite*: good **3** *adj* **harmful**, adverse, detrimental, unfavorable, unpropitious, inauspicious, ominous, bad [➡ DANGEROUS; 236] *Opposite*: good **4** *adj* **wicked**, evil, immoral, bad, iniquitous, sinful, reprobate [➡ MORALLY BAD OR IMPROPER; 775] *Opposite*: good **5** *adv* **unkindly**, hostilely, harshly, cruelly, unpleasantly, poorly, shoddily, amiss, inadequately, inappropriately, badly [➡ BAD AND BADLY; 223] *Opposite*: well **6** *adv* **unfavorably**, adversely, unpropitiously, inauspiciously, ominously, badly, harmfully, detrimentally [➡ DANGEROUS; 236] *Opposite*: well **7** *adv* **hardly**, barely, scarcely [➡ TO A CERTAIN EXTENT; 136] *Opposite*: well **8** *n* **harm**, evil, misfortune, trouble, mischief, bad luck, ill luck, injury [➡ NUISANCES; 253] *Opposite*: good

ill-advised *adj* **foolish**, foolhardy, misguided, rash, reckless, hasty, unwise, imprudent, incautious, ill-considered, ill-judged, injudicious, risky, irresponsible [➡ THE NATURE OF IDEAS; 771] *Opposite*: well-advised

ill-advisedly *adv* **foolishly**, foolhardily, misguidedly, rashly, recklessly, hastily, unwisely, incautiously, injudiciously, riskily, irresponsibly, imprudently (*formal*) [➡ THE NATURE OF IDEAS; 771] *Opposite*: sensibly

ill-assorted *adj* **incompatible**, mismatched, unsuited, incongruous, antagonistic, clashing [➡ DISHARMONY; 156] *Opposite*: compatible

ill at ease *adj* **uncomfortable**, anxious, awkward, uneasy, edgy, on edge, jumpy, jittery, tense, self-conscious, nervous [➡ INSECURITY AND LOSS OF COMPOSURE; 544] *Opposite*: relaxed

ill-bred *adj* **rude**, impolite, boorish, bad-mannered, ill-mannered, ignorant, insensitive, inconsiderate, coarse, vulgar, common [➡ BAD MANNERS AND SOCIAL SKILLS; 521] *Opposite*: well-bred

ill-conceived *adj* **doomed**, impractical, vague, ill-judged, half-baked (*informal*), crackpot (*informal*) [➡ THE NATURE OF IDEAS; 771]

ill-considered *adj* **careless**, reckless, irresponsible, rash, hasty, imprudent, unwise, ill-advised, ill-judged, foolhardy, foolish [➡ THE NATURE OF IDEAS; 771] *Opposite*: prudent

ill-defined *adj* **imprecise**, vague, hazy, unclear, nebulous, blurred, inexact, inaccurate [➡ VAGUENESS; 243] *Opposite*: clear

ill-disguised *adj* **obvious**, blatant, clear, apparent, plain, undisguised, unconcealed, glaring, visible, undoubted [➡ KNOWN AND FAMOUS; 181] *Opposite*: concealed

ill-disposed *adj* **hostile**, unfriendly, cold, cool, antagonistic, negative, aggressive [➡ IRRITATION AND ANGER; 541] *Opposite*: well-disposed

illegal *adj* **against the law**, unlawful, illicit, illegitimate, prohibited, banned, proscribed, forbidden, criminal, dishonest [➡ ILLEGAL; 816] *Opposite*: legal

See Compare and Contrast at **unlawful**.

illegality **1** *n* **unlawfulness**, illicitness, illegitimacy, impropriety, wrongfulness, criminality, dishonesty [➡ ILLEGAL; 816] *Opposite*: legality **2** *n* **crime**, misdemeanor, felony, infraction, offense, transgression, contravention, violation, infringement [➡ CRIMES; 817]

illegible *adj* **unreadable**, indecipherable, scrawled, scribbled, spidery, obscured [➡ DIFFICULTY AND COMPLEXITY; 242] *Opposite*: legible

illegitimate *adj* **unlawful**, illegal, illicit, prohibited, banned, proscribed, forbidden, criminal, dishonest [➡ ILLEGAL; 816] *Opposite*: legitimate

ill-fated *adj* **doomed**, ill-starred, unlucky, unfortunate, hapless, star-crossed, fateful, ill-omened, disastrous [➡ BAD LUCK AND UNLUCKY; 784] *Opposite*: lucky

ill-favored *adj* **unattractive**, ugly, unpleasant, repulsive, horrible, repellent, hideous [➡ PEOPLE'S PHYSICAL APPEARANCE; 475] *Opposite*: good-looking

ill feeling *n* **animosity**, hostility, ill will, antagonism, enmity, malice, resentment, antipathy, bitterness, hard feelings [➡ ANTAGONISM; 552] *Opposite*: friendliness

ill-founded *adj* **illogical**, false, inaccurate, trumped-up, unreliable, dubious, unsubstantiated, unsound [➡ THE NATURE OF IDEAS; 771] *Opposite*: reliable

ill-gotten *adj* **illegal**, illicit, fraudulent, contraband, unlawful, false, dishonest [➡ ILLEGAL; 816]

ill-gotten gains *n* [➡ PROCEEDS OF CRIME; 427]

ill health *n* **infirmity**, illness, sickness, disease, frailty, weakness, debility, disability [➡ ILL AND SICK; 740] *Opposite*: good health

ill humor *n* **grouchiness**, bad mood, mood, bad temper, foul mood, sulk, pet, downer (*UK informal*), grumps (*UK informal*) [➡ IRRITATION AND ANGER; 541]

ill-humored *adj* [➡ NEGATIVITY OF OUTLOOK; 514]

illiberal **1** *adj* **intolerant**, bigoted, narrow-minded, reactionary, parochial, conservative, proscriptive (*formal*) [➡ NEGATIVE INTELLECTUAL CHARACTERISTICS; 525] *Opposite*: liberal **2** *adj* (*formal*) **mean**, parsimonious, stingy, miserly, niggardly, tight, grudging, tightfisted, penny-pinching (*informal*) [➡ GRASPING AND FINANCIALLY MEAN; 519] *Opposite*: generous

illicit *adj* **illegal**, unlawful, illegitimate, dishonest, crim-

inal, against the law, prohibited, banned, forbidden, proscribed [➡ ILLEGAL; 816] *Opposite*: legal

See Compare and Contrast at **unlawful**.

illicitness *n* [➡ ILLEGAL; 816]

illiterate *adj* **uneducated**, untaught, unschooled, untrained, uninformed, ignorant [➡ UNSKILLED; 529] *Opposite*: literate

ill-judged *adj* **misguided**, injudicious, inappropriate, unwise, imprudent, rash, hasty, careless, thoughtless, ill-advised, ill-considered, ill-conceived [➡ THE NATURE OF IDEAS; 771] *Opposite*: prudent

ill-mannered *adj* **rude**, bad-mannered, impolite, discourteous, disrespectful, common, ill-bred, vulgar, coarse, boorish, ignorant [➡ BAD MANNERS AND SOCIAL SKILLS; 521] *Opposite*: well-mannered

ill-natured *adj* **unpleasant**, disagreeable, ill-tempered, bad-tempered, ill-humored, irascible, irritable, surly, sulky, gruff, grumpy, cross, moody, crabby, curt, brusque, short, cantankerous, prickly (*informal*), snippy (*informal*), grouchy (*informal*), crotchety (*informal*) [➡ AGGRESSIVE AND BELLIGERENT; 518] *Opposite*: good-natured

illness **1** *n* **disease**, sickness, complaint, ailment, infection, virus, disorder, syndrome, malady, affliction, bug (*informal*) [➡ ILL AND SICK; 740] **2** *n* **ill health**, sickness, disease, infirmity, disability, weakness, debility [➡ ILL AND SICK; 740] *Opposite*: good health

illogical **1** *adj* **irrational**, unreasoned, unscientific, specious, unsound, unfounded, inconsistent, contradictory, invalid, irreconcilable, incongruous [➡ THE NATURE OF IDEAS; 771] *Opposite*: logical **2** *adj* **unreasonable**, senseless, absurd, ludicrous, nonsensical, perverse [➡ THE NATURE OF IDEAS; 771] *Opposite*: logical

illogicality **1** *n* **irrationality**, speciousness, unsoundness, inconsistency, contradiction, invalidity, irreconcilability, incongruity [➡ THE NATURE OF IDEAS; 771] **2** *n* **unreasonableness**, senselessness, absurdity, ludicrousness, nonsensicality, perverseness [➡ THE NATURE OF IDEAS; 771]

ill-omened *adj* **inauspicious**, unlucky, unfortunate, ominous, fateful, unpropitious, ill-starred, ill-fated, doomed, hapless [➡ BAD LUCK AND UNLUCKY; 784] *Opposite*: blessed

ill-starred *adj* **unlucky**, doomed, ill-fated, unfortunate, hapless, star-crossed, fateful, ill-omened, inauspicious, disastrous [➡ BAD LUCK AND UNLUCKY; 784] *Opposite*: lucky

ill-tempered *adj* **bad-tempered**, ill-humored, short-tempered, irascible, irritable, grumpy, cross, moody, sulky, gruff, cantankerous, prickly (*informal*), snippy (*informal*), grouchy (*informal*), crotchety (*informal*) [➡ AGGRESSIVE AND BELLIGERENT; 518] *Opposite*: good-tempered

ill-timed *adj* **inopportune**, mistimed, untimely, inconvenient, intrusive, unfortunate, inappropriate, misjudged, ill-judged [➡ PROMPTNESS: BADLY TIMED; 101] *Opposite*: opportune

ill-treat *v* **abuse**, harm, mistreat, maltreat, ill-use, misuse, hurt, harass, torment, oppress, neglect, batter, knock around (*informal*) [➡ WOUND A PERSON OR ANIMAL; 383] *Opposite*: look after

See Compare and Contrast at **misuse**.

ill-treated *adj* **abused**, harmed, mistreated, maltreated, ill-used, misused, hurt, harassed, tormented, oppressed, neglected, battered, knocked around (*informal*) [➡ INJURED; 742] *Opposite:* cherished

ill-treatment *n* **abuse**, harm, maltreatment, mistreatment, cruelty, ill-use, misuse, hurt, harassment, torment, oppression, neglect [➡ MALICIOUS ACTIONS OR BEHAVIOR; 296] *Opposite:* care

illuminate **1** *v* **light up**, light, brighten, lighten, irradiate, illumine (*formal*), illume (*archaic or literary*) [➡ LIGHT EMISSION; 368] *Opposite:* darken **2** *v* **clarify**, elucidate, explain, clear up, illustrate [➡ EXPLAIN AND CLARIFY; 610] *Opposite:* confuse

illuminating *adj* **enlightening**, revealing, informative, instructive, educational, helpful [➡ INTERESTING AND MEANINGFUL; 190] *Opposite:* confusing

illumination **1** *n* **light**, lighting, lights, brightness, brilliance, radiance [➡ LIGHT; 1164] **2** *n* **enlightenment**, clarification, explanation, insight, knowledge, elucidation (*formal*) [➡ EXPLAIN AND CLARIFY; 610] *Opposite:* confusion

illuminations *n* **lights**, Christmas lights, colored lights, decorations, fairy lights (*UK*) [➡ LIGHT; 1164]

illumine (*formal*) *v* [➡ LIGHT EMISSION; 368]

ill-use *v* **abuse**, harm, mistreat, maltreat, treat badly, be cruel to, ill-treat, misuse, hurt, harass, torment, oppress, neglect, batter, knock around (*informal*) [➡ WOUND A PERSON OR ANIMAL; 383] *Opposite:* look after

ill-used *adj* **mistreated**, maltreated, badly treated, abused, hurt, harmed, ill-treated, misused, harassed, tormented, oppressed, neglected, battered, knocked around (*informal*) [➡ INJURED; 742] *Opposite:* cherished

illusion **1** *n* **delusion**, impression, misapprehension, deception, misconception, magic, trickery, sleight of hand, artifice (*formal*) [➡ DECEPTION AND LIES; 660] **2** *n* **impression**, semblance, appearance, feeling, sensation, sense, idea, effect [➡ IDEAS AND THOUGHTS; 770] **3** *n* **fantasy**, daydream, figment of your imagination, chimera, mirage, dream, trick, deception, hallucination, figment [➡ NONEXISTENT THINGS; 23] *Opposite:* reality

illusionist *n* [➡ WORKERS IN ENTERTAINMENT AND MEDIA; 873]

illusive *adj* **illusory**, deceptive, false, misleading, imagined, unreal, erroneous, sham [➡ FALSE AND UNREAL; 173] *Opposite:* real

illusoriness *n* [➡ FALSE AND UNREAL; 173]

illusory *adj* **deceptive**, false, illusive, imagined, misleading, unreal, sham, erroneous [➡ FALSE AND UNREAL; 173] *Opposite:* real

illustrate *v* **exemplify**, demonstrate, show, point up, prove, explain, clarify, elucidate, illuminate, point out [➡ REPRESENT SOMETHING OR SOMEBODY; 59]

illustration **1** *n* **picture**, drawing, design, figure, diagram, sketch, photograph, photo, image, graphic, artwork, visual, visual aid [➡ DRAWINGS, CHARTS, AND TABLES; 594] **2** *n* **example**, demonstration, instance, case in point, exemplification, model, specimen, sample, representative [➡ REPRESENTATIONS AND GENERAL EXAMPLES; 65]

illustrations *n* [➡ DRAWINGS, CHARTS, AND TABLES; 594]

illustrative *adj* **descriptive**, explanatory, graphic, expressive, demonstrative [➡ REPRESENTATIVE; 66]

illustrious *adj* **distinguished**, celebrated, renowned, famous, eminent, great, grand, glorious, admired, well-known [➡ KNOWN AND FAMOUS; 181] *Opposite:* obscure

ill will *n* **animosity**, hostility, ill feeling, antagonism, enmity, malice, resentment, antipathy, bitterness, hard feelings [➡ ANTAGONISM; 552] *Opposite:* goodwill

image **1** *n* **picture**, representation, drawing, icon, figure, likeness, illustration, reflection [➡ ARTWORKS; 898] **2** *n* **impression**, picture, idea, concept, notion, vision, view [➡ IDEAS AND THOUGHTS; 770] **3** *n* **copy**, twin, double, duplicate, carbon copy, doppelgänger, spitting image (*informal*) [➡ REPRESENTATIONS AND GENERAL EXAMPLES; 65] **4** *n* **appearance**, look, persona, aura, air, aspect, semblance [➡ APPEARANCE AND ATMOSPHERE; 1237]

imagery *n* **images**, pictures, imaginings, descriptions, metaphors, similes [➡ REPRESENTATIONS AND GENERAL EXAMPLES; 65]

imaginable *adj* **conceivable**, possible, thinkable, supposable, presumable, comprehensible [➡ POSSIBLE AND PROBABLE; 177] *Opposite:* unimaginable

imaginariness *n* [➡ FALSE AND UNREAL; 173]

imaginary *adj* **fantasy**, make-believe, made-up, unreal, invented, pretend, imagined, fictional, illusory [➡ FALSE AND UNREAL; 173] *Opposite:* real

imagination **1** *n* **mind's eye**, mind, head, thoughts, imaginings, dreams, fancy [➡ DREAM, IMAGINE, AND FANTASIZE; 749] **2** *n* **resourcefulness**, ingenuity, creativity, powers of invention, vision, inspiration, inventiveness [➡ POSITIVE INTELLECTUAL CHARACTERISTICS; 524]

imaginative *adj* **creative**, inventive, original, ingenious, inspired, artistic, resourceful, visionary, inspirational [➡ POSITIVE INTELLECTUAL CHARACTERISTICS; 524] *Opposite:* unimaginative

imaginativeness *n* **creativeness**, inventiveness, originality, ingeniousness, resourcefulness [➡ POSITIVE INTELLECTUAL CHARACTERISTICS; 524]

imagine **1** *v* **picture**, envisage, visualize, see, conjure up, envision, conceive, fancy [➡ DREAM, IMAGINE, AND FANTASIZE; 749] **2** *v* **make up**, dream, dream up, invent, make believe, think up, think of, conceive of, concoct [➡ DREAM, IMAGINE, AND FANTASIZE; 749] **3** *v* **suppose**, think, expect, assume, presume, guess, dare say, understand, reckon [➡ DEVELOP THEORIES AND REASON; 744]

imagined *adj* **fictional**, imaginary, abstract, unreal, illusory, fantasy, make-believe, made-up, invented, pretend [➡ FALSE AND UNREAL; 173] *Opposite:* real

imago *type of* **stage of insect development** [➡ INSECT STAGES; 1020]

imbalance *n* **inequity**, disparity, unevenness, disproportion, inequality, difference, discrepancy, one-sidedness [➡ DIFFERENCE; 149] *Opposite:* balance

imbibe (*formal or humorous*) *v* **drink**, down, swallow, take in, absorb, gulp, sip, taste, guzzle (*informal*) [➡ DRINK; 711]

imbroglio *n* **mess**, embarrassment, entanglement, complication, enmeshment, confusion [➡ DIFFICULT SITUATIONS; 72]

imbue *v* **instill**, fill, permeate, infuse, saturate, impregnate [➡ FILL; 406]

imitate 1 *v* **mimic**, copy, impersonate, ape, pretend to be, do an impression, take off (*informal*) [➡ PRETEND AND MIMIC; 60] 2 *v* **copy**, reproduce, emulate, duplicate, replicate, try to be like, rip off (*informal*) [➡ PRETEND AND MIMIC; 60]

Compare and Contrast: *imitate, copy, emulate, mimic, take off, ape*

CORE MEANING: to adopt the behavior of another person

imitate to copy another's behavior, voice, or manner, sometimes in order to make fun of him or her; *copy* to do exactly what somebody else does; *emulate* to try to equal or surpass somebody else who is successful or admired; *mimic* to imitate somebody in a deliberate and exaggerated way, especially to amuse people; *take off* (*informal*) to imitate somebody to amuse people; *ape* to imitate somebody in an absurd or grotesque way.

---

imitation 1 *n* **simulation**, reproduction, replication, copy, facsimile, mock-up, rip-off (*informal*) [➡ REPRESENTATIONS AND GENERAL EXAMPLES; 65] 2 *n* **impersonation**, impression, skit, parody, sendup (*informal*), takeoff (*informal*) [➡ REPRESENTATIONS AND GENERAL EXAMPLES; 65] 3 *adj* **mock**, fake, simulated, artificial, pretend, synthetic, ersatz [➡ FALSE AND UNREAL; 173] *Opposite*: real

imitative *adj* **unoriginal**, derivative, plagiarized, copied, secondhand, clichéd, commonplace, trite [➡ RELATED; 142] *Opposite*: original

imitator 1 *n* **impersonator**, impressionist, mimic, double, actor, look-alike (*informal*) [➡ WORKERS IN ENTERTAINMENT AND MEDIA; 873] 2 *n* **follower**, sheep, copier, clone, imitation, pale imitation, copycat (*informal*) [➡ REPRESENTATIONS AND GENERAL EXAMPLES; 65] *Opposite*: original

immaculate 1 *adj* **spotless**, perfect, neat and tidy, clean, spick-and-span, tidy [➡ CLEAN AND HYGIENIC; 1233] *Opposite*: messy 2 *adj* **perfect**, flawless, faultless, pristine, pure, impeccable [➡ IN GOOD REPAIR; 1232] *Opposite*: flawed

immanent (*formal*) *adj* **inherent**, intrinsic, innate, ingrained, internal, essential [➡ PRESENT AND AVAILABLE; 11]

immaterial *adj* **irrelevant**, unimportant, of no importance, of no consequence, inconsequential, beside the point, neither here nor there, makes no difference [➡ UNIMPORTANT AND UNNECESSARY; 238] *Opposite*: relevant

immateriality *n* [➡ UNIMPORTANT AND UNNECESSARY; 238]

immaterialness *n* [➡ UNIMPORTANT AND UNNECESSARY; 238]

immature 1 *adj* **young**, undeveloped, small, unformed, juvenile, adolescent, unripe [➡ BABYHOOD, CHILDHOOD, AND ADOLESCENCE; 917] *Opposite*: mature 2 *adj* **childish**, babyish, infantile, juvenile, adolescent, puerile [➡ BAD MANNERS AND SOCIAL SKILLS; 521] *Opposite*: mature

immaturely *adv* **childishly**, babyishly, puerilely [➡ BAD MANNERS AND SOCIAL SKILLS; 521] *Opposite*: maturely

immaturity 1 *n* **adolescence**, infancy, reproductive immaturity, youth, babyhood, childhood [➡ BABYHOOD, CHILDHOOD, AND ADOLESCENCE; 917] *Opposite*: maturity 2 *n* **childishness**, irresponsibility, naiveté, ingenuousness, silliness, stupidity, puerility, fatuity (*formal*) [➡ BAD MANNERS AND SOCIAL SKILLS; 521] *Opposite*: maturity 3 *n* **inexperience**, greenness, naiveté, rawness, awkwardness, crudeness, heavy-handedness [➡ NEGATIVE INTELLECTUAL CHARACTERISTICS; 525] *Opposite*: maturity

immeasurable *adj* **vast**, beyond measure, endless, infinite, incalculable, inestimable, immense, untold, massive, great, colossal, huge, enormous, considerable [➡ LARGE; 1193] *Opposite*: slight

immeasurably *adv* **infinitely**, vastly, incalculably, inestimably, immensely, greatly, colossally, hugely, enormously, considerably, massively (*informal*) [➡ TO A GREAT EXTENT; 132] *Opposite*: slightly

immediate 1 *adj* **instant**, direct, instantaneous, abrupt, fast, speedy [➡ HAPPENING QUICKLY; 104] 2 *adj* **direct**, close, near, proximate [➡ CLOSENESS; 159] *Opposite*: distant 3 *adj* **urgent**, current, pressing, high priority, burning, important [➡ IMPORTANT; 194]

immediately 1 *adv* **right away**, at once, without delay, instantly, directly, instantaneously, without further ado, right now, just now, straightaway [➡ HAPPENING QUICKLY; 104] 2 *adv* **directly**, closely, nearly, proximately [➡ CLOSENESS; 159] 3 *conj* **as soon as**, the moment, the instant, the minute, the second [➡ CONCURRENT AND CONTEMPORANEOUS; 164]

immemorial *adj* **ancient**, age-old, old, centuries old, timeworn, long-established [➡ PERMANENCE: WITHOUT END; 94]

immense *adj* **huge**, vast, enormous, massive, gigantic, mammoth, giant, colossal, immeasurable, great, incalculable [➡ LARGE; 1193] *Opposite*: tiny

immensely *adv* **hugely**, vastly, enormously, immeasurably, greatly, incalculably, very, extremely, gigantically, colossally, infinitely, massively (*informal*) [➡ TO A GREAT EXTENT; 132]

immenseness *n* [➡ LARGE; 1193]

immensity *n* **hugeness**, vastness, enormity, sheer size, extent [➡ LARGE; 1193]

immerse 1 *v* **submerge**, dip, plunge, duck, dunk, submerge [➡ MOVE SOMETHING: DOWNWARD; 329] 2 *v* **engross**, throw yourself into, absorb yourself in, engage, occupy [➡ CHANGE OF MOOD AND COMPOSURE; 580]

immersed *adj* **engrossed**, wrapped up, absorbed, deep, occupied [➡ PENSIVENESS AND INTEREST; 538] *Opposite*: distracted

immersion 1 *n* **involvement**, engagement, absorption, entanglement, preoccupation, obsession [➡ POSITIVE IMPATIENCE, ENTHUSIASM, AND ALERTNESS; 537] 2 *n* **dipping**, soaking, wetting, dunking, steeping, bathing, rinsing, submersion, covering [➡ WET; 1240]

immersion heater *type of* **heating appliance** [➡ HEATING, REFRIGERATION, AND VENTILATION; 1142]

immigrant *n* **settler**, émigré, migrant, refugee, colonist, colonizer [➤ PEOPLE LIVING AWAY FROM HOME; 887] *Opposite:* emigrant

immigrate *v* **settle**, arrive, colonize, discover, found, establish [➤ TRAVEL: WAYS OF TRAVELING; 320] *Opposite:* emigrate

immigration *n* **migration**, settlement, arrival, entry, colonization [➤ ARRIVAL; 13]

imminence *n* [➤ FUTURE; 86]

imminent *adj* **impending**, forthcoming, pending, looming, about to happen, coming up, in the offing, on the agenda, on the horizon, in the stars, in the pipeline, at hand, just around the corner [➤ ABOUT TO HAPPEN; 33]. *Opposite:* distant

immobile 1 *adj* **motionless**, stationary, still, stock-still, inert, static, at a halt, at a standstill, at rest [➤ LACK OF ACTIVITY OR MOTION; 342] *Opposite:* mobile　2 *adj* **fixed**, immovable, secure, steady, permanent [➤ RIGID AND HARD; 1211] *Opposite:* mobile

immobility *n* **stillness**, motionlessness, immovability, fixity, stasis, rigidity [➤ LACK OF ACTIVITY OR MOTION; 342] *Opposite:* mobility

immobilize *v* **stop**, halt, restrain, arrest, bring to a halt, put out of action [➤ CAUSE TO STOP; 266] *Opposite:* mobilize

immoderate *adj* **excessive**, extreme, intemperate, extravagant, unrestrained, debauched, wild, violent, riotous, uncontrolled, out of control, decadent, over-the-top (*informal*) [➤ PLEASURE-SEEKING AND EXCESS; 885] *Opposite:* moderate

immoderateness (*formal*) *see* **immoderation**

immoderation (*formal*) *n* **excess**, intemperance, extravagance, prodigality, abandon, decadence, debauchery, riotousness, lack of control, immoderateness [➤ PLEASURE-SEEKING AND EXCESS; 885] *Opposite:* moderation

immodest *adj* **boastful**, arrogant, conceited, ostentatious, bombastic, pretentious, bigheaded (*informal*) [➤ POMPOUS, LOUD, AND OVERCONFIDENT; 635] *Opposite:* modest

immodestly *adv* **boastfully**, arrogantly, conceitedly, ostentatiously, pretentiously, bombastically, bigheadedly (*informal*) [➤ POMPOUS, LOUD, AND OVERCONFIDENT; 635] *Opposite:* modestly

immodesty *n* **arrogance**, conceit, boastfulness, pretentiousness, ostentatiousness, showing off, bigheadedness (*informal*) [➤ POMPOUS, LOUD, AND OVERCONFIDENT; 635] *Opposite:* modesty

immolate (*literary*) *v* **sacrifice**, offer up, slaughter, make an offering of, kill, burn [➤ KILL; 923]

immolation (*formal*) *n* [➤ CAUSES OF DEATH; 921]

immoral *adj* **wicked**, depraved, corrupt, dissolute, dishonest, dissipated, decadent, debauched, sinful, iniquitous [➤ MORALLY BAD OR IMPROPER; 775] *Opposite:* moral

immorality *n* **wickedness**, sin, depravity, corruption, dissoluteness, dishonesty, dissipation, decadence, iniquity, debauchery [➤ MORALLY BAD OR IMPROPER; 775] *Opposite:* morality

immortal 1 *adj* **eternal**, everlasting, undying, perpetual, enduring, never-ending, endless, unending, abiding, that will live forever, that will never die [➤ PERMANENCE: WITHOUT END; 94] *Opposite:* mortal　2 *adj* **memorable**, well-known, famous, illustrious, unforgettable, remarkable [➤ KNOWN AND FAMOUS; 181] *Opposite:* forgotten

immortality *n* [➤ PERMANENCE: WITHOUT END; 94]

immortalize *v* **commemorate**, celebrate, preserve, make immortal, memorialize, eternalize, exalt (*formal*) [➤ REPRESENT SOMETHING OR SOMEBODY; 59]

immortally *adv* [➤ PERMANENCE: WITHOUT END; 94]

immovable 1 *adj* **fixed**, immobile, secure, steady, permanent [➤ RIGID AND HARD; 1211] *Opposite:* movable　2 *adj* **resolute**, unbending, rigid, stubborn, obstinate, inflexible, adamant, firm, steadfast, obdurate, set [➤ UNWILLINGNESS AND STUBBORNNESS; 564] *Opposite:* irresolute

immune 1 *adj* **resistant**, protected, invulnerable, safe, insusceptible (*formal*) [➤ SAFE AND SAFETY; 191] *Opposite:* susceptible　2 *adj* **exempt**, excepted, absolved, excused, not liable [➤ FREEDOM AND LIBERTY; 208] *Opposite:* liable　3 *adj* **impervious**, invulnerable, untouchable, untouched, unaffected, safe, proof [➤ SAFE AND SAFETY; 191] *Opposite:* vulnerable

immune system *n* **body's defenses**, natural defenses, immune response, white blood cells, natural resistance, antibodies, white corpuscles [➤ HEALING; 730]

immunity 1 *n* **resistance**, protection, invulnerability, insusceptibility (*formal*) [➤ HEALING; 730] *Opposite:* susceptibility　2 *n* **invulnerability**, imperviousness, freedom, exception, protection [➤ SAFE AND SAFETY; 191] *Opposite:* vulnerability　3 *n* **exemption**, exception, liberty, freedom, liberation [➤ FREEDOM AND LIBERTY; 208] *Opposite:* liability

immunization 1 *n* **vaccination**, inoculation, injection, shot (*informal*) [➤ HEALING; 730]　2 *type of* **medical procedure** [➤ REMEDIES, TREATMENTS, AND OPERATIONS; 731]

immunize *v* **vaccinate**, inoculate, inject, protect [➤ BECOME SICK, TREAT, AND RECOVER; 728]

immure (*literary*) *v* **imprison**, confine, shut away, shut up, hold captive, seclude, incarcerate (*formal*) [➤ CAPTIVITY AND LOSS OF FREEDOM; 248] *Opposite:* free

immutability *n* [➤ PERMANENCE: WITHOUT CHANGE; 95]

immutable *adj* **unchanging**, irreversible, fixed, absolute, unchangeable, unalterable, permanent [➤ PERMANENCE: WITHOUT CHANGE; 95] *Opposite:* mercurial

imp 1 *n* **elf**, goblin, pixie, sprite, fairy, demon, gremlin (*informal*) [➤ MYTHICAL BEINGS; 789]　2 *n* **mischief**, urchin, scamp (*informal*), scalawag (*dated informal*), rascal (*humorous*), rapscallion (*archaic or humorous*) [➤ MISCHIEVOUS OR BADLY BEHAVED CHILD; 946]

impact 1 *n* **crash**, collision, shock, bang, blow, force, contact, brunt [➤ CONTACT: IMPACT; 413]　2 *n* **influence**, impression, effect, bearing, power, control, sway [➤ RESULTS AND OUTCOMES; 83]

impacted *adj* **wedged**, stuck, jammed, squeezed, obstructed, crushed, compressed [➤ LACK OF ACTIVITY OR MOTION; 342]

impair *v* **damage**, harm, spoil, weaken, worsen, prejudice, blight, ruin, mar, mess up (*informal*) [➤ WORSEN SOMETHING; 380] *Opposite:* enhance

impaired *adj* **reduced**, lessened, decreased, weakened, diminished, compromised [➞IN BAD REPAIR; 1234] *Opposite:* unimpaired

impairment *n* **damage**, injury, hurt, loss, weakening, deficiency, diminishing [➞FAULTS, FLAWS, AND WEAKNESSES; 251] *Opposite:* enhancement

impala *type of* **deer or antelope** [➞DEER AND ANTELOPES; 981]

impale *v* **spear**, pierce, stab, bayonet, spike, skewer, run through (*literary*) [➞STAB; 416]

impalpability (*formal*) *n* [➞IMPERCEPTIBLE; 26]

impalpable (*formal*) *adj* **intangible**, shadowy, vague, unclear, indefinable, imperceptible, obscure, indescribable, mysterious [➞IMPERCEPTIBLE; 26] *Opposite:* palpable

impart *v* **communicate**, inform, tell, convey, report, teach, instruct, divulge, disclose, reveal, expose, pass on [➞INFORM, ANNOUNCE, AND ISSUE; 611]

impartial *adj* **neutral**, fair, unbiased, independent, objective, detached, unprejudiced, disinterested, open-minded, evenhanded, balanced, nonaligned [➞NEUTRALITY AND INDIFFERENCE; 553] *Opposite:* biased

impartiality *n* **neutrality**, fairness, independence, objectivity, detachment, lack of prejudice, disinterest, open-mindedness, nonalignment, balance, evenhandedness [➞NEUTRALITY AND INDIFFERENCE; 553] *Opposite:* bias

impassable *adj* **blocked**, impenetrable, treacherous, closed, obstructed, inaccessible [➞IN BAD REPAIR; 1234] *Opposite:* open

impasse *n* **stalemate**, standoff, deadlock, gridlock, bottleneck, dead end [➞DIFFICULT SITUATIONS; 72]

impassioned *adj* **emotional**, ardent, fervent, passionate, heated, excited, heartfelt, from the heart, moving, touching [➞ENTHUSIASTIC AND INQUISITIVE; 628] *Opposite:* impassive

impassive 1 *adj* **expressionless**, blank, inexpressive, poker-faced, unrevealing, deadpan [➞FACIAL EXPRESSIONS AND BLUSHING; 651] *Opposite:* expressive 2 *adj* **emotionless**, unemotional, unmoved, stolid, stoical, phlegmatic, apathetic [➞NEUTRALITY AND INDIFFERENCE; 553]

> ### Compare and Contrast: *impassive, apathetic, phlegmatic, stolid, stoic, unmoved*
>
> CORE MEANING: showing no emotional response or interest
>
> *impassive* showing no outward sign of emotion, especially on the face; *apathetic* not taking any interest in anything, or not bothering to do anything; *phlegmatic* generally unemotional and difficult to arouse; *stolid* solemn, unemotional, and not easily excited or upset; *stoic* showing admirable patience and endurance in the face of adversity without complaining or getting upset; *unmoved* showing no emotion, surprise, or excitement when this would normally have been expected.

impassively *adv* **unemotionally**, blankly, without emotion, coolly, emotionlessly, aloofly [➞UNINTERESTED AND DETACHED; 629] *Opposite:* expressively

impassiveness *n* [➞NEUTRALITY AND INDIFFERENCE; 553]

impassivity *n* [➞NEUTRALITY AND INDIFFERENCE; 553]

impatience 1 *n* **annoyance**, irritation, edginess, intolerance, pique, displeasure, exasperation, touchiness, tetchiness (*informal*) [➞IRRITATION AND ANGER; 541] *Opposite:* patience 2 *n* **eagerness**, anxiety, hurry, haste, impulsiveness, impetuosity, rashness, zeal, enthusiasm, excitement, keenness [➞FEELINGS ABOUT THE FUTURE; 533] *Opposite:* patience

impatient 1 *adj* **annoyed**, irritated, edgy, intolerant, exasperated, aggravated, irked, piqued, irascible, touchy, querulous, tetchy (*informal*) [➞IRRITATION AND ANGER; 541] *Opposite:* patient 2 *adj* **eager**, raring, anxious, in a hurry, hurried, hasty, impulsive, impetuous, rash, enthusiastic, excited, hotheaded, zealous, keen [➞POSITIVE IMPATIENCE, ENTHUSIASM, AND ALERTNESS; 537] *Opposite:* patient

impeach *v* **indict**, accuse, arraign, charge, inculpate (*formal*), denunciate (*formal*) [➞TRIAL, PUNISHMENT, AND LEGAL OUTCOMES; 819]

impeccability *n* [➞GOOD, WELL, BETTER; 183]

impeccable *adj* **perfect**, flawless, faultless, unimpeachable, above reproach, immaculate, spotless, unsullied [➞CORRECT AND FAULTLESS; 182] *Opposite:* flawed

impecunious *adj* **poor**, impoverished, penniless, struggling, underprivileged, deprived, disadvantaged, poverty-stricken, below the poverty line, needy, badly off, ruined, destitute, insolvent, bankrupt, broke (*informal*), strapped (*informal*), hard up (*informal*), cleaned out (*informal*), indigent (*formal*), on the breadline (*UK*) [➞POVERTY AND POOR; 892] *Opposite:* wealthy

impecuniousness (*formal*) *n* [➞POVERTY AND POOR; 892]

impede *v* **obstruct**, hinder, hamper, slow down, delay, hold back, hold up, encumber, inhibit, block, get in the way of [➞AVOID, PREVENT, LIMIT, AND CONTROL; 277] *Opposite:* facilitate

> *See Compare and Contrast at* **hinder**.

impediment 1 *n* **impairment**, disablement, weakness, disorder, inhibition [➞PROBLEMS; 256] 2 *n* **obstacle**, obstruction, barrier, hurdle, hindrance, block, drawback, holdup, let (*formal*) [➞PROBLEMS; 256]

impel 1 *v* **compel**, urge, force, drive, coerce, make, oblige, require, induce [➞CAUSE OR COMPEL TO ACT; 271] *Opposite:* hold back 2 *v* (*formal*) **propel**, force, drive, throw, push, fling, hurl, thrust [➞PUSH, PULL, AND SLIDE; 335]

impend 1 *v* (*formal*) **loom**, approach, be on the horizon, be imminent, be in the offing, appear, be close, be in the cards (*informal*) [➞ABOUT TO HAPPEN; 33] *Opposite:* recede 2 *v* (*literary*) **menace**, loom, threaten, hover, hang, overshadow [➞PUT AT RISK; 384]

impending *adj* **imminent**, looming, in the near future, awaiting, approaching, future, coming, on the horizon, just around the corner, at hand, forthcoming [➞ABOUT TO HAPPEN; 33] *Opposite:* far-off

impenetrability 1 *n* **impassability**, impermeability, density, denseness, thickness, darkness, murkiness [➞DENSITY AND CONSISTENCY; 1207] 2 *n* **incomprehensibility**, complexity, opacity, intricacy, obscurity, denseness,

inaccessibility, inscrutability [➡ DIFFICULTY AND COMPLEXITY; 242]
Opposite: lucidity

impenetrable 1 *adj* **impassable**, dense, tightly packed, thick, solid, impermeable, dark, murky [➡ DENSITY AND CONSISTENCY; 1207] **2** *adj* **incomprehensible**, unfathomable, indecipherable, inscrutable, unsolvable, obscure, mysterious, sphinxlike, enigmatic [➡ DIFFICULTY AND COMPLEXITY; 242] *Opposite*: understandable

impenitent *adj* **unrepentant**, unremorseful, unapologetic, defiant, shameless, brazen [➡ RUDE AND HOSTILE; 625] *Opposite*: remorseful

imperative 1 *adj* **necessary**, vital, crucial, essential, urgent, of the essence, important [➡ NECESSARY AND ESSENTIAL; 196] *Opposite*: unimportant **2** *adj* (*formal*) **commanding**, domineering, bossy, imperious, overbearing, authoritative [➡ BOSSY AND OVERBEARING; 516] *Opposite*: subservient **3** *n* **priority**, essential, requirement, necessity, rule, constraint, obligation, must, need [➡ MOST IMPORTANT THING; 197] *Opposite*: option

imperativeness *n* [➡ IMPORTANCE AND SIGNIFICANCE; 192]

imperceptibility *n* [➡ IMPERCEPTIBLE; 26]

imperceptible *adj* **slight**, gradual, subtle, invisible, barely visible, faint, indiscernible, undetectable, light, small, little, tiny, unnoticeable [➡ IMPERCEPTIBLE; 26] *Opposite*: obvious

imperceptibly *adv* **slightly**, gradually, invisibly, subtly, little by little, bit by bit, slowly, faintly, indiscernibly, undetectably, lightly, a little [➡ TO A CERTAIN EXTENT; 136] *Opposite*: obviously

imperceptive *adj* [➡ NEGATIVE INTELLECTUAL CHARACTERISTICS; 525]

imperfect *adj* **faulty**, defective, deficient, damaged, flawed, unsatisfactory, inadequate, incomplete, limited [➡ IN BAD REPAIR; 1234] *Opposite*: perfect

imperfection 1 *n* **fault**, defect, deficiency, blemish, flaw, limitation, blot, failing, shortcoming, weakness [➡ FAULTS, FLAWS, AND WEAKNESSES; 251] **2** *n* **faultiness**, inadequacy, limitation, deficiency, failure, defectiveness [➡ FAULTS, FLAWS, AND WEAKNESSES; 251] *Opposite*: perfection

> See Compare and Contrast at **flaw**.

imperial *adj* **grand**, majestic, imposing, regal, stately, lordly, magnificent, royal [➡ ROYALNESS; 825]

imperialism *n* **expansionism**, colonialism, empire-building, colonization, interventionism, domination [➡ STYLES AND SYSTEMS OF GOVERNMENT; 806]

imperil (*formal*) *v* **endanger**, put in danger, risk, put at risk, jeopardize, expose, hazard, chance [➡ PUT AT RISK; 384] *Opposite*: protect

imperiled (*formal*) *adj* [➡ IN DANGER; 237]

imperious *adj* **domineering**, authoritative, commanding, arrogant, superior, haughty, high-handed, overbearing, bossy [➡ BOSSY AND OVERBEARING; 516] *Opposite*: humble

imperiously *adv* **domineeringly**, authoritatively, commandingly, arrogantly, superiorly, haughtily, high-handedly, overbearingly, bossily [➡ BOSSY AND OVERBEARING; 516] *Opposite*: meekly

imperiousness *n* **haughtiness**, overbearingness, arrogance, superiority, bossiness, high-handedness [➡ BOSSY AND OVERBEARING; 516] *Opposite*: humility

imperishability 1 *n* **durability**, resilience, stability, endurance, hardiness, indestructibility [➡ DURABLE; 1210] **2** *n* (*literary*) **permanence**, immortality, everlastingness, enduringness [➡ PERMANENCE: WITHOUT END; 94] *Opposite*: transience

imperishable 1 *adj* **permanent**, durable, indestructible, resilient, stable, enduring, hardy [➡ DURABLE; 1210] **2** *adj* (*literary*) **enduring**, eternal, everlasting, permanent, immortal, perpetual, inextinguishable [➡ PERMANENCE: WITHOUT END; 94] *Opposite*: transient

imperishably (*literary*) *adv* **enduringly**, eternally, everlastingly, immortally, perpetually, permanently, indestructibly [➡ PERMANENCE: WITHOUT END; 94]

impermanence *n* **transience**, transitoriness, evanescence, ephemerality, temporariness, insubstantiality, incorporeity [➡ FINITENESS, VARIABILITY, AND TRANSIENCE; 96] *Opposite*: permanence

impermanent *adj* **temporary**, transitory, passing, transient, evanescent, ephemeral [➡ FINITENESS, VARIABILITY, AND TRANSIENCE; 96] *Opposite*: permanent

impermeability *n* **watertightness**, airtightness, waterproofness, protection, impenetrability, security [➡ DENSITY AND CONSISTENCY; 1207] *Opposite*: permeability

impermeable *adj* **resistant**, impervious, waterproof, water-resistant, rainproof, watertight, solid [➡ DENSITY AND CONSISTENCY; 1207] *Opposite*: permeable

impersonal 1 *adj* **objective**, cool, detached, measured, careful, neutral [➡ UNINTERESTED AND DETACHED; 629] *Opposite*: personal **2** *adj* **anonymous**, faceless, soulless, featureless, depersonalized, impassive, bureaucratic, monolithic, gray, inhuman [➡ BORING AND UNINTERESTING; 234] **3** *adj* **unfriendly**, cool, cold, aloof, frosty, distant, remote, uncongenial, unwelcoming, inhospitable, formal [➡ RETICENT AND UNFORTHCOMING; 631] *Opposite*: friendly

impersonate 1 *v* **mimic**, imitate, ape, copy, satirize, make fun of, take off (*informal*) [➡ PRETEND AND MIMIC; 60] **2** *v* **pretend to be**, pose as, masquerade as, personate, pass off [➡ PRETEND AND MIMIC; 60]

impersonation 1 *n* **impression**, parody, caricature, takeoff (*informal*), sendup (*informal*) [➡ REPRESENTATIONS AND GENERAL EXAMPLES; 65] **2** *n* **imitation**, pretense, masquerade, personation, imposture (*formal*) [➡ REPRESENTATIONS AND GENERAL EXAMPLES; 65]

impertinence *n* **impudence**, insolence, disrespect, impoliteness, brazenness, cheekiness, cheek (*informal*), sass (*informal*), sauce (*informal*), lip (*slang*) [➡ BAD MANNERS AND SOCIAL SKILLS; 521] *Opposite*: respect

impertinent (*formal*) *adj* **impudent**, insolent, disrespectful, impolite, brazen, brash, rude, cheeky (*informal*), sassy (*informal*) [➡ BAD MANNERS AND SOCIAL SKILLS; 521] *Opposite*: respectful

impertinently (*formal*) *adv* **impudently**, insolently, disrespectfully, impolitely, brazenly, cheekily (*informal*) [➡ BAD MANNERS AND SOCIAL SKILLS; 521] *Opposite*: respectfully

imperturbability *n* [➡ CONFIDENCE AND COMPOSURE; 499]

imperturbable *adj* **calm**, cool, unflappable, collected, composed, steady, serene, unflustered, level-headed, unruffled [➡ CONFIDENCE AND COMPOSURE; 499] *Opposite*: excitable

impervious **1** *adj* **unreceptive**, unbending, unyielding, unwavering, rigid, obdurate, unmovable, unmoved, unaffected, unfeeling [➡ NEUTRALITY AND INDIFFERENCE; 553] *Opposite*: responsive **2** *adj* **impermeable**, solid, resistant, waterproof, water-resistant, rainproof, invulnerable, watertight, proof [➡ DENSITY AND CONSISTENCY; 1207] *Opposite*: permeable

imperviousness **1** *n* **unreceptiveness**, unyieldingness, rigidity, obduracy, inflexibility [➡ NEUTRALITY AND INDIFFERENCE; 553] *Opposite*: responsiveness **2** *n* **impermeability**, resistance, invulnerability, watertightness, solidity [➡ DENSITY AND CONSISTENCY; 1207] *Opposite*: permeability

impetuosity *n* **impulsiveness**, rashness, hastiness, suddenness, recklessness, spontaneity, impetuousness, hotheadedness [➡ LACK OF COMMITMENT AND UNRELIABILITY; 509] *Opposite*: consideration

impetuous *adj* **impulsive**, rash, hasty, hotheaded, unthinking, sudden, reckless, spontaneous [➡ LACK OF COMMITMENT AND UNRELIABILITY; 509] *Opposite*: considered

impetuousness *n* **impulsiveness**, rashness, hastiness, hotheadedness, suddenness, recklessness, spontaneity, impetuosity [➡ LACK OF COMMITMENT AND UNRELIABILITY; 509] *Opposite*: consideration

impetus **1** *n* **force**, momentum, impulsion, thrust, forward motion, motion, movement [➡ ENERGY; 1161] *Opposite*: inertia **2** *n* **push**, motivation, incentive, energy, stimulus, drive, impulse, spur, will [➡ CAUSATION; 168]

impiety *n* **irreverence**, sinfulness, sin, wickedness, transgression, immorality, ungodliness, badness [➡ MORALLY BAD OR IMPROPER; 775] *Opposite*: piety

impinge (*formal*) *v* **impose**, intrude, interrupt, encroach, invade, impact, have a bearing on, affect, have an effect on [➡ CHANGE; 372]

impious *adj* **sinful**, irreverent, wicked, bad, immoral, irreligious, ungodly [➡ MORALLY BAD OR IMPROPER; 775] *Opposite*: pious

impiousness *n* **sinfulness**, irreverence, sin, wickedness, transgression, immorality, ungodliness, badness [➡ MORALLY BAD OR IMPROPER; 775] *Opposite*: piety

impish *adj* **mischievous**, naughty, wicked, playful, puckish, roguish, waggish (*informal*), rascally (*humorous*) [➡ LACK OF COMMITMENT AND UNRELIABILITY; 509]

impishness *n* **mischievousness**, naughtiness, wickedness, playfulness, puckishness, roguishness, mischief, waggishness (*informal*) [➡ LACK OF COMMITMENT AND UNRELIABILITY; 509]

implacability (*formal*) *n* **pitilessness**, mercilessness, relentlessness, ruthlessness, cruelty, hardheartedness, cold-heartedness, callousness, rigidity, unyieldingness, obduracy [➡ UNWILLINGNESS AND STUBBORNNESS; 564] *Opposite*: kindness

implacable *adj* **pitiless**, merciless, relentless, ruthless,

cruel, hardhearted, cold-hearted, callous, rigid, unbending, unyielding, obdurate [➡ UNWILLINGNESS AND STUBBORNNESS; 564] *Opposite*: kind

implant *v* **establish**, embed, instill, plant, place, insert, lodge, fix [➡ POSITION SOMETHING: BETWEEN, BESIDE, OR INSIDE SOMETHING; 326]

implantation *n* **embedding**, establishment, grafting, attaching, joining, splicing, inserting, attachment, insertion, fixing [➡ FASTEN, LINK, AND JOIN; 408]

implausibility *n* **improbability**, unlikelihood, inconceivability, inconceivableness, doubtfulness, questionability, unlikeliness [➡ IMPOSSIBLE AND IMPROBABLE; 178] *Opposite*: plausibility

implausible *adj* **unlikely**, improbable, unbelievable, incredible, fantastic, far-fetched, doubtful, questionable [➡ IMPOSSIBLE AND IMPROBABLE; 178] *Opposite*: plausible

implement **1** *n* **tool**, device, gadget, instrument, contrivance, appliance, gizmo (*informal*) [➡ DEVICES; 1115] **2** *v* **carry out**, put into practice, apply, realize, execute, employ, put into operation, put into service, put into action, instigate, put into effect, fulfill, effect (*formal*) [➡ CARRY OUT AN ACTION; 269]

implementation *n* **carrying out**, application, putting into practice, operation, employment, execution, enactment [➡ CARRY OUT AN ACTION; 269] *Opposite*: proposal

implicate *v* **connect**, involve, associate, link, incriminate, bring in, point to, point the finger at, finger (*slang*) [➡ ACCUSE, BLAME, AND CRITICIZE; 641] *Opposite*: clear

implication *n* **insinuation**, inference, suggestion, allegation, consequence, repercussion, effect, association [➡ MEANING; 690]

implicit **1** *adj* **understood**, implied, unspoken, tacit, hidden, embedded, indirect, inherent [➡ KNOWN AND FAMOUS; 181] *Opposite*: explicit **2** *adj* **unreserved**, absolute, total, complete, utter, perfect, unconditional, unqualified [➡ WHOLENESS AND COMPLETENESS; 198] *Opposite*: qualified

implicitly **1** *adv* **unreservedly**, absolutely, totally, completely, wholly, utterly, perfectly, unconditionally, without reservation [➡ TO A GREAT EXTENT; 132] **2** *adv* **indirectly**, covertly, tacitly, obliquely, subtly, subliminally, discreetly [➡ SECRET AND UNKNOWN; 179]

implied *adj* **indirect**, understood, implicit, unspoken, tacit, veiled, oblique [➡ KNOWN AND FAMOUS; 181]

implode *v* **collapse**, fail, cave in, fall in, subside, shrink, crash, founder, break down [➡ CEASE TO EXIST; 22] *Opposite*: explode

implore (*formal*) *v* **beg**, plead, pray, appeal, entreat, beseech (*literary*) [➡ REQUEST AND DEMAND; 663]

imploring (*formal*) *adj* **pleading**, desperate, longing, heartfelt, suppliant (*formal*), supplicatory (*formal*), beseeching (*literary*) [➡ REQUEST AND DEMAND; 663]

implosion *n* **collapse**, falling-in, subsidence, cave-in, disintegration, crumbling [➡ SUDDEN EVENTS; 52] *Opposite*: explosion

imply **1** *v* **suggest**, infer, hint at, point toward [➡ SUGGEST, HINT, AND COMMENT; 612] **2** *v* **involve**, entail, mean, indicate, denote [➡ MEAN SOMETHING; 61]

impolite *adj* **rude**, ill-mannered, bad-mannered, loutish, boorish, ignorant, disrespectful, indecorous, discourteous [➡ BAD MANNERS AND SOCIAL SKILLS; 521] *Opposite*: polite

impoliteness *n* **rudeness**, bad manners, loutishness, boorishness, coarseness, discourteousness [➡ BAD MANNERS AND SOCIAL SKILLS; 521] *Opposite*: politeness

impolitic *adj* **unwise**, inappropriate, misguided, ill-advised, ill-judged, injudicious, imprudent [➡ THE NATURE OF IDEAS; 771] *Opposite*: wise

imponderable 1 *adj* **unknown**, unquantifiable, incalculable, indeterminable, inestimable, immeasurable [➡ SECRET AND UNKNOWN; 179] 2 *n* **unknown**, mystery, enigma, paradox, uncertainty [➡ SECRETS AND MYSTERIES; 180]

import 1 *v* **bring in**, introduce, trade in, smuggle [➡ PURCHASE; 422] *Opposite*: export 2 *n* **introduction**, importation, ingress (*formal*) [➡ BUSINESS ACTIVITIES AND PHENOMENA; 794] *Opposite*: export 3 *n* **significance**, importance, meaning, consequence (*formal*) [➡ IMPORTANCE AND SIGNIFICANCE; 192]

importance 1 *n* **significance**, meaning, weight, magnitude, import, substance, value, worth, consequence (*formal*) [➡ IMPORTANCE AND SIGNIFICANCE; 192] *Opposite*: triviality 2 *n* **rank**, position, standing, status, reputation, prominence [➡ STATUS; 888]

important 1 *adj* **significant**, vital, imperative, central, chief, key, main, essential, principal, critical, crucial, weighty [➡ IMPORTANT; 194] *Opposite*: trivial 2 *adj* **high-ranking**, eminent, worthy, notable, prominent, influential [➡ KNOWN AND FAMOUS; 181] *Opposite*: insignificant

importantly *adv* **significantly**, notably, crucially, critically, vitally, relevantly, seriously [➡ IMPORTANT; 194]

importation *n* **import**, introduction, ingress (*formal*) [➡ BUSINESS ACTIVITIES AND PHENOMENA; 794] *Opposite*: export

importer *n* **trader**, shipper, carrier, hauler, distributor, wholesaler, retailer, broker, dealer [➡ BUSINESS PEOPLE; 793]

importunate (*formal*) *adj* **persistent**, demanding, unrelenting, annoying, overeager, forceful, avid [➡ BOSSY AND OVERBEARING; 516]

importune (*formal*) *v* **bother**, pester, badger, harass, plague, annoy, beleaguer, pursue [➡ COMPLAIN AND NAG; 686]

importunity (*formal*) 1 *n* **persistence**, demanding, pestering, insistence, begging, clamoring, supplication (*formal*) [➡ DIFFICULT TO PLEASE; 515] 2 *n* **demand**, request, entreaty, appeal, petition, plea [➡ REQUEST AND DEMAND; 663]

impose 1 *v* **enforce**, levy, exact, execute, carry out, enact [➡ FUNDS, PAYMENTS, AND CHARGES; 800] 2 *v* **inflict**, force, foist, dump, insist, insist on [➡ GIVE TOO MUCH AND OVERBURDEN; 437] 3 *v* **intrude**, be in the way, be a nuisance, be a burden, disturb, trespass, inconvenience [➡ INTERRUPT AND BUTT IN; 619]

imposing *adj* **impressive**, striking, grand, magnificent, stately, arresting, commanding [➡ EXTRAORDINARY: UNCOMMON; 205] *Opposite*: unimpressive

imposition *n* **burden**, nuisance, annoyance, obligation, bother, hassle (*informal*) [➡ NUISANCES; 253]

impossibility *n* **unfeasibility**, impracticality, hopelessness, ridiculousness, unlikelihood [➡ IMPOSSIBLE AND IMPROBABLE; 178] *Opposite*: possibility

impossible 1 *adj* **irresolvable**, irresoluble, unfeasible, impracticable, unattainable, unachievable, unworkable, out of the question, unviable, impractical, hopeless, ridiculous, not on (*UK*) [➡ IMPOSSIBLE AND IMPROBABLE; 178] *Opposite*: possible 2 *adj* **unbearable**, incredible, terrible, dreadful, intolerable, difficult, awkward, unmanageable, insufferable, unreasonable [➡ EMOTIONALLY UNPLEASANT AND UPSETTING; 227] *Opposite*: manageable

impossibly *adv* **dreadfully**, terribly, hopelessly, unbearably, ridiculously, intolerably, insufferably, unbelievably, incredibly, extremely, unreasonably, unfeasibly [➡ TO A GREAT EXTENT; 132] *Opposite*: reasonably

impostor *n* **deceiver**, imitator, impersonator, pretender, masquerader, fake, fraud, sham, charlatan, plant (*informal*) [➡ PEOPLE WHO DECEIVE; 661] *Opposite*: the real McCoy (*informal*)

imposture (*formal*) *n* **deception**, impersonation, masquerade, imitation, pretense, faking, sham [➡ DECEPTION AND LIES; 660]

impotence *n* **ineffectiveness**, incapability, ineffectualness, feebleness, powerlessness, weakness, helplessness, inability, incapacity [➡ UNSKILLED; 529] *Opposite*: strength

impotent *adj* **powerless**, weak, helpless, unable, incapable, ineffective, ineffectual, feeble [➡ UNSKILLED; 529] *Opposite*: powerful

impound *v* **confiscate**, seize, lock up, take away, hold, store, possess [➡ TAKE SOMETHING AWAY; 425] *Opposite*: release

impoverish *v* **deprive**, ruin, bankrupt, diminish, weaken, deplete, drain [➡ TAKE SOMETHING AWAY; 425] *Opposite*: enrich

impoverished *adj* **needy**, poor, penniless, disadvantaged, underprivileged, insolvent, bankrupt, impecunious, destitute, deprived, broke (*informal*), hard up (*informal*), indigent (*formal*), penurious (*literary*) [➡ POVERTY AND POOR; 892] *Opposite*: rich

impoverishment 1 *n* **destitution**, failure, disadvantage, poverty, insolvency, penury, privation, hardship, deprivation, bankruptcy, ruin [➡ POVERTY AND POOR; 892] *Opposite*: prosperity 2 *n* **diminishment**, ruination, decline, depletion, degeneration, deterioration [➡ WORSEN SOMETHING; 380] *Opposite*: enrichment

impracticability *n* **unworkability**, impossibility, impracticality, impracticableness, unworkableness, uselessness [➡ IMPOSSIBLE AND IMPROBABLE; 178] *Opposite*: feasibility

impracticable *adj* **unviable**, useless, unrealistic, unfeasible, unpractical, unrealizable, unworkable, impossible, impractical [➡ IMPOSSIBLE AND IMPROBABLE; 178] *Opposite*: viable

impractical 1 *adj* **unpractical**, unreasonable, unviable, unfeasible, unworkable, unrealizable, unusable, impossible, impracticable [➡ IMPOSSIBLE AND IMPROBABLE; 178] *Opposite*: practical 2 *adj* **unrealistic**, idealistic, useless, hopeless, inept, incompetent, clueless (*informal*) [➡ NEGATIVE INTELLECTUAL CHARACTERISTICS; 525] *Opposite*: realistic

impracticality *n* **unviability**, unfeasibility, impracticableness, inconvenience, hopelessness, impossibility [➡ IMPOSSIBLE AND IMPROBABLE; 178] *Opposite*: practicality

imprecate (*formal*) *v* curse, revile, call down, execrate (*literary or formal*), maledict (*literary*) [→INSULTS, ABUSE, AND SWEARING; 658]

imprecation (*formal*) **1** *n* oath, insult, swearword, expletive, curse, malediction (*formal*), execration (*literary or formal*) [→INSULTS, ABUSE, AND SWEARING; 658] **2** *n* swearing, cursing, blasphemy, profanity, cussing (*informal*), execration (*literary or formal*) [→INSULTS, ABUSE, AND SWEARING; 658]

imprecise *adj* sketchy, vague, inexact, blurred, rough, inaccurate, hazy, fuzzy, indefinite, unfocused, unclear, ill-defined, indistinct, loose, woolly [→VAGUENESS; 243] *Opposite*: precise

impreciseness *n* [→VAGUENESS; 243]

imprecision *n* fuzziness, roughness, sketchiness, inaccuracy, inexactitude, haziness, woolliness, vagueness, indistinctness, sloppiness (*informal*) [→VAGUENESS; 243] *Opposite*: accuracy

impregnable *adj* unassailable, invincible, secure, unconquerable, impenetrable, invulnerable, indestructible [→STRENGTH; 201] *Opposite*: vulnerable

impregnate *v* saturate, soak, steep, infuse, permeate, fill, imbue [→FILL; 406] *Opposite*: dry out

impresario *n* manager, producer, promoter, agent, entrepreneur, organizer, business manager, entertainer [→BUSINESS PEOPLE; 793]

impress **1** *v* excite, move, amaze, influence, affect, sway, astound, astonish, electrify, strike, stir [→SURPRISE AND IMPRESS; 574] *Opposite*: disappoint **2** *v* emphasize, stress, drive home, drum into, din in, underline, highlight, imprint [→CLAIM, INSIST, AND EMPHASIZE; 614] *Opposite*: gloss over

impressed *adj* [→SURPRISE, SHOCK, AND AMAZEMENT; 545]

impression **1** *n* feeling, idea, notion, thought, sense, intuition, inkling, consciousness, fancy [→IDEAS AND THOUGHTS; 770] *Opposite*: certainty **2** *n* imprint, dent, mark, dint, hollow, dip, dimple, depression, brand, stamp, ding (*informal*), impress (*literary*) [→HOLES, GAPS, AND FORKS; 1252] **3** *n* mark, impact, effect, influence, reaction, sway, vestige [→RESULTS AND OUTCOMES; 83] **4** *n* impersonation, imitation, parody, takeoff (*informal*), sendup (*informal*) [→REPRESENTATIONS AND GENERAL EXAMPLES; 65]

impressionability *n* [→NEGATIVE INTELLECTUAL CHARACTERISTICS; 525]

impressionable *adj* susceptible, suggestible, vulnerable, receptive, sensitive, gullible, pliable [→NEGATIVE INTELLECTUAL CHARACTERISTICS; 525] *Opposite*: unreceptive

impressionableness *n* [→NEGATIVE INTELLECTUAL CHARACTERISTICS; 525]

impressionism *type of* pre-20th-century art movement [→ARTISTIC MOVEMENTS AND STYLES; 899]

impressionist *n* impersonator, mimic, imitator, comic, entertainer, performer [→WORKERS IN ENTERTAINMENT AND MEDIA; 873]

impressionistic *adj* ill-defined, rough, loose, unfocused, imprecise, blurred, generalized, hazy, sketchy, vague, indistinct, inexplicit, undetailed [→VAGUENESS; 243] *Opposite*: detailed

impressive *adj* imposing, inspiring, striking, remark-

able, notable, extraordinary, exciting, moving, stirring [→EXTRAORDINARY: AMAZING; 204] *Opposite*: unimpressive

impressiveness *n* grandeur, magnificence, brilliance, eminence, powerfulness, effectiveness, splendor [→EXTRAORDINARY: AMAZING; 204]

imprint **1** *n* impression, print, mark, indentation, hollow, dent, dint, depression, impress (*literary*) [→HOLES, GAPS, AND FORKS; 1252] **2** *n* stamp, inscription, name, print, printer's mark, watermark, colophon [→SYMBOLS, SIGNS, AND NUMBERS; 596] **3** *n* hallmark, emblem, stamp, seal, sign, symbol, identification mark, mark [→REPRESENTATIONS AND GENERAL EXAMPLES; 65] **4** *n* indication, mark, impression, effect, sign, impress (*literary*) [→APPEARANCE AND ATMOSPHERE; 1237] **5** *v* impress, fix, establish, drive home, drum into, din in [→INSTRUCT AND TEACH; 609]

imprison *v* confine, detain, intern, lock up, lock away, jail, put away (*informal*), put inside (*informal*), incarcerate (*formal*) [→THE POLICE, ARREST, AND PRETRIAL PROCEEDINGS; 818]

imprisoned *adj* confined, jailed, captive, restrained, trapped, caged, bound, held, shut in, constricted, inside (*informal*) [→CAPTIVITY AND LOSS OF FREEDOM; 248] *Opposite*: free

imprisonment *n* custody, captivity, detention, sentence, term, internment, confinement, jail term, time (*informal*), incarceration (*formal*) [→CAPTIVITY AND LOSS OF FREEDOM; 248]

improbability *n* unlikelihood, implausibility, dubiousness, doubtfulness, questionability, improbableness, incredibility, dubiety (*formal*) [→IMPOSSIBLE AND IMPROBABLE; 178] *Opposite*: probability

improbable *adj* unlikely, doubtful, implausible, questionable, dubious, impracticable, unconvincing, unbelievable, incredible [→IMPOSSIBLE AND IMPROBABLE; 178] *Opposite*: likely

improbably *adv* strangely, implausibly, unconvincingly, unbelievably, weirdly, doubtfully, oddly, unusually, surprisingly, incredibly, questionably [→BIZARRE AND PECULIAR; 257] *Opposite*: usually

improbity *n* [→MORALLY BAD OR IMPROPER; 775]

impromptu *adj* unprepared, unrehearsed, unplanned, spontaneous, spur-of-the-moment, unarranged, off-the-cuff, ad lib, improvised, unpremeditated, extempore, ad hoc [→UNPLANNED AND UNEXPECTED; 281] *Opposite*: prepared

improper **1** *adj* (*formal*) indecorous, inappropriate, unsuitable, out of place, unfitting, inopportune, inadequate, wrong, incorrect [→INAPPROPRIATE AND UNSUITABLE; 224] *Opposite*: fitting **2** *adj* rude, shocking, indecent, inappropriate, unacceptable, unseemly, offensive, reprehensible [→UNACCEPTABLE AND UNFORGIVABLE; 225] *Opposite*: proper **3** *adj* dishonest, irregular, illegal, criminal, unlawful, shady, illicit, crooked (*informal*) [→MORALLY BAD OR IMPROPER; 775] *Opposite*: honest

improperly **1** *adv* rudely, shockingly, inappropriately, unacceptably, offensively, reprehensively, indecently [→UNACCEPTABLE AND UNFORGIVABLE; 225] *Opposite*: properly **2** *adv* dishonestly, irregularly, illegally, unlawfully, shadily, illicitly, criminally, crookedly (*informal*) [→MORALLY BAD OR IMPROPER; 775] *Opposite*: honestly **3** *adv* (*formal*) indecorously, unsuitably, inappropriately, inadequately, wrongly, incorrectly, unfittingly, inopportunely [➡ INAPPROPRIATE AND UNSUITABLE; 224] *Opposite*: fittingly

impropriety *n* **rudeness**, indecency, unseemliness, immodesty, bad behavior, indecorum, offensiveness [➡ BAD MANNERS AND SOCIAL SKILLS; 521] *Opposite*: propriety

improve **1** *v* **look up**, perk up, get better, rally, mend, recover, advance, progress, develop, expand, increase, pick up (*informal*) [➡ GET BETTER; 375] *Opposite*: worsen **2** *v* **better**, build up, enhance, perfect, develop, expand, further, enrich, upgrade, increase [➡ IMPROVE SOMETHING; 374] *Opposite*: deteriorate **3** *v* **correct**, adjust, touch up, titivate, amend, tweak (*informal*) [➡ IMPROVE SOMETHING; 374]

improved *adj* **better**, enhanced, amended, better-quality, upgraded, developed, value-added, enriched, perfected [➡ GOOD, WELL, BETTER; 183] *Opposite*: deteriorated

improvement **1** *n* **amendment**, correction, development, step-up, upgrade, enhancement, advancement, progress, expansion, enlargement, increase [➡ PROGRESS AND ADVANCEMENT; 213] *Opposite*: deterioration **2** *n* **recovery**, recuperation, progress, advance, upturn, convalescence [➡ PROGRESS AND ADVANCEMENT; 213] *Opposite*: decline

improve on *v* **better**, go one better, top, beat, exceed, surpass, transcend, cap, outdo, outshine, outperform [➡ BEAT AND DEFEAT; 80]

improvident *adj* **imprudent**, careless, reckless, negligent, irresponsible, wasteful, spendthrift, profligate, rash, extravagant [➡ INCAUTIOUS AND CARELESS; 283] *Opposite*: prudent

improvisation **1** *n* **inventiveness**, invention, creativeness, lateral thinking [➡ WAYS OF DOING THINGS; 294] **2** *n* **extemporization**, ad-libbing, standup [➡ ONE-WAY COMMUNICATION; 49]

improvise **1** *v* **ad-lib**, extemporize, create, make up, invent, rely on your wits, wing it (*informal*) [➡ UTTER AND PRONOUNCE; 608] **2** *v* **contrive**, concoct, invent, create, devise, make up, cobble together, rig, knock together (*UK informal*) [➡ CREATION; 346]

improvised *adj* **unpremeditated**, ad hoc, unplanned, makeshift, spontaneous, offhand, spur-of-the-moment, unprepared, unarranged, unrehearsed, ad lib, impromptu, off-the-cuff, extempore [➡ UNPLANNED AND UNEXPECTED; 281] *Opposite*: prepared

imprudence *n* **profligacy**, carelessness, indiscretion, rashness, injudiciousness, unwariness, haste, bad judgment, impulsiveness, recklessness, incaution, extravagance, foolishness, irresponsibility [➡ NEGATIVE INTELLECTUAL CHARACTERISTICS; 525] *Opposite*: prudence

imprudent *adj* **foolish**, impulsive, indiscreet, irresponsible, rash, hasty, unwise, unconsidered, thoughtless, careless, improvident, ill-considered, unwary, incautious, reckless [➡ INCAUTIOUS AND CARELESS; 283] *Opposite*: prudent

impudence *n* **impertinence**, boldness, insolence, nerve, effrontery, audacity, rudeness, disrespect, impoliteness, presumption, sassiness, mouthiness (*informal*), cheek (*informal*) [➡ BAD MANNERS AND SOCIAL SKILLS; 521] *Opposite*: respect

impudent *adj* **bold**, brazen, insolent, rude, disrespectful, impolite, presumptuous, ill-mannered, sassy, mouthy

(*informal*), cheeky (*informal*), impertinent (*formal*) [➡ BAD MANNERS AND SOCIAL SKILLS; 521] *Opposite*: respectful

impugn (*formal*) *v* **question**, dispute, call into question, doubt, query, challenge, assail [➡ QUESTION THINGS; 751]

impulse **1** *n* **instinct**, desire, urge, whim, compulsion, wish, itch, yen, yearning, bent, fancy, inclination [➡ DESIRE AND WANT; 579] *Opposite*: aversion (*formal*) **2** *n* **propulsion**, motive power, drive, stimulus, pressure, impetus, goad, spur, force, catalyst, incentive, motivation [➡ CAUSATION; 168] **3** *n* **tick**, pulse, nerve, pulsation, beat, signal, thrust [➡ ENERGY; 1161]

impulsion **1** *n* **push**, propulsion, thrust, momentum, impetus, spur, drive [➡ BEGINNINGS; 53] **2** *n* **desire**, yen, compulsion, instinct, whim, urge, inclination, impulse, wish, stimulus, motivation [➡ DESIRE AND WANT; 579] *Opposite*: aversion (*formal*)

impulsive *adj* **unwary**, thoughtless, impetuous, imprudent, precipitate, spontaneous, rash, brash, reckless, hasty, irresponsible, offhand, madcap [➡ INCAUTIOUS AND CARELESS; 283] *Opposite*: cautious

impulsively *adv* **unwarily**, thoughtlessly, on impulse, impetuously, spontaneously, on a whim, precipitately, rashly, hastily, unwisely, irresponsibly, imprudently (*formal*) [➡ CAUTIOUS AND CAREFUL; 282] *Opposite*: deliberately

impulsiveness *n* **precipitateness**, suddenness, thoughtlessness, impetuosity, spontaneity, recklessness, rashness, hastiness, irresponsibility [➡ LACK OF COMMITMENT AND UNRELIABILITY; 509] *Opposite*: deliberation (*formal*)

impunity *n* **license**, exemption, freedom, liberty, latitude, immunity [➡ FREEDOM AND LIBERTY; 208]

impure *adj* **contaminated**, adulterated, mixed, tainted, polluted, dirty, infected, poisoned, unclean [➡ DIRTY; 1235] *Opposite*: pure

impurity *n* **contamination**, pollution, adulteration, uncleanness, infection, dirtiness, dirt [➡ UNPLEASANT, DIRTY, AND TOXIC SUBSTANCES; 1268] *Opposite*: purity

imputation *n* **accusation**, assertion, attribution, citation, reproach, complaint, allegation, insinuation, suggestion, charge [➡ CRITICISMS AND ANGRY OUTBURSTS; 50]

impute **1** *v* **credit**, chalk up, attribute, accredit, assign, ascribe (*formal*) [➡ CREATING CONNECTIONS; 144] **2** *v* **complain**, accuse, implicate, allege, assert, challenge, cite, charge [➡ ACCUSE, BLAME, AND CRITICIZE; 641]

in **1** *prep* **inside**, within, around [➡ RELATIVE LOCATION; 161] *Opposite*: outside **2** *adv* **around**, inside, accessible, available, at home, here, arrived, indoors, inward [➡ GENERAL LOCATIONS; 158] *Opposite*: out **3** *adj* **cutting-edge**, fashionable, popular, now, in vogue, voguish, modish, all the rage, stylish, trendy (*informal*), happening (*informal*), hip (*slang*) [➡ NEW, MODERN; 166] *Opposite*: out

in a bad mood *adj* [➡ IRRITATION AND ANGER; 541]

in abeyance *adj* **suspended**, withdrawn, withheld, inoperative, out of action, pending, in remission, on ice, on the back burner, in limbo [➡ NOT HAPPENING; 34] *Opposite*: ongoing

in a big way *adv* [➡ TO A GREAT EXTENT; 132]

inability *n* **incapability**, incapacity, powerlessness, helplessness, failure, incompetence, hopelessness [➥ UNSKILLED; 529] *Opposite*: ability

in a bind *adj* [➥ IN TROUBLE AND DISADVANTAGED; 73]

in a bit *adv* [➥ FUTURE; 86]

in abundance *adv* **abundantly**, in great quantities, in large quantities, in profusion, aplenty, galore [➥ MANY, MUCH, LARGE AMOUNT; 117] *Opposite*: in short supply

inaccessibility **1** *n* **unreachability**, remoteness, distance, isolation, unapproachability, solitariness, aloneness [➥ DISTANCE; 160] *Opposite*: approachability **2** *n* **unattainability**, unavailability, unaffordability, unobtainability, confidentiality, impossibility [➥ IMPOSSIBLE AND IMPROBABLE; 178] *Opposite*: accessibility **3** *n* **difficulty**, obscurity, obscureness, obliqueness, impenetrability, opaqueness [➥ DIFFICULTY AND COMPLEXITY; 242] *Opposite*: lucidity

inaccessible **1** *adj* **unreachable**, out-of-the-way, unapproachable, difficult to get to, hard to find, remote, distant, faraway, isolated [➥ DISTANCE; 160] *Opposite*: approachable **2** *adj* **difficult**, obscure, esoteric, abstruse, challenging, difficult to understand, hard to follow, oblique, impenetrable, opaque [➥ DIFFICULTY AND COMPLEXITY; 242] *Opposite*: simple

in accordance *adj* **in conformity**, in line, in compliance, in keeping, in step [➥ APPROPRIATE, SUITABLE, AND ADVISABLE; 184] *Opposite*: at odds

inaccuracy **1** *n* **imprecision**, inexactness, mistakenness, wrongness, erroneousness, incorrectness, impreciseness, inexactitude [➥ INCORRECT AND ERRONEOUS; 222] *Opposite*: precision **2** *n* **error**, mistake, slip, flaw, blunder, miscalculation, slip-up (*informal*) [➥ MISTAKES; 250]

> *See Compare and Contrast at* **mistake.**

inaccurate *adj* **imprecise**, inexact, mistaken, erroneous, wrong, incorrect, out, way-out (*informal*) [➥ INCORRECT AND ERRONEOUS; 222] *Opposite*: precise

in a cleft stick (*UK*) *adj* [➥ UNCERTAINTY; 559]

inaction **1** *n* **failure to act**, indecision, procrastination, fumbling, delay, dithering, indecisiveness [➥ UNCERTAINTY; 559] *Opposite*: decisiveness **2** *n* **inactivity**, laziness, idleness, inertia, apathy, immobility, lethargy, sluggishness, sloth [➥ LACK OF ACTIVITY OR MOTION; 342] *Opposite*: energy

inactivate *v* **deactivate**, put out of action, incapacitate, disable, render inoperative, render inactive, render inoperable, turn off, unplug, disarm, idle [➥ CAUSE TO STOP; 266] *Opposite*: set in motion

inactive **1** *adj* **motionless**, stationary, unmoving, immobile, stopped, still [➥ LACK OF ACTIVITY OR MOTION; 342] *Opposite*: moving **2** *adj* **idle**, dormant, out of action, reserve, unused, inoperative, out of order, static [➥ LACK OF ACTIVITY OR MOTION; 342] *Opposite*: working **3** *adj* **sedentary**, lazy, slothful, indolent, sluggish, deskbound, lethargic, quiet, sleepy, torpid [➥ LIFELESS, LAZY, AND UNENTHUSIASTIC; 506] *Opposite*: energetic

inactivity **1** *n* **motionlessness**, immobility, stillness [➥ LACK OF ACTIVITY OR MOTION; 342] *Opposite*: motion **2** *n* **idleness**, dormancy, inoperativeness [➥ LACK OF ACTIVITY OR MOTION; 342] *Opposite*: activity **3** *n* **sedentariness**, laziness, sloth, indolence, sluggishness, lethargy, quietness, sleepiness, torpidity, torpor, slothfulness (*formal*) [➥ LIFELESS, LAZY, AND UNENTHUSIASTIC; 506] *Opposite*: energy

in actual fact *adv* **actually**, in fact, in reality, in truth, really, as it happens, in point of fact [➥ WORDS AND PHRASES EMPHASIZING THE TRUTH OF A MATTER; 172]

in a daze *adj* [➥ SURPRISE, SHOCK, AND AMAZEMENT; 545]

in addition *adv* **furthermore**, moreover, as well, also, too, additionally, on top, besides, into the bargain, to boot [➥ EXPRESSIONS INTRODUCING EXTRA INFORMATION; 139]

in addition to *prep* **as well as**, along with, on top of, besides, over and above, not counting, other than [➥ ALSO; 138]

inadequacy **1** *n* **insufficiency**, meagerness, scantiness, lack, shortage, shortfall [➥ TOO FEW, TOO LITTLE; 122] *Opposite*: sufficiency **2** *n* **fault**, failure, failing, incompetence, defectiveness, hopelessness, shortcoming, defect, problem [➥ FAULTS, FLAWS, AND WEAKNESSES; 251] *Opposite*: asset

inadequate **1** *adj* **insufficient**, scarce, too little, derisory, laughable, poor, short, scant, scanty [➥ TOO FEW, TOO LITTLE; 122] *Opposite*: sufficient **2** *adj* **incompetent**, lacking, deficient, ineffective, inefficient, ineffectual, defective, imperfect, hopeless, unsatisfactory, incapable [➥ UNSKILLED; 529] *Opposite*: capable

in a dilemma *adj* [➥ UNCERTAINTY; 559]

inadmissible *adj* **unacceptable**, prohibited, excluded, barred, disallowed, irrelevant, banned, censored, precluded (*formal*) [➥ REFUSE PERMISSION AND NOT ALLOW; 670] *Opposite*: acceptable

in advance *adv* **beforehand**, before, prior to, ahead, earlier [➥ BEFORE, FIRST, AND PRECEDING; 163] *Opposite*: afterward

inadvertence **1** *n* **carelessness**, inattention, negligence, thoughtlessness, laxity, forgetfulness, inadvertency [➥ NEGATIVE INTELLECTUAL CHARACTERISTICS; 525] **2** *n* **oversight**, omission, error, mistake, blunder, inadvertency, fallacy, slip-up (*informal*), miscue (*informal*), faux pas (*literary*) [➥ MISTAKES; 250]

inadvertency *see* **inadvertence**

inadvertent *adj* **unintentional**, careless, unintended, involuntary, unplanned, accidental [➥ UNPLANNED AND UNEXPECTED; 281] *Opposite*: intentional

inadvisable *adj* **ill-advised**, imprudent, unwise, foolish, injudicious, impolitic, stupid (*informal*), inexpedient (*formal*) [➥ THE NATURE OF IDEAS; 771] *Opposite*: wise

in a fix (*informal*) *adj* **in trouble**, in difficulties, in a tight spot, in extremis, in dire straits, in hot water (*informal*), in a jam (*informal*), up the creek (*informal*), in the soup (*informal*) [➥ IN TROUBLE AND DISADVANTAGED; 73]

in a flap (*informal*) *adj* [➥ CONFUSION, ANXIETY, AND WORRY; 540]

in a flash **1** *adv* **rapidly**, quickly, in (less than) no time, in the twinkling of an eye, hastily, like a bat out of hell (*informal*) [➥ MOVING QUICKLY; 103] *Opposite*: slowly **2** *adv* **suddenly**, immediately, right away, without hesitation, all of a sudden, like a bolt from the blue, straight away [➥ HAPPENING QUICKLY; 104] *Opposite*: gradually

in a frenzy *adj* [➡ CONFUSION, ANXIETY, AND WORRY; 540]

in a funk (*informal*) *adj* [➡ SADNESS, DISTRESS, AND DESPAIR; 539]

in agreement *adv* [➡ HARMONY; 155]

in a huff (*informal*) *adj* **annoyed**, piqued, offended, affronted, put out, vexed, in high dudgeon, nettled (*informal*), peeved (*informal*) [➡ SADNESS, DISTRESS, AND DESPAIR; 539] *Opposite*: unconcerned

in a hurry 1 *adj* **rushed**, pressed for time, short of time, in a rush, late [➡ IN TROUBLE AND DISADVANTAGED; 73] *Opposite*: unrushed 2 *adv* **in a rush**, hurriedly, quickly, rapidly, hastily, fast, at speed, with no time to spare, in a flash [➡ MOVING QUICKLY; 103] *Opposite*: slowly

in a jam (*informal*) *adj* **in trouble**, in difficulties, in a tight spot, in extremis, in dire straits, in hot water (*informal*), in a fix (*informal*), up the creek (*informal*), in the soup (*informal*) [➡ IN TROUBLE AND DISADVANTAGED; 73]

in a jiffy (*informal*) *adv* **in a moment**, in a minute, in a second, shortly, right away, directly, in (less than) no time, immediately, forthwith, straightaway [➡ FUTURE; 86]

in a jumble *adj* [➡ DISORDER AND CHAOS; 245]

in a lather (*informal*) *adj* [➡ CONFUSION, ANXIETY, AND WORRY; 540]

inalienable (*formal*) *adj* **unchallengeable**, absolute, immutable, unassailable, incontrovertible, indisputable, undeniable [➡ CERTAIN; 174] *Opposite*: disputable

in a little while *adv* [➡ FUTURE; 86]

in all *adv* **ultimately**, altogether, all in all, as a whole, all told, overall [➡ ALL; 128]

in all fairness *adv* [➡ EXPRESSIONS OF OPINION; 623]

in all honesty *adv* [➡ EXPRESSIONS OF OPINION; 623]

in all likelihood *adv* [➡ EXPRESSIONS OF OPINION; 623]

in all probability *adv* [➡ EXPRESSIONS OF OPINION; 623]

in a minute *adv* [➡ FUTURE; 86]

in a mood *adj* [➡ SADNESS, DISTRESS, AND DESPAIR; 539]

inamorata (*literary*) *n* [➡ SEXUAL AND ROMANTIC RELATIONSHIPS; 964]

inane *adj* **silly**, unintelligent, absurd, ridiculous, stupid, frivolous, childish, immature, mindless, crass [➡ THE NATURE OF IDEAS; 771] *Opposite*: sensible

inaneness *n* [➡ THE NATURE OF IDEAS; 771]

inanimate 1 *adj* **lifeless**, dead, nonliving, inorganic, inert, extinct, deceased (*formal*) [➡ DEAD AND DYING; 925] *Opposite*: alive 2 *adj* **inactive**, dull, unresponsive, apathetic, impassive, listless, lethargic, spiritless, insensate, vacant [➡ LIFELESS, LAZY, AND UNENTHUSIASTIC; 506] *Opposite*: spirited

inanity 1 *n* **meaninglessness**, senselessness, stupidity, ridiculousness, absurdity [➡ THE NATURE OF IDEAS; 771] *Opposite*: logic 2 *n* **silliness**, foolishness, frivolousness, stupidity, ridiculousness, childishness, immaturity, mindlessness, crassness [➡ NEGATIVE INTELLECTUAL CHARACTERISTICS; 525] *Opposite*: sensibleness

in a nutshell *adv* **in short**, briefly, in a word, in brief, concisely, succinctly, to sum up, in a few words, all

things considered, when all's said and done, in summary, to cut a long story short [➡ SUMMARIZING EXPRESSIONS; 622] *Opposite*: at length

in any case 1 *adv* **anyway**, all in all, moreover, furthermore, besides, anyhow, at any rate, in any event [➡ EXPRESSIONS INTRODUCING EXTRA INFORMATION; 139] 2 *adv* **regardless**, anyway, nevertheless, nonetheless, whatever, in any event, come rain or shine, no matter what [➡ ALTHOUGH, NEVERTHELESS, AND DESPITE; 169]

in any event *adv* **anyhow**, anyway, in any case, at any rate, besides, moreover, furthermore, whatever happens, regardless, no matter what, even so [➡ EXPRESSIONS INTRODUCING EXTRA INFORMATION; 139]

in a panic *adj* [➡ FEAR AND PANIC; 543]

inapplicability *n* **unsuitability**, inappropriateness, irrelevance, inaptness, wrongness, inappositeness (*formal*) [➡ INAPPROPRIATE AND UNSUITABLE; 224] *Opposite*: suitability

inapplicable *adj* **unsuitable**, irrelevant, inappropriate, inapposite, inapt, wrong, misplaced [➡ INAPPROPRIATE AND UNSUITABLE; 224] *Opposite*: suitable

inapposite *adj* **unsuitable**, out of place, inappropriate, inapt, unfitting, wrong, misplaced, misguided, irrelevant, inapplicable [➡ INAPPROPRIATE AND UNSUITABLE; 224] *Opposite*: suitable

inappositeness (*formal*) *n* **unsuitability**, inappropriateness, inaptness, wrongness, misguidedness, irrelevance, inapplicability [➡ INAPPROPRIATE AND UNSUITABLE; 224] *Opposite*: suitability

inappreciable *adj* **insignificant**, imperceptible, unperceivable, negligible, unimportant, immaterial, microscopic, minute [➡ IMPERCEPTIBLE; 26] *Opposite*: significant

inappreciably *adv* **insignificantly**, imperceptibly, unperceivably, negligibly, unimportantly, immaterially, microscopically, minutely [➡ UNIMPORTANT AND UNNECESSARY; 238] *Opposite*: significantly

inappropriate *adj* **unsuitable**, unfitting, untimely, unfortunate, inapt, wrong, incorrect, incongruous, inapplicable, inapposite, ill-chosen, ill-timed, insensitive, misplaced, improper, tasteless, unseemly, tactless, unbecoming, unacceptable [➡ INAPPROPRIATE AND UNSUITABLE; 224] *Opposite*: fitting

inappropriateness *n* **unsuitability**, impropriety, wrongness, incorrectness, unseemliness, untimeliness, unfortunateness, inaptness, incongruity, indelicacy, indecorousness, tastelessness, unacceptability, insensitivity, inapplicability, inappositeness (*formal*) [➡ INAPPROPRIATE AND UNSUITABLE; 224] *Opposite*: appropriateness

in a predicament *adj* [➡ IN TROUBLE AND DISADVANTAGED; 73]

inapt *adj* [➡ INAPPROPRIATE AND UNSUITABLE; 224]

inaptness *n* [➡ INAPPROPRIATE AND UNSUITABLE; 224]

in a quandary *adj* [➡ UNCERTAINTY; 559]

in a roundabout way *adv* **indirectly**, expansively, laboriously, circuitously, discursively, tangentially, long-windedly, obliquely, evasively [➡ INARTICULATE, RAMBLING, AND AWKWARD; 633] *Opposite*: directly

in a row *adv* **one after the other**, one behind the other, in single file, end to end, in succession, back-to-back, consecutively, in line, on the trot (*UK*) [➠AFTER, LAST, AND FOLLOWING; 165]

in arrears *adj* **behind**, overdue, late, in the red, behindhand [➠POVERTY AND POOR; 892] *Opposite:* ahead

inarticulacy 1 *n* **incoherence**, hesitation, lack of fluency, stumbling, stuttering, stammering, speechlessness, awkwardness, clumsiness [➠INARTICULATE, RAMBLING, AND AWKWARD; 633] *Opposite:* eloquence   2 *n* **unintelligibility**, incomprehensibility, inaudibility, indistinctness, unclearness [➠IMPERCEPTIBLE; 26] *Opposite:* clarity

inarticulate 1 *adj* **tongue-tied**, incoherent, mumbling, hesitant, faltering, speechless, stuttering, stammering, stumbling, clumsy, awkward [➠INARTICULATE, RAMBLING, AND AWKWARD; 633] *Opposite:* eloquent   2 *adj* **garbled**, muttered, incoherent, unintelligible, incomprehensible, mumbled, inaudible, indistinct, unclear [➠IMPERCEPTIBLE; 26] *Opposite:* clear

inarticulateness *n* [➠INARTICULATE, RAMBLING, AND AWKWARD; 633]

in a rush 1 *adj* **in a hurry**, rushed, short of time, pressed for time, late [➠IN TROUBLE AND DISADVANTAGED; 73] *Opposite:* unrushed   2 *adv* **hurriedly**, hastily, quickly, at speed, rapidly, fast, swiftly, at the last minute [➠HAPPENING QUICKLY; 104] *Opposite:* slowly

in a rut *adj* **bored**, stagnant, in the doldrums, unchanging, fixed, inflexible [➠PERMANENCE: WITHOUT CHANGE; 95] *Opposite:* dynamic

in a second *adv* [➠FUTURE; 86]

in a short time *adv* [➠FUTURE; 86]

inasmuch as *conj* **because**, insofar as, considering that, since, as, seeing that, as long as, whereas (*formal*) [➠CAUSATION; 168]

in a state of shock *adj* [➠SURPRISE, SHOCK, AND AMAZEMENT; 545]

in a tight corner *adj* [➠IN TROUBLE AND DISADVANTAGED; 73]

in a tight spot *adj* [➠IN TROUBLE AND DISADVANTAGED; 73]

in a tizzy (*informal*) *adj* [➠SADNESS, DISTRESS, AND DESPAIR; 539]

in a trice *adv* [➠FUTURE; 86]

in attendance *adj* [➠PRESENT AND AVAILABLE; 11]

inattention *n* **inattentiveness**, daydreaming, woolgathering, distraction, abstraction, carelessness, negligence, absent-mindedness, doziness [➠NOT PAY ATTENTION; 764] *Opposite:* concentration

inattentive *adj* **careless**, daydreaming, distracted, abstracted, woolgathering, negligent, unmindful, absent-minded, dreamy, dozy, out of it (*informal*) [➠INCAUTIOUS AND CARELESS; 283] *Opposite:* careful

inattentiveness *n* **carelessness**, inattention, daydreaming, distraction, abstraction, negligence, doziness, absent-mindedness, woolgathering [➠NOT PAY ATTENTION; 764] *Opposite:* attention

inaudibility *n* **quietness**, faintness, imperceptibility, noiselessness, silence, quiet, softness, stillness, soundlessness [➠IMPERCEPTIBLE; 26] *Opposite:* audibility

inaudible *adj* **quiet**, out of earshot, low, faint, soft, silent, noiseless, imperceptible, soundless, still [➠IMPERCEPTIBLE; 26] *Opposite:* perceptible

inaugural *adj* **opening**, initial, first, introductory, foundational, maiden, original, primary, germinal (*formal*) [➠BEFORE, FIRST, AND PRECEDING; 163]

inaugurate 1 *v* **swear in**, install, induct, instate, initiate, invest (*formal*) [➠CONFER STATUS; 458] *Opposite:* dismiss   2 *v* **open**, launch, dedicate, initiate, unveil, start up, introduce, institute [➠INSTITUTE AND INAUGURATE; 348] *Opposite:* close   3 *v* **initiate**, establish, put in place, get underway, set up, start up, create, introduce, bring into being [➠CAUSE TO START; 265] *Opposite:* terminate (*formal*)

inauguration 1 *n* **induction**, investiture, installation, swearing in, inaugural ceremony, appointment [➠CEREMONIES AND ANNIVERSARIES; 38] *Opposite:* dismissal   2 *n* **opening**, launch, opening ceremony, initiation ceremony, start, unveiling [➠BEGINNINGS; 53] *Opposite:* closure   3 *n* **initiation**, creation, introduction, setting up, conception, invention [➠BEGINNINGS; 53] *Opposite:* closedown

inauspicious *adj* **unpromising**, discouraging, ill-starred, ill-fated, unfavorable, ominous, gloomy, fateful, adverse [➠UNSUCCESSFUL AND UNPROMISING; 76] *Opposite:* promising

inauthentic *adj* **false**, imitation, fake, forged, counterfeit, mock, synthetic, ersatz [➠FALSE AND UNREAL; 173] *Opposite:* genuine

in awe of *adj* **frightened**, overcome, overwhelmed, impressed, daunted, intimidated, fearful, awed [➠SURPRISE, SHOCK, AND AMAZEMENT; 545] *Opposite:* unimpressed

in a while *adv* **soon**, shortly, afterward, later, later on, before long, in good time, in your own good time, presently (*formal or literary*) [➠FUTURE; 86] *Opposite:* immediately

in a world of your own *adj* **in a dream**, in a daze, daydreaming, lost in thought, preoccupied, engrossed, absent-minded, far away [➠NEUTRALITY AND INDIFFERENCE; 553]

in back *adv* [➠GENERAL LOCATIONS; 158]

in bad odor *adj* [➠IN TROUBLE AND DISADVANTAGED; 73]

in bad repair *adj* [➠IN BAD REPAIR; 1234]

in bad shape *adj* **in bad condition**, unhealthy, unfit, out of condition, out of shape, in poor health, flabby (*informal*) [➠UNFIT AND WEAK; 739] *Opposite:* in good shape

in bad taste *adj* **offensive**, tasteless, in poor taste, distasteful, ill-chosen, tactless, indelicate, insensitive, vulgar, crude, nasty, unpleasant [➠IN POOR TASTE AND OVERSENTIMENTAL; 229] *Opposite:* tasteful

in between *prep* **between**, amidst, next to, sandwiched by, in the middle of, amid, among, amongst [➠RELATIVE LOCATION; 161]

in-between 1 *adj* **intermediate**, separating, isolating, halfway, indeterminate, vague, inconclusive, fuzzy [➠RELATIVE LOCATION; 161]   2 *adv* **meanwhile**, in the interval, in the intervening time, between times, at the same time, intermediately, vaguely, inconclusively, fuzzily [➠PRESENT; 85]

in bits *adj* [➠IN BAD REPAIR; 1234]

inborn *adj* **innate**, natural, instinctive, intuitive, inherited, congenital, inherent [➡ REPRODUCTION AND HEREDITY; 725] *Opposite*: acquired

inbound *adj* **incoming**, arriving, inward bound, coming in, heading toward [➡ DIRECTION OF MOTION; 345]

in-box *n* **tray**, pigeonhole, mailbox, in-tray (*UK*) [➡ CONTAINERS, RECEPTACLES, AND PACKAGING; 1245]

inbred *adj* **congenital**, inherited, hereditary, ingrained, deep-seated, inborn [➡ REPRODUCTION AND HEREDITY; 725] *Opposite*: acquired

in brief *adv* **briefly**, in a few words, in short, to sum up, everything considered, when all's said and done, in a word, in summary, in a nutshell, to cut a long story short, to be brief, to come to the point, concisely [➡ SUMMARIZING EXPRESSIONS; 622] *Opposite*: at length

in broad daylight *adv* **visibly**, noticeably, conspicuously, perceptibly, plainly, boldly, in full view, before your very eyes, right under your nose, openly [➡ PERCEPTIBLE; 25] *Opposite*: surreptitiously

in-built **1** *adj* **innate**, natural, inborn, inherent, instinctive, unlearned, intrinsic, intuitive, ingrained [➡ REPRODUCTION AND HEREDITY; 725] *Opposite*: learned **2** *adj* (*UK*) **incorporated**, integral, intrinsic, included, integrated, built-in, inboard, onboard, fitted (*UK*) [➡ RELATED; 142] *Opposite*: add-on

in bulk *adv* **in large quantities**, wholesale [➡ MANY, MUCH, LARGE AMOUNT; 117] *Opposite*: piecemeal

incalculable **1** *adj* **countless**, without number, innumerable, infinite, multitudinous, vast, huge, immense, untold, inestimable, immeasurable, limitless [➡ MANY, MUCH, LARGE AMOUNT; 117] *Opposite*: finite **2** *adj* **unpredictable**, unforeseeable, indeterminable, uncertain, haphazard, hit-or-miss [➡ UNCERTAIN; 175] *Opposite*: predictable

incalculably **1** *adv* **countlessly**, innumerably, immeasurably, infinitely, inestimably, immensely, multitudinously, hugely, vastly [➡ TO A GREAT EXTENT; 132] **2** *adv* **unpredictably**, unforeseeably, indeterminably, uncertainly, haphazardly [➡ UNCERTAIN; 175] *Opposite*: predictably

in camera *adv* **in private**, in secret, clandestinely, covertly, confidentially, privately, secretly, behind closed doors [➡ SECRET AND UNKNOWN; 179] *Opposite*: openly

incandesce *v* **glow**, radiate, shine, luminesce, fluoresce, burn, flame, beam, flare [➡ LIGHT EMISSION; 368]

incandescence *n* **glow**, luminosity, light, luminescence, fluorescence, burning, radiance, luster [➡ LIGHT; 1164]

incandescent *adj* **glowing**, radiant, luminous, shining, bright, luminescent, aglow, burning, fluorescent, flaming, beaming, flaring [➡ DESCRIBING LIGHT; 1228]

incantation *n* **chant**, invocation, prayer, spell, charm, summons [➡ RELIGIONS AND RELIGIOUS PRACTICES; 777]

incapable **1** *adj* **unable**, powerless, inept, inexpert, unqualified, incompetent [➡ UNSKILLED; 529] *Opposite*: able **2** *adj* **helpless**, weak, vulnerable, feeble, frail, dependent, incapacitated [➡ UNFIT AND WEAK; 739] *Opposite*: strong

incapacitate *v* **debilitate**, injure, harm, disable, lay up,

weaken, undermine [➡ WOUND A PERSON OR ANIMAL; 383] *Opposite*: enable

incapacitated *adj* **debilitated**, injured, harmed, disabled, laid up, weakened, undermined [➡ UNFIT AND WEAK; 739] *Opposite*: fit

incapacitating *adj* [➡ PHYSICALLY UNPLEASANT; 226]

incapacity *n* **inability**, ineffectiveness, injury, incapability, powerlessness, failure, disability, weakness [➡ UNSKILLED; 529] *Opposite*: ability

incarcerate (*formal*) *v* **imprison**, jail, lock up, hold prisoner, intern, detain, put in prison, send to prison, keep under lock and key [➡ THE POLICE, ARREST, AND PRETRIAL PROCEEDINGS; 818] *Opposite*: free

incarcerated (*formal*) *adj* [➡ CAPTIVITY AND LOSS OF FREEDOM; 248]

incarceration *n* **imprisonment**, confinement, custody, captivity, internment, detention [➡ CAPTIVITY AND LOSS OF FREEDOM; 248] *Opposite*: freedom

incarnate *adj* **personified**, in person, in the flesh, alive, embodied, in material form, come to life, made flesh [➡ REPRESENTATIVE; 66]

incarnation *n* **personification**, embodiment, manifestation, avatar, living form, life, materialization [➡ REPRESENTATIONS AND GENERAL EXAMPLES; 65]

in case *conj* **just in case**, in the event, lest, if, whether or no, whether or not [➡ UNCERTAIN; 175]

incautious *adj* **careless**, rash, reckless, impetuous, impulsive, unwary, unthinking, imprudent, indiscreet, hasty [➡ INCAUTIOUS AND CARELESS; 283] *Opposite*: careful

incendiary **1** *adj* **inflammable**, combustible, flammable [➡ FIRE, FLAMMABILITY, AND BURNING; 1165] **2** *adj* **inflammatory**, provocative, rabble-rousing, aggressive, stirring, rousing [➡ REBELLIOUSNESS AND DISOBEDIENCE; 565] *Opposite*: conciliatory **3** *n* (*formal*) **troublemaker**, agitator, demagogue, activist, firebrand, agent provocateur, rabble-rouser [➡ UNCOOPERATIVE OR REBELLIOUS PEOPLE; 566] **4** *n* **arsonist**, pyromaniac, burner, firebomber, torcher (*slang*), firebug (*slang*), fire raiser (*UK*) [➡ CRIMINALS; 821]

incense *v* **enrage**, anger, exasperate, infuriate, annoy, rile (*informal*) [➡ ANGER AND ANNOY; 569] *Opposite*: calm

incensed *adj* **enraged**, angry, exasperated, infuriated, annoyed, irate, furious, riled (*informal*) [➡ IRRITATION AND ANGER; 541] *Opposite*: calm

incentive *n* **inducement**, enticement, motivation, encouragement, spur, reason [➡ CAUSATION; 168] *Opposite*: disincentive

See Compare and Contrast at **motive**.

inception (*formal*) *n* **beginning**, start, inauguration, initiation, foundation, origin, launch, establishment, commencement (*formal*) [➡ BEGINNINGS; 53] *Opposite*: culmination

incertitude *n* [➡ UNCERTAINTY; 559]

incessant *adj* **nonstop**, never-ending, ceaseless, continuous, continual, unremitting, relentless, persistent, constant [➡ PERMANENCE: WITHOUT END; 94] *Opposite*: sporadic

inch 1 *v* **creep**, crawl, shuffle, edge [➡ MOVE SLOWLY; 314] **2** *type of* **nonmetric unit** [➡ SIZE AND DIMENSIONS; 1192]

in charge *adj* **in command**, in control, at the helm, responsible, giving the orders, liable [➡ SUPERIORITY; 152]

inchoate (*formal*) *adj* **undeveloped**, incipient, immature, beginning, starting, budding, developing, emergent, early, embryonic [➡ VAGUENESS; 243] *Opposite*: mature

in chorus *adv* **together**, in unison, all together, in harmony, harmoniously, as one, in concert, jointly [➡ ACTING WITH OTHERS; 285] *Opposite*: individually

incidence *n* **occurrence**, frequency, rate, commonness, prevalence [➡ FREQUENT AND OFTEN; 107]

incident 1 *n* **event**, occurrence, occasion, happening, episode, instance, case [➡ EVENTS AND OCCURRENCES; 35] **2** *n* **confrontation**, clash, skirmish, fight, episode, scene [➡ ARGUMENTS; 47]

incidental *adj* **related**, accompanying, secondary, subsidiary, supplementary, attendant, minor [➡ RELATED; 142] *Opposite*: essential

incidentally *adv* **by the way**, by the by, while we're on the subject, before I forget, parenthetically [➡ EXPRESSIONS INTRODUCING EXTRA INFORMATION; 139]

incinerate *v* **burn**, burn up, set fire to, cremate, reduce to ashes, destroy [➡ FIRE, FLAMMABILITY, AND BURNING; 1165]

incineration *n* [➡ FIRE, FLAMMABILITY, AND BURNING; 1165]

incinerator *n* **furnace**, brazier, kiln, oven, burner, firebox [➡ FIRE, FLAMMABILITY, AND BURNING; 1165]

incipient *adj* **emerging**, initial, embryonic, budding, early, developing, emergent, inchoate (*formal*) [➡ VAGUENESS; 243] *Opposite*: final

incise *v* **cut**, slit, notch, score, carve, chisel, engrave [➡ TEAR, BREAK, AND CUT; 360]

incision *n* **cut**, slit, opening, notch, scratch, score [➡ HOLES, GAPS, AND FORKS; 1252]

incisive *adj* **keen**, perceptive, insightful, sharp, penetrating, razor-sharp [➡ POSITIVE INTELLECTUAL CHARACTERISTICS; 524] *Opposite*: dull

incisiveness *n* [➡ POSITIVE INTELLECTUAL CHARACTERISTICS; 524]

incisor *type of* **tooth** [➡ THE MOUTH; 702]

incite *v* **provoke**, inflame, rouse, goad, spur, egg on, stimulate, motivate, push, stir up, instigate, whip up, breed, cause [➡ CAUSE OR COMPEL TO ACT; 271] *Opposite*: quell

incitement *n* **provocation**, stimulation, agitation, encouragement, goad, spur, stimulus, motivation [➡ BEGINNINGS; 53] *Opposite*: deterrent

incivility *n* **rudeness**, impoliteness, discourteousness, discourtesy, lack of respect, bad manners, coarseness, vulgarity [➡ BAD MANNERS AND SOCIAL SKILLS; 521] *Opposite*: politeness

inclement *adj* **intemperate**, extreme, severe, bad, foul, rough, harsh, stormy, rainy, windy, squally [➡ COLD WEATHER; 1051] *Opposite*: pleasant

inclination 1 *n* **feeling**, predisposition, disposition, leaning, proclivity, penchant, preference, liking, partiality, fondness, tendency [➡ LIKE, LOVE, VALUE, AND ENJOY; 578] *Opposite*: antipathy **2** *n* **slope**, slant, incline, gradient, pitch, steepness [➡ ORIENTATION AND ALIGNMENT; 1223]

incline 1 *v* **slant**, slope, tilt, rise, fall, lean [➡ TAKE UP A NEW POSITION; 312] **2** *v* **dispose**, persuade, prejudice, bias, bring around, lean, verge, favor, show a preference for, predispose (*formal*) [➡ LIKE, LOVE, VALUE, AND ENJOY; 578] *Opposite*: deter **3** *n* **slope**, slant, gradient, rise, ascent, hill [➡ MOUNTAINS AND HILLS; 1044]

inclined 1 *adj* **motivated**, persuaded, tending, disposed, apt, liable, prone, of a mind, having half a mind to (*informal*) [➡ APPRECIATION AND GRATITUDE; 535] *Opposite*: averse (*formal*) **2** *adj* **leaning**, sloping, slanting, tilting, orientated, oriented [➡ ORIENTATION AND ALIGNMENT; 1223]

in close proximity *adv* [➡ CLOSENESS; 159]

in clover *adj* **well-off**, wealthy, affluent, rich, comfortable, in the lap of luxury, living high on the hog (*slang*) [➡ WEALTH AND WEALTHY; 891]

include 1 *v* **contain**, comprise, take in, consist of, take account of, embrace [➡ POSSESS; 444] *Opposite*: omit **2** *v* **bring in**, incorporate, add in, enter, involve, rope in [➡ COMBINE AND MIX; 400] *Opposite*: reject

included *adj* **contained within**, counted in, comprised, encompassed, involved [➡ PRESENT AND AVAILABLE; 11] *Opposite*: omitted

including *prep* **counting**, as well as, with, together with, plus [➡ ALSO; 138] *Opposite*: excluding

inclusion *n* **presence**, addition, enclosure, insertion, annexation, attachment [➡ MORE AND EXCESS; 124] *Opposite*: absence

inclusive *adj* **comprehensive**, wide-ranging, all-encompassing, complete, broad, general [➡ WHOLENESS AND COMPLETENESS; 198] *Opposite*: restricted

incognito *adv* **in disguise**, disguised, undercover, anonymously, secretly, in secret [➡ SECRET AND UNKNOWN; 179] *Opposite*: openly

incoherence *n* **unintelligibility**, inarticulateness, disjointedness, illogicality, confusedness, confusion, disorganization [➡ VAGUENESS; 243] *Opposite*: coherence

incoherent 1 *adj* **disjointed**, confused, jumbled, illogical, all over the place (*informal*) [➡ THE NATURE OF IDEAS; 771] *Opposite*: clear **2** *adj* **inarticulate**, unintelligible, incomprehensible, garbled, mumbled, slurred, rambling [➡ INARTICULATE, RAMBLING, AND AWKWARD; 633] *Opposite*: articulate

in cold blood *adv* **mercilessly**, deliberately, premeditatedly, unemotionally, coolly, cruelly, cold-heartedly, pitilessly [➡ INTENTIONAL AND DELIBERATE; 279]

incombustible *adj* **fireproof**, flameproof, fire-resistant, flame-resistant, fire-retardant, flame-retardant [➡ FIRE, FLAMMABILITY, AND BURNING; 1165] *Opposite*: flammable

income *n* **profits**, proceeds, returns, revenue, earnings,

wages, pay, salary, take-home pay, takings [➡ INCOME; 460]
Opposite: expenditure

incomer (*UK*) *n* **settler**, immigrant, colonist, migrant, newcomer [➡ STRANGERS; 972]

income tax *n* **tax**, VAT, toll, duty, excise, tariff, levy, charge [➡ TAX AND TAXATION; 802]

incoming 1 *adj* **inbound**, inward bound, homeward bound, arriving, entering, inward [➡ DIRECTION OF MOTION; 345] *Opposite*: outgoing   2 *adj* **new**, next, succeeding, newly appointed, newly elected, returning [➡ NEW, MODERN; 166] *Opposite*: outgoing

incommensurate *adj* **disproportionate**, unequal, inadequate, insufficient, lacking parity, out of line (*informal*) [➡ DIFFERENCE; 149] *Opposite*: proportionate

in commission *adj* **in service**, in use, operating, working, functioning [➡ HAPPENING AND IN PROGRESS; 32]

incommode (*formal*) *v* **inconvenience**, trouble, disturb, bother, put out, put to some trouble [➡ UPSET, DISTRESS, AND HUMILIATE; 567]

incommodious (*formal*) 1 *adj* **cramped**, restricted, confined, tiny, small [➡ SMALL; 1195] *Opposite*: roomy   2 *adj* **inconvenient**, troublesome, awkward, annoying, bothersome, difficult [➡ PHYSICALLY UNPLEASANT; 226]

incommunicado *adj* **not in contact**, out of touch, not in communication, not able to communicate, unwilling to communicate, in solitary confinement [➡ SOLITARINESS; 941]

incomparable *adj* **unequaled**, unrivaled, unparalleled, unsurpassed, unmatched, outstanding, unique [➡ EXTRAORDINARY; AMAZING; 204] *Opposite*: ordinary

incompatibility 1 *n* **mismatch**, unsuitability, discordancy, inharmoniousness, irreconcilability [➡ DISHARMONY; 156]   2 *n* **inconsistency**, illogicality, irreconcilability, incongruity, mismatch, conflict [➡ DISHARMONY; 156] *Opposite*: consistency

incompatible *adj* **mismatched**, unsuited, discordant, unharmonious, dissenting, irreconcilable, ill-assorted [➡ DISHARMONY; 156] *Opposite*: like-minded

incompetence *n* **ineptitude**, unskillfulness, inability, ineffectiveness, stupidity, uselessness [➡ UNSKILLED; 529] *Opposite*: ability

incompetent *adj* **inept**, useless, unskilled, ineffectual, hopeless, unapt, unable, incapable, bungling (*informal*) [➡ UNSKILLED; 529] *Opposite*: able

incomplete 1 *adj* **imperfect**, partial, unfinished, inadequate, half-finished, piecemeal, lacking [➡ UNFINISHEDNESS; 239] *Opposite*: entire   2 *adj* **unfinished**, undeveloped, curtailed, shortened, deficient, inchoate (*formal*) [➡ UNFINISHEDNESS; 239] *Opposite*: finished

incomprehensibility *n* [➡ DIFFICULTY AND COMPLEXITY; 242]

incomprehensible *adj* **unintelligible**, unfathomable, impenetrable, inexplicable, inconceivable, perplexing [➡ DIFFICULTY AND COMPLEXITY; 242] *Opposite*: understandable

incomprehension *n* **disbelief**, incredulity, incredulousness, perplexity, blankness [➡ SURPRISE, SHOCK, AND AMAZEMENT; 545] *Opposite*: understanding

inconceivable *adj* **unimaginable**, unthinkable, beyond belief, unbelievable, incredible, implausible, mind-blowing (*informal*), mind-boggling (*informal*) [➡ IMPOSSIBLE AND IMPROBABLE; 178] *Opposite*: imaginable

in concert 1 *adv* **performing**, presenting, in recital, live, playing, singing, in performance, onstage, before a live audience [➡ MUSICAL TERMS; 912]   2 *adv* **in chorus**, harmoniously, together, as one, in unison, all together, jointly [➡ ACTING WITH OTHERS; 285] *Opposite*: individually

inconclusive *adj* **indecisive**, questionable, unconvincing, unsatisfying, unsettled, inadequate, lacking, unfounded, groundless, unsound, uncertain [➡ UNCERTAIN; 175] *Opposite*: decisive

in confidence *adv* **in secret**, confidentially, between ourselves, in private, privately, secretly, off the record [➡ SECRET AND UNKNOWN; 179] *Opposite*: openly

incongruence *n* [➡ BIZARRE AND PECULIAR; 257]

incongruent *adj* [➡ BIZARRE AND PECULIAR; 257]

incongruity *n* **oddness**, strangeness, absurdity, inappropriateness, inaptness, unsuitableness, incompatibility, inconsistency, bizarreness, unsuitability, inharmoniousness [➡ BIZARRE AND PECULIAR; 257] *Opposite*: consistency

incongruous *adj* **odd**, strange, out of place, incompatible, inappropriate, inconsistent, absurd, bizarre, unsuitable, inharmonious [➡ BIZARRE AND PECULIAR; 257] *Opposite*: consistent

incongruousness *n* [➡ BIZARRE AND PECULIAR; 257]

in conjunction with *prep* **together with**, combined with, along with, with, in addition to, in tandem with, alongside, next to [➡ ALSO; 138] *Opposite*: apart from

in consequence (*formal*) *adv* **accordingly**, as a result, consequently, therefore, so, hence (*formal*), thus (*formal*) [➡ RESULTS AND OUTCOMES; 83]

inconsequence *n* **unimportance**, irrelevance, insignificance, triviality, inconsequentiality, frivolity, inappropriateness, worthlessness [➡ UNIMPORTANT AND UNNECESSARY; 238] *Opposite*: importance

inconsequential *adj* **unimportant**, trivial, petty, negligible, minor, insignificant, irrelevant, frivolous, inappropriate, worthless [➡ UNIMPORTANT AND UNNECESSARY; 238] *Opposite*: important

inconsequentiality *n* **unimportance**, insignificance, triviality, frivolity, inconsequence, irrelevance, inappropriateness, worthlessness [➡ UNIMPORTANT AND UNNECESSARY; 238] *Opposite*: importance

inconsiderable *adj* **small**, minor, tiny, paltry, negligible, trivial, petty, trifling, dinky (*informal*) [➡ UNIMPORTANT AND UNNECESSARY; 238] *Opposite*: sizable

inconsiderate *adj* **selfish**, thoughtless, insensitive, uncharitable, unkind, uncaring, careless, discourteous [➡ SELFISH AND UNKIND; 505] *Opposite*: caring

inconsiderateness *n* [➡ SELFISH AND UNKIND; 505]

inconsistency *n* **discrepancy**, contradiction, variation, irregularity, changeability, unpredictability, conflict [➠ DIFFERENCE; 149]

inconsistent 1 *adj* **conflicting**, contradictory, incompatible, incoherent, incongruous, paradoxical, irreconcilable [➠ DISHARMONY; 156] *Opposite*: consistent **2** *adj* **unpredictable**, varying, unreliable, erratic, uneven, shifting, fickle, changeable, variable, inconstant, mercurial, capricious [➠ FINITENESS, VARIABILITY, AND TRANSIENCE; 96] *Opposite*: constant

inconsolable *adj* **grief-stricken**, brokenhearted, devastated, desolate, despairing, heartbroken, wretched [➠ SADNESS, DISTRESS, AND DESPAIR; 539] *Opposite*: ecstatic

inconspicuous *adj* **unobtrusive**, discreet, unremarkable, ordinary, modest, quiet, low-key, unassuming [➠ IMPERCEPTIBLE; 26] *Opposite*: obvious

inconspicuousness *n* [➠ IMPERCEPTIBLE; 26]

inconstancy *n* [➠ FINITENESS, VARIABILITY, AND TRANSIENCE; 96]

inconstant 1 *adj* (*literary*) **unfaithful**, disloyal, fickle, deceitful, false, two-timing (*informal*) [➠ DECEITFUL; 513] *Opposite*: faithful **2** *adj* **changeable**, variable, irregular, unpredictable, fluctuating, varying [➠ FINITENESS, VARIABILITY, AND TRANSIENCE; 96] *Opposite*: unchanging

incontestable *adj* **indisputable**, incontrovertible, irrefutable, unquestionable, indubitable, undeniable, unarguable, obvious, undoubted [➠ CERTAIN; 174] *Opposite*: arguable

incontrovertible *adj* **undeniable**, unquestionable, irrefutable, incontestable, indisputable, indubitable, unarguable, unassailable [➠ CERTAIN; 174] *Opposite*: questionable

inconvenience 1 *n* **troublesomeness**, tiresomeness, inopportuneness, untimeliness, awkwardness, embarrassment [➠ NUISANCES; 253] *Opposite*: benefit **2** *n* **problem**, trouble, bother, difficulty, nuisance, annoyance, hassle (*informal*) [➠ NUISANCES; 253] **3** *v* **disrupt**, put out, trouble, bother, disturb, incommode (*formal*), discommode (*formal*) [➠ ANGER AND ANNOY; 569] *Opposite*: help

inconvenient *adj* **troublesome**, tiresome, inopportune, problematic, untimely, awkward, ill-timed, bothersome, difficult, embarrassing [➠ IRRITATING; 228] *Opposite*: beneficial

inconveniently *adv* **awkwardly**, troublesomely, inopportunely, tiresomely, problematically, embarrassingly [➠ PROMPTNESS: BADLY TIMED; 101] *Opposite*: beneficially

in cooperation with *prep* **together with**, in association with, in collaboration with, alongside, in conjunction with [➠ ALSO; 138]

incorporate 1 *v* **join**, slot in, fit in, add in, slip in, include, integrate, unite, combine [➠ POSITION SOMETHING: BETWEEN, BESIDE, OR INSIDE SOMETHING; 326] *Opposite*: exclude **2** *v* **merge**, combine, feature, contain, include, encompass, absorb, assimilate [➠ COMBINE AND MIX; 400] *Opposite*: divide

incorporated *adj* **combined**, united, unified, merged, fused, assimilated, amalgamated, integrated [➠ RELATED; 142] *Opposite*: separate

incorporation *n* **combination**, amalgamation, integration, assimilation, merger, fusion, unification, absorption, union [➠ COMBINE AND MIX; 400] *Opposite*: separation

incorporeal (*formal*) *adj* **intangible**, ethereal, spiritual, unreal, disembodied, ghostly [➠ FALSE AND UNREAL; 173] *Opposite*: tangible

incorrect 1 *adj* **erroneous**, wrong, mistaken, untrue, inaccurate, false [➠ INCORRECT AND ERRONEOUS; 222] *Opposite*: right **2** *adj* **improper**, unfitting, inappropriate, unseemly, unbecoming, indecorous, indelicate, indecent, impolite, offensive, unsuitable [➠ INAPPROPRIATE AND UNSUITABLE; 224] *Opposite*: proper

incorrectness 1 *n* **erroneousness**, error, fallacy, wrongness, mistakenness, falseness, inaccuracy [➠ INCORRECT AND ERRONEOUS; 222] *Opposite*: correctness **2** *n* **impropriety**, inappropriateness, unsuitability, unseemliness, indecorousness, indelicacy, indecency, impoliteness [➠ INAPPROPRIATE AND UNSUITABLE; 224] *Opposite*: propriety

incorrigible *adj* **irredeemable**, habitual, inveterate, dyed-in-the-wool, persistent, incurable, hopeless [➠ UNWILLINGNESS AND STUBBORNNESS; 564] *Opposite*: tractable

incorruptibility *n* [➠ HONEST AND RELIABLE; 502]

incorruptible 1 *adj* **moral**, principled, just, straight, honorable, honest, upright [➠ HONEST AND RELIABLE; 502] *Opposite*: venal **2** *adj* **imperishable**, everlasting, immortal, indestructible, unchanging, constant [➠ PERMANENCE: WITHOUT CHANGE; 95] *Opposite*: perishable

increase 1 *v* **enlarge**, extend, boost, amplify, swell, expand, multiply, improve, intensify, raise, augment (*formal*) [➠ CHANGE OF SIZE: BIGGER; 392] *Opposite*: decrease **2** *n* **upsurge**, surge, rise, growth, intensification, escalation, proliferation, upturn, spread, expansion, multiplication, buildup [➠ CHANGE OF INTENSITY: MORE; 394] *Opposite*: decrease

---

Compare and Contrast: *increase, expand, enlarge, extend, augment, intensify, amplify*

CORE MEANING: to make larger or greater

increase to become or cause to become larger in number, quantity, degree, or scope; *expand* to become or cause to become larger or more extensive; *enlarge* to become or cause to become larger generally, or to broaden in scope and detail; *extend* to make larger in terms of length, area, period of time, or other existing limits; *augment* (*formal*) to add to something in order to make it larger or more substantial; *intensify* to become or cause to become greater in strength or degree; *amplify* to become or cause to become louder, or greater in intensity or scope.

---

incredible 1 *adj* **unbelievable**, implausible, improbable, far-fetched, absurd, inconceivable [➠ IMPOSSIBLE AND IMPROBABLE; 178] *Opposite*: believable **2** *adj* **amazing**, astonishing, extraordinary, staggering, unbelievable, fantastic, remarkable, mind-blowing (*informal*), mind-boggling (*informal*) [➠ EXTRAORDINARY: AMAZING; 204] *Opposite*: unremarkable **3** *adj* (*informal*) **excellent**, superb, tremendous, prodigious, phenomenal [➠ MANY, MUCH, LARGE AMOUNT; 117] *Opposite*: mediocre

incredibly 1 *adv* **unbelievably**, implausibly, inconceivably, absurdly, improbably [➠ IMPOSSIBLE AND IMPROBABLE; 178] *Opposite*: believably **2** *adv* (*informal*) **very**, extremely, unbelievably, amazingly, really, exceedingly, extraordinarily, exceptionally, awfully [➡ TO A GREAT EXTENT; 132]

incredulity *n* **disbelief**, amazement, astonishment, doubt, skepticism, wonder, suspicion [➡ SURPRISE, SHOCK, AND AMAZEMENT; 545] *Opposite*: belief

incredulous *adj* **disbelieving**, skeptical, unbelieving, doubtful, doubting, unconvinced, suspicious [➡ SURPRISE, SHOCK, AND AMAZEMENT; 545] *Opposite*: believing

increment *n* **increase**, addition, augmentation, raise, rise, growth, boost [➡ CHANGE OF INTENSITY: MORE; 394] *Opposite*: cut

incriminate *v* **implicate**, impeach, give away, lay the blame on, convict, point the finger, drop somebody in it (*UK*) [➡ ACCUSE, BLAME, AND CRITICIZE; 641] *Opposite*: exonerate

in-crowd (*informal*) *n* **inner circle**, beau monde, high society, clique, elite, in-group, beautiful people, jet set (*informal*) [➡ RICH PEOPLE; 895]

incrustation *n* **coating**, crust, layer, covering, accumulation, shell, veneer [➡ COVERS AND COATINGS; 1246]

incubate *v* **hatch**, gestate, raise, rear, nurture, protect, nurse [➡ REPRODUCTION AND HEREDITY; 725]

incubation *n* **development**, gestation, cultivation, nurture, growth, increase, maturation, evolution [➡ PROGRESS AND ADVANCEMENT; 213] *Opposite*: destruction

incubus *n* [➡ MYTHICAL BEINGS; 789]

inculcate *v* **impress upon**, teach, drum into, instruct, drill into, din, hammer into, coach, train, instill, indoctrinate [➡ INSTRUCT AND TEACH; 609]

incumbency (*formal*) **1** *n* **tenure**, period of office, term of office, term, time, period [➡ WORK-RELATED ACTIVITIES; 834] **2** *n* **post**, position, office, appointment [➡ JOB; 833] **3** *n* **duty**, obligation, responsibility, office, task, role, commitment, charge [➡ RESPONSIBILITY; 170]

incumbent **1** *adj* (*formal*) **obligatory**, mandatory, compulsory, binding, unavoidable, inescapable [➡ NECESSARY AND ESSENTIAL; 196] *Opposite*: optional **2** *n* **official**, office holder, occupant, appointee, officer, executive [➡ POLITICAL OFFICES AND POLITICIANS; 808]

incur **1** *v* **experience**, suffer, sustain, bring upon yourself, lay yourself open to, invite, acquire, earn, gain, deserve, meet with, encounter, come in for [➡ CAUSE TO HAPPEN; 31] *Opposite*: avoid **2** *v* **sustain**, meet with, encounter, experience, suffer, come in for [➡ EXPERIENCE AND ENCOUNTER; 582]

incurable **1** *adj* **terminal**, fatal, deadly, inoperable, untreatable, grave, permanent [➡ SICKNESS; 729] *Opposite*: curable **2** *adj* **irredeemable**, inveterate, incorrigible, hopeless, undying, dyed-in-the-wool, irrepressible, eternal [➡ UNWILLINGNESS AND STUBBORNNESS; 564] *Opposite*: redeemable

incurious *adj* **uninterested**, indifferent, unmoved, unconcerned, detached, apathetic [➡ NEUTRALITY AND INDIFFERENCE; 553] *Opposite*: inquisitive

incursion **1** *n* **raid**, night raid, attack, sortie, invasion, foray [➡ AGGRESSIVE EVENTS; 39] *Opposite*: retreat **2** *n* (*formal*) **intrusion**, invasion, spread, infiltration, movement, arrival, inroad [➡ ARRIVAL; 13]

incus *part of* **ear** [➡ THE EAR; 706]

in custody *n* **under arrest**, in prison, in detention, detained, remanded, arrested [➡ CAPTIVITY AND LOSS OF FREEDOM; 248]

in danger *adj* [➡ IN DANGER; 237]

in debit *adj* **in the red**, in debt, overdrawn, in arrears, insolvent [➡ POVERTY AND POOR; 892] *Opposite*: in credit

in debt *adj* **in the red**, overdrawn, insolvent, in arrears, owing money, in debit, bankrupt, broke (*informal*) [➡ POVERTY AND POOR; 892] *Opposite*: in credit

indebted *adj* **obligated**, obliged, grateful, thankful, in somebody's debt, beholden, owing a favor, appreciative [➡ APPRECIATION AND GRATITUDE; 535] *Opposite*: ungrateful

indebtedness *n* **obligation**, gratitude, appreciation, thankfulness, gratefulness, acknowledgement [➡ APPRECIATION AND GRATITUDE; 535] *Opposite*: ingratitude

indecency **1** *n* **offensiveness**, coarseness, crudeness, lewdness, obscenity, rudeness, filth, licentiousness (*formal*) [➡ MORALLY BAD OR IMPROPER; 775] *Opposite*: decency **2** *n* **impropriety**, unsuitability, unseemliness, indecorousness, indelicacy, inappropriateness [➡ INAPPROPRIATE AND UNSUITABLE; 224] *Opposite*: propriety

indecent **1** *adj* **offensive**, coarse, rude, crude, filthy, lewd, licentious [➡ MORALLY BAD OR IMPROPER; 775] *Opposite*: decorous **2** *adj* **improper**, unsuitable, unseemly, indecorous, unbecoming, indelicate, shocking, inappropriate [➡ INAPPROPRIATE AND UNSUITABLE; 224] *Opposite*: proper

indecipherable **1** *adj* **illegible**, incomprehensible, unintelligible, unreadable, indistinct, unclear [➡ DIFFICULTY AND COMPLEXITY; 242] *Opposite*: legible **2** *adj* **impenetrable**, inscrutable, obscure, unfathomable, enigmatic, cryptic, incomprehensible, unintelligible [➡ DIFFICULTY AND COMPLEXITY; 242] *Opposite*: clear

indecision *n* **irresolution**, hesitancy, indecisiveness, uncertainty, vacillation, wavering [➡ UNCERTAINTY; 559] *Opposite*: decisiveness

indecisive **1** *adj* **irresolute**, vacillating, wavering, hesitant, unsure, faltering, dithering, uncertain, of two minds [➡ NEGATIVE INTELLECTUAL CHARACTERISTICS; 525] *Opposite*: decisive **2** *adj* **inconclusive**, indefinite, indeterminate, tentative, unclear [➡ UNCERTAIN; 175] *Opposite*: conclusive

indecisively *adv* **irresolutely**, vacillatingly, waveringly, hesitantly, uncertainly, ditheringly [➡ NEGATIVE INTELLECTUAL CHARACTERISTICS; 525] *Opposite*: decisively

indecisiveness **1** *n* **irresolution**, hesitancy, hesitation, vacillation, uncertainty [➡ UNCERTAINTY; 559] *Opposite*: decisiveness **2** *n* **indefiniteness**, inconclusiveness, woolliness, vagueness, indeterminacy, tentativeness, unclearness, uncertainty [➡ UNCERTAIN; 175] *Opposite*: certainty

indecorous *adj* **impolite**, rude, shocking, inappropriate, unseemly, improper, undignified, ill-mannered [➡ BAD MANNERS AND SOCIAL SKILLS; 521] *Opposite*: polite

indecorousness *n* [➡ BAD MANNERS AND SOCIAL SKILLS; 521]

indecorum *n* **impoliteness**, bad behavior, rudeness, shockingness, offensiveness, impropriety, unseemliness, untowardness, solecism [➡ BAD MANNERS AND SOCIAL SKILLS; 521] *Opposite*: politeness

indeed **1** *adv* **certainly**, really, to be sure, undeniably, definitely, without a doubt, truly [➡ CERTAIN; 174] **2** *adv* **in reality**, in fact, actually, in truth, as a matter of fact, in actual fact, if truth be told [➡ WORDS AND PHRASES EMPHASIZING THE TRUTH OF A MATTER; 172]

in deep trouble *adj* [➡ IN TROUBLE AND DISADVANTAGED; 73]

in deep water *adj* [➡ IN TROUBLE AND DISADVANTAGED; 73]

indefatigable *adj* **untiring**, unflagging, unrelenting, remorseless, unfaltering, dogged, determined, inexorable (*formal*) [➡ STRENGTH OF WILL; 501] *Opposite*: half-hearted

indefensible **1** *adj* **inexcusable**, unpardonable, unforgivable, unjustifiable, unwarrantable, reprehensible, uncalled-for [➡ UNACCEPTABLE AND UNFORGIVABLE; 225] *Opposite*: excusable **2** *adj* **unprotected**, exposed, vulnerable, undefended, defenseless, unfortified, weak [➡ WEAKNESS; 241] *Opposite*: impregnable **3** *adj* **invalid**, untenable, unsustainable, shaky, weak, wrong [➡ MORALLY BAD OR IMPROPER; 775] *Opposite*: valid

indefensibly **1** *adv* **inexcusably**, unforgivably, unpardonably, unjustifiably, reprehensibly, shamefully [➡ UNACCEPTABLE AND UNFORGIVABLE; 225] *Opposite*: excusably **2** *adv* **invalidly**, untenably, unsustainably, shakily, weakly, wrongly [➡ IMPOSSIBLE AND IMPROBABLE; 178]

indefinable *adj* **indescribable**, inexpressible, vague, indefinite, obscure, impalpable (*formal*) [➡ VAGUENESS; 243]

indefinite **1** *adj* **unlimited**, unfixed, unspecified, unknown, indeterminate, open-ended, undefined, undetermined [➡ SECRET AND UNKNOWN; 179] *Opposite*: specified **2** *adj* **unclear**, imprecise, vague, hazy, woolly, indistinct, blurred [➡ VAGUENESS; 243] *Opposite*: precise **3** *adj* **vague**, uncertain, undecided, unclear, noncommittal, unsure [➡ UNCERTAIN; 175] *Opposite*: certain

indefinite article *type of* **word class** [➡ ASPECTS OF LANGUAGE; 682]

indefinitely *adv* **until further notice**, for the foreseeable future, for life, forever, ad infinitum, indeterminately, open-endedly [➡ PERMANENCE: WITHOUT END; 94]

indelible **1** *adj* **permanent**, fixed, ineradicable, fast, stubborn [➡ PERMANENCE: WITHOUT END; 94] *Opposite*: temporary **2** *adj* **unforgettable**, deep-seated, deep-rooted, lasting, enduring, ingrained [➡ PERMANENCE: WITHOUT END; 94] *Opposite*: temporary

indelibly *adv* **permanently**, ineradicably, lastingly, forever, for good, for always [➡ PERMANENCE: WITHOUT END; 94] *Opposite*: temporarily

indelicacy *n* **tactlessness**, offensiveness, tastelessness, crudeness, unseemliness, coarseness, impropriety, indecency, bad manners [➡ BAD MANNERS AND SOCIAL SKILLS; 521] *Opposite*: politeness

indelicate *adj* **tactless**, offensive, improper, unseemly, impolite, indecent, coarse, bad-mannered, crude [➡ BAD MANNERS AND SOCIAL SKILLS; 521] *Opposite*: polite

indelicateness *n* [➡ BAD MANNERS AND SOCIAL SKILLS; 521]

in demand *adj* [➡ POPULAR AND WANTED; 220]

indemnify **1** *v* **insure**, underwrite, cover, assure, protect, guarantee [➡ INSURANCE; 801] **2** *v* **reimburse**, compensate, repay, pay, refund, remunerate, settle [➡ GIVE MONEY; 433]

indemnity **1** *n* **insurance**, protection, cover, life insurance, security, guarantee, coverage, life assurance (*UK*) [➡ SAFE AND SAFETY; 191] **2** *n* **compensation**, reimbursement, remuneration, reparation, payment, repayment, settlement [➡ REWARDS AND AWARDS; 439]

indent **1** *v* **hollow out**, dent, depress, stave in, scoop, gouge, pockmark, pit [➡ CHANGE OF SHAPE; 385] **2** *v* **notch**, serrate, nick, pink, incise, score [➡ TEAR, BREAK, AND CUT; 360]

indentation **1** *n* **notch**, groove, serration, nick, incision [➡ HOLES, GAPS, AND FORKS; 1252] **2** *n* **hollow**, dent, depression, scoop, gouge, dimple, pockmark [➡ HOLES, GAPS, AND FORKS; 1252]

indenture *n* **contract**, arrangement, pact, deal, agreement, accord [➡ OFFICIAL DOCUMENTS; 586]

independence **1** *n* **self-sufficiency**, self-reliance, self-determination, freedom, autonomy, individualism [➡ RELATIONSHIP TO ANOTHER; 973] *Opposite*: helplessness **2** *n* **self-government**, sovereignty, autonomy, self-rule, self-determination, freedom, liberty [➡ FREEDOM AND LIBERTY; 208] *Opposite*: subjection **3** *n* **individuality**, freedom, liberation, unconventionality [➡ FREEDOM AND LIBERTY; 208] *Opposite*: conventionality **4** *n* **impartiality**, objectivity, disinterest, neutrality, disinterestedness, nonalignment [➡ NEUTRALITY AND INDIFFERENCE; 553] *Opposite*: partiality

independent **1** *adj* **self-governing**, sovereign, autonomous, self-determining, self-regulating, free, liberated [➡ FREEDOM AND LIBERTY; 208] *Opposite*: dependent **2** *adj* **self-sufficient**, self-reliant, autonomous, self-supporting, self-contained [➡ RELATIONSHIP TO ANOTHER; 973] *Opposite*: dependent **3** *adj* **free**, liberated, individual, individualistic, unconventional, unconstrained, unfettered [➡ FREEDOM AND LIBERTY; 208] *Opposite*: conventional **4** *adj* **impartial**, detached, objective, dispassionate, neutral, nonpartisan, unbiased, unprejudiced, nonaligned [➡ NEUTRALITY AND INDIFFERENCE; 553] *Opposite*: partial

independently **1** *adv* **sovereignly**, autonomously, freely [➡ FREEDOM AND LIBERTY; 208] **2** *adv* **self-sufficiently**, self-reliantly, autonomously [➡ ACTING INDEPENDENTLY; 284] *Opposite*: helplessly **3** *adv* **individualistically**, freely, individually, unconventionally [➡ FREEDOM AND LIBERTY; 208] *Opposite*: conventionally **4** *adv* **impartially**, detachedly, dispassionately, objectively, disinterestedly, neutrally [➡ NEUTRALITY AND INDIFFERENCE; 553] *Opposite*: partially

in depth *adv* **at length**, painstakingly, in detail, thoroughly, exhaustively, fully, comprehensively, profoundly, deeply, carefully [➡ WHOLENESS AND COMPLETENESS; 198] *Opposite*: superficially

in-depth *adj* **painstaking**, detailed, exhaustive, thorough, comprehensive, considered, full, profound, careful, deep, extensive, far-reaching [➡ WHOLENESS AND COMPLETENESS; 198] *Opposite*: superficial

indescribable **1** *adj* **indefinable**, inexpressible, unutterable, incommunicable, unspeakable, ineffable (*formal*) [➡ DIFFICULTY AND COMPLEXITY; 242] **2** *adj* **extreme**, great, tremendous, intense, dramatic, powerful [➡ EXTRAORDINARY: AMAZING; 204]

indescribably **1** *adv* **indefinably**, unspeakably, inexpressibly, unutterably, incommunicably, ineffably (*formal*) [➡ DIFFICULTY AND COMPLEXITY; 242] **2** *adv* **extremely**, greatly, tremendously, intensely, dramatically, powerfully [➡ TO A GREAT EXTENT; 132]

in despair adj [➡ SADNESS, DISTRESS, AND DESPAIR; 539]

indestructibility n [➡ DURABLE; 1210]

indestructible 1 adj **abiding**, durable, everlasting, imperishable, eternal, immortal, enduring, unyielding [➡ PERMANENCE: WITHOUT END; 94] Opposite: perishable 2 adj **unbreakable**, nonbreaking, resistant, shatterproof, rock-solid, reinforced, armored, durable [➡ DURABLE; 1210] Opposite: fragile

in detail adv **fully**, in depth, thoroughly, exhaustively, comprehensively, carefully, painstakingly, meticulously, scrupulously [➡ WHOLENESS AND COMPLETENESS; 198] Opposite: cursorily

indeterminable 1 adj **unknowable**, indefinable, indescribable, impalpable (formal) [➡ UNCERTAIN; 175] Opposite: knowable 2 adj **unresolvable**, unanswerable, uncountable [➡ VAGUENESS; 243] Opposite: answerable

indeterminacy n [➡ UNCERTAIN; 175]

indeterminate 1 adj **unknown**, unspecified, unstipulated, unstated, unclassified, uncategorized [➡ UNCERTAIN; 175] Opposite: known 2 adj **undefined**, vague, undetermined, indefinite, unfixed, imprecise, unclear, uncertain [➡ VAGUENESS; 243] Opposite: definite

indeterminately adv [➡ UNCERTAIN; 175]

index 1 n **catalog**, directory, guide, file, key, table [➡ LISTS AND SCHEDULES; 587] 2 n **indication**, indicator, symbol, pointer, sign, mark [➡ PERFECT EXAMPLES AND EMBODIMENTS; 67]

index finger part of **arm or hand** [➡ PARTS OF THE BODY: ARM AND HAND; 605]

Indiaman type of **historical vessel** [➡ SHIPS AND BOATS; 1150]

Indian summer n [➡ HOT WEATHER; 1050]

indicate 1 v **point to**, point toward, point at, show, point out, direct (formal) [➡ GESTURES AND GESTICULATION; 653] 2 v **denote**, signify, be a sign of, imply, suggest, hint at, show, reveal, be a symptom of, signpost (UK) [➡ MEAN SOMETHING; 61] 3 v (UK) **signal**, wink, flash [➡ LIGHT EMISSION; 368]

indication n **sign**, suggestion, signal, hint, warning, clue, symptom [➡ INDICATIONS, SIGNS, AND WARNINGS; 68]

indicative 1 adj **revealing**, symptomatic, telling, telltale, suggestive, symbolic [➡ REPRESENTATIVE; 66] 2 type of **grammatical term** [➡ ASPECTS OF LANGUAGE; 682]

indicator n **pointer**, needle, gauge, dial, display, meter [➡ PARTS OF MACHINES AND TOOLS; 1118]

indict v **accuse**, impeach, summons, prosecute, arraign, charge [➡ TRIAL, PUNISHMENT, AND LEGAL OUTCOMES; 819] Opposite: exonerate

indictable adj **criminal**, unlawful, illegal, chargeable, felonious, prosecutable [➡ ILLEGAL; 816]

indictment 1 n **accusation**, impeachment, summons, prosecution, arraignment, charge [➡ TRIAL, PUNISHMENT, AND LEGAL OUTCOMES; 819] Opposite: exoneration 2 n **condemnation**, denunciation, criticism, comment, censure, blame [➡ CRITICISMS AND ANGRY OUTBURSTS; 50] Opposite: praise

indie (informal) type of **rock music** [➡ MUSIC, SONGS, AND SINGING; 907]

indifference 1 n **apathy**, coldness, coolness, unconcern, disinterest, uninterest [➡ NEUTRALITY AND INDIFFERENCE; 553] Opposite: concern 2 n **unimportance**, insignificance, inconsequence, meaninglessness, irrelevance, triviality [➡ UNIMPORTANT AND UNNECESSARY; 238] Opposite: importance

indifferent 1 adj **uncaring**, uninterested, unresponsive, apathetic, unsympathetic, unconcerned, unmoved, cold, cool [➡ NEUTRALITY AND INDIFFERENCE; 553] Opposite: concerned 2 adj **average**, mediocre, moderate, undistinguished, middling, tolerable, fair, unexceptional, poor, so-so (informal) [➡ ORDINARINESS; 244] Opposite: exceptional

in difficulty adj [➡ IN TROUBLE AND DISADVANTAGED; 73]

indigence (formal) n **poverty**, need, penury, deprivation, destitution, impoverishment, pennilessness, impecuniousness (formal) [➡ POVERTY AND POOR; 892] Opposite: wealth

indigenous adj **native**, original, aboriginal, homegrown, local, ethnic [➡ COUNTRIES AND REGIONS; 1067] Opposite: immigrant

See Compare and Contrast at **native**.

indigent (formal) adj **poor**, needy, impoverished, poverty-stricken, penniless, destitute, impecunious, deprived, below the poverty line, penurious (literary) [➡ POVERTY AND POOR; 892] Opposite: wealthy

indigestible 1 adj **heavy**, rich, tough, inedible, stodgy (informal) [➡ FOOD; 1167] Opposite: edible 2 adj **incomprehensible**, impenetrable, unreadable, complex, obscure, dense, dry [➡ DIFFICULTY AND COMPLEXITY; 242] Opposite: readable

indigestion n **heartburn**, stomachache, upset stomach, colic, gastritis, dyspepsia [➡ DISORDERS OF THE DIGESTIVE SYSTEM; 713]

indignant adj **angry**, furious, vexed, irate, outraged, incensed, put out, annoyed, piqued, cross, in a huff (informal) [➡ IRRITATION AND ANGER; 541] Opposite: mollified

indignantly adv **angrily**, furiously, irately, heatedly, crossly, huffily [➡ IRRITATION AND ANGER; 541] Opposite: delightedly

indignation n **anger**, resentment, outrage, annoyance, crossness, exasperation, pique, irritation [➡ IRRITATION AND ANGER; 541] Opposite: delight

See Compare and Contrast at **anger**.

indignity n **humiliation**, shame, disgrace, mortification, embarrassment, ignominy, dishonor [➡ DIFFICULT SITUATIONS; 72] Opposite: glory

indigo type of **blue** [➡ COLORS; 1224]

indirect 1 adj **circuitous**, roundabout, rambling, circumlocutory, tortuous, meandering [➡ DIRECTION OF MOTION; 345] Opposite: straight 2 adj **unintended**, unplanned, secondary, ancillary, subsidiary, incidental, unforeseen [➡ UNPLANNED AND UNEXPECTED; 281] Opposite: intended 3 adj **devious**, oblique, implicit, tacit, implied, understood, inferred, hinted at [➡ RETICENT AND UNFORTHCOMING; 631] Opposite: overt

indirectly 1 adv **circuitously**, ramblingly, tortuously, meanderingly [➡ DIRECTION OF MOTION; 345] Opposite: straight 2 adv **incidentally**, secondarily, subsidiarily [➡ UNPLANNED AND UNEXPECTED; 281] 3 adv **deviously**, obliquely, implicitly, tacitly, subtly, tactfully, subliminally [➡RETICENT AND UNFORTHCOMING; 631] *Opposite:* overtly

in dire straits *adj* **in difficulties**, in extremis, in a tight spot, in trouble, in hot water, in a jam (*informal*), in a fix (*informal*), up the creek (*informal*), in the soup (*informal*) [➡IN TROUBLE AND DISADVANTAGED; 73]

in disarray *adj* **confused**, in a mess, chaotic, in pieces, in a jumble, in a muddle, untidy, disorganized, disordered, all over the place (*informal*) [➡DISORDER AND CHAOS; 245] *Opposite:* orderly

in disbelief *adj* **incredulous**, disbelieving, unbelieving, shocked, dumbfounded [➡SURPRISE, SHOCK, AND AMAZEMENT; 545]

indiscernibility *n* [➡IMPERCEPTIBLE; 26]

indiscernible *adj* **imperceptible**, invisible, inaudible, unnoticeable, unfathomable, undetectable, impalpable (*formal*) [➡IMPERCEPTIBLE; 26] *Opposite:* perceptible

indiscipline *n* **disorderliness**, rowdiness, unruliness, insubordination, disruptiveness [➡REBELLIOUSNESS AND DISOBEDIENCE; 565] *Opposite:* control

indiscreet 1 *adj* **careless**, injudicious, imprudent, incautious, unthinking, reckless, rash [➡INCAUTIOUS AND CARELESS; 283] *Opposite:* careful 2 *adj* **tactless**, undiplomatic, unsubtle, garrulous, indelicate [➡BAD MANNERS AND SOCIAL SKILLS; 521] *Opposite:* tactful

indiscretion 1 *n* **carelessness**, injudiciousness, imprudence, lack of caution, recklessness, rashness, incaution, thoughtlessness, unthinkingness [➡NEGATIVE INTELLECTUAL CHARACTERISTICS; 525] *Opposite:* carefulness 2 *n* **tactlessness**, garrulousness, indelicateness, nosiness (*informal*) [➡NOSY AND INTERFERING; 512] 3 *n* **transgression**, impropriety, peccadillo, misdemeanor, misdeed, lapse, folly, blunder, gaffe, slip, faux pas (*literary*) [➡BAD BEHAVIOR OR ACTIONS; 254]

indiscriminate 1 *adj* **unselective**, undiscriminating, undiscerning, undifferentiating, uncritical, catholic [➡NEGATIVE INTELLECTUAL CHARACTERISTICS; 525] *Opposite:* selective 2 *adj* **haphazard**, random, arbitrary, wholesale, blanket, unsystematic [➡DISORDER AND CHAOS; 245] *Opposite:* planned

in disgrace *adj* [➡IN TROUBLE AND DISADVANTAGED; 73]

indispensable *adj* **necessary**, essential, crucial, vital, required, obligatory, imperative, key [➡NECESSARY AND ESSENTIAL; 196] *Opposite:* unnecessary

See Compare and Contrast at **necessary.**

indispensably *adv* **necessarily**, essentially, crucially, vitally, imperatively, obligatorily [➡NECESSARY AND ESSENTIAL; 196] *Opposite:* unnecessarily

indisposed (*formal*) 1 *adj* **sick**, unwell, ill, laid up, under the weather [➡ILL AND SICK; 740] *Opposite:* well 2 *adj* **unwilling**, disinclined, reluctant, loath, loth [➡UNWILLINGNESS AND STUBBORNNESS; 564] *Opposite:* willing

indisposition 1 *n* **illness**, complaint, condition, problem, debility, sickness [➡ILL AND SICK; 740] *Opposite:* health 2 *n* **reluctance**, unwillingness, disinclination, refusal, resistance [➡UNWILLINGNESS AND STUBBORNNESS; 564] *Opposite:* willingness

indisputability *n* [➡CERTAIN; 174]

indisputable *adj* **indubitable**, unquestionable, undeniable, beyond doubt, incontrovertible, irrefutable, certain, unarguable, incontestable [➡CERTAIN; 174] *Opposite:* debatable

indissoluble *adj* **binding**, unbreakable, enduring, everlasting, eternal, permanent [➡PERMANENCE: WITHOUT END; 94] *Opposite:* temporary

indistinct 1 *adj* **unclear**, blurry, hazy, dim, misty, inaudible, inarticulate, slurred, faint, muffled, low, mumbled, soft [➡IMPERCEPTIBLE; 26] *Opposite:* clear 2 *adj* **vague**, imprecise, indistinguishable, indefinite, unintelligible [➡VAGUENESS; 243] *Opposite:* definite

indistinctive *adj* **ordinary**, dull, everyday, unexceptional, unmemorable, undistinguished, unidentified, unspecified [➡BORING AND UNINTERESTING; 234] *Opposite:* unique

indistinctness 1 *n* **unclearness**, inarticulacy, faintness, softness [➡VAGUENESS; 243] *Opposite:* clarity 2 *n* **blurriness**, haziness, fuzziness, mistiness, dimness, faintness, imprecision, indefiniteness, inaudibility, unintelligibility [➡IMPERCEPTIBLE; 26] *Opposite:* clarity

indistinguishable 1 *adj* **undifferentiated**, homogeneous, identical, the same, interchangeable, like two peas in a pod [➡SAMENESS; 150] *Opposite:* separable 2 *adj* **vague**, blurry, hazy, fuzzy, misty, dim, faint [➡VAGUENESS; 243] *Opposite:* clear 3 *adj* **inaudible**, inarticulate, unintelligible, faint, soft, low [➡IMPERCEPTIBLE; 26] *Opposite:* clear

indistinguishably *adv* [➡IMPERCEPTIBLE; 26]

in distress *adj* [➡SADNESS, DISTRESS, AND DESPAIR; 539]

individual 1 *n* **person**, human being, entity, character, personality, being, creature, personage (*formal*), party (*formal*) [➡PERSON; 931] 2 *adj* **separable**, singular, separate, discrete, distinct, single, specific, different [➡UNRELATEDNESS AND SEPARATENESS; 146] 3 *adj* **particularized**, special, private, exclusive, particular, specific, personal [➡BELONGING OR RELATING TO INDIVIDUALS; 944] *Opposite:* collective 4 *adj* **unusual**, distinctive, original, idiosyncratic, individualistic, characteristic, peculiar, unique, singular, personal [➡EXTRAORDINARY: UNCOMMON; 205] *Opposite:* ordinary

individualism *n* **uniqueness**, egoism, individuality, independence, selfishness, distinctiveness, eccentricity [➡UNRELATEDNESS AND SEPARATENESS; 146] *Opposite:* conformity

individualist *n* **free spirit**, nonconformist, eccentric, rebel, maverick, loner [➡SOLITARY PEOPLE AND MISFITS; 942] *Opposite:* conformist

individuality *n* **independence**, uniqueness, eccentricity, personality, distinctiveness, originality, individualism [➡UNRELATEDNESS AND SEPARATENESS; 146] *Opposite:* conformity

individualize *v* **adapt**, modify, customize, personalize, convert, change, tailor, adjust [➡CHANGE; 372]

individually *adv* **separately**, independently, alone, on your own, by yourself, in isolation, exclusively, discretely [➡ACTING INDEPENDENTLY; 284] *Opposite:* together

indivisible *adj* **inseparable**, undividable, united, amalgamated, blended, conjoined (*formal*) [➡RELATED; 142] *Opposite:* separable

indoctrinate *v* **instruct**, program, train, teach, coach, brainwash, proselytize, propagandize [➡ INSTRUCT AND TEACH; 609]

indoctrination *n* **instruction**, programming, propaganda, brainwashing, training, teaching, coaching, proselytization [➡ TEACHING; 839]

indolence *n* **laziness**, idleness, lethargy, sloth, inactivity, torpor, lassitude, apathy, sluggishness [➡ LIFELESS, LAZY, AND UNENTHUSIASTIC; 506] *Opposite*: energy

indolent *adj* **lazy**, lethargic, idle, sluggish, slothful, apathetic, torpid, lax, languid, laid-back (*informal*) [➡ LIFELESS, LAZY, AND UNENTHUSIASTIC; 506] *Opposite*: energetic

indomitability *n* [➡ STRENGTH OF WILL; 501]

indomitable *adj* **unconquerable**, strong, resolute, determined, stubborn, tough, spirited, invincible, steadfast, staunch, doughty (*archaic*) [➡ STRENGTH OF WILL; 501] *Opposite*: submissive

indoor *adj* **inside**, interior, covered, enclosed, internal [➡ GENERAL LOCATIONS; 158] *Opposite*: outdoor

indoors *adv* **inside**, in, within, at home, in the house [➡ GENERAL LOCATIONS; 158] *Opposite*: outside

in doubt *adj* **open to question**, in question, undecided, doubtful, dubious, unresolved, insecure, at risk, uncertain [➡ UNCERTAIN; 175] *Opposite*: assured

See Compare and Contrast at **doubtful**.

indubitable *adj* **unquestionable**, definite, certain, positive, concrete, undoubted, undeniable, conclusive, irrefutable, sure-fire (*informal*) [➡ CERTAIN; 174] *Opposite*: questionable

induce 1 *v* **persuade**, encourage, tempt, make, bring, talk into, prevail upon, convince, prompt [➡ CAUSE OR COMPEL TO ACT; 271] *Opposite*: dissuade 2 *v* **bring on**, bring about, provoke, stimulate, produce, cause, generate, engender [➡ CAUSE TO HAPPEN; 31] *Opposite*: deter

inducement *n* **stimulus**, incentive, encouragement, carrot, enticement, bribe, lure, bait [➡ BRIBES; 440] *Opposite*: disincentive

See Compare and Contrast at **motive**.

induct 1 *v* **inaugurate**, swear in, initiate, welcome, receive, instate, install, invest (*formal*) [➡ CONFER STATUS; 458] 2 *v* **introduce**, initiate, train, instruct, educate, acquaint [➡ INSTRUCT AND TEACH; 609]

induction 1 *n* **introduction**, initiation, training, instruction, orientation, education [➡ TEACHING; 839] 2 *n* **inauguration**, investiture, reception, installment, swearing in [➡ CEREMONIES AND ANNIVERSARIES; 38] 3 *n* **bringing on**, stimulation, generation, production, provocation, initiation, bringing about, setting off [➡ BEGINNINGS; 53]

in due course *adv* **afterward**, eventually, in good time, ultimately, in the end, sooner or later, finally, in a while, later [➡ FUTURE; 86]

indulge *v* **treat**, spoil, pamper, pander, cosset, make a fuss of, coddle, humor [➡ TAKE CARE OF AND SPOIL; 300] *Opposite*: deny

indulgence 1 *n* **treat**, luxury, extravagance, pleasure [➡ AMAZING THINGS; 211] *Opposite*: necessity 2 *n* **tolerance**, lenience, understanding, clemency, sympathy, pardon, absolution, leniency, forbearance (*formal*) [➡ KIND ACTIONS OR BEHAVIOR; 295] *Opposite*: strictness

indulgent *adj* **permissive**, kind, lenient, tolerant, generous, nonjudgmental, easygoing, understanding, forbearing (*formal*) [➡ GENEROSITY AND KINDNESS; 495] *Opposite*: strict

Indus *type of* **constellation** [➡ HEAVENLY BODIES; 1061]

industrial 1 *adj* **manufacturing**, engineering, trade, business, work [➡ BUSINESS; 791] 2 *adj* **developed**, built-up, industrialized, mechanized, manufacturing, modern [➡ DESCRIBING TECHNOLOGY; 1160]

industrial action (*UK*) *n* **strike**, stoppage, job action, slowdown, lightning strike, general strike, wildcat strike, work-to-rule (*UK*), go-slow (*UK*) [➡ WORK-RELATED ACTIVITIES; 834]

industrial espionage *n* **espionage**, spying, intelligence gathering, surveillance, bugging, phone tapping [➡ BUSINESS ACTIVITIES AND PHENOMENA; 794]

industrial estate (*UK*) *n* **industrial zone**, enterprise zone, business park, industrial development, science park, development, industrial park, trading estate (*UK*) [➡ URBAN OUTDOOR SPACES; 1072]

industrialist *n* **manufacturer**, entrepreneur, businessperson, factory owner, capitalist, owner, mogul [➡ BUSINESS PEOPLE; 793]

industrialization *n* **industrial development**, economic development, development, economic growth, progress, social change, mechanization, mass production, automation [➡ SOCIAL, POLITICAL, AND ECONOMIC CHANGE; 373]

industrialize *v* **change**, mechanize, develop, mass-produce, automate [➡ SOCIAL, POLITICAL, AND ECONOMIC CHANGE; 373]

industrialized *adj* **industrial**, developed, technologically advanced, manufacturing, commercial [➡ STYLES AND SYSTEMS OF GOVERNMENT; 806] *Opposite*: agrarian

industrial park *n* **industrial zone**, enterprise zone, business park, industrial development, science park, development, industrial estate (*UK*), trading estate (*UK*) [➡ INDUSTRIAL BUILDINGS; 1087]

industrial site *n* [➡ INDUSTRIAL BUILDINGS; 1087]

industrial site

◆ *types of industrial sites*
business park, coalfield, coalmine, colliery, depot, dock, dockyard, enterprise zone, garage, gasworks, industrial park, industrial zone, lab (*informal*), laboratory, mine, nuclear power plant, nuclear reprocessing plant, office block, oil rig, pit, pithead, power plant, quarry, refinery, rig, shipyard, slaughterhouse, tannery, winery

industrial tribunal (*UK*) *n* **tribunal**, hearing, court, law court, magistrates' court, high court [➡ TRIAL, PUNISHMENT, AND LEGAL OUTCOMES; 819]

industrial unit *n* [➡ INDUSTRIAL BUILDINGS; 1087]

industrial zone *type of* **industrial site** [➡ INDUSTRIAL BUILDINGS; 1087]

industrious *adj* **diligent**, hard-working, busy, productive, conscientious, active, assiduous, energetic, bustling [➡ HARD-WORKING AND COMMITTED; 500] *Opposite:* indolent

industriousness *n* **diligence**, hard work, application, conscientiousness, productiveness, energy, industry (*formal or literary*) [➡ HARD-WORKING AND COMMITTED; 500] *Opposite:* indolence

industry 1 *n* **manufacturing**, business, commerce, trade, engineering, production [➡ BUSINESS; 791] 2 *n* (*formal or literary*) **hard work**, diligence, productiveness, conscientiousness, activity, industriousness [➡ HARD-WORKING AND COMMITTED; 500] *Opposite:* indolence

in earnest *adv* **genuinely**, seriously, sincerely, earnestly, for real, passionately, intensely, wholeheartedly [➡ TRUE AND REAL; 171] *Opposite:* jokingly

in easy reach *adv* [➡ CLOSENESS; 159]

inebriated *adj* **drunk**, intoxicated, liquored up (*informal*), plastered (*informal*), smashed (*informal*), under the influence (*informal*), wasted (*slang*), bombed (*slang*), stewed (*slang*), loaded (*slang*), tanked (*slang*), sloshed (*slang*), soused (*slang*), crocked (*slang*) [➡ UNDER THE INFLUENCE OF DRUGS OR ALCOHOL; 741] *Opposite:* sober

inebriation *n* [➡ UNDER THE INFLUENCE OF DRUGS OR ALCOHOL; 741]

inedible *adj* **uneatable**, indigestible, unpalatable, revolting, bad, disgusting, poisonous, unfit for human consumption, noxious, tough as old boots (*UK*) [➡ FOOD; 1167] *Opposite:* edible

ineffable (*formal*) *adj* **indescribable**, inexpressible, unutterable, beyond words, overwhelming, deep, unspeakable, indefinable [➡ EXTRAORDINARY: AMAZING; 204]

in effect *adv* **basically**, essentially, in fact, effectively, to all intents and purposes, really, actually [➡ TRUE AND REAL; 171]

ineffective *adj* **unsuccessful**, unproductive, useless, vain, futile, hopeless, fruitless, ineffectual, abortive, feeble [➡ REDUNDANT AND USELESS; 240] *Opposite:* successful

ineffectiveness *n* **unsuccessfulness**, unproductiveness, uselessness, futility, hopelessness, vanity, feebleness [➡ REDUNDANT AND USELESS; 240] *Opposite:* success

ineffectual *adj* **incompetent**, indecisive, weak, feeble, unimpressive, unsuccessful, useless, hopeless, inadequate, inefficient, inept, fruitless [➡ NEGATIVE INTELLECTUAL CHARACTERISTICS; 525] *Opposite:* competent

ineffectuality *n* **incompetence**, indecisiveness, futility, fruitlessness, inadequacy, uselessness, feebleness, hopelessness, inefficiency, ineptness [➡ NEGATIVE INTELLECTUAL CHARACTERISTICS; 525] *Opposite:* competence

ineffectualness *n* [➡ NEGATIVE INTELLECTUAL CHARACTERISTICS; 525]

inefficiency *n* **disorganization**, incompetence, inadequacy, wastefulness, ineptitude, ineffectiveness, uselessness [➡ WASTEFUL AND UNECONOMICAL; 246] *Opposite:* competence

inefficient *adj* **disorganized**, unproductive, wasteful, inept, useless, uneconomical, incompetent, ineffective,

bungling (*informal*) [➡ WASTEFUL AND UNECONOMICAL; 246] *Opposite:* competent

inelastic *adj* **inflexible**, rigid, unbendable, stiff, unyielding, hard, brittle [➡ RIGID AND HARD; 1211] *Opposite:* stretchy

inelegance 1 *n* **unstylishness**, unsophistication, tastelessness, bad taste, vulgarity [➡ IN POOR TASTE AND OVERSENTIMENTAL; 229] *Opposite:* stylishness 2 *n* **clumsiness**, awkwardness, gracelessness, coarseness, roughness, uncouthness, gawkiness (*informal*) [➡ AGILITY OF THE BODY; 476] *Opposite:* grace

inelegant 1 *adj* **unstylish**, unsophisticated, tasteless, vulgar, unpolished [➡ IN POOR TASTE AND OVERSENTIMENTAL; 229] *Opposite:* stylish 2 *adj* **clumsy**, awkward, ungainly, maladroit, graceless, splay, uncouth, gawky (*informal*) [➡ AGILITY OF THE BODY; 476] *Opposite:* graceful

ineligible *adj* **unentitled**, unqualified, disqualified, barred, disallowed, unable, not qualified, banned [➡ REFUSE PERMISSION AND NOT ALLOW; 670] *Opposite:* entitled

ineluctable (*literary*) *adj* **unavoidable**, inescapable, inevitable, unpreventable, certain, sure, inexorable (*formal*) [➡ CERTAIN; 174] *Opposite:* avoidable

inept *adj* **incompetent**, inexpert, clumsy, maladroit, useless, hopeless, unskilled, heavy-handed, ham-fisted (*informal*), bungling (*informal*), ham-handed (*informal*) [➡ UNSKILLED; 529] *Opposite:* competent

ineptitude *n* **incompetence**, ineptness, clumsiness, uselessness, ineffectiveness, lack of ability, lack of skill, maladroitness (*formal*) [➡ UNSKILLED; 529] *Opposite:* competence

ineptness *n* **incompetence**, clumsiness, uselessness, ineffectiveness, lack of ability, lack of skill, ineptitude, maladroitness (*formal*) [➡ UNSKILLED; 529] *Opposite:* competence

inequality *n* **disparity**, dissimilarity, variation, difference, discrimination, inequity, disproportion, imbalance, unfairness [➡ DIFFERENCE; 149] *Opposite:* parity

inequitable *adj* **unfair**, unjust, unbalanced, undemocratic, unequal, discriminatory, prejudiced, biased [➡ MORALLY BAD OR IMPROPER; 775] *Opposite:* fair

inequity (*formal*) *n* **unfairness**, injustice, discrimination, inequality, bias, disproportion, imbalance [➡ MORALLY BAD OR IMPROPER; 775] *Opposite:* fairness

ineradicable *adj* **indelible**, enduring, lasting, ingrained, stubborn, deep-seated, unforgettable, deep-rooted, permanent, ineffaceable (*formal*) [➡ PERMANENCE: WITHOUT END; 94] *Opposite:* fleeting

inert 1 *adj* **motionless**, still, lifeless, immobile, unmoving, static [➡ LACK OF ACTIVITY OR MOTION; 342] *Opposite:* moving 2 *adj* **sluggish**, unmotivated, slow, inactive, passive, torpid, indolent, lethargic, phlegmatic, stolid, unwilling [➡ LIFELESS, LAZY, AND UNENTHUSIASTIC; 506] *Opposite:* active

inert gas *type of* **gas** [➡ GASES; 1275]

inertia *n* **apathy**, inactivity, torpor, lethargy, inaction, indolence, sluggishness, unwillingness [➡ LACK OF ACTIVITY OR MOTION; 342] *Opposite:* activity

inescapable *adj* **inevitable**, unavoidable, bound to happen, certain, unpreventable, patent, manifest, obvious, inexorable (*formal*) [➡ CERTAIN; 174] *Opposite*: avoidable

in essence *adv* **fundamentally**, intrinsically, basically, essentially, at heart, inherently, quintessentially, in reality, in effect, really, to all intents and purposes [➡ MAINLY AND PRIMARILY; 140]

inessential *adj* **unnecessary**, unneeded, superfluous, redundant, dispensable, extra, surplus [➡ UNIMPORTANT AND UNNECESSARY; 238] *Opposite*: necessary

inestimable *adj* **incalculable**, immeasurable, great, fathomless, enormous, invaluable, infinite, tremendous [➡ LARGE; 1193] *Opposite*: measurable

inestimably *adv* **incalculably**, immeasurably, enormously, immensely, tremendously, infinitely [➡ TO A GREAT EXTENT; 132] *Opposite*: measurably

in evidence *adj* [➡ PRESENT AND AVAILABLE; 11]

inevitability *n* **unavoidability**, predictability, certainty, inescapability, irrevocability, inexorableness (*formal*) [➡ CERTAIN; 174]

inevitable *adj* **unavoidable**, predictable, expected, foreseeable, to be expected, to be anticipated, certain, inescapable, preordained, inexorable (*formal*) [➡ CERTAIN; 174] *Opposite*: avoidable

inevitably *adv* **unavoidably**, inescapably, without doubt, certainly, predictably, unsurprisingly, inexorably (*formal*) [➡ CERTAIN; 174]

inexact *adj* **imprecise**, inaccurate, vague, rough, approximate, indefinite, indistinct [➡ APPROXIMATELY; 135] *Opposite*: precise

inexactness *n* **imprecision**, vagueness, uncertainty, roughness, approximation, inaccuracy, indefiniteness [➡ VAGUENESS; 243] *Opposite*: precision

in excess of *prep* **more than**, beyond, above, over and above, exceeding, greater than [➡ MORE AND EXCESS; 124] *Opposite*: below

inexcusable *adj* **unpardonable**, unforgivable, uncalled-for, intolerable, indefensible, unjustifiable, unwarrantable, rude, impolite [➡ UNACCEPTABLE AND UNFORGIVABLE; 225] *Opposite*: excusable

inexhaustible *adj* **everlasting**, infinite, unlimited, never-ending, bottomless, endless, limitless, vast, boundless [➡ MANY, MUCH, LARGE AMOUNT; 117] *Opposite*: limited

in existence *adj* [➡ PRESENT AND AVAILABLE; 11]

inexorability (*formal*) *n* **inevitability**, unavoidability, inescapability, relentlessness, certainty, obdurateness, inflexibility, inexorableness (*formal*) [➡ CERTAIN; 174]

inexorable 1 *adj* (*formal*) **unstoppable**, inevitable, unavoidable, inescapable, unchangeable, relentless, inflexible [➡ CERTAIN; 174] 2 *adj* **adamant**, obstinate, obdurate, unyielding, unbending, unwavering, immovable, stubborn [➡ UNWILLINGNESS AND STUBBORNNESS; 564]

inexorableness (*formal*) *n* **unavoidability**, inescapability, relentlessness, inevitability, certainty, obdurateness, inflexibility, inexorability (*formal*) [➡ CERTAIN; 174]

inexorably (*formal*) *adv* **inevitably**, inescapably, relentlessly, unavoidably, unalterably, adamantly, unstoppably, obdurately [➡ CERTAIN; 174]

inexpedient 1 *adj* **inconvenient**, impractical, inopportune, untimely, ill-timed [➡ PROMPTNESS: BADLY TIMED; 101] *Opposite*: convenient 2 *adj* (*formal*) **inadvisable**, inappropriate, unwise, unsuitable, injudicious, ill-judged, imprudent [➡ INAPPROPRIATE AND UNSUITABLE; 224] *Opposite*: advisable

inexpensive *adj* **cheap**, low-cost, low-priced, economical, budget, reasonable, cheapo (*informal*) [➡ CHEAP AND INEXPENSIVE; 221] *Opposite*: costly

inexperience *n* **greenness**, rawness, innocence, immaturity, naiveté, ingenuousness, unsophistication, amateurishness [➡ UNSKILLED; 529] *Opposite*: experience

inexperienced *adj* **green**, inexpert, raw, new, innocent, untried, untested, unproven, unsophisticated, amateurish, naive [➡ UNSKILLED; 529] *Opposite*: seasoned

inexpert *adj* **unskilled**, clumsy, inept, inexperienced, untrained, unprofessional, awkward, amateurish, hamfisted (*informal*), bungling (*informal*), ham-handed (*informal*) [➡ UNSKILLED; 529] *Opposite*: skilled

inexplicable *adj* **unaccountable**, mysterious, incomprehensible, unfathomable, bizarre, curious, strange, perplexing, mystifying, puzzling, baffling, enigmatic [➡ BIZARRE AND PECULIAR; 257] *Opposite*: explicable

inexplicit *adj* **imprecise**, vague, ambiguous, hazy, sketchy, indistinct, impressionistic, fuzzy, indefinite [➡ VAGUENESS; 243] *Opposite*: precise

inexpressible *adj* **indescribable**, beyond words, overwhelming, deep, indefinable, unutterable, unspeakable, ineffable (*formal*) [➡ EXTRAORDINARY: AMAZING; 204]

inexpressive *adj* **emotionless**, impassive, soulless, deadpan, unemotional, expressionless, blank, wooden, flat, bland [➡ UNINTERESTED AND DETACHED; 629] *Opposite*: animated

inextinguishable *adj* [➡ PERMANENCE: WITHOUT END; 94]

in extremis 1 *adj* **in trouble**, in difficulty, in distress, struggling, failing, in the soup (*informal*), up the creek (*informal*) [➡ IN TROUBLE AND DISADVANTAGED; 73] 2 *adj* **critical**, dire, near-death, dying, at death's door, moribund [➡ DEAD AND DYING; 925] *Opposite*: alive and kicking (*informal*)

inextricable *adj* **complicated**, complex, tricky, involved, knotty, tangled, indissoluble, inseparable, indivisible [➡ DIFFICULTY AND COMPLEXITY; 242] *Opposite*: simple

inextricably *adv* **indissolubly**, inseparably, indistinguishably, intimately, indivisibly, intricately [➡ RECIPROCITY AND INTERDEPENDENCE; 147]

in fact 1 *adv* **actually**, in actual fact, in effect, in reality, really, in truth, indeed [➡ WORDS AND PHRASES EMPHASIZING THE TRUTH OF A MATTER; 172] 2 *adv* **truthfully**, actually, in effect, in reality, really, as a matter of fact, in point of fact [➡ TRUE AND REAL; 171]

infallibility 1 *n* **dependability**, soundness, reliability, trustworthiness, steadiness, solidity, sureness [➡ CERTAIN; 174] *Opposite*: fallibility 2 *n* **perfection**, rightness, flawlessness, correctness, exactitude, accuracy [➡ CORRECT AND FAULTLESS; 182] *Opposite*: inaccuracy

infallible 1 *adj* **dependable**, unfailing, foolproof, watertight, reliable, sound, fail-safe, trustworthy, steady, solid, sure, certain, sure-fire (*informal*) [➡ CERTAIN; 174] *Opposite*: unreliable **2** *adj* **perfect**, right, flawless, correct, exact, accurate, faultless, unerring, unfailing [➡ CORRECT AND FAULTLESS; 182] *Opposite*: imperfect

infallibly *adv* **dependably**, unfailingly, without fail, reliably, always, perfectly, unerringly, faultlessly [➡ CERTAIN; 174] *Opposite*: unreliably

infamous 1 *adj* **notorious**, disreputable, ill-famed, ill-reputed, dishonorable, scandalous, shameful [➡ KNOWN AND FAMOUS; 181] *Opposite*: reputable **2** *adj* **abominable**, villainous, wicked, iniquitous, loathsome, outrageous, evil, shameful, nefarious, ignoble, heinous [➡ MORALLY BAD OR IMPROPER; 775] *Opposite*: illustrious

infamy 1 *n* **notoriety**, ill repute, ill fame, shame, disrepute, ignominy, dishonor [➡ KNOWN AND FAMOUS; 181] *Opposite*: repute (*formal*) **2** *n* **disgrace**, scandal, outrage, abomination, atrocity, villainy [➡ BAD BEHAVIOR OR ACTIONS; 254] *Opposite*: good deed

infancy 1 *n* **babyhood**, childhood, early years, youth, immaturity, early life, formative years [➡ BABYHOOD, CHILDHOOD, AND ADOLESCENCE; 917] *Opposite*: adulthood **2** *n* **beginning**, early stages, embryonic stage, initial stages, first phase, start [➡ BEGINNINGS; 53] *Opposite*: conclusion

infant *n* **baby**, child, newborn, babe in arms, toddler, preschooler, nursling, suckling, tot (*informal*), kid (*informal*) [➡ CHILD OR YOUTH; 945] *Opposite*: adult

infantile 1 *adj* **childish**, babyish, immature, puerile, juvenile, silly [➡ BAD MANNERS AND SOCIAL SKILLS; 521] *Opposite*: mature **2** *adj* **childhood**, juvenile, infant, baby, youthful [➡ BABYHOOD, CHILDHOOD, AND ADOLESCENCE; 917] *Opposite*: adult

infantry *n* [➡ THE ARMED FORCES; 827]

infatuated *adj* **in love**, lovesick, obsessed, besotted, captivated, enamored, enchanted, crazy about (*informal*), enraptured (*formal*), smitten (*humorous or literary*) [➡ APPRECIATION AND GRATITUDE; 535] *Opposite*: disenchanted

infatuation *n* **passion**, obsession, craze, love, fascination, fixation, rapture, enchantment, crush (*informal*) [➡ FADS, FETISHES, AND IDOLATRY; 555] *Opposite*: disenchantment

See Compare and Contrast at **love**.

in favor *adj* [➡ APPRECIATION AND GRATITUDE; 535]

in favor of *prep* **for**, all for, supporting, on the side of, supportive of, in support of, pro, with, rooting for [➡ LIKE, LOVE, VALUE, AND ENJOY; 578] *Opposite*: against

infect 1 *v* **contaminate**, pollute, taint, poison, blight, dirty [➡ DIRTY AND CONTAMINATE; 404] *Opposite*: cleanse **2** *v* **pervert**, corrupt, deprave, debase, defile (*formal*), debauch (*formal*) [➡ WORSEN SOMETHING; 380] *Opposite*: redeem **3** *v* **influence**, affect, afflict, touch, inspire, move, overwhelm, enthuse [➡ APPEAL TO AND AROUSE INTEREST; 575]

infected 1 *adj* **contaminated**, polluted, tainted, poisoned, impure, diseased, dirty, blighted [➡ DECAYING OR INFESTED; 1236] *Opposite*: pure **2** *adj* **ill**, diseased, sick, infested, disease-ridden, plague-ridden [➡ ILL AND SICK; 740] *Opposite*: healthy

3 *adj* **septic**, festering, weeping, pus-filled, purulent, suppurating, pussy (*UK*) [➡ DECAYING OR INFESTED; 1236] *Opposite*: healthy **4** *adj* **affected**, influenced, touched, inspired, moved, overwhelmed, enthused [➡ PLEASURE, EXCITEMENT, AND ELATION; 534] *Opposite*: untouched

infection 1 *n* **contagion**, contamination, pollution, taint, poison, impurity, dirt, septicity, toxicity [➡ DIRTY AND CONTAMINATE; 404] **2** *n* **disease**, illness, virus, blight, bug (*informal*), pestilence (*archaic*) [➡ ILLNESSES AND DISORDERS; 732] **3** *n* **corruption**, perversion, depravity, debasement, debauchery, defilement (*formal*) [➡ MORALLY BAD OR IMPROPER; 775]

infectious 1 *adj* **communicable**, catching, transferable, transmittable, transmissible, contagious, infective, virulent, catchable [➡ SICKNESS; 729] **2** *adj* **irresistible**, compelling, catching, contagious [➡ INTERESTING AND MEANINGFUL; 190]

infective *adj* **infectious**, communicable, catching, transferable, transmittable, transmissible, virulent, catchable, contagious [➡ SICKNESS; 729]

infer 1 *v* **conclude**, deduce, suppose, gather, understand, conjecture, surmise, assume, extrapolate, reckon, reason, judge, work out, figure out [➡ SOLVE AND INTERPRET; 760] *Opposite*: guess **2** *v* **imply**, suggest, insinuate, hint [➡ SUGGEST, HINT, AND COMMENT; 612]

See Compare and Contrast at **deduce**.

inference 1 *n* **implication**, extrapolation, corollary, interpretation, reading, insinuation [➡ SUGGEST, HINT, AND COMMENT; 612] **2** *n* **conclusion**, deduction, supposition, conjecture, presumption, assumption, reasoning, reckoning, judgement [➡ IDEAS AND THOUGHTS; 770] *Opposite*: guess

inferior 1 *adj* **mediocre**, lesser, lower, substandard, poorer, low-grade, second-rate, not up to snuff (*informal*) [➡ INFERIORITY; 153] *Opposite*: superior **2** *adj* **lower**, junior, secondary, subordinate, subsidiary, minor, subservient [➡ RELATIONSHIP TO ANOTHER; 973] *Opposite*: superior **3** *n* **junior**, subordinate, underling, vassal, menial (*formal*), minion (*archaic or literary*) [➡ SUBORDINATES AND ASSISTANTS; 966] *Opposite*: superior

inferiority 1 *n* **mediocrity**, weakness, inadequacy, shoddiness, meanness, poor quality [➡ FAULTS, FLAWS, AND WEAKNESSES; 251] *Opposite*: superiority **2** *n* **lowliness**, humbleness, subordination, subservience, subsidiarity, dependency [➡ INFERIORITY; 153] *Opposite*: superiority

inferiority complex *n* **inadequacy**, anxiety, phobia, depression, obsession, fixation, neurosis (*dated*) [➡ PSYCHOLOGY AND THE MIND; 769]

inferno 1 *n* **conflagration**, blaze, fire, firestorm, flames, oven, furnace [➡ FIRE, FLAMMABILITY, AND BURNING; 1165] **2** *n* **hellhole**, hell, underworld, perdition, fire and brimstone, Hades (*informal*) [➡ RELIGIOUS CONCEPTS; 776] *Opposite*: heaven

See Compare and Contrast at **fire**.

infertile *adj* **sterile**, unproductive, barren, unfruitful, childless, arid, bare [➡ REPRODUCTION AND HEREDITY; 725] *Opposite*: fertile

infertility *n* **sterility**, barrenness, poverty, childlessness, aridity, unproductiveness, unfruitfulness [➡ REPRODUCTION AND HEREDITY; 725] *Opposite*: fertility

infest v **overrun**, fill, invade, crowd, infiltrate, pervade, permeate, infect, plague, overwhelm, riddle [➡ MOVE PAST, INTO, OR THROUGH SOMETHING; 331]

infestation n **plague**, invasion, swarm, influx, infiltration, incursion [➡ ARRIVAL; 13]

infested adj [➡ DECAYING OR INFESTED; 1236]

infidelity n **unfaithfulness**, faithlessness, disloyalty, betrayal, adultery, cheating, perfidy (formal) [➡ MORALLY BAD OR IMPROPER; 775] Opposite: faithfulness

infighting n **internal strife**, backbiting, squabbling, bickering, wrangling, power struggle [➡ ARGUMENTS; 47]

infiltrate v **penetrate**, permeate, gain access to, break into, creep into, subvert, intrude, insinuate [➡ MOVE PAST, INTO, OR THROUGH SOMETHING; 331]

infiltration n **penetration**, permeation, access, intrusion, insinuation, subversion [➡ ARRIVAL; 13]

infiltrator n **mole**, spy, secret agent, double agent, subversive, undercover agent, plant (informal) [➡ INTERFERING PEOPLE AND TATTLETALES; 950]

in fine fettle adj [➡ FIT AND STRONG; 736]

infinite 1 adj **immeasurable**, never-ending, endless, countless, unbounded, boundless, vast, inestimable, unlimited, interminable, limitless [➡ PERMANENCE: WITHOUT END; 94] Opposite: limited 2 adj **extreme**, stupendous, great, immense, large, huge, tremendous, vast [➡ LARGE; 1193] Opposite: slight

infinitely adv **extremely**, enormously, markedly, a great deal, substantially, noticeably, interminably, by a long shot (informal), by a long way (UK), by a long chalk (UK) [➡ TO A GREAT EXTENT; 132] Opposite: slightly

infinitesimal adj **tiny**, minute, minuscule, microscopic, insignificant, inconsiderable, diminutive, indiscernible, teeny (informal) [➡ SMALL; 1195] Opposite: huge

infinitive type of **grammatical term** [➡ ASPECTS OF LANGUAGE; 682]

infinitude n [➡ PERMANENCE: WITHOUT END; 94]

infinity n **eternity**, immensity, endlessness, infinitude, boundlessness, limitlessness, perpetuity [➡ PERMANENCE: WITHOUT END; 94]

infirm adj **unwell**, sick, ill, frail, in poor health, weak, feeble, sickly, ailing (dated) [➡ ILL AND SICK; 740] Opposite: healthy

See Compare and Contrast at **weak**.

infirmary n **hospital**, sanatorium, sickbay, hospice, medical center, medical wing, nursing home [➡ HOSPITALS AND CLINICS; 826]

infirmity n **ill health**, illness, frailty, disability, weakness, susceptibility, ailment, malady, indisposition, frailness, sickness [➡ ILL AND SICK; 740] Opposite: health

in flagrante delicto adv **red-handed**, committing a crime, lawbreaking, offending, violating, committing an offense [➡ HAPPENING AND IN PROGRESS; 32]

inflame 1 v **arouse**, anger, fan, provoke, stir up, agitate,

ignite, kindle [➡ ANGER AND ANNOY; 569] Opposite: calm 2 v **exacerbate**, aggravate, fuel, intensify, increase, worsen [➡ WORSEN SOMETHING; 380] Opposite: diminish

inflamed adj **reddened**, swollen, irritated, tender, sore, angry [➡ ILL AND SICK; 740]

in flames adj **burning**, alight, aflame, raging, ablaze, on fire [➡ FIRE, FLAMMABILITY, AND BURNING; 1165]

inflammable adj **flammable**, combustible, ignitable, burnable, incendiary [➡ FIRE, FLAMMABILITY, AND BURNING; 1165] Opposite: nonflammable

inflammation n **irritation**, swelling, soreness, tenderness, redness, infection [➡ ILL AND SICK; 740]

inflammatory adj **provocative**, seditious, rabble-rousing, fiery, stirring, inspiring, incendiary, inciting, demagogic [➡ ELOQUENT, TALKATIVE, AND LONG-WINDED; 632] Opposite: placatory

inflatable adj **blow-up**, pump-up, expandable [➡ CHANGE OF SHAPE; 385]

inflate 1 v **blow up**, pump up, fill with air, expand, fill, puff up, swell, bloat [➡ CHANGE OF SIZE: BIGGER; 392] Opposite: deflate 2 v **exaggerate**, amplify, embellish, magnify, overestimate, overstate [➡ DECEPTION AND LIES; 660] Opposite: understate 3 v **increase**, go up, drive up, escalate, boost, raise [➡ CHANGE OF INTENSITY: MORE; 394] Opposite: deflate

inflated adj **exaggerated**, overstated, overblown, puffed up, magnified, extravagant, overestimated, bloated, swollen [➡ BIZARRE AND PECULIAR; 257] Opposite: understated

inflation 1 n **price rises**, rise, increase, price increases [➡ MARKET FORCES; 803] Opposite: deflation 2 type of **economic condition** [➡ FINANCE AND ECONOMICS; 796]

inflationary adj **price-raising**, price-increasing, spiraling [➡ FINANCE AND ECONOMICS; 796]

inflationary spiral type of **economic condition** [➡ FINANCE AND ECONOMICS; 796]

inflect v **change**, modulate, vary, adjust, modify, transform [➡ CHANGE; 372]

inflection n **modulation**, nuance, variation, variety, shade, accent, articulation, enunciation, intonation, tone, timbre, tonality [➡ ASPECTS OF LANGUAGE; 682]

inflexibility 1 n **stubbornness**, obstinacy, intransigence, rigor, rigidity, dogmatism, pigheadedness [➡ UNWILLINGNESS AND STUBBORNNESS; 564] Opposite: tractability 2 n **rigidity**, stiffness, hardness, firmness, tautness, tension, solidness [➡ RIGID AND HARD; 1211] Opposite: flexibility

inflexible 1 adj **unbending**, stubborn, obstinate, uncompromising, strict, fixed, set in your ways, unyielding, intransigent, rigid, hidebound, obdurate, pigheaded, recalcitrant [➡ UNWILLINGNESS AND STUBBORNNESS; 564] Opposite: tractable 2 adj **rigid**, stiff, hard, unbendable, firm, unyielding, solid, taut [➡ RIGID AND HARD; 1211] Opposite: bendable

inflexibly adv **unbendingly**, unyieldingly, stubbornly, obstinately, intransigently, dogmatically, uncompromisingly, rigidly [➡ WITHOUT ENTHUSIASM; 287]

inflict v **impose**, exact, mete out, wreak, perpetrate,

visit, lay on, bring to bear, dump on [➡ CAUSE TO HAPPEN; 31]
Opposite: remove

in-flight *adj* **onboard**, mid-flight, airborne, midair
[➡ GENERAL LOCATIONS; 158]

in floods (*UK*) *adj* [➡ CRYING; 650]

in floods of tears (*UK*) *adj* [➡ CRYING; 650]

inflow *n* **influx**, arrival, invasion, incursion, introduction, entry [➡ ARRIVAL; 13] *Opposite*: outflow

influence 1 *n* **effect**, inspiration, impact, stimulus,
encouragement, guidance [➡ PSYCHOLOGY AND THE MIND; 769]
2 *n* **power**, sway, authority, weight, control, pressure,
hold, pull (*informal*) [➡ STRENGTH; 201] 3 *v* **sway**, manipulate,
persuade, induce, win over, prompt, impel [➡ CAUSE OR COMPEL
TO ACT; 271] 4 *v* **affect**, motivate, inspire, shape, have an effect
on, guide, change [➡ CHANGE; 372]

influential *adj* **powerful**, important, significant, persuasive, dominant, leading, prominent, effective, instrumental, forceful [➡ STRENGTH; 201] *Opposite*: ineffectual

influenza *n* **flu**, cold, virus, infection, respiratory tract
infection, bug (*informal*) [➡ ILLNESSES AND DISORDERS; 732]

influx *n* **arrival**, invasion, incursion, flood, entry, inflow
[➡ ARRIVAL; 13] *Opposite*: outflow

info (*informal*) 1 *n* **information**, data, statistics, facts,
figures [➡ BASIC DETAILS; 688] 2 *n* **news**, report, tidings, word,
communication, intelligence, knowledge [➡ BASIC DETAILS; 688]

in focus *adj* **sharp**, focused, clear, well-defined, crystal
clear, distinct [➡ CONCISE AND CLEAR; 202] *Opposite*: blurred

infomediary *n* [➡ E-COMMERCE; 1129]

infomercial 1 *n* **commercial**, ad, advertisement, promotional film, promo (*informal*) [➡ ADVERTISING AND PUBLICITY; 604]
2 *type of* **broadcast** [➡ TELEVISION AND RADIO; 606]

in for *adj* **due**, heading for, in line for [➡ ABOUT TO HAPPEN; 33]

in force 1 *adj* **effective**, valid, serviceable, working,
applicable, in operation, in use, operational, in effect
[➡ HAPPENING AND IN PROGRESS; 32] *Opposite*: invalid 2 *adv* **strongly**,
powerfully, monumentally, forcefully, solidly, in large
numbers, in strength [➡ MANY, MUCH, LARGE AMOUNT; 117] *Opposite*:
feebly

inform 1 *v* **tell**, notify, let know, update, bring up-to-
date, put in the picture, enlighten, report to, advise, tip
off, apprise (*formal*) [➡ INFORM, ANNOUNCE, AND ISSUE; 611] *Opposite*:
keep in the dark 2 *v* **blow the whistle on**, betray, denounce,
tell on, tattle, snitch (*slang*), squeal (*slang*), sneak on
(*UK*) [➡ BETRAY CONFIDENCES AND GOSSIP; 618] *Opposite*: keep mum
(*informal*)

informal 1 *adj* **relaxed**, casual, familiar, easy, comfortable, unceremonious, easygoing, natural [➡ LEVELS OF
FORMALITY; 522] *Opposite*: ceremonious 2 *adj* **unofficial**, off-the-
record, unauthorized, unsanctioned, confidential, unconfirmed [➡ SECRET AND UNKNOWN; 179] *Opposite*: official 3 *adj* **colloquial**, idiomatic, vernacular, everyday, familiar [➡ ASPECTS
OF LANGUAGE; 682] *Opposite*: formal

informality *n* **casualness**, familiarity, ease, unpretentiousness, lack of formality, lack of ceremony [➡ LEVELS
OF FORMALITY; 522] *Opposite*: formality

informally 1 *adv* **casually**, nonchalantly, easily, unceremoniously, offhandedly, familiarly [➡ LEVELS OF FORMALITY; 522]
Opposite: ceremoniously 2 *adv* **unofficially**, off the record,
confidentially [➡ SECRET AND UNKNOWN; 179] *Opposite*: officially

informant 1 *n* **source**, guide, interpreter, adviser,
tipster, supplier of information [➡ ADVISERS, JUDGES, AND ARBITERS;
971] 2 *n* **informer**, spy, mole, tattletale, stool pigeon (*slang*),
snitch (*slang*), rat (*slang*), squealer (*slang*), sneak (*UK*)
[➡ INTERFERING PEOPLE AND TATTLETALES; 950]

information 1 *n* **data**, statistics, facts, figures, material,
evidence, info (*informal*) [➡ BASIC DETAILS; 688] 2 *n* **news**, report,
tidings, word, communication, intelligence, knowledge
[➡ BASIC DETAILS; 688]

See Compare and Contrast at **knowledge**.

information processing *n* **data processing**, data handling, data manipulation, data analysis, data transmission, computer processing, computing [➡ COMPUTERS AND
COMPUTING; 1127]

information retrieval *n* **data storage and retrieval**, data
storage, data retrieval, data processing, computer processing [➡ COMPUTERS AND COMPUTING; 1127]

information sheet *n* **newsletter**, brochure, leaflet, bulletin, communiqué, press release, handout [➡ MANUALS AND
INSTRUCTIONS; 589]

information superhighway *n* **superhighway**, worldwide computer network, electronic telecommunication,
the Internet, electronic networks, computer networks,
electronic communications, electronic communications
network, the World Wide Web, the Net (*informal*), the
Web (*informal*) [➡ THE INTERNET; 1128]

information technology *n* **IT**, computing, telecommunications, computer technology, electronic technology [➡ COMPUTERS AND COMPUTING; 1127]

informative *adj* **educational**, revealing, edifying,
enlightening, useful, helpful, instructive, explanatory,
illuminating [➡ INTERESTING AND MEANINGFUL; 190] *Opposite*: uncommunicative

informed *adj* **knowledgeable**, well-versed, conversant,
up-to-date, educated, abreast, primed, learned, cognizant
(*formal*) [➡ KNOWLEDGE AND WISDOM; 558] *Opposite*: ignorant

informer *n* **informant**, spy, mole, tattletale, stool pigeon
(*slang*), snitch (*slang*), rat (*slang*), squealer (*slang*), sneak
(*UK*) [➡ INTERFERING PEOPLE AND TATTLETALES; 950]

infotainment *type of* **broadcast** [➡ TELEVISION AND RADIO; 606]

infraction *n* **breach**, violation, infringement, contravention, transgression, flouting, lawbreaking, trespass [➡ CRIMES; 817]

infra dig (*informal*) *adj* **beneath one's dignity**, undignified,
unacceptable, improper, inappropriate, unsuitable
[➡ INAPPROPRIATE AND UNSUITABLE; 224] *Opposite*: appropriate

infrastructure 1 *n* **substructure**, organization, structure, setup, arrangement, frame, groundwork, foun-
dation, base [➡ COMMUNICATION NETWORKS; 1105] 2 *n* **public services**,
communications, public transport, power supplies, water

supplies, broadcasting, radio, telecommunications, road and rail networks, transportation [➡ INSTITUTIONS; 790]

infrequency *n* rarity, irregularity, uncommonness, paucity, scarcity, scarceness [➡ NEVER AND INFREQUENCY; 97] *Opposite*: frequency

infrequent *adj* rare, uncommon, occasional, intermittent, sporadic, irregular, scarce, few, fitful, few and far between (*informal*) [➡ NEVER AND INFREQUENCY; 97] *Opposite*: frequent

infringe 1 *v* **encroach on**, intrude on, interfere with, trespass, invade, overstep, impinge on (*formal*) [➡ INTERRUPT AND BUTT IN; 619] *Opposite*: respect 2 *v* **disobey**, disregard, breach, break, violate, contravene, flout, transgress [➡ DISOBEY; 302] *Opposite*: obey

infringement 1 *n* **breach**, violation, contravention, transgression, flouting, infraction [➡ CRIMES; 817] *Opposite*: compliance 2 *n* **encroachment**, intrusion, invasion, interference, trespass, incursion [➡ ARRIVAL; 13]

in front 1 *adv* **ahead**, leading, in the lead, before, further on, at the front [➡ GENERAL LOCATIONS; 158] *Opposite*: behind 2 *adv* **in the lead**, ahead, winning, beating, leading, up on, defeating, outplaying, outrunning, outpacing [➡ SUCCESSFUL AND PROMISING; 81] *Opposite*: losing

in front of 1 *prep* **before**, ahead of, facing, opposite [➡ RELATIVE LOCATION; 161] *Opposite*: behind 2 *prep* **in the presence of**, with, in the company of, before, watched by [➡ RELATIVE LOCATION; 161]

in full *adv* **completely**, fully, totally, in total, wholly, entirely, in its entirety, absolutely, one hundred percent [➡ WHOLENESS AND COMPLETENESS; 198] *Opposite*: in part

in full swing *adj* **well under way**, in progress, up and running, well-advanced [➡ HAPPENING AND IN PROGRESS; 32]

in full view *adv* [➡ PERCEPTIBLE; 25]

in funds (*UK*) *adj* [➡ WEALTH AND WEALTHY; 891]

infuriate *v* **enrage**, madden, incense, make your blood boil, annoy, irritate, anger, make see red, irk, exasperate, inflame, rile (*informal*), wind up (*UK informal*) [➡ ANGER AND ANNOY; 569] *Opposite*: calm

infuriated *adj* **enraged**, exasperated, furious, angry, incensed, irate, up in arms, inflamed, mad, irked, riled (*informal*), wound up (*UK informal*) [➡ IRRITATION AND ANGER; 541] *Opposite*: calm

infuriating *adj* **maddening**, annoying, irritating, exasperating, galling, vexatious [➡ IRRITATING; 228] *Opposite*: calming

infuse 1 *v* **pervade**, fill, permeate, suffuse, imbue, bathe [➡ FILL; 406] 2 *v* **instill**, impart, introduce, inculcate, imbue, implant, inspire, fortify [➡ INSTRUCT AND TEACH; 609] 3 *v* **steep**, soak, brew, immerse, saturate, souse [➡ SOFTEN, LIQUEFY, AND DAMPEN; 388] *Opposite*: drain

infusion *n* **brew**, tea, distillation, fermentation, drink, mixture, potion [➡ COLLECTIONS AND MIXTURES OF THINGS; 1244]

in future *adv* [➡ FUTURE; 86]

in general 1 *adv* **as a whole**, generally, altogether, overall [➡ USUALLY; 108] *Opposite*: in particular 2 *adv* **in most**

cases, generally, mainly, normally, usually, ordinarily, on the whole [➡ USUALLY; 108] *Opposite*: occasionally

ingenious 1 *adj* **inventive**, clever, imaginative, resourceful, original, creative [➡ TALENTED AND SKILLFUL; 527] *Opposite*: unimaginative 2 *adj* **effective**, cunning, inspired, nifty (*informal*), clever (*UK*) [➡ INTERESTING AND MEANINGFUL; 190]

ingeniously *adv* **inventively**, imaginatively, cleverly, resourcefully, skillfully, creatively, cunningly, niftily (*informal*) [➡ TALENTED AND SKILLFUL; 527] *Opposite*: unimaginatively

ingenuity *n* **inventiveness**, cleverness, resourcefulness, imagination, originality, skill, creativity, cunning, initiative [➡ POSITIVE INTELLECTUAL CHARACTERISTICS; 524] *Opposite*: unimaginativeness

ingenuous 1 *adj* **innocent**, unworldly, artless, unsophisticated, gullible, inexperienced, naive, trusting, simple [➡ NEGATIVE INTELLECTUAL CHARACTERISTICS; 525] *Opposite*: artful 2 *adj* **honest**, direct, frank, open, straightforward, sincere, candid [➡ HONEST AND OPEN; 630] *Opposite*: dishonest

ingenuously 1 *adv* **innocently**, artlessly, unpretentiously, gullibly, unsophisticatedly, simply, naively [➡ NEGATIVE INTELLECTUAL CHARACTERISTICS; 525] *Opposite*: artfully 2 *adv* **honestly**, frankly, candidly, openly, directly, straightforwardly, sincerely [➡ HONEST AND OPEN; 630] *Opposite*: dishonestly

ingenuousness 1 *n* **openness**, straightforwardness, directness, honesty, candor, artlessness, frankness, sincerity [➡ NATURALNESS; 497] *Opposite*: dishonesty 2 *n* **innocence**, unpretentiousness, unworldliness, gullibility, simplicity, naiveté [➡ LEVELS OF EDUCATION AND SOPHISTICATION; 894] *Opposite*: artfulness

ingest *v* **absorb**, swallow, take in, consume, eat, drink, devour, gulp down, sip, gulp, swig (*informal*) [➡ EAT AND NOT EAT; 710] *Opposite*: vomit

inglenook *n* **hearthside**, fireside, nook, corner, recess, fireplace [➡ ALCOVES, CUBICLES, AND COMPARTMENTS; 1096]

inglorious *adj* **shameful**, dishonorable, disgraceful, humiliating, unsuccessful, ignominious, ignoble [➡ UNACCEPTABLE AND UNFORGIVABLE; 225] *Opposite*: glorious

ingoing *adj* **incoming**, new, inward, moving [➡ DIRECTION OF MOTION; 345] *Opposite*: outgoing

in good condition *adj* [➡ FIT AND STRONG; 736]

in good form *adj* [➡ FIT AND STRONG; 736]

in good health *adj* [➡ FIT AND STRONG; 736]

in good shape *adj* **in good condition**, healthy, fit, in good health, hale and hearty, well [➡ FIT AND STRONG; 736] *Opposite*: in bad shape

in good spirits *adj* [➡ PLEASURE, EXCITEMENT, AND ELATION; 534]

in good taste *adv* [➡ APPROPRIATE, SUITABLE, AND ADVISABLE; 184]

in good time *adv* [➡ PROMPTNESS: ON TIME; 99]

ingot *n* **slab**, nugget, lump, brick, block, bar [➡ AMOUNTS OF SOLID OR SEMISOLID; 115]

ingrain *v* **impress**, etch, drill in, fix, root, hammer in, drum into, set, indoctrinate, instill [➡ INSTRUCT AND TEACH; 609]

ingrained *adj* **deep-seated**, in-built, entrenched, fixed, deep-rooted, rooted [➡PERMANENCE: WITHOUT END; 94] *Opposite:* superficial

ingratiate *v* **curry favor**, insinuate yourself, toady, get in with, grovel, cozy up, suck up (*informal*), crawl (*informal*) [➡ESTABLISHING RELATIONSHIPS WITH OTHERS; 974] *Opposite:* alienate

ingratiating *adj* **sycophantic**, insinuative, obsequious, smarmy, deferential [➡INGRATIATING; 638] *Opposite:* proud

ingratitude *n* **rudeness**, unmannerliness, unappreciativeness, ungratefulness, thanklessness, boorishness [➡BAD MANNERS AND SOCIAL SKILLS; 521] *Opposite:* gratitude

ingredient *n* **element**, component, part, constituent, factor, feature, item [➡PHYSICAL OBJECTS; 1243]

ingress (*formal*) *n* **entry**, entrance, opening, door, admission, doorway, right of way [➡DOORS AND ACCESS POINTS; 1101]

in-group *n* **clique**, gang, faction, circle, elite, coterie, camp, cabal, clan (*informal*) [➡FRIENDS AND ACQUAINTANCES; 936]

ingrowing *adj* **ingrown**, impacted, malformed, deformed [➡PAIN AND OTHER PHYSICAL SENSATIONS; 733]

inhabit *v* **live**, reside, populate, occupy, squat, dwell (*literary*) [➡INHABIT; 20]

inhabitable *adj* **habitable**, civilized, usable, hospitable, livable, residential, up to scratch (*informal*) [➡IN GOOD REPAIR; 1232] *Opposite:* uninhabitable

inhabitant *n* **occupant**, resident, citizen, native, denizen, tenant, occupier, dweller (*literary*) [➡INHABITANTS; 857]

inhabited *adj* **populated**, populous, tenanted [➡FULL; 1239] *Opposite:* uninhabited

inhalation *n* **breath**, gulp, gasp, pant, mouthful [➡BREATHE AND NOT BREATHE; 716]

inhale *v* **gasp**, gulp, huff, pant [➡BREATHE AND NOT BREATHE; 716] *Opposite:* exhale

inhaler *n* **bronchodilator**, nebulizer, spray [➡REMEDIES, TREATMENTS, AND OPERATIONS; 731]

in half a shake (*UK*) *adv* [➡FUTURE; 86]

in hand 1 *adj* **under control**, receiving attention, under consideration, under deliberation, being dealt with [➡HAPPENING AND IN PROGRESS; 32] *Opposite:* pending 2 *adj* **unused**, remaining, spare, superfluous, available, to play with, over, extra, free, surplus, left over [➡PRESENT AND AVAILABLE; 11]

inharmonious 1 *adj* **discordant**, clashing, unpleasant, harsh, jarring, unmusical, unmelodious, tuneless, dissonant, cacophonous [➡LOUD, HIGH, OR UNPLEASANT SOUNDS; 1266] *Opposite:* harmonious 2 *adj* **argumentative**, clashing, incompatible, disagreeable, antagonistic, conflicting, contradictory, discordant, at odds, at variance [➡DISHARMONY; 156] *Opposite:* cordial

in harmony *adv* [➡HARMONY; 155]

in haste *adv* [➡HAPPENING QUICKLY; 104]

inherent *adj* **characteristic**, essential, innate, natural, intrinsic, inborn, in-built, integral, fundamental [➡REPRODUCTION AND HEREDITY; 725] *Opposite:* acquired

inherit *v* **receive**, accede to, come into, succeed to, take over, get [➡GET MONEY OR REWARD; 421] *Opposite:* bequeath

inheritance *n* **heirloom**, tradition, legacy, bequest, birthright, heritage [➡BEQUEATH AND BEQUESTS; 432]

inhibit 1 *v* **slow**, stop, hold back, restrain, hinder, hamper, stall, reduce [➡AVOID, PREVENT, LIMIT, AND CONTROL; 277] 2 *v* **constrain**, hinder, prevent, impede, obstruct, deter, bar [➡MAKE IMPOSSIBLE; 276]

inhibited *adj* **self-conscious**, reserved, introverted, repressed, subdued, withdrawn, shy, reticent [➡RETICENT AND UNFORTHCOMING; 631] *Opposite:* uninhibited

inhibition *n* **reserve**, shyness, embarrassment, self-consciousness, reticence, hang-up (*informal*) [➡RETICENT AND UNFORTHCOMING; 631] *Opposite:* spontaneity

in high dudgeon *adj* [➡CONFUSION, ANXIETY, AND WORRY; 540]

in high spirits *adj* [➡PLEASURE, EXCITEMENT, AND ELATION; 534]

inhospitable 1 *adj* **unwelcoming**, unfriendly, unreceptive, uncongenial, uninviting, hostile, cold [➡UNFRIENDLINESS AND UNSOCIABILITY; 504] *Opposite:* hospitable 2 *adj* **harsh**, forbidding, bleak, desolate, barren, hostile [➡PHYSICALLY UNPLEASANT; 226] *Opposite:* inviting

in hot water *adj* **in trouble**, in difficulties, in extremis, in dire straits, in the soup (*informal*), up the creek (*informal*), in a jam (*informal*), in a fix (*informal*) [➡IN TROUBLE AND DISADVANTAGED; 73]

inhuman 1 *adj* **cruel**, vicious, cold-blooded, inhumane, brutal, ruthless [➡BEASTLY AND BRUTISH; 510] *Opposite:* kind 2 *adj* **cold-hearted**, unfeeling, insensitive, merciless, callous, heartless [➡SELFISH AND UNKIND; 505] *Opposite:* sensitive 3 *adj* **otherworldly**, weird, strange, unearthly, eerie, uncanny [➡BIZARRE AND PECULIAR; 257] *Opposite:* earthly

inhumane *adj* **cold-hearted**, cold-blooded, cruel, callous, brutal, merciless, sadistic, vicious, heartless, atrocious, appalling [➡BEASTLY AND BRUTISH; 510] *Opposite:* humane

inhumanity *n* **cruelty**, cold-heartedness, mercilessness, viciousness, ruthlessness, cold-bloodedness, brutality, sadism, heartlessness, atrociousness, callousness [➡SELFISH AND UNKIND; 505] *Opposite:* humanity

inimical 1 *adj* **unfavorable**, contrary, opposed, adverse, detrimental, disadvantageous [➡DANGEROUS; 236] *Opposite:* favorable 2 *adj* **hostile**, unfriendly, unwelcoming, cold, ill-disposed [➡IRRITATION AND ANGER; 541] *Opposite:* friendly

inimitable *adj* **unique**, matchless, unmatched, incomparable, peerless, one and only, one-off (*UK*) [➡EXTRAORDINARY: AMAZING; 204] *Opposite:* common

iniquitous *adj* **wicked**, heinous, sinful, bad, evil, unjust, immoral, naughty [➡MORALLY BAD OR IMPROPER; 775] *Opposite:* good

iniquity *n* **wickedness**, evil, sin, vice, immorality, injustice, crime, heinousness [➡MORALLY BAD OR IMPROPER; 775] *Opposite:* goodness

in isolation *adv* **separately**, out of context, alone, individually, independently [➡UNRELATEDNESS AND SEPARATENESS; 146] *Opposite:* together

initial *adj* **first**, early, original, preliminary, opening, primary [→ BEFORE, FIRST, AND PRECEDING; 163] *Opposite*: final

initialize *v* **reset**, prime, prepare, set, make ready, adjust, modify [→ COMPUTERS AND COMPUTING; 1127] *Opposite*: disable

initiate 1 *v* **start**, introduce, originate, begin, open, commence, set off, instigate, kick off (*informal*) [→ START AN ACTION; 260] *Opposite*: finish 2 *v* **instruct**, induct, admit, introduce, teach, tutor, coach, train, catechize [→ INSTRUCT AND TEACH; 609] *Opposite*: expel

initiation 1 *n* **beginning**, start, opening, instigation, launch, origination, introduction, commencement (*formal*) [→ BEGINNINGS; 53] *Opposite*: end 2 *n* **introduction**, admission, induction, admittance, instruction, training, catechesis [→ TEACHING; 839] *Opposite*: expulsion

initiative 1 *n* **inventiveness**, creativity, wits, enterprise, resourcefulness, ingenuity [→ POSITIVE INTELLECTUAL CHARACTERISTICS; 524] 2 *n* **plan**, proposal, scheme, program, idea, project [→ IDEAS AND THOUGHTS; 770] 3 *n* **pole position**, upper hand, advantage, edge, lead, ascendancy [→ SOURCE OF HAPPINESS, PLEASURE, OR IMPROVEMENT; 209]

initiator *n* **motivator**, inventor, originator, author, creator, architect, prime mover, spur [→ DESIGNERS, CREATORS, AND INSTIGATORS; 347]

in its entirety *adv* [→ ALL; 128]

inject 1 *v* **vaccinate**, inoculate, insert, give a shot (*informal*) [→ BECOME SICK, TREAT, AND RECOVER; 728] 2 *v* **bring**, add, introduce, instill, infuse [→ POSITION SOMETHING: BETWEEN, BESIDE, OR INSIDE SOMETHING; 326] *Opposite*: remove

injection 1 *n* **inoculation**, dose, vaccination, booster, shot (*informal*) [→ REMEDIES, TREATMENTS, AND OPERATIONS; 731] 2 *n* **addition**, instillation, insertion, introduction, infusion, instillment [→ COMBINE AND MIX; 400] *Opposite*: removal

in jeopardy *adj* [→ IN DANGER; 237]

in jest *adv* [→ JOKES AND TEASING; 674]

in-joke *n* **private joke**, joke, running joke, prank, witticism, jest (*literary*) [→ JOKES AND TEASING; 674]

injudicious *adj* **ill-advised**, unwise, foolish, imprudent, careless, indiscreet, inadvisable [→ THE NATURE OF IDEAS; 771] *Opposite*: judicious

injudiciousness *n* **indiscretion**, imprudence, foolishness, rashness, impulsiveness, hastiness, carelessness, misjudgment [→ THE NATURE OF IDEAS; 771] *Opposite*: prudence

injunction *n* **ban**, sanction, embargo, restriction, order, command, ruling [→ LEGISLATIVE BODIES AND LEGISLATION; 809]

injure *v* **damage**, harm, hurt, wound, cut, scar, burn [→ WOUND A PERSON OR ANIMAL; 383] *Opposite*: heal

> See Compare and Contrast at **harm**.

injured *adj* **hurt**, incapacitated, wounded, battered, bruised, damaged, gammy (*UK*) [→ INJURED; 742] *Opposite*: unscathed

injurious *adj* **harmful**, distressing, damaging, adverse, detrimental, deleterious, ruinous [→ DANGEROUS; 236] *Opposite*: beneficial

injury *n* **wound**, damage, grievance, wrong, hurt, harm [→ PAIN AND OTHER PHYSICAL SENSATIONS; 733]

injury time (*UK*) *n* **overtime**, extension, extra time (*UK*) [→ SPORTS TERMS; 877]

injustice *n* **discrimination**, unfairness, inequality, bias, prejudice, wrong [→ MORALLY BAD OR IMPROPER; 775] *Opposite*: justice

in keeping *adj* **consistent with**, suitable for, in accordance with, in line with, according to, compliant with, in agreement with [→ HARMONY; 155]

inkling *n* **suspicion**, hint, clue, hunch, feeling, idea, notion [→ IDEAS AND THOUGHTS; 770] *Opposite*: certainty

inkwell *n* **jar**, inkstand, pot, container, well, receptacle [→ CONTAINERS, RECEPTACLES, AND PACKAGING; 1245]

inky *type of* **black** [→ COLORS; 1224]

inky cap *type of* **fungus** [→ MICROORGANISMS, FUNGI, AND ALGAE; 1023]

inlaid *adj* **decorated**, veneered, enameled, ornamented, mosaic, tessellated, tiled, inset [→ DESCRIBING PATTERNS; 1227]

inland 1 *adj* **interior**, internal, upcountry, inward, central [→ GENERAL LOCATIONS; 158] 2 *adv* **within**, inshore, upcountry, inside, inward, centrally, toward [→ DIRECTION OF MOTION; 345]

inlay 1 *n* **stone**, glass, ivory, wood, enamel, tile, piece, ornament, inset [→ ORNAMENTS AND DECORATIONS; 1248] 2 *n* **pattern**, enameling, decoration, ornament, mosaic, marquetry, veneer [→ ORNAMENTS AND DECORATIONS; 1248]

in less than no time *adv* **immediately**, at once, quickly, rapidly, instantly, in an instant, in a flash, in a jiffy (*informal*) [→ HAPPENING QUICKLY; 104] *Opposite*: slowly

inlet *n* **bay**, cove, fjord, creek, tidal creek [→ THE SEAS, OCEANS, AND SHORES; 1041]

in lieu *adv* **instead**, in place, in the place of, to compensate for, to make up for, as a replacement for, for [→ DIFFERENCE; 149]

in limbo *adj* **in abeyance**, suspended, on hold, on the back burner, up in the air, on ice [→ NOT HAPPENING; 34] *Opposite*: on the move

in line 1 *adv* **in a row**, in order, in sequence, in turn, in rank, in formation, in single file [→ ORIENTATION AND ALIGNMENT; 1223] 2 *adv* **in keeping**, in accordance, in agreement, in step, in harmony, in concordance [→ HARMONY; 155] *Opposite*: against

in line for *adj* **due**, due for, owed, worthy of, entitled to, in for, up for [→ OWE AND DESERVE; 465]

in-line skating *type of* **extreme sport** [→ HOBBIES, GAMES, AND SPORTS; 875]

in line with *prep* **in agreement with**, according to, in keeping with, corresponding to, consistent with, along the lines of, in proportion to [→ HARMONY; 155]

in love *adj* [→ APPRECIATION AND GRATITUDE; 535]

in low spirits *adj* [➡ SADNESS, DISTRESS, AND DESPAIR; 539]

in luck *adj* [➡ LUCK; 783]

inmate *n* **prisoner**, internee, patient, convict, jailbird (*slang*) [➡ CAPTIVES AND PRISONERS; 249]

in memoriam *prep* **in memory of**, in remembrance of, as a memorial to, in commemoration of, for [➡ FOREIGN WORDS AND PHRASES; 672]

in moderation *adv* **within reason**, a little, within limits, within bounds, moderately, reasonably, sensibly, a bit (*informal*) [➡ TO A CERTAIN EXTENT; 136] *Opposite*: excessively

inmost *adj* **innermost**, deepest, private, secret, intimate, personal [➡ SECRET AND UNKNOWN; 179] *Opposite*: outermost

in most cases *adv* [➡ USUALLY; 108]

in mourning *adj* [➡ DEATH AND BEREAVEMENT; 927]

in my book *adv* **to my mind**, in my opinion, if you ask me, as far as I'm concerned, personally, in my view [➡ EXPRESSIONS OF OPINION; 623]

in my opinion *adv* [➡ EXPRESSIONS OF OPINION; 623]

in my view *adv* [➡ EXPRESSIONS OF OPINION; 623]

inn *type of* **hotel** [➡ HOTELS, RESTAURANTS, AND CLUBS; 1082]

in name only *adv* **theoretically**, supposedly, officially, in theory, on paper, in principle, nominally, notionally, technically [➡ FALSE AND UNREAL; 173] *Opposite*: really

innards (*informal*) *n* **entrails**, guts, intestines, bowels, viscera, insides (*informal*) [➡ THE DIGESTIVE TRACT; 709]

innate *adj* **essential**, inborn, native, distinctive, natural, characteristic, instinctive, inherent, intrinsic [➡ REPRODUCTION AND HEREDITY; 725]

in need *adj* [➡ POVERTY AND POOR; 892]

inner 1 *adj* **innermost**, inward, internal, inside, central, middle, interior [➡ CENTRAL PARTS OF PHYSICAL OBJECTS; 1251] *Opposite*: outer   2 *adj* **private**, secret, intimate, deep, hidden, personal, innermost [➡ SECRET AND UNKNOWN; 179] *Opposite*: public

inner city *n* **downtown**, city center, center, town center [➡ HUMAN SETTLEMENTS; 1070]

inner-city *adj* **city**, metropolitan, town, downtown, central, inner, urban, built-up [➡ HUMAN SETTLEMENTS; 1070] *Opposite*: suburban

innermost *adj* **inmost**, deepest, private, secret, intimate, personal [➡ SECRET AND UNKNOWN; 179] *Opposite*: outermost

in next to no time *adv* [➡ HAPPENING QUICKLY; 104]

innings *n* **runs**, turn, batting, score, round, go, shot [➡ SPORTS TERMS; 877]

innocence 1 *n* **blamelessness**, goodness, guiltlessness, incorruptibility, virtue, virtuousness, purity [➡ MORALLY GOOD; 774] *Opposite*: guilt   2 *n* **inexperience**, unworldliness, naiveté, unsophistication, gullibility, ingenuousness, artlessness, simplicity [➡ LEVELS OF EDUCATION AND SOPHISTICATION; 894] *Opposite*: experience

innocent 1 *adj* **blameless**, acquitted, guiltless, cleared, not guilty, above suspicion, in the clear [➡ MORALLY GOOD; 774]

Opposite: guilty   2 *adj* **harmless**, unknowing, unintended, unintentional, inoffensive, innocuous, safe [➡ SAFE AND SAFETY; 191] *Opposite*: malicious   3 *adj* **virtuous**, untouched, unsullied, chaste, immaculate, spotless, pure (*literary*) [➡ MORALLY GOOD; 774] *Opposite*: tainted   4 *adj* **unsophisticated**, unworldly, artless, harmless, naive, childlike, gullible, ingenuous, simple, pure (*literary*) [➡ LEVELS OF EDUCATION AND SOPHISTICATION; 894] *Opposite*: worldly

innocuous *adj* **inoffensive**, harmless, innocent, safe, mild, bland [➡ SAFE AND SAFETY; 191] *Opposite*: offensive

in no doubt *adj* [➡ CERTAINTY; 561]

in no time *adv* [➡ HAPPENING QUICKLY; 104]

innovate *v* **invent**, modernize, originate, revolutionize, transform, update, renovate, renew, remodel [➡ IMPROVE SOMETHING; 374] *Opposite*: stagnate

innovation *n* **novelty**, invention, revolution, modernization, origination, improvement, advance [➡ NEW, MODERN; 166] *Opposite*: stagnation

innovative *adj* **groundbreaking**, advanced, state-of-the-art, pioneering, inventive, original, new, novel, modern, innovatory [➡ NEW, MODERN; 166] *Opposite*: outdated

innuendo *n* **insinuation**, ambiguity, double entendre, inference, intimation, suggestion, allusion, hint, overtone [➡ SUGGEST, HINT, AND COMMENT; 612]

innumerable *adj* **countless**, uncountable, numerous, incalculable, immeasurable, untold, inestimable, infinite [➡ MANY, MUCH, LARGE AMOUNT; 117]

inoculate *v* **immunize**, vaccinate, inject, protect, give a shot (*informal*) [➡ BECOME SICK, TREAT, AND RECOVER; 728] *Opposite*: infect

inoculation *n* **vaccination**, injection, booster, immunization, shot (*informal*) [➡ REMEDIES, TREATMENTS, AND OPERATIONS; 731]

inoffensive *adj* **innocuous**, harmless, bland, dull, safe, mild, unoffending [➡ SAFE AND SAFETY; 191] *Opposite*: offensive

inoffensively *adv* **innocuously**, harmlessly, innocently, mildly, blandly, safely [➡ SAFE AND SAFETY; 191] *Opposite*: offensively

in one fell swoop *adv* [➡ HAPPENING QUICKLY; 104]

inoperable 1 *adj* **incurable**, untreatable, terminal, grave, fatal, deadly [➡ SICKNESS; 729] *Opposite*: operable   2 *adj* **impracticable**, unworkable, unfeasible, impossible, unachievable, impractical [➡ IMPOSSIBLE AND IMPROBABLE; 178] *Opposite*: doable

inoperative *adj* **out of action**, out of order, out of use, broken, broken down, defective [➡ IN BAD REPAIR; 1234] *Opposite*: operative

inopportune *adj* **ill-timed**, unfortunate, inconvenient, mistimed, untimely, inappropriate, unpropitious [➡ PROMPTNESS: BADLY TIMED; 101] *Opposite*: opportune

inopportunely *adv* **inconveniently**, unsuitably, inappropriately, unfortunately, awkwardly, regrettably [➡ PROMPTNESS: BADLY TIMED; 101] *Opposite*: conveniently

in opposition *adj* [➡ DISHARMONY; 156]

in order 1 *adj* **correct**, appropriate, acceptable, all right,

permissible, permitted, satisfactory, adequate, OK (*informal*), okay (*informal*) [➡ ACCEPTABLE AND PASSABLE; 219] *Opposite*: incorrect **2** *adv* **in turn**, in sequence, in line, in rank, consecutively, one at a time, one by one, sequentially, one after the other [➡ AFTER, LAST, AND FOLLOWING; 165] *Opposite*: out of order

in order to *conj* **so as to**, to, with the intention of, with the purpose of, with the aim of, that, so that [➡ CAUSATION; 168]

inordinate *adj* **excessive**, undue, unwarranted, immoderate, unreasonable, extravagant, disproportionate, unconscionable, exorbitant [➡ TOO MUCH; 119] *Opposite*: moderate

inordinately *adv* [➡ TO A GREAT EXTENT; 132]

inorganic *adj* **mineral**, inanimate, inert, lifeless [➡ RAW AND NATURAL; 1214] *Opposite*: organic

in other words *adv* [➡ SUMMARIZING EXPRESSIONS; 622]

in pain *adj* [➡ PAIN AND OTHER PHYSICAL SENSATIONS; 733]

in part *adv* **to some extent**, partly, partially, in some measure, in some way, to a certain extent, comparatively, relatively, to some degree, somewhat [➡ TO A CERTAIN EXTENT; 136] *Opposite*: completely

in particular *adv* **specifically**, especially, specially, particularly, above all, singularly, expressly [➡ MAINLY AND PRIMARILY; 140] *Opposite*: in general

in peak condition *adj* [➡ FIT AND STRONG; 736]

in peril *adj* [➡ IN DANGER; 237]

in perpetuity *adv* [➡ PERMANENCE: WITHOUT END; 94]

in person *adv* **personally**, yourself, in the flesh, physically, individually [➡ ACTING INDEPENDENTLY; 284]

in pieces *adj* [➡ IN BAD REPAIR; 1234]

in plain sight *adj* [➡ PERCEPTIBLE; 25]

in plenty of time *adv* [➡ PROMPTNESS: EARLY; 98]

in point of fact *adv* **genuinely**, irrefutably, in truth, in reality, in fact, as it happens, as a matter of fact, actually, really [➡ WORDS AND PHRASES EMPHASIZING THE TRUTH OF A MATTER; 172]

in poor condition *adj* [➡ UNFIT AND WEAK; 739]

in poor health *adj* [➡ ILL AND SICK; 740]

in poor taste *adj* [➡ IN POOR TASTE AND OVERSENTIMENTAL; 229]

in principle *adv* **in theory**, theoretically, hypothetically, on paper, technically, in name only, notionally, supposedly, officially [➡ POSSIBLE AND PROBABLE; 177]

in print *adv* **published**, printed, available, in book form [➡ WRITING; 583]

in prison *adj* [➡ CAPTIVITY AND LOSS OF FREEDOM; 248]

in progress *adj* [➡ HAPPENING AND IN PROGRESS; 32]

input **1** *n* **contribution**, effort, say, participation, involvement, idea, feedback, response [➡ BASIC DETAILS; 688] **2** *v* **enter**, key, key in, record, store [➡ RECORD SOMETHING; 371]

inquest *n* **investigation**, inquiry, examination, post-mortem, autopsy, probe, review [➡ BURIAL AND PREPARATION FOR BURIAL; 929]

in question *adj* [➡ UNCERTAIN; 175]

inquire *v* **ask**, query, request, question, find out, make inquiries [➡ ASK PEOPLE QUESTIONS; 666]

inquire into *v* **investigate**, go into, delve into, look into, probe into, research [➡ QUESTION THINGS; 751]

inquiring **1** *adj* **inquisitive**, interested, curious, questioning, analytical, probing, examining, investigative, speculative [➡ ENTHUSIASTIC AND INQUISITIVE; 628] *Opposite*: incurious **2** *adj* **searching**, questioning, penetrating, probing, prying, intrusive, quizzical [➡ NOSY AND INTERFERING; 512]

inquiry **1** *n* **review**, postmortem, autopsy, investigation, examination, analysis, survey, probe, inquest, study [➡ EXAMINE AND ASSESS; 753] **2** *n* **request**, question, query, interrogation, quiz [➡ ASK PEOPLE QUESTIONS; 666]

inquisition *n* **inquiry**, inquest, investigation, examination, interrogation, cross-examination, cross-questioning [➡ ASK PEOPLE QUESTIONS; 666]

inquisitive **1** *adj* **curious**, inquiring, interested, questioning, probing, keen [➡ RETICENT AND UNFORTHCOMING; 631] *Opposite*: indifferent **2** *adj* **prying**, intrusive, prurient, meddlesome, officious, inquisitorial, interfering, nosy (*informal*), snooping (*informal*) [➡ NOSY AND INTERFERING; 512] *Opposite*: incurious

inquisitiveness **1** *n* **curiosity**, interest, keenness, desire for knowledge, thirst for knowledge, imagination [➡ POSITIVE INTELLECTUAL CHARACTERISTICS; 524] *Opposite*: indifference **2** *n* **prurience**, meddlesomeness, prying, questioning, officiousness, intrusiveness, nosiness (*informal*) [➡ NOSY AND INTERFERING; 512] *Opposite*: indifference

inquisitor *n* **cross-examiner**, examiner, investigator, interrogator, questioner, interviewer [➡ QUESTIONERS; 667]

inquisitorial *adj* **interrogational**, cross-examining, investigative, interviewing, questioning, interrogative [➡ ENTHUSIASTIC AND INQUISITIVE; 628]

in rags *adj* [➡ IN BAD REPAIR; 1234]

in raptures *adj* [➡ PLEASURE, EXCITEMENT, AND ELATION; 534]

in reality *adv* **in actual fact**, really, actually, in fact, in effect, as a matter of fact, in point of fact, in truth [➡ TRUE AND REAL; 171]

in retrospect **1** *adj* **on reflection**, with the benefit of hindsight, on second thought, all together, looking back, with hindsight [➡ PAST; 84] **2** *adv* **with hindsight**, looking back, retrospectively, on second thought, with the benefit of hindsight, on review [➡ PAST; 84]

in ruins *adj* [➡ IN BAD REPAIR; 1234]

in safe hands *adj* [➡ SAFE AND SAFETY; 191]

insalubrious (*formal*) *adj* **unhealthy**, unsavory, unwholesome, harmful, unhygienic, seedy [➡ DIRTY; 1235] *Opposite*: healthy

ins and outs *n* **details**, fine points, particulars, facts, minutiae, circumstances, nitty-gritty (*informal*), nuts and bolts (*informal*) [➡ BASIC DETAILS; 688] *Opposite*: generalities

insane *adj* **foolish**, silly, stupid, impractical, ridiculous, senseless, unreasonable, crazy (*informal*) [➡ BIZARRE AND PECULIAR; 257] *Opposite*: sensible

insanitary *adj* **unhygienic**, dirty, unclean, contaminated, unhealthy, unwholesome, septic, toxic, unsanitary [➡ DIRTY; 1235] *Opposite*: hygienic

insanity *n* **foolishness**, stupidity, irrationality, folly, senselessness, recklessness, absurdity, craziness (*informal*) [➡ ECCENTRICITY AND IRRATIONALITY; 562] *Opposite*: common sense

insatiability *n* **voraciousness**, greed, greediness, gluttony, ravenousness, avidity [➡ GRASPING AND FINANCIALLY MEAN; 519]

insatiable *adj* **voracious**, greedy, avid, ravenous, unquenchable, unappeasable, unsatisfiable, limitless [➡ GRASPING AND FINANCIALLY MEAN; 519]

inscribe 1 *v* **engrave**, carve, etch, cut, scratch, incise, mark, print, pen, write, imprint, chisel, impress [➡ CREATE IMAGES; 356] *Opposite*: erase 2 *v* **list**, enter, record, register, enroll, add [➡ RECORD SOMETHING; 371] *Opposite*: delete 3 *v* **dedicate**, autograph, address, sign, assign, consecrate [➡ NAME AND DESCRIBE; 665]

inscription 1 *n* **writing**, caption, label, engraving, legend, words, lettering, imprinting, impression [➡ LETTERS AND WRITTEN MESSAGES; 584] 2 *n* **dedication**, autograph, signature, personal note, initials [➡ NAME AND DESCRIBE; 665]

inscrutability *n* **mystique**, mystery, mysteriousness, enigma, incomprehensibility, impenetrability [➡ RETICENT AND UNFORTHCOMING; 631] *Opposite*: clarity

inscrutable *adj* **enigmatic**, sphinx-like, unfathomable, mysterious, impenetrable, unreadable, incomprehensible, indecipherable, unknowable, inexplicable [➡ RETICENT AND UNFORTHCOMING; 631] *Opposite*: transparent

in secrecy *adv* [➡ SECRET AND UNKNOWN; 179]

in secret *adv* **secretly**, privately, in private, confidentially, clandestinely, surreptitiously, furtively, in confidence, between ourselves, unbeknownst to others [➡ SECRET AND UNKNOWN; 179] *Opposite*: openly

insect *n* **butterfly**, moth, ant, bug, pest, creature, fly, beetle, creepy-crawly (*informal*) [➡ INSECTS; 1012]

---

insect

◆ *parts of an insect*
abdomen, antenna, feeler, proboscis, thorax, wing

◆ *types of stages of insect development*
caterpillar, chrysalis, glowworm, grub, imago, larva, maggot, nit, pupa, silkworm, woodworm

---

insecure 1 *adj* **unconfident**, anxious, self-doubting, uncertain, lacking confidence, timid, doubtful, apprehensive, diffident [➡ INSECURITY AND LOSS OF COMPOSURE; 544] *Opposite*: confident 2 *adj* **vulnerable**, unprotected, unguarded, undefended, at risk, unsafe, endangered, exposed, precarious [➡ DANGEROUS; 236] *Opposite*: secure 3 *adj* **shaky**, rickety, unstable, unsteady, loose, wobbly, unsound, frail, unreliable, tottering [➡ IN BAD REPAIR; 1234] *Opposite*: steady

insecurely *adv* **anxiously**, uncertainly, tentatively,

apprehensively, timidly, diffidently, doubtfully [➡ INSECURITY AND LOSS OF COMPOSURE; 544] *Opposite*: confidently

insecurity *n* **lack of confidence**, anxiety, uncertainty, timidity, self-doubt, diffidence [➡ INSECURITY AND LOSS OF COMPOSURE; 544] *Opposite*: confidence

inseminate *v* [➡ REPRODUCTION AND HEREDITY; 725]

insemination *n* [➡ REPRODUCTION AND HEREDITY; 725]

insensate 1 *adj* **unconscious**, comatose, inert, numbed, numb, knocked out, insentient, insensible, anesthetized [➡ TIRED, ASLEEP, AND UNCONSCIOUS; 738] *Opposite*: animate 2 *adj* (*literary*) **heartless**, callous, cold, insensitive, unsympathetic, hardhearted, unfeeling, uncaring [➡ SELFISH AND UNKIND; 505] *Opposite*: sympathetic 3 *adj* (*literary*) **thoughtless**, inconsiderate, inattentive, heedless, unthinking, selfish [➡ SELFISH AND UNKIND; 505] *Opposite*: considerate

insensible 1 *adj* **unaware**, unresponsive, insensitive, oblivious, numb, unfeeling [➡ IGNORANCE; 557] *Opposite*: sensitive 2 *adj* **unconscious**, comatose, inert, insentient, numb, numbed, knocked out, anesthetized, insensate [➡ TIRED, ASLEEP, AND UNCONSCIOUS; 738] *Opposite*: conscious 3 *adj* **imperceptible**, indiscernible, unnoticeable, indistinguishable, inappreciable, invisible [➡ IMPERCEPTIBLE; 26] *Opposite*: obvious

insensitive 1 *adj* **unresponsive**, impervious, oblivious, unmoved, inured to, indifferent, obtuse, unaffected, blasé [➡ NEUTRALITY AND INDIFFERENCE; 553] *Opposite*: responsive 2 *adj* **tactless**, thoughtless, inconsiderate, uncaring, unsympathetic, thick-skinned, inattentive, hardened, cold, callous [➡ SELFISH AND UNKIND; 505] *Opposite*: sensitive 3 *adj* **numb**, unfeeling, insensate, insensible, dead, impervious, impassive [➡ IGNORANCE; 557] *Opposite*: sensitive

insensitively *adv* **tactlessly**, thoughtlessly, inconsiderately, inattentively, undiplomatically, coldly, callously [➡ SELFISH AND UNKIND; 505] *Opposite*: considerately

insensitivity *n* **selfishness**, thoughtlessness, inconsiderateness, tactlessness, inattentiveness, coldness, callousness [➡ SELFISH AND UNKIND; 505] *Opposite*: sensitivity

insentient *adj* **lifeless**, inert, inanimate, insensate, unconscious, numbed, comatose, knocked out, insensible, numb [➡ TIRED, ASLEEP, AND UNCONSCIOUS; 738] *Opposite*: sentient

inseparable 1 *adj* **close**, devoted, intimate, joined at the hip, in each other's pocket, thick as thieves, attached [➡ RELATIONSHIP TO ANOTHER; 973] *Opposite*: distant 2 *adj* **indivisible**, indissoluble, undividable, inextricable, united, conjoined (*formal*) [➡ RECIPROCITY AND INTERDEPENDENCE; 147] *Opposite*: independent

in sequence *adv* [➡ AFTER, LAST, AND FOLLOWING; 165]

in serious trouble *adj* [➡ IN TROUBLE AND DISADVANTAGED; 73]

insert 1 *v* **introduce**, implant, inject, put in, place in, slot in, interleave, set in, pop in (*informal*) [➡ POSITION SOMETHING: BETWEEN, BESIDE, OR INSIDE SOMETHING; 326] *Opposite*: take out 2 *v* **add**, include, enclose, append, incorporate, introduce [➡ POSITION SOMETHING: BETWEEN, BESIDE, OR INSIDE SOMETHING; 326] *Opposite*: extract 3 *n* **supplement**, pullout, addition, enclosure, inset, insertion, attachment [➡ PARTS OF BOOKS AND DOCUMENTS; 593]

insertion 1 *n* **supplement**, pullout, addition, inset, insert, enclosure, attachment [➡ PARTS OF BOOKS AND DOCUMENTS; 593]

2 *n* **addition**, inclusion, incorporation, enclosure, attachment, introduction [➡ COMBINE AND MIX; 400]

in-service *adj* **work-related**, occupational, professional, vocational, job-related, on-the-job [➡ TYPES OF WORK; 835]

inset 1 *v* **insert**, put in, add, include, incorporate, place, position [➡ POSITION SOMETHING: BETWEEN, BESIDE, OR INSIDE SOMETHING; 326] *Opposite*: extract **2** *n* **supplement**, insert, pullout, insertion, inclusion, addition, enclosure [➡ PARTS OF BOOKS AND DOCUMENTS; 593]

in seventh heaven *adj* [➡ PLEASURE, EXCITEMENT, AND ELATION; 534]

in shape *adj* [➡ FIT AND STRONG; 736]

in sharp contrast *adv* [➡ DIFFERENCE; 149]

in shock *adj* [➡ SURPRISE, SHOCK, AND AMAZEMENT; 545]

inshore *adv* **landward**, coastward, ashore, shoreward [➡ DIRECTION OF MOTION; 345]

in short *adv* **in brief**, briefly, in a word, in summary, in a nutshell, to sum up, to cut a long story short, to be brief, to come to the point, concisely [➡ SUMMARIZING EXPRESSIONS; 622] *Opposite*: at length

in short supply *adj* **rare**, running low, at a premium, insufficient, lacking, scarce, scant, few and far between (*informal*) [➡ TOO FEW, TOO LITTLE; 122] *Opposite*: plentiful

in shreds *adj* [➡ IN BAD REPAIR, 1234]

inside 1 *adv* **indoors**, in, within, in the interior, at home [➡ GENERAL LOCATIONS, 158] *Opposite*: outside **2** *adj* **confidential**, privileged, secret, private, exclusive, classified, esoteric, intimate, internal [➡ SECRET AND UNKNOWN; 179] **3** *adj* **inner**, innermost, inmost, inward [➡ RELATIVE LOCATION; 161] *Opposite*: outer **4** *adj* **indoor**, interior, internal [➡ GENERAL LOCATIONS; 158] *Opposite*: outside **5** *adj* (*informal*) **locked up**, imprisoned, put away (*informal*), doing time (*slang*) [➡ CAPTIVITY AND LOSS OF FREEDOM; 248] **6** *n* **interior**, inner recesses, inner parts, contents [➡ CENTRAL PARTS OF PHYSICAL OBJECTS; 1251] *Opposite*: outside **7** *prep* **in**, within, surrounded by, contained by [➡ RELATIVE LOCATION; 161] *Opposite*: outside

inside out 1 *adj* **the wrong way around**, inverted, reversed, topsy-turvy, transposed, back to front (*UK*) [➡ ORIENTATION AND ALIGNMENT; 1223] **2** *adv* **really well**, like the back of your hand, thoroughly, backward, exhaustively, back to front (*UK*) [➡ WHOLENESS AND COMPLETENESS; 198] *Opposite*: superficially

insides (*informal*) *n* **internal organs**, guts, entrails, bowels, viscera, intestines, innards (*informal*) [➡ THE DIGESTIVE TRACT; 709]

insidious *adj* **sinister**, treacherous, crafty, sneaky, deceptive, devious, stealthy, underhand [➡ DANGEROUS; 236] *Opposite*: harmless

insidiousness *n* [➡ DANGER; 235]

in sight *adv* [➡ PERCEPTIBLE; 25]

insight *n* **vision**, understanding, awareness, intuition, perception, acumen, comprehension, discernment, perceptiveness [➡ POSITIVE INTELLECTUAL CHARACTERISTICS; 524]

insightful *adj* **perceptive**, astute, shrewd, understanding, discerning, aware, intuitive [➡ POSITIVE INTELLECTUAL CHARACTERISTICS; 524] *Opposite*: unperceptive

insightfulness *n* **perspicacity**, perceptiveness, astuteness, discernment, sensitivity, understanding, insight, comprehension [➡ POSITIVE INTELLECTUAL CHARACTERISTICS; 524]

insignia *n* **emblem**, crest, badge, sign, symbol, motif, logo, decoration [➡ SYMBOLS, SIGNS, AND NUMBERS; 596]

insignificance *n* **unimportance**, irrelevance, inconsequentiality, triviality, paltriness, pettiness [➡ UNIMPORTANT AND UNNECESSARY; 238] *Opposite*: significance

insignificant *adj* **unimportant**, irrelevant, immaterial, inconsequential, trivial, minor, paltry, petty, trifling, slight [➡ UNIMPORTANT AND UNNECESSARY; 238] *Opposite*: significant

insincere *adj* **dishonest**, two-faced, hypocritical, disingenuous, deceitful, devious, double-dealing, dissembling (*formal*) [➡ DECEITFUL; 513] *Opposite*: sincere

insincerity *n* **dishonesty**, disingenuousness, hypocrisy, deceit, mendacity, deviousness [➡ DECEITFUL; 513] *Opposite*: sincerity

insinuate 1 *v* **imply**, suggest, hint, intimate, indicate, allude, whisper [➡ SUGGEST, HINT, AND COMMENT; 612] *Opposite*: declare **2** *v* **ingratiate yourself**, worm your way in, wheedle, cozy up, curry favor, get in with [➡ ESTABLISHING RELATIONSHIPS WITH OTHERS; 974] *Opposite*: insult

insinuation *n* **suggestion**, implication, hint, intimation, allusion, indication, whisper [➡ SUGGEST, HINT, AND COMMENT; 612] *Opposite*: statement

insipid 1 *adj* **dull**, bland, characterless, colorless, trite, tame, unexciting, uninteresting, boring, lifeless, inane, banal, wishy-washy (*informal*) [➡ BORING AND UNINTERESTING; 234] *Opposite*: exciting **2** *adj* **bland**, tasteless, unappetizing, flavorless, watery, weak, wishy-washy (*informal*), savorless [➡ TASTE; 703] *Opposite*: tasty

insipidly *adv* **boringly**, uninterestingly, dully, blandly, feebly, unexcitingly, weakly, lifelessly, inanely, banally [➡ BORING AND UNINTERESTING; 234] *Opposite*: interestingly

insipidness 1 *n* **dullness**, blandness, feebleness, characterlessness, colorlessness, lifelessness, banality, inanity [➡ BORING AND UNINTERESTING; 234] **2** *n* **tastelessness**, blandness, wateriness, weakness, flavorlessness, staleness, savorlessness [➡ TASTE; 703] *Opposite*: tastiness

insist 1 *v* **maintain**, claim, assert, contend, swear, vow, hold, aver (*formal*) [➡ CLAIM, INSIST, AND EMPHASIZE; 614] *Opposite*: deny **2** *v* **require**, demand, press for, stipulate, enforce, claim [➡ REQUEST AND DEMAND; 663]

insistence *n* **persistence**, resolve, firmness, perseverance, doggedness, determination [➡ HARD-WORKING AND COMMITTED; 500]

insistent 1 *adj* **adamant**, firm, persistent, unrelenting, resolute, persevering, demanding, clamorous, imperative [➡ STRENGTH OF WILL; 501] *Opposite*: half-hearted **2** *adj* **incessant**, repeated, persistent, relentless, unrelenting, monotonous [➡ PERMANENCE: WITHOUT END; 94] *Opposite*: occasional

in situ *adj* [➡ PRESENT AND AVAILABLE; 11]

insofar as *conj* **inasmuch as**, insomuch as, to the extent that, to the degree that, because, since, in that [➡ CAUSATION; 168]

insolence *n* **impudence**, cheekiness, impertinence, rudeness, audacity, disrespect, cheek (*informal*) [➡ BAD MANNERS AND SOCIAL SKILLS; 521] *Opposite*: respect

insolent *adj* **impudent**, rude, audacious, disrespectful, brazen, cheeky (*informal*), impertinent (*formal*) [➡ BAD MANNERS AND SOCIAL SKILLS; 521] *Opposite*: respectful

insolently *adv* **impudently**, rudely, audaciously, disrespectfully, brazenly, impertinently (*formal*) [➡ BAD MANNERS AND SOCIAL SKILLS; 521] *Opposite*: respectfully

insolubility *n* **mysteriousness**, insolvability, indecipherability, intricacy, difficulty, impenetrability, enigma, mystery, unfathomableness [➡ DIFFICULTY AND COMPLEXITY; 242] *Opposite*: solubility

insoluble *adj* **inexplicable**, mysterious, insolvable, unfathomable, indecipherable, impenetrable, difficult, intricate, enigmatic [➡ DIFFICULTY AND COMPLEXITY; 242] *Opposite*: solvable

insolvency *n* **bankruptcy**, liquidation, indebtedness, ruin, collapse, failure [➡ ACCOUNTING, BANKING, AND BUDGETING; 799] *Opposite*: solvency

insolvent *adj* **bankrupt**, ruined, in debt, in receivership, broke (*informal*), bust (*informal*) [➡ POVERTY AND POOR; 892] *Opposite*: solvent

insomnia *n* **sleeplessness**, wakefulness, restlessness [➡ SLEEP AND DREAM; 723]

insomuch as *conj* **insofar as**, inasmuch as, to the extent that, to the degree that, because, since, in that [➡ CAUSATION; 168]

insouciance *n* **carefreeness**, nonchalance, indifference, happiness, unconcern [➡ NEUTRALITY AND INDIFFERENCE; 553] *Opposite*: worry

insouciant *adj* [➡ NEUTRALITY AND INDIFFERENCE; 553]

inspect *v* **look at**, review, examine, scrutinize, look over, study, check, give the once-over (*informal*) [➡ EXAMINE AND ASSESS; 753] *Opposite*: ignore

inspection *n* **review**, examination, scrutiny, checkup, assessment, check, going-over (*informal*) [➡ EXAMINE AND ASSESS; 753]

inspector *n* **examiner**, superintendent, overseer, assessor, supervisor, checker [➡ SURVEYORS, EXAMINERS, AND JUDGES; 853]

inspiration 1 *n* **stimulus**, spur, motivation, stimulation, encouragement [➡ CAUSATION; 168] *Opposite*: disincentive 2 *n* **creativeness**, inventiveness, brilliance, vision, creativity, muse [➡ POSITIVE INTELLECTUAL CHARACTERISTICS; 524] 3 *n* **insight**, flash, idea, revelation, brainstorm (*informal*) [➡ IDEAS AND THOUGHTS; 770]

inspirational *adj* **stimulating**, inspiring, stirring, rousing, moving, encouraging, motivating [➡ INTERESTING AND MEANINGFUL; 190] *Opposite*: boring

inspire *v* **stimulate**, motivate, stir, instigate, encourage, enthuse, move, arouse, rouse [➡ APPEAL TO AND AROUSE INTEREST; 575] *Opposite*: bore

inspired 1 *adj* **brilliant**, outstanding, superb, exceptional, virtuosic, dazzling [➡ EXTRAORDINARY: AMAZING; 204] *Opposite*: uninspired 2 *adj* **stimulated**, stirred, moved, encouraged, motivated [➡ POSITIVE IMPATIENCE, ENTHUSIASM, AND ALERTNESS; 537] *Opposite*: uninspired

inspiring *adj* **inspirational**, stirring, rousing, moving, exciting, stimulating [➡ INTERESTING AND MEANINGFUL; 190] *Opposite*: uninspiring

in spite of *prep* **despite**, regardless of, in the face of, notwithstanding (*formal*) [➡ ALTHOUGH, NEVERTHELESS, AND DESPITE; 169]

instability *n* **unpredictability**, variability, uncertainty, unsteadiness, volatility, shakiness, insecurity, flux [➡ DANGER; 235] *Opposite*: stability

install 1 *v* **connect**, fit, put in, set up, fix, mount, bed in [➡ EQUIP AND SUPPLY; 435] *Opposite*: remove 2 *v* **ordain**, establish, inaugurate, instate, induct, appoint, invest (*formal*) [➡ CONFER STATUS; 458] *Opposite*: oust 3 *v* **settle in**, settle, settle down, ensconce, position [➡ POSITION SOMETHING; 325]

installation 1 *n* **connection**, fitting, setting up, fixing, putting in, putting in place [➡ FASTEN, LINK, AND JOIN; 408] *Opposite*: removal 2 *n* **system**, mechanism, machinery, equipment, apparatus [➡ DEVICES; 1115] 3 *n* **appointment**, ordination, inauguration, investiture, instatement, induction [➡ BEGINNINGS; 53] *Opposite*: removal 4 *n* [➡ INDUSTRIAL BUILDINGS; 1087]

installment 1 *n* **payment**, portion, part, section, segment [➡ FUNDS, PAYMENTS, AND CHARGES; 800] 2 *n* **part**, episode, chapter [➡ PAUSES AND PHASES; 56]

instance *n* **example**, case, case in point, occurrence, illustration, occasion [➡ REPRESENTATIONS AND GENERAL EXAMPLES; 65]

instant 1 *adj* **prompt**, immediate, sudden, rapid, swift, instantaneous, on the spot, direct [➡ HAPPENING QUICKLY; 104] *Opposite*: gradual 2 *adj* **prepared**, precooked, premixed, powdered, microwavable, fast [➡ STATE OF PREPARED FOOD; 1171] 3 *adj* **urgent**, pressing, immediate [➡ IMPORTANT; 194] 4 *n* **moment**, second, split second, the twinkling of an eye, minute, time [➡ SHORT PERIODS OF TIME; 93]

instantaneous *adj* **prompt**, rapid, sudden, immediate, instant, direct, on the spot [➡ HAPPENING QUICKLY; 104] *Opposite*: gradual

instantly *adv* **promptly**, rapidly, suddenly, right away, instantaneously, immediately, directly, at once, straightaway [➡ HAPPENING QUICKLY; 104] *Opposite*: gradually

instant messaging *n* [➡ THE INTERNET; 1128]

instate *v* **appoint**, ordain, inaugurate, establish, install, invest (*formal*) [➡ CONFER STATUS; 458] *Opposite*: oust

instead *adv* **in its place**, as an alternative, as a substitute, as a replacement for [➡ DIFFERENCE; 149]

instead of *prep* **in place of**, rather than, as opposed to, in preference to [➡ DIFFERENCE; 149]

in step 1 *adv* **in line**, in accordance, in harmony, in concordance, in agreement, in keeping, correspondingly [➡ HARMONY; 155] 2 *adv* **keeping pace**, in time, in synchronization, keeping up, in harmony, simultaneously, in sync (*informal*) [➡ ACTING WITH OTHERS; 285]

instep *part of* **leg or foot** [➡ PARTS OF THE BODY: LEG AND FOOT; 694]

instigate *v* **bring about**, prompt, initiate, start, activate, set off, originate [➡ CAUSE TO HAPPEN; 31] *Opposite*: stifle

instigation 1 *n* **start**, beginning, initiation, establishment, commencement (*formal*) [➡ BEGINNINGS; 53] *Opposite*: end 2 *n* **initiation**, prompting, urging, encouragement, provocation [➡ BEGINNINGS; 53] *Opposite*: discouragement

instigator *n* **initiator**, prime mover, mastermind, troublemaker, ringleader, leader [➡ DESIGNERS, CREATORS, AND INSTIGATORS; 347]

instill 1 *v* **impart**, implant, inculcate, introduce, drum into, drive into, impress upon, teach, drill, school [➡ INSTRUCT AND TEACH; 609] 2 *v* **drip**, pour, infuse, inject, introduce [➡ MOVE PAST, INTO, OR THROUGH SOMETHING; 331]

instinct 1 *n* **nature**, character, makeup, predisposition, disposition, constitution [➡ TEMPERAMENT AND BEHAVIOR; 492] 2 *n* **drive**, reflex, feeling, impulse, urge, compulsion, need [➡ FEELINGS; 531] *Opposite*: reason 3 *n* **feeling**, intuition, gut feeling, sixth sense, sense [➡ FEELINGS; 531] 4 *n* **talent**, knack, gift, flair, ability, aptitude, feeling [➡ SKILLS, TALENTS, AND ABILITIES; 526]

instinctive 1 *adj* **involuntary**, automatic, reflex, natural, unconscious, intuitive [➡ AUTOMATIC AND INSTINCTIVE; 280] *Opposite*: conscious 2 *adj* **natural**, intuitive, innate, inherent, inborn [➡ REPRODUCTION AND HEREDITY; 725] *Opposite*: learned

instinctively *adv* **impulsively**, mechanically, on impulse, automatically, unconsciously, intuitively [➡ AUTOMATIC AND INSTINCTIVE; 280]

institute 1 *v* **introduce**, establish, set up, bring about, found, start, inaugurate [➡ INSTITUTE AND INAUGURATE; 348] 2 *n* **organization**, institution, establishment, foundation, association, society [➡ INSTITUTIONS; 790]

institution 1 *n* **establishment**, organization, body, association, society, foundation, institute [➡ INSTITUTIONS; 790] 2 *n* **tradition**, custom, convention, ritual [➡ WAYS OF DOING THINGS; 294] 3 *n* **introduction**, establishment, setting up, foundation, creation [➡ BEGINNINGS; 53]

institutional 1 *adj* **official**, recognized, formal, established, organized, influential [➡ KNOWN AND FAMOUS; 181] *Opposite*: unofficial 2 *adj* **utilitarian**, uniform, dull, functional, ugly, ordinary, standard issue [➡ BORING AND UNINTERESTING; 234] *Opposite*: unique

institutionalized *adj* **established**, existing, long-standing, traditional, entrenched, customary [➡ OLD, OLD-FASHIONED; 167] *Opposite*: innovative

in store 1 *adj* [➡ ABOUT TO HAPPEN; 33] 2 *adv* **to come**, coming up, in the making, for the future, waiting, in the offing, before you, ahead of you [➡ ABOUT TO HAPPEN; 33]

in strength *adv* **in force**, in large numbers, in their thousands, in crowds, in throngs, in floods [➡ MANY, MUCH, LARGE AMOUNT; 117]

instruct 1 *v* **teach**, train, coach, tutor, educate, drill, inculcate, initiate [➡ INSTRUCT AND TEACH; 609] 2 *v* **command**, order, tell, give orders to, charge, direct (*formal*) [➡ CAUSE OR COMPEL TO ACT; 271]

*See Compare and Contrast at **teach**.*

instruction 1 *n* **teaching**, training, lessons, tuition, education, coaching, tutoring [➡ TEACHING; 839] 2 *n* **order**, command, direction, directive [➡ REQUEST AND DEMAND; 663]

instructive *adj* **informative**, educational, useful, helpful, enlightening, edifying [➡ INTERESTING AND MEANINGFUL; 190]

instructor *n* **teacher**, coach, tutor, trainer, mentor, lecturer [➡ EDUCATORS; 840]

instrument 1 *n* **tool**, gadget, device, utensil, apparatus, appliance, implement, mechanism, contraption [➡ DEVICES; 1115] 2 *n* **means**, channel, vehicle, method, medium, mechanism, catalyst [➡ WAYS OF DOING THINGS; 294]

instrumental *adj* **contributory**, active, involved, helpful, influential [➡ RELATED; 142] *Opposite*: tangential

instrumentalist *n* **musician**, player, performer [➡ MUSICIANS AND SINGERS; 908]

instrumentation 1 *n* **arrangement**, composition, musical arrangement, music, score [➡ NOTES AND CHORDS; 909] 2 *n* **instrument panel**, equipment, instruments, controls, console, dials, control panel, dashboard [➡ MACHINERY; 1114]

instrument panel *n* [➡ PARTS OF MACHINES AND TOOLS; 1118]

insubordinate *adj* **disobedient**, defiant, rebellious, mutinous, unruly, noncompliant [➡ REBELLIOUSNESS AND DISOBEDIENCE; 565] *Opposite*: obedient

insubordination *n* **disobedience**, defiance, rebelliousness, mutiny, unruliness, noncompliance [➡ REBELLIOUSNESS AND DISOBEDIENCE; 565] *Opposite*: obedience

insubstantial *adj* **flimsy**, light, slight, weak, frail, thin [➡ WEAKNESS; 241] *Opposite*: weighty

insubstantiality *n* **weakness**, fragility, thinness, flimsiness, lightness, delicacy [➡ WEAKNESS; 241] *Opposite*: robustness

in succession *adv* [➡ AFTER, LAST, AND FOLLOWING; 165]

insufferable *adj* **excruciating**, unbearable, intolerable, insupportable, unendurable, beyond the pale, unspeakable [➡ IRRITATING; 228]

insufficiency 1 *n* **lack**, deficiency, dearth, absence, shortage, scarcity, paucity [➡ TOO FEW, TOO LITTLE; 122] 2 *n* **inadequacy**, deficiency, unfitness, failure, inefficiency, ineffectuality [➡ INAPPROPRIATE AND UNSUITABLE; 224] *Opposite*: adequacy

insufficient *adj* **inadequate**, deficient, lacking, in short supply, unsatisfactory, scarce [➡ TOO FEW, TOO LITTLE; 122]

insular *adj* **inward-looking**, blinkered, narrow-minded, narrow, limited [➡ NEGATIVE INTELLECTUAL CHARACTERISTICS; 525] *Opposite*: open-minded

insularity *n* **narrow-mindedness**, narrowness, blinkeredness [➡ NEGATIVE INTELLECTUAL CHARACTERISTICS; 525]

insulate 1 *v* **lag**, wad, line, fill, pad [➡ DECORATE, ADORN, AND APPLY COATINGS; 405] 2 *v* **cloister**, protect, shield, cut off, isolate, separate, segregate, sequester (*formal*) [➡ SEPARATE AND DIVIDE; 401] *Opposite*: expose

insulation 1 *n* **lining**, lagging, wadding, padding, filling [➡ COVERS AND COATINGS; 1246] 2 *n* **protection**, isolation, separation, segregation, sequestration [➡ SEPARATE AND DIVIDE; 401] *Opposite*: exposure

insulator *n* **soundproofing**, heatproofing, padding, lagging [➤ BUILDING MATERIALS; 1077]

insult **1** *v* **offend**, affront, abuse, slur, slight, upset [➤ INSULTS, ABUSE, AND SWEARING; 658] *Opposite*: praise **2** *n* **affront**, slight, slur, offense, rudeness [➤ INSULTS, ABUSE, AND SWEARING; 658]

insulted *adj* [➤ SADNESS, DISTRESS, AND DESPAIR; 539]

insulting *adj* **abusive**, offensive, rude, insolent, wounding, discourteous, slighting, impertinent (*formal*) [➤ INSULTS, ABUSE, AND SWEARING; 658] *Opposite*: polite

in sum *adv* [➤ SUMMARIZING EXPRESSIONS; 622]

in summary *adv* [➤ SUMMARIZING EXPRESSIONS; 622]

insuperability *n* [➤ DIFFICULTY AND COMPLEXITY; 242]

insuperable *adj* **insurmountable**, impossible, unbeatable, challenging, undefeatable, overwhelming [➤ DIFFICULTY AND COMPLEXITY; 242] *Opposite*: easy

insupportable *adj* **unbearable**, intolerable, unendurable, insufferable, unspeakable, unacceptable [➤ IRRITATING; 228] *Opposite*: bearable

insurance *n* **cover**, indemnity, assurance, protection, coverage, indemnification [➤ INSURANCE; 801]

insurance policy **1** *n* **document**, contract, cover, agreement, guarantee, warranty [➤ OFFICIAL DOCUMENTS; 586] **2** *n* **safety net**, safeguard, precaution, protection, provision [➤ INSURANCE; 801]

insure *v* **protect**, cover, assure, indemnify, underwrite [➤ INSURANCE; 801]

insurer *n* **underwriter**, broker, guarantor [➤ INSURANCE; 801]

insurgence *n* **uprising**, rebellion, revolt, revolution, mutiny, riot [➤ AGGRESSIVE EVENTS; 39]

insurgency *n* **insurrection**, insurgence, rebellion, revolution, revolt, uprising, mutiny, riot [➤ AGGRESSIVE EVENTS; 39]

insurgent **1** *n* **rebel**, insurrectionary, revolutionary, guerrilla, mutineer, rioter, protester [➤ UNCOOPERATIVE OR REBELLIOUS PEOPLE; 566] **2** *adj* **mutinous**, rebellious, rebel, insurrectionary [➤ REBELLIOUSNESS AND DISOBEDIENCE; 565]

insurmountable *adj* **unbeatable**, insuperable, impossible, undefeatable, overwhelming [➤ DIFFICULTY AND COMPLEXITY; 242] *Opposite*: easy

insurrection *n* **insurgence**, insurgency, rebellion, revolution, revolt, mutiny, uprising, rising, civil disobedience [➤ AGGRESSIVE EVENTS; 39]

in suspense *adj* [➤ POSITIVE IMPATIENCE, ENTHUSIASM, AND ALERTNESS; 537]

in sync (*informal*) *adv* [➤ HARMONY; 155]

intact *adj* **complete**, whole, unbroken, in one piece, integral, undamaged, unharmed, together [➤ WHOLENESS AND COMPLETENESS; 198] *Opposite*: broken

intake **1** *n* **consumption**, eating, drinking, ingestion [➤ EAT AND NOT EAT; 710] **2** *n* **opening**, pipe, tube, aperture, entry, inlet, duct [➤ WATERCOURSES; 1111] *Opposite*: outlet **3** *n* **entry**, entrants, students [➤ STUDENTS AND PUPILS; 841]

in tandem *adv* **in partnership**, together, concurrently, jointly, as a pair, as a team, with each other, collectively [➤ ACTING WITH OTHERS; 285] *Opposite*: independently

intangibility **1** *n* **imperceptibility**, immateriality, immaterialness, untouchability, insubstantiality, impalpability (*formal*) [➤ IMPERCEPTIBLE; 26] *Opposite*: tangibility **2** *n* **indescribability**, elusiveness, vagueness, subtlety, unquantifiability, abstractness, ethereality [➤ VAGUENESS; 243]

intangible **1** *adj* **imperceptible**, immaterial, insubstantial, incorporeal (*formal*), impalpable (*formal*) [➤ IMPERCEPTIBLE; 26] *Opposite*: concrete **2** *adj* **unquantifiable**, elusive, vague, ethereal, subtle, indefinable, indescribable [➤ VAGUENESS; 243]

intangibly *adv* **elusively**, imperceptibly, unsubstantially, impalpably [➤ IMPERCEPTIBLE; 26]

in tatters *adj* [➤ IN BAD REPAIR; 1234]

in tears *adj* [➤ CRYING; 650]

integer *n* **whole number**, number, numeral, digit, figure [➤ MATH; 597] *Opposite*: fraction

integral **1** *adj* **essential**, vital, important, basic, fundamental, primary, central [➤ FUNDAMENTAL; 195] **2** *adj* **connected**, internal, central, at the heart of [➤ RELATED; 142] *Opposite*: unimportant **3** *adj* **complete**, whole, intact, undivided, unbroken, full [➤ WHOLENESS AND COMPLETENESS; 198]

integrate **1** *v* **mix**, fit in, join in, assimilate, take part, participate [➤ PARTICIPATE; 292] **2** *v* **put together**, mix, incorporate, add, join together, amalgamate, combine, assimilate [➤ COMBINE AND MIX; 400] *Opposite*: separate **3** *v* **open up**, desegregate, combine, mix, assimilate [➤ ESTABLISHING RELATIONSHIPS WITH OTHERS; 974]

integrated **1** *adj* **combined**, united, joined, unified, cohesive, assimilated, incorporated, included, amalgamated [➤ RELATED; 142] *Opposite*: separated **2** *adj* **open**, desegregated, multiethnic, multicultural, multilingual, interracial [➤ HARMONY; 155] *Opposite*: segregated

integrated circuit *type of* **hardware** [➤ COMPUTERS AND COMPUTING; 1127]

integration *n* **addition**, mixing, incorporation, combination, amalgamation, assimilation [➤ COMBINE AND MIX; 400]

integrity *n* **honesty**, truth, truthfulness, honor, veracity, reliability, uprightness [➤ MORALLY GOOD; 774] *Opposite*: dishonesty

integument *n* [➤ THE SKIN; 720]

intellect *n* **intelligence**, brainpower, brain, brains, mind, understanding [➤ DESCRIBING SOMEBODY'S INTELLECT; 523] *Opposite*: emotion

intellectual **1** *adj* **knowledgeable**, intelligent, highbrow, academic, rational, logical, cerebral, scholarly [➤ POSITIVE INTELLECTUAL CHARACTERISTICS; 524] **2** *n* **philosopher**, thinker, academic, scholar, highbrow, brain (*informal*), egghead (*informal*) [➤ LEVELS OF EDUCATION AND SOPHISTICATION; 894]

intellectualize *v* [➤ THINK AND REFLECT; 743]

intelligence **1** *n* **brain**, cleverness, aptitude, intellect, brains, astuteness, brainpower, acumen [➤ DESCRIBING SOMEBODY'S INTELLECT; 523] *Opposite*: stupidity **2** *n* **information**, news, reports, communication, word, details [➤ BASIC DETAILS; 688]

intelligence quotient *n* **IQ**, mental ability, measure, measurement, degree, aptitude [➡ DESCRIBING SOMEBODY'S INTELLECT; 523]

intelligent 1 *adj* **clever**, bright, gifted, intellectual, sharp, quick, able, smart, scholarly, knowledgeable, brainy (*informal*) [➡ POSITIVE INTELLECTUAL CHARACTERISTICS; 524] *Opposite*: stupid 2 *adj* **sensible**, rational, wise, logical, perceptive, shrewd, judicious, cerebral [➡ POSITIVE INTELLECTUAL CHARACTERISTICS; 524] *Opposite*: irrational

Compare and Contrast: *intelligent, bright, quick, smart, clever, able, gifted*

CORE MEANING: having the ability to learn and understand easily

intelligent quick to learn and understand; *bright* showing an ability to think, learn, or respond quickly, especially used of younger people; *quick* alert, perceptive, and able to respond quickly; *smart* showing intelligence and mental alertness; *clever* having sharp mental abilities, sometimes suggesting showy or superficial cleverness; *able* capable or talented, also used in educational circles of children who are intelligent; *gifted* talented, especially artistically or creatively, also used in educational circles of children who are exceptionally intelligent.

intelligentsia *n* **intellectuals**, academics, highbrows, cognoscenti, literati (*formal*) [➡ LEVELS OF EDUCATION AND SOPHISTICATION; 894]

intelligible *adj* **comprehensible**, understandable, clear, plain, lucid, logical [➡ CONCISE AND CLEAR; 202] *Opposite*: unintelligible

intemperance *n* **self-indulgence**, overindulgence, excess, hedonism, gluttony, greed [➡ PLEASURE-SEEKING AND EXCESS; 885] *Opposite*: moderation

intemperate *adj* **self-indulgent**, uncontrolled, unrestrained, inordinate, immoderate, unbalanced, extreme, severe, excessive, greedy, extravagant, unreasonable [➡ PLEASURE-SEEKING AND EXCESS; 885] *Opposite*: moderate

intemperately *adv* **greedily**, excessively, self-indulgently, inordinately, extravagantly, unreasonably, extremely, severely, immoderately (*formal*) [➡ PLEASURE-SEEKING AND EXCESS; 885] *Opposite*: temperately

intend *v* **mean**, aim, propose, plan, have it in mind, anticipate, expect [➡ PREPARE FOR ACTION; 289]

intended 1 *adj* **envisioned**, future, planned, proposed, projected, wished-for, anticipated [➡ FUTURE; 86] 2 *adj* **planned**, intentional, deliberate, on purpose, premeditated, calculated [➡ INTENTIONAL AND DELIBERATE; 279] *Opposite*: accidental 3 *n* (*dated or humorous*) **fiancé**, fiancée, husband-to-be, wife-to-be, girlfriend, boyfriend, betrothed (*formal*) [➡ RELATIVES BY MARRIAGE; 960]

intense *adj* **penetrating**, strong, powerful, forceful, concentrated, deep, passionate, extreme, severe [➡ STRENGTH; 201] *Opposite*: moderate

intensely *adv* **forcefully**, penetratingly, powerfully, strongly, deeply, very much, extremely, hugely, passionately, severely [➡ TO A GREAT EXTENT; 132] *Opposite*: mildly

intensification *n* **strengthening**, increase, rise, spiral-ing, escalation, growth, amplification [➡ CHANGE OF INTENSITY: MORE; 394] *Opposite*: reduction

intensify *v* **strengthen**, deepen, step up, exaggerate, increase, heap on, build up, pile on (*UK*) [➡ CHANGE OF INTENSITY: MORE; 394] *Opposite*: weaken

*See Compare and Contrast at **increase**.*

intensity *n* **strength**, concentration, power, force, passion, amount, greatness [➡ STRENGTH; 201] *Opposite*: moderation

intensive *adj* **concentrated**, rigorous, exhaustive, severe, thorough, demanding, serious [➡ STRENGTH; 201] *Opposite*: easy

intensive care 1 *n* **monitoring**, nursing, 24-hour care, one-to-one care, specialist care (*UK*) [➡ HOSPITALS AND CLINICS; 826] 2 *n* **ward**, ICU, intensive care unit [➡ HOSPITALS AND CLINICS; 826]

intensive care unit *n* **intensive care**, ICU, ward [➡ HOSPITALS AND CLINICS; 826]

intent 1 *n* (*formal*) **intention**, aim, goal, target, objective, plan, meaning, purpose [➡ INTENTIONS AND PURPOSES; 772] 2 *adj* **concentrated**, absorbed, focused, directed, fixed, rapt, engaged [➡ PENSIVENESS AND INTEREST; 538] 3 *adj* **intending to**, bent on, determined, resolved, set on, committed [➡ DESIRE AND WANT; 579]

intention *n* **aim**, purpose, goal, target, objective, plan, intent (*formal*) [➡ INTENTIONS AND PURPOSES; 772]

intentional *adj* **deliberate**, planned, intended, premeditated, calculated, purposeful [➡ INTENTIONAL AND DELIBERATE; 279] *Opposite*: accidental

intently *adv* **closely**, fixedly, carefully, keenly, attentively, absorbedly, raptly [➡ PENSIVENESS AND INTEREST; 538] *Opposite*: abstractedly

intentness *n* **attentiveness**, concentration, focus, attention, close attention, raptness, fixedness, absorption [➡ ATTENTION AND ATTENTIVENESS; 763] *Opposite*: abstraction

inter *v* **bury**, entomb, lay to rest [➡ BURIAL AND PREPARATION FOR BURIAL; 929]

interact *v* **interrelate**, act together, cooperate, relate, intermingle, network [➡ CREATING CONNECTIONS; 144]

interaction *n* **communication**, contact, interface, dealings, relations, collaboration [➡ COMMUNICATION; 602]

interactive *adj* **communicating**, collaborating, cooperating, collaborative, cooperative, shared [➡ RELATED; 142]

inter alia (*formal*) *adv* **among others**, among other things, and others, et cetera, and so on [➡ WRITTEN CONVENTIONS; 599]

interbreed *v* **breed**, reproduce, multiply, mate, produce, propagate, spawn [➡ REPRODUCTION AND HEREDITY; 725]

intercalate *v* **insert**, introduce, interpolate, add, interpose, place [➡ POSITION SOMETHING: BETWEEN, BESIDE, OR INSIDE SOMETHING; 326] *Opposite*: extrapolate

intercede *v* **intervene**, mediate, plead, negotiate, arbitrate [➡ PARTICIPATE; 292]

intercept *v* **cut off**, catch, interrupt, stop, seize, capture, divert [➡ CAUSE TO STOP; 266]

interception *n* **capture**, seizure, interruption, interference, intervention [➡ PAUSES AND PHASES; 56]

intercession *n* **intervention**, mediation, arbitration, negotiation [➡ NEGOTIATION AND DEBATE; 46]

interchange **1** *v* **switch**, trade, exchange, substitute, trade off, swap (*informal*) [➡ EXCHANGE AND INTERCHANGE; 448] **2** *n* **trading**, exchange, transaction, swapping, substitution, tradeoff, swap (*informal*) [➡ EXCHANGE AND INTERCHANGE; 448] **3** *n* **crossroads**, junction, intersection [➡ BRIDGES, TUNNELS, CROSSINGS, AND JUNCTIONS; 1112]

interchangeable *adj* **substitutable**, identical, the same, similar, compatible, transposable, exchangeable, switchable, swappable [➡ SAMENESS; 150] *Opposite*: incompatible

intercity *adj* **interurban**, long-distance [➡ COMMUNICATION NETWORKS; 1105] *Opposite*: local

intercollegiate *adj* **intercollege**, interuniversity, interschool, intermural [➡ CLASSES, COURSEWORK, AND EXAMINATIONS; 842] *Opposite*: intramural

intercom *type of* **telecommunications equipment** [➡ TELECOMMUNICATIONS; 1130]

intercommunicate *v* **talk**, communicate, converse, discuss, contact [➡ TWO-WAY COMMUNICATION; 607]

interconnect *v* **join**, intersect, connect, interrelate, interlock, communicate [➡ CREATING CONNECTIONS; 144]

intercontinental *adj* **international**, transnational, global, worldwide, large-scale [➡ COUNTRIES AND REGIONS; 1067] *Opposite*: national

intercourse *n* **dealings**, contact, communication, interaction, association [➡ COMMUNICATION; 602]

intercut *v* **interpose**, insert, alternate, interweave, interject, interpolate [➡ POSITION SOMETHING: BETWEEN, BESIDE, OR INSIDE SOMETHING; 326]

interdenominational *adj* **interfaith**, interreligion, ecumenical, inclusive, mixed [➡ RELIGIONS AND RELIGIOUS PRACTICES; 777]

interdependent *adj* **symbiotic**, dependent, reliant, codependent [➡ RECIPROCITY AND INTERDEPENDENCE; 147]

interdict **1** *n* **order**, court order, ban, prohibition, veto, injunction, restraining order, exclusion order, embargo, sanction, restriction, proscription (*formal*) [➡ REFUSE PERMISSION AND NOT ALLOW; 670] **2** *v* **ban**, prohibit, forbid, veto, embargo, exclude, proscribe, bar, preclude (*formal*) [➡ REFUSE PERMISSION AND NOT ALLOW; 670] *Opposite*: permit

interest **1** *n* **attention**, notice, curiosity, concentration, awareness, attentiveness, concern [➡ ATTENTION AND ATTENTIVENESS; 763] *Opposite*: indifference **2** *n* **concern**, importance, significance, relevance, note, consequence (*formal*) [➡ IMPORTANCE AND SIGNIFICANCE; 192] **3** *n* **hobby**, activity, pursuit, pastime, leisure activity, leisure pursuit [➡ LEISURE AND RECREATION; 874] **4** *n* **good**, advantage, benefit, gain, profit [➡ SOURCE OF HAPPINESS, PLEASURE, OR IMPROVEMENT; 209] **5** *v* **attract**, draw, appeal, fascinate, be of interest, catch your eye [➡ APPEAL TO AND AROUSE INTEREST; 575] *Opposite*: bore

interested *adj* **absorbed**, attentive, involved, concerned,

attracted, fascinated, engrossed, intent, entranced, captivated, riveted (*informal*) [➡ PENSIVENESS AND INTEREST; 538] *Opposite*: indifferent

interest group **1** *n* **alliance**, association, society, cartel, trade union, league, pressure group, lobby, faction, group, lobby group (*UK*) [➡ GROUPS WITH A COMMON INTEREST; 938] **2** *n* **club**, association, group, society [➡ CLUBS AND SOCIETIES; 939]

interesting *adj* **stimulating**, attractive, thought-provoking, motivating, exciting, fascinating, attention-grabbing, out of the ordinary, remarkable, worthy of note, curious, noteworthy [➡ INTERESTING AND MEANINGFUL; 190] *Opposite*: boring

interface **1** *n* **border**, boundary, line, crossing point, edge [➡ EXTREMITIES OF PHYSICAL OBJECTS; 1250] **2** *type of* **software** [➡ COMPUTERS AND COMPUTING; 1127] **3** *type of* **hardware** [➡ COMPUTERS AND COMPUTING; 1127]

interfere **1** *v* **delay**, inhibit, restrict, affect, get in the way, hinder, obstruct, impede, hold up, hamper [➡ AVOID, PREVENT, LIMIT, AND CONTROL; 277] **2** *v* **pry**, intrude, meddle, disturb, intervene, stick your nose in, interlope, snoop (*informal*), stick your oar in (*UK*) [➡ INTERRUPT AND BUTT IN; 619]

interference **1** *n* **meddling**, intrusion, prying, interfering, intervention, interloping, nosiness (*informal*), snooping (*informal*) [➡ BAD BEHAVIOR OR ACTIONS; 254] **2** *n* **restriction**, obstruction, hindrance, obstacle, delay, impediment, holdup [➡ PROBLEMS; 256]

interfere with (*UK*) *v* [➡ WOUND A PERSON OR ANIMAL; 383]

interfering *adj* **intrusive**, meddlesome, prying, inquisitive, meddling, interloping, nosy (*informal*), snooping (*informal*) [➡ NOSY AND INTERFERING; 512]

intergalactic *adj* **interstellar**, interplanetary, space [➡ THE SOLAR SYSTEM AND ASTRONOMY; 1060]

intergovernmental *adj* **interstate**, international, diplomatic, foreign, high-level, transnational, geopolitical [➡ COUNTRIES AND REGIONS; 1067]

interim **1** *adj* **temporary**, provisional, short-term, intervening, acting, pro tem, ad hoc [➡ FINITENESS, VARIABILITY, AND TRANSIENCE; 96] *Opposite*: permanent **2** *n* **interlude**, pause, break, interval, pause in the action, intermezzo [➡ PAUSES AND PHASES; 56]

interior **1** *n* **inside**, core, center, heart [➡ CENTRAL PARTS OF PHYSICAL OBJECTS; 1251] *Opposite*: outside **2** *adj* **internal**, inner, central, inland, inside [➡ GENERAL LOCATIONS; 158] *Opposite*: peripheral

interior decoration *n* **decoration**, furnishings, decorating scheme, interior design, decor, color scheme [➡ ORNAMENTS AND DECORATIONS; 1248]

interject *v* **butt in**, exclaim, interrupt, throw in, interpose, cut in, interpolate, speak [➡ INTERRUPT AND BUTT IN; 619]

interjection **1** *n* **exclamation**, outburst, cry, utterance, shout [➡ ONE-WAY COMMUNICATION; 49] **2** *n* **interruption**, interpolation, introduction, addition, insertion [➡ ONE-WAY COMMUNICATION; 49] **3** *type of* **word class** [➡ ASPECTS OF LANGUAGE; 682]

interlace *v* **interweave**, intertwine, interlock, entwine, knit, connect, intermingle, link, interconnect, interlink, join, intermesh, mesh [➡ POSITION SOMETHING: BETWEEN, BESIDE, OR INSIDE SOMETHING; 326]

interlard v **interpose**, insert, introduce, intersperse, interweave, intertwine, alternate, interpolate, vary [➡ POSITION SOMETHING: BETWEEN, BESIDE, OR INSIDE SOMETHING; 326]

interleave v **slot in**, put in, enclose, interweave, add, incorporate, include, insert [➡ POSITION SOMETHING: BETWEEN, BESIDE, OR INSIDE SOMETHING; 326]

interlink v **interweave**, intertwine, interlace, insert, intersperse, add, link, entwine, interconnect, knit, connect, intermingle, intermesh, mesh, join [➡ POSITION SOMETHING: BETWEEN, BESIDE, OR INSIDE SOMETHING; 326]

interlock v **mesh**, dovetail, link, join, interconnect, connect, intertwine, knit, intermingle, interlink, interweave, intermesh [➡ POSITION SOMETHING: BETWEEN, BESIDE, OR INSIDE SOMETHING; 326]

interlocutor n **speaker**, talker, discusser, panelist, converser, debater [➡ SPEAKERS AND ORATORS; 603]

interloper 1 n **intruder**, trespasser, gatecrasher, persona non grata, impostor [➡ STRANGERS; 972] 2 n **meddler**, busybody (*informal*), snoop (*informal*) [➡ INTERFERING PEOPLE AND TATTLETALES; 950]

interlude n **interval**, break, rest, pause, interim, intermission, intermezzo [➡ PAUSES AND PHASES; 56]

intermediary 1 n **intercessor**, arbitrator, negotiator, go-between, mediator, liaison, agent, conciliator, intermediate [➡ REPRESENTATIVES AND PATRONS; 968] 2 adj **intermediate**, middle, midway, in-between, transitional, halfway [➡ RELATIVE LOCATION; 161]

intermediate adj **middle**, midway, in between, transitional, halfway, intermediary [➡ RELATIVE LOCATION; 161] Opposite: extreme

interment n **burial**, entombment, committal, funeral, funeral rites [➡ BURIAL AND PREPARATION FOR BURIAL; 929]

intermesh v **join**, interlink, knit, mesh, interconnect, interlock, interlace, intertwine, intersperse, link, entwine [➡ POSITION SOMETHING: BETWEEN, BESIDE, OR INSIDE SOMETHING; 326]

intermezzo type of **musical form** [➡ MUSIC, SONGS, AND SINGING; 907]

interminable adj **endless**, ceaseless, everlasting, perpetual, never-ending, incessant [➡ PERMANENCE: WITHOUT END; 94] Opposite: finite

intermingle v **intermix**, mingle, interact, combine, fuse, meld, amalgamate, coalesce [➡ COMBINE AND MIX; 400]

intermission n **intermezzo**, interval, break, interlude, pause, rest [➡ PAUSES AND PHASES; 56]

intermittent adj **spasmodic**, recurrent, erratic, irregular, sporadic, discontinuous, broken, alternating, occasional [➡ FINITENESS, VARIABILITY, AND TRANSIENCE; 96] Opposite: constant

See Compare and Contrast at **periodic**.

intermix v **meld**, intermingle, mix, mingle, blend, amal-

gamate, fuse, merge, combine, coalesce [➡ COMBINE AND MIX; 400] Opposite: separate

intern 1 v **imprison**, detain, confine, hold, jail [➡ THE POLICE, ARREST, AND PRETRIAL PROCEEDINGS; 818] Opposite: release 2 n **medical student**, med student, doctor, student doctor, medic (*informal*) [➡ STUDENTS AND PUPILS; 841]

internal 1 adj **interior**, inner, inside, core, heart, center [➡ CENTRAL PARTS OF PHYSICAL OBJECTS; 1251] Opposite: external 2 adj **domestic**, in-house, home, intramural [➡ BELONGING OR RELATING TO INDIVIDUALS; 944] Opposite: external

internal ear part of **ear** [➡ THE EAR; 706]

internalize 1 v **adopt**, affect, take on, assume, co-opt [➡ LEARN AND DISCOVER; 762] 2 v **stew**, mull over, bottle up, suppress [➡ WITHHOLD INFORMATION; 687] Opposite: externalize

international adj **global**, worldwide, intercontinental, universal, transnational [➡ COUNTRIES AND REGIONS; 1067] Opposite: domestic

internationalist adj **open-minded**, unprejudiced, unbigoted, unnationalistic [➡ STYLES AND SYSTEMS OF GOVERNMENT; 806] Opposite: nationalist

internecine 1 adj **internal**, inner, civil, domestic [➡ BELONGING OR RELATING TO INDIVIDUALS; 944] 2 adj **destructive**, devastating, decimating, deadly, injurious, costly, havoc-wreaking [➡ DANGEROUS; 236]

internee n **prisoner**, captive, detainee, hostage, inmate, political prisoner [➡ CAPTIVES AND PRISONERS; 249]

Internet n [➡ THE INTERNET; 1128]

internment n **imprisonment**, captivity, confinement, custody, detention, incarceration (*formal*) [➡ CAPTIVITY AND LOSS OF FREEDOM; 248] Opposite: release

internship n **residency**, medical training, practicum, medical school, training period, position, placement, job [➡ JOB; 833]

interpersonal adj **relational**, social, personal, interactive [➡ RELATIONSHIP TO ANOTHER; 973] Opposite: solitary

interplanetary adj **space**, planetary, interstellar, intergalactic, astronomical [➡ THE SOLAR SYSTEM AND ASTRONOMY; 1060]

interplay n **chemistry**, interaction, relationship, interchange, back-and-forth [➡ CONNECTIONS; 143]

interpolate 1 v **insert**, interpose, intercalate, incorporate, include, add, introduce [➡ POSITION SOMETHING: BETWEEN, BESIDE, OR INSIDE SOMETHING; 326] 2 v **interrupt**, interject, interpose, throw in, cut in, butt in [➡ INTERRUPT AND BUTT IN; 619]

interpose 1 v **interrupt**, cut in, throw in, interpolate, interject, butt in [➡ INTERRUPT AND BUTT IN; 619] 2 v **intervene**, interfere, intercede, meddle, butt in, mediate, negotiate, arbitrate [➡ PARTICIPATE; 292]

interpret 1 v **explain**, clarify, account for, elucidate, make clear, shed light on, illuminate [➡ EXPLAIN AND CLARIFY; 610] 2 v **take to mean**, understand, read, construe, infer, read between the lines, deduce, take [➡ SOLVE AND INTERPRET; 760] 3 v **translate**, decode, decipher, unravel, figure out [➡ SOLVE AND INTERPRET; 760]

interpretation n **clarification**, understanding, reading, explanation, analysis, version, construal, elucidation (*formal*) [➡ EXPLAIN AND CLARIFY; 610]

interpretative *adj* **explanatory**, revelatory, informational, informative, revealing, interpretive [➡ EXPLAIN AND CLARIFY; 610]

interpreter 1 *n* **translator**, linguist, transcriber, polyglot, explainer, paraphraser, commentator, exegetist, explicator [➡ PEOPLE WHO WORK WITH LANGUAGE AND CODE; 854] **2** *n* **performer**, portrayer, exponent, promoter, medium, player, actor, musician, reader [➡ ARTISTS; 900]

interpretive *adj* **explanatory**, revelatory, informational, informative, revealing, interpretative [➡ EXPLAIN AND CLARIFY; 610]

interracial *adj* **mixed**, of mixed race, multicultural, multiethnic, integrated, mixed-race, multiracial [➡ RECIPROCITY AND INTERDEPENDENCE; 147] *Opposite*: segregated

interregnum *n* **interval**, pause, lag, lapse, wait, period, interruption, hiatus [➡ PAUSES AND PHASES; 56]

interrelate *v* **interconnect**, relate, connect, link up, correlate, join up, interdepend [➡ CREATING CONNECTIONS; 144]

interrogate *v* **question**, cross-examine, quiz, interview, debrief, catechize, probe, grill (*informal*), give the third degree (*informal*) [➡ ASK PEOPLE QUESTIONS; 666]

See Compare and Contrast at **question**.

interrogation *n* **questioning**, examination, cross-examination, grilling, interview, debriefing [➡ ASK PEOPLE QUESTIONS; 666]

interrogative *adj* **questioning**, curious, inquisitive, inquiring, probing [➡ ENTHUSIASTIC AND INQUISITIVE; 628]

interrogator *n* **questioner**, interviewer, investigator, examiner [➡ QUESTIONERS; 667]

interrupt 1 *v* **butt in**, barge in, interject, disturb, intrude, interpose, intersect, interfere, cut in on [➡ INTERRUPT AND BUTT IN; 619] **2** *v* **break off**, cut short, disrupt, break up, stop, suspend, discontinue, disconnect [➡ CAUSE TO STOP; 266]

interruption *n* **break**, pause, disruption, stoppage, disturbance, intrusion, intermission, interlude, interval, disconnection [➡ PAUSES AND PHASES; 56]

intersect *v* **cross**, interconnect, meet, traverse, overlap, crisscross, pass across, transect [➡ CREATING CONNECTIONS; 144]

intersection 1 *n* **connection**, meeting, node, joint, joining, crossing, coming together, juncture (*formal*) [➡ CONNECTIONS; 143] **2** *n* **junction**, crossroads, fork, interchange, cloverleaf, exit, traffic circle, rotary, gyratory (*UK*), roundabout (*UK*), T-junction (*UK*) [➡ BRIDGES, TUNNELS, CROSSINGS, AND JUNCTIONS; 1112]

intersperse *v* **mix together**, combine, scatter, spread, intermingle, sprinkle, interpose, pepper, intermix, punctuate, break up, dot, disperse, broadcast, commingle (*literary*) [➡ COMBINE AND MIX; 400]

interstate 1 *adj* **regional**, national, federal, political, administrative, judicial [➡ GOVERNMENT AND POLITICS; 805] **2** *type of* **highway** [➡ ROADS; 1106]

interstellar *adj* **interplanetary**, space, star, intergalactic, stellar, astronomical [➡ THE SOLAR SYSTEM AND ASTRONOMY; 1060]

interstice *n* **space**, gap, crack, opening, aperture, chink, cranny, crevice, cleft, fissure [➡ HOLES, GAPS, AND FORKS; 1252]

intertwine *v* **interweave**, entwine, interlace, link, interleave, interlink, interlock, knit, interconnect, intermingle, connect, braid, crisscross, mesh [➡ POSITION SOMETHING: BETWEEN, BESIDE, OR INSIDE SOMETHING; 326] *Opposite*: divide

intertwined *adj* [➡ RELATIVE LOCATION; 161]

interval 1 *n* **gap**, space, distance, hiatus, separation, rift, breach [➡ HOLES, GAPS, AND FORKS; 1252] **2** *n* (*UK*) **intermission**, break, pause, interlude, recess, rest, wait, interim [➡ PAUSES AND PHASES; 56]

intervene 1 *v* **intercede**, arbitrate, mediate, interfere, get involved, intrude, interpose, butt in (*informal*) [➡ PARTICIPATE; 292] *Opposite*: hold back **2** *v* **happen**, occur, take place, ensue, succeed, arise, come to pass (*archaic or literary*), befall (*archaic or literary*) [➡ HAPPEN; 27]

intervention *n* **interference**, involvement, intrusion, intercession, interposition, interpolation, mediation, intermediation [➡ NEGOTIATION AND DEBATE; 46]

interview 1 *n* **meeting**, talk, consultation, conference, discussion, question and answer session, conversation, dialogue, roundtable [➡ MEETINGS AND ASSEMBLIES; 43] **2** *v* **question**, interrogate, talk to, converse with, put questions to, cross-examine, quiz [➡ ASK PEOPLE QUESTIONS; 666]

interviewee *n* **applicant**, candidate, hopeful, aspirant, contender, entrant, examinee [➡ SUBORDINATES AND ASSISTANTS; 966] *Opposite*: interviewer

interviewer 1 *n* **examiner**, assessor, questioner, interrogator, evaluator, investigator, cross-examiner [➡ QUESTIONERS; 667] *Opposite*: interviewee **2** *n* **questioner**, correspondent, personality, journalist, presenter (*UK*) [➡ WORKERS IN ENTERTAINMENT AND MEDIA; 873]

interweave *v* **intertwine**, interlace, mingle, intermingle, entwine, link, interleave, interlink, interlock, knit, interconnect, connect, crisscross, braid, mesh [➡ POSITION SOMETHING: BETWEEN, BESIDE, OR INSIDE SOMETHING; 326]

interwoven *adj* [➡ RELATIVE LOCATION; 161]

intestate *adj* **without a will**, unrepresented, unaccounted for, voiceless, unheard [➡ LACK OF POSSESSION; 445]

intestinal *adj* **duodenal**, colonic, abdominal, stomach, bowel, celiac, gastric, gut, ventral, visceral [➡ THE DIGESTIVE TRACT; 709]

intestine *part of* **digestive tract** [➡ THE DIGESTIVE TRACT; 709]

in that *conj* **because**, as, since, given that [➡ CAUSATION; 168]

in the air *adj* **imminent**, about to happen, in the pipeline, forthcoming, coming, near, happening, threatening, in preparation [➡ ABOUT TO HAPPEN; 33]

in the altogether (*informal*) *adj* **naked**, nude, bare, unclothed, stark-naked, stripped, undressed, buck naked, with nothing on, in the buff (*informal*), in your birthday suit (*slang humorous*) [➡ DRESS, WEAR, AND UNDRESS; 868] *Opposite*: clothed

in the area *adv* [➡ PRESENT AND AVAILABLE; 11]

in the ascendant *adj* [➡ PLEASANT SITUATIONS; 74]

in the background *adv* [➡ GENERAL LOCATIONS; 158]

in the bag (*informal*) *adj* **certain**, guaranteed, assured, definite, a sure thing (*informal*) [➡ CERTAIN; 174] *Opposite*: uncertain

in the black *adj* **in credit**, solvent, in the money, in clover, flush (*informal*) [➡ WEALTH AND WEALTHY; 891] *Opposite*: in the red

in the blink of an eye *adv* [➡ HAPPENING QUICKLY; 104]

in the buff (*informal*) *adj* [➡ DRESS, WEAR, AND UNDRESS; 868]

in the cards (*informal*) *adj* [➡ POSSIBLE AND PROBABLE; 177]

in the chips *adj* [➡ WEALTH AND WEALTHY; 891]

in the clear *adj* **innocent**, let off, free of blame, cleared, guiltless, blameless, free to go, scot free, exonerated, off the hook (*informal*) [➡ FREEDOM AND LIBERTY; 208] *Opposite*: guilty

in the course of *prep* [➡ CONCURRENT AND CONTEMPORANEOUS; 164]

in the distance *adv* [➡ DISTANCE; 160]

in the doghouse (*informal*) *adj* **in disgrace**, in trouble, out of favor, disgraced, in bad odor, under a cloud [➡ IN TROUBLE AND DISADVANTAGED; 73] *Opposite*: popular

in the doldrums *adj* [➡ SADNESS, DISTRESS, AND DESPAIR; 539]

in the dumps *adj* [➡ SADNESS, DISTRESS, AND DESPAIR; 539]

in the end *adv* **finally**, eventually, after some time, at long last, after a while, ultimately, at last, at the end of the day [➡ AFTER, LAST, AND FOLLOWING; 165] *Opposite*: initially

in the event *adv* **as it turned out**, as it was, unexpectedly, surprisingly, when it came to it, as it happened, anyway, anyhow, the thing was [➡ RESULTS AND OUTCOMES; 83]

in the face of *prep* **despite**, in spite of, notwithstanding (*formal*), regardless of [➡ ALTHOUGH, NEVERTHELESS, AND DESPITE; 169]

in the family way (*dated informal*) *adj* [➡ REPRODUCTION AND HEREDITY; 725]

in the flesh *adv* **in person**, personally, in real life, physically, individually, yourself [➡ ACTING INDEPENDENTLY; 284]

in the fullness of time *adv* [➡ FUTURE; 86]

in the future *adv* [➡ FUTURE; 86]

in the know *adj* **informed**, in the picture, well-informed, aware, primed, enlightened, with it (*informal*), on the ball (*informal*) [➡ KNOWLEDGE AND WISDOM; 558] *Opposite*: ignorant

in the lap of luxury *adj* [➡ PLEASANT SITUATIONS; 74]

in the lead *adj* [➡ PLEASANT SITUATIONS; 74]

in the light of *prep* **taking into consideration**, in view of, considering, taking into account, with regard to, given that, all in all [➡ CAUSATION; 168]

in the limelight *adj* [➡ KNOWN AND FAMOUS; 181]

in the long run *adv* [➡ FUTURE; 86]

in the lurch *adj* [➡ IN TROUBLE AND DISADVANTAGED; 73]

in the main *adv* **largely**, in general, on the whole, generally, generally speaking, for the most part, by and large, when all's said and done, as a rule, ordinarily, commonly, usually [➡ SUMMARIZING EXPRESSIONS; 622] *Opposite*: in part

in the making *adj* **future**, potential, budding, prospective, to be, to come, upcoming, up and coming, promising [➡ FUTURE; 86] *Opposite*: established

in the midst of *adv* **in the middle of**, at the heart of, amid, among, between, in, amongst, within, inside [➡ GENERAL LOCATIONS; 158]

in the money *adj* **rich**, in clover, well-off, affluent, prosperous, not short, in the black, rolling in it (*informal*), flush (*informal*), loaded (*slang*) [➡ WEALTH AND WEALTHY; 891] *Opposite*: poor

in the name of *prep* **on behalf of**, for, for the benefit of, for the sake of, on the authority of [➡ CAUSATION; 168]

in the near future *adv* [➡ FUTURE; 86]

in the nick of time *adv* [➡ PROMPTNESS: ON TIME; 99]

in the nude *adj* [➡ DRESS, WEAR, AND UNDRESS; 868]

in the offing *adj* **imminent**, coming up, on the agenda, on the horizon, forthcoming, in the pipeline, pending, looming, expected, likely, upcoming, in the cards (*informal*) [➡ ABOUT TO HAPPEN; 33]

in the open **1** *adj* **unhidden**, unconcealed, revealed, on show, public, public knowledge, known, in the public domain [➡ KNOWN AND FAMOUS; 181] *Opposite*: concealed **2** *adv* **openly**, publicly, in full view, for everyone to see, in public, without fear, unashamedly [➡ PERCEPTIBLE; 25] *Opposite*: furtively

in theory *adv* **theoretically**, technically, in principle, hypothetically, on paper, ideally [➡ POSSIBLE AND PROBABLE; 177] *Opposite*: in fact

in the past *adv* [➡ PAST; 84]

in the picture *adj* [➡ KNOWLEDGE AND WISDOM; 558]

in the pink (*dated*) *adj* [➡ FIT AND STRONG; 736]

in the pipeline *adj* **in preparation**, on the way, underway, on the go, planned, under discussion, coming up, forthcoming, imminent, on the agenda, up and coming, in the offing, on the horizon, upcoming, in the cards (*informal*) [➡ ABOUT TO HAPPEN; 33]

in the public domain *adj* [➡ KNOWN AND FAMOUS; 181]

in the raw (*informal*) *adj* **naked**, stark-naked, nude, in the nude, with nothing on, in a state of undress, stripped, unclothed, in the buff (*informal*), in your birthday suit (*slang humorous*), au naturel (*humorous*) [➡ DRESS, WEAR, AND UNDRESS; 868] *Opposite*: dressed

in the rear *adv* [➡ GENERAL LOCATIONS; 158]

in the red *adj* **overdrawn**, in debt, insolvent, in arrears, bankrupt, indebted, broke (*informal*) [➡ POVERTY AND POOR; 892] *Opposite*: in the black

in the region of *adv* [➡ APPROXIMATELY; 135]

in the right *adj* **correct**, right, justified, blameless, not to blame, vindicated [➡ MORALLY GOOD; 774] *Opposite*: wrong

in the running *adj* **in contention**, in competition, up there, in with a shout (*informal*) [➡ POSSIBLE AND PROBABLE; 177]

in the short term *adv* [➡ FUTURE; 86]

in the soup (*informal*) *adj* **in trouble**, in hot water, in a tight spot, in a tight corner, in a predicament, in dire straits, in difficulties, in a jam (*informal*), up the creek (*informal*), in a fix (*informal*) [➡ IN TROUBLE AND DISADVANTAGED; 73]

in the stars *adj* [➡ ABOUT TO HAPPEN; 33]

in the throes of *adv* **in the process of**, in the middle of, in the midst of, in the thick of, involved in [➡ HAPPENING AND IN PROGRESS; 32]

in the twinkling of an eye *adv* [➡ HAPPENING QUICKLY; 104]

in the vicinity *adv* [➡ CLOSENESS; 159]

in the wind (*UK*) *adj* [➡ HAPPENING AND IN PROGRESS; 32]

in the works *adj* [➡ HAPPENING AND IN PROGRESS; 32]

in the wrong 1 *adj* **to blame**, at fault, culpable, responsible, blameworthy, guilty, blamable, out of line (*informal*) [➡ MORALLY BAD OR IMPROPER; 775] *Opposite*: in the right 2 *adj* **mistaken**, incorrect, wide of the mark, off beam, wrong, not thinking straight [➡ INCORRECT AND ERRONEOUS; 222] *Opposite*: in the right

in this day and age *adv* [➡ PRESENT; 85]

in throngs *adv* [➡ MANY, MUCH, LARGE AMOUNT; 117]

intimacy 1 *n* **familiarity**, closeness, understanding, confidence, caring, tenderness, affection [➡ RELATIONSHIP TO ANOTHER; 973] *Opposite*: distance 2 *n* **quietness**, seclusion, privacy, informality, friendliness, warmth [➡ LEVELS OF FORMALITY; 522] *Opposite*: formality

intimate 1 *adj* **close**, dear, near, warm, friendly, bosom, cherished, familiar [➡ RELATIONSHIP TO ANOTHER; 973] *Opposite*: distant 2 *adj* **quiet**, cozy, informal, friendly, warm, snug, comfortable, relaxed [➡ LEVELS OF FORMALITY; 522] *Opposite*: formal 3 *adj* **personal**, confidential, private, secret, innermost, guarded [➡ SECRET AND UNKNOWN; 179] *Opposite*: public 4 *adj* **thorough**, detailed, in-depth, profound, firsthand, exhaustive, deep, special, close [➡ WHOLENESS AND COMPLETENESS; 198] *Opposite*: superficial 5 *v* **suggest**, hint, insinuate, imply, indicate, infer, allude, rumor [➡ SUGGEST, HINT, AND COMMENT; 612]

intimately 1 *adv* **closely**, warmly, familiarly, confidentially, personally, well [➡ RELATIONSHIP TO ANOTHER; 973] *Opposite*: distantly 2 *adv* **quietly**, informally, cozily, warmly, comfortably, snugly [➡ LEVELS OF FORMALITY; 522] *Opposite*: coldly 3 *adv* **thoroughly**, very well, fully, in detail, closely, through and through, deeply [➡ WHOLENESS AND COMPLETENESS; 198] *Opposite*: superficially

intimation *n* **hint**, allusion, insinuation, suggestion, warning, inkling, indication, rumor [➡ SUGGEST, HINT, AND COMMENT; 612]

in time 1 *adv* **early enough**, soon enough, before you know it, early [➡ PROMPTNESS: EARLY; 98] *Opposite*: late 2 *adv* **eventually**, after a while, over time, in the end, in due course, in the fullness of time, sooner or later, ultimately, at the end of the day [➡ FUTURE; 86] *Opposite*: instantly 3 *adv*

in step, keeping pace, in synchronization, keeping up, together, synchronously, all together, in sync (*informal*) [➡ HARMONY; 155]

intimidate *v* **threaten**, frighten, scare, bully, coerce, terrorize, overawe, daunt, put off, terrify, alarm, browbeat [➡ FRIGHTEN AND SHOCK; 568]

intimidated *adj* **daunted**, scared, frightened, overwhelmed, unsettled, afraid, overawed, apprehensive, nervous, alarmed, terrified, browbeaten [➡ FEAR AND PANIC; 543] *Opposite*: relaxed

intimidating *adj* **threatening**, unapproachable, frightening, daunting, menacing, nerve-racking, overwhelming, alarming, terrifying, browbeating, scary (*informal*) [➡ FRIGHTENING; 231] *Opposite*: approachable

intimidation *n* **coercion**, pressure, bullying, threats, terrorization, extortion [➡ CRITICISMS AND ANGRY OUTBURSTS; 50]

in tiptop condition *adj* [➡ IN GOOD REPAIR; 1232]

into *adj* **addicted to**, interested in, obsessed by, mad about, crazy about (*informal*), hooked on (*slang*), keen on (*UK*) [➡ APPRECIATION AND GRATITUDE; 535]

intolerable *adj* **unbearable**, insufferable, impossible, unendurable, painful, insupportable, excruciating, inexcusable [➡ EMOTIONALLY UNPLEASANT AND UPSETTING; 227] *Opposite*: bearable

intolerance *n* **bigotry**, prejudice, narrow-mindedness, fanaticism, narrowness, bias, xenophobia, chauvinism, racism [➡ PREJUDICE; 550] *Opposite*: tolerance

intolerant *adj* **bigoted**, prejudiced, narrow-minded, fanatical, blinkered, biased, chauvinistic, xenophobic, racist [➡ SELFISH AND UNKIND; 505] *Opposite*: tolerant

intolerantly *adv* **narrow-mindedly**, bigotedly, prejudicially, illiberally, unfairly, chauvinistically [➡ SELFISH AND UNKIND; 505] *Opposite*: tolerantly

intonation 1 *n* **pitch**, inflection, lilt, cadence, timbre, modulation, tone, stress, accentuation [➡ THE SPOKEN WORD; 671] 2 *n* **chanting**, chant, incantation, invocation, intoning, singing, humming [➡ MUSIC, SONGS, AND SINGING; 907]

intone 1 *v* (*formal*) **chant**, sing, croon, drone, hum [➡ MUSIC, SONGS, AND SINGING; 907] 2 *v* **say**, utter, speak, articulate, pronounce, declare [➡ UTTER AND PRONOUNCE; 608]

in total *adv* [➡ ALL; 128]

into the bargain *adv* [➡ EXPRESSIONS INTRODUCING EXTRA INFORMATION; 139]

intoxicated *adj* [➡ UNDER THE INFLUENCE OF DRUGS OR ALCOHOL; 741]

intoxicating 1 *adj* (*formal*) **alcoholic**, strong, powerful, heady, mind-altering, inebriating, hallucinogenic, hard [➡ STRENGTH; 201] *Opposite*: soft 2 *adj* **exciting**, invigorating, stimulating, exhilarating, fascinating, enthralling, compulsive, enchanting, elating [➡ EMOTIONALLY PLEASANT; 187] *Opposite*: dull

intoxication *n* **alcoholism**, drunkenness, inebriation, intemperance, heavy drinking, boozing (*slang*) [➡ UNDER THE INFLUENCE OF DRUGS OR ALCOHOL; 741]

intractability 1 *n* (*formal*) **unmanageability**, uncontrollability, obstinacy, stubbornness, pigheadedness, rebelliousness, recalcitrance, recidivism [➡UNWILLINGNESS AND STUBBORNNESS; 564] *Opposite*: tractability **2** *n* **difficulty**, knottiness, insolvability, complexity, awkwardness, unwieldiness [➡DIFFICULTY AND COMPLEXITY; 242] *Opposite*: simplicity

intractable 1 *adj* (*formal*) **stubborn**, obstinate, obdurate, willful, inflexible, pigheaded, headstrong, perverse, mulish [➡UNWILLINGNESS AND STUBBORNNESS; 564] *Opposite*: easygoing **2** *adj* **difficult**, problematic, troublesome, awkward, thorny, knotty [➡DIFFICULTY AND COMPLEXITY; 242] *Opposite*: easy

See Compare and Contrast at **unruly.**

intramural *adj* **internal**, inner, in-house, college, school [➡EDUCATION; 838] *Opposite*: extramural

intransigence *n* **inflexibility**, stubbornness, narrow-mindedness, obstinacy, unyieldingness, obduracy [➡UNWILLINGNESS AND STUBBORNNESS; 564] *Opposite*: flexibility

intransigent 1 *adj* **inflexible**, stubborn, obdurate, narrow-minded, obstinate, uncompromising, unyielding, unbending, intractable (*formal*) [➡UNWILLINGNESS AND STUBBORNNESS; 564] *Opposite*: flexible **2** *n* (*formal*) **conservative**, dinosaur, diehard, reactionary, extremist, bigot [➡UNCOOPERATIVE OR REBELLIOUS PEOPLE; 566] *Opposite*: progressive

intransitive *type of* **grammatical term** [➡ASPECTS OF LANGUAGE; 682]

intrapreneur *n* [➡BUSINESS PEOPLE; 793]

intravenous *adj* **venous**, vein, arterial, blood, circulatory [➡THE BLOOD AND CIRCULATION; 717]

in-tray (*UK*) *n* **in-box**, mailbox, tray, pigeonhole [➡CONTAINERS, RECEPTACLES, AND PACKAGING; 1245]

intrepid *adj* **fearless**, bold, courageous, valiant, heroic, daring, resolute, audacious, plucky, gallant (*literary*), dauntless (*literary*), brave [➡COURAGE; 498] *Opposite*: cowardly

intrepidity *n* [➡COURAGE; 498]

intricacies *n* **details**, ins and outs, workings, particulars, minutiae, niceties, complexities, twists and turns, convolutions [➡BASIC DETAILS; 688]

intricacy *n* **complexity**, difficulty, obscurity, sophistication, convolutedness, multifariousness [➡DIFFICULTY AND COMPLEXITY; 242]

intricate *adj* **complicated**, complex, involved, difficult, elaborate, convoluted, sophisticated, tricky, knotty [➡DIFFICULTY AND COMPLEXITY; 242] *Opposite*: simple

intrigue 1 *n* **plotting**, conspiracy, trickery, scheming, maneuvering, secrecy [➡DECEPTION AND LIES; 660] **2** *n* **conspiracy**, plot, deception, scheme, stratagem, maneuver, ruse [➡WAYS OF DOING THINGS; 294] **3** *v* **interest**, fascinate, charm, attract, captivate, absorb, enthrall, titillate, tickle your fancy (*informal*) [➡APPEAL TO AND AROUSE INTEREST; 575]

intriguer *n* [➡PEOPLE WHO DECEIVE; 661]

intriguing *adj* **interesting**, fascinating, exciting, stimulating, absorbing, captivating, enthralling, titillating [➡INTERESTING AND MEANINGFUL; 190] *Opposite*: uninteresting

intrinsic *adj* **basic**, essential, inherent, fundamental,

central, core, key, deep-down, deep-seated, deep-rooted, innate, underlying [➡FUNDAMENTAL; 195] *Opposite*: acquired

intro (*informal*) *n* [➡BEGINNINGS; 53]

introduce 1 *v* **present**, make known to, acquaint with, familiarize, announce, bring together [➡INFORM, ANNOUNCE, AND ISSUE; 611] **2** *v* **host**, present, preside over, lead, head [➡ENTERTAINMENT; 872] **3** *v* **bring in**, set up, initiate, usher in, begin, commence, pioneer, launch, establish, institute, start, propose, advance, create [➡INSTITUTE AND INAUGURATE; 348] *Opposite*: conclude **4** *v* **make somebody aware of**, bring to somebody's attention, acquaint somebody with, turn somebody on to, get somebody into, give somebody a taste for, familiarize, initiate, inform [➡INSTRUCT AND TEACH; 609]

introduction 1 *n* **foreword**, opening, preface, prologue, preamble, beginning, overture [➡PARTS OF BOOKS AND DOCUMENTS; 593] *Opposite*: conclusion **2** *n* **outline**, overview, primer, summary, starter, rough guide, taster (*UK*) [➡MANUALS AND INSTRUCTIONS; 589] **3** *n* **institution**, presentation, insertion, ushering in [➡BEGINNINGS; 53]

introductory 1 *adj* **preliminary**, initial, opening, starting, early, first, preparatory, exploratory, prefatory [➡BEFORE, FIRST, AND PRECEDING; 163] *Opposite*: final **2** *adj* **basic**, entry-level, preliminary, first, simple [➡EASE AND SIMPLICITY; 200]

introspection *n* **self-examination**, contemplation, brooding, meditation, self-analysis, reflection, navel-gazing, solipsism, soul-searching [➡THINK AND REFLECT; 743]

introspective *adj* **self-examining**, self-absorbed, inward-looking, contemplative, brooding, solipsistic, lost in thought, deep in thought, meditative, thoughtful, soul-searching [➡PENSIVENESS AND INTEREST; 538]

in trouble *adj* **in difficulty**, having problems, struggling, failing, in distress, liable, in the soup (*informal*), up the creek (*informal*) [➡IN TROUBLE AND DISADVANTAGED; 73]

introversion *n* **introspection**, self-absorption, inwardness, contemplation, navel-gazing, shyness, timidity, reserve, musing, soul-searching [➡PSYCHOLOGY AND THE MIND; 769] *Opposite*: extroversion

introvert 1 *n* **recluse**, hermit, loner, homebody (*informal*), shrinking violet (*informal*) [➡SOLITARY PEOPLE AND MISFITS; 942] *Opposite*: extrovert **2** *adj* **introverted**, shy, withdrawn, reclusive, reserved, reticent, timid, quiet [➡RETICENT AND UNFORTHCOMING; 631] *Opposite*: extrovert

introverted *adj* **shy**, withdrawn, reclusive, reserved, reticent, timid, quiet, introvert [➡RETICENT AND UNFORTHCOMING; 631]

intrude *v* **encroach**, break in, interrupt, interfere, impose, butt in, intervene, interlope, meddle [➡INTERRUPT AND BUTT IN; 619]

intruder *n* **interloper**, burglar, trespasser, prowler, stalker, invader, partycrasher, impostor, cuckoo in the nest, gatecrasher (*UK*) [➡STRANGERS; 972]

intrusion *n* **disturbance**, interruption, imposition, interference, invasion, incursion, meddling, interloping, intervention [➡BAD BEHAVIOR OR ACTIONS; 254]

intrusive *adj* **invasive**, indiscreet, interfering, unpleasant, insensitive, upsetting, disturbing, meddling, pushy (*informal*) [➡NOSY AND INTERFERING; 512] *Opposite*: discreet

intrusiveness *n* **invasiveness**, insensitivity, indiscreetness, inappropriateness, tactlessness, pushiness (*informal*) [➡ NOSY AND INTERFERING; 512] *Opposite*: discretion

in truth *adv* [➡ WORDS AND PHRASES EMPHASIZING THE TRUTH OF A MATTER; 172]

intuit *v* **sense**, perceive, discern, feel, understand, be aware of [➡ UNDERSTAND AND GRASP; 759]

intuition 1 *n* **instinct**, perception, insight, sixth sense, awareness, sensitivity, clairvoyance [➡ THE SUPERNATURAL; 787] 2 *n* **hunch**, feeling, inkling, suspicion, sense, presentiment, instinct, surmise, flash [➡ FEELINGS; 531]

intuitive 1 *adj* **instinctive**, spontaneous, innate, in-built, instinctual, untaught, natural, native, inborn [➡ THE NATURE OF IDEAS; 771] 2 *adj* **perceptive**, sensitive, shrewd, discerning, insightful, perspicacious [➡ POSITIVE INTELLECTUAL CHARACTERISTICS; 524]

intuitively *adv* **instinctively**, automatically, by instinct, spontaneously, naturally, unthinkingly, subconsciously, subliminally, innately [➡ THE NATURE OF IDEAS; 771]

intuitiveness *n* **instinctiveness**, instinct, perceptiveness, perception, insightfulness, insight, awareness, sensitivity, intuition [➡ POSITIVE INTELLECTUAL CHARACTERISTICS; 524]

in tune *adj* [➡ HARMONY; 155]

in turmoil *adj* [➡ SADNESS, DISTRESS, AND DESPAIR; 539]

in two shakes of a lamb's tail *adv* [➡ HAPPENING QUICKLY; 104]

inundate *v* **flood**, overwhelm, snow under, swamp, deluge, engulf, submerge, drown [➡ GIVE TOO MUCH AND OVERBURDEN; 437] *Opposite*: starve

inundated 1 *adj* **snowed under**, flooded, swamped, overwhelmed, besieged, overcome, drowned [➡ TOO MUCH; 119] *Opposite*: starved 2 *adj* **flooded**, immersed, waterlogged, submerged, submersed, covered, engulfed [➡ WET; 1240] *Opposite*: drained

inundation (*formal*) 1 *n* **deluge**, flood, sea, stream, shower, tidal wave [➡ TOO MUCH; 119] *Opposite*: trickle 2 *n* **flood**, blizzard, sea, wave, barrage, mound, heap, backlog, accumulation [➡ MANY, MUCH, LARGE AMOUNT; 117]

in unison *adv* [➡ ACTING WITH OTHERS; 285]

inure *v* **harden**, toughen, accustom, season, habituate, acclimatize, desensitize, familiarize, naturalize [➡ SOOTHE AND CALM; 573]

inured to *adj* **accustomed to**, used to, conditioned to, insensible of, insensitive to, familiarized [➡ NEUTRALITY AND INDIFFERENCE; 553] *Opposite*: unaccustomed

inurement *n* **hardening**, toughening, acclimatization, seasoning, desensitization, habituation (*formal*) [➡ CHANGE; 372]

invade 1 *v* **attack**, occupy, enter, conquer, annex, march into, assault, overrun [➡ ARRIVE; 12] 2 *v* **overrun**, infect, infest, plague, colonize, parasitize [➡ ARRIVE; 12]

invader *n* **attacker**, aggressor, raider, intruder, assailant, trespasser, interloper [➡ ENEMIES AND TORMENTORS; 969]

in vain *adv* **without success**, unsuccessfully, uselessly, hopelessly, with little hope, fruitlessly, for nothing, to no avail, to no purpose, ineffectively, vainly, for no good reason, pointlessly, futilely [➡ UNSUCCESSFUL AND UNPROMISING; 76] *Opposite*: successfully

invalid 1 *adj* **null and void**, unacceptable, unenforceable, illegal, worthless, unsound, void [➡ REDUNDANT AND USELESS; 240] *Opposite*: valid 2 *adj* **unsound**, untrue, unfounded, illogical, untenable, worthless, unsustainable, null, void, unconvincing, fallacious [➡ FALSE AND UNREAL; 173] *Opposite*: valid 3 *adj* **infirm**, enfeebled, debilitated, disabled, sick, incapacitated, ailing (*dated*) [➡ UNFIT AND WEAK; 739] *Opposite*: well 4 *n* **convalescent**, patient, sick person [➡ UNFIT AND WEAK; 739]

invalidate *v* **overturn**, cancel, annul, nullify, undo, quash, overthrow, undermine, refute, countermand, discredit, abrogate (*formal*) [➡ ABOLISH AND ANNUL; 452] *Opposite*: validate

See Compare and Contrast at **nullify**.

invalidation *n* **annulment**, undoing, overthrow, nullification, cancellation, refutation, countermanding, discrediting, abrogation (*formal*) [➡ ENDS AND DEPARTURES; 54] *Opposite*: validation

invalidity 1 *n* **unsoundness**, inaccuracy, baselessness, unjustifiability, irrationality, falsehood, inadequacy, fallaciousness, faultiness, unconvincingness [➡ INCORRECT AND ERRONEOUS; 222] *Opposite*: validity 2 *n* **illegality**, inoperativeness, ineffectiveness, unenforceability, voidness, unsoundness, unsustainability, abrogation (*formal*) [➡ REDUNDANT AND USELESS; 240] *Opposite*: legality

invaluable *adj* **priceless**, irreplaceable, vital, instrumental, helpful, important, valuable, precious, unique, treasured, inestimable, rare, choice [➡ USEFULNESS; 199] *Opposite*: worthless

invaluableness *n* **pricelessness**, irreplaceability, helpfulness, importance, value, preciousness, uniqueness, rareness, choiceness [➡ IMPORTANCE AND SIGNIFICANCE; 192] *Opposite*: worthlessness

invariability *n* [➡ PERMANENCE: WITHOUT CHANGE; 95]

invariable *adj* **constant**, set, unchanging, inflexible, rigid, consistent, unwavering, habitual, uniform, unvarying, undeviating, unchangeable [➡ PERMANENCE: WITHOUT CHANGE; 95] *Opposite*: erratic

invasion *n* **attack**, assault, incursion, raid, foray, offensive, annexation, conquest, subjugation, penetration, infiltration, aggression [➡ AGGRESSIVE EVENTS; 39] *Opposite*: withdrawal

invasive 1 *adj* **aggressive**, offensive, hostile, warlike, bellicose, martial [➡ AGGRESSIVE AND BELLIGERENT; 518] 2 *adj* **intrusive**, disturbing, interfering, insensitive, imposing, annoying [➡ NOSY AND INTERFERING; 512] *Opposite*: discreet

invective (*formal*) *n* **diatribe**, tirade, attack, broadside, counterblast, polemic, abuse, criticism, vituperation, denunciation, vilification, execration (*literary or formal*) [➡ CRITICISMS AND ANGRY OUTBURSTS; 50] *Opposite*: eulogy

inveigh *v* **protest**, complain, fulminate, criticize, rail, rant, denounce, abuse, castigate (*formal*) [➡PROTEST AND EXPRESS DISAPPROVAL; 642]

inveigle *v* **persuade**, entice, charm, cajole, trick, deceive, con, wheedle, influence, convince, beguile, allure, seduce [➡CAUSE OR COMPEL TO ACT; 271]

invent **1** *v* **create**, devise, formulate, originate, conceive, design, discover, develop, contrive, fashion [➡CREATION; 346] **2** *v* **make up**, think up, concoct, fabricate, contrive, dream up, conjure up, cook up (*Informal*) [➡DREAM, IMAGINE, AND FANTASIZE; 749]

invented *adj* **false**, made-up, fictitious, imaginary, pretend, concocted, hypothetical, make-believe, fabricated, fictional, contrived [➡FALSE AND UNREAL; 173] *Opposite*: real

invention **1** *n* **creation**, discovery, development, brainchild, origination, baby (*slang*) [➡CREATION; 346] **2** *n* **device**, innovation, contraption, gadget, design, contrivance, implement, apparatus [➡DEVICES; 1115] **3** *n* **creativity**, imagination, ingenuity, inventiveness, resourcefulness, originality, innovativeness, fertility [➡POSITIVE INTELLECTUAL CHARACTERISTICS; 524] **4** *n* **fabrication**, forgery, falsehood, deceit, lies, sham, fake, fiction, fantasy [➡DECEPTION AND LIES; 660] *Opposite*: truth

inventive *adj* **creative**, imaginative, ingenious, resourceful, original, innovative, fertile [➡POSITIVE INTELLECTUAL CHARACTERISTICS; 524] *Opposite*: unimaginative

inventiveness *n* **ingenuity**, resourcefulness, originality, creativity, imagination, invention, initiative, cleverness, fertility [➡POSITIVE INTELLECTUAL CHARACTERISTICS; 524]

inventor *n* **discoverer**, originator, creator, architect, author, designer, maker [➡DESIGNERS, CREATORS, AND INSTIGATORS; 347]

inventory **1** *n* **list**, record, account, register, catalog, portfolio, stock list, roster, roll [➡LISTS AND SCHEDULES; 587] **2** *n* **supply**, range, array, stock, accounting, stock-taking [➡COLLECTIONS AND MIXTURES OF THINGS; 1244]

inverse **1** *adj* **opposite**, converse, reverse, contrary, other, counter, transposed, inverted, backward, antithetical (*formal*) [➡OPPOSITE; 157] *Opposite*: same **2** *n* **reverse**, opposite, other, contrary, converse, antithesis, flip side, counterpoint [➡OPPOSITE; 157]

inversion **1** *n* **reversal**, overturn, downturn, upturn, capsizal, transposal, transposition [➡CHANGE; 372] **2** *n* **reverse**, transposition, antithesis, contrary, converse [➡OPPOSITE; 157]

invert *v* **turn over**, upset, capsize, overturn, reverse, upturn, turn upside down, double back, upend, flip-flop (*informal*) [➡MOVE SOMETHING INTO A NEW POSITION OR OVERTURN; 330] *Opposite*: right

invertebrate *n* [➡LIVING THINGS AND LIVING; 976]

invertebrate

◆ *types of aquatic invertebrates*
abalone, barnacle, bivalve, clam, cockle, conch, coral, crustacean, cuttlefish, jellyfish, limpet, mollusk, mussel, octopus, oyster, Portuguese man-of-war, quahog, scallop, sea anemone, sea urchin, sponge, squid, starfish, whelk, winkle

◆ *types of crustaceans*
crab, crayfish, hermit crab, horseshoe crab, langoustine, lobster, prawn, sand flea, shrimp, water flea

◆ *types of land invertebrates*
centipede, earthworm, millipede, mollusk, slug, snail, wood louse, worm

invest **1** *v* **capitalize**, put in, devote, advance, finance [➡GIVE MONEY; 433] **2** *v* **endow**, provide, supply, empower, authorize, arm, license, enable [➡PERMIT AND ALLOW; 669] **3** *v* (*formal*) **appoint**, ordain, instate, inaugurate, establish, install [➡CONFER STATUS; 458]

investigate *v* **examine**, look into, explore, inspect, study, consider, probe, scrutinize, poke around, reconnoiter, research, delve into, recce (*slang*) [➡EXAMINE AND ASSESS; 753]

investigation *n* **study**, examination, search, exploration, analysis, research, survey, scrutiny, inspection, inquiry, reconnaissance, enquiry, probe, review, recce (*slang*) [➡EXAMINE AND ASSESS; 753]

investigative *adj* **analytical**, exploratory, undercover, fact-finding, research, probing, inspective [➡EXAMINE AND ASSESS; 753]

investigator *n* **detective**, private detective, private investigator, agent, plainclothesman, private eye (*informal*), sleuth (*informal*), gumshoe (*dated Informal*), dick (*dated slang*) [➡THE POLICE, ARREST, AND PRETRIAL PROCEEDINGS; 818]

investiture *n* **installation**, inauguration, swearing-in, instatement, admission, enthronement, investment (*formal*) [➡CONFER STATUS; 458]

investment **1** *n* (*formal*) **investiture**, swearing-in, instatement, installation, enthronement [➡CONFER STATUS; 458] **2** *n* **savings**, speculation, venture, deal, asset, stock, share, venture capital, security, outlay, investing, capital spending, financing [➡EXPENDITURE; 423]

investor **1** *n* **saver**, shareholder, depositor, stakeholder, stockholder, nominee, financier, venture capitalist [➡PEOPLE INVOLVED IN FINANCE; 804] **2** *n* **backer**, sponsor, patron, guarantor, security [➡PEOPLE INVOLVED IN FINANCE; 804]

inveterate *adj* **chronic**, confirmed, hardened, ingrained, incurable, incorrigible, seasoned, entrenched, habitual, deep-rooted, diehard, adamant [➡UNWILLINGNESS AND STUBBORNNESS; 564] *Opposite*: occasional

invidious *adj* **unpleasant**, discriminatory, unenviable, unfair, undesirable, tricky, odious, difficult, offensive, awkward, horrible, impossible, insulting, spiteful, malevolent [➡EMOTIONALLY UNPLEASANT AND UPSETTING; 227] *Opposite*: pleasant

in view of *prep* **considering**, bearing in mind, taking into consideration, taking into account, in consideration of (*formal*) [➡CAUSATION; 168] *Opposite*: notwithstanding (*formal*)

invigilate *v* **supervise**, monitor, inspect, observe, check, police, keep an eye on [➡LOOKING AND LOOKS; 700]

invigilator *n* **supervisor**, inspector, monitor, overseer, scrutineer, examiner, official, verifier, observer [➡ONLOOKERS AND SPECTATORS; 701]

invigorate *v* **energize**, revitalize, refresh, stimulate, enliven, animate, rejuvenate, strengthen, liven up, galvanize, exhilarate, fortify, quicken [➡IMPROVE STRENGTH AND DURABILITY; 378] *Opposite*: exhaust

invigorated *adj* **strengthened**, fortified, energized, refreshed, restored, revitalized, rejuvenated, exhilarated, perked up, galvanized, motivated, quickened, pepped up (*informal*) [➡WIDE AWAKE AND CONSCIOUS; 735] *Opposite*: weakened

invigorating *adj* **bracing**, brisk, stimulating, refreshing, revitalizing, energizing, reviving, vitalizing, enlivening, exhilarating, restorative, animating, rejuvenating [➡PHYSICALLY PLEASANT; 186] *Opposite*: enervating

invincibility *n* **strength**, insuperability, invulnerability, impregnability, indomitability, unassailability, indestructability, dauntlessness (*literary*) [➡STRENGTH; 201] *Opposite*: vulnerability

invincible *adj* **unbeatable**, invulnerable, unconquerable, indomitable, impregnable, unassailable, insuperable, indestructible, supreme, unshakable, insurmountable, irrepressible [➡STRENGTH; 201] *Opposite*: vulnerable

inviolable *adj* **unbreakable**, sacred, sacrosanct, firm, uninfringeable, unchallengeable, inviolate [➡STRENGTH; 201] *Opposite*: breakable

inviolate 1 *adj* **unaltered**, unchanged, unbroken, intact, entire, perfect, immune, inviolable, infrangible (*formal*) [➡STRENGTH; 201] *Opposite*: altered 2 *adj* **pure**, unsullied, untouched, whole, intact, virgin, perfect, unspoiled, unadulterated, uncontaminated [➡IN GOOD REPAIR; 1232] *Opposite*: contaminated

invisibility *n* **hiddenness**, inconspicuousness, indiscernibility, faintness, indistinctness [➡IMPERCEPTIBLE; 26] *Opposite*: visibility

invisible 1 *adj* **imperceptible**, unseen, indistinguishable, indiscernible, undetectable, obscure, unseeable [➡IMPERCEPTIBLE; 26] *Opposite*: visible 2 *adj* **hidden**, concealed, disguised, unnoticed, obscured, out of sight, covered, masked, covert, veiled [➡SECRET AND UNKNOWN; 179] *Opposite*: obvious 3 *adj* **imaginary**, nonexistent, intangible, shadowy, insubstantial, ghostly, impalpable (*formal*) [➡FALSE AND UNREAL; 173] *Opposite*: palpable

invisibly *adv* **imperceptibly**, indiscernibly, unnoticeably, undetectably, intangibly, impalpably (*formal*) [➡IMPERCEPTIBLE; 26] *Opposite*: visibly

invitation 1 *n* **offer**, request, call, summons, bidding, solicitation, invite (*informal*) [➡REQUEST AND DEMAND; 663] 2 *n* **encouragement**, inducement, provocation, incitement, enticement, challenge, temptation, lure [➡ADVICE; 689] *Opposite*: discouragement

invite 1 *n* (*informal*) **invitation**, request, call, summons,

offer, bidding [➡REQUEST AND DEMAND; 663] 2 *v* **ask**, request, call, summon, bid (*archaic*) [➡REQUEST AND DEMAND; 663] *Opposite*: blackball 3 *v* **provoke**, incite, induce, attract, encourage, tempt, lure, welcome [➡APPEAL TO AND AROUSE INTEREST; 575] *Opposite*: forbid

inviting *adj* **attractive**, appealing, alluring, tempting, pleasing, fascinating, engaging, welcoming, enticing [➡INTERESTING AND MEANINGFUL; 190] *Opposite*: unappealing

invocation *n* **prayer**, call, request, entreaty, petition, appeal, solicitation, plea, supplication (*formal*) [➡REQUEST AND DEMAND; 663]

in vogue *adj* [➡DESCRIBING CLOTHES; 869]

invoice 1 *n* **bill**, account, statement, demand, proof of purchase [➡RECEIPTS AND INVOICES; 591] 2 *v* **bill**, debit, charge [➡SELL; 441]

invoke 1 *v* **appeal**, call upon, call up, pray, beg, summon, entreat, petition, raise, implore (*formal*), beseech (*literary*) [➡REQUEST AND DEMAND; 663] 2 *v* **cite**, quote, use, refer, mention, bring up, resort to [➡NAME AND DESCRIBE; 665] 3 *v* **evoke**, call to mind, conjure up, incite, arouse, call forth, remind [➡CAUSE TO APPEAR; 5]

involucre *part of* **flower** [➡FLOWERS; 1032]

involuntarily *adv* **unwillingly**, reluctantly, unhappily, against your will, compulsorily, obligatorily [➡WITHOUT ENTHUSIASM; 287] *Opposite*: willingly

involuntary 1 *adj* **compulsory**, obligatory, forced, unwilling, reluctant, unchosen [➡CAPTIVITY AND LOSS OF FREEDOM; 248] *Opposite*: willing 2 *adj* **instinctive**, spontaneous, reflex, unintentional, automatic, unconscious, unthinking, uncontrolled [➡AUTOMATIC AND INSTINCTIVE; 280] *Opposite*: intentional

involve 1 *v* **contain**, include, take in, comprise, consist of, encompass [➡CREATING CONNECTIONS; 144] 2 *v* **concern**, have to do with, affect, interest, encompass, embrace [➡BE ABOUT SOMETHING; 62] 3 *v* **implicate**, draw in, mix up, get into, embroil, entangle, enmesh [➡CAUSE OR COMPEL TO ACT; 271] 4 *v* **engage**, engross, absorb, grip, occupy, preoccupy, rivet (*informal*) [➡APPEAL TO AND AROUSE INTEREST; 575] *Opposite*: bore 5 *v* **imply**, mean, entail, necessitate, require [➡NEED AND REQUIRE; 464]

involved 1 *adj* **complicated**, complex, intricate, elaborate, knotty, tangled, convoluted, tortuous, difficult, labyrinthine [➡DIFFICULTY AND COMPLEXITY; 242] *Opposite*: simple 2 *adj* **concerned**, caught up, mixed up, occupied, implicated, drawn in, immersed, enmeshed, entangled [➡RELATED; 142] *Opposite*: uninvolved

involvement 1 *n* **participation**, association, connection, contribution, engrossment, immersion, envelopment [➡CONNECTIONS; 143] 2 *n* **attachment**, interest, concern, enthusiasm, connection, commitment, preoccupation, engagement [➡ATTENTION AND ATTENTIVENESS; 763] *Opposite*: detachment

invulnerability *n* [➡SAFE AND SAFETY; 191]

invulnerable *adj* **untouchable**, invincible, unassailable, safe, impenetrable, secure, indestructible, unconquerable, unbeatable, indomitable [➡SAFE AND SAFETY; 191] *Opposite*: vulnerable

inward 1 *adj* **inner**, innermost, inmost, interior,

internal, private, deep, deepest, secret, hidden, confidential [➡ SECRET AND UNKNOWN; 179] *Opposite*: external **2** *adj* **internal**, interior, inner, inner-directed, innermost, within, inmost [➡ GENERAL LOCATIONS; 158] *Opposite*: outer **3** *adj* **incoming**, ingoing, entering, inward bound, inflowing, return [➡ DIRECTION OF MOTION; 345] *Opposite*: outward **4** *adv* **within**, inwardly, inside, in [➡ DIRECTION OF MOTION; 345] *Opposite*: outward

inwardly *adv* **secretly**, privately, to yourself, silently, deeply, interiorly [➡ SECRET AND UNKNOWN; 179] *Opposite*: openly

in work (*UK*) *adj* [➡ EMPLOYMENT STATUS; 831]

in working order *adj* [➡ IN GOOD REPAIR; 1232]

in-your-face (*slang*) *adj* **direct**, forthright, provocative, outspoken, shocking, aggressive, full-on (*UK*) [➡ POMPOUS, LOUD, AND OVERCONFIDENT; 635] *Opposite*: indirect

in your own right *adv* **independently**, voluntarily, for yourself, by yourself, solo [➡ ACTING INDEPENDENTLY; 284]

in your prime *adj* [➡ FIT AND STRONG; 736]

Ionic *type of* **pre-20th-century architecture** [➡ BUILDING AND ARCHITECTURE; 1076]

ionosphere *n* [➡ THE EARTH'S ATMOSPHERE; 1040]

iota *n* **jot**, bit, scrap, speck, grain, particle, scintilla, smidgen (*informal*) [➡ FEW, LITTLE, SMALL AMOUNT; 120] *Opposite*: lot

ipso facto *adv* **as a result**, therefore, so, consequently, in view of, hence (*formal*), thus (*formal*), in consequence (*formal*) [➡ CAUSATION; 168]

I.Q. *n* **intelligence quotient**, level of intelligence, degree of intelligence, intelligence [➡ PSYCHOLOGY AND THE MIND; 769]

irascibility *n* [➡ AGGRESSIVE AND BELLIGERENT; 518]

irascible *adj* **quick-tempered**, irritable, petulant, hot-tempered, short-tempered, grumpy, snappy, touchy, snappish, cantankerous, cross, testy (*informal*), ornery (*informal*) [➡ AGGRESSIVE AND BELLIGERENT; 518] *Opposite*: easygoing

irate *adj* **angry**, incensed, furious, mad, irritated, enraged, fuming, infuriated, annoyed [➡ IRRITATION AND ANGER; 541] *Opposite*: calm

ire (*formal*) *n* **fury**, rage, anger, wrath, annoyance, indignation, bile (*literary*) [➡ IRRITATION AND ANGER; 541] *Opposite*: calmness

See Compare and Contrast at **anger**.

ireful (*literary*) *adj* [➡ IRRITATION AND ANGER; 541]

iridescent *adj* **lustrous**, rainbowlike, shimmering, rainbow, shimmery, shot, dazzling, kaleidoscopic, glittering, sparkling, shining, gleaming, glistening, flickering, colorful, shiny, opalescent, prismatic [➡ VISUAL TEXTURE; 1221] *Opposite*: monochrome

iridology *type of* **complementary therapy** [➡ REMEDIES, TREATMENTS, AND OPERATIONS; 731]

iris 1 *type of* **flower grown from bulbs** [➡ FLOWERS FROM BULBS; 1030] **2** *part of* **eye** [➡ THE EYE; 698]

Irish coffee *type of* **coffee** [➡ DRINKS; 1187]

Irish moss *type of* **marine alga** [➡ MICROORGANISMS, FUNGI, AND ALGAE; 1023]

Irish stew *type of* **cooked dish** [➡ PREPARED DISHES; 1170]

irk *v* **annoy**, vex, displease, trouble, bother, nag, rankle, gall, irritate, exasperate, rile (*informal*), peeve (*informal*), bug (*informal*) [➡ ANGER AND ANNOY; 569] *Opposite*: please

See Compare and Contrast at **annoy**.

irked *adj* [➡ IRRITATION AND ANGER; 541]

irksome *adj* **annoying**, irritating, exasperating, tiresome, wearing, tedious, bothersome, trying, galling, vexing [➡ IRRITATING; 228] *Opposite*: pleasant

iron 1 *type of* **metal** [➡ METALS; 1276] **2** *type of* **appliance** [➡ HOUSEHOLD APPLIANCES; 1117] **3** *v* **press**, smooth out, iron out, smooth, flatten, steam, even out [➡ CHANGE OF SHAPE; 385] *Opposite*: crumple **4** *adj* **firm**, hard, strong, determined, tough, steely, rock-hard [➡ STRENGTH OF WILL; 501] *Opposite*: soft

iron-clad *adj* **definite**, firm, sure, watertight, unimpeachable, unshakable, cast-iron [➡ UNWILLINGNESS AND STUBBORNNESS; 564]

iron curtain *n* **obstacle**, impediment, hurdle, line, border [➡ PROBLEMS; 256]

ironic 1 *adj* **caustic**, dry, biting, sarcastic, satirical, sardonic, mocking, ironical, tongue-in-cheek [➡ MOCKING AND DISMISSIVE; 636] **2** *adj* **incongruous**, paradoxical, poignant, peculiar, odd, strange, weird, atypical, contradictory, curious [➡ BIZARRE AND PECULIAR; 257]

See Compare and Contrast at **sarcastic**.

ironical *see* **ironic**

iron out *v* **sort out**, resolve, smooth over, clear up, settle, end [➡ CORRECT AND PUT RIGHT; 377]

iron-willed *adj* [➡ UNWILLINGNESS AND STUBBORNNESS; 564]

ironwork *n* **wrought iron**, metalwork, ironware, iron object, hardware, ironmongery (*UK*) [➡ ORNAMENTS AND DECORATIONS; 1248]

irony 1 *n* **satire**, dryness, causticness, sardonicism, sarcasm, mockery, insincerity, wit, humor, double meaning [➡ MOCKING AND DISMISSIVE; 636] *Opposite*: sincerity **2** *n* **paradox**, incongruity, fatefulness, dramatic irony, contrariety, contrariness, absurdity [➡ BIZARRE AND PECULIAR; 257]

irradiate 1 *v* **light up**, light, illuminate, brighten, cast light on, illumine (*formal*) [➡ LIGHT EMISSION; 368] *Opposite*: darken **2** *v* **enlighten**, clarify, inform, instruct, inspire, explain [➡ EXPLAIN AND CLARIFY; 610] *Opposite*: obfuscate

irradiation 1 *n* **radioactivity**, radiation, contamination, X-ray, treatment [➡ LIGHT; 1164] **2** *n* **preservation**, treatment, sterilization, purification [➡ CLEAN AND POLISH; 403]

irrational *adj* **illogical**, unreasonable, foolish, ridiculous, absurd, silly, senseless, unfounded, groundless, unsound, baseless, nonsensical, crazy (*informal*) [➡ BIZARRE AND PECULIAR; 257] *Opposite*: rational

irrationality *n* **illogicality**, unreasonableness, foolishness, ludicrousness, absurdity, ridiculousness, sense-

lessness, pointlessness, craziness (*informal*) [➡ BIZARRE AND PECULIAR; 257] *Opposite*: sense

irreconcilable *adj* **incompatible**, irresoluble, conflicting, opposing, opposed, clashing, contradictory [➡ DISHARMONY; 156] *Opposite*: compatible

irrecoverable 1 *adj* **irretrievable**, gone, lost, given up, written off (*informal*) [➡ ABSENT AND UNAVAILABLE; 7] 2 *adj* **irreparable**, beyond repair, irreversible, irredeemable, irremediable, irrevocable [➡ BAD AND BADLY; 223]

irredeemable *adj* **hopeless**, unalterable, absolute, complete, incorrigible, inveterate, incurable, lost [➡ UNWILLINGNESS AND STUBBORNNESS; 564] *Opposite*: redeemable

irredentist *n* [➡ UNCOOPERATIVE OR REBELLIOUS PEOPLE; 566]

irreducible *adj* **complex**, complicated, involved, intricate, difficult [➡ POSITIVELY COMPLEX OR COMPLICATED; 217]

irrefutable *adj* **indisputable**, certain, unquestionable, overwhelming, unassailable, convincing, undeniable, incontrovertible, watertight, proven [➡ CERTAIN; 174] *Opposite*: disputable

irregular 1 *adj* **uneven**, unequal, asymmetrical, unbalanced, rough, crooked, jagged, bumpy, lopsided, broken [➡ ANGULAR SHAPE; 1217] *Opposite*: even 2 *adj* **erratic**, variable, random, haphazard, intermittent, sporadic, patchy, fluctuating, fitful [➡ FINITENESS, VARIABILITY, AND TRANSIENCE; 96] *Opposite*: regular 3 *adj* **improper**, unacceptable, abnormal, wrong, unsuitable, inappropriate, unconventional, unorthodox, unusual, nonconforming [➡ INAPPROPRIATE AND UNSUITABLE; 224] *Opposite*: proper

irregularity 1 *n* **indiscretion**, abnormality, wrongdoing, misdeed, anomaly, loophole, peccadillo [➡ BAD BEHAVIOR OR ACTIONS; 254] 2 *n* **unevenness**, inequality, variability, randomness, haphazardness, patchiness, disproportion, asymmetry, roughness [➡ DIFFERENCE; 149] *Opposite*: regularity

irrelevance 1 *n* **insignificance**, unimportance, inappropriateness, worthlessness, inconsequence, triviality, inappositeness (*formal*) [➡ UNIMPORTANT AND UNNECESSARY; 238] *Opposite*: relevance 2 *n* **inconsequence**, side issue, detail, technicality, red herring, diversion [➡ UNIMPORTANT AND UNNECESSARY; 238]

irrelevant *adj* **immaterial**, neither here nor there, unrelated, inappropriate, extraneous, beside the point, unconnected, inapt, off base [➡ UNIMPORTANT AND UNNECESSARY; 238] *Opposite*: relevant

irreligious *adj* **ungodly**, unspiritual, nonreligious, blasphemous, sacrilegious, unbelieving, godless, impious, profane (*formal*) [➡ RELIGIOUS CONCEPTS; 776] *Opposite*: devout

irremediable *adj* **irreparable**, irreversible, irredeemable, beyond repair, irrevocable, irretrievable, unsalvageable [➡ BAD AND BADLY; 223]

irreparable *adj* **beyond repair**, irreversible, irretrievable, severe, lasting, irrevocable, irremediable, irredeemable, uncorrectable, unsalvageable [➡ BAD AND BADLY; 223]

irreplaceable *adj* **unique**, inimitable, matchless, exceptional, rare, nonpareil, one-off (*UK*) [➡ EXTRAORDINARY: UNCOMMON; 205] *Opposite*: common

irrepressible *adj* **uncontrollable**, out of control, uncon-

tainable, wild, unruly, disorderly, incorrigible, unmanageable, willful, unrestrainable, unquenchable, intractable (*formal*) [➡ ENERGY AND ENTHUSIASM; 496] *Opposite*: contained

irreproachability *n* [➡ MORALLY GOOD; 774]

irreproachable *adj* **blameless**, faultless, flawless, perfect, impeccable, spotless, immaculate, stainless, unimpeachable [➡ MORALLY GOOD; 774] *Opposite*: blameworthy

irreproachably *adv* [➡ MORALLY GOOD; 774]

irresistible 1 *adj* **overwhelming**, overpowering, uncontrollable, compelling, strong, overriding, uncontainable, powerful [➡ STRENGTH; 201] *Opposite*: weak 2 *adj* **desirable**, tempting, appealing, enticing, alluring, mouthwatering, seductive, tantalizing [➡ INTERESTING AND MEANINGFUL; 190] *Opposite*: unappealing

irresistibly *adv* **overwhelmingly**, overpoweringly, uncontrollably, compellingly, powerfully, strongly, seductively, tantalizingly [➡ STRENGTH; 201] *Opposite*: weakly

irresolute *adj* **indecisive**, vacillating, unsure, weak, undetermined, wavering, procrastinating, unsteady, wishy-washy (*informal*) [➡ UNCERTAINTY; 559] *Opposite*: determined

irresoluteness *n* [➡ UNCERTAINTY; 559]

irresolution *n* **indecision**, indecisiveness, vacillation, weakness, hesitancy, changeableness [➡ UNCERTAINTY; 559] *Opposite*: determination

irrespective *adv* **regardless**, nevertheless, nonetheless, heedlessly, unrelatedly, notwithstanding (*formal*) [➡ ALTHOUGH, NEVERTHELESS, AND DESPITE; 169]

irrespective of *prep* **regardless of**, despite, no matter, in spite of, heedless of, notwithstanding (*formal*) [➡ ALTHOUGH, NEVERTHELESS, AND DESPITE; 169] *Opposite*: considering

irresponsibility *n* **recklessness**, carelessness, inattention, negligence, rashness, imprudence, frivolity, flippancy, unreliability [➡ BAD BEHAVIOR OR ACTIONS; 254] *Opposite*: responsibility

irresponsible *adj* **reckless**, careless, negligent, rash, foolish, immature, undependable, unreliable, imprudent [➡ LACK OF COMMITMENT AND UNRELIABILITY; 509] *Opposite*: responsible

irretrievable *adj* **irreparable**, irreversible, irrevocable, lasting, severe, irrecoverable, lost [➡ PERMANENCE: WITHOUT CHANGE; 95]

irreverence *n* **disrespect**, mockery, derision, impertinence, impudence, discourtesy, ridicule, sauciness, cheek (*informal*) [➡ MOCKING AND DISMISSIVE; 636] *Opposite*: respect

irreverent *adj* **disrespectful**, mocking, derisive, rude, impudent, flippant, bold, saucy, discourteous, sassy (*informal*), cheeky (*informal*), impertinent (*formal*) [➡ MOCKING AND DISMISSIVE; 636] *Opposite*: respectful

irreversible *adj* **irreparable**, irretrievable, irrevocable, unalterable, irremediable, permanent [➡ PERMANENCE: WITHOUT CHANGE; 95] *Opposite*: temporary

irrevocable *adj* **binding**, irreversible, final, unalterable, unchangeable, immutable, irretrievable, fixed, per-

manent, conclusive [➞PERMANENCE: WITHOUT CHANGE; 95] *Opposite*: flexible

irrevocably *adv* **irreversibly**, forever, permanently, once and for all, for all time, irretrievably, conclusively [➞PERMANENCE: WITHOUT CHANGE; 95]

irrigate *v* **water**, flood, wet, moisten, hose down, hose [➞SOFTEN, LIQUEFY, AND DAMPEN; 388] *Opposite*: dry out

irritability *n* **touchiness**, bad temper, petulance, cantankerousness, tetchiness (*informal*), prickliness (*informal*) [➞IRRITATION AND ANGER; 541] *Opposite*: equanimity (*formal*)

irritable *adj* **bad-tempered**, short-tempered, ill-tempered, petulant, cantankerous, irascible, cross, touchy, prickly (*informal*), tetchy (*informal*), testy (*informal*), grouchy (*informal*) [➞IRRITATION AND ANGER; 541] *Opposite*: easygoing

irritant *n* **nuisance**, annoyance, aggravation, irritation, pain (*informal*), bane, vexation [➞NUISANCES; 253] *Opposite*: balm

irritate **1** *v* **annoy**, get on somebody's nerves, infuriate, bother, exasperate, rub the wrong way, vex, irk, wind up, peeve (*informal*), aggravate (*informal*) [➞ANGER AND ANNOY; 569] *Opposite*: soothe **2** *v* **inflame**, rub, chafe, sting, hurt, worsen, aggravate (*informal*) [➞PAIN AND OTHER PHYSICAL SENSATIONS; 733] *Opposite*: soothe

See Compare and Contrast at **annoy**.

irritated *adj* **annoyed**, cross, angry, exasperated, maddened, vexed, wound up (*informal*), peeved (*informal*) [➞IRRITATION AND ANGER; 541] *Opposite*: unperturbed

irritating *adj* **annoying**, exasperating, irksome, infuriating, frustrating, grating, nauseating, galling, vexing, peeving (*informal*) [➞IRRITATING; 228] *Opposite*: soothing

irritation **1** *n* **annoyance**, crossness, frustration, impatience, exasperation, anger, irascibility, touchiness, indignation, testiness (*informal*) [➞IRRITATION AND ANGER; 541] *Opposite*: calmness **2** *n* **nuisance**, bother, irritant, bane, pain, pest (*informal*) [➞NUISANCES; 253] **3** *n* **inflammation**, soreness, tenderness, itchiness, rash, prickliness (*informal*) [➞PAIN AND OTHER PHYSICAL SENSATIONS; 733]

See Compare and Contrast at **anger**.

island *n* **isle**, islet, atoll, desert island, key, landmass [➞THE CONTINENTS AND ISLANDS; 1048]

islander *n* **inhabitant**, local, resident, occupant, native, dweller (*literary*) [➞INHABITANTS; 857]

island-hop *v* **travel around**, tour, sail around, sail, cruise, visit [➞TRAVEL: WAYS OF TRAVELING; 320]

isle *n* **island**, islet, atoll, desert island, key [➞THE CONTINENTS AND ISLANDS; 1048]

islet *see* **isle**

ism (*informal*) *n* **doctrine**, ideology, belief, belief system, principles, creed, philosophy, movement, practice [➞IDEAS AND THOUGHTS; 770]

isobar *n* **line**, weather symbol, front, low, low front, high, high front [➞WEATHER AND CLIMATE; 1049]

isolate *v* **cut off**, separate, segregate, detach, divorce, set apart, insulate, quarantine, sequester (*formal*) [➞SEPARATE AND DIVIDE; 401] *Opposite*: include

isolated **1** *adj* **remote**, cut off, inaccessible, lonely, secluded, out-of-the-way, insulated, quarantined, sequestered (*formal*) [➞DISTANCE; 160] *Opposite*: nearby **2** *adj* **exceptional**, unique, solitary, unrepeated, special, rare, one-off (*UK*) [➞UNRELATEDNESS AND SEPARATENESS; 146] *Opposite*: common **3** *adj* **lonely**, alone, solitary, insular, friendless, single [➞SOLITARINESS; 941]

isolation *n* **separation**, segregation, remoteness, loneliness, seclusion, inaccessibility, sequestration, quarantine [➞DISTANCE; 160] *Opposite*: inclusion

isolationism *n* **separateness**, remoteness, seclusion, independence, standoffishness, pride [➞STYLES AND SYSTEMS OF GOVERNMENT; 806]

isometrics *n* **exercise**, workout, bodybuilding [➞HOBBIES, GAMES, AND SPORTS; 875]

isotherm *n* **line**, weather symbol, front, warm front, cold front [➞WEATHER AND CLIMATE; 1049]

isotope *n* **element**, form, variant, version [➞VARIETIES, TYPES, AND KINDS; 145]

ISP *n* [➞THE INTERNET; 1128]

issue **1** *n* **subject**, matter, question, topic, problem, concern, dispute [➞SUBJECT AREAS; 768] **2** *n* **copy**, number, edition, installment, back number, back issue, back copy [➞NEWSPAPERS AND MAGAZINES; 605] **3** *n* **production**, release, distribution, circulation, publication, delivery, issuance [➞DISPENSE, RATION, AND DISTRIBUTE; 434] **4** *n* **progeny**, offspring, children, young, descendants, heirs, posterity (*formal*) [➞YOUNGER GENERATION RELATIVES; 958] **5** *v* **supply**, give out, hand out, deliver, distribute, deal out, dispense, allot [➞DISPENSE, RATION, AND DISTRIBUTE; 434] **6** *v* **announce**, broadcast, send out, make, declare, put out [➞INFORM, ANNOUNCE, AND ISSUE; 611] **7** *v* **publish**, release, broadcast, disseminate, distribute, deliver, circulate [➞INFORM, ANNOUNCE, AND ISSUE; 611] *Opposite*: withdraw **8** *v* **originate**, stem, come forth, spring, arise, rise, proceed, result, follow [➞GRADUALLY COME INTO EXISTENCE; 1] **9** *v* **emanate**, emerge, issue forth, gush, flow, come out, erupt [➞EMIT AND EMANATE; 361]

isthmus *n* **strip**, neck, bridge, peninsula, spit, bar, promontory, headland [➞THE SEAS, OCEANS, AND SHORES; 1041]

IT *n* **information technology**, computer science, data processing, information processing, data retrieval [➞COMPUTERS AND COMPUTING; 1127]

italic *adj* **sloping**, slanted, oblique [➞PRINTING; 600] *Opposite*: roman

itch **1** *v* **irritate**, prickle, scratch, tickle, crawl, tingle, creep [➞PAIN AND OTHER PHYSICAL SENSATIONS; 733] *Opposite*: soothe **2** *v* **long**, desire, wish, hanker, yearn, ache, burn, have a yen for, pine for, crave [➞DESIRE AND WANT; 579] **3** *n* **itchiness**, tickle, irritation, prickling, tingling, prickliness [➞PAIN AND OTHER PHYSICAL SENSATIONS; 733] **4** *n* **desire**, longing, wish, eagerness, hankering, yearning, craving, pining, yen, appetite [➞DESIRE AND WANT; 579]

itchiness *n* **irritation**, tickle, inflammation, tingling, prickliness, prickling, prickly heat, heat rash, discomfort [➡ CONDITIONS AFFECTING THE SKIN; 721]

itching *adj* **eager**, longing, dying, keen, burning, impatient [➡ POSITIVE IMPATIENCE, ENTHUSIASM, AND ALERTNESS; 537] *Opposite:* reluctant

itchy *adj* **prickly**, tickly, scratchy, uncomfortable, irritated, inflamed [➡ PAIN AND OTHER PHYSICAL SENSATIONS; 733]

itchy feet *n* [➡ POSITIVE IMPATIENCE, ENTHUSIASM, AND ALERTNESS; 537]

item 1 *n* **thing**, article, piece, entry, point, element, note, detail, particular [➡ PHYSICAL OBJECTS; 1243] **2** *n* (*informal*) **couple**, pair, twosome, match, duo, lovers [➡ SEXUAL AND ROMANTIC RELATIONSHIPS; 964]

itemize *v* **list**, detail, enumerate, record, document, catalog, note, enter, specify [➡ RECORD SOMETHING; 371]

iterate *v* **repeat**, restate, reiterate, go over, retell, do again, rehearse, redo, recapitulate (*formal*) [➡ RECITE, REPEAT, AND NARRATE; 620]

iteration *n* **repetition**, restatement, reiteration, rehearsal, duplication, recapitulation (*formal*) [➡ CLAIM, INSIST, AND EMPHASIZE; 614]

itinerant *adj* **peripatetic**, roving, wandering, nomadic, roaming, migrant, traveling, wayfaring (*literary*) [➡ NOMADIC AND ROOTLESS LIFESTYLES; 884] *Opposite:* settled

itinerary *n* **route**, schedule, journey, circuit, tour, program, travel plan [➡ SUMMARIES, OUTLINES, AND EXCERPTS; 588]

itsy-bitsy (*informal*) *adj* **tiny**, little, small, minute, minuscule, wee, teeny (*informal*), teeny-weeny (*informal*), itty-bitty (*informal*) [➡ SMALL; 1195] *Opposite:* huge

itty-bitty (*informal*) *adj* [➡ SMALL; 1195]

ivory *type of* **white** [➡ COLORS; 1224]

ivory tower *n* **seclusion**, isolation, retreat, remoteness, academic world, academe (*formal*) [➡ EDUCATIONAL INSTITUTIONS; 813] *Opposite:* real world

ivy *type of* **climber** [➡ CLIMBERS; 1033]

J

jab 1 *v* **stab**, prod, thrust, dig, poke, nudge, tap, punch [→CONTACT: TOUCH; 412] **2** *n* **prod**, stab, thrust, dig, poke, nudge, tap, blow, hit [→CONTACT: TOUCH; 412]

jabber *v* **chatter**, babble, prattle, gabble, ramble, prate, natter (*informal*), blather (*informal*), gab (*informal*) [→CHATTER AND BABBLE; 617]

jack 1 *type of* **game piece** [→GAME PIECES; 878] **2** *type of* **general tool** [→HAND TOOLS; 1119]

jackal *type of* **canine** [→CANINES; 979]

jackass *type of* **male animal** [→MALE OR FEMALE ANIMALS; 978]

jackboot *type of* **boot** [→FOOTWEAR; 871]

jackdaw *type of* **scavenger** [→BIRDS; 997]

jacket 1 *n* **cover**, covering, casing, sheathing, sheath, sleeve, skin, coat, insulation, lagging, wrapper, wrapping, envelope [→COVERS AND COATINGS; 1246] **2** *type of* **jacket** [→GARMENTS AND OUTFITS; 866]

jack-in-the-box *type of* **toy** [→TOYS; 880]

jackknife 1 *v* **turn**, skid, swerve, veer, swivel, twist [→CHANGE DIRECTION OF MOTION; 344] **2** *type of* **knife** [→CUTTING TOOLS; 1120]

jackpot *n* **prize**, bonanza, winnings, windfall, pool, rollover (*UK*) [→INCOME; 460]

Jack Russell *type of* **small dog** [→DOGS; 980]

jack up 1 *v* **lift**, lift up, raise, raise up, put up, lever up [→MOVE SOMETHING: UPWARD; 328] *Opposite:* lower **2** *v* **increase**, raise, put up, hike up, boost, push up [→CHANGE OF INTENSITY: MORE; 394] *Opposite:* slash

jade 1 *type of* **gemstone** [→PRECIOUS STONES; 1278] **2** *type of* **green** [→COLORS; 1224]

jaded 1 *adj* **bored**, world-weary, jaundiced, cynical, tired, weary, overstimulated, fed up (*informal*) [→NEGATIVITY OF OUTLOOK; 514] *Opposite:* enthusiastic **2** *adj* **tired**, weary, exhausted, worn-out, burned-out, lackluster [→TIRED, ASLEEP, AND UNCONSCIOUS; 738] *Opposite:* fresh

jade green *type of* **green** [→COLORS; 1224]

jagged 1 *adj* **sharp**, pointed, pointy, rough, serrated, spiky, toothed [→PHYSICAL TEXTURE; 1222] *Opposite:* smooth **2** *adj* **uneven**, rough, ragged, crude, irregular, bumpy, coarse, angular [→PHYSICAL TEXTURE; 1222] *Opposite:* even

jaggedness 1 *n* **sharpness**, pointedness, pointiness, roughness, serration, serratedness, spikiness, toothiness [→PHYSICAL TEXTURE; 1222] *Opposite:* smoothness **2** *n* **unevenness**, raggedness, roughness, irregularity, bumpiness, coarseness, angularity [→PHYSICAL TEXTURE; 1222] *Opposite:* evenness

jaguar *type of* **cat** [→FELINES; 983]

jai alai *type of* **court game** [→HOBBIES, GAMES, AND SPORTS; 875]

jail 1 *n* **prison**, penitentiary, lockup, detention home, open prison, correctional institution, dungeon, secure unit, borstal (*UK*), remand home (*UK*) [→BUILDINGS FOR CONFINING PEOPLE; 1094] **2** *v* **imprison**, lock up, lock away, put behind bars, confine, detain, put away (*informal*), incarcerate (*formal*) [→THE POLICE, ARREST, AND PRETRIAL PROCEEDINGS; 818] *Opposite:* free

jailbird (*slang*) *n* **convict**, prisoner, inmate, detainee, offender, con (*slang*) [→CAPTIVES AND PRISONERS; 249]

jailbreak *n* **breakout**, escape, getaway, exodus, flight [→SUDDEN EVENTS; 52]

jailed *adj* [→CAPTIVITY AND LOSS OF FREEDOM; 248]

jailer *n* **prison officer**, guard, warden, governor, keeper, prison guard, screw (*slang*), warder (*UK*) [→PEOPLE WHO GUARD AND PROTECT; 846] *Opposite:* liberator

jalopy (*dated informal*) *n* **wreck**, tin lizzie (*informal*), rattletrap (*informal*), beater (*informal*), crate (*dated informal*), heap (*slang*) [→BIKES, CARS, AND CARRIAGES; 1149]

jam 1 *v* **push**, squash, cram, stuff, pack, ram, shove, force, wedge, crush, squeeze, press [→CONTACT: EXERT PRESSURE; 414] **2** *v* **fill**, fill up, throng, pack, block, congest [→FILL; 406] **3** *v* **stop**, seize, seize up, grind to a halt, stick, block, clog [→FAIL OR CEASE TO FUNCTION; 470] **4** *n* **traffic jam**, gridlock, bottleneck, logjam, roadblock, queue (*UK*), tailback (*UK*) [→TRAVEL: TRAFFIC PROBLEMS AND TRAFFIC MANAGEMENT; 323] **5** *n* (*informal*) **predicament**, mess, quandary, pickle (*informal*), fix (*informal*), scrape (*informal*) [→DIFFICULT SITUATIONS; 72] **6** *type of* **preserve** [→SUGAR AND PRESERVES; 1184]

jamb *n* **upright**, post, support, column, doorpost, vertical, side [→SUPPORTS AND BASES; 1255]

jamboree *n* **celebration**, party, fete, carnival, garden party, block party, shindig (*informal*) [→PARTIES, DANCES, AND CELEBRATIONS; 37]

jammed 1 *adj* **stuck**, wedged, stuck fast, lodged, caught, trapped [→LACK OF ACTIVITY OR MOTION; 342] *Opposite:* free **2** *adj* **blocked**, congested, thronged, packed, crammed, full [→FULL; 1239] *Opposite:* deserted

jam-pack (*informal*) *v* [→FILL; 406]

jam-packed (*informal*) *adj* **crowded**, full, full up, packed, filled to capacity, filled to the brim, chock-full (*informal*), heaving (*UK*), chock-a-block (*UK informal*), packed out (*UK informal*) [→FULL; 1239] *Opposite:* empty

jangle 1 *v* **rattle**, jingle, clank, clink, clatter, clang [→EMIT SOUNDS THROUGH IMPACT AND ABRASION; 365] **2** *n* **jingle**, rattle, clank, clink, clatter, clang [→RINGING AND HOOTING SOUNDS; 1259]

janitor *n* [→PEOPLE WHO GUARD AND PROTECT; 846]

Japanese beetle *type of* **beetle** [→BEETLES AND WEEVILS; 1016]

Japanese garden *type of* **garden** [→GARDENS; 1074]

jape (*archaic or literary*) **1** *n* **prank**, trick, practical joke, joke, lark, caper, escapade, setup (*informal*), jest (*literary*) [➡ JOKES AND TEASING; 674] **2** *v* **joke**, fool around, make mischief, trick, play with, mess around (*informal*), set up (*informal*), josh (*informal*) [➡ JOKES AND TEASING; 674]

jar 1 *n* **pot**, container, vessel, crock, urn, cruse (*archaic*), jam jar (*UK*) [➡ CONTAINERS, RECEPTACLES, AND PACKAGING; 1245] **2** *v* **shake**, jolt, jerk, bump, hit, shudder, vibrate, judder, bash (*informal*) [➡ MOVE SOMETHING: ON THE SPOT; 336] **3** *v* **irritate**, grate, annoy, irk, get on somebody's nerves, vex, nettle (*informal*) [➡ ANGER AND ANNOY; 569]

jargon 1 *n* **terminology**, slang, argot, parlance, language, lingo (*informal*) [➡ ASPECTS OF LANGUAGE; 682] **2** *n* **nonsense**, verbiage, cant, gobbledygook (*informal*), mumbo jumbo (*informal*), waffle (*informal*), guff (*informal*) [➡ MEANINGLESS SPEECH OR WRITING; 676]

> See Compare and Contrast at **language**.

jarring 1 *adj* **irritating**, grating, annoying, unpleasant, unbearable [➡ EMOTIONALLY UNPLEASANT AND UPSETTING; 227] *Opposite*: calming **2** *adj* **disturbing**, unsettling, shocking, destabilizing, uncomfortable, worrying, upsetting [➡ EMOTIONALLY UNPLEASANT AND UPSETTING; 227] *Opposite*: reassuring **3** *adj* **clashing**, incongruous, uncharacteristic, discordant, inharmonious, uncomfortable, inappropriate, disturbing [➡ LOUD, HIGH, OR UNPLEASANT SOUNDS; 1266] *Opposite*: harmonious

jasmine *type of* **climber** [➡ CLIMBERS; 1033]

jaundiced *adj* **cynical**, pessimistic, skeptical, unenthusiastic, jaded, negative [➡ NEGATIVITY OF OUTLOOK; 514]

jaunt *n* **outing**, trip, excursion, break, day out, spree, day away, away day (*UK*) [➡ TRAVEL: JOURNEYS AND TRIPS; 318]

jauntiness *n* **cheerfulness**, jolliness, gaiety, dash, spryness, cheeriness, self-confidence, briskness, chirpiness (*informal*) [➡ PLEASURE, EXCITEMENT, AND ELATION; 534]

jaunty *adj* **carefree**, cheerful, cheery, jolly, spry, lively, brisk, merry, sprightly, chipper (*informal*), chirpy (*informal*) [➡ PLEASURE, EXCITEMENT, AND ELATION; 534]

javelin 1 *n* **spear**, projectile, missile, lance, harpoon [➡ PROJECTILES; 1159] **2** *type of* **sports equipment** [➡ SPORTS EQUIPMENT; 879] **3** *type of* **track and field** [➡ HOBBIES, GAMES, AND SPORTS; 875]

jaw 1 *n* **chin**, jawbone, jawline, jowl, mouth, mandible, maxilla, chops (*informal*) [➡ PARTS OF THE BODY: HEAD; 692] **2** *v* (*slang*) **chat**, chatter, gossip, talk, prattle, blather, rabbit on (*informal*) [➡ TWO-WAY COMMUNICATION; 607]

jawbone *n* **jaw**, chin, maxilla, mandible [➡ THE BONES AND JOINTS; 719]

jawbreaker *type of* **confectionery** [➡ CONFECTIONERY; 1182]

jawline *part of* **face** [➡ PARTS OF THE BODY: HEAD; 692]

jaywalk *v* **cross**, cross over, walk across, stroll across, go across, traverse [➡ PROCEED AND GO; 305]

jaywalker *n* **pedestrian**, walker, crosser, traverser, stroller [➡ TRAVEL: TRAVELERS AND WALKERS; 319]

jazz 1 *n* (*slang*) **stuff**, things, paraphernalia, belongings, tackle, equipment, gear (*informal*) [➡ PHYSICAL OBJECTS; 1243] **2** *n* (*slang*) **nonsense**, rubbish, rigmarole, stuff, stuff and nonsense, verbiage, drivel, talk, gobbledygook (*informal*), guff (*informal*), waffle (*informal*), blather (*informal*), flimflam (*slang*), jive (*slang*) [➡ MEANINGLESS SPEECH OR WRITING; 676] **3** *n* (*slang*) **liveliness**, vivacity, enthusiasm, energy, joie de vivre, oomph (*informal*), pizazz (*informal*), zip (*informal*), zing (*informal*), pep (*informal*) [➡ ENERGY AND ENTHUSIASM; 496] **4** *type of* **jazz music** [➡ MUSIC, SONGS, AND SINGING; 907]

jazz band *type of* **band** [➡ MUSICIANS AND SINGERS; 908]

jazz funk *type of* **jazz music** [➡ MUSIC, SONGS, AND SINGING; 907]

jazz fusion *type of* **jazz music** [➡ MUSIC, SONGS, AND SINGING; 907]

jazz rock *type of* **jazz music** [➡ MUSIC, SONGS, AND SINGING; 907]

jazz up (*informal*) *v* **enhance**, spice, spice up, liven up, enliven, add zing to, add zest to, zest, brighten up, pep up (*informal*) [➡ IMPROVE APPEARANCE; 379]

jazzy (*slang*) *adj* **showy**, bright, flashy, gaudy, glitzy, smart, fancy, psychedelic, colorful [➡ DESCRIBING COLORS; 1226] *Opposite*: somber

jealous 1 *adj* **envious**, covetous, resentful, green with envy, green, green-eyed, bitter, desirous (*formal*) [➡ ENVY AND JEALOUSY; 548] **2** *adj* **protective**, suspicious, wary, watchful, mistrustful, possessive [➡ INSECURITY AND LOSS OF COMPOSURE; 544] *Opposite*: trusting

jealousy 1 *n* **envy**, covetousness, resentment, resentfulness, desirousness (*formal*) [➡ ENVY AND JEALOUSY; 548] **2** *n* **protectiveness**, suspicion, suspiciousness, wariness, watchfulness, mistrustfulness, distrust, possessiveness [➡ INSECURITY AND LOSS OF COMPOSURE; 544]

jeans *type of* **pants** [➡ GARMENTS AND OUTFITS; 865]

jeep *type of* **military vehicle** [➡ VEHICLES; 1145]

jeepers (*dated informal*) *interj* [➡ EXPRESSIONS OF SURPRISE AND PLEASURE; 546]

jeer 1 *v* **boo**, hiss, heckle, catcall, taunt, laugh at, mock, abuse, call names [➡ INSULTS, ABUSE, AND SWEARING; 658] *Opposite*: applaud **2** *n* **hiss**, boo, taunt, catcall, hoot, Bronx cheer (*informal*), raspberry (*informal*) [➡ INSULTS, ABUSE, AND SWEARING; 658]

jeer at *v* **insult**, taunt, sneer, mock, deride, ridicule, scoff [➡ INSULTS, ABUSE, AND SWEARING; 658] *Opposite*: cheer

jeering 1 *n* **derision**, mockery, name-calling, mocking, taunting, scoffing, heckling, booing, hissing [➡ INSULTS, ABUSE, AND SWEARING; 658] *Opposite*: applause **2** *adj* **derisive**, scornful, mocking, sardonic, contemptuous, sneering, taunting [➡ MOCKING AND DISMISSIVE; 636]

jejune 1 *adj* **boring**, undemanding, uninteresting, lightweight, insubstantial, superficial [➡ BORING AND UNINTERESTING; 234] *Opposite*: interesting **2** *adj* **childish**, immature, adolescent, unsophisticated, crude, simplistic [➡ NEGATIVE INTELLECTUAL CHARACTERISTICS; 525] *Opposite*: mature

jell 1 *v* **solidify**, set, congeal, firm, harden, thicken, gel [➡ HARDEN, CONGEAL, AND DRY; 387] *Opposite*: liquefy **2** *v* **take shape**, shape up, crystallize, come together, firm up, become clear, gel (*informal*) [➡ GRADUALLY COME INTO EXISTENCE; 1] *Opposite*: disintegrate **3** *v* **bond**, be compatible, be on the same wavelength, get along, click (*informal*), hit it off (*informal*), gel (*informal*), get on (*UK*) [➡ ESTABLISHING RELATIONSHIPS WITH OTHERS; 974] *Opposite*: clash

jellied *adj* **gelatinous**, set, solid, congealed [➡ STATE OF PREPARED FOOD; 1171]

jellify *v* **set**, jelly, gelatinize, congeal, jell, gel [➡ HARDEN, CONGEAL, AND DRY; 387] *Opposite:* liquefy

jelly 1 *n* **gelatin**, aspic, gel [➡ CAKES, COOKIES, AND DESSERTS; 1181] 2 *n* **petroleum jelly**, lubricant, ointment [➡ LOTIONS, PASTES, AND GELS; 1272] 3 *v* **set**, thicken, jellify, gelatinize, congeal, jell, gel, firm [➡ HARDEN, CONGEAL, AND DRY; 387] *Opposite:* liquefy 4 *type of* **preserve** [➡ SUGAR AND PRESERVES; 1184]

jellybean *type of* **confectionery** [➡ CONFECTIONERY; 1182]

jellyfish *type of* **aquatic invertebrate** [➡ AQUATIC INVERTEBRATES; 1022]

jellylike *adj* [➡ MALLEABLE AND ELASTIC; 1212]

jelly roll *type of* **cake** [➡ CAKES, COOKIES, AND DESSERTS; 1181]

je ne sais quoi *n* [➡ FOREIGN WORDS AND PHRASES; 672]

jenny *type of* **female animal** [➡ MALE OR FEMALE ANIMALS; 978]

jeopardize *v* **put at risk**, risk, put in danger, endanger, expose, threaten [➡ PUT AT RISK; 384]

jeopardy *n* **danger**, risk, threat, peril, hazard, difficulty, trouble [➡ DANGER; 235]

jerboa *type of* **rodent** [➡ RODENTS; 989]

jeremiad (*formal*) *n* [➡ CRITICISMS AND ANGRY OUTBURSTS; 50]

jerk 1 *v* **yank**, tug, pull, wrench, haul [➡ PUSH, PULL, AND SLIDE; 335] 2 *v* **lurch**, jolt, shudder, judder, bump, shake [➡ MOVE SOMETHING: ON THE SPOT; 336] 3 *v* **twitch**, shudder, tremble, shake [➡ PHYSICAL REACTIONS; 316] 4 *n* **pull**, tug, yank, wrench, haul [➡ CONTACT, TOUCH; 412] 5 *n* **jolt**, bump, shudder, judder, lurch, shake [➡ MOVE SOMETHING: ON THE SPOT; 336] 6 *n* **spasm**, twitch, shudder, tremble, shake [➡ PHYSICAL REACTIONS; 316]

jerkin *n* **jacket**, body warmer, tunic, vest, gilet, waistcoat (*UK*) [➡ GARMENTS AND OUTFITS; 865]

jerkiness *n* **bumpiness**, jumpiness, bounciness, lurching, shuddering, juddering, jolting, irregularity [➡ DESCRIBING BODY MOVEMENTS; 288] *Opposite:* smoothness

jerky 1 *adj* **irregular**, spasmodic, erratic, fitful, bumpy, jumpy, bouncy, rough, shuddering, juddering, lurching, jolting [➡ DESCRIBING BODY MOVEMENTS; 288] *Opposite:* smooth 2 *type of* **processed meat** [➡ TYPES AND CUTS OF MEAT; 1177]

jerrybuild *v* **throw up**, fling up, throw together (*informal*), knock together (*informal*) [➡ BUILD; 352]

jerrybuilt *adj* **badly built**, poor, poor quality, shoddy, flimsy, slapdash, ramshackle, cheap and nasty, thrown together (*informal*), knocked together (*informal*) [➡ IN BAD REPAIR; 1234]

jerry can *n* **can**, container, canister [➡ CONTAINERS, RECEPTACLES, AND PACKAGING; 1245]

jerry-rigged *adj* [➡ IN BAD REPAIR; 1234]

jersey 1 *type of* **sweater** [➡ GARMENTS AND OUTFITS; 865] 2 *type of* **fabric from animals** [➡ FABRICS; 1132]

jest (*literary*) 1 *n* **joke**, prank, hoax, quip, spoof, gag (*informal*), canard (*literary*), jape (*archaic or literary*)

[➡ JOKES AND TEASING; 674] 2 *v* **banter**, joke, kid, tease, quip, clown [➡ JOKES AND TEASING; 674]

jester *n* **fool**, clown, comedian, entertainer, comic, joker [➡ JOKERS AND TEASES; 675]

jesting (*literary*) 1 *adj* **jokey**, lighthearted, flippant, funny, humorous, playful [➡ GOOD-TEMPERED AND HUMOROUS; 627] *Opposite:* serious 2 *n* **joking**, clowning, kidding, slapstick, fun, humor, banter [➡ JOKES AND TEASING; 674]

jet 1 *n* **spurt**, spout, fountain, squirt, stream, gush [➡ AMOUNTS OF LIQUID; 114] 2 *type of* **civil aircraft** [➡ AIRCRAFT; 1148] 3 *type of* **mineral** [➡ MINERALS; 1277]

jet black *type of* **black** [➡ COLORS; 1224]

jet engine *part of* **aircraft** [➡ AIRCRAFT; 1148]

jetsam *n* **odds and ends**, flotsam, debris, detritus, rubbish, miscellanea, trash, bits and pieces (*informal*), junk (*informal*) [➡ JUNK AND USELESS OBJECTS; 1249]

jet set (*informal*) *n* **glitterati**, high society, rich and famous, beautiful people, idle rich, café society [➡ RICH PEOPLE; 895] *Opposite:* hoi polloi

jetsetter (*informal*) *n* [➡ TRAVEL: TRAVELERS AND WALKERS; 319]

jettison *v* **throw away**, throw out, get rid of, abandon, discard, dump, chuck (*informal*), chuck out (*informal*), ditch (*informal*) [➡ GET RID OF SOMETHING; 451] *Opposite:* keep

jetty *n* **dock**, breakwater, quay, landing stage, pier, quayside, wharf [➡ WATERWAYS AND SEAWAYS; 1108]

jewel 1 *n* **gemstone**, gem, precious stone, semiprecious stone, crystal, rock (*informal*), sparkler (*informal*) [➡ PRECIOUS STONES; 1278] 2 *n* **ornament**, trinket, accessory [➡ ORNAMENTS AND DECORATIONS; 1248]

jewel case *type of* **container** [➡ CONTAINERS, RECEPTACLES, AND PACKAGING; 1245]

jewel in the crown (*UK*) *n* [➡ AMAZING THINGS; 211]

jewelry *type of* **accessory** [➡ ACCESSORIES, MILLINERY, AND LINGERIE; 867]

jewelry

◆ *types of jewelry*
anklet, armlet, badge, bangle, bracelet, brooch, cameo, charm, cuff link, eardrop, earring, necklace, nose ring, nose stud, pin, ring, stud, tiara, tie clasp, tie tack, wristlet

◆ *types of necklaces*
beads, chain, choker, collar, locket, medallion, pendant, torque

jib 1 *part of* **sailing vessel** [➡ PARTS OF A SHIP OR BOAT; 1151] 2 *v* (*UK*) **balk**, stop short, pull up, recoil, retreat, shy [➡ NOT DO AND REFUSE TO DO; 274]

jibe 1 *n* **taunt**, dig, sneer, insult, gibe, crack (*informal*) [➡ INSULTS, ABUSE, AND SWEARING; 658] 2 *v* **sneer**, taunt, mock, ridicule, insult, belittle, gibe [➡ JOKES AND TEASING; 674]

jiff (*informal*) *n* [➡ SHORT PERIODS OF TIME; 93]

jiffy (*informal*) *n* **moment**, second, minute, flash, instant, sec (*informal*) [➡ SHORT PERIODS OF TIME; 93]

jig 1 *type of* **dance** [➡DANCE; 903] **2** *v* **jerk**, skip, hop, caper, leap, spring, dance [➡FIDGET AND FROLIC; 311]

jiggle *v* **wiggle**, waggle, shake, joggle, rattle, agitate, jostle [➡MOVE SOMETHING: ON THE SPOT; 336]

jigsaw 1 *n* **puzzle**, jigsaw puzzle, picture puzzle, Chinese puzzle, tangram [➡TOYS; 880] **2** *type of* **carpentry tool** [➡HAND TOOLS; 1119]

jigsaw puzzle *see* **jigsaw**

jilt *v* **reject**, turn down, break up, split up, walk out, leave, leave in the lurch, desert, abandon, drop (*informal*), ditch (*informal*) [➡REFUSING OR REJECTING RELATIONS; 975] *Opposite*: stick by

jim-dandy (*informal*) *n* [➡AMAZING THINGS; 211]

jimmy 1 *v* **lever**, open, force, pry, prize, crowbar [➡UNFASTEN AND UNDO; 409] **2** *type of* **general tool** [➡HAND TOOLS; 1119]

jimsonweed *type of* **weed** [➡WEEDS AND THISTLES; 1034]

jingle 1 *n* **ringing**, ring, tinkle, tinkling, clink, clinking, clank, clanking, clatter, clattering, rattle, rattling [➡RINGING AND HOOTING SOUNDS; 1259] **2** *n* **tune**, song, refrain, chorus, ditty [➡MUSIC, SONGS, AND SINGING; 907] **3** *v* **tinkle**, rattle, ring, clink, clank, clatter [➡EMIT SOUNDS THROUGH IMPACT AND ABRASION; 365]

jingoism *n* **chauvinism**, patriotism, nationalism, xenophobia, hostility, antipathy, antagonism, flag-waving, wrapping yourself in the flag [➡PREJUDICE; 550]

jingoist *n* [➡SELF-IMPORTANT AND SELF-SEEKING PEOPLE; 949]

jingoistic *adj* **chauvinistic**, patriotic, nationalistic, xenophobic, hostile, antagonistic [➡NEGATIVE INTELLECTUAL CHARACTERISTICS; 525]

jinne *n* [➡MYTHICAL BEINGS; 789]

jinx *n* **curse**, plague, evil eye, spell, bad luck, misfortune, bugaboo, gremlin (*informal*), whammy (*informal*) [➡PROBLEMS; 256]

jinxed *adj* **unlucky**, luckless, hapless, unfortunate, star-crossed, ill-fated, ill-starred (*formal*) [➡BAD LUCK AND UNLUCKY; 784] *Opposite*: lucky

jitney *type of* **public service vehicle** [➡VEHICLES; 1145]

jitterbug *type of* **dance** [➡DANCE; 903]

jitteriness *n* [➡CONFUSION, ANXIETY, AND WORRY; 540]

jitters (*informal*) *n* **nervousness**, agitation, uneasiness, anxiety, apprehension, fright, fear, shakes, nerves (*informal*), butterflies (*informal*), shivers (*informal*), heebie-jeebies (*slang*) [➡CONFUSION, ANXIETY, AND WORRY; 540] *Opposite*: calmness

jittery *adj* **nervous**, jumpy, on edge, edgy, fidgety, skittish, stressed out (*informal*), frazzled (*informal*) [➡CONFUSION, ANXIETY, AND WORRY; 540] *Opposite*: calm

jive 1 *type of* **dance** [➡DANCE; 903] **2** *n* (*slang*) **flattery**, smooth talk, sweet talk (*informal*), soft soap (*informal*), weasel words (*informal*), blarney (*informal*), blandishment (*formal*) [➡INGRATIATING; 638] **3** *type of* **jazz music** [➡MUSIC, SONGS, AND SINGING; 907]

job 1 *n* **occupation**, work, trade, profession, career,

employment, contract, business [➡PROFESSIONS; 845] **2** *n* **position**, post, appointment, vacancy, role, function, engagement, slot, opening [➡JOB; 833] **3** *n* **task**, duty, responsibility, chore, assignment, activity, mission, affair, charge [➡WORK IN GENERAL; 297]

Compare and Contrast: *job*, *assignment*, *task*, *chore*, *duty*

CORE MEANING: a piece of work to be done

job somebody's employment, or a piece of work that somebody has chosen to do or one that he or she is obliged to do, for example, because it is part of his or her employment; *assignment* a set piece of work given to somebody as part of the workload of an occupation or course of study, often with a deadline, or a post or position that has been allocated to somebody; *task* a piece of work that requires effort, often imposed by an employer or someone in authority, and usually quite short in duration or with a deadline; *chore* a relatively short routine undertaking, either imposed by somebody in authority or self-imposed, requiring effort and considered tedious and even unpleasant; *duty* something that has to be done because of obligations to other individuals or to society.

jobbing *adj* **casual**, occasional, freelance, part-time, temporary, self-employed [➡EMPLOYMENT STATUS; 831] *Opposite*: regular

jobless *adj* **unemployed**, out of work, on welfare, laid off, unwaged (*UK*), on benefit (*UK*), redundant (*UK*) [➡EMPLOYMENT STATUS; 831] *Opposite*: employed

joblessness *n* [➡WORK-RELATED ACTIVITIES; 834]

job-sharer *n* [➡WORKERS; 836]

job-sharing *n* **part-time work**, work-sharing, sharing [➡WORK-RELATED ACTIVITIES; 834]

jockey 1 *n* **rider**, equestrian, steeplechaser, show-jumper, competitor, point-to-pointer, eventer (*UK*) [➡PEOPLE IN SPORTS AND LEISURE; 876] **2** *v* **ride**, race, steeplechase, show jump, compete, show, event (*UK*) [➡HOBBIES, GAMES, AND SPORTS; 875] **3** *v* **compete**, contend, fight, struggle, juggle, jostle, maneuver [➡COMPETE, CONTEND, AND COMBAT; 303] **4** *v* **manipulate**, cajole, trick, deceive, talk into, con, pressure, press, coax, persuade [➡CAUSE OR COMPEL TO ACT; 271]

jockstrap *type of* **lower body underwear** [➡ACCESSORIES, MILLINERY, AND LINGERIE; 867]

jocose (*literary*) *adj* [➡GOOD-TEMPERED AND HUMOROUS; 627]

jocular *adj* **funny**, joking, jokey, jovial, playful, witty, flippant, lighthearted, frivolous, sportive, facetious, roguish, humorous, good-humored, flip (*informal*), waggish (*informal*), jocose (*literary*) [➡GOOD-TEMPERED AND HUMOROUS; 627] *Opposite*: solemn

jocularity *n* **wittiness**, comicality, playfulness, jokiness, humorousness, facetiousness, cheerfulness, joviality, sportiveness, roguishness, humor, waggishness (*informal*) [➡GOOD-TEMPERED AND HUMOROUS; 627] *Opposite*: solemnity

jocund (*literary*) *adj* **cheerful**, good-humored, cheery, merry, ebullient, hearty [➡GOOD-TEMPERED AND HUMOROUS; 627]

jocundity (*literary*) *n* [➡ GOOD-TEMPERED AND HUMOROUS; 627]

jodhpurs *type of* **pants** [➡ GARMENTS AND OUTFITS; 865]

joey *type of* **young animal** [➡ YOUNG ANIMALS; 977]

jog 1 *v* **trot**, run, train, exercise, sprint [➡ MOVE FAST; 313] 2 *v* **nudge**, prod, bump, push, bang, hit, shake, jerk, pull, twitch [➡ CONTACT: IMPACT; 413]

jogger *n* **runner**, sprinter, cross-country runner, athlete, harrier (*UK*) [➡ PEOPLE IN SPORTS AND LEISURE; 876]

jogging suit *type of* **sportswear** [➡ GARMENTS AND OUTFITS; 865]

joggle *v* **shake**, wiggle, waggle, jiggle, jerk, bump, knock [➡ MOVE SOMETHING: ON THE SPOT; 336]

John Dory *type of* **ocean fish** [➡ OCEAN FISH; 1009]

John Hancock (*informal*) *n* **signature**, autograph, name, mark [➡ NAME AND DESCRIBE; 665]

johnnycake *type of* **pancake** [➡ CAKES, COOKIES, AND DESSERTS; 1181]

joie de vivre *n* **vitality**, enthusiasm, liveliness, exuberance, high-spiritedness, spiritedness, energy, élan (*literary*) [➡ PLEASURE, EXCITEMENT, AND ELATION; 534] *Opposite*: lethargy

join 1 *v* **link**, unite, connect, stick, fasten, fix, adhere, bond, bind, paste [➡ FASTEN, LINK, AND JOIN; 408] *Opposite*: separate 2 *v* **connect**, link up, merge, bring together, unite, link, put in touch, bridge, unify, consolidate [➡ CREATING CONNECTIONS; 144] *Opposite*: disengage 3 *v* **sign up**, enroll, enlist, join up, go in with, enter, subscribe to [➡ PARTICIPATE; 292] *Opposite*: leave 4 *n* **joint**, seam, connection, intersection, link, junction [➡ FASTENERS, LINKS, AND NETWORKS; 1247]

joined 1 *adj* **bonded**, fixed together, hinged, hitched, linked, tied, bound, attached, coupled, connected, yoked [➡ FASTEN, LINK, AND JOIN; 408] *Opposite*: detached 2 *adj* **associated**, allied, affiliated, twinned, connected, bound [➡ RELATED; 142] *Opposite*: independent

joinery *n* **woodworking**, cabinetmaking, furniture making, carving, carpentry, woodcraft [➡ CRAFTS AND CARVING; 355]

join forces *v* **team up**, collaborate, get together, come together, rally, merge, amalgamate, combine, consolidate [➡ ESTABLISHING RELATIONSHIPS WITH OTHERS; 974] *Opposite*: split

join in *v* **participate**, become involved, take part, enter into, play, contribute, have a go (*informal*) [➡ PARTICIPATE; 292] *Opposite*: leave

joint 1 *adj* **combined**, dual, shared, multiparty, united, mutual, common, cooperative, communal, collaborative, allied [➡ ACTING WITH OTHERS; 285] *Opposite*: individual 2 *n* **join**, linkage, link, junction, intersection, seam, connection, coupling, hinge, juncture (*formal*) [➡ FASTENERS, LINKS, AND NETWORKS; 1247] 3 *type of* **cut** [➡ TYPES AND CUTS OF MEAT; 1177] 4 *n* (*slang*) **venue**, place, establishment, locale, location, hangout (*informal*), dive (*informal*) [➡ HOTELS, RESTAURANTS, AND CLUBS; 1082]

join together *v* **merge**, amalgamate, integrate, dovetail, associate, federate, unite, consolidate, cooperate [➡ ESTABLISHING RELATIONSHIPS WITH OTHERS; 974] *Opposite*: split

joint-stock company *n* [➡ BUSINESS ENTERPRISES AND RELATED BODIES; 792]

joint venture *n* [➡ BUSINESS ENTERPRISES AND RELATED BODIES; 792]

join up 1 *v* **enlist**, enroll, sign up, join, subscribe, enter, go in with [➡ PARTICIPATE; 292] *Opposite*: quit 2 *v* (*UK*) **meet up**, link, team up, come together, get together, combine, pair, unite, consolidate, amalgamate [➡ ESTABLISHING RELATIONSHIPS WITH OTHERS; 974]

joist *n* **beam**, spar, truss, support [➡ BUILDING MATERIALS; 1077]

joke 1 *n* **witticism**, tall story, pun, anecdote, tale, tall tale, shaggy-dog story, gag (*informal*), yarn (*informal*), put-on (*informal*), jest (*literary*) [➡ JOKES AND TEASING; 674] 2 *n* **prank**, trick, practical joke, stunt, hoax, act, caper, lark [➡ JOKES AND TEASING; 674] 3 *n* **butt**, laughingstock, object of ridicule, fool, buffoon [➡ LAZY OR UNSUCCESSFUL PEOPLE; 948] 4 *v* **kid**, pretend, clown, play the fool, pull somebody's leg (*informal*), mess around (*informal*), josh (*informal*), jest (*literary*) [➡ JOKES AND TEASING; 674]

joker *n* **clown**, fool, buffoon, comedian, comic, prankster, entertainer, wit, jester, wag (*informal*) [➡ JOKERS AND TEASES; 675]

jokey *adj* **amusing**, lighthearted, flippant, funny, witty, comical, humorous, facetious, good-humored, flip (*informal*), joshing (*informal*), jesting (*literary*) [➡ GOOD-TEMPERED AND HUMOROUS; 627] *Opposite*: serious

jokily *adv* **amusingly**, good-humoredly, jokingly, humorously, drolly, facetiously, wittily, comically, entertainingly, flippantly [➡ GOOD-TEMPERED AND HUMOROUS; 627] *Opposite*: seriously

jokiness *n* [➡ GOOD-TEMPERED AND HUMOROUS; 627]

joking 1 *adj* **jokey**, playful, flippant, lighthearted, facetious, funny, teasing, jesting (*literary*) [➡ GOOD-TEMPERED AND HUMOROUS; 627] *Opposite*: serious 2 *n* **clowning**, teasing, raillery, fooling around, horseplay, playing the fool, high jinks (*informal*) [➡ JOKES AND TEASING; 674]

jollification *n* **festivity**, revelry, celebration, merrymaking, party, revel, feast, carousal (*literary*) [➡ PARTIES, DANCES, AND CELEBRATIONS; 37]

jolliness *see* **jollity**

jollity *n* **cheerfulness**, fun, hilarity, joviality, jolliness, gaiety, high-spiritedness, jauntiness, gleefulness, merriness, high spirits, playfulness, ebullience [➡ PLEASURE, EXCITEMENT, AND ELATION; 534] *Opposite*: seriousness

jolly *adj* **cheerful**, happy, fun, jovial, bright, ebullient, cheery, good-humored, merry, gleeful, playful [➡ CHEERFULNESS OF OUTLOOK; 503] *Opposite*: sad

jolt 1 *v* **shake**, jerk, bump, joggle, nudge, push, shove, lurch, quake [➡ MOVE SOMETHING: ON THE SPOT; 336] 2 *n* **shock**, surprise, bolt from the blue, blow, reminder, jar, thunderbolt, trauma, bombshell (*informal*) [➡ SUDDEN EVENTS; 52] 3 *n* **bump**, shake, jerk, joggle, bounce, judder, shudder, lurch, quake (*informal*) [➡ MOVE SOMETHING: ON THE SPOT; 336]

jonquil *type of* **flower grown from bulbs** [➡ FLOWERS FROM BULBS; 1030]

josh (*informal*) *v* **tease**, make fun of, chaff, ridicule, mock, rib (*informal*), pull somebody's leg (*informal*), set up (*informal*) [➡ JOKES AND TEASING; 674]

josher (*informal*) *n* [➡ JOKERS AND TEASES; 675]

joshing (*informal*) *n* [→ JOKES AND TEASING; 674]

jostle *v* **push**, knock, bump, push, shove, elbow, manhandle, crowd, butt, shoulder, push around (*informal*) [→ CONTACT: IMPACT; 413]

jot *n* **iota**, atom, bit, speck, tittle, dot, mite, smidgen (*informal*), whit (*dated*) [→ FEW, LITTLE, SMALL AMOUNT; 120]

jot down *v* **write down**, make a note of, scribble down, put on paper, put down, note, list, record, enter [→ RECORD SOMETHING; 371]

jotter (*UK*) *n* **notepad**, notebook, pad, personal organizer, writing pad [→ WRITING AND DRAWING IMPLEMENTS, AND MEDIA; 601]

joule *type of* **SI unit** [→ SIZE AND DIMENSIONS; 1192]

journal 1 *n* **periodical**, magazine, paper, weekly, monthly, quarterly, bulletin, newsletter [→ NEWSPAPERS AND MAGAZINES; 605] 2 *n* **diary**, log, chronicle, record, register, daybook [→ RECORDS; 585]

journalism *n* **reporting**, reportage, broadcasting, commentary, fourth estate, press [→ NEWSPAPERS AND MAGAZINES; 605]

journalist *n* **correspondent**, reporter, broadcaster, columnist, newscaster, commentator, press officer, newswriter [→ WORKERS IN ENTERTAINMENT AND MEDIA; 873]

journalistic *adj* **reporting**, editorial, newspaper, broadsheet, tabloid, weekly, monthly, quarterly, magazine [→ NEWSPAPERS AND MAGAZINES; 605]

journey 1 *n* **trip**, voyage, expedition, ride, flight, passage, crossing, excursion, drive, tour, trek, outing [→ TRAVEL: JOURNEYS AND TRIPS; 318] 2 *v* **travel**, tour, go, trek, voyage, fly, sail, sightsee, cruise, roam [→ TRAVEL: WAYS OF TRAVELING; 320]

joust *v* **fight**, tilt, compete, battle, engage, contest, contend, spar, bicker, squabble, dispute, argue, wrangle [→ ARGUE AND FIGHT; 643] *Opposite*: agree

jovial *adj* **cheerful**, jolly, fun-loving, breezy, happy, cheery, buoyant, merry, ebullient, good-humored, hearty, full of beans (*informal*), jocund (*literary*), blithe (*literary*) [→ CHEERFULNESS OF OUTLOOK; 503] *Opposite*: glum

joviality *n* **cheerfulness**, jollity, jolliness, cheeriness, bonhomie, merriness, good humor, ebullience, jocundity (*literary*), blitheness (*literary*) [→ CHEERFULNESS OF OUTLOOK; 503] *Opposite*: glumness

jovialness *see* **joviality**

jowl *n* **jaw**, chin, jawbone, jawline, muzzle, mandible, chops (*informal*) [→ PARTS OF THE BODY: HEAD; 692]

joy 1 *n* **happiness**, delight, enjoyment, bliss, ecstasy, elation, joyfulness, thrill, pleasure, gladness, exultation, rapture [→ PLEASURE, EXCITEMENT, AND ELATION; 534] *Opposite*: sadness 2 *n* **delight**, jewel, treasure, pearl, angel, wonder, prize, pride, gem (*informal*) [→ TREATS; 210]

joyful 1 *adj* **happy**, elated, ecstatic, thrilled, pleased, jubilant, glad, delighted, exultant [→ PLEASURE, EXCITEMENT, AND ELATION; 534] *Opposite*: sad 2 *adj* **wonderful**, blissful, pleasurable, fantastic, enjoyable, carefree, pleasant, happy, pleasing, heartwarming, delightful, welcome [→ EMOTIONALLY PLEASANT; 187] *Opposite*: unpleasant

joyfully *adv* **happily**, ecstatically, blissfully, merrily,

gladly, cheerily, elatedly, jubilantly, exuberantly [→ GOOD-TEMPERED AND HUMOROUS; 627] *Opposite*: sadly

joyfulness *n* **happiness**, enjoyment, bliss, ecstasy, merriment, cheerfulness, jubilation, pleasure, gladness, exultation, rapture [→ PLEASURE, EXCITEMENT, AND ELATION; 534] *Opposite*: sadness

joyless *adj* **miserable**, cheerless, depressing, bleak, desolate, unhappy, dreary, gloomy, dour [→ EMOTIONALLY UNPLEASANT AND UPSETTING; 227] *Opposite*: happy

joylessness *n* **cheerlessness**, misery, gloom, unhappiness, bleakness, desolation, despondency, dreariness, gloominess, dourness [→ SADNESS, DISTRESS, AND DESPAIR; 539] *Opposite*: happiness

joyous *adj* **happy**, merry, blissful, festive, cheerful, jubilant, exuberant, delighted, elated, exultant [→ PLEASURE, EXCITEMENT, AND ELATION; 534] *Opposite*: glum

joyousness *n* **happiness**, pleasure, bliss, joyfulness, jubilation, cheerfulness, elation, exuberance, joy, gladness, exultation, rapture [→ PLEASURE, EXCITEMENT, AND ELATION; 534] *Opposite*: glumness

joyride *v* **carjack**, speed, hot-rod (*slang*) [→ STEAL AND ROB; 426]

joyrider *n* **carjacker**, car thief, speeder, hot-rodder (*slang*) [→ CRIMINALS; 821]

joyriding *n* **carjacking**, car theft, speeding, hot-rodding (*slang*) [→ CRIMES; 817]

joystick 1 *type of* **hardware** [→ COMPUTERS AND COMPUTING; 1127] 2 *part of* **aircraft** [→ AIRCRAFT; 1148]

JP *n* **Justice of the Peace**, magistrate, justice, official, judge, arbitrator, administrator [→ PEOPLE IN LAW COURTS; 820]

jubilant *adj* **triumphant**, proud, thrilled, ecstatic, delighted, euphoric, glad, overjoyed, joyful, exultant, joyous, over the moon (*UK informal*) [→ PLEASURE, EXCITEMENT, AND ELATION; 534] *Opposite*: disappointed

jubilation *n* **elation**, triumph, joyousness, euphoria, delight, joy [→ PLEASURE, EXCITEMENT, AND ELATION; 534] *Opposite*: disappointment

jubilee *n* **anniversary**, celebration, commemoration, festival, festivity, silver jubilee, golden jubilee, diamond jubilee [→ CEREMONIES AND ANNIVERSARIES; 38]

Judas tree *type of* **deciduous tree** [→ DECIDUOUS TREES; 1028]

judder 1 *v* **shake**, vibrate, shudder, quiver, tremble, quaver, roll, rock, jerk [→ MOVE SOMETHING: ON THE SPOT; 336] 2 *n* **shudder**, vibration, quiver, tremor, jerk, quaver [→ MOVE SOMETHING: ON THE SPOT; 336]

judge 1 *n* **magistrate**, justice, justice of the peace, judge advocate [→ PEOPLE IN LAW COURTS; 820] 2 *n* **arbitrator**, adjudicator, moderator, umpire, referee [→ SURVEYORS, EXAMINERS, AND JUDGES; 853] 3 *n* **evaluator**, critic, reviewer, arbiter, expert, authority, connoisseur, assessor, appraiser [→ SURVEYORS, EXAMINERS, AND JUDGES; 853] 4 *v* **arbitrate**, adjudicate, mediate, referee, umpire, rule on, try, adjudge [→ ASSESS QUALITY; 755] 5 *v* **estimate**, guess, consider, say, assess, think, decide, find, resolve, ascertain (*formal*) [→ ASSESS QUANTITY; 757] 6 *v* **condemn**, criticize, sneer at, belittle, pass judgment on [→ ACCUSE, BLAME, AND CRITICIZE; 641] 7 *v* **assess**, evaluate, weigh, look at, appraise, rate, rank, estimate, weigh up (*UK*) [→ EXAMINE AND ASSESS; 753] 8 *v* **con-**

sider, reckon, think, believe, maintain, conclude, deem (*formal*) [➡ HAVE AN OPINION OF SOMETHING; 756]

judgment 1 *n* **verdict**, ruling, decision, finding, sentence, conclusion, result, decree, adjudication, arbitration [➡ RESULTS AND OUTCOMES; 83] 2 *n* **discernment**, good sense, shrewdness, wisdom, common sense, discrimination, prudence, intelligence, judiciousness, perceptiveness, acumen [➡ DESCRIBING SOMEBODY'S INTELLECT; 523] 3 *n* **opinion**, view, considered opinion, feeling, thoughts, way of thinking, reasoning, belief, assessment, appraisal, conviction [➡ POINTS OF VIEW; 767]

judgmental *adj* **critical**, hypercritical, condemnatory, negative, disapproving, disparaging, pejorative (*formal*) [➡ SELFISH AND UNKIND; 505] *Opposite*: complimentary

Judgment Day *n* [➡ RELIGIOUS CONCEPTS; 776]

judicial *adj* **legal**, court, justice, official [➡ LEGAL AND LEGITIMATE; 815]

judicial proceedings *n* [➡ TRIAL, PUNISHMENT, AND LEGAL OUTCOMES; 819]

judiciary *n* **judges**, bench, courts, magistrates [➡ THE LAW AND LEGAL AUTHORITY; 814]

judicious *adj* **sensible**, wise, careful, shrewd, astute, prudent, cautious, thoughtful, sagacious, just, discriminating [➡ POSITIVE INTELLECTUAL CHARACTERISTICS; 524] *Opposite*: foolish

judiciousness *n* **wisdom**, prudence, shrewdness, sense, care, caution, judgment, discrimination, sagacity [➡ POSITIVE INTELLECTUAL CHARACTERISTICS; 524] *Opposite*: foolishness

judo *type of* **combat sport** [➡ HOBBIES, GAMES, AND SPORTS; 875]

jug *n* **pitcher**, ewer, carafe, crock [➡ TABLEWARE, FLATWARE, AND KITCHENWARE; 861]

juggernaut (*UK*) *n* **giant**, titan, leviathan, behemoth, goliath, hulk, colossus [➡ BIG THINGS; 1194]

juggle 1 *v* **fit in**, manage, cope with, run, deal with, organize [➡ CARRY OUT AN ACTION; 269] 2 *v* **manipulate**, falsify, alter, misrepresent, tamper with, disguise, rearrange [➡ FALSIFY AND CHEAT; 176]

juggler *type of* **entertainer** [➡ WORKERS IN ENTERTAINMENT AND MEDIA; 873]

jugular vein *type of* **blood vessel** [➡ THE BLOOD AND CIRCULATION; 717]

juice 1 *n* **extract**, sap, liquid, fluid, liquor, nectar, essence [➡ LIQUIDS; 1269] 2 *part of* **fruit** [➡ FRUIT AND VEGETABLES; 1176]

juice extractor *type of* **utensil** [➡ TABLEWARE, FLATWARE, AND KITCHENWARE; 861]

juicer *type of* **appliance** [➡ HOUSEHOLD APPLIANCES; 1117]

juiciness *n* **succulence**, ripeness, lusciousness, moistness [➡ TASTE; 703] *Opposite*: dryness

juicy 1 *adj* **succulent**, luscious, thirst-quenching, moist, ripe [➡ TASTE; 703] *Opposite*: dry 2 *adj* (*informal*) **titillating**, scandalous, salacious, exciting, sensational, vivid, racy, lurid, spicy (*informal*) [➡ INTERESTING AND MEANINGFUL; 190] *Opposite*: dull

juju *n* [➡ LUCKY CHARMS; 785]

jukebox *type of* **audio equipment** [➡ AUDIO EQUIPMENT; 1139]

julienne 1 *type of* **soup** [➡ SOUPS; 1186] 2 *type of* **food presentation** [➡ COOKING AND FOOD PREPARATION; 353]

jumble 1 *v* **mix up**, muddle, clutter, disarrange, shuffle, strew, mess up (*informal*) [➡ CREATE DISORDER AND CAUSE CHAOS; 358] *Opposite*: tidy 2 *n* **muddle**, heap, clutter, hodgepodge, mishmash, mixture, mess, confusion, disarray, tangle [➡ DISORDER AND CHAOS; 245] 3 *n* (*UK*) **unwanted items**, secondhand goods, odds and ends, castoffs, junk (*informal*) [➡ JUNK AND USELESS OBJECTS; 1249]

jumbled *adj* **untidy**, topsy-turvy, muddled, chaotic, disorderly, random, messy, tangled, cluttered, confused, higgledy-piggledy, disarrayed, mixed-up (*informal*) [➡ DISORDER AND CHAOS; 245] *Opposite*: orderly

jumble sale (*UK*) *n* [➡ SALES AND SHOWS; 443]

jumbo *adj* **oversize**, oversized, outsize, outsized, huge, gigantic, giant, massive, immense, mammoth, colossal, stupendous, whopping (*informal*), super (*informal*) [➡ LARGE; 1193] *Opposite*: tiny

jump 1 *v* **bound**, leap, hop, skip, soar, shoot, fly, hurdle, vault, spring, bounce [➡ BOUNCE, UNDULATE, AND VIBRATE; 308] 2 *v* **be startled**, be surprised, start, get a fright, be frightened, jerk, flinch, recoil [➡ PHYSICAL REACTIONS; 316] 3 *v* (*informal*) **obey**, do as you are told, conform, toe the line, play the game, kowtow [➡ OBEY AND ABIDE BY; 301] 4 *n* **leap**, bound, hop, skip, spring, caper, vault [➡ BOUNCE, UNDULATE, AND VIBRATE; 308] 5 *n* **obstacle**, hurdle, fence, wall, hedge, obstruction, barrier, barricade [➡ BARRIERS; 1113] 6 *n* **start**, jolt, jerk, lurch, jar, flinch [➡ PHYSICAL REACTIONS; 316]

jump back *v* **rebound**, recoil, bounce back, ricochet [➡ GO BACKWARD; 309]

jumper 1 *n* **athlete**, high jumper, long jumper, hurdler, steeplechaser, showjumper [➡ PEOPLE IN SPORTS AND LEISURE; 876] 2 *type of* **dress** [➡ GARMENTS AND OUTFITS; 865]

jump in *v* **make a start**, take the plunge, get going, leap in, take the bull by the horns, take action, be decisive [➡ START AN ACTION; 260]

jumpiness 1 *n* **jitteriness**, anxiety, nervousness, agitation, edginess, restlessness, apprehensiveness, uneasiness, nerves (*informal*) [➡ CONFUSION, ANXIETY, AND WORRY; 540] *Opposite*: calmness 2 *n* **jerkiness**, erraticism, unsteadiness, suddenness, abruptness, shakiness, fitfulness [➡ DESCRIBING BODY MOVEMENTS; 288] *Opposite*: smoothness

jumping spider *type of* **arachnid** [➡ ARACHNIDS; 1018]

jump ship *v* [➡ RUN AWAY AND AVOID; 10]

jump-start 1 *v* **kick-start**, start up, start, get going, set in motion, rev up (*informal*), bump-start (*UK*), push-start (*UK*) [➡ CAUSE TO START; 265] 2 *v* **stimulate**, trigger, set off, start up, kick-start, spark, spark off, rouse, spur, bring about [➡ CAUSE TO HAPPEN; 31] 3 *n* **kick-start**, startup, start, bump-start (*UK*), push-start (*UK*) [➡ BEGINNINGS; 53] 4 *n* **stimulus**, momentum, spur, start, impetus, thrust, push, drive [➡ SOURCE OF HAPPINESS, PLEASURE, OR IMPROVEMENT; 209]

jumpsuit *type of* **suit** [➡ GARMENTS AND OUTFITS; 865]

jumpy 1 *adj* **jittery**, anxious, nervous, worried, tense, scared, frightened, agitated, on edge, edgy, restless, fidgety, skittish [➡CONFUSION, ANXIETY, AND WORRY; 540] *Opposite*: calm **2** *adj* **jerky**, erratic, unsteady, sudden, abrupt, shaky, fitful, jolting, lurching [➡DESCRIBING BODY MOVEMENTS; 288] *Opposite*: smooth

junction *n* **connection**, intersection, seam, link, joint, join, confluence, interchange, convergence, linkup [➡FASTENERS, LINKS, AND NETWORKS; 1247]

juncture 1 *n* **point in time**, stage, moment, occasion, interval, pass [➡PAUSES AND PHASES; 56] **2** *n* (*formal*) **join**, connection, joint, link, seam, junction, confluence, intersection [➡FASTENERS, LINKS, AND NETWORKS; 1247]

jungle 1 *n* **tropical forest**, rain forest, forest, wilderness, bush, wilds [➡WOODS, FORESTS, AND JUNGLES; 1047] **2** *n* **tangle**, muddle, maze, jumble, mess, confusion, mass [➡DISORDER AND CHAOS; 245] **3** *type of* **dance music** [➡MUSIC, SONGS, AND SINGING; 907]

junior 1 *adj* **low-ranking**, subordinate, inferior, lower, low-grade, lesser, secondary, minor [➡INFERIORITY; 153] *Opposite*: senior **2** *n* **subordinate**, underling, beginner, trainee, novice, apprentice [➡UNSKILLED PEOPLE; 530]

junior high *type of* **school** [➡EDUCATIONAL INSTITUTIONS; 813]

juniper 1 *type of* **berry** [➡FRUIT AND VEGETABLES; 1176] **2** *type of* **evergreen tree** [➡EVERGREEN AND CONIFEROUS TREES; 1029]

junk 1 *n* (*informal*) **secondhand goods**, unwanted items, castoffs, odds and ends, jumble (*UK*) [➡JUNK AND USELESS OBJECTS; 1249] **2** *n* (*informal*) **rubbish**, trash, scrap, debris, litter, refuse, garbage, waste [➡JUNK AND USELESS OBJECTS; 1249] **3** *type of* **sailing vessel** [➡SHIPS AND BOATS; 1150] **4** *v* (*informal*) **discard**, throw away, throw out, get rid of, scrap, jettison, dump, chuck (*informal*), ditch (*informal*) [➡GET RID OF SOMETHING; 451] *Opposite*: keep

junket 1 *n* **trip**, excursion, visit, outing, spree, freebie (*informal*) [➡TRAVEL: JOURNEYS AND TRIPS; 318] **2** *type of* **dessert** [➡CAKES, COOKIES, AND DESSERTS; 1181]

junk food *n* **snack food**, convenience food, fast food, TV dinner [➡FOOD; 1167]

junk mail *n* **fliers**, leaflets, brochures, direct mail, mailshot (*UK*) [➡ADVERTISING AND PUBLICITY; 604]

junta 1 *n* **military government**, military rule, regime, martial law, government, leadership, dictatorship [➡STYLES AND SYSTEMS OF GOVERNMENT; 806] **2** *n* **cabal**, faction, clique, gang, band [➡GROUPS WITH A COMMON INTEREST; 938] **3** *n* **council**, committee, legislative body, assembly, forum, cabinet [➡LEGISLATIVE BODIES AND LEGISLATION; 809]

Jupiter *type of* **planet** [➡HEAVENLY BODIES; 1061]

Jurassic *type of* **period** [➡EPOCHS AND ERAS; 89]

jurisdiction 1 *n* **authority**, dominion, influence, power, control, prerogative, rule, say [➡THE LAW AND LEGAL AUTHORITY; 814] **2** *n* **area**, state, extent of power, territory, province, dominion, bailiwick, precinct, district, circuit, patch, preserve [➡SUBJECT AREAS; 768]

juror *n* **jury member**, assessor, estimator, judge, adjudicator, panel member [➡PEOPLE IN LAW COURTS; 820]

jury *n* **adjudicators**, judges, bench, panel, board [➡PEOPLE IN LAW COURTS; 820]

just 1 *adv* **a minute ago**, a moment ago, a second ago, only this minute, in the past few minutes, a short time ago, recently, lately, not long ago [➡AFTER, LAST, AND FOLLOWING; 165] **2** *adv* **at this moment**, now, immediately, presently, in a minute, very soon, right now, straightaway [➡PRESENT; 85] **3** *adv* **only**, merely, simply, solely, purely [➡TO A CERTAIN EXTENT; 136] **4** *adv* **barely**, hardly, scarcely, slightly [➡TO A CERTAIN EXTENT; 136] **5** *adv* **simply**, really, truly, definitely, emphatically, clearly, entirely, absolutely, completely, perfectly [➡ABSOLUTE AND ABSOLUTELY; 133] **6** *adv* **exactly**, precisely, absolutely, emphatically, completely, totally [➡EXACT; 203] **7** *adj* **fair**, impartial, objective, unbiased, unprejudiced, disinterested, evenhanded [➡HONEST AND RELIABLE; 502] *Opposite*: unfair **8** *adj* **correct**, moral, ethical, good, appropriate, proper, right, fitting [➡MORALLY GOOD; 774] *Opposite*: unjust **9** *adj* **reasonable**, valid, sensible, sound, balanced, justified, well-grounded, merited, unreasonable [➡THE NATURE OF IDEAS; 771]

just about *adv* **almost**, practically, approximately, virtually, nearly, around, about, not quite, pretty nearly (*informal*), pretty well (*informal*), pretty much (*informal*) [➡APPROXIMATELY; 135]

just deserts *n* **comeuppance** (*informal*), what you deserve, what was coming to you, just reward [➡RESULTS AND OUTCOMES; 83]

just-folks (*informal*) *adj* **unaffected**, unsophisticated, folksy, simple, friendly, informal, relaxed, unpretentious [➡NATURALNESS; 497] *Opposite*: pretentious

justice 1 *n* **fairness**, reasonableness, impartiality, evenhandedness, righteousness, fair dealing, honesty, integrity, uprightness, rightness, justness [➡MORALLY GOOD; 774] *Opposite*: unfairness **2** *n* **validity**, legitimacy, rightfulness, acceptability, reasonableness, legitimateness, lawfulness [➡TRUE AND REAL; 171] **3** *n* **judge**, magistrate, justice of the peace, judge advocate [➡PEOPLE IN LAW COURTS; 820]

Justice of the Peace *n* [➡PEOPLE IN LAW COURTS; 820]

justifiable *adj* **defensible**, admissible, justified, reasonable, correct, right, acceptable, permissible, understandable, valid, fit, sound, proper, fair, arguable, maintainable [➡ACCEPTABLE AND PASSABLE; 219] *Opposite*: indefensible

justification *n* **defense**, reason, reasoning, explanation, validation, rationalization, excuse, account, confirmation, support [➡EXPLAIN AND CLARIFY; 610]

justified *adj* **warranted**, defensible, vindicated, correct, right, acceptable, reasonable, necessary, befitting, validated, confirmed, supportable (*literary*) [➡ACCEPTABLE AND PASSABLE; 219] *Opposite*: unwarranted

justify 1 *v* **defend**, validate, explain, rationalize, excuse, vindicate, substantiate, warrant, support [➡EXPLAIN AND CLARIFY; 610] **2** *v* **align**, adjust, straighten up, line up [➡ARRANGE AND CREATE ORDER; 357]

just-in-time *n* [➡BUSINESS ACTIVITIES AND PHENOMENA; 794]

justly 1 *adv* **fairly**, impartially, rightly, reasonably, honorably, honestly, truthfully, righteously, morally, evenhandedly, equitably (*formal*) [➡MORALLY GOOD; 774] *Opposite*: unfairly **2** *adv* **correctly**, morally, deservedly, reasonably, justifiably, with reason, with good reason, rightly, excus-

kahikatea *type of* **evergreen tree** [➡ EVERG...
TREES; 1029]

kahuna (*informal*) *n* [➡ IMPORTANT OR FAMOUS PEOPLE; 893]

kaiten sushi restaurant *type of* **eating place** [➡ HO...
RESTAURANTS, AND CLUBS; 1082]

ka... *n* [➡ BUSINESS ACTIVITIES ... PHENOM... 794]

kale *type of* **veg...** FRUIT A...

kaleidoscope 1 *n* **complex patterns**...176...phanta...
display, mixture, medley, changing sc...ne [➡ COLLE...
MIXTURES OF THINGS; 1244] 2 *n* **series**, web, set, chain react...
domino effect, chain of events [➡ CHAIN OF EVENTS; 162] 3 *type o...
toy [➡ TOYS; 880]

kaleidoscopic *adj* **colorful**, variegated, multicolored,
many-colored, motley, psychedelic, phantasmagoric,
parti-colored [➡ DESCRIBING COLORS; 1226] *Opposite:* monochromatic

kangaroo *type of* **marsupial** [➡ MARSUPIALS; 992]

kanji *type of* **alphabet** [➡ SYMBOLS, SIGNS, AND NUMBERS; 596]

kaolin *n* **clay**, kaolinite, argil, potter's clay, potter's
earth [➡ MINERALS; 1277]

kaon *type of* **elementary particle** [➡ ELEMENTARY PARTICLES; 1279]

kapok *type of* **fiber** [➡ PLANT MATERIALS; 1133]

kaput (*informal*) *adj* **broken**, ruined, wrecked, finished,
ended, useless, defunct [➡ IN BAD REPAIR; 1234] *Opposite:*
working

karaoke *n* **sing-along**, singing, karaoke night, music,
entertainment, singsong (*UK*) [➡ ENTERTAINMENT; 872]

karate *type of* **combat sport** [➡ HOBBIES, GAMES, AND SPORTS; 875]

karma 1 *n* **destiny**, fate, kismet, fortune, providence,
predestination [➡ RELIGIOUS CONCEPTS; 776] 2 *n* (*informal*) **atmosphere**, aura, feeling, ambiance, vibrations (*informal*),
vibes (*slang*) [➡ APPEARANCE AND ATMOSPHERE; 1237]

katakana *type of* **alphabet** [➡ SYMBOLS, SIGNS, AND NUMBERS; 596]

kauri *type of* **evergreen tree** [➡ EVERGREEN AND CONIFEROUS TREES;
1029]

kayak *type of* **small vessel** [➡ SHIPS AND BOATS; 1150]

kebab *n* **skewer**, brochette, satay, shish kebab, souv-
lakia, grill stick (*UK*) [➡ TYPES AND CUTS OF MEAT; 1177]

kedgeree *type of* **cooked dish** [➡ PREPARED DISHES; 1170]

keel 1 *part of* **ship or boat** [➡ PARTS OF A SHIP OR BOAT; 1151]
2 *v* **capsize**, turn upside down, upset, overturn, turn over,
tip over, roll over, tip, upturn, keel over (*informal*) [➡ MOVE
SOMETHING: INTO A NEW POSITION OR OVERTURN; 330] *Opposite:* right

keel over (*informal*) 1 *v* **collapse**, fall over, faint, pass

consciousness, swoon, conk out (*informal*)
...TREAT, AND RECOVER; 728] *Opposite:* come to 2 *v* **capsize**,
...upside down, upset, overturn, turn over, tip
...er, tip, upturn, upset [➡ MOVE SOMETHING: INTO A NEW POSITION OR
...*Opposite:* right

...**tense**, strong, acute, deep, powerful, pro-
...[➡ STRENGTH; 201] *Opposite:* mild
...ardent, lively [➡ STRENGTH...] ...perceptive,
...sharp, precise, accurate, acute, perceptive,
...ly honed, finely tuned, well-developed
...site: insensitive 3 *adj* (*literary*) **sharp**,
INTELL...ed, bright, steely, well-honed, razor
[➡ PHYSICAL TEXTURE; 122] *Opposite:* blunt
petitive, ...stic, willing, fan... desl, dedicated,
AND INEXPENSIVE; 207... earnest, desl, ...ren... (*formal*)
...osite: indifferen... **icy**,
howl, weep, sob, lam...zing, glacial, bi...
...mild 6 *adj* **acute**,...
...stute, sharp (*UK*) cu...
keenly 1 *adv* **intensely**, strongly, ...effective [➡ CHEAP
fully, profoundly, extremely, clearly, p... **out**, ...
...2011 *Opposite:* faintly 2 *adv* **eagerly**, enthusiastica... wor-
ingly, fanatically, devotedly, ardently, zealously, ent...
estly [➡ ENERGY AND ENTHUSIASM; 496] *Opposite:* indifferently

keenness 1 *n* **enthusiasm**, eagerness, zeal, passion, willingness, zest, gusto, ardor, interest, fervor [➡ ENERGY AND
ENTHUSIASM; 496] *Opposite:* reluctance 2 *n* **intensity**, intenseness, strength, acuteness, depth, powerfulness, profundity [➡ STRENGTH; 201] *Opposite:* mildness 3 *n* **sensitivity**,
sharpness, precision, accuracy, acuity, responsiveness,
perceptiveness [➡ POSITIVE INTELLECTUAL CHARACTERISTICS; 524] *Opposite:* insensitivity 4 *n* (*literary*) **sharpness**, razor-sharp-
ness, brightness, steeliness [➡ PHYSICAL TEXTURE; 1222] *Opposite:*
bluntness 5 *n* **iciness**, bitterness, coldness, chill, wintriness, bitter cold [➡ COLD WEATHER; 1051] *Opposite:* mildness
6 *n* **acuteness**, perception, quickness, cleverness, perceptiveness, sensitivity, alertness, acuity, intelligence,
astuteness [➡ POSITIVE INTELLECTUAL CHARACTERISTICS; 524] *Opposite:*
dullness 7 *n* (*UK*) **fondness**, attraction, enthusiasm, devotion, partiality, liking, love, affection, attachment, soft
spot [➡ LIKE, LOVE, VALUE, AND ENJOY; 578] *Opposite:* aversion (*formal*)
8 *n* (*UK*) **competitiveness**, lowness, cheapness, attractiveness, affordability [➡ ECONOMICAL AND RESOURCEFUL; 207]

keen on (*UK*) *adj* **partial to**, taken with, fond of, wild
about, gone on (*informal*), stuck on (*informal*), smitten
with (*humorous or literary*) [➡ APPRECIATION AND GRATITUDE; 535]

keen-sighted *adj* **sharp-sighted**, sharp-eyed, eagle-eyed,
hawk-eyed [➡ SEE; 699]

keep 1 *v* **hold onto**, hang onto, save, retain, have, possess,
cling to, preserve [➡ STORE AND KEEP; 453] *Opposite:* let go
2 *v* **maintain**, hold, sustain, preserve, conserve, fix [➡ STORE

...andably, legitimately,
site: unjustly

adv **a minute ago**, a mom... ...s minute, in the past fe... ...ot long ago, recently, la... **2** *adv* **at this moment**, now,... ...tly, in a minute, very

...ard *n* **comeuppance** (*in...* ...hat was coming to you, ...83]

...ght *adj* **perfect**, as it should... ...s, on the button, spot-on (*U...* ...TER; 183]

...the same *adv* **neverthe...** ...., be that as it may, in ... ...ESPITE; 169]

...out, protrude, overhang, p... ...o beyond [➡ EXIST IN A PLACE; 19]

...ype of **fiber** [➡ PLANT MATERIALS: 1133]

...enile 1 *adj* **youthful**, young, immatur... ...aby-faced, fresh-faced [➡ BABYHOOD, CHILDHOOD, AND... Opposite: mature **2** *adj* **childish**, infant... puerile, immature, adolescent [➡ NEGATIVE INT... ACTERISTICS; 525] *Opposite:* grown-up **3** *n* **youngster**, young person, teenager, youth, child, m... (informal) [➡ CHILD OR YOUTH; 945] *Opposite:* adult

juxtapose *v* **put side by side**, put ...e alongside, c... put beside, set against, put adjacent to, [➡ POSITI... OMETHING: BETWEEN, BESIDE... ...com...ison, contras... ...nnection [➡ CONNECTIONS; 43] ...association, ap...os...

AND KEEP; 453] *Opposite*: abandon **3** *v* **hide**, conceal, repress, withhold, hold back, hold in, keep to yourself, stifle [➠ WITHHOLD INFORMATION; 687] *Opposite*: let out **4** *v* **store**, hold, stash, stack, shelve, file, deposit, stock [➠ STORE AND KEEP; 453] *Opposite*: get rid of **5** *v* **continue**, go on, keep on, persist in, persevere with, carry on [➠ CONTINUE AN ACTION; 262] *Opposite*: stop **6** *v* **detain**, delay, hold up, hold back, keep back, retard [➠ AVOID, PREVENT, LIMIT, AND CONTROL; 277] *Opposite*: release **7** *v* **take care of**, care for, tend, look after, watch over, mind, sit, watch, guard, house [➠ TAKE CARE OF AND SPOIL; 300] **8** *v* **honor**, fulfill, carry out, comply with, obey, adhere to, observe, respect [➠ OBEY AND ABIDE BY; 301] *Opposite*: break **9** *v* **stay**, remain, be, keep yourself [➠ CONTINUE TO EXIST; 17] *Opposite*: become **10** *v* **own**, look after, care for, farm, rear, breed [➠ POSSESS; 444]

keep abreast *v* **stay current**, keep up, keep up to date, be well-informed, stay in touch, keep in touch, keep in contact, follow [➠ UNDERSTAND AND GRASP; 759]

keep an eye on 1 *v* **watch closely**, keep a close watch on, observe, spy on, watch, monitor, keep track of, check, keep tabs on (*informal*) [➠ LOOKING AND LOOKS; 700] **2** *v* **look after**, watch over, keep in check, mind, take care of, watch [➠ TAKE CARE OF AND SPOIL; 300]

keep a secret *v* **not tell a soul**, be discreet, keep quiet, be the soul of discretion, keep mum (*informal*), button your lip (*slang*) [➠ WITHHOLD INFORMATION; 687] *Opposite*: spill the beans (*informal*)

keep a straight face *v* **have a poker face**, look blank, dissemble, show no emotion [➠ FACIAL EXPRESSIONS AND BLUSHING; 651]

keep at *v* **persevere**, persist, soldier on, plow through, keep your nose to the grindstone, plow on, stick to, beaver (*informal*), plug away (*informal*) [➠ CONTINUE AN ACTION; 262] *Opposite*: give up

keep at bay *v* **hold off**, keep away, ward off, stave off, fend off, repel, discourage [➠ AVOID OR ESCAPE CONTACT; 418] *Opposite*: encourage

keep at it *v* [➠ CONTINUE AN ACTION; 262]

keep away *v* **hold off**, ward off, keep at bay, stave off, fend off, repel, discourage [➠ AVOID OR ESCAPE CONTACT; 418] *Opposite*: encourage

keep back 1 *v* **restrain**, curb, control, restrict, limit, check [➠ AVOID, PREVENT, LIMIT, AND CONTROL; 277] **2** *v* **withhold**, keep secret, suppress, omit, hide, conceal, retain, keep to yourself, sit on, hush up (*informal*) [➠ WITHHOLD INFORMATION; 687] *Opposite*: reveal **3** *v* **reserve**, conserve, hold on to, save, withhold, set aside, put by [➠ STORE AND KEEP; 453] *Opposite*: use up

keep count *v* **record**, note, keep a record of, note down, keep a note of, keep track of, remember [➠ REMEMBER; 746] *Opposite*: lose track of

keep down 1 *v* **oppress**, suppress, repress, subjugate, subdue, keep under [➠ CAPTIVITY AND LOSS OF FREEDOM; 248] *Opposite*: liberate **2** *v* **limit**, curb, restrain, control, check, keep in check, keep a tight rein on [➠ AVOID, PREVENT, LIMIT, AND CONTROL; 277]

keeper *n* **custodian**, guard, guardian, caretaker, attendant, curator, ranger, groundskeeper, warden, warder (*UK*), groundsman (*UK*) [➠ PEOPLE WHO GUARD AND PROTECT; 846]

keep from 1 *v* **prevent**, restrain, stop, deter, prohibit, put off, discourage [➠ MAKE IMPOSSIBLE; 276] *Opposite*: allow **2** *v* **protect**, shield, shelter, save, cushion, safeguard, guard [➠ PREVENT CONTACT OR ATTACK; 419] *Opposite*: expose **3** *v* **withhold**, omit, hide, conceal, keep back, retain, keep to yourself, save, hush up (*informal*) [➠ WITHHOLD INFORMATION; 687] *Opposite*: reveal

keep going *v* **persevere**, carry on, persist, hold up, last, sustain, survive, spin out, chug away (*informal*), plug away (*informal*) [➠ CONTINUE AN ACTION; 262] *Opposite*: stop

keep in *v* **hold in**, repress, withhold, hold back, retain, suppress, rein in, stifle [➠ WITHHOLD INFORMATION; 687] *Opposite*: let out

keep in check *v* **control**, restrict, restrain, curb, limit, keep an eye on, monitor [➠ AVOID, PREVENT, LIMIT, AND CONTROL; 277]

keeping *n* **charge**, custody, possession, care, trust, protection, guardianship [➠ STORE AND KEEP; 453]

keep in mind *v* **bear in mind**, remember, recall, retain [➠ REMEMBER; 746] *Opposite*: forget

keep in the dark *v* **keep in ignorance**, withhold information from, keep something back from, hold something back from, conceal something from [➠ WITHHOLD INFORMATION; 687] *Opposite*: inform

keep mum (*informal*) *v* **keep quiet**, not tell a soul, be discreet, keep secret, keep under wraps, keep under your hat, be the soul of discretion, button your lip (*slang*) [➠ WITHHOLD INFORMATION; 687] *Opposite*: spill the beans (*informal*)

keep off 1 *v* **abstain**, do without, go without, avoid, not touch, lay off (*informal*) [➠ FORGO AND DENY ONESELF; 449] *Opposite*: indulge **2** *v* **hold off**, hold back, separate, shut out, ward off, prevent [➠ EJECT AND EXCLUDE; 340] *Opposite*: encourage

keep on *v* **continue**, persist, persevere, carry on, go on, soldier on [➠ CONTINUE AN ACTION; 262] *Opposite*: give up

keep out *v* **exclude**, shut out, bar, ban, deny entry, proscribe, ostracize [➠ REFUSE PERMISSION AND NOT ALLOW; 670] *Opposite*: admit

keep quiet *v* [➠ WITHHOLD INFORMATION; 687]

keepsake *n* **memento**, reminder, souvenir, gift, token, relic, remembrance [➠ ORNAMENTS AND DECORATIONS; 1248]

keep secret *v* **withhold**, suppress, sit on, keep from, keep under wraps, keep to yourself, keep under your hat, keep back, keep quiet [➠ WITHHOLD INFORMATION; 687] *Opposite*: let slip

keep the ball rolling *v* **continue**, keep things moving, keep things going, keep up the momentum, maintain momentum, go on, carry on [➠ CAUSE TO CONTINUE; 267] *Opposite*: stop

keep the lid on *v* **keep under control**, contain, control, suppress, restrain, check, curb, keep in check [➠ AVOID, PREVENT, LIMIT, AND CONTROL; 277]

keep to *v* **obey**, comply with, abide by, stick to, adhere to, go along with [➠ OBEY AND ABIDE BY; 301]

keep to yourself *v* [➠ WITHHOLD INFORMATION; 687]

keep track of *v* **follow**, keep an eye on, keep up with, contain, keep up to date with, monitor [➡ REMEMBER; 746] *Opposite*: lose track of

keep under control *v* **keep in check**, restrain, contain, keep the lid on, suppress, curb, check [➡ AVOID, PREVENT, LIMIT, AND CONTROL; 277]

keep under wraps *v* **keep secret**, keep to yourself, keep back, keep quiet, hide, conceal, cover up, suppress, draw a veil over [➡ WITHHOLD INFORMATION; 687] *Opposite*: reveal

keep under your hat *v* [➡ WITHHOLD INFORMATION; 687]

keep up 1 *v* **continue**, sustain, maintain, carry on, persevere, preserve [➡ CONTINUE AN ACTION; 262] *Opposite*: stop 2 *v* **stay beside**, keep abreast, keep pace, stay even, match, stay shoulder to shoulder [➡ ACCOMPANY AND FOLLOW; 337] *Opposite*: fall behind 3 *v* **stay in touch**, keep in touch, keep in contact, keep abreast, keep up to date, stay informed [➡ UNDERSTAND AND GRASP; 759]

keep your chin up *v* **make the best of things**, take the bad with the good, look on the bright side, not let things get the better of you, make the best of a bad job (*UK*), take the rough with the smooth (*UK*) [➡ TOLERATE AND ENDURE; 766] *Opposite*: go under

keep your cool (*informal*) *v* **stay calm**, keep your head, calm down, simmer down, cool off, chill out (*slang*), cool it (*slang*) [➡ TOLERATE AND ENDURE; 766]

keep your word *v* **be as good as your word**, stand by your promise, deliver on a promise, be true to your word, keep your side of the bargain [➡ PROMISE AND ASSURE; 684]

keg *n* **barrel**, cask, tub, firkin, drum, vat, puncheon [➡ CONTAINERS, RECEPTACLES, AND PACKAGING; 1245]

keiretsu *n* [➡ BUSINESS ENTERPRISES AND RELATED BODIES; 792]

kelp *type of* **marine alga** [➡ MICROORGANISMS, FUNGI, AND ALGAE; 1023]

ken *n* **knowledge**, acquaintance, understanding, awareness, comprehension, wit, cognizance (*formal*) [➡ KNOWLEDGE AND WISDOM; 558]

kendo *type of* **combat sport** [➡ HOBBIES, GAMES, AND SPORTS; 875]

kennel 1 *n* **house**, hut, shelter, lair, den [➡ ANIMAL OR BIRD ACCOMMODATIONS; 1079] 2 *type of* **herd** [➡ GROUPS OF ANIMALS; 993]

Kentucky bluegrass *type of* **grass** [➡ GRASS; 1031]

kernel 1 *n* **pip**, pit, stone [➡ FRUIT AND VEGETABLES; 1176] 2 *n* **core**, nub, root, heart, essence, crux, gist, marrow, pith [➡ CENTRAL PARTS OF PHYSICAL OBJECTS; 1251]

kerosene *n* **fuel**, oil, fuel oil, lamp oil, paraffin (*UK*), paraffin oil (*UK*) [➡ ENERGY SOURCES; 1162]

kerosine *see* **kerosene**

kestrel *type of* **bird of prey** [➡ BIRDS OF PREY; 998]

ketch *type of* **sailing vessel** [➡ SHIPS AND BOATS; 1150]

ketchup *type of* **seasonings, sauces, and dips** [➡ SEASONINGS AND SAUCES; 1174]

kettle 1 *n* **pot**, pan, caldron, steamer, fish kettle, teakettle [➡ TABLEWARE, FLATWARE, AND KITCHENWARE; 861] 2 *type of* **flock** [➡ GROUPS OF BIRDS; 1007]

kettledrum *type of* **percussion instrument** [➡ MUSICAL INSTRUMENTS; 910]

kettle of fish *n* **mess**, predicament, difficulty, problem, quagmire, crisis, situation [➡ DIFFICULT SITUATIONS; 72]

key 1 *n* **skeleton key**, master key, passe-partout, passkey, latchkey, opener [➡ FASTENERS, LINKS, AND NETWORKS; 1247] 2 *n* **pitch**, register, tone, scale, note [➡ NOTES AND CHORDS; 909] 3 *n* **button**, knob, control [➡ PARTS OF MACHINES AND TOOLS; 1118] 4 *n* **solution**, answer, explanation, means, secret, meaning, interpretation, source, resolution, basis, recipe [➡ SOLUTIONS; 215] 5 *adj* **important**, main, crucial, significant, vital, major, strategic, basic, fundamental, central, keynote, essential, quintessential [➡ IMPORTANT; 194] *Opposite*: unimportant 6 *v* **input**, keyboard, enter, key in, type, set, typeset [➡ RECORD SOMETHING; 371]

keyboard 1 *n* **control panel**, console, controls [➡ PARTS OF MACHINES AND TOOLS; 1118] 2 *v* **type**, key, key in, input, enter, typeset, set, input data [➡ RECORD SOMETHING; 371] 3 *type of* **hardware** [➡ COMPUTERS AND COMPUTING; 1127]

keyboarder *n* **keyboard operator**, typist, data entry clerk, typesetter, inputter, secretary [➡ OFFICE WORKERS; 847]

keyed up (*informal*) *adj* **nervous**, tense, excited, jumpy, anxious, edgy, jittery, twitchy, hyper (*informal*) [➡ CONFUSION, ANXIETY, AND WORRY; 540] *Opposite*: relaxed

keyhole *n* **hole**, aperture, spyhole, peephole, opening, orifice (*literary*) [➡ HOLES, GAPS, AND FORKS; 1252]

keyhole surgery *type of* **medical procedure** [➡ REMEDIES, TREATMENTS, AND OPERATIONS; 731]

key in *v* **key**, type, input, enter, typeset, input data, keyboard [➡ RECORD SOMETHING; 371]

key lime pie *type of* **cake** [➡ CAKES, COOKIES, AND DESSERTS; 1181]

keynote 1 *n* **theme**, essence, idea, gist, core, heart [➡ MOST IMPORTANT THING; 197] 2 *adj* **important**, crucial, major, essential, defining, significant, central [➡ IMPORTANT; 194]

key player *n* **leading light**, principal, kingpin (*informal*), big cheese (*informal*), honcho (*slang*) [➡ IMPORTANT OR FAMOUS PEOPLE; 893]

keystone *n* **foundation**, basis, bedrock, underpinning, grounding, root, source, base, principle, cornerstone [➡ MOST IMPORTANT THING; 197]

khaki *type of* **brown** [➡ COLORS; 1224]

khakis *type of* **pants** [➡ GARMENTS AND OUTFITS; 865]

khamsin *type of* **wind** [➡ WINDY AND STORMY WEATHER; 1053]

kibbutz *n* **collective**, commune, cooperative, community, settlement, village, kolkhoz, ashram [➡ HUMAN SETTLEMENTS; 1070]

kick 1 *v* **boot**, strike, hack, put the boot in (*UK*) [➡ PHYSICAL ATTACK AND PUNISHMENT; 415] 2 *v* **dribble**, punt, placekick, kick off [➡ CONTACT: IMPACT; 413] 3 *v* **jolt**, jerk, recoil, flex, reflex, thrust, hit out, strike out [➡ PHYSICAL REACTIONS; 316] 4 *v* (*informal*) **give up**, quit, end, cease, stop, abandon, forsake [➡ FORGO AND DENY ONESELF; 449] *Opposite*: take up 5 *n* **recoil**, rebound, return, reaction, reflex, backlash, jolt, jerk [➡ PHYSICAL REACTIONS; 316] 6 *n* (*informal*) **thrill**, boost, pleasure, excitement, frisson, shudder, buzz (*informal*), high (*informal*) [➡ TREATS; 210]

kickback *n* **bribe**, softener, payment, reward, inducement, share, commission, sweetener (*informal*), cut (*informal*), boodle (*slang*) [➡BRIBES; 440]

kickboxing *type of* **combat sport** [➡HOBBIES, GAMES, AND SPORTS; 875]

kick in 1 *v* (*informal*) **take effect**, come on-line, get going, get underway, start, begin, commence, come on-stream [➡SUDDENLY COME INTO EXISTENCE; 2] *Opposite*: run out 2 *v* **break down**, smash, demolish, flatten, destroy, knock down, batter [➡PHYSICAL ATTACK AND PUNISHMENT; 415]

kick in the teeth *n* **setback**, blow, shock, betrayal, letdown, body blow, knock (*informal*) [➡PROBLEMS; 256] *Opposite*: boost

kick off (*informal*) *v* **start**, begin, start the ball rolling, get underway, commence, open [➡START AN ACTION; 260] *Opposite*: end

kickoff (*informal*) *n* **start**, beginning, opening, initiation, commencement (*formal*), inception (*formal*) [➡BEGINNINGS; 53] *Opposite*: end

kick out (*informal*) *v* **throw out**, sling out, eject, force out, show the door, chuck out (*informal*), sack (*informal*), ax (*informal*), fire (*informal*), give the bum's rush (*slang*), cast out (*formal*), make redundant (*UK*) [➡EJECT AND EXCLUDE; 340] *Opposite*: appoint

kick-start 1 *v* **start up**, start, get going, turn over, crank up, rev up (*informal*) [➡CAUSE TO START; 265] *Opposite*: stop 2 *v* **restart**, start, revive, resuscitate, jump-start, revitalize, resurrect, rejuvenate, inject new life into [➡CAUSE TO START; 265] *Opposite*: kill off 3 *n* (*informal*) **fillip**, shot in the arm, spur, stimulus, boost, reactivation, jump-start, kickoff (*informal*) [➡SOURCE OF HAPPINESS, PLEASURE, OR IMPROVEMENT; 209] 4 *n* **kick-starter**, pedal, starter, foot pedal, lever, treadle [➡EXTERNAL PARTS OF A VEHICLE; 1147]

kick the bucket (*slang*) *v* **die**, pass away, expire [➡DIE; 922]

kick up a fuss *v* **protest**, rampage, make a scene, make a fuss, complain, go on about, grumble, kick up a storm, grouse (*informal*), make a song and dance (*informal*), kick up a rumpus (*UK*) [➡PROTEST AND EXPRESS DISAPPROVAL; 642] *Opposite*: smooth over

kick up a rumpus (*UK*) *v* [➡PROTEST AND EXPRESS DISAPPROVAL; 642]

kick up a storm *v* [➡PROTEST AND EXPRESS DISAPPROVAL; 642]

kick up your heels *v* [➡FIDGET AND FROLIC; 311]

kid 1 *type of* **young animal** [➡YOUNG ANIMALS; 977] 2 *type of* **leather** [➡FABRICS; 1132] 3 *n* (*informal*) **child**, teenager, adolescent, youngster, toddler, tyke, tot (*informal*), young'un (*informal*), kiddie (*informal*), teen (*informal*), rugrat (*informal humorous*) [➡CHILD OR YOUTH; 945] *Opposite*: adult 4 *v* **tease**, joke, poke fun at, make fun of, mock, ridicule, rib (*informal*), pull somebody's leg (*informal*), josh (*informal*), yank somebody's chain (*informal*), rag on (*informal*) [➡JOKES AND TEASING; 674] 5 *v* (*informal*) **fool**, trick, delude, hoodwink, con, mislead, deceive, bamboozle (*informal*) [➡DECEPTION AND LIES; 660]

See Compare and Contrast at **youth**.

kidder *n* **joker**, tease, trickster, clown, prankster [➡JOKERS AND TEASES; 675]

kiddie (*informal*) *n* [➡CHILD OR YOUTH; 945]

kiddo (*informal*) *n* [➡ENDEARMENTS; 656]

kidnap *v* **abduct**, take hostage, capture, take prisoner, hijack, shanghai, snatch (*informal*) [➡CAPTIVITY AND LOSS OF FREEDOM; 248] *Opposite*: release

kidnapper *n* [➡CRIMINALS; 821]

kidney 1 *part of* **digestive tract** [➡THE DIGESTIVE TRACT; 709] 2 *type of* **rounded shape** [➡ROUNDED SHAPE; 1218]

kidney bean *type of* **pulse** [➡PEAS AND BEANS; 1189]

kid's stuff *n* **child's play**, piece of cake, pushover, doddle (*UK informal*) [➡EASY WORK; 299]

kill *v* **murder**, assassinate, execute, put to death, slaughter, dispatch, massacre, put to sleep, destroy, exterminate, eradicate, bump off (*slang*), slay (*formal or literary*) [➡KILL; 923] *Opposite*: revive

Compare and Contrast: *kill, murder, assassinate, execute, put to death, slaughter, slay, put to sleep*

CORE MEANING: to deprive of life

kill to cause the death of a person or animal; *murder* to take the life of another person deliberately and not in self-defense in a serious criminal act; *assassinate* to murder a public figure in a sudden violent attack; *execute* to take somebody's life as part of a judicial or extrajudicial process; *put to death* to deliberately take somebody's life, especially in accordance with a legal death sentence; *slaughter* to kill farm animals for food, or to kill a person or large numbers of people brutally; *slay* (*formal or literary*) to kill a person or animal; *put down or put to sleep* to kill a sick or injured animal, especially when done by a vet.

killer 1 *n* **murderer**, assassin, slaughterer, executioner, exterminator, eradicator, hit man (*slang*), hatchet man (*slang*), slayer (*formal or literary*) [➡PEOPLE WHO KILL; 924] 2 *n* **disease**, destroyer, natural disaster, predator [➡DISASTERS; 252]

killer whale *type of* **whale** [➡WHALES; 991]

killing *n* **murder**, assassination, butchery, slaughter, carnage, homicide, massacre, slaying, extermination, liquidation [➡CAUSES OF DEATH; 921]

killjoy *n* **spoilsport**, party pooper (*informal*), sourpuss (*informal*), wet blanket (*informal*) [➡GRUMPY AND NEGATIVE PEOPLE; 953]

kill off *v* **put an end to**, stop, halt, destroy, end, ruin, eradicate, scotch, finish (*informal*) [➡CAUSE TO STOP; 266] *Opposite*: set up

kill time *v* **pass the time**, waste time, wait, loiter, twiddle your thumbs, idle away the hours, fill in time, hang around [➡LACK OF ACTIVITY OR MOTION; 342]

kill yourself *v* **commit suicide**, end it all, take your own life, top yourself (*UK slang*) [➡DIE; 922]

kill yourself laughing *v* **laugh your head off**, double over, have hysterics (*informal*), split your sides (*informal*), crease up (*UK informal*) [➡ LAUGHTER; 649]

kiln *n* **oven**, furnace, forge [➡ FIRE, FLAMMABILITY, AND BURNING; 1165]

kilogram *type of* **metric unit** [➡ SIZE AND DIMENSIONS; 1192]

kiloliter *type of* **metric unit** [➡ SIZE AND DIMENSIONS; 1192]

kilt 1 *type of* **skirt** [➡ GARMENTS AND OUTFITS; 865] **2** *v* (*UK*) **pleat**, gather, fold, crease, smock, corrugate [➡ CHANGE OF SHAPE; 385]

kimono 1 *type of* **dress** [➡ GARMENTS AND OUTFITS; 865] **2** *n* **dressing gown**, peignoir, bathrobe, robe, negligee [➡ GARMENTS AND OUTFITS; 865]

kin *n* **family**, relatives, relations, nearest and dearest, kith and kin, folks, kinsfolk, flesh and blood, people (*informal*), clan (*informal*), kinfolk [➡ THE FAMILY; 956]

kina *type of* **currency** [➡ CURRENCIES; 798]

kind 1 *adj* **caring**, nice, generous, gentle, compassionate, thoughtful, benevolent, kindhearted, sympathetic, humane, humanitarian, considerate, benign, kindly, charitable [➡ GENEROSITY AND KINDNESS; 495] *Opposite:* inhumane **2** *n* **type**, sort, class, variety, category, breed, manner, style, nature, form, hue, caste, brand, genre, make [➡ VARIETIES, TYPES, AND KINDS; 145]

See Compare and Contrast at **type**.

kindhearted *adj* **kind**, friendly, generous, sympathetic, caring, tenderhearted, benevolent, gentle, compassionate, thoughtful, humane, considerate, benign, kindly, nice, charitable [➡ GENEROSITY AND KINDNESS; 495] *Opposite:* cruel

kindheartedness *n* **kindness**, sympathy, compassion, benevolence, thoughtfulness, humanity, consideration, kindliness, helpfulness, charity [➡ GENEROSITY AND KINDNESS; 495] *Opposite:* cruelty

kindle 1 *v* **encourage**, stimulate, stir up, fire up, promote, inspire, rouse, awaken, ignite, instill, provoke, incite [➡ CAUSE TO HAPPEN; 31] *Opposite:* quench **2** *v* **spark**, light, set alight, burn, ignite, set on fire, torch (*slang*) [➡ FIRE, FLAMMABILITY, AND BURNING; 1165] *Opposite:* douse

kindliness *n* **kindness**, compassion, sympathy, amiability, gentleness, thoughtfulness, kindheartedness, sensitivity, warmth, humanity, consideration, graciousness, charity [➡ GENEROSITY AND KINDNESS; 495] *Opposite:* cruelty

kindly 1 *adj* **friendly**, sympathetic, generous, kindhearted, caring, kind, compassionate, benevolent, nice, thoughtful, gentle, humane, considerate, benign, helpful, charitable [➡ GENEROSITY AND KINDNESS; 495] **2** *adv* **gently**, compassionately, sympathetically, benevolently, kindheartedly, nicely, thoughtfully, humanely, considerately, benignly, helpfully [➡ GENEROSITY AND KINDNESS; 495] *Opposite:* cruelly

kindness *n* **compassion**, gentleness, sympathy, kindheartedness, benevolence, thoughtfulness, humanity, consideration, helpfulness, charity [➡ GENEROSITY AND KINDNESS; 495] *Opposite:* cruelty

kind of (*informal*) *adv* **rather**, somewhat, fairly, in a way, sort of (*informal*), a bit (*informal*), quite (*UK*) [➡ TO A CERTAIN EXTENT; 136]

kindred 1 *adj* **associated**, close, like, alike, allied, corresponding, akin, similar, matching, analogous [➡ RELATED; 142] *Opposite:* dissimilar **2** *n* **kinship**, family, kin, blood, ties, parentage, relatedness [➡ THE FAMILY; 956] **3** *n* **family**, relations, relatives, kinsfolk, nearest and dearest, kin, kith and kin, folks, kinfolk, people (*informal*) [➡ THE FAMILY; 956]

kinesiology *type of* **complementary therapy** [➡ REMEDIES, TREATMENTS, AND OPERATIONS; 731]

king 1 *n* **monarch**, sovereign, ruler, rajah, tsar, liege, suzerain [➡ RULERS AND ARISTOCRACY; 823] *Opposite:* subject **2** *n* **ruler**, chief, head, leader, dictator, despot [➡ RULERS AND ARISTOCRACY; 823] **3** *n* **leader**, star, superstar, luminary, leading light, principal, maven, kingpin (*informal*), ace (*informal*), honcho (*slang*) [➡ IMPORTANT OR FAMOUS PEOPLE; 893]

kingdom *n* **realm**, empire, monarchy, territory, domain, dominion, nation, estate, demesne (*formal*) [➡ REALMS AND RULES; 824]

kingfish *type of* **tropical fish** [➡ OCEAN FISH; 1009]

kingfisher *type of* **freshwater bird** [➡ FRESHWATER BIRDS; 1000]

kingly *adj* **magnificent**, stately, grand, majestic, regal, splendid, royal, imperial, monarchal [➡ ROYALNESS; 825]

kingpin (*informal*) *n* **key player**, leading light, principal, superstar, linchpin, top dog (*informal*), number one (*informal*), ace (*informal*), honcho (*slang*) [➡ IMPORTANT OR FAMOUS PEOPLE; 893]

kingship *n* **monarchy**, sovereignty, crown, power, authority, supremacy, reign, rule [➡ ROYALNESS; 825]

king-size *adj* **extra-large**, outsize, enormous, huge, giant, massive, vast, immense, mammoth [➡ LARGE; 1193] *Opposite:* miniature

king-size bed *type of* **bed** [➡ FURNITURE; 858]

king snake *type of* **nonpoisonous snake** [➡ SNAKES; 995]

kink *n* **bend**, twist, crook, hook, bow, knot, snarl, crimp, crinkle, curve [➡ ROUNDED SHAPE; 1218]

kinky 1 *adj* **crinkled**, crinkly, twisty, knotted, twisted, warped [➡ IN BAD REPAIR; 1234] *Opposite:* straight **2** *adj* (*informal*) **unusual**, strange, idiosyncratic, quirky, unnatural, unconventional, odd, peculiar, eccentric, unorthodox [➡ BIZARRE AND PECULIAR; 257] *Opposite:* conventional

kinsfolk 1 *n* **family**, relatives, relations, kindred, kith and kin, nearest and dearest, kin, kinfolk, folks, people (*informal*) [➡ THE FAMILY; 956] **2** *n* **family**, relatives, relations, kindred, kith and kin, nearest and dearest, kin, kinfolk, folks, people (*informal*) [➡ THE FAMILY; 956]

kinship 1 *n* **relationship**, connection, tie, link, bond [➡ RELATIONSHIP TO ANOTHER; 973] **2** *n* **relatedness**, understanding, empathy, affiliation, affinity, connection, similarity, likeness [➡ CONNECTIONS; 143]

kinship

◆ *types of in-laws*
brother-in-law, daughter-in-law, father-in-law, mother-in-law, sister-in-law, son-in-law

◆ *types of older relatives*
adoptive parent, aunt, biological parent, dad (*informal*), father, gramps (*informal*), gran (*informal*), granddad (*informal*), grandfather, grandma (*informal*), grandmother, grandpa (*informal*), grandparent, granny (*informal*), great-aunt, great-grandfather, great-grandmother, great-grandparent, great-uncle, lone parent, ma (*informal*), mama (*informal*), mammy (*informal*), mom, momma (*informal*), mommy (*informal*), mother, nan (*informal*), nana (*informal*), nanna (*informal*), papa (*dated*), parent, poppa (*informal*), single parent, stepfather, stepmother, step-parent, uncle

◆ *types of same-generation relatives*
brother, cousin, second cousin, senior, sibling, sister, stepbrother, stepsister

◆ *types of younger relatives*
child, daughter, dependent, grandchild, granddaughter, grandson, great-grandchild, great-granddaughter, great-grandson, great-nephew, great-niece, nephew, niece, son, stepchild, stepdaughter, stepson

kinsman (*formal*) *n* **relative**, relation, family member [➡ THE FAMILY; 956]

kinswoman (*formal*) *n* **relative**, relation, family member [➡ THE FAMILY; 956]

kiosk 1 *n* **booth**, stall, stand, hut [➡ RETAIL OUTLETS; 1083] 2 *type of* **outbuilding** [➡ ANCILLARY BUILDINGS; 1080]

kismet *n* **fate**, fortune, luck, destiny, doom, lot, providence, end, karma, portion (*literary*) [➡ FATE, DESTINY, AND ASTROLOGY; 782]

kiss 1 *v* **peck**, make out (*informal*), smooch (*informal*), canoodle (*informal*), neck (*informal*), osculate (*formal or humorous*), buss (*dated*) [➡ PHYSICAL CONTACT AS COMMUNICATION; 655] 2 *v* **touch**, brush, glance, graze, caress, skim, rub [➡ CONTACT: TOUCH; 412] 3 *n* **caress**, light touch, contact, graze, pat, stroke [➡ PHYSICAL CONTACT AS COMMUNICATION; 655] 4 *n* **peck**, embrace, smacker (*informal*), smooch (*informal*), canoodle (*informal*), osculation (*formal or humorous*) [➡ PHYSICAL CONTACT AS COMMUNICATION; 655]

kiss-and-tell (*informal*) *adj* **revealing**, exposing, divulging, sensational, scandalous, lurid, juicy (*informal*) [➡ IN POOR TASTE AND OVERSENTIMENTAL; 229]

kit 1 *n* **tackle**, tools, equipment, implements, supplies, gear (*informal*), necessaries (*informal*) [➡ DEVICES; 1115] 2 *n* **set of clothes**, dress, apparel, costume, clothing, outfit, uniform, gear (*informal*), strip (*UK*) [➡ CLOTHES AND ACCESSORIES; 864] 3 *n* **belongings**, things, stuff, baggage, luggage, personal belongings, personal effects, possessions, trappings, paraphernalia, accouterments, gear (*informal*) [➡ POSSESSIONS; 461]

kit bag *n* **canvas bag**, duffel bag, backpack, knapsack, rucksack, carryall, tote bag, holdall (*UK*) [➡ CONTAINERS, RECEPTACLES, AND PACKAGING; 1245]

kitchen *n* **kitchenette**, galley, scullery [➡ TYPES OF ROOMS; 1097]

kitchenette *type of* **room in the home** [➡ TYPES OF ROOMS; 1097]

kitchen garden *type of* **garden** [➡ GARDENS; 1074]

kite 1 *type of* **toy** [➡ TOYS; 880] 2 *type of* **bird of prey** [➡ BIRDS OF PREY; 998]

kith and kin *n* **relatives**, family, relations, folks, kinsfolk, flesh and blood, nearest and dearest, kinfolk, people (*informal*) [➡ THE FAMILY; 956]

kit out (*UK*) *v* **equip**, prepare, provide, fit out, supply, give, fix up, rig out (*informal*), furnish (*formal*) [➡ EQUIP AND SUPPLY; 435]

kitsch 1 *n* **vulgarity**, tastelessness, sentimentality, ostentation, showiness, brashness, tackiness (*informal*) [➡ IN POOR TASTE AND OVERSENTIMENTAL; 229] *Opposite:* tastefulness 2 *n* **trash**, frippery, junk (*informal*), tack (*informal*) [➡ JUNK AND USELESS OBJECTS; 1249] 3 *adj* **tasteless**, in poor taste, vulgar, brash, common, loud, cheap, tacky (*informal*), crummy (*informal*), cheesy (*informal*) [➡ IN POOR TASTE AND OVERSENTIMENTAL; 229] *Opposite:* tasteful

kitschy *adj* **tasteless**, vulgar, loud, in poor taste, common, cheap, cheesy (*informal*), tacky (*informal*) [➡ IN POOR TASTE AND OVERSENTIMENTAL; 229] *Opposite:* tasteful

kitten *type of* **young animal** [➡ YOUNG ANIMALS; 977]

kittenish 1 *adj* **playful**, frisky, lively, coltish, frolicsome, fun-loving, mischievous, impish, sportive [➡ ENERGY AND ENTHUSIASM; 496] *Opposite:* staid 2 *adj* **flirtatious**, coy, frisky, cute, coquettish (*literary*) [➡ FLIRTATIOUS; 639]

kittiwake *type of* **sea bird** [➡ SEA BIRDS; 1002]

kitty 1 *n* (*informal*) **cat**, kitten, puss (*informal*), pussy (*informal*), pussycat (*informal*) [➡ FELINES; 983] 2 *n* **fund**, pool, stake, ante, pot (*informal*) [➡ MONEY; 797]

kitty-cornered *adv* **cater-cornered**, crosswise, crossways, sideways, catty-cornered, diagonally, across, corner to corner, on the cross, obliquely [➡ ORIENTATION AND ALIGNMENT; 1223]

kiwi *type of* **flightless bird** [➡ BIRDS; 997]

kiwi fruit *type of* **fruit** [➡ FRUIT AND VEGETABLES; 1176]

Klaxon *n* **horn**, siren, alarm, signal, buzzer, bell [➡ SIGNALING; 1140]

knack *n* **ability**, skill, talent, flair, aptitude, gift, capability, capacity, propensity, facility, dexterity, expertise [➡ SKILLS, TALENTS, AND ABILITIES; 526]

See Compare and Contrast at **talent**.

knapsack *n* **bag**, shoulder bag, rucksack, backpack, daypack, duffel bag [➡ CONTAINERS, RECEPTACLES, AND PACKAGING; 1245]

knead *v* **massage**, rub, work, manipulate, press, mold, squeeze [➡ CONTACT: EXERT PRESSURE; 414]

knee *part of* **leg or foot** [➡ PARTS OF THE BODY: LEG AND FOOT; 694]

kneecap *type of* **bone** [➡ THE BONES AND JOINTS; 719]

knee-deep *adj* **involved**, occupied, engrossed, absorbed, immersed, submerged, up to your ears, up to your elbows, up to your eyes, sunk, entangled [➡ PENSIVENESS AND INTEREST; 538] *Opposite*: uninvolved

knee-high *adj* [➡ DESCRIBING CLOTHES; 869]

knee-highs *type of* **lower body underwear** [➡ ACCESSORIES, MILLINERY, AND LINGERIE; 867]

knee-jerk (*informal*) **1** *adj* **unthinking**, automatic, reflex, habitual, immediate, thoughtless, mindless [➡ AUTOMATIC AND INSTINCTIVE; 280] *Opposite*: considered **2** *adj* **predictable**, prejudging, prejudiced, biased, dyed-in-the-wool, unchanging [➡ THE NATURE OF IDEAS; 771] *Opposite*: unpredictable

kneel *v* **go down on your knees**, genuflect, kneel down, kowtow [➡ ASSUME A POSITION; 317] *Opposite*: rise

knee-length *adj* [➡ DESCRIBING CLOTHES; 869]

knell **1** *n* **toll**, ring, peal, sound, ringing, tolling [➡ RINGING AND HOOTING SOUNDS; 1259] **2** *v* **ring**, toll, sound, peal, chime, strike, resound, reverberate [➡ EMIT RINGING AND HOOTING SOUNDS; 367]

knickerbockers *type of* **pants** [➡ GARMENTS AND OUTFITS; 865]

knickknack *n* **trinket**, curio, souvenir, object, decoration, ornament, trifle, bauble, gewgaw, tchotchke [➡ ORNAMENTS AND DECORATIONS; 1248]

knife **1** *type of* **flatware** [➡ TABLEWARE, FLATWARE, AND KITCHENWARE; 861] **2** *type of* **cutting tool** [➡ CUTTING TOOLS; 1120] **3** *v* **stab**, spear, stick, wound, lacerate, cut, slash [➡ WOUND A PERSON OR ANIMAL; 383]

knife

◆ *types of knives*
bread knife, butcher knife, carving knife, clasp knife, cleaver, jackknife, paperknife, penknife, pocketknife, switchblade, table knife

knife-edge *n* **critical point**, decisive point, turning point, watershed, crisis, crux, crunch [➡ DECISIVE MOMENTS; 44]

knight **1** *n* **cavalier**, caballero, knight-errant, adventurer [➡ NOMADIC AND ROOTLESS LIFESTYLES; 884] **2** *type of* **aristocrat** [➡ RULERS AND ARISTOCRACY; 823]

knight in shining armor *n* [➡ PEOPLE WHO ARE APPROVED OF; 955]

knish *type of* **processed potato** [➡ FRUIT AND VEGETABLES; 1176]

knit **1** *v* **unite**, join, interweave, weave, interlace, bind, tie, braid, plait, interlock [➡ FASTEN, LINK, AND JOIN; 408] **2** *v* **heal**, mend, set, join, meld, get better, bond, attach [➡ REPAIR AND MEND; 376]

knitting *type of* **handicraft** [➡ CRAFTS AND CARVING; 355]

knit your brow *v* [➡ FACIAL EXPRESSIONS AND BLUSHING; 651]

knob **1** *n* **handle**, doorknob, dial, button, handhold, hold, grip [➡ PARTS OF MACHINES AND TOOLS; 1118] **2** *n* **lump**, bump, bulge, protuberance, protrusion, hump, knot, knurl, nub [➡ ROUNDED SHAPE; 1218]

knobby *adj* **lumpy**, bumpy, ridged, bony, protuberant, uneven, rough, textured, knotty [➡ PHYSICAL TEXTURE; 1222]

knock **1** *v* **hit**, bump, collide, bang, thump, crack, clout, whack, strike, slam, hammer, pound, tap, rap, beat, bash (*informal*), smite (*archaic or literary*) [➡ CONTACT: IMPACT; 413]

2 *v* (*slang*) **criticize**, disparage, censure, condemn, belittle, deprecate, abuse, slam (*informal*), put down (*informal*), pan (*informal*) [➡ ACCUSE, BLAME, AND CRITICIZE; 641] *Opposite*: praise **3** *n* (*informal*) **blow**, setback, upset, kick in the teeth, misfortune [➡ PROBLEMS; 256] **4** *n* **blow**, collision, hit, bump, bang, thump, clout, whack, stroke, thwack, rap, tap, bash (*informal*), crack (*informal*) [➡ PHYSICAL ATTACK AND PUNISHMENT; 415]

knockabout **1** *adj* **physical**, slapstick, boisterous, rowdy, rough, visual, lively, spontaneous [➡ DISORDER AND CHAOS; 245] *Opposite*: decorous **2** *adj* **sturdy**, stout, strong, solid, substantial, tough, casual, informal, everyday [➡ DESCRIBING CLOTHES; 869] *Opposite*: flimsy **3** *n* **slapstick**, physical comedy, visual comedy, clowning, buffoonery, farce [➡ JOKES AND TEASING; 674]

knock around (*informal*) **1** *v* **hit**, beat, mistreat, abuse, batter, beat up (*informal*) [➡ PHYSICAL ATTACK AND PUNISHMENT; 415] **2** *v* **hang around**, spend time, relax, hang out (*informal*), kick around (*informal*), chill (*slang*) [➡ LACK OF ACTIVITY OR MOTION; 342]

knock back (*informal*) *v* **down**, gulp, swallow, drink, put back, toss back, swig (*informal*), chug (*slang*), quaff (*literary or humorous*), swill [➡ DRINK; 711]

knock down **1** *v* **floor**, fell, knock over, hit, strike, pound, smash, deck (*informal*), smite (*archaic or literary*) [➡ MOVE SOMETHING: INTO A NEW POSITION OR OVERTURN; 330] **2** *v* **destroy**, demolish, dismantle, bulldoze, pull down, tear down, take down, flatten, raze, level [➡ DESTRUCTION AND DEMOLITION; 359] *Opposite*: build **3** *v* **reduce the price of**, discount, mark down, lower, reduce [➡ SELL; 441] *Opposite*: put up

knockdown *adj* **cheap**, reduced, low, rock-bottom, bargain, budget, giveaway (*informal*) [➡ CHEAP AND INEXPENSIVE; 221] *Opposite*: inflated

knock down with a feather *v* [➡ SURPRISE AND IMPRESS; 574]

knocked out **1** *adj* **unconscious**, stunned, anesthetized, comatose, out cold, out for the count, under (*informal*) [➡ TIRED, ASLEEP, AND UNCONSCIOUS; 738] **2** *adj* (*informal*) **bowled over**, awestruck, dazzled, amazed, blown away (*slang*) [➡ SURPRISE, SHOCK, AND AMAZEMENT; 545] *Opposite*: unimpressed

knocker **1** *n* **door fixture**, knob, handle, bell, doorbell [➡ ORNAMENTS AND DECORATIONS; 1248] **2** *n* (*UK informal*) **critic**, faultfinder, detractor, carper, caviler, whiner (*informal*), moaner (*UK informal*) [➡ GRUMPY AND NEGATIVE PEOPLE; 953] *Opposite*: admirer

knock off **1** *v* (*informal*) **stop work**, finish, call it a day, leave, head off, pack in (*informal*), down tools (*UK*) [➡ STOP ACTING; 264] *Opposite*: start **2** *v* (*informal*) **deduct**, take off, discount, subtract, reduce [➡ SELL; 441] *Opposite*: add on **3** *v* (*informal*) **mass-produce**, churn out, knock out, turn out, rattle off, produce [➡ MANUFACTURE; 349] **4** *v* (*slang*) **kill**, murder, assassinate, eliminate, liquidate, do in (*informal*), do away with (*informal*) [➡ KILL; 923] **5** *v* (*slang*) **steal**, rob, pilfer, thieve, make off with, embezzle, appropriate, filch (*informal*), lift (*informal*) [➡ STEAL AND ROB; 426]

knockoff (*informal*) *n* **copy**, fake, forgery, reproduction, counterfeit, rip-off (*informal*) [➡ COPIES AND REPLICAS; 151] *Opposite*: original

knock-on effect (*UK*) *n* **consequence**, outcome, result, upshot, conclusion, chain reaction, chain of events, domino effect [➡ RESULTS AND OUTCOMES; 83]

knowing 1 *adj* **meaningful**, significant, expressive, elo-
...nt, perceptive, shrewd [➡ KNOWLEDGE AND WISDOM; 558] *Oppo-*
...ocent 2 *adj* **deliberate**, intentional, intended,
...lculating, aware [➡ INTENTIONAL AND DELIBERATE; 279]
...ious

...nal) *n* **smart aleck** (*informal*), smarty
...se guy (*informal*), wiseacre (*informal*)
...LF-SEEKING PEOPLE; 949]

...l *n* **acquaintance**, familiarity, awareness,
...g, comprehension, realization, experience,
...ill, know-how (*informal*) [➡ KNOWLEDGE AND WISDOM;
...e: ignorance 2 *n* **information**, facts, data [➡ BASIC
...3 *n* **wisdom**, learning, education, scholarship,
...n, intelligence [➡ KNOWLEDGE AND WISDOM; 558]

...mpare and Contrast: *knowledge, erudition, infor-*
...tion, learning, scholarship, wisdom

...ORE MEANING: what can be known

knowledge what can be known through observation,
investigation, reasoning, and experience as well as
study; *erudition* advanced academic learning, often of
a specialized or difficult nature; *information* facts or
data; *learning* what is known through formal study,
especially study of quite an advanced nature; *schol-*
arship advanced academic learning, especially when
this is specialized; *wisdom* the ability to use knowledge
or learning prudently and combine it with experience
and good judgment.

knowledgeable *adj* **well-informed**, au fait, conversant,
familiar, informed, educated, erudite, experienced,
expert, on the ball (*informal*) [➡ KNOWLEDGE AND WISDOM; 558] *Oppo-*
site: ignorant

known 1 *adj* **recognized**, identified, acknowledged,
branded, well-known, famous, celebrated, renowned
[➡ KNOWN AND FAMOUS; 181] 2 *adj* **accepted**, acknowledged, established, recognized, proven [➡ KNOWN AND FAMOUS; 181]

knuckle 1 *n* **protuberance**, projection, lump, prominence, bulge, knob, nub, knot [➡ ROUNDED SHAPE; 1218] 2 *part*
of **arm or hand** [➡ PARTS OF THE BODY: ARM AND HAND; 695]

knuckle down (*informal*) *v* **work hard**, apply yourself,
get down to it, buckle down (*informal*), get your head
down (*UK*) [➡ HARD WORK OR EFFORT; 298]

knuckle under *v* **give in**, give up, admit defeat, concede
defeat, concede, surrender, give way, yield, throw in the
towel (*informal*), throw in your hand (*informal*) [➡ FAIL OR BE
UNSUCCESSFUL; 75] *Opposite*: continue

KO (*informal*) *v* [➡ PHYSICAL ATTACK AND PUNISHMENT; 415]

koala *type of* **marsupial** [➡ MARSUPIALS; 992]

kohl *n* **eyeliner**, eye pencil, mascara [➡ MAKEUP AND BEAUTY
PRODUCTS; 490]

Komodo dragon *type of* **reptile** [➡ REPTILES; 994]

koruna *type of* **currency** [➡ CURRENCIES; 798]

kosher 1 *adj* [➡ FOOD; 1167] (*informal*) 2 *adj* **lawful**, acceptable, legitimate, aboveboard, proper [➡ APPROPRIATE, SUITABLE, AND
ADVISABLE; 184] *Opposite*: unlawful 3 *adj* **genuine**, authentic,
true, real, bona fide [➡ TRUE AND REAL; 171] *Opposite*: fake

---

...et, esteem [➡ SOURCE OF HAPPINESS, PLEASURE,
...e: discredit
...➡ CLIMBERS; 1033]
...FRUIT AND VEGETABLES; 1176]
...URRENCIES; 798]
...ort [➡ HOBBIES, GAMES, AND SPORTS; 875]
...ain, whine, grumble, moan
...URRENCIES; 798]
...RENCIES; 798]
...; 798]

al,

...UNTAINS

...nny knot
...mp, bulge,
...ster, huddle,
...group, bunch,
...d, tether, secure

...GARDENS; 1074]

..., secured, taut, tangled, tight,
...ned, clenched, drawn, furrowed,
...RD; 1211] *Opposite*: relaxed

...cky, awkward, complicated, complex,
...problematic, hard, difficult [➡ DIFFICULTY AND
...posite: simple

...nderstand, be aware of, be knowledgeable
...rehend, appreciate, realize, grasp, recognize,
...formal) [➡ KNOWLEDGE AND WISDOM; 558] 2 *v* **experience**,
...gh, undergo [➡ EXPERIENCE AND ENCOUNTER; 582] 3 *v* **be**
...d with, be familiar with, distinguish, see, have
...ge of, be friendly with [➡ KNOWLEDGE AND WISDOM; 558]

...ble *adj* **intelligible**, comprehensible, under-
..., coherent, identifiable, recognizable, fatho-
...CISE AND CLEAR; 202] *Opposite*: unknowable

...out **ward and forward** *v* **know well**, know
...ards (*UK*) like the back of your hand, know
...58] ...know back to front (*UK*) [➡ KNOWLEDGE AND

...ow (*inform*... *n* **knowledge**, experience, expert-
...voir-faire, proficiency, competence, savvy
...) [➡ SKILLS, TALENTS, AND ABILITIES; 526]

kowtow 1 *v* **kneel**, bow, genuflect, prostrate oneself, salaam, stoop, bend [➡GESTURES AND GESTICULATION; 653] **2 *v* grovel**, be servile, be obsequious, show deference, bow and scrape, fawn, humble oneself [➡FLATTER AND FAWN; 621] **3 *n* bow**, genuflection, prostration, salaam, homage, obeisance (*formal*) [➡GESTURES AND GESTICULATION; 653]

krona *type of* **currency** [➡CURRENCIES; 798]

krone *type of* **currency** [➡CURRENCIES; 798]

kroon *type of* **currency** [➡CURRENCIES; 798]

krouźek *type of* **diacritic** [➡ASPECTS OF LANGUAGE; 682]

kudos *n* **glory**, praise, credit, fame, admiration, acclaim,

honor, prestige, cach
OR IMPROVEMENT; 209] *Oppos*

kudzu *type of* **climber**

kumquat *type of* **fruit** [

kuna *type of* **currency** [➡C

kung fu *type of* **combat sp**

kvetch (*informal*) *v* **comp**
[➡COMPLAIN AND NAG; 686]

kwacha *type of* **currency** [➡C

kwanza *type of* **currency** [➡CU

kyat *type of* **currency** [➡CURRENCIE

L

laager *n* **camp**, encampment, settlement, defensive position, shelter, stronghold [➡ HUMAN SETTLEMENTS; 1070]

lab (*informal*) *n* **workroom**, workshop, test center, test bed, laboratory [➡ INDUSTRIAL BUILDINGS; 1087]

label 1 *n* **tag**, ticket, sticker, marker, sticky tag, sticky label (*UK*) [➡ NAME AND DESCRIBE; 665] 2 *n* **make**, brand name, trade name, trademark, mark, marque, brand [➡ NAME AND DESCRIBE; 665] 3 *n* **description**, categorization, classification, characterization [➡ NAME AND DESCRIBE; 665] 4 *v* **put a label on**, mark, identify, stamp [➡ NAME AND DESCRIBE; 665] 5 *v* **consider**, regard, describe, categorize, class, characterize, pigeonhole, brand, write off as (*informal*) [➡ NAME AND DESCRIBE; 665]

labor 1 *n* **work**, toil, hard work, manual labor, efforts, employment, exertions, hard labor, blood, sweat, and tears, industry (*formal or literary*) [➡ HARD WORK OR EFFORT; 298] 2 *n* **workers**, work force, employees, labor force, hands, staff, personnel, manual workers, blue-collar workers, working class [➡ THE WORK FORCE; 837] *Opposite*: management 3 *n* **task**, job, chore, effort, exertion, mission, duty, activity, occupation [➡ JOB; 833] 4 *n* **childbirth**, delivery, giving birth, confinement (*dated*) [➡ REPRODUCTION AND HEREDITY; 725] 5 *v* **strive**, strain, grind away, keep at it, burn the candle at both ends, toil, slog, sweat blood, work like a dog, break your back, struggle, sweat (*informal*), plug away (*informal*), endeavor (*formal*) [➡ HARD WORK OR EFFORT; 298] *Opposite*: laze around 6 *v* **struggle**, exert, grapple, wrestle, agonize [➡ COMPETE, CONTEND, AND COMBAT; 303] 7 *v* **malfunction**, struggle, complain, seize up, falter, crash, strain, stall, play up (*UK*) [➡ FAIL OR CEASE TO FUNCTION; 470] *Opposite*: run smoothly 8 *v* **drag yourself**, stagger, struggle, plod, trudge, trail, slog [➡ WALK UNSTEADILY; 315] *Opposite*: skip 9 *v* **overemphasize**, go on, dwell on, exaggerate, drive home, overdo, stress, underline, accentuate, belabor, labor the point [➡ CLAIM, INSIST, AND EMPHASIZE; 614] *Opposite*: pass over

> *See Compare and Contrast at* **work**.

laboratory *n* **workroom**, workshop, test bed, test center, research laboratory, test site [➡ INDUSTRIAL BUILDINGS; 1087]

labored *adj* **tortured**, tortuous, difficult, strenuous, arduous, awkward, contrived, artificial, forced, leaden [➡ DIFFICULTY AND COMPLEXITY; 242] *Opposite*: effortless

laborer *n* **manual worker**, blue-collar worker, hand, workhand, drudge, worker, employee [➡ WORKERS; 836]

labor-intensive *adj* [➡ DIFFICULTY AND COMPLEXITY; 242]

laborious *adj* **arduous**, backbreaking, painstaking, protracted, lengthy, strenuous, hard, tough, painful, difficult [➡ DIFFICULTY AND COMPLEXITY; 242] *Opposite*: easy

> *See Compare and Contrast at* **hard**.

laboriousness *n* **difficulty**, arduousness, hardness, toughness, tedium [➡ DIFFICULTY AND COMPLEXITY; 242] *Opposite*: ease

laborsaving *adj* [➡ EASE AND SIMPLICITY; 200]

labor the point *v* [➡ CLAIM, INSIST, AND EMPHASIZE; 614]

labor under *v* **suffer from**, struggle with, be disadvantaged by, be burdened with, be swayed by, be influenced by, persist, suffer, experience [➡ EXPERIENCE AND ENCOUNTER; 582]

labor union *n* **workers' association**, organized labor, staff association, syndicate, union, trade union (*UK*) [➡ BUSINESS ENTERPRISES AND RELATED BODIES; 792]

Labrador *type of* **large dog** [➡ DOGS; 980]

laburnum *type of* **deciduous tree** [➡ DECIDUOUS TREES; 1028]

labyrinth *n* **maze**, warren, web, tangle, jumble, muddle [➡ DISORDER AND CHAOS; 245]

labyrinthine *adj* **complex**, convoluted, intricate, complicated, tortuous, obscure, tangled, involved [➡ DIFFICULTY AND COMPLEXITY, 242] *Opposite*: straightforward

lace 1 *n* **tie**, shoelace, bootlace, cord [➡ FASTENERS, LINKS, AND NETWORKS; 1247] 2 *part of* **garment** [➡ PARTS OF A GARMENT; 870] 3 *v* **do up**, tie up, lace up, fasten [➡ FASTEN, LINK, AND JOIN; 408] *Opposite*: undo 4 *v* **spike**, mix, fortify [➡ COMBINE AND MIX; 400]

lacemaking *type of* **handicraft** [➡ CRAFTS AND CARVING; 355]

lacerate *v* **slash**, tear, cut, score, scratch, shred, gash, rip, slit, slice, hack [➡ TEAR, BREAK, AND CUT; 360]

laceration *n* **cut**, slash, graze, scratch, tear, gash, rip, slit [➡ HOLES, GAPS, AND FORKS; 1252]

Lacerta *type of* **constellation** [➡ HEAVENLY BODIES; 1061]

lachrymose (*literary*) 1 *adj* **tearful**, crying, easily moved, in tears, in floods of tears, with tears in your eyes, close to tears, weepy (*informal*) [➡ SADNESS, DISTRESS, AND DESPAIR; 539] *Opposite*: dry-eyed 2 *adj* **sad**, tragic, unhappy, moving, dismal, mournful, sorrowful [➡ EMOTIONALLY UNPLEASANT AND UPSETTING; 227] *Opposite*: cheerful

lack 1 *n* **shortage**, absence, want, dearth, deficiency, deficit [➡ TOO FEW, TOO LITTLE; 122] 2 *v* **be short of**, not have, be deficient in, want for, need, require [➡ NEED AND REQUIRE; 464] *Opposite*: have

Compare and Contrast: *lack, shortage, deficiency, deficit, want, dearth*

CORE MEANING: an insufficiency or absence of something

lack a complete absence of a particular thing; *shortage* a lack of something that is needed or required; *deficiency* a shortfall in the amount of something necessary, e.g., a particular nutrient in the human body, or an inadequacy in the supply or performance of something; *deficit* the amount by which something falls short of a target amount or level; *want* or *dearth* a scarcity or absence of something.

lackadaisical *adj* **apathetic**, careless, lazy, relaxed, half-hearted, easygoing, laissez-faire, lax, casual, slapdash, laid-back (*informal*) [➡ NEUTRALITY AND INDIFFERENCE; 553] *Opposite*: energetic

lackey 1 *n* **minion**, lapdog, sycophant, toady, creature, yes man [➡ SUBORDINATES AND ASSISTANTS; 966] 2 (*archaic*) *type of* **servant** [➡ DOMESTIC AND KITCHEN WORKERS; 850]

lacking *adj* **missing**, not there, wanting, absent [➡ ABSENT AND UNAVAILABLE; 7] *Opposite*: present

lacking in *adj* **short of**, without, not having, bereft of, devoid of, deficient in [➡ TOO FEW, TOO LITTLE; 122] *Opposite*: full of

lackluster *adj* **dull**, lifeless, dreary, unexciting, uninspiring, tame, bland, undistinguished, flat, leaden [➡ BORING AND UNINTERESTING; 234] *Opposite*: brilliant

laconic *adj* **terse**, brief, short, concise, economical, curt, to the point [➡ SUCCINCT AND TO THE POINT; 640] *Opposite*: long-winded

laconicism *n* [➡ SUCCINCT AND TO THE POINT; 640]

lacquer *n* **polish**, varnish, gloss [➡ COVERS AND COATINGS; 1246]

lacrosse *type of* **ball game** [➡ HOBBIES, GAMES, AND SPORTS; 875]

lacrosse stick *type of* **sports equipment** [➡ SPORTS EQUIPMENT; 879]

lactose *type of* **nutrient** [➡ FOOD COMPONENTS; 1188]

lacuna (*literary*) *n* **space**, empty space, void, hole, omission, gap [➡ HOLES, GAPS, AND FORKS; 1252]

lacy *adj* **delicate**, lacelike, net, filigree, fine [➡ VISUAL TEXTURE; 1221]

lad 1 *n* **boy**, young man, youngster, youth, teenager, adolescent, son, kid (*informal*), laddie (*informal*) [➡ CHILD OR YOUTH; 945] *Opposite*: lass 2 *n* (*informal*) **man**, fellow, guy (*informal*), fella (*informal*) [➡ MALE PERSON; 934] *Opposite*: lass

ladder 1 *n* **ranking**, tree, standings, pecking order, hierarchy [➡ CONNECTIONS; 143] 2 *n* **stepladder**, folding ladder, loft ladder, roof ladder, rope ladder, steps (*UK*) [➡ STAIRS AND STORIES; 1102]

ladder-back *type of* **seating** [➡ FURNITURE; 858]

laddie (*informal*) *see* **lad**

laden *adj* **weighed down**, burdened, overloaded, loaded [➡ FULL; 1239] *Opposite*: empty

la-di-da (*informal*) *adj* **affected**, pretentious, snobbish, put-on, full of airs and graces, upper-class, genteel, refined, precious, highfalutin (*informal*) [➡ AFFECTATION, SELF-SATISFACTION, AND SNOBBISHNESS; 507] *Opposite*: common

ladle *n* [➡ SPOONS, SCOOPS, AND SHOVELS; 1121]

lady *n* **woman**, female, matron [➡ FEMALE PERSON; 933]

ladybug *type of* **beetle** [➡ BEETLES AND WEEVILS; 1016]

lady friend (*informal*) *n* **female companion**, girlfriend, partner [➡ SEXUAL AND ROMANTIC RELATIONSHIPS; 964]

lag 1 *v* **drop back**, drop behind, fall back, fall behind, trail, hang back, dawdle, loiter, linger, crawl, straggle, drag your feet, bring up the rear, dally [➡ MOVE SLOWLY; 314] *Opposite*: lead 2 *v* **insulate**, wrap, wad, protect, pad [➡ DECORATE, ADORN, AND APPLY COATINGS; 405] 3 *n* **interval**, wait, delay, intermission, pause, halt [➡ PAUSES AND PHASES; 56]

laggard *n* **straggler**, dawdler, shirker, slacker, idler, foot-dragger (*informal*), lazybones (*informal*), slowpoke (*informal*) [➡ LAZY OR UNSUCCESSFUL PEOPLE; 948] *Opposite*: leader

lagging *n* **insulation**, wadding, padding, sleeve, skin, sheathing, covering, coat, casing, protection [➡ COVERS AND COATINGS; 1246]

lagoon 1 *n* **inlet**, cove, bay, creek [➡ THE SEAS, OCEANS, AND SHORES; 1041] 2 *n* **lake**, pond, pool, mere (*archaic or literary*), lough (*UK*), loch (*UK*) [➡ RIVERS, LAKES, AND STREAMS; 1042]

lah-di-dah (*informal*) *see* **la-di-da**

laid-back (*informal*) *adj* **relaxed**, easygoing, easy, phlegmatic, cool, casual, calm, chilled (*slang*), chilled out (*slang*) [➡ COOL AND CALM; 536] *Opposite*: tense

laid off *adj* **out of work**, jobless, unemployed [➡ EMPLOYMENT STATUS; 831] *Opposite*: employed

laid up *adj* **unwell**, ill, sick, bedridden, under the weather, injured, ailing (*dated*) [➡ ILL AND SICK; 740] *Opposite*: well

lair 1 *n* (*informal*) **hideout**, den, haunt, retreat, hideaway, hangout (*informal*) [➡ UNDESIRABLE ACCOMMODATIONS; 856] 2 *type of* **den or nest** [➡ ANIMAL OR BIRD ACCOMMODATIONS; 1079]

laird (*UK*) *n* **landowner**, owner, proprietor, property owner, landlord, lord [➡ OWNERS; 446]

laissez-faire 1 *n* **noninterventionism**, nonintervention, noninvolvement, laxity [➡ NEUTRALITY AND INDIFFERENCE; 553] *Opposite*: intervention 2 *adj* **noninterventionist**, unrestrictive, permissive, freewheeling, lax, hands-off, relaxed, laid-back [➡ PERMIT AND ALLOW; 669] *Opposite*: proactive

laity 1 *n* **laypeople**, congregation, worshipers [➡ RELIGIOUS PEOPLE; 778] *Opposite*: clergy 2 *n* **nonprofessionals**, outsiders, amateurs, uninitiated [➡ UNSKILLED PEOPLE; 530]

lake *n* **pond**, lagoon, tarn, water, sea, mere (*archaic or literary*), lough (*UK*), loch (*UK*) [➡ RIVERS, LAKES, AND STREAMS; 1042]

lakeside *n* **shore**, waterside, water's edge, bank, land, beach [➡ THE SEAS, OCEANS, AND SHORES; 1041]

lama *n* **monk**, priest, brother, father, clergyman [➡ RELIGIOUS PEOPLE; 778]

lamb 1 *type of* **meat** [➡ TYPES AND CUTS OF MEAT; 1177] 2 *type of* **young animal** [➡ YOUNG ANIMALS; 977]

lambada *n* [➡ DANCE; 903]

lambaste *v* **attack**, upbraid, reprimand, criticize, reprove, scold, deride, lash, condemn, lay into (*informal*), tell off (*informal*), castigate (*formal*), excoriate (*formal*), slate (*UK*), have your knife in (*UK*) [➡ ACCUSE, BLAME, AND CRITICIZE; 641]

lambent 1 *adj* (*literary*) **gleaming**, glowing, radiant, luminous, shining, shimmering, glimmering, soft [➡ DESCRIBING LIGHT; 1228] *Opposite*: dull 2 *adj* **brilliant**, scintillating, witty, sharp, rapier-like, quick [➡ POSITIVE INTELLECTUAL CHARACTERISTICS; 524] *Opposite*: leaden

lambswool *type of* **fabric from animals** [➡ FABRICS; 1132]

lamé *type of* **synthetic fabric** [➡ FABRICS; 1132]

lame duck *n* [➡ LAZY OR UNSUCCESSFUL PEOPLE; 948]

lament **1** *v* mourn, grieve, cry for, weep, bemoan, howl, moan (*informal*), bewail (*formal*) [➡ GIVING VENT TO EMOTIONS; 679] *Opposite*: celebrate **2** *n* **lamentation**, cry, dirge, crying, weeping, howling, wailing [➡ SOUNDS MADE BY PEOPLE; 1262] *Opposite*: celebration

lamentable **1** *adj* **regrettable**, deplorable, inexcusable, appalling, dreadful, hopeless, terrible, bad, unsatisfactory, pitiful, disappointing, execrable (*formal*) [➡ BAD AND BADLY; 223] *Opposite*: laudable **2** *adj* (*literary*) **woeful**, sad, mournful, pitiful [➡ EMOTIONALLY UNPLEASANT AND UPSETTING; 227]

lamentation *n* lament, dirge, cry, weeping, crying, howling, mourning [➡ SOUNDS MADE BY PEOPLE; 1262] *Opposite*: celebration

laminaria *type of* **marine alga** [➡ MICROORGANISMS, FUNGI, AND ALGAE; 1023]

laminate *v* **cover**, seal, coat, protect, enclose [➡ DECORATE, ADORN, AND APPLY COATINGS; 405]

laminated *adj* **plastic-coated**, coated, covered, bonded, composite, layered, veneered [➡ PHYSICAL TEXTURE; 1222]

lammergeier *type of* **scavenger** [➡ BIRDS; 997]

lammergeyer *see* **lammergeier**

lamp *type of* **light** [➡ LIGHT; 1164]

lampoon **1** *v* ridicule, satirize, make fun of, parody, caricature, send up (*informal*) [➡ JOKES AND TEASING; 674] **2** *n* **satire**, parody, skit, sketch, caricature, sendup (*informal*) [➡ JOKES AND TEASING; 674]

lamppost *n* **streetlight**, streetlamp, light [➡ LIGHT; 1164]

lampshade *n* [➡ FURNISHING AND HOUSEHOLD LINENS; 860]

lanai *n* [➡ STAGES, PLATFORMS, AND RAISED AREAS; 1098]

lance **1** *n* **spear**, weapon, bayonet, javelin [➡ PROJECTILES; 1159] **2** *v* **cut**, pierce, prick, slice into, slice open, puncture, incise, hack [➡ TEAR, BREAK, AND CUT; 360]

lancet *type of* **medical instrument** [➡ HAND TOOLS; 1119]

lancet window *type of* **window** [➡ WINDOWS; 1100]

land **1** *n* **earth**, ground, terrain, countryside [➡ THE COUNTRYSIDE AND OUTDOOR SPACES; 1071] **2** *n* **homeland**, nation, country, territory [➡ COUNTRIES AND REGIONS; 1067] **3** *n* **property**, plot, parcel, lot, acreage, estate, spread (*informal*) [➡ HUMAN SETTLEMENTS; 1070] **4** *v* **arrive**, set down, alight, come down, touch down [➡ ARRIVE BY TRANSPORT; 14] *Opposite*: take off **5** *v* **acquire**, get, annex, gain, obtain, procure, secure, win [➡ GET; 420] *Opposite*: lose

landau *type of* **wagon or carriage** [➡ VEHICLES; 1145]

landaulet *type of* **wagon or carriage** [➡ VEHICLES; 1145]

landed *adj* **property-owning**, landowning, wealthy, propertied, rich, moneyed, powerful [➡ CLASS STATUS; 889] *Opposite*: landless

landed gentry *n* [➡ CLASS STATUS; 889]

lander *type of* **spacecraft** [➡ SPACE VEHICLES; 1063]

landfall **1** *n* **arrival**, landing, touchdown, docking, mooring [➡ ARRIVAL; 13] **2** *n* **land**, dry land, mainland, terra firma, shore, coast [➡ THE SEAS, OCEANS, AND SHORES; 1041]

landfill *type of* **storage space** [➡ STORES AND STORAGE BUILDINGS; 1088]

land forces *n* **army**, ground forces, troops, infantry, soldiers, foot soldiers, land army [➡ THE ARMED FORCES; 827]

landholder *n* **landowner**, landlord, property-owner, proprietor, owner [➡ OWNERS; 446]

landing **1** *n* **arrival**, alighting, touchdown, docking, mooring [➡ ARRIVAL; 13] **2** *n* **mooring**, pier, jetty, quay, landing stage [➡ WATERWAYS AND SEAWAYS; 1108] **3** *n* **mezzanine**, half floor, top of the stairs [➡ STAIRS AND STORIES; 1102] **4** *part of* **building** [➡ PARTS OF A BUILDING; 1095]

landing field *n* **airstrip**, landing strip, runway, airfield, airdrome, aerodrome (*UK*) [➡ AIRWAYS; 1109]

landing gear *part of* **aircraft** [➡ AIRCRAFT; 1148]

landing stage *n* **jetty**, quay, mooring, landing [➡ WATERWAYS AND SEAWAYS; 1108]

landing strip *n* **runway**, airstrip, landing field, airfield, airdrome, aerodrome (*UK*) [➡ AIRWAYS; 1109]

landlady **1** *n* **property owner**, landowner, landholder, proprietor, owner, lessor [➡ OWNERS; 446] *Opposite*: tenant **2** *n* **licensee**, proprietor, manager, hotelier, innkeeper, lessee [➡ BUSINESS PEOPLE; 793]

landless *adj* **dispossessed**, evicted, ousted, powerless [➡ POVERTY AND POOR; 892] *Opposite*: landed

landline *n* **cable**, line, phone line, wire, link [➡ TELECOMMUNICATIONS; 1130]

landlocked *adj* **closed in**, blocked-in, noncoastal, interior [➡ THE SEAS, OCEANS, AND SHORES; 1041] *Opposite*: coastal

landlord **1** *n* **property-owner**, landowner, landholder, proprietor, owner, lessor [➡ OWNERS; 446] *Opposite*: tenant **2** *n* **licensee**, proprietor, manager, hotelier, innkeeper, lessee [➡ BUSINESS PEOPLE; 793]

landmark **1** *n* **marker**, sight, attraction, sign, signpost, pointer, cairn [➡ PLACE; 1065] **2** *n* **breakthrough**, milestone, revolution, innovation, benchmark, standard, development [➡ DECISIVE MOMENTS; 44] **3** *adj* **milestone**, breakthrough, momentous, revolutionary, innovative, innovatory, groundbreaking, radical, pioneering, historic, significant [➡ MOST IMPORTANT AND MAIN; 193] *Opposite*: run-of-the-mill

landmass *n* **continent**, land, landform, island, mainland [➡ THE CONTINENTS AND ISLANDS; 1048]

land of make-believe *n* [➡ NONEXISTENT PLACES; 1066]

land on your feet *v* **come out on top**, succeed, get lucky, come through unscathed, find yourself, survive, finish up, wind up (*informal*) [➡ SUCCEED AND WIN; 79] *Opposite*: fail

landowner *n* **property owner**, landlord, owner, proprietor, landlady [➡ OWNERS; 446] *Opposite*: tenant

landscape **1** *n* **scenery**, countryside, land, site, scene, setting, background, backdrop, backcloth, panorama, view, topography, geography, terrain, environment, sur-roundings [➥ THE COUNTRYSIDE AND OUTDOOR SPACES; 1071] **2** *n* **back-ground**, backdrop, circumstances, situation, setting, scene [➥ SITUATIONS; 71] **3** *v* **design**, model, form, shape, plan out, improve, camouflage, disguise [➥ IMPROVE APPEARANCE; 379]

landslide 1 *n* **mudslide**, avalanche, landslip, rock fall [➥ EROSION AND WEATHERING; 1055] **2** *n* **victory**, rout, win, success, triumph, clean sweep [➥ SUCCESS; 82]

landslip *see* **landslide**

landward 1 *adj* **inland**, inward, inward-looking, inner, innermost [➥ ORIENTATION AND ALIGNMENT; 1223] **2** *adv* **ashore**, inland, inward, in [➥ DIRECTION OF MOTION; 345]

land yacht *type of* **leisure vehicle** [➥ VEHICLES; 1145]

lane *n* **traffic lane**, fast lane, inside lane, passing lane, left-hand lane, right-hand lane, right lane, slow lane (*UK*), overtaking lane (*UK*), outside lane (*UK*) [➥ ROADS; 1106]

langlauf *type of* **winter sport** [➥ HOBBIES, GAMES, AND SPORTS; 875]

langoustine *type of* **crustacean** [➥ AQUATIC INVERTEBRATES; 1022]

language 1 *n* **communication**, speech, talking [➥ THE SPOKEN WORD; 671] **2** *n* **tongue**, idiom, dialect, patois, argot, con-versation, vernacular, jargon, lingua franca, idiolect, par-lance, lingo (*informal*) [➥ ASPECTS OF LANGUAGE; 682] **3** *n* **words**, vocabulary, writing, prose, poetry, style, expression [➥ ASPECTS OF LANGUAGE; 682]

Compare and Contrast: *language, vocabulary, idio-lect, tongue, dialect, slang, jargon, parlance, lingo, -speak, -ese*

CORE MEANING: communication by words

language the human use of spoken or written words as a communication system, or the particular system of communication prevailing in a specific country, nation, or community; *vocabulary* the body of words that make up a particular language; *idiolect* an indi-vidual person's speech habits or vocabulary; *tongue* a particular language used by a specific country, nation, or community; *dialect* a regional variety of a language, or a form of a language spoken by members of a particular social class or profession; *slang* words, expressions, and turns of phrase used instead of stand-ard terms in casual speech or writing, or by a par-ticular group of people; *jargon* terms associated with a particular specialized activity, profession, or culture, especially terms that are not generally understood by outsiders; *parlance* the style of speech or writing used by people in a particular context or profession; *lingo* (*informal*) the way of speaking associated with a par-ticular, usually specialized, group of people; *-speak* a suffix added to nouns to describe the language used by a particular group of people or in a particular context, suggesting that this way of speaking or writing is obscure or difficult to follow; *-ese* a suffix added to nouns to describe the language associated with a group of people, especially when it resembles jargon.

languid *adj* **unhurried**, relaxed, languorous, lazy, indo-lent, lethargic, slow, dreamy, droopy, sleepy, somnolent,

drowsy, leisurely [➥ TIRED, ASLEEP, AND UNCONSCIOUS; 738] *Opposite*: vigorous

languish 1 *v* **suffer**, weaken, fail, flag, deteriorate, waste away, ail (*archaic or literary*) [➥ GET WORSE; 381] *Opposite*: thrive **2** *v* **pine**, pine away, fade away, long for, grieve [➥ DESIRE AND WANT; 579] **3** *v* **decline**, fail, sink, teeter, diminish [➥ CEASE TO EXIST; 22] *Opposite*: thrive

languishing *adj* [➥ TIRED, ASLEEP, AND UNCONSCIOUS; 738]

languor *n* **tiredness**, listlessness, lethargy, sluggishness, dreaminess, slowness, stillness, torpor, sleepiness [➥ TIRED, ASLEEP, AND UNCONSCIOUS; 738] *Opposite*: vigor

languorous *adj* **tired**, listless, lethargic, languid, slug-gish, dreamy, slow, still, torpid, sleepy, unhurried, relaxed [➥ TIRED, ASLEEP, AND UNCONSCIOUS; 738] *Opposite*: vigorous

laniard *see* **lanyard**

lank *adj* **limp**, lifeless, dull, thin, floppy [➥ DESCRIBING HAIR; 486]

lankiness *n* [➥ BUILD; 477]

lanky *adj* **gangling**, gangly, long-legged, leggy, angular [➥ BUILD; 477] *Opposite*: rotund

lantern *type of* **light** [➥ LIGHT; 1164]

lanyard *n* **rope**, cord, line, cable, halyard, vang, ratline [➥ FASTENERS, LINKS, AND NETWORKS; 1247]

lap 1 *part of* **leg or foot** [➥ PARTS OF THE BODY: LEG AND FOOT; 694] **2** *n* **circuit**, tour, round, circle [➥ SPORTS TERMS; 877] **3** *n* **stage**, leg, part, segment, section, heat, phase [➥ PAUSES AND PHASES; 56] **4** *v* **lick up**, slurp, lap up, drink [➥ DRINK; 711]

laparoscopy *type of* **medical procedure** [➥ REMEDIES, TREAT-MENTS, AND OPERATIONS; 731]

lapdog *n* **minion**, toady, sycophant, lackey, creature, yes man [➥ SUPERFICIAL OR INSINCERE PEOPLE; 951]

lapel *part of* **garment** [➥ PARTS OF A GARMENT; 870]

lapis lazuli 1 *type of* **blue** [➥ COLORS; 1224] **2** *type of* **gemstone** [➥ PRECIOUS STONES; 1278]

lap of luxury *n* **bed of roses**, the life of Riley, life of ease, Easy Street [➥ PLEASANT SITUATIONS; 74]

lapse 1 *n* **error**, slip, failure, mistake, blunder, slip-up (*informal*), hiccup (*informal*) [➥ MISTAKES; 250] **2** *n* **interval**, space, break, delay, pause, wait, hiatus, gap, time lag [➥ PAUSES AND PHASES; 56] **3** *v* **decline**, tumble, descend, drop, fall, slide [➥ GO DOWNWARD; 307] *Opposite*: rise **4** *v* **come to an end**, end, fail, give up, lose, stop [➥ CEASE TO EXIST; 22] *Opposite*: renew **5** *v* **slip**, tail off, trail off, drift, falter, fade, fail [➥ GET WORSE; 381] *Opposite*: start up

lapsed *adj* **failed**, onetime, former, erstwhile, recent, has-been (*informal*) [➥ PAST; 84] *Opposite*: current

lapse into 1 *v* **slide into**, slip into, fall into, drift into, resort to [➥ START AN ACTION; 260] *Opposite*: choose **2** *v* **revert**, regress, backslide, relapse, fall back, go back to, slide back, return to [➥ GET WORSE; 381] *Opposite*: progress

laptop *type of* **computer** [➥ COMPUTERS AND COMPUTING; 1127]

lap up 1 *v* **lick up**, slurp up, lap [➥ DRINK; 711] **2** *v* **enjoy**, soak up, bask in, love, glory in, get a kick out of [➡ LIKE, LOVE, VALUE, AND ENJOY; 578] *Opposite*: hate **3** *v* **swallow**, fall for, believe, be fooled by, take in, accept, eat up (*informal*) [➡ FORGET, FORGIVE, AND ACCEPT; 748] *Opposite*: disbelieve

larcenist *n* [➡ CRIMINALS; 821]

larcenous *adj* [➡ ILLEGAL; 816]

larceny *n* **theft**, robbery, burglary, stealing, thieving, appropriation, pilfering, breaking and entering, shoplifting, embezzlement [➡ CRIMES; 817]

larch *type of* **evergreen tree** [➡ EVERGREEN AND CONIFEROUS TREES; 1029]

lard *type of* **cooking fat and oil** [➡ FATS AND OILS; 1173]

larder *n* **pantry**, storeroom, room, cupboard, store, cold storage, cold-room (*UK*), cold store (*UK*) [➡ STORES AND STORAGE BUILDINGS; 1088]

large **1** *adj* **big**, great big, huge, fat, bulky, hefty, outsized, enormous, great (*UK*) [➡ LARGE; 1193] *Opposite*: tiny **2** *adj* **well-built**, big, larger, outsized, overweight, fat, chubby, obese, corpulent, heavy, portly, generously proportioned [➡ BUILD; 477] *Opposite*: small **3** *adj* **sizable**, considerable, not inconsiderable, great, greater, significant, substantial, generous, copious [➡ MANY, MUCH, LARGE AMOUNT; 117] *Opposite*: insignificant

large amount *n* [➡ MANY, MUCH, LARGE AMOUNT; 117]

large-hearted *adj* **generous**, giving, kind, kindly, kind-hearted, warm-hearted, soft-hearted, big-hearted, understanding, sympathetic [➡ GENEROSITY AND KINDNESS; 495] *Opposite*: mean-spirited

large intestine *part of* **digestive tract** [➡ THE DIGESTIVE TRACT; 709]

largely *adv* **mainly**, in the main, mostly, for the most part, principally, basically, chiefly, on the whole, by and large, generally [➡ MAINLY AND PRIMARILY; 140] *Opposite*: particularly

largeness *n* **size**, bulk, expansiveness, mass, extent, scale [➡ LARGE; 1193] *Opposite*: smallness

larger-than-life *adj* **flamboyant**, confident, impressive, exaggerated, overstated, blown up, attention-grabbing, arresting, over-the-top (*informal*) [➡ TOO MUCH; 119] *Opposite*: understated

large-scale *adj* **major**, important, significant, extensive, sweeping, comprehensive, across-the-board, all-encompassing, far-reaching, wide-ranging, broad, wholesale, global, international, intercontinental, worldwide, leading, detailed [➡ IMPORTANT; 194] *Opposite*: small-scale

largesse **1** *n* **generosity**, charity, liberality, munificence, benevolence, bounty (*literary*) [➡ GENEROSITY AND KINDNESS; 495] *Opposite*: miserliness **2** *n* **gifts**, handouts, aid, assistance, donations, favors, money [➡ GIFTS; 438]

larghetto *type of* **musical term** [➡ MUSICAL TERMS; 912]

largo *type of* **musical term** [➡ MUSICAL TERMS; 912]

lari *type of* **currency** [➡ CURRENCIES; 798]

lariat *n* **lasso**, noose, loop, rope, tether, riata [➡ FASTENERS, LINKS, AND NETWORKS; 1247]

lark **1** *n* **game**, joke, prank, caper, shines, high jinks (*informal*), laugh (*UK informal*) [➡ JOKES AND TEASING; 674] **2** *type of* **songbird** [➡ SONGBIRDS; 1003]

lark around *v* **fool around**, play the fool, mess around (*informal*), goof around (*informal*), goof off (*informal*), have a lark (*UK*) [➡ JOKES AND TEASING; 674] *Opposite*: behave

larva *type of* **stage of insect development** [➡ INSECT STAGES; 1020]

larynx *part of* **respiratory system** [➡ RESPIRATORY ORGANS; 715]

lasagna *type of* **pasta** [➡ PASTA; 1180]

lasagne *type of* **cooked dish** [➡ PREPARED DISHES; 1170]

lascivious *adj* [➡ MORALLY BAD OR IMPROPER; 775]

laser *type of* **optical instrument** [➡ OPTICAL INSTRUMENTS; 1124]

lash **1** *n* **hit**, whip, blow, stroke, whiplash, belt (*informal*) [➡ PHYSICAL ATTACK AND PUNISHMENT; 415] **2** *n* **cat-o'-nine-tails**, cat, whip, belt, switch, strap, horsewhip [➡ BLUNT INSTRUMENTS AND WHIPS; 1158] **3** *v* **smash**, pound, beat, impact, bump, slam [➡ CONTACT: IMPACT; 413] **4** *v* **criticize**, lambaste, upbraid, condemn, lay into (*informal*), castigate (*formal*), slate (*UK*) [➡ ACCUSE, BLAME, AND CRITICIZE; 641] **5** *v* **whip**, flog, flay, thrash, strike, hit, beat, punish, belt (*informal*) [➡ PHYSICAL ATTACK AND PUNISHMENT; 415] **6** *v* **shake**, jerk, thrash, twitch, thump, whisk, beat [➡ MOVE SOMETHING: ON THE SPOT; 336] **7** *v* **tie**, bind, fasten, knot, secure, rope, tie up, fix, attach [➡ FASTEN, LINK, AND JOIN; 408] *Opposite*: loosen

lash out **1** *v* **attack**, strike out, hit out, let fly, flail around, go for, set on, lay into (*informal*) [➡ PHYSICAL ATTACK AND PUNISHMENT; 415] **2** *v* **criticize**, lambaste, berate, hit out, tear into, round on, lay into (*informal*), take apart (*informal*) [➡ ACCUSE, BLAME, AND CRITICIZE; 641]

lass *n* **girl**, miss, young woman, daughter, teenager, adolescent, mademoiselle [➡ FEMALE PERSON; 933] *Opposite*: lad

lassitude *n* **weariness**, listlessness, apathy, lethargy, fatigue, tiredness, exhaustion, inertia, ennui, jadedness, inactivity, torpor [➡ TIRED, ASLEEP, AND UNCONSCIOUS; 738] *Opposite*: vigor

lasso *n* **noose**, rope, lariat, loop, tether, riata [➡ FASTENERS, LINKS, AND NETWORKS; 1247]

last **1** *adj* **previous**, latter, past, preceding, latest, former [➡ BEFORE, FIRST, AND PRECEDING; 163] *Opposite*: next **2** *adj* **final**, end, ultimate, closing, concluding, finishing [➡ AFTER, LAST, AND FOLLOWING; 165] *Opposite*: first **3** *adj* **remaining**, surviving, extant, final, sole remaining [➡ MORE AND EXCESS; 124] *Opposite*: original **4** *v* **keep**, stay fresh, keep going, carry on, go on, last out [➡ CONTINUE TO EXIST; 17]

last-ditch *adj* **final**, last-minute, one last, eleventh-hour, desperate, last [➡ AFTER, LAST, AND FOLLOWING; 165]

lasting *adj* **permanent**, long-lasting, long-term, lifelong, eternal, durable, enduring, fixed, undying, unchanging, ongoing, continuing [➡ PERMANENCE: WITHOUT END; 94] *Opposite*: temporary

last leg *n* [➡ ENDS AND DEPARTURES; 54]

lastly *adv* **finally**, last of all, to finish, to conclude, to end, in conclusion, to sum up [➡ SUMMARIZING EXPRESSIONS; 622] *Opposite*: firstly

last minute *n* **eleventh hour**, final moment, last ditch, last gasp [➡ PROMPTNESS: LATE; 100]

last-minute *adj* **eleventh-hour**, final, last, last-ditch, emergency, rushed [➡ PROMPTNESS: LATE; 100] *Opposite:* early

last nail in the coffin *n* [➡ ENDS AND DEPARTURES; 54]

last name *n* **surname**, family name, name, patronymic, matronymic [➡ NAME AND DESCRIBE; 665] *Opposite:* given name

last out *v* **survive**, live, go on, continue, persist, keep on, keep up, carry on, persevere [➡ CONTINUE TO EXIST; 17] *Opposite:* fail

last resort *n* **last chance**, only hope, last-ditch effort, fallback [➡ ENDS AND DEPARTURES; 54]

last straw *n* **final straw**, limit, end, breaking point, finishing touch, deciding factor, end of the line, end of the road, coup de grâce [➡ ENDS AND DEPARTURES; 54]

lat *type of* **currency** [➡ CURRENCIES; 798]

latch *n* **fastener**, handle, bolt, key, bar, clasp [➡ FASTENERS, LINKS, AND NETWORKS; 1247]

latch onto (*informal*) **1** *v* **fall in with**, befriend, take to, get in good with, take up with, hit on (*slang*) [➡ ESTABLISHING RELATIONSHIPS WITH OTHERS; 974] *Opposite:* abandon **2** *v* **take up**, discover, get into, pursue, go in for [➡ LIKE, LOVE, VALUE, AND ENJOY; 578] *Opposite:* give up

late 1 *adj* **delayed**, tardy, overdue, belated, unpunctual, last-minute [➡ PROMPTNESS: LATE; 100] *Opposite:* early **2** *adj* **later**, delayed, deferred, postponed [➡ PROMPTNESS: LATE; 100] *Opposite:* early **3** *adj* **late-night**, nighttime, evening, twilight [➡ TIMES OF DAY; 87] *Opposite:* early **4** *adj* **dead**, much lamented, late lamented, deceased (*formal*), dear departed (*formal or literary*) [➡ DEAD AND DYING; 925] *Opposite:* living **5** *adj* **last-minute**, eleventh-hour, last-ditch, final [➡ PROMPTNESS: LATE; 100] *Opposite:* early **6** *adv* **recently**, until recently, lately, of late, latterly [➡ AFTER, LAST, AND FOLLOWING; 165] **7** *adv* **belatedly**, unpunctually, tardily, behind schedule, behind time [➡ PROMPTNESS: LATE; 100] *Opposite:* early **8** *adv* **at the last minute**, too late, finally, at the end, in the nick of time, late on (*UK*) [➡ PROMPTNESS: LATE; 100] *Opposite:* early **9** *adv* **at night**, in the small hours, in the dead of night, in the evening, after dark, in the wee hours [➡ PAST; 84] *Opposite:* early

*See Compare and Contrast at **dead**.*

latecomer *n* **straggler**, dawdler, laggard [➡ LAZY OR UNSUCCESSFUL PEOPLE; 948]

lately *adv* **recently**, of late, these days, latterly, currently, just, just now, today, up till now, until now [➡ PAST; 84]

latency *n* **dormancy**, inexpression, inactivity, potential, expectancy, underdevelopment, unconsciousness, invisibility [➡ IMPERCEPTIBLE; 26] *Opposite:* expression

lateness *n* **tardiness**, unpunctuality, delay, belatedness, deferment, postponement [➡ PROMPTNESS: LATE; 100] *Opposite:* promptness

latent 1 *adj* **hidden**, covert, buried, concealed, invisible, imperceptible, unseen, undiscovered [➡ IMPERCEPTIBLE; 26] *Opposite:* manifest **2** *adj* **dormant**, inactive, lurking, embryonic, underlying, suppressed, undeveloped [➡ SECRET AND UNKNOWN; 179]

later *adv* **afterward**, later on, in a while, shortly, soon, presently (*formal or literary*), anon (*archaic or literary*) [➡ FUTURE; 86]

lateral *adj* **side**, on the side, adjacent, crossways, horizontal, cross, sideways [➡ ORIENTATION AND ALIGNMENT; 1223]

lateral thinking *n* [➡ PSYCHOLOGY AND THE MIND; 769]

latest *adj* **newest**, up-to-the-minute, hottest, state-of-the-art, modern, up-to-date, cutting-edge [➡ NEW, MODERN; 166] *Opposite:* outdated

latex 1 *n* **sap**, fluid, liquid [➡ PARTS OF TREES AND PLANTS; 1026] **2** *type of* **plastic** [➡ PLASTICS; 1134]

lathe *type of* **general tool** [➡ HAND TOOLS; 1119]

lather 1 *n* **foam**, suds, froth, bubbles, soapsuds [➡ FOAM; 1273] **2** *n* (*informal*) **agitation**, anxiety, panic, dither, pother, flap (*informal*), tizzy (*informal*), state (*informal*) [➡ FEAR AND PANIC; 543] *Opposite:* calmness **3** *v* **soap**, lather up, soap up [➡ FROTH AND EFFERVESCE; 389]

latin *type of* **world music** [➡ MUSIC, SONGS, AND SINGING; 907]

latitude 1 *n* **parallel**, position, location, coordinate [➡ NAVIGATION; 1141] *Opposite:* longitude **2** *n* **leeway**, freedom, autonomy, liberty, room, scope, opportunity, rope, breathing space, room for maneuver, space (*informal*) [➡ FREEDOM AND LIBERTY; 208]

latke *type of* **processed potato** [➡ FRUIT AND VEGETABLES; 1176]

latte *type of* **coffee** [➡ DRINKS; 1187]

latter *adj* **last**, final, concluding, second, end, later [➡ AFTER, LAST, AND FOLLOWING; 165] *Opposite:* former

latter-day *adj* **modern**, modern-day, contemporary, current [➡ PRESENT; 85]

latterly 1 *adv* **recently**, lately, up till now, currently, of late, in recent times, these days, until now [➡ PAST; 84] *Opposite:* formerly **2** *adv* **at the end**, in the last part, toward the end, finally [➡ AFTER, LAST, AND FOLLOWING; 165] *Opposite:* initially

lattice *n* **frame**, mesh, framework, web, matrix, trellis, wood frame, open-mesh frame [➡ FASTENERS, LINKS, AND NETWORKS; 1247]

laud *v* **praise**, applaud, extol, acclaim, glorify, sing the praises of, praise to the skies, speak well of, pay tribute to, rave about, wax lyrical (*literary*) [➡ PRAISE AND ENCOURAGE; 647] *Opposite:* criticize

laudable *adj* **admirable**, praiseworthy, creditable, worthy, commendable, impressive, meritorious [➡ ADMIRABLE AND COMMENDABLE; 185] *Opposite:* despicable

laudatory *adj* **admiring**, congratulatory, praising, sycophantic, complimentary, approving, approbatory, acclamatory [➡ EXPRESSING RESPECT AND APPROVAL; 637] *Opposite:* damning

laugh 1 *v* **chuckle**, chortle, guffaw, giggle, hoot, snort, cackle, titter, double up, roll in the aisles, snicker, fall down laughing, snigger, have hysterics (*informal*), laugh your head off (*informal*), lose it (*informal*) [➡ LAUGHTER; 649] *Opposite:* cry **2** *n* **chuckle**, chortle, guffaw, giggle, hoot, snort, cackle, titter, snigger [➡ LAUGHTER; 649] **3** *n* (*informal*)

fun, joke, teasing, giggle, prank, game, hoot (*slang*) [➡JOKES AND TEASING; 674]

laughable *adj* **pathetic**, pitiful, derisory, inadequate, ridiculous, absurd, preposterous, ludicrous, embarrassing, unsatisfactory, unimpressive [➡INAPPROPRIATE AND UNSUITABLE; 224] *Opposite*: impressive

laugh at *v* **sneer**, jeer, mock, make fun of, tease, deride, disparage, ridicule, poke fun at, scoff at, put down (*informal*) [➡JOKES AND TEASING; 674] *Opposite*: respect

See Compare and Contrast at **ridicule**.

laughingstock *n* **figure of fun**, joke, fool, buffoon, butt, clown (*informal*) [➡JOKES AND TEASING; 674]

laugh off *v* **downplay**, trivialize, shrug off, joke about, dismiss, discount, take no notice of, ignore, pass over [➡FORGET, FORGIVE, AND ACCEPT; 748] *Opposite*: face up to

laugh out of court *v* **ridicule**, mock, make fun of, scoff at, pour scorn on, poke fun at, laugh at, deride, scorn [➡JOKES AND TEASING; 674]

laughter *n* **happiness**, amusement, hilarity, mirth, merriment, glee, enjoyment [➡LAUGHTER; 649] *Opposite*: sadness

laugh your head off *v* [➡LAUGHTER; 649]

launch 1 *v* **dispatch**, send off, send, shoot, fire, release, loose, let fly, unleash, discharge (*formal*) [➡DISPATCH AND SEND; 333] 2 *v* **open**, start, begin, commence, initiate, instigate, get underway, embark on, depart, start on (*informal*) [➡START AN ACTION; 260] 3 *v* **introduce**, present, inaugurate, unveil, reveal, bring out [➡INSTITUTE AND INAUGURATE; 348] 4 *v* **hurl**, throw, toss, fling, propel, spring, jump, leap [➡MOVE SOMETHING THROUGH THE AIR; 334] 5 *n* **presentation**, introduction, promotion, unveiling, inauguration [➡BEGINNINGS; 53] 6 *type of* **motor vessel** [➡SHIPS AND BOATS; 1150]

launching pad *n* **take off point**, springboard, start, base, foundation [➡BEGINNINGS; 53]

launch into *v* **embark on**, get going on, break into, begin, commence, start on (*informal*) [➡START AN ACTION; 260]

launch out (*UK*) *v* **start**, start afresh, start anew, start out, begin, give it a try [➡START AN ACTION; 260] *Opposite*: finish

launch vehicle *type of* **spacecraft** [➡SPACE VEHICLES; 1063]

launder 1 *v* **wash**, clean, dry-clean, valet [➡CLEAN AND POLISH; 403] 2 *v* **legalize**, filter, clean, decontaminate [➡STEAL AND ROB; 426]

laundry *n* **washing**, wash, clean wash, dirty wash, clean washing (*UK*), dirty washing (*UK*) [➡CLOTHES AND ACCESSORIES; 864]

laundry room *type of* **room in the home** [➡TYPES OF ROOMS; 1097]

laurel 1 *type of* **shrub or bush** [➡BUSHES AND SHRUBS; 1027] 2 *type of* **evergreen tree** [➡EVERGREEN AND CONIFEROUS TREES; 1029]

laurels *n* **success**, glory, honor, achievements [➡SUCCESS; 82]

lava *type of* **stone** [➡STONES, ROCKS, AND BOULDERS; 1057]

lavatory *type of* **room in public buildings** [➡TYPES OF ROOMS; 1097]

lavender 1 *type of* **shrub or bush** [➡BUSHES AND SHRUBS; 1027] 2 *type of* **purple** [➡COLORS; 1224]

lavish 1 *adj* **abundant**, plentiful, sumptuous, copious, prolific, fulsome, rich, generous, unstinting, bountiful (*literary*) [➡MANY, MUCH, LARGE AMOUNT; 117] *Opposite*: scanty 2 *adj* **extravagant**, profligate, wasteful, unrestrained, excessive, prodigal, over-the-top (*informal*), immoderate (*formal*) [➡TOO MUCH; 119] *Opposite*: frugal 3 *v* **heap**, pour, smother, cover, load, shower, bestow (*formal*) [➡GIVE TOO MUCH AND OVERBURDEN; 437] *Opposite*: deprive

lavishness 1 *n* **abundance**, richness, generosity, fulsomeness, profusion, copiousness [➡MANY, MUCH, LARGE AMOUNT; 117] *Opposite*: scantiness 2 *n* **extravagance**, profligacy, wastefulness, excess, prodigality, immoderation (*formal*) [➡TOO MUCH; 119] *Opposite*: frugality

law 1 *n* **rule**, regulation, decree, act, edict, ruling, commandment, directive, bylaw [➡THE LAW AND LEGAL AUTHORITY; 814] 2 *n* **principle**, theory, formula, rule [➡WAYS OF DOING THINGS; 294]

law-abiding *adj* **honest**, straight, upright, upstanding, peaceable, decent, just, respectable [➡MORALLY GOOD; 774] *Opposite*: crooked (*informal*)

law and order 1 *n* **law enforcement**, keeping the peace, order, orderliness, policing [➡THE LAW AND LEGAL AUTHORITY; 814] *Opposite*: crime 2 *n* **stability**, harmony, peace, peace and quiet, peacefulness, cooperation [➡PEACEFULNESS AND GENTLENESS; 214] *Opposite*: unrest

lawbreaker *n* **criminal**, felon, wrongdoer, convict, offender, delinquent [➡CRIMINALS; 821]

law enforcement agency *n* [➡THE POLICE, ARREST, AND PRETRIAL PROCEEDINGS; 818]

law enforcement officer *n* [➡THE POLICE, ARREST, AND PRETRIAL PROCEEDINGS; 818]

lawful *adj* **legal**, legalized, legitimate, official, endorsed, allowed, permitted, permissible, decriminalized, licit, legit (*slang*) [➡LEGAL AND LEGITIMATE; 815] *Opposite*: unlawful

See Compare and Contrast at **legal**.

lawgiver *n* **lawmaker**, legislator, policymaker [➡PEOPLE IN LAW COURTS; 820]

lawless *adj* **unruly**, anarchic, uncontrolled, unregulated, ungovernable, anarchistic, uncontrollable [➡DISORDER AND CHAOS; 245] *Opposite*: law-abiding

lawlessness *n* **anarchy**, chaos, disorder, unruliness, mayhem (*informal*) [➡CHAOS AND UPROAR; 51] *Opposite*: order

lawmaker *n* **lawgiver**, legislator, policymaker [➡PEOPLE IN LAW COURTS; 820]

lawn 1 *type of* **fabric from plants** [➡FABRICS; 1132] 2 *part of* **garden** [➡GARDENS; 1074]

lawn bowling *type of* **target ball game** [➡HOBBIES, GAMES, AND SPORTS; 875]

lawsuit *n* **court case**, proceedings, litigation, process [➡TRIAL, PUNISHMENT, AND LEGAL OUTCOMES; 819]

lawyer *n* **legal representative**, attorney, notary, trial lawyer, public prosecutor, solicitor (*UK*), barrister (*UK*) [➡ PEOPLE IN LAW COURTS; 820]

lax 1 *adj* **lenient**, soft, tolerant, permissive, accepting, nonjudgmental [➡ PERMIT AND ALLOW; 669] 2 *adj* **negligent**, slack, careless, slipshod, sloppy, indifferent, laid-back (*informal*) [➡ NEUTRALITY AND INDIFFERENCE; 553] *Opposite*: strict 3 *adj* **limp**, loose, flaccid, relaxed, floppy, slack [➡ MALLEABLE AND ELASTIC; 1212] *Opposite*: tense

laxity 1 *n* **leniency**, tolerance, permissiveness, softness, forbearance (*formal*) [➡ GENEROSITY AND KINDNESS; 495] *Opposite*: severity 2 *n* **carelessness**, negligence, sloppiness, slackness, indifference, laxness [➡ NEUTRALITY AND INDIFFERENCE; 553] *Opposite*: vigilance

laxness *see* **laxity**

lay 1 *v* **put down**, place, rest, put, arrange, leave, set, position [➡ MOVE SOMETHING: DOWNWARD; 329] *Opposite*: pick up 2 *adj* **untrained**, amateur, nonprofessional, uninitiated, unqualified [➡ UNSKILLED; 529] *Opposite*: professional

lay about (*UK*) *v* **strike out**, hit out, flail around, hit, strike, beat, set on, attack, lay into, thrash about (*UK*) [➡ PHYSICAL ATTACK AND PUNISHMENT; 415]

layabout *n* **slacker**, shirker, timewaster, idler, lounger, lazybones (*informal*), slouch (*informal*), bum (*informal*), goldbrick (*informal*) [➡ LAZY OR UNSUCCESSFUL PEOPLE; 948] *Opposite*: go-getter (*informal*)

lay a wager *v* [➡ GAMBLE AND TAKE RISKS; 466]

lay bare *v* **reveal**, explain, show, expose, display, bare, uncover [➡ CAUSE TO APPEAR; 5] *Opposite*: cover up

lay before *v* **set before**, present, put before, submit, set out, show, propose, suggest [➡ PROFFER AND HAND OVER; 431]

lay bets *v* **bet**, gamble, wager, stake, money on, lay a wager [➡ GAMBLE AND TAKE RISKS; 466]

lay claim to *v* **appropriate**, claim, stake a claim to, demand, insist on, request, annex, assume, take possession of, take over [➡ REQUEST AND DEMAND; 663] *Opposite*: renounce

lay down 1 *v* **put down**, lay aside, put aside, give up, surrender, let fall, set down [➡ MOVE SOMETHING: DOWNWARD; 329] *Opposite*: take up 2 *v* **decree**, set down, put down, formulate, rule, dictate, ordain (*formal*) [➡ REQUEST AND DEMAND; 663]

lay down the law *v* **order**, boss, order around, boss around, dictate to, throw your weight around, call the tune [➡ REQUEST AND DEMAND; 663]

layer 1 *n* **coating**, coat, sheet, film, deposit, cover [➡ COVERS AND COATINGS; 1246] 2 *n* **level**, tier, seam, gradation, stratum (*formal*) [➡ DEGREE AND EXTENT; 110]

layette *n* **baby clothes**, babywear, baby linen, nursery equipment [➡ GARMENTS AND OUTFITS; 865]

lay in *v* **store**, acquire, hoard, save, stock up, stockpile, squirrel, put by, salt away, gather [➡ GET; 420]

lay into 1 *v* (*informal*) **criticize**, attack, lambaste, get at, round on, hit out, lash out (*informal*), tell off (*informal*) [➡ ACCUSE, BLAME, AND CRITICIZE; 641] 2 *v* **hit**, attack, beat, thump, thrash, strike, set on [➡ PHYSICAL ATTACK AND PUNISHMENT; 415]

lay it on *v* **exaggerate**, embroider, embellish, overdo, overstate, lay it on thick, boast, ham it up, lay on with a shovel (*informal*), pile on (*UK*), lay it on with a trowel (*UK*) [➡ BOAST; 616] *Opposite*: understate

lay it on the line (*informal*) *v* **be honest**, be direct, be blunt, be straight, be clear, give somebody an ultimatum, be frank, not beat around the bush, tell it how it is (*informal*), come clean (*informal*) [➡ EXPLAIN AND CLARIFY; 610] *Opposite*: lie

lay it on thick *v* [➡ CLAIM, INSIST, AND EMPHASIZE; 614]

lay it on with a trowel (*informal*) *v* [➡ CLAIM, INSIST, AND EMPHASIZE; 614]

lay off 1 *v* **dismiss**, suspend, sack, let go, discharge (*formal*), make redundant (*UK*) [➡ REVOKE STATUS; 459] *Opposite*: hire 2 *v* (*informal*) **stop**, cease, desist, discontinue, cut out, call a halt [➡ STOP ACTING; 264] *Opposite*: continue

layoff 1 *n* **dismissal**, downsizing, streamlining, sacking (*informal*), discharge (*formal*), redundancy (*UK*), rationalization (*UK*) [➡ WORK-RELATED ACTIVITIES; 834] 2 *n* **unemployment**, career break, inactivity, rest, joblessness [➡ WORK-RELATED ACTIVITIES; 834] *Opposite*: employment

lay of the land (*informal*) *n* **general state**, general situation, prospect, state of affairs, picture, look of things, state of things, circumstances, appearance, how the land lies, how things stand [➡ SITUATIONS; 71]

lay on *v* **provide**, supply, make available, organize, cater [➡ EQUIP AND SUPPLY; 435]

lay out 1 *v* **explain**, present, describe, outline, set out, detail [➡ EXPLAIN AND CLARIFY; 610] 2 *v* **design**, plan, arrange, organize, prepare, draft [➡ POSITION SOMETHING; 325]

layout *n* **plan**, design, arrangement, outline, draft, blueprint [➡ DRAWINGS, CHARTS, AND TABLES; 594]

layover *n* **stopover**, stop, halt, break, stay [➡ PAUSES AND PHASES; 56]

lay to rest *v* **bury**, entomb, inter (*formal*) [➡ BURIAL AND PREPARATION FOR BURIAL; 929]

lay waste *v* [➡ DESTRUCTION AND DEMOLITION; 359]

laze 1 *v* **idle**, lounge, loaf, bask, relax, lie, hang around, kill time [➡ LACK OF ACTIVITY OR MOTION; 342] 2 *v* **laze around**, bask, loaf around, lie around, lounge around, loll around, take it easy, waste time, twiddle your thumbs [➡ LACK OF ACTIVITY OR MOTION; 342]

laze around *see* **laze**

lazily *adv* **idly**, indolently, slowly, languidly, sluggishly, lethargically, slothfully (*formal*) [➡ LIFELESS, LAZY, AND UNENTHUSIASTIC; 506] *Opposite*: energetically

laziness *n* **idleness**, lethargy, indolence, languor, sluggishness, sloth, slothfulness (*formal*) [➡ LIFELESS, LAZY, AND UNENTHUSIASTIC; 506] *Opposite*: energy

lazy *adj* **indolent**, idle, lethargic, languid, sluggish, slothful [➡ LIFELESS, LAZY, AND UNENTHUSIASTIC; 506] *Opposite*: energetic

lazybones (*informal*) *n* **layabout**, slacker, shirker, loafer, idler, parasite, slouch (*informal*), bum (*informal*), goldbrick (*informal*), lollygagger (*dated*) [➡ LAZY OR UNSUCCESSFUL PEOPLE; 948] *Opposite*: worker

LBO *n* [➡ BUSINESS ACTIVITIES AND PHENOMENA; 794]

lea (*literary*) *n* **meadow**, field, pasture, grassland [➡ THE COUNTRYSIDE AND OUTDOOR SPACES; 1071]

leach *v* **leak**, filter, percolate, trickle, seep [➡ LIQUID EMISSION; 370]

lead 1 *v* **guide**, indicate, direct, escort, pilot, precede, steer, front, head, conduct, usher [➡ ACCOMPANY AND FOLLOW; 337] *Opposite*: follow 2 *v* **be in charge of**, run, control, command, direct, manage, head, steer [➡ CAUSE TO HAPPEN; 31] 3 *v* **be in the lead**, take the lead, be the forerunner, be in front, have an advantage [➡ SUCCEED AND WIN; 79] *Opposite*: trail 4 *n* **leader**, spearhead, leading light, trailblazer, groundbreaker, frontrunner (*informal*) [➡ IMPORTANT OR FAMOUS PEOPLE; 893] 5 *n* **advantage**, advance, start, head start, flying start [➡ SOURCE OF HAPPINESS, PLEASURE, OR IMPROVEMENT; 209] 6 *n* **precedent**, example, style, pattern, model, practice [➡ INDICATIONS, SIGNS, AND WARNINGS; 68] 7 *n* **clue**, tip, indication, information, hint, pointer [➡ EVIDENCE AND PROOF; 69] 8 *n* **leash**, chain, tether, restraint, rope, halter, string [➡ FASTENERS, LINKS, AND NETWORKS; 1247] 9 *type of* **metal** [➡ METALS; 1276] 10 *adj* **principal**, chief, main, central, prime, top [➡ MOST IMPORTANT AND MAIN; 193]

See Compare and Contrast at **guide**.

lead astray *v* **mislead**, misinform, lead on, hoodwink, delude, deceive, trick, seduce, corrupt, lead down the garden path [➡ DECEPTION AND LIES; 660]

lead down the garden path *v* [➡ DECEPTION AND LIES; 660]

leaden 1 *adj* **gray**, steely, ashen, dull, grim, dark, gloomy, somber, cloudy, overcast [➡ CLOUDY AND RAINY WEATHER; 1052] *Opposite*: bright 2 *adj* **heavy**, ponderous, weighty, sluggish, stodgy (*informal*) [➡ WEIGHT: HEAVY; 1206] *Opposite*: light 3 *adj* **sluggish**, labored, slow, dragging, crawling, plodding, unhurried, leisurely [➡ MOVING SLOWLY; 105] *Opposite*: quick 4 *adj* **lifeless**, dull, dreary, flat, monotonous, boring, uninteresting, unexciting, forced, stodgy (*informal*) [➡ BORING AND UNINTERESTING; 234] *Opposite*: lively

leader 1 *n* **guide**, director, organizer, mentor, guru, adviser [➡ IMPORTANT OR FAMOUS PEOPLE; 893] 2 *n* **spearhead**, leading light, trailblazer, groundbreaker, lead, forerunner, frontrunner (*informal*) [➡ IMPORTANT OR FAMOUS PEOPLE; 893] 3 *n* **head**, chief, manager, superior, principal, boss, supervisor, kingpin (*informal*), top dog (*informal*) [➡ BOSSES AND MANAGEMENT; 965]

leadership *n* **management**, control, guidance, headship, direction, governance (*formal*) [➡ RELATIONSHIP TO ANOTHER; 973]

lead glass *type of* **glass** [➡ GLASS; 1136]

lead-in *n* **introduction**, preamble, preface, prelude, preliminary, way in, opener [➡ BEGINNINGS; 53] *Opposite*: conclusion

leading *adj* **prominent**, foremost, important, principal, chief, top, primary [➡ MOST IMPORTANT AND MAIN; 193] *Opposite*: secondary

leading article (*UK*) *n* **editorial**, opinion, view, comment, piece, leader (*UK*) [➡ NEWSPAPERS AND MAGAZINES; 605]

leading edge *n* **forefront**, cutting edge, sharp end, vanguard, avant-garde, van, front, lead, spearhead, fore (*literary*) [➡ BEGINNINGS; 53]

leading light *n* **big name**, top name, star, superstar, celebrity, luminary, expert, authority, leader, top dog (*informal*), kingpin (*informal*), VIP (*informal*) [➡ IMPORTANT OR FAMOUS PEOPLE; 893] *Opposite*: nobody

lead off *v* **begin**, start, start off, commence, open, set in motion, set the ball rolling, get going, kick off (*informal*) [➡ START AN ACTION; 260] *Opposite*: end

lead on *v* **entice**, lure, tempt, seduce, attract, cajole, persuade [➡ APPEAL TO AND AROUSE INTEREST; 575]

lead the way *v* **blaze a trail**, set a trend, originate, break new ground, break through, spearhead [➡ START AN ACTION; 260]

lead time *n* **notice**, advance notice, warning, notification, foreknowledge, run-up (*UK*) [➡ FUTURE; 86]

lead to *v* **cause**, bring about, make possible, initiate, set in motion, produce, result in [➡ CAUSE TO HAPPEN; 31]

lead up to 1 *v* **prepare for**, prepare the way, prepare the ground, sow the seeds, gear up, make ready, precede [➡ PREPARE FOR ACTION; 289] 2 *v* **approach**, get around to, come to, get to [➡ START AN ACTION; 260]

leaf 1 *n* **foliage**, greenery, sprig, spray, frond, shoot [➡ PARTS OF TREES AND PLANTS; 1026] 2 *n* **page**, sheet, folio, side [➡ PARTS OF BOOKS AND DOCUMENTS; 593] 3 *n* **sheet**, foil, plate, lamina, film, coating, patina [➡ COVERS AND COATINGS; 1246] 4 *n* **flap**, foldout, projection, section, piece [➡ EXTREMITIES OF PHYSICAL OBJECTS; 1250]

leafcutter ant *type of* **ant** [➡ ANTS; 1014]

leaflet *n* **booklet**, brochure, pamphlet, flier, handbill, handout, circular [➡ ADVERTISING AND PUBLICITY; 604]

leaf through *v* **look through**, flick through, skim, browse, flip, scan, riffle [➡ LOOKING AND LOOKS; 700]

leafy *adj* **green**, verdant, lush, luxuriant, rank [➡ VEGETATION; 1025] *Opposite*: bare

league *n* **association**, group, union, confederation, club, alliance, coalition, federation, confederacy [➡ GROUPS WITH A COMMON INTEREST; 938]

leak 1 *n* **escape**, seepage, leakage, outflow, drip, trickle [➡ EMIT AND EMANATE; 361] 2 *n* **disclosure**, betrayal, giveaway, revelation, release [➡ INFORM, ANNOUNCE, AND ISSUE; 611] 3 *v* **seep**, escape, pour out, trickle, drip, ooze [➡ LIQUID EMISSION; 370] 4 *v* **disclose**, reveal, give away, betray, uncover, let slip [➡ BETRAY CONFIDENCES AND GOSSIP; 618]

leakage *n* **leak**, escape, seepage, outflow, drip, trickle [➡ EMIT AND EMANATE; 361]

leak out *v* **emerge**, get out, slip out, come out, come to light, get around [➡ APPEAR AND EMERGE; 3]

leakproof *adj* **watertight**, waterproof, sealed, hermetic, rainproof, showerproof, damp-proof [➡ IN GOOD REPAIR; 1232] *Opposite*: leaky

leaky 1 *adj* **leaking**, holey, sieve-like, dripping, drippy, permeable [➡ IN BAD REPAIR; 1234] *Opposite*: watertight 2 *adj* (*informal*) **unsecured**, unsafe, indiscreet, loose, lax [➡ DANGEROUS; 236] *Opposite*: secure

lean 1 *v* **bend**, bend over, bend forward, incline, tilt, tip, slant, bow, slope [➡ ASSUME A POSITION; 317] 2 *v* **rest**, prop, support, place, put [➡ MOVE SOMETHING: INTO A NEW POSITION OR OVERTURN; 330] 3 *v* **tend**, incline, be disposed, favor, prefer, like better [➡ LIKE, LOVE, VALUE, AND ENJOY; 578] 4 *adj* **thin**, slender, slim, wiry, sinewy, spare, trim, bony, angular [➡ BUILD; 477] *Opposite*: stout

See Compare and Contrast at **thin**.

leaning *n* **inclination**, tendency, bent, affinity, preference, proclivity, propensity, liking, penchant, predilection (*formal*) [➡ LIKE, LOVE, VALUE, AND ENJOY; 578] *Opposite*: aversion (*formal*)

lean on 1 *v* **depend on**, rely on, trust, count on [➡ CERTAINTY; 561] 2 *v* (*informal*) **intimidate**, pressurize, put pressure on, oblige, coerce, induce, require [➡ CAUSE OR COMPEL TO ACT; 271]

lean-to *type of* **outbuilding** [➡ ANCILLARY BUILDINGS; 1080]

leap 1 *v* **jump**, bound, dive, soar, fly, hurdle, bounce, hop, spring, vault [➡ BOUNCE, UNDULATE, AND VIBRATE; 308] 2 *v* **increase**, rise, shoot up, go up, jump, mount, ascend, surge [➡ CHANGE OF INTENSITY: MORE; 394] *Opposite*: drop 3 *n* **bound**, jump, dive, spring, hop [➡ BOUNCE, UNDULATE, AND VIBRATE; 308] 4 *n* **rise**, increase, jump, hike, climb, spike, surge [➡ CHANGE OF INTENSITY: MORE; 394] *Opposite*: drop

leap at *v* **jump at**, seize, grab, clutch, accept, go for (*informal*) [➡ TAKE SOMETHING AWAY; 425] *Opposite*: balk

leapfrog 1 *v* **jump**, vault, leap, bound, spring [➡ BOUNCE, UNDULATE, AND VIBRATE; 308] 2 *v* **advance**, shoot ahead, get ahead, pull ahead, catapult, jump ahead, make strides, get on (*UK*) [➡ MOVE PAST, INTO, OR THROUGH SOMETHING; 331] 3 *v* **overtake**, pass, leave behind, outstrip, leave standing, step over [➡ BEAT AND DEFEAT; 80] 4 *v* **circumvent**, evade, avoid, sidestep, bypass, dodge [➡ NOT DO AND REFUSE TO DO; 274]

leap out at *v* **stand out**, stick out, jump out, hit somebody in the face, impact, strike [➡ APPEAR AND EMERGE; 3] *Opposite*: hide

leap year *type of* **time period** [➡ TIMES OF YEAR; 88]

learn 1 *v* **study**, absorb, pick up, acquire, hit the books (*informal*), cram (*informal*) [➡ STUDYING; 844] 2 *v* **find out**, hear, discover, realize, gather, understand, come to know, ascertain (*formal*) [➡ LEARN AND DISCOVER; 762]

learned *adj* **erudite**, educated, scholarly, academic, cultured, well-read, well-educated, knowledgeable [➡ KNOWLEDGE AND WISDOM; 558] *Opposite*: uneducated

learner *n* **beginner**, apprentice, student, pupil, novice, greenhorn, initiate [➡ UNSKILLED PEOPLE; 530] *Opposite*: expert

learning *n* **knowledge**, education, erudition, scholarship, culture, wisdom, book learning [➡ KNOWLEDGE AND WISDOM; 558] *Opposite*: ignorance

See Compare and Contrast at **knowledge**.

lease *v* **rent**, rent out, hire, hire out, let, charter, lease out, let out [➡ LEND, LEASE, AND BORROW; 428]

lease out *see* **lease**

leash 1 *n* **lead**, chain, tether, string, rope, restraint, halter [➡ FASTENERS, LINKS, AND NETWORKS; 1247] 2 *type of* **herd** [➡ GROUPS OF ANIMALS; 993]

least *adj* **smallest**, slightest, tiniest, minimum [➡ FEW, LITTLE, SMALL AMOUNT; 120] *Opposite*: most

leastways (*informal*) *adv* **in any case**, anyway, at least, at any rate, in spite of [➡ ALTHOUGH, NEVERTHELESS, AND DESPITE; 169]

leastwise (*informal*) *adv* **in any case**, anyway, at least, at any rate, in spite of [➡ ALTHOUGH, NEVERTHELESS, AND DESPITE; 169]

leather 1 *n* [➡ TEXTILES AND THREADS; 1131] 2 *type of* **fabric from animals** [➡ FABRICS; 1132]

leather

◆ *types of leather*
buckskin, calf, calfskin, chamois, hide, kid, morocco, patent leather, pigskin, rawhide, sheepskin, suede

leave 1 *v* **go away**, depart, go, run off, abscond, disappear, exit, vamoose (*slang*), quit (*archaic*) [➡ LEAVE AND GO AWAY; 8] *Opposite*: stay 2 *v* **put down**, set down, put, put away, place, leave behind [➡ POSITION SOMETHING; 325] *Opposite*: remove 3 *v* **set aside**, allow, give, permit, assign, allot, hand over [➡ PERMIT AND ALLOW; 669] 4 *v* **result in**, cause, bring about, effect (*formal*) [➡ CAUSE TO HAPPEN; 31] 5 *v* **bequeath**, pass on, hand down, donate, legate, consign, entrust, will [➡ BEQUEATH AND BEQUESTS; 432] 6 *v* **abandon**, desert, renounce, forsake, ditch (*informal*), dump (*informal*), drop (*informal*) [➡ REFUSING OR REJECTING RELATIONS; 975] 7 *v* **delay**, defer, put off, avoid, hold off, put aside [➡ SHIRK AND DELAY; 273] 8 *n* **sabbatical**, time off, leave of absence, time out, vacation, holiday (*UK*) [➡ PERIODS OF REST; 91] 9 *n* (*formal*) **permission**, consent, authority, authorization, dispensation [➡ PERMIT AND ALLOW; 669]

leave alone *v* **let be**, let be, leave in peace, leave well enough alone, pay no attention, ignore, disregard, leave somebody to himself/herself, get off somebody's back (*slang*), get off somebody's case (*slang*) [➡ NOT PAY ATTENTION; 764] *Opposite*: harass

leave be *v* **let alone**, let be, leave in peace, leave well enough alone, pay no attention, ignore, disregard, leave somebody to himself/herself, get off somebody's back (*slang*), get off somebody's case (*slang*) [➡ REFUSING OR REJECTING RELATIONS; 975] *Opposite*: harass

leave behind 1 *v* **overtake**, outstrip, outpace, leave in the dust, surpass, leave standing, shake off, outdo, move ahead of, get ahead of, outrun [➡ BEAT AND DEFEAT; 80] *Opposite*: fall behind 2 *v* **put behind you**, escape, evade, get away from, put to one side, put away, dismiss, forget, free yourself of, shed [➡ FORGET, FORGIVE, AND ACCEPT; 748] 3 *v* **abandon**, get rid of, cast off, leave, forget, forsake, desert, shed, walk out on (*informal*) [➡ GET RID OF SOMETHING; 451] *Opposite*: retain

leave in peace *v* **leave alone**, let be, let alone, leave somebody to himself/herself, go away, leave well enough alone, pay no attention, ignore, disregard, leave somebody to his/her own devices, get off somebody's back (*slang*), get off somebody's case (*slang*) [➡ NOT PAY ATTENTION; 764] *Opposite*: harass

leave much to be desired *v* **be unsatisfactory**, disappoint, let down, not make the grade, fall short, not be up to scratch (*informal*) [➡ FAIL OR BE UNSUCCESSFUL; 75] *Opposite:* pass muster

leave no stone unturned *v* **do all you can**, do your utmost, pull out all the stops, spare no effort, try everything, move heaven and earth, try your best, stop at nothing [➡ HARD WORK OR EFFORT; 298]

leave of absence *n* **sabbatical**, time off, time out, leave [➡ PERIODS OF REST; 91]

leave off *v* **stop**, desist, cease, refrain, discontinue [➡ STOP ACTING; 264] *Opposite:* carry on

leave out *v* **omit**, exclude, count out, ignore, overlook, except (*formal*) [➡ NOT PAY ATTENTION; 764] *Opposite:* include

leave-taking (*literary*) *n* **farewell**, goodbye, sendoff, departure, separation, parting, adieu, exit, going, valediction (*formal*) [➡ ENDS AND DEPARTURES; 54] *Opposite:* greeting

leavings *n* **leftovers**, scraps, remnants, remains, castoffs, orts, dregs [➡ REMAINDER AND REMAINDERS; 125]

lecherous *adj* **lewd**, lustful, lascivious, libidinous, lusty, randy (*informal*) [➡ MORALLY BAD OR IMPROPER; 775]

lectern *n* **bookstand**, reading stand, reading desk, stand, bookrest [➡ FURNITURE; 858]

lecture 1 *n* **talk**, address, sermon, speech, homily, oration, discourse, allocution (*formal*) [➡ ONE-WAY COMMUNICATION; 49] 2 *n* **reprimand**, dressing-down, scolding, tongue-lashing, telling-off (*informal*) [➡ CRITICISMS AND ANGRY OUTBURSTS; 50] 3 *v* **teach**, address, instruct, talk, hold forth, pontificate [➡ INSTRUCT AND TEACH; 609] 4 *v* **harangue**, criticize, scold, reprove, censure, reprimand, upbraid, tell off (*informal*), castigate (*formal*) [➡ ACCUSE, BLAME, AND CRITICIZE; 641]

lecture hall *n* [➡ BUILDINGS FOR PUBLIC ENTERTAINMENT; 1084]

lecturer *n* **speaker**, public speaker, speechmaker, orator, spokesperson, debater [➡ EDUCATORS; 840]

lecture room *n* [➡ BUILDINGS FOR PUBLIC ENTERTAINMENT; 1084]

lecture theater *n* [➡ BUILDINGS FOR PUBLIC ENTERTAINMENT; 1084]

LED *type of* **light** [➡ LIGHT; 1164]

lederhosen *type of* **pants** [➡ GARMENTS AND OUTFITS; 865]

ledge 1 *n* **shelf**, sill, niche, ridge, rack, bookshelf, mantelpiece, window ledge, windowsill, bracket [➡ SUPPORTS AND BASES; 1255] 2 *n* **outcrop**, ridge, sill, shelf, foothold, projection, protrusion, protuberance, bulge, extension [➡ EXTREMITIES OF PHYSICAL OBJECTS; 1250] 3 *n part of* **window** [➡ WINDOWS; 1100]

ledger *n* **book**, account book, record book, record, register, archive, journal [➡ RECORDS; 585]

lee *n* **shelter**, cover, protection, shadow, shade [➡ SAFE BUILDINGS OR PLACES; 1093]

leech *n* [➡ SUPERFICIAL OR INSINCERE PEOPLE; 951]

leek *type of* **vegetable** [➡ FRUIT AND VEGETABLES; 1176]

leer 1 *v* **smirk**, ogle, eye, sneer, stare, make eyes [➡ FACIAL EXPRESSIONS AND BLUSHING; 651] 2 *n* **sneer**, grimace, smirk, evil eye, stare [➡ FACIAL EXPRESSIONS AND BLUSHING; 651]

leery *adj* **suspicious**, wary, doubting, doubtful, circumspect, cautious, untrusting, watchful [➡ UNCERTAINTY; 559]

lees *n* **dregs**, remains, leftovers, remnants [➡ REMAINDER AND REMAINDERS; 125]

leeward *adj* **protected**, sheltered, shielded [➡ GENERAL LOCATIONS; 158]

leeway *n* **scope**, flexibility, margin, freedom, latitude, breathing space, breathing room [➡ FREEDOM AND LIBERTY; 208]

left-hand *adj* **left**, leftward, port [➡ GENERAL LOCATIONS; 158] *Opposite:* right-hand

left-handed *adj* **counterclockwise**, right to left, circular, round, helical, spiral, anticlockwise (*UK*) [➡ DIRECTION OF MOTION; 345] *Opposite:* right-handed

leftie (*informal*) *n* [➡ PHILOSOPHICAL AND POLITICAL THINKERS; 781]

leftism *n* [➡ PHILOSOPHIES AND BELIEFS; 780]

leftist *n* [➡ PHILOSOPHICAL AND POLITICAL THINKERS; 781]

leftover *n* **relic**, hangover, vestige, remnant, remainder, residue, legacy, inheritance [➡ REMAINDER AND REMAINDERS; 125]

leftovers *n* **scraps**, remains, what's left, leavings, remnants, orts, dregs, lees [➡ REMAINDER AND REMAINDERS; 125]

left-wing *adj* **progressive**, reformist, leftist [➡ STYLES AND SYSTEMS OF GOVERNMENT; 806] *Opposite:* right-wing

left-winger *n* **progressive**, reformist, leftist [➡ PHILOSOPHICAL AND POLITICAL THINKERS; 781] *Opposite:* right-winger

leg 1 *n* **limb**, foreleg, hindleg, peg (*informal*), pins (*informal*) [➡ PARTS OF THE BODY: LEG AND FOOT; 694] 2 *n* **pole**, foot, support, stand, base, prop, rod, shaft, brace, bracket [➡ SUPPORTS AND BASES; 1255] 3 *n* **stage**, phase, lap, step, part, section, segment [➡ PAUSES AND PHASES; 56] 4 *type of* **cut** [➡ TYPES AND CUTS OF MEAT; 1177] 5 *part of* **garment** [➡ PARTS OF A GARMENT; 870]

leg

◆ *parts of a leg or foot*

ankle, big toe, calf, haunch, heel, instep, knee, lap, little toe, shin, sole, thigh, toe, toenail

legacy 1 *n* **bequest**, inheritance, heirloom, heritage, birthright, gift, money [➡ BEQUEATH AND BEQUESTS; 432] 2 *n* **relic**, hangover, vestige, remnant, remainder, residue, remains, consequence, leftover [➡ REMAINDER AND REMAINDERS; 125]

legal *adj* **lawful**, permissible, permitted, allowed, authorized, aboveboard, legitimate, official, licit, rightful, legalized, decriminalized [➡ LEGAL AND LEGITIMATE; 815] *Opposite:* illegal

Compare and Contrast: *legal, lawful, decriminalized, legalized, legitimate, licit*

CORE MEANING: describes something that is permitted, recognized, or required by law

legal permitted, recognized, or required by law; *lawful* a less common word meaning legal; *decriminalized* no longer categorized as a criminal offense; *legalized* previously categorized as illegal and now declared legal; *legitimate* complying with the law, or under the law; *licit* a rarely used word meaning legal.

legal eagle (*slang*) *n* **lawyer**, advocate, counsel, attorney, barrister (*UK*), solicitor (*UK*) [➡ PEOPLE IN LAW COURTS; 820]

legalese *n* **jargon**, cant, mumbo jumbo (*informal*), gobbledygook (*informal*) [➡ MEANINGLESS SPEECH OR WRITING; 676]

legality *n* **validity**, lawfulness, rightfulness, legitimacy [➡ LEGAL AND LEGITIMATE; 815]

legalization *n* **ratification**, authorization, certification, validation, endorsement [➡ TRIAL, PUNISHMENT, AND LEGAL OUTCOMES; 819] *Opposite*: criminalization

legalize *v* **decriminalize**, authorize, sanction, allow, permit, validate, enact, decree [➡ TRIAL, PUNISHMENT, AND LEGAL OUTCOMES; 819] *Opposite*: prohibit

legalized *adj* [➡ LEGAL AND LEGITIMATE; 815]

See Compare and Contrast at **legal**.

legate *n* **representative**, envoy, ambassador, emissary, diplomat, messenger [➡ REPRESENTATIVES AND PATRONS; 968]

legato *type of* **musical term** [➡ MUSICAL TERMS; 912]

legend 1 *n* **fable**, myth, tale, lore, folklore, fairy tale, folk tale [➡ THE ORAL TRADITION; 677] 2 *n* **star**, celebrity, big name, icon, personality, prodigy, superstar [➡ IMPORTANT OR FAMOUS PEOPLE; 893]

legendary 1 *adj* **fabled**, mythical, mythological, imaginary, fabulous [➡ FALSE AND UNREAL; 173] 2 *adj* **famous**, renowned, well-known, celebrated, great, illustrious, eminent [➡ KNOWN AND FAMOUS; 181]

legerdemain *n* [➡ SKILLS, TALENTS, AND ABILITIES; 526]

leggings *type of* **pants** [➡ GARMENTS AND OUTFITS; 865]

leggy *adj* [➡ BUILD; 477]

legible *adj* **clear**, readable, intelligible, decipherable, understandable, comprehensible [➡ CONCISE AND CLEAR; 202] *Opposite*: illegible

legion *n* **multitude**, host, team, crowd, throng, mass, gang, band, group [➡ GROUPS OF PEOPLE; 935]

legionnaire *n* [➡ MILITARY PERSONNEL; 828]

legislate *v* **enact**, pass, establish, lay down the law, decree, authorize, constitute (*formal*), promulgate (*formal*) [➡ TRIAL, PUNISHMENT, AND LEGAL OUTCOMES; 819]

legislation 1 *n* **lawmaking**, lawgiving, legislature, regulation [➡ THE LAW AND LEGAL AUTHORITY; 814] 2 *n* **laws**, legal code, body of law, bill, rule, guidelines, statute, decree, code, law [➡ THE LAW AND LEGAL AUTHORITY; 814]

legislative *adj* **lawmaking**, parliamentary, governmental, judicial, jurisdictive, statutory [➡ GOVERNMENT AND POLITICS; 805]

legislator *n* [➡ LEGISLATIVE BODIES AND LEGISLATION; 809]

legislature *n* **government**, parliament, administration, senate, assembly, council [➡ LEGISLATIVE BODIES AND LEGISLATION; 809]

leg it (*informal*) *v* [➡ RUN AWAY AND AVOID; 10]

legit (*slang*) 1 *adj* **legitimate**, lawful, legal, valid, rightful [➡ LEGAL AND LEGITIMATE; 815] *Opposite*: unlawful 2 *adj* **genuine**, sincere, real, valid, authentic, appropriate, reasonable [➡ TRUE AND REAL; 171] *Opposite*: spurious

legitimacy 1 *n* **legality**, lawfulness, validity, rightfulness, justice [➡ LEGAL AND LEGITIMATE; 815] 2 *n* **acceptability**, rightfulness, correctness [➡ CORRECT AND FAULTLESS; 182] 3 *n* **sincerity**, genuineness, realness, authenticity, validity, fairness [➡ TRUE AND REAL; 171]

legitimate 1 *adj* **lawful**, rightful, valid, legal [➡ LEGAL AND LEGITIMATE; 815] *Opposite*: unlawful 2 *adj* **reasonable**, acceptable, justifiable, logical, valid, sensible, recognized [➡ CORRECT AND FAULTLESS; 182] *Opposite*: unreasonable 3 *adj* **genuine**, sincere, real, valid, authentic, appropriate, reasonable [➡ TRUE AND REAL; 171] *Opposite*: spurious

See Compare and Contrast at **legal**.

legitimately 1 *adv* **legally**, lawfully, rightfully, validly [➡ LEGAL AND LEGITIMATE; 815] *Opposite*: unlawfully 2 *adv* **reasonably**, acceptably, justifiably, logically, validly, sensibly [➡ CORRECT AND FAULTLESS; 182] *Opposite*: unreasonably

legroom *n* **room**, space, freedom, elbowroom (*informal*) [➡ FREEDOM AND LIBERTY; 208]

legume *n* **leguminous plant**, pulse, pea, bean [➡ PEAS AND BEANS; 1189]

leguminous plant *n* [➡ PEAS AND BEANS; 1189]

legwarmer *n* **sock**, stocking, legging, gaiter, puttee, anklewarmer [➡ ACCESSORIES, MILLINERY, AND LINGERIE; 867]

legwork (*informal*) *n* **research**, preparation, homework, groundwork, spadework, dirty work [➡ HARD WORK OR EFFORT; 298]

lei *n* **garland**, wreath [➡ ORNAMENTS AND DECORATIONS; 1248]

leisure *n* **spare time**, time off, leisure time, time out, freedom, relaxation, rest, ease, R & R, vacation, free time, holiday (*UK*) [➡ LEISURE AND RECREATION; 874] *Opposite*: work

leisured *adj* **rich**, wealthy, affluent, moneyed, propertied, well-off, well-to-do, prosperous, comfortable, well-heeled (*informal*) [➡ WEALTH AND WEALTHY; 891] *Opposite*: poor

leisurely *adj* **unhurried**, easy, relaxed, restful, relaxing, slow, gentle, laid-back (*informal*) [➡ MOVING SLOWLY; 105] *Opposite*: frantic

leisure pursuit *n* [➡ LEISURE AND RECREATION; 874]

leisure time *n* [➡ PERIODS OF REST; 91]

leisurewear *n* **sportswear**, casualwear, casual clothes, mufti, casuals (*UK*) [➡ GARMENTS AND OUTFITS; 865]

leitmotif *n* **motif**, theme, strand, element, topic, subject, subject matter [➡ SUBJECT AREAS; 768]

lek *type of* **currency** [➡ CURRENCIES; 798]

lekvar *type of* **preserve** [➡ SUGAR AND PRESERVES; 1184]

lemma *part of* **flower** [➡ FLOWERS; 1032]

lemming 1 *n* **conformist**, sheep, imitator, follower, copycat (*informal*) [➡ LAZY OR UNSUCCESSFUL PEOPLE; 948] *Opposite:* nonconformist 2 *type of* **rodent** [➡ RODENTS; 989]

lemon 1 *n* (*informal*) **failure**, dud (*informal*), nonstarter (*informal*), washout (*informal*), flop (*informal*) [➡ FAILURE; 77] *Opposite:* winner 2 *type of* **citrus fruit** [➡ FRUIT AND VEGETABLES; 1176] 3 *type of* **yellow** [➡ COLORS; 1224]

lemonade *n* [➡ DRINKS; 1187]

lemon curd *type of* **preserve** [➡ SUGAR AND PRESERVES; 1184]

lemongrass *type of* **herb** [➡ HERBS AND SPICES; 1175]

lemon sole *type of* **flatfish** [➡ OCEAN FISH; 1009]

lemony *adj* **lemon-flavored**, lemon, citrus [➡ TASTE; 703] *Opposite:* sweet

lemon yellow *type of* **yellow** [➡ COLORS; 1224]

lempira *type of* **currency** [➡ CURRENCIES; 798]

lemur *type of* **primate** [➡ PRIMATES; 988]

lend 1 *v* **loan**, advance, give, offer [➡ LEND, LEASE, AND BORROW; 428] *Opposite:* borrow 2 *v* **provide**, offer, give, impart, add, inject, contribute, afford (*formal*), bestow (*formal*) [➡ GIVE AND PROVIDE; 430] *Opposite:* take away

lend a hand *v* **help**, help out, give somebody a hand, do your bit, assist, pull your weight, do your part, chip in (*informal*) [➡ HELP; 293] *Opposite:* hinder

lend an ear *v* **listen**, pay attention, hang on somebody's words, listen up (*slang*) [➡ LISTEN AND LISTENERS; 708]

lender *n* **giver**, moneylender, financier, creditor, investor, savings and loan, bank, building society (*UK*) [➡ PEOPLE INVOLVED IN FINANCE; 804]

length 1 *n* **distance**, span, measurement, extent, dimension, size, interval, stretch [➡ LENGTH: LONG; 1197] 2 *n* **duration**, time, timespan, extent [➡ PERIODS OF TIME; 90] 3 *n* **piece**, strip, segment, section, bit, quantity, amount, part, chunk [➡ AMOUNTS OF SOLID OR SEMISOLID; 115]

lengthen *v* **grow**, increase, extend, elongate, stretch, pull out, draw out, prolong, drag out [➡ CHANGE OF SIZE: BIGGER; 392] *Opposite:* shorten

lengthiness *n* [➡ LENGTH: LONG; 1197]

lengthwise 1 *adv* **lengthways**, along, end to end, sideways, laterally [➡ ORIENTATION AND ALIGNMENT; 1223] *Opposite:* endwise 2 *adv* **lengthways** [➡ ORIENTATION AND ALIGNMENT; 1223]

lengthy *adj* **long**, long-lasting, extensive, prolonged, protracted, extended, drawn-out, overlong, interminable, long-winded [➡ HAPPENING SLOWLY; 106] *Opposite:* brief

lenience *n* **clemency**, leniency, mercy, compassion, humanity, tolerance, indulgence, kindness, forgiveness, mildness, moderation, forbearance (*formal*) [➡ GENEROSITY AND KINDNESS; 495] *Opposite:* severity

leniency *n* **clemency**, lenience, mercy, compassion, humanity, tolerance, indulgence, kindness, forgiveness, mildness, moderation, forbearance (*formal*) [➡ GENEROSITY AND KINDNESS; 495] *Opposite:* severity

lenient *adj* **compassionate**, merciful, humane, tolerant, indulgent, kind, forgiving, mild, temperate, moderate, soft, light, forbearing (*formal*) [➡ GENEROSITY AND KINDNESS; 495] *Opposite:* severe

Leninism *n* [➡ PHILOSOPHIES AND BELIEFS; 780]

Leninist *adj* [➡ PHILOSOPHIES AND BELIEFS; 780]

lens 1 *part of* **camera** [➡ PHOTOGRAPHY AND PHOTOGRAPHIC EQUIPMENT; 1122] 2 *part of* **eye** [➡ THE EYE; 698]

lens cap *part of* **camera** [➡ PHOTOGRAPHY AND PHOTOGRAPHIC EQUIPMENT; 1122]

lentil *type of* **pulse** [➡ PEAS AND BEANS; 1189]

lentissimo *type of* **musical term** [➡ MUSICAL TERMS; 912]

lento *type of* **musical term** [➡ MUSICAL TERMS; 912]

Leo 1 *type of* **astrological sign** [➡ FATE, DESTINY, AND ASTROLOGY; 782] 2 *type of* **constellation** [➡ HEAVENLY BODIES; 1061]

Leo Minor *type of* **constellation** [➡ HEAVENLY BODIES; 1061]

leone *type of* **currency** [➡ CURRENCIES; 798]

leonine *adj* **impressive**, imposing, majestic, proud, dignified, magnificent [➡ EXTRAORDINARY: AMAZING; 204]

leopard *type of* **cat** [➡ FELINES; 983]

leper *n* **outcast**, untouchable, pariah, outsider, exile [➡ SOLITARY PEOPLE AND MISFITS; 942]

leprechaun *n* **sprite**, elf, imp, pixie, dwarf, gnome, goblin [➡ MYTHICAL BEINGS; 789]

lepton *type of* **elementary particle** [➡ ELEMENTARY PARTICLES; 1279]

Lepus *type of* **constellation** [➡ HEAVENLY BODIES; 1061]

lèse majesté *see* **lese majesty**

lese majesty 1 *n* **disrespect**, disregard, dishonor, contempt, disdain, irreverence, disparagement, belittlement [➡ ANTAGONISM; 552] *Opposite:* respect 2 *n* **treason**, high treason, sedition, betrayal, treachery, traitorousness, disloyalty, perfidy (*formal*), perfidiousness (*literary*) [➡ DECEPTION AND LIES; 660] *Opposite:* loyalty

lesion *n* **wound**, injury, cut, graze, scratch, laceration, abrasion, gash [➡ ILLNESSES AND DISORDERS; 732]

less 1 *adj* **a smaller amount of**, not as much of, a lesser amount of, a reduced amount of [➡ LESS; 126] *Opposite:* more 2 *prep* **minus**, take away, with a reduction of, excluding [➡ LESS; 126] *Opposite:* plus

lessen *v* **diminish**, decrease, decline, tail off, ease off, let up, die down, slacken, lower, cut, reduce, minimize [➡ CHANGE OF INTENSITY: LESS; 395] *Opposite:* increase

lesser *adj* **smaller**, slighter, minor, reduced [➡ INFERIORITY; 153] *Opposite:* greater

lesson 1 *n* **class**, lecture, session, tutorial, seminar, period [➡ CLASSES, COURSEWORK, AND EXAMINATIONS; 842] 2 *n* **example**, message, moral, warning, object lesson, experience, punishment [➡ MEANING; 690]

lest *conj* **in case**, for fear that, so as not to [➡ UNCERTAIN; 175]

let 1 *v* **allow**, give permission, permit, agree to, consent to, authorize, assent to, accede to, give leave (*formal*) [➡ PERMIT AND ALLOW; 669] *Opposite*: forbid 2 *v* **rent**, rent out, lease, lease out, hire, hire out, sublet, sublease [➡ LEND, LEASE, AND BORROW; 428] 3 *n* (*formal*) **problem**, difficulty, hindrance, impediment, complication, hurdle, hitch, stumbling block [➡ NUISANCES; 253] 4 *n* (*UK*) **lease**, tenancy, occupancy, rent, agreement, contract [➡ ACCOMMODATIONS; 855]

let alone *v* **leave be**, leave alone, let be, leave to yourself, leave in peace, leave off, get off somebody's back (*slang*) [➡ NOT PAY ATTENTION; 764] *Opposite*: pester

let be *v* **leave alone**, leave in peace, leave be, let alone, leave to yourself, leave off, leave well enough alone, pay no attention, ignore, disregard, leave somebody to himself/herself, leave somebody to his/her own devices, get off somebody's back (*slang*) [➡ NOT PAY ATTENTION; 764] *Opposite*: bother

let bygones be bygones *v* [➡ FORGET, FORGIVE, AND ACCEPT; 748]

let down 1 *v* **disappoint**, fail, abandon, betray, disillusion, desert, forsake [➡ UPSET, DISTRESS, AND HUMILIATE; 567] 2 *v* **lower**, drop, sink, let fall, move down, take down [➡ MOVE SOMETHING: DOWNWARD; 329] *Opposite*: raise 3 *v* **lengthen**, extend, let out, expand, enlarge [➡ CHANGE OF SIZE: BIGGER; 392] *Opposite*: take up 4 *v* (*UK*) **deflate**, empty, drain [➡ CHANGE OF SIZE: SMALLER; 393] *Opposite*: inflate

letdown *n* **disappointment**, anticlimax, failure, disillusionment, discouragement, washout (*informal*), flop (*informal*) [➡ FAILURE; 77] *Opposite*: success

let drop *v* **disclose**, reveal, divulge, let slip, let out, give away, leak [➡ BETRAY CONFIDENCES AND GOSSIP; 618]

let fly 1 *v* **throw**, fling, toss, hurl, pitch, launch, propel [➡ MOVE SOMETHING: THROUGH THE AIR; 334] 2 *v* **lose your temper**, hit the roof, explode, rage, see red (*informal*), go crazy (*informal*), go nuts (*slang*) [➡ GIVING VENT TO EMOTIONS; 679] *Opposite*: keep your cool

let go *v* **release**, liberate, set free, free, set loose, unchain, unleash, drop, relinquish, give up, surrender, discard, shed [➡ FREEDOM AND LIBERTY; 208] *Opposite*: retain

lethal *adj* **deadly**, fatal, mortal, poisonous, toxic, dangerous, harmful, disastrous, destructive, ruinous [➡ DANGEROUS; 236]

See Compare and Contrast at **deadly**.

lethally *adv* **fatally**, mortally, terminally, gravely, severely, seriously, incurably, critically, acutely, dangerously, disastrously [➡ CRITICALLY AND SERIOUSLY; 134] *Opposite*: slightly

lethargic *adj* **sluggish**, tired, weary, lackluster, exhausted, lazy, languid, indolent, slow, dull, lifeless, listless [➡ TIRED, ASLEEP, AND UNCONSCIOUS; 738] *Opposite*: energetic

lethargically *adv* **sluggishly**, tiredly, wearily, lazily, languidly, indolently, slowly, dully, lifelessly, listlessly [➡ TIRED, ASLEEP, AND UNCONSCIOUS; 738] *Opposite*: energetically

lethargy *n* **sluggishness**, tiredness, weariness, exhaustion, fatigue, lassitude, laziness, indolence, stupor, slowness, dullness, lifelessness, listlessness [➡ TIRED, ASLEEP, AND UNCONSCIOUS; 738] *Opposite*: energy

let in *v* **admit**, allow in, open the door to, show in, receive, let past, invite in, usher in, welcome in, take in [➡ PERMIT AND ALLOW; 669] *Opposite*: keep out

let in for (*informal*) *v* **involve in**, entangle in, ensnare in, mix up in, entrap in, catch up in, embroil in [➡ CAUSE OR COMPEL TO ACT; 271] *Opposite*: get out of

let in on *v* **make aware of**, tell, acquaint with, reveal to, disclose to, share, fill in on, inform of, put in the picture (*UK*), let into (*UK*) [➡ INFORM, ANNOUNCE, AND ISSUE; 611] *Opposite*: keep from

let into 1 *v* **allow into**, admit to, receive into, welcome into, take into, invite into, show into, usher into [➡ PERMIT AND ALLOW; 669] 2 *v* **admit to**, accept into, receive into, welcome into, take into, allow into, enlist into, induct into, enroll into [➡ PERMIT AND ALLOW; 669] 3 *v* (*UK*) **let in on**, fill in on, share, tell, inform of, notify of, acquaint with, disclose to, let know, reveal to [➡ INFORM, ANNOUNCE, AND ISSUE; 611] *Opposite*: keep from

let know *v* **tell**, inform, advise, alert, warn, update, put in the picture, acquaint, impart, pass on, apprise (*formal*) [➡ INFORM, ANNOUNCE, AND ISSUE; 611] *Opposite*: keep in the dark

let loose *v* **let out**, let go, set free, set loose, release, free, liberate, unchain, unleash, unfetter [➡ FREEDOM AND LIBERTY; 208] *Opposite*: confine

let off 1 *v* **excuse**, pardon, release, free, acquit, discharge (*formal*) [➡ FORGET, FORGIVE, AND ACCEPT; 748] *Opposite*: punish 2 *v* (*UK*) **fire**, explode, detonate, set off, shoot, put a match to, discharge (*formal*) [➡ FIRE, FLAMMABILITY, AND BURNING; 1165]

let off steam *v* [➡ GIVING VENT TO EMOTIONS; 679]

let on 1 *v* **admit**, disclose, divulge, reveal, declare, say, acknowledge, confess, tell, own up, avow (*formal*) [➡ ADMIT AND CONFESS; 615] *Opposite*: conceal 2 *v* **pretend**, make out, claim, profess, act, affect, fake [➡ PRETEND AND MIMIC; 60] *Opposite*: come clean (*informal*)

let out 1 *v* **emit**, give, utter, release, produce, give out, give off, give forth [➡ EMIT AND EMANATE; 361] *Opposite*: suppress 2 *v* **free**, let go, release, set free, let loose, liberate, set loose [➡ FREEDOM AND LIBERTY; 208] *Opposite*: keep in 3 *v* **enlarge**, expand, extend, widen, broaden, unfasten, release [➡ CHANGE OF SIZE: BIGGER; 392] *Opposite*: take in 4 *v* **let slip**, reveal, divulge, disclose, blurt out, give away, leak [➡ BETRAY CONFIDENCES AND GOSSIP; 618] *Opposite*: conceal

let-out (*UK*) *n* **loophole**, escape clause, way out, technicality, window, opening [➡ ADVANTAGES; 212]

let pass 1 *v* **ignore**, let go, overlook, let ride, pay no attention to, take no notice of, disregard, close your eyes to, turn a blind eye to, pass over, forgive, excuse [➡ NOT PAY ATTENTION; 764] *Opposite*: pick up on (*informal*) 2 *v* **let through**, let by, let past, stand aside for, make way for, clear the way for, admit, allow in, let in, usher in, welcome in [➡ PERMIT AND ALLOW; 669] *Opposite*: bar

let ride *v* **ignore**, close your eyes to, turn a blind eye to, let go, let pass, take no notice of, pay no attention to, pass over, disregard, forgive, excuse [➡ NOT PAY ATTENTION; 764] *Opposite*: stop

let slip 1 *v* **reveal**, disclose, divulge, give away, let out, blurt out, tell, leak, betray [➡BETRAY CONFIDENCES AND GOSSIP; 618] *Opposite*: hold back 2 *v* **let go**, lose, lose track of, lose sight of, take your eyes off, miss, waste [➡LOSE AND FORFEIT; 447]

letter 1 *n* **communication**, note, message, memo, dispatch, document, missive, epistle (*formal*), notelet (*UK*) [➡LETTERS AND WRITTEN MESSAGES; 584] 2 *n* **character**, symbol, sign, capital, capital letter, uppercase, lowercase [➡SYMBOLS, SIGNS, AND NUMBERS; 596]

letterbox (*UK*) *n* **mailbox**, post office box, maildrop, postbox (*UK*) [➡CONTAINERS, RECEPTACLES, AND PACKAGING; 1245]

letter card (*UK*) *n* **note card**, notelet (*UK*) [➡LETTERS AND WRITTEN MESSAGES; 584]

lettered *adj* **educated**, knowledgeable, cultured, cultivated, literary, literate, scholarly, erudite, learned, well-read, intellectual [➡LEVELS OF EDUCATION AND SOPHISTICATION; 894] *Opposite*: uneducated

lettering *n* **writing**, print, calligraphy, letters, inscription, script, words, characters, graffiti [➡WRITING; 583]

letter-perfect *adj* **exact**, precise, perfect, faultless, flawless, impeccable, consummate, prepared, word-perfect (*UK*) [➡EXACT; 203] *Opposite*: unprepared

letters *n* **literature**, culture, cultivation, knowledge, education, literacy, erudition [➡LEVELS OF EDUCATION AND SOPHISTICATION; 894]

let the cat out of the bag *v* **talk**, let on, tell a secret, tell, spill the beans (*informal*), blab (*informal*), squeal (*slang*) [➡BETRAY CONFIDENCES AND GOSSIP; 618] *Opposite*: keep mum (*informal*)

let through *v* **make way for**, stand aside for, clear the way for, let pass, let past, let by, admit, allow in, let in, usher in, welcome in [➡PERMIT AND ALLOW; 669] *Opposite*: block

lettuce *type of* **salad vegetable** [➡FRUIT AND VEGETABLES; 1176]

let up *v* **ease off**, ease, ease up, lessen, slacken, relent, relax, slow down, die down, tail off, abate (*formal or literary*) [➡CHANGE OF INTENSITY: LESS; 395] *Opposite*: intensify

letup (*informal*) *n* **respite**, break, rest, relief, interval, lull, relaxation, remission [➡PAUSES AND PHASES; 56] *Opposite*: intensification

let up on *v* **ease up on**, ease off on, slack off on, soften up on, spare, go easy on (*informal*) [➡TAKE CARE OF AND SPOIL; 300]

let your hair down *v* **relax**, have a good time, enjoy yourself, let yourself go, have fun, party (*informal*) [➡CHANGE OF MOOD AND COMPOSURE; 580]

let yourself go 1 *v* **unwind**, relax, mellow, let your hair down, throw caution to the winds, lighten up (*informal*), chill out (*slang*) [➡LEISURE AND RECREATION; 874] 2 *v* **give up**, lose heart, go downhill, lose your self-respect, go to the dogs (*informal*) [➡CHANGE OF MOOD AND COMPOSURE; 580]

leu *type of* **currency** [➡CURRENCIES; 798]

lev *type of* **currency** [➡CURRENCIES; 798]

levanter *type of* **wind** [➡WINDY AND STORMY WEATHER; 1053]

levee 1 *n* **embankment**, earthwork, bank, wall, rampart, protection [➡BARRIERS; 1113] 2 *n* **reception**, royal reception, royal function, court reception, court function [➡PARTIES, DANCES, AND CELEBRATIONS; 37]

level 1 *adj* **flat**, smooth, flat as a pancake, even, dead flat [➡PHYSICAL TEXTURE; 1222] *Opposite*: bumpy 2 *adj* **horizontal**, parallel with the ground, even, flat [➡ORIENTATION AND ALIGNMENT; 1223] 3 *adj* **equal**, neck and neck, side by side, close, near [➡EQUALITY; 154] 4 *n* **height**, altitude, stage, point, plane, echelon, rank [➡DEGREE AND EXTENT; 110] 5 *n* **intensity**, quantity, concentration, amount, degree, reading [➡DEGREE AND EXTENT; 110] 6 *type of* **measuring device** [➡MEASURING DEVICES; 1123] 7 *v* **flatten**, smooth, steamroll, press flat, even out [➡CHANGE OF SHAPE; 385] 8 *v* **aim**, direct, point, turn [➡MOVE SOMETHING UPWARD; 328] 9 *v* **demolish**, knock down, raze, blow up, raze to the ground [➡DESTRUCTION AND DEMOLITION; 359] *Opposite*: rebuild

level crossing (*UK*) *n* **railroad crossing**, grade crossing, crossing [➡BRIDGES, TUNNELS, CROSSINGS, AND JUNCTIONS; 1112]

level-headed *adj* **sensible**, calm, sound, even-tempered, reliable, equable, composed, rational, dispassionate, unperturbed [➡CONFIDENCE AND COMPOSURE; 499] *Opposite*: rash

level-headedness *n* **composure**, calmness, good sense, reliability, balance, equanimity (*formal*) [➡CONFIDENCE AND COMPOSURE; 499] *Opposite*: rashness

levelly 1 *adv* **calmly**, steadily, sensibly, evenly, equably, unemotionally [➡CONFIDENCE AND COMPOSURE; 499] *Opposite*: excitedly 2 *adv* **smoothly**, flatly, evenly [➡PHYSICAL TEXTURE; 1222] *Opposite*: unevenly

level off *v* **stabilize**, even out, settle, settle down, smooth out, steady [➡CHANGE; 372]

level out *v* **settle down**, stabilize, settle, even out, even up, balance out, steady [➡CHANGE; 372]

level pegging (*UK*) *n* **equality**, parity, draw, dead heat, same score, tie [➡EQUALITY; 154] *Opposite*: inequality

lever 1 *n* **handle**, control, regulator, knob [➡PARTS OF MACHINES AND TOOLS; 1118] 2 *part of* **engine** [➡PARTS OF AN ENGINE; 1144]

leverage 1 *n* **influence**, power, force, control, weight, pull (*informal*), clout (*informal*) [➡STRENGTH; 201] 2 *n* [➡OWE AND DESERVE; 465]

leveraged buyout *n* [➡BUSINESS ACTIVITIES AND PHENOMENA; 794]

leveret *type of* **young animal** [➡YOUNG ANIMALS; 977]

leviathan *n* **giant**, colossus, behemoth, monster [➡BIG THINGS; 1194]

levitate *v* **float**, rise up, ascend, drift up, soar, take off, fly up [➡GO UPWARD; 306] *Opposite*: sink

levitation *n* **defiance of gravity**, rising, raising, hovering, floating, flying [➡GO UPWARD; 306]

levity *n* **lightheartedness**, cheerfulness, humor, lightness, flippancy, jokiness [➡GOOD-TEMPERED AND HUMOROUS; 627] *Opposite*: gravity

levy 1 *v* **impose**, tax, collect, put, charge [➡FUNDS, PAYMENTS, AND CHARGES; 800] 2 *n* **tax**, rates, toll, duty, tariff, charge [➡TAX AND TAXATION; 802]

lewd *adj* **salacious**, obscene, crude, vulgar, indecent, rude [➡MORALLY BAD OR IMPROPER; 775]

lewdness *n* [➡ MORALLY BAD OR IMPROPER; 775]

lexical *adj* **verbal**, word, vocabulary, philological, etymological [➡ ASPECTS OF LANGUAGE; 682]

lexicon 1 *n* **dictionary**, monolingual dictionary, bilingual dictionary, foreign language dictionary, reference book [➡ BOOKS AND BOOKLETS; 590] **2** *n* **vocabulary**, vocabulary list, word list, lexis, idiolect, glossary, concordance [➡ LISTS AND SCHEDULES; 587]

lexis *n* [➡ ASPECTS OF LANGUAGE; 682]

liability 1 *n* **legal responsibility**, obligation, accountability, responsibility, charge [➡ RESPONSIBILITY; 170] **2** *n* **disadvantage**, problem, burden, millstone, jinx, disaster area (*informal*) [➡ PROBLEMS; 256]

liable 1 *adj* **legally responsible**, accountable, answerable, responsible [➡ RESPONSIBILITY; 170] *Opposite:* unaccountable **2** *adj* **likely**, apt, predisposed, prone [➡ THE WILL AND WILLINGNESS; 563] *Opposite:* unlikely

liaise *v* **act as a go-between**, communicate, link, bridge, mediate, coordinate, interact, get together with, network [➡ NEGOTIATION AND DEBATE; 46]

liaison *n* **link**, connection, contact, cooperation, relationship, association [➡ CONNECTIONS; 143]

liana *type of* **climber** [➡ CLIMBERS; 1033]

liar *n* **deceiver**, fast talker, perjurer, fibber (*informal*), storyteller (*informal*), dissembler (*formal*) [➡ PEOPLE WHO DECEIVE; 661]

libation 1 *n* (*humorous*) **drink**, alcoholic drink, potion, brew (*informal*), beverage (*formal*), potation (*literary*) [➡ DRINKS; 1187] **2** *n* **offering**, oblation, offertory, sacrifice, tribute [➡ RELIGIOUS CONCEPTS; 776]

libel 1 *n* **defamation**, vilification, slander, smear, denigration, character assassination [➡ INSULTS, ABUSE, AND SWEARING; 658] *Opposite:* praise **2** *v* **defame**, vilify, sully, tarnish, malign, slander [➡ INSULTS, ABUSE, AND SWEARING; 658] *Opposite:* praise

> *See Compare and Contrast at* **malign**.

libelous *adj* **defamatory**, vilifying, slanderous, unfounded [➡ INSULTS, ABUSE, AND SWEARING; 658] *Opposite:* admiring

liberal 1 *adj* **open-minded**, broad-minded, moderate, noninterventionist, freethinking, tolerant, laissez-faire [➡ POSITIVE INTELLECTUAL CHARACTERISTICS; 524] *Opposite:* narrow-minded **2** *adj* **generous**, copious, abundant, profuse, substantial, large [➡ MANY, MUCH, LARGE AMOUNT; 117] *Opposite:* meager

> *See Compare and Contrast at* **generous**.

liberalism *n* **tolerance**, broad-mindedness, open-mindedness, moderation, freethinking, laissez-faire [➡ POSITIVE INTELLECTUAL CHARACTERISTICS; 524] *Opposite:* narrow-mindedness

liberalize *v* **relax**, slacken, loosen, ease up, open, free up [➡ CHANGE OF INTENSITY: LESS; 395] *Opposite:* tighten

liberally *adv* **open-mindedly**, broad-mindedly, moderately, tolerantly [➡ POSITIVE INTELLECTUAL CHARACTERISTICS; 524] *Opposite:* narrow-mindedly

liberate *v* **release**, free, set free, unshackle, unfetter [➡ FREEDOM AND LIBERTY; 208]

liberated *adj* **unconventional**, open-minded, freethinking, modern, enlightened, progressive [➡ POSITIVE INTELLECTUAL CHARACTERISTICS; 524] *Opposite:* unenlightened

liberation *n* **freedom**, liberty, release, discharge, emancipation, deliverance (*formal*) [➡ FREEDOM AND LIBERTY; 208] *Opposite:* captivity

liberator *n* **deliverer**, savior, emancipator, releaser [➡ PEOPLE WHO ARE APPROVED OF; 955] *Opposite:* captor

libertine *n* [➡ PLEASURE-SEEKERS AND HEDONISTS; 886]

liberty 1 *n* **freedom**, independence, autonomy, emancipation, liberation [➡ FREEDOM AND LIBERTY; 208] *Opposite:* captivity **2** *n* **right**, freedom, authorization, authority, permission [➡ FREEDOM AND LIBERTY; 208] *Opposite:* suppression

libidinous *adj* **lustful**, lecherous, lusty, lascivious, salacious [➡ MORALLY BAD OR IMPROPER; 775]

Libra 1 *type of* **astrological sign** [➡ FATE, DESTINY, AND ASTROLOGY; 782] **2** *type of* **constellation** [➡ HEAVENLY BODIES; 1061]

library 1 *n* **collection**, archive, books, papers, records [➡ RECORDS; 585] **2** *n* **3** *type of* **room in public buildings** [➡ TYPES OF ROOMS; 1097]

librettist *n* **libretto writer**, lyricist, songwriter, writer, author [➡ WRITERS AND STYLES; 914]

libretto *n* [➡ MUSICAL TERMS; 912]

license 1 *v* **certify**, permit, allow, authorize, accredit [➡ PERMIT AND ALLOW; 669] **2** *n* **certificate**, authorization, pass, card, permit, ticket, warrant [➡ OFFICIAL DOCUMENTS; 586] **3** *n* **excess**, abandon, lawlessness, unrestraint, intemperance, immoderation (*formal*) [➡ PLEASURE-SEEKING AND EXCESS; 885] **4** *n* **freedom**, liberty, carte blanche, dispensation, authority, privilege, permission, right [➡ FREEDOM AND LIBERTY; 208]

licensed *adj* **approved**, qualified, certified, accredited, registered [➡ PERMIT AND ALLOW; 669]

license plate *type of* **external feature** [➡ EXTERNAL PARTS OF A VEHICLE; 1147]

licentiate *n* **license holder**, licensee, certified professional, qualified practitioner [➡ OWNERS; 446]

licentious *adj* **immoral**, degenerate, decadent, dissipated, depraved, corrupt [➡ MORALLY BAD OR IMPROPER; 775]

licentiousness (*formal*) *n* [➡ MORALLY BAD OR IMPROPER; 775]

lichen *type of* **fungus** [➡ MICROORGANISMS, FUNGI, AND ALGAE; 1023]

licit *adj* **lawful**, legitimate, legal, valid, right, proper, acceptable, permissible, admissible, accepted, permitted, admitted, authorized, sanctioned by law [➡ LEGAL AND LEGITIMATE; 815] *Opposite:* illegal

> *See Compare and Contrast at* **legal**.

lick (*informal*) *v* **defeat**, conquer, get the better of, overcome, thrash, clobber (*informal*), beat, cream (*slang*) [➡ BEAT AND DEFEAT; 80]

lickety-split (*informal*) *adv* **quickly**, fast, at high speed, swiftly, rapidly, speedily, quick as a wink, at a rate of knots (*UK*) [➡HAPPENING QUICKLY; 104] *Opposite:* sluggishly

licking (*informal*) *n* **trouncing**, thrashing, drubbing, hammering (*informal*), pasting (*informal*), walloping (*informal*) [➡BEAT AND DEFEAT; 80]

lick your lips *v* **relish**, salivate, drool, anticipate, await, look forward to, hope for, long for [➡PREDICT AND ANTICIPATE; 750]

licorice *type of* **confectionery** [➡CONFECTIONERY; 1182]

lid *n* **top**, cover, cap, closure [➡COVERS AND COATINGS; 1246]

lido (*UK*) **1** *n* **outdoor pool**, outdoor swimming pool, open-air pool, public swimming pool [➡URBAN OUTDOOR SPACES; 1072] **2** *n* **public beach**, bathing beach, beach [➡THE SEAS, OCEANS, AND SHORES; 1041]

lie 1 *v* **recline**, stretch out, lounge, lie down, slouch, laze, loll [➡ASSUME A POSITION; 317] **2** *v* **be positioned**, be arranged, be placed, be situated, sit, rest [➡EXIST IN A PLACE; 19] **3** *v* **remain**, rest, stay, be, stop, keep [➡CONTINUE TO EXIST; 17] **4** *v* **tell untruths**, perjure yourself, tell stories, be economical with the truth, fib (*informal*) [➡DECEPTION AND LIES; 660] *Opposite:* tell the truth **5** *n* **untruth**, falsehood, tall tale, fabrication, white lie, invention, fib (*informal*), story (*informal*) [➡DECEPTION AND LIES; 660] *Opposite:* truth

---

Compare and Contrast: *lie, untruth, falsehood, fabrication, fib, white lie*

CORE MEANING: something that is not true

lie a false statement made deliberately; *untruth* something that is presented as being true but is actually false; *falsehood* a lie or an untruth; *fabrication* an invented statement, story, or account devised with intent to deceive; *fib* (*informal*) an insignificant harmless lie; *white lie* a minor harmless lie, usually told to avoid hurting somebody's feelings.

---

lie around (*informal*) **1** *v* **laze**, bask, lounge around, sit around, laze around, flop around, loaf, relax, sprawl, flop about (*UK*) [➡LACK OF ACTIVITY OR MOTION; 342] **2** *v* **be scattered about**, be all over the place, clutter up the place, be distributed, litter, be dispersed, be spread, mess up the place (*informal*), lie about (*UK*) [➡EXIST IN A PLACE; 19]

lie back *v* **recline**, stretch out, lounge, sprawl, relax, rest, lie, loll, slump, flop [➡ASSUME A POSITION; 317]

lie down *v* **recline**, rest, stretch out, relax, lounge, sprawl [➡ASSUME A POSITION; 317] *Opposite:* stand up

lie in wait *v* **lurk**, hide, conceal yourself, ambush, prowl, stalk, wait in the shadows [➡LACK OF ACTIVITY OR MOTION; 342]

lieutenant *n* [➡SUBORDINATES AND ASSISTANTS; 966]

life 1 *n* **existence**, being, living [➡THE STAGES OF LIFE; 916] *Opposite:* death **2** *n* **lifetime**, life span, life cycle, life expectancy, natural life [➡THE STAGES OF LIFE; 916] **3** *n* **verve**, vivacity, animation, energy, excitement, soul, sparkle, kick (*informal*), go (*informal*), get-up-and-go (*informal*) [➡ENERGY AND ENTHUSIASM; 496]

life-and-death *adj* **critical**, crucial, vital, pivotal, para-

mount, momentous, fateful, life-or-death [➡IMPORTANT; 194] *Opposite:* unimportant

life and soul of the party *n* [➡PEOPLE WHO ARE APPROVED OF; 955]

lifeblood 1 *n* (*literary*) **blood**, sap, essence, life force, élan vital, vital spark, spark of life, vital signs [➡THE BLOOD AND CIRCULATION; 717] **2** *n* **essential**, essence, quintessence, sine qua non, necessity, basic [➡MOST IMPORTANT THING; 197]

lifeboat *type of* **motor vessel** [➡SHIPS AND BOATS; 1150]

life cycle *n* **life span**, development, maturation, growth [➡THE STAGES OF LIFE; 916]

life expectancy *n* **life span**, lifetime, allotted span, natural life [➡THE STAGES OF LIFE; 916]

life form *n* [➡LIVING THINGS AND LIVING; 976]

lifeguard *n* **rescuer**, beach attendant, swimming pool attendant, pool attendant, lifesaver (*informal*) [➡PEOPLE WHO GUARD AND PROTECT; 846]

lifeless 1 *adj* **dead**, unconscious, unresponsive, unmoving, inert, motionless, comatose, limp, insensible [➡TIRED, ASLEEP, AND UNCONSCIOUS; 738] *Opposite:* alive **2** *adj* **unexciting**, dull, uninteresting, tedious, listless, flat [➡BORING AND UNINTERESTING; 234] *Opposite:* animated

---

See Compare and Contrast at **dead**.

---

lifelessly *adv* **inertly**, motionlessly, insensibly, limply, unresponsively, unconsciously [➡TIRED, ASLEEP, AND UNCONSCIOUS; 738]

lifelessness *n* **motionlessness**, limpness, listlessness, unresponsiveness, inertness, unconsciousness, insensibility [➡TIRED, ASLEEP, AND UNCONSCIOUS; 738] *Opposite:* animation

lifelike *adj* **realistic**, natural, believable, convincing, credible, authentic, faithful [➡TRUE AND REAL; 171] *Opposite:* unrealistic

lifeline *n* **salvation**, link, help, support, helping hand, sustenance [➡KIND ACTIONS OR BEHAVIOR; 295]

lifelong *adj* **enduring**, all-time, permanent, ultimate, lasting, constant, lifetime (*informal*) [➡PERMANENCE: WITHOUT END; 94] *Opposite:* temporary

life of ease *n* [➡PLEASANT SITUATIONS; 74]

life of Riley *n* [➡PLEASANT SITUATIONS; 74]

life-or-death *see* **life-and-death**

life raft *type of* **small vessel** [➡SHIPS AND BOATS; 1150]

lifesaver (*informal*) *n* [➡SOLUTIONS; 215]

life-size *adj* **full-scale**, full-size, actual size [➡LARGE; 1193] *Opposite:* miniature

life span *n* **natural life**, lifetime, life cycle, life expectancy, life [➡THE STAGES OF LIFE; 916]

lifestyle *n* **way of life**, standard of living, existence, routine, life, daily life, everyday life, regime [➡LIFESTYLE; 881]

life-support system *part of* **spacecraft** [➡ SPACE VEHICLES; 1063]

life-threatening *adj* **dangerous**, serious, severe, grave, incurable, critical, acute, mortal, lethal, deadly, fatal [➡ DEADLY; 928]

lifetime 1 *n* **life**, time, life span, natural life, life cycle, life expectancy [➡ THE STAGES OF LIFE; 916] 2 *n* (*informal*) **eternity**, days, forever (*informal*), ages (*informal*) [➡ LONG PERIODS OF TIME; 92] 3 *n* **era**, generation, time, period, days, epoch [➡ EPOCHS AND ERAS; 89]

lifework *n* **product of working life**, result of working life, achievement, accomplishment, success, attainment, life's work (*UK*) [➡ SUCCESS; 82]

lift 1 *v* **winch up**, haul up, elevate, boost, raise, pick up [➡ MOVE SOMETHING: UPWARD; 328] 2 *v* **revoke**, cancel, take back, relax, rescind, repeal [➡ APOLOGIZE AND RETRACT; 683] *Opposite*: impose 3 *v* **lighten**, buoy up, brighten, elate, uplift, raise [➡ ENCOURAGE; 576] 4 *v* (*informal*) **steal**, walk off with, help yourself, pocket, take, plagiarize, filch (*informal*) [➡ STEAL AND ROB; 426] 5 *n* **boost**, revitalization, tonic, encouragement, kick (*informal*), high (*informal*), buzz (*informal*) [➡ TREATS; 210]

See Compare and Contrast at **raise**.

liftoff *n* [➡ BEGINNINGS; 53]

ligature 1 *n* **cord**, string, rope, tie, line, lace, thong, band [➡ FASTENERS, LINKS, AND NETWORKS; 1247] 2 *n* (*formal*) **bond**, connection, link, linkage, union, tie [➡ CONNECTIONS; 143]

light 1 *n* **glow**, beam, brightness, luminosity, daylight, illumination, radiance [➡ DESCRIBING LIGHT; 1228] *Opposite*: darkness 2 *n* [➡ LIGHT; 1164] 3 *adj* **bright**, sunny, sunlit, well-lit [➡ DESCRIBING LIGHT; 1228] *Opposite*: dark 4 *adj* **pastel**, subtle, neutral, fair, pale, muted [➡ DESCRIBING COLORS; 1226] *Opposite*: dark 5 *adj* **weightless**, buoyant, fluffy, insubstantial, frothy, wispy, feathery, flimsy [➡ WEIGHT: LIGHT; 1206] *Opposite*: heavy 6 *adj* **gentle**, delicate, soft, noiseless, featherlike, imperceptible [➡ IMPERCEPTIBLE; 26] *Opposite*: heavy 7 *adj* **nimble**, graceful, dainty, elegant, agile, sprightly [➡ AGILITY OF THE BODY; 476] *Opposite*: heavy 8 *adj* **carefree**, happy, cheerful, untroubled, joyful, blithe (*literary*) [➡ PLEASURE, EXCITEMENT, AND ELATION; 534] *Opposite*: heavy 9 *adj* **easy**, manageable, undemanding, simple, effortless, unexacting [➡ EASE AND SIMPLICITY; 200] *Opposite*: heavy 10 *adj* **entertaining**, lightweight, fun, frivolous, amusing, playful, undemanding [➡ FUNNY AND AMUSING; 216] *Opposite*: heavy 11 *v* **set alight**, set on fire, ignite, strike, set fire to [➡ FIRE, FLAMMABILITY, AND BURNING; 1165] *Opposite*: extinguish

light

♦ *types of lights*
arc lamp, chandelier, flashlight, floodlight, fluorescent lamp, footlights, headlight, hurricane lamp, lamp, lamppost, lantern, LED, light bulb, neon light, nightlight, penlight, searchlight, spotlight, standard lamp, streetlamp, streetlight, striplight, sunlamp, traffic light

light bulb *type of* **light** [➡ LIGHT; 1164]

light-colored *adj* **pale**, light, pastel, subtle, fair, neutral, blonde, blond [➡ DESCRIBING COLORS; 1226]

lighten 1 *v* **ease**, lessen, alleviate, reduce, lift, relieve, allay, assuage [➡ CHANGE OF INTENSITY: LESS; 395] 2 *v* **cheer up**, improve, lift, refresh, buoy up, relax, loosen up, lighten up (*informal*) [➡ CHANGE OF MOOD AND COMPOSURE; 580]

lighten up (*informal*) *v* **relax**, take it easy, cool it (*slang*), loosen up, unwind, chill out (*slang*) [➡ CHANGE OF MOOD AND COMPOSURE; 580]

lighter *type of* **motor vessel** [➡ SHIPS AND BOATS; 1150]

lightface *adj* **faint**, light [➡ PRINTING; 600] *Opposite*: boldface

light-fingered *adj* **thieving**, kleptomaniacal, larcenous, dishonest [➡ MORALLY BAD OR IMPROPER; 775]

light-footed *adj* **nimble**, graceful, dainty, elegant, agile [➡ AGILITY OF THE BODY; 476] *Opposite*: clumsy

lightheaded *adj* **dizzy**, faint, giddy, woozy, unsteady, groggy, wobbly (*informal*) [➡ ILL AND SICK; 740]

lighthearted 1 *adj* **carefree**, happy-go-lucky, happy, cheerful, cheery, relaxed, merry, buoyant, upbeat (*informal*), blithe (*literary*) [➡ PLEASURE, EXCITEMENT, AND ELATION; 534] *Opposite*: troubled 2 *adj* **enjoyable**, entertaining, amusing, diverting, fun, delightful, pleasant, pleasing [➡ FUNNY AND AMUSING; 216] *Opposite*: serious 3 *adj* **cheerful**, jokey, cheery, funny, bright, frivolous, jocular, flippant, facetious, humorous [➡ GOOD-TEMPERED AND HUMOROUS; 627] *Opposite*: gloomy

lightheartedly *adv* **cheerfully**, cheerily, brightly, happily, gaily, blithely (*literary*) [➡ GOOD-TEMPERED AND HUMOROUS; 627] *Opposite*: gloomily

lighting *n* **illumination**, light, lights [➡ LIGHT; 1164]

light into (*informal*) *v* **attack**, tear into, set upon, lay into, let have it, let fly at, maul, pitch into (*informal*) [➡ PHYSICAL ATTACK AND PUNISHMENT; 415] *Opposite*: defend

lightly 1 *adv* **gently**, softly, delicately, imperceptibly, quietly, noiselessly [➡ IMPERCEPTIBLE; 26] *Opposite*: heavily 2 *adv* **flippantly**, frivolously, jokily, informally, casually, carelessly, nonchalantly, without due consideration, blithely (*literary*) [➡ INCAUTIOUS AND CARELESS; 283] 3 *adv* **nimbly**, gracefully, trippingly, adeptly, dexterously, daintily [➡ AGILITY OF THE BODY; 476] *Opposite*: heavily

light-minded *adj* **frivolous**, silly, foolish, vacuous, inane [➡ NEGATIVE INTELLECTUAL CHARACTERISTICS; 525] *Opposite*: serious-minded

lightness 1 *n* **weightlessness**, buoyancy, fluffiness, frothiness, flimsiness [➡ WEIGHT: LIGHT; 1206] *Opposite*: heaviness 2 *n* **nimbleness**, precision, grace, agility, dexterity, subtlety [➡ AGILITY OF THE BODY; 476] *Opposite*: clumsiness

lightning 1 *n* **flash of lightning**, sheet lightning, heat lightning, lightning bolt, lightning strike, fulguration (*formal*), coruscation (*literary*), forked lightning (*UK*) [➡ WINDY AND STORMY WEATHER; 1053] 2 *adj* **fast**, quick, speedy, whirlwind, sudden, precipitous, headlong [➡ HAPPENING QUICKLY; 104] *Opposite*: slow

light out (*informal*) *v* **run away**, run off, leave in a hurry, cut and run, run for it, bolt, flee, take flight, take to your heels, make yourself scarce (*informal*), skedaddle (*slang*) [➡ RUN AWAY AND AVOID; 10]

light plane *type of* **civil aircraft** [➡ AIRCRAFT; 1148]

lightship *type of* **motor vessel** [➡ SHIPS AND BOATS; 1150]

lights out 1 *n* **bedtime**, time for bed, sleep time, bye-bye (*informal*) [➡ TIMES OF DAY; 87] **2** *n* **signal**, taps, bugle call, curfew, last post (*UK*) [➡ TIMES OF DAY; 87] *Opposite*: reveille

light up 1 *v* **illuminate**, light, cast light on, shed light on, shine a light on, brighten, illumine (*formal*) [➡ LIGHT EMISSION; 368] *Opposite*: darken **2** *v* **cheer up**, brighten up, perk up, liven up, brighten, animate, gladden, buck up (*informal*) [➡ CHANGE OF MOOD AND COMPOSURE; 580] **3** *v* **shine**, glow, gleam, beam, burn, glimmer, flare, blaze, flame [➡ LIGHT EMISSION; 368] *Opposite*: darken

lightweight 1 *adj* **frivolous**, trivial, insubstantial, inconsequential, unimportant, frothy [➡ UNIMPORTANT AND UNNECESSARY; 238] *Opposite*: serious **2** *n* **person of little consequence**, small fry, little man, little guy, pawn [➡ LAZY OR UNSUCCESSFUL PEOPLE; 948] *Opposite*: heavyweight

ligneous *adj* [➡ RIGID AND HARD; 1211]

likable *adj* **pleasant**, nice, affable, agreeable, amiable, genial, easygoing, congenial, friendly [➡ FRIENDLINESS AND SOCIABILITY; 494] *Opposite*: abominable

like 1 *prep* **similar to**, akin to, approximating to, in the vein of, reminiscent of, resembling [➡ SIMILARITY; 148] *Opposite*: unlike **2** *adj* **similar**, comparable, alike, corresponding, identical [➡ SIMILARITY; 148] **3** *v* **be fond of**, love, enjoy, be partial to, adore, be keen on (*UK*) [➡ LIKE, LOVE, VALUE, AND ENJOY; 578] *Opposite*: dislike

like a bat out of hell (*informal*) *adv* [➡ MOVING QUICKLY; 103]

like a bolt from the blue *adv* [➡ HAPPENING QUICKLY; 104]

like a cat on a hot tin roof *adj* [➡ POSITIVE IMPATIENCE, ENTHUSIASM, AND ALERTNESS; 537]

like a shot *adv* **quickly**, eagerly, enthusiastically, keenly, willingly, avidly [➡ POSITIVE IMPATIENCE, ENTHUSIASM, AND ALERTNESS; 537] *Opposite*: reluctantly

like clockwork *adv* **smoothly**, without a hitch, regularly, efficiently, routinely, perfectly [➡ ORDER AND ORGANIZATION; 206]

like greased lightning *adv* **quick as a flash**, like the wind, in the twinkling of an eye, in a trice, with alacrity, in a flash, like a bat out of hell (*informal*), in a jiffy (*informal*) [➡ HAPPENING QUICKLY; 104]

likelihood *n* **probability**, possibility, prospect, chance, chances, odds [➡ POSSIBLE AND PROBABLE; 177]

likely 1 *adj* **probable**, possible, expected, prospective, to be expected, in the offing, in the cards (*informal*) [➡ POSSIBLE AND PROBABLE; 177] *Opposite*: unlikely **2** *adj* **liable**, apt, prone, tending, having a tendency to [➡ THE WILL AND WILLINGNESS; 563]

like mad *adv* **like crazy**, madly, intensely, like anything, like fury, energetically [➡ POSITIVE IMPATIENCE, ENTHUSIASM, AND ALERTNESS; 537]

like-minded *adj* **in agreement**, concurring, compatible, in accord, of one mind, on the same wavelength, on the same page (*slang*) [➡ HARMONY; 155]

liken *v* **compare**, equate, relate, associate [➡ CREATING CONNECTIONS; 144] *Opposite*: contrast

likeness 1 *n* **similarity**, resemblance, correspondence [➡ SIMILARITY; 148] **2** *n* **portrait**, image, reproduction, picture, rendering, representation [➡ REPRESENTATIONS AND GENERAL EXAMPLES; 65]

like so *adv* **like this**, this way, in this way, in this fashion, thus (*formal*) [➡ WAYS OF DOING THINGS; 294]

like the back of your hand *adv* **thoroughly**, backward and forward, inside out, backward, back to front (*UK*) [➡ KNOWLEDGE AND WISDOM; 558]

like the wind *adv* [➡ MOVING QUICKLY; 103]

like two peas in a pod *adj* [➡ SAMENESS; 150]

likewise *adv* **similarly**, the same, equally, also, as well, too [➡ SIMILARITY; 148]

liking *n* **taste**, fondness, partiality, love, penchant, weakness, fancy, soft spot, predilection (*formal*) [➡ APPRECIATION AND GRATITUDE; 535] *Opposite*: dislike

See Compare and Contrast at **love**.

lilac 1 *type of* **purple** [➡ COLORS; 1224] **2** *type of* **shrub or bush** [➡ BUSHES AND SHRUBS; 1027]

lilangeni *type of* **currency** [➡ CURRENCIES; 798]

lilt *n* **intonation**, inflection, rise and fall, cadence, stress [➡ THE SPOKEN WORD; 671]

lily *type of* **flower grown from bulbs** [➡ FLOWERS FROM BULBS; 1030]

lily-livered (*dated*) *adj* **cowardly**, faint-hearted, spineless, weak, chicken (*informal*), craven (*literary*) [➡ COWARDICE AND WEAKNESS OF WILL; 508] *Opposite*: courageous

lily of the valley *type of* **perennial flower** [➡ FLOWERS; 1032]

lima bean *type of* **pulse** [➡ PEAS AND BEANS; 1189]

limb 1 *n* **member**, appendage, extremity, projection, branch, bough [➡ SUBDIVISIONS AND OFFSHOOTS; 1253] **2** *n* **extremity**, appendage, member [➡ PARTS OF THE BODY: TORSO; 693]

limber *adj* **lithe**, supple, agile, nimble, lissom, flexible [➡ AGILITY OF THE BODY; 476] *Opposite*: stiff

limber up *v* **warm up**, loosen up, exercise, practice, prepare [➡ PREPARE FOR ACTION; 289]

limbo 1 *n* [➡ RELIGIOUS CONCEPTS; 776] **2** *type of* **dance** [➡ DANCE; 903]

lime 1 *type of* **citrus fruit** [➡ FRUIT AND VEGETABLES; 1176] **2** *type of* **mineral** [➡ MINERALS; 1277] **3** *type of* **deciduous tree** [➡ DECIDUOUS TREES; 1028]

lime green *type of* **green** [➡ COLORS; 1224]

limelight *n* **attention**, public interest, public eye, fame, renown, publicity, glare of publicity [➡ KNOWN AND FAMOUS; 181]

limerick *n* [➡ POETRY AND VERSE; 915]

limestone *type of* **stone** [➡ STONES, ROCKS, AND BOULDERS; 1057]

limit 1 *n* **boundary**, bounds, border, edge, perimeter, frontier [➡ EXTREMITIES OF PHYSICAL OBJECTS; 1250] **2** *n* **threshold**, cutoff point, check, cap, constraint, maximum value, maximum, ceiling, minimum value, floor [➡ MAJORITY AND MAXIMUM; 141] **3** *v* **control**, regulate, restrain, curb, constrain, ration, keep a tight rein on, restrict, reduce, check [➡ AVOID, PREVENT, LIMIT, AND CONTROL; 277] *Opposite*: deregulate

limitation *n* **drawback**, inadequacy, imperfection, weakness, weak point, shortcoming, snag [➡ FAULTS, FLAWS, AND WEAKNESSES; 251]

limited *adj* **incomplete**, imperfect, partial, inadequate, restricted, narrow [➡ UNFINISHEDNESS; 239] *Opposite*: boundless

limited-access highway *type of* **highway** [➡ ROADS; 1106]

limited company *n* **public limited company**, joint-stock company, company, corporation, firm, enterprise, PLC (*UK*) [➡ BUSINESS ENTERPRISES AND RELATED BODIES; 792]

limited edition *n* **special edition**, limited printing, limited issue, limited print run, deluxe edition [➡ BOOKS AND BOOKLETS; 590]

limiter *n* **regulator**, controller, control, restraint, check [➡ ELECTRONICS AND ELECTRICS; 1137]

limitless *adj* **boundless**, unbounded, immeasurable, infinite, vast, inexhaustible, never-ending, unlimited [➡ PERMANENCE: WITHOUT END; 94] *Opposite*: limited

limitlessness *n* [➡ PERMANENCE: WITHOUT END; 94]

limits *n* **bounds**, restrictions, confines, parameters, boundaries [➡ EXTREMITIES OF PHYSICAL OBJECTS; 1250]

limo (*informal*) *type of* **car** [➡ BIKES, CARS, AND CARRIAGES; 1149]

Limoges *type of* **pottery** [➡ POTTERY; 1135]

limousine *type of* **car** [➡ BIKES, CARS, AND CARRIAGES; 1149]

limp 1 *v* **hobble**, shuffle, shamble, stagger, wobble, hitch [➡ WALK UNSTEADILY; 315] 2 *adj* **floppy**, wilted, flaccid, lifeless, drooping, sagging, wilting, loose, bendy (*UK*) [➡ MALLEABLE AND ELASTIC; 1212] *Opposite*: stiff

limpet *type of* **aquatic invertebrate** [➡ AQUATIC INVERTEBRATES; 1022]

limpid 1 *adj* **transparent**, clear, translucent, diaphanous, see-through, sheer, crystalline, crystal, pellucid (*literary*) [➡ VISUAL TEXTURE; 1221] *Opposite*: opaque 2 *adj* **lucid**, clear, crystal clear, clear as day, understandable, intelligible, comprehensible, unambiguous [➡ CONCISE AND CLEAR; 202] *Opposite*: obscure

limpness *n* **floppiness**, flaccidity, droopiness, lifelessness, sagginess, softness, flabbiness (*informal*) [➡ MALLEABLE AND ELASTIC; 1212] *Opposite*: stiffness

limy *adj* **lime-flavored**, lime, citrus [➡ TASTE; 703]

linchpin *n* **kingpin** (*informal*), fulcrum, cornerstone, hub, essential, prerequisite, sine qua non, requirement [➡ MOST IMPORTANT THING; 197] *Opposite*: accessory

Lincoln green *type of* **green** [➡ COLORS; 1224]

lindy hop *n* [➡ DANCE; 903]

line 1 *n* **streak**, stripe, contour, mark, stroke [➡ PATTERNS; 1225] 2 *n* **edge**, profile, contour, outline, silhouette, delineation [➡ EXTREMITIES OF PHYSICAL OBJECTS; 1250] 3 *n* **boundary**, limit, border, edge, frontier [➡ EXTREMITIES OF PHYSICAL OBJECTS; 1250] 4 *n* **link**, route, track, connection, course, way, passage [➡ RAILROADS; 1107] 5 *n* **string**, cable, rope, thread, twine, wire, lead, cord, flex (*UK*) [➡ FASTENERS, LINKS, AND NETWORKS; 1247] 6 *n* **ancestry**, family,

lineage, descent, race, parentage, stock, heritage [➡ THE FAMILY; 956] 7 *n* **policy**, attitude, method, approach, ideology, position, stance, course, procedure [➡ POINTS OF VIEW; 767] 8 *n* **area**, occupation, field, interest, specialty, specialization, specialism, work, job, calling, pursuit [➡ SUBJECT AREAS; 768] 9 *n* **row**, column, procession, lineup, queue (*UK*) [➡ AREA AND RANGE; 111] 10 *v* **coat**, cover, face, reinforce, pad [➡ DECORATE, ADORN, AND APPLY COATINGS; 405]

lineage *n* **ancestry**, family, line, heredity, extraction, pedigree, roots, family tree, stock, descent [➡ THE FAMILY; 956]

lineament (*literary*) *n* **facial feature**, feature, contour [➡ FACIAL CHARACTERISTICS; 481]

linear 1 *adj* **in lines**, lined, line [➡ ORIENTATION AND ALIGNMENT; 1223] 2 *adj* **straight**, rectilinear, direct, undeviating, right, true [➡ ORIENTATION AND ALIGNMENT; 1223]

lined 1 *adj* **wrinkled**, creased, wizened, furrowed, crinkled [➡ FACIAL CHARACTERISTICS; 481] *Opposite*: smooth 2 *adj* **ruled**, feint [➡ DESCRIBING PATTERNS; 1227] *Opposite*: plain

line dancing *type of* **dance** [➡ DANCE; 903]

line manager *n* **manager**, production manager, sales manager, boss, superior, supervisor [➡ BOSSES AND MANAGEMENT; 965]

linen *type of* **fabric from plants** [➡ FABRICS; 1132]

line of attack *n* **stratagem**, tactic, technique, method, modus operandi, game plan, approach [➡ WAYS OF DOING THINGS; 294]

line officer *n* **combat officer**, frontline officer, fighting officer, field officer, officer, combatant [➡ MILITARY PERSONNEL; 828]

line of sight *n* **sightline**, line of vision, view [➡ SEE; 699]

line of work *n* **profession**, career, job, occupation [➡ PROFESSIONS; 845]

liner *n* **lining**, pool liner, facing, insert, bin liner (*UK*) [➡ COVERS AND COATINGS; 1246]

line up 1 *v* **arrange**, collect, order, organize, place, array (*formal*) [➡ ARRANGE AND CREATE ORDER; 357] *Opposite*: disarrange 2 *v* **form ranks**, fall into line, marshal, order, align [➡ POSITION SOMETHING; 325] 3 *v* **assemble**, queue, gather together, collect, align, organize [➡ ARRANGE AND CREATE ORDER; 357] 4 *v* **plan**, organize, arrange, prepare, set up, get ready, sort, systematize, provide [➡ PREPARE FOR ACTION; 289]

lineup 1 *n* **team list**, roster, team, listing, side, cast [➡ GROUPS WITH A COMMON INTEREST; 938] 2 *n* **schedule**, listing, program [➡ WORKERS IN ENTERTAINMENT AND MEDIA; 873] 3 *n* **group**, team, alliance, association, league, union, assembly, band, ensemble [➡ GROUPS OF PEOPLE; 935]

ling *type of* **ocean fish** [➡ OCEAN FISH; 1009]

linger *v* **remain**, stay behind, hang on, loiter, stay, delay, dawdle, hang back, hang around, stick around (*informal*) [➡ MOVE SLOWLY; 314] *Opposite*: leave

lingerie *n* **underwear**, underclothes, underclothing, undergarments, undies (*informal*) [➡ ACCESSORIES, MILLINERY, AND LINGERIE; 867]

lingering 1 *adj* **lasting**, remaining, persistent, enduring,

haunting [➡PERMANENCE: WITHOUT END; 94] **2** *adj* **drawn-out**, slow, protracted, long-drawn-out, prolonged, spun-out (*UK*) [➡HAPPENING SLOWLY; 106] *Opposite:* quick

lingo (*informal*) *n* **language**, speech, idiom, vernacular, jargon, argot, dialect, patois, patter [➡ASPECTS OF LANGUAGE; 682]

See Compare and Contrast at **language**.

lingua franca *n* [➡ASPECTS OF LANGUAGE; 682]

linguine *type of* **pasta** [➡PASTA; 1180]

linguist *n* [➡PEOPLE WHO WORK WITH LANGUAGE AND CODE; 854]

linguistic *adj* **language**, verbal, philological, dialectal, etymological, phonological, morphological, semantic, grammatical, syntactical [➡ASPECTS OF LANGUAGE; 682]

linguistics *n* **dialectology**, etymology, phonology, morphology, semantics, grammar, syntax [➡ASPECTS OF LANGUAGE; 682]

liniment *n* **ointment**, cream, unguent, rub, salve, lotion, balm, emollient, gel [➡LOTIONS, PASTES, AND GELS; 1272]

lining **1** *n* **coating**, liner, insert, facing [➡COVERS AND COATINGS; 1246] **2** *part of* **garment** [➡PARTS OF A GARMENT; 870]

link **1** *n* **connection**, relation, association, relationship, linkage, tie, bond, yoke, nexus [➡CONNECTIONS; 143] **2** *v* **connect**, relate, associate, bring together, link up, network, join, combine, couple, conjoin (*formal*) [➡CREATING CONNECTIONS; 144] *Opposite:* separate

linkage *n* **connection**, relation, association, relationship, link, bond, tie, yoke, nexus [➡CONNECTIONS; 143]

linked *adj* **related**, connected, accompanying, allied, associated, interconnected, interrelated, concomitant, concurrent, attendant [➡RELATED; 142] *Opposite:* unrelated

linkup *n* **connection**, association, link, linkage, bond, union, tie-up, hookup (*informal*) [➡CONNECTIONS; 143] *Opposite:* separation

linnet *type of* **songbird** [➡SONGBIRDS; 1003]

lion *type of* **cat** [➡FELINES; 983]

lioness *type of* **female animal** [➡MALE OR FEMALE ANIMALS; 978]

lionhearted *adj* **brave**, courageous, stouthearted, bold, audacious, daring, fearless, unafraid, plucky, valorous, valiant, heroic, intrepid (*literary or humorous*), dauntless (*literary*), doughty (*literary*), gallant (*literary*) [➡COURAGE; 498] *Opposite:* cowardly

lionheartedness *n* [➡COURAGE; 498]

lionize *v* **glorify**, idolize, praise, fete, celebrate, acclaim, applaud, hail, extol [➡PRAISE AND ENCOURAGE; 647] *Opposite:* censure

lion's share *n* **largest part**, bulk, most, majority, mass, vast majority [➡MAJORITY AND MAXIMUM; 141]

lip **1** *part of* **mouth** [➡THE MOUTH; 702] **2** *n* **edge**, rim, brim, brink [➡EXTREMITIES OF PHYSICAL OBJECTS; 1250] **3** *n* (*slang*) **impertinence**, impudence, rudeness, attitude, back talk, sass (*informal*), mouth (*informal*), cheek (*informal*) [➡BAD MANNERS AND SOCIAL SKILLS; 521] *Opposite:* respect **4** *part of* **flower** [➡FLOWERS; 1032]

lip pencil *type of* **cosmetic** [➡MAKEUP AND BEAUTY PRODUCTS; 490]

lips *part of* **face** [➡PARTS OF THE BODY: HEAD; 692]

lip-smacking *adj* **delicious**, delectable, tasty, flavorful, flavorsome, mouthwatering [➡TASTE; 703]

lipstick *n* [➡MAKEUP AND BEAUTY PRODUCTS; 490]

liquefied *adj* [➡FLUID AND NONSOLID; 1213]

liquefy *v* **dissolve**, soften, melt, run, thaw, deliquesce [➡SOFTEN, LIQUEFY, AND DAMPEN; 388] *Opposite:* solidify

liquescence *n* [➡FLUID AND NONSOLID; 1213]

liquescent *adj* **melting**, runny, gooey, liquefying [➡FLUID AND NONSOLID; 1213] *Opposite:* solid

liqueur *n* [➡DRINKS; 1187]

liquid **1** *n* **fluid**, water, juice, solution, liquor [➡LIQUIDS; 1269] **2** *adj* **runny**, fluid, gooey, watery, melted, liquescent, molten, liquefied [➡FLUID AND NONSOLID; 1213] *Opposite:* solid

liquid assets *n* [➡FINANCIAL ASSETS; 462]

liquidate **1** *v* **settle**, clear up, pay, pay off, satisfy, square, honor, discharge (*formal*), quit (*archaic*) [➡GIVE MONEY; 433] **2** *v* **shut down**, sell out, sell off, bankrupt, wind up [➡BUSINESS ACTIVITIES AND PHENOMENA; 794] **3** *v* **kill**, murder, execute, eliminate, assassinate, exterminate, dispose of, bump off (*slang*), knock off (*slang*), take out (*slang*) [➡KILL; 923]

liquidation *n* **insolvency**, bankruptcy, closing, winding up, selling out, shutting down [➡BUSINESS ACTIVITIES AND PHENOMENA; 794]

liquidator *n* **receiver**, official receiver, administrative receiver, overseer, sequestrator (*UK*) [➡PEOPLE INVOLVED IN FINANCE; 804]

liquidity **1** *n* **liquidness**, fluidity, fluidness, wateriness, runniness, liquescence, liquescency [➡FLUID AND NONSOLID; 1213] *Opposite:* solidity **2** *n* **assets**, liquid assets, convertible assets, resources, financial resources, cash, cash flow, funds, reserves, monies (*formal*) [➡FINANCIAL ASSETS; 462]

liquidize *v* **purée**, blend, pulverize, mash, pulp, mix, intermix, liquefy [➡COOKING AND FOOD PREPARATION; 353]

liquidizer *type of* **utensil** [➡TABLEWARE, FLATWARE, AND KITCHENWARE; 861]

liquor **1** *n* **alcohol**, spirits, strong drink [➡DRINKS; 1187] **2** *n* **liquid**, fluid, solution, juice [➡LIQUIDS; 1269]

liquor cabinet *type of* **cabinet** [➡FURNITURE; 858]

liquored up (*informal*) *adj* [➡UNDER THE INFLUENCE OF DRUGS OR ALCOHOL; 741]

lira *type of* **currency** [➡CURRENCIES; 798]

lissom **1** *adj* **lithe**, supple, flexible, willowy, svelte, limber [➡BUILD; 477] *Opposite:* stiff **2** *adj* **agile**, nimble, lively, quick, light, deft, graceful, adroit, spry, light on your feet, sprightly [➡AGILITY OF THE BODY; 476] *Opposite:* awkward

lissome *see* **lissom**

list **1** *n* **catalog**, register, record, roll, listing, directory, file, inventory [➡LISTS AND SCHEDULES; 587] **2** *n* **tilt**, slant, slope, gradient, lean, grade, incline, angle [➡ORIENTATION AND ALIGNMENT;

1223] **3** *v* **record**, catalog, register, itemize, enumerate, inventory [➡RECORD SOMETHING; 371] **4** *v* **slant**, tilt, incline, lean, bank, decline, recline, slope [➡TAKE UP A NEW POSITION; 312]

listed *adj* **registered**, recorded, itemized, enumerated [➡PRESENT AND AVAILABLE; 11] *Opposite*: unlisted

listen *v* **lend an ear**, pay attention, take note, attend, give heed, hang on somebody's words, listen up (*slang*) [➡LISTEN AND LISTENERS; 708] *Opposite*: ignore

listener *n* **hearer**, radio listener, audience member, audiophile, eavesdropper, auditor (*formal*) [➡LISTEN AND LISTENERS; 708]

listen in *v* **eavesdrop**, monitor, wiretap, bug, snoop (*informal*) [➡LISTEN AND LISTENERS; 708]

listening post *n* **observation post**, lookout post, surveillance post, sentry post [➡TOWERS; 1099]

listen up (*slang*) *v* **listen**, pay attention, attend, heed, pay heed, give heed, take notice, concentrate, lend an ear [➡PAY ATTENTION; 765] *Opposite*: ignore

listeria *type of* **microorganism** [➡MICROORGANISMS, FUNGI, AND ALGAE; 1023]

listing 1 *n* **list**, catalog, register, record, roll, inventory, directory [➡LISTS AND SCHEDULES; 587] **2** *n* **citation**, item, entry [➡SUMMARIES, OUTLINES, AND EXCERPTS; 588]

listings *n* **schedule**, program, guide [➡LISTS AND SCHEDULES; 587]

listless *adj* **languid**, lethargic, indolent, enervated, limp, apathetic, inactive, inert [➡TIRED, ASLEEP, AND UNCONSCIOUS; 738] *Opposite*: energetic

listlessness *n* [➡TIRED, ASLEEP, AND UNCONSCIOUS; 738]

litany 1 *n* **prayers**, liturgical prayers, petitions, invocations, responses, supplications (*formal*) [➡RELIGIONS AND RELIGIOUS PRACTICES; 777] **2** *n* **list**, listing, catalog, series, recital, recitation, enumeration, inventory [➡COLLECTIONS AND MIXTURES OF THINGS; 1244]

litas *type of* **currency** [➡CURRENCIES; 798]

liter *type of* **metric unit** [➡SIZE AND DIMENSIONS; 1192]

literacy 1 *n* **literateness**, reading ability, three Rs [➡KNOWLEDGE AND WISDOM; 558] **2** *n* **knowledge**, learning, mastery, savvy (*informal*), nous (*UK*) [➡KNOWLEDGE AND WISDOM; 558]

literal 1 *adj* **factual**, truthful, honest, exact, accurate, unembroidered, unembellished, plain, bare, unvarnished [➡TRUE AND REAL; 171] *Opposite*: figurative **2** *adj* **word for word**, verbatim, accurate, exact, correct, precise [➡EXACT; 203] *Opposite*: inaccurate

literally *adv* **factually**, accurately, exactly, plainly [➡TRUE AND REAL; 171] *Opposite*: figuratively

literary 1 *adj* **fictional**, mythical, legendary, storybook, fictitious [➡FALSE AND UNREAL; 173] *Opposite*: historical **2** *adj* **bookish**, erudite, scholarly, well-read, literate [➡LEVELS OF EDUCATION AND SOPHISTICATION; 894]

literate *adj* **well-educated**, well-read, knowledgeable, cultured, erudite, literary, informed, scholarly, scholastic, learned [➡LEVELS OF EDUCATION AND SOPHISTICATION; 894] *Opposite*: illiterate

literati (*formal*) **1** *n* **intellectuals**, intellects, highbrows, intelligentsia, academics, scholars [➡LEVELS OF EDUCATION AND SOPHISTICATION; 894] **2** *n* **authors**, writers, poets, playwrights, editors, publishers, littérateurs (*archaic*) [➡WRITERS AND STYLES; 914]

literature 1 *n* **writings**, works, collected works, texts, books, words, prose, poetry, fiction [➡FICTION AND DRAMA; 913] **2** *n* **information**, sources, reading matter, brochures, pamphlets, leaflets, fliers, info (*informal*) [➡BOOKS AND BOOKLETS; 590]

lithe *adj* **supple**, flexible, lissom, agile, nimble, limber [➡AGILITY OF THE BODY; 476] *Opposite*: stiff

litheness *n* [➡AGILITY OF THE BODY; 476]

lithesome (*archaic or literary*) *adj* **lithe**, supple, flexible, limber, lissom, loose-limbed, willowy [➡AGILITY OF THE BODY; 476] *Opposite*: stiff

lithograph *n* [➡DRAWINGS, CHARTS, AND TABLES; 594]

litigable *adj* **responsible**, liable, accountable, answerable, actionable, disputable, suable, arguable [➡RESPONSIBILITY; 170]

litigant *n* [➡THE POLICE, ARREST, AND PRETRIAL PROCEEDINGS; 818]

litigate *v* **take proceedings**, sue, contest, file, petition, prosecute, implead, arraign, impeach, accuse, charge, press charges [➡TRIAL, PUNISHMENT, AND LEGAL OUTCOMES; 819]

litigation *n* **court case**, proceedings, lawsuit, legal action, legal process, trial, hearing, process [➡TRIAL, PUNISHMENT, AND LEGAL OUTCOMES; 819]

litmus test *n* **acid test**, proof, confirmation, test, measure [➡PERFECT EXAMPLES AND EMBODIMENTS; 67]

litotes *type of* **figure of speech** [➡FIGURES OF SPEECH; 673]

litter 1 *n* **waste**, rubbish, trash, garbage, debris, refuse [➡JUNK AND USELESS OBJECTS; 1249] **2** *n* **disorder**, confusion, jumble, clutter, untidiness, mess [➡DISORDER AND CHAOS; 245] **3** *n* **offspring**, young, progeny, brood, family [➡GROUPS OF ANIMALS; 993] **4** *v* **drop litter**, scatter, spoil, strew, clutter [➡WORSEN APPEARANCE; 382] *Opposite*: clean up

litterbug (*informal*) *n* **litterer**, dumper, fly-tipper (*UK*) [➡DIRTY AND SLOVENLY PEOPLE; 954]

little 1 *adj* **small**, slight, petite, diminutive, tiny, minute, bantam, miniature, pocket-sized, pint-sized (*informal*) [➡SMALL; 1195] *Opposite*: large **2** *adj* **unimportant**, trivial, slight, petty, trifling, inconsequential, negligible, insignificant, minor, piddling (*informal*) [➡UNIMPORTANT AND UNNECESSARY; 238] *Opposite*: major **3** *pron* **bit**, touch, spot, some, pittance, minimum, trace, tad (*informal*) [➡FEW, LITTLE, SMALL AMOUNT; 120] *Opposite*: lot **4** *adv* **not very**, not much, not sufficiently, insufficiently, inadequately, not enough, barely, hardly, slightly, scarcely [➡TO A CERTAIN EXTENT; 136] *Opposite*: well

little by little *adv* **gradually**, bit by bit, inch by inch, slowly, incrementally, imperceptibly, by degrees [➡HAPPENING SLOWLY; 106] *Opposite*: all at once

little finger *part of* **arm or hand** [➡PARTS OF THE BODY: ARM AND HAND; 695]

little folk *see* **little people**

little green man (*humorous*) *n* **alien**, Martian, extra-terrestrial [➡ SCIENCE FICTION; 1064]

little-known *adj* [➡ SECRET AND UNKNOWN; 179]

little owl *type of* **owl** [➡ OWLS; 1001]

little people *n* **little folk**, supernatural beings, imaginary beings, fairies, elves, pixies, leprechauns, gnomes [➡ MYTHICAL BEINGS; 789]

little toe *part of* **leg or foot** [➡ PARTS OF THE BODY: LEG AND FOOT; 694]

littoral 1 *adj* **coastal**, shoreline, seaside [➡ THE SEAS, OCEANS, AND SHORES; 1041] *Opposite*: inland 2 *n* **shore**, coast, seaside, shoreline, beach, seafront, shorefront, oceanfront [➡ THE SEAS, OCEANS, AND SHORES; 1041]

liturgy *n* **church service**, mass, ritual, religious ceremony, rite, worship [➡ RELIGIONS AND RELIGIOUS PRACTICES; 777]

livable 1 *adj* **habitable**, functional, civilized, comfortable, agreeable, pleasant, convenient, enjoyable, accommodating, suitable, cozy [➡ PHYSICALLY PLEASANT; 186] *Opposite*: uninhabitable 2 *adj* **bearable**, endurable, acceptable, tolerable, worthwhile, passable, supportable (*literary*) [➡ ACCEPTABLE AND PASSABLE; 219] *Opposite*: intolerable

live 1 *v* **exist**, be alive, be in this world, survive, subsist, breathe, be, be animate [➡ EXIST; 15] *Opposite*: die 2 *v* **reside**, stay, have your home, inhabit, settle, occupy, dwell (*literary*), abide (*archaic*) [➡ INHABIT; 20] 3 *adj* **living**, animate, conscious, breathing, aware, sentient, alive, vital, quick (*archaic*), existent (*formal*) [➡ LIVING THINGS AND LIVING; 976] *Opposite*: dead

liveable *see* **livable**

lived-in 1 *adj* **comfortable**, relaxed, disheveled, untidy, homey, laid-back (*informal*), homely (*UK*) [➡ IN GOOD REPAIR; 1232] 2 *adj* **careworn**, haggard, worn, lined, tired, weatherbeaten, rundown [➡ FACIAL CHARACTERISTICS; 481]

live down *v* **get over**, recover, shake off, forget, survive, outlast [➡ FORGET, FORGIVE, AND ACCEPT; 748]

live it up (*slang*) *v* **enjoy life**, have a good time, have fun, paint the town red (*informal*), have a blast (*slang*), have a ball (*dated slang*) [➡ LEISURE AND RECREATION; 874]

livelihood 1 *n* **employment**, occupation, trade, business, work, job [➡ JOB; 833] 2 *n* **living**, income, source of revenue, means of support, maintenance, funds [➡ INCOME; 460]

liveliness *n* **energy**, sparkle, joie de vivre, vivacity, dynamism, spirit, vigor, get-up-and-go (*informal*) [➡ ENERGY AND ENTHUSIASM; 496] *Opposite*: lethargy

lively *adj* **energetic**, vigorous, sparkling, active, vivacious, animated, sprightly, dynamic, bouncy, bubbly, buoyant, spirited [➡ ENERGY AND ENTHUSIASM; 496] *Opposite*: lethargic

liven *v* **perk up**, cheer up, boost, quicken, energize, enliven [➡ IMPROVE SOMETHING; 374] *Opposite*: depress

liven up *v* **enliven**, stimulate, revive, cheer up, perk up, brighten up, raise, lift [➡ IMPROVE SOMETHING; 374]

live off *v* **rely on**, depend on, impose on, sponge, mooch (*informal*), leech (*informal*) [➡ RECIPROCITY AND INTERDEPENDENCE; 147]

live on 1 *v* **survive on**, get by on, exist on, subsist on,

eke out a living, make ends meet [➡ CONTINUE TO EXIST; 17] 2 *v* **remain**, continue, survive, persist, prevail, persevere [➡ CONTINUE TO EXIST; 17] *Opposite*: die away

liver 1 *type of* **brown** [➡ COLORS; 1224] 2 *part of* **digestive tract** [➡ THE DIGESTIVE TRACT; 709]

liveried *adj* **uniformed**, costumed, dressed up, caparisoned [➡ DRESS, WEAR, AND UNDRESS; 868]

liverish *adj* **irritable**, bad-tempered, moody, irascible, volatile, hotheaded, ill-humored, touchy, tetchy (*informal*) [➡ IRRITATION AND ANGER; 541]

liverwurst *type of* **processed meat** [➡ TYPES AND CUTS OF MEAT; 1177]

livery 1 *n* **uniform**, dress, costume, vestments, regalia, attire (*formal*) [➡ GARMENTS AND OUTFITS; 865] 2 *n* (*literary*) **insignia**, colors, corporate colors, racing colors [➡ PATTERNS; 1225]

livestock *n* **animals**, cattle, stock [➡ FARM ANIMALS; 982]

live through *v* **survive**, come through, get through, experience, undergo, go through, weather, withstand, brave, ride out [➡ EXPERIENCE AND ENCOUNTER; 582] *Opposite*: succumb

live up to *v* **match**, achieve, reach, come up to, meet, compare [➡ SUCCEED AND WIN; 79]

live wire (*informal*) *n* **doer**, activist, high-flier, extrovert, go-getter (*informal*), live one (*informal*) [➡ PEOPLE WHO ARE APPROVED OF; 955]

live with *v* **tolerate**, put up with, bear, endure, manage, cope, accept [➡ TOLERATE AND ENDURE; 766]

livid 1 *adj* **furious**, enraged, up in arms, beside yourself, incensed, fuming, outraged, irate, mad, angry [➡ IRRITATION AND ANGER; 541] *Opposite*: pleased 2 *adj* **bruised**, purple, discolored, black and blue, contused [➡ INJURED; 742]

lividly *adv* **furiously**, angrily, irately, exasperatedly [➡ IRRITATION AND ANGER; 541]

living 1 *adj* **alive**, breathing, existing, live, active, animate, incarnate, corporeal, organic, extant, quick (*archaic*) [➡ LIVING THINGS AND LIVING; 976] *Opposite*: dead 2 *n* **livelihood**, income, living wage, source of revenue, subsistence, means of support, funds [➡ INCOME; 460]

Compare and Contrast: *living*, *alive*, *animate*, *extant*

CORE MEANING: having life or existence

living not dead, or, of inanimate things, still in existence; *alive* not dead; *animate* physically alive, used especially to distinguish animals and plants from inanimate objects such as rocks, water, or buildings; *extant* still in existence.

living being *n* [➡ LIVING THINGS AND LIVING; 976]

living quarters *n* [➡ ACCOMMODATIONS; 855]

living room *type of* **room in the home** [➡ TYPES OF ROOMS; 1097]

living thing *n* **creature**, being, living being, life form, organism, animal, beast, human, human being [➡ LIVING THINGS AND LIVING; 976]

lizard *type of* **reptile** [➡ REPTILES; 994]

llama *type of* **large mammal** [➡ LARGE MAMMALS; 986]

loach *type of* **freshwater fish** [➡ FRESHWATER FISH; 1010]

load 1 *n* **weight**, cargo, freight, consignment, shipment, burden, capacity, contents [➡ TRANSPORTATION, TRANSPORTERS, AND CARGOS; 322] **2** *v* **fill**, pack, stack, load up, pile, heap, stock, stuff, charge (*formal*) [➡ FILL; 406] *Opposite:* unload **3** *v* **put in**, insert, slot in, pop in (*informal*) [➡ POSITION SOMETHING; 325] *Opposite:* eject **4** *v* **burden**, encumber, weigh down, overload, oppress, worry, overwhelm, crush, hamper [➡ GIVE TOO MUCH AND OVERBURDEN; 437] *Opposite:* alleviate

loaded 1 *adj* **laden**, weighed down, encumbered, burdened, overloaded, full, overburdened [➡ FULL; 1239] *Opposite:* empty **2** *adj* **biased**, leading, deceptive, trick, manipulative, unfair [➡ FALSE AND UNREAL; 173] *Opposite:* innocent **3** *adj* (*slang*) **rich**, wealthy, well-off, affluent, well-heeled (*informal*), rolling in it (*informal*) [➡ WEALTH AND WEALTHY; 891] *Opposite:* poor

loads (*informal*) *n* **many**, much, lots, heaps (*informal*), oodles (*informal*), tons (*informal*) [➡ MANY, MUCH, LARGE AMOUNT; 117] *Opposite:* handful

load up *v* **fill up**, stack, pack, pile, fill, cram, stuff, heap up, load, charge (*formal*) [➡ FILL; 406] *Opposite:* unload

loaf *v* **be idle**, be unoccupied, laze, loiter, loll, malinger, hang out (*informal*), lie around (*informal*), mooch (*slang*) [➡ LACK OF ACTIVITY OR MOTION; 342]

loaf around *v* [➡ LACK OF ACTIVITY OR MOTION; 342]

loafer *n* **idler**, slacker, shirker, sloth, loiterer, malingerer, bum (*informal*), slouch (*informal*), lazybones (*informal*), goldbrick (*informal*), lollygagger (*dated*) [➡ LAZY OR UNSUCCESSFUL PEOPLE; 948]

loam *n* [➡ EROSION PRODUCTS AND SOIL; 1058]

loan 1 *n* **advance**, credit, finance, mortgage [➡ ACCOUNTING, BANKING, AND BUDGETING; 799] **2** *v* **lend**, advance, give a loan, give an advance, allow [➡ LEND, LEASE, AND BORROW; 428] *Opposite:* borrow

loath *adj* **wary**, unwilling, reluctant, chary, against, opposed, disinclined, averse (*formal*) [➡ UNWILLINGNESS AND STUBBORNNESS; 564] *Opposite:* eager

See Compare and Contrast at **unwilling**.

loathe *v* **hate**, dislike, detest, despise, scorn, disdain, abhor (*formal*), abominate (*formal*) [➡ DISLIKE AND HATE; 577] *Opposite:* adore

loathed *adj* [➡ UNPOPULAR AND UNWANTED; 258]

loathing *n* **hate**, hatred, dislike, antipathy, repugnance, detestation, abhorrence, disgust, revulsion, animus, animosity, hostility, aversion (*formal*) [➡ DISLIKE AND HATE; 577] *Opposite:* love

See Compare and Contrast at **dislike**.

loathsome *adj* **hateful**, despicable, disgusting, repugnant, detestable, nasty, vile, odious, obnoxious, repulsive, revolting, offensive, abhorrent (*formal*) [➡ DISGUSTING AND REPULSIVE; 230] *Opposite:* delightful

lob 1 *v* **throw**, toss, fling, pitch, hurl, chuck (*informal*) [➡ MOVE SOMETHING: THROUGH THE AIR; 334] **2** *v* **hit**, knock, strike, bat, whack [➡ CONTACT: IMPACT; 413] **3** *n* **toss**, throw, pitch, hit, ball [➡ MOVE SOMETHING: THROUGH THE AIR; 334]

lobby 1 *n* **entrance hall**, foyer, reception area, vestibule, atrium, entrance, hall, antechamber, anteroom, waiting room [➡ DOORS AND ACCESS POINTS; 1101] **2** *type of* **room in public buildings** [➡ TYPES OF ROOMS; 1097] **3** *n* **pressure group**, interest group, ginger group, campaign group, special interest group, faction, alliance, lobby group (*UK*) [➡ GROUPS WITH A COMMON INTEREST; 938] **4** *v* **petition**, press your case, try to influence, apply pressure, sway opinion, push, promote, urge, pull strings [➡ REQUEST AND DEMAND; 663]

lobby group (*UK*) *n* **pressure group**, campaign group, interest group, lobby, alliance, faction, special interest group [➡ GROUPS WITH A COMMON INTEREST; 938]

lobe 1 *n* [➡ THE EAR; 706] **2** *n* **part**, section, portion, hemisphere [➡ EXTREMITIES OF PHYSICAL OBJECTS; 1250]

lobelia *type of* **annual flower** [➡ FLOWERS; 1032]

lobster *type of* **crustacean** [➡ AQUATIC INVERTEBRATES; 1022]

local 1 *adj* **home**, neighboring, neighborhood, community, district, regional, area, provincial [➡ COUNTRIES AND REGIONS; 1067] *Opposite:* national **2** *adj* **native**, indigenous, resident, homegrown [➡ COUNTRIES AND REGIONS; 1067] *Opposite:* foreign **3** *adj* **restricted**, limited, confined, narrow, insular, parochial [➡ CLOSENESS; 159] *Opposite:* universal **4** *n* **resident**, inhabitant, citizen, native [➡ INHABITANTS; 857] *Opposite:* stranger

locale *n* **location**, setting, place, milieu, area, locality, site, spot [➡ PLACE; 1065]

locality 1 *n* **area**, district, neighborhood, region, zone, section, vicinity, quarter, ghetto [➡ PLACE; 1065] **2** *n* **position**, place, site, spot, setting, environment, locale [➡ PLACE; 1065]

localize 1 *v* **restrict**, confine, limit, focus, contain, concentrate [➡ CAPTIVITY AND LOSS OF FREEDOM; 248] **2** *v* **pinpoint**, locate, identify, find exactly, narrow down, specify [➡ FIND; 463]

localized *adj* **contained**, limited, restricted, confined, local [➡ CAPTIVITY AND LOSS OF FREEDOM; 248] *Opposite:* generalized

locally *adv* **nearby**, close by, in the vicinity, in the neighborhood [➡ CLOSENESS; 159]

locate 1 *v* **find**, trace, discover, track down, detect, pinpoint, localize, ferret out, uncover [➡ FIND; 463] *Opposite:* lose **2** *v* **place**, put, position, situate, set, establish, station, post, fix (*informal*) [➡ POSITION SOMETHING; 325]

location *n* **site**, place, position, spot, setting, scene, locality, whereabouts, situation, locale [➡ PLACE; 1065]

loch (*UK*) 1 *n* **lake**, tarn, water, mere (*archaic or literary*), lough (*UK*), broad (*UK*) [➡ RIVERS, LAKES, AND STREAMS; 1042] **2** *n* **inlet**, fjord, sound, estuary, creek, firth (*UK*), sea loch (*UK*) [➡ THE SEAS, OCEANS, AND SHORES; 1041]

lock 1 *n* **security device**, padlock, combination lock, latch, bolt, catch, deadlock, dead bolt, mortise lock (*UK*), safety catch (*UK*) [➡ FASTENERS, LINKS, AND NETWORKS; 1247] **2** *n* **curl**, strand, tuft, wisp, ringlet, tress, hank, skein [➡ HAIR; 484] **3** *v* **fasten**, bolt, secure, lock up, padlock, bar [➡ FASTEN, LINK, AND JOIN; 408] *Opposite:* unlock **4** *v* **fix in place**, lodge, wedge,

secure, confine [➡ BAR AND OBSTRUCT ACCESS; 410] *Opposite:* free
5 *v* **brace,** clench, stiffen, tighten [➡ PHYSICAL REACTIONS; 316] *Opposite:* flex **6** *v* **link,** clasp, intertwine, join, unite, interlink, clinch, interlock [➡ FASTEN, LINK, AND JOIN; 408]

lock away 1 *v* **imprison,** lock up, jail, send to prison, sentence to prison, intern, pen, cage, send up the river, put away (*informal*), put inside (*informal*), incarcerate (*formal*) [➡ CAPTIVITY AND LOSS OF FREEDOM; 248] **2** *v* **shut away,** keep safe, secure, seal up, hide away, conceal, put in store, squirrel, put away, store, stash (*informal*) [➡ STORE AND KEEP; 453] *Opposite:* bring out

locked up *adj* [➡ CAPTIVITY AND LOSS OF FREEDOM; 248]

locket *type of* **necklace** [➡ JEWELRY; 866]

lock horns *v* **argue,** row, disagree, fight, contest, dispute, struggle [➡ ARGUE AND FIGHT; 643]

lock on *v* **home in on,** track, follow, shadow [➡ ACCOMPANY AND FOLLOW; 337]

lock, stock, and barrel *adv* **completely,** entirely, totally [➡ ALL; 128]

lock up *v* **imprison,** put in jail, put in prison, put behind bars, confine, detain, pen, coop up, put away (*informal*), incarcerate (*formal*) [➡ CAPTIVITY AND LOSS OF FREEDOM; 248] *Opposite:* release

lockup *n* **jail,** prison, reformatory, penitentiary, detention center, slammer (*slang*) [➡ BUILDINGS FOR CONFINING PEOPLE; 1094]

locomotion *n* **movement,** motion, propulsion, kinetic energy, kinesis, drive [➡ SELF-PROPULSION; 304] *Opposite:* immobility

locomotive *n* **train,** engine, steam engine, tank engine [➡ RAILROADS, 1107]

locum *n* [➡ SUBORDINATES AND ASSISTANTS; 966]

locus *n* [➡ PLACE; 1065]

locust *type of* **flying insect** [➡ FLYING INSECTS; 1013]

locution *n* [➡ ASPECTS OF LANGUAGE; 682]

loden *type of* **fabric from animals** [➡ FABRICS; 1132]

lodge 1 *n* **small house,** cabin, cottage, chalet, hunting lodge, shooting lodge, gatehouse [➡ RESIDENTIAL BUILDINGS; 1078] **2** *n* **hotel,** inn, resort, motel [➡ HOTELS, RESTAURANTS, AND CLUBS; 1082] **3** *type of* **outbuilding** [➡ ANCILLARY BUILDINGS; 1080] **4** *type of* **den or nest** [➡ ANIMAL OR BIRD ACCOMMODATIONS; 1079] **5** *v* **stay,** live, board, be a lodger, take lodgings, stop, put up, room, sojourn (*literary*) [➡ INHABIT; 20] **6** *v* **accommodate,** board, billet, put up, quarter, entertain, harbor, shelter [➡ TAKE CARE OF AND SPOIL; 300] **7** *v* **fix in place,** embed, implant, stick, catch, settle, become fixed [➡ FASTEN, LINK, AND JOIN; 408]

lodger *n* **tenant,** boarder, paying guest, cotenant, lessee, occupier, resident, occupant, roomer, renter [➡ INHABITANTS; 857]

lodging *n* **accommodations,** room, space, place to stay, housing, billet, bed and board [➡ ACCOMMODATIONS; 855]

lodgings (*dated*) *n* **rooms,** quarters, accommodations [➡ ACCOMMODATIONS; 855]

loft 1 *type of* **apartment** [➡ RESIDENTIAL BUILDINGS; 1078] **2** *type of* **room in the home** [➡ TYPES OF ROOMS; 1097] **3** *type of* **storage space** [➡ STORES AND STORAGE BUILDINGS; 1088]

loftily *adv* **superciliously,** in a superior way, disdainfully, arrogantly, proudly, haughtily, snootily (*informal*) [➡ POMPOUS, LOUD, AND OVERCONFIDENT; 635] *Opposite:* humbly

loftiness *n* **haughtiness,** superior manner, disdain, arrogance, condescension, superciliousness [➡ POMPOUS, LOUD, AND OVERCONFIDENT; 635] *Opposite:* humility

lofty 1 *adj* **supercilious,** superior, disdainful, lordly, arrogant, aloof, proud, haughty, condescending, patronizing, snooty (*informal*) [➡ POMPOUS, LOUD, AND OVERCONFIDENT; 635] *Opposite:* humble **2** *adj* **grand,** elevated, noble, admirable, distinguished, dignified, imposing, stately, majestic, exalted (*formal*), sublime (*formal*) [➡ SUPERIORITY; 152] *Opposite:* base **3** *adj* **tall,** high, towering, soaring, high-ceilinged, elevated [➡ HEIGHT: HIGH; 1203] *Opposite:* short

log 1 *n* **record,** journal, notes, minutes, logbook, daybook, calendar, diary [➡ RECORDS; 585] **2** *v* **make a note of,** chart, record, note down, note, register, list [➡ RECORD SOMETHING; 371]

loganberry *type of* **berry** [➡ FRUIT AND VEGETABLES; 1176]

logbook *n* **record,** record book, log, journal, report, register, diary [➡ RECORDS; 585]

loge *n* **box,** enclosure, box seat, skybox [➡ ALCOVES, CUBICLES, AND COMPARTMENTS; 1096]

loggia *n* [➡ ALCOVES, CUBICLES, AND COMPARTMENTS; 1096]

logic *n* **reason,** judgment, sense, common sense, lucidity, reasoning, rationality, sensibleness, soundness [➡ IDEAS AND THOUGHTS; 770]

logical 1 *adj* **rational,** reasonable, sound, commonsense, commonsensical, consistent, coherent, valid, analytical, cogent, lucid [➡ POSITIVE INTELLECTUAL CHARACTERISTICS; 524] *Opposite:* illogical **2** *adj* **plausible,** reasonable, obvious, sensible, understandable, likely, compelling [➡ POSSIBLE AND PROBABLE; 177] *Opposite:* implausible

log in *v* **gain access,** open up, start, switch on, sign in, start up, commence, begin, access, log on, initiate [➡ USE TOOLS AND MACHINERY; 468]

logjam 1 *n* **deadlock,** standstill, standoff, stalemate, impasse, gridlock [➡ LACK OF ACTIVITY OR MOTION; 342] **2** *n* **traffic jam,** holdup, buildup, snarl, tailback (*UK*), snarl-up (*UK*) [➡ TRAVEL: TRAFFIC PROBLEMS AND TRAFFIC MANAGEMENT; 323]

logo *n* **symbol,** sign, emblem, badge, insignia, design [➡ SYMBOLS, SIGNS, AND NUMBERS; 596]

log off *v* **leave,** quit, exit, log out, close down, shut down [➡ USE TOOLS AND MACHINERY; 468] *Opposite:* log on

logogram *type of* **wordplay** [➡ JOKES AND TEASING; 674]

log on *v* **gain access,** open up, start, switch on, sign in, start up, commence, begin, access, log in, initiate [➡ USE TOOLS AND MACHINERY; 468]

log out *v* **log off,** close, exit, sign off, leave [➡ USE TOOLS AND MACHINERY; 468]

logy *adj* **tired,** run-down, enervated, sleepy, washed out, bushed (*informal*), wiped out (*slang*) [➡ TIRED, ASLEEP, AND UNCONSCIOUS; 738]

loin *type of* **cut** [➡ TYPES AND CUTS OF MEAT; 1177]

loiter 1 *v* **amble**, stroll, wander, drift, dally, dawdle, idle [➡ MOVE SLOWLY; 314] 2 *v* **wait**, linger, lurk, skulk, hang around, hang out (*informal*) [➡ LACK OF ACTIVITY OR MOTION; 342]

loll 1 *v* **lie**, lounge, lie back, sprawl, slouch, slump, recline, flop [➡ ASSUME A POSITION; 317] 2 *v* **droop**, hang down, dangle, sag, flop [➡ TAKE UP A NEW POSITION; 312]

loll around *v* [➡ LACK OF ACTIVITY OR MOTION; 342]

lollipop *type of* **confectionery on a stick** [➡ CONFECTIONERY; 1182]

lollop 1 *v* **bound**, bounce, bumble, stride, lope, walk [➡ PROCEED AND GO; 305] 2 *v* (*UK*) **relax**, take it easy, lounge, veg out (*informal*), chill out (*slang*) [➡ LACK OF ACTIVITY OR MOTION; 342]

lollygag (*dated*) *v* [➡ LACK OF ACTIVITY OR MOTION; 342]

lollygagger (*dated*) *n* **loafer**, dawdler, idler, lazybones (*informal*) [➡ LAZY OR UNSUCCESSFUL PEOPLE; 948]

lone 1 *adj* **solitary**, single, single-handed, solo [➡ ACTING INDEPENDENTLY; 284] *Opposite*: accompanied 2 *adj* **only**, sole, unique, singular [➡ UNRELATEDNESS AND SEPARATENESS; 146] 3 *adj* **isolated**, lonely, separate, distinct, discrete, detached, solitary [➡ SOLITARINESS; 941]

loneliness *n* **aloneness**, solitude, isolation, lonesomeness, seclusion [➡ SOLITARINESS; 941] *Opposite*: companionship

lonely 1 *adj* **forlorn**, lost, alone, friendless, without a friend in the world, abandoned, deserted, lonesome [➡ SOLITARINESS; 941] 2 *adj* **isolated**, solitary, secluded, cut off, deserted, remote, desolate, lonesome, lone [➡ DISTANCE; 160]

lone parent *type of* **older relative** [➡ OLDER GENERATION RELATIVES; 959]

loner *n* **recluse**, hermit, lone wolf, outsider [➡ SOLITARY PEOPLE AND MISFITS; 942]

lonesome 1 *adj* **lonely**, forlorn, lost, alone, friendless, without a friend in the world, abandoned, deserted [➡ SOLITARINESS; 941] 2 *adj* **solitary**, isolated, secluded, lonely, cut off, deserted, remote, desolate [➡ DISTANCE; 160]

lonesomeness *n* [➡ SOLITARINESS; 941]

lone wolf *n* [➡ SOLITARY PEOPLE AND MISFITS; 942]

long 1 *adj* **extended**, extensive, elongated, lengthy, stretched [➡ LENGTH: LONG; 1197] *Opposite*: short 2 *adj* **time-consuming**, protracted, lengthy, slow, prolonged, lingering, sustained [➡ HAPPENING SLOWLY; 106] *Opposite*: brief

long ago *n* [➡ PAST; 84]

long-ago *adj* **past**, old, historic, early, prehistoric, ancient, primitive, olden (*archaic or literary*) [➡ PAST; 84] *Opposite*: modern

longboat *type of* **historical vessel** [➡ SHIPS AND BOATS; 1150]

long bone *type of* **bone** [➡ THE BONES AND JOINTS; 719]

longbow *type of* **bow** [➡ WEAPONS FOR SHOOTING; 1156]

long-drawn-out *adj* **protracted**, prolonged, lengthy,

drawn-out, dragged-out, long-winded, rambling, tedious, boring [➡ HAPPENING SLOWLY; 106] *Opposite*: brief

long-eared owl *type of* **owl** [➡ OWLS; 1001]

longed-for *adj* [➡ POPULAR AND WANTED; 220]

long-established *adj* **age-old**, time-honored, timeworn, ancient, old, traditional, established, deep-rooted, customary, usual [➡ OLD, OLD-FASHIONED; 167] *Opposite*: new

longevity *n* **long life**, permanence, durability, endurance [➡ PERMANENCE: WITHOUT END; 94]

long face *n* [➡ FACIAL EXPRESSIONS AND BLUSHING; 651]

long for *v* **want**, yearn, crave, desire, hunger, ache, pine [➡ DESIRE AND WANT; 579]

See Compare and Contrast at **want**.

long-gone *adj* [➡ ABSENT AND UNAVAILABLE; 7]

long haul (*informal*) 1 *n* **ordeal**, marathon, trial, struggle, endurance test, uphill battle [➡ HARD WORK OR EFFORT; 298] 2 *n* **trek**, hike, distance, way, schlep (*informal*) [➡ TRAVEL: JOURNEYS AND TRIPS; 318]

longing *n* **desire**, wish, yearning, hunger, craving, ache, pining, lust [➡ DESIRE AND WANT; 579]

longitude *n* **position**, meridian, coordinate, location [➡ NAVIGATION; 1141] *Opposite*: latitude

long johns *type of* **lower body underwear** [➡ ACCESSORIES, MILLINERY, AND LINGERIE; 867]

long jump *type of* **track and field** [➡ HOBBIES, GAMES, AND SPORTS; 875]

long-lasting *adj* **long-term**, continuing, enduring, lifelong, abiding, ongoing [➡ PERMANENCE: WITHOUT END; 94] *Opposite*: short-lived

long-lived *adj* **long-lasting**, long-standing, prolonged, abiding, long-term, enduring [➡ PERMANENCE: WITHOUT END; 94] *Opposite*: short-lived

long-lost (*humorous*) *adj* **lost**, gone, forgotten, missing [➡ ABSENT AND UNAVAILABLE; 7]

long-range *adj* **long-term**, future, distant, far-off [➡ FUTURE; 86]

longship *type of* **historical vessel** [➡ SHIPS AND BOATS; 1150]

long shot *n* **slim chance**, long odds, poor prospect, remote possibility, outside chance, fat chance (*informal*) [➡ IMPOSSIBLE AND IMPROBABLE; 178]

long-standing *adj* **established**, long-lasting, age-old, ancient, enduring, time-honored [➡ PERMANENCE: WITHOUT END; 94]

long-suffering *adj* **forgiving**, resigned, tolerant, accommodating, patient, selfless [➡ GENEROSITY AND KINDNESS; 495] *Opposite*: intolerant

long-term *adj* **lasting**, long-standing, enduring, continuing, durable, abiding [➡ PERMANENCE: WITHOUT END; 94] *Opposite*: short-term

long-winded *adj* **long-drawn-out**, rambling, interminable, lengthy, prolix, loquacious, wordy, verbose, discursive, circuitous, expansive [➡ ELOQUENT, TALKATIVE, AND LONG-WINDED; 632] *Opposite*: concise

See Compare and Contrast at **wordy**.

long-windedness *n* **verbosity**, wordiness, volubility, prolixity, verbiage, discursiveness, circumlocution, circuitousness, lengthiness, expansiveness, loquaciousness (*formal*) [➡ ELOQUENT, TALKATIVE, AND LONG-WINDED; 632] *Opposite*: conciseness

loofa *n* **sponge**, scrubber, exfoliator [➡ PERSONAL HYGIENE; 491]

look 1 *v* **seem**, appear, come across, seem to be [➡ SEEM TO BE SOMETHING; 58] 2 *v* **observe**, watch, see, view, regard, eye, gaze, contemplate, consider (*formal*), behold (*archaic or literary*) [➡ LOOKING AND LOOKS; 700] 3 *v* **examine**, inspect, scrutinize, pore over, study, scan, survey, eyeball (*informal*) [➡ EXAMINE AND ASSESS; 753] 4 *v* **focus on**, gaze, stare, glare, glance, peep, peek, peer, gawk (*informal*) [➡ LOOKING AND LOOKS; 700] 5 *v* **explore**, investigate, examine, consider, discuss, tackle [➡ EXAMINE AND ASSESS; 753] 6 *n* **appearance**, expression, air, aspect, guise, mien (*formal*) [➡ APPEARANCE AND ATMOSPHERE; 1237]

look after *v* **care for**, take care of, see to, watch over, guard, tend, oversee, mind [➡ TAKE CARE OF AND SPOIL; 300]

look ahead *v* **look forward**, project, plan, anticipate, think about, look to the future [➡ PREDICT AND ANTICIPATE; 750]

look-alike (*informal*) *n* **double**, twin, doppelgänger, mirror image, duplicate, match [➡ COPIES AND REPLICAS; 151]

look back 1 *v* **remember**, reminisce, recall, recollect, relive [➡ REMEMBER; 746] *Opposite*: look ahead 2 *v* **review**, check, return, revisit [➡ LOOKING AND LOOKS; 700]

look daggers *v* **glare**, glower, scowl, give somebody a dirty look [➡ FACIAL EXPRESSIONS AND BLUSHING; 651]

look down on *v* **scorn**, disdain, despise, frown on, abhor (*formal*) [➡ DISLIKE AND HATE; 577] *Opposite*: look up to

looked-for *adj* **anticipated**, expected, awaited, foreseen, hoped-for, desired, wanted, required, necessary [➡ POPULAR AND WANTED; 220] *Opposite*: unexpected

looker *n* **observer**, watcher, spectator, viewer, onlooker, bystander [➡ ONLOOKERS AND SPECTATORS; 701]

look for *v* **search for**, seek, hunt for, rummage [➡ SEEK POSSESSION AND SEARCH; 456]

look forward to *v* **anticipate**, hope for, expect, await, wait for, long for [➡ PREDICT AND ANTICIPATE; 750] *Opposite*: dread

looking glass *n* **mirror**, glass, hand mirror, shaving mirror [➡ FIXTURES; 859]

look into *v* **investigate**, go into, check out, research, study, examine, explore, delve, dig, probe, inquire [➡ QUESTION THINGS; 751]

look like *v* **resemble**, be like, be similar to, mimic [➡ PRETEND AND MIMIC; 60]

look on the bright side *v* **be positive**, be optimistic, make the best of something, make the best of things, hope for the best, keep your chin up, grin and bear it (*informal*), make the best of a bad job (*UK*) [➡ TOLERATE AND ENDURE; 766] *Opposite*: despair

look out 1 *v* **watch out**, beware, take care, pay attention, be alert, be watchful, keep your eyes open, mind [➡ PAY ATTENTION; 765] 2 *v* **look over**, look on to, look out on, overlook, face, give on to (*UK*), front (*UK*) [➡ EXIST IN A PLACE; 19]

lookout 1 *n* **guard**, sentry, sentinel, watch [➡ PEOPLE WHO GUARD AND PROTECT; 846] 2 *n* **viewpoint**, vantage point, lookout tower, crow's nest, belvedere [➡ TOWERS; 1099]

lookout tower *n* [➡ TOWERS; 1099]

look over *v* **inspect**, examine, check, peruse, scan, flick through, skim, flip through, give the once-over (*informal*) [➡ EXAMINE AND ASSESS; 753]

lookover (*informal*) *n* **inspection**, examination, scan, glance, skim, once-over (*informal*) [➡ LOOKING AND LOOKS; 700]

look-see (*informal*) *n* **look**, glance, inspection, scan, examination, skim, once-over (*informal*) [➡ LOOKING AND LOOKS; 700]

look through *v* **ignore**, take no notice of, give the cold shoulder, snub, cut, walk by, pass by, sail by [➡ REFUSING OR REJECTING RELATIONS; 975] *Opposite*: acknowledge

look up 1 *v* **search**, hunt, research, find, consult [➡ FIND; 463] 2 *v* **get better**, improve, take a turn for the better, mend, recuperate, convalesce, pick up (*informal*), be on the up (*informal*) [➡ GET BETTER; 375] *Opposite*: worsen 3 *v* **visit**, call on, contact, get in touch, locate [➡ INITIATE AND ESTABLISH COMMUNICATION; 680]

look up to *v* **admire**, respect, esteem, worship, adore, revere [➡ LIKE, LOVE, VALUE, AND ENJOY; 578] *Opposite*: look down on

loom 1 *v* **appear**, emerge, come out, materialize, show, reveal [➡ APPEAR AND EMERGE; 3] *Opposite*: recede 2 *v* **hang over**, approach, come up, threaten, menace, impend (*formal*) [➡ ABOUT TO HAPPEN; 33] *Opposite*: recede

looming *adj* **impending**, pending, forthcoming, coming up, approaching, imminent, future, on the horizon, in the offing, at hand, upcoming [➡ ABOUT TO HAPPEN; 33]

loon *type of* **freshwater bird** [➡ FRESHWATER BIRDS; 1000]

loop 1 *n* **ring**, coil, twist, circlet, hoop, eye, circle [➡ ROUNDED SHAPE; 1218] 2 *v* **wind**, twist, coil, entwine, encircle, encompass, ring, surround, circle [➡ POSITION SOMETHING: AROUND SOMETHING; 327]

loophole *n* **dodge**, gap, ambiguity, excuse, escape, get-out (*UK*) [➡ FAULTS, FLAWS, AND WEAKNESSES; 251]

loose 1 *adj* **movable**, slack, wobbly, unfastened, free, unattached [➡ MALLEABLE AND ELASTIC; 1212] *Opposite*: fixed 2 *adj* **floppy**, relaxed, supple, slack, droopy, sagging, limp [➡ SHAPELESSNESS; 1219] *Opposite*: tight 3 *adj* **loose-fitting**, baggy, unrestricting, flowing, roomy, voluminous, ample, shapeless, formless [➡ DESCRIBING CLOTHES; 869] *Opposite*: tight 4 *adj* **free**, freed, at liberty, unchained, untied, flowing, unconfined, at large [➡ FREEDOM AND LIBERTY; 208] *Opposite*: secure 5 *adj* **assorted**, diverse, free, miscellaneous, eclectic [➡ DIFFERENCE; 149] 6 *adj* (*dated*) **irresponsible**, lax, slack, relaxed, free, unprofessional, careless, weak, sloppy [➡ INCAUTIOUS AND CARELESS; 283] *Opposite*: strict

loose-fitting *adj* **loose**, baggy, voluminous, roomy, ample, floppy, shapeless, formless [➡ DESCRIBING CLOTHES; 869] *Opposite*: tight

loose-limbed *adj* **supple**, lissom, agile, lithe, elastic [➡ AGILITY OF THE BODY; 476] *Opposite:* stiff

loosely (*dated*) *adv* **inaccurately**, sloppily, freely, carelessly, laxly [➡ INCAUTIOUS AND CARELESS; 283] *Opposite:* accurately

loosen *v* **come loose**, work loose, untie, undo, release, relax, slacken, slacken off [➡ UNFASTEN AND UNDO; 409] *Opposite:* tighten

looseness 1 *n* (*dated*) **irresponsibility**, laxity, slackness, freeness, carelessness, sloppiness, negligence [➡ LACK OF COMMITMENT AND UNRELIABILITY; 509] *Opposite:* strictness 2 *n* **bagginess**, shapelessness, roominess, ampleness [➡ SHAPELESSNESS; 1219] *Opposite:* tightness

loosen up 1 *v* **warm up**, limber up, stretch, exercise, prepare [➡ PREPARE FOR ACTION; 289] 2 *v* **relax**, kick back (*informal*), let your hair down, take it easy, chill out (*slang*) [➡ CHANGE OF MOOD AND COMPOSURE; 580]

loot 1 *n* **booty**, spoils, plunder, swag (*slang*) [➡ PROCEEDS OF CRIME; 427] 2 *n* (*informal*) **money**, cash, wealth, assets, dough (*slang*) [➡ MONEY; 797] 3 *v* **burgle**, plunder, ransack, pillage, rob, sack [➡ STEAL AND ROB; 426]

looter *n* **robber**, raider, plunderer, burglar, thief, pillager [➡ CRIMINALS; 821]

lop 1 *v* **cut**, chop, hack, sever, crop, trim, slice, prune, pare [➡ EXTRACT AND SEVER; 341] *Opposite:* graft 2 *v* **cut off**, chop off, slice off, remove, amputate [➡ EXTRACT AND SEVER; 341] *Opposite:* attach 3 *v* **deduct**, take off, subtract, discount, reduce, decrease, lower [➡ REMOVE SOMETHING; 338] *Opposite:* add

lope 1 *n* **pace**, stride, step, gait, tread, walk [➡ PROCEED AND GO; 305] 2 *v* **stride**, move, walk, lollop, yomp (*UK informal*) [➡ PROCEED AND GO; 305]

lopsided *adj* **uneven**, askew, crooked, cockeyed, disproportionate, skewed, unequal, irregular [➡ ORIENTATION AND ALIGNMENT; 1223] *Opposite:* even

lopsidedness *n* **unevenness**, crookedness, skewedness, imbalance, disproportionateness, irregularity [➡ ORIENTATION AND ALIGNMENT; 1223] *Opposite:* evenness

loquacious *adj* **talkative**, garrulous, chatty, voluble, verbose, prolix, long-winded, wordy, effusive, noisy, talky, gabby (*informal*), windy (*UK informal*) [➡ ELOQUENT, TALKATIVE, AND LONG-WINDED; 632] *Opposite:* silent

See Compare and Contrast at **talkative**.

loquaciousness (*formal*) *n* [➡ ELOQUENT, TALKATIVE, AND LONG-WINDED; 632]

lore *n* **wisdom**, tradition, teachings, knowledge, experience, beliefs, legends, folklore [➡ THE ORAL TRADITION; 677]

lose 1 *v* **misplace**, be unable to find, mislay, drop, miss [➡ LOSE AND FORFEIT; 447] *Opposite:* find 2 *v* **be defeated**, be beaten, go under, fail, suffer defeat, go down (*informal*), take a licking (*informal*) [➡ FAIL OR BE UNSUCCESSFUL; 75] *Opposite:* win 3 *v* **shake off**, evade, give somebody the slip, leave behind, get away from, elude, escape, drop [➡ GET RID OF SOMETHING; 451] 4 *v* **waste**, squander, exhaust, use up, consume, spend [➡ USE UP AND WASTE; 474] *Opposite:* save

lose consciousness *v* **faint**, blackout, pass out, swoon, collapse [➡ BECOME SICK, TREAT, AND RECOVER; 728] *Opposite:* come to

lose control *v* **get carried away**, go berserk, hit the roof, lose it (*informal*), blow up (*informal*), see red (*informal*), blow your top (*informal*), lose your cool (*informal*) [➡ GIVING VENT TO EMOTIONS; 679] *Opposite:* stay calm

lose heart *v* **become despondent**, become demoralized, give up, give in, lose motivation, falter, flag [➡ CHANGE OF MOOD AND COMPOSURE; 580] *Opposite:* take heart

lose it (*informal*) *v* **lose your temper**, hit the roof, lose control, blow up (*informal*), blow your top (*informal*), see red (*informal*), lose your cool (*informal*) [➡ GIVING VENT TO EMOTIONS; 679] *Opposite:* keep your cool (*informal*)

lose out (*informal*) *v* **miss out**, get the worst of it, come off second best, fail to benefit, miss the boat, miss an opportunity, miss a chance [➡ FAIL OR BE UNSUCCESSFUL; 75] *Opposite:* gain

loser *n* **failure**, also-ran, underdog, dud (*informal*), has-been (*informal*) [➡ LAZY OR UNSUCCESSFUL PEOPLE; 948]

lose the thread *v* **get off the point**, lose the point, digress, go off on a tangent, deviate, stray, drift, lose concentration, falter, hesitate [➡ HESITATE; 272] *Opposite:* follow

lose track of *v* **misplace**, lose sight of, lose, be unable to follow, mislay, forget [➡ LOSE AND FORFEIT; 447] *Opposite:* keep track of

lose weight *v* **diet**, go on a diet, slim, watch your weight, count the calories, cut down, fast [➡ EAT AND NOT EAT; 710]

lose your bearings *v* **get lost**, lose your way, stray, become disoriented, take a wrong turn [➡ AIMLESS AND ERRANT MOTION; 343]

lose your cool (*informal*) *v* **go off the deep end**, go berserk, lose control, hit the roof, lose your head, lose it (*informal*), see red (*informal*), blow up (*informal*), blow your top (*informal*) [➡ GIVING VENT TO EMOTIONS; 679] *Opposite:* keep your cool (*informal*)

lose your footing *v* **stumble**, trip, trip up, fall over, slip, tumble, take a tumble, falter, fall, lose your balance [➡ GO DOWNWARD; 307]

lose your nerve *v* **go to pieces**, break down, get flustered, give up, fall apart, crack up (*informal*), chicken out (*slang*) [➡ CHANGE OF MOOD AND COMPOSURE; 580] *Opposite:* keep your cool (*informal*)

lose your patience *v* **flare up**, snap, hit the roof, lose your cool (*informal*), lose it (*informal*), see red (*informal*), blow up (*informal*), blow your top (*informal*) [➡ GIVING VENT TO EMOTIONS; 679] *Opposite:* keep your cool (*informal*)

lose your temper *v* **fly into a rage**, explode, hit the roof, fly off the handle (*informal*), blow your top (*informal*), see red (*informal*), lose it (*informal*), go nuts (*slang*), go crazy [➡ GIVING VENT TO EMOTIONS; 679] *Opposite:* keep your cool (*informal*)

lose your way *v* **lose your bearings**, get lost, become disoriented, stray, take a wrong turn, go wrong [➡ AIMLESS AND ERRANT MOTION; 343]

losing *adj* **behind**, trailing, bringing up the rear, down [➡ IN TROUBLE AND DISADVANTAGED; 73] *Opposite*: winning

loss 1 *n* **deprivation**, removal, withdrawal, forfeiture, depletion, erosion [➡ REMOVE SOMETHING; 338] 2 *n* **bereavement**, passing, passing away, death, demise (*formal*) [➡ DEATH AND BEREAVEMENT; 927] 3 *n* **deficit**, debit, deficiency, shortfall [➡ TOO FEW, TOO LITTLE; 122] *Opposite*: profit 4 *n* **damage**, harm, injury, cost, hurt [➡ NUISANCES; 253] 5 *n* **defeat**, beating, thrashing, trouncing, hammering (*informal*), pasting (*informal*), slaughter (*slang*) [➡ FAILURE; 77] *Opposite*: victory

lossmaking (*UK*) *adj* **running at a loss**, unprofitable, not viable, uneconomic, inefficient, impracticable [➡ FINANCE AND ECONOMICS; 796] *Opposite*: profitable

loss of consciousness *n* **blackout**, faint, fainting fit, swoon, collapse [➡ TIRED, ASLEEP, AND UNCONSCIOUS; 738]

lost 1 *adj* **misplaced**, mislaid, missing, gone, nowhere to be found, gone astray, vanished, absent [➡ ABSENT AND UNAVAILABLE; 7] *Opposite*: found 2 *adj* **disoriented**, adrift, astray, off-course (*UK*) [➡ AIMLESS AND ERRANT MOTION; 343] 3 *adj* **deep in thought**, spellbound, entranced, rapt, engrossed, absorbed, preoccupied [➡ PENSIVENESS AND INTEREST; 538] 4 *adj* **confused**, bewildered, bemused, at sea, stumped, puzzled, perplexed, mystified, baffled, flummoxed (*informal*) [➡ CONFUSION, ANXIETY, AND WORRY; 540] 5 *adj* **forlorn**, vulnerable, abandoned, alone, aimless, helpless [➡ IN TROUBLE AND DISADVANTAGED; 73]

lost in thought *adj* **faraway**, dreamy, engrossed, absorbed, deep in thought, pensive, distant, bemused, miles away (*UK*) [➡ PENSIVENESS AND INTEREST; 538]

lot 1 *n* **batch**, set, assortment, grouping, bundle, delivery, quantity, group, bunch (*informal*) [➡ COLLECTIONS AND MIXTURES OF THINGS; 1244] 2 *n* **ration**, share, slice, proportion, percentage, allocation, allotment, allowance, measure, quota, portion (*literary*) [➡ AMOUNTS AND QUANTITIES; 112] 3 *n* **fate**, destiny, luck, kismet, fortune, plight [➡ FATE, DESTINY, AND ASTROLOGY; 782]

loth *see* **loath**

Lothario (*literary*) *n* [➡ PLEASURE-SEEKERS AND HEDONISTS; 886]

loti *type of* **currency** [➡ CURRENCIES; 798]

lotion *n* **oil**, ointment, liniment, unguent, rub, salve, gel, balm, cream [➡ LOTIONS, PASTES, AND GELS; 1272]

lots *n* **plenty**, many, heaps (*informal*), loads (*informal*), oodles (*informal*), tons (*informal*), stacks (*informal*), bags of (*UK informal*) [➡ MANY, MUCH, LARGE AMOUNT; 117] *Opposite*: few

lottery 1 *n* **draw**, sweepstakes, raffle, lotto, bingo, tombola (*UK*) [➡ GAMBLE AND TAKE RISKS; 466] 2 *n* **risk**, gamble, chance, fortune, luck, the luck of the draw [➡ LUCK; 783] *Opposite*: certainty

lotus *type of* **perennial flower** [➡ FLOWERS; 1032]

lotus-eater *n* **lazy person**, hedonist, dreamer, daydreamer, idler [➡ LAZY OR UNSUCCESSFUL PEOPLE; 948]

louche *adj* **disreputable**, shady, dubious, immoral, suspect, corrupt [➡ MORALLY BAD OR IMPROPER; 775] *Opposite*: respectable

loud 1 *adj* **noisy**, deafening, piercing, strident, thunderous, booming, shrill, earsplitting [➡ LOUD, HIGH, OR UNPLEASANT SOUNDS; 1266] *Opposite*: quiet 2 *adj* **vociferous**, rowdy, bois-

terous, raucous, noisy, forceful, voluble, riotous, blaring, loudmouthed (*informal*) [➡ POMPOUS, LOUD, AND OVERCONFIDENT; 635] *Opposite*: gentle 3 *adj* **lurid**, flamboyant, brash, flashy, gaudy, vulgar, garish, showy, ostentatious [➡ IN POOR TASTE AND OVERSENTIMENTAL; 229] *Opposite*: muted

loudly 1 *adv* **noisily**, deafeningly, piercingly, stridently, at the top of your voice, at full volume [➡ LOUD, HIGH, OR UNPLEASANT SOUNDS; 1266] *Opposite*: quietly 2 *adv* **vociferously**, rowdily, boisterously, raucously, noisily, forcefully, brashly [➡ POMPOUS, LOUD, AND OVERCONFIDENT; 635] *Opposite*: quietly

loudmouth (*informal*) *n* [➡ SELF-IMPORTANT AND SELF-SEEKING PEOPLE; 949]

loudmouthed (*informal*) *adj* **blustering**, loud, noisy, vociferous, voluble, brash [➡ POMPOUS, LOUD, AND OVERCONFIDENT; 635] *Opposite*: quiet

loudness *n* **volume**, noise, decibels, level, intensity [➡ LOUD, HIGH, OR UNPLEASANT SOUNDS; 1266] *Opposite*: quietness

loudspeaker *part of* **audio equipment** [➡ AUDIO EQUIPMENT; 1139]

lough (*UK*) 1 *n* **lake**, tarn, water, mere (*archaic or literary*), broad (*UK*), loch (*UK*) [➡ RIVERS, LAKES, AND STREAMS; 1042] 2 *n* **inlet**, fjord, sound, estuary, creek, sea loch (*UK*), firth (*UK*) [➡ THE SEAS, OCEANS, AND SHORES; 1041]

lounge 1 *n* **living room**, drawing room, sitting room, family room, salon [➡ TYPES OF ROOMS; 1097] 2 *v* **sprawl**, recline, laze, loaf, loll, relax, take it easy, idle, dawdle, lie around (*informal*), veg out (*slang*), hang (*slang*), chill (*slang*) [➡ LACK OF ACTIVITY OR MOTION; 342] 3 *type of* **pop and vocal music** [➡ MUSIC, SONGS, AND SINGING; 907]

lounge around *v* [➡ LACK OF ACTIVITY OR MOTION; 342]

lounger *n* **reclining seat**, recliner, tanning bed, folding chair, deck chair, sunbed (*UK*) [➡ FURNITURE; 858]

louse *type of* **parasitic insect** [➡ PARASITES; 1017]

louse-ridden *adj* [➡ DECAYING OR INFESTED; 1236]

lousy (*informal*) 1 *adj* **useless**, worthless, stupid, second-rate, mean, inferior, horrible, crummy (*informal*) [➡ BAD AND BADLY; 223] *Opposite*: great (*informal*) 2 *adj* **awful**, rotten, miserable, dreadful, abysmal, nasty, terrible, fed up (*informal*) [➡ SADNESS, DISTRESS, AND DESPAIR; 539] *Opposite*: great (*informal*)

lout *n* **hulk**, oaf, ox (*informal*), lug (*informal*), lummox (*informal*), lump (*informal*), meathead (*slang*) [➡ LAZY OR UNSUCCESSFUL PEOPLE; 948]

loutish *adj* **coarse**, impolite, rough, uncouth, rude, ill-mannered, boorish [➡ BAD MANNERS AND SOCIAL SKILLS; 521] *Opposite*: genteel

loutishness *n* **uncouthness**, rudeness, incivility, vulgarity, bad behavior, boorishness [➡ BAD MANNERS AND SOCIAL SKILLS; 521] *Opposite*: politeness

lovable *adj* **endearing**, adorable, enchanting, attractive, delightful, affable, congenial, amiable, engaging, winning, captivating, cute [➡ BEAUTY AND ATTRACTIVENESS; 189]

lovage *type of* **herb** [➡ HERBS AND SPICES; 1175]

lovat *type of* **green** [➡ COLORS; 1224]

love 1 *n* **affection**, friendship, feeling, adoration, tenderness, fondness, devotion, passion, liking, ardor, amity (*formal*) [➡ LOVE, RESPECT, AND GOODWILL; 549] *Opposite:* hatred **2** *n* **darling**, dear, dearest, sweetheart, honey (*informal*) [➡ ENDEARMENTS; 656] **3** *v* **feel affection for**, adore, worship, be in love with, be devoted to, care for, find irresistible, be fond of, hold dear, be keen on (*UK*) [➡ LIKE, LOVE, VALUE, AND ENJOY; 578] *Opposite:* hate **4** *v* **like**, enjoy, appreciate, be partial to, have a weakness for, be attracted to, go for (*informal*), have a thing for (*informal*), be keen on (*UK*) [➡ LIKE, LOVE, VALUE, AND ENJOY; 578] *Opposite:* dislike

---

Compare and Contrast: *love, liking, affection, fondness, passion, infatuation, crush*

CORE MEANING: a strong positive feeling toward somebody or something

love an intense feeling of tender affection and compassion, especially strong romantic or sexual feelings between people; *liking* a feeling of enjoying something or or finding it pleasant, or personal taste or choice; *affection* fond or tender feelings toward somebody or something; *fondness* a feeling of affection or preference; *passion* intense or overpowering emotion, either love for somebody, usually of a strong sexual nature, or strong liking or enthusiasm for something; *infatuation* an intense but short-lived, often unrealistic love for somebody, usually of a romantic or sexual nature; *crush* (*informal*) a temporary romantic *infatuation*, especially in teenagers and young people.

---

lovebird *type of* **pet bird** [➡ BIRDS; 997]

loved *adj* **precious**, treasured, respected, important, adored, worshipped, valued, esteemed, prized [➡ POPULAR AND WANTED; 220] *Opposite:* detested

loved ones *n* **family**, nearest and dearest, relations, relatives, kin, kith and kin [➡ THE FAMILY; 956]

love handles (*informal*) *n* [➡ EXTRA WEIGHT; 478]

loveless *adj* **harsh**, hard, unhappy, unkind, cruel, insensitive, unsympathetic, callous [➡ SELFISH AND UNKIND; 505] *Opposite:* loving

loveliness *n* **beauty**, attractiveness, good looks, exquisiteness, charm, allure, comeliness (*archaic or literary*) [➡ PEOPLE'S PHYSICAL APPEARANCE; 475] *Opposite:* ugliness

lovely **1** *adj* **beautiful**, attractive, pretty, good-looking, gorgeous, exquisite, charming, handsome, adorable, fetching, enchanting, divine (*informal or humorous*), comely (*archaic or literary*) [➡ BEAUTY AND ATTRACTIVENESS; 189] *Opposite:* ugly **2** *adj* **pleasant**, agreeable, delightful, perfect, wonderful, superb, nice, good, splendid, fine [➡ EMOTIONALLY PLEASANT; 187] *Opposite:* unpleasant

See Compare and Contrast at **good-looking**.

love seat *type of* **seating** [➡ FURNITURE; 858]

lovesick *adj* **infatuated**, sentimental, overly affectionate, obsessed, pining, overemotional, yearning, longing, icky (*informal*), sloppy (*informal*), sappy (*informal*) [➡ APPRECIATION AND GRATITUDE; 535]

love-struck *adj* [➡ APPRECIATION AND GRATITUDE; 535]

loving *adj* **affectionate**, tender, fond, devoted, caring,

warm, adoring, amorous, doting, sympathetic, benevolent, solicitous [➡ FRIENDLINESS AND SOCIABILITY; 494] *Opposite:* cold

low **1** *adj* **near to the ground**, close to the ground, low down, short, small, little, squat, low-slung, stumpy, truncated [➡ HEIGHT: LOW; 1204] *Opposite:* high **2** *adj* **depleted**, at a low level, down, short, in short supply, dwindling, minimal, run-down [➡ TOO FEW, TOO LITTLE; 122] *Opposite:* high **3** *adj* **soft**, muted, soothing, muffled, subdued, gentle, subtle, hushed, faint, quiet [➡ SOFT, LOW, OR PLEASANT SOUNDS; 1265] *Opposite:* loud **4** *adj* **sad**, miserable, unhappy, down, depressed, gloomy, sorry for yourself, glum, despondent, downcast, forlorn, dejected, disheartened, dispirited, down in the dumps (*informal*), fed up (*informal*), blue (*informal*) [➡ SADNESS, DISTRESS, AND DESPAIR; 539] *Opposite:* cheerful **5** *n* **low point**, slump, depression, depths, nadir, trough [➡ INTERMEDIATE STAGES; 55] *Opposite:* peak

See Compare and Contrast at **mean**.

lowboy *type of* **cabinet** [➡ FURNITURE; 858]

lowbrow *adj* **popular**, mass-market, philistine, undemanding, middle-of-the-road [➡ THE NATURE OF IDEAS; 771] *Opposite:* highbrow

low-cut *adj* [➡ DESCRIBING CLOTHES; 869]

lowdown (*informal*) *n* **facts**, fundamentals, basics, ins and outs, particulars, info (*informal*), 411 (*slang*) [➡ BASIC DETAILS; 688]

lower **1** *adj* **inferior**, subordinate, lesser, junior, poorer, worse, minor [➡ INFERIORITY; 153] *Opposite:* superior **2** *v* **let down**, drop, let fall, hand down, sink, pull down, depress, take down [➡ MOVE SOMETHING: DOWNWARD; 329] *Opposite:* raise **3** *v* **lessen**, drop, cut, bring down, decrease, slash, reduce [➡ CHANGE OF INTENSITY: LESS; 395] *Opposite:* raise

lower class *n* **working class**, masses, hoi polloi, lower classes, proletariat [➡ CLASS STATUS; 889] *Opposite:* upper class

lower-class *adj* **working-class**, blue-collar, plebeian, popular [➡ CLASS STATUS; 889] *Opposite:* aristocratic

lower ground floor *n* [➡ STAIRS AND STORIES; 1102]

lowermost *adj* **lowest**, bottommost, deepest, bottom, last [➡ RELATIVE LOCATION; 161]

lower yourself *v* **deign**, condescend, cheapen yourself, stoop, humiliate yourself, humble yourself [➡ CHANGE OF MOOD AND COMPOSURE; 580]

low-grade *adj* **low-quality**, inferior, cheap, substandard, second-rate [➡ ORDINARINESS; 244] *Opposite:* premium

low-key *adj* **simple**, unglamorous, unspectacular, understated, subdued, discreet, unpretentious, muted, restrained, toned-down [➡ PLAIN; 232] *Opposite:* elaborate

lowland *n* **plain**, fen, flat, valley, swamp, wetland [➡ DESERTS, PLAINS, AND MOORLAND; 1045]

lowliness *n* **humbleness**, meekness, submissiveness, inferiority, commonness, modesty [➡ CLASS STATUS; 889] *Opposite:* eminence

lowly *adj* **humble**, poor, deprived, ordinary, modest, simple, common, meek, submissive, mean (*archaic*) [➡ CLASS STATUS; 889] *Opposite:* exalted (*formal*)

low-lying adj **low**, lowland, sea-level, below sea level, coastal, sunken [➡ HEIGHT: LOW; 1204] *Opposite*: high

low-minded adj **coarse**, common, vulgar, base, uncouth, rude [➡ BAD MANNERS AND SOCIAL SKILLS; 521] *Opposite*: refined

low-necked adj [➡ DESCRIBING CLOTHES; 869]

low-pitched adj **low**, deep, throaty, gruff [➡ SOFT, LOW, OR PLEASANT SOUNDS; 1265] *Opposite*: high

low point n **low**, all-time low, nadir, rock bottom [➡ INTERMEDIATE STAGES; 55] *Opposite*: high point

low-rise adj **single-story**, two-story, small, three-story, low [➡ HEIGHT: LOW; 1204] *Opposite*: high-rise

loyal adj **faithful**, trustworthy, devoted, reliable, dependable, dedicated, steadfast, trusty, constant [➡ HONEST AND RELIABLE; 502] *Opposite*: disloyal

loyalist n **stalwart**, partisan, supporter, devotee, advocate, proponent [➡ DEVOTEES AND ADDICTED PEOPLE; 556] *Opposite*: rebel

loyalty n **faithfulness**, allegiance, constancy, fidelity, devotion, trustworthiness, reliability, dependability, steadfastness [➡ HONEST AND RELIABLE; 502] *Opposite*: disloyalty

lozenge 1 n **pastille**, tablet, pill [➡ REMEDIES, TREATMENTS, AND OPERATIONS; 731] 2 *type of* **angular shape** [➡ ANGULAR SHAPE; 1217]

LP n [➡ RECORDINGS AND PLAYERS; 911]

lubricate v **oil**, grease, loosen [➡ DECORATE, ADORN, AND APPLY COATINGS; 405]

lucid 1 adj **articulate**, clear, well-spoken, silver-tongued, smooth-tongued, eloquent, thought through, coherent, plain, simple, sound [➡ CONCISE AND CLEAR; 202] *Opposite*: incoherent 2 adj **rational**, sane, sober, clear-headed, compos mentis, in your right mind, logical, cogent, reasoned [➡ COOL AND CALM; 536] *Opposite*: delirious 3 adj **luminous**, shining, luminescent, limpid, translucent, bright [➡ DESCRIBING LIGHT; 1228] *Opposite*: dull

lucidity 1 n **intelligibility**, lucidness, unambiguousness, perspicuity, fluency, eloquence, articulacy [➡ CONCISE AND CLEAR; 202] *Opposite*: ambiguousness 2 n **rationality**, lucidness, clarity, reason, sanity, logic, saneness, soberness [➡ COOL AND CALM; 536] *Opposite*: confusion 3 n **luminousness**, luminescence, limpidness, lucidness, translucence, brightness [➡ DESCRIBING LIGHT; 1228] *Opposite*: dullness

lucidly adv **clearly**, logically, coherently, cogently, plainly, simply, soundly, intelligibly [➡ CONCISE AND CLEAR; 202] *Opposite*: incoherently

lucidness 1 n **clarity**, logic, intelligibleness, coherence, plainness, simplicity, clearness [➡ CONCISE AND CLEAR; 202] *Opposite*: incoherence 2 n **saneness**, soberness, clear-headedness, rationality, judgment, cogency [➡ COOL AND CALM; 536] *Opposite*: irrationality

luck 1 n **good fortune**, good luck, stroke of luck, windfall, blessing, godsend, providence, fluke (*informal*), break (*informal*) [➡ LUCK; 783] *Opposite*: misfortune 2 n **chance**, fate, fortune, destiny, providence, accident, coincidence, kismet [➡ FATE, DESTINY, AND ASTROLOGY; 782]

luckless adj **hapless**, unlucky, unfortunate, jinxed, ill-fated, doomed, unsuccessful [➡ BAD LUCK AND UNLUCKY; 784] *Opposite*: lucky

luck of the draw n [➡ LUCK; 783]

lucky adj **fortunate**, blessed, auspicious, propitious, providential, timely, happy, fluky (*informal*) [➡ LUCK; 783] *Opposite*: unlucky

lucky break n **opportunity**, opening, chance, blessing, boon, break (*informal*) [➡ PROGRESS AND ADVANCEMENT; 213]

lucky charm n **amulet**, mascot, good luck charm, juju, talisman [➡ LUCKY CHARMS; 785]

lucky dip (*UK*) n **raffle**, draw, lottery, drawing, lotto, grab bag, tombola (*UK*) [➡ LUCK; 783]

lucrative adj **profitable**, well-paid, rewarding, worthwhile, beneficial, productive [➡ ECONOMICAL AND RESOURCEFUL; 207] *Opposite*: unprofitable

ludicrous adj **absurd**, ridiculous, preposterous, nonsensical, comical, farcical, foolish, stupid, outrageous [➡ BIZARRE AND PECULIAR; 257] *Opposite*: sensible

ludicrousness n **absurdity**, ridiculousness, unreasonableness, foolishness, nonsensicalness, irrationality, illogicality, preposterousness, farce, silliness, stupidity [➡ BIZARRE AND PECULIAR; 257] *Opposite*: sensibleness

lug v **drag**, heave, cart, carry, haul, pull, tow, tug, draw [➡ PUSH, PULL, AND SLIDE; 335]

luge *type of* **leisure vehicle** [➡ VEHICLES; 1145]

luggage n **baggage**, bags, cases, suitcases, stuff, belongings, gear (*informal*), kit (*UK*) [➡ CONTAINERS, RECEPTACLES, AND PACKAGING; 1245]

luggage compartment 1 n **hold**, trunk, locker, boot (*UK*) [➡ STORES AND STORAGE BUILDINGS; 1088] 2 *part of* **train** [➡ RAILROADS; 1107]

luggage rack *type of* **external feature** [➡ EXTERNAL PARTS OF A VEHICLE; 1147]

lugubrious adj **sad**, mournful, gloomy, depressing, doleful, melancholic, somber, cheerless, miserable, dismal, morose [➡ SADNESS, DISTRESS, AND DESPAIR; 539] *Opposite*: cheerful

lugubriousness n **moroseness**, gloominess, melancholy, depression, sadness, misery, mournfulness, dolefulness, somberness, cheerlessness [➡ SADNESS, DISTRESS, AND DESPAIR; 539] *Opposite*: cheerfulness

lukewarm 1 adj **tepid**, warm, cool, hand-hot (*UK*) [➡ TEMPERATURE: MEDIUM; 1230] 2 adj **unenthusiastic**, half-hearted, cool, unexcited, indifferent, subdued, apathetic, uninterested [➡ NEUTRALITY AND INDIFFERENCE; 553] *Opposite*: enthusiastic

lull 1 v **soothe**, calm, reassure, quiet, settle down, comfort, pacify, hush [➡ SOOTHE AND CALM; 573] *Opposite*: rouse 2 n **quiet**, calm, stillness, silence, pause, break, respite, hiatus, letup (*informal*) [➡ PAUSES AND PHASES; 56] *Opposite*: flare-up (*informal*)

lullaby n **cradlesong**, song, ditty, child's bedtime song, serenade, chorus [➡ MUSIC, SONGS, AND SINGING; 907]

lumbago n **backache**, back pain, bad back [➡ PAIN AND OTHER PHYSICAL SENSATIONS; 733]

lumber 1 *n* **wood**, boards, planks, logs, timber (*UK*) [➡ BUILDING MATERIALS; 1077] **2** *v* **trudge**, shamble, hobble, plod, clump, stagger [➡ WALK UNSTEADILY; 315]

lumbering *adj* **awkward**, clumsy, unwieldy, hulking, graceless, bumbling (*informal*) [➡ AGILITY OF THE BODY; 476] *Opposite*: dainty

lumen *type of* **SI unit** [➡ SIZE AND DIMENSIONS; 1192]

luminary *n* **celebrity**, star, achiever, personality, personage, name, VIP, leading light, face (*informal*) [➡ IMPORTANT OR FAMOUS PEOPLE; 893] *Opposite*: nobody

luminesce *v* [➡ LIGHT EMISSION; 368]

luminescence *n* [➡ DESCRIBING LIGHT; 1228]

luminescent *adj* [➡ DESCRIBING LIGHT; 1228]

luminosity *n* **glow**, light, brilliance, radiance, shine, sheen, brightness, glare, incandescence, gleam [➡ DESCRIBING LIGHT; 1228]

luminous *adj* **glowing**, shining, brilliant, bright, radiant, gleaming, shimmering, incandescent, resplendent [➡ DESCRIBING LIGHT; 1228] *Opposite*: dull

lump 1 *n* **piece**, chunk, morsel, block, section, hunk, mass, slab, slice [➡ AMOUNTS OF SOLID OR SEMISOLID; 115] **2** *n* **bump**, swelling, protuberance, knob, inflammation, bulge, tumor [➡ ROUNDED SHAPE; 1218] **3** *v* (*informal*) **put up with**, deal with, take, endure, bear, suffer, grin and bear it (*informal*) [➡ TOLERATE AND ENDURE; 766] **4** *v* **group**, collect, combine, join, amalgamate, mass, consolidate, conjoin (*formal*) [➡ COMBINE AND MIX; 400] *Opposite*: split

lumpenproletariat *n* [➡ CLASS STATUS; 889]

lump together *v* [➡ COMBINE AND MIX; 400]

lumpy 1 *adj* **clumpy**, uneven, bumpy, unsmooth [➡ PHYSICAL TEXTURE; 1222] **2** *adj* **cumbersome**, awkward, lumbering, unwieldy, graceless, bumbling (*informal*) [➡ AGILITY OF THE BODY; 476] *Opposite*: graceful

luna moth *type of* **moth** [➡ MOTHS AND BUTTERFLIES; 1015]

lunar *adj* **lunate**, semilunar, lunular [➡ THE SOLAR SYSTEM AND ASTRONOMY; 1060]

lunar module *type of* **spacecraft** [➡ SPACE VEHICLES; 1063]

lunar month *type of* **time period** [➡ TIMES OF YEAR; 88]

lunch *type of* **meal** [➡ MEALS AND PARTS OF MEALS; 1169]

lunch break *n* [➡ PERIODS OF REST; 91]

lunch counter *type of* **eating place** [➡ HOTELS, RESTAURANTS, AND CLUBS; 1082]

luncheonette *type of* **eating place** [➡ HOTELS, RESTAURANTS, AND CLUBS; 1082]

lunchroom *type of* **eating place** [➡ HOTELS, RESTAURANTS, AND CLUBS; 1082]

lunchtime *n* [➡ TIMES OF DAY; 87]

lung *part of* **respiratory system** [➡ RESPIRATORY ORGANS; 715]

lunge 1 *n* **swipe**, grab, swing, thrust, stab, plunge [➡ CONTACT: HOLD; 411] **2** *v* **attack**, dive, spring, leap, charge,

pounce, plunge, pitch [➡ MOVE FAST; 313] **3** *v* **grab**, swipe, swing, thrust, stab, make for [➡ CONTACT: HOLD; 411]

lupine *type of* **perennial flower** [➡ FLOWERS; 1032]

Lupus *type of* **constellation** [➡ HEAVENLY BODIES; 1061]

lurch 1 *v* **pitch**, stagger, rock, tilt, list, reel, roll, sway, wobble, heave, yaw, lean [➡ TAKE UP A NEW POSITION; 312] **2** *v* **totter**, stagger, stumble, sway, reel, falter [➡ AIMLESS AND ERRANT MOTION; 343]

lure 1 *v* **entice**, tempt, attract, decoy, draw in, ensnare, allure, trap, persuade [➡ APPEAL TO AND AROUSE INTEREST; 575] **2** *n* **bait**, trap, decoy, enticement, temptation, appeal, attraction, allure, pull (*informal*) [➡ BEAUTY AND ATTRACTIVENESS; 189]

lurid 1 *adj* **shocking**, explicit, sensational, vivid, juicy (*informal*) [➡ IN POOR TASTE AND OVERSENTIMENTAL; 229] *Opposite*: bland **2** *adj* **loud**, garish, gaudy, bright, vivid, colorful, striking, shocking [➡ DESCRIBING COLORS; 1226] *Opposite*: dull

luridness 1 *n* **explicitness**, sensationalism, vividness, juiciness (*informal*) [➡ IN POOR TASTE AND OVERSENTIMENTAL; 229] **2** *n* **garishness**, brightness, vividness, gaudiness, colorfulness [➡ DESCRIBING COLORS; 1226]

lurk *v* **lie in wait for**, loiter, prowl, skulk, wait, creep around [➡ LACK OF ACTIVITY OR MOTION; 342]

luscious *adj* **juicy**, moist, delicious, succulent, sweet, tasty, scrumptious (*informal*) [➡ TASTE; 703] *Opposite*: dry

lusciousness *n* **juiciness**, succulence, moistness, palatability, sweetness, tastiness, scrumptiousness (*informal*) [➡ TASTE; 703] *Opposite*: dryness

lush 1 *adj* **verdant**, abundant, green, flourishing, thriving, luxuriant, fertile, blossoming, grassy, leafy, blooming [➡ VEGETATION; 1025] *Opposite*: arid **2** *adj* **luxurious**, lavish, opulent, sumptuous, deluxe, upscale, rich, posh (*informal*), plush (*informal*), swanky (*informal*) [➡ EXPENSIVE AND LUXURIOUS; 218] *Opposite*: downscale

lushness 1 *n* **greenness**, abundance, fertility, leafiness, luxuriance, verdure, grassiness [➡ VEGETATION; 1025] *Opposite*: aridity **2** *n* **luxury**, lavishness, sumptuousness, opulence, richness, magnificence, extravagance, luxuriance, plushness (*informal*), swankiness (*informal*) [➡ EXPENSIVE AND LUXURIOUS; 218]

lust 1 *n* **desire**, envy, covetousness, longing, yearning, hankering, hunger, thirst, itch [➡ DESIRE AND WANT; 579] **2** *v* **yearn**, desire, long, hanker, hunger, ache, covet, thirst, itch [➡ DESIRE AND WANT; 579]

luster *n* **sheen**, shine, gleam, patina, glint, gloss, polish [➡ VISUAL TEXTURE; 1221] *Opposite*: lusterless

lusterless *adj* **dull**, mat, drab, faded, unpolished, lackluster, lifeless [➡ VISUAL TEXTURE; 1221] *Opposite*: shiny

lustful *adj* **lecherous**, libidinous, lascivious, passionate, amorous, craving [➡ DESIRE AND WANT; 579]

lustrous *adj* **shiny**, glossy, radiant, gleaming, shimmering, glistening [➡ DESCRIBING LIGHT; 1228] *Opposite*: dull

lusty *adj* **hearty**, healthy, vigorous, forceful, robust, strong [➡ FIT AND STRONG; 736] *Opposite*: feeble

lute *type of* **stringed instrument** [➡ MUSICAL INSTRUMENTS; 910]

lux *type of* **SI unit** [➡ SIZE AND DIMENSIONS; 1192]

luxuriance *n* **lavishness**, luxury, extravagance, abundance, richness, lushness, opulence [➡ EXPENSIVE AND LUXURIOUS; 218]

luxuriant 1 *adj* **lush**, flourishing, thriving, fertile, rich, dense, verdant [➡ VEGETATION; 1025] *Opposite*: sparse 2 *adj* **abundant**, lavish, plentiful, copious, ample [➡ EXPENSIVE AND LUXURIOUS; 218] *Opposite*: meager

luxuriate *v* **enjoy**, wallow, indulge, bask, relish, revel, delight [➡ LIKE, LOVE, VALUE, AND ENJOY; 578]

luxurious 1 *adj* **deluxe**, sumptuous, opulent, expensive, lavish, well-appointed, posh (*informal*), plush (*informal*) [➡ EXPENSIVE AND LUXURIOUS; 218] *Opposite*: simple 2 *adj* **extravagant**, indulgent, decadent, prodigal, epicurean, bohemian, sensual, pleasure-loving [➡ PLEASURE-SEEKING AND EXCESS; 885] *Opposite*: simple

luxuriousness *n* **expensiveness**, luxury, sumptuousness, magnificence, fulsomeness, richness, extravagance, opulence, lavishness, grandness, splendor [➡ EXPENSIVE AND LUXURIOUS; 218]

luxury 1 *n* **treat**, extra, extravagance, indulgence, bonus, amenity, frill, superfluity [➡ AMAZING THINGS; 211] 2 *n* **lavishness**, comfort, sumptuousness, opulence, magnificence, extravagance [➡ EXPENSIVE AND LUXURIOUS; 218]

lychee *type of* **fruit** [➡ FRUIT AND VEGETABLES; 1176]

lying 1 *adj* **deceitful**, dishonest, two-faced, insincere, untruthful, mendacious, double-dealing, false, two-timing [➡ DECEITFUL; 513] *Opposite*: truthful 2 *n* **dishonesty**, deceit, duplicity, falseness, untruthfulness, insincerity, mendacity, mendaciousness [➡ DECEPTION AND LIES; 660] *Opposite*: truthfulness

lyme grass *type of* **grass** [➡ GRASS; 1031]

lymph *n* [➡ EXCRETION AND EXCRETA; 722]

lynch *v* **hang**, string up, murder, mob, assassinate, kill [➡ KILL; 923]

lynchpin *see* **linchpin**

lynx *type of* **cat** [➡ FELINES; 983]

lyonnaise *type of* **food presentation** [➡ COOKING AND FOOD PREPARATION; 353]

Lyra *type of* **constellation** [➡ HEAVENLY BODIES; 1061]

lyre *type of* **stringed instrument** [➡ MUSICAL INSTRUMENTS; 910]

lyric 1 *adj* **poetic**, romantic, emotional, expressive, inspired, sentimental [➡ EMOTIONALLY PLEASANT; 187] 2 *adj* **musical**, melodic, harmonious, tuneful, lilting [➡ SOFT, LOW, OR PLEASANT SOUNDS; 1265]

lyrical *adj* **poetic**, romantic, emotional, expressive, inspired, sentimental [➡ EMOTIONALLY PLEASANT; 187]

lyricism *n* **poeticality**, expressiveness, eloquence, floweriness [➡ ELOQUENT, TALKATIVE, AND LONG-WINDED; 632]

lyricist *n* [➡ MUSICIANS AND SINGERS; 908]

lyrics *n* **words**, lines, libretto, stanza [➡ MUSIC, SONGS, AND SINGING; 907]

M

ma *n* (*informal*) **mother**, mom (*informal*), mommy (*informal*), mama (*informal*), mammy (*informal*), mamma (*informal*), momma (*informal*) [➥OLDER GENERATION RELATIVES; 959]

macabre *adj* **ghoulish**, ghastly, grisly, chilling, gruesome, horrid, morbid, horrific, deathly, cadaverous (*formal or literary*) [➥FRIGHTENING; 231]

macadam *n* **asphalt**, tar, paving, blacktop, pavement [➥COVERS AND COATINGS; 1246]

macadamia nut *type of* **nut** [➥NUTS; 1185]

macaque *type of* **primate** [➥PRIMATES; 988]

macarena *type of* **dance** [➥DANCE; 903]

macaroni *type of* **pasta** [➥PASTA; 1180]

macaroon *type of* **cake** [➥CAKES, COOKIES, AND DESSERTS; 1181]

macaw *type of* **pet bird** [➥BIRDS; 997]

mace 1 *type of* **club** [➥BLUNT INSTRUMENTS AND WHIPS; 1158] 2 *type of* **spice** [➥HERBS AND SPICES; 1175]

macerate 1 *v* **soften**, soak, steep, marinate, marinade, drench, saturate, infuse [➥SOFTEN, LIQUEFY, AND DAMPEN; 388] 2 *v* **break up**, separate, soak, mash, pulp, puree, deliquesce [➥CHANGE OF SHAPE; 385] 3 *v* **waste away**, starve, fast, slim down, lose weight, shed pounds, reduce, slim (*UK*) [➥CHANGE OF SIZE: SMALLER; 393]

machete 1 *type of* **cutting tool** [➥CUTTING TOOLS; 1120] 2 *type of* **sword or knife** [➥SWORDS AND KNIVES; 1157]

Machiavellian *adj* **cunning**, unscrupulous, tricky, amoral, devious, treacherous, deceitful, opportunist, scheming, conniving [➥DECEITFUL; 513] *Opposite*: honest

machinate *v* **plot**, scheme, conspire, intrigue, hatch, maneuver, cook up (*informal*) [➥DEVELOP THEORIES AND REASON; 744]

machination *n* **intrigue**, plotting, maneuvering, scheming, planning [➥DECEPTION AND LIES; 660]

machine 1 *n* **mechanism**, engine, appliance, apparatus, contraption, device, instrument, contrivance [➥DEVICES; 1115] 2 *n* **system**, machinery, structure, procedure, mechanism, organization [➥WAYS OF DOING THINGS; 294] 3 *n* **automaton**, robot, cyborg, android [➥MACHINES AND MACHINE PARTS; 1116]

machine gun *type of* **gun** [➥WEAPONS FOR SHOOTING; 1156]

machine-gun 1 *v* **shoot**, kill, fire at, blaze, strafe, attack, mow down [➥KILL; 923] 2 *adj* **staccato**, rapid, abrupt, fast, quick, rapid-fire, speedy [➥HAPPENING QUICKLY; 104] *Opposite*: slow

machinery 1 *n* **machines**, apparatus, tackle, gear, technology, equipment [➥MACHINERY; 1114] 2 *n* **mechanism**, moving parts, workings, works, cogs [➥PARTS OF MACHINES AND TOOLS; 1118] 3 *n* **organization**, system, procedure, machine, structure, mechanism, arrangement [➥WAYS OF DOING THINGS; 294]

machine shop *type of* **factory** [➥INDUSTRIAL BUILDINGS; 1087]

machine tool *type of* **general tool** [➥HAND TOOLS; 1119]

machinist *n* **machine operator**, operator, factory worker, operative, technician, mechanic [➥FARMERS, GARDENERS, AND MANUAL WORKERS; 849]

machismo *n* **manliness**, masculinity, masculineness, maleness, virility [➥GENDER IDENTITY AND SEXUALITY; 932]

macho *adj* **manly**, masculine, virile, laddish [➥GENDER IDENTITY AND SEXUALITY; 932]

mackerel *type of* **ocean fish** [➥OCEAN FISH; 1009]

macramé *type of* **handicraft** [➥CRAFTS AND CARVING; 355]

macro *n* **instruction**, command, key code, function, shortcut [➥COMPUTERS AND COMPUTING; 1127]

macrobiotic *adj* **wholefood**, vegan, vegetarian, organic, wholegrain, natural, unrefined, unprocessed [➥RAW AND NATURAL; 1214]

macrocosm *n* **system**, structure, formation, composition, whole [➥REPRESENTATIONS AND GENERAL EXAMPLES; 65] *Opposite*: microcosm

macula *part of* **eye** [➥THE EYE; 698]

mad 1 *adj* **angry**, furious, livid, irate, infuriated, fuming, annoyed, beside yourself, up in arms, wrathful, outraged, ireful (*literary*), choleric (*literary*) [➥IRRITATION AND ANGER; 541] *Opposite*: calm 2 *adj* **uncontrolled**, frenzied, frenetic, panic-stricken, frantic, wild, crazy (*informal*) [➥DISORDER AND CHAOS; 245] *Opposite*: calm 3 *adj* **passionate**, wild about, infatuated with, enthusiastic, crazy about (*informal*), nuts about (*slang*) [➥APPRECIATION AND GRATITUDE; 535] *Opposite*: indifferent

madcap *adj* **silly**, zany, chaotic, wild, crazy (*informal*), wacky (*informal*), goofy (*informal*) [➥FUNNY AND AMUSING; 216] *Opposite*: sensible

madden *v* **infuriate**, enrage, annoy, anger, irritate, exasperate, make somebody's blood boil, frustrate, gall, drive somebody crazy, rile (*informal*), drive somebody up the wall (*informal*) [➥ANGER AND ANNOY; 569] *Opposite*: pacify

maddened *adj* **infuriated**, incensed, annoyed, angered, enraged, exasperated, irritated, frustrated [➥IRRITATION AND ANGER; 541] *Opposite*: calm

maddening *adj* **infuriating**, annoying, irritating, exasperating, frustrating, enraging, vexing, galling [➥IRRITATING; 228] *Opposite*: pleasing

Madeira cake *type of* **cake** [➥CAKES, COOKIES, AND DESSERTS; 1181]

madeleine *type of* **cake** [➥CAKES, COOKIES, AND DESSERTS; 1181]

mademoiselle *n* [➥FEMALE PERSON; 933]

made-to-measure *adj* **tailor-made**, custom-made,

made-to-order, customized, custom-built, bespoke (*UK*) [➡ EXTRAORDINARY: UNCOMMON; 205] *Opposite*: off-the-rack

made-to-order *adj* **custom-made**, custom-built, made-to-measure, tailor-made, bespoke (*UK*) [➡ EXTRAORDINARY: UNCOMMON; 205] *Opposite*: mass-produced

made-up *adj* **pretend**, invented, concocted, fictional, fictitious, imaginary, make-believe [➡ FALSE AND UNREAL; 173] *Opposite*: real

madly **1** *adv* **intensely**, extremely, strongly, deeply, very, utterly, totally [➡ TO A GREAT EXTENT; 132] **2** *adv* **wildly**, frantically, frenetically, rashly, riotously, uncontrollably [➡ DISORDER AND CHAOS; 245] *Opposite*: calmly

madness *n* **folly**, foolishness, stupidity, foolhardiness [➡ NEGATIVE INTELLECTUAL CHARACTERISTICS; 525]

madras *type of* **fabric from plants** [➡ FABRICS; 1132]

madrigal *type of* **musical form** [➡ MUSIC, SONGS, AND SINGING; 907]

maelstrom *n* **tumult**, turbulence, flurry, whirl, turmoil, scramble, frenzy, vortex [➡ DISORDER AND CHAOS; 245]

maestro *n* **genius**, talent, virtuoso, marvel, expert, wonder, wunderkind, ace (*informal*), whiz (*informal*), whiz kid (*informal*) [➡ TALENTED OR INTELLIGENT PEOPLE; 528] *Opposite*: amateur

mafia *n* **clique**, gang, coterie, faction, set, circle [➡ CRIMINALS; 821]

Mafioso *n* [➡ CRIMINALS; 821]

mag (*informal*) *n* [➡ NEWSPAPERS AND MAGAZINES; 605]

magazine **1** *n* **periodical**, publication, slick, journal, weekly, monthly, quarterly, fortnightly, mag (*informal*), glossy magazine (*UK*) [➡ NEWSPAPERS AND MAGAZINES; 605] **2** *n* **arsenal**, depot, repository, ordnance, stockpile, storeroom, storehouse [➡ STORES AND STORAGE BUILDINGS; 1088]

magenta *type of* **red** [➡ COLORS; 1224]

maggot *type of* **stage of insect development** [➡ INSECT STAGES; 1020]

maggoty *adj* [➡ DECAYING OR INFESTED; 1236]

magic **1** *n* **enchantment**, sorcery, witchcraft, voodoo, augury, alchemy [➡ THE SUPERNATURAL; 787] **2** *n* **conjuring**, tricks, trickery, illusion, sleight of hand, artifice (*formal*) [➡ FALSE AND UNREAL; 173] **3** *n* **mystery**, charm, appeal, allure, attraction, fascination, charisma, magnetism, sparkle, je ne sais quoi [➡ BEAUTY AND ATTRACTIVENESS; 189] **4** *adj* **enchanted**, magical, fairylike, charmed, dreamlike, mystic, fairy-tale [➡ FALSE AND UNREAL; 173] **5** *adj* **supernatural**, magical, paranormal, mysterious, miraculous [➡ THE SUPERNATURAL; 787] *Opposite*: normal **6** *adj* **thrilling**, magical, enchanting, delightful, wonderful, lovely, captivating, charming, astonishing, breathtaking [➡ EXTRAORDINARY: AMAZING; 204] *Opposite*: mundane **7** *adj* **powerful**, special, key, all-important, famous [➡ MOST IMPORTANT AND MAIN; 193]

magical **1** *adj* **enchanted**, magic, fairylike, charmed, dreamlike, mystic, fairy-tale [➡ FALSE AND UNREAL; 173] **2** *adj* **supernatural**, magic, paranormal, mysterious, miraculous [➡ THE SUPERNATURAL; 787] *Opposite*: normal **3** *adj* **thrilling**, magic, enchanting, delightful, wonderful, lovely, captivating,

charming, astonishing, breathtaking [➡ EXTRAORDINARY: AMAZING; 204] *Opposite*: mundane

magician **1** *n* **conjurer**, illusionist, entertainer, escape artist, performer, prestidigitator (*formal*) [➡ WORKERS IN ENTERTAINMENT AND MEDIA; 873] **2** *n* **sorcerer**, wizard, warlock, enchanter, necromancer (*literary*) [➡ PEOPLE WITH SUPERNATURAL POWERS; 788] **3** *n* **genius**, virtuoso, expert, wizard, marvel, wonder, wunderkind, whiz (*informal*), whiz kid (*informal*), ace (*informal*) [➡ TALENTED OR INTELLIGENT PEOPLE; 528]

magisterial **1** *adj* **overbearing**, arrogant, superior, domineering, imperious, dictatorial [➡ BOSSY AND OVERBEARING; 516] *Opposite*: diffident **2** *adj* **commanding**, authoritative, majestic, stately, dignified, imposing, regal, august (*formal*) [➡ EXTRAORDINARY: AMAZING; 204] *Opposite*: lightweight **3** *adj* **authoritative**, expert, able, knowledgeable, scholarly [➡ TALENTED AND SKILLFUL; 527]

magistrate *n* **law officer**, justice of the peace, judge, JP, justice, public officer, judicial officer, official [➡ PEOPLE IN LAW COURTS; 820]

magma *n* **molten rock**, lava, tuff, igneous rock, pumice [➡ STONES, ROCKS, AND BOULDERS; 1057]

magnanimity *n* **nobility**, high-mindedness, fairness, generousness, generosity, benevolence, altruism [➡ GENEROSITY AND KINDNESS; 495] *Opposite*: pettiness

magnanimous *adj* **generous**, high-minded, noble, big, worthy, upright, benevolent, altruistic, considerate, kindly, forgiving [➡ GENEROSITY AND KINDNESS; 495] *Opposite*: petty

See *Compare and Contrast* at **generous**.

magnate *n* **tycoon**, mogul, entrepreneur, industrialist, baron, plutocrat, kahuna (*slang*), big cheese (*slang*), honcho (*slang*), fat cat (*slang*) [➡ RICH PEOPLE; 895]

magnesium *type of* **metal** [➡ METALS; 1276]

magnet **1** *n* **magnetic body**, lodestone, horseshoe magnet, electromagnet, bar magnet, refrigerator magnet, fridge magnet (*UK*) [➡ ENERGY; 1161] **2** *n* **lure**, draw, attraction, pull, enticement, inducement, center of attention, crowd puller (*UK*) [➡ TREATS; 210]

magnetic *adj* **attractive**, charming, compelling, alluring, captivating, charismatic, irresistible, mesmeric, fascinating, hypnotic [➡ INTERESTING AND MEANINGFUL; 190] *Opposite*: repellent

magnetism **1** *n* **magnetic field**, attraction, pull [➡ ENERGY; 1161] **2** *n* **charisma**, appeal, allure, charm, magic, fascination, draw, enticement, attraction, mesmerism, pull (*informal*) [➡ INTERESTING AND MEANINGFUL; 190]

magnetize *v* **attract**, charm, influence, draw, fascinate, entice, pull (*informal*) [➡ APPEAL TO AND AROUSE INTEREST; 575] *Opposite*: repel

magnification *n* **exaggeration**, intensification, enlargement, increase, amplification [➡ CHANGE OF SIZE: BIGGER; 392] *Opposite*: reduction

magnificence *n* **splendor**, glory, brilliance, radiance, majesty, grandeur, grandness, impressiveness, marvelousness, beauty [➡ BEAUTY AND ATTRACTIVENESS; 189]

magnificent *adj* **superb**, wonderful, splendid, glorious, brilliant, outstanding, superlative, bravura, stunning, marvelous, resplendent, grand, beautiful, impressive [➡ EXTRAORDINARY: AMAZING; 204] *Opposite*: unimpressive

magnify 1 *v* enlarge, blow up, expand, amplify, increase, extend, heighten, boost, augment (*formal*) [➡ CHANGE OF SIZE: BIGGER; 392] *Opposite*: shrink **2** *v* (*formal*) **worship**, praise, extol, laud, glorify, venerate, bless, adore, exalt (*formal*) [➡ PRAISE AND ENCOURAGE; 647]

magnifying glass *type of* **optical instrument** [➡ OPTICAL INSTRUMENTS; 1124]

magniloquence *n* [➡ POMPOUS, LOUD, AND OVERCONFIDENT; 635]

magniloquent *adj* [➡ POMPOUS, LOUD, AND OVERCONFIDENT; 635]

magnitude 1 *n* **greatness**, size, extent, degree, amount, enormousness, level, scale [➡ DEGREE AND EXTENT; 110] **2** *n* **importance**, significance, enormity, weight, consequence (*formal*), moment (*formal*) [➡ IMPORTANCE AND SIGNIFICANCE; 192] *Opposite*: triviality

magnolia 1 *type of* **white** [➡ COLORS; 1224] **2** *type of* **shrub or bush** [➡ BUSHES AND SHRUBS; 1027] **3** *type of* **deciduous tree** [➡ DECIDUOUS TREES; 1028]

magnum 1 *n* **bottle**, jeroboam, demijohn [➡ CONTAINERS, RECEPTACLES, AND PACKAGING; 1245] **2** *type of* **gun** [➡ WEAPONS FOR SHOOTING; 1156]

magnum opus *n* [➡ ARTWORKS; 898]

magpie 1 *n* (*informal*) **collector**, hoarder, saver, accumulator, pack rat (*informal*), squirrel (*informal*) [➡ PEOPLE WHO COLLECT THINGS; 454] **2** *n* (*informal*) **chatterer**, babbler, prattler, talker, gossip, chatterbox (*informal*), yammerer (*informal*), yapper (*informal*) [➡ INTERFERING PEOPLE AND TATTLETALES; 950] **3** *type of* **scavenger** [➡ BIRDS; 997]

magus *n* [➡ PEOPLE WITH SUPERNATURAL POWERS; 788]

maharajah *type of* **aristocrat** [➡ RULERS AND ARISTOCRACY; 823]

maharani *type of* **aristocrat** [➡ RULERS AND ARISTOCRACY; 823]

maharishi *n* **religious teacher**, guru, mahatma, prophet, evangelist, swami, sage (*literary*) [➡ RELIGIOUS PEOPLE; 778] *Opposite*: follower

mahi-mahi *type of* **tropical fish** [➡ OCEAN FISH; 1009]

mahogany 1 *type of* **brown** [➡ COLORS; 1224] **2** *type of* **evergreen tree** [➡ EVERGREEN AND CONIFEROUS TREES; 1029]

maid *type of* **servant** [➡ DOMESTIC AND KITCHEN WORKERS; 850]

maiden 1 *n* **girl**, lass, young woman, young lady, damsel (*archaic or literary*) [➡ FEMALE PERSON; 933] **2** *adj* **first**, earliest, initial, original [➡ BEFORE, FIRST, AND PRECEDING; 163]

maidservant *type of* **servant** [➡ DOMESTIC AND KITCHEN WORKERS; 850]

mail 1 *n* **letters**, correspondence, packages, parcels, junk mail, circulars, bulk mail, post (*UK*) [➡ LETTERS AND WRITTEN MESSAGES; 584] **2** *v* **send**, dispatch, transmit, email, post (*UK*) [➡ DISPATCH AND SEND; 333]

mailbag 1 *n* **mail sack**, sack, bag, satchel, shoulder bag, mail pouch, postbag (*UK*) [➡ CONTAINERS, RECEPTACLES, AND PACKAGING; 1245] **2** *n* **correspondence**, feedback, mail, letters, com-munications, messages, post (*UK*), postbag (*UK*) [➡ LETTERS AND WRITTEN MESSAGES; 584]

mailbox *n* **maildrop**, post office box, mail slot, box, in-box, pillar box (*UK*), post box (*UK*), letterbox (*UK*) [➡ CONTAINERS, RECEPTACLES, AND PACKAGING; 1245]

maildrop *n* [➡ CONTAINERS, RECEPTACLES, AND PACKAGING; 1245]

mailer 1 *n* **envelope**, padded envelope, carton, mailing tube, container [➡ CONTAINERS, RECEPTACLES, AND PACKAGING; 1245] **2** *n* **advertisement**, circular, flier, leaflet, brochure, hand-bill [➡ ADVERTISING AND PUBLICITY; 604]

mailing list *n* **distribution list**, register, circulation list, newsgroup, address book, clientele [➡ LISTS AND SCHEDULES; 587]

mail order *n* **cybershopping**, electronic shopping, home shopping, online shopping, teleshopping, virtual shopping, teleordering (*UK*) [➡ PURCHASE; 422]

mailshot (*UK*) *n* **advertisement**, circular, leaflet, letter, brochure, pamphlet, junk mail [➡ ADVERTISING AND PUBLICITY; 604]

mail slot *n* [➡ HOLES, GAPS, AND FORKS; 1252]

maim *v* **wound**, injure, hurt, mutilate, damage, lacerate [➡ WOUND A PERSON OR ANIMAL; 383]

main *adj* **major**, chief, key, foremost, core, focal, central, highest, leading, principal, head [➡ MOST IMPORTANT AND MAIN; 193] *Opposite*: minor

main course *part of* **meal** [➡ MEALS AND PARTS OF MEALS; 1169]

Maine coon *type of* **cat** [➡ FELINES; 983]

mainframe *type of* **computer** [➡ COMPUTERS AND COMPUTING; 1127]

mainland *n* **landmass**, continent, land [➡ THE CONTINENTS AND ISLANDS; 1048] *Opposite*: island

main line *n* **rail route**, principal route, trunk route, major route, line [➡ RAILROADS; 1107]

mainline (*UK*) *adj* **main**, chief, central, inter-city, principal [➡ COMMUNICATION NETWORKS; 1105] *Opposite*: local

mainly *adv* **mostly**, largely, chiefly, for the most part, primarily, principally, generally, essentially, above all, predominantly, first and foremost [➡ USUALLY; 108]

main road *type of* **highway** [➡ ROADS; 1106]

mainsail *part of* **sailing vessel** [➡ PARTS OF A SHIP OR BOAT; 1151]

mainspring *n* **driving force**, motive force, motivating force, chief reason, chief motive, impelling cause, impetus, dynamo [➡ MOST IMPORTANT THING; 197]

mainstay 1 *n* **cornerstone**, linchpin, keystone, foundation, basis, backbone [➡ MOST IMPORTANT THING; 197] **2** *part of* **sailing vessel** [➡ PARTS OF A SHIP OR BOAT; 1151]

mainstream *adj* **normal**, typical, conventional, ordinary, middle-of-the-road, majority, vanilla (*informal*), white-bread (*informal*) [➡ ORDINARINESS; 244] *Opposite*: unconventional

maintain 1 *v* **uphold**, keep, keep up, continue, sustain, retain, conserve, keep alive, preserve [➡ CAUSE TO CONTINUE; 267] *Opposite*: destroy **2** *v* **look after**, care for, take care of, keep up, keep in good condition, continue, support [➡ REPAIR

AND MEND; 376] *Opposite*: neglect   **3** *v* **argue**, claim, insist, assert, hold, swear, be adamant, declare, affirm, state, avow (*formal*) [➡ CLAIM, INSIST, AND EMPHASIZE; 614] *Opposite*: deny

maintenance   **1** *n* **repairs**, upkeep, looking after, care, keep, conservation, preservation [➡ WORK IN GENERAL; 297] *Opposite*: neglect   **2** *n* **preservation**, upholding, protection, continuation, continuance, safeguarding [➡ PERMANENCE: WITHOUT END; 94] *Opposite*: destruction   **3** *n* **alimony**, allowance, child support, child maintenance, grant [➡ FUNDS, PAYMENTS, AND CHARGES; 800]

maître d' *type of* **person who works in restaurants** [➡ DOMESTIC AND KITCHEN WORKERS; 850]

majestic   **1** *adj* **impressive**, superb, grand, wonderful, splendid, awesome, sublime, magnificent [➡ EXTRAORDINARY: AMAZING; 204] *Opposite*: modest   **2** *adj* **regal**, royal, grand, stately, imposing, grandiose, resplendent, impressive, august (*formal*) [➡ LEVELS OF FORMALITY; 522] *Opposite*: humble

majesty *n* **magnificence**, splendor, dignity, grandeur, illustriousness, stateliness, gravitas [➡ EXTRAORDINARY: AMAZING; 204]

major   **1** *adj* **main**, chief, key, foremost, leading, greatest, principal [➡ MOST IMPORTANT AND MAIN; 193] *Opposite*: minor   **2** *adj* **significant**, important, weighty, substantial, crucial, big [➡ IMPORTANT; 194] *Opposite*: trivial   **3** *adj* **serious**, grave, life-threatening [➡ DANGEROUS; 236] *Opposite*: minor

major-domo *type of* **servant** [➡ DOMESTIC AND KITCHEN WORKERS; 850]

majority   **1** *n* **bulk**, preponderance, mass, greater part, lion's share, best part [➡ MAJORITY AND MAXIMUM; 141]   **2** *n* **margin**, difference, gap, advantage, lead, edge [➡ MAJORITY AND MAXIMUM; 141]   **3** *n* **adulthood**, maturity, manhood, womanhood, adult years, independence, seniority, legal age [➡ ADULTHOOD; 918] *Opposite*: childhood   **4** *adj* **mainstream**, popular, common, widely held, middle-of-the-road [➡ ORDINARINESS; 244] *Opposite*: minority

make   **1** *v* **create**, fashion, compose, craft, build, construct, formulate [➡ CREATION; 346] *Opposite*: destroy   **2** *v* **put together**, assemble, make up, put up, cobble together, knock together (*informal*) [➡ BUILD; 352]   **3** *v* **manufacture**, produce, fabricate, churn out, yield, turn out [➡ MANUFACTURE; 349] *Opposite*: consume   **4** *v* **cook**, prepare, concoct, produce, create, brew, bake, rustle up (*informal*), throw together (*informal*) [➡ COOKING AND FOOD PREPARATION; 353]   **5** *v* **cause**, bring about, create, give rise to, occasion, generate, effect (*formal*), render (*formal*) [➡ CAUSE TO HAPPEN; 31]   **6** *v* **earn**, bring in, get, take home, get paid, receive [➡ GET MONEY OR REWARD; 421] *Opposite*: spend   **7** *v* **force**, compel, pressure, command, cause, oblige, constrain, require, pressurize (*UK*) [➡ CAUSE OR COMPEL TO ACT; 271] *Opposite*: ask   **8** *v* **become**, turn into, change into, be [➡ GRADUALLY COME INTO EXISTENCE; 1]   **9** *v* **appoint**, elect, designate, nominate, name [➡ CONFER STATUS; 458]   **10** *v* **manage**, accomplish, find time for, fit in, finish, do [➡ COMPLETE AN ACTION; 263]   **11** *v* **achieve**, get into, get on to, succeed, progress to, be selected for [➡ SUCCEED AND WIN; 79] *Opposite*: miss   **12** *v* **form**, make up, constitute, comprise, be, add up to [➡ AMOUNT TO AND EQUAL; 70]   **13** *v* **reach**, get to, make it to, get as far as, arrive at, attain [➡ ARRIVE; 12]   **14** *n* **sort**, type, kind, style, variety, mark, brand [➡ VARIETIES, TYPES, AND KINDS; 145]

Compare and Contrast: *make*, *produce*, *create*, *fashion*, *manufacture*

CORE MEANING: to bring something into existence

make to bring something into existence; *produce* to make something in large quantities or in a commercial setting; *create* to make something using imagination and artistic skill, or to cause something such as a job or opportunity to exist; *fashion* to make something by shaping and working raw materials, especially when using only the hands or handheld tools; *manufacture* to make something in large numbers, usually in a factory using machinery, or to make something quickly and cynically, especially something that normally requires time and artistic skill.

make a beeline for *v* **make straight for**, go directly to, head for, target [➡ MOVE FAST; 313]

make a big thing of *v* **make a mountain out of a molehill**, make a point of, make a show of, make a big deal out of (*informal*) [➡ CLAIM, INSIST, AND EMPHASIZE; 614] *Opposite*: play down

make a break for it *v* [➡ RUN AWAY AND AVOID; 10]

make a clean breast of things *v* **admit**, confess, own up, tell all, tell the truth, come clean (*informal*), fess up (*slang*) [➡ ADMIT AND CONFESS; 610]

make a dash for it *v* [➡ RUN AWAY AND AVOID; 10]

make a difference *v* **have an effect**, matter, be important, change things [➡ CHANGE; 372]

make a dog's breakfast/dinner of (*UK*) *v* **botch**, make a mess of, bungle (*informal*), foul up (*informal*), mess up (*informal*), make a pig's ear of (*UK*) [➡ MESS UP AND MAKE MISTAKES; 472]

make a fool of *v* **con**, deceive, dupe, fool, make somebody look an idiot, mislead, take for a ride, trick, make a monkey of (*informal*) [➡ DECEPTION AND LIES; 660]

make a fool of yourself *v* **appear foolish**, embarrass yourself, expose yourself to ridicule, humiliate yourself, make an exhibition of yourself, put your foot in it (*informal*) [➡ CHANGE OF MOOD AND COMPOSURE; 580]

make a fuss *v* **complain**, fuss, make a scene, kick up a fuss, make a mountain out of a molehill, make a song and dance (*informal*) [➡ COMPLAIN AND NAG; 686]

make a fuss of *v* **make much of**, indulge, spoil, cosset, coddle, pamper, fuss over, baby [➡ TAKE CARE OF AND SPOIL; 300] *Opposite*: ignore

make a hash of (*informal*) *v* **muddle**, confuse, jumble, spoil, mix up, mess up (*informal*) [➡ MESS UP AND MAKE MISTAKES; 472]

make allowances *v* **take into account**, bear in mind, consider, take into consideration, cut somebody some slack (*slang*) [➡ TOLERATE AND ENDURE; 766]

make amends *v* **compensate for**, make reparations, make up for, pay back, recompense, redress the balance, repent, atone (*formal*) [➡ APOLOGIZE AND RETRACT; 683]

make a mess of *v* **botch**, botch up, do badly, manage badly, mishandle, mismanage, ruin, spoil, bungle (*informal*), foul up (*informal*), make a hash of (*informal*), mess up (*informal*), throw a monkey wrench into (*informal*), make a dog's dinner of (*UK*), put a spanner in the works (*UK*) [➡ MESS UP AND MAKE MISTAKES; 472]

make a mistake *v* [➡ MESS UP AND MAKE MISTAKES; 472]

make a monkey of (*informal*) *v* [➡ DECEPTION AND LIES; 660]

make a mountain out of a molehill *v* exaggerate, make a big thing of, make a fuss, make too much of, overstate, make a big deal out of (*informal*), make a song and dance about (*informal*) [➡ CLAIM, INSIST, AND EMPHASIZE; 614]

make a name for yourself *v* succeed, rise to fame, make it to the top, become known, gain respect [➡ SUCCEED AND WIN; 79]

make an effort *v* attempt, put yourself out, try, work hard, endeavor (*formal*) [➡ HARD WORK OR EFFORT; 298]

make an exhibition of yourself *v* make a fool of yourself, expose yourself to ridicule, embarrass yourself, behave foolishly, show off [➡ CHANGE OF MOOD AND COMPOSURE; 580]

make a note of 1 *v* mark, memorize, notice, observe, remark upon, pick up on (*informal*) [➡ REMEMBER; 746] 2 *v* write down, jot down, take down, keep a record [➡ RECORD SOMETHING; 371]

make a pig's ear of (*UK*) *v* [➡ MESS UP AND MAKE MISTAKES; 472]

make a point of 1 *v* make sure to, not forget to, take care to, remember to, make an effort to, try to [➡ REMEMBER; 746] 2 *v* let people know about, make a big thing of, make a fuss, make a show of, make a song and dance about (*informal*) [➡ OVERDO SOMETHING; 290]

make a racket *v* n [➡ SOUND EMISSION; 362]

make a run for it *v* [➡ RUN AWAY AND AVOID; 10]

make a scene *v* be angry, carry on, make an exhibition of yourself, make a fuss, throw a tantrum, have hysterics (*informal*), have kittens (*informal*) [➡ GIVING VENT TO EMOTIONS; 679]

make a sharp exit *v* [➡ RUN AWAY AND AVOID; 10]

make a splash *v* make an impression, impress, get noticed, make an impact, turn heads, make your presence felt [➡ SUCCEED AND WIN; 79]

make a stab at (*informal*) *v* attempt, try, strive at, take a stab at (*informal*), endeavor (*formal*), essay (*formal*), assay (*literary*) [➡ ATTEMPT AN ACTION; 261]

make a start *v* begin, get going, jump in, start, get cracking (*informal*) [➡ START AN ACTION; 260] *Opposite:* procrastinate

make a statement *v* say something, send a message, catch the eye, turn heads, make an impact [➡ MEAN SOMETHING; 61]

make available *v* free up, find, set aside, release, provide, grant access to, supply [➡ DISPENSE, RATION, AND DISTRIBUTE; 434] *Opposite:* refuse

make believe *v* pretend, imagine, fantasize, daydream, muse [➡ DREAM, IMAGINE, AND FANTASIZE; 749]

make-believe 1 *n* fantasy, pretense, role-playing, play-acting, story, game [➡ DREAM, IMAGINE, AND FANTASIZE; 749] *Opposite:*

reality 2 *adj* pretend, imaginary, fantasy, made-up, invented, fake, mock [➡ FALSE AND UNREAL; 173] *Opposite:* real

make better *v* cure, heal, treat, alleviate, relieve, improve, remedy, palliate, ameliorate (*formal*) [➡ IMPROVE SOMETHING; 374]

make certain *v* check, double-check, ensure, make sure, be in no doubt, ascertain (*formal*) [➡ APPROVE AND CONFIRM; 646]

make clear *v* clarify, elucidate, spell out, explain, give details, illuminate, shed light on, make obvious, ram home [➡ EXPLAIN AND CLARIFY; 610] *Opposite:* obscure

make contact *v* speak to, approach, communicate, touch base, get in touch, contact [➡ INITIATE AND ESTABLISH COMMUNICATION; 680] *Opposite:* drop

make contacts *v* meet people, exchange cards, introduce yourself, make friends, network, schmooze (*slang*) [➡ ESTABLISHING RELATIONSHIPS WITH OTHERS; 974]

make do *v* manage, put up with, cope, accept, tolerate, live with, cut your coat according to your cloth [➡ CONTINUE TO EXIST; 17]

make ends meet *v* cope, manage, pay your bills, break even, get by, eke out a living [➡ CONTINUE TO EXIST; 17]

make enquiries *see* make inquiries

make for 1 *v* head for, head toward, go toward, proceed toward, aim for, approach [➡ PROCEED AND GO; 305] 2 *v* produce, create, bring about, give rise to, generate, occasion, effect (*formal*) [➡ CAUSE TO HAPPEN; 31]

make friends *v* befriend, take up with, get in with, get to know, become acquainted, strike up a friendship, win peoples' hearts, make contacts [➡ ESTABLISHING RELATIONSHIPS WITH OTHERS; 974] *Opposite:* repel

make fun of *v* mock, poke fun at, laugh at, tease, ridicule, scoff at, satirize, burlesque, lampoon, send up (*informal*) [➡ JOKES AND TEASING; 674] *Opposite:* respect

make good *v* succeed, arrive, be somebody, do well, become successful, come out on top, make it (*informal*) [➡ SUCCEED AND WIN; 79] *Opposite:* fail

make happen *v* cause, bring about, realize, make real, produce, effect (*formal*) [➡ CAUSE TO HAPPEN; 31]

make headway *v* make progress, progress, get somewhere, get on, make ground, make inroads [➡ SUCCEED AND WIN; 79]

make inquiries *v* research, investigate, explore, look into, inspect, analyze [➡ ASK PEOPLE QUESTIONS; 666]

make inroads 1 *v* produce a result, have an effect on, get somewhere, make something happen, make headway, make progress [➡ SUCCEED AND WIN; 79] 2 *v* encroach, creep up on, dent, overstep, infringe, intrude, trespass [➡ APPEAR AND EMERGE; 3]

make it (*informal*) *v* succeed, achieve, accomplish, attain, manage, make good, come out on top, do well, pull off (*informal*), hit the big time (*slang*) [➡ SUCCEED AND WIN; 79] *Opposite:* give up

make known *v* **publicize**, announce, communicate, proclaim, broadcast [➡INFORM, ANNOUNCE, AND ISSUE; 611]

make light of *v* **play down**, make little of, minimize, underestimate, understate, slough off, dismiss, belittle, underplay, underrate, talk down [➡UNDERDO SOMETHING; 291] *Opposite:* overstate

make merry *v* [➡LEISURE AND RECREATION; 874]

make mincemeat of *v* **defeat heavily**, thrash, rout, overwhelm, overpower, crush, hammer (*informal*), cream (*slang*), slaughter (*slang*) [➡BEAT AND DEFEAT; 80]

make much of *v* **make a fuss of**, mollycoddle, baby, pet, pat, fuss over, indulge, spoil, cosset, pamper [➡TAKE CARE OF AND SPOIL; 300]

make off *v* **run away**, run off, decamp, make a break for it, make a run for it, head off, flee, bolt, beat a hasty retreat, escape, take off (*informal*), vamoose (*slang*) [➡RUN AWAY AND AVOID; 10] *Opposite:* come back

make off with *v* **appropriate**, run away with, steal, remove, pilfer, thieve, take, lift (*informal*) [➡STEAL AND ROB; 426] *Opposite:* return

make out **1** *v* **distinguish**, see, hear, perceive, pick out, recognize, discern [➡LOOKING AND LOOKS; 700] **2** *v* **understand**, work out, decipher, decode, figure out, comprehend [➡SOLVE AND INTERPRET; 760] **3** *v* **fill in**, write out, make, compose, draw up, complete, write [➡RECORD SOMETHING; 371] **4** *v* **imply**, suggest, give the impression, make somebody believe, insinuate, hint [➡SUGGEST, HINT, AND COMMENT; 612] **5** *v* **get by**, get on, manage, fare, do, get along [➡SUCCEED AND WIN; 79] **6** *v* (*informal*) **kiss**, make love, embrace, smooch (*informal*), canoodle (*informal*), pet (*informal*), neck (*informal*) [➡PHYSICAL CONTACT AS COMMUNICATION; 655]

makeover **1** *n* **transformation**, change, restyling, cosmetic treatment, beautification, alteration [➡IMPROVE APPEARANCE; 379] **2** *n* **remodeling**, renovation, restoration, transformation, alteration, conversion, rehab (*informal*) [➡IMPROVE APPEARANCE; 379]

makeover program *type of* **broadcast** [➡TELEVISION AND RADIO; 606]

make overtures *v* [➡INITIATE AND ESTABLISH COMMUNICATION; 680]

make points with *v* **get on the good side of**, get in good with, pander to, ingratiate yourself, flatter, suck up to (*informal*), butter up (*informal*) [➡FLATTER AND FAWN; 621]

make preparations *v* [➡PREPARE FOR ACTION; 289]

make progress **1** *v* **make headway**, progress, advance, get somewhere, forge ahead, make inroads, come on, proceed [➡SUCCEED AND WIN; 79] *Opposite:* stall **2** *v* **recover**, get well, get better, improve, be on the mend [➡GET BETTER; 375] *Opposite:* deteriorate

make public *v* **publicize**, publish, release, put out, reveal, make known, expose, air, announce [➡INFORM, ANNOUNCE, AND ISSUE; 611]

maker *n* **creator**, manufacturer, fabricator, producer, architect, cause [➡DESIGNERS, CREATORS, AND INSTIGATORS; 347] *Opposite:* destroyer

make redundant (*UK*) *v* [➡REVOKE STATUS; 459]

make reparations *v* [➡APOLOGIZE AND RETRACT; 683]

make sense *v* **add up**, fit, seem sensible, seem right [➡MEAN SOMETHING; 61]

make sense of *v* **understand**, decode, decipher, follow, grasp, work out, comprehend, figure out, get (*informal*) [➡SOLVE AND INTERPRET; 760] *Opposite:* misunderstand

makeshift *adj* **rough-and-ready**, crude, temporary, improvised, provisional, do-it-yourself, ersatz [➡IN BAD REPAIR; 1234] *Opposite:* permanent

make short work of *v* **make short shrift of**, do quickly, dash through, rush through, dash off (*informal*) [➡CARRY OUT AN ACTION; 269]

make small talk *v* [➡TWO-WAY COMMUNICATION; 607]

make somebody's acquaintance *v* **meet for the first time**, meet, get to know, become acquainted, bump into, come across [➡ESTABLISHING RELATIONSHIPS WITH OTHERS; 974]

make somebody's blood boil *v* **anger**, annoy, exasperate, irritate, enrage, infuriate, incense, madden, drive crazy [➡ANGER AND ANNOY; 569] *Opposite:* delight

make somebody's hackles rise *v* **anger**, antagonize, get up somebody's nose, annoy, get somebody's back up, infuriate, incense, enrage [➡ANGER AND ANNOY; 569] *Opposite:* placate

make sure *v* **validate**, confirm, certify, take care, ensure, verify, make certain, check [➡APPROVE AND CONFIRM; 646] *Opposite:* assume

make the best of a bad job (*UK*) *v* **make the best of things**, keep smiling, keep your chin up, take the bad with the good, look on the bright side, grin and bear it (*informal*), take the rough with the smooth (*UK*) [➡TOLERATE AND ENDURE; 766] *Opposite:* complain

make the best of things *v* **take the bad with the good**, look on the bright side, keep your chin up, keep smiling, grin and bear it (*informal*), take the rough with the smooth (*UK*), make the best of a bad job (*UK*) [➡TOLERATE AND ENDURE; 766] *Opposite:* complain

make the grade *v* **meet the standards**, be good enough, measure up, hit the mark, come up with the goods, satisfy, deliver, come up to scratch (*informal*) [➡SUCCEED AND WIN; 79] *Opposite:* fail

make the most of *v* **capitalize on**, take advantage of, maximize, profit from, make hay while the sun shines (*informal*) [➡MAKE GOOD USE OF SOMETHING; 473] *Opposite:* squander

make tracks (*informal*) *v* **leave**, depart, go away, vamoose (*slang*), make a move, hit the road, take off (*informal*) [➡LEAVE AND GO AWAY; 8] *Opposite:* stay

make up **1** *v* **prepare**, make ready, get ready, set up, put together [➡CREATION; 346] **2** *v* **contribute**, add, supply, come up with, provide, chip in (*informal*) [➡GIVE AND PROVIDE; 430] *Opposite:* deduct **3** *v* **form**, comprise, constitute, add up to, make, be, join up, compose [➡AMOUNT TO AND EQUAL; 70] **4** *v* **invent**, concoct, forge, fabricate, think up, dream up [➡DREAM, IMAGINE, AND FANTASIZE; 749] **5** *v* **top up**, subsidize, complete, supplement, round up, bring up, augment (*formal*) [➡CHANGE OF SIZE: BIGGER; 392] **6** *v* **be reconciled**, make peace, forgive and forget, kiss and make up, bury the hatchet, settle your differences

[➡ FORGET, FORGIVE, AND ACCEPT; 748] *Opposite*: fall out **7** *v* **compensate**, make amends, make good, recompense, redeem, balance, offset, atone for (*formal*) [➡ CORRECT AND PUT RIGHT; 377]

makeup **1** *n* **cosmetics**, face paint, greasepaint, powder and paint, maquillage, face (*informal*) [➡ MAKEUP AND BEAUTY PRODUCTS; 490] **2** *n* **composition**, constitution, structure, formation, construction [➡ QUALITIES AND CHARACTERISTICS; 1191] **3** *n* **temperament**, character, personality, nature, disposition, complexion, humor, individuality [➡ TEMPERAMENT AND BEHAVIOR; 492]

makeup remover *n* [➡ MAKEUP AND BEAUTY PRODUCTS; 490]

make up your mind *v* **decide**, come to a decision, resolve, determine [➡ MAKE DECISIONS AND CHOICES; 752]

make use of *v* **utilize**, use, draw on, take advantage of, avail yourself of, exploit [➡ USE; 467]

See Compare and Contrast at **use**.

make waves *v* **kick up a fuss**, create a stir, rock the boat, dissent, revolt, rebel, disturb, criticize [➡ PROTEST AND EXPRESS DISAPPROVAL; 642]

makeweight **1** *n* **counterpoise**, weight, counterbalance, ballast, counterweight [➡ WEIGHT: HEAVY; 1205] **2** *n* **extra**, complement, supplement, compensation, reinforcement, offset [➡ MORE AND EXCESS; 124]

make your mark *v* **succeed**, arrive, make an impact, make an impression, make your presence felt, impact, impress, make it (*informal*) [➡ SUCCEED AND WIN; 79]

make yourself known *v* **introduce yourself**, say who you are, identify yourself, give your name, come forward, show yourself [➡ INITIATE AND ESTABLISH COMMUNICATION; 680]

make yourself scarce (*informal*) *v* [➡ LEAVE AND GO AWAY; 8]

make yourself useful *v* **help out**, be of service, lend a hand, assist, rally round [➡ HELP; 293] *Opposite*: hinder

make your way *v* **go**, move, head, wend your way, pick your way, progress, proceed [➡ PROCEED AND GO; 305]

making *n* **creation**, manufacture, production, construction, assembly, building [➡ CREATION; 346]

makings **1** *n* **ingredients**, requirements, components, elements, materials, pieces, parts [➡ PHYSICAL OBJECTS; 1243] **2** *n* **qualities**, potential, wherewithal, what it takes, assets, ability, talent [➡ SKILLS, TALENTS, AND ABILITIES; 526]

malachite *type of* **stone** [➡ STONES, ROCKS, AND BOULDERS; 1057]

maladjusted *adj* **disturbed**, neurotic, unstable, confused, alienated, estranged [➡ PSYCHOLOGY AND THE MIND; 769] *Opposite*: well-adjusted

maladjustment *n* **instability**, disturbance, confusion, alienation, estrangement, neurosis (*dated*) [➡ PSYCHOLOGY AND THE MIND; 769] *Opposite*: balance

maladroit *adj* **awkward**, clumsy, inept, gauche, ungainly, inelegant, graceless, unskillful, insensitive, ham-fisted (*informal*), ham-handed (*informal*), gawky (*informal*) [➡ UNSKILLED; 529] *Opposite*: dexterous

maladroitness (*formal*) *n* **clumsiness**, insensitivity, awkwardness, ineptitude, gaucheness, inelegance, gra-

celessness, gawkiness (*informal*), ham-handedness (*informal*), ham-fistedness (*informal*) [➡ UNSKILLED; 529]

malady *n* **sickness**, illness, disease, disorder, condition, malaise [➡ SICKNESS; 729]

malaise **1** *n* **sickness**, illness, disease, disorder, condition, malady [➡ SICKNESS; 729] **2** *n* **dissatisfaction**, discontent, unease, disquiet, anxiety, depression, discomfort [➡ SADNESS, DISTRESS, AND DESPAIR; 539]

malapropism *type of* **wordplay** [➡ JOKES AND TEASING; 674]

malarkey (*informal*) *n* [➡ MEANINGLESS SPEECH OR WRITING; 676]

malcontent **1** *n* **complainer**, mischief-maker, protester, rebel, whiner, agitator, troublemaker, dissident, grouch (*informal*) [➡ UNCOOPERATIVE OR REBELLIOUS PEOPLE; 566] **2** *adj* **discontented**, disgruntled, dissatisfied, unhappy, complaining, rebellious, grumbling [➡ SADNESS, DISTRESS, AND DESPAIR; 539] *Opposite*: happy

male **1** *adj* **masculine**, mannish, manlike, manly, virile, macho [➡ GENDER IDENTITY AND SEXUALITY; 932] *Opposite*: feminine **2** *n* **man**, fellow, boy, guy (*informal*), fella (*informal*), dude (*slang*) [➡ MALE PERSON; 934] *Opposite*: female

malediction (*formal*) *n* **curse**, spell, blight, charm, hex [➡ BAD LUCK AND UNLUCKY; 784] *Opposite*: blessing

malefactor (*formal*) *n* **lawbreaker**, wrongdoer, criminal, outlaw, offender, villain, miscreant (*literary*) [➡ CRIMINALS; 821]

maleficence *n* [➡ MORALLY BAD OR IMPROPER; 775]

maleficent *adj* [➡ MORALLY BAD OR IMPROPER; 775]

malevolence *n* **wickedness**, malice, ill will, evil, spite, nastiness, unkindness, meanness [➡ MORALLY BAD OR IMPROPER; 775] *Opposite*: benevolence

malevolent *adj* **malicious**, spiteful, wicked, nasty, mean, unkind, vindictive, malign, malignant, evil [➡ MORALLY BAD OR IMPROPER; 775] *Opposite*: benevolent

malfeasance (*formal*) *n* [➡ MORALLY BAD OR IMPROPER; 775]

malformation *n* **deformity**, defect, fault, abnormality, distortion, disfigurement, aberration, crookedness, twistedness [➡ FAULTS, FLAWS, AND WEAKNESSES; 251]

malformed *adj* **misshapen**, deformed, abnormal, crooked, distorted, twisted [➡ ORIENTATION AND ALIGNMENT; 1223] *Opposite*: perfect

malfunction **1** *v* **act up**, break down, crash, fail, go wrong, bomb (*informal*), flop (*informal*), play up (*UK*) [➡ FAIL OR CEASE TO FUNCTION; 470] **2** *n* **fault**, breakdown, failure, error, blip, glitch [➡ FAILURE; 77]

malice *n* **hatred**, spite, malevolence, meanness, nastiness, cruelty, wickedness, mischievousness, evil [➡ SELFISH AND UNKIND; 505] *Opposite*: kindness

malicious *adj* **hateful**, spiteful, malevolent, mean, nasty, cruel, wicked, mischievous, evil [➡ SELFISH AND UNKIND; 505] *Opposite*: kind

maliciousness *n* [➡ SELFISH AND UNKIND; 505]

malign **1** *v* **criticize**, slander, defame, denigrate, disparage, libel, smear, badmouth (*slang*), asperse (*formal*),

vilify, slur [→INSULTS, ABUSE, AND SWEARING; 658] *Opposite*: praise
2 *adj* **harmful**, hurtful, damaging, destructive, negative, evil, injurious, aspersive (*formal*) [→DANGEROUS; 236] *Opposite*: benign

Compare and Contrast: *malign, defame, slander, libel, vilify*

CORE MEANING: to say or write something damaging about somebody

malign to criticize somebody in a spiteful and false or misleading way; *defame* to make an attack on somebody's good name or reputation with a view to damaging or destroying it; *slander* in legal terms, to make spoken false damaging accusations about somebody injurious to the person's reputation; *libel* in legal terms, to make false damaging accusations about somebody in writing, signs, or pictures; *vilify* to make viciously defamatory statements about somebody.

malignancy **1** *n* **spite**, malevolence, menace, evil, malice, enmity, hostility, unkindness, vindictiveness [→SELFISH AND UNKIND; 505] *Opposite*: kindness **2** *n* **melanoma**, tumor, disease, growth, cancer, sarcoma [→SICKNESS; 729]

malignant **1** *adj* **evil**, malevolent, hateful, spiteful, malicious, menacing, wicked, nasty, unkind, vindictive, cruel, mean [→SELFISH AND UNKIND; 505] *Opposite*: kind **2** *adj* **cancerous**, spreading, harmful, fatal [→SICKNESS; 729]

malignantly *adv* **malevolently**, menacingly, malignly, maliciously, unkindly, spitefully, vindictively, meanly, nastily, wickedly [→SELFISH AND UNKIND; 505] *Opposite*: kindly

malignly *adv* **malevolently**, maliciously, spitefully, unkindly, harmfully, nastily, vindictively, malignantly [→SELFISH AND UNKIND; 505] *Opposite*: benignly

malinger *v* **shirk**, be AWOL, duck, sidestep, shun, play hooky (*informal*) [→NOT DO AND REFUSE TO DO; 274]

malingerer *n* [→LAZY OR UNSUCCESSFUL PEOPLE; 948]

mall *n* **shopping mall**, plaza, shopping precinct (*UK*), shopping centre (*UK*) [→RETAIL OUTLETS; 1083]

mallard *type of* **freshwater bird** [→FRESHWATER BIRDS; 1000]

malleability **1** *n* **ductility**, flexibility, plasticity, pliability, softness, suppleness, bendiness (*UK*) [→MALLEABLE AND ELASTIC; 1212] *Opposite*: rigidity **2** *n* **impressionability**, pliability, manipulability, compliance, acquiescence [→THE WILL AND WILLINGNESS; 563] *Opposite*: inflexibility

malleable **1** *adj* **soft**, supple, flexible, pliable, ductile, plastic, bendy (*UK*) [→MALLEABLE AND ELASTIC; 1212] *Opposite*: rigid **2** *adj* **impressionable**, compliant, acquiescent, manipulable, biddable, persuadable, pliable [→THE WILL AND WILLINGNESS; 563]

See Compare and Contrast at **pliable**.

mallet *type of* **carpentry tool** [→HAND TOOLS; 1119]

malleus *part of* **ear** [→THE EAR; 706]

malnourished *adj* **underfed**, undernourished, underweight, starving, famished, half-starved, hungry, emaciated, wasted, thin [→EAT AND NOT EAT; 710] *Opposite*: well-fed

malnourishment *n* [→DISORDERS OF THE DIGESTIVE SYSTEM; 713]

malnutrition *n* **undernourishment**, malnourishment, underfeeding, starvation, famine, hunger [→DISORDERS OF THE DIGESTIVE SYSTEM; 713]

malodorous *adj* **fetid**, foul, foul-smelling, offensive, putrid, reeking, smelly, stinking, ripe (*informal*), rank (*literary*) [→SMELL AND SMELLING; 705] *Opposite*: sweet-smelling

malpractice *n* **misconduct**, negligence, abuse, dereliction, mismanagement, misuse [→MISUSE AND ABUSE; 471]

maltreat *v* **mistreat**, hurt, injure, harm, damage, abuse, neglect, misuse [→WOUND A PERSON OR ANIMAL; 383]

See Compare and Contrast at **misuse**.

maltreatment *n* **mistreatment**, abuse, ill-treatment, harm, damage, cruelty, injury, hurt, neglect [→MALICIOUS ACTIONS OR BEHAVIOR; 296]

mama *n* (*informal*) **mother**, mom (*informal*), momma (*informal*), mommy (*informal*), mammy (*informal*), mamma (*informal*), ma (*informal*) [→OLDER GENERATION RELATIVES; 959]

mamba *type of* **poisonous snake** [→SNAKES; 995]

mambo *type of* **dance** [→DANCE; 903]

mamma (*informal*) *see* **mama**

mammal *n* **animal**, marsupial, placental mammal, marine mammal [→LIVING THINGS AND LIVING; 976]

mammal

◆ *types of large mammals*
alpaca, bactrian camel, bear, bison, boar, buffalo, camel, dromedary, elephant, giraffe, hippopotamus, llama, panda, polar bear, rhinoceros, wart hog

◆ *types of marine mammals*
dolphin, dugong, grampus, manatee, porpoise, sea lion, seal, walrus, whale

◆ *types of small mammals*
anteater, armadillo, badger, ferret, hare, hedgehog, hyrax, marten, mink, mongoose, otter, pine marten, polecat, porcupine, rabbit, raccoon, skunk, sloth, stoat, weasel, wolverine

mammon *n* **ambition**, greed, loot, money, riches, wealth, lucre (*dated or humorous*) [→FINANCIAL ASSETS; 462]

mammoth *adj* **enormous**, huge, massive, immense, epic, gargantuan, colossal, vast, titanic [→LARGE; 1193] *Opposite*: tiny

mammy (*informal*) *type of* **older relative** [→OLDER GENERATION RELATIVES; 959]

man **1** *n* **gentleman**, male, fellow, fella (*informal*), guy (*informal*), gent (*informal*), dude (*slang*), brother (*slang*) [→MALE PERSON; 934] *Opposite*: woman **2** *v* **operate**, staff, crew, work, manage, handle [→USE TOOLS AND MACHINERY; 468]

manacle **1** *n* **handcuff**, chain, shackle, bond, fetter, irons [→FASTENERS, LINKS, AND NETWORKS; 1247] **2** *v* **bind**, chain, chain up, fetter, handcuff, shackle, pinion, enchain (*formal or literary*) [→CAPTIVITY AND LOSS OF FREEDOM; 248] *Opposite*: release

manage 1 *v* **achieve**, accomplish, succeed, be able to, bring about [➡ SUCCEED AND WIN; 79] *Opposite*: fail 2 *v* **cope**, fare, get on, do, get by, get along, make do, survive, muddle through [➡ CONTINUE TO EXIST; 17] *Opposite*: give up 3 *v* **run**, direct, administer, supervise, be in charge, oversee, operate, govern [➡ BE IN CHARGE; 270] 4 *v* **handle**, deal with, control, cope with [➡ CARRY OUT AN ACTION; 269] 5 *v* **control**, discipline, master, dominate, boss [➡ AVOID, PREVENT, LIMIT, AND CONTROL; 277]

manageable *adj* **controllable**, handy, untroublesome, practicable, adaptable, wieldy [➡ USEFULNESS; 199] *Opposite*: unwieldy

management 1 *n* **organization**, running, administration, supervision, managing, controlling [➡ BUSINESS ACTIVITIES AND PHENOMENA; 794] 2 *n* **directors**, managers, executives, employers, board, bosses [➡ BOSSES AND MANAGEMENT; 965]

management buyout *n* [➡ BUSINESS ACTIVITIES AND PHENOMENA; 794]

manager *n* **boss**, director, executive, administrator, supervisor, leader, chief, superior [➡ BOSSES AND MANAGEMENT; 965]

managerial *adj* **executive**, management, supervisory, directorial, decision-making, organizational, administrative, professional, white-collar [➡ TYPES OF WORK; 835]

managing director (*UK*) *n* [➡ BUSINESS PEOPLE; 793]

manat *type of* **currency** [➡ CURRENCIES; 798]

manatee *type of* **marine mammal** [➡ MARINE MAMMALS; 987]

mandarin 1 *n* **bureaucrat**, official, public servant, civil servant, manager [➡ POLITICAL OFFICES AND POLITICIANS; 808] 2 *type of* **citrus fruit** [➡ FRUIT AND VEGETABLES; 1176]

mandate 1 *n* **order**, command, directive, decree, dictate, instruction, fiat, obligation [➡ REQUEST AND DEMAND; 663] 2 *n* **authority**, authorization, consent, permission, support, go-ahead (*informal*) [➡ PERMIT AND ALLOW; 669] 3 *n* **term of office**, reign, tenure, stay [➡ POLITICAL OFFICES AND POLITICIANS; 808] 4 *v* **assign**, authorize, command, delegate, instruct, require, direct (*formal*) [➡ REQUEST AND DEMAND; 663]

mandatory *adj* **obligatory**, compulsory, required, fixed, binding, needed [➡ NECESSARY AND ESSENTIAL; 196] *Opposite*: optional

mandible 1 *n* **jaw**, jawbone, maxilla, mouth, mouthpiece, bill, beak [➡ PARTS OF THE BODY: HEAD; 692] 2 *type of* **bone** [➡ THE BONES AND JOINTS; 719]

mandolin *type of* **stringed instrument** [➡ MUSICAL INSTRUMENTS; 910]

mandrill *type of* **primate** [➡ PRIMATES; 988]

mane 1 *n* (*literary or informal*) **tresses**, curls, shock, head of hair, locks (*literary*) [➡ HAIR; 484] 2 *part of* **horse** [➡ HORSES; 985]

man-eating *adj* **carnivorous**, ferocious, fierce, wild, aggressive [➡ DANGEROUS; 236]

maneuver 1 *n* **move**, movement, operation, exercise [➡ ACTIONS OR UNDERTAKINGS; 259] 2 *n* **ploy**, trick, plot, scheme, device, tactic, plan, move, stratagem, gambit, ruse, feint, artifice (*formal*) [➡ WAYS OF DOING THINGS; 294] 3 *v* **manipulate**, plot,

scheme, contrive, plan, finesse, play, machinate [➡ FALSIFY AND CHEAT; 176]

man friend (*informal*) *n* **male companion**, boyfriend, partner [➡ SEXUAL AND ROMANTIC RELATIONSHIPS; 964]

manful *adj* **brave**, strong, resolute, bold, determined, courageous, intrepid (*literary or humorous*) [➡ COURAGE; 498] *Opposite*: cowardly

mangel-wurzel *type of* **root vegetable** [➡ FRUIT AND VEGETABLES; 1176]

manger *n* **trough**, feeding-box, container, crib [➡ CONTAINERS, RECEPTACLES, AND PACKAGING; 1245]

mangle *v* **crush**, mash, smash, contort, twist, batter, maul, injure, mar, disfigure [➡ CHANGE OF SHAPE; 385]

mangled *adj* [➡ IN BAD REPAIR; 1234]

mango *type of* **fruit** [➡ FRUIT AND VEGETABLES; 1176]

mangrove *type of* **evergreen tree** [➡ EVERGREEN AND CONIFEROUS TREES; 1029]

mangy (*informal*) *adj* **unpleasant**, dirty, shabby, disgusting, filthy, foul, sticky, messy, mucky (*informal*), grungy (*informal*), gunky (*informal*), scuzzy (*slang*) [➡ DIRTY; 1235] *Opposite*: pristine

manhandle *v* **push**, shove, jostle, hustle, move, bundle (*informal*) [➡ PHYSICAL ATTACK AND PUNISHMENT; 415]

manhood 1 *n* **maturity**, independence, adulthood [➡ ADULTHOOD; 918] 2 *n* **men**, menfolk, males [➡ MALE PERSON; 934] 3 *n* **strength**, courage, determination, virility, boldness, manliness [➡ COURAGE; 498]

mania *n* **obsession**, desire, love, craze, passion, fad, fashion, enthusiasm, hysteria, fever, thing (*informal*) [➡ FADS, FETISHES, AND IDOLATRY; 555]

maniac *n* **enthusiast**, fanatic, zealot, fiend, freak (*informal*), nut (*informal*) [➡ DEVOTEES AND ADDICTED PEOPLE; 556]

manic (*informal*) *adj* **overexcited**, agitated, hectic, frenzied, busy, hysterical, feverish, frantic, excited, hyper (*informal*) [➡ PLEASURE, EXCITEMENT, AND ELATION; 534] *Opposite*: calm

manicure *v* **trim**, file, shape, cut, clip, pare, crop [➡ IMPROVE APPEARANCE; 379]

manifest 1 *adj* **apparent**, unmistakable, clear, obvious, distinct, noticeable [➡ PERCEPTIBLE; 25] *Opposite*: unclear 2 *v* **make plain**, establish, demonstrate, display, reveal, show, exhibit, express [➡ CAUSE TO APPEAR; 5]

manifestation *n* **sign**, indication, index, indicator, appearance, display, exhibition, expression, demonstration [➡ REPRESENTATIONS AND GENERAL EXAMPLES; 65]

manifestly *adv* **apparently**, unmistakably, clearly, obviously, distinctly, noticeably [➡ PERCEPTIBLE; 25]

manifesto *n* **declaration**, statement, policy, guidelines, proposal, philosophy, plan, platform, program, beliefs, strategy [➡ OFFICIAL DOCUMENTS; 586]

manifold 1 *adj* **various**, diverse, many, multiple, assorted, multifarious [➡ MANY, MUCH, LARGE AMOUNT; 117] *Opposite*: uniform 2 *part of* **engine** [➡ PARTS OF AN ENGINE; 1144]

manipulate 1 *v* **operate**, work, use, deploy, employ, handle [→USE; 467] **2** *v* **influence**, control, bias, direct, sway, affect, impress [→CAUSE OR COMPEL TO ACT; 271] **3** *v* **maneuver**, direct, control, stage-manage, engineer [→CARRY OUT AN ACTION; 269]

manipulation 1 *n* **operation**, handling, management, use, guidance, influence, employment [→USE; 467] **2** *n* **running**, control, maneuvering, exploitation, persuasion, scheming, capitalizing on, wheeler-dealing (*informal*) [→CARRY OUT AN ACTION; 269] **3** *n* **falsification**, forgery, alteration, misuse, tampering with, misapplication, tweaking (*informal*) [→MISUSE AND ABUSE; 471] **4** *n* **osteopathy**, massage, movement, flexing, rub, kneading, therapy, treatment, physiotherapy (*UK*) [→REMEDIES, TREATMENTS, AND OPERATIONS; 731]

manipulative *adj* **scheming**, calculating, controlling, devious, unscrupulous, cunning, Machiavellian, serpentine (*literary*) [→DECEITFUL; 513]

manipulator *n* **Machiavelli**, exploiter, schemer, Svengali, wheeler-dealer (*informal*), spin doctor (*slang*) [→PEOPLE WHO DECEIVE; 661]

mankind 1 *n* (*dated*) **men**, menfolk, manhood, males [→MALE PERSON; 934] **2** *n* **human race**, humankind, humanity, human beings, people [→PERSON; 931]

manliness *n* **masculinity**, machismo, manhood [→GENDER IDENTITY AND SEXUALITY; 932]

manly *adj* **virile**, mannish, male, masculine, macho [→GENDER IDENTITY AND SEXUALITY; 932] *Opposite*: womanly

man-made *adj* **artificial**, synthetic, manufactured, substitute, imitation, faux [→FALSE AND UNREAL; 173] *Opposite*: natural

manna 1 *n* **food**, sustenance, victuals, fodder, provisions, provender (*literary or humorous*), vittles (*archaic*) [→FOOD; 1167] **2** *n* **godsend**, blessing, boon, gift, help, benefit, lifesaver (*informal*) [→SOURCE OF HAPPINESS, PLEASURE, OR IMPROVEMENT; 209]

mannequin *n* **dummy**, model, figure, tailor's dummy, dressmaker's dummy, figurine, manikin [→REPRESENTATIONS AND GENERAL EXAMPLES; 65]

manner 1 *n* **way**, means, method, style, custom, routine, mode, fashion, modus [→WAYS OF DOING THINGS; 294] **2** *n* **type**, kind, sort, class, category, variety [→VARIETIES, TYPES, AND KINDS; 145] **3** *n* **behavior**, conduct, demeanor, bearing, comportment (*formal*), deportment (*formal*), behaviour (*UK*) [→TEMPERAMENT AND BEHAVIOR; 492]

mannered *adj* **affected**, artificial, put-on, false, simpering, genteel [→AFFECTATION, SELF-SATISFACTION, AND SNOBBISHNESS; 507] *Opposite*: natural

mannerism 1 *n* **gesture**, trait, characteristic, gesticulation, habit, idiosyncrasy, quirk, trick [→GESTURES AND GESTICULATION; 653] **2** *n* **affectation**, show, act, display, pretense, parade [→DECEPTION AND LIES; 660]

Mannerism *type of* **pre-20th-century art movement** [→ARTISTIC MOVEMENTS AND STYLES; 899]

mannerly *adj* **well-behaved**, polite, refined, well-mannered, respectful, decent, gallant, polished, gracious, well-bred, decorous, courteous, respectable, civilized,

well brought-up, courtly [→GOOD MANNERS AND SOCIAL SKILLS; 520] *Opposite*: rude

manners 1 *n* **etiquette**, protocol, good manners [→GOOD MANNERS AND SOCIAL SKILLS; 520] **2** *n* **behavior**, conduct, demeanor, deportment, manner, comportment (*formal*) [→TEMPERAMENT AND BEHAVIOR; 492]

man-of-war *type of* **historical vessel** [→SHIPS AND BOATS; 1150]

manor *type of* **house** [→RESIDENTIAL BUILDINGS; 1078]

manor house *type of* **house** [→RESIDENTIAL BUILDINGS; 1078]

manqué *adj* **failed**, near, would-be, unfulfilled, unsuccessful, wannabe (*informal*), ersatz [→UNSUCCESSFUL AND UNPROMISING; 76] *Opposite*: successful

mansard *n* **attic**, loft, roof, eaves, rafters [→ROOFS, ROOF PARTS, AND CEILINGS; 1103]

manse *n* **vicarage**, rectory, parsonage, residence, church house [→RELIGIOUS BUILDINGS; 1085]

mansion *type of* **house** [→RESIDENTIAL BUILDINGS; 1078]

manslaughter *n* **murder**, homicide, killing, assassination, slaying, slaughter, unlawful death, massacre [→CAUSES OF DEATH; 921]

manta *type of* **flatfish** [→OCEAN FISH; 1009]

mantel *type of* **general fixtures** [→FIXTURES; 859]

mantelpiece *type of* **general fixtures** [→FIXTURES; 859]

mantilla *type of* **headgear** [→ACCESSORIES, MILLINERY, AND LINGERIE; 867]

mantle 1 *n* (*literary*) **layer**, blanket, covering, shroud, veil, cloak [→COVERS AND COATINGS; 1246] **2** *n* (*formal*) **responsibility**, function, role, position, duty, onus [→RESPONSIBILITY; 170]

mantra *n* **chant**, intonation, repetition, refrain, sacred word, hymn, song, word [→RELIGIONS AND RELIGIOUS PRACTICES; 777]

manual 1 *adj* **physical**, labor-intensive, blue-collar [→TYPES OF WORK; 835] *Opposite*: mental **2** *n* **instruction booklet**, guide, handbook, guidebook, instruction manual, booklet, instructions [→MANUALS AND INSTRUCTIONS; 589]

manual labor *n* [→TYPES OF WORK; 835]

manual laborer *n* [→WORKERS; 836]

manual worker *n* [→WORKERS; 836]

manufacture 1 *v* **build**, assemble, construct, produce, create, turn out, make, form, fashion, fabricate [→MANUFACTURE; 349] **2** *n* **production**, making, creation, building, assembly, manufacturing, construction, fabrication [→CREATION; 346]

See Compare and Contrast at **make**.

manufactured *adj* **factory-made**, mass-produced, industrial, man-made, synthetic, artificial [→NOT IN A NATURAL STATE; 1215]

manufacturer *n* **builder**, producer, constructor, creator, industrialist, maker [→DESIGNERS, CREATORS, AND INSTIGATORS; 347]

manufacturing *n* production, manufacture, making, assembly, construction, building, fabrication, creation [➡ CREATION; 346]

manumission (*formal*) *n* [➡ FREEDOM AND LIBERTY; 208]

manure *n* dung, compost, guano, muck, fertilizer, droppings [➡ EXCRETION AND EXCRETA; 722]

manuscript *n* document, copy, text, script [➡ BOOKS AND BOOKLETS; 590]

Manx cat *type of* cat [➡ FELINES; 983]

many *adj* a lot of, lots of, numerous, countless, several, various, scores of, sundry, loads of (*informal*) [➡ MANY, MUCH, LARGE AMOUNT; 117] *Opposite*: few

many-colored *adj* [➡ DESCRIBING COLORS; 1226]

many-hued *adj* [➡ DESCRIBING COLORS; 1226]

many-sided *adj* multifaceted, complex, complicated, deep, multidimensional [➡ POSITIVELY COMPLEX OR COMPLICATED; 217] *Opposite*: one-dimensional

Maoism *n* [➡ PHILOSOPHIES AND BELIEFS; 780]

Maoist *adj* [➡ PHILOSOPHIES AND BELIEFS; 780]

map 1 *n* plan, plot, chart, atlas, record, drawing, diagram [➡ DRAWINGS, CHARTS, AND TABLES; 594] 2 *v* chart, plot, plan, record, draw, represent [➡ CREATE IMAGES; 356]

maple *type of* deciduous tree [➡ DECIDUOUS TREES; 1028]

maple syrup *n* [➡ SUGAR AND PRESERVES; 1184]

map out *v* work out, plan, devise, outline, arrange, design [➡ CREATION; 346]

map reading *n* route-planning, routing, direction-finding, orienteering, triangulation [➡ NAVIGATION; 1141]

maquiladora *type of* factory [➡ INDUSTRIAL BUILDINGS; 1087]

maquillage *n* [➡ MAKEUP AND BEAUTY PRODUCTS; 490]

mar *v* deface, ruin, mutilate, damage, disfigure, stain, injure, blemish, harm, impair [➡ WORSEN APPEARANCE; 382] *Opposite*: repair

marabou *type of* scavenger [➡ BIRDS; 997]

maraca *type of* percussion instrument [➡ MUSICAL INSTRUMENTS; 910]

marathon 1 *adj* lengthy, epic, long-drawn-out, grueling, difficult, long-winded [➡ HAPPENING SLOWLY; 106] 2 *type of* track and field [➡ HOBBIES, GAMES, AND SPORTS; 875]

maraud *v* raid, plunder, ransack, loot, pillage [➡ STEAL AND ROB; 426]

marauder *n* raider, robber, bandit, pillager, plunderer, brigand (*literary*) [➡ VILLAINS AND THUGS; 947]

marble 1 *n* toy, glass ball, agate, cat's eye [➡ TOYS; 880] 2 *type of* stone [➡ STONES, ROCKS, AND BOULDERS; 1057]

marbled *adj* veined, streaked, mottled, lined, shot through, patterned, moiré [➡ DESCRIBING PATTERNS; 1227]

marbles (*slang*) *n* wits, mind, reason, sense, commonsense [➡ PSYCHOLOGY AND THE MIND; 769]

march 1 *v* parade, file, step, troop, process, walk [➡ PROCEED AND GO; 305] 2 *v* stride, stomp, storm, sweep, flounce, stalk [➡ PROCEED AND GO; 305] 3 *n* hike, trek, walk, tramp, trudge [➡ TRAVEL: JOURNEYS AND TRIPS; 318] 4 *n* protest, picket, mass lobby, rally, demonstration, campaign, demo (*informal*) [➡ AGGRESSIVE EVENTS; 39]

marcher *n* demonstrator, protester, walker, campaigner, supporter, activist, picketer [➡ UNCOOPERATIVE OR REBELLIOUS PEOPLE; 566]

marchioness *type of* aristocrat [➡ RULERS AND ARISTOCRACY; 823]

march-past *n* parade, review, muster, procession [➡ PERFORMANCES AND SHOWS; 42]

mare *type of* female animal [➡ MALE OR FEMALE ANIMALS; 978]

mare's-tail *type of* cloud [➡ CLOUDY AND RAINY WEATHER; 1052]

margarine *type of* cooking fat and oil [➡ FATS AND OILS; 1173]

margin 1 *n* boundary, border, brim, sideline, edge, verge, fringe, side, perimeter [➡ EXTREMITIES OF PHYSICAL OBJECTS; 1250] 2 *n* surplus, room, leeway, allowance, scope, space, play, latitude, slack [➡ DEGREE AND EXTENT; 110]

marginal 1 *adj* negligible, minimal, low, minor, slight, small, tiny [➡ FEW, LITTLE, SMALL AMOUNT; 120] *Opposite*: major 2 *adj* irrelevant, insignificant, unimportant, borderline, fringe [➡ UNIMPORTANT AND UNNECESSARY; 238] *Opposite*: central

marginalization *n* relegation, sidelining, demotion, downgrading, disregarding, freezing out, ostracism, banishment [➡ SEPARATE AND DIVIDE; 401]

marginalize *v* relegate, sideline, demote, downgrade, disregard, freeze out, banish, ostracize [➡ SEPARATE AND DIVIDE; 401] *Opposite*: include

marginally *adv* slightly, a little, a touch, a bit (*informal*), a tad (*informal*) [➡ TO A CERTAIN EXTENT; 136]

mariachi *type of* band [➡ MUSICIANS AND SINGERS; 908]

marigold *type of* annual flower [➡ FLOWERS; 1032]

marimba *type of* percussion instrument [➡ MUSICAL INSTRUMENTS; 910]

marina *n* harbor, port, dock, quay [➡ THE SEAS, OCEANS, AND SHORES; 1041]

marinade 1 *n* dressing, sauce, flavoring, juices, infusion [➡ SEASONINGS AND SAUCES; 1174] 2 *see* **marinate**

marinate *v* steep, soak, infuse, immerse, douse [➡ COOKING AND FOOD PREPARATION; 353]

marinated *adj* [➡ STATE OF PREPARED FOOD; 1171]

marine 1 *adj* saltwater, seawater, sea, aquatic [➡ THE SEAS, OCEANS, AND SHORES; 1041] 2 *adj* nautical, oceangoing, naval, seafaring, seagoing, oceanic, maritime [➡ THE SEAS, OCEANS, AND SHORES; 1041]

mariner *n* sailor, seafarer, seadog, old salt, tar (*archaic informal*) [➡ TRAVEL: TRAVELERS AND WALKERS; 319]

marinière *type of* food presentation [➡ COOKING AND FOOD PREPARATION; 353]

marital *adj* conjugal, nuptial, wedded, spousal, matrimonial, connubial (*literary*) [➡ MARRIED STATE; 961]

maritime 1 *adj* **nautical**, naval, oceanic, seafaring, seagoing, marine [➡ THE SEAS, OCEANS, AND SHORES; 1041] **2** *adj* **seaside**, coastal, shoreline, littoral [➡ THE SEAS, OCEANS, AND SHORES; 1041]

marjoram *type of* **herb** [➡ HERBS AND SPICES; 1175]

mark 1 *n* **spot**, scratch, dent, stain, smear, blot, smudge, streak [➡ FAULTS, FLAWS, AND WEAKNESSES; 251] **2** *n* **sign**, indication, feature, characteristic, symbol, indicator, index, symptom, evidence [➡ INDICATIONS, SIGNS, AND WARNINGS; 68] **3** *n* **score**, point, assessment, evaluation, grade [➡ SCORES AND EVALUATIONS; 598] **4** *v* **stain**, scratch, smudge, smear, blot, taint, besmear, soil, streak, tarnish, mar, sully (*literary*) [➡ DIRTY AND CONTAMINATE; 404] **5** *v* **correct**, assess, grade, evaluate, score [➡ ASSESS QUALITY; 755] **6** *v* **indicate**, denote, show, demonstrate, evidence, exhibit [➡ MEAN SOMETHING; 61] **7** *v* **celebrate**, commemorate, keep, observe, solemnize [➡ PRAISE AND ENCOURAGE; 647]

marka *type of* **currency** [➡ CURRENCIES; 798]

markdown *n* **discount**, price cutting, reduction, concession (*UK*) [➡ FUNDS, PAYMENTS, AND CHARGES; 800] *Opposite:* markup

marked *adj* **clear**, apparent, evident, noticeable, conspicuous, pronounced, blatant, obvious, arresting, prominent, striking, significant, decided, distinct [➡ PERCEPTIBLE; 25]

marker 1 *n* **indicator**, sign, indication, symbol, pointer [➡ INDICATIONS, SIGNS, AND WARNINGS; 68] **2** *type of* **pen** [➡ WRITING AND DRAWING IMPLEMENTS, AND MEDIA; 601]

market 1 *n* **marketplace**, souk, bazaar, arcade, fair, flea market [➡ URBAN OUTDOOR SPACES; 1072] **2** *v* **sell**, promote, advertise, peddle, trade, merchandise, package [➡ SELL; 441]

marketable *adj* **in demand**, sought-after, wanted, vendible, merchantable, salable, merchandisable [➡ POPULAR AND WANTED; 220]

market analyst *n* [➡ PEOPLE INVOLVED IN FINANCE; 804]

market economy *type of* **economic system** [➡ FINANCE AND ECONOMICS; 796]

market garden (*UK*) *n* [➡ AGRICULTURE AND FARMING; 1075]

marketing *n* **advertising**, selling, presentation, publicizing, promotion [➡ ADVERTISING AND PUBLICITY; 604]

marketplace 1 *n* **bazaar**, market, souk, flea market, open market, covered market, square, fair [➡ URBAN OUTDOOR SPACES; 1072] **2** *n* **trading floor**, sphere, arena, market [➡ BUSINESS; 791]

market square *n* [➡ URBAN OUTDOOR SPACES; 1072]

marking *n* **pattern**, coloration, design [➡ PATTERNS; 1225]

markka *type of* **currency** [➡ CURRENCIES; 798]

mark out 1 *v* **outline**, demarcate, sketch, delimit, delineate, map out, establish, define, draw, set down, bound, determine [➡ NAME AND DESCRIBE; 665] **2** *v* **distinguish**, differentiate, single out, identify, characterize, highlight [➡ NAME AND DESCRIBE; 665]

markup *n* **price increase**, rise, hike, profit, profit margin [➡ FUNDS, PAYMENTS, AND CHARGES; 800] *Opposite:* markdown

marlin *type of* **tropical fish** [➡ OCEAN FISH; 1009]

marmalade *type of* **preserve** [➡ SUGAR AND PRESERVES; 1184]

marmoset *type of* **primate** [➡ PRIMATES; 988]

marmot *type of* **rodent** [➡ RODENTS; 989]

maroon 1 *v* **abandon**, leave high and dry, leave, cast aside, cast adrift, isolate, forsake, strand, desert [➡ REFUSING OR REJECTING RELATIONS; 975] **2** *type of* **red** [➡ COLORS; 1224]

marooned *adj* **stranded**, deserted, abandoned, isolated, stuck, forsaken, left [➡ SOLITARINESS; 941]

marque *n* **make**, label, trademark, brand [➡ NAME AND DESCRIBE; 665]

marquee *n* **tent**, pavilion, canvas, shelter, erection (*formal*) [➡ BUILDINGS FOR PUBLIC ENTERTAINMENT; 1084]

marquess *type of* **aristocrat** [➡ RULERS AND ARISTOCRACY; 823]

marquetry 1 *n* **inlay**, pattern, design, veneer [➡ ORNAMENTS AND DECORATIONS; 1248] **2** *type of* **woodworking** [➡ CRAFTS AND CARVING; 355]

marram *type of* **grass** [➡ GRASS; 1031]

marred *adj* **blemished**, flawed, stained, disfigured, tarnished, tainted, soiled, smudged, scratched, spoiled [➡ IN BAD REPAIR; 1234] *Opposite:* unblemished

marriage 1 *n* **wedding**, matrimony, wedding ceremony, marriage ceremony, nuptials (*formal*) [➡ CEREMONIES AND ANNIVERSARIES; 38] *Opposite:* divorce **2** *n* **union**, fusion, combination, coming together, alliance, coalition, merger [➡ COLLECTIONS AND MIXTURES OF THINGS; 1244] *Opposite:* separation

marriageability *n* **eligibility**, suitability, availability, fitness [➡ MARITAL STATUS; 890]

marriageable *adj* **eligible**, suitable, available, adult, grown-up [➡ MARITAL STATUS; 890]

married *adj* **wedded**, matrimonial, nuptial, conjugal, marital, connubial (*literary*) [➡ MARRIED STATE; 961]

marrow (*literary*) *n* **core**, heart, soul, spirit, essence, substance, center, nucleus [➡ MOST IMPORTANT THING; 197]

marrow squash *type of* **vegetable** [➡ FRUIT AND VEGETABLES; 1176]

marry *v* **get married**, walk down the aisle, join in matrimony, tie the knot (*informal*), wed (*formal or literary*), espouse (*archaic*) [➡ ESTABLISHING RELATIONSHIPS WITH OTHERS; 974]

Mars *type of* **planet** [➡ HEAVENLY BODIES; 1061]

marsh *n* **bog**, swamp, quagmire, swampland, marshland, fen, fenland, everglade, peat bog, wetland, morass [➡ WETLANDS; 1043]

marshal 1 *n* **officer**, sheriff, deputy, law officer [➡ THE POLICE, ARREST, AND PRETRIAL PROCEEDINGS; 818] **2** *v* **assemble**, position, gather together, collect, shepherd, line up, group, organize [➡ COMBINE AND MIX; 400] *Opposite:* disperse **3** *v* **arrange**, order, sort out, put in order, organize, rationalize [➡ ARRANGE AND CREATE ORDER; 357] *Opposite:* muddle

marsh gas *type of* **gas** [➡ GASES; 1275]

marshland *n* **bog**, swamp, swampland, marsh, wetland, fen, fenland, peat bog, quagmire, everglade [➡ WETLANDS; 1043]

marshmallow *type of* **confectionery** [➡CONFECTIONERY; 1182]

marshy *adj* **boggy**, swampy, soggy, muddy, peaty, squelchy [➡WET; 1240] *Opposite:* dry

marsupial *n* [➡LIVING THINGS AND LIVING; 976]

marsupial

◆ *types of marsupials*
bandicoot, bettong, bilby, kangaroo, koala, opossum, phalanger, potoroo, Tasmanian devil, thylacine, wallaby, wombat

mart *n* **auction**, sale, market, store, trading place, saleroom (*UK*) [➡RETAIL OUTLETS; 1083]

marten *type of* **small mammal** [➡SMALL MAMMALS; 990]

martial 1 *adj* **military**, soldierly, warlike, battle-hardened, fighting, paramilitary [➡MILITARY; 829] *Opposite:* civilian 2 *adj* **warlike**, fierce, aggressive, belligerent, hostile, antagonistic, bellicose [➡AGGRESSIVE AND BELLIGERENT; 518] *Opposite:* peaceful

martial law *n* **state of emergency**, militarism, junta, dictatorship, emergency powers, military rule, stratocracy (*formal*) [➡STYLES AND SYSTEMS OF GOVERNMENT; 806]

Martian *n* **alien**, extraterrestrial, ET, spaceman, invader, space invader, little green man (*humorous*) [➡SCIENCE FICTION; 1064] *Opposite:* terrestrial

martinet *n* **disciplinarian**, stickler, despot, hardliner, perfectionist, tyrant [➡GRUMPY AND NEGATIVE PEOPLE; 953] *Opposite:* softy (*informal*)

martyr 1 *n* **sacrifice**, sacrificial victim, victim, scapegoat, ransom (*literary*) [➡DEAD PERSON; 926] 2 *n* **idealist**, witness, believer, supporter [➡RELIGIOUS PEOPLE; 778] 3 *n* **sufferer**, invalid, patient [➡UNFIT AND WEAK; 739]

martyrdom 1 *n* **death**, killing, slaughter, torture, ritual murder, execution [➡CAUSES OF DEATH; 921] 2 *n* **suffering**, misery, pain, sacrifice, torment, agony, passion, persecution, endurance [➡SADNESS, DISTRESS, AND DESPAIR; 539]

marvel 1 *n* **wonder**, miracle, spectacle, sight, curiosity, phenomenon, sensation [➡AMAZING THINGS; 211] 2 *n* **genius**, prodigy, phenomenon, wunderkind, whiz (*informal*), ace (*informal*) [➡TALENTED OR INTELLIGENT PEOPLE; 528] 3 *v* **be amazed**, be surprised, be impressed, admire, wonder, be awed, gaze in awe [➡PRAISE AND ENCOURAGE; 647] *Opposite:* deride

marvellous *see* **marvelous**

marvelous 1 *adj* **amazing**, impressive, remarkable, magnificent, superb, stunning, outstanding, excellent, spectacular, awe-inspiring, splendid [➡EXTRAORDINARY: AMAZING; 204] *Opposite:* ordinary 2 *adj* **great**, brilliant, wonderful, fantastic, fabulous, cool (*slang*), groovy (*dated slang*) [➡EXTRAORDINARY: AMAZING; 204]

Marxism *n* [➡PHILOSOPHIES AND BELIEFS; 780]

Marxist *adj* [➡PHILOSOPHIES AND BELIEFS; 780]

marzipan *type of* **confectionery** [➡CONFECTIONERY; 1182]

mascara *n* [➡MAKEUP AND BEAUTY PRODUCTS; 490]

mascarpone *type of* **soft cheese** [➡DAIRY PRODUCTS AND CHEESES; 1183]

mascot *n* **symbol**, charm, talisman, amulet, periapt [➡LUCKY CHARMS; 785] *Opposite:* hex

masculine *adj* **male**, manly, mannish, macho, virile, boyish [➡GENDER IDENTITY AND SEXUALITY; 932] *Opposite:* feminine

masculinity *n* **maleness**, manliness, mannishness, manhood, boyhood, boyishness, virility, machismo [➡GENDER IDENTITY AND SEXUALITY; 932] *Opposite:* femininity

mash 1 *n* **purée**, pulp, mush [➡PREPARED DISHES; 1170] 2 *v* **pulp**, squash, pound, crush, smash, purée, mush, pulverize [➡CHANGE OF SHAPE; 385]

mask 1 *n* **cover**, disguise, guise, façade, front, veneer, concealment [➡CLOTHES AND ACCESSORIES; 864] 2 *v* **hide**, conceal, disguise, cover, camouflage, screen, veil, cloak [➡CAUSE TO DISAPPEAR; 6] *Opposite:* expose

masked 1 *adj* **disguised**, incognito, camouflaged, concealed, screened, veiled, covered [➡IMPERCEPTIBLE; 26] *Opposite:* exposed 2 *adj* **undetectable**, imperceptible, latent, hidden, invisible, concealed, disguised, covered up [➡IMPERCEPTIBLE; 26] *Opposite:* detectable

masonry *n* **stonework**, brickwork, building materials, granite, sandstone, stone, brick, bricks and mortar [➡BUILDING MATERIALS; 1077]

masque 1 *n* **performance**, allegory, theatricals, play, opera, entertainment, show [➡PERFORMANCES AND SHOWS; 42] 2 *n* **dance**, ball, masked ball [➡PARTIES, DANCES, AND CELEBRATIONS; 37]

masquerade 1 *n* **pretense**, deception, cover-up, subterfuge, ruse, charade, trick, concealment [➡DECEPTION AND LIES; 660] 2 *v* **pretend to be**, impersonate, pose, disguise yourself, make-believe, make as if, imitate [➡PRETEND AND MIMIC; 60]

mass 1 *n* **form**, figure, frame, physique, build, bulk [➡SHAPE; 1216] 2 *n* **quantity**, corpus, amount, area, reservoir, supply [➡SIZE AND DIMENSIONS; 1192] 3 *n* **bulk**, main part, essence, majority, better part, lion's share [➡MAJORITY AND MAXIMUM; 141] 4 *type of* **musical form** [➡MUSIC, SONGS, AND SINGING; 907] 5 *v* **gather**, assemble, group, congregate, collect, huddle [➡GET CLOSER TOGETHER; 310] *Opposite:* disperse 6 *adj* **general**, widespread, common, universal, wholesale, large [➡WHOLENESS AND COMPLETENESS; 198]

massacre 1 *n* **extermination**, annihilation, carnage, butchery, mass slaughter, holocaust, destruction, bloodbath, genocide [➡CAUSES OF DEATH; 921] 2 *v* **slaughter**, murder, exterminate, butcher, mow down, annihilate, decimate, wipe out (*informal*), blow away (*slang*) [➡KILL; 923]

massage 1 *n* **manipulation**, pressure, kneading, rubbing, reflexology, acupressure, shiatsu, bodywork [➡CONTACT: EXERT PRESSURE; 414] 2 *v* **knead**, manipulate, rub, rub down [➡CONTACT: EXERT PRESSURE; 414] 3 *v* **falsify**, manipulate, alter, amend, misrepresent, fiddle (*informal*) [➡FALSIFY AND CHEAT; 176] 4 *type of* **complementary therapy** [➡REMEDIES, TREATMENTS, AND OPERATIONS; 731]

masses *n* **common people**, crowd, multitude, commonality, hoi polloi, the many, the multitude, the people, grassroots [➡CLASS STATUS; 889] *Opposite:* elite

massif *n* **mountain range**, chain, sierra, ridge, line [➡MOUNTAINS AND HILLS; 1044]

massive 1 *adj* **bulky**, heavy, solid, weighty, hulking, mighty [➡ WEIGHT: HEAVY; 1205] *Opposite*: slight 2 *adj* **huge**, enormous, gigantic, immense, colossal, substantial, considerable, great, vast, mammoth, giant [➡ LARGE; 1193] *Opposite*: tiny

massively (*informal*) *adv* **enormously**, immensely, hugely, tremendously, vastly, greatly, colossally, extremely, very [➡ TO A GREAT EXTENT; 132] *Opposite*: slightly

mass-produce *v* **churn out**, turn out, manufacture, process, knock out, spit out [➡ MANUFACTURE; 349]

mass-produced *adj* **ready-to-wear**, off-the-shelf, off-the-rack, ready-made, machine-made, high-street (*UK*) [➡ ORDINARINESS; 244] *Opposite*: custom-made

mast 1 *part of* **sailing vessel** [➡ PARTS OF A SHIP OR BOAT; 1151] 2 *type of* **telecommunications equipment** [➡ TELECOMMUNICATIONS; 1130]

mastectomy *type of* **medical procedure** [➡ REMEDIES, TREATMENTS, AND OPERATIONS; 731]

master 1 *n* **controller**, ruler, leader, chief, boss [➡ BOSSES AND MANAGEMENT; 965] *Opposite*: underling 2 *n* **teacher**, guru, tutor, instructor, guide, leader, trainer [➡ EDUCATORS; 840] *Opposite*: pupil 3 *n* **expert**, virtuoso, maestro, genius, prodigy, wonder, wunderkind, wizard (*informal*), ace (*informal*) [➡ TALENTED OR INTELLIGENT PEOPLE; 528] 4 *adj* **chief**, principal, main, major, leading, dominant, controlling, directing [➡ MOST IMPORTANT AND MAIN; 193] *Opposite*: secondary 5 *v* **become skilled at**, become proficient at, grasp, learn, understand, get to grips with [➡ UNDERSTAND AND GRASP; 759] *Opposite*: fail 6 *v* **conquer**, gain control of, overcome, subdue, get the better of, control, surmount [➡ BEAT AND DEFEAT; 80]

masterful 1 *adj* **expert**, skilled, proficient, skillful, accomplished, adept, consummate [➡ TALENTED AND SKILLFUL; 527] *Opposite*: incompetent 2 *adj* **authoritative**, commanding, imposing, assured, forceful, firm [➡ STRENGTH; 201] *Opposite*: weak

masterly *adj* **skilled**, skillful, proficient, talented, gifted, accomplished, expert [➡ TALENTED AND SKILLFUL; 527] *Opposite*: incompetent

mastermind 1 *n* **brains**, architect, organizer, instigator, brain (*informal*) [➡ TALENTED OR INTELLIGENT PEOPLE; 528] 2 *v* **plan**, engineer, oversee, organize, devise, instigate, think up, conceive, come up with, hatch [➡ INSTITUTE AND INAUGURATE; 348] *Opposite*: carry out

masterpiece *n* **work of art**, masterwork, magnum opus, tour de force, stroke of genius, chef-d'oeuvre (*formal*) [➡ ARTWORKS; 898]

masterwork *n* **masterpiece**, magnum opus, tour de force, stroke of genius, work of art, chef-d'oeuvre (*formal*) [➡ ARTWORKS; 898]

mastery 1 *n* **expertise**, skill, knowledge, proficiency, command, ability [➡ SKILLS, TALENTS, AND ABILITIES; 526] 2 *n* **control**, power, supremacy, authority, command, sway [➡ STRENGTH; 201]

masthead *n* **title**, banner, strip, logo, header, spread (*informal*) [➡ NEWSPAPERS AND MAGAZINES; 605]

masticate *v* **chew**, munch, crunch, champ, grind, pulverize, eat, chomp (*informal*) [➡ EAT AND NOT EAT; 710]

mastication *n* **chewing**, munching, eating, grinding, champing, chomping (*informal*) [➡ EAT AND NOT EAT; 710]

mastiff *type of* **large dog** [➡ DOGS; 980]

mat 1 *n* **rug**, carpet, doormat, bathmat, floorcovering, runner [➡ FURNISHING AND HOUSEHOLD LINENS; 860] 2 *n* **table mat**, place mat, doily, coaster, pad [➡ FURNISHING AND HOUSEHOLD LINENS; 860] 3 *v* **tangle**, entwine, entangle, intertwine, knot, snarl, tangle up [➡ COMBINE AND MIX; 400] *Opposite*: disentangle 4 *adj* **dull**, lusterless, nonglossy, muted [➡ VISUAL TEXTURE; 1221] *Opposite*: glossy

match 1 *n* **competition**, bout, contest, game, tie, cup tie (*UK*) [➡ NON-AGGRESSIVE/SPORTING EVENTS; 40] 2 *n* **equal**, counterpart, equivalent, pair, partner [➡ EQUALITY; 154] 3 *v* **go with**, complement, harmonize, accord, coordinate, agree with, be compatible [➡ HARMONY; 155] *Opposite*: clash 4 *v* **be alike**, correspond, be identical, tally, fit, equal, pair, match up, marry up, partner [➡ EQUALITY; 154] *Opposite*: differ

matching 1 *adj* **corresponding**, identical, similar, alike, same, equivalent [➡ SAMENESS; 150] *Opposite*: different 2 *adj* **toning**, harmonizing, complementary, coordinative, coordinating, accordant (*formal*) [➡ HARMONY; 155] *Opposite*: clashing

matchless *adj* **peerless**, outstanding, unparalleled, incomparable, unrivaled, perfect, unique, inimitable, without equal, beyond compare [➡ EXTRAORDINARY: AMAZING; 204] *Opposite*: ordinary

matchmaker *n* **marriage broker**, go-between, fixer, intermediary, cupid [➡ SEXUAL AND ROMANTIC RELATIONSHIPS; 964]

mate 1 *n* **helper**, assistant, colleague, partner, coworker [➡ COLLEAGUES AND EQUALS; 967] 2 *n* (*UK*) **friend**, companion, comrade, pal (*informal*), buddy (*informal*), chum (*informal*) [➡ FRIENDS AND GUESTS; 963] *Opposite*: rival 3 *v* **breed**, reproduce, couple (*formal*), copulate (*formal*) [➡ REPRODUCTION AND HEREDITY; 725]

materfamilias (*formal*) *n* [➡ OLDER GENERATION RELATIVES; 959]

material 1 *n* **substance**, matter, raw material, stuff [➡ SUBSTANCES; 1267] 2 *n* **data**, information, ideas, facts, notes, background [➡ BASIC DETAILS; 688] 3 *n* **fabric**, textile, stuff, cloth, yard goods, piece goods [➡ TEXTILES AND THREADS; 1131] 4 *adj* **physical**, substantial, solid, factual, quantifiable, sensible, measurable, visible [➡ TRUE AND REAL; 171] *Opposite*: insubstantial 5 *adj* **significant**, relevant, pertinent, important, central, associated, substantive [➡ IMPORTANT; 194] *Opposite*: immaterial

materialism *n* **acquisitiveness**, avariciousness, avarice, covetousness, avidity, greediness, greed, cupidity (*formal*) [➡ GRASPING AND FINANCIALLY MEAN; 519] *Opposite*: detachment

materialistic *adj* **money-oriented**, grasping, acquisitive, avaricious, covetous, greedy, worldly [➡ GRASPING AND FINANCIALLY MEAN; 519] *Opposite*: spiritual

materialization *n* **appearance**, arrival, advent, embodiment, manifestation, incarnation, realization, emergence [➡ BEGINNINGS; 53] *Opposite*: disappearance

materialize 1 *v* **appear**, turn up, show up, arrive, reveal yourself, emerge, pop up (*informal*) [➡ APPEAR AND EMERGE; 3] *Opposite*: disappear 2 *v* **come into existence**, happen, occur, exist, take shape, come about, become manifest, shape up, emerge [➡ GRADUALLY COME INTO EXISTENCE; 1] *Opposite*: evaporate

materially *adv* **significantly**, considerably, substantially, importantly, essentially, greatly, immensely, pertinently, centrally, substantively [➡ IMPORTANT; 194] *Opposite*: slightly

materials *n* **resources**, supplies, ingredients, constituents, equipment, tackle, tools, provisions, things, stuff [➡ PHYSICAL OBJECTS; 1243]

maternal 1 *adj* **motherly**, parental, nurturing, protective, guiding [➡ RELATIONSHIP TO ANOTHER; 973] 2 *adj* **caring**, devoted, kind, tender, gentle, affectionate, warm, loving [➡ GENEROSITY AND KINDNESS; 495] *Opposite*: uncaring

maternally *adv* **caringly**, tenderly, devotedly, protectively, gently, warmly, lovingly, affectionately [➡ GENEROSITY AND KINDNESS; 495] *Opposite*: neglectfully

maternity *n* **motherhood**, childbearing, parenthood [➡ RELATIONSHIP TO ANOTHER; 973]

matey (*UK*) *adj* **friendly**, comradely, companionable, warm, amiable, genial, pally (*informal*), chummy (*informal*), buddy-buddy (*informal*) [➡ FRIENDLINESS AND SOCIABILITY; 494] *Opposite*: unfriendly

mathematical 1 *adj* **arithmetical**, numerical, arithmetic, geometric, algebraic, statistical [➡ MATH; 597] 2 *adj* **exact**, precise, scientific, accurate, measured, calculated [➡ EXACT; 203] *Opposite*: random

mathematics *n* **calculation**, reckoning, math, algebra, arithmetic, calculus, geometry, statistics, trigonometry [➡ MATH; 597]

matinée *n* **afternoon showing**, show, performance, presentation [➡ PERFORMANCES AND SHOWS; 42]

matiness (*UK*) *n* [➡ FRIENDLINESS AND SOCIABILITY; 494]

matriarch *n* **mother**, matron, grandmother, older woman, materfamilias (*formal*) [➡ OLDER GENERATION RELATIVES; 959] *Opposite*: patriarch

matriculate 1 *v* **admit**, register, enlist, enroll, inscribe, enter [➡ RECORD SOMETHING; 371] *Opposite*: strike off 2 *v* **enroll**, be admitted, sign up, join, be enrolled, register, enter [➡ PARTICIPATE; 292] *Opposite*: drop out

matriculation *n* **enrollment**, admission, registration, admittance, enlistment, inscription, entry, signing up [➡ CLASSES, COURSEWORK, AND EXAMINATIONS; 842] *Opposite*: expulsion

matrimonial *adj* **marital**, wedded, married, nuptial, conjugal, spousal, connubial (*literary*) [➡ MARRIED STATE; 961]

matrimony *n* **marriage**, wedlock, wedding, ceremony, service, ritual, vows, nuptials (*formal*), marriage vows [➡ MARRIED STATE; 961] *Opposite*: divorce

matrix 1 *n* **substance**, medium, carrier, solution, base, bed, ground [➡ SUBSTANCES; 1267] 2 *n* **situation**, environment, milieu, conditions, background [➡ PLACE; 1065] 3 *n* **template**, mold, format, pattern, mint, plate [➡ EXTREMITIES OF PHYSICAL OBJECTS; 1250]

matron *n* **older woman**, mature woman, middle-aged woman, matriarch, doyenne, woman of a certain age [➡ FEMALE PERSON; 933]

matronly *adj* **full-figured**, plump, portly, stout, well-rounded, mature [➡ BUILD; 477]

matronymic *n* [➡ NAME AND DESCRIBE; 665]

matte *see* **mat**

matted *adj* **tangled**, entwined, entangled, disheveled, intertwined, knotted, knotty [➡ IN BAD REPAIR; 1234]

matter 1 *n* **substance**, stuff, stock, staple, material [➡ SUBSTANCES; 1267] 2 *n* **trouble**, problem, difficulty, worry, concern, complication [➡ PROBLEMS; 256] 3 *n* **subject**, topic, theme, issue, affair, question [➡ SUBJECT AREAS; 768] 4 *v* **be of importance**, be important, count, signify, be significant, carry some weight, make a difference, have a bearing, be relevant [➡ MEAN SOMETHING; 61]

See Compare and Contrast at **subject**.

matter-of-fact 1 *adj* **down-to-earth**, straightforward, rational, unemotional, realistic, practical, sensible, nonsense, pragmatic, straight-thinking, hardheaded, with both feet on the ground, literal [➡ HONEST AND OPEN; 630] 2 *adj* **factual**, unvarnished, down-to-earth, literal, unembroidered, unembellished, plain, exact, accurate, faithful, undistorted, truthful [➡ TRUE AND REAL; 171] *Opposite*: fictional

matter-of-factness *n* [➡ HONEST AND OPEN; 630]

matting *n* **floorcovering**, tatami, mats, coconut matting, rush matting, sisal, coir, jute [➡ PLANT MATERIALS; 1133]

mattress *n* **futon**, air mattress, cushion, pad, bed, paillasse, air bed (*UK*) [➡ FURNISHING AND HOUSEHOLD LINENS; 860]

maturation *n* **maturing**, ripening, mellowing, development, growth, evolution, progress, fruition [➡ PROGRESS AND ADVANCEMENT; 213]

mature 1 *adj* **established**, developed, advanced, settled, matured, complete [➡ IN GOOD REPAIR; 1232] *Opposite*: undeveloped 2 *adj* **experienced**, responsible, prudent, wise, sensible, stable, settled [➡ POSITIVE INTELLECTUAL CHARACTERISTICS; 524] *Opposite*: naive 3 *adj* **grown-up**, adult, full-grown, middle-aged, older, in your prime [➡ ADULTHOOD; 918] *Opposite*: immature 4 *adj* **ripe**, mellow, ready, strong, sweet, aged, flavorsome, flavorful [➡ TASTE; 703] *Opposite*: young 5 *v* **grow up**, develop, ripen, mellow, age, season [➡ CHANGE; 372]

matured *adj* **mature**, ripe, ripened, mellowed, aged, seasoned, developed [➡ OLD, OLD-FASHIONED; 167] *Opposite*: young

maturely *adv* **wisely**, sensibly, responsibly, prudently [➡ POSITIVE INTELLECTUAL CHARACTERISTICS; 524] *Opposite*: immaturely

maturity 1 *n* **adulthood**, prime of life, middle age, old age [➡ ADULTHOOD; 918] *Opposite*: youth 2 *n* **ripeness**, mellowness, development, age [➡ OLD, OLD-FASHIONED; 167] *Opposite*: youth 3 *n* **wisdom**, experience, responsibility, reliability, sensibleness [➡ POSITIVE INTELLECTUAL CHARACTERISTICS; 524] *Opposite*: inexperience

matzo *type of* **bread** [➡ BREAD, FLOUR, AND BREAD PRODUCTS; 1179]

maudlin *adj* **oversentimental**, mawkish, slushy, mushy, syrupy, overemotional, self-pitying, tearful, saccharine, soppy (*informal*), weepy (*informal*) [➡ IN POOR TASTE AND OVERSENTIMENTAL; 229] *Opposite*: unemotional

maul 1 *v* **claw**, attack, ill-treat, paw, mangle, batter, injure, assault, beat, savage, knock around (*informal*), rough up (*informal*) [➡ PHYSICAL ATTACK AND PUNISHMENT; 415] **2** *v* **criticize**, attack, savage, slam (*informal*), pan (*informal*), put down (*informal*), badmouth (*slang*), slate (*UK*) [➡ ACCUSE, BLAME, AND CRITICIZE; 641]

mauling *n* **criticism**, disparagement, censure, barrage, blast, panning (*slang*) [➡ CRITICISMS AND ANGRY OUTBURSTS; 50]

maunder *v* [➡ MOVE SLOWLY; 314]

mausoleum *n* **tomb**, vault, crypt, resting place, grave, burial chamber, burial place, catacomb, sepulcher, last resting place [➡ MONUMENTS; 1092]

mauve *type of* **purple** [➡ COLORS; 1224]

maven *n* **expert**, doyen, doyenne, enthusiast, pundit, connoisseur, aficionado, aficionada, devotee, ace (*informal*) [➡ TALENTED OR INTELLIGENT PEOPLE; 528]

maverick *n* **nonconformist**, eccentric, individualist, rebel, odd one out, dissident, one of a kind [➡ SOLITARY PEOPLE AND MISFITS; 942] *Opposite*: conformist

maw *n* [➡ THE MOUTH; 702]

mawkish *adj* **oversentimental**, slushy, mushy, syrupy, overemotional, weepy (*informal*), soppy (*informal*) [➡ IN POOR TASTE AND OVERSENTIMENTAL; 229] *Opposite*: unemotional

mawkishness *n* **sentimentality**, oversentimentality, tearfulness, mushiness, slushiness, weepiness (*informal*), soppiness (*informal*) [➡ IN POOR TASTE AND OVER-SENTIMENTAL; 229]

max (*slang*) **1** *v* **win**, succeed, come first, come out on top, triumph, pass with flying colors, ace (*slang*) [➡ SUCCEED AND WIN; 79] **2** *adv* **at the most**, maximum, as a maximum, at most, tops (*informal*) [➡ MAJORITY AND MAXIMUM; 141]

maxi *adj* **large**, mega, big, jumbo, king-size, giant [➡ LARGE; 1193] *Opposite*: mini

maxilla **1** *n* [➡ PARTS OF THE BODY: HEAD; 692] **2** *type of* **bone** [➡ THE BONES AND JOINTS; 719]

maxim **1** *n* **saying**, adage, proverb, saw, aphorism, truism, axiom, motto, dictum (*formal*) [➡ FIGURES OF SPEECH; 673] **2** *n* **rule**, tenet, guideline, truth, principle, precept (*formal*) [➡ IDEAS AND THOUGHTS; 770]

maximal *adj* **best**, greatest, most, utmost, highest, top, leading, biggest, first-rate, first-class, maximum [➡ GOOD, WELL, BETTER; 183] *Opposite*: minimal

maximization *n* **expansion**, growth, enlargement, extension, intensification, boosting [➡ CHANGE OF SIZE: BIGGER; 392]

maximize **1** *v* **make the most of**, make best use of, exploit, take full advantage of, capitalize on, get the most out of, take advantage of, get the best out of, exhaust the possibilities, use to the full [➡ MAKE GOOD USE OF SOMETHING; 473] *Opposite*: minimize **2** *v* **increase**, expand, amplify, make bigger, boost, extend, enlarge, raise, augment (*formal*) [➡ CHANGE OF SIZE: BIGGER; 392] *Opposite*: minimize

maximum **1** *n* **limit**, ceiling, greatest extent, top figure, upper limit [➡ MAJORITY AND MAXIMUM; 141] *Opposite*: minimum **2** *n* **most**, greatest, highest, utmost [➡ MANY, MUCH, LARGE AMOUNT; 117] *Opposite*: minimum

maximum-security prison *n* [➡ BUILDINGS FOR CONFINING PEOPLE; 1094]

maxi skirt *type of* **skirt** [➡ GARMENTS AND OUTFITS; 865]

maybe *adv* **perhaps**, possibly, it could be, perchance (*archaic or literary*), mayhap (*archaic*) [➡ POSSIBLE AND PROBABLE; 177] *Opposite*: definitely

mayday *n* **SOS**, distress signal, emergency call, distress call, alert, call for help, 911 call, 999 call (*UK*) [➡ SIGNPOSTS, SIGNALS, AND BILLBOARDS; 595]

mayfly *type of* **flying insect** [➡ FLYING INSECTS; 1013]

mayhem (*informal*) *n* **chaos**, disorder, confusion, turmoil, havoc, pandemonium, bedlam, anarchy [➡ DISORDER AND CHAOS; 245] *Opposite*: order

mayonnaise *type of* **seasonings, sauces, and dips** [➡ SEASONINGS AND SAUCES; 1174]

maypole *n* **column**, post, pole, support [➡ STICKS, POLES, AND WEDGES; 1254]

maze **1** *n* **labyrinth**, warren, web, network [➡ FASTENERS, LINKS, AND NETWORKS; 1247] **2** *n* **confusion**, muddle, jumble, mess, intricacy, tangle [➡ DISORDER AND CHAOS; 245] *Opposite*: order

MBO *n* [➡ BUSINESS ACTIVITIES AND PHENOMENA; 794]

MC *n* **host**, toastmaster, moderator, emcee (*informal*), presenter (*UK informal*) [➡ WORKERS IN ENTERTAINMENT AND MEDIA; 873]

m-commerce *n* [➡ E-COMMERCE; 1129]

MD (*UK*) *n* [➡ BOSSES AND MANAGEMENT; 965]

meadow *n* **field**, pasture, paddock, grazing land, lea (*literary*) [➡ THE COUNTRYSIDE AND OUTDOOR SPACES; 1071]

meadow fescue *type of* **grass** [➡ GRASS; 1031]

meadowland *n* [➡ THE COUNTRYSIDE AND OUTDOOR SPACES; 1071]

meadowlark *type of* **songbird** [➡ SONGBIRDS; 1003]

meager *adj* **small**, slight, insufficient, inadequate, sparse, poor, scant, miserable, paltry, mean, skimpy, dinky (*informal*), measly (*informal*) [➡ TOO FEW, TOO LITTLE; 122] *Opposite*: plentiful

meagerness *n* **insufficiency**, inadequacy, scantness, stinginess, sparseness [➡ TOO FEW, TOO LITTLE; 122] *Opposite*: abundance

meal **1** *n* **food**, bite, snack, something to eat [➡ MEALS AND PARTS OF MEALS; 1169] **2** *type of* **flour** [➡ BREAD, FLOUR, AND BREAD PRODUCTS; 1179]

meal

◆ *types of meals*
clambake, cookout, banquet, barbecue, breakfast, brunch, buffet, dinner, English breakfast, lunch, picnic, ready-made meal, snack, supper, takeout, tea, tidbit, TV dinner

◆ *parts of a meal*
antipasto, aperitif, appetizer, canapé, delicacy, dessert, entrée, hors d'oeuvre, main course, meze, side dish, starter, tapas

mealtime *n* **breakfast time**, lunchtime, dinnertime, suppertime, teatime (*UK*) [➡ TIMES OF DAY; 87]

mealy-mouthed *adj* **diffident**, restrained, hypocritical, insincere, euphemistic, indirect, devious [➡ RETICENT AND UNFORTHCOMING; 631] *Opposite*: frank

mean 1 *v* **denote**, signify, indicate, stand for, represent, connote, imply, suggest, insinuate, presage, portend, purport (*formal*) [➡ MEAN SOMETHING; 61] 2 *v* **intend**, propose, aim, plan, want, wish, have in mind, be thinking about [➡ PREPARE FOR ACTION; 289] 3 *v* **entail**, involve, require, lead to, necessitate, cause, result in [➡ CAUSE TO HAPPEN; 31] 4 *adj* **nasty**, unkind, cruel, callous, uncaring, malicious, despicable, vile, shameful, unpleasant [➡ SELFISH AND UNKIND; 505] *Opposite*: kind 5 *adj* **poor**, shabby, squalid, humble, lowly, miserable, wretched [➡ IN BAD REPAIR; 1234] *Opposite*: comfortable 6 *adj* (*archaic*) **humble**, lowly, poor, simple, underprivileged [➡ POVERTY AND POOR; 892] 7 *adj* **paltry**, measly (*informal*), derisory, meager, miserable, scanty, insufficient, inadequate, skimpy, scant, small [➡ TOO FEW, TOO LITTLE; 122] *Opposite*: plentiful 8 *adj* (*UK*) **miserly**, stingy, niggardly, tightfisted, parsimonious, ungenerous, closefisted (*informal*), penny-pinching (*informal*) [➡ GRASPING AND FINANCIALLY MEAN; 519] *Opposite*: generous 9 *adj* **middle**, mid, average, normal, standard, median [➡ MATH; 597] *Opposite*: extreme 10 *n* **average**, norm, median, middle, midpoint [➡ MEASURABLE PORTIONS; 127] *Opposite*: extremity

---

Compare and Contrast: *mean, nasty, vile, low, base, ignoble*

CORE MEANING: referring to somebody or something below normal standards of decency

mean unkind or malicious; *nasty* showing spitefulness, malice, or ill-nature; *vile* despicable or shameful; *low* without principles or morals; *base* lacking proper social values or moral principles; *ignoble* dishonorable and contrary to the high standards of conduct expected.

---

mean business *v* **be serious**, mean what you say, mean it, be determined, be deadly serious, be in earnest, not be joking, be resolute [➡ MAKE DECISIONS AND CHOICES; 752]

meander 1 *v* **wind**, zigzag, twist and turn, twist, snake, bend, curve [➡ CHANGE DIRECTION OF MOTION; 344] 2 *v* **wander**, roam, amble, ramble, stroll, rove [➡ AIMLESS AND ERRANT MOTION; 343] *Opposite*: rush

meandering *adj* **twisting**, winding, twisty, tortuous, snaking, windy, snaky, zigzagging, curving, sinuous, circuitous, indirect, zigzag, roundabout, meandrous, bendy (*UK*) [➡ ROUNDED SHAPE; 1218] *Opposite*: straight

meaning 1 *n* **sense**, connotation, denotation, import, gist [➡ MEANING; 690] 2 *n* **significance**, importance, implication, worth, value, consequence (*formal*) [➡ IMPORTANCE AND SIGNIFICANCE; 192] *Opposite*: insignificance

meaningful 1 *adj* **expressive**, evocative, telling, eloquent, speaking, feeling [➡ INTERESTING AND MEANINGFUL; 190] 2 *adj* **significant**, important, consequential, momentous, deep, profound [➡ IMPORTANT; 194] *Opposite*: meaningless

meaningfulness *n* **meaning**, importance, significance, seriousness, relevance, consequence (*formal*) [➡ IMPORTANCE AND SIGNIFICANCE; 192] *Opposite*: meaninglessness

meaningless 1 *adj* **empty**, worthless, throwaway, hollow, pointless, futile, insincere, vain [➡ REDUNDANT AND USELESS; 240] *Opposite*: meaningful 2 *adj* **unimportant**, trivial, inconsequential, irrelevant, insignificant [➡ UNIMPORTANT AND UNNECESSARY; 238] *Opposite*: significant

meaninglessness *n* **emptiness**, insignificance, futility, purposelessness, worthlessness, vanity [➡ UNIMPORTANT AND UNNECESSARY; 238] *Opposite*: importance

mean it *v* **be in earnest**, not be joking, be deadly serious, mean business, mean what you say, be determined [➡ MAKE DECISIONS AND CHOICES; 752]

meanly 1 *adv* **cruelly**, unkindly, spitefully, callously, despicably, shamefully, contemptibly [➡ SELFISH AND UNKIND; 505] *Opposite*: kindly 2 *adv* **squalidly**, humbly, miserably, poorly [➡ POVERTY AND POOR; 892] *Opposite*: affluently 3 *adv* (*UK*) **stingily**, niggardly, parsimoniously, tightfistedly, ungenerously, grudgingly [➡ GRASPING AND FINANCIALLY MEAN; 519] *Opposite*: generously

mean-minded *adj* [➡ SELFISH AND UNKIND; 505]

mean-mindedness *n* [➡ SELFISH AND UNKIND; 505]

meanness 1 *n* **nastiness**, unkindness, cruelty, callousness, spitefulness, malice, heartlessness [➡ SELFISH AND UNKIND; 505] *Opposite*: kindness 2 *n* (*UK*) **miserliness**, stinginess, niggardliness, parsimoniousness, tightfistedness, close-fistedness (*informal*) [➡ GRASPING AND FINANCIALLY MEAN; 519] *Opposite*: generosity

means 1 *n* **way**, method, process, measures, channel, course, instrument, agency [➡ WAYS OF DOING THINGS; 294] 2 *n* **income**, earnings, resources, revenue, funds, capital, wealth, worth [➡ INCOME; 460]

mean-spirited *adj* **ungenerous**, uncharitable, harsh, mean, unkind, cruel, uncaring, spiteful, nasty, heartless, malicious [➡ SELFISH AND UNKIND; 505] *Opposite*: generous

mean-spiritedness *n* [➡ SELFISH AND UNKIND; 505]

meant 1 *adj* **intended**, designed, planned, aimed, purposed, targeted [➡ INTENTIONAL AND DELIBERATE; 279] *Opposite*: unexpected 2 *adj* **inevitable**, preordained, fated, predestined, destined, ordained (*formal*) [➡ FATE, DESTINY, AND ASTROLOGY; 782] *Opposite*: accidental

meantime *n* **interim**, intervening time, period in-between, the time being [➡ PAUSES AND PHASES; 56]

mean well *v* **have good intentions**, have your heart in the right place, try to do the right thing, try hard, have the best intentions, have the right intentions [➡ ATTEMPT AN ACTION; 261]

meanwhile *adv* **in the meantime**, for the meantime, in the interim, in the intervening time, for now, for the time being, temporarily, for the moment [➡ PRESENT; 85]

measly (*informal*) *adj* **stingy**, ungenerous, meager, mean, derisory, paltry, miserable, small, inadequate, insufficient [➡ TOO FEW, TOO LITTLE; 122] *Opposite*: ample

measurable 1 *adj* **quantifiable**, assessable, gaugeable, computable, calculable, determinate, reckonable [➡ ASSESS QUANTITY; 757] *Opposite*: indeterminate 2 *adj* **considerable**, appreciable, noticeable, detectable, perceptible, discernible, significant [➡ PERCEPTIBLE; 25] *Opposite*: imperceptible

measurably *adv* **noticeably**, evidently, significantly, demonstrably, obviously, visibly, detectably [➡ TO A GREAT EXTENT; 132] *Opposite*: insignificantly

measure 1 *n* **amount**, degree, quantity, portion, ration, quota, size, extent [➡ DEGREE AND EXTENT; 110] **2** *n* **measuring device**, gauge, meter, counter [➡ MEASURING DEVICES; 1123] **3** *v* **gauge**, calculate, compute, determine, assess, quantify, evaluate, appraise, rate [➡ ASSESS QUANTITY; 757]

measured 1 *adj* **slow**, unhurried, unrushed, restrained, stately, dignified, sedate, leisurely [➡ MOVING SLOWLY; 105] *Opposite*: hurried **2** *adj* **deliberate**, calculated, precise, exact, careful, considered, reasonable [➡ CAUTIOUS AND CAREFUL; 282] *Opposite*: unthinking

measureless *adj* **incalculable**, immeasurable, immense, vast, without limit, boundless, unbounded, great, limitless [➡ LARGE; 1193] *Opposite*: negligible

measurement *n* **dimension**, size, extent, quantity, amount, capacity, height, depth, width, breadth, length, weight, volume, area, magnitude [➡ SIZE AND DIMENSIONS; 1192]

measurement

◆ *types of metric units*
centigram, centiliter, centimeter, decagram, decaliter, decameter, decigram, deciliter, decimeter, gram, hectare, hectogram, hectoliter, hectometer, kilogram, kiloliter, kilometer, liter, meter, microgram, micrometer, milligram, milliliter, millimeter, tonne

◆ *types of nonmetric units*
acre, barrel, bushel, degree Fahrenheit, dram, fluid dram, fluid ounce, foot, gallon, gill, inch, mile, ounce, peck, pint, pound, quart, rod, ton, yard

◆ *types of SI units*
becquerel (radioactivity), coulomb (electric charge), degree Celsius (temperature), farad (capacitance), gray (radiation dose), henry (inductance), hertz (frequency), joule (energy), lumen (luminous flux), lux (illuminance), newton (force), ohm (electric resistance), pascal (pressure), siemens (electric conductance), sievert (radiation effects), tesla (magnetic flux density), volt (electric potential), watt (power), weber (magnetic flux)

measure up *v* **hit the mark**, satisfy, deliver, do, meet the required standards, be good enough, be alright, be satisfactory, fulfill requirements, come up to scratch (*informal*), be okay (*informal*) [➡ ACCEPTABLE AND PASSABLE; 219] *Opposite*: fall short

measuring device *n* **gauge**, measure, meter, counter [➡ MEASURING DEVICES; 1123]

measuring device

◆ *types of measuring devices*
altimeter, anemometer, aneroid barometer, balance, barograph, barometer, calipers, clock, compass, dipstick, dividers, dropper, Geiger counter, level, measuring tape, micrometer, odometer, pipette, protractor, quadrant, rule, scale, speedometer, statoscope, tachometer, tape, tape measure, theodolite, thermometer, weather vane, weighing machine, weighing scale, wind gauge, windsock

measuring tape *type of* **measuring device** [➡ MEASURING DEVICES; 1123]

meat 1 *n* **flesh**, food, carrion [➡ TYPES AND CUTS OF MEAT; 1177] **2** *n* **substance**, heart, gist, pith, kernel, essence, core, nub [➡ MOST IMPORTANT THING; 197]

meat

◆ *types of cuts*
breast, brisket, chop, chuck, cutlet, drumstick, flank, foreshank, hock, joint, leg, loin, neck, rasher, rib, round, scrag end, shoulder, side, sparerib, steak, top round, wing

◆ *types of meats*
beef, chicken, duck, gammon, goat, goose, grouse, hare, lamb, mutton, partridge, pheasant, pork, rabbit, turkey, veal, venison, wild boar

◆ *types of processed meats*
bacon, beefburger, bologna, bratwurst, bresaola, burger, chorizo, foie gras, frankfurter, ground beef, ground meat, ham, hamburger, jerky, liverwurst, meat loaf, meatball, merguez, mincemeat, mortadella, pancetta, parma ham, pastrami, pâté, patty, pepperoni, rissole, salami, sausage, saveloy, wiener, wienerwurst

◆ *types of steaks*
Chateaubriand, fillet, porterhouse steak, rump, sirloin, T-bone steak, tenderloin

meat-and-potatoes *adj* **basic**, fundamental, essential, primary, central, principal, key, critical [➡ FUNDAMENTAL; 195]

meatball *type of* **processed meat** [➡ TYPES AND CUTS OF MEAT; 1177]

meat loaf 1 *type of* **processed meat** [➡ TYPES AND CUTS OF MEAT; 1177] **2** *type of* **cooked dish** [➡ PREPARED DISHES; 1170]

meat locker *n* [➡ STORES AND STORAGE BUILDINGS; 1088]

meat pie *n* [➡ PREPARED DISHES; 1170]

meaty 1 *adj* **substantial**, profound, deep, weighty, solid, interesting, significant, full of meaning [➡ INTERESTING AND MEANINGFUL; 190] *Opposite*: lightweight **2** *adj* **brawny**, burly, muscular, fleshy, husky, hunky (*informal*), chunky (*informal*), buff (*slang*) [➡ MUSCLES AND MUSCULATURE; 479] *Opposite*: weedy

mecca *n* **center**, focus, focal point, magnet, hub, seat, heart [➡ CENTRAL PARTS OF PHYSICAL OBJECTS; 1251]

mechanic *n* [➡ FARMERS, GARDENERS, AND MANUAL WORKERS; 849]

mechanical 1 *adj* **motorized**, powered, power-driven, machine-driven, automated, automatic [➡ ENGINES AND HYDRAULICS; 1143] *Opposite*: manual **2** *adj* **automatic**, perfunctory, unconscious, unthinking, reflex, involuntary, routine, machine-like, mechanistic, robotic, systematic, knee-jerk (*informal*) [➡ AUTOMATIC AND INSTINCTIVE; 280]

mechanics *n* **workings**, technicalities, procedure, mechanism, process, method, ins and outs, system [➡ WAYS OF DOING THINGS; 294]

mechanism 1 *n* **device**, instrument, apparatus, machine, machinery, appliance, tool, contrivance, gadget [➡ DEVICES; 1115] **2** *n* **means**, method, system, procedure, process, way, structure [➡ WAYS OF DOING THINGS; 294]

mechanistic *adj* **automatic**, mechanical, machine-like, automatous, robotic, systematic, cold, unfeeling, perfunctory, unthinking, routine [➡ AUTOMATIC AND INSTINCTIVE; 280]

mechanization *n* **automation**, computerization, streamlining, modernization, systematization, industrialization [➡ MACHINERY; 1114]

mechanize *v* **automate**, power, systematize, industrialize, program, preset, computerize [➡ MANUFACTURE; 349]

mechanized *adj* **automated**, mechanical, industrialized, automatic, computerized, modern, programmed, preset, streamlined [➡ MACHINERY; 1114]

medal *n* **award**, decoration, honor, distinction, laurel, accolade [➡ REWARDS AND AWARDS; 439]

medalist *n* **winner**, champion, runner-up, gold medalist, silver medalist, bronze medalist, prizewinner, victor [➡ COMPETITORS; 41]

medallion 1 *n* **medal**, decoration, pendant, ornament, rondure (*archaic*) [➡ ORNAMENTS AND DECORATIONS; 1248] 2 *type of* **necklace** [➡ JEWELRY; 866]

meddle *v* **interfere**, butt in, stick your nose in, intrude, pry, stir, gossip, invade, snoop (*informal*), horn in (*informal*), put your oar in (*UK*) [➡ INTERRUPT AND BUTT IN; 619]

meddler *n* **troublemaker**, nuisance, gossip, interferer, busybody (*informal*), pest (*informal*), snoop (*informal*) [➡ INTERFERING PEOPLE AND TATTLETALES; 950]

meddlesome *adj* **interfering**, intrusive, meddling, officious, prying, snoopy, gossipy, nosy (*informal*) [➡ NOSY AND INTERFERING; 512] *Opposite:* detached

meddle with *v* [➡ MISUSE AND ABUSE; 471]

meddling 1 *n* **interference**, inquisitiveness, intrusion, prying, intrusiveness, officiousness, intervention, nosiness (*informal*) [➡ NOSY AND INTERFERING; 512] 2 *adj* **interfering**, meddlesome, inquisitive, intrusive, prying, officious, nosy (*informal*), snooping (*informal*) [➡ NOSY AND INTERFERING; 512] *Opposite:* uninterested

media *n* **mass media**, television, radio, newspapers, magazines, broadcasting [➡ ADVERTISING AND PUBLICITY; 604]

median *n* **mean**, midpoint, middle, norm, standard, par, golden mean, average, center [➡ MATH; 597]

median strip *n* [➡ BARRIERS; 1113]

mediate *v* **arbitrate**, intercede, facilitate, intermediate, referee, umpire, intervene, reconcile, negotiate, resolve [➡ TWO-WAY COMMUNICATION; 607] *Opposite:* provoke

mediation *n* **arbitration**, intercession, conciliation, intervention, negotiation, facilitation, intermediation [➡ NEGOTIATION AND DEBATE; 46] *Opposite:* provocation

mediator *n* **go-between**, intermediary, third party, arbitrator, negotiator, moderator, facilitator, referee, umpire, intercessor, conciliator [➡ ADVISERS, JUDGES, AND ARBITERS; 971]

medic (*informal*) *n* **doctor**, medical student, physician, surgeon, general practitioner, specialist, resident, medical practitioner, GP, family practitioner, intern, houseman (*UK*), registrar (*UK*), consultant (*UK*) [➡ PEOPLE WHO WORK IN MEDICINE; 848]

medical 1 *adj* **medicinal**, remedial, health, homeopathic, curative, therapeutic, healing, restorative [➡ REMEDIES, TREATMENTS, AND OPERATIONS; 731] 2 *n* **checkup**, health check, examination [➡ REMEDIES, TREATMENTS, AND OPERATIONS; 731]

medical

◆ *types of complementary therapies*
acupressure, acupuncture, Alexander technique, Ayurvedic medicine, Bach flower remedy, chiropractic, color therapy, cranial osteopathy, flotation, herbal medicine, homeopathy, hydrotherapy, hypnotherapy, iridology, kinesiology, massage, music therapy, naturopathy, neurolinguistic programming, osteopathy, Pilates, reflexology, reiki, shiatsu, tai chi, yoga

◆ *types of medical procedures*
amniocentesis, amputation, anesthesia, angioplasty, appendectomy, biopsy, booster, bypass, CAT scan, Cesarean section, checkup, chemotherapy, diagnosis, dialysis, endoscopy, facelift, graft, hysterectomy, immunization, keyhole surgery, laparoscopy, manipulation, mastectomy, operation, physical therapy, plastic surgery, radiotherapy, resuscitation, sedation, tracheotomy, transfusion, ultrasound scan, vaccination, vasectomy, X-ray

medical practitioner *n* [➡ PEOPLE WHO WORK IN MEDICINE; 848]

medical school *n* [➡ EDUCATIONAL INSTITUTIONS; 813]

medical student *n* [➡ STUDENTS AND PUPILS; 841]

medical training *n* [➡ CLASSES, COURSEWORK, AND EXAMINATIONS; 842]

medicament *n* **medicine**, remedy, treatment, pharmaceutical, curative, drug, ointment, unguent, lotion, salve, balm [➡ REMEDIES, TREATMENTS, AND OPERATIONS; 731]

medicated *adj* **medicinal**, antiseptic, antibacterial, antiviral, analgesic, therapeutic, curative, tonic [➡ REMEDIES, TREATMENTS, AND OPERATIONS; 731]

medication *n* **drug**, pharmaceutical, pill, tablet, capsule, suppository, medicine [➡ REMEDIES, TREATMENTS, AND OPERATIONS; 731]

medicinal *adj* **medicated**, remedial, healing, therapeutic, curative, homeopathic, pharmaceutical, restorative, tonic [➡ REMEDIES, TREATMENTS, AND OPERATIONS; 731]

medicine *n* **drug**, remedy, medication, treatment, prescription, dose [➡ REMEDIES, TREATMENTS, AND OPERATIONS; 731]

medieval *adj* **old-fashioned**, out-of-date, primitive, feudal, unenlightened, barbaric, passé, benighted [➡ OLD, OLD-FASHIONED; 167] *Opposite:* modern

mediocre *adj* **middling**, average, unexceptional, ordinary, middle-of-the-road, run-of-the-mill, second-rate, pedestrian, commonplace [➡ ORDINARINESS; 244] *Opposite:* excellent

mediocrity *n* **patchiness**, unevenness, poorness, weakness, averageness, ordinariness [➡ ORDINARINESS; 244] *Opposite:* excellence

meditate *v* **contemplate**, ponder, think, consider, delib-

r, mull over, reflect, ruminate, muse [➡THINK

on n **thought**, consideration, contemplation, ..., rumination, musing, introspection, con-..., deliberation (formal) [➡THINK AND REFLECT; 743]

tative adj **thoughtful**, reflective, contemplative, ...sive, introspective, preoccupied, serious, absorbed, ...t in thought, brooding, wistful [➡PENSIVENESS AND INTEREST; ...8] Opposite: active

medium 1 adj **average**, intermediate, middle, middling, standard, mediocre, moderate [➡ORDINARINESS; 244] Opposite: extraordinary 2 n **means**, vehicle, channel, mode, method, way, avenue, form, agent, instrument, organ [➡WAYS OF DOING THINGS; 294]

medium-large adj [➡MEDIUM; 1196]

medium-security prison n [➡BUILDINGS FOR CONFINING PEOPLE; 1094]

medium-sized adj [➡MEDIUM; 1196]

medley n **mixture**, combination, assortment, mix, jumble, variety, miscellany, pastiche, patchwork [➡COL-LECTIONS AND MIXTURES OF THINGS; 1244]

meek 1 adj **mild**, quiet, humble, gentle, docile, modest, lowly [➡RETICENT AND UNFORTHCOMING; 631] Opposite: overbearing 2 adj **timid**, compliant, weak, cowed, fearful, tame, sub-missive [➡THE WILL AND WILLINGNESS; 563] Opposite: assertive

meekness 1 n **humbleness**, quietness, docility, humil-ity, gentleness, modesty, mildness [➡RETICENT AND UNFORTH-COMING; 631] 2 n **timidity**, submissiveness, fearfulness, compliance, weakness, tameness [➡THE WILL AND WILLINGNESS; 563] Opposite: assertiveness

meet 1 adj (archaic) [➡APPROPRIATE, SUITABLE, AND ADVISABLE; 184] 2 v **come across**, encounter, bump into, run into, chance on, see, happen, chance, light [➡EXPERIENCE AND ENCOUNTER; 582] Opposite: avoid 3 v **gather**, get together, come together, convene, assemble, congregate, rally, meet up, reunite [➡GET CLOSER TOGETHER; 310] Opposite: disperse 4 v **be introduced to**, make somebody's acquaintance, get to know, greet, become acquainted with, know [➡ESTABLISHING RELATIONSHIPS WITH OTHERS; 974] 5 v **touch**, contact, connect, join, converge, come together, unite, link, cross, intersect [➡CREATING CONNECTIONS; 144] Opposite: separate 6 v **experience**, encounter, come across, endure, go through, suffer, undergo, sustain [➡EXPERIENCE AND ENCOUNTER; 582]

meeting 1 n **business meeting**, conference, assembly, summit, seminar, workshop, board meeting, con-sultation, gathering, convention, get-together (informal) [➡MEETINGS AND ASSEMBLIES; 43] 2 n **encounter**, introduction, reunion, appointment, engagement, date, assignation [➡MEETINGS AND ASSEMBLIES; 43]

meetinghouse n **assembly hall**, church, building, con-...nticle (formal) [➡RELIGIOUS BUILDINGS; 1085]

...eeting room type of **room in public buildings** [➡TYPES OF ...S; 1097]

...a adj [➡LARGE; 1193]

...lith n **prehistoric monument**, standing stone,

menhir, dolmen, sarsen, stele, plinth, monolith [➡ANCIENT MANMADE STRUCTURES; 1089]

megalomania n **power lust**, overbearingness, tyranny, totalitarianism, autocracy, despotism [➡BOSSY AND OVERBEARING; 516]

megalomaniac 1 n **tyrant**, dictator, autocrat, despot [➡SELF-IMPORTANT AND SELF-SEEKING PEOPLE; 949] 2 adj **power-hungry**, power-crazy, self-important, tyrannical, dictatorial, des-potic, totalitarian, autocratic [➡BOSSY AND OVERBEARING; 516]

megalosaur type of **dinosaur** [➡DINOSAURS; 996]

megaphone n **loudspeaker**, bullhorn, amplifier, public-address system, PA, microphone, mike (informal), loud-hailer (UK) [➡AUDIO EQUIPMENT; 1139]

megastar n [➡IMPORTANT OR FAMOUS PEOPLE; 893]

meiosis type of **figure of speech** [➡FIGURES OF SPEECH; 673]

Meissen type of **pottery** [➡POTTERY; 1135]

melamine type of **plastic** [➡PLASTICS; 1134]

melancholic adj **dejected**, sad, unhappy, miserable, forlorn, gloomy, mournful, despondent, sorrowful, lam-enting, morose, nostalgic, dark, moody, down, blue, plaintive, elegiac (formal) [➡SADNESS, DISTRESS, AND DESPAIR; 539] Opposite: cheerful

melancholy 1 adj **sad**, downhearted, miserable, down, low, glum, gloomy, unhappy, despondent, dejected, dismal, blue, down in the dumps (informal) [➡SADNESS, DISTRESS, AND DESPAIR; 539] Opposite: cheerful 2 n **sadness**, unhap-piness, dejection, sorrow, the blues, downheartedness, depression, gloominess, despondency [➡SADNESS, DISTRESS, AND DESPAIR; 539] Opposite: cheerfulness

melange (literary or formal) n **mixture**, mix, jumble, potpourri, mishmash, medley, blend, hodgepodge, muddle, assortment, mixed bag, crazy quilt [➡COLLECTIONS AND MIXTURES OF THINGS; 1244]

mélange (literary or formal) see **melange**

melanoma n [➡CONDITIONS AFFECTING THE SKIN; 721]

meld 1 v **mix**, merge, blend, fuse, combine, amalgamate, mingle, commingle (literary) [➡COMBINE AND MIX; 400] Opposite: separate 2 n **combination**, mix, mixture, blend, amal-gamation, fusion, mingling [➡COLLECTIONS AND MIXTURES OF THINGS; 1244]

melding n [➡COLLECTIONS AND MIXTURES OF THINGS; 1244]

melee 1 n **fight**, commotion, brawl, fracas, uproar, riot, tussle, skirmish, scuffle, confusion, clash, struggle, rumpus, ruckus, hullabaloo, fray, donnybrook, free-for-all (informal), scrap (informal), to-do (informal) [➡AGGRESSIVE EVENTS; 39] 2 n **muddle**, jumble, mix, confusion, mixture, mishmash, medley, hodgepodge, blend, miscellany, pot-pourri, hash [➡COLLECTIONS AND MIXTURES OF THINGS; 1244]

mêlée see **melee**

mellifluous adj **pleasant**, soothing, sweet, melodious, honeyed, mellow, dulcet, musical [➡SOFT, LOW, OR PLEASANT SOUNDS; 1265] Opposite: jarring

mellifluousness n [➡SOFT, LOW, OR PLEASANT SOUNDS; 1265]

mellow 1 *adj* **smooth**, rich, full, warm, soft, deep, mellifluous [➡ SOFT, LOW, OR PLEASANT SOUNDS; 1265] *Opposite*: harsh **2** *adj* **mature**, full-flavored, ripe, aged, strong, full-bodied [➡ TASTE; 703] *Opposite*: young **3** *adj* **easygoing**, tolerant, approachable, genial, equable, affable, relaxed, placid, calm, sedate, good-humored, laid-back (*informal*) [➡ CONFIDENCE AND COMPOSURE; 499] *Opposite*: uptight (*informal*) **4** *v* **calm down**, ease up, settle down, relax, mature, soften, expand [➡ CHANGE OF MOOD AND COMPOSURE; 580] **5** *v* **mature**, soften, develop, ripen, improve, fill out, age, grow [➡ IMPROVE SOMETHING; 374] *Opposite*: deteriorate

mellowness 1 *n* **smoothness**, richness, warmth, fullness, mellifluousness, pleasantness, softness [➡ SOFT, LOW, OR PLEASANT SOUNDS; 1265] *Opposite*: harshness **2** *n* **ripeness**, sweetness, fullness, matureness, maturity, softness [➡ TASTE; 703] *Opposite*: rawness **3** *n* **geniality**, amiability, warmth, affability, expansiveness, good humor, kindheartedness, equanimity (*formal*) [➡ GENEROSITY AND KINDNESS; 495]

melodic *adj* **tuneful**, harmonious, musical, melodious, easy on the ear, mellow, euphonious, pleasant, lyrical, dulcet [➡ SOFT, LOW, OR PLEASANT SOUNDS; 1265] *Opposite*: discordant

melodious *adj* **tuneful**, harmonious, musical, melodic, easy on the ear, mellow, euphonious, pleasant, lyrical, dulcet [➡ SOFT, LOW, OR PLEASANT SOUNDS; 1265] *Opposite*: discordant

melodiousness *n* **tunefulness**, musicalness, pleasantness, euphoniousness, euphony, melody, harmoniousness, lyricism [➡ SOFT, LOW, OR PLEASANT SOUNDS; 1265]

melodrama 1 *n* **play**, drama, tragedy, comedy, farce, stage show, act [➡ FICTION AND DRAMA; 913] **2** *n* **fuss**, drama, scene, exaggeration, commotion, stir, ruckus, quarrel, tempest in a teapot, to-do (*informal*), storm in a teacup (*UK*) [➡ CHAOS AND UPROAR; 51]

melodramatic *adj* **histrionic**, overdramatic, overemotional, exaggerated, sensational, theatrical, acting up, over-the-top (*informal*) [➡ AFFECTATION, SELF-SATISFACTION, AND SNOBBISHNESS; 507] *Opposite*: low-key

melody *n* **tune**, song, air, phrase, strain, descant [➡ MUSIC, SONGS, AND SINGING; 907]

melon *type of* **fruit** [➡ FRUIT AND VEGETABLES; 1176]

melt 1 *v* **thaw**, thaw out, dissolve, soften, liquefy, melt down, flux [➡ SOFTEN, LIQUEFY, AND DAMPEN; 388] *Opposite*: freeze **2** *v* **disappear**, dissolve, fade, vanish, evaporate, vaporize, dissipate [➡ DISAPPEAR; 4] *Opposite*: materialize

melt away *v* [➡ DISAPPEAR; 4]

meltdown (*informal*) *n* **collapse**, breakdown, failure, disaster, disintegration, ruin, destruction, decay, extinction [➡ FAILURE; 77] *Opposite*: success

melting *adj* **tender**, sweet, loving, sentimental, soft, gentle, soppy (*informal*) [➡ EMOTIONALLY PLEASANT; 187] *Opposite*: harsh

melting pot *n* **mixture**, mix, mishmash, blend, hodgepodge, fusion, jumble, medley [➡ COLLECTIONS AND MIXTURES OF THINGS; 1244]

member 1 *n* **associate**, affiliate, fellow, adherent, participant, follower, supporter, colleague, partner, representative, delegate [➡ BUSINESS PEOPLE; 793] **2** *n* **limb**, appendage, organ, extremity, leg, arm [➡ PARTS OF THE BODY: TORSO;

693] **3** *n* **part**, constituent, item, unit [➡ PHYSICAL OBJECTS;

member of parlian
808]

membership 1
connection, re)
belonging, inclusi.
exclusion **2** *n* **memb**
adherents, participants,
leagues, partners, representati
COMMON INTEREST; 988]

membrane *n* **skin**, film, sheath, casing, covering, coating, layer, rind, peel [➡ COVERS AND

memento *n* **souvenir**, reminder, vestige, keepsa token, relic [➡ ORNAMENTS AND DECORATIONS; 1248]

memo *n* **memorandum**, note, minute, letter, message, communication, document, dispatch, missive [➡ LETTERS AND WRITTEN MESSAGES; 584]

memoir 1 *n* **account**, biography, history, chronicle, description, record, diary, journal, dossier [➡ RECORDS; 585] **2** *n* **essay**, article, report, paper, thesis, dissertation, treatise, study [➡ ANALYTICAL NONFICTION WRITING; 592]

memoirist *n* [➡ WRITERS AND STYLES; 914]

memoirs *n* **autobiography**, journal, life story, life history, diary, account, chronicle, record, reminiscences, recollections, confessions [➡ BOOKS AND BOOKLETS; 590]

memorabilia *n* **collectables**, collector's items, souvenirs, mementos, ephemera, keepsakes, personal effects, possessions, tokens, relics [➡ COLLECTIONS AND MIXTURES OF THINGS; 1244]

memorability *n* **importance**, note, momentousness, uncommonness, impressiveness, fame, consequence (*formal*), moment (*formal*) [➡ EXTRAORDINARY: UNCOMMON; 205] *Opposite*: inconsequence

memorable *adj* **unforgettable**, notable, remarkable, outstanding, impressive, striking, extraordinary, haunting, stamped on your memory, noteworthy [➡ EXTRAORDINARY: AMAZING; 204] *Opposite*: forgettable

memorandum *n* **memo**, note, minute, letter, message, communication, document, dispatch, missive [➡ LETTERS AND WRITTEN MESSAGES; 584]

memorial *n* **monument**, cenotaph, statue, bust, plaq stone, memorial stone [➡ MONUMENTS; 1092]

memorial stone *n* [➡ MONUMENTS; 1092]

memorize *v* **learn by heart**, learn by rote, learr to memory, remember [➡ REMEMBER; 746] *Opposite*

memory 1 *n* **reminiscence**, recollection, r brance, retention [➡ MEMORY; 745] **2** *n* **commem** brance, celebration, memorial [➡ CEREMONIE **3** *type of* **hardware** [➡ COMPUTERS AND COMPUTING

menace 1 *n* **threat**, danger, hazard [➡ DANGER; 235] *Opposite*: reassurance in the flesh, nuisance, troublema' thorn in one's side, pain in the (*informal*) [➡ NUISANCES; 253] **3** *v* **endanger**, thre

hang over, loom over, imperil (*formal*) [➡ PUT AT RISK; 384]
4 *v* **threaten**, intimidate, terrorize, frighten, alarm, scare, bully, pick on [➡ FRIGHTEN AND SHOCK; 568] *Opposite*: reassure

menacing *adj* **threatening**, ominous, frightening, alarming, intimidating, looming, foreboding, dark, ugly, scary (*informal*) [➡ FRIGHTENING; 231] *Opposite*: reassuring

menagerie *n* **zoo**, zoological gardens, petting zoo, farm park, city farm (*UK*) [➡ URBAN OUTDOOR SPACES; 1072]

mend **1** *v* **repair**, fix, put right, put back together, restore, patch up, stick, glue [➡ REPAIR AND MEND; 376] *Opposite*: break **2** *v* **stitch**, sew, sew up, patch, patch up, darn, repair [➡ REPAIR AND MEND; 376] *Opposite*: rip **3** *v* **improve**, amend, rectify, reform, transform, work on, make better [➡ CORRECT AND PUT RIGHT; 377] **4** *v* **recover**, get better, get well, recuperate, heal [➡ GET BETTER; 375] *Opposite*: deteriorate **5** *n* **patch**, darn, repair [➡ REPAIR AND MEND; 376]

mendacious **1** *adj* **untruthful**, dishonest, deceitful, unreliable, lying, inaccurate [➡ DECEITFUL; 513] *Opposite*: truthful **2** *adj* **untrue**, misleading, false, spurious, untruthful, dishonest, deceitful, unreliable [➡ FALSE AND UNREAL; 173] *Opposite*: true

mendaciously *adv* **untruthfully**, dishonestly, deceitfully, falsely, unreliably, misleadingly, spuriously, inaccurately [➡ DECEITFUL; 513] *Opposite*: truthfully

mendaciousness *n* [➡ DECEPTION AND LIES; 660]

mendacity *n* **lies**, deception, deceit, falsehood, fabrication, dishonesty, deceitfulness, untruthfulness, unreliability, spuriousness, inaccuracy [➡ DECEITFUL; 513] *Opposite*: truthfulness

mendicant **1** *adj* **homeless**, vagrant, vagabond, begging, penniless, indigent (*formal*) [➡ POVERTY AND POOR; 892] **2** *n* (*formal*) **beggar**, vagrant, panhandler, tramp, down-and-out, homeless person, hobo, street person, vagabond [➡ POOR PEOPLE; 896]

mending *n* **sewing**, darning, stitching, fixing, patching, repairing, needlecraft, needlework, hemming [➡ REPAIR AND MEND; 376]

menfolk *n* **kinsmen**, men, boys, husbands, sons, brothers [➡ THE FAMILY; 956]

menial *adj* **unskilled**, boring, tedious, basic, lowly, humble, low [➡ BORING AND UNINTERESTING; 234] *Opposite*: skilled

mensch (*informal*) *n* [➡ PERSON; 931]

men's clothing *n* [➡ GARMENTS AND OUTFITS; 865]

men's room *type of* **room in public buildings** [➡ TYPES OF ROOMS; 1097]

menswear *n* **men's clothing**, sportswear, outerwear, haberdashery [➡ GARMENTS AND OUTFITS; 865]

mental *adj* **psychological**, cerebral, rational, intellectual, spiritual, emotional, conceptual, perceptual, abstract [➡ PSYCHOLOGY AND THE MIND; 769] *Opposite*: physical

mental image *n* [➡ IDEAS AND THOUGHTS; 770]

mentality *n* **attitude**, approach, outlook, mindset, state of mind, frame of mind, point of view, temperament, character, personality [➡ POINTS OF VIEW; 767]

mental picture *n* [➡ IDEAS AND THOUGHTS; 770]

mention **1** *v* **talk about**, state, say, cite, bring up, comment on, remark on, touch on, refer to, allude to, declare, reveal, point out [➡ SUGGEST, HINT, AND COMMENT; 612] *Opposite*: conceal **2** *n* **reference**, indication, discussion, remark, comment, allusion, declaration, statement, citation [➡ SUGGEST, HINT, AND COMMENT; 612]

mento *type of* **world music** [➡ MUSIC, SONGS, AND SINGING; 907]

mentor *n* **adviser**, counselor, guide, tutor, teacher, guru, supporter [➡ ADVISERS, JUDGES, AND ARBITERS; 971] *Opposite*: pupil

menu *n* **bill of fare**, carte du jour, tariff, blackboard, set menu [➡ LISTS AND SCHEDULES; 587]

meow **1** *n* **mew**, purr, cry, caterwaul, whimper, yowl, whine, howl, screech, wail [➡ SOUNDS MADE BY ANIMALS; 1261] **2** *v* **cry**, purr, mew, whimper, caterwaul, yowl, whine, howl, screech, wail [➡ SOUND EMISSION BY ANIMALS OR BIRDS; 364]

mephitic (*formal*) *adj* [➡ DANGEROUS; 236]

mercantile *adj* **merchant**, commercial, trade, trading, business [➡ BUSINESS; 791]

mercenary **1** *n* **soldier of fortune**, soldier, legionnaire, freedom fighter, guerrilla, dog of war (*UK*) [➡ MILITARY PERSONNEL; 828] **2** *adj* **acquisitive**, grasping, greedy, avaricious, covetous, gold-digging, moneygrubbing, venal [➡ GRASPING AND FINANCIALLY MEAN; 519] *Opposite*: altruistic

merchandise **1** *n* **goods**, products, produce, commodities, stock, range [➡ BUSINESS PRODUCTS; 795] **2** *v* **sell**, retail, trade in, deal in, handle, buy, import, export, market, promote [➡ SELL; 441]

merchant **1** *n* **wholesaler**, dealer, trader, supplier, broker, importer, exporter [➡ BUSINESS PEOPLE; 793] **2** *n* **retailer**, seller, vendor, storekeeper, shopkeeper (*UK*), tradesperson (*UK*) [➡ SELLERS; 442]

merchant navy (*UK*) *n* [➡ THE ARMED FORCES; 827]

merciful **1** *adj* **compassionate**, kind, kindhearted, lenient, humane, generous, sympathetic, understanding, forgiving, gracious, benevolent, forbearing (*formal*) [➡ GENEROSITY AND KINDNESS; 495] *Opposite*: hardhearted **2** *adj* **thankful**, fortunate, welcome, lucky, happy, timely, opportune [➡ LUCK; 783] *Opposite*: unfortunate

mercifulness *n* [➡ GENEROSITY AND KINDNESS; 495]

merciless *adj* **cruel**, hardhearted, pitiless, harsh, heartless, unpitying, ruthless, unforgiving, severe, unsympathetic, uncompromising, hard, unfeeling, callous, cold-blooded [➡ SELFISH AND UNKIND; 505] *Opposite*: kind

mercilessness *n* **cruelty**, hardheartedness, pitilessness, harshness, heartlessness, ruthlessness, severity, callousness, cold-bloodedness, unkindness, nastiness [➡ SELFISH AND UNKIND; 505] *Opposite*: kindness

mercurial *adj* **changeable**, unpredictable, lively, active, impulsive, inconstant, volatile, witty, fast-talking, brilliant [➡ LACK OF COMMITMENT AND UNRELIABILITY; 509] *Opposite*: consistent

mercury *type of* **metal** [➡ METALS; 1276]

Mercury *type of* **planet** [➡ HEAVENLY BODIES; 1061]

mercy 1 *n* **compassion**, pity, clemency, kindness, leniency, humanity, generosity, sympathy, understanding, forgiveness, grace, benevolence, forbearance (*formal*) [➥ COMPASSION AND FORGIVENESS; 551] *Opposite*: cruelty **2** *n* **blessing**, relief, kindness, stroke of luck, piece of luck, godsend [➥ TREATS; 210] *Opposite*: blow

mere 1 *adj* **ordinary**, simple, sheer, plain, unadorned [➥ PLAIN; 232] **2** *adj* **scant**, paltry, mean, miserable, meager [➥ TOO FEW, TOO LITTLE; 122] **3** *n* (*archaic or literary*) **lake**, lagoon, tarn, lough (*UK*), broad (*UK*), loch (*UK*) [➥ RIVERS, LAKES, AND STREAMS; 1042]

merely *adv* **just**, only, simply, purely [➥ TO A CERTAIN EXTENT; 136]

merengue *n* [➥ DANCE; 903]

meretricious 1 *adj* (*formal*) **superficial**, flashy, vulgar, tawdry, showy, glitzy, kitschy [➥ IN POOR TASTE AND OVERSENTIMENTAL; 229] **2** *adj* **plausible**, specious, glib, persuasive, insincere, deceiving, deceptive, false [➥ FALSE AND UNREAL; 173] *Opposite*: genuine

merganser *type of* **freshwater bird** [➥ FRESHWATER BIRDS; 1000]

merge 1 *v* **combine**, unite, come together, join, amalgamate, become one, join together, team up, unify [➥ ESTABLISHING RELATIONSHIPS WITH OTHERS; 974] *Opposite*: separate **2** *v* **blend**, meld, blur, fuse, unify, mix, mingle, conflate [➥ COMBINE AND MIX; 400] *Opposite*: separate

merger 1 *n* **amalgamation**, union, combination, joining, fusion, unification [➥ BUSINESS ACTIVITIES AND PHENOMENA; 794] *Opposite*: separation **2** *n* **blend**, meld, blur, fusion, union, unification, mix, mixture, conflation, amalgamation, combination [➥ COLLECTIONS AND MIXTURES OF THINGS; 1244] *Opposite*: separation

merguez *type of* **processed meat** [➥ TYPES AND CUTS OF MEAT; 1177]

meridian (*literary*) *n* **zenith**, height, high point, peak, apogee, apex [➥ EXTREMITIES OF PHYSICAL OBJECTS; 1250] *Opposite*: nadir

meringue *type of* **dessert** [➥ CAKES, COOKIES, AND DESSERTS; 1181]

merit 1 *n* **value**, worth, quality, excellence, distinction, virtue, importance, weight [➥ IMPORTANCE AND SIGNIFICANCE; 192] *Opposite*: worthlessness **2** *n* **ability**, accomplishment, capability, aptitude, skill [➥ SKILLS, TALENTS, AND ABILITIES; 526] *Opposite*: worthlessness **3** *n* **advantage**, good point, pro, asset, virtue, quality, redeeming feature, plus (*informal*), plus point (*UK*) [➥ SOURCE OF HAPPINESS, PLEASURE, OR IMPROVEMENT; 209] *Opposite*: disadvantage **4** *v* **deserve**, warrant, earn, call for, be worthy of, be deserving of, be entitled to [➥ OWE AND DESERVE; 465]

meritocracy *n* [➥ STYLES AND SYSTEMS OF GOVERNMENT; 806]

meritorious *adj* **commendable**, praiseworthy, estimable, admirable, laudable, worthy [➥ ADMIRABLE AND COMMENDABLE; 185] *Opposite*: despicable

mermaid *type of* **mythological creature** [➥ MYTHICAL CREATURES; 1036]

merriment *n* **cheerfulness**, happiness, fun, high spirits, jollity, gaiety, laughter, glee, joy, joyfulness, cheer, amusement [➥ PLEASURE, EXCITEMENT, AND ELATION; 534] *Opposite*: misery

merry *adj* **cheerful**, happy, cheery, jolly, joyful, joyous, laughing, lively [➥ PLEASURE, EXCITEMENT, AND ELATION; 534] *Opposite*: miserable

merry-go-round *n* **whirl**, round, series, succession, string, sequence, flurry [➥ EVENTS AND OCCURRENCES; 35]

merrymaker *n* **reveler**, partygoer, party guest, life and soul of the party, social butterfly, raver (*informal*), carouser (*literary*) [➥ PLEASURE-SEEKERS AND HEDONISTS; 886] *Opposite*: killjoy

merrymaking *n* **celebration**, revels, partying, jollification, jollity, fun, fun and games, enjoyment, high jinks (*informal*), carousing (*literary*) [➥ PARTIES, DANCES, AND CELEBRATIONS; 37] *Opposite*: misery

mesa *n* **butte**, hill, mound, tor, peak, cliff, rock formation [➥ MOUNTAINS AND HILLS; 1044]

mesh 1 *n* **net**, web, network, netting, webbing, wire, weave, lattice, trellis [➥ FASTENERS, LINKS, AND NETWORKS; 1247] **2** *v* **interlock**, interconnect, engage, fit together, enmesh, tangle, entangle, interlace, knit [➥ FASTEN, LINK, AND JOIN; 408] *Opposite*: separate

mesmeric *adj* **mesmerizing**, fascinating, absorbing, attractive, compelling, compulsive, enthralling, entrancing, spellbinding, captivating, alluring, appealing, enticing, magnetic, gripping, charming, hypnotic (*informal*), riveting (*informal*) [➥ INTERESTING AND MEANINGFUL; 190] *Opposite*: boring

mesmerize *v* **hypnotize**, fascinate, enthrall, absorb, entrance, spellbind, captivate, excite, charm, thrill, rivet (*informal*) [➥ APPEAL TO AND AROUSE INTEREST; 575] *Opposite*: bore

mesmerized *adj* [➥ PENSIVENESS AND INTEREST; 538]

mesmerizing *adj* **mesmeric**, fascinating, absorbing, attractive, compelling, compulsive, enthralling, entrancing, spellbinding, captivating, alluring, appealing, enticing, magnetic, gripping, charming, hypnotic (*informal*), riveting (*informal*) [➥ INTERESTING AND MEANINGFUL; 190] *Opposite*: boring

meson *type of* **elementary particle** [➥ ELEMENTARY PARTICLES; 1279]

mesosphere *n* [➥ THE EARTH'S ATMOSPHERE; 1040]

Mesozoic *type of* **era** [➥ EPOCHS AND ERAS; 89]

mesquite *type of* **deciduous tree** [➥ DECIDUOUS TREES; 1028]

mess 1 *n* **untidiness**, muddle, chaos, confusion, clutter, jumble, disorder, disarray, tip, heap, tangle, state (*informal*) [➥ DISORDER AND CHAOS; 245] *Opposite*: order **2** *n* **tight spot**, disaster, predicament, plight, bind, tight corner, trouble, fix (*informal*), jam (*informal*), hole (*informal*), scrape (*informal*), pickle (*informal*), stew (*informal*) [➥ DIFFICULT SITUATIONS; 72] **3** *n* **canteen**, refectory, dining room, dining hall, restaurant, mess hall, cafeteria [➥ HOTELS, RESTAURANTS, AND CLUBS; 1082]

message 1 *n* **communication**, memo, memorandum, note, letter, missive, dispatch [➥ LETTERS AND WRITTEN MESSAGES; 584] **2** *n* **meaning**, significance, point, lesson, moral, idea, implication [➥ MEANING; 690]

mess around (*informal*) 1 *v* **waste time**, fool around, play, mooch (*slang*) [➥ LEISURE AND RECREATION; 874] *Opposite*: behave **2** *v* **relax**, laze around, lounge around, loll around,

rest up, chill out (*slang*) [➡LACK OF ACTIVITY OR MOTION; 342]
3 *v* **tamper**, fiddle, meddle, interfere, mess, tinker, play [➡CONTACT: TOUCH; 412] **4** *v* **hang around**, associate, go around, go out, spend time [➡ESTABLISHING RELATIONSHIPS WITH OTHERS; 974] **5** *v* **joke**, fool around, play the fool, act the fool, tease, kid, clown around, clown, pull somebody's leg (*informal*), josh (*informal*), have a laugh (*UK*), lark around (*UK*), have a lark (*UK*) [➡JOKES AND TEASING; 674] **6** *v* **mistreat**, treat badly, treat unfairly, fool with, toy with [➡MISUSE AND ABUSE; 471] **7** *v* **putter**, tinker, dabble, fiddle, play around, toy with [➡CONTACT: TOUCH; 412]

messed up (*informal*) *adj* [➡IN BAD REPAIR; 1234]

messenger *n* **courier**, envoy, go-between, emissary, herald, runner, dispatch rider [➡MESSENGERS AND COURIERS; 852]

messiah *n* **champion**, liberator, leader, defender, savior, guardian angel (*informal*) [➡PEOPLE WHO ARE APPROVED OF; 955]

messiness **1** *n* **untidiness**, disorderliness, scruffiness, dirtiness, scrappiness, disarray, muddle, chaos, confusion, clutter, disorganization, disorder, state (*informal*) [➡DISORDER AND CHAOS; 245] *Opposite*: neatness **2** *n* **unpleasantness**, acrimony, bitterness, awkwardness, complexity, nastiness, trickiness, difficulty, distress, painfulness [➡EMOTIONALLY UNPLEASANT AND UPSETTING; 227]

mess up (*informal*) **1** *v* **spoil**, ruin, wreck, botch, scupper, blunder, make a mistake, muck up (*informal*), bungle (*informal*), flub (*slang*) [➡MESS UP AND MAKE MISTAKES; 472] **2** *v* **make untidy**, muddle up, mix up, make a mess, clutter, dirty [➡CREATE DISORDER AND CAUSE CHAOS; 358] *Opposite*: tidy up **3** *v* **upset**, confuse, put out, put somebody off their stride, throw (*informal*) [➡CONFUSE AND BEWILDER; 571] *Opposite*: sort out

mess-up (*informal*) *n* **muddle**, mix-up, mess, confusion, blunder, mistake, botch (*informal*), bungle (*informal*), muddle-up (*UK*) [➡MISTAKES; 250]

messy **1** *adj* **untidy**, muddled, chaotic, confused, cluttered, in disarray, disorganized, disordered, scruffy, dirty, scrappy, in a state (*informal*) [➡DISORDER AND CHAOS; 245] *Opposite*: neat **2** *adj* **unpleasant**, acrimonious, bitter, awkward, complicated, complex, tricky, difficult, problematic, distressing, painful, nasty (*informal*) [➡EMOTIONALLY UNPLEASANT AND UPSETTING; 227] *Opposite*: amicable

metabolism *n* **breakdown**, absorption, digestion, uptake, use, metabolic rate [➡EAT AND NOT EAT; 710]

metabolize *v* **break down**, absorb, digest, take up, make use of, process [➡EAT AND NOT EAT; 710]

metacarpal *type of* **bone** [➡THE BONES AND JOINTS; 719]

metal **1** *n* [➡SUBSTANCES; 1267] **2** *type of* **rock music** [➡MUSIC, SONGS, AND SINGING; 907]

metal

◆ *types of metals*
aluminum, brass, chromium, copper, gold, iron, lead, magnesium, mercury, molybdenum, nickel, pewter, platinum, radium, silver, stainless steel, steel, tin, titanium, tungsten, uranium, zinc

metallic **1** *adj* **metal**, iron, steel, copper, brass, stainless steel, gold, silver, pewter, platinum, titanium [➡METALS; 1276] **2** *adj* **shiny**, reflective, glossy, glittering, polished [➡VISUAL TEXTURE; 1221] *Opposite*: dull **3** *adj* **tinny**, brassy, ringing, clanging, sharp, hard, harsh, unpleasant, jarring [➡LOUD, HIGH, OR UNPLEASANT SOUNDS; 1266] *Opposite*: soft

metallophone *type of* **percussion instrument** [➡MUSICAL INSTRUMENTS; 910]

metamorphose *v* **change**, transform, transmute, mutate, alter, convert, become, turn, morph, transfigure [➡CHANGE; 372]

metamorphosis *n* **transformation**, change, mutation, conversion, alteration, transmutation, transfiguration [➡CHANGE; 372]

metaphor *n* **symbol**, image, figure of speech, allegory, comparison, representation [➡FIGURES OF SPEECH; 673]

metaphoric *adj* [➡REPRESENTATIVE; 66]

metaphorical *adj* **figurative**, symbolic, allegorical, emblematic, representational [➡REPRESENTATIVE; 66] *Opposite*: literal

metaphysical *adj* **abstract**, theoretical, philosophical, hypothetical, conjectural, philosophic, supernatural, speculative, ontological, incorporeal (*formal*) [➡PHILOSOPHIES AND BELIEFS; 780]

metatarsal *type of* **bone** [➡THE BONES AND JOINTS; 719]

meteor *type of* **heavenly body** [➡HEAVENLY BODIES; 1061]

meteoric *adj* **dramatic**, sudden, swift, spectacular, impressive, rapid, brilliant, dazzling, speedy, quick, fast [➡HAPPENING QUICKLY; 104] *Opposite*: gradual

meteorite *type of* **heavenly body** [➡HEAVENLY BODIES; 1061]

meteorological *adj* **climatological**, climatic, atmospheric, weather, weather-related, barometric [➡WEATHER AND CLIMATE; 1049]

meteorology *n* **weather forecasting**, climatology, weather prediction, weathercasting [➡WEATHER AND CLIMATE; 1049]

mete out *v* **give out**, deal out, allocate, impose, exact, wreak, dispense, dole out (*informal*), dish out (*informal*), bestow (*formal*) [➡DISPENSE, RATION, AND DISTRIBUTE; 434]

meter **1** *n* **rhythm**, beat, tempo, pulse, pattern, stress, cadence, measure, rhyme [➡NOTES AND CHORDS; 909] **2** *type of* **metric unit** [➡SIZE AND DIMENSIONS; 1192] **3** *n* **measuring device**, gauge, counter [➡MEASURING DEVICES; 1123]

methane *type of* **gas** [➡GASES; 1275]

method **1** *n* **means**, way, process, system, procedure, approach, practice, technique, modus [➡WAYS OF DOING THINGS; 294] **2** *n* **orderliness**, organization, order, form, structure, pattern, design [➡WAYS OF DOING THINGS; 294]

methodical *adj* **systematic**, logical, disciplined, precise, orderly, regular, meticulous, careful, painstaking [➡CAUTIOUS AND CAREFUL; 282] *Opposite*: haphazard

methodological *adj* **procedural**, organizational, working, running, operational, practical [➡ORDER AND ORGANIZATION; 206]

methodology *n* **organizing system**, practice, procedure, organization, policy, method, approach, style, system [➡WAYS OF DOING THINGS; 294]

metical *type of* **currency** [➡ CURRENCIES; 798]

meticulous *adj* **careful**, scrupulous, thorough, particular, painstaking, duteous, punctilious, assiduous, conscientious [➡ HARD-WORKING AND COMMITTED; 500] *Opposite*: careless

See Compare and Contrast at **careful**.

meticulously *adv* **exactly**, accurately, precisely, squarely, methodically, punctiliously, fastidiously [➡ CAUTIOUS AND CAREFUL; 282] *Opposite*: carelessly

meticulousness *n* **care**, thoroughness, strictness, diligence, perfectionism, precision, exactness, fastidiousness, punctiliousness, scrupulousness [➡ HARD-WORKING AND COMMITTED; 500] *Opposite*: carelessness

métier *n* **vocation**, occupation, profession, calling, sphere, pursuit, lifework [➡ PROFESSIONS; 845]

metonymy *type of* **figure of speech** [➡ FIGURES OF SPEECH; 673]

metric unit *n* [➡ SIZE AND DIMENSIONS; 1192]

metronome *n* [➡ CLOCKS AND TIMERS; 1126]

metropolis *n* **city**, conurbation, capital, metropolitan area, megalopolis, municipality [➡ HUMAN SETTLEMENTS; 1070]

See Compare and Contrast at **city**.

metropolitan *adj* **city**, urban, municipal, civic [➡ HUMAN SETTLEMENTS; 1070]

mettle *n* **courage**, bravery, determination, spirit, grit, nerve, pluck, resolve, valor, vigor, guts (*slang*), cojones (*slang*) [➡ COURAGE; 498]

See Compare and Contrast at **courage**.

mettlesome *adj* **lively**, spirited, high-spirited, courageous, plucky, frisky, energetic, fiery, spunky (*informal*) [➡ ENERGY AND ENTHUSIASM; 496] *Opposite*: lethargic

meunière *type of* **food presentation** [➡ COOKING AND FOOD PREPARATION; 353]

mew 1 *v* **cry**, meow, sob, whimper, yowl, whine, howl, screech, wail [➡ SOUND EMISSION BY ANIMALS OR BIRDS; 364] **2** *n* **meow**, cry, sob, whimper, yowl, whine, howl, screech, wail [➡ SOUNDS MADE BY ANIMALS; 1261]

meze *part of* **meal** [➡ MEALS AND PARTS OF MEALS; 1169]

mezzanine *n* **mezzanine floor**, entresol, story, level [➡ STAIRS AND STORIES; 1102]

mezzanine floor *n* [➡ STAIRS AND STORIES; 1102]

mezzo-soprano *type of* **musical register** [➡ MUSICAL TERMS; 912]

miasma *n* **mist**, fog, haze, cloud, murk, steam, pall, film, mistiness, brume (*literary*) [➡ GASES; 1275]

mica *type of* **mineral** [➡ MINERALS; 1277]

microbe *n* **microorganism**, germ, bug (*informal*) [➡ MICROORGANISMS, FUNGI, AND ALGAE; 1023]

microbial *adj* [➡ MICROORGANISMS, FUNGI, AND ALGAE; 1023]

microbiological *adj* **biological**, bacteriological, fungal, viral, microparasitic [➡ BIOLOGICAL SCIENCES; 1037]

microbiology *type of* **bioscience** [➡ BIOLOGICAL SCIENCES; 1037]

microchip *type of* **hardware** [➡ COMPUTERS AND COMPUTING; 1127]

microcomputer *type of* **computer** [➡ COMPUTERS AND COMPUTING; 1127]

microcosm *n* **small-scale version**, version in miniature, miniature copy, miniature [➡ REPRESENTATIONS AND GENERAL EXAMPLES; 65] *Opposite*: macrocosm

microfiche *type of* **photographic equipment** [➡ PHOTOGRAPHY AND PHOTOGRAPHIC EQUIPMENT; 1122]

microfilm *type of* **photographic equipment** [➡ PHOTOGRAPHY AND PHOTOGRAPHIC EQUIPMENT; 1122]

microgram *type of* **metric unit** [➡ SIZE AND DIMENSIONS; 1192]

micromanage *v* **interfere**, intervene, nitpick, breathe down somebody's neck, control, meddle [➡ AVOID, PREVENT, LIMIT, AND CONTROL; 277]

micrometer 1 *type of* **measuring device** [➡ MEASURING DEVICES; 1123] **2** *type of* **metric unit** [➡ SIZE AND DIMENSIONS; 1192]

microorganism *n* **microbe**, germ, bug (*informal*) [➡ MICROORGANISMS, FUNGI, AND ALGAE; 1023]

microorganism

◆ *types of microorganisms*
amoeba, bacteriophage, bacterium, botulinum, candida, ciliate, coccus, E. coli, flagellate, listeria, mycoplasma, protozoan, rhizopod, salmonella, spirillum, spirochete, staphylococcus, stentor, streptococcus, virus

microphone *part of* **audio equipment** [➡ AUDIO EQUIPMENT; 1139]

microprocessor *type of* **hardware** [➡ COMPUTERS AND COMPUTING; 1127]

microscope *type of* **optical instrument** [➡ OPTICAL INSTRUMENTS; 1124]

microscopic *adj* **tiny**, minute, infinitesimal, minuscule, atomic, minuscular, mini (*informal*) [➡ SMALL; 1195] *Opposite*: gigantic

microscopically *adv* **meticulously**, minutely, closely, carefully, painstakingly, scrupulously, diligently, thoroughly [➡ HARD-WORKING AND COMMITTED; 500]

microwave 1 *v* **heat**, heat up, warm, warm up, cook, zap (*informal*), nuke (*informal*), warm through (*UK*) [➡ COOKING AND FOOD PREPARATION; 353] **2** *type of* **appliance** [➡ HOUSEHOLD APPLIANCES; 1117]

microwaved *adj* [➡ STATE OF PREPARED FOOD; 1171]

microwave oven *type of* **appliance** [➡ HOUSEHOLD APPLIANCES; 1117]

mid *adj* **middle**, median, medium, midway, central, halfway, equidistant, medial, midmost [➡ RELATIVE LOCATION; 161] *Opposite*: extreme

midair 1 *adj* **in the air**, up in the air, in the sky, overhead, above the ground, aloft, high up [➡ GENERAL LOCATIONS; 158] 2 *adj* **air**, airborne, in-flight, mid-flight, midcourse [➡ GENERAL LOCATIONS; 158]

midday *n* **noon**, noontime, twelve noon, lunchtime, the middle of the day [➡ TIMES OF DAY; 87]

middle 1 *adj* **central**, mid, internal, intermediate, inside, medium, interior, inner, equidistant, midmost [➡ RELATIVE LOCATION; 161] 2 *adj* **median**, average, intermediate, medium, middling, moderate [➡ ACCEPTABLE AND PASSABLE; 219] 3 *n* **midpoint**, halfway point, median, mean, norm [➡ CENTRAL PARTS OF PHYSICAL OBJECTS; 1251] 4 *n* **center**, heart, focus, core, hub, central point, focal point [➡ CENTRAL PARTS OF PHYSICAL OBJECTS; 1251]

middlebrow (*informal*) *adj* **unintellectual**, conventional, unchallenging, middle-of-the-road, mediocre, unexceptional, bourgeois [➡ ORDINARINESS; 244]

middle-class *adj* [➡ CLASS STATUS; 889]

middle ear *part of* **ear** [➡ THE EAR; 706]

middle finger *part of* **arm or hand** [➡ PARTS OF THE BODY: ARM AND HAND; 695]

middleman 1 *n* **trader**, distributor, wholesaler, retailer, broker, shopkeeper [➡ BUSINESS PEOPLE; 793] 2 *n* **intermediary**, agent, go-between, mediator, negotiator, envoy [➡ REPRESENTATIVES AND PATRONS; 968]

middle name *n* [➡ NAME AND DESCRIBE; 665]

middle-of-the-road *adj* **normal**, mainstream, majority, standard, typical, run-of-the-mill, ordinary [➡ ORDINARINESS; 244]

middle school *type of* **school** [➡ EDUCATIONAL INSTITUTIONS; 813]

middling 1 *adj* **usual**, typical, ordinary, average, run-of-the-mill, moderate, medium [➡ ORDINARINESS; 244] 2 *adj* **adequate**, all right, tolerable, fair, passable, average, mediocre, modest, satisfactory, unexceptional, so-so (*informal*), okay (*informal*) [➡ ACCEPTABLE AND PASSABLE; 219] Opposite: exceptional

midge *type of* **flying insect** [➡ FLYING INSECTS; 1013]

midnight *n* **twelve o'clock**, twelve midnight, middle of the night, night, nighttime, the wee small hours, the wee hours [➡ TIMES OF DAY; 87]

midnight blue *type of* **blue** [➡ COLORS; 1224]

midpoint *n* **center**, middle, nucleus, median, mean [➡ CENTRAL PARTS OF PHYSICAL OBJECTS; 1251]

midriff *n* **waist**, stomach, belly, middle, abdomen, diaphragm, love handles (*informal*), tummy (*informal*) [➡ PARTS OF THE BODY: TORSO; 693]

midst *n* **middle**, center, heart, focus, core, hub [➡ CENTRAL PARTS OF PHYSICAL OBJECTS; 1251]

midstream *adv* **halfway through**, midway, in the middle, in full flow [➡ HAPPENING AND IN PROGRESS; 32]

midsummer *n* **middle of the summer**, summertime, summer solstice, dog days, the height of summer [➡ TIMES OF YEAR; 88] Opposite: midwinter

midway 1 *adv* **central**, middle, mid, halfway [➡ GENERAL LOCATIONS; 158] 2 *adv* **halfway**, in the middle, midstream, in full flow, halfway through [➡ HAPPENING AND IN PROGRESS; 32]

midweek *n* **the middle of the week**, the midweek period, weekdays [➡ TIMES OF YEAR; 88]

midwife toad *type of* **amphibian** [➡ AMPHIBIANS; 1008]

midwinter *n* **middle of winter**, wintertime, winter solstice, the winter months, the depths of winter [➡ TIMES OF YEAR; 88] Opposite: midsummer

mien (*formal*) *n* **appearance**, bearing, expression, manner, look, aspect, demeanor, air, deportment, presence [➡ TEMPERAMENT AND BEHAVIOR; 492]

miff (*informal*) *v* **irritate**, upset, annoy, vex, peeve (*informal*), irk [➡ ANGER AND ANNOY; 569]

miffed (*informal*) *adj* **annoyed**, displeased, put out, chagrined, bothered, irked, hurt, perturbed, agitated, peeved (*informal*) [➡ IRRITATION AND ANGER; 541]

might *n* **strength**, power, force, capacity, valor, potency, powerfulness, influence [➡ STRENGTH; 201]

mightily *adv* **tremendously**, greatly, extremely, awfully, decidedly, exceedingly, terribly, hugely, strongly, powerfully [➡ TO A GREAT EXTENT; 132] Opposite: slightly

mighty 1 *adj* **powerful**, strong, forceful, potent, great, almighty, impressive, grand, influential [➡ STRENGTH; 201] Opposite: weak 2 *adj* **huge**, enormous, vast, expansive, massive, monumental, colossal, immense, gigantic, large, titanic, gargantuan [➡ LARGE; 1193] Opposite: insignificant

migrant 1 *n* **refugee**, immigrant, emigrant, asylum seeker [➡ PEOPLE LIVING AWAY FROM HOME; 887] 2 *n* **wanderer**, traveler, nomad, itinerant, wayfarer (*literary*) [➡ NOMADIC AND ROOTLESS LIFESTYLES; 884] Opposite: resident 3 *adj* **migratory**, traveling, wandering, drifting, itinerant, nomadic, seasonal, mobile [➡ NOMADIC AND ROOTLESS LIFESTYLES; 884] Opposite: resident

migrant worker *n* [➡ WORKERS; 836]

migrate *v* **travel**, journey, wander, drift, roam, move about, transfer, voyage, rove, trek, move around [➡ TRAVEL: WAYS OF TRAVELING; 320]

migration *n* **relocation**, immigration, passage, exodus, movement, journey, voyage, trek, resettlement [➡ TRAVEL: JOURNEYS AND TRIPS; 318]

migratory *adj* **traveling**, wandering, drifting, migrant, itinerant, nomadic, seasonal [➡ NOMADIC AND ROOTLESS LIFESTYLES; 884]

mild 1 *adj* **slight**, unimportant, insignificant, trifling, trivial, minor [➡ UNIMPORTANT AND UNNECESSARY; 238] Opposite: serious 2 *adj* **gentle**, kind, soft, easygoing, meek, placid, calm, serene, docile, lenient, peaceable [➡ GENEROSITY AND KINDNESS; 495] Opposite: harsh 3 *adj* **warm**, balmy, pleasant, clement, temperate, moderate, benign [➡ HOT WEATHER; 1050] 4 *adj* **weak**, bland, tasteless, insipid, flat, distasteful [➡ TASTE; 703] Opposite: strong

mildew *type of* **fungus** [➡ MICROORGANISMS, FUNGI, AND ALGAE; 1023]

mildewed *adj* [➡ DECAYING OR INFESTED; 1236]

mildewy *adj* [➡ DECAYING OR INFESTED; 1236]

mildly 1 *adv* **slightly**, a little, somewhat, a touch, unimportantly, insignificantly, a bit (*informal*) [➡ TO A CERTAIN EXTENT; 136] *Opposite*: considerably **2** *adv* **gently**, kindly, meekly, placidly, calmly, serenely, leniently [➡ GENEROSITY AND KINDNESS; 495] *Opposite*: harshly

mild-mannered *adj* **gentle**, kind, polite, good-natured, placid, calm, easygoing, affable, amiable, genial [➡ GOOD MANNERS AND SOCIAL SKILLS; 520] *Opposite*: fierce

mildness *n* **gentleness**, kindness, leniency, tenderness, warmth, mercy, compassion, consideration, clemency [➡ PEACEFULNESS AND GENTLENESS; 214] *Opposite*: harshness

mile *type of* **nonmetric unit** [➡ SIZE AND DIMENSIONS; 1192]

mileage 1 *n* **distance**, traveling distance, range, extent, way, stretch [➡ AREA AND RANGE; 111] **2** *n* (*informal*) **benefit**, profit, advantage, usefulness, assistance, gain, good [➡ SOURCE OF HAPPINESS, PLEASURE, OR IMPROVEMENT; 209]

milepost *n* **marker**, sign, mark, indicator, signpost, landmark, milestone [➡ SIGNPOSTS, SIGNALS, AND BILLBOARDS; 595]

miles (*informal*) *n* **a long way**, a great distance, miles and miles, miles away, a long way away, a long way off [➡ DISTANCE; 160]

miles away *adj* [➡ NEUTRALITY AND INDIFFERENCE; 553]

milestone 1 *n* **sign**, signpost, indicator, mark, marker, milepost [➡ SIGNPOSTS, SIGNALS, AND BILLBOARDS; 595] **2** *n* **landmark**, highlight, high point, achievement, record, goal, target, objective, aim, purpose, ambition [➡ DECISIVE MOMENTS; 44]

milieu *n* **setting**, environment, scene, background, surroundings, situation, location, locale, ambiance, atmosphere, climate [➡ PLACE; 1065]

militancy *n* **aggressiveness**, combativeness, belligerence, forcefulness, violence, pugnaciousness [➡ AGGRESSIVE AND BELLIGERENT; 518]

militant 1 *adj* **confrontational**, aggressive, radical, revolutionary, combative, rebellious, belligerent, bellicose, pugnacious [➡ AGGRESSIVE AND BELLIGERENT; 518] *Opposite*: peaceable **2** *n* **activist**, revolutionary, radical, fighter, supporter, rebel [➡ UNCOOPERATIVE OR REBELLIOUS PEOPLE; 566]

militarism *n* **belligerence**, aggression, aggressiveness, pugnaciousness, bellicosity, hostility, hawkishness [➡ AGGRESSIVE AND BELLIGERENT; 518]

militarist *adj* **bellicose**, militaristic, aggressive, warmongering, martial, military, belligerent, pugnacious, hawkish, warlike [➡ AGGRESSIVE AND BELLIGERENT; 518] *Opposite*: pacific

militaristic *adj* **militarist**, martial, bellicose, aggressive, warmongering, military, belligerent, pugnacious, warlike, hawkish [➡ AGGRESSIVE AND BELLIGERENT; 518] *Opposite*: pacific

militarized *adj* **mobilized**, armed, battle-ready, prepared, organized, trained, equipped, on a war footing [➡ MILITARY; 829]

military 1 *adj* **armed**, martial, soldierly, fighting [➡ MILITARY; 829] *Opposite*: civilian **2** *n* **services**, forces, armed forces, military establishment, army, navy, air force [➡ THE ARMED FORCES; 827]

military attaché *n* [➡ MILITARY PERSONNEL; 828]

military establishment *n* [➡ THE ARMED FORCES; 827]

military government *n* [➡ STYLES AND SYSTEMS OF GOVERNMENT; 806]

military rule *n* [➡ STYLES AND SYSTEMS OF GOVERNMENT; 806]

military unit *n* [➡ THE ARMED FORCES; 827]

militate *v* **influence**, inspire, affect, work, act on, count, have an effect on, weigh [➡ CHANGE; 372]

militia *n* **reservists**, local militia, paramilitaries, mercenaries, soldiers, guerrillas, soldiers of fortune, legionnaires, territorial army (*UK*) [➡ THE ARMED FORCES; 827]

milk 1 *v* (*informal*) **exploit**, drain, tap, take advantage of, cash in on, profit, benefit, extract, make the most of, bleed (*informal*) [➡ MAKE GOOD USE OF SOMETHING; 473] **2** *n* [➡ DAIRY PRODUCTS AND CHEESES; 1183]

milkshake *n* [➡ DRINKS; 1187]

milk tooth *type of* **tooth** [➡ THE MOUTH; 702]

milky *adj* **cloudy**, chalky, creamy, pale, translucent, whitish, opaque [➡ VISUAL TEXTURE; 1221] *Opposite*: clear

Milky Way *n* [➡ THE SOLAR SYSTEM AND ASTRONOMY; 1060]

mill 1 *type of* **factory** [➡ INDUSTRIAL BUILDINGS; 1087] **2** *type of* **utensil** [➡ TABLEWARE, FLATWARE, AND KITCHENWARE; 861]

millennial *adj* **utopian**, idealistic, visionary, romantic, optimistic, futuristic, millenarian, millenary, revolutionary [➡ EXTRAORDINARY: UNCOMMON; 205]

millennium *n* **epoch**, era, age, period, time [➡ EPOCHS AND ERAS; 89]

millet *type of* **cereal** [➡ CEREAL FOODS; 1178]

milligram *type of* **metric unit** [➡ SIZE AND DIMENSIONS; 1192]

milliliter *type of* **metric unit** [➡ SIZE AND DIMENSIONS; 1192]

millimeter *type of* **metric unit** [➡ SIZE AND DIMENSIONS; 1192]

millionaire *n* **tycoon**, mogul, magnate, billionaire, baron [➡ RICH PEOPLE; 895] *Opposite*: pauper

millions *n* **lots**, masses, many, loads (*informal*), heaps (*informal*), oodles (*informal*) [➡ MANY, MUCH, LARGE AMOUNT; 117]

millipede *type of* **land invertebrate** [➡ LAND INVERTEBRATES; 1021]

millpond *n* [➡ THE COUNTRYSIDE AND OUTDOOR SPACES; 1071]

millstone *n* **burden**, weight, dead weight, albatross, shackle, chain, load, responsibility [➡ PROBLEMS; 256]

mime 1 *v* **act out**, represent, simulate, express, symbolize [➡ REPRESENT SOMETHING OR SOMEBODY; 59] **2** *v* **mimic**, satirize, caricature, parody, ape, mock, ridicule, take off (*informal*) [➡ PRETEND AND MIMIC; 60] **3** *type of* **entertainer** [➡ WORKERS IN ENTERTAINMENT AND MEDIA; 873]

mimeograph *n* [➡ SYMBOLS, SIGNS, AND NUMBERS; 596]

mimetic *adj* **imitative**, derivative, copied, representational, simulated, faked [➡ SIMILARITY; 148] *Opposite*: original

mimic 1 *v* **imitate**, impersonate, represent, mirror, simulate, copy, take off (*informal*) [➡ PRETEND AND MIMIC; 60] **2** *v* caricature, ape, satirize, parody, mock, ridicule, make fun of [➡ JOKES AND TEASING; 674] **3** *n* **impersonator**, impressionist, imitator, caricaturist, parodist, satirist, simulator, copycat (*informal*) [➡ JOKERS AND TEASES; 675]

See Compare and Contrast at **imitate.**

mimicry *n* **imitation**, impersonation, impression, parody, caricature, simulation, act [➡ JOKES AND TEASING; 674]

mimosa *type of* **deciduous tree** [➡ DECIDUOUS TREES; 1028]

minaret *n* **turret**, tower, spire [➡ TOWERS; 1099]

mince *v* **shred**, cut up, chop up, crumble, hash, grind, chop [➡ TEAR, BREAK, AND CUT; 360]

mincemeat *type of* **preserve** [➡ SUGAR AND PRESERVES; 1184]

mince pie *type of* **cake** [➡ CAKES, COOKIES, AND DESSERTS; 1181]

mincing *adj* **dainty**, prim, fussy, precious, affected, foppish [➡ AGILITY OF THE BODY; 476]

mind **1** *n* **brain**, intellect, wits, brains, brainpower, psyche, mentality, intelligence [➡ DESCRIBING SOMEBODY'S INTELLECT; 523] **2** *n* **attention**, concentration, thoughts, awareness, observance, notice, cognizance (*formal*) [➡ ATTENTION AND ATTENTIVENESS; 763] **3** *n* **thinker**, intellect, intellectual, brain (*informal*), egghead (*informal*) [➡ TALENTED OR INTELLIGENT PEOPLE; 528] **4** *n* **point of view**, mentality, opinion, thinking, view, viewpoint, approach, attitude, belief, conviction, sentiment [➡ POINTS OF VIEW; 767] **5** *v* **pay attention**, take care, beware, heed, be careful, watch out, look out [➡ PAY ATTENTION; 765] **6** *v* **object**, care, demur, take offense, resent, disagree, disapprove, be bothered, be offended [➡ BE CONCERNED AND CARE; 581] *Opposite:* approve **7** *v* **look after**, tend, care for, attend to, take care of, watch, look out for, guard, keep an eye on [➡ TAKE CARE OF AND SPOIL; 300]

mind-bending *see* **mind-boggling**

mind-blowing (*informal*) *adj* **astonishing**, amazing, incredible, inconceivable, astounding, stupefying, staggering [➡ EXTRAORDINARY: AMAZING; 204] *Opposite:* unexceptional

mind-boggling (*informal*) *adj* **overwhelming**, complex, difficult, complicated, puzzling, baffling, confusing, challenging, mind-bending (*informal*) [➡ DIFFICULTY AND COMPLEXITY; 242] *Opposite:* simple

minded (*formal*) *adj* **inclined**, of a mind to, intent, set, prepared, ready, willing [➡ THE WILL AND WILLINGNESS; 563] *Opposite:* disinclined

minder (*UK*) *n* **sitter**, baby-sitter, child minder (*UK*), carer (*UK*) [➡ PEOPLE WHO GUARD AND PROTECT; 846]

mindful *adj* **watchful**, aware, wary, heedful, alert, careful, attentive, chary, thoughtful, conscious, sensible (*formal*) [➡ POSITIVE IMPATIENCE, ENTHUSIASM, AND ALERTNESS; 537] *Opposite:* unwary

See Compare and Contrast at **aware.**

mindfulness *n* [➡ POSITIVE IMPATIENCE, ENTHUSIASM, AND ALERTNESS; 537]

mindless **1** *adj* **tedious**, dull, boring, monotonous, mechanical, undemanding, humdrum, mind-numbing [➡ BORING AND UNINTERESTING; 234] *Opposite:* enthralling **2** *adj* **senseless**, gratuitous, unnecessary, pointless, needless, meaningless, uncalled-for, purposeless, motiveless [➡ REDUNDANT AND USELESS; 240]

mindlessly **1** *adv* **automatically**, mechanically, unconsciously, unthinkingly, robotically, instinctively, routinely [➡ INCAUTIOUS AND CARELESS; 283] **2** *adv* **senselessly**, stupidly, thoughtlessly, carelessly, foolishly, idiotically, crassly, asininely [➡ BAD AND BADLY; 223] *Opposite:* thoughtfully

mindlessness *n* [➡ REDUNDANT AND USELESS; 240]

mind-numbing *adj* **boring**, dull, tedious, tiresome, wearisome, monotonous, tiring, humdrum, uninteresting, mindless [➡ BORING AND UNINTERESTING; 234] *Opposite:* interesting

mindset *n* **attitude**, outlook, mind, mentality, way of thinking, approach, frame of mind, belief, conviction [➡ POINTS OF VIEW; 767]

mind your own business *v* **keep it to yourself**, keep your nose out of it, keep off, keep out of it, mind your own beeswax, butt out (*slang*), keep yourself to yourself (*UK*) [➡ NOT PAY ATTENTION; 764]

mine **1** *n* **pit**, excavation, colliery, coalfield, coalmine, pithead, coalface (*UK*) [➡ INDUSTRIAL BUILDINGS; 1087] **2** *n* **source**, repository, fund, gold mine, store, abundance, reserve, hoard, wealth [➡ MANY, MUCH, LARGE AMOUNT; 117] *Opposite:* dearth **3** *type of* **explosive weapon** [➡ EXPLOSIVES; 1155] **4** *v* **extract**, excavate, quarry, dig, dig out, unearth, burrow, drill, scoop [➡ CAUSE TO APPEAR; 5]

minefield *n* **problem**, trial, test, ordeal, hazard, obstacle, block [➡ DIFFICULT SITUATIONS; 72]

miner *n* **sapper**, coalminer, collier, tunneler, driller, mineworker, pit worker [➡ FARMERS, GARDENERS, AND MANUAL WORKERS; 849]

mineral **1** *n* [➡ SUBSTANCES; 1267] **2** *type of* **nutrient** [➡ FOOD COMPONENTS; 1188]

mineral

♦ *types of minerals*
arsenic, asbestos, asphalt, bauxite, carbon, clay, coal, coke, feldspar, fluorite, graphite, gypsum, jet, kaolin, lime, mica, pyrite, quartz, silicate, sulfur

mineralogy *type of* **earth science** [➡ EARTH SCIENCES; 1059]

minestrone *type of* **soup** [➡ SOUPS; 1186]

minesweeper *type of* **military vessel** [➡ SHIPS AND BOATS; 1150]

mingle **1** *v* **mix**, blend, fuse, join, unite, fold in, stir in, dilute [➡ COMBINE AND MIX; 400] *Opposite:* separate **2** *v* **circulate**, associate, intermingle, socialize, mix, move around [➡ ESTABLISHING RELATIONSHIPS WITH OTHERS; 974]

mini (*informal*) *adj* **small**, miniature, baby, diminutive, tiny, minute, little, minuscule [➡ SMALL; 1195] *Opposite:* maxi

miniature *adj* **small-scale**, small, tiny, minute, little, baby, minuscule, diminutive, mini (*informal*) [➡ SMALL; 1195]

miniaturist *n* [➡ ARTISTS; 900]

miniaturization *n* **reduction**, shrinking, contraction, diminishment [➡CHANGE OF SIZE: SMALLER; 393] *Opposite*: enlargement

miniaturize *v* reduce, scale down, shrink, contract, diminish [➡CHANGE OF SIZE: SMALLER; 393] *Opposite*: enlarge

minibar *n* bar, fridge, cupboard, cooler, cocktail cabinet [➡HOUSEHOLD APPLIANCES; 1117]

minibus *type of* public service vehicle [➡VEHICLES; 1145]

minicomputer *type of* computer [➡COMPUTERS AND COMPUTING; 1127]

minimal 1 *adj* negligible, trifling, slight, nominal, token, insignificant, marginal [➡FEW, LITTLE, SMALL AMOUNT; 120] *Opposite*: large 2 *adj* least, smallest, minimum, tiniest, minutest, infinitesimal [➡SMALL; 1195] *Opposite*: maximum

minimalism 1 *n* simplicity, plainness, unfussiness, cleanness, austereness, starkness, restraint [➡EASE AND SIMPLICITY; 200] *Opposite*: elaboration 2 *type of* 20th-century art movement [➡ARTISTIC MOVEMENTS AND STYLES; 899]

minimalist 1 *adj* simple, uncluttered, understated, discreet, plain, unfussy, austere, restrained, stark, clean [➡EASE AND SIMPLICITY; 200] *Opposite*: baroque 2 *type of* 20th-century architecture [➡BUILDING AND ARCHITECTURE; 1076]

minimally *adv* slightly, negligibly, triflingly, marginally, nominally, insignificantly [➡TO A CERTAIN EXTENT; 136] *Opposite*: significantly

minimize 1 *v* minimalize, diminish, curtail, lessen, reduce, abate (*formal or literary*) [➡CHANGE OF INTENSITY: LESS; 395] *Opposite*: maximize 2 *v* play down, make light of, reduce, dismiss, shrug off, brush off, belittle, disparage, write off (*informal*) [➡UNDERDO SOMETHING; 291] *Opposite*: exaggerate

minimum 1 *n* least, bare minimum, smallest amount, iota, jot, modicum, speck, smidgen (*informal*) [➡FEW, LITTLE, SMALL AMOUNT; 120] *Opposite*: maximum 2 *adj* smallest, least, lowest, tiniest, minutest, slightest, bottom [➡SMALL; 1195] *Opposite*: maximum

minion *n* follower, assistant, hanger-on, crony, underling, subordinate, slave, sycophant, toady, gofer (*informal*) [➡SUBORDINATES AND ASSISTANTS; 966] *Opposite*: superior

miniseries *n* series, serial, soap, drama, serialization [➡TELEVISION AND RADIO; 606]

miniskirt *type of* skirt [➡GARMENTS AND OUTFITS; 865]

minister 1 *n* priest, vicar, rector, parson, reverend, clergyman, clergywoman, cleric [➡RELIGIOUS PEOPLE; 778] 2 *v* (*formal*) attend, look after, care for, tend, nurse, wait on, comfort, aid, support [➡TAKE CARE OF AND SPOIL; 300] *Opposite*: neglect

ministerial *adj* governmental, parliamentary, cabinet, official, legislative, departmental, executive [➡GOVERNMENT AND POLITICS; 805]

ministration (*formal*) *n* care, support, attention, nurture, aid, assistance, comfort, help, treatment, service [➡KIND ACTIONS OR BEHAVIOR; 295] *Opposite*: neglect

ministry *n* office, bureau, department, agency, organization, government [➡PLACE OF EMPLOYMENT; 832]

minivan *type of* car [➡BIKES, CARS, AND CARRIAGES; 1149]

mink *type of* small mammal [➡SMALL MAMMALS; 990]

minke whale *type of* whale [➡WHALES; 991]

minnow 1 *type of* freshwater fish [➡FRESHWATER FISH; 1010] 2 *n* small fry, little man, little guy, nobody, sprat, spear carrier (*informal*) [➡LAZY OR UNSUCCESSFUL PEOPLE; 948]

minor 1 *adj* slight, small, negligible, inconsequential, trivial, unimportant, trifling, petty, inconsiderable, minimal, marginal, insignificant [➡FEW, LITTLE, SMALL AMOUNT; 120] *Opposite*: major 2 *adj* lesser, inferior, junior, secondary, minor-league, lower, insignificant [➡INFERIORITY; 153] *Opposite*: major 3 *n* juvenile, youth, adolescent, child, teenager, youngster [➡CHILD OR YOUTH; 945] *Opposite*: adult

minority 1 *n* section, faction, interest group, subgroup, sector, component, element [➡GROUPS WITH A COMMON INTEREST; 938] 2 *adj* alternative, underground, marginal, sectional, pressure, smaller, lesser [➡BELONGING OR RELATING TO INDIVIDUALS; 944] *Opposite*: majority

minster *type of* church [➡RELIGIOUS BUILDINGS; 1085]

minstrel *n* musician, troubadour, wandering minstrel, player, entertainer, singer, songster, versifier, poet [➡MUSICIANS AND SINGERS; 908]

mint 1 *type of* herb [➡HERBS AND SPICES; 1175] 2 *type of* factory [➡INDUSTRIAL BUILDINGS; 1087] 3 *n* (*informal*) fortune, millions, billions, pile (*informal*), bundle (*slang*) [➡LARGE AMOUNTS OF MONEY; 118] *Opposite*: pittance 4 *v* cast, issue, imprint, make, strike, coin, produce, stamp [➡MANUFACTURE; 349]

mint sauce *type of* seasonings, sauces, and dips [➡SEASONINGS AND SAUCES; 1174]

minuet *type of* dance [➡DANCE; 903]

minus 1 *prep* less, take away, excluding, reduced by, with the subtraction of [➡NOT; 137] *Opposite*: plus 2 *prep* without, lacking, excluding, exclusive of, with the exception of, wanting, excepting (*formal*), sans (*literary or humorous*) [➡LACK OF POSSESSION; 445] *Opposite*: including 3 *n* disadvantage, detriment, handicap, hindrance, drawback, demerit [➡FAULTS, FLAWS, AND WEAKNESSES; 251] *Opposite*: plus 4 *n* deficiency, loss, drop, fall, decrease, difference, deduction [➡LESS; 126] *Opposite*: addition

minuscule *adj* tiny, minute, microscopic, infinitesimal, little, miniature, diminutive [➡SMALL; 1195] *Opposite*: gigantic

minute 1 *n* moment, instant, second, flash, sec (*informal*), jiffy (*informal*) [➡SHORT PERIODS OF TIME; 93] *Opposite*: ages (*informal*) 2 *v* record, summarize, write down, précis, transcribe, log, report, take notes [➡RECORD SOMETHING; 371] 3 *adj* miniature, tiny, minuscule, microscopic, infinitesimal, little, small, diminutive, insignificant [➡SMALL; 1195] *Opposite*: enormous 4 *adj* close, detailed, thorough, exhaustive, painstaking, meticulous, exact, precise [➡EXACT; 203] *Opposite*: cursory

minutely *adv* closely, thoroughly, carefully, meticulously, painstakingly, microscopically, exhaustively, exactly, in great detail, precisely, with a fine-tooth comb [➡CAUTIOUS AND CAREFUL; 282] *Opposite*: cursorily

minuteness *n* smallness, tininess, shortness, compactness [➡SMALL; 1195]

minutes *n* **notes**, record, proceedings, transcript, transcription, summary, résumé, follow-up, log, report [➡ RECORDS; 585]

minutiae *n* **details**, niceties, intricacies, particulars, ins and outs, workings [➡ BASIC DETAILS; 688] *Opposite*: gist

Miocene *type of* **epoch** [➡ EPOCHS AND ERAS; 89]

miracle *n* **wonder**, phenomenon, marvel, sensation, vision, dream [➡ AMAZING THINGS; 211]

miraculous *adj* **amazing**, astounding, astonishing, incredible, unbelievable, phenomenal, marvelous, extraordinary, inexplicable, wonderful, wondrous, mind-blowing (*informal*) [➡ EXTRAORDINARY: AMAZING; 204] *Opposite*: mundane

mirage *n* **hallucination**, optical illusion, illusion, vision, delusion, fantasy, figment, imagining, phantasm [➡ NON-EXISTENT THINGS; 23] *Opposite*: reality

mire *n* **swamp**, marsh, mud, sludge, slush, morass, bog, quagmire [➡ WETLANDS; 1043]

mired *adj* [➡ CONFUSION, ANXIETY, AND WORRY; 540]

mirror 1 *n* **glass**, hand mirror, shaving mirror, looking glass (*dated*) [➡ FIXTURES; 859] 2 *v* **reflect**, echo, copy, parallel, emulate, imitate [➡ PRETEND AND MIMIC; 60] 3 *v* **represent**, symbolize, illustrate, typify, signify, correspond, embody, epitomize [➡ REPRESENT SOMETHING OR SOMEBODY; 59]

mirror image *n* **double**, twin, copy, replica, likeness, spitting image (*informal*), chip off the old block (*informal*), dead ringer (*informal*) [➡ COPIES AND REPLICAS; 151]

mirth *n* **laughter**, hilarity, humor, jollity, fun, merriment, entertainment, delight, glee, joy, joyfulness, cheer, merrymaking [➡ LAUGHTER; 649] *Opposite*: sadness

mirthful *adj* **joyful**, merry, gleeful, jovial, cheery, jolly, happy [➡ PLEASURE, EXCITEMENT, AND ELATION; 534] *Opposite*: mirthless

mirthfully *adv* **merrily**, cheerily, laughingly, gleefully, happily, brightly, joyfully, jovially [➡ PLEASURE, EXCITEMENT, AND ELATION; 534] *Opposite*: mirthlessly

mirthfulness *n* [➡ LAUGHTER; 649]

mirthless *adj* **cheerless**, dour, gloomy, grim, dismal, dreary, humorless [➡ NEGATIVITY OF OUTLOOK; 514] *Opposite*: cheerful

misadventure *n* **accident**, mishap, misfortune, disaster, calamity, catastrophe [➡ DISASTERS; 252]

misaligned *adj* **askew**, skewed, awry, cockeyed, crooked, uneven, out of true, asymmetrical, twisted, disorderly, lopsided [➡ ORIENTATION AND ALIGNMENT; 1223] *Opposite*: straight

misalliance *n* **mismatch**, inequality, bad match, disparity, mésalliance, incongruity, incompatibility [➡ DISHARMONY; 156]

misanthrope *n* **pessimist**, recluse, loner, cynic, malcontent, misanthropist [➡ GRUMPY AND NEGATIVE PEOPLE; 953] *Opposite*: philanthropist

misanthropic *adj* **cynical**, pessimistic, distrustful, disdainful, sardonic, reclusive [➡ UNFRIENDLINESS AND UNSOCIABILITY; 504] *Opposite*: philanthropic

misanthropist *n* **misanthrope**, recluse, loner, pessimist, cynic, malcontent [➡ GRUMPY AND NEGATIVE PEOPLE; 953] *Opposite*: philanthropist

misanthropy *n* **cynicism**, pessimism, distrust, disdain, sardonicism, reclusiveness [➡ UNFRIENDLINESS AND UNSOCIABILITY; 504] *Opposite*: philanthropy

misapplication *n* **misuse**, abuse, misemployment, mishandling, exploitation, mismanagement, misappropriation [➡ MISUSE AND ABUSE; 471]

misapply *v* **misuse**, abuse, misemploy, mishandle, mismanage, misappropriate, exploit [➡ MISUSE AND ABUSE; 471]

misapprehend *v* **mistake**, misunderstand, misinterpret, misconstrue, misjudge, misread, get the wrong end of the stick, get the wrong idea, confuse, get the wrong impression, miscomprehend, get wrong [➡ MISUNDERSTAND AND FAIL TO GRASP; 761]

misapprehension *n* **misunderstanding**, misinterpretation, wrong idea, false impression, misconception, delusion, misreading [➡ MISUNDERSTAND AND FAIL TO GRASP; 761] *Opposite*: comprehension

misappropriate *v* **steal**, embezzle, pocket, take, help yourself, siphon off, defraud, misuse, fiddle (*informal*) [➡ STEAL AND ROB; 426] *Opposite*: reimburse

See Compare and Contrast at **steal**.

misappropriation *n* **embezzlement**, misuse, stealing, dishonesty, fraud, deceit, appropriation, cheating, double-dealing, fiddling (*informal*) [➡ CRIMES; 817]

misbegotten *adj* **ill-conceived**, bad, inappropriate, foolish, deplorable, improper, malapropos (*formal*) [➡ THE NATURE OF IDEAS; 771]

misbehave *v* **be naughty**, be bad, act up, behave badly, disobey, cut up (*slang*), play up (*UK*) [➡ DISOBEY; 302] *Opposite*: behave

misbehavior *n* **naughtiness**, misconduct, mischief, disobedience, waywardness, mischievousness, troublesomeness [➡ BAD BEHAVIOR OR ACTIONS; 254]

miscalculate *v* **misjudge**, underestimate, overestimate, get it wrong, misconstrue, overvalue, overrate, undervalue, underrate, misunderstand [➡ MISUNDERSTAND AND FAIL TO GRASP; 761]

miscalculation *n* **error**, mistake, inaccuracy, blunder, slip, fault, oversight, misstep, slip-up (*informal*), faux pas (*literary*) [➡ MISTAKES; 250]

miscarriage 1 *n* [➡ REPRODUCTION AND HEREDITY; 725] 2 *n* (*formal*) **failure**, lapse, breakdown, insufficiency, mistake, blunder, debacle [➡ MISTAKES; 250]

miscarriage of justice *n* **wrongful conviction**, unfair ruling, injustice, judicial error, mistake, error, travesty [➡ TRIAL, PUNISHMENT, AND LEGAL OUTCOMES; 819]

miscarry (*formal*) *v* **fail**, founder, backfire, go wrong, go amiss, come to nothing, fall through, fall short [➡ FAIL OR BE UNSUCCESSFUL; 75]

miscellanea *n* [➡ COLLECTIONS AND MIXTURES OF THINGS; 1244]

miscellaneous *adj* **various**, varied, assorted, mixed, diverse, sundry, jumbled, disparate [➡DIFFERENCE; 149] *Opposite*: homogeneous

miscellany *n* **assortment**, collection, selection, grouping, medley, pastiche, variety, diversity, hodgepodge, jumble, mixed bag, mishmash, mixture [➡COLLECTIONS AND MIXTURES OF THINGS; 1244]

mischance *n* **misfortune**, ill fortune, bad luck, ill luck, misadventure [➡BAD LUCK AND UNLUCKY; 784]

mischief **1** *n* **misbehavior**, naughtiness, trouble, disobedience, waywardness, troublesomeness, monkey business (*informal*), tomfoolery (*informal*) [➡BAD BEHAVIOR OR ACTIONS; 254] **2** *n* **harm**, damage, trouble, disruption, injury, hurt, malice [➡NUISANCES; 253] **3** *n* **troublemaker**, nuisance, scamp (*informal*), monkey (*informal*), pest (*informal*), rascal (*humorous*) [➡MISCHIEVOUS OR BADLY BEHAVED CHILD; 946]

mischief-maker *n* **meddler**, troublemaker, gossip, ringleader, instigator, rabble-rouser (*informal*) [➡UNCOOPERATIVE OR REBELLIOUS PEOPLE; 566]

mischievous **1** *adj* **naughty**, playful, impish, roguish, badly behaved, bad, tricksy, disobedient, rascally (*humorous*) [➡REBELLIOUSNESS AND DISOBEDIENCE; 565] *Opposite*: well-behaved **2** *adj* (*formal*) **harmful**, damaging, malicious, wicked, negative, hurtful, bad, malign, spiteful, nasty (*informal*) [➡SELFISH AND UNKIND; 505] *Opposite*: harmless

*See Compare and Contrast at **bad**.*

mischievousness **1** *n* **naughtiness**, bad behavior, impishness, playfulness, disobedience [➡REBELLIOUSNESS AND DISOBEDIENCE; 565] **2** *n* (*formal*) **malice**, hatred, harm, animosity, spite, ill will, damage [➡UNFRIENDLINESS AND UNSOCIABILITY; 504]

miscomprehend *v* [➡MISUNDERSTAND AND FAIL TO GRASP; 761]

misconceive *v* **misunderstand**, misapprehend, misinterpret, get the wrong impression, get the wrong idea, get the wrong end of the stick, miscomprehend, mistake, misconstrue [➡MISUNDERSTAND AND FAIL TO GRASP; 761] *Opposite*: understand

misconceived *adj* **ill-conceived**, ill-thought-out, flawed, misguided, inappropriate, doomed, misjudged, misunderstood, misconstrued, mistaken [➡THE NATURE OF IDEAS; 771]

misconception *n* **fallacy**, delusion, misapprehension, misconstruction, mistaken belief, false impression, misunderstanding, misreading, error [➡MISTAKES; 250] *Opposite*: fact

misconduct *n* **bad behavior**, misbehavior, delinquency, transgression, wrongdoing [➡BAD BEHAVIOR OR ACTIONS; 254]

misconstruction *n* **misinterpretation**, misunderstanding, misreading, false impression, misjudgment, wrong idea, error, fallacy [➡MISUNDERSTAND AND FAIL TO GRASP; 761] *Opposite*: understanding

misconstrue *v* **misinterpret**, misunderstand, misread, get the wrong idea about, get the wrong impression about, get the wrong end of the stick, misapprehend, miscomprehend [➡MISUNDERSTAND AND FAIL TO GRASP; 761] *Opposite*: understand

miscount *v* **lose count**, miscalculate, make a mistake, err, underestimate, overestimate [➡ASSESS QUANTITY; 757]

miscreant (*literary*) *n* **troublemaker**, scoundrel, mischief-maker, wrongdoer, criminal, reprobate, offender, villain, lowlife (*informal*), malefactor (*formal*) [➡VILLAINS AND THUGS; 947]

misdeed *n* **crime**, offense, wrong, transgression, misdemeanor, fault, error [➡BAD BEHAVIOR OR ACTIONS; 254]

misdemeanor **1** *n* **petty larceny**, crime, offense, transgression, infringement, violation, malfeasance (*formal*) [➡CRIMES; 817] **2** *n* **misdeed**, wrongdoing, indiscretion, lapse, transgression, foul, wrong, breach, misconduct, slip, misbehavior, faux pas (*literary*) [➡BAD BEHAVIOR OR ACTIONS; 254]

misdirect **1** *v* **point in the wrong direction**, lead astray, send off course, send on a wild goose chase [➡DISPATCH AND SEND; 333] *Opposite*: direct **2** *v* **misallocate**, misuse, misapply, waste, misemploy, mismanage [➡MISUSE AND ABUSE; 471]

misemploy *v* [➡MISUSE AND ABUSE; 471]

miser **1** *n* **hoarder**, accumulator, saver, collector, squirrel (*informal*), magpie (*informal*) [➡PEOPLE WHO COLLECT THINGS; 454] **2** *n* **skinflint**, pinchpenny, niggard, penny pincher (*informal*), cheapskate (*informal*), scrooge (*informal*) [➡FINANCIALLY MEAN PEOPLE; 952]

miserable **1** *adj* **unhappy**, sad, depressed, down, despondent, dejected, wretched, glum, dismal, low, woeful, fed up (*informal*) [➡SADNESS, DISTRESS, AND DESPAIR; 539] *Opposite*: happy **2** *adj* **depressing**, cheerless, wretched, desolate, gloomy, dismal, glum, melancholy [➡EMOTIONALLY UNPLEASANT AND UPSETTING; 227] *Opposite*: cheery **3** *adj* **inadequate**, paltry, derisory, miserly, mean, meager, contemptible, pitiable, measly (*informal*), piddling (*informal*) [➡TOO FEW, TOO LITTLE; 122] *Opposite*: generous **4** *adj* **gloomy**, dull, gray, overcast, dreary [➡COLD WEATHER; 1051] *Opposite*: bright

miserably *adv* **unhappily**, sadly, despondently, dejectedly, wretchedly, glumly, gloomily, desolately, sorrowfully [➡SADNESS, DISTRESS, AND DESPAIR; 539] *Opposite*: happily

miserliness *n* **stinginess**, greed, greediness, parsimoniousness, tightfistedness, avariciousness, meanness, tightness, close-fistedness (*informal*) [➡GRASPING AND FINANCIALLY MEAN; 519] *Opposite*: generosity

miserly **1** *adj* **mean**, stingy, tightfisted, parsimonious, tight, niggardly, penny-pinching (*informal*), close-fisted (*informal*), scrounging (*informal*) [➡GRASPING AND FINANCIALLY MEAN; 519] *Opposite*: generous **2** *adj* **paltry**, derisory, meager, mean, stingy, miserable, measly (*informal*), piddling (*informal*) [➡SMALL; 1195] *Opposite*: generous

misery **1** *n* **unhappiness**, sadness, depression, desolation, gloom, wretchedness, melancholy, despair, grief, sorrow, agony [➡SADNESS, DISTRESS, AND DESPAIR; 539] *Opposite*: happiness **2** *n* **deprivation**, destitution, distress, poverty, privation, misfortune, suffering, indigence (*formal*) [➡POVERTY AND POOR; 892]

misfire *v* **go wrong**, backfire, fail, fall through, miscarry, not come off, fall flat [➡FAIL OR BE UNSUCCESSFUL; 75] *Opposite*: succeed

misfit *n* **oddity**, eccentric, loner, odd one out, nonconformist [➡SOLITARY PEOPLE AND MISFITS; 942] *Opposite*: conformist

misfortune *n* **disaster**, calamity, trial, tribulation, misadventure, catastrophe, accident [➡ DISASTERS; 252] *Opposite:* opportunity

misgiving *n* **scruple**, qualm, doubt, suspicion, hesitation, worry, unease, mistrust, reservation, uncertainty, fear, niggle (*UK*) [➡ FEELINGS ABOUT THE FUTURE; 533]

misguided *adj* **mistaken**, foolish, ill-advised, unwise, erroneous, injudicious, wrong, imprudent [➡ THE NATURE OF IDEAS; 771] *Opposite:* wise

mishandle 1 *v* **mismanage**, make a mess of, botch, misapply, misuse, abuse, bungle (*informal*), mess up (*informal*), make a hash of (*informal*) [➡ MESS UP AND MAKE MISTAKES; 472] **2** *v* **abuse**, mistreat, exploit, ill-treat, rough up (*informal*), knock around (*informal*) [➡ MISUSE AND ABUSE; 471]

mishap *n* **accident**, calamity, misfortune, disaster, catastrophe, misadventure, casualty [➡ DISASTERS; 252]

mishear *v* **hear wrong**, get wrong, pick up wrong, not get, be mistaken, get the wrong end of the stick, misunderstand [➡ MISUNDERSTAND AND FAIL TO GRASP; 761]

mishit 1 *v* **botch**, miss, nick, clip, hit a foul, foul, slice, hook, fluff (*informal*) [➡ MESS UP AND MAKE MISTAKES; 472] **2** *n* **error**, slice, hook, miss, nick, clip, foul, foul ball [➡ MISTAKES; 250]

mishmash *n* **hodgepodge**, jumble, muddle, miscellany, mixture, mixed bag, pastiche, assortment, collection [➡ COLLECTIONS AND MIXTURES OF THINGS; 1244]

misinform *v* **mislead**, deceive, lie to, lead on, lead astray, delude, misrepresent, distort, fabricate, propagandize, hoodwink, bamboozle (*informal*) [➡ DECEPTION AND LIES; 660]

misinformation *n* **propaganda**, dishonesty, distortion, fabrication, bending of the truth, half truth, misrepresentation, deception, spin (*slang*) [➡ DECEPTION AND LIES; 660] *Opposite:* fact

misinterpret *v* **misconstrue**, misunderstand, misread, get the wrong idea about, get the wrong impression about, get the wrong end of the stick, miss the point, mistake, misjudge, misapprehend [➡ MISUNDERSTAND AND FAIL TO GRASP; 761] *Opposite:* understand

misinterpretation *n* **misunderstanding**, misconception, misapprehension, misreading, confusion, mix-up, misconstruction [➡ MISUNDERSTAND AND FAIL TO GRASP; 761] *Opposite:* understanding

misjudge *v* **miscalculate**, underestimate, overestimate, be wrong about, get the wrong idea, get the wrong impression, misapprehend, mistake, misinterpret [➡ MISUNDERSTAND AND FAIL TO GRASP; 761]

misjudgment 1 *n* **poor judgment**, error of judgment, error, miscalculation, slip, mistake, oversight, slip-up (*informal*), faux pas (*literary*) [➡ MISUNDERSTAND AND FAIL TO GRASP; 761] **2** *n* **wrong impression**, misinterpretation, misconstruction, false reading, prejudice, prejudgment, irrationality [➡ MISTAKES; 250] *Opposite:* understanding

mislaid *adj* **lost**, missing, nowhere to be found, gone astray, misplaced [➡ ABSENT AND UNAVAILABLE; 7]

mislay *v* **lose**, misplace, be unable to find, miss, put in the wrong place, drop, leave behind, forget [➡ LOSE AND FORFEIT; 447] *Opposite:* find

mislead *v* **give the wrong impression**, misinform, deceive, lie, delude, take in, lead on, misrepresent, distort, fabricate, hoodwink, bamboozle (*informal*) [➡ DECEPTION AND LIES; 660]

misleading *adj* **deceptive**, ambiguous, confusing, false, disingenuous, misrepresentative, distorted [➡ FALSE AND UNREAL; 173] *Opposite:* truthful

mismanage *v* **mishandle**, make a mess of, botch, misuse, manage badly, mess up (*informal*), make a hash of (*informal*), bungle (*informal*) [➡ MISUSE AND ABUSE; 471]

mismanagement *n* **mishandling**, misconduct, negligence, malpractice, maladministration, bungling (*informal*) [➡ MISUSE AND ABUSE; 471] *Opposite:* efficiency

mismatch *n* **incongruity**, discrepancy, gap, disparity, misalliance, bad fit, divergence, incompatibility [➡ DISHARMONY; 156] *Opposite:* harmony

mismatched *adj* **incompatible**, unequal, uneven, unjust, one-sided, inequitable, lopsided, asymmetric, off-balance [➡ DISHARMONY; 156]

misnomer *n* **misleading term**, inaccurate term, poor description, loose term, contradiction, inaccuracy, incongruity [➡ NAME AND DESCRIBE; 665]

miso *type of* **cooked dish** [➡ PREPARED DISHES; 1170]

misperceive *v* [➡ MISUNDERSTAND AND FAIL TO GRASP; 761]

misplace *v* **lose**, mislay, be unable to put your hands on, drop, leave behind, forget [➡ LOSE AND FORFEIT; 447] *Opposite:* find

misplaced 1 *adj* **mislaid**, nowhere to be found, missing, lost, gone astray, absent [➡ ABSENT AND UNAVAILABLE; 7] **2** *adj* **inappropriate**, erroneous, misdirected, out-of-place, inapt, improper, illogical [➡ INAPPROPRIATE AND UNSUITABLE; 224] *Opposite:* appropriate

misprint *n* **typographical error**, error, mistake, blunder, oversight, typo (*informal*), literal (*UK*) [➡ MISTAKES; 250]

mispronounce *v* **say wrong**, distort, mangle, make a mess of, stumble through, misstate, mess up (*informal*) [➡ CHATTER AND BABBLE; 617] *Opposite:* articulate

mispronunciation *n* **distortion**, error, misstatement, slip, blunder, mistake [➡ THE SPOKEN WORD; 671]

misquote *v* **put words in somebody's mouth**, misreport, misrepresent, misattribute, quote out of context, overstate [➡ RECITE, REPEAT, AND NARRATE; 620]

misread *v* **misjudge**, misinterpret, misunderstand, misconstrue, get the wrong idea, get the wrong impression, miss the point, get the wrong end of the stick, mistake, garble, misapprehend [➡ MISUNDERSTAND AND FAIL TO GRASP; 761] *Opposite:* interpret

misrepresent *v* **parody**, pervert, twist, distort, pass off, bias, falsify, slant [➡ FALSIFY AND CHEAT; 176]

misrepresentation *n* **parody**, caricature, distortion, falsification, twisting, slanting, perversion [➡ REPRESENTATIONS AND GENERAL EXAMPLES; 65]

misrule 1 *n* **misgovernment**, mishandling, corruption, maladministration, mismanagement, tyranny, abuse of power [➡ MISUSE AND ABUSE; 471] **2** *n* **lawlessness**, anarchy, unruliness, chaos, turmoil, disorder [➡ DISORDER AND CHAOS; 245] *Opposite*: order

miss **1** *v* **overlook**, fail to spot, let pass, fail to notice, fail to see, neglect, ignore, fail to catch [➡ MISUNDERSTAND AND FAIL TO GRASP; 761] *Opposite*: see **2** *v* **skip**, fail to attend, escape, avoid, forget, pass on [➡ FORGET, FORGIVE, AND ACCEPT; 748] *Opposite*: attend **3** *v* **forego**, lose, pass up, let pass, let go, let slip, disregard [➡ FORGO AND DENY ONESELF; 449] *Opposite*: take up **4** *v* **pine for**, long for, yearn for, wish for, want, lack [➡ DESIRE AND WANT; 579] **5** *n* **failure**, false step, error, slip, miscue, blunder [➡ MISTAKES; 250] **6** *n* **omission**, oversight, delinquency, neglect, mistake, loss [➡ MISTAKES; 250]

missal *n* **service book**, prayer book, liturgical book, breviary, psalter, hymn book, hymnal [➡ RELIGIOUS OBJECTS; 779]

misshapen *adj* **distorted**, twisted, deformed, malformed, warped, contorted, disproportionate, crooked, irregular [➡ ORIENTATION AND ALIGNMENT; 1223] *Opposite*: shapely

misshapenness *n* [➡ SHAPELESSNESS; 1219]

missile *type of* **explosive weapon** [➡ EXPLOSIVES; 1155]

missing *adj* **lost**, absent, gone astray, misplaced, mislaid, gone, omitted, disappeared, unaccounted for, AWOL [➡ ABSENT AND UNAVAILABLE; 7] *Opposite*: present

mission **1** *n* **assignment**, task, job, work, undertaking, duty, operation, exercise, errand, enterprise, quest, charge [➡ WORK IN GENERAL; 297] **2** *n* **delegation**, deputation, task force, legation, embassy, group [➡ ADMINISTRATIVE OFFICERS; 811] **3** *n* **calling**, vocation, purpose, goal, aim, objective, duty, pursuit, raison d'être [➡ PROFESSIONS; 845]

Mission *type of* **pre-20th-century architecture** [➡ BUILDING AND ARCHITECTURE; 1076]

missionary **1** *n* **evangelist**, proselytizer, preacher, minister, priest, apostle, teacher [➡ RELIGIOUS PEOPLE; 778] **2** *n* **campaigner**, champion, crusader, proselytizer, propagandist, activist [➡ PHILOSOPHICAL AND POLITICAL THINKERS; 781]

missive *n* **letter**, communiqué, note, communication, memo, memorandum, notification, dispatch, message, epistle (*formal*) [➡ LETTERS AND WRITTEN MESSAGES; 584]

miss out **1** *v* **fail to benefit from**, forego, miss the boat, miss an opportunity, miss a chance, lose out (*informal*) [➡ LOSE AND FORFEIT; 447] *Opposite*: benefit **2** *v* (*UK*) **omit**, leave out, disregard, miss, exclude, overlook [➡ NOT PAY ATTENTION; 764] *Opposite*: include

misspelling *n* **spelling mistake**, wrong spelling, slip, error, orthographical error, mistake [➡ MISTAKES; 250]

misspend *v* **squander**, fritter away, waste, throw away, misuse, dissipate [➡ MISUSE AND ABUSE; 471] *Opposite*: save

misspent *adj* **wasted**, squandered, frittered away, misused, thrown away, dissipated, misapplied [➡ WASTEFUL AND UNECONOMICAL; 246] *Opposite*: profitable

misstep *n* **mistake**, slip, gaffe, blunder, error, lapse, solecism, shortcoming, indiscretion, miscalculation,

slip-up (*informal*), boo-boo (*informal*), blooper (*informal humorous*), faux pas (*literary*) [➡ MISTAKES; 250]

miss the boat *v* **miss an opportunity**, miss a chance, miss out, fail to benefit from, forego, lose out (*informal*) [➡ LOSE AND FORFEIT; 447]

miss the point *v* **misunderstand**, misinterpret, misconstrue, fail to understand, misread, not get the point, get hold of the wrong end of the stick, misapprehend [➡ MISUNDERSTAND AND FAIL TO GRASP; 761] *Opposite*: understand

mist *n* **haze**, fog, smog, vapor, spray, steam, film [➡ CLOUDY AND RAINY WEATHER; 1052]

mistake **1** *n* **blunder**, gaffe, slip, lapse, miscalculation, misstep, slip-up (*informal*), blooper (*informal humorous*), faux pas (*literary*) [➡ MISTAKES; 250] **2** *n* **error**, fault, inaccuracy, oversight, misspelling, misprint [➡ MISTAKES; 250] **3** *v* **misunderstand**, misjudge, misinterpret, misconstrue, confuse, miscalculate, misapprehend [➡ MISUNDERSTAND AND FAIL TO GRASP; 761] *Opposite*: understand **4** *v* **confuse with**, take for, mix up with, confound, mix, muddle up, misidentify [➡ MISUNDERSTAND AND FAIL TO GRASP; 761] *Opposite*: recognize

> **Compare and Contrast:** *mistake, error, inaccuracy, slip, blunder, faux pas*
>
> CORE MEANING: something incorrect or improper
>
> **mistake** an unwise decision or an error resulting from a lack of care; **error** something that unintentionally deviates from a recognized standard or guide; **inaccuracy** something that is incorrect because it has been measured, calculated, copied, or conveyed incorrectly; **slip** a minor mistake or oversight, especially one caused by carelessness; **blunder** a serious or embarrassing mistake, usually the result of carelessness or ignorance; **faux pas** (*literary*) an embarrassing mistake that breaks a social convention.

mistaken *adj* **wrong**, incorrect, false, erroneous, faulty, flawed, fallacious, inaccurate, unfounded [➡ INCORRECT AND ERRONEOUS; 222] *Opposite*: correct

mistime *v* **misjudge**, miss the boat, anticipate, jump the gun, preempt, lag behind [➡ MESS UP AND MAKE MISTAKES; 472] *Opposite*: coordinate

mistimed *adj* [➡ PROMPTNESS: BADLY TIMED; 101]

mistiness **1** *n* **haziness**, murkiness, duskiness, cloudiness, fogginess, darkness, smogginess [➡ CLOUDY AND RAINY WEATHER; 1052] *Opposite*: clarity **2** *n* **vagueness**, indistinctness, obscurity, opacity, lack of clarity, fuzziness [➡ VAGUENESS; 243] *Opposite*: clarity

mist over *v* **mist**, mist up, fog over, become hazy, become clouded, cloud up, cloud over, glaze over, film over, become indistinct, become obscure [➡ CAUSE TO DISAPPEAR; 6] *Opposite*: clear

mistral *type of* **wind** [➡ WINDY AND STORMY WEATHER; 1053]

mistreat *v* **abuse**, maltreat, ill-treat, harm, mishandle, misuse, ill-use, oppress, rough up (*informal*), knock around (*informal*) [➡ MISUSE AND ABUSE; 471] *Opposite*: pamper

See Compare and Contrast at **misuse**.

mistreated *adj* **abused**, neglected, wronged, injured, victimized, ill-treated, maltreated, ill-used, oppressed [➞ IN TROUBLE AND DISADVANTAGED; 73] *Opposite:* pampered

mistreatment *n* **maltreatment**, exploitation, abuse, ill-treatment, neglect, harm, oppression, ill-use [➞ MALICIOUS ACTIONS OR BEHAVIOR; 296] *Opposite:* pampering

mistress **1** *n* **lover**, concubine, courtesan, kept woman, lady friend (*informal*), paramour (*literary*) [➞ SEXUAL AND ROMANTIC RELATIONSHIPS; 964] *Opposite:* wife **2** *n* **manager**, employer, controller, proprietor, owner, boss, ruler [➞ BOSSES AND MANAGEMENT; 965] *Opposite:* servant **3** *n* **expert**, specialist, queen, doyenne, leading exponent, authority [➞ TALENTED OR INTELLIGENT PEOPLE; 528] *Opposite:* novice **4** *n* **owner**, trainer, keeper, rider [➞ OWNERS; 446] **5** *n* (*UK*) **teacher**, schoolmistress, governess, instructress, schoolteacher, tutor [➞ EDUCATORS; 840] *Opposite:* pupil

mistrial *n* **invalid trial**, unfair trial, miscarriage of justice, travesty, injustice, unfairness [➞ TRIAL, PUNISHMENT, AND LEGAL OUTCOMES; 819]

mistrust **1** *n* **suspicion**, distrust, doubt, wariness, uncertainty, caution, misgiving, skepticism, caginess (*informal*) [➞ UNCERTAINTY; 559] *Opposite:* trust **2** *v* **distrust**, doubt, suspect, be wary of, be suspicious of, have doubts about, disbelieve [➞ QUESTION THINGS; 751] *Opposite:* trust

mistrustful *adj* **distrustful**, wary, suspicious, doubtful, skeptical, cautious, chary, cagey (*informal*) [➞ INSECURITY AND LOSS OF COMPOSURE; 544] *Opposite:* trusting

misty **1** *adj* **hazy**, foggy, murky, cloudy, steamy, vaporous, dewy [➞ CLOUDY AND RAINY WEATHER; 1052] *Opposite:* clear **2** *adj* **indistinct**, vague, obscure, dim, opaque, unclear, fuzzy, murky, nebulous, cloudy [➞ VAGUENESS; 243] *Opposite:* clear

misty-eyed **1** *adj* **tearful**, emotional, teary, teary-eyed, close to tears, sad, weepy (*informal*), lachrymose (*literary*) [➞ CRYING; 650] *Opposite:* dry-eyed **2** *adj* **sentimental**, nostalgic, romantic, weepy (*informal*), sloppy (*informal*), soppy (*informal*) [➞ IN POOR TASTE AND OVERSENTIMENTAL; 229] *Opposite:* unsentimental

misunderstand *v* **get the wrong idea**, misinterpret, misread, misconstrue, get the wrong impression, get the wrong end of the stick, miss the point, misjudge, mistake, miscalculate, misapprehend [➞ MISUNDERSTAND AND FAIL TO GRASP; 761] *Opposite:* understand

misunderstanding **1** *n* **mistake**, mix-up, confusion, misinterpretation, misconstruction, misapprehension, miscalculation, false impression [➞ MISUNDERSTAND AND FAIL TO GRASP; 761] **2** *n* **quarrel**, row, argument, difference of opinion, disagreement, falling-out, squabble, dispute, rift, fight [➞ ARGUMENTS; 47] *Opposite:* agreement

misunderstood *adj* **unacknowledged**, unrecognized, unappreciated, undervalued, misjudged, unvalued [➞ IN TROUBLE AND DISADVANTAGED; 73] *Opposite:* valued

misuse **1** *n* **misappropriation**, misapplication, waste, ill use, mismanagement [➞ MISUSE AND ABUSE; 471] **2** *v* **abuse**, exploit, mistreat, maltreat, ill-treat, ill-use, wrong, rough up (*informal*), knock around (*informal*) [➞ WOUND A PERSON OR ANIMAL; 383] *Opposite:* cherish **3** *v* **waste**, misappropriate, squander, misapply, mishandle, mismanage [➞ MISUSE AND ABUSE; 471]

Compare and Contrast: *misuse, abuse, ill-treat, maltreat, mistreat*

CORE MEANING: to treat somebody or something wrongly or badly

misuse to put something to an inappropriate use or purpose, or to treat a person or animal badly or harshly; *abuse* to use in a wrong or inappropriate way something that should be used responsibly, for example, a power, privilege, or a substance such as alcohol or a drug. It is also used to refer to cruel or violent treatment of a person or animal, especially on a regular or habitual basis; *ill-treat* or *maltreat* to behave cruelly toward a person or animal, or to treat something roughly and carelessly; *mistreat* to treat a person badly, inconsiderately, or unfairly, not necessarily in a way involving physical cruelty, or to treat something roughly and carelessly.

mite **1** *n* (*dated*) **jot**, bit, scrap, speck, grain, iota, scintilla, smidgen (*informal*) [➞ FEW, LITTLE, SMALL AMOUNT; 120] **2** *type of* **arachnid** [➞ ARACHNIDS; 1018] **3** *type of* **parasitic insect** [➞ PARASITES; 1017]

mitigate *v* **alleviate**, lessen, ease, allay, moderate, take the edge off, diminish, tone down, dull, soften, assuage, relieve, mollify, palliate, abate (*formal or literary*) [➞ CHANGE OF INTENSITY: LESS; 395] *Opposite:* aggravate

mitigating *adj* **justifying**, extenuating, modifying, qualifying, vindicating, moderating, alleviating [➞ CALMING; 188] *Opposite:* aggravating

mitigation **1** *n* **extenuation**, vindication, justification, qualification, moderation, modification [➞ CAUSATION; 168] **2** *n* **alleviation**, easing, improvement, lessening, relief, palliation [➞ CHANGE OF INTENSITY: LESS; 395] *Opposite:* intensification

mitt **1** *n* (*slang*) **hand**, appendage, paw (*informal*) [➞ PARTS OF THE BODY: ARM AND HAND; 695] **2** *type of* **sports equipment** [➞ SPORTS EQUIPMENT; 879] **3** *type of* **accessory** [➞ ACCESSORIES, MILLINERY, AND LINGERIE; 867]

mitten *type of* **accessory** [➞ ACCESSORIES, MILLINERY, AND LINGERIE; 867]

mix **1** *v* **mix up**, mingle, intermingle, blend, intersperse, combine, jumble, stir together, admix [➞ COMBINE AND MIX; 400] *Opposite:* separate **2** *v* **combine**, blend, unite, merge, join, amalgamate, mingle, fuse [➞ COMBINE AND MIX; 400] *Opposite:* separate out **3** *v* **fraternize**, mingle, associate, get together, socialize, hang out (*informal*), hobnob (*informal*), consort (*formal*) [➞ ESTABLISHING RELATIONSHIPS WITH OTHERS; 974] **4** *v* **go together**, accord, agree, fit, harmonize, match [➞ HARMONY; 155] *Opposite:* clash **5** *n* **combination**, mixture, blend, assortment, fusion, amalgam, synthesis, mingling, assembly [➞ COLLECTIONS AND MIXTURES OF THINGS; 1244]

mixed **1** *adj* **varied**, diverse, assorted, sundry, miscellaneous, motley, diversified, variegated, hybrid [➞ DIFFERENCE; 149] *Opposite:* uniform **2** *adj* **cosmopolitan**, integrated, international, interracial, unsegregated, multiracial, blended, multicultural, multinational, mingled [➞ DIFFERENCE; 149] *Opposite:* segregated

mixed bag *n* **ragbag**, assortment, combination, jumble, variety, hodgepodge [➞ COLLECTIONS AND MIXTURES OF THINGS; 1244]

mixed economy *type of* **economic system** [➞ FINANCE AND ECONOMICS; 796]

mixed-up (*informal*) **1** *adj* **confused**, muddled, bewildered, puzzled, perplexed, upset [➡ CONFUSION, ANXIETY, AND WORRY; 540] *Opposite:* clear **2** *adj* **disturbed**, maladjusted, confused, troubled, rebellious, alienated [➡ PSYCHOLOGY AND THE MIND; 769] *Opposite:* well-adjusted

mixer *type of* **appliance** [➡ HOUSEHOLD APPLIANCES; 1117]

mixture *n* **combination**, mix, blend, assortment, concoction, jumble, muddle, fusion, admixture, amalgam [➡ COLLECTIONS AND MIXTURES OF THINGS; 1244]

Compare and Contrast: *mixture, blend, combination, compound, alloy, amalgam*

CORE MEANING: something formed by mixing materials

mixture a number of elements or ingredients brought together; *blend* something formed by putting together two or more different kinds of things, especially in a skilled way, to form a new whole in which the original elements lose their distinctness; *combination* something formed by the association of two or more things that retain their distinctness; *compound* a technical word for a chemical formed from two or more elements, also used generally to describe anything composed of two or more separate parts; *alloy* a technical word for a metal such as steel that is formed by combining two or more different metallic elements; *amalgam* a technical word for an alloy formed by combining mercury with another metal, also used generally to describe something that is a mixture of two or more elements or characteristics.

---

mix up **1** *v* **confuse**, misunderstand, muddle, confound, mistake, muddle up [➡ MISUNDERSTAND AND FAIL TO GRASP; 761] *Opposite:* straighten out **2** *v* **mix**, combine, merge, blend, fuse, unite, incorporate, mingle, amalgamate [➡ COMBINE AND MIX; 400] *Opposite:* separate

mix-up *n* **mistake**, muddle, misunderstanding, confusion, error, tangle [➡ MISTAKES; 250]

mizzen *part of* **sailing vessel** [➡ PARTS OF A SHIP OR BOAT; 1151]

mizzle *n* [➡ CLOUDY AND RAINY WEATHER; 1052]

mnemonic *n* **memory aid**, reminder, prompt, cue, aide-mémoire (*formal*) [➡ NAME AND DESCRIBE; 665]

moan **1** *v* **groan**, sigh, whine, whimper, mutter, wail, lament, bemoan, keen [➡ SOUND EMISSION BY PEOPLE; 363] **2** *v* (*informal*) **complain**, grumble, whine, gripe (*informal*), grouse (*informal*) [➡ COMPLAIN AND NAG; 686] **3** *n* **sigh**, groan, whine, whimper, sob, wail, lament, keening [➡ SOUNDS MADE BY PEOPLE; 1262] **4** *n* (*informal*) **complaint**, grumble, gripe (*informal*), grouse (*informal*) [➡ COMPLAIN AND NAG; 686] *Opposite:* compliment

moaner (*informal*) *n* **grumbler**, complainer, whiner, wailer, objector, protester, grouch (*informal*) [➡ GRUMPY AND NEGATIVE PEOPLE; 953]

moat *n* **ditch**, trench, fosse, channel, dyke, earthwork, defense [➡ WATERCOURSES; 1111] *Opposite:* bank

mob **1** *n* **crowd**, horde, mass, multitude, throng, gang, pack, flock, crush, herd, rabble [➡ GROUPS OF PEOPLE; 935] **2** *n* (*informal*) **populace**, plebs, hoi polloi, rabble, the masses, rank and file, proletariat, the great unwashed [➡ CLASS STATUS; 889] *Opposite:* elite **3** *type of* **flock** [➡ GROUPS OF

BIRDS; 1007] **4** *type of* **herd** [➡ GROUPS OF ANIMALS; 993] **5** *v* **besiege**, descend on, crowd around, surround, swarm around, encircle, converge [➡ GET CLOSER TOGETHER; 310] *Opposite:* avoid **6** *v* **attack**, jostle, pester, set upon, set about, assail [➡ PHYSICAL ATTACK AND PUNISHMENT; 415] *Opposite:* defend

mobcap *type of* **headgear** [➡ ACCESSORIES, MILLINERY, AND LINGERIE; 867]

mobile **1** *adj* **movable**, portable, transportable, itinerant, peripatetic, traveling, ambulatory, rootless, nomadic [➡ TRANSPORTATION, TRANSPORTERS, AND CARGOS; 322] *Opposite:* fixed **2** *adj* **active**, flexible, limber, supple, agile, energetic [➡ FIT AND STRONG; 736] *Opposite:* immobile **3** *adj* **expressive**, changing, changeable, lively, communicative, eloquent [➡ FACIAL EXPRESSIONS AND BLUSHING; 651] *Opposite:* inexpressive **4** *adj* **upwardly mobile**, successful, ambitious, aspiring, rising [➡ SUCCESSFUL AND PROMISING; 81] *Opposite:* unambitious

mobile home **1** *type of* **house** [➡ RESIDENTIAL BUILDINGS; 1078] **2** *type of* **leisure vehicle** [➡ VEHICLES; 1145]

mobility **1** *n* **flexibility**, freedom of movement, agility, suppleness, movement, motion, kinesis [➡ SELF-PROPULSION; 304] *Opposite:* stasis **2** *n* **progress**, social mobility, upward mobility, success, promotion, social climbing [➡ SUCCESS; 82]

mobilization *n* **enlistment**, deployment, armament, organization, utilization, conscription, recruitment, enrollment, draft [➡ BEGINNINGS; 53] *Opposite:* demobilization

mobilize *v* **rally**, assemble, muster, drum up, gather together, marshal, activate, call up, organize, summon, call to arms [➡ GET CLOSER TOGETHER; 310] *Opposite:* demobilize

mobster (*informal*) *n* **gangster**, hoodlum, thug, tough, racketeer, crook (*informal*), heavy (*slang*) [➡ VILLAINS AND THUGS; 947]

moccasin *type of* **shoe** [➡ FOOTWEAR; 871]

mocha **1** *type of* **coffee** [➡ DRINKS; 1187] **2** *type of* **brown** [➡ COLORS; 1224]

mochaccino *type of* **coffee** [➡ DRINKS; 1187]

mock **1** *v* **ridicule**, tease, make fun of, laugh at, poke fun at, scorn, scoff at, deride, taunt, jeer at, burlesque, lampoon, send up (*informal*) [➡ JOKES AND TEASING; 674] *Opposite:* praise **2** *v* **mimic**, imitate, parody, ape, simulate, caricature, satirize [➡ PRETEND AND MIMIC; 60] **3** *adj* **fake**, pretend, simulated, imitation, artificial, ersatz, pseudo, faux [➡ FALSE AND UNREAL; 173] *Opposite:* genuine

---

See Compare and Contrast at **ridicule**.

---

mocker *n* **ridiculer**, derider, scorner, scoffer, caricaturist, satirist, lampooner [➡ JOKERS AND TEASES; 675]

mockery **1** *n* **ridicule**, scorn, derision, contempt, disdain, sarcasm, jeering [➡ JOKES AND TEASING; 674] *Opposite:* respect **2** *n* **travesty**, charade, farce, sham, caricature, parody, lampoon, burlesque [➡ DECEPTION AND LIES; 660] *Opposite:* exemplar (*literary*)

mocking *adj* **scornful**, derisive, contemptuous, disdainful, sardonic, sarcastic, disrespectful, insulting, jeering [➡ MOCKING AND DISMISSIVE; 636] *Opposite:* respectful

mockingbird *type of* **common bird** [➡ BIRDS; 997]

mock turtle *type of* **sweater** [➡ GARMENTS AND OUTFITS; 865]

mock-up *n* **replica**, copy, model, sample, dummy, facsimile, likeness, prototype, simulation, test case, beta version [➡ REPRESENTATIONS AND GENERAL EXAMPLES; 65]

modal *type of* **grammatical term** [➡ ASPECTS OF LANGUAGE; 682]

modal jazz *type of* **jazz music** [➡ MUSIC, SONGS, AND SINGING; 907]

mode *n* **form**, style, manner, method, means, approach, type, sort, way, kind, genre, fashion, course, rule [➡ VARIETIES, TYPES, AND KINDS; 145]

model **1** *n* **replica**, mock-up, representation, copy, reproduction, facsimile, prototype, simulation, dummy [➡ REPRESENTATIONS AND GENERAL EXAMPLES; 65] **2** *n* **type**, sort, style, kind, version, mode, genre, brand [➡ VARIETIES, TYPES, AND KINDS; 145] **3** *n* **example**, paradigm, pattern, standard, prototype, template, exemplar (*literary*) [➡ PERFECT EXAMPLES AND EMBODIMENTS; 67] **4** *v* **demonstrate**, show, exhibit, display, show off [➡ CAUSE TO APPEAR; 5] **5** *v* **sculpt**, mold, form, shape, fashion, develop, pattern, cast [➡ CRAFTS AND CARVING; 355] **6** *adj* **perfect**, classical, prototypical, typical, archetypal, classic, exemplary, ideal, consummate, standard, representative [➡ REPRESENTATIVE; 66] *Opposite*: atypical

modem **1** *type of* **hardware** [➡ COMPUTERS AND COMPUTING; 1127] **2** *type of* **telecommunications equipment** [➡ TELECOMMUNICATIONS; 1130]

moderate **1** *adj* **reasonable**, modest, sensible, restrained, judicious, fair, temperate, enough, adequate, sufficient, relative, mild, rational, measured [➡ ENOUGH AND SUFFICIENT; 131] *Opposite*: excessive **2** *adj* **average**, medium, normal, balanced, middling, ordinary, adequate, modest [➡ ORDINARINESS; 244] *Opposite*: extraordinary **3** *v* **curb**, control, tone down, play down, diminish, restrain, regulate, temper, lessen, subdue, tame [➡ CHANGE OF INTENSITY: LESS; 395] *Opposite*: intensify **4** *v* **arbitrate**, mediate, referee, facilitate, umpire, orchestrate, regulate, direct, manage, conduct [➡ AVOID, PREVENT, LIMIT, AND CONTROL; 277]

moderately *adv* **reasonably**, rather, somewhat, fairly, comparatively, quite [➡ TO A CERTAIN EXTENT; 136] *Opposite*: excessively

moderation *n* **restraint**, control, self-control, temperance, fairness, balance, reasonableness, equability [➡ GOOD MANNERS AND SOCIAL SKILLS; 520] *Opposite*: excess

moderato *type of* **musical term** [➡ MUSICAL TERMS; 912]

moderator *n* **mediator**, go-between, arbiter, arbitrator, diplomat, referee, broker, representative, intermediary, agent, facilitator [➡ ADVISERS, JUDGES, AND ARBITERS; 971]

modern **1** *adj* **contemporary**, current, up-to-date, up-to-the-minute, recent, new, present, fresh, prevailing, modern-day [➡ NEW, MODERN; 166] *Opposite*: old-fashioned **2** *adj* **state-of-the-art**, latest, cutting-edge, leading-edge, novel, innovative [➡ NEW, MODERN; 166] *Opposite*: outdated **3** *adj* **progressive**, enlightened, forward-looking, avant-garde, advanced, novel [➡ THE NATURE OF IDEAS; 771] *Opposite*: traditional

See Compare and Contrast at **new.**

modern-day *adj* **contemporary**, modern, current, recent, present-day, today's, new [➡ PRESENT; 85] *Opposite*: past

moderne *type of* **20th-century architecture** [➡ BUILDING AND ARCHITECTURE; 1076]

modernism **1** *n* **innovation**, innovativeness, novelty, originality, modernization, radicalism, progress, avant-gardism [➡ NEW, MODERN; 166] *Opposite*: traditionalism **2** *type of* **20th-century art movement** [➡ ARTISTIC MOVEMENTS AND STYLES; 899]

modernist *type of* **20th-century architecture** [➡ BUILDING AND ARCHITECTURE; 1076]

modernistic *adj* **ultramodern**, modern, radical, futuristic, avant-garde, high-tech, state-of-the-art [➡ NEW, MODERN; 166] *Opposite*: traditional

modernity *n* **modernism**, innovation, innovativeness, freshness, newness, stylishness, avant-gardism, contemporaneousness, trendiness (*informal*) [➡ NEW, MODERN; 166] *Opposite*: traditionalism

modernization *n* **transformation**, upgrading, innovation, reconstruction, renewal, rejuvenation, renovation, rebuilding, development [➡ IMPROVE SOMETHING; 374]

modernize *v* **update**, renovate, streamline, revolutionize, reform, improve, remodel, redevelop, upgrade, transform [➡ IMPROVE SOMETHING; 374]

modernizer *n* **innovator**, pacesetter, trendsetter, new broom, visionary, avant-gardist, reformer [➡ PHILOSOPHICAL AND POLITICAL THINKERS; 781]

modern pentathlon *type of* **track and field** [➡ HOBBIES, GAMES, AND SPORTS; 875]

modest **1** *adj* **self-effacing**, humble, reserved, discreet, unpretentious, unassuming [➡ NATURALNESS; 497] *Opposite*: arrogant **2** *adj* **shy**, meek, diffident, quiet, reserved, unsure, uncertain, retiring, unassertive [➡ RETICENT AND UNFORTHCOMING; 631] *Opposite*: overbearing **3** *adj* **unexceptional**, ordinary, humble, unpretentious, plain, simple, discreet [➡ ORDINARINESS; 244] *Opposite*: showy **4** *adj* **moderate**, reasonable, acceptable, small, low, token, fair [➡ ENOUGH AND SUFFICIENT; 131] *Opposite*: excessive

modestly **1** *adv* **humbly**, diffidently, discreetly, unassumingly, self-effacingly, unpretentiously, unassertively [➡ RETICENT AND UNFORTHCOMING; 631] *Opposite*: arrogantly **2** *adv* **moderately**, reasonably, acceptably, fairly [➡ TO A CERTAIN EXTENT; 136] *Opposite*: excessively

modesty *n* **humility**, reserve, reticence, diffidence, shyness, unpretentiousness, decorum, restraint, simplicity, discretion [➡ GOOD MANNERS AND SOCIAL SKILLS; 520] *Opposite*: arrogance

modicum *n* **little**, bit, degree, scrap, ounce, measure, mite, drop, smidgen (*informal*) [➡ FEW, LITTLE, SMALL AMOUNT; 120]

modification *n* **change**, alteration, adjustment, amendment, reform, revision, reformation, adaptation, adaption, conversion, variation [➡ CHANGE; 372]

modified *adj* **adapted**, altered, changed, improved, revised, reformed, adjusted, amended [➡ CHANGE; 372] *Opposite*: unmodified

modifier *type of* **word class** [➡ ASPECTS OF LANGUAGE; 682]

modify **1** *v* **alter**, change, adapt, adjust, amend, vary, transform, revise, refashion, rework [➡ CHANGE; 372] *Opposite*: maintain **2** *v* **lessen**, reduce, restrain, moderate, curb, control, tone down, play down, temper, modulate, lower, restrict, limit [➡ CHANGE OF INTENSITY: LESS; 395] *Opposite:* intensify

See Compare and Contrast at **change**.

modish *adj* **fashionable**, stylish, in, chic, up-to-the-minute, in vogue, voguish, current, faddish, smart, trendy (*informal*), classy (*informal*), à la mode (*dated*) [➡ NEW, MODERN; 166] *Opposite:* unfashionable

modular *adj* **linked**, flexible, integrated, prefabricated, segmental, sectional [➡ RECIPROCITY AND INTERDEPENDENCE; 147]

modulate 1 *v* **adjust**, alter, amend, vary, modify, change, adapt, revise, temper, shift [➡ CHANGE; 372] 2 *v* **moderate**, curb, control, tone down, play down, temper, lessen, restrain, modify, reduce, regulate, lower [➡ CHANGE OF INTENSITY: LESS; 395] *Opposite:* intensify

modulation 1 *n* **inflection**, intonation, accent, lilt, cadence [➡ THE SPOKEN WORD; 671] *Opposite:* flatness 2 *n* **adjustment**, change, alteration, swing, variation, tempering [➡ CHANGE; 372]

module *n* **unit**, component, part, element, section, segment, building block [➡ AREA AND RANGE; 111]

modus *n* [➡ WAYS OF DOING THINGS; 294]

modus operandi *n* **method**, formula, technique, way, protocol, procedure, approach, plan, practice, means [➡ WAYS OF DOING THINGS; 294]

modus vivendi 1 *n* **compromise**, arrangement, settlement, deal, bargain, truce, agreement [➡ WAYS OF DOING THINGS; 294] 2 *n* **practice**, way of life, lifestyle, standard of living, habit, routine, pattern, wont (*formal*) [➡ LIFESTYLE; 881]

mogul *n* **tycoon**, entrepreneur, magnate, industrialist, dynast, power, czar, big shot (*informal*), kingpin (*informal*) [➡ RICH PEOPLE; 895]

mohair *type of* **fabric from animals** [➡ FABRICS; 1132]

mohawk *type of* **hairstyle** [➡ HAIRSTYLES AND HAIRPIECES; 488]

moist *adj* **damp**, wet, humid, soggy, clammy [➡ MOIST; 1241] *Opposite:* dry

See Compare and Contrast at **wet**.

moisten *v* **dampen**, wet, moisturize, humidify, sprinkle, spray, irrigate [➡ SOFTEN, LIQUEFY, AND DAMPEN; 388] *Opposite:* dry

moistness *n* **dampness**, humidity, wetness, clamminess, sogginess, mugginess, dankness [➡ MOIST; 1241] *Opposite:* aridity

moisture *n* **damp**, dampness, wetness, humidity, moistness, vapor [➡ MOIST; 1241] *Opposite:* dryness

moisturize 1 *v* **cream**, nourish, soothe, oil, condition, treat, massage, cleanse [➡ CLEAN AND POLISH; 403] *Opposite:* dry 2 *v* **moisten**, dampen, wet, humidify, spray, sprinkle, irrigate [➡ SOFTEN, LIQUEFY, AND DAMPEN; 388]

moisturizer *n* **cold cream**, cream, lotion, conditioner, night cream [➡ MAKEUP AND BEAUTY PRODUCTS; 490]

molar *type of* **tooth** [➡ THE MOUTH; 702]

molasses *n* **blackstrap molasses**, syrup, treacle (*UK*) [➡ SUGAR AND PRESERVES; 1184]

mold 1 *n* **container**, cast, form, die, shape, dish, bowl, tin (*UK*) [➡ CONTAINERS, RECEPTACLES, AND PACKAGING; 1245] 2 *n* **impression**, cast, plaster cast, molding, prototype, form, shape [➡ PERFECT EXAMPLES AND EMBODIMENTS; 67] 3 *n* **frame**, pattern, template, stencil, outline, guide, matrix, shell, die [➡ EXTREMITIES OF PHYSICAL OBJECTS; 1250] 4 *n* **character**, type, variety, kind, shape, line, contour, conformation [➡ VARIETIES, TYPES, AND KINDS; 145] 5 *n* **mildew**, fungus, growth, decay, rot, blight, rust [➡ UNPLEASANT, DIRTY, AND TOXIC SUBSTANCES; 1268] 6 *type of* **fungus** [➡ MICROORGANISMS, FUNGI, AND ALGAE; 1023] 7 *v* **shape**, make, fashion, cast, style, form, create, sculpt, model, construct, forge [➡ MANUFACTURE; 349] 8 *v* **influence**, affect, change, shape, fashion, forge, create, modify, guide, form [➡ CHANGE; 372] 9 *v* **cling**, hug, follow, fit, press, wrap, encase [➡ EXIST IN CLOSE PROXIMITY; 21]

molder *v* **rot**, gather dust, disintegrate, crumble, decay, mildew, fester, decompose, break down, perish (*UK*) [➡ GO BAD AND CORRODE; 390]

moldering *adj* [➡ DECAYING OR INFESTED; 1236]

moldiness *n* **decay**, mustiness, mildew, rottenness, disintegration, putrefaction, state of decay [➡ DECAYING OR INFESTED; 1236]

molding *n* **decoration**, detail, cornice, dado, beading, edging, ceiling rose [➡ ORNAMENTS AND DECORATIONS; 1248]

moldy 1 *adj* **fungal**, decaying, decayed, rotting, rotten, growing, sprouting, mildewed, festering [➡ DECAYING OR INFESTED; 1236] *Opposite:* fresh 2 *adj* **stale**, neglected, dingy, seedy, shabby, crumbling, dirty, fusty, old [➡ DIRTY; 1235] *Opposite:* fresh

mole 1 *n* **spy**, infiltrator, secret agent, undercover agent, plant [➡ INTERFERING PEOPLE AND TATTLETALES; 950] 2 *type of* **rodent** [➡ RODENTS; 989]

molecular biology *type of* **bioscience** [➡ BIOLOGICAL SCIENCES; 1037]

molecule *n* **particle**, bit, iota, speck, shred, smidgen (*informal*) [➡ SMALL PIECES; 129]

moleskin *type of* **fabric from plants** [➡ FABRICS; 1132]

molest 1 *v* **assault**, mistreat, abuse, attack, feel up (*informal*) [➡ PHYSICAL ATTACK AND PUNISHMENT; 415] 2 *v* **bother**, pester, annoy, torment, harass, tease, disturb, harry, trouble, bug (*informal*) [➡ ANGER AND ANNOY; 569]

mollify *v* **pacify**, calm, placate, appease, calm down, soothe, moderate, quell, still [➡ SOOTHE AND CALM; 573] *Opposite:* enrage

mollusk 1 *type of* **aquatic invertebrate** [➡ AQUATIC INVERTEBRATES; 1022] 2 *type of* **land invertebrate** [➡ LAND INVERTEBRATES; 1021]

mollycoddle *v* **pamper**, fuss over, spoil, overprotect, cosset, indulge, humor, pander to, overindulge, baby, pet [➡ TAKE CARE OF AND SPOIL; 300]

moloch *type of* **reptile** [➡ REPTILES; 994]

Molotov cocktail *type of* **explosive weapon** [➡ EXPLOSIVES; 1155]

molt *v* **shed**, cast, peel, skin, slough, scale, flake [➡ LOSE AND FORFEIT; 447] *Opposite:* grow

molten *adj* **melted**, liquefied, liquid, fluid, heated, flowing, smelted, igneous, red-hot [➡ FLUID AND NONSOLID; 1213] *Opposite*: solid

molybdenum *type of* **metal** [➡ METALS; 1276]

mom (*informal*) *type of* **older relative** [➡ OLDER GENERATION RELATIVES; 959]

mom-and-pop store *type of* **retail outlet** [➡ RETAIL OUTLETS; 1083]

moment 1 *n* **instant**, second, minute, split second, flash, twinkling, trice, jiffy (*informal*) [➡ SHORT PERIODS OF TIME; 93] *Opposite*: age 2 *n* (*formal*) **importance**, significance, weight, import, substance, consequence (*formal*) [➡ IMPORTANCE AND SIGNIFICANCE; 192]

momentarily 1 *adv* **for a moment**, briefly, temporarily, fleetingly, transitorily, quickly [➡ HAPPENING QUICKLY; 104] 2 *adv* **soon**, right away, in a moment, before long, any time now, in next to no time, presently (*formal or literary*) [➡ FUTURE; 86]

momentariness *n* [➡ SPEED; 102]

momentary *adj* **brief**, fleeting, passing, temporary, transitory, short-lived, quick, short, transient, ephemeral [➡ HAPPENING QUICKLY; 104] *Opposite*: interminable

momentous *adj* **important**, significant, historic, earth-shattering, crucial, vital, meaningful, big, considerable, critical, decisive, fateful [➡ IMPORTANT; 194] *Opposite*: insignificant

momentousness *n* [➡ IMPORTANCE AND SIGNIFICANCE; 192]

momentum *n* **impetus**, thrust, energy, force, drive, motion, push [➡ ENERGY; 1161] *Opposite*: brake

momma *type of* **older relative** (*informal*) [➡ OLDER GENERATION RELATIVES; 959]

mommy *type of* **older relative** (*informal*) [➡ OLDER GENERATION RELATIVES; 959]

monarch *n* **ruler**, sovereign, crowned head, emperor, king, queen, tsar, imperator [➡ RULERS AND ARISTOCRACY; 823] *Opposite*: subject

monarch butterfly *type of* **butterfly** [➡ MOTHS AND BUTTERFLIES; 1015]

monarchism *n* **royalism**, imperialism, elitism, anti-republicanism, tsarism, traditionalism, absolutism, divine right [➡ STYLES AND SYSTEMS OF GOVERNMENT; 806] *Opposite*: republicanism

monarchist *n* **royalist**, loyalist, counterrevolutionary, traditionalist, imperialist, old guard [➡ DEVOTEES AND ADDICTED PEOPLE; 556] *Opposite*: revolutionary

monarchy *n* **realm**, kingdom, dominion, domain, empire, demesne (*formal*) [➡ REALMS AND RULES; 824] *Opposite*: republic

monastery *n* **religious foundation**, religious community, cloister, friary, abbey, priory, hermitage, convent, nunnery [➡ RELIGIOUS BUILDINGS; 1085]

monastic *adj* **austere**, reclusive, simple, Spartan, frugal, ascetic, hermetic, monkish, cloistral [➡ SELF-DENIAL; 882]

monetary *adj* **financial**, fiscal, economic, monetarist, pecuniary, budgetary, regulatory [➡ FINANCE AND ECONOMICS; 796]

money 1 *n* **cash**, currency, ready money, ready cash, coins, coinage, change, bucks (*informal*), greenbacks (*slang*), dough (*slang*), bread (*dated slang*) [➡ MONEY; 797] 2 *n* **capital**, funds, riches, means, wherewithal, wealth, income, earnings, wages, stock, equities, assets, affluence, big bucks (*slang*) [➡ FINANCIAL ASSETS; 462]

moneybags (*informal*) *n* **millionaire**, multimillionaire, billionaire, tycoon, mogul, bankroller (*informal*), fat cat (*slang*) [➡ RICH PEOPLE; 895]

money box *n* **piggy bank**, cash box, collecting box, safe [➡ CONTAINERS, RECEPTACLES, AND PACKAGING; 1245]

moneyed *adj* **wealthy**, rich, affluent, prosperous, comfortable, well-off, successful, well-heeled (*informal*), well-fixed (*informal*) [➡ WEALTH AND WEALTHY; 891]

moneygrubbing *adj* [➡ GRASPING AND FINANCIALLY MEAN; 519]

moneylender *n* **lender**, usurer, financier, banker, loan shark, pawnbroker, bankroller (*informal*) [➡ PEOPLE INVOLVED IN FINANCE; 804]

moneymaker 1 *n* **tycoon**, speculator, magnate, investor, mogul, millionaire, multimillionaire, billionaire [➡ RICH PEOPLE; 895] 2 *n* **hit**, success, gold mine, profit center, cash cow (*slang*) [➡ ADVANTAGES; 212]

moneymaking *adj* **profitable**, commercial, economic, fruitful, lucrative, worthwhile, helpful, gainful, beneficial, productive, well-paying, remunerative [➡ SUCCESSFUL AND PROMISING; 81]

money spider *type of* **arachnid** [➡ ARACHNIDS; 1018]

mongoose *type of* **small mammal** [➡ SMALL MAMMALS; 990]

mongrel *n* **dog**, cur, hound, crossbreed, pye-dog, pooch (*informal*), mutt (*slang*) [➡ DOGS; 980] *Opposite*: pedigree

moniker (*slang*) *n* **name**, first name, signature, nickname, given name, Christian name, surname, initials, sobriquet, handle (*slang*), cognomen (*formal*), appellation (*formal*) [➡ NAME AND DESCRIBE; 665]

monitor 1 *n* **screen**, display, video display unit, television set, closed-circuit television, CCTV, VDU (*UK*) [➡ COMPUTERS AND COMPUTING; 1127] 2 *n* **observer**, supervisor, overseer, inspector, invigilator, duty officer, proctor, disciplinarian [➡ ADVISERS, JUDGES, AND ARBITERS; 971] 3 *v* **observe**, keep an eye on, supervise, scrutinize, examine, check, watch, censor [➡ EXAMINE AND ASSESS; 753]

monitor lizard *type of* **reptile** [➡ REPTILES; 994]

monk *n* **holy man**, religious, monastic, friar, abbot, prior, brother, hermit [➡ RELIGIOUS PEOPLE; 778]

monkey 1 *n* (*informal*) **mischief**, rogue, rascal (*humorous*), scamp (*informal*), scalawag (*dated informal*) [➡ MISCHIEVOUS OR BADLY BEHAVED CHILD; 946] 2 *n* (*informal*) **fool**, dupe, laughingstock, ass, butt, buffoon, figure of fun (*UK*) [➡ VICTIMS OF DECEIT; 662] 3 *type of* **primate** [➡ PRIMATES; 988]

monkey around *v* **fool around**, joke, play the fool, clown around, lark, horse around, mess around (*informal*) [➡ JOKES AND TEASING; 674]

monkey business (*informal*) *n* tricks, mischief, trouble, pranks, monkeyshines, high jinks (*informal*), tomfoolery (*informal*), shenanigans (*informal*) [➡ BAD BEHAVIOR OR ACTIONS; 254]

monkey puzzle *type of* **evergreen tree** [➡ EVERGREEN AND CONIFEROUS TREES; 1029]

monkey with *v* tamper, meddle, interfere, fiddle, tinker, mess, mess around (*informal*) [➡ CONTACT: TOUCH; 412]

monkfish *type of* **ocean fish** [➡ OCEAN FISH; 1009]

monkish *adj* **reclusive**, austere, withdrawn, cloistered, simple, ascetic, self-denying [➡ SOLITARINESS; 941] *Opposite*: worldly

mono 1 *n* **monophonic sound reproduction**, monophonic sound, monaural sound, audio [➡ ACOUSTICS; 1138] *Opposite*: stereo **2** *adj* **monophonic**, monaural, audio, one-track, simple [➡ ACOUSTICS; 1138] *Opposite*: stereo

Monoceros *type of* **constellation** [➡ HEAVENLY BODIES; 1061]

monochromatic 1 *adj* **one-color**, homochromous, unicolor, homochromatic, shaded, self-colored, monochrome, black-and-white, monotone, tinted [➡ DESCRIBING COLORS; 1226] **2** *adj* **dull**, indistinct, undistinctive, neutral, uniform, boring, insipid, monotonous, unvarying [➡ BORING AND UNINTERESTING; 234] *Opposite*: colorful

monochrome 1 *adj* **unicolor**, self-colored, homochromous, homochromatic, monochromatic, shaded [➡ DESCRIBING COLORS; 1226] **2** *adj* **neutral**, colorless, dull, undistinctive, indeterminate, toneless, uniform, monotonous, unvarying [➡ BORING AND UNINTERESTING; 234]

monocle *n* **eyeglass**, glass, lens [➡ GLASSES AND SPECTACLES; 1125]

monogamous *adj* **faithful**, exclusive, committed, married, steady, one-on-one [➡ RELATIONSHIP TO ANOTHER; 973]

monogamy *n* **exclusivity**, fidelity, commitment, marriage, coupledom, stability [➡ RELATIONSHIP TO ANOTHER; 973]

monogram 1 *n* **initials**, signet, logo, seal, stamp, symbol, design, emblem [➡ ORNAMENTS AND DECORATIONS; 1248] **2** *v* **mark**, initial, sign, seal, identify, brand, stamp, decorate [➡ CREATE IMAGES; 356]

monograph *n* **book**, article, paper, essay, thesis, profile, critique [➡ BOOKS AND BOOKLETS; 590]

monolith *n* **standing stone**, menhir, megalith, sarsen, stone, monument, pillar, column, stele [➡ ANCIENT MANMADE STRUCTURES; 1089]

monolithic *adj* **colossal**, monumental, massive, uniform, immovable, solid, huge, gigantic [➡ LARGE; 1193]

monologue 1 *n* **soliloquy**, speech, prologue, epilogue, aside, solo, oration, address, lecture [➡ THE SPOKEN WORD; 671] *Opposite*: dialogue **2** *n* **harangue**, rant, speech, running commentary, lecture [➡ ONE-WAY COMMUNICATION; 49] *Opposite*: conversation

monophonic *adj* [➡ ACOUSTICS; 1138]

monoplane *type of* **civil aircraft** [➡ AIRCRAFT; 1148]

monopolistic *adj* **anticompetitive**, unchallenged, controlling, autocratic, exploitative, dominant [➡ BOSSY AND OVERBEARING; 516] *Opposite*: competitive

monopolization *n* **control**, domination, appropriation, takeover, expropriation, exploitation, seizure [➡ MISUSE AND ABUSE; 471] *Opposite*: cooperation

monopolize *v* **control**, dominate, take over, corner, exploit, cartelize, hog (*informal*) [➡ BE IN CHARGE; 270] *Opposite*: share

monopoly *n* **control**, domination, cartel, trust, corner [➡ BUSINESS ACTIVITIES AND PHENOMENA; 794]

monorail *type of* **railroad** [➡ RAILROADS; 1107]

monosyllabic *adj* **uncommunicative**, curt, gruff, brief, short, terse, abrupt, laconic [➡ RETICENT AND UNFORTHCOMING; 631] *Opposite*: verbose

monosyllable *n* **word**, syllable, grunt, squeak [➡ ASPECTS OF LANGUAGE; 682]

monotheism *n* **theism**, deism [➡ RELIGIOUS CONCEPTS; 776] *Opposite*: polytheism

monotone *n* **drone**, whine, chant, intonation, mutter [➡ LOUD, HIGH, OR UNPLEASANT SOUNDS; 1266]

monotonous *adj* **dull**, repetitious, uninteresting, droning, repetitive, boring, tedious, wearisome, unvaried, colorless, dreary, pedestrian [➡ BORING AND UNINTERESTING; 234] *Opposite*: varied

See Compare and Contrast at **boring**.

monotony 1 *n* **tedium**, dullness, wearisomeness, boredom, flatness, dreariness, deadliness (*informal*) [➡ BORING AND UNINTERESTING; 234] *Opposite*: excitement **2** *n* **uniformity**, repetitiousness, sameness, repetitiveness, predictability [➡ SAMENESS; 150] *Opposite*: variety

monsoon 1 *n* **rainy season**, wet season, rains [➡ CLOUDY AND RAINY WEATHER; 1052] **2** *type of* **wind** [➡ WINDY AND STORMY WEATHER; 1053]

monster 1 *n* **fiend**, ogre, beast, brute [➡ VILLAINS AND THUGS; 947] **2** *n* **giant**, behemoth, leviathan, whopper (*informal*), biggie (*informal*) [➡ BIG THINGS; 1194] **3** *adj* **huge**, enormous, giant, monstrous, gigantic, massive, mammoth, colossal, prodigious [➡ LARGE; 1193] *Opposite*: small

monstrosity *n* **eyesore**, blot on the landscape, atrocity, sight, horror, miscreation [➡ UGLINESS AND UNATTRACTIVENESS; 233]

monstrous 1 *adj* **atrocious**, outrageous, horrific, immoral, evil, shocking, scandalous, lurid, grisly, unfair [➡ UNACCEPTABLE AND UNFORGIVABLE; 225] **2** *adj* **huge**, enormous, giant, monster, gigantic, massive, colossal, mammoth, prodigious [➡ LARGE; 1193] *Opposite*: small **3** *adj* **hideous**, grotesque, gruesome, ugly, horrible, horrid, ghastly [➡ UGLINESS AND UNATTRACTIVENESS; 233] *Opposite*: lovely

monstrously *adv* **preposterously**, shockingly, offensively, unbelievably, prodigiously, horribly, enormously, dreadfully, hugely [➡ TO A GREAT EXTENT; 132] *Opposite*: unexceptionally

montage *n* **mosaic**, tableau, medley, mixture, pastiche, hodgepodge, assortment, mishmash, collage [➡ COLLECTIONS AND MIXTURES OF THINGS; 1244]

Monterey Jack *type of* **hard cheese** [➡ DAIRY PRODUCTS AND CHEESES; 1183]

month *type of* **time period** [➡ TIMES OF YEAR; 88]

monthly 1 *adj* **regular**, periodic, frequent, once-a-month, scheduled, continuing, prearranged, recurrent, cyclic [➡ FREQUENT AND OFTEN; 107] *Opposite:* occasional 2 *adj* **month-long**, 30-day, period, season, medium-term [➡ TIMES OF YEAR; 88] 3 *adv* **regularly**, once a month, periodically, frequently, at monthly intervals, every month, by the month, cyclically [➡ FREQUENT AND OFTEN; 107] *Opposite:* irregularly 4 *n* **magazine**, publication, periodical, journal, bulletin, review [➡ NEWS-PAPERS AND MAGAZINES; 605]

monument 1 *n* **memorial**, testimonial, testament, tribute [➡ MONUMENTS; 1092] 2 *n* **headstone**, marker, tombstone, gravestone [➡ BURIAL AND PREPARATION FOR BURIAL; 929]

monumental 1 *adj* **colossal**, epic, immense, massive, enormous, huge, mammoth, vast, titanic, prodigious [➡ LARGE; 1193] *Opposite:* small 2 *adj* **historic**, classic, significant, important, epic, towering, overwhelming [➡ IMPORTANT; 194] *Opposite:* minor

monumentally *adv* **hugely**, overwhelmingly, intensely, prodigiously, enormously, extremely, massively (*informal*) [➡ TO A GREAT EXTENT; 132] *Opposite:* moderately

moo *type of* **animal sound** [➡ SOUNDS MADE BY ANIMALS; 1261]

mooch 1 *v* (*slang*) **wander**, amble, meander, roam, ramble, saunter, walk, drift, range, knock around (*informal*), mosey (*informal*) [➡ MOVE SLOWLY; 314] 2 *v* (*informal*) **wheedle**, sponge, beg, cadge (*informal*), scrounge (*informal*), freeload (*informal*) [➡ OBTAIN POSSESSION BY PERSUASION; 457] 3 *v* (*slang*) **steal**, take, rob, pilfer, make away with, swipe (*informal*) [➡ STEAL AND ROB; 426] 4 *v* (*slang*) **sneak**, steal, prowl, lurk, stalk, loiter [➡ LACK OF ACTIVITY OR MOTION; 342]

moocher (*informal*) *n* **scrounger**, taker, cadger (*informal*), freeloader (*informal*), sponger (*informal*) [➡ LAZY OR UNSUCCESSFUL PEOPLE; 948]

mood 1 *n* **frame of mind**, disposition, temper, attitude, temperament, vein, humor [➡ FEELINGS; 531] 2 *n* **atmosphere**, feel, ambiance, air, feeling, aura, tone, vibes (*slang*) [➡ APPEARANCE AND ATMOSPHERE; 1237] 3 *n* **temper**, bad temper, sulk, the doldrums, anger, state (*informal*) [➡ IRRITATION AND ANGER; 541]

moodily *adv* **sulkily**, sullenly, glumly, irritably, grumpily, morosely [➡ DIFFICULT TO PLEASE; 515] *Opposite:* cheerily

moodiness *n* **sulkiness**, changeableness, sullenness, grumpiness, glumness, irritability [➡ DIFFICULT TO PLEASE; 515] *Opposite:* cheeriness

moody *adj* **temperamental**, morose, sulky, sullen, glum, irritable, short-tempered, grumpy, unstable [➡ DIFFICULT TO PLEASE; 515] *Opposite:* predictable

moon 1 *type of* **heavenly body** [➡ HEAVENLY BODIES; 1061] 2 *v* **wander**, drift, meander, amble, dawdle, mosey (*informal*), mooch (*slang*) [➡ MOVE SLOWLY; 314] 3 *v* (*literary or humorous*) **fantasize**, dream, daydream, languish, pine, long, yearn [➡ DREAM, IMAGINE, AND FANTASIZE; 749]

moonbeam *n* **ray**, moonlight, shaft of light, moonshine, glint, glimmer, shimmer, beam, gleam [➡ LIGHT; 1164] *Opposite:* sunbeam

moonlight (*informal*) *v* **do work on the side**, do two jobs, supplement your income, have a second job, have a night job, make some pocket money, work double, work illegally, burn the midnight oil [➡ WORK-RELATED ACTIVITIES; 834]

moonscape *n* **wasteland**, desert, wilderness, barren land, waste, dust bowl [➡ DESERTS, PLAINS, AND MOORLAND; 1045]

moonshine 1 *n* (*informal*) **poteen**, bootleg alcohol, homebrew, white lightning, mountain dew (*informal*), hooch (*slang*), firewater (*dated slang*) [➡ DRINKS; 1187] 2 *n* **nonsense**, fantasy, silliness, fiction, gibberish, drivel, balderdash, corn (*informal*) [➡ MEANINGLESS SPEECH OR WRITING; 676]

moonshot *n* **rocket launch**, launch, lunar expedition, lunar exploration, mission, space mission, liftoff [➡ SPACE TRAVEL AND EXPLORATION; 1062]

moonstone *type of* **gemstone** [➡ PRECIOUS STONES; 1278]

moonstruck (*informal humorous*) *adj* **dazed**, confused, irrational, distracted, in a daze, in another world, dreamy [➡ CONFUSION, ANXIETY, AND WORRY; 540] *Opposite:* alert

moor 1 *n* **heath**, moorland, common, upland, hill, fell (*UK*) [➡ DESERTS, PLAINS, AND MOORLAND; 1045] 2 *v* **tie**, fix, secure, chain, attach, fasten, cable, anchor [➡ FASTEN, LINK, AND JOIN; 408] *Opposite:* untie

moorhen *type of* **freshwater bird** [➡ FRESHWATER BIRDS; 1000]

mooring *n* **anchorage**, berth, tie-up, bay, reserved space, parking bay, parking space [➡ WATERWAYS AND SEAWAYS; 1108]

Moorish *type of* **pre-20th-century architecture** [➡ BUILDING AND ARCHITECTURE; 1076]

moorland *n* **heath**, moor, common, upland, hill, fell (*UK*) [➡ DESERTS, PLAINS, AND MOORLAND; 1045]

moose *type of* **deer or antelope** [➡ DEER AND ANTELOPES; 981]

moot 1 *adj* **debatable**, arguable, doubtful, controversial, unresolved, disputable, unlikely, unsettled [➡ UNCERTAIN; 175] *Opposite:* established 2 *v* **propose**, put forward, suggest, bring up, introduce, present [➡ SUGGEST, HINT, AND COMMENT; 612]

mop 1 *n* [➡ HAND TOOLS; 1119] 2 *v* **wipe**, clean, swab, dust, mop up, wipe up, clear up, wash, clean up [➡ CLEAN AND POLISH; 403]

mope *v* **brood**, languish, pine, sulk, pout, despond (*archaic or literary*) [➡ THINK AND REFLECT; 743]

moped *type of* **bike** [➡ BIKES, CARS, AND CARRIAGES; 1149]

moppet (*informal*) *n* **child**, toddler, little one, tot (*informal*), kid (*informal*), kiddie (*informal*) [➡ CHILD OR YOUTH; 945]

mop up 1 *v* **wipe up**, clear up, mop, wipe, swab, clean up, wash [➡ CLEAN AND POLISH; 403] 2 *v* (*informal*) **finish off**, dispose of, see to, deal with, polish off, complete, wrap up (*informal*) [➡ COMPLETE AN ACTION; 263]

moquette *type of* **synthetic fabric** [➡ FABRICS; 1132]

moraine *n* **glacial deposit**, debris, rubble, residue, lateral moraine, terminal moraine [➡ EROSION PRODUCTS AND SOIL; 1058]

moral 1 *adj* **ethical**, good, right, honest, decent, proper, honorable, just, principled [➡ MORALLY GOOD; 774] *Opposite:* immoral 2 *n* **message**, meaning, significance, rule, maxim, point, lesson, truism, aphorism, axiom, dictum (*formal*) [➡ MEANING; 690]

morale *n* **confidence**, self-esteem, spirits, self-confidence, assurance, optimism, drive, determination [➡ FEELINGS; 531] *Opposite*: aimlessness

moralist 1 *n* **moralizer**, censor, preacher, critic, philosopher [➡ PHILOSOPHICAL AND POLITICAL THINKERS; 781] 2 *n* **virtuous person**, upright person, puritan, saint, prude [➡ ASCETIC PEOPLE; 883]

moralistic *adj* **moralizing**, didactic, strait-laced, serious, upright, high-minded [➡ ACCUSATORY AND DISAPPROVING; 634]

morality 1 *n* **ethics**, morals, principles, standards, scruples, mores [➡ MORAL CONCEPTS; 773] 2 *n* **goodness**, decency, probity, honesty, integrity, honor, virtue, godliness, saintliness [➡ MORALLY GOOD; 774] *Opposite*: wickedness

moralize *v* **preach**, lecture, sermonize, criticize, nag, advise [➡ ACCUSE, BLAME, AND CRITICIZE; 641]

moralizing 1 *n* **lecturing**, sermonizing, instruction, remonstration, admonishment, censure, criticism [➡ CRITICISMS AND ANGRY OUTBURSTS; 50] 2 *adj* **lecturing**, critical, preaching, exhorting, hectoring, improving, sanctimonious, holier-than-thou (*informal*) [➡ ACCUSATORY AND DISAPPROVING; 634] *Opposite*: unprincipled

morals *n* **ethics**, morality, standards, scruples, principles, mores [➡ MORAL CONCEPTS; 773]

morass 1 *n* **bog**, marsh, mire, swamp, wetland [➡ WETLANDS; 1043] 2 *n* **mess**, chaos, muddle, quagmire, mire, tangle, knot, jungle [➡ DISORDER AND CHAOS; 245]

moratorium *n* **suspension**, freeze, halt, pause, cessation, standstill, delay [➡ PAUSES AND PHASES; 56]

morbid 1 *adj* **morose**, gloomy, dark, moody, melancholic, sullen, saturnine [➡ SADNESS, DISTRESS, AND DESPAIR; 539] *Opposite*: cheerful 2 *adj* **gruesome**, dark, sinister, macabre, perverse, gloomy, grisly, ominous, baleful, maleficent [➡ FRIGHTENING; 231]

morbidity *n* **illness**, injury, disease, ill health, indisposition, sickness [➡ ILL AND SICK; 740] *Opposite*: health

mordant *adj* **caustic**, astringent, acerbic, penetrating, sarcastic, biting, scathing, corrosive, harsh, sardonic, acid, acrid [➡ RUDE AND HOSTILE; 625] *Opposite*: gentle

more *adj* **additional**, extra, supplementary, added, further, new, other [➡ MORE AND EXCESS; 124] *Opposite*: less

morel *type of* **fungus** [➡ MICROORGANISMS, FUNGI, AND ALGAE; 1023]

more often than not *adv* **usually**, typically, routinely, normally, frequently, as a rule, customarily [➡ USUALLY; 108]

more or less *adv* **relatively**, comparatively, essentially, roughly, thereabouts, approximately, almost [➡ APPROXIMATELY; 135]

moreover *adv* **furthermore**, what is more, in addition, besides, also, additionally, likewise [➡ EXPRESSIONS INTRODUCING EXTRA INFORMATION; 139]

mores *n* **customs**, values, habits, traditions, patterns, behavior, ethics, morals, standards, principles, scruples [➡ WAYS OF DOING THINGS; 294]

morgue *n* **mortuary**, funeral parlor, funeral home, undertaker's (*UK*) [➡ STORES AND STORAGE BUILDINGS; 1088]

moribund 1 *adj* **dying**, failing, expiring, on your last legs, at death's door, on your deathbed [➡ DEAD AND DYING; 925] *Opposite*: well 2 *adj* **declining**, on the way out, waning, on its last legs, dilapidated, seen better days, past its best (*UK*) [➡ IN BAD REPAIR; 1234] *Opposite*: thriving

mornay *type of* **food presentation** [➡ COOKING AND FOOD PREPARATION; 353]

morning *n* **dawn**, daybreak, sunrise, break of day, first light, sunup, crack of dawn, daylight, cockcrow (*archaic or literary*) [➡ TIMES OF DAY; 87]

morning glory *type of* **climber** [➡ CLIMBERS; 1033]

morocco *type of* **leather** [➡ FABRICS; 1132]

morose *adj* **miserable**, glum, depressed, down, low, gloomy, pessimistic, sad, sullen, down in the dumps (*informal*), blue (*informal*) [➡ SADNESS, DISTRESS, AND DESPAIR; 539] *Opposite*: cheery

moroseness *n* [➡ SADNESS, DISTRESS, AND DESPAIR; 539]

morph *v* **transform**, alter, switch, convert, adapt, change, mutate, transmute, metamorphose [➡ CHANGE; 372]

morphology *n* **shape**, form, contours, formation [➡ SHAPE; 1216]

morris dancing *type of* **dance** [➡ DANCE; 903]

morsel *n* **scrap**, crumb, bit, piece, fragment, speck, ort, tidbit [➡ SMALL PIECES; 129] *Opposite*: chunk

mortadella *type of* **processed meat** [➡ TYPES AND CUTS OF MEAT; 1177]

mortal 1 *adj* **earthly**, worldly, human, corporeal, finite, temporal [➡ RELIGIOUS CONCEPTS; 776] *Opposite*: immortal 2 *adj* **deadly**, fatal, lethal, life-threatening, terminal, pestilent [➡ DEADLY; 928] 3 *adj* **extreme**, great, grave, severe, serious, excessive, inordinate, intense [➡ ABSOLUTE AND ABSOLUTELY; 133] *Opposite*: mild 4 *n* **human being**, human, person, individual, soul, man, woman, body (*informal*) [➡ PERSON; 931]

See Compare and Contrast at **deadly**.

mortality *n* **humanity**, death, transience, impermanence [➡ THE STAGES OF LIFE; 916]

mortally 1 *adv* **fatally**, lethally, incurably, terminally [➡ CRITICALLY AND SERIOUSLY; 134] 2 *adv* **extremely**, severely, seriously, greatly, very, highly, gravely [➡ TO A GREAT EXTENT; 132] *Opposite*: mildly

mortar 1 *n* [➡ BUILDING MATERIALS; 1077] 2 *type of* **gun** [➡ WEAPONS FOR SHOOTING; 1156] 3 *type of* **utensil** [➡ TABLEWARE, FLATWARE, AND KITCHENWARE; 861]

mortgage 1 *n* **loan**, bank loan, advance, secured loan, debt, home equity loan, second mortgage, bridging loan, remortgage, hypothecation [➡ ACCOUNTING, BANKING, AND BUDGETING; 799] 2 *v* **pledge**, forfeit, offer as security, use as a guarantee, pawn, hypothecate, promise, guarantee [➡ ACCOUNTING, BANKING, AND BUDGETING; 799]

mortician *n* [➡ BURIAL AND PREPARATION FOR BURIAL; 929]

mortification *n* **shame**, degradation, indignity, embarrassment, chagrin, humiliation, loss of face [➡ EMBARRASSMENT AND HUMILIATION; 542]

mortified *adj* **ashamed**, embarrassed, humiliated, horrified, offended, affronted, chagrined [➡ EMBARRASSMENT AND HUMILIATION; 542] *Opposite*: proud

mortify *v* **degrade**, humiliate, take down, embarrass, crush, confound, shame, humble, put down (*informal*), abase (*literary*) [➡ UPSET, DISTRESS, AND HUMILIATE; 567]

mortifying *adj* **humiliating**, shameful, embarrassing, degrading, chastening, appalling, ignominious [➡ EMOTIONALLY UNPLEASANT AND UPSETTING; 227] *Opposite*: uplifting

mortuary *n* **morgue**, funeral parlor, funeral home, undertaker's (*UK*) [➡ STORES AND STORAGE BUILDINGS; 1088]

mosaic *n* **medley**, assortment, mixture, variety, montage, miscellany [➡ COLLECTIONS AND MIXTURES OF THINGS; 1244]

mosasaur *type of* **dinosaur** [➡ DINOSAURS; 996]

mosey (*informal*) *v* **saunter**, wander, amble, stroll, dawdle, drift, mooch (*slang*) [➡ MOVE SLOWLY; 314] *Opposite*: rush

mosque *type of* **place of worship** [➡ RELIGIOUS BUILDINGS; 1085]

mosquito *type of* **flying insect** [➡ FLYING INSECTS; 1013]

moss *type of* **foliage plant** [➡ FOLIAGE PLANTS; 1035]

mossy *adj* **moss-covered**, moss-grown, moss-topped, overgrown, green [➡ VEGETATION; 1025]

most **1** *pron* **the majority**, nearly everyone, nearly all, a good number, a large amount, the largest part, maximum, majority [➡ MAJORITY AND MAXIMUM; 141] *Opposite*: few **2** *adv* **very**, highly, extremely, really, truly, terribly, best [➡ TO A GREAT EXTENT; 132] *Opposite*: fairly

most likely *adv* [➡ POSSIBLE AND PROBABLE; 177]

mostly **1** *adv* **for the most part**, above all, mainly, generally, on the whole, principally, largely, in general, particularly, chiefly, predominantly, primarily, greatly [➡ MAINLY AND PRIMARILY; 140] **2** *adv* **usually**, more often than not, normally, typically, commonly, generally, as a rule, more or less [➡ USUALLY; 108] *Opposite*: rarely

most of all *adv* [➡ MAINLY AND PRIMARILY; 140]

most probably *adv* [➡ POSSIBLE AND PROBABLE; 177]

mote *n* **speck**, particle, jot, iota, bit, grain, spot, piece [➡ SMALL PIECES; 129] *Opposite*: mass

motel *type of* **hotel** [➡ HOTELS, RESTAURANTS, AND CLUBS; 1082]

moth *n* [➡ INSECTS; 1012]

moth

◆ *types of moths*
cinnabar moth, clearwing, clothes moth, death's head moth, emperor moth, goat moth, gypsy moth, hawk moth, luna moth, peppered moth, pyralid, tiger moth, tussock moth, underwing

mothball **1** *v* **postpone**, delay, put on the back burner, put aside, put on ice, defer, put off, suspend, table [➡ DELAY ACTION OR OCCURRENCE; 278] **2** *v* **shut up**, pack away, decommission, put into storage, put out of commission [➡ CAUSE TO STOP; 266] *Opposite*: open up

moth-eaten *adj* **tattered**, threadbare, tatty, dog-eared, worn, holey, decrepit, ragged, shabby [➡ IN BAD REPAIR; 1234] *Opposite*: brand-new

mother **1** *type of* **older relative** [➡ OLDER GENERATION RELATIVES; 959] **2** *v* **look after**, care for, protect, nurse, tend, cherish, pamper, cosset, nurture, raise, rear, mind [➡ TAKE CARE OF AND SPOIL; 300] *Opposite*: neglect

motherboard *type of* **hardware** [➡ COMPUTERS AND COMPUTING; 1127]

motherhood *n* **maternity**, parenthood, kinship [➡ REPRODUCTION AND HEREDITY; 725] *Opposite*: fatherhood

mother-in-law *type of* **in-law** [➡ RELATIVES BY MARRIAGE; 960]

motherland *n* **mother country**, native country, birthplace, homeland, fatherland, native land, native soil, land of your birth, place of origin, home [➡ COUNTRIES AND REGIONS; 1067]

motherly *adj* **maternal**, protective, caring, loving, kind, kindly, tender, devoted [➡ GENEROSITY AND KINDNESS; 495] *Opposite*: uncaring

mother-of-pearl *type of* **gemstone** [➡ PRECIOUS STONES; 1278]

motif **1** *n* **design**, pattern, image, decoration, shape, ornamentation, logo [➡ ARTWORKS; 898] **2** *n* **theme**, idea, subject, topic, keynote, style, treatment [➡ SUBJECT AREAS; 768]

motion **1** *n* **gesture**, wave, signal, sign, gesticulation, nod, indication, cue [➡ GESTURES AND GESTICULATION; 653] **2** *n* **movement**, action, activity, change, mobility, flow, kinesis [➡ SELF-PROPULSION; 304] *Opposite*: stillness **3** *n* **proposal**, suggestion, proposition, submission, recommendation, presentation, request [➡ SUGGEST, HINT, AND COMMENT; 612] **4** *v* **signal**, indicate, wave, gesture, beckon, gesticulate, nod [➡ GESTURES AND GESTICULATION; 653]

motionless *adj* **stationary**, immobile, still, stock-still, static, frozen, unmoving, quiet, inert, immovable, fixed [➡ LACK OF ACTIVITY OR MOTION; 342] *Opposite*: moving

motionlessness *n* **stillness**, calm, immobility, paralysis, rigidity, lifelessness, inertness [➡ LACK OF ACTIVITY OR MOTION; 342] *Opposite*: mobility

motion picture *n* **film**, movie, picture, feature film, video, flick (*informal*), talkie (*dated*) [➡ FILM; 901]

motion sick *adj* [➡ ILL AND SICK; 740]

motivate **1** *v* **inspire**, stimulate, encourage, egg on, persuade, arouse, provoke, influence, prompt [➡ CAUSE OR COMPEL TO ACT; 271] *Opposite*: discourage **2** *v* **cause**, prompt, provoke, induce, spur, trigger off, impel, activate, move [➡ CAUSE TO HAPPEN; 31] *Opposite*: deter

motivated *adj* **interested**, driven, inspired, moved, stirred, encouraged, enthused, striving, determined, ambitious [➡ ENERGY AND ENTHUSIASM; 496] *Opposite*: unmotivated

motivating *adj* **stimulating**, interesting, inspiring, galvanizing, encouraging, fascinating, exciting, moving, stirring, rousing, provoking, influencing, prompting [➡ INTERESTING AND MEANINGFUL; 190] *Opposite*: uninspiring

motivation **1** *n* **incentive**, inspiration, enthusiasm, impetus, stimulus, provocation, spur, impulse, drive, driving force [➡ CAUSATION; 168] *Opposite*: disincentive

2 *n* **reason**, cause, motive, purpose, rationale, aim, goal [➡ CAUSATION; 168]

motivator *n* **instigator**, persuader, stimulus, cheerleader, driving force, promoter, reason, carrot, influence, inspiration [➡ CAUSATION; 168]

motive *n* **reason**, motivation, motivating force, incentive, inducement, spur, goad, stimulus, cause [➡ CAUSATION; 168] *Opposite*: deterrent

Compare and Contrast: *motive, incentive, inducement, spur, goad*

CORE MEANING: something that prompts action

motive the reason for doing something or behaving in a particular way; *incentive* something external, often some kind of reward, that inspires extra enthusiasm or effort; *inducement* something external that persuades or attracts somebody to a particular course of action, especially something that is offered as a reward; *spur* something such as the hope of a reward or the fear of punishment that encourages action or effort or energy; *goad* a stimulus that motivates somebody or stirs somebody into action, often against his or her will.

motiveless *adj* **unprovoked**, gratuitous, wanton, senseless, unwarranted, needless, groundless, mindless [➡ REDUNDANT AND USELESS; 240] *Opposite*: justified

motley *adj* **assorted**, miscellaneous, diverse, varied, mixed, contrasting, dissimilar, heterogeneous, disparate, variegated [➡ DIFFERENCE; 149] *Opposite*: uniform

motocross *n* **scrambling**, MX, cross-country, trail biking, motorcycle racing, motorcycle race [➡ HOBBIES, GAMES, AND SPORTS; 875]

motor **1** *n* **engine**, diesel engine, gasoline engine, internal combustion engine, electric motor, petrol engine (*UK*) [➡ ENGINES AND HYDRAULICS; 1143] **2** *adj* **motorized**, motor-powered, gas-powered, diesel-powered, electrically powered, mechanical, petrol-powered (*UK*) [➡ ENGINES AND HYDRAULICS; 1143] **3** *v* (*formal*) **drive**, travel, proceed, journey, ride, cruise [➡ TRAVEL: WAYS OF TRAVELING; 320]

motorboat *type of* **motor vessel** [➡ SHIPS AND BOATS; 1150]

motorcade *n* **convoy**, procession, parade, file, escort, cavalcade, cortege [➡ GROUPS OF VEHICLES; 1152]

motor home *type of* **leisure vehicle** [➡ VEHICLES; 1145]

motorist *n* **driver**, car driver, car user, car owner, chauffeur [➡ DRIVERS; 1153] *Opposite*: passenger

motorized *adj* **motor**, motor-powered, gas-powered, diesel-powered, electrically powered, mechanical, petrol-powered (*UK*) [➡ ENGINES AND HYDRAULICS; 1143]

motor scooter *type of* **bike** [➡ BIKES, CARS, AND CARRIAGES; 1149]

Motown *type of* **pop and vocal music** [➡ MUSIC, SONGS, AND SINGING; 907]

mottle *v* [➡ DECORATE, ADORN, AND APPLY COATINGS; 405]

mottled *adj* **dappled**, spotted, blotchy, speckled, stippled, motley, parti-colored, varicolored, spotty (*UK*) [➡ DESCRIBING PATTERNS; 1227] *Opposite*: plain

motto *n* **slogan**, saying, maxim, aphorism, adage, watchword, proverb, byword, axiom, dictum (*formal*) [➡ FIGURES OF SPEECH; 673]

mound **1** *n* **pile**, stack, mass, bundle, mountain, heap, load [➡ MANY, MUCH, LARGE AMOUNT; 117] **2** *n* **knoll**, hillock, embankment, bank, hill, rise, dune, mount [➡ MOUNTAINS AND HILLS; 1044] *Opposite*: valley

mount **1** *v* **rise**, mount up, increase, accumulate, grow, get bigger, swell, escalate, multiply, intensify, build up, soar, surge [➡ CHANGE OF INTENSITY: MORE; 394] *Opposite*: decrease **2** *v* **climb**, ascend, go up, climb up, clamber up, scale [➡ GO UPWARD; 306] *Opposite*: descend **3** *v* **prepare**, set up, produce, launch, arrange, organize [➡ INSTITUTE AND INAUGURATE; 348] **4** *v* **get on**, climb on, jump on, board, go on, clamber on, straddle [➡ ASSUME A POSITION; 317] *Opposite*: dismount **5** *v* **frame**, box, encase, inset, affix, exhibit, display, install, fit, equip [➡ FASTEN, LINK, AND JOIN; 408] **6** *n* **base**, stand, support, pedestal, plinth, post [➡ SUPPORTS AND BASES; 1255] **7** *n* **horse**, mule, ass, donkey, pony, mare, steed (*literary*) [➡ HORSES; 985]

mountain **1** *n* **peak**, mount, crag, massif, foothill, elevation, highland, alp, fell (*UK*) [➡ MOUNTAINS AND HILLS; 1044] *Opposite*: valley **2** *n* **pile**, mass, stack, bundle, mound, heap, load [➡ MANY, MUCH, LARGE AMOUNT; 117]

Mountain *type of* **time zone** [➡ TIMES OF DAY; 87]

mountain bike *type of* **bike** [➡ BIKES, CARS, AND CARRIAGES; 1149]

mountain biking *type of* **extreme sport** [➡ HOBBIES, GAMES, AND SPORTS; 875]

mountain climbing *n* [➡ HOBBIES, GAMES, AND SPORTS; 875]

mountaineer *n* **climber**, alpinist, rock climber [➡ PEOPLE IN SPORTS AND LEISURE; 876]

mountaineering *n* [➡ HOBBIES, GAMES, AND SPORTS; 875]

mountain lion *type of* **cat** [➡ FELINES; 983]

mountainous **1** *adj* **hilly**, high, steep, precipitous, rocky, rugged [➡ MOUNTAINS AND HILLS; 1044] *Opposite*: flat **2** *adj* **huge**, enormous, immense, monumental, gigantic, colossal, massive, vast [➡ LARGE; 1193] *Opposite*: tiny

mountainside *n* **slope**, shoulder, gradient, incline, ramp [➡ MOUNTAINS AND HILLS; 1044] *Opposite*: foothill

mountaintop *n* **peak**, summit, crest, hilltop, pinnacle, pike (*UK*) [➡ MOUNTAINS AND HILLS; 1044] *Opposite*: bottom

mountebank (*literary*) *n* **fraud**, deceiver, trickster, cheat, charlatan, quack, huckster, con artist (*slang*), fraudster (*UK*) [➡ PEOPLE WHO DECEIVE; 661]

mounted **1** *adj* **on horseback**, equestrian, astride, straddling, riding, on [➡ TRAVEL: WAYS OF TRAVELING; 320] *Opposite*: on foot **2** *adj* **attached**, fixed, affixed, screwed on, displayed, framed, set, fitted, installed [➡ FASTEN, LINK, AND JOIN; 408] *Opposite*: loose

mounting *adj* **rising**, increasing, growing, swelling, escalating, intensifying [➡ CHANGE OF INTENSITY: MORE; 394] *Opposite*: decreasing

mourn *v* **grieve**, lament, grieve for, grieve over, weep for, bemoan, pine, keen, bewail (*formal*), sorrow (*literary*) [➡ GIVING VENT TO EMOTIONS; 679] *Opposite*: rejoice (*literary*)

mourner *n* **bereaved person**, funeral-goer, griever, widow, widower, pallbearer [➡ DEATH AND BEREAVEMENT; 927]

mournful *adj* **sad**, sorrowful, somber, woeful, doleful, despondent, desolate [➡ SADNESS, DISTRESS, AND DESPAIR; 539] *Opposite*: cheerful

mournfulness *n* **sadness**, somberness, melancholy, gloominess, despondency, dolefulness [➡ SADNESS, DISTRESS, AND DESPAIR; 539] *Opposite*: cheerfulness

mourning *n* **grief**, bereavement, sorrow, sadness, lamentation, woe, grieving [➡ DEATH AND BEREAVEMENT; 927] *Opposite*: rejoicing

mourning cloak *type of* **butterfly** [➡ MOTHS AND BUTTERFLIES; 1015]

mourning dove *type of* **common bird** [➡ BIRDS; 997]

mouse 1 *type of* **rodent** [➡ RODENTS; 989] 2 *type of* **hardware** [➡ COMPUTERS AND COMPUTING; 1127]

moussaka *type of* **cooked dish** [➡ PREPARED DISHES; 1170]

mousse *type of* **dessert** [➡ CAKES, COOKIES, AND DESSERTS; 1181]

mousy *type of* **brown** [➡ COLORS; 1224]

mouth 1 *part of* **face** [➡ PARTS OF THE BODY: HEAD; 692] 2 *n* **maw**, trap (*informal*) [➡ THE MOUTH; 702] 3 *n* **entrance**, opening, door, doorway, aperture, gate, gateway, means of access, entry, way in, way out, exit [➡ DOORS AND ACCESS POINTS; 1101] 4 *n* **estuary**, outlet, bay, inlet [➡ THE SEAS, OCEANS, AND SHORES; 1041] 5 *n* (*informal*) **insolence**, impertinence, rudeness, back talk, cheek (*informal*), lip (*slang*) [➡ BAD MANNERS AND SOCIAL SKILLS; 521] 6 *v* **say**, mime, state, utter, reply, pronounce, speak [➡ UTTER AND PRONOUNCE; 608]

mouth

♦ parts of a mouth
adenoids, denture, gum, lip, palate, roof, soft palate, taste bud, tongue, tonsils, tooth, uvula

mouthful 1 *n* **bite**, taste, piece, spoonful, forkful, sip, gulp, draft, swallow, swig (*informal*), slurp (*informal*) [➡ DRINK; 711] 2 *n* **harangue**, sermon, lecture, tirade, earful (*informal*), invective (*formal*) [➡ CRITICISMS AND ANGRY OUTBURSTS; 50]

mouthiness (*informal*) *n* [➡ POMPOUS, LOUD, AND OVERCONFIDENT; 635]

mouth off (*informal*) *v* [➡ BOAST; 616]

mouthpiece *n* **spokesperson**, representative, agent, ambassador, delegate, messenger [➡ REPRESENTATIVES AND PATRONS; 968]

mouth-to-mouth *n* **artificial respiration**, kiss of life, resuscitation, cardiopulmonary resuscitation, CPR, rescue, emergency procedure, mouth-to-mouth resuscitation [➡ BREATHE AND NOT BREATHE; 716]

mouthwash *n* **gargle**, rinse, breath freshener, mouth spray [➡ MAKEUP AND BEAUTY PRODUCTS; 490]

mouthwatering *adj* **delicious**, delectable, lip-smacking, luscious, tasty, appetizing, yummy, succulent, scrumptious (*informal*) [➡ TASTE; 703] *Opposite*: revolting

mouthy (*informal*) *adj* [➡ POMPOUS, LOUD, AND OVERCONFIDENT; 635]

movable 1 *adj* **portable**, transportable, transferable, mobile, detachable, flexible, removable [➡ TRANSPORTATION, TRANSPORTERS, AND CARGOS; 322] *Opposite*: fixed 2 *adj* **changeable**, variable, mutable, impermanent, adjustable, alterable, separable [➡ FINITENESS, VARIABILITY, AND TRANSIENCE; 96] *Opposite*: fixed

move 1 *v* **reposition**, shift, budge, shove, stir, push, pull, rearrange, move about, transfer, redistribute [➡ POSITION SOMETHING; 325] 2 *v* **go**, progress, transport, walk, shuffle, step, jump, run, travel, turn, dance, proceed, advance [➡ PROCEED AND GO; 305] 3 *v* **transfer**, progress, relocate, refocus, redeploy, change, shift, transplant [➡ MOVE SOMETHING TO ANOTHER LOCATION; 324] *Opposite*: stay put 4 *v* **cause**, provoke, persuade, encourage, prod, nudge, propose, suggest, influence, induce, lead [➡ CAUSE OR COMPEL TO ACT; 271] 5 *n* **change**, transfer, traffic, interchange, passage, travel, transport, exchange [➡ CHANGE; 372] 6 *n* **attempt**, effort, step, start, action, movement [➡ ACTIONS OR UNDERTAKINGS; 259] 7 *n* **shift**, step, realignment, rearrangement, repositioning, relocation, change, movement [➡ MOVE SOMETHING TO ANOTHER LOCATION; 324]

move ahead *v* **progress**, move on, press forward, go on, move forward, get going, go forward, press on, proceed, advance, make headway, forge ahead [➡ PROCEED AND GO; 305] *Opposite*: retreat

move along 1 *v* **proceed**, hasten, go on, advance, press on, hurry, go forward, run [➡ PROCEED AND GO; 305] 2 *v* **move aside**, move over, make way, make room, shift, change position, change places [➡ TAKE UP A NEW POSITION; 312] *Opposite*: stay put

move away *v* **retreat**, back off, diverge, distance, deviate, regress, remove [➡ GO BACKWARD; 309]

move back *v* **recoil**, recede, shrink back, retreat, regress, draw back, shy away, fall back, return [➡ GO BACKWARD; 309] *Opposite*: advance

move fast *v* **streak**, zoom, speed, tear, whiz, fly, zip (*informal*) [➡ MOVE FAST; 313]

move forward *v* **advance**, progress, push on, go ahead, proceed, move ahead, go forward, forge ahead, make headway [➡ PROCEED AND GO; 305] *Opposite*: fall back

move heaven and earth *v* **do your utmost**, pull out all the stops, make every effort, move mountains, leave no stone unturned [➡ HARD WORK OR EFFORT; 298]

move in on *v* **approach**, surround, converge, come closer, draw near, sneak up on, creep up on, move toward [➡ GET CLOSER TOGETHER; 310] *Opposite*: retreat

move into *v* **enter**, start, enter on, begin, set the ball rolling, initiate, take the first step [➡ START AN ACTION; 260] *Opposite*: back out

movement 1 *n* **motion**, mobility, locomotion, circulation [➡ SELF-PROPULSION; 304] 2 *n* **drive**, crusade, program, undertaking, measure, effort [➡ WAYS OF DOING THINGS; 294] 3 *n* **pressure group**, association, society, lobby, faction, group, sect, cult, action group, interest group, organization [➡ GROUPS WITH A COMMON INTEREST; 938] 4 *n* **progress**, advance, development, improvement, headway, increase, rise, change, deterioration, drop, fall, decrease [➡ PROGRESS AND ADVANCEMENT; 213]

movements *n* **actions**, activities, travels, schedule, arrangements, appointments, engagements, whereabouts, program [➡ ACTIONS OR UNDERTAKINGS; 259]

move mountains v [➡ HARD WORK OR EFFORT; 298]

move on 1 v **leave**, depart, go, make off, set off, move out, take off (*informal*) [➡ LEAVE AND GO AWAY; 8] *Opposite*: stay put 2 v **progress**, get going, go on, take the next step, uproot, advance, move ahead [➡ PROCEED AND GO; 305] *Opposite*: backtrack

move out v **leave**, depart, go, relocate, move on, move away [➡ LEAVE AND GO AWAY; 8] *Opposite*: stay put

move over v **move aside**, make way, make room, shift, move along, change position [➡ TAKE UP A NEW POSITION; 312] *Opposite*: stay put

mover 1 n **motivator**, driving force, agent, doer, goer, force, mover and shaker, animator, powerhouse (*informal*) [➡ IMPORTANT OR FAMOUS PEOPLE; 893] 2 n **initiator**, proposer, introducer, advocate, sponsor, presenter (*UK*) [➡ SUGGEST, HINT, AND COMMENT; 612] *Opposite*: seconder

mover and shaker n [➡ IMPORTANT OR FAMOUS PEOPLE; 893]

move toward v **draw near**, move in on, approach, converge, creep up on, come closer [➡ GET CLOSER TOGETHER; 310] *Opposite*: move away

move up v **go up**, rise, increase, progress, advance, shift up, ascend [➡ GO UPWARD; 306] *Opposite*: drop

movie n **moving picture**, show, picture, picture show, film, motion picture, flick (*informal*) [➡ FILM; 901]

movie camera type of **photographic equipment** [➡ PHOTOGRAPHY AND PHOTOGRAPHIC EQUIPMENT; 1122]

movies n **cinema**, big screen, silver screen, movie industry, pictures (*dated informal*), flicks (*dated informal*) [➡ FILM; 901]

movie star type of **entertainer** [➡ WORKERS IN ENTERTAINMENT AND MEDIA; 873]

moving adj **touching**, poignant, affecting, stirring, heartrending, heartwarming, emotional, inspiring, pathetic, tender, emotive [➡ EMOTIONALLY UNPLEASANT AND UPSETTING; 227]

Compare and Contrast: *moving, pathetic, pitiful, poignant, touching, heartwarming, heartrending*

CORE MEANING: arousing emotion

moving causing deep feelings, especially of sadness or compassion; *pathetic* arousing feelings of compassion and pity, often centered on somebody who is vulnerable, helpless, or unfortunate; *pitiful* arousing compassion and pity, or arousing contempt or derision; *poignant* causing strong, often bittersweet feelings of sadness, pity, or regret; *touching* causing feelings of warmth, sympathy, and tenderness; *heartwarming* inspiring warm or kindly feelings, usually by showing life and human nature in a positive and reassuring light; *heartrending* causing intense sadness or distress, especially in sympathy with somebody else's unhappiness or hardship because it involves suffering or tragic events.

---

moving parts n **mechanism**, machinery, workings, components, gears, apparatus, works [➡ PARTS OF MACHINES AND TOOLS; 1118]

moving picture n [➡ FILM; 901]

mow v **cut**, scythe, cut down, shear, trim, clip [➡ EXTRACT AND SEVER; 341]

mow down 1 v **shoot**, kill, slaughter, massacre, butcher, shoot down, gun down (*informal*), wipe out (*slang*), blow away (*slang*) [➡ KILL; 923] 2 v **knock down**, run over, knock over, floor, topple, deck (*informal*) [➡ MOVE SOMETHING INTO A NEW POSITION OR OVERTURN; 330]

moxie (*slang*) n [➡ POSITIVE INTELLECTUAL CHARACTERISTICS; 524]

mozzarella type of **soft cheese** [➡ DAIRY PRODUCTS AND CHEESES; 1183]

MP n [➡ POLITICAL OFFICES AND POLITICIANS; 808]

much 1 adv **significantly**, noticeably, considerably, greatly, substantially, extensively, sizably, largely [➡ MANY, MUCH, LARGE AMOUNT; 117] 2 adv **often**, frequently, over and over again, time and again, repeatedly, habitually, a lot, regularly [➡ FREQUENT AND OFTEN; 107] 3 adj **a good deal**, a great deal, lots, abundant, ample, considerable, copious, plentiful, loads (*informal*), heaps (*informal*) [➡ MANY, MUCH, LARGE AMOUNT; 117]

much-admired adj [➡ POPULAR AND WANTED; 220]

much-loved adj **adored**, favorite, preferred, chosen, desired, sought after, singled out [➡ POPULAR AND WANTED; 220]

muck 1 n **manure**, sewage, waste, sludge, dung [➡ UNPLEASANT, DIRTY, AND TOXIC SUBSTANCES; 1268] 2 n (*informal*) **dirt**, mess, grime, mud, filth, grunge (*informal*) [➡ UNPLEASANT, DIRTY, AND TOXIC SUBSTANCES; 1268]

muck around (*informal*) v **fool around**, waste time, be silly, mess around (*informal*), lark about (*UK*) [➡ LEISURE AND RECREATION; 874]

muckiness (*informal*) n **filthiness**, muddiness, dirtiness, grubbiness, griminess [➡ DIRTY; 1235]

muckraker n **scandalmonger**, gossipmonger, troublemaker, mudslinger, slanderer [➡ INTERFERING PEOPLE AND TATTLETALES; 950]

muckraking n **scandalmongering**, dishing the dirt, mudslinging, slander, libel, exposure, exposé [➡ GOSSIP; 678]

muck up (*informal*) v **spoil**, ruin, make a mess of, botch, damage, muddy up, mess up (*informal*) [➡ MESS UP AND MAKE MISTAKES; 472]

mucky (*informal*) adj **dirty**, muddy, messy, grubby, smeared, tarnished, filthy, grimy, soiled, unclean, grotty (*UK*) [➡ DIRTY; 1235] *Opposite*: clean

mucous adj **self-lubricating**, slimy, slippery, lubricated [➡ PHYSICAL TEXTURE; 1222]

mucus n **slime**, secretion, saliva, lubricant, phlegm, coating, liquid [➡ EXCRETION AND EXCRETA; 722]

mud n **mire**, sludge, dirt, muck (*informal*) [➡ EROSION PRODUCTS AND SOIL; 1058]

muddiness 1 n **dirtiness**, grubbiness, filthiness, griminess, muckiness (*informal*) [➡ DIRTY; 1235] *Opposite*: cleanness 2 n **cloudiness**, murkiness, dullness, opacity, thickness, darkness [➡ VISUAL TEXTURE; 1221] *Opposite*: clarity

muddle 1 v **mix up**, jumble, disorder, disorganize, tangle, spoil, muff, botch, fumble, mistake, mess up (*informal*) [➡ CREATE DISORDER AND CAUSE CHAOS; 358] *Opposite*: disentangle

2 *v* **confuse**, bewilder, baffle, puzzle, perplex, stupefy, nonplus, confound, bamboozle (*informal*) [➡ CONFUSE AND BEWILDER; 571] *Opposite*: clarify **3** *n* **disorder**, jumble, confusion, mix-up, chaos, bewilderment, tangle, upheaval, commotion, shambles, mess, disorganization, disarray, clutter [➡ DISORDER AND CHAOS; 245] *Opposite*: order

muddled 1 *adj* **jumbled**, scrambled, mixed up, topsy-turvy, upside down, higgledy-piggledy, disarrayed, cluttered [➡ DISORDER AND CHAOS; 245] *Opposite*: ordered **2** *adj* **confused**, befuddled, bewildered, bemused, perplexed, mixed up, puzzled, baffled, stupefied, nonplussed, confounded, bamboozled (*informal*) [➡ CONFUSION, ANXIETY, AND WORRY; 540] *Opposite*: clear

muddleheaded 1 *adj* **baffled**, mixed up, confused, befuddled, bewildered, bemused, perplexed, puzzled, stupefied, nonplussed, confounded [➡ CONFUSION, ANXIETY, AND WORRY; 540] *Opposite*: clear-headed **2** *adj* **inept**, illogical, impractical, random, ineffective, disordered, confusing, unclear [➡ THE NATURE OF IDEAS; 771] *Opposite*: logical

muddle up *v* **confuse**, disturb, mix up, mistake, disorder, spoil, muff, tangle, mess up (*informal*) [➡ CREATE DISORDER AND CAUSE CHAOS; 358]

muddy 1 *adj* **mud-spattered**, dirty, grubby, grimy, filthy, slimy, mucky (*informal*) [➡ DIRTY; 1235] *Opposite*: clean **2** *adj* **cloudy**, murky, unclear, opaque, thick, dark [➡ VISUAL TEXTURE; 1221] *Opposite*: clear

mud flap *n* **mudguard**, splashguard, flap, shield, guard, cover [➡ EXTERNAL PARTS OF A VEHICLE; 1147]

mudflat *n* [➡ WETLANDS; 1043]

mudguard *type of* **external feature** [➡ EXTERNAL PARTS OF A VEHICLE; 1147]

mudpack *n* **face mask**, facial, face pack, treatment, beauty treatment [➡ MAKEUP AND BEAUTY PRODUCTS; 490]

mudslide *n* [➡ EROSION AND WEATHERING; 1055]

mudslinger *n* **slanderer**, defamer, denigrator, character assassin, attacker, backbiter, exposer [➡ INTERFERING PEOPLE AND TATTLETALES; 950]

mudslinging *n* **defamation**, backbiting, slander, denigration, character assassination, libel [➡ GOSSIP; 678] *Opposite*: praise

mud-spattered *adj* [➡ DIRTY; 1235]

muff 1 *v* **miss**, drop, fumble, mishit, mishandle [➡ MESS UP AND MAKE MISTAKES; 472] **2** *v* **get wrong**, botch, mishandle, bungle (*informal*), mess up (*informal*), make a hash of (*informal*), fluff (*informal*), foul up (*informal*), blow (*slang*) [➡ MESS UP AND MAKE MISTAKES; 472] **3** *type of* **accessory** [➡ ACCESSORIES, MILLINERY, AND LINGERIE; 867]

muffin *type of* **cake** [➡ CAKES, COOKIES, AND DESSERTS; 1181]

muffle *v* **deaden**, dampen, quiet, silence, mute, stifle [➡ CHANGE OF INTENSITY: LESS; 395] *Opposite*: amplify

muffled *adj* **stifled**, muted, inaudible, soft, lowered, silenced, subdued, hushed, quiet [➡ SOFT, LOW, OR PLEASANT SOUNDS; 1265] *Opposite*: loud

muffler 1 *type of* **external feature** [➡ EXTERNAL PARTS OF A VEHICLE; 1147] **2** *type of* **accessory** [➡ ACCESSORIES, MILLINERY, AND LINGERIE; 867]

mufti *n* **civvies**, civilian clothes, ordinary clothes, street clothes, casual wear, casuals (*UK*) [➡ GARMENTS AND OUTFITS; 865] *Opposite*: uniform

mug 1 *n* (*slang*) **face**, countenance, features, visage (*literary*) [➡ PARTS OF THE BODY: HEAD; 692] **2** *v* **attack**, assault, rob, ambush, hold up, jump (*informal*) [➡ PHYSICAL ATTACK AND PUNISHMENT; 415]

mugger 1 *n* **robber**, assailant, thug, attacker, assaulter, aggressor, thief, bag-snatcher, pickpocket [➡ CRIMINALS; 821] **2** *type of* **reptile** [➡ REPTILES; 994]

mugginess *n* **humidity**, closeness, clamminess, oppressiveness, warmth, moistness, dampness, heat, stickiness, sweatiness, stifling heat [➡ HOT WEATHER; 1050] *Opposite*: freshness

mugging *n* **attack**, assault, robbery, ambush, theft, purse-snatch, holdup, bag-snatch (*UK*) [➡ CRIMES; 817]

muggy *adj* **humid**, close, sultry, clammy, oppressive, stifling, warm, sticky, sweaty, moist, damp, steamy [➡ HOT WEATHER; 1050] *Opposite*: fresh

mug shot *n* **photo**, portrait, close-up, passport photo, photograph, snap, snapshot [➡ PHOTOGRAPHY AND PHOTOGRAPHIC EQUIPMENT; 1122]

mukluk *type of* **boot** [➡ FOOTWEAR; 871]

mulberry 1 *type of* **berry** [➡ FRUIT AND VEGETABLES; 1176] **2** *type of* **deciduous tree** [➡ DECIDUOUS TREES; 1028]

mulch 1 *n* **covering**, protection, insulation, organic matter, leaves, straw, bark, peat, plastic sheeting [➡ COVERS AND COATINGS; 1246] **2** *v* **cover**, protect, insulate, dress, top dress [➡ GROW AND CULTIVATE; 351]

mule 1 *type of* **shoe** [➡ FOOTWEAR; 871] **2** *n* (*slang*) [➡ CRIMINALS; 821] **3** *type of* **farm animal** [➡ FARM ANIMALS; 982]

mulish *adj* **stubborn**, obstinate, defiant, headstrong, obdurate, determined, willful, pigheaded, recalcitrant [➡ UNWILLINGNESS AND STUBBORNNESS; 564] *Opposite*: amenable

mulishness *n* **stubbornness**, obstinacy, defiance, obduracy, determination, pigheadedness, willfulness [➡ UNWILLINGNESS AND STUBBORNNESS; 564] *Opposite*: amenability

mull *v* **reflect**, think, consider, dwell on, ponder, muse, deliberate, cogitate (*formal*) [➡ THINK AND REFLECT; 743]

mulled *adj* **spiced**, warmed, sweetened, warm, heated, hot, flavored [➡ STATE OF PREPARED FOOD; 1171]

mullet 1 *type of* **freshwater fish** [➡ FRESHWATER FISH; 1010] **2** *type of* **hairstyle** [➡ HAIRSTYLES AND HAIRPIECES; 488]

mulligatawny *type of* **soup** [➡ SOUPS; 1186]

mull over *v* **think over**, consider, dwell on, think about, reflect, ponder, muse, think through, contemplate, ruminate, meditate, chew over, deliberate, weigh, pore over, reflect on, cogitate (*formal*), weigh up (*UK*) [➡ THINK AND REFLECT; 743]

multicolor *adj* **colorful**, rainbow, rainbow-colored, many-hued, variegated, polychrome, parti-colored, iridescent, multicolored [➡ DESCRIBING COLORS; 1226]

multicultural *adj* **diverse**, multiethnic, multiracial, inclusive, all-inclusive, open, culturally diverse, multinational [➞DIFFERENCE; 149]

multifaceted *adj* **multilayered**, complex, complicated, many-sided, polygonal, manifold, multidimensional [➞POSITIVELY COMPLEX OR COMPLICATED; 217] *Opposite:* simple

multifarious *adj* **diverse**, varied, assorted, mixed, miscellaneous, different, manifold, diversified, various, heterogeneous [➞DIFFERENCE; 149] *Opposite:* homogeneous

multifariousness *n* [➞DIFFERENCE; 149]

multilateral 1 *adj* **many-sided**, polygonal, multifaceted, multidimensional [➞POSITIVELY COMPLEX OR COMPLICATED; 217] **2** *adj* **mutual**, all-party, multiparty, joint, bilateral, simultaneous [➞RECIPROCITY AND INTERDEPENDENCE; 147] *Opposite:* unilateral

multilingual *adj* **polyglot**, trilingual, bilingual [➞ASPECTS OF LANGUAGE; 682]

multimedia 1 *n* **hypermedia**, software, interactive program, program [➞COMPUTERS AND COMPUTING; 1127] **2** *n* **collage**, combination, montage, assemblage, construction [➞COLLECTIONS AND MIXTURES OF THINGS; 1244]

multimillionaire *n* **millionaire**, magnate, billionaire, tycoon, mogul, moneybags (*informal*) [➞RICH PEOPLE; 895]

multinational 1 *adj* **international**, cosmopolitan, transnational, global, worldwide, offshore [➞COUNTRIES AND REGIONS; 1067] *Opposite:* national **2** *n* **conglomerate**, transnational, corporation, international business, international company, group, holding company [➞BUSINESS ENTERPRISES AND RELATED BODIES; 792]

multipartite *adj* **multiple**, multifarious, multifaceted, composite, compound, manifold [➞POSITIVELY COMPLEX OR COMPLICATED; 217]

multiple *adj* **manifold**, numerous, many, several, various, compound [➞MANY, MUCH, LARGE AMOUNT; 117] *Opposite:* few

multiplex *n* **movie theater complex**, cinema complex (*UK*), multiscreen cinema (*UK*) [➞BUILDINGS FOR PUBLIC ENTERTAINMENT; 1084]

multiplication *n* **increase**, growth, development, reproduction, duplication, proliferation, exponentiation [➞CHANGE OF INTENSITY: MORE; 394] *Opposite:* decrease

multiplicity *n* **array**, diversity, variety, large quantity, range, assortment, collection, wealth [➞MANY, MUCH, LARGE AMOUNT; 117] *Opposite:* dearth

multiply *v* **increase**, grow, reproduce, swell, proliferate, enlarge, magnify, augment (*formal*), burgeon (*literary*) [➞CHANGE OF SIZE: BIGGER; 392] *Opposite:* decrease

multipurpose *adj* **versatile**, flexible, adaptable, multiuse [➞USEFULNESS; 199] *Opposite:* dedicated

multiracial *adj* **interracial**, multicultural, multiethnic, inclusive, all-inclusive, all-embracing [➞DIFFERENCE; 149] *Opposite:* exclusive

multistage rocket *type of* **spacecraft** [➞SPACE VEHICLES; 1063]

multistory *adj* **high-rise**, multistoried, tall, high, towering [➞HEIGHT: HIGH; 1203] *Opposite:* low-rise

multitalented *adj* [➞TALENTED AND SKILLFUL; 527]

multitude 1 *n* **crowd**, horde, host, mass, throng, swarm, assembly, gathering, congregation, mob, legion [➞GROUPS OF PEOPLE; 935] *Opposite:* handful **2** *n* **variety**, assortment, array, collection, wealth, large quantity, multiplicity [➞MANY, MUCH, LARGE AMOUNT; 117] *Opposite:* few

multitudinous *adj* [➞MANY, MUCH, LARGE AMOUNT; 117]

mum (*informal*) *adj* **silent**, tight-lipped, mute, quiet, dumb, wordless, still, closemouthed, taciturn [➞RETICENT AND UNFORTHCOMING; 631] *Opposite:* communicative

mumble *v* **mutter**, murmur, drone, intone, gabble, stammer, stutter, slur, babble, garble [➞CHATTER AND BABBLE; 617] *Opposite:* enunciate

mumbled *adj* **muttered**, murmured, muffled, inaudible, slurred, low, incomprehensible, unintelligible, incoherent, faint, inarticulate, garbled, stammered, stuttered [➞INARTICULATE, RAMBLING, AND AWKWARD; 633] *Opposite:* enunciated

mumbo jumbo (*informal*) *n* **jargon**, gibberish, doublespeak, cant, technobabble, legalese, gobbledygook (*informal*) [➞MEANINGLESS SPEECH OR WRITING; 676] *Opposite:* sense

mummify 1 *v* **embalm**, preserve, wrap up, pickle, prepare, dress [➞BURIAL AND PREPARATION FOR BURIAL; 929] **2** *v* **shrivel**, dry out, dry up, wrinkle, wither, desiccate [➞HARDEN, CONGEAL, AND DRY; 387] *Opposite:* flourish

mummy *n* **mummified body**, body, cadaver, corpse [➞BURIAL AND PREPARATION FOR BURIAL; 929]

munch *v* **chew**, masticate, crunch, grind, eat, champ, chomp (*informal*) [➞EAT AND NOT EAT; 710]

mundane *adj* **ordinary**, dull, routine, everyday, commonplace, boring, unexciting, humdrum, dreary, monotonous, tedious, prosaic, banal, uninteresting [➞BORING AND UNINTERESTING; 234] *Opposite:* exotic

mundaneness *n* **routineness**, tedium, flatness, ordinariness, unimaginativeness, dullness [➞BORING AND UNINTERESTING; 234] *Opposite:* excitement

mung bean *type of* **pulse** [➞PEAS AND BEANS; 1189]

municipal *adj* **civic**, public, community, urban, metropolitan [➞HUMAN SETTLEMENTS; 1070] *Opposite:* private

municipality *n* **city**, metropolis, town, borough, burg [➞HUMAN SETTLEMENTS; 1070]

See Compare and Contrast at **city***.*

munificence *n* **generosity**, largesse, benevolence, kindness, philanthropy, charity, magnanimousness, bounty (*literary*) [➞GENEROSITY AND KINDNESS; 495] *Opposite:* miserliness

munificent *adj* **generous**, liberal, magnanimous, unstinting, unsparing, freehanded, openhanded, charitable, bountiful (*literary*) [➞GENEROSITY AND KINDNESS; 495] *Opposite:* miserly

See Compare and Contrast at **generous***.*

munitions *n* **weaponry**, ammunition, arms, guns, armaments, firepower, military capability [➞WEAPONS; 1154]

muon *type of* **elementary particle** [➡ ELEMENTARY PARTICLES; 1279]

mural *n* **wall painting**, fresco, frieze, painting [➡ ARTWORKS; 898]

murder **1** *n* **homicide**, manslaughter, assassination, killing, slaying, unlawful death, contract killing, slaughter, massacre, wasting (*slang*) [➡ CAUSES OF DEATH; 921] **2** *v* **kill**, assassinate, execute, put to death, slaughter, massacre, snuff (*informal*), slay (*formal or literary*), bump off (*slang*), waste (*slang*), do (*slang*) [➡ KILL; 923]

See Compare and Contrast at **kill**.

murderer *n* **killer**, assassin, butcher, slaughterer, executioner, contract killer, slayer (*formal or literary*) [➡ PEOPLE WHO KILL; 924]

murderous **1** *adj* **fatal**, lethal, mortal, deadly, homicidal, brutal, vicious, cruel [➡ DEADLY; 928] **2** *adj* (*informal*) **difficult**, testing, arduous, rigorous, exhausting, strenuous [➡ PHYSICALLY UNPLEASANT; 226] *Opposite*: easy

murk *n* **gloom**, darkness, shadows, dark, dimness, shade, obscurity [➡ DESCRIBING LIGHT; 1228] *Opposite*: light

murkiness *n* **darkness**, fogginess, mistiness, cloudiness, gloom, shadows, dark, dimness, shade [➡ CLOUDY AND RAINY WEATHER; 1052] *Opposite*: brightness

murky *adj* **dark**, gloomy, foggy, misty, cloudy, muddy, shadowy, dim, overcast [➡ CLOUDY AND RAINY WEATHER; 1052] *Opposite*: clear

murmur **1** *v* **whisper**, mutter, mumble, purr, croon, susurrate, babble [➡ CHATTER AND BABBLE; 617] **2** *v* **complain**, grumble, grouch, mutter, grouse (*informal*), bellyache (*informal*) [➡ COMPLAIN AND NAG; 686] **3** *type of* **human sound** [➡ SOUNDS MADE BY PEOPLE; 1262]

murmuration (*literary*) *type of* **flock** [➡ GROUPS OF BIRDS; 1007]

murmured *adj* [➡ SOFT, LOW, OR PLEASANT SOUNDS; 1265]

Murphy bed *type of* **bed** [➡ FURNITURE; 858]

Musca *type of* **constellation** [➡ HEAVENLY BODIES; 1061]

muscle **1** *n* **sinew**, brawn, musculature, thew (*archaic*) [➡ THE MUSCLES; 718] **2** *n* **influence**, power, authority, force, control, weight, sway, pressure, pull [➡ STRENGTH; 201] **3** *n* (*informal*) **strength**, vigor, power, force, elbow grease (*informal*) [➡ STRENGTH; 201] **4** *n* (*slang*) **bodyguard**, guard, heavy (*slang*), minder (*UK informal*) [➡ PEOPLE WHO GUARD AND PROTECT; 846]

muscle

◆ *types of muscles or tendons*
abdominals, Achilles tendon, biceps, diaphragm, hamstring, pectoral, quadriceps, sinew, smooth muscle, sphincter, striated muscle, tendon, triceps

muscle in (*informal*) *v* **intrude**, intervene, barge in, butt in, interfere, push in, get involved [➡ INTERRUPT AND BUTT IN; 619]

muscly *adj* [➡ MUSCLES AND MUSCULATURE; 479]

muscular *adj* **brawny**, beefy, well-built, burly, well-developed, powerfully built, strong, powerful, strapping (*informal*) [➡ MUSCLES AND MUSCULATURE; 479] *Opposite*: puny

muscularity *n* [➡ MUSCLES AND MUSCULATURE; 479]

muse *v* **think**, ponder, consider, mull over, deliberate, reflect on, chew over, ruminate, contemplate, recollect, meditate, cogitate (*formal*) [➡ THINK AND REFLECT; 743]

museum *n* **gallery**, exhibition hall, arts center, academy, institution [➡ BUILDINGS FOR PUBLIC ENTERTAINMENT; 1084]

mush **1** *n* **pap**, purée, mash, paste, slop, slush, pulp [➡ LOTIONS, PASTES, AND GELS; 1279] **2** *n* **sentimentality**, sentimentalism, slush, sugariness, slop (*informal*), schmaltz (*informal*), goo (*informal*), soppiness (*informal*) [➡ IN POOR TASTE AND OVERSENTIMENTAL; 229]

mushiness *n* [➡ FLUID AND NONSOLID; 1213]

mushroom **1** *type of* **fungus** [➡ MICROORGANISMS, FUNGI, AND ALGAE; 1023] **2** *v* **grow**, increase, expand, flourish, swell, thrive, spread out, proliferate, burgeon (*literary*) [➡ CHANGE OF SIZE: BIGGER; 392] *Opposite*: decline

mushy **1** *adj* **soggy**, soft, squashy, squishy, spongy, squidgy (*UK*) [➡ MALLEABLE AND ELASTIC; 1212] *Opposite*: firm **2** *adj* **soppy**, oversentimental, mawkish, maudlin, syrupy, bathetic, romantic, slushy, gooey (*informal*), schmaltzy (*informal*), sloppy (*informal*) [➡ IN POOR TASTE AND OVERSENTIMENTAL; 229]

music *n* **melody**, tune, harmony, composition, song [➡ MUSIC, SONGS, AND SINGING; 907]

music

◆ *types of musical forms*
anthem, aria, bagatelle, ballad, cantata, canticle, capriccio, chorale, coloratura, concerto, étude, fantasia, fugue, hymn, intermezzo, madrigal, mass, nocturne, oratorio, overture, prelude, requiem, rondo, scherzo, sinfonia, sonata, song, suite, symphony, tone poem, waltz

◆ *types of musical registers*
alto, baritone, bass, countertenor, falsetto, mezzo-soprano, soprano, tenor

◆ *types of musical terms*
a cappella, adagio, allegro, andante, appassionato, arpeggio, capriccioso, con brio, con moto, crescendo, decrescendo, diminuendo, forte, fortissimo, grave, larghetto, largo, legato, lentissimo, lento, moderato, pianissimo, piano, pizzicato, rubato, sotto voce, staccato

◆ *types of classical music*
Baroque, chamber music, comic opera, early music, opera, operetta, Romantic, twelve-tone

◆ *types of dance music*
acid house, acid jazz, big beat, boogie, broken beat, disco, drum 'n' bass, funk, garage, hardcore, hip hop, house, jungle, ragga, raggamuffin, rap, rave, reggae, rock steady, ska, speed garage, techno, trance, two step

◆ *types of electronic music*
ambient, breakbeat, breaks and beats, chillout, downbeat, dub, electro, electronica, new age, trip hop

◆ *types of jazz music*
bebop, boogie-woogie, cool jazz, Dixieland, honky-tonk, jazz, jazz funk, jazz fusion, jazz rock, jive, modal jazz, New Orleans jazz, ragtime, swing

◆ *types of pop and vocal music*
bluegrass, blues, country and western, doowop, easy listening, folk, gangsta rap, gospel, lounge, Motown, new wave, pop, R&B, rap metal, rare soul, rockabilly, soul, spiritual, urban

◆ *types of rock music*
grunge, heavy metal, indie, metal, punk, rock, rock 'n' roll, thrash metal

◆ *types of world music*
afrobeat, bhangra, calypso, flamenco, latin, mento, raga, rai, roots, salsa, yodel

musical *adj* **melodic**, harmonious, melodious, tuneful, easy on the ear, pleasant-sounding, pleasing, sweet [➡ SOFT, LOW, OR PLEASANT SOUNDS; 1265] *Opposite*: discordant

musical instrument *n* [➡ MUSIC, SONGS, AND SINGING; 907]

musical instrument

◆ *types of brass instruments*
bugle, cornet, euphonium, flugelhorn, French horn, horn, post horn, saxhorn, saxophone, sousaphone, trombone, trumpet, tuba

◆ *types of keyboards*
accordion, baby grand, celesta, clavichord, concertina, grand piano, harpsichord, organ, piano, pianoforte, spinet, synthesizer, upright piano

◆ *types of percussion instruments*
bass drum, bongo drums, castanet, chimes, conga drum, cymbal, drum, gamelan, glockenspiel, gong, kettledrum, maraca, marimba, metallophone, snare drum, steel drum, tabla, tabor, tambourine, timpani, tom-tom, triangle, tubular bells, vibraphone, xylophone

◆ *types of stringed instruments*
balalaika, banjo, bass guitar, bouzouki, cello, double bass, electric guitar, fiddle, guitar, harp, Hawaiian guitar, lute, lyre, mandolin, sitar, Spanish guitar, steel guitar, ukulele, viol, viola, viola da gamba, violin, violoncello, zither

◆ *types of wind instruments*
bagpipes, bassoon, clarinet, crumhorn, didgeridoo, English horn, fife, fipple flute, flute, harmonica, nose flute, oboe, ocarina, panpipes, penny whistle, piccolo, recorder

music hall *n* [➡ BUILDINGS FOR PUBLIC ENTERTAINMENT; 1084]

musician 1 *n* **performer**, instrumentalist, player, artiste, composer, singer, conductor, picker (*informal*) [➡ MUSICIANS AND SINGERS; 908] **2** *type of* **entertainer** [➡ WORKERS IN ENTERTAINMENT AND MEDIA; 873]

music therapy *type of* **complementary therapy** [➡ REMEDIES, TREATMENTS, AND OPERATIONS; 731]

musing 1 *n* **thinking**, reflection, reverie, daydream, consideration, contemplation, ponderings, recollection, meditation, cogitation (*formal*), deliberation (*formal*) [➡ IDEAS AND THOUGHTS; 770] **2** *adj* **thoughtful**, reflective, pensive, contemplative, absorbed, speculative [➡ PENSIVENESS AND INTEREST; 538]

musk *n* **perfume**, scent, smell, fragrance, aroma, bouquet [➡ SMELL AND SMELLING; 705]

musket *type of* **gun** [➡ WEAPONS FOR SHOOTING; 1156]

muskrat *type of* **rodent** [➡ RODENTS; 989]

musky *adj* **pungent**, perfumed, scented, odorous, aromatic, spicy [➡ SMELL AND SMELLING; 705]

muslin *type of* **fabric from plants** [➡ FABRICS; 1132]

mussel *type of* **aquatic invertebrate** [➡ AQUATIC INVERTEBRATES; 1022]

must 1 *v* **have to**, have got to, be obliged to, ought to, should, be required to, need, want [➡ NEED AND REQUIRE; 464] **2** *n* **necessity**, obligation, duty, essential, requirement, need, commitment, precondition, requisite (*formal*) [➡ MOST IMPORTANT THING; 197] *Opposite*: option

mustache *n* **whiskers**, walrus mustache, pencil mustache, handlebar mustache, mustachio (*archaic or humorous*) [➡ FACIAL HAIR; 489]

mustang *type of* **horse** [➡ HORSES; 985]

mustard 1 *type of* **spice** [➡ HERBS AND SPICES; 1175] **2** *type of* **yellow** [➡ COLORS; 1224]

mustard gas *type of* **gas** [➡ GASES; 1275]

muster 1 *v* **gather**, gather together, congregate, collect, get together, assemble, meet, rally, marshal, rendezvous, aggregate [➡ GET CLOSER TOGETHER; 310] *Opposite*: disperse **2** *n* **gathering**, assembly, meeting, congregation, congress, assemblage, collection, aggregation [➡ MEETINGS AND ASSEMBLIES; 43] **3** *type of* **flock** [➡ GROUPS OF BIRDS; 1007]

mustiness *n* **dankness**, staleness, moldiness, stuffiness, fustiness, fetidness, rankness (*literary*) [➡ DIRTY; 1235] *Opposite*: freshness

musty *adj* **mildewed**, moldy, stale, fusty, stuffy, fetid, malodorous, smelly, rank (*literary*) [➡ DIRTY; 1235] *Opposite*: fresh

mutability *n* [➡ FINITENESS, VARIABILITY, AND TRANSIENCE; 96]

mutable *adj* **changeable**, alterable, changing, variable, fluctuating, inconsistent, unsettled, capricious [➡ FINITENESS, VARIABILITY, AND TRANSIENCE; 96] *Opposite*: fixed

mutant *adj* **distorted**, misshapen, malformed, transformed, altered, changed, transmuted, modified [➡ ORIENTATION AND ALIGNMENT; 1223]

mutate *v* **change**, alter, transform, transmute, metamorphose, transfigure, modify [➡ CHANGE; 372]

mutation *n* **change**, alteration, transformation, transmutation, metamorphosis, transfiguration, modification [➡ CHANGE; 372]

mute *adj* **silent**, speechless, voiceless, unspeaking, quiet, taciturn, dumb, wordless, mum (*informal*) [➡ ABSENCE OF SOUND; 1257] *Opposite*: vocal

muted *adj* **subdued**, hushed, soft, quiet, gentle, low-key, muffled [➡ SOFT, LOW, OR PLEASANT SOUNDS; 1265] *Opposite*: loud

mutilate *v* maim, injure, hurt, disfigure, harm, damage, spoil, deface, mar, dismember [➡ DESTRUCTION AND DEMOLITION; 359]

mutilated *adj* [➡ IN BAD REPAIR; 1234]

mutilation *n* disfigurement, defacement, damage, injury, maiming, dismemberment, hurt [➡ DESTRUCTION AND DEMOLITION; 359]

mutineer *n* rebel, insurgent, rioter, radical, insurrectionist, revolutionary [➡ UNCOOPERATIVE OR REBELLIOUS PEOPLE; 566]

mutinous *adj* rebellious, revolutionary, seditious, subversive, disobedient, insubordinate, defiant, recalcitrant, unruly, wayward, riotous (*formal*) [➡ REBELLIOUSNESS AND DISOBEDIENCE; 565] *Opposite:* obedient

mutiny *n* rebellion, revolt, sedition, uprising, insubordination, defiance, recalcitrance, revolution, riot, insurgence, insurrection [➡ AGGRESSIVE EVENTS; 39]

mutt (*slang*) *n* [➡ DOGS; 980]

mutter 1 *v* mumble, murmur, drone, burble, slur, gabble [➡ CHATTER AND BABBLE; 617] 2 *v* complain, grouch, grumble, murmur, grouse (*informal*), bellyache (*informal*) [➡ COMPLAIN AND NAG; 686] 3 *type of* human sound [➡ SOUNDS MADE BY PEOPLE; 1262]

mutton *type of* meat [➡ TYPES AND CUTS OF MEAT; 1177]

muttonchops *n* [➡ FACIAL HAIR; 489]

mutual *adj* joint, shared, common, communal, reciprocated, reciprocal, conjoint, related [➡ RECIPROCITY AND INTERDEPENDENCE; 147]

muumuu *type of* dress [➡ GARMENTS AND OUTFITS; 865]

muzzily *adv* woozily, confusedly, vaguely, dazedly, groggily, dizzily, blearily [➡ ILL AND SICK; 740]

muzzle *v* silence, gag, hush, quiet, stifle, suppress, shut up (*informal*) [➡ MAKE IMPOSSIBLE; 276]

muzzy 1 *adj* fuzzy, woozy, groggy, bleary, shaky, dizzy, wobbly (*informal*) [➡ ILL AND SICK; 740] *Opposite:* clear-headed 2 *adj* vague, fuzzy, out of focus, bleary, indistinct, faint, shadowy [➡ VAGUENESS; 243] *Opposite:* clear

my *interj* [➡ EXPRESSIONS OF SURPRISE AND PLEASURE; 546]

mycoplasma *type of* microorganism [➡ MICROORGANISMS, FUNGI, AND ALGAE; 1023]

my goodness *interj* [➡ EXPRESSIONS OF SURPRISE AND PLEASURE; 546]

mynah *type of* pet bird [➡ BIRDS; 997]

Mynx *type of* constellation [➡ HEAVENLY BODIES; 1061]

myopia 1 *n* nearsightedness, poor sight, short-sightedness [➡ SEE; 699] 2 *n* bigotry, prejudice, bias, intolerance, narrow-mindedness [➡ NEGATIVE INTELLECTUAL CHARACTERISTICS; 525]

myopic 1 *adj* short-sighted, nearsighted, owlish [➡ SEE; 699] 2 *adj* narrow-minded, bigoted, parochial, prejudiced, intolerant, biased [➡ NEGATIVE INTELLECTUAL CHARACTERISTICS; 525] *Opposite:* broad-minded

myriad 1 *adj* countless, innumerable, numberless, numerous, many, uncountable, unnumbered, untold [➡ MANY, MUCH, LARGE AMOUNT; 117] *Opposite:* few 2 *n* multitude, mass, host, army, crowd, wealth, variety, heap (*informal*) [➡ MANY, MUCH, LARGE AMOUNT; 117] *Opposite:* few

mysterious 1 *adj* strange, unexplained, inexplicable, unsolved, odd, puzzling, mystifying, baffling, peculiar, weird [➡ BIZARRE AND PECULIAR; 257] 2 *adj* secretive, enigmatic, shadowy, furtive, cryptic, covert, stealthy, surreptitious, cagey (*informal*) [➡ RETICENT AND UNFORTHCOMING; 631] *Opposite:* open

mysteriousness *n* strangeness, oddness, weirdness, curiousness, inexplicableness, peculiarity [➡ BIZARRE AND PECULIAR; 257] *Opposite:* normality

mystery 1 *n* problem, puzzle, conundrum, enigma, riddle [➡ SECRETS AND MYSTERIES; 180] 2 *n* secrecy, obscurity, ambiguity, inscrutability, vagueness, anonymity [➡ SECRET AND UNKNOWN; 179] 3 *n* whodunit, detective novel, thriller, crime novel [➡ FICTION AND DRAMA; 913] 4 *adj* unknown, anonymous, unidentified, secret, clandestine, furtive, enigmatic, covert, cryptic [➡ SECRET AND UNKNOWN; 179]

See Compare and Contrast at **problem**.

mystic 1 *n* spiritualist, medium, shaman, sorcerer, wizard, sage (*literary*) [➡ PEOPLE WITH SUPERNATURAL POWERS; 788] 2 *adj* mystical, spiritual, supernatural, magical, cabalistic, sorcerous, numinous (*formal*) [➡ THE SUPERNATURAL; 787]

mystical *adj* spiritual, mystic, magical, supernatural, magic, transcendent, preternatural, numinous (*formal*) [➡ THE SUPERNATURAL; 787]

mystification *n* bewilderment, confusion, perplexity, bafflement, puzzlement, stupefaction, incomprehension, disorientation [➡ CONFUSION, ANXIETY, AND WORRY; 540]

mystified *adj* puzzled, confused, bewildered, baffled, perplexed, bamboozled (*informal*) [➡ CONFUSION, ANXIETY, AND WORRY; 540] *Opposite:* enlightened

mystify *v* puzzle, confuse, bewilder, confound, baffle, stump, perplex, stymie, stupefy, floor, muddle, bamboozle (*informal*) [➡ CONFUSE AND BEWILDER; 571]

mystifying *adj* mysterious, baffling, inexplicable, puzzling, confusing, strange, perplexing, enigmatic, stupefying [➡ BIZARRE AND PECULIAR; 257]

mystique *n* air of mystery, air of secrecy, aura, charisma, magic, charm, inscrutability, mysteriousness, secretiveness [➡ SECRET AND UNKNOWN; 179]

myth 1 *n* legend, fable, saga, fairy tale, allegory, parable, lore, mythos, apologue, fairy story (*UK*) [➡ THE ORAL TRADITION; 677] 2 *n* falsehood, fiction, illusion, invention, fabrication, untruth, figment, creation [➡ NONEXISTENT THINGS; 23] *Opposite:* fact

mythic *see* **mythical**

mythical 1 *adj* legendary, mythological, fabled, fabulous, storybook, fairy-tale [➡ FALSE AND UNREAL; 173] *Opposite:* factual 2 *adj* imaginary, untrue, fictitious, fictional, made-up, make-believe, invented, unreal, false [➡ FALSE AND UNREAL; 173] *Opposite:* real

mythological *adj* mythical, mythic, fabulous, fairy-tale, fabled, storybook, allegorical, epic [➡ FALSE AND UNREAL; 173] *Opposite:* factual

mythological creature

◆ *types of mythological creatures*
centaur, Chimera, dragon, griffin, mermaid, sphinx,
unicorn, vampire, werewolf

mythology *n* **myths**, legends, folklore, tradition,
mythos, lore [➡ THE ORAL TRADITION; 677]

my word (*dated*) *interj* [➡ EXPRESSIONS OF SURPRISE AND PLEASURE;
546]

N

nab 1 *v* (*informal*) **arrest**, seize, capture, detain, catch, hold, apprehend [➡ THE POLICE, ARREST, AND PRETRIAL PROCEEDINGS; 818] 2 *v* **steal**, walk off with, rip off (*informal*), swipe (*informal*), lift (*informal*), snitch (*slang*) [➡ STEAL AND ROB; 426]

nachos *type of* **cooked dish** [➡ PREPARED DISHES; 1170]

nadir *n* **lowest point**, all-time low, depths of despair, depths, base, foot, rock bottom, pits (*informal*) [➡ DIFFICULT SITUATIONS; 72] *Opposite*: zenith

naevus (*UK*) *n* [➡ CONDITIONS AFFECTING THE SKIN; 721]

nag 1 *v* **badger**, pester, plague, harass, harry, carp at, needle, hassle (*informal*) [➡ COMPLAIN AND NAG; 686] 2 *v* **criticize**, find fault, carp, grumble, complain, grouse (*informal*) [➡ ACCUSE, BLAME, AND CRITICIZE; 641] 3 *v* **irritate**, annoy, worry, trouble, torment, irk, disturb, vex, bother, distress [➡ ANGER AND ANNOY; 569]

See Compare and Contrast at **complain***.*

nagging *adj* **irritating**, niggling, troublesome, distressing, irksome, harassing, pesky (*informal*) [➡ IRRITATING; 228]

naiad *n* [➡ MYTHICAL BEINGS; 789]

nail 1 *n* **pin**, spike, tack, peg [➡ FASTENERS, LINKS, AND NETWORKS; 1247] 2 *v* **tack**, pin, fix, fasten, attach, secure [➡ FASTEN, LINK, AND JOIN; 408]

nail-biting *adj* **nerve-racking**, tense, exciting, stressful, anxious, worrying, scary (*informal*) [➡ FRIGHTENING; 231] *Opposite*: relaxing

nail bomb *type of* **explosive weapon** [➡ EXPLOSIVES; 1155]

nailbrush *type of* **cosmetic tool** [➡ HAND TOOLS; 1119]

nail clippers *type of* **cosmetic tool** [➡ HAND TOOLS; 1119]

nail down *v* **pin down**, get an agreement on, get a decision on, settle, confirm, agree, decide [➡ EXPLAIN AND CLARIFY; 610]

nail file *type of* **cosmetic tool** [➡ HAND TOOLS; 1119]

nail polish *n* [➡ MAKEUP AND BEAUTY PRODUCTS; 490]

nail scissors *type of* **cosmetic tool** [➡ HAND TOOLS; 1119]

naira *type of* **currency** [➡ CURRENCIES; 798]

naissance *n* [➡ BEGINNINGS; 53]

naive 1 *adj* **simple**, trusting, innocent, childlike, inexperienced, ingenuous, guileless [➡ NATURALNESS; 497] *Opposite*: suspicious 2 *adj* **unsophisticated**, gullible, wet behind the ears, green, foolish, credulous, unwise [➡ NEGATIVE INTELLECTUAL CHARACTERISTICS; 525] *Opposite*: shrewd

naiveté *n* **innocence**, ingenuousness, candor, art-

lessness, naturalness, inexperience, gullibility, simplicity [➡ NATURALNESS; 497] *Opposite*: sophistication

naked 1 *adj* **bare**, nude, unclothed, stark-naked, stripped, undressed, buck naked, with nothing on, in the altogether (*informal*), in the buff (*informal*), in your birthday suit (*informal humorous*) [➡ DRESS, WEAR, AND UNDRESS; 868] *Opposite*: clothed 2 *adj* **uncovered**, unprotected, exposed, unsheathed, unwrapped, unguarded [➡ PERCEPTIBLE; 25] *Opposite*: covered 3 *adj* **open**, undisguised, unadorned, unadulterated, unvarnished, blatant, stark, obvious, plain, simple, overt [➡ PERCEPTIBLE; 25] *Opposite*: hidden

> **Compare and Contrast:** *naked*, *bare*, *nude*, *undressed*, *unclothed*
>
> CORE MEANING: devoid of clothes or covering
>
> *naked* not covered or concealed, especially not covered by clothing on any part of the body; *bare* without the usual furnishings or decorations, or not covered by clothing; *nude* not wearing any clothes at all, especially in artistic contexts; *undressed* not wearing any or many clothes, used especially when clothes have just been removed or are about to be put on; *unclothed* not wearing any clothes.

nakedly *adv* **openly**, blatantly, starkly, obviously, overtly, plainly, simply [➡ INTENTIONAL AND DELIBERATE; 279] *Opposite*: covertly

nakedness 1 *n* **nudity**, bareness, state of undress [➡ DRESS, WEAR, AND UNDRESS; 868] 2 *n* **defenselessness**, helplessness, exposure, vulnerability [➡ DANGER; 235] 3 *n* **blatancy**, obviousness, openness, overtness, starkness, plainness, evidence [➡ PERCEPTIBLE; 25] *Opposite*: covertness

nakfa *type of* **currency** [➡ CURRENCIES; 798]

namby-pamby (*informal insult*) *adj* **feeble**, soft, spineless, ineffectual, pathetic (*informal*), wishy-washy (*informal*) [➡ COWARDICE AND WEAKNESS OF WILL; 508] *Opposite*: tough

name 1 *n* **first name**, Christian name, forename, given name, surname, family name, middle name, maiden name, pet name, nickname, last name, handle (*slang*), moniker (*slang*) [➡ NAME AND DESCRIBE; 665] 2 *n* **designation**, term, tag, title, label, appellation (*formal*), style (*formal*) [➡ NAME AND DESCRIBE; 665] 3 *n* **reputation**, renown, character, respectability, honor, fame, celebrity, repute (*formal*) [➡ KNOWN AND FAMOUS; 181] *Opposite*: notoriety 4 *n* **celebrity**, star, big name, public figure, VIP, luminary, famous person, bigwig (*informal*) [➡ IMPORTANT OR FAMOUS PEOPLE; 893] *Opposite*: nobody 5 *v* **call**, christen, baptize, nickname, label, term, dub, entitle [➡ NAME AND DESCRIBE; 665] 6 *v* **identify**, specify, refer to, mention, cite, brand [➡ NAME AND DESCRIBE; 665] *Opposite*: conceal 7 *v* **nominate**, appoint, assign, choose, suggest, propose, select [➡ CONFER STATUS; 458] *Opposite*: reject

name-calling *n* **abuse**, insults, foul language, swearing, invective (*formal*) [➡ INSULTS, ABUSE, AND SWEARING; 658]

named *adj* **called**, baptized, christened, entitled, titled, known as, so-called, termed [⟹ NAME AND DESCRIBE; 665] *Opposite*: nameless

name-drop *v* **boast**, brag, show off, vaunt [⟹ BOAST; 616]

name-dropper *n* **boaster**, bragger, braggart, show-off (*informal*), blower (*informal*), bigmouth (*informal*) [⟹ SELF-IMPORTANT AND SELF-SEEKING PEOPLE; 949]

nameless 1 *adj* **anonymous**, unknown, unidentified, unnamed, unspecified, mysterious, shadowy [⟹ SECRET AND UNKNOWN; 179] *Opposite*: named 2 *adj* **indescribable**, awful, dreadful, horrible, ghastly, fearsome, terrible [⟹ EMOTIONALLY UNPLEASANT AND UPSETTING; 227]

namely *adv* **that is**, that is to say, viz., specifically, explicitly, to be exact, to be precise, i.e., to wit, for example, such as [⟹ EXPRESSIONS INTRODUCING EXAMPLES; 64]

nameplate *n* **plate**, sign, plaque, notice, panel [⟹ SIGNPOSTS, SIGNALS, AND BILLBOARDS; 595]

naming *n* **identification**, designation, nomenclature, christening, baptism [⟹ NAME AND DESCRIBE; 665]

nan 1 *type of* **bread** [⟹ BREAD, FLOUR, AND BREAD PRODUCTS; 1179] 2 *type of* **older relative** (*informal*) [⟹ OLDER GENERATION RELATIVES; 959]

nana *type of* **older relative** (*informal*) [⟹ OLDER GENERATION RELATIVES; 959]

nanna *type of* **older relative** (*informal*) [⟹ OLDER GENERATION RELATIVES; 959]

nanny 1 *n* **caretaker**, au pair, caregiver, minder (*UK*), child minder (*UK*), carer (*UK*) [⟹ PEOPLE WHO GUARD AND PROTECT; 846] 2 *n* (*informal*) **grandmother**, nana (*informal*), nan (*informal*), granny (*informal*), gran (*informal*), grandma (*informal*) [⟹ OLDER GENERATION RELATIVES; 959]

nanny goat *type of* **female animal** [⟹ MALE OR FEMALE ANIMALS; 978]

nanosecond *n* **moment**, split second, second, instant, trice, jiffy (*informal*) [⟹ SHORT PERIODS OF TIME; 93]

nap 1 *n* **doze**, catnap, siesta, sleep, rest, snooze (*informal*), shuteye (*informal*), forty winks (*informal*) [⟹ SLEEP AND DREAM; 723] 2 *n* **pile**, surface, finish, weave, texture, down, shag, fiber [⟹ TEXTURE; 1220] 3 *v* **sleep**, catnap, have a siesta, doze, drowse, snooze (*informal*), have forty winks (*informal*), get some shuteye (*informal*), catch some z's (*informal*) [⟹ SLEEP AND DREAM; 723]

napalm *type of* **explosive material** [⟹ EXPLOSIVES; 1155]

napkin *n* **bib**, paper towel, table linen, napery (*archaic*), serviette (*UK*) [⟹ FURNISHING AND HOUSEHOLD LINENS; 860]

narcissism *n* **self-love**, self-admiration, self-absorption, egotism, conceit, self-importance, selfishness, vanity, self-centeredness [⟹ AFFECTATION, SELF-SATISFACTION, AND SNOBBISHNESS; 507] *Opposite*: selflessness

narcissist *n* [⟹ SELF-IMPORTANT AND SELF-SEEKING PEOPLE; 949]

narcissistic *adj* **vain**, self-absorbed, egotistic, egotistical, selfish, conceited, self-important, self-loving, self-admiring [⟹ AFFECTATION, SELF-SATISFACTION, AND SNOBBISHNESS; 507] *Opposite*: selfless

narcissus *type of* **flower grown from bulbs** [⟹ FLOWERS FROM BULBS; 1030]

narrate *v* **relate**, recount, tell, describe, recite, report [⟹ RECITE, REPEAT, AND NARRATE; 620]

narration 1 *n* **telling**, recitation, relating, unfolding, recounting, describing [⟹ ONE-WAY COMMUNICATION; 49] 2 *n* **tale**, account, description, chronicle, history, story [⟹ THE ORAL TRADITION; 677]

narrative 1 *n* **tale**, account, description, chronicle, history, story [⟹ THE ORAL TRADITION; 677] 2 *n* **plot**, story line, sequence of events [⟹ THE ORAL TRADITION; 677]

narrator *n* **storyteller**, speaker, raconteur, teller of tales, relator, chronicler, reporter [⟹ THE ORAL TRADITION; 677] *Opposite*: listener

narrow 1 *adj* **thin**, fine, slim, slender, slight, tapered, contracted, constricted, tight, limited, restricted [⟹ WIDTH: NARROW AND THIN; 1200] *Opposite*: wide 2 *v* **get thinner**, get smaller, taper, contract, tighten, constrict [⟹ CHANGE OF SIZE: SMALLER; 393] *Opposite*: widen 3 *v* **restrict**, limit, narrow down, confine, focus, reduce [⟹ CHANGE OF SIZE: SMALLER; 393] *Opposite*: broaden

narrow down *v* **focus**, restrict, limit, confine, concentrate, fix on, center on, zero in [⟹ CHANGE OF SIZE: SMALLER; 393] *Opposite*: broaden

narrow escape *n* **close call**, near miss, narrow squeak, close shave, lucky escape [⟹ RESULTS AND OUTCOMES; 83]

narrowing *n* **tapering**, contraction, thinning, reduction, tightening, lessening [⟹ CHANGE OF SIZE: SMALLER; 393]

narrowly 1 *adv* **only just**, barely, hardly, scarcely, by a hair's breadth, by a whisker [⟹ TO A CERTAIN EXTENT; 136] 2 *adv* **closely**, intently, carefully, attentively, assiduously, with care [⟹ CAUTIOUS AND CAREFUL; 282]

narrow-minded *adj* **bigoted**, blinkered, insular, intolerant, prejudiced, biased, reactionary, parochial, provincial, pigheaded [⟹ NEGATIVE INTELLECTUAL CHARACTERISTICS; 525] *Opposite*: broad-minded

narrow-mindedness *n* **bigotry**, insularity, prejudice, bias, intolerance, parochialism, provinciality [⟹ NEGATIVE INTELLECTUAL CHARACTERISTICS; 525] *Opposite*: broad-mindedness

narrowness *n* **thinness**, fineness, slimness, slightness, constriction, tightness, slenderness, restriction [⟹ WIDTH: NARROW AND THIN; 1200] *Opposite*: width

narrow squeak *n* **narrow escape**, close shave, close call, lucky escape, near miss [⟹ RESULTS AND OUTCOMES; 83]

narwhal *type of* **whale** [⟹ WHALES; 991]

nasal *adj* [⟹ THE NOSE; 704]

nascent *adj* **budding**, promising, embryonic, emerging, blossoming, burgeoning, growing [⟹ FUTURE; 86] *Opposite*: moribund

nasi goreng *type of* **cooked dish** [⟹ PREPARED DISHES; 1170]

nastily *adv* **spitefully**, meanly, maliciously, viciously, cruelly, horribly, unkindly, unpleasantly, obnoxiously, objectionably, offensively [⟹ SELFISH AND UNKIND; 505] *Opposite*: kindly

nastiness *n* **spite**, meanness, malice, viciousness, cruelty, unkindness, unpleasantness, offensiveness, maliciousness, spitefulness, malevolence, wickedness, obnoxiousness [➡ MALICIOUS ACTIONS OR BEHAVIOR; 296] *Opposite*: kindness

nasturtium *type of* **annual flower** [➡ FLOWERS; 1032]

nasty 1 *adj* **spiteful**, mean, malicious, vicious, cruel, horrible, malevolent, wicked [➡ SELFISH AND UNKIND; 505] *Opposite*: kind 2 *adj* **foul**, horrid, horrible, revolting, offensive, bad, disgusting, nauseating, sickening, vile, ghastly, unpleasant, repugnant [➡ DISGUSTING AND REPULSIVE; 230] *Opposite*: pleasant 3 *adj* **severe**, painful, horrible, serious, grave, worrying, dangerous [➡ DANGEROUS; 236] *Opposite*: slight 4 *adj* (*informal*) **obscene**, offensive, indecent, vulgar, crude, vile [➡ MORALLY BAD OR IMPROPER; 775] 5 *adj* (*informal*) **difficult**, tricky, hard, complicated, knotty, thorny, complex [➡ DIFFICULTY AND COMPLEXITY; 242]

See Compare and Contrast at **mean**.

nation 1 *n* **state**, country, land, realm, homeland, nation-state [➡ COUNTRIES AND REGIONS; 1067] 2 *n* **people**, population, inhabitants, residents, populace [➡ GROUPS IN SOCIETY; 940]

national 1 *adj* **nationwide**, countrywide, state, general, coast-to-coast, domestic, home [➡ GENERAL LOCATIONS; 158] *Opposite*: local 2 *adj* **state**, public, nationalized, state-run, state-owned, federal [➡ BELONGING OR RELATING TO PEOPLE; 943] *Opposite*: private 3 *n* **resident**, citizen, inhabitant, subject, native [➡ INHABITANTS; 857] *Opposite*: visitor

national guard *n* [➡ THE ARMED FORCES; 827]

nationalism 1 *n* **independence**, autonomy, home rule, self-rule, self-government, separatism [➡ STYLES AND SYSTEMS OF GOVERNMENT; 806] 2 *n* **patriotism**, chauvinism, jingoism, xenophobia [➡ PHILOSOPHIES AND BELIEFS; 780] *Opposite*: internationalism

nationalist *n* **separatist**, autonomist, separationist [➡ UNCOOPERATIVE OR REBELLIOUS PEOPLE; 566]

nationalistic *adj* **patriotic**, jingoistic, chauvinistic, xenophobic [➡ PHILOSOPHIES AND BELIEFS; 780] *Opposite*: internationalist

nationality *n* **people**, population, race, ethnic group [➡ COUNTRIES AND REGIONS; 1067]

nationalize *v* **make public**, take over, municipalize [➡ SOCIAL, POLITICAL, AND ECONOMIC CHANGE; 373] *Opposite*: privatize

nationalized *adj* **state-owned**, publicly owned, public sector, state, national [➡ BELONGING OR RELATING TO PEOPLE; 943] *Opposite*: private

nationally *adv* **countrywide**, all over the country, on a national scale, nationwide, generally [➡ COUNTRIES AND REGIONS; 1067] *Opposite*: locally

national park *n* [➡ THE COUNTRYSIDE AND OUTDOOR SPACES; 1071]

nation-state *n* **state**, country, land, nation, sovereign state, realm [➡ COUNTRIES AND REGIONS; 1067]

nationwide 1 *adj* **countrywide**, general, national, state, coast-to-coast, from Land's End to John O'Groats (*UK*) [➡ GENERAL LOCATIONS; 158] *Opposite*: local 2 *adv* **nationally**, countrywide, all over the country, on a national scale, generally [➡ COUNTRIES AND REGIONS; 1067] *Opposite*: locally

native 1 *adj* **innate**, natural, inborn, instinctive, inherent, built-in, intrinsic, intuitive [➡ TRUE AND REAL; 171] *Opposite*: acquired 2 *adj* **indigenous**, local, aboriginal, resident, autochthonous [➡ COUNTRIES AND REGIONS; 1067] *Opposite*: foreign 3 *n* **inhabitant**, resident, local, citizen, subject, national, aboriginal [➡ INHABITANTS; 857] *Opposite*: foreigner

Compare and Contrast: *native, aboriginal, indigenous, autochthonous*

CORE MEANING: originating in a particular place

native born or originating in a particular place; *aboriginal* existing in a region from the earliest known times; *indigenous* originating in and typical of a region or country; *autochthonous* originating where currently found, especially used of rocks and minerals that were formed in their present position, or flora, fauna, or inhabitants descended from those present in a region from earliest times.

native land *n* **land of origin**, land of birth, birthplace, native country, motherland, fatherland, mother country, home, homeland [➡ COUNTRIES AND REGIONS; 1067]

nativity *n* **origin**, birth, genesis, conception, dawn, beginning [➡ BEGINNINGS; 53] *Opposite*: demise (*formal*)

natter (*informal*) *v* **have a chat**, chat, chatter, gossip, talk, prattle, blather (*informal*), jaw (*slang*) [➡ TWO-WAY COMMUNICATION; 607]

nattering (*informal*) *n* [➡ INFORMAL COMMUNICATION; 45]

natterjack toad *type of* **amphibian** [➡ AMPHIBIANS; 1008]

natty *adj* **smart**, fashionable, trim, dapper, chic, spruce, neat, nifty (*informal*), snazzy (*informal*), trendy (*informal*) [➡ WELL-GROOMED; 482] *Opposite*: unfashionable

natural 1 *adj* **usual**, normal, ordinary, accepted, expected, regular, likely [➡ ORDINARINESS; 244] *Opposite*: unusual 2 *adj* **physical**, biological, environmental, ecological, geographic, geological [➡ BIOLOGICAL SCIENCES; 1037] *Opposite*: technological 3 *adj* **innate**, native, inborn, instinctive, effortless, inherent [➡ TRUE AND REAL; 171] *Opposite*: learned 4 *adj* **unaffected**, unpretentious, spontaneous, genuine, artless, sincere, relaxed, open [➡ NATURALNESS; 497] *Opposite*: affected 5 *adj* **untreated**, unprocessed, pure, raw, crude, organic [➡ RAW AND NATURAL; 1214] *Opposite*: artificial 6 *adj* **biological**, physical, birth, true, actual, real [➡ TRUE AND REAL; 171] *Opposite*: adoptive

natural ability *n* [➡ SKILLS, TALENTS, AND ABILITIES; 526]

natural disaster *n* [➡ DISASTERS; 252]

natural fiber *n* [➡ TEXTILES AND THREADS; 1131]

natural gas *type of* **gas** [➡ GASES; 1275]

natural gift *n* [➡ SKILLS, TALENTS, AND ABILITIES; 526]

naturalistic *adj* **realistic**, real, true-to-life, natural, lifelike, representational, real-life [➡ TRUE AND REAL; 171]

naturalize 1 *v* **accept**, adopt, enfranchise [➡ ELECTIONS AND VOTING; 807] 2 *v* **adapt**, become established, grow wild, grow naturally, acclimatize [➡ CHANGE; 372]

naturally 1 *adv* **of course**, obviously, logically, as expected, unsurprisingly, certainly, indeed [➡ EXPRESSIONS OF AGREEMENT; 648] *Opposite:* surprisingly **2** *adv* **innately**, inherently, instinctively, intuitively, effortlessly [➡ TRUE AND REAL; 171] **3** *adv* **unaffectedly**, unpretentiously, spontaneously, genuinely, artlessly, sincerely, in a relaxed manner, openly, easily, effortlessly [➡ NATURALNESS; 497] *Opposite:* pretentiously **4** *adv* **in nature**, physically, biologically, geographically, geologically, organically, purely [➡ RAW AND NATURAL; 1214] *Opposite:* artificially

naturalness *n* **unaffectedness**, spontaneity, genuineness, artlessness, sincerity, openness [➡ NATURALNESS; 497] *Opposite:* affectedness

natural resource *n* **raw material**, mineral, mineral deposit, reserve, resource [➡ SUBSTANCES; 1267]

natural world *n* **environment**, nature, biosphere, ecosphere [➡ NATURE AND THE ENVIRONMENT; 1038]

nature 1 *n* **Mother Nature**, countryside, natural surroundings, wildlife, flora, fauna, landscape, natural world, environment [➡ NATURE AND THE ENVIRONMENT; 1038] **2** *n* **class**, kind, sort, type, description, character, quality, characteristics, features, ilk, stripe [➡ VARIETIES, TYPES, AND KINDS; 145] **3** *n* **character**, personality, temperament, disposition, spirit, makeup, complexion, humor [➡ TEMPERAMENT AND BEHAVIOR; 492]

nature preserve *n* [➡ THE COUNTRYSIDE AND OUTDOOR SPACES; 1071]

nature reserve *n* [➡ THE COUNTRYSIDE AND OUTDOOR SPACES; 1071]

naturopath *n* [➡ PEOPLE WHO WORK IN MEDICINE; 848]

naturopathy *type of* **complementary therapy** [➡ REMEDIES, TREATMENTS, AND OPERATIONS; 731]

naught *n* **zero**, nil, nothing, zilch (*informal*) [➡ NONE; 123]

naughtiness *n* **disobedience**, bad behavior, wickedness, ill-discipline, waywardness, mischief, impishness [➡ REBELLIOUSNESS AND DISOBEDIENCE; 565] *Opposite:* obedience

naughty *adj* **disobedient**, bad, badly behaved, wicked, ill-disciplined, wayward, mischievous, impish [➡ REBELLIOUSNESS AND DISOBEDIENCE; 565] *Opposite:* good

See Compare and Contrast at **bad**.

nausea 1 *n* **biliousness**, queasiness, sickness, vomiting, unsettled stomach, seasickness, motion sickness [➡ ILL AND SICK; 740] **2** *n* (*literary*) **revulsion**, repugnance, repulsion, abhorrence, disgust, detestation, hatred, aversion (*formal*) [➡ DISLIKE AND HATE; 577]

nauseate *v* **sicken**, disgust, repel, revolt, turn your stomach, make you feel sick, upset, put off [➡ UPSET, DISTRESS, AND HUMILIATE; 567] *Opposite:* please

nauseated *adj* [➡ ILL AND SICK; 740]

nauseating *adj* **disgusting**, sickening, repellent, revolting, repulsive, hideous, upsetting, off-putting, gross [➡ DISGUSTING AND REPULSIVE; 230] *Opposite:* pleasant

nauseous 1 *adj* **sick**, bilious, queasy, unwell, nauseated, woozy, seasick [➡ ILL AND SICK; 740] *Opposite:* well **2** *adj* **disgusting**, sickening, repellent, revolting, repulsive, upsetting, gross, detestable, hideous [➡ DISGUSTING AND REPULSIVE; 230] *Opposite:* pleasant

nautical *see* **naval**

naval *adj* **nautical**, maritime, seafaring, sailing, marine, navigational [➡ THE SEAS, OCEANS, AND SHORES; 1041]

nave *n* [➡ PARTS OF RELIGIOUS BUILDINGS; 1086]

navel *n* **umbilicus**, bellybutton (*informal*) [➡ PARTS OF THE BODY: TORSO; 693]

navel-gazing *n* **self-analysis**, reflection, rumination, brooding, self-absorption, meditation, contemplation, daydreaming, woolgathering [➡ THINK AND REFLECT; 743]

navigable 1 *adj* **passable**, negotiable, crossable, traversable [➡ IN GOOD REPAIR; 1232] *Opposite:* impassable **2** *adj* **maneuverable**, controllable, pilotable, seaworthy, sturdy, steerable [➡ IN GOOD REPAIR; 1232]

navigate 1 *v* **find the way**, plot a course, plot a route, map read, follow the map [➡ TRAVEL: WAYS OF TRAVELING; 320] **2** *v* **sail across**, circumnavigate, steer, pilot, take the helm, direct, pass through, travel through, cross, traverse [➡ TRAVEL: WAYS OF TRAVELING; 320]

navigation *n* **direction finding**, steering, course plotting, map reading, celestial navigation, triangulation [➡ NAVIGATION; 1141]

navigational *adj* **directional**, direction-finding, course-plotting, route-finding [➡ NAVIGATION; 1141]

navigator *n* **guide**, autopilot, skipper, pilot, direction finder, route finder [➡ NAVIGATION; 1141]

navvy (*dated*) *n* **manual worker**, laborer, manual laborer, worker, hand [➡ FARMERS, GARDENERS, AND MANUAL WORKERS; 849]

navy *n* **fleet**, armada, flotilla, merchant marine, merchant navy (*UK*) [➡ THE ARMED FORCES; 827]

navy bean *type of* **pulse** [➡ PEAS AND BEANS; 1189]

navy blue *type of* **blue** [➡ COLORS; 1224]

nay (*archaic or literary*) *adv* **or rather**, and also, more correctly, indeed, even, truly, verily (*archaic*) [➡ EXPRESSIONS INTRODUCING EXTRA INFORMATION; 139]

naysay *v* [➡ DENY AND REJECT; 644]

N.B. *adv* [➡ WRITTEN CONVENTIONS; 599]

near 1 *prep* **close to**, by, next to, in close proximity to, in the vicinity of, in the neighborhood, in front of [➡ CLOSENESS; 159] *Opposite:* far from **2** *prep* **like**, close to, similar to, resembling, approaching [➡ SIMILARITY; 148] **3** *prep* **on the verge of**, approaching, nearing, close to, bordering on, touching on [➡ CLOSENESS; 159] **4** *adv* **nearby**, close, close by, close to, close at hand, in close proximity, hard by, to hand, in the vicinity, in the neighborhood, nigh [➡ CLOSENESS; 159] **5** *adv* **almost**, nearly, virtually, practically, just about, all but, not quite, about [➡ TO A CERTAIN EXTENT; 136] **6** *adj* **close**, nearby, neighboring, adjacent, adjoining, immediate, nigh, proximate [➡ CLOSENESS; 159] *Opposite:* far **7** *v* **approach**, reach, draw up to, draw near to, go up to, come up to, border on, verge on, touch on, come close to [➡ PROCEED AND GO; 305] *Opposite:* leave

nearby 1 *adj* **close**, near, neighboring, adjacent, adjoining, proximate, immediate, nigh [➡CLOSENESS; 159] *Opposite*: distant 2 *adv* **near**, close, close by, close to, close at hand, in close proximity, hard by, to hand, in the vicinity, in the neighborhood, nigh [➡CLOSENESS; 159]

near enough *adv* [➡APPROXIMATELY; 135]

nearest and dearest *n* [➡THE FAMILY; 956]

nearly *adv* **closely**, approximately, almost, near, virtually, practically, all but, just about, not quite, more or less [➡TO A CERTAIN EXTENT; 136]

near miss *n* **lucky escape**, close thing, close call, close shave, narrow escape, narrow squeak [➡RESULTS AND OUTCOMES; 83]

nearness *n* **immediacy**, imminence, proximity, closeness, juxtaposition, propinquity (*formal*), contiguity (*formal*) [➡CLOSENESS; 159] *Opposite*: distance

nearside (*UK*) *adj* **passenger**, inside, curbside [➡RELATIVE LOCATION; 161]

nearsighted *adj* **short-sighted**, myopic, owlish [➡SEE; 699] *Opposite*: farsighted

nearsightedness *n* [➡SEE; 699]

neat 1 *adj* **well-ordered**, in order, straight, arranged, immaculate, spotless, shipshape, spick-and-span, tidy, orderly, trim [➡ORDER AND ORGANIZATION; 206] *Opposite*: untidy 2 *adj* **well-organized**, organized, methodical, systematic, careful, painstaking, orderly, tidy, efficient, precise, regular [➡ORDER AND ORGANIZATION; 206] *Opposite*: disorganized 3 *adj* **straight**, undiluted, unmixed, full-strength, pure, plain, unadulterated [➡RAW AND NATURAL; 1214] *Opposite*: diluted 4 *adj* **simple**, ingenious, elegant, convenient, effective, well-thought-out, handy, useful, nifty (*informal*), clever (*UK*) [➡THE NATURE OF IDEAS; 771] 5 *adj* **graceful**, effortless, practiced, precise, deft, skillful [➡DESCRIBING BODY MOVEMENTS; 288] *Opposite*: clumsy 6 *adj* **natty**, trim, compact, well-designed, elegant, simple, handy [➡SMALL; 1195] *Opposite*: cumbersome

neat and tidy *adj* [➡IN GOOD REPAIR; 1232]

neaten *v* **order**, tidy, tidy up, arrange, sort out, put in order [➡ARRANGE AND CREATE ORDER; 357] *Opposite*: mess up (*informal*)

neatly 1 *adv* **carefully**, tidily, in order, efficiently, precisely, painstakingly, trimly, nattily, immaculately [➡ORDER AND ORGANIZATION; 206] *Opposite*: messily 2 *adv* **ingeniously**, elegantly, cleverly, effectively, handily, usefully, conveniently [➡THE NATURE OF IDEAS; 771] *Opposite*: ineffectively 3 *adv* **gracefully**, effortlessly, deftly, precisely, skillfully [➡DESCRIBING BODY MOVEMENTS; 288] *Opposite*: clumsily

neatness 1 *n* **tidiness**, orderliness, carefulness, efficiency, precision, trimness, immaculateness [➡ORDER AND ORGANIZATION; 206] *Opposite*: messiness 2 *n* **ingeniousness**, elegance, cleverness, effectiveness, handiness, usefulness, convenience [➡THE NATURE OF IDEAS; 771] *Opposite*: ineffectiveness 3 *n* **gracefulness**, effortlessness, preciseness, deftness, skillfulness [➡DESCRIBING BODY MOVEMENTS; 288] *Opposite*: clumsiness 4 *n* **simplicity**, elegance, nattiness, trimness, compactness, handiness [➡EASE AND SIMPLICITY; 200]

nebula *type of* **star or star system** [➡HEAVENLY BODIES; 1061]

nebulous *adj* **unclear**, vague, imprecise, hazy, unformulated, tenuous, ill-defined, indefinable [➡VAGUENESS; 243] *Opposite*: precise

nebulousness *n* [➡VAGUENESS; 243]

necessary *adj* **essential**, needed, required, compulsory, obligatory, indispensable, basic, crucial, vital, mandatory, requisite (*formal*), de rigueur (*formal*) [➡NECESSARY AND ESSENTIAL; 196] *Opposite*: optional

> **Compare and Contrast:** *necessary, essential, vital, indispensable, requisite, needed*
>
> CORE MEANING: describes something that is required
>
> *necessary* important in order to achieve a desired result, or required by authority or convention; *essential* of the highest importance for achieving something; *vital* extremely important to the survival or continuing effectiveness of something; *indispensable* absolutely essential, or extremely desirable or useful; *requisite* (*formal*) necessary for a particular purpose; *needed* required or desired.

necessitate *v* **require**, demand, need, call for, dictate, force, impose, oblige, compel, take [➡NEED AND REQUIRE; 464]

necessitous (*formal*) *adj* [➡NECESSARY AND ESSENTIAL; 196]

necessitude *n* **need**, necessity, demand, requirement, want, obligation, requisite (*formal*) [➡MOST IMPORTANT THING; 197]

necessity 1 *n* **essential**, requirement, prerequisite, basic, necessary, must, requisite (*formal*) [➡MOST IMPORTANT THING; 197] *Opposite*: luxury 2 *n* **need**, requirement, inevitability, obligation, stipulation, compulsion [➡NECESSARY AND ESSENTIAL; 196]

neck 1 *part of* **torso** [➡PARTS OF THE BODY: TORSO; 693] 2 *type of* **cut** [➡TYPES AND CUTS OF MEAT; 1177] 3 *part of* **garment** [➡PARTS OF A GARMENT; 870] 4 *n* **narrow part**, stem, shank, shaft [➡EXTREMITIES OF PHYSICAL OBJECTS; 1250] 5 *v* (*informal*) **kiss**, cuddle, hug, embrace, smooch (*informal*), canoodle (*informal*) [➡PHYSICAL CONTACT AS COMMUNICATION; 655]

neck and neck (*informal*) *adv* **equal**, level, close, too close to call, with nothing to choose between them, even-steven (*informal*), level pegging (*UK*) [➡EQUALITY; 154]

neckband *part of* **garment** [➡PARTS OF A GARMENT; 870]

neckerchief *n* **bandanna**, cravat, scarf, tie, band [➡ACCESSORIES, MILLINERY, AND LINGERIE; 867]

necklace *n* **chain**, string, choker, band, rope, necklet (*UK*) [➡JEWELRY; 866]

neckline *part of* **garment** [➡PARTS OF A GARMENT; 870]

neck of the woods *n* [➡PLACE; 1065]

necktie *n* **tie**, scarf, bandanna, cravat [➡ACCESSORIES, MILLINERY, AND LINGERIE; 867]

necrophobia *type of* **phobia** [➡FEARS AND PHOBIAS; 554]

necropolis *n* **cemetery**, burial ground, graveyard, resting place, churchyard, catacomb, boneyard (*informal*) [➡BURIAL PLACES AND ACCESSORIES; 930]

nectar *n* **liquid**, juice, sap, fluid, syrup [➡PARTS OF TREES AND PLANTS; 1026]

nectarine *type of* **fruit** [➡ FRUIT AND VEGETABLES; 1176]

nectary *part of* **flower** [➡ FLOWERS; 1032]

née *adj* **formerly**, previously, originally [➡ NAME AND DESCRIBE; 665]

need 1 *v* **demand**, require, call for, want, necessitate, crave, take [➡ NEED AND REQUIRE; 464] 2 *v* **have to**, must, should, ought [➡ NEED AND REQUIRE; 464] 3 *n* **essential**, necessity, requirement, want, prerequisite, basic, necessary, must, demand, requisite (*formal*) [➡ MOST IMPORTANT THING; 197] *Opposite*: option 4 *n* **privation**, poverty, want, hardship, neediness, penury, destitution, indigence (*formal*) [➡ POVERTY AND POOR; 892] *Opposite*: luxury

needed *adj* [➡ NECESSARY AND ESSENTIAL; 196]

See Compare and Contrast at **necessary**.

needful 1 *adj* (*formal or archaic*) **necessary**, obligatory, compulsory, mandatory, essential, vital, prerequisite, requisite (*formal*) [➡ NECESSARY AND ESSENTIAL; 196] 2 *adj* (*formal*) **requiring**, necessitating, demanding, calling for, needing, lacking, without [➡ LACK OF POSSESSION; 445]

neediness *n* **need**, poverty, want, penury, destitution, privation, hardship, deprivation, poorness, indigence (*formal*) [➡ POVERTY AND POOR; 892]

needle 1 *n* **pointer**, indicator, hand [➡ PARTS OF MACHINES AND TOOLS; 1118] 2 *n* **spine**, spike, prickle, barb, sticker, pine needle [➡ PARTS OF TREES AND PLANTS; 1026] 3 *v* (*informal*) **irritate**, provoke, annoy, pester, niggle, enrage, bedevil, irk, gnaw, tease, nettle (*informal*), rile (*informal*), aggravate (*informal*), hassle (*informal*) [➡ ANGER AND ANNOY; 569]

needlecraft *n* [➡ CRAFTS AND CARVING; 355]

needlepoint *type of* **handicraft** [➡ CRAFTS AND CARVING; 355]

needless *adj* **unnecessary**, pointless, uncalled-for, useless, unneeded, unwanted, inessential, unrequired [➡ REDUNDANT AND USELESS; 240] *Opposite*: necessary

needlessness *n* **uselessness**, unhelpfulness, fruitlessness, impracticality, pointlessness, senselessness [➡ REDUNDANT AND USELESS; 240] *Opposite*: usefulness

needlework *type of* **handicraft** [➡ CRAFTS AND CARVING; 355]

needy *adj* **poor**, in need, deprived, disadvantaged, destitute, indigent (*formal*), penurious (*literary*) [➡ POVERTY AND POOR; 892]

ne'er-do-well *n* **layabout**, waster, idler, slacker, shirker, lazybones (*informal*), scalawag (*dated informal*) [➡ LAZY OR UNSUCCESSFUL PEOPLE; 948]

nefarious *adj* **wicked**, evil, despicable, immoral, reprehensible, disreputable, degenerate, infamous, perverse [➡ MORALLY BAD OR IMPROPER; 775] *Opposite*: reputable

nefariousness *n* [➡ MORALLY BAD OR IMPROPER; 775]

negate (*formal*) 1 *v* **refute**, contradict, disprove, disavow, deny, repudiate, contravene, disaffirm (*formal*) [➡ DENY AND REJECT; 644] *Opposite*: affirm 2 *v* **invalidate**, cancel, reverse, render null and void, annul, remove, wipe out, cancel out, abolish, nullify, abrogate (*formal*) [➡ DENY AND REJECT; 644] *Opposite*: validate

See Compare and Contrast at **nullify**.

negation 1 *n* **denial**, annulment, nullification, repudiation, cancellation, reversal, disavowal (*formal*) [➡ DENY AND REJECT; 644] *Opposite*: affirmation 2 *n* **opposite**, contrary, absence, lack, antithesis [➡ OPPOSITE; 157] *Opposite*: confirmation

negative 1 *adj* **unenthusiastic**, unconstructive, unhelpful, pessimistic, downbeat, disapproving, off-putting, discouraging, depressing [➡ NEGATIVITY OF OUTLOOK; 514] *Opposite*: encouraging 2 *adj* **bad**, undesirable, adverse, harmful, damaging, destructive, deleterious [➡ BAD AND BADLY; 223] *Opposite*: positive 3 *n* **rejection**, rebuff, veto, no, refusal, denial, thumbs down (*informal*), nix (*dated slang*) [➡ REFUSE PERMISSION AND NOT ALLOW; 670] *Opposite*: approval

negatively 1 *adv* **in the negative**, with a no, with a refusal, with a denial [➡ NOT; 137] *Opposite*: affirmatively 2 *adv* **damagingly**, harmfully, destructively, undesirably, depressingly, adversely, deleteriously [➡ BAD AND BADLY; 223] *Opposite*: positively 3 *adv* **offputtingly**, discouragingly, unenthusiastically, unconstructively, unhelpfully, pessimistically, disapprovingly [➡ NEGATIVITY OF OUTLOOK; 514] *Opposite*: encouragingly

negativity *n* **unconstructiveness**, unhelpfulness, pessimism, disapproval [➡ FEELINGS ABOUT THE FUTURE; 533] *Opposite*: enthusiasm

neglect 1 *v* **abandon**, desert, forget, forsake, ignore, pass over [➡ NOT PAY ATTENTION; 764] *Opposite*: look after 2 *v* **omit**, forget, overlook, ignore, disregard, fail [➡ NOT DO AND REFUSE TO DO; 274] 3 *n* **negligence**, abandonment, desertion, disregard, inattention, mistreatment, lack of care, carelessness [➡ NOT PAY ATTENTION; 764] *Opposite*: care

Compare and Contrast: *neglect, forget, omit, overlook*

CORE MEANING: to fail to do something

neglect to fail to give the proper or required care and attention to somebody or something, or to fail to do something, especially because of carelessness, forgetfulness, or indifference; *forget* to fail, or fail to remember, to give due attention to somebody or something; *omit* to fail to do something, either deliberately or accidentally; *overlook* to fail to notice or check something as a result of inattention, preoccupation, or haste.

neglected *adj* **deserted**, abandoned, unkempt, uncared for, mistreated, ignored, unloved [➡ IN TROUBLE AND DISADVANTAGED; 73] *Opposite*: looked after

neglectful *adj* **negligent**, careless, slipshod, remiss, lax, slack, casual, forgetful, inattentive [➡ LACK OF COMMITMENT AND UNRELIABILITY; 509] *Opposite*: attentive

negligee *n* **nightdress**, nightgown, dressing gown, peignoir, nightie (*informal*) [➡ GARMENTS AND OUTFITS; 865]

negligence *n* **neglect**, inattention, abandonment, disregard, laxity, slackness, casualness, forgetfulness, carelessness [➡ NOT PAY ATTENTION; 764] *Opposite*: attention

negligent 1 *adj* **neglectful**, careless, inattentive, slipshod, remiss, lax, slack, casual, forgetful [➡ LACK OF COMMITMENT

AND UNRELIABILITY; 509] *Opposite*: careful　**2** *adj* (*literary*) **nonchalant**, relaxed, casual, informal, easy, indifferent [➡ NEUTRALITY AND INDIFFERENCE; 553] *Opposite*: attentive

negligible *adj* **insignificant**, tiny, small, slight, unimportant, minor, trifling, trivial [➡ UNIMPORTANT AND UNNECESSARY; 238] *Opposite*: significant

negligibly *adv* **not noticeably**, unimportantly, just, insignificantly, trivially, marginally, slightly [➡ TO A CERTAIN EXTENT; 136] *Opposite*: significantly

negotiable **1** *adj* **open to discussion**, unfixed, flexible, open-ended, up for grabs (*informal*) [➡ UNCERTAIN; 175] *Opposite*: nonnegotiable　**2** *adj* **transferable**, exchangeable, convertible, assignable, movable, flexible [➡ FINANCE AND ECONOMICS; 796]　**3** *adj* **passable**, navigable, crossable, traversable, accessible, reachable, open [➡ IN GOOD REPAIR; 1232] *Opposite*: impassable

negotiate **1** *v* **talk**, discuss, confer, consult, bargain, parley, agree, settle, cooperate, collaborate [➡ TWO-WAY COMMUNICATION; 607]　**2** *v* **sell**, transfer, exchange, convert, convey, assign [➡ ACCOUNTING, BANKING, AND BUDGETING; 799]　**3** *v* **get past**, pass, navigate, go around, cross, cope with, traverse, deal with [➡ MOVE PAST, INTO, OR THROUGH SOMETHING; 331]

negotiation *n* **arbitration**, mediation, discussion, cooperation, diplomacy, intercession, intervention [➡ NEGOTIATION AND DEBATE; 46]

negotiations *n* **talks**, discussions, conference, consultation, dialogue, debate, parley [➡ NEGOTIATION AND DEBATE; 46]

negotiator *n* **speaker**, representative, envoy, delegate, mediator, diplomat [➡ REPRESENTATIVES AND PATRONS; 968]

Nehru jacket *type of* **jacket** [➡ GARMENTS AND OUTFITS; 865]

neigh *type of* **animal sound** [➡ SOUNDS MADE BY ANIMALS; 1261]

neighbor *v* [➡ EXIST IN CLOSE PROXIMITY; 21]

neighborhood *n* **area**, district, barrio, region, locality, zone, quarter, community, vicinity, environs, proximity [➡ PLACE; 1065]

neighboring *adj* **adjacent**, adjoining, bordering, next door, near, next, nearby, close, immediate, local [➡ CLOSENESS; 159] *Opposite*: distant

neighborliness *n* **friendliness**, kindness, helpfulness, consideration, sociability, hospitality, care, cooperation [➡ FRIENDLINESS AND SOCIABILITY; 494] *Opposite*: unfriendliness

neither here nor there *adj* **beside the point**, irrelevant, inappropriate, unimportant, inconsequential, not worth worrying about, not the issue [➡ UNIMPORTANT AND UNNECESSARY; 238] *Opposite*: to the point

nemesis (*literary*) **1** *n* **punishment**, vengeance, retribution, fate, doom, revenge [➡ FATE, DESTINY, AND ASTROLOGY; 782]　**2** *n* **opponent**, archenemy, archrival, adversary, competitor, rival, antagonist, foe (*formal*) [➡ ENEMIES AND TORMENTORS; 969]　**3** *n* **avenger**, retaliator, revenger, vindicator [➡ ENEMIES AND TORMENTORS; 969]

neoclassical *type of* **pre-20th-century architecture** [➡ BUILDING AND ARCHITECTURE; 1076]

neologism *n* **new word**, coinage, buzzword (*informal*) [➡ ASPECTS OF LANGUAGE; 682]

neon *type of* **gas** [➡ GASES; 1275]

neonatal *adj* **newborn**, new, brand-new [➡ BABYHOOD, CHILDHOOD, AND ADOLESCENCE; 917]

neonate *n* [➡ CHILD OR YOUTH; 945]

neon light *type of* **light** [➡ LIGHT; 1164]

neophyte *n* **novice**, beginner, recruit, learner, trainee, raw recruit, newcomer, greenhorn, amateur, apprentice, tyro, tenderfoot (*informal*), rookie (*informal*) [➡ UNSKILLED PEOPLE; 530]

neoprene *type of* **plastic** [➡ PLASTICS; 1134]

nephew *type of* **younger relative** [➡ YOUNGER GENERATION RELATIVES; 958]

ne plus ultra *n* [➡ GOOD, WELL, BETTER; 183]

nepotism *n* **favoritism**, preferential treatment, partiality, bias, preference, discrimination, prejudice, one-sidedness [➡ PREJUDICE; 550]

Neptune *type of* **planet** [➡ HEAVENLY BODIES; 1061]

nerve **1** *n* **courage**, bravery, spirit, audacity, bravado, daring, pluck, mettle, fearlessness, guts (*slang*) [➡ COURAGE; 498] *Opposite*: cowardice　**2** *n* **boldness**, impudence, insolence, effrontery, bravado, audacity, face (*informal*), cheek (*informal*) [➡ BAD MANNERS AND SOCIAL SKILLS; 521]

See Compare and Contrast at **courage**.

nerve center *n* **hub**, control room, headquarters, H.Q., nexus, command post, head office, control center [➡ PLACE OF EMPLOYMENT; 832]

nerve gas *type of* **gas** [➡ GASES; 1275]

nerve-racking *adj* **anxious**, nervous, worrying, tense, panicky, terrifying, nail-biting, menacing, intimidating, scary (*informal*) [➡ EMOTIONALLY UNPLEASANT AND UPSETTING; 227]

nerves (*informal*) *n* **anxiety**, worry, tension, stress, mental strain, nervous tension, concern, uneasiness, nervousness [➡ FEELINGS ABOUT THE FUTURE; 533]

nerve-wracking *see* **nerve-racking**

nerve yourself *v* [➡ CHANGE OF MOOD AND COMPOSURE; 580]

nerviness *n* **edginess**, anxiety, jumpiness, tenseness, uneasiness, nervousness, tension [➡ FEELINGS ABOUT THE FUTURE; 533] *Opposite*: calmness

nervous *adj* **anxious**, worried, edgy, jumpy, panicky, tense, uneasy [➡ CONFUSION, ANXIETY, AND WORRY; 540] *Opposite*: calm

nervous breakdown *n* [➡ PSYCHOLOGY AND THE MIND; 769]

nervousness *n* **anxiety**, edginess, jumpiness, tenseness, uneasiness, apprehension, tension, nerviness (*informal*), nerves (*informal*) [➡ FEELINGS ABOUT THE FUTURE; 533] *Opposite*: calmness

nervous tension *n* [➡ PSYCHOLOGY AND THE MIND; 769]

nervy (*informal*) *adj* **fearless**, brave, daring, bold, gutsy (*informal*) [➡ COURAGE; 498]

nest *n* [➡ ANIMAL OR BIRD ACCOMMODATIONS; 1079]

nest egg *n* **savings**, reserve, capital, fund, store, contingency, something for a rainy day, stash (*informal*) [➡ MONEY; 797]

nestle 1 *v* **cuddle up**, cozy up, huddle, nuzzle, settle, burrow, snuggle [➡ GET CLOSER TOGETHER; 310] 2 *v* **cushion**, place, lie, soften, shelter, protect [➡ AVOID OR ESCAPE CONTACT; 418]

nestling *type of* **young bird** [➡ YOUNG BIRDS; 1004]

net 1 *n* **mesh**, web, netting, lattice, grid, meshwork, network [➡ FASTENERS, LINKS, AND NETWORKS; 1247] 2 *v* (*informal*) **get**, catch, achieve, obtain, procure, acquire, win [➡ GET; 420] 3 *v* **earn**, make, gain, make a profit of, profit, clear (*informal*) [➡ GET MONEY OR REWARD; 421] 4 *adj* **remaining**, disposable, clear, after deductions, left, take-home [➡ LESS; 126] *Opposite*: gross

netball *type of* **ball game** [➡ HOBBIES, GAMES, AND SPORTS; 875]

nether (*formal*) *adj* **rear**, hind, hinder, back, after, posterior (*formal*), hindmost (*literary*) [➡ RELATIVE LOCATION; 161]

netherworld 1 *n* (*literary*) [➡ CRIMINALS; 821] 2 *n* (*formal*) **hell**, inferno, purgatory, underworld, perdition [➡ RELIGIOUS CONCEPTS; 776]

net income *n* [➡ INCOME; 460]

netphone *type of* **telecommunications equipment** [➡ TELECOMMUNICATIONS; 1130]

netting *n* **mesh**, net, web, fabric, meshwork [➡ FASTENERS, LINKS, AND NETWORKS; 1247]

nettle 1 *type of* **weed** [➡ WEEDS AND THISTLES; 1034] 2 *v* (*informal*) **irritate**, annoy, infuriate, bother, exasperate, irk, get on somebody's nerves, aggravate (*informal*) [➡ ANGER AND ANNOY; 569]

nettled (*informal*) *adj* [➡ IRRITATION AND ANGER; 541]

network 1 *n* **net**, system, grid, web, link, linkage [➡ FASTENERS, LINKS, AND NETWORKS; 1247] 2 *type of* **hardware** [➡ COMPUTERS AND COMPUTING; 1127]

neurolinguistic programming *type of* **complementary therapy** [➡ REMEDIES, TREATMENTS, AND OPERATIONS; 731]

neurological *adj* **nervous**, nerve, neural [➡ PSYCHOLOGY AND THE MIND; 769]

neurosis (*dated*) *n* **quirk**, complex, obsession, inhibition, idiosyncrasy, phobia, problem, fixation, hang-up (*informal*) [➡ PSYCHOLOGY AND THE MIND; 769]

neurosurgeon *n* [➡ PEOPLE WHO WORK IN MEDICINE; 848]

neurotic *adj* **anxious**, fearful, phobic, fixated, disturbed, irrational, obsessed, overanxious, hung up (*informal*) [➡ PSYCHOLOGY AND THE MIND; 769] *Opposite*: rational

neuter *v* **spay**, sterilize, castrate, fix [➡ STERILIZE; 726]

neutral 1 *adj* **unbiased**, impartial, disinterested, dispassionate, middle-of-the-road, not taking sides, on the fence, impersonal, nonaligned [➡ NEUTRALITY AND INDIFFERENCE; 553] *Opposite*: biased 2 *adj* **drab**, light-colored, indistinct, indeterminate, pale, colorless, wishy-washy (*informal*) [➡ DESCRIBING COLORS; 1226] *Opposite*: colorful

neutrality *n* **impartiality**, detachment, objectivity, non-involvement, disinterest, nonalignment [➡ NEUTRALITY AND INDIFFERENCE; 553] *Opposite*: bias

neutralization *n* **canceling out**, nullification, off-setting, frustration, counteraction, removal, counterbalancing, deactivation [➡ ENDS AND DEPARTURES; 54] *Opposite*: activation

neutralize *v* **counteract**, counterbalance, defuse, deactivate, nullify, offset, cancel out, counterweight [➡ CORRECT AND PUT RIGHT; 377]

neutrally *adv* **impartially**, disinterestedly, dispassionately, objectively, without taking sides, impersonally [➡ NEUTRALITY AND INDIFFERENCE; 553]

neutrino *type of* **elementary particle** [➡ ELEMENTARY PARTICLES; 1279]

neutron *type of* **elementary particle** [➡ ELEMENTARY PARTICLES; 1279]

neutron bomb *type of* **explosive weapon** [➡ EXPLOSIVES; 1155]

never 1 *adv* **not ever**, not once, on no occasion, at no time [➡ NEVER AND INFREQUENCY; 97] *Opposite*: always 2 *adv* **certainly not**, under no circumstances, by no means, in no way, not at all, on no account, for no reason, no way (*informal*) [➡ NOT; 137]

never-ending *adj* **endless**, everlasting, continual, continuous, nonstop, constant, incessant, interminable, unremitting, eternal, infinite, permanent [➡ PERMANENCE: WITHOUT END; 94]

never-never land *n* [➡ NONEXISTENT PLACES; 1066]

nevertheless *adv* **yet**, but, however, nonetheless, on the other hand, all the same, even so, still, though [➡ ALTHOUGH, NEVERTHELESS, AND DESPITE; 169]

never-to-be-repeated *adj* [➡ EXTRAORDINARY: UNCOMMON; 205]

nevus *n* [➡ CONDITIONS AFFECTING THE SKIN; 721]

new 1 *adj* **novel**, newfangled, original, innovative, fresh, different, firsthand [➡ EXTRAORDINARY: UNCOMMON; 205] *Opposite*: old 2 *adj* **recent**, latest, up-to-the-minute, contemporary, up-to-date, modern, modernistic, neoteric [➡ NEW, MODERN; 166] *Opposite*: outmoded 3 *adj* **another**, additional, extra, further, different, fresh, more, other [➡ MORE AND EXCESS; 124] 4 *adj* **brand-new**, pristine, newborn, in mint condition, newfound, spanking [➡ IN GOOD REPAIR; 1232] *Opposite*: used 5 *adj* **inexperienced**, new to the job, just starting out, wet behind the ears, green, recent, unfamiliar, unaccustomed [➡ UNSKILLED; 529] *Opposite*: experienced

Compare and Contrast: *new, fresh, modern, newfangled, novel, original*

CORE MEANING: never experienced before or having recently come into being

new recently invented, discovered, made, bought, experienced, or not previously known or encountered; *fresh* excitingly or refreshingly different from what has been done or experienced previously; *modern* of the latest kind, or characterized by up-to-date ideas, techniques, design, or equipment; *newfangled* puzzlingly or worryingly new or different, especially because it seems gimmicky or overcomplicated; *novel* new and different, often in an interesting, unusual, or inventive way; *original* unique and not copied or derived from anything else.

new age *type of* **electronic music** [➡ MUSIC, SONGS, AND SINGING; 907]

New Age traveler *n* [➡ TRAVEL: TRAVELERS AND WALKERS; 319]

newborn 1 *adj* **new**, brand-new, neonatal [➡ BABYHOOD, CHILD-HOOD, AND ADOLESCENCE; 917] **2** *adj* **newfound**, new, brand-new, fresh, recent [➡ NEW, MODERN; 166] *Opposite*: established **3** *n* **baby**, infant, child, neonate, babe (*literary or archaic*) [➡ CHILD OR YOUTH; 945]

Newburg *type of* **food presentation** [➡ COOKING AND FOOD PREPARATION; 353]

newcomer 1 *n* **new arrival**, stranger, Johnny-come-lately (*informal*) [➡ STRANGERS; 972] **2** *n* **novice**, recruit, beginner, neophyte, trainee, greenhorn, apprentice, tenderfoot (*informal*) [➡ UNSKILLED PEOPLE; 530] *Opposite*: old hand

new economy *type of* **economic system** [➡ FINANCE AND ECONOMICS; 796]

newfangled *adj* **novel**, new, innovative, up-to-date, up-to-the-minute, modern [➡ NEW, MODERN; 166] *Opposite*: old-fashioned

> *See Compare and Contrast at* **new**.

Newfoundland *type of* **large dog** [➡ DOGS; 980]

newly 1 *adv* **recently**, lately, freshly, just now, just this minute, only just [➡ PRESENT; 85] **2** *adv* **afresh**, anew, again, once more [➡ AGAIN; 109]

newlyweds *n* **just marrieds**, wedding couple, happy couple, bride and groom, bride, groom, couple [➡ RELATIVES BY MARRIAGE; 960]

newness *n* **novelty**, innovation, originality, freshness, inventiveness, individuality [➡ EXTRAORDINARY: UNCOMMON; 205]

New Orleans jazz *type of* **jazz music** [➡ MUSIC, SONGS, AND SINGING; 907]

new potato *type of* **root vegetable** [➡ FRUIT AND VEGETABLES; 1176]

news 1 *n* **information**, reports, intelligence, gossip, rumor, hearsay [➡ BASIC DETAILS; 688] **2** *n* **news bulletin**, news broadcast, newscast, news summary, news flash, news update, bulletin, broadcast, update, summary, news report, news hour [➡ TELEVISION AND RADIO; 606]

newscast *n* **news**, news bulletin, news broadcast, news summary, news flash, news update, news hour, broadcast, bulletin, update, summary, news report [➡ TELEVISION AND RADIO; 606]

newscaster *n* **broadcaster**, telecaster, anchor, announcer [➡ WORKERS IN ENTERTAINMENT AND MEDIA; 873]

news flash *n* **news update**, news bulletin, news broadcast, newscast [➡ TELEVISION AND RADIO; 606]

newsgroup *n* [➡ THE INTERNET; 1128]

newshawk (*informal*) *n* **reporter**, journalist, investigative reporter, correspondent, newsgatherer [➡ WORKERS IN ENTERTAINMENT AND MEDIA; 873]

newshound (*informal*) *n* **reporter**, journalist, investigative journalist, newsgatherer, correspondent, newshawk (*informal*) [➡ WORKERS IN ENTERTAINMENT AND MEDIA; 873]

newsletter *n* **information sheet**, bulletin, circular, news-sheet (*UK*) [➡ NEWSPAPERS AND MAGAZINES; 605]

newsman *n* **reporter**, journalist, broadcaster, correspondent, newspaperman, newshound (*informal*), newshawk (*informal*) [➡ WORKERS IN ENTERTAINMENT AND MEDIA; 873]

newspaper 1 *n* **paper**, broadsheet, daily, weekly, broadside, rag (*informal*), tabloid (*UK*) [➡ NEWSPAPERS AND MAGAZINES; 605] **2** *n* **newsprint**, printing paper, coarse paper [➡ NEWSPAPERS AND MAGAZINES; 605]

newspaperman *n* **reporter**, journalist, correspondent, newsman, newshound (*informal*), newshawk (*informal*) [➡ WORKERS IN ENTERTAINMENT AND MEDIA; 873]

newspaperwoman *n* **reporter**, journalist, correspondent, newswoman, newshound (*informal*), newshawk (*informal*) [➡ WORKERS IN ENTERTAINMENT AND MEDIA; 873]

newsprint *n* **newspaper**, printing paper, coarse paper [➡ NEWSPAPERS AND MAGAZINES; 605]

newsreel *n* **news film**, documentary, news movie, news report, news bulletin, news footage [➡ TELEVISION AND RADIO; 606]

newsroom *n* **news studio**, broadcasting studio, TV studio [➡ TELEVISION AND RADIO; 606]

newssheet (*UK*) *n* **newsletter**, bulletin, press release, information sheet, data sheet, fact file, newspaper [➡ NEWSPAPERS AND MAGAZINES; 605]

newsstand *n* **kiosk**, stand, stall, booth [➡ RETAIL OUTLETS; 1083]

newswoman *n* **reporter**, broadcaster, correspondent, journalist, newspaperwoman, newshound (*informal*), newshawk (*informal*) [➡ WORKERS IN ENTERTAINMENT AND MEDIA; 873]

newsworthy *adj* **interesting**, exciting, remarkable, out of the ordinary, extraordinary, important [➡ INTERESTING AND MEANINGFUL; 190] *Opposite*: unremarkable

newsy *adj* **chatty**, gossipy, friendly, interesting, informative, explanatory, informational [➡ INTERESTING AND MEANINGFUL; 190]

newt *type of* **amphibian** [➡ AMPHIBIANS; 1008]

newton *type of* **SI unit** [➡ SIZE AND DIMENSIONS; 1192]

new wave *type of* **pop and vocal music** [➡ MUSIC, SONGS, AND SINGING; 907]

next *adv* **after that**, then, afterward, after, thereafter, consequently, subsequently, behind, later [➡ AFTER, LAST, AND FOLLOWING; 165] *Opposite*: first

next door *adv* **nearby**, close, in the vicinity, around the corner [➡ CLOSENESS; 159]

next-door *adj* **adjacent**, adjoining, neighboring, flanking, next, nearby [➡ CLOSENESS; 159]

next of kin *n* **close relative**, blood relation, blood relative, spouse, partner, parent, kinsman, kinswoman, kin, kinsfolk, kinfolk [➡ THE FAMILY; 956]

next to last *adj* [➡ AFTER, LAST, AND FOLLOWING; 165]

next world *n* [➡ RELIGIOUS CONCEPTS; 776]

nexus *n* **connection**, link, tie, relationship, node, join, interconnection, bond, yoke [➡ CONNECTIONS; 143]

ngultrum *type of* **currency** [➡ CURRENCIES; 798]

nib *n* **tip**, point, end [➡ EXTREMITIES OF PHYSICAL OBJECTS; 1250]

nibble 1 *v* **chew**, nip, peck, gnaw, bite [➡ EAT AND NOT EAT; 710] *Opposite*: chomp (*informal*) 2 *n* **bite**, morsel, tidbit, crumb, speck, particle, fragment [➡ SMALL PIECES; 129]

nice 1 *adj* **enjoyable**, agreeable, pleasant, good, lovely, amusing, wonderful, fine (*informal*) [➡ EMOTIONALLY PLEASANT; 187] *Opposite*: unpleasant 2 *adj* **polite**, considerate, friendly, courteous, charming, kind, sympathetic, warm-hearted, cordial [➡ GENEROSITY AND KINDNESS; 495] *Opposite*: nasty 3 *adj* **respectable**, proper, refined, virtuous, genteel, correct, seemly, acceptable [➡ GOOD MANNERS AND SOCIAL SKILLS; 520] *Opposite*: improper 4 *adj* **attractive**, lovely, pleasant, delightful, appealing, good-looking, fine (*informal*) [➡ BEAUTY AND ATTRACTIVENESS; 189] *Opposite*: unattractive 5 *adj* **precise**, exact, fine-drawn, meticulous, narrow, subtle, fine (*informal*) [➡ CONCISE AND CLEAR; 202] *Opposite*: broad 6 *adj* **discriminating**, painstaking, particular, scrupulous, precise, fastidious, meticulous, fussy, exact, finicky, careful, choosy (*informal*) [➡ DIFFICULT TO PLEASE; 515]

nice-looking *adj* **good-looking**, pretty, attractive, handsome, appealing, pleasing, lovely, striking, beautiful [➡ PEOPLE'S PHYSICAL APPEARANCE; 475] *Opposite*: unattractive

nicely 1 *adv* **agreeably**, kindly, well, politely, courteously, attractively, pleasantly [➡ GOOD MANNERS AND SOCIAL SKILLS; 520] *Opposite*: unpleasantly 2 *adv* **suitably**, effectively, satisfactorily, accurately, carefully, adequately, exactly, well, agreeably, properly [➡ CORRECT AND FAULTLESS; 182] *Opposite*: unsatisfactorily 3 *adv* **carefully**, meticulously, finely, subtly, narrowly, precisely, fastidiously, neatly [➡ CONCISE AND CLEAR; 202] *Opposite*: broadly

nicety 1 *n* **distinction**, precision, detail, small point, refinement, subtlety [➡ BASIC DETAILS; 688] 2 *n* **delicacy**, tactfulness, particularity, finesse, polish, subtlety, meticulousness, exactness [➡ CONCISE AND CLEAR; 202]

niche 1 *n* **place**, position, slot, function, role, forte, calling, vocation, métier [➡ PROFESSIONS; 845] 2 *n* **alcove**, bay, nook, cubbyhole, recess, cranny, corner, hollow, hidey-hole (*informal*) [➡ ALCOVES, CUBICLES, AND COMPARTMENTS; 1096]

nick 1 *n* **incision**, groove, mark, notch, cut, scratch, score, chip [➡ HOLES, GAPS, AND FORKS; 1252] 2 *v* **score**, incise, mark, cut, scratch, notch, dent, deface [➡ TEAR, BREAK, AND CUT; 360]

See Compare and Contrast at **steal**.

nickel 1 *type of* **metal** [➡ METALS; 1276] 2 *n* [➡ CURRENCIES; 798]

nicknack *see* **knickknack**

nickname 1 *n* **name**, pet name, epithet, sobriquet, diminutive, moniker (*slang*), handle (*slang*), cognomen (*formal*) [➡ NAME AND DESCRIBE; 665] 2 *v* **label**, call, name, designate, dub, tag [➡ NAME AND DESCRIBE; 665]

niece *type of* **younger relative** [➡ YOUNGER GENERATION RELATIVES; 958]

niftiness (*informal*) *n* [➡ USEFULNESS; 199]

nifty 1 *adj* (*informal*) **useful**, handy, convenient, effective, ingenious, neat, clever (*UK*) [➡ USEFULNESS; 199] *Opposite*: useless 2 *adj* **smart**, attractive, well-designed, neat, natty, stylish [➡ BEAUTY AND ATTRACTIVENESS; 189] *Opposite*: unattractive

3 *adj* **good**, quick, clever, neat, slick, agile, adroit, deft, skillful [➡ DESCRIBING BODY MOVEMENTS; 288] *Opposite*: clumsy

niggard *n* **miser**, skinflint, pinchpenny, penny pincher (*informal*), scrooge (*informal*), cheapskate (*informal*) [➡ FINANCIALLY MEAN PEOPLE; 952]

niggardliness *n* [➡ GRASPING AND FINANCIALLY MEAN; 519]

niggardly 1 *adj* **ungenerous**, stingy, mean, miserly, tight, cheap, parsimonious, measly (*informal*) [➡ GRASPING AND FINANCIALLY MEAN; 519] *Opposite*: generous 2 *adj* **miserable**, meager, wretched, insufficient, paltry, poor, beggarly, sorry [➡ TOO FEW, TOO LITTLE; 122]

niggle 1 *v* **criticize**, cavil, carp, nag, nitpick, find fault, grouse (*informal*) [➡ COMPLAIN AND NAG; 686] 2 *v* **trouble**, bother, nag, annoy, irritate, worry [➡ ANGER AND ANNOY; 569] 3 *n* **complaint**, grumble, objection, grievance, criticism [➡ COMPLAIN AND NAG; 686] 4 *n* **doubt**, anxiety, twinge, misgiving, concern, worry [➡ CONFUSION, ANXIETY, AND WORRY; 540]

niggling 1 *adj* **trivial**, petty, unimportant, inconsequential, insignificant, minor, small, trifling, piddling (*informal*) [➡ UNIMPORTANT AND UNNECESSARY; 238] *Opposite*: important 2 *adj* **irritating**, awkward, finicky, troublesome, difficult, nagging, tricky, bothersome, worrying, troubling [➡ IRRITATING; 228]

nigh *adj* **imminent**, close, near, at hand, approaching, coming, nearly here, pending, impending [➡ CLOSENESS; 159] *Opposite*: remote

night 1 *n* **nighttime**, hours of darkness, dark, darkness, nightfall, dusk [➡ TIMES OF DAY; 87] *Opposite*: day 2 *n* **early hours**, small hours, middle of the night [➡ TIMES OF DAY; 87] 3 *interj* (*informal*) **good night**, sleep well, sleep tight [➡ GREETINGS, FAREWELLS, AND SALUTATIONS; 659]

nightcap 1 *n* **drink**, bedtime drink, hot drink, hot toddy [➡ DRINKS; 1187] 2 *n* **bedcap**, sleeping cap, hat [➡ GARMENTS AND OUTFITS; 865]

nightclothes *n* **pajamas**, sleepwear, nightwear [➡ GARMENTS AND OUTFITS; 865]

nightclub *type of* **bar or club** [➡ HOTELS, RESTAURANTS, AND CLUBS; 1082]

nightfall *n* **dusk**, twilight, evening, sunset, end of the day, sundown, eventide (*literary*) [➡ TIMES OF DAY; 87] *Opposite*: daybreak

nightgown *n* **negligee**, nightshirt, nightie (*informal*), nightdress (*UK*) [➡ GARMENTS AND OUTFITS; 865]

nightie *see* **nightgown**

nightingale *type of* **songbird** [➡ SONGBIRDS; 1003]

nightjar *type of* **songbird** [➡ SONGBIRDS; 1003]

nightlife *n* **nightspots**, social life, entertainment, club scene, discos, bars, nightclubs, pubs and clubs (*UK*) [➡ ENTERTAINMENT; 872]

nightlight *type of* **light** [➡ LIGHT; 1164]

nightly 1 *adj* **night**, evening, nocturnal [➡ TIMES OF DAY; 87] 2 *adv* **every night**, night by night, once a night, through the night [➡ FREQUENT AND OFTEN; 107]

nightmare 1 *n* **dream**, bad dream, hallucination, vision, incubus [➞SLEEP AND DREAM; 723] **2** *adj* **traumatic**, frightening, dreadful, terrible, nightmarish, horrendous, terrifying [➞FRIGHTENING; 231] *Opposite*: wonderful

nightmarish *adj* **nightmare**, frightening, terrifying, horrendous, terrible, dreadful [➞FRIGHTENING; 231] *Opposite*: lovely

nightshirt *type of* **sleepwear** [➞GARMENTS AND OUTFITS; 865]

nightspot *n* **bar**, nightclub, disco, club [➞HOTELS, RESTAURANTS, AND CLUBS; 1082]

nightstick *type of* **club** [➞BLUNT INSTRUMENTS AND WHIPS; 1158]

night table *type of* **table** [➞FURNITURE; 858]

nighttime *n* **night**, evening, dark, hours of darkness, middle of the night, early hours [➞TIMES OF DAY; 87] *Opposite*: daytime

night watchman *n* [➞PEOPLE WHO GUARD AND PROTECT; 846]

nightwear *n* **sleepwear**, nightclothes, pajamas [➞GARMENTS AND OUTFITS; 865]

nihilism *n* **negativism**, pessimism, nothingness, emptiness, anarchism, skepticism [➞PHILOSOPHIES AND BELIEFS; 780]

nihilist *n* **pessimist**, existentialist, anarchist, revolutionary, radical, rebel, destroyer [➞PHILOSOPHICAL AND POLITICAL THINKERS; 781]

nihilistic *adj* **negativistic**, pessimistic, existentialist, destructive, anarchic, revolutionary, rebellious, radical [➞PHILOSOPHIES AND BELIEFS; 780]

nil *n* **nothing**, zero, none, naught, null, nullity, zilch (*informal*), nix (*dated slang*) [➞NONE; 123]

Nile green *type of* **green** [➞COLORS; 1224]

Nile perch *type of* **freshwater fish** [➞FRESHWATER FISH; 1010]

nimble *adj* **sprightly**, lithe, deft, agile, quick, dexterous, lively, lissom, light-footed, spry [➞AGILITY OF THE BODY; 476] *Opposite*: awkward

nimbleness *n* **sprightliness**, litheness, agility, quickness, dexterity, liveliness, spryness [➞AGILITY OF THE BODY; 476] *Opposite*: awkwardness

nimbus 1 *n* **circle of light**, halo, corona, aura, radiance [➞LIGHT; 1164] **2** *type of* **cloud** [➞CLOUDY AND RAINY WEATHER; 1052]

nip 1 *v* **squeeze**, compress, grasp, grab, grip, pinch, tweak [➞CONTACT: TOUCH; 412] **2** *v* **peck**, nibble, snap, gnaw, bite, lop, snip, clip, dock [➞TEAR, BREAK, AND CUT; 360] **3** *v* **steal**, snatch, pilfer, make off with, make away with, lift (*informal*), swipe (*informal*), purloin (*formal or humorous*) [➞STEAL AND ROB; 426] **4** *n* **pinch**, tweak, grasp, grab, squeeze [➞CONTACT: TOUCH; 412] **5** *n* **peck**, bite, nibble, snippet, clipping, cutting [➞SMALL PIECES; 129] **6** *n* **sip**, drink, swallow, tot, swig (*informal*), shot (*informal*) [➞DRINKS; 1187]

nip in the bud (*informal*) *v* **stop**, prevent, hinder, block, thwart, stymie, abort, nix (*slang*) [➞CAUSE TO STOP; 266] *Opposite*: encourage

nipper *n* **pincer**, claw, gripper, appendage [➞PARTS OF THE BODY: ARM AND HAND; 695]

nipple *part of* **torso** [➞PARTS OF THE BODY: TORSO; 693]

nippy 1 *adj* **cold**, chilly, freezing, biting, icy, cool [➞COLD WEATHER; 1051] *Opposite*: warm **2** *adj* (*UK*) **quick**, fast, speedy, rapid, swift [➞MOVING QUICKLY; 103] *Opposite*: slow

nirvana 1 *n* **enlightenment**, spiritual enlightenment, state of grace [➞RELIGIOUS CONCEPTS; 776] **2** *n* **bliss**, heaven, joy, paradise, pleasure, glory, Eden, seventh heaven, promised land [➞PLEASANT SITUATIONS; 74] *Opposite*: hell

nit *type of* **stage of insect development** [➞INSECT STAGES; 1020]

nitpick *v* **cavil**, complain, quibble, find fault, criticize, carp, pick holes, take apart (*informal*) [➞COMPLAIN AND NAG; 686]

See Compare and Contrast at **criticize**.

nitpicker *n* **faultfinder**, critic, carper, nagger, pedant [➞GRUMPY AND NEGATIVE PEOPLE; 953]

nitpicking 1 *n* **criticism**, faultfinding, carping, hairsplitting, quibbling, fussiness, pickiness [➞DIFFICULT TO PLEASE; 515] **2** *adj* **critical**, faultfinding, carping, finicky, fussy, hypercritical, unfavorable, disapproving [➞DIFFICULT TO PLEASE; 515]

nitrogen *type of* **gas** [➞GASES; 1275]

nitroglycerin *type of* **explosive material** [➞EXPLOSIVES; 1155]

nitrous oxide *type of* **gas** [➞GASES; 1275]

nitty-gritty (*informal*) *n* **essentials**, brass tacks, fundamentals, basics, crux of the matter, details, nuts and bolts (*informal*) [➞BASIC DETAILS; 688]

nix 1 *n* (*dated slang*) **zero**, nil, nothing, naught, none, null, nullity, zilch (*informal*) [➞NONE; 123] **2** *v* (*slang*) **refuse**, forbid, veto, overturn, nullify, annul, reverse, invalidate, negate (*formal*) [➞CAUSE TO STOP; 266]

no 1 *adv* **on no account**, not at all, certainly not, definitely not, by no means, no way (*informal*), nope (*slang*) [➞NOT; 137] **2** *n* **rejection**, negative, denial, rebuff, refusal, veto, thumbs down (*informal*) [➞REFUSE PERMISSION AND NOT ALLOW; 670] **3** *adj* **not any**, not one, not at all [➞NONE; 123]

no ball (*UK*) *n* **foul throw**, misthrow, foul ball [➞SPORTS TERMS; 877]

nobility 1 *n* **aristocracy**, upper class, landed gentry, upper crust (*informal*) [➞CLASS STATUS; 889] **2** *n* **dignity**, graciousness, decency, goodness, nobleness, superiority [➞MORALLY GOOD; 774]

noble 1 *adj* **honorable**, principled, moral, decent, upright, gallant, polite, self-sacrificing, magnanimous, virtuous, just [➞MORALLY GOOD; 774] *Opposite*: unprincipled **2** *adj* **magnificent**, impressive, imposing, fine, splendid, gracious, great, superior [➞SUPERIORITY; 152] *Opposite*: unimpressive **3** *adj* **aristocratic**, patrician, blue-blooded, titled, upper-class, princely, highborn (*literary*) [➞CLASS STATUS; 889] **4** *n* **nobleman**, noblewoman, lord, lady, earl, duke, duchess, baron, baronet, baroness, aristocrat, peer, patrician [➞RULERS AND ARISTOCRACY; 823] *Opposite*: commoner

noble gas *type of* **gas** [➞GASES; 1275]

nobleman *n* **noble**, aristocrat, lord, patrician, peer [➞RULERS AND ARISTOCRACY; 823] *Opposite*: commoner

nobleness *n* honorableness, honor, morality, magnanimity, dignity, decency, goodness, gallantry, nobility, righteousness, graciousness, greatness, superiority [➡ MORALLY GOOD; 774]

noblewoman *n* noble, peer, lady, aristocrat, patrician [➡ RULERS AND ARISTOCRACY; 823]

nobody 1 *pron* **not one person**, not a single person, no one, not a soul [➡ NONE; 123] *Opposite*: everybody 2 *n* **nonentity**, mediocrity, unknown, upstart, nothing [➡ LAZY OR UNSUCCESSFUL PEOPLE; 948]

nocturnal *adj* **nighttime**, night, nightly [➡ TIMES OF DAY; 87] *Opposite*: diurnal

nocturne *type of* **musical form** [➡ MUSIC, SONGS, AND SINGING; 907]

nod 1 *v* **move**, bow, bob, jiggle, dip, waggle, move up and down, shake [➡ MOVE SOMETHING: ON THE SPOT; 336] 2 *n* **permission**, affirmation, signal, sign, gesture, go-ahead (*informal*), okay (*informal*), thumbs up (*informal*) [➡ GESTURES AND GESTICULATION; 653]

noddle (*dated informal*) *n* **head**, nut (*informal*), noodle (*slang*), noggin (*dated informal*) [➡ PARTS OF THE BODY: HEAD; 692]

node 1 *n* **bulge**, protuberance, lump, swelling, bump, knob, knot, nodule, burl, bud [➡ ROUNDED SHAPE; 1218] 2 *n* **meeting point**, join, connection, intersection, point, joint [➡ FASTENERS, LINKS, AND NETWORKS; 1247]

no different *adj* **identical**, the same, equal, alike, equivalent [➡ SAMENESS; 150]

nod off *v* **doze off**, fall asleep, drift off, doze, catnap, nap, drowse, drop off (*informal*), snooze (*informal*) [➡ SLEEP AND DREAM; 723] *Opposite*: wake up

no doubt *adv* **undoubtedly**, surely, certainly, without a doubt, for sure (*informal*) [➡ CERTAIN; 174]

nod to *v* **acknowledge**, greet, signal to, salute [➡ GESTURES AND GESTICULATION; 653]

nodule *n* **node**, knot, knob, lump, bump, protuberance, swelling [➡ ROUNDED SHAPE; 1218]

no end of (*informal*) *pron* **a lot of**, a great deal of, very much, lots of, plenty of [➡ MANY, MUCH, LARGE AMOUNT; 117]

no-frills (*informal*) *adj* **basic**, utilitarian, unadorned, economy, generic, plain, straightforward [➡ PLAIN; 232] *Opposite*: luxury

noggin (*dated informal*) *n* **head**, nut (*informal*), noodle (*slang*), noddle (*dated informal*) [➡ PARTS OF THE BODY: HEAD; 692]

no good *adj* [➡ REDUNDANT AND USELESS; 240]

no great shakes *adj* [➡ REDUNDANT AND USELESS; 240]

no holds barred *adv* **unrestrained**, unconstrained, uninhibited, free, without restraint, without fear or favor [➡ INCAUTIOUS AND CARELESS; 283]

noise *n* **sound**, din, racket, clamor, clatter, blast, blare, uproar, hullabaloo, commotion [➡ SOUNDS; 1256] *Opposite*: silence

noiseless *adj* **soundless**, silent, muted, hushed, quiet, still, inaudible [➡ ABSENCE OF SOUND; 1257] *Opposite*: noisy

noiselessness *n* [➡ ABSENCE OF SOUND; 1257]

noisiness *n* [➡ LOUD, HIGH, OR UNPLEASANT SOUNDS; 1266]

noisome *adj* **foul**, offensive, disgusting, repulsive, repellent, repugnant, horrible, awful, putrid [➡ DISGUSTING AND REPULSIVE; 230] *Opposite*: pleasant

noisy *adj* **loud**, deafening, earsplitting, piercing, raucous, strident, boisterous, blaring [➡ LOUD, HIGH, OR UNPLEASANT SOUNDS; 1266] *Opposite*: quiet

no joke *adj* **a serious matter**, no laughing matter, not a trivial issue, hard work [➡ DIFFICULTY AND COMPLEXITY; 242]

no longer with us *adj* [➡ DEAD AND DYING; 925]

nomad *n* **wanderer**, traveler, itinerant, migrant, drifter, rover [➡ NOMADIC AND ROOTLESS LIFESTYLES; 884]

nomadic *adj* **itinerant**, traveling, roaming, wandering, roving, drifting [➡ NOMADIC AND ROOTLESS LIFESTYLES; 884]

no matter what *adv* **come what may**, anyhow, regardless, by hook or by crook, anyway, in any case [➡ ALTHOUGH, NEVERTHELESS, AND DESPITE; 169]

nom de guerre *n* [➡ NAME AND DESCRIBE; 665]

nom de plume *n* **pen name**, pseudonym, alias, assumed name, nom de guerre [➡ NAME AND DESCRIBE; 665]

nomenclature 1 *n* **classification**, taxonomy, codification, categorization, organization, arrangement, catalog [➡ NAME AND DESCRIBE; 665] 2 *n* **terminology**, vocabulary, language, terms, jargon [➡ ASPECTS OF LANGUAGE; 682]

nominal 1 *adj* **supposed**, ostensible, so-called, in name only, titular [➡ FALSE AND UNREAL; 173] *Opposite*: actual 2 *adj* **small**, trifling, token, minimal, insignificant, minor, peppercorn [➡ SMALL; 1195] *Opposite*: great

nominally *adv* **supposedly**, ostensibly, by name, technically, in name only [➡ FALSE AND UNREAL; 173]

nominate 1 *v* **propose**, put forward, suggest, name, submit, recommend [➡ CONFER STATUS; 458] *Opposite*: reject 2 *v* **appoint**, elect, designate, choose, select, pick, commission [➡ CONFER STATUS; 458] *Opposite*: reject

nomination 1 *n* **proposal**, suggestion, recommendation, submission [➡ APPROVE AND CONFIRM; 646] 2 *n* **choice**, selection, appointment, nominee, candidate [➡ CONFER STATUS; 458]

nominative *type of* **grammatical term** [➡ ASPECTS OF LANGUAGE; 682]

nominee *n* **candidate**, entrant, applicant, nomination, contender [➡ COMPETITORS; 41]

nonaggression *n* **pacifism**, peaceful coexistence, nonbelligerence, nonviolence, inaction [➡ PEACEFULNESS AND GENTLENESS; 214] *Opposite*: aggression

nonalcoholic *adj* **soft**, lite, low-alcohol [➡ DRINKS; 1187] *Opposite*: alcoholic

nonaligned *adj* **neutral**, independent, unallied, unconnected, unrelated, autonomous, impartial [➡ NEUTRALITY AND INDIFFERENCE; 553] *Opposite*: aligned

nonalignment *n* **neutrality**, independence, autonomy, self-determination, impartiality [➡ NEUTRALITY AND INDIFFERENCE; 553] *Opposite*: alignment

nonattendance 1 *n* truancy, default, playing truant, playing hooky, cutting class [➡ ABSENT AND UNAVAILABLE; 7] *Opposite*: attendance 2 *n* **absence**, default, absenteeism, nonappearance [➡ ABSENT AND UNAVAILABLE; 7] *Opposite*: presence

nonbeliever *n* **disbeliever**, unbeliever, doubter, skeptic, agnostic, atheist [➡ PHILOSOPHICAL AND POLITICAL THINKERS; 781] *Opposite*: believer

nonchalance *n* **indifference**, detachment, disinterest, calmness, dispassion, casualness, insouciance [➡ NEUTRALITY AND INDIFFERENCE; 553] *Opposite*: interest

nonchalant *adj* **casual**, offhand, cool, calm, relaxed, blasé, indifferent, detached, unconcerned, dispassionate, imperturbable, unflappable, insouciant, laid-back (*informal*) [➡ NEUTRALITY AND INDIFFERENCE; 553] *Opposite*: concerned

noncombatant *n* **civilian**, citizen, nonfighter [➡ MILITARY PERSONNEL; 828] *Opposite*: soldier

noncommittal *adj* **guarded**, evasive, vague, wary, tactful, reserved, cautious, careful, discreet, unrevealing, ambiguous [➡ RETICENT AND UNFORTHCOMING; 631] *Opposite*: definite

noncompliance *n* **nonfulfillment**, nonconformity, refusal, failure, denial, defiance, disobedience, rebellion, rebelliousness [➡ REBELLIOUSNESS AND DISOBEDIENCE; 565] *Opposite*: compliance

noncompliant *adj* **disobedient**, recalcitrant, rebellious, uncooperative, dissenting, nonconforming, defiant [➡ REBELLIOUSNESS AND DISOBEDIENCE; 565] *Opposite*: cooperative

nonconformist 1 *adj* **unconventional**, eccentric, alternative, rebellious, radical, individualistic, way-out (*informal*) [➡ REBELLIOUSNESS AND DISOBEDIENCE; 565] *Opposite*: conformist 2 *n* **rebel**, dissenter, maverick, radical, eccentric, free spirit, individualist [➡ UNCOOPERATIVE OR REBELLIOUS PEOPLE; 566] *Opposite*: conformist

nonconformity 1 *n* **unconventionality**, originality, eccentricity, idiosyncrasy, individuality, free-spiritedness, individualism, rebelliousness [➡ DIFFERENCE; 149] *Opposite*: conformity 2 *n* **noncooperation**, noncompliance, divergence, variation, difference, disobedience, rebellion, variance [➡ REBELLIOUSNESS AND DISOBEDIENCE; 565] *Opposite*: conformity

noncooperation *n* **defiance**, disobedience, insubordination, rebellion, rebelliousness, nonconformity, insolence, boldness, noncompliance [➡ REBELLIOUSNESS AND DISOBEDIENCE; 565] *Opposite*: cooperation

nondescript *adj* **unremarkable**, ordinary, unexceptional, dull, uninteresting, commonplace, characterless, plain [➡ PLAIN; 232] *Opposite*: special

nondiscriminatory *adj* **fair**, equal, unbiased, evenhanded, just, fair-minded [➡ EQUALITY; 154] *Opposite*: discriminatory

none 1 *pron* **no one**, nobody, not a soul, not a single person [➡ NONE; 123] 2 *pron* **not any**, nothing, not a bit, not an iota, not a hint [➡ NONE; 123] *Opposite*: some

nonentity *n* **nobody**, unknown, mediocrity, nothing [➡ LAZY OR UNSUCCESSFUL PEOPLE; 948] *Opposite*: somebody

nonessential 1 *adj* **luxury**, extra, supplementary, additional, dispensable, unnecessary, unneeded [➡ UNIMPORTANT AND UNNECESSARY; 238] *Opposite*: essential 2 *n* **extra**, luxury, perk [➡ AMAZING THINGS; 211] *Opposite*: essential

nonetheless *adv* **however**, nevertheless, even so, on the other hand [➡ ALTHOUGH, NEVERTHELESS, AND DESPITE; 169]

nonevent *n* **failure**, anticlimax, disappointment, letdown, flop, dud (*informal*), bomb (*informal*), bummer (*slang*) [➡ DISASTERS; 252] *Opposite*: success

nonexistence 1 *n* **absence**, lack, want, dearth, deficiency [➡ TOO FEW, TOO LITTLE; 122] 2 *n* **nothingness**, unreality, fictionality [➡ NONEXISTENCE; 24] *Opposite*: existence

nonexistent *adj* **missing**, unreal, fictional, imaginary, absent [➡ FALSE AND UNREAL; 173] *Opposite*: existent (*formal*)

nonfatal *adj* [➡ SAFE AND SAFETY; 191]

nonfiction *adj* **factual**, true-life, reference, fact-based [➡ TRUE AND REAL; 171] *Opposite*: fiction

nonflammable *adj* **noninflammable**, fireproof, flameproof, fire-retardant, fire-resistant [➡ FIRE, FLAMMABILITY, AND BURNING; 1165] *Opposite*: inflammable

nonhazardous *adj* [➡ SAFE AND SAFETY; 191]

nonintervention *n* **inaction**, noninvolvement, noninterventionism, laissez-faire, abstention, neutrality [➡ NEUTRALITY AND INDIFFERENCE; 553] *Opposite*: intervention

noninterventionist *adj* **laissez-faire**, noninterfering, neutral, nonaligned, nonpartisan [➡ NEUTRALITY AND INDIFFERENCE; 553]

noniron (*UK*) *adj* **crease-resistant**, easy-care, drip-dry, wash-and-wear, permanent-press [➡ DESCRIBING CLOTHES; 869]

nonjudgmental *adj* **indulgent**, lax, easygoing, relaxed, lenient, open-minded, broad-minded, liberal, unprejudiced, tolerant [➡ POSITIVE INTELLECTUAL CHARACTERISTICS; 524] *Opposite*: judgmental

nonmember *n* **outsider**, visitor, guest [➡ STRANGERS; 972] *Opposite*: member

nonmetric unit *n* [➡ SIZE AND DIMENSIONS; 1192]

nonnegotiable 1 *adj* **firm**, immutable, unchanging, inflexible, fixed [➡ PERMANENCE: WITHOUT CHANGE; 95] *Opposite*: negotiable 2 *adj* **nontransferable**, unmarketable, nonsalable, nonexchangeable, nonconvertible [➡ FINANCE AND ECONOMICS; 796] *Opposite*: transferable

no-no (*informal*) *n* **impossibility**, hopeless case, nonstarter (*informal*), no-go (*informal*) [➡ PROBLEMS; 256] *Opposite*: possibility

no-nonsense *adj* **straightforward**, plain, practical, down-to-earth, plain-speaking, blunt [➡ HONEST AND OPEN; 630]

nonpareil *adj* **unparalleled**, peerless, best, unequalled, unique, matchless, choice, elite [➡ EXTRAORDINARY: UNCOMMON; 205] *Opposite*: common

nonpartisan *adj* **unbiased**, impartial, unprejudiced, independent, neutral, nonaligned [➡ NEUTRALITY AND INDIFFERENCE; 553] *Opposite:* partisan

nonpayment *n* **defaulting**, evasion, default, avoidance [➡ ACCOUNTING, BANKING, AND BUDGETING; 799] *Opposite:* payment

nonperformance *n* **delinquency**, default, arrears [➡ FUNDS, PAYMENTS, AND CHARGES; 800]

nonplus *v* **unnerve**, befuddle, stump, bewilder, mystify, baffle, puzzle, alarm, bemuse, confuse, perplex, throw (*informal*), flummox (*informal*) [➡ CONFUSE AND BEWILDER; 571]

nonplussed *adj* **confused**, baffled, bewildered, puzzled, stumped, at a loss, mystified, perplexed, bemused, befuddled, thrown (*informal*), flummoxed (*informal*) [➡ CONFUSION, ANXIETY, AND WORRY; 540]

nonprofessional *adj* **amateur**, blue-collar, manual, lay [➡ EMPLOYMENT STATUS; 831] *Opposite:* professional

nonprofit *adj* **not-for-profit**, public, state, charitable [➡ CHARITY AND CHARITABLE INSTITUTIONS; 822] *Opposite:* profitmaking

nonproliferation *n* **limitation**, reduction, control, prevention [➡ AVOID, PREVENT, LIMIT, AND CONTROL; 277] *Opposite:* proliferation

nonresident **1** *adj* **transient**, visiting, commuting, vacationing, holidaying (*UK*) [➡ NOMADIC AND ROOTLESS LIFESTYLES; 884] *Opposite:* resident **2** *n* **visitor**, transient, guest, vacationer, tourist, holidaymaker (*UK*) [➡ STRANGERS; 972] *Opposite:* resident

nonsense *n* **rubbish**, drivel, gibberish, noise, babble, balderdash, jabber, garbage, twaddle (*informal*), claptrap (*informal*), gobbledygook (*informal*), hot air (*informal*), baloney (*informal*), poppycock (*dated informal*) [➡ MEANINGLESS SPEECH OR WRITING; 676] *Opposite:* sense

nonsensical *adj* **ridiculous**, stupid, senseless, absurd, illogical, silly, ludicrous, preposterous, unreasonable, asinine, irrational [➡ BIZARRE AND PECULIAR; 257] *Opposite:* sensible

nonspecific *adj* **generic**, general, broad, broad-based, broad-spectrum, common, basic [➡ VAGUENESS; 243] *Opposite:* specific

nonstandard *adj* **unusual**, out of the ordinary, atypical, special, modified, altered, special-order, custom-made, custom-built, nonconforming [➡ EXTRAORDINARY: UNCOMMON; 205] *Opposite:* standard

nonstarter (*informal*) *n* **hopeless case**, loser, failure, dud (*informal*) [➡ FAILURE; 77] *Opposite:* winner

nonstick *adj* **coated**, protected, surfaced, covered [➡ DECORATE, ADORN, AND APPLY COATINGS; 405]

nonstop *adj* **continuous**, never-ending, uninterrupted, around-the-clock, constant, round-the-clock, unending, endless, interminable, ceaseless, unbroken, relentless, unceasing, incessant, steady [➡ PERMANENCE: WITHOUT END; 94] *Opposite:* intermittent

nontoxic *adj* **harmless**, safe, nonhazardous, innocuous, risk-free [➡ SAFE AND SAFETY; 191] *Opposite:* toxic

nonverbal communication *n* [➡ COMMUNICATION; 602]

nonviolence *n* **pacifism**, passivity, nonaggression, civil disobedience [➡ PEACEFULNESS AND GENTLENESS; 214] *Opposite:* violence

nonviolent *adj* **peaceful**, nonaggressive, pacific, peaceable, passive [➡ PEACEFULNESS AND GENTLENESS; 214] *Opposite:* violent

noodle (*slang*) *n* [➡ PARTS OF THE BODY: HEAD; 692]

nook *n* **corner**, alcove, cranny, niche, recess [➡ ALCOVES, CUBICLES, AND COMPARTMENTS; 1096]

noon *n* **midday**, twelve noon, noontime, noonday (*literary*) [➡ TIMES OF DAY; 87]

noonday (*literary*) *n* **noon**, midday, twelve o'clock, middle of the day [➡ TIMES OF DAY; 87] *Opposite:* midnight

no one *pron* **not one person**, not a single person, nobody, not a soul [➡ NONE; 123] *Opposite:* everyone

noose **1** *n* **loop**, lasso, lariat, halter, rope, riata [➡ FASTENERS, LINKS, AND NETWORKS; 1247] **2** *n* **snare**, trap, booby trap, trick, con, ruse [➡ DECEPTION AND LIES; 660]

no problem (*informal*) *interj* **you're welcome**, all right, don't mention it, yes, it's no trouble, sure, it was nothing, certainly, my pleasure, agreed, not at all, of course, okay (*informal*), fair enough (*informal*), that's okay (*informal*) [➡ EXPRESSIONS OF AGREEMENT; 648]

Nordic skiing *type of* **winter sport** [➡ HOBBIES, GAMES, AND SPORTS; 875]

norm *n* **standard**, average, custom, rule, model, type, pattern [➡ PERFECT EXAMPLES AND EMBODIMENTS; 67]

normal *adj* **usual**, standard, ordinary, typical, customary, common, average, natural, habitual, routine, conventional, regular [➡ ACCEPTABLE AND PASSABLE; 219] *Opposite:* abnormal

normalcy *see* **normality**

normality *n* **routine**, regularity, normalcy, status quo [➡ ORDER AND ORGANIZATION; 206]

normalization *n* **regularization**, standardization, stabilization, regulation, control [➡ CHANGE; 372] *Opposite:* deviation

normalize *v* **regularize**, standardize, regulate, put on a normal footing, control, stabilize [➡ IMPROVE SOMETHING; 374] *Opposite:* destabilize

normally **1** *adv* **usually**, in general, as a rule, on the whole, by and large, more often than not, on average, generally, typically, customarily, ordinarily, habitually, routinely [➡ USUALLY; 108] *Opposite:* rarely **2** *adv* **as normal**, as usual, naturally, unexceptionally, conventionally [➡ ACCEPTABLE AND PASSABLE; 219] *Opposite:* abnormally

Norman *type of* **pre-20th-century architecture** [➡ BUILDING AND ARCHITECTURE; 1076]

northeaster *type of* **wind** [➡ WINDY AND STORMY WEATHER; 1053]

northwester *type of* **wind** [➡ WINDY AND STORMY WEATHER; 1053]

Norwegian forest cat *type of* **cat** [➡ FELINES; 983]

nose **1** *n* **snout**, muzzle, beak, proboscis, hooter (*slang humorous*), schnozzle (*slang*) [➡ THE NOSE; 704] **2** *part of* **face**

nose around (*informal*) poke around, watch, sneak, pry, snoop (*informal*), nose around (*informal*) ► SEEK
► PARTS OF THE BODY: HEAD; 692] **3** v (*informal*) poke around, watch,
POSSESSION AND SEARCH; 456]

nosebag n feedbag, bag, container ► CONTAINERS; RECEPTACLES;
AND PACKAGING; 1245] v ► SEEK POSSESSION AND SEARCH; 456]

nosebleed n bloody nose, blood, hemorrhage, blood
LOSS ► THE BLOOD AND CIRCULATION; 717]

nose cone 1 part of aircraft ► AIRCRAFT; 1148] **2** part of
spacecraft ► SPACE VEHICLES; 1063]

nosedive 1 n drop, fall, dive, plunge, tumble, plummet
► GO DOWNWARD; 307] Opposite: ascent **2** n decrease, fall, deteri-
oration, drop, crash, tumble, slump, plunge, dive, collapse
► DISASTERS; 252] Opposite: increase

nose-dive 1 v plummet, drop, plunge, dive, tumble, fall
► GO DOWNWARD; 307] Opposite: ascend **2** v decrease, deteriorate
plummet, drop, slump, crash, rumble, plunge, dive ► COL-

-nosh (*informal*)...

type of flying insect ► FLYING INSECTS; 1013]
type of wind instrument ► MUSICAL INSTRUMENTS; 910]
spray, bouquet, buch, sprig ► COL-

notch 1 n ... gash, scratch ...
step, stage, ...
3 v (*slang*) attain...

not counting besides, except, ...
tion of, over and ...
► NOT 137]

note 1 n letter, me...
munication, reminder,...
2 n footnote, annotation, ...
mentary ► PART- OF BOOKS AND D...
shade, hint, suggestion ►...
of, see, perceive ► LEARN AND DISC...
5 v mention, observe, sta...
COMMENT; 612] **6** v make a note of,
record, jot down, log, write, doc...

network type of computer ►...

notepad n ... pad, scr...
AND DRAWING IMPLEMEN...

notepaper n ...
-headed paper, leather/(K)...

noteworthy adj of note, ...
... significant, worth...

...ness, void,
[→...; 24]

[→ORDINARINESS; 244]

...ent, advertisement,
...) 2 n warning, noti-
...unication [→ADVICE; 689]
observe, perceive, note,
...ght, make out [→SEE; 699]

...f, visible, perceptible, con-
...in plain sight, in full view,
...e: inconspicuous

...tin board, display board, infor-
...NALS, AND BILLBOARDS; 595]

...cement, notice, warning, state-
...[→...AND ISSUE; 611]

...advise, warn, report, let know,
...uaint, tip off [→INFORM, ANNOUNCE, AND ISSUE;

...view, concept, belief, conception,
...tion, perception, thought [→IDEAS AND
...pulse, urge, whim, fancy, instinct [→FEEL-

...j **theoretical**, estimated, speculative, a...
...etical, abstract [→UNCERTAIN; 175] **2** adj i...
...ncied, fanciful, whimsical [→...173] Opposite: rea...
...FALSE AND UNREAL; 173]

...adv **theoretically**, on paper, hypothetically,
...[→UNCERTAIN; 175]

...y adj [→FEW, LITTLE, SMALL AMOUNT; 120]

...ce words v h... **direct**, speak plain...
...spade, be blunt, speak... [→EXPLAIN AND
...ormal]

...uch adj [...

...n (UK) [...

...iety n **disrep**... ...ame, ill repute

...ous 1 adj **infa**...
...ed [→MORALLY ...chaic) **fa**...ly, esp...
celeb...

nougat type of confectionery [→CONFECTIONERY; 1182]

noun type of word class [→ASPECTS OF LANGUAGE; 682]

nourish 1 v nurture, give food to, sustain, suckle, feed [→EAT AND NOT EAT; 710] **2** v encourage, promote, cultivate, support, foster, develop [→IMPROVE STRENGTH AND DURABILITY; 378]

nourishing adj nutritious, wholesome, beneficial, healthful [→FOOD; 1167] Opposite: unhealthy

nourishment n food, sustenance, diet, nutrition [→FOOD; 1167]

nous n intellect, ability, intelligence, rationality, reason, mind [→POSITIVE INTELLECTUAL CHARACTERISTICS; 524]

no use adj [→REDUNDANT AND USELESS; 240]

nouveau riche adj [→WEALTH AND WEALTHY; 891]

nova type of star or star system [→HEAVENLY BODIES; 10...]

novel 1 n book, narrative, work of f... fable [→FICTION AND DRAMA; 913] **2** adj original, innovative, unusual, unique [→... STYLES; ...] Opposite: well-worn ... fable

See Compare and Contrast

novelette short nov...ness, [→FICTION AND DRAMA; 913]

novelist write... reen- [→...; 530]

novel... [→FIC...

n...

...nesick...
...oly [→FE...

sentimental, [→PENSIVENESS AN...

[→THE NOSE; 704]

...m **remedy**, plan, sche... [→...SOONS; 215]
(infrmal) adj **inquisitive**, ...meddlesome, intrusive, snoo... [→...RING; 512]

no...ty 1 n **famous person**, celebri... not... (for...rsonality, public figure, som... [→IMPORTANT OR FAMOUS PEOPLE; 893] O... **2** n ...ficance, importance, relevance, [→IMPORTANCE AND SIGNIFICANCE; 192]

...otab... **1** adj **noteworthy**, distinguished, ...minent, extraordinary, famous, remarka... att..., significant, noted [→IMPORTANT; 194] ...nificant **2** n celebrity, dignity, VIP, personality, [→...

...ost, virtually, a... ...pproximately, nigh o... [→...LARITY; 148]

...ormal] **1** prep **despite**, i... ...setting aside, ...all the same... [→DESPITE; 16...

venomous, injurious, deleterious, pernicious [➡DANGEROUS; 236] *Opposite:* harmless **2** *adj* **nasty**, unpleasant, offensive, foul, horrible, disgusting [➡DISGUSTING AND REPULSIVE; 230] *Opposite:* pleasant

noxiousness *n* [➡DANGER; 235]

nozzle *n* **spout**, jet, control valve, spigot, outlet, tap [➡FIXTURES; 859]

nuance *n* **tone**, gradation, distinction, tinge, hint, degree, touch, trace, note, shade [➡FEW, LITTLE, SMALL AMOUNT; 120]

nub *n* **crux**, crucial point, essence, core, heart, root, gist, nitty-gritty (*informal*) [➡MOST IMPORTANT THING; 197]

nubbin *n* [➡EXTREMITIES OF PHYSICAL OBJECTS; 1250]

nub end *n* [➡EXTREMITIES OF PHYSICAL OBJECTS; 1250]

nuclear *adj* **atomic**, nuclear-powered, fissile, fissionable [➡ENERGY SOURCES; 1162]

nuclear family *n* [➡THE FAMILY; 956]

nuclear missile *type of* **explosive weapon** [➡EXPLOSIVES; 1155]

nuclear power plant *type of* **industrial site** [➡INDUSTRIAL BUILDINGS; 1087]

nuclear reprocessing plant *type of* **industrial site** [➡INDUSTRIAL BUILDINGS; 1087]

nuclear warhead *type of* **explosive weapon** [➡EXPLOSIVES; 1155]

nuclear weapon *type of* **explosive weapon** [➡EXPLOSIVES; 1155]

nucleus *n* **center**, basis, core, heart, nub, focus [➡CENTRAL PARTS OF PHYSICAL OBJECTS; 1251]

nude *adj* **unclothed**, in the nude, undressed, in a state of undress, stripped, stark-naked, bare, naked, with nothing on, buck naked, in the buff (*informal*), in your birthday suit (*slang humorous*) [➡DRESS, WEAR, AND UNDRESS; 868] *Opposite:* clothed

See Compare and Contrast at **naked**.

nudge **1** *v* **push**, bump, elbow, shove, jolt, prod [➡CONTACT: TOUCH; 412] **2** *n* **prod**, push, shove, bump, jolt [➡CONTACT: TOUCH; 412]

nudity *n* **bareness**, nakedness, undress, dishabille [➡DRESS, WEAR, AND UNDRESS; 868]

nugatory *adj* **trifling**, petty, insignificant, trivial, unimportant, irrelevant [➡UNIMPORTANT AND UNNECESSARY; 238] *Opposite:* significant

nugget *n* **piece**, bit, chunk, lump, hunk, tidbit [➡AMOUNTS OF SOLID OR SEMISOLID; 115]

nuisance *n* **irritation**, annoyance, bother, trouble, irritant, pest (*informal*), pain (*informal*) [➡NUISANCES; 253]

nuke (*slang*) *v* **bomb**, obliterate, blow up, destroy, annihilate, wipe out (*informal*) [➡DESTRUCTION AND DEMOLITION; 359]

null **1** *adj* **invalid**, null and void, void, unacceptable, unsound, untrue [➡ILLEGAL; 816] *Opposite:* valid **2** *adj* **worth**-less, valueless, unimportant, insignificant, useless [➡UNIMPORTANT AND UNNECESSARY; 238]

null and void *adj* **invalid**, void, null, unacceptable, flawed [➡ILLEGAL; 816] *Opposite:* valid

nullify *v* **invalidate**, annul, cancel out, abolish, reverse, repeal, quash, abrogate (*formal*), negate (*formal*) [➡ABOLISH AND ANNUL; 452] *Opposite:* validate

Compare and Contrast: *nullify, abrogate, annul, repeal, invalidate, negate*

CORE MEANING: to put an end to the effective existence of something

nullify to make something legally invalid or ineffective, or to cancel something out; *abrogate* (*formal*) to end an agreement or contract formally and publicly; *annul* to declare something officially or legally invalid or ineffective; *repeal* to end a law officially; *invalidate* to deprive something of its legal force or value, e.g., by failing to comply with certain terms and conditions; *negate* (*formal*) to render something ineffective, e.g., by doing something that counterbalances its force or effectiveness.

numb **1** *adj* **frozen**, anesthetized, dead, deadened, unfeeling, insensitive, sensationless [➡PAIN AND OTHER PHYSICAL SENSATIONS; 733] **2** *adj* **emotionless**, shocked, dazed, traumatized, disoriented, distressed [➡NEUTRALITY AND INDIFFERENCE; 553] *Opposite:* animated **3** *v* **deaden**, freeze, anesthetize, stun, dull, blunt [➡PAIN AND OTHER PHYSICAL SENSATIONS; 733]

number **1** *n* **figure**, numeral, digit, integer [➡SYMBOLS, SIGNS, AND NUMBERS; 596] **2** *n* **amount**, quantity, sum [➡AMOUNTS AND QUANTITIES; 112] **3** *v* **come to**, add up to, total, amount to, run to [➡AMOUNT TO AND EQUAL; 70]

number-cruncher (*slang*) *n* [➡PEOPLE INVOLVED IN FINANCE; 804]

numberless *adj* **countless**, innumerable, numerous, endless, myriad [➡MANY, MUCH, LARGE AMOUNT; 117] *Opposite:* few

number one **1** *n* (*informal*) **important person**, key player, linchpin, leader, prime candidate, main contender, top dog (*informal*) [➡IMPORTANT OR FAMOUS PEOPLE; 893] **2** *n* (*informal*) **chief executive officer**, chief executive, boss, chief, head, head honcho, managing director (*UK*) [➡BOSSES AND MANAGEMENT; 965] **3** *adj* (*informal*) **excellent**, high quality, first-rate, top, top quality, top-class, top-grade, bestselling, first-class, world-class [➡ADMIRABLE AND COMMENDABLE; 185] **4** *adj* **first**, top, leading, best, most important, favored, chosen, successful, winning [➡MOST IMPORTANT AND MAIN; 193]

numbing **1** *adj* **deadening**, freezing, anesthetizing [➡PAIN AND OTHER PHYSICAL SENSATIONS; 733] **2** *adj* **shocking**, distressing, dazing, upsetting, disorienting, traumatic [➡EMOTIONALLY UNPLEASANT AND UPSETTING; 227]

numbly *adv* **dazedly**, dully, torpidly, emotionlessly, impassively, expressionlessly [➡NEUTRALITY AND INDIFFERENCE; 553] *Opposite:* animatedly

numbness **1** *n* **deadness**, unresponsiveness, lack of sensation [➡PAIN AND OTHER PHYSICAL SENSATIONS; 733] *Opposite:* sensation **2** *n* **emotionlessness**, impassiveness, coldness, detachment, shock [➡NEUTRALITY AND INDIFFERENCE; 553]

numeracy *n* **mathematical ability**, numerical competence, skill, proficiency, expertise, accomplishment, facility [➡ KNOWLEDGE AND WISDOM; 558]

numeral *n* **number**, figure, digit, cipher [➡ SYMBOLS, SIGNS, AND NUMBERS; 596]

numerate *adj* **mathematically competent**, good with numbers, proficient, accomplished, competent [➡ KNOWLEDGE AND WISDOM; 558]

numerical *adj* **mathematical**, arithmetic, arithmetical, statistical [➡ MATH; 597]

numeric keypad *type of* **hardware** [➡ COMPUTERS AND COMPUTING; 1127]

numerous *adj* **many**, frequent, plentiful, abundant, several, copious, various [➡ MANY, MUCH, LARGE AMOUNT; 117] *Opposite*: few

numerousness *n* [➡ MANY, MUCH, LARGE AMOUNT; 117]

nun *n* [➡ RELIGIOUS PEOPLE; 778]

nunnery *n* **convent**, monastery, abbey, religious foundation, religious community [➡ RELIGIOUS BUILDINGS; 1085]

nuptial *adj* **marriage**, wedding, bridal, matrimonial, marital, conjugal, connubial (*literary*) [➡ CEREMONIES AND ANNIVERSARIES; 38]

nuptials (*formal*) *n* **wedding**, marriage, happy day [➡ CEREMONIES AND ANNIVERSARIES; 38]

nurse 1 *n* [➡ PEOPLE WHO WORK IN MEDICINE; 848] **2** *v* **care for**, take care of, tend, foster, nurture, look after [➡ TAKE CARE OF AND SPOIL; 300] *Opposite*: neglect **3** *v* **harbor**, cherish, nurture, have, foster, indulge [➡ CAUSE TO CONTINUE; 267]

nursery 1 *n* **nursery school**, day nursery, playgroup, kindergarten [➡ EDUCATIONAL INSTITUTIONS; 813] **2** *n* **plant sales outlet**, garden center, plant market [➡ RETAIL OUTLETS; 1083]

nursery school *type of* **school** [➡ EDUCATIONAL INSTITUTIONS; 813]

nursing home *n* [➡ HOSPITALS AND CLINICS; 826]

nurture 1 *v* **care for**, take care of, raise, rear, foster, look after [➡ TAKE CARE OF AND SPOIL; 300] **2** *v* **cultivate**, cherish, develop, support, encourage, foster [➡ CAUSE TO CONTINUE; 267]

nut 1 *n* [➡ PARTS OF TREES AND PLANTS; 1026] **2** *n* (*informal*) **skull**, cranium, dome, crown, bean (*slang*), noodle (*slang*), pate (*archaic or humorous*) [➡ PARTS OF THE BODY: HEAD; 692] **3** *n* (*informal*) **enthusiast**, fan, aficionado, aficionada, buff, devotee, follower, admirer [➡ DEVOTEES AND ADDICTED PEOPLE; 556]

nut

◆ *types of nuts*
acorn, almond, brazil nut, cashew, chestnut, cob, cobnut, coconut, cola nut, groundnut, hazelnut, hickory nut, horse chestnut, macadamia nut, peanut, pecan, pine nut, pistachio, walnut

nut-brown *type of* **brown** [➡ COLORS; 1224]

nutcracker *type of* **utensil** [➡ TABLEWARE, FLATWARE, AND KITCHENWARE; 861]

nuthatch *type of* **common bird** [➡ BIRDS; 997]

nutmeg *type of* **spice** [➡ HERBS AND SPICES; 1175]

nutrient *n* [➡ FOOD; 1167]

nutrient

◆ *types of nutrients*
amino acid, carbohydrate, dextrose, fat, fiber, fructose, glucose, lactose, mineral, protein, salt, starch, sucrose, sugar, vitamin

nutrition *n* **nourishment**, diet, food, sustenance [➡ FOOD; 1167]

nutritional *adj* **nutritious**, nourishing, nutritive, dietary, alimentary, dietetic, food [➡ FOOD; 1167]

nutritious *adj* **nourishing**, healthy, wholesome, healthful, beneficial, nutritive [➡ FOOD; 1167] *Opposite*: unhealthy

nutritive 1 *adj* **nutritional**, dietary, dietetic, alimentary, food [➡ FOOD; 1167] **2** *adj* **nutritious**, nourishing, healthy, wholesome, healthful, beneficial [➡ FOOD; 1167] *Opposite*: unhealthy

nuts (*slang*) *adj* [➡ ECCENTRICITY AND IRRATIONALITY; 562]

nuts and bolts (*informal*) *n* **basics**, brass tacks, practicalities, fundamentals, details, foundations, nitty-gritty (*informal*) [➡ BASIC DETAILS; 688]

nutshell *n* **husk**, casing, shell [➡ COVERS AND COATINGS; 1246]

nuzzle *v* **nestle**, cuddle, burrow, snuggle, push, rub [➡ CONTACT: TOUCH; 412]

nyctophobia *type of* **phobia** [➡ FEARS AND PHOBIAS; 554]

nye (*literary*) *type of* **flock** [➡ GROUPS OF BIRDS; 1007]

nylon *type of* **synthetic fabric** [➡ FABRICS; 1132]

NY-LON *n* [➡ TRAVEL: TRAVELERS AND WALKERS; 319]

nylons *type of* **lower body underwear** [➡ ACCESSORIES, MILLINERY, AND LINGERIE; 867]

nymph *n* **fairy**, sprite, spirit, dryad, elf, leprechaun [➡ MYTHICAL BEINGS; 789]

O

oaf *n* **buffoon**, bumbler, lummox (*informal*), klutz (*slang*) [➡ LAZY OR UNSUCCESSFUL PEOPLE; 948]

oak *type of* **deciduous tree** [➡ DECIDUOUS TREES; 1028]

oar *n* **paddle**, scull, sweep, blade [➡ PARTS OF A SHIP OR BOAT; 1151]

oarlock *part of* **ship or boat** [➡ PARTS OF A SHIP OR BOAT; 1151]

oasis *n* **retreat**, refuge, haven, sanctuary, escape [➡ SAFE BUILDINGS OR PLACES; 1093]

oat *type of* **cereal** [➡ CEREAL FOODS; 1178]

oath 1 *n* **promise**, pledge, vow, word, assurance, word of honor [➡ PROMISE AND ASSURE; 684] 2 *n* **curse**, swearword, expletive, four-letter word, cussword (*informal*), imprecation (*formal*) [➡ INSULTS, ABUSE, AND SWEARING; 658]

oatmeal *type of* **beige** [➡ COLORS; 1224]

obduracy *n* **obstinacy**, stubbornness, inflexibility, mulishness, pigheadedness, determination, immovability, implacability (*formal*) [➡ UNWILLINGNESS AND STUBBORNNESS; 564] *Opposite*: compliance

obdurate 1 *adj* **obstinate**, stubborn, inflexible, unyielding, unbending, pigheaded, adamant, immovable, implacable, mulish, stiff-necked [➡ UNWILLINGNESS AND STUBBORNNESS; 564] *Opposite*: compliant 2 *adj* **hardhearted**, callous, unfeeling, heartless, pitiless, ruthless, unsympathetic, hard-boiled (*informal*) [➡ SELFISH AND UNKIND; 505] *Opposite*: warm-hearted

obdurately *adv* **obstinately**, stubbornly, mulishly, inflexibly, unbendingly, unyieldingly, pigheadedly, adamantly, immovably, implacably (*formal*) [➡ WITHOUT ENTHUSIASM; 287] *Opposite*: compliantly

obdurateness *n* [➡ UNWILLINGNESS AND STUBBORNNESS; 564]

obedience *n* **compliance**, agreement, submission, respect, duty, deference, tractability, docility, conformity, subservience, meekness [➡ THE WILL AND WILLINGNESS; 563] *Opposite*: disobedience

obedient *adj* **compliant**, dutiful, submissive, respectful, biddable, deferential, well-trained, docile, tractable, amenable, subservient, meek, tame, unquestioning [➡ THE WILL AND WILLINGNESS; 563] *Opposite*: disobedient

obeisance 1 *n* (*formal*) **bow**, curtsy, bob, nod, genuflection, kowtow [➡ GESTURES AND GESTICULATION; 653] 2 *n* **homage**, respect, deference, duty, loyalty, genuflection [➡ LOVE, RESPECT, AND GOODWILL; 549]

obelisk *n* **pillar**, column, pylon, needle, tower, monument [➡ MONUMENTS; 1092]

obese *adj* **fat**, overweight, heavy, stout, plump, large, corpulent, chunky (*informal*) [➡ BUILD; 477] *Opposite*: underweight

obesity *n* **plumpness**, fatness, stoutness, portliness, corpulence, fleshiness, largeness, heaviness [➡ BUILD; 477] *Opposite*: thinness

obey *v* **do as you are told**, submit, follow, comply with, act upon, observe, abide by, conform, mind, defer to [➡ OBEY AND ABIDE BY; 301] *Opposite*: disobey

obfuscate *v* **obscure**, complicate, confuse, muddy, cloud, mystify, muddle, befuddle, befog (*literary*) [➡ CREATE DISORDER AND CAUSE CHAOS; 358] *Opposite*: clarify

obfuscation *n* **complication**, mystification, confusion, muddying, clouding, smoke screen [➡ DECEPTION AND LIES; 660] *Opposite*: clarification

obituary 1 *n* **tribute**, article, announcement, eulogy, epitaph, obit (*informal*) [➡ BURIAL AND PREPARATION FOR BURIAL; 929] 2 *adj* **funerary**, funereal, memorial, epitaphic, death, valedictory (*formal*) [➡ BURIAL AND PREPARATION FOR BURIAL; 929]

object 1 *n* **thing**, article, item, entity, body, piece [➡ PHYSICAL OBJECTS; 1243] 2 *n* **purpose**, objective, aim, point, idea, goal, intention, reason, intent (*formal*) [➡ INTENTIONS AND PURPOSES; 772] 3 *type of* **grammatical term** [➡ ASPECTS OF LANGUAGE; 682] 4 *v* **oppose**, protest, complain, challenge, demur, balk, remonstrate, expostulate, take exception to, grumble, carp [➡ PROTEST AND EXPRESS DISAPPROVAL; 642] *Opposite*: approve

Compare and Contrast: *object, protest, demur, remonstrate, expostulate*

CORE MEANING: to indicate opposition to something

object to be opposed or averse to something, or express opposition to it; ***protest*** to express strong disapproval of or disagreement with something, or to refuse to obey or accept something, often by making a formal statement or taking action in public; ***demur*** to raise objections in a hesitant or tentative way; ***remonstrate*** to reason or argue forcefully with somebody about something; ***expostulate*** to express disagreement or disapproval vehemently, or to attempt to dissuade somebody from doing something.

See Compare and Contrast at **complain, disapprove**.

objectify 1 *v* **actualize**, realize, represent, portray, reify, symbolize [➡ REPRESENT SOMETHING OR SOMEBODY; 59] 2 *v* **diminish**, reduce, simplify, trivialize [➡ CHANGE; 372]

objection 1 *n* **opposition**, protest, protestation, hostility, demurral, complaint [➡ CRITICISMS AND ANGRY OUTBURSTS; 50] *Opposite*: approval 2 *n* **doubt**, concern, problem, worry, difficulty, niggle (*UK*) [➡ PROBLEMS; 256] *Opposite*: confidence

objectionable *adj* **offensive**, obnoxious, horrible, unpleasant, intolerable, distasteful, disagreeable, loathsome, unacceptable, abhorrent (*formal*) [➡ DISGUSTING AND REPULSIVE; 230] *Opposite*: inoffensive

objective 1 *adj* **impartial**, detached, neutral, unbiased, unprejudiced, independent, dispassionate, disinterested, fair [➡ NEUTRALITY AND INDIFFERENCE; 553] *Opposite*: subjective **2** *adj* **factual**, actual, tangible, fact-based, demonstrable, quantitative, empirical, real [➡ TRUE AND REAL; 171] *Opposite*: subjective **3** *n* **object**, purpose, aim, point, idea, goal, intention, reason, intent (*formal*) [➡ INTENTIONS AND PURPOSES; 772]

objectivity *n* **impartiality**, detachment, independence, neutrality, fairness [➡ NEUTRALITY AND INDIFFERENCE; 553] *Opposite*: subjectivity

objet d'art *n* **work of art**, masterpiece, creation, piece, ornament, curio [➡ ARTWORKS; 898]

obligate *v* **compel**, oblige, force, make, require, coerce, necessitate [➡ CAUSE OR COMPEL TO ACT; 271] *Opposite*: request

obligated *adj* [➡ APPRECIATION AND GRATITUDE; 535]

obligation 1 *n* **duty**, responsibility, requirement, compulsion, commitment, onus [➡ RESPONSIBILITY; 170] *Opposite*: option **2** *n* **debt**, contract, commitment, promise, agreement, understanding [➡ PROMISE AND ASSURE; 684]

obligatory 1 *adj* **compulsory**, required, necessary, essential, de rigueur (*formal*), requisite (*formal*) [➡ NECESSARY AND ESSENTIAL; 196] *Opposite*: optional **2** *adj* **required**, statutory, mandatory, binding, the law [➡ NECESSARY AND ESSENTIAL; 196] *Opposite*: discretionary

oblige 1 *v* **compel**, obligate, force, make, require, coerce, necessitate [➡ CAUSE OR COMPEL TO ACT; 271] *Opposite*: request **2** *v* **gratify**, please, indulge, accommodate, help, assist [➡ PLEASE AND AMUSE; 572] *Opposite*: disappoint

obliged *adj* **grateful**, thankful, appreciative, gratified, indebted [➡ APPRECIATION AND GRATITUDE; 535]

obliging *adj* **helpful**, kind, considerate, willing, agreeable, polite, courteous, accommodating, cooperative [➡ THE WILL AND WILLINGNESS; 563] *Opposite*: unhelpful

oblique 1 *adj* **slanting**, slanted, tilted, sloping, leaning, askew, diagonal [➡ ORIENTATION AND ALIGNMENT; 1223] *Opposite*: upright **2** *adj* **indirect**, implicit, implied, roundabout, circuitous, backhanded [➡ INARTICULATE, RAMBLING, AND AWKWARD; 633] *Opposite*: direct

obliqueness 1 *n* **tilt**, inclination, slant, steepness, lean, slope, cant [➡ ORIENTATION AND ALIGNMENT; 1223] **2** *n* **indirectness**, circuitousness, circumlocution, obscureness, opaqueness, opacity [➡ VAGUENESS; 243] *Opposite*: directness

obliterate *v* **destroy**, demolish, eliminate, eradicate, annihilate, abolish, wipe out (*informal*) [➡ DESTRUCTION AND DEMOLITION; 359] *Opposite*: create

obliteration *n* **destruction**, annihilation, eradication, elimination, abolition, demolition [➡ DESTRUCTION AND DEMOLITION; 359] *Opposite*: creation

oblivion 1 *n* **forgetfulness**, unconsciousness, stupor, insensibility, obliviousness [➡ IGNORANCE; 557] *Opposite*: awareness **2** *n* **obscurity**, extinction, the past, the annals of history, nothingness, silence [➡ NONEXISTENCE; 24] *Opposite*: existence

oblivious *adj* **unaware**, unconscious, unmindful, ignorant, insensible [➡ IGNORANCE; 557] *Opposite*: conscious

oblong *type of* **angular shape** [➡ ANGULAR SHAPE; 1217]

obloquy (*formal or literary*) 1 *n* **censure**, criticism, defamation, blame, opprobrium, bad press, attack, character assassination [➡ CRITICISMS AND ANGRY OUTBURSTS; 50] *Opposite*: praise **2** *n* **disgrace**, shame, infamy, ignominy, disfavor, dishonor, humiliation, odium, disrepute [➡ DIFFICULT SITUATIONS; 72]

obnoxious *adj* **loathsome**, hateful, horrible, insufferable, intolerable, detestable, unbearable, abominable, despicable, repugnant, repellent, offensive, unpleasant, abhorrent (*formal*) [➡ DISGUSTING AND REPULSIVE; 230] *Opposite*: delightful

obnoxiousness *n* [➡ DISGUSTING AND REPULSIVE; 230]

oboe *type of* **wind instrument** [➡ MUSICAL INSTRUMENTS; 910]

obscene 1 *adj* **indecent**, lewd, explicit, offensive, crude, rude, blue (*informal*), X-rated (*informal*) [➡ MORALLY BAD OR IMPROPER; 775] *Opposite*: decent **2** *adj* **disgusting**, nauseating, sickening, offensive, rude, crass, excessive, beyond the pale [➡ DISGUSTING AND REPULSIVE; 230] *Opposite*: decent **3** *adj* **tasteless**, foul-mouthed, crude, loutish, boorish, gross, crass [➡ BAD MANNERS AND SOCIAL SKILLS; 521]

obscenity 1 *n* **offensiveness**, atrocity, tastelessness, vulgarity, rudeness, crassness [➡ IN POOR TASTE AND OVERSENTIMENTAL; 229] *Opposite*: tastefulness **2** *n* **indecency**, lewdness, offensiveness, explicitness, crudeness, rudeness [➡ MORALLY BAD OR IMPROPER; 775] *Opposite*: decency **3** *n* **curse**, swearword, four-letter word, expletive, cuss word (*informal*) [➡ INSULTS, ABUSE, AND SWEARING; 658]

obscurantism *n* **conservatism**, traditionalism, dogmatism, reaction, illiberalism, opposition [➡ PHILOSOPHIES AND BELIEFS; 780] *Opposite*: liberalism

obscurantist 1 *adj* **reactionary**, conservative, backward-looking, traditionalist, old-fashioned, diehard, hidebound, doctrinaire, illiberal [➡ UNADVENTUROUS AND DULL; 517] *Opposite*: liberal **2** *n* **conservative**, reactionary, traditionalist, diehard, dogmatist, obscurant [➡ UNCOOPERATIVE OR REBELLIOUS PEOPLE; 566] *Opposite*: liberal

obscure 1 *adj* **incomprehensible**, unclear, vague, ambiguous, abstruse, enigmatic, cryptic, unintelligible, arcane, recondite [➡ DIFFICULTY AND COMPLEXITY; 242] *Opposite*: clear **2** *adj* **indistinct**, faint, shadowy, murky, blurry, dim, foggy, muddy, opaque [➡ IMPERCEPTIBLE; 26] *Opposite*: clear **3** *adj* **unknown**, little-known, minor, unseen, unheard of, humble [➡ SECRET AND UNKNOWN; 179] *Opposite*: famous **4** *v* **confuse**, disguise, conceal, complicate, obfuscate, muddy, muddle [➡ CREATE DISORDER AND CAUSE CHAOS; 358] *Opposite*: clarify **5** *v* **darken**, cloak, mask, hide, shroud, veil, eclipse, block out [➡ CAUSE TO DISAPPEAR; 6] *Opposite*: disclose

Compare and Contrast: *obscure, abstruse, recondite, arcane, cryptic, enigmatic*

CORE MEANING: difficult to understand

obscure difficult to understand because it is expressed in a complicated way or because it involves areas of knowledge or study that are not known to most people; *abstruse* not easy to understand, often because it involves specialist knowledge or is expressed in specialist language; *recondite* requiring a high degree of scholarship or specialist knowledge to be understood; *arcane* requiring information that is secret or known only to a few people in order to be understood; *cryptic* deliberately mysterious or ambiguous and seeming to have a hidden meaning; *enigmatic* having a quality of mystery and ambiguity that makes it difficult to understand or interpret.

obscurely 1 *adv* **incomprehensibly**, unclearly, vaguely, ambiguously, abstrusely, murkily, unintelligibly [➡ DIF-FICULTY AND COMPLEXITY; 242] *Opposite*: clearly 2 *adv* **indistinctly**, faintly, murkily, blurrily, dimly [➡ IMPERCEPTIBLE; 26] *Opposite*: clearly

obscurity 1 *n* **anonymity**, insignificance, unimportance, inconspicuousness, oblivion [➡ SECRET AND UNKNOWN; 179] *Oppo-site*: fame 2 *n* **incomprehensibility**, vagueness, ambigu-ousness, doubt, opacity, abstruseness, murkiness, unintelligibility [➡ VAGUENESS; 243] *Opposite*: clarity

obsequious *adj* **servile**, sycophantic, flattering, toady-ing, submissive, fawning, compliant, deferential, rev-erential, groveling, unctuous, smarmy [➡ INGRATIATING; 638] *Opposite*: assertive

obsequiousness *n* **sycophancy**, servility, flattery, sub-missiveness, compliance, deference, unctuousness, smarminess, reverence, sweet talk (*informal*) [➡ INGRATIATING; 638] *Opposite*: assertiveness

observable *adj* **noticeable**, visible, apparent, evident, obvious, discernible, recognizable, perceptible, plain, clear, detectable [➡ PERCEPTIBLE; 25] *Opposite*: imperceptible

observance 1 *n* **adherence**, compliance, execution, per-formance, observation, fulfillment, obedience [➡ THE WILL AND WILLINGNESS; 563] *Opposite*: violation 2 *n* **ritual**, ceremony, ceremonial, rite, celebration, practice [➡ CEREMONIES AND ANNI-VERSARIES; 38]

observant *adj* **sharp-eyed**, alert, attentive, watchful, vigilant, wide-awake, perceptive, on the ball (*informal*) [➡ POSITIVE INTELLECTUAL CHARACTERISTICS; 524] *Opposite*: unobservant

observation 1 *n* **surveillance**, scrutiny, watching, inspection, examination, study [➡ SEE; 699] *Opposite*: neglect 2 *n* **remark**, comment, opinion, thought, reflection, state-ment [➡ SUGGEST, HINT, AND COMMENT; 612]

observation car *part of* **train** [➡ RAILROADS; 1107]

observation tower *n* [➡ TOWERS; 1099]

observatory *n* **building**, station, laboratory, telescope, viewpoint [➡ TOWERS; 1099]

observe 1 *v* **detect**, perceive, witness, see, spot, note, discern, notice [➡ SEE; 699] *Opposite*: miss 2 *v* **watch**, view, scrutinize, monitor, study, examine, survey [➡ LOOKING AND LOOKS; 700] *Opposite*: ignore 3 *v* **remark**, comment, say, declare, state, reflect, opine (*formal*) [➡ UTTER AND PRONOUNCE; 608] 4 *v* **abide by**, respect, follow, comply with, heed, conform to, keep, adhere to [➡ OBEY AND ABIDE BY; 301] *Opposite*: violate 5 *v* **celebrate**, keep, remember, take part in, perform [➡ PAR-TICIPATE; 292] *Opposite*: break

observer *n* **spectator**, witness, viewer, onlooker, bystander, eyewitness [➡ ONLOOKERS AND SPECTATORS; 701] *Opposite*: participant

obsess *v* **preoccupy**, grip, consume, fixate, possess, fas-cinate [➡ APPEAL TO AND AROUSE INTEREST; 575] *Opposite*: bore

obsessed *adj* **fanatical**, gripped, preoccupied, infatu-ated, fixated, passionate, possessed [➡ PENSIVENESS AND INTEREST; 538] *Opposite*: indifference

obsession *n* **mania**, fascination, fixation, passion, pre-occupation, thing (*informal*) [➡ FADS, FETISHES, AND IDOLATRY; 555] *Opposite*: indifference

obsessional *adj* [➡ NEGATIVE INTELLECTUAL CHARACTERISTICS; 525]

obsessive *adj* **compulsive**, fanatical, fixated, infatuated, neurotic, preoccupied, possessed [➡ NEGATIVE INTELLECTUAL CHAR-ACTERISTICS; 525] *Opposite*: easygoing

obsessiveness *n* [➡ FADS, FETISHES, AND IDOLATRY; 555]

obsolescence *n* **uselessness**, undesirability, out-modedness, oldness, unfashionableness, desuetude (*formal*) [➡ OLD, OLD-FASHIONED; 167] *Opposite*: modernity

obsolescent *adj* **dated**, old, antiquated, out of date, passé, unfashionable, old-fashioned, outmoded, archaic, superseded, obsolete, undesirable, antediluvian (*informal*) [➡ OLD, OLD-FASHIONED; 167] *Opposite*: up-to-date

obsolete *adj* **archaic**, superseded, outmoded, anti-quated, passé, unfashionable, outdated, out-of-date, obso-lescent, dated, old, old-fashioned, antediluvian (*informal*) [➡ OLD, OLD-FASHIONED; 167] *Opposite*: up-to-date

See Compare and Contrast at **old-fashioned**.

obstacle 1 *n* **problem**, difficulty, hindrance, impedi-ment, complication, hurdle, hitch, stumbling block [➡ PROB-LEMS; 256] *Opposite*: help 2 *n* **obstruction**, barrier, blockage, blockade, impediment [➡ PROBLEMS; 256] *Opposite*: passage

obstinacy *n* **stubbornness**, determination, pig-headedness, inflexibility, unreasonableness, persistence, tenacity, intransigence, mulishness, wrong-headedness [➡ UNWILLINGNESS AND STUBBORNNESS; 564] *Opposite*: compliance

obstinate *adj* **stubborn**, determined, pigheaded, fixed, inflexible, adamant, unmoved, persistent, tenacious, mulish, headstrong, wrong-headed [➡ UNWILLINGNESS AND STUB-BORNNESS; 564] *Opposite*: compliant

obstreperous *adj* **disruptive**, rowdy, disorderly, loud, noisy, undisciplined, unruly, rough [➡ REBELLIOUSNESS AND DIS-OBEDIENCE; 565] *Opposite*: demure

See Compare and Contrast at **unruly**.

obstreperousness *n* [➡ REBELLIOUSNESS AND DISOBEDIENCE; 565]

obstruct 1 *v* **block**, barricade, impede, hold up, stop, bar [➡ BAR AND OBSTRUCT ACCESS; 410] *Opposite*: clear 2 *v* **hinder**, thwart, frustrate, hamper, complicate, prohibit, check [➡ AVOID, PREVENT, LIMIT, AND CONTROL; 277] *Opposite*: assist

See Compare and Contrast at **hinder**.

obstruction *n* **obstacle**, barrier, block, blockade, bar-ricade, impediment, hindrance, stumbling block, hitch, difficulty [➡ PROBLEMS; 256] *Opposite*: help

obstructionism *n* **timewasting**, stalling, filibustering, sabotage, hindrance, blocking [➡ AVOID, PREVENT, LIMIT, AND CONTROL; 277] *Opposite*: helpfulness

obstructionist 1 *adj* **stalling**, timewasting, fili-bustering, delaying, delay [➡ AVOID, PREVENT, LIMIT, AND CONTROL; 277]

2 *n* **staller**, timewaster, filibusterer, wrecker, saboteur, delayer [➡ INTERFERING PEOPLE AND TATTLETALES; 950]

obstructive *adj* **disruptive**, uncooperative, unhelpful, obstreperous, awkward, hindering, frustrating [➡ REBELLIOUSNESS AND DISOBEDIENCE; 565] *Opposite*: helpful

obstructiveness *n* [➡ REBELLIOUSNESS AND DISOBEDIENCE; 565]

obtain *v* **get**, get hold of, acquire, procure, attain, secure, gain, achieve [➡ GET; 420] *Opposite*: lose

See Compare and Contrast at **get**.

obtainable *adj* **available**, accessible, reachable, attainable [➡ PRESENT AND AVAILABLE; 11] *Opposite*: unavailable

obtrude **1** *v* **interfere**, impose, meddle, pry, interrupt, interpose, intercede, horn in (*informal*) [➡ INTERRUPT AND BUTT IN; 619] **2** *v* **extend**, thrust, stick out, push out [➡ APPEAR AND EMERGE; 3]

obtrusive **1** *adj* **conspicuous**, unmistakable, blatant, prominent, garish, flagrant, flashy, obvious, bald, sheer [➡ PERCEPTIBLE; 25] *Opposite*: inconspicuous **2** *adj* **interfering**, intruding, meddlesome, forward, presumptuous, pushy (*informal*) [➡ NOSY AND INTERFERING; 512]

obtuse *adj* **insensitive**, dull-witted, simple-minded, imperceptive, stupid, dull [➡ NEGATIVE INTELLECTUAL CHARACTERISTICS; 525] *Opposite*: astute

obtuseness *n* [➡ DIFFICULTY AND COMPLEXITY; 242]

obverse **1** *n* **front**, head, heads, side, face, top [➡ EXTREMITIES OF PHYSICAL OBJECTS; 1250] **2** *n* **counterpart**, complement, opposite, equivalent, opposite number, supplement [➡ OPPOSITE; 157] **3** *adj* **front**, forward-facing, opposite, visible, anterior [➡ OPPOSITE; 157] *Opposite*: reverse **4** *adj* **equivalent**, complementary, opposite, other, opposing [➡ OPPOSITE; 157]

obviate *v* **do away with**, avoid, remove, forestall, prevent, avert, ward off, stave off, fend off, preclude (*formal*) [➡ AVOID, PREVENT, LIMIT, AND CONTROL; 277]

obvious *adj* **clear**, understandable, palpable, noticeable, apparent, evident, observable, recognizable, discernible [➡ PERCEPTIBLE; 25] *Opposite*: obscure

obviousness *n* **clearness**, undoubtedness, certainty, patentness, overtness, unmistakableness, conspicuousness, plainness, inevitability, unavoidability, blatancy [➡ PERCEPTIBLE; 25] *Opposite*: obscurity

ocarina *type of* **wind instrument** [➡ MUSICAL INSTRUMENTS; 910]

occasion **1** *n* **time**, juncture, case, instance, event, incident, occurrence, circumstance, point, spot, position [➡ EVENTS AND OCCURRENCES; 35] **2** *n* **possibility**, opportunity, opening, season, contingency, stage, chance [➡ POSSIBLE AND PROBABLE; 177] **3** *n* **reason**, cause, motive, justification, rationale, explanation, excuse, basis, ground [➡ CAUSATION; 168] **4** *v* **cause**, motivate, give rise to, bring about, induce, prompt, elicit, effect (*formal*) [➡ CAUSE TO HAPPEN; 31]

occasional *adj* **infrequent**, irregular, chance, sporadic, rare, intermittent, random [➡ NEVER AND INFREQUENCY; 97] *Opposite*: regular

See Compare and Contrast at **periodic**.

occasional table *type of* **table** [➡ FURNITURE; 858]

occlude **1** *v* **block**, stop up, close off, seal, shut off, obstruct, clog up, cork [➡ BAR AND OBSTRUCT ACCESS; 410] *Opposite*: free **2** *v* **cut off**, cut out, close, block off, shut, block out, seal, stem, stop, obscure [➡ BAR AND OBSTRUCT ACCESS; 410] *Opposite*: open

occlusion **1** *n* **blocking**, obstruction, closing off, sealing, shutting off, clogging up, constriction, stopping up [➡ FASTEN, LINK, AND JOIN; 408] **2** *n* **cutting off**, cutting out, closure, blocking, sealing, blocking off, blocking out, stemming, stopping, obscuring [➡ ENDS AND DEPARTURES; 54]

occult *adj* [➡ THE SUPERNATURAL; 787]

occultist *n* [➡ PEOPLE WITH SUPERNATURAL POWERS; 788]

occupancy *n* **tenancy**, tenure, habitation, possession, residence, use [➡ POSSESS; 444] *Opposite*: vacancy

occupant *n* **inhabitant**, tenant, lodger, resident, occupier, denizen, dweller (*literary*) [➡ INHABITANTS; 857]

occupation **1** *n* **job**, profession, work, career, livelihood, living, employment, business, vocation, calling, position, post [➡ PROFESSIONS; 845] **2** *n* **activity**, pursuit, enterprise, task [➡ WORK IN GENERAL; 297]

occupational *adj* **work-related**, job-related, professional, industrial, working, business [➡ TYPES OF WORK; 835]

occupied **1** *adj* **busy**, engaged, employed, unavailable, working [➡ ABSENT AND UNAVAILABLE; 7] *Opposite*: free **2** *adj* **in use**, full, engaged, tied down, taken, tied up [➡ ABSENT AND UNAVAILABLE; 7] *Opposite*: empty **3** *adj* **conquered**, subjugated, subject, dominated, ruled, captured, seized, oppressed [➡ CAPTIVITY AND LOSS OF FREEDOM; 248] *Opposite*: liberated

occupier *n* **inhabitant**, resident, tenant, occupant, lodger, dweller (*literary*) [➡ INHABITANTS; 857]

occupy **1** *v* **live in**, inhabit, reside in, dwell in (*literary*), lodge (*dated*) [➡ INHABIT; 20] *Opposite*: vacate **2** *v* **interest**, engage, divert, take up, entertain, absorb, amuse, concern [➡ APPEAL TO AND AROUSE INTEREST; 575] **3** *v* **conquer**, subjugate, dominate, rule, seize, oppress, capture [➡ CAPTIVITY AND LOSS OF FREEDOM; 248] *Opposite*: liberate

occur **1** *v* **happen**, take place, arise, come about, transpire, ensue, follow, crop up (*informal*), befall (*archaic or literary*) [➡ HAPPEN; 27] **2** *v* **hit**, strike, cross your mind, appear, come to mind [➡ APPEAR AND EMERGE; 3]

occurrence **1** *n* **incidence**, rate, amount, existence, manifestation [➡ FREQUENT AND OFTEN; 107] **2** *n* **happening**, event, incident, episode, occasion, circumstance, fact, experience [➡ EVENTS AND OCCURRENCES; 35]

ocean **1** *n* **sea**, deep, water, briny (*UK*) [➡ THE SEAS, OCEANS, AND SHORES; 1041] **2** *adj* **marine**, sea, deep-sea, oceanic [➡ THE SEAS, OCEANS, AND SHORES; 1041]

oceangoing *adj* **seagoing**, sea, seaworthy, maritime, seafaring [➡ TRANSPORTATION, TRANSPORTERS, AND CARGOS; 322]

oceanic *adj* **sea**, deep-sea, ocean, saltwater, marine [➡ THE SEAS, OCEANS, AND SHORES; 1041]

ocelot *type of* **cat** [➡ FELINES; 983]

ocher *type of* **orange** [➡ COLORS; 1224]

ochlocracy *n* [➡ STYLES AND SYSTEMS OF GOVERNMENT; 806]

OCR *type of* **software** [➡ COMPUTERS AND COMPUTING; 1127]

octagonal *adj* [➡ ANGULAR SHAPE; 1217]

Octans *type of* **constellation** [➡ HEAVENLY BODIES; 1061]

octet *type of* **band** [➡ MUSICIANS AND SINGERS; 908]

octopus *type of* **aquatic invertebrate** [➡ AQUATIC INVERTEBRATES; 1022]

ocular *adj* **visual**, optical, ophthalmic [➡ SEE; 699]

odd *adj* **strange**, peculiar, unusual, abnormal, anomalous, weird, funny, offbeat, incongruous, eccentric, idiosyncratic, unconventional, uncommon, unorthodox, individual [➡ BIZARRE AND PECULIAR; 257] *Opposite*: ordinary

oddball (*informal*) *adj* [➡ BIZARRE AND PECULIAR; 257]

oddity **1** *n* **peculiarity**, quirk, foible, idiosyncrasy, twist, kink, tic, eccentricity [➡ PERSONAL ECCENTRICITIES; 493] **2** *n* **strangeness**, peculiarity, quirkiness, oddness, bizarreness, abnormality, incongruousness [➡ BIZARRE AND PECULIAR; 257] *Opposite*: normality **3** *n* **eccentric**, character, original, exception, misfit, case (*informal*) [➡ SOLITARY PEOPLE AND MISFITS; 942] **4** *n* **curiosity**, rarity, phenomenon, freak [➡ BIZARRE AND PECULIAR; 257]

oddments **1** *n* **odds and ends**, leftovers, offcuts, bits, fragments, bits and pieces (*informal*), odds and sods (*UK*) [➡ REMAINDER AND REMAINDERS; 125] **2** *n* **knickknacks**, notions, sundries, curios, gewgaws, novelties [➡ ORNAMENTS AND DECORATIONS; 1248]

oddness *n* **strangeness**, peculiarity, mysteriousness, incongruity, weirdness, abnormality, quaintness, deviation, aberration [➡ BIZARRE AND PECULIAR; 257] *Opposite*: normality

odd one out *n* [➡ DIFFERENCE; 149]

odds *n* **chances**, probability, likelihood, balance [➡ GAMBLE AND TAKE RISKS; 466]

odds and ends *n* **remnants**, leftovers, loose ends, offcuts, fragments, bits and pieces (*informal*) [➡ REMAINDER AND REMAINDERS; 125]

odds and sods (*UK*) *n* [➡ REMAINDER AND REMAINDERS; 125]

odds-on (*informal*) *adv* **probably**, most likely, likely, dependably, reliably, like enough (*UK*) [➡ POSSIBLE AND PROBABLE; 177] *Opposite*: unlikely

ode *n* **poem**, elegy, verse, sonnet, song (*literary*) [➡ POETRY AND VERSE; 915]

odious *adj* **hateful**, horrible, loathsome, revolting, detestable, repellent, repulsive, obnoxious, abominable, abhorrent (*formal*), execrable (*formal*) [➡ DISGUSTING AND REPULSIVE; 230] *Opposite*: delightful

odium *n* **abhorrence**, hatred, disgust, revulsion, hate, loathing, abomination, detestation, execration (*literary or formal*) [➡ DISLIKE AND HATE; 577] *Opposite*: approval

odometer *type of* **measuring device** [➡ MEASURING DEVICES; 1123]

odor **1** *n* **scent**, perfume, aroma, redolence, fragrance, bouquet, stink, stench [➡ SMELL AND SMELLING; 705] **2** *n* **air**, aura, atmosphere, flavor, spirit, feeling, quality, sense, essence [➡ APPEARANCE AND ATMOSPHERE; 1237]

See Compare and Contrast at **smell**.

odoriferous *adj* [➡ SMELL AND SMELLING; 705]

odorless *adj* **unscented**, fragrance-free, neutral [➡ SMELL AND SMELLING; 705] *Opposite*: scented

odorous (*literary*) *adj* **scented**, aromatic, redolent, fragrant, perfumed, odoriferous [➡ SMELL AND SMELLING; 705]

odyssey *n* **journey**, trek, crusade, pilgrimage, wanderings, travels, peregrination (*literary*) [➡ TRAVEL: JOURNEYS AND TRIPS; 318]

OEM *n* [➡ BUSINESS ENTERPRISES AND RELATED BODIES; 792]

oeuvre (*formal*) *n* **work**, piece, composition, opus, works, legacy, productions, creations [➡ ARTWORKS; 898]

of a kind *adj* [➡ SIMILARITY; 148]

of course **1** *adv* **obviously**, unquestionably, undeniably, certainly, indubitably (*formal*) [➡ CERTAIN; 174] **2** *adv* **yes**, certainly, naturally, evidently, no problem (*informal*), sure (*informal*), for sure (*informal*) [➡ EXPRESSIONS OF AGREEMENT; 648] **3** *adv* **naturally**, not surprisingly, sure enough, needless to say [➡ CERTAIN; 174] *Opposite*: surprisingly

off *adj* **rotten**, rancid, bad, moldy, tainted, sour, inedible [➡ DECAYING OR INFESTED; 1236] *Opposite*: fresh

offal *n* [➡ TYPES AND CUTS OF MEAT, 1177]

off and on *adv* **intermittently**, infrequently, by fits and starts, discontinuously [➡ FINITENESS, VARIABILITY, AND TRANSIENCE; 96] *Opposite*: regularly

off balance *adv* [➡ ORIENTATION AND ALIGNMENT; 1223]

off beam *adj* **mistaken**, inaccurate, wrong, wide of the mark, off course, off track, erroneous, incorrect [➡ INCORRECT AND ERRONEOUS; 222]

offbeat *adj* **unusual**, unconventional, eccentric, quirky, off-center, bizarre, different, off-the-wall (*informal*) [➡ BIZARRE AND PECULIAR; 257] *Opposite*: typical

off center *adv* [➡ ORIENTATION AND ALIGNMENT; 1223]

off-center **1** *adj* **asymmetrical**, skewed, uneven, unbalanced, eccentric [➡ ORIENTATION AND ALIGNMENT; 1223] **2** *adj* **quirky**, eccentric, unconventional, odd, out in left field (*informal*), off-the-wall (*informal*) [➡ BIZARRE AND PECULIAR; 257]

off chance *n* **likelihood**, probability, possibility, chance, prospect, outside chance [➡ POSSIBLE AND PROBABLE; 177]

off-color **1** *adj* (*informal*) **risqué**, indecorous, improper, indiscreet, racy, suggestive, broad, dirty, adult, bawdy, raunchy (*informal*), spicy (*informal*), smutty (*informal*), blue (*informal*) [➡ MORALLY BAD OR IMPROPER; 775] **2** *adj* (*UK*) **unwell**, under the weather, unfit, sick, ill [➡ ILL AND SICK; 740] *Opposite*: well

off course *adj* **disoriented**, lost, out, astray, adrift, at sea [➡ AIMLESS AND ERRANT MOTION; 343]

off duty *adj* **on vacation**, on leave, not working, having a break, on holiday (*UK*) [➡ EMPLOYMENT STATUS; 831]

offend 1 v **hurt somebody's feelings**, upset, insult, affront, be rude to, cause offense, rub the wrong way [➡ UPSET, DISTRESS, AND HUMILIATE; 567] 2 v **commit an offense**, commit a crime, commit a felony, transgress, break the law [➡ DISOBEY; 302]

offended adj **affronted**, insulted, hurt, upset, slighted, snubbed [➡ SADNESS, DISTRESS, AND DESPAIR; 539]

offender n **criminal**, wrongdoer, reprobate, delinquent, lawbreaker [➡ CRIMINALS; 821]

offense 1 n **crime**, wrongdoing, felony, fault, transgression, violation, infraction, breach, infringement, misdemeanor, sin [➡ CRIMES; 817] 2 n **insult**, affront, outrage, slight, slur, dig, barb, aspersion [➡ INSULTS, ABUSE, AND SWEARING; 658] 3 n **umbrage**, resentment, pique, indignation [➡ IRRITATION AND ANGER; 541] 4 n **attack**, offensive, assault, onslaught, bombardment, aggression [➡ AGGRESSIVE EVENTS; 39] Opposite: defense

offensive 1 adj **unpleasant**, distasteful, disgusting, odious, hateful, nasty (informal) [➡ DISGUSTING AND REPULSIVE; 230] Opposite: agreeable 2 adj **insulting**, rude, impolite, provoking, provocative, abusive, impertinent (formal) [➡ RUDE AND HOSTILE; 625] Opposite: courteous 3 adj **aggressive**, attacking, violent, invasive, belligerent, bellicose [➡ AGGRESSIVE AND BELLIGERENT; 518] Opposite: peaceful

offensively adv **rudely**, abusively, impolitely, indecently, unpleasantly, vulgarly, nastily, outrageously, disgracefully, impertinently (formal) [➡ RUDE AND HOSTILE; 625] Opposite: politely

offensiveness n **rudeness**, impoliteness, indecency, vulgarity, abusiveness, tastelessness, unpleasantness, nastiness (informal) [➡ BAD MANNERS AND SOCIAL SKILLS; 521] Opposite: politeness

offer 1 v **proffer**, tender, present, bid [➡ DISPENSE, RATION, AND DISTRIBUTE; 434] 2 v **propose**, suggest, pose, recommend, put forward, submit, propound, extend, advance, move [➡ SUGGEST, HINT, AND COMMENT; 612] Opposite: withdraw 3 n **proposal**, suggestion, bid, proposition, bargain, agreement, compromise, deal, submission, motion, advance, approach, overture [➡ SUGGEST, HINT, AND COMMENT; 612]

offering n **contribution**, gift, donation, present, submission, subscription [➡ GIFTS; 438]

off-guard adj **unready**, unawares, napping, unprepared [➡ NEUTRALITY AND INDIFFERENCE; 553] Opposite: ready

offhand 1 adj **impromptu**, extemporaneous, improvised, unrehearsed, spontaneous [➡ UNPLANNED AND UNEXPECTED; 281] Opposite: premeditated 2 adj **informal**, casual, nonchalant, easygoing, indifferent, blasé [➡ UNINTERESTED AND DETACHED; 629] Opposite: serious

offhandedly 1 adv **extemporaneously**, spontaneously [➡ UNPLANNED AND UNEXPECTED; 281] Opposite: deliberately 2 adv **informally**, casually, nonchalantly [➡ UNINTERESTED AND DETACHED; 629] Opposite: seriously

offhandedness n [➡ UNINTERESTED AND DETACHED; 629]

office 1 n **bureau**, workplace, administrative center, headquarters, agency [➡ PLACE OF EMPLOYMENT; 832] 2 type of **room in public buildings** [➡ TYPES OF ROOMS; 1097]

office assistant n [➡ OFFICE WORKERS; 847]

office block type of **industrial site** [➡ INDUSTRIAL BUILDINGS; 1087]

office holder n **official**, officer, politician, public servant, elected official, civil servant [➡ POLITICAL OFFICES AND POLITICIANS; 808]

officer 1 n **major**, captain, colonel, brigadier, field marshal, general, soldier of rank [➡ MILITARY PERSONNEL; 828] 2 n **constable**, sergeant, police officer, detective, policeman, policewoman, peace officer, patrolman, cop (slang) [➡ THE POLICE, ARREST, AND PRETRIAL PROCEEDINGS; 818] 3 n **official**, bureaucrat, representative, administrator, office holder, executive, manager, exec (informal) [➡ ADMINISTRATIVE OFFICERS; 811]

office worker n [➡ WORKERS; 836]

official 1 n **bureaucrat**, administrator, representative, spokesperson, officer, executive, exec (informal) [➡ ADMINISTRATIVE OFFICERS; 811] 2 adj **authorized**, certified, endorsed, sanctioned, allowed, approved, formal, authoritative, legitimate [➡ LEGAL AND LEGITIMATE; 815] Opposite: informal

officialdom (informal) n **the powers that be**, bureaucracy, administrative system, red tape (informal) [➡ ADMINISTRATIVE OFFICERS; 811]

officiate v **preside**, manage, perform official duties, carry out official duties, solemnize, celebrate, oversee, be in charge [➡ BE IN CHARGE; 270]

officious adj **meddlesome**, bossy, bureaucratic, self-important, overbearing, interfering, intrusive, fussy [➡ BOSSY AND OVERBEARING; 516]

officiousness n [➡ BOSSY AND OVERBEARING; 516]

off-key 1 adj **out of key**, tuneless, out of tune, discordant, screeching, caterwauling, unmusical [➡ LOUD, HIGH, OR UNPLEASANT SOUNDS; 1266] Opposite: melodious 2 adv **tunelessly**, out of tune, discordantly, unmusically [➡ LOUD, HIGH, OR UNPLEASANT SOUNDS; 1266] Opposite: melodiously

off-limits adj **forbidden**, prohibited, proscribed, outlawed, verboten, out of bounds [➡ REFUSE PERMISSION AND NOT ALLOW; 670] Opposite: permitted

off-line adj **off**, disconnected, down [➡ COMPUTERS AND COMPUTING; 1127] Opposite: online

offload 1 v (informal) **relieve of**, divest, rid, free from, unburden [➡ GET RID OF SOMETHING; 451] 2 v **discharge**, unload, deposit, dump, leave, unlade, debark, disburden (archaic) [➡ MOVE SOMETHING TO ANOTHER LOCATION; 324] Opposite: load 3 v **pass on**, get rid of, dump, deposit, devolve, unload, leave, abandon, delegate, distribute [➡ GET RID OF SOMETHING; 451] Opposite: keep

off-peak adj [➡ TIMES OF DAY; 87]

off-putting 1 adj **repellent**, repulsive, disgusting, distasteful, offensive [➡ DISGUSTING AND REPULSIVE; 230] Opposite: attractive 2 adj **forbidding**, disconcerting, upsetting, disturbing, daunting [➡ EMOTIONALLY UNPLEASANT AND UPSETTING; 227] Opposite: comforting

off-roader (informal) type of **car** [➡ BIKES, CARS, AND CARRIAGES; 1149]

offset 1 n **counterbalance**, balance, counterpoise, counterweight, equalizer, compensation, equipoise (formal) [➡ EQUALITY; 154] 2 v **counterweigh**, counterbalance, make up

offshoot 1 *n* **sideshoot**, sprout, sucker, branch, twig, sprig, shoot, outgrowth [➡ PARTS OF TREES AND PLANTS; 1026] **2** *n* **derivative**, subsidiary, consequence, result, outcome, development, branch, byproduct, spinoff [➡ RESULTS AND OUTCOMES; 83]

offspring *n* **descendants**, progeny, children, issue, young, brood, litter, kids (*informal*), posterity (*formal*) [➡ YOUNGER GENERATION RELATIVES; 958]

offspring

◆ *types of offspring*
only child, quadruplet, quintuplet, singleton, triplet, twin

off the beam *adj* [➡ ORIENTATION AND ALIGNMENT; 1223]

off the beaten path *adj* [➡ DISTANCE; 160]

off the beaten track (*informal*) *adj* **secluded**, remote, isolated, out-of-the-way, far-flung, distant [➡ DISTANCE; 160]

off-the-cuff *adj* **impromptu**, spontaneous, improvised, unprepared, unrehearsed, unscripted, ad lib, ad hoc [➡ UNPLANNED AND UNEXPECTED, 281]

off-the-rack *adj* **ready-made**, ready-to-wear, mass-produced, prêt-à-porter, off-the-peg (*UK*) [➡ DESCRIBING CLOTHES; 869] *Opposite*: made-to-measure

off the record *adj* **private**, confidential, secret, unofficial, privy (*archaic*) [➡ SECRET AND UNKNOWN; 179] *Opposite*: official

off-the-shelf *adj* **standard**, regular, mass-produced, ordinary, run-of-the-mill, garden-variety, common, common or garden (*UK*) [➡ ORDINARINESS; 244]

off-the-wall (*informal*) *adj* **bizarre**, strange, eccentric, unusual, unconventional, funny, weird, offbeat, out in left field (*informal*), wacky (*informal*) [➡ BIZARRE AND PECULIAR; 257]

off-white *type of* **white** [➡ COLORS; 1224]

of interest *adj* [➡ INTERESTING AND MEANINGFUL; 190]

of its own accord *adv* **by itself**, on its own, unaided, voluntarily [➡ AUTOMATIC AND INSTINCTIVE; 280]

of late *adv* **lately**, recently, latterly [➡ PAST; 84]

of necessity *adv* **necessarily**, unavoidably, automatically, inevitably [➡ NECESSARY AND ESSENTIAL; 196]

of no account *adj* **unimportant**, of no consequence, inconsequential, insignificant, minor [➡ UNIMPORTANT AND UNNECESSARY; 238] *Opposite*: important

of no consequence *adj* **irrelevant**, insignificant, a minor point, inconsequential, immaterial, neither here nor there, beside the point, unimportant, trivial [➡ UNIMPORTANT AND UNNECESSARY; 238] *Opposite*: important

of no importance *adj* [➡ UNIMPORTANT AND UNNECESSARY; 238]

of note *adj* **important**, well-known, worth mentioning,

notable, acclaimed, famous, noteworthy [➡ IMPORTANT; 194] *Opposite*: unknown

of no use *adj* [➡ REDUNDANT AND USELESS; 240]

of no value *adj* [➡ REDUNDANT AND USELESS; 240]

of one mind *adj* [➡ HARMONY; 155]

often *adv* **frequently**, over and over again, time and again, repeatedly, habitually, a lot, regularly, all the time [➡ FREQUENT AND OFTEN, 107] *Opposite*: seldom

of the essence *adj* **vital**, very important, crucial, imperative [➡ NECESSARY AND ESSENTIAL; 196] *Opposite*: unimportant

of the order of (*UK*) *adv* [➡ APPROXIMATELY; 135]

of use *adj* [➡ USEFULNESS; 199]

of your own accord *adv* **voluntarily**, willingly, spontaneously, independently, by choice, autonomously [➡ THE WILL AND WILLINGNESS; 563]

ogle *v* **scrutinize**, eye, look at, stare, gaze, keep an eye on, gawk, rubberneck (*informal*) [➡ LOOKING AND LOOKS; 700] *Opposite*: ignore

> *See Compare and Contrast at* **gaze**.

ogonek *type of* **diacritic** [➡ ASPECTS OF LANGUAGE; 682]

ogre *n* **giant**, troll, tyrant, monster, fiend [➡ MYTHICAL BEINGS; 789]

ohm *type of* **SI unit** [➡ SIZE AND DIMENSIONS; 1192]

oh my (*informal*) *interj* [➡ EXPRESSIONS OF SURPRISE AND PLEASURE; 546]

oil **1** *n* **lubricant**, emollient, grease [➡ LIQUIDS; 1269] **2** *n* **grease**, fat, lard [➡ FATS AND OILS; 1173] **3** *v* **apply oil**, lubricate, smear with oil, grease, loosen [➡ DECORATE, ADORN, AND APPLY COATINGS; 405]

oil

◆ *types of cooking fats and oils*
butter, canola oil, corn oil, dripping, ghee, lard, margarine, olive oil, peanut oil, rape oil, sesame oil, shortening, suet, sunflower oil, vegetable oil

oil burner *type of* **heating appliance** [➡ HEATING, REFRIGERATION, AND VENTILATION; 1142]

oil painting *n* [➡ ARTWORKS; 898]

oil pan *part of* **engine** [➡ PARTS OF AN ENGINE; 1144]

oil rig *type of* **industrial site** [➡ INDUSTRIAL BUILDINGS; 1087]

oily *adj* **greasy**, fatty, slick, slippery, oleaginous, unctuous [➡ PHYSICAL TEXTURE; 1222]

oink *type of* **animal sound** [➡ SOUNDS MADE BY ANIMALS; 1261]

ointment *n* **gel**, liniment, lotion, balm, salve, cream, unguent [➡ LOTIONS, PASTES, AND GELS; 1272]

OK (*informal*) *adv* [➡ EXPRESSIONS OF AGREEMENT; 648]

okapi *type of* **deer or antelope** [➡ DEER AND ANTELOPES; 981]

okay (*informal*) **1** *interj* **all right**, of course, certainly, yes, agreed, fine (*informal*), sure (*informal*), no problem (*informal*), yep (*informal*) [➡ EXPRESSIONS OF AGREEMENT; 648] **2** *adj* **satisfactory**, acceptable, all right, tolerable, passable, up to par, up to scratch (*informal*) [➡ ACCEPTABLE AND PASSABLE; 219] *Opposite*: unacceptable **3** *v* **green light**, approve, agree to, sanction, give the nod to, endorse, authorize, certify, give the go-ahead to (*informal*) [➡ APPROVE AND CONFIRM; 646] *Opposite*: veto **4** *n* **approval**, consent, permission, sanction, endorsement, go-ahead (*informal*) [➡ APPROVE AND CONFIRM; 646]

okeydokey (*informal*) *adv* [➡ EXPRESSIONS OF AGREEMENT; 648]

okra *type of* **vegetable** [➡ FRUIT AND VEGETABLES; 1176]

old 1 *adj* **aged**, elderly, older, mature, getting on, not getting any younger [➡ OLD AGE; 919] *Opposite*: young **2** *adj* **from the past**, ancient, from way back, long-standing, long forgotten, deep-rooted, hoary, timeworn [➡ OLD, OLD-FASHIONED; 167] *Opposite*: recent **3** *adj* **previous**, last, other, former, erstwhile, onetime, archaic, dated, outmoded, antiquated [➡ PAST; 84] *Opposite*: current

olden (*archaic or literary*) *adj* **past**, ancient, historic, bygone, aged, hoary, age-old [➡ OLD, OLD-FASHIONED; 167] *Opposite*: modern

Old English sheepdog *type of* **large dog** [➡ DOGS; 980]

old-fashioned 1 *adj* **antiquated**, archaic, unfashionable, behind the times, outmoded, passé, out-of-date, outdated, obsolete, antediluvian (*informal*) [➡ OLD, OLD-FASHIONED; 167] *Opposite*: up-to-date **2** *adj* **fogyish**, traditional, conservative, conventional, old-school [➡ OLD, OLD-FASHIONED; 167] *Opposite*: modern

Compare and Contrast: *old-fashioned, outdated, antiquated, archaic, obsolete, passé, antediluvian*

CORE MEANING: no longer in current use or no longer considered fashionable

old-fashioned no longer considered fashionable or suitable because of changes in taste or technology, or nostalgically favoring or maintaining the style of a former time; *outdated* no longer relevant to modern life because it has been superseded by something better, more fashionable, or more technologically advanced; *antiquated* regarded as in need of updating or replacing, though still functioning or in use; *archaic* belonging to a much earlier period of time, often suggesting a lack of relevance to modern life; *obsolete* superseded by something new, and in some cases therefore no longer in use; *passé* dismissed as no longer current or fashionable; *antediluvian* (*informal*) extremely old-fashioned and outdated.

old flame (*informal*) *n* [➡ SEXUAL AND ROMANTIC RELATIONSHIPS; 964]

old fogy *n* [➡ OLD PEOPLE; 920]

old gold *type of* **orange** [➡ COLORS; 1224]

old hand *n* **veteran**, expert, professional, connoisseur, authority [➡ TALENTED OR INTELLIGENT PEOPLE; 528] *Opposite*: novice

old hat (*informal*) *adj* **outmoded**, obsolete, clichéd, out-of-date, dated, anachronistic, ancient, old-fashioned, corny [➡ OLD, OLD-FASHIONED; 167] *Opposite*: up-to-date

old master *n* [➡ ARTWORKS; 898]

old person *n* [➡ OLD PEOPLE; 920]

old-style *adj* **traditional**, outdated, outmoded, out-of-date, old, old-fashioned [➡ OLD, OLD-FASHIONED; 167] *Opposite*: modern

old-time *adj* **old-fashioned**, outdated, outmoded, traditional, old-style, quaint, old-world [➡ OLD, OLD-FASHIONED; 167] *Opposite*: modern

old-timer *n* [➡ OLD PEOPLE; 920]

old-world *adj* **outdated**, outmoded, quaint, traditional, old-style, old-fashioned [➡ OLD, OLD-FASHIONED; 167] *Opposite*: modern

oleaginous *adj* [➡ PHYSICAL TEXTURE; 1222]

oleaginousness *n* [➡ PHYSICAL TEXTURE; 1222]

Oligocene *type of* **epoch** [➡ EPOCHS AND ERAS; 89]

olive *type of* **fruit** [➡ FRUIT AND VEGETABLES; 1176]

olive branch *n* **peace offering**, compromise, concession, gesture, apology, reconciliation [➡ APOLOGIZE AND RETRACT; 683]

olive green *type of* **green** [➡ COLORS; 1224]

olive oil *type of* **cooking fat and oil** [➡ FATS AND OILS; 1173]

olive-skinned *adj* [➡ COMPLEXION; 480]

ombudsman *n* [➡ SURVEYORS, EXAMINERS, AND JUDGES; 853]

omen *n* **sign**, portent, warning, forecast, premonition, augury, presage, foretoken (*literary*) [➡ INDICATIONS, SIGNS, AND WARNINGS; 68]

ominous *adj* **threatening**, warning, worrying, gloomy, portentous, menacing, ill-omened, unpromising [➡ DANGEROUS; 236] *Opposite*: promising

omission 1 *n* **oversight**, lapse, slip, error, blunder, inadvertence, faux pas (*literary*) [➡ MISTAKES; 250] **2** *n* **exclusion**, exception, absence, leaving out, noninclusion, hiatus, blank, gap, lacuna (*literary*) [➡ ABSENT AND UNAVAILABLE; 7] *Opposite*: inclusion

omit 1 *v* **leave out**, miss out, pass over, skip, skip over, exclude [➡ EJECT AND EXCLUDE; 340] *Opposite*: include **2** *v* **neglect**, forget, not take the trouble, not bother, overlook, ignore, fail [➡ NOT DO AND REFUSE TO DO; 274] *Opposite*: remember

See Compare and Contrast at **neglect**.

omitted *adj* [➡ ABSENT AND UNAVAILABLE; 7]

omnibus *n* **compilation**, collection, anthology, edition, album, florilegium (*archaic*) [➡ COLLECTIONS AND MIXTURES OF THINGS; 1244]

omnipotence *n* **authority**, power, all-powerfulness, supremacy, influence, control, might, invincibility [➡ STRENGTH; 201] *Opposite*: powerlessness

omnipotent *adj* **almighty**, all-powerful, invincible, unstoppable, supreme, godlike [➡ STRENGTH; 201] *Opposite*: powerless

omnipresent *adj* **ubiquitous**, all-pervading, universal, ever-present, pervasive, all over [➡ PRESENT AND AVAILABLE; 11] *Opposite*: absent

omniscience *n* **knowledge**, awareness, insight, wisdom, sapience, sagacity [➡ KNOWLEDGE AND WISDOM; 558] *Opposite*: ignorance

omniscient *adj* **all-knowing**, all-seeing, wise, well-informed, sagacious [➡ KNOWLEDGE AND WISDOM; 558]

on 1 *prep* **sitting on**, on top of, resting on, lying on, upon, atop (*literary*) [➡ RELATIVE LOCATION; 161] *Opposite*: under 2 *prep* **at**, next to, by the side of, by [➡ RELATIVE LOCATION; 161] 3 *adv* **happening**, taking place, scheduled, arranged, proceeding, going on [➡ HAPPENING AND IN PROGRESS; 32] *Opposite*: off 4 *adv* **without stopping**, continuously, without a break, never-endingly [➡ PERMANENCE: WITHOUT END; 94]

on account of *prep* **owing to**, because of, due to, through, as a result of, in view of, in consequence of (*formal*) [➡ CAUSATION; 168]

on and off *adv* **occasionally**, intermittently, sporadically, with breaks, now and then, now and again [➡ NEVER AND INFREQUENCY; 97] *Opposite*: continuously

on an even keel *adj* **stable**, well-balanced, reliable, dependable, steady, poised, steadfast [➡ ORDER AND ORGANIZATION; 206] *Opposite*: unstable

on a par *adj* [➡ EQUALITY; 154]

on a par with *adj* **on an equal footing with**, equal to, similar to, parallel to, equivalent to, level pegging with (*UK*) [➡ EQUALITY; 154]

on a roll (*informal*) *adj* [➡ SUCCESSFUL AND PROMISING; 81]

on a shoestring *adv* **cheaply**, on a tight budget, inexpensively, economically, for next to nothing, frugally, on the cheap (*informal*) [➡ CHEAP AND INEXPENSIVE; 221] *Opposite*: extravagantly

on a slope *adj* [➡ ORIENTATION AND ALIGNMENT; 1223]

on a tight rein *adj* **under control**, restricted, closely controlled, regimented, disciplined [➡ CAPTIVITY AND LOSS OF FREEDOM; 248]

on a whim *adv* [➡ UNPLANNED AND UNEXPECTED; 281]

on balance *adv* **all things considered**, all in all, at the end of the day, taking everything into account [➡ SUMMARIZING EXPRESSIONS; 622]

on benefit (*UK*) *adj* [➡ EMPLOYMENT STATUS; 831]

on board *adj* **involved**, committed, on the team, on the project, on our side [➡ PRESENT AND AVAILABLE; 11]

onboard *adj* **aboard**, on the ship, on the train, on the bus [➡ TRAVEL: WAYS OF TRAVELING; 320]

on call *adj* **on duty**, working, available, on hand, on standby, on call-out (*UK*) [➡ EMPLOYMENT STATUS; 831] *Opposite*: off duty

once 1 *adv* **some time ago**, formerly, previously, a long time ago, once upon a time, in the past, then [➡ PAST; 84] *Opposite*: now 2 *adv* **as soon as**, when, after, the minute [➡ AFTER, LAST, AND FOLLOWING; 165]

once again *adv* [➡ AGAIN; 109]

once in a blue moon (*informal*) *adv* [➡ NEVER AND INFREQUENCY; 97]

once-in-a-lifetime *adj* [➡ NEVER AND INFREQUENCY; 97]

once in a while *adv* **every so often**, every now and then, now and again, from time to time, occasionally, sometimes, on occasion, infrequently [➡ NEVER AND INFREQUENCY; 97] *Opposite*: frequently

once more *adv* [➡ AGAIN; 109]

once-over (*informal*) *n* **examination**, inspection, check, review, survey, going-over (*informal*) [➡ EXAMINE AND ASSESS; 753]

once upon a time *adv* [➡ PAST; 84]

on cloud nine (*informal*) *adj* **happy**, elated, excited, ecstatic, pleased, in seventh heaven, joyful, in raptures, delighted, enraptured (*formal*) [➡ PLEASURE, EXCITEMENT, AND ELATION; 534] *Opposite*: down in the dumps

oncoming *adj* **approaching**, looming, nearing, advancing, onrushing [➡ ABOUT TO HAPPEN; 33]

on display *adj* [➡ PERCEPTIBLE; 25]

one *adj* **unique**, single, solitary, lone, individual, one and only [➡ EXTRAORDINARY: UNCOMMON; 205]

one after another *adv* **one by one**, consecutively, in sequence, in succession, back-to-back, end-to-end, sequentially, one after the other, singly, in turn [➡ AFTER, LAST, AND FOLLOWING; 165]

one after the other *adv* **in a row**, one by one, consecutively, in sequence, in succession, back-to-back, end-to-end, sequentially, one after another, singly, in turn [➡ AFTER, LAST, AND FOLLOWING; 165]

one and all *pron* **everyone**, everybody, all, all and sundry, ladies and gentlemen [➡ ALL; 128] *Opposite*: nobody

one and only *adj* **unique**, inimitable, incomparable, amazing, incredible [➡ EXTRAORDINARY: UNCOMMON; 205] *Opposite*: common

one and the same *adj* **identical**, the same, the very same [➡ SAMENESS; 150] *Opposite*: different

one by one *adv* **one after another**, one after the other, one at a time, sequentially, separately, consecutively, in succession, singly, in sequence, in turn [➡ AFTER, LAST, AND FOLLOWING; 165] *Opposite*: all together

on edge *adj* **edgy**, irritated, touchy, jumpy, tense, uneasy, jittery, nervous, anxious [➡ CONFUSION, ANXIETY, AND WORRY; 540] *Opposite*: calm

one-dimensional *adj* **superficial**, lacking in depth, simplistic, simple-minded, basic [➡ ORDINARINESS; 244]

one-liner *n* **joke**, witticism, quip, bon mot, epigram, gag (*informal*), wisecrack (*informal*), crack (*informal*), jest (*literary*) [➡ JOKES AND TEASING; 674]

on end *adv* **successively**, consecutively, continuously, continually, without end, running, on the run, on the trot (*UK*) [➡ AFTER, LAST, AND FOLLOWING; 165]

oneness 1 *n* **singleness**, cohesion, coherence [➡ SAMENESS; 150] *Opposite*: diversity 2 *n* **agreement**, unanimity, unity, togetherness, solidarity [➡ HARMONY; 155] *Opposite*: divergence

one of a kind *adj* **unique**, exceptional, irreplaceable, special, inimitable, incomparable [➡EXTRAORDINARY: UNCOMMON; 205] *Opposite*: commonplace

one-off (*UK*) **1** *adj* unique, once-in-a-lifetime, never-to-be-repeated, limited-edition, special, unrepeatable [➡EXTRAORDINARY: UNCOMMON; 205] **2** *n* rarity, limited edition, one in a million [➡EXTRAORDINARY: UNCOMMON; 205]

one of these days *adv* [➡FUTURE; 86]

one-on-one 1 *adj* individual, private, personal, intimate, personalized, individualized [➡BELONGING OR RELATING TO INDIVIDUALS; 944] **2** *adv* individually, privately, personally, alone [➡BELONGING OR RELATING TO INDIVIDUALS; 944] **3** *n* [➡INFORMAL COMMUNICATION; 45]

one or two *adj* a few, a couple, a handful, some, not many [➡FEW, LITTLE, SMALL AMOUNT; 120] *Opposite*: lots

one-piece *n* [➡GARMENTS AND OUTFITS; 865]

onerous *adj* difficult, burdensome, arduous, heavy, tiring, time-consuming, tedious [➡DIFFICULTY AND COMPLEXITY; 242] *Opposite*: easy

onerousness *n* [➡DIFFICULTY AND COMPLEXITY; 242]

one-sided *adj* biased, unfair, prejudiced, weighted, unrepresentative, misleading, partisan, partial, inequitable [➡THE NATURE OF IDEAS; 771] *Opposite*: balanced

one-sidedness *n* bias, biasedness, partiality, unfairness, prejudice, inequity, unrepresentativeness [➡THE NATURE OF IDEAS; 771]

onetime *adj* former, previous, ex, past, old, erstwhile [➡PAST; 84] *Opposite*: current

one-way *adj* single, outward [➡DIRECTION OF MOTION; 345] *Opposite*: round-trip

on fire 1 *adj* burning, alight, ablaze, blazing, in flames, afire, fiery [➡FIRE, FLAMMABILITY, AND BURNING; 1165] **2** *adj* passionate, enthusiastic, fervent, ardent, bubbling over, fired up, fiery, eager [➡PLEASURE, EXCITEMENT, AND ELATION; 534] *Opposite*: apathetic

on foot *adv* walking, under your own steam, by shank's pony (*UK*) [➡TRAVEL: WAYS OF TRAVELING; 320]

ongoing *adj* continuing, rolling, in progress, current, open-ended, constant [➡PERMANENCE: WITHOUT END; 94]

on hand *adj* nearby, available, to hand, at hand, close by, convenient, there, around, close at hand [➡PRESENT AND AVAILABLE; 11] *Opposite*: unavailable

on hold *adj* [➡NOT HAPPENING; 34]

on ice *adj* [➡NOT HAPPENING; 34]

on impulse *adv* [➡UNPLANNED AND UNEXPECTED; 281]

onion *type of* vegetable [➡FRUIT AND VEGETABLES; 1176]

on its last legs *adj* falling apart, dilapidated, run-down, decrepit, ramshackle, crumbling [➡IN BAD REPAIR; 1234]

online *adj* connected, on, operational, working, available, accessible, wired, virtual, cyber-, real-time, on-screen, electronic [➡COMPUTERS AND COMPUTING; 1127]

online banking *n* [➡E-COMMERCE; 1129]

on loan *adj* borrowed, lent, rented, loaned out, hired out (*UK*) [➡ABSENT AND UNAVAILABLE; 7]

onlooker *n* bystander, spectator, viewer, observer, witness, watcher [➡ONLOOKERS AND SPECTATORS; 701]

only 1 *adv* merely, simply, just, barely, no more than [➡TO A CERTAIN EXTENT; 136] **2** *adj* single, lone, solitary, individual, one [➡SOLITARINESS; 941]

only child *type of* offspring [➡YOUNGER GENERATION RELATIVES; 958]

on no account *adv* in no way, for no reason, by no means, certainly not, never, under no circumstances [➡NOT; 137]

on paper *adv* in theory, theoretically, notionally, hypothetically, conjecturally, suppositionally, abstractly [➡POSSIBLE AND PROBABLE; 177] *Opposite*: in reality

on purpose *adv* consciously, knowingly, deliberately, purposely, intentionally, by design, with intent, explicitly [➡INTENTIONAL AND DELIBERATE; 279] *Opposite*: accidentally

onrush *n* surge, rush, wave, tide, deluge, flood [➡SUDDEN EVENTS; 52]

onrushing *adj* oncoming, surging, rushing, approaching, nearing, advancing [➡ABOUT TO HAPPEN; 33]

on sale *adj* being sold, available, for sale, reduced, discounted, selling at knockdown prices, in a promotion, on offer (*UK*), on special offer (*UK*) [➡PRESENT AND AVAILABLE; 11]

on-screen *adj* televised, television, live, on-air, televisual, public, TV (*informal*) [➡TELEVISION AND RADIO; 606]

onset *n* start, beginning, arrival, inception (*formal*), commencement (*formal*) [➡BEGINNINGS; 53] *Opposite*: conclusion

on show *adj* [➡PERCEPTIBLE; 25]

onside 1 *adj* legal, safe, clear, in the clear [➡SAFE AND SAFETY; 191] **2** *adv* legally, safely, legitimately [➡SAFE AND SAFETY; 191]

onslaught *n* attack, assault, offensive, ambush, blitz, blitzkrieg [➡AGGRESSIVE EVENTS; 39]

on stand-by *adj* on call, standing by, ready to step in, as backup, in case of emergency, available [➡PRESENT AND AVAILABLE; 11]

on tap *adj* at hand, on hand, ready, obtainable, available, accessible, attainable, procurable [➡PRESENT AND AVAILABLE; 11]

on tenterhooks *adj* in suspense, excited, anxious, apprehensive, on edge, agitated, nervous [➡CONFUSION, ANXIETY, AND WORRY; 540]

on the agenda *adj* [➡ABOUT TO HAPPEN; 33]

on the air *adj* live, being broadcast, on air, recording, on TV, on the radio [➡TELEVISION AND RADIO; 606]

on the alert *adj* on the lookout, aware, wary, vigilant, observant, prepared, on guard, attentive, alert, heedful, watchful, on the ball (*informal*) [➡POSITIVE IMPATIENCE, ENTHUSIASM, AND ALERTNESS; 537]

on the back burner *adj* [➡NOT HAPPENING; 34]

on the ball (*informal*) *adj* aware, clued-in, alert, with your wits about you, on your toes, awake, apprehensive, sensible, with it (*informal*), clued up (*UK*) [➡POSITIVE IMPATIENCE, ENTHUSIASM, AND ALERTNESS; 537]

on the blink (*informal*) *adj* **broken**, out of order, not working, faulty, acting up, malfunctioning, brokendown, busted (*informal*) [➡IN BAD REPAIR; 1234]

on the breadline (*UK*) *adj* [➡POVERTY AND POOR; 892]

on the button (*informal*) *adv* **exactly**, precisely, dead right, on the nail, on the nose, dead on, plumb (*informal*) [➡EXACT; 203]

on the cheap (*informal*) *adv* **discounted**, cheaply, economically, inexpensively, for next to nothing, on a shoestring, for a song, at a low price [➡CHEAP AND INEXPENSIVE; 221]

on the contrary *adv* **quite the reverse**, in contrast, quite the opposite, not at all, absolutely not [➡NOT; 137]

on the cross (*UK*) *adv* [➡ORIENTATION AND ALIGNMENT; 1223]

on the dot *adv* **on time**, punctually, precisely, promptly, exactly, squarely [➡PROMPTNESS: ON TIME; 99] *Opposite*: late

on the double *adv* **straightaway**, quickly, immediately, now, in double time, instantly [➡MOVING QUICKLY; 103] *Opposite*: slowly

on the face of it *adv* [➡EXPRESSIONS OF UNCERTAINTY; 560]

on the fence *adj* **undecided**, noncommittal, hedging your bets, equivocal, indecisive, unsettled [➡UNCERTAINTY; 559] *Opposite*: decided

on the go *adj* **occupied**, bustling, active, busy, on the move, lively [➡HAPPENING AND IN PROGRESS; 32]

on the horizon *adj* [➡ABOUT TO HAPPEN; 33]

on the horns of a dilemma *adj* **in a quandary**, between a rock and a hard place, at a stalemate, in a predicament, in a bind, in a cleft stick (*UK*) [➡IN TROUBLE AND DISADVANTAGED; 73]

on the house *adj* **free of charge**, for free, free, complimentary, gratis [➡GIFTS; 438]

on the level (*informal*) *adj* **trustworthy**, honest, straight, telling the truth, reliable, truthful [➡HONEST AND RELIABLE; 502] *Opposite*: underhanded

on the loose *adj* **at large**, free, roaming freely, running wild, loose, unrestrained, unconfined [➡FREEDOM AND LIBERTY; 208]

on the market *adj* **on sale**, on offer, for sale, available, purchasable, obtainable [➡PRESENT AND AVAILABLE; 11]

on the mend *adj* **getting better**, on the road to recovery, improving, recovering, recuperating, getting your strength back, convalescing [➡HEALING; 730]

on the move 1 *adv* **traveling**, touring, traveling around, on the road, moving about (*UK*) [➡TRAVEL: WAYS OF TRAVELING; 320] 2 *adv* **moving ahead**, succeeding, making headway, progressing, making progress, forging ahead [➡SUCCESSFUL AND PROMISING; 81] 3 *adj* **bustling**, on the go, active, busy, moving, lively, energetic [➡HAPPENING AND IN PROGRESS; 32]

on the nail *adv* [➡EXACT; 203]

on the nose (*informal*) *adv* **exactly**, precisely, on the button, on the nail, squarely, dead on [➡EXACT; 203]

on the order of *adv* [➡APPROXIMATELY; 135]

on the other hand *adv* **instead**, conversely, alternatively, then again, in contrast, oppositely, contrariwise [➡OPPOSITE; 157]

on the point of *adj* **about to**, near to, bordering on, on the threshold of, considering, all set to, set to, getting ready to, on the verge of, close to, just going to, ready to, likely to [➡ABOUT TO HAPPEN; 33]

on the road *adj* **on the move**, traveling, touring, on tour, doing a tour [➡TRAVEL: WAYS OF TRAVELING; 320]

on the rocks (*informal*) *adj* **in trouble**, in danger, failing, collapsing, breaking up [➡IN DANGER; 237]

on the run *adj* **runaway**, escaping, absconding, fleeing, running scared, in retreat, in flight, routed [➡ABSENT AND UNAVAILABLE; 7]

on the same wavelength *adj* **compatible**, in tune, similar, coming from the same direction, singing the same song, consistent, consonant (*formal*) [➡HARMONY; 155] *Opposite*: incompatible

on the skids (*slang*) *adj* [➡POVERTY AND POOR; 892]

on the slant *adv* [➡ORIENTATION AND ALIGNMENT; 1223]

on the sly *adv* **secretly**, behind your back, slyly, surreptitiously, sneakily, covertly [➡SECRET AND UNKNOWN; 179] *Opposite*: openly

on the spot 1 *adv* **immediately**, instantly, then and there, there and then, without delay, at once, right away [➡HAPPENING QUICKLY; 104] *Opposite*: later 2 *adj* **in a difficult situation**, in a tight corner, under pressure, in a tricky situation [➡IN TROUBLE AND DISADVANTAGED; 73] *Opposite*: in the clear

on the spur of the moment *adv* **impulsively**, on impulse, suddenly, impetuously, on a whim, spontaneously, off the cuff, abruptly [➡AUTOMATIC AND INSTINCTIVE; 280] *Opposite*: deliberately

on the streets *adj* [➡POVERTY AND POOR; 892]

on the strength of *prep* **because of**, on the basis of, on account of, by reason of, by virtue of, due to [➡CAUSATION; 168] *Opposite*: notwithstanding (*formal*)

on the subject of *prep* **concerning**, with reference to, regarding, as regards, re, about, as to, apropos (*formal*) [➡EXPRESSIONS OF REFERENCE; 63]

on the surface *adv* **superficially**, on the face of it, at first glance, at first sight, to the outsider, from the outside, apparently, ostensibly [➡PERCEPTIBLE; 25] *Opposite*: in reality

on the threshold of *prep* **on the brink of**, on the point of, at the start of, verging on, bordering on, on the cusp of [➡FUTURE; 86]

on the trot (*UK*) *adv* **consecutively**, in succession, without a break, nonstop, successively, running, one after the other, sequentially, in a row, without stopping [➡AFTER, LAST, AND FOLLOWING; 165]

on the up and up (*informal*) 1 *adv* **doing well**, successful, up and coming, doing nicely, prosperous, wealthy, improving, on the increase, shooting up, rocketing, on an upward curve, on a winning streak, on the way, rising, on the up (*UK*) [➡ SUCCESSFUL AND PROMISING; 81] **2 see on the up**

on the verge of *adj* **on the brink of**, on the edge of, bordering on, on the threshold of, on the point of, close to, near [➡ ABOUT TO HAPPEN; 33]

on the wagon *adj* [➡ SELF-DENIAL; 882]

on the warpath (*informal*) *adj* **furious**, looking for trouble, gunning for somebody, spoiling for a fight, in high dudgeon, up in arms, on the offensive [➡ AGGRESSIVE AND BELLIGERENT; 518]

on the way *adj* **imminent**, near, close, about to happen, under discussion, on the horizon, in the offing, in the pipeline, in the cards (*informal*) [➡ ABOUT TO HAPPEN; 33]

on the whole *adv* **in general**, overall, generally, generally speaking, usually, mostly, for the most part, largely, by and large [➡ USUALLY; 108]

on time **1** *adj* **punctual**, prompt, in time, in good time [➡ PROMPTNESS: ON TIME; 99] *Opposite*: late **2** *adv* **punctually**, promptly, in good time, with time to spare, in plenty of time, on the dot, in time [➡ PROMPTNESS: ON TIME; 99] *Opposite*: late

on top *adv* **ahead**, leading, with the upper hand, in the lead, in front, in pole position, in control, in the driver's seat [➡ SUCCESSFUL AND PROMISING; 81]

on top form *adj* [➡ FIT AND STRONG; 736]

on top of **1** *prep* **over**, lying on, resting on, on, above, covering, across [➡ RELATIVE LOCATION; 161] *Opposite*: beneath **2** *adj* **ahead of**, in control of, dealing with, abreast of, aware of [➡ KNOWLEDGE AND WISDOM; 558]

on tour *adv* **on the road**, touring, traveling [➡ TRAVEL: WAYS OF TRAVELING; 320]

on track *adj* [➡ HAPPENING AND IN PROGRESS; 32]

on unemployment *adj* [➡ EMPLOYMENT STATUS; 831]

onus *n* **responsibility**, burden, obligation, duty [➡ RESPONSIBILITY; 170]

on view *adj* [➡ PERCEPTIBLE; 25]

onward **1** *adj* **forward**, headlong [➡ DIRECTION OF MOTION; 345] *Opposite*: backward **2** *adv* **on**, forward, ahead, headlong, straight on [➡ DIRECTION OF MOTION; 345] *Opposite*: backward

onwards *see* **onward**

on welfare *adj* [➡ EMPLOYMENT STATUS; 831]

on your mettle *adj* **alert**, with all your wits about you, on your toes, on top form, ready for anything, on guard [➡ POSITIVE IMPATIENCE, ENTHUSIASM, AND ALERTNESS; 537]

on your own **1** *adv* **alone**, all alone, by yourself, unaccompanied, single-handedly, unaided, solo, single-handed [➡ ACTING INDEPENDENTLY; 284] **2** *adj* **by yourself**, alone, all alone, unmarried, unattached, single [➡ SOLITARINESS; 941]

onyx *type of* **gemstone** [➡ PRECIOUS STONES; 1278]

oodles (*informal*) *n* **plenty**, lots, piles (*informal*), tons (*informal*), loads (*informal*), heaps (*informal*) [➡ MANY, MUCH, LARGE AMOUNT; 117]

oomph *n* **energy**, enthusiasm, life, dynamism, vivacity, liveliness, gusto, verve, vigor, go (*informal*), get-up-and-go (*informal*), vim (*informal*), brio (*literary*) [➡ ENERGY AND ENTHUSIASM; 496]

ooze **1** *v* **seep**, leach, leak, trickle, dribble, drip, exude, come out of, emerge [➡ LIQUID EMISSION; 370] **2** *v* **exude**, be full of, reek of, radiate, overflow with, be bursting with, be brimming with [➡ EMIT AND EMANATE; 361]

opacity **1** *n* **opaqueness**, imperviousness, impenetrability, denseness, cloudiness, muddiness, mistiness, smokiness, milkiness, dullness [➡ VISUAL TEXTURE; 1221] *Opposite*: transparency **2** *n* **obscurity**, obtuseness, impenetrability, complexity, vagueness, difficulty [➡ DIFFICULTY AND COMPLEXITY; 242] *Opposite*: transparency

opal *type of* **gemstone** [➡ PRECIOUS STONES; 1278]

opalescent *adj* [➡ VISUAL TEXTURE; 1221]

opaque **1** *adj* **impervious**, cloudy, muddy, milky, misty, smoky, dense, solid, thick [➡ VISUAL TEXTURE; 1221] *Opposite*: transparent **2** *adj* **obscure**, unclear, incomprehensible, impenetrable, difficult, hard, dense [➡ DIFFICULTY AND COMPLEXITY; 242] *Opposite*: clear

opaqueness *n* [➡ VISUAL TEXTURE; 1221]

op art *type of* **20th-century art movement** [➡ ARTISTIC MOVEMENTS AND STYLES; 899]

open **1** *adj* **unlocked**, ajar, wide open, gaping [➡ UNFASTEN AND UNDO; 409] *Opposite*: closed **2** *adj* **exposed**, uncluttered, sweeping, undeveloped, unspoilt [➡ THE COUNTRYSIDE AND OUTDOOR SPACES; 1071] *Opposite*: built-up **3** *adj* **approachable**, friendly, amenable, receptive, amicable [➡ FRIENDLINESS AND SOCIABILITY; 494] *Opposite*: standoffish **4** *adj* **honest**, unguarded, direct, straight, frank, sincere, candid [➡ HONEST AND OPEN; 630] *Opposite*: guarded **5** *adj* **vulnerable**, exposed, undefended, unprotected, unguarded [➡ IN DANGER; 237] *Opposite*: safe **6** *adj* **accessible**, public, unrestricted, free [➡ PRESENT AND AVAILABLE; 11] *Opposite*: restricted **7** *v* **unlock**, unbolt, undo, unfasten, release, untie, unwrap, unseal [➡ UNFASTEN AND UNDO; 409] *Opposite*: close **8** *v* **begin**, start, commence, initiate, launch, set off, kick off (*informal*) [➡ START AN ACTION; 260] *Opposite*: conclude

open-air *adj* **outside**, outdoor, alfresco, uncovered [➡ GENERAL LOCATIONS; 158] *Opposite*: indoor

open-and-shut *adj* **simple**, clear, straightforward, clear-cut, obvious [➡ EASE AND SIMPLICITY; 200] *Opposite*: ambiguous

open-ended *adj* **open**, flexible, undecided, unrestricted, fluid [➡ VAGUENESS; 243] *Opposite*: fixed

opener **1** *n* **bottle opener**, can opener, corkscrew, tin opener (*UK*) [➡ TABLEWARE, FLATWARE, AND KITCHENWARE; 861] **2** *n* (*informal*) **starter**, introduction, icebreaker, preamble [➡ BEGINNINGS; 53]

openhanded *adj* **generous**, unstinting, lavish, unselfish, philanthropic, bountiful (*literary*) [➡ GENEROSITY AND KINDNESS; 495] *Opposite*: ungenerous

openhandedness *n* **generosity**, lavishness, unselfish-

work, manage, run, carry on, carry out, conduct, direct,
~rganize [➡ CARRY OUT AN ACTION; 269]

~ting 1 *n* **running**, functioning, managing, per-
~rking [➡ USE; 467] **2** *adj* **functional**, functioning,
~ional, in service, going, effective, working,
~perative [➡ HAPPENING AND IN PROGRESS; 32]

of **room in public buildings** [➡ TYPES

ype of **software** [➡ COMPUTERS AND COM-

~**rocess**, action, act, procedure, man-
~etup [➡ WAYS OF DOING THINGS; 294] **2** *n* **campaign**,
~d, attack, strategy, tactic, maneuver
~; 830] **3** *n* **control**, management, use, con-
~neuvering, working [➡ USE; 467] **4** *n* **business**,
~venture, undertaking, outfit (*informal*) [➡ BUSINESS
~ AND RELATED BODIES; 792] **5** *type of* **medical procedure**
~ES, TREATMENTS, AND OPERATIONS; 731]

~perational *adj* **in use**, in operation, in order, working,
active, in force, operative, in effect, effective, functioning, operating [➡ HAPPENING AND IN PROGRESS; 32]

operative 1 *adj* **in effect**, functioning, working, effective, operational, running, active, in force, in operation
[➡ HAPPENING AND IN PROGRESS; 32] *Opposite:* inoperative **2** *n* **worker**,
operator, machinist, hand, technician [➡ WORKERS; 836]

operator *n* **worker**, operative, machinist, hand [➡ WORKERS;
836]

operetta *type of* **classical music** [➡ MUSIC, SONGS, AND SINGING; 907]

operose (*formal*) *adj* **arduous**, taxing, difficult, strenuous, hard, back-breaking, exacting [➡ PHYSICALLY UNPLEASANT; 226]
Opposite: easy

Ophiuchus 1 *type of* **constellation** [➡ HEAVENLY BODIES; 1061]

ophthalmic *adj* [➡ SEE; 699]

opine (*formal*) *v* **pronounce**, hold forth, discourse,
lecture, preach, rant, speak out [➡ CLAIM, INSIST, AND EMPHASIZE;
614]

opinion *n* **view**, estimation, belief, judgment, attitude,
~tlook [➡ POINTS OF VIEW; 767]

~ionated *adj* **voluble**, bigoted, narrow-minded, par-
~ejudiced, biased, rigid [➡ NEGATIVE INTELLECTUAL CHAR-
~] *Opposite:* open-minded

~l *n* **survey**, poll, questionnaire, inves-
~E QUESTIONS; 666]

of **marsupial** [➡ MARSUPIALS; 992]

~ *n* **adversary**, enemy, rival, challenger, antag-
~ (*formal*) [➡ ENEMIES AND TORMENTORS; 969] *Opposite:* ally

~portune *adj* **fitting**, favorable, appropriate, apt, right,
suitable, timely, well-timed, convenient, auspicious, propitious, lucky [➡ APPROPRIATE, SUITABLE, AND ADVISABLE; 184] *Opposite:*
inopportune

opportuneness *n* [➡ APPROPRIATE, SUITABLE, AND ADVISABLE; 184]

opportunism *n* **resourcefulness**, unscrupulousness,

cunning, deviousness, speculation, buccaneering, carpetbaggery [➡ MORALLY BAD OR IMPROPER; 775]

opportunist *n* **freebooter**, speculator, fortune hunter, buccaneer, swashbuckler, carpetbagger [➡ SUPERFICIAL OR INSINCERE PEOPLE; 951]

opportunistic *adj* **unscrupulous**, resourceful, unprincipled, devious, cunning, adaptable [➡ MORALLY BAD OR IMPROPER; 775] *Opposite*: principled

opportunity *n* **occasion**, opening, prospect, chance, break (*informal*) [➡ PROGRESS AND ADVANCEMENT; 213]

oppose 1 *v* **be against**, resist, fight, contest, combat, counter, disagree with, dissent, dispute [➡ PROTEST AND EXPRESS DISAPPROVAL; 642] 2 *v* **compete with**, face, compete against, do battle with, clash with, be in conflict with, be in competition with, be pitted against [➡ COMPETE, CONTEND, AND COMBAT; 303]

opposed *adj* **opposite**, different, contrasting, divergent, conflicting, disparate [➡ OPPOSITE; 157] *Opposite*: similar

opposed to *adj* **against**, hostile to, antagonistic to, resistant to, anti (*informal*) [➡ UNWILLINGNESS AND STUBBORNNESS; 564] *Opposite*: in favor of

opposing 1 *adj* **opposite**, contrasting, differing, disparate, conflicting, divergent, contradictory [➡ OPPOSITE; 157] *Opposite*: similar 2 *adj* **rival**, opposite, hostile, competing, antagonistic, opposed [➡ UNWILLINGNESS AND STUBBORNNESS; 564] *Opposite*: allied

opposite 1 *adj* **conflicting**, contradictory, differing, reverse, contrary, opposed, contrasting, antithetical (*formal*) [➡ OPPOSITE; 157] *Opposite*: matching 2 *adj* **far**, other, furthest, facing, opposing, parallel [➡ DISTANCE; 160] *Opposite*: adjacent 3 *n* **contrary**, reverse, converse, inverse, opposite number, counterpart [➡ OPPOSITE; 157] *Opposite*: same 4 *prep* **facing**, across from, in front of, overlooking [➡ RELATIVE LOCATION; 161] *Opposite*: beside

opposite number *n* **counterpart**, equivalent, parallel, equal, match, partner [➡ COLLEAGUES AND EQUALS; 967]

opposition 1 *n* **resistance**, antagonism, hostility, disapproval, disagreement, obstruction, unfriendliness [➡ UNWILLINGNESS AND STUBBORNNESS; 564] *Opposite*: friendliness 2 *n* **opponent**, challenger, competitor, enemy, rival, adversary, foe (*formal*) [➡ ENEMIES AND TORMENTORS; 969]

oppress 1 *v* **keep down**, coerce, tyrannize, dominate, repress, subjugate, persecute, harry, harass, hound, beset [➡ CAPTIVITY AND LOSS OF FREEDOM; 248] *Opposite*: liberate 2 *v* **afflict**, worry, torment, depress, distress, burden [➡ UPSET, DISTRESS, AND HUMILIATE; 567] *Opposite*: relieve

oppressed *adj* [➡ IN TROUBLE AND DISADVANTAGED; 73]

oppression *n* **domination**, coercion, cruelty, tyranny, repression, subjugation, persecution, harassment [➡ MALICIOUS ACTIONS OR BEHAVIOR; 296]

oppressive 1 *adj* **cruel**, harsh, domineering, tyrannical, repressive, despotic, unfair, unjust, overbearing [➡ MORALLY BAD OR IMPROPER; 775] *Opposite*: fair 2 *adj* **humid**, hot, close, muggy, stifling, sticky, airless [➡ HOT WEATHER; 1050] *Opposite*: fresh 3 *adj* **overwhelming**, crushing, depressing, distressing, stressful, burdensome, worrying, troubling,

uncomfortable, [UNPLEASANT AND UPSETTING]

oppressively *ad* tyrannically, despo ineeringly, overbear *site*: fairly

oppressor *n* **autocrat** dictator, tormentor, in [➡ VILLAINS AND THUGS; 947] *Oppo*

opprobrious 1 *adj* **sco** dismissive, reproachful, approving, excoriating (*for* 634] *Opposite*: approving 2 *ad* minious, embarrassing, belitt disgraceful, dishonorable, ing AND UPSETTING; 227] *Opposite*: gloriou

opprobriousness 1 *n* s soriousness, dismissiveness, approval [➡ IRRITATION AND ANGER; 54 2 *n* **shamefulness**, shame, humiliat rassment, ingloriousness, degrad disgrace, dishonor [➡ EMBARRASSMENT AND H glory

opprobrium 1 *n* **scorn**, contempt,co cism, reproach, censure, disaprov (*formal*) [➡ IRRITATION AND ANGER; 541] *Oppo* 2 *n* **shame**, disgrace, ignominy, umil rassment, mortification, dishonor [➡BARRAS ATION; 542] *Opposite*: glory

opt *v* **choose**, elect, decide, determi lump on, select, pick, go for (*informal*) [➡DECISIONS 752]

optical *adj* **visual**, ocular, hthal photo [➡ SEE; 699]

optical glass *type of* **glass**

optical illusion 1 *n* **illusion** effect, mirage, will-o'-the-wi [➡ NONEXISTENT THINGS; 23] 2 *n* **trick** special effect, visual effect, c [➡ NONEXISTENT THINGS; 23]

optical instrument

◆ *types of optical instrume* astronomical telescope, l scope, laser, magnifying g periscope, spyglass, telesc

optic nerve *part of* **eye**

optimal *adj* **best**, ideal, prime [➡ GOOD, WELL, BETTER; 183

optimism 1 *n* **hopefuln** tiveness, assurance, p *Opposite*: pessimism ancy, sunniness, br *Opposite*: pessimis

optimist *n* **idealis** [➡ PEOPLE WHO ARE APPRO

optimistic *adj* **hopeful**, positive, bright, cheerful, expectant, sanguine, confident, buoyant, enthusiastic [➡ CHEERFULNESS OF OUTLOOK; 503] *Opposite:* pessimistic

optimize *v* **enhance**, improve, adjust, heighten, elevate, raise, boost, augment (*formal*) [➡ IMPROVE SOMETHING; 374]

optimum 1 *n* **ideal situation**, best-case scenario, goal, ideal, best, target [➡ GOOD, WELL, BETTER; 183] 2 *adj* **best**, ideal, optimal, top, finest, peak, prime [➡ GOOD, WELL, BETTER; 183] *Opposite:* worst

option *n* **choice**, alternative, possibility, route, opportunity, preference, selection, decision [➡ MAKE DECISIONS AND CHOICES; 752]

optional *adj* **elective**, noncompulsory, voluntary, discretionary, possible, uncompelled, free [➡ POSSIBLE AND PROBABLE; 177] *Opposite:* compulsory

optometer *type of* **optical instrument** [➡ OPTICAL INSTRUMENTS; 1124]

opt out (*informal*) *v* **bow out**, bail out, withdraw, get out, leave, wriggle out, decline, refuse, abandon [➡ NOT DO AND REFUSE TO DO; 274]

opulence 1 *n* **lavishness**, luxury, richness, magnificence, sumptuousness, abundance [➡ EXPENSIVE AND LUXURIOUS; 218] *Opposite:* simplicity 2 *n* **wealth**, affluence, riches, prosperity, fortune [➡ WEALTH AND WEALTHY; 891] *Opposite:* poverty

opulent 1 *adj* **wealthy**, lavish, luxurious, rich, magnificent, affluent, sumptuous, prosperous [➡ EXPENSIVE AND LUXURIOUS; 218] *Opposite:* poor 2 *adj* **abundant**, ample, lavish, profuse, rich, plentiful [➡ MANY, MUCH, LARGE AMOUNT; 117] *Opposite:* sparse

opus *n* **composition**, work, piece, production, brainchild, creation, oeuvre (*formal*) [➡ ARTWORKS; 898]

oracle 1 *n* **prophesy**, vision, revelation, foreshadowing, prediction, answer, truth, advice, forewarning [➡ PREDICT AND ANTICIPATE; 750] 2 *n* **prophet**, augur, soothsayer, seer, visionary, psychic, sibyl, sage (*literary*) [➡ PEOPLE WITH SUPERNATURAL POWERS; 788]

oracular *adj* [➡ THE SUPERNATURAL; 787]

oral *adj* **spoken**, verbal, uttered, said, verbalized, voiced, viva voce, sounded [➡ THE SPOKEN WORD; 671] *Opposite:* written

See Compare and Contrast at **verbal**.

oral tradition *n* [➡ THE ORAL TRADITION; 677]

orange 1 *type of* **citrus fruit** [➡ FRUIT AND VEGETABLES; 1176] 2 *type of* **color** [➡ COLORS; 1224]

orange

◆ *types of orange*
amber, apricot, flame, ginger, gold, golden, ocher, old gold, peach, tangerine, titian

orange-peel fungus *type of* **fungus** [➡ MICROORGANISMS, FUNGI, AND ALGAE; 1023]

orangery *n* **greenhouse**, hothouse, conservatory, winter garden, glasshouse (*UK*) [➡ ANCILLARY BUILDINGS; 1080]

orangutan *type of* **primate** [➡ PRIMATES; 988]

orate 1 *v* **speak**, lecture, make a speech, take the floor, discourse, speechify (*informal*) [➡ INSTRUCT AND TEACH; 609] 2 *v* (*formal*) **hold forth**, preach, lecture, speak, declaim, pronounce, moralize, sermonize, rant [➡ UTTER AND PRONOUNCE; 608]

oration *n* **speech**, discourse, address, lecture, sermon, proclamation [➡ ONE-WAY COMMUNICATION; 49]

orator *n* **speaker**, debater, lecturer, raconteur, storyteller, speechmaker, declaimer [➡ SPEAKERS AND ORATORS; 603]

oratorical *adj* **rhetorical**, debating, declamatory, speechmaking, eloquent, silver-tongued, high-flown, fluent [➡ ELOQUENT, TALKATIVE, AND LONG-WINDED; 632] *Opposite:* halting

oratorio *type of* **musical form** [➡ MUSIC, SONGS, AND SINGING; 907]

oratory 1 *n* **debating**, discussion, rhetoric, declamation, speechifying (*informal*) [➡ COMMUNICATION; 602] 2 *n* **eloquence**, persuasiveness, cogency, skill, style, technique [➡ ELOQUENT, TALKATIVE, AND LONG-WINDED; 632] 3 *n* **pomposity**, prolixity, grandiloquence, verbosity, speechifying (*informal*), hot air (*informal*) [➡ MEANINGLESS SPEECH OR WRITING; 676]

orb *n* **globe**, sphere, planet, ball, round, circle [➡ ROUNDED SHAPE; 1218]

orbicular (*formal*) *adj* [➡ ROUNDED SHAPE; 1218]

orbit 1 *n* **path**, track, trajectory, flight path, course, revolution, range, circle, circuit [➡ DIRECTION OF MOTION; 345] 2 *n* **scope**, range, compass, influence, ambit, circle [➡ DEGREE AND EXTENT; 110] 3 *n* [➡ THE EYE; 698] 4 *v* **circle**, circumnavigate, loop, encircle, revolve [➡ TRAVEL: WAYS OF TRAVELING; 320]

orbital space station *type of* **spacecraft** [➡ SPACE VEHICLES; 1063]

orbiter *type of* **spacecraft** [➡ SPACE VEHICLES; 1063]

orchard 1 *n* **plantation**, wood, copse, grove, coppice, spinney (*UK*) [➡ WOODS, FORESTS, AND JUNGLES; 1047] 2 *type of* **garden** [➡ GARDENS; 1074]

orchestra *type of* **band** [➡ MUSICIANS AND SINGERS; 908]

orchestral *adj* **instrumental**, classical, symphonic, musical [➡ MUSICAL TERMS; 912]

orchestrate 1 *v* **score**, arrange, compose, write, rewrite [➡ INSTITUTE AND INAUGURATE; 348] 2 *v* **plan out**, work out, arrange, coordinate, organize, stage-manage, plan, preplan, choreograph, devise [➡ ARRANGE AND CREATE ORDER; 357] *Opposite:* improvise

orchestration 1 *n* **instrumentation**, transposition, arrangement, scoring, composition, adaptation [➡ MUSIC, SONGS, AND SINGING; 907] 2 *n* **planning**, organization, stage-management, arrangement, preplanning, choreography [➡ ARRANGE AND CREATE ORDER; 357] *Opposite:* improvisation

orchid 1 *type of* **perennial flower** [➡ FLOWERS; 1032] 2 *type of* **purple** [➡ COLORS; 1224]

ordain 1 *v* [➡ CONFER STATUS; 458] 2 *v* (*formal*) **order**, decree, proclaim, enact, command, lay down, rule, adjudge, determine, establish [➡ REQUEST AND DEMAND; 663] *Opposite:* suggest

ordeal *n* **trial**, torment, suffering, tribulation, test, nightmare, trouble, affliction [➡ DIFFICULT SITUATIONS; 72]

order 1 *n* **instruction**, command, directive, direction, demand, edict, mandate, imperative [➡ REQUEST AND DEMAND; 663] *Opposite*: suggestion 2 *n* **stability**, calm, harmony, peace, peacefulness, tranquility, lawfulness, serenity [➡ PEACE-FULNESS AND GENTLENESS; 214] *Opposite*: upheaval 3 *n* **orderliness**, neatness, tidiness, method, regulation, uniformity, regularity, symmetry, organization [➡ ORDER AND ORGANIZATION; 206] *Opposite*: disorder 4 *n* **sequence**, succession, rank, classification, arrangement, categorization, series [➡ CONNECTIONS; 143] *Opposite*: chaos 5 *n* **contract**, purchase, sale, request, requisition, demand [➡ PURCHASE; 422] 6 *n* **sect**, organization, group, class, lodge, society, fraternity, sisterhood, fellowship, company, association, union [➡ CLUBS AND SOCIETIES; 939] 7 *v* **arrange**, organize, regulate, classify, categorize, sort, tidy, systematize, sort out, array (*formal*) [➡ ARRANGE AND CREATE ORDER; 357] *Opposite*: confuse 8 *v* **command**, instruct, tell, require, charge, direct (*formal*), enjoin (*formal*), bid (*archaic*) [➡ REQUEST AND DEMAND; 663] *Opposite*: request 9 *v* **requisition**, request, ask for, send for, send off for, buy [➡ PURCHASE; 422] *Opposite*: supply

order around *v* **boss around**, bully, lord it over, push around (*informal*), boss about (*UK*) [➡ CAUSE OR COMPEL TO ACT; 271]

ordered 1 *adj* **well-ordered**, neat, tidy, methodical, well-organized, well thought-out, well-arranged, orderly, systematic [➡ ORDER AND ORGANIZATION; 206] *Opposite*: disorganized 2 *adj* **controlled**, regimented, consistent, steady, efficient, regular, strict, rigid, structured, disciplined, self-controlled [➡ ORDER AND ORGANIZATION; 206] *Opposite*: irregular

orderliness *n* **neatness**, order, tidiness, method, organization, regulation, uniformity, regularity, symmetry [➡ ORDER AND ORGANIZATION; 206] *Opposite*: disorderliness

orderly 1 *adj* **arranged**, tidy, methodical, neat, logical, systematic, organized, well-ordered [➡ ORDER AND ORGANIZATION; 206] *Opposite*: disorderly 2 *adj* **obedient**, disciplined, well-behaved, decorous, compliant, amenable [➡ HONEST AND RELIABLE; 502] *Opposite*: disorderly

ordinance *n* **decree**, order, rule, regulation, law, edict, writ, dictate, injunction, fiat, sanction, dictum (*formal*) [➡ REQUEST AND DEMAND; 663]

ordinarily *adv* **normally**, usually, generally, customarily, in general, as a rule, typically [➡ USUALLY; 108] *Opposite*: unusually

ordinariness 1 *n* **normality**, commonplaceness, usualness, commonness, familiarity, routineness, customariness, averageness [➡ ORDINARINESS; 244] 2 *n* **dullness**, triteness, drabness, dreariness, predictability, staleness, monotony [➡ BORING AND UNINTERESTING; 234]

ordinary 1 *adj* **normal**, commonplace, usual, regular, common, everyday, conventional, average, familiar, routine [➡ ORDINARINESS; 244] *Opposite*: out of the ordinary 2 *adj* **dull**, trite, drab, dreary, predictable, stale, monotonous, boring, routine, commonplace [➡ BORING AND UNINTERESTING; 234] *Opposite*: extraordinary

ordination *n* **investiture**, consecration, ceremony, conferment, installation, initiation [➡ RELIGIONS AND RELIGIOUS PRACTICES; 777]

ordnance *n* **weapons**, artillery, arms, guns, weaponry, armaments [➡ WEAPONS; 1154]

Ordovician *type of* **period** [➡ EPOCHS AND ERAS; 89]

ordure (*formal*) *n* **excrement**, filth, dung, manure, feces, dirt, muck [➡ UNPLEASANT, DIRTY, AND TOXIC SUBSTANCES; 1268]

ore *n* **mineral**, rock, metal, element, aggregate, raw material [➡ STONES, ROCKS, AND BOULDERS; 1057]

oregano *type of* **herb** [➡ HERBS AND SPICES; 1175]

organ 1 *type of* **keyboard** [➡ MUSICAL INSTRUMENTS; 910] 2 *n* **body part**, tissue, structure [➡ BODY; 691] 3 *n* (*formal*) **publication**, mouthpiece, newspaper, magazine, periodical, newsletter, journal [➡ NEWSPAPERS AND MAGAZINES; 605] 4 *n* (*formal*) **agency**, organization, body, representative, voice, front, cover, means, medium, vehicle [➡ WAYS OF DOING THINGS; 294]

organdy *type of* **fabric from plants** [➡ FABRICS; 1132]

organic 1 *adj* **carbon-based**, biological, living, animate, animal, plant [➡ LIVING THINGS AND LIVING; 976] *Opposite*: inorganic 2 *adj* **natural**, unprocessed, unrefined, untreated, raw, non-chemical, green, GM-free [➡ RAW AND NATURAL; 1214] *Opposite*: synthetic 3 *adj* **gradual**, natural, spontaneous, slow, unforced, free [➡ HAPPENING SLOWLY; 106] *Opposite*: artificial

organic matter *n* [➡ LIVING THINGS AND LIVING; 976]

organism *n* **living thing**, creature, animal, plant, virus, bacterium, being, beast, entity [➡ LIVING THINGS AND LIVING; 976]

organization 1 *n* **group**, body, society, association, party, union, institute, business, company, corporation, establishment [➡ CLUBS AND SOCIETIES; 939] 2 *n* **orderliness**, order, method, regulation, neatness, tidiness [➡ ORDER AND ORGANIZATION; 206] *Opposite*: chaos 3 *n* **arrangement**, configuration, design, format, composition, constitution, make-up, pattern, structure [➡ QUALITIES AND CHARACTERISTICS; 1191]

organizational *adj* **structural**, administrative, legislative, executive, logistic, managerial, directorial, governmental, clerical [➡ TYPES OF WORK; 835]

organize 1 *v* **establish**, form, shape, unify, unite, consolidate, bring together, start up, get off the ground [➡ CAUSE TO HAPPEN; 31] 2 *v* **systematize**, arrange, sort out, classify, categorize, combine, structure [➡ ARRANGE AND CREATE ORDER; 357] *Opposite*: disarrange 3 *v* **coordinate**, manage, control, run, set up, fix (*informal*) [➡ AVOID, PREVENT, LIMIT, AND CONTROL; 277]

organized 1 *adj* **prearranged**, structured, ordered, systematized, well thought-out, controlled, planned, prepared [➡ ORDER AND ORGANIZATION; 206] *Opposite*: spontaneous 2 *adj* **methodical**, logical, orderly, reasonable, sensible, systematic, regular [➡ HARD-WORKING AND COMMITTED; 500] *Opposite*: disorganized

organized crime *n* [➡ CRIMES; 817]

organizer 1 *n* **manager**, director, coordinator, planner, controller, arranger [➡ BOSSES AND MANAGEMENT; 965] 2 *n* **diary**, agenda, schedule, daybook, log book [➡ LISTS AND SCHEDULES; 587]

orgy *n* [➡ PARTIES, DANCES, AND CELEBRATIONS; 37]

orient 1 *v* **familiarize**, adjust, learn about, orientate, adapt, accommodate [➡ LEARN AND DISCOVER; 762] 2 *v* **position**, turn, angle, place, face, orientate [➡ MOVE SOMETHING INTO A NEW POSITION OR OVERTURN; 330]

orientate 1 *v* **familiarize**, adjust, learn about, orient, adapt, accommodate [➡ LEARN AND DISCOVER; 762] 2 *v* **position**, turn, angle, face, place, orient [➡ MOVE SOMETHING: INTO A NEW POSITION OR OVERTURN; 330]

orientation 1 *n* **location**, alignment, direction, positioning, angle, bearings, placement, coordination [➡ NAVIGATION; 1141] 2 *n* **emphasis**, focus, character, slant, thrust, inclination [➡ ORIENTATION AND ALIGNMENT; 1223] 3 *n* **leaning**, tendency, proclivity, preference, inclination, nature [➡ LIKE, LOVE, VALUE, AND ENJOY; 578] 4 *n* **adjustment**, acclimatization, assimilation, acclimation, settling in, finding your feet [➡ CHANGE; 372] 5 *n* **initiation**, briefing, reception, welcome, induction, training [➡ BEGINNINGS; 53]

oriented *adj* **concerned with**, focused on, preoccupied with, slanted toward, adapted to, in favor of [➡ THE NATURE OF IDEAS; 771]

orienteering *n* [➡ HOBBIES, GAMES, AND SPORTS; 875]

orifice (*literary*) *n* **opening**, hole, vent, cavity, outlet, slit [➡ HOLES, GAPS, AND FORKS; 1252]

origin *n* **source**, derivation, provenance, beginning, cause, root, basis, foundation [➡ BEGINNINGS; 53]

Compare and Contrast: *origin, source, derivation, provenance, root*

CORE MEANING: the beginning of something

origin the beginning of something in terms of the time, place, situation, or idea from which it arose, or somebody's ancestry, social background, or country; *source* the place, person, or thing through which something has come into being or from which it has been obtained; *derivation* the origin or source of something, especially a word, phrase, or name; *provenance* the place of origin of something, or the source and ownership history of a work of art or archaeological artifact; *root* the fundamental cause, basis, or origin of something, especially a feeling or a problem.

original 1 *adj* **unique**, innovative, novel, inventive, creative, new, unusual, imaginative, unprecedented, singular, special [➡ EXTRAORDINARY: UNCOMMON; 205] *Opposite:* unoriginal 2 *adj* **first**, initial, previous, fundamental, primary, prime [➡ BEFORE, FIRST, AND PRECEDING; 163] *Opposite:* last 3 *n* **prototype**, genuine article, pattern, archetype, template, form, mold, real McCoy (*informal*), exemplar (*literary*) [➡ PERFECT EXAMPLES AND EMBODIMENTS; 67] *Opposite:* copy

See Compare and Contrast at **new**.

originality *n* **innovation**, novelty, uniqueness, inventiveness, creativity, freshness, imagination, ingenuity [➡ EXTRAORDINARY: AMAZING; 204] *Opposite:* unoriginality

originally *adv* **first**, initially, in the beginning, formerly, at first, firstly [➡ PAST; 84] *Opposite:* eventually

originate 1 *v* **create**, invent, initiate, instigate, inaugurate, start off, make, devise, patent, coin [➡ INSTITUTE AND INAUGURATE; 348] 2 *v* **begin**, derive, stem from, start, commence [➡ GRADUALLY COME INTO EXISTENCE; 1] *Opposite:* finish

origination *n* [➡ BEGINNINGS; 53]

originator *n* **inventor**, creator, instigator, designer, maker, discoverer, initiator, prime mover [➡ DESIGNERS, CREATORS, AND INSTIGATORS; 347]

oriole *type of* **songbird** [➡ SONGBIRDS; 1003]

Orion *type of* **constellation** [➡ HEAVENLY BODIES; 1061]

ornament 1 *n* **decoration**, adornment, embellishment, pattern, enhancement, enrichment, trimming, garnish, beautification [➡ ORNAMENTS AND DECORATIONS; 1248] 2 *n* **knick knack**, figurine, objet d'art, bauble, decoration, trinket [➡ ORNAMENTS AND DECORATIONS; 1248] 3 *v* **adorn**, decorate, beautify, embellish, paint, prettify, smarten up, trim, embroider, elaborate, festoon, deck out [➡ DECORATE, ADORN, AND APPLY COATINGS; 405]

ornamental *adj* **decorative**, attractive, for show, ornate, patterned, embellished [➡ BEAUTY AND ATTRACTIVENESS; 189] *Opposite:* functional

ornamentation *n* **decoration**, adornment, embellishment, enhancement, garnishing, beautification, trimming [➡ IMPROVE APPEARANCE; 379]

ornate 1 *adj* **decorative**, overelaborate, baroque, elaborate, ornamental, sumptuous, rich, opulent, lavish [➡ EXPENSIVE AND LUXURIOUS; 218] *Opposite:* unadorned 2 *adj* **high-flown**, flowery, wordy, verbose, loquacious, elaborate, complex, overelaborate, metaphorical, highly wrought, complicated, flamboyant [➡ DIFFICULTY AND COMPLEXITY; 242] *Opposite:* plain

ornately *adv* **elaborately**, overelaborately, baroquely, lavishly, richly, sumptuously, opulently, ornamentally, flamboyantly [➡ EXPENSIVE AND LUXURIOUS; 218]

ornateness *n* [➡ EXPENSIVE AND LUXURIOUS; 218]

ornery (*informal*) *adj* **irritable**, crabby, cantankerous, bad-tempered, awkward, uncooperative, grouchy (*informal*), cranky (*informal*) [➡ DIFFICULT TO PLEASE; 515] *Opposite:* good-tempered

ornithologist *n* [➡ PEOPLE IN SPORTS AND LEISURE; 876]

orology *type of* **earth science** [➡ EARTH SCIENCES; 1059]

orotund (*formal*) 1 *adj* **loud**, clear, strong, ringing, stentorian, robust [➡ LOUD, HIGH, OR UNPLEASANT SOUNDS; 1266] *Opposite:* soft 2 *adj* **wordy**, verbose, grandiloquent, pompous, bombastic, long-winded, self-important [➡ POMPOUS, LOUD, AND OVERCONFIDENT; 635] *Opposite:* humble

orotundity (*formal*) *n* [➡ POMPOUS, LOUD, AND OVERCONFIDENT; 635]

orotundly (*formal*) *adv* [➡ POMPOUS, LOUD, AND OVERCONFIDENT; 635]

orphan 1 *n* **child**, baby, boy, girl, waif, urchin, foundling (*dated*) [➡ CHILD OR YOUTH; 945] 2 *v* **bereave**, leave alone, leave all alone, leave, make an orphan, leave parentless [➡ REFUSING OR REJECTING RELATIONS; 975]

orphanage *n* **home**, residential home, hostel, poorhouse, workhouse, institution, children's home, residential care [➡ CHARITY AND CHARITABLE INSTITUTIONS; 822]

or so *adv* [➡ APPROXIMATELY; 135]

ort *n* [➡ REMAINDER AND REMAINDERS; 125]

ortanique *type of* **citrus fruit** [➡ FRUIT AND VEGETABLES; 1176]

orthodox *adj* **conventional**, accepted, traditional, mainstream, conformist, standard, approved, established [➡ ACCEPTABLE AND PASSABLE; 219] *Opposite:* unorthodox

orthodoxy *n* **accepted view**, convention, accepted belief, prevailing attitude, tenet, belief, canon, custom [➡ POINTS OF VIEW; 767]

OS *type of* **software** [➡ COMPUTERS AND COMPUTING; 1127]

oscillate 1 *v* **swing**, move back and forth, move to and fro, move backward and forward, fluctuate, vacillate, alternate, undulate [➡ BOUNCE, UNDULATE, AND VIBRATE; 308] 2 *v* **waver**, hesitate, vacillate, blow hot and cold, dither, equivocate, be indecisive, run hot and cold, fluctuate [➡ HESITATE; 272]

oscillation *n* **swaying**, fluctuation, vacillation, alternation, swinging, undulation, wavering [➡ BOUNCE, UNDULATE, AND VIBRATE; 308]

osculate (*formal or humorous*) *v* **kiss**, give a kiss, French kiss, give a smacker (*informal*), canoodle with (*informal*), smooch (*informal*) [➡ PHYSICAL CONTACT AS COMMUNICATION; 655]

osculation (*formal or humorous*) *n* [➡ PHYSICAL CONTACT AS COMMUNICATION; 655]

osprey 1 *type of* **bird of prey** [➡ BIRDS OF PREY; 998] 2 *type of* **sea bird** [➡ SEA BIRDS; 1002]

ossification *n* [➡ HARDEN, CONGEAL, AND DRY; 387]

ossified *adj* [➡ RIGID AND HARD; 1211]

ossify *v* **petrify**, fossilize, harden, become inflexible, become fixed, solidify, fix, paralyze [➡ HARDEN, CONGEAL, AND DRY; 387]

ossuary (*formal*) *n* **vault**, grave, tomb, crypt, charnel house, urn, catacomb [➡ BURIAL PLACES AND ACCESSORIES; 930]

ostensible *adj* **ostensive**, apparent, professed, supposed, perceived, seeming, alleged, superficial [➡ UNCERTAIN; 175] *Opposite*: real

ostensive *adj* [➡ UNCERTAIN; 175]

ostentation *n* **flashiness**, showiness, display, flamboyance, pretension, affectation, brazenness, vulgarity [➡ IN POOR TASTE AND OVERSENTIMENTAL; 229] *Opposite*: modesty

ostentatious *adj* **flashy**, showy, flamboyant, affected, pretentious, grandiose, brazen [➡ IN POOR TASTE AND OVERSENTIMENTAL; 229] *Opposite*: modest

ostentatiousness *n* [➡ IN POOR TASTE AND OVERSENTIMENTAL; 229]

osteopathy *type of* **complementary therapy** [➡ REMEDIES, TREATMENTS, AND OPERATIONS; 731]

ostinato *n* [➡ MUSICAL TERMS; 912]

ostracism *n* **shunning**, snubbing, exclusion, barring, keeping out, banishment, isolation, excommunication, expulsion, sending to Coventry (*UK*) [➡ MALICIOUS ACTIONS OR BEHAVIOR; 296] *Opposite*: inclusion

ostracize *v* **coldshoulder**, exclude, banish, shun, ignore, snub, excommunicate, expel, blackball, blacklist, send to Coventry (*UK*) [➡ REFUSING OR REJECTING RELATIONS; 975] *Opposite*: include

ostracized *adj* [➡ IN TROUBLE AND DISADVANTAGED; 73]

ostrich *type of* **flightless bird** [➡ BIRDS; 997]

other *adj* **additional**, new, more, fresh, extra, another, further [➡ MORE AND EXCESS; 124]

other half *n* [➡ SEXUAL AND ROMANTIC RELATIONSHIPS; 964]

otherness *n* **strangeness**, difference, uniqueness, distinctiveness, oddness, apartness, dissimilarity, unlikeness [➡ UNRELATEDNESS AND SEPARATENESS; 146] *Opposite*: normality

otherwise *adv* **or else**, if not, else, alternatively [➡ ALTHOUGH, NEVERTHELESS, AND DESPITE; 169]

otherworldliness *n* [➡ BIZARRE AND PECULIAR; 257]

otherworldly *adj* [➡ BIZARRE AND PECULIAR; 257]

otiose *adj* **futile**, ineffectual, useless, impractical, ineffective, hopeless [➡ REDUNDANT AND USELESS; 240] *Opposite*: effective

OTT (*informal*) *adj* [➡ TOO MUCH; 119]

otter *type of* **small mammal** [➡ SMALL MAMMALS; 990]

ottoman *n* **divan**, couch, day bed, chaise longue, settee, sofa, seat, footstool [➡ FURNITURE; 858]

oubliette *n* **prison cell**, dungeon, prison, cell [➡ BUILDINGS FOR CONFINING PEOPLE; 1094]

ouguiya *type of* **currency** [➡ CURRENCIES; 798]

ounce 1 *type of* **nonmetric unit** [➡ SIZE AND DIMENSIONS; 1192] 2 *n* **grain**, jot, scrap, small amount, modicum, iota, particle, speck, smidgeon (*informal*) [➡ FEW, LITTLE, SMALL AMOUNT; 120]

oust *v* **expel**, throw out, get rid of, drive out, exile, overthrow, eject, force out, banish, deport, cast out (*formal*) [➡ EJECT AND EXCLUDE; 340] *Opposite*: appoint

ousted *adj* [➡ IN TROUBLE AND DISADVANTAGED; 73]

ouster *n* **removal**, ejection, dismissal, expulsion, coup, upheaval, overthrow [➡ AGGRESSIVE EVENTS; 39]

out 1 *adv* **outdoors**, out-of-doors, in the open, in the open air, alfresco, outside, without (*archaic*) [➡ GENERAL LOCATIONS; 158] 2 *adj* **elsewhere**, not in, not at home, away, away from home, absent, gone [➡ ABSENT AND UNAVAILABLE; 7] *Opposite*: in 3 *adj* **available**, on view, obtainable, ready, on show, on sale, purchasable [➡ PRESENT AND AVAILABLE; 11] *Opposite*: unavailable 4 *adj* **banned**, prohibited, disallowed, barred, prevented, vetoed, not permitted, forbidden, contraband, censored [➡ REFUSE PERMISSION AND NOT ALLOW; 670] *Opposite*: legitimate 5 *adj* **unacceptable**, impossible, improbable, not worth it, unthinkable, not on (*UK*) [➡ IMPOSSIBLE AND IMPROBABLE; 178] *Opposite*: acceptable 6 *adj* **unconscious**, out cold, asleep, comatose, dazed, in a daze, out for the count (*informal*) [➡ TIRED, ASLEEP, AND UNCONSCIOUS; 738] *Opposite*: conscious 7 *adj* **old-fashioned**, unfashionable, outdated, dated, passé, outmoded, antiquated, old hat (*informal*) [➡ OLD, OLD-FASHIONED; 167] *Opposite*: fashionable 8 *adj* **exposed**, revealed, given away, made known, shown, publicized, open, uncovered [➡ KNOWN AND FAMOUS; 181] *Opposite*: hidden

out-and-out *adj* **complete**, blatant, obvious, outright, utter, absolute, total, shameless, brazen, glaring [➡ ABSOLUTE AND ABSOLUTELY; 133]

outback *n* **wilderness**, scrubland, wilds, desert, badlands [➡ REMOTE PLACES; 1046]

outbid *v* **offer more than**, outspend, outdo, leave standing, overpay, up the ante (*informal*) [➡ GAMBLE AND TAKE RISKS; 466]

outboard *adj* **external**, on the outside, outside, outward, exterior [➡ GENERAL LOCATIONS; 158]

outboard motor *part of* **ship or boat** [➡ PARTS OF A SHIP OR BOAT; 1151]

outbound *adj* [➡ DIRECTION OF MOTION; 345]

outbrave (*archaic*) *v* **defy**, confront, brave, stand up to, face up to, outface, face, resist [➡ COMPETE, CONTEND, AND COMBAT; 303]

outbreak *n* **eruption**, outburst, epidemic, occurrence, rash, spate, plague, burst [➡ SUDDEN EVENTS; 52]

outbuilding *n* **shed**, outhouse, lean-to, barn, shack [➡ ANCILLARY BUILDINGS; 1080]

outbuilding

◆ *types of outbuildings*
barn, booth, carport, conservatory, cowshed, garage, garden shed, gatehouse, gazebo, greenhouse, guardhouse, hothouse, hut, kiosk, lean-to, lodge, orangery, outhouse, pavilion, privy (*informal*), sentry box, shed, stall, stand, summerhouse

outburst *n* **outpouring**, upsurge, surge, eruption, explosion, outbreak, burst, gust, frenzy, flare-up (*informal*) [➡ SUDDEN EVENTS; 52]

outcast *n* **untouchable**, exile, pariah, recluse, outsider, castaway, leper [➡ SOLITARY PEOPLE AND MISFITS; 942]

outclass *v* **surpass**, outshine, excel, do better than, better, outdo, exceed, outstep, outrun [➡ BEAT AND DEFEAT; 80]

out cold *adj* [➡ TIRED, ASLEEP, AND UNCONSCIOUS; 738]

outcome *n* **consequence**, result, ending, product, conclusion, upshot, effect, aftermath, sequel, aftereffect [➡ RESULTS AND OUTCOMES; 83]

outcrop *n* **rocky outcrop**, crag, ridge, bluff, boulder, outlier, protrusion, protuberance, projection [➡ GEOLOGIC FEATURES; 1056]

outcry **1** *n* **protest**, disagreement, objection, chorus of disapproval, quarrel [➡ CRITICISMS AND ANGRY OUTBURSTS; 50] *Opposite*: acceptance **2** *n* **uproar**, hullabaloo, hue and cry, turmoil, clamor, row, din, commotion, tumult [➡ CHAOS AND UPROAR; 51]

outdated *adj* **antiquated**, passé, outmoded, obsolete, dated, archaic, out-of-date, old-fashioned [➡ OLD, OLD-FASHIONED; 167] *Opposite*: up-to-date

See Compare and Contrast at **old-fashioned**.

outdistance *v* **outdo**, beat, do better than, outrun, outstrip, leave behind, overtake [➡ BEAT AND DEFEAT; 80]

outdo *v* **exceed**, surpass, top, outdistance, outshine, outclass, do better than, outstrip, beat, excel [➡ BEAT AND DEFEAT; 80]

outdoor *adj* **outside**, open-air, out-of-doors, alfresco [➡ GENERAL LOCATIONS; 158] *Opposite*: indoor

outdoors *adv* **out-of-doors**, outside, in the open, in the open air, alfresco [➡ GENERAL LOCATIONS; 158] *Opposite*: indoors

outer *adj* **outside**, external, on the outside, surface, superficial, exterior, outward [➡ EXTREMITIES OF PHYSICAL OBJECTS; 1250] *Opposite*: inner

outer ear *n* [➡ THE EAR; 706]

outermost *adj* **furthest**, farthest, remotest, outmost [➡ DISTANCE; 160] *Opposite*: innermost

outer space *n* **space**, the heavens, the universe, the solar system, the cosmos, interstellar space [➡ THE SOLAR SYSTEM AND ASTRONOMY; 1060]

outerwear *n* [➡ GARMENTS AND OUTFITS; 865]

outface **1** *v* **stare down**, outstare, stare out (*UK*) [➡ COMPETE, CONTEND, AND COMBAT; 303] *Opposite*: give in **2** *v* **brave**, stand up to, face up to, defy, confront, beat, overcome, outbrave (*archaic*) [➡ BEAT AND DEFEAT; 80] *Opposite*: capitulate

outfall *n* **vent**, mouth, duct, channel, culvert, drain, waste pipe, outlet [➡ WATERCOURSES; 1111]

outfit **1** *n* **suit**, clothes, clothing, ensemble, dress, guise, getup (*informal*) [➡ CLOTHES AND ACCESSORIES; 864] **2** *n* (*informal*) **company**, team, business, group, unit, setup, party, corps, troop [➡ GROUPS OF PEOPLE; 935] **3** *v* **supply**, equip, fit out, arm, furnish (*formal*), kit out (*UK*) [➡ EQUIP AND SUPPLY; 435]

outflank **1** *v* **go around**, attack from behind, attack from the rear, outmaneuver [➡ WARFARE AND WAR; 830] **2** *v* **outwit**, outmaneuver, outdo, bypass, outclass, outfox, beat, outthink, outsmart [➡ BEAT AND DEFEAT; 80]

outflow **1** *n* **discharge**, drainage, seepage, leakage, depletion, loss [➡ EMIT AND EMANATE; 361] *Opposite*: influx **2** *n* **expenditure**, debit, expenses, spending, outlay, disbursement [➡ EXPENDITURE; 423] *Opposite*: income

out for the count (*informal*) **1** *adj* **asleep**, dead to the world, sleeping, sound asleep, out, unconscious [➡ TIRED, ASLEEP, AND UNCONSCIOUS; 738] *Opposite*: awake **2** *adj* **unconscious**, out, out cold, knocked out, comatose, dazed, insensible [➡ TIRED, ASLEEP, AND UNCONSCIOUS; 738] *Opposite*: conscious

outfox *v* **defeat**, outwit, get the better of, outflank, take in, con, outsmart, outthink [➡ BEAT AND DEFEAT; 80]

outgo *n* **expense**, expenditure, cost, overhead, outlay, disbursement [➡ EXPENDITURE; 423] *Opposite*: income

outgoing **1** *adj* **outward-bound**, outbound, outward, departing, leaving [➡ DIRECTION OF MOTION; 345] *Opposite*: incoming **2** *adj* **retiring**, leaving, departing, withdrawing, resigning [➡ PAST; 84] *Opposite*: incoming **3** *adj* **sociable**, friendly, gregarious, extrovert, genial, affable, demonstrative, expansive [➡ FRIENDLINESS AND SOCIABILITY; 494] *Opposite*: introvert

outgoings (*UK*) *n* **expenses**, expenditure, costs, overhead, outlay, spending, disbursement [➡ EXPENDITURE; 423] *Opposite*: income

outgrow **1** *v* **get too large for**, grow too big for, get too big for, enlarge, grow up, expand, fill out [➡ CHANGE OF SIZE: BIGGER; 392] **2** *v* **move beyond**, be too grown-up for, be too old for, mature, develop, surpass [➡ GET BETTER; 375] **3** *v* **grow bigger than**, grow larger than, grow faster than, grow quicker than, outnumber, outstrip, overwhelm, exceed [➡ BEAT AND DEFEAT; 80]

outgrowth *n* **extension**, result, development, product, consequence, effect, outcome [➡ RESULTS AND OUTCOMES; 83]

outhouse *n* **outdoor toilet**, latrine, toilet, privy (*informal*) [➡ ANCILLARY BUILDINGS; 1080]

outing *n* **visit**, excursion, trip, day trip, jaunt, day out, junket, getaway [➡ TRAVEL: JOURNEYS AND TRIPS; 318]

out in left field (*informal*) *adj* [➡ BIZARRE AND PECULIAR; 257]

out in the open *adj* [➡ KNOWN AND FAMOUS; 181]

outjockey *v* **outfox**, outdo, outwit, outmaneuver, outflank, beat [➡ BEAT AND DEFEAT; 80]

outlandish *adj* **unusual**, bizarre, peculiar, strange, eccentric, weird, odd [➡ BIZARRE AND PECULIAR; 257] *Opposite:* usual

outlandishness *n* [➡ BIZARRE AND PECULIAR; 257]

outlast *v* **outlive**, survive, live longer than, last longer than, endure, carry on [➡ CONTINUE TO EXIST; 17]

outlaw 1 *n* **runaway**, criminal, fugitive, bandit, desperado, brigand (*literary*) [➡ RUNAWAYS AND ABSENTEES; 9] 2 *v* **forbid**, ban, prohibit, proscribe, veto, bar, censure, suppress [➡ REFUSE PERMISSION AND NOT ALLOW; 670] *Opposite:* allow

outlay 1 *n* **expenditure**, expense, cost, spending, sum, amount, disbursement [➡ EXPENDITURE; 423] 2 *v* **expend**, spend, lay out, pay out, disburse, shell out (*informal*), fork out (*informal*) [➡ GIVE MONEY; 433]

outlet 1 *n* **opening**, passage, vent, exit, channel, hole, pipe, aperture, egress (*formal*), orifice (*literary*) [➡ HOLES, GAPS, AND FORKS; 1252] 2 *n* **means**, channel, conduit, vent, instrument, vehicle [➡ WAYS OF DOING THINGS; 294] 3 *n* **department store**, shop, retailer, market, store, showroom [➡ BUSINESS ENTERPRISES AND RELATED BODIES; 792]

outline 1 *n* **shape**, form, figure, contour, silhouette, profile [➡ SHAPE; 1216] 2 *n* **plan**, rough draft, summary, sketch, rough idea, skeleton, framework [➡ SUMMARIES, OUTLINES, AND EXCERPTS; 588] 3 *v* **draw round**, sketch, draw, delineate, chart, border, bound, define, edge [➡ CREATE IMAGES; 356] *Opposite:* fill in 4 *v* **summarize**, sketch out, delineate, run through, give a rough idea, make a rough draft [➡ EXPLAIN AND CLARIFY; 610] *Opposite:* expand

outlive *v* **live longer than**, outlast, survive, last longer than, endure, carry on [➡ CONTINUE TO EXIST; 17]

outlook 1 *n* **viewpoint**, view, attitude, position, point of view, stance [➡ POINTS OF VIEW; 767] 2 *n* **future**, prospect, time to come, time ahead [➡ FUTURE; 86] 3 *n* **view**, panorama, vista [➡ VIEWS AND OUTLOOKS; 1073]

out loud *adv* **loudly**, audibly, distinctly, aloud, vocally [➡ PERCEPTIBLE; 25] *Opposite:* inaudibly

outlying *adj* **remote**, out-of-the-way, distant, faraway, far-off, far-flung [➡ DISTANCE; 160] *Opposite:* neighboring

outmaneuver *v* **outsmart**, outfox, outwit, outflank, beat, outdo, get the better of [➡ BEAT AND DEFEAT; 80]

outmoded 1 *adj* **unfashionable**, dated, passé, old-fashioned, out-of-date, outdated [➡ OLD, OLD-FASHIONED; 167] *Opposite:* fashionable 2 *adj* **obsolete**, out of use, out of commission, archaic, antiquated, worn-out [➡ REDUNDANT AND USELESS; 240]

outmodedness *n* [➡ OLD, OLD-FASHIONED; 167]

outmost *adj* **outermost**, remotest, furthest, most remote, extreme, furthermost, utmost [➡ DISTANCE; 160]

outnumber *v* **be more than**, be more numerous than, outstrip [➡ BEAT AND DEFEAT; 80]

out of bounds *adj* **off-limits**, forbidden, prohibited, banned, barred, not accessible, inaccessible [➡ REFUSE PERMISSION AND NOT ALLOW; 670] *Opposite:* open

out of breath *adj* **breathless**, panting, gasping, puffing, winded, wheezy [➡ BREATHE AND NOT BREATHE; 716]

out of cash *adj* [➡ POVERTY AND POOR; 892]

out of commission *adj* **out of order**, out of action, not working, not in use, broken-down, broken, inoperative, inactive, incapacitated, busted (*informal*) [➡ IN BAD REPAIR; 1234] *Opposite:* functional

out of condition *adj* [➡ UNFIT AND WEAK; 739]

out-of-date *adj* **outdated**, obsolete, outmoded, old-fashioned, dated, archaic, passé, antiquated [➡ OLD, OLD-FASHIONED; 167] *Opposite:* up-to-date

out-of-doors *adv* **outdoors**, outside, in the open, in the open air, alfresco [➡ GENERAL LOCATIONS; 158] *Opposite:* indoors

out of fashion *adj* [➡ OLD, OLD-FASHIONED; 167]

out of favor *adj* [➡ IN TROUBLE AND DISADVANTAGED; 73]

out of focus *adj* [➡ IMPERCEPTIBLE; 26]

out of harm's way *adj* [➡ SAFE AND SAFETY; 191]

out of it *adj* [➡ UNDER THE INFLUENCE OF DRUGS OR ALCOHOL; 741]

out of kilter *adj* [➡ ORIENTATION AND ALIGNMENT; 1223]

out of order *adj* **not working**, unusable, broken, out of commission, out of use, inoperative, incapacitated, inactive, busted (*informal*), bust (*informal*) [➡ IN BAD REPAIR; 1234] *Opposite:* functional

out of shape *adj* [➡ UNFIT AND WEAK; 739]

out of sight *adj* **out of view**, hidden, hidden from view, hidden from sight, obscured, concealed, veiled [➡ IMPERCEPTIBLE; 26]

out of sorts 1 *adj* **unwell**, not yourself, sick, ill, down in the mouth (*informal*) [➡ ILL AND SICK; 740] *Opposite:* well 2 *adj* **grumpy**, ill-tempered, cross, impatient, touchy, irritable, grouchy (*informal*), tetchy (*informal*) [➡ IRRITATION AND ANGER; 541] *Opposite:* good-tempered

out of stock *adj* [➡ ABSENT AND UNAVAILABLE; 7]

out of sync *adj* [➡ PROMPTNESS: BADLY TIMED; 101]

out of the blue *adv* **unexpectedly**, without warning, all of a sudden, suddenly, surprisingly, from nowhere [➡ HAPPENING QUICKLY; 104]

out of the ordinary *adj* **unusual**, exceptional, atypical, extraordinary, uncommon, rare, remarkable [➡ EXTRAORDINARY: UNCOMMON; 205] *Opposite:* ordinary

out of the question *adj* **impossible**, unthinkable, unacceptable, highly unlikely, improbable, not feasible [➡ IMPOSSIBLE AND IMPROBABLE; 178] *Opposite:* possible

out-of-the-way 1 *adj* **distant**, off the beaten path, off the beaten track, remote, isolated, desolate, outlying, faraway [➡ DISTANCE; 160] *Opposite:* accessible 2 *adj* **uncommon**, unconventional, different, out of the ordinary, special, unusual, singular, unique, extraordinary [➡ EXTRAORDINARY: UNCOMMON; 205] *Opposite:* common

out of this world (*informal*) *adj* **exceptional**, superb, wonderful, fabulous, amazing, marvelous, terrific (*informal*) [➡ EXTRAORDINARY: AMAZING; 204] *Opposite:* unexceptional

out of true *adj* [➡ ORIENTATION AND ALIGNMENT; 1223]

out of view *adj* [➡ IMPERCEPTIBLE; 26]

outpace *v* **outstrip**, outperform, overtake, outdo, beat, leave standing, leave behind [➡ BEAT AND DEFEAT; 80]

outperform *v* **outdo**, outstrip, outpace, outclass, beat, overtake, leave behind [➡ BEAT AND DEFEAT; 80] *Opposite:* underperform

outpost *n* **garrison**, base, station, settlement, colony, post [➡ HUMAN SETTLEMENTS; 1070]

outpouring *n* **expression**, outburst, torrent, spate, flood, deluge, inundation (*formal*) [➡ SUDDEN EVENTS; 52]

output *n* **production**, productivity, amount produced, yield, harvest, crop [➡ CREATION; 346]

outrage 1 *n* **crime**, barbarity, disgrace, scandal, horror, atrocity, violence [➡ BAD BEHAVIOR OR ACTIONS; 254] 2 *n* **indignation**, anger, rage, fury, annoyance, wrath, ire (*formal*) [➡ IRRITATION AND ANGER; 541] 3 *v* **infuriate**, offend, insult, anger, enrage, affront, wrong, incense [➡ ANGER AND ANNOY; 569] *Opposite:* placate

outraged *adj* **angry**, incensed, livid, infuriated, furious, shocked, scandalized [➡ IRRITATION AND ANGER; 541] *Opposite:* calm

outrageous *adj* **disgraceful**, shameful, shocking, offensive, contemptible, despicable, extreme [➡ UNACCEPTABLE AND UNFORGIVABLE; 225] *Opposite:* commendable

outré *adj* **shocking**, eccentric, unconventional, excessive, too much, beyond the pale, de trop, outrageous, over-the-top (*informal*) [➡ UNACCEPTABLE AND UNFORGIVABLE; 225]

outride 1 *v* **outpace**, outstrip, outclass, beat, overtake, leave behind [➡ BEAT AND DEFEAT; 80] 2 *v* **survive**, last out, endure, ride out, make it through, last [➡ CONTINUE TO EXIST; 17]

outrider *n* **patrol**, guard, bodyguard, attendant, escort [➡ SUPPORTERS, PROTECTORS, AND COMPATRIOTS; 970]

outrigger *part of* **ship or boat** [➡ PARTS OF A SHIP OR BOAT; 1151]

outright 1 *adv* **completely**, entirely, totally, fully, absolutely, wholly [➡ ABSOLUTE AND ABSOLUTELY; 133] *Opposite:* partially 2 *adv* **immediately**, straightaway, right away, without hesitation, at once, instantly [➡ HAPPENING QUICKLY; 104] *Opposite:* hesitantly 3 *adv* **openly**, unreservedly, frankly, forthrightly, unequivocally, candidly [➡ HONEST AND OPEN; 630] *Opposite:* equivocally 4 *adj* **absolute**, complete, total, utter, out-and-out, entire, consummate, downright [➡ ABSOLUTE AND ABSOLUTELY; 133] *Opposite:* partial 5 *adj* **out-and-out**, clear, transparent, obvious, direct, overt [➡ PERCEPTIBLE; 25]

outrun 1 *v* **outpace**, outstrip, outclass, beat, overtake, leave behind, run faster than [➡ BEAT AND DEFEAT; 80] 2 *v* **leave behind**, flee, run faster than, elude, get away from, escape

[➡ AVOID OR ESCAPE CONTACT; 418] 3 *v* **go beyond**, overrun, exceed, excel, surpass, outshine, outdo [➡ BEAT AND DEFEAT; 80]

outsell *v* **beat**, overtake, outpace, outstrip, sell more than, outperform [➡ SELL; 441] *Opposite:* underperform

outset *n* **beginning**, start, onset, kickoff (*informal*), inception (*formal*) [➡ BEGINNINGS; 53]

outshine *v* **surpass**, outdo, outstrip, outperform, do better than, overtake, beat [➡ BEAT AND DEFEAT; 80]

outside 1 *adv* **outdoors**, in the open air, alfresco, out of doors, in the fresh air, in the street, in the road, in the yard [➡ GENERAL LOCATIONS; 158] 2 *adv* **beyond**, out there, elsewhere, yonder [➡ GENERAL LOCATIONS; 158] 3 *adj* **outdoor**, external, separate, open-air, exterior, freestanding [➡ GENERAL LOCATIONS; 158] 4 *adj* **external**, unknown, unfamiliar, independent, freelance, foreign [➡ SECRET AND UNKNOWN; 179] 5 *adj* **slight**, faint, remote, scarce, slim [➡ IMPOSSIBLE AND IMPROBABLE; 178] *Opposite:* strong 6 *prep* **beyond**, out of, further than, farther than, past, in front of, beside [➡ RELATIVE LOCATION; 161] *Opposite:* within 7 *n* **exterior**, outer surface, surface, external surface [➡ EXTREMITIES OF PHYSICAL OBJECTS; 1250] *Opposite:* inside

outsider *n* **stranger**, foreigner, unknown, interloper, outcast, recluse [➡ SOLITARY PEOPLE AND MISFITS; 942] *Opposite:* native

outsize *adj* **enormous**, massive, vast, huge, immense, gigantic, capacious, extra-large, big, giant-sized, oversize, hefty, giant, whopping (*informal*) [➡ LARGE; 1193]

outsized *see* **outsize**

outskirts *n* **border**, fringes, periphery, bounds, outer reaches, environs, suburbs, limit [➡ HUMAN SETTLEMENTS; 1070] *Opposite:* center

outsmart *v* **outwit**, outfox, outmaneuver, get the better of, overcome, best, beat [➡ BEAT AND DEFEAT; 80]

outspoken *adj* **frank**, opinionated, honest, candid, open, blunt, forthright [➡ HONEST AND OPEN; 630] *Opposite:* tactful

outspokenness *n* **frankness**, honesty, candor, openness, bluntness, forthrightness [➡ HONEST AND OPEN; 630] *Opposite:* tact

outspread 1 *adj* **extended**, spread-out, stretched, widely spread, open, outstretched, unfolded [➡ ORIENTATION AND ALIGNMENT; 1223] *Opposite:* folded 2 *v* **extend**, expand, stretch, spread, spread out, hold out [➡ CHANGE OF SIZE: BIGGER; 392] *Opposite:* close in

outstanding 1 *adj* **exceptional**, wonderful, stupendous, dazzling, marvelous, excellent, great, superior, remarkable, terrific (*informal*) [➡ EXTRAORDINARY: AMAZING; 204] *Opposite:* abysmal 2 *adj* **unresolved**, unsettled, unpaid, remaining, owing, due [➡ OWE AND DESERVE; 465] *Opposite:* settled

outstandingly *adv* **exceptionally**, terrifically, wonderfully, stupendously, marvelously, dazzlingly, excellently, staggeringly [➡ EXTRAORDINARY: AMAZING; 204] *Opposite:* abysmally

outstay *v* **outlast**, outlive, survive, stay longer than [➡ CONTINUE TO EXIST; 17]

outstretched *adj* **outspread**, extended, stretched out, spread-out, stretched, widely spread, open, unfolded [➠ ORIENTATION AND ALIGNMENT; 1223] *Opposite*: folded

outstrip *v* outdo, outshine, surpass, exceed, do better than, outperform, better, beat, overtake [➠ BEAT AND DEFEAT; 80] *Opposite*: fall behind

out to lunch (*slang*) *adj* [➠ BIZARRE AND PECULIAR; 257]

outward 1 *adj* visible, external, apparent, obvious, noticeable [➠ PERCEPTIBLE; 25] *Opposite*: inward 2 *adv* out, away, centrifugally [➠ DIRECTION OF MOTION; 345] *Opposite*: inward

outward-bound *adj* [➠ DIRECTION OF MOTION; 345]

outweigh *v* overshadow, be more important than, prevail over, be greater than, dwarf [➠ MOST IMPORTANT AND MAIN; 193]

outwit *v* outsmart, outfox, outmaneuver, get the better of, take in, beat [➠ BEAT AND DEFEAT; 80]

outworker (*UK*) *n* [➠ WORKERS; 836]

outworking (*UK*) *n* [➠ TYPES OF WORK; 835]

outworn *adj* obsolete, outmoded, out-of-date, antiquated, archaic, ancient, old [➠ OLD, OLD-FASHIONED; 167] *Opposite*: current

ova *n* [➠ EGGS, SPERM, AND SPAWN; 727]

oval *type of* rounded shape [➠ ROUNDED SHAPE; 1218]

ovary 1 *n* [➠ REPRODUCTION AND HEREDITY; 725] 2 *part of* flower [➠ FLOWERS; 1032]

ovate *adj* oval, egg-shaped, ellipsoid [➠ ROUNDED SHAPE; 1218]

ovation *n* standing ovation, cheer, vote of confidence, endorsement, thumbs up (*informal*) [➠ APPLAUSE; 652]

oven dish (*UK*) *n* [➠ TABLEWARE, FLATWARE, AND KITCHENWARE; 861]

oven tray *n* [➠ TABLEWARE, FLATWARE, AND KITCHENWARE; 861]

ovenware *n* [➠ TABLEWARE, FLATWARE, AND KITCHENWARE; 861]

over 1 *prep* in excess of, more than, greater than, larger than, above, older than, faster than, heavier than, taller than, longer than [➠ MORE AND EXCESS; 124] *Opposite*: under 2 *prep* throughout, around, the length and breadth of, round, across, all around, all across [➠ RELATIVE LOCATION; 161] 3 *prep* on top of, above, on, upon [➠ RELATIVE LOCATION; 161] *Opposite*: beneath 4 *adj* ended, finished, done, completed, concluded, terminated [➠ PAST; 84]

overabundance *n* excess, surplus, glut, superfluity, flood, surfeit, plethora, oversupply [➠ TOO MUCH; 119] *Opposite*: shortage

overabundant *adj* [➠ TOO MUCH; 119]

overact *v* ham it up, ham, overdo it, exaggerate, overplay [➠ OVERDO SOMETHING; 290]

overactive *adj* feverish, overexcited, overcharged, intense, fervid, fanciful, febrile [➠ NEGATIVE INTELLECTUAL CHARACTERISTICS; 525]

over again *adv* [➠ AGAIN; 109]

overall 1 *adj* general, complete, total, global, inclusive, whole [➠ WHOLENESS AND COMPLETENESS; 198] 2 *adv* on the whole, in general, generally, taken as a whole, largely, by and large [➠ USUALLY; 108] *Opposite*: in particular

overalls 1 *type of* suit [➠ GARMENTS AND OUTFITS; 865] 2 *type of* pants [➠ GARMENTS AND OUTFITS; 865]

over and above *prep* in addition to, besides, as well as, added to, on top of [➠ ALSO; 138]

over and done with *adj* over, finished, done, ended, complete, completed, concluded, done with (*UK*) [➠ PAST; 84]

over and over *adv* [➠ AGAIN; 109]

over and over again *adv* [➠ AGAIN; 109]

overarching *adj* all-embracing, main, all-encompassing, predominant, principal, primary, central, supreme, key [➠ MOST IMPORTANT AND MAIN; 193]

overawe *v* intimidate, scare, impress, subdue [➠ FRIGHTEN AND SHOCK; 568]

overawed *adj* [➠ SURPRISE, SHOCK, AND AMAZEMENT; 545]

overbearing *adj* arrogant, domineering, bossy, imperious, pompous, haughty [➠ BOSSY AND OVERBEARING; 516] *Opposite*: meek

overbearingness *n* [➠ BOSSY AND OVERBEARING; 516]

overblown 1 *adj* overdone, excessive, exaggerated, unrestrained, immoderate, extravagant, overstated, inflated [➠ TOO MUCH; 119] *Opposite*: understated 2 *adj* pretentious, pompous, puffed-up, extravagant [➠ POMPOUS, LOUD, AND OVERCONFIDENT; 635] *Opposite*: unassuming

overburden *v* overload, overtax, overstrain, burden, load, tax, overstretch [➠ GIVE TOO MUCH AND OVERBURDEN; 437]

overburdened *adj* [➠ IN TROUBLE AND DISADVANTAGED; 73]

overcast *adj* cloudy, gray, gloomy, dark, dull, dreary [➠ CLOUDY AND RAINY WEATHER; 1052] *Opposite*: bright

overcharge *v* charge too much, take advantage of, cheat, swindle, rip off (*informal*), fleece (*informal*) [➠ STEAL AND ROB; 426]

overcoat *type of* overcoat [➠ GARMENTS AND OUTFITS; 865]

overcome 1 *v* overwhelm, overpower, incapacitate, disable, knock out, kill, asphyxiate, choke, poison [➠ WOUND A PERSON OR ANIMAL; 383] 2 *v* carry away, affect, move to tears, reduce to tears, grip, seize [➠ UPSET, DISTRESS, AND HUMILIATE; 567] 3 *v* surmount, prevail over, rise above, triumph over, conquer, defeat [➠ BEAT AND DEFEAT; 80] *Opposite*: yield 4 *v* conquer, defeat, beat, trounce, triumph over, vanquish [➠ BEAT AND DEFEAT; 80] *Opposite*: lose

See Compare and Contrast at **defeat***.*

overcompensate *v* overreact, overcorrect, overplay, give too much weight to, try too hard [➠ OVERDO SOMETHING; 290]

overconfidence *n* arrogance, overoptimism, boldness, pride, nerve, self-confidence, brashness, bullishness (*informal*) [➠ BOSSY AND OVERBEARING; 516] *Opposite*: caution

overconfident *adj* arrogant, full of yourself, brash,

overoptimistic, bullish (*informal*) [➡ BOSSY AND OVERBEARING; 516] *Opposite*: modest

overcook *v* **overdo**, stew, burn, char, spoil, ruin [➡ COOKING AND FOOD PREPARATION; 353] *Opposite*: undercook

overcooked *adj* **overdone**, burnt, well done, chewy, hard, stewed, charred, tough [➡ STATE OF PREPARED FOOD; 1171] *Opposite*: underdone

overcritical *adj* **harsh**, hypercritical, censorious, severe, critical, contemptuous, disapproving, stern, judgmental, disparaging [➡ DIFFICULT TO PLEASE; 515]

overcrowded *adj* **filled to capacity**, congested, overloaded, teeming, swarming, jammed, clogged, stuffed (*informal*), heaving (*UK*) [➡ FULL; 1239] *Opposite*: empty

overcrowding *n* **congestion**, overloading, overpopulation, excess, excess numbers [➡ TOO MUCH; 119]

overdo 1 *v* **overcook**, burn, stew, char, spoil, ruin [➡ COOKING AND FOOD PREPARATION; 353] *Opposite*: undercook 2 *v* **exaggerate**, overstate, overplay, overemphasize [➡ OVERDO SOMETHING; 290] *Opposite*: play down

overdo it *v* [➡ OVERDO SOMETHING; 290]

overdone *adj* **overcooked**, stewed, charred, spoilt, spoiled, burned, ruined [➡ STATE OF PREPARED FOOD; 1171] *Opposite*: underdone

overdo things *v* **strain yourself**, burn the candle at both ends, overtax yourself, overexert yourself, overdo it, overwork, work too hard, burn the midnight oil [➡ OVERDO SOMETHING; 290] *Opposite*: relax

overdramatize *v* [➡ OVERDO SOMETHING; 290]

overdrawn *adj* **in debt**, in the red, overspent, insolvent, over your limit [➡ POVERTY AND POOR; 892] *Opposite*: in credit

overdue *adj* **late**, tardy, unpaid, unsettled, belated [➡ PROMPTNESS: LATE; 100] *Opposite*: early

overeat *v* **overindulge**, eat too much, gorge, stuff yourself, binge, overdose [➡ OVERDO SOMETHING; 290]

over-egg the pudding (*UK*) *v* [➡ OVERDO SOMETHING; 290]

overemotional *adj* **emotional**, sentimental, melodramatic, maudlin, histrionic, mawkish, slushy, mushy, syrupy, tearful, gushing, weepy (*informal*) [➡ EXCESSIVE SENSITIVITY; 511] *Opposite*: unemotional

overemphasize *v* **exaggerate**, overstate, overstress, stress, go over the top about, go on and on about, lay it on with a trowel (*informal*) [➡ CLAIM, INSIST, AND EMPHASIZE; 614]

overenthusiasm *n* **fanaticism**, mania, obsessiveness, obsession, fever, feverishness, ardor, fervor, zeal [➡ FADS, FETISHES, AND IDOLATRY; 555]

overenthusiastic *adj* **overzealous**, carried away, fanatical, obsessive, obsessional, ardent, fervent, feverish, over-the-top (*informal*), manic (*informal*) [➡ ENERGY AND ENTHUSIASM; 496]

overestimate 1 *v* **misjudge**, overrate, miscalculate, overvalue, allow too much for [➡ ASSESS QUALITY; 755] *Opposite*: underestimate 2 *v* **overrate**, expect too much of, misjudge, miscalculate, overemphasize [➡ OVERDO SOMETHING; 290] *Opposite*: underestimate

overexcite *v* **work up**, excite, get in a state, get carried away, wind up (*informal*), get in a lather (*informal*) [➡ APPEAL TO AND AROUSE INTEREST; 575]

overexcited *adj* **carried away**, high, frenzied, in a frenzy, feverish, nervous, anxious, worked up (*informal*), in a lather (*informal*), in a state (*informal*), hyper (*informal*), keyed up (*informal*), manic (*informal*) [➡ PLEASURE, EXCITEMENT, AND ELATION; 534] *Opposite*: calm

overexcitement *n* **frenzy**, mania, feverishness, anxiety, emotion, excitement, hyperactivity [➡ PLEASURE, EXCITEMENT, AND ELATION; 534]

overextend *v* **overstretch**, overreach, go too far, bite off more than you can chew, exceed your limit [➡ OVERDO SOMETHING; 290]

overflow 1 *v* **run over**, flood, spill over, brim over, pour out, burst [➡ FILL; 406] 2 *n* **excess**, runoff, extra, surfeit, surplus, overspill [➡ MORE AND EXCESS; 124] *Opposite*: lack

overflowing *adj* **spilling over**, teeming, swarming, brimming, abundant, brimful [➡ FULL; 1239] *Opposite*: empty

overflow with *v* **be full of**, brim with, abound with, bubble with, be bursting at the seams with, exude, be brimming with [➡ PROSPER AND ABOUND; 16] *Opposite*: lack

overgrown *adj* **dense**, thick, overrun, lush, untidy, unkempt, wild [➡ IN BAD REPAIR; 1234] *Opposite*: tidy

overhang 1 *v* **project**, extend, jut out, hang over, extend beyond, jut out over [➡ EXIST IN A PLACE; 19] 2 *n* **projection**, extension, outcrop, ledge, outcropping [➡ GEOLOGIC FEATURES; 1056]

overhaul 1 *v* **repair**, renovate, fix, refit, refurbish, service, revamp, strip down [➡ REPAIR AND MEND; 376] 2 *v* **overtake**, surpass, leave behind, outdo, pass, go past [➡ BEAT AND DEFEAT; 80] *Opposite*: fall behind 3 *n* **service**, refit, refurbishment [➡ REPAIR AND MEND; 376]

overhead 1 *adv* **above**, in the air, upstairs, directly above, above your head [➡ GENERAL LOCATIONS; 158] *Opposite*: below 2 *n* **cost**, expense, payment, business cost, bill [➡ EXPENDITURE; 423]

overheads (*UK*) *n* **costs**, expenses, payments, business costs, bills, outgoings (*UK*) [➡ EXPENDITURE; 423]

overhear *v* **eavesdrop**, listen in, hear, eavesdrop on, listen to [➡ LISTEN AND LISTENERS; 708]

overheated *adj* **excited**, impassioned, agitated, inflamed, hot and bothered, upset, worked up (*informal*), hot under the collar (*informal*) [➡ IRRITATION AND ANGER; 541] *Opposite*: cool

overindulge *v* **overeat**, eat too much, stuff yourself, gorge, gorge yourself, binge [➡ OVERDO SOMETHING; 290]

overindulgence *n* **excess**, greed, intemperance, hedonism, gluttony, dissipation, debauchery, gourmandise, abandonment, overkill, immoderation (*formal*) [➡ MORALLY BAD OR IMPROPER; 775]

overindulgent *adj* **excessive**, greedy, immoderate, intemperate, hedonistic, debauched, dissipated [➡ MORALLY BAD OR IMPROPER; 775]

overjoyed *adj* **delighted**, joyful, elated, ecstatic, jubilant, thrilled, over the moon (*UK informal*) [➡ PLEASURE, EXCITEMENT, AND ELATION; 534] *Opposite*: disappointed

overkill *n* excess, too much, overstatement, too much of a good thing, heavy-handedness, overindulgence, overload, overegging the pudding (*UK*) [➡ TOO MUCH; 119] *Opposite*: restraint

overladen *adj* **overloaded**, overfilled, crammed, overburdened, weighed down, stuffed (*informal*) [➡ FULL; 1239]

overlap 1 *v* **partly cover**, overlie, meet, touch, cover [➡ EXIST IN CLOSE PROXIMITY; 21] 2 *v* **coincide**, correspond, intersect, meet, come together, interrelate, correspond with, bring together [➡ CREATING CONNECTIONS; 144] 3 *n* **overlay**, intersection, edge, join, connection [➡ EXTREMITIES OF PHYSICAL OBJECTS; 1250] 4 *n* **correspondence**, intersection, connection, similarity, common ground, commonality [➡ CONNECTIONS; 143]

overlay *v* **cover**, coat, put over, overlap, drape, shroud, blanket [➡ DECORATE, ADORN, AND APPLY COATINGS; 405]

overlie *v* [➡ EXIST IN CLOSE PROXIMITY; 21]

overload 1 *v* **overburden**, overwork, tax, weigh down, overexert, strain [➡ GIVE TOO MUCH AND OVERBURDEN; 437] 2 *n* **excess**, surplus, overwork, burden, overkill [➡ TOO MUCH; 119] *Opposite*: lack

overloaded *adj* **weighed down**, weighted down, loaded, laden, full, burdened, encumbered, bogged down (*informal*) [➡ FULL; 1239]

overlook 1 *v* **ignore**, miss, forget, skip, neglect, omit [➡ NOT PAY ATTENTION; 764] *Opposite*: notice 2 *v* **excuse**, condone, spare, let pass, pardon, forgive, wink at (*informal*) [➡ FORGET, FORGIVE, AND ACCEPT; 748] *Opposite*: punish 3 *v* **give onto**, be opposite, face [➡ EXIST IN A PLACE; 19] 4 *v* **supervise**, oversee, superintend, boss, observe, manage, direct, administer, guide, watch, regulate [➡ BE IN CHARGE; 270] 5 *v* **inspect**, survey, examine, peruse, scan [➡ LOOKING AND LOOKS; 700]

See Compare and Contrast at **neglect**.

overlooked *adj* [➡ IN TROUBLE AND DISADVANTAGED; 73]

overly *adv* **excessively**, too, desperately, exaggeratedly, exceedingly, very [➡ TOO MUCH; 119] *Opposite*: slightly

overmuch 1 *adv* **excessively**, too much, very much, unnecessarily, overly, extravagantly, unduly, inordinately, immoderately (*formal*) [➡ TOO MUCH; 119] 2 *adj* **excessive**, extreme, too much, immoderate, extravagant, undue, inordinate [➡ TOO MUCH; 119] 3 *n* **excess**, superfluity, surplus, overage [➡ TOO MUCH; 119]

overnight 1 *adv* **suddenly**, at once, quickly, instantly, abruptly, immediately, instantaneously [➡ HAPPENING QUICKLY; 104] *Opposite*: gradually 2 *adj* **instant**, immediate, abrupt, instantaneous, sudden, rapid, dramatic, meteoric [➡ HAPPENING QUICKLY; 104] *Opposite*: gradual

overnight bag *type of* **baggage** [➡ CONTAINERS, RECEPTACLES, AND PACKAGING; 1245]

overpass 1 *type of* **bridge** [➡ BRIDGES, TUNNELS, CROSSINGS, AND JUNCTIONS; 1112] 2 *type of* **highway** [➡ ROADS; 1106]

overpitch *v* **exaggerate**, overdo, overcompensate, over-

play, overemphasize, overstress, make too much of, overstate, give too much weight to [➡ CLAIM, INSIST, AND EMPHASIZE; 614]

overplay *v* **overemphasize**, exaggerate, overdo, overstress, overstate [➡ CLAIM, INSIST, AND EMPHASIZE; 614] *Opposite*: underplay

overpower 1 *v* **subdue**, override, suppress, subjugate, conquer, subsume, stretch, defeat, overcome, overdevelop, overdraw, master, prevail [➡ BEAT AND DEFEAT; 80] *Opposite*: yield 2 *v* **overwhelm**, overshadow, floor, overcome, dumbfound, daze, stagger, stun, overawe, throw (*informal*) [➡ UPSET, DISTRESS, AND HUMILIATE; 567]

overpowered *adj* [➡ BEATEN AND DEFEATED; 78]

overpowering *adj* **overwhelming**, intense, overriding, uncontrollable, consuming, unbearable, overshadowing, strong [➡ STRENGTH; 201] *Opposite*: weak

overpoweringly *adv* **irresistibly**, overwhelmingly, devastatingly, strongly, intensely, extremely, powerfully, distinctly, tremendously, greatly, deeply, keenly, very much, fearsomely, astonishingly, formidably, strikingly, amazingly, awesomely [➡ TO A GREAT EXTENT; 132]

overprice *v* **overrate**, overvalue, hike up, write up, mark up [➡ FUNDS, PAYMENTS, AND CHARGES; 800] *Opposite*: underprice

overpriced *adj* **high-priced**, costly, extortionate, expensive, exorbitant, dear, stiff, steep (*informal*) [➡ EXPENSIVE AND OVERPRICED; 247] *Opposite*: cheap

overprotect *v* **fuss over**, cocoon, indulge, protect, mollycoddle, baby, coddle, pamper, spoil, cosset [➡ TAKE CARE OF AND SPOIL; 300] *Opposite*: neglect

overrate *v* **overprize**, overestimate, exaggerate, overvalue [➡ CLAIM, INSIST, AND EMPHASIZE; 614] *Opposite*: underrate

overrated *adj* **overvalued**, overestimated, hyped, puffed up, glorified [➡ ORDINARINESS; 244] *Opposite*: underrated

overreach 1 *v* **overdo**, bite off more than you can chew, overstretch, overextend, outreach, strain [➡ OVERDO SOMETHING; 290] 2 *v* **outwit**, outsmart, outfox, outplay, deceive, trick [➡ DECEPTION AND LIES; 660]

overreact *v* **exaggerate**, react excessively, make a big deal, overdramatize, overplay, overstretch, go over the top (*informal*) [➡ OVERDO SOMETHING; 290]

override 1 *v* **disregard**, overrule, defy, flout, countermand, reverse, ignore [➡ ABOLISH AND ANNUL; 452] *Opposite*: follow 2 *v* **supersede**, dominate, prevail, predominate, overrule, outweigh [➡ CHANGE ONE THING FOR ANOTHER; 398]

overriding *adj* **overruling**, superseding, intervening, dominant, prevailing, prime, principal, preponderant, paramount, supreme [➡ MOST IMPORTANT AND MAIN; 193] *Opposite*: insignificant

overrule 1 *v* **override**, cancel, rule against, refuse, make null and void, annul, reject, disallow, veto [➡ ABOLISH AND ANNUL; 452] 2 *v* **master**, exercise authority, domineer, pull rank [➡ BE IN CHARGE; 270]

overrun 1 *v* **invade**, attack, assail, assault, besiege, ravage, plunder [➡ PHYSICAL ATTACK AND PUNISHMENT; 415] 2 *adj* **swarming**, infested, teeming, flooded, swamped, choked, clogged, filled [➡ FULL; 1239]

overseas 1 *adj* **foreign**, external, ultramarine (*literary*) [➡ COUNTRIES AND REGIONS; 1067] **2** *adv* **abroad**, out of the country, in foreign parts [➡ COUNTRIES AND REGIONS; 1067]

oversee *v* **supervise**, manage, superintend, run, direct, watch over, administer, mastermind, keep an eye on [➡ BE IN CHARGE; 270]

overseer *n* **supervisor**, manager, administrator, chief, boss, superintendent [➡ BOSSES AND MANAGEMENT; 965]

oversell *v* **overpraise**, overvalue, overrate, exaggerate, hype [➡ CLAIM, INSIST, AND EMPHASIZE; 614] *Opposite*: undersell

oversensitive *adj* **emotional**, thin-skinned, hypersensitive, vulnerable, touchy, prickly (*informal*) [➡ EXCESSIVE SENSITIVITY; 511] *Opposite*: thick-skinned

oversensitivity *n* [➡ EXCESSIVE SENSITIVITY; 511]

oversentimental *adj* **mawkish**, syrupy, maudlin, sad, mushy, overemotional, tearful, emotional, slushy, gooey (*informal*), weepy (*informal*), schmaltzy (*informal*) [➡ IN POOR TASTE AND OVERSENTIMENTAL; 229] *Opposite*: callous

overshadow *v* **outshine**, outdo, dominate, surpass, eclipse, dwarf, put in the shade, minimize, reduce, detract from [➡ BEAT AND DEFEAT; 80]

overshoot *v* **pass**, exceed, overreach, overpass, overrun, overextend, miss [➡ MOVE PAST, INTO, OR THROUGH SOMETHING; 331] *Opposite*: hit

oversight 1 *n* **mistake**, failure to notice, slip, omission, misunderstanding, error, lapse, inaccuracy, bungle (*informal*), flub (*slang*) [➡ MISTAKES; 250] **2** *n* **supervision**, control, overseeing, management, administration, managing, surveillance [➡ LOOKING AND LOOKS; 700]

oversimplify *v* **generalize**, overgeneralize, simplify, distort [➡ OVERDO SOMETHING; 290] *Opposite*: complicate

oversize *adj* **oversized**, king-size, extra large, large, huge, monster, gigantic, extremely large, enormous, gargantuan, colossal, massive, maxi [➡ LARGE; 1193]

oversized *see* **oversize**

oversleep *v* **sleep in**, sleep late [➡ SLEEP AND DREAM; 723]

overspill 1 *n* **flood**, overflow, runoff, excess, surplus, extra [➡ TOO MUCH; 119] **2** *v* **spill over**, overflow, brim over, pour out, flood, run over [➡ EMPTY AND UNLOAD; 407]

overstate *v* **exaggerate**, make too much of, overdo, overstress, overemphasize, overplay [➡ CLAIM, INSIST, AND EMPHASIZE; 614] *Opposite*: understate

overstated *adj* **exaggerated**, extravagant, excessive, inflated, overelaborate, loud, blown up, flamboyant, larger-than-life, overdone, garish, puffed up, gaudy, overblown, showy, flashy, attention-grabbing, overemphasized, over-the-top (*informal*) [➡ IN POOR TASTE AND OVERSENTIMENTAL; 229] *Opposite*: understated

overstatement *n* **exaggeration**, hyperbole, overemphasis [➡ CLAIM, INSIST, AND EMPHASIZE; 614] *Opposite*: understatement

overstay *v* **prolong**, protract, spin out, extend [➡ OVERDO SOMETHING; 290]

overstep 1 *v* **exceed**, go beyond, pass, surpass, step over [➡ OVERDO SOMETHING; 290] **2** *v* **transgress**, violate, disregard, disobey, contravene, break [➡ DISOBEY; 302] *Opposite*: obey

overstrain *v* **overstretch**, overstress, overreach, overtax, overload, burden, overdo [➡ GIVE TOO MUCH AND OVERBURDEN; 437]

overstress 1 *v* **overstretch**, overstrain, overreach, overtax, overload, overburden [➡ GIVE TOO MUCH AND OVERBURDEN; 437] **2** *v* **overemphasize**, overplay, overpitch, overstate, overdo, dwell on [➡ CLAIM, INSIST, AND EMPHASIZE; 614] **3** *n* **overstating**, overplaying, overdoing, dwelling on, going on about [➡ CLAIM, INSIST, AND EMPHASIZE; 614]

overstretch *v* **overstrain**, overstress, overreach, overtax, overload, overdo, go too far, bite off more than you can chew, strain, tax [➡ OVERDO SOMETHING; 290]

overstretched *adj* [➡ IN TROUBLE AND DISADVANTAGED; 73]

overstrung *adj* **nervous**, tense, oversensitive, high-strung, temperamental, excitable, touchy, emotional, volatile [➡ EXCESSIVE SENSITIVITY; 511] *Opposite*: placid

overstuffed *adj* **brimming**, overfilled, brimful, overflowing, bursting at the seams, packed [➡ FULL; 1239] *Opposite*: empty

oversupply 1 *n* **overflow**, excess, surplus, glut, superfluity, flood, surfeit [➡ TOO MUCH; 119] **2** *v* **glut**, overwhelm, flood, inundate, swamp, saturate [➡ GIVE TOO MUCH AND OVERBURDEN; 437]

overt *adj* **obvious**, unconcealed, explicit, evident, open, clear, plain, manifest, blatant, apparent [➡ PERCEPTIBLE; 25] *Opposite*: covert

overtake 1 *v* **pass**, go beyond, go past, overhaul, leave behind, outdo, surpass, run by, reach [➡ BEAT AND DEFEAT; 80] *Opposite*: fall behind **2** *v* **hit**, sweep over, engulf, assail, strike, catch off-guard [➡ UPSET, DISTRESS, AND HUMILIATE; 567]

overtax *v* **strain**, overload, overdo it, overstretch, overstrain, overburden, burn the candle at both ends, overwork, load, overextend, burden, exhaust [➡ GIVE TOO MUCH AND OVERBURDEN; 437]

over-the-hill *adj* **old**, past your prime, ancient, decrepit (*archaic or humorous*), past your sell-by date (*UK*) [➡ OLD AGE; 919]

over the moon (*UK informal*) *adj* **overjoyed**, delighted, thrilled, ecstatic, exultant, jubilant, glad, pleased [➡ PLEASURE, EXCITEMENT, AND ELATION; 534]

over-the-top (*informal*) *adj* **exaggerated**, excessive, overdone, extravagant, overblown, melodramatic, theatrical, overemotional, dramatic, overdramatic, histrionic, unrestrained, immoderate, OTT (*informal*) [➡ TOO MUCH; 119] *Opposite*: understated

overthrow *v* **conquer**, defeat, dethrone, bring down, depose, oust, topple [➡ BEAT AND DEFEAT; 80] *Opposite*: uphold

overtime 1 *n* **extra pay**, extra hours, time and a half, additional hours, double time, extra work, bonus, late shift, flextime, graveyard shift [➡ WORK-RELATED ACTIVITIES; 834] **2** *adv* **energetically**, tirelessly, actively, strenuously, intensely [➡ ENERGY AND ENTHUSIASM; 496]

overtness *n* [➡ PERCEPTIBLE; 25]

overtone *n* **implication**, association, hint, undertone, connotation, nuance, insinuation, tinge, suggestion [➡ SUGGEST, HINT, AND COMMENT; 612]

overture *type of* **musical form** [➡ MUSIC, SONGS, AND SINGING; 907]

overturn 1 *v* **turn over**, knock over, tip over, upend, capsize, upset, spill over, topple, keel over (*informal*) [➡ MOVE SOMETHING: INTO A NEW POSITION OR OVERTURN; 330] *Opposite*: right 2 *v* **nullify**, abolish, invalidate, annul, reverse, throw out, cancel, veto, nix (*slang*), negate (*formal*) [➡ ABOLISH AND ANNUL; 452]

overturned *adj* [➡ ORIENTATION AND ALIGNMENT; 1223]

overuse 1 *n* **overemployment**, overdoing, misuse, abuse, overplay [➡ USE UP AND WASTE; 474] 2 *v* **overemploy**, overdo, go to extremes, run riot, misuse, abuse [➡ OVERDO SOMETHING; 290]

overused *adj* **overworked**, clichéd, hackneyed, commonplace, trite, corny, stereotyped [➡ BORING AND UNINTERESTING; 234]

overvalue *v* **overrate**, overprize, overestimate [➡ OVERDO SOMETHING; 290] *Opposite*: undervalue

overview *n* **indication**, summary, outline, gestalt, synopsis [➡ SUMMARIES, OUTLINES, AND EXCERPTS; 588]

overweening *adj* **arrogant**, conceited, pompous, presumptuous, haughty [➡ BOSSY AND OVERBEARING; 516] *Opposite*: unassuming

overweight *adj* **heavy**, big, large, weighty, cumbersome, bulky, overheavy [➡ BUILD; 477] *Opposite*: underweight

overwhelm *v* **overpower**, overcome, engulf, devastate, crush, rout, overthrow, annihilate, beat [➡ BEAT AND DEFEAT; 80]

overwhelmed 1 *adj* **overcome**, overawed, speechless, dazed, stunned, incredulous, astounded, amazed, dumbfounded, flabbergasted (*informal*) [➡ SURPRISE, SHOCK, AND AMAZEMENT; 545] *Opposite*: unimpressed 2 *adj* **overpowered physically**, overcome, beaten, conquered, crushed, subjugated, routed, vanquished, trounced [➡ BEATEN AND DEFEATED; 78] 3 *adj* **inundated**, snowed under, swamped, flooded, exhausted [➡ SADNESS, DISTRESS, AND DESPAIR; 539]

overwhelming *adj* **irresistible**, overpowering, devastating, crushing, awe-inspiring, awesome, prodigious, vast, great, tremendous [➡ STRENGTH; 201] *Opposite*: insignificant

overwhelmingly *adv* **overpoweringly**, devastatingly, crushingly, prodigiously, tremendously, awesomely [➡ TO A GREAT EXTENT; 132] *Opposite*: insignificantly

overwinter *v* **hibernate**, lie dormant, stagnate, vegetate, lie fallow, hide away, hole up (*slang*) [➡ CONTINUE TO EXIST; 17]

overwork *v* **burn the midnight oil**, overdo it, overburden, overtax, overtask, overextend, overstrain, overload, burn the candle at both ends [➡ HARD WORK OR EFFORT; 298]

overworked *adj* [➡ IN TROUBLE AND DISADVANTAGED; 73]

overwrought *adj* **tense**, stressed, distraught, emotional, strained, overexcited, excitable, jumpy, fidgety, touchy, nervous, high-strung [➡ EXCESSIVE SENSITIVITY; 511] *Opposite*: calm

oviraptor *type of* **dinosaur** [➡ DINOSAURS; 996]

ovoid *adj* [➡ ROUNDED SHAPE; 1218]

ovule 1 *n* [➡ EGGS, SPERM, AND SPAWN; 727] 2 *part of* **flower** [➡ FLOWERS; 1032]

ovum *n* [➡ EGGS, SPERM, AND SPAWN; 727]

owe *v* **be beholden**, be obligated [➡ OWE AND DESERVE; 465] *Opposite*: repay

owed *adj* **owing**, unpaid, outstanding, due, payable, remaining, unsettled, in arrears, in the red [➡ OWE AND DESERVE; 465] *Opposite*: paid

owing *adj* **in arrears**, owed, due, in the red [➡ OWE AND DESERVE; 465] *Opposite*: paid

owing to *prep* **because of**, due to, on account of, thanks to, as a result of, in consequence of (*formal*) [➡ CAUSATION; 168]

owl *type of* **bird of prey** [➡ BIRDS OF PREY; 998]

owl

◆ *types of owls*
barn owl, fish owl, hoot owl, little owl, long-eared owl, screech owl, short-eared owl, snowy owl, tawny owl

owlet *type of* **young bird** [➡ YOUNG BIRDS; 1004]

owlish *adj* **owl-like**, serious, wise, solemn, bespectacled, myopic [➡ FACIAL CHARACTERISTICS; 481]

owl-like *adj* [➡ FACIAL CHARACTERISTICS; 481]

own 1 *adj* **individual**, private, particular, peculiar, specific, identifiable, personal [➡ BELONGING OR RELATING TO INDIVIDUALS; 944] 2 *v* **possess**, have, have possession of, keep, retain, preserve, maintain, hold, be in possession of [➡ POSSESS; 444] 3 *v* (*formal*) **confess**, admit, own up, acknowledge, profess, express, utter, declare, accept, concede [➡ ADMIT AND CONFESS; 615] *Opposite*: deny

owner *n* **proprietor**, landlord, possessor, holder, titleholder, vendor [➡ OWNERS; 446]

ownership *n* **possession**, rights, tenure, title, proprietorship [➡ POSSESS; 444]

own goal (*UK*) *n* **self-defeating action**, blunder, mistake, misjudgment, miscalculation, slip up (*informal*), faux pas (*literary*) [➡ MISTAKES; 250]

own up *v* **confess**, admit, profess, express, utter, declare [➡ ADMIT AND CONFESS; 615]

ox *n* **bull**, bullock, steer [➡ FARM ANIMALS; 982]

oxblood *type of* **red** [➡ COLORS; 1224]

oxford *type of* **shoe** [➡ FOOTWEAR; 871]

oxidation *n* [➡ GO BAD AND CORRODE; 390]

oxidization *n* **reaction**, rust, tarnishing, corrosion, verdigris, decomposition [➡ GO BAD AND CORRODE; 390]

oxidize *v* **react**, rust, tarnish, corrode, dissolve, flake, crumble [➡ GO BAD AND CORRODE; 390]

oxygen *type of* **gas** [➡ GASES; 1275]

oxymoron 1 *n* [➡ ASPECTS OF LANGUAGE; 682] **2** *type of* **figure of speech** [➡ FIGURES OF SPEECH; 673]

oyster 1 *type of* **white** [➡ COLORS; 1224] **2** *type of* **aquatic invertebrate** [➡ AQUATIC INVERTEBRATES; 1022]

oystercatcher *type of* **sea bird** [➡ SEA BIRDS; 1002]

oyster mushroom *type of* **fungus** [➡ MICROORGANISMS, FUNGI, AND ALGAE; 1023]

ozonosphere *n* [➡ THE EARTH'S ATMOSPHERE; 1040]

P

P2P *adj* [➡E-COMMERCE; 1129]

PA *n* **public-address system**, loudspeaker, speaker, amplifier, amp [➡AUDIO EQUIPMENT; 1139]

pa'anga *type of* **currency** [➡CURRENCIES; 798]

pace 1 *n* **speed**, rapidity, swiftness, velocity, rate of knots [➡SPEED; 102] 2 *n* **rate**, speed, tempo, time, regularity, frequency [➡SPEED; 102] 3 *n* **step**, stride, leap, bound, hop, skip, jump [➡PROCEED AND GO; 305] 4 *v* **walk**, stride, march, walk back and forth, walk up and down, walk to and fro, patrol, wander [➡PROCEED AND GO; 305] 5 *v* **govern**, regulate, restrict, manage, limit, control, monitor [➡BE IN CHARGE; 270]

pacemaker *n* **leader**, pacesetter, pacer, innovator, trendsetter, leading light, modernizer, pioneer [➡IMPORTANT OR FAMOUS PEOPLE; 893]

pacer *type of* **horse** [➡HORSES; 985]

pacific 1 *adj* **soothing**, appeasing, conciliatory, comforting, placatory [➡EMOTIONALLY PLEASANT; 187] *Opposite:* antagonistic 2 *adj* **tranquil**, peaceful, calm, untroubled, gentle, relaxing [➡PEACEFULNESS AND GENTLENESS; 214] *Opposite:* violent

Pacific *type of* **time zone** [➡TIMES OF DAY; 87]

pacifist 1 *n* **peace lover**, conscientious objector, dove, peacemaker, peacekeeper [➡PHILOSOPHICAL AND POLITICAL THINKERS; 781] 2 *adj* **pacific**, appeasing, conciliatory, placatory, comforting, soothing [➡EMOTIONALLY PLEASANT; 187] *Opposite:* antagonistic

pacify *v* **calm**, soothe, mollify, placate, calm down, appease [➡SOOTHE AND CALM; 573] *Opposite:* antagonize

pack 1 *v* **store**, arrange, put, place, sort, put away [➡ARRANGE AND CREATE ORDER; 357] 2 *v* **package**, wrap, wrap up, box, bundle, parcel [➡DECORATE, ADORN, AND APPLY COATINGS; 405] *Opposite:* unpack 3 *v* **fill**, cram, stuff, jam, load, cover [➡FILL; 406] 4 *v* **compact**, press, compress, squash, flatten, tamp [➡CONTACT: EXERT PRESSURE; 414] 5 *n* **carton**, packet, box, parcel, container, package, drum [➡CONTAINERS, RECEPTACLES, AND PACKAGING; 1245] 6 *n* **folder**, packet, wallet, dossier, file, portfolio [➡CONTAINERS, RECEPTACLES, AND PACKAGING; 1245] 7 *n* **set**, bunch, group, quantity, collection, bundle, wad [➡COLLECTIONS AND MIXTURES OF THINGS; 1244] 8 *n* **bag**, backpack, rucksack, haversack, daypack, bundle [➡CONTAINERS, RECEPTACLES, AND PACKAGING; 1245] 9 *n* **crowd**, horde, mob, gang, bunch, group, herd, flock, army [➡GROUPS OF PEOPLE; 935] 10 *type of* **herd** [➡GROUPS OF ANIMALS; 993]

package 1 *n* **parcel**, packet, box, envelope, padded bag (*UK*) [➡CONTAINERS, RECEPTACLES, AND PACKAGING; 1245] 2 *n* **set**, bundle, suite, raft, compendium, platform, file, array [➡COLLECTIONS AND MIXTURES OF THINGS; 1244] 3 *v* **pack**, wrap, wrap up, parcel, box, bundle [➡DECORATE, ADORN, AND APPLY COATINGS; 405] *Opposite:* unwrap 4 *v* **promote**, present, market, advertise, put across, portray [➡BUSINESS ACTIVITIES AND PHENOMENA; 794]

packaging *n* **wrapping**, packing, wrapper, packet, box,

bag, pack, container [➡CONTAINERS, RECEPTACLES, AND PACKAGING; 1245]

packed *adj* **crowded**, crammed, full, full to capacity, filled, bursting, overflowing, jam-packed (*informal*), chock-full (*informal*), chock-a-block (*informal*), heaving (*UK*) [➡FULL; 1239] *Opposite:* empty

packet *n* **pack**, package, sachet, container, carton, envelope, wallet, box [➡CONTAINERS, RECEPTACLES, AND PACKAGING; 1245]

packhorse *type of* **horse** [➡HORSES; 985]

pack in 1 *v* (*informal*) **stop**, give up, quit, abandon, drop, ditch (*informal*), dump (*informal*) [➡STOP ACTING; 264] *Opposite:* take up 2 *v* **attract**, interest, excite, fill the seats, be a box office success [➡APPEAL TO AND AROUSE INTEREST; 575] *Opposite:* flop (*informal*)

packing *n* **stuffing**, filling, filler, wadding, padding [➡CENTRAL PARTS OF PHYSICAL OBJECTS; 1251]

pack up *v* **stop**, give up, quit, abandon, drop, cease [➡STOP ACTING; 264] *Opposite:* start

pact *n* **deal**, agreement, treaty, contract, accord, concord, concordat, settlement, compact [➡PROMISE AND ASSURE; 684]

pad 1 *n* **cushion**, cloth, wad, swab, plug (*informal*), pack [➡CENTRAL PARTS OF PHYSICAL OBJECTS; 1251] 2 *type of* **sports equipment** [➡SPORTS EQUIPMENT; 879] 3 *n* **notepad**, sketchpad, notebook, sketchbook, scratchpad, jotter (*UK*) [➡WRITING AND DRAWING IMPLEMENTS, AND MEDIA; 601] 4 *n* **mat**, place mat, coaster, doily, table mat (*UK*) [➡FURNISHING AND HOUSEHOLD LINENS; 860] 5 *n* (*slang dated*) **place**, house, apartment, lodgings (*dated*), flat (*UK*), bedsit (*UK*) [➡ACCOMMODATIONS; 855] 6 *v* **creep**, tiptoe, steal, walk, sneak [➡MOVE SLOWLY; 314] 7 *v* **line**, cover, fill, stuff, wad, cushion, lag, protect [➡IMPROVE STRENGTH AND DURABILITY; 378] 8 *v* **fill out**, flesh out, amplify, lengthen, expand, stretch out, embellish [➡CHANGE OF SIZE: BIGGER; 392]

padding 1 *n* **stuffing**, filling, wadding, lining, packing, packaging, insulation [➡CENTRAL PARTS OF PHYSICAL OBJECTS; 1251] 2 *n* **verbiage**, circumlocution, periphrasis, garbage, rubbish, gobbledygook (*informal*), waffle (*UK informal*) [➡MEANINGLESS SPEECH OR WRITING; 676]

paddle 1 *n* **oar**, scull, sweep, blade [➡PARTS OF A SHIP OR BOAT; 1151] 2 *v* **row**, scull, propel [➡TRAVEL: WAYS OF TRAVELING; 320]

paddock *n* [➡THE COUNTRYSIDE AND OUTDOOR SPACES; 1071]

padlock *n* [➡FASTENERS, LINKS, AND NETWORKS; 1247]

pad out *v* [➡FILL; 406]

padre *n* [➡RELIGIOUS PEOPLE; 778]

paella *type of* **cooked dish** [➡PREPARED DISHES; 1170]

page 1 *n* **sheet**, piece of paper, sheet of paper, leaf, folio, side (*UK*) [➡WRITING AND DRAWING IMPLEMENTS, AND MEDIA; 601] 2 *v* **call**, contact, beep, summon, bleep (*UK*) [➡TELEPHONE, PAGE, AND TEXT; 681]

pageant *n* **procession**, parade, cavalcade, display, carnival, spectacle, show, play [➡PARTIES, DANCES, AND CELEBRATIONS; 37]

pageantry *n* **spectacle**, display, pomp, ceremony, ritual, tradition [➡PARTIES, DANCES, AND CELEBRATIONS; 37]

pageboy *type of* **hairstyle** [➡HAIRSTYLES AND HAIRPIECES; 488]

pager *type of* **telecommunications equipment** [➡TELECOMMUNICATIONS; 1130]

paid *adj* **salaried**, professional, funded, waged (*UK*) [➡TYPES OF WORK; 835] *Opposite:* unpaid

pail *n* [➡CONTAINERS, RECEPTACLES, AND PACKAGING; 1245]

paillasse *n* [➡FURNISHING AND HOUSEHOLD LINENS; 860]

pain 1 *n* **discomfort**, agony, aching, hurt, ache, sting, soreness, throbbing, smarting, stinging, twinge [➡PAIN AND OTHER PHYSICAL SENSATIONS; 733] *Opposite:* pleasure **2** *n* **grief**, sorrow, anguish, ache, torture, agony, heartache [➡SADNESS, DISTRESS, AND DESPAIR; 539] *Opposite:* joy **3** *n* (*informal*) **nuisance**, bother, bind, menace, drag (*informal*), pest (*informal*) [➡NUISANCES; 253] *Opposite:* pleasure **4** *v* **sadden**, distress, upset, disturb, grieve, displease, worry [➡UPSET, DISTRESS, AND HUMILIATE; 567] *Opposite:* hearten

pain au chocolat *type of* **cake** [➡CAKES, COOKIES, AND DESSERTS; 1181]

pained *adj* **hurt**, aggrieved, indignant, wounded, injured, disappointed [➡SADNESS, DISTRESS, AND DESPAIR; 539]

painful 1 *adj* **tender**, aching, raw, throbbing, excruciating, hurting, agonizing, burning, sore, uncomfortable [➡PAIN AND OTHER PHYSICAL SENSATIONS; 733] *Opposite:* painless **2** *adj* **sorrowful**, distressing, anguished, heartbreaking, upsetting, harrowing, heartrending [➡EMOTIONALLY UNPLEASANT AND UPSETTING; 227] *Opposite:* pleasant **3** *adj* **laborious**, troublesome, awkward, labored, tedious, slow [➡DIFFICULTY AND COMPLEXITY; 242] *Opposite:* easy **4** *adj* **awful**, excruciating, dire, dreadful, agonizing, embarrassing, terrible [➡BAD AND BADLY; 223] *Opposite:* wonderful

pain in the neck (*informal*) *n* [➡NUISANCES; 253]

painkiller *n* **analgesic**, sedative, anesthetic, drug [➡REMEDIES, TREATMENTS, AND OPERATIONS; 731]

painkilling *adj* **analgesic**, calming, sedative, deadening, numbing, palliative, soothing [➡PHYSICALLY PLEASANT; 186]

painless *adj* **effortless**, easy, trouble-free, simple, unproblematic, straightforward [➡EASE AND SIMPLICITY; 200] *Opposite:* problematic

pains *n* **care**, effort, trouble, lengths [➡HARD WORK OR EFFORT; 298]

painstaking *adj* **thorough**, careful, meticulous, conscientious, scrupulous, particular, assiduous [➡HARDWORKING AND COMMITTED; 500] *Opposite:* careless

See Compare and Contrast at **careful.**

paint 1 *v* **coat**, decorate, smear, daub, splatter, undercoat, brush [➡DECORATE, ADORN, AND APPLY COATINGS; 405] **2** *v* **portray**, capture, catch, show, render (*formal*) [➡NAME AND DESCRIBE; 665]

painted lady *type of* **butterfly** [➡MOTHS AND BUTTERFLIES; 1015]

painter *n* **artist**, watercolorist, portraitist, miniaturist [➡ARTISTS; 900]

painting 1 *n* **picture**, work of art, image, canvas, oil painting, landscape, portrait, still life [➡ARTWORKS; 898] **2** *n* **art**, fine art, portraiture, landscape, oils, acrylics [➡THE PICTORIAL ARTS; 897]

paint the town red (*informal*) *v* **celebrate**, have a good time, have fun, revel, go out, socialize, let your hair down, have a night on the town, whoop it up (*informal*), party (*informal*), go out on the town (*informal*), live it up (*slang*), have a ball (*dated slang*) [➡LEISURE AND RECREATION; 874]

pair 1 *n* **couple**, duo, twosome, brace, set [➡AMOUNTS AND QUANTITIES; 112] **2** *v* **pair off**, team up, join up, match up, put together, combine [➡CREATING CONNECTIONS; 144] *Opposite:* separate

paisley *n* [➡PATTERNS; 1225]

pajamas *type of* **sleepwear** [➡GARMENTS AND OUTFITS; 865]

pal (*informal*) *n* **friend**, comrade, crony, chum (*informal*), buddy (*informal*), mate (*UK*) [➡FRIENDS AND GUESTS; 963]

palace *type of* **house** [➡RESIDENTIAL BUILDINGS; 1078]

palatable 1 *adj* **edible**, pleasant, tasty, appetizing, toothsome, delicious [➡TASTE; 703] *Opposite:* inedible **2** *adj* **acceptable**, agreeable, satisfactory, pleasant, passable [➡ACCEPTABLE AND PASSABLE; 219] *Opposite:* disagreeable

palate *part of* **mouth** [➡THE MOUTH; 702]

palatial *adj* **luxurious**, lavish, grand, impressive, splendid, regal, extravagant, opulent [➡EXPENSIVE AND LUXURIOUS; 218] *Opposite:* miserable

palaver 1 *n* **chatter**, chat, gossip, talk, chitchat (*informal*), nattering (*informal*) [➡INFORMAL COMMUNICATION; 45] **2** *n* (*UK*) **fuss**, bother, trouble, nuisance, commotion, uproar, hassle (*informal*), to-do (*informal*) [➡CHAOS AND UPROAR; 51]

palazzo pants *type of* **pants** [➡GARMENTS AND OUTFITS; 865]

pale 1 *adj* **light**, pastel, soft, whitish, insipid, watery, wishy-washy (*informal*) [➡DESCRIBING COLORS; 1226] *Opposite:* dark **2** *adj* **pallid**, colorless, fair, ashen, white, pasty, sallow, anemic, wan [➡COMPLEXION; 480] **3** *adj* **faint**, dim, feeble, weak, watery [➡DESCRIBING LIGHT; 1228] *Opposite:* strong **4** *v* **diminish**, reduce, recede, lessen, fade [➡CHANGE OF INTENSITY: LESS; 395] *Opposite:* intensify **5** *v* **fade**, lose color, become washed out, soften, lighten [➡CHANGE OF COLOR; 391] *Opposite:* deepen **6** *v* **go white**, whiten, go pale, blanch, bleach [➡CHANGE OF COLOR; 391] *Opposite:* color

palea *part of* **flower** [➡FLOWERS; 1032]

Paleocene *type of* **epoch** [➡EPOCHS AND ERAS; 89]

Paleozoic *type of* **era** [➡EPOCHS AND ERAS; 89]

palimpsest *n* [➡BOOKS AND BOOKLETS; 590]

palindrome *type of* **wordplay** [➡JOKES AND TEASING; 674]

paling *n* [➡BARRIERS; 1113]

palisade *n* [➡BARRIERS; 1113]

pall 1 *v* **lose its attraction**, fade, diminish, wither, go sour, outstay its welcome [➡ GET WORSE; 381] **2** *n* **cloud**, blanket, shroud, sheet, wall, column [➡ AMOUNTS OF GAS; 116] **3** *n* **gloom**, despair, sadness, depression, melancholy, despondency [➡ SADNESS, DISTRESS, AND DESPAIR; 539]

Palladian *type of* **pre-20th-century architecture** [➡ BUILDING AND ARCHITECTURE; 1076]

pallbearer *n* [➡ BURIAL AND PREPARATION FOR BURIAL; 929]

pallet *n* [➡ FURNISHING AND HOUSEHOLD LINENS; 860]

palliate *v* [➡ IMPROVE SOMETHING; 374]

palliation *n* [➡ IMPROVE SOMETHING; 374]

palliative 1 *adj* **soothing**, calming, relaxing, comforting, mollifying, reassuring [➡ CALMING; 188] **2** *adj* **analgesic**, pain-killing, anesthetic, sedative [➡ PHYSICALLY PLEASANT; 186]

pallid *adj* **pale**, white, ashen, pasty, colorless, sallow, anemic, wan [➡ COMPLEXION; 480] *Opposite*: dark

pallor *n* **paleness**, whiteness, pastiness, wanness, sallowness [➡ COMPLEXION; 480]

pally (*informal*) *adj* [➡ RELATIONSHIP TO ANOTHER; 973]

palm *part of* **arm or hand** [➡ PARTS OF THE BODY: ARM AND HAND; 695]

palmcorder *type of* **video equipment** [➡ PHOTOGRAPHY AND PHOTOGRAPHIC EQUIPMENT; 1122]

palm off *v* [➡ GET RID OF SOMETHING; 451]

palmtop *type of* **computer** [➡ COMPUTERS AND COMPUTING; 1127]

palpability *n* [➡ PERCEPTIBLE; 25]

palpable 1 *adj* **intense**, tangible, physical, real, deep, profound, substantial [➡ PERCEPTIBLE; 25] *Opposite*: intangible **2** *adj* **obvious**, clear, demonstrable, unmistakable, evident, self-evident, unambiguous, definite [➡ PERCEPTIBLE; 25] *Opposite*: hidden

palpitate *v* **flutter**, pound, race, tremble, quiver, twitch [➡ PHYSICAL REACTIONS; 316]

paltriness *n* [➡ TOO FEW, TOO LITTLE; 122]

paltry 1 *adj* **worthless**, trivial, trifling, miserable, insignificant, measly (*informal*) [➡ TOO FEW, TOO LITTLE; 122] *Opposite*: substantial **2** *adj* **despicable**, wretched, mean, miserable, contemptible, low, poor, base [➡ UNACCEPTABLE AND UNFORGIVABLE; 225]

pampas *n* [➡ DESERTS, PLAINS, AND MOORLAND; 1045]

pampas grass *type of* **grass** [➡ GRASS; 1031]

pamper *v* **spoil**, indulge, coddle, mollycoddle, cosset, baby, treat [➡ TAKE CARE OF AND SPOIL; 300]

pamphlet *n* **leaflet**, brochure, booklet, guide, tract, fact sheet (*UK*) [➡ BOOKS AND BOOKLETS; 590]

pan 1 *n* **pot**, saucepan, casserole, wok, frying pan, skillet, pressure cooker [➡ TABLEWARE, FLATWARE, AND KITCHENWARE; 861] **2** *v* (*informal*) **criticize**, berate, disparage, deride, slam (*informal*), roast (*informal*), slate (*UK*) [➡ ACCUSE, BLAME, AND CRITICIZE; 641] *Opposite*: praise

panacea *n* **cure-all**, cure, solution, answer, remedy, magic potion, magic bullet [➡ SOLUTIONS; 215]

panache *n* **flair**, flamboyance, style, spirit, confidence, elegance, élan (*literary*) [➡ CONFIDENCE AND COMPOSURE; 499] *Opposite*: awkwardness

Panama hat *type of* **hat** [➡ ACCESSORIES, MILLINERY, AND LINGERIE; 867]

pancake *n* [➡ CAKES, COOKIES, AND DESSERTS; 1181]

pancake

◆ *types of pancakes*
battercake, blini, blintz, crepe, flapjack, griddlecake, hotcake, johnnycake, waffle

pancetta *type of* **processed meat** [➡ TYPES AND CUTS OF MEAT; 1177]

pancreas *part of* **digestive tract** [➡ THE DIGESTIVE TRACT; 709]

panda *type of* **large mammal** [➡ LARGE MAMMALS; 986]

pandemic *n* **epidemic**, plague, contagion, sickness, disease, illness [➡ SICKNESS; 729]

pandemonium *n* **chaos**, bedlam, uproar, hubbub, racket, mayhem (*informal*) [➡ CHAOS AND UPROAR; 51]

pander to *v* **indulge**, satisfy, gratify, bow to, go along with, be a slave to [➡ TAKE CARE OF AND SPOIL; 300] *Opposite*: resist

pane *n* **windowpane**, glass, window, sheet, panel, piece [➡ WINDOWS; 1100]

panegyric *n* [➡ ONE-WAY COMMUNICATION; 49]

panegyrize (*archaic*) *v* [➡ PRAISE AND ENCOURAGE; 647]

panel 1 *n* **piece**, board, pane, sheet, plate, section, square, rectangle [➡ AREA AND RANGE; 111] **2** *n* **board**, team, jury, group, council, committee [➡ GROUPS WITH A COMMON INTEREST; 938]

pan-fry *v* [➡ COOKING AND FOOD PREPARATION; 353]

pang *n* **twinge**, spasm, paroxysm, shooting pain, cramp, stitch, pain, wrench [➡ PAIN AND OTHER PHYSICAL SENSATIONS; 733]

panhandler *n* [➡ POOR PEOPLE; 896]

panic 1 *n* **fear**, anxiety, fright, terror, dread, alarm, horror [➡ FEAR AND PANIC; 543] *Opposite*: calm **2** *v* **be frightened**, be terrified, lose your nerve, go to pieces, get flustered, lose it (*informal*), freak (*slang*) [➡ GIVING VENT TO EMOTIONS; 679] *Opposite*: calm down **3** *v* **terrify**, unnerve, scare, frighten, fluster, throw into disarray, spook, rattle [➡ FRIGHTEN AND SHOCK; 568]

panicked *adj* [➡ FEAR AND PANIC; 543]

panicky *adj* **frightened**, scared, alarmed, fearful, anxious, unnerved, jumpy, edgy [➡ FEAR AND PANIC; 543] *Opposite*: calm

panic-stricken *adj* **terrified**, unnerved, frightened, fearful, scared out of your wits, shocked [➡ FEAR AND PANIC; 543] *Opposite*: calm

pannacotta *type of* **dessert** [➡ CAKES, COOKIES, AND DESSERTS; 1181]

panoply *n* **display**, array, show, parade, exhibition [➡ COLLECTIONS AND MIXTURES OF THINGS; 1244]

panorama *n* **view**, scene, vista, outlook, landscape, prospect [➡ VIEWS AND OUTLOOKS; 1073]

pan out (*informal*) *v* **turn out**, work out, develop, end up, resolve itself, conclude, end [➡ HAPPEN; 27]

panpipes *type of* **wind instrument** [➡ MUSICAL INSTRUMENTS; 910]

pansy *type of* **annual flower** [➡ FLOWERS; 1032]

pant *v* **gasp**, puff, wheeze, blow, gasp for air, huff [➡ BREATHE AND NOT BREATHE; 716]

pantheism *n* [➡ PHILOSOPHIES AND BELIEFS; 780]

panther *type of* **cat** [➡ FELINES; 983]

panties (*informal*) *type of* **lower body underwear** [➡ ACCESSORIES, MILLINERY, AND LINGERIE; 867]

pantry *type of* **storage space** [➡ STORES AND STORAGE BUILDINGS; 1088]

pants *n* **trousers**, slacks [➡ GARMENTS AND OUTFITS; 865]

pants

◆ *types of pants*
bell-bottom pants, Bermuda shorts, breeches, capri pants, cargo pants, chaps, chinos, clam diggers, cords, culottes, cutoffs, fatigues, harem pants, hip-huggers, hot pants, jeans, jodhpurs, khakis, knickerbockers, lederhosen, leggings, overalls, palazzo pants, pedal pushers, plus fours, shorts, slacks, trews

pantsuit *type of* **suit** [➡ GARMENTS AND OUTFITS; 865]

pantyhose *type of* **lower body underwear** [➡ ACCESSORIES, MILLINERY, AND LINGERIE; 867]

pap *n* **drivel**, nonsense, rubbish, trash, garbage, dreck [➡ JUNK AND USELESS OBJECTS; 1249]

papa *type of* **older relative** (*dated*) [➡ OLDER GENERATION RELATIVES; 959]

paparazzo *n* [➡ WORKERS IN ENTERTAINMENT AND MEDIA; 873]

papaya *type of* **fruit** [➡ FRUIT AND VEGETABLES; 1176]

paper **1** *n* **newspaper**, daily, weekly, broadsheet, broadside, tabloid, rag (*informal*) [➡ NEWSPAPERS AND MAGAZINES; 605] **2** *n* **document**, manuscript, thesis, term paper, dissertation, essay, article, piece, lecture [➡ ANALYTICAL NONFICTION WRITING; 592]

paperback *n* **book**, softback, softcover, novel [➡ BOOKS AND BOOKLETS; 590]

paperclip *n* [➡ FASTENERS, LINKS, AND NETWORKS; 1247]

paperknife *type of* **knife** [➡ CUTTING TOOLS; 1120]

paper over **1** *v* **wallpaper**, cover, cover up, obscure, disguise, hide [➡ DECORATE, ADORN, AND APPLY COATINGS; 405] *Opposite*: strip **2** *v* **conceal**, sweep under the carpet, hide, cover up, make light of, minimize [➡ CAUSE TO DISAPPEAR; 6] *Opposite*: highlight

paper-pusher (*informal*) *n* [➡ WORKERS; 836]

paper-thin *adj* [➡ WIDTH: NARROW AND THIN; 1200]

paperwork *n* **form-filling**, accounts, bookkeeping, correspondence, administration, filing [➡ WORK-RELATED ACTIVITIES; 834]

papery *adj* **flimsy**, frail, thin, paper-thin, delicate, dry, diaphanous [➡ FRAGILE; 1209]

paprika *type of* **spice** [➡ HERBS AND SPICES; 1175]

papyrus *n* [➡ WRITING AND DRAWING IMPLEMENTS, AND MEDIA; 601]

par *n* **average**, standard, norm, the usual [➡ SCORES AND EVALUATIONS; 598]

parable *n* **allegory**, fable, moral tale, folk tale, tale, legend, story [➡ THE ORAL TRADITION; 677]

parade **1** *n* **procession**, pageant, cavalcade, display, carnival, spectacle, line [➡ PARTIES, DANCES, AND CELEBRATIONS; 37] **2** *v* **process**, march, file, strut, turn out [➡ PROCEED AND GO; 305] **3** *v* **show off**, exhibit, display, trumpet, flaunt, flourish [➡ CAUSE TO APPEAR; 5] *Opposite*: hide **4** *v* **walk**, stalk, march, strut, stroll, posture [➡ PROCEED AND GO; 305] *Opposite*: skulk

paradiddle (*UK*) *n* [➡ IMPACT SOUNDS; 1260]

paradigm **1** *n* **epitome**, archetype, model, example, exemplar (*literary*) [➡ PERFECT EXAMPLES AND EMBODIMENTS; 67] *Opposite*: antithesis **2** *n* **model**, template, prototype, standard, pattern, example [➡ PERFECT EXAMPLES AND EMBODIMENTS; 67]

paradise **1** *n* **heaven**, seventh heaven, nirvana, happy hunting ground [➡ RELIGIOUS CONCEPTS; 776] *Opposite*: hell **2** *n* (*informal*) **dreamworld**, wonderland, cloud nine, utopia, bliss [➡ NONEXISTENT PLACES; 1066]

paradisiac *adj* [➡ PHYSICALLY PLEASANT; 186]

paradox *n* **inconsistency**, absurdity, irony, contradiction, contradiction in terms, oxymoron, enigma, puzzle [➡ SECRETS AND MYSTERIES; 180]

paradoxical *adj* **inconsistent**, absurd, ironic, contradictory, illogical, impossible, enigmatic, puzzling [➡ BIZARRE AND PECULIAR; 257] *Opposite*: logical

paradoxically **1** *adv* **illogically**, absurdly, inconsistently, puzzlingly, unexpectedly, in contradiction [➡ BIZARRE AND PECULIAR; 257] *Opposite*: logically **2** *adv* **strangely enough**, oddly enough, funnily enough, surprisingly, ironically, bizarrely, in actual fact [➡ EXPRESSIONS OF SURPRISE AND PLEASURE; 546]

paraffin oil (*UK*) *n* [➡ ENERGY SOURCES; 1162]

paraglider *type of* **civil aircraft** [➡ AIRCRAFT; 1148]

paragon *n* **model**, shining example, epitome, archetype, quintessence, paradigm, ideal, exemplar (*literary*) [➡ PERFECT EXAMPLES AND EMBODIMENTS; 67]

paragraph **1** *n* **section**, subsection, passage, part, clause [➡ ASPECTS OF LANGUAGE; 682] **2** *n* **article**, piece, item, story, editorial, column [➡ NEWSPAPERS AND MAGAZINES; 605]

parakeet *type of* **pet bird** [➡ BIRDS; 997]

parallel **1** *adj* **similar**, equivalent, corresponding, analogous, matching, comparable [➡ SIMILARITY; 148] *Opposite*: dissimilar **2** *n* **counterpart**, match, equal, equivalent, peer, twin, like [➡ EQUALITY; 154] *Opposite*: opposite **3** *n* **similarity**, correspondence, equivalence, resemblance, analogy, comparison, congruence [➡ SIMILARITY; 148] *Opposite*: dissimilarity **4** *type of* **hardware** [➡ COMPUTERS AND COMPUTING; 1127]

parallelogram *type of* **angular shape** [➡ANGULAR SHAPE; 1217]

paralyze *v* [➡MAKE IMPOSSIBLE; 276]

parameter *n* **limit**, boundary, limitation, restriction, constraint, bound, factor, consideration, stricture (*formal*) [➡DEGREE AND EXTENT; 110]

paramilitary 1 *adj* **guerrilla**, rebel, revolutionary, terrorist [➡MILITARY; 829] 2 *n* **rebel**, revolutionary, terrorist, guerrilla, fighter, partisan, soldier [➡MILITARY PERSONNEL; 828]

paramount *adj* **supreme**, utmost, dominant, chief, principal, top, overriding, vital [➡MOST IMPORTANT AND MAIN; 193] *Opposite*: minimal

paramour (*literary*) *n* [➡SEXUAL AND ROMANTIC RELATIONSHIPS; 964]

paranoia *n* **fear**, suspicion, mistrust, distrust, obsession, terror [➡FEARS AND PHOBIAS; 554] *Opposite*: confidence

paranoid *adj* **suspicious**, fearful, mistrustful, distrustful, obsessed, unreasonable [➡INSECURITY AND LOSS OF COMPOSURE; 544] *Opposite*: trusting

paranormal *adj* [➡THE SUPERNATURAL; 787]

parapet *n* [➡PARTS OF FORTRESSES; 1091]

paraphernalia *n* **things**, stuff, equipment, kit, trappings, odds and ends, accouterments, bits and pieces (*informal*), gear (*informal*) [➡POSSESSIONS; 461]

paraphrase 1 *v* **rephrase**, summarize, reword, interpret, translate, restate [➡RECITE, REPEAT, AND NARRATE; 620] 2 *n* **summary**, rewording, précis, translation, interpretation, restatement [➡SUMMARIES, OUTLINES, AND EXCERPTS; 588]

parapsychological *adj* [➡THE SUPERNATURAL; 787]

parapsychologist *n* [➡PEOPLE WITH SUPERNATURAL POWERS; 788]

parasite 1 *n* **pest**, bug, bloodsucker, insect, flea, louse [➡PARASITES; 1017] *Opposite*: host 2 *n* **leech**, scrounger (*informal*), sponger (*informal*), sponge (*informal*), freeloader (*informal*) [➡LAZY OR UNSUCCESSFUL PEOPLE; 948]

parasite

◆ *types of parasitic insects*
bedbug, botfly, chigger, chigoe, crab louse, deer tick, flea, gadfly, harvest mite, head louse, horsefly, louse, mite, sand flea, sandfly, tapeworm, tick

parasitic 1 *adj* **biting**, bloodsucking, dependent, opportunistic [➡PARASITES; 1017] *Opposite*: host 2 *adj* **dependent**, lazy, scrounging (*informal*), sponging (*informal*), freeloading (*informal*) [➡SELFISH AND UNKIND; 505]

parasol *n* **sunshade**, umbrella, shade [➡COVERS AND COATINGS; 1246]

parboil *v* [➡COOKING AND FOOD PREPARATION; 353]

parcel 1 *n* **package**, packet, bundle, carton, box, pack [➡CONTAINERS, RECEPTACLES, AND PACKAGING; 1245] 2 *n* **tract**, plot, piece, section, portion, lot, allotment (*UK*) [➡AREA AND RANGE; 111] 3 *v* **pack**, package, wrap, wrap up, box, bundle [➡DECORATE, ADORN, AND APPLY COATINGS; 405] *Opposite*: unwrap

parcel out *v* **distribute**, divide, give out, hand out,

apportion, dispense, allocate, allot, share out (*UK*) [➡DISPENSE, RATION, AND DISTRIBUTE; 434]

parcel up (*UK*) *v* **wrap up**, wrap, parcel, bundle, pack, box, package [➡DECORATE, ADORN, AND APPLY COATINGS; 405] *Opposite*: unwrap

parch *v* **dry**, dry out, scorch, dehydrate, desiccate [➡HARDEN, CONGEAL, AND DRY; 387]

parched 1 *adj* (*informal*) **thirsty**, gasping, dehydrated, dry, panting, thirsting [➡DRINK; 711] *Opposite*: refreshed 2 *adj* **dry**, arid, dried up, dried out, scorched, dehydrated, desiccated, waterless [➡DRY; 1242] *Opposite*: waterlogged

See Compare and Contrast at **dry**.

parchment *n* [➡WRITING AND DRAWING IMPLEMENTS, AND MEDIA; 601]

pardon 1 *v* **forgive**, absolve, exonerate, let off, acquit, release, let go [➡FORGET, FORGIVE, AND ACCEPT; 748] *Opposite*: condemn 2 *v* **excuse**, forgive, overlook, let pass, take no notice of, ignore [➡NOT PAY ATTENTION; 764] *Opposite*: resent 3 *n* **forgiveness**, absolution, exoneration, amnesty, mercy, acquittal, release, remission [➡COMPASSION AND FORGIVENESS; 551]

pare 1 *v* **peel**, skin, strip, trim, shave, prepare [➡COOKING AND FOOD PREPARATION; 353] 2 *v* **cut**, trim, clip, cut back, tidy up [➡EXTRACT AND SEVER; 341] *Opposite*: grow

pare down *v* **cut back**, cut down, reduce, scale down, pare, shave, trim [➡CHANGE OF SIZE: SMALLER; 393] *Opposite*: increase

parent *type of* **older relative** [➡OLDER GENERATION RELATIVES; 959]

parentage 1 *n* **parents**, paternity, maternity [➡RELATIONSHIP TO ANOTHER; 973] 2 *n* **ancestry**, background, pedigree, origin, derivation, descent, family, line [➡THE FAMILY; 956]

parental *adj* **parent**, maternal, paternal [➡THE FAMILY; 956]

parenthesis 1 *type of* **punctuation mark** [➡ASPECTS OF LANGUAGE; 682] 2 *n* **digression**, afterthought, addition, aside, comment, interpolation [➡FIGURES OF SPEECH; 673]

parenthood *n* **parentage**, fatherhood, motherhood, parenting, paternity, maternity, guardianship [➡RELATIONSHIP TO ANOTHER; 973]

parenting *n* **childcare**, child-rearing, babycare, nurturing, child raising, education [➡TEACHING; 839]

parget *n* [➡BUILDING MATERIALS; 1077]

pargeting *n* [➡BUILDING MATERIALS; 1077]

pariah *n* [➡SOLITARY PEOPLE AND MISFITS; 942]

parings *n* [➡REMAINDER AND REMAINDERS; 125]

parish *n* **community**, district, village, locality, area, neighborhood [➡HUMAN SETTLEMENTS; 1070]

parish priest *n* [➡RELIGIOUS PEOPLE; 778]

parity *n* **equivalence**, equality, uniformity, similarity, correspondence [➡EQUALITY; 154] *Opposite*: disparity

park 1 *n* **gardens**, botanical gardens, common, green, grounds, country park, estate [➡URBAN OUTDOOR SPACES; 1072] 2 *v* (*slang*) **sit**, settle, plonk, plunk, put, be seated, settle down [➡POSITION SOMETHING; 325]

parka *type of* **overcoat** [➡ GARMENTS AND OUTFITS; 865]

parking *n* **parking lot**, parking space, parking bay, parking place, car park (*UK*) [➡ URBAN OUTDOOR SPACES; 1072]

parking light *type of* **external feature** [➡ EXTERNAL PARTS OF A VEHICLE; 1147]

parking lot *n* [➡ URBAN OUTDOOR SPACES; 1072]

parkland *n* **grassland**, land, fields, meadows, estate, reserve [➡ THE COUNTRYSIDE AND OUTDOOR SPACES; 1071]

parkway *type of* **highway** [➡ ROADS; 1106]

parlance *n* **idiom**, turn of phrase, phraseology, phrasing, jargon, vernacular, dialect [➡ THE SPOKEN WORD; 671]

See Compare and Contrast at **language.**

parley 1 *v* **confer**, negotiate, talk, discuss, deliberate, consult [➡ NEGOTIATION AND DEBATE; 46] **2** *n* **conference**, meeting, discussion, negotiations, consultation, talks, confab (*informal*), huddle (*informal*), deliberations (*formal*) [➡ NEGOTIATION AND DEBATE; 46]

parliament *n* **government**, legislative body, legislature, assembly, MPs (*UK*) [➡ LEGISLATIVE BODIES AND LEGISLATION; 809]

parliamentarian *n* **member of parliament**, politician, backbencher, legislator, minister, MP (*UK*), front-bencher (*UK*) [➡ POLITICAL OFFICES AND POLITICIANS; 808]

parliamentary *adj* **governmental**, legislative, law-making, congressional, senatorial, legislatorial, deliberative (*formal*) [➡ STYLES AND SYSTEMS OF GOVERNMENT; 806]

parliamentary government *n* [➡ STYLES AND SYSTEMS OF GOVERNMENT; 806]

parlor 1 *n* **business premises**, salon, store, business establishment, studio, shop [➡ RETAIL OUTLETS; 1083] **2** *type of* **room in the home** [➡ TYPES OF ROOMS; 1097]

parlous (*archaic or humorous*) *adj* **dangerous**, perilous, risky, unsafe, uncertain, difficult [➡ DANGEROUS; 236] *Opposite*: comfortable

parma ham *type of* **processed meat** [➡ TYPES AND CUTS OF MEAT; 1177]

Parmesan *type of* **hard cheese** [➡ DAIRY PRODUCTS AND CHEESES; 1183]

parochial *adj* **narrow**, narrow-minded, closed-minded, provincial, insular, hidebound, unsophisticated [➡ NEGATIVE INTELLECTUAL CHARACTERISTICS; 525] *Opposite*: broad-minded

parochialism *n* **narrow-mindedness**, provincialism, insularity, closed-mindedness, narrowness [➡ NEGATIVE INTELLECTUAL CHARACTERISTICS; 525] *Opposite*: broad-mindedness

parodist *n* **satirist**, humorist, imitator, lampooner, burlesquer, impersonator, caricaturist [➡ WRITERS AND STYLES; 914]

parody 1 *n* **caricature**, imitation, lampoon, satire, burlesque, spoof, mockery, takeoff (*informal*) [➡ JOKES AND TEASING; 674] **2** *n* **distortion**, travesty, misrepresentation, perversion, pale imitation, insult [➡ REPRESENTATIONS AND GENERAL EXAMPLES; 65] *Opposite*: model **3** *v* **distort**, pervert, misrepresent, twist [➡ PRETEND AND MIMIC; 60] **4** *v* **lampoon**, imitate, caricature, sat-

irize, burlesque, make fun of, mock, ape, take the mickey (*UK informal*) [➡ JOKES AND TEASING; 674]

parole 1 *n* **conditional release**, early release, bail, liberation [➡ TRIAL, PUNISHMENT, AND LEGAL OUTCOMES; 819] **2** *v* **release on parole**, release conditionally, liberate, bail, give terms [➡ TRIAL, PUNISHMENT, AND LEGAL OUTCOMES; 819]

paroxysm 1 *n* **convulsion**, spasm, fit, seizure, attack, outbreak [➡ PAIN AND OTHER PHYSICAL SENSATIONS; 733] **2** *n* **outburst**, fit, frenzy, outpouring, explosion, eruption [➡ CRITICISMS AND ANGRY OUTBURSTS; 50]

paroxysmal *adj* **convulsive**, violent, spasmodic, uncontrollable, involuntary [➡ PAIN AND OTHER PHYSICAL SENSATIONS; 733]

parp (*UK*) *v* [➡ EMIT RINGING AND HOOTING SOUNDS; 367]

parquet *n* **flooring**, parquetry, floor, floorboards, inlay [➡ BUILDING MATERIALS; 1077]

parquetry *n* [➡ BUILDING MATERIALS; 1077]

parricide *n* [➡ CAUSES OF DEATH; 921]

parrot 1 *type of* **pet bird** [➡ BIRDS; 997] **2** *n* **imitator**, mimic, impersonator, impressionist, copier, copycat (*informal*) [➡ JOKERS AND TEASES; 675] **3** *v* **mimic**, imitate, copy, impersonate, echo, ape, repeat back [➡ PRETEND AND MIMIC; 60]

parry 1 *v* **deflect**, block, fend off, shield yourself from, dodge, duck [➡ AVOID OR ESCAPE CONTACT; 418] *Opposite*: take **2** *v* **evade**, avoid, dodge, elude, sidestep, deflect, circumvent [➡ WITHHOLD INFORMATION; 687] *Opposite*: answer

parse *v* **analyze**, describe, break down, explain, construe, deconstruct [➡ EXAMINE AND ASSESS; 753]

parsimonious *adj* **stingy**, thrifty, frugal, ungenerous, miserly, tightfisted, tight, sparing, penny-pinching (*informal*), mean (*UK*) [➡ GRASPING AND FINANCIALLY MEAN; 519] *Opposite*: extravagant

parsimoniousness *n* **stinginess**, thrift, thriftiness, frugality, ungenerousness, miserliness, tightfistedness, parsimony, penny-pinching (*informal*), meanness (*UK*) [➡ GRASPING AND FINANCIALLY MEAN; 519] *Opposite*: extravagance

parsimony *n* **stinginess**, thrift, thriftiness, meanness, frugality, ungenerousness, miserliness, tightfistedness, parsimoniousness, penny-pinching (*informal*) [➡ GRASPING AND FINANCIALLY MEAN; 519] *Opposite*: extravagance

parsley *type of* **herb** [➡ HERBS AND SPICES; 1175]

parsnip *type of* **root vegetable** [➡ FRUIT AND VEGETABLES; 1176]

parson *n* **cleric**, priest, minister, pastor, parish priest, rector, vicar, preacher, beneficiary [➡ RELIGIOUS PEOPLE; 778]

parsonage *n* **church house**, rectory, vicarage, manse, residence [➡ RELIGIOUS BUILDINGS; 1085]

part 1 *n* **portion**, division, section, fraction, piece, bit, segment [➡ AREA AND RANGE; 111] *Opposite*: whole **2** *n* **feature**, ingredient, element, component, bit, piece [➡ AMOUNTS OF SOLID OR SEMISOLID; 115] **3** *n* **share**, portion, fragment, slice, chunk, amount, quantity, measure, cut (*informal*) [➡ AMOUNTS AND QUANTITIES; 112] *Opposite*: whole **4** *n* **function**, role, duty, job, position, capacity, involvement [➡ JOB; 833] **5** *v* **divide**, separate, open, split, segregate, draw apart, put asunder (*formal*) [➡ SEPARATE AND DIVIDE; 401] *Opposite*: join

partake 1 *v* **consume**, dine, eat, drink, taste, touch [➡ EAT AND NOT EAT; 710] *Opposite*: abstain 2 *v* **participate**, share, contribute, take part, play a part, join [➡ PARTICIPATE; 292] *Opposite*: refrain

Parthian shot *n* [➡ CRITICISMS AND ANGRY OUTBURSTS; 50]

partial 1 *adj* **incomplete**, fractional, limited, restricted, unfinished, half- [➡ UNFINISHEDNESS; 239] *Opposite*: complete 2 *adj* **biased**, prejudiced, subjective, one-sided, inequitable, preferential [➡ THE NATURE OF IDEAS; 771] *Opposite*: impartial

partiality 1 *n* **fondness**, liking, penchant, inclination, affection, soft spot, predilection (*formal*) [➡ LIKE, LOVE, VALUE, AND ENJOY; 578] *Opposite*: dislike 2 *n* **bias**, prejudice, preference, leaning, favoritism, subjectivity, one-sidedness [➡ THE NATURE OF IDEAS; 771] *Opposite*: impartiality

partially *adv* **partly**, in part, incompletely, to some extent, somewhat, moderately, to a degree, in some measure [➡ TO A CERTAIN EXTENT; 136] *Opposite*: completely

partially sighted *adj* [➡ SEE; 699]

partial to *adj* **fond of**, keen on, into [➡ APPRECIATION AND GRATITUDE; 535]

participant *n* **member**, contributor, contestant, applicant, partaker, accomplice [➡ COMPETITORS; 41] *Opposite*: observer

participate *v* **contribute**, partake, take part, join, join in, share, play a part, chip in (*informal*) [➡ PARTICIPATE; 292] *Opposite*: observe

participation *n* **contribution**, input, sharing, partaking, involvement, membership [➡ CONNECTIONS; 143] *Opposite*: observation

participatory *adj* **taking part**, participating, sharing, partaking, hands-on, involved [➡ PRESENT AND AVAILABLE; 11]

participle *type of* **grammatical term** [➡ ASPECTS OF LANGUAGE; 682]

particle 1 *n* **bit**, speck, spot, crumb, grain, fragment, fleck, flake, shard [➡ SMALL PIECES; 129] 2 *n* **iota**, bit, jot, scrap, shred, smidgen (*informal*), whit (*dated*) [➡ FEW, LITTLE, SMALL AMOUNT; 120] 3 *type of* **word class** [➡ ASPECTS OF LANGUAGE; 682]

parti-colored *adj* **variegated**, multicolored, pied, piebald, rainbow, motley [➡ DESCRIBING COLORS; 1226] *Opposite*: monochrome

particular 1 *adj* **specific**, precise, certain, exact, actual, individual [➡ EXACT; 203] *Opposite*: vague 2 *adj* **individual**, distinct, noteworthy, special, unique, specific [➡ EXTRAORDINARY; UNCOMMON; 205] *Opposite*: general 3 *adj* **exacting**, meticulous, scrupulous, fastidious, fussy, finicky, picky [➡ DIFFICULT TO PLEASE; 515] *Opposite*: relaxed

particularity 1 *n* **fastidiousness**, meticulousness, fussiness, carefulness, discrimination, exactitude, accuracy [➡ DIFFICULT TO PLEASE; 515] *Opposite*: recklessness 2 *n* **peculiarity**, characteristic, trait, idiosyncrasy, quirk, eccentricity [➡ PERSONAL ECCENTRICITIES; 493] 3 *n* **individuality**, distinctiveness, idiosyncrasy, singularity, originality, specialness, difference [➡ DIFFERENCE; 149] *Opposite*: similarity

particularize *v* **detail**, itemize, specify, enumerate, stipulate, spell out, describe, list, relate, delineate (*formal*) [➡ NAME AND DESCRIBE; 665]

particularly 1 *adv* **chiefly**, mainly, above all, predominantly, mostly, on the whole, principally [➡ MAINLY AND PRIMARILY; 140] 2 *adv* **exceptionally**, intensely, acutely, especially, specifically, remarkably, outstandingly, markedly [➡ TO A GREAT EXTENT; 132] *Opposite*: unexceptionally

particulars *n* **details**, facts, information, essentials, basics, statistics, data, the whole story, nitty-gritty (*informal*) [➡ BASIC DETAILS; 688]

parting *n* **leaving**, departure, separation, going, goodbye, sendoff, farewell, leave-taking (*literary*), valediction (*formal*) [➡ ENDS AND DEPARTURES; 54] *Opposite*: reunion

parting shot *n* **Parthian shot**, last word, final remark, retort, hostile remark, valediction (*formal*) [➡ CRITICISMS AND ANGRY OUTBURSTS; 50]

partisan 1 *n* **supporter**, follower, adherent, fan, member, enthusiast, devotee, sponsor, backer, champion [➡ DEVOTEES AND ADDICTED PEOPLE; 556] *Opposite*: opponent 2 *adj* **biased**, prejudiced, opinionated, one-sided, bigoted, limited, parochial, narrow-minded [➡ NEGATIVE INTELLECTUAL CHARACTERISTICS; 525] *Opposite*: impartial

partisanship 1 *n* **support**, devotion, membership, sponsorship, adherence, allegiance [➡ CONNECTIONS; 143] 2 *n* **bias**, prejudice, bigotry, narrow-mindedness, one-sidedness [➡ PREJUDICE; 550] *Opposite*: impartiality

partition 1 *n* **divider**, panel, dividing wall, screen, sliding doors, room divider, wall, barrier [➡ WALLS AND PARTITIONS; 1104] 2 *n* **separation**, division, rift, split, dividing up, detachment, breaking up, severance [➡ SEPARATE AND DIVIDE; 401] 3 *v* **divide**, separate, wall off, fence off, split, segregate, break up, divide up, subdivide, apportion, divvy up (*informal*) [➡ SEPARATE AND DIVIDE; 401]

partly *adv* **partially**, in part, somewhat, partway, moderately, comparatively, fairly, relatively, incompletely [➡ TO A CERTAIN EXTENT; 136] *Opposite*: wholly

partner 1 *n* **spouse**, wife, husband, other half, lover, mate, companion, significant other [➡ SEXUAL AND ROMANTIC RELATIONSHIPS; 964] 2 *n* **associate**, colleague, collaborator, equal, coworker, affiliate, mate (*UK*) [➡ COLLEAGUES AND EQUALS; 967] *Opposite*: superior 3 *v* **team up**, unite, join, link up, accompany, escort, consort (*formal*) [➡ ACCOMPANY AND FOLLOW; 337]

partner in crime *n* **accessory**, accomplice, crony, associate, sidekick (*informal*), buddy (*informal*) [➡ COLLEAGUES AND EQUALS; 967]

partnership 1 *n* **company**, business, firm, corporation, enterprise, joint venture, conglomerate, trust, syndicate, cartel, combine, organization [➡ BUSINESS ENTERPRISES AND RELATED BODIES; 792] 2 *n* **affiliation**, association, collaboration, companionship, alliance, relationship, interest, connection, cooperation [➡ RELATIONSHIP TO ANOTHER; 973] *Opposite*: opposition

partridge 1 *type of* **fowl** [➡ FOOD BIRDS; 999] 2 *type of* **meat** [➡ TYPES AND CUTS OF MEAT; 1177]

part-time *adj* **job-sharing**, evening, weekend, freelance, casual [➡ EMPLOYMENT STATUS; 831] *Opposite*: full-time

part-timer *n* **part-time worker**, job-sharer, freelance, freelancer, casual, employee [➡ WORKERS; 836] *Opposite*: full-timer

part-time work *n* [➡ TYPES OF WORK; 835]

part-time worker n [⇒WORKERS; 836]

parturition (formal) n [⇒REPRODUCTION AND HEREDITY; 725]

partway adv **partly**, partially, halfway, in part, somewhat, incompletely [⇒TO A CERTAIN EXTENT; 136] Opposite: completely

party 1 n **social gathering**, gathering, festivity, revelry, event, social, merrymaking, celebration, bash, get-together (informal), shindig (informal), thrash (dated informal) [⇒PARTIES, DANCES, AND CELEBRATIONS; 37] 2 n **faction**, political party, interest group, society, splinter group, cabal, caucus, coalition, bloc, group, organization [⇒GROUPS WITH A COMMON INTEREST; 938] 3 n **participant**, accomplice, accessory, partaker, contributor, assistant, associate, partner [⇒SUPPORTERS, PROTECTORS, AND COMPATRIOTS; 970] 4 n **company**, band, gang, crew, contingent, team, sector, faction, section, delegation, sect, troop, denomination, side, group, outfit (informal) [⇒GROUPS OF PEOPLE; 935] 5 n (formal) **individual**, person, one, person concerned, someone [⇒PERSON; 931] 6 v (informal) **celebrate**, have fun, revel, whoop it up (informal), paint the town red (informal), let your hair down (informal), hang loose (informal), get down (informal dated), groove (informal dated) [⇒LEISURE AND RECREATION; 874]

party animal (informal) n [⇒PLEASURE-SEEKERS AND HEDONISTS; 886]

party crasher n **interloper**, trespasser, invader, persona non grata, gatecrasher (UK) [⇒STRANGERS; 972] Opposite: guest

partygoer n **celebrator**, socializer, guest, sociable person, attendee, partyer, socialite, party animal (informal) [⇒PLEASURE-SEEKERS AND HEDONISTS; 886]

party line n **official policy**, official position, party policy, official line, dogma, doctrine, policy [⇒GOVERNMENT POLICIES; 810]

party piece n [⇒ENTERTAINMENT; 872]

party pooper (informal) n **spoilsport**, killjoy, nonparticipant, bore, wet blanket (informal) [⇒GRUMPY AND NEGATIVE PEOPLE; 953]

parvenu n **upstart**, nouveau riche, social climber, arriviste, pretender [⇒CLASS STATUS; 889]

pascal type of **SI unit** [⇒SIZE AND DIMENSIONS; 1192]

pashmina type of **accessory** [⇒ACCESSORIES, MILLINERY, AND LINGERIE; 867]

pass 1 v **go by**, overtake, exceed, outdo, surpass, overstep, bypass [⇒MOVE PAST, INTO, OR THROUGH SOMETHING; 331] Opposite: stop 2 v **elapse**, go by, pass by, lapse, go, slip away [⇒HAPPEN; 27] 3 v **hand over**, give, deliver, hand, forward, hand out, distribute, dispatch, spread, circulate, disseminate, send on (UK) [⇒DISPENSE, RATION, AND DISTRIBUTE; 434] Opposite: withhold 4 v **happen**, occur, arise, take place, come about, appear, come up, issue, ensue, befall (archaic or literary) [⇒HAPPEN; 27] 5 v **approve**, ratify, adopt, permit, accept, authorize [⇒APPROVE AND CONFIRM; 646] 6 v **succeed**, qualify, make the grade, excel, exceed, surpass [⇒SUCCEED AND WIN; 79] Opposite: fail 7 v **throw**, kick, hit, toss, lob, pitch, fling, flip, cast, hurl, chuck (informal) [⇒MOVE SOMETHING THROUGH THE AIR; 334] 8 n **permit**, license, authorization, card, documentation, badge, clearance, permission [⇒OFFICIAL DOCUMENTS; 586] Opposite: ban 9 n **passage**, gorge, route, corridor, valley, road, way, gap [⇒MOUNTAINS AND HILLS; 1044] 10 n **toss**, kick, hit, throw, lob, fling, pitch, cast, hurl, flip [⇒MOVE SOMETHING THROUGH THE AIR; 334]

11 n **state of affairs**, state, plight, predicament, circumstances, condition, situation, fix (informal), jam (informal) [⇒DIFFICULT SITUATIONS; 72]

passable 1 adj **traversable**, crossable, drivable, safe, penetrable, okay (informal) [⇒IN GOOD REPAIR; 1232] Opposite: impassable 2 adj **acceptable**, adequate, good enough, all right, respectable, tolerable, satisfactory, fair, decent [⇒ACCEPTABLE AND PASSABLE; 219] Opposite: unacceptable

passably adv **acceptably**, adequately, tolerably, reasonably, respectably, satisfactorily [⇒ACCEPTABLE AND PASSABLE; 219] Opposite: inadequately

passage 1 n **way through**, way, road, channel, course, means of access, route, opening, path, track, trail [⇒PATHWAYS; 1110] 2 n **section**, part, chapter, paragraph, segment, bit, extract, article, clause, piece [⇒PARTS OF BOOKS AND DOCUMENTS; 593] 3 n **corridor**, pathway, walkway, hall, hallway, gangway, path, passageway [⇒PATHWAYS; 1110] 4 n **approval**, enactment, passing, ratification, acceptance, establishment, validation, legitimization [⇒APPROVE AND CONFIRM; 646] 5 n **journey**, voyage, transfer, run, crossing, expedition, transit, trip [⇒TRAVEL: JOURNEYS AND TRIPS; 318] 6 n **migration**, movement, exodus, flood, transit, progress, growth, motion [⇒TRAVEL: JOURNEYS AND TRIPS; 318]

passageway n **passage**, corridor, pathway, hallway, hall, walkway, gangway [⇒PATHWAYS; 1110]

pass away 1 v **die**, expire, succumb, pass on, kick the bucket (slang), depart (formal) [⇒DIE; 922] 2 v **come to an end**, finish, end, cease, terminate [⇒CEASE TO EXIST; 221]

pass by 1 v **disregard**, overlook, pass over, ignore, look the other way, let pass, close the eyes to [⇒NOT PAY ATTENTION; 764] 2 v **overtake**, go by, pass, surpass, leave behind, overstep, elude, outstrip, outrun, exceed [⇒MOVE PAST, INTO, OR THROUGH SOMETHING; 331] 3 v **reject**, turn down, decline, refuse, ignore, decide against [⇒DENY AND REJECT; 644]

pass down v [⇒BEQUEATH AND BEQUESTS; 432]

passé adj **out-of-date**, old, faded, aged, worn-out, archaic, done to death, obsolescent, unfashionable, obsolete, dated, old-fashioned, outdated, outmoded, behind the times, antiquated, outworn, old hat (informal) [⇒OLD, OLD-FASHIONED; 167] Opposite: fashionable

See Compare and Contrast at **old-fashioned**.

passed on adj [⇒DEAD AND DYING; 925]

passenger n **traveler**, customer, fare, commuter, rail user [⇒TRAVEL: TRAVELERS AND WALKERS; 319]

passenger seat type of **internal feature** [⇒INTERNAL PARTS OF A VEHICLE; 1146]

passer-by n **onlooker**, bystander, spectator, witness, passer, pedestrian, watcher [⇒STRANGERS; 972]

pass for v **impersonate**, pass as, look like, go as, do as, pose as, masquerade, carry off [⇒PRETEND AND MIMIC; 60]

passim (formal) adv **here and there**, throughout, frequently, in various places, in several places, everywhere [⇒WRITTEN CONVENTIONS; 599]

passing 1 adj **transitory**, short-lived, ephemeral, fleeting, fly-by-night, momentary, temporary, perishable, impermanent, fugitive, transient [➡ HAPPENING QUICKLY; 104] *Opposite*: permanent **2** *adj* **cursory**, quick, casual, superficial, surface, hasty, shallow, slight, slapdash [➡ HAPPENING QUICKLY; 104] *Opposite*: in depth **3** *n* **departure**, departing, leaving, disappearance, desertion, leave-taking (*literary*) [➡ ENDS AND DEPARTURES; 54] **4** *n* **death**, dying, passing away, end, departure, passing on, demise (*formal*) [➡ DEATH AND BEREAVEMENT; 927]

See Compare and Contrast at **temporary**.

passing comment *n* [➡ ONE-WAY COMMUNICATION; 49]

passion **1** *n* **fervor**, ardor, obsession, infatuation, excitement, enthusiasm, zeal, craze, delight, fervidness, emotion, fervency [➡ POSITIVE IMPATIENCE, ENTHUSIASM, AND ALERTNESS; 537] **2** *n* **desire**, hunger, thirst, appetite, craving, lust, urge, ache [➡ DESIRE AND WANT; 579] **3** *n* **rage**, fury, outburst, fever, anger, fit, paroxysm, storm, dudgeon, wrath, temper, furor, ire (*formal*), choler (*literary or archaic*) [➡ IRRITATION AND ANGER; 541]

See Compare and Contrast at **love**.

passionate **1** *adj* **fervent**, ardent, zealous, avid, obsessive, fanatical, adoring, loving, impassioned, vehement, fervid, enthusiastic [➡ POSITIVE IMPATIENCE, ENTHUSIASM, AND ALERTNESS; 537] *Opposite*: indifferent **2** *adj* **fiery**, quick-tempered, incensed, inflamed, enraged, fuming, infuriated, raving, hot-blooded [➡ EXCESSIVE SENSITIVITY; 511] *Opposite*: easygoing

passionately *adv* **fervently**, ardently, avidly, single-mindedly, overpoweringly, keenly, zealously, vehemently, fervidly, enthusiastically [➡ POSITIVE IMPATIENCE, ENTHUSIASM, AND ALERTNESS; 537] *Opposite*: indifferently

passionflower *type of* **climber** [➡ CLIMBERS; 1033]

passion fruit *type of* **fruit** [➡ FRUIT AND VEGETABLES; 1176]

passionless *adj* **loveless**, detached, unromantic, emotionless, frigid, dispassionate, unloving, calm, unemotional, cold, cold-blooded, insensitive, impervious, thick-skinned [➡ NEUTRALITY AND INDIFFERENCE; 553] *Opposite*: passionate

passive *adj* **inert**, inactive, unreceptive, reflexive, flaccid, lifeless, submissive, impassive, unresponsive, docile [➡ LIFELESS, LAZY, AND UNENTHUSIASTIC; 506] *Opposite*: active

passiveness *n* **inactiveness**, inaction, inactivity, non-participation, indifference, apathy, impassiveness, unresponsiveness, passivity, submissiveness, docility [➡ LIFELESS, LAZY, AND UNENTHUSIASTIC; 506] *Opposite*: activeness

passivity *n* **inactivity**, inactiveness, inaction, non-participation, indifference, apathy, unresponsiveness, impassiveness, passiveness, docility [➡ LIFELESS, LAZY, AND UNENTHUSIASTIC; 506] *Opposite*: activeness

pass judgment *v* **give opinion**, judge, criticize, condemn, deliver judgment, adjudicate [➡ PROTEST AND EXPRESS DISAPPROVAL; 642]

pass muster *v* **measure up**, be all right, check out, qualify, do, be okay (*informal*), be up to scratch (*informal*) [➡ ACCEPTABLE AND PASSABLE; 219]

pass off *v* **masquerade**, pretend, misrepresent, palm off, falsify, fob off [➡ DECEPTION AND LIES; 660]

pass on *v* **convey**, send, forward, impart, communicate, transmit [➡ INFORM, ANNOUNCE, AND ISSUE; 611]

pass out **1** *v* **faint**, black out, lose consciousness, have a fainting fit, swoon, keel over (*informal*), conk out (*informal*) [➡ BECOME SICK, TREAT, AND RECOVER; 728] *Opposite*: come to **2** *v* **distribute**, hand out, give out, assign, deal out, administer, circulate, dispense, spread, dish out (*informal*), share out (*UK*) [➡ DISPENSE, RATION, AND DISTRIBUTE; 434]

pass over *v* **ignore**, neglect, discount, disregard, let go, omit [➡ NOT PAY ATTENTION; 764] *Opposite*: consider

passport **1** *n* **official document**, travel document, ID, papers, permit, visa, pass, travel permit, credentials [➡ OFFICIAL DOCUMENTS; 586] **2** *n* **access**, gateway, entry, opening, door, key, entrance, channel, admission, avenue, portal (*literary*) [➡ BEGINNINGS; 53]

pass the buck (*informal*) *v* **shift the blame**, evade responsibility, lay something at somebody's door [➡ ACCUSE, BLAME, AND CRITICIZE; 641]

pass through *v* **cross**, go through, lead through, traverse, move across, navigate [➡ TRAVEL: WAYS OF TRAVELING; 320]

pass up *v* [➡ FORGO AND DENY ONESELF; 449]

pass with flying colors *v* [➡ SUCCEED AND WIN; 79]

password *n* **code word**, open sesame, secret word, PIN, key, secret code, watchword, keyword [➡ ASPECTS OF LANGUAGE; 682]

past **1** *adj* **previous**, historical, earlier, former, bygone, ancient, older, preceding, long-ago, early, late, prior [➡ BEFORE, FIRST, AND PRECEDING; 163] *Opposite*: future **2** *adj* **elapsed**, completed, accomplished, over and done, done, ended, gone, forgotten, over, ancient history, spent [➡ PAST; 84] *Opposite*: ongoing **3** *n* **history**, earlier period, ancient times, times of yore, antiquity, long ago, yesterday, yesteryear, bygone days [➡ PAST; 84] *Opposite*: future

pasta *n* [➡ BREAD, FLOUR, AND BREAD PRODUCTS; 1179]

pasta

◆ *types of pasta*
cannelloni, capellini, cappelletti, conchiglie, fettuccine, fusilli, lasagna, linguine, macaroni, penne, ravioli, rigatoni, spaghetti, tagliatelle, tortellini, vermicelli

paste **1** *n* **adhesive**, glue, gum, fixative, wallpaper paste, cement [➡ ADHESIVES; 1271] **2** *n* **slime**, gunk (*informal*), goo (*informal*), glop (*informal*), goop (*informal*) [➡ LOTIONS, PASTES, AND GELS; 1272] **3** *v* **glue**, stick, gum, fix, bond, attach [➡ FASTEN, LINK, AND JOIN; 408]

pastel **1** *adj* **pale**, light, soft, muted, neutral, gentle, wishy-washy (*informal*) [➡ DESCRIBING COLORS; 1226] *Opposite*: vivid **2** *n* **crayon**, colored chalk, chalk, oil pastel [➡ WRITING AND DRAWING IMPLEMENTS, AND MEDIA; 601]

pastern *part of* **horse** [➡ HORSES; 985]

pasteurization *n* **sterilization**, heat treatment, purification, decontamination, disinfection, sanitization [➡ CLEAN AND POLISH; 403]

pasteurize v **sterilize**, heat, purify, decontaminate, disinfect, sanitize [➡ COOKING AND FOOD PREPARATION; 353]

pasteurized adj **sterilized**, treated, purified, decontaminated, disinfected, sanitized [➡ NOT IN A NATURAL STATE; 1215]

past history n [➡ PAST; 84]

pastiche n **imitation**, spoof, satire, lampoon, parody, takeoff (informal) [➡ JOKES AND TEASING; 674]

pastime n **hobby**, interest, activity, pursuit, amusement, distraction, diversion, entertainment [➡ LEISURE AND RECREATION; 874]

pastiness n [➡ COMPLEXION; 480]

pasting (informal) n **beating**, defeat, thrashing, drubbing, pounding, battering, hammering (informal), licking (informal), hiding (informal), whipping (informal) [➡ BEAT AND DEFEAT; 80]

past love n **first love**, ex (informal), old flame (informal), blast from the past (informal) [➡ SEXUAL AND ROMANTIC RELATIONSHIPS; 964]

pastor n **minister**, priest, vicar, clergyman, cleric [➡ RELIGIOUS PEOPLE; 778]

pastoral adj **rural**, rustic, countryside, countrified, idyllic, bucolic [➡ THE COUNTRYSIDE AND OUTDOOR SPACES; 1071] Opposite: urban

pastrami type of **processed meat** [➡ TYPES AND CUTS OF MEAT; 1177]

pastry 1 n **dough**, shortcrust pastry, puff pastry, flaky pastry, choux pastry, filo pastry, crust [➡ BREAD, FLOUR, AND BREAD PRODUCTS; 1179] 2 n **pie**, tart, tartlet, flan, Danish pastry [➡ CAKES, COOKIES, AND DESSERTS; 1181]

pastry chef type of **person who works in restaurants** [➡ DOMESTIC AND KITCHEN WORKERS; 850]

pastry fork type of **flatware** [➡ TABLEWARE, FLATWARE, AND KITCHENWARE; 861]

pastry slice type of **flatware** [➡ TABLEWARE, FLATWARE, AND KITCHENWARE; 861]

pasturage n [➡ THE COUNTRYSIDE AND OUTDOOR SPACES; 1071]

pasture n **meadow**, meadowland, fallow, grassland, prairie, grass [➡ THE COUNTRYSIDE AND OUTDOOR SPACES; 1071]

pastureland n [➡ THE COUNTRYSIDE AND OUTDOOR SPACES; 1071]

pasty 1 adj **pale**, unhealthy-looking, ashen, pallid, wan, sickly, white, pasty-faced, gray, anemic [➡ COMPLEXION; 480] 2 n (UK) **turnover**, meat pie, pie, pastry, Cornish pasty (UK), sausage roll (UK), steak pie (UK) [➡ BREAD, FLOUR, AND BREAD PRODUCTS; 1179]

pasty-faced adj **pasty**, pale, unhealthy-looking, ashen, pallid, wan, sickly, gray, white, anemic [➡ COMPLEXION; 480]

pat 1 v **tap**, touch, stroke, caress, massage, slap, palm [➡ CONTACT: TOUCH; 412] 2 v **shape**, smooth, work, knead, mold, flatten [➡ CONTACT: EXERT PRESSURE; 414] 3 n **touch**, tap, stroke [➡ CONTACT: TOUCH; 412] 4 adv **perfectly**, faultlessly, fluently, impeccably, by heart, word for word, verbatim [➡ EXACT; 203]

pataca type of **currency** [➡ CURRENCIES; 798]

patch 1 n **cover**, reinforcement, covering, square [➡ COVERS AND COATINGS; 1246] 2 n **area**, spot, blotch, bit, smear, piece, stain [➡ AREA AND RANGE; 111] 3 n **badge**, award, stripe, tag, square, decoration, insignia [➡ SYMBOLS, SIGNS, AND NUMBERS; 596] 4 type of **software** [➡ COMPUTERS AND COMPUTING; 1127] 5 v **repair**, cover, mend, strengthen, reinforce, fix, patch up [➡ REPAIR AND MEND; 376]

patchiness 1 n **unevenness**, intermittence, bittiness, sparseness [➡ UNFINISHEDNESS; 239] Opposite: evenness 2 n **variability**, inconsistency, unreliability, irregularity, unevenness [➡ FINITENESS, VARIABILITY, AND TRANSIENCE; 96] Opposite: consistency

patchouli n **aromatic oil**, oil, perfume, scent, essential oil, aromatherapy oil, fragrance [➡ PERSONAL HYGIENE; 491]

patch up v **mend**, repair, fix, strengthen, reinforce, cover, sew up, patch [➡ REPAIR AND MEND; 376]

patchwork 1 n **mixture**, mix, collage, assortment, potpourri, mixed bag, mess, crazy quilt, hodgepodge, mélange (literary or formal) [➡ COLLECTIONS AND MIXTURES OF THINGS; 1244] 2 adj **pieced together**, jury-rigged, makeshift, collaged, jerrybuilt, piecemeal, jerry-rigged [➡ IN BAD REPAIR; 1234]

patchy 1 adj **occasional**, irregular, sporadic, intermittent, sparse [➡ UNFINISHEDNESS; 239] 2 adj **variable**, inconsistent, unreliable, erratic, unpredictable, irregular, intermittent [➡ FINITENESS, VARIABILITY, AND TRANSIENCE; 96]

pate (archaic or humorous) n **head**, crown, cranium, skull, noggin (dated informal), bean (dated informal), poll (archaic) [➡ PARTS OF THE BODY: HEAD; 692]

pâté type of **processed meat** [➡ TYPES AND CUTS OF MEAT; 1177]

patella type of **bone** [➡ THE BONES AND JOINTS; 719]

paten n [➡ RELIGIOUS OBJECTS; 779]

patent 1 n **copyright**, charter, right [➡ OFFICIAL DOCUMENTS; 586] 2 adj **clear**, obvious, blatant, bald-faced, flagrant, barefaced, out-and-out, manifest, self-evident, arrant [➡ PERCEPTIBLE; 25] Opposite: unclear

patent leather type of **leather** [➡ FABRICS; 1132]

paterfamilias n **father**, head of household, head, headman, paternalist [➡ OLDER GENERATION RELATIVES; 959]

paternal adj **fatherly**, parental, nurturing, protective, guiding [➡ RELATIONSHIP TO ANOTHER; 973]

paternalism n **authoritarianism**, interventionism, protectiveness, overprotectiveness, control [➡ RELATIONSHIP TO ANOTHER; 973]

paternalistic adj **authoritarian**, patriarchal, protective, overprotective [➡ RELATIONSHIP TO ANOTHER; 973]

paternal name n [➡ NAME AND DESCRIBE; 665]

paternity n **fatherhood**, parenthood, role, status, responsibility [➡ RELATIONSHIP TO ANOTHER; 973]

paternoster 1 n **elevator**, platform, compartment, lift (UK) [➡ STAIRS AND STORIES; 1102] 2 part of **building** [➡ PARTS OF A BUILDING; 1095]

path 1 n **track**, trail, pathway, footpath, route [➡ PATHWAYS; 1110] 2 n **course**, route, way, orbit, direction, line [➡ DIRECTION OF MOTION; 345] 3 type of **secondary road** [➡ ROADS; 1106]

pathetic 1 *adj* **pitiful**, sad, moving, tragic, doleful, pitiable, wretched, touching, distressing, heartbreaking, heartrending [➡ EMOTIONALLY UNPLEASANT AND UPSETTING; 227] **2** *adj* (*informal*) **contemptible**, useless, risible, derisory, laughable, feeble, woeful, pitiful, ridiculous, lamentable, absurd, ludicrous [➡ INAPPROPRIATE AND UNSUITABLE; 224]

See Compare and Contrast at **moving**.

pathfinder *n* **leader**, trailblazer, scout, pioneer, guide [➡ TRAVEL: TRAVELERS AND WALKERS; 319]

pathological 1 *adj* **extreme**, compulsive, uncontrolled, unreasonable, unreasoning, obsessive, irrational, neurotic [➡ ECCENTRICITY AND IRRATIONALITY; 562] **2** *adj* **medical**, clinical, scientific, diagnostic, immunological, biochemical, cellular [➡ SICKNESS; 729] **3** *adj* **morbid**, systemic, allergic, viral, bacteriological [➡ SICKNESS; 729]

pathos *n* **sadness**, tragedy, bleakness, despair, anguish [➡ SADNESS, DISTRESS, AND DESPAIR; 539]

pathway *n* **trail**, path, way, lane, alleyway, conduit, corridor, passageway, route [➡ PATHWAYS; 1110]

patience 1 *n* **endurance**, staying power, stamina, persistence, perseverance [➡ STRENGTH OF WILL; 501] *Opposite*: impatience **2** *n* **tolerance**, fortitude, serenity, imperturbability, unflappability, placidity, forbearance (*formal*) [➡ CONFIDENCE AND COMPOSURE; 499] *Opposite*: impatience

patient 1 *adj* **enduring**, persistent, persevering, easygoing [➡ STRENGTH OF WILL; 501] **2** *adj* **tolerant**, long-suffering, serene, fortitudinous, imperturbable, unflappable, good-natured, understanding, uncomplaining, forbearing (*formal*) [➡ CONFIDENCE AND COMPOSURE; 499]

patiently *adv* **uncomplainingly**, long-sufferingly, tolerantly, good-naturedly, unwearyingly [➡ CONFIDENCE AND COMPOSURE; 499] *Opposite*: impatiently

patina 1 *n* **discoloration**, tarnishing, staining, coating, verdigris [➡ DESCRIBING COLORS; 1226] **2** *n* **sheen**, shine, gloss, luster [➡ VISUAL TEXTURE; 1221] **3** *n* **layer**, veneer, covering, coating, coat, skin [➡ COVERS AND COATINGS; 1246]

patio *part of* **garden** [➡ GARDENS; 1074]

patois 1 *n* **dialect**, vernacular, idiom, language, speech, lingo (*informal*) [➡ THE SPOKEN WORD; 671] **2** *n* **jargon**, slang, cant, patter, lingo (*informal*), argot [➡ ASPECTS OF LANGUAGE; 682]

pat on the back (*informal*) *n* **handshake**, round of applause, endorsement, seal of approval [➡ GESTURES AND GESTICULATION; 653]

patriarch 1 *n* **head of family**, paterfamilias, father, head, headman [➡ OLDER GENERATION RELATIVES; 959] *Opposite*: matriarch **2** *n* **bishop**, archbishop, prelate, leader [➡ RELIGIOUS PEOPLE; 778]

patriarchal *adj* **male-controlled**, male, masculine, macho [➡ STYLES AND SYSTEMS OF GOVERNMENT; 806]

patrician 1 *adj* **aristocratic**, refined, upper-class, noble, blue-blooded, titled, well-bred, highborn (*literary*) [➡ CLASS STATUS; 889] **2** *n* **aristocrat**, noble, peer, squire [➡ RULERS AND ARISTOCRACY; 823]

patricide 1 *n* **murder**, killing, parricide, slaughter, manslaughter, homicide [➡ CAUSES OF DEATH; 921] **2** *n* **murderer**, killer, parricide, slaughterer, homicide, slayer (*formal or literary*) [➡ PEOPLE WHO KILL; 924]

patriot *n* **nationalist**, loyalist, flag-waver [➡ DEVOTEES AND ADDICTED PEOPLE; 556]

patriotic *adj* **nationalistic**, loyal, jingoistic, xenophobic, chauvinistic [➡ PHILOSOPHIES AND BELIEFS; 780]

patriotism *n* **loyalty**, partisanship, nationalism, jingoism, xenophobia, chauvinism [➡ PHILOSOPHIES AND BELIEFS; 780]

patrol 1 *n* **tour**, round, beat, circuit, perambulation, guard, duty [➡ WORK-RELATED ACTIVITIES; 834] **2** *n* **unit**, detachment, squad, troop, group [➡ MILITARY PERSONNEL; 828] **3** *v* **guard**, watch, tour, make the rounds, walk the beat, traverse [➡ PROCEED AND GO; 305]

patron 1 *n* **sponsor**, benefactor, supporter, investor, backer, donor [➡ REPRESENTATIVES AND PATRONS; 968] **2** *n* **customer**, client, diner, user, shopper [➡ PURCHASER; 424]

See Compare and Contrast at **backer**.

patronage *n* **investment**, backing, aid, sponsorship, benefaction, pork barrel (*slang*), pap (*slang*) [➡ GIFTS; 438]

patronize 1 *v* (*formal*) **frequent**, shop at, use, utilize, visit, go to [➡ EXIST IN A PLACE; 19] **2** *v* **be condescending to**, demean, denigrate, belittle, talk down to [➡ INSULTS, ABUSE, AND SWEARING; 658]

patronizing *adj* **condescending**, superior, denigrating, belittling, full of yourself, supercilious [➡ MOCKING AND DISMISSIVE; 636]

patronymic *n* [➡ NAME AND DESCRIBE; 665]

patter 1 *n* **tapping**, drumming, beating, pitter-patter, rhythm, drumbeat [➡ IMPACT SOUNDS; 1260] **2** *n* **speech**, script, talk, spiel (*informal*) [➡ ONE-WAY COMMUNICATION; 49] **3** *n* **jargon**, slang, cant, patois, argot, lingo (*informal*) [➡ ASPECTS OF LANGUAGE; 682] **4** *v* **tap**, drum, beat, pitter-patter, knock, clatter [➡ EMIT SOUNDS THROUGH IMPACT AND ABRASION; 365] **5** *v* **jabber**, prattle, rattle on, rant, go on and on, burble (*informal*) [➡ CHATTER AND BABBLE; 617]

pattern 1 *n* **prototype**, outline, model, example, blueprint, mold, guide, sample, precedent, archetype [➡ REPRESENTATIONS AND GENERAL EXAMPLES; 65] **2** *n* **design**, decoration, shape, outline, form, arrangement, configuration, array, display, repetition, tessellation [➡ PATTERNS; 1225]

patterned *adj* **decorated**, spotted, lined, squared, dotted, checked, striped, tartan, plaid, paisley, psychedelic, speckled, floral, flowery, decorative, checkered, mottled, marbled, stippled, dappled, veined [➡ DESCRIBING PATTERNS; 1227]

patty 1 *n* **pie**, pastry, meat pie, pasty (*UK*) [➡ BREAD, FLOUR, AND BREAD PRODUCTS; 1179] **2** *n* **cake**, burger, rissole [➡ TYPES AND CUTS OF MEAT; 1177]

paucity *n* **dearth**, scarcity, rareness, scantiness, lack, rarity, scarceness [➡ TOO FEW, TOO LITTLE; 122]

paunch *n* **stomach**, belly, gut, potbelly, pot (*informal*), beer gut (*slang*), beer belly (*slang*), bay window (*slang*) [➡ EXTRA WEIGHT; 478]

paunchy *adj* **potbellied**, portly, corpulent, fleshy, plump, tubby (*informal*) [➡ BUILD; 477]

pauper *n* **poor person**, down-and-out, bankrupt, indigent (*formal*) [➡ POOR PEOPLE; 896]

pause 1 *v* **stop**, wait, break off, rest, stop what you're doing, adjourn, hesitate [➡ STOP ACTING; 264] *Opposite*: continue **2** *v* **hesitate**, falter, waver, wait, hold back, stall [➡ HESITATE; 272] **3** *v* **linger**, stop, rest, tarry, halt, hang back [➡ STOP ACTING; 264] *Opposite*: move on **4** *n* **silence**, awkward moment, hiatus, gap [➡ PAUSES AND PHASES; 56] **5** *n* **break**, recess, suspension, intermission, hiatus, stop, breather (*informal*) [➡ PERIODS OF REST; 91] *Opposite*: continuation

See Compare and Contrast at **hesitate**.

pave *v* **cover**, surface, floor, tile, flag, concrete [➡ DECORATE, ADORN, AND APPLY COATINGS; 405]

paved *adj* **cemented**, flagged, surfaced, covered, tiled, concreted, concrete [➡ DECORATE, ADORN, AND APPLY COATINGS; 405]

pavement **1** *n* **road surface**, roadway, asphalt, street, tarmac [➡ ROADS; 1106] **2** *n* (*UK*) **path**, footpath, roadside, pathway, sidewalk, walkway [➡ PATHWAYS; 1110]

pave the way *v* [➡ PREPARE FOR ACTION; 289]

pavilion *type of* **outbuilding** [➡ ANCILLARY BUILDINGS; 1080]

paving *n* **flagging**, pavement, tiling, flooring, concrete, stonework [➡ BUILDING MATERIALS; 1077]

paving slab *n* [➡ BUILDING MATERIALS; 1077]

paving stone *n* [➡ BUILDING MATERIALS; 1077]

pavlova *type of* **dessert** [➡ CAKES, COOKIES, AND DESSERTS; 1181]

Pavo *type of* **constellation** [➡ HEAVENLY BODIES; 1061]

paw **1** *n* (*informal*) **hand**, appendage, mitt (*slang*) [➡ PARTS OF THE BODY: ARM AND HAND; 695] **2** *v* **maul**, molest, fondle, stroke, touch, grope (*slang*), pet (*UK*) [➡ CONTACT: TOUCH; 412]

pawl *n* [➡ PARTS OF MACHINES AND TOOLS; 1118]

pawn *v* **trade in**, wager, put up, place as collateral, pledge, forfeit, stake, hock (*slang*) [➡ SELL; 441] *Opposite*: redeem

pay **1** *v* **disburse**, reimburse, compensate, forfeit, recompense, give, remunerate, repay, shell out (*informal*) [➡ GIVE MONEY; 433] *Opposite*: receive **2** *n* **wage**, salary, recompense, reimbursement, earnings, compensation, remuneration, fee, hire, stipend, emolument (*formal or humorous*) [➡ INCOME; 460]

See Compare and Contrast at **wage**.

payable *adj* **owed**, billed, due, allocated, to be paid, mature, outstanding, unsettled [➡ OWE AND DESERVE; 465]

pay-as-you-earn *n* [➡ TAX AND TAXATION; 802]

pay attention *v* [➡ PAY ATTENTION; 765]

pay back **1** *v* **repay**, reimburse, pay off, settle up, restore, ante up (*informal*) [➡ GIVE MONEY; 433] *Opposite*: keep **2** *v* **retaliate**, get even, take revenge, give tit for tat, settle scores, make somebody pay, square, get somebody (*informal*) [➡ VENGEANCE AND REVENGE; 685]

payback **1** *n* **return**, reimbursement, profit, remu-

neration, repayment, settlement, benefits [➡ INCOME; 460] **2** *n* (*informal*) **revenge**, retaliation, retribution, vengeance, reprisal, settling of scores [➡ VENGEANCE AND REVENGE; 685]

paycheck *n* **wages**, salary, pay, payment, earnings, income [➡ INCOME; 460]

pay court to (*dated*) *v* [➡ ESTABLISHING RELATIONSHIPS WITH OTHERS; 974]

PAYE (*UK*) *n* **pay-as-you-earn**, income tax, revenue, tax, tax at source, direct tax [➡ TAX AND TAXATION; 802]

payee *n* **recipient**, beneficiary, receiver, collector, acceptor, heir [➡ SELLERS; 442] *Opposite*: payer

pay envelope *n* **wages**, salary, paycheck, earnings, income, payment [➡ INCOME; 460]

payer *n* **spender**, financier, customer, client, paymaster, bursar [➡ PURCHASER; 424] *Opposite*: payee

pay heed *v* [➡ PAY ATTENTION; 765]

pay homage to *v* [➡ PRAISE AND ENCOURAGE; 647]

pay in *v* **deposit**, bank, put away, put in, save, invest, lay aside, coffer [➡ ACCOUNTING, BANKING, AND BUDGETING; 799] *Opposite*: withdraw

paying guest *n* [➡ INHABITANTS; 857]

payload *n* **cargo**, load, freight, shipment, consignment, goods, contents, lading, burden [➡ TRANSPORTATION, TRANSPORTERS, AND CARGOS; 322]

payment *n* **sum**, expense, compensation, recompense, disbursement, fee [➡ INCOME; 460]

payment gateway *n* [➡ E-COMMERCE; 1129]

pay no attention *v* [➡ NOT PAY ATTENTION; 764]

pay no heed *v* [➡ NOT PAY ATTENTION; 764]

pay off **1** *v* **settle**, square, repay, pay back, reimburse, compensate, recompense, amortize, liquidate, discharge (*formal*) [➡ GIVE MONEY; 433] **2** *v* **succeed**, bear fruit, work, be effective, prosper, flourish [➡ SUCCEED AND WIN; 79]

payoff (*informal*) **1** *n* **payment**, settlement, reckoning, payout, remuneration [➡ INCOME; 460] **2** *n* **bribe**, graft, take, inducement, bribery, fix (*informal*) [➡ BRIBES; 440]

payola (*informal*) *n* **payment**, bribe, bribery, inducement, graft, palm greasing (*informal*), payoff (*informal*), fix (*informal*) [➡ BRIBES; 440]

payout **1** *n* **disbursement**, expenditure, expenses, outgoing, charge, overhead [➡ EXPENDITURE; 423] *Opposite*: income **2** *n* **payment**, pay, wages, money, cash, salary, payoff (*informal*) [➡ INCOME; 460]

payphone *type of* **telecommunications equipment** [➡ TELECOMMUNICATIONS; 1130]

payroll *n* **employees**, personnel, staff, workforce, workers, labor force [➡ THE WORK FORCE; 837]

paystub *n* **statement**, stub, record, note, pay, paycheck, payment, pay envelope, pay slip (*UK*) [➡ RECEIPTS AND INVOICES; 591]

pay tribute *v* [➡ PRAISE AND ENCOURAGE; 647]

PC 1 *type of* **computer** [➡COMPUTERS AND COMPUTING; 1127] **2** *n* (*UK*) [➡ THE POLICE, ARREST, AND PRETRIAL PROCEEDINGS; 818]

PDA *type of* **computer** [➡COMPUTERS AND COMPUTING; 1127]

pdq (*informal*) *adv* **immediately**, at once, quickly, fast, right away, ASAP, stat, forthwith, instantly, pretty damn quick (*informal*) [➡HAPPENING QUICKLY; 104] *Opposite*: at your leisure

pea *type of* **pulse** [➡PEAS AND BEANS; 1189]

peace 1 *n* **concord**, peacetime, harmony, armistice, reconciliation, ceasefire, accord, goodwill, amity (*formal*) [➡HARMONY; 155] *Opposite*: war **2** *n* **harmony**, calm, quiet, tranquility, stillness, silence, serenity [➡PEACEFULNESS AND GENTLENESS; 214] *Opposite*: uproar

peaceable 1 *adj* **peace-loving**, amiable, agreeable, easygoing, willing to please, compliant, unwarlike, nonbelligerent, nonviolent, diplomatic [➡FRIENDLINESS AND SOCIABILITY; 494] *Opposite*: aggressive **2** *adj* **tranquil**, peaceful, serene, harmonious, calm, quiet, ordered, restful [➡PEACEFULNESS AND GENTLENESS; 214] *Opposite*: chaotic

peaceably 1 *adv* **peacefully**, quietly, amiably, placidly, nonviolently, nonbelligerently, agreeably, compliantly, diplomatically [➡FRIENDLINESS AND SOCIABILITY; 494] *Opposite*: belligerently **2** *adv* **tranquilly**, peacefully, calmly, quietly, serenely, restfully, harmoniously [➡PEACEFULNESS AND GENTLENESS; 214] *Opposite*: noisily

peace agreement *n* **treaty**, truce, ceasefire, armistice, agreement [➡HARMONY; 155]

peace and quiet *n* [➡PEACEFULNESS AND GENTLENESS; 214]

peaceful 1 *adj* **quiet**, serene, calm, still, peaceable, undisturbed [➡PEACEFULNESS AND GENTLENESS; 214] *Opposite*: disordered **2** *adj* **nonviolent**, passive, diplomatic, peaceable, pacific [➡FRIENDLINESS AND SOCIABILITY; 494] *Opposite*: violent

peaceful coexistence *n* [➡RELATIONSHIP TO ANOTHER; 973]

peacefully *adv* **quietly**, serenely, calmly, peaceably, tranquilly [➡PEACEFULNESS AND GENTLENESS; 214] *Opposite*: manically (*informal*)

peacefulness *n* **serenity**, tranquillity, repose, placidity, quietness, quiet, hush [➡PEACEFULNESS AND GENTLENESS; 214]

peacekeeper *n* **intermediary**, mediator, go-between, diplomat, pacifist, negotiator, broker, interceder, conciliator [➡ADVISERS, JUDGES, AND ARBITERS; 971]

peacekeeping *n* **mediation**, intermediation, diplomacy, pacification, negotiation, international relations [➡NEGOTIATION AND DEBATE; 46]

peace-loving *adj* [➡FRIENDLINESS AND SOCIABILITY; 494]

peacemaker *n* **negotiator**, arbitrator, diplomat, mediator, intermediary, go-between, appeaser, pacifier [➡ADVISERS, JUDGES, AND ARBITERS; 971] *Opposite*: fighter

peacemaking *n* **reconciliation**, conciliation, mediation, arbitration, appeasement, pacification [➡NEGOTIATION AND DEBATE; 46]

peace offering *n* **olive branch**, apology, overture, approach, gesture, flag of truce [➡APOLOGIZE AND RETRACT; 683]

peace of mind *n* [➡PEACEFULNESS AND GENTLENESS; 214]

peacetime *n* **peace**, harmony, armistice, truce, ceasefire, reconciliation, amity (*formal*) [➡PEACEFULNESS AND GENTLENESS; 214]

peach 1 *n* (*informal*) **beauty**, pearl, wow (*informal*), honey (*informal*), jim-dandy (*informal*), humdinger (*slang*), dilly (*slang*) [➡AMAZING THINGS; 211] **2** *type of* **orange** [➡COLORS; 1224] **3** *type of* **fruit** [➡FRUIT AND VEGETABLES; 1176]

peach Melba *type of* **dessert** [➡CAKES, COOKIES, AND DESSERTS; 1181]

peachy 1 *adj* **peachlike**, downy, fuzzy, velvety, soft, smooth [➡PHYSICAL TEXTURE; 1222] **2** *adj* (*informal*) **excellent**, wonderful, nice, splendid, great (*informal*), fine (*informal*), cool (*slang*) [➡GOOD, WELL, BETTER; 183] *Opposite*: terrible

pea coat *type of* **overcoat** [➡GARMENTS AND OUTFITS; 865]

peacock 1 *n* **egoist**, exhibitionist, fop, show-off (*informal*), dandy (*dated*), coxcomb (*archaic*) [➡SELF-IMPORTANT AND SELF-SEEKING PEOPLE; 949] **2** *type of* **flightless bird** [➡BIRDS; 997]

peacock blue *type of* **blue** [➡COLORS; 1224]

peacock butterfly *type of* **butterfly** [➡MOTHS AND BUTTERFLIES; 1015]

pea green *type of* **green** [➡COLORS; 1224]

peak 1 *n* **mountain**, mountaintop, summit, crest, point, height, mount, alp [➡MOUNTAINS AND HILLS; 1044] *Opposite*: valley **2** *n* **tip**, pinnacle, zenith, top, summit, height, apex, apogee [➡EXTREMITIES OF PHYSICAL OBJECTS; 1250] *Opposite*: base **3** *v* **climax**, crest, max out, top [➡GO UPWARD; 306] *Opposite*: dip **4** *adj* **top**, highest, crowning, topmost, ultimate, greatest, uttermost [➡SUPERIORITY; 152] *Opposite*: bottom

peaked 1 *adj* **pointed**, sharp, pointy, spiky, tipped [➡ANGULAR SHAPE; 1217] *Opposite*: rounded **2** *adj* **sickly-looking**, pale, thin, wan, emaciated, drawn, sickly, peaky (*UK*) [➡UNFIT AND WEAK; 739]

peal 1 *n* **clangor**, ringing, tolling, din, clang, ding-dong, knell, chime [➡RINGING AND HOOTING SOUNDS; 1259] **2** *v* **ring**, toll, clang, sound, resonate, boom, bong, knell [➡EMIT RINGING AND HOOTING SOUNDS; 367]

peanut *type of* **nut** [➡NUTS; 1185]

peanut butter *type of* **preserve** [➡SUGAR AND PRESERVES; 1184]

peanut oil *type of* **cooking fat and oil** [➡FATS AND OILS; 1173]

peanuts (*informal*) *n* **a small sum**, a trifling amount, a trifle, a trifling sum, a paltry sum, chicken feed (*informal*) [➡SMALL AMOUNTS OF MONEY; 121] *Opposite*: fortune

pear *type of* **fruit** [➡FRUIT AND VEGETABLES; 1176]

pearl 1 *n* **treasure**, precious thing, nugget, prize, gem (*informal*) [➡AMAZING THINGS; 211] *Opposite*: dud (*informal*) **2** *type of* **white** [➡COLORS; 1224] **3** *type of* **gemstone** [➡PRECIOUS STONES; 1278]

pearl gray *type of* **gray** [➡COLORS; 1224]

pearly *adj* **iridescent**, lustrous, gleaming, shining, translucent, glowing, burnished, glistening, sheeny, nacreous [➡VISUAL TEXTURE; 1221] *Opposite*: dull

pear-shaped *adj* **bottom-heavy**, broadening, widening, bulging, billowing, rotund, plump, thickset [➡BUILD; 477] *Opposite*: top-heavy

peasant 1 *n* **farmer**, laborer, farm hand, farmworker, crofter [➡FARMERS, GARDENERS, AND MANUAL WORKERS; 849] 2 *n* **country-dweller**, rustic, provincial, hillbilly (*informal*), bumpkin (*informal*) [➡CLASS STATUS; 889]

pea soup *type of* **soup** [➡SOUPS; 1186]

peasouper (*UK*) *n* [➡CLOUDY AND RAINY WEATHER; 1052]

peat *n* mulch, moss, compost, fertilizer, turf [➡EROSION PRODUCTS AND SOIL; 1058]

pebble *n* stone, nugget, grit, shingle [➡STONES, ROCKS, AND BOULDERS; 1057]

pebbledash (*UK*) *n* facing, finish, plaster, roughcast, encrustation, pebbles, cladding [➡BUILDING MATERIALS; 1077]

pecan *type of* nut [➡NUTS; 1185]

peccadillo *n* sin, offense, failing, indulgence, crime, transgression, wrong, wrongdoing, fault, infringement, breach [➡MORALLY BAD OR IMPROPER; 775] *Opposite*: virtue

peck 1 *v* strike, bite, jab, poke, dig, tap, hit [➡CONTACT: TOUCH; 412] 2 *v* nibble, pick at, eat, play with, toy with, sniff at [➡EAT AND NOT EAT; 710] *Opposite*: gobble 3 *v* (*informal*) kiss, brush, caress, osculate (*formal or humorous*), buss (*dated*) [➡PHYSICAL CONTACT AS COMMUNICATION; 655] 4 *n* bite, blow, stroke, jab, dig, poke [➡CONTACT: TOUCH; 412] 5 *type of* nonmetric unit [➡SIZE AND DIMENSIONS; 1192] 6 *n* (*informal*) kiss, brush, caress, smack, osculation (*formal or humorous*), buss (*dated*) [➡PHYSICAL CONTACT AS COMMUNICATION; 655]

pecking order *n* hierarchy, class structure, social order, social structure, ladder, society [➡CONNECTIONS; 143]

peckish (*informal*) *adj* hungry, famished, ravenous, starving (*informal*), starved (*informal*) [➡EAT AND NOT EAT; 710] *Opposite*: full

pecorino *type of* hard cheese [➡DAIRY PRODUCTS AND CHEESES; 1183]

pectoral *type of* muscle or tendon [➡THE MUSCLES; 718]

pectoral fin *part of* fish [➡PARTS OF A FISH; 1011]

peculate (*formal*) *v* [➡STEAL AND ROB; 426]

peculiar 1 *adj* unusual, odd, strange, weird, irregular, abnormal, uncharacteristic, atypical, curious, eccentric, unconventional [➡BIZARRE AND PECULIAR; 257] *Opposite*: normal 2 *adj* unique, idiosyncratic, local, individual, special, distinctive, particular, inimitable [➡EXTRAORDINARY: UNCOMMON; 205] *Opposite*: universal

peculiarity 1 *n* individuality, idiosyncrasy, distinctiveness, particularity, uniqueness, inimitableness [➡EXTRAORDINARY: UNCOMMON; 205] 2 *n* oddness, strangeness, weirdness, eccentricity, abnormality, irregularity, curiousness [➡BIZARRE AND PECULIAR; 257] *Opposite*: normality

peculiarly 1 *adv* uniquely, abnormally, unusually, curiously, strangely, markedly, noticeably [➡BIZARRE AND PECULIAR; 257] *Opposite*: typically 2 *adv* particularly, especially, extremely, very, extraordinarily, massively (*informal*) [➡TO A GREAT EXTENT; 132] *Opposite*: slightly

pecuniary *adj* monetary, financial, fiscal, economic, commercial, budgetary [➡FINANCE AND ECONOMICS; 796]

pedagogic *see* **pedagogical**

pedagogical *adj* educational, academic, instructive, tutorial, didactic, informative, instructional, pedagogic, teaching, scholastic [➡EDUCATION; 838]

pedagogics (*formal*) *n* [➡TEACHING; 839]

pedagogue *n* teacher, educator, schoolteacher, instructor, tutor, lecturer [➡EDUCATORS; 840]

pedagogy *n* teaching, education, instruction, training, tutoring, schooling, pedagogics (*formal*) [➡TEACHING; 839]

pedal 1 *part of* bike [➡BIKES, CARS, AND CARRIAGES; 1149] 2 *n* lever, device, control, treadle [➡PARTS OF MACHINES AND TOOLS; 1118] 3 *type of* controls [➡INTERNAL PARTS OF A VEHICLE; 1146] 4 *v* cycle, ride, drive, steer, travel, bike (*informal*) [➡TRAVEL: WAYS OF TRAVELING; 320] 5 *v* ride, operate, propel, control, guide, steer, impel [➡TRAVEL: WAYS OF TRAVELING; 320]

pedal pushers *type of* pants [➡GARMENTS AND OUTFITS; 865]

pedant *n* doctrinaire, obfuscator, nitpicker, sophist, hairsplitter, scholar, theoretician [➡GRUMPY AND NEGATIVE PEOPLE; 953] *Opposite*: dilettante

pedantic *adj* finicky, plodding, obscure, arcane, dull, doctrinaire, sophistic, hairsplitting, nitpicking, fussy [➡NEGATIVE INTELLECTUAL CHARACTERISTICS; 525] *Opposite*: dilettante

pedantry *n* literalism, laboriousness, sophistry, meticulousness, thoroughness, unimaginativeness [➡NEGATIVE INTELLECTUAL CHARACTERISTICS; 525] *Opposite*: creativity

peddle 1 *v* sell, tout, hawk, vend, retail, market, get rid of, push (*slang*) [➡SELL; 441] 2 *v* promote, market, hype, espouse, advocate, publicize, push (*slang*) [➡SELL; 441]

peddler *n* seller, dealer, trader, vendor, hawker, supplier, retailer, wholesaler, merchant, salesperson, pusher (*slang*), purveyor (*formal*), street trader (*UK*) [➡SELLERS; 442]

pedestal *n* base, plinth, stand, dais, platform, podium, support, foundation, understructure, foot [➡SUPPORTS AND BASES; 1255]

pedestrian 1 *n* rambler, walker, ambler, hiker, strider, foot-traveler [➡TRAVEL: TRAVELERS AND WALKERS; 319] 2 *adj* dull, ordinary, unimaginative, uninspired, prosaic, everyday, humdrum, unexciting, boring, tedious [➡ORDINARINESS; 244] *Opposite*: exciting

pedestrian crossing *n* crosswalk, crossing, pelican crossing (*UK*), zebra crossing (*UK*) [➡BRIDGES, TUNNELS, CROSSINGS, AND JUNCTIONS; 1112]

pedestrianized *adj* pedestrian, converted, nonvehicle, nonvehicular, closed off [➡PATHWAYS; 1110]

pedestrian precinct (*UK*) *n* [➡PATHWAYS; 1110]

pedicel *part of* flower [➡FLOWERS; 1032]

pedicure *n* beauty treatment, foot massage, cosmetic treatment, cosmetic session, chiropody treatment, chiropody session [➡PERSONAL HYGIENE; 491]

pedigree 1 *n* lineage, family background, ancestry, derivation, history, bloodline, birth, extraction, parentage [➡THE FAMILY; 956] 2 *adj* purebred, full-blooded, thoroughbred, noble, aristocratic, blue-blooded [➡ CLASS STATUS; 889]

pedology *type of* **earth science** [➡ EARTH SCIENCES; 1059]

peduncle *part of* **flower** [➡ FLOWERS; 1032]

peek 1 *v* **peep**, glance, peer, steal a look, have a look-see, sneak a quick look [➡ LOOKING AND LOOKS; 700] *Opposite:* stare 2 *n* **look**, glance, peep, glimpse, once-over (*informal*), gander (*informal*), look-see (*informal*) [➡ LOOKING AND LOOKS; 700] *Opposite:* gaze

peel 1 *v* **unpeel**, skin, strip, unwrap, pare, hull, bark, flay, shed [➡ COOKING AND FOOD PREPARATION; 353] 2 *n* **skin**, rind, peelings, covering, shell, crust, wrapping, bark, husk [➡ FRUIT AND VEGETABLES; 1176]

peeler *n* **potato peeler**, carrot peeler, paring knife, scraper [➡ TABLEWARE, FLATWARE, AND KITCHENWARE; 861]

peeling *adj* **flaking**, shedding, cracking, coming off, coming loose, detaching [➡ IN BAD REPAIR; 1234] *Opposite:* smooth

peelings *n* **parings**, skin, peel, rind, shavings, bark, husk, wrapping, covering, shell [➡ REMAINDER AND REMAINDERS; 125]

peep 1 *v* **peek**, peer, steal a look, glance, sneak a look, glimpse [➡ LOOKING AND LOOKS; 700] *Opposite:* gaze 2 *v* **chirp**, twitter, chirrup, squeak, beep, cheep, tweet (*UK*) [➡ SOUND EMISSION BY ANIMALS OR BIRDS; 364] 3 *n* **look**, peek, glance, glimpse, gander (*informal*), gawk (*informal*) [➡ LOOKING AND LOOKS; 700] 4 *n* **chirp**, cheep, twitter, squeak, tweet, beep, chirrup [➡ SOUNDS MADE BY BIRDS; 1263] 5 *n* **sound**, utterance, noise, word [➡ SOUNDS MADE BY PEOPLE; 1262]

peephole 1 *n* **opening**, crack, hole, aperture, knothole [➡ HOLES, GAPS, AND FORKS; 1252] 2 *n* **spyhole**, eyehole, keyhole [➡ HOLES, GAPS, AND FORKS; 1252]

Peeping Tom *n* [➡ CRIMINALS; 821]

peer 1 *n* **equal**, colleague, contemporary, friend, match, like, partner, associate, fellow (*dated*), mate (*UK*) [➡ COLLEAGUES AND EQUALS; 967] 2 *n* **noble**, aristocrat, lord, earl, duke, viscount, patrician, peer of the realm (*UK*) [➡ RULERS AND ARISTOCRACY; 823] 3 *v* **look**, scrutinize, gaze, stare, examine, look closely, go over, take in, squint [➡ LOOKING AND LOOKS; 700] *Opposite:* glance

peerage (*UK*) 1 *n* **dukedom**, title, honor, hereditary peerage (*UK*), life peerage (*UK*) [➡ CLASS STATUS; 889] 2 *n* **aristocracy**, nobility, nobles, aristocrats, peers, upper classes, peers of the realm (*UK*) [➡ RULERS AND ARISTOCRACY; 823]

peer group *n* **cohort**, coequals, generation, age group, classmates, colleagues, contemporaries, equals [➡ COLLEAGUES AND EQUALS; 967]

peerless *adj* **incomparable**, unequaled, matchless, unrivaled, without equal, nonpareil, unsurpassed, unmatched [➡ SUPERIORITY; 152] *Opposite:* commonplace

peer of the realm (*UK*) *n* **earl**, duke, viscount, noble, aristocrat, patrician, lord, peer (*UK*) [➡ RULERS AND ARISTOCRACY; 823]

peeve (*informal*) 1 *v* **vex**, annoy, irritate, irk, upset, pique, provoke, chafe, nettle (*informal*), miff (*informal*), rile (*informal*) [➡ ANGER AND ANNOY; 569] *Opposite:* please 2 *n* **gripe**

(*informal*), bugbear, irritation, vexation, nuisance, bother, annoyance, irritant, headache (*informal*), hassle (*informal*) [➡ NUISANCES; 253] *Opposite:* pleasure

peeved (*informal*) *adj* **annoyed**, irritated, irked, piqued, upset, put out, vexed, provoked, nettled (*informal*), miffed (*informal*), riled (*informal*) [➡ IRRITATION AND ANGER; 541] *Opposite:* pleased

peevish *adj* **irritable**, crabby, bad-tempered, cross, grumpy, spiteful, petulant, touchy, cranky (*informal*), testy (*informal*), grouchy (*informal*) [➡ IRRITATION AND ANGER; 541] *Opposite:* good-tempered

peevishness *n* **irritability**, crabbiness, spitefulness, crossness, grumpiness, pettiness, grouchiness (*informal*), crankiness (*informal*) [➡ IRRITATION AND ANGER; 541]

peewee (*informal*) *adj* **miniature**, toy, undersized, tiny, small, mini (*informal*), pint-size (*informal*) [➡ SMALL; 1195] *Opposite:* jumbo

peg 1 *n* **pin**, fastener, dowel, hook, bolt, hanger, nail, spike, tack [➡ FASTENERS, LINKS, AND NETWORKS; 1247] 2 *n* (*informal*) [➡ PARTS OF THE BODY: LEG AND FOOT; 694] 3 *v* **fasten**, secure, attach, fix, hang, nail, make fast [➡ FASTEN, LINK, AND JOIN; 408] *Opposite:* detach 4 *v* **mark**, keep score, track, gauge, measure, note down [➡ ASSESS QUALITY; 755] 5 *v* **freeze**, fix, set, control, limit [➡ AVOID, PREVENT, LIMIT, AND CONTROL; 277] *Opposite:* free

Pegasus *type of* **constellation** [➡ HEAVENLY BODIES; 1061]

peignoir *type of* **sleepwear** [➡ GARMENTS AND OUTFITS; 865]

pejorative (*formal*) *adj* **disapproving**, judgmental, harsh, scornful, derogatory, uncomplimentary, negative, depreciative, deprecatory, critical, sneering, sniping, disparaging, belittling, downgrading [➡ ACCUSATORY AND DISAPPROVING; 634] *Opposite:* positive

Pekingese *type of* **small dog** [➡ DOGS; 980]

pelargonium *type of* **perennial flower** [➡ FLOWERS; 1032]

pelican *type of* **sea bird** [➡ SEA BIRDS; 1002]

pelican crossing (*UK*) *n* **crossing**, crosswalk, zebra crossing (*UK*), pedestrian crossing (*UK*) [➡ BRIDGES, TUNNELS, CROSSINGS, AND JUNCTIONS; 1112]

pellet *type of* **projectile** [➡ PROJECTILES; 1159]

pell-mell 1 *adv* **helter-skelter**, hurriedly, headlong, recklessly, tumultuously, precipitously, impulsively, rashly, impetuously [➡ HAPPENING QUICKLY; 104] *Opposite:* carefully 2 *adv* **untidily**, higgledy-piggledy, haphazardly, chaotically, topsy-turvily, randomly [➡ DISORDER AND CHAOS; 245] *Opposite:* neatly

pellucid (*literary*) *adj* [➡ VISUAL TEXTURE; 1221]

pellucidity (*literary*) *n* [➡ VISUAL TEXTURE; 1221]

pelmet (*UK*) *n* **valance**, decoration, drapery, board, frill [➡ FURNISHING AND HOUSEHOLD LINENS; 860]

pelt 1 *n* **hide**, fur, skin, hair, coat, covering, fleece [➡ THE SKIN; 720] 2 *v* **bombard**, assail, assault, strafe, attack, shell, mortar, shower [➡ MOVE SOMETHING: THROUGH THE AIR; 334] 3 *v* **pour**, cascade, come down in sheets (*informal*), rain cats and dogs (*informal*) [➡ CLOUDY AND RAINY WEATHER; 1052] *Opposite:* drizzle

pelt down *v* [➡ CLOUDY AND RAINY WEATHER; 1052]

pelvic *adj* **pubic**, lumbar, sacral, genital, iliac [➡ THE BONES AND JOINTS; 719]

pelvic fin *part of* **fish** [➡ PARTS OF A FISH; 1011]

pelvis *type of* **bone** [➡ THE BONES AND JOINTS; 719]

pelycosaur *type of* **dinosaur** [➡ DINOSAURS; 996]

Pembroke table *type of* **table** [➡ FURNITURE; 858]

pen 1 *n* [➡ WRITING AND DRAWING IMPLEMENTS, AND MEDIA; 601] 2 *n* **enclosure**, run, cage, coop [➡ ANIMAL OR BIRD ACCOMMODATIONS; 1079] 3 *type of* **male or female bird** [➡ MALE OR FEMALE BIRDS; 1005] 4 *n* (*slang*) [➡ BUILDINGS FOR CONFINING PEOPLE; 1094] 5 *v* **dash off** (*informal*), scribble, jot, compose, scrawl, write, author [➡ RECORD SOMETHING; 371] 6 *v* **confine**, shut in, hold in, trap, capture, hem in, keep, imprison, cage in, corral [➡ CAPTIVITY AND LOSS OF FREEDOM; 248] *Opposite*: release

pen

◆ *types of pens*
ballpoint, felt-tipped pen, fountain pen, highlighter, marker, quill, rollerball

penal *adj* **punitive**, punishing, disciplinary, corrective [➡ TRIAL, PUNISHMENT, AND LEGAL OUTCOMES; 819]

penal colony *n* [➡ BUILDINGS FOR CONFINING PEOPLE; 1094]

penal complex *n* [➡ BUILDINGS FOR CONFINING PEOPLE; 1094]

penal institution *n* [➡ BUILDINGS FOR CONFINING PEOPLE; 1094]

penalization *n* **castigation** (*formal*), imprisonment, punishment, disciplining, fining, discipline, correction [➡ THE LAW AND LEGAL AUTHORITY; 814] *Opposite*: rewarding

penalize *v* **punish**, discipline, fine, reprimand, correct, chasten, imprison, castigate (*formal*) [➡ ACCUSE, BLAME, AND CRITICIZE; 641] *Opposite*: let off

penalty 1 *n* **punishment**, fine, sentence, penalization [➡ TRIAL, PUNISHMENT, AND LEGAL OUTCOMES; 819] 2 *n* **consequence**, disadvantage, drawback, forfeit, price [➡ RESULTS AND OUTCOMES; 83] *Opposite*: advantage

penance *n* **self-punishment**, reparation, forfeit, atonement, amends, propitiation, repentance, contrition, self-flagellation [➡ APOLOGIZE AND RETRACT; 683]

penchant *n* **liking**, fondness, partiality, taste, proclivity, desire, weakness, inclination, predilection (*formal*) [➡ APPRECIATION AND GRATITUDE; 535] *Opposite*: antipathy

pencil *v* **write**, draw, mark, color, sketch, trace, outline, delineate [➡ RECORD SOMETHING; 371]

pencil case *type of* **container** [➡ CONTAINERS, RECEPTACLES, AND PACKAGING; 1245]

pencil mustache *n* [➡ FACIAL HAIR; 489]

pencil pusher *n* [➡ WORKERS; 836]

pencil skirt *type of* **skirt** [➡ GARMENTS AND OUTFITS; 865]

pendant *type of* **necklace** [➡ JEWELRY; 866]

pendent 1 *adj* **hanging**, suspended, dangling, sagging, pendulous, trailing, overhanging, drooping [➡ ORIENTATION AND ALIGNMENT; 1223] 2 *adj* (*formal or literary*) **pending**, incomplete, unresolved, awaiting, undecided [➡ ABOUT TO HAPPEN; 33]

pending 1 *adj* **undecided**, incomplete, awaiting, unresolved, pendent (*formal or literary*) [➡ ABOUT TO HAPPEN; 33] 2 *adj* **imminent**, impending, expected, around the corner, approaching, forthcoming [➡ ABOUT TO HAPPEN; 33] 3 *prep* **awaiting**, until, till [➡ FUTURE; 86] 4 *prep* **during**, throughout, in the course of [➡ CONCURRENT AND CONTEMPORANEOUS; 164]

pendulous 1 *adj* **hanging**, swinging, overhanging, drooping, loose, sagging, oscillating, pendent, dangling [➡ ORIENTATION AND ALIGNMENT; 1223] 2 *adj* **undecided**, wavering, vacillating, uncommitted, uncertain, unsure [➡ UNCERTAINTY; 559] *Opposite*: decided

pendulum *n* **weight**, bob, plumb, swing [➡ PARTS OF MACHINES AND TOOLS; 1118]

penetrability *n* [➡ DENSITY AND CONSISTENCY; 1207]

penetrable *adj* [➡ DENSITY AND CONSISTENCY; 1207]

penetrate 1 *v* **enter**, pass through, go through, go in, break in, break through, pierce, infiltrate, access, broach, stab, gore, spear, lance, spike [➡ MOVE PAST, INTO, OR THROUGH SOMETHING; 331] 2 *v* **diffuse**, seep in, soak in, infiltrate, imbue, invade, infuse, seep into, permeate, creep into, saturate, filter through, transfuse [➡ MOVE PAST, INTO, OR THROUGH SOMETHING; 331] 3 *v* **grasp**, see into, perceive, figure out, comprehend, understand, apprehend, discern [➡ UNDERSTAND AND GRASP; 759] 4 *v* **work out**, solve, decipher, figure out, understand, fathom, apprehend, crack (*informal*) [➡ SOLVE AND INTERPRET; 760]

penetrating 1 *adj* **all-pervading**, powerful, pungent, sharp, piercing, strong [➡ STRENGTH; 201] 2 *adj* **probing**, piercing, searching, questioning, inquiring, sharp, penetrative [➡ FACIAL EXPRESSIONS AND BLUSHING; 651] 3 *adj* **sharp**, intelligent, astute, perceptive, insightful, clever, acute, keen, discriminating [➡ POSITIVE INTELLECTUAL CHARACTERISTICS; 524] *Opposite*: obtuse 4 *adj* **piercing**, shrill, high-pitched, ear-splitting, sharp, strident, loud [➡ LOUD, HIGH, OR UNPLEASANT SOUNDS; 1266]

penetration 1 *n* **diffusion**, infiltration, saturation, dispersion, dissemination, permeation [➡ DISPENSE, RATION, AND DISTRIBUTE; 434] 2 *n* **perception**, astuteness, understanding, discernment, comprehension, insight, acumen, shrewdness, intelligence [➡ POSITIVE INTELLECTUAL CHARACTERISTICS; 524] 3 *n* **incursion**, access, breach, entrance, infringement, invasion [➡ ARRIVAL; 13]

penetrative 1 *adj* **penetrating**, piercing, penetrant, permeating, pervasive [➡ STRENGTH; 201] 2 *adj* **keen**, perceptive, insightful, acute, sharp, discerning [➡ POSITIVE INTELLECTUAL CHARACTERISTICS; 524] *Opposite*: unperceptive

pen friend (*UK*) *n* **correspondent**, letter writer, friend, acquaintance, pal (*informal*), pen pal (*informal*) [➡ FRIENDS AND GUESTS; 963]

penguin *type of* **flightless bird** [➡ BIRDS; 997]

peninsula *n* **neck of land**, finger of land, cape, point, headland [➡ THE CONTINENTS AND ISLANDS; 1048]

penitence *n* **shame**, repentance, contrition, atonement, remorse, regret, sorrow, compunction [➡ APOLOGIZE AND RETRACT; 683] *Opposite*: shamelessness

penitent *adj* **repentant**, repenting, contrite, remorseful, regretful, apologetic, rueful, conscience-stricken, sorry [➡EMBARRASSMENT AND HUMILIATION; 542] *Opposite:* unrepentant

penitential *adj* **penitent**, sorrowful, repentant, penitentiary, atoning, regretful, contrite, remorseful [➡EMBARRASSMENT AND HUMILIATION; 542] *Opposite:* unrepentant

penitentiary *n* **prison**, penal colony, labor camp, house of correction, reformatory, penal institution, jail, pen (*slang*) [➡BUILDINGS FOR CONFINING PEOPLE; 1094]

penknife *type of* **knife** [➡CUTTING TOOLS; 1120]

penlight *type of* **light** [➡LIGHT; 1164]

pen name *n* **pseudonym**, nom de plume, alias, nom de guerre [➡NAME AND DESCRIBE; 665]

pennant 1 *n* **banner**, flag, ensign, emblem, streamer, pennon, bunting [➡SYMBOLS, SIGNS, AND NUMBERS; 596] 2 *part of* **sailing vessel** [➡PARTS OF A SHIP OR BOAT; 1151]

penne *type of* **pasta** [➡PASTA; 1180]

penniless *adj* **poor**, impoverished, impecunious, destitute, bankrupt, ruined, insolvent, broke (*informal*), flat broke (*informal*), cleaned out (*informal*) [➡POVERTY AND POOR; 892] *Opposite:* rich

pennilessness *n* [➡POVERTY AND POOR; 892]

pennon *n* **flag**, pennant, banner, standard, emblem, streamer, bunting [➡SYMBOLS, SIGNS, AND NUMBERS; 596]

penny pincher (*informal*) *n* **skinflint**, miser, niggard, pinchpenny, cheapskate (*informal*), scrooge (*informal*) [➡FINANCIALLY MEAN PEOPLE; 952] *Opposite:* spendthrift

penny-pinching (*informal*) *adj* **frugal**, thrifty, tight-fisted, stingy, parsimonious, economizing [➡GRASPING AND FINANCIALLY MEAN; 519] *Opposite:* generous

penny whistle *type of* **wind instrument** [➡MUSICAL INSTRUMENTS; 910]

penny-wise *adj* [➡GRASPING AND FINANCIALLY MEAN; 519]

pen pal (*informal*) *n* **correspondent**, letter writer, friend, acquaintance, pal (*informal*), pen friend (*UK*) [➡FRIENDS AND GUESTS; 963]

pension 1 *n* **retirement pension**, retirement fund, annuity, income, retirement income, fixed income, allowance, social security [➡FUNDS, PAYMENTS, AND CHARGES; 800] 2 *type of* **hotel** [➡HOTELS, RESTAURANTS, AND CLUBS; 1082]

pensioner *n* **retiree**, retired person, senior citizen, senior, OAP (*UK*) [➡OLD PEOPLE; 920]

pension fund *n* [➡ACCOUNTING, BANKING, AND BUDGETING; 799]

pensive *adj* **thoughtful**, meditative, contemplative, thinking, brooding, pondering, preoccupied, lost in thought, absorbed, engrossed, reflective [➡PENSIVENESS AND INTEREST; 538]

pensiveness *n* **thoughtfulness**, dreaminess, wistfulness, meditativeness, reflectiveness, preoccupation, contemplativeness, musing [➡THINK AND REFLECT; 743]

pentagon *type of* **angular shape** [➡ANGULAR SHAPE; 1217]

pentagonal *adj* [➡ANGULAR SHAPE; 1217]

penthouse *type of* **apartment** [➡RESIDENTIAL BUILDINGS; 1078]

pent-up *adj* **repressed**, stifled, unexpressed, contained, constrained, bottled up, curbed, restrained [➡SECRET AND UNKNOWN; 179] *Opposite:* voiced

penultimate *adj* **second to last**, one before the last, next to last, last but one (*UK*) [➡AFTER, LAST, AND FOLLOWING; 165]

penumbra 1 *n* **shadow**, shade, darkness [➡DESCRIBING LIGHT; 1228] 2 *n* **obscurity**, uncertainty, cloudiness, indistinctness [➡VAGUENESS; 243]

pen up *v* **cage**, round up, shut within, corral, enclose, hold, trap, capture, hem in, keep, imprison [➡CAPTIVITY AND LOSS OF FREEDOM; 248] *Opposite:* free

penurious (*literary*) 1 *adj* **poor**, impoverished, destitute, needy, penniless, impecunious, broke (*informal*), strapped (*informal*), indigent (*formal*) [➡POVERTY AND POOR; 892] *Opposite:* well-off 2 *adj* **stingy**, grudging, cheap, miserly, niggardly, frugal, mean [➡GRASPING AND FINANCIALLY MEAN; 519] *Opposite:* generous

penury *n* **poverty**, pennilessness, destitution, neediness, impoverishment, indigence (*formal*), impecuniousness (*formal*) [➡POVERTY AND POOR; 892] *Opposite:* luxury

peon *n* [➡WORKERS; 836]

peony *type of* **perennial flower** [➡FLOWERS; 1032]

people 1 *n* **nation**, community, nationality, populace, population, inhabitants [➡INHABITANTS; 857] 2 *n* **persons**, folks, individuals, public, general public, society [➡GROUPS IN SOCIETY; 940] 3 *n* (*informal*) **relatives**, relations, family, folks, ancestors [➡THE FAMILY; 956] 4 *v* **populate**, fill, inhabit, immigrate, colonize, pioneer, occupy [➡INHABIT; 20]

pep (*informal*) *n* **energy**, liveliness, vigor, perkiness, zest, verve, activeness, potency, vim (*informal*), moxie (*slang*) [➡ENERGY AND ENTHUSIASM; 496]

pepper 1 *v* **sprinkle**, shower, spray, scatter, speckle, dot, stipple [➡SPREAD AND SCATTER; 332] 2 *v* **scatter**, intersperse, sprinkle, interleave, infuse, interrupt, interfuse, interlace [➡SPREAD AND SCATTER; 332] 3 *type of* **spice** [➡HERBS AND SPICES; 1175] 4 *type of* **salad vegetable** [➡FRUIT AND VEGETABLES; 1176]

peppercorn *type of* **spice** [➡HERBS AND SPICES; 1175]

peppered moth *type of* **moth** [➡MOTHS AND BUTTERFLIES; 1015]

pepperiness *n* [➡TASTE; 703]

peppermint *type of* **confectionery** [➡CONFECTIONERY; 1182]

pepperoni *type of* **processed meat** [➡TYPES AND CUTS OF MEAT; 1177]

peppery *adj* **spicy**, piquant, hot, fiery, pungent, strong, zesty, gingery [➡TASTE; 703] *Opposite:* mild

peppy (*informal*) *adj* **lively**, vigorous, sprightly, perky, frisky, playful, spry, animated, vivacious, energetic [➡ENERGY AND ENTHUSIASM; 496] *Opposite:* lethargic

pep talk (*informal*) *n* **team talk**, speech, support, encouragement, inspiration, boost, talking-to (*informal*) [➡ONE-WAY COMMUNICATION; 49]

peptic *adj* [➡THE DIGESTIVE TRACT; 709]

pep up (*informal*) *v* **spice up**, add zest, liven up, make something swing, give a bit of zing (*informal*), jazz up (*informal*), make something go with a bang (*UK informal*) [➡ IMPROVE SOMETHING; 374]

per *prep* **for each**, apiece, for every, each, per capita [➡ APPORTIONMENT; 113]

perambulate (*formal*) *v* [➡ PROCEED AND GO; 305]

perambulator (*UK formal*) *n* **baby carriage**, stroller, baby buggy, buggy, pram (*UK*), pushchair (*UK*) [➡ BIKES, CARS, AND CARRIAGES; 1149]

per annum *adv* **each year**, by year, yearly, annually, every year, once a year [➡ TIMES OF YEAR; 88]

percale *type of* **synthetic fabric** [➡ FABRICS; 1132]

per capita *adj* **each one**, each person, per person, per head, apiece, per [➡ APPORTIONMENT; 113]

perceivable *adj* [➡ PERCEPTIBLE; 25]

perceive 1 *v* **notice**, observe, see, take in, remark, distinguish, recognize, pick out, identify, make out [➡ SEE; 699] *Opposite*: ignore 2 *v* **understand**, comprehend, sense, feel, become aware of, realize [➡ UNDERSTAND AND GRASP; 759]

percent 1 *adv* **out of a hundred**, out of each hundred, in each hundred, in a hundred, per hundred [➡ APPORTIONMENT; 113] 2 *n* **percentage**, part, proportion, ratio, percentile, fraction [➡ MEASURABLE PORTIONS; 127]

percentage 1 *n* **fraction**, proportion, ratio, part, section, measurement, calculation [➡ MEASURABLE PORTIONS; 127] 2 *n* (*informal*) **commission**, proportion, fraction, take, profit, entitlement, gain, cut (*informal*) [➡ MEASURABLE PORTIONS; 127]

percentile *n* [➡ MEASURABLE PORTIONS; 127]

perceptibility *n* [➡ PERCEPTIBLE; 25]

perceptible *adj* **noticeable**, traceable, observable, appreciable, visible, definite, distinguishable, distinctive, perceivable, detectable [➡ PERCEPTIBLE; 25] *Opposite*: invisible

perception 1 *n* **reading**, view, opinion, picture, take, slant, assessment, experience [➡ POINTS OF VIEW; 767] 2 *n* **insight**, acuity, awareness, discernment, observation, sensitivity [➡ THE SENSES; 696]

perceptive *adj* **discerning**, sensitive, insightful, keen, observant, understanding, aware, sharp [➡ POSITIVE INTELLECTUAL CHARACTERISTICS; 524] *Opposite*: insensitive

perceptiveness *n* **insight**, insightfulness, understanding, intuition, discernment, astuteness, acuity, sensitivity, discrimination, sharpness [➡ POSITIVE INTELLECTUAL CHARACTERISTICS; 524]

perch 1 *v* **rest**, sit, settle, balance, alight, land, light [➡ EXIST IN A PLACE; 19] 2 *type of* **freshwater fish** [➡ FRESHWATER FISH; 1010]

perchance (*archaic or literary*) *adv* **perhaps**, maybe, possibly, by chance, conceivably, feasibly [➡ POSSIBLE AND PROBABLE; 177] *Opposite*: definitely

percipience *n* **insight**, insightfulness, perceptiveness, discernment, understanding, intuition [➡ POSITIVE INTELLECTUAL CHARACTERISTICS; 524] *Opposite*: insensitivity

percipient *adj* **insightful**, perceptive, observant, discerning, understanding, intuitive [➡ POSITIVE INTELLECTUAL CHARACTERISTICS; 524] *Opposite*: insensitive

percolate 1 *v* **drip**, filter, trickle, ooze, leach [➡ LIQUID EMISSION; 370] 2 *v* **seep into**, infiltrate, permeate, penetrate, get into, infect, saturate [➡ MOVE PAST, INTO, OR THROUGH SOMETHING; 331]

percolator *n* **coffeepot**, coffee maker, coffee machine [➡ HOUSEHOLD APPLIANCES; 1117]

per contra *adv* **on the contrary**, in contrast, quite the reverse, quite the opposite, not at all, absolutely not [➡ FOREIGN WORDS AND PHRASES; 672]

percussion (*formal*) *n* **drumming**, beating, striking, hitting, bass beat, thumping, tapping [➡ IMPACT SOUNDS; 1260]

per diem *adj* **by the day**, daily, day-by-day, part-time, day-to-day, every day, quotidian (*formal*) [➡ TIMES OF DAY; 87]

perdition *n* **hell**, purgatory, punishment, damnation, abyss, inferno, underworld, hades (*informal*), netherworld (*formal*) [➡ RELIGIOUS CONCEPTS; 776]

peregrination (*literary*) *n* **journey**, voyage, passage, traversing, crossing, trip, expedition, excursion, pilgrimage, safari [➡ TRAVEL: JOURNEYS AND TRIPS; 318]

peregrine falcon *type of* **bird of prey** [➡ BIRDS OF PREY; 998]

peremptorily *adv* **dictatorially**, imperatively, imperiously, urgently, dogmatically, commandingly, authoritatively, definitively, emphatically, positively [➡ POMPOUS, LOUD, AND OVERCONFIDENT; 635] *Opposite*: meekly

peremptory 1 *adj* **dictatorial**, authoritative, unconditional, absolute, dogmatic, imperious, commanding, definite [➡ POMPOUS, LOUD, AND OVERCONFIDENT; 635] *Opposite*: polite 2 *adj* **decisive**, no-nonsense, quick, hasty, direct, unthinking, snap, determined, resolute [➡ CERTAINTY; 561] *Opposite*: roundabout

perennial *adj* **recurrent**, returning, perpetual, constant, persistent, lasting, continuing, permanent, enduring, regular, unfailing [➡ PERMANENCE: WITHOUT END; 94] *Opposite*: occasional

perestroika *n* **restructuring**, reform, reconstruction, reorganization, modernization, transformation [➡ SOCIAL, POLITICAL, AND ECONOMIC CHANGE; 373]

perfect 1 *adj* **faultless**, flawless, textbook, picture-perfect, seamless, unspoiled, unadulterated, impeccable, unflawed [➡ IN GOOD REPAIR; 1232] *Opposite*: flawed 2 *adj* **complete**, absolute, unqualified, whole, finished, total, entire, intact [➡ WHOLENESS AND COMPLETENESS; 198] *Opposite*: incomplete 3 *adj* **ideal**, just right, just the thing, wonderful, just what the doctor ordered, great (*informal*) [➡ GOOD, WELL, BETTER; 183] *Opposite*: wrong 4 *adj* **precise**, exact, accurate, on target, just right [➡ EXACT; 203] 5 *v* **achieve**, finish, complete, finalize, reach the summit of, top off [➡ COMPLETE AN ACTION; 263] 6 *v* **improve**, refine, hone, tighten up, work on, sharpen, round off, put the finishing touches to [➡ IMPROVE SOMETHING; 374] *Opposite*: spoil

perfection 1 *n* **excellence**, rightness, faultlessness, exactness, precision, flawlessness, aptness [➡ CORRECT AND

FAULTLESS; 182] **2** *n* **accomplishment**, fulfillment, completion, realization, achievement, working out [➡ENDS AND DEPARTURES; 54] *Opposite*: abandonment

perfectionism *n* **fastidiousness**, fussiness, nitpicking, hairsplitting, pedantry, meticulousness, conscientiousness, rigorousness [➡DIFFICULT TO PLEASE; 515] *Opposite*: carelessness

perfectionist *n* **stickler**, purist, pedant, obsessive, quibbler, hairsplitter, fussbudget (*informal*) [➡GRUMPY AND NEGATIVE PEOPLE; 953]

perfectly **1** *adv* **flawlessly**, faultlessly, impeccably, effortlessly, seamlessly, like a dream, without a glitch, dreamily [➡GOOD, WELL, BETTER; 183] *Opposite*: badly **2** *adv* **completely**, entirely, wholly, absolutely, utterly, thoroughly, extremely [➡WHOLENESS AND COMPLETENESS; 198] *Opposite*: partially

perfidious (*formal*) *adj* **disloyal**, treacherous, deceitful, dishonest, lying, untrue, base, low [➡DECEITFUL; 513] *Opposite*: honest

perfidiousness (*formal*) *n* [➡DECEITFUL; 513]

perfidy (*formal*) *n* **treachery**, disloyalty, deceit, duplicity, betrayal, lying, dishonesty [➡DECEITFUL; 513] *Opposite*: honesty

perforate *v* **puncture**, prick, pierce, hole, go through, burst, punch [➡TEAR, BREAK, AND CUT; 360]

perforation *n* **hole**, puncture, tear, rip, slash, gap [➡HOLES, GAPS, AND FORKS; 1252]

perforce (*literary*) *adv* **unavoidably**, inevitably, of necessity, necessarily, inescapably, helplessly [➡NECESSARY AND ESSENTIAL; 196]

perform **1** *v* **do**, carry out, fulfill, achieve, execute, complete, accomplish, implement, act upon, make, discharge (*formal*) [➡CARRY OUT AN ACTION; 269] **2** *v* **present**, act, play, put on, stage, do, enact, impersonate [➡THE PERFORMING ARTS; 904] **3** *v* **function**, work, behave, act, go, run, operate, react [➡CARRY OUT AN ACTION; 269]

Compare and Contrast: *perform*, *do*, *carry out*, *fulfill*, *discharge*, *execute*

CORE MEANING: to complete a task

perform to complete an action or accomplish a task, especially when this requires skill or care or when it forms part of a set procedure; *do* to complete an action or accomplish a task of any kind; *carry out* to complete any action or task; *fulfill* to do what is necessary to achieve the successful accomplishment or realization of something planned, promised, or anticipated; *discharge* (*formal*) to complete duties or responsibilities successfully; *execute* to put an instruction or plan into effect, or to complete an action or procedure that requires skill and expertise.

---

performance **1** *n* **presentation**, recital, act, routine, concert, show, piece, enactment [➡PERFORMANCES AND SHOWS; 42] **2** *n* **functioning**, implementation, execution, performing, carrying out, operation, running, working [➡CARRY OUT AN ACTION; 269] **3** *n* **feat**, deed, act, accomplishment, occurrence [➡ACTIONS OR UNDERTAKINGS; 259]

performance art *n* [➡THE PERFORMING ARTS; 904]

performer **1** *n* **doer**, perpetrator, executor, architect, operator [➡WORKERS; 836] **2** *n* **player**, actor, musician, recitalist, actress, artist, entertainer [➡PERFORMERS; 905] *Opposite*: spectator

performing arts *n* [➡THE PERFORMING ARTS; 904]

perfume **1** *n* **fragrance**, scent, cologne, body spray, toilet water, body mist, balm, incense [➡PERSONAL HYGIENE; 491] **2** *n* **smell**, aroma, scent, odor, fragrance, essence, whiff, bouquet, redolence [➡SMELL AND SMELLING; 705] **3** *v* **scent**, fragrance, imbue, freshen, lace, anoint, aromatize [➡DECORATE, ADORN, AND APPLY COATINGS; 405]

See Compare and Contrast at **smell**.

---

perfumed *adj* **scented**, sweet-smelling, sweet-scented, aromatic, fragrant, fragranced, pleasant-smelling, sweetly perfumed, odorous (*literary*) [➡SMELL AND SMELLING; 705]

perfunctory **1** *adj* **unthinking**, automatic, mechanical, dutiful, obligatory, token, routine, careless, cursory [➡AUTOMATIC AND INSTINCTIVE; 280] *Opposite*: thoughtful **2** *adj* **hasty**, superficial, quick, fleeting, hurried, passing, rapid, brief [➡INCAUTIOUS AND CARELESS; 283] *Opposite*: thorough

pergola *n* **arch**, trellis, framework, arbor, structure, passageway, pavilion, arcade, walkway, bower [➡GARDENS; 1074]

perhaps *adv* **maybe**, possibly, conceivably, feasibly, imaginably, perchance (*archaic or literary*) [➡POSSIBLE AND PROBABLE; 177] *Opposite*: definitely

per head *adj* [➡APPORTIONMENT; 113]

perianth *part of* **flower** [➡FLOWERS; 1032]

peril *n* **danger**, threat, risk, hazard, jeopardy, liability, exposure [➡DANGER; 235] *Opposite*: safety

perilous *adj* **dangerous**, unsafe, hazardous, risky, death-defying, terrifying, exposed, extreme [➡DANGEROUS; 236] *Opposite*: safe

perilousness *n* [➡DANGER; 235]

perimeter *n* **boundary**, border, edge, limit, outskirts, outside [➡EXTREMITIES OF PHYSICAL OBJECTS; 1250]

perinatal *adj* [➡REPRODUCTION AND HEREDITY; 725]

period **1** *n* **era**, age, epoch, stage, phase, time, day [➡EPOCHS AND ERAS; 89] **2** *n* **interval**, episode, interlude, phase, cycle, time, extent [➡PERIODS OF TIME; 90]

periodic **1** *adj* **episodic**, intermittent, interrupted, sporadic, occasional, broken, intervallic [➡FINITENESS, VARIABILITY, AND TRANSIENCE; 96] *Opposite*: constant **2** *adj* **cyclic**, recurring, recurrent, serial, regular, continuing, seasonal [➡FREQUENT AND OFTEN; 107] *Opposite*: irregular

ecute, perform, pull off (*informal*),
OUT AN ACTION; 269]

mmission, enactment, transaction,
, performance, execution [➡CARRY OUT

lprit, criminal, wrongdoer, guilty
mitter, agent, perp (*slang*) [➡CRIMINALS;

tinuous, everlasting, uninterrupted,
ong-lasting, eternal, continual, per-
nduring, undying [➡PERMANENCE: WITHOUT
orary

tinue, preserve, prolong, carry on,
e, keep up, maintain, keep alive,
mmortalize [➡CAUSE TO CONTINUE; 267] *Oppo-*

continuation, continuance, pre-
tion, spread, dissemination, main-
ation, endurance, extension,
RMANENCE: WITHOUT END; 94] *Opposite*: ending

ity, time without end, all time, infin-
endlessness, timelessness, imper-
CE: WITHOUT END; 94]

baffle, confuse, stun, mystify, con-
bewilder, befuddle, disconcert, throw
x (*informal*), bamboozle (*informal*)
71] *Opposite*: enlighten

uzzled, baffled, confused, at a loss,
, confounded, stumped, foxed, bewild-
sconcerted, blank, uncomprehending,
al), bamboozled (*informal*), thrown
ON, ANXIETY, AND WORRY; 540] *Opposite*: com-

puzzling, baffling, confusing, mys-
ding, bewildering, disconcerting,
icult, befuddling [➡DIFFICULTY AND COMPLEXITY;
le

zzlement, bafflement, confusion, bewil-
cation, blankness, incomprehension
WORRY; 540] *Opposite*: comprehension

al) n **privilege**, gratuity, perk, bonus,
dvantage, incentive, plus, sweetener
(*informal*), plus point (*UK*) [➡REWARDS AND
: disadvantage

adv **as such**, by itself, for itself, in
ically [➡FOREIGN WORDS AND PHRASES; 672]

ppress, hound, harass, maltreat, pursue,
discriminate against, bully, torture,
ze, intimidate [➡UPSET, DISTRESS, AND HUMILIATE;
ect 2 v **pester**, harass, torment, bother,
y, irritate, hassle (*informal*) [➡COMPLAIN AND
eave alone

j [➡IN TROUBLE AND DISADVANTAGED; 73]

n **oppression**, harassment, maltreatment,
nination, torture, torment, tyranny,
bjection [➡MALICIOUS ACTIONS OR BEHAVIOR; 296]

---

tly, self-assuredly, cockily, bump-
ND OVERCONFIDENT; 635] *Opposite*: timidly

ness, cheerfulness, energy, jaunti-
htliness, zest, verve, vigor, hap-
uoyancy, bounciness, spryness,
s, spirit, vibrancy, pep (*informal*)
] 2 n **overconfidence**, confidence,
nportance, self-assurance, cocki-
mptiousness [➡POMPOUS, LOUD, AND OVER-
midity

cheer up, brighten up, wake up,
nto the mood, spice up, enliven,
(*informal*) [➡ENCOURAGE; 576] 2 v **stick**
pop up, straighten up, cock up
site: droop

eerful, energetic, jaunty, pert,
nated, buoyant, bouncy, spry,
[➡ENERGY AND ENTHUSIASM; 490] *Opposite*:
nfident, confident, self-confident,
red, cocksure, bumptious, cocky
ND OVERCONFIDENT; 635] *Opposite*: timid

, crimp, frizz [➡CHANGE OF SHAPE; 385]

RODUCTS AND SOIL; 1058]

ty, durability, durableness, lon-
immovability, lastingness, per-
UT END; 94] *Opposite*: transience

nence

al, enduring, lasting, eternal,
undying, stable, undeviating,
NENCE: WITHOUT END; 94] *Opposite*: tem-

DESCRIBING CLOTHES; 869]

usness, penetrability, per-
sorptivity, sponginess [➡DENSITY
impermeability

netrable, pervious, absorbent,
leaky [➡DENSITY AND CONSISTENCY; 1207]

ade, flood, fill, saturate, soak,
rough [➡FILL; 406] 2 v **filter**, seep,
soak, percolate, impregnate,
AST, INTO, OR THROUGH SOMETHING; 331]

pervasion, flood, saturation,
d [➡MORE AND EXCESS; 124] 2 n **fil-**
pervasion, entrance, pene-
nation, diffusion [➡DENSITY AND

CHS AND ERAS; 89]

allowed, permitted, accept-
lerated, approved, admis-
[➡PERMIT AND ALLOW; 669] *Opposite*:

orization, approval, agree-
ight, clearance, sanction,

blessing, carte blanche, OK (*informal*), say-so (*informal*), go-ahead (*informal*), leave (*formal*) [➡ PERMIT AND ALLOW; 669]

permissive *adj* **tolerant**, lenient, liberal, accommodating, lax, laissez-faire, hands-off, broad-minded, nonjudgmental, free, loose, indulgent, progressive, openminded [➡ POSITIVE INTELLECTUAL CHARACTERISTICS; 524] *Opposite*: strict

permissively *adv* **tolerantly**, leniently, liberally, accommodatingly, laxly, broad-mindedly, nonjudgmentally, freely, loosely, indulgently, progressively, open-mindedly [➡ POSITIVE INTELLECTUAL CHARACTERISTICS; 524] *Opposite*: strictly

permissiveness *n* **tolerance**, leniency, liberalism, laxness, laxity, broad-mindedness, indulgence, progressiveness, open-mindedness, flexibility, openness, license [➡ POSITIVE INTELLECTUAL CHARACTERISTICS; 524] *Opposite*: strictness

permit 1 *v* **authorize**, allow, let, approve, consent to, agree to, sanction, acquiesce to, pass, clear, give the go-ahead, give your blessing, give the green light, give carte blanche, tolerate, enable, facilitate, OK (*informal*), give leave (*formal*) [➡ PERMIT AND ALLOW; 669] *Opposite*: forbid 2 *n* **license**, document, certification, certificate, authorization, authority, warrant, card, badge [➡ OFFICIAL DOCUMENTS; 586]

permitted *adj* **allowed**, allowable, permissible, acceptable, accepted, approved, tolerable, tolerated, admissible, legitimate, legal, lawful [➡ PERMIT AND ALLOW; 669] *Opposite*: forbidden

permutation *n* **variation**, transformation, version, arrangement, rearrangement, combination, alternative, change, vicissitude, mutation [➡ CHANGE; 372]

pernicious 1 *adj* **malicious**, wicked, evil, malevolent, malign, malignant, maleficent, spiteful, bad [➡ MORALLY BAD OR IMPROPER; 775] *Opposite*: benign 2 *adj* **destructive**, harmful, deadly, fatal, insidious, ruinous, malignant, damaging, deleterious, noxious [➡ DANGEROUS; 236] *Opposite*: harmless

perniciousness 1 *n* **maliciousness**, malice, wickedness, evil, malevolence, malignity, maleficence, spite, badness [➡ MORALLY BAD OR IMPROPER; 775] *Opposite*: benignity 2 *n* **destructiveness**, harmfulness, deadliness, insidiousness, ruinousness, malignancy, deleteriousness (*formal*), noxiousness [➡ DANGER; 235] *Opposite*: harmlessness

perorate (*formal*) *v* [➡ INSTRUCT AND TEACH; 609]

peroration (*formal*) *n* **speech**, oration, discourse, address, talk, lecture, declamation [➡ ONE-WAY COMMUNICATION; 49]

peroxide 1 *n* **hydrogen peroxide**, bleaching agent, bleach, tint [➡ DYES AND COLORANTS; 1270] 2 *v* **bleach**, tint, lighten, dye, discolor, rinse, fade, color [➡ CHANGE OF COLOR; 391]

perp (*slang*) *n* [➡ CRIMINALS; 821]

perpend (*archaic*) *v* [➡ THINK AND REFLECT; 743]

perpendicular 1 *adj* **vertical**, at right angles, upright, bolt upright, erect, sheer, abrupt, steep [➡ ORIENTATION AND ALIGNMENT; 1223] *Opposite*: parallel 2 *type of* **pre-20th-century architecture** [➡ BUILDING AND ARCHITECTURE; 1076]

per person *adj* [➡ APPORTIONMENT; 113]

perpetrate *v* **commit**, carry out, do, be responsible for,

be behind, enact, ex effect (*formal*) [➡ CARRY

perpetration *n* c action, responsibilit AN ACTION; 269]

perpetrator *n* cu party, offender, com 821]

perpetual *adj* con lasting, unending, l manent, constant, e END; 94] *Opposite*: tem

perpetuate *v* co spread, disseminat propagate, extend, i *site*: stop

perpetuation servation, prolong tenance, propa immortalization [➡ F

perpetuity *n* eter ity, permanence, ishability [➡ PERMANEN

perplex *v* **puzzle**, found, stump, fox, (*informal*), flumm [➡ CONFUSE AND BEWILDER;

perplexed *adj* stunned, mystified ered, befuddled, d flummoxed (*infor* (*informal*) [➡ CONFUS prehending

perplexing *adj* tifying, confou impenetrable, dif 242] *Opposite*: simp

perplexity *n* pu derment, mystifi [➡ CONFUSION, ANXIETY, AN

perquisite (*for* benefit, extra, a (*informal*), freebi AWARDS; 439] *Opposit*

per se (*formal* isolation, intrins

persecute 1 *v* o hunt, single out torment, tyrann 567] *Opposite*: pro bait, badger, ann NAG; 686] *Opposite*:

persecuted a

persecution 1 pursuit, discrin intimidation, s

Opposite: protection **2** *n* **harassment**, torment, annoyance, irritation, suffering, vexation, hassle (*informal*) [➡ IRRITATION AND ANGER; 541]

persecutor **1** *n* **oppressor**, harasser, pursuer, bully, torturer, tormentor, tyrant, intimidator [➡ ENEMIES AND TORMENTORS; 969] *Opposite*: protector **2** *n* **pesterer**, harasser, tormentor, nuisance, baiter, heckler, aggravator, gadfly, a thorn in somebody's flesh [➡ ENEMIES AND TORMENTORS; 969]

Perseus *type of* **constellation** [➡ HEAVENLY BODIES; 1061]

perseverance *n* **persistence**, determination, resolve, resolution, doggedness, diligence, grit, insistence, tenacity, obstinacy, stubbornness, tirelessness, endurance, steadfastness, purpose, dedication, devotion, drive [➡ STRENGTH OF WILL; 501]

persevere *v* **persist**, continue, keep at, keep it up, keep on, carry on, stick it out, stick at, insist, endure, proceed, press on [➡ CONTINUE AN ACTION; 262] *Opposite*: give up

persevering *adj* **persistent**, determined, resolute, resolved, dogged, diligent, insistent, tenacious, obstinate, stubborn, tireless, enduring, steadfast, purposeful, dedicated, devoted, driven, staunch, unrelenting, unwavering, indomitable, single-minded [➡ STRENGTH OF WILL; 501] *Opposite*: irresolute

Persian cat *type of* **cat** [➡ FELINES; 983]

persist **1** *v* **persevere**, continue, keep at, keep it up, keep on, carry on, stick it out, stick at [➡ CONTINUE AN ACTION; 262] *Opposite*: give up **2** *v* **continue**, endure, live on, stay, go on, hang on, refuse to go away, stick around (*informal*) [➡ CONTINUE TO EXIST; 17] *Opposite*: fade away

persistence **1** *n* **perseverance**, determination, tenacity, resolve, resolution, doggedness, diligence, insistence, obstinacy, stubbornness, tirelessness, endurance, steadfastness, purpose, dedication, devotion, drive, grit, pushiness (*informal*), importunity (*formal*) [➡ STRENGTH OF WILL; 501] **2** *n* **continuance**, continuation, endurance, permanence, preservation, maintenance, continuity, durability [➡ PERMANENCE: WITHOUT END; 94] *Opposite*: transience

persistent **1** *adj* **tenacious**, determined, obstinate, insistent, dogged, stubborn, tireless, untiring, assiduous, steadfast, pushy (*informal*), importunate (*formal*) [➡ STRENGTH OF WILL; 501] *Opposite*: irresolute **2** *adj* **continuing**, continual, continued, unrelenting, incessant, constant, relentless, permanent, lasting, remaining, enduring [➡ PERMANENCE: WITHOUT END; 94] *Opposite*: fleeting

persnicketiness (*informal*) *n* [➡ DIFFICULT TO PLEASE; 515]

persnickety (*informal*) **1** *adj* **painstaking**, meticulous, demanding, exacting, finicky, fussy, picky, nitpicking, pedantic, particular, fastidious, punctilious, nice, choosy (*informal*) [➡ DIFFICULT TO PLEASE; 515] *Opposite*: slapdash **2** *adj* **exacting**, detailed, precise, painstaking, finicky, fine, complex, complicated [➡ DIFFICULTY AND COMPLEXITY; 242] *Opposite*: straightforward

person **1** *n* **being**, human being, individual, creature, soul, type, one, somebody, anybody, human, party (*formal*) [➡ PERSON; 931] **2** *n* **body**, form, frame, figure [➡ BODY; 691] **3** *n* (*formal*) **appearance**, persona, personality, character, ego, mien (*formal*) [➡ TEMPERAMENT AND BEHAVIOR; 492]

persona **1** *n* **character**, figure, person, role, part, personage (*formal*) [➡ PERSON; 931] **2** *n* **identity**, role, guise, personality, character, qualities, façade, front, face, image [➡ TEMPERAMENT AND BEHAVIOR; 492]

personable *adj* **amiable**, friendly, pleasant, affable, agreeable, likable, charming, attractive [➡ FRIENDLINESS AND SOCIABILITY; 494] *Opposite*: disagreeable

personage (*formal*) *n* **VIP**, celebrity, star, public figure, dignitary, somebody, notable, grandee [➡ IMPORTANT OR FAMOUS PEOPLE; 893] *Opposite*: nobody

personal **1** *adj* **individual**, private, own, special, particular, peculiar, subjective, respective, delicate, intimate [➡ BELONGING OR RELATING TO INDIVIDUALS; 944] *Opposite*: public **2** *adj* **offensive**, rude, derogatory, familiar, intrusive, cheeky (*informal*), impertinent (*formal*) [➡ EMOTIONALLY UNPLEASANT AND UPSETTING; 227] *Opposite*: complimentary **3** *n* **ad**, advertisement, announcement, public notice, personal ad (*UK*) [➡ ADVERTISING AND PUBLICITY; 604]

personal ad (*UK*) *n* **ad**, advertisement, announcement, public notice, personal [➡ ADVERTISING AND PUBLICITY; 604]

personal assistant *n* **secretary**, assistant, administrative assistant, administrator, right arm, aide, PA (*UK*) [➡ SUBORDINATES AND ASSISTANTS; 966]

personal belongings *n* [➡ POSSESSIONS; 461]

personal computer *n* **PC**, computer, terminal, laptop, notebook, palmtop, workstation, word processor [➡ COMPUTERS AND COMPUTING; 1127]

personal digital assistant *type of* **computer** [➡ COMPUTERS AND COMPUTING; 1127]

personal effects *n* **belongings**, possessions, personal property, things, stuff, gear (*informal*), effects (*formal*) [➡ POSSESSIONS; 461]

personal hygiene *n* [➡ PERSONAL HYGIENE; 491]

personality **1** *n* **character**, nature, disposition, behavior, temperament, makeup, traits, qualities, persona [➡ TEMPERAMENT AND BEHAVIOR; 492] **2** *n* **celebrity**, star, public figure, somebody, VIP, dignitary [➡ IMPORTANT OR FAMOUS PEOPLE; 893] *Opposite*: nobody

personalize **1** *v* **initial**, monogram, mark, engrave, identify, brand, tattoo [➡ DECORATE, ADORN, AND APPLY COATINGS; 405] **2** *v* **customize**, individualize, differentiate, distinguish, specify, change, modify [➡ CHANGE; 372] *Opposite*: generalize

personally **1** *adv* **for myself**, in my opinion, in my view, for my part, myself [➡ EXPRESSIONS OF OPINION; 623] *Opposite*: generally **2** *adv* **in person**, face to face, individually, myself, directly [➡ BELONGING OR RELATING TO INDIVIDUALS; 944] *Opposite*: indirectly

personal organizer **1** *n* **planner**, appointment book, address book, engagement book, datebook, calendar, aide-mémoire (*formal*), diary (*UK*) [➡ LISTS AND SCHEDULES; 587] **2** *n* **hand-held computer**, electronic planner, palmtop, electronic organizer (*UK*) [➡ COMPUTERS AND COMPUTING; 1127]

personal possessions *n* [➡ POSSESSIONS; 461]

personal property *n* [➡ POSSESSIONS; 461]

personal stereo *type of* **audio equipment** [➡ AUDIO EQUIPMENT; 1139]

persona non grata *n* [➡ LAZY OR UNSUCCESSFUL PEOPLE; 948]

personate *v* [➡ REPRESENT SOMETHING OR SOMEBODY; 59]

personation *n* [➡ REPRESENTATIONS AND GENERAL EXAMPLES; 65]

personification 1 *n* **epitome**, image, embodiment, incarnation, representation, characterization, distillation, exemplification [➡ REPRESENTATIONS AND GENERAL EXAMPLES; 65] 2 *type of* **figure of speech** [➡ FIGURES OF SPEECH; 673]

personify 1 *v* **epitomize**, embody, incarnate, exemplify, characterize, typify, represent, show [➡ REPRESENT SOMETHING OR SOMEBODY; 59] 2 *v* **anthropomorphize**, humanize, personalize, give a human face, bring alive [➡ PRETEND AND MIMIC; 60]

personnel *n* **workers**, staff, employees, work force, human resources, people, recruits, laborers [➡ THE WORK FORCE; 837]

perspective 1 *n* **viewpoint**, standpoint, outlook, view, perception, point of view, side, angle, take, evaluation, assessment [➡ POINTS OF VIEW; 767] 2 *n* **proportion**, scale, ratio, size, depth, range, distance [➡ DEGREE AND EXTENT; 110] 3 *n* **vista**, view, prospect, scene, lookout, outlook, overlook [➡ VIEWS AND OUTLOOKS; 1073]

perspicacious *adj* **discerning**, perceptive, astute, insightful, wise, sagacious, sharp, smart, clear-sighted [➡ POSITIVE INTELLECTUAL CHARACTERISTICS; 524] *Opposite*: obtuse

perspicacity *n* **discernment**, perceptiveness, astuteness, shrewdness, clear-sightedness, cleverness, intelligence, insightfulness, wisdom, acuity, sharpness [➡ POSITIVE INTELLECTUAL CHARACTERISTICS; 524]

perspicuity *n* [➡ POSITIVE INTELLECTUAL CHARACTERISTICS; 524]

perspicuous *adj* [➡ POSITIVE INTELLECTUAL CHARACTERISTICS; 524]

perspiration *n* **sweat**, fluid, exudate, secretion, moisture, dampness, wetness [➡ EXCRETION AND EXCRETA; 722]

perspire *v* **sweat**, exude, ooze, swelter, drip, secrete [➡ EXCRETION AND EXCRETA; 722]

persuade 1 *v* **encourage**, coax, influence, induce, motivate, convince, prevail upon, sway, plead with [➡ CAUSE OR COMPEL TO ACT; 271] *Opposite*: dissuade 2 *v* **convince**, win over, sway, convert, bring around [➡ ENCOURAGE; 576]

persuaded *adj* [➡ CERTAINTY; 561]

persuasion 1 *n* **persuading**, encouragement, coaxing, influence, urging, arguments, wiles, inducement, conversion [➡ ELOQUENT, TALKATIVE, AND LONG-WINDED; 632] 2 *n* **affiliation**, belief, order, denomination, faith, conviction, opinion, view, creed, credo [➡ POINTS OF VIEW; 767]

persuasive *adj* **convincing**, influential, winning, swaying, believable, credible, cogent [➡ ELOQUENT, TALKATIVE, AND LONG-WINDED; 632] *Opposite*: unconvincing

persuasiveness *n* **persuasion**, influence, cogency, smoothness, eloquence, articulateness, slickness [➡ ELOQUENT, TALKATIVE, AND LONG-WINDED; 632]

pert *adj* **lively**, flippant, impudent, perky, breezy, animated, jaunty, vivacious, sassy, cheeky (*informal*), chirpy (*informal*), flip (*informal*), impertinent (*formal*) [➡ CHEERFULNESS OF OUTLOOK; 503]

pertain to *v* **relate**, refer to, apply to, belong to, affect, connect to [➡ BE ABOUT SOMETHING; 62]

pertinacious *adj* **resolute**, stubborn, obstinate, persistent, headstrong, perverse, tenacious, willful, obdurate, mulish, unshakable [➡ STRENGTH OF WILL; 501] *Opposite*: malleable

pertinence *n* **relevance**, relatedness, appositeness, appropriateness, suitability, aptness, applicability, germaneness (*formal*) [➡ APPROPRIATE, SUITABLE, AND ADVISABLE; 184] *Opposite*: irrelevance

pertinent *adj* **relevant**, related, apposite, appropriate, germane, applicable, relatable, apt, valid [➡ APPROPRIATE, SUITABLE, AND ADVISABLE; 184] *Opposite*: irrelevant

pertly *adv* **flippantly**, perkily, breezily, animatedly, impudently, jauntily, vivaciously, sassily, chirpily (*informal*), impertinently (*formal*) [➡ CHEERFULNESS OF OUTLOOK; 503] *Opposite*: bashfully

pertness *n* **cheekiness**, liveliness, flippancy, perkiness, breeziness, jauntiness, vivacity, sassiness, impudence, impertinence, chirpiness (*informal*) [➡ CHEERFULNESS OF OUTLOOK; 503]

perturb *v* **trouble**, bother, disturb, worry, agitate, upset, shake up, ruffle, fluster, flurry, discompose (*formal*) [➡ UPSET, DISTRESS, AND HUMILIATE; 567]

perturbation *n* **alarm**, worry, agitation, disquiet, trepidation, discomposure, disconcertion, uneasiness, unrest, distress [➡ CONFUSION, ANXIETY, AND WORRY; 540] *Opposite*: composure

perturbed *adj* **troubled**, disturbed, worried, anxious, disconcerted, agitated, uneasy, distressed, nervous [➡ CONFUSION, ANXIETY, AND WORRY; 540] *Opposite*: composed

perturbing *adj* [➡ EMOTIONALLY UNPLEASANT AND UPSETTING; 227]

perusal *n* **examination**, scrutiny, inspection, checking, read-through, survey, review [➡ EXAMINE AND ASSESS; 753]

peruse *v* **read**, examine, scan, pore over, scrutinize, inspect, check [➡ EXAMINE AND ASSESS; 753] *Opposite*: skim

pervade *v* **permeate**, pass through, saturate, spread through, infuse, suffuse, diffuse, transfuse, infiltrate [➡ MOVE PAST, INTO, OR THROUGH SOMETHING; 331]

pervasive *adj* **extensive**, universal, general, inescapable, prevalent, widespread, ubiquitous, omnipresent, persistent, rife [➡ PRESENT AND AVAILABLE; 11] *Opposite*: localized

pervasiveness *n* **extensiveness**, universality, generality, ubiquity, ubiquitousness, inescapability, prevalence, omnipresence, rifeness, commonness [➡ PRESENT AND AVAILABLE; 11]

perverse 1 *adj* **obstinate**, willful, stubborn, headstrong, pertinacious, tenacious, dogged, obdurate, awkward (*UK*) [➡ UNWILLINGNESS AND STUBBORNNESS; 564] *Opposite*: malleable 2 *adj* **aberrant**, irrational, deviant, abnormal, unreasonable, contrary, rebellious, disobedient, contradictory, difficult [➡ REBELLIOUSNESS AND DISOBEDIENCE; 565] *Opposite*: obliging

perverseness 1 *n* **aberrance**, irrationality, deviance, disobedience, unreasonableness, contrariness, rebelliousness [➡ REBELLIOUSNESS AND DISOBEDIENCE; 565] 2 *n* **willfulness**, stubbornness, contrariness, recalcitrance [➡ UNWILLINGNESS AND STUBBORNNESS; 564] *Opposite*: malleability

perversion *n* **distortion**, misinterpretation, twisting, corruption, misapplication, falsification [➡ MISUSE AND ABUSE; 471]

perversity *n* **obstinacy**, willfulness, stubbornness, unreasonableness, contrariness, intransigence [➡ UNWILLINGNESS AND STUBBORNNESS, 564] *Opposite:* malleability

pervert 1 *v* **deprave**, corrupt, lead astray, spoil, warp, debauch (*formal*) [➡ WORSEN SOMETHING; 380] 2 *v* **distort**, misinterpret, twist, misrepresent, alter, spoil, change, garble [➡ FALSIFY AND CHEAT; 176]

perverted 1 *adj* **distorted**, misinterpreted, twisted, garbled, changed, misrepresented, altered [➡ FALSE AND UNREAL; 173] *Opposite:* undistorted 2 *adj* **depraved**, corrupt, debauched, warped, degenerate, wayward, deviant, deviate, aberrant, spoiled, abnormal [➡ MORALLY BAD OR IMPROPER; 775]

pervious 1 *adj* **porous**, penetrable, absorbent, permeable [➡ DENSITY AND CONSISTENCY; 1207] *Opposite:* impervious 2 *adj* **receptive**, amenable, responsive, flexible, open [➡ POSITIVE INTELLECTUAL CHARACTERISTICS; 524] *Opposite:* impervious

perviousness *n* [➡ DENSITY AND CONSISTENCY; 1207]

peseta *type of* **currency** [➡ CURRENCIES; 798]

pesky (*informal*) *adj* **irritating**, troublesome, annoying, harassing, bothersome, irksome, vexatious, galling, chafing [➡ IRRITATING; 228]

peso *type of* **currency** [➡ CURRENCIES; 798]

pessimism *n* **negativity**, cynicism, doubt, distrust, gloom, glumness, nihilism, suspicion, hopelessness [➡ FEELINGS ABOUT THE FUTURE; 533] *Opposite:* optimism

pessimist *n* **cynic**, doubter, worrier, nihilist, defeatist, doomsayer, gloomy Gus, worrywart (*informal*), wet blanket (*informal*), naysayer (*literary*), doom merchant (*UK*) [➡ GRUMPY AND NEGATIVE PEOPLE; 953] *Opposite:* optimist

pessimistic *adj* **negative**, cynical, doubtful, distrustful, gloomy, glum, unenthusiastic, suspicious [➡ NEGATIVITY OF OUTLOOK; 514] *Opposite:* optimistic

pest 1 *n* **vermin**, bug, insect, fly, mosquito [➡ INSECTS; 1012] 2 *n* (*informal*) **bother**, nuisance, annoyance, vexation, irritant, hassle (*informal*), pain in the neck (*informal*) [➡ NUISANCES; 253]

pester *v* **annoy**, harass, worry, beleaguer, disturb, bedevil, tease, hector, hound, dog, nag, pick on, ride (*informal*) [➡ ANGER AND ANNOY; 569] *Opposite:* delight

pestilence (*archaic*) *n* **plague**, epidemic, virus, disease, bubonic plague, endemic, pandemic [➡ SICKNESS; 729]

pestilent 1 *adj* **deadly**, lethal, fatal, virulent, killer, pestilential, infectious, contagious [➡ DANGEROUS; 236] *Opposite:* mild 2 *adj* **infected**, plague-ridden, contaminated, polluted, bug-ridden, infested, toxic, diseased [➡ DECAYING OR INFESTED; 1236] *Opposite:* healthy 3 *adj* (*literary or humorous*) **annoying**, irksome, irritating, bothersome, troublesome, pesky (*informal*) [➡ IRRITATING; 228] *Opposite:* pleasing

pestilential *adj* [➡ DECAYING OR INFESTED; 1236]

pestle *type of* **utensil** [➡ TABLEWARE, FLATWARE, AND KITCHENWARE; 861]

pest-ridden *adj* [➡ DECAYING OR INFESTED; 1236]

pet 1 *n* **animal**, domestic animal, domesticated animal, tame animal, companion, four-legged friend [➡ LIVING THINGS AND LIVING; 976] 2 *n* **favorite**, darling, treasure, jewel, idol, beloved, apple of somebody's eye [➡ PEOPLE WHO ARE APPROVED OF; 955] 3 *n* **dear**, love, darling, precious, dearest, sweetheart, sweetie (*informal*), honey (*informal*), babe (*slang*), baby (*slang*) [➡ ENDEARMENTS; 656] 4 *n* **sulk**, huff, pique, temper, tantrum, tiff, miff (*informal*) [➡ IRRITATION AND ANGER; 541] 5 *adj* **favorite**, special, cherished, indulged, preferred, beloved, dearest, precious, prized, dear [➡ POPULAR AND WANTED; 220] 6 *v* **stroke**, pat, fondle, caress, nuzzle, rub [➡ CONTACT: TOUCH; 412] 7 *v* **indulge**, pamper, cosset, mollycoddle, spoil, fuss over, make a fuss of, coddle [➡ TAKE CARE OF AND SPOIL; 300]

petal *part of* **flower** [➡ FLOWERS; 1032]

peter out *v* **disappear**, dwindle, fade, recede, decrease, go away, diminish, die out, melt away, dissolve [➡ DISAPPEAR; 4] *Opposite:* grow

petite *adj* **small**, diminutive, short, little, tiny, elfin [➡ BUILD; 477]

petit four *type of* **cake** [➡ CAKES, COOKIES, AND DESSERTS; 1181]

petition 1 *n* **request**, appeal, entreaty, requisition, application, plea, supplication (*formal*) [➡ REQUEST AND DEMAND; 663] 2 *v* **appeal**, lobby, request, beg, plead, ask, solicit, implore (*formal*) [➡ REQUEST AND DEMAND; 663]

petitioner *n* **lobbyist**, activist, campaigner, requester, asker, suitor, solicitor, supplicant (*formal*) [➡ PEOPLE WHO MAKE REQUESTS; 664]

petits pois *type of* **pulse** [➡ PEAS AND BEANS; 1189]

pet name *n* **name**, nickname, sobriquet, diminutive, epithet, moniker (*slang*), handle (*slang*) [➡ NAME AND DESCRIBE; 665]

petrification *n* [➡ HARDEN, CONGEAL, AND DRY; 387]

petrified 1 *adj* **frightened**, terrified, scared, alarmed, scared stiff, horrified [➡ FEAR AND PANIC; 543] *Opposite:* reassured 2 *adj* **fossilized**, hardened, solidified, fixed, calcified, rigidified, ossified [➡ RIGID AND HARD; 1211]

petrify 1 *v* **frighten**, terrify, scare, alarm, fill with fear, horrify [➡ FRIGHTEN AND SHOCK; 568] *Opposite:* reassure 2 *v* **fossilize**, harden, solidify, ossify, fix, rigidify, turn into stone, calcify, set [➡ HARDEN, CONGEAL, AND DRY; 387]

petrifying *adj* **frightening**, terrifying, horrifying, shocking, spine-chilling, bloodcurdling, chilling, startling, terrorizing, scary (*informal*) [➡ FRIGHTENING; 231] *Opposite:* reassuring

petrol (*UK*) *n* [➡ ENERGY SOURCES; 1162]

petroleum *n* [➡ ENERGY SOURCES; 1162]

petrology *type of* **earth science** [➡ EARTH SCIENCES; 1059]

petrol station (*UK*) *n* **filling station**, garage, service station, gas station [➡ RETAIL OUTLETS; 1083]

petticoat *type of* **lower body underwear** [➡ ACCESSORIES, MILLINERY, AND LINGERIE; 867]

pettifoggery *n* [➡ NEGATIVE INTELLECTUAL CHARACTERISTICS; 525]

pettifogging *adj* **trivial**, petty, unimportant, minor, insignificant, trifling, niggling, picayune (*informal*) [➡ UNIMPORTANT AND UNNECESSARY; 238] *Opposite*: important

pettiness 1 *n* **triviality**, unimportance, inconsequence, paltriness, irrelevance, insignificance [➡ UNIMPORTANT AND UNNECESSARY; 238] *Opposite*: importance 2 *n* **petty-mindedness**, mean-mindedness, triviality, pettifoggery, narrow-mindedness [➡ NEGATIVE INTELLECTUAL CHARACTERISTICS; 525] 3 *n* **spitefulness**, grudgingness, resentfulness, maliciousness, vindictiveness, mean-spiritedness, meanness [➡ SELFISH AND UNKIND; 505]

pettish *adj* **peevish**, irritable, sulky, bad-tempered, petulant, irascible, touchy, testy (*informal*), grouchy (*informal*), cranky (*informal*), sore (*informal*) [➡ IRRITATION AND ANGER; 541] *Opposite*: even-tempered

petty 1 *adj* **trivial**, unimportant, inconsequential, insignificant, paltry, irrelevant, trifling, small, niggling, minor, little [➡ UNIMPORTANT AND UNNECESSARY; 238] *Opposite*: important 2 *adj* **petty-minded**, mean-minded, niggling, narrow-minded, trivial [➡ NEGATIVE INTELLECTUAL CHARACTERISTICS; 525] 3 *adj* **spiteful**, grudging, resentful, malicious, vindictive, mean-spirited, mean [➡ SELFISH AND UNKIND; 505] *Opposite*: generous

petty cash *n* **cash fund**, office fund, coffee fund, float (*UK*) [➡ FUNDS, PAYMENTS, AND CHARGES; 800]

petty larceny *n* [➡ CRIMES; 817]

petty-minded *adj* [➡ NEGATIVE INTELLECTUAL CHARACTERISTICS; 525]

petty-mindedness *n* [➡ NEGATIVE INTELLECTUAL CHARACTERISTICS; 525]

petty thief *n* [➡ CRIMINALS; 821]

petulance *n* **sulkiness**, crabbiness, peevishness, sullenness, moodiness, cantankerousness, bad temper, irritability, grumpiness, tantrums, touchiness, querulousness, grouchiness (*informal*), testiness (*informal*) [➡ IRRITATION AND ANGER; 541] *Opposite*: affability

petulant *adj* **sulky**, crabby, peevish, grumpy, sullen, moody, cantankerous, bad-tempered, irritable, touchy, querulous, snappy, ill-tempered, huffy, snappish, testy (*informal*), grouchy (*informal*) [➡ IRRITATION AND ANGER; 541] *Opposite*: affable

petunia *type of* **annual flower** [➡ FLOWERS; 1032]

pew *n* **bench**, form, seat, bleacher [➡ FURNITURE; 858]

pewter 1 *type of* **metal** [➡ METALS; 1276] 2 *type of* **gray** [➡ COLORS; 1224]

phaeton *type of* **wagon or carriage** [➡ VEHICLES; 1145]

phalanger *type of* **marsupial** [➡ MARSUPIALS; 992]

phalanx *n* **group**, body, mass, unit, formation, assemblage [➡ GROUPS OF PEOPLE; 935]

Phanerozoic *type of* **eon** [➡ EPOCHS AND ERAS; 89]

phantasm *n* **ghost**, spirit, apparition, specter, phantom, spook (*informal*), shade (*literary*) [➡ THE SUPERNATURAL; 787]

phantasmagoria *n* **image**, dream, hallucination, optical illusion, mirage, fantasy [➡ NONEXISTENT THINGS; 23]

phantasmagoric *adj* **dreamlike**, bizarre, surreal, psychedelic, fantastical, hallucinatory [➡ BIZARRE AND PECULIAR; 257]

phantasmagory *see* **phantasmagoria**

phantom *n* **ghost**, apparition, spirit, specter, phantasm, spook (*informal*), shade (*literary*) [➡ THE SUPERNATURAL; 787]

Pharaoh *n* **ruler**, king, sovereign, monarch, emperor, sultan [➡ RULERS AND ARISTOCRACY; 823]

Pharaoh ant *type of* **ant** [➡ ANTS; 1014]

pharmaceutical 1 *adj* **medicinal**, medical, pharmacological, therapeutic, curative [➡ REMEDIES, TREATMENTS, AND OPERATIONS; 731] 2 *n* **drug**, medicine, medication, treatment, narcotic, analgesic, antibiotic [➡ REMEDIES, TREATMENTS, AND OPERATIONS; 731]

pharmacist *n* **druggist**, pharmacologist, posologist, apothecary (*archaic*), chemist (*UK*), dispensing chemist (*UK*) [➡ PEOPLE WHO WORK IN MEDICINE; 848]

pharmacologist *n* [➡ PEOPLE WHO WORK IN MEDICINE; 848]

pharmacy *n* **drugstore**, dispensary, druggist's, apothecary (*archaic*), chemist's (*UK*), dispensing chemist's (*UK*) [➡ RETAIL OUTLETS; 1083]

pharynx *part of* **respiratory system** [➡ RESPIRATORY ORGANS; 715]

phase *n* **stage**, point, chapter, time, segment, part, period, level, rung [➡ PAUSES AND PHASES; 56]

phase in *v* [➡ CAUSE TO START; 265]

phase out *v* [➡ CAUSE TO STOP; 266]

pheasant 1 *type of* **fowl** [➡ FOOD BIRDS; 999] 2 *type of* **meat** [➡ TYPES AND CUTS OF MEAT; 1177]

phenomenal 1 *adj* **remarkable**, extraordinary, impressive, prodigious, outstanding, astonishing, unbelievable, incredible, astounding, exceptional, unique, unusual, rare, extra special, out of the ordinary, unparalleled [➡ EXTRAORDINARY: UNCOMMON; 205] *Opposite*: unremarkable 2 *adj* (*informal*) **fantastic**, marvelous, wonderful, amazing, brilliant, sensational, huge (*informal*), great (*informal*) [➡ EXTRAORDINARY: AMAZING; 204] *Opposite*: moderate

phenomenon 1 *n* **occurrence**, fact, experience, happening, incident, event, trend [➡ EVENTS AND OCCURRENCES; 35] 2 *n* **marvel**, wonder, singularity, miracle, spectacle, sensation, portent (*formal*) [➡ AMAZING THINGS; 211] 3 *n* **prodigy**, genius, bright star, enfant terrible, whiz kid (*informal*) [➡ TALENTED OR INTELLIGENT PEOPLE; 528]

phial *n* **vial**, bottle, vessel, flask, flagon, ampoule [➡ CONTAINERS, RECEPTACLES, AND PACKAGING; 1245]

philanderer *n* **flirt**, Casanova, adulterer, ladies' man, lady-killer, Romeo, womanizer, stud (*informal*), wolf (*informal*), Lothario (*literary*) [➡ PLEASURE-SEEKERS AND HEDONISTS; 886]

philandering *adj* [➡ PLEASURE-SEEKING AND EXCESS; 885]

philanthropic *adj* **charitable**, benevolent, humanitarian, generous, big-hearted, giving, goodhearted, altruistic [➡ GENEROSITY AND KINDNESS; 495] *Opposite*: misanthropic

philanthropist *n* **patron**, humanitarian, donor, sponsor, promoter, contributor, backer, guarantor [➡ REPRESENTATIVES AND PATRONS; 968] *Opposite*: misanthropist

philanthropy *n* **charity**, compassion, humanity, patronage, generosity, benevolence, altruism, clemency, goodwill, amity (*formal*) [➡ KIND ACTIONS OR BEHAVIOR; 295] *Opposite*: misanthropy

philharmonic *adj* [➡ MUSICAL TERMS; 912]

philippic *n* **diatribe**, tirade, discourse, denunciation, insult, harangue, rant, invective (*formal*), jeremiad (*formal*) [➡ CRITICISMS AND ANGRY OUTBURSTS; 50]

philistine 1 *n* **vulgarian**, boor [➡ VILLAINS AND THUGS; 947] *Opposite*: aesthete 2 *adj* **uncultured**, unsophisticated, uninformed, untutored, boorish [➡ LEVELS OF EDUCATION AND SOPHISTICATION; 894] *Opposite*: cultured

philistinism *n* **barbarism**, unsophistication, boorishness, ignorance [➡ LEVELS OF EDUCATION AND SOPHISTICATION; 894]

philosopher *n* **theorist**, thinker, logician, truth-seeker, academic, dreamer [➡ PHILOSOPHICAL AND POLITICAL THINKERS; 781] *Opposite*: realist

philosophic 1 *adj* **logical**, ethical, metaphysical, moral, theoretical, rational [➡ PHILOSOPHIES AND BELIEFS; 780] 2 *adj* **deep-thinking**, learned, thoughtful, studious, enlightened, wise, erudite, scholarly, rational [➡ POSITIVE INTELLECTUAL CHARACTERISTICS; 524] *Opposite*: shallow 3 *adj* **calm**, resigned, restrained, stoical, patient, uncomplaining, wise, accepting, unruffled [➡ COOL AND CALM; 536] *Opposite*: emotional

philosophical 1 *adj* **logical**, ethical, metaphysical, moral, theoretical, rational [➡ PHILOSOPHIES AND BELIEFS; 780] 2 *adj* **deep-thinking**, learned, thoughtful, studious, enlightened, wise, erudite, scholarly, rational [➡ POSITIVE INTELLECTUAL CHARACTERISTICS; 524] *Opposite*: shallow 3 *adj* **calm**, resigned, restrained, stoical, patient, uncomplaining, wise, accepting, unruffled [➡ COOL AND CALM; 536] *Opposite*: emotional

philosophize *v* **moralize**, speculate, theorize, pronounce, meditate, reason [➡ DEVELOP THEORIES AND REASON; 744]

philosophy *n* **beliefs**, viewpoint, thinking, values, attitude, idea, way of life [➡ PHILOSOPHIES AND BELIEFS; 780]

philter (*literary*) *n* **potion**, charm, drug, aphrodisiac, magic potion, draft (*dated*) [➡ LUCKY CHARMS; 785]

phlegm 1 *n* **mucus**, catarrh, rheum [➡ EXCRETION AND EXCRETA; 722] 2 *n* **calmness**, composure, unflappability, self-possession, imperturbability, coolness, equanimity (*formal*) [➡ CONFIDENCE AND COMPOSURE; 499] *Opposite*: nervousness

phlegmatic *adj* **calm**, unemotional, composed, unflappable, apathetic, indifferent, unconcerned, undemonstrative, matter-of-fact, placid, impassive, dry, stoic, stolid [➡ COOL AND CALM; 536] *Opposite*: nervous

See Compare and Contrast at **impassive**.

phobia *n* **fear**, terror, dread, horror, fright, obsession, paranoia, anxiety, thing (*informal*) [➡ FEARS AND PHOBIAS; 554]

phobia

◆ *types of phobias*
acrophobia (fear of high places), agoraphobia (fear of public or open spaces), ailurophobia (fear of cats), arachnophobia (fear of spiders), claustrophobia (fear of confined or enclosed spaces), hydrophobia (fear of water), necrophobia (fear of death or dead bodies), nyctophobia (fear of night or darkness), photophobia (fear of light or lighted spaces), pyrophobia (fear of fire), technophobia (fear of new technology or computerization), zoophobia (fear of animals)

phobic 1 *adj* **fearful**, scared, terrified, nervous, anxious, neurotic, overanxious, paranoid [➡ FEAR AND PANIC; 543] 2 *adj* **irrational**, neurotic, obsessed, disturbed, fixated, paranoid, hung up (*informal*) [➡ FEARS AND PHOBIAS; 554]

Phoenix *type of* **constellation** [➡ HEAVENLY BODIES; 1061]

phone 1 *n* **telephone**, touchtone phone, mobile phone, mobile, cellphone, cellular phone [➡ TELECOMMUNICATIONS; 1130] 2 *v* **call**, ring, ring up, telephone, make a call, call up, buzz (*informal*), give a ring (*UK*) [➡ TELEPHONE, PAGE, AND TEXT; 681]

phone call *n* [➡ TELEPHONE COMMUNICATION; 48]

phonecard *type of* **telecommunications equipment** [➡ TELECOMMUNICATIONS; 1130]

phonetic alphabet *type of* **alphabet** [➡ SYMBOLS, SIGNS, AND NUMBERS; 596]

phone up (*UK*) *v* [➡ TELEPHONE, PAGE, AND TEXT; 681]

phoney *see* **phony**

phoniness *n* [➡ FALSE AND UNREAL; 173]

phonograph *type of* **audio equipment** [➡ AUDIO EQUIPMENT; 1139]

phony 1 *adj* **false**, fake, counterfeit, bogus, artificial, feigned, forged, spurious, sham, ersatz [➡ FALSE AND UNREAL; 173] *Opposite*: genuine 2 *adj* **affected**, pretentious, deceiving, insincere, deceptive, sham, put-on, mannered [➡ DECEITFUL; 513] *Opposite*: sincere 3 *n* **fake**, counterfeit, impostor, hypocrite, forgery, fraud, sham, charlatan, hoax, pretender, dissembler (*formal*) [➡ PEOPLE WHO DECEIVE; 661]

photo *n* **photograph**, picture, snapshot, print, snap, shot [➡ PHOTOGRAPHY AND PHOTOGRAPHIC EQUIPMENT; 1122]

photocopy 1 *n* **copy**, duplicate, reproduction, print [➡ PHOTOGRAPHY AND PHOTOGRAPHIC EQUIPMENT; 1122] 2 *v* **copy**, reproduce, make a copy of, run off, duplicate, replicate, reduplicate [➡ COPY AND DUPLICATE; 402]

photo finish *n* **close contest**, close thing, tie, neck-and-neck finish (*informal*) [➡ SPORTS TERMS; 877]

photogenic *adj* **camera-friendly**, attractive, picturesque, appealing, good-looking, striking, beautiful, pretty [➡ PEOPLE'S PHYSICAL APPEARANCE; 475]

photograph 1 *n* **photo**, picture, snap, shot, snapshot, print [➡ PHOTOGRAPHY AND PHOTOGRAPHIC EQUIPMENT; 1122] 2 *v* **photo**, snap, shoot, get on film [➡ CREATE IMAGES; 356]

photographer *n* **professional photographer**, press photographer, paparazzo, amateur photographer, photojournalist, shutterbug (*informal*), snapper (*informal*) [➡ARTISTS; 900]

photographic 1 *adj* **pictorial**, graphic, picturesque, photogenic, camera-friendly [➡ARTISTIC MOVEMENTS AND STYLES; 899] 2 *adj* **vivid**, clear, accurate, exact, detailed, precise, graphic, acute, rich, intense [➡EXACT; 203]

photography *n* **cinematography**, filmmaking, picture making, shooting, camerawork [➡THE PICTORIAL ARTS; 897]

photography

◆ *parts of a camera*
autofocus, diaphragm, exposure meter, film, filter, fisheye lens, flash, lens, lens cap, rangefinder, shutter, telephoto lens, viewfinder, zoom lens

◆ *types of photographic equipment*
box camera, camera, darkroom, developer, disc camera, enlarger, microfiche, microfilm, movie camera, pinhole camera, printer, projector, reflex camera, single-lens reflex, speed camera, tripod, twin-lens reflex

photojournalism *n* **photography**, news photography, reportage, camerawork, filmmaking, journalism [➡NEWS-PAPERS AND MAGAZINES; 605]

photon *type of* **elementary particle** [➡ELEMENTARY PARTICLES; 1279]

photo opportunity *n* **publicity stunt**, photo shoot, photo op, media event, public-relations exercise, press interview, TV interview, interview, publicity event [➡TELEVISION AND RADIO; 606]

photophobia *type of* **phobia** [➡FEARS AND PHOBIAS; 554]

photorealism *type of* **20th-century art movement** [➡ARTISTIC MOVEMENTS AND STYLES; 899]

photosensitive *adj* **light sensitive**, sensitive, reactive, light reactive, hypersensitive, photophobic [➡SEE; 699]

phrasal *adj* **linguistic**, verbal, expressive, semantic, phraseological, terminological [➡ASPECTS OF LANGUAGE; 682]

phrasal verb *type of* **word class** [➡ASPECTS OF LANGUAGE; 682]

phrase 1 *n* **expression**, saying, idiom, axiom, slogan, turn of phrase, locution, catch phrase, watchword [➡ASPECTS OF LANGUAGE; 682] 2 *v* **express**, couch, put, say, put into words, verbalize, formulate, word [➡UTTER AND PRONOUNCE; 608]

phrase book *n* **glossary**, bilingual dictionary, foreign-language dictionary, dictionary, lexicon, vocabulary list, thesaurus [➡BOOKS AND BOOKLETS; 590]

phraseology *n* **phrasing**, wording, choice of words, word choice, terminology, turn of phrase, expression, style [➡ASPECTS OF LANGUAGE; 682]

phrasing *n* **wording**, turn of phrase, style, word choice, diction, language, idiom, expression, phraseology, choice of words, manner of speaking [➡ASPECTS OF LANGUAGE; 682]

physical 1 *adj* **bodily**, corporeal, animal, corporal, fleshly, somatic, carnal (*formal*) [➡LIVING THINGS AND LIVING; 976] *Opposite*: mental 2 *adj* **substantial**, material, objective, natural, real, tangible, sensible, touchable [➡PERCEPTIBLE; 25] *Opposite*: ethereal 3 *adj* **brute**, instinctive, visceral,

instinctual, basic, base [➡AUTOMATIC AND INSTINCTIVE; 280] *Opposite*: refined

physical education *n* **sports**, gymnastics, athletics, exercise, aerobics, games (*UK*) [➡CLASSES, COURSEWORK, AND EXAMINATIONS; 842]

physically *adv* **bodily**, actually, in the flesh, really, materially, substantially, tangibly [➡TRUE AND REAL; 171] *Opposite*: mentally

physical therapy *n* **treatment**, remedial exercise, rehabilitation, exercise, physiotherapy (*UK*), physical exercises (*UK*) [➡REMEDIES, TREATMENTS, AND OPERATIONS; 731]

physician *n* **doctor**, medical doctor, doctor of medicine, general practitioner, GP, surgeon [➡PEOPLE WHO WORK IN MEDICINE; 848]

physics *n* **dynamics**, forces, physical processes, interactions, properties, behavior [➡QUALITIES AND CHARACTERISTICS; 1191]

physiognomy *n* **appearance**, face, features, characteristics, physical appearance, physical characteristics [➡PARTS OF THE BODY: HEAD; 692]

physiological *adj* **physical**, bodily, biological, functional [➡BIOLOGICAL SCIENCES; 1037]

physiology *type of* **bioscience** [➡BIOLOGICAL SCIENCES; 1037]

physique *n* **build**, body type, physical type, figure, form, body, shape, size, structure, frame [➡BODY; 691]

phytoplankton *type of* **marine alga** [➡MICROORGANISMS, FUNGI, AND ALGAE; 1023]

pianissimo *type of* **musical term** [➡MUSICAL TERMS; 912]

piano 1 *type of* **musical term** [➡MUSICAL TERMS; 912] 2 *type of* **keyboard** [➡MUSICAL INSTRUMENTS; 910]

pianoforte (*formal*) *type of* **keyboard** [➡MUSICAL INSTRUMENTS; 910]

piazza *n* **square**, forum, gathering place, village square, town square, quadrangle, market square [➡URBAN OUTDOOR SPACES; 1072]

picaresque *adj* **roguish**, mischievous, rascally, impish, villainous, cheating [➡BAD MANNERS AND SOCIAL SKILLS; 521]

picayune (*informal*) *adj* [➡NEGATIVE INTELLECTUAL CHARACTERISTICS; 525]

piccalilli *type of* **relish** [➡SEASONINGS AND SAUCES; 1174]

piccolo *type of* **wind instrument** [➡MUSICAL INSTRUMENTS; 910]

pick 1 *v* **harvest**, gather, cut, collect, pluck, reap [➡GROW AND CULTIVATE; 351] 2 *v* **select**, single out, choose, pick and choose, accept, make a choice, elect to choose, decide on, settle on, elect, opt [➡MAKE DECISIONS AND CHOICES; 752] 3 *n* **best choice**, top choice, choice, cream of the crop, pick of the litter, preference, prize, best, elite [➡SOURCE OF HAPPINESS, PLEASURE, OR IMPROVEMENT; 209]

pick and choose *v* [➡MAKE DECISIONS AND CHOICES; 752]

pickax *type of* **cutting tool** [➡CUTTING TOOLS; 1120]

picked *adj* **chosen**, selected, select, elect, handpicked, elite, exclusive [➡SUPERIORITY; 152]

picket 1 *n* **stake**, post, fence post, peg, rod, pole, stick, paling [➡ STICKS, POLES, AND WEDGES; 1254] 2 *n* **lookout**, sentinel, watch, sentry, guard, patrol [➡ UNCOOPERATIVE OR REBELLIOUS PEOPLE; 566] 3 *n* **striker**, protester, boycotter, blockader [➡ WORK-RELATED ACTIVITIES; 834] 4 *v* **enclose**, fence, corral, restrain, hedge in, pen in [➡ BAR AND OBSTRUCT ACCESS; 410] 5 *v* **protest**, strike, demonstrate, strike against, demonstrate at, blockade, besiege [➡ PROTEST AND EXPRESS DISAPPROVAL; 642]

pick holes in *v* **find fault with**, fault, criticize, attack, tear to shreds, disparage, slam (*informal*) [➡ ACCUSE, BLAME, AND CRITICIZE; 641] *Opposite*: praise

See Compare and Contrast at **criticize**.

pickiness *n* [➡ DIFFICULT TO PLEASE; 515]

pickings *n* **earnings**, profits, takings, proceeds, spoils, loot, plunder, ill-gotten gains, booty, swag (*slang*) [➡ PROCEEDS OF CRIME; 427]

pickle 1 *n* (*informal*) **difficulty**, bind, predicament, plight, quandary, mess, fix (*informal*), jam (*informal*), scrape (*informal*), spot (*informal*), tight spot (*informal*) [➡ DIFFICULT SITUATIONS; 72] 2 *v* **preserve**, marinate, cure, keep, conserve, soak, store [➡ COOKING AND FOOD PREPARATION; 353]

pickled *adj* **preserved**, marinated, soused [➡ STATE OF PREPARED FOOD; 1171]

pickled cucumber *type of* **relish** [➡ SEASONINGS AND SAUCES; 1174]

pick-me-up (*informal*) *n* **refreshment**, stimulant, shot in the arm, drink, hair of the dog, tonic, catalyst, impetus, incentive, motivation [➡ TREATS; 210]

pick of the bunch *n* [➡ SOURCE OF HAPPINESS, PLEASURE, OR IMPROVEMENT; 209]

pick of the litter *n* [➡ SOURCE OF HAPPINESS, PLEASURE, OR IMPROVEMENT; 209]

pick on *v* **tease**, make fun of, bully, harass, criticize, be critical of, single out, persecute, annoy, harry, pester, bedevil [➡ JOKES AND TEASING; 674]

pick out 1 *v* **choose**, make a choice, select, pick, pull out, single out, elect, opt [➡ MAKE DECISIONS AND CHOICES; 752] 2 *v* **identify**, distinguish, isolate, recognize, single out, discern, differentiate, discriminate [➡ NAME AND DESCRIBE; 665] 3 *v* **highlight**, outline, emphasize [➡ MAKE DECISIONS AND CHOICES; 752]

pickpocket *n* **thief**, sneak thief, robber, bag-snatcher, purse snatcher, crook (*informal*) [➡ CRIMINALS; 821]

pick up 1 *v* **lift**, raise, hoist, raise up, elevate, uplift [➡ MOVE SOMETHING UPWARD; 328] *Opposite*: put down 2 *v* (*informal*) **improve**, recover, bounce back, buck up, change for the better, look up, get better, rally [➡ GET BETTER; 375] *Opposite*: deteriorate 3 *v* **give a ride to**, give a lift to, come and get somebody, call for somebody, stop for somebody, come by, take on, load up, transport, convey, carry, collect (*UK*) [➡ ACCOMPANY AND FOLLOW; 337] *Opposite*: drop off (*informal*) 4 *v* **learn**, understand, grasp, get the hang of, remember, become familiar with, master, memorize, realize [➡ UNDERSTAND AND GRASP; 759] 5 *v* **speed up**, accelerate, go faster, get better, improve, be more exciting, liven up, quicken, stimulate [➡ CHANGE OF SPEED: MORE; 396] *Opposite*: slow down

6 *v* **restart**, take up again, continue, carry on, jump back in [➡ CONTINUE AN ACTION; 262] *Opposite*: drop

pickup *type of* **commercial or industrial vehicle** [➡ VEHICLES; 1145]

pick up on (*informal*) *v* **notice**, point out, focus on, single out, call attention to, mention, raise, remark on, comment on [➡ SUGGEST, HINT, AND COMMENT; 612] *Opposite*: miss

pick up speed *v* [➡ CHANGE OF SPEED: MORE; 396]

pick up the pace *v* [➡ CHANGE OF SPEED: MORE; 396]

picky *adj* **fastidious**, fussy, hard to please, finicky, particular, exacting, choosy (*informal*), persnickety (*informal*) [➡ DIFFICULT TO PLEASE; 515] *Opposite*: easygoing

picnic 1 *type of* **meal** [➡ MEALS AND PARTS OF MEALS; 1169] 2 *n* (*informal*) **nothing**, walkover (*informal*), cinch (*informal*), piece of cake (*informal*), breeze (*informal*) [➡ EASY WORK; 299] 3 *v* **have a picnic**, eat al fresco, eat outside [➡ LEISURE AND RECREATION; 874]

pictogram *n* [➡ SYMBOLS, SIGNS, AND NUMBERS; 596]

pictograph *n* **symbol**, hieroglyph, primitive writing, character, drawing, picture [➡ SYMBOLS, SIGNS, AND NUMBERS; 596]

pictographic *adj* **graphic**, symbolic, pictorial, illustrative, visual [➡ ARTISTIC MOVEMENTS AND STYLES; 899]

Pictor *type of* **constellation** [➡ HEAVENLY BODIES; 1061]

pictorial *adj* **graphic**, symbolic, illustrative, pictographic, clear, vivid [➡ ARTISTIC MOVEMENTS AND STYLES; 899]

picture 1 *n* **image**, depiction, portrait, representation, photograph, photo, print, painting, drawing, sketch, delineation, portrayal, illustration, likeness [➡ ARTWORKS; 898] 2 *n* **movie**, film, feature, motion picture, flick (*informal*) [➡ FILM; 901] 3 *n* **embodiment**, epitome, perfect example, essence, personification, archetype, image, living example, model, mold, paragon, mirror [➡ PERFECT EXAMPLES AND EMBODIMENTS; 67] 4 *v* **imagine**, create in your mind, visualize, see, conceive of, see in your mind's eye, conjure up, dream of, evoke, fancy [➡ DREAM, IMAGINE, AND FANTASIZE; 749] 5 *v* **describe**, depict, illustrate, draw, show, give, portray, represent, delineate [➡ NAME AND DESCRIBE; 665]

picture book *n* **illustrated book**, children's book, story book, annual, coffee-table book, comic book [➡ BOOKS AND BOOKLETS; 590]

picture hat *type of* **hat** [➡ ACCESSORIES, MILLINERY, AND LINGERIE; 867]

picture molding *type of* **general fixtures** [➡ FIXTURES; 859]

picture-perfect *adj* [➡ BEAUTY AND ATTRACTIVENESS; 189]

picture-postcard *adj* **picturesque**, attractive, pretty, chocolate-box, scenic, charming, appealing, pleasant, quaint, twee (*UK*) [➡ BEAUTY AND ATTRACTIVENESS; 189] *Opposite*: unattractive

picturesque 1 *adj* **attractive**, pretty, scenic, charming, chocolate-box, striking, quaint, pleasing [➡ BEAUTY AND ATTRACTIVENESS; 189] *Opposite*: unattractive 2 *adj* **pictorial**, graphic, symbolic, pictographic, vivid, colorful [➡ ARTISTIC MOVEMENTS AND STYLES; 899]

picturesquely *adv* **attractively**, prettily, scenically, charmingly, appealingly, pleasantly [➡BEAUTY AND ATTRACT-IVENESS; 189] *Opposite:* unattractively

picturesqueness *n* [➡BEAUTY AND ATTRACTIVENESS; 189]

picture window *type of* **window** [➡WINDOWS; 1100]

piddling (*informal*) *adj* **small**, petty, puny, paltry, trifling, trivial, unimportant, insignificant, minor, skimpy, slight, measly (*informal*), picayune (*informal*), piffling (*informal*) [➡FEW, LITTLE, SMALL AMOUNT; 120] *Opposite:* enormous

pidgin *n* **lingua franca**, creole, patois, dialect, lingo (*informal*) [➡THE SPOKEN WORD; 671]

pie *type of* **dessert** [➡CAKES, COOKIES, AND DESSERTS; 1181]

piebald *adj* **parti-colored**, pied, skewbald, spotted, mottled, speckled, dappled, flecked, two-colored [➡DESCRIBING PATTERNS; 1227] *Opposite:* plain

piece 1 *n* **part**, fragment, bit, member, part of a set, part of the pack, section [➡AREA AND RANGE; 111] *Opposite:* whole 2 *n* **bit**, portion, hunk, wedge, slice, chunk, fragment, amount, quantity, cut (*informal*) [➡AMOUNTS OF SOLID OR SEMISOLID; 115] *Opposite:* whole 3 *n* **example**, case, sample, instance, occurrence, specimen [➡REPRESENTATIONS AND GENERAL EXAMPLES; 65] 4 *v* **patch**, mend, repair, restore, fix [➡REPAIR AND MEND; 376]

pièce de résistance *n* [➡SOURCE OF HAPPINESS, PLEASURE, OR IMPROVEMENT; 209]

piecemeal 1 *adv* **gradually**, by degrees, little by little, a little at a time, a bit at a time, slowly, inchmeal, progressively [➡HAPPENING SLOWLY; 106] *Opposite:* all at once 2 *adv* **piece by piece**, bit by bit, one by one, separately, one at a time, individually, fractionally [➡APPORTIONMENT; 113] 3 *adj* **fragmentary**, disjointed, disconnected, disorganized, haphazard, fractional, spasmodic, bitty (*UK*) [➡UNFINISHEDNESS; 239] *Opposite:* cohesive

piece of cake (*informal*) *n* **snap**, child's play, nothing, breeze (*informal*), cinch (*informal*), gift (*informal*) [➡EASY WORK; 299]

piece of music *n* **composition**, creation, tune, melody, work, piece [➡MUSIC, SONGS, AND SINGING; 907]

piece of writing *n* **article**, essay, composition, report, discourse, treatise, thesis, book [➡ANALYTICAL NONFICTION WRITING; 592]

piece out 1 *v* **piece together**, work out, reconstruct, restore, make sense of, rationalize [➡DEVELOP THEORIES AND REASON; 744] 2 *v* (*UK*) **apportion**, mete out, share out, dispense, hand out, distribute [➡DISPENSE, RATION, AND DISTRIBUTE; 434]

piece together 1 *v* **work out**, piece out, reconstruct, make sense of, rationalize [➡DEVELOP THEORIES AND REASON; 744] 2 *v* **assemble**, join, fix, repair, mend, put together, reconstruct, patch, restore [➡BUILD; 352] *Opposite:* take apart

piecework *n* **freelance work**, part-time work, casual work, commission [➡TYPES OF WORK; 835]

piechart *n* **graph**, chart, diagram, illustration, figure [➡DRAWINGS, CHARTS, AND TABLES; 594]

pied *adj* **multicolored**, variegated, mottled, piebald, flecked, brindled, dappled, parti-colored [➡DESCRIBING PATTERNS; 1227] *Opposite:* plain

pied-à-terre *n* **second home**, vacation home, apartment, city apartment, studio, holiday home (*UK*), town flat (*UK*) [➡RESIDENTIAL BUILDINGS; 1078]

pied wagtail *type of* **songbird** [➡SONGBIRDS; 1003]

pier *n* **dock**, wharf, berth, jetty, landing-stage, quay, landing place, landing, levee, piling, slip [➡WATERWAYS AND SEAWAYS; 1108]

pierce 1 *v* **bore into**, stab, impale, cut, slice, slice open, penetrate, prick, perforate, puncture, drill, stick, spear, lance [➡TEAR, BREAK, AND CUT; 360] 2 *v* **hurt**, sting, pain, wound, affront, grieve, distress [➡UPSET, DISTRESS, AND HUMILIATE; 567] *Opposite:* heal

piercing 1 *adj* **penetrating**, intense, sharp, loud, ear-splitting, high-pitched, shrill, deafening, discordant, strident, acute, stabbing, painful, keen, cutting, knife-like [➡LOUD, HIGH, OR UNPLEASANT SOUNDS; 1266] *Opposite:* soothing 2 *adj* **perceptive**, searching, shrewd, acute, keen, penetrating, intense, sharp [➡POSITIVE INTELLECTUAL CHARACTERISTICS; 524] *Opposite:* gentle 3 *adj* **cold**, bitter, freezing, wintry, raw, biting, chilling, penetrating [➡COLD WEATHER; 1051] *Opposite:* mild

piercingly 1 *adv* **penetratingly**, intensely, sharply, loudly, earsplittingly, shrilly, deafeningly, discordantly, stridently, acutely, painfully, keenly [➡LOUD, HIGH, OR UNPLEASANT SOUNDS; 1266] *Opposite:* soothingly 2 *adv* **perceptively**, searchingly, shrewdly, acutely, keenly, penetratingly, intensely, sharply [➡POSITIVE INTELLECTUAL CHARACTERISTICS; 524] *Opposite:* gently

piety 1 *n* **piousness**, devoutness, devotion, religiousness, virtue, goodness, faithfulness, holiness, reverence, respect, godliness (*formal*) [➡MORALLY GOOD; 774] *Opposite:* impiety 2 *n* **sanctimoniousness**, moralizing, hypocrisy, smugness, self-righteousness [➡AFFECTATION, SELF-SATISFACTION, AND SNOBBISHNESS; 507]

piffle (*informal*) *n* **nonsense**, garbage, twaddle (*informal*), bunkum (*informal*), tripe (*informal*), claptrap (*informal*), rot (*informal*), rubbish (*UK*) [➡MEANINGLESS SPEECH OR WRITING; 676] *Opposite:* sense

piffling (*informal*) *adj* **trifling**, unimportant, trivial, insignificant, petty, minor, small, paltry [➡UNIMPORTANT AND UNNECESSARY; 238] *Opposite:* important

pig 1 *n* (*informal*) **glutton**, gourmand, greedy pig (*informal*), guzzler (*informal*) [➡PLEASURE-SEEKERS AND HEDONISTS; 886] 2 *n* (*informal*) **brute**, beast, monster, rat (*slang*) [➡VILLAINS AND THUGS; 947] 3 *type of* **farm animal** [➡FARM ANIMALS; 982]

pigeon 1 *n* (*informal*) **easy target**, dupe, sitting duck (*informal*), sucker (*informal*), chump (*informal*), mark (*slang*) [➡VICTIMS OF DECEIT; 662] 2 *type of* **fowl** [➡FOOD BIRDS; 999] 3 *type of* **common bird** [➡BIRDS; 997]

pigeon-breasted *adj* **barrel-chested**, top-heavy, stout [➡BUILD; 477]

pigeonhole 1 *n* **cubbyhole**, compartment, box, shelf, slot, niche, cubicle [➡CONTAINERS, RECEPTACLES, AND PACKAGING; 1245] 2 *n* **category**, class, slot, classification, compartment, label [➡VARIETIES, TYPES, AND KINDS; 145] 3 *v* **categorize**, class, classify, label, compartmentalize, sort, slot, partition, rank, break down, sort out, group [➡NAME AND DESCRIBE; 665]

piggery *type of* **pen or cage** [➡ANIMAL OR BIRD ACCOMMODATIONS; 1079]

piggish 1 *adj* **greedy**, gluttonous, hoggish, self-indulgent [➡ BEASTLY AND BRUTISH; 510] *Opposite*: abstemious **2** *adj* **stubborn**, uncooperative, obstructive, selfish, self-centered [➡ SELFISH AND UNKIND; 505] *Opposite*: considerate

piggy *adj* **greedy**, piggish, gluttonous, hoggish, self-indulgent [➡ BEASTLY AND BRUTISH; 510] *Opposite*: abstemious

piggyback *adj* **allied**, attached, associated, linked, added [➡ RELATED; 142]

piggy bank *n* **money box**, cash box, collecting box, savings box [➡ CONTAINERS, RECEPTACLES, AND PACKAGING; 1245]

piggy in the middle (*UK*) *n* **go-between**, mediator, intermediary, negotiator, peacemaker, pig in the middle (*UK*) [➡ ADVISERS, JUDGES, AND ARBITERS; 971]

pigheaded *adj* **stubborn**, obstinate, mulish, dogged, single-minded, intransigent, obdurate, inflexible, unyielding, tenacious, headstrong, willful, intractable (*formal*) [➡ UNWILLINGNESS AND STUBBORNNESS; 564] *Opposite*: flexible

pigheadedness *n* **stubbornness**, obstinacy, mulishness, single-mindedness, intransigence, obduracy, inflexibility, unyieldingness, tenacity, perseverance, doggedness, persistence, intractability (*formal*) [➡ UNWILLINGNESS AND STUBBORNNESS; 564] *Opposite*: flexibility

piglet *type of* **young animal** [➡ YOUNG ANIMALS; 977]

pigment *n* **color**, dye, stain, tint, coloring, tincture, colorant, dyestuff [➡ DYES AND COLORANTS; 1270]

pigmentation *n* **coloring**, coloration, skin-color, pigment, color, natural coloring, skin coloring [➡ PATTERNS; 1225]

pig out (*informal*) *v* **gobble**, gorge, devour, eat, scarf (*informal*), scarf down (*informal*), scoff (*informal*), guzzle (*informal*) [➡ EAT AND NOT EAT; 710]

pigpen **1** *type of* **pen or cage** [➡ ANIMAL OR BIRD ACCOMMODATIONS; 1079] **2** *n* **filthy surroundings**, mess, dump (*informal*), hole (*informal*), pigsty (*UK*) [➡ UNDESIRABLE ACCOMMODATIONS; 856]

pigskin **1** *n* **football**, ball, oval [➡ SPORTS EQUIPMENT; 879] **2** *type of* **leather** [➡ FABRICS; 1132]

pigswill (*UK*) *n* **slops**, pig food, scraps, mash, leftovers [➡ ANIMAL FEED; 1168]

pigtail *type of* **hairstyle** [➡ HAIRSTYLES AND HAIRPIECES; 488]

pike *type of* **freshwater fish** [➡ FRESHWATER FISH; 1010]

pilaf *type of* **cooked dish** [➡ PREPARED DISHES; 1170]

pilaster *n* [➡ SUPPORTS AND BASES; 1255]

Pilates *type of* **complementary therapy** [➡ REMEDIES, TREATMENTS, AND OPERATIONS; 731]

pilchard *type of* **ocean fish** [➡ OCEAN FISH; 1009]

pile **1** *n* **mound**, mountain, quantity, mass, heap, stack, load, batch, accumulation, hoard [➡ MANY, MUCH, LARGE AMOUNT; 117] **2** *n* (*informal*) **big money**, fortune, mint (*informal*), wad (*informal*), megabucks (*slang*) [➡ LARGE AMOUNTS OF MONEY; 118] **3** *n* **stake**, post, support, pillar, column, piling, upright [➡ STICKS, POLES, AND WEDGES; 1254] **4** *n* **soft surface**, fiber, down, nap, fur [➡ TEXTURE; 1220] **5** *v* **heap**, load, stack, pile up, amass, superimpose, swell, assemble, accumulate [➡ POSITION SOMETHING; 325] *Opposite*: scatter

pile up *v* **stack**, heap up, amass, mound, collect, pile, heap, accumulate, assemble, load [➡ POSITION SOMETHING; 325] *Opposite*: scatter

pileup (*informal*) *n* **crash**, car crash, collision, road accident, accident, smashup, bump, smash [➡ TRAFFIC ACCIDENTS; 255]

pilfer *v* **steal**, rob, thieve, poach, take, swipe (*informal*), filch (*informal*), knock off (*slang*), purloin (*formal or humorous*) [➡ STEAL AND ROB; 426]

See Compare and Contrast at **steal**.

pilferer *n* **thief**, petty thief, sneak thief, robber, shoplifter, burglar, crook (*informal*) [➡ CRIMINALS; 821]

pilfering *n* [➡ CRIMES; 817]

pilgrim *n* **traveler**, hajji, tourist, visitor, wayfarer (*literary*) [➡ TRAVEL: TRAVELERS AND WALKERS; 319]

pilgrimage *n* **journey**, trip, visit, hajj, tour, excursion [➡ TRAVEL: JOURNEYS AND TRIPS; 318]

pill *n* **tablet**, capsule, medication [➡ REMEDIES, TREATMENTS, AND OPERATIONS; 731]

pillage **1** *v* **plunder**, sack, rob, loot, steal, embezzle, despoil [➡ STEAL AND ROB; 426] **2** *n* **loot**, spoils, plunder, booty, prize, takings [➡ PROCEEDS OF CRIME; 427]

pillager *n* **plunderer**, robber, looter, raider, thief, burglar, rustler [➡ CRIMINALS; 821]

pillar **1** *n* **support**, column, post, prop, mast, stake [➡ SUPPORTS AND BASES; 1255] **2** *n* **rock**, mainstay, tower of strength, stalwart [➡ PEOPLE WHO ARE APPROVED OF; 955]

pillar box (*UK*) *n* **mailbox**, maildrop, postbox (*UK*), letterbox (*UK*) [➡ CONTAINERS, RECEPTACLES, AND PACKAGING; 1245]

pillbox **1** *n* **box**, tin, container, étui [➡ CONTAINERS, RECEPTACLES, AND PACKAGING; 1245] **2** *n* **lookout post**, shelter, gun emplacement, gun shelter [➡ FORTRESSES AND FORTIFICATIONS; 1090] **3** *type of* **hat** [➡ ACCESSORIES, MILLINERY, AND LINGERIE; 867]

pillory *v* **ridicule**, denounce, scorn, deride, humiliate, brand, pour scorn on, tear to pieces [➡ ACCUSE, BLAME, AND CRITICIZE; 641] *Opposite*: praise

pillow **1** *n* **cushion**, support, throw cushion, pad, throw pillow, bolster, head rest, padding [➡ FURNISHING AND HOUSEHOLD LINENS; 860] **2** *v* **protect**, support, prop up, hold up [➡ PREVENT CONTACT OR ATTACK; 419]

pillowcase *n* **pillowslip**, pillow sham, sham, slipcover, slipcase, bedding, slip [➡ FURNISHING AND HOUSEHOLD LINENS; 860]

pillow sham *n* [➡ FURNISHING AND HOUSEHOLD LINENS; 860]

pillowslip *n* [➡ FURNISHING AND HOUSEHOLD LINENS; 860]

pilot **1** *n* [➡ DRIVERS; 1153] **2** *v* **guide**, conduct, control, navigate, lead, direct, steer, handle [➡ TRAVEL: WAYS OF TRAVELING; 320]

3 *adj* **experimental**, trial, model, test, preliminary, initial [➡ DESCRIBING TECHNOLOGY; 1160]

pilot whale *type of* **whale** [➡ WHALES; 991]

pimple *n* **spot**, blemish, blackhead, boil, pustule, zit (*slang*) [➡ CONDITIONS AFFECTING THE SKIN; 721]

pimpled *adj* [➡ COMPLEXION; 480]

pimply *adj* **spotty**, blemished, acned [➡ COMPLEXION; 480] *Opposite*: clear

pin **1** *n* **brooch**, badge, stick pin [➡ JEWELRY; 866] **2** *n* (*dated informal*) **iota**, tittle, pinch, bit, dash, soupçon, touch, jot, smidgen (*informal*) [➡ FEW, LITTLE, SMALL AMOUNT; 120] **3** *v* **fasten**, attach, fix, secure [➡ FASTEN, LINK, AND JOIN; 408] **4** *v* **hold**, pin down, hold down, restrain, stick, pinion, trap, immobilize [➡ CAPTIVITY AND LOSS OF FREEDOM; 248]

pinafore *n* **apron**, overall [➡ GARMENTS AND OUTFITS; 865]

pince-nez *type of* **glasses** [➡ GLASSES AND SPECTACLES; 1125]

pincers *type of* **general tool** [➡ HAND TOOLS; 1119]

pinch **1** *v* **squeeze**, nip, tweak, grasp, press, grip [➡ CONTACT: EXERT PRESSURE; 414] **2** *v* **steal**, take, thieve, pilfer, make off with [➡ STEAL AND ROB; 426] **3** *n* **touch**, dash, soupçon, bit, taste, jot, iota, tittle, smidgen (*informal*) [➡ FEW, LITTLE, SMALL AMOUNT; 120]

See Compare and Contrast at **steal**.

pinched *adj* **haggard**, gaunt, drawn, pale, thin, tired, shrunken, withered, wan, tense, careworn, strained, drained [➡ FACIAL CHARACTERISTICS; 481]

pinchpenny **1** *adj* **stingy**, ungenerous, miserly, tight-fisted, niggardly, mean [➡ GRASPING AND FINANCIALLY MEAN; 519] *Opposite*: generous **2** *n* **miser**, skinflint, niggard, penny pincher (*informal*), scrooge (*informal*), cheapskate (*informal*) [➡ FINANCIALLY MEAN PEOPLE; 952]

pin down **1** *v* **identify**, determine, locate, pinpoint, isolate, find [➡ FIND; 463] **2** *v* **hold down**, restrain, trap, pinion, pin, hold, immobilize [➡ CAPTIVITY AND LOSS OF FREEDOM; 248]

pine **1** *type of* **evergreen tree** [➡ EVERGREEN AND CONIFEROUS TREES; 1029] **2** *v* **long**, yearn, ache, want, wish for, crave, hunger [➡ DESIRE AND WANT; 579] **3** *v* **waste away**, fade, fade away, suffer, go downhill, languish, mope, fail [➡ GET WORSE; 381] *Opposite*: thrive

pineapple *type of* **fruit** [➡ FRUIT AND VEGETABLES; 1176]

pine cone *n* **cone**, fir cone, seed case [➡ PARTS OF TREES AND PLANTS; 1026]

pine marten *type of* **small mammal** [➡ SMALL MAMMALS; 990]

pine nut *type of* **nut** [➡ NUTS; 1185]

ping **1** *v* **sound**, ring, ding, beep, tinkle, chime, clang, bleep, peep [➡ EMIT RINGING AND HOOTING SOUNDS; 367] **2** *v* [➡ THE INTERNET; 1128] **3** *type of* **ringing sound** [➡ RINGING AND HOOTING SOUNDS; 1259]

pinhole camera *type of* **photographic equipment** [➡ PHOTOGRAPHY AND PHOTOGRAPHIC EQUIPMENT; 1122]

pinion *v* **hold down**, trap, restrain, pin down, immobilize, hold, pin [➡ CAPTIVITY AND LOSS OF FREEDOM; 248]

pink **1** *adj* **flushed**, red, rosy, glowing, blushing, ruddy, healthy-looking [➡ COMPLEXION; 480] **2** *adj* **undercooked**, rare, underdone, raw [➡ STATE OF PREPARED FOOD; 1171] **3** *type of* **perennial flower** [➡ FLOWERS; 1032] **4** *type of* **color** [➡ COLORS; 1224]

pink

◆ *types of pink*
cerise, coral, fuchsia, raspberry, rose, salmon pink, shell pink, shocking pink

pinkie (*informal*) *part of* **arm or hand** [➡ PARTS OF THE BODY: ARM AND HAND; 695]

pin money *n* **pocket money**, spending money, allowance, change, small change, chump change (*slang*) [➡ SMALL AMOUNTS OF MONEY; 121]

pinnacle **1** *n* **summit**, peak, height, top, apex [➡ EXTREMITIES OF PHYSICAL OBJECTS; 1250] *Opposite*: base **2** *n* **high point**, peak, acme, zenith, apex [➡ PLEASANT SITUATIONS; 74] *Opposite*: nadir

pinpoint *v* **locate**, identify, pin down, isolate, find, determine [➡ FIND; 463]

pinprick *n* **hole**, puncture, pinhole, perforation, prick, cut, incision [➡ HOLES, GAPS, AND FORKS; 1252]

pins (*informal*) *n* [➡ PARTS OF THE BODY: LEG AND FOOT; 694]

pins and needles *n* **tingling**, prickling, numbness [➡ PAIN AND OTHER PHYSICAL SENSATIONS; 733]

pinstripe suit *type of* **suit** [➡ GARMENTS AND OUTFITS; 865]

pint *type of* **nonmetric unit** [➡ SIZE AND DIMENSIONS; 1192]

pinto bean *type of* **pulse** [➡ PEAS AND BEANS; 1189]

pint-size (*informal*) *adj* **miniature**, pocket-sized, pocket-size, little, minuscule, minute, undersized, undersize, tiny, small, diminutive, pint-sized (*informal*), mini (*informal*) [➡ SMALL; 1195]

pint-sized (*informal*) *adj* [➡ SMALL; 1195]

pinwheel *type of* **firework** [➡ EXPLOSIVES; 1155]

pion *type of* **elementary particle** [➡ ELEMENTARY PARTICLES; 1279]

pioneer **1** *n* **innovator**, inventor, forerunner, developer, creator, discoverer [➡ DESIGNERS, CREATORS, AND INSTIGATORS; 347] **2** *v* **lead the way**, open up, forge, found, initiate, break new ground, establish, prepare [➡ START AN ACTION; 260]

pioneering *adj* **groundbreaking**, revolutionary, original, new, inventive, innovative [➡ NEW, MODERN; 166]

pious **1** *adj* **devout**, religious, virtuous, moral, sincere, spiritual, reverent, holy, saintly, godly (*formal*) [➡ RELIGIOUS CONCEPTS; 776] *Opposite*: impious **2** *adj* **self-righteous**, sanctimonious, moralizing, hypocritical, smug, holier-than-thou (*informal*), goody-goody (*informal*) [➡ AFFECTATION, SELF-SATISFACTION, AND SNOBBISHNESS; 507]

piousness **1** *n* **piety**, devoutness, devotion, religiousness, virtue, holiness, spirituality, saintliness, godliness (*formal*) [➡ MORALLY GOOD; 774] *Opposite*: impiety **2** *n* **self-righteousness**, sanctimoniousness, moralizing, hypocrisy, smugness [➡ AFFECTATION, SELF-SATISFACTION, AND SNOBBISHNESS; 507]

pip **1** *n* **seed**, pit, fruit seed, stone, nut, kernel [➡ FRUIT AND

fixing, hanging, setting, laying [➡ MOVE SOMETHING TO ANOTHER LOCATION; 324]

place of safety n [➡ SAFE BUILDINGS OR PLACES; 1093]

place of worship n [➡ RELIGIOUS BUILDINGS; 1085]

place of worship

◆ *types of places of worship*
church, gurdwara, mosque, shrine, synagogue, temple

place setting n **setting**, cover, place, tableware, flatware, utensils, glassware [➡ TABLEWARE, FLATWARE, AND KITCHENWARE; 861]

placid adj **calm**, equable, even-tempered, imperturbable, easygoing, docile, good-natured, mild, peaceful, serene, tranquil, still, quiet, gentle, sedate [➡ COOL AND CALM; 536] *Opposite*: excitable

placidity n **calmness**, equability, serenity, imperturbability, even-temperedness, mildness, good-naturedness, tranquillity, docility, peacefulness, stillness, quietness, gentleness, sedateness [➡ COOL AND CALM; 536] *Opposite*: excitability

plagiarism n **copy**, piracy, theft, bootlegging, fraud, thieving, stealing, imitation, deception, lifting (*informal*) [➡ CRIMES; 817]

plagiarist n **copyist**, pirate, bootlegger, imitator, cheat, fraud, deceiver, thief, purloiner (*formal*) [➡ CRIMINALS; 821] *Opposite*: originator

plagiarize v **copy**, pirate, bootleg, steal, pass off as your own, imitate, purloin, lift (*informal*) [➡ COPY AND DUPLICATE; 402] *Opposite*: originate

plague 1 n **epidemic**, disease, infection, pandemic, wave, outbreak, pestilence (*archaic*) [➡ SICKNESS; 729] 2 n **curse**, affliction, scourge, blight, visitation, calamity, adversity [➡ NUISANCES; 253] *Opposite*: blessing 3 v **afflict**, trouble, pursue, hound, harass, torture, torment, persecute, dog [➡ UPSET, DISTRESS, AND HUMILIATE; 567] *Opposite*: bless 4 v **pester**, badger, bother, harass, trouble, agitate, upset, perturb, annoy, beleaguer, vex, dog [➡ ANGER AND ANNOY; 569] *Opposite*: leave off

plague-ridden adj [➡ DECAYING OR INFESTED; 1236]

plaice type of **flatfish** [➡ OCEAN FISH; 1009]

plaid adj **checkered**, checked, tartan [➡ DESCRIBING PATTERNS; 1227] *Opposite*: plain

plain 1 adj **simple**, basic, unadorned, natural, pure, bare, ordinary, normal, stark, everyday, austere, dull, commonplace [➡ PLAIN; 232] *Opposite*: elaborate 2 adj **clear**, evident, obvious, apparent, pronounced, manifest, palpable, tangible, patent, unmistakable, transparent, unambiguous, comprehensible, lucid [➡ PERCEPTIBLE; 25] *Opposite*: obscure 3 adj **blunt**, straightforward, direct, frank, open, blatant, forthright, candid, bald [➡ HONEST AND OPEN; 630] *Opposite*: evasive 4 adj **plain-featured**, ordinary, homely, unattractive, unappealing [➡ PEOPLE'S PHYSICAL APPEARANCE; 475] *Opposite*: pretty 5 n **prairie**, savanna, steppe, pampas [➡ DESERTS, PLAINS, AND MOORLAND; 1045]

plain as a pikestaff (*UK*) adj [➡ CONCISE AND CLEAR; 202]

plain-clothes adj **undercover**, ununiformed, secret, disguised, out of uniform [➡ DESCRIBING CLOTHES; 869]

plain flour type of **flour** [➡ BREAD, FLOUR, AND BREAD PRODUCTS; 1179]

plainly 1 adv **simply**, normally, basically, naturally, purely, barely [➡ PLAIN; 232] *Opposite*: elaborately 2 adv **clearly**, evidently, obviously, apparently, pronouncedly, palpably, tangibly, patently, unmistakably, manifestly [➡ PERCEPTIBLE; 25] *Opposite*: obscurely 3 adv **bluntly**, straightforwardly, directly, frankly, openly, blatantly, forthrightly, candidly, baldly, straight from the shoulder [➡ HONEST AND OPEN; 630] *Opposite*: evasively

plainness 1 n **simplicity**, ordinariness, naturalness, purity, bareness, starkness, everydayness, austerity, dullness, commonplaceness [➡ ORDINARINESS; 244] 2 n **clarity**, clearness, palpability, tangibility, transparency, unambiguousness, comprehensibility, lucidity [➡ PERCEPTIBLE; 25] *Opposite*: obscurity 3 n **bluntness**, straightforwardness, directness, frankness, openness, forthrightness, candidness, baldness [➡ HONEST AND OPEN; 630] *Opposite*: evasiveness

plain sailing adj [➡ EASE AND SIMPLICITY; 200]

plain-speaking adj [➡ HONEST AND OPEN; 630]

plain-spoken adj **direct**, frank, blunt, forthright, bald, candid, open, honest, straight-talking, straightforward [➡ HONEST AND OPEN; 630] *Opposite*: mealy-mouthed

plain-spokenness n [➡ HONEST AND OPEN; 630]

plaint n **plea**, charge, accusation, complaint, action, suit, indictment, grievance [➡ TRIAL, PUNISHMENT, AND LEGAL OUTCOMES; 819] *Opposite*: defense

plaintiff n **accuser**, applicant, complainant, petitioner, litigant, claimant, appellant [➡ TRIAL, PUNISHMENT, AND LEGAL OUTCOMES; 819] *Opposite*: defendant

plaintive adj **mournful**, lamenting, nostalgic, sorrowful, wistful, sad, melancholy, elegiac (*formal*) [➡ SADNESS, DISTRESS, AND DESPAIR; 539] *Opposite*: cheerful

plait 1 type of **hairstyle** [➡ HAIRSTYLES AND HAIRPIECES; 488] 2 v **braid**, interweave, weave, intertwine, crisscross, interlace, splice, twill [➡ FASTEN, LINK, AND JOIN; 408] *Opposite*: unravel

plan 1 n **strategy**, scheme, idea, proposal, plot, design, disposition, organization, blueprint, ground plan [➡ WAYS OF DOING THINGS; 294] 2 v **work out**, arrange, scheme, plot, organize, design, devise, develop, form, formulate, shape, fashion, conceive, mold [➡ CAUSE TO HAPPEN; 31] *Opposite*: improvise 3 v **intend**, propose, mean, line up, schedule, project, set up, arrange, organize, prearrange, prepare [➡ ARRANGE AND CREATE ORDER; 357]

plane 1 n **aircraft**, airplane, aeroplane (*UK*) [➡ AIRCRAFT; 1148] 2 type of **carpentry tool** [➡ HAND TOOLS; 1119]

planet 1 n [➡ THE SOLAR SYSTEM AND ASTRONOMY; 1060] 2 n **earth**, world, globe [➡ THE EARTH; 1039] 3 type of **heavenly body** [➡ HEAVENLY BODIES; 1061]

planet

◆ *types of planets*
Earth, Jupiter, Mars, Mercury, Neptune, Pluto, Saturn, Uranus, Venus

planetarium *n* [➡ BUILDINGS FOR PUBLIC ENTERTAINMENT; 1084]

planetary *adj* **terrestrial**, earthly, environmental, global, universal, world [➡ THE SOLAR SYSTEM AND ASTRONOMY; 1060]

plane tree *type of* **deciduous tree** [➡ DECIDUOUS TREES; 1028]

plangent *adj* [➡ LOUD, HIGH, OR UNPLEASANT SOUNDS; 1266]

plank *n* [➡ BUILDING MATERIALS; 1077]

planking *n* [➡ BUILDING MATERIALS; 1077]

planned *adj* **deliberate**, intentional, prearranged, strategic, premeditated, on purpose, scheduled, intended, calculated, designed, organized, prepared [➡ INTENTIONAL AND DELIBERATE; 279] *Opposite*: unplanned

planned economy *type of* **economic system** [➡ FINANCE AND ECONOMICS; 796]

planner **1** *n* **town planner**, organizer, developer, city planner, designer, arranger, proposer, architect, engineer, manager, schemer, director, urban planner [➡ DESIGNERS, CREATORS, AND INSTIGATORS; 347] **2** *n* **diary**, calendar, appointment book, wall chart, planning aid, chart, notebook [➡ LISTS AND SCHEDULES; 587]

planning *n* **preparation**, setting up, development, arrangement, scheduling, design, forecasting, organization, formation, projection, provision [➡ BEGINNINGS; 53]

plant **1** *n* **shrub**, bush, flower, herb, vegetable, potted plant, houseplant, cutting, seedling, pot plant (*UK*) [➡ PLANTS AND TREES; 1024] **2** *n* **factory**, works, installation, industrial unit, manufacturing plant, shop floor (*UK*) [➡ INDUSTRIAL BUILDINGS; 1087] **3** *n* (*informal*) **spy**, informant, infiltrator, secret agent, agent [➡ PEOPLE WHO DECEIVE; 661] **4** *v* **introduce**, lodge, establish, implant, fix, embed, ingrain, root [➡ POSITION SOMETHING; 325] *Opposite*: erase **5** *v* **place**, fix, stand, transplant, deposit, set, lodge [➡ POSITION SOMETHING; 325] **6** *v* **sow**, seed, scatter, root, transplant, pot, replant, put in, bed [➡ GROW AND CULTIVATE; 351] **7** *v* (*informal*) **conceal**, hide, bury [➡ CAUSE TO DISAPPEAR; 6]

plantation *n* **estate**, farm, homestead, farmstead, manor [➡ THE COUNTRYSIDE AND OUTDOOR SPACES; 1071]

planter **1** *n* **pot**, flower pot, container, window box, urn, plant-holder [➡ CONTAINERS, RECEPTACLES, AND PACKAGING; 1245] **2** *part of* **garden** [➡ GARDENS; 1074]

plaque *n* **sign**, panel, commemoration, inscription, plate, tablet, tile [➡ SIGNPOSTS, SIGNALS, AND BILLBOARDS; 595]

plasma *n* [➡ THE BLOOD AND CIRCULATION; 717]

plasma engine *part of* **spacecraft** [➡ SPACE VEHICLES; 1063]

plaster **1** *n* [➡ BUILDING MATERIALS; 1077] **2** *n* (*UK*) **adhesive bandage**, covering, dressing, bandage, sticking plaster (*UK*) [➡ COVERS AND COATINGS; 1246] **3** *v* **surface**, coat, cover, face, plaster over, mortar, daub [➡ DECORATE, ADORN, AND APPLY COATINGS; 405]

plasterboard *n* [➡ BUILDING MATERIALS; 1077]

plastered (*informal*) *adj* [➡ UNDER THE INFLUENCE OF DRUGS OR ALCOHOL; 741]

plasterwork *n* **plaster**, molding, stuccowork, stucco, pargeting, frieze, decoration, parget, scagliola [➡ BUILDING MATERIALS; 1077]

plastic **1** *adj* **malleable**, soft, pliable, elastic, flexible, manipulable [➡ MALLEABLE AND ELASTIC; 1212] *Opposite*: hard **2** *adj* **artificial**, fake, synthetic, false, forced, unnatural [➡ FALSE AND UNREAL; 173] *Opposite*: genuine

plastic

◆ *types of plastic*
acetate, celluloid, epoxide, latex, melamine, neoprene, polyethylene, polystyrene, polyurethane, vinyl

plastic bullet *type of* **projectile** [➡ PROJECTILES; 1159]

plastic explosive *type of* **explosive material** [➡ EXPLOSIVES; 1155]

plasticity *n* **malleability**, softness, pliability, elasticity, flexibility, manipulability [➡ MALLEABLE AND ELASTIC; 1212] *Opposite*: hardness

plastic surgeon *n* [➡ PEOPLE WHO WORK IN MEDICINE; 848]

plastic surgery *type of* **medical procedure** [➡ REMEDIES, TREATMENTS, AND OPERATIONS; 731]

plate **1** *n* **dish**, platter, salver, serving dish, bowl [➡ TABLEWARE, FLATWARE, AND KITCHENWARE; 861] **2** *n* **license plate**, registration, number plate (*UK*) [➡ EXTERNAL PARTS OF A VEHICLE; 1147] **3** *v* **cover**, coat, overlay, protect, shield, laminate, sheet, finish, electroplate [➡ DECORATE, ADORN, AND APPLY COATINGS; 405]

plateau **1** *n* **upland**, highland, hill, mesa, tableland, table [➡ DESERTS, PLAINS, AND MOORLAND; 1045] **2** *n* **level**, stage, period, phase [➡ PAUSES AND PHASES; 56]

plated *adj* **coated**, overlaid, gold-plated, covered, finished, electroplated, silver-plated, gilded [➡ METALS; 1276] *Opposite*: solid

plateful *n* [➡ AMOUNTS OF SOLID OR SEMISOLID; 115]

plate glass *type of* **glass** [➡ GLASS; 1136]

platform **1** *n* **stage**, display place, raised area, podium, stand, dais, boards [➡ STAGES, PLATFORMS, AND RAISED AREAS; 1098] **2** *n* **policy**, proposal, manifesto, program [➡ GOVERNMENT POLICIES; 810] **3** *type of* **shoe** [➡ FOOTWEAR; 871] **4** *type of* **computer feature** [➡ COMPUTERS AND COMPUTING; 1127] **5** *type of* **hardware** [➡ COMPUTERS AND COMPUTING; 1127]

plating **1** *n* **electroplating**, silver-plating, gilding, coating, luster [➡ COVERS AND COATINGS; 1246] **2** *n* **armor**, armor plate, cladding, metal casing, outer casing, reinforcement, strengthening, protection [➡ EXTREMITIES OF PHYSICAL OBJECTS; 1250] *Opposite*: core

platinum **1** *type of* **metal** [➡ METALS; 1276] **2** *type of* **white** [➡ COLORS; 1224]

platitude **1** *n* **cliché**, inanity, tired expression, commonplace, banality, prosaicism, bromide (*dated*) [➡ FIGURES OF SPEECH; 673] **2** *n* **dullness**, boredom, insipidity, triteness, plainness, vapidity, inaneness [➡ BORING AND UNINTERESTING; 234]

platitudinous *adj* **clichéd**, trite, banal, corny, hackneyed, unoriginal, prosaic, old hat (*informal*) [➡ BORING AND UNINTERESTING; 234] *Opposite*: original

platonic *adj* **spiritual**, companionable, friendly, nonsexual, nonphysical, sexless, amicable, neighborly [➡ RELATIONSHIP TO ANOTHER; 973]

platoon *n* **squad**, legion, team, detachment, subdivision, section, unit, group [➞MILITARY PERSONNEL; 828]

platter *n* **plate**, serving dish, salver, dish, tray [➞TABLEWARE, FLATWARE, AND KITCHENWARE; 861]

plaudit *n* **applause**, approval, praise, positive feedback, appreciation, recognition, acclaim [➞PRAISE AND ENCOURAGE; 647] *Opposite*: criticism

plausibility *n* **believability**, credibility, reasonableness, probability, conceivability, likelihood, possibility, acceptability, plausibleness [➞POSSIBLE AND PROBABLE; 177] *Opposite*: implausibility

plausible *adj* **believable**, credible, reasonable, probable, conceivable, likely, possible, acceptable [➞POSSIBLE AND PROBABLE; 177] *Opposite*: implausible

play 1 *v* **enjoy yourself**, occupy yourself, amuse yourself, have fun, frolic, fool around [➞LEISURE AND RECREATION; 874] 2 *v* **joke**, tease, fool around, mess around (*informal*), kid (*informal*), jest (*literary*) [➞JOKES AND TEASING; 674] 3 *v* **participate**, take part, join in, compete, engage in, cooperate [➞PARTICIPATE; 292] 4 *v* **perform**, act, play-act, portray, star as, be, enact [➞PRETEND AND MIMIC; 60] 5 *n* **recreation**, amusement, fun, diversion, games, sport, sports [➞LEISURE AND RECREATION; 874] *Opposite*: work 6 *n* **production**, drama, show, piece, performance, comedy, tragedy, composition, work [➞PERFORMANCES AND SHOWS; 42] 7 type of **broadcast** [➞TELEVISION AND RADIO; 606]

play-act (*informal*) *v* **pretend**, ham it up, put it on, put on an act, play to the gallery, fake, sham, posture, make believe [➞PRETEND AND MIMIC; 60]

play a part *v* [➞PARTICIPATE; 292]

playback *n* **replay**, rerun, reshowing, repetition, reproduction [➞RECORDINGS AND PLAYERS; 911] *Opposite*: recording

play down *v* **minimize**, make light of, underplay, underestimate, make little of [➞UNDERDO SOMETHING; 291] *Opposite*: accentuate

player 1 *n* **participant**, team member, competitor, contestant [➞PEOPLE IN SPORTS AND LEISURE; 876] 2 *n* **actor**, thespian, performer, entertainer, play-actor, trouper [➞PERFORMERS; 905]

playfellow (*archaic*) *n* **friend**, playmate, chum (*informal*), pal (*informal*), buddy (*informal*), mate (*UK*) [➞FRIENDS AND GUESTS; 963] *Opposite*: enemy

playful 1 *adj* **lively**, bouncy, full of fun, full of life, frisky, spirited, full of beans (*informal*) [➞ENERGY AND ENTHUSIASM; 496] *Opposite*: subdued 2 *adj* **good-humored**, lighthearted, good-natured, teasing, jokey, mischievous, humorous, impish, naughty, roguish [➞GOOD-TEMPERED AND HUMOROUS; 627] *Opposite*: serious

playfulness 1 *n* **liveliness**, bounce, bounciness, friskiness, spirit [➞ENERGY AND ENTHUSIASM; 496] 2 *n* **lightheartedness**, good humor, teasing, mischief, impishness, mischievousness, naughtiness, roguishness [➞GOOD-TEMPERED AND HUMOROUS; 627] *Opposite*: seriousness

play games with *v* **deceive**, trick, confuse, mistreat, abuse, mess around (*informal*), string along (*informal*) [➞DECEPTION AND LIES; 660]

playgoer *n* **theatergoer**, theater buff, spectator [➞IN THE THEATER; 906]

playground 1 *n* **park**, play area, community playground, adventure playground, outdoor play area [➞URBAN OUTDOOR SPACES; 1072] 2 *n* (*UK*) **school yard**, school grounds, play area, recreation area, concourse, forecourt [➞URBAN OUTDOOR SPACES; 1072] *Opposite*: classroom

play hooky (*informal*) *v* **play truant**, truant, skip classes, miss school, absent yourself [➞RUN AWAY AND AVOID; 10] *Opposite*: attend

playhouse 1 *n* **theater**, auditorium, studio, venue [➞BUILDINGS FOR PUBLIC ENTERTAINMENT; 1084] 2 *n* **tree house**, den, Wendy house (*UK*) [➞TOYS; 880]

playing field *n* **sports grounds**, sports field, park, ground, field, court, pitch (*UK*) [➞URBAN OUTDOOR SPACES; 1072]

playmate *n* **friend**, pal (*informal*), chum (*informal*), buddy (*informal*), playfellow (*archaic*), mate (*UK*) [➞FRIENDS AND GUESTS; 963] *Opposite*: enemy

play off *v* **oppose**, set against, pit against, go against, challenge [➞COMPETE, CONTEND, AND COMBAT; 303]

playoff *n* **final**, final round, semifinal, quarterfinal, tiebreaker, competition, contest, game, match [➞NON-AGGRESSIVE/SPORTING EVENTS; 40]

playroom type of **room in the home** [➞TYPES OF ROOMS; 1097]

play safe *v* **take no risks**, hedge your bets, take care, be cautious, be careful, go easy (*informal*) [➞PAY ATTENTION; 765] *Opposite*: gamble

playschool *n* **playgroup**, nursery, kindergarten, preschool [➞EDUCATIONAL INSTITUTIONS; 813]

play the game *v* **toe the line**, follow the rules, conform, comply, obey, act honestly [➞OBEY AND ABIDE BY; 301] *Opposite*: act up

plaything *n* **toy**, doll, bauble, curio, game, knickknack [➞TOYS; 880]

playtime *n* **break**, recess, interval, free time, leisure time, lunchtime [➞PERIODS OF REST; 91]

play to the gallery *v* **show off**, play up, posture, perform, play to the crowd, ham it up, put on an act [➞OVERDO SOMETHING; 290]

play truant *v* [➞RUN AWAY AND AVOID; 10]

play up 1 *v* **exaggerate**, emphasize, embellish, highlight, draw attention to, stress [➞CLAIM, INSIST, AND EMPHASIZE; 614] *Opposite*: play down 2 *v* (*UK*) **misbehave**, act up, malfunction, go wrong [➞FAIL OR CEASE TO FUNCTION; 470] *Opposite*: behave

play up to *v* **flatter**, toady, ingratiate yourself with, win the favor of, butter up (*informal*), crawl (*informal*), suck up to (*informal*) [➞FLATTER AND FAWN; 621]

playwright *n* **dramatist**, writer, author, tragedian, dramaturge, scriptwriter [➞WRITERS AND STYLES; 914]

play your cards close to your chest *v* **be secretive**, be a dark horse, keep quiet, keep mum (*informal*) [➞WITHHOLD INFORMATION; 687]

plaza 1 *n* **square**, piazza, mall, marketplace, court [➞URBAN

OUTDOOR SPACES; 1072] **2** *n* **shopping center**, arcade, mall, precinct (*UK*) [➡ RETAIL OUTLETS; 1083]

PLC (*UK*) *n* [➡ BUSINESS ENTERPRISES AND RELATED BODIES; 792]

plea **1** *n* **appeal**, entreaty, prayer, request, petition, supplication (*formal*), imploration (*formal*) [➡ REQUEST AND DEMAND; 663] *Opposite*: demand **2** *n* **statement**, claim, defense, declaration, assertion [➡ TRIAL, PUNISHMENT, AND LEGAL OUTCOMES; 819] *Opposite*: denial **3** *n* **excuse**, pretext, reason, explanation, alibi [➡ EXPLAIN AND CLARIFY; 610]

plea-bargain *v* **plead guilty**, do a deal, negotiate, come to an agreement, contract, compromise, cop a plea (*slang*) [➡ TRIAL, PUNISHMENT, AND LEGAL OUTCOMES; 819]

plead **1** *v* **beg**, appeal, pray, entreat, request, petition, implore (*formal*), importune (*formal*), supplicate (*formal*), beseech (*literary*) [➡ REQUEST AND DEMAND; 663] *Opposite*: demand **2** *v* **declare**, assert, claim, state, put forward, allege [➡ CLAIM, INSIST, AND EMPHASIZE; 614] **3** *v* **support**, defend, argue, contend, vindicate, assert [➡ APPROVE AND CONFIRM; 646]

pleading *adj* **begging**, piteous, persuasive, suppliant (*formal*), imploring (*formal*), entreating (*formal*), beseeching (*literary*) [➡ REQUEST AND DEMAND; 663]

pleasant **1** *adj* **enjoyable**, agreeable, pleasing, lovely, nice, pleasurable, satisfying, amusing [➡ EMOTIONALLY PLEASANT; 187] *Opposite*: unpleasant **2** *adj* **amiable**, friendly, congenial, likable, genial, affable, nice, cheery, good-humored, good-natured [➡ FRIENDLINESS AND SOCIABILITY; 494] *Opposite*: nasty

pleasantness **1** *n* **appeal**, loveliness, niceness, pleasurableness, satisfaction, enjoyableness, agreeableness [➡ EMOTIONALLY PLEASANT; 187] *Opposite*: unpleasantness **2** *n* **amiability**, friendliness, congeniality, likability, likableness, niceness, geniality, affableness, cheeriness, good humor, good-naturedness [➡ FRIENDLINESS AND SOCIABILITY; 494] *Opposite*: nastiness

pleasantries *n* **small talk**, chat, gossip, banter, conversation, chitchat (*informal*) [➡ INFORMAL COMMUNICATION; 45]

pleasantry *n* **remark**, civility, banality, politeness, observation, comment, passing comment [➡ ONE-WAY COMMUNICATION; 49] *Opposite*: insult

please **1** *v* **satisfy**, gratify, make happy, delight, thrill, entertain, content, make somebody's day [➡ PLEASE AND AMUSE; 572] *Opposite*: displease **2** *v* **like**, prefer, choose, desire, wish, want [➡ LIKE, LOVE, VALUE, AND ENJOY; 578] *Opposite*: dislike

pleased *adj* **satisfied**, happy, content, delighted, contented, thrilled [➡ PLEASURE, EXCITEMENT, AND ELATION; 534] *Opposite*: displeased

pleasing *adj* **agreeable**, pleasant, enjoyable, lovely, nice, pleasurable, satisfying, gratifying, delightful, welcome [➡ EMOTIONALLY PLEASANT; 187] *Opposite*: disagreeable

pleasing to the eye *adj* [➡ BEAUTY AND ATTRACTIVENESS; 189]

pleasurable *adj* **agreeable**, enjoyable, pleasing, pleasant, gratifying, satisfying, congenial, delightful [➡ EMOTIONALLY PLEASANT; 187] *Opposite*: disagreeable

pleasure **1** *n* **enjoyment**, happiness, delight, bliss, contentment, satisfaction, gratification, joy [➡ PLEASURE, EXCITEMENT, AND ELATION; 534] *Opposite*: displeasure **2** *n* **gratification**,

indulgence, hedonism, decadence, sensuality, carnality [➡ PLEASURE, EXCITEMENT, AND ELATION; 534] **3** *n* **amusement**, recreation, fun, leisure, diversion, relaxation, delectation (*formal*) [➡ ENTERTAINMENT; 872] *Opposite*: work **4** *n* (*formal or literary*) **desire**, preference, wish, choice, liking, inclination, will [➡ LIKE, LOVE, VALUE, AND ENJOY; 578] *Opposite*: displeasure

pleasure-lover *n* [➡ PLEASURE-SEEKERS AND HEDONISTS; 886]

pleasure-loving *adj* [➡ PLEASURE-SEEKING AND EXCESS; 885]

pleasure-seeker *n* [➡ PLEASURE-SEEKERS AND HEDONISTS; 886]

pleasure-seeking *adj* [➡ PLEASURE-SEEKING AND EXCESS; 885]

pleat **1** *n* **crease**, fold, tuck, gather, crimp, corrugation, furrow, wrinkle [➡ CHANGE OF SHAPE; 385] **2** *v* **fold**, crease, tuck, gather, crimp, wrinkle [➡ CHANGE OF SHAPE; 385]

plebe *n* [➡ STUDENTS AND PUPILS; 841]

plebiscite *n* **referendum**, poll, vote, ballot, opinion poll, survey, direct vote [➡ ELECTIONS AND VOTING; 807]

pledge **1** *n* **vow**, oath, promise, assurance, guarantee, word of honor, undertaking, word [➡ PROMISE AND ASSURE; 684] **2** *n* **initiate**, new member, recruit, freshman, inductee, newcomer, pledgee [➡ UNSKILLED PEOPLE; 530] **3** *n* **security**, deposit, guarantee, warranty, collateral, down payment, advance, guaranty, token [➡ FUNDS, PAYMENTS, AND CHARGES; 800] **4** *v* **promise**, vow, swear, guarantee, give your word, swear an oath, assure, vouchsafe, covenant, plight, undertake [➡ PROMISE AND ASSURE; 684]

Pleistocene *type of* **epoch** [➡ EPOCHS AND ERAS; 89]

plenary **1** *adj* (*formal*) **full**, complete, entire, whole, quorate, unlimited [➡ WHOLENESS AND COMPLETENESS; 198] **2** *n* **meeting**, session, general assembly, plenary meeting, plenary session, plenum, lecture [➡ MEETINGS AND ASSEMBLIES; 43]

plenary meeting *n* [➡ MEETINGS AND ASSEMBLIES; 43]

plenary session *n* [➡ MEETINGS AND ASSEMBLIES; 43]

plenipotentiary **1** *adj* **presiding**, all-powerful, in charge, officiating, supreme, absolute, authoritative [➡ STRENGTH; 201] *Opposite*: powerless **2** *n* **minister**, minister plenipotentiary, ambassador, special envoy, envoy, delegate, representative [➡ REPRESENTATIVES AND PATRONS; 968] *Opposite*: pawn

plenteous (*literary*) *adj* **plentiful**, abundant, copious, overflowing, ample, profuse, lavish, bounteous (*literary*), bountiful (*literary*) [➡ MANY, MUCH, LARGE AMOUNT; 117] *Opposite*: sparse

plentiful *adj* **abundant**, copious, overflowing, ample, lavish, profuse, plenteous (*literary*), bountiful (*literary*), bounteous (*literary*) [➡ MANY, MUCH, LARGE AMOUNT; 117] *Opposite*: scarce

plenty **1** *n* **prosperity**, abundance, copiousness, profusion, plethora, bounty (*literary*) [➡ MANY, MUCH, LARGE AMOUNT; 117] *Opposite*: insufficiency **2** *adj* (*informal*) **ample**, a lot, lots, a load, sufficient, enough, adequate, loads (*informal*), heaps (*informal*), stacks (*informal*) [➡ ENOUGH AND SUFFICIENT; 131] *Opposite*: inadequate **3** *adv* (*informal*) **sufficiently**, adequately, amply, abundantly, profusely, copiously, quite, very, loads (*informal*), plenteously (*literary*) [➡ ENOUGH AND SUFFICIENT; 131] *Opposite*: insufficiently

plenum n **general assembly**, meeting, session, plenary meeting, plenary session, plenary [➡ MEETINGS AND ASSEMBLIES; 43]

pleonasm n [➡ MEANINGLESS SPEECH OR WRITING; 676]

plesiosaur type of **dinosaur** [➡ DINOSAURS; 996]

plethora n **overabundance**, excess, surfeit, glut, surplus, superfluity [➡ TOO MUCH; 119] Opposite: shortage

pleural adj [➡ RESPIRATORY ORGANS; 715]

pliability 1 n **flexibility**, bendability, suppleness, pliancy, elasticity, malleability, plasticity, softness, bendiness (UK) [➡ MALLEABLE AND ELASTIC; 1212] Opposite: rigidity 2 n **compliance**, pliancy, adaptability, flexibility, meekness, obedience, docility, manipulability, suggestibility, tractability, impressionability [➡ THE WILL AND WILLINGNESS; 563] Opposite: inflexibility

pliable 1 adj **flexible**, bendable, supple, workable, pliant, elastic, malleable, plastic, ductile, soft, bendy (UK) [➡ MALLEABLE AND ELASTIC; 1212] Opposite: rigid 2 adj **compliant**, pliant, adaptable, adjustable, flexible, agreeable, accommodating, meek, obedient, docile, manipulable, yielding, easily swayed, biddable, suggestible, tractable, impressionable [➡ THE WILL AND WILLINGNESS; 563] Opposite: inflexible

---

Compare and Contrast: *pliable, ductile, malleable, elastic, pliant*

CORE MEANING: able to be bent or molded

pliable flexible and easily bent or molded; *ductile* describes metals that can be easily drawn out into a long continuous wire or hammered into thin sheets; *malleable* describes metals that can be hammered or pressed into various shapes without breaking or cracking; *elastic* describes substances or materials that can be stretched without breaking and then return to their original shape; *pliant* supple and springy and therefore easily bent.

---

pliancy 1 n **pliability**, flexibility, bendability, suppleness, elasticity, malleability, plasticity, softness, bendiness (UK) [➡ MALLEABLE AND ELASTIC; 1212] Opposite: stiffness 2 n **compliance**, pliability, adaptability, adjustability, flexibility, meekness, obedience, docility, manipulability, suggestibility, tractability, impressionability [➡ THE WILL AND WILLINGNESS; 563] Opposite: obstinacy

pliant 1 adj **pliable**, flexible, bendable, supple, workable, elastic, plastic, malleable, soft, bendy (UK) [➡ MALLEABLE AND ELASTIC; 1212] Opposite: inflexible 2 adj **compliant**, pliable, adaptable, adjustable, flexible, agreeable, accommodating, meek, obedient, docile, manipulable, yielding, easily swayed, biddable, suggestible, tractable, impressionable [➡ THE WILL AND WILLINGNESS; 563] Opposite: inflexible

See Compare and Contrast at **pliable**.

pliers type of **general tool** [➡ HAND TOOLS; 1119]

plight n **dilemma**, trouble, predicament, difficulty, quandary, scrape (informal) [➡ DIFFICULT SITUATIONS; 72]

plinth n **pedestal**, platform, base, stand, support, podium, dais [➡ SUPPORTS AND BASES; 1255]

Pliocene type of **epoch** [➡ EPOCHS AND ERAS; 89]

plod v **trudge**, slog, tread, lumber, tramp, clump, clomp, walk, traipse (informal) [➡ MOVE SLOWLY; 314] Opposite: race

plodder n **snail**, toiler, slogger, idler, slowpoke (informal) [➡ LAZY OR UNSUCCESSFUL PEOPLE; 948] Opposite: high-flier

plodding adj **slow**, dull, slow but sure, ponderous, tedious, steady, slow-moving, labored [➡ MOVING SLOWLY; 105] Opposite: rapid

plonk v **place**, put, put down, set down, dump, lay, stick (informal), pop (informal), plop (informal) [➡ POSITION SOMETHING; 325]

plop 1 v (informal) **place**, put, put down, set down, plonk, dump, lay, stick (informal), pop (informal) [➡ POSITION SOMETHING; 325] 2 type of **impact sound** [➡ IMPACT SOUNDS; 1260]

plop down v **sit**, sit down, plunk down, settle, flop down, plonk down (informal) [➡ ASSUME A POSITION; 317]

plot 1 n **conspiracy**, plan, scheme, subversion, strategy, design, intrigue, stratagem [➡ WAYS OF DOING THINGS; 294] 2 n **story line**, action, scenario, outline, narrative, story [➡ THE ORAL TRADITION; 677] 3 n **area**, section, parcel, piece, lot [➡ AREA AND RANGE; 111] 4 v **plan**, scheme, strategize, conspire, design, contrive, intrigue, connive [➡ CAUSE TO HAPPEN; 31] 5 v **chart**, map, draw, mark, map out, outline, calculate [➡ RECORD SOMETHING; 371]

plotter n **schemer**, conspirator, conniver, contriver, strategist, planner [➡ PEOPLE WHO DECEIVE; 661]

plover type of **sea bird** [➡ SEA BIRDS; 1002]

plow 1 v **cultivate**, till, turn over, work [➡ USE TOOLS AND MACHINERY; 468] 2 type of **cutting tool** [➡ CUTTING TOOLS; 1120]

plow into v **crash into**, bang into, drive into, run into, career into, collide with [➡ CONTACT: IMPACT; 413]

plow on v **keep at it**, struggle on, persevere, persist, keep your nose to the grindstone, plug away (informal) [➡ CONTINUE AN ACTION; 262]

plow through v **keep at**, struggle on, plow on, persevere, persist, plug away (informal) [➡ CONTINUE AN ACTION; 262]

plow under v **overwhelm**, inundate, snow under, overburden, deluge, engulf, swamp [➡ GIVE TOO MUCH AND OVERBURDEN; 437]

ploy n **trick**, maneuver, strategy, plan, ruse, tactic, scheme, gambit, stratagem [➡ WAYS OF DOING THINGS; 294]

pluck 1 v **pull**, tug, pick at, grasp, take, grab [➡ REMOVE SOMETHING; 338] 2 v **pull out**, remove, yank, tweak, uproot [➡ EXTRACT AND SEVER; 341] 3 v **pick**, collect, gather, harvest [➡ GET; 420] 4 v **strum**, play, twang, plunk, pick [➡ MUSIC, SONGS, AND SINGING; 907] 5 n **courage**, determination, bravery, fortitude, resolve, nerve, backbone, fearlessness, guts (slang) [➡ COURAGE; 498] Opposite: cowardice

See Compare and Contrast at **courage**.

pluckiness n **bravery**, courage, pluck, fearlessness, boldness, audacity, audaciousness, spirit, intrepidity, daring, determination, guts (slang) [➡ COURAGE; 498] Opposite: cowardice

pluck up courage *v* **dare**, screw up, take the plunge, brace yourself, take a deep breath, steel yourself, get up, muster [➡ PREPARE FOR ACTION; 289] *Opposite:* chicken out (*slang*)

plucky *adj* **brave**, courageous, fearless, bold, audacious, spirited, intrepid, daring, determined, gutsy (*informal*) [➡ COURAGE; 498] *Opposite:* cowardly

plug 1 *n* **stopper**, cork, cap, bung, top [➡ COVERS AND COATINGS; 1246] 2 *n* **wad**, mass, lump, wadding, padding, pad [➡ AMOUNTS OF SOLID OR SEMISOLID; 115] 3 *n* **sample**, core, piece, wedge, extract, section, cross section [➡ REPRESENTATIONS AND GENERAL EXAMPLES; 65] 4 *n* (*informal*) **socket**, outlet, wall outlet, power point (*UK*), point (*UK*) [➡ ELECTRONICS AND ELECTRICS; 1137] 5 *n* (*informal*) **advertisement**, ad, mention, promotion, publicity [➡ ADVERTISING AND PUBLICITY; 604] 6 *v* **stop**, cap, bung, cork, seal, block, close, clog, congest, plug up [➡ FILL; 406] *Opposite:* unplug 7 *v* (*informal*) **work**, carry on, keep at it, keep going, persevere, press on, soldier on, keep your nose to the grindstone, struggle, persist, labor, plow, beaver (*informal*), keep your head down (*UK*) [➡ CONTINUE AN ACTION; 262] 8 *v* (*informal*) **puff**, hype, sell, push, spin, endorse, advertise, promote, publicize [➡ ADVERTISING AND PUBLICITY; 604] *Opposite:* run down

plug away (*informal*) *v* [➡ CONTINUE AN ACTION; 262]

plughole (*UK*) *n* **outlet**, drainhole, bunghole, drain, hole [➡ HOLES, GAPS, AND FORKS; 1252]

plug in *v* **connect**, link up, hook up (*informal*) [➡ FASTEN, LINK, AND JOIN; 408] *Opposite:* unplug

plum 1 *type of* **fruit** [➡ FRUIT AND VEGETABLES; 1176] 2 *type of* **purple** [➡ COLORS; 1224] 3 *n* (*informal*) **reward**, award, bonus, windfall, trophy, catch, prize [➡ AMAZING THINGS; 211] 4 *adj* (*informal*) **desirable**, choice, covetable, prestigious, profitable, preferable [➡ ADMIRABLE AND COMMENDABLE; 185]

plumage *n* **feathers**, down, fluff, fuzz [➡ PARTS OF A BIRD; 1006]

plumb 1 *adv* (*informal*) **exactly**, precisely, right, bang, slap (*informal*), smack-dab (*informal*) [➡ EXACT; 203] 2 *adv* (*informal*) **completely**, truly, totally, absolutely, utterly, entirely, very, extremely [➡ ABSOLUTE AND ABSOLUTELY; 133] 3 *adj* **perpendicular**, upright, vertical, true, aligned, straight [➡ ORIENTATION AND ALIGNMENT; 1223] *Opposite:* horizontal 4 *v* **comprehend**, understand, fathom, grasp, know, follow [➡ UNDERSTAND AND GRASP; 759] 5 *v* **experience**, undergo, face, suffer, go through, live through [➡ EXPERIENCE AND ENCOUNTER; 582]

plumbing *n* **drains**, sanitation, drainage system, water system, heating system, pipes, fixtures [➡ FIXTURES; 859]

plumb line *type of* **general tool** [➡ HAND TOOLS; 1119]

plume 1 *n* **trail**, cloud, spiral, column, curl [➡ AMOUNTS OF GAS; 116] 2 *part of* **bird** [➡ PARTS OF A BIRD; 1006]

plummet *v* **plunge**, drop, dive, tumble, crash, nose-dive, fall [➡ GO DOWNWARD; 307] *Opposite:* climb

plummy 1 *adj* **resonant**, mellow, rich, sonorous [➡ SOFT, LOW, OR PLEASANT SOUNDS; 1265] *Opposite:* reedy 2 *adj* (*UK*) **upper-class**, patrician, affected, public-school (*UK*) [➡ AFFECTATION, SELF-SATISFACTION, AND SNOBBISHNESS; 507] *Opposite:* common

plump 1 *adj* **fat**, overweight, chubby, stout, fleshy, curvy, obese, round [➡ BUILD; 477] *Opposite:* slender 2 *v* **flop down**, drop, plop down, flop, fall, collapse, plunk down,

plonk down (*informal*) [➡ ASSUME A POSITION; 317] *Opposite:* stand up

plump down *v* [➡ ASSUME A POSITION; 317]

plump for 1 *v* **support**, root for, cheer on, pull for, encourage, give moral support for, champion [➡ PRAISE AND ENCOURAGE; 647] 2 *v* (*UK*) **choose**, decide on, opt for, take, settle on, go for (*informal*) [➡ MAKE DECISIONS AND CHOICES; 752]

plumpness *n* **fatness**, chubbiness, fleshiness, curviness, obesity, roundness [➡ BUILD; 477] *Opposite:* slenderness

plump up *v* **fatten**, shake up, plump, fluff up [➡ CHANGE OF SIZE: BIGGER; 392]

plunder 1 *v* **steal**, rob, loot, pillage, raid, ransack [➡ STEAL AND ROB; 426] 2 *n* **stolen goods**, loot, booty, spoils, ill-gotten gains, swag [➡ PROCEEDS OF CRIME; 427]

plunge 1 *v* **thrust**, force, throw, push, pitch, sink, stab [➡ MOVE SOMETHING: DOWNWARD; 329] 2 *v* **rush**, jump, leap, lurch, throw yourself, immerse yourself, rush headlong, charge, embark [➡ MOVE FAST; 313] *Opposite:* hesitate 3 *v* **drop**, dive, plummet, sink, nose-dive, fall, dip, tumble [➡ GO DOWNWARD; 307] *Opposite:* soar 4 *n* **dive**, drop, plummet, fall, nosedive [➡ GO DOWNWARD; 307] *Opposite:* climb

plunger *type of* **general tool** [➡ HAND TOOLS; 1119]

plunging 1 *adj* **plummeting**, dipping, dropping, tumbling, reducing, falling, sinking, downward [➡ MOVING QUICKLY; 103] *Opposite:* rising 2 *adj* **low**, low-cut, revealing, décolleté [➡ DESCRIBING CLOTHES; 869] *Opposite:* high

plunk 1 *v* **twang**, strum, plonk, play, pick, pluck [➡ EMIT SOUNDS THROUGH IMPACT AND ABRASION; 365] 2 *v* **throw**, push, drop, toss, fall, dump [➡ POSITION SOMETHING; 325] 3 *n* **twang**, strum, plonk [➡ IMPACT SOUNDS; 1260]

plunk down *v* **plump down**, flop down, plop down, drop down, collapse, fall, plonk down (*informal*) [➡ ASSUME A POSITION; 317] *Opposite:* stand up

plural *type of* **grammatical term** [➡ ASPECTS OF LANGUAGE; 682]

pluralism *n* **variety**, diversity, multiplicity, heterogeneity [➡ DIFFERENCE; 149] *Opposite:* homogeneity

pluralistic *adj* **varied**, mixed, diverse, multicultural, multiethnic, pluralist [➡ DIFFERENCE; 149] *Opposite:* homogeneous

plurality 1 *n* **number**, range, variety, multiplicity, multitude, group [➡ MANY, MUCH, LARGE AMOUNT; 117] *Opposite:* single 2 *n* **majority**, landslide, margin [➡ MAJORITY AND MAXIMUM; 141]

plus 1 *prep* **in addition to**, added to, as well as, along with, together with, and also, and [➡ ALSO; 138] *Opposite:* minus 2 *adj* **and above**, and over, and more [➡ ALSO; 138] 3 *adj* **desirable**, positive, advantageous, favorable, good [➡ ADMIRABLE AND COMMENDABLE; 185] *Opposite:* minus 4 *n* (*informal*) **advantage**, bonus, benefit, good thing, boon, pro, good point [➡ SOURCE OF HAPPINESS, PLEASURE, OR IMPROVEMENT; 209] *Opposite:* minus

plus fours *type of* **pants** [➡ GARMENTS AND OUTFITS; 865]

plush (*informal*) *adj* **lush**, luxurious, expensive, rich, lavish, luxury, deluxe, swanky (*informal*) [➡ EXPENSIVE AND LUXURIOUS; 218]

plus point (*UK*) *n* **advantage**, good point, bonus, good thing, pro, benefit, boon, plus (*informal*) [➡ SOURCE OF HAPPINESS, PLEASURE, OR IMPROVEMENT; 209]

Pluto *type of* **planet** [➡ HEAVENLY BODIES; 1061]

plutocrat *n* **tycoon**, magnate, mogul, big shot (*informal*) [➡ RICH PEOPLE; 895]

ply **1** *v* **work**, practice, pursue, carry out, wage, carry on, exercise [➡ CARRY OUT AN ACTION; 269] **2** *v* **use**, work with, apply, utilize, employ [➡ USE; 467] **3** *v* **supply**, pile, load, provide, furnish (*formal*) [➡ EQUIP AND SUPPLY; 435] **4** *v* **badger**, hound, harass, overwhelm, bombard, barrage [➡ COMPLAIN AND NAG; 686] **5** *n* **layer**, thickness, strand, tier [➡ COVERS AND COATINGS; 1246]

plywood *n* [➡ BUILDING MATERIALS; 1077]

PM *n* [➡ POLITICAL OFFICES AND POLITICIANS; 808]

p.m. *adj* **afternoon**, after lunch, evening, night [➡ TIMES OF DAY; 87] *Opposite*: a.m.

pneumatic *adj* **air-filled**, inflated, inflatable, air [➡ DESCRIBING TECHNOLOGY; 1160] *Opposite*: solid

poach **1** *v* **steal**, thieve, rustle, pilfer, plunder, rob [➡ STEAL AND ROB; 426] **2** *v* **simmer**, boil, steam, braise [➡ COOKING AND FOOD PREPARATION; 353]

poached *adj* [➡ STATE OF PREPARED FOOD; 1171]

poacher *n* **thief**, rustler, robber, pilferer [➡ CRIMINALS; 821]

pocked *adj* **pitted**, pockmarked, dented, cratered, scarred, marked, blemished [➡ CONDITIONS AFFECTING THE SKIN; 721] *Opposite*: unblemished

pocket **1** *n* **pouch**, compartment, receptacle, sack, bag [➡ CONTAINERS, RECEPTACLES, AND PACKAGING; 1245] **2** *part of* **garment** [➡ PARTS OF A GARMENT; 870] **3** *v* **help yourself**, steal, appropriate, take, purloin (*formal or humorous*) [➡ STEAL AND ROB; 426] **4** *adj* **concise**, abridged, reduced, short, small, compact, portable, pocket-sized, little, handy, mini (*informal*) [➡ SMALL; 1195]

pocketbook **1** *n* **shoulder bag**, handbag, purse [➡ CONTAINERS, RECEPTACLES, AND PACKAGING; 1245] **2** *n* **notecase** (*dated*), wallet, purse, case, organizer [➡ CONTAINERS, RECEPTACLES, AND PACKAGING; 1245]

pocketknife *type of* **knife** [➡ CUTTING TOOLS; 1120]

pocket money *n* **spending money**, pin money, expenses, extra cash, personal money [➡ SMALL AMOUNTS OF MONEY; 121]

pocket-size *see* **pocket-sized**

pocket-sized *adj* **little**, small, handy, compact, portable, pocket, mini (*informal*) [➡ SMALL; 1195] *Opposite*: bulky

pocket watch *type of* **clock** [➡ CLOCKS AND TIMERS; 1126]

pockmark *n* **blemish**, scar, indentation, hollow, blotch, pit [➡ CONDITIONS AFFECTING THE SKIN; 721]

pockmarked *adj* **pitted**, pocked, dented, cratered, scarred, marked, blemished [➡ CONDITIONS AFFECTING THE SKIN; 721] *Opposite*: unblemished

pod **1** *n* **shell**, husk, peapod, case, hull, shuck [➡ PARTS OF

TREES AND PLANTS; 1026] **2** *part of* **spacecraft** [➡ SPACE VEHICLES; 1063] **3** *type of* **herd** [➡ GROUPS OF ANIMALS; 993]

podginess (*UK*) *n* [➡ BUILD; 477]

podgy (*UK*) *adj* **fat**, overweight, chubby, stout, fleshy, curvy, obese, round, pudgy (*informal*) [➡ BUILD; 477] *Opposite*: slim

podium **1** *n* **dais**, platform, stage, plinth [➡ STAGES, PLATFORMS, AND RAISED AREAS; 1098] **2** *n* **lectern**, pedestal, stand, support [➡ SUPPORTS AND BASES; 1255]

poem *n* **verse**, rhyme, ode, sonnet, elegy, limerick, couplet, epic [➡ POETRY AND VERSE; 915] *Opposite*: prose

poesy (*archaic or literary*) *n* [➡ POETRY AND VERSE; 915]

poet *n* **writer**, lyricist, rhymester, versifier, composer, bard (*literary or humorous*) [➡ WRITERS AND STYLES; 914]

poetaster *n* [➡ WRITERS AND STYLES; 914]

poetic **1** *adj* **lyrical**, elegiac, graceful, rhythmical, flowing, expressive, whimsical, romantic, elevated, uplifting [➡ ELOQUENT, TALKATIVE, AND LONG-WINDED; 632] *Opposite*: prosaic **2** *adj* **sensitive**, full of feeling, profound, deep, moving, perceptive, insightful, imaginative [➡ EMOTIONALLY PLEASANT; 187] *Opposite*: insensitive

poeticality *n* **lyricism**, expressivity, eloquence [➡ ELOQUENT, TALKATIVE, AND LONG-WINDED; 632]

poetry *n* **verse**, rhyme, poems, rhymes, lyrics, poesy (*archaic or literary*) [➡ POETRY AND VERSE; 915] *Opposite*: prose

po-faced (*UK*) *adj* **humorless**, disapproving, solemn, serious, strait-laced, dour [➡ BAD-TEMPERED AND HUMORLESS; 626] *Opposite*: jovial

pogo (*UK*) *v* [➡ BOUNCE, UNDULATE, AND VIBRATE; 308]

pogrom *n* **persecution**, extermination, massacre, devastation, slaughter, holocaust, ethnic cleansing [➡ CAUSES OF DEATH; 921]

poignance *n* **pathos**, sadness, tragedy, nostalgia, expressiveness, tenderness [➡ SADNESS, DISTRESS, AND DESPAIR; 539]

poignancy *n* **pathos**, sadness, tragedy, nostalgia, tenderness, expressiveness [➡ SADNESS, DISTRESS, AND DESPAIR; 539]

poignant *adj* **moving**, emotional, touching, distressing, sad, affecting, heartrending, heartbreaking, upsetting, tender, agonizing, expressive, nostalgic [➡ SADNESS, DISTRESS, AND DESPAIR; 539] *Opposite*: unemotional

See Compare and Contrast at **moving**.

poinsettia *type of* **foliage plant** [➡ FOLIAGE PLANTS; 1035]

point **1** *n* **opinion**, fact, idea, argument, theme, topic [➡ SUBJECT AREAS; 768] **2** *n* **instant**, time, stage, moment, juncture (*formal*) [➡ SHORT PERIODS OF TIME; 93] **3** *n* **aim**, meaning, central theme, intention, heart, crux, thrust [➡ MEANING; 690] **4** *n* **purpose**, advantage, use, sense, object, objective, aim, goal, usefulness [➡ INTENTIONS AND PURPOSES; 772] **5** *n* **argument**, statement, line of reasoning, thrust, viewpoint, view [➡ POINTS OF VIEW; 767] **6** *n* **detail**, item, feature, aspect, thing, article, element, step [➡ SUBJECT AREAS; 768] **7** *n* **position**, spot, place, situation, site, location, locus, station [➡ PLACE; 1065] **8** *n* **tip**, end, top, summit, peak, apex, cusp, prong [➡ EXTREM-

ITIES OF PHYSICAL OBJECTS; 1250] **9** *n* **headland**, cape, promontory, spit, peninsula, foreland, head [➡THE SEAS, OCEANS, AND SHORES; 1041] **10** *n* (*UK*) **socket**, plug, contact, outlet, power point (*UK*) [➡ELECTRONICS AND ELECTRICS; 1137] **11** *v* **direct**, aim, face, indicate, draw attention to, steer, train [➡POSITION SOMETHING; 325]

point and click agreement *n* [➡E-COMMERCE; 1129]

point-blank **1** *adv* **at close range**, straight on, dead on, close up, close to, closely, immediately [➡CLOSENESS; 159] **2** *adv* **frankly**, bluntly, outright, straightforwardly, directly, abruptly, straight out (*UK*) [➡HONEST AND OPEN; 630] *Opposite*: indirectly

pointed **1** *adj* **sharp**, piercing, keen, pointy, jagged [➡ANGULAR SHAPE; 1217] *Opposite*: blunt **2** *adj* **barbed**, critical, meaningful, incisive, sharp, cutting, trenchant, acerbic, emphatic, insightful [➡RUDE AND HOSTILE; 625] *Opposite*: mild

pointedly *adv* **deliberately**, purposely, intentionally, meaningfully, openly, emphatically [➡RUDE AND HOSTILE; 625] *Opposite*: subtly

pointer **1** *n* **cane**, baton, stick, pole [➡STICKS, POLES, AND WEDGES; 1254] **2** *n* **needle**, indicator, hand, cursor [➡PARTS OF MACHINES AND TOOLS; 1118] **3** *n* **tip**, advice, hint, suggestion, warning, indication [➡ADVICE; 689]

pointillism *type of* **pre-20th-century art movement** [➡ARTISTIC MOVEMENTS AND STYLES; 899]

pointiness *n* [➡ANGULAR SHAPE; 1217]

pointing (*UK*) *n* **mortar**, cement, grout, filling [➡BUILDING MATERIALS; 1077]

pointless *adj* **useless**, futile, senseless, meaningless, worthless, stupid, inane, purposeless, hopeless, needless, aimless, vain [➡REDUNDANT AND USELESS; 240] *Opposite*: useful

pointlessness *n* **uselessness**, futility, senselessness, meaninglessness, worthlessness, stupidity, inanity, purposelessness, hopelessness, needlessness, aimlessness, vanity [➡REDUNDANT AND USELESS; 240] *Opposite*: usefulness

point of departure *n* [➡BEGINNINGS; 53]

point of no return *n* [➡DECISIVE MOMENTS; 44]

point of view *n* **opinion**, attitude, standpoint, viewpoint, position, approach, judgment, perspective [➡POINTS OF VIEW; 767]

point out **1** *v* **indicate**, show, reveal, point at, identify [➡INFORM, ANNOUNCE, AND ISSUE; 611] **2** *v* **call attention to**, draw attention to, highlight, indicate, mention, spotlight, emphasize [➡CLAIM, INSIST, AND EMPHASIZE; 614] *Opposite*: hide

point the finger *v* [➡ACCUSE, BLAME, AND CRITICIZE; 641]

point-to-point *n* **steeplechase**, horserace, equestrian event, cross-country racing [➡NON-AGGRESSIVE/SPORTING EVENTS; 40]

point up *v* **emphasize**, draw attention to, underline, make clear, show, reveal, underscore, put the accent on, highlight, demonstrate, accentuate, focus [➡CLAIM, INSIST, AND EMPHASIZE; 614]

pointy *adj* [➡ANGULAR SHAPE; 1217]

pointy-headed (*slang*) *adj* [➡NEGATIVE INTELLECTUAL CHARACTERISTICS; 525]

poise **1** *n* **composure**, dignity, self-assurance, self-confidence, self-control, sang-froid, aplomb, self-possession, gracefulness, calm, cool [➡CONFIDENCE AND COMPOSURE; 499] **2** *n* **grace**, bearing, deportment, good posture, composure, carriage (*formal*), mien (*formal*) [➡TEMPERAMENT AND BEHAVIOR; 492] **3** *v* **hover**, balance, float, perch, hang, suspend [➡ASSUME A POSITION; 317]

poised **1** *adj* **ready**, prepared, primed, in position, in place [➡ABOUT TO HAPPEN; 33] *Opposite*: unprepared **2** *adj* **balanced**, suspended, hovering, on the edge, on the brink, perched, hanging, floating [➡LACK OF ACTIVITY OR MOTION; 342] **3** *adj* **composed**, dignified, self-assured, self-confident, controlled, self-possessed, graceful, calm, cool, easygoing, placid [➡CONFIDENCE AND COMPOSURE; 499] *Opposite*: insecure

poison **1** *n* **venom**, toxin, contagion, toxic substance [➡UNPLEASANT, DIRTY, AND TOXIC SUBSTANCES; 1268] **2** *v* **kill**, murder, exterminate, destroy, harm, injure, assassinate, slaughter, attack [➡KILL; 923] **3** *v* **pollute**, taint, corrupt, contaminate, adulterate, spoil, dirty, sully, debase, turn [➡DIRTY AND CONTAMINATE; 404]

poisoner *n* **murderer**, killer, exterminator, assassin, slaughterer, attacker [➡PEOPLE WHO KILL; 924]

poison gas *type of* **gas** [➡GASES; 1275]

poison ivy *type of* **weed** [➡WEEDS AND THISTLES; 1034]

poison oak *type of* **weed** [➡WEEDS AND THISTLES; 1034]

poisonous **1** *adj* **toxic**, venomous, noxious, fatal, lethal, deadly, pestilential, mephitic (*formal*) [➡DEADLY; 928] *Opposite*: harmless **2** *adj* **malicious**, evil, wicked, ill-intentioned, nasty, spiteful, vicious, hostile, venomous, malevolent, vituperative [➡AGGRESSIVE AND BELLIGERENT; 518] *Opposite*: kindly

poisonously *adv* **maliciously**, evilly, wickedly, nastily, spitefully, viciously, hostilely, venomously, malevolently, vituperatively [➡AGGRESSIVE AND BELLIGERENT; 518]

poke **1** *v* **jab**, stab, push, prod, thrust, dig, nudge, punch, stick [➡CONTACT: TOUCH; 412] **2** *v* **protrude**, stick out, project, jut, extend [➡ARRIVE; 12] **3** *v* **search through**, look through, root, browse, rummage, search, nose around (*informal*), ferret about (*UK*) [➡SEEK POSSESSION AND SEARCH; 456] **4** *n* **stab**, jab, push, prod, thrust, dig, nudge [➡CONTACT: TOUCH; 412]

poke around *v* [➡SEEK POSSESSION AND SEARCH; 456]

poke fun at *v* **make fun of**, ridicule, tease, mock, laugh at, razz (*informal*), rag (*dated*) [➡JOKES AND TEASING; 674]

poker *type of* **general tool** [➡HAND TOOLS; 1119]

poker-faced *adj* **expressionless**, reactionless, blank, impassive, emotionless, deadpan, straight-faced [➡FACIAL EXPRESSIONS AND BLUSHING; 651] *Opposite*: expressive

pokey (*slang*) *n* [➡BUILDINGS FOR CONFINING PEOPLE; 1094]

poky (*informal*) **1** *adj* **slow**, plodding, sluggish, leaden, dilatory [➡MOVING SLOWLY; 105] *Opposite*: quick **2** *adj* **frumpy**, dowdy, shabby, drab, plain, unfashionable, old-fashioned [➡OLD, OLD-FASHIONED; 167] **3** *adj* **small**, tiny, cramped, restricted, tight, boxy [➡SMALL; 1195] *Opposite*: spacious

polar *adj* **glacial**, Arctic, Antarctic [➡COLD WEATHER; 1051] *Opposite*: tropical

polar bear *type of* **large mammal** [➡ LARGE MAMMALS; 986]

Polaris *type of* **constellation** [➡ HEAVENLY BODIES; 1061]

polarity *n* **division**, split, schism, divergence, polarization, separation, opposition [➡ SEPARATE AND DIVIDE; 401] *Opposite*: convergence

polarization *n* **divergence**, separation, division, opposition, schism, split, polarity [➡ SEPARATE AND DIVIDE; 401] *Opposite*: union

polarize *v* **diverge**, split, drive apart, separate, create a rift in, differentiate, divide, oppose [➡ SEPARATE AND DIVIDE; 401] *Opposite*: unite

pole 1 *n* **opposite**, extreme, extremity, limit, end [➡ OPPOSITE; 157] 2 *n* **rod**, shaft, stick, post, dowel, staff, baton, stake [➡ STICKS, POLES, AND WEDGES; 1254] 3 *v* **push**, propel, raft, punt, shove, thrust, drive [➡ PUSH, PULL, AND SLIDE; 335]

poleax 1 *v* **astonish**, amaze, stupefy, stun, shock, dumbfound [➡ CONFUSE AND BEWILDER; 571] 2 *type of* **sword or knife** [➡ SWORDS AND KNIVES; 1157]

polecat *type of* **small mammal** [➡ SMALL MAMMALS; 990]

polemic 1 *n* **argument**, plea, diatribe, speech, discourse, attack, defense [➡ CRITICISMS AND ANGRY OUTBURSTS; 50] 2 *adj* **controversial**, outspoken, impassioned, uncompromising, bold, polemical, passionate, persuasive [➡ HONEST AND OPEN; 630] *Opposite*: dispassionate

polemicist *n* **debater**, orator, speaker, essayist, lecturer, thinker, campaigner, activist [➡ SPEAKERS AND ORATORS; 603]

pole position *n* **prime position**, lead, front, advantage, catbird seat (*informal*) [➡ SOURCE OF HAPPINESS, PLEASURE, OR IMPROVEMENT; 209] *Opposite*: rear

poles apart *adj* **complete opposites**, diametrically opposed, nothing like each other, completely different [➡ DIFFERENCE; 149]

pole vault *type of* **track and field** [➡ HOBBIES, GAMES, AND SPORTS; 875]

pole-vault *v* **jump**, vault, leap, bound [➡ GO UPWARD; 306]

police 1 *n* **police department**, law enforcement agency, police force, force, constabulary, law, crime squad, drug squad, vice squad, fraud squad, riot police [➡ THE POLICE, ARREST, AND PRETRIAL PROCEEDINGS; 818] 2 *v* **regulate**, control, keep watch over, monitor, patrol, supervise, watch [➡ AVOID, PREVENT, LIMIT, AND CONTROL; 277]

police cadet *n* [➡ THE POLICE, ARREST, AND PRETRIAL PROCEEDINGS; 818]

police car *type of* **public service vehicle** [➡ VEHICLES; 1145]

police constable (*UK*) *n* [➡ THE POLICE, ARREST, AND PRETRIAL PROCEEDINGS; 818]

police department *n* [➡ THE POLICE, ARREST, AND PRETRIAL PROCEEDINGS; 818]

police force *n* **law enforcement agency**, police department, crime squad, drug squad, vice squad, fraud squad, riot police, police, force, constabulary, law [➡ THE POLICE, ARREST, AND PRETRIAL PROCEEDINGS; 818]

policeman *see* **police officer**

police officer *n* **copper**, sheriff, peace officer, policeman, policewoman, detective, law enforcement officer, sergeant, cop (*slang*), WPC (*UK*), police constable (*UK*), PC (*UK*) [➡ THE POLICE, ARREST, AND PRETRIAL PROCEEDINGS; 818]

policewoman *see* **police officer**

policy 1 *n* **course of action**, rule, strategy, plan, guiding principle, guidelines, procedure, dogma, program [➡ WAYS OF DOING THINGS; 294] 2 *n* **contract**, document, certificate, statement, papers, testament, record, schedule [➡ OFFICIAL DOCUMENTS; 586]

polish 1 *v* **shine**, buff, buff up, rub, clean, dust, furbish [➡ CLEAN AND POLISH; 403] *Opposite*: tarnish 2 *v* **improve**, enhance, refine, perfect, hone, brush up, work on, practice, mend [➡ IMPROVE SOMETHING; 374] 3 *n* **shine**, luster, gleam, sheen, brilliance, smoothness, gloss [➡ VISUAL TEXTURE; 1221] *Opposite*: dullness 4 *n* **refinement**, skill, control, sophistication, grace, style, sparkle, culture, elegance [➡ GOOD MANNERS AND SOCIAL SKILLS; 520]

polished 1 *adj* **smooth**, shiny, gleaming, glossy, slippery, bright [➡ VISUAL TEXTURE; 1221] *Opposite*: dull 2 *adj* **practiced**, skillful, accomplished, professional, impeccable, expert [➡ TALENTED AND SKILLFUL; 527] *Opposite*: amateur 3 *adj* **refined**, elegant, cultured, sophisticated, graceful, genteel [➡ GOOD MANNERS AND SOCIAL SKILLS; 520] *Opposite*: coarse

polish off *v* **finish**, finish off, dispose of, complete, eliminate, eat, eat up, gobble, wolf, bolt, demolish (*informal*), scarf down (*slang*) [➡ EAT AND NOT EAT; 710] *Opposite*: leave

polish up 1 *v* **shine**, buff, rub, clean, dust, furbish [➡ CLEAN AND POLISH; 403] *Opposite*: tarnish 2 *v* **refine**, improve, practice, brush up, work on, perfect, hone, enhance [➡ IMPROVE SOMETHING; 374] *Opposite*: let go

polish up on *v* **refine**, improve, practice, brush up, work on, perfect, hone, enhance [➡ IMPROVE SOMETHING; 374] *Opposite*: let go

polite 1 *adj* **well-mannered**, good-mannered, civil, well-bred, gracious, courteous, respectful, mannerly [➡ GOOD MANNERS AND SOCIAL SKILLS; 520] *Opposite*: rude 2 *adj* **refined**, cultured, sophisticated, polished, elegant, genteel, urbane, poised [➡ LEVELS OF EDUCATION AND SOPHISTICATION; 894] *Opposite*: coarse

politely *adv* **civilly**, graciously, courteously, respectfully [➡ GOOD MANNERS AND SOCIAL SKILLS; 520] *Opposite*: rudely

politeness *n* **good manners**, graciousness, manners, civility, breeding, courtesy, respect [➡ GOOD MANNERS AND SOCIAL SKILLS; 520] *Opposite*: rudeness

politesse *n* [➡ GOOD MANNERS AND SOCIAL SKILLS; 520]

politic *adj* **tactful**, diplomatic, prudent, wise, expedient, sensible, discreet, shrewd, astute, crafty, canny, cunning, sly [➡ POSITIVE INTELLECTUAL CHARACTERISTICS; 524] *Opposite*: foolish

political 1 *adj* **governmental**, administrative, electoral, civil, diplomatic, constitutional, doctrinal, ethical, civic [➡ GOVERNMENT AND POLITICS; 805] 2 *adj* **politically aware**, radical, partisan, dogmatic, party-political [➡ THE NATURE OF IDEAS; 771]

political correctness *n* **appropriateness**, sensitivity, awareness, tactfulness, inclusiveness, inoffensiveness [➡ GOOD MANNERS AND SOCIAL SKILLS; 520] *Opposite*: insensitivity

politically correct *adj* **inclusive**, appropriate, sensitive, aware, tactful, inoffensive, right-on (*dated informal*) [➡ GOOD MANNERS AND SOCIAL SKILLS; 520] *Opposite*: politically incorrect

politically incorrect *adj* **exclusive**, insensitive, inappropriate, unaware, tactless, prejudiced, offensive, insulting, inconsiderate [➡ BAD MANNERS AND SOCIAL SKILLS; 521] *Opposite*: politically correct

politician *n* **political figure**, representative, candidate, official, legislator, statesman, stateswoman, office-bearer (*UK*) [➡ POLITICAL OFFICES AND POLITICIANS; 808]

politicization *n* **awareness raising**, consciousness raising, lobbying [➡ SOCIAL, POLITICAL, AND ECONOMIC CHANGE; 373]

politicize *v* **raise awareness of**, put on the agenda, debate, discuss, air, lobby, campaign [➡ SOCIAL, POLITICAL, AND ECONOMIC CHANGE; 373] *Opposite*: depoliticize

politicking *n* **campaigning**, speechmaking, lobbying, politics, scheming, intriguing [➡ GOVERNMENT AND POLITICS; 805]

politics 1 *n* **government**, political affairs, affairs of state, policy, policymaking, legislation [➡ GOVERNMENT AND POLITICS; 805] 2 *n* **beliefs**, principles, opinions, views, theory, philosophy, dogma [➡ POINTS OF VIEW; 767]

polity *n* **political entity**, organization, institution, state, society, community [➡ INSTITUTIONS; 790]

polka *type of* **dance** [➡ DANCE; 903]

poll 1 *n* **election**, census, survey, opinion poll, sample, ballot, referendum, market research [➡ ELECTIONS AND VOTING; 807] 2 *v* **sample**, survey, question, ask, interview, ballot [➡ ASK PEOPLE QUESTIONS; 666]

pollinate *v* **fertilize**, cross-fertilize, self-fertilize, cross-pollinate, self-pollinate [➡ GROW AND CULTIVATE; 351]

pollination *n* **fertilization**, cross-fertilization, self-fertilization, cross-pollination, self-pollination, allogamy, autogamy [➡ GROW AND CULTIVATE; 351]

polling *n* **voting**, casting your vote, balloting, going to the polls [➡ ELECTIONS AND VOTING; 807]

polling booth *n* **cubicle**, voting booth, booth, stall, box, compartment [➡ ELECTIONS AND VOTING; 807]

pollutant *n* **contaminant**, impurity, toxin, poison, waste product, chemical [➡ UNPLEASANT, DIRTY, AND TOXIC SUBSTANCES; 1268]

pollute 1 *v* **contaminate**, poison, adulterate, infest, infect, foul, spoil, litter, dirty, taint [➡ DIRTY AND CONTAMINATE; 404] *Opposite*: clean 2 *v* **corrupt**, pervert, demoralize, violate, damage, impair, blight, defile (*formal*) [➡ MISUSE AND ABUSE; 471] *Opposite*: purify

polluted *adj* **contaminated**, dirty, poisoned, adulterated, unclean, insanitary, unhygienic, diseased, infested, infected, fouled, foul, fetid, impure, tainted, rank (*literary*) [➡ DIRTY; 1235] *Opposite*: clean

polluter *n* **contaminator**, dumper, poisoner, emitter, discharger, fly-tipper (*UK*) [➡ DIRTY AND SLOVENLY PEOPLE; 954] *Opposite*: environmentalist

pollution 1 *n* **contamination**, infection, adulteration, corruption [➡ DIRTY AND CONTAMINATE; 404] 2 *n* **contaminant**, toxic waste, effluence, greenhouse gasses, smog, fumes, litter, trash [➡ UNPLEASANT, DIRTY, AND TOXIC SUBSTANCES; 1268]

polo shirt *type of* **top** [➡ GARMENTS AND OUTFITS; 865]

poltergeist *n* **ghost**, spirit, manifestation, apparition, specter, phantom, presence [➡ THE SUPERNATURAL; 787]

polychromatic *adj* [➡ DESCRIBING COLORS; 1226]

polychrome *adj* [➡ DESCRIBING COLORS; 1226]

polyester *type of* **synthetic fabric** [➡ FABRICS; 1132]

polyethylene *type of* **plastic** [➡ PLASTICS; 1134]

polyglot *n* **linguist**, multilingual person, bilingual person [➡ PEOPLE WHO WORK WITH LANGUAGE AND CODE; 854]

polygon *type of* **angular shape** [➡ ANGULAR SHAPE; 1217]

polygonal *adj* **many-sided**, multilateral, triangular, quadrilateral, pentagonal, hexagonal, octagonal, geometric [➡ ANGULAR SHAPE; 1217]

polygraph *n* **detector**, lie detector, recorder, tester [➡ THE POLICE, ARREST, AND PRETRIAL PROCEEDINGS; 818]

polymath *n* **fount of knowledge**, Renaissance man, Renaissance woman, walking encyclopedia, mine of information, sage (*literary*) [➡ TALENTED OR INTELLIGENT PEOPLE; 528] *Opposite*: specialist

polyp *n* **growth**, tumor, cyst, nodule, swelling, lump [➡ ILLNESSES AND DISORDERS; 732]

polystyrene *type of* **plastic** [➡ PLASTICS; 1134]

polysyllabic *adj* **long**, compound, complex, multisyllabic [➡ ASPECTS OF LANGUAGE; 682] *Opposite*: monosyllabic

polysyllable *n* **long word**, compound, complex word [➡ ASPECTS OF LANGUAGE; 682] *Opposite*: monosyllable

polytechnic *n* **college**, technical college, university, tech (*informal*) [➡ EDUCATIONAL INSTITUTIONS; 813]

polytheism *n* **dualism**, animism, pantheism [➡ RELIGIOUS CONCEPTS; 776] *Opposite*: monotheism

polyurethane *type of* **plastic** [➡ PLASTICS; 1134]

pomegranate *type of* **fruit** [➡ FRUIT AND VEGETABLES; 1176]

pomelo *type of* **citrus fruit** [➡ FRUIT AND VEGETABLES; 1176]

pomeranian *type of* **small dog** [➡ DOGS; 980]

pomfret *type of* **tropical fish** [➡ OCEAN FISH; 1009]

pomp *n* **splendor**, spectacle, display, ceremony, show, showiness, pageantry, solemnity, magnificence, grandeur [➡ EXTRAORDINARY: AMAZING; 204] *Opposite*: understatement

pompadour *type of* **hairstyle** [➡ HAIRSTYLES AND HAIRPIECES; 488]

pompano *type of* **flatfish** [➡ OCEAN FISH; 1009]

pom-pom *n* **tassel**, decoration, detail, ball, bobble (*UK*) [➡ ORNAMENTS AND DECORATIONS; 1248]

pomposity *n* **self-importance**, arrogance, pretentiousness, pretension, snobbishness, affectation, affectedness, ostentation, portentousness, haughtiness, exaggeration, pompousness, grandiosity, vanity [➡ AFFECTATION, SELF-SATISFACTION, AND SNOBBISHNESS; 507] *Opposite:* modesty

pompous 1 *adj* **self-important**, arrogant, pretentious, snobbish, affected, ostentatious, portentous, haughty, exaggerated, grandiose, vain [➡ AFFECTATION, SELF-SATISFACTION, AND SNOBBISHNESS; 507] *Opposite:* modest 2 *adj* **showy**, flaunting, spectacular, magnificent, grand, splendid, overstated [➡ IN POOR TASTE AND OVERSENTIMENTAL; 229] *Opposite:* modest

pompousness 1 *n* **self-importance**, arrogance, pretentiousness, pretension, snobbishness, affectedness, ostentation, portentousness, haughtiness, pomposity, grandiosity, vanity [➡ AFFECTATION, SELF-SATISFACTION, AND SNOBBISHNESS; 507] *Opposite:* modesty 2 *n* **spectacle**, magnificence, pomp, grandeur, ceremony, pageantry, splendor, display, show, showiness, overstatement [➡ IN POOR TASTE AND OVERSENTIMENTAL; 229] *Opposite:* modesty

poncho *n* **cloak**, cape, wrap [➡ GARMENTS AND OUTFITS; 865]

pond *n* **pool**, tarn, fishpond, millpond, mere (*archaic or literary*) [➡ RIVERS, LAKES, AND STREAMS; 1042]

ponder *v* **consider**, think about, think over, contemplate, deliberate, wonder about, muse, brood over, mull over, meditate upon, weigh up (*UK*) [➡ THINK AND REFLECT; 743]

ponderable *adj* **appreciable**, significant, considerable, substantial, weighty, palpable [➡ IMPORTANT; 194] *Opposite:* insignificant

ponderous 1 *adj* **heavy**, laborious, lumbering, weighty, unwieldy, cumbersome, bulky, hefty [➡ WEIGHT: HEAVY; 1205] *Opposite:* light 2 *adj* **tedious**, boring, laborious, tiresome, dull, slow, verbose, long-winded [➡ BORING AND UNINTERESTING; 234] *Opposite:* lively

ponderously *adv* **heavily**, laboriously, slowly, tediously, boringly, tiresomely [➡ BORING AND UNINTERESTING; 234] *Opposite:* briskly

ponderousness *n* [➡ BORING AND UNINTERESTING; 234]

pond scum *type of* **marine alga** [➡ MICROORGANISMS, FUNGI, AND ALGAE; 1023]

pontiff *n* **pope**, bishop of Rome, Holy Father [➡ RELIGIOUS PEOPLE; 778]

pontifical 1 *adj* **episcopal**, papal, prelatic [➡ RELIGIONS AND RELIGIOUS PRACTICES; 777] 2 *adj* **pompous**, self-important, pontificating, grandiose, portentous, pretentious, swaggering [➡ AFFECTATION, SELF-SATISFACTION, AND SNOBBISHNESS; 507] *Opposite:* humble

pontificate *v* **hold forth**, preach, go on, sound off [➡ UTTER AND PRONOUNCE; 608]

pontoon *n* **platform**, float, buoy, support, base, raft [➡ SUPPORTS AND BASES; 1255]

pontoon bridge *type of* **bridge** [➡ BRIDGES, TUNNELS, CROSSINGS, AND JUNCTIONS; 1112]

pony *type of* **horse** [➡ HORSES; 985]

ponytail *type of* **hairstyle** [➡ HAIRSTYLES AND HAIRPIECES; 488]

pony-trekking (*UK*) *n* **hacking**, horseback riding, riding, riding out, equitation (*formal*), horse-riding (*UK*) [➡ HOBBIES, GAMES, AND SPORTS; 875]

pooch (*informal*) *n* **dog**, lapdog, canine companion, canine, hound, pet, doggy (*babytalk*) [➡ DOGS; 980]

poodle *type of* **small dog** [➡ DOGS; 980]

pooh-pooh *v* **reject**, dismiss, spurn, scorn, scoff at, express contempt, undermine, turn your nose up at, put down (*informal*) [➡ DENY AND REJECT; 644] *Opposite:* praise

pool 1 *n* **pond**, puddle, lake, swimming pool, tarn, mere (*archaic or literary*), loch (*UK*) [➡ RIVERS, LAKES, AND STREAMS; 1042] 2 *n* **team**, band, collection, consortium, collective, group [➡ GROUPS OF PEOPLE; 935] 3 *n* **kitty**, fund, pot (*informal*) [➡ MONEY; 797] 4 *type of* **target ball game** [➡ HOBBIES, GAMES, AND SPORTS; 875] 5 *v* **share**, combine, bring together, put together, assemble, merge, amalgamate [➡ COMBINE AND MIX; 400]

poop *part of* **ship or boat** [➡ PARTS OF A SHIP OR BOAT; 1151]

pooped (*informal*) *adj* **exhausted**, tired out, worn out, drained, ready to drop, bushed (*informal*), dog-tired (*informal*), done in (*informal*), wiped out (*slang*), shattered (*UK*) [➡ TIRED, ASLEEP, AND UNCONSCIOUS; 738] *Opposite:* invigorated

poor 1 *adj* **destitute**, needy, poverty-stricken, impoverished, penniless, badly off, broke (*informal*), hard up (*informal*), indigent (*formal*) [➡ POVERTY AND POOR; 892] *Opposite:* rich 2 *adj* **deprived**, unfortunate, underprivileged, meager, reduced, pitiable, humble, lowly, modest [➡ IN TROUBLE AND DISADVANTAGED; 73] *Opposite:* privileged 3 *adj* **weak**, inadequate, feeble, meager, bad, inferior, scanty, deficient, mediocre [➡ WEAKNESS; 241] *Opposite:* superior 4 *adj* **humble**, lowly, modest, insignificant [➡ CLASS STATUS; 889] *Opposite:* noble

poorly *adv* **badly**, inadequately, weakly, feebly, scantily, defectively, unsuccessfully, disappointingly [➡ WEAKNESS; 241] *Opposite:* well

poorly maintained *adj* [➡ IN BAD REPAIR; 1234]

poorness 1 *n* **poverty**, impoverishment, destitution, pennilessness, neediness, deprivation, indigence (*formal*) [➡ POVERTY AND POOR; 892] *Opposite:* wealth 2 *n* **weakness**, inadequacy, feebleness, inferiority, poor quality, poor standard, deficiency, mediocrity [➡ ORDINARINESS; 244] *Opposite:* superiority

poor person *n* [➡ POOR PEOPLE; 896]

poor quality *n* **cheapness**, tawdriness, mediocrity, inferiority, weakness, worthlessness, atrociousness [➡ IN BAD REPAIR; 1234] *Opposite:* quality

poor-quality *adj* **cheap**, shoddy, trashy, jerrybuilt, second-class, second-rate, mediocre, rubbishy, substandard, thrown together (*informal*) [➡ IN BAD REPAIR; 1234] *Opposite:* first-rate

pop 1 *n* **explosion**, bang, crack, report, snap [➡ IMPACT SOUNDS; 1260] 2 *type of* **pop and vocal music** [➡ MUSIC, SONGS, AND SINGING; 907] 3 *v* **explode**, burst, go off, crack [➡ EMIT SOUNDS THROUGH IMPACT AND ABRASION; 365] 4 *v* (*informal*) **dash**, dart, go, call, nip (*informal*) [➡ MOVE FAST; 313] 5 *v* (*informal*) **put**, place, insert, drop, shove, push, stick (*informal*) [➡ POSITION SOMETHING; 325] 6 *adj* (*informal*) **popular**, modern, current, accessible, easy, simple, contemporary, superficial [➡ NEW, MODERN; 166]

pop art *type of* **20th-century art movement** [➡ ARTISTIC MOVEMENTS AND STYLES; 899]

pop by (*UK*) *v* [➡ ARRIVE; 12]

pope *n* **pontiff**, bishop of Rome, Holy Father [➡ RELIGIOUS PEOPLE; 778]

popeyed *adj* **goggle-eyed**, swollen-eyed, wide-eyed, bug-eyed (*informal*) [➡ FACIAL CHARACTERISTICS; 481]

pop group *type of* **band** [➡ MUSICIANS AND SINGERS; 908]

popgun *type of* **toy** [➡ TOYS; 880]

pop in (*informal*) *v* **visit**, go, stop at, look in on, drop in on, call in (*UK*), call round (*UK*) [➡ ARRIVE; 12]

poplar *type of* **deciduous tree** [➡ DECIDUOUS TREES; 1028]

poplin *type of* **fabric from plants** [➡ FABRICS; 1132]

poppa (*informal*) *type of* **older relative** [➡ OLDER GENERATION RELATIVES; 959]

poppadom *type of* **bread** [➡ BREAD, FLOUR, AND BREAD PRODUCTS; 1179]

popper (*UK*) *n* [➡ FASTENERS, LINKS, AND NETWORKS; 1247]

poppy *type of* **annual flower** [➡ FLOWERS; 1032]

poppycock (*dated informal*) *n* **nonsense**, absurdity, untruth, rubbish, twaddle (*informal*) [➡ MEANINGLESS SPEECH OR WRITING; 676]

pop round (*informal*) *v* [➡ ARRIVE; 12]

populace *n* **public**, population, general public, common people, lay people, masses, inhabitants [➡ GROUPS IN SOCIETY; 940]

popular **1** *adj* **well-liked**, accepted, admired, in style, all the rage, fashionable, trendy (*informal*) [➡ POPULAR AND WANTED; 220] *Opposite*: unpopular **2** *adj* **common**, general, prevalent, widely held, current, widespread, standard [➡ PRESENT AND AVAILABLE; 11] *Opposite*: rare

popularity *n* **admiration**, approval, acceptance, fame, status, reputation, attractiveness, regard, esteem, recognition [➡ KNOWN AND FAMOUS; 181] *Opposite*: infamy

popularization **1** *n* **promotion**, spread, commercialization, propagation, universalization, dissemination [➡ INFORM, ANNOUNCE, AND ISSUE; 611] **2** *n* **simplification**, vulgarization, interpretation, explanation, universalization [➡ EXPLAIN AND CLARIFY; 610]

popularize **1** *v* **make popular**, promote, spread, propagate, commercialize, disseminate [➡ INFORM, ANNOUNCE, AND ISSUE; 611] **2** *v* **simplify**, interpret, vulgarize, put in layperson's terms, explain, gloss, universalize [➡ EXPLAIN AND CLARIFY; 610]

popularly *adv* **generally**, commonly, prevalently, readily, widely, usually, universally, traditionally [➡ USUALLY; 108] *Opposite*: rarely

populate *v* **inhabit**, people, settle, colonize, fill, crowd, occupy [➡ INHABIT; 20] *Opposite*: desert

population *n* **inhabitants**, populace, people, residents [➡ GROUPS IN SOCIETY; 940]

populist *adj* **antielitist**, majority, mainstream, democratic, general, accessible [➡ STYLES AND SYSTEMS OF GOVERNMENT; 806] *Opposite*: elitist

populous *adj* **crowded**, overcrowded, populated, full of people, packed [➡ FULL; 1239]

pop-up *adj* **spring-operated**, automatic, self-opening, folding, foldaway [➡ CHANGE OF SHAPE; 385]

porcelain *type of* **pottery** [➡ POTTERY; 1135]

porch *part of* **building** [➡ PARTS OF A BUILDING; 1095]

porcine *adj* **piggy**, piggish, swinish, hoglike [➡ BEASTLY AND BRUTISH; 510]

porcupine *type of* **small mammal** [➡ SMALL MAMMALS; 990]

pore *n* **hole**, opening, aperture, stoma [➡ HOLES, GAPS, AND FORKS; 1252]

pore over *v* **examine**, scour, read, study, go over, go through, scrutinize, peruse [➡ EXAMINE AND ASSESS; 753]

pork *type of* **meat** [➡ TYPES AND CUTS OF MEAT; 1177]

porkpie hat *type of* **hat** [➡ ACCESSORIES, MILLINERY, AND LINGERIE; 867]

porosity *n* [➡ DENSITY AND CONSISTENCY; 1207]

porous *adj* **absorbent**, permeable, leaky, spongy [➡ DENSITY AND CONSISTENCY; 1207] *Opposite*: impermeable

porousness *n* [➡ DENSITY AND CONSISTENCY; 1207]

porpoise *type of* **marine mammal** [➡ MARINE MAMMALS; 987]

porridge (*UK*) *n* **breakfast cereal**, gruel, oatmeal, oats [➡ CEREAL FOODS; 1178]

port **1** *n* **seaport**, anchorage, dock, harbor, haven (*literary*) [➡ THE SEAS, OCEANS, AND SHORES; 1041] **2** *type of* **hardware** [➡ COMPUTERS AND COMPUTING; 1127]

portability *n* **movability**, transportability, transferability, lightness, compactness, handiness, convenience, manageability [➡ WEIGHT: LIGHT; 1206] *Opposite*: bulkiness

portable *adj* **movable**, transportable, transferable, handy, convenient, manageable, compact, light [➡ WEIGHT: LIGHT; 1206] *Opposite*: fixed

portal **1** *n* [➡ THE INTERNET; 1128] **2** *n* (*literary*) **gateway**, doorway, porch, entrance, entry, threshold, portico, entryway, entranceway [➡ DOORS AND ACCESS POINTS; 1101]

portcullis *n* **gate**, door, grating, drawbridge, entry, entryway [➡ PARTS OF FORTRESSES; 1091]

portend *v* **foreshadow**, foretell, signify, mean, warn of, herald, threaten, indicate, presage [➡ MEAN SOMETHING; 61]

portent **1** *n* **omen**, sign, presage, warning, indication, signal, augury, threat, foreshadowing, herald [➡ INDICATIONS, SIGNS, AND WARNINGS; 68] **2** *n* (*formal*) **marvel**, phenomenon, prodigy, wonder, miracle [➡ AMAZING THINGS; 211]

portentous **1** *adj* **significant**, important, crucial, ominous, fateful, threatening [➡ IMPORTANT; 194] *Opposite*: trivial **2** *adj* **pompous**, pretentious, self-important, haughty, arrogant, solemn, grave, serious [➡ AFFECTATION, SELF-SATISFACTION, AND SNOBBISHNESS; 507] *Opposite*: modest

portentously **1** *adv* **significantly**, importantly, crucially, ominously, fatefully, threateningly [➡ IMPORTANT; 194] **2** *adv* **pompously**, pretentiously, self-importantly, haughtily, solemnly, gravely, arrogantly, seriously [➡AFFECTATION, SELF-SAT-ISFACTION, AND SNOBBISHNESS; 507] *Opposite*: modestly

portentousness *n* [➡AFFECTATION, SELF-SATISFACTION, AND SNOBBISHNESS; 507]

porter *n* **gatekeeper**, doorkeeper, concierge, janitor, receptionist, caretaker (*UK*) [➡PEOPLE WHO GUARD AND PROTECT; 846]

porterhouse steak *type of* **steak** [➡TYPES AND CUTS OF MEAT; 1177]

portfolio 1 *n* **case**, folder, file, wallet [➡CONTAINERS, RECEPTACLES, AND PACKAGING; 1245] 2 *n* (*formal*) **range**, collection, selection, group, set, assortment [➡COLLECTIONS AND MIXTURES OF THINGS; 1244]

portfolio worker *n* [➡WORKERS; 836]

porthole *type of* **window** [➡WINDOWS; 1100]

portico *n* **porch**, entrance, doorway, entry, entryway, entranceway [➡DOORS AND ACCESS POINTS; 1101]

portion 1 *n* **helping**, share, slice, serving, percentage, quota, ration, lot, measure, quantity, allotment [➡DEGREE AND EXTENT; 110] 2 *n* **fraction**, piece, bit, part, segment, section, fragment, scrap, division [➡AMOUNTS AND QUANTITIES; 112] *Opposite*: whole 3 *n* (*literary*) **fate**, destiny, lot, karma, kismet [➡FATE, DESTINY, AND ASTROLOGY; 782] 4 *v* **divide**, distribute, allocate, assign, share out, apportion, mete out, parcel out, dole out (*informal*) [➡DISPENSE, RATION, AND DISTRIBUTE; 434]

portliness *n* **stoutness**, stockiness, roundness, heaviness, heftiness, chubbiness [➡BUILD; 477] *Opposite*: slimness

portly *adj* **overweight**, stout, stocky, round, heavy, hefty, chubby [➡BUILD; 477] *Opposite*: slim

portmanteau 1 *n* **suitcase**, case, bag, valise, holdall, carryall [➡CONTAINERS, RECEPTACLES, AND PACKAGING; 1245] 2 *adj* (*UK*) **multiple**, combination, hybrid, blended, general-purpose, multipurpose [➡DIFFERENCE; 149]

portrait *n* **picture**, representation, portrayal, likeness, photograph, sketch, depiction, study, painting, drawing [➡REPRESENTATIONS AND GENERAL EXAMPLES; 65]

portraitist *n* [➡ARTISTS; 900]

portraiture *n* **portrait making**, portrait painting, photography, painting, drawing, self-portraiture [➡THE PICTORIAL ARTS; 897]

portray *v* **depict**, represent, describe, show, interpret, picture, render (*formal*) [➡REPRESENT SOMETHING OR SOMEBODY; 59]

portrayal *n* **representation**, interpretation, depiction, picture, description, rendering, reading [➡REPRESENTATIONS AND GENERAL EXAMPLES; 65]

Portuguese man-of-war *type of* **aquatic invertebrate** [➡AQUATIC INVERTEBRATES; 1022]

pose 1 *v* **model**, stand, sit, sit for, posture, position yourself [➡ASSUME A POSITION; 317] 2 *v* **impersonate**, pretend, play the part of, masquerade, profess, disguise yourself, pass off, feign [➡PRETEND AND MIMIC; 60] 3 *v* **present**, cause, create, set, establish, throw up, proffer, tender [➡CREATION; 346] 4 *v* **ask**, put, put forward, present, propound, inquire, question, propose [➡ASK PEOPLE QUESTIONS; 666] 5 *n* **posture**, stance, position, attitude, carriage (*formal*) [➡TEMPERAMENT AND BEHAVIOR; 492]

6 *n* **pretense**, sham, fake, front, façade, masquerade, affectation [➡DECEPTION AND LIES; 660]

poser 1 *n* (*informal*) **poseur**, show-off, exhibitionist, posturer, narcissist, swaggerer, peacock [➡SUPERFICIAL OR INSINCERE PEOPLE; 951] 2 *n* **problem**, question, puzzle, conundrum, challenge, riddle, enigma [➡SECRETS AND MYSTERIES; 180]

poseur *n* **exhibitionist**, posturer, narcissist, swaggerer, peacock, poser (*informal*), show-off (*informal*) [➡SUPERFICIAL OR INSINCERE PEOPLE; 951]

posh (*informal*) *adj* **upmarket**, elegant, fashionable, expensive, luxurious, exclusive, smart [➡EXPENSIVE AND LUXURIOUS; 218] *Opposite*: downmarket

posit (*formal*) *v* **put forward**, postulate, suggest, theorize, speculate, hypothesize, advance [➡DEVELOP THEORIES AND REASON; 744]

position 1 *n* **location**, place, site, spot, point, situation, locus, station [➡PLACE; 1065] 2 *n* **posture**, stance, pose, arrangement, attitude [➡TEMPERAMENT AND BEHAVIOR; 492] 3 *n* **rank**, status, standing, station [➡STATUS; 888] 4 *n* **view**, opinion, policy, stance, perception, side, attitude, thinking, outlook, standpoint, take [➡POINTS OF VIEW; 767] 5 *v* **put**, place, locate, stand, sit, set, arrange [➡POSITION SOMETHING; 325]

positive 1 *adj* **sure**, certain, clear, convinced, assured, confident [➡CERTAINTY; 561] *Opposite*: uncertain 2 *adj* **irrefutable**, definite, explicit, clear-cut, conclusive, categorical, decisive, unquestionable, confirmed, certain [➡CERTAIN; 174] *Opposite*: dubious 3 *adj* **optimistic**, confident, constructive, helpful, encouraging, affirmative, progressive, up, upbeat (*informal*) [➡CHEERFULNESS OF OUTLOOK; 503] *Opposite*: negative

positively 1 *adv* **definitely**, absolutely, completely, really, certainly, surely, confidently, clearly [➡CERTAIN; 174] 2 *adv* **encouragingly**, confidently, optimistically, supportively, constructively, helpfully, progressively [➡CHEERFULNESS OF OUTLOOK; 503] *Opposite*: negatively

positron *type of* **elementary particle** [➡ELEMENTARY PARTICLES; 1279]

posse (*informal*) *n* **gang**, band, party, group, company, body of people, clique, crew (*informal*) [➡FRIENDS AND ACQUAINTANCES; 936]

possess 1 *v* **own**, have, hold, enjoy, keep, retain [➡POSSESS; 444] *Opposite*: lack 2 *v* **take control**, influence, take, occupy, seize, hold, have power over, take over, control, dominate [➡BE IN CHARGE; 270]

possessed *adj* **controlled**, influenced, obsessed, crazed, overcome, infatuated, haunted [➡ECCENTRICITY AND IRRATIONALITY; 562]

possession *n* **ownership**, control, tenure, custody, proprietorship [➡POSSESS; 444]

possessions *n* **property**, belongings, wealth, goods, assets, personal effects, chattels, movables [➡POSSESSIONS; 461]

possessive 1 *adj* **domineering**, jealous, controlling, overprotective, covetous, suspicious, envious [➡ENVY AND JEALOUSY; 548] *Opposite*: trusting 2 *adj* **selfish**, greedy, grasping, tightfisted, mean, stingy, ungenerous [➡SELFISH AND UNKIND; 505] *Opposite*: generous

possessiveness 1 *n* **selfishness**, greed, tightfistedness, meanness, stinginess, greediness [➡ SELFISH AND UNKIND; 505] *Opposite*: generosity 2 *n* **jealousy**, jealousness, suspiciousness, overprotectiveness, insecurity, covetousness, suspicion, envy, enviousness [➡ ENVY AND JEALOUSY; 548]

possessor *n* **owner**, holder, bearer, keeper, proprietor, inheritor [➡ OWNERS; 446]

possibility *n* **likelihood**, prospect, risk, chance, probability [➡ POSSIBLE AND PROBABLE; 177]

possible 1 *adj* **likely**, conceivable, imaginable, thinkable, probable, potential, promising [➡ POSSIBLE AND PROBABLE; 177] *Opposite*: unlikely 2 *adj* **achievable**, doable, feasible, viable, workable, in the cards (*informal*) [➡ POSSIBLE AND PROBABLE; 177] *Opposite*: impossible

possibly *adv* **perhaps**, maybe, probably, conceivably, feasibly, perchance (*archaic or literary*) [➡ POSSIBLE AND PROBABLE; 177] *Opposite*: certainly

post 1 *n* **pole**, column, stake, upright, marker, boundary marker, pillar, support [➡ STICKS, POLES, AND WEDGES; 1254] 2 *n* **position**, placement, job, station, place, workplace [➡ JOB; 833] 3 *v* **display**, announce, advertise, put up, publish, declare, publicize [➡ INFORM, ANNOUNCE, AND ISSUE; 611] 4 *v* (*UK*) **send**, dispatch, mail, forward, airmail [➡ DISPATCH AND SEND; 333] *Opposite*: receive

postage *n* **stamp price**, postage fee, postage charge, postage cost, first-class postage (*UK*), second-class postage (*UK*) [➡ EXPENDITURE; 423]

postbox (*UK*) *n* **mailbox**, posting box, collection box, collection point, maildrop, letterbox (*UK*), pillar box (*UK*) [➡ CONTAINERS, RECEPTACLES, AND PACKAGING; 1245]

postcard *n* **card**, picture postcard, message, note, letter, missive [➡ LETTERS AND WRITTEN MESSAGES; 584]

poster 1 *n* **picture**, print, reproduction, artwork, photograph [➡ SIGNPOSTS, SIGNALS, AND BILLBOARDS; 595] 2 *n* **advertisement**, placard, notice, bill, announcement [➡ ADVERTISING AND PUBLICITY; 604]

posterior (*formal*) *adj* **latter**, subsequent, following, next, later, after [➡ AFTER, LAST, AND FOLLOWING; 165] *Opposite*: earlier

posterity *n* **future generations**, later generations, generations to come, successors, future, years to come, descendants, children, heirs [➡ FUTURE; 86]

postgrad (*informal*) *n* [➡ STUDENTS AND PUPILS; 841]

postgraduate *n* **student**, postgraduate student, graduate student, PhD student, graduate, postgrad (*informal*) [➡ STUDENTS AND PUPILS; 841]

posthaste *adv* **fast**, immediately, right away, quickly, straight away, without delay [➡ HAPPENING QUICKLY; 104] *Opposite*: slowly

post horn *type of* **brass instrument** [➡ MUSICAL INSTRUMENTS; 910]

posthumous *adj* **subsequent**, retrospective, delayed, following, postmortem, post-obit (*formal*) [➡ BURIAL AND PREPARATION FOR BURIAL; 929]

postimpressionism *type of* **pre-20th-century art movement** [➡ ARTISTIC MOVEMENTS AND STYLES; 899]

posting *n* **placement**, relocation, position, post, military posting, stationing, appointment [➡ JOB; 833]

postmark 1 *n* **date stamp**, frank, stamp, mark, rubber stamp, proof of posting [➡ RECEIPTS AND INVOICES; 591] 2 *v* **frank**, stamp, date, mark, rubber-stamp, validate [➡ CREATE IMAGES; 356]

postmodern *type of* **20th-century architecture** [➡ BUILDING AND ARCHITECTURE; 1076]

postmodernism *type of* **20th-century art movement** [➡ ARTISTIC MOVEMENTS AND STYLES; 899]

postmortem 1 *n* **autopsy**, postmortem examination, medical examination, examination, inquest [➡ BURIAL AND PREPARATION FOR BURIAL; 929] 2 *n* **investigation**, analysis, examination, inquest, review, debriefing [➡ EXAMINE AND ASSESS; 753]

postmortem examination *n* [➡ BURIAL AND PREPARATION FOR BURIAL; 929]

postnatal *adj* **postpartum**, post-delivery, perinatal [➡ REPRODUCTION AND HEREDITY; 725]

post-obit (*formal*) *adj* [➡ BURIAL AND PREPARATION FOR BURIAL; 929]

post office 1 *n* **PO**, mail depot, mailroom, GPO (*UK*), sorting office (*UK*) [➡ RETAIL OUTLETS; 1083] 2 *n* **mail system**, mail service, postal service, postal communications, mail [➡ RETAIL OUTLETS; 1083]

postpartum *adj* [➡ REPRODUCTION AND HEREDITY; 725]

postpone *v* **delay**, put off, put back, shelve, put on the back burner, defer, suspend, stall, reschedule, adjourn, take a rain check on (*informal*) [➡ DELAY ACTION OR OCCURRENCE; 278] *Opposite*: bring forward

postponed *adj* [➡ NOT HAPPENING; 34]

postponement *n* **delay**, rescheduling, rearrangement, deferment, adjournment, deferral, suspension [➡ DELAY ACTION OR OCCURRENCE; 278]

postscript *n* **afterthought**, addition, supplement, afterword, epilogue, message [➡ PARTS OF BOOKS AND DOCUMENTS; 593] *Opposite*: preface

postulate *v* **assume**, guess, hypothesize, suggest, claim, put forward, propose, advance [➡ DEVELOP THEORIES AND REASON; 744]

posture *n* **bearing**, stance, attitude, position, pose, deportment, carriage (*formal*), mien (*formal*) [➡ TEMPERAMENT AND BEHAVIOR; 492]

posturing *n* **self-importance**, pomposity, swagger, bravado, bluster, airs, posing, affectation, pretense, pretentiousness, pretension [➡ AFFECTATION, SELF-SATISFACTION, AND SNOBBISHNESS; 507]

posy 1 *n* **bouquet**, bunch of flowers, spray, nosegay, arrangement, boutonniere (*formal*), buttonhole (*UK*) [➡ COLLECTIONS AND MIXTURES OF THINGS; 1244] 2 *n* **blossom**, flower, bloom (*literary*) [➡ PARTS OF TREES AND PLANTS; 1026]

pot 1 *n* **container**, pan, vessel, jar, tub, crock [➡ CONTAINERS, RECEPTACLES, AND PACKAGING; 1245] 2 *n* (*informal*) **potbelly**, paunch, beer belly (*slang*) [➡ EXTRA WEIGHT; 478] 3 *v* **shoot**, bag, catch, get, hit [➤GET; 420] **4** *v* **preserve**, seal, pickle, can, tin (*UK*) [➤COOKING AND FOOD PREPARATION; 353]

potable *adj* **drinkable**, clean, filtered, fit to drink, drinking [➤ACCEPTABLE AND PASSABLE; 219]

potage *type of* **soup** [➤SOUPS; 1186]

potation (*literary*) *n* [➤DRINKS; 1187]

potato *n* **tuber**, new potato, seed potato, spud (*informal*), tater (*informal*), murphy (*dated informal*) [➤FRUIT AND VEGETABLES; 1176]

potato

◆ *types of processed potatoes*
chip, croquette, French fries, fries, hash browns, home fries, knish, latke, potato cake, potato chip, potato pancake, rösti

potato cake *type of* **processed potato** [➤FRUIT AND VEGETABLES; 1176]

potato chip *type of* **processed potato** [➤FRUIT AND VEGETABLES; 1176]

potato pancake *type of* **processed potato** [➤FRUIT AND VEGETABLES; 1176]

potbellied *adj* [➤BUILD; 477]

potbelly *n* [➤EXTRA WEIGHT; 478]

potbelly stove *n* [➤HOUSEHOLD APPLIANCES; 1117]

potboiler *n* [➤WRITERS AND STYLES; 914]

poteen *n* **bootleg alcohol**, spirit, bootleg whiskey, whiskey, white lightning, moonshine (*informal*), mountain dew (*informal*), hooch (*slang*), firewater (*dated slang*) [➤DRINKS; 1187]

potency *n* **strength**, force, power, might, vigor, energy, muscle (*informal*) [➤STRENGTH; 201] *Opposite*: **weakness**

potent **1** *adj* **strong**, effective, powerful, forceful, mighty, vigorous, puissant (*literary*) [➤STRENGTH; 201] *Opposite*: **weak** **2** *adj* **persuasive**, convincing, influential, forceful [➤STRENGTH; 201]

potentate *n* **monarch**, ruler, leader, emperor, sovereign, tsar, king, queen, empress [➤RULERS AND ARISTOCRACY; 823]

potential **1** *n* **ability**, capacity, possibility, makings, what it takes, aptitude, capability [➤SKILLS, TALENTS, AND ABILITIES; 526] **2** *adj* **possible**, hypothetical, conceivable, likely, probable, imaginable, thinkable [➤POSSIBLE AND PROBABLE; 177] *Opposite*: **unlikely**

pothole **1** *n* **rut**, hole, dip, depression, fault, fissure [➤HOLES, GAPS, AND FORKS; 1252] **2** *n* **cave**, cavern, catacomb, pit, hole [➤GEOLOGIC FEATURES; 1056]

potholed *adj* **rutted**, pitted, holed, eroded, uneven, bumpy, rough, broken [➤PHYSICAL TEXTURE; 1222] *Opposite*: **smooth**

potholer *n* **speleologist**, caver, spelunker [➤PEOPLE IN SPORTS AND LEISURE; 876]

potion *n* **liquid**, medicine, concoction, mixture, brew, tonic, remedy [➤DRINKS; 1187]

potluck *n* **luck of the draw**, whatever is going, whatever is on offer, chance, whatever is available [➤LUCK; 783]

potoroo *type of* **marsupial** [➤MARSUPIALS; 992]

pot plant (*UK*) *n* [➤FOLIAGE PLANTS; 1035]

potpourri *n* **miscellany**, mixture, assortment, hodgepodge, collection, jumble, variety, medley, assembly, ragbag (*informal*) [➤COLLECTIONS AND MIXTURES OF THINGS; 1244]

pots (*informal*) *n* **bags**, heaps (*informal*), piles (*informal*), tons (*informal*), loads (*informal*) [➤MANY, MUCH, LARGE AMOUNT; 117]

potshot *n* **shot**, pot, go, aim, try, attempt [➤ATTEMPT AN ACTION; 261]

potted *adj* **preserved**, sealed, conserved, pickled, canned, tinned (*UK*) [➤STATE OF PREPARED FOOD; 1171] *Opposite*: **fresh**

potted plant *n* [➤FOLIAGE PLANTS; 1035]

potter (*UK*) *v* **go slowly**, dawdle, shuffle, amble, toddle (*informal*) [➤MOVE SLOWLY; 314] *Opposite*: **hurry**

pottery **1** *n* **ceramic objects**, earthenware, stoneware, ceramics [➤POTTERY; 1135] **2** *type of* **factory** [➤INDUSTRIAL BUILDINGS; 1087]

pottery

◆ *types of pottery*
bone china, ceramic, china, delft, earthenware, enamel, faience, Limoges, Meissen, porcelain, Sèvres, stoneware, terra cotta

potty (*UK informal*) *adj* **foolish**, irrational, eccentric, silly, ridiculous, absurd, crazy (*informal*), batty (*informal*) [➤ECCENTRICITY AND IRRATIONALITY; 562] *Opposite*: **sensible**

potty-train (*informal*) *v* **toilet train**, housetrain, socialize, train, bring up, raise, housebreak [➤INSTRUCT AND TEACH; 609]

potty-training (*informal*) *n* **toilet training**, continence training, housetraining, housebreaking, personal hygiene, socialization [➤TEACHING; 839]

pouch *n* **bag**, pocket, money bag, purse, sack [➤CONTAINERS, RECEPTACLES, AND PACKAGING; 1245]

pouf (*UK*) *n* **stool**, beanbag, seat, cushion, floor cushion, footrest, hassock [➤FURNITURE; 858]

poultice *n* **dressing**, compress, bandage, plaster (*UK*) [➤COVERS AND COATINGS; 1246]

pounce **1** *v* **attack**, seize upon, seize, tackle, ambush, snatch, grab [➤PHYSICAL ATTACK AND PUNISHMENT; 415] **2** *v* **spring**, swoop, leap, jump, dive, bound [➤BOUNCE, UNDULATE, AND VIBRATE; 308] *Opposite*: **recoil** **3** *n* **leap**, jump, spring, bound, swoop, dive [➤BOUNCE, UNDULATE, AND VIBRATE; 308]

pound **1** *n* **pound sterling** [➤CURRENCIES; 798] **2** *type of* **pen or cage** [➤ANIMAL OR BIRD ACCOMMODATIONS; 1079] **3** *type of* **nonmetric unit** [➤SIZE AND DIMENSIONS; 1192] **4** *v* **hit**, strike, batter, beat, hammer, thump, pummel, buffet, thrash, clobber (*informal*) [➤CONTACT: IMPACT; 413] **5** *v* **throb**, thump, beat, pulsate, pulse, palpitate, hammer [➤PHYSICAL REACTIONS; 316] **6** *v* **grind**, crush, pulverize, bruise, mash, squash, smash, stamp [➤TEAR, BREAK, AND CUT; 360]

pounding 1 *n* **beating**, thrashing, drubbing, defeat, pasting (*informal*), hammering (*informal*), whitewash (*informal*) [➡ BEAT AND DEFEAT; 80] **2** *n* **throbbing**, thumping, pulsation, pulse, hammering, beating, beat [➡ PHYSICAL REACTIONS; 316]

pour 1 *v* **decant**, drizzle, dispense, discharge, transfer, empty, tip [➡ EMPTY AND UNLOAD; 407] **2** *v* **spill out**, gush, stream, flow, rush, surge, cascade, course [➡ LIQUID EMISSION; 370] *Opposite*: trickle **3** *v* **swarm**, crowd, teem, stream, rush, flow [➡ MOVE FAST; 313] *Opposite*: trickle **4** *v* **rain**, drench, lash, rain cats and dogs (*informal*), sheet down (*UK*) [➡ CLOUDY AND RAINY WEATHER; 1052] *Opposite*: drizzle

pouring *adj* **torrential**, heavy, hammering, driving, sheeting down (*UK*) [➡ CLOUDY AND RAINY WEATHER; 1052] *Opposite*: light

pour out *v* **reveal**, blurt out, disclose, give away, tell [➡ BETRAY CONFIDENCES AND GOSSIP; 618]

pour scorn on *v* **disparage**, ridicule, deride, sneer at, mock, show contempt for [➡ PROTEST AND EXPRESS DISAPPROVAL; 642]

pour with rain *v* **pour down**, teem, come down in torrents, rain cats and dogs (*informal*), bucket (*UK informal*), bucket down (*UK informal*), chuck down (*UK informal*) [➡ CLOUDY AND RAINY WEATHER; 1052]

pout 1 *v* **purse your lips**, pucker, frown, scowl, glower, grimace [➡ FACIAL EXPRESSIONS AND BLUSHING; 651] *Opposite*: smile **2** *v* **sulk**, mope, glower, scowl, grouch (*informal*) [➡ FACIAL EXPRESSIONS AND BLUSHING; 651] *Opposite*: smile

poverty 1 *n* **lack**, deficiency, scarcity, shortage, dearth, paucity, scarceness, insufficiency [➡ TOO FEW, TOO LITTLE; 122] *Opposite*: surplus **2** *n* **neediness**, destitution, hardship, deprivation, privation, penury, impoverishment, want, indigence (*formal*), impecuniousness (*formal*), impecuniosity (*formal*) [➡ POVERTY AND POOR; 892] *Opposite*: affluence

poverty-stricken *adj* **destitute**, in need, poor, penniless, impoverished, impecunious, needy, broke (*informal*), indigent (*formal*), penurious (*literary*) [➡ POVERTY AND POOR; 892] *Opposite*: rich

powder 1 *n* **fine particles**, dust, residue, precipitate, ash, shavings, concentrate, face powder, gunpowder, triturate [➡ SOLIDS; 1274] **2** *type of* **cosmetic** [➡ MAKEUP AND BEAUTY PRODUCTS; 490] **3** *v* **crush**, grind, pound, pulverize, mill, process, triturate, comminute [➡ CHANGE OF SHAPE; 385]

powder blue *type of* **blue** [➡ COLORS; 1224]

powdered *adj* **ground**, crushed, pulverized, milled, processed, pounded, triturated, comminuted [➡ PHYSICAL TEXTURE; 1222] *Opposite*: whole

powder keg *n* **tinderbox**, minefield, time bomb, recipe for disaster, explosive combination [➡ DANGER; 235]

powder room *type of* **room in public buildings** [➡ TYPES OF ROOMS; 1097]

powdery *adj* **fine**, crumbly, chalky, dusty, dry, powdered, granular [➡ PHYSICAL TEXTURE; 1222]

power 1 *n* **control**, influence, authority, supremacy, rule, command, sway, dominance, dominion, sovereignty, clout (*informal*), muscle (*informal*) [➡ RELATIONSHIP TO ANOTHER; 973] *Opposite*: powerlessness **2** *n* **ability**, capacity, faculty, potential, capability, competence, function, aptitude,

skill [➡ SKILLS, TALENTS, AND ABILITIES; 526] *Opposite*: inability **3** *n* **authority**, right, prerogative, license, privilege, ability [➡ PERMIT AND ALLOW; 669] *Opposite*: powerlessness **4** *n* **nation**, country, state, player, superpower, world power, nation-state, sovereign state [➡ TERRITORIES AND GROUPS OF NATIONS; 1068] **5** *n* **strength**, force, might, energy, brawn, weight, potency, muscle (*informal*), sinew (*literary*) [➡ STRENGTH; 201] *Opposite*: weakness

power base *n* **stronghold**, seat of power, headquarters, home base, base [➡ PLACE; 1065]

powerboat *type of* **motor vessel** [➡ SHIPS AND BOATS; 1150]

powerful 1 *adj* **influential**, commanding, authoritative, controlling, prevailing, dominant, potent, great, mighty, formidable, weighty [➡ STRENGTH; 201] *Opposite*: powerless **2** *adj* **strong**, mighty, brawny, muscular, sturdy, robust, hard, vigorous, sinewy [➡ MUSCLES AND MUSCULATURE; 479] *Opposite*: weak **3** *adj* **effective**, potent, strong, pungent, overwhelming, overpowering, intense, distinct [➡ STRENGTH; 201] *Opposite*: impotent **4** *adj* **persuasive**, compelling, forceful, effective, convincing, impressive, moving, evocative, eloquent, deep, haunting, emotive, effectual (*formal*) [➡ EXTRAORDINARY: AMAZING; 204] *Opposite*: unimpressive

powerfully 1 *adv* **strongly**, mightily, sturdily, muscularly, robustly, forcefully, hard, vigorously, violently [➡ STRENGTH; 201] *Opposite*: weakly **2** *adv* **effectively**, potently, intensely, strongly, overpoweringly, overwhelmingly, distinctly, pungently, very, extremely [➡ TO A GREAT EXTENT; 132] *Opposite*: somewhat **3** *adv* **persuasively**, compellingly, forcefully, effectively, convincingly, impressively, eloquently, movingly, evocatively, hauntingly, emotively [➡ EXTRAORDINARY: AMAZING; 204] *Opposite*: weakly

powerhouse (*informal*) *n* **driving force**, heart, center, dynamo, live wire (*informal*) [➡ TALENTED OR INTELLIGENT PEOPLE; 528]

powerless *adj* **helpless**, incapable, unable, weak, feeble, ineffective, defenseless [➡ WEAKNESS; 241] *Opposite*: powerful

powerlessness *n* **helplessness**, hopelessness, weakness, feebleness, ineffectiveness, subjection, incapability, inability, incapacity, defenselessness [➡ WEAKNESS; 241]

power line *n* **electricity cable**, overhead cable, cable, wire, overhead wire, high-voltage line [➡ ELECTRONICS AND ELECTRICS; 1137]

power plant *type of* **industrial site** [➡ INDUSTRIAL BUILDINGS; 1087]

power point (*UK*) *n* **socket**, point, electric socket, plug, hookup, outlet [➡ ELECTRONICS AND ELECTRICS; 1137]

power struggle *n* [➡ ARGUMENTS; 47]

powwow (*informal*) *n* [➡ MEETINGS AND ASSEMBLIES; 43]

practicability *n* **feasibility**, viability, workability, attainability, operability, possibility, practicality, achievability [➡ POSSIBLE AND PROBABLE; 177] *Opposite*: impossibility

practicable *adj* **feasible**, realistic, possible, workable, attainable, operable, achievable, practical, viable, doable [➡ POSSIBLE AND PROBABLE; 177] *Opposite*: impossible

practical 1 *adj* **applied**, real-world, hands-on, everyday, real, useful [➡ TRUE AND REAL; 171] *Opposite*: theoretical **2** *adj* **realistic**, down-to-earth, level-headed, sensible, pragmatic, reasonable, hardheaded, rational, businesslike, matter-of-fact, sober [➡ POSITIVE INTELLECTUAL CHARACTERISTICS; 524] *Opposite:* unrealistic **3** *adj* **useful**, sensible, feasible, sound, workable, practicable, handy, step-by-step, helpful, user-friendly, realistic, viable [➡ USEFULNESS; 199] *Opposite:* useless **4** *adj* **everyday**, workaday, serviceable, functional, plain, useful, convenient, utilitarian [➡ USEFULNESS; 199] *Opposite:* decorative

practicality **1** *n* **realism**, common sense, level-headedness, pragmatism, sensibleness, reasonableness, soberness [➡ POSITIVE INTELLECTUAL CHARACTERISTICS; 524] *Opposite:* impracticality **2** *n* **usefulness**, sensibleness, feasibility, soundness, workability, reasonableness, helpfulness, applicability, practicability, user-friendliness [➡ USEFULNESS; 199] *Opposite:* uselessness

practical joke *n* **trick**, prank, joke, lark, hoax, escapade, caper, shenanigan (*informal*) [➡ JOKES AND TEASING; 674]

practically **1** *adv* **almost**, nearly, virtually, just about, well-nigh, all but, as good as, essentially, in effect, nigh on to [➡ TO A CERTAIN EXTENT; 136] **2** *adv* **realistically**, sensibly, rationally, reasonably, level-headedly, pragmatically, expediently [➡ POSITIVE INTELLECTUAL CHARACTERISTICS; 524]

practice **1** *n* **repetition**, rehearsal, exercise, preparation, training, run-through, drill [➡ PREPARATORY EVENTS; 57] **2** *n* **habit**, custom, tradition, way, system, routine, procedure, ritual, manner, method, praxis (*formal*) [➡ WAYS OF DOING THINGS; 294] **3** *v* **rehearse**, prepare, exercise, repeat, try, attempt, drill, go through, run through [➡ PREPARE FOR ACTION; 289] **4** *v* **live out**, carry out, perform, apply, follow, observe, do, put into practice [➡ CARRY OUT AN ACTION; 269] *Opposite:* reject

See Compare and Contrast at **habit**.

practiced *adj* **skillful**, experienced, trained, expert, adept, proficient, accomplished, able [➡ TALENTED AND SKILLFUL; 527] *Opposite:* untrained

practice session *n* [➡ PREPARATORY EVENTS; 57]

practitioner *n* **doctor**, medical practitioner, general practitioner, GP, physician, consultant, health worker [➡ PEOPLE WHO WORK IN MEDICINE; 848]

praenomen *n* [➡ NAME AND DESCRIBE; 665]

pragmatic *adj* **practical**, realistic, logical, rational, reasonable, sensible, hardheaded, matter-of-fact, no-nonsense, down-to-earth, hard-nosed (*informal*) [➡ POSITIVE INTELLECTUAL CHARACTERISTICS; 524] *Opposite:* idealistic

pragmatism *n* **practicality**, realism, logicality, rationality, reasonableness, common sense, uncomplicatedness, matter-of-factness, hardheadedness [➡ POSITIVE INTELLECTUAL CHARACTERISTICS; 524] *Opposite:* idealism

pragmatist *n* **practical person**, down-to-earth person, realist, doer, rationalist, logician [➡ PEOPLE WHO ARE APPROVED OF; 955] *Opposite:* idealist

prairie *n* **plain**, savanna, steppe, pampas [➡ DESERTS, PLAINS, AND MOORLAND; 1045]

prairie dog *type of* **rodent** [➡ RODENTS; 989]

prairie schooner *type of* **wagon or carriage** [➡ VEHICLES; 1145]

praise **1** *n* **admiration**, commendation, approval, acclaim, tribute, applause, compliment, recommendation [➡ PRAISE AND ENCOURAGE; 647] *Opposite:* criticism **2** *n* **worship**, honor, adoration, devotion, thanks, glory, celebration, blessing [➡ RELIGIONS AND RELIGIOUS PRACTICES; 777] *Opposite:* vilification **3** *v* **admire**, commend, extol, honor, compliment, eulogize, congratulate, pay tribute to, go into raptures over, applaud, acclaim, hail [➡ PRAISE AND ENCOURAGE; 647] *Opposite:* criticize **4** *v* **glorify**, honor, laud, worship, adore, bless, celebrate, extol, exalt (*formal*), magnify (*formal*) [➡ RELIGIONS AND RELIGIOUS PRACTICES; 777] *Opposite:* vilify

praise to the skies *v* [➡ PRAISE AND ENCOURAGE; 647]

praiseworthy *adj* **admirable**, commendable, laudable, worthy, exemplary, creditable [➡ ADMIRABLE AND COMMENDABLE; 185] *Opposite:* blameworthy

praline *type of* **confectionery** [➡ CONFECTIONERY; 1182]

pram (*UK*) *n* **buggy**, stroller, baby carriage, perambulator (*formal*), pushchair (*UK*) [➡ BIKES, CARS, AND CARRIAGES; 1149]

prance **1** *v* **cavort**, dance, frolic, gambol, caper, frisk, romp, revel [➡ FIDGET AND FROLIC; 311] **2** *v* **swagger**, strut, parade, flounce, sashay (*humorous*) [➡ MOVE FAST; 313]

prank *n* **trick**, practical joke, hoax, joke, lark [➡ JOKES AND TEASING; 674]

prankster *n* **trickster**, joker, practical joker, mischief-maker, imp, Puck [➡ JOKERS AND TEASES; 675]

prate *v* **chatter**, gibber, prattle, babble, jabber, rant, burble (*informal*), natter (*informal*), blather (*informal*), jaw (*slang*) [➡ CHATTER AND BABBLE; 617]

prattle **1** *v* **prate**, gibber, chatter, jabber, babble, burble (*informal*), natter (*informal*), blather (*informal*) [➡ CHATTER AND BABBLE; 617] **2** *n* **chatter**, gibber, drivel, nonsense, jabber, babble, burble (*informal*), nattering (*informal*), blather (*informal*) [➡ MEANINGLESS SPEECH OR WRITING; 676]

prattling *adj* [➡ INARTICULATE, RAMBLING, AND AWKWARD; 633]

prawn *type of* **crustacean** [➡ AQUATIC INVERTEBRATES; 1022]

praxis (*formal*) *n* [➡ WAYS OF DOING THINGS; 294]

pray **1** *v* **request**, plead, beg, crave, ask, entreat, urge, appeal, implore (*formal*), importune (*formal*), beseech (*literary*) [➡ REQUEST AND DEMAND; 663] **2** *v* **hope**, wish, cross your fingers, hope against hope, yearn, long, ache, yen [➡ DESIRE AND WANT; 579] **3** *v* **meditate**, contemplate, say your prayers, call upon, invoke, call up, summon [➡ RELIGIONS AND RELIGIOUS PRACTICES; 777]

prayer **1** *n* **entreaty**, appeal, plea, request, desire, hope, wish, supplication, petition, imploration (*formal*) [➡ REQUEST AND DEMAND; 663] **2** *n* **invocation**, meditation, contemplation, devotions, chant, petition, appeal, supplication (*formal*), imploration (*formal*) [➡ RELIGIONS AND RELIGIOUS PRACTICES; 777]

prayer book *n* [➡ RELIGIOUS OBJECTS; 779]

preach **1** *v* **give a sermon**, speak, discourse, talk, deliver an address, address, expound, orate (*formal*) [➡ INSTRUCT AND TEACH; 609] **2** *v* **advise**, lecture, sermonize, moralize, advocate, urge, persuade [➡ ADVISE AND WARN; 613]

preacher *n* **minister**, pastor, missionary, lay preacher, vicar, celebrant, parson, evangelist [➡ RELIGIOUS PEOPLE; 778]

preadolescent *adj* [➡ BABYHOOD, CHILDHOOD, AND ADOLESCENCE; 917]

preamble *n* **introduction**, preface, foreword, prelude, overture, opening, explanation [➡ PARTS OF BOOKS AND DOCUMENTS; 593] *Opposite:* postscript

preamplifier *type of* **audio equipment** [➡ AUDIO EQUIPMENT; 1139]

pre-Archean *type of* **eon** [➡ EPOCHS AND ERAS; 89]

prearrange *v* **organize**, set up, arrange, plan, settle upon, decide upon, preset, schedule, agree [➡ CAUSE TO HAPPEN; 31]

prearranged *adj* **planned**, arranged, agreed, preset, programmed, controled, specified, established, selected, given, intended, scheduled, determined, allotted, chosen, fixed, set [➡ INTENTIONAL AND DELIBERATE; 279] *Opposite:* chance

prebake *v* [➡ COOKING AND FOOD PREPARATION; 353]

precarious *adj* **shaky**, unstable, insecure, wobbly, unsteady, uncertain, unsafe [➡ DANGEROUS; 236] *Opposite:* stable

precariousness *n* [➡ DANGER; 235]

precatory (*formal*) *adj* [➡ RELIGIOUS CONCEPTS; 776]

precaution *n* **protection**, safety measure, preventive measure, insurance, safeguard, provision, security, deterrent [➡ ACTIONS OR UNDERTAKINGS; 259]

precautionary *adj* **protective**, defensive, safety, cautionary, preventive, preventative, counteractive, prophylactic, anticipatory [➡ SAFE AND SAFETY; 191] *Opposite:* remedial

precede *v* **lead**, come first, go before, pave the way, herald, head [➡ BEFORE, FIRST, AND PRECEDING; 163] *Opposite:* follow

precedence *n* **superiority**, priority, preference, primacy, antecedence, precedency [➡ SUPERIORITY; 152]

precedent *n* **example**, model, guide, pattern, standard, instance, practice [➡ REPRESENTATIONS AND GENERAL EXAMPLES; 65]

preceding *adj* **previous**, earlier, prior, former, past, above, foregoing, antecedent, anterior [➡ BEFORE, FIRST, AND PRECEDING; 163] *Opposite:* following

precept (*formal*) *n* **principle**, teaching, rule, guideline, instruction, edict, law, dictum (*formal*) [➡ IDEAS AND THOUGHTS; 770]

precinct *n* **district**, zone, area, sector, quarter, division, ward, borough [➡ PLACE; 1065]

precious 1 *adj* **valuable**, costly, expensive, dear, treasurable, exquisite, priceless, prized [➡ EXPENSIVE AND LUXURIOUS; 218] *Opposite:* worthless 2 *adj* **valued**, loved, beloved, important, dear, treasured, cherished, favorite [➡ POPULAR AND WANTED; 220] *Opposite:* despised 3 *adj* **fastidious**, affected, overrefined, fussy, self-conscious, dainty, pretentious, artificial [➡ AFFECTATION, SELF-SATISFACTION, AND SNOBBISHNESS; 507] *Opposite:* natural

preciously *adv* **fastidiously**, affectedly, fussily, self-consciously, daintily, pretentiously, artificially [➡ AFFECTATION, SELF-SATISFACTION, AND SNOBBISHNESS; 507] *Opposite:* naturally

preciousness 1 *n* **valuableness**, value, costliness, expensiveness, dearness, exquisiteness, pricelessness [➡ EXPENSIVE AND LUXURIOUS; 218] *Opposite:* worthlessness 2 *n* **fastidiousness**, affectation, fussiness, self-consciousness, daintiness, overrefinement, pretentiousness, artificiality [➡ AFFECTATION, SELF-SATISFACTION, AND SNOBBISHNESS; 507] *Opposite:* naturalness

precious stone *n* **gemstone**, jewel, stone, gem, sparkler (*informal*), rock (*informal*) [➡ PRECIOUS STONES; 1278]

precipice *n* **rock face**, cliff, crag, sheer drop, abyss, height, face [➡ GEOLOGIC FEATURES; 1056]

precipitate 1 *adj* **rash**, impulsive, impetuous, careless, reckless [➡ INCAUTIOUS AND CARELESS; 283] *Opposite:* considered 2 *adj* **abrupt**, sudden, unexpected, surprising, unforeseen [➡ HAPPENING QUICKLY; 104] *Opposite:* expected 3 *adj* **hurried**, hasty, swift, quick, rapid, precipitous [➡ MOVING QUICKLY; 103] *Opposite:* slow 4 *v* **hasten**, bring on, cause, lead to, occasion, give rise to, trigger, advance [➡ CAUSE TO HAPPEN; 31] *Opposite:* retard

precipitateness *n* [➡ SPEED; 102]

precipitation *n* **rain**, rainfall, snow, sleet, hail, drizzle [➡ CLOUDY AND RAINY WEATHER; 1052]

precipitous 1 *adj* **rash**, quick, hurried, swift, impulsive, hasty, precipitate [➡ INCAUTIOUS AND CARELESS; 283] *Opposite:* careful 2 *adj* **steep**, sheer, abrupt, high, vertical, lofty [➡ ORIENTATION AND ALIGNMENT; 1223] *Opposite:* gentle

precipitousness *n* [➡ SPEED; 102]

précis 1 *n* **summary**, synopsis, résumé, abstract, sketch, thumbnail sketch, digest, compendium [➡ SUMMARIES, OUTLINES, AND EXCERPTS; 588] 2 *v* **summarize**, sum up, condense, outline, abridge, digest [➡ EXPLAIN AND CLARIFY; 610] *Opposite:* expand

precise 1 *adj* **exact**, detailed, accurate, specific, particular, clear-cut, defined, fixed, correct, complete [➡ EXACT; 203] *Opposite:* vague 2 *adj* **meticulous**, scrupulous, particular, careful, fastidious, strict [➡ HARD-WORKING AND COMMITTED; 500] *Opposite:* careless

preciseness *n* [➡ EXACT; 203]

precision *n* **exactness**, accuracy, exactitude, care, meticulousness, correctness, fastidiousness, strictness [➡ EXACT; 203] *Opposite:* vagueness

preclude (*formal*) *v* **prevent**, impede, stop, rule out, exclude, disqualify, prohibit, bar [➡ MAKE IMPOSSIBLE; 276] *Opposite:* permit

preclusion (*formal*) *n* **prevention**, exclusion, disqualification, prohibition, deterrence, impediment, bar, hindrance, obstacle [➡ AVOID, PREVENT, LIMIT, AND CONTROL; 277] *Opposite:* permission

precocious *adj* **advanced**, developed, intelligent, bright, gifted, talented, mature, articulate, clever [➡ TALENTED AND SKILLFUL; 527] *Opposite:* immature

precociousness *n* **talent**, cleverness, brightness, intelligence, precocity, maturity, giftedness [➡ SKILLS, TALENTS, AND ABILITIES; 526] *Opposite:* immaturity

precocity *n* **talent**, cleverness, brightness, intelligence, precociousness, maturity, giftedness [➡ SKILLS, TALENTS, AND ABILITIES; 526] *Opposite:* immaturity

precognition *n* **clairvoyance**, foreknowledge, premonition, foresight, second sight, sixth sense [➡ THE SUPERNATURAL; 787]

preconceived *adj* **fixed**, set, defined, rigid, inflexible, predetermined, prejudiced, biased [➡ THE NATURE OF IDEAS; 771] *Opposite:* unprejudiced

preconception *n* **prejudice**, bias, fixed idea, presumption, notion, predetermination [➡ PREJUDICE; 550]

precondition *n* **condition**, requirement, prerequisite, qualification, must, necessity [➡ NECESSARY AND ESSENTIAL; 196]

precook *v* **parboil**, boil, cook, prepare, soften, simmer [➡ COOKING AND FOOD PREPARATION; 353]

precooked *adj* [➡ STATE OF PREPARED FOOD; 1171]

precursor *n* **forerunner**, ancestor, predecessor, antecedent, pioneer, herald, originator, sign, foundation, foretaste [➡ BEFORE, FIRST, AND PRECEDING; 163] *Opposite:* successor

predate *v* **precede**, go before, antedate, exist before, preexist, antecede, prelude, come before [➡ BEFORE, FIRST, AND PRECEDING; 163]

predator *n* **marauder**, killer, hunter, pillager, raider, slayer (*formal or literary*) [➡ VILLAINS AND THUGS; 947]

predatory *adj* **greedy**, destructive, rapacious, grasping, voracious, vulturine, predacious (*formal*) [➡ SELFISH AND UNKIND; 505]

predecessor *n* **precursor**, forerunner, ancestor, antecedent, prototype [➡ BEFORE, FIRST, AND PRECEDING; 163] *Opposite:* successor

predestination *n* **destiny**, fate, doom, kismet, lot, predetermination, preordination, preordainment, foreordination (*formal*), foreordainment (*formal*) [➡ FATE, DESTINY, AND ASTROLOGY; 782] *Opposite:* free will

predestine *v* **destine**, fate, preordain, doom, predetermine, decide, prearrange, foreordain (*formal*) [➡ CAUSE TO HAPPEN; 31]

predestined *adj* **fated**, destined, bound, preordained, appointed, predetermined, prearranged, inevitable, foreordained (*formal*), inexorable (*formal*) [➡ FATE, DESTINY, AND ASTROLOGY; 782]

predetermination **1** *n* **prearrangement**, arrangement, intention, decision, resolution, resolve, agreement, plan, intent (*formal*) [➡ INTENTIONS AND PURPOSES; 772] **2** *n* **predestination**, preordination, preordainment, lot, destiny, fate, doom, kismet, foreordination (*formal*), foreordainment (*formal*) [➡ FATE, DESTINY, AND ASTROLOGY; 782] *Opposite:* free will

predetermine **1** *v* **set**, program, encode, determine, decide, fix, prearrange, schedule [➡ MAKE DECISIONS AND CHOICES; 752] **2** *v* **predestine**, destine, fate, preordain, doom, foreordain (*formal*) [➡ CAUSE TO HAPPEN; 31]

predetermined **1** *adj* **prearranged**, programmed, encoded, fixed, determined, set, preset, scheduled [➡ BEFORE, FIRST, AND PRECEDING; 163] **2** *adj* **predestined**, destined, fated, bound, preordained, inevitable, foreordained (*formal*), inexorable (*formal*) [➡ FATE, DESTINY, AND ASTROLOGY; 782]

predicament *n* **difficulty**, quandary, dilemma, tight spot, tight corner, mess, jam (*informal*), pickle (*informal*), fix (*informal*) [➡ DIFFICULT SITUATIONS; 72]

predicate **1** *v* (*formal*) **base**, establish, found, ground, build, center, rest [➡ INSTITUTE AND INAUGURATE; 348] **2** *type of grammatical term* [➡ ASPECTS OF LANGUAGE; 682]

predict *v* **forecast**, foresee, envisage, expect, guess, calculate, foretell, see coming, prophesy [➡ PREDICT AND ANTICIPATE; 750]

predictability **1** *n* **expectedness**, obviousness, certainty, likelihood, probability, liability, sureness, predictableness [➡ CERTAIN; 174] *Opposite:* unlikelihood **2** *n* **unoriginality**, banality, triteness, obviousness, staleness, tiredness, predictableness [➡ BORING AND UNINTERESTING; 234] *Opposite:* originality

predictable **1** *adj* **foreseeable**, expectable, expected, likely, probable, liable, anticipated, sure, certain [➡ POSSIBLE AND PROBABLE; 177] *Opposite:* unlikely **2** *adj* **unsurprising**, unoriginal, banal, trite, obvious, stale, tired, hackneyed [➡ BORING AND UNINTERESTING; 234] *Opposite:* original

predictableness **1** *n* **likelihood**, obviousness, expectedness, probability, predictability, liability, sureness, certainty [➡ CERTAIN; 174] *Opposite:* unlikelihood **2** *n* **unoriginality**, banality, triteness, obviousness, staleness, tiredness, predictability [➡ BORING AND UNINTERESTING; 234] *Opposite:* originality

predicted *adj* **foretold**, forecast, foreseen, prophesied, projected, expected, anticipated [➡ PREDICT AND ANTICIPATE; 750] *Opposite:* unforeseen

prediction *n* **forecast**, guess, calculation, estimate, prophecy, expectation, likelihood, extrapolation, prognostication, projection [➡ PREDICT AND ANTICIPATE; 750]

predictive *adj* **prognostic**, extrapolative, prophetic, projecting, foretelling [➡ PREDICT AND ANTICIPATE; 750]

predilection (*formal*) *n* **liking**, preference, fondness, partiality, penchant, taste, weakness, tendency [➡ APPRECIATION AND GRATITUDE; 535] *Opposite:* dislike

predispose (*formal*) *v* **incline**, dispose, prompt, influence, prejudice, bias, affect [➡ ENCOURAGE; 576]

predisposed (*formal*) *adj* **inclined**, disposed, subject, liable, susceptible, prone, given [➡ THE WILL AND WILLINGNESS; 563] *Opposite:* unwilling

predisposition *n* **tendency**, disposition, inclination, penchant, bias, susceptibility, predilection (*formal*) [➡ TEMPERAMENT AND BEHAVIOR; 492]

predominance **1** *n* **superiority**, power, dominance, control, supremacy, leadership [➡ SUPERIORITY; 152] **2** *n* **majority**, prevalence, preponderance, numerousness [➡ MANY, MUCH, LARGE AMOUNT; 117] *Opposite:* minority

predominant *adj* **main**, major, chief, principal, prime, biggest, largest, leading, prevalent [➡ MOST IMPORTANT AND MAIN; 193] *Opposite:* minor

predominantly *adv* **mainly**, mostly, largely, chiefly, principally, primarily, in the main, for the most part [➡ MAINLY AND PRIMARILY; 140] *Opposite:* partially

predominate *v* **prevail**, dominate, outweigh, preponderate, be in the majority, lead [➡ PROSPER AND ABOUND; 16]

preeminence *n* **superiority**, authority, excellence, eminence, renown, prestige, prominence [➡SUPERIORITY; 152] *Opposite*: obscurity

preeminent *adj* **distinguished**, outstanding, famous, well-known, foremost, leading, dominant, excellent, eminent, renowned, prestigious, prominent, exalted (*formal*) [➡KNOWN AND FAMOUS; 181] *Opposite*: obscure

preempt *v* **forestall**, anticipate, obstruct, block, prevent, head off, avert, deter, stave off [➡AVOID, PREVENT, LIMIT, AND CONTROL; 277] *Opposite*: react

preemption *n* **preemptive action**, preventive action, preventive measures, prevention, anticipation [➡AVOID, PREVENT, LIMIT, AND CONTROL; 277] *Opposite*: reaction

preemptive *adj* **preventive**, preventative, proactive, anticipatory, blocking, defensive, tactical [➡AVOID, PREVENT, LIMIT, AND CONTROL; 277] *Opposite*: reactive

preen *v* **groom**, smarten, clean, tidy, smooth, trim [➡IMPROVE APPEARANCE; 379]

preexist *v* **predate**, precede, antecede, go before, prelude, antedate, forerun [➡BEFORE, FIRST, AND PRECEDING; 163]

preexisting *adj* **previous**, prior, earlier, former, established, preexistent, foregoing, antecedent, preceding [➡BEFORE, FIRST, AND PRECEDING; 163] *Opposite*: new

prefabricate *v* **manufacture**, make up, assemble, produce, mass-produce [➡MANUFACTURE; 349]

preface 1 *n* **foreword**, preamble, introduction, prologue, prelude [➡PARTS OF BOOKS AND DOCUMENTS; 593] *Opposite*: postscript 2 *v* **prefix**, precede, introduce, start, begin [➡BEFORE, FIRST, AND PRECEDING; 163]

prefect *n* **senior pupil**, monitor, captain, head boy (*UK*), head girl (*UK*) [➡STUDENTS AND PUPILS; 841]

prefer *v* **favor**, have a preference, like better, rather, wish, desire, choose, select, single out [➡LIKE, LOVE, VALUE, AND ENJOY; 578]

preferable *adj* **better**, desirable, nicer, superior, choice [➡GOOD, WELL, BETTER; 183] *Opposite*: inferior

preference *n* **favorite**, first choice, partiality, penchant, fondness, liking, inclination, predilection (*formal*) [➡LIKE, LOVE, VALUE, AND ENJOY; 578] *Opposite*: dislike

preferential *adj* **special**, favored, privileged, superior, better, partisan [➡SUPERIORITY; 152] *Opposite*: disadvantageous

preferment (*formal*) *n* **promotion**, upgrading, appointment, advancement, elevation [➡CONFER STATUS; 458] *Opposite*: demotion

preferred *adj* **favored**, favorite, chosen, number one, in, ideal [➡POPULAR AND WANTED; 220]

prefigure *v* **anticipate**, herald, foreshadow, portend, presage, predict, suggest [➡BEFORE, FIRST, AND PRECEDING; 163]

prefix 1 *v* **preface**, precede, begin, start, start off, attach, put in front, introduce, add [➡BEFORE, FIRST, AND PRECEDING; 163] 2 *type of* **grammatical term** [➡ASPECTS OF LANGUAGE; 682]

pregnancy 1 *n* **gestation**, prenatal period, perinatal period, gravidity, gravidness, confinement (*dated*), lying-in (*archaic*), antenatal period (*UK*) [➡REPRODUCTION AND HEREDITY; 725] 2 *n* **significance**, importance, import, meaning [➡IMPORTANCE AND SIGNIFICANCE; 192]

pregnant 1 *adj* **expectant**, antenatal, prenatal, gravid, expecting (*informal*), in the family way (*dated informal*), with child (*archaic or literary*), heavy with child (*archaic or literary*) [➡REPRODUCTION AND HEREDITY; 725] 2 *adj* **charged**, significant, weighty, meaningful, pointed, loaded [➡INTERESTING AND MEANINGFUL; 190]

preheat *v* **heat**, heat up, warm, warm up, turn on [➡COOKING AND FOOD PREPARATION; 353] *Opposite*: cool

prehistoric 1 *adj* **primeval**, primitive, antediluvian, early, ancient, old, primordial, primal [➡PAST; 84] 2 *adj* **old-fashioned**, out-of-date, ancient, old, antiquated, archaic, outmoded, antediluvian [➡OLD, OLD-FASHIONED; 167] *Opposite*: modern

prehistory *n* **early history**, olden days, times gone by, dawn of time, Stone Age, Bronze Age, Iron Age, ancient history [➡PAST; 84]

prejudge *v* **jump to conclusions**, presume, presuppose, anticipate, assume, posit (*formal*) [➡PREDICT AND ANTICIPATE; 750]

prejudice 1 *n* **bias**, preconception, prejudgment, predisposition, partiality [➡THE NATURE OF IDEAS; 771] *Opposite*: impartiality 2 *n* **bigotry**, chauvinism, narrow-mindedness, discrimination, intolerance, injustice, unfairness, partisanship [➡PREJUDICE; 550] *Opposite*: tolerance 3 *v* **influence**, bias, sway, slant, distort, incline, prepossess, predispose (*formal*) [➡APPEAL TO AND AROUSE INTEREST; 575]

prejudiced *adj* **biased**, intolerant, bigoted, narrow-minded, discriminatory, unfair, opinionated, partisan, blinkered, unjust [➡NEGATIVE INTELLECTUAL CHARACTERISTICS; 525] *Opposite*: tolerant

prejudicial *adj* **harmful**, detrimental, hurtful, damaging, injurious, deleterious [➡DANGEROUS; 236] *Opposite*: helpful

prelate *n* **bishop**, archbishop, cardinal, abbot, prior, cleric, minister [➡RELIGIOUS PEOPLE; 778]

preliminary 1 *adj* **initial**, first, opening, pilot, introductory, maiden, primary, earliest [➡BEFORE, FIRST, AND PRECEDING; 163] *Opposite*: closing 2 *n* **beginning**, first round, introduction, opening, groundwork, preface, prelude, initiation, inception (*formal*) [➡BEGINNINGS; 53] *Opposite*: finale

prelude 1 *n* **introduction**, overture, prologue, preface, foreword, preamble, run-up (*UK*) [➡BEGINNINGS; 53] *Opposite*: finale 2 *type of* **musical form** [➡MUSIC, SONGS, AND SINGING; 907]

premature *adj* **early**, untimely, hasty, rash, precipitate, impulsive, previous (*informal*) [➡PROMPTNESS: EARLY; 98] *Opposite*: overdue

premeditated *adj* **planned**, deliberate, intentional, calculated, thought-out, intended, conscious, studied [➡INTENTIONAL AND DELIBERATE; 279] *Opposite*: spontaneous

premeditation 1 *n* **planning**, calculation, cold-bloodedness, coldness, contemplation, scheming, design [➡THINK AND REFLECT; 743] *Opposite*: impulsiveness 2 *n* **reflection**, contemplation, thought, consideration, cogitation (*formal*), deliberation (*formal*) [➡IDEAS AND THOUGHTS; 770] *Opposite*: spontaneity

premier 1 *adj* **best**, first, leading, foremost, highest, chief, primary, principal, arch [➡SUPERIORITY; 152] *Opposite:* worst **2** *n* **prime minister**, PM, leader, head of state, ruler, head of government, minister [➡POLITICAL OFFICES AND POLITICIANS; 808]

premiere *n* **opening**, first night, first performance, first showing, debut [➡PERFORMANCES AND SHOWS; 42]

premiership 1 *n* **leadership**, prime ministership, presidency, chancellorship, office, tenure [➡POLITICAL OFFICES AND POLITICIANS; 808] **2** *n* (*UK*) **league championship**, championship competition, championship, premier league championship (*UK*), premier championship (*UK*), premier league (*UK*) [➡NON-AGGRESSIVE/SPORTING EVENTS; 40]

premise 1 *n* **evidence**, principle, idea, foundation, ground, statement [➡IDEAS AND THOUGHTS; 770] **2** *n* **proposition**, supposition, hypothesis, assertion, thesis, presupposition, grounds, basis, assumption, postulate, presumption [➡POINTS OF VIEW; 767]

premises *n* **building**, grounds, location, site, property, place [➡PLACE; 1065]

premium 1 *n* **payment**, percentage, bonus, reward, perk, extra, dividend, prize [➡FUNDS, PAYMENTS, AND CHARGES; 800] **2** *adj* **best**, top, finest, quality, first-class, first-rate, superior, exceptional [➡SUPERIORITY; 152] *Opposite:* low-grade

premolar *type of* **tooth** [➡THE MOUTH; 702]

premonition 1 *n* **intuition**, presentiment, feeling, hunch, fear, sense, suspicion, foreboding [➡FEELINGS ABOUT THE FUTURE; 533] **2** *n* **warning**, omen, sign, portent, indication, admonition, forewarning [➡THE SUPERNATURAL; 787]

premonitory 1 *adj* **intuitive**, predictive, clairvoyant, prophetic, precognitive, psychic, mantic, vatic [➡PREDICT AND ANTICIPATE; 750] **2** *adj* **warning**, prognostic, precautionary, cautionary, sobering, worrying, ominous, admonitory [➡ADVISE AND WARN; 613]

prenatal *adj* [➡REPRODUCTION AND HEREDITY; 725]

prenominal *type of* **grammatical term** [➡ASPECTS OF LANGUAGE; 682]

preoccupation *n* **worry**, obsession, anxiety, concern, fixation, bee in your bonnet, care, uneasiness, niggle (*UK*) [➡CONFUSION, ANXIETY, AND WORRY; 540]

preoccupied *adj* **worried**, anxious, lost in thought, elsewhere, inattentive, in a world of your own, distant, thoughtful, pensive, engrossed, absent-minded [➡CONFUSION, ANXIETY, AND WORRY; 540] *Opposite:* carefree

preoccupy *v* **worry**, concern, disturb, trouble, consume, possess, eat away at, get to, haunt, grip, obsess, bug (*informal*) [➡UPSET, DISTRESS, AND HUMILIATE; 567]

preordained *adj* **inevitable**, fated, predetermined, destined, doomed, predicted, inescapable, certain, unavoidable, foreordained (*formal*) [➡CERTAIN; 174]

preparation 1 *n* **groundwork**, training, grounding, homework, research, tuition [➡TEACHING; 839] **2** *n* **planning**, provision, arrangement, formulation, organization [➡BEGINNINGS; 53]

preparatory *adj* **introductory**, foundation, preliminary, elementary, opening, preparative (*formal*) [➡BEFORE, FIRST, AND PRECEDING; 163] *Opposite:* final

prepare 1 *v* **get ready**, arrange, organize, plan, set up, practice, put in order [➡PREPARE FOR ACTION; 289] **2** *v* **train**, groom, coach, prime, make ready, warm up [➡INSTRUCT AND TEACH; 609] **3** *v* **make**, cook, get ready, concoct, formulate, fix (*informal*) [➡MEAL PREPARATION; 354]

prepared *adj* **ready**, set, equipped, geared up, organized, arranged, all set, primed, willing, able [➡POSITIVE IMPATIENCE, ENTHUSIASM, AND ALERTNESS; 537]

preparedness *n* **readiness**, preparation, alertness, attentiveness, awareness, vigilance [➡POSITIVE IMPATIENCE, ENTHUSIASM, AND ALERTNESS; 537]

prepare the ground *v* [➡PREPARE FOR ACTION; 289]

prepare the way *v* [➡PREPARE FOR ACTION; 289]

prepare yourself *v* **steel yourself**, brace yourself, nerve yourself, compose yourself, get ready [➡PREPARE FOR ACTION; 289]

prepayment *n* **advance payment**, down payment, payment, advance, deposit, installment [➡EXPENDITURE; 423] *Opposite:* debt

prep cook *type of* **person who works in restaurants** [➡DOMESTIC AND KITCHEN WORKERS; 850]

preplan *v* [➡PREPARE FOR ACTION; 289]

preponderance (*formal*) 1 *n* **majority**, mass, great number, multitude, many [➡MANY, MUCH, LARGE AMOUNT; 117] *Opposite:* minority **2** *n* **dominance**, superiority, prevalence, predominance, weight, majority, supremacy [➡IMPORTANCE AND SIGNIFICANCE; 192]

preponderant *adj* **greater**, more numerous, more powerful, more important, more significant, preeminent [➡MOST IMPORTANT AND MAIN; 193] *Opposite:* lesser

preponderantly *adv* **generally**, largely, in the main, by and large, for the most part, on the whole [➡MAINLY AND PRIMARILY; 140]

preposition *type of* **word class** [➡ASPECTS OF LANGUAGE; 682]

prepossessing (*formal*) *adj* **attractive**, pleasant, alluring, good-looking, eye-catching, beautiful, handsome, striking, pleasing, nice-looking [➡PEOPLE'S PHYSICAL APPEARANCE; 475] *Opposite:* unattractive

preposterous *adj* **outrageous**, absurd, ridiculous, ludicrous, unbelievable, laughable, silly, outlandish, unreasonable [➡BIZARRE AND PECULIAR; 257] *Opposite:* sensible

preposterousness *n* **outrageousness**, absurdity, ridiculousness, ludicrousness, silliness, outlandishness, unreasonableness [➡BIZARRE AND PECULIAR; 257] *Opposite:* sensibleness

preppy (*informal*) *adj* **yuppie**, conservative, classic, traditional, tailored, well-groomed, neat, smart [➡DESCRIBING CLOTHES; 869]

preproduction *n* **planning**, groundwork, organization, scheduling, planning stage, preparation [➡BEGINNINGS; 53]

prep school *type of* **school** [➡EDUCATIONAL INSTITUTIONS; 813]

prepubescent 1 *adj* **preadolescent**, preteen, pre-teenager, young, childish, childlike, juvenile [➡ BABYHOOD, CHILDHOOD, AND ADOLESCENCE; 917] *Opposite*: adult 2 *n* **youngster**, preadolescent, preteenager, preteen, subteen, child, youth, kid (*informal*), moppet (*informal*) [➡ CHILD OR YOUTH; 945] *Opposite*: adult

prequel *n* **prelude**, prologue, spinoff [➡ FICTION AND DRAMA; 913] *Opposite*: sequel

Pre-Raphaelitism *type of* **pre-20th-century art movement** [➡ ARTISTIC MOVEMENTS AND STYLES; 899]

prerecord *v* **record**, tape, film, copy, video (*UK*) [➡ RECORD SOMETHING; 371]

prerequisite *n* **precondition**, requirement, condition, qualification, criterion, essential, must, necessity [➡ NECESSARY AND ESSENTIAL; 196]

prerogative *n* **right**, privilege, due, entitlement, birthright, perquisite [➡ FREEDOM AND LIBERTY; 208]

presage 1 *n* **portent**, omen, sign, warning, signal, indication, augury, herald [➡ THE SUPERNATURAL; 787] 2 *v* **foretell**, foreshadow, portend, bode, augur, signify, betoken (*literary*) [➡ MEAN SOMETHING; 61]

presbyter *n* [➡ RELIGIOUS PEOPLE; 778]

preschool 1 *adj* **young**, toddler, infant, kindergarten, nursery, infantile [➡ BABYHOOD, CHILDHOOD, AND ADOLESCENCE; 917] 2 *type of* **school** [➡ EDUCATIONAL INSTITUTIONS; 813]

preschooler *n* **young child**, preschool child, toddler, infant, baby, youngster, child, tot (*informal*), under-five (*UK*) [➡ CHILD OR YOUTH; 945]

prescience *n* **foresight**, precognition, clairvoyance, prophecy, prediction, divination, insight, intuition, fore-knowledge [➡ PREDICT AND ANTICIPATE; 750] *Opposite*: hindsight

prescient *adj* **prophetic**, psychic, clairvoyant, discerning, perceptive, mantic, vatic, revelatory [➡ THE SUPERNATURAL; 787]

prescribe 1 *v* **recommend**, suggest, advise, propose, advocate, commend, counsel (*formal or literary*) [➡ ADVISE AND WARN; 613] 2 *v* **lay down**, stipulate, impose, order, set down, demand, fix, specify, particularize [➡ REQUEST AND DEMAND; 663]

prescribed *adj* **set**, agreed, arranged, prearranged, given, approved [➡ BEFORE, FIRST, AND PRECEDING; 163]

prescript (*formal*) *n* **rule**, regulation, law, convention, canon, decree, edict, ordinance, statute [➡ REQUEST AND DEMAND; 663]

prescription *n* **medicine**, treatment, drug, preparation, remedy, medicament [➡ REMEDIES, TREATMENTS, AND OPERATIONS; 731]

prescriptive *adj* **narrow**, rigid, strict, unbending, inflexible, dogmatic, doctrinaire, authoritarian [➡ THE NATURE OF IDEAS; 771] *Opposite*: lax

prescriptiveness *n* **narrowness**, rigidity, strictness, inflexibility, dogmatism, authoritarianism [➡ THE NATURE OF IDEAS; 771] *Opposite*: laxity

presence 1 *n* **attendance**, company, occurrence, incidence, existence, manifestation [➡ PRESENT AND AVAILABLE; 11] *Opposite*: absence 2 *n* **dignity**, charisma, aura, authority,

poise, air, bearing, comportment (*formal*), mien (*formal*) [➡ TEMPERAMENT AND BEHAVIOR; 492] 3 *n* **ghost**, apparition, spirit, ghoul, manifestation, specter, phantom, phantasm [➡ THE SUPERNATURAL; 787]

presence of mind *n* **nerve**, composure, level-head-edness, common sense, sense, alertness, gumption (*informal*) [➡ CONFIDENCE AND COMPOSURE; 499]

present 1 *v* **give**, hand over, award, donate, offer, give away, hand out, bestow (*formal*) [➡ PROFFER AND HAND OVER; 431] *Opposite*: deny 2 *v* **stage**, show, put on, exhibit, organize, display, mount, perform [➡ CAUSE TO APPEAR; 5] 3 *v* **cause**, represent, raise, throw up, produce, bring about, pose [➡ CAUSE TO HAPPEN; 31] 4 *v* **introduce**, acquaint with, put forward [➡ INFORM, ANNOUNCE, AND ISSUE; 611] 5 *v* **portray**, represent, depict, cast, describe, render (*formal*) [➡ REPRESENT SOMETHING OR SOMEBODY; 59] 6 *v* (*formal*) **submit**, impart, offer, put forward, expound, state, communicate [➡ SUGGEST, HINT, AND COMMENT; 612] 7 *v* **appear**, report, arrive, turn up, visit, attend [➡ ARRIVE; 12] 8 *n* **gift**, offering, grant, dowry, largesse, benevolence [➡ GIFTS; 438] 9 *n* **now**, here and now, present day, today, nowadays, this day and age, these days [➡ PRESENT; 85] *Opposite*: past 10 *adj* **current**, contemporary, present-day, existing, extant, contemporaneous, existent (*formal*) [➡ PRESENT; 85] *Opposite*: past 11 *adj* **there**, here, in attendance, at hand, near, nearby [➡ PRESENT AND AVAILABLE; 11] *Opposite*: absent

See Compare and Contrast at **give**.

presentable 1 *adj* **respectable**, personable, fit to be seen, smart, well-dressed, neat, tidy, well-turned-out (*UK*) [➡ WELL-GROOMED; 482] *Opposite*: scruffy 2 *adj* **reasonable**, acceptable, satisfactory, good enough, passable, tolerable, OK (*informal*), okay (*informal*) [➡ ACCEPTABLE AND PASSABLE; 219] *Opposite*: unsatisfactory

presentation 1 *n* **performance**, exhibition, demonstration, appearance, arrangement, staging, production, management, exposition [➡ SALES AND SHOWS; 443] 2 *n* **award**, donation, giving, offer, bestowal, benefaction, contribution, bestowment (*formal*) [➡ GIFTS; 438] 3 *n* **talk**, lecture, seminar, speech, address, report, allocution (*formal*) [➡ ONE-WAY COMMUNICATION; 49]

present circumstances *n* [➡ SITUATIONS; 71]

present day *n* **now**, here and now, present, today, nowadays, this day and age, these days [➡ PRESENT; 85] *Opposite*: past

present-day *adj* **contemporary**, current, existing, present, modern, extant [➡ PRESENT; 85] *Opposite*: past

presenter (*UK*) *n* **announcer**, broadcaster, anchor, host, newscaster, TV presenter (*UK*), radio presenter (*UK*) [➡ WORKERS IN ENTERTAINMENT AND MEDIA; 873]

presentiment *n* **feeling**, intuition, foreboding, fear, sense, hunch, premonition, suspicion, awareness [➡ FEELINGS ABOUT THE FUTURE; 533]

presently *adv* **currently**, at the moment, at present, right now, now [➡ PRESENT; 85]

preservation 1 *n* **protection**, conservation, safeguarding, defense, conservancy, salvation [➡ PREVENT CONTACT OR ATTACK; 419] *Opposite*: destruction 2 *n* **maintenance**, continuation, perpetuation, keeping, upholding, support [➡ PERMANENCE: WITHOUT END; 94] *Opposite*: abolition

preservative 1 *adj* **preserving**, conserving, protective, antibacterial, antifungal, stabilizing [➡ SAFE AND SAFETY; 191] *Opposite*: destructive **2** *n* **additive**, preserver, stabilizer, E number (*UK*) [➡ ADDITIVES; 1172]

preserve 1 *v* **maintain**, uphold, keep, continue, carry on, sustain, save, conserve [➡ STORE AND KEEP; 453] *Opposite*: destroy **2** *n* [➡ SUGAR AND PRESERVES; 1184] **3** *n* **realm**, domain, sphere, field, territory, ambit, compass, orbit, purview [➡ SUBJECT AREAS; 768] **4** *n* **game reserve**, reservation, sanctuary, game preserve, reserve (*UK*) [➡ THE COUNTRYSIDE AND OUTDOOR SPACES; 1071]

preserve

◆ *types of preserves*
compote, conserve, honey, jam, jelly, lekvar, lemon curd, marmalade, mincemeat, peanut butter

preserved 1 *adj* **conserved**, well-looked-after, well-maintained, well-preserved, well-kept-up, well-kept, unspoiled [➡ IN GOOD REPAIR; 1232] *Opposite*: dilapidated **2** *adj* **treated**, pickled, frozen, dried, salted, canned, smoked, bottled, cured, tinned (*UK*) [➡ STATE OF PREPARED FOOD; 1171] *Opposite*: fresh

preserver *n* **protector**, guard, guardian, savior, conserver [➡ SUPPORTERS, PROTECTORS, AND COMPATRIOTS; 970] *Opposite*: destroyer

preset *adj* **set**, predetermined, fixed, stipulated, specific, stated, firm, certain [➡ BEFORE, FIRST, AND PRECEDING; 163]

preshrunk *adj* [➡ DESCRIBING CLOTHES; 869]

preside *v* **take the chair**, chair, control, supervise, head, lead, manage, direct, run, oversee, reign, govern [➡ BE IN CHARGE; 270]

presidency 1 *n* **premiership**, position, job, function, term, term of office, role, tenure [➡ POLITICAL OFFICES AND POLITICIANS; 808] **2** *n* **post**, status, function, office, authority, responsibility [➡ JOB; 833]

president 1 *n* **leader**, premier, head, head of state, chair, chief, commander [➡ POLITICAL OFFICES AND POLITICIANS; 808] **2** *n* [➡ BUSINESS PEOPLE; 793]

presidential 1 *adj* **political**, constitutional, high-level, governmental, top-level, diplomatic, official, executive [➡ STYLES AND SYSTEMS OF GOVERNMENT; 806] **2** *adj* **dignified**, authoritative, monarchic, judicious, regal, diplomatic, imperial, powerful, authoritarian, awe-inspiring, self-assured, commanding [➡ CONFIDENCE AND COMPOSURE; 499]

presidentially *adv* **authoritatively**, monarchically, judiciously, regally, powerfully, imperially, confidently, commandingly, with dignity [➡ CONFIDENCE AND COMPOSURE; 499]

presidium *n* **executive committee**, committee, council, group, body, authority [➡ BUSINESS ENTERPRISES AND RELATED BODIES; 792]

press 1 *v* **push**, depress, force down, bear down on, compress, squash [➡ CONTACT: EXERT PRESSURE; 414] *Opposite*: pull **2** *v* **force**, urge, push, compel, oblige, hound, pressure [➡ CAUSE OR COMPEL TO ACT; 271] **3** *v* **pursue**, lobby, beg, entreat, enjoin, bug (*informal*), implore (*formal*), importune

(*formal*) [➡ REQUEST AND DEMAND; 663] **4** *v* (*literary*) **surge**, crowd, swarm, mill, cluster, herd, huddle, throng [➡ GET CLOSER TOGETHER; 310] **5** *v* **iron**, smooth, steam, flatten, hot-press [➡ CHANGE OF SHAPE; 385] **6** *n* **journalists**, media, reporters, newspapers, correspondents, fourth estate, print media [➡ WORKERS IN ENTERTAINMENT AND MEDIA; 873] **7** *n* **crowd**, horde, throng, mob, multitude, swarm, host, crush [➡ GROUPS OF PEOPLE; 935] **8** *type of* **cabinet** [➡ FURNITURE; 858]

press ahead *v* [➡ CONTINUE AN ACTION; 262]

press conference *n* **news conference**, question and answer session, interview, conference, photo opportunity, meeting [➡ MEETINGS AND ASSEMBLIES; 43]

pressed *adj* **busy**, pushed, hard-pressed, constrained, compelled, forced [➡ IN TROUBLE AND DISADVANTAGED; 73]

pressed for time *adj* [➡ IN TROUBLE AND DISADVANTAGED; 73]

press for *v* **demand**, seek, urge, push for, campaign for, lobby for, advocate [➡ REQUEST AND DEMAND; 663]

press-gang *v* **force**, coerce, bully, pressure, make, compel, shanghai, bulldoze (*informal*), pressurize (*UK*) [➡ CAUSE OR COMPEL TO ACT; 271]

pressing 1 *adj* **urgent**, important, serious, crucial, vital, burning, imperative, necessary, critical [➡ IMPORTANT; 194] *Opposite*: unimportant **2** *adj* **persistent**, insistent, unrelenting, unyielding, demanding, irresistible, tenacious, persuasive, crying, clamoring, importunate (*formal*) [➡ STRENGTH OF WILL; 501] *Opposite*: half-hearted

press officer *n* **spokesperson**, media spokesperson, press liaison officer, press agent [➡ WORKERS IN ENTERTAINMENT AND MEDIA; 873]

press on *v* **continue**, push on, forge ahead, keep going, press ahead, persist, persevere, carry on [➡ CONTINUE AN ACTION; 262] *Opposite*: give up

press release *n* **statement**, document, announcement, bulletin [➡ ADVERTISING AND PUBLICITY; 604]

press stud (*UK*) *n* **fastening**, fastener, stud, snap, popper (*UK*), press fastener (*UK*) [➡ FASTENERS, LINKS, AND NETWORKS; 1247]

press together *v* **squeeze together**, force together, clamp, join together, close, purse, clump, crowd, cluster, huddle [➡ GET CLOSER TOGETHER; 310] *Opposite*: pull apart

pressure 1 *n* **force**, weight, heaviness, burden, compression, gravity, density [➡ ENERGY; 1161] **2** *n* **stress**, anxiety, weight, strain, tension, demands, care, difficulty, burden, load, hassle (*informal*) [➡ DIFFICULT SITUATIONS; 72] **3** *v* **coerce**, force, bully, insist, compel, bulldoze (*informal*), hassle (*informal*), pressurize (*UK*) [➡ CAUSE OR COMPEL TO ACT; 271]

pressure cooker *n* [➡ TABLEWARE, FLATWARE, AND KITCHENWARE; 861]

pressured *adj* **worried**, stressed, under pressure, overstretched, edgy, distressed, tense, anxious, careworn, strung out (*informal*) [➡ SADNESS, DISTRESS, AND DESPAIR; 539] *Opposite*: relaxed

pressure sore *n* [➡ CONDITIONS AFFECTING THE SKIN; 721]

pressurize (*UK*) *v* **press**, coerce, compel, make, pressure, bully, press-gang, force, bulldoze (*informal*) [➡ CAUSE OR COMPEL TO ACT; 271]

prestige *n* **status**, standing, stature, kudos, esteem, reputation, regard, cachet, fame, celebrity, notability, distinction, respect, repute (*formal*) [➡ STATUS; 888] *Opposite:* notoriety

prestigious *adj* **admired**, respected, significant, important, impressive, high-status, prominent, esteemed, celebrated, influential, major, famed, notable, respectable, exalted (*formal*) [➡ KNOWN AND FAMOUS; 181] *Opposite:* insignificant

presumably *adv* **most probably**, I assume, I imagine, in all probability, most likely, it would seem, seemingly, apparently, doubtless, probably, likely, ostensibly, assumedly [➡ POSSIBLE AND PROBABLE; 177]

presume 1 *v* **believe**, assume, guess, deduce, imagine, suppose, take as read, take for granted, postulate, gather, think, posit (*formal*) [➡ PREDICT AND ANTICIPATE; 750] *Opposite:* know 2 *v* **venture**, dare, be so bold, take the liberty, make free, have the audacity, have the nerve [➡ ATTEMPT AN ACTION; 261]

presumption 1 *n* **belief**, assumption, conjecture, supposition, presupposition, guess, deduction, opinion, hypothesis, premise, speculation [➡ POINTS OF VIEW; 767] 2 *n* **impertinence**, audacity, nerve, gall, impudence, boldness, effrontery, rudeness, brass (*informal*), cheek (*informal*), chutzpah (*informal*), front (*UK*) [➡ BAD MANNERS AND SOCIAL SKILLS; 521]

presumptive (*formal*) *adj* **probable**, likely, plausible, convincing, reasonable, possible, ostensible, apparent [➡ POSSIBLE AND PROBABLE; 177] *Opposite:* implausible

presumptuous *adj* **overfamiliar**, rude, presuming, audacious, insolent, bold, rash, disrespectful, inconsiderate, overconfident, arrogant, improper, impolite, inappropriate, shameless, pushy (*informal*) [➡ BAD MANNERS AND SOCIAL SKILLS; 521] *Opposite:* modest

presumptuousness *n* **rudeness**, arrogance, impropriety, disrespect, inappropriateness, presumption, audacity, insolence, boldness, rashness, inconsiderateness, overfamiliarity, overconfidence, shamelessness, pushiness (*informal*), chutzpah (*informal*) [➡ BAD MANNERS AND SOCIAL SKILLS; 521] *Opposite:* modesty

presuppose *v* **assume**, take for granted, take as read, take as fact, presume, suppose, accept [➡ PREDICT AND ANTICIPATE; 750]

presupposition *n* **assumption**, supposition, conjecture, belief, guess, deduction, presumption, premise, opinion, hypothesis [➡ POINTS OF VIEW; 767]

prêt-à-porter *adj* **off-the-rack**, ready-made, ready-to-wear, mass-produced [➡ DESCRIBING CLOTHES; 869] *Opposite:* made-to-measure

preteen *n* [➡ CHILD OR YOUTH; 945]

preteenager *n* [➡ CHILD OR YOUTH; 945]

pretend 1 *v* **make believe**, imagine, fantasize, make up, play, play-act (*informal*) [➡ DREAM, IMAGINE, AND FANTASIZE; 749] 2 *v* **feign**, put on, affect, profess, simulate, fake, imitate, sham [➡ PRETEND AND MIMIC; 60] 3 *adj* **imaginary**, make-believe, made-up, invented, false, sham, fictitious [➡ FALSE AND UNREAL; 173] *Opposite:* real

pretended *adj* [➡ FALSE AND UNREAL; 173]

pretender *n* **aspirant**, aspiring leader, candidate, opponent, claimant [➡ COMPETITORS; 41]

pretend to be *v* **impersonate**, masquerade as, pose as, imitate, pass for, pass yourself off as, mimic, play-act [➡ PRETEND AND MIMIC; 60]

pretense 1 *n* **trick**, con, sham, hoax, fabrication, invention, deception, subterfuge, cover, pretext, deceit, charade, façade [➡ DECEPTION AND LIES; 660] 2 *n* **make-believe**, fantasy, fancy, imagination, castles in the air, nonsense [➡ NONEXISTENT THINGS; 23] *Opposite:* reality 3 *n* **claim**, suggestion, allegation, hint, supposition, presumption, pretension [➡ POINTS OF VIEW; 767]

pretension *n* **affectation**, pretentiousness, airs, posing, posturing, pretense, self-importance [➡ AFFECTATION, SELF-SATISFACTION, AND SNOBBISHNESS; 507] *Opposite:* humility

pretentious *adj* **affected**, ostentatious, showy, exaggerated, pompous, conceited, hollow, fake [➡ AFFECTATION, SELF-SATISFACTION, AND SNOBBISHNESS; 507] *Opposite:* down-to-earth

pretentiousness *see* **pretension**

preterit *type of* **grammatical term** [➡ ASPECTS OF LANGUAGE; 682]

preternatural (*literary*) *adj* **supernatural**, paranormal, uncanny, unnatural, otherworldly, occult, unearthly, weird, bizarre [➡ THE SUPERNATURAL; 787] *Opposite:* natural

pretext *n* **excuse**, cause, con, ploy, ruse, grounds [➡ CAUSATION; 168]

prettify *v* **smarten up**, do up, beautify, improve, adorn, decorate, gentrify, ornament [➡ IMPROVE APPEARANCE; 379] *Opposite:* mess up (*informal*)

prettiness *n* **good looks**, handsomeness, attractiveness, beauty, cuteness, loveliness [➡ PEOPLE'S PHYSICAL APPEARANCE; 475] *Opposite:* ugliness

pretty 1 *adj* **attractive**, beautiful, handsome, cute, good-looking, appealing, lovely, sweet, nice-looking, comely (*archaic or literary*) [➡ PEOPLE'S PHYSICAL APPEARANCE; 475] *Opposite:* unattractive 2 *adv* **rather**, fairly, reasonably, quite, moderately, somewhat, adequately, satisfactorily [➡ TO A CERTAIN EXTENT; 136]

See Compare and Contrast at **good-looking**.

pretty up *v* [➡ IMPROVE APPEARANCE; 379]

prevail 1 *v* **triumph**, succeed, be victorious, overcome, win out, conquer, carry the day, win through (*UK*) [➡ SUCCEED AND WIN; 79] *Opposite:* fail 2 *v* (*formal*) **exist**, reign, be happening, occur, predominate, abound, be present, be current [➡ PROSPER AND ABOUND; 16]

prevailing 1 *adj* **usual**, main, dominant, predominant, principal, fundamental, prevalent, normal, preponderant [➡ MOST IMPORTANT AND MAIN; 193] *Opposite:* underlying 2 *adj* **current**, existing, customary, established, popular, general, widespread [➡ PRESENT AND AVAILABLE; 11]

prevail on *v* **persuade**, convince, cajole, sway, coax into, influence, talk into, induce, nag into [➡ CAUSE OR COMPEL TO ACT; 271]

prevail upon v [➡ CAUSE OR COMPEL TO ACT; 271]

prevalence n occurrence, commonness, pervasiveness, incidence, frequency, popularity [➡ PRESENT AND AVAILABLE; 11]

prevalent adj common, dominant, predominant, widespread, rampant, ubiquitous, established, customary, prevailing, numerous, frequent [➡ PRESENT AND AVAILABLE; 11] Opposite: rare

See Compare and Contrast at **widespread**.

prevaricate v hedge, evade, beat around the bush, lie, quibble, stall, dither, dissemble, misstate, fib (informal), fudge (informal), put off (UK) [➡ DECEPTION AND LIES; 660]

prevarication n evasiveness, evasion, equivocation, avoidance, hedging, lying, stonewalling (informal), fudging (informal) [➡ DECEPTION AND LIES; 660] Opposite: forthrightness

prevaricator n [➡ PEOPLE WHO DECEIVE; 661]

prevent v stop, avert, avoid, foil, thwart, put a stop to, forestall, inhibit, counteract, block, ward off, check, nip in the bud (informal), preclude (formal) [➡ MAKE IMPOSSIBLE; 276] Opposite: encourage

preventable adj avoidable, needless, unnecessary, avertible, escapable [➡ UNIMPORTANT AND UNNECESSARY; 238] Opposite: inevitable

prevention 1 n avoidance, deterrence, stoppage, inhibition, hindrance, preclusion (formal) [➡ AVOID, PREVENT, LIMIT, AND CONTROL; 277] Opposite: promotion 2 n obstacle, hindrance, impediment, inhibition, restraint, bar [➡ PROBLEMS; 258]

preventive 1 adj anticipatory, preemptive, defensive, prophylactic, deterrent, protective, proactive [➡ AVOID, PREVENT, LIMIT, AND CONTROL; 277] 2 n protection, anticipatory measure, preemptive measure, deterrent, disincentive, preventative, defense [➡ AVOID, PREVENT, LIMIT, AND CONTROL; 277]

preview 1 n showing, performance, broadcast, screening, opening [➡ PERFORMANCES AND SHOWS; 42] 2 n trailer, ad, clip, foretaste, extract, coming attraction, promo (informal), teaser (informal), taster (UK) [➡ ADVERTISING AND PUBLICITY; 604] 3 v show, perform, broadcast, screen, promote, advertise [➡ CAUSE TO APPEAR; 5] 4 v review, describe, introduce, advertise, trail [➡ NAME AND DESCRIBE; 665]

previous adj preceding, earlier, prior, former, past, foregoing, erstwhile, aforementioned (formal) [➡ BEFORE, FIRST, AND PRECEDING; 163] Opposite: subsequent

prey n quarry, victim, target, kill, game [➡ DEAD PERSON; 926]

prey on 1 v live on, live off, feed on, hunt, kill, exploit [➡ KILL; 923] 2 v worry, preoccupy, bother, haunt, oppress, depress, bug (informal) [➡ UPSET, DISTRESS, AND HUMILIATE; 567] 3 v take advantage of, exploit, victimize, intimidate, bully [➡ MISUSE AND ABUSE; 471]

price 1 n cost, worth, fee, face value, amount, bill, rate, expense, value, charge [➡ EXPENDITURE; 423] 2 n penalty, cost, punishment, consequences, fine [➡ RESULTS AND OUTCOMES; 83] 3 v set a price, assess, estimate, rate, evaluate, appraise, value [➡ ASSESS QUALITY; 755]

priceless 1 adj invaluable, inestimable, beyond price, incalculable, costly, expensive, irreplaceable, incom-

parable, peerless, precious [➡ EXPENSIVE AND LUXURIOUS; 218] Opposite: worthless 2 adj (informal) hilarious, funny, comic, amusing, entertaining, sidesplitting [➡ FUNNY AND AMUSING; 216]

price tag n [➡ NAME AND DESCRIBE; 665]

pricey (informal) adj costly, expensive, dear, high-priced, exorbitant, overpriced, steep (informal) [➡ EXPENSIVE AND OVERPRICED; 247] Opposite: cheap

prick 1 v pierce, stab, puncture, perforate, jab, make a hole in, cut, lance [➡ TEAR, BREAK, AND CUT; 360] 2 n hole, puncture, perforation, pinhole [➡ HOLES, GAPS, AND FORKS; 1252]

prickle 1 n spike, spine, barb, thorn, quill, needle [➡ EXTREMITIES OF PHYSICAL OBJECTS; 1250] 2 n itch, tickle, sting, irritation, tingling [➡ CONDITIONS AFFECTING THE SKIN; 721] 3 v sting, itch, tickle, prick, irritate, tingle [➡ PAIN AND OTHER PHYSICAL SENSATIONS; 733]

prickling n scratchiness, pricking, itchiness, itching, prickle, tingling, sting, tickle, irritation [➡ CONDITIONS AFFECTING THE SKIN; 721]

prickly 1 adj spiny, thorny, barbed, bristly, spiky [➡ PHYSICAL TEXTURE; 1222] Opposite: smooth 2 adj itchy, tickly, scratchy, stinging, tingling [➡ CONDITIONS AFFECTING THE SKIN; 721] 3 adj (informal) sensitive, snappy, irritable, grumpy, snappish, cantankerous, touchy, tetchy (informal) [➡ EXCESSIVE SENSITIVITY; 511] Opposite: impervious

prickly heat n [➡ CONDITIONS AFFECTING THE SKIN; 721]

pride 1 n arrogance, conceit, smugness, superiority, self-importance, egotism, vanity, immodesty [➡ MORALLY BAD OR IMPROPER; 775] Opposite: humility 2 n self-respect, dignity, self-esteem, honor [➡ CONFIDENCE AND COMPOSURE; 499] 3 n satisfaction, delight, gratification, enjoyment, joy, happiness, pleasure, self-satisfaction [➡ APPRECIATION AND GRATITUDE; 535] 4 type of herd [➡ GROUPS OF ANIMALS; 993]

pride and joy n most prized possession, the apple of your eye, poster child, treasure, pride, showpiece, obsession [➡ TREATS; 210]

pride yourself on v be proud of, take satisfaction in, revel in, take pride in, glory in, exult [➡ LIKE, LOVE, VALUE, AND ENJOY; 578]

priest n minister, pastor, vicar, rector, presbyter, celebrant, chief priest, high priest, cleric, ecclesiastic [➡ RELIGIOUS PEOPLE; 778]

priesthood n clergy, ministry, cloth [➡ RELIGIOUS PEOPLE; 778] Opposite: laity

prim 1 adj prudish, prissy, strait-laced, puritanical, moralistic, uptight (informal) [➡ EXCESSIVE SENSITIVITY; 511] Opposite: broad-minded 2 adj formal, proper, dignified, starchy, stiff, correct, demure, snobbish [➡ LEVELS OF FORMALITY; 522] Opposite: informal 3 adj tidy, orderly, precise, meticulous, fussy, fastidious, neat [➡ ORDER AND ORGANIZATION; 206] Opposite: messy

primacy 1 n preeminence, importance, predominance, dominance, prevalence, superiority, supremacy, priority [➡ IMPORTANCE AND SIGNIFICANCE; 192] 2 n archbishopric, bishopric [➡ RELIGIOUS PEOPLE; 778]

prima facie 1 adv at first glance, on the face of it, apparently, ostensibly, seemingly, superficially [➡ FOREIGN

WORDS AND PHRASES; 672] **2** *adj* **apparent**, clear, clear-cut, obvious, unambiguous [➡CONCISE AND CLEAR; 202]

primal *adj* **primitive**, primeval, aboriginal, primordial, prehistoric, original, ancient [➡OLD, OLD-FASHIONED; 167] *Opposite*: new

primarily *adv* **first and foremost**, above all, chiefly, mainly, principally, for the most part, mostly, largely, predominantly [➡MAINLY AND PRIMARILY; 140]

primary **1** *adj* **first**, initial, top, leading, foremost [➡BEFORE, FIRST, AND PRECEDING; 163] *Opposite*: last **2** *adj* **main**, chief, most important, key, prime, principal, major, crucial [➡MOST IMPORTANT AND MAIN; 193] *Opposite*: secondary **3** *adj* **basic**, core, central, fundamental, essential, important [➡FUNDAMENTAL; 195] *Opposite*: minor

primary school *type of* **school** [➡EDUCATIONAL INSTITUTIONS; 813]

primate **1** *n* [➡LIVING THINGS AND LIVING; 976] **2** *n* **archbishop**, bishop, prelate, cardinal [➡RELIGIOUS PEOPLE; 778]

---

primate

◆ *types of primates*
ape, aye-aye, baboon, Barbary ape, bonnet monkey, capuchin, chimp, chimpanzee, colobus, gibbon, gorilla, human, lemur, macaque, mandrill, marmoset, monkey, orangutan, proboscis monkey, rhesus monkey, spider monkey

---

prime **1** *adj* **top**, superior, superlative, best, premier, first-class, foremost, first-rate [➡SUPERIORITY; 152] *Opposite*: inferior **2** *adj* **major**, main, key, chief, leading, primary, principal, crucial [➡MOST IMPORTANT AND MAIN; 193] **3** *n* **peak**, zenith, heyday, summit, high point, pinnacle, best part [➡INTERMEDIATE STAGES; 55] *Opposite*: nadir **4** *v* **prepare**, ready, get ready, make ready [➡PREPARE FOR ACTION; 289] **5** *v* **brief**, fill in, instruct, give somebody the lowdown (*informal*) [➡INSTRUCT AND TEACH; 609]

primed **1** *adj* **aware**, well-informed, geared up, informed, in the picture, clued in, au courant, with it (*informal*), on the ball (*informal*) [➡KNOWLEDGE AND WISDOM; 558] *Opposite*: unprepared **2** *adj* **prepared**, ready, set, in position, poised, in place, at the ready [➡ABOUT TO HAPPEN; 33]

prime minister *n* **premier**, chief minister, head of cabinet, PM, head of government [➡POLITICAL OFFICES AND POLITICIANS; 808]

prime of life *n* [➡ADULTHOOD; 918]

primer *n* **textbook**, reader, grammar, introduction, how-to (*informal*) [➡MANUALS AND INSTRUCTIONS; 589]

primeval **1** *adj* **prehistoric**, original, ancient, archaic [➡OLD, OLD-FASHIONED; 167] *Opposite*: modern **2** *adj* **primitive**, primordial, primal, basic, instinctive, intuitive [➡PSYCHOLOGY AND THE MIND; 769] *Opposite*: considered

primitive **1** *adj* **embryonic**, primeval, original, aboriginal, nascent [➡PAST; 84] *Opposite*: developed **2** *adj* **simple**, basic, uncomplicated, unsophisticated, crude, rough, coarse [➡ORDINARINESS; 244] *Opposite*: sophisticated **3** *adj* **prehistoric**, ancient, primordial, primal, archaic, primeval, original [➡OLD, OLD-FASHIONED; 167] *Opposite*: modern

primitiveness **1** *n* **antiquity**, ancientness, primitive

stage, early stage, primeval stage, early stage of development, earliness [➡OLD, OLD-FASHIONED; 167] **2** *n* **crudeness**, simplicity, roughness, coarseness, unsophisticatedness, plainness [➡ORDINARINESS; 244] *Opposite*: sophistication

primness **1** *n* **prudishness**, narrowness, shockability, oversensitivity, strait-lacedness, politeness, prissiness [➡EXCESSIVE SENSITIVITY; 511] *Opposite*: broad-mindedness **2** *n* **formality**, properness, starchiness, propriety, stiffness, correctness, demureness [➡LEVELS OF FORMALITY; 522] *Opposite*: informality **3** *n* **neatness**, tidiness, orderliness, fastidiousness, meticulousness, fussiness [➡ORDER AND ORGANIZATION; 206] *Opposite*: messiness

primordial **1** *adj* **primeval**, prehistoric, primal, ancient, primitive, elemental, aboriginal [➡OLD, OLD-FASHIONED; 167] **2** *adj* **embryonic**, developing, early, nascent [➡FUTURE; 86]

primp *v* **fuss**, fuss over, groom, preen, adorn, admire, gussy up (*informal*) [➡IMPROVE APPEARANCE; 379]

primrose *type of* **perennial flower** [➡FLOWERS; 1032]

primrose path (*literary*) *n* [➡DECEPTION AND LIES; 660]

prince **1** *n* **leader**, leading figure, leading light, doyen, big shot (*informal*), big gun (*informal*) [➡IMPORTANT OR FAMOUS PEOPLE; 893] **2** *n* (*informal*) **gentleman**, mensch (*informal*), trump (*informal*) [➡PEOPLE WHO ARE APPROVED OF; 955] *Opposite*: egotist **3** *type of* **aristocrat** [➡RULERS AND ARISTOCRACY; 823]

princely *adj* **generous**, handsome, large, significant, huge, sizable, substantial [➡MANY, MUCH, LARGE AMOUNT; 117] *Opposite*: measly (*informal*)

princess *type of* **aristocrat** [➡RULERS AND ARISTOCRACY; 823]

principal **1** *adj* **main**, major, chief, most important, primary, prime, key, foremost, basic, fundamental [➡MOST IMPORTANT AND MAIN; 193] **2** *n* **leader**, chief, doyenne, doyen, head, leading light, big shot (*informal*), big gun (*informal*) [➡IMPORTANT OR FAMOUS PEOPLE; 893] *Opposite*: follower **3** *n* **head of school**, headmaster, headmistress, dean, provost, superintendent, head teacher (*UK*), head (*UK*) [➡BOSSES AND MANAGEMENT; 965]

principality *n* **princedom**, territory, country, domain [➡COUNTRIES AND REGIONS; 1067]

principally *adv* **mainly**, chiefly, above all, first and foremost, primarily, predominantly, mostly, largely, essentially, for the most part [➡MAINLY AND PRIMARILY; 140]

principle **1** *n* **rule**, theory, notion, concept, tenet, dogma, assumption, law [➡WAYS OF DOING THINGS; 294] **2** *n* **code**, standard, belief, attitude, value, opinion, norm [➡IDEAS AND THOUGHTS; 770] **3** *n* **source**, wellspring, origin, cause, basis, antecedent, determinant [➡BEGINNINGS; 53]

principled *adj* **honorable**, righteous, upright, ethical, just, moral, good [➡MORALLY GOOD; 774] *Opposite*: unethical

print **1** *n* **pattern**, design, motif [➡ARTWORKS; 898] **2** *n* **reproduction**, copy, lithograph, photograph, photocopy, facsimile, duplication, imitation, replica, version [➡PHOTOGRAPHY AND PHOTOGRAPHIC EQUIPMENT; 1122] **3** *v* **turn out**, produce, make, issue, run off [➡CREATE IMAGES; 356] **4** *v* **publish**, carry, make known, advertise, broadcast, disseminate, feature [➡UTTER AND PRONOUNCE; 608] **5** *v* **stamp**, imprint, engrave, emboss [➡CREATE IMAGES; 356]

printed *adj* **in print**, in black and white, on paper, published, reproduced [➡ WRITING; 583]

printed circuit *type of* **hardware** [➡ COMPUTERS AND COMPUTING; 1127]

printer 1 *type of* **hardware** [➡ COMPUTERS AND COMPUTING; 1127] 2 *type of* **photographic equipment** [➡ PHOTOGRAPHY AND PHOTOGRAPHIC EQUIPMENT; 1122]

printing 1 *n* **production**, reproduction, lithography, offset lithography, letterpress, photogravure, laser printing, silk-screening, block printing [➡ PRINTING; 600] 2 *n* **text**, lettering, words, writing, wording, information [➡ PRINTING; 600] 3 *n* lettering, capitals, upper case, lower case, block lettering, print [➡ WRITING; 583] *Opposite*: script 4 *n* **edition**, print run, run, impression [➡ PRINTING; 600]

prior *adj* **previous**, preceding, past, erstwhile, former, earlier, aforementioned (*formal*) [➡ BEFORE, FIRST, AND PRECEDING; 163] *Opposite*: subsequent

prioritization *n* **ordering**, ranking, arranging, arrangement, listing, prioritizing [➡ ARRANGE AND CREATE ORDER; 357]

prioritize 1 *v* **order**, rank, arrange, list, line up, place in order [➡ ARRANGE AND CREATE ORDER; 357] 2 *v* **concentrate on**, give precedence to, select, highlight, rank first, spotlight, focus on [➡ MAKE DECISIONS AND CHOICES; 752]

priority *n* **importance**, precedence, urgency, import, significance, primacy [➡ MOST IMPORTANT THING; 197]

prior to *prep* **before**, previous to, earlier than, preceding, in advance of [➡ BEFORE, FIRST, AND PRECEDING; 163] *Opposite*: after

priory *n* **monastery**, convent, religious community, abbey, ashram [➡ RELIGIOUS BUILDINGS; 1085]

prismatic *adj* [➡ DESCRIBING COLORS; 1226]

prison 1 *n* **jail**, penitentiary, top-security prison, penal complex, detention center, house of correction, reformatory, juvenile hall, pen (*slang*), slammer (*slang*), pokey (*slang*), clink (*dated slang*), young offenders' institution (*UK*), secure unit (*UK*) [➡ BUILDINGS FOR CONFINING PEOPLE; 1094] 2 *n* **imprisonment**, confinement, solitary confinement, detention, custody, incarceration (*formal*) [➡ CAPTIVITY AND LOSS OF FREEDOM; 248]

prison cell *n* [➡ BUILDINGS FOR CONFINING PEOPLE; 1094]

prison chaplain *n* [➡ RELIGIOUS PEOPLE; 778]

prisoner 1 *n* **detainee**, inmate, convict, political prisoner, prisoner of war, prisoner of conscience, recidivist, jailbird (*slang*) [➡ CAPTIVES AND PRISONERS; 249] 2 *n* **captive**, hostage, kidnap victim [➡ CAPTIVES AND PRISONERS; 249]

prissiness *n* **primness**, prudishness, properness, starchiness, stiffness, formality, strait-lacedness [➡ LEVELS OF FORMALITY; 522] *Opposite*: informality

prissy *adj* **prim**, prudish, proper, starchy, stiff, formal, strait-laced, uptight (*informal*) [➡ LEVELS OF FORMALITY; 522] *Opposite*: informal

pristine 1 *adj* **immaculate**, perfect, faultless, spotless, pure, unsullied [➡ CLEAN AND HYGIENIC; 1233] *Opposite*: soiled 2 *adj* **unspoiled**, untouched, primeval, original, virgin [➡ IN GOOD REPAIR; 1232] *Opposite*: developed

privacy 1 *n* **solitude**, time alone, space, seclusion, isolation, retreat [➡ SOLITARINESS; 941] *Opposite*: company 2 *n* **confidentiality**, discretion, secrecy, concealment [➡ SECRET AND UNKNOWN; 179] *Opposite*: disclosure

private 1 *adj* **confidential**, secret, concealed, undisclosed, classified, clandestine, personal, hush-hush (*informal*) [➡ SECRET AND UNKNOWN; 179] *Opposite*: public 2 *adj* **secluded**, set apart, isolated, remote, cloistered, sequestered (*formal*) [➡ DISTANCE; 160] 3 *adj* **privileged**, restricted, not in the public domain, exclusive, reserved [➡ BELONGING OR RELATING TO INDIVIDUALS; 944] *Opposite*: public 4 *adj* **reserved**, secretive, reticent, tight-lipped, self-contained, unrevealing [➡ RETICENT AND UNFORTHCOMING; 631] *Opposite*: forthcoming

private banking *n* [➡ ACCOUNTING, BANKING, AND BUDGETING; 799]

private detective *n* **private investigator**, PI, private eye (*informal*), gumshoe (*dated informal*), dick (*dated slang*) [➡ THE POLICE, ARREST, AND PRETRIAL PROCEEDINGS; 818]

private economy *type of* **economic system** [➡ FINANCE AND ECONOMICS; 796]

private eye (*informal*) *n* **private detective**, private investigator, PI, gumshoe (*dated informal*), dick (*dated slang*) [➡ THE POLICE, ARREST, AND PRETRIAL PROCEEDINGS; 818]

private investigator *n* **private detective**, operative, PI, private eye (*informal*), gumshoe (*dated informal*), dick (*dated slang*) [➡ THE POLICE, ARREST, AND PRETRIAL PROCEEDINGS; 818]

private joke *n* [➡ JOKES AND TEASING; 674]

privately *adv* **confidentially**, in confidence, in private, secretly, in secret, behind closed doors, surreptitiously, on the sly [➡ SECRET AND UNKNOWN; 179] *Opposite*: publicly

private residence *n* [➡ ACCOMMODATIONS; 855]

private school *type of* **school** [➡ EDUCATIONAL INSTITUTIONS; 813]

privation *n* **hardship**, deprivation, adversity, poverty, need, misery [➡ POVERTY AND POOR; 892]

privatization *n* **sale**, transfer, denationalization [➡ BUSINESS ACTIVITIES AND PHENOMENA; 794]

privatize *v* **sell**, transfer, denationalize, go public [➡ BUSINESS ACTIVITIES AND PHENOMENA; 794] *Opposite*: nationalize

privet *type of* **shrub or bush** [➡ BUSHES AND SHRUBS; 1027]

privilege 1 *n* **freedom**, license, opportunity, dispensation, advantage, benefit, concession, right [➡ FREEDOM AND LIBERTY; 208] 2 *n* **honor**, source of pride, treat, pleasure, joy [➡ TREATS; 210] 3 *v* **favor**, show partiality toward, benefit [➡ LIKE, LOVE, VALUE, AND ENJOY; 578]

privileged 1 *adj* **advantaged**, lucky, fortunate, honored [➡ WEALTH AND WEALTHY; 891] *Opposite*: disadvantaged 2 *adj* **confidential**, private, restricted, controlled, limited, top secret [➡ SECRET AND UNKNOWN; 179] *Opposite*: public

privy 1 *adj* **in the know**, sharing in, aware of, party to, partaking of, in on [➡ KNOWLEDGE AND WISDOM; 558] 2 *n* (*informal*) **outside toilet**, outhouse, outside lavatory, latrine, toilet, lavatory, outside loo (*UK*), garderobe (*UK*) [➡ ANCILLARY BUILDINGS; 1080]

prize 1 *n* **award**, reward, trophy, medal, accolade, honor [➡ REWARDS AND AWARDS; 439] 2 *v* **lever**, open, work loose, work free, force, pry, jimmy [➡ UNFASTEN AND UNDO; 409] **3** v **extract**, drag out, pry out of, wheedle, coax, cajole, force, bully, squeeze [➡ OBTAIN POSSESSION BY PERSUASION; 457] **4** v **treasure**, cherish, value, respect, esteem, appreciate, hold dear [➡ LIKE, LOVE, VALUE, AND ENJOY; 578]

prized adj **award-winning**, high-quality, valued, respected, esteemed, appreciated, cherished [➡ POPULAR AND WANTED; 220]

prize open v [➡ UNFASTEN AND UNDO; 409]

prizewinning adj **award-winning**, victorious, successful, triumphant, winning, number-one, champion [➡ SUCCESSFUL AND PROMISING; 81] Opposite: unsuccessful

pro 1 prep **for**, in favor of, all for, in support of [➡ EXPRESSING RESPECT AND APPROVAL; 637] Opposite: against **2** n **professional**, authority, maven, expert, specialist, ace (informal) [➡ TALENTED OR INTELLIGENT PEOPLE; 528] Opposite: amateur

proactive adj **practical**, taking the initiative, hands-on, active, down to business, positive, preemptive, upbeat (informal) [➡ ENERGY AND ENTHUSIASM; 496] Opposite: passive

probability n **likelihood**, prospect, odds, possibility, chance [➡ POSSIBLE AND PROBABLE; 177]

probable adj **likely**, credible, possible, feasible, plausible, apparent [➡ POSSIBLE AND PROBABLE; 177] Opposite: unlikely

probate n **certification**, validation, confirmation, validity [➡ THE LAW AND LEGAL AUTHORITY; 814]

probation n **trial**, test, audition, experimentation, tryout [➡ PREPARATORY EVENTS; 57]

probationary adj **provisional**, trial, test, experimental, sample, introductory, exploratory [➡ EMPLOYMENT STATUS; 831] Opposite: permanent

probe 1 n **investigation**, inquiry, review, examination, analysis, postmortem [➡ EXAMINE AND ASSESS; 753] **2** type of **medical instrument** [➡ HAND TOOLS; 1119] **3** v **investigate**, research, delve, inquire, look into, explore, examine, study [➡ EXAMINE AND ASSESS; 753]

probing adj **searching**, penetrating, analytical, inquisitive, curious, investigative, exploratory, examining, interested, pointed, thorough, researching, incisive, inquiring [➡ EXAMINE AND ASSESS; 753] Opposite: cursory

probity n **correctness**, scrupulousness, rectitude, righteousness, integrity, justice, morality, honor [➡ MORALLY GOOD; 774] Opposite: immorality

problem 1 n **difficulty**, setback, hitch, drawback, glitch, hindrance, obstruction, snag, obstacle, catch (informal) [➡ PROBLEMS; 256] **2** n **puzzle**, question, conundrum, challenge, poser, mystery, enigma, riddle [➡ SECRETS AND MYSTERIES; 180] **3** adj **problematic**, tricky, unruly, badly-behaved, delinquent, difficult [➡ REBELLIOUSNESS AND DISOBEDIENCE; 565]

Compare and Contrast: problem, mystery, puzzle, riddle, conundrum, enigma

CORE MEANING: something difficult to solve or understand

problem a difficult situation, matter, or person; **mystery** an event or situation that has never been fully explained or understood, or a person who is puzzling or mysterious; **puzzle** a problem whose solution requires ingenuity, or a situation that it is difficult to resolve, or somebody whose behavior or motives are difficult to understand; **riddle** a perplexing or confusing issue; **conundrum** something puzzling, confusing, or mysterious; **enigma** somebody or something that is mysterious and hard to understand.

problematic adj **tricky**, challenging, sticky, awkward, knotty, problematical, difficult [➡ DIFFICULTY AND COMPLEXITY; 242] Opposite: easy

problematical see **problematic**

problematically adv **not without difficulty**, awkwardly, trickily, challengingly, ticklishly, knottily [➡ DIFFICULTY AND COMPLEXITY; 242] Opposite: easily

pro bono adj [➡ FOREIGN WORDS AND PHRASES; 672]

proboscis n **nose**, snout, feeler, trunk, antenna [➡ PARTS OF AN INSECT; 1019]

proboscis monkey type of **primate** [➡ PRIMATES; 988]

procedural adj **technical**, practical, bureaucratic, routine, ritual, ceremonial [➡ ORDER AND ORGANIZATION; 206]

procedure n **process**, modus operandi, way, technique, method, course of action, system, formula, route, practice [➡ WAYS OF DOING THINGS; 294]

proceed v **go on**, carry on, continue, ensue, advance, keep, keep on, progress [➡ PROCEED AND GO; 305] Opposite: recede

proceedings 1 n **events**, actions, measures, trial, procedures, dealings [➡ EVENTS AND OCCURRENCES; 35] **2** n **minutes**, record, account, report, chronicle [➡ RECORDS; 585]

proceeds n **profits**, income, earnings, gate, box office, takings [➡ INCOME; 460]

process 1 n **procedure**, course, activity, development, progression, method, route, course of action, manner, means [➡ WAYS OF DOING THINGS; 294] **2** v **deal with**, handle, treat, sort out, administer, see to, manage [➡ CARRY OUT AN ACTION; 269]

processed adj [➡ NOT IN A NATURAL STATE; 1215]

procession 1 n **march**, parade, pageant, demonstration, march past, convoy, motorcade, demo (informal) [➡ MEETINGS AND ASSEMBLIES; 43] **2** n **sequence**, succession, string, series, line, chain, row [➡ COLLECTIONS AND MIXTURES OF THINGS; 1244]

processional adj **ceremonial**, ritual, commemorative, celebratory, sacred, formal, regimented [➡ CEREMONIES AND ANNIVERSARIES; 38]

processor type of **hardware** [➡ COMPUTERS AND COMPUTING; 1127]

proclaim v **state publicly**, announce, declare, state, make known, decree, assert, pronounce, broadcast [➡ INFORM, ANNOUNCE, AND ISSUE; 611]

proclamation n **public statement**, announcement, declaration, decree, assertion, edict [➡ INFORM, ANNOUNCE, AND ISSUE; 611]

proclivity *n* **liking**, appetite, taste, penchant, inclination, tendency, bent [➡ APPRECIATION AND GRATITUDE; 535]

procrastinate *v* **put off**, delay, postpone, adjourn, dally, drag your feet, hang fire, defer, dawdle, take a raincheck (*informal*) [➡ SHIRK AND DELAY; 273]

procrastination *n* **deferment**, putting off, postponement, stalling, delay, adjournment [➡ DELAY ACTION OR OCCURRENCE; 278] *Opposite*: action

procreate *v* [➡ REPRODUCTION AND HEREDITY; 725]

procreation *n* [➡ REPRODUCTION AND HEREDITY; 725]

procreative *adj* [➡ REPRODUCTION AND HEREDITY; 725]

procurable *adj* [➡ PRESENT AND AVAILABLE; 11]

procure *v* **obtain**, acquire, secure, get hold of, get, land, buy, gain, attain, pick up [➡ GET; 420]

See Compare and Contrast at **get**.

procurement 1 *n* **gaining**, obtaining, finding, locating, tracking down, winning, earning, attaining [➡ FIND; 463] *Opposite*: giving up 2 *n* **buying**, purchasing, ordering, obtaining [➡ BUSINESS ACTIVITIES AND PHENOMENA; 794] *Opposite*: selling

procurer *n* **buyer**, purchaser, customer, client, consumer [➡ PURCHASER; 424]

prod 1 *v* **elbow**, nudge, dig, jab, push, poke [➡ CONTACT: TOUCH; 412] 2 *v* **urge**, stimulate, stir, prompt, provoke, egg on [➡ CAUSE OR COMPEL TO ACT; 271] 3 *n* **nudge**, elbow, dig, jab, push, poke [➡ CONTACT: TOUCH; 412]

prodigal *adj* **wasteful**, reckless, dissolute, profligate, uncontrolled, extravagant [➡ PLEASURE-SEEKING AND EXCESS; 885] *Opposite*: cautious

prodigality *n* [➡ PLEASURE-SEEKING AND EXCESS; 885]

prodigal son *n* [➡ PEOPLE WHO ARE APPROVED OF; 955]

prodigious 1 *adj* **huge**, vast, copious, giant, gigantic, immense, enormous, profuse, massive [➡ LARGE; 1193] *Opposite*: small 2 *adj* **abnormal**, extraordinary, phenomenal, unusual, exceptional, remarkable, wonderful, amazing, impressive [➡ EXTRAORDINARY: AMAZING; 204] *Opposite*: average

prodigiously 1 *adv* **enormously**, hugely, immensely, tremendously, colossally, inordinately, vastly, stupendously, massively (*informal*) [➡ TO A GREAT EXTENT; 132] *Opposite*: minutely 2 *adv* **amazingly**, exceptionally, extraordinarily, remarkably, fabulously, fantastically, phenomenally, strikingly, marvelously [➡ EXTRAORDINARY: AMAZING; 204] *Opposite*: ordinarily

prodigiousness 1 *n* **hugeness**, enormousness, vastness, massiveness, immenseness, immensity, tremendousness [➡ LARGE; 1193] *Opposite*: smallness 2 *n* **stupendousness**, remarkableness, amazingness, exceptional nature, fabulousness, marvelousness [➡ EXTRAORDINARY: AMAZING; 204] *Opposite*: ordinariness

prodigy *n* **genius**, sensation, phenomenon, wonder, star, wunderkind, child prodigy [➡ TALENTED OR INTELLIGENT PEOPLE; 528]

produce 1 *v* **create**, make, manufacture, construct, fabricate, bring into being, turn out, generate [➡ CREATION; 346] 2 *v* **give**, give off, yield, churn out, be the source of, engender, emit, supply, deliver [➡ EMIT AND EMANATE; 361] 3 *n* **crop**, foodstuffs, harvest, products, goods, food, yield [➡ FOOD; 1167]

See Compare and Contrast at **make**.

producer *n* **creator**, manufacturer, maker, fabricator [➡ DESIGNERS, CREATORS, AND INSTIGATORS; 347]

product 1 *n* **manufactured article**, creation, produce, item for consumption, invention, merchandise, artifact [➡ PHYSICAL OBJECTS; 1243] 2 *n* **result**, outcome, upshot, consequence, effect [➡ RESULTS AND OUTCOMES; 83]

production *n* **manufacture**, making, construction, creation, invention, fabrication, assembly [➡ CREATION; 346]

productive 1 *adj* **creative**, prolific, fecund, industrious, fruitful, dynamic [➡ ECONOMICAL AND RESOURCEFUL; 207] *Opposite*: destructive 2 *adj* **useful**, helpful, constructive, beneficial, valuable, practical, positive [➡ USEFULNESS; 199] *Opposite*: negative

productiveness *n* **usefulness**, constructiveness, use, utility, fruitfulness, productivity [➡ USEFULNESS; 199]

productivity *n* **output**, efficiency, yield, production, throughput [➡ BUSINESS PRODUCTS; 795]

profanation (*formal*) *n* [➡ MORALLY BAD OR IMPROPER; 775]

profane (*formal*) *adj* **irreverent**, blasphemous, irreligious, disrespectful, wicked, sacrilegious [➡ MORALLY BAD OR IMPROPER; 775] *Opposite*: sacred

profanely (*formal*) *adv* [➡ MORALLY BAD OR IMPROPER; 775]

profaner *n* [➡ RELIGIOUS CONCEPTS; 776]

profanity *n* **blasphemy**, oath, vulgarity, curse, swearword, expletive, sacrilege [➡ INSULTS, ABUSE, AND SWEARING; 658]

profess *v* **admit**, own up, confess, acknowledge, agree, recognize, own (*formal*), allow (*formal*) [➡ ADMIT AND CONFESS; 615]

professed 1 *adj* **declared**, acknowledged, open, stated, blatant, avowed (*formal*) [➡ KNOWN AND FAMOUS; 181] *Opposite*: unspoken 2 *adj* **supposed**, alleged, so-called, ostensible, seeming, apparent, ersatz, soi-disant (*literary*) [➡ UNCERTAIN; 175] *Opposite*: proven

profession *n* **job**, work, occupation, line of work, career, vocation, business, living [➡ PROFESSIONS; 845]

professional 1 *adj* **specialized**, qualified, proficient, skilled, trained, certified, practiced, licensed, expert, career [➡ EMPLOYMENT STATUS; 831] *Opposite*: amateur 2 *n* [➡ WORKERS; 836] 3 *n* **specialist**, expert, authority, pro, maven [➡ TALENTED OR INTELLIGENT PEOPLE; 528] *Opposite*: amateur

professionalism *n* **skill**, competence, expertise, proficiency, efficiency, experience, effectiveness, ability, know-how (*informal*) [➡ SKILLS, TALENTS, AND ABILITIES; 526] *Opposite*: incompetence

professor *n* **university teacher**, lecturer, tutor, instructor, dean, fellow (*UK*), don (*UK*) [➡ EDUCATORS; 840]

professorial *adj* **academic**, pedagogical, intellectual, educational, senior [➡ EDUCATION; 838]

proffer *v* **offer**, hold out, extend, tender, volunteer, submit, give [➡ PROFFER AND HAND OVER; 431] *Opposite*: withdraw

proficiency *n* **skill**, ability, talent, expertise, aptitude, knack, adeptness, competence, know-how (*informal*) [➡ SKILLS, TALENTS, AND ABILITIES; 526] *Opposite*: incompetence

proficient *adj* **capable**, talented, expert, gifted, adroit, skilled, dexterous, competent, adept, skillful, practiced [➡ TALENTED AND SKILLFUL; 527] *Opposite*: incompetent

profile 1 *n* **outline**, side view, shape, silhouette, contour [➡ SHAPE; 1216] 2 *n* **summary**, sketch, outline, report, précis, rundown, synopsis [➡ SUMMARIES, OUTLINES, AND EXCERPTS; 588] 3 *v* **summarize**, sketch, outline, report, sum up, describe [➡ NAME AND DESCRIBE; 665]

profit 1 *n* **income**, earnings, revenue, proceeds, turnover, return, yield, takings [➡ INCOME; 460] *Opposite*: loss 2 *n* **advantage**, gain, benefit, use, reward, good [➡ REWARDS AND AWARDS; 439] *Opposite*: loss 3 *v* **earn**, bring in, make, make money on, turn a profit [➡ GET MONEY OR REWARD; 421] *Opposite*: lose 4 *v* **benefit**, gain, be of advantage to, help, aid, serve [➡ IMPROVE SOMETHING; 374]

profitability 1 *n* **success**, effectiveness, productivity, viability, cost-effectiveness, lucrativeness [➡ ECONOMICAL AND RESOURCEFUL; 207] 2 *n* **usefulness**, worth, fruitfulness, use, value, point [➡ USEFULNESS; 199] *Opposite*: uselessness

profitable 1 *adj* **lucrative**, moneymaking, gainful, commercial, cost-effective, successful [➡ ECONOMICAL AND RESOURCEFUL; 207] *Opposite*: unprofitable 2 *adj* **advantageous**, beneficial, rewarding, useful, valuable, worthwhile, helpful [➡ USEFULNESS; 199] *Opposite*: unhelpful

profit and loss *n* [➡ ACCOUNTING, BANKING, AND BUDGETING; 799]

profiteer 1 *v* **exploit**, take advantage of, make use of, racketeer, abuse [➡ MISUSE AND ABUSE; 471] 2 *n* **swindler**, racketeer, embezzler, crook (*informal*), con man (*slang*), con artist (*slang*), scammer (*slang*) [➡ PEOPLE WHO DECEIVE; 661]

profiteroles *type of* **dessert** [➡ CAKES, COOKIES, AND DESSERTS; 1181]

profitmaking *adj* **profitable**, viable, moneymaking, economic, cost-effective, lucrative, commercial, going, prosperous [➡ ECONOMICAL AND RESOURCEFUL; 207] *Opposite*: draining

profit margin *n* [➡ ACCOUNTING, BANKING, AND BUDGETING; 799]

profligacy *n* **wastefulness**, recklessness, dissolution, decadence, extravagance, licentiousness (*formal*) [➡ WASTEFUL AND UNECONOMICAL; 246] *Opposite*: parsimony

profligate 1 *adj* **wasteful**, reckless, spendthrift, squandering, decadent, extravagant [➡ WASTEFUL AND UNECONOMICAL; 246] *Opposite*: parsimonious 2 *adj* **dissolute**, licentious, immoral, wicked, shameless [➡ MORALLY BAD OR IMPROPER; 775]

pro forma *n* [➡ FOREIGN WORDS AND PHRASES; 672]

profound 1 *adj* **deep**, thoughtful, reflective, philosophical, weighty, insightful [➡ THE NATURE OF IDEAS; 771] *Opposite*: superficial 2 *adj* **intense**, great, overpowering, overwhelming, extreme, acute, sincere [➡ STRENGTH; 201] *Opposite*: shallow

profoundly *adv* **intensely**, greatly, overpoweringly, overwhelmingly, extremely, strongly, very much, severely [➡ TO A GREAT EXTENT; 132] *Opposite*: superficially

profoundness 1 *n* **degree**, extent, intensity, strength, depth, completeness, acuteness, profundity [➡ STRENGTH; 201] 2 *n* **perceptiveness**, wisdom, acuity, insight, depth, weight, perspicacity, profundity [➡ THE NATURE OF IDEAS; 771] 3 *n* **depth**, immensity, cavernousness, fathomlessness, extent, reach, profundity [➡ DEPTH: DEEP; 1201]

profundity 1 *n* **understanding**, perceptiveness, wisdom, acuity, perspicacity, profoundness, insight, insightfulness, depth [➡ THE NATURE OF IDEAS; 771] *Opposite*: superficiality 2 *n* **complexity**, abstruseness, difficulty, depth, intricacy [➡ DIFFICULTY AND COMPLEXITY; 242] *Opposite*: simplicity 3 *n* **intensity**, greatness, strength, seriousness, enormity, extensiveness, extent [➡ STRENGTH; 201] *Opposite*: mildness 4 *n* **depth**, immensity, cavernousness, fathomlessness, extent, reach [➡ DEPTH: DEEP; 1201]

profuse *adj* **plentiful**, copious, abundant, teeming, generous, prolific, bountiful (*literary*) [➡ MANY, MUCH, LARGE AMOUNT; 117] *Opposite*: scanty

profusion *n* **abundance**, large amount, excess, cornucopia, plethora, glut, surplus, wealth [➡ MANY, MUCH, LARGE AMOUNT; 117] *Opposite*: dearth

progenitor 1 *n* **ancestor**, forerunner, forebear, antecedent, predecessor, precursor [➡ OLDER GENERATION RELATIVES; 959] *Opposite*: descendant 2 *n* **antecedent**, originator, forerunner, prototype, predecessor, precursor [➡ BEFORE, FIRST, AND PRECEDING; 163] *Opposite*: copy

progeny *n* **offspring**, children, young, descendants, issue, scions, posterity (*formal*) [➡ YOUNGER GENERATION RELATIVES; 958]

prognosis *n* **forecast**, prediction, projection, scenario, diagnosis, prospects [➡ PREDICT AND ANTICIPATE; 750]

prognosticate 1 *v* **predict**, divine, foresee, foretell, forecast, prophesy, soothsay, portend [➡ PREDICT AND ANTICIPATE; 750] *Opposite*: recall 2 *v* **indicate**, suggest, point to, augur, signify, herald, portend, presage, betoken (*literary*) [➡ MEAN SOMETHING; 61] *Opposite*: prove

prognostication 1 *n* **prediction**, prognosis, projection, divination, foreseeing, foretelling, forecast, prophecy, soothsaying [➡ PREDICT AND ANTICIPATE; 750] *Opposite*: recollection 2 *n* **indication**, suggestion, pointer, token, portent, augury, foretoken (*literary*) [➡ INDICATIONS, SIGNS, AND WARNINGS; 68] *Opposite*: proof

prognosticator *n* **predictor**, diviner, prophet, seer, clairvoyant, psychic, forecaster, haruspex, soothsayer [➡ PEOPLE WITH SUPERNATURAL POWERS; 788]

program 1 *n* **plan**, agenda, schedule, timetable, list, curriculum, syllabus, rubric, calendar, docket [➡ LISTS AND SCHEDULES; 587] 2 *n* **broadcast**, presentation, production, performance, show, game show, talk show, quiz show [➡ TELEVISION AND RADIO; 606] 3 *n* **brochure**, booklet, pamphlet, listing, synopsis, timetable, itinerary [➡ LISTS AND SCHEDULES; 587] 4 *n* **system**, procedure, course, series, setup [➡ WAYS OF DOING THINGS; 294] 5 *type of* **software** [➡ COMPUTERS AND COMPUTING; 1127]

6 *n* **setting**, option, cycle, mode, instruction, set of instructions [➡ COMPUTERS AND COMPUTING; 1127] **7** *v* **schedule**, arrange, book, plan, line up, lay on, design, map out [➡ ARRANGE AND CREATE ORDER; 357] **8** *v* **train**, condition, compel, brainwash, hypnotize, manipulate, order [➡ CAUSE TO HAPPEN; 31] **9** *v* **write instructions**, load instructions, write software, load software, set, adjust, calibrate [➡ COMPUTERS AND COMPUTING; 1127]

programmed *adj* **automatic**, involuntary, planned, automated, set, preset [➡ INTENTIONAL AND DELIBERATE; 279] *Opposite:* spontaneous

programmer *n* **computer operator**, computer programmer, computer scientist, program writer, systems analyst, IT worker, techie (*informal*) [➡ COMPUTERS AND COMPUTING; 1127]

programming *n* **software design**, program design, program writing, user interface design, software development [➡ COMPUTERS AND COMPUTING; 1127]

progress **1** *n* **development**, improvement, advancement, evolution, growth, headway, steps forward, movement, advances, evolvement [➡ PROGRESS AND ADVANCEMENT; 213] *Opposite:* regression **2** *v* **improve**, develop, advance, evolve, increase, grow, move on, get better, make progress, make headway [➡ GET BETTER; 375] *Opposite:* regress **3** *v* **move forward**, advance, proceed, continue, make progress, move on, march, forge ahead [➡ PROCEED AND GO; 305] *Opposite:* retreat

progression **1** *n* **development**, evolution, movement, advance, advancement, progress, headway [➡ PROGRESS AND ADVANCEMENT; 213] *Opposite:* regression **2** *n* **series**, sequence, succession, string, chain, cycle, sequel, train [➡ CHAIN OF EVENTS; 162]

progressive **1** *adj* **liberal**, reformist, open-minded, broad-minded, radical, enlightened, advanced, tolerant [➡ POSITIVE INTELLECTUAL CHARACTERISTICS; 524] *Opposite:* reactionary **2** *adj* **gradual**, ongoing, increasing, continuing, developing, advancing, step-by-step [➡ HAPPENING AND IN PROGRESS; 32] *Opposite:* acute

progressively *adv* **increasingly**, more and more, with time, gradually, little by little, ever more [➡ HAPPENING AND IN PROGRESS; 32] *Opposite:* suddenly

progressiveness *n* **liberalism**, reformism, progressivism, modernism, tolerance, open-mindedness, permissiveness, broad-mindedness, enlightenment, radicalism [➡ POSITIVE INTELLECTUAL CHARACTERISTICS; 524]

progressivism *n* **liberalism**, reformism, modernism, radicalism, leftism [➡ PHILOSOPHIES AND BELIEFS; 780]

prohibit *v* **forbid**, ban, proscribe, disallow, veto, outlaw, bar, exclude, rule out, interdict [➡ REFUSE PERMISSION AND NOT ALLOW; 670] *Opposite:* permit

prohibited *adj* **forbidden**, banned, verboten, illegal, proscribed, taboo, outlawed, illicit, barred [➡ ILLEGAL; 816] *Opposite:* permitted

prohibition *n* **ban**, exclusion, embargo, prevention, ruling out, veto, injunction, bar, proscription (*formal*) [➡ REFUSE PERMISSION AND NOT ALLOW; 670] *Opposite:* permission

prohibitive *adj* **high-priced**, excessive, exorbitant, extortionate, unaffordable, unreasonable, expensive [➡ EXPENSIVE AND OVERPRICED; 247] *Opposite:* affordable

project **1** *n* **assignment**, task, undertaking, job, plan, blueprint, design, scheme, strategy [➡ ACTIONS OR UNDERTAKINGS; 259] **2** *v* **forecast**, predict, estimate, foresee, foretell, envisage, envision [➡ PREDICT AND ANTICIPATE; 750] **3** *v* **stick out**, jut out, protrude, bulge, distend [➡ EXIST IN A PLACE; 19] **4** *v* **throw**, launch, shoot, propel, cast, impel, send off, fling, hurl, pitch [➡ MOVE SOMETHING THROUGH THE AIR; 334] **5** *v* **plan**, envisage, propose, intend, anticipate, expect, plan ahead [➡ PREDICT AND ANTICIPATE; 750]

projected *adj* **estimated**, planned, proposed, outlined, expected, anticipated, future [➡ FUTURE; 86] *Opposite:* actual

projectile *n* [➡ WEAPONS; 1154]

projectile

◆ *types of projectiles*
arrow, arrowhead, assegai, bolt, boomerang, brickbat, buckshot, bullet, cannonball, dart, dumdum bullet, grenade, harpoon, javelin, lance, pellet, plastic bullet, rubber bullet, shell, shot, slug, spear

projection **1** *n* **forecast**, prediction, plan, prognosis, estimate, prognostication [➡ PREDICT AND ANTICIPATE; 750] *Opposite:* outcome **2** *n* **outcrop**, protuberance, bulge, protrusion, ledge, shelf, ridge, jut, overhang [➡ EXTREMITIES OF PHYSICAL OBJECTS; 1250]

projector *type of* **photographic equipment** [➡ PHOTOGRAPHY AND PHOTOGRAPHIC EQUIPMENT; 1122]

prole (*slang*) *n* [➡ CLASS STATUS; 889]

proletarian *adj* **popular**, grassroots, people's, working-class, blue-collar, plebeian, democratic [➡ CLASS STATUS; 889] *Opposite:* aristocratic

proletariat *n* **hoi polloi**, rank and file, grassroots, working class, workers, masses, blue-collars, public [➡ CLASS STATUS; 889] *Opposite:* gentry

proliferate **1** *v* **multiply**, thrive, flourish, boom, increase, bloom, grow, mushroom, burgeon (*literary*) [➡ PROSPER AND ABOUND; 16] *Opposite:* dwindle **2** *v* **reproduce**, propagate, multiply, breed, procreate, beget, replicate [➡ REPRODUCTION AND HEREDITY; 725] *Opposite:* die out

proliferation *n* **propagation**, explosion, spread, multiplying, production, creation, increase, rise [➡ MORE AND EXCESS; 124]

prolific **1** *adj* **productive**, creative, fertile, inexhaustible, high-volume, fruitful [➡ SUCCESSFUL AND PROMISING; 81] *Opposite:* unproductive **2** *adj* **abundant**, abounding, plentiful, copious, profuse, teeming, fruitful, rich, bountiful (*literary*) [➡ MANY, MUCH, LARGE AMOUNT; 117] *Opposite:* scarce

prolix *adj* **wordy**, verbose, long-winded, flowery, protracted, rambling, diffuse [➡ INARTICULATE, RAMBLING, AND AWKWARD; 633] *Opposite:* concise

See Compare and Contrast at **wordy**.

prolixity *n* [➡ INARTICULATE, RAMBLING, AND AWKWARD; 633]

prologue *n* **introduction**, preface, foreword, preamble, opening, prelude [➡ BEGINNINGS; 53] *Opposite:* epilogue

prolong *v* **extend**, lengthen, protract, draw out, spin out, delay, stretch, elongate, persist [➡ CAUSE TO CONTINUE; 267] *Opposite*: curtail

prolongation *n* **continuation**, perpetuation, drawing out, protraction, extension, maintenance, elongation [➡ PERMANENCE: WITHOUT END; 94] *Opposite*: curtailment

prolonged *adj* **lengthy**, protracted, long, continued, extended, sustained, elongated, persistent [➡ PERMANENCE: WITHOUT END; 94] *Opposite*: curtailed

prom 1 *n* **dance**, college dance, high-school dance, formal dance, ball [➡ PARTIES, DANCES, AND CELEBRATIONS; 37] **2** *n* (*UK informal*) **walkway**, path, esplanade, boardwalk, promenade [➡ PATHWAYS; 1110]

promenade 1 *n* **walkway**, path, boardwalk, esplanade, prom (*UK*) [➡ PATHWAYS; 1110] **2** *n* (*formal*) **stroll**, walk, saunter, amble, constitutional [➡ PROCEED AND GO; 305] **3** *v* (*formal*) **walk**, stroll, amble, saunter, wander, roam, drift, mosey (*informal*) [➡ PROCEED AND GO; 305]

prominence 1 *n* **fame**, importance, distinction, celebrity, eminence, reputation, standing, status, notoriety [➡ KNOWN AND FAMOUS; 181] *Opposite*: obscurity **2** *n* **bump**, lump, bulge, swelling, protrusion, protuberance, projection [➡ ROUNDED SHAPE; 1218] *Opposite*: crater

prominent 1 *adj* **protuberant**, protruding, projecting, bulbous, bulging [➡ ROUNDED SHAPE; 1218] *Opposite*: flat **2** *adj* **noticeable**, conspicuous, obvious, blatant, flagrant, pronounced, glaring [➡ PERCEPTIBLE; 25] *Opposite*: subtle **3** *adj* **famous**, well-known, important, high-flying, top, major, outstanding, leading, foremost, notorious, renowned [➡ KNOWN AND FAMOUS; 181] *Opposite*: obscure

prominently *adv* **conspicuously**, obviously, blatantly, flagrantly, glaringly [➡ PERCEPTIBLE; 25] *Opposite*: subtly

promiscuous *adj* **immoral**, loose, licentious, wanton, uninhibited, unrestrained, philandering [➡ MORALLY BAD OR IMPROPER; 775]

promise 1 *v* **assure**, swear, vow, undertake, guarantee, give your word, pledge, confirm, engage, ensure [➡ PROMISE AND ASSURE; 684] **2** *v* **suggest**, augur, bode, look like, show all the signs, indicate, imply, insinuate, hint at, forebode, foreshadow [➡ MEAN SOMETHING; 61] **3** *n* **assurance**, undertaking, guarantee, agreement, contract, word, oath, pledge, vow [➡ PROMISE AND ASSURE; 684] **4** *n* **potential**, possibilities, aptitude, ability, capacity, talent [➡ SKILLS, TALENTS, AND ABILITIES; 526]

promised land *n* [➡ RELIGIOUS CONCEPTS; 776]

promising 1 *adj* **talented**, gifted, capable, able [➡ TALENTED AND SKILLFUL; 527] **2** *adj* **auspicious**, hopeful, likely, encouraging, favorable [➡ SUCCESSFUL AND PROMISING; 81] *Opposite*: disappointing

promisingly *adv* **favorably**, auspiciously, hopefully, well, nicely, encouragingly [➡ SUCCESSFUL AND PROMISING; 81] *Opposite*: disappointingly

promo (*informal*) *n* **promotion**, advertisement, publicity stunt, publicity, profile-raiser, photo-shoot, photo op, sound bite, hook (*informal*) [➡ ADVERTISING AND PUBLICITY; 604]

promontory *n* **cape**, headland, peninsula, outcrop, point, cliff [➡ THE SEAS, OCEANS, AND SHORES; 1041]

promote 1 *v* **advance**, upgrade, further, elevate, put forward, raise [➡ CONFER STATUS; 458] *Opposite*: demote **2** *v* **endorse**, encourage, help, support, stimulate, sponsor, campaign for, uphold, prop up, foster [➡ APPROVE AND CONFIRM; 646] *Opposite*: suppress **3** *v* **advertise**, publicize, make known, market, tout, push, disseminate, advocate, boost, propagandize, plug (*informal*) [➡ ADVERTISING AND PUBLICITY; 604] *Opposite*: defame **4** *v* **further**, progress, move forward, stage, put on, organize, arrange [➡ CAUSE TO HAPPEN; 31] *Opposite*: prevent

promoter *n* **organizer**, agent, sponsor, advocate, supporter, publicist, marketer, developer, backer, PR man, PR woman, flack (*slang*) [➡ SUPPORTERS, PROTECTORS, AND COMPATRIOTS; 970]

promotion 1 *n* **upgrade**, raise, advancement, elevation, preferment (*formal*) [➡ CONFER STATUS; 458] *Opposite*: demotion **2** *n* **advertising**, marketing, publicity, publicity campaign, public relations, hype [➡ ADVERTISING AND PUBLICITY; 604] **3** *n* **endorsement**, encouragement, help, support, stimulation, sponsorship, backup, backing [➡ APPROVE AND CONFIRM; 646] **4** *n* **offer**, special promotion, deal, loss leader, plug (*informal*) [➡ ADVERTISING AND PUBLICITY; 604]

promotional *adj* **publicity**, advertising, public relations, P.R., positive, profile-raising, persuasive, marketing [➡ ADVERTISING AND PUBLICITY; 604]

prompt 1 *adj* **punctual**, on time, at the appointed time, without delay, timely [➡ PROMPTNESS: ON TIME; 99] *Opposite*: late **2** *adj* **quick**, rapid, swift, without delay, speedy, hasty, early, ready, apt [➡ HAPPENING QUICKLY; 104] *Opposite*: slow **3** *v* **stimulate**, encourage, provoke, incite, urge, inspire, pressure, motivate, exhort, prod, pressurize (*UK*) [➡ CAUSE OR COMPEL TO ACT; 271] *Opposite*: prevent **4** *v* **bring about**, induce, occasion, set off, trigger, start off, prevail, persuade, effect (*formal*) [➡ CAUSE TO HAPPEN; 31] *Opposite*: prevent **5** *n* **stimulus**, prod, goad, reminder, heads-up, aide-mémoire (*formal*) [➡ BEGINNINGS; 53]

prompting *n* **encouragement**, warning, pressure, motivation, instigation [➡ BEGINNINGS; 53]

promptness 1 *n* **speed**, rapidity, swiftness, alacrity, velocity, pace, haste, celerity (*literary*) [➡ SPEED; 102] *Opposite*: slowness **2** *n* **punctuality**, timeliness, timekeeping [➡ PROMPTNESS: ON TIME; 99] *Opposite*: tardiness

promulgate (*formal*) 1 *v* **publicize**, spread, disseminate, circulate, transmit, broadcast, propagate [➡ INFORM, ANNOUNCE, AND ISSUE; 611] *Opposite*: suppress **2** *v* **declare**, proclaim, decree, announce, pronounce, endorse, state [➡ INFORM, ANNOUNCE, AND ISSUE; 611] *Opposite*: withdraw

promulgation (*formal*) 1 *n* **declaration**, proclamation, decree, announcement, pronouncement, statement, endorsement [➡ INFORM, ANNOUNCE, AND ISSUE; 611] *Opposite*: withdrawal **2** *n* **publicizing**, spreading, dissemination, circulation, broadcasting, transmission, propagation [➡ INFORM, ANNOUNCE, AND ISSUE; 611] *Opposite*: suppression

prone 1 *adj* **disposed to**, predisposed to, susceptible to, inclined to, likely to, liable to [➡ THE WILL AND WILLINGNESS; 563] **2** *adj* **flat**, horizontal, flat out, face down, motionless [➡ ORIENTATION AND ALIGNMENT; 1223] *Opposite*: upright

prong *n* **point**, spike, spine, tine [➡ EXTREMITIES OF PHYSICAL OBJECTS; 1250]

pronoun *type of* **word class** [➡ ASPECTS OF LANGUAGE; 682]

pronounce 1 *v* **say**, speak, utter, articulate, voice, enunciate, phonate [➡ UTTER AND PRONOUNCE; 608] **2** *v* **state**, assert, declare, announce, decree, lay down the law, proclaim, maintain, pontificate [➡ INFORM, ANNOUNCE, AND ISSUE; 611]

pronounced *adj* **marked**, noticeable, distinct, definite, obvious, prominent, evident, unmistakable, manifest [➡ PERCEPTIBLE; 25] *Opposite*: subtle

pronouncement *n* **statement**, assertion, declaration, announcement, decree, verdict, proclamation [➡ INFORM, ANNOUNCE, AND ISSUE; 611]

pronto (*informal*) *adv* **straightaway**, right away, quick, on the double, quickly, at once, promptly, immediately, right now, this instant, rapidly, ASAP [➡ HAPPENING QUICKLY; 104] *Opposite*: sluggishly

pronunciation *n* **articulation**, accent, elocution, intonation, enunciation, diction, phonation [➡ THE SPOKEN WORD; 671]

proof 1 *n* **evidence**, testimony, verification, confirmation, attestation, corroboration, substantiation, testimonial, witness [➡ EVIDENCE AND PROOF; 69] **2** *adj* **resistant**, resilient, impervious, immune [➡ STRENGTH; 201] *Opposite*: vulnerable

proof of identity *n* [➡ EVIDENCE AND PROOF; 69]

proof of ownership *n* [➡ EVIDENCE AND PROOF; 69]

proof of posting *n* [➡ RECEIPTS AND INVOICES; 591]

proof of purchase *n* [➡ RECEIPTS AND INVOICES; 591]

proof positive *n* [➡ EVIDENCE AND PROOF; 69]

proofread *v* **check**, correct, check through, check over, look through, look over, mark up, edit [➡ READ; 758]

proofreader *n* **checker**, reader, editor, copy editor, corrector [➡ WORKERS IN ENTERTAINMENT AND MEDIA; 873]

prop 1 *n* **support**, leg, crutch, buttress, pile, strut, brace, underpinning [➡ SUPPORTS AND BASES; 1255] **2** *v* **hold up**, support, prop up, sustain, buttress, bolster, uphold, buoy, brace [➡ IMPROVE STRENGTH AND DURABILITY; 378] *Opposite*: destabilize

propaganda 1 *n* **publicity**, advertising, marketing, literature, information, hype, buildup, puffery (*informal*), hoopla (*informal*) [➡ ADVERTISING AND PUBLICITY; 604] **2** *n* **misinformation**, disinformation, party line, half truths, cant, indoctrination [➡ DECEPTION AND LIES; 660]

propagandist 1 *n* **publicist**, polemicist, essayist, writer, speaker, orator, satirist [➡ WRITERS AND STYLES; 914] **2** *n* **partisan**, apologist, mouthpiece, sophist, spin doctor (*slang*) [➡ SPEAKERS AND ORATORS; 603] **3** *adj* **slanted**, distorted, one-sided, polemical, partisan, extremist, manipulative [➡ FALSE AND UNREAL; 173]

propagate 1 *v* **breed**, grow, raise, reproduce, proliferate, generate [➡ GROW AND CULTIVATE; 351] **2** *v* **spread**, broadcast, proliferate, circulate, disseminate, transmit, publicize, promulgate (*formal*) [➡ INFORM, ANNOUNCE, AND ISSUE; 611]

propagation 1 *n* **breeding**, reproduction, proliferation, procreation [➡ GROW AND CULTIVATE; 351] **2** *n* **spread**, proliferation, circulation, dissemination, transmission, promulgation (*formal*) [➡ INFORM, ANNOUNCE, AND ISSUE; 611]

propagator 1 *n* **spreader**, broadcaster, transmitter, communicator, diffuser [➡ DESIGNERS, CREATORS, AND INSTIGATORS; 347] **2** *n* **tray**, box, seed tray, cloche, cold frame, pan [➡ CONTAINERS, RECEPTACLES, AND PACKAGING; 1245]

propel *v* **push**, drive, force, boost, thrust, impel [➡ MOVE SOMETHING THROUGH THE AIR; 334]

propellant 1 *type of* **explosive material** [➡ EXPLOSIVES; 1155] **2** *type of* **gas** [➡ GASES; 1275]

propeller *part of* **aircraft** [➡ AIRCRAFT; 1148]

propensity *n* **tendency**, inclination, partiality, bent, proclivity, predisposition, susceptibility, penchant, predilection (*formal*) [➡ TEMPERAMENT AND BEHAVIOR; 492]

proper 1 *adj* **good**, correct, appropriate, suitable, right, apt, apposite, accurate, fitting [➡ APPROPRIATE, SUITABLE, AND ADVISABLE; 184] *Opposite*: wrong **2** *adj* **polite**, modest, decorous, prim, genteel, respectable, courteous [➡ GOOD MANNERS AND SOCIAL SKILLS; 520] *Opposite*: improper **3** *adj* **own**, personal, characteristic, identifiable, individual [➡ BELONGING OR RELATING TO INDIVIDUALS; 944]

properly *adv* **correctly**, right, appropriately, as it should be, by the book, suitably, accurately, well [➡ APPROPRIATE, SUITABLE, AND ADVISABLE; 184] *Opposite*: incorrectly

proper noun *type of* **word class** [➡ ASPECTS OF LANGUAGE; 682]

propertied *adj* **property-owning**, land-owning, landed, affluent, moneyed, titled [➡ WEALTH AND WEALTHY; 891] *Opposite*: dispossessed

property 1 *n* **possessions**, belongings, goods, assets, material goods, chattels, things, stuff [➡ POSSESSIONS; 461] **2** *n* **land**, home, house, estate, acreage [➡ PLACE; 1065]

property owner *n* **proprietor**, owner, landowner, homeowner, property holder, landholder [➡ OWNERS; 446] *Opposite*: tenant

prophecy *n* **prediction**, forecast, divination, foretelling, insight, foresight [➡ PREDICT AND ANTICIPATE; 750]

prophesy *v* **predict**, forecast, divine, foretell, see the future, prefigure, portend, presage, envisage [➡ PREDICT AND ANTICIPATE; 750]

prophet *n* **clairvoyant**, forecaster, fortune teller, seer, prescient, psychic, diviner, mystic, telepathist, spiritualist, parapsychologist, sibyl [➡ PEOPLE WITH SUPERNATURAL POWERS; 788]

prophetic *adj* **visionary**, farsighted, predictive, foretelling, forewarning, oracular, divinatory [➡ PREDICT AND ANTICIPATE; 750]

propinquity (*formal*) *n* **nearness**, closeness, proximity, convenience, relationship [➡ CLOSENESS; 159] *Opposite*: remoteness

propitiate *v* **appease**, placate, mollify, pacify, soothe, calm down, conciliate [➡ SOOTHE AND CALM; 573] *Opposite*: aggravate (*informal*)

propitiation (*formal*) *n* **placation**, appeasement, mollification, pacification, soothing, calming, conciliation [➡ APOLOGIZE AND RETRACT; 683] *Opposite*: provocation

propitiatory *adj* **placatory**, conciliatory, soothing, mollifying, calming, pacifying [➡CALMING; 188] *Opposite*: provocative

propitious *adj* [➡SUCCESSFUL AND PROMISING; 81]

propitiousness *n* [➡SUCCESS; 82]

proponent *n* **advocate**, supporter, exponent, protagonist, follower, fan, champion [➡SUPPORTERS, PROTECTORS, AND COMPATRIOTS; 970] *Opposite*: opponent

proportion **1** *n* **amount**, quantity, part, share, percentage, fraction [➡DEGREE AND EXTENT; 110] **2** *n* **ratio**, comparison, relative amount, relationship [➡MEASURABLE PORTIONS; 127]

proportional *adj* **relative**, comparative, relational, related, proportionate [➡EQUALITY; 154]

proportionate *adj* **balanced**, proportional, comparable, equal, equivalent [➡EQUALITY; 154]

proportions *n* [➡SIZE AND DIMENSIONS; 1192]

proposal *n* **suggestion**, offer, application, tender, bid, plan, scheme, request, proposition [➡SUGGEST, HINT, AND COMMENT; 612]

propose **1** *v* **suggest**, offer, recommend, proposition, advise, put forward [➡SUGGEST, HINT, AND COMMENT; 612] **2** *v* **intend**, plan, have in mind, aim, mean [➡PREPARE FOR ACTION; 289]

proposer *n* **nominator**, supporter, sponsor, advocate, advocator, backer, exponent, champion [➡SUPPORTERS, PROTECTORS, AND COMPATRIOTS; 970]

proposition *n* **proposal**, plan, scheme, intention, suggestion, offer [➡SUGGEST, HINT, AND COMMENT; 612]

propound *v* **put forward**, advocate, submit, set out, offer, bring forward, yield, propose, promote, promulgate (*formal*) [➡SUGGEST, HINT, AND COMMENT; 612]

proprietary **1** *adj* **branded**, exclusive, patented, registered, trademarked, copyrighted, named, brand-named [➡FINANCE AND ECONOMICS; 796] *Opposite*: generic **2** *adj* **private**, privately owned, privately run, privately operated, commercial [➡BELONGING OR RELATING TO INDIVIDUALS; 944] **3** *adj* **protective**, jealous, territorial, possessive, suspicious, watchful [➡ENVY AND JEALOUSY; 548]

proprietor *n* **owner**, manager, administrator, landowner, property owner, landlord [➡OWNERS; 446]

proprietorial *adj* **possessive**, protective, jealous, suspicious, territorial, proprietary [➡ENVY AND JEALOUSY; 548]

propriety **1** *n* **politeness**, decorum, modesty, good manners, respectability, decency [➡GOOD MANNERS AND SOCIAL SKILLS; 520] *Opposite*: impropriety **2** *n* **correctness**, aptness, appropriateness, decency, suitability [➡MORALLY GOOD; 774] *Opposite*: impropriety

propulsion *n* **force**, forward motion, thrust, impulsion, momentum, impetus, driving force [➡ENERGY; 1161]

prop up *v* **hold up**, support, prop, sustain, buttress, bolster, uphold, stand, place, set [➡IMPROVE STRENGTH AND DURABILITY; 378] *Opposite*: destabilize

pro rata *adv* [➡FOREIGN WORDS AND PHRASES; 672]

prosaic **1** *adj* **straightforward**, matter-of-fact, simple, plain, ordinary, routine [➡ORDINARINESS; 244] **2** *adj* **banal**, mundane, everyday, dull, humdrum, colorless, run-of-the-mill, pedestrian, plain, vanilla, characterless, ordinary, commonplace [➡BORING AND UNINTERESTING; 234] *Opposite*: extraordinary

prosaicness *n* **plainness**, dullness, flatness, woodenness, pedestrianism [➡BORING AND UNINTERESTING; 234] *Opposite*: poeticality

proscribe *v* **ban**, bar, forbid, exclude, make illegal, veto, disallow, rule out, prohibit [➡REFUSE PERMISSION AND NOT ALLOW; 670] *Opposite*: permit

proscribed *adj* **prohibited**, banned, forbidden, verboten, inadmissible, barred, illegal, illicit, unacceptable, taboo, outlawed [➡REFUSE PERMISSION AND NOT ALLOW; 670] *Opposite*: permissible

proscription (*formal*) *n* **prohibition**, banning, exclusion, forbidding, interdiction, outlawing, veto [➡REFUSE PERMISSION AND NOT ALLOW; 670]

proscriptive (*formal*) *adj* [➡REFUSE PERMISSION AND NOT ALLOW; 670]

prose *n* **writing style**, style, text [➡FICTION AND DRAMA; 913]

prosecute *v* **put on trial**, act against, impeach, arraign, indict, take legal action, accuse, bring to court, sue [➡TRIAL, PUNISHMENT, AND LEGAL OUTCOMES; 819]

prosecuting attorney *n* [➡PEOPLE IN LAW COURTS; 820]

prosecution *n* **trial**, action, suit, case, examination, hearing, tribunal [➡TRIAL, PUNISHMENT, AND LEGAL OUTCOMES; 819]

prosecutor *n* **prosecuting attorney**, DA, district attorney, public prosecutor [➡PEOPLE IN LAW COURTS; 820]

proselyte *n* [➡SUPPORTERS, PROTECTORS, AND COMPATRIOTS; 970]

proselytization *n* **preaching**, evangelization, agitation, propagandizing, campaigning, tireless support, boundless enthusiasm [➡APPROVE AND CONFIRM; 646]

proselytize *v* **preach**, agitate, evangelize, persuade, cajole, spread the word, convert, make see the light, lecture, bend somebody's ear [➡INSTRUCT AND TEACH; 609]

proselytizer *n* **preacher**, evangelist, missionary, zealot, agitator, lecturer, tireless campaigner, polemicist [➡SPEAKERS AND ORATORS; 603]

prosopopeia *type of* **figure of speech** [➡FIGURES OF SPEECH; 673]

prospect **1** *n* **view**, scene, vision, outlook, panorama, vista, viewpoint, overlook [➡VIEWS AND OUTLOOKS; 1073] **2** *n* **hope**, possibility, expectation, outlook, vision, likelihood, probability, potential, option, chance [➡POSSIBLE AND PROBABLE; 177] **3** *v* **search**, mine, dig, seek, pan, hunt [➡SEEK POSSESSION AND SEARCH; 456]

prospective *adj* **potential**, future, forthcoming, likely, probable, soon-to-be, eventual, approaching, upcoming, latent [➡FUTURE; 86]

prospectus *n* **brochure**, list, document, catalog, booklet, leaflet, pamphlet [➡MANUALS AND INSTRUCTIONS; 589]

prosper **1** *v* **flourish**, thrive, do well, get on, grow, burgeon (*literary*) [➡PROSPER AND ABOUND; 16] *Opposite*: decline

lingering, expanded, lengthy, lengthened, delayed, stretched out [➡ PERMANENCE: WITHOUT END; 94] *Opposite*: brief

protraction 1 *n* **extension**, lengthening, drawing out, continuation [➡ PERMANENCE: WITHOUT END; 94] *Opposite*: shortening 2 *n* **scale drawing**, plan, elevation, blueprint, diagram, drawing [➡ DRAWINGS, CHARTS, AND TABLES; 594]

protractor *type of* **measuring device** [➡ MEASURING DEVICES; 1123]

protrude *v* **stick out**, jut, project, overhang, obtrude, extend beyond, bulge, swell [➡ EXIST IN A PLACE; 19]

protruding *adj* [➡ PERCEPTIBLE; 25]

protrusion *n* **lump**, lip, flange, overhang, outcrop, protuberance, projection, bulge, extension, overlap [➡ EXTREMITIES OF PHYSICAL OBJECTS; 1250]

protrusive 1 *adj* **prominent**, bulging, swelling, jutting, extending, proud (*UK*) [➡ PERCEPTIBLE; 25] *Opposite*: sunken 2 *adj* **brash**, forward, presumptuous, rude, fresh (*informal*), impertinent (*formal*) [➡ POMPOUS, LOUD, AND OVERCONFIDENT; 635] *Opposite*: retiring

protuberance *n* **swelling**, bulge, bump, lump, knob, distension, protrusion, prominence, projection, convexity [➡ ROUNDED SHAPE; 1218]

protuberant *adj* **sticking out**, prominent, bulging, swelling, popping, bulgy, swollen, convex [➡ ROUNDED SHAPE; 1218] *Opposite*: concave

proud 1 *adj* **pleased**, satisfied, gratified, honored, delighted, fulfilled [➡ PLEASURE, EXCITEMENT, AND ELATION; 534] *Opposite*: ashamed 2 *adj* **independent**, self-sufficient, honorable, dignified, scrupulous, self-respecting [➡ GOOD MANNERS AND SOCIAL SKILLS; 520] 3 *adj* **rewarding**, satisfying, pleasurable, pleasing, uplifting, fulfilling [➡ EMOTIONALLY PLEASANT; 187] 4 *adj* **arrogant**, conceited, smug, superior, self-important, pompous, self-righteous, vain, egotistic, self-satisfied, overbearing, bigheaded (*informal*) [➡ AFFECTATION, SELF-SATISFACTION, AND SNOBBISHNESS; 507] *Opposite*: humble 5 *adj* **impressive**, stately, majestic, noble, magnificent, great, grand, lordly [➡ EXTRAORDINARY: UNCOMMON; 205] 6 *adj* (*UK*) **projecting**, prominent, jutting, bulging, protrusive, sticking out [➡ PERCEPTIBLE; 25] *Opposite*: sunken

Compare and Contrast: *proud, arrogant, conceited, egotistic, vain*

CORE MEANING: describing somebody who is pleased with himself or herself

proud justifiably pleased and satisfied about a situation, or self-satisfied and having an exaggerated opinion of self-worth; *arrogant* feeling or showing self-importance and contempt for others; *conceited* showing excessive satisfaction with one's personal qualities or abilities; *egotistic* having an inflated sense of self-importance, especially when this is shown through constantly talking or thinking about oneself; *vain* excessively self-satisfied, especially suggesting that somebody is overly concerned with and admires his or her own personal appearance.

proudly 1 *adv* **delightedly**, happily, triumphantly, joyfully, ashamedly [➡ PLEASURE, EXCITEMENT, AND ELATION; 534] 2 *adv* **arrogantly**, conceitedly, smugly, self-importantly, pompously, bigheadedly (*informal*) [➡ AFFECTATION, SELF-SATISFACTION, AND SNOBBISHNESS; 507] *Opposite*: humbly

provable *adj* **demon** testable, unarguable

prove 1 *v* **show**, esta evidence, attest, be uphold, support, sus CONFIRM; 646] *Opposite*: d grow up, be, show yo ENCE; 1]

proven *adj* **establishe** fied, recognized, su [➡ CERTAIN; 174] *Opposite*: u

provenance *n* **origi** birthplace, backgroun

See Compare and Con

provender 1 *n* (*archa* [➡ ANIMAL FEED; 1168] 2 *n* (provisions, victuals, gr ables (*informal*), chow (*formal*) [➡ FOOD; 1167]

proverb *n* **maxim**, axio truth, epigram [➡ FIGURES

proverbial 1 *adj* **w** legendary, famous, fam [➡ KNOWN AND FAMOUS; 181] 2 regular, common, usual, *site*: novel

provide 1 *v* **give**, supply offer, bestow (*formal*), f 435] *Opposite*: withhold 2 arrange for, run, be resp AND PROVIDE; 430] *Opposite*: wi specify, require [➡ REQUEST support, look after, care f arrange, plan, cater [➡ TAK neglect

provided *see* **provided tha**

provided that *conj* **on c** as, so long as, providing [➡ CAUSATION; 168]

provide for *v* [➡ TAKE CARE OF

providence 1 *n* **fate**, lu intervention, outside influe 2 *n* **wisdom**, foresight, prud farsightedness, forethought CHARACTERISTICS; 524]

provident 1 *adj* **prudent**, wise, careful, sensible, fars ACTERISTICS; 524] *Opposite*: impr cautious, careful, sparing, miserly, mean (*UK*) [➡ ECONOMIC spendthrift

providential 1 *adj* **fortunat** tageous [➡ LUCK; 783] *Opposite*: ur destined, fated, God-given, DESTINY, AND ASTROLOGY; 782] *Opposite*:

providentially *adv* **fortunately**, luckily, conveniently, beneficially, advantageously, opportunely [➡LUCK; 783] *Opposite*: unfortunately

provider 1 *n* **breadwinner**, wage-earner, earner, worker, billpayer, benefactor [➡SUPPORTERS, PROTECTORS, AND COMPATRIOTS; 970] *Opposite*: dependent 2 *n* **supplier**, source, contributor, donor, bringer, giver [➡REPRESENTATIVES AND PATRONS; 968] *Opposite*: beneficiary

providing *conj* **on condition that**, if, only if, as long as, so long as, provided that, in case, granted [➡CAUSATION; 168]

province 1 *n* **region**, area, state, county, prefecture, territory, district, realm, department (*informal*) [➡COUNTRIES AND REGIONS; 1067] 2 *n* **area**, sphere, field, jurisdiction, domain, bailiwick, authority [➡SUBJECT AREAS; 768]

provinces *n* **outlying areas**, countryside, backwaters, hinterland, sticks (*informal*), boonies (*informal*), boondocks (*informal*), shires (*UK*) [➡COUNTRIES AND REGIONS; 1067] *Opposite*: capital

provincial 1 *adj* **local**, regional, county, district, small-town, rural, bucolic, rustic, country [➡HUMAN SETTLEMENTS; 1070] *Opposite*: central 2 *adj* **unsophisticated**, unfashionable, simple, outmoded, parochial, narrow-minded, insular [➡LEVELS OF EDUCATION AND SOPHISTICATION; 894] *Opposite*: worldly

provincialism *n* **lack of sophistication**, lack of refinement, parochialism, narrow-mindedness, insularity [➡LEVELS OF EDUCATION AND SOPHISTICATION; 894] *Opposite*: worldliness

provision 1 *n* **delivery**, facility, running, setting up, establishment, providing, endowment, donation [➡DISPENSE, RATION, AND DISTRIBUTE; 434] 2 *n* **anticipation**, prearrangement, forethought, wherewithal, readiness, precaution [➡POSITIVE INTELLECTUAL CHARACTERISTICS; 524] 3 *n* **stipulation**, rider, condition, proviso, if, prerequisite, specification, requirement, obligation, but (*informal*) [➡NECESSARY AND ESSENTIAL; 196]

provisional *adj* **temporary**, interim, conditional, makeshift, short-term, impermanent, draft, outline, rough [➡FINITENESS, VARIABILITY, AND TRANSIENCE; 96] *Opposite*: permanent

provisions *n* **supplies**, necessities, requirements, food, rations, sustenance, eatables (*informal*), comestibles (*formal*) [➡FOOD; 1167]

proviso *n* **stipulation**, rider, condition, provision, if, disclaimer, prerequisite, specification, requirement, limitation, but (*informal*) [➡NECESSARY AND ESSENTIAL; 196]

provisory *adj* **conditional**, subject to, dependent upon, provisional, contingent, limited [➡FINITENESS, VARIABILITY, AND TRANSIENCE; 96] *Opposite*: unconditional

provocation 1 *n* **incitement**, needling, goading, baiting, niggling, hassle (*informal*) [➡NUISANCES; 253] 2 *n* **vexation**, frustration, irritation, annoyance, affront [➡IRRITATION AND ANGER; 541]

provocative 1 *adj* **challenging**, provoking, stimulating, inflammatory, incendiary, confrontational, instigating, rabble-rousing, aggressive, offensive, insulting, annoying, vexing, aggravating (*informal*) [➡RUDE AND HOSTILE; 625] *Opposite*: conciliatory 2 *adj* **suggestive**, enticing, seductive, alluring, encouraging, tantalizing, beguiling, bewitching, cheeky (*informal*) [➡INTERESTING AND MEANINGFUL; 190] *Opposite*: forbidding

provoke 1 *v* **incite**, needle, goad, bait, irritate, niggle, inflame, rouse, whip up, aggravate (*informal*), hassle (*informal*) [➡ANGER AND ANNOY; 569] *Opposite*: soothe 2 *v* **cause**, elicit, produce, trigger, bring about, stir, activate, prompt, instigate [➡CAUSE TO HAPPEN; 31] *Opposite*: prevent

provoked *adj* **irritated**, annoyed, angered, goaded, frustrated, aggravated (*informal*) [➡IRRITATION AND ANGER; 541] *Opposite*: unaffected

provoking *adj* **infuriating**, irritating, annoying, frustrating, maddening, aggravating (*informal*) [➡IRRITATING; 228] *Opposite*: soothing

Provolone *type of* **hard cheese** [➡DAIRY PRODUCTS AND CHEESES; 1183]

provost *n* **principal**, director, head, chancellor, leader, dean, chief [➡EDUCATORS; 840]

prow *part of* **ship or boat** [➡SHIPS AND BOATS; 1150]

prowess 1 *n* **ability**, skill, expertise, competence, dexterity, competency, aptitude, proficiency, knack, talent, know-how (*informal*) [➡SKILLS, TALENTS, AND ABILITIES; 526] *Opposite*: incompetence 2 *n* **bravery**, valor, heroism, gallantry, courage, daring [➡COURAGE; 498] *Opposite*: cowardice

prowl *v* **stalk**, lurk, skulk, lie in wait, hang around, scavenge [➡PROCEED AND GO; 305]

prowl car *type of* **public service vehicle** [➡VEHICLES; 1145]

prowler *n* **stalker**, pursuer, intruder, tormentor, Peeping Tom, lurker [➡VILLAINS AND THUGS; 947]

proximate *adj* [➡CLOSENESS; 159]

proximity *n* **nearness**, closeness, juxtaposition, vicinity, immediacy, propinquity (*formal*), contiguity (*formal*) [➡CLOSENESS; 159] *Opposite*: remoteness

proxy 1 *n* **substitute**, alternate, stand-in, deputy, delegate, understudy, surrogate, replacement [➡REPRESENTATIVES AND PATRONS; 968] 2 *n* **indirect means**, substitution, deputation, commission, delegation, representation [➡REPRESENTATIONS AND GENERAL EXAMPLES; 65]

prudence *n* **practicality**, carefulness, caution, cautiousness, discretion, forethought, farsightedness, judiciousness, good sense, common sense, shrewdness, judgment, pragmatism, wisdom, calculation, foresight, providence, care [➡POSITIVE INTELLECTUAL CHARACTERISTICS; 524] *Opposite*: imprudence

prudent *adj* **practical**, careful, cautious, sensible, discreet, wise, judicious, farsighted, shrewd, pragmatic [➡POSITIVE INTELLECTUAL CHARACTERISTICS; 524] *Opposite*: imprudent

See Compare and Contrast at **cautious**.

prudential *adj* **sensible**, wise, sagacious, provident, practical, commonsensical [➡POSITIVE INTELLECTUAL CHARACTERISTICS; 524] *Opposite*: foolish

prudery *n* **prudishness**, primness, stuffiness, reserve, puritanism, prissiness, narrow-mindedness [➡EXCESSIVE SENSITIVITY; 511] *Opposite*: permissiveness

prudish *adj* **prim**, stuffy, strait-laced, starchy, formal, proper, prissy, squeamish, puritanical, narrow-minded, uptight [➡ EXCESSIVE SENSITIVITY; 511] *Opposite*: relaxed

prudishness *see* prudery

prune
1 *v* **clip**, trim, snip, cut back, cut, thin, lop, crop [➡ EXTRACT AND SEVER; 341] **2** *v* **shorten**, cut, abridge, condense, tighten up, curtail, reduce, trim, abbreviate [➡ CHANGE OF SIZE: SMALLER; 393] *Opposite*: expand

prurience *n* [➡ MORALLY BAD OR IMPROPER; 775]

prurient
adj **unwholesome**, unhealthy, immodest, indecent, salacious, voyeuristic, lustful, libidinous, lascivious [➡ MORALLY BAD OR IMPROPER; 775] *Opposite*: healthy

Prussian blue *type of* **blue** [➡ COLORS; 1224]

pry
1 *v* **interfere**, poke your nose in, meddle, inquire, peer, be inquisitive, snoop (*informal*), be nosy (*informal*) [➡ ASK PEOPLE QUESTIONS; 666] *Opposite*: leave alone **2** *v* **lever open**, force, force open, wrench, wrest, prize [➡ UNFASTEN AND UNDO; 409]

prying
adj **interfering**, inquisitive, curious, meddling, peeping, peering, snooping (*informal*), nosy (*informal*) [➡ NOSY AND INTERFERING; 512] *Opposite*: incurious

pry open *v* [➡ UNFASTEN AND UNDO; 409]

P.S.
n **postscript**, addendum, afterthought, addition, coda, stop press (*UK*) [➡ WRITTEN CONVENTIONS; 599]

psalm
n **sacred song**, hymn, poem, canticle, prayer, song, song of praise [➡ RELIGIONS AND RELIGIOUS PRACTICES; 777]

psalter
n **book of psalms**, prayer book, breviary, hymnal, missal [➡ RELIGIOUS OBJECTS; 779]

pseud
(*UK*) *n* **fraud**, fake, pseudointellectual, know-it-all (*informal*), poser (*informal*) [➡ SUPERFICIAL OR INSINCERE PEOPLE; 951]

pseudo *adj* [➡ FALSE AND UNREAL; 173]

pseudonym
n **alias**, false name, assumed name, fictitious name, stage name, pen name, nom de plume [➡ NAME AND DESCRIBE; 665]

psych
1 *v* **panic**, frighten, scare, worry, trouble, bother [➡ UPSET, DISTRESS, AND HUMILIATE; 567] **2** *v* **nerve**, steel, brace, motivate, gear up, wind up, prepare, get ready [➡ PREPARE FOR ACTION; 289]

psyche
1 *n* **soul**, spirit, inner self, essence, being [➡ PSYCHOLOGY AND THE MIND; 769] **2** *n* **mind**, consciousness, awareness, ego, intellect, mentality, personality [➡ PSYCHOLOGY AND THE MIND; 769]

psychedelic
1 *adj* **hallucinogenic**, mind-altering, mind-expanding, mood-altering, mind-blowing (*informal*), intoxicating (*formal*) [➡ PAIN AND OTHER PHYSICAL SENSATIONS; 733] **2** *adj* **colored**, patterned, vibrant, vivid, loud, exuberant, kaleidoscopic [➡ DESCRIBING COLORS; 1226] *Opposite*: dull

psychiatrist *n* [➡ PEOPLE WHO WORK IN MEDICINE; 848]

psychiatry *n* [➡ PSYCHOLOGY AND THE MIND; 769]

psychic
1 *adj* **mental**, cerebral, intellectual, cognitive, psychosomatic, emotional [➡ PSYCHOLOGY AND THE MIND; 769] **2** *adj* **supernatural**, extrasensory, mysterious, unexplained, paranormal, spiritual, out-of-body [➡ THE SUPERNATURAL; 787]

Opposite: physical **3** *adj* **telepathic**, clairvoyant, intuitive, second-sighted, stargazing, spiritualistic [➡ THE SUPERNATURAL; 787] **4** *n* **clairvoyant**, spiritualist, soothsayer, sensitive, diviner, medium [➡ PEOPLE WITH SUPERNATURAL POWERS; 788]

psychical
adj **supernatural**, paranormal, spiritual, extrasensory, subliminal, subconscious, clairvoyant [➡ THE SUPERNATURAL; 787] *Opposite*: physical

psychoanalysis *n* [➡ PSYCHOLOGY AND THE MIND; 769]

psychoanalyst *n* [➡ PEOPLE WHO WORK IN MEDICINE; 848]

psychological
adj **mental**, emotional, inner, spiritual, psychosomatic [➡ PSYCHOLOGY AND THE MIND; 769] *Opposite*: physical

psychology
n **mind**, thinking, mindset, makeup, sensibility, consciousness, attitude, feeling [➡ PSYCHOLOGY AND THE MIND; 769]

psychosis *n* [➡ PSYCHOLOGY AND THE MIND; 769]

psychosomatic
adj **self-induced**, mental, psychological, inner, all in the mind [➡ PSYCHOLOGY AND THE MIND; 769]

psychotherapist *n* [➡ PEOPLE WHO WORK IN MEDICINE; 848]

psychotherapy *n* [➡ PSYCHOLOGY AND THE MIND; 769]

PT
(*UK*) *n* **physical training**, physical education, P.E., gymnastics, sports education, games (*UK*) [➡ HOBBIES, GAMES, AND SPORTS; 875]

PT boat *type of* **military vessel** [➡ SHIPS AND BOATS; 1150]

pteranodon *type of* **dinosaur** [➡ DINOSAURS; 996]

pterodactyl *type of* **dinosaur** [➡ DINOSAURS; 996]

pterosaur *type of* **dinosaur** [➡ DINOSAURS; 996]

P.T.O. *n* [➡ WRITTEN CONVENTIONS; 599]

pubertal *adj* [➡ BABYHOOD, CHILDHOOD, AND ADOLESCENCE; 917]

puberty
n **sexual maturity**, adolescence, youth, teens [➡ BABYHOOD, CHILDHOOD, AND ADOLESCENCE; 917]

pubescent
adj **pubertal**, teenage, adolescent, teen (*informal*) [➡ BABYHOOD, CHILDHOOD, AND ADOLESCENCE; 917]

pubis *type of* **bone** [➡ THE BONES AND JOINTS; 719]

public
1 *adj* **community**, civic, communal, municipal, free, open, unrestricted [➡ BELONGING OR RELATING TO PEOPLE; 943] *Opposite*: private **2** *adj* **freely available**, shared, known, open, in the public domain, broadcast [➡ KNOWN AND FAMOUS; 181] *Opposite*: secret **3** *n* **everyone**, people, populace, community, society, nation, the world at large [➡ GROUPS IN SOCIETY; 940]

public amenities *n* [➡ SOCIAL WELFARE; 812]

publication
n **book**, magazine, newspaper, journal, periodical, pamphlet, newsletter [➡ BOOKS AND BOOKLETS; 590]

public defender *n* [➡ PEOPLE IN LAW COURTS; 820]

public disgrace
n **dishonor**, disgrace, ignominy, humiliation, exposure, shaming, embarrassment, naming and shaming (*UK*) [➡ CRITICISMS AND ANGRY OUTBURSTS; 50]

public disturbance *n* [➡ CRIMES; 817]

public figure *n* celebrity, name, personality, personage, household name, VIP, star [➡ IMPORTANT OR FAMOUS PEOPLE; 893]

public holiday (*UK*) *n* [➡ PERIODS OF REST; 91]

public image *n* façade, front, public face, persona, identity [➡ TEMPERAMENT AND BEHAVIOR; 492]

publicity *n* advertising, promotion, exposure, hype, media hype, public relations, coverage, ink (*slang*) [➡ ADVERTISING AND PUBLICITY; 604]

publicize *v* make public, make known, broadcast, advertise, announce, expose, publish, air [➡ INFORM, ANNOUNCE, AND ISSUE; 611] *Opposite*: suppress

public limited company *n* [➡ BUSINESS ENTERPRISES AND RELATED BODIES; 792]

publicly *adv* openly, in public, overtly, widely, freely, visibly [➡ PERCEPTIBLE; 25] *Opposite*: secretly

public nuisance *n* [➡ CRIMES; 817]

public prosecutor *n* [➡ PEOPLE IN LAW COURTS; 820]

public relations *n* image management, publicity, media, relations, self-promotion, spin doctoring (*slang*) [➡ ADVERTISING AND PUBLICITY; 604]

public school *type of* school [➡ EDUCATIONAL INSTITUTIONS; 813]

public services *n* [➡ SOCIAL WELFARE; 812]

public-spirited *adj* philanthropic, charitable, altruistic, humanitarian, benevolent, unselfish [➡ GENEROSITY AND KINDNESS; 495] *Opposite*: selfish

public transport *n* [➡ SOCIAL WELFARE; 812]

publish 1 *v* issue, put out, bring out, print, distribute, circulate [➡ INFORM, ANNOUNCE, AND ISSUE; 611] 2 *v* make public, make known, announce, broadcast, advertise [➡ INFORM, ANNOUNCE, AND ISSUE; 611] *Opposite*: keep secret

publisher *n* producer, originator, commissioner, editor, issuer [➡ WORKERS IN ENTERTAINMENT AND MEDIA; 873]

publishing *n* publication, printing, issuing, reproducing, dissemination, broadcasting [➡ INFORM, ANNOUNCE, AND ISSUE; 611]

puce *type of* red [➡ COLORS; 1224]

puck *type of* sports equipment [➡ SPORTS EQUIPMENT; 879]

pucker 1 *v* wrinkle, crease, gather, pull together, ruck up, crumple [➡ CHANGE OF SHAPE; 385] *Opposite*: smooth 2 *n* gather, wrinkle, crease, ruck, pull [➡ CHANGE OF SHAPE; 385]

puckish *adj* mischievous, playful, naughty, impish, elfin, cheeky (*informal*), rascally (*humorous*) [➡ CHEERFULNESS OF OUTLOOK; 503]

pudding *type of* dessert [➡ CAKES, COOKIES, AND DESSERTS; 1181]

puddle 1 *n* pool, slick, wet patch [➡ AMOUNTS OF LIQUID; 114] 2 *v* splash, dabble, paddle, wade, splosh (*UK*) [➡ PROCEED AND GO; 305] 3 *v* (*UK*) putter, mosey around, dawdle, idle, lounge around, mooch (*slang*) [➡ AIMLESS AND ERRANT MOTION; 343]

pudginess (*informal*) *n* [➡ BUILD; 477]

pudgy (*informal*) *adj* fat, chubby, stubby, heavy, round, obese, overweight, portly, stocky, tubby, podgy (*UK*) [➡ BUILD; 477]

puerile *adj* childish, immature, infantile, foolish, silly, trivial, trifling, fatuous, inane [➡ NEGATIVE INTELLECTUAL CHARACTERISTICS; 525] *Opposite*: mature

puerility *n* immaturity, childishness, silliness, foolishness, inanity, fatuousness, fatuity (*formal*) [➡ NEGATIVE INTELLECTUAL CHARACTERISTICS; 525]

puff 1 *n* gust, breath, draft, current, flurry [➡ WINDY AND STORMY WEATHER; 1053] 2 *n* cloud, wisp, waft, billow [➡ AMOUNTS OF GAS; 116] 3 *n* praise, recommendation, advertisement, publicity, blurb (*slang*) [➡ PRAISE AND ENCOURAGE; 647] 4 *v* blow, exhale, breathe out, breathe [➡ BREATHE AND NOT BREATHE; 716] *Opposite*: inhale 5 *v* pant, breathe heavily, wheeze, gasp, gasp for breath, be short of breath [➡ BREATHE AND NOT BREATHE; 716]

puff adder *type of* poisonous snake [➡ SNAKES; 995]

puffball *type of* fungus [➡ MICROORGANISMS, FUNGI, AND ALGAE; 1023]

puffed (*UK*) *adj* out of breath, breathless, breathing heavily, panting, gasping, winded, puffed out (*UK*) [➡ BREATHE AND NOT BREATHE; 716]

puffed out (*UK*) *adj* [➡ BREATHE AND NOT BREATHE; 716]

puffed-up *adj* pompous, self-important, arrogant, conceited, boastful, self-satisfied, swaggering, superior, swollen with pride, haughty, proud, egotistic [➡ POMPOUS, LOUD, AND OVERCONFIDENT; 635] *Opposite*: humble

puffin *type of* sea bird [➡ SEA BIRDS; 1002]

puffiness 1 *n* swelling, enlargement, inflammation, edema, distension, engorgement [➡ ILL AND SICK; 740] 2 *n* pomposity, pompousness, arrogance, haughtiness, pride, egotism [➡ POMPOUS, LOUD, AND OVERCONFIDENT; 635] *Opposite*: humility

puffing 1 *n* wheezing, wheeziness, breathlessness, heavy breathing, breathing, panting, gasping [➡ BREATHE AND NOT BREATHE; 716] 2 *adj* breathless, out of breath, panting, gasping, winded, wheezy, fighting for breath [➡ BREATHE AND NOT BREATHE; 716]

puff out *v* enlarge, swell, expand, puff up, distend, bulge [➡ CHANGE OF SIZE: BIGGER; 392] *Opposite*: deflate

puff pastry *n* [➡ BREAD, FLOUR, AND BREAD PRODUCTS; 1179]

puff up *v* enlarge, swell, inflate, expand, puff out, bulge [➡ CHANGE OF SIZE: BIGGER; 392] *Opposite*: deflate

puffy *adj* swollen, distended, inflated, bloated, bulbous, bulging [➡ ILL AND SICK; 740]

pug 1 *type of* small dog [➡ DOGS; 980] 2 *n* (*slang*) pugilist, boxer, fighter, prizefighter [➡ PEOPLE IN SPORTS AND LEISURE; 876]

pugilism *n* boxing, fighting, prizefighting [➡ HOBBIES, GAMES, AND SPORTS; 875]

pugilist *n* boxer, fighter, prizefighter, pug (*informal*) [➡ PEOPLE IN SPORTS AND LEISURE; 876]

pugnacious *adj* aggressive, confrontational, belligerent, truculent, argumentative, contentious, hostile [➡ AGGRESSIVE AND BELLIGERENT; 518] *Opposite*: peaceable

pugnaciousness *see* **pugnacity**

pugnacity *n* **aggression**, fierceness, forcefulness, hostility, confrontational attitude, intimidating manner, pugnaciousness [➡ AGGRESSIVE AND BELLIGERENT; 518]

pug-nosed *adj* [➡ FACIAL CHARACTERISTICS; 481]

puissant (*literary*) *adj* [➡ STRENGTH; 201]

puke (*slang*) **1** *v* **vomit**, be sick, spew, retch, bring up, gag, throw up (*informal*), upchuck (*informal*), toss your cookies (*slang humorous*) [➡ VOMIT AND BELCH; 712] **2** *n* **vomit**, spew, sick (*UK*) [➡ VOMIT AND BELCH; 712]

pukka *adj* **fine**, well-made, excellent, high-quality, first-class, topnotch (*informal*) [➡ ADMIRABLE AND COMMENDABLE; 185]

pula *type of* **currency** [➡ CURRENCIES; 798]

pull **1** *v* **drag**, draw, heave, haul, tow, lug, cart [➡ PUSH, PULL, AND SLIDE; 335] *Opposite*: push **2** *v* **tug**, jerk, yank, wrench, pluck, twitch [➡ CONTACT: EXERT PRESSURE; 414] **3** *v* **attract**, draw, bring in, pull in, lure, entice [➡ APPEAL TO AND AROUSE INTEREST; 575] *Opposite*: put off **4** *v* **strain**, sprain, damage, injure, tear [➡ WOUND A PERSON OR ANIMAL; 383] **5** *v* **remove**, extract, withdraw, draw out, pluck out, pull out [➡ EXTRACT AND SEVER; 341] *Opposite*: put in **6** *n* (*informal*) **attraction**, appeal, power, influence, draw, magnetism, allure [➡ INTERESTING AND MEANINGFUL; 190] **7** *n* **jerk**, tug, yank, twitch, tweak, wrench [➡ PUSH, PULL, AND SLIDE; 335]

> **Compare and Contrast:** *pull, drag, draw, haul, tow, tug, yank*
>
> CORE MEANING: to move something toward you or in the same direction as you
>
> *pull* to move something toward you or in the same direction as you; *drag* to move something large or heavy with effort across a surface; *draw* to pull something with a smooth movement; *haul* to pull something with a steady strong movement, often involving strenuous effort; *tow* to pull something along behind by means of a rope or chain; *tug* to pull at something with a sharp forceful movement, without necessarily moving the object; *yank* to pull something suddenly and sharply with a single strong movement.

pull a face *v* [➡ FACIAL EXPRESSIONS AND BLUSHING; 651]

pull a fast one (*slang*) *v* **deceive**, trick, con, swindle, put one over (*informal*), bamboozle (*informal*) [➡ DECEPTION AND LIES; 660]

pull apart *v* **disintegrate**, tear apart, dismantle, pull to pieces, demolish, separate [➡ DESTRUCTION AND DEMOLITION; 359] *Opposite*: assemble

pull away *v* [➡ LEAVE AND GO AWAY; 8]

pull back *v* **recoil**, shrink, shrink away, back off, retract, balk [➡ GO BACKWARD; 309]

pull down *v* **demolish**, tear down, destroy, fell, flatten, raze [➡ DESTRUCTION AND DEMOLITION; 359] *Opposite*: build up

pullet *type of* **young bird** [➡ YOUNG BIRDS; 1004]

pulley *n* **winch**, hoist, block and tackle [➡ PARTS OF MACHINES AND TOOLS; 1118]

pull in **1** *v* (*slang*) **arrest**, take into custody, detain, hold, take in for questioning, nab (*informal*) [➡ THE POLICE, ARREST, AND PRETRIAL PROCEEDINGS; 818] **2** *v* **attract**, draw, bring in, pull, encourage, entice [➡ APPEAL TO AND AROUSE INTEREST; 575] *Opposite*: put off

Pullman *part of* **train** [➡ RAILROADS; 1107]

pull off (*informal*) *v* **achieve**, succeed, be successful, accomplish, carry out, execute, realize [➡ SUCCEED AND WIN; 79] *Opposite*: fail

See Compare and Contrast at **accomplish**.

pull out **1** *v* **remove**, extract, withdraw, draw out, pluck out, pull [➡ EXTRACT AND SEVER; 341] *Opposite*: insert **2** *v* **leave**, depart, abandon, drop out, go away, draw out, take off [➡ LEAVE AND GO AWAY; 8] *Opposite*: remain

pullout **1** *n* **insert**, flier, supplement, enclosure, addendum [➡ PARTS OF BOOKS AND DOCUMENTS; 593] **2** *n* **retreat**, withdrawal, departure [➡ ENDS AND DEPARTURES; 54]

pull out all the stops *v* **do your utmost**, go all-out, move heaven and earth, make a supreme effort, do all you can, give your all, go for it (*slang*) [➡ HARD WORK OR EFFORT; 298]

pullover *type of* **sweater** [➡ GARMENTS AND OUTFITS; 865]

pull somebody's leg (*informal*) *v* **tease somebody**, joke, have a joke on somebody, have a laugh, tell stories, kid somebody (*informal*) [➡ JOKES AND TEASING; 674]

pull the plug *v* **end**, discontinue, close down, cut off, wind up, finish off (*informal*), terminate (*formal*) [➡ CAUSE TO STOP; 266]

pull the wool over somebody's eyes *v* **deceive**, delude, hoodwink, swindle, con, cheat [➡ DECEPTION AND LIES; 660]

pull through *v* **recover**, get better, pick up, survive, get through, get over, rally, revive [➡ GET BETTER; 375]

pull together **1** *v* **unite**, join forces, rally, cooperate, team up, collaborate, pool your resources [➡ HELP; 293] **2** *v* **organize**, arrange, assemble, draw together, bring together, form [➡ ARRANGE AND CREATE ORDER; 357]

pull to pieces **1** *v* **dismantle**, pull to bits, pull apart, take to pieces, rip to pieces, rip to shreds [➡ TEAR, BREAK, AND CUT; 360] **2** *v* **criticize**, vilify, make short work of, make mincemeat of, shoot down, rip to shreds, hammer (*informal*), slate (*UK*) [➡ ACCUSE, BLAME, AND CRITICIZE; 641]

pull up **1** *v* **stop**, halt, draw to a halt, brake, pull in [➡ ARRIVE BY TRANSPORT; 14] **2** *v* (*UK*) **criticize**, reprimand, rebuke, take to task, have words with, tell off (*informal*) [➡ ACCUSE, BLAME, AND CRITICIZE; 641]

pull yourself together (*informal*) *v* **compose yourself**, regain your composure, think straight, calm down, regain your self-control, control yourself, get a hold of yourself, get a grip (*informal*) [➡ CHANGE OF MOOD AND COMPOSURE; 580]

pulmonary *adj* **pulmonic**, lung, respiratory [➡ RESPIRATORY ORGANS; 715]

pulp **1** *n* **soft tissue**, fleshy tissue, tissue, flesh [➡ CENTRAL

PARTS OF PHYSICAL OBJECTS; 1251] **2** *part of* **fruit** [➡ FRUIT AND VEGETABLES; 1176] **3** *n* **paste**, mush, mash, blend, soft mass, smooth mixture [➡ LOTIONS, PASTES, AND GELS; 1272] **4** *v* **mash**, crush, squash, pound, grind, pulverize [➡ CHANGE OF SHAPE; 385]

pulpit **1** *n* **podium**, dais, stand, lectern, reading desk [➡ RELIGIOUS OBJECTS; 779] **2** *n* **clergy**, church, church authorities [➡ RELIGIOUS PEOPLE; 778]

pulsar *type of* **star or star system** [➡ HEAVENLY BODIES; 1061]

pulsate *v* **throb**, beat, pulse, thump, thud, pound [➡ PHYSICAL REACTIONS; 316]

pulsation *n* **throb**, beat, pulse, rhythm, pounding, thump [➡ PHYSICAL REACTIONS; 316]

pulse **1** *n* **throb**, pulsation, rhythm, pounding, thump, beat [➡ PHYSICAL REACTIONS; 316] **2** *n* **legume**, leguminous plant, bean, pea [➡ PEAS AND BEANS; 1189] **3** *v* **throb**, beat, pulsate, pound, palpitate, vibrate [➡ PHYSICAL REACTIONS; 316]

pulse

◆ *types of pulses*
bean, black bean, black-eyed pea, broad bean, butter bean, chickpea, fava bean, French bean, garbanzo, haricot, kidney bean, lentil, lima bean, mung bean, navy bean, pea, petits pois, pinto bean, runner bean, snow pea, soybean, string bean

pulverization **1** *n* **maceration**, liquidation, crushing, reduction, grinding [➡ DESTRUCTION AND DEMOLITION; 359] **2** *n* (*informal*) **defeat**, humiliation, thrashing, beating, whipping, drubbing [➡ BEAT AND DEFEAT; 80]

pulverize **1** *v* **grind**, crush, macerate, pulp, mash, chop up, chop into pieces, pound [➡ DESTRUCTION AND DEMOLITION; 359] **2** *v* (*informal*) **thrash**, crush, annihilate, destroy, defeat, trounce, lick (*informal*), hammer (*informal*) [➡ BEAT AND DEFEAT; 80]

pumice *type of* **stone** [➡ STONES, ROCKS, AND BOULDERS; 1057]

pummel *v* **beat**, thump, thrash, pound, punch, bash (*informal*), wallop (*informal*) [➡ PHYSICAL ATTACK AND PUNISHMENT; 415]

pummeling *n* [➡ PHYSICAL ATTACK AND PUNISHMENT; 415]

pump **1** *v* **force**, drive, impel, propel, thrust, push, send [➡ PUSH, PULL, AND SLIDE; 335] **2** *v* **question**, interrogate, quiz, probe, debrief, cross examine (*informal*), grill (*informal*) [➡ ASK PEOPLE QUESTIONS; 666] **3** *part of* **engine** [➡ PARTS OF AN ENGINE; 1144] **4** *type of* **shoe** [➡ FOOTWEAR; 871] **5** *type of* **general tool** [➡ HAND TOOLS; 1119]

pumpernickel *type of* **bread** [➡ BREAD, FLOUR, AND BREAD PRODUCTS; 1179]

pumpkin *type of* **vegetable** [➡ FRUIT AND VEGETABLES; 1176]

pump out *v* **produce**, give off, generate, churn out, emit, expel, broadcast, disseminate, release [➡ EMIT AND EMANATE; 361]

pump up *v* **inflate**, blow up, puff up, puff out, expand, fill, dilate, distend [➡ CHANGE OF SIZE: BIGGER; 392] *Opposite*: deflate

pun **1** *n* **witticism**, joke, double entendre, quip, bon mot, gag (*informal*), jest (*literary*) [➡ JOKES AND TEASING; 674] **2** *v* **play with words**, joke, quip, make a joke, banter, jest (*literary*) [➡ JOKES AND TEASING; 674]

punch **1** *v* **stamp**, press, perforate, cut, pierce [➡ TEAR, BREAK, AND CUT; 360] **2** *v* **hit**, beat, strike, pummel, thump, clout, cuff, box, whack, clobber, sock (*informal*), smite (*archaic or literary*) [➡ PHYSICAL ATTACK AND PUNISHMENT; 415] **3** *n* **blow**, hit, thump, clout, knock, cuff, stroke, box, sock (*informal*) [➡ PHYSICAL ATTACK AND PUNISHMENT; 415] **4** *n* **vigor**, drive, energy, power, verve, punchiness, liveliness, oomph (*informal*), pizzazz (*informal*), vim (*informal*), pep (*informal*) [➡ ENERGY AND ENTHUSIASM; 496] **5** *type of* **general tool** [➡ HAND TOOLS; 1119]

punch-drunk (*informal*) *adj* **dazed**, confused, bewildered, stupefied, stunned, punchy (*informal*) [➡ CONFUSION, ANXIETY, AND WORRY; 540] *Opposite*: alert

punchiness *n* **vigor**, energy, verve, liveliness, drive, power, oomph (*informal*), pizzazz (*informal*), vim (*informal*), pep (*informal*) [➡ ENERGY AND ENTHUSIASM; 496] *Opposite*: lethargy

punchy **1** *adj* **pithy**, hard-hitting, forceful, terse, effective, succinct, direct [➡ SUCCINCT AND TO THE POINT; 640] *Opposite*: bland **2** *adj* **dazed**, confused, bewildered, stupefied, stunned, punch-drunk (*informal*) [➡ CONFUSION, ANXIETY, AND WORRY; 540] *Opposite*: alert

punctilious **1** *adj* **fastidious**, scrupulous, painstaking, assiduous, meticulous, conscientious, thorough, exact, precise, correct [➡ HARD-WORKING AND COMMITTED; 500] *Opposite*: sloppy (*informal*) **2** *adj* **correct**, seemly, courteous, polite, civil, proper [➡ GOOD MANNERS AND SOCIAL SKILLS; 520] *Opposite*: boorish

See Compare and Contrast at **careful**.

punctiliousness **1** *n* **fastidiousness**, precision, correctness, exactitude, efficiency, assiduity, thoroughness, attention to detail, nitpicking, rectitude (*formal*), sedulousness (*literary*) [➡ HARD WORKING AND COMMITTED; 500] *Opposite*: carelessness **2** *n* **propriety**, courteousness, correctness, politeness, decorum [➡ GOOD MANNERS AND SOCIAL SKILLS; 520] *Opposite*: boorishness

punctual *adj* **on time**, in good time, prompt, on the dot [➡ PROMPTNESS: ON TIME; 99] *Opposite*: late

punctuality *n* **promptness**, timekeeping, reliability, regularity [➡ PROMPTNESS: ON TIME; 99] *Opposite*: lateness

punctuate **1** *v* **interrupt**, intersperse, scatter, interpose, pepper, dot, litter, speckle, disrupt, break, sprinkle, lace [➡ SPREAD AND SCATTER; 332] **2** *v* **mark**, edit, correct, mark up, proofread, proof, hyphenate, bracket [➡ RECORD SOMETHING; 371]

punctuation *n* [➡ ASPECTS OF LANGUAGE; 682]

punctuation

◆ *types of punctuation marks*
asterisk, backslash, bracket, colon, comma, dash, exclamation mark, hyphen, semicolon

puncture **1** *n* **hole**, perforation, wound, lesion, pinhole, cut, break, rupture [➡ HOLES, GAPS, AND FORKS; 1252] **2** *v* **pierce**, stab, perforate, prick, stick in, penetrate, wound, nick [➡ TEAR, BREAK, AND CUT; 360] **3** *v* **undermine**, deflate, erode, ruin, destroy, shoot down, demolish (*informal*) [➡ WORSEN SOMETHING; 380] *Opposite*: inflate

punctured *adj* [➡ IN BAD REPAIR; 1234]

pundit *n* **expert**, specialist, authority, commentator, guru, analyst [➡ TALENTED OR INTELLIGENT PEOPLE; 528]

pungency 1 *n* **spiciness**, strong flavor, bitterness, sharpness, tanginess, acidity, hotness [➡ TASTE; 703] *Opposite*: blandness 2 *n* **pithiness**, pointedness, wit, force, bite, causticness [➡ ELOQUENT, TALKATIVE, AND LONG-WINDED; 632] *Opposite*: mildness

pungent 1 *adj* **strong**, powerful, spicy, hot, overpowering, sharp, bitter, sharp-tasting, piquant, stimulating [➡ TASTE; 703] *Opposite*: bland 2 *adj* **caustic**, pithy, pointed, witty, forceful, biting, cutting, acerbic, trenchant, sharp, piercing [➡ ELOQUENT, TALKATIVE, AND LONG-WINDED; 632] *Opposite*: mild

punish *v* **chastise**, discipline, penalize, reprove, rebuke, reprimand, correct, admonish, chasten, castigate (*formal*) [➡ ACCUSE, BLAME, AND CRITICIZE; 641] *Opposite*: commend

punishable *adj* **serious**, indictable, bookable, hanging, capital, disciplinary [➡ UNACCEPTABLE AND UNFORGIVABLE; 225]

punishing *adj* **grueling**, exhausting, demanding, tiring, arduous, laborious, strenuous, harsh, severe, unremitting [➡ PHYSICALLY UNPLEASANT; 226] *Opposite*: undemanding

punishment 1 *n* **sentence**, penalty, reprimand, retribution, penance, price, deserts, chastisement (*formal*), castigation (*formal*) [➡ RESULTS AND OUTCOMES; 83] *Opposite*: reward 2 *n* **rough treatment**, abuse, mistreatment, heavy use, ill-use, maltreatment [➡ MALICIOUS ACTIONS OR BEHAVIOR; 296]

punitive *adj* **disciplinary**, penal, corrective, retaliatory, retributive, retributory, punishing, revengeful, vindictive, castigatory (*formal*) [➡ VENGEANCE AND REVENGE; 685]

punk 1 *adj* (*informal*) **inferior**, second rate, cheap, nasty, poor, rotten, weak, unimpressive [➡ IN POOR TASTE AND OVERSENTIMENTAL; 229] 2 *type of* **rock music** [➡ MUSIC, SONGS, AND SINGING; 907]

punkie *type of* **flying insect** [➡ FLYING INSECTS; 1013]

punning *adj* [➡ JOKES AND TEASING; 674]

punster *n* [➡ JOKERS AND TEASES; 675]

punt 1 *type of* **small vessel** [➡ SHIPS AND BOATS; 1150] 2 *type of* **currency** [➡ CURRENCIES; 798] 3 *n* (*UK*) **bet**, gamble, stake, wager, flutter [➡ GAMBLE AND TAKE RISKS; 466] 4 *v* **kick**, hit, strike, boot, shoot, send, lob [➡ MOVE SOMETHING: THROUGH THE AIR; 334]

puny 1 *adj* **small**, weak, tiny, feeble, frail, stunted, scrawny, undersized, underdeveloped, pint-sized (*informal*) [➡ BUILD; 477] *Opposite*: robust 2 *adj* **inadequate**, trifling, paltry, minor, feeble, insignificant, useless, worthless, meager [➡ REDUNDANT AND USELESS; 240] *Opposite*: considerable

pup 1 *type of* **young animal** [➡ YOUNG ANIMALS; 977] 2 *n* **upstart**, brat, puppy (*informal*), smart aleck (*informal*), know-it-all (*informal*), whippersnapper (*dated*) [➡ MISCHIEVOUS OR BADLY BEHAVED CHILD; 946] 3 *v* **whelp**, litter, bear, deliver, give birth, drop [➡ REPRODUCTION AND HEREDITY; 725]

pupa *type of* **stage of insect development** [➡ INSECT STAGES; 1020]

pupil 1 *n* **acolyte**, understudy, follower, apprentice, student, scholar, learner, beginner, novice, trainee, protégé [➡ STUDENTS AND PUPILS; 841] *Opposite*: teacher 2 *part of* **eye** [➡ THE EYE; 698]

pupillage (*formal*) *n* [➡ CLASSES, COURSEWORK, AND EXAMINATIONS; 842]

puppet 1 *n* **marionette**, dummy, doll, hand puppet, finger-puppet, string-puppet, mannequin, glove puppet (*UK*) [➡ TOYS; 880] 2 *n* **pawn**, lackey, instrument, tool, lapdog, creature, minion, cat's-paw, flunky (*informal*) [➡ SUBORDINATES AND ASSISTANTS; 966]

Puppis *type of* **constellation** [➡ HEAVENLY BODIES; 1061]

puppy 1 *n* **upstart**, brat, pup, smart aleck (*informal*), know-it-all (*informal*), whippersnapper (*dated*) [➡ MISCHIEVOUS OR BADLY BEHAVED CHILD; 946] 2 *type of* **young animal** [➡ YOUNG ANIMALS; 977]

pup tent *n* [➡ RESIDENTIAL BUILDINGS; 1078]

purchase 1 *v* **buy**, pay for, acquire, obtain, procure, get, pick up [➡ PURCHASE; 422] *Opposite*: sell 2 *v* **obtain**, win, gain, secure, acquire [➡ GET; 420] 3 *n* **acquisition**, buying, obtaining, procurement, securing, consumption [➡ BUSINESS ACTIVITIES AND PHENOMENA; 422] 4 *n* **buy**, acquisition, goods, merchandise, item [➡ PURCHASE; 422] 5 *n* **grip**, grasp, hold, leverage, foothold, firm footing, toehold [➡ CONTACT: HOLD; 411]

purchaser *n* **buyer**, procurer, customer, client, consumer, payer [➡ PURCHASER; 424] *Opposite*: seller

purdah 1 *n* **seclusion**, withdrawal, separation, retirement, isolation, exclusion, restriction [➡ RELIGIONS AND RELIGIOUS PRACTICES; 777] 2 *n* **screen**, curtain, barrier, divider, shield [➡ WALLS AND PARTITIONS; 1104]

pure 1 *adj* **uncontaminated**, unadulterated, unpolluted, clean, untainted, wholesome, unalloyed [➡ CLEAN AND HYGIENIC; 1233] *Opposite*: tainted 2 *adj* (*literary*) **chaste**, unsullied, uncorrupted, innocent, sinless, moral, virtuous, virginal [➡ MORALLY GOOD; 774] *Opposite*: corrupt 3 *adj* **theoretical**, abstract, fundamental, basic, higher [➡ THE NATURE OF IDEAS; 771] *Opposite*: applied 4 *adj* **unmixed**, one hundred percent, genuine, real, authentic, natural [➡ TRUE AND REAL; 171] 5 *adj* **sheer**, complete, utter, absolute, downright, out-and-out, total [➡ ABSOLUTE AND ABSOLUTELY; 133] 6 *adj* **clear**, vivid, strong, vibrant, rich, deep [➡ SOFT, LOW, OR PLEASANT SOUNDS; 1265] *Opposite*: weak

purebred *adj* **thoroughbred**, pedigree, pure [➡ CLASS STATUS; 889]

purée 1 *n* **pulp**, paste, mush, pap, sauce, coulis [➡ PREPARED DISHES ; 1170] 2 *v* **mash**, blend, process, liquidize, pound [➡ COOKING AND FOOD PREPARATION; 353]

purely 1 *adv* **entirely**, wholly, totally, thoroughly, completely, absolutely [➡ ABSOLUTE AND ABSOLUTELY; 133] *Opposite*: partly 2 *adv* **merely**, only, simply, just, solely, essentially [➡ MAINLY AND PRIMARILY; 140] 3 *adv* **chastely**, virtuously, decently, morally, innocently, virginally [➡ MORALLY GOOD; 774] *Opposite*: indecently

pureness 1 *n* **cleanliness**, wholesomeness, spotlessness, clarity, transparency, limpidness, cleanness, stainlessness [➡ CLEAN AND HYGIENIC; 1233] *Opposite*: dirtiness 2 *n* **clarity**, vividness, strength, vibrancy, richness, depth [➡ SOFT, LOW, OR PLEASANT SOUNDS; 1265]

purgative (*formal*) 1 *n* **enema**, emetic, suppository, laxative, purge, cathartic [➡ REMEDIES, TREATMENTS, AND OPERATIONS; 731] 2 *adj* **cleansing**, emetic, laxative, emptying, purging [➡ EXCRETION AND EXCRETA; 722]

purgatory *n* **agony**, limbo, hell, anguish, despair, suffering, torment, torture [➡ SADNESS, DISTRESS, AND DESPAIR; 539]

purge 1 *v* **get rid of**, eliminate, remove, eradicate, do away with, expel, expunge, liquidate, oust, dismiss [➡ GET RID OF SOMETHING; 451] 2 *v* **wash out**, cleanse, clean, flush out, sluice, clean up, purify [➡ CLEAN AND POLISH; 403] 3 *v* (*formal*) **pardon**, exonerate, absolve, forgive, excuse, shrive, atone for (*formal*) [➡ FORGET, FORGIVE, AND ACCEPT; 748] *Opposite*: castigate (*formal*) 4 *n* **laxative**, cathartic, emetic, purgative (*formal*) [➡ REMEDIES, TREATMENTS, AND OPERATIONS; 731] 5 *n* **elimination**, removal, eradication, expulsion, ridding, shakeup, housecleaning (*informal*) [➡ REMOVE SOMETHING; 338]

puri *type of* **bread** [➡ BREAD, FLOUR, AND BREAD PRODUCTS; 1179]

purification *n* **cleansing**, sanitization, decontamination, distillation, sterilization, refinement, refining, ablution [➡ CLEAN AND POLISH; 403]

purified *adj* [➡ NOT IN A NATURAL STATE; 1215]

purifier *n* **cleanser**, filter, sterilizer, disinfectant, antiseptic, decontaminant [➡ CLEANING AGENTS; 863]

purify *v* **cleanse**, disinfect, sanitize, decontaminate, clean, get rid of impurities, filter, distill, refine, sterilize [➡ CLEAN AND POLISH; 403] *Opposite*: contaminate

purist *n* **traditionalist**, perfectionist, stickler, pedant, conformist, conservative [➡ GRUMPY AND NEGATIVE PEOPLE; 953]

puritan *n* [➡ ASCETIC PEOPLE; 883]

puritanical *adj* [➡ SELF-DENIAL; 882]

puritanism *n* [➡ SELF-DENIAL; 882]

purity 1 *n* **cleanliness**, spotlessness, clarity, transparency, limpidness, concentration, pureness [➡ CLEAN AND HYGIENIC; 1233] *Opposite*: dirtiness 2 *n* **innocence**, wholesomeness, virtue, virtuousness, chasteness, chastity [➡ MORALLY GOOD; 774]

purl 1 *n* **thread**, gold thread, silver thread, wire, filigree [➡ TEXTILES AND THREADS; 1131] 2 *n* **border**, edge, frill, trim, fringe, decoration [➡ ORNAMENTS AND DECORATIONS; 1248] 3 *n* (*literary*) **ripple**, babble, murmur, gurgle, tinkle, plash (*literary*) [➡ CONTINUOUS SOUNDS; 1258] 4 *v* (*literary*) **flow**, ripple, babble, murmur, gurgle, tinkle, plash (*literary*) [➡ EMIT CONTINUOUS SOUNDS; 366]

purlieu *n* **suburb**, exurb, outskirts, suburbia, vicinity, neighborhood, district, commuter belt (*UK*) [➡ PLACE; 1065]

purloin (*formal or humorous*) *v* **steal**, appropriate, walk off with, pocket, help yourself to, thieve, shoplift, pilfer, filch (*informal*), lift (*informal*), swipe (*informal*) [➡ STEAL AND ROB; 426]

See Compare and Contrast at **steal**.

purple 1 *adj* **elaborate**, exaggerated, florid, overwritten, ornate, excessive, overheated, over-the-top (*informal*) [➡ IN POOR TASTE AND OVERSENTIMENTAL; 229] 2 *type of* **color** [➡ COLORS; 1224]

purple

◆ *types of purple*
amethyst, aubergine, heliotrope, lavender, lilac, mauve, orchid, plum, violet

purport 1 *v* (*formal*) **intend**, aim, mean, plan [➡ PREPARE FOR ACTION; 289] 2 *v* **claim**, assert, allege, profess, contend, maintain, declare, seem [➡ CLAIM, INSIST, AND EMPHASIZE; 614] 3 *n* (*formal*) **sense**, significance, importance, meaning, implication, relevance, import, reason, rationale [➡ IMPORTANCE AND SIGNIFICANCE; 192] 4 *n* (*formal*) **purpose**, intention, aim, design, plan, end, object, objective, intent (*formal*) [➡ INTENTIONS AND PURPOSES; 772]

purported *adj* **supposed**, claimed, alleged, ostensible, unsupported, unsubstantiated, professed, maintained [➡ FALSE AND UNREAL; 173]

purpose 1 *n* **intention**, aim, object, objective, goal, target, end, intent (*formal*) [➡ INTENTIONS AND PURPOSES; 772] 2 *n* **determination**, resolution, resolve, persistence, perseverance, tenacity, single-mindedness, commitment, purposefulness, devotion, dedication, drive [➡ POSITIVE IMPATIENCE, ENTHUSIASM, AND ALERTNESS; 537] *Opposite*: indifference

purpose-built (*UK*) *adj* **tailor-made**, custom-made, custom-built, individual, exclusive, unique, one-off (*UK*) [➡ BUILDING AND ARCHITECTURE; 1076] *Opposite*: standard

purposeful *adj* **focused**, determined, decisive, resolute, firm, fixed, decided, persistent [➡ POSITIVE IMPATIENCE, ENTHUSIASM, AND ALERTNESS; 537] *Opposite*: indecisive

purposefully *adv* **decisively**, firmly, resolutely, persistently, tenaciously [➡ WITH ENTHUSIASM; 286] *Opposite*: aimlessly

purposefulness *n* **determination**, resolution, single-mindedness, commitment, tenacity, devotion, dedication, drive, resolve, persistence, perseverance, purpose [➡ HARD-WORKING AND COMMITTED; 500] *Opposite*: aimlessness

purposeless 1 *adj* **pointless**, irrational, useless, illogical, unreasonable [➡ REDUNDANT AND USELESS; 240] 2 *adj* **empty**, aimless, meaningless, pointless, senseless, useless [➡ REDUNDANT AND USELESS; 240] *Opposite*: meaningful

purposelessly *adv* [➡ REDUNDANT AND USELESS; 240]

purposelessness *n* [➡ REDUNDANT AND USELESS; 240]

purposely *adv* **deliberately**, intentionally, on purpose, knowingly, wittingly, with intent, expressly [➡ INTENTIONAL AND DELIBERATE; 279] *Opposite*: accidentally

purr 1 *n* **purring**, hum, buzz, whir, vibration, drone [➡ CONTINUOUS SOUNDS; 1258] 2 *type of* **animal sound** [➡ SOUNDS MADE BY ANIMALS; 1261] 3 *v* **vibrate**, hum, rumble, whir, buzz, drone [➡ EMIT CONTINUOUS SOUNDS; 366]

purse 1 *type of* **bag** [➡ CONTAINERS, RECEPTACLES, AND PACKAGING; 1245] 2 *n* **handbag**, bag, pocketbook [➡ CONTAINERS, RECEPTACLES, AND PACKAGING; 1245] 3 *n* **change purse**, wallet, pouch, money bag [➡ CONTAINERS, RECEPTACLES, AND PACKAGING; 1245] 4 *n* **reward**, winnings, takings, prize [➡ INCOME; 460] 5 *v* **pucker**, tighten, squeeze, press, compress [➡ CHANGE OF SHAPE; 385] *Opposite*: relax

purse-snatch *v* [➡ STEAL AND ROB; 426]

purse snatcher *n* [➡ CRIMINALS; 821]

purse your lips *v* [➡ FACIAL EXPRESSIONS AND BLUSHING; 651]

pursuance (*formal*) *n* **enactment**, undertaking, fulfillment, achievement, acquirement, carrying out [➡ CARRY OUT AN ACTION; 269]

pursue 1 v **follow**, chase, hunt, trail, track, tail, shadow, dog, hound, stalk [➡ACCOMPANY AND FOLLOW; 337] 2 v **practice**, engage in, work at, go in for, take up, carry out [➡CARRY OUT AN ACTION; 269]

See Compare and Contrast at **follow**.

pursuer n **follower**, chaser, hunter, trailer, tracker, shadow, tail (*informal*) [➡ENEMIES AND TORMENTORS; 969]

pursuit 1 n **chase**, hunt, search, quest, detection [➡SEEK POSSESSION AND SEARCH; 456] 2 n **hobby**, recreation, activity, pastime, interest [➡LEISURE AND RECREATION; 874]

purulent adj **infected**, pus-filled, pussy, weeping, oozing [➡CONDITIONS AFFECTING THE SKIN; 721]

purvey 1 v (*formal*) **sell**, provide, supply, deal in, furnish (*formal*) [➡SELL; 441] *Opposite*: buy 2 v **gossip**, tattle, whisper, spread, tell [➡GOSSIP; 678]

purveyor (*formal*) 1 n **supplier**, seller, vendor, outlet, source, stockist (*UK*) [➡SELLERS; 442] 2 n **spreader**, gossipmonger, teller, tattler, source, scandalmonger, whisperer [➡INTERFERING PEOPLE AND TATTLETALES; 950]

pus n **discharge**, secretion, excretion, fluid, infection [➡EXCRETION AND EXCRETA; 722]

pus-filled adj [➡DECAYING OR INFESTED; 1236]

push 1 v **shove**, thrust, ram, press on, set in motion, drive, move forward [➡PUSH, PULL, AND SLIDE; 335] *Opposite*: pull 2 v **impel**, urge, goad, force, make, coerce, induce, exhort, persuade, press [➡CAUSE OR COMPEL TO ACT; 271] *Opposite*: restrain 3 v **advocate**, promote, advance, endorse, boost, get behind, back, plug (*informal*) [➡APPROVE AND CONFIRM; 646] *Opposite*: oppose 4 v (*slang*) **sell**, vend, hawk, peddle, tout [➡SELL; 441] *Opposite*: buy 5 n **ambition**, energy, force, vigor, impetus, motivation, drive, get-up-and-go (*informal*) [➡CAUSATION; 168] *Opposite*: apathy

push-button adj **automatic**, high-tech, remote-control, electronic [➡MACHINERY; 1114] *Opposite*: manual

pushcart n **cart**, handcart, trolley, wagon, barrow (*UK*) [➡BIKES, CARS, AND CARRIAGES; 1149]

pushchair (*UK*) n **stroller**, buggy, baby carriage, carriage [➡BIKES, CARS, AND CARRIAGES; 1149]

pushed (*informal*) 1 adj **lacking**, short, short of cash, strapped (*informal*), hard up (*informal*), broke (*informal*) [➡POVERTY AND POOR; 892] 2 adj **hard-pressed**, pressed, busy, struggling, hard at it [➡IN TROUBLE AND DISADVANTAGED; 73]

pusher (*slang*) n **dealer**, supplier, peddler, hawker [➡SELLERS; 442]

push for v [➡REQUEST AND DEMAND; 663]

push in v **cut in**, barge in, shove in, squeeze in, cut in line, butt in, muscle in (*informal*), jump the queue (*UK*), skip the queue (*UK*) [➡MOVE PAST, INTO, OR THROUGH SOMETHING; 331]

pushiness n **forcefulness**, nerve, aggressiveness, assertiveness, brashness, insistence, cheek (*informal*), front (*UK*) [➡BOSSY AND OVERBEARING; 516] *Opposite*: reluctance

pushing 1 adj **assertive**, forceful, aggressive, strident, brash, insistent, nervy (*informal*), loudmouthed

(*informal*) [➡BOSSY AND OVERBEARING; 516] *Opposite*: retiring 2 adj **approaching**, nearly, almost, just about, roughly, near enough, close to [➡APPROXIMATELY; 135]

push into v [➡CAUSE OR COMPEL TO ACT; 271]

push off 1 v **cast off**, shove off, embark, depart, set sail [➡LEAVE AND GO AWAY; 8] 2 v (*informal*) **go away**, leave, depart, get going, set out, head off, shove off (*informal*), split (*slang*) [➡LEAVE AND GO AWAY; 8] *Opposite*: remain

pushover (*informal*) n **dupe**, soft touch, gull, target, softy (*informal*), sucker (*informal*), mark (*slang*) [➡VICTIMS OF DECEIT; 662]

push-start (*UK*) n [➡BEGINNINGS; 53]

push through v **put into force**, enforce, enact, introduce, force through, drive through, rush through, railroad [➡CAUSE TO HAPPEN; 31]

pushy (*informal*) adj **assertive**, forceful, aggressive, strident, brash, insistent, overbearing, bossy, loudmouthed (*informal*), nervy (*informal*) [➡BOSSY AND OVERBEARING; 516] *Opposite*: retiring

pusillanimity n **timidity**, fear, cowardliness, nervousness, hesitation, trepidation, spinelessness, tremulousness, fearfulness, faint-heartedness [➡COWARDICE AND WEAKNESS OF WILL; 508] *Opposite*: confidence

pusillanimous adj **timid**, cowardly, faint-hearted, weak, spineless, fearful, tremulous, nervous, gutless, craven, lily-livered (*dated*) [➡COWARDICE AND WEAKNESS OF WILL; 508] *Opposite*: brave

See Compare and Contrast at **cowardly**.

puss 1 n (*slang*) **face**, mug (*informal*), phiz (*slang*), phizog (*slang*) [➡PARTS OF THE BODY: HEAD; 692] 2 n (*informal*) **cat**, kitten, pussy (*informal*), pussycat (*informal*), kitty (*informal*) [➡FELINES; 983]

pussy 1 n (*informal*) **cat**, kitten, puss (*informal*), pussycat (*informal*), kitty (*informal*) [➡FELINES; 983] 2 adj **infected**, purulent, pus-filled, weeping, oozing [➡DECAYING OR INFESTED; 1236]

pussycat 1 n **cat**, kitten, pussy (*informal*), puss (*informal*), kitty (*informal*) [➡FELINES; 983] 2 n (*informal*) **dear**, soft touch, pushover, softy (*informal*), sweetie (*informal*) [➡PEOPLE WHO ARE APPROVED OF; 955]

pussyfoot (*informal*) 1 v **hesitate**, waver, wander, prevaricate, procrastinate, sit on the fence, fudge (*informal*) [➡HESITATE; 272] 2 v **tiptoe**, creep, steal, pick your way, ghost, glide [➡MOVE SLOWLY; 314]

pussy willow *type of* **shrub or bush** [➡BUSHES AND SHRUBS; 1027]

pustule n **boil**, abscess, eruption, pimple, carbuncle, spot, furuncle [➡CONDITIONS AFFECTING THE SKIN; 721]

put v **place**, set, lay, position, situate, locate, plant, deposit, leave, plonk, plunk [➡POSITION SOMETHING; 325] *Opposite*: remove

put about v **spread**, circulate, tell, inform, give out, make known, disseminate, leak [➡INFORM, ANNOUNCE, AND ISSUE; 611] *Opposite*: keep secret

put across *v* **get across**, express, transmit, articulate, explain, communicate [➠ EXPLAIN AND CLARIFY; 610]

put a damper on *v* **deflate**, spoil, mar, subdue, depress, mess up (*informal*) [➠ WORSEN SOMETHING; 380] *Opposite*: enliven

put a match to *v* **set alight**, set fire to, set on fire, light, ignite, burn, burn down, set light to (*UK*) [➠ FIRE, FLAMMABILITY, AND BURNING; 1165] *Opposite*: put out

put an end to *v* **stop**, discontinue, halt, suspend, call a halt, bring to an end, put a stop to, pull the plug on, terminate (*formal*) [➠ CAUSE TO STOP; 266] *Opposite*: continue

put a premium on *v* **value**, appreciate, prize, favor, rate highly [➠ LIKE, LOVE, VALUE, AND ENJOY; 578]

put aside **1** *v* **save**, earmark, allocate, put by, set aside, put to one side, reserve, put away, stash away [➠ STORE AND KEEP; 453] **2** *v* **disregard**, ignore, close your eyes to, forget, waive, set aside [➠ NOT PAY ATTENTION; 764] **3** *v* **set down**, set aside, deposit, lay down, put down, put to one side [➠ MOVE SOMETHING TO ANOTHER LOCATION; 324]

put a spanner in the works (*UK*) *v* [➠ MAKE IMPOSSIBLE; 276]

put a spoke in somebody's wheel (*UK*) *v* **foil**, thwart, frustrate, put a wrench in the works, sabotage, wreak havoc, cause havoc, put a spanner in the works (*UK*) [➠ MAKE IMPOSSIBLE; 276] *Opposite*: help

put a stop to *v* **put an end to**, stop, bring to an end, pull the plug on, call a halt, discontinue, halt, suspend, terminate (*formal*) [➠ CAUSE TO STOP; 266] *Opposite*: continue

putative **1** *adj* **accepted**, acknowledged, recognized, known, believed [➠ KNOWN AND FAMOUS; 181] **2** *adj* **supposed**, reputed, alleged, assumed, presumed [➠ UNCERTAIN; 175]

put at risk *v* **endanger**, jeopardize, gamble with, risk, imperil (*formal*) [➠ PUT AT RISK; 384]

put away **1** *v* **tidy up**, pack away, clear up, store, pack up, stow, tidy away (*UK*) [➠ ARRANGE AND CREATE ORDER; 357] *Opposite*: scatter **2** *v* **save**, put aside, keep, stash away, put by, reserve, set aside, earmark, allocate, put to one side [➠ STORE AND KEEP; 453] **3** *v* (*informal*) **consume**, eat, drink, swallow, devour, wolf, bolt, chow down (*informal*), scarf down (*slang*) [➠ EAT AND NOT EAT; 710] **4** *v* (*informal*) **imprison**, jail, commit, confine [➠ THE POLICE, ARREST, AND PRETRIAL PROCEEDINGS; 818]

put a wrench in the works *v* **foil**, thwart, cause havoc, frustrate, wreak havoc, sabotage, put a spanner in the works (*UK*), put a spoke in somebody's wheel (*UK*) [➠ MAKE IMPOSSIBLE; 276] *Opposite*: help

put back **1** *v* **put away**, replace, pack away, return, clear away, tidy [➠ MOVE SOMETHING TO ANOTHER LOCATION; 324] **2** *v* **pay back**, repay, reimburse, compensate, recompense, remunerate [➠ GIVE MONEY; 433] **3** *v* **postpone**, defer, suspend, put on hold, put off, reschedule, delay, hold up, set back, retard [➠ DELAY ACTION OR OCCURRENCE; 278] **4** *v* **drink**, throw back, put away, gulp down, swallow down, quaff (*literary or humorous*) [➠ DRINK; 711]

put back together *v* **mend**, repair, reassemble, rebuild, reconstruct [➠ REPAIR AND MEND; 376] *Opposite*: take apart

put behind bars *v* [➠ THE POLICE, ARREST, AND PRETRIAL PROCEEDINGS; 818]

put behind you *v* **forget**, get over, recover from, put down to experience, get out of your system, turn your back on [➠ FORGET, FORGIVE, AND ACCEPT; 748] *Opposite*: brood

put by *v* **save**, put aside, stash away, earmark, put away, allocate, set aside, put to one side [➠ STORE AND KEEP; 453]

put down **1** *v* **set down**, lay down, down, deposit, leave, plonk, put aside, plop (*informal*) [➠ MOVE SOMETHING: DOWNWARD; 329] *Opposite*: pick up **2** *v* **enter**, write down, put in writing, record, log, note, file [➠ RECORD SOMETHING; 371] **3** *v* (*informal*) **ridicule**, mock, criticize, deride, disparage, deprecate [➠ ACCUSE, BLAME, AND CRITICIZE; 641] *Opposite*: praise **4** *v* **quell**, crush, suppress, quash, repress [➠ CAUSE TO STOP; 266]

putdown (*informal*) *n* **insult**, attack, jibe, criticism, dig, slap in the face (*informal*) [➠ CRITICISMS AND ANGRY OUTBURSTS; 50] *Opposite*: compliment

put forth (*formal*) **1** *v* **state**, make known, publish, present, give, propose, submit, offer, set forth (*formal*) [➠ INFORM, ANNOUNCE, AND ISSUE; 611] **2** *v* **leave**, set out, depart, head off, start out, move off [➠ LEAVE AND GO AWAY; 8]

put forward **1** *v* **state**, make known, publish, present, give, set forth (*formal*) [➠ INFORM, ANNOUNCE, AND ISSUE; 611] **2** *v* **suggest**, propose, present, submit, offer [➠ SUGGEST, HINT, AND COMMENT; 612]

put in **1** *v* **donate**, contribute, dedicate, allocate, give, spend [➠ GIVE MONEY; 433] **2** *v* **present**, submit, offer, make, claim, apply, request [➠ SUGGEST, HINT, AND COMMENT; 612] **3** *v* **interrupt**, break in, interpose, interject, butt in [➠ INTERRUPT AND BUTT IN; 619]

put in an appearance *v* **attend**, drop in, appear, turn up, be present, roll up, arrive, show your face, show up (*informal*), show (*informal*) [➠ ARRIVE; 12]

put in danger *v* **endanger**, jeopardize, hazard, risk, compromise, menace, imperil (*formal*) [➠ PUT AT RISK; 384]

put in jail *v* [➠ THE POLICE, ARREST, AND PRETRIAL PROCEEDINGS; 818]

put in prison *v* [➠ THE POLICE, ARREST, AND PRETRIAL PROCEEDINGS; 818]

put in the shade *v* **outshine**, be head and shoulders above, eclipse, be way ahead of, humiliate, surpass, overshadow, be streets ahead of (*UK*) [➠ BEAT AND DEFEAT; 80]

put into (*UK*) *v* **invest in**, devote to, give to, donate to, sink in, tie up in, plow into [➠ GIVE MONEY; 433]

put into action *v* **implement**, put into practice, apply, realize, carry out, put into effect, enforce, exercise [➠ CARRY OUT AN ACTION; 269]

put into effect *v* **enforce**, put into practice, exercise, apply, carry out, put into action, implement, realize [➠ CARRY OUT AN ACTION; 269]

put into operation *v* **implement**, put into action, put into practice, apply, set up, put into effect, carry out [➠ CARRY OUT AN ACTION; 269]

put into practice *v* **carry out**, practice, do, realize, implement, put into effect, achieve, accomplish, put into action [➠ CARRY OUT AN ACTION; 269]

put into words *v* **phrase**, articulate, formulate, express, convey, say [➤UTTER AND PRONOUNCE; 608]

put in writing *v* **put down on paper**, put down in black and white, put down, confirm in writing, write down, record [➤RECORD SOMETHING; 371]

put money on *v* [➤GAMBLE AND TAKE RISKS; 466]

put off **1** *v* **postpone**, delay, defer, shelve, suspend, adjourn, hold over, leave to another time, put on the back burner, put on ice, put on hold [➤DELAY ACTION OR OCCURRENCE; 278] *Opposite*: bring forward **2** *v* **hinder**, discourage, delay, obstruct, prevent, impede [➤MAKE IMPOSSIBLE; 276] **3** *v* **disgust**, repel, offend, sicken, revolt, repulse [➤UPSET, DISTRESS, AND HUMILIATE; 567] *Opposite*: attract **4** *v* (*UK*) **confuse**, distract, divert, disconcert, fluster, put somebody off his or her stride [➤CONFUSE AND BEWILDER; 571]

put on **1** *v* **dress in**, wear, change into, get into, don [➤DRESS, WEAR, AND UNDRESS; 868] *Opposite*: take off **2** *v* **stage**, present, produce, mount, direct, dramatize, show [➤CAUSE TO HAPPEN; 31] **3** *v* **gain**, add, increase, accumulate, acquire [➤CHANGE OF SIZE: BIGGER; 392] *Opposite*: lose **4** *v* **pretend**, feign, simulate, fake, play-act, sham, assume, adopt [➤PRETEND AND MIMIC; 60]

put-on **1** *adj* **pretend**, false, fake, sham, feigned, artificial, assumed, phony [➤FALSE AND UNREAL; 173] *Opposite*: genuine **2** *n* (*informal*) **deception**, simulation, trick, hoax, con, act, pose, scam (*slang*) [➤DECEPTION AND LIES; 660]

put on a brave front *v* **put a brave face on it**, keep up appearances, be brave, keep your chin up [➤TOLERATE AND ENDURE; 766]

put on an act *v* **pretend**, put it on, put on a pretense, sham, feign, play-act, ham, play to the gallery [➤PRETEND AND MIMIC; 60]

put on a pedestal *v* **elevate**, idolize, worship, admire, regard highly, look up to, lionize, adulate [➤PRAISE AND ENCOURAGE; 647]

put on hold *v* **put off**, delay, postpone, adjourn, defer, set aside, put to one side, shelve, put on the back burner, put on ice [➤DELAY ACTION OR OCCURRENCE; 278]

put on ice *v* **put off**, delay, postpone, adjourn, defer, set aside, shelve, put on hold, put on the back burner [➤DELAY ACTION OR OCCURRENCE; 278]

put on the back burner *v* **put off**, delay, postpone, adjourn, defer, set aside, put to one side, shelve, put on hold, put on ice [➤DELAY ACTION OR OCCURRENCE; 278]

put on the market *v* **offer for sale**, put up for sale, market, advertise [➤SELL; 441]

put out **1** *v* **extinguish**, douse, snuff out, stifle, snuff [➤CAUSE TO STOP; 266] *Opposite*: light **2** *v* **annoy**, irritate, slight, offend, exasperate, inconvenience, disturb, vex, provoke, niggle, aggravate (*informal*) [➤ANGER AND ANNOY; 569] *Opposite*: please **3** *v* **make public**, make known, publicize, circulate, spread, issue, publish, release, put about, disseminate [➤INFORM, ANNOUNCE, AND ISSUE; 611] *Opposite*: keep secret

put pressure on *v* [➤CAUSE OR COMPEL TO ACT; 271]

putrefaction *n* **decay**, decomposition, rot, breakdown, corruption, degeneration [➤DECAYING OR INFESTED; 1236]

putrefied *adj* [➤DECAYING OR INFESTED; 1236]

putrefy *v* **rot**, decay, decompose, go moldy, go bad, deteriorate, become rancid, spoil, turn, go off (*UK*) [➤GO BAD AND CORRODE; 390]

putrescent *adj* [➤DECAYING OR INFESTED; 1236]

putrid *adj* **rotten**, rotting, decayed, decaying, decomposed, decomposing, tainted, putrescent, moldy, bad, spoiled, rancid, fetid, smelly, stinky, off, rank (*literary*) [➤DECAYING OR INFESTED; 1236] *Opposite*: fresh

put right *v* **repair**, fix, mend, rectify, restore, redress, correct, straighten out [➤CORRECT AND PUT RIGHT; 377]

putsch *n* **coup**, insurrection, uprising, revolution, revolt, overthrow [➤AGGRESSIVE EVENTS; 39]

put somebody's back up (*informal*) *v* **annoy**, irritate, get on somebody's nerves, get on the wrong side of somebody, alienate, provoke, bother, vex, put out, aggravate (*informal*) [➤ANGER AND ANNOY; 569]

putt **1** *v* **hit**, tap, stroke, knock, push, drive [➤PUSH, PULL, AND SLIDE; 335] **2** *n* **tap**, stroke, hit, knock, push, shove [➤PUSH, PULL, AND SLIDE; 335]

putter *v* **dawdle**, idle, do nothing much, fiddle, fool around, dilly-dally, mosey (*informal*), mess around (*informal*), mooch (*slang*) [➤LACK OF ACTIVITY OR MOTION; 342]

put the arm on (*informal*) *v* [➤CAUSE OR COMPEL TO ACT; 271]

put the lid on *v* [➤CAUSE TO STOP; 266]

put to death *v* **kill**, execute, murder, assassinate, liquidate, decapitate, guillotine, exterminate, massacre, slaughter, waste (*slang*), do (*slang*), off (*slang*), hit (*slang*), bump off (*slang*), slay (*formal or literary*) [➤KILL; 923]

See Compare and Contrast at **kill**.

put together **1** *v* **assemble**, piece together, construct, build, fabricate, make [➤BUILD; 352] **2** *v* **draw up**, formulate, devise, develop, prepare, run up, concoct, make up, invent, rustle up (*informal*) [➤CREATION; 346]

put to good use *v* **use**, apply, exploit, exercise, make use of, utilize, find a use for [➤MAKE GOOD USE OF SOMETHING; 473] *Opposite*: discard

put to sleep **1** *v* [➤KILL; 923] **2** *v* **knock out**, sedate, put under, put out, numb, dope [➤REMEDIES, TREATMENTS, AND OPERATIONS; 731]

See Compare and Contrast at **kill**.

put to use *v* [➤USE; 467]

putty **1** *n* [➤BUILDING MATERIALS; 1077] **2** *type of gray* [➤COLORS; 1224]

put under *v* **sedate**, put to sleep, put out, knock out, anesthetize [➤REMEDIES, TREATMENTS, AND OPERATIONS; 731] *Opposite*: bring around

put up **1** *v* **erect**, raise, build, construct, create [➤BUILD; 352] *Opposite*: tear down **2** *v* **accommodate**, house, lodge, take in [➤TAKE CARE OF AND SPOIL; 300] *Opposite*: evict **3** *v* **offer**, provide, proffer, extend, advance, give, stand [➡GIVE MONEY; 433]

put-upon *adj* **overburdened**, exploited, used, overworked, abused, exhausted [➡IN TROUBLE AND DISADVANTAGED; 73]

put up to *v* **induce**, persuade, encourage, make, cause, incite, prompt, urge, challenge, dare [➡CAUSE OR COMPEL TO ACT; 271] *Opposite*: dissuade

put up with *v* **tolerate**, endure, bear, stand, submit, swallow, stomach, suffer, shoulder [➡TOLERATE AND ENDURE; 766]

put your back into *v* **try hard**, give your all, work hard, give it your best shot, give it all you've got, slog, go all out, buckle down (*informal*), use elbow grease (*informal*), go for it (*slang*) [➡HARD WORK OR EFFORT; 298]

put your faith in *v* **trust**, rely on, count on, have confidence in, bank on, believe [➡CERTAINTY; 561]

put your feet up *v* **relax**, rest, nap, stop, lounge around, lie down, take a break, take it easy, take five (*informal*), catch forty winks (*informal*), take a breather (*informal*), catch some z's (*informal*), chill out (*slang*), put your head down (*UK*) [➡STOP ACTING; 264]

put your foot down *v* **demand**, stand firm, stand fast, be resolute, be determined, insist [➡CLAIM, INSIST, AND EMPHASIZE; 614]

put your foot in it (*informal*) *v* **blunder**, err, goof, speak out of turn, be indiscreet, be tactless, put your foot in your mouth (*informal*), slip up (*informal*) [➡BETRAY CONFIDENCES AND GOSSIP; 618]

put your foot in your mouth (*informal*) *v* **blunder**, be indiscreet, be tactless, speak out of turn, goof, err, put your foot in it (*informal*), slip up (*informal*), blow it (*slang*) [➡BETRAY CONFIDENCES AND GOSSIP; 618]

put your oar in (*UK*) *v* **interfere**, meddle, stick your nose in, intrude, intervene, butt in [➡INTERRUPT AND BUTT IN; 619]

puzzle 1 *v* **mystify**, bewilder, perplex, baffle, confuse, stump, bamboozle (*informal*) [➡CONFUSE AND BEWILDER; 571] 2 *v* **wonder**, mull, brood, ponder [➡THINK AND REFLECT; 743] 3 *n* **mystery**, enigma, conundrum, problem, dilemma, brainteaser, riddle, poser, puzzler [➡SECRETS AND MYSTERIES; 180] *Opposite*: explanation

See Compare and Contrast at **problem**.

puzzled *adj* **mystified**, bewildered, perplexed, baffled, confused, stumped, all at sea, at a complete loss, nonplussed, confounded, bamboozled (*informal*) [➡CONFUSION, ANXIETY, AND WORRY; 540] *Opposite*: enlightened

puzzlement *n* **bafflement**, perplexity, uncertainty, disorientation, bemusement, confusion, bewilderment, mystification [➡CONFUSION, ANXIETY, AND WORRY; 540] *Opposite*: understanding

puzzle out *v* **work out**, solve, figure out, resolve, decipher, find the answer, decode, untangle [➡SOLVE AND INTERPRET; 760]

puzzler *n* **conundrum**, puzzle, mystery, riddle, brainteaser, challenge, poser, toughie (*informal*) [➡SECRETS AND MYSTERIES; 180]

puzzling *adj* **mystifying**, bewildering, perplexing, baffling, confusing, bamboozling (*informal*) [➡DIFFICULTY AND COMPLEXITY; 242] *Opposite*: enlightening

PVC *type of* **synthetic fabric** [➡FABRICS; 1132]

pye-dog *n* [➡DOGS; 980]

pygmy *adj* **miniature**, small, tiny, dwarf, little, undersized, diminutive, midget, toy [➡SMALL; 1195]

pylon *n* **tower**, mast, post, pillar [➡TOWERS; 1099]

pyralid *type of* **moth** [➡MOTHS AND BUTTERFLIES; 1015]

pyramid *type of* **angular shape** [➡ANGULAR SHAPE; 1217]

pyre *n* **fire**, bonfire, furnace [➡FIRE, FLAMMABILITY, AND BURNING; 1165]

Pyrenean mountain dog *type of* **large dog** [➡DOGS; 980]

pyrite *type of* **mineral** [➡MINERALS; 1277]

pyromania *n* [➡FADS, FETISHES, AND IDOLATRY; 555]

pyromaniac *n* **fire setter**, arsonist, torcher, fire raiser (*UK*) [➡DEVOTEES AND ADDICTED PEOPLE; 556]

pyrophobia *type of* **phobia** [➡FEARS AND PHOBIAS; 554]

pyrotechnics *n* [➡FIRE, FLAMMABILITY, AND BURNING; 1165]

python *type of* **nonpoisonous snake** [➡SNAKES; 995]

Pyxis *type of* **constellation** [➡HEAVENLY BODIES; 1061]

Q

quack 1 *type of* **bird sound** [➡ SOUNDS MADE BY BIRDS; 1263] 2 *n* **charlatan**, fraud, fake, sham, pretender, con artist (*slang*), mountebank (*literary*) [➡ PEOPLE WHO DECEIVE; 661]

quackery *n* **deception**, trickery, dishonesty, fraud, deceit, charlatanism, flimflam (*slang*) [➡ DECEPTION AND LIES; 660] *Opposite*: honesty

quad (*informal*) *n* **quadrangle**, yard, courtyard, square, patio, piazza, plaza [➡ URBAN OUTDOOR SPACES; 1072]

quadrangle 1 *n* **courtyard**, yard, square, piazza, plaza, patio, quad (*informal*) [➡ URBAN OUTDOOR SPACES; 1072] 2 *n* **four-sided figure**, rectangle, oblong, quadrilateral, parallelogram, rhombus, lozenge, diamond, square [➡ ANGULAR SHAPE; 1217]

quadrant *type of* **measuring device** [➡ MEASURING DEVICES; 1123]

quadriceps *type of* **muscle or tendon** [➡ THE MUSCLES; 718]

quadrilateral 1 *n* **rectangle**, oblong, square, parallelogram, rhombus, lozenge, diamond, four-sided figure, tetragon, trapezoid, trapezium [➡ ANGULAR SHAPE; 1217] 2 *adj* **four-sided**, quadrangular, quadrate, rectangular, square, rhomboid, diamond, trapezoidal [➡ ANGULAR SHAPE; 1217]

quadrille *type of* **dance** [➡ DANCE; 903]

quadruped *n* **animal**, four-footed animal, tetrapod [➡ LIVING THINGS AND LIVING; 976]

quadruple *v* **increase fourfold**, multiply, times, magnify, augment, expand [➡ CHANGE OF SIZE: BIGGER; 392] *Opposite*: decrease

quadruplet *type of* **offspring** [➡ YOUNGER GENERATION RELATIVES; 958]

quaff (*literary or humorous*) *v* **drink**, gulp down, put away, throw back, swallow down, swill, swig (*informal*), guzzle (*informal*), knock back (*informal*), imbibe (*formal or humorous*) [➡ DRINK; 711]

quagmire 1 *n* **swamp**, marsh, bog, mire, quicksand, morass [➡ WETLANDS; 1043] 2 *n* **predicament**, dilemma, quandary, sticky situation, muddle, imbroglio, crisis, perplexity, entanglement [➡ DIFFICULT SITUATIONS; 72]

quahog *type of* **aquatic invertebrate** [➡ AQUATIC INVERTEBRATES; 1022]

quail 1 *v* **flinch**, recoil, cringe, balk [➡ PHYSICAL REACTIONS; 316] 2 *type of* **fowl** [➡ FOOD BIRDS; 999]

See Compare and Contrast at **recoil**.

quaint 1 *adj* **old-world**, old-fashioned, picturesque, antiquated, charming, pretty, attractive, appealing [➡ BEAUTY AND ATTRACTIVENESS; 189] *Opposite*: modern 2 *adj* **strange**, peculiar, odd, curious, bizarre, weird, extraordinary, unusual [➡ BIZARRE AND PECULIAR; 257] *Opposite*: ordinary

quaintness 1 *n* **picturesqueness**, antiquatedness, antiqueness, charm, appeal, attraction, attractiveness, prettiness [➡ BEAUTY AND ATTRACTIVENESS; 189] *Opposite*: modernity 2 *n* **strangeness**, peculiarity, oddness, weirdness, curiousness, curiosity [➡ BIZARRE AND PECULIAR; 257] *Opposite*: ordinariness

quake 1 *v* **quail**, tremble, shudder, quaver, cower, flinch, cringe, show fear, take fright [➡ PHYSICAL REACTIONS; 316] 2 *v* **shake**, tremble, quiver, shudder, shiver, wobble, vibrate [➡ BOUNCE, UNDULATE, AND VIBRATE; 308] 3 *n* (*informal*) **earthquake**, tremor, temblor, seismic wave, seismic activity, seism [➡ VOLCANOES AND EARTHQUAKES; 1054]

qualification 1 *n* **skill**, quality, attribute, ability, aptitude, talent, characteristic, fitness, experience [➡ SKILLS, TALENTS, AND ABILITIES; 526] *Opposite*: failing 2 *n* **credential**, diploma, certificate, license [➡ QUALIFICATIONS; 843] 3 *n* **requirement**, condition, prerequisite, criterion, sine qua non, stipulation, proviso, rider [➡ NECESSARY AND ESSENTIAL; 196] 4 *n* **restriction**, reservation, modification, limitation, tempering [➡ CHANGE OF INTENSITY: LESS; 395]

qualified 1 *adj* **eligible**, short-listed, accepted, nominated, seeded, authorized, certified, licensed, enrolled [➡ QUALIFICATIONS; 843] *Opposite*: unqualified 2 *adj* **suitable**, fitted, eligible, capable, competent, skilled, trained, experienced, practiced [➡ APPROPRIATE, SUITABLE, AND ADVISABLE; 184] *Opposite*: unsuitable 3 *adj* **limited**, contingent, modified [➡ CHANGE; 372] *Opposite*: unconditional

qualifier *type of* **word class** [➡ ASPECTS OF LANGUAGE; 682]

qualify 1 *v* **be suitable**, be in the running, meet the requirements, be eligible, make the grade, be nominated, succeed, be licensed, be certified [➡ SUCCEED AND WIN; 79] *Opposite*: fail 2 *v* **train**, certify, license, empower, entitle, enable, allow, permit, authorize [➡ PERMIT AND ALLOW; 669] 3 *v* **restrict**, limit, modify, temper, moderate, lessen, soften, reduce [➡ CHANGE OF INTENSITY: LESS; 395]

quality 1 *n* **characteristic**, feature, attribute, property, trait, condition [➡ QUALITIES AND CHARACTERISTICS; 1191] 2 *n* **standard**, grade, level, caliber, class, kind, type [➡ VARIETIES, TYPES, AND KINDS; 145] 3 *n* **excellence**, superiority, caliber, class, eminence, worth, value [➡ GOOD, WELL, BETTER; 183] *Opposite*: inferiority

qualm 1 *n* **misgiving**, doubt, pang, fear, apprehensiveness, uneasiness, foreboding, trepidation, disquiet [➡ FEELINGS ABOUT THE FUTURE; 533] 2 *n* **scruple**, pang of conscience, remorse, contrition, compunction, regret, repentance, shame [➡ FEELINGS ABOUT THE PAST; 532]

quandary *n* **dilemma**, predicament, difficulty, Catch-22, fix (*informal*), jam (*informal*), cleft stick (*UK*) [➡ DIFFICULT SITUATIONS; 72]

quantifiable *adj* **calculable**, computable, measurable, assessable, reckonable, finite, countable, specifiable, ratable [➡ ASSESS QUANTITY; 757] *Opposite*: unquantifiable

quantifier *type of* **word class** [➡ ASPECTS OF LANGUAGE; 682]

quantify *v* **calculate**, count, enumerate, measure, compute, tell, reckon, put a figure on [➡ASSESS QUANTITY; 757]

quantitative 1 *adj* **measurable**, quantifiable, calculable, numerical, computable, assessable, reckonable, ratable [➡MATH; 597] *Opposite*: unquantifiable 2 *adj* **numerical**, enumerative, finite, arithmetical, mathematical, variable [➡ASSESS QUANTITY; 757]

quantity *n* **amount**, number, measure, extent, size, magnitude, capacity, mass [➡AMOUNTS AND QUANTITIES; 112]

quantum *adj* **major**, dramatic, significant, important, considerable, substantial, huge [➡MOST IMPORTANT AND MAIN; 193] *Opposite*: minor

quarantine 1 *n* **isolation**, seclusion, confinement, solitary confinement, cordon sanitaire, separation [➡REMEDIES, TREATMENTS, AND OPERATIONS; 731] *Opposite*: integration 2 *v* **isolate**, seclude, set apart, confine, separate, cordon off [➡BECOME SICK, TREAT, AND RECOVER; 728] *Opposite*: integrate 3 *v* **detain**, imprison, hold, lock up, intern, confine, keep under lock and key, put in solitary [➡CAPTIVITY AND LOSS OF FREEDOM; 248] *Opposite*: release

quark 1 *n* [➡DAIRY PRODUCTS AND CHEESES; 1183] 2 *type of* **elementary particle** [➡ELEMENTARY PARTICLES; 1279]

quarrel 1 *n* **argument**, dispute, squabble, disagreement, row, tiff, difference of opinion, clash, fight, spat, wrangle [➡ARGUMENTS; 47] *Opposite*: reconciliation 2 *n* **complaint**, grievance, grumble, problem (*informal*), bone to pick (*informal*), issue (*informal*) [➡COMPLAIN AND NAG; 686] 3 *v* **argue**, row, fall out, clash, fight, wrangle, have a tiff [➡ARGUE AND FIGHT; 643] *Opposite*: make up

quarrelsome *adj* **argumentative**, cantankerous, irritable, petulant, confrontational, querulous, hot-tempered, difficult, cranky (*informal*), grouchy (*informal*) [➡DIFFICULT TO PLEASE; 515] *Opposite*: agreeable

quarry 1 *n* **mine**, excavation, pit, diggings [➡INDUSTRIAL BUILDINGS; 1087] 2 *n* **prey**, victim, target, kill, game, objective [➡DEAD PERSON; 926] *Opposite*: hunter 3 *v* **mine**, dig out, extract, excavate, dig up, gouge out, cut [➡EXTRACT AND SEVER; 341]

quart *type of* **nonmetric unit** [➡SIZE AND DIMENSIONS; 1192]

quarter 1 *n* **fourth**, division, part, section, quadrant, quartile [➡MEASURABLE PORTIONS; 127] 2 *type of* **time period** [➡TIMES OF YEAR; 88] 3 *n* [➡CURRENCIES; 798] 4 *n* **district**, neighborhood, sector, zone, section, part, area, barrio, quartier [➡HUMAN SETTLEMENTS; 1070] 5 *v* **divide**, subdivide, cut up, section, split up, slice [➡SEPARATE AND DIVIDE; 401] 6 *v* **lodge**, house, billet, accommodate, put up, find a bed for [➡TAKE CARE OF AND SPOIL; 300] *Opposite*: evict

quarterfinal *n* **round**, heat, leg, match, game [➡NON-AGGRESSIVE/SPORTING EVENTS; 40]

quarterly 1 *adj* **three-monthly**, trimestral, four times a year [➡TIMES OF YEAR; 88] 2 *n* **magazine**, periodical, journal, publication, slick, glossy magazine (*UK*) [➡NEWSPAPERS AND MAGAZINES; 605]

quarters *n* **rooms**, accommodations, billet, housing, lodgings (*dated*), accommodation (*UK*) [➡ACCOMMODATIONS; 855]

quartet *type of* **band** [➡MUSICIANS AND SINGERS; 908]

quartile *n* [➡MEASURABLE PORTIONS; 127]

quartz *type of* **mineral** [➡MINERALS; 1277]

quartz clock *type of* **clock** [➡CLOCKS AND TIMERS; 1126]

quartz glass *type of* **glass** [➡GLASS; 1136]

quartz heater *type of* **heating appliance** [➡HEATING, REFRIGERATION, AND VENTILATION; 1142]

quartzite *type of* **stone** [➡STONES, ROCKS, AND BOULDERS; 1057]

quasar *type of* **star or star system** [➡HEAVENLY BODIES; 1061]

quash 1 *v* **put down**, suppress, quell, subdue, crush, repress, overwhelm, defeat, conquer [➡BEAT AND DEFEAT; 80] *Opposite*: allow 2 *v* **nullify**, cancel, repeal, overturn, annul, invalidate, make void [➡ABOLISH AND ANNUL; 452] *Opposite*: validate

quasi *adj* **virtual**, to all intents and purposes, pseudo, would-be, self-styled, mock, wannabe (*informal*), as it were (*formal*) [➡FALSE AND UNREAL; 173] *Opposite*: through and through

Quaternary *type of* **period** [➡EPOCHS AND ERAS; 891]

quatrain *n* **verse**, stanza, rhyme [➡POETRY AND VERSE; 915]

quaver 1 *v* **tremble**, shudder, shake, quiver, quake, quail, flinch [➡PHYSICAL REACTIONS; 316] 2 *v* **trill**, warble, wobble, vibrate, quiver, waver [➡EMIT RINGING AND HOOTING SOUNDS; 367]

quavering *adj* [➡SOFT, LOW, OR PLEASANT SOUNDS; 1265]

quay *n* **dockside**, wharf, quayside, dock, pier, harbor, seafront, jetty [➡WATERWAYS AND SEAWAYS; 1108]

quayside *n* **dock**, quay, dockside, wharf, harbor, seafront [➡WATERWAYS AND SEAWAYS; 1108]

queasily *adv* **nauseously**, biliously, dizzily, groggily, woozily [➡ILL AND SICK; 740]

queasiness *n* **nausea**, sickness, biliousness, vomiting, upset stomach, dizziness, faintness [➡ILL AND SICK; 740]

queasy 1 *adj* **nauseous**, sick, ill, indisposed, seasick, odd, groggy, woozy, unsettled, green around the gills (*informal*), queer (*dated*) [➡ILL AND SICK; 740] *Opposite*: well 2 *adj* **uneasy**, uncomfortable, doubtful, dubious, troubling, unsettling [➡INSECURITY AND LOSS OF COMPOSURE; 544] *Opposite*: reassuring

queen 1 *n* **monarch**, sovereign, ruler, crowned head, empress [➡RULERS AND ARISTOCRACY; 823] 2 *n* **icon**, star, prima donna, doyenne [➡IMPORTANT OR FAMOUS PEOPLE; 893] 3 *n* **epitome**, model, essence, crème de la crème, ideal [➡PERFECT EXAMPLES AND EMBODIMENTS; 67]

queenly *adj* **majestic**, royal, regal, dignified, stately, noble [➡ROYALNESS; 825]

Queen's Counsel *n* [➡PEOPLE IN LAW COURTS; 820]

queen-size *adj* **large**, largish, medium-large [➡LARGE; 1193]

queen-size bed *type of* **bed** [➡FURNITURE; 858]

queer (*dated*) 1 *adj* **unusual**, unexpected, strange, surprising, funny, odd, peculiar, out of the ordinary, atypical, fishy [➡BIZARRE AND PECULIAR; 257] *Opposite*: commonplace 2 *adj* **eccentric**, unconventional, idiosyncratic, curious, bizarre, unusual, cranky (*informal*) [➡ECCENTRICITY AND IRRATIONALITY; 562] *Opposite*: normal 3 *adj* **unwell**, sick, nauseous, queasy, faint, dizzy, groggy, woozy [➞ILL AND SICK; 740] *Opposite*: well

queerness (*dated*) *n* **eccentricity**, oddness, strangeness, peculiarity, abnormality, bizarreness, crankiness (*informal*) [➞BIZARRE AND PECULIAR; 257] *Opposite*: normality

quell 1 *v* **suppress**, put down, subdue, crush, quash, repress, control, overwhelm, defeat, conquer [➞CAUSE TO STOP; 266] *Opposite*: incite 2 *v* **allay**, assuage, alleviate, mollify, mitigate, soothe, calm, disperse [➞CHANGE OF INTENSITY: LESS; 395] *Opposite*: aggravate

quench 1 *v* **slake**, satisfy, satiate, reduce, sate, appease [➞DRINK; 711] *Opposite*: stimulate 2 *v* **extinguish**, put out, douse, smother, stifle, snuff out [➞CAUSE TO STOP; 266] *Opposite*: ignite

querulous 1 *adj* **complaining**, carping, critical, difficult, hard to please, fussy, negative, censorious [➞ACCUSATORY AND DISAPPROVING; 634] *Opposite*: equable 2 *adj* **whining**, cantankerous, grumbling, complaining, moaning (*informal*), grouchy (*informal*), cranky (*informal*) [➞BAD-TEMPERED AND HUMORLESS; 626] *Opposite*: good-natured

querulousness *n* **peevishness**, negativity, cantankerousness, criticalness, argumentativeness, quarrelsomeness, provocativeness, petulance, crankiness (*informal*) [➞BAD-TEMPERED AND HUMORLESS; 626]

query 1 *n* **inquiry**, question, request, interrogation, demand, probe [➞ASK PEOPLE QUESTIONS; 666] *Opposite*: answer 2 *n* **doubt**, uncertainty, reservation, question, question mark, objection [➞UNCERTAINTY; 559] *Opposite*: certainty 3 *v* **question**, cast doubt on, doubt, suspect, challenge, mistrust, distrust, have reservations about [➞QUESTION THINGS; 751] *Opposite*: trust 4 *v* **inquire**, ask, interrogate, quiz, demand, question, probe, look into, grill (*informal*) [➞ASK PEOPLE QUESTIONS; 666] *Opposite*: answer

quest 1 *n* **mission**, expedition, pursuit, search, hunt, journey [➞SEEK POSSESSION AND SEARCH; 456] 2 *v* **search**, hunt, seek, chase, pursue, go in search of [➞SEEK POSSESSION AND SEARCH; 456] *Opposite*: find

question 1 *n* **inquiry**, query, interrogation, request, demand [➞ASK PEOPLE QUESTIONS; 666] *Opposite*: answer 2 *n* **issue**, subject, matter, point at issue, problem, difficulty [➞SUBJECT AREAS; 768] *Opposite*: resolution 3 *n* **uncertainty**, doubt, reservation, query, question mark, hesitation, anxiety [➞UNCERTAINTY; 559] *Opposite*: certainty 4 *v* **interrogate**, quiz, ask, debrief, probe, examine, look into, grill (*informal*), give somebody the third degree (*informal*) [➞ASK PEOPLE QUESTIONS; 666] *Opposite*: reply 5 *v* **doubt**, suspect, mistrust, distrust, query, have reservations about, cast doubt on [➞QUESTION THINGS; 751] *Opposite*: trust

---

Compare and Contrast: *question, quiz, interrogate, grill, give somebody the third degree*

CORE MEANING: to ask for information

question to ask for information on a particular subject, especially formally or officially; *quiz* to subject somebody to persistent questions; *interrogate* to question somebody systematically and intensively in a formal or official context, such as in a police investigation or court case; *grill* (*informal*) to question somebody intensively; *give somebody the third degree* (*informal*) to question somebody intensively, especially in an aggressive way.

---

questionable *adj* **dubious**, doubtful, open to discussion, open to doubt, moot, disputed, problematic, debatable, uncertain [➞UNCERTAIN; 175] *Opposite*: indisputable

questioner *n* **interviewer**, interrogator, cross-examiner, asker, inquirer, examiner [➞QUESTIONERS; 667] *Opposite*: interviewee

questioning *adj* **interrogative**, inquisitorial, searching, quizzical, inquiring, probing, prying, inquisitive, curious, nosy (*informal*) [➞ENTHUSIASTIC AND INQUISITIVE; 628] *Opposite*: responsive

question mark *n* **doubt**, uncertainty, reservation, query, question, issue [➞UNCERTAINTY; 559] *Opposite*: certainty

question master (*UK*) *n* **host**, quiz master, interviewer, questioner, chair, examiner, emcee (*informal*) [➞QUESTIONERS; 667] *Opposite*: contestant

questionnaire *n* **survey**, opinion poll, inquiry form, form, feedback form [➞ASK PEOPLE QUESTIONS; 666]

quetzal *type of* **currency** [➞CURRENCIES; 798]

queue 1 *n* (*UK*) **line**, file, column, train, row, crocodile (*UK*) [➞AREA AND RANGE; 111] 2 *n* (*UK*) **backlog**, logjam, tailback (*UK*) [➞TRAVEL: TRAFFIC PROBLEMS AND TRAFFIC MANAGEMENT; 323] 3 *v* **line up**, get in line, wait your turn, stand in line, wait in line, form a queue (*UK*), queue up (*UK*) [➞GET CLOSER TOGETHER; 310]

queue-jump (*UK*) *v* **leapfrog**, push in, gain an advantage, move ahead, overtake, butt in, push ahead [➞ARRIVE; 12]

quibble 1 *v* **equivocate**, hedge, split hairs, nitpick, cavil, be pedantic [➞PROTEST AND EXPRESS DISAPPROVAL; 642] *Opposite*: agree 2 *n* **objection**, cavil, equivocation, quiddity (*formal*) [➞DISHARMONY; 156]

quiche *n* **tart**, egg pie, flan, tartlet, pastry [➞PREPARED DISHES; 1170]

quick 1 *adj* **rapid**, fast, speedy, swift, hasty, hurried, snappy, nippy (*UK*) [➞MOVING QUICKLY; 103] *Opposite*: slow 2 *adj* **sudden**, immediate, instant, prompt, abrupt, swift, rapid [➞HAPPENING QUICKLY; 104] *Opposite*: delayed 3 *adj* **brief**, short, cursory, fleeting, momentary, passing, transient [➞FINITENESS, VARIABILITY, AND TRANSIENCE; 96] *Opposite*: lasting 4 *adj* **alert**, clever, bright, quick-thinking, quick-witted, sharp-witted, smart, adroit, shrewd, astute, intelligent, quick off the mark, quick on the uptake (*informal*), on the ball (*informal*) [➞POSITIVE INTELLECTUAL CHARACTERISTICS; 524] 5 *adj* **nimble**, lively, sprightly, spry, agile, nifty (*informal*) [➞DESCRIBING BODY MOVEMENTS; 288] *Opposite*: sluggish

See Compare and Contrast at **intelligent**.

quick as a flash *adv* [➞HAPPENING QUICKLY; 104]

quicken *v* **speed up**, accelerate, hasten, pick up speed, go faster, get faster, open up (*informal*) [➞CHANGE OF SPEED: MORE; 396] *Opposite*: slow down

quick-fire *adj* **rapid**, swift, successive, automatic, fast, brisk, speedy, quick [➞HAPPENING QUICKLY; 104] *Opposite*: measured

quickly 1 *adv* **rapidly**, fast, speedily, swiftly, hurriedly, hastily, nippily (*UK*) [➞MOVING QUICKLY; 103] *Opposite*: slowly 2 *adv* **suddenly**, immediately, promptly, without delay, at once, instantly, abruptly, hurriedly, hastily [➡HAPPENING QUICKLY; 104] *Opposite:* slowly **3** *adv* briefly, cursorily, fleetingly, momentarily, passingly, transiently [➡FINITENESS, VARIABILITY, AND TRANSIENCE; 96] *Opposite:* lastingly

quickness 1 *n* **rapidity**, speed, speediness, swiftness, promptness, nippiness (*UK*) [➡SPEED; 102] *Opposite:* sluggishness **2** *n* **alertness**, cleverness, quick-wittedness, adroitness, sharpness, responsiveness, intelligence [➡POSITIVE INTELLECTUAL CHARACTERISTICS; 524]

quick off the mark *adj* [➡POSITIVE INTELLECTUAL CHARACTERISTICS; 524]

quick on the uptake (*informal*) *adj* **bright**, smart, quick-witted, alert, intelligent, sharp, quick, on the ball (*informal*), with it (*informal*) [➡POSITIVE INTELLECTUAL CHARACTERISTICS; 524]

quicksand *n* **swamp**, marsh, quagmire, bog, mire, morass [➡WETLANDS; 1043]

quicksilver *adj* **volatile**, mercurial, changeable, inconstant, unpredictable, unstable [➡LACK OF COMMITMENT AND UNRELIABILITY; 509] *Opposite:* constant

quickstep *type of* **dance** [➡DANCE; 903]

quick-tempered *adj* **fiery**, temperamental, excitable, volatile, passionate, hotheaded, hot-blooded [➡EXCESSIVE SENSITIVITY; 511] *Opposite:* calm

quick-thinking *adj* [➡POSITIVE INTELLECTUAL CHARACTERISTICS; 524]

quick-witted *adj* **smart**, intelligent, clever, bright, sharp, quick, brilliant, alert, adroit, inventive, perceptive, astute [➡POSITIVE INTELLECTUAL CHARACTERISTICS; 524]

quick-wittedness *n* **adroitness**, inventiveness, sharpness, intelligence, cleverness, perceptiveness, keenness, astuteness [➡POSITIVE INTELLECTUAL CHARACTERISTICS; 524]

quid pro quo *n* **deal**, trade, agreement, exchange, tradeoff, bribe, tit for tat, an eye for an eye [➡EXCHANGE AND INTERCHANGE; 448]

quiescence *n* **dormancy**, latency, rest, inertness, calm, stillness, motionlessness, inactivity, inertia, lifelessness, stagnation, sluggishness [➡LACK OF ACTIVITY OR MOTION; 342] *Opposite:* action

quiescent *adj* **calm**, inactive, dormant, gentle, sluggish, inert, still, motionless, latent, lifeless [➡LACK OF ACTIVITY OR MOTION; 342] *Opposite:* active

quiet 1 *adj* **silent**, noiseless, inaudible, low, soft, discreet, unobtrusive, soundless [➡ABSENCE OF SOUND; 1257] *Opposite:* noisy **2** *adj* **peaceful**, still, tranquil, uninterrupted, undisturbed, serene, calm, halcyon (*literary*) [➡PEACEFULNESS AND GENTLENESS; 214] *Opposite:* noisy **3** *adj* **private**, discreet, unofficial, off-the-record, confidential, intimate [➡SECRET AND UNKNOWN; 179] *Opposite:* public **4** *adj* **trouble-free**, straightforward, uncomplicated, simple, easy, hassle-free (*informal*) [➡EASE AND SIMPLICITY; 200] **5** *adj* **relaxing**, restful, leisurely, peaceful, pleasant, untroubled, relaxed [➡EMOTIONALLY PLEASANT; 187] *Opposite:* busy **6** *adj* **discreet**, modest, subtle, subdued, muted, understated, restrained, unobtrusive [➡IMPERCEPTIBLE; 26] *Opposite:* showy **7** *n* **silence**, hush, peace, stillness, tranquillity, peace and quiet, quietude [➡ABSENCE OF SOUND; 1257] *Opposite:* noise **8** *v* **fall silent**, calm down, settle down, calm, hush, silence [➡CHANGE OF INTENSITY: LESS; 395] *Opposite:*

animate **9** *v* **alleviate**, allay, soothe, assuage, quell, mollify, banish, dispel, still [➡CHANGE OF INTENSITY: LESS; 395] *Opposite:* aggravate

See Compare and Contrast at **silent**.

quiet down *v* **stop talking**, fall silent, keep it down, shut up (*informal*), shush (*informal*), cool it (*slang*) [➡CHANGE OF INTENSITY: LESS; 395]

quietly 1 *adv* **silently**, gently, inaudibly, softly, in silence, soundlessly, noiselessly, unobtrusively [➡ABSENCE OF SOUND; 1257] *Opposite:* loudly **2** *adv* **calmly**, peacefully, tranquilly, serenely, uninterrupted, undisturbed [➡PEACEFULNESS AND GENTLENESS; 214] *Opposite:* noisily **3** *adv* **peacefully**, tranquilly, pleasantly, agreeably, restfully [➡EMOTIONALLY PLEASANT; 187]

quietness 1 *n* **silence**, softness, quiet, noiselessness, inaudibility, lowness, discreetness, unobtrusiveness, soundlessness [➡ABSENCE OF SOUND; 1257] *Opposite:* noise **2** *n* **peace**, stillness, tranquillity, serenity, calm, quiet [➡PEACEFULNESS AND GENTLENESS; 214]

quill 1 *n* **feather**, plume, barb, spine, spike [➡PARTS OF A BIRD; 1006] **2** *type of* **pen** [➡WRITING AND DRAWING IMPLEMENTS, AND MEDIA; 601]

quilt *n* **comforter**, patchwork quilt, bedspread, eiderdown, coverlet, duvet, counterpane (*dated*), bedcover (*UK*) [➡FURNISHING AND HOUSEHOLD LINENS; 860]

quince *type of* **fruit** [➡FRUIT AND VEGETABLES; 1176]

quintessence *n* **essence**, embodiment, epitome, personification, soul, heart, ideal [➡PERFECT EXAMPLES AND EMBODIMENTS; 67]

quintessential *adj* **typical**, essential, archetypal, prototypical, model, exemplary, classic, ideal [➡REPRESENTATIVE; 66] *Opposite:* atypical

quintet *type of* **band** [➡MUSICIANS AND SINGERS; 908]

quintuplet *type of* **offspring** [➡YOUNGER GENERATION RELATIVES; 958]

quip 1 *n* **witticism**, joke, jibe, one-liner, clever remark, pun, retort, bon mot, comeback, wisecrack (*informal*) [➡JOKES AND TEASING; 674] **2** *v* **joke**, jibe, remark, banter, retort, kid, come back, wisecrack (*informal*), jest (*literary*) [➡JOKES AND TEASING; 674]

quirk 1 *n* **twist of fate**, coincidence, accident, chance, oddity, twist, fluke (*informal*) [➡CHANCE EVENTS; 36] **2** *n* **idiosyncrasy**, peculiarity, foible, oddity, habit, eccentricity, trait, whim [➡PERSONAL ECCENTRICITIES; 493]

quirkiness *n* **strangeness**, oddness, nonconformity, eccentricity, weirdness, peculiarity, idiosyncrasy [➡ECCENTRICITY AND IRRATIONALITY; 562] *Opposite:* normality

quirky *adj* **idiosyncratic**, individual, unusual, peculiar, odd, strange, eccentric, unpredictable [➡ECCENTRICITY AND IRRATIONALITY; 562] *Opposite:* normal

quit 1 *v* **resign**, leave, walk out, abandon, vacate, give notice, desert, give up [➡LEAVE AND GO AWAY; 8] *Opposite:* stay **2** *v* **give up**, stop, relinquish, refrain from, renounce, suspend, call it quits (*informal*) [➡STOP ACTING; 264] *Opposite:* take up

quite 1 *adv* **very**, entirely, completely, totally, utterly, absolutely, extremely, fully, wholly [➡ ABSOLUTE AND ABSOLUTELY; 133] *Opposite*: slightly **2** *adv* **fairly**, rather, moderately, relatively, reasonably, somewhat, pretty (*informal*) [➡ TO A CERTAIN EXTENT; 136] *Opposite*: extremely

quits (*informal*) *adj* **even**, square, settled, level, even-steven (*informal*) [➡ EQUALITY; 154]

quitter (*informal*) *n* **defeatist**, deserter, loser, pessimist, coward, fatalist [➡ LAZY OR UNSUCCESSFUL PEOPLE; 948] *Opposite*: go-getter (*informal*)

quiver **1** *v* **tremble**, shake, shudder, shiver, quake, vibrate, quaver [➡ PHYSICAL REACTIONS; 316] **2** *n* **shudder**, shiver, tremble, palpitation, tremor, spasm, vibration [➡ PHYSICAL REACTIONS; 316]

quivering **1** *adj* **trembling**, quaking, quavering, unsteady, shaky, shaking, wobbly, weak [➡ DESCRIBING BODY MOVEMENTS; 288] *Opposite*: steady **2** *n* **pulsation**, vibration, spasm, palpitation, tremor [➡ PHYSICAL REACTIONS; 316]

quixotic *adj* **romantic**, unrealistic, idealistic, impractical, dreamy [➡ NEGATIVE INTELLECTUAL CHARACTERISTICS; 525] *Opposite*: down-to-earth

quiz **1** *n* **test**, puzzle, game, contest, competition, exercise, examination [➡ NON-AGGRESSIVE/SPORTING EVENTS; 40] **2** *v* **question**, interrogate, cross-examine, interview, examine, sound out, cross-question, debrief, query, catechize, grill (*informal*) [➡ ASK PEOPLE QUESTIONS; 666]

See Compare and Contrast at **question**.

quiz master *n* **host**, emcee, interviewer, questioner, chair, examiner, question master (*UK*) [➡ WORKERS IN ENTERTAINMENT AND MEDIA; 873] *Opposite*: contestant

quizzical *adj* **questioning**, curious, puzzled, surprised, perplexed, inquiring, amused, sardonic, ironic [➡ ENTHUSIASTIC AND INQUISITIVE; 628]

quorum *n* **minimum**, minimum number, least, required number, lower limit [➡ ENOUGH AND SUFFICIENT; 131]

quota *n* **share**, allocation, allowance, part, ration, slice, proportion, measure, lot, portion [➡ MEASURABLE PORTIONS; 127]

quotation **1** *n* **quote**, citation, line, passage, extract, reference, excerpt, reading [➡ SUMMARIES, OUTLINES, AND EXCERPTS; 588] **2** *n* **estimate**, price, figure, costing, quote, appraisal, estimation, assessment [➡ SCORES AND EVALUATIONS; 598]

quote **1** *v* **cite**, recite, repeat, refer to, mention, allude to, parrot [➡ RECITE, REPEAT, AND NARRATE; 620] **2** *v* **give an estimate**, estimate, bid, give a price of, give a figure of, price, offer [➡ ASSESS QUANTITY; 757] **3** *n* **quotation**, citation, line, passage, extract, reference, excerpt [➡ SUMMARIES, OUTLINES, AND EXCERPTS; 588] **4** *n* **estimate**, price, figure, costing, quotation, appraisal, estimation, assessment, bid [➡ SCORES AND EVALUATIONS; 598]

quotidian (*formal*) *adj* [➡ TIMES OF DAY; 87]

quotient *n* **proportion**, measure, amount, share, percentage [➡ MEASURABLE PORTIONS; 127]

ragtag 1 *adj* **motley**, disparate, assorted, miscellaneous, multifarious [➡ DIFFERENCE; 149] **2** *adj* **untidy**, shabby, unkempt, scruffy, ragged, raggedy, messy, sloppy [➡ BADLY GROOMED; 483] *Opposite*: neat

ragtime *type of* **jazz music** [➡ MUSIC, SONGS, AND SINGING; 907]

ragweed *type of* **weed** [➡ WEEDS AND THISTLES; 1034]

rai *type of* **world music** [➡ MUSIC, SONGS, AND SINGING; 907]

raid 1 *n* **attack**, search, forced entry, break-in, incursion, invasion, foray, swoop, bust (*slang*) [➡ SUDDEN EVENTS; 52] **2** *v* **storm**, attack, invade, search, break into, ransack, maraud, swoop, assault, bust (*slang*) [➡ ARRIVE; 12] **3** *v* **rob**, loot, plunder, hold up, burgle, burglarize, knock off (*slang*) [➡ STEAL AND ROB; 426]

raider *n* **attacker**, thief, robber, marauder, invader, plunderer, ravager, looter [➡ CRIMINALS; 821]

rail 1 *n* **railing**, handrail, banister, bar, support, barrier, fence [➡ BARRIERS; 1113] **2** *v* **protest**, complain, object, criticize, condemn, denounce, attack, inveigh, vociferate, fulminate, kick (*informal*), kick up (*informal*) [➡ PROTEST AND EXPRESS DISAPPROVAL; 642] *Opposite*: accept

railhead *n* **terminus**, starting point, end of the line [➡ RAILROADS; 1107]

railing *n* **fence**, paling, barrier, balustrade, boundary line, rails, rail [➡ BARRIERS; 1113]

raillery *n* **teasing**, joking, banter, repartee, kidding, badinage, joshing (*informal*), sport (*formal*), jesting (*literary*) [➡ JOKES AND TEASING; 674] *Opposite*: bullying

rail line *n* [➡ RAILROADS; 1107]

rail network *n* [➡ RAILROADS; 1107]

railroad 1 *n* **track**, line, train track, route, rail, rail line, railway (*UK*) [➡ RAILROADS; 1107] **2** *n* **rail network**, network, train system, train network, rail transportation system, railway (*UK*), rail transport system (*UK*) [➡ RAILROADS; 1107] **3** *v* (*informal*) **push**, force, steamroller, bulldoze, shove, press [➡ CAUSE OR COMPEL TO ACT; 271]

---

railroad

◆ *types of railroads*
cable railroad, monorail, streetcar line, subway, underground

◆ *types of rail vehicles*
cable car, funicular, locomotive, steam engine, streetcar, train

◆ *parts of a train*
box car, cabin, caboose, car, coach, compartment, dining car, freight car, locomotive, luggage compartment, observation car, Pullman, sleeper, sleeping car, smoker, smoking car, smoking compartment, steam engine, tank engine, wagon

---

railroad station *n* [➡ RAILROADS; 1107]

rail route *n* [➡ RAILROADS; 1107]

rail terminal *n* [➡ RAILROADS; 1107]

rail transportation system *n* [➡ RAILROADS; 1107]

raiment (*archaic or literary*) *n* **clothing**, apparel, clothes, wear, dress, costume, garments, attire (*formal*), habiliment (*formal*) [➡ CLOTHES AND ACCESSORIES; 864]

rain 1 *n* **rainfall**, drizzle, shower, torrent, precipitation, rainwater, raindrops, driving rain, sprinkle, mizzle, Scotch mist (*UK*) [➡ CLOUDY AND RAINY WEATHER; 1052] **2** *n* **volley**, hail, stream, torrent, flood, deluge, shower, barrage, fall, spate, plethora [➡ SUDDEN EVENTS; 52] **3** *v* **pour**, drizzle, pelt down, shower, sprinkle, spit, rain cats and dogs (*informal*) [➡ CLOUDY AND RAINY WEATHER; 1052] **4** *v* **lavish**, shower, pour, deluge, overwhelm, bombard [➡ GIVE TOO MUCH AND OVERBURDEN; 437]

rain barrel *n* [➡ CONTAINERS, RECEPTACLES, AND PACKAGING; 1245]

rainbow 1 *n* **arc**, arch, bow [➡ CLOUDY AND RAINY WEATHER; 1052] **2** *adj* **multicolored**, colorful, variegated, spectral, polychromatic, kaleidoscopic [➡ DESCRIBING COLORS; 1226] *Opposite*: monochrome

rainbow-colored *adj* [➡ DESCRIBING COLORS; 1226]

rain cats and dogs (*informal*) *v* **pour with rain**, teem, pour down, come down in torrents, come down in buckets, come down in sheets (*informal*) [➡ CLOUDY AND RAINY WEATHER; 1052]

rain check (*informal*) *n* [➡ DELAY ACTION OR OCCURRENCE; 278]

rain cloud *type of* **cloud** [➡ CLOUDY AND RAINY WEATHER; 1052]

raincoat *type of* **overcoat** [➡ GARMENTS AND OUTFITS; 865]

raindrops *n* [➡ CLOUDY AND RAINY WEATHER; 1052]

rainfall *n* **rain**, shower, drizzle, torrent, precipitation, rainwater, raindrops, sprinkle, mizzle, Scotch mist (*UK*) [➡ CLOUDY AND RAINY WEATHER; 1052] *Opposite*: sunshine

rain forest *n* [➡ WOODS, FORESTS, AND JUNGLES; 1047]

rain hat *type of* **hat** [➡ ACCESSORIES, MILLINERY, AND LINGERIE; 867]

rainmaker (*informal*) *n* **achiever**, triumph, success, star, celebrity, somebody, winner [➡ PEOPLE WHO ARE APPROVED OF; 955] *Opposite*: failure

rain off (*UK*) *v* **postpone**, put back, call off, move on, move forward, cancel, rain out [➡ MAKE IMPOSSIBLE; 276] *Opposite*: bring forward

rain on somebody's parade (*informal*) *v* [➡ WORSEN SOMETHING; 380]

rain out *v* **postpone**, put back, call off, move on, move forward, cancel, rain off (*UK*) [➡ DELAY ACTION OR OCCURRENCE; 278] *Opposite*: bring forward

rainproof *adj* **impermeable**, water-resistant, waterproof, showerproof, impervious, watertight, impregnable [➡ IN GOOD REPAIR; 1232] *Opposite*: permeable

rainstorm *n* **cloudburst**, downpour, deluge, thunderstorm, shower, squall, gullywasher (*informal*) [➡ CLOUDY AND RAINY WEATHER; 1052]

rainwater *n* **rain**, precipitation, rainfall, raindrops [➡ CLOUDY AND RAINY WEATHER; 1052]

rainy *adj* **wet**, raining, drizzling, showery, drizzly, damp, sprinkling, pouring, inclement [➡ CLOUDY AND RAINY WEATHER; 1052] *Opposite*: dry

rainy season n [➟ CLOUDY AND RAINY WEATHER; 1052]

raise 1 v **hoist**, lift up, uplift, elevate, move up, lift [➟ MOVE SOMETHING: UPWARD; 328] *Opposite*: let down 2 v **look after**, bring up, foster, grow, breed, produce, educate, cultivate, nurse, develop, nurture, rear [➟ TAKE CARE OF AND SPOIL; 300] *Opposite*: neglect 3 v **increase**, put up, inflate, boost, jack up, augment (*formal*) [➟ CHANGE OF SIZE: BIGGER; 392] *Opposite*: lower 4 v **build**, erect, set up, construct, put up [➟ BUILD; 352] 5 v **mention**, bring up, present, put forward, moot, broach, introduce [➟ SUGGEST, HINT, AND COMMENT; 612] *Opposite*: withdraw 6 v **solicit**, canvass, obtain, bring in, procure, amass, muster, scrape together (*informal*) [➟ OBTAIN POSSESSION BY PERSUASION; 457] 7 v **lift**, end, terminate, conclude [➟ CAUSE TO STOP; 266] 8 v **improve**, better, enhance, uplift, advance, upgrade, augment (*formal*) [➟ IMPROVE SOMETHING; 374] *Opposite*: deteriorate 9 v **cause**, elicit, stimulate, induce, excite, rouse, precipitate, result in, provoke, produce, create [➟ CAUSE TO HAPPEN; 31] *Opposite*: quell 10 n **increase**, promotion, advance, elevation [➟ CHANGE OF INTENSITY: MORE; 394]

Compare and Contrast: raise, elevate, lift, hoist

CORE MEANING: to place something in a higher position

raise to move something to a higher position, usually by means of physical effort. It does not suggest great physical effort; **elevate** a formal word meaning the same as **raise**; **lift** to raise something either by means of physical effort or using a mechanism; **hoist** to raise something by mechanical means, sometimes by heavy manual effort.

raise a fuss v [➟ PROTEST AND EXPRESS DISAPPROVAL; 642]

raise a ruckus v [➟ PROTEST AND EXPRESS DISAPPROVAL; 642]

raised bed garden type of **garden** [➟ GARDENS; 1074]

raised crossing n [➟ TRAVEL: TRAFFIC PROBLEMS AND TRAFFIC MANAGEMENT; 323]

raised ranch type of **house** [➟ RESIDENTIAL BUILDINGS; 1078]

raise objections v **object**, protest about, demur, remonstrate, contest, disagree, oppose [➟ PROTEST AND EXPRESS DISAPPROVAL; 642] *Opposite*: agree

raise the spirits v [➟ ENCOURAGE; 576]

raise your spirits v **cheer up**, lift your spirits, gladden, hearten, buoy up, liven up, inspire, give confidence, cheer [➟ ENCOURAGE; 576] *Opposite*: depress

raison d'état n **national interest**, realpolitik, expediency, diplomacy, politics, consideration [➟ STYLES AND SYSTEMS OF GOVERNMENT; 806]

raison d'être n **meaning**, purpose, rationale, motivation, inspiration, ethos, philosophy, belief, hope [➟ INTENTIONS AND PURPOSES; 772]

raita type of **seasonings, sauces, and dips** [➟ SEASONINGS AND SAUCES; 1174]

rajah n **king**, prince, maharajah, chief, ruler, sovereign, leader [➟ RULERS AND ARISTOCRACY; 823] *Opposite*: subject

rake 1 v **gather**, clear up, scrape, collect, scrape up, rake over, rake up (*informal*) [➟ USE TOOLS AND MACHINERY; 468] *Opposite*: scatter 2 v **enfilade**, pepper, spray, shoot [➟ SPREAD AND SCATTER; 332] 3 v **search through**, go through, sift, rummage, comb,

hunt for, scour, ransack [➟ SEEK POSSESSION AND SEARCH; 456] *Opposite*: find 4 n **reprobate**, degenerate, prodigal, profligate, squanderer, drunkard, gambler, playboy, voluptuary, libertine, roué (*literary*), inebriate (*archaic or literary*) [➟ VILLAINS AND THUGS; 947] *Opposite*: paragon

rake it in (*informal*) v [➟ GET MONEY OR REWARD; 421]

rake-off (*informal*) n **bribe**, kickback, favor, sweetener (*informal*), cut (*informal*), payoff (*informal*) [➟ FUNDS, PAYMENTS, AND CHARGES; 800] *Opposite*: cost

rake over the coals v [➟ ACCUSE, BLAME, AND CRITICIZE; 641]

rake up (*informal*) v **mention**, drag up, dredge up, bring up, dig up, allude to [➟ SUGGEST, HINT, AND COMMENT; 612] *Opposite*: keep mum (*informal*)

rakish 1 adj **dashing**, stylish, natty, sporty, jaunty, casual, confident, breezy, dapper, spruce, debonair [➟ WELL-GROOMED; 482] *Opposite*: bland 2 adj **dissolute**, profligate, degenerate, louche, dubious, disreputable, depraved, lecherous, dissipated, raffish [➟ MORALLY BAD OR IMPROPER; 775] *Opposite*: upright

rally 1 n **resurgence**, revival, comeback, recovery, revitalization, improvement [➟ PROGRESS AND ADVANCEMENT; 213] 2 n **gathering**, meeting, assembly, convention, demonstration, march, caucus, demo (*informal*) [➟ MEETINGS AND ASSEMBLIES; 43] 3 v **come together**, gather, call together, bring together, unite, assemble, collect, support, join forces, reassemble, reconvene, reunite [➟ GET CLOSER TOGETHER; 310] *Opposite*: disperse 4 v **revive**, improve, recover, pull through, get better, recuperate, perk up, make a comeback, pick up [➟ GET BETTER; 375] *Opposite*: decline

rally round v [➟ HELP; 293]

ram 1 v **strike**, hit, bump, slam, collide with, crash into, hammer, pound [➟ CONTACT: IMPACT; 413] 2 v **force**, stuff, jam, cram, compress, pack, push [➟ FILL; 406] 3 type of **male animal** [➟ MALE OR FEMALE ANIMALS; 978]

RAM type of **hardware** [➟ COMPUTERS AND COMPUTING; 1127]

ramble 1 v **go on**, digress, go off on a tangent, ramble on, blather (*informal*), rattle on (*UK*) [➟ CHATTER AND BABBLE; 617] *Opposite*: focus 2 v **walk**, hike, wander, roam, go for a walk, stroll, saunter, amble, traipse, drift, perambulate (*formal*) 3 n **hike**, walk, roam, stroll, wander, amble, saunter [➟ PROCEED AND GO; 305] [➟ PROCEED AND GO; 305]

ramble on v **go on**, ramble, digress, go off on a tangent, blather (*informal*), rattle on (*UK*) [➟ CHATTER AND BABBLE; 617] *Opposite*: focus

rambler n **walker**, hiker, backpacker, roamer, wanderer, stroller [➟ TRAVEL: TRAVELERS AND WALKERS; 319]

rambling 1 adj **pointless**, inconsequential, confused, incoherent, tedious, wordy, long-winded, prolix, digressive, discursive [➟ INARTICULATE, RAMBLING, AND AWKWARD; 633] *Opposite*: concise 2 adj **spread out**, sprawling, trailing, straggling, irregular, shaggy, all over the place (*informal*) [➟ LARGE; 1193] *Opposite*: compact

See Compare and Contrast at **wordy**.

rambunctious adj **rowdy**, high-spirited, lively, dis-

zling, glowing, resplendent [➡ DESCRIBING LIGHT; 1228] *Opposite*: dull

radiate 1 *v* **give out**, give off, emit, discharge, issue, release [➡ EMIT AND EMANATE; 361] 2 *v* **exude**, emanate, glow with, bristle with, brim with, overflow with, burst with [➡ EMIT AND EMANATE; 361] 3 *v* **spread out**, branch out, diverge, spread, circulate, diffuse, strew [➡ CHANGE DIRECTION OF MOTION; 344]

radiation *n* **particle emission**, energy, radioactivity, fallout, contamination, pollution [➡ ENERGY SOURCES; 1162]

radiator 1 *n* **heater**, room heater, storage heater, space heater [➡ HEATING, REFRIGERATION, AND VENTILATION; 1142] 2 *part of* **engine** [➡ PARTS OF AN ENGINE; 1144] 3 *type of* **general fixtures** [➡ FIXTURES; 859]

radical 1 *adj* **basic**, fundamental, essential, profound, deep-seated, deep-rooted [➡ FUNDAMENTAL; 195] 2 *adj* **sweeping**, pervasive, thorough, far-reaching, wide-ranging, profound, drastic, major [➡ WHOLENESS AND COMPLETENESS; 198] *Opposite*: minor 3 *adj* **revolutionary**, extreme, extremist, uncompromising, militant, fanatical [➡ REBELLIOUSNESS AND DISOBEDIENCE; 565] *Opposite*: conservative 4 *n* **extremist**, activist, militant, revolutionary, fanatic [➡ UNCOOPERATIVE OR REBELLIOUS PEOPLE; 566] *Opposite*: conservative

radicalism *n* **extremism**, militancy, fanaticism, zealotry, radicalness, ardor [➡ PHILOSOPHIES AND BELIEFS; 780]

radically *adv* **very**, fundamentally, thoroughly, drastically, completely, totally, deeply, profoundly [➡ ABSOLUTE AND ABSOLUTELY; 133] *Opposite*: superficially

radicchio *type of* **salad vegetable** [➡ FRUIT AND VEGETABLES; 1176]

radio *n* **radio set**, transistor, receiver, hi-fi, boom box (*informal*), wireless (*dated*) [➡ AUDIO EQUIPMENT; 1139]

radioactive *adj* **emitting radiation**, dangerous, harmful, hot, active [➡ ENERGY SOURCES; 1162]

radioactivity *n* **radiation**, particle emission, energy, fallout [➡ ENERGY SOURCES; 1162]

radio-controlled *adj* **remote-controlled**, automatic, remote [➡ DESCRIBING TECHNOLOGY; 1160]

radio presenter (*UK*) *n* [➡ WORKERS IN ENTERTAINMENT AND MEDIA; 873]

radio set *type of* **audio equipment** [➡ AUDIO EQUIPMENT; 1139]

radiotherapy *type of* **medical procedure** [➡ REMEDIES, TREATMENTS, AND OPERATIONS; 731]

radish *type of* **salad vegetable** [➡ FRUIT AND VEGETABLES; 1176]

radium *type of* **metal** [➡ METALS; 1276]

radius 1 *n* **area**, range, circle, ambit, extent, bounds, span, limit, compass, purview [➡ ROUNDED SHAPE; 1218] 2 *n* **line**, distance, length [➡ WIDTH: WIDE; 1199] 3 *n* **scope**, range, area of influence, umbrella, reach, sweep, remit (*UK*) [➡ DEGREE AND EXTENT; 110] 4 *type of* **bone** [➡ THE BONES AND JOINTS; 719]

raffia *n* **straw**, fiber, grass, natural fiber [➡ PLANT MATERIALS; 1133]

raffish 1 *adj* **unconventional**, dashing, rakish, disreputable, louche, free-spirited, colorful, individual, unusual [➡ MORALLY BAD OR IMPROPER; 775] *Opposite*: conventional 2 *adj* **showy**, ostentatious, gaudy, loud, garish, brash [➡ IN POOR TASTE AND OVERSENTIMENTAL; 229] *Opposite*: discreet

raffle 1 *n* **lottery**, draw, sweepstakes, drawing, tombola (*UK*) [➡ GAMBLE AND TAKE RISKS; 466] 2 *v* **offer**, give away, award, present, donate, proffer, tender [➡ GIVE AND PROVIDE; 430]

raft 1 *type of* **small vessel** [➡ SHIPS AND BOATS; 1150] 2 *n* (*informal*) **bundle**, number, tranche, portfolio, range, host, amount [➡ MANY, MUCH, LARGE AMOUNT; 117]

rafter *n* **beam**, roof beam, support, joist, strut, girder, timber [➡ BUILDING MATERIALS; 1077]

rag 1 *n* **cloth**, duster, scrap, shred, wisp, tatter, thread [➡ JUNK AND USELESS OBJECTS; 1249] 2 *n* (*informal*) **newspaper**, paper, tabloid [➡ NEWSPAPERS AND MAGAZINES; 605] 3 *v* (*dated*) **tease**, taunt, make fun of, call names, poke fun at, bait, mock, rib (*informal*), razz (*informal*) [➡ JOKES AND TEASING; 674]

raga *type of* **world music** [➡ MUSIC, SONGS, AND SINGING; 907]

ragamuffin (*dated*) *n* **urchin**, waif, child [➡ CHILD OR YOUTH; 945]

ragbag (*informal*) *n* **mixture**, mixed bag, miscellany, hodgepodge, jumble, assortment, potpourri, melange (*literary or formal*) [➡ COLLECTIONS AND MIXTURES OF THINGS; 1244]

rag doll *type of* **toy** [➡ TOYS; 880]

rage 1 *n* **fury**, anger, wrath, temper, frenzy, indignation, ire (*formal*) [➡ IRRITATION AND ANGER; 541] *Opposite*: calmness 2 *v* **fume**, rant and rave, storm, seethe, thunder, fulminate, explode, erupt, hit the roof (*informal*), blow your top (*informal*), blow your stack (*informal*), lose it (*informal*), see red (*informal*) [➡ GIVING VENT TO EMOTIONS; 679]

See Compare and Contrast at **anger**.

ragga *type of* **dance music** [➡ MUSIC, SONGS, AND SINGING; 907]

raggamuffin *type of* **dance music** [➡ MUSIC, SONGS, AND SINGING; 907]

ragged 1 *adj* **tattered**, torn, worn-out, raggedy, in tatters, frayed, worn to shreds, shabby [➡ IN BAD REPAIR; 1234] *Opposite*: pristine 2 *adj* **jagged**, serrated, uneven, irregular, rough, notched [➡ PHYSICAL TEXTURE; 1222] *Opposite*: even 3 *adj* **unkempt**, untidy, shabby, raggedy, in rags, scruffy, tatty, ragtag [➡ BADLY GROOMED; 483] *Opposite*: neat

raggedly 1 *adv* **untidily**, shabbily, scruffily, sloppily, messily, tattily [➡ BADLY GROOMED; 483] *Opposite*: neatly 2 *adv* **unevenly**, jaggedly, roughly, irregularly, sharply, ruggedly, brokenly [➡ PHYSICAL TEXTURE; 1222] *Opposite*: smoothly

raggedness 1 *n* **untidiness**, shabbiness, scruffiness, sloppiness, messiness, dishevelment [➡ BADLY GROOMED; 483] *Opposite*: neatness 2 *n* **unevenness**, jaggedness, roughness, irregularity, sharpness, serration, ruggedness, brokenness [➡ PHYSICAL TEXTURE; 1222] *Opposite*: smoothness

raggedy 1 *adj* **ragged**, torn, worn out, in tatters, frayed, worn to shreds, old, shabby, tattered [➡ IN BAD REPAIR; 1234] *Opposite*: pristine 2 *adj* **unkempt**, untidy, shabby, ragged, in rags, scruffy, tatty, ragtag [➡ BADLY GROOMED; 483] *Opposite*: neat

raging *adj* **powerful**, intense, furious, strong, rampant, violent, uncontrolled, wild [➡ STRENGTH; 201] *Opposite*: mild

ragout *type of* **cooked dish** [➡ PREPARED DISHES; 1170]

R

rabbi *n* **religious leader**, scholar, teacher, official, leader [➡ RELIGIOUS PEOPLE; 778]

rabbit 1 *n* **bunny**, coney, cottontail [➡ SMALL MAMMALS; 990] 2 *type of* **meat** [➡ TYPES AND CUTS OF MEAT; 1177]

rabble *n* **mob**, crowd, swarm, throng, horde, multitude, army, herd, hoi polloi [➡ GROUPS OF PEOPLE; 935]

rabble-rouser *n* **troublemaker**, agitator, demagogue, activist, firebrand, agent provocateur [➡ UNCOOPERATIVE OR REBELLIOUS PEOPLE; 566]

rabble-rousing 1 *n* **troublemaking**, sedition, provocation, agitation, activism [➡ BAD BEHAVIOR OR ACTIONS; 254] 2 *adj* **provocative**, inflammatory, seditious, incendiary, troublemaking [➡ REBELLIOUSNESS AND DISOBEDIENCE; 565]

rabid 1 *adj* **foaming at the mouth**, diseased, sick, ill, infected, unwell [➡ ILL AND SICK; 740] *Opposite*: well 2 *adj* **fanatical**, extreme, radical, uncompromising, militant, dedicated [➡ APPRECIATION AND GRATITUDE; 535] *Opposite*: lukewarm 3 *adj* **intense**, fervent, ardent, violent, zealous [➡ STRENGTH; 201] *Opposite*: moderate

rabidly *adv* **fervently**, ardently, intensely, single-mindedly, zealously [➡ APPRECIATION AND GRATITUDE; 535] *Opposite*: moderately

raccoon *type of* **small mammal** [➡ SMALL MAMMALS; 990]

race 1 *n* **contest**, competition, heat, sprint, marathon, steeplechase, relay race [➡ NON-AGGRESSIVE/SPORTING EVENTS; 40] 2 *n* **ethnic group**, nation, tribe, line, people (*informal*) [➡ GROUPS IN SOCIETY; 940] 3 *n* **competition**, contest, battle, duel, fight, rivalry, meeting [➡ NON-AGGRESSIVE/SPORTING EVENTS; 40] 4 *v* **compete**, take part, run, sprint, contest, battle, vie [➡ COMPETE, CONTEND, AND COMBAT; 303] *Opposite*: withdraw 5 *v* **speed**, go fast, run, sprint, hurry, dash, rush, gallop, fly, zip (*informal*) [➡ MOVE FAST; 313] *Opposite*: crawl

racecourse *n* **track**, stadium, running track, circuit, speedway, drag strip [➡ URBAN OUTDOOR SPACES; 1072]

racehorse *type of* **horse** [➡ HORSES; 985]

racer *n* **competitor**, contender, entrant, sprinter, runner, athlete [➡ PEOPLE IN SPORTS AND LEISURE; 876]

racetrack *n* **track**, turf, course, hippodrome [➡ URBAN OUTDOOR SPACES; 1072]

raceway 1 *n* **channel**, race, conduit, canal, course, gutter, trough, aqueduct [➡ WATERCOURSES; 1111] 2 *n* **track**, circuit, course, stadium, racecourse [➡ URBAN OUTDOOR SPACES; 1072]

racial *adj* **ethnic**, cultural, tribal, national [➡ BELONGING OR RELATING TO PEOPLE; 943]

racing bike *type of* **bike** [➡ BIKES, CARS, AND CARRIAGES; 1149]

racing car *type of* **car** [➡ BIKES, CARS, AND CARRIAGES; 1149]

racism *n* **racial discrimination**, discrimination, prejudice, bigotry, intolerance, xenophobia, bias [➡ PREJUDICE; 550]

racist *adj* **chauvinistic**, bigoted, xenophobic, prejudiced, discriminatory [➡ NEGATIVE INTELLECTUAL CHARACTERISTICS; 525] *Opposite*: tolerant

rack 1 *n* **stand**, frame, framework, holder, shelf, support [➡ SUPPORTS AND BASES; 1255] 2 *v* **afflict**, torment, plague, torture, beset, disturb, pain, agonize, try [➡ UPSET, DISTRESS, AND HUMILIATE; 567] *Opposite*: comfort 3 *v* **shake**, rock, devastate, play havoc with, wreck, damage [➡ DESTRUCTION AND DEMOLITION; 359] *Opposite*: restore 4 *v* **store**, shelve, stack, stow, put away, keep, pack [➡ POSITION SOMETHING; 325] *Opposite*: unpack

racket 1 *n* **noise**, din, rumpus, commotion, hullabaloo, clamor, uproar, row [➡ CHAOS AND UPROAR; 51] 2 *n* **swindle**, con, fraud, scheme, fiddle (*informal*), scam (*slang*) [➡ CRIMES; 817] 3 *type of* **sports equipment** [➡ SPORTS EQUIPMENT; 879]

racketeer *n* **criminal**, swindler, hoodlum, shark (*informal*), con artist (*slang*), hood (*slang*), fraudster (*UK*) [➡ CRIMINALS; 821]

racketeering *n* [➡ CRIMES; 817]

rackets *type of* **court game** [➡ HOBBIES, GAMES, AND SPORTS; 875]

racking *adj* [➡ PHYSICALLY UNPLEASANT; 226]

rack up (*informal*) *v* **accumulate**, chalk up, score, make, achieve, collect, notch up (*slang*) [➡ GET MONEY OR REWARD; 421]

rack your brains *v* **try to remember**, think hard, concentrate, make an effort, focus [➡ THINK AND REFLECT; 743]

raconteur *n* **narrator**, storyteller, conversationalist, after-dinner speaker, wit [➡ SPEAKERS AND ORATORS; 603]

racquets *see* **rackets**

racy *adj* **indecent**, risqué, indelicate, improper, sexy, rude, shocking, lewd, lascivious, smutty (*informal*), spicy (*informal*), off-color (*informal*) [➡ MORALLY BAD OR IMPROPER; 775] *Opposite*: clean

radar *n* **detector**, locater, sensor, locating system, position finder [➡ NAVIGATION; 1141]

raddled *adj* **haggard**, debauched, worn-out, unkempt, disheveled, worn [➡ BADLY GROOMED; 483] *Opposite*: fresh

radial *adj* **circular**, outward, centrifugal, radiated, outspread, radiating [➡ ORIENTATION AND ALIGNMENT; 1223]

radiance 1 *n* **happiness**, sparkle, joy, vivacity, joie de vivre, warmth, glow [➡ PLEASURE, EXCITEMENT, AND ELATION; 534] *Opposite*: dullness 2 *n* **light**, brightness, glow, luminosity, brilliance, gleam, glare [➡ LIGHT; 1164]

radiant 1 *adj* **happy**, healthy, glowing, beaming, sunny, joyful, ecstatic [➡ PLEASURE, EXCITEMENT, AND ELATION; 534] *Opposite*: unhappy 2 *adj* **shining**, luminous, brilliant, bright, daz-

raring *adj* **enthusiastic**, eager, keen, ready, impatient, revitalized, refreshed, restored, game, impetuous, in a hurry [➡ THE WILL AND WILLINGNESS; 563] *Opposite:* reluctant

rarity 1 *n* **infrequency**, shortage, scarcity, uncommonness, fewness, intermittence, paucity [➡ TOO FEW, TOO LITTLE; 122] 2 *n* **find**, unusual object, curiosity, oddity, singularity, gem (*informal*), one-off (*UK*) [➡ EXTRAORDINARY: UNCOMMON; 205]

rascal 1 *n* **rogue**, mischief, mischief-maker, scoundrel, scamp (*informal*), scalawag (*dated informal*) [➡ MISCHIEVOUS OR BADLY BEHAVED CHILD; 946] 2 *n* (*humorous*) **tease**, joker, prankster, trickster, jester, puck, imp [➡ JOKERS AND TEASES; 675]

rascally 1 *adj* (*humorous*) **mischievous**, impish, naughty, puckish, playful, elfin [➡ BAD MANNERS AND SOCIAL SKILLS; 521] *Opposite:* well-behaved 2 *adj* **dishonest**, wicked, bad, mean, untrustworthy, evil [➡ MORALLY BAD OR IMPROPER; 775] *Opposite:* good

rash 1 *adj* **impetuous**, thoughtless, hasty, impulsive, reckless, foolish, sudden, careless, imprudent, precipitous, brash [➡ INCAUTIOUS AND CARELESS; 283] *Opposite:* sensible 2 *n* **eruption**, spots, reaction, itchiness, inflammation, irritation, pimples, hives, heat rash, diaper rash [➡ CONDITIONS AFFECTING THE SKIN; 721] 3 *n* **outbreak**, flush, spate, string, eruption, wave, flood, epidemic [➡ SUDDEN EVENTS; 52] *Opposite:* incident

rasher *type of* **cut** [➡ TYPES AND CUTS OF MEAT; 1177]

rashness *n* **impetuousness**, thoughtlessness, haste, recklessness, foolishness, imprudence, impulsiveness, indiscretion, lack of caution, carelessness, precipitousness, hastiness, brashness [➡ LACK OF COMMITMENT AND UNRELIABILITY; 509] *Opposite:* prudence

rasp 1 *n* **file**, scraper, tool [➡ HAND TOOLS; 1119] 2 *n* **scraping**, rasping, rubbing, grating, grinding, scratching [➡ CONTINUOUS SOUNDS; 1258] 3 *v* **scrape**, rub, grate, chafe, grind, scratch, file, abrade [➡ USE TOOLS AND MACHINERY; 468] *Opposite:* smooth 4 *v* **grate**, bark, snarl, growl [➡ EMIT SOUNDS THROUGH IMPACT AND ABRASION; 365] *Opposite:* murmur

raspberry 1 *type of* **berry** [➡ FRUIT AND VEGETABLES; 1176] 2 *type of* **pink** [➡ COLORS; 1224] 3 *type of* **fruit** [➡ FRUIT AND VEGETABLES; 1176] 4 *n* (*slang*) [➡ UNFAVORABLE NONVERBAL RESPONSES; 654]

rasping *adj* **harsh**, rough, grating, hoarse, jarring [➡ LOUD, HIGH, OR UNPLEASANT SOUNDS; 1266] *Opposite:* smooth

rat 1 *type of* **rodent** [➡ RODENTS; 989] 2 *n* (*slang*) **swine**, scoundrel, good-for-nothing, rogue, traitor, sneak (*UK*) [➡ VILLAINS AND THUGS; 947]

rat-a-tat-tat *type of* **impact sound** [➡ IMPACT SOUNDS; 1260]

ratatouille *type of* **cooked dish** [➡ PREPARED DISHES; 1170]

ratchet 1 *n* **notch**, tooth, cog, wheel, pawl [➡ PARTS OF MACHINES AND TOOLS; 1118] 2 *v* **intensify**, inflame, step up, stir up, increase, heighten, force up [➡ CHANGE OF INTENSITY: MORE; 394] *Opposite:* lessen

rate 1 *n* **speed**, tempo, pace, velocity [➡ SPEED; 102] 2 *n* **amount**, frequency, level, degree, proportion, percentage, ratio, quotient, scale [➡ DEGREE AND EXTENT; 110] 3 *n* **charge**, fee, price, tariff, toll, cost, figure [➡ EXPENDITURE; 423] 4 *v* **value**, regard, rank, esteem, appraise, evaluate, grade, assess, measure, assay, valuate [➡ ASSESS QUALITY; 755]

rather 1 *adv* **somewhat**, to a certain extent, slightly, pretty, fairly, kind of, sort of, relatively, moderately [➡ TO A CERTAIN EXTENT; 136] 2 *adv* **very**, considerably, significantly, noticeably, extremely [➡ TO A GREAT EXTENT; 132] *Opposite:* hardly 3 *adv* **sooner**, preferably, instead, by preference [➡ DIFFERENCE; 149]

ratification *n* **approval**, sanction, endorsement, confirmation, authorization, agreement, consent, permission [➡ APPROVE AND CONFIRM; 646] *Opposite:* rejection

ratify *v* **approve**, sanction, endorse, confirm, authorize, consent, back, be behind [➡ APPROVE AND CONFIRM; 646] *Opposite:* reject

rat-infested *adj* [➡ DECAYING OR INFESTED; 1236]

rating 1 *n* **assessment**, score, evaluation, grade, ranking, mark [➡ SCORES AND EVALUATIONS; 598] 2 *n* (*UK*) **sailor**, seaman, hand [➡ MILITARY PERSONNEL; 828]

ratio *n* **proportion**, relative amount, relation, percentage, share, part, fraction, quotient, relationship [➡ MEASURABLE PORTIONS; 127]

ratiocination (*formal*) *n* [➡ IDEAS AND THOUGHTS; 770]

ration 1 *n* **share**, portion, allowance, quota, allotment, helping, measure, allocation [➡ AMOUNTS AND QUANTITIES; 112] 2 *v* **restrict**, control, limit, put a ceiling on, regulate, curb, prorate, allocate, allot [➡ DISPENSE, RATION, AND DISTRIBUTE; 434] *Opposite:* lavish

rational 1 *adj* **reasonable**, sensible, logical, realistic, sound, wise, judicious [➡ THE NATURE OF IDEAS; 771] *Opposite:* illogical 2 *adj* **lucid**, balanced, sane, normal, cogent, coherent [➡ POSITIVE INTELLECTUAL CHARACTERISTICS; 524] *Opposite:* irrational

rationale *n* **reasoning**, basis, foundation, justification, motivation, grounds, raison d'être, validation, logic [➡ EXPLAIN AND CLARIFY; 610]

rationalist *n* [➡ PEOPLE WHO ARE APPROVED OF; 955]

rationality *n* **logic**, reason, shrewdness, judgment, lucidity, clear-headedness, wisdom, sensibleness, saneness, level-headedness, reasonableness, equanimity (*formal*) [➡ POSITIVE INTELLECTUAL CHARACTERISTICS; 524] *Opposite:* irrationality

rationalization 1 *n* **justification**, explanation, reasoning, validation, excuse, reason [➡ EXPLAIN AND CLARIFY; 610] 2 *n* **streamlining**, restructuring, reorganization, rearrangement, reshuffling [➡ ARRANGE AND CREATE ORDER; 357]

rationalize 1 *v* **justify**, give good reason for, vindicate, excuse, explain, account for [➡ EXPLAIN AND CLARIFY; 610] 2 *v* **streamline**, make more efficient, downsize, slim down, scale down, reduce [➡ ARRANGE AND CREATE ORDER; 357] *Opposite:* increase 3 *v* **adjust**, tune, level, straighten out, unravel, improve, enhance [➡ CORRECT AND PUT RIGHT; 377]

ration out *v* **distribute**, share out, apportion, divide up, allot, allocate, dispense, hand out, give out, assign, dole out (*informal*) [➡ DISPENSE, RATION, AND DISTRIBUTE; 434] *Opposite:* pool

rations *n* **provisions**, supplies, food, consignment, distribution [➡ FOOD; 1167]

rat on (*informal*) *v* **betray**, tell on, inform on, set up, spill the beans on (*informal*), squeal on (*slang*) [➡BETRAY CONFIDENCES AND GOSSIP; 618]

rat snake *type of* **nonpoisonous snake** [➡SNAKES; 995]

rattan 1 *type of* **fiber** [➡PLANT MATERIALS; 1133] 2 *type of* **climber** [➡CLIMBERS; 1033]

rattily (*informal*) *adv* **messily**, shabbily, tattily, raggedly, scruffily, untidily [➡BADLY GROOMED; 483] *Opposite*: tidily

rattle 1 *v* **shake**, clatter, bang, crash, jangle, knock [➡EMIT SOUNDS THROUGH IMPACT AND ABRASION; 365] 2 *v* **unnerve**, fluster, faze, shock, disconcert, perturb, disturb, unsettle, put off your stride, throw (*informal*), put off (*UK*) [➡UPSET, DISTRESS, AND HUMILIATE; 567] *Opposite*: calm 3 *n* **clatter**, jangle, bang, crash, commotion [➡IMPACT SOUNDS; 1260] 4 *type of* **continuous sound** [➡CONTINUOUS SOUNDS; 1258]

rattle off *v* **say quickly**, reel off, run through, list, recite, repeat [➡RECITE, REPEAT, AND NARRATE; 620] *Opposite*: stammer

rattle on *v* **chatter**, go on and on, drone on, talk nineteen to the dozen, jabber, blabber, blather (*informal*) [➡CHATTER AND BABBLE; 617] *Opposite*: clam up (*informal*)

rattler *type of* **poisonous snake** [➡SNAKES; 995]

rattlesnake *type of* **poisonous snake** [➡SNAKES; 995]

rattle through (*UK*) *v* **rush through**, dash through, make short work of, dash off (*informal*) [➡MOVE FAST; 313] *Opposite*: labor

rattletrap (*informal*) *n* **wreck**, clunker (*informal*), rust bucket (*informal humorous*), heap (*slang*), junker (*slang*), jalopy (*dated informal*) [➡BIKES, CARS, AND CARRIAGES; 1149]

rattling *adj* **fast**, brisk, lively, speedy, fast-moving, rapid-fire, quick-fire (*UK*), pacey (*UK*) [➡MOVING QUICKLY; 103] *Opposite*: plodding

ratty (*informal*) 1 *adj* **messy**, unkempt, shabby, seedy, tatty, ragged [➡BADLY GROOMED; 483] *Opposite*: tidy 2 *adj* **shabby**, dilapidated, worn, seedy, decrepit, falling apart, ragged, tattered, tatty, rundown [➡IN BAD REPAIR; 1234] *Opposite*: pristine

raucous *adj* **loud**, harsh, rough, hoarse, disorderly, boisterous, unruly, riotous, rowdy, noisy, wild [➡REBELLIOUSNESS AND DISOBEDIENCE; 565] *Opposite*: subdued

raucousness *n* **boisterousness**, wildness, disorderliness, unruliness, riotousness, rowdiness, noisiness, loudness, roughness, harshness, hoarseness [➡CHAOS AND UPROAR; 51] *Opposite*: quietness

raunchy (*informal*) *adj* [➡MORALLY BAD OR IMPROPER; 775]

ravage 1 *v* **wreck**, devastate, destroy, ruin, damage, wreak havoc on, raze, desolate [➡DESTRUCTION AND DEMOLITION; 359] *Opposite*: create 2 *v* **despoil**, pillage, plunder, sack, lay waste, ransack [➡DESTRUCTION AND DEMOLITION; 359] *Opposite*: restore

ravages *n* **effects**, consequences, results, aftereffects [➡RESULTS AND OUTCOMES; 83]

rave 1 *v* **rant**, rage, fume, fulminate, hold forth, thunder, babble [➡GIVING VENT TO EMOTIONS; 679] *Opposite*: reason 2 *v* **enthuse**, praise, go on about, laud, extol [➡PRAISE AND ENCOURAGE; 647] *Opposite*: criticize 3 *n* **party**, bash, event,

revelry, festivity, celebration, shindig (*informal*), thrash (*dated informal*) [➡PARTIES, DANCES, AND CELEBRATIONS; 37] 4 *type of* **dance music** [➡MUSIC, SONGS, AND SINGING; 907]

ravel *v* **tangle**, knot, twist, snag, catch, snarl [➡COMBINE AND MIX; 400] *Opposite*: untangle

raven 1 *type of* **scavenger** [➡BIRDS; 997] 2 *type of* **black** [➡COLORS; 1224] 3 *v* (*literary*) **wolf**, wolf down, gobble, gobble up, bolt, gulp, gulp down, scarf (*informal*), scarf down (*informal*), scoff (*informal*) [➡EAT AND NOT EAT; 710]

ravening *adj* **voracious**, greedy, hungry, predatory, vicious, ravenous, insatiable [➡GRASPING AND FINANCIALLY MEAN; 519] *Opposite*: sated

ravenous 1 *adj* **hungry**, famished, starving (*informal*), starved (*informal*) [➡EAT AND NOT EAT; 710] *Opposite*: sated 2 *adj* **greedy**, voracious, rapacious, ravening, predatory, gluttonous, insatiable [➡GRASPING AND FINANCIALLY MEAN; 519] *Opposite*: generous

ravenousness *n* **greediness**, insatiability, hunger, greed, gluttony, voraciousness [➡EAT AND NOT EAT; 710]

raver (*informal*) *n* **partygoer**, hedonist, sybarite, clubber, party animal (*informal*), carouser (*literary*), bon viveur (*literary*) [➡PLEASURE-SEEKERS AND HEDONISTS; 886]

ravine *n* **valley**, gorge, gap, gully, canyon, gulch, chasm, abyss, rift [➡GEOLOGIC FEATURES; 1056]

raving *adj* **frenzied**, gibbering, crazed, raging, delirious, rampant, frantic, furious, wild, uncontrollable, irrational, angry [➡ECCENTRICITY AND IRRATIONALITY; 562] *Opposite*: controlled

ravioli *type of* **pasta** [➡PASTA; 1180]

ravish *v* **overwhelm**, overcome, transport, overpower, delight, entrance, enchant, stun, bewitch, enrapture (*formal*) [➡APPEAL TO AND AROUSE INTEREST; 575]

ravishing *adj* **beautiful**, stunning, gorgeous, striking, eye-catching, entrancing, delightful, enchanting [➡PEOPLE'S PHYSICAL APPEARANCE; 475] *Opposite*: plain

raw 1 *adj* **uncooked**, fresh, rare, red, underdone, pink, blue [➡STATE OF PREPARED FOOD; 1171] *Opposite*: cooked 2 *adj* **unprocessed**, unrefined, untreated, crude, basic, natural [➡RAW AND NATURAL; 1214] *Opposite*: processed 3 *adj* **painful**, sore, sensitive, tender, bleeding, bloody, inflamed, angry, red [➡PAIN AND OTHER PHYSICAL SENSATIONS; 733] 4 *adj* **inexperienced**, green, untrained, wet behind the ears, untried, new [➡UNSKILLED; 529] *Opposite*: experienced 5 *adj* **bitter**, chilly, bleak, freezing, inclement, icy, cold, harsh, perishing (*UK*) [➡COLD WEATHER; 1051] *Opposite*: mild 6 *adj* **visceral**, brutal, crude, rude, primal, atavistic, primitive, simple, gut-wrenching, direct, authentic, no-holds-barred, vivid, intense [➡STRENGTH; 201] *Opposite*: bland

rawboned *adj* [➡BUILD; 477]

rawhide *type of* **leather** [➡FABRICS; 1132]

raw material *n* [➡SUBSTANCES; 1267]

rawness 1 *n* **inflammation**, painfulness, soreness, pain, redness, abrasion [➡CONDITIONS AFFECTING THE SKIN; 721] 2 *n* **inexperience**, naiveté, ingenuousness, innocence, immaturity, greenness [➡UNSKILLED; 529] *Opposite*: poise 3 *n* **cold**, chill, bitterness, iciness, chilliness, coldness [➡COLD WEATHER; 1051]

Opposite: mildness **4** *n* **brutality**, crudeness, rudeness, primitiveness, atavism, simplicity, directness, authenticity, vividness, intensity [➦STRENGTH; 201] *Opposite*: polish

raw recruit *n* [➦UNSKILLED PEOPLE; 530]

ray 1 *n* **beam**, shaft, gleam, glimmer, flicker, spark [➦LIGHT; 1164] **2** *type of* **flatfish** [➦OCEAN FISH; 1009]

ray of sunshine *n* [➦PEOPLE WHO ARE APPROVED OF; 955]

rayon *type of* **synthetic fabric** [➦FABRICS; 1132]

raze *v* **destroy**, demolish, annihilate, level, flatten, bulldoze, lay waste, wreck, ruin, devastate, knock down, tear down [➦DESTRUCTION AND DEMOLITION; 359] *Opposite*: build

raze to the ground *v* [➦DESTRUCTION AND DEMOLITION; 359]

razor 1 *v* **shave**, cut, trim, style, clip, shear [➦TEAR, BREAK, AND CUT; 360] **2** *type of* **cosmetic tool** [➦HAND TOOLS; 1119]

razor blade *type of* **cutting tool** [➦CUTTING TOOLS; 1120]

razz (*informal*) *v* **tease**, taunt, make fun of, poke fun at, ridicule, mock [➦JOKES AND TEASING; 674]

razzle-dazzle *n* [➦INTERESTING AND MEANINGFUL; 190]

razzmatazz *n* **showiness**, flashiness, hype, razzle-dazzle, glitziness, snazziness (*informal*) [➦INTERESTING AND MEANINGFUL; 190] *Opposite*: dullness

re *prep* **on the subject of**, with regard to, with reference to, in re, concerning, regarding, about, pertaining to, relating to, apropos (*formal*) [➦EXPRESSIONS OF REFERENCE; 63]

reach 1 *v* **stretch**, touch, get hold of, grasp, extend, get (*informal*) [➦GET; 420] **2** *v* **go**, move, feel, fumble, lunge, dive, grasp, grab [➦CONTACT: HOLD; 411] **3** *v* **arrive at**, get to, attain, make, achieve, accomplish, turn up, show up (*informal*) [➦ARRIVE; 12] **4** *v* **influence**, touch, affect, impact on, get to, speak to, sway, move [➦APPEAL TO AND AROUSE INTEREST; 575] **5** *v* **contact**, get in touch with, access, get through to, get hold of, make contact with, get a message to, connect with, catch, communicate [➦INITIATE AND ESTABLISH COMMUNICATION; 680] **6** *n* **scope**, spread, range, orbit, grasp, influence, extent [➦DEGREE AND EXTENT; 110]

reachable *adj* **within reach**, on hand, nearby, easy to get to, accessible, local, at hand [➦PRESENT AND AVAILABLE; 11] *Opposite*: remote

react 1 *v* **respond**, counter, retort, answer, reply, rejoin [➦REPLY AND ANSWER; 668] *Opposite*: ignore **2** *v* **change**, alter, oxidize, reduce, bond, ionize [➦CHANGE; 372]

reaction *n* **response**, reply, answer, feedback, retort, return, comeback, rejoinder (*formal*), antiphon (*literary*) [➦REPLY AND ANSWER; 668]

reactionary 1 *adj* **backward-looking**, conservative, right-wing, illiberal, unreceptive, unreasonable, intolerant, bigoted, intransigent, diehard, medieval, prehistoric, outdated [➦NEGATIVE INTELLECTUAL CHARACTERISTICS; 525] *Opposite*: progressive **2** *n* **conservative**, right-winger, dinosaur, diehard, extremist, bigot, intransigent (*formal*) [➦UNCOOPERATIVE OR REBELLIOUS PEOPLE; 566] *Opposite*: progressive

reactivate *v* **restart**, reboot, galvanize, resuscitate, revitalize, revive, resurrect, reenergize [➦RECOMMENCE AND RESUME; 268] *Opposite*: deactivate

reactive *adj* **responsive**, sensitive, oversensitive, volatile, mercurial, touchy, irritable, combative [➦EXCESSIVE SENSITIVITY; 511] *Opposite*: phlegmatic

reactor *n* **device**, apparatus, vessel, container, receptacle, cauldron [➦ENERGY STORAGE AND GENERATION; 1163]

read 1 *v* **interpret**, study, examine, translate, convert, understand, comprehend, make sense of [➦READ; 758] **2** *v* **read out**, recite, deliver, speak, declaim, reel off, state [➦RECITE, REPEAT, AND NARRATE; 620] **3** *v* **peruse**, scan, glance at, look at, study, look through, look over, skim, browse, leaf through, flick through, inspect, examine, go through [➦LOOKING AND LOOKS; 700] **4** *v* **interpret**, understand, comprehend, decipher, figure out, make sense of, follow [➦SOLVE AND INTERPRET; 760] **5** *v* **study**, take, research, take a degree in [➦STUDYING; 844]

readable *adj* **clear**, legible, decipherable, understandable, comprehensible [➦CONCISE AND CLEAR; 202] *Opposite*: illegible

read between the lines *v* [➦SOLVE AND INTERPRET; 760]

reader *n* **booklover**, bibliophile, bookworm (*informal*) [➦DEVOTEES AND ADDICTED PEOPLE; 556]

readership *n* **circulation**, audience, distribution, market share, niche [➦GROUPS WITH A COMMON INTEREST; 938]

readily 1 *adv* **willingly**, gamely, eagerly, voluntarily, gladly, with good grace, with pleasure, enthusiastically, cheerfully, freely, graciously, ungrudgingly [➦WITH ENTHUSIASM; 286] *Opposite*: grudgingly **2** *adv* **promptly**, unhesitatingly, quickly, at once, without delay, swiftly, speedily, immediately, instantly, right away, straightaway, pronto (*informal*) [➦HAPPENING QUICKLY; 104] *Opposite*: belatedly **3** *adv* **without difficulty**, easily, effortlessly, with no trouble, smoothly, facilely, dexterously [➦EASE AND SIMPLICITY; 200] *Opposite*: painfully

readiness 1 *n* **willingness**, gameness, eagerness, keenness, enthusiasm, inclination [➦THE WILL AND WILLINGNESS; 563] *Opposite*: unwillingness **2** *n* **promptness**, speediness, quickness, alacrity, skill, ease [➦SPEED; 102] *Opposite*: delay

reading 1 *n* **understanding**, comprehension, construing, interpretation, analysis, appraisal, evaluation, impression, sense, imagination, conception [➦EXAMINE AND ASSESS; 753] **2** *n* **recitation**, recital, rendition, performance, presentation, delivery [➦PERFORMANCES AND SHOWS; 42]

reading desk *n* [➦FURNITURE; 858]

reading stand *n* [➦FURNITURE; 858]

readjust 1 *v* **get used to**, readapt, settle, settle in, accommodate, come to terms with [➦CHANGE; 372] **2** *v* **rearrange**, realign, modify, calibrate, rectify, straighten, change, manipulate [➦ARRANGE AND CREATE ORDER; 357] *Opposite*: leave alone

readjustment *n* **rearrangement**, change, modification, alteration, reformation, revision [➦CHANGE; 372]

read out *v* **announce**, recite, deliver, declaim, reel off, read, state, orate [➦RECITE, REPEAT, AND NARRATE; 620]

readout 1 *n* **data**, information, figures, statistics, details, info (*informal*) [➦COMPUTERS AND COMPUTING; 1127] **2** *n* **display**, retrieval, record, screen, monitor [➦RECORDS; 585]

read the riot act v [➡ACCUSE, BLAME, AND CRITICIZE; 641]

read up v **study**, find out about, look into, investigate, research [➡STUDYING; 844]

ready 1 adj **prepared**, set, all set, complete, standing by, geared up, equipped, organized, arranged [➡COOL AND CALM; 536] Opposite: unprepared 2 adj **likely to**, about to, on the verge of, on the point of, liable to, close to, on the brink of, just about [➡FUTURE; 86] Opposite: unlikely 3 adj **willing**, eager, prepared, disposed, keen, glad, raring to go, inclined, game, prone [➡THE WILL AND WILLINGNESS; 563] Opposite: unwilling 4 adj **quick**, prompt, apt, timely, swift, flexible, immediate, alacritous, punctual, speedy, expeditious [➡HAPPENING QUICKLY; 104] Opposite: slow 5 adj **perceptive**, discerning, attentive, wide-awake, astute, acute [➡POSITIVE INTELLECTUAL CHARACTERISTICS; 524] Opposite: dull 6 v **prepare**, set, arrange, prime, make plans for, lay out, organize, equip, fit out [➡PREPARE FOR ACTION; 289]

ready and waiting adj [➡COOL AND CALM; 536]

ready cash n [➡MONEY; 797]

ready for action adj [➡COOL AND CALM; 536]

ready for anything adj [➡COOL AND CALM; 536]

ready-made adj **off-the-rack**, ready-to-wear, prêt-à-porter, retail, convenient, handy, high-street (UK) [➡DESCRIBING CLOTHES; 869] Opposite: custom-made

ready-made meal type of **meal** [➡MEALS AND PARTS OF MEALS; 1169]

ready money n [➡MONEY; 797]

ready to drop adj [➡TIRED, ASLEEP, AND UNCONSCIOUS; 738]

ready-to-wear adj **off-the-rack**, ready-made, mass-produced, retail, convenient, prêt-à-porter, high-street (UK) [➡DESCRIBING CLOTHES; 869] Opposite: custom-made

ready yourself v [➡PREPARE FOR ACTION; 289]

reaffirm v **repeat**, reassert, confirm, reiterate, endorse, restate [➡CLAIM, INSIST, AND EMPHASIZE; 614] Opposite: contradict

reaffirmation n **restatement**, repetition, reiteration, endorsement, confirmation, reassertion [➡CLAIM, INSIST, AND EMPHASIZE; 614] Opposite: contradiction

reagent n **substance**, component, element, chemical, mixture [➡SUBSTANCES; 1267]

real 1 adj **existent** (formal), physical, actual, factual, material, tangible [➡TRUE AND REAL; 171] Opposite: nonexistent 2 adj **genuine**, original, authentic, bona fide, valid, true, unquestionable [➡TRUE AND REAL; 171] Opposite: false 3 adj **sincere**, unfeigned, genuine, frank, heartfelt, unaffected, authentic, truthful, honest [➡HONEST AND RELIABLE; 502] Opposite: artificial 4 adv (informal) **very**, truly, extremely, honestly, really, absolutely [➡TO A GREAT EXTENT; 132] Opposite: hardly 5 type of **currency** [➡CURRENCIES; 798]

real estate n **land**, property, realty, commercial property, houses [➡POSSESSIONS; 461]

realign v **readjust**, straighten, manipulate, rearrange, restore, calibrate [➡ARRANGE AND CREATE ORDER; 357] Opposite: disarrange

realignment n **readjustment**, rearrangement, shift, repositioning, relocation, change, manipulation [➡ARRANGE AND CREATE ORDER; 357]

realism 1 n **practicality**, pragmatism, level-headedness, common sense, sanity, saneness [➡POSITIVE INTELLECTUAL CHARACTERISTICS; 524] Opposite: impracticality 2 type of **pre-20th-century art movement** [➡ARTISTIC MOVEMENTS AND STYLES; 899]

realist n **pragmatist**, doer, experimenter, radical, stoic, humanist [➡PHILOSOPHICAL AND POLITICAL THINKERS; 781] Opposite: idealist

realistic 1 adj **practical**, sensible, pragmatic, down-to-earth, level-headed, reasonable, rational, matter-of-fact, no-nonsense [➡POSITIVE INTELLECTUAL CHARACTERISTICS; 524] Opposite: impractical 2 adj **convincing**, lifelike, representative, truthful, accurate, faithful, genuine, true, credible, true-to-life, natural, authentic [➡TRUE AND REAL; 171] Opposite: unnatural

reality 1 n **realism**, authenticity, truth, certainty, veracity, genuineness, representativeness [➡TRUE AND REAL; 171] Opposite: idealism 2 n **actuality**, the everyday, experience, existence, life, the here and now, corporeality, materiality [➡TRUE AND REAL; 171] Opposite: make-believe

reality show type of **broadcast** [➡TELEVISION AND RADIO; 606]

realizable adj **achievable**, attainable, realistic, viable, possible, doable, reachable, practicable, feasible [➡POSSIBLE AND PROBABLE; 177] Opposite: unattainable

realization 1 n **understanding**, comprehension, consciousness, awareness, recognition, apprehension, insight, grasp [➡UNDERSTAND AND GRASP; 759] 2 n **achievement**, accomplishment, carrying out, attainment, completion, fulfillment [➡SUCCESS; 82] Opposite: failure

realize 1 v **understand**, comprehend, become conscious, appreciate, grasp, apprehend, recognize, take in, gather, fathom, get (informal) [➡UNDERSTAND AND GRASP; 759] Opposite: misunderstand 2 v **fulfill**, achieve, accomplish, carry out, bring to fruition, make happen, complete, reach, attain, consummate, execute, do [➡CARRY OUT AN ACTION; 269] Opposite: fail

See Compare and Contrast at **accomplish**.

real life n [➡TRUE AND REAL; 171]

real-life adj **actual**, true, factual, real, realistic, genuine, everyday, tangible, palpable [➡TRUE AND REAL; 171] Opposite: imaginary

reallocate v **redistribute**, reshuffle, reorganize, transfer, rationalize, sort out, restructure, rearrange, change around, reorder [➡ARRANGE AND CREATE ORDER; 357]

really 1 adv **actually**, in fact, in truth, in reality, truly, in actual fact, if truth be told, certainly, indeed, categorically, surely [➡WORDS AND PHRASES EMPHASIZING THE TRUTH OF A MATTER; 172] Opposite: on the contrary 2 adv **very**, thoroughly, truly, genuinely, sincerely, exceedingly, especially, truthfully [➡TO A GREAT EXTENT; 132] Opposite: hardly

realm 1 n **kingdom**, monarchy, dominion, empire, land, territory, jurisdiction, country, state, demesne (formal) [➡TERRITORIES AND GROUPS OF NATIONS; 1068] 2 n **scope**, area, range, domain, sphere, field, ambit, province, orbit [➡SUBJECT AREAS; 768]

realness *n* **reality**, actuality, authenticity, genuineness, sincerity, trueness, truth [➡ TRUE AND REAL; 171]

realpolitik *n* [➡ STYLES AND SYSTEMS OF GOVERNMENT; 806]

real-time *adj* [➡ COMPUTERS AND COMPUTING; 1127]

realty *n* **real estate**, real property, land, property, estate [➡ POSSESSIONS; 461]

real world *n* **reality**, life, everyday, the world, actuality, hurly-burly, real life, everyday life, the big bad world [➡ TRUE AND REAL; 171] *Opposite*: ivory tower

real-world *adj* **practical**, actual, everyday, real, real-life, true [➡ TRUE AND REAL; 171] *Opposite*: imaginary

ream *n* **quantity**, amount, pack, pile [➡ AMOUNTS OF SOLID OR SEMISOLID; 115]

reamer *type of* **utensil** [➡ TABLEWARE, FLATWARE, AND KITCHENWARE; 861]

reanimate *v* **revive**, restore, reawaken, awaken, resuscitate, resurrect, bring around [➡ IMPROVE STRENGTH AND DURABILITY; 378] *Opposite*: deaden

reap 1 *v* **gather**, harvest, garner, collect, pick, bring in, get in, glean [➡ GET; 420] *Opposite*: sow 2 *v* **obtain**, acquire, gain, earn, secure, win, get in, procure, realize, derive [➡ GET MONEY OR REWARD; 421] *Opposite*: lose

reaper *n* **gatherer**, harvester, cutter, gleaner, mower, farmer [➡ FARMERS, GARDENERS, AND MANUAL WORKERS; 849]

reappear *v* **come back**, recur, resurface, return, come again, reemerge, repeat [➡ HAPPEN AGAIN; 28] *Opposite*: disappear

reappearance *n* **recurrence**, repetition, reemergence, return, comeback, revival [➡ REPETITION; 29] *Opposite*: disappearance

reappraisal *n* **reassessment**, review, reconsideration, check, second look, reevaluation, revision, reexamination [➡ SCORES AND EVALUATIONS; 598]

reappraise *v* **reassess**, check, reevaluate, reconsider, reexamine, review [➡ EXAMINE AND ASSESS; 753]

rear 1 *v* **raise**, bring up, care for, nurture, take care of, tend, look after, watch over, train, educate, cultivate [➡ GROW AND CULTIVATE; 351] *Opposite*: neglect 2 *n* **back**, stern, tail, tail end, back end, end, posterior (*formal*) [➡ EXTREMITIES OF PHYSICAL OBJECTS; 1250] *Opposite*: front

rear-end *v* **crash into**, bang into, bump into, collide, hit, smash into [➡ CONTACT: IMPACT; 413]

rear-ender (*informal*) *n* [➡ TRAFFIC ACCIDENTS; 255]

rearguard *n* **tail end**, rear, back end, tail, back, rear end [➡ EXTREMITIES OF PHYSICAL OBJECTS; 1250] *Opposite*: vanguard

rear its head *v* **appear**, loom, turn up, materialize, rise up, crop up (*informal*) [➡ APPEAR AND EMERGE; 3] *Opposite*: disappear

rearm 1 *v* **arm**, equip, provide, supply, sell, trade [➡ EQUIP AND SUPPLY; 435] 2 *v* **build up**, upgrade, reinforce, fortify, secure, reequip [➡ IMPROVE STRENGTH AND DURABILITY; 378] *Opposite*: disarm

rearmament 1 *n* **equipment**, armament, provision, supply, sale, trade, arming [➡ WARFARE AND WAR; 830] 2 *n* **buildup**, upgrade, fortification, reinforcement, securement, reequipment, reequipping [➡ IMPROVE STRENGTH AND DURABILITY; 378] *Opposite*: disarmament

rearmost *adj* **backmost**, last, final, ultimate, terminal, end, posterior (*formal*), hindmost (*literary*), hinder (*UK*) [➡ RELATIVE LOCATION; 161] *Opposite*: foremost

rearrange 1 *v* **reorder**, reorganize, reposition, move, redispose, relocate, readjust, reshuffle [➡ ARRANGE AND CREATE ORDER; 357] 2 *v* **reschedule**, change the date, postpone, delay, adjourn, put off [➡ DELAY ACTION OR OCCURRENCE; 278] *Opposite*: bring forward

rearrangement 1 *n* **reorganization**, reordering, movement, redisposition, change, relocation, readjustment, reshuffle [➡ ARRANGE AND CREATE ORDER; 357] 2 *n* **rescheduling**, postponement, change of date, delay, adjournment, transferal [➡ DELAY ACTION OR OCCURRENCE; 278]

rearview mirror *type of* **internal feature** [➡ INTERNAL PARTS OF A VEHICLE; 1146]

rearward 1 *adv* **backward**, toward the rear, behind, back, to the rear, over your shoulder [➡ DIRECTION OF MOTION; 345] *Opposite*: forward 2 *adj* **backward**, to the rear, toward the rear, back, behind, rear [➡ RELATIVE LOCATION; 161] *Opposite*: forward

reason 1 *n* **justification**, explanation, basis, grounds, cause, excuse, rationale, pretext, occasion [➡ CAUSATION; 168] 2 *n* **motive**, cause, aim, end, goal, purpose, object, intention, motivation [➡ INTENTIONS AND PURPOSES; 772] 3 *n* **thought**, judgment, logic, sense, mind, brains, intelligence, wit, comprehension [➡ DESCRIBING SOMEBODY'S INTELLECT; 523] 4 *n* **sanity**, right mind, mind, wits, senses, intelligence, brains, faculties [➡ PSYCHOLOGY AND THE MIND; 769] *Opposite*: insanity 5 *v* **think**, rationalize, deduce, analyze, work out, infer, apply your mind, figure out, solve, conclude [➡ DEVELOP THEORIES AND REASON; 744] 6 *v* **argue**, debate, discuss, influence, persuade, talk through, talk over, dispute [➡ CLAIM, INSIST, AND EMPHASIZE; 614]

See Compare and Contrast at **deduce**.

reasonable 1 *adj* **sensible**, rational, judicious, practical, realistic, level-headed, sound, intelligent, wise, logical, evenhanded [➡ POSITIVE INTELLECTUAL CHARACTERISTICS; 524] *Opposite*: unreasonable 2 *adj* **not bad**, quite good, passable, tolerable, all right, sufficient, acceptable, good enough, satisfactory, fair [➡ ACCEPTABLE AND PASSABLE; 219] *Opposite*: appalling 3 *adj* **inexpensive**, affordable, cheap, moderate, economical, equitable (*formal*) [➡ CHEAP AND INEXPENSIVE; 221] *Opposite*: expensive

See Compare and Contrast at **valid**.

reasonableness *n* **sensibleness**, rationality, fairness, common sense, level-headedness, practicality, moderation, balance, intelligence, wisdom, logicality, equanimity (*formal*) [➡ POSITIVE INTELLECTUAL CHARACTERISTICS; 524] *Opposite*: irrationality

reasonably 1 *adv* **sensibly**, rationally, judiciously, level-headedly, soundly, practically, realistically, commonsensically, intelligently, wisely, logically, equitably (*formal*) [➡ POSITIVE INTELLECTUAL CHARACTERISTICS; 524] *Opposite*: irrationally 2 *adv* **quite**, fairly, moderately, rather, relatively, tolerably, acceptably, satisfactorily, well enough, somewhat [➡ TO A CERTAIN EXTENT; 136] *Opposite:* extremely

reasoned *adj* **rational**, coherent, logical, lucid, analytic, well-structured, consistent, articulate, systematic, clear, thought through, plain, sound, cogent, methodical [➡ THE NATURE OF IDEAS; 771] *Opposite:* illogical

reasoning *n* **analysis**, logic, calculation, reckoning, interpretation, deduction, thought, thinking, ratiocination (*formal*) [➡ IDEAS AND THOUGHTS; 770]

reassemble 1 *v* **put back together**, reconstruct, rebuild, repair, mend, restore [➡ BUILD; 352] *Opposite:* take apart 2 *v* **meet again**, reconvene, reunite, get back together, congregate, collect [➡ GET CLOSER TOGETHER; 310] *Opposite:* disperse

reassert *v* **restate**, reaffirm, repeat, reiterate, confirm, insist [➡ CLAIM, INSIST, AND EMPHASIZE; 614] *Opposite:* abandon

reassertion *n* **reaffirmation**, restatement, repetition, reiteration, confirmation, insistence, saying again [➡ CLAIM, INSIST, AND EMPHASIZE; 614] *Opposite:* abandonment

reassess *v* **reconsider**, review, have another look at, think again, check, go back over, reevaluate, go over, reexamine [➡ EXAMINE AND ASSESS; 753]

reassessment *n* **reconsideration**, review, reexamination, check, revision, second look, reevaluation [➡ SCORES AND EVALUATIONS; 598]

reassurance *n* **comfort**, assurance, support, encouragement, hope, faith, guarantee [➡ COOL AND CALM; 536] *Opposite:* discouragement

reassure *v* **assure**, comfort, support, encourage, set your mind at rest, soothe, calm, bolster, uplift, cheer [➡ SOOTHE AND CALM; 573] *Opposite:* discourage

reassured *adj* [➡ COOL AND CALM; 536]

reassuring *adj* **encouraging**, comforting, supportive, cheering, heartening, soothing, calming, uplifting [➡ CALMING; 188] *Opposite:* discouraging

reawaken *v* **stir up**, revive, bring back, rekindle, resuscitate, recall, resurrect [➡ RECOMMENCE AND RESUME; 268] *Opposite:* obliterate

rebadge *v* **rebrand**, rename, retitle, change name, give another name [➡ BUSINESS ACTIVITIES AND PHENOMENA; 794]

rebarbative (*formal*) *adj* **unpleasant**, unattractive, objectionable, annoying, forbidding, antipathetic, repugnant [➡ DISGUSTING AND REPULSIVE; 230] *Opposite:* pleasant

rebate *n* **refund**, repayment, return, discount, reimbursement, allowance, reduction [➡ FUNDS, PAYMENTS, AND CHARGES; 800] *Opposite:* supplement

rebel 1 *n* **protester**, objector, campaigner, agitator, radical, dissenter, revolutionary, mutineer, insurgent, maverick, renegade, iconoclast, nonconformist [➡ UNCOOPERATIVE OR REBELLIOUS PEOPLE; 566] *Opposite:* loyalist 2 *v* **revolt**, rise up, mutiny, resist, mount the barricades, take up arms, fight [➡ NOT DO AND REFUSE TO DO; 274] *Opposite:* comply 3 *v* **protest**, campaign, agitate, defy, dissent, take on, fight [➡ COMPETE, CONTEND, AND COMBAT; 303] *Opposite:* obey

rebellion *n* **revolt**, uprising, insurgence, upheaval, mutiny, revolution, rising, agitation, insurrection [➡ AGGRESSIVE EVENTS; 39] *Opposite:* compliance

rebellious 1 *adj* **disobedient**, unruly, insubordinate, recalcitrant, defiant, stubborn, unmanageable, uncontrollable, refractory, contrary, fractious, iconoclastic, nonconformist [➡ UNWILLINGNESS AND STUBBORNNESS; 564] *Opposite:* obedient 2 *adj* **revolutionary**, militant, armed, treacherous, mutinous, disloyal, seditious [➡ REBELLIOUSNESS AND DISOBEDIENCE; 565] *Opposite:* law-abiding

rebelliousness 1 *n* **disobedience**, unruliness, recalcitrance, insubordination, defiance, noncompliance [➡ UNWILLINGNESS AND STUBBORNNESS; 564] *Opposite:* obedience 2 *n* **revolution**, insurrection, sedition, mutiny, treachery, seditiousness, disloyalty, dissent, iconoclasm, nonconformity [➡ REBELLIOUSNESS AND DISOBEDIENCE; 565] *Opposite:* compliance

rebirth 1 *n* **revival**, renaissance, reawakening, renascence, return, resurgence [➡ REPETITION; 29] *Opposite:* disappearance 2 *n* **regeneration**, renewal, restoration, revitalization, rejuvenation, new beginning, revival [➡ BEGINNINGS; 53] *Opposite:* degeneration

reboot *v* **restart**, start up again, open again, boot up [➡ COMPUTERS AND COMPUTING; 1127] *Opposite:* shut down

reborn *adj* **born again**, recreated, regenerated, renewed, revitalized, brought back to life, resurrected, reincarnated [➡ NEW, MODERN; 166]

rebound 1 *v* **spring back**, recoil, ricochet, jump back, return [➡ CHANGE DIRECTION OF MOTION; 344] 2 *v* **recover**, bounce back, rally, pick up, return to normal, get back, make a comeback [➡ BECOME SICK, TREAT, AND RECOVER; 728]

rebuff 1 *v* **reject**, snub, refuse, repulse, slight, spurn, give the cold shoulder, decline, turn down [➡ REFUSING OR REJECTING RELATIONS; 975] *Opposite:* accept 2 *n* **rejection**, refusal, snub, slight, denial, putdown (*informal*) [➡ DENY AND REJECT; 644] *Opposite:* acceptance

rebuild 1 *v* **reconstruct**, build, restructure, reerect, remake, reconstitute, reestablish [➡ BUILD; 352] *Opposite:* destroy 2 *v* **restore**, renovate, recreate, reconstitute, do up, remodel, reform, overhaul [➡ REPAIR AND MEND; 376] *Opposite:* neglect

rebuke 1 *v* **reprimand**, reprove, censure, reproach, take to task, tell off, haul over the coals, scold, admonish, criticize, chide (*literary*), give a talking-to (*UK*) [➡ ACCUSE, BLAME, AND CRITICIZE; 641] *Opposite:* praise 2 *n* **reproach**, reproof, censure, reprimand, scolding, admonition, lecture, criticism, telling-off (*informal*), slap on the wrist (*informal*) [➡ CRITICISMS AND ANGRY OUTBURSTS; 50] *Opposite:* compliment

rebut *v* **refute**, disprove, deny, invalidate, confute (*formal*), contradict, controvert (*formal*) [➡ DENY AND REJECT; 644] *Opposite:* accept

rebuttal *n* **refutation**, disproof, denial, negation, contradiction, confutation (*formal*) [➡ DENY AND REJECT; 644] *Opposite:* endorsement

recalcitrance *n* **resistance**, noncooperation, stubbornness, obstinacy, obduracy, defiance, insubordination, mutiny, rebellion, disobedience, waywardness [➡ REBELLIOUSNESS AND DISOBEDIENCE; 565] *Opposite:* cooperation

recalcitrant *adj* **unruly**, refractory, disobedient,

wayward, headstrong, obstinate, unmanageable, non-compliant, stubborn, uncooperative, intractable (*formal*) [➡REBELLIOUSNESS AND DISOBEDIENCE; 565] *Opposite*: cooperative

See Compare and Contrast at **unruly.**

recall 1 *v* **remember**, bring to mind, evoke, call to mind, recollect, summon up, bear in mind, elicit, educe (*formal*) [➡REMEMBER; 746] *Opposite*: forget **2** *v* **call back**, call in, take back, withdraw, take out, retract, abjure, recant [➡APOLOGIZE AND RETRACT; 683] **3** *n* **memory**, recollection, remembrance, reminiscence [➡MEMORY; 745] *Opposite*: amnesia

recant *v* **take back**, renounce, repudiate, disavow, retract, renege, withdraw, deny, revoke [➡APOLOGIZE AND RETRACT; 683] *Opposite*: avow (*formal*)

recantation *n* **denial**, withdrawal, repudiation, retraction, revocation, negation [➡APOLOGIZE AND RETRACT; 683] *Opposite*: affirmation

recap 1 *v* **sum up**, summarize, go over, run through, review, repeat, reiterate, restate, recapitulate (*formal*) [➡EXPLAIN AND CLARIFY; 610] **2** *n* **summary**, outline, summing up, review, restatement, repetition, recapitulation (*formal*) [➡SUMMARIES, OUTLINES, AND EXCERPTS; 588]

recapitulate (*formal*) *v* **sum up**, recap, summarize, run through, review, go over, repeat, reiterate [➡EXPLAIN AND CLARIFY; 610]

recapitulation (*formal*) *n* **recap**, summary, restatement, review, outline, repetition [➡SUMMARIES, OUTLINES, AND EXCERPTS; 588]

recapture 1 *v* **regain**, retake, take back, reclaim, repossess, recover [➡REGAIN POSSESSION; 429] **2** *v* **summon up**, recall, evoke, bring back, recollect, take back, educe (*formal*) [➡REMEMBER; 746]

recast 1 *v* **reorganize**, re-present, re-form, modify, alter, change, vary [➡CHANGE; 372] **2** *v* **reassign**, reallocate, reselect, redistribute [➡THE PERFORMING ARTS; 904]

recce (*slang*) 1 *n* **reconnaissance**, exploration, look, lookout, watch, patrol [➡LOOKING AND LOOKS; 700] **2** *v* **reconnoiter**, explore, look out, look, watch, patrol [➡LOOKING AND LOOKS; 700]

recede 1 *v* **move away**, retreat, go back, withdraw, draw back, draw away, ebb, retrocede, regress [➡GO BACKWARD; 309] *Opposite*: advance **2** *v* **diminish**, lessen, decline, wane, fade, dwindle, decrease, abate (*formal or literary*) [➡CHANGE OF INTENSITY: LESS; 395] *Opposite*: increase

receding *adj* **retreating**, withdrawing, disappearing, ebbing, declining, waning, fading [➡DIRECTION OF MOTION; 345] *Opposite*: growing

receipt 1 *n* **acknowledgment**, proof of purchase, note, tab (*informal*), slip, voucher, chit (*dated*) [➡RECEIPTS AND INVOICES; 591] *Opposite*: invoice **2** *n* **receiving**, reception, delivery, unloading, acceptance [➡ACCEPT POSSESSION; 450] *Opposite*: dispatch

receive 1 *v* **get**, obtain, accept, take, have, take delivery of, be given, collect [➡ACCEPT POSSESSION; 450] *Opposite*: dispatch **2** *v* **hear**, catch, sense, gather, grasp, pick up, convert [➡HEAR; 707] **3** *v* **entertain**, greet, welcome, meet [➡ESTABLISHING RELATIONSHIPS WITH OTHERS; 974]

Received Pronunciation *n* [➡ASPECTS OF LANGUAGE; 682]

receiver *type of* **telecommunications equipment** [➡TELECOMMUNICATIONS; 1130]

receivership *n* **bankruptcy**, insolvency, liquidation, failure, ruin, dissolution, Chapter 7, Chapter 11 [➡BUSINESS ACTIVITIES AND PHENOMENA; 794]

recent *adj* **new**, of late, fresh, current, topical, hot, modern, up to date, latest, contemporary [➡NEW, MODERN; 166] *Opposite*: old

recently *adv* **lately**, in recent times, a moment ago, a short time ago, newly, freshly, not long ago, just now [➡PAST; 84]

receptacle 1 *n* **container**, vessel, holder, repository, magazine, depot, store [➡CONTAINERS, RECEPTACLES, AND PACKAGING; 1245] **2** *part of* **flower** [➡FLOWERS; 1032]

reception 1 *n* **party**, function, cocktail party, gathering, get-together (*informal*), bash (*informal*), soirée (*formal*), drinks party (*UK*), do (*UK informal*) [➡PARTIES, DANCES, AND CELEBRATIONS; 37] **2** *n* **welcome**, greeting, reaction, response, treatment [➡GREETINGS, FAREWELLS, AND SALUTATIONS; 659] **3** *n* **signal**, clarity, picture, sound [➡TELEVISION AND RADIO; 606] **4** *n* **receipt**, receiving, delivery, unloading, acceptance [➡ACCEPT POSSESSION; 450] *Opposite*: dispatch

receptionist *n* **receiver**, welcomer, greeter, telephonist, switchboard operator, administrator [➡OFFICE WORKERS; 847]

reception room *type of* **room in public buildings** [➡TYPES OF ROOMS; 1097]

receptive 1 *adj* **open**, amenable, accessible, interested, approachable, friendly, sympathetic [➡FRIENDLINESS AND SOCIABILITY; 494] *Opposite*: hostile **2** *adj* **alert**, sensitive, responsive, sharp, bright, quick [➡POSITIVE INTELLECTUAL CHARACTERISTICS; 524] *Opposite*: slow

receptively *adv* **openly**, amenably, accessibly, approachably, sympathetically [➡FRIENDLINESS AND SOCIABILITY; 494] *Opposite*: antagonistically

receptiveness 1 *n* **receptivity**, openness, accessibility, interest, approachability, friendliness [➡FRIENDLINESS AND SOCIABILITY; 494] *Opposite*: hostility **2** *n* **alertness**, sensitivity, responsiveness, acuteness, brightness, sharpness [➡POSITIVE INTELLECTUAL CHARACTERISTICS; 524] *Opposite*: slowness

receptivity *n* **receptiveness**, openness, accessibility, interest, approachability, friendliness, sociableness [➡FRIENDLINESS AND SOCIABILITY; 494] *Opposite*: hostility

recess 1 *n* **break**, vacation, time off, rest, retreat, leave, respite, adjournment, holiday (*UK*) [➡PERIODS OF REST; 91] **2** *n* **alcove**, nook, indentation, niche, bay, depression [➡ALCOVES, CUBICLES, AND COMPARTMENTS; 1096]

recession 1 *n* **depression**, slump, downturn, collapse, decline, stagnation [➡MARKET FORCES; 803] *Opposite*: boom **2** *type of* **economic condition** [➡FINANCE AND ECONOMICS; 796]

recessionary *adj* **falling**, declining, failing, in slump, in depression, in recession [➡FINANCE AND ECONOMICS; 796] *Opposite*: booming

recessive 1 *adj* **receding**, falling, retreating, ebbing, declining, lowering [➡DIRECTION OF MOTION; 345] *Opposite*:

growing **2** *adj* **latent**, suppressed, dormant, hidden, masked, unrevealed [➡ IMPERCEPTIBLE; 26] *Opposite*: dominant

recharge *v* **renew**, refresh, boost, revive, revitalize, restore, rejuvenate [➡ IMPROVE STRENGTH AND DURABILITY; 378] *Opposite*: drain

recherché *adj* **rare**, exotic, obscure, exquisite, unusual, extraordinary [➡ EXTRAORDINARY: UNCOMMON; 205] *Opposite*: ordinary

recidivism *n* **reoffending**, reoffense, repetition, habit, tendency, backsliding [➡ TRIAL, PUNISHMENT, AND LEGAL OUTCOMES; 819]

recidivist *n* **reoffender**, hardened criminal, repeat offender, backslider, lawbreaker, criminal, malefactor (*formal*) [➡ CRIMINALS; 821]

recipe *n* **formula**, guidelines, instructions, method, steps, way, procedure, technique, process [➡ WAYS OF DOING THINGS; 294]

recipe for disaster *n* [➡ DANGER; 235]

recipient *n* **receiver**, beneficiary, heir, addressee, inheritor, heritor (*archaic*) [➡ OWNERS; 446] *Opposite*: donor

reciprocal *adj* **mutual**, joint, shared, equal, common, communal, give-and-take (*informal*) [➡ RECIPROCITY AND INTERDEPENDENCE; 147] *Opposite*: one-sided

reciprocate *v* **give in return**, respond, return, give back, counter, reply, share, interchange [➡ GIVE AND PROVIDE; 430]

reciprocation *n* **giving in return**, correspondence, exchange, trade, interchange, sharing [➡ RECIPROCITY AND INTERDEPENDENCE; 147]

reciprocity *n* **mutual benefit**, mutuality, exchange, trade, tradeoff, logrolling, interchange, switch [➡ RECIPROCITY AND INTERDEPENDENCE; 147] *Opposite*: isolation

recital *n* **performance**, concert, presentation, reading, recitation, narration, solo [➡ PERFORMANCES AND SHOWS; 42]

recitation *n* **recital**, reading, performance, narration, presentation, oration [➡ PERFORMANCES AND SHOWS; 42]

recitative *n* **declamation**, narrative, oratorio, opera, singing [➡ PERFORMANCES AND SHOWS; 42]

recite **1** *v* **declaim**, narrate, perform, rehearse, speak publicly, deliver, recount, relate [➡ RECITE, REPEAT, AND NARRATE; 620] **2** *v* **list**, enumerate, reel off, regurgitate, itemize, detail, count, number [➡ RECITE, REPEAT, AND NARRATE; 620]

reckless *adj* **irresponsible**, wild, thoughtless, uncontrolled, out of control, inattentive, hasty, careless, rash, heedless [➡ INCAUTIOUS AND CARELESS; 283] *Opposite*: cautious

recklessness *n* **irresponsibility**, unruliness, wildness, thoughtlessness, carelessness, haste, rashness [➡ LACK OF COMMITMENT AND UNRELIABILITY; 509] *Opposite*: caution

reckon **1** *v* **regard**, consider, judge, rate, deem (*formal*) [➡ HAVE AN OPINION OF SOMETHING; 756] **2** *v* **think**, believe, suppose, imagine, feel, guess, surmise [➡ DEVELOP THEORIES AND REASON; 744] *Opposite*: know

reckonable *adj* **calculable**, countable, quantifiable, finite, measurable, assessable [➡ ASSESS QUANTITY; 757] *Opposite*: incalculable

reckoning **1** *n* **calculation**, estimate, weighing up, computation, arithmetic [➡ MATH; 597] **2** *n* **opinion**, judgment, view, estimation [➡ POINTS OF VIEW; 767]

reckon on (*informal*) *v* **depend**, rely, count on, bank on, be prepared, bargain for, anticipate, assume, expect [➡ PREDICT AND ANTICIPATE; 750]

reckon with *v* **allow for**, bargain for, be prepared for, expect, anticipate, take into account, take seriously [➡ PREDICT AND ANTICIPATE; 750]

reclaim *v* **get back**, regain, retrieve, recover, repossess, recoup, salvage, rescue [➡ REGAIN POSSESSION; 429]

reclamation *n* **recovery**, retrieval, repossession, recuperation, renovation, salvage [➡ REGAIN POSSESSION; 429]

recline *v* **lie down**, lie back, stretch out, loll, lounge, tilt back, rest, sprawl [➡ ASSUME A POSITION; 317] *Opposite*: stand

recliner *type of* **seating** [➡ FURNITURE; 858]

recluse *n* **hermit**, loner, outsider, lone wolf, solitary, anchorite, eremite (*literary*) [➡ SOLITARY PEOPLE AND MISFITS; 942]

reclusive *adj* **isolated**, cloistered, solitary, withdrawn, secluded, lone, antisocial [➡ SOLITARINESS; 941] *Opposite*: sociable

reclusiveness *n* [➡ SOLITARINESS; 941]

recognition **1** *n* **identification**, detection, distinguishing, perception, differentiation, establishing, apperception [➡ KNOWLEDGE AND WISDOM; 558] **2** *n* **credit**, gratitude, acknowledgment, thanks, appreciation, respect [➡ APPRECIATION AND GRATITUDE; 535] *Opposite*: blame

recognizable *adj* **familiar**, identifiable, decipherable, detectable, distinguishable, perceptible, noticeable [➡ KNOWN AND FAMOUS; 181] *Opposite*: unfamiliar

recognize **1** *v* **know**, identify, distinguish, make out, be familiar with, be aware of, be acquainted with, be on familiar terms with, diagnose, spot [➡ KNOWLEDGE AND WISDOM; 558] **2** *v* **accept**, acknowledge, appreciate, understand, admit, comprehend, concede, grant, realize, see, agree [➡ UNDERSTAND AND GRASP; 759] *Opposite*: deny **3** *v* **acknowledge**, credit, cherish, value, have appreciation for, attach importance to, be grateful for, be thankful for [➡ PRAISE AND ENCOURAGE; 647]

recognized **1** *adj* **documented**, familiar, known, standard, predictable, renowned, accepted, acknowledged, well-known, recognizable [➡ KNOWN AND FAMOUS; 181] *Opposite*: unknown **2** *adj* **established**, acclaimed, professional, accepted, important, highly praised, much-admired [➡ POPULAR AND WANTED; 220]

recoil **1** *v* **shrink back**, withdraw, quail, draw back, jump back, back away, wince, react, flinch, dodge [➡ GO BACKWARD; 309] *Opposite*: confront **2** *n* **shrinking**, wince, withdrawal, start, retreat, hesitation, shudder [➡ PHYSICAL REACTIONS; 316]

recollect v **remember**, recall, call to mind, summon up, think of, reminisce [→REMEMBER; 746] *Opposite:* forget

recollection n **memory**, recall, remembrance, reminiscence, calling to mind [→MEMORY; 745]

recommence v **begin again**, restart, resume, take up again, continue, carry on, pick up where you left off, start again, pick up, carry on with [→RECOMMENCE AND RESUME; 268]

recommencement n [→REPETITION; 29]

recommend 1 v **suggest**, advocate, propose, advise, urge, counsel (*formal or literary*) [→ADVISE AND WARN; 613] *Opposite:* oppose 2 v **endorse**, commend, vouch for, mention, put in a good word for, acclaim, applaud, praise [→APPROVE AND CONFIRM; 646] *Opposite:* criticize

recommendation 1 n **advice**, proposal, suggestion, counsel (*formal or literary*) [→ADVICE; 689] 2 n **reference**, endorsement, commendation, blessing, approval, sanction, good word [→APPROVE AND CONFIRM; 646] *Opposite:* disparagement

recompense 1 v **reward**, compensate, repay, pay, remunerate, reimburse, make up for, requite [→REWARD; 436] *Opposite:* charge 2 n **payment**, reward, remuneration, repayment, return, compensation, reparation, restitution, quittance [→REWARDS AND AWARDS; 439] *Opposite:* cost

reconcile v **settle**, bring together, square, reunite, resolve, merge, patch up, put to rights, join [→CORRECT AND PUT RIGHT; 377] *Opposite:* fall out

reconciliation n **settlement**, understanding, squaring off, resolution, compromise, reunion, ceasefire, bringing together, appeasement [→HARMONY; 155] *Opposite:* conflict

recondite adj **obscure**, abstruse, complex, out-of-the-way, little known, esoteric, hidden, concealed [→SECRET AND UNKNOWN; 179] *Opposite:* mainstream

See Compare and Contrast at **obscure**.

recondition v **overhaul**, service, tune, clean, repair, mend, get into shape, renovate [→REPAIR AND MEND; 376]

See Compare and Contrast at **renew**.

reconnaissance n **investigation**, scouting, inspection, exploration, survey, recce (*slang*) [→LOOKING AND LOOKS; 700]

reconnect v **connect up**, rewire, rejoin, relink, recouple, recombine [→FASTEN, LINK, AND JOIN; 408] *Opposite:* sever

reconnection n **connecting again**, connecting up, rejoining, relinking, rewiring, recoupling, recombination [→FASTEN, LINK, AND JOIN; 408] *Opposite:* severance

reconnoiter 1 v **explore**, look out, patrol, watch, search, spy, keep an eye out, survey, scout, probe, investigate, inspect [→EXAMINE AND ASSESS; 753] 2 n **exploration**, reconnaissance, look, lookout, watch, patrol, investigation, survey, search, inspection [→LOOKING AND LOOKS; 700]

reconsider v **reassess**, review, think again, go back over, reexamine, reevaluate [→EXAMINE AND ASSESS; 753]

reconsideration n **reassessment**, reevaluation, review, reexamination [→EXAMINE AND ASSESS; 753]

reconstitute 1 v **reconstruct**, rebuild, re-form, put back together, build again, make again [→BUILD; 352] *Opposite:* take apart 2 v **alter**, change, reorganize, modify, revise, vary, refashion [→CHANGE; 372]

reconstitution 1 n **reconstruction**, rebuilding, re-formation, putting back together, building again, making again [→CREATION; 346] *Opposite:* breakup 2 n **alteration**, modification, reorganization, revision, change, rearrangement [→CHANGE; 372]

reconstruct v **rebuild**, renovate, recreate, redo, restructure, modernize, re-form [→BUILD; 352] *Opposite:* take apart

reconstructed adj **rebuilt**, recreated, reassembled, restored, renovated, remodeled [→CHANGE; 372] *Opposite:* original

reconstruction n **rebuilding**, renovation, reform, modernization, renewal, restoration, refurbishment, reestablishment [→CREATION; 346]

reconvene v **resume**, come together again, call together again, gather again, call again, reunite, bring together again, convene again, begin again, continue, carry on, restart, pick up where you left off, start again, pick up, carry on with, take up again [→RECOMMENCE AND RESUME; 268]

recook v [→COOKING AND FOOD PREPARATION; 353]

record 1 n **account**, report, archive, chronicle, document, file [→RECORDS; 585] 2 n **past performance**, track record, reputation, background, history, profile [→SCORES AND EVALUATIONS; 598] 3 n **personal best**, top score, high, world record, best [→ADVANTAGES; 212] 4 part of **audio equipment** [→AUDIO EQUIPMENT; 1139] 5 v **note down**, make a note, keep a note, take notes, keep details, keep information, write down, log, chronicle, note, verify, document, detail [→RECORD SOME-

THING; 371] **6** *v* **make a recording**, tape, video, film, pick up [➥RECORD SOMETHING; 371]

recorder *type of* **wind instrument** [➥MUSICAL INSTRUMENTS; 910]

recording *n* **footage**, video recording, copy, soundtrack, demo (*informal*), tape, cassette, CD, record [➥RECORDINGS AND PLAYERS; 911]

record player *type of* **audio equipment** [➥AUDIO EQUIPMENT; 1139]

recount *v* **tell**, narrate, relate, report, describe, give an account, communicate, detail [➥RECITE, REPEAT, AND NARRATE; 620]

re-count **1** *n* **verification**, second opinion, check [➥SCORES AND EVALUATIONS; 598] **2** *v* **count again**, verify, tally up, check [➥ASSESS QUANTITY; 757]

recoup *v* **get back**, earn, make back, recover, regain, make good, recuperate, retrieve, recapture [➥REGAIN POSSESSION; 429] *Opposite*: lose

recouple *v* [➥FASTEN, LINK, AND JOIN; 408]

recourse *n* **option**, alternative, remedy, way out, choice, route, resort [➥SOLUTIONS; 215]

recover **1** *v* **get back**, claim, regain, recuperate, recoup, retrieve, salvage, recapture, repossess [➥REGAIN POSSESSION; 429] *Opposite*: lose **2** *v* **get well**, get better, pull through, recuperate, make progress, convalesce, improve, mend, heal, restore your health, pick up [➥BECOME SICK, TREAT, AND RECOVER; 728] *Opposite*: deteriorate

recovery **1** *n* **revival**, upturn, recuperation, mending, healing, improvement, resurgence, revitalization, renewal [➥PROGRESS AND ADVANCEMENT; 213] *Opposite*: deterioration **2** *n* **retrieval**, salvage, recapture, repossession, regaining, rescue, reclamation [➥REGAIN POSSESSION; 429] *Opposite*: loss **3** *type of* **economic condition** [➥FINANCE AND ECONOMICS; 796]

re-create *v* **reproduce**, copy, redesign, redevise, reinvent, reconstruct, rebuild, remake, reestablish, restructure, restore, re-form, redo [➥CREATION; 346]

See Compare and Contrast at **copy**.

recreation **1** *n* **leisure**, hobby, pastime, exercise, play, activity, amusement, sport [➥LEISURE AND RECREATION; 874] *Opposite*: work **2** *n* **regeneration**, rebirth, reformation, restoration, restitution, refreshment [➥CREATION; 346] *Opposite*: exhaustion

recreational *adj* **leisure**, spare time, fun, frivolous, entertaining, amusing [➥EMOTIONALLY PLEASANT; 187]

recreation area *n* [➥URBAN OUTDOOR SPACES; 1072]

recreation ground *n* [➥URBAN OUTDOOR SPACES; 1072]

recreation room *n* **rec room**, family room, living room, playroom, den, game room [➥TYPES OF ROOMS; 1097]

recrimination *n* **accusation**, blame, reproach, allegation, retort, retaliation [➥CRITICISMS AND ANGRY OUTBURSTS; 50] *Opposite*: appeasement

recriminatory *adj* **counter-accusatory**, accusing, retali-

atory, counterattacking [➥VENGEANCE AND REVENGE; 685] *Opposite*: placatory

rec room *type of* **room in the home** [➥TYPES OF ROOMS; 1097]

recrudescence *n* **reactivation**, recurrence, breaking out again, repetition, happening again, renaissance, rebirth, revival [➥REPETITION; 29]

recruit **1** *v* **employ**, take on, enlist, engage, draft, conscript, hire, sign up, enroll [➥WORK-RELATED ACTIVITIES; 834] *Opposite*: fire (*informal*) **2** *n* **employee**, trainee, beginner, novice, newcomer, apprentice, convert, greenhorn, tyro, rookie (*informal*) [➥UNSKILLED PEOPLE; 530] *Opposite*: old hand

recruitment *n* **staffing**, employment, enrollment, conscription, enlistment [➥WORK-RELATED ACTIVITIES; 834] *Opposite*: dismissal

rectangle *type of* **angular shape** [➥ANGULAR SHAPE; 1217]

rectangular *adj* **four-sided**, quadrilateral, quadrangular, oblong [➥ANGULAR SHAPE; 1217]

rectification *n* **correction**, improvement, adjustment, minor adjustment, modification, alteration, refinement, amendment, tweak [➥IMPROVE SOMETHING; 374]

rectify *v* **put right**, set right, correct, remedy, cure, repair, fix, resolve, mend [➥CORRECT AND PUT RIGHT; 377] *Opposite*: damage

rectilinear *adj* **straight-lined**, with straight lines, direct, unbending, uncurving, straight [➥ANGULAR SHAPE; 1217] *Opposite*: serpentine

rectitude **1** *n* **righteousness**, morality, goodness, correctness, decency, integrity, uprightness [➥MORALLY GOOD; 774] *Opposite*: immorality **2** *n* (*formal*) **correctness**, rightness, precision, accuracy, exactness, exactitude, infallibility [➥CORRECT AND FAULTLESS; 182]

rector **1** *n* **minister**, cleric, parson, priest, vicar, reverend [➥RELIGIOUS PEOPLE; 778] **2** *n* **principal**, director, chancellor, dean, president, provost, head (*UK*) [➥EDUCATORS; 840]

rectory *n* **vicarage**, manse, church house, residence [➥RELIGIOUS BUILDINGS; 1085]

rectum *part of* **digestive tract** [➥THE DIGESTIVE TRACT; 709]

recumbent (*literary*) *adj* **lying down**, leaning, lying back, reclining, resting, horizontal, supine, prone [➥ORIENTATION AND ALIGNMENT; 1223] *Opposite*: upright

recuperate **1** *v* **convalesce**, build up your strength, recover, get better, get well, heal, improve, pull through, mend, restore your form (*UK*) [➥BECOME SICK, TREAT, AND RECOVER; 728] *Opposite*: deteriorate **2** *v* **get back**, retrieve, reclaim, recover, recapture, salvage, regain, rescue, claim, recoup, repossess [➥REGAIN POSSESSION; 429] *Opposite*: lose

recuperation **1** *n* **convalescence**, healing, recovery, getting better, restoration, improvement, rehabilitation [➥HEALING; 730] *Opposite*: deterioration **2** *n* **retrieval**, recovery, repossession, salvage, reclamation, recapture, regaining, rescue [➥REGAIN POSSESSION; 429] *Opposite*: loss

recuperative *adj* **curative**, restorative, invigorating, convalescent, healing, recovering, soothing, uplifting [➥HEALING; 730]

recur *v* **happen again**, persist, return, come back, reappear, come again, relapse, repeat [➞HAPPEN AGAIN; 28] *Opposite*: cease

recurrence *n* **reappearance**, return, repetition, relapse [➞REPETITION; 29] *Opposite*: cessation

recurrent *adj* **recurring**, repeated, persistent, frequent, periodic, intermittent, continuing, continual, chronic, regular, spasmodic [➞FREQUENT AND OFTEN; 107] *Opposite*: finished

recurring *adj* **recurrent**, periodic, frequent, repeated, habitual, repetitive, regular, cyclical [➞FREQUENT AND OFTEN; 107] *Opposite*: finished

recurvate *adj* **curved**, bowed, arched, rounded, bent [➞ROUNDED SHAPE; 1218] *Opposite*: straight

recyclable *adj* [➞ECONOMICAL AND RESOURCEFUL; 207]

recycle *v* **reprocess**, salvage, reuse, recover, reutilize, recondition [➞MAKE GOOD USE OF SOMETHING; 473] *Opposite*: throw away

recycled *adj* [➞ECONOMICAL AND RESOURCEFUL; 207]

red *type of* **color** [➞COLORS; 1224]

red

◆ *types of red*
blood red, brick red, burgundy, carmine, carnation, cherry red, claret, crimson, damask, garnet, magenta, maroon, oxblood, puce, ruby, scarlet, vermilion, wine

red admiral *type of* **butterfly** [➞MOTHS AND BUTTERFLIES; 1015]

red alga *type of* **marine alga** [➞MICROORGANISMS, FUNGI, AND ALGAE; 1023]

red ant *type of* **ant** [➞ANTS; 1014]

redback *type of* **arachnid** [➞ARACHNIDS; 1018]

red-blooded *adj* **vigorous**, strong, robust, hearty, lusty, hale [➞FIT AND STRONG; 736] *Opposite*: weak

red-carpet *adj* **preferential**, VIP, no-expense-spared, special, favored, privileged, superior [➞SUPERIORITY; 152]

red corpuscle *n* [➞THE BLOOD AND CIRCULATION; 717]

red currant *type of* **berry** [➞FRUIT AND VEGETABLES; 1176]

redden *v* **flush**, blush, color, glow [➞CHANGE OF COLOR; 391]

redecorate *v* **revamp**, spruce up, refurbish, restore, repaint, repaper, renovate, transform [➞DECORATE, ADORN, AND APPLY COATINGS; 405]

redeem 1 *v* **compensate for**, make up for, make amends for, restore, redress [➞REWARD; 436] 2 *v* **cash in**, cash, trade in, exchange, convert, use, buy back, transfer [➞EXCHANGE AND INTERCHANGE; 448] *Opposite*: keep 3 *v* **release**, liberate, free, emancipate, deliver, rescue, save [➞FREEDOM AND LIBERTY; 208] *Opposite*: arrest

redeemable *adj* **exchangeable**, valid, good, convertible, equivalent, tradable [➞USEFULNESS; 199] *Opposite*: irredeemable

redeeming *adj* **saving**, good, positive, abiding, compensatory, restorative [➞GOOD, WELL, BETTER; 183]

redeeming feature *n* [➞SOURCE OF HAPPINESS, PLEASURE, OR IMPROVEMENT; 209]

redeeming quality *n* [➞SOURCE OF HAPPINESS, PLEASURE, OR IMPROVEMENT; 209]

redemption 1 *n* **improvement**, recovery, renovation, reclamation, refurbishment, revitalization, restoration [➞IMPROVE SOMETHING; 374] *Opposite*: deterioration 2 *n* **salvation**, rescue, release, liberation, emancipation, deliverance (*formal*) [➞FREEDOM AND LIBERTY; 208] *Opposite*: downfall 3 *n* **exchange**, use, conversion, trade-in, buying back, swap (*informal*) [➞EXCHANGE AND INTERCHANGE; 448]

redemptive *adj* **liberating**, redeeming, saving, rescuing, delivering, emancipating, releasing [➞FREEDOM AND LIBERTY; 208]

redeploy *v* **redistribute**, divert, post, send, dispatch, reassign, reorganize [➞POSITION SOMETHING; 325]

redeployment *n* **redistribution**, posting, reorganization, relocation, rearrangement, reassignment [➞MOVE SOMETHING TO ANOTHER LOCATION; 324]

redesign *v* [➞CREATION; 346]

redevelop *v* **improve**, revitalize, renovate, revamp, restore, regenerate, renew, revive, rekindle [➞BUILD; 352] *Opposite*: neglect

redevelopment *n* **improvement**, renovation, revitalization, revamping, restoration, regeneration, renewal, revival, rekindling [➞CREATION; 346] *Opposite*: neglect

redevise *v* [➞INSTITUTE AND INAUGURATE; 348]

red-faced 1 *adj* **blushing**, flushed, embarrassed, hot and bothered, sweating, ashamed [➞EMBARRASSMENT AND HUMILIATION; 542] 2 *adj* **ruddy**, weather-beaten, rosy, florid, rubicund (*literary*) [➞COMPLEXION; 480]

red giant *type of* **star or star system** [➞HEAVENLY BODIES; 1061]

redheaded *adj* **auburn**, chestnut-haired, auburn-haired, strawberry blond, sandy, ginger (*UK*) [➞HAIR COLOR; 485]

red herring *n* **decoy**, trick, ploy, lure, diversion, deviation, device [➞DECEPTION AND LIES; 660]

red-hot *adj* **burning**, boiling, scalding, fiery, scorching (*informal*), sizzling (*informal*) [➞TEMPERATURE: HOT; 1229] *Opposite*: cold

redirect *v* **forward**, send, readdress, transmit, convey, relay, send on (*UK*), pass on [➞DISPATCH AND SEND; 333]

redirection *n* **sending on**, resending, redispatch, rerouting, transferal, forwarding, redistribution [➞MOVE SOMETHING TO ANOTHER LOCATION; 324]

rediscover *v* **find again**, revive, experience again, remember, relive, reexperience [➞REMEMBER; 746]

rediscovery *n* **finding again**, discovering again, reawakening, seeing afresh, rekindling, renewal, renaissance [➞REPETITION; 29]

redistribute *v* **reallocate**, reorder, sort out, restructure, rearrange, redeploy, reorganize [➡DISPENSE, RATION, AND DISTRIBUTE; 434]

redistribution *n* **redeployment**, rearrangement, relocation, reorganization, restructuring, reallocation [➡DISPENSE, RATION, AND DISTRIBUTE; 434]

red-letter day *n* **special day**, day to remember, occasion, event, turning point [➡DECISIVE MOMENTS; 44]

red light 1 *n* **traffic light**, stop light, warning signal, warning light, stop sign, signal [➡SIGNALING; 1140] *Opposite*: green light 2 *n* (*informal*) **rejection**, disapproval, refusal, no, prohibition, declining, thumbs down (*informal*) [➡REFUSE PERMISSION AND NOT ALLOW; 670] *Opposite*: approval

redness 1 *n* **blush**, flush, rosiness, glow, pinkness, ruddiness, color, reddishness [➡COMPLEXION; 480] *Opposite*: pallor 2 *n* **soreness**, rawness, tenderness, inflammation, painfulness, irritation [➡CONDITIONS AFFECTING THE SKIN; 721]

redo *v* **rebuild**, do from scratch, do again, recreate, start again, go back to the beginning, repeat, restart [➡RECOMMENCE AND RESUME; 268]

redolence 1 *n* **suggestion**, hint, trace, evocation, reminiscence, idea, whisper [➡REPRESENTATIONS AND GENERAL EXAMPLES; 65] 2 *n* (*literary*) **fragrance**, scent, aroma, odor, smell, bouquet [➡SMELL AND SMELLING; 705]

redolent 1 *adj* **suggestive**, reminiscent, evocative, indicative, recalling [➡REPRESENTATIVE; 66] 2 *adj* **scented**, aromatic, fragrant, sweet-smelling, perfumed, smelling, odorous (*literary*) [➡SMELL AND SMELLING; 705]

redouble *v* **intensify**, renew, increase, multiply, amplify, augment (*formal*) [➡CHANGE OF INTENSITY: MORE; 394] *Opposite*: reduce

redoubt (*literary*) *n* **stronghold**, castle, fortification, fort, fortress, citadel, keep [➡FORTRESSES AND FORTIFICATIONS; 1090]

redoubtable *adj* **formidable**, impressive, terrible, mighty, fearsome, awesome [➡EXTRAORDINARY: AMAZING; 204] *Opposite*: unimpressive

redraft 1 *n* **rewrite**, reworking, alteration, modification, change, revision, amendment [➡CHANGE; 372] 2 *v* **rewrite**, reword, rework, revise, rephrase, alter, modify, change, say differently, reshape, amend [➡CORRECT AND PUT RIGHT; 377]

redress 1 *n* **compensation**, reparation, damages, recompense, reimbursement, amends [➡REWARDS AND AWARDS; 439] 2 *v* **reimburse**, repay, pay damages, pay reparations, remunerate, compensate [➡GIVE MONEY; 433] 3 *v* **restore**, level out, equalize, right, rectify, remedy, put right, even out, set right, balance out [➡CORRECT AND PUT RIGHT; 377]

red tape (*informal*) *n* **formalities**, bureaucracy, paperwork, official procedure, rules and regulations, procedures, regulations, rules [➡WAYS OF DOING THINGS; 294]

reduce 1 *v* **decrease**, lessen, diminish, cut, trim down, condense, shrink, ease, moderate, lower [➡CHANGE OF INTENSITY: LESS; 395] *Opposite*: increase 2 *v* **downgrade**, cut down, demote, degrade, slash, bring down, drive down, relegate [➡WORSEN SOMETHING; 380] *Opposite*: upgrade 3 *v* **lose weight**, slim, slim down, go on a diet, diet, slenderize (*dated*) [➡EAT AND NOT EAT; 710]

reduced *adj* **cheap**, bargain, low-price, cut-rate, on sale, cut-price (*UK*) [➡CHEAP AND INEXPENSIVE; 221]

reduce speed *v* [➡CHANGE OF SPEED: LESS; 397]

reduce to ashes *v* [➡DESTRUCTION AND DEMOLITION; 359]

reduce to rubble *v* [➡DESTRUCTION AND DEMOLITION; 359]

reduce to tears *v* [➡UPSET, DISTRESS, AND HUMILIATE; 567]

reduce to the ranks *v* [➡REVOKE STATUS; 459]

reduction *n* **discount**, decrease, lessening, drop, saving, bargain, fall, decline, diminution, cutback, cut [➡CHANGE OF SIZE: SMALLER; 393] *Opposite*: increase

redundancy (*UK*) *n* **unemployment**, job loss, dismissal, severance, laying-off, termination, firing [➡WORK-RELATED ACTIVITIES; 834] *Opposite*: employment

redundant 1 *adj* **superfluous**, outmoded, disused, surplus, unneeded, unnecessary, uncalled-for, unwanted [➡REDUNDANT AND USELESS; 240] *Opposite*: needed 2 *adj* (*UK*) **laid off**, let go, out of work, out of a job, jobless, fired, dismissed, terminated [➡EMPLOYMENT STATUS; 831] *Opposite*: employed

redundantly *adv* **superfluously**, unnecessarily, excessively, in surplus [➡REDUNDANT AND USELESS; 240] *Opposite*: necessarily

reduplicate *v* **repeat**, double, copy, redo, recast, duplicate, reproduce, imitate [➡COPY AND DUPLICATE; 402]

reduplication *n* **repetition**, copying, imitation, doubling, duplication, reproduction [➡SAMENESS; 150]

redwood *type of* **evergreen tree** [➡EVERGREEN AND CONIFEROUS TREES; 1029]

reecho *v* [➡RECITE, REPEAT, AND NARRATE; 620]

reed *n* **cane**, stalk, stem [➡GRASS; 1031]

reediness *n* **squeakiness**, shrillness, stridency, screechiness, squawkiness, thinness [➡LOUD, HIGH, OR UNPLEASANT SOUNDS; 1266] *Opposite*: sonority

reeducate *v* **retrain**, reskill, retool, requalify, reinstruct, rehabilitate, reorient [➡INSTRUCT AND TEACH; 609]

reeducation *n* **retraining**, reskilling, retooling, reequipping, requalification, reinstruction, rehabilitation, reorientation [➡TEACHING; 839]

reedy 1 *adj* **high-pitched**, thin, shrill, high, feeble [➡LOUD, HIGH, OR UNPLEASANT SOUNDS; 1266] *Opposite*: full-bodied 2 *adj* **thin**, narrow, slim, skinny, long, elongated, flexible [➡BUILD; 477] *Opposite*: squat

reef *n* **ridge**, bar, bank, mound, range [➡THE SEAS, OCEANS, AND SHORES; 1041]

reefer *type of* **jacket** [➡GARMENTS AND OUTFITS; 865]

reek 1 *v* **stink**, smell [➡SMELL EMISSION; 369] 2 *v* **show signs**, smack, smell, suggest, be redolent of, stink, evidence [➡SEEM TO BE SOMETHING; 58] 3 *n* **stench**, stink, smell, odor, whiff [➡SMELL AND SMELLING; 705]

See Compare and Contrast at **smell**.

reel 1 *n* roll, spool, cylinder, bobbin, roller, winder [➤ CONTAINERS, RECEPTACLES, AND PACKAGING; 1245] **2** *v* **lurch**, stagger, totter, stumble, wobble, sway [➤ WALK UNSTEADILY; 315] **3** *v* **wind**, whirl, spin, go round and round, revolve, twirl [➤ MOVE SOMETHING: ON THE SPOT; 336]

reelect *v* **appoint again**, vote in again, reappoint, reconfirm, endorse, reinstate, reinstall [➤ CONFER STATUS; 458]

reelection *n* **reappointment**, endorsement, confirmation [➤ CONFER STATUS; 458] *Opposite*: defeat

reel off *v* **recite**, rattle off, list, repeat, go through, enumerate [➤ RECITE, REPEAT, AND NARRATE; 620]

reemerge *v* [➤ ARRIVE; 12]

reemergence *n* [➤ REPETITION; 29]

reengineering *n* [➤ BUSINESS ACTIVITIES AND PHENOMENA; 794]

reenter *v* **return**, go back into, withdraw into, retire into, turn back into, retrace your steps, come back [➤ ARRIVE; 12] *Opposite*: leave

reentry *n* **return**, going back into, going into again, going in again [➤ ARRIVAL; 13]

reestablish *v* **establish again**, create again, regenerate, reinvent, rebuild, recreate, restore, reconstruct, reinstate, reproduce, redevise, remake, redesign, put back [➤ CREATION; 346]

reexamination *n* **reappraisal**, reconsideration, reassessment, reevaluation, verification, rechecking, examining again, review, revision, check, second look [➤ EXAMINE AND ASSESS; 753]

reexamine *v* **reconsider**, go back over, review, reassess, go over, return to, reevaluate, take another look at, revisit, go back to, make another study of, revise [➤ EXAMINE AND ASSESS; 753]

ref (*informal*) *n* **referee**, umpire, arbitrator, adjudicator, mediator, arbiter, judge [➤ ADVISERS, JUDGES, AND ARBITERS; 971]

refectory 1 *n* **cafeteria**, dining hall, mess hall, lunchroom [➤ TYPES OF ROOMS; 1097] **2** *type of* **eating place** [➤ HOTELS, RESTAURANTS, AND CLUBS; 1082]

refer 1 *v* **mention**, denote, talk about, bring up, speak of, state, comment on, discuss, raise [➤ SUGGEST, HINT, AND COMMENT; 612] **2** *v* **signify**, mean, indicate, suggest, insinuate, stand for, represent, imply, denote, describe [➤ MEAN SOMETHING; 61] **3** *v* **apply to**, relate to, concern, belong, be relevant to, connect with [➤ BE ABOUT SOMETHING; 62] **4** *v* **consult**, check, turn to, look up, examine, search [➤ EXAMINE AND ASSESS; 753] **5** *v* **send to**, direct to, pass on to, consign to, turn over to, deliver to, hand over, transfer [➤ DISPATCH AND SEND; 333]

referee 1 *n* **umpire**, arbitrator, judge, arbiter, adjudicator, ref (*informal*) [➤ ADVISERS, JUDGES, AND ARBITERS; 971] *Opposite*: partisan **2** *v* **arbitrate**, adjudicate, umpire, mediate, judge, decide [➤ EXAMINE AND ASSESS; 753]

reference 1 *n* **allusion**, mention, suggestion, indication, citation, quotation, note [➤ SUGGEST, HINT, AND COMMENT; 612] **2** *n* **recommendation**, testimonial, character reference, endorsement, commendation, good word [➤ LETTERS AND WRITTEN MESSAGES; 584] **3** *n* **orientation**, position, situation, location, locus, place [➤ NAVIGATION; 1141]

referendum *n* **vote**, poll, plebiscite, survey, ballot [➤ ELECTIONS AND VOTING; 807]

referral *n* **transfer**, recommendation, appointment, medical appointment [➤ EXCHANGE AND INTERCHANGE; 448]

refill *v* **replenish**, top up, fill up, restock, stock up [➤ FILL; 406] *Opposite*: empty

refine 1 *v* **purify**, process, treat, filter, distill, get rid of impurities [➤ CLEAN AND POLISH; 403] *Opposite*: contaminate **2** *v* **improve**, polish, perfect, hone, enhance, sharpen up, upgrade, make better, cultivate [➤ IMPROVE SOMETHING; 374] *Opposite*: coarsen

refined 1 *adj* **sophisticated**, advanced, superior, polished, distinguished, developed, experienced, cultured, gracious, cultivated [➤ GOOD MANNERS AND SOCIAL SKILLS; 520] *Opposite*: coarse **2** *adj* **purified**, processed, treated, filtered, distilled, pure [➤ NOT IN A NATURAL STATE; 1215]

refinement 1 *n* **sophistication**, finesse, class, maturity, delicacy, subtlety, culture, style, taste, civility, elegance [➤ GOOD MANNERS AND SOCIAL SKILLS; 520] *Opposite*: coarseness **2** *n* **modification**, alteration, minor change, improvement, enhancement, tweak, fine-tuning [➤ IMPROVE SOMETHING; 374]

refinery *type of* **industrial site** [➤ INDUSTRIAL BUILDINGS; 1087]

refining 1 *n* **purifying**, sanitizing, decontaminating, cleansing, filtering [➤ CLEAN AND POLISH; 403] *Opposite*: adulterating **2** *n* **improving**, cultivating, educating, taming, enlightening, improvement, refinement, civilizing [➤ IMPROVE SOMETHING; 374] *Opposite*: coarsening **3** *adj* **improving**, educating, cultivating, civilizing, enlightening, taming [➤ MORALLY GOOD; 774] *Opposite*: coarsening

refit 1 *v* **overhaul**, renovate, service, reequip, repair, refurbish, fit out, revamp, set up, kit out (*UK*) [➤ REPAIR AND MEND; 376] **2** *n* **overhaul**, reequipping, repair, refurbishment, service, fitting out, renovation, fitting up (*UK*), kitting out (*UK*) [➤ REPAIR AND MEND; 376]

reflate *v* **expand**, increase, stimulate, spur on, build up, boost, inject [➤ ACCOUNTING, BANKING, AND BUDGETING; 799] *Opposite*: deflate

reflation 1 *n* **expansion**, increase, stimulation, boost, advance, broadening [➤ MARKET FORCES; 803] *Opposite*: deflation **2** *type of* **economic condition** [➤ FINANCE AND ECONOMICS; 796]

reflect 1 *v* **reproduce**, mirror, imitate, replicate, redirect, echo, return [➤ PRETEND AND MIMIC; 60] **2** *v* **be a sign of**, reveal, expose, suggest, signal, indicate, point toward, show, display, manifest, exhibit, signify [➤ REPRESENT SOMETHING OR SOMEBODY; 59] **3** *v* **think**, consider, ponder, mull over, contemplate, ruminate, wonder, think about, chew over, cogitate (*formal*) [➤ THINK AND REFLECT; 743]

reflection 1 *n* **mirror image**, likeness, echo, image, replication, reproduction [➤ COPIES AND REPLICAS; 151] **2** *n* **consideration**, thinking, thought, contemplation, meditation, musing, rumination, deliberation (*formal*) [➤ THINK AND REFLECT; 743] *Opposite*: impulse **3** *n* **indication**, sign, manifestation, suggestion, expression, evidence, signal [➤ REPRESENTATIONS AND GENERAL EXAMPLES; 65]

reflective *adj* **thoughtful**, pensive, wistful, meditative, contemplative, deep, profound, studious, serious, quiet, sober [➤ PENSIVENESS AND INTEREST; 538] *Opposite*: impulsive

reflector *part of* **bike** [➡ BIKES, CARS, AND CARRIAGES; 1149]

reflex *n* **reaction**, impulse, instinct, spontaneous effect, response [➡ RESULTS AND OUTCOMES; 83]

reflex camera *type of* **photographic equipment** [➡ PHOTOGRAPHY AND PHOTOGRAPHIC EQUIPMENT; 1122]

reflexive *adj* **automatic**, impulsive, spontaneous, involuntary, instinctive, knee-jerk (*informal*) [➡ AUTOMATIC AND INSTINCTIVE; 280] *Opposite*: premeditated

reform 1 *v* **improve**, restructure, revolutionize, remodel, modernize, rearrange, upgrade, amend, restore, ameliorate (*formal*), reorganize [➡ IMPROVE SOMETHING; 374] 2 *n* **improvement**, reorganization, restructuring, modification, transformation, alteration, development, amendment, change [➡ PROGRESS AND ADVANCEMENT; 213]

re-form *v* **recreate**, reconstruct, refashion, reinvent, refabricate [➡ CHANGE; 372]

reformat *v* [➡ CHANGE; 372]

reformation *n* **improvement**, renovation, reorganization, restructuring, overhaul, restoration, rectification [➡ PROGRESS AND ADVANCEMENT; 213]

reformatory *n* **institution**, reform school, detention center, jail, penitentiary, penal complex, prison, pokey (*slang*), secure unit (*UK*) [➡ BUILDINGS FOR CONFINING PEOPLE; 1094]

reformed *adj* **rehabilitated**, transformed, changed, converted, renewed, new, improved [➡ GOOD, WELL, BETTER; 183]

reformer *n* **improver**, campaigner, activist, crusader, agitator, reorganizer [➡ PHILOSOPHICAL AND POLITICAL THINKERS; 781] *Opposite*: conservative

reformist *n* **supporter of reform**, improver, corrector, campaigner, activist, crusader, agitator, reorganizer [➡ PHILOSOPHICAL AND POLITICAL THINKERS; 781] *Opposite*: conservative

reform school *n* [➡ EDUCATIONAL INSTITUTIONS; 813]

refract *v* **bend**, divert, change course, detour, deflect, alter [➡ CHANGE DIRECTION OF MOTION; 344]

refraction *n* **bending**, change of direction, change of course, diversion, detour, deflection, alteration [➡ CHANGE DIRECTION OF MOTION; 344]

refractory *adj* **headstrong**, stubborn, rebellious, obstinate, wayward, recalcitrant, noncompliant, unruly, unmanageable, disobedient, intractable (*formal*) [➡ REBELLIOUSNESS AND DISOBEDIENCE; 565] *Opposite*: placid

refrain 1 *v* **desist**, abstain, hold back, leave off, cease, renounce, avoid doing [➡ STOP ACTING; 264] *Opposite*: persist 2 *n* **catch phrase**, chorus, buzzword (*informal*), exhortation (*formal*) [➡ FIGURES OF SPEECH; 673]

refresh *v* **revive**, cool down, enliven, invigorate, rejuvenate, energize, restore, recharge, revitalize, pep up (*informal*) [➡ IMPROVE STRENGTH AND DURABILITY; 378] *Opposite*: wear out

refreshed *adj* [➡ WIDE AWAKE AND CONSCIOUS; 735]

refresher *n* **reminder**, revision, update, review [➡ SUMMARIES, OUTLINES, AND EXCERPTS; 588]

refreshing *adj* **stimulating**, uplifting, inspirational, invigorating, energizing, bracing, revitalizing, cool, thirst-quenching [➡ PHYSICALLY PLEASANT; 186] *Opposite*: draining

refreshingly *adv* **pleasingly**, excitingly, unusually, thrillingly, differently, interestingly, stirringly, bracingly [➡ INTERESTING AND MEANINGFUL; 190] *Opposite*: mundanely

refreshment *n* **drink**, food, nourishment, sustenance, nutriment, nutrition [➡ FOOD; 1167]

refreshment break *n* [➡ PERIODS OF REST; 91]

refreshments *n* **food and drink**, snacks, drinks, nibbles, hors d'oeuvres, appetizers, finger foods [➡ FOOD; 1167]

refreshment stand *type of* **food outlet** [➡ RETAIL OUTLETS; 1083]

refrigerate *v* **keep cold**, store at a low temperature, cool, ice, chill [➡ CHANGE OF TEMPERATURE; 386] *Opposite*: heat

refrigeration *n* **cooling**, chilling, preservation, freezing, conserving [➡ HEATING, REFRIGERATION, AND VENTILATION; 1142]

refrigerator *type of* **cooling appliance** [➡ HEATING, REFRIGERATION, AND VENTILATION; 1142]

refrigerator magnet *n* [➡ ORNAMENTS AND DECORATIONS; 1248]

refry *v* [➡ COOKING AND FOOD PREPARATION; 353]

refuel *v* **refill**, replenish, top up, restock, resupply [➡ FILL; 406] *Opposite*: run down

refuge *n* **haven**, sanctuary, harbor, shelter, protection, place of safety, bolthole, asylum, retreat [➡ SAFE BUILDINGS OR PLACES; 1093]

refugee *n* **person in exile**, immigrant, migrant, expatriate, exile, evacuee, emigrant, émigré, displaced person, expat (*informal*) [➡ PEOPLE LIVING AWAY FROM HOME; 887]

refulgence (*literary*) *n* **brilliance**, splendor, shine, brightness, glitter, luster [➡ DESCRIBING LIGHT; 1228] *Opposite*: dullness

refulgent (*literary*) *adj* **brilliant**, shining, bright, sparkling, glittering, lustrous [➡ DESCRIBING LIGHT; 1228] *Opposite*: dull

refund 1 *v* **repay**, reimburse, give back, pay back, compensate, restore, return [➡ GIVE MONEY; 433] *Opposite*: keep 2 *n* **repayment**, reimbursement, money back, compensation, recompense [➡ FUNDS, PAYMENTS, AND CHARGES; 800] *Opposite*: payment

refurbish *v* **renovate**, restore, refit, fix up, spruce up, do up, smarten up, redecorate, renew, revamp, overhaul, repair [➡ REPAIR AND MEND; 376]

refurbishment *n* **restoration**, renovation, overhaul, renewal, repair, refit, redecoration, revamp [➡ REPAIR AND MEND; 376]

refusal *n* **negative response**, snub, denial, rejection, negation, rebuttal, repudiation, rebuff [➡ DENY AND REJECT; 644] *Opposite*: acceptance

refuse 1 *v* **say no**, decline, reject, snub, rebuff, turn down, repudiate, deny, pass up (*informal*), negate (*formal*) [➡ DENY AND REJECT; 644] *Opposite*: accept 2 *n* **waste**, garbage, rubbish, trash, litter, debris, junk (*informal*) [➡ JUNK AND USELESS OBJECTS; 1249]

refutation *n* **repudiation**, disproof, negation, rejection, contradiction, rebuff, retraction, dismissal, denial, disclaimer, refusal, confutation (*formal*), disavowal (*formal*) [➡DENY AND REJECT; 644] *Opposite:* confirmation

refute *v* **disprove**, contest, rebut, counter, repudiate, negate (*formal*), contradict [➡DENY AND REJECT; 644] *Opposite:* prove

regain *v* **recover**, get back, recuperate, recoup, reclaim, salvage, take back, recapture, redeem [➡REGAIN POSSESSION; 429] *Opposite:* lose

regain consciousness *v* [➡WAKE AND REGAIN CONSCIOUSNESS; 724]

regal *adj* **royal**, majestic, noble, imperial, stately, magnificent, kingly [➡ROYALNESS; 825]

regale *v* **entertain**, amuse, delight, divert [➡PLEASE AND AMUSE; 572]

regalia *n* **symbols of office**, ceremonial objects, ceremonial dress, insignia [➡ORNAMENTS AND DECORATIONS; 1248]

regard **1** *v* **consider**, hold, think, see, view, interpret, deem (*formal*) [➡HAVE AN OPINION OF SOMETHING; 756] **2** *v* **look upon**, stare, observe, gaze at, view, watch [➡LOOKING AND LOOKS; 700] **3** *v* **relate to**, concern, touch on, connect with, have to do with, involve, pertain to [➡BE ABOUT SOMETHING; 62] **4** *n* **respect**, esteem, favor, affection, honor, admiration, repute (*formal*) [➡LOVE, RESPECT, AND GOODWILL; 549] **5** *n* (*formal*) **look**, stare, gaze, glance [➡SEE; 699]

> **Compare and Contrast:** *regard, admiration, esteem, favor, respect, reverence, veneration*
>
> CORE MEANING: appreciation of the worth of somebody or something
>
> *regard* a mixture of liking and appreciation of somebody or something; *admiration* warm approval and appreciation of somebody or something, often suggesting a desire to copy or resemble somebody; *esteem* a high opinion and appreciation of somebody or something; *favor* a liking and preference for somebody or something; *respect* a strong acknowledgment and appreciation of somebody's abilities and achievements; *reverence* a feeling of deep respect and devotion combined with a slight sense of awe; *veneration* a profound feeling of respect and awe.

regard highly *v* [➡LIKE, LOVE, VALUE, AND ENJOY; 578]

regarding *prep* **concerning**, about, on the subject of, on the topic of, as regards, re, in re, vis-à-vis, apropos (*formal*) [➡EXPRESSIONS OF REFERENCE; 63]

regardless *adv* **anyway**, anyhow, no matter what, whatever happens, nevertheless [➡ALTHOUGH, NEVERTHELESS, AND DESPITE; 169]

regardless of *prep* **in spite of**, despite, apart from, not considering, not withstanding [➡ALTHOUGH, NEVERTHELESS, AND DESPITE; 169]

regatta *n* **boat race competition**, race, gala, competition, contest, competitive event, meet [➡NON-AGGRESSIVE/SPORTING EVENTS; 40]

regenerate *v* **renew**, restore, revive, redevelop,

reinforce, stimulate, restart, rejuvenate, revitalize, rekindle [➡IMPROVE SOMETHING; 374] *Opposite:* degenerate

regeneration *n* **renewal**, rebirth, revival, renaissance, rejuvenation, restoration, redevelopment, reinforcement [➡PROGRESS AND ADVANCEMENT; 213]

regenerative *adj* **growing back**, reformative, recreating, re-forming, recovering, renewing [➡GOOD, WELL, BETTER; 183] *Opposite:* degenerative

regent *n* **substitute**, proxy, replacement, protector [➡RULERS AND ARISTOCRACY; 823]

reggae *type of* **dance music** [➡MUSIC, SONGS, AND SINGING, 907]

regime **1** *n* **government**, command, rule, administration, management, leadership, system, establishment, organization [➡GOVERNMENT AND POLITICS; 805] **2** *n* **routine**, system, regimen, treatment, course of therapy, schedule, procedure, method, scheme (*UK*) [➡WAYS OF DOING THINGS; 294]

regimen *n* **routine**, schedule, treatment, regime, course of therapy, procedure, program [➡WAYS OF DOING THINGS; 294]

regiment **1** *n* **military unit**, troop, squadron, battalion, brigade, company, team, contingent, squad, division, corps [➡MILITARY PERSONNEL; 828] **2** *v* **control strictly**, regulate, oppress, suppress, order, discipline, control [➡AVOID, PREVENT, LIMIT, AND CONTROL; 277] *Opposite:* liberate **3** *v* **organize systematically**, arrange, order, file, organize, group, categorize [➡ARRANGE AND CREATE ORDER; 357]

regimental *adj* **strict**, rigid, disciplined, harsh, ordered, severe [➡ORDER AND ORGANIZATION; 206] *Opposite:* lax

regimentation *n* **control**, regulation, oppression, suppression, organization, arrangement, order [➡ARRANGE AND CREATE ORDER; 357]

regimented *adj* **strictly controlled**, well-ordered, disciplined, on a tight rein, restricted, closely controlled, strict, rigid, ordered, well-organized, regular [➡ORDER AND ORGANIZATION; 206] *Opposite:* undisciplined

region *n* **area**, district, county, section, province, state, constituency, borough, territory, zone, locality [➡COUNTRIES AND REGIONS; 1067]

regional *adj* **local**, area, district, provincial, county [➡COUNTRIES AND REGIONS; 1067] *Opposite:* national

regionalism **1** *n* **regional loyalty**, regional prejudice, decentralization, home loyalty, area loyalty [➡STYLES AND SYSTEMS OF GOVERNMENT; 806] **2** *n* **linguistic feature**, local expression, dialect word [➡ASPECTS OF LANGUAGE; 682]

regionalization *n* [➡SOCIAL, POLITICAL, AND ECONOMIC CHANGE; 373]

regionalize *v* [➡SOCIAL, POLITICAL, AND ECONOMIC CHANGE; 373]

register **1** *n* **list**, record, catalog, roll, index, inventory, chronicle, schedule, roster, calendar [➡LISTS AND SCHEDULES; 587] **2** *v* **enter**, list, record, catalog, keep details, put in, chronicle [➡RECORD SOMETHING; 371] **3** *v* **enroll**, join, sign up, matriculate, enlist, sign on, go into, put your name down [➡PARTICIPATE; 292] **4** *v* **reveal**, disclose, show, convey, score, express, transmit, display [➡CAUSE TO APPEAR; 5] *Opposite:* hide **5** *v* **reach**, touch, record, measure, indicate [➡CAUSE TO APPEAR; 5]

registrar **1** *n* **administrative officer**, school administrator, university official, administrator, bursar [➡ADMINISTRATIVE OFFICERS; 811] **2** *n* **public official**, recorder, public administrator, record-keeper, clerk [➡ADMINISTRATIVE OFFICERS; 811] **3** *n* (*UK*) **senior hospital doctor**, specialist, consultant [➡PEOPLE WHO WORK IN MEDICINE; 848]

registration **1** *n* **registering**, recording, record-keeping, cataloguing, listing, chronicling [➡ADMINISTRATIVE OFFICES; 811] **2** *n* **enrollment**, enlisting, course enrollment, signing up, class enrollment, school enrollment, signing on [➡LISTS AND SCHEDULES; 587] **3** *n* **roll call**, register, muster, check, entry, list [➡TEACHING; 839]

registry *n* **records office**, registrar's office, archive, administrative office, office, register office (*UK*) [➡ADMINISTRATIVE OFFICES; 811]

regress **1** *v* **relapse**, revert, lapse, backslide, retrogress, degenerate [➡GET WORSE; 381] *Opposite*: progress **2** *v* **go back**, lose headway, lose ground, retreat, move back, fall back [➡GO BACKWARD; 309] *Opposite*: advance

regression **1** *n* **reversion**, deterioration, relapse, worsening, getting worse, lapse [➡WORSEN SOMETHING; 380] *Opposite*: progression **2** *n* **going backward**, recession, retreat, retrogression, return, movement backward [➡GO BACKWARD; 309] *Opposite*: advance

regressive *adj* **reverting**, returning, going back, degenerating, deteriorating, backsliding, relapsing [➡WORSEN SOMETHING; 380] *Opposite*: progressive

regret **1** *v* **be sorry**, be apologetic, apologize for, be repentant, feel sorry [➡CHANGE OF MOOD AND COMPOSURE; 580] **2** *v* (*formal*) **be disappointed**, be unhappy, lament, be remorseful, express grief, mourn, grieve over, bemoan [➡APOLOGIZE AND RETRACT; 683] **3** *n* **remorse**, guilt, repentance, compunction, pang of conscience, shame, pang of guilt [➡FEELINGS ABOUT THE PAST; 532] *Opposite*: shamelessness **4** *n* **disappointment**, sorrow, unhappiness, grief, distress [➡SADNESS, DISTRESS, AND DESPAIR; 539] *Opposite*: contentment

regretful **1** *adj* **apologetic**, remorseful, repentant, sorry, penitent, ashamed, contrite [➡EMBARRASSMENT AND HUMILIATION; 542] *Opposite*: unapologetic **2** *adj* **disappointed**, unhappy, sorrowful, sad [➡SADNESS, DISTRESS, AND DESPAIR; 539] *Opposite*: content

regrettable *adj* **unfortunate**, deplorable, lamentable, undesirable, unwelcome, inopportune, disappointing [➡EMOTIONALLY UNPLEASANT AND UPSETTING; 227] *Opposite*: fortunate

regroup *v* **re-form**, recover, rearrange, recuperate, reorder, change around, reorganize [➡ARRANGE AND CREATE ORDER; 357] *Opposite*: scatter

regular **1** *adj* **usual**, normal, standard, ordinary, customary, habitual, expected, accepted, conventional, common [➡ACCEPTABLE AND PASSABLE; 219] *Opposite*: unusual **2** *adj* **even**, steady, unvarying, consistent, systematic, fixed [➡ORDER AND ORGANIZATION; 206] *Opposite*: irregular **3** *adj* **recurring**, recurrent, frequent, repeated, fixed, uniform, set [➡FREQUENT AND OFTEN; 107] *Opposite*: intermittent **4** *adj* **ordered**, methodical, even, consistent, reliable, steady, routine [➡ORDER AND ORGANIZATION; 206] *Opposite*: inconsistent **5** *n* **soldier**, combatant, legionnaire, GI [➡MILITARY PERSONNEL; 828]

regularity *n* **orderliness**, symmetry, uniformity, consistency, constancy, sameness, monotony, predictability [➡SAMENESS; 150] *Opposite*: inconsistency

regularize *v* **standardize**, normalize, make conform, legalize, regulate, systematize [➡ARRANGE AND CREATE ORDER; 357]

regularly **1** *adv* **frequently**, often, usually, generally, on a regular basis, habitually, repeatedly, recurrently, commonly [➡FREQUENT AND OFTEN; 107] *Opposite*: rarely **2** *adv* **consistently**, evenly, smoothly, methodically, systematically, steadily [➡ORDER AND ORGANIZATION; 206] *Opposite*: irregularly

regulate **1** *v* **control**, order, adjust, set, synchronize, standardize, regularize, normalize [➡AVOID, PREVENT, LIMIT, AND CONTROL; 277] **2** *v* (*formal*) **direct**, control, guide, manage, handle, govern, legalize, supervise [➡ARRANGE AND CREATE ORDER; 357]

regulation **1** *n* **rule**, directive, guideline, parameter, instruction, ruling, bylaw, law, decree, order [➡WAYS OF DOING THINGS; 294] **2** *n* **control**, adjustment, adaptation, alteration, management, supervision, government, organizing [➡CHANGE; 372]

regulator **1** *n* **watchdog**, controller, supervisory body, manager, supervisor, official [➡ADVISERS, JUDGES, AND ARBITERS; 971] **2** *n* **device**, valve, mechanism, controller, rheostat, circuit breaker, governor, switch [➡PARTS OF MACHINES AND TOOLS; 1118]

regulatory *adj* **controlling**, supervisory, governing, monitoring, directing, adjusting, guiding [➡ORDER AND ORGANIZATION; 206]

regurgitate **1** *v* **bring up**, vomit, spew up, spit up, throw up (*informal*), heave (*informal*), upchuck (*slang*) [➡VOMIT AND BELCH; 712] **2** *v* **repeat**, rehearse, go over, do again, reiterate, say again, restate, recite, churn out, parrot [➡RECITE, REPEAT, AND NARRATE; 620]

regurgitation **1** *n* **bringing up**, vomiting, spitting out, spewing, spewing out, spitting up, throwing up (*informal*), sicking up (*UK*) [➡VOMIT AND BELCH; 712] **2** *n* **repetition**, rehearsal, restating, churning out, recitation, reiteration [➡ONE-WAY COMMUNICATION; 49]

rehab (*informal*) *n* [➡HEALING; 730]

rehabilitate **1** *v* **restore**, recover, mend, repair, revitalize, reestablish, regenerate [➡IMPROVE SOMETHING; 374] **2** *v* **assimilate**, acclimatize, reeducate, naturalize, reorient, socialize [➡INSTRUCT AND TEACH; 609]

rehabilitation *n* **reintegration**, restoration, therapy, recuperation, convalescence, physical therapy, analysis, recovery, psychotherapy, help, remedy, psychoanalysis, rehab (*informal*), physiotherapy (*UK*) [➡HEALING; 730]

rehash *v* **rework**, reuse, do again, go over, repeat, return to, revise, go back to [➡RECOMMENCE AND RESUME; 268]

rehearsal *n* **practice**, preparation, trial, run-through, tryout, dry run, dummy run (*UK*) [➡PREPARATORY EVENTS; 57] *Opposite*: performance

rehearse *v* **practice**, go over, run through, prepare, train, repeat, study, review [➡PREPARE FOR ACTION; 289]

rehearsed *adj* **practiced**, prepared, learned, studied, planned out, thought out [➡INTENTIONAL AND DELIBERATE; 279] *Opposite*: ad-lib

reheat *v* **heat up**, warm up, warm, heat, refry, recook, rewarm, warm through (*UK*) [➡COOKING AND FOOD PREPARATION; 353]

rehoboam n [➡ CONTAINERS, RECEPTACLES, AND PACKAGING; 1245]

rehouse v **move**, transfer, relocate, resettle [➡ MOVE SOMETHING TO ANOTHER LOCATION; 324]

reign 1 n **rule**, sovereignty, control, supremacy, sway, time in power, period in office, period of influence [➡ REALMS AND RULES; 824] 2 v **rule**, hold sway, govern, control, lead, administrate, be in power [➡ BE IN CHARGE; 270]

reiki type of **complementary therapy** [➡ REMEDIES, TREATMENTS, AND OPERATIONS; 731]

reimburse v **repay**, pay back, give money back, compensate, refund, recompense [➡ GIVE MONEY; 433]

reimbursement n **repayment**, compensation, recompense, settlement, damages, refund [➡ FUNDS, PAYMENTS, AND CHARGES; 800]

rein n **bridle**, restraint, harness, leash, lead, strap, restriction [➡ FASTENERS, LINKS, AND NETWORKS; 1247]

rein back v [➡ AVOID, PREVENT, LIMIT, AND CONTROL; 277]

reincarnate v **revive**, bring back, revitalize, rejuvenate, reawaken, restore, re-embody [➡ IMPROVE STRENGTH AND DURABILITY; 378]

reincarnation n **re-embodiment**, rebirth, re-creation, reawakening, restoration [➡ RELIGIOUS CONCEPTS; 776]

reindeer type of **deer or antelope** [➡ DEER AND ANTELOPES; 981]

reinforce 1 v **strengthen**, support, underpin, buttress, bolster, fortify, shore up [➡ IMPROVE STRENGTH AND DURABILITY; 378] Opposite: weaken 2 v **emphasize**, underline, highlight, add force to, boost [➡ CLAIM, INSIST, AND EMPHASIZE; 614] Opposite: weaken

reinforcement 1 n **strengthening**, support, underpinning, fortification, buttressing, shoring up, bolstering [➡ IMPROVE STRENGTH AND DURABILITY; 378] Opposite: weakening 2 n **emphasis**, underlining, underscoring, corroboration, backup, highlighting, boosting [➡ CLAIM, INSIST, AND EMPHASIZE; 614] Opposite: weakening

reinforcements n [➡ MORE AND EXCESS; 124]

rein in v **hold back**, cut back, restrain, reduce, decrease, temper, curb, contain, inhibit, control [➡ AVOID, PREVENT, LIMIT, AND CONTROL; 277] Opposite: unleash

reinstate v **restore**, return, give back, put back, replace, reestablish, recall [➡ CONFER STATUS; 458]

reinstatement n **restoration**, return, recall, replacement, reestablishment [➡ REPETITION; 29]

reinsurance n **provision**, protection, additional coverage, extra cover (UK) [➡ INSURANCE; 801]

reinsure v **transfer**, make extra provision, take out extra cover (UK) [➡ INSURANCE; 801]

reintroduce v **introduce again**, bring into effect again, reinstate, restore, reestablish, bring back [➡ INSTITUTE AND INAUGURATE; 348]

reintroduction n **reinstatement**, restoration, reestablishment [➡ BEGINNINGS; 53]

reinvent v [➡ CHANGE; 372]

reinvigorated adj [➡ WIDE AWAKE AND CONSCIOUS; 735]

reissue 1 v **rerelease**, redistribute, recirculate, republish, send out again, reprint, reproduce [➡ INFORM, ANNOUNCE, AND ISSUE; 611] 2 n **new issue**, reprint, rerelease, new edition, new copy [➡ BEGINNINGS; 53]

reiterate v **repeat**, go over, restate, stress, reinforce, do again, recap, retell, echo [➡ RECITE, REPEAT, AND NARRATE; 620]

reiteration n **repetition**, replication, restatement, echo, recap [➡ REPETITION; 29]

reject v **refuse**, rebuff, decline, snub, throw out, discard, disallow, eliminate, deny [➡ DENY AND REJECT; 644] Opposite: accept

rejection n **refusal**, denial, rebuff, denunciation, refutation, dismissal, elimination, negative [➡ DENY AND REJECT; 644] Opposite: acceptance

rejigger (informal) v **rearrange**, alter, readjust, reorganize, change, juggle [➡ ARRANGE AND CREATE ORDER; 357]

rejoice (literary) v **celebrate**, be pleased about, cheer, exult, be glad, delight [➡ GIVING VENT TO EMOTIONS; 679]

rejoin (formal) v **reply**, answer, respond, retort, return, come back with [➡ REPLY AND ANSWER; 668]

rejoinder (formal) n **response**, answer, reply, comeback, retort, riposte, return [➡ REPLY AND ANSWER; 668]

See Compare and Contrast at **answer**.

rejuvenate v **revitalize**, invigorate, revive, make younger, revivify, refresh, renew, restore, regenerate [➡ IMPROVE STRENGTH AND DURABILITY; 378]

rejuvenated adj [➡ WIDE AWAKE AND CONSCIOUS; 735]

rejuvenating adj [➡ PHYSICALLY PLEASANT; 186]

rejuvenation n **revitalization**, reinvigoration, regeneration, renewal, renovation, restoration, rebirth, restitution, revival [➡ IMPROVE SOMETHING; 374]

rekindle v **renew**, reawaken, revive, regenerate, relight, revitalize, refresh, restore [➡ CAUSE TO HAPPEN; 31] Opposite: kill

rekindling n [➡ REPETITION; 29]

relapse 1 v **go back to**, revert, deteriorate, degenerate, fall back, worsen, lapse [➡ GET WORSE; 381] Opposite: improve 2 n **deterioration**, decline, degeneration, reversion, waning, setback [➡ PROBLEMS; 256] Opposite: improvement

relate 1 v **tell**, narrate, speak about, recount, relay, transmit, communicate, share, convey, report [➡ RECITE, REPEAT, AND NARRATE; 620] 2 v **connect**, link, associate, correlate, link up, join, attach [➡ CREATING CONNECTIONS; 144] 3 v **interact**, form a relationship, connect, cooperate, get along, associate, hit it off (informal), get on (UK) [➡ ESTABLISHING RELATIONSHIPS WITH OTHERS; 974]

related adj **connected**, linked, associated, correlated, interrelated, allied, interconnected [➡ RELATED; 142] Opposite: unconnected

relatedness n [➡ CONNECTIONS; 143]

relating to prep **about**, regarding, re, apropos of, in relation to, pertaining to, with regard to, vis-à-vis, in connection with, as regards, in connection to, respecting, with respect to, with reference to, in respect of, concerning, on the subject of [➡ EXPRESSIONS OF REFERENCE; 63]

relation *n* **family member**, relative, next of kin [➡ THE FAMILY; 956]

relations 1 *n* **kith and kin**, kin, family members, relatives, family, kindred [➡ THE FAMILY; 956] 2 *n* **relationships**, dealings, associations, affairs, contact, interaction [➡ RELATIONSHIP TO ANOTHER; 973]

relationship *n* **association**, connection, affiliation, rapport, liaison, link, correlation, bond [➡ CONNECTIONS; 143]

relative 1 *adj* **comparative**, qualified, virtual [➡ TO A CERTAIN EXTENT; 136] *Opposite*: absolute 2 *n* **family member**, relation, next of kin [➡ THE FAMILY; 956]

relative to *prep* **in relation to**, compared with, proportionate to, corresponding to [➡ EXPRESSIONS OF REFERENCE; 63]

relativism *n* **contingency**, belief, doctrine [➡ PHILOSOPHIES AND BELIEFS; 780] *Opposite*: absolutism

relativist 1 *n* **equivocator**, fence sitter, trimmer, agnostic, waverer, vacillator [➡ PHILOSOPHICAL AND POLITICAL THINKERS; 781] 2 *adj* (*UK*) **contingent**, dependent, relative [➡ PHILOSOPHIES AND BELIEFS; 780]

relativity *n* **relativeness**, dependence, contingency [➡ CONNECTIONS; 143]

relax 1 *v* **unwind**, calm down, slow down, let go, loosen up, settle down, lighten up (*informal*) [➡ CHANGE OF MOOD AND COMPOSURE; 580] 2 *v* **rest**, put your feet up, take it easy, have a break, lie down, be calm, chill out (*slang*) [➡ LACK OF ACTIVITY OR MOTION; 342] 3 *v* **loosen**, slacken, ease, let up on, let out [➡ CHANGE OF INTENSITY: LESS; 395] *Opposite*: tense 4 *v* **lessen**, decrease, diminish, lower, ease, reduce [➡ CHANGE OF INTENSITY: LESS; 395] *Opposite*: increase

relaxation 1 *n* **recreation**, leisure, entertainment, rest, repose, respite [➡ LEISURE AND RECREATION; 874] 2 *n* **reduction**, lessening, easing, slackening, letup (*informal*), moderation [➡ LESS; 126] *Opposite*: increase

relaxed 1 *adj* **tranquil**, calm, comfortable, stress-free, unperturbed, peaceful, undisturbed, cozy, hassle-free (*informal*) [➡ EMOTIONALLY PLEASANT; 187] *Opposite*: tense 2 *adj* **lenient**, easygoing, untroubled, casual, laid-back (*informal*) [➡ PEACEFULNESS AND GENTLENESS; 214] *Opposite*: strict 3 *adj* [➡ DESCRIBING HAIR; 486]

relaxing *adj* **calming**, soothing, comforting, peaceful, tranquil [➡ CALMING; 188]

relay *v* **communicate**, pass on, transmit, spread, convey, impart, dispatch, send [➡ INFORM, ANNOUNCE, AND ISSUE; 611]

relay race *type of* **track and field** [➡ HOBBIES, GAMES, AND SPORTS; 875]

release 1 *v* **let go**, free, discharge, liberate, let loose, leave go of, emancipate [➡ FREEDOM AND LIBERTY; 208] *Opposite*: hold 2 *v* **make public**, make available, announce, publish, circulate, issue, emit, publicize, distribute [➡ INFORM, ANNOUNCE, AND ISSUE; 611] *Opposite*: withhold 3 *n* **relief**, discharge, freedom, liberation, emancipation, delivery

[➡ FREEDOM AND LIBERTY; 208] 4 *n* **announcement**, issue, statement, publication, proclamation [➡ INFORM, ANNOUNCE, AND ISSUE; 611]

release on bail *n* [➡ TRIAL, PUNISHMENT, AND LEGAL OUTCOMES; 819]

release on parole *v* [➡ TRIAL, PUNISHMENT, AND LEGAL OUTCOMES; 819]

relegate *v* **demote**, downgrade, transfer, consign, refer, reduce in importance, lower [➡ REVOKE STATUS; 459] *Opposite*: promote

relegation *n* **demotion**, sending down, transfer down, lowering of rank, downgrade, being demoted [➡ REVOKE STATUS; 459] *Opposite*: promotion

relent *v* **give in**, cave in, change your mind, concede, yield, take a softer line, give up, surrender, sympathize [➡ FORGET, FORGIVE, AND ACCEPT; 748] *Opposite*: stand firm

relentless 1 *adj* **ceaseless**, unremitting, persistent, endless, steady, remorseless (*formal*) [➡ PERMANENCE: WITHOUT END; 94] 2 *adj* **remorseless**, merciless, pitiless, ruthless, heartless, cold-blooded, harsh, implacable (*informal*), inexorable (*formal*) [➡ SELFISH AND UNKIND; 505]

relentlessness 1 *n* **ceaselessness**, unremittingness, persistence, remorselessness, intensity, steadiness, endlessness [➡ PERMANENCE: WITHOUT END; 94] 2 *n* **remorselessness**, mercilessness, pitilessness, ruthlessness, harshness, strictness, heartlessness, cold-bloodedness, implacability (*formal*), inexorability (*formal*) [➡ SELFISH AND UNKIND; 505]

relevance *n* **significance**, bearing, application, importance, weight, applicability, consequence (*formal*), germaneness (*formal*) [➡ IMPORTANCE AND SIGNIFICANCE; 192] *Opposite*: irrelevance

relevancy *see* **relevance**

relevant *adj* **pertinent**, applicable, germane, related, appropriate, significant, important [➡ IMPORTANT; 194] *Opposite*: unrelated

reliability *n* **dependability**, consistency, steadfastness, trustworthiness [➡ HONEST AND RELIABLE; 502] *Opposite*: untrustworthiness

reliable *adj* **dependable**, consistent, steadfast, unswerving, unfailing, trustworthy [➡ HONEST AND RELIABLE; 502] *Opposite*: unreliable

reliance *n* **dependence**, confidence, trust, belief, faith, support [➡ RECIPROCITY AND INTERDEPENDENCE; 147] *Opposite*: independence

reliant *adj* **dependent**, needful, conditional, subject to, contingent, trusting [➡ RELATIONSHIP TO ANOTHER; 973] *Opposite*: independent

relic *n* **historical object**, artifact, remnant, remains, vestige, leftover [➡ REMAINDER AND REMAINDERS; 125]

relief 1 *n* **respite**, release, reprieve, break, liberation [➡ FREEDOM AND LIBERTY; 208] 2 *n* **assistance**, aid, help, reinforcement, support, alleviation [➡ KIND ACTIONS OR BEHAVIOR; 295]

relieve 1 *v* **ease**, release, alleviate, reduce, mitigate, lessen, lighten, allay [➡ CHANGE OF INTENSITY: LESS; 395] *Opposite*: exacerbate 2 *v* **take somebody's place**, take over for, substitute for, stand in for, replace, pinch-hit for [➡ CHANGE ONE THING FOR ANOTHER; 398] 3 *v* **dismiss**, release, let go, discharge, get rid of, fire (*informal*), boot out (*informal*), sack (*informal*) [➡ REVOKE STATUS; 459] *Opposite*: appoint

relieved *adj* **reassured**, thankful, calmed, pleased, comforted [➡ COOL AND CALM; 536] *Opposite*: worried

religion *n* **faith**, belief, creed, conviction, denomination, persuasion [➡ RELIGIONS AND RELIGIOUS PRACTICES; 777]

religious 1 *adj* **theological**, sacred, holy, consecrated, church, spiritual [➡ RELIGIOUS CONCEPTS; 776] *Opposite*: secular 2 *adj* **spiritual**, devout, pious, holy, observant, God-fearing, godly (*formal*) [➡ RELIGIOUS CONCEPTS; 776] *Opposite*: irreligious 3 *adj* **thorough**, conscientious, dutiful, faithful, reliable, loyal [➡ HONEST AND RELIABLE; 502] *Opposite*: unreliable

religious education *n* [➡ CLASSES, COURSEWORK, AND EXAMINATIONS; 842]

religious fervor *n* [➡ FADS, FETISHES, AND IDOLATRY; 555]

religious instruction *n* [➡ CLASSES, COURSEWORK, AND EXAMINATIONS; 842]

religiously *adv* **dutifully**, faithfully, consistently, thoroughly, conscientiously, unfailingly, devotedly, loyally, reliably [➡ HONEST AND RELIABLE; 502] *Opposite*: carelessly

religiousness *n* **devoutness**, piousness, spirituality, sense of God, faithfulness, conscientiousness [➡ RELIGIOUS CONCEPTS; 776]

religious studies *n* [➡ CLASSES, COURSEWORK, AND EXAMINATIONS; 842]

religious zeal *n* [➡ FADS, FETISHES, AND IDOLATRY; 555]

relinquish *v* **give up**, surrender, hand over, abandon, renounce, resign, turn down, let go by, let pass [➡ FORGO AND DENY ONESELF; 449] *Opposite*: retain

reliquary *n* **repository**, casket, container, shrine [➡ RELIGIOUS OBJECTS; 779]

relish 1 *v* **enjoy**, delight in, savor, take pleasure in, like, appreciate [➡ LIKE, LOVE, VALUE, AND ENJOY; 578] *Opposite*: dislike 2 *n* **enjoyment**, delight, pleasure, elation, appreciation, bliss, gusto, zest [➡ PLEASURE, EXCITEMENT, AND ELATION; 534] *Opposite*: displeasure

relish

◆ *types of relishes*
caponata, chow-chow, chutney, cornichon, gherkin, piccalilli, pickled cucumber

relive *v* **experience again**, go through again, live through again, remember, recall, reexperience, recreate [➡ REMEMBER; 746] *Opposite*: forget

reload *v* **refill**, fill, load again, replenish, recharge, fill up [➡ FILL; 406] *Opposite*: unload

relocate *v* **move**, change place, reposition, transfer, displace, shuffle, put somewhere else, rearrange [➡ MOVE SOMETHING TO ANOTHER LOCATION; 324] *Opposite*: remain

relocation *n* **transfer**, moving, rearrangement, repositioning, replacement, removal, move [➡ MOVE SOMETHING TO ANOTHER LOCATION; 324]

reluctance *n* **unwillingness**, lack of enthusiasm, disinclination, hesitancy, foot-dragging (*informal*), aver-

seness (*formal*) [➡ UNWILLINGNESS AND STUBBORNNESS; 564] *Opposite*: enthusiasm

reluctant *adj* **unwilling**, unenthusiastic, disinclined, loath, hesitant, indisposed (*formal*), averse (*formal*) [➡ UNWILLINGNESS AND STUBBORNNESS; 564] *Opposite*: enthusiastic

See Compare and Contrast at **unwilling**.

reluctantly *adv* **unwillingly**, unenthusiastically, half-heartedly, grudgingly, hesitantly, aversely (*formal*) [➡ WITHOUT ENTHUSIASM; 287] *Opposite*: willingly

rely *v* **depend on**, bank on, count on, trust, be sure of, be dependent on, have faith in, put your faith in, be certain about, have confidence in [➡ RECIPROCITY AND INTERDEPENDENCE; 147] *Opposite*: distrust

remain 1 *v* **stay**, stay put, stay behind, stay on, linger, wait, hang around [➡ EXIST IN A PLACE; 19] *Opposite*: leave 2 *v* **continue**, keep on, endure, persist, go on [➡ CONTINUE TO EXIST; 17] *Opposite*: stop

remainder *n* **rest**, residue, remnants, remains, leftovers, what's left, balance [➡ REMAINDER AND REMAINDERS; 125]

remainders *n* [➡ REMAINDER AND REMAINDERS; 125]

remaining *adj* **residual**, outstanding, left over, excess, lingering, enduring, lasting, left behind [➡ PERMANENCE: WITHOUT END; 94]

remains 1 *n* **leftovers**, remnants, relics, remainder, ruins, vestiges, residue, what's left, rest, scraps, orts [➡ REMAINDER AND REMAINDERS; 125] 2 *n* **dead body**, corpse, cadaver, ashes, cremains, carcass, skeleton, body [➡ DEAD PERSON; 926]

remake 1 *n* **new version**, cover version, cover, new edition, re-creation [➡ ARTWORKS; 898] 2 *v* **produce again**, re-create, re-form, change the format, reshape, reconstruct, redesign, remodel, restyle, reproduce, reformat [➡ CREATION; 346]

remand 1 *v* **return to custody**, return to prison, commit to custody, imprison, jail, incarcerate (*formal*) [➡ TRIAL, PUNISHMENT, AND LEGAL OUTCOMES; 819] 2 *n* **return to custody**, return to prison, committal to custody, custody, prison, imprisonment [➡ TRIAL, PUNISHMENT, AND LEGAL OUTCOMES; 819]

remand home (*UK*) *n* [➡ BUILDINGS FOR CONFINING PEOPLE; 1094]

remark 1 *n* **comment**, statement, observation, aside, mention, quip [➡ SUGGEST, HINT, AND COMMENT; 612] 2 *v* **say**, comment, state, observe, pronounce, mention [➡ SUGGEST, HINT, AND COMMENT; 612]

remarkability *n* [➡ EXTRAORDINARY: AMAZING; 204]

remarkable *adj* **extraordinary**, amazing, notable, outstanding, noteworthy, significant, incredible, astonishing, awesome (*informal*) [➡ EXTRAORDINARY: AMAZING; 204] *Opposite*: ordinary

remarkableness *n* [➡ EXTRAORDINARY: AMAZING; 204]

remarry *v* **get married again**, marry again, get wed again, re-wed, wed again (*formal or literary*) [➡ ESTABLISHING RELATIONSHIPS WITH OTHERS; 974]

rematch *n* **replay**, another game, a second go (*UK*) [➡ NON-AGGRESSIVE/SPORTING EVENTS; 40]

rematerialize *v* [➡APPEAR AND EMERGE; 3]

remedial *adj* **corrective**, counteractive, helpful, educative, curative [➡USEFULNESS; 199]

remedy **1** *n* **medicine**, medication, preparation, mixture, therapy, cure, tonic, remedying [➡REMEDIES, TREATMENTS, AND OPERATIONS; 731] **2** *n* **solution**, cure, answer, antidote, resolution, alleviation, treatment [➡SOLUTIONS; 215] **3** *v* **cure**, relieve, improve, alleviate, ease, treat, fix [➡BECOME SICK, TREAT, AND RECOVER; 728] **4** *v* **resolve**, deal with, correct, improve, make better, sort out, take care of, fix [➡CORRECT AND PUT RIGHT; 377] *Opposite:* exacerbate

remember **1** *v* **recall**, think of, recollect, dredge up, hark back to, reminisce, evoke, summon up, bring to mind [➡REMEMBER; 746] *Opposite:* forget **2** *v* **keep in mind**, bear in mind, retain, memorize, learn, have down pat, commit to memory, consider, take into account, have off pat (*UK*) [➡REMEMBER; 746] *Opposite:* forget

remembrance *n* **commemoration**, memory, tribute, recollection, reminiscence, celebration [➡MEMORY; 745]

remind **1** *v* **be reminiscent**, strike a chord, take you back, jog your memory, ring a bell (*informal*) [➡REMIND; 747] **2** *v* **repeat**, retell, prompt, recap, run by again, hark back, tell again [➡INFORM, ANNOUNCE, AND ISSUE; 611]

reminder **1** *n* **cue**, notice, prompt, recap, aide-mémoire (*formal*) [➡INDICATIONS, SIGNS, AND WARNINGS; 68] **2** *n* **souvenir**, token, memento, knickknack, keepsake, remembrance [➡ORNAMENTS AND DECORATIONS; 1248]

reminisce *v* **recall**, talk about, hark back to, muse over, evoke, recollect, bring to mind, ponder, ruminate [➡REMEMBER; 746]

reminiscence **1** *n* **nostalgia**, recollection, looking back, musing, rumination [➡MEMORY; 745] **2** *n* **memory**, recollection, reminder [➡MEMORY; 745]

reminiscent *adj* **suggestive**, evocative, resonant, redolent, similar, like [➡SIMILARITY; 148]

remiss *adj* **careless**, negligent, lax, slipshod, slapdash, sloppy, inattentive, thoughtless, inconsistent [➡INCAUTIOUS AND CARELESS; 283] *Opposite:* diligent

remission *n* **reduction**, decrease, lessening, diminution, cutback, retardation [➡CHANGE OF SIZE: SMALLER; 393]

remissive *adj* **pardoning**, forgiving, absolving, exonerating [➡GENEROSITY AND KINDNESS; 495]

remit **1** *v* **send**, forward, dispatch, pay, settle, square [➡DISPATCH AND SEND; 333] **2** *v* **submit**, refer, pass on [➡GIVE MONEY; 433] *Opposite:* handle **3** *v* **slacken**, decrease, lessen, diminish, cancel, reduce, abate (*formal or literary*) [➡CHANGE OF INTENSITY: LESS; 395] *Opposite:* increase **4** *n* (*UK*) **responsibility**, concern, sphere of activity, job, brief, sphere, scope [➡DISPENSE, RATION, AND DISTRIBUTE; 434]

remittance **1** *n* **payment**, transfer of funds, transmittal, fee, transfer, settlement [➡FUNDS, PAYMENTS, AND CHARGES; 800] **2** *n* **release**, dispatch, discharge (*formal*) [➡FREEDOM AND LIBERTY; 208]

remix **1** *v* **produce new version**, rehash, reproduce, alter, change, revise, rejigger (*informal*) [➡CREATION; 346] **2** *n* **new**

recording, different version, new version, latest version, revised version [➡RECORDINGS AND PLAYERS; 911]

remnant *n* **remainder**, remains, relic, residue, trace, vestige, scrap, end, last part, leftover [➡REMAINDER AND REMAINDERS; 125]

remnants *n* [➡REMAINDER AND REMAINDERS; 125]

remodel *v* **alter**, modify, modernize, adapt, adjust, amend, transform, renovate, change, refashion [➡IMPROVE SOMETHING; 374]

remonstrance **1** *n* **argument**, evidence, backup, proof, case, point [➡POINTS OF VIEW; 767] **2** *n* **protest**, complaint, objection, petition, dispute, civil disobedience [➡CRITICISMS AND ANGRY OUTBURSTS; 50]

remonstrate *v* **argue**, protest, object, oppose, complain, squabble, bicker, dispute, gripe (*informal*) [➡PROTEST AND EXPRESS DISAPPROVAL; 642] *Opposite:* agree

See Compare and Contrast at **object**.

remorse *n* **regret**, sorrow, repentance, penitence, guilt, compunction, shame [➡FEELINGS ABOUT THE PAST; 532]

remorseful *adj* **regretful**, repentant, penitent, contrite, apologetic, rueful, sorry [➡EMBARRASSMENT AND HUMILIATION; 542] *Opposite:* unrepentant

remorseless **1** *adj* **pitiless**, ruthless, merciless, callous, cruel, hard, brutal, compassionless, unforgiving, coldhearted [➡SELFISH AND UNKIND; 505] *Opposite:* merciful **2** *adj* **inexorable**, implacable, indefatigable, unbending, unyielding, unstoppable, relentless [➡PERMANENCE: WITHOUT END; 94]

remote **1** *adj* **distant**, isolated, inaccessible, far-flung, far-off, in the sticks, secluded, out-of-the-way, faraway, apart, in the boondocks (*informal*) [➡DISTANCE; 160] *Opposite:* nearby **2** *adj* **slight**, outside, slim, unlikely, improbable, faint, small [➡IMPOSSIBLE AND IMPROBABLE; 178] *Opposite:* likely **3** *adj* **aloof**, detached, withdrawn, reserved, cool, cold, frosty, uninvolved, inaccessible, diffident [➡UNFRIENDLINESS AND UNSOCIABILITY; 504] *Opposite:* approachable

remotely **1** *adv* **distantly**, tenuously, slightly, a little, somewhat, vaguely [➡TO A CERTAIN EXTENT; 136] *Opposite:* closely **2** *adv* **at all**, in the least, the least bit, the slightest bit [➡TO A CERTAIN EXTENT; 136] *Opposite:* greatly

remoteness **1** *n* **isolation**, seclusion, distance, solitude, inaccessibility [➡DISTANCE; 160] *Opposite:* closeness **2** *n* **aloofness**, detachment, reserve, inaccessibility, coolness, frostiness, diffidence [➡UNFRIENDLINESS AND UNSOCIABILITY; 504] *Opposite:* approachability

remount *v* **get on again**, get back on, mount again, ride again, get back in the saddle, climb on again [➡ASSUME A POSITION; 317]

removable *adj* **detachable**, not fixed, can be removed, changeable, transferable [➡UNRELATEDNESS AND SEPARATENESS; 146] *Opposite:* attached

removal *n* **taking away**, elimination, exclusion, subtraction, deletion, amputation, confiscation, deduction, abstraction, ejection [➡REMOVE SOMETHING; 338] *Opposite:* addition

remove **1** *v* **take away**, get rid of, eliminate, do away with, eradicate, take out, confiscate [➡REMOVE SOMETHING; 338] *Opposite*: add **2** *v* **take off**, detach, cut off, amputate, disconnect, strip off, subtract, delete [➡DELETE AND ERASE; 339]

remunerate *v* **pay**, reward, compensate, recompense, repay, reimburse [➡GIVE MONEY; 433]

remuneration *n* **payment**, fee, salary, wage, compensation, recompense, pay, reward, return, stipend, reimbursement [➡INCOME; 460]

See Compare and Contrast at **wage**.

renaissance *n* **rebirth**, new start, new beginning, resurgence, revitalization, revival, regeneration, recovery, reawakening [➡REPETITION; 29] *Opposite*: decline

Renaissance 1 *type of* **pre-20th-century art movement** [➡ARTISTIC MOVEMENTS AND STYLES; 899] **2** *type of* **pre-20th-century architecture** [➡BUILDING AND ARCHITECTURE; 1076]

rename *v* **name again**, give a new name, retitle, rechristen, give a name again, change name, give another name [➡NAME AND DESCRIBE; 665]

renascent *adj* **becoming active**, budding, burgeoning, appearing, becoming popular, reviving, reemerging [➡SUCCESSFUL AND PROMISING; 81]

rend *v* **tear**, tear apart, rip, come apart, split, slash, shred, slit [➡TEAR, BREAK, AND CUT; 360] *Opposite*: mend

See Compare and Contrast at **tear**.

render 1 *v* (*formal*) **portray**, depict, represent, execute, translate, perform [➡CAUSE TO APPEAR; 5] **2** *v* (*formal*) **decide**, decree, judge, adjudicate, declare [➡MAKE DECISIONS AND CHOICES; 752] **3** *v* (*formal*) **provide**, give, deliver, submit, make available, hand over, supply, afford (*formal*), bestow (*formal*) [➡EQUIP AND SUPPLY; 435] **4** *v* **melt down**, reduce, condense, concentrate, boil down, purify, extract [➡SOFTEN, LIQUEFY, AND DAMPEN; 388] *Opposite*: solidify

rendering 1 *n* **portrayal**, depiction, picture, image, portrait, shooting, reproduction, description, delivery [➡REPRESENTATIONS AND GENERAL EXAMPLES; 65] **2** *n* **version**, translation, interpretation, interpreting, execution, representation, transcription, adaptation [➡ONE-WAY COMMUNICATION; 49] **3** *n* **plaster coating**, plaster, coating, cladding, siding, coat, pebbledash (*UK*) [➡COVERS AND COATINGS; 1246]

render speechless *v* [➡CONFUSE AND BEWILDER; 571]

rendezvous 1 *n* **engagement**, meeting, appointment, tryst, assignation, date [➡MEETINGS AND ASSEMBLIES; 43] **2** *n* **meeting place**, meeting point, assembly point, location, site, resort, muster, station, hangout (*informal*) [➡PUBLIC BUILDINGS AND MEETING PLACES; 1081] **3** *v* **meet**, come together, make contact, get together, assemble, gather, congregate [➡INITIATE AND ESTABLISH COMMUNICATION; 680]

rendition *n* **version**, interpretation, performance, rendering, execution, delivery [➡ONE-WAY COMMUNICATION; 49]

renegade *n* **apostate**, traitor, rebel, turncoat, betrayer, defector, deserter [➡VILLAINS AND THUGS; 947] *Opposite*: loyalist

renege *v* **go back on**, break your word, break a promise, back out, default [➡NOT DO AND REFUSE TO DO; 274]

renew 1 *v* **return to**, reintroduce, repeat, restart, begin again, recommence (*formal*) [➡RECOMMENCE AND RESUME; 268] **2** *v* **recondition**, renovate, refurbish, repair, restore, mend, make good, revamp [➡REPAIR AND MEND; 376] **3** *v* **restore**, rekindle, revitalize, rejuvenate, refresh, recharge, revive, regenerate, reinstate, recall [➡IMPROVE SOMETHING; 374]

Compare and Contrast: *renew, recondition, renovate, restore, revamp*

CORE MEANING: to improve the condition of something

renew to replace something worn or broken; *recondition* to bring something such as a machine or appliance back to a good condition or working state by means of repairs or replacement of parts; *renovate* to bring something such as a building back to a former better state by means of repairs, redecoration, or refurbishment; *restore* to bring something back to an original state after it has been damaged or fallen into a bad condition; *revamp* to improve the appearance or condition of something.

renewal *n* **regeneration**, restitution, rekindling, revitalization, rejuvenation, rebirth, replenishment, restoration, repair [➡IMPROVE SOMETHING; 374]

renounce 1 *v* **relinquish**, surrender, hand over, turn down, disown, refuse, give up, abdicate, demit [➡FORGO AND DENY ONESELF; 449] *Opposite*: accept **2** *v* **disavow**, repudiate, give up, reject, abandon, forsake, desert, quit [➡DENY AND REJECT; 644] *Opposite*: embrace

renovate *v* **renew**, recondition, modernize, refurbish, repair, restore, mend, do up, revamp, remodel, redecorate, fix up [➡REPAIR AND MEND; 376]

See Compare and Contrast at **renew**.

renovated *adj* [➡IN GOOD REPAIR; 1232]

renovation *n* **face-lift**, revamp, makeover, restoration, redecoration, repair, overhaul, renewal, reformation, transformation, reconstruction [➡IMPROVE SOMETHING; 374]

renown *n* **fame**, celebrity, notoriety, prominence, popularity, reputation, recognition, distinction, repute (*formal*) [➡KNOWN AND FAMOUS; 181] *Opposite*: obscurity

renowned *adj* **famous**, well-known, celebrated, prominent, popular, distinguished, legendary, recognized, established, VIP [➡KNOWN AND FAMOUS; 181] *Opposite*: unknown

rent 1 *n* **rental**, rent payment, hire charge, fee, payment, charge [➡FUNDS, PAYMENTS, AND CHARGES; 800] **2** *v* **let**, hire out, lend out, rent out, charter, lease [➡LEND, LEASE, AND BORROW; 428] **3** *n* **hole**, tear, rip, split, slash, fissure, gash, crack, cleft, slit, divide [➡HOLES, GAPS, AND FORKS; 1252]

rental *n* **rent payment**, fee, payment, hire charge, charge, rent [➡FUNDS, PAYMENTS, AND CHARGES; 800]

rent out *v* [➡LEND, LEASE, AND BORROW; 428]

renunciation 1 *n* **repudiation**, abandonment, denial, renouncement, rejection, disavowal (*formal*) [➡DENY AND REJECT; 644] *Opposite*: acceptance **2** *n* **rejection**, repudiation, abandonment, denial, refusal, disallowance, refutation [➡REFUSE PERMISSION AND NOT ALLOW; 670] *Opposite*: acceptance

3 *n* **surrender**, disowning, refusal, resignation, abdication, relinquishment [➡ FORGO AND DENY ONESELF; 449]

reoccurrence *n* [➡ REPETITION; 29]

reoffender *n* [➡ CRIMINALS; 821]

reorder *v* **rearrange**, reorganize, regroup, restructure, move around, alter, change around, mix up, sort out [➡ ARRANGE AND CREATE ORDER; 357]

reorganization *n* **reform**, restructuring, reshuffle, redeployment, reformation, shake-up, sort-out (*UK*) [➡ ARRANGE AND CREATE ORDER; 357]

reorganize *v* **regroup**, move around, reorder, rearrange, restructure, alter, change around, reschedule, sort out, tidy up, change [➡ ARRANGE AND CREATE ORDER; 357]

rep (*informal*) *n* **representative**, agent, courier, delegate, deputy, sales rep (*informal*) [➡ REPRESENTATIVES AND PATRONS; 968]

repaint *v* **redecorate**, renovate, touch up, patch up, freshen the paint, recoat [➡ DECORATE, ADORN, AND APPLY COATINGS; 405]

repair **1** *v* **mend**, fix, patch up, restore, overhaul, darn, put back together, get working again [➡ REPAIR AND MEND; 376] **2** *n* **overhaul**, reparation, restoration, patch-up, mending, healing, renovation, darning [➡ REPAIR AND MEND; 376]

repaper *v* [➡ DECORATE, ADORN, AND APPLY COATINGS; 405]

reparation *n* **amends**, compensation, damages, recompense, reimbursement, restitution [➡ FUNDS, PAYMENTS, AND CHARGES; 800]

repartee *n* **banter**, wit, wordplay, badinage, raillery [➡ JOKES AND TEASING; 674]

repast (*literary*) *n* **meal**, banquet, feast, buffet, collation, spread (*informal*), refection (*literary*) [➡ MEALS AND PARTS OF MEALS; 1169]

repatriate *v* **send home**, deport, send back, banish, exile, expel, oust [➡ EJECT AND EXCLUDE; 340]

repatriation *n* **sending home**, going home, deportation, return, exile, banishment, expulsion, ouster [➡ MOVE SOMETHING TO ANOTHER LOCATION; 324]

repay *v* **pay**, pay back, reimburse, refund, pay off, settle up, recompense, square [➡ REWARD; 436]

repayment *n* **payment**, refund, reimbursement, settlement, compensation, recompense [➡ FUNDS, PAYMENTS, AND CHARGES; 800]

repeal *v* **cancel**, revoke, rescind, annul, retract, abolish, dismantle, reverse [➡ ABOLISH AND ANNUL; 452] *Opposite*: enact

See Compare and Contrast at **nullify**.

repeat **1** *v* **reiterate**, recap, go over, echo, retell, say again, recite, resay, restate, iterate [➡ RECITE, REPEAT, AND NARRATE; 620] **2** *v* **do again**, replicate, duplicate, show again, copy, imitate [➡ RECOMMENCE AND RESUME; 268] **3** *n* **recurrence**, replication, reiteration, duplication, reappearance, echo, recap, reprise, repetition [➡ REPETITION; 29]

repeated *adj* **recurrent**, frequent, recurring, repetitive, constant, continual [➡ FREQUENT AND OFTEN; 107] *Opposite*: rare

repeat offender *n* [➡ CRIMINALS; 821]

repel **1** *v* **disgust**, revolt, nauseate, repulse, make you feel sick, sicken [➡ UPSET, DISTRESS, AND HUMILIATE; 567] **2** *v* **keep away**, fend off, drive back, keep at bay, deter, resist, prevent, hold off, ward off [➡ AVOID OR ESCAPE CONTACT; 418] *Opposite*: attract

repellant *adj* [➡ DISGUSTING AND REPULSIVE; 230]

repelled *adj* [➡ IRRITATION AND ANGER; 541]

repellent **1** *adj* **disgusting**, revolting, nauseating, repulsive, repugnant, off-putting, sickening, hideous, vile, disconcerting [➡ DISGUSTING AND REPULSIVE; 230] *Opposite*: attractive **2** *adj* **impervious**, impermeable, resistant, proof, tight [➡ SAFE AND SAFETY; 191]

repent *v* **regret**, be sorry, apologize, ask forgiveness, feel sorrow, be penitent, be remorseful, atone (*formal*) [➡ APOLOGIZE AND RETRACT; 683]

repentance *n* **regret**, sorrow, remorse, penitence, atonement, shame, contrition, penance, contriteness [➡ FEELINGS ABOUT THE PAST; 532]

repentant *adj* **regretful**, remorseful, apologetic, penitent, rueful, contrite, sorry [➡ EMBARRASSMENT AND HUMILIATION; 542] *Opposite*: unrepentant

repercussion *n* **consequence**, effect, upshot, impact, aftermath, outcome, ramification, corollary, influence, implication, result [➡ RESULTS AND OUTCOMES; 83]

repertoire *n* **repertory**, collection, selection, series, stock, range, group [➡ COLLECTIONS AND MIXTURES OF THINGS; 1244]

repertory **1** *n* **theater**, company, theater company, theater group, repertory company, repertory theater [➡ THE PERFORMING ARTS; 904] **2** *n* **repertoire**, selection, series, stock, range, collection, store [➡ COLLECTIONS AND MIXTURES OF THINGS; 1244] **3** *n* (*UK*) **staging**, production, performance [➡ PERFORMANCES AND SHOWS; 42]

repertory company *n* [➡ THE PERFORMING ARTS; 904]

repertory theater *n* [➡ THE PERFORMING ARTS; 904]

repetition *n* **recurrence**, replication, duplication, reiteration, reappearance, echo, reverberation, reprise, repeat [➡ REPETITION; 29]

repetitious *adj* **repetitive**, boring, monotonous, tedious, dull, tiresome, pedestrian, dreary [➡ BORING AND UNINTERESTING; 234] *Opposite*: innovative

repetitiousness *n* [➡ REPETITION; 29]

repetitive *adj* **boring**, dull, monotonous, tedious, tiresome, uninteresting, pedestrian, dreary [➡ BORING AND UNINTERESTING; 234] *Opposite*: varied

repetitively *adv* **repeatedly**, continually, over and over again, cyclically, frequently [➡ FREQUENT AND OFTEN; 107] *Opposite*: infrequently

repetitiveness *n* [➡ REPETITION; 29]

repetitive strain injury *n* [➡ THE BONES AND JOINTS; 719]

rephrase *v* **restate**, retell, say differently, put another way, reshape, rearticulate, resay [➡ RECITE, REPEAT, AND NARRATE; 620]

replace 1 *v* **substitute**, trade, use instead, exchange, switch, interchange, take the place of, supplant, change, supersede, swap (*informal*) [➡ EXCHANGE AND INTERCHANGE; 448] **2** *v* **replenish**, put back, restore, return, reinstate, restitute [➡ POSITION SOMETHING; 325]

replacement *n* **substitute**, stand-in, substitution, proxy, surrogate, alternative, alternate, understudy [➡ SUBSTITUTES AND STAND-INS; 399] *Opposite*: original

replay 1 *v* **play again**, rerun, repeat, retell, reiterate, restate [➡ RECOMMENCE AND RESUME; 268] **2** *n* **rerun**, repetition, reiteration, echo, repeat [➡ REPETITION; 29]

replenish *v* **replace**, refill, fill, stock up, top up, restock, reload [➡ FILL; 406] *Opposite*: deplete

replenishment *n* **replacement**, refill, renewal, top up (*UK*) [➡ MORE AND EXCESS; 124]

replete 1 *adj* **full**, complete, supplied, abounding, brimming, awash, rife, chock-full (*informal*) [➡ FULL; 1239] *Opposite*: lacking **2** *adj* **sated**, satisfied, satiated, full, full up, stuffed (*informal*) [➡ EAT AND NOT EAT; 710] *Opposite*: hungry

repletion *n* **fullness**, surfeit, glut, satiety [➡ FULL; 1239]

replica *n* **copy**, reproduction, imitation, model, facsimile, duplication, mock-up, carbon copy [➡ COPIES AND REPLICAS; 151] *Opposite*: original

replicate *v* **duplicate**, repeat, copy, imitate, reproduce, photocopy, redo [➡ COPY AND DUPLICATE; 402]

See Compare and Contrast at **copy**.

replication *n* **repetition**, duplication, imitation, copying, reproduction [➡ REPETITION; 29]

reply 1 *v* **respond**, answer, retort, answer back, react, counter, come back with, rejoin (*formal*) [➡ REPLY AND ANSWER; 668] **2** *n* **response**, account, answer, retort, riposte, comeback, reaction, rejoinder (*formal*) [➡ REPLY AND ANSWER; 668]

See Compare and Contrast at **answer**.

repo (*informal*) *n* [➡ BUSINESS ACTIVITIES AND PHENOMENA; 794]

report 1 *v* **give an account**, tell, state, describe, give details, testify, convey, inform, recount, relate, narrate [➡ RECITE, REPEAT, AND NARRATE; 620] **2** *v* **register**, check in, present yourself, turn up, show up, arrive [➡ ARRIVE; 12] **3** *n* **tale**, statement, description, testimony, story, account, chronicle, narrative, version [➡ ONE-WAY COMMUNICATION; 49] **4** *n* **loud noise**, bang, boom, crash, explosion, shot, noise, echo [➡ IMPACT SOUNDS; 1260]

reportage *n* **news coverage**, reporting, coverage, mention, analysis, exposure [➡ NEWSPAPERS AND MAGAZINES; 605]

reportedly *adv* **allegedly**, supposedly, apparently, seemingly, so they say, purportedly (*formal*) [➡ UNCERTAIN; 175] *Opposite*: in fact

reporter *n* **foreign correspondent**, special correspondent, journalist, correspondent, writer, newsperson [➡ WORKERS IN ENTERTAINMENT AND MEDIA; 873]

repose 1 *n* **inactivity**, sleep, rest, relaxation, restfulness,

ease, leisure [➡ PERIODS OF REST; 91] *Opposite*: activity **2** *n* **calmness**, peace, stillness, tranquillity, calm, peacefulness [➡ LACK OF ACTIVITY OR MOTION; 342] *Opposite*: agitation **3** *v* (*formal*) **relax**, rest, take it easy, recline, put your feet up, lounge, stretch out, lie, lie down [➡ LACK OF ACTIVITY OR MOTION; 342]

reposition *v* **shift**, transpose, move, relocate [➡ MOVE SOMETHING TO ANOTHER LOCATION; 324]

repositioning *n* **transposition**, relocation, moving, move [➡ MOVE SOMETHING TO ANOTHER LOCATION; 324]

repository 1 *n* **store**, container, storage area, storage place, receptacle, storeroom, vessel, storehouse, warehouse [➡ STORES AND STORAGE BUILDINGS; 1088] **2** *n* **source**, fountain, mine, storehouse, origin, fount (*literary*) [➡ BEGINNINGS; 53]

repossess 1 *v* **recoup**, take back, reclaim, recover, recuperate, retrieve, recall, get back, regain [➡ REGAIN POSSESSION; 429] **2** *v* [➡ BUSINESS ACTIVITIES AND PHENOMENA; 794]

repossession 1 *n* **recovery**, reclamation, retrieval, taking back, seizure, recouping [➡ REGAIN POSSESSION; 429] **2** *n* [➡ BUSINESS ACTIVITIES AND PHENOMENA; 794]

repot *v* **transplant**, transfer, replant, pot, pot on (*UK*), pot up (*UK*) [➡ GROW AND CULTIVATE; 351]

reprehend *v* [➡ ACCUSE, BLAME, AND CRITICIZE; 641]

reprehensible *adj* **wrong**, bad, disgraceful, shameful, inexcusable, unacceptable, heinous [➡ UNACCEPTABLE AND UNFORGIVABLE; 225] *Opposite*: praiseworthy

reprehension *n* **criticism**, censure, condemnation, telling off, admonition, reproof, censoriousness [➡ IRRITATION AND ANGER; 541] *Opposite*: praise

reprehensive *adj* **condemnatory**, reproachful, accusing, reproving, blameful, critical, censorious [➡ ACCUSATORY AND DISAPPROVING; 634] *Opposite*: praiseworthy

represent 1 *v* **act for**, speak for, stand for, stand in for [➡ REPRESENT SOMETHING OR SOMEBODY; 59] **2** *v* **stand for**, symbolize, correspond to, signify, exemplify, characterize, embody, be a symbol of, denote, epitomize [➡ REPRESENT SOMETHING OR SOMEBODY; 59] *Opposite*: misrepresent

representation 1 *n* **picture**, image, symbol, depiction, illustration, demonstration, sign, exemplification [➡ REPRESENTATIONS AND GENERAL EXAMPLES; 65] **2** *n* **statement**, complaint, submission, argument [➡ CLAIM, INSIST, AND EMPHASIZE; 614] **3** *n* **account**, version, portrayal, description, interpretation, depiction [➡ REPRESENTATIONS AND GENERAL EXAMPLES; 65]

representational *adj* **mimetic**, representative, figurative, depictive, realistic [➡ REPRESENTATIVE; 66] *Opposite*: abstract

representative 1 *n* **envoy**, delegate, agent, spokesperson, diplomat, commissioner, ambassador [➡ REPRESENTATIVES AND PATRONS; 968] **2** *n* **agent**, courier, delegate, deputy, rep (*informal*), sales rep (*informal*) [➡ SUBORDINATES AND ASSISTANTS; 966] **3** *adj* **illustrative**, typical, characteristic, demonstrative, archetypal [➡ REPRESENTATIVE; 66] **4** *adj* **symbolic**, descriptive, illustrative, evocative, expressive [➡ REPRESENTATIVE; 66]

repress 1 *v* **curb**, block, suppress, contain, keep inside, hold back, bottle up, limit, inhibit, stifle, internalize [➡ WITHHOLD INFORMATION; 687] *Opposite*: express **2** *v* **dominate**, subdue, overpower, subjugate, quell, suppress, crush [➡ CAPTIVITY AND LOSS OF FREEDOM; 248]

repressed 1 *adj* **stifled**, bottled-up, suppressed, blocked, curbed, inhibited [➡ SECRET AND UNKNOWN; 179] *Opposite*: expressed 2 *adj* **intimidated**, crushed, suppressed, subjugated, overpowered, oppressed [➡ CAPTIVITY AND LOSS OF FREEDOM; 248] *Opposite*: liberated

repression *n* **suppression**, subjugation, domination, authoritarianism, tyranny, despotism, cruelty, control, oppression [➡ CAPTIVITY AND LOSS OF FREEDOM; 248]

repressive *adj* **oppressive**, suppressive, tyrannical, authoritarian, brutal, cruel, exploitive, despotic [➡ CAPTIVITY AND LOSS OF FREEDOM; 248] *Opposite*: liberal

reprieve 1 *v* **let off**, pardon, grant a stay of execution, acquit, stay, remit, excuse, liberate [➡ TRIAL, PUNISHMENT, AND LEGAL OUTCOMES; 819] *Opposite*: punish 2 *n* **official pardon**, stay of execution, amnesty, pardon, acquittal, absolution, exoneration, stay, exculpation (*formal*) [➡ TRIAL, PUNISHMENT, AND LEGAL OUTCOMES; 819]

reprimand 1 *v* **chastise**, reproach, lecture, scold, admonish, reprove, criticize, bawl out (*informal*), chew out (*informal*), tell off (*informal*), castigate (*formal*), chide (*literary*) [➡ ACCUSE, BLAME, AND CRITICIZE; 641] *Opposite*: praise 2 *n* **rebuke**, admonishment, warning, dressing-down, reproof, lecture, telling off, scolding, talking-to (*informal*), slap on the wrist (*informal*) [➡ CRITICISMS AND ANGRY OUTBURSTS; 50]

reprint 1 *v* **reissue**, print again, publish again, produce again, republish, reproduce, recopy, redistribute [➡ COPY AND DUPLICATE; 402] 2 *n* **reissue**, copy, edition, new copy, new edition, new version [➡ COPIES AND REPLICAS; 151]

reprisal *n* **retaliation**, revenge, act of vengeance, punishment, payback (*informal*) [➡ VENGEANCE AND REVENGE; 685]

reprise 1 *n* **reappearance**, echo, recap, repeat, repetition, return, recurrence [➡ REPETITION; 29] 2 *v* **repeat**, reinterpret, reenact, re-present [➡ RECOMMENCE AND RESUME; 268]

reproach 1 *v* **admonish**, accuse, reprove, criticize, scold, rebuke, reprimand, blame, point the finger at, chide (*literary*) [➡ ACCUSE, BLAME, AND CRITICIZE; 641] *Opposite*: praise 2 *n* **criticism**, censure, reprimand, blame, accusation, reproof, rebuke, scolding [➡ CRITICISMS AND ANGRY OUTBURSTS; 50] *Opposite*: praise

reproachful *adj* **censorious**, accusing, disapproving, reproving, critical, judgmental, faultfinding [➡ ACCUSATORY AND DISAPPROVING; 634] *Opposite*: approving

reproachfulness *n* [➡ ANTAGONISM; 552]

reprobate *n* **degenerate**, rascal, troublemaker, ne'er-do-well, sinner, wrongdoer [➡ VILLAINS AND THUGS; 947]

reprocess *v* **process again**, reuse, recycle, recover, reclaim, salvage [➡ MAKE GOOD USE OF SOMETHING; 473]

reproduce 1 *v* **copy**, replicate, duplicate, repeat, imitate, mimic, clone, re-create [➡ COPY AND DUPLICATE; 402] 2 *v* **have children**, produce offspring, produce young, breed, give birth, procreate, produce [➡ REPRODUCTION AND HEREDITY; 725]

See Compare and Contrast at **copy**.

reproduction 1 *n* **copy**, imitation, replica, duplicate,

facsimile, model [➡ COPIES AND REPLICAS; 151] *Opposite*: original 2 *n* **breeding**, procreation, propagation, generation, multiplication [➡ REPRODUCTION AND HEREDITY; 725] 3 *adj* **imitation**, replica, fake, faux [➡ FALSE AND UNREAL; 173] *Opposite*: genuine

reproductive *adj* **generative**, multiplicative, procreative, procreant, propagative [➡ REPRODUCTION AND HEREDITY; 725]

reproductive cell *n* [➡ EGGS, SPERM, AND SPAWN; 727]

reproof *n* **criticism**, blame, accusation, rebuke, scolding, reprimand, telling off, dressing-down, admonition, chastisement (*formal*) [➡ CRITICISMS AND ANGRY OUTBURSTS; 50] *Opposite*: compliment

reprove *v* **criticize**, take to task, accuse, rebuke, scold, reprimand, admonish, haul over the coals, reproach, chastise, tell off (*informal*), chide (*literary*) [➡ ACCUSE, BLAME, AND CRITICIZE; 641]

reproving *adj* **disapproving**, condemnatory, reproachful, admonitory, censorious, withering, contemptuous, critical [➡ ACCUSATORY AND DISAPPROVING; 634] *Opposite*: approving

reptile *n* [➡ LIVING THINGS AND LIVING; 976]

reptile

◆ *types of reptiles*
alligator, basilisk, bearded dragon, cayman, chameleon, crocodile, gecko, gila monster, glass snake, goanna, horned lizard, iguana, Komodo dragon, lizard, moloch, monitor lizard, mugger, skink, slowworm, terrapin, tortoise, turtle

reptilian *adj* **cold-blooded**, unfriendly, emotionless, inhuman, stony, cold [➡ BEASTLY AND BRUTISH; 510] *Opposite*: warm

republic *n* **state**, nation, democracy [➡ COUNTRIES AND REGIONS; 1067] *Opposite*: monarchy

republican 1 *n* **antiroyalist**, antimonarchist [➡ POLITICAL OFFICES AND POLITICIANS; 808] *Opposite*: monarchist 2 *adj* **pro-republic**, antiroyalist, antimonarchist [➡ STYLES AND SYSTEMS OF GOVERNMENT; 806] *Opposite*: monarchist

republicanism *n* **antimonarchism**, antiroyalism, political belief [➡ STYLES AND SYSTEMS OF GOVERNMENT; 806] *Opposite*: monarchism

repudiate *v* **reject**, disclaim, renounce, deny, not accept, rebut, retract, disavow, turn your back on, wash your hands of [➡ DENY AND REJECT; 644] *Opposite*: acknowledge

repudiation 1 *n* **refutation**, retraction, renunciation, rejection, disavowal (*formal*) [➡ DENY AND REJECT; 644] *Opposite*: acknowledgment 2 *n* **denial**, refutation, negation, disclaimer, rejection, abandonment, refusal, disallowance [➡ DENY AND REJECT; 644] *Opposite*: acceptance

repugnance *n* **disgust**, revulsion, hatred, dislike, hate, abhorrence, repulsion, loathing, aversion (*formal*) [➡ DISLIKE AND HATE; 577] *Opposite*: attraction

See Compare and Contrast at **dislike**.

repugnant 1 *adj* **disgusting**, revolting, nauseating, repulsive, hideous, vile, foul, repellent, loathsome, abominable, heinous, sickening, gross (*slang*), abhorrent (*formal*) [➡ DISGUSTING AND REPULSIVE; 230] *Opposite*: attractive **2** *adj* **offensive**, objectionable, distasteful, unacceptable, obnoxious, obscene, shocking [➡ UNACCEPTABLE AND UNFORGIVABLE; 225] *Opposite*: agreeable

repulse **1** *v* **repel**, drive away, force away, hold back, hold off, ward off, resist, deter, force back, fight off, keep at bay, drive back [➡ AVOID OR ESCAPE CONTACT; 418] *Opposite*: yield **2** *v* **reject**, rebuff, resist, spurn, snub, turn away [➡ REFUSING OR REJECTING RELATIONS; 975] *Opposite*: welcome

repulsed *adj* **disgusted**, nauseated, revolted, repelled, sickened [➡ IRRITATION AND ANGER; 541] *Opposite*: attracted

repulsion *n* **disgust**, revulsion, nausea, loathing, repugnance, dislike, abhorrence [➡ DISLIKE AND HATE; 577] *Opposite*: attraction

repulsive *adj* **disgusting**, revolting, nauseating, hideous, vile, foul, repellent, stomach-turning, gross (*slang*), abhorrent (*formal*) [➡ DISGUSTING AND REPULSIVE; 230] *Opposite*: attractive

repulsiveness *n* **hideousness**, repugnance, foulness, abhorrence, vileness, grossness, offensiveness [➡ DISGUSTING AND REPULSIVE; 230] *Opposite*: attractiveness

reputable *adj* **highly regarded**, trustworthy, well-thought-of, sound, upright, honest, decent, dependable, reliable, respectable, of good standing, of good repute (*formal*) [➡ ADMIRABLE AND COMMENDABLE; 185] *Opposite*: disreputable

reputation *n* **standing**, status, name, character, repute (*formal*) [➡ STATUS; 888]

repute (*formal*) *n* **standing**, status, name, reputation, character [➡ STATUS; 888]

reputed *adj* **supposed**, alleged, presumed, apparent, believed, fabled [➡ UNCERTAIN; 175] *Opposite*: actual

request **1** *v* **ask for**, demand, apply for, call for, entreat, invite, wish, bid (*archaic*) [➡ REQUEST AND DEMAND; 663] **2** *n* **appeal**, call, demand, application, entreaty, invitation, wish, bid [➡ REQUEST AND DEMAND; 663]

requiem **1** *n* **service**, Mass, funeral, funeral Mass, service for the dead [➡ RELIGIONS AND RELIGIOUS PRACTICES; 777] **2** *n* **funeral music**, lament, dirge, funeral hymn, funeral song [➡ MUSIC, SONGS, AND SINGING; 907]

require **1** *v* **need**, necessitate, want, have need of, entail, involve, call for [➡ NEED AND REQUIRE; 464] **2** *v* **oblige**, compel, demand, expect, force, make, command [➡ CAUSE OR COMPEL TO ACT; 271]

required *adj* **necessary**, obligatory, compulsory, mandatory, essential, vital, prerequisite, requisite (*formal*) [➡ NECESSARY AND ESSENTIAL; 196] *Opposite*: optional

requirement *n* **obligation**, condition, prerequisite, must, necessity, constraint, requisite (*formal*) [➡ NECESSARY AND ESSENTIAL; 196] *Opposite*: option

requisite (*formal*) *adj* **necessary**, mandatory, vital, essential, indispensable, basic, required, obligatory, prerequisite, called for [➡ NECESSARY AND ESSENTIAL; 196] *Opposite*: optional

requisition **1** *n* **demand**, request, application, summons [➡ REQUEST AND DEMAND; 663] **2** *v* **take over**, commandeer, seize, take possession of, appropriate, occupy [➡ TAKE SOMETHING AWAY; 425] *Opposite*: relinquish **3** *v* **demand**, apply for, call for, request, put in for, summons [➡ REQUEST AND DEMAND; 663]

reread *v* **revisit**, look back over, check through, go through, read again, come back to, review, revise (*UK*) [➡ READ; 758]

rerun **1** *v* **replay**, repeat, play again, air again, show again [➡ TELEVISION AND RADIO; 606] **2** *n* **repeat**, repeat showing, replay [➡ TELEVISION AND RADIO; 606]

reschedule *v* **postpone**, rearrange, defer, reorganize, suspend, carryover [➡ DELAY ACTION OR OCCURRENCE; 278] *Opposite*: bring forward

rescheduling *n* **postponement**, deferment, putting off, rearrangement, rearranging, reorganizing [➡ DELAY ACTION OR OCCURRENCE; 278]

rescind *v* **withdraw**, annul, cancel, repeal, overturn, quash, void, retract, revoke, make null and void [➡ ABOLISH AND ANNUL; 452] *Opposite*: authorize

rescue **1** *v* **save**, free, set free, liberate, release, salvage, let go [➡ FREEDOM AND LIBERTY; 208] *Opposite*: abandon **2** *n* **release**, liberation, saving, salvage [➡ FREEDOM AND LIBERTY; 208]

rescuer *n* **savior**, champion, liberator, salvation, redeemer [➡ SUPPORTERS, PROTECTORS, AND COMPATRIOTS; 970]

research **1** *n* **investigation**, study, exploration, examination, inquiries [➡ EXAMINE AND ASSESS; 753] **2** *v* **investigate**, study, explore, do research, delve into, examine, make inquiries, follow a line of investigation, seek, look into [➡ EXAMINE AND ASSESS; 753]

researcher *n* **investigator**, academic, scholar, scientist, student, assistant [➡ STUDENTS AND PUPILS; 841]

resemblance *n* **similarity**, likeness, semblance, sameness, alikeness, closeness, similitude (*formal*) [➡ SIMILARITY; 148] *Opposite*: difference

resemble *v* **look like**, bear a resemblance to, be similar to, be like, look a lot like, remind somebody of, take after, bring to mind, seem like, smack of [➡ SEEM TO BE SOMETHING; 58] *Opposite*: differ

resembling *adj* **like**, similar to, not unlike, close to, reminiscent of, bordering on, approaching, in the vein of, approximating, akin to [➡ SIMILARITY; 148]

resent **1** *v* **dislike**, not like, hate, be offended by, show antipathy towards, take exception to, rail against [➡ DISLIKE AND HATE; 577] *Opposite*: like **2** *v* **begrudge**, bear a grudge, feel bitter about, have hard feelings about, feel aggrieved [➡ DISLIKE AND HATE; 577] *Opposite*: accept

resentful *adj* **angry**, bitter, indignant, offended, aggrieved, annoyed, insulted [➡ IRRITATION AND ANGER; 541]

resentfulness *n* [➡ ANTAGONISM; 552]

resentment *n* **anger**, bitterness, dislike, hatred, antipathy, offense, umbrage, bile (*literary*) [➡ ANTAGONISM; 552]

*See Compare and Contrast at **necessary**.*

*See Compare and Contrast at **anger**.*

reservable adj [➞ PRESENT AND AVAILABLE; 11]

reservation 1 n **advance booking**, booking, registration, reserved seat, arrangement, reserved table, reserved room, reserved ticket [➞ BUSINESS ACTIVITIES AND PHENOMENA; 794] 2 n **condition**, proviso, rider, corollary, stipulation [➞ NECESSARY AND ESSENTIAL; 196] 3 n **unwillingness**, reluctance, hesitation, distance, aloofness, formality, reserve, shyness, coolness, detachment, coldness, diffidence [➞ UNFRIENDLINESS AND UNSOCIABILITY; 504] Opposite: enthusiasm 4 n **protected area**, game park, game reserve, preserve, sanctuary, wildlife sanctuary, wildlife refuge, refuge, park, reserve [➞ THE COUNTRYSIDE AND OUTDOOR SPACES; 1071]

reservations n **misgivings**, doubts, hesitation, questions, uncertainties, difficulties, issues, objections [➞ UNCERTAINTY; 559]

reserve 1 v **set aside**, keep, keep back, hold back, put to one side, store, salt away, hoard, stockpile, save, stash, preserve [➞ STORE AND KEEP; 453] Opposite: use 2 v **book**, retain, put your name down for, make a reservation [➞ LEND, LEASE, AND BORROW; 428] Opposite: cancel 3 n **store**, cache, hoard, stock, emergency supply, supply, stockpile, stash (informal) [➞ COLLECTIONS AND MIXTURES OF THINGS; 1244] 4 n **reservation**, park, game park, protected area, game reserve, sanctuary, wildlife sanctuary, wildlife refuge, preserve [➞ THE COUNTRYSIDE AND OUTDOOR SPACES; 1071] 5 n **substitute**, stand-in, locum, extra, fallback, replacement, alternate [➞ SUBSTITUTES AND STAND-INS; 399]

reserved 1 adj **booked**, retained, taken, engaged [➞ ABSENT AND UNAVAILABLE; 7] Opposite: free 2 adj **earmarked**, kept, set aside, held in reserve, kept back [➞ ABSENT AND UNAVAILABLE; 7] Opposite: used 3 adj **aloof**, reticent, standoffish, snobbish, distant, unfriendly, cold, detached, cool, shy, diffident [➞ RETICENT AND UNFORTHCOMING; 631] Opposite: outgoing

reserves 1 n **assets**, funds, contingency fund, financial resources, capital, investments, cash, nest egg, money, stash (informal), monies (formal) [➞ FINANCIAL ASSETS; 462] 2 n **stocks**, supplies, hoard, resources, stores [➞ COLLECTIONS AND MIXTURES OF THINGS; 1244]

reservist n **soldier**, reserve, reserve member, part-time soldier, Territorial (UK) [➞ MILITARY PERSONNEL; 828]

reservoir n **tank**, pool, basin, lake, artificial lake [➞ RIVERS, LAKES, AND STREAMS; 1042]

reset v **rearrange**, reorganize, retune, change, right, set something to rights [➞ CHANGE; 372]

resettle v **relocate**, transfer, transplant, emigrate, immigrate, migrate, move, shift [➞ MOVE SOMETHING TO ANOTHER LOCATION; 324]

resettlement n **relocation**, immigration, emigration, migration, transfer, transplantation, movement [➞ MOVE SOMETHING TO ANOTHER LOCATION; 324]

reshape v **redesign**, reform, rewrite, restructure, reformat, restyle, remodel, remake [➞ CHANGE; 372]

reshuffle 1 n **reorganization**, rearrangement, rationalization, reallocation, reordering, restructuring [➞ ARRANGE AND CREATE ORDER; 357] 2 v **reorganize**, rearrange, rationalize, reallocate, reorder, restructure, change [➞ ARRANGE AND CREATE ORDER; 357]

reside 1 v **exist in**, be inherent in, be located in, be a feature of, be present in, be vested in, belong to [➞ EXIST IN A PLACE; 19] 2 v **live**, live in, inhabit, have your home, be a resident of, dwell (literary) [➞ INHABIT; 20]

residence n **house**, home, seat, habitation, dwelling (formal), abode (literary) [➞ ACCOMMODATIONS; 855]

residency n **placement**, position, job, post, internship [➞ JOB; 833]

resident n **occupant**, inhabitant, denizen, tenant, occupier, dweller (literary) [➞ INHABITANTS; 857]

residential adj **domestic**, suburban, housing, domiciliary [➞ HUMAN SETTLEMENTS; 1070] Opposite: business

residential area n [➞ HUMAN SETTLEMENTS; 1070]

residential care n [➞ HOSPITALS AND CLINICS; 826]

residential home n [➞ HOSPITALS AND CLINICS; 826]

residual adj **left over**, remaining, lingering, left behind, outstanding, lasting, enduring [➞ MORE AND EXCESS; 124]

residue n **remains**, remainder, rest, deposit, scum, lees, dregs, filtrate, excess [➞ REMAINDER AND REMAINDERS; 125]

resign v **leave**, leave your job, quit, walk out, give notice, hand in your notice, give up your job, step down [➞ WORK-RELATED ACTIVITIES; 834] Opposite: sign on

resignation 1 n **notice**, notification, letter of resignation [➞ LETTERS AND WRITTEN MESSAGES; 584] 2 n **acceptance**, acquiescence, acknowledgment, submission, forbearance (formal) [➞ FEELINGS ABOUT THE PAST; 532] Opposite: defiance

resigned adj **reconciled**, accepting, acquiescent, submissive, stoic, fatalistic, long-suffering, forbearing (formal) [➞ THE WILL AND WILLINGNESS; 563] Opposite: resistant

resignedly adv **reluctantly**, long-sufferingly, stoically, with a sigh, wearily, despairingly, unenthusiastically, tiredly [➞ WITHOUT ENTHUSIASM; 287] Opposite: enthusiastically

resign yourself v **accept**, acknowledge, give in to, yield to, reconcile yourself, come to terms [➞ FORGET, FORGIVE, AND ACCEPT; 748] Opposite: resist

resilience 1 n **buoyancy**, spirit, hardiness, toughness, resistance, strength [➞ STRENGTH OF WILL; 501] Opposite: defeatism 2 n **pliability**, flexibility, elasticity, suppleness, bounciness, springiness [➞ MALLEABLE AND ELASTIC; 1212] Opposite: rigidity

resilient 1 adj **hardy**, strong, tough, robust, buoyant, irrepressible, spirited, resistant [➞ STRENGTH OF WILL; 501] Opposite: defeatist 2 adj **elastic**, pliable, flexible, supple, resistant, tough, durable, sturdy [➞ MALLEABLE AND ELASTIC; 1212] Opposite: rigid

resin n **mastic**, gum, balm, kauri gum, gamboge, dammar, pitch, tolu [➞ PARTS OF TREES AND PLANTS; 1026]

resinous adj **sticky**, viscous, tacky, gummy [➞ PHYSICAL TEXTURE; 1222]

resist 1 v **fight**, battle, struggle, fight back, attack, counterattack, repel [➞ PREVENT CONTACT OR ATTACK; 419] Opposite: surrender 2 v **oppose**, defy, stand firm, contest, challenge, forbear (formal) [➞ COMPETE, CONTEND, AND COMBAT; 303] Opposite: accept 3 v **withstand**, survive, endure, weather, be proof against [➞ TOLERATE AND ENDURE; 766] Opposite: succumb 4 v **keep**

from, avoid, refuse, refrain, withstand, abstain [➡ NOT DO AND REFUSE TO DO; 274] *Opposite*: give in

resistance 1 *n* **confrontation**, fight, battle, fighting, struggle, conflict, opposition [➡ AGGRESSIVE EVENTS; 39] *Opposite*: surrender 2 *n* **opposition**, defiance, challenge, endurance [➡ REBELLIOUSNESS AND DISOBEDIENCE; 565] *Opposite*: acceptance

resistant 1 *adj* **opposed**, dead set against, unwilling, defiant, challenging, opposing, anti (*informal*) [➡ REBELLIOUSNESS AND DISOBEDIENCE; 565] *Opposite*: accepting 2 *adj* **resilient**, hardy, unaffected, impervious, tough, strong, sturdy [➡ STRENGTH; 201] *Opposite*: weak

resistor *n* **device**, controller, regulator, rheostat [➡ ELECTRONICS AND ELECTRICS; 1137]

resit (*UK*) 1 *n* **retake**, reexamination, retest, repeat [➡ CLASSES, COURSEWORK, AND EXAMINATIONS; 842] 2 *v* **take again**, retake, repeat, sit again [➡ RECOMMENCE AND RESUME; 268]

resolute *adj* **firm**, staunch, unyielding, stubborn, unbendable, definite, determined, unwavering, steadfast, tenacious, persevering, purposeful [➡ STRENGTH OF WILL; 501] *Opposite*: irresolute

resoluteness *n* **firmness**, determination, steadfastness, staunchness, single-mindedness, sense of purpose, confidence, stubbornness, decisiveness [➡ STRENGTH OF WILL; 501] *Opposite*: indecisiveness

resolution 1 *n* **decree**, declaration, decision, motion, ruling [➡ MAKE DECISIONS AND CHOICES; 752] 2 *n* **promise**, pledge, oath, vow [➡ PROMISE AND ASSURE; 684] 3 *n* **resolve**, determination, steadfastness, tenacity, firmness, perseverance, doggedness, purpose [➡ STRENGTH OF WILL; 501] *Opposite*: indecision 4 *n* **solution**, answer, end, upshot, outcome [➡ SOLUTIONS; 215]

resolve 1 *v* **make up your mind**, decide, determine, make a decision, undertake, agree [➡ MAKE DECISIONS AND CHOICES; 752] 2 *v* **solve**, come to a decision, get to the bottom of, sort out, put an end to, settle, answer, work out [➡ SOLVE AND INTERPRET; 760] 3 *n* **resolution**, determination, steadfastness, tenacity, doggedness, firmness [➡ STRENGTH OF WILL; 501] *Opposite*: indecision

resolved *adj* **determined**, set, resolute, fixed, committed [➡ STRENGTH OF WILL; 501] *Opposite*: undecided

resonance 1 *n* **timbre**, character, quality, tone, reverberation, echo [➡ QUALITY OF SOUNDS; 1264] 2 *n* **significance**, meaning, importance, suggestion, echo, hint, reverberation, reminiscence [➡ MEANING; 690]

resonant 1 *adj* **booming**, ringing, echoing, reverberating, resounding, deep, rich [➡ LOUD, HIGH, OR UNPLEASANT SOUNDS; 1266] *Opposite*: tinny 2 *adj* **significant**, meaningful, important, evocative, indicative, reminiscent [➡ IMPORTANT; 194] *Opposite*: insignificant

resonate *v* **reverberate**, vibrate, resound, ring, echo, boom [➡ EMIT RINGING AND HOOTING SOUNDS; 367]

resonating *adj* [➡ LOUD, HIGH, OR UNPLEASANT SOUNDS; 1266]

resort *n* **option**, recourse, alternative, course of action, possibility, choice, help [➡ SOLUTIONS; 215]

resort to *v* **turn to**, give in to, have recourse to, fall back on, avail yourself of, employ, make use of, use [➡ USE; 467]

resound *v* **echo**, resonate, boom, ring, reverberate [➡ SOUND EMISSION; 362]

resounding 1 *adj* **unqualified**, categorical, unambiguous, definite, unquestionable, decisive [➡ CERTAIN; 174] *Opposite*: qualified 2 *adj* **loud**, booming, echoing, ringing, resonant, reverberating, deep, rich [➡ LOUD, HIGH, OR UNPLEASANT SOUNDS; 1266] *Opposite*: weak

resource *n* **reserve**, supply, source, means, store [➡ COLLECTIONS AND MIXTURES OF THINGS; 1244]

resourceful *adj* **ingenious**, imaginative, inventive, practical, quick-witted, creative, capable [➡ POSITIVE INTELLECTUAL CHARACTERISTICS; 524] *Opposite*: unimaginative

resourcefulness *n* **ingenuity**, imagination, inventiveness, wits, originality, creativity [➡ POSITIVE INTELLECTUAL CHARACTERISTICS; 524]

resources *n* **capital**, income, possessions, wealth, property, funds, assets, wherewithal, means [➡ FINANCIAL ASSETS; 462]

respect 1 *n* **admiration**, high opinion, deference, esteem, reverence, veneration [➡ LOVE, RESPECT, AND GOODWILL; 549] *Opposite*: disrespect 2 *n* **detail**, regard, matter, particular, point, way, sense, manner, characteristic [➡ SUBJECT AREAS; 768] 3 *v* **value**, revere, think a lot of, esteem, defer to, have a high opinion of, look up to, admire, venerate [➡ LIKE, LOVE, VALUE, AND ENJOY; 578] *Opposite*: disrespect 4 *v* **show consideration for**, appreciate, regard, have a high regard for, recognize, pay attention to [➡ PAY ATTENTION; 765] *Opposite*: disregard 5 *v* **follow**, abide by, comply with, obey, acknowledge, accept [➡ OBEY AND ABIDE BY; 301] *Opposite*: deny

See Compare and Contrast *at* **regard**.

respectability *n* **decency**, propriety, uprightness, decorum, morality [➡ MORALLY GOOD; 774] *Opposite*: indecency

respectable 1 *adj* **reputable**, highly regarded, well-thought-of, decent, good, upright, proper, suitable [➡ ADMIRABLE AND COMMENDABLE; 185] *Opposite*: disreputable 2 *adj* **adequate**, decent, reasonable, acceptable, satisfactory, fair [➡ ACCEPTABLE AND PASSABLE; 219] *Opposite*: inadequate

respected *adj* **reliable**, authoritative, distinguished, venerable, esteemed, valued, appreciated, prized [➡ POPULAR AND WANTED; 220]

respectful *adj* **deferential**, reverential, reverent, humble, dutiful [➡ GOOD MANNERS AND SOCIAL SKILLS; 520] *Opposite*: disrespectful

respectfulness *n* **deference**, respect, consideration, regard, honor, veneration [➡ LOVE, RESPECT, AND GOODWILL; 549] *Opposite*: contemptuousness

respecting *prep* **with regard to**, regarding, with respect to, in respect of, relating to, about, concerning [➡ EXPRESSIONS OF REFERENCE; 63]

respective *adj* **own**, individual, particular, separate, corresponding, one-on-one [➡ BELONGING OR RELATING TO INDIVIDUALS; 944]

respects *n* **compliments**, good wishes, greetings, salutations (*formal*) [➡ PRAISE AND ENCOURAGE; 647]

respiration *n* **breathing**, inhalation, exhalation [➡BREATHE AND NOT BREATHE; 716]

respirator *n* **breathing apparatus**, ventilator, gas mask, oxygen mask [➡BREATHE AND NOT BREATHE; 716]

respiratory *adj* **breathing**, lung, respirational [➡BREATHE AND NOT BREATHE; 716]

respiratory

◆ *parts of a respiratory system*
air sac, airway, alveolus, bronchial tube, bronchiole, bronchus, larynx, lung, pharynx, throat, trachea, vocal cords, voice box, windpipe

respire *v* **breathe**, take breaths, inhale, exhale [➡BREATHE AND NOT BREATHE; 716]

respite **1** *n* **interval**, break, breathing space, lull, relief, breathing room, breather (*informal*), letup (*informal*) [➡PERIODS OF REST; 91] **2** *n* **reprieve**, delay, adjournment, hiatus, break, postponement [➡PAUSES AND PHASES; 56]

resplendent *adj* **splendid**, dazzling, magnificent, glorious, brilliant, stunning, glittering, impressive [➡BEAUTY AND ATTRACTIVENESS; 189] *Opposite*: unimpressive

respond **1** *v* **reply**, answer, retort, answer back, rejoin, return [➡REPLY AND ANSWER; 668] **2** *v* **react**, act in response, take action, counter, act, act on [➡CARRY OUT AN ACTION; 269] *Opposite*: ignore

respondent *n* **defendant**, accused, plaintiff [➡PEOPLE IN LAW COURTS; 820]

response *n* **reply**, answer, retort, comeback, reaction, riposte, rejoinder (*formal*) [➡REPLY AND ANSWER; 668]

See Compare and Contrast at **answer**.

responsibility **1** *n* **accountability**, duty, charge, concern, obligation, onus, bond, restraint [➡RESPONSIBILITY; 170] **2** *n* **blame**, liability, guilt, answerability, fault [➡RESPONSIBILITY; 170] **3** *n* **task**, brief, assignment, concern, job, commission, remit (*UK*) [➡WORK IN GENERAL; 297]

responsible **1** *adj* **accountable**, in charge, in control, in authority, answerable [➡RESPONSIBILITY; 170] **2** *adj* **dependable**, conscientious, trustworthy, reliable, sensible, mature [➡HONEST AND RELIABLE; 502] *Opposite*: irresponsible **3** *adj* **to blame**, liable, guilty, at fault, blamable [➡MORALLY BAD OR IMPROPER; 775]

responsive *adj* **receptive**, open, approachable, reactive, quick to respond, alert [➡FRIENDLINESS AND SOCIABILITY; 494] *Opposite*: sluggish

responsively *adv* **quickly**, quick-wittedly, instinctively, rapidly, swiftly, instantaneously [➡HAPPENING QUICKLY; 104] *Opposite*: sluggishly

responsiveness *n* **receptiveness**, openness, reaction, sensitivity, awareness, approachability, alertness [➡FRIENDLINESS AND SOCIABILITY; 494] *Opposite*: sluggishness

rest **1** *n* **break**, respite, time out, relaxation, recreation, cessation, repose, breather (*informal*) [➡PERIODS OF REST; 91] **2** *n* **remainder**, residue, leftovers, remnants, surplus, balance, excess [➡REMAINDER AND REMAINDERS; 125] **3** *n* **stand**,

support, holder, rack, frame [➡SUPPORTS AND BASES; 1255] **4** *v* **relax**, take it easy, have a rest, take a break, have a break, put your feet up, repose, sleep [➡LACK OF ACTIVITY OR MOTION; 342] **5** *v* **lie**, lean, lay, place, put, support, uphold [➡MOVE SOMETHING INTO A NEW POSITION OR OVERTURN; 330]

restart **1** *v* **resume**, take up, start again, pick up, start over [➡RECOMMENCE AND RESUME; 268] **2** *v* **revive**, resurrect, save, renew, reopen, regenerate [➡CAUSE TO HAPPEN; 31] *Opposite*: wind down

restate *v* **repeat**, reaffirm, reiterate, say again, regurgitate, paraphrase, iterate [➡RECITE, REPEAT, AND NARRATE; 620]

restaurant *n* [➡HOTELS, RESTAURANTS, AND CLUBS; 1082]

restaurant

◆ *types of eating places*
bistro, brasserie, café, cafeteria, canteen, chophouse, coffee bar, coffee shop, commons, cybercafé, diner, drive-in, eatery, gastrodome, greasy spoon, hole-in-the-wall (*informal*), kaiten sushi restaurant, lunch counter, luncheonette, lunchroom, mess, pizzeria, refectory, roadside café, salad bar, snack bar, steakhouse, sushi bar, tearoom, trattoria, truck stop

◆ *types of people who work in restaurants*
barista, bartender, busboy, chef, greeter, headwaiter, maître d', pastry chef, prep cook, short-order cook, sommelier, sous-chef, waiter, waitron (*slang*), wine waiter

rested *adj* **refreshed**, relaxed, restored, reinvigorated, revitalized, raring to go [➡FIT AND STRONG; 736] *Opposite*: exhausted

restful *adj* **soothing**, relaxing, soporific, calming, peaceful, quiet [➡CALMING; 188] *Opposite*: stimulating

restfulness *n* [➡PEACEFULNESS AND GENTLENESS; 214]

rest home *n* [➡HOSPITALS AND CLINICS; 826]

resting place *n* [➡BURIAL PLACES AND ACCESSORIES; 930]

restitution **1** *n* **compensation**, recompense, reimbursement, amends, repayment, refund [➡REWARDS AND AWARDS; 439] **2** *n* **restoration**, return, reinstatement [➡REGAIN POSSESSION; 429]

restive *adj* **restless**, fidgety, antsy, twitchy, agitated, edgy, impatient, on edge, uneasy [➡POSITIVE IMPATIENCE, ENTHUSIASM, AND ALERTNESS; 537] *Opposite*: calm

restiveness *n* **restlessness**, impatience, agitation, edginess, nervousness, uneasiness [➡POSITIVE IMPATIENCE, ENTHUSIASM, AND ALERTNESS; 537] *Opposite*: calmness

restless *adj* **fidgety**, restive, twitchy, agitated, edgy, impatient, on edge [➡POSITIVE IMPATIENCE, ENTHUSIASM, AND ALERTNESS; 537] *Opposite*: relaxed

restlessness *n* **agitation**, impatience, restiveness, edginess, anxiety, disquiet [➡POSITIVE IMPATIENCE, ENTHUSIASM, AND ALERTNESS; 537] *Opposite*: calmness

restock *v* **refill**, replenish, top off, top up, fill up, replace [➡FILL; 406]

rest on *v* **hinge on**, turn on, depend on, rely, hang on, pend [➡RECIPROCITY AND INTERDEPENDENCE; 147]

restoration 1 *n* reinstatement, reestablishment, return, restitution, reinstallation [➡ CONFER STATUS; 458] *Opposite*: abolition 2 *n* refurbishment, renovation, repair, renewal, rebuilding [➡ REPAIR AND MEND; 376]

restorative *adj* healing, uplifting, invigorating, soothing, recuperative, curative [➡ CALMING; 188] *Opposite*: draining

restore 1 *v* reinstate, reestablish, bring back, return, give back [➡ INSTITUTE AND INAUGURATE; 348] 2 *v* refurbish, renovate, repair, do up, rebuild, recondition, touch up, fix, fix up [➡ REPAIR AND MEND; 376]

See Compare and Contrast at **renew**.

restrain 1 *v* hold back, prevent, stop, keep, deter, inhibit, forestall [➡ AVOID, PREVENT, LIMIT, AND CONTROL; 277] 2 *v* control, bring under control, keep under control, keep in check, check, curtail, limit, restrict, stem, contain [➡ AVOID, PREVENT, LIMIT, AND CONTROL; 277] 3 *v* confine, detain, jail, lock up, imprison, put away [➡ CAPTIVITY AND LOSS OF FREEDOM; 248] *Opposite*: free

restrained *adj* reserved, controlled, in control of yourself, self-possessed, calm, unemotional, undemonstrative, nonaggressive [➡ RETICENT AND UNFORTHCOMING; 631] *Opposite*: demonstrative

restraining order *n* injunction, court order, gag order, stay [➡ TRIAL, PUNISHMENT, AND LEGAL OUTCOMES; 819]

restraint 1 *n* self-control, control, command, self-possession, self-discipline, moderation [➡ CONFIDENCE AND COMPOSURE; 499] *Opposite*: self-indulgence 2 *n* limit, limitation, curb, ceiling, restriction, control, check [➡ CAPTIVITY AND LOSS OF FREEDOM; 248] 3 *n* captivity, arrest, imprisonment, confinement, detention [➡ CAPTIVITY AND LOSS OF FREEDOM; 248] *Opposite*: freedom 4 *n* belt, chain, shackle, fetter, bond, attachment [➡ FASTENERS, LINKS, AND NETWORKS; 1247]

restrict *v* limit, confine, put a ceiling on, curb, control, contain, hamper, hold back, constrain, impede, inhibit, keep a tight rein on, check, constrict, cramp [➡ AVOID, PREVENT, LIMIT, AND CONTROL; 277] *Opposite*: loosen

restricted 1 *adj* limited, controlled, constrained, regulated, delimited (*formal*), circumscribed (*formal*) [➡ CAPTIVITY AND LOSS OF FREEDOM; 248] *Opposite*: open 2 *adj* classified, top-secret, secret, confidential, privileged [➡ SECRET AND UNKNOWN; 179] *Opposite*: public

restriction *n* limit, constraint, restraint, control, ceiling, curb, limitation, check [➡ CAPTIVITY AND LOSS OF FREEDOM; 248]

restrictive *adj* preventive, obstructive, limiting, deterring, restraining, constricting, cramping, holding back, restricting, hampering, off-putting [➡ CAPTIVITY AND LOSS OF FREEDOM; 248] *Opposite*: free

restroom *type of* room in public buildings [➡ TYPES OF ROOMS; 1097]

restructure *v* rearrange, reorganize, reform, reshuffle, redistribute, streamline [➡ ARRANGE AND CREATE ORDER; 357]

restructuring *n* rearrangement, reorganization, shake-up, reform, reshuffle, streamlining, reformation [➡ ARRANGE AND CREATE ORDER; 357]

rest up *v* [➡ LACK OF ACTIVITY OR MOTION; 342]

result 1 *n* consequence, outcome, upshot, effect, product, end result, end [➡ RESULTS AND OUTCOMES; 83] 2 *n* mark, grade, score, outcome [➡ SCORES AND EVALUATIONS; 598] 3 *n* calculation, solution, answer, findings, conclusion [➡ SOLUTIONS; 215] 4 *v* cause, bring about, give rise to, occasion, lead to [➡ CAUSE TO HAPPEN; 31] 5 *v* ensue, be caused by, stem, rise, be brought about by, develop, follow [➡ HAPPEN; 27]

resultant *adj* subsequent, ensuing, resulting, consequential, follow-on, secondary [➡ AFTER, LAST, AND FOLLOWING; 165]

resulting *adj* subsequent, resultant, ensuing, consequential, follow-on [➡ AFTER, LAST, AND FOLLOWING; 165]

resume 1 *v* recommence, start again, continue, begin again, pick up where you left off, restart, take up again, carry on [➡ RECOMMENCE AND RESUME; 268] *Opposite*: stop 2 *v* return, go back, reoccupy, take up again [➡ RECOMMENCE AND RESUME; 268]

resume see **résumé**

résumé *n* précis, review, outline, rundown, summary, potted version [➡ SUMMARIES, OUTLINES, AND EXCERPTS; 588]

resumption *n* recommencement, continuation, carrying on, renewal, reopening [➡ REPETITION; 29]

resurface 1 *v* float up, come up, break the surface, rise, reappear, reemerge [➡ GO UPWARD; 306] *Opposite*: sink 2 *v* reappear, come back, rematerialize, reemerge, return [➡ APPEAR AND EMERGE; 3] 3 *v* coat, cover, skim, overlay, surface [➡ DECORATE, ADORN, AND APPLY COATINGS; 405]

resurgence *n* revival, renaissance, rebirth, resurrection, recovery, reappearance [➡ REPETITION; 29] *Opposite*: disappearance

resurgent *adj* burgeoning, growing, rising, increasing, reviving, renascent, on the up (*UK*) [➡ SUCCESSFUL AND PROMISING; 81]

resurrect 1 *v* resuscitate, bring back to life, raise from the dead, restore to life, revive [➡ BECOME SICK, TREAT, AND RECOVER; 728] *Opposite*: kill 2 *v* save, breathe new life into, revive, revivify, restart, resuscitate, revitalize [➡ IMPROVE STRENGTH AND DURABILITY; 378]

resurrection *n* revival, renaissance, rebirth, revivification, reappearance, restoration, resurgence, renewal, revitalization [➡ REPETITION; 29]

resuscitate 1 *v* give artificial respiration to, bring around, save, give the kiss of life to [➡ BECOME SICK, TREAT, AND RECOVER; 728] *Opposite*: asphyxiate 2 *v* breathe new life into, revive, revivify, resurrect, boost, save, revitalize, renew [➡ IMPROVE STRENGTH AND DURABILITY; 378]

resuscitation 1 *n* artificial respiration, cardiac massage, revival, recovery [➡ HEALING; 730] 2 *n* restoration, resurgence, renewal, revival, revitalization, resurrection [➡ REPETITION; 29] 3 *type of* medical procedure [➡ REMEDIES, TREATMENTS, AND OPERATIONS; 731]

retail 1 *n* trade, selling, marketing, merchandising, wholesale, sales [➡ BUSINESS ACTIVITIES AND PHENOMENA; 794] 2 *v* sell, trade, put on the market, put up for sale, vend [➡ SELL; 441]

retailer 1 *n* shop, store, retail outlet [➡ RETAIL OUTLETS; 1083] 2 *n* seller, vendor, merchant, trader, dealer [➡ SELLERS; 442]

retail outlet *n* [➡ RETAIL OUTLETS; 1083]

retail store *n* [➡ RETAIL OUTLETS; 1083]

retain 1 *v* **keep**, keep hold of, hold on to, hold, hang on to, maintain, save, preserve [➡ STORE AND KEEP; 453] *Opposite*: let go **2** *v* **recall**, recollect, keep in mind, remember, hold [➡ REMEMBER; 746]

retainer *n* **deposit**, down payment, fee, payment [➡ FUNDS, PAYMENTS, AND CHARGES; 800]

retake 1 *v* **take back**, recapture, regain, reconquer, win back [➡ GET; 420] **2** *v* **repeat**, redo, resit (*UK*) [➡ RECOMMENCE AND RESUME; 268] **3** *n* **exam**, examination, repeat, resit (*UK*) [➡ CLASSES, COURSEWORK, AND EXAMINATIONS; 842]

retaliate *v* **hit back**, strike back, get even, even the score, react, get revenge, give as good as you get, get back at, give tit for tat, get your own back (*UK*) [➡ VENGEANCE AND REVENGE; 685] *Opposite*: forgive

retaliation *n* **reprisal**, revenge, vengeance, retribution [➡ VENGEANCE AND REVENGE; 685] *Opposite*: forgiveness

retaliatory *adj* **tit-for-tat**, reciprocal, reactive, punitive, revengeful, vengeful, avenging [➡ VENGEANCE AND REVENGE; 685] *Opposite*: forgiving

retard *v* **delay**, slow down, hold up, hold back, hinder, impede, check [➡ DELAY ACTION OR OCCURRENCE; 278] *Opposite*: speed up

retardation *n* **delay**, check, obstruction, hindrance, obstacle, impedance (*formal*) [➡ PROBLEMS; 256] *Opposite*: acceleration

retarded *adj* **underdeveloped**, slow, stunted, arrested, lagging [➡ HAPPENING SLOWLY; 106] *Opposite*: accelerated

retch *v* **vomit**, gag, be sick, heave (*informal*), throw up (*informal*), puke (*slang*) [➡ VOMIT AND BELCH; 712]

retell *v* **repeat**, restate, go over, reiterate, recite [➡ RECITE, REPEAT, AND NARRATE; 620]

retention 1 *n* **holding**, retaining, preservation, withholding, maintenance, custody [➡ STORE AND KEEP; 453] *Opposite*: release **2** *n* **remembering**, memorizing, recalling, memory, recollection [➡ MEMORY; 745] *Opposite*: forgetting

retentive *adj* **retaining**, absorbent, spongy [➡ DENSITY AND CONSISTENCY; 1207]

rethink 1 *v* **reconsider**, change your mind, change direction, change tack, change course, think again, start afresh, have second thoughts, do an about-face, do a volte-face, do an about-turn (*UK*) [➡ MAKE DECISIONS AND CHOICES; 752] **2** *n* **reconsideration**, change of mind, change of heart, second thoughts, volte-face, about-face, consideration, about-turn (*UK*), changeround (*UK*) [➡ MAKE DECISIONS AND CHOICES; 752]

reticence 1 *n* **reserve**, silence, uncommunicativeness, discretion, restraint, caginess (*informal*) [➡ RETICENT AND UNFORTHCOMING; 631] *Opposite*: openness **2** *n* **shyness**, bashfulness, reserve, quietness, modesty, introversion [➡ RETICENT AND UNFORTHCOMING; 631] *Opposite*: boldness

reticent *adj* **reserved**, discreet, restrained, unforthcoming, uncommunicative, taciturn, silent, quiet, cagey (*informal*) [➡ RETICENT AND UNFORTHCOMING; 631] *Opposite*: talkative

See Compare and Contrast at **silent**.

reticule *n* **bag**, handbag, purse, container [➡ CONTAINERS, RECEPTACLES, AND PACKAGING; 1245]

retina *part of eye* [➡ THE EYE; 698]

retinue *n* **entourage**, followers, attendants, servants, aides, cortege [➡ FRIENDS AND ACQUAINTANCES; 936]

retire 1 *v* **give up work**, stop working, step down, be pensioned off, be superannuated, be put out to pasture [➡ WORK-RELATED ACTIVITIES; 834] **2** *v* **leave**, take your leave, withdraw, go away, go off, retreat [➡ LEAVE AND GO AWAY; 8] **3** *v* **go to bed**, call it a day, turn in (*informal*), hit the sack (*informal*), hit the hay (*informal*), crash (*slang*) [➡ SLEEP AND DREAM; 723]

retired *adj* **superannuated**, pensioned off, discharged, emeritus, emerita, elderly, aged, old [➡ EMPLOYMENT STATUS; 831] *Opposite*: working

retirement 1 *n* **superannuation**, departure, leaving, giving up work, stepping down [➡ PERIODS OF REST; 91] **2** *n* **withdrawal**, retreat, sequestration, seclusion [➡ ENDS AND DEPARTURES; 54]

retiring *adj* **reticent**, self-effacing, unassuming, shy, reserved, timid, diffident, introverted [➡ RETICENT AND UNFORTHCOMING; 631]

retort 1 *v* **respond**, snap, rejoin, come back, counter, bite back [➡ REPLY AND ANSWER; 668] **2** *n* **reply**, response, riposte, answer, rejoinder (*formal*), squelch (*slang*) [➡ REPLY AND ANSWER; 668]

See Compare and Contrast at **answer**.

retouch *v* **touch up**, correct, restore, renovate, improve [➡ IMPROVE APPEARANCE; 379]

retrace *v* **review**, redo, go back over, repeat [➡ GO BACKWARD; 309]

retract 1 *v* **draw in**, draw back, pull in, pull back, withdraw [➡ MOVE SOMETHING: INTO A NEW POSITION OR OVERTURN; 330] *Opposite*: extend **2** *v* **deny**, take back, withdraw, apologize, recant, rescind [➡ APOLOGIZE AND RETRACT; 683] *Opposite*: stand by

retractable *adj* **telescopic**, folding, able to be drawn in, sheathable, coverable [➡ CHANGE OF SHAPE; 385]

retraction *n* **withdrawal**, refutation, disclaimer, denial, negation, renunciation, repudiation, disavowal (*formal*) [➡ APOLOGIZE AND RETRACT; 683] *Opposite*: confirmation

retreat 1 *n* **departure**, withdrawal, flight, evacuation [➡ ENDS AND DEPARTURES; 54] *Opposite*: advance **2** *n* **haven**, hideaway, sanctuary, refuge, shelter [➡ SAFE BUILDINGS OR PLACES; 1093] **3** *v* **move away**, move back, draw back, back away, run away, recoil, withdraw, leave, give ground, flee [➡ GO BACKWARD; 309] *Opposite*: advance

retrench *v* **cut back**, economize, save, save money, tighten your belt, make savings, make economies, make cuts, draw in your horns (*UK*) [➡ BUSINESS ACTIVITIES AND PHENOMENA; 794]

retrenchment *n* **cutback**, economizing, cuts, cost-cutting, belt-tightening [➡ BUSINESS ACTIVITIES AND PHENOMENA; 794]

retribution *n* **vengeance**, revenge, reprisal, reckoning, justice, payback (*informal*) [➡VENGEANCE AND REVENGE; 685]

retributive *adj* **punitive**, retaliatory, vengeful, punishing, revengeful, avenging [➡VENGEANCE AND REVENGE; 685]

retrieval *n* **recovery**, repossession, rescue, reclamation, salvage [➡REGAIN POSSESSION; 429] *Opposite*: loss

retrieve *v* **save**, get back, recover, regain, repossess, salvage, rescue, reclaim, take back [➡REGAIN POSSESSION; 429] *Opposite*: lose

retriever *type of* **large dog** [➡DOGS; 980]

retro *adj* **period**, old-fashioned, dated, historical, passé [➡OLD, OLD-FASHIONED; 167]

retroactive *adj* **backdated**, retrospective, ex post facto [➡PAST; 84]

retrograde 1 *adj* **backward**, reversing, rearward [➡DIRECTION OF MOTION; 345] *Opposite*: forward 2 *adj* **regressive**, declining, worsening, getting worse, deteriorating, reverting [➡WORSEN SOMETHING; 380] *Opposite*: improving

retrogress 1 *v* **regress**, decline, revert, degenerate, worsen, get worse, deteriorate [➡GET WORSE; 381] *Opposite*: progress 2 *v* **move backward**, reverse, go back, retreat, draw back, withdraw, move back [➡GO BACKWARD; 309] *Opposite*: move forward

retrogression *n* **decline**, regression, return, relapse, deterioration, worsening, lapse [➡WORSEN SOMETHING; 380] *Opposite*: progression

retrogressive 1 *adj* **regressive**, reverting, degenerating, worsening, getting worse, deteriorating, declining [➡WORSEN SOMETHING; 380] *Opposite*: progressive 2 *adj* **reversing**, retreating, withdrawing, moving back, drawing back [➡DIRECTION OF MOTION, 345]

retropack *part of* **spacecraft** [➡SPACE VEHICLES; 1063]

retrospect *n* **recollection**, remembrance, review, reconsideration, survey [➡MEMORY; 745] *Opposite*: prospect

retrospective 1 *adj* **backward-looking**, nostalgic, retrograde, traditional, conservative [➡THE NATURE OF IDEAS; 771] *Opposite*: forward-thinking 2 *adj* **reviewing**, reflective, surveying, reconsidering [➡EXAMINE AND ASSESS; 753] 3 *adj* **retroactive**, backdated, ex post facto [➡PAST; 84] 4 *n* **exhibition**, show, presentation, showcase, display, demonstration, exposition, showing [➡PERFORMANCES AND SHOWS; 42]

retrospectively *adv* **on reflection**, in retrospect, with hindsight, with the benefit of hindsight, on second thought, looking back [➡PAST; 84]

return 1 *v* **revisit**, come back, go again, come again, go back [➡ARRIVE; 12] *Opposite*: depart 2 *v* **repay**, pay back, refund, reimburse, give back [➡GIVE AND PROVIDE; 430] *Opposite*: keep 3 *v* **resume**, go back, revert, revisit, begin again [➡GO BACKWARD; 309] *Opposite*: stop 4 *v* **send back**, take back, replace, restore [➡DISPATCH AND SEND; 333] *Opposite*: remove 5 *n* **coming back**, reappearance, reoccurrence, arrival, homecoming [➡ARRIVAL; 13] *Opposite*: departure 6 *n* **profit**, earnings, yield, revenue, proceeds, gain, benefit [➡INCOME; 460]

returns *n* **revenue**, earnings, yield, proceeds, takings, income, profits [➡INCOME; 460] *Opposite*: outlay

reunification *n* **reunion**, reconsolidation, amalgamation, recombination, reintegration [➡STYLES AND SYSTEMS OF GOVERNMENT; 806]

reunify *v* **reunite**, come together, rejoin, bring together, reintegrate, reassemble, reconcile, recombine [➡CREATING CONNECTIONS; 144]

reunion 1 *n* **gathering**, meeting, event, get-together (*informal*) [➡MEETINGS AND ASSEMBLIES; 43] 2 *n* **reunification**, reintegration, recombination, reconsolidation [➡HARMONY; 155]

reunite *v* **reunify**, unite, bring together, unify, come together, join up [➡CREATING CONNECTIONS; 144] *Opposite*: split

reusable *adj* **refillable**, returnable, recyclable, green, ecofriendly, environmentally friendly, ecological [➡ECONOMICAL AND RESOURCEFUL; 207] *Opposite*: disposable

reuse *v* **recycle**, reclaim, reprocess, salvage [➡MAKE GOOD USE OF SOMETHING; 473] *Opposite*: discard

rev 1 *n* **revolution**, cycle, rotation, turn, revolution per minute, rpm [➡MOVE SOMETHING: ON THE SPOT; 336] 2 *v* **race**, roar, scream, increase power, accelerate, throttle, open up (*informal*), gun (*informal*) [➡CHANGE OF SPEED: MORE; 396]

revaluation *n* **revision**, reappraisal, reassessment, readjustment, redefinition, adjustment [➡EXAMINE AND ASSESS; 753]

revalue 1 *v* **raise**, increase, up, enhance, augment (*formal*) [➡BUSINESS ACTIVITIES AND PHENOMENA; 794] *Opposite*: devalue 2 *v* **reappraise**, reevaluate, adjust, reset, change, reassess [➡EXAMINE AND ASSESS; 753]

revamp 1 *v* **makeover**, do up, refurbish, restore, give a face-lift, overhaul, titivate [➡IMPROVE APPEARANCE; 379] 2 *n* **face-lift**, refurbishment, restoration, renovation, overhaul, makeover [➡IMPROVE APPEARANCE; 379]

> *See Compare and Contrast at* **renew.**

rev counter (*informal*) *type of* **controls** [➡INTERNAL PARTS OF A VEHICLE; 1146]

reveal 1 *v* **make known**, disclose, divulge, expose, make public, let slip, tell [➡BETRAY CONFIDENCES AND GOSSIP; 618] *Opposite*: conceal 2 *v* **expose**, uncover, show, bare, bring to light [➡CAUSE TO APPEAR; 5] *Opposite*: cover up

revealing 1 *adj* **skimpy**, see-through, figure-hugging, close-fitting, tight-fitting [➡DESCRIBING CLOTHES; 869] 2 *adj* **enlightening**, illuminating, telling, telltale, informative, educational [➡INTERESTING AND MEANINGFUL; 190] *Opposite*: obscure

revealingly *adv* **tellingly**, significantly, interestingly, importantly, conspicuously, noticeably [➡INTERESTING AND MEANINGFUL; 190]

reveille 1 *n* **wake-up call**, early-morning call, bugle call [➡SIGNALING; 1140] 2 *n* **early morning**, daybreak, dawn, sunrise, the crack of dawn, sun up, cockcrow (*archaic or literary*) [➡TIMES OF DAY; 87]

revel 1 *v* **make merry**, celebrate, have fun, let your hair down, socialize, party (*informal*), go to town (*informal*), rejoice (*literary*), carouse (*literary*) [➡LEISURE AND RECREATION; 874] 2 *v* **delight**, enjoy, take pleasure in, luxuriate, bask, wallow, take pride, take satisfaction, lap up, glory, exult [➡LIKE, LOVE, VALUE, AND ENJOY; 578] 3 *n* **celebration**, party, festivities, carnival, merrymaking, carousal (*literary*) [➡PARTIES, DANCES, AND CELEBRATIONS; 37]

revelation 1 *n* **exposé**, exposure, disclosure, leak, admission [➡INFORM, ANNOUNCE, AND ISSUE; 611] 2 *n* **surprise**, shock, eye opener [➡DECISIVE MOMENTS; 44]

reveler *n* **partygoer**, roisterer, merrymaker, pleasure-seeker, celebrator, drinker, party animal (*informal*), carouser (*literary*) [➡PLEASURE-SEEKERS AND HEDONISTS; 886]

revelry *n* **festivities**, revels, celebrations, partying, merriment, gaiety, carousing (*literary*) [➡PARTIES, DANCES, AND CELEBRATIONS; 37]

revels *n* [➡PARTIES, DANCES, AND CELEBRATIONS; 37]

revenge 1 *n* **retaliation**, vengeance, retribution, settling of scores, reprisal, payback (*informal*) [➡VENGEANCE AND REVENGE; 685] 2 *v* **requite**, avenge, even the score, get back, retaliate, get your own back (*UK*) [➡VENGEANCE AND REVENGE; 685]

revengeful *adj* [➡VENGEANCE AND REVENGE; 685]

revenue *n* **income**, proceeds, profits, returns, takings [➡INCOME; 460] *Opposite*: expenses

revenue system *n* [➡TAX AND TAXATION; 802]

reverberant *adj* [➡LOUD, HIGH, OR UNPLEASANT SOUNDS; 1266]

reverberate *v* **echo**, resound, ring, vibrate, resonate [➡SOUND EMISSION; 362]

reverberating *adj* **resounding**, echoing, resonant, rich, rumbling, ringing, booming, deep, loud [➡LOUD, HIGH, OR UNPLEASANT SOUNDS; 1266]

reverberation *n* **echo**, sound, noise, boom [➡SOUNDS; 1256]

reverberations *n* **aftershock**, aftereffects, impact, shock [➡RESULTS AND OUTCOMES; 83]

revere *v* **admire**, respect, look up to, hold in the highest regard, be in awe of, worship, venerate [➡LIKE, LOVE, VALUE, AND ENJOY; 578] *Opposite*: despise

revered 1 *adj* **respected**, valued, illustrious, distinguished, esteemed, well-regarded, admired, honored, celebrated, august (*formal*) [➡POPULAR AND WANTED; 220] *Opposite*: vilified 2 *adj* **holy**, sacred, blessed, venerated, hallowed, consecrated, sanctified [➡RELIGIOUS CONCEPTS; 776] *Opposite*: vilified

reverence *n* **respect**, admiration, worship, awe, veneration, amazement, devotion [➡LOVE, RESPECT, AND GOODWILL; 549] *Opposite*: contempt

See Compare and Contrast at **regard***.*

reverend 1 *n* **vicar**, priest, cleric, minister, parson [➡RELIGIOUS PEOPLE; 778] 2 *adj* **ecclesiastical**, clerical, priestly, ministerial [➡RELIGIONS AND RELIGIOUS PRACTICES; 777] 3 *adj* (*formal*) **respected**, revered, venerated, worthy, noble, hallowed [➡POPULAR AND WANTED; 220]

reverent *adj* **deferential**, reverential, respectful, worshipful, awed, humble [➡EXPRESSING RESPECT AND APPROVAL; 637] *Opposite*: irreverent

reverential *adj* **respectful**, deferential, reverent, humble, awed [➡EXPRESSING RESPECT AND APPROVAL; 637] *Opposite*: disrespectful

reverie *n* **daydream**, dream, trance, musing, contemplation, brown study [➡DREAM, IMAGINE, AND FANTASIZE; 749]

reversal 1 *n* **turnaround**, U-turn, about-face, volte-face, about-turn (*UK*) [➡DECISIVE MOMENTS; 44] 2 *n* **setback**, hitch, problem, reverse, blow, snag, misfortune, difficulty [➡PROBLEMS; 256]

reverse 1 *v* **overturn**, turn around, undo, annul, invalidate, repeal, quash, render null and void [➡ABOLISH AND ANNUL; 452] *Opposite*: carry out 2 *v* **move backward**, back up, drive backward, go backward, retreat, withdraw [➡GO BACKWARD; 309] *Opposite*: advance 3 *v* **transpose**, switch, invert, reorder, rearrange, change, swap (*informal*) [➡CHANGE ONE THING FOR ANOTHER; 398] 4 *n* **contrary**, opposite, antithesis, converse [➡OPPOSITE; 157] 5 *n* **back**, rear, underneath, other side, opposite side [➡EXTREMITIES OF PHYSICAL OBJECTS; 1250] *Opposite*: front 6 *n* **setback**, reversal, hitch, problem, misfortune, difficulty, blow, snag [➡PROBLEMS; 256] 7 *adj* **opposite**, contrary, converse, inverse [➡OPPOSITE; 157] *Opposite*: same

reversible 1 *adj* **rescindable**, revocable, alterable, adjustable, changeable, mutable, flexible [➡FINITENESS, VARIABILITY, AND TRANSIENCE; 96] *Opposite*: irreversible 2 *adj* **two-sided**, dual-purpose, multipurpose, double-sided, two-in-one [➡DESCRIBING CLOTHES; 869]

reversion 1 *n* **return**, decline, deterioration, degeneration, retreat, relapse, lapse [➡WORSEN SOMETHING; 380] 2 *n* **reversal**, turnaround, about-face, U-turn, change of direction, volte-face, about-turn (*UK*) [➡DECISIVE MOMENTS; 44]

revert 1 *v* **return**, go back, take a step back, relapse, regress, lapse [➡GO BACKWARD; 309] 2 *v* **go back**, revisit, go over again, take another look at, return, reinvestigate, reexamine, retrace your steps, reopen [➡EXAMINE AND ASSESS; 753] 3 *v* **regress**, change back, return, mutate, degenerate, deteriorate [➡GET WORSE; 381] 4 *v* **lapse**, backslide, go back to your old ways, slip back, reoffend, slide back [➡GET WORSE; 381] 5 *v* **be returned**, pass, pass back, return, go back [➡GO BACKWARD; 309]

review 1 *v* **study**, go over, go through, look over, reread, brush up, revise (*UK*) [➡STUDYING; 844] 2 *v* **appraise**, evaluate, assess, look at, examine, study, go through [➡EXAMINE AND ASSESS; 753] 3 *v* **reconsider**, reassess, go over, check, make another study of, have another look at, reevaluate, reexamine [➡EXAMINE AND ASSESS; 753] 4 *n* **appraisal**, evaluation, assessment, examination, analysis, criticism [➡EXAMINE AND ASSESS; 753] 5 *n* **publication**, magazine, journal, periodical [➡NEWSPAPERS AND MAGAZINES; 605] 6 *n* **reconsideration**, reassessment, check, reexamination, revision, reevaluation [➡EXAMINE AND ASSESS; 753]

reviewer *n* **critic**, commentator, assessor, referee [➡ADVISERS, JUDGES, AND ARBITERS; 971]

revile *v* **insult**, abuse, scorn, condemn, censure, despise, berate, disparage [➡INSULTS, ABUSE, AND SWEARING; 658] *Opposite*: praise

reviled *adj* [➡UNPOPULAR AND UNWANTED; 258]

revise 1 *v* **amend**, modify, adjust, alter, change, correct, improve, rework [➡CORRECT AND PUT RIGHT; 377] 2 *v* (*UK*) **review**, study, brush up, go over, look over, go through, reread, bone up (*informal*) [➡STUDYING; 844]

revision 1 *n* **amendment**, reconsideration, modification, adjustment, alteration, correction, improvement, review, change [➥IMPROVE SOMETHING; 374]

revisionism *n* **reassessment**, reconsideration, reinterpretation, pragmatism, alteration, modification, readjustment, heresy, heterodoxy (*formal*) [➥PHILOSOPHIES AND BELIEFS; 780]

revisionist 1 *adj* **pragmatic**, heretical, progressive, modernizing, ideological, political, controversial, heterodox (*formal*) [➥THE NATURE OF IDEAS; 771] 2 *n* **pragmatist**, modernizer, heretic, liberal [➥PHILOSOPHICAL AND POLITICAL THINKERS; 781]

revisit 1 *v* **return to**, go back to, come back to, retreat to, reenter [➥ARRIVE; 12] *Opposite*: abandon 2 *v* **reconsider**, reexamine, reassess, reevaluate, rethink, reopen [➥EXAMINE AND ASSESS; 753]

revitalization *n* **renewal**, renaissance, revival, new life, recovery, regeneration [➥IMPROVE SOMETHING; 374] *Opposite*: decline

revitalize *v* **refresh**, invigorate, revive, rejuvenate, regenerate, renew, give a new lease on life [➥IMPROVE STRENGTH AND DURABILITY; 378] *Opposite*: wear out

revitalized *adj* [➥WIDE AWAKE AND CONSCIOUS; 735]

revitalizing *adj* **energizing**, vitalizing, stimulating, uplifting, invigorating, refreshing, thirst-quenching, bracing, inspirational, fortifying, reviving, restorative, enlivening [➥PHYSICALLY PLEASANT; 186]

revival 1 *n* **revitalization**, renewal, restoration, stimulation, reinforcement, recovery, resumption, resurgence, rebirth, rehabilitation [➥IMPROVE SOMETHING; 374] *Opposite*: disappearance 2 *n* **resuscitation**, recovery, waking, coming to, bringing around [➥HEALING; 730] *Opposite*: relapse

revive 1 *v* **revitalize**, renew, breathe life into, restore, refresh, restart, stimulate, reinforce, reawaken [➥IMPROVE STRENGTH AND DURABILITY; 378] *Opposite*: kill 2 *v* **recover**, pick up, perk up, resume, develop, flourish [➥GET BETTER; 375] *Opposite*: die down 3 *v* **resuscitate**, come around, recover, come to, bring around, regain consciousness, recuperate, wake up [➥BECOME SICK, TREAT, AND RECOVER; 728] *Opposite*: lose consciousness 4 *v* **put on**, stage, restage, perform, redo, repeat, show again [➥CAUSE TO APPEAR; 5]

revived *adj* [➥WIDE AWAKE AND CONSCIOUS; 735]

revivify *v* **rejuvenate**, breathe new life into, refresh, resurrect, resuscitate, give a boost to [➥IMPROVE STRENGTH AND DURABILITY; 378] *Opposite*: exhaust

revocation *n* **cancellation**, withdrawal, reversal, overturning, annulment [➥CHANGE; 372] *Opposite*: enactment

revoke *v* **cancel**, annul, rescind, withdraw, retract, repeal, invalidate [➥ABOLISH AND ANNUL; 452]

revolt 1 *v* **rebel**, rise up, mutiny, riot [➥PROTEST AND EXPRESS DISAPPROVAL; 642] 2 *v* **repel**, repulse, sicken, nauseate, turn your stomach, put off, turn off (*informal*) [➥UPSET, DISTRESS, AND HUMILIATE; 567] *Opposite*: attract 3 *n* **rebellion**, revolution, uprising, upheaval, insurgency, insurrection, mutiny, riot [➥AGGRESSIVE EVENTS; 39]

revolted *adj* **nauseated**, appalled, horror-struck, horror-stricken, dismayed, sickened, aghast, disgusted, shocked, offended, repelled, repulsed [➥IRRITATION AND ANGER; 541] *Opposite*: charmed

revolting *adj* **disgusting**, repellent, repulsive, sickening, nauseating, horrible, horrendous, awful, dreadful, horrid [➥DISGUSTING AND REPULSIVE; 230] *Opposite*: appealing

revolution 1 *n* **rebellion**, revolt, uprising, upheaval, insurgency, insurrection, mutiny, riot [➥AGGRESSIVE EVENTS; 39] 2 *n* **transformation**, upheaval, conversion, alteration, development, change, reform, innovation, modernization [➥CHANGE; 372] 3 *n* **rotation**, turn, spin, cycle, circle, orbit, gyration [➥MOVE SOMETHING: ON THE SPOT; 336]

revolutionary 1 *adj* **rebellious**, radical, insurgent, mutinous, anarchist, riotous (*formal*) [➥REBELLIOUSNESS AND DISOBEDIENCE; 565] 2 *adj* **radical**, groundbreaking, world-shattering, innovative, innovatory, new, avant-garde, progressive [➥EXTRAORDINARY: UNCOMMON; 205] *Opposite*: conventional 3 *n* **rebel**, radical, insurgent, rioter, mutineer, anarchist, insurrectionist [➥UNCOOPERATIVE OR REBELLIOUS PEOPLE; 566]

revolutionize *v* **transform**, transfigure, reform, alter, change, modernize, update [➥CHANGE; 372] *Opposite*: maintain

revolve *v* **rotate**, turn, spin, circle, orbit, turn around, gyrate [➥MOVE SOMETHING: ON THE SPOT; 336]

revolver *type of* **gun** [➥WEAPONS FOR SHOOTING; 1156]

revolving *adj* **rotating**, turning, spinning, circling, gyrating, gyratory [➥DIRECTION OF MOTION; 345]

revue *n* **variety show**, show, skit, sketch show, satire, lampoon, vaudeville, burlesque, cabaret [➥PERFORMANCES AND SHOWS; 42]

revulsion *n* **disgust**, repulsion, repugnance, nausea, distaste, horror, loathing, dislike, aversion (*formal*) [➥DISLIKE AND HATE; 577] *Opposite*: attraction

See Compare and Contrast at **dislike**.

revulsive *adj* [➥DISGUSTING AND REPULSIVE; 230]

reward 1 *n* **recompense**, payment, repayment, return, remuneration, incentive, compensation, gift, bonus, prize [➥REWARDS AND AWARDS; 439] *Opposite*: penalty 2 *v* **recompense**, pay, repay, remunerate, compensate [➥REWARD; 436] *Opposite*: penalize

rewarding *adj* **satisfying**, worthwhile, gratifying, pleasing, fulfilling [➥EMOTIONALLY PLEASANT; 187] *Opposite*: disappointing

rewind *v* **wind back**, spool back, reverse [➥MOVE SOMETHING: ON THE SPOT; 336]

rewire *v* **redo**, renovate, renew, refurbish, revamp, modernize [➥REPAIR AND MEND; 376]

reword *v* **rephrase**, redraft, rewrite, rework, revise, amend, alter, modify, change [➥CORRECT AND PUT RIGHT; 377]

rework *v* **revise**, redraft, rephrase, rewrite, reword, amend, alter, modify, change [➥CORRECT AND PUT RIGHT; 377]

rewrite 1 *v* **redraft**, rephrase, reword, rework, revise, amend, alter, modify, change, reshape, adjust [➥CORRECT AND

PUT RIGHT; 377] **2** *n* **revision**, amendment, alteration, modification [➥CHANGE; 372]

rhapsodic *adj* **ecstatic**, enthusiastic, lyrical, rapturous, fervent, ardent, passionate, extravagant, eulogistic, over-the-top (*informal*) [➥ENTHUSIASTIC AND INQUISITIVE; 628] *Opposite:* unenthusiastic

rhapsodize *v* **enthuse**, be ecstatic, go on, eulogize, wax lyrical (*literary*), go over the top (*informal*) [➥PRAISE AND ENCOURAGE; 647]

rhapsody *n* **ecstasy**, rapture, bliss, enthusiasm, eagerness, joy [➥PLEASURE, EXCITEMENT, AND ELATION; 534] *Opposite:* gloom

rheostat *n* **control**, regulator, resistor, controller [➥ELECTRONICS AND ELECTRICS; 1137]

rhesus monkey *type of* **primate** [➥PRIMATES; 988]

rhetoric **1** *n* **oratory**, public speaking, speechmaking, speechifying (*informal*) [➥THE SPOKEN WORD; 671] **2** *n* **bombast**, pomposity, grandiloquence, fustian, orotundity, magniloquence (*formal*) [➥BOAST; 616] **3** *n* **language**, expression, style, idiom, words, vocabulary, speech, writing [➥ASPECTS OF LANGUAGE; 682]

rhetorical **1** *adj* **oratorical**, verbal, linguistic, stylistic [➥ASPECTS OF LANGUAGE; 682] **2** *adj* **bombastic**, pompous, pretentious, periphrastic, voluble, showy, flashy, declamatory, theatrical, contrived, effusive, high-flown, highfalutin (*informal*) [➥POMPOUS, LOUD, AND OVERCONFIDENT; 635]

rhetorician *n* **orator**, speaker, public speaker, debater, advocate [➥SPEAKERS AND ORATORS; 603]

rheum *n* [➥BREATHE AND NOT BREATHE; 716]

rheumatic *adj* **stiff**, aching, sore, inflexible, rigid, unbending [➥THE BONES AND JOINTS; 719] *Opposite:* flexible

rheumy *adj* [➥BREATHE AND NOT BREATHE; 716]

rhinestone *n* **paste**, strass, diamanté [➥ORNAMENTS AND DECORATIONS; 1248]

rhinoceros *type of* **large mammal** [➥LARGE MAMMALS; 986]

rhinoceros beetle *type of* **beetle** [➥BEETLES AND WEEVILS; 1016]

rhizome *n* **stem**, shoot, root, tuber, corm, bulb [➥PARTS OF TREES AND PLANTS; 1026]

rhizopod *type of* **microorganism** [➥MICROORGANISMS, FUNGI, AND ALGAE; 1023]

rhododendron *type of* **shrub or bush** [➥BUSHES AND SHRUBS; 1027]

rhomboid *n* **parallelogram**, diamond, lozenge [➥ANGULAR SHAPE; 1217]

rhombus *n* **diamond**, lozenge, parallelogram [➥ANGULAR SHAPE; 1217]

rhubarb *n* **argument**, quarrel, fight, disagreement, dispute, row [➥ARGUMENTS; 47]

rhyme **1** *n* **poem**, verse, nursery rhyme, jingle, limerick, couplet, quatrain [➥POETRY AND VERSE; 915] **2** *n* **assonance**, consonance, rhyming [➥POETRY AND VERSE; 915]

rhyme or reason *n* **sense**, logic, meaning, pattern [➥IDEAS AND THOUGHTS; 770]

rhythm **1** *n* **beat**, pace, tempo, time, measure, cadence, pulse [➥NOTES AND CHORDS; 909] **2** *n* **regularity**, pattern, progression, sequence [➥FREQUENT AND OFTEN; 107]

rhythmic **1** *adj* **musical**, cadenced, metrical [➥MUSICAL TERMS; 912] **2** *adj* **recurring**, regular, periodic, recurrent [➥FREQUENT AND OFTEN; 107]

rial *type of* **currency** [➥CURRENCIES; 798]

rib **1** *type of* **bone** [➥THE BONES AND JOINTS; 719] **2** *type of* **cut** [➥TYPES AND CUTS OF MEAT; 1177] **3** *n* **beam**, strut, spoke, spine, spar [➥BUILDING MATERIALS; 1077] **4** *v* (*informal*) **tease**, make fun of, laugh at, mock, kid, ride (*informal*), josh (*informal*), razz (*informal*), rag (*dated*) [➥JOKES AND TEASING; 674]

ribald *adj* **coarse**, vulgar, bawdy, rude, lewd, funny, humorous [➥MORALLY BAD OR IMPROPER; 775] *Opposite:* refined

ribaldry *n* **ribaldry** [➥MORALLY BAD OR IMPROPER; 775]

ribbed *adj* **grooved**, corrugated, ridged, bumpy, uneven, textured, striped [➥PHYSICAL TEXTURE; 1222]

ribbing (*informal*) *n* [➥JOKES AND TEASING; 674]

ribbon **1** *n* **band**, tie, trimming, decoration, tape [➥ORNAMENTS AND DECORATIONS; 1248] **2** *n* **decoration**, award, honor, badge of honor, medal, badge, emblem [➥ORNAMENTS AND DECORATIONS; 1248] **3** *n* **strip**, stretch, band, length, taper [➥AMOUNTS OF SOLID OR SEMISOLID; 115]

rib cage *part of* **torso** [➥PARTS OF THE BODY: TORSO; 693]

rib-tickling (*informal*) *adj* [➥FUNNY AND AMUSING; 216]

rice *type of* **cereal** [➥CEREAL FOODS; 1178]

rich **1** *adj* **wealthy**, well-off, affluent, prosperous, moneyed, well-to-do, rolling in it (*informal*), well-heeled (*informal*), loaded (*slang*) [➥WEALTH AND WEALTHY; 891] *Opposite:* poor **2** *adj* **opulent**, gorgeous, lush, luxuriant, splendid, valuable, expensive, ornate, costly, fine, precious, plush (*informal*) [➥EXPENSIVE AND LUXURIOUS; 218] *Opposite:* shabby **3** *adj* **full**, abounding, plentiful, stuffed, heavy, dripping, loaded (*slang*) [➥MANY, MUCH, LARGE AMOUNT; 117] *Opposite:* lacking **4** *adj* **productive**, fertile, abundant, plentiful, fruitful, lush, full, prolific [➥ECONOMICAL AND RESOURCEFUL; 207] *Opposite:* infertile **5** *adj* **heavy**, indigestible, calorific, cloying, unhealthy, creamy, buttery, fatty, sweet [➥TASTE; 703] *Opposite:* light **6** *adj* **intense**, deep, strong, full, powerful, vivid, resonant, full-bodied [➥STRENGTH; 201] *Opposite:* weak **7** *adj* (*informal*) **ironic**, amusing, irritating, annoying, ridiculous, unlikely [➥FUNNY AND AMUSING; 216]

rich and famous *n* [➥RICH PEOPLE; 895]

riches *n* **resources**, treasures, reserves, materials, raw materials, assets, possessions [➥FINANCIAL ASSETS; 462]

richly **1** *adv* **opulently**, luxuriantly, luxuriously, splendidly, ornately, handsomely, abundantly, elaborately [➥EXPENSIVE AND LUXURIOUS; 218] *Opposite:* shabbily **2** *adv* **thoroughly**, fully, completely, totally, deeply, well, absolutely, suitably [➥TO A GREAT EXTENT; 132] *Opposite:* barely

richness **1** *n* **prosperity**, fortune, affluence, wealth [➥WEALTH AND WEALTHY; 891] *Opposite:* poverty **2** *n* **opulence**, luxury, sumptuousness, splendor, luxuriousness, lavishness, magnificence [➥EXPENSIVE AND LUXURIOUS; 218] *Opposite:* shabbiness **3** *n* **fertility**, fruitfulness, productivity, lushness, fullness, abundance [➥USEFULNESS; 199] *Opposite:* infer-

tility 4 *n* **intensity**, depth, strength, fullness, power, vibrancy, vividness, resonance [➡ STRENGTH; 201] *Opposite*: weakness

rick (*UK*) *v* **twist**, pull, wrench, sprain, crick, dislocate, injure, strain, put out [➡ WOUND A PERSON OR ANIMAL; 383]

ricketiness *n* [➡ IN BAD REPAIR; 1234]

rickety *adj* **shaky**, unsteady, unstable, rocky, unbalanced, unsound, insecure, wobbly (*informal*) [➡ IN BAD REPAIR; 1234] *Opposite*: firm

rickshaw *type of* **bike** [➡ BIKES, CARS, AND CARRIAGES; 1149]

ricochet 1 *v* **recoil**, rebound, glance off, bounce off, reflect, reverberate, echo [➡ CHANGE DIRECTION OF MOTION; 344] **2** *n* **rebound**, recoil, reverberation, reflection, echo, bounce [➡ CHANGE DIRECTION OF MOTION; 344]

ricotta *type of* **soft cheese** [➡ DAIRY PRODUCTS AND CHEESES; 1183]

rictus *n* **grimace**, grin, fixed expression, contortion [➡ FACIAL EXPRESSIONS AND BLUSHING; 651]

rid *v* **free**, clear, purge, liberate, divest, do away with, relieve, exonerate, get rid of [➡ GET RID OF SOMETHING; 451]

riddle 1 *n* **puzzle**, conundrum, question, mystery, enigma, brainteaser, challenge [➡ SECRETS AND MYSTERIES; 180] **2** *v* **pierce**, perforate, puncture, pepper, damage, poke [➡ TEAR, BREAK, AND CUT; 360] **3** *v* **sift**, screen, sieve, separate [➡ SEPARATE AND DIVIDE; 401]

See Compare and Contrast at **problem**.

ride 1 *v* **gallop**, canter, trot, jockey [➡ TRAVEL: WAYS OF TRAVELING; 320] **2** *v* **travel**, journey, go, be carried, be conveyed [➡ PROCEED AND GO; 305] *Opposite*: walk **3** *v* (*informal*) **tease**, torment, criticize, mock, provoke, bother [➡ JOKES AND TEASING; 674] **4** *v* **depend on**, rest on, center on, rely on, be contingent on, be affected by, be decided by [➡ RECIPROCITY AND INTERDEPENDENCE; 147] **5** *n* **trip**, outing, jaunt, journey, drive, cycle [➡ TRAVEL: JOURNEYS AND TRIPS; 318]

ride out *v* **endure**, brave, stick out, survive, live through, weather, come through, withstand, pass through [➡ TOLERATE AND ENDURE; 766] *Opposite*: succumb

rider *n* **proviso**, qualification, provision, condition, stipulation, requirement, criterion, clause, specification, prerequisite, disclaimer [➡ PARTS OF BOOKS AND DOCUMENTS; 593]

ridership *n* [➡ TRANSPORTATION, TRANSPORTERS, AND CARGOS; 322]

ride up *v* **roll up**, slide up, wriggle up, move up, wrinkle, pucker [➡ GO UPWARD; 306] *Opposite*: fall down

ridge 1 *n* **edge**, point, crest, rim, elevation, range [➡ EXTREMITIES OF PHYSICAL OBJECTS; 1250] **2** *v* **fold**, crumple, crinkle, crease, wrinkle, pucker, pleat [➡ CHANGE OF SHAPE; 385]

ridicule 1 *v* **mock**, deride, scorn, scoff at, laugh at, make fun of, poke fun at, jeer at, tease, send up (*informal*) [➡ JOKES AND TEASING; 674] **2** *n* **mockery**, scorn, derision, laughter, mimicry [➡ JOKES AND TEASING; 674]

Compare and Contrast: *ridicule, deride, laugh at, mock, send up*

CORE MEANING: to belittle or make fun of somebody or something

ridicule to make fun of somebody or something in a cruel contemptuous way in order to make that person or thing an object of fun; *deride* (*formal*) to ridicule somebody or something in harsh terms; *laugh at* to ridicule somebody in an amused or contemptuous way; *mock* to treat somebody or something with scorn or contempt, often involving cruel mimicking. It can suggest something more subtle than *ridicule* or *deride*; *send up* (*informal*) to make fun of or mock somebody or something, usually by means of parody or mimicking.

ridiculed *adj* [➡ UNPOPULAR AND UNWANTED; 258]

ridiculous *adj* **ludicrous**, preposterous, absurd, silly, outlandish, outrageous, bizarre, unreasonable, incredible, nonsensical [➡ BIZARRE AND PECULIAR; 257] *Opposite*: sensible

ridiculousness *n* **ludicrousness**, preposterousness, absurdity, nonsensicality, irrationality, outlandishness, silliness, outrageousness [➡ BIZARRE AND PECULIAR; 257] *Opposite*: sense

riding *n* **show jumping**, racing, hunting, dressage, cross-country, pony-trekking (*UK*) [➡ HOBBIES, GAMES, AND SPORTS; 875]

riel *type of* **currency** [➡ CURRENCIES; 798]

rife 1 *adj* **widespread**, common, endemic, extensive, prevalent, ubiquitous, predominant, rampant, plentiful [➡ PRESENT AND AVAILABLE; 11] *Opposite*: rare **2** *adj* **full**, abounding, bursting, laden, loaded, packed, stuffed (*informal*) [➡ FULL; 1239] *Opposite*: lacking

See Compare and Contrast at **widespread**.

riff 1 *n* **phrase**, refrain, melody, tune, groove, loop, sample, ostinato [➡ NOTES AND CHORDS; 909] **2** *v* **play**, jam, improvise, strum, perform, noodle (*slang*) [➡ MUSIC, SONGS, AND SINGING; 907]

riffle 1 *v* **flick through**, turn pages, peruse, glance at, scan, skim through, cast your eyes over, browse, leaf through, thumb [➡ LOOKING AND LOOKS; 700] **2** *v* **shuffle**, mix, mix up, randomize, jumble up, recombine [➡ CREATE DISORDER AND CAUSE CHAOS; 358] **3** *v* **ripple**, roughen, undulate, get choppy, ruffle, dimple [➡ CHANGE OF SHAPE; 385] **4** *n* **flick**, quick look, glance, perusal, skim, scan, browse [➡ LOOKING AND LOOKS; 700]

rifle 1 *v* **ransack**, search, search through, rummage, go through, scour, shuffle through, turn over [➡ SEEK POSSESSION AND SEARCH; 456] **2** *type of* **gun** [➡ WEAPONS FOR SHOOTING; 1156]

rifleman *n* [➡ MILITARY PERSONNEL; 828]

rift 1 *n* **crack**, hole, fissure, split, crevice, cleft, aperture, fracture, opening, gap, fault, rupture [➡ HOLES, GAPS, AND FORKS; 1252] **2** *n* **disagreement**, difference, conflict, falling-out, quarrel, dispute [➡ ARGUMENTS; 47]

rig 1 *v* **fix**, engineer, arrange, prepare, fit, put together, assemble, equip, furnish (*formal*) [➡ BUILD; 352] **2** *v* **improvise**, fix up, invent, set up, assemble, provide, slap together, make up [➡ ARRANGE AND CREATE ORDER; 357] *Opposite*: plan

3 *v* **manipulate**, falsify, mock up, fix, set up, arrange, swindle, trick [➡ FALSIFY AND CHEAT; 176] **4** *n* **oil rig**, platform, derrick [➡ INDUSTRIAL BUILDINGS; 1087] **5** *n* (*informal*) **dress**, clothes, clothing, outfit, getup (*informal*), gear (*informal*), togs (*informal*), threads (*slang*), attire (*formal*), rigout (*UK*) [➡ CLOTHES AND ACCESSORIES; 864]

rigamarole *see* **rigmarole**

rigatoni *type of pasta* [➡ PASTA; 1180]

rigging *n* **ropes**, chains, wires, supports, pulleys, controls [➡ FASTENERS, LINKS, AND NETWORKS; 1247]

right **1** *adj* **correct**, accurate, true, exact, precise, factual, veracious, dead-on (*informal*) [➡ CORRECT AND FAULTLESS; 182] *Opposite*: wrong **2** *adj* **just**, proper, fair, moral, honorable, upright, righteous, acceptable, justified, nondiscriminatory [➡ MORALLY GOOD; 774] *Opposite*: immoral **3** *adj* **appropriate**, respectable, fitting, proper, desirable, best, reasonable, suited, decent, suitable [➡ APPROPRIATE, SUITABLE, AND ADVISABLE; 184] *Opposite*: inappropriate **4** *adj* **well**, healthy, in shape, fit, very well, satisfactory, hale, fine (*informal*) [➡ SAFE AND SOUND; 737] *Opposite*: ill **5** *adv* **appropriately**, as it should be, acceptably, suitably, properly, aptly, reasonably, well [➡ APPROPRIATE, SUITABLE, AND ADVISABLE; 184] *Opposite*: unsuitably **6** *adv* **correctly**, exactly, accurately, precisely, directly, perfectly, dead on, plumb (*informal*), on the nose (*informal*) [➡ CORRECT AND FAULTLESS; 182] *Opposite*: inexactly **7** *adv* **utterly**, entirely, completely, absolutely, totally, straight, intensely, very [➡ TO A GREAT EXTENT; 132] **8** *n* **truth**, honesty, goodness, morality, fairness, justice [➡ MORALLY GOOD; 774] *Opposite*: wrong **9** *n* **entitlement**, privilege, due, birthright, justification, claim, permission, merit [➡ THE LAW AND LEGAL AUTHORITY; 814] **10** *v* **redress**, rectify, amend, remedy, correct, restore [➡ CORRECT AND PUT RIGHT; 377]

right and proper *adj* [➡ MORALLY GOOD; 774]

right-angled *adj* **angled**, square, rectilinear, ninety-degree, right-angle [➡ ANGULAR SHAPE; 1217]

right away *adv* **immediately**, at once, instantaneously, right now, just now, without ado, at this instant, without delay, straightaway, pronto (*informal*) [➡ HAPPENING QUICKLY; 104]

righteous *adj* **virtuous**, moral, good, just, blameless, upright, honorable, honest, respectable, decent [➡ MORALLY GOOD; 774] *Opposite*: sinful

righteousness *n* **virtue**, morality, justice, decency, uprightness, rectitude, honesty, blamelessness [➡ MORALLY GOOD; 774] *Opposite*: wickedness

rightful *adj* **fair**, correct, legal, due, just, apt, in principle, equitable (*formal*) [➡ LEGAL AND LEGITIMATE; 815] *Opposite*: unlawful

rightfulness *n* **truth**, fairness, correctness, legality, lawfulness, justice, impartiality, legitimacy [➡ LEGAL AND LEGITIMATE; 815]

right hand *n* **assistant**, aide, deputy, lieutenant, helper, helping hand [➡ SUBORDINATES AND ASSISTANTS; 966]

right-hand **1** *adj* **right**, rightward, starboard [➡ GENERAL LOCATIONS; 158] *Opposite*: left-hand **2** *adj* **trusted**, important, reliable, principal, main, favorite [➡ RELATIONSHIP TO ANOTHER; 973]

right-handed *adj* **clockwise**, left to right, circular, round, helical, spiral [➡ DIRECTION OF MOTION; 345] *Opposite*: left-handed

rightist *adj* **right-wing**, conservative, traditionalist [➡ STYLES AND SYSTEMS OF GOVERNMENT; 806]

rightly **1** *adv* **correctly**, truly, exactly, accurately, precisely, properly, appropriately [➡ CORRECT AND FAULTLESS; 182] *Opposite*: wrongly **2** *adv* **justly**, fittingly, justifiably, suitably, rightfully, legally, lawfully, correctly, duly, fairly, equitably (*formal*) [➡ LEGAL AND LEGITIMATE; 815] *Opposite*: unreasonably **3** *adv* (*informal*) **for certain**, without a shadow of a doubt, for sure, certainly, positively, absolutely [➡ CERTAIN; 174]

right-minded *adj* **reasonable**, sensible, fair-minded, decent, rational, right-thinking [➡ POSITIVE INTELLECTUAL CHARACTERISTICS; 524]

rightness **1** *n* **rectitude**, correctness, faultlessness, truth, precision, accuracy, exactness [➡ CORRECT AND FAULTLESS; 182] **2** *n* **aptness**, suitability, appropriateness, timeliness, properness, equitableness (*formal*) [➡ APPROPRIATE, SUITABLE, AND ADVISABLE; 184] *Opposite*: inappropriateness

right now *adv* [➡ PRESENT; 85]

right-size *v* [➡ BUSINESS ACTIVITIES AND PHENOMENA; 794]

right-thinking *adj* [➡ POSITIVE INTELLECTUAL CHARACTERISTICS; 524]

rightward *adj* [➡ DIRECTION OF MOTION; 345]

right whale *type of whale* [➡ WHALES; 991]

right-wing *adj* **conservative**, rightist, traditionalist [➡ STYLES AND SYSTEMS OF GOVERNMENT; 806] *Opposite*: left-wing

right-winger *n* **conservative**, rightist, traditionalist [➡ PHILOSOPHICAL AND POLITICAL THINKERS; 781] *Opposite*: liberal

rigid **1** *adj* **unbending**, inflexible, stiff, firm, set, unyielding, inelastic [➡ RIGID AND HARD; 1211] *Opposite*: floppy **2** *adj* **severe**, strict, harsh, stern, inflexible [➡ DIFFICULT TO PLEASE; 515] *Opposite*: lax

rigidity **1** *n* **stiffness**, inflexibility, inelasticity, firmness, rigor [➡ RIGID AND HARD; 1211] *Opposite*: floppiness **2** *n* **inflexibility**, firmness, severity, strictness, stringency [➡ DIFFICULT TO PLEASE; 515] *Opposite*: laxness

rigmarole **1** *n* **fuss**, bother, ritual, business, hassle (*informal*), to-do (*informal*) [➡ NUISANCES; 253] **2** *n* **explanation**, account, excuse, palaver, verbiage, overelaboration, waffle (*informal*), gobbledygook (*informal*) [➡ MEANINGLESS SPEECH OR WRITING; 676]

rigor **1** *n* **severity**, strictness, harshness, intransigence, dogmatism, rigidity, intolerance, inflexibility, sternness [➡ DIFFICULT TO PLEASE; 515] *Opposite*: flexibility **2** *n* **thoroughness**, consistency, attention to detail, precision, accuracy, care, objectivity, exactitude [➡ POSITIVE INTELLECTUAL CHARACTERISTICS; 524] *Opposite*: negligence **3** *n* **hardship**, difficulty, hard time, difficult time, demand, restriction, adversity, trial, trouble, stricture (*formal*) [➡ DIFFICULTY AND COMPLEXITY; 242] *Opposite*: mildness **4** *n* **stiffness**, rigidity, unresponsiveness, stiffening, rigor mortis [➡ RIGID AND HARD; 1211] *Opposite*: flexibility

rigor mortis *n* [➡ DEATH AND BEREAVEMENT; 927]

rigorous **1** *adj* **hard**, severe, harsh, demanding, laborious, rough, arduous, difficult [➡ DIFFICULTY AND COMPLEXITY; 242] *Opposite*: mild **2** *adj* **exact**, thorough, precise, meticulous, painstaking, accurate, careful, scrupulous [➡ EXACT; 203] *Opposite*: slapdash

rigorousness **1** *n* **strictness**, discipline, severity, harshness, difficulty, arduousness [➡ DIFFICULTY AND COMPLEXITY; 242] *Opposite*: lenience **2** *n* **exactness**, thoroughness, discipline, meticulousness, scrupulousness, carefulness [➡ EXACT; 203] *Opposite*: negligence

rig out (*informal*) **1** *v* **equip**, provide, prepare, arrange, fit out, furnish (*formal*) [➡ EQUIP AND SUPPLY; 435] **2** *v* **dress up**, clothe, get up (*informal*), attire (*formal*), kit out (*UK*) [➡ DRESS, WEAR, AND UNDRESS; 868]

rigout (*UK*) *n* [➡ CLOTHES AND ACCESSORIES; 864]

rig up *v* **improvise**, cobble together, set up, assemble, fix up, provide [➡ CREATION; 346] *Opposite*: plan

rile (*informal*) *v* **anger**, enrage, annoy, irritate, irk, vex, bug (*informal*), peeve (*informal*), aggravate (*informal*) [➡ ANGER AND ANNOY; 569] *Opposite*: placate

riled (*informal*) *adj* [➡ IRRITATION AND ANGER; 541]

rim *n* **edge**, border, lip, perimeter, circumference, brim [➡ EXTREMITIES OF PHYSICAL OBJECTS; 1250] *Opposite*: center

rime *n* **frost**, hoar frost, ice [➡ COLD WEATHER; 1051]

rind *n* **peel**, skin, husk, crust, coat, coating, outer layer, integument [➡ FRUIT AND VEGETABLES; 1176] *Opposite*: flesh

ring **1** *n* **circle**, loop, hoop, band, halo [➡ ROUNDED SHAPE; 1218] **2** *type of* **jewelry** [➡ JEWELRY; 866] **3** *n* **group**, band, gang, organization, team, cartel, mob [➡ CRIMINALS; 821] **4** *type of* **ringing sound** [➡ RINGING AND HOOTING SOUNDS; 1259] **5** *n* **impression**, semblance, appearance, feel, air [➡ APPEARANCE AND ATMOSPHERE; 1237] **6** *n* **call**, phone call, telephone call, buzz (*informal*) [➡ TELEPHONE COMMUNICATION; 481] **7** *v* **encircle**, enclose, circle, surround [➡ EXIST IN CLOSE PROXIMITY; 21] **8** *v* **peal**, tinkle, chime, toll, ding-dong, jingle [➡ EMIT RINGING AND HOOTING SOUNDS; 367] **9** *v* **resonate**, resound, ring out, reverberate, echo, reecho [➡ SOUND EMISSION; 362] **10** *v* (*UK*) **call**, phone, telephone, give a ring, give a bell (*informal*), ring up (*UK*) [➡ TELEPHONE, PAGE, AND TEXT; 681]

ring a bell (*informal*) *v* **strike a chord**, jog somebody's memory, sound familiar, be reminiscent, remind [➡ REMIND; 747]

ring-fence (*UK*) **1** *v* **set aside**, isolate, restrict, stipulate, protect, separate, specify, limit [➡ AVOID, PREVENT, LIMIT, AND CONTROL; 277] **2** *n* **restriction**, limitation, specification, separation, reservation, agreement [➡ CAPTIVITY AND LOSS OF FREEDOM; 248] **3** *n* **fence**, barrier, boundary, perimeter, border [➡ BARRIERS; 1113]

ring finger *part of* **arm or hand** [➡ PARTS OF THE BODY: ARM AND HAND; 695]

ringgit *type of* **currency** [➡ CURRENCIES; 798]

ringhals *type of* **poisonous snake** [➡ SNAKES; 995]

ringleader *n* **gang leader**, leader of the pack, agitator, instigator, inciter, leader [➡ UNCOOPERATIVE OR REBELLIOUS PEOPLE; 566]

ringlet **1** *n* **curl**, lock, twist, coil, spiral, wisp, whorl,

wave [➡ HAIR; 484] **2** *type of* **hairstyle** [➡ HAIRSTYLES AND HAIRPIECES; 488]

ringlets *n* **curls**, locks, coils, spirals [➡ HAIR; 484]

ringmaster *n* **master of ceremonies**, MC, host, chair, chairperson, emcee (*informal*), presenter (*UK*) [➡ WORKERS IN ENTERTAINMENT AND MEDIA; 873]

ring off (*UK*) *v* **hang up**, put the receiver down, finish, go [➡ TELEPHONE, PAGE, AND TEXT; 681] *Opposite*: hang on

ring out *v* **be heard**, sound, rise, pierce the silence, blast out, blare out, peal out [➡ EMIT RINGING AND HOOTING SOUNDS; 367]

ringside *adj* **front row**, grandstand, unimpeded, unobstructed, clear, good, perfect, touchline (*UK*) [➡ GOOD, WELL, BETTER; 183]

ring up (*UK*) *v* **phone**, call, telephone, give a bell (*informal*), ring (*UK*), give a tinkle (*UK*) [➡ TELEPHONE, PAGE, AND TEXT; 681]

rink *n* **arena**, floor, space, area [➡ BUILDINGS FOR PUBLIC ENTERTAINMENT; 1084]

rinse **1** *n* **wash**, clean, bathe, sluice, dip, wet, soak, douse, sponge down, bath [➡ CLEAN AND POLISH; 403] **2** *n* **solution**, dye, tint, bleach, stain, colorant [➡ DYES AND COLORANTS; 1270]

riot **1** *n* **uprising**, insurrection, disturbance, unrest, demonstration, protest, insurgence, mutiny, rebellion, revolt, revolution [➡ AGGRESSIVE EVENTS; 39] **2** *n* (*informal*) **laugh** (*informal*), scream (*informal*), hoot (*slang*), gas (*slang*) [➡ FUNNY AND AMUSING; 216] **3** *v* **mutiny**, demonstrate, run riot, rebel, protest, revolt, rampage, rise up, run amok, take to the streets [➡ PROTEST AND EXPRESS DISAPPROVAL; 642]

rioter *n* **demonstrator**, rebel, revolutionary, insurgent, protester, mutineer, marcher, dissident [➡ UNCOOPERATIVE OR REBELLIOUS PEOPLE; 566]

riotous **1** *adj* **violent**, disorderly, unruly, uncontrolled, uncontained, lawless, mutinous, rebellious, revolutionary, anarchic [➡ REBELLIOUSNESS AND DISOBEDIENCE; 565] *Opposite*: peaceful **2** *adj* **wild**, debauched, uncontrolled, out of control, hedonistic, intemperate, immoderate, rowdy, rambunctious [➡ DISORDER AND CHAOS; 245] *Opposite*: subdued

riotously **1** *adv* **hilariously**, madly, side-splittingly, screamingly, wildly, raucously [➡ FUNNY AND AMUSING; 216] **2** *adv* **raucously**, rowdily, wildly, rambunctiously, noisily, uproariously [➡ DISORDER AND CHAOS; 245] *Opposite*: quietly

riotousness *n* [➡ DISORDER AND CHAOS; 245]

riot police *n* [➡ THE POLICE, ARREST, AND PRETRIAL PROCEEDINGS; 818]

rip **1** *v* **tear**, split, cleave, shred, scratch, slash, slit, break, gash [➡ TEAR, BREAK, AND CUT; 360] **2** *v* **snatch**, tear, seize, grab, pluck, pull [➡ TAKE SOMETHING AWAY; 425] **3** *v* **speed**, tear, dash, rush, fly, pelt, zoom, whiz, dart, zip (*informal*) [➡ MOVE FAST; 313] **4** *n* **tear**, split, scratch, cleft, slash, slit, gash, opening, break, rupture [➡ APPROPRIATE, SUITABLE, AND ADVISABLE; 184]

See Compare and Contrast at **tear**.

rip apart *v* [➡ TEAR, BREAK, AND CUT; 360]

ripcord *n* **cord**, line, string, cable, rope, release, handle [➡ FASTENERS, LINKS, AND NETWORKS; 1247]

ripe **1** *adj* (*informal*) **pungent**, strong, sour, strong-smelling, off, smelly [➡ SMELL AND SMELLING; 705] *Opposite*: sweet **2** *adj* **mature**, ready, grown, fully grown, matured, seasoned, developed, ripened [➡ IN GOOD REPAIR; 1232] *Opposite*: unripe **3** *adj* **ready**, suitable, prepared, crying out, disposed, apt, set, developed [➡ ORDER AND ORGANIZATION; 206]

ripen *v* **mature**, season, grow, develop, evolve [➡ CHANGE; 372]

ripeness *n* **maturity**, readiness, mellowness, age [➡ OLD, OLD-FASHIONED; 167]

ripieno *type of* **food presentation** [➡ COOKING AND FOOD PREPARATION; 353]

rip off (*informal*) *v* **overcharge**, cheat, swindle, dupe, deceive, fleece (*informal*), do (*informal*), diddle (*slang*) [➡ STEAL AND ROB; 426]

rip-off (*informal*) *n* **swindle**, con, cheat, diddle (*slang*), swizz (*UK*) [➡ DECEPTION AND LIES; 660]

rip open *v* [➡ TEAR, BREAK, AND CUT; 360]

riposte **1** *n* **reply**, retort, comeback, response, answer, return, wisecrack (*informal*), rejoinder (*formal*) [➡ REPLY AND ANSWER; 668] **2** *v* **retort**, reply, come back, return, counter, answer, fight back, respond, rejoin (*formal*) [➡ REPLY AND ANSWER; 668]

See Compare and Contrast at **answer**.

ripped *adj* [➡ IN BAD REPAIR; 1234]

ripple **1** *v* **undulate**, swell, flow, move, rise and fall, heave [➡ BOUNCE, UNDULATE, AND VIBRATE; 308] **2** *n* **wave**, undulation, swell, current, wrinkle [➡ BOUNCE, UNDULATE, AND VIBRATE; 308] *Opposite*: stillness

rip-roaring (*informal*) *adj* **exciting**, uproarious, boisterous, rollicking, energetic, riotous, adrenaline-fueled [➡ EXTRAORDINARY: UNCOMMON; 205] *Opposite*: boring

rip to pieces *v* [➡ TEAR, BREAK, AND CUT; 360]

rip to shreds *v* [➡ TEAR, BREAK, AND CUT; 360]

rip up *v* **tear up**, shred, pull apart, chew up, pull to pieces, destroy [➡ TEAR, BREAK, AND CUT; 360] *Opposite*: piece together

rise **1** *v* **stand up**, get up, get to your feet, arise (*archaic or literary*) [➡ ASSUME A POSITION; 317] *Opposite*: sit down **2** *v* **go up**, increase, climb, mount, get higher, ascend, grow, escalate, levitate, soar, rocket, augment (*formal*) [➡ GO UPWARD; 306] *Opposite*: drop **3** *v* **rebel**, revolt, mutiny, rise up, riot [➡ PROTEST AND EXPRESS DISAPPROVAL; 642] **4** *v* **originate**, begin, start, come out of, be set in motion [➡ GRADUALLY COME INTO EXISTENCE; 1] *Opposite*: end **5** *v* **emerge**, come up, appear, arise, be apparent, tower, come into view, materialize, come out [➡ APPEAR AND EMERGE; 3] *Opposite*: disappear **6** *v* **wake up**, get up, get out of bed, arise, awaken, come to life [➡ GO UPWARD; 306] *Opposite*: retire **7** *n* **increase**, growth, upsurge, intensification, escalation, upswing, augmentation, enlargement [➡ CHANGE OF INTENSITY: MORE; 394] *Opposite*: decrease **8** *n* **growth**, spread, development, expansion, advance, progress, improvement, amelioration, upturn [➡ SUCCESS; 82] *Opposite*: decline **9** *n* **hill**, slope, incline, acclivity, elevation, gradient, bank, mount, hillock, mound, knoll [➡ MOUNTAINS AND HILLS; 1044] *Opposite*: hollow **10** *n* **climb**, ascent, elevation [➡ GO UPWARD; 306] *Opposite*: fall

rise above *v* **surmount**, overcome, conquer, triumph over, surpass [➡ BEAT AND DEFEAT; 80]

rise and fall *n* **swell**, undulation, ripple, movement, rolling, fluctuation [➡ BOUNCE, UNDULATE, AND VIBRATE; 308] *Opposite*: stability

rise to (*informal*) *v* **respond**, meet, shine, succeed, perform, behave [➡ SUCCEED AND WIN; 79]

rise to the bait *v* **respond**, react, get angry, be provoked, answer, retort, rejoin (*formal*) [➡ CHANGE OF MOOD AND COMPOSURE; 580] *Opposite*: ignore

rise up **1** *v* **rebel**, revolt, riot, rise, mutiny, rampage, run amok, run riot, demonstrate [➡ PROTEST AND EXPRESS DISAPPROVAL; 642] **2** *v* **emerge**, stand up, float up, soar, arise (*archaic or literary*) [➡ APPEAR AND EMERGE; 3] *Opposite*: sink

risibility **1** *n* (*formal*) **humorousness**, sense of humor, happiness, wit, humor [➡ CHEERFULNESS OF OUTLOOK; 503] *Opposite*: soberness **2** *n* **ridiculousness**, ludicrousness, absurdity, laughableness, stupidity, foolishness [➡ BIZARRE AND PECULIAR; 257] *Opposite*: seriousness

risible **1** *adj* **laughable**, ludicrous, absurd, ridiculous, stupid, foolish [➡ BIZARRE AND PECULIAR; 257] *Opposite*: serious **2** *adj* (*formal*) **humorous**, good-humored, happy, cheerful, cheery, hearty [➡ CHEERFULNESS OF OUTLOOK; 503] *Opposite*: somber

rising **1** *adj* **increasing**, growing, going up, mounting, getting higher, getting bigger, intensifying, expanding, escalating, climbing [➡ CHANGE OF INTENSITY: MORE; 394] *Opposite*: falling **2** *n* **uprising**, rebellion, revolt, mutiny, riot, insurrection, revolution, insurgence [➡ AGGRESSIVE EVENTS; 39]

risk **1** *n* **danger**, jeopardy, peril, hazard, menace, threat [➡ DANGER; 235] *Opposite*: safety **2** *n* **possibility**, chance, danger, hazard, gamble, probability, stake, consequence [➡ POSSIBLE AND PROBABLE; 177] **3** *v* **endanger**, jeopardize, lay bare, expose, imperil (*formal*) [➡ PUT AT RISK; 384] *Opposite*: protect **4** *v* **chance**, hazard, attempt, gamble, venture, run the risk of, take the risk of, take a chance [➡ GAMBLE AND TAKE RISKS; 466] *Opposite*: play safe

risk factor *n* [➡ DANGER; 235]

risk-free *adj* [➡ SAFE AND SAFETY; 191]

riskiness *n* **hazardousness**, perilousness, precariousness, dangerousness, audaciousness, insecurity [➡ DANGER; 235] *Opposite*: safety

risky *adj* **dangerous**, hazardous, chancy, precarious, perilous, unsafe, uncertain, dicey (*informal*), dodgy (*informal*) [➡ DANGEROUS; 236] *Opposite*: safe

risotto *type of* **cooked dish** [➡ PREPARED DISHES; 1170]

risqué *adj* **racy**, rude, lewd, salacious, naughty, suggestive, bawdy, ribald, smutty (*informal*), blue (*informal*) [➡ MORALLY BAD OR IMPROPER; 775] *Opposite*: decorous

rissole *type of* **processed meat** [➡ TYPES AND CUTS OF MEAT; 1177]

rite **1** *n* **ritual**, ceremony, formal procedure, service, sacrament, formality [➡ CEREMONIES AND ANNIVERSARIES; 38] **2** *n* **custom**, habit, practice, routine, procedure, convention, tradition, usage [➡ WAYS OF DOING THINGS; 294]

ritual **1** *n* **rite**, ceremony, service, formal procedure, sacrament, formality, ceremonial [➡ CEREMONIES AND ANNI-

VERSARIES; 38] **2** *n* **custom**, habit, practice, routine, procedure, schedule, convention, tradition, usage [➥WAYS OF DOING THINGS; 294] **3** *adj* **ceremonial**, procedural, ceremonious, sacramental, formal [➥CEREMONIES AND ANNIVERSARIES; 38] **4** *adj* **customary**, habitual, usual, normal, expected, predictable, routine, traditional, conventional [➥ORDINARINESS; 244]

ritualistic *adj* **ceremonial**, formalized, formulaic, ritualized, sacred [➥CEREMONIES AND ANNIVERSARIES; 38]

ritzy (*informal*) *adj* [➥EXPENSIVE AND LUXURIOUS; 218]

rival **1** *n* **competitor**, opponent, adversary, contender, challenger, enemy, foe (*formal*) [➥ENEMIES AND TORMENTORS; 969] *Opposite*: ally **2** *n* **equal**, match, counterpart, peer, equivalent [➥EQUALITY; 154] **3** *v* **match**, equal, be the equal of, be similar to, compare with, resemble [➥EQUALITY; 154] **4** *v* **oppose**, compete with, challenge, go up against, be against, contest, confront [➥COMPETE, CONTEND, AND COMBAT; 303] **5** *v* **outdo**, surpass, exceed, beat, top, outshine [➥BEAT AND DEFEAT; 80] **6** *adj* **competing**, opposing, challenging, contending, enemy, conflicting [➥RELATIONSHIP TO ANOTHER; 973]

rivalry *n* **competition**, opposition, contention, competitiveness, enmity, conflict, challenge, jealousy [➥RELATIONSHIP TO ANOTHER; 973] *Opposite*: cooperation

riven (*literary*) *adj* **split**, torn apart, divided, fragmented, torn asunder (*formal*), rent asunder (*formal*) [➥IN BAD REPAIR; 1234] *Opposite*: united

river *n* **stream**, waterway, tributary, canal, watercourse, brook (*literary*) [➥RIVERS, LAKES, AND STREAMS; 1042]

riverbank *n* [➥RIVERS, LAKES, AND STREAMS; 1042]

riverside *n* **waterside**, water's edge, bank, shore [➥RIVERS, LAKES, AND STREAMS; 1042]

rivet **1** *n* **pin**, nail, fastener, bolt, screw, snap, press stud (*UK*) [➥FASTENERS, LINKS, AND NETWORKS; 1247] **2** *v* (*informal*) **fascinate**, enthrall, entrance, interest, mesmerize [➥APPEAL TO AND AROUSE INTEREST; 575] *Opposite*: bore **3** *v* **fasten**, hold, pin, bolt, nail, fix, attach, join, weld, screw [➥FASTEN, LINK, AND JOIN; 408]

riveted (*informal*) *adj* [➥PENSIVENESS AND INTEREST; 538]

riveting (*informal*) *adj* **fascinating**, enthralling, exciting, spellbinding, entrancing, interesting, mesmeric, exhilarating, thrilling, captivating [➥INTERESTING AND MEANINGFUL; 190] *Opposite*: boring

rivulet *n* **stream**, creek, gully, brook (*literary*), burn (*UK*) [➥RIVERS, LAKES, AND STREAMS; 1042]

riyal *type of* **currency** [➥CURRENCIES; 798]

RNA *n* **nucleic acid**, ribonucleic acid, genetic material [➥REPRODUCTION AND HEREDITY; 725]

roach **1** (*informal*) *type of* **beetle** [➥BEETLES AND WEEVILS; 1016] **2** *type of* **freshwater fish** [➥FRESHWATER FISH; 1010]

road *n* **street**, thoroughfare, lane, way [➥ROADS; 1106]

road

◆ *types of highways*
artery, avenue, beltway, boulevard, bypass, divided highway, expressway, freeway, highway, interstate, limited-access highway, main road, overpass, parkway, speedway, superhighway, thruway, toll road, trunk route, turnpike

◆ *types of secondary roads*
access road, access strip, alley, alleyway, backstreet, blind alley, byroad, byway, corniche, cul-de-sac, dead end, dirt track, driveway, esplanade, lane, parade, path, service road, side street, slip road, street, track

roadblock *n* **barricade**, barrier, sentry post, obstruction, blockade [➥BARRIERS; 1113]

roadhouse *n* **hotel**, motel, inn, tavern, bar, greasy spoon (*informal*), pub (*UK*), transport café (*UK*) [➥HOTELS, RESTAURANTS, AND CLUBS; 1082]

road show **1** *n* **radio show**, live broadcast, open-air broadcast, broadcast, tour [➥PERFORMANCES AND SHOWS; 42] **2** *n* **campaign**, publicity campaign, advertising campaign, tour, circus [➥ADVERTISING AND PUBLICITY; 604]

roadside café *type of* **eating place** [➥HOTELS, RESTAURANTS, AND CLUBS; 1082]

road sign *n* **sign**, signpost, notice, stop sign, yield sign, one-way sign, signal, chevrons (*UK*) [➥SIGNPOSTS, SIGNALS, AND BILLBOARDS; 595]

roadster *type of* **car** (*dated*) [➥BIKES, CARS, AND CARRIAGES; 1149]

road test **1** *n* **test**, drive, test drive [➥PREPARATORY EVENTS; 57] **2** *n* **controlled test**, test, trial, field test, experiment, assay, analysis [➥EXAMINE AND ASSESS; 753]

road-test *v* **try out**, test, test drive, trial, run, analyze [➥EXAMINE AND ASSESS; 753]

roadway *n* **road**, street, thoroughfare, highway [➥ROADS; 1106]

roadworthiness *n* **safety**, soundness, reliability, working order [➥SAFE AND SAFETY; 191]

roadworthy *adj* **safe**, fit, legal, driveable, suitable, sound [➥SAFE AND SAFETY; 191]

roam *v* **wander**, rove, travel, journey, stray, ramble, meander [➥AIMLESS AND ERRANT MOTION; 343] *Opposite*: settle

roamer *n* **wanderer**, traveler, rover, itinerant, nomad, drifter [➥TRAVEL: TRAVELERS AND WALKERS; 319]

roaming *adj* **wandering**, roving, itinerant, nomadic, peripatetic, drifting, traveling [➥NOMADIC AND ROOTLESS LIFESTYLES; 884] *Opposite*: stationary

roan *type of* **brown** [➥COLORS; 1224]

roar **1** *type of* **continuous sound** [➥CONTINUOUS SOUNDS; 1258] **2** *type of* **animal sound** [➥SOUNDS MADE BY ANIMALS; 1261]

roaring **1** *adj* **noisy**, loud, deafening, boisterous, thunderous [➥LOUD, HIGH, OR UNPLEASANT SOUNDS; 1266] *Opposite*: quiet **2** *adj* **busy**, thriving, prosperous, active [➥SUCCESSFUL AND PROMISING; 81] *Opposite*: slack

roast *v* **bake**, cook, heat [➡ COOKING AND FOOD PREPARATION; 353]

roasting (*informal*) *adj* **boiling**, hot, red-hot, sweltering, burning up, burning, scorching (*informal*) [➡ TEMPERATURE: HOT; 1229] *Opposite*: cool

rob 1 *v* **steal from**, take from, hold up, raid, pickpocket, mug, stick up (*informal*) [➡ STEAL AND ROB; 426] **2** *v* **deprive**, cheat, strip, drain, fleece (*informal*) [➡ TAKE SOMETHING AWAY; 425]

robber *n* **thief**, burglar, pickpocket, shoplifter, mugger, raider [➡ CRIMINALS; 821]

robbery *n* **theft**, burglary, break-in, mugging, stealing, raid, shoplifting, pilfering [➡ CRIMES; 817]

robe *n* **dressing gown**, negligee, housecoat, bathrobe, gown, kimono [➡ GARMENTS AND OUTFITS; 865]

robin *type of* **common bird** [➡ BIRDS; 997]

robot 1 *n* **automaton**, android, machine, computer, mechanical device [➡ DEVICES; 1115] **2** *n* [➡ THE INTERNET; 1128]

robotic 1 *adj* **mechanical**, mechanized, automated, automatic, cybernetic, computerized [➡ MACHINERY; 1114] **2** *adj* **machinelike**, mechanical, unresponsive, unfeeling, humorless, unemotional, cold [➡ NEUTRALITY AND INDIFFERENCE; 553] *Opposite*: warm

robotics *n* **cybernetics**, automation, engineering, manufacturing, science, computing [➡ MACHINERY; 1114]

robust *adj* **healthy**, vigorous, hearty, strong, tough, forceful, stout, hardy [➡ FIT AND STRONG; 736] *Opposite*: weak

robustness *n* **heftiness**, sturdiness, strength, toughness, forcefulness, stoutness, healthiness, vigor, hardiness [➡ FIT AND STRONG; 736] *Opposite*: weakness

rock 1 *n* **stone**, boulder, pebble [➡ STONES, ROCKS, AND BOULDERS; 1057] **2** *n* **pillar**, mainstay, tower of strength, stalwart [➡ PEOPLE WHO ARE APPROVED OF; 955] **3** *type of* **rock music** [➡ MUSIC, SONGS, AND SINGING; 907] **4** *v* (*informal*) **astound**, shock, shake, stun, disturb, upset [➡ SURPRISE AND IMPRESS; 574] **5** *v* **sway**, swing, shake, move up and down, pitch [➡ MOVE SOMETHING: ON THE SPOT; 336]

rockabilly *type of* **pop and vocal music** [➡ MUSIC, SONGS, AND SINGING; 907]

rock bottom *n* **the lowest**, the bottom, the depths, all-time low, nadir, the pits (*informal*) [➡ DIFFICULT SITUATIONS; 72]

rock candy *type of* **confectionery** [➡ CONFECTIONERY; 1182]

rock climber *n* [➡ PEOPLE IN SPORTS AND LEISURE; 876]

rock climbing *n* [➡ HOBBIES, GAMES, AND SPORTS; 875]

rocker 1 *n* (*informal*) **rock star**, rock musician, rock singer, rock and roller, guitarist, bassist, singer, drummer, pop star [➡ MUSICIANS AND SINGERS; 908] **2** *n* (*informal*) **rock fan**, fan, teddy boy, devotee, aficionado, aficionada, music lover [➡ DEVOTEES AND ADDICTED PEOPLE; 556] **3** *n* (*UK*) **biker**, greaser, Hell's Angel, motorcyclist, youth, teenager [➡ PEOPLE IN SPORTS AND LEISURE; 876]

rockery *n* **garden**, rock garden, alpine garden, terrace [➡ GARDENS; 1074]

rocket 1 *type of* **spacecraft** [➡ SPACE VEHICLES; 1063] **2** *type of* **firework** [➡ EXPLOSIVES; 1155] **3** *v* **speed**, whiz, hurtle, fly, zoom, career [➡ MOVE FAST; 313] **4** *v* (*informal*) **shoot up**, soar, increase rapidly, go through the roof, go sky-high [➡ CHANGE OF SIZE: BIGGER; 392] *Opposite*: plummet

rocket engine *part of* **spacecraft** [➡ SPACE VEHICLES; 1063]

rocket ship *type of* **spacecraft** [➡ SPACE VEHICLES; 1063]

rock face *n* **cliff face**, face, precipice, crag, cliff, overhang, sheer drop, sea cliff [➡ MOUNTAINS AND HILLS; 1044]

rock garden *n* **garden**, rockery, alpine garden, terrace [➡ GARDENS; 1074]

rock-hard *adj* **solid**, firm, cast-iron, hard as nails, like granite, indestructible [➡ RIGID AND HARD; 1211] *Opposite*: soft

rockiness *n* **shakiness**, unsteadiness, uncertainty, insecurity, instability [➡ DANGER; 235] *Opposite*: steadiness

rocking chair *type of* **seating** [➡ FURNITURE; 858]

rocking horse *type of* **toy** [➡ TOYS; 880]

rock musician *n* [➡ MUSICIANS AND SINGERS; 908]

rock 'n' roll *type of* **rock music** [➡ MUSIC, SONGS, AND SINGING; 907]

rock singer *n* [➡ MUSICIANS AND SINGERS; 908]

rock-solid 1 *adj* **firm**, unshakable, solid, rigid, unyielding, unwavering [➡ SAFE AND SAFETY; 191] *Opposite*: shaky **2** *adj* **durable**, unbreakable, strong, firm, enduring, permanent [➡ DURABLE; 1210] *Opposite*: breakable

rock star *n* [➡ MUSICIANS AND SINGERS; 908]

rock steady *type of* **dance music** [➡ MUSIC, SONGS, AND SINGING; 907]

rock-strewn *adj* **stony**, rocky, gravelly, pebbly, rough [➡ PHYSICAL TEXTURE; 1222] *Opposite*: smooth

rock the boat (*informal*) *v* **cause an argument**, cause an upset, cause trouble [➡ PROTEST AND EXPRESS DISAPPROVAL; 642]

rockweed *type of* **marine alga** [➡ MICROORGANISMS, FUNGI, AND ALGAE; 1023]

rocky 1 *adj* **stony**, rock-strewn, pebbly, gravelly [➡ PHYSICAL TEXTURE; 1222] **2** *adj* **shaky**, unsteady, wobbly, unsound, insecure, unstable, inconstant, wavering, quaking [➡ DANGEROUS; 236] *Opposite*: stable **3** *adj* **difficult**, troubled, uncertain, not easy, hard, trying, strenuous, tough [➡ DIFFICULTY AND COMPLEXITY; 242] *Opposite*: easy

rococo *type of* **pre-20th-century architecture** [➡ BUILDING AND ARCHITECTURE; 1076]

rod 1 *n* **bar**, pole, stick, shaft, dowel, fishing rod [➡ STICKS, POLES, AND WEDGES; 1254] **2** *type of* **nonmetric unit** [➡ SIZE AND DIMENSIONS; 1192] **3** *part of* **eye** [➡ THE EYE; 698]

rodent *n* [➡ LIVING THINGS AND LIVING; 976]

rodent

◆ *types of rodents*
beaver, capybara, chinchilla, chipmunk, coypu, dormouse, gerbil, gopher, groundhog, guinea pig, hamster, jerboa, lemming, marmot, mole, mouse, muskrat, prairie dog, rat, shrew, squirrel, vole, woodchuck

rodeo *n* **competition**, display, festival, meet, fair, trial [➡ NON-AGGRESSIVE/SPORTING EVENTS; 40]

roe *part of* **fish** [➡ EGGS, SPERM, AND SPAWN; 727]

roger (*informal*) *interj* **fine**, yes, OK (*informal*), right (*informal*), yeah (*informal*), great (*informal*) [➡ EXPRESSIONS OF AGREEMENT; 648]

rogue *n* **scoundrel**, rascal, reprobate, ne'er-do-well, cad (*dated*), scalawag (*dated informal*) [➡ VILLAINS AND THUGS; 947]

roguery **1** *n* **dishonesty**, deceit, unscrupulousness, double-dealing, sharp practice, criminality, cheating, knavery (*archaic*) [➡ DECEITFUL; 513] *Opposite*: honesty **2** *n* **mischief**, mischievousness, playfulness, naughtiness, tricks, pranks [➡ BAD BEHAVIOR OR ACTIONS; 254]

roguish **1** *adj* **mischievous**, naughty, impish, wicked, malicious, wayward [➡ BAD MANNERS AND SOCIAL SKILLS; 521] **2** *adj* **dishonest**, deceitful, unscrupulous, double-dealing, criminal, cheating [➡ DECEITFUL; 513] *Opposite*: honest

roguishness **1** *n* **unscrupulousness**, dishonesty, deceit, double-dealing, sharp practice, criminality, cheating, knavery (*archaic*) [➡ DECEITFUL; 513] *Opposite*: honesty **2** *n* **mischievousness**, mischief, playfulness, naughtiness, tricks, pranks [➡ BAD BEHAVIOR OR ACTIONS; 254]

roister **1** *v* **revel**, make merry, celebrate, drink, party (*informal*), carouse (*literary*) [➡ LEISURE AND RECREATION; 874] **2** *v* **brag**, boast, show off, swagger, gloat, exult [➡ BOAST; 616]

roisterer **1** *n* **reveler**, partygoer, merrymaker, pleasure-seeker, celebrator, drinker, party animal (*informal*), carouser (*literary*) [➡ PLEASURE-SEEKERS AND HEDONISTS; 886] **2** *n* **braggart**, boaster, show-off (*informal*), loudmouth (*informal*), bigmouth (*informal*) [➡ SELF-IMPORTANT AND SELF-SEEKING PEOPLE; 949]

role **1** *n* **position**, function, responsibility, job, task, part [➡ JOB; 833] **2** *n* **part**, character, person, title role, starring role, hero, heroine, protagonist [➡ PERFORMERS; 905]

role model *n* **example**, model, paradigm, exemplar (*literary*) [➡ PERFECT EXAMPLES AND EMBODIMENTS; 67]

role-play *v* **act**, act out, enact, play, imagine, work through, work out [➡ PRETEND AND MIMIC; 60]

role-playing *n* **acting**, acting out, game-playing, imagination, play-acting, role-play [➡ THE PERFORMING ARTS; 904]

roll **1** *v* **bowl**, trundle, troll, set rolling, roll along, move [➡ PUSH, PULL, AND SLIDE; 335] **2** *v* **revolve**, turn, turn over, turn around, spin, rotate [➡ MOVE SOMETHING: ON THE SPOT; 336] **3** *n* **reel**, cylinder, spool, tube [➡ CONTAINERS, RECEPTACLES, AND PACKAGING; 1245] **4** *type of* **roll or bun** [➡ BREAD, FLOUR, AND BREAD PRODUCTS; 1179]

roll call **1** *n* **attendance check**, register check, checkup, check, monitoring, supervision [➡ LISTS AND SCHEDULES; 587] **2** *n* **time**, slot, period, session, allotted time, regular time [➡ TIMES OF DAY; 87]

roller *n* **breaker**, wave, whitecap [➡ THE SEAS, OCEANS, AND SHORES; 1041]

rollerball *type of* **pen** [➡ WRITING AND DRAWING IMPLEMENTS, AND MEDIA; 601]

roller-skate *v* **skate**, blade, skateboard [➡ HOBBIES, GAMES, AND SPORTS; 875]

rollicking *adj* **boisterous**, rowdy, loud, carefree, swashbuckling, noisy, thumping (*informal*) [➡ EXTRAORDINARY: UNCOMMON; 205]

roll in *v* **arrive**, enter, land, roll up, appear, breeze in [➡ ARRIVE; 12] *Opposite*: leave

rolling **1** *adj* **undulating**, rising and falling, gently sloping [➡ ROUNDED SHAPE; 1218] *Opposite*: steep **2** *adj* **progressing**, continuing, systematic, regular, developing [➡ HAPPENING AND IN PROGRESS; 32]

rolling in it (*informal*) *adj* **rich**, wealthy, in the money, loaded (*slang*) [➡ WEALTH AND WEALTHY; 891] *Opposite*: broke (*informal*)

roll in the aisles *v* [➡ LAUGHTER; 649]

roll out *v* **introduce**, launch, inaugurate, issue, bring out [➡ INSTITUTE AND INAUGURATE; 348]

roll out the red carpet *v* **treat like royalty**, give a hero's welcome, lionize, make a fuss of, welcome [➡ TAKE CARE OF AND SPOIL; 300]

roll-top desk *type of* **table** [➡ FURNITURE; 858]

roll up **1** *v* **appear**, turn up, ride up, show up, roll in [➡ ARRIVE; 12] *Opposite*: leave **2** *v* **turn up**, push back, furl [➡ CHANGE OF SHAPE; 385] *Opposite*: unroll

ROM *type of* **hardware** [➡ COMPUTERS AND COMPUTING; 1127]

roman **1** *adj* **upright**, straight, plain [➡ PRINTING; 600] *Opposite*: italic **2** *adj* **in classical style**, classical, ancient [➡ OLD, OLD-FASHIONED; 167]

Roman alphabet *type of* **alphabet** [➡ SYMBOLS, SIGNS, AND NUMBERS; 596]

Roman candle *type of* **firework** [➡ EXPLOSIVES; 1155]

romance **1** *n* **love**, passion, amorousness, sex, eroticism, ardor, desire, sexual love [➡ SEXUAL AND ROMANTIC RELATIONSHIPS; 964] **2** *n* **relationship**, love affair, affair, involvement, fling (*informal*) [➡ RELATIONSHIP TO ANOTHER; 973] **3** *n* **allure**, excitement, adventure, nostalgia, feeling, sensation, exoticism, sense of adventure, sense of excitement, sense of history [➡ FEELINGS ABOUT THE PAST; 532] **4** *n* **fascination**, enthusiasm, passion, love, love affair, involvement, association [➡ PLEASURE, EXCITEMENT, AND ELATION; 534] **5** *n* **love story**, romantic story, romantic novel, romantic short story, romantic film, romantic comedy, romantic tale, weepie (*informal*) [➡ FICTION AND DRAMA; 913] *Opposite*: tragedy **6** *n* **adventure story**, adventure, tale, story, narrative, yarn (*informal*), romp (*informal*) [➡ FICTION AND DRAMA; 913] **7** *n* **fantasy**, story, tall tale, fiction, daydream, tissue of lies [➡ DECEPTION AND LIES; 660] **8** *n* **short piece of music**, song, piece [➡ MUSIC, SONGS, AND SINGING; 907] **9** *v* **tell stories**, fantasize, romanticize [➡ DREAM, IMAGINE, AND FANTASIZE; 749] **10** *v* **be romantic**, act romantically, swoon, daydream, be in love, gush, moon (*literary or humorous*) [➡ LIKE, LOVE, VALUE, AND ENJOY; 578] **11** *v* **court** (*dated*), put on a pedestal, woo (*literary*), pay court to (*dated*) [➡ ESTABLISHING RELATIONSHIPS WITH OTHERS; 974] **12** *v* **have an affair with**, have a love affair with, have a relationship with, date, have a fling with, be involved with, step out with (*informal*), sleep with (*informal*) [➡ ESTABLISHING RELATIONSHIPS WITH OTHERS; 974]

Romanesque *type of* **pre-20th-century architecture** [➡ BUILDING AND ARCHITECTURE; 1076]

romantic 1 *adj* **idealistic**, dreamy, quixotic, impractical, starry-eyed [➡NEGATIVE INTELLECTUAL CHARACTERISTICS; 525] *Opposite:* prosaic 2 *adj* **loving**, passionate, tender, amorous, adoring, sexual [➡APPRECIATION AND GRATITUDE; 535] *Opposite:* platonic

Romantic *type of* **classical music** [➡MUSIC, SONGS, AND SINGING; 907]

romanticism *n* **idealization**, fantasy, nostalgia, soft focus, rose-tinted glasses, invention, idealism, naiveté [➡DREAM, IMAGINE, AND FANTASIZE; 749]

Romanticism *type of* **pre-20th-century art movement** [➡ARTISTIC MOVEMENTS AND STYLES; 899]

romanticize 1 *v* **idealize**, glamorize, sentimentalize, put on a pedestal, look at through rose-colored glasses, view through rose-tinted glasses, exaggerate [➡LIKE, LOVE, VALUE, AND ENJOY; 578] 2 *v* **daydream**, swoon, gush, dream, rhapsodize, moon (*literary or humorous*) [➡DREAM, IMAGINE, AND FANTASIZE; 749]

Romeo *n* **Don Juan**, Casanova, seducer, wolf, womanizer, Lothario (*literary*) [➡PLEASURE-SEEKERS AND HEDONISTS; 886]

romp 1 *v* **cavort**, frolic, horse around, caper, prance, play, gambol, leap about, let off steam, bound about, kick up your heels [➡FIDGET AND FROLIC; 311] 2 *v* **sail**, steam, coast, cruise, whiz, zip (*informal*) [➡MOVE FAST; 313] *Opposite:* struggle 3 *v* (*informal*) **win**, coast, excel yourself, surpass yourself [➡SUCCEED AND WIN; 79] *Opposite:* lose 4 *n* **frolic**, frisk, gambol, run, scramble, caper [➡FIDGET AND FROLIC; 311] 5 *n* (*informal*) **frolic**, page-turner, thriller, chiller, potboiler [➡FICTION AND DRAMA; 913] *Opposite:* bore 6 *n* (*informal*) **foregone conclusion**, one-horse race, piece of cake (*informal*), cinch (*informal*), walkover (*informal*) [➡EASY WORK; 299]

rondo *type of* **musical form** [➡MUSIC, SONGS, AND SINGING; 907]

rondure (*archaic*) *n* [➡ROUNDED SHAPE; 1218]

roof 1 *part of* **building** [➡PARTS OF A BUILDING; 1095] 2 *part of* **mouth** [➡THE MOUTH; 702]

roofed *adj* **covered**, enclosed, vaulted, ceiled, topped [➡BUILDING AND ARCHITECTURE; 1076] *Opposite:* open

roofing *n* **tiling**, slating, tiles, slates, shingles, thatch, guttering, gutters [➡BUILDING MATERIALS; 1077]

roof space *n* [➡ROOFS, ROOF PARTS, AND CEILINGS; 1103]

rooftop *n* **roof**, top, tiles, slates, gable, ridge [➡ROOFS, ROOF PARTS, AND CEILINGS; 1103]

rook *type of* **scavenger** [➡BIRDS; 997]

rookery 1 *type of* **flock** [➡GROUPS OF BIRDS; 1007] 2 *type of* **herd** [➡GROUPS OF ANIMALS; 993]

rookie (*informal*) *n* **beginner**, novice, recruit, trainee, learner, apprentice, neophyte, greenhorn, tyro [➡UNSKILLED PEOPLE; 530] *Opposite:* old hand

room 1 *n* **space**, scope, accommodation, extent, span, capacity [➡DEGREE AND EXTENT; 110] 2 *n* **area**, apartment (*formal*), chamber (*archaic or literary*) [➡TYPES OF ROOMS; 1097] 3 *n* **scope**, opportunity, possibility, occasion, chance, leeway [➡POSSIBLE AND PROBABLE; 177]

room

◆ *types of rooms in public buildings*
antechamber, anteroom, ballroom, banqueting hall, boardroom, bunkhouse, cell, classroom, dining hall, dormitory, dressing room, entrance hall, foyer, gallery, games room, hall, lavatory, library, lobby, lounge, meeting room, men's room, office, operating room, powder room, reception room, refectory, restroom, schoolroom, stateroom, vault, waiting room, ward, washroom

◆ *types of rooms in the home*
atelier, attic, bathroom, bedchamber (*archaic or literary*), bedroom, boudoir, closet, day room, den, dining room, drawing room, family room, garret, guestroom, kitchen, kitchenette, laundry room, living room, loft, parlor, playroom, rec room, recreation room, salon, scullery, sitting room, sleeping quarters, spare room, study, sunroom, toilet, utility room

roomer *n* **lodger**, tenant, occupant, resident, renter, dweller (*literary*) [➡INHABITANTS; 857] *Opposite:* landlord

roomie (*informal*) *n* **roommate**, cotenant, lodger, buddy (*informal*), pal (*informal*), flatmate (*UK*) [➡COLLEAGUES AND EQUALS; 967]

roominess *n* **spaciousness**, largeness, capaciousness, generousness, sizableness, voluminousness [➡LARGE; 1193] *Opposite:* smallness

rooming house *type of* **hotel** [➡HOTELS, RESTAURANTS, AND CLUBS; 1082]

roommate *n* **cotenant**, housemate, lodger, roomie (*informal*), buddy (*informal*), flatmate (*UK*) [➡COLLEAGUES AND EQUALS; 967]

rooms *n* **housing**, accommodations, quarters, place, lodgings (*dated*) [➡ACCOMMODATIONS; 855]

roomy *adj* **spacious**, large, generous, sizable, capacious, voluminous [➡LARGE; 1193] *Opposite:* cramped

roost *v* **settle**, rest, stay, perch, sleep, nestle [➡EXIST IN A PLACE; 19]

rooster *type of* **male or female bird** [➡MALE OR FEMALE BIRDS; 1005]

root 1 *n* **stem**, rhizome, tuber, radicle, radix, corm [➡PARTS OF TREES AND PLANTS; 1026] 2 *n* **origin**, cause, source, basis, starting place, derivation, core, essence, foundation [➡BEGINNINGS; 53] 3 *v* **dig**, grub, forage, delve, burrow, rootle (*UK*) [➡SEEK POSSESSION AND SEARCH; 456] 4 *v* **search**, rummage, delve, rifle, burrow, nose (*informal*) [➡SEEK POSSESSION AND SEARCH; 456] 5 *v* **cheer**, shout, applaud, yell, clap [➡PRAISE AND ENCOURAGE; 647] *Opposite:* jeer

See Compare and Contrast at **origin**.

rooted *adj* **entrenched**, ingrained, fixed, deep-rooted, deep-seated, embedded, established [➡PERMANENCE: WITHOUT END; 94]

root for *v* [➡PRAISE AND ENCOURAGE; 647]

rootle (*UK*) *v* [➡SEEK POSSESSION AND SEARCH; 456]

rootless *adj* **drifting**, freewheeling, roving, nomadic, itinerant, traveling, disenfranchised, peripatetic, homeless [➡ NOMADIC AND ROOTLESS LIFESTYLES; 884] *Opposite*: rooted

root out 1 *v* **eradicate**, remove, get rid of, do away with, eliminate, obliterate, wipe out (*informal*) [➡ GET RID OF SOMETHING; 451] 2 *v* **find**, discover, locate, turn up, unearth, produce [➡ FIND; 463] *Opposite*: hide

roots 1 *n* **origins**, ancestry, background, heritage, pedigree, stock [➡ BEGINNINGS; 53] 2 *type of* **world music** [➡ MUSIC, SONGS, AND SINGING; 907]

root to the spot *v* [➡ FRIGHTEN AND SHOCK; 568]

rope 1 *n* **cord**, line, cable, lead, twine, string [➡ FASTENERS, LINKS, AND NETWORKS; 1247] 2 *v* **tie**, fasten, lash, secure, attach, moor, link, bind [➡ FASTEN, LINK, AND JOIN; 408] *Opposite*: untie

rope in *v* [➡ CAUSE OR COMPEL TO ACT; 271]

Roquefort *type of* **soft cheese** [➡ DAIRY PRODUCTS AND CHEESES; 1183]

rose 1 *type of* **perennial flower** [➡ FLOWERS; 1032] 2 *type of* **shrub or bush** [➡ BUSHES AND SHRUBS; 1027] 3 *type of* **pink** [➡ COLORS; 1224] 4 *n* **design**, rosette, ornament, representation, emblem, badge [➡ ORNAMENTS AND DECORATIONS; 1248] 5 *n* **sprinkler**, jet, nozzle, spray, attachment, irrigator [➡ FIXTURES; 859] 6 *n* **ceiling rose**, fitting, boss, connector, socket [➡ ROOFS, ROOF PARTS, AND CEILINGS; 1103]

roseate *adj* **reddish**, rose, fuchsia, magenta, rose-colored, pink [➡ DESCRIBING COLORS; 1226]

rosebud *n* **bud**, bloom, rose, flower, blossom, floret [➡ PARTS OF TREES AND PLANTS; 1026]

rose-colored *adj* **idealistic**, assured, sanguine, trusting, optimistic, hopeful [➡ EMOTIONALLY PLEASANT; 187] *Opposite*: pessimistic

rose garden *type of* **garden** [➡ GARDENS; 1074]

rosemary *type of* **herb** [➡ HERBS AND SPICES; 1175]

rose-tinted *adj* **rose-colored**, optimistic, idealistic, sanguine, trusting, hopeful [➡ EMOTIONALLY PLEASANT; 187] *Opposite*: pessimistic

rosette 1 *n* **badge**, decoration, prize, emblem, insignia, ornament [➡ ORNAMENTS AND DECORATIONS; 1248] 2 *n* **ornament**, design, rose, shape, representation, decoration [➡ ORNAMENTS AND DECORATIONS; 1248]

rose window *type of* **window** [➡ WINDOWS; 1100]

rosiness *n* **blush**, flush, pinkness, redness, glow, color, ruddiness [➡ COMPLEXION; 480]

roster *n* **list**, schedule, roll, register, rota (*UK*) [➡ LISTS AND SCHEDULES; 587]

rösti *type of* **processed potato** [➡ FRUIT AND VEGETABLES; 1176]

rostrum *n* **platform**, podium, stage, dais, stand, pulpit [➡ STAGES, PLATFORMS, AND RAISED AREAS; 1098]

rosy 1 *adj* **pink**, rose-colored, reddish, pinkish, rose, roseate [➡ DESCRIBING COLORS; 1226] 2 *adj* **blushing**, flushed, glowing, healthy, ruddy, rubicund (*literary*) [➡ COMPLEXION; 480] *Opposite*: pale 3 *adj* **promising**, auspicious, successful, happy, favorable, bright [➡ SUCCESSFUL AND PROMISING; 81] *Opposite*: unpromising 4 *adj* **optimistic**, idealistic, unrealistic,

hopeful, encouraging, sunny [➡ EMOTIONALLY PLEASANT; 187] *Opposite*: pessimistic

rot 1 *v* **decompose**, decay, putrefy, disintegrate, break down, go off (*UK*), perish (*UK*) [➡ GO BAD AND CORRODE; 390] 2 *n* (*informal*) **nonsense**, balderdash, rubbish, twaddle (*informal*), claptrap (*informal*), poppycock (*dated informal*) [➡ MEANINGLESS SPEECH OR WRITING; 676] *Opposite*: sense 3 *n* **decay**, deterioration, putrefaction, decomposition, corrosion, corruption [➡ GO BAD AND CORRODE; 390]

rota (*UK*) *n* **roster**, list, schedule, register, roll [➡ LISTS AND SCHEDULES; 587]

rotary *adj* **rotating**, turning, revolving, rotational, gyratory, rotatory [➡ DIRECTION OF MOTION; 345]

rotate 1 *v* **turn**, revolve, go, spin, swivel, pivot [➡ MOVE SOMETHING ON THE SPOT; 336] 2 *v* **alternate**, take turns, interchange, switch, revolve, swap (*informal*) [➡ EXCHANGE AND INTERCHANGE; 448] 3 *v* **replace**, switch, interchange, alternate, exchange, swap (*informal*) [➡ CHANGE ONE THING FOR ANOTHER; 398]

rotation 1 *n* **revolution**, turning, spin, gyration [➡ MOVE SOMETHING ON THE SPOT; 336] 2 *n* **alternation**, variation, interchange, replacement, cycle, sequence [➡ EXCHANGE AND INTERCHANGE; 448]

rote *n* **repetition**, memorization, routine, habit, rotation, conditioning [➡ MEMORY; 745]

roti *type of* **bread** [➡ BREAD, FLOUR, AND BREAD PRODUCTS; 1179]

rotisserie *n* **spit**, skewer, brochette, grill, barbecue, tandoor [➡ HOUSEHOLD APPLIANCES; 1117]

rotor *n* **blade**, propeller, airfoil [➡ AIRCRAFT; 1148]

rotten 1 *adj* **decayed**, putrid, bad, decomposed, moldy, rotted, disintegrating, off (*UK*) [➡ DECAYING OR INFESTED; 1236] *Opposite*: fresh 2 *adj* (*informal*) **awful**, bad, nasty, terrible, unpleasant, unfortunate, foul (*informal*) [➡ EMOTIONALLY UNPLEASANT AND UPSETTING; 227] *Opposite*: pleasant 3 *adj* (*informal*) **inferior**, poor, bad, dreadful, incompetent, inadequate [➡ BAD AND BADLY; 223] *Opposite*: good 4 *adj* (*informal*) **unhappy**, uncomfortable, guilty, embarrassed, bad, wretched [➡ SADNESS, DISTRESS, AND DESPAIR; 539] *Opposite*: happy 5 *adj* (*informal*) **unwell**, ill, sick, seedy (*informal*) [➡ ILL AND SICK; 740] *Opposite*: fine (*informal*) 6 *adv* (*informal*) **terribly**, unduly, excessively, overly, outrageously, dreadfully [➡ TO A GREAT EXTENT; 132] *Opposite*: slightly

rottenly (*informal*) *adv* **shabbily**, badly, terribly, awfully, dreadfully, appallingly, poorly, unfairly, atrociously [➡ BAD AND BADLY; 223] *Opposite*: well

rottenness 1 *n* **decay**, moldiness, dry rot, wet rot, badness, decomposition, degradation, disintegration [➡ DECAYING OR INFESTED; 1236] *Opposite*: freshness 2 *n* (*informal*) **unpleasantness**, awfulness, dreadfulness, hideousness, ghastliness, nastiness [➡ DISGUSTING AND REPULSIVE; 230] *Opposite*: pleasantness 3 *n* (*informal*) **beastliness**, nastiness, cruelness, cruelty, horridness, awfulness, unpleasantness [➡ BAD BEHAVIOR OR ACTIONS; 254] *Opposite*: goodness

rotter (*dated informal*) *n* **scoundrel**, liar, swindler, cheat, cad (*dated*) [➡ VILLAINS AND THUGS; 947] *Opposite*: angel

rotting *adj* **decomposing**, decaying, putrid, bad, contaminated, tainted [➡ DECAYING OR INFESTED; 1236] *Opposite*: fresh

rottweiler *type of* **large dog** [➡ DOGS; 980]

rotund *adj* **overweight**, stout, fat, plump, curved, corpulent, round [➡ BUILD; 477] *Opposite:* slender

rotunda *n* **pavilion**, tower, dome, cupola [➡ TOWERS; 1099]

rotundity *n* **roundness**, sphericalness, rotundness, overweight, stoutness, fatness, plumpness [➡ BUILD; 477] *Opposite:* slenderness

rotundness *n* [➡ BUILD; 477]

roué (*literary*) *n* [➡ PLEASURE-SEEKERS AND HEDONISTS; 886]

rouge **1** *n* (*dated*) **lipstick**, blush, makeup, face paint, coloring, red [➡ MAKEUP AND BEAUTY PRODUCTS; 490] **2** *v* (*dated*) **make up**, redden, color, highlight, paint, beautify [➡ CHANGE OF COLOR; 391]

rough **1** *adj* **uneven**, coarse, bumpy, irregular, jagged, lumpy [➡ PHYSICAL TEXTURE; 1222] *Opposite:* even **2** *adj* **coarse**, shaggy, hairy, bristly, bushy, tangled [➡ PHYSICAL TEXTURE; 1222] *Opposite:* smooth **3** *adj* **turbulent**, stormy, tempestuous, squally, wild [➡ WINDY AND STORMY WEATHER; 1053] *Opposite:* calm **4** *adj* **rugged**, wild, uncultivated, rocky, hilly, craggy [➡ PHYSICAL TEXTURE; 1222] *Opposite:* level **5** *adj* **violent**, forceful, tough, physical, forcible, brutal [➡ PHYSICALLY UNPLEASANT; 226] *Opposite:* gentle **6** *adj* **unrefined**, impolite, rough-and-ready, coarse, crude, uncultured [➡ BAD MANNERS AND SOCIAL SKILLS; 521] *Opposite:* refined **7** *adj* **harsh**, grating, jarring, discordant, rasping [➡ LOUD, HIGH, OR UNPLEASANT SOUNDS; 1266] *Opposite:* smooth **8** *adj* **approximate**, sketchy, vague, estimated, imprecise, ballpark (*informal*) [➡ APPROXIMATELY; 135] *Opposite:* exact **9** *adj* **rowdy**, boisterous, noisy, violent, tough, tempestuous [➡ DISORDER AND CHAOS; 245] *Opposite:* quiet **10** *n* **outline**, sketch, summary, draft, mock-up, cartoon [➡ DRAWINGS, CHARTS, AND TABLES; 594]

roughage *n* **fiber**, bulk, cellulose, bran [➡ FOOD COMPONENTS; 1188]

rough-and-ready **1** *adj* **crude**, simple, basic, primitive, serviceable, practical, usable, rustic [➡ IN BAD REPAIR; 1234] *Opposite:* sophisticated **2** *adj* **down-to-earth**, unpretentious, honest, rough-hewn, decent, kindhearted, warm, unsophisticated, unrefined, homely, downhome (*informal*) [➡ LEVELS OF EDUCATION AND SOPHISTICATION; 894] *Opposite:* refined

rough-and-tumble *n* **hurly-burly**, cut and thrust, infighting, sparring, fracas, free-for-all (*informal*) [➡ CHAOS AND UPROAR; 51]

roughcast *n* **coating**, cladding, facing, plasterwork, rendering, pebbledash (*UK*) [➡ BUILDING MATERIALS; 1077]

rough copy *n* **outline**, sketch, summary, draft, rough, mock-up [➡ SUMMARIES, OUTLINES, AND EXCERPTS; 588]

roughen *v* **coarsen**, toughen, scratch, abrade, rough, crumple [➡ WORSEN APPEARANCE; 382] *Opposite:* soften

rough-hewn **1** *adj* **rough**, unfinished, undressed, incomplete [➡ PHYSICAL TEXTURE; 1222] **2** *adj* **crude**, basic, primitive, simple, rough, unfinished [➡ RAW AND NATURAL; 1214] *Opposite:* polished **3** *adj* **rugged**, rough, unrefined, coarse, crude, uncouth [➡ BAD MANNERS AND SOCIAL SKILLS; 521]

roughhouse (*informal*) *n* **rowdiness**, boisterousness,

rough-and-tumble, horseplay, roughness, high spirits [➡ CHAOS AND UPROAR; 51]

roughly **1** *adv* **approximately**, about, around, more or less, almost, nearly [➡ APPROXIMATELY; 135] *Opposite:* exactly **2** *adv* **violently**, physically, forcefully, forcibly, brutally, rudely [➡ PHYSICALLY UNPLEASANT; 226] *Opposite:* gently **3** *adv* **unevenly**, coarsely, jaggedly, bumpily, crudely, incompletely [➡ PHYSICAL TEXTURE; 1222] *Opposite:* evenly

roughly speaking *adv* [➡ APPROXIMATELY; 135]

roughneck (*informal*) *n* **thug**, hoodlum, rowdy, hooligan (*informal*), ruffian (*dated*) [➡ VILLAINS AND THUGS; 947]

roughness **1** *n* **unevenness**, coarseness, bumpiness, irregularity, jaggedness, lumpiness [➡ PHYSICAL TEXTURE; 1222] *Opposite:* smoothness **2** *n* **coarseness**, shagginess, hairiness, bristliness, bushiness, fuzziness [➡ TEXTURE; 1220] *Opposite:* smoothness **3** *n* **turbulence**, storminess, tempestuousness, wildness [➡ WINDY AND STORMY WEATHER; 1053] *Opposite:* calmness **4** *n* **ruggedness**, wildness, rockiness, hilliness, cragginess, stoniness [➡ PHYSICAL TEXTURE; 1222] *Opposite:* evenness **5** *n* **violence**, force, toughness, power, brutality, severity [➡ PHYSICALLY UNPLEASANT; 226] *Opposite:* gentleness **6** *n* **brusqueness**, rudeness, gruffness, harshness, coarseness [➡ BAD MANNERS AND SOCIAL SKILLS; 521] *Opposite:* refinement **7** *n* **harshness**, discordance, astringency, gruffness, raucousness [➡ LOUD, HIGH, OR UNPLEASANT SOUNDS; 1266] *Opposite:* smoothness **8** *n* **vagueness**, sketchiness, ambiguity, inexactness, haziness, imprecision [➡ VAGUENESS; 243] *Opposite:* exactness **9** *n* (*informal*) **sickliness**, illness, sickness, seediness (*informal*) [➡ ILL AND SICK; 740] *Opposite:* healthiness **10** *n* **rowdiness**, boisterousness, noisiness, violence, toughness, tempestuousness [➡ DISORDER AND CHAOS; 245] *Opposite:* quietness

rough out *v* **draft**, outline, prepare, sketch, block out, plan [➡ RECORD SOMETHING; 371] *Opposite:* finalize

rough up (*informal*) *v* **maltreat**, mistreat, abuse, batter, manhandle, beat, harm, ill-treat, beat up (*informal*), knock around (*informal*) [➡ WOUND A PERSON OR ANIMAL; 383] *Opposite:* take care of

round **1** *n* **circle**, disk, slice, ring, band [➡ ROUNDED SHAPE; 1218] **2** *type of* **cut** [➡ TYPES AND CUTS OF MEAT; 1177] **3** *v* **turn**, circumnavigate, negotiate, skirt, pass [➡ PROCEED AND GO; 305] **4** *prep* **surrounding**, around, about, encircling, encompassing, on all sides of [➡ RELATIVE LOCATION; 161] **5** *adv* **around**, about, near, on all sides [➡ DIRECTION OF MOTION; 345]

round about *prep* **around**, circa, say, in the neighborhood of, in the region of, nigh on to [➡ APPROXIMATELY; 135]

roundabout **1** *n* **merry-go-round**, carousel, ride, attraction [➡ ENTERTAINMENT; 872] **2** *n* (*UK*) **traffic junction**, junction, intersection, crossroads, traffic circle, rotary, traffic island (*UK*) [➡ BRIDGES, TUNNELS, CROSSINGS, AND JUNCTIONS; 1112] **3** *adj* **indirect**, oblique, circuitous, winding, meandering, ambiguous [➡ INARTICULATE, RAMBLING, AND AWKWARD; 633] *Opposite:* direct

rounded *adj* **curved**, smoothed, smooth-edged, round, curvy, plump [➡ ROUNDED SHAPE; 1218] *Opposite:* pointed

rounders *type of* **ball game** [➡ HOBBIES, GAMES, AND SPORTS; 875]

round-eyed *adj* **open-mouthed**, amazed, gaping, staring, fascinated, disbelieving [➡ FACIAL EXPRESSIONS AND BLUSHING; 651]

round here (*UK*) *adv* [➡ CLOSENESS; 159]

roundly *adv* **severely**, forcefully, completely, utterly, bluntly, outright, plainly [➡ ABSOLUTE AND ABSOLUTELY; 133]

roundness *n* **roundedness**, plumpness, chubbiness [➡ BUILD; 477]

round of applause *n* [➡ APPLAUSE; 652]

round-shouldered *adj* **stooping**, hunched, slouching, bent, bent over, huddled [➡ BUILD; 477] *Opposite:* erect

roundtable *n* **discussion**, negotiation, debate, forum, meeting, consultation [➡ MEETINGS AND ASSEMBLIES; 43]

round-the-clock *adj* **24-hour**, day-and-night, continuous, permanent, constant, unceasing, ceaseless [➡ PERMANENCE: WITHOUT END; 94]

round trip *n* **both ways**, circuit, tour, return journey (*UK*), return (*UK*) [➡ TRAVEL: JOURNEYS AND TRIPS; 318]

round up *v* **capture**, gather together, collect, arrest, amass, bring together [➡ GET; 420] *Opposite:* disperse

roundup 1 *n* **assembly**, capture, hunt, herding, rodeo, muster [➡ CAPTIVITY AND LOSS OF FREEDOM; 248] *Opposite:* release 2 *n* **summary**, rundown, review, summing up, recap, overview [➡ SUMMARIES, OUTLINES, AND EXCERPTS; 588]

rouse 1 *v* **stir**, wake up, revive, awaken, disturb, arouse [➡ APPEAL TO AND AROUSE INTEREST; 575] *Opposite:* lull 2 *v* **stir up**, provoke, incite, move, galvanize, wind up (*informal*) [➡ CAUSE OR COMPEL TO ACT; 271] *Opposite:* lull

rousing *adj* **stirring**, inspiring, moving, exciting, stimulating, upbeat (*informal*) [➡ EMOTIONALLY PLEASANT; 187] *Opposite:* soothing

rout 1 *n* **retreat**, flight, stampede, surrender, collapse, disarray [➡ FAILURE; 77] *Opposite:* advance 2 *n* **defeat**, massacre, landslide, thrashing, beating, pasting (*informal*) [➡ BEAT AND DEFEAT; 80] *Opposite:* victory 3 *n* **tumult**, disorder, riot, disturbance, hubbub [➡ CHAOS AND UPROAR; 51] 4 *v* **beat back**, overpower, overwhelm, beat, defeat, overthrow, crush, trounce [➡ BEAT AND DEFEAT; 80] *Opposite:* retreat

route 1 *n* **road**, path, way, track, itinerary [➡ ROADS; 1106] 2 *n* **course**, means, method, way, direction, path [➡ WAYS OF DOING THINGS; 294] 3 *v* **direct**, send, transmit, move, channel, guide [➡ DISPATCH AND SEND; 333]

router *n* [➡ THE INTERNET; 1128]

routine 1 *n* **procedure**, practice, habit, custom, sequence, schedule [➡ WAYS OF DOING THINGS; 294] 2 *adj* **usual**, standard, everyday, normal, customary, habitual, regular, scheduled [➡ ORDINARINESS; 244] *Opposite:* unusual 3 *adj* **monotonous**, dull, tedious, repetitive, humdrum, mundane, predictable, unchanging [➡ BORING AND UNINTERESTING; 234] *Opposite:* exciting

See Compare and Contrast at **habit, usual**.

routinely *adv* **regularly**, as a matter of course, normally, habitually, usually, customarily, consistently, characteristically [➡ USUALLY; 108] *Opposite:* unusually

routineness *n* [➡ ORDINARINESS; 244]

rove *v* **wander**, roam, range, meander, travel, journey, ramble, stray [➡ AIMLESS AND ERRANT MOTION; 343]

rover 1 *n* **wanderer**, traveler, rolling stone, nomad, drifter, itinerant, rambler [➡ TRAVEL: TRAVELERS AND WALKERS; 319] 2 *type of* **spacecraft** [➡ SPACE VEHICLES; 1063]

roving 1 *adj* **roaming**, traveling, wandering, rambling, nomadic, itinerant, drifting, peripatetic, meandering, moving, rootless [➡ NOMADIC AND ROOTLESS LIFESTYLES; 884] *Opposite:* stationary 2 *adj* **erratic**, wandering, fickle, capricious, inconsistent, whimsical [➡ LACK OF COMMITMENT AND UNRELIABILITY; 509] *Opposite:* steady

row 1 *n* **line**, chain, string, file, rank, strip, queue (*UK*) [➡ AREA AND RANGE; 111] 2 *n* **disagreement**, dispute, quarrel, controversy, argument, fight, wrangle [➡ ARGUMENTS; 47] *Opposite:* agreement 3 *n* **noise**, racket, rumpus, din, commotion, disorder, clamor, disturbance, ruckus [➡ CHAOS AND UPROAR; 51] *Opposite:* lull 4 *v* **paddle**, scull, punt, take the oars, propel, maneuver [➡ TRAVEL: WAYS OF TRAVELING; 320] 5 *v* **fight**, quarrel, have a row, disagree, argue, dispute, wrangle [➡ ARGUE AND FIGHT; 643] *Opposite:* agree

rowan 1 *type of* **berry** [➡ FRUIT AND VEGETABLES; 1176] 2 *type of* **deciduous tree** [➡ DECIDUOUS TREES; 1028]

rowboat *type of* **small vessel** [➡ SHIPS AND BOATS; 1150]

rowdiness *n* **disorderliness**, unruliness, noisiness, loudness, raucousness, disruptiveness, boisterousness [➡ CHAOS AND UPROAR; 51] *Opposite:* restraint

rowdy *adj* **disorderly**, unruly, noisy, loud, raucous, disruptive, boisterous, wild [➡ REBELLIOUSNESS AND DISOBEDIENCE; 565] *Opposite:* restrained

rower *n* **oarsperson**, sculler, coxswain, cox, sportsperson [➡ PEOPLE IN SPORTS AND LEISURE; 876]

row house *n* **row home**, terrace, town house, terraced house (*UK*) [➡ RESIDENTIAL BUILDINGS; 1078]

royal 1 *adj* **regal**, imperial, majestic, stately, noble, kingly, queenly [➡ ROYALNESS; 825] 2 *adj* **magnificent**, splendid, noble, excellent, grand, extravagant [➡ EXPENSIVE AND LUXURIOUS; 218] *Opposite:* ordinary

royal blue *type of* **blue** [➡ COLORS; 1224]

royal family *n* [➡ RULERS AND ARISTOCRACY; 823]

royalist *n* **monarchist**, traditionalist, constitutionalist, conservative, loyal subject [➡ DEVOTEES AND ADDICTED PEOPLE; 556] *Opposite:* republican

royals *n* **royalty**, crowned heads, monarchs, sovereigns, royal family, heads of state [➡ RULERS AND ARISTOCRACY; 823]

royalty 1 *n* **royals**, crowned heads, monarchs, sovereigns, royal family, heads of state [➡ RULERS AND ARISTOCRACY; 823] 2 *n* **fee**, payment, percentage, credit, token, cut (*informal*) [➡ INCOME; 460]

R.P. *n* **Received Pronunciation**, BBC English, the Queen's English, Standard English [➡ ASPECTS OF LANGUAGE; 682]

RSI *n* **repetitive strain injury**, industrial injury, work-related injury, tenosynovitis, injury, strain [➡ THE BONES AND JOINTS; 719]

R.S.V.P. 1 *n* **reply**, acknowledgment, answer, response [➡ REPLY AND ANSWER; 668] 2 *v* **answer**, reply, acknowledge, respond [➡ REPLY AND ANSWER; 668]

rub 1 *v* **massage**, stroke, caress, knead, pat [➡CONTACT: EXERT PRESSURE; 414] **2** *v* **polish**, wipe, buff, shine, clean, dry [➡CLEAN AND POLISH; 403] **3** *v* **chafe**, hurt, gall, irritate, scrape, squeeze [➡WOUND A PERSON OR ANIMAL; 383] *Opposite*: soothe

rubato *type of* **musical term** [➡MUSICAL TERMS; 912]

rubber 1 *n* **foam rubber**, neoprene, gum, elastic, latex, sap, vulcanized rubber, India rubber [➡SOLIDS; 1274] **2** *type of* **boot** [➡FOOTWEAR; 871]

rubber bullet *type of* **projectile** [➡PROJECTILES; 1159]

rubberneck (*informal*) *v* **stare**, gape, goggle, gaze, gawk (*informal*) [➡LOOKING AND LOOKS; 700]

See Compare and Contrast at **gaze**.

rubbernecked (*informal*) *adj* **staring**, gazing, ogling, gaping, gawking (*informal*) [➡NOSY AND INTERFERING; 512]

rubbernecking (*informal*) *n* [➡LOOKING AND LOOKS; 700]

rubber plant *type of* **foliage plant** [➡FOLIAGE PLANTS; 1035]

rubber stamp *n* **stamping device**, stamp, seal, stamper, signet, office stamp [➡WRITING AND DRAWING IMPLEMENTS, AND MEDIA; 601]

rubber-stamp *v* **approve**, agree to, authorize, consent to, sanction, okay (*informal*) [➡APPROVE AND CONFIRM; 646] *Opposite*: veto

rubbery *adj* **tough**, elastic, chewy, hard, overcooked, overdone [➡STATE OF PREPARED FOOD; 1171] *Opposite*: tender

rubbing 1 *n* **impression**, brass rubbing, copy, reproduction, relief [➡COPIES AND REPLICAS; 151] **2** *n* **friction**, scraping, abrasion, resistance, chafing, drag [➡ENERGY; 1161] **3** *n* **soreness**, chafing, irritation, blistering, saddle sores, pressure sores [➡CONDITIONS AFFECTING THE SKIN; 721]

rubbish 1 *n* **refuse**, debris, litter, waste, garbage, trash, junk (*informal*) [➡JUNK AND USELESS OBJECTS; 1249] **2** *n* **nonsense**, drivel, dross, claptrap (*informal*), hogwash (*informal*), twaddle (*informal*) [➡MEANINGLESS SPEECH OR WRITING; 676]

rubbishy *adj* **inferior**, poor quality, poor, bad [➡IN BAD REPAIR; 1234] *Opposite*: quality

rubble *n* **debris**, ruins, wreckage, remains, bricks, stones [➡JUNK AND USELESS OBJECTS; 1249]

rub down 1 *v* **dry**, rub, dry off, towel dry, towel [➡CLEAN AND POLISH; 403] **2** *v* **massage**, rub, go over, oil, stroke, caress [➡CONTACT: EXERT PRESSURE; 414] **3** *v* **finish**, wipe down, sand, scour, prepare, scrub [➡CLEAN AND POLISH; 403]

rubel *type of* **currency** [➡CURRENCIES; 798]

rubicund (*literary*) *adj* **red**, rosy, ruddy, red-faced, flushed, healthy, hale, hearty, reddish [➡COMPLEXION; 480] *Opposite*: pale

ruble *type of* **currency** [➡CURRENCIES; 798]

rub out *v* **erase**, delete, wipe, expunge, efface, remove [➡DELETE AND ERASE; 339]

rubric 1 *n* **title**, heading, header, head, introduction, preface [➡PARTS OF BOOKS AND DOCUMENTS; 593] **2** *n* **rules**, instructions, guidelines, directions, rulebook, procedures, comments, documentation [➡MANUALS AND INSTRUCTIONS; 589]

3 *n* **custom**, tradition, practice, system, convention, rule [➡WAYS OF DOING THINGS; 294] **4** *n* **class**, category, classification, division, type, family [➡VARIETIES, TYPES, AND KINDS; 145]

rub the wrong way *v* **irritate**, annoy, make somebody's hackles rise, get on the wrong side of somebody, offend, make an enemy of somebody, aggravate (*informal*) [➡ANGER AND ANNOY; 569]

ruby 1 *type of* **gemstone** [➡PRECIOUS STONES; 1278] **2** *type of* **red** [➡COLORS; 1224]

ruched *adj* **pleated**, gathered, frilled, frilly, edged, fancy [➡PHYSICAL TEXTURE; 1222] *Opposite*: plain

ruck 1 *n* **mass**, pile, heap, accumulation, conglomeration, number [➡AMOUNTS OF SOLID OR SEMISOLID; 115] **2** *v* **wrinkle**, crease, fold, crumple, gather, pucker, rumple, ruck up [➡CHANGE OF SHAPE; 385] *Opposite*: smooth **3** *n* **crease**, wrinkle, fold, crumple, rumple [➡CHANGE OF SHAPE; 385]

rucksack *n* **backpack**, haversack, knapsack, frame rucksack, daypack [➡CONTAINERS, RECEPTACLES, AND PACKAGING; 1245]

ruckus *n* **commotion**, disturbance, rumpus, riot, uproar, turmoil [➡CHAOS AND UPROAR; 51]

ruction *n* **quarrel**, fight, dispute, disturbance, row, scene [➡CHAOS AND UPROAR; 51]

ructions *n* **rumpus**, fuss, uproar, dispute, controversy, disturbance, to-do (*informal*) [➡CHAOS AND UPROAR; 51]

rudder 1 *part of* **aircraft** [➡AIRCRAFT; 1148] **2** *part of* **ship or boat** [➡PARTS OF A SHIP OR BOAT; 1151]

ruddiness *n* **redness**, rosiness, glow, blush, flush, reddishness [➡COMPLEXION; 480] *Opposite*: pallor

ruddy *adj* **reddish**, rosy, flushed, glowing, healthy-looking, red [➡COMPLEXION; 480] *Opposite*: pale

rude 1 *adj* **impolite**, discourteous, insolent, bad-mannered, ill-mannered, uncouth, boorish, disrespectful, offensive, vulgar [➡RUDE AND HOSTILE; 625] *Opposite*: polite **2** *adj* **foul**, crude, offensive, vulgar, foul-mouthed, obscene, indecent [➡BAD MANNERS AND SOCIAL SKILLS; 521] *Opposite*: polite

rudeness *n* **impoliteness**, insolence, discourtesy, offensiveness, vulgarity, boorishness, disrespect [➡BAD MANNERS AND SOCIAL SKILLS; 521] *Opposite*: politeness

rudimentary *adj* **basic**, elementary, simple, fundamental, primary, undeveloped [➡EASE AND SIMPLICITY; 200] *Opposite*: advanced

rudiments *n* **basics**, essentials, fundamentals, principles, beginnings, bare bones (*informal*) [➡BASIC DETAILS; 688]

rue *v* **regret**, lament, repent, deplore, feel sorry about, be sorry for [➡CHANGE OF MOOD AND COMPOSURE; 580]

rueful *adj* **regretful**, remorseful, apologetic, repentant, contrite, sheepish, doleful [➡EMBARRASSMENT AND HUMILIATION; 542] *Opposite*: cheerful

ruff *part of* **bird** [➡PARTS OF A BIRD; 1006]

ruffian (*dated*) *n* **thug**, tough guy, gangster, hooligan (*informal*), hood (*slang*) [➡VILLAINS AND THUGS; 947]

ruffle 1 *v* **disturb**, tousle, rumple, upset, dishevel, make a mess of, mess up (*informal*) [➡WORSEN APPEARANCE; 382] *Opposite*:

smooth **2** *v* **perturb**, upset, annoy, disrupt, distress, unsettle [➡ UPSET, DISTRESS, AND HUMILIATE; 567] *Opposite*: calm

rufiyaa *type of* **currency** [➡ CURRENCIES; 798]

rug **1** *n* **carpet**, mat, hearth rug, sheepskin, runner [➡ FURNISHING AND HOUSEHOLD LINENS; 860] **2** *n* (*informal*) **wig**, toupee, hairpiece, periwig [➡ HAIRSTYLES AND HAIRPIECES; 488] **3** *n* **blanket**, car rug, throw, cover, bedspread [➡ FURNISHING AND HOUSEHOLD LINENS; 860]

rugby *type of* **ball game** [➡ HOBBIES, GAMES, AND SPORTS; 875]

rugged **1** *adj* **rocky**, rough, craggy, uneven, jagged, sharp, harsh, bleak [➡ PHYSICAL TEXTURE; 1222] *Opposite*: rolling **2** *adj* **strong-featured**, craggy, weathered, furrowed, rough, masculine, manly, chiseled [➡ COMPLEXION; 480] **3** *adj* **strong**, hardy, tough, robust, resilient, muscular, sinewy [➡ STRENGTH; 201] *Opposite*: weak **4** *adj* **testing**, demanding, difficult, harsh, tough, severe, punishing, unforgiving [➡ PHYSICALLY UNPLEASANT; 226] *Opposite*: easy **5** *adj* **well-built**, sturdy, tough, robust, strong, resilient [➡ STRENGTH; 201] *Opposite*: flimsy

ruggedness **1** *n* **roughness**, rockiness, harshness, jaggedness, cragginess, unevenness, sharpness, bleakness [➡ PHYSICAL TEXTURE; 1222] *Opposite*: smoothness **2** *n* **strong features**, cragginess, handsomeness, manliness, masculinity [➡ BUILD; 477] *Opposite*: roundness **3** *n* **toughness**, resilience, stamina, endurance, strength, survival skills, staying power [➡ COMPLEXION; 480] *Opposite*: weakness **4** *n* **unforgiving nature**, difficulty, harshness, toughness, severity, punishing nature, demanding nature [➡ PHYSICALLY UNPLEASANT; 226] **5** *n* **resilience**, sturdiness, toughness, robustness, strength, rugged construction [➡ STRENGTH; 201] *Opposite*: flimsiness

rug rat (*informal humorous*) *n* [➡ CHILD OR YOUTH; 945]

ruin **1** *n* **remains**, wreck, debris, wreckage, shell [➡ REMAINDER AND REMAINDERS; 125] **2** *n* **devastation**, shambles, decay, destruction, collapse, disintegration, deterioration, loss [➡ DIFFICULT SITUATIONS; 72] *Opposite*: regeneration **3** *n* **decline**, downfall, defeat, fall, disaster, death [➡ FAILURE; 77] *Opposite*: improvement **4** *v* **damage**, wreck, spoil, destroy, devastate, reduce to rubble, impair, trash (*informal*), mess up (*informal*) [➡ DESTRUCTION AND DEMOLITION; 359] *Opposite*: mend

ruination **1** *n* **undoing**, downfall, ruin, curse, destruction, nemesis (*literary*) [➡ FAILURE; 77] *Opposite*: making **2** *n* **destruction**, loss, ruin, calamity, devastation, perdition (*archaic or literary*) [➡ DIFFICULT SITUATIONS; 72] *Opposite*: salvation

ruined **1** *adj* **bankrupt**, insolvent, out of business, broke (*informal*), cleaned out (*informal*), bust (*informal*) [➡ POVERTY AND POOR; 892] *Opposite*: solvent **2** *adj* **tumbledown**, crumbling, derelict, abandoned, uninhabited, in ruins [➡ IN BAD REPAIR; 1234] *Opposite*: renovated

ruinous *adj* **disastrous**, damaging, harmful, devastating, catastrophic, dire [➡ DANGEROUS; 236] *Opposite*: advantageous

rule **1** *n* **instruction**, law, regulation, decree, statute, imperative, canon, tenet, ruling, directive [➡ THE LAW AND LEGAL AUTHORITY; 814] **2** *n* **regime**, power, control, leadership, reign, government, management, administration [➡ REALMS AND RULES; 824] **3** *type of* **measuring device** [➡ MEASURING DEVICES; 1123] **4** *v* **govern**, reign, run, administrate, have power over, lead, control, preside over, direct, manage [➡ BE IN CHARGE; 270] *Opposite*: follow

rulebook *n* **manual**, rules, instructions, directory, rubric, guidelines, directions, procedures [➡ MANUALS AND INSTRUCTIONS; 589]

rule out **1** *v* **exclude**, dismiss, reject, discount, discard, forget about [➡ NOT PAY ATTENTION; 764] *Opposite*: consider **2** *v* **prevent**, exclude, ban, prohibit, forbid, preclude (*formal*) [➡ MAKE IMPOSSIBLE; 276] *Opposite*: facilitate

ruler *n* **monarch**, sovereign, leader, head of state, potentate [➡ RULERS AND ARISTOCRACY; 823] *Opposite*: subject

rules and regulations *n* [➡ WAYS OF DOING THINGS; 294]

rule the roost *v* **be in control**, be in charge, reign supreme, be in the saddle, be in the driver's seat, be top dog (*informal*) [➡ BE IN CHARGE; 270]

ruling **1** *n* **decision**, verdict, edict, judgment, declaration, decree [➡ MAKE DECISIONS AND CHOICES; 752] **2** *adj* **presiding**, reigning, governing, dominant, sovereign, chief [➡ MOST IMPORTANT AND MAIN; 193] *Opposite*: subordinate

ruling body *n* **council**, administration, government, assembly, legislative body [➡ LEGISLATIVE BODIES AND LEGISLATION; 809]

rumba *type of* **dance** [➡ DANCE; 903]

rumble **1** *v* **grumble**, thunder, crash, growl, roll, roar, reverberate, resound, boom [➡ EMIT CONTINUOUS SOUNDS; 366] **2** *n* **roar**, thunder, crash, growl, grumble, roll, reverberation, boom [➡ CONTINUOUS SOUNDS; 1258]

rumble strip *n* [➡ TRAVEL: TRAFFIC PROBLEMS AND TRAFFIC MANAGEMENT; 323]

rumbling (*informal*) *n* **indication**, early sign, beginning, warning sign, rumor, intimation, hint, suggestion, whispering [➡ SUGGEST, HINT, AND COMMENT; 612]

rumbustious *adj* **boisterous**, exuberant, unruly, swashbuckling, cavalier, swaggering [➡ POMPOUS, LOUD, AND OVERCONFIDENT; 635] *Opposite*: reticent

ruminant *adj* **reflective**, thoughtful, contemplative, speculative, deep, meditative, philosophical, calculating, retrospective, pensive, musing, deliberative (*formal*), cogitative (*formal*) [➡ PENSIVENESS AND INTEREST; 538] *Opposite*: thoughtless

ruminate **1** *v* **ponder**, think over, reflect, chew over, meditate, mull over, deliberate, contemplate, muse, cogitate (*formal*) [➡ THINK AND REFLECT; 743] **2** *v* **chew**, graze, browse, crop, pasture, chew the cud [➡ EAT AND NOT EAT; 710]

rumination **1** *n* **reflection**, pondering, contemplation, musing, thought, meditation, cogitation (*formal*) [➡ THINK AND REFLECT; 743] **2** *n* **chewing**, grazing, browsing, chewing the cud [➡ EAT AND NOT EAT; 710]

ruminative *adj* **thoughtful**, pensive, reflective, contemplative, speculative, deep, meditative, philosophical, calculating, retrospective, cogitative (*formal*), deliberative (*formal*) [➡ PENSIVENESS AND INTEREST; 538] *Opposite*: thoughtless

rummage *v* **search**, look through, grope, fumble, poke around, delve, ferret out [➡ SEEK POSSESSION AND SEARCH; 456]

rummage sale *n* **sale**, yard sale, garage sale, jumble sale (*UK*), car boot sale (*UK*) [➡ SALES AND SHOWS; 443]

rumor 1 *n* **claim**, report, unconfirmed report, belief, allegation, opinion, story (*informal*) [➡ THE ORAL TRADITION; 677] *Opposite*: fact **2** *n* **speculation**, opinion, gossip, talk, tittle-tattle, word, the word on the street, chitchat (*informal*), buzz (*informal*) [➡ THE ORAL TRADITION; 677] **3** *v* **say**, believe, allege, claim, speculate, spread the word, opine (*formal*) [➡ GOSSIP; 678] *Opposite*: confirm

rumored *adj* **supposed**, thought, whispered, alleged, held, believed, said, understood, assumed [➡ UNCERTAIN; 175] *Opposite*: true

rumor has it that *adv* [➡ EXPRESSIONS OF UNCERTAINTY; 560]

rumor mill *n* **grapevine**, network, newsmongers, gossips, tattlers, word on the street, bush telegraph (*informal*) [➡ INTERFERING PEOPLE AND TATTLETALES; 950]

rumormonger *n* **gossip**, tattletale, scandalmonger, gossipmonger, telltale [➡ INTERFERING PEOPLE AND TATTLETALES; 950]

rumormongering *n* [➡ GOSSIP; 678]

rump 1 *n* **hindquarters**, back end, rear, buttocks, rear end [➡ PARTS OF THE BODY: TORSO; 693] **2** *type of* **steak** [➡ TYPES AND CUTS OF MEAT; 1177]

rumple *v* **wrinkle**, crumple, crease, crinkle, pucker, scrunch up, mess up (*informal*) [➡ CHANGE OF SHAPE; 385] *Opposite*: tidy

rumpled *adj* **crumpled**, creased, untidy, messy, bedraggled, disheveled, puckered, unkempt, scruffy, wrinkled [➡ IN BAD REPAIR; 1234] *Opposite*: tidy

rumpus *n* **disturbance**, commotion, furor, brouhaha, fuss, stir, hullabaloo, tumult, outcry, to-do (*informal*) [➡ CHAOS AND UPROAR; 51]

run 1 *v* **sprint**, jog, lope, scuttle, scamper, dart, dash, scurry, rush, hurry [➡ MOVE FAST; 313] **2** *v* **flow**, stream, trickle, course, pour out, seep, gush, flood, spill [➡ MOVE FAST; 313] **3** *v* **proceed**, happen, go, progress, move along, pass, go by, pass by, move forward [➡ HAPPEN; 27] **4** *v* **manage**, administer, govern, administrate, lead, control, be in charge, be in power, handle, manipulate, direct, rule, organize [➡ BE IN CHARGE; 270] **5** *v* **operate**, function, process [➡ USE; 467] **6** *v* **move**, pass, cast, throw [➡ MOVE SOMETHING TO ANOTHER LOCATION; 324] **7** *v* **continue**, extend, reach, stretch, go, last, carry on, persist, keep on, go on [➡ CONTINUE TO EXIST; 17] **8** *v* **compete**, enter, participate, take part, contend [➡ COMPETE, CONTEND, AND COMBAT; 303] **9** *n* **course**, track, route, lane, path [➡ PATHWAYS; 1110] **10** *n* **sequence**, series, chain, string, list, spate, succession, cycle, train [➡ PERIODS OF TIME; 90] **11** *n* **enclosure**, pen, cage, coop, paddock [➡ ANIMAL OR BIRD ACCOMMODATIONS; 1079] **12** *n* **outing**, trip, ride, excursion, visit [➡ TRAVEL: JOURNEYS AND TRIPS; 318] **13** *n* **sprint**, race, lope, dart, dash, scuttle [➡ PROCEED AND GO; 305]

runabout 1 *type of* **car** [➡ BIKES, CARS, AND CARRIAGES; 1149] **2** *n* **wanderer**, rover, rolling stone, nomad, traveler, drifter [➡ NOMADIC AND ROOTLESS LIFESTYLES; 884]

run after *v* **pursue**, chase, go after, follow, hound [➡ ACCOMPANY AND FOLLOW; 337]

run aground *adj* [➡ LACK OF ACTIVITY OR MOTION; 342]

run along *v* **go away**, go, leave, depart, take leave, take off (*informal*), scram (*informal*), split (*slang*) [➡ LEAVE AND GO AWAY; 8] *Opposite*: stay

run amok *v* **go berserk**, be in a frenzy, run riot, go on the rampage, go wild, rampage, riot [➡ GIVING VENT TO EMOTIONS; 679]

run a risk *v* **take a risk**, play a dangerous game, sail close to the wind, court disaster, play Russian roulette [➡ GAMBLE AND TAKE RISKS; 466]

run around *v* **associate**, spend time, keep company, hang out (*informal*), hang (*slang*) [➡ ESTABLISHING RELATIONSHIPS WITH OTHERS; 974]

run around after *v* [➡ TAKE CARE OF AND SPOIL; 300]

run away *v* **escape**, flee, run off, abscond, elope, abandon, turn your back on [➡ RUN AWAY AND AVOID; 10]

runaway 1 *n* **escapee**, absentee, absconder, fugitive [➡ RUNAWAYS AND ABSENTEES; 9] **2** *adj* (*informal*) **bestselling**, blockbusting, hit, roaring, huge [➡ SUCCESSFUL AND PROMISING; 81]

runaway success *n* **big hit**, smash, smash hit, blockbuster (*informal*), barnburner (*informal*) [➡ SUCCESS; 82]

runaway victory *n* [➡ SUCCESS; 82]

run by *v* **explain**, describe, tell, impart, acquaint, pass on, apprise (*formal*) [➡ EXPLAIN AND CLARIFY; 610]

run counter to *v* [➡ DIFFERENCE; 149]

run down 1 *v* **belittle**, criticize, knock, disparage, put down, rubbish (*UK*) [➡ ACCUSE, BLAME, AND CRITICIZE; 641] *Opposite*: praise **2** *v* **bring to an end**, close down, wind up, shut down, peter out [➡ CAUSE TO STOP; 266] *Opposite*: start

rundown *n* **details**, list, listing, inventory, record, account, enumeration [➡ SUMMARIES, OUTLINES, AND EXCERPTS; 588]

run-down 1 *adj* **dilapidated**, ramshackle, shabby, neglected, derelict, in bad repair, in bad condition, badly maintained, tumbledown, ragged, worn, seedy, beat-up (*informal*) [➡ IN BAD REPAIR; 1234] *Opposite*: well-kept **2** *adj* **exhausted**, tired, weak, wearied, worn-out, beat (*informal*), fried (*slang*), shattered (*UK*) [➡ TIRED, ASLEEP, AND UNCONSCIOUS; 738] *Opposite*: energetic **3** *adj* **under the weather**, worn out, tired, weary, washed out [➡ UNFIT AND WEAK; 739] *Opposite*: well

rune *n* **character**, letter, symbol, sign, hieroglyph, hieroglyphic [➡ SYMBOLS, SIGNS, AND NUMBERS; 596]

run for it *v* [➡ RUN AWAY AND AVOID; 10]

rung *n* **step**, stair, tread, stage [➡ SUPPORTS AND BASES; 1255]

runic *type of* **alphabet** [➡ SYMBOLS, SIGNS, AND NUMBERS; 596]

run-in (*informal*) *n* **argument**, confrontation, quarrel, clash, disagreement, altercation, face-off, fight, tiff, row [➡ ARGUMENTS; 47]

run into 1 *v* **come across**, bump into, meet by chance, encounter [➡ EXPERIENCE AND ENCOUNTER; 582] **2** *v* **hit**, bump into, crash into, collide with, run over, smash into, knock down [➡ CONTACT: IMPACT; 413] *Opposite*: miss

runnel *n* [➡ WATERCOURSES; 1111]

runner 1 *n* **sprinter**, jogger, racer, contender, competitor [➡ PEOPLE IN SPORTS AND LEISURE; 876] **2** *n* **messenger**, courier, gofer (*informal*) [➡ MESSENGERS AND COURIERS; 852] **3** *n* **candidate**, contender, entrant, participant, competitor, contestant [➡ COMPETITORS; 41]

runner-up n **second place**, person in second place, silver medalist, second to finish, next best person, person with consolation prize [➡ PEOPLE IN SPORTS AND LEISURE; 876]

runniness n [➡ FLUID AND NONSOLID; 1213]

running 1 n **management**, administration, organization, operation, controlling, overseeing [➡ CARRY OUT AN ACTION; 269] 2 adv **in a row**, consecutively, successively, in succession, seriatim, on the trot (UK) [➡ AFTER, LAST, AND FOLLOWING; 165]

running joke n [➡ JOKES AND TEASING; 674]

runny adj **liquid**, fluid, gooey, soft, thin [➡ FLUID AND NONSOLID; 1213] Opposite: set

run off v **flee**, escape, run away, decamp [➡ RUN AWAY AND AVOID; 10]

run-of-the-mill adj **mediocre**, ordinary, middling, average, undistinguished, basic, unremarkable, commonplace, everyday, plain, mundane, regular, no-frills (informal), common or garden (UK) [➡ ORDINARINESS; 244] Opposite: extraordinary

run on v **go on**, carry on, continue, keep going [➡ CONTINUE AN ACTION; 262] Opposite: stop

run out v **end**, expire, come to an end, finish [➡ DISAPPEAR; 4]

run over 1 v **crush**, hit, squash, flatten, collide with, run into, knock down [➡ CONTACT: IMPACT; 413] 2 v **explain**, summarize, go over, run through, cover, recap, recapitulate (formal) [➡ EXPLAIN AND CLARIFY; 610]

run rings around v **outshine**, beat, outdo, outstrip, outperform, surpass, trample over, thrash, walk over (informal), hammer (informal) [➡ BEAT AND DEFEAT; 80]

run riot v **run amok**, go on the rampage, riot, go berserk, go wild, rampage [➡ GIVING VENT TO EMOTIONS; 679]

runt n **smallest**, weakest, littlest [➡ LAZY OR UNSUCCESSFUL PEOPLE; 948]

run the gauntlet v **undergo**, experience, face, suffer, endure, bear [➡ EXPERIENCE AND ENCOUNTER; 582]

run through 1 v **use up**, exhaust, eat through, go through, deplete, get through, waste [➡ USE UP AND WASTE; 474] Opposite: conserve 2 v **review**, go over, examine, consider, look over [➡ READ; 758] 3 v **pervade**, spread through, underlie, permeate [➡ EXIST IN A PLACE; 19] 4 v **rehearse**, practice, try out, go through [➡ CARRY OUT AN ACTION; 269] 5 v **infect**, contaminate, pollute [➡ DIRTY AND CONTAMINATE; 404] 6 v (literary) **spear**, impale, stab, jab [➡ MOVE PAST, INTO, OR THROUGH SOMETHING; 331]

run-through 1 n **rehearsal**, practice, dry run, test run, test, tryout, trial, drill [➡ PREPARATORY EVENTS; 57] 2 n **review**, survey, summary, overview, résumé [➡ SUMMARIES, OUTLINES, AND EXCERPTS; 588]

run to v [➡ AMOUNT TO AND EQUAL; 70]

run to ground v [➡ GET; 420]

run up 1 v **accumulate**, amass, collect, incur, build up [➡ GET; 420] Opposite: discharge 2 v **sew**, create, make, put together [➡ CRAFTS AND CARVING; 355]

run-up 1 n **run**, approach, advance [➡ PAST; 84] 2 n (UK) **approach**, lead-in, introduction, buildup [➡ BEGINNINGS; 53]

runway n **landing strip**, airstrip, landing field, taxiway, flight strip, takeoff strip [➡ AIRWAYS; 1109]

rupee type of **currency** [➡ CURRENCIES; 798]

rupiah type of **currency** [➡ CURRENCIES; 798]

rupture 1 n **break**, crack, tear, split, fissure, opening, gash, breach, gap [➡ HOLES, GAPS, AND FORKS; 1252] 2 n **disagreement**, falling-out, split, breakup, separation, estrangement, division, break, breach, rift [➡ ARGUMENTS; 47] 3 v **break**, crack, burst, come apart, rip apart, rip open, shatter [➡ TEAR, BREAK, AND CUT; 360]

rural adj **country**, rustic, pastoral, bucolic, countryside [➡ THE COUNTRYSIDE AND OUTDOOR SPACES; 1071] Opposite: urban

ruse n **trick**, dodge, subterfuge, wile, con, hoax, deception, ploy, stunt, plot, scam (slang) [➡ DECEPTION AND LIES; 660]

rush 1 v **run**, hurry, dash, sprint, flash, scurry, scuttle, tear, charge, get a move on (informal) [➡ MOVE FAST; 313] Opposite: dawdle 2 v **hurry**, precipitate, hasten, dash, bolt, hustle (informal) [➡ OVERDO SOMETHING; 290] 3 n **haste**, hurry, urgency, flash [➡ SPEED; 102] 4 n **blast**, current, gale, gust, blow, stream, draft [➡ SUDDEN EVENTS; 52]

rushed adj **hurried**, quick, swift, hasty [➡ HAPPENING QUICKLY; 104] Opposite: leisurely

rushes n **unedited prints**, dailies, first prints, raw footage, footage [➡ FILM; 901]

russet type of **brown** [➡ COLORS; 1224]

rust 1 n **corrosion**, oxidation, erosion, corruption, decomposition, tarnishing [➡ GO BAD AND CORRODE; 390] 2 v **corrode**, oxidize, tarnish, erode, decompose, corrupt [➡ GO BAD AND CORRODE; 390]

rust bucket (informal humorous) n [➡ BIKES, CARS, AND CARRIAGES; 1149]

rust-free adj [➡ IN GOOD REPAIR; 1232]

rustic adj **rural**, country, pastoral, bucolic, countryside [➡ THE COUNTRYSIDE AND OUTDOOR SPACES; 1071] Opposite: urban

rustle n **crackle**, crunch, whisper, swish [➡ CONTINUOUS SOUNDS; 1258]

rustler n **thief**, poacher, robber, horse thief, cattle thief, livestock thief [➡ CRIMINALS; 821]

rustle up (informal) v **prepare**, concoct, put together, make, produce, find, whip up, knock together (informal) [➡ MEAL PREPARATION; 354]

rustproof 1 adj **nonrusting**, rust-free, rustproofed, stainless-steel, corrosion-proof, nonreactive, inert, coated, sealed, waterproofed [➡ DURABLE; 1210] 2 v **seal**, make rustproof, waterproof, coat, paint, prime, proof, treat [➡ DECORATE, ADORN, AND APPLY COATINGS; 405]

rusty 1 adj **corroded**, oxidized, tarnished, eroded [➡ IN BAD REPAIR; 1234] 2 adj **out of practice**, unpracticed, unaccustomed, off form, unhabituated, out of shape [➡ UNSKILLED; 529]

rut n **furrow**, groove, channel, runnel, pothole [➡ HOLES, GAPS, AND FORKS; 1252]

rutabaga type of **root vegetable** [➡ FRUIT AND VEGETABLES; 1176]

ruthless *adj* **cruel**, callous, brutal, pitiless, merciless, cold-blooded, unfeeling, hardhearted, heartless, hard-nosed (*informal*) [➡ SELFISH AND UNKIND; 505] *Opposite*: merciful

ruthlessness *n* **callousness**, cruelty, mercilessness, brutality, heartlessness, cold-bloodedness, hard-heartedness [➡ SELFISH AND UNKIND; 505] *Opposite*: mercy

rutted *adj* **uneven**, furrowed, potholed, bumpy [➡ PHYSICAL TEXTURE; 1222] *Opposite*: smooth

RV *n* **recreational vehicle**, camper, motor home, mobile home, trailer, motor caravan (*UK*) [➡ VEHICLES; 1145]

rye *type of* **cereal** [➡ CEREAL FOODS; 1178]

rye bread *type of* **bread** [➡ BREAD, FLOUR, AND BREAD PRODUCTS; 1179]

rye grass *type of* **grass** [➡ GRASS; 1031]

S

sabbatical *n* **study leave**, leave, time off, retreat, time out, leave of absence [➡ PERIODS OF REST; 91]

saber *type of* **sword or knife** [➡ SWORDS AND KNIVES; 1157]

saber-rattler *n* [➡ UNCOOPERATIVE OR REBELLIOUS PEOPLE; 566]

saber rattling *n* **display of force**, bravado, empty threats, bluffing, aggression [➡ CRITICISMS AND ANGRY OUTBURSTS; 50]

sable *type of* **black** [➡ COLORS; 1224]

sabotage **1** *n* **disruption**, damage, vandalism, interference, interruption [➡ BAD BEHAVIOR OR ACTIONS; 254] **2** *v* **disrupt**, damage, vandalize, interfere with, interrupt, harm, incapacitate, impair, undermine [➡ MAKE IMPOSSIBLE; 276]

saboteur *n* **vandal**, terrorist, ecowarrior, computer hacker, hunt saboteur [➡ UNCOOPERATIVE OR REBELLIOUS PEOPLE; 566]

sac *n* **bag**, sack, pouch, case, pod, bladder [➡ CONTAINERS, RECEPTACLES, AND PACKAGING; 1245]

saccharine **1** *adj* **sugary**, sickly, sweet, syrupy, treacly [➡ TASTE; 703] *Opposite:* sour **2** *adj* **sentimental**, slushy, gushy, mawkish, cloying, sickly, sickly-sweet, treacly [➡ IN POOR TASTE AND OVERSENTIMENTAL; 229] *Opposite:* unsentimental

sacerdotal *adj* **priestly**, clerical, ecclesiastic, religious, spiritual [➡ RELIGIONS AND RELIGIOUS PRACTICES; 777]

sachet *n* **envelope**, packet, pouch [➡ CONTAINERS, RECEPTACLES, AND PACKAGING; 1245]

sack **1** *n* **bag**, brown bag, gunnysack, carryall, pouch, sac [➡ CONTAINERS, RECEPTACLES, AND PACKAGING; 1245] **2** *n* (*informal*) **dismissal**, termination, layoff, pink slip, discharge [➡ REVOKE STATUS; 459] **3** *v* (*informal*) **dismiss**, give somebody notice, throw out, terminate, lay off, fire (*informal*), kick out (*informal*), give somebody the boot (*informal*), boot out (*informal*), give somebody a pink slip (*informal*), give somebody their walking papers (*informal*), give somebody the hook (*slang*), can (*slang*), discharge (*formal*), give somebody their cards (*UK*) [➡ REVOKE STATUS; 459] *Opposite:* employ **4** *v* **ransack**, plunder, destroy, pillage, tear apart, ruin, despoil [➡ DESTRUCTION AND DEMOLITION, 359]

sacking (*informal*) **1** *n* **dismissal**, discharge, job loss, notice, termination, layoff, firing (*informal*), the boot (*informal*), walking papers (*informal*), pink slip (*informal*) [➡ REVOKE STATUS; 459] **2** *type of* **fabric from plants** [➡ FABRICS; 1132]

sacrament *n* **rite**, ceremony, ritual, service, mass [➡ RELIGIONS AND RELIGIOUS PRACTICES; 777]

sacred *adj* **holy**, blessed, consecrated, hallowed, revered, sanctified, sacrosanct [➡ RELIGIOUS CONCEPTS; 776] *Opposite:* secular

sacredness *n* [➡ RELIGIOUS CONCEPTS; 776]

sacrifice **1** *n* **price**, toll, cost, loss, expense, forfeiture, penalty [➡ FORGO AND DENY ONESELF; 449] **2** *v* **give up**, forgo, forfeit, let go, surrender, lose [➡ FORGO AND DENY ONESELF; 449]

sacrilege *n* **blasphemy**, desecration, profanity, irreverence, violation, disrespect [➡ RELIGIOUS CONCEPTS; 776] *Opposite:* reverence

sacrilegious *adj* **blasphemous**, irreverent, heretical, impious, disrespectful, profane (*formal*) [➡ RELIGIOUS CONCEPTS; 776] *Opposite:* reverent

sacrosanct **1** *adj* **sacred**, revered, holy, sanctified [➡ RELIGIOUS CONCEPTS; 776] **2** *adj* **inviolable**, untouchable, off limits, protected [➡ STRENGTH; 201]

sacrum *type of* **bone** [➡ THE BONES AND JOINTS; 719]

sad **1** *adj* **unhappy**, miserable, depressed, gloomy, down, low, wretched, dejected, despondent, desolate, forlorn, sorrowful, melancholy, woeful, blue (*informal*) [➡ SADNESS, DISTRESS, AND DESPAIR; 539] *Opposite:* happy **2** *adj* **depressing**, gloomy, miserable, cheerless, distressing, heartbreaking, poignant, moving [➡ EMOTIONALLY UNPLEASANT AND UPSETTING; 227] *Opposite:* cheerful

sadden *v* **depress**, distress, upset, dismay, pain, bring down [➡ UPSET, DISTRESS, AND HUMILIATE; 567] *Opposite:* cheer

saddened *adj* [➡ SADNESS, DISTRESS, AND DESPAIR; 539]

saddening *adj* [➡ EMOTIONALLY UNPLEASANT AND UPSETTING; 227]

saddlebag *n* **basket**, bag, pannier, carrier, holdall (*UK*) [➡ CONTAINERS, RECEPTACLES, AND PACKAGING; 1245]

saddle horse *type of* **horse** [➡ HORSES; 985]

saddle with *v* **burden**, encumber, weigh down, dump on, land, load, leave, impose, stick with (*informal*), lumber (*UK*) [➡ GIVE TOO MUCH AND OVERBURDEN; 437]

sadism *n* [➡ MALICIOUS ACTIONS OR BEHAVIOR; 296]

sadistic *adj* **cruel**, nasty, callous, heartless, vicious, brutal, aggressive, inhuman, violent, merciless, gloating [➡ AGGRESSIVE AND BELLIGERENT; 518] *Opposite:* empathetic

sadly **1** *adv* **unhappily**, miserably, gloomily, wretchedly, dejectedly, despondently, desolately, forlornly, sorrowfully, woefully [➡ SADNESS, DISTRESS, AND DESPAIR; 539] *Opposite:* happily **2** *adv* **unfortunately**, unluckily, regrettably, alas [➡ EXPRESSIONS OF REGRET; 547] *Opposite:* luckily

sadness *n* **unhappiness**, misery, depression, gloom, wretchedness, dejection, despondency, desolation, heartache, sorrow, melancholy, grief, woe, blues (*informal*) [➡ SADNESS, DISTRESS, AND DESPAIR; 539] *Opposite:* happiness

safari *n* **trek**, expedition, trip, search, quest, field trip, camera safari [➡ TRAVEL: JOURNEYS AND TRIPS; 318]

safari jacket *type of* **jacket** [➡ GARMENTS AND OUTFITS; 865]

safari park *n* [➡ THE COUNTRYSIDE AND OUTDOOR SPACES; 1071]

safe **1** *adj* **harmless**, benign, innocuous, innocent, nonviolent, nontoxic, anodyne (*literary*) [➡ SAFE AND SAFETY; 191]

Opposite: dangerous **2** *adj* **secure**, protected, sheltered, in safe hands, out of harm's way, safe and sound, in one piece [➡ SAFE AND SAFETY; 191] *Opposite*: unsafe **3** *adj* **unharmed**, undamaged, uninjured, unhurt, unscathed, safe and sound, secure, alive and well, untouched, all right [➡ SAFE AND SOUND; 737] **4** *adj* **reliable**, dependable, trustworthy, careful, cautious, prudent, sound [➡ HONEST AND RELIABLE; 502] *Opposite*: unsafe **5** *n* **strongbox**, lockbox, safe-deposit box, vault [➡ CONTAINERS, RECEPTACLES, AND PACKAGING; 1245]

safe and sound *adj* **unharmed**, undamaged, uninjured, unhurt, unscathed, safe, secure, alive and well, untouched, all right, in one piece [➡ SAFE AND SOUND; 737]

safe as houses (*UK*) *adj* [➡ SAFE AND SAFETY; 191]

safe bet *n* [➡ CERTAIN; 174]

safeguard 1 *n* **protection**, precaution, defense, safety measure, safety device, safety net [➡ SAFE AND SAFETY; 191] **2** *v* **defend**, protect, preserve, maintain, uphold, guard, look after, shield [➡ PREVENT CONTACT OR ATTACK; 419] *Opposite*: endanger

> **Compare and Contrast:** *safeguard, protect, defend, guard, shield*
>
> CORE MEANING: to keep safe from actual or potential damage or attack
>
> *safeguard* to take steps to prevent somebody or something from being harmed or damaged; *protect* to keep somebody or something from any kind of harm or damage; *defend* to deter an actual or threatened attack; *guard* to work to prevent damage, loss, or attack by being vigilant and taking defensive measures; *shield* to prevent harm, damage, or attack by using a physical barrier or by intervening in a protective way.

safeguarding *n* **protection**, preservation, conservation, maintenance, upkeep, continuation, continuance, defense [➡ PREVENT CONTACT OR ATTACK; 419] *Opposite*: destruction

safe haven *n* **refuge**, asylum, haven, sanctuary [➡ SAFE BUILDINGS OR PLACES; 1093]

safe house *n* **hideout**, hideaway, retreat, refuge, hidey-hole (*informal*) [➡ SAFE BUILDINGS OR PLACES; 1093]

safekeeping *n* **protection**, care, security, custody, charge, safety, trust, good hands [➡ SAFE AND SAFETY; 191]

safely *adv* **securely**, carefully, firmly [➡ SAFE AND SAFETY; 191] *Opposite*: unsafely

safe place *n* **refuge**, safe haven, hideaway, haven, sanctuary, retreat, asylum [➡ SAFE BUILDINGS OR PLACES; 1093]

safety *n* **care**, security, protection, shelter, well-being, welfare [➡ SAFE AND SAFETY; 191] *Opposite*: danger

safety belt *n* **seat belt**, strap, restraint, harness, safety harness [➡ FASTENERS, LINKS, AND NETWORKS; 1247]

safety glass *type of* **glass** [➡ GLASS; 1136]

safety net *n* **safety device**, safeguard, fail-safe, guard, shield, screen, fallback [➡ SAFE AND SAFETY; 191]

safety valve 1 *n* **fail-safe**, valve, safety device, safety

precaution, overflow [➡ PARTS OF MACHINES AND TOOLS; 1118] **2** *n* **release**, channel, outlet [➡ SAFE AND SAFETY; 191]

saffron 1 *type of* **spice** [➡ HERBS AND SPICES; 1175] **2** *type of* **yellow** [➡ COLORS; 1224]

sag 1 *v* **droop**, wilt, slump, flag, drop, hang down, loll, bend [➡ CHANGE OF SHAPE; 385] **2** *n* **drop**, slump, dip, fall, depression, slackness [➡ CHANGE OF INTENSITY: LESS; 395]

saga *n* **epic**, account, chronicle, tale, legend, narrative, history, story, yarn (*informal*) [➡ THE ORAL TRADITION; 677]

sagacious *adj* **wise**, knowledgeable, learned, erudite, perceptive, intelligent, astute, clever, shrewd, discerning, sage (*literary*) [➡ KNOWLEDGE AND WISDOM; 558] *Opposite*: foolish

sagaciousness (*formal*) *see* **sagacity**

sagacity *n* **wisdom**, knowledge, erudition, perceptiveness, intelligence, insight, shrewdness, understanding, discernment, prudence, sagaciousness (*formal*) [➡ KNOWLEDGE AND WISDOM; 558] *Opposite*: stupidity

sage 1 *n* (*literary*) **adviser**, mentor, elder, savant, statesman, wise man, solon (*literary*) [➡ TALENTED OR INTELLIGENT PEOPLE; 528] **2** *type of* **herb** [➡ HERBS AND SPICES; 1175] **3** *adj* (*literary*) **learned**, erudite, perceptive, intelligent, astute, clever, shrewd, discerning, sagacious (*formal*) [➡ KNOWLEDGE AND WISDOM; 558]

sagebrush *type of* **shrub or bush** [➡ BUSHES AND SHRUBS; 1027]

sage green *type of* **green** [➡ COLORS; 1224]

sagginess *n* [➡ SHAPELESSNESS; 1219]

sagging *adj* **drooping**, wilting, flaccid, floppy, slumped, bending, baggy, saggy, shapeless, flabby (*informal*) [➡ SHAPELESSNESS; 1219]

saggy *see* **sagging**

Sagitta *type of* **constellation** [➡ HEAVENLY BODIES; 1061]

Sagittarius 1 *type of* **astrological sign** [➡ FATE, DESTINY, AND ASTROLOGY; 782] **2** *type of* **constellation** [➡ HEAVENLY BODIES; 1061]

said *adj* **alleged**, supposed, assumed, above, previously mentioned, aforesaid (*formal*), aforementioned (*formal*) [➡ EXPRESSIONS OF REFERENCE; 63]

sail 1 *v* **set sail**, navigate, cruise, voyage, put out to sea, cast off [➡ TRAVEL: WAYS OF TRAVELING; 320] **2** *v* **glide**, float, flow, drift, fly [➡ MOVE FAST; 313]

sailboat *type of* **sailing vessel** [➡ SHIPS AND BOATS; 1150]

sailcloth *type of* **fabric from plants** [➡ FABRICS; 1132]

sailfish *type of* **tropical fish** [➡ OCEAN FISH; 1009]

sailing *n* **boating**, cruising, yachting, navigation [➡ HOBBIES, GAMES, AND SPORTS; 875]

sailor *n* **seafarer**, mariner, navigator, deckhand, salt (*informal*), tar (*informal*) [➡ TRAVEL: TRAVELERS AND WALKERS; 319]

sailor hat *type of* **hat** [➡ ACCESSORIES, MILLINERY, AND LINGERIE; 867]

sail through *v* **do well**, do with ease, pass with flying colors, breeze through, ace (*slang*) [➡ SUCCEED AND WIN; 79] *Opposite*: fail

saint n [➡RELIGIOUS PEOPLE; 778]

Saint Bernard type of **large dog** [➡DOGS; 980]

saintliness n **virtue**, goodness, piety, holiness, devoutness, righteousness, godliness [➡RELIGIOUS CONCEPTS; 776] Opposite: evil

saintly adj **virtuous**, good, holy, pious, devout, righteous, godly, angelic [➡RELIGIOUS CONCEPTS; 776] Opposite: evil

saint's day n [➡RELIGIOUS CONCEPTS; 776]

salaam 1 n **greeting**, salutation, bow, nod, acknowledgment [➡GREETINGS, FAREWELLS, AND SALUTATIONS; 659] 2 v **greet**, bow, salute, nod, acknowledge [➡GESTURES AND GESTICULATION; 653]

salacious adj **risqué**, indecent, crude, improper, obscene, smutty, prurient [➡MORALLY BAD OR IMPROPER; 775]

salad n [➡PREPARED DISHES; 1170]

salad

◆ types of salad vegetables
alfalfa, arugula, bean sprout, capsicum, carrot, celery, cherry tomato, chicory, cress, cucumber, endive, green onion, lettuce, pepper, radicchio, radish, scallion, sorrel, sweet pepper, tomato, watercress

salad bar type of **eating place** [➡HOTELS, RESTAURANTS, AND CLUBS; 1082]

salad days (dated) n **youth**, prime, heyday [➡PLEASANT SITUATIONS; 74]

salamander type of **amphibian** [➡AMPHIBIANS; 1008]

salami type of **processed meat** [➡TYPES AND CUTS OF MEAT; 1177]

salaried adj **remunerated**, on the payroll, on the books, paid, compensated, waged (UK) [➡EMPLOYMENT STATUS; 831]

salary n **income**, pay, earnings, remuneration, payment, wages, wage, money [➡INCOME; 460]

See Compare and Contrast at **wage**.

sale 1 n **transaction**, deal, selling, retailing, vending, trade [➡BUSINESS ACTIVITIES AND PHENOMENA; 794] Opposite: purchase 2 n **auction**, clearance sale, rummage sale, garage sale, tag sale, yard sale, closeout sale, fire sale, closing-down sale (UK), jumble sale (UK), car boot sale (UK) [➡SALES AND SHOWS, 443]

sales assistant n **salesperson**, salesclerk, cashier, floorwalker, shop assistant (UK) [➡SELLERS; 442]

salesclerk see **sales assistant**

sales manager n [➡SELLERS; 442]

salesperson 1 n **rep**, seller, trader, marketer, peddler, vendor, hawker, sales rep (informal), purveyor (formal) [➡SELLERS; 442] 2 n **sales assistant**, salesclerk, cashier, floorwalker, shop assistant (UK) [➡SELLERS; 442]

sales rep (informal) n [➡SELLERS; 442]

sales representative n **salesperson**, rep, seller, trader, marketer, vendor, peddler, hawker, sales rep (informal), purveyor (formal) [➡SELLERS; 442]

salesroom type of **retail outlet** [➡RETAIL OUTLETS; 1083]

salient adj **noticeable**, striking, prominent, outstanding, relevant, significant, leading, main [➡MOST IMPORTANT AND MAIN; 193] Opposite: minor

saline adj **salty**, salt, brackish, briny, salted [➡TASTE; 703]

saliva n **spittle**, spit, drool, dribble, slobber, slaver [➡EXCRETION AND EXCRETA; 722]

salivate v **drool**, dribble, slobber, slaver [➡EXCRETION AND EXCRETA; 722]

sallow adj **yellow**, sickly, wan, washed-out, ashen, pallid, pale [➡COMPLEXION; 480]

sallowness n [➡COMPLEXION; 480]

sally 1 n **attack**, sortie, breakout, breakthrough, raid, strike, incursion [➡SUDDEN EVENTS; 52] 2 n **rush**, charge, dash, push [➡SUDDEN EVENTS; 52] 3 v **attack**, charge, raid, strike [➡PHYSICAL ATTACK AND PUNISHMENT; 415] 4 v **go forth**, go out, venture forth, venture out, set out [➡LEAVE AND GO AWAY; 8] Opposite: retreat

salmon type of **ocean fish** [➡OCEAN FISH; 1009]

salmonella type of **microorganism** [➡MICROORGANISMS, FUNGI, AND ALGAE; 1023]

salmon pink type of **pink** [➡COLORS; 1224]

salon 1 n **soiree**, gathering, rendezvous, meeting, group, get-together (informal) [➡MEETINGS AND ASSEMBLIES; 43] 2 n **beauty parlor**, beauty salon, hair salon, hairdresser's, barbershop, hairdresser, barber [➡RETAIL OUTLETS; 1083] 3 type of **room in the home** [➡TYPES OF ROOMS; 1097]

saloon type of **bar or club** [➡HOTELS, RESTAURANTS, AND CLUBS; 1082]

salsa 1 type of **seasonings, sauces, and dips** [➡SEASONINGS AND SAUCES; 1174] 2 type of **dance** [➡DANCE; 903] 3 type of **world music** [➡MUSIC, SONGS, AND SINGING; 907]

salt type of **nutrient** [➡FOOD COMPONENTS; 1188]

salt-and-pepper adj **flecked**, streaked, grizzled, graying, patchy, mottled [➡DESCRIBING PATTERNS; 1227]

salt away v **hoard**, save, squirrel away, put by, set aside, amass, accumulate, stash (informal) [➡STORE AND KEEP; 453] Opposite: fritter away

salt flat n [➡WETLANDS; 1043]

salt water n **brine**, sea water, saline [➡LIQUIDS; 1269]

salty adj **salt**, saline, brackish, salted, briny [➡TASTE; 703] Opposite: sweet

salubrious (formal) adj **healthy**, wholesome, respectable, decent, hygienic, clean [➡CLEAN AND HYGIENIC; 1233] Opposite: insalubrious (formal)

salutary adj **beneficial**, helpful, useful, valuable, constructive, productive [➡USEFULNESS; 199]

salutation n **greeting**, acknowledgment, welcome, gesture, salute, nod, salaam [➡GREETINGS, FAREWELLS, AND SALUTATIONS; 659]

salutations (formal) n [➡GREETINGS, FAREWELLS, AND SALUTATIONS; 659]

salute 1 *v* **acknowledge**, greet, welcome, gesture, wave, nod [➤ GESTURES AND GESTICULATION; 653] **2** *n* **sign of respect**, salutation, greeting, acknowledgment, signal, gesture [➤ GESTURES AND GESTICULATION; 653]

salvage *v* **save**, recover, rescue, retrieve, reclaim, recoup, pick up [➤ REGAIN POSSESSION; 429]

salvation *n* **redemption**, rescue, recovery, escape, deliverance (*formal*) [➤ FREEDOM AND LIBERTY; 208]

salve 1 *n* **lotion**, ointment, balm, balsam, liniment, unguent, cream [➤ LOTIONS, PASTES, AND GELS; 1272] *Opposite:* irritant **2** *v* **appease**, soothe, comfort, mollify, calm, ease, relieve, pacify [➤ SOOTHE AND CALM; 573] *Opposite:* irritate

salver *n* **tray**, platter, plate, serving dish, dish, paten [➤ TABLEWARE, FLATWARE, AND KITCHENWARE; 861]

salvo *n* **barrage**, bombardment, round, torrent, hail, deluge, volley [➤ SUDDEN EVENTS; 52]

samba *type of* **dance** [➤ DANCE; 903]

sambal *type of* **cooked dish** [➤ PREPARED DISHES; 1170]

same 1 *adj* **identical**, alike, matching, similar, equal, equivalent [➤ SAMENESS; 150] *Opposite:* different **2** *adj* **unchanged**, constant, consistent, uniform, even, invariable, unaffected [➤ PERMANENCE: WITHOUT CHANGE; 95] *Opposite:* changed

sameness 1 *n* **similarity**, likeness, resemblance, uniformity, equivalence, equality, identicalness, similitude (*formal*) [➤ SAMENESS; 150] *Opposite:* difference **2** *n* **monotony**, repetitiveness, uniformity, consistency, evenness, regularity, similarity [➤ BORING AND UNINTERESTING; 234] *Opposite:* variety

Samoa *type of* **time zone** [➤ TIMES OF DAY; 87]

samovar *n* **tea urn**, urn, teapot, jug, kettle [➤ TABLEWARE, FLATWARE, AND KITCHENWARE; 861]

sampan *type of* **small vessel** [➤ SHIPS AND BOATS; 1150]

sample 1 *n* **example**, model, trial, illustration, mock-up, tester, prototype, tryout, taste, taster (*UK*) [➤ REPRESENTATIONS AND GENERAL EXAMPLES; 65] **2** *v* **test**, try, appraise, try out, check out, taste, experiment [➤ EXAMINE AND ASSESS; 753]

sampler 1 *n* **technician**, tester, analyst, quality control analyst, laboratory technician [➤ SURVEYORS, EXAMINERS, AND JUDGES; 853] **2** *n* **selection**, sample, cross section, sampling, representative selection, test group, control group [➤ REPRESENTATIONS AND GENERAL EXAMPLES; 65] **3** *n* **sample**, tryout, example, taste, illustration, taster (*UK*) [➤ REPRESENTATIONS AND GENERAL EXAMPLES; 65] **4** *n* **embroidery**, sewing, needlework, handwork [➤ CRAFTS AND CARVING; 355]

sampling *n* **sample**, specimen, cross section, selection, test group, sampler, control group, random sample, straw poll, straw vote [➤ REPRESENTATIONS AND GENERAL EXAMPLES; 65]

sanatorium *n* **clinic**, hospital, infirmary, hospice, spa, health resort [➤ HOSPITALS AND CLINICS; 826]

sanctification *n* [➤ RELIGIOUS CONCEPTS; 776]

sanctified *adj* **sacred**, holy, blessed, consecrated, hallowed, dedicated, purified [➤ RELIGIOUS CONCEPTS; 776] *Opposite:* desecrated

sanctify *v* **bless**, consecrate, hallow, dedicate, purify [➤ RELIGIONS AND RELIGIOUS PRACTICES; 777] *Opposite:* desecrate

sanctimonious *adj* **self-righteous**, smug, pious, pompous, self-satisfied, superior, censorious, holier-than-thou (*informal*) [➤ AFFECTATION, SELF-SATISFACTION, AND SNOBBISHNESS; 507] *Opposite:* humble

sanctimoniousness *n* **self-righteousness**, smugness, pomposity, superiority [➤ AFFECTATION, SELF-SATISFACTION, AND SNOBBISHNESS; 507]

sanction 1 *n* **authorization**, permission, approval, agreement, consent, endorsement, green light [➤ PERMIT AND ALLOW; 669] *Opposite:* prohibition **2** *n* **support**, approval, encouragement, agreement, affirmation, favor [➤ APPROVE AND CONFIRM; 646] **3** *n* **restriction**, penalty, ban, punishment, injunction, measure, action [➤ REFUSE PERMISSION AND NOT ALLOW; 670] **4** *v* **authorize**, permit, approve, allow, pass, endorse, OK (*informal*) [➤ PERMIT AND ALLOW; 669] *Opposite:* veto

sanctity *n* **holiness**, blessedness, sacredness, inviolability, purity, sacrosanctity [➤ RELIGIOUS CONCEPTS; 776] *Opposite:* profanity

sanctuary 1 *n* **refuge**, asylum, shelter, safe haven, haven, safe house, retreat [➤ SAFE BUILDINGS OR PLACES; 1093] **2** *n* **reserve**, reservation, national park, nature reserve, preserve, nature preserve [➤ THE COUNTRYSIDE AND OUTDOOR SPACES; 1071] **3** *n* **safety**, protection, refuge, asylum, shelter, immunity [➤ SAFE AND SAFETY; 191]

sanctum 1 *n* **holy of holies**, sanctum sanctorum, temple, altar, shrine [➤ RELIGIOUS BUILDINGS; 1085] **2** *n* **retreat**, den, refuge, study, hideaway, office, sanctum sanctorum, lair (*informal*) [➤ SAFE BUILDINGS OR PLACES; 1093]

sand 1 *n* [➤ BUILDING MATERIALS; 1077] **2** *n* **shingle**, grit, gravel, powder, silt, soil [➤ EROSION PRODUCTS AND SOIL; 1058] **3** *n* **beach**, strand, dune, shore, shoreline [➤ THE SEAS, OCEANS, AND SHORES; 1041] **4** *v* **rub down**, smooth, sandpaper, polish, rub, scrape [➤ CLEAN AND POLISH; 403]

sandal *type of* **shoe** [➤ FOOTWEAR; 871]

sandalwood *type of* **evergreen tree** [➤ EVERGREEN AND CONIFEROUS TREES; 1029]

sandbank *n* **sandbar**, dune, mound, bank, hummock, hill, ridge [➤ THE SEAS, OCEANS, AND SHORES; 1041]

sandbar *n* **sandbank**, ridge, shallows, shoal [➤ THE SEAS, OCEANS, AND SHORES; 1041]

sander *type of* **carpentry tool** [➤ HAND TOOLS; 1119]

sand flea 1 *type of* **parasitic insect** [➤ PARASITES; 1017] **2** *type of* **crustacean** [➤ AQUATIC INVERTEBRATES; 1022]

sandfly *type of* **parasitic insect** [➤ PARASITES; 1017]

S&L *n* [➤ ACCOUNTING, BANKING, AND BUDGETING; 799]

sandpaper *v* **rub down**, smooth, sand, polish, rub, scrape [➤ CLEAN AND POLISH; 403]

sandstone *type of* **stone** [➤ STONES, ROCKS, AND BOULDERS; 1057]

sandwich 1 *n* **snack**, club sandwich, double-decker, hoagie, roll, submarine [➤ PREPARED DISHES; 1170] **2** *v* **squeeze in**, squash in, pack in, cram, slot in, insert, fit in [➤ POSITION SOMETHING: BETWEEN, BESIDE, OR INSIDE SOMETHING; 326]

sane 1 *adj* **well-balanced**, compos mentis, rational, stable, healthy, lucid, of sound mind [➡ POSITIVE INTELLECTUAL CHARACTERISTICS; 524] *Opposite*: insane 2 *adj* **sensible**, reasonable, rational, sound, wise, commonsensical [➡ THE NATURE OF IDEAS; 771] *Opposite*: irrational

saneness *see* **sanity**

sang-froid *n* **self-possession**, calmness, poise, aplomb, self-assurance, self-control, composure, cool (*informal*) [➡ CONFIDENCE AND COMPOSURE; 499] *Opposite*: anxiety

sanguinary (*formal*) 1 *adj* **bloody**, gory, brutal, grim, gruesome, bloodied [➡ DISGUSTING AND REPULSIVE; 230] 2 *adj* **bloodthirsty**, murderous, ruthless, savage, cruel, merciless, homicidal [➡ SELFISH AND UNKIND; 505]

sanguine *adj* **confident**, optimistic, cheerful, hopeful, positive, upbeat (*informal*) [➡ COOL AND CALM; 536] *Opposite*: pessimistic

sanguineness *n* [➡ COOL AND CALM; 536]

sanguinity *n* [➡ COOL AND CALM; 536]

sanitariness *n* [➡ CLEAN AND HYGIENIC; 1233]

sanitarium *n* **clinic**, rest home, convalescent home, hospital, infirmary, hospice, spa, health resort [➡ HOSPITALS AND CLINICS; 826]

sanitary *adj* **hygienic**, clean, healthy, wholesome, sterile, salubrious (*formal*) [➡ CLEAN AND HYGIENIC; 1233] *Opposite*: insanitary

sanitation *n* **hygiene**, cleanliness, cleanness, public health, health [➡ SOCIAL WELFARE; 812]

sanitize 1 *v* **purify**, fumigate, disinfect, clean, cleanse, wash, sterilize, decontaminate [➡ CLEAN AND POLISH; 403] *Opposite*: contaminate 2 *v* **censor**, clean up, bowdlerize, water down [➡ WITHHOLD INFORMATION; 687] *Opposite*: spice up

sanitized *adj* [➡ CLEAN AND HYGIENIC; 1233]

sanity 1 *n* **saneness**, rationality, stability, lucidity, reason, mental health [➡ POSITIVE INTELLECTUAL CHARACTERISTICS; 524] *Opposite*: insanity 2 *n* **reasonableness**, sense, rationality, soundness, wisdom, understanding, common sense, reason, judgment [➡ THE NATURE OF IDEAS; 771] *Opposite*: unreasonableness

sans (*literary or humorous*) *prep* **without**, lacking, missing, wanting, less, minus [➡ NOT; 137]

sansevieria *type of* **foliage plant** [➡ FOLIAGE PLANTS; 1035]

Santa Ana *type of* **wind** [➡ WINDY AND STORMY WEATHER; 1053]

santim *type of* **currency** [➡ CURRENCIES; 798]

sap 1 *n* **juice**, fluid, liquid, latex [➡ PARTS OF TREES AND PLANTS; 1026] 2 *n* **energy**, vitality, health, strength, life, vigor [➡ ENERGY AND ENTHUSIASM; 496] 3 *v* **dig down**, burrow, bore, tunnel, mine [➡ SEEK POSSESSION AND SEARCH; 456] 4 *v* **weaken**, drain, undermine, deplete, eat away, debilitate, reduce [➡ CHANGE OF INTENSITY: LESS; 395] *Opposite*: boost

sapience *n* [➡ KNOWLEDGE AND WISDOM; 558]

sapient *adj* **wise**, learned, educated, intelligent, knowing, discerning, sage (*literary*) [➡ KNOWLEDGE AND WISDOM; 558] *Opposite*: ignorant

sapling 1 *n* **tree**, seedling, plantlet, sprout, scion, sprig [➡ PLANTS AND TREES; 1024] 2 *n* (*literary*) **youth**, adolescent, youngster, juvenile, teenager, teen (*informal*) [➡ CHILD OR YOUTH; 945]

sapphire 1 *type of* **gemstone** [➡ PRECIOUS STONES; 1278] 2 *type of* **blue** [➡ COLORS; 1224]

sarcasm *n* **irony**, mockery, cynicism, derision, acerbity, scorn, disdain [➡ MOCKING AND DISMISSIVE; 636]

sarcastic *adj* **ironic**, mocking, sardonic, cynical, acerbic, mordant, derisive, dismissive, caustic [➡ MOCKING AND DISMISSIVE; 636]

> ## Compare and Contrast: *sarcastic*, *ironic*, *sardonic*, *satirical*, *caustic*
>
> CORE MEANING: used to describe remarks that are designed to hurt or mock
>
> *sarcastic* contemptuous, scornful, or mocking and intended to hurt or belittle; *ironic* deliberately stating the opposite of the truth, usually with the intention of being amusing; *sardonic* mocking and cynical or disdainful, though not deliberately hurtful; *satirical* using ridicule, especially in a work of art, to criticize somebody's or something's faults, especially in the arts; *caustic* harsh and bitter and intended to mock, offend, or belittle.

sarcoma *n* [➡ ILLNESSES AND DISORDERS; 732]

sarcophagus *n* **coffin**, tomb, casket [➡ BURIAL PLACES AND ACCESSORIES; 930]

sard *type of* **gemstone** [➡ PRECIOUS STONES; 1278]

sardine *type of* **ocean fish** [➡ OCEAN FISH; 1009]

sardonic *adj* **mocking**, scornful, ironic, sarcastic, derisive, satirical, cutting, mordant, scathing, disdainful [➡ MOCKING AND DISMISSIVE; 636]

> *See Compare and Contrast at* **sarcastic**.

sardonicism *n* [➡ MOCKING AND DISMISSIVE; 636]

sari *type of* **dress** [➡ GARMENTS AND OUTFITS; 865]

sarong *type of* **skirt** [➡ GARMENTS AND OUTFITS; 865]

sarsaparilla *type of* **climber** [➡ CLIMBERS; 1033]

sarsen *n* **rock**, boulder, stone, cairn, block [➡ STONES, ROCKS, AND BOULDERS; 1057]

sartorial *adj* **dress**, fashion, clothing [➡ WELL-GROOMED; 482]

sash 1 *n* **band**, ribbon, belt, cummerbund, tie, girdle [➡ PARTS OF A GARMENT; 870] 2 *type of* **accessory** [➡ ACCESSORIES, MILLINERY, AND LINGERIE; 867]

sashay (*humorous*) *v* **flounce**, sway, strut, prance, swagger, shimmy [➡ MOVE FAST; 313]

sashimi *n* [➡ PREPARED DISHES; 1170]

sash window *type of* **window** [➡ WINDOWS; 1100]

sasquatch *n* **humanoid**, Bigfoot [➡ MYTHICAL BEINGS; 789]

sass (*informal*) *n* **impertinence**, impudence, rudeness, attitude, cheek, back talk, mouth (*informal*), lip (*slang*) [➡ BAD MANNERS AND SOCIAL SKILLS; 521]

sassafras *type of* **deciduous tree** [➡ DECIDUOUS TREES; 1028]

sassiness 1 *n* **impudence**, impertinence, brazenness, insolence, impishness, mischief, disrespect, nerve, cheekiness, cheek (*informal*) [➡ BAD MANNERS AND SOCIAL SKILLS; 521] *Opposite*: respectfulness **2** *n* **liveliness**, high spirits, jauntiness, vivacity, vivaciousness, bubbliness, playfulness, feistiness (*informal*) [➡ ENERGY AND ENTHUSIASM; 496] *Opposite*: quietness

sassy 1 *adj* **impudent**, brazen, insolent, impish, mischievous, disrespectful, cheeky (*informal*), impertinent (*formal*) [➡ BAD MANNERS AND SOCIAL SKILLS; 521] *Opposite*: respectful **2** *adj* **lively**, high-spirited, spirited, jaunty, vivacious, bubbly, playful, frisky, feisty (*informal*) [➡ ENERGY AND ENTHUSIASM; 496] *Opposite*: subdued

satay 1 *type of* **seasonings, sauces, and dips** [➡ SEASONINGS AND SAUCES; 1174] **2** *type of* **cooked dish** [➡ PREPARED DISHES; 1170]

satchel *n* **bag**, shoulder bag, haversack, school bag, backpack, briefcase, bookbag, knapsack, valise [➡ CONTAINERS, RECEPTACLES, AND PACKAGING; 1245]

sate *v* **fill up**, fill, satiate, stuff, gorge, satisfy, feed, glut [➡ EAT AND NOT EAT; 710]

sated *adj* **full**, satiated, gorged, bursting, satisfied, replete, surfeited, full up, stuffed (*informal*) [➡ EAT AND NOT EAT; 710] *Opposite*: hungry

sateen *type of* **synthetic fabric** [➡ FABRICS; 1132]

satellite 1 *n* **dependency**, protectorate, colony, overseas territory, subject population [➡ TERRITORIES AND GROUPS OF NATIONS; 1068] **2** *n* **satellite television**, satellite TV, satellite broadcasting, digital television, digital TV, cable [➡ TELEVISION AND RADIO; 606] **3** *type of* **spacecraft** [➡ SPACE VEHICLES; 1063] **4** *type of* **telecommunications equipment** [➡ TELECOMMUNICATIONS; 1130]

satellite dish *type of* **telecommunications equipment** [➡ TELECOMMUNICATIONS; 1130]

satellite television *n* [➡ TELEVISION AND RADIO; 606]

satiate 1 *v* **gratify**, satisfy, quench, sate, slake, assuage, appease [➡ CHANGE OF INTENSITY: LESS; 395] **2** *v* **glut**, fill, satisfy, sate, fill up, overindulge [➡ EAT AND NOT EAT; 710]

satiated 1 *adj* **gratified**, satisfied, quenched, sated, slaked, assuaged, appeased [➡ PLEASURE, EXCITEMENT, AND ELATION; 534] **2** *adj* **full**, satisfied, replete, sated, full up [➡ EAT AND NOT EAT; 710] *Opposite*: unsatisfied

satiety *n* **fullness**, surfeit, glut, repletion [➡ FULL; 1239]

satin *type of* **synthetic fabric** [➡ FABRICS; 1132]

satiny *adj* **lustrous**, luminous, shiny, radiant, glossy, smooth, glowing, sheeny [➡ VISUAL TEXTURE; 1221] *Opposite*: dull

satire 1 *n* **mockery**, irony, sarcasm, ridicule, wit, parody, invective (*formal*) [➡ MOCKING AND DISMISSIVE; 636] **2** *n* **parody**, lampoon, burlesque, caricature, travesty, spoof, sendup (*informal*), mockery [➡ JOKES AND TEASING; 674]

satirical *adj* **mocking**, ironic, sardonic, humorous, sarcastic, tongue-in-cheek, spoof, irreverent [➡ MOCKING AND DISMISSIVE; 636]

See Compare and Contrast at **sarcastic**.

satirist *n* **humorist**, wit, joker, satirizer, comic, lampooner, wag (*informal*) [➡ WORKERS IN ENTERTAINMENT AND MEDIA; 873]

satirize *v* **mock**, ridicule, parody, lampoon, deride, caricature, send up (*informal*) [➡ JOKES AND TEASING; 674]

satisfaction 1 *n* **contentment**, pleasure, happiness, joy, enjoyment, pride [➡ PLEASURE, EXCITEMENT, AND ELATION; 534] *Opposite*: dissatisfaction **2** *n* **gratification**, consummation, fulfillment [➡ PLEASURE, EXCITEMENT, AND ELATION; 534] **3** *n* **approval**, liking, taste, contentment, agreement, pleasure [➡ APPRECIATION AND GRATITUDE; 535] *Opposite*: dissatisfaction **4** *n* **redress**, reparation, compensation, settlement, repayment, recompense [➡ REWARDS AND AWARDS; 439]

satisfactory *adj* **acceptable**, reasonable, pleasing, fitting, agreeable, adequate, sufficient, suitable, all right [➡ ACCEPTABLE AND PASSABLE; 219] *Opposite*: unsatisfactory

satisfied *adj* **content**, pleased, happy, gratified, fulfilled, contented, complacent [➡ PLEASURE, EXCITEMENT, AND ELATION; 534] *Opposite*: dissatisfied

satisfy 1 *v* **content**, please, gratify, mollify, placate, fulfill [➡ PLEASE AND AMUSE; 572] *Opposite*: dissatisfy **2** *v* **gratify**, satiate, quench, sate, slake, assuage, appease [➡ CAUSE TO STOP; 266] **3** *v* **convince**, assure, persuade, reassure, win over [➡ SOOTHE AND CALM; 573] **4** *v* **fulfill**, comply with, meet, suit, fill, fit, answer, discharge (*formal*) [➡ OBEY AND ABIDE BY; 301]

satisfying 1 *adj* **pleasing**, gratifying, fulfilling, rewarding, enjoyable, agreeable [➡ EMOTIONALLY PLEASANT; 187] *Opposite*: dissatisfying **2** *adj* **filling**, sustaining, nourishing, substantial, satiating, sufficient, adequate [➡ ENOUGH AND SUFFICIENT; 131] *Opposite*: insufficient

satsuma *type of* **citrus fruit** [➡ FRUIT AND VEGETABLES; 1176]

saturate 1 *v* **soak**, drench, wet through, douse, steep, marinate, flood, inundate, waterlog [➡ SOFTEN, LIQUEFY, AND DAMPEN; 388] *Opposite*: dry out **2** *v* **oversupply**, overwhelm, overload, flood, inundate, overfill, fill [➡ GIVE TOO MUCH AND OVERBURDEN; 437]

saturated 1 *adj* **soaked**, soaking, drenched, wet through, wet, wringing wet, dripping wet, flooded, inundated, waterlogged, steeped, marinated [➡ WET; 1240] *Opposite*: dry **2** *adj* **packed**, full, brimming, brimful, overfull, flooded, inundated, overwhelmed, replete, overloaded [➡ FULL; 1239] *Opposite*: empty

See Compare and Contrast at **wet**.

saturated fat *n* [➡ FOOD COMPONENTS; 1188]

saturated fatty acid *n* [➡ FOOD COMPONENTS; 1188]

saturation 1 *n* **wetness**, soaking, drenching, wetting, moistening [➡ WET; 1240] *Opposite*: dryness **2** *n* **fullness**, capacity, overload, satiety, permeation, inundation (*formal*) [➡ FULL; 1239]

saturation bombing *n* [➡ WARFARE AND WAR; 830]

Saturn *type of* **planet** [➡ HEAVENLY BODIES; 1061]

saturnalia *n* **orgy**, celebration, bacchanalia, revel, party, debauch (*formal*), carousal (*literary*) [➡ PARTIES, DANCES, AND CELEBRATIONS; 37]

saturnine *adj* **melancholy**, morose, gloomy, sad, sullen, dejected, depressed [➡ SADNESS, DISTRESS, AND DESPAIR; 539] *Opposite:* cheerful

satyr *n* [➡ PLEASURE-SEEKERS AND HEDONISTS; 886]

sauce 1 *n* (*informal*) **impudence**, impertinence, rudeness, insolence, nerve, sauciness, insouciance, sass (*informal*), cheek (*informal*) [➡ BAD MANNERS AND SOCIAL SKILLS; 521] **2** *n* [➡ SEASONINGS AND SAUCES; 1174]

---

sauce

◆ *types of seasonings, sauces, and dips*
aioli, applesauce, barbecue sauce, béarnaise, béchamel sauce, chili sauce, coulis, dressing, French dressing, gravy, guacamole, hollandaise, hummus, ketchup, marinade, mayonnaise, mint sauce, raita, ranch dressing, salsa, satay, soy sauce, tabasco, tahini, taramasalata, tartar sauce, Thousand Island dressing, vinegar, wasabi, Worcestershire sauce

---

saucepan *n* **pan**, pot, cooking pot [➡ TABLEWARE, FLATWARE, AND KITCHENWARE; 861]

saucer *n* **plate**, bowl, dish [➡ TABLEWARE, FLATWARE, AND KITCHENWARE; 861]

saucy *adj* **impudent**, smart, rude, sassy, cheeky (*informal*), snippy (*informal*), fresh (*informal*), smart-alecky (*informal*), impertinent (*formal*) [➡ BAD MANNERS AND SOCIAL SKILLS; 521]

sauerkraut *type of* **cooked dish** [➡ PREPARED DISHES; 1170]

sault *n* **waterfall**, rapids, race, chute, white water [➡ RIVERS, LAKES, AND STREAMS; 1042]

sauna *n* **steam bath**, Turkish bath [➡ FIXTURES; 859]

saunter 1 *v* **stroll**, walk, amble, meander, ramble, wander, mosey (*informal*), promenade (*formal*) [➡ MOVE SLOWLY; 314] *Opposite:* hurry **2** *n* **walk**, stroll, amble, ramble, meander, wander, promenade (*formal*) [➡ PROCEED AND GO; 305]

sausage *type of* **processed meat** [➡ TYPES AND CUTS OF MEAT; 1177]

sauté *v* **fry**, stir-fry, pan-fry, brown [➡ COOKING AND FOOD PREPARATION; 353]

sautéed *adj* [➡ STATE OF PREPARED FOOD; 1171]

savage 1 *adj* **violent**, unrestrained, vicious, fierce, ferocious, brutal [➡ SELFISH AND UNKIND; 505] *Opposite:* gentle **2** *adj* **severe**, harsh, drastic, stringent, ruthless, brutal, unsparing [➡ PHYSICALLY UNPLEASANT; 226] *Opposite:* mild **3** *adj* **undomesticated**, wild, ferocious, fierce, feral, untamed [➡ DANGEROUS; 236] *Opposite:* tame **4** *v* **attack**, brutalize, mug, maul, mangle, jump (*informal*) [➡ PHYSICAL ATTACK AND PUNISHMENT; 415] **5** *v* **criticize**, tear apart, maul, destroy, attack, weigh into (*informal*), blast (*informal*), castigate (*formal*) [➡ ACCUSE, BLAME, AND CRITICIZE; 641] *Opposite:* praise

savagely 1 *adv* **violently**, unrestrainedly, viciously, fiercely, ferociously, brutally [➡ SELFISH AND UNKIND; 505] *Opposite:* gently **2** *adv* **severely**, harshly, ruthlessly, brutally, cruelly, callously [➡ TO A GREAT EXTENT; 132] *Opposite:* mildly

savagery *n* **cruelty**, violence, barbarity, viciousness, barbarism, ferocity [➡ MALICIOUS ACTIONS OR BEHAVIOR; 296] *Opposite:* gentleness

savanna *n* **grassland**, pampas, plains, prairie [➡ DESERTS, PLAINS, AND MOORLAND; 1045]

savant *n* **guru**, philosopher, thinker, pundit, expert, scholar, maven, sage (*literary*) [➡ TALENTED OR INTELLIGENT PEOPLE; 528]

save 1 *v* **rescue**, recover, salvage, bail out, revive, resuscitate [➡ FREEDOM AND LIBERTY; 208] *Opposite:* abandon **2** *v* **accumulate**, bank, salt away, collect [➡ STORE AND KEEP; 453] *Opposite:* spend **3** *v* **keep back**, set aside, put aside, put away, hold back, hoard [➡ STORE AND KEEP; 453] *Opposite:* use up **4** *v* **avoid**, prevent, stop, avert, bar, spare, preclude (*formal*) [➡ AVOID, PREVENT, LIMIT, AND CONTROL; 277] **5** *prep* **but**, except, apart from, with the exception of, excluding, bar, save for [➡ NOT; 137] *Opposite:* including

save for *prep* **but**, except, apart from, with the exception of, excluding, bar, save [➡ NOT; 137]

saveloy *type of* **processed meat** [➡ TYPES AND CUTS OF MEAT; 1177]

saver *n* **investor**, collector, hoarder, gatherer, squirrel (*informal*), magpie (*informal*) [➡ PEOPLE WHO COLLECT THINGS; 454]

saving *n* **economy**, reduction, cutback, discount, cut [➡ FUNDS, PAYMENTS, AND CHARGES; 800] *Opposite:* increase

saving grace *n* **merit**, advantage, strong point, strong suit, virtue, compensation, redeeming feature, redeeming quality [➡ SOURCE OF HAPPINESS, PLEASURE, OR IMPROVEMENT; 209] *Opposite:* failing

savings *n* **investments**, reserves, nest egg, funds, hoard, money, assets, stash (*informal*) [➡ FINANCIAL ASSETS; 462] *Opposite:* expenditure

savings and loan association *n* [➡ ACCOUNTING, BANKING, AND BUDGETING; 799]

savior *n* **redeemer**, rescuer, knight in shining armor, liberator, deliverer, protector [➡ PEOPLE WHO ARE APPROVED OF; 955]

savoir-faire *n* **confidence**, style, flair, poise, sense, savvy (*informal*), know-how (*informal*) [➡ KNOWLEDGE AND WISDOM; 558] *Opposite:* gaucheness

savor 1 *n* **taste**, smell, flavor, aroma, tang, bouquet [➡ TASTE; 703] **2** *v* **enjoy**, relish, appreciate, delight in, cherish, treasure, value [➡ LIKE, LOVE, VALUE, AND ENJOY; 578]

savorless *adj* **tasteless**, insipid, bland, flavorless [➡ TASTE; 703] *Opposite:* flavorful

savorlessness *n* **tastelessness**, insipidness, blandness, flavorlessness [➡ TASTE; 703] *Opposite:* tastiness

savory 1 *adj* **appetizing**, tasty, flavorful, palatable, delicious, delectable, mouthwatering, zesty [➡ TASTE; 703] *Opposite:* insipid **2** *adj* **salty**, salt, spicy, piquant, pungent, aromatic, sharp [➡ TASTE; 703] *Opposite:* sweet **3** *adj* **respectable**, pleasant, acceptable, nice, wholesome, congenial [➡ APPROPRIATE, SUITABLE, AND ADVISABLE; 184] *Opposite:* unsavory **4** *type of* **herb** [➡ HERBS AND SPICES; 1175]

savvy (*informal*) *n* **shrewdness**, practicality, knowledge, perception, understanding, know-how (*informal*), smarts (*informal*) [➡ KNOWLEDGE AND WISDOM; 558] *Opposite:* ignorance

saw 1 *type of* **carpentry tool** [➡ HAND TOOLS; 1119] **2** *n* **saying**, proverb, adage, maxim, motto, aphorism, axiom [➡ FIGURES OF SPEECH; 673] **3** *v* **cut**, slice, sever, divide, chop, rip [➡ USE TOOLS AND MACHINERY; 468]

sawed-off shotgun *type of* **gun** [➡ WEAPONS FOR SHOOTING; 1156]

sawfish *type of* **tropical fish** [➡ OCEAN FISH; 1009]

sawmill *type of* **factory** [➡ INDUSTRIAL BUILDINGS; 1087]

saxe blue *type of* **blue** [➡ COLORS; 1224]

saxhorn *type of* **brass instrument** [➡ MUSICAL INSTRUMENTS; 910]

saxophone *type of* **brass instrument** [➡ MUSICAL INSTRUMENTS; 910]

say 1 *v* **speak**, utter, articulate, declare, pronounce, state, cry, verbalize, exclaim [➡ UTTER AND PRONOUNCE; 608] **2** *v* **convey**, indicate, reveal, give away, tell, disclose, express, display, impart [➡ BETRAY CONFIDENCES AND GOSSIP; 618] **3** *n* **input**, voice, opinion, view, two cents' worth, right of speech, penny-worth (*UK*) [➡ POINTS OF VIEW; 767] **4** *adv* **approximately**, roughly, about, around, give or take, round about, at a guess [➡ APPROXIMATELY; 135] *Opposite*: exactly

saying *n* **proverb**, adage, maxim, axiom, motto, saw, aphorism, dictum (*formal*) [➡ FIGURES OF SPEECH; 673]

sayonara *interj* **goodbye**, so long, bye (*informal*), bye-bye (*informal*), see you (*informal*), later (*informal*), ciao (*informal*), hasta la vista (*informal*), adios (*informal*), farewell (*literary*) [➡ GREETINGS, FAREWELLS, AND SALUTATIONS; 659] *Opposite*: hello

say-so (*informal*) *n* **authorization**, authority, permission, approval, agreement, sanction, accord, consent, endorsement, acquiescence [➡ PERMIT AND ALLOW; 669] *Opposite*: veto

say yes *v* **agree**, accept, consent, acquiesce, assent, jump at the chance [➡ AGREE; 645] *Opposite*: refuse

say you're sorry *v* **apologize**, excuse yourself, crawl, grovel, beg forgiveness, swallow your pride [➡ APOLOGIZE AND RETRACT; 683]

say your piece *v* **speak out**, speak up, protest, take a stand, make a stand, stand your ground, fight your corner (*UK*) [➡ PROTEST AND EXPRESS DISAPPROVAL; 642] *Opposite*: hold back

scab *n* **crust**, layer, skin, shell, covering, casing, coating [➡ COVERS AND COATINGS; 1246]

scabbard *n* **sheath**, case, covering, cover, casing, holster [➡ CONTAINERS, RECEPTACLES, AND PACKAGING; 1245]

scabby 1 *adj* **mangy**, scaly, diseased, shabby, dirty, moth-eaten, grotty (*UK*) [➡ IN BAD REPAIR; 1234] *Opposite*: unblemished 2 *adj* (*slang*) **despicable**, dislikable, contemptible, detestable, low, shabby [➡ UNACCEPTABLE AND UNFORGIVABLE; 225] *Opposite*: admirable

scabrous *adj* **rough**, flaky, scaly, mangy, leprous [➡ CONDITIONS AFFECTING THE SKIN; 721] *Opposite*: smooth

scads (*informal*) *n* **lots**, scores, tons (*informal*), heaps (*informal*), buckets (*informal*), piles (*informal*), loads (*informal*) [➡ MANY, MUCH, LARGE AMOUNT; 117] *Opposite*: none

scaffold 1 *n* **support**, framework, frame, platform, shell,

skeleton, scaffolding [➡ SUPPORTS AND BASES; 1255] **2** *n* **gallows**, gibbet, halter, noose [➡ ANCIENT MANMADE STRUCTURES; 1089]

scaffolding *n* **support**, framework, frame, platform, shell, skeleton, scaffold [➡ SUPPORTS AND BASES; 1255]

scalawag (*dated informal*) *n* **mischief-maker**, rogue, scoundrel, imp, monkey (*informal*), scamp (*informal*), rascal (*humorous*), rapscallion (*archaic or humorous*) [➡ MISCHIEVOUS OR BADLY BEHAVED CHILD; 946] *Opposite*: angel

scald 1 *v* **burn**, blister, singe, sear, injure, hurt, damage, scorch [➡ FIRE, FLAMMABILITY, AND BURNING; 1165] **2** *v* **sterilize**, boil, steam, autoclave, heat, disinfect, clean, sanitize [➡ CLEAN AND POLISH; 403] *Opposite*: contaminate **3** *v* **bring to the boil**, boil, heat, warm, simmer [➡ COOKING AND FOOD PREPARATION; 353] *Opposite*: chill

scalding 1 *adj* **boiling**, piping hot, baking, burning, blistering, searing, broiling, sweltering, torrid, red-hot, hot, scorching (*informal*), roasting (*informal*) [➡ TEMPERATURE: HOT; 1229] *Opposite*: icy **2** *adj* **scathing**, blistering, critical, fierce, scornful, withering, caustic, cutting, biting [➡ ACCUSATORY AND DISAPPROVING; 634] *Opposite*: complimentary

scale 1 *n* **weighing machine**, balance, scales, measure, weighbridge (*UK*) [➡ MEASURING DEVICES; 1123] **2** *n* **gradation**, tier, band, ratio, progression, calibration, measurement [➡ SIZE AND DIMENSIONS; 1192] **3** *n* **range**, extent, size, degree, level, amount, magnitude, dimension, hierarchy, gamut [➡ AREA AND RANGE; 111] **4** *n* **deposit**, crust, fur, covering, plaque, tartar [➡ COVERS AND COATINGS; 1246] **5** *n* **plate**, flake, skin, scab, scurf, piece [➡ SMALL PIECES; 129] **6** *part of* **fish** [➡ PARTS OF A FISH; 1011] **7** *v* **ascend**, climb, mount, go up, clamber up, shin [➡ GO UPWARD; 306] **8** *v* **peel**, pare, skin, exfoliate, flake [➡ TEAR, BREAK, AND CUT; 360]

scale down *v* **reduce**, decrease, lower, cut back, cut down, trim, shave, pare, scale back, step down [➡ CHANGE OF INTENSITY: LESS; 395] *Opposite*: scale up

scale up *v* **increase**, expand, extend, raise, step up, upgrade, improve, develop, widen, broaden [➡ CHANGE OF INTENSITY: MORE; 394] *Opposite*: scale down

scallion *type of* **salad vegetable** [➡ FRUIT AND VEGETABLES; 1176]

scallop 1 *type of* **aquatic invertebrate** [➡ AQUATIC INVERTEBRATES; 1022] **2** *n* **pinking**, edging, scalloping, piping, border, decoration [➡ ORNAMENTS AND DECORATIONS; 1248]

scallywag *see* **scalawag**

scalpel *type of* **medical instrument** [➡ HAND TOOLS; 1119]

scaly *adj* **flaking**, peeling, crusty, encrusted, scabby, rough, scabrous [➡ PHYSICAL TEXTURE; 1222] *Opposite*: smooth

scam (*slang*) 1 *n* **con**, swindle, trick, cheat, dodge, rip-off (*informal*), fiddle (*informal*), sting (*slang*) [➡ DECEPTION AND LIES; 660] **2** *v* **cheat**, trick, con, swindle, rip off (*informal*), fiddle (*informal*) [➡ DECEPTION AND LIES; 660]

scammer (*slang*) *n* **swindler**, racketeer, embezzler, crook (*informal*), con man (*slang*) [➡ PEOPLE WHO DECEIVE; 661]

scamp (*informal*) *n* **rogue**, imp, urchin, mischief-maker, scoundrel, scalawag (*dated informal*), monkey (*informal*), rascal (*humorous*), rapscallion (*archaic or humorous*) [➡ MISCHIEVOUS OR BADLY BEHAVED CHILD; 946] *Opposite*: angel

scamper *v* **scurry**, scuttle, run, hurry, dash, dart, tear, scoot (*informal*), zip (*informal*) [➥ MOVE FAST; 313] *Opposite*: dawdle

scampi *n* [➥ SEAFOOD; 1190]

scan 1 *v* **scrutinize**, examine, look into, pore over, inspect, search, look at, check [➥ EXAMINE AND ASSESS; 753] 2 *v* **skim**, skim through, glance at, glance over, peruse, browse, page through, look over, flick through, cast an eye over [➥ LOOKING AND LOOKS; 700] *Opposite*: study 3 *v* **examine**, photograph, visualize, image, X-ray, shoot, probe, test [➥ CREATE IMAGES; 356] 4 *n* **image**, X-ray, CT scan, MRI, PET scan, ultrasound, examination, photograph, shot, test, probe [➥ PHOTOGRAPHY AND PHOTOGRAPHIC EQUIPMENT; 1122] 5 *n* **perusal**, skim, examination, inspection, look, glance, once over (*informal*) [➥ LOOKING AND LOOKS; 700]

scandal 1 *n* **disgrace**, shame, dishonor, humiliation, outrage, indignity [➥ NUISANCES; 253] 2 *n* **gossip**, tittle-tattle, rumor, talk, rumormongering, scandalmongering [➥ GOSSIP; 678]

scandalize *v* **horrify**, outrage, shock, disgust, dismay, appall [➥ FRIGHTEN AND SHOCK; 568] *Opposite*: impress

scandalized *adj* [➥ SURPRISE, SHOCK, AND AMAZEMENT; 545]

scandalmonger *n* **gossip**, rumormonger, gossipmonger, newsmonger, snoop (*informal*) [➥ INTERFERING PEOPLE AND TATTLETALES; 950]

scandalmongering *n* [➥ GOSSIP; 678]

scandalous *adj* **shocking**, outrageous, disgraceful, immoral, shameful, indecent, disreputable, appalling, reprehensible, wicked [➥ MORALLY BAD OR IMPROPER; 775] *Opposite*: admirable

scanner *type of* **hardware** [➥ COMPUTERS AND COMPUTING; 1127]

scant *adj* **slight**, limited, negligible, little, scarce, inadequate, insufficient, meager, measly (*informal*) [➥ TOO FEW, TOO LITTLE; 122] *Opposite*: extensive

scantiness *n* [➥ TOO FEW, TOO LITTLE; 122]

scantness *n* [➥ TOO FEW, TOO LITTLE; 122]

scanty 1 *adj* **revealing**, flimsy, light, low-cut, tight, short, small [➥ DESCRIBING CLOTHES; 869] 2 *adj* **insufficient**, inadequate, meager, little, scarce, sparse, negligible, limited, miserable, measly (*informal*) [➥ TOO FEW, TOO LITTLE; 122] *Opposite*: abundant

scapegoat 1 *n* **stooge**, victim, accused, culprit, fall guy (*slang*) [➥ SOLITARY PEOPLE AND MISFITS; 942] 2 *v* **blame**, incriminate, condemn, accuse, reproach, censure, single out [➥ ACCUSE, BLAME, AND CRITICIZE; 641] *Opposite*: exonerate

scar 1 *n* **mark**, blemish, mutilation, scratch, wound, scab, wheal, welt, burn [➥ CONDITIONS AFFECTING THE SKIN; 721] 2 *n* **effect**, wound, trauma, hurt, aftereffect, hangover, legacy, trace, damage [➥ RESULTS AND OUTCOMES; 83] 3 *v* **damage**, mark, blemish, mutilate, disfigure, scratch, scrape, score, wound [➥ WORSEN APPEARANCE; 382] 4 *v* **traumatize**, hurt, affect, damage, mark, devastate [➥ UPSET, DISTRESS, AND HUMILIATE; 567]

scarab *type of* **beetle** [➥ BEETLES AND WEEVILS; 1016]

scarce 1 *adj* **in short supply**, limited, insufficient, inadequate, scant, meager, sparse [➥ TOO FEW, TOO LITTLE; 122] *Opposite*: abundant 2 *adj* **rare**, uncommon, unusual,

infrequent, threatened, occasional [➥ EXTRAORDINARY: UNCOMMON; 205] *Opposite*: common

scarcely *adv* **barely**, hardly, not quite, only just, just, narrowly, not at all [➥ TO A CERTAIN EXTENT; 136] *Opposite*: fully

scarceness 1 *n* **shortage**, lack, dearth, insufficiency, scarcity, paucity, inadequacy [➥ TOO FEW, TOO LITTLE; 122] *Opposite*: abundance 2 *n* **rarity**, uncommonness, infrequency, lack, want, absence [➥ ABSENT AND UNAVAILABLE; 7] *Opposite*: commonness

scarcity 1 *n* **shortage**, lack, dearth, insufficiency, scarceness, paucity, inadequacy [➥ TOO FEW, TOO LITTLE; 122] *Opposite*: abundance 2 *n* **rarity**, uncommonness, infrequency, lack, want, absence [➥ ABSENT AND UNAVAILABLE; 7] *Opposite*: commonness

scare 1 *v* **frighten**, terrify, startle, alarm, panic, worry, shock, intimidate, jolt, shake up, spook, scarify (*informal*) [➥ FRIGHTEN AND SHOCK; 568] *Opposite*: reassure 2 *n* **fright**, shock, start, jolt, alarm, panic, worry, anxiety [➥ FEAR AND PANIC; 543] *Opposite*: reassurance

scarecrow *n* **figure**, effigy, mannequin, guy (*UK*) [➥ REPRESENTATIONS AND GENERAL EXAMPLES; 65]

scared *adj* **frightened**, afraid, fearful, terrified, nervous, startled, alarmed, worried, anxious, shaken up, timid, timorous [➥ FEAR AND PANIC; 543] *Opposite*: fearless

scared rigid (*UK*) *adj* [➥ FEAR AND PANIC; 543]

scared stiff *adj* [➥ FEAR AND PANIC; 543]

scared to death *adj* [➥ FEAR AND PANIC; 543]

scaremonger *n* **alarmist**, doomsayer, troublemaker, rumormonger, newsmonger, gossip [➥ GRUMPY AND NEGATIVE PEOPLE; 953] *Opposite*: optimist

scare off *v* **frighten away**, drive away, chase off, scare away, frighten, warn off, deter, discourage, put off [➥ FRIGHTEN AND SHOCK; 568] *Opposite*: welcome

scare up (*informal*) 1 *v* **get**, get hold of, lay hands on, rustle up, search out, locate, find [➥ GET; 420] 2 *v* **prepare**, concoct, put together, whip up, rustle up (*informal*), knock together (*informal*) [➥ MEAL PREPARATION; 354]

scarf 1 *n* **muffler**, headscarf, bandana, cravat, shawl, stole, wrap, pashmina, mantilla [➥ ACCESSORIES, MILLINERY, AND LINGERIE; 867] 2 *v* (*informal*) **gobble**, wolf, bolt, devour, scarf down (*informal*), scoff (*informal*) [➥ EAT AND NOT EAT; 710] *Opposite*: refuse

scarf down (*informal*) *v* **gobble**, wolf, bolt, devour, scarf (*informal*), scoff (*informal*) [➥ EAT AND NOT EAT; 710] *Opposite*: refuse

scarify 1 *v* (*informal*) **scare**, frighten, alarm, worry, startle, terrify, petrify, panic, shock [➥ FRIGHTEN AND SHOCK; 568] *Opposite*: reassure 2 *v* **lacerate**, scratch, incise, cut, score, lance [➥ TEAR, BREAK, AND CUT; 360]

scariness *n* **menace**, creepiness (*informal*), spookiness (*informal*) [➥ FRIGHTENING; 231] *Opposite*: reassurance

scarlet *type of* **red** [➥ COLORS; 1224]

scarp *n* **escarpment**, ridge, cliff, bluff, crag, incline, slope [➥ MOUNTAINS AND HILLS; 1044]

scarred 1 *adj* **mutilated**, disfigured, marked, injured, wounded, pockmarked [➡ CONDITIONS AFFECTING THE SKIN; 721] **2** *adj* **damaged**, defaced, blemished, marked, scratched, scraped, scored [➡ IN BAD REPAIR; 1234]

scary (*informal*) *adj* **frightening**, chilling, terrifying, petrifying, daunting, forbidding, bloodcurdling, intimidating, menacing, startling, alarming, worrying, creepy (*informal*) [➡ FRIGHTENING; 231] *Opposite:* reassuring

scat (*informal*) *v* **run away**, run off, escape, flee, abscond, fly, beat it (*informal*) [➡ RUN AWAY AND AVOID; 10]

scathing *adj* **scornful**, mocking, derisive, sarcastic, contemptuous, cutting, biting, wounding, hurtful, caustic, scalding, critical, blistering, withering, fierce [➡ MOCKING AND DISMISSIVE; 636] *Opposite:* complimentary

scatter 1 *v* **throw**, strew, fling, toss, sprinkle, distribute, disseminate, broadcast, dot [➡ SPREAD AND SCATTER; 332] *Opposite:* collect **2** *v* **disperse**, spread out, spread, flee, take flight, break up, fly away, fly apart [➡ SEPARATE AND DIVIDE; 401] *Opposite:* gather

Compare and Contrast: *scatter*, *broadcast*, *distribute*, *disseminate*

CORE MEANING: to spread around

scatter to spread things around physically, especially in a random widespread manner; *broadcast* to spread or transmit information, especially by means of radio or television, or to scatter seeds over the ground; *distribute* to allocate, share, or give out something in a structured or organized way, or to spread something over a particular surface or area; *disseminate* to spread ideas, information, or attitudes such as goodwill.

scatterbrained *adj* **absent-minded**, vague, forgetful, harebrained, woolly-headed, careless, unreliable, dizzy (*informal*) [➡ NEGATIVE INTELLECTUAL CHARACTERISTICS; 525] *Opposite:* focused

scattered 1 *adj* **dispersed**, distributed, strewn, sprinkled, disseminated, spread, speckled, spread out, dotted, here and there, few and far between [➡ GENERAL LOCATIONS; 158] *Opposite:* concentrated **2** *adj* **infrequent**, isolated, discrete, separate, occasional, sporadic, rare [➡ NEVER AND INFREQUENCY; 97] *Opposite:* frequent

scattering *n* **handful**, sprinkling, trickle, bit, smattering, dusting, sprinkle, dash [➡ FEW, LITTLE, SMALL AMOUNT; 120]

scattershot *adj* **disorganized**, indiscriminate, random, chaotic, slapdash, careless, haphazard, unfocused [➡ DISORDER AND CHAOS; 245] *Opposite:* focused

scavenge *v* **hunt**, forage, search, rummage, sift, go through [➡ SEEK POSSESSION AND SEARCH; 456]

scenario *n* **situation**, state of affairs, state, setup, circumstances, setting, picture, development, consequence [➡ SITUATIONS; 71]

scene 1 *n* **act**, division, part, section, passage, extract [➡ PARTS OF BOOKS AND DOCUMENTS; 593] **2** *n* **setting**, site, place, background, backdrop, location, area, field, arena [➡ PLACE; 1065] **3** *n* **sight**, prospect, picture, panorama, view, landscape, outlook, vista, tableau [➡ VIEWS AND OUTLOOKS; 1073] **4** *n* **fuss**, commotion, exhibition, incident, spectacle, display, outburst, to-do (*informal*) [➡ CHAOS AND UPROAR; 51]

scenery 1 *n* **set**, backdrop, backcloth, background, decor, setting, staging [➡ IN THE THEATER; 906] **2** *n* **landscape**, panorama, vista, outlook, view, countryside [➡ VIEWS AND OUTLOOKS; 1073]

scenic *adj* **picturesque**, beautiful, attractive, lovely, charming, pretty [➡ BEAUTY AND ATTRACTIVENESS; 189] *Opposite:* unsightly

scent 1 *n* **smell**, odor, aroma, perfume, bouquet, whiff [➡ SMELL AND SMELLING; 705] **2** *n* **trail**, trace, track, spoor, aroma, odor [➡ EVIDENCE AND PROOF; 69] **3** *n* **perfume**, fragrance, cologne, toilet water, eau de cologne, eau de toilette, aftershave [➡ PERSONAL HYGIENE; 491] **4** *n* **hint**, trace, air, whiff, suggestion, indication [➡ FEW, LITTLE, SMALL AMOUNT; 120] **5** *v* **sniff**, smell, detect, sense, pick up, perceive [➡ SMELL AND SMELLING; 705] **6** *v* **predict**, foresee, foretell, sense, feel, expect [➡ PREDICT AND ANTICIPATE; 750] **7** *v* **imbue**, perfume, fill, infuse, suffuse, tinge [➡ DECORATE, ADORN, AND APPLY COATINGS; 405]

See Compare and Contrast at **smell**.

scented *adj* **perfumed**, fragrant, aromatic, sweet-smelling, smelly, spicy [➡ SMELL AND SMELLING; 705]

scepter *n* **staff**, staff of office, mace, rod, insignia, wand [➡ STICKS, POLES, AND WEDGES; 1254]

schedule 1 *n* **agenda**, timetable, diary, calendar, list, plan, roster, program, to-do list, rota (*UK*) [➡ LISTS AND SCHEDULES; 587] **2** *v* **arrange**, plan, program, book, organize, list, reserve, slate, timetable (*UK*) [➡ PREPARE FOR ACTION; 289] *Opposite:* cancel

scheduled *adj* **arranged**, planned, programmed, listed, booked, slated, organized, reserved, timetabled (*UK*) [➡ INTENTIONAL AND DELIBERATE; 279] *Opposite:* unplanned

schema *n* **plan**, diagram, scheme, schematic, representation, graphic, chart, outline, draft [➡ DRAWINGS, CHARTS, AND TABLES; 594]

schematize *v* **systematize**, arrange, structure, organize, draft, set out, outline [➡ ARRANGE AND CREATE ORDER; 357] *Opposite:* disarrange

scheme 1 *n* **plot**, plan, conspiracy, ploy, ruse, intrigue [➡ INTENTIONS AND PURPOSES; 772] **2** *n* **plan**, method, stratagem, format, program, idea, proposal, design, policy, arrangement, system [➡ WAYS OF DOING THINGS; 294] **3** *n* **arrangement**, system, structure, outline, organization, pattern, order [➡ ORDER AND ORGANIZATION; 206] *Opposite:* chaos **4** *n* **diagram**, plan, schematic, graphic, representation, chart, schema [➡ DRAWINGS, CHARTS, AND TABLES; 594] **5** *v* **plot**, conspire, intrigue, connive, plan, machinate [➡ PREPARE FOR ACTION; 289]

schemer *n* **plotter**, conspirator, conniver, traitor, intriguer [➡ PEOPLE WHO DECEIVE; 661]

scheming *adj* **devious**, calculating, conniving, conspiratorial, treacherous, cunning, underhand, wily, tricky [➡ DECEITFUL; 513] *Opposite:* honest

scherzo *type of* **musical form** [➡ MUSIC, SONGS, AND SINGING; 907]

schilling *type of* **currency** [➡ CURRENCIES; 798]

schism *n* **split**, break, division, rupture, rift, gulf, breakup, faction, factionalism [➡ DISHARMONY; 156] *Opposite:* union

schismatic *adj* **factional**, divisive, clashing, conflicting, controversial, polemical, dissonant, dissenting [➔ DIS-HARMONY; 156] *Opposite*: unifying

schist *type of* **stone** [➔ STONES, ROCKS, AND BOULDERS; 1057]

schlep (*informal*) **1** *v* **lug**, haul, heave, drag, cart [➔ MOVE SLOWLY; 314] **2** *n* **trek**, trudge, hike, bore, bind, chore [➔ HARD WORK OR EFFORT; 298]

schlock (*slang*) *n* **garbage**, trash, rubbish, junk (*informal*), crud (*informal*), tripe (*informal*) [➔ JUNK AND USELESS OBJECTS; 1249]

schlocky (*slang*) *adj* **junky**, cheap, worthless, garbagy, trashy, rubbishy, tacky (*informal*), cruddy (*informal*) [➔ IN BAD REPAIR; 1234]

schmaltz (*informal*) *n* **sentimentality**, slush, mush, corniness, mawkishness, emotionalism [➔ IN POOR TASTE AND OVER-SENTIMENTAL; 229]

schmaltziness (*informal*) *n* [➔ IN POOR TASTE AND OVER-SENTIMENTAL; 229]

schmaltzy (*informal*) *adj* **sentimental**, cloying, sugary, saccharine, slushy, mushy, corny, mawkish, emotional, soft, soppy (*informal*) [➔ IN POOR TASTE AND OVERSENTIMENTAL; 229] *Opposite*: hardheaded

schmooze (*slang*) **1** *v* **chat**, chatter, socialize, converse, banter, talk, gossip, chitchat (*informal*), yak (*informal*) [➔ TWO-WAY COMMUNICATION; 607] **2** *n* **conversation**, chat, talk, gossip, dialogue, chitchat (*informal*), yak (*informal*) [➔ INFORMAL COM-MUNICATION; 45]

schmoozer (*slang*) *n* **conversationalist**, chatterer, talker, gossip, banterer, raconteur, speaker [➔ SPEAKERS AND ORATORS; 603]

schnozzle (*slang*) *n* [➔ THE NOSE; 704]

scholar *n* **academic**, researcher, professor, doctor, intellectual, specialist, sage (*literary*), don (*UK*) [➔ TALENTED OR INTELLIGENT PEOPLE; 528]

scholarly *adj* **learned**, academic, erudite, intellectual, educated, studious, bookish, cerebral, knowledgeable, well-read, highbrow, donnish (*UK*) [➔ LEVELS OF EDUCATION AND SOPHISTICATION; 894] *Opposite*: lowbrow

scholarship **1** *n* **grant**, bursary, studentship, subsidy, allowance [➔ FUNDS, PAYMENTS, AND CHARGES; 800] **2** *n* **learning**, erudition, study, knowledge, research, skill, science [➔ KNOWLEDGE AND WISDOM; 558] *Opposite*: ignorance

See Compare and Contrast at **knowledge**.

scholastic *adj* **educational**, academic, pedagogic, school, college, collegiate, university [➔ EDUCATION; 838]

school **1** *n* **educational institution**, place of learning [➔ EDUCATIONAL INSTITUTIONS; 813] **2** *n* **university**, college, seminary, conservatory, graduate school, institute [➔ EDUCATIONAL INSTITUTIONS; 813] **3** *n* **group**, set, coterie, brotherhood, sisterhood [➔ GROUPS OF PEOPLE; 935] *Opposite*: individual **4** *v* **train**, instruct, educate, discipline, teach, tutor, drill, coach, prepare [➔ INSTRUCT AND TEACH; 609] **5** *type of* **herd** [➔ GROUPS OF ANIMALS; 993]

school

◆ *types of schools*
academy, boarding school, elementary school, grade school, grammar school, high school, junior high, kindergarten, middle school, nursery school, prep school, preschool, primary school, private school, public school, trade school, vocational school

See Compare and Contrast at **teach**.

schoolboy *n* [➔ STUDENTS AND PUPILS; 841]

schoolchild *n* **pupil**, student, scholar, schoolkid (*informal*), schoolboy, schoolgirl, schoolmate [➔ STUDENTS AND PUPILS; 841]

schoolgirl *n* [➔ STUDENTS AND PUPILS; 841]

schooling *n* **education**, teaching, training, instruction, tuition, coaching [➔ TEACHING; 839]

schoolkid (*informal*) *n* [➔ STUDENTS AND PUPILS; 841]

schoolmate *n* [➔ FRIENDS AND GUESTS; 963]

school of dance *n* [➔ EDUCATIONAL INSTITUTIONS; 813]

school of the arts *n* [➔ EDUCATIONAL INSTITUTIONS; 813]

school of thought *n* **philosophy**, doctrine, ideology, outlook, attitude, viewpoint [➔ POINTS OF VIEW; 767]

schoolroom *type of* **room in public buildings** [➔ TYPES OF ROOMS; 1097]

schoolteacher *n* [➔ EDUCATORS; 840]

schoolwork *n* [➔ CLASSES, COURSEWORK, AND EXAMINATIONS; 842]

school yard *n* [➔ URBAN OUTDOOR SPACES; 1072]

schooner *type of* **sailing vessel** [➔ SHIPS AND BOATS; 1150]

sciatica *n* [➔ ILLNESSES AND DISORDERS; 732]

science *n* **discipline**, knowledge, skill, learning, scholarship [➔ KNOWLEDGE AND WISDOM; 558]

science fiction *n* [➔ FICTION AND DRAMA; 913]

science park *n* [➔ URBAN OUTDOOR SPACES; 1072]

scientific *adj* **technical**, methodical, systematic, logical, precise, exact, controlled [➔ EXACT; 203] *Opposite*: unscientific

scimitar *type of* **sword or knife** [➔ SWORDS AND KNIVES; 1157]

scintilla *n* **jot**, iota, scrap, shred, speck, ounce, bit, spark, trace, particle [➔ FEW, LITTLE, SMALL AMOUNT; 120]

scintillate **1** *v* **sparkle**, glitter, gleam, flash, glint, glisten, twinkle, shine [➔ LIGHT EMISSION; 368] **2** *v* **fascinate**, dazzle, charm, shine, sparkle, stimulate, delight, bewitch [➔ APPEAL TO AND AROUSE INTEREST; 575] *Opposite*: bore

scintillating *adj* **sparkling**, dazzling, brilliant, bright, shining, glittering, amusing, entertaining, fascinating, stimulating, witty, animated, lively [➔ INTERESTING AND MEANINGFUL; 190] *Opposite*: dull

scintillation *n* **sparkling**, glittering, gleaming, flashing, glinting, glistening, twinkling [➡ LIGHT; 1164] *Opposite*: dullness

scion 1 *n* **cutting**, graft, shoot, implant, implantation, insert, splice [➡ PARTS OF TREES AND PLANTS; 1026] 2 *n* **offspring**, child, heir, descendant, son, daughter [➡ YOUNGER GENERATION RELATIVES; 958] *Opposite*: parent

scirocco *see* **sirocco**

scissors *type of* **cutting tool** [➡ CUTTING TOOLS; 1120]

scoff 1 *v* **jeer**, sneer, mock, ridicule, make fun of, laugh at, poke fun at, pooh-pooh, deride [➡ PROTEST AND EXPRESS DISAPPROVAL; 642] *Opposite*: praise 2 *v* (*informal*) **eat**, gobble, stuff your face, bolt, wolf, scarf down, guzzle (*informal*) [➡ EAT AND NOT EAT; 710] *Opposite*: nibble

scoffing *adj* **mocking**, jeering, sneering, dismissive, contemptuous, scornful [➡ MOCKING AND DISMISSIVE; 636]

scold *v* **tell off** (*informal*), admonish, reprimand, reproach, rebuke, caution, discipline, haul over the coals, yell at, chew out (*informal*) [➡ ACCUSE, BLAME, AND CRITICIZE; 641] *Opposite*: praise

scolding *n* **admonishment**, reprimand, reproach, rebuke, caution, dressing-down, telling-off (*informal*), tongue-lashing [➡ CRITICISMS AND ANGRY OUTBURSTS; 50] *Opposite*: praise

sconce *n* **light fixture**, bracket, wall lamp, candleholder, light fitting (*UK*), lamp fitting (*UK*) [➡ LIGHTING; 862]

scoop 1 *n* **ladle**, dipper, serving spoon, server, soup ladle, punch ladle [➡ SPOONS, SCOOPS, AND SHOVELS; 1121] 2 *n* (*informal*) **news story**, story, exclusive, revelation, exposé, sensation [➡ NEWSPAPERS AND MAGAZINES; 605] 3 *v* **dig**, hollow, scrape, shovel, excavate, gouge [➡ USE TOOLS AND MACHINERY; 468] *Opposite*: fill 4 *v* **lift**, gather up, pick up, raise, take, bundle (*informal*) [➡ GET; 420] *Opposite*: drop

scoot (*informal*) 1 *v* **move quickly**, rush, hurry, scurry, dash, run, race, career, zip (*informal*) [➡ MOVE FAST; 313] *Opposite*: dawdle 2 *v* **go away**, leave, scat (*informal*), make yourself scarce (*informal*), skedaddle (*slang*), vamoose (*slang*) [➡ RUN AWAY AND AVOID; 10] *Opposite*: arrive

scooter *type of* **bike** [➡ BIKES, CARS, AND CARRIAGES; 1149]

scope 1 *n* **possibility**, choice, room, opportunity, space, latitude [➡ POSSIBLE AND PROBABLE; 177] *Opposite*: constraint 2 *n* **range**, extent, capacity, span, reach, compass, bounds [➡ DEGREE AND EXTENT; 110]

scorch *v* **burn**, singe, sear, char, blacken, mark, brand [➡ FIRE, FLAMMABILITY, AND BURNING; 1165]

scorched 1 *adj* **burned**, singed, seared, charred, blackened, marked, branded [➡ IN BAD REPAIR; 1234] 2 *adj* **dried**, dry as a bone, dry, parched, baked, dried up, dried out, bone dry, desiccated, arid [➡ DRY; 1242] *Opposite*: drenched

scorching (*informal*) *adj* **boiling**, baking, sweltering, sizzling (*informal*), blazing, burning, blistering, roasting (*informal*) [➡ HOT WEATHER; 1050] *Opposite*: freezing

score 1 *n* **total**, tally, mark, result, count, grade [➡ SCORES AND EVALUATIONS; 598] 2 *n* **notch**, cut, slash, groove, nick, mark [➡ HOLES, GAPS, AND FORKS; 1252] 3 *v* **achieve**, chalk up, attain, make, gain, get, notch up (*slang*) [➡ GET MONEY OR REWARD; 421] 4 *v* **keep count**, keep a tally, keep score, count, tot up, record [➡ ASSESS QUANTITY; 757] 5 *v* **cut into**, slash, notch, nick,

slice, cut, mark, carve [➡ TEAR, BREAK, AND CUT; 360] 6 *v* **scratch**, etch, carve, mark, scrape, cut [➡ TEAR, BREAK, AND CUT; 360]

scoreboard *n* **display**, board, panel, bulletin board, notice board (*UK*) [➡ SIGNPOSTS, SIGNALS, AND BILLBOARDS; 595]

scorecard *n* **tally**, scoresheet, record, card [➡ RECORDS; 585]

scores *n* **lots**, tons (*informal*), heaps (*informal*), buckets (*informal*), piles (*informal*), loads (*informal*) [➡ MANY, MUCH, LARGE AMOUNT; 117] *Opposite*: none

scoresheet *n* **sheet**, scorecard, tally, record [➡ RECORDS; 585]

scorn 1 *n* **contempt**, disdain, disrespect, derision, scornfulness, disparagement, ridicule, sneering, mockery [➡ ANTAGONISM; 552] *Opposite*: admiration 2 *v* **show contempt for**, despise, disdain, belittle, deride, pour scorn on, disparage, ridicule, sneer at, mock, revile [➡ PROTEST AND EXPRESS DISAPPROVAL; 642] *Opposite*: admire 3 *v* **reject**, spurn, rebuff, turn down, refuse, disdain, disregard, hate [➡ DENY AND REJECT; 644] *Opposite*: choose

scorned 1 *adj* **despised**, disdained, belittled, derided, disparaged, reviled [➡ UNPOPULAR AND UNWANTED; 258] *Opposite*: admired 2 *adj* **rejected**, spurned, rebuffed, turned down, refused, disdained, disregarded [➡ UNPOPULAR AND UNWANTED; 258] *Opposite*: chosen

scornful *adj* **contemptuous**, disdainful, disrespectful, mocking, derisive, disparaging, sneering [➡ MOCKING AND DISMISSIVE; 636] *Opposite*: admiring

scornfulness *n* **contempt**, disdain, disrespect, mockery, derision, disparagement [➡ ANTAGONISM; 552]

Scorpio *type of* **astrological sign** [➡ FATE, DESTINY, AND ASTROLOGY; 782]

scorpion *type of* **arachnid** [➡ ARACHNIDS; 1018]

Scorpius *type of* **constellation** [➡ HEAVENLY BODIES; 1061]

scotch *v* **stop**, spoil, foil, scuttle, scupper, mess up (*informal*), ruin [➡ MAKE IMPOSSIBLE; 276] *Opposite*: initiate

Scotch broth *type of* **soup** [➡ SOUPS; 1186]

scot-free *adv* **unpunished**, without punishment, with impunity, lightly, easily, without a scratch [➡ FREEDOM AND LIBERTY; 208]

Scottie *type of* **small dog** [➡ DOGS; 980]

scoundrel *n* **rogue**, rascal, villain, cheat, crook (*informal*), rat (*slang*) [➡ VILLAINS AND THUGS; 947] *Opposite*: hero

scour 1 *v* **scrub**, rub, clean, wash, polish, burnish [➡ CLEAN AND POLISH; 403] *Opposite*: dirty 2 *v* **search**, comb, hunt, go over with a fine-tooth comb, rake through [➡ SEEK POSSESSION AND SEARCH; 456]

scourge 1 *n* **bane**, blight, plague, curse, menace, thorn in your flesh, thorn in your side, tormentor [➡ NUISANCES; 253] *Opposite*: blessing 2 *v* **plague**, curse, afflict, terrorize, torment, devastate [➡ UPSET, DISTRESS, AND HUMILIATE; 567] *Opposite*: bless

scout 1 *n* **lookout**, spy, watch, undercover agent, detective, emissary, pathfinder, guide, mole [➡ PEOPLE WHO GUARD AND PROTECT; 846] 2 *v* **search**, hunt, scout around, look around, cast around, scout out, seek, look for, look out for, search for, nose around (*informal*) [➧SEEK POSSESSION AND SEARCH; 456] *Opposite*: find **3** *v* **check out**, survey, investigate, spy out, explore, reconnoiter, recce (*slang*) [➧LOOKING AND LOOKS; 700]

scout around *v* **search**, hunt, scout, look around, scout out, seek, look for, look out for, search for, cast around, forage, nose around (*informal*) [➧SEEK POSSESSION AND SEARCH; 456]

scowl **1** *n* **glare**, frown, glower, grimace, stare, pout, dirty look [➧FACIAL EXPRESSIONS AND BLUSHING; 651] *Opposite*: smile **2** *v* **look daggers**, glare, frown, glower, grimace, pout [➧FACIAL EXPRESSIONS AND BLUSHING; 651] *Opposite*: smile

scrabble **1** *v* **scratch**, dig, scrape, claw, pick, worry [➧CONTACT: TOUCH; 412] **2** *v* **grope**, fumble, clutch, rummage, scrape around, feel, forage, rootle (*UK*) [➧SEEK POSSESSION AND SEARCH; 456]

scrag end *type of* **cut** [➧TYPES AND CUTS OF MEAT; 1177]

scragginess *n* **scrawniness**, boniness, gauntness, skinniness, thinness [➧BUILD; 477] *Opposite*: plumpness

scraggly *adj* **messy**, disheveled, untidy, unkempt, tangled, tousled, bedraggled [➧BADLY GROOMED; 483] *Opposite*: tidy

scraggy *adj* **scrawny**, bony, thin, emaciated, gaunt, skinny [➧BUILD; 477] *Opposite*: plump

See Compare and Contrast at **thin**.

scram (*informal*) *v* **run off**, run away, get out, get away, bolt, scat (*informal*), skedaddle (*slang*), beat it (*slang*), vamoose (*slang*) [➧RUN AWAY AND AVOID; 10]

scramble **1** *v* **climb**, clamber, crawl, scrabble, struggle, swarm, scale [➧GO UPWARD; 306] *Opposite*: descend **2** *v* **move quickly**, rush, run, scuttle, jostle, push, stampede, dash [➧MOVE FAST; 313] *Opposite*: plod **3** *v* **mix up**, jumble, mix, muddle, confuse, disorganize [➧CREATE DISORDER AND CAUSE CHAOS; 358] *Opposite*: unscramble **4** *n* **ascent**, climb, clamber, hike [➧GO UPWARD; 306] *Opposite*: descent **5** *n* **rush**, run, stampede, commotion, dash, free-for-all (*informal*) [➧SUDDEN EVENTS; 52] *Opposite*: calm

scrambler *type of* **bike** [➧BIKES, CARS, AND CARRIAGES; 1149]

scrap **1** *n* **piece**, bit, fragment, slip, wisp, particle, crumb, morsel [➧SMALL PIECES; 129] **2** *n* (*informal*) **fight**, scuffle, tussle, row, clash, fracas, brawl [➧AGGRESSIVE EVENTS; 39] **3** *v* **cancel**, abandon, get rid of, do away with, give up, write off (*informal*), ditch (*informal*), bin (*UK*) [➧ABOLISH AND ANNUL; 452] *Opposite*: adopt **4** *v* **scuffle**, fight, tussle, spar, brawl, wrestle, come to blows, clash [➧COMPETE, CONTEND, AND COMBAT; 303]

scrape **1** *v* **rub**, scratch, scuff, abrade, scour, rasp, scrub [➧WORSEN APPEARANCE; 382] **2** *v* **graze**, scratch, scuff, mark, abrade, chafe, bark, skin, cut [➧TEAR, BREAK, AND CUT; 360] **3** *n* **scratch**, scuff, graze, mark, abrasion, cut [➧HOLES, GAPS, AND FORKS; 1252] **4** *n* (*informal*) **predicament**, plight, problem, fix (*informal*), pickle (*informal*), jam (*informal*) [➧DIFFICULT SITUATIONS; 72] **5** *n* (*informal*) **fight**, brawl, clash, fracas, scuffle, tussle [➧AGGRESSIVE EVENTS; 39]

scrape by *v* **make do**, survive, make ends meet, get by, scratch a living, eke out a living, scrape out a living [➧CONTINUE TO EXIST; 17] *Opposite*: prosper

scrape out *v* **hollow out**, scoop out, gouge out, carve out, gouge, scoop, dig out [➧EMPTY AND UNLOAD; 407] *Opposite*: fill

scrape together *v* **collect**, amass, put by, put aside, scrape up, save, gather, assemble, garner, glean, scratch together, scrounge (*informal*) [➧GET; 420] *Opposite*: disperse

scrapheap *n* **garbage dump**, junkyard, landfill, tip (*UK*) [➧URBAN OUTDOOR SPACES; 1072]

scrappy **1** *adj* **fragmentary**, fragmented, patchy, piecemeal, incomplete, patchwork, bitty (*UK*) [➧UNFINISHEDNESS; 239] *Opposite*: complete **2** *adj* **disjointed**, inconsistent, disconnected, incoherent, patchy, untidy [➧DISORDER AND CHAOS; 245] *Opposite*: uniform **3** *adj* (*informal*) **plucky**, courageous, determined, spirited, spunky (*informal*) [➧COURAGE; 498] *Opposite*: timid **4** *adj* (*informal*) **argumentative**, contrary, confrontational, hotheaded, quarrelsome, belligerent [➧AGGRESSIVE AND BELLIGERENT; 518] *Opposite*: docile

scraps *n* **leftovers**, scrapings, slops, crumbs, leavings, odds and ends, remainders, orts [➧REMAINDER AND REMAINDERS; 125]

scrapyard (*UK*) *n* [➧URBAN OUTDOOR SPACES; 1072]

scratch **1** *v* **scrape**, graze, grate, rub, cut, score, nick, scuff, abrade, mark [➧WORSEN APPEARANCE; 382] **2** *v* **itch**, rub, scrape, worry at [➧CONTACT: TOUCH; 412] **3** *v* **cancel**, abandon, forget, scrap, leave out, delete, scrub (*informal*) [➧ABOLISH AND ANNUL; 452] *Opposite*: keep **4** *v* **pull out**, drop out, bow out, withdraw, abandon, leave [➧NOT DO AND REFUSE TO DO; 274] *Opposite*: continue **5** *n* **cut**, scrape, graze, score, nick, scuff, abrasion, mark [➧HOLES, GAPS, AND FORKS; 1252]

scratched *adj* **scuffed**, scored, scraped, scored, marked, damaged [➧IN BAD REPAIR; 1234]

scratchpad *n* [➧WRITING AND DRAWING IMPLEMENTS, AND MEDIA; 601]

scratch together *v* **collect**, amass, put by, put aside, scratch up, scrape together, save, gather, assemble, garner, glean, scrounge (*informal*) [➧GET; 420] *Opposite*: disperse

scratchy *adj* **itchy**, prickly, tickly, irritating, uncomfortable, rough [➧PHYSICAL TEXTURE; 1222] *Opposite*: soft

scrawl **1** *v* **scribble**, doodle, pencil, write, draw, jot, dash off (*informal*) [➧RECORD SOMETHING; 371] **2** *n* **illegible writing**, scribble, doodle, graffiti, squiggle, writing [➧WRITING; 583]

scrawled *adj* **indecipherable**, illegible, incomprehensible, scribbled, untidy, messy [➧WRITING; 583] *Opposite*: neat

scrawniness *n* **gauntness**, skinniness, boniness, scragginess, thinness, emaciation [➧BUILD; 477] *Opposite*: plumpness

scrawny *adj* **skinny**, scraggy, gaunt, bony, undernourished, emaciated, thin, skeletal [➧BUILD; 477] *Opposite*: plump

See Compare and Contrast at **thin**.

screak **1** *v* **screech**, howl, yowl, yell, scream, squeal, holler (*informal*) [➧SOUND EMISSION BY PEOPLE; 363] *Opposite*: murmur **2** *v* **creak**, groan, grate, squeak, squeal, squawk [➧SOUND EMISSION BY ANIMALS OR BIRDS; 364] **3** *type of* **human sound**

[➡SOUNDS MADE BY PEOPLE; 1262] **4** *type of* **bird sound** [➡SOUNDS MADE BY BIRDS; 1263]

scream 1 *n* **shriek**, yell, cry, yelp, shout, screech, squeal, squawk [➡SOUNDS MADE BY PEOPLE; 1262] *Opposite:* murmur **2** *n* (*informal*) **laugh** (*informal*), riot (*informal*), card (*dated informal*), gas (*slang*), hoot (*slang*) [➡JOKERS AND TEASES; 675] **3** *v* **shout**, shriek, yell, cry, screech, bawl, squeal, squawk [➡SOUND EMISSION BY PEOPLE; 363] *Opposite:* whisper

scream with laughter *v* [➡LAUGHTER; 649]

scree *n* **rock debris**, talus, rubble, gravel, stones, rock [➡EROSION PRODUCTS AND SOIL; 1058]

screech 1 *n* **scream**, shriek, squeal, cry, yelp, yell, squawk, shout [➡SOUND EMISSION BY PEOPLE; 363] *Opposite:* whisper **2** *type of* **human sound** [➡SOUNDS MADE BY PEOPLE; 1262] **3** *type of* **bird sound** [➡SOUNDS MADE BY BIRDS; 1263] **4** *v* **shriek**, scream, squeal, cry, yelp, yell, squawk, shout [➡SOUND EMISSION BY ANIMALS OR BIRDS; 364] *Opposite:* whisper **5** *v* **skid**, judder, shudder, squeal, scream, career [➡MOVE FAST; 313] *Opposite:* glide

screech owl *type of* **owl** [➡OWLS; 1001]

screen 1 *n* **partition**, divider, panel, shield, guard, barrier [➡WALLS AND PARTITIONS; 1104] **2** *n* **shade**, awning, canopy, shelter, curtain, blind [➡COVERS AND COATINGS; 1246] **3** *n* **monitor**, VDT, display, computer screen, television, VDU (*UK*) [➡COMPUTERS AND COMPUTING; 1127] **4** *v* **hide**, conceal, cover, protect, shelter, shield, guard [➡CAUSE TO DISAPPEAR; 6] *Opposite:* reveal **5** *v* **partition**, separate, divide, mark off, curtain [➡SEPARATE AND DIVIDE; 401] *Opposite:* open out **6** *v* **broadcast**, put on, show, transmit, project, air, put on air (*UK*) [➡TELEVISION AND RADIO; 606] **7** *v* **test**, inspect, examine, diagnose, check, check out [➡EXAMINE AND ASSESS; 753] **8** *v* **vet**, select, assess, investigate, inspect, test, examine, check out, sift, weed out [➡EXAMINE AND ASSESS; 753]

screening 1 *n* **show**, showing, viewing, program, projection, matinée [➡PERFORMANCES AND SHOWS; 42] **2** *n* **broadcast**, showing, transmission, run, airing, repeat, rerun [➡FILM; 901] **3** *n* **inspection**, testing, examination, diagnosis, checking, check [➡EXAMINE AND ASSESS; 753] **4** *n* **selection**, vetting, assessment, investigation, inspection, examination, review [➡EXAMINE AND ASSESS; 753]

screenplay *n* **script**, dialogue, scenario, text, writing [➡FILM; 901]

screensaver *type of* **software** [➡COMPUTERS AND COMPUTING; 1127]

screen test *n* [➡FILM; 901]

screenwriter *n* **scriptwriter**, writer, dramatist, author, playwright [➡WRITERS AND STYLES; 914]

screw 1 *v* **attach**, bolt, fasten, fix, secure [➡FASTEN, LINK, AND JOIN; 408] *Opposite:* unscrew **2** *v* **twist**, rotate, coil, turn, wind, spin [➡MOVE SOMETHING: ON THE SPOT; 336] *Opposite:* unscrew **3** *v* **crumple**, twist, distort, contort, crinkle, fold, scrunch, crunch, wrinkle, furrow [➡CHANGE OF SHAPE; 385] *Opposite:* smooth

screwdriver *type of* **general tool** [➡HAND TOOLS; 1119]

screw up *v* **muster**, gather, summon, call up, pluck up, concentrate, get up [➡GET; 420] *Opposite:* lose

scribble 1 *v* **scrawl**, jot, write, dash off (*informal*) [➡RECORD

SOMETHING; 371] **2** *v* **draw**, doodle, scrawl, squiggle [➡CREATE IMAGES; 356] **3** *n* **writing**, handwriting, scrawl, lettering [➡WRITING; 583] **4** *n* **doodle**, scrawl, jotting, squiggle, design, cartoon, drawing [➡DRAWINGS, CHARTS, AND TABLES; 594]

scribbled *adj* **scrawled**, jotted, untidy, illegible, indecipherable, unreadable, incomprehensible, hurried, dashed off (*informal*) [➡WRITING; 583] *Opposite:* neat

scribbler *n* [➡WRITING AND DRAWING IMPLEMENTS, AND MEDIA; 601]

scribbling pad *n* [➡WRITING AND DRAWING IMPLEMENTS, AND MEDIA; 601]

scribe *n* **transcriber**, copyist, clerk, illuminator [➡WRITERS AND STYLES; 914]

scrimmage 1 *n* **struggle**, tussle, fray, ruckus, free-for-all (*informal*), scrum (*UK*) [➡CHAOS AND UPROAR; 51] **2** *n* **fight**, battle, skirmish, clash, fray, brawl, scuffle, affray [➡AGGRESSIVE EVENTS; 39]

scrimp *v* **economize**, save, skimp, tighten your belt, pull in your horns, go easy (*informal*), draw in your horns (*UK*) [➡FORGO AND DENY ONESELF; 449] *Opposite:* squander

script 1 *n* **screenplay**, text, dialogue, words, libretto, play, speech [➡FICTION AND DRAMA; 913] **2** *n* **writing**, calligraphy, handwriting, hand, cursive, lettering [➡WRITING; 583]

scriptwriter *n* **writer**, author, playwright, screenwriter, dramatist [➡WRITERS AND STYLES; 914]

scroll *n* **roll**, parchment, document, certificate, manuscript, spool [➡OFFICIAL DOCUMENTS; 586]

scrooge (*informal*) *n* **miser**, skinflint, niggard, pinchpenny, cheapskate (*informal*), penny pincher (*informal*) [➡FINANCIALLY MEAN PEOPLE; 952]

scrounge (*informal*) **1** *v* **beg**, borrow, sponge, solicit, cadge (*informal*), bum (*informal*) [➡OBTAIN POSSESSION BY PERSUASION; 457] *Opposite:* give **2** *v* **scavenge**, rummage, forage, go through, search, hunt, garner, glean, scratch together [➡GET; 420]

scrounger (*informal*) *n* **beggar**, borrower, cadger (*informal*), sponger (*informal*), bum (*informal*), freeloader (*informal*) [➡LAZY OR UNSUCCESSFUL PEOPLE; 948] *Opposite:* donor

scrub 1 *v* **clean**, rub, scour, polish, brush, cleanse, burnish [➡CLEAN AND POLISH; 403] *Opposite:* dirty **2** *v* (*informal*) **cancel**, delete, erase, forget about, scratch, postpone [➡ABOLISH AND ANNUL; 452] *Opposite:* schedule **3** *n* **undergrowth**, brush, bush, brushwood, vegetation, thicket, scrubland [➡VEGETATION; 1025] **4** *n* **rub**, clean, scour, polish, brush, burnish [➡CLEAN AND POLISH; 403]

scrubby 1 *adj* [➡VEGETATION; 1025] **2** *adj* [➡IN BAD REPAIR; 1234]

scrubland *n* [➡DESERTS, PLAINS, AND MOORLAND; 1045]

scruffy *adj* **untidy**, shabby, tatty, unkempt, disheveled, messy, grubby, sloppy, ratty (*informal*) [➡BADLY GROOMED; 483] *Opposite:* tidy

scrum (*UK*) *n* **tussle**, fray, scuffle, free-for-all (*informal*), scrimmage, jostle, struggle [➡CHAOS AND UPROAR; 51]

scrumptious (*informal*) *adj* **delicious**, delectable, mouthwatering, tasty, delightful, yummy, gorgeous, delish (*slang*) [➡TASTE; 703] *Opposite:* revolting

scrumptiousness (*informal*) *n* [→ TASTE; 703]

scrunch *v* **crumple**, crush, crunch, crease, wrinkle, squeeze [→ CHANGE OF SHAPE; 385] *Opposite*: smooth

scruple *n* **misgiving**, doubt, qualm, compunction, hesitation, regret, second thought, pang of conscience [→ UNCERTAINTY; 559]

scrupulous 1 *adj* **honorable**, trustworthy, reliable, dependable, trusty, upright [→ HONEST AND RELIABLE; 502] 2 *adj* **conscientious**, meticulous, thorough, careful, rigorous, painstaking, fussy, fastidious, punctilious, assiduous [→ HARD-WORKING AND COMMITTED; 500] *Opposite*: sloppy

See Compare and Contrast at **careful**.

scrupulousness 1 *n* **honesty**, reliability, dependability, trustworthiness, decency, uprightness [→ HONEST AND RELIABLE; 502] 2 *n* **conscientiousness**, meticulousness, thoroughness, carefulness, rigor, fastidiousness, punctiliousness [→ HARD-WORKING AND COMMITTED; 500]

scrutinize *v* **examine**, inspect, study, pore over, analyze, dissect, search [→ EXAMINE AND ASSESS; 753] *Opposite*: glance at

scrutiny *n* **examination**, inspection, study, analysis, search, inquiry [→ EXAMINE AND ASSESS; 753]

scuba dive *v* [→ HOBBIES, GAMES, AND SPORTS; 875]

scuba diver *n* [→ PEOPLE IN SPORTS AND LEISURE; 876]

scud *v* **speed**, sweep, fly, sail, rush, hurry, tear, zoom, zip (*informal*), bowl along (*UK*) [→ MOVE FAST; 313] *Opposite*: crawl

scuff 1 *v* **scrape**, wear away, rub, graze, scratch, abrade [→ WORSEN APPEARANCE; 382] 2 *n* **scratch**, scrape, graze, abrasion [→ FAULTS, FLAWS, AND WEAKNESSES; 251]

scuffle 1 *n* **fight**, brawl, fracas, fray, scrap (*informal*), punch-up (*UK*) [→ AGGRESSIVE EVENTS; 39] 2 *v* **wrestle**, fight, come to blows, exchange blows, scrap [→ COMPETE, CONTEND, AND COMBAT; 303]

scull 1 *n* **oar**, paddle, blade, sweep [→ PARTS OF A SHIP OR BOAT; 1151] 2 *type of* **small vessel** [→ SHIPS AND BOATS; 1150] 3 *v* **row**, paddle, propel, canoe [→ TRAVEL: WAYS OF TRAVELING; 320]

scullery *type of* **room in the home** [→ TYPES OF ROOMS; 1097]

sculpt *v* **carve**, shape, mold, form, fashion, chisel [→ CRAFTS AND CARVING; 355]

sculptor *n* [→ ARTISTS; 900]

Sculptor *type of* **constellation** [→ HEAVENLY BODIES; 1061]

sculpture *n* **statue**, statuette, figure, figurine, carving, monument, relief, cast, maquette [→ SCULPTURE; 902]

scum *n* **froth**, foam, impurities, filth, crust, skin [→ UNPLEASANT, DIRTY, AND TOXIC SUBSTANCES; 1268]

scummy *adj* [→ DIRTY; 1235]

scupper *v* **wreck**, stymie, thwart, ruin, spoil, foil, scuttle, damage, scotch, undo, mess up (*informal*) [→ MAKE IMPOSSIBLE; 276]

scurf 1 *n* **dandruff**, dander, dead skin, flakes [→ CONDITIONS AFFECTING THE SKIN; 721] 2 *n* **encrustation**, scale, crust, deposit, coat, coating, layer [→ COVERS AND COATINGS; 1246]

scurrilous *adj* **scandalous**, slanderous, defamatory, outrageous, abusive, libelous, insulting [→ RUDE AND HOSTILE; 625] *Opposite*: complimentary

scurry *v* **dash**, scuttle, scamper, dart, rush, hurry, bustle [→ MOVE FAST; 313] *Opposite*: saunter

scuttle 1 *v* **destroy**, stymie, thwart, spoil, ruin, foil, scupper, wreck, scotch, mess up (*informal*) [→ MAKE IMPOSSIBLE; 276] 2 *v* **scurry**, scamper, dart, dash, rush [→ MOVE FAST; 313] *Opposite*: saunter

scuttlebutt (*slang*) *n* **rumor**, hearsay, tittle-tattle, scandal, chitchat [→ GOSSIP; 678]

scuzzy (*slang*) *adj* **dirty**, filthy, foul, unclean [→ DIRTY; 1235]

scythe 1 *type of* **cutting tool** [→ CUTTING TOOLS; 1120] 2 *v* **cut**, cut down, hack, slice, sweep, mow, reap [→ USE TOOLS AND MACHINERY; 468]

sea 1 *n* **ocean**, deep, depths, briny (*UK*) [→ THE SEAS, OCEANS, AND SHORES; 1041] 2 *adj* **maritime**, aquatic, oceanic, marine, nautical [→ THE SEAS, OCEANS, AND SHORES; 1041] *Opposite*: land

sea anemone *type of* **aquatic invertebrate** [→ AQUATIC INVERTEBRATES; 1022]

seaboard *n* **coast**, coastline, shore, seashore, shoreline, seacoast, seaside [→ THE SEAS, OCEANS, AND SHORES; 1041] *Opposite*: interior

sea bream *type of* **ocean fish** [→ OCEAN FISH; 1009]

sea change *n* **transformation**, metamorphosis, shift, turnaround, U-turn, reversal, volte-face, conversion, alteration, about-face, total change, change, about-turn (*UK*) [→ CHANGE; 372]

seacoast *n* **shore**, shoreline, coast, coastline, seaboard, seashore, beach [→ THE SEAS, OCEANS, AND SHORES; 1041] *Opposite*: interior

sea eagle *type of* **bird of prey** [→ BIRDS OF PREY; 998]

seafaring *adj* **maritime**, nautical, oceangoing, seagoing, marine [→ TRANSPORTATION, TRANSPORTERS, AND CARGOS; 322]

seafront *n* **waterfront**, esplanade, boardwalk, beach, seashore, shore, promenade, shoreline, prom (*UK*), coast [→ THE SEAS, OCEANS, AND SHORES; 1041]

seagoing *adj* **seafaring**, oceangoing, maritime, nautical, marine [→ TRANSPORTATION, TRANSPORTERS, AND CARGOS; 322] *Opposite*: land

seagrass *type of* **fiber** [→ PLANT MATERIALS; 1133]

sea green *type of* **green** [→ COLORS; 1224]

seagull *type of* **sea bird** [→ SEA BIRDS; 1002]

seal 1 *n* **closure**, cover, stopper, lid, cap [→ COVERS AND COATINGS; 1246] 2 *part of* **engine** [→ PARTS OF AN ENGINE; 1144] 3 *n* **stamp**, hallmark, impression, signet, sigil, impress (*literary*) [→ WRITING AND DRAWING IMPLEMENTS, AND MEDIA; 601] 4 *type of* **marine mammal** [→ MARINE MAMMALS; 987] 5 *v* **close**, fasten, stick, close up, shut, stop, stick down [→ FASTEN, LINK, AND JOIN; 408] *Opposite*: open 6 *v* **guarantee**, settle, finalize, wrap up, confirm, clinch [→ COMPLETE AN ACTION; 263]

sea lane *n* **seaway**, shipping lane, sea route, channel, corridor, passage [➡ WATERWAYS AND SEAWAYS; 1108]

sealant *n* [➡ BUILDING MATERIALS; 1077]

sealed 1 *adj* **closed**, stuck down, wrapped, taped up [➡ FASTEN, LINK, AND JOIN; 408] *Opposite*: unsealed **2** *adj* **impenetrable**, hermetically sealed, vacuum-packed, airtight, watertight, coated [➡ IN GOOD REPAIR; 1232] *Opposite*: unsealed

sea lettuce *type of* **marine alga** [➡ MICROORGANISMS, FUNGI, AND ALGAE; 1023]

sea lion *type of* **marine mammal** [➡ MARINE MAMMALS; 987]

seal off *v* **close off**, cordon off, fence off, isolate, quarantine, block, enclose, shut in [➡ BAR AND OBSTRUCT ACCESS; 410] *Opposite*: open

sealyham *type of* **small dog** [➡ DOGS; 980]

seam 1 *n* **join**, closure, ridge [➡ EXTREMITIES OF PHYSICAL OBJECTS; 1250] **2** *n* **layer**, join, joint, stratum, vein, lode [➡ COVERS AND COATINGS; 1246]

seaman *n* **sailor**, mariner, seafarer, navigator, deckhand, salt (*informal*), tar (*informal*) [➡ GRASPING AND FINANCIALLY MEAN; 519]

seamless 1 *adj* **unified**, all-in-one, one-piece, whole, continuous, unbroken [➡ IN GOOD REPAIR; 1232] *Opposite*: joined **2** *adj* **smooth**, perfect, faultless, uniform, unified, harmonious [➡ GOOD, WELL, BETTER; 183]

seamy *adj* **unpleasant**, degenerate, sordid, unsavory, squalid, seedy, debauched, rough [➡ DISGUSTING AND REPULSIVE; 230] *Opposite*: wholesome

seaplane *type of* **civil aircraft** [➡ AIRCRAFT; 1148]

seaport *n* **harbor**, port, coastal town, anchorage, dock, haven (*literary*) [➡ THE SEAS, OCEANS, AND SHORES; 1041]

sear *v* **burn**, scorch, solder, singe, char, broil, flame, blister [➡ FIRE, FLAMMABILITY, AND BURNING; 1165]

search 1 *v* **examine**, rifle, comb, look for, seek, hunt, explore, seek out, investigate, rummage [➡ SEEK POSSESSION AND SEARCH; 456] **2** *n* **examination**, hunt, quest, pursuit, exploration, inquiry [➡ SEEK POSSESSION AND SEARCH; 456]

search engine 1 *n* [➡ THE INTERNET; 1128] **2** *type of* **software** [➡ COMPUTERS AND COMPUTING; 1127]

searching *adj* **thorough**, penetrating, incisive, probing, pointed, sharp [➡ ENTHUSIASTIC AND INQUISITIVE; 628] *Opposite*: superficial

searchlight *n* **light**, spotlight, beam, lamp, flashlight, torch (*UK*) [➡ LIGHT; 1164]

search out *v* **discover**, uncover, find out, find, research, reveal, get, get ahold of (*informal*) [➡ FIND; 463]

search party *n* **searchers**, rescue party, rescuers, rescue patrol, emergency workers, posse, volunteers [➡ GROUPS WITH A COMMON INTEREST; 938]

search through *v* **sift through**, sort through, rummage, hunt through, ransack, rifle, scour, comb [➡ SEEK POSSESSION AND SEARCH; 456]

searing 1 *adj* **blistering**, sweltering, scorching (*in-*

formal), sizzling (*informal*), roasting (*informal*) [➡ HOT WEATHER; 1050] *Opposite*: freezing **2** *adj* **intense**, shooting, stabbing, agonizing, burning [➡ PHYSICALLY UNPLEASANT; 226] *Opposite*: mild

sea serpent *n* [➡ SNAKES; 995]

seashore *n* **coastline**, seaboard, shore, shoreline, coast, beach, sand, seaside [➡ THE SEAS, OCEANS, AND SHORES; 1041]

seasick *adj* **sick**, nauseous, queasy, travel-sick, ill, green around the gills (*informal*) [➡ ILL AND SICK; 740]

seaside *n* **seashore**, coast, shore, beach, seafront [➡ THE SEAS, OCEANS, AND SHORES; 1041]

sea snake *type of* **poisonous snake** [➡ SNAKES; 995]

season 1 *n* **period**, term, spell, time, time of year [➡ TIMES OF YEAR; 88] **2** *v* **flavor**, spice, spike, pepper, salt [➡ COOKING AND FOOD PREPARATION; 353]

seasonable *adj* **appropriate**, fitting, timely, opportune, suitable [➡ APPROPRIATE, SUITABLE, AND ADVISABLE; 184] *Opposite*: unseasonable

seasonal 1 *adj* **cyclical**, periodic, cyclic, recurrent, regular, spring, summer, autumn, fall, winter [➡ TIMES OF YEAR; 88] *Opposite*: year-round **2** *adj* **limited**, sporadic, intermittent, temporary, casual [➡ FINITENESS, VARIABILITY, AND TRANSIENCE; 96] *Opposite*: permanent

seasonal worker *n* [➡ WORKERS; 836]

seasoned *adj* **experienced**, veteran, hardened, tested, weathered, expert, versed in, well up in, au fait [➡ TALENTED AND SKILLFUL; 527] *Opposite*: inexperienced

seasoning *n* **zest**, flavoring, flavor, zing (*informal*) [➡ SEASONINGS AND SAUCES; 1174]

seat 1 *n* **chair**, bench, couch, pew, stool, throne, armchair [➡ FURNITURE; 858] **2** *part of* **bike** [➡ BIKES, CARS, AND CARRIAGES; 1149] **3** *n* **base**, HQ, headquarters, center, station, capital [➡ PLACE; 1065] **4** *v* **place**, sit, sit down, set, install, settle [➡ POSITION SOMETHING; 325] **5** *v* **accommodate**, hold, sit, contain, take [➡ HOLD AND CONTAIN; 455]

seat belt *type of* **internal feature** [➡ INTERNAL PARTS OF A VEHICLE; 1146]

seating *n* **seats**, chairs, spaces, places, places to sit, seating accommodations [➡ FURNITURE; 858]

seating

◆ *types of seating*
Adirondack chair, armchair, beach chair, bench, bleachers, Boston rocker, bucket seat, carver, chair, chaise longue, chesterfield, couch, davenport, deck chair, easy chair, highchair, ladder-back, lounger, love seat, pew, recliner, rocking chair, settee, sofa, stall, stool, swivel chair, Windsor chair, wing chair

sea urchin *type of* **aquatic invertebrate** [➡ AQUATIC INVERTEBRATES; 1022]

sea wall *n* **dike**, jetty, breakwater, groin, embankment, barricade, barrier, dam [➡ BARRIERS; 1113]

seaward *adv* [➡ DIRECTION OF MOTION; 345]

seaway *n* **channel**, sea lane, shipping lane, sea route, canal, corridor, passage [➡ WATERWAYS AND SEAWAYS; 1108]

seaweed *type of* **marine alga** [➡ MICROORGANISMS, FUNGI, AND ALGAE; 1023]

sea wrack *type of* **marine alga** [➡ MICROORGANISMS, FUNGI, AND ALGAE; 1023]

secede *v* **withdraw**, break away, break from, disaffiliate, pull out, split, separate, become independent [➡ SEPARATE AND DIVIDE; 401] *Opposite*: affiliate

secession *n* **withdrawal**, departure, separation, retreat, retirement, resignation, breakaway [➡ ENDS AND DEPARTURES; 54]

seclude *v* **isolate**, separate, keep away, keep apart, remove, pull out, withdraw, split off, segregate [➡ SEPARATE AND DIVIDE; 401]

secluded *adj* **private**, sheltered, quiet, isolated, out-of-the-way [➡ SECRET AND UNKNOWN; 179] *Opposite*: public

seclusion *n* **privacy**, shelter, isolation, quiet, solitude [➡ SECRET AND UNKNOWN; 179]

second **1** *adj* **additional**, another, next, subsequent, following, succeeding [➡ AFTER, LAST, AND FOLLOWING; 165] **2** *n* **moment**, minute, instant, trice, flash, jiffy (*informal*) [➡ SHORT PERIODS OF TIME; 93] *Opposite*: age **3** *v* **support**, agree with, endorse, subscribe, uphold, back, go along with, be with, back up [➡ APPROVE AND CONFIRM; 646] *Opposite*: oppose **4** *v* (*UK*) **transfer**, assign, post, attach, send [➡ DISPATCH AND SEND; 333]

secondary **1** *adj* **subordinate**, minor, inferior, lesser, tributary, ancillary, unimportant [➡ INFERIORITY; 153] *Opposite*: primary **2** *adj* **derived**, derivative, resulting, resultant, consequent, consequential [➡ AFTER, LAST, AND FOLLOWING; 165] *Opposite*: original

second best *adj* **second-rate**, second class, second choice, next best, minor, inferior [➡ INFERIORITY; 153] *Opposite*: best

second class *adj* **second-rate**, mediocre, indifferent, middling, second best, substandard, inferior, shoddy [➡ INFERIORITY; 153] *Opposite*: first class

second cousin *type of* **same-generation relative** [➡ SAME-GENERATION RELATIVES; 957]

seconder *n* **supporter**, endorser, backer, advocate, assenter, follower, sponsor, subscriber [➡ SUPPORTERS, PROTECTORS, AND COMPATRIOTS; 970]

second-guess *v* **predict**, guess, foretell, anticipate, work out (*UK*) [➡ PREDICT AND ANTICIPATE; 750]

secondhand **1** *adj* **used**, nearly new, hand-me-down, preowned [➡ OLD, OLD-FASHIONED; 167] *Opposite*: new **2** *adv* **indirectly**, circuitously, through the grapevine, in a roundabout way, on the rumor mill [➡ GOSSIP; 678] *Opposite*: firsthand

secondly *adv* **then**, furthermore, in addition, what is more, also, next, moreover, again, in the second place [➡ EXPRESSIONS INTRODUCING EXTRA INFORMATION; 139] *Opposite*: firstly

second name (*UK*) *n* **surname**, family name, last name [➡ NAME AND DESCRIBE; 665]

second-rate *adj* **inadequate**, mediocre, unsatisfactory,

poor, below standard, inferior, shoddy, cheap, tawdry, second class, tacky (*informal*) [➡ INFERIORITY; 153] *Opposite*: first-rate

second sight *n* **clairvoyance**, foresight, foreknowledge, precognition, intuition, prediction [➡ THE SUPERNATURAL; 787]

second-sighted *adj* [➡ THE SUPERNATURAL; 787]

second thoughts *n* **reconsideration**, pangs, doubts, qualms, misgivings, regrets, compunction, reservations [➡ FEELINGS ABOUT THE FUTURE; 533]

secrecy *n* **concealment**, confidentiality, privacy, mystery, silence [➡ SECRET AND UNKNOWN; 179] *Opposite*: openness

secret **1** *adj* **clandestine**, covert, undisclosed, surreptitious, furtive, stealthy, cloak-and-dagger, underhand, closet, underground, hush-hush (*informal*), hole-and-corner (*UK*) [➡ SECRET AND UNKNOWN; 179] *Opposite*: open **2** *adj* **confidential**, private, classified, top-secret, restricted, hush-hush (*informal*) [➡ SECRET AND UNKNOWN; 179] *Opposite*: public **3** *n* **confidence**, skeleton in the closet, mystery, riddle, enigma [➡ SECRETS AND MYSTERIES; 180]

Compare and Contrast: *secret, clandestine, covert, furtive, stealthy, surreptitious*

CORE MEANING: conveying a desire or need for concealment

secret intentionally withheld from general knowledge; *clandestine* describes an activity that needs to be concealed, usually because it is illegal or unauthorized; *covert* not intended to be known, seen, or found out, suggesting a lack of honesty or openness; *furtive* cautious and careful in order to escape notice; *stealthy* quiet, slow, and cautious in order to escape notice; *surreptitious* done in a concealed or underhand way to escape notice.

secret agent *n* **spy**, undercover agent, double agent, mole, infiltrator, detective, private eye (*informal*) [➡ INTERFERING PEOPLE AND TATTLETALES; 950]

secretary **1** *n* **clerical worker**, administrative assistant, personal assistant, office assistant, typist, stenographer, clerk, administrator, PA (*UK*) [➡ OFFICE WORKERS; 847] **2** *type of* **cabinet** [➡ FURNITURE; 858]

secretary-general *n* **chief executive officer**, C.E.O., head, chief, chair, chairperson, president [➡ BOSSES AND MANAGEMENT; 965]

secret ballot *n* [➡ ELECTIONS AND VOTING; 807]

secrete **1** *v* **hide**, hide away, conceal, stow, squirrel away, stash (*informal*) [➡ CAUSE TO DISAPPEAR; 6] *Opposite*: display **2** *v* **exude**, ooze, emit, produce, squirt, discharge (*formal*) [➡ LIQUID EMISSION; 370] *Opposite*: absorb

secreted *adj* [➡ IMPERCEPTIBLE; 26]

secretion *n* **discharge**, excretion, exudation, emission, ooze [➡ EMIT AND EMANATE; 361]

secretive *adj* **private**, mysterious, enigmatic, guarded, reticent, reserved, cautious, cagey (*informal*) [➡ RETICENT AND UNFORTHCOMING; 631] *Opposite*: open

secretiveness *n* [➡ RETICENT AND UNFORTHCOMING; 631]

secretly *adv* **clandestinely**, covertly, in secret, furtively, surreptitiously, furtively, stealthily, behind somebody's back, behind closed doors, on the sly, on the q.t. (*informal*) [➞ SECRET AND UNKNOWN; 179] *Opposite*: openly

sect 1 *n* **group**, clique, faction, camp, party, cult, division, offshoot, branch [➞ GROUPS WITH A COMMON INTEREST; 938] 2 *n* **religious group**, religious persuasion, denomination, cult, movement [➞ RELIGIOUS PEOPLE; 778]

sectarian 1 *adj* **religious**, denominational, sectional, factional [➞ RELIGIONS AND RELIGIOUS PRACTICES; 777] 2 *adj* **dogmatic**, intolerant, bigoted, biased, partisan, prejudiced, narrow-minded, rigid [➞ NEGATIVE INTELLECTUAL CHARACTERISTICS; 525] *Opposite*: tolerant

section 1 *n* **part**, unit, piece, segment, slice, sector, division, subdivision, fragment, portion [➞ AREA AND RANGE; 111] *Opposite*: whole 2 *v* **divide**, divide up, partition, split, segment [➞ SEPARATE AND DIVIDE; 401] *Opposite*: combine

sector 1 *n* **part**, division, subdivision, segment, area [➞ AREA AND RANGE; 111] *Opposite*: whole 2 *n* **area**, zone, region, quarter, district [➞ COUNTRIES AND REGIONS; 1067]

secular *adj* **earthly**, worldly, nonspiritual, profane, lay, material, temporal, irreligious, of this world, materialistic [➞ RELIGIOUS CONCEPTS; 776] *Opposite*: spiritual

secure 1 *adj* **confident**, assured, self-confident, sure of yourself, self-assured, together [➞ CONFIDENCE AND COMPOSURE; 499] *Opposite*: insecure 2 *adj* **fixed firmly**, closed, fastened, locked [➞ IN GOOD REPAIR; 1232] *Opposite*: unfastened 3 *adj* **dependable**, reliable, safe, stable, steady [➞ SAFE AND SAFETY; 191] *Opposite*: unreliable 4 *adj* **safe**, protected, safe and sound, sheltered, safe as houses (*UK*) [➞ SAFE AND SAFETY; 191] *Opposite*: vulnerable 5 *v* **fix**, fasten, make fast, position, attach, tighten [➞ FASTEN, LINK, AND JOIN; 408] *Opposite*: loosen 6 *v* **make safe**, safeguard, fortify, lock, lock up [➞ BAR AND OBSTRUCT ACCESS; 410] 7 *v* **obtain**, acquire, get, get hold of, capture, procure, get your hands on [➞ GET; 420] *Opposite*: lose 8 *v* **guarantee**, ensure, give security, indemnify, assure [➞ INSURANCE; 801]

*See Compare and Contrast at **get**.*

secure electronic transaction *n* [➞ E-COMMERCE; 1129]

securely *adv* **firmly**, steadily, tightly, strongly, safely, fast [➞ SAFE AND SAFETY; 191]

secure unit (*UK*) *n* [➞ BUILDINGS FOR CONFINING PEOPLE; 1094]

securities broker *n* [➞ PEOPLE INVOLVED IN FINANCE; 804]

security 1 *n* **safety**, refuge, sanctuary, haven, safekeeping, retreat [➞ SAFE AND SAFETY; 191] *Opposite*: danger 2 *n* **confidence**, well-being, self-assurance, reassurance, self-confidence [➞ CONFIDENCE AND COMPOSURE; 499] *Opposite*: insecurity 3 *n* **precautions**, safety measures, defense, protection [➞ SAFE AND SAFETY; 191] 4 *n* **guarantee**, collateral, surety, insurance, indemnity, underwriting [➞ FUNDS, PAYMENTS, AND CHARGES; 800]

security guard *n* [➞ PEOPLE WHO GUARD AND PROTECT; 846]

security officer *n* [➞ PEOPLE WHO GUARD AND PROTECT; 846]

sedan *type of* **car** [➞ BIKES, CARS, AND CARRIAGES; 1149]

sedate 1 *adj* **dignified**, calm, cool, demure, serene, stately, placid, composed, unflappable [➞ CONFIDENCE AND COMPOSURE; 499] *Opposite*: boisterous 2 *adj* **staid**, unexciting,

dull, slow-moving, slow [➞ UNADVENTUROUS AND DULL; 517] *Opposite*: exciting 3 *v* **anesthetize**, tranquilize, drug, put under sedation, knock out [➞ BECOME SICK, TREAT, AND RECOVER; 728] *Opposite*: revive

sedated *adj* [➞ UNDER THE INFLUENCE OF DRUGS OR ALCOHOL; 741]

sedateness 1 *n* **dignity**, calmness, coolness, demureness, composedness [➞ CONFIDENCE AND COMPOSURE; 499] 2 *n* **staidness**, dullness, slowness [➞ UNADVENTUROUS AND DULL; 517]

sedation *n* **calm**, restfulness, drowsiness, torpor, tranquility, peacefulness [➞ REMEDIES, TREATMENTS, AND OPERATIONS; 731] *Opposite*: excitement

sedative 1 *n* **tranquilizer**, narcotic, barbiturate, downer (*slang*) [➞ REMEDIES, TREATMENTS, AND OPERATIONS; 731] 2 *adj* **tranquilizing**, calming, soothing, relaxing, soporific [➞ CALMING; 188] *Opposite*: stimulating

sedentary *adj* **sitting**, inactive, deskbound, desk [➞ TYPES OF WORK; 835] *Opposite*: active

sediment *n* **residue**, deposit, dregs, remains, grounds, silt [➞ SUBSTANCES; 1267]

sedimentary *adj* [➞ EROSION PRODUCTS AND SOIL; 1058]

sedition 1 *n* **incitement to rebellion**, agitation, treason, subversion, rabble-rousing, troublemaking [➞ UNWILLINGNESS AND STUBBORNNESS; 564] 2 *n* **rebellion**, mutiny, defiance, unrest, civil disobedience [➞ AGGRESSIVE EVENTS; 39]

seditious *adj* **rebellious**, subversive, treasonable, disloyal, mutinous, up in arms [➞ UNWILLINGNESS AND STUBBORNNESS; 564] *Opposite*: loyal

seditiousness *n* [➞ UNWILLINGNESS AND STUBBORNNESS; 564]

seduce 1 *v* **entice**, lead astray, lure, allure, tempt, attract [➞ CAUSE OR COMPEL TO ACT; 271] 2 *v* **persuade**, wheedle, inveigle, talk into, coax, influence, induce [➞ CAUSE OR COMPEL TO ACT; 271]

sedulity (*literary*) *n* [➞ HARD-WORKING AND COMMITTED; 500]

sedulous (*literary*) *adj* **zealous**, assiduous, diligent, hard-working, keen, conscientious, determined, painstaking, careful [➞ HARD-WORKING AND COMMITTED; 500] *Opposite*: lazy

sedulousness (*literary*) *n* [➞ HARD-WORKING AND COMMITTED; 500]

see 1 *v* **perceive**, observe, distinguish, notice, witness, spot, glimpse, catch sight of, catch a glimpse of, set eyes on, make out, discern [➞ SEE; 699] 2 *v* **understand**, realize, perceive, grasp, appreciate, get the drift, comprehend, recognize, get (*informal*), get the message (*informal*) [➞ UNDERSTAND AND GRASP; 759] *Opposite*: misunderstand 3 *v* **meet**, visit, pay a visit to, go to see, call on [➞ INITIATE AND ESTABLISH COMMUNICATION; 680] 4 *v* **find out**, establish, investigate, look into, check, attend to, ascertain (*formal*) [➞ LEARN AND DISCOVER; 762] 5 *v* **imagine**, picture, envisage, predict, foresee, envision [➞ DREAM, IMAGINE, AND FANTASIZE; 749] 6 *v* **make sure**, see to it, ensure, make certain, guarantee [➞ CAUSE TO HAPPEN; 31] 7 *v* **consider** it, think about it, refer it to, give it some thought, think it over, reflect on it, mull it over, chew it over [➞ THINK AND REFLECT; 743] 8 *v* **date**, escort, accompany, go with, go out with [➞ ACCOMPANY AND FOLLOW; 337] 9 *v* **look at**, refer to, consult, view, regard [➞ LOOKING AND LOOKS; 700]

see about *v* **take care of**, look into, investigate, find out about, attend to [➞ EXAMINE AND ASSESS; 753] *Opposite*: leave alone

seed 1 *n* **kernel**, pip, spore, germ, stone, pit [➡ FRUIT AND VEGETABLES; 1176] **2** *n* **source**, beginning, start, starting point, nucleus, germ [➡ BEGINNINGS; 53] **3** *v* **sow**, plant, broadcast, scatter [➡ GROW AND CULTIVATE; 351] *Opposite:* harvest

seedcake *type of* **cake** [➡ CAKES, COOKIES, AND DESSERTS; 1181]

seed capital (*UK*) *n* **startup funds**, venture capital, initial investment, working capital, seed money, pump priming funds (*UK*) [➡ FUNDS, PAYMENTS, AND CHARGES; 800]

seed case *n* [➡ PARTS OF TREES AND PLANTS; 1026]

seed husk *n* [➡ PARTS OF TREES AND PLANTS; 1026]

seediness 1 *n* **dinginess**, grubbiness, shabbiness, squalor, tattiness [➡ BAD AND BADLY; 223] **2** *n* (*informal*) **sickliness**, poorliness, roughness (*informal*) [➡ ILL AND SICK; 740]

seedling *n* **sprout**, sapling, plantlet, slip, twig [➡ PLANTS AND TREES; 1034]

seed money *n* **startup funds**, venture capital, initial investment, working capital, seed capital (*UK*), pump priming funds (*UK*) [➡ FUNDS, PAYMENTS, AND CHARGES; 800]

seedpod *n* [➡ PARTS OF TREES AND PLANTS; 1026]

seedy 1 *adj* **dingy**, sordid, shabby, squalid, sleazy, seamy [➡ BAD AND BADLY; 223] *Opposite:* respectable **2** *adj* (*informal*) **unwell**, ill, sick, pale, wan, sickly [➡ ILL AND SICK; 740] *Opposite:* healthy

see eye to eye *v* **agree**, see things the same way, have the same opinion, be of the same mind [➡ AGREE; 645] *Opposite:* disagree

seeing *conj* **considering**, bearing in mind, as, since, in view of [➡ EXPRESSIONS OF REFERENCE; 63]

seeing as *conj* [➡ EXPRESSIONS OF REFERENCE; 63]

seeing that *conj* [➡ EXPRESSIONS OF REFERENCE; 63]

see into *v* **discern**, understand, penetrate, comprehend, figure out, grasp, get a handle on [➡ UNDERSTAND AND GRASP; 759]

see in your mind's eye *v* **imagine**, picture, visualize, envision, see, conjure up [➡ DREAM, IMAGINE, AND FANTASIZE; 749]

seek 1 *v* **search for**, try to find, hunt for, pursue, seek out, look for [➡ SEEK POSSESSION AND SEARCH; 456] *Opposite:* find **2** *v* **strive for**, try for, go after, work toward, pursue, go for (*informal*) [➡ ATTEMPT AN ACTION; 261] *Opposite:* achieve **3** *v* **ask for**, request, inquire about [➡ REQUEST AND DEMAND; 663] *Opposite:* obtain

seek out *v* **look for**, seek, search for, try to find, hunt for [➡ SEEK POSSESSION AND SEARCH; 456] *Opposite:* find

seek to *v* **try to**, aspire to, aim to, attempt to, strive to, endeavor to (*formal*) [➡ ATTEMPT AN ACTION; 261] *Opposite:* succeed

seem *v* **appear**, give the impression, seem like, look, look as if, look like [➡ SEEM TO BE SOMETHING; 58]

seeming *adj* **apparent**, outward, ostensible, surface, superficial, to all appearances [➡ UNCERTAIN; 175] *Opposite:* real

seemingly 1 *adv* **by all accounts**, on the face of it, rumor has it, or so it seems, at first glance, at first sight [➡ EXPRESSIONS OF UNCERTAINTY; 560] **2** *adv* **apparently**, outwardly, ostensibly, superficially [➡ UNCERTAIN; 175] *Opposite:* really

seemliness *n* [➡ APPROPRIATE, SUITABLE, AND ADVISABLE; 184]

seemly *adj* **appropriate**, decorous, fitting, fit, decent, proper, becoming, right [➡ APPROPRIATE, SUITABLE, AND ADVISABLE; 184] *Opposite:* unseemly

seen better days *adj* [➡ IN BAD REPAIR; 1234]

see off 1 *v* **say goodbye to**, bid farewell to, send off, take to the station, take to the airport, go with, accompany [➡ ACCOMPANY AND FOLLOW; 337] *Opposite:* welcome **2** *v* (*UK*) **defeat**, beat, withstand, fend off [➡ BEAT AND DEFEAT; 80]

see out 1 *v* **show to the door**, show out, say goodbye to, accompany, go with, escort out, escort [➡ ACCOMPANY AND FOLLOW; 337] **2** *v* **stay**, last, last out, live out, survive, endure [➡ CONTINUE TO EXIST; 17]

seep *v* **leak**, ooze, trickle, dribble, soak, leach, bleed, percolate, escape [➡ LIQUID EMISSION; 370]

seepage *n* **leakage**, leak, outflow, waste, escape, ooze, discharge [➡ EMIT AND EMANATE; 361]

seer *n* **prophet**, soothsayer, clairvoyant, oracle, fortune-teller, psychic [➡ PEOPLE WITH SUPERNATURAL POWERS; 788]

see red (*informal*) *v* **lose your temper**, go berserk, be enraged, fly into a rage, go wild, rage, lose your head, fly off the handle (*informal*), lose it (*informal*) [➡ GIVING VENT TO EMOTIONS; 679] *Opposite:* calm down

seersucker *type of* **fabric from plants** [➡ FABRICS; 1132]

seesaw *v* **alternate**, go up and down, oscillate, fluctuate, swing [➡ BOUNCE, UNDULATE, AND VIBRATE; 308] *Opposite:* stabilize

seethe 1 *v* **boil**, bubble, froth, foam, churn [➡ FROTH AND EFFERVESCE; 389] **2** *v* **fume**, rage, be furious, be livid, boil with rage, be hopping mad (*informal*) [➡ GIVING VENT TO EMOTIONS; 679] *Opposite:* calm down **3** *v* **teem**, swarm, be alive with, be crawling with [➡ PROSPER AND ABOUND; 16]

seething 1 *adj* **fuming**, furious, livid, beside yourself, enraged, incensed, apoplectic, irate, hopping mad (*informal*) [➡ IRRITATION AND ANGER; 541] *Opposite:* calm **2** *adj* **boiling**, bubbling, foaming, simmering, on the boil (*UK*) [➡ FLUID AND NONSOLID; 1213] *Opposite:* still **3** *adj* **bustling**, busy, frantic, teeming, packed, crowded, full to bursting, bursting at the seams, jam-packed (*informal*), heaving (*UK*) [➡ FULL; 1239] *Opposite:* quiet

see through 1 *v* **understand**, get to the bottom of, be wise to, know inside out, read like a book, penetrate [➡ UNDERSTAND AND GRASP; 759] **2** *v* **persevere with**, persist at, stick at, stay with, carry out, finish, continue [➡ CONTINUE AN ACTION; 262] *Opposite:* quit

see-through *adj* **transparent**, translucent, sheer, diaphanous, gauzy, filmy [➡ VISUAL TEXTURE; 1221] *Opposite:* opaque

see to *v* **deal with**, sort out, handle, take care of, manage, attend to, do [➡ CARRY OUT AN ACTION; 269]

see to it *v* **make sure**, see, ensure, make certain, guarantee [➡ CAUSE TO HAPPEN; 31]

see you (*informal*) *interj* [➡ GREETINGS, FAREWELLS, AND SALUTATIONS; 659]

see you later (*informal*) *interj* [➡ GREETINGS, FAREWELLS, AND SALUTATIONS; 659]

segment 1 *n* **section**, part, piece, slice, sector, division, subdivision, fragment, portion, bit, wedge [➡ AREA AND RANGE; 111] *Opposite*: whole 2 *v* **divide**, split, subdivide, section, portion, carve up (*informal*) [➡ SEPARATE AND DIVIDE; 401]

segmentation *n* **division**, subdivision, separation, splitting up, dissection, breakdown [➡ SEPARATE AND DIVIDE; 401] *Opposite*: integration

segregate *v* **separate**, separate out, isolate, keep apart, set apart, set aside [➡ EJECT AND EXCLUDE; 340] *Opposite*: integrate

segregation *n* **separation**, isolation, exclusion, setting apart, apartheid, seclusion, discrimination [➡ EJECT AND EXCLUDE; 340] *Opposite*: integration

seismic *adj* [➡ VOLCANOES AND EARTHQUAKES; 1054]

seismic activity *n* [➡ VOLCANOES AND EARTHQUAKES; 1054]

seismic wave *n* [➡ VOLCANOES AND EARTHQUAKES; 1054]

seize 1 *v* **take hold of**, grab, grab hold of, get hold of, snatch, grasp, clutch [➡ CONTACT: HOLD; 411] *Opposite*: relinquish 2 *v* **appropriate**, confiscate, take away, sequester, remove, take possession of, commandeer [➡ TAKE SOMETHING AWAY; 425] *Opposite*: return 3 *v* **take control of**, capture, take, take over, annex, overrun, conquer [➡ BEAT AND DEFEAT; 80] *Opposite*: lose 4 *v* **arrest**, capture, take into custody, apprehend, take hostage, snatch, abduct, kidnap [➡ CAPTIVITY AND LOSS OF FREEDOM; 248] *Opposite*: release 5 *v* **take advantage of**, grab, jump at, take [➡ GET; 420]

seize up 1 *v* **grind to a halt**, jam, fail, stop working, stall, pack up, conk out (*informal*) [➡ FAIL OR CEASE TO FUNCTION; 470] 2 *v* **stiffen**, stiffen up, stop working, freeze up, stick, cramp [➡ FAIL OR CEASE TO FUNCTION; 470]

seizure 1 *n* **attack**, fit, spasm, convulsion [➡ PHYSICAL REACTIONS; 316] 2 *n* **capture**, arrest, abduction, apprehension [➡ CAPTIVITY AND LOSS OF FREEDOM; 248] *Opposite*: release 3 *n* **appropriation**, confiscation, commandeering, annexation, capture, removal [➡ TAKE SOMETHING AWAY; 425] *Opposite*: return

seldom *adv* **not often**, hardly ever, rarely, infrequently, occasionally, scarcely, once in a while [➡ NEVER AND INFREQUENCY; 97] *Opposite*: often

select 1 *v* **choose**, pick, pick out, decide on, opt for, go for (*informal*), plump for (*UK*) [➡ MAKE DECISIONS AND CHOICES; 752] 2 *adj* **choice**, top quality, first-class, excellent, first-rate, handpicked [➡ SUPERIORITY; 152] *Opposite*: inferior 3 *adj* **exclusive**, elite, privileged, cliquey, restricted, limited [➡ EXPENSIVE AND LUXURIOUS; 218]

selected *adj* **carefully chosen**, designated, nominated, particular, certain, a number of, a selection of [➡ AMOUNTS AND QUANTITIES; 112] *Opposite*: all

selection *n* **range**, assortment, collection, choice, variety, miscellany, mixture, medley [➡ COLLECTIONS AND MIXTURES OF THINGS; 1244]

selective *adj* **discerning**, discriminating, discriminatory, careful, choosy (*informal*) [➡ POSITIVE INTELLECTUAL CHARACTERISTICS; 524] *Opposite*: indiscriminate

selectivity *n* **discrimination**, discernment, choosiness (*informal*) [➡ POSITIVE INTELLECTUAL CHARACTERISTICS; 524]

selector *n* **chooser**, picker, committee member, jury member, panel member, member of selection panel [➡ SURVEYORS, EXAMINERS, AND JUDGES; 853]

self *n* **personality**, nature, character, psyche, identity, person, ego [➡ PSYCHOLOGY AND THE MIND; 769]

self-abasement *n* **humbling**, humiliation, mortification, prostration, eating humble pie, self-effacement, crawling (*informal*) [➡ EMBARRASSMENT AND HUMILIATION; 542] *Opposite*: self-aggrandizement

self-absorbed *adj* **full of yourself**, self-regarding, self-centered, narcissistic, egocentric, egoistic, egotistic, egotistical, selfish [➡ SELFISH AND UNKIND; 505] *Opposite*: considerate

self-absorption *n* **self-preoccupation**, egotism, egoism, egocentricity, self-centeredness, narcissism, self-importance, self-interest, self-regard, selfishness [➡ SELFISH AND UNKIND; 505] *Opposite*: generosity

self-acting *adj* **self-operating**, automatic, automated, mechanized, mechanical, robotic [➡ DESCRIBING TECHNOLOGY; 1160]

self-admiring *adj* [➡ POMPOUS, LOUD, AND OVERCONFIDENT; 635]

self-aggrandizement *n* **ambition**, self-promotion, braggadocio, self-importance, self-glorification, self-glory, self-flattery, boasting, bragging [➡ BOAST; 616]

self-aggrandizing *adj* [➡ POMPOUS, LOUD, AND OVERCONFIDENT; 635]

self-assertive *adj* **confident**, self-confident, forceful, assured, aggressive, bossy, strong, pushy (*informal*), in-your-face (*slang*) [➡ CONFIDENCE AND COMPOSURE; 499] *Opposite*: timid

self-assurance *n* **confidence**, self-confidence, self-possession, poise, assurance, composure [➡ CONFIDENCE AND COMPOSURE; 499] *Opposite*: timidity

self-assured *adj* **confident**, self-confident, poised, assured, self-possessed, sure of yourself, well-balanced [➡ CONFIDENCE AND COMPOSURE; 499] *Opposite*: timid

self-assuredness *n* [➡ CONFIDENCE AND COMPOSURE; 499]

self-centered *adj* **selfish**, self-interested, egocentric, egoistic, egotistic, egotistical, self-absorbed, self-seeking, narcissistic [➡ SELFISH AND UNKIND; 505] *Opposite*: altruistic

self-centeredness *n* **selfishness**, self-interest, egocentricity, egoism, egotism, self-regard, self-absorption, narcissism [➡ SELFISH AND UNKIND; 505] *Opposite*: altruism

self-colored *adj* **uniform**, plain, single-color, unpatterned [➡ DESCRIBING COLORS; 1226] *Opposite*: patterned

self-conceit *n* **smugness**, arrogance, boastfulness, conceit, superiority, superciliousness, pride, swollen head (*UK*) [➡ AFFECTATION, SELF-SATISFACTION, AND SNOBBISHNESS; 507] *Opposite*: modesty

self-confessed *adj* **admitted**, by your own admission, self-proclaimed, acknowledged, known [➡ TRUE AND REAL; 171] *Opposite*: closet

self-confidence *n* **confidence**, self-assurance, self-possession, poise, assurance [➡ CONFIDENCE AND COMPOSURE; 499] *Opposite*: insecurity

self-confident *adj* **confident**, self-assured, self-possessed, poised, assured [➡CONFIDENCE AND COMPOSURE; 499] *Opposite*: insecure

self-congratulation *n* **self-satisfaction**, smugness, self-praise, self-glorification, self-flattery, self-love, self-regard [➡AFFECTATION, SELF-SATISFACTION, AND SNOBBISHNESS; 507] *Opposite*: self-hatred

self-conscious *adj* **ill at ease**, awkward, uncomfortable, embarrassed, insecure, unsure of yourself [➡INSECURITY AND LOSS OF COMPOSURE; 544] *Opposite*: self-confident

self-consciousness *n* [➡INSECURITY AND LOSS OF COMPOSURE; 544]

self-contained *adj* **independent**, self-sufficient, self-reliant, autonomous [➡RELATIONSHIP TO ANOTHER; 973] *Opposite*: dependent

self-contempt *n* [➡INSECURITY AND LOSS OF COMPOSURE; 544]

self-contradictory *adj* **inconsistent**, self-contradicting, contradictory, illogical, unreasonable, incongruous [➡DISORDER AND CHAOS; 245] *Opposite*: consistent

self-control *n* **self-discipline**, discipline, willpower, restraint, strength of mind, strength of will, self-will [➡STRENGTH OF WILL; 501] *Opposite*: self-indulgence

self-controlled *adj* [➡STRENGTH OF WILL; 501]

self-critical *adj* **self-deprecatory**, self-deprecating, self-effacing, reticent, humble, modest, hard on yourself (*informal*) [➡RETICENT AND UNFORTHCOMING; 631]

self-defense *n* **self-protection**, self-preservation, defense, resistance [➡SAFE AND SAFETY; 191]

self-denial *n* **abstinence**, abstemiousness, frugality, asceticism, self-discipline, austerity [➡SELF-DENIAL; 882] *Opposite*: self-indulgence

self-denying *adj* [➡SELF-DENIAL; 882]

self-deprecating *adj* **self-critical**, self-deprecatory, self-effacing, modest, humble, overly modest, reticent [➡RETICENT AND UNFORTHCOMING; 631] *Opposite*: boastful

self-deprecation *n* **self-criticism**, self-depreciation, self-effacement, modesty, humility, reticence, hiding your light under a bushel, selling yourself short [➡RETICENT AND UNFORTHCOMING; 631] *Opposite*: boasting

self-determination *n* **autonomy**, self-rule, self-government, freedom, independence, sovereignty, free will [➡STYLES AND SYSTEMS OF GOVERNMENT; 806]

self-discipline *n* **self-control**, discipline, willpower, restraint, strength of mind, strength of will, self-will [➡STRENGTH OF WILL; 501] *Opposite*: self-indulgence

self-disciplined *adj* [➡STRENGTH OF WILL; 501]

self-disgust *n* [➡INSECURITY AND LOSS OF COMPOSURE; 544]

self-dislike *n* [➡INSECURITY AND LOSS OF COMPOSURE; 544]

self-doubt *n* **uncertainty**, lack of confidence, insecurity, self-loathing, self-hatred [➡INSECURITY AND LOSS OF COMPOSURE; 544] *Opposite*: self-confidence

self-effacing *adj* **modest**, quiet, meek, diffident, unassuming, shy, humble [➡NATURALNESS; 497] *Opposite*: brash

self-employed *adj* **freelance**, your own boss, working for yourself, independent, freelancing, entrepreneurial, self-starting [➡EMPLOYMENT STATUS; 831] *Opposite*: employed

self-esteem *n* **confidence**, self-confidence, self-worth, sense of worth, self-respect, self-image, self-regard, self-assurance, pride [➡PSYCHOLOGY AND THE MIND; 769] *Opposite*: insecurity

self-evident *adj* **obvious**, clear, plain, manifest, undeniable, indisputable, palpable, incontrovertible, explicit [➡CERTAIN; 174] *Opposite*: unclear

self-explanatory *adj* **clear**, easy to understand, easy to follow, transparent, understandable, palpable, plain [➡CONCISE AND CLEAR; 202] *Opposite*: unclear

self-expression *n* **creativity**, making a statement, assertiveness, individualism, expressing yourself, making yourself heard, expressiveness [➡COMMUNICATION; 602]

self-fertilization *n* **self-fertilizing**, self-pollination, self-pollinating, autogamy, hermaphroditism, androgyny [➡REPRODUCTION AND HEREDITY; 725] *Opposite*: cross-fertilization

self-flattery *n* **self-congratulation**, self-satisfaction, self-praise, self-glorification, self-aggrandizement, self-glory, self-promotion, boasting, bragging, vanity, conceit [➡BOAST; 616] *Opposite*: self-abasement

self-glorification *n* **self-promotion**, self-congratulation, self-satisfaction, self-praise, self-flattery, self-aggrandizement, boasting, bragging, braggadocio, vanity, conceit [➡BOAST; 616] *Opposite*: self-deprecation

self-governing *adj* **autonomous**, independent, sovereign, self-determining, self-sufficient [➡STYLES AND SYSTEMS OF GOVERNMENT; 806] *Opposite*: dependent

self-government *n* **autonomy**, independence, self-governance, sovereignty, self-rule, self-determination, self-sufficiency [➡STYLES AND SYSTEMS OF GOVERNMENT; 806] *Opposite*: dependence

self-gratification *n* **self-indulgence**, hedonism, pleasure-seeking, high living, selfishness, pleasure, over-indulgence, intemperance [➡PLEASURE-SEEKING AND EXCESS; 885] *Opposite*: self-sacrifice

self-hatred *n* **self-contempt**, self-loathing, self-disgust, self-denigration, self-dislike, self-abasement [➡INSECURITY AND LOSS OF COMPOSURE; 544] *Opposite*: self-love

self-help *n* **support**, mutual support, group support, help, counseling, do-it-yourself [➡PSYCHOLOGY AND THE MIND; 769]

self-help group *n* [➡GROUPS WITH A COMMON INTEREST; 938]

self-image *n* **opinion of yourself**, self-perception, self-esteem, self-regard, self-respect, sense of worth [➡PSYCHOLOGY AND THE MIND; 769]

self-immolation *n* **suicide**, self-sacrifice, hara-kiri, suttee, martyrdom, self-destruction, ultimate sacrifice [➡CAUSES OF DEATH; 921]

self-importance *n* **arrogance**, pride, egotism, haughtiness, pomposity, conceit, bumptiousness, officiousness, swagger, narcissism [➡POMPOUS, LOUD, AND OVERCONFIDENT; 635] *Opposite*: humility

self-important *adj* **arrogant**, pompous, conceited, egotistic, bumptious, officious, self-opinionated, full of yourself, puffed-up, swaggering [➡ POMPOUS, LOUD, AND OVERCONFIDENT; 635] *Opposite*: humble

self-imposed *adj* **chosen**, voluntary, self-inflicted, self-induced, of your own free will [➡ INTENTIONAL AND DELIBERATE; 279] *Opposite*: enforced

self-incrimination *n* **self-accusation**, self-implication, confession, admission of guilt, self-blame [➡ ADMIT AND CONFESS; 615]

self-indulgence 1 *n* **decadence**, indulgence, hedonism, pleasure, luxury, pleasure-seeking, high living, intemperance, abandon, dissipation [➡ PLEASURE-SEEKING AND EXCESS; 885] *Opposite*: restraint 2 *n* **self-pity**, childishness, selfishness, self-centeredness, self-absorption [➡ SELFISH AND UNKIND; 505] *Opposite*: restraint

self-indulgent 1 *adj* **decadent**, indulgent, hedonistic, epicurean, luxurious, pleasure-seeking, abandoned [➡ PLEASURE-SEEKING AND EXCESS; 885] *Opposite*: restrained 2 *adj* **self-pitying**, wallowing, childish, selfish, self-centered, self-absorbed [➡ SELFISH AND UNKIND; 505] *Opposite*: restrained

self-interest *n* **selfishness**, self-centeredness, egotism, self-regard, egocentricity, self-absorption [➡ SELFISH AND UNKIND; 505] *Opposite*: altruism

self-interested *adj* **selfish**, self-centered, self-seeking, egocentric, egoistic, egotistic, egotistical, self-absorbed, self-regarding [➡ SELFISH AND UNKIND; 505] *Opposite*: altruistic

selfish *adj* **self-centered**, self-seeking, self-interested, egotistical, egotistic, egoistic, egocentric, self-regarding, greedy, venal, mercenary [➡ SELFISH AND UNKIND; 505] *Opposite*: selfless

selfishness *n* **self-centeredness**, self-interest, egotism, egoism, egocentricity, egocentrism, self-regard, greediness [➡ SELFISH AND UNKIND; 505] *Opposite*: selflessness

selfless *adj* **unselfish**, self-sacrificing, altruistic, generous, noble, gallant, self-effacing, disinterested [➡ GENEROSITY AND KINDNESS; 495] *Opposite*: selfish

selflessness *n* **unselfishness**, self-sacrifice, altruism, generosity, gallantry, self-abnegation [➡ GENEROSITY AND KINDNESS; 495] *Opposite*: selfishness

self-loathing *n* [➡ INSECURITY AND LOSS OF COMPOSURE; 544]

self-love *n* **egotism**, selfishness, egocentricity, narcissism, egoism, self-centeredness, self-interest, vanity, conceit, amour-propre (*formal*) [➡ SELFISH AND UNKIND; 505] *Opposite*: modesty

self-motivated *adj* **energetic**, dynamic, keen, enthusiastic, driven, committed, forceful, vigorous, ambitious, self-directed, self-starting, go-ahead (*informal*) [➡ ENERGY AND ENTHUSIASM; 496] *Opposite*: unmotivated

self-obsessed *adj* **self-centered**, egocentric, egomaniacal, egotistical, narcissistic, self-absorbed, self-seeking [➡ SELFISH AND UNKIND; 505]

self-opinionated 1 *adj* **overconfident**, sure of yourself, cocksure, self-confident, opinionated, pompous, bumptious, arrogant, overbearing, self-opinioned [➡ BOSSY AND OVERBEARING; 516] *Opposite*: diffident 2 *adj* **conceited**, vain, full of yourself, self-satisfied, self-opinioned, bigheaded (*informal*), too big for your britches (*informal*), too big

for your boots (*informal*) [➡ POMPOUS, LOUD, AND OVERCONFIDENT; 635] *Opposite*: self-deprecating

self-opinioned *see* **self-opinionated**

self-pity *n* **self-indulgence**, misery, unhappiness, defeatism, self-absorption, depression [➡ SADNESS, DISTRESS, AND DESPAIR; 539] *Opposite*: cheerfulness

self-pitying *adj* **self-absorbed**, wallowing, defeatist, sorry for yourself, miserable, melancholic, self-indulgent [➡ SADNESS, DISTRESS, AND DESPAIR; 539] *Opposite*: happy-go-lucky

self-possessed *adj* **confident**, self-assured, self-confident, assured, poised, well-balanced, sure of yourself [➡ CONFIDENCE AND COMPOSURE; 499] *Opposite*: insecure

self-possession *n* **confidence**, self-assurance, self-confidence, assurance, poise, composure, coolness [➡ CONFIDENCE AND COMPOSURE; 499] *Opposite*: insecurity

self-preservation *n* **self-protection**, self-defense, survival, preservation instinct, survival instinct [➡ PSYCHOLOGY AND THE MIND; 769]

self-promotion *n* **self-aggrandizement**, self-importance, self-glorification, self-glory, self-praise, self-flattery, boasting, bragging [➡ BOAST; 616] *Opposite*: self-deprecation

self-regard 1 *n* **self-interest**, self-centeredness, selfishness, egotism, egocentricity, egoism, narcissism, self-absorption [➡ SELFISH AND UNKIND; 505] *Opposite*: altruism 2 *n* **self-respect**, self-esteem, self-worth, dignity, pride, sense of self [➡ CONFIDENCE AND COMPOSURE; 499] *Opposite*: self-hatred

self-regarding *adj* **selfish**, self-centered, egocentric, egotistical, egotistic, self-absorbed, self-interested, vain, conceited [➡ SELFISH AND UNKIND; 505] *Opposite*: selfless

self-reliance *n* **independence**, self-sufficiency, autonomy, self-confidence, self-assurance, self-containment, resourcefulness [➡ RELATIONSHIP TO ANOTHER; 973] *Opposite*: dependence

self-reliant *adj* **independent**, self-sufficient, autonomous, self-confident, self-assured, self-contained, self-starting, resourceful, enterprising [➡ RELATIONSHIP TO ANOTHER; 973] *Opposite*: dependent

self-reproach *n* **self-criticism**, remorse, contrition, shame, guilt, regret [➡ FEELINGS ABOUT THE PAST; 532] *Opposite*: self-congratulation

self-respect *n* **self-esteem**, self-confidence, confidence, dignity, pride, self-worth, sense of worth [➡ CONFIDENCE AND COMPOSURE; 499] *Opposite*: self-hatred

self-restraint *n* **self-control**, self-discipline, discipline, willpower, moderation, restraint [➡ STRENGTH OF WILL; 501] *Opposite*: abandon

self-righteous *adj* **sanctimonious**, smug, self-satisfied, complacent, pious, haughty, supercilious, pompous, hypocritical, pretentious, holier-than-thou (*informal*), hoity-toity (*informal*) [➡ AFFECTATION, SELF-SATISFACTION, AND SNOBBISHNESS; 507] *Opposite*: humble

self-righteousness *n* **sanctimoniousness**, smugness, complacency, piety, superciliousness, haughtiness, pomposity, conceit, self-satisfaction, pretentiousness, hypocrisy [➡ AFFECTATION, SELF-SATISFACTION, AND SNOBBISHNESS; 507] *Opposite:* humility

self-rising flour *type of* **flour** [➡ BREAD, FLOUR, AND BREAD PRODUCTS; 1179]

self-rule *n* **self-government**, independence, self-determination, autonomy, self-governance, sovereignty [➡ STYLES AND SYSTEMS OF GOVERNMENT; 806] *Opposite:* dependence

self-sacrifice *n* **altruism**, unselfishness, selflessness, self-denial, martyrdom [➡ GENEROSITY AND KINDNESS; 495] *Opposite:* selfishness

self-sacrificing *adj* **altruistic**, unselfish, selfless, noble, self-denying [➡ GENEROSITY AND KINDNESS; 495] *Opposite:* selfish

selfsame *adj* **very same**, identical, very, exact, same [➡ SAMENESS; 150] *Opposite:* different

self-satisfaction *n* **smugness**, complacency, self-righteousness, conceit, arrogance, pride, self-assurance, narcissism [➡ AFFECTATION, SELF-SATISFACTION, AND SNOBBISHNESS; 507] *Opposite:* self-doubt

self-satisfied *adj* **smug**, pleased with yourself, self-righteous, conceited, arrogant, proud, self-assured, narcissistic, complacent [➡ AFFECTATION, SELF-SATISFACTION, AND SNOBBISHNESS; 507]

self-seeker *n* [➡ SELF-IMPORTANT AND SELF-SEEKING PEOPLE; 949]

self-seeking *adj* **selfish**, self-centered, self-regarding, egocentric, egoistic, egotistic, egotistical, self-absorbed, self-interested [➡ SELFISH AND UNKIND; 505] *Opposite:* selfless

self-serving *adj* **selfish**, egotistic, egotistical, self-centered, narcissistic, egocentric, self-absorbed, self-interested [➡ SELFISH AND UNKIND; 505] *Opposite:* altruistic

self-starter *n* [➡ PEOPLE WHO ARE APPROVED OF; 955]

self-starting *adj* [➡ HARD-WORKING AND COMMITTED; 500]

self-styled *adj* **self-appointed**, self-proclaimed, so-called, professed, would-be, soi-disant (*literary*) [➡ NAME AND DESCRIBE; 665] *Opposite:* certified

self-sufficiency *n* **independence**, autonomy, self-reliance, self-support [➡ RELATIONSHIP TO ANOTHER; 973] *Opposite:* dependence

self-sufficient *adj* **independent**, autonomous, self-reliant, self-supporting, self-financing, self-contained [➡ RELATIONSHIP TO ANOTHER; 973] *Opposite:* dependent

self-supporting *adj* **self-sufficient**, self-financing, profitable, healthy, successful, self-sustaining, economically viable [➡ ECONOMICAL AND RESOURCEFUL; 207] *Opposite:* struggling

self-sustaining *adj* [➡ ECONOMICAL AND RESOURCEFUL; 207]

self-will *n* **determination**, obstinacy, stubbornness, willfulness, pigheadedness, intransigence, inflexibility [➡ UNWILLINGNESS AND STUBBORNNESS; 564] *Opposite:* weakness

self-willed *adj* **headstrong**, obstinate, determined, stubborn, pigheaded, willful [➡ UNWILLINGNESS AND STUBBORNNESS; 564] *Opposite:* weak-willed

self-worth *n* **self-esteem**, self-respect, self-confidence,

pride, dignity, positive self-image, amour-propre (*formal*) [➡ CONFIDENCE AND COMPOSURE; 499]

sell 1 *v* **vend**, wholesale, trade, retail [➡ SELL; 441] *Opposite:* buy 2 *v* **put up for sale**, market, offer, deal in, auction, have, put on sale, handle, peddle, traffic in, hawk, dump, unload, get rid of, push (*slang*) [➡ SELL; 441] *Opposite:* buy 3 *v* **be bought**, go, sell like hotcakes, be snapped up, be popular, be in demand [➡ SELL; 441] 4 *v* **persuade people to buy**, market, promote, advertise, traffic in, hawk, plug (*informal*) [➡ ADVERTISING AND PUBLICITY; 604]

seller *n* **vendor**, retailer, wholesaler, supplier, merchant, shopkeeper, trader, broker, dealer, hawker, peddler, trafficker, purveyor (*formal*) [➡ SELLERS; 442] *Opposite:* buyer

selling *n* **vending**, sales, marketing, trade, retailing, auctioning, export, hawking, peddling, trafficking [➡ BUSINESS ACTIVITIES AND PHENOMENA; 794] *Opposite:* buying

sell out 1 *v* **run out**, be out of stock, be snapped up, go, be unavailable [➡ USE UP AND WASTE; 474] *Opposite:* stock up 2 *v* **give in**, give up, sell your soul, betray your principles, be co-opted, cave in, surrender, deliver up [➡ FAIL OR BE UNSUCCESSFUL; 75]

sellout 1 *n* **box-office hit**, hit, smash hit, smash, bestseller, success, triumph [➡ SUCCESS; 82] *Opposite:* flop (*informal*) 2 *n* (*informal*) **betrayal**, treachery, disloyalty, apostasy, co-optation, stab in the back (*informal*) [➡ MALICIOUS ACTIONS OR BEHAVIOR; 296] *Opposite:* loyalty 3 *n* (*informal*) **traitor**, opportunist, turncoat, renegade, apostate [➡ LAZY OR UNSUCCESSFUL PEOPLE; 948] *Opposite:* loyalist

semantic *adj* [➡ ASPECTS OF LANGUAGE; 682]

semantics *n* [➡ ASPECTS OF LANGUAGE; 682]

semblance 1 *n* **appearance**, impression, air, resemblance, façade, veneer, aspect, likeness, look [➡ APPEARANCE AND ATMOSPHERE; 1237] 2 *n* **trace**, shred, fragment, measure, modicum, hint [➡ FEW, LITTLE, SMALL AMOUNT; 120]

semen *n* [➡ EGGS, SPERM, AND SPAWN; 727]

semester *type of* **time period** [➡ TIMES OF YEAR; 88]

semi *see* **semitrailer**

semiautomatic *type of* **gun** [➡ WEAPONS FOR SHOOTING; 1156]

semicircle *type of* **rounded shape** [➡ ROUNDED SHAPE; 1218]

semicircular *adj* [➡ ROUNDED SHAPE; 1218]

semicolon *type of* **punctuation mark** [➡ ASPECTS OF LANGUAGE; 682]

semiconscious *adj* **half-conscious**, half-awake, half-asleep, surfacing, dazed, stunned, knocked out, insensible [➡ TIRED, ASLEEP, AND UNCONSCIOUS; 738]

semidarkness *n* **twilight**, half-light, dusk, dimness, gloom, shadow, shade, dark, gloaming (*literary*) [➡ DESCRIBING LIGHT; 1228]

semidesert *n* [➡ DESERTS, PLAINS, AND MOORLAND; 1045]

semidetached *type of* **house** [➡ RESIDENTIAL BUILDINGS; 1078]

semifinal *n* **round**, heat, leg, game, match [➡ NON-AGGRESSIVE/SPORTING EVENTS; 40]

seminal *adj* **influential**, important, formative, pivotal, inspiring, inspirational, groundbreaking, epoch-making, original, creative, germinal (*formal*) [➡ IMPORTANT; 194] *Opposite*: insignificant

seminal moment *n* [➡ DECISIVE MOMENTS; 44]

seminar 1 *n* **meeting**, session, roundtable, discussion, conference, assembly, talk, colloquium, forum [➡ MEETINGS AND ASSEMBLIES; 43] **2** *n* **discussion group**, tutorial, class, evening class, talk, colloquium [➡ CLASSES, COURSEWORK, AND EXAMINATIONS; 842]

seminary *n* **theological college**, divinity school, college, academy, institute, university, school, training college (*UK*) [➡ EDUCATIONAL INSTITUTIONS; 813]

semiprecious stone *n* [➡ PRECIOUS STONES; 1278]

semiskilled worker *n* [➡ WORKERS; 836]

semitrailer *type of* **commercial or industrial vehicle** [➡ VEHICLES; 1145]

senate *n* **governing body**, legislature, congress, parliament, diet, assembly, ruling body, committee, board, council [➡ LEGISLATIVE BODIES AND LEGISLATION; 809]

senator *n* **senate member**, politician, representative, legislator, congresswoman, congressman, stateswoman, statesman, governor, political figure [➡ POLITICAL OFFICES AND POLITICIANS; 808]

send 1 *v* **mail**, transmit, dispatch, forward, convey, remit, consign, send off, send out, ship, express, relay, post (*UK*) [➡ DISPATCH AND SEND; 333] *Opposite*: receive **2** *v* **direct**, refer, guide, show, lead, conduct [➡ ACCOMPANY AND FOLLOW; 337] **3** *v* **propel**, hurl, fling, throw, fire, launch, drive, deliver, shoot, cast [➡ MOVE SOMETHING THROUGH THE AIR; 334] *Opposite*: bring **4** *v* **transmit**, project, broadcast, disseminate, give off, emit [➡ EMIT AND EMANATE; 361]

send down (*UK*) *v* **expel**, rusticate, suspend, banish, dismiss, send away [➡ REVOKE STATUS; 459]

send for *v* **request**, summon, call for, order, assemble, gather [➡ INITIATE AND ESTABLISH COMMUNICATION; 680] *Opposite*: dismiss

send forth (*archaic or literary*) *v* **produce**, give out, emit, spout, put out, sprout, issue [➡ EMIT AND EMANATE; 361] *Opposite*: retract

send off *v* **dispatch**, send, send away, transmit, forward, circulate, convey, consign, mail, ship, remit, post (*UK*) [➡ DISPATCH AND SEND; 333] *Opposite*: receive

sendoff *n* **goodbye**, farewell, leaving party, leaving do (*UK*), valediction (*formal*), leave-taking (*literary*) [➡ ENDS AND DEPARTURES; 54] *Opposite*: welcome

send on (*UK*) *v* **redirect**, readdress, pass on, forward, transfer, relay [➡ DISPATCH AND SEND; 333] *Opposite*: return

send over the edge *v* **derange**, unhinge, unsettle, stress out (*informal*) [➡ UPSET, DISTRESS, AND HUMILIATE; 567]

send packing (*informal*) *v* **dismiss**, discharge (*formal*), expel, evict, turn out, throw out, drive out, send home, send away, banish [➡ EJECT AND EXCLUDE; 340] *Opposite*: welcome

send to Coventry (*UK*) *v* **ostracize**, ignore, freeze out, give the cold shoulder to, exclude, boycott, blackball [➡ REFUSING OR REJECTING RELATIONS; 975]

send up 1 *v* **raise**, elevate, heighten, boost, bump up (*informal*), augment (*formal*) [➡ MOVE SOMETHING: UPWARD; 328] *Opposite*: lower **2** *v* (*informal*) **lampoon**, satirize, mock, parody, mimic, impersonate, ape, make fun of, burlesque, caricature, ridicule, take somebody off (*informal*) [➡ JOKES AND TEASING; 674]

*See Compare and Contrast at **ridicule**.*

sendup (*informal*) *n* **parody**, lampoon, takeoff, imitation, impersonation, caricature, mockery, satire, spoof, burlesque, skit [➡ JOKES AND TEASING; 674]

send your apologies *v* [➡ RUN AWAY AND AVOID; 10]

senile *adj* **confused**, disoriented, forgetful, failing, absent-minded, doddering [➡ CONFUSION, ANXIETY, AND WORRY; 540]

senior 1 *adj* **older**, elder, oldest, eldest, first-born [➡ OLD, OLD-FASHIONED; 167] *Opposite*: junior **2** *adj* **high-ranking**, high-grade, superior, higher, leading, chief, major, primary, above, over [➡ CLASS STATUS; 889] *Opposite*: junior **3** *n* **senior citizen**, pensioner, golden ager, retiree, retired person, OAP (*UK*) [➡ OLD PEOPLE; 920] **4** *n* **elder**, first-born, elder sibling, big brother, big sister [➡ SAME-GENERATION RELATIVES; 957] *Opposite*: junior **5** *n* **boss**, superior, chief, manager, leader, director, head, higher-up (*informal*) [➡ BOSSES AND MANAGEMENT; 965] *Opposite*: junior

senior citizen *n* **pensioner**, retired person, golden ager, senior, OAP (*UK*) [➡ OLD PEOPLE; 920]

seniority *n* **superiority**, supremacy, precedence, priority, position, tenure, rank [➡ SUPERIORITY; 152]

sensation 1 *n* **feeling**, sense, impression, awareness, consciousness, perception, responsiveness [➡ THE SENSES; 696] *Opposite*: numbness **2** *n* **commotion**, stir, fuss, uproar, rumpus, ruckus, thrill, to-do (*informal*), buzz (*informal*) [➡ CHAOS AND UPROAR; 51] *Opposite*: lull **3** *n* **phenomenon**, miracle, wonder, marvel, spectacle, runaway success [➡ AMAZING THINGS; 211]

sensational 1 *adj* (*informal*) **amazing**, astounding, marvelous, exciting, thrilling, breathtaking, out of this world, magnificent, incredible, striking, spectacular, remarkable [➡ EXTRAORDINARY: AMAZING; 204] *Opposite*: boring **2** *adj* **extraordinary**, dramatic, astonishing, unbelievable, historic, memorable [➡ EXTRAORDINARY: UNCOMMON; 205] *Opposite*: predictable **3** *adj* **startling**, shocking, scandalous, melodramatic, lurid, sensationalist, exaggerated [➡ IN POOR TASTE AND OVERSENTIMENTAL; 229] *Opposite*: understated

sensationalism *n* **exaggeration**, overstatement, luridness, scandal, melodrama, shock tactics [➡ IN POOR TASTE AND OVERSENTIMENTAL; 229] *Opposite*: understatement

sensationalist *adj* **startling**, shocking, scandalous, melodramatic, lurid, sensational, exaggerated [➡ IN POOR TASTE AND OVERSENTIMENTAL; 229] *Opposite*: understated

sense 1 *n* **feeling**, sensation, awareness, perception [➡ THE SENSES; 696] **2** *n* **appreciation**, impression, consciousness, awareness, feeling, perception [➡ FEELINGS; 531] **3** *n* **intelligence**, brains, intellect, wisdom, sagacity, common sense, logic, good judgment, wit [➡ DESCRIBING SOMEBODY'S INTELLECT; 523] *Opposite*: folly **4** *n* **purpose**, point, reason, function, end, advantage [➡ INTENTIONS AND PURPOSES; 772] **5** *n* **opinion**, view, viewpoint, consensus, mood, feeling [➡ POINTS OF VIEW; 767]

6 *n* **gist**, substance, drift, nub, idea, essence [➡ MEANING; 690]
7 *n* **meaning**, denotation, significance, signification, implication, connotation [➡ MEANING; 690] **8** *v* **detect**, identify, distinguish, recognize, know, pick up [➡ DEVELOP THEORIES AND REASON; 744] **9** *v* **perceive**, feel, have a feeling, get the impression, discern, be aware of [➡ USING THE SENSES; 697] *Opposite*: observe **10** *v* **intuit**, guess, suspect, pick up, feel, feel in your bones, infer [➡ UNDERSTAND AND GRASP; 759]

senseless **1** *adj* **pointless**, ridiculous, absurd, meaningless, futile, vain, nonsensical, useless, irrational [➡ REDUNDANT AND USELESS; 240] *Opposite*: worthwhile **2** *adj* **stupid**, silly, foolish, mindless, idiotic, inane, fatuous, mad, crazy (*informal*) [➡ BIZARRE AND PECULIAR; 257] *Opposite*: sensible **3** *adj* **unconscious**, comatose, numb, deadened, knocked out, passed out, insensible [➡ TIRED, ASLEEP, AND UNCONSCIOUS; 738] *Opposite*: conscious

senselessness **1** *n* **pointlessness**, ridiculousness, absurdity, irrationality, meaninglessness, futility, uselessness [➡ REDUNDANT AND USELESS; 240] **2** *n* **stupidity**, silliness, foolishness, madness, idiocy, inanity, mindlessness [➡ BIZARRE AND PECULIAR; 257] *Opposite*: sense

sense of humor *n* [➡ CHEERFULNESS OF OUTLOOK; 503]

sense of smell *n* [➡ THE SENSES; 696]

sense of taste *n* [➡ THE SENSES; 696]

senses *n* [➡ THE SENSES; 696]

sensibility *n* **responsiveness**, deep feeling, emotional response, receptivity, susceptibility, feeling, awareness [➡ FEELINGS; 531] *Opposite*: insensitivity

sensible **1** *adj* **level-headed**, sane, rational, reasonable, shrewd, wise, sagacious, prudent, judicious [➡ POSITIVE INTELLECTUAL CHARACTERISTICS; 524] *Opposite*: foolish **2** *adj* **practical**, serviceable, workable, functional, utilitarian, no-nonsense [➡ USEFULNESS; 199] *Opposite*: impractical **3** *adj* (*formal*) **aware**, conscious, mindful, cognizant (*formal*) [➡ WIDE AWAKE AND CONSCIOUS; 735]

See Compare and Contrast at **aware**.

sensibleness *n* **rationality**, level-headedness, reasonableness, shrewdness, wisdom, sagacity, prudence, judiciousness [➡ POSITIVE INTELLECTUAL CHARACTERISTICS; 524] *Opposite*: foolishness

sensibly *adv* **level-headedly**, rationally, reasonably, wisely, shrewdly, prudently, judiciously, sagaciously (*formal*), sagely (*literary*) [➡ POSITIVE INTELLECTUAL CHARACTERISTICS; 524] *Opposite*: foolishly

sensitive **1** *adj* **responsive**, receptive, susceptible, aware, perceptive, impressionable [➡ POSITIVE INTELLECTUAL CHARACTERISTICS; 524] *Opposite*: indifferent **2** *adj* **delicate**, irritable, susceptible, allergic, difficult, problematic [➡ WEAKNESS; 241] *Opposite*: robust **3** *adj* **subtle**, delicate, complex, searching, penetrating, profound [➡ THE NATURE OF IDEAS; 771] *Opposite*: superficial **4** *adj* **thoughtful**, sympathetic, understanding, perceptive, considerate, caring [➡ GENEROSITY AND KINDNESS; 495] *Opposite*: unsympathetic **5** *adj* **thin-skinned**, easily upset, easily hurt, hypersensitive, vulnerable, touchy [➡ EXCESSIVE SENSITIVITY; 511] *Opposite*: impervious **6** *adj* **secret**, confidential, classified, top secret, restricted, hush-hush (*informal*) [➡ SECRET AND UNKNOWN; 179] *Opposite*: public

7 *adj* **awkward**, tricky, difficult, sticky, delicate, embarrassing [➡ EMOTIONALLY UNPLEASANT AND UPSETTING; 227] *Opposite*: straightforward **8** *adj* **precise**, exact, delicate, finely tuned, responsive [➡ EXACT; 203] *Opposite*: imprecise

sensitivity *n* **compassion**, sympathy, understanding, kindliness, warmth, feeling, thoughtfulness [➡ GENEROSITY AND KINDNESS; 495] *Opposite*: indifference

sensitize **1** *v* **alert**, make aware, inform, explain, brief, warn, prepare [➡ INFORM, ANNOUNCE, AND ISSUE; 611] *Opposite*: desensitize **2** *v* **expose**, make sensitive, irritate, trigger, induce, provoke, set off [➡ CAUSE TO HAPPEN; 31] *Opposite*: desensitize

sensor *n* **device**, measuring device, instrument, radar, beam, feeler, antenna, pickup, bug [➡ DEVICES; 1115]

sensual **1** *adj* **sensory**, carnal, bodily, physical, corporeal, fleshly, animal [➡ LIVING THINGS AND LIVING; 976] *Opposite*: intellectual **2** *adj* **sexual**, erotic, voluptuous, fleshly, carnal, sexy [➡ PHYSICALLY PLEASANT; 186] *Opposite*: ascetic

sensualist *n* [➡ PLEASURE-SEEKERS AND HEDONISTS; 886]

sensuous *adj* **sumptuous**, opulent, rich, deep, intense, voluptuous, lush, luxurious [➡ EXPENSIVE AND LUXURIOUS; 218] *Opposite*: ascetic

sentence **1** *type of* **grammatical term** [➡ ASPECTS OF LANGUAGE; 682] **2** *n* **judgment**, verdict, ruling, decree, condemnation, punishment, prison term, stretch [➡ TRIAL, PUNISHMENT, AND LEGAL OUTCOMES; 819] **3** *v* **pass judgment on**, condemn, punish, send to prison, pronounce judgment on, penalize, send down (*UK informal*) [➡ TRIAL, PUNISHMENT, AND LEGAL OUTCOMES; 819] *Opposite*: acquit

sentence structure *n* [➡ ASPECTS OF LANGUAGE; 682]

sententious *adj* **moralizing**, moralistic, judgmental, critical, censorious, disapproving [➡ ACCUSATORY AND DISAPPROVING; 634] *Opposite*: approving

sentience *n* [➡ WIDE AWAKE AND CONSCIOUS; 735]

sentient **1** *adj* **conscious**, animate, flesh-and-blood, alive, living, live, breathing, aware, alert [➡ LIVING THINGS AND LIVING; 976] *Opposite*: inanimate **2** *adj* **emotional**, responsive, sensitive, perceptive, feeling, sentimental [➡ POSITIVE INTELLECTUAL CHARACTERISTICS; 524] *Opposite*: intellectual

sentiment **1** *n* **feeling**, emotion, response, reaction, attitude, opinion, outlook [➡ FEELINGS; 531] **2** *n* **sentimentality**, mawkishness, gush, romanticism, corn (*informal*), soppiness (*informal*) [➡ IN POOR TASTE AND OVERSENTIMENTAL; 229]

sentimental *adj* **mawkish**, romantic, slushy, gushy, mushy, maudlin, syrupy, emotional, corny, sloppy (*informal*), schmaltzy (*informal*), soppy (*informal*) [➡ IN POOR TASTE AND OVERSENTIMENTAL; 229] *Opposite*: cynical

sentimentality *n* **mawkishness**, corniness, slushiness, mushiness, romanticism, soppiness (*informal*), sloppiness (*informal*), schmaltziness (*informal*) [➡ IN POOR TASTE AND OVERSENTIMENTAL; 229] *Opposite*: cynicism

sentimentalize *v* **gush**, emotionalize, romanticize, wax lyrical (*literary*) [➡ DREAM, IMAGINE, AND FANTASIZE; 749]

sentinel *n* **sentry**, lookout, guard, watch, watchman, picket, custodian, patrol [➡ PEOPLE WHO GUARD AND PROTECT; 846]

sentry *n* **guard**, sentinel, patrol, lookout, watch, watchman, picket, custodian [➤ PEOPLE WHO GUARD AND PROTECT; 846]

sentry box *type of* **outbuilding** [➤ ANCILLARY BUILDINGS; 1080]

sepal *part of* **flower** [➤ FLOWERS; 1032]

separable *adj* **divisible**, distinguishable, detachable, removable, discrete, separate, independent [➤ UNRELATEDNESS AND SEPARATENESS; 146] *Opposite*: inseparable

separate 1 *adj* **unconnected**, disconnected, individual, independent, unattached, autonomous, solitary [➤ RELATIONSHIP TO ANOTHER; 973] *Opposite*: connected 2 *adj* **distinct**, discrete, detached, loose, dispersed, isolated, single [➤ UNRELATEDNESS AND SEPARATENESS; 146] *Opposite*: attached 3 *v* **divide**, part, disconnect, undo, split, split up, break up, take apart, detach [➤ SEPARATE AND DIVIDE; 401] *Opposite*: unite 4 *v* **break away**, secede, branch out, break free, break, split up, withdraw, pull out [➤ LEAVE AND GO AWAY; 8] *Opposite*: join 5 *v* **split up**, split, divorce, part, part company, become estranged [➤ REFUSING OR REJECTING RELATIONS; 975]

separately 1 *adv* **distinctly**, unconnectedly, disjointedly, discretely, severally [➤ UNRELATEDNESS AND SEPARATENESS; 146] *Opposite*: together 2 *adv* **independently**, alone, individually, one at a time, singly, one by one, on their own [➤ ACTING INDEPENDENTLY; 284] *Opposite*: together

separateness *n* **distinctness**, disconnectedness, separation, distinctiveness, difference, discreteness [➤ UNRELATEDNESS AND SEPARATENESS; 146]

separate off *v* **divide**, divide off, split off, detach, sever, set apart, set aside, keep apart, isolate, segregate [➤ SEPARATE AND DIVIDE; 401]

separate out *v* **strain**, filter, pass through a filter, sieve, extract [➤ SEPARATE AND DIVIDE; 401] *Opposite*: cohere (*formal*)

separates *n* [➤ GARMENTS AND OUTFITS; 865]

separation 1 *n* **division**, severance, taking apart, partition, disjunction, disconnection [➤ SEPARATE AND DIVIDE; 401] *Opposite*: unification 2 *n* **parting**, departure, goodbye, farewell, leave-taking (*literary*) [➤ ENDS AND DEPARTURES; 54] *Opposite*: meeting 3 *n* **split-up**, split, divorce, estrangement, rift, parting [➤ ENDS AND DEPARTURES; 54]

separatist *n* **dissenter**, secessionist, protester, rebel, freedom fighter, separationist [➤ UNCOOPERATIVE OR REBELLIOUS PEOPLE; 566]

separator 1 *n* **divider**, barrier, partition, dividing wall, screen, wedge [➤ WALLS AND PARTITIONS; 1104] 2 *n* **sieve**, strainer, filter, extractor, centrifuge [➤ PARTS OF MACHINES AND TOOLS; 1118] *Opposite*: blender

septet *type of* **band** [➤ MUSICIANS AND SINGERS; 908]

septic *adj* **poisoned**, infected, festering, gangrenous, diseased, putrefying [➤ SICKNESS; 729] *Opposite*: healthy

septic tank *n* [➤ CONTAINERS, RECEPTACLES, AND PACKAGING; 1245]

sepulcher *n* **vault**, tomb, grave, crypt, burial chamber, mausoleum, resting place [➤ BURIAL PLACES AND ACCESSORIES; 930]

sepulchral *adj* **funereal**, sad, dismal, somber, melancholy, gloomy [➤ EMOTIONALLY UNPLEASANT AND UPSETTING; 227] *Opposite*: cheery

sequel 1 *n* **follow-on**, continuation, conclusion, follow-up [➤ AFTER, LAST, AND FOLLOWING; 165] *Opposite*: prequel 2 *n* **consequence**, development, result, outcome, upshot, effect [➤ RESULTS AND OUTCOMES; 83] *Opposite*: prelude

sequence 1 *n* **series**, succession, run, progression, chain, string, cycle [➤ CHAIN OF EVENTS; 162] 2 *n* **order**, arrangement, classification, categorization, system, structure [➤ COLLECTIONS AND MIXTURES OF THINGS; 1244] *Opposite*: disarray

sequence of events *n* [➤ CHAIN OF EVENTS; 162]

sequential 1 *adj* **in sequence**, consecutive, in order, successive, chronological, serial, progressive [➤ CHAIN OF EVENTS; 162] *Opposite*: jumbled 2 *adj* **consequent**, resulting, resultant, ensuing, following, subsequent [➤ AFTER, LAST, AND FOLLOWING; 165] *Opposite*: previous

sequentially *adv* **in sequence**, in succession, successively, in order, consecutively, one after another, serially, chronologically, one after the other [➤ AFTER, LAST, AND FOLLOWING; 165] *Opposite*: out of order

sequester 1 *v* (*formal*) **isolate**, separate, segregate, cut off, set apart, keep apart, insulate, quarantine [➤ SEPARATE AND DIVIDE; 401] 2 *v* **confiscate**, requisition, appropriate, impound, seize, repossess [➤ TAKE SOMETHING AWAY; 425] *Opposite*: restore

sequestered (*formal*) *adj* [➤ SECRET AND UNKNOWN; 179]

sequestrate (*UK*) *v* **confiscate**, seize, appropriate, repossess, impound, take, requisition [➤ TAKE SOMETHING AWAY; 425] *Opposite*: release

sequestration *n* **confiscation**, appropriation, impounding, seizure, requisitioning, repossession [➤ TAKE SOMETHING AWAY; 425] *Opposite*: restoration

sequin *n* **spangle**, bead, bauble, star, decoration, trimming [➤ ORNAMENTS AND DECORATIONS; 1248]

sequoia *type of* **evergreen tree** [➤ EVERGREEN AND CONIFEROUS TREES; 1029]

seraph *n* [➤ RELIGIOUS CONCEPTS; 776]

sere (*literary*) *adj* [➤ DRY; 1242]

See Compare and Contrast at **dry**.

serenade *v* **sing**, croon, court, entertain, divert, regale [➤ MUSIC, SONGS, AND SINGING; 907]

serendipitous *adj* **fortunate**, lucky, happy, fortuitous, providential [➤ LUCK; 783]

serendipity *n* **fate**, destiny, karma, providence, luck, fortune, coincidence, accident, kismet, chance [➤ LUCK; 783] *Opposite*: design

serene 1 *adj* **calm**, composed, unruffled, cool, unflustered, equable, laid-back (*informal*) [➤ COOL AND CALM; 536] *Opposite*: agitated 2 *adj* **tranquil**, calm, peaceful, still, quiet, placid [➤ PEACEFULNESS AND GENTLENESS; 214] *Opposite*: bustling

serenity 1 *n* **composure**, coolness, peace of mind, poise, contentment, repose, mellowness, equanimity (*formal*) [➤ COOL AND CALM; 536] *Opposite*: panic 2 *n* **tranquility**, calmness, peacefulness, quietude, quietness, stillness [➤ PEACEFULNESS AND GENTLENESS; 214] *Opposite*: bustle

serial 1 *adj* **sequential**, successive, consecutive, ongoing, in order, in sequence [➡ AFTER, LAST, AND FOLLOWING; 165] *Opposite:* out of order **2** *type of* **hardware** [➡ COMPUTERS AND COMPUTING; 1127]

series *n* **sequence**, succession, run, chain, string, cycle, progression [➡ CHAIN OF EVENTS; 162]

series of events *n* [➡ CHAIN OF EVENTS; 162]

serious 1 *adj* **dangerous**, acute, life-threatening, critical, grave, severe, worrying [➡ DANGEROUS; 236] *Opposite:* minor **2** *adj* **important**, momentous, significant, crucial, vital, critical, considerable, major, fundamental [➡ IMPORTANT; 194] *Opposite:* trivial **3** *adj* **thoughtful**, grave, solemn, somber, stern, grim, severe, staid, sober, unsmiling, quiet, humorless, serious-minded [➡ NEGATIVITY OF OUTLOOK; 514] *Opposite:* light-hearted **4** *adj* **thought-provoking**, meaningful, intense, deep, profound, powerful [➡ THE NATURE OF IDEAS; 771] *Opposite:* lightweight **5** *adj* **earnest**, sincere, genuine, honest, resolute, decided, determined [➡ HONEST AND OPEN; 630] *Opposite:* flippant

seriously 1 *adv* **badly**, dangerously, critically, fatally, acutely, gravely [➡ CRITICALLY AND SERIOUSLY; 134] *Opposite:* slightly **2** *adv* **earnestly**, truly, sincerely, genuinely, honestly, really [➡ HONEST AND RELIABLE; 502] *Opposite:* jokingly **3** *adv* (*informal*) **extremely**, very, really, totally, utterly, completely [➡ TO A GREAT EXTENT; 132]

serious-minded *adj* **earnest**, sensible, sedate, steady, determined, resolute, serious [➡ POSITIVE INTELLECTUAL CHARACTERISTICS; 524] *Opposite:* frivolous

seriousness 1 *n* **importance**, significance, gravity, weightiness, momentousness, solemnity, urgency [➡ IMPORTANCE AND SIGNIFICANCE; 192] *Opposite:* triviality **2** *n* **earnestness**, sincerity, genuineness, honesty, resoluteness, determination [➡ HONEST AND RELIABLE; 502] *Opposite:* flippancy

sermon 1 *n* **talk**, address, homily, discourse, oration, lecture [➡ RELIGIONS AND RELIGIOUS PRACTICES; 777] *Opposite:* conversation **2** *n* **lecture**, harangue, homily, talking-to (*informal*), ticking-off (*informal*), telling-off (*informal*) [➡ CRITICISMS AND ANGRY OUTBURSTS; 50] *Opposite:* praise

sermonize *v* **preach**, pontificate, moralize, hold forth, lecture, harangue [➡ INSTRUCT AND TEACH; 609] *Opposite:* flatter

Serpens 1 *type of* **constellation** [➡ HEAVENLY BODIES; 1061] **2** *type of* **constellation** [➡ HEAVENLY BODIES; 1061]

serpent 1 *n* (*literary*) **snake**, sea serpent, sea snake, reptile, viper [➡ SNAKES; 995] **2** *n* **traitor**, liar, cheat, trouble-maker, snake in the grass, schemer, sneak (*UK*) [➡ PEOPLE WHO DECEIVE; 661] *Opposite:* friend

serpentine *adj* **winding**, meandering, twisting, sinuous, bending, roundabout, circuitous, indirect [➡ DIRECTION OF MOTION; 345] *Opposite:* straight

serrated *adj* **jagged**, toothed, notched, ragged, saw-toothed [➡ PHYSICAL TEXTURE; 1222] *Opposite:* smooth

servant *n* **domestic**, retainer, help [➡ DOMESTIC AND KITCHEN WORKERS; 850] *Opposite:* employer

servant

◆ *types of servants*
butler, chambermaid, cleaner, cook, factotum, flunky, footman, lackey, maid, maidservant, major-domo, valet

serve 1 *v* **work for**, help, aid, attend, assist, oblige [➡ HELP; 293] **2** *v* **function**, work, operate, act, perform, behave [➡ FUNCTION SUCCESSFULLY; 469] **3** *v* **supply**, dish up, serve up, hand out, give out, provide, distribute, dole out (*informal*), hand round (*UK*) [➡ DISPENSE, RATION, AND DISTRIBUTE; 434] **4** *v* **wait on**, wait, attend, tend, minister to, wait at table (*UK*) [➡ WORK-RELATED ACTIVITIES; 834]

server *type of* **hardware** [➡ COMPUTERS AND COMPUTING; 1127]

service 1 *n* **help**, assistance, aid, use, benefit, advantage, good turn [➡ KIND ACTIONS OR BEHAVIOR; 295] *Opposite:* disservice **2** *n* **facility**, provision, package, deal, amenity [➡ USEFULNESS; 199] **3** *n* **overhaul**, examination, check, tune-up, maintenance, once-over (*informal*) [➡ REPAIR AND MEND; 376] **4** *n* **ceremony**, ritual, rite, sacrament, mass, observance [➡ RELIGIONS AND RELIGIOUS PRACTICES; 777] **5** *v* **repair**, overhaul, examine, tune, check, retune [➡ REPAIR AND MEND; 376]

serviceable 1 *adj* **durable**, strong, stout, tough, sturdy, hard-wearing [➡ STRENGTH; 201] *Opposite:* flimsy **2** *adj* **working**, operative, functional, in working order, usable, workable [➡ IN GOOD REPAIR; 1232] *Opposite:* broken **3** *adj* **effective**, helpful, practical, useful, practicable, utilitarian, convenient, efficient [➡ USEFULNESS; 199] *Opposite:* impractical

service economy *type of* **economic system** [➡ FINANCE AND ECONOMICS; 796]

service for the dead *n* [➡ BURIAL AND PREPARATION FOR BURIAL; 929]

service provider *n* [➡ THE INTERNET; 1128]

service road *type of* **secondary road** [➡ ROADS; 1106]

services 1 *n* **service station**, gas station, service area, filling station, facilities, amenities, rest stop, rest area, motorway facilities (*UK*), motorway service station (*UK*) [➡ RETAIL OUTLETS; 1083] **2** *n* **service industries**, nonmanufacturing industries, service sector, service jobs, customer services [➡ BUSINESS PRODUCTS; 795] *Opposite:* manufacturing **3** *n* **public amenities**, civic amenities, amenities, public services, essential services, local services, council services (*UK*) [➡ SOCIAL WELFARE; 812] **4** *n* **armed forces**, forces, military, armed services, security forces, defense [➡ THE ARMED FORCES; 827]

service station *type of* **retail outlet** [➡ RETAIL OUTLETS; 1083]

servile *adj* **submissive**, abject, fawning, subservient, sycophantic, obsequious, groveling, toadying [➡ INGRATIATING; 638] *Opposite:* proud

servility *n* [➡ INGRATIATING; 638]

serving *n* **portion**, helping, plateful, ration, quota, allocation [➡ AMOUNTS AND QUANTITIES; 112]

serving dish *n* **platter**, salver, plate, tray, dish, bowl [➡ TABLEWARE, FLATWARE, AND KITCHENWARE; 861]

serving spoon *type of* **flatware** [➡ TABLEWARE, FLATWARE, AND KITCHENWARE; 861]

servitude 1 *n* **slavery**, bondage, serfdom, enslavement, vassalage, thralldom [➡ CAPTIVITY AND LOSS OF FREEDOM; 248] *Opposite*: freedom 2 *n* **subjection**, subjugation, subordination, dependence, dependency, subservience [➡ RELATIONSHIP TO ANOTHER; 973] *Opposite*: liberty

sesame oil *type of* **cooking fat and oil** [➡ FATS AND OILS; 1173]

session 1 *n* **meeting**, sitting, assembly, conference, gathering, hearing [➡ MEETINGS AND ASSEMBLIES; 43] 2 *n* **term**, period, semester, trimester, quarter, year, academic year [➡ CLASSES, COURSEWORK, AND EXAMINATIONS; 842] 3 *n* **shift**, stint, go, spell, turn, phase [➡ PERIODS OF TIME; 90]

set 1 *v* **put**, place, locate, position, situate, deposit, stand, lay down, rest, plonk, plunk, stick (*informal*), park (*slang*) [➡ POSITION SOMETHING; 325] *Opposite*: pick up 2 *v* **become hard**, harden, solidify, congeal, coagulate, gel, freeze, go hard (*UK*) [➡ HARDEN, CONGEAL, AND DRY; 387] *Opposite*: liquefy 3 *v* **establish**, fix, agree on, appoint, decide, settle on, arrange [➡ MAKE DECISIONS AND CHOICES; 752] *Opposite*: change 4 *v* **adjust**, regulate, synchronize, align, program, calibrate, tune [➡ CHANGE; 372] 5 *n* **scenery**, stage set, movie set, setting, location, backdrop [➡ IN THE THEATER; 906] 6 *n* **collection**, group, arrangement, array, series, suite [➡ COLLECTIONS AND MIXTURES OF THINGS; 1244] *Opposite*: individual 7 *n* **circle**, group, clique, gang, crowd [➡ FRIENDS AND ACQUAINTANCES; 936] 8 *adj* **established**, usual, customary, traditional, conventional, agreed, fixed, regular, arranged, prearranged, normal [➡ ORDER AND ORGANIZATION; 206] *Opposite*: changing 9 *adj* **inflexible**, obstinate, determined, resolute, resolved, rigid, stubborn, unbending, hardheaded, unyielding, set in your ways [➡ UNWILLINGNESS AND STUBBORNNESS; 564] *Opposite*: flexible 10 *adj* **ready**, prepared, fit, primed, organized, geared up [➡ ORDER AND ORGANIZATION; 206] *Opposite*: unprepared 11 *adj* **firm**, congealed, solid, hard, fixed, jelled, frozen [➡ DENSITY AND CONSISTENCY; 1207] *Opposite*: liquid 12 *see* **sett**

set about *v* **begin**, tackle, start, launch into, get down to, make a start [➡ START AN ACTION; 260]

set against 1 *v* **compare**, contrast, consider, set side by side, oppose, juxtapose [➡ EXAMINE AND ASSESS; 753] 2 *v* **pit against**, turn against, set as rivals, set in opposition, alienate, disaffect, make unfriendly, estrange [➡ ACCUSE, BLAME, AND CRITICIZE; 641] *Opposite*: bring together

set alight *v* **kindle**, light, ignite, set fire to, set on fire, put a match to, burn, set light to (*UK*) [➡ FIRE, FLAMMABILITY, AND BURNING; 1165] *Opposite*: put out

set apart 1 *v* **reserve**, put aside, keep on one side, set aside, separate, keep apart, isolate, sequester (*formal*) [➡ STORE AND KEEP; 453] 2 *v* **distinguish**, differentiate, single out, make something stand out, mark out, isolate, identify, characterize, typify, pinpoint [➡ DIFFERENCE; 149]

set aside 1 *v* **reserve**, save, keep back, put to one side, lay by, set apart, leave behind [➡ STORE AND KEEP; 453] *Opposite*: use up 2 *v* **forget**, break free from, shake off, reject, dismiss, put on the back burner [➡ FORGET, FORGIVE, AND ACCEPT; 748]

set back *v* **delay**, hinder, hold up, impede, slow down, retard, arrest [➡ DELAY ACTION OR OCCURRENCE; 278] *Opposite*: facilitate

setback *n* **hindrance**, holdup, delay, impediment, stumbling block, obstruction, obstacle, hiccup (*informal*) [➡ PROBLEMS; 256] *Opposite*: boost

set down 1 *v* **put down**, lay down, place, deposit, put, plonk, plunk [➡ MOVE SOMETHING: DOWNWARD; 329] 2 *v* **write down**, report, record, chronicle, write out, transcribe, draft, jot down, note, set forth (*formal*) [➡ RECORD SOMETHING; 3711]

set eyes on *v* **catch sight of**, observe, notice, sight, spot, see [➡ SEE; 699]

set fire to *v* **kindle**, light, ignite, set alight, set on fire, put a match to, burn, set light to (*UK*) [➡ FIRE, FLAMMABILITY, AND BURNING; 1165] *Opposite*: put out

set foot in *v* **enter**, go in, come into, show your face, turn up, show up (*informal*) [➡ ARRIVE; 12]

set forth 1 *v* (*formal*) **state**, describe, express, lay down, present, submit, propose, lay out, set down [➡ EXPLAIN AND CLARIFY; 610] 2 *v* (*literary*) **leave**, depart, set out, set off, start out, head off, go [➡ LEAVE AND GO AWAY; 8] *Opposite*: arrive

set free 1 *v* **liberate**, free, release, discharge, let go, let out, emancipate, deliver (*literary*) [➡ FREEDOM AND LIBERTY; 208] *Opposite*: imprison 2 *v* **untie**, unloose, unshackle, unleash, let loose, unfetter [➡ UNFASTEN AND UNDO; 409] *Opposite*: tie up

set in *v* **come to stay**, be here to stay, take root, become established, become entrenched, continue [➡ CONTINUE TO EXIST; 17] *Opposite*: pass

set in motion *v* **start**, initiate, begin, kick-start, set off, trigger, activate, set up, cause, start off [➡ CAUSE TO START; 265] *Opposite*: stop

set in train (*UK*) *v* [➡ CAUSE TO START; 265]

set light to (*UK*) *v* [➡ FIRE, FLAMMABILITY, AND BURNING; 1165]

set of circumstances *n* [➡ SITUATIONS; 71]

set off 1 *v* **start out**, set out, go, depart, arrive, leave, get going, hit the road, head out [➡ LEAVE AND GO AWAY; 8] 2 *v* **detonate**, explode, light, ignite, trigger, let off, arm, blow up, fire [➡ CAUSE TO START; 265] *Opposite*: defuse 3 *v* **start**, begin, commence, start off, burst out, break into, embark on [➡ START AN ACTION; 260] *Opposite*: finish 4 *v* **initiate**, instigate, launch, inaugurate, begin, start, introduce [➡ CAUSE TO START; 265] 5 *v* **draw attention to**, display, bring out, highlight, enhance, show to advantage, emphasize [➡ CAUSE TO APPEAR; 5]

set on *v* **attack**, set upon, assault, lay into, terrorize, beat up (*informal*) [➡ PHYSICAL ATTACK AND PUNISHMENT; 415]

set on fire *v* **kindle**, light, ignite, set alight, set fire to, put a match to, burn, set light to (*UK*) [➡ FIRE, FLAMMABILITY, AND BURNING; 1165] *Opposite*: put out

set out 1 *v* **leave**, set off, depart, go, move off, start out, head off, set forth (*literary*) [➡ LEAVE AND GO AWAY; 8] *Opposite*: arrive 2 *v* **embark on**, start, begin, commence, set off, start off [➡ START AN ACTION; 260] *Opposite*: finish 3 *v* **plan**, aim, intend, determine, design [➡ ATTEMPT AN ACTION; 261] 4 *v* **display**, lay out, arrange, present, show, exhibit [➡ CAUSE TO APPEAR; 5] 5 *v* **explain**, specify, define, describe, detail, give particulars of, give an account of, outline, elaborate, illustrate [➡ EXPLAIN AND CLARIFY; 610]

set phrase *n* **expression**, phrase, idiom, turn of phrase, saying, stock phrase, formula, cliché, term [➡ FIGURES OF SPEECH; 673]

set right *v* **correct**, rectify, right, put right, put to rights, sort out, put on the right track [➡ CORRECT AND PUT RIGHT; 377]

set rolling v [➡ CAUSE TO START; 265]

set sail v [➡ LEAVE AND GO AWAY; 8]

set store by v **deem important**, value, esteem, prize, regard highly, put a premium on, rate, appreciate [➡ LIKE, LOVE, VALUE, AND ENJOY; 578]

sett 1 n **paving stone**, paving slab, paver, stone, slab, flag, flagstone, cobble, cobblestone, tile [➡ BUILDING MATERIALS; 1077] **2** *type of* **den or nest** [➡ ANIMAL OR BIRD ACCOMMODATIONS; 1079]

settee n **sofa**, couch, loveseat, chaise longue, divan, futon, davenport, day bed [➡ FURNITURE; 858]

setter *type of* **large dog** [➡ DOGS; 980]

set the ball rolling v [➡ CAUSE TO START; 265]

setting n **location**, surroundings, scenery, situation, background, set, locale, site, venue, backdrop [➡ PLACE; 1065]

settle 1 v **resolve**, reconcile, clear up, straighten out, mend, patch up [➡ CORRECT AND PUT RIGHT; 377] **2** v **stay**, inhabit, put down roots, set up house, establish yourself, homestead, colonize, stay on, remain [➡ INHABIT; 20] **3** v **sink**, drop, descend, fall, go to the bottom, lie [➡ GO DOWNWARD; 307] *Opposite*: rise **4** v **pay**, defray, discharge, clear, foot, settle up, square [➡ GIVE MONEY; 433] *Opposite*: owe **5** v **land**, perch, alight, roost, come to rest [➡ GO DOWNWARD; 307] *Opposite*: take off **6** v **become peaceful**, become calm, settle down, calm down, relax, slow down [➡ CHANGE OF MOOD AND COMPOSURE; 580] *Opposite*: fluster

settled *adj* **established**, stable, solid, firm, steady, mature [➡ CERTAIN; 174] *Opposite*: unsettled

settle down 1 v **become less restless**, quiet down, relax, calm down, snuggle down, slow down, take it easy [➡ CHANGE OF MOOD AND COMPOSURE; 580] *Opposite*: agitate **2** v **sink**, drop, descend, fall, stabilize, settle [➡ GO DOWNWARD; 307] *Opposite*: rise

settle for v **agree to**, accept, make do with, take, be happy with, compromise on [➡ ACCEPT POSSESSION; 450] *Opposite*: refuse

settle in 1 v **adapt**, acclimatize, adjust, get used to it, find your feet, fit in [➡ CHANGE; 372] **2** v **get comfortable**, get comfy, snuggle down, ensconce yourself, remain, park yourself (*slang*) [➡ CHANGE OF MOOD AND COMPOSURE; 580]

settlement 1 n **resolution**, conclusion, completion, decision, agreement, arrangement [➡ SOLUTIONS; 215] **2** n **payment**, defrayal, clearance, clearing, reimbursement, disbursement, expenditure [➡ FUNDS, PAYMENTS, AND CHARGES; 800] *Opposite*: receipt **3** n **community**, village, town, township, colony, commune, hamlet, neighborhood, suburb [➡ HUMAN SETTLEMENTS; 1070]

settle on v **choose**, pick, select, decide on, agree on, go for (*informal*) [➡ MAKE DECISIONS AND CHOICES; 752] *Opposite*: reject

settler n **colonizer**, colonist, pioneer, pilgrim, immigrant, early settler, incomer (*UK*) [➡ PEOPLE LIVING AWAY FROM HOME; 887]

settle up v **pay the bill**, pay, pay up, settle the debt, settle your account, cough up (*informal*), ante up (*informal*), shell out (*informal*), fork out (*informal*) [➡ GIVE MONEY; 433] *Opposite*: quibble

settling of scores n [➡ VENGEANCE AND REVENGE; 685]

set to 1 v **get on with it**, put your shoulder to the wheel, make a start, get started, start work, start, get going, buckle down (*informal*), knuckle down (*informal*) [➡ START AN ACTION; 260] **2** v **come to blows**, start fighting, lay into, grapple, tussle, skirmish, scuffle, brawl, wrestle, go for, raise your fists [➡ COMPETE, CONTEND, AND COMBAT; 303]

set-to (*informal*) n **confrontation**, quarrel, altercation, disagreement, difference of opinion, row, war of words, debate, squabble, argument, fight, skirmish, scuffle, brawl, flare-up (*informal*) [➡ ARGUMENTS; 47] *Opposite*: reconciliation

set up 1 v **erect**, raise, build, construct, put up, assemble [➡ BUILD; 352] **2** v **establish**, inaugurate, found, institute, launch, organize, prepare [➡ INSTITUTE AND INAUGURATE; 348] **3** v (*informal*) **frame**, trap, entrap, trick, entice, con, fix (*informal*) [➡ DECEPTION AND LIES; 660]

setup 1 n **system**, arrangement, format, situation, circumstance, structure, operation, framework, way things work, organization [➡ WAYS OF DOING THINGS; 294] **2** n (*informal*) **frame**, trap, trick, deception, con, fraud, swindle, confidence game, con game (*informal*), sting (*slang*), confidence trick (*UK*) [➡ DECEPTION AND LIES; 660]

set upon v **attack**, assault, lay into, assail, pounce on, ambush [➡ PHYSICAL ATTACK AND PUNISHMENT; 415] *Opposite*: defend

seventh heaven n **bliss**, ecstasy, heaven, nirvana, cloud nine, rapture, delight, elation, joy, happiness [➡ PLEASANT SITUATIONS; 74] *Opposite*: despair

sever 1 v **cut**, split, separate, undo, disunite, dissolve, break [➡ SEPARATE AND DIVIDE; 401] *Opposite*: unite **2** v **cut off**, chop off, lop off, shear off, slice off, amputate, remove [➡ EXTRACT AND SEVER; 341] *Opposite*: attach

several *adj* **some**, quite a lot of, a number of, numerous, many, more than a few, quite a few (*informal*) [➡ AMOUNTS AND QUANTITIES; 112]

severally *adv* **separately**, individually, singly, one at a time, one by one, in turn, respectively, discretely [➡ UNRELATEDNESS AND SEPARATENESS; 146] *Opposite*: together

severance 1 n **separation**, detachment, disconnection, division, taking apart, cutting off, uncoupling, partition (*formal*) [➡ SEPARATE AND DIVIDE; 401] *Opposite*: joining **2** n **compensation**, severance pay, golden handshake (*informal*), golden parachute (*informal*), redundancy pay (*UK*), redundancy money (*UK*) [➡ FUNDS, PAYMENTS, AND CHARGES; 800]

severe 1 *adj* **harsh**, stern, strict, cruel, brutal, ruthless, relentless, rigid, uncompromising, rigorous, difficult [➡ EMOTIONALLY UNPLEASANT AND UPSETTING; 227] *Opposite*: gentle **2** *adj* **acute**, grave, critical, mortal, serious, dangerous, awful, terrible [➡ DANGEROUS; 236] *Opposite*: slight **3** *adj* **plain**, simple, Spartan, unadorned, unembellished, undecorated, stark, austere [➡ PLAIN; 232] *Opposite*: ornate

severity 1 n **harshness**, sternness, strictness, cruelty, brutality, ruthlessness, relentlessness, rigorousness, difficulty [➡ EMOTIONALLY UNPLEASANT AND UPSETTING; 227] *Opposite*: gentleness **2** n **gravity**, seriousness, acuteness, dangerousness, awfulness [➡ DANGER; 235] *Opposite*: insignificance **3** n **plainness**, simplicity, starkness, bareness, austerity [➡ PLAIN; 232] *Opposite*: ornateness

Sèvres *type of* **pottery** [➡ POTTERY; 1135]

sew *v* **stitch**, seam, baste, tack, hem, embroider, darn [➡ CRAFTS AND CARVING; 355] *Opposite:* unpick

sewage *n* [➡ UNPLEASANT, DIRTY, AND TOXIC SUBSTANCES; 1268]

sewer *n* **drain**, septic tank, cesspit, cesspool, open drain, gutter, culvert, sink, sump [➡ WATERCOURSES; 1111]

sewing *n* **stitching**, embroidery, tapestry, needlework, needlepoint, hemming, darning, basting [➡ CRAFTS AND CARVING; 355]

sew up 1 *v* **settle**, clinch, tie up, finalize, finish, complete [➡ COMPLETE AN ACTION; 263] 2 *v* **stitch up**, sew, stitch, darn, repair, mend [➡ REPAIR AND MEND; 376] *Opposite:* unpick

sex *n* **gender**, sexual category, masculinity, femininity [➡ GENDER IDENTITY AND SEXUALITY; 932]

sexism *n* [➡ PREJUDICE; 550]

sexless *adj* [➡ GENDER IDENTITY AND SEXUALITY; 932]

Sextans *type of* **constellation** [➡ HEAVENLY BODIES; 1061]

sextet *type of* **band** [➡ MUSICIANS AND SINGERS; 908]

sexual *adj* [➡ REPRODUCTION AND HEREDITY; 725]

sexual category *n* [➡ GENDER IDENTITY AND SEXUALITY; 932]

sexual characteristics *n* [➡ GENDER IDENTITY AND SEXUALITY; 932]

sexual maturity *n* [➡ REPRODUCTION AND HEREDITY; 725]

sexy 1 *adj* **erotic**, sensual, sexual, suggestive, pleasurable [➡ PHYSICALLY PLEASANT; 186] 2 *adj* **voluptuous**, curvaceous, sensuous, alluring, attractive [➡ BUILD; 477]

shabbiness 1 *n* **scruffiness**, untidiness, dilapidation, seediness, raggedness, grunginess (*informal*) [➡ BADLY GROOMED; 483] *Opposite:* elegance 2 *n* **inconsiderateness**, unfairness, meanness, disrespect, negligence [➡ MALICIOUS ACTIONS OR BEHAVIOR; 296] *Opposite:* decency

shabby 1 *adj* **scruffy**, untidy, ragged, tattered, worn out, threadbare, dilapidated, unkempt, poorly maintained, ratty (*informal*), grungy (*informal*) [➡ BADLY GROOMED; 483] *Opposite:* elegant 2 *adj* **inconsiderate**, unjust, mean, dishonorable, contemptible, despicable, unfair, rotten, disrespectful [➡ SELFISH AND UNKIND; 505] *Opposite:* decent

shack *n* **hut**, shanty, hovel, lean-to, shed [➡ RESIDENTIAL BUILDINGS; 1078]

shackle 1 *v* **fetter**, manacle, handcuff, chain, put in irons, bind [➡ CAPTIVITY AND LOSS OF FREEDOM; 248] *Opposite:* free 2 *v* **constrain**, restrict, impede, hamper, hinder, obstruct, thwart [➡ AVOID, PREVENT, LIMIT, AND CONTROL; 277] *Opposite:* facilitate

shackles *n* **fetters**, manacles, chains, restraints, irons, handcuffs [➡ FASTENERS, LINKS, AND NETWORKS; 1247]

shade 1 *n* **shadow**, dark, darkness, gloom, gloominess, dimness [➡ DESCRIBING LIGHT; 1228] *Opposite:* light 2 *n* **blind**, screen, awning, canopy, cover, shield [➡ COVERS AND COATINGS; 1246] 3 *n* **hue**, tint, tinge, color, tone [➡ DESCRIBING COLORS; 1226] 4 *n* **hint**, trace, suggestion, touch, dash, little bit, shadow, flicker [➡ FEW, LITTLE, SMALL AMOUNT; 120] 5 *v* **cover**, shield, protect, screen, veil, mask, shelter, hide, conceal [➡ CAUSE TO DISAPPEAR; 6] *Opposite:* expose 6 *v* **darken**, eclipse, blot out, shadow,

block out [➡ CHANGE OF COLOR; 391] *Opposite:* brighten 7 *v* **fill in**, hatch, color, color in, block in [➡ CHANGE OF COLOR; 391]

shades (*informal*) *n* **sunglasses**, dark glasses, tinted lenses [➡ GLASSES AND SPECTACLES; 1125]

shadiness 1 *n* **dishonesty**, crookedness, underhandedness, shiftiness, suspiciousness, deviousness, dubiousness [➡ MORALLY BAD OR IMPROPER; 775] *Opposite:* honesty 2 *n* **dimness**, dark, darkness, shadowiness, obscurity, shade [➡ DESCRIBING LIGHT; 1228] *Opposite:* brightness

shadow 1 *n* **shade**, silhouette, outline, dark, darkness, gloom, gloominess, dusk, dimness [➡ SHAPE; 1216] *Opposite:* light 2 *n* **hint**, trace, suggestion, touch, shade, flicker [➡ FEW, LITTLE, SMALL AMOUNT; 120] 3 *n* **constant companion**, alter ego, sidekick, other self, double, doppelgänger [➡ SUPPORTERS, PROTECTORS, AND COMPATRIOTS; 970] 4 *n* **private investigator**, private detective, private eye (*informal*), sleuth (*informal*), gumshoe (*dated informal*) [➡ ENEMIES AND TORMENTORS; 969] 5 *n* **follower**, stalker, pursuer, tracker, tail (*informal*) [➡ ENEMIES AND TORMENTORS; 969] 6 *n* **ghost**, specter, spirit, wraith, apparition, phantom [➡ THE SUPERNATURAL; 787] 7 *v* **follow**, trail, track, stalk, observe, pursue, go after, chase, tail (*informal*) [➡ ACCOMPANY AND FOLLOW; 337] 8 *v* **darken**, eclipse, blot out, shade [➡ CAUSE TO DISAPPEAR; 6] *Opposite:* brighten

See Compare and Contrast at **follow.**

shadows *n* **shade**, dark, darkness, obscurity, dimness, gloom, murk [➡ DESCRIBING LIGHT; 1228] *Opposite:* light

shadowy 1 *adj* **indistinct**, obscure, vague, indistinguishable, unclear, dim, faint [➡ IMPERCEPTIBLE; 26] *Opposite:* distinct 2 *adj* **dim**, dark, murky, gloomy, poorly lit, shady [➡ DESCRIBING LIGHT; 1228] *Opposite:* bright 3 *adj* **ghostly**, spectral, ethereal, sinister, mysterious, shrouded in mystery, eerie [➡ SECRET AND UNKNOWN; 179] *Opposite:* material

shady 1 *adj* **out of the sun**, in the shade, shaded, under the trees, cool, dappled, sheltered [➡ DESCRIBING LIGHT; 1228] *Opposite:* sunny 2 *adj* **dishonest**, underhand, shifty, suspicious, devious, dubious, doubtful, disreputable, questionable, suspect, crooked (*informal*), fishy (*informal*) [➡ MORALLY BAD OR IMPROPER; 775] *Opposite:* aboveboard

shaft *part of* **engine** [➡ PARTS OF AN ENGINE; 1144]

shagginess *n* **hairiness**, unkemptness, dishevelment, untidiness, bushiness [➡ HAIR; 484] *Opposite:* neatness

shaggy *adj* **hairy**, unkempt, disheveled, bushy, unshaven, untrimmed, unshorn, hirsute [➡ DESCRIBING HAIR; 486] *Opposite:* tidy

shaggy-dog story *n* [➡ DECEPTION AND LIES; 660]

shahtoosh *type of* **fabric from animals** [➡ FABRICS; 1132]

shake 1 *v* **agitate**, stir, blend, move up and down, jiggle, waggle, mix [➡ COMBINE AND MIX; 400] *Opposite:* steady 2 *v* **tremble**, quiver, quake, jolt, shudder, shiver, judder, wobble, vibrate, quaver [➡ PHYSICAL REACTIONS; 316] 3 *v* **unsettle**, unnerve, disturb, distress, upset, alarm [➡ UPSET, DISTRESS, AND HUMILIATE; 567] *Opposite:* reassure 4 *v* **brandish**, flourish, flaunt, wave, wield [➡ MOVE SOMETHING: ON THE SPOT; 336] 5 *n* **jiggle**, wobble, agitation, vibration, quiver, tremor, shudder, jolt [➡ MOVE SOMETHING: ON THE SPOT; 336]

shakedown (*slang*) *n* [➡ CRIMES; 817]

shaken *adj* [➥ CONFUSION, ANXIETY, AND WORRY; 540]

shake off 1 *v* **get rid of**, get away from, lose, elude, leave behind, give somebody the slip [➥ AVOID OR ESCAPE CONTACT; 418] 2 *v* **recover from**, recuperate from, get over, get rid of [➥ BECOME SICK, TREAT, AND RECOVER; 728] *Opposite*: succumb

shakeout *n* **transformation**, radical change, overhaul, reorganization, reform, revamp, rethink, rearrangement, reshuffle, restructuring, shake-up [➥ CHANGE; 372]

shake up 1 *v* **transform**, overhaul, change drastically, revamp, rethink, modify, alter, improve, rejigger (*informal*) [➥ CHANGE; 372] *Opposite*: leave alone 2 *v* **upset**, disturb, distress, shock, alarm, traumatize, devastate, stun, perturb, unsettle, worry [➥ FRIGHTEN AND SHOCK; 568] *Opposite*: calm down 3 *v* **mix**, blend, combine, agitate, shake, stir [➥ COMBINE AND MIX; 400]

shake-up *n* **transformation**, radical change, upheaval, overhaul, reorganization, reform, revamp, rethink, rearrangement, reshuffle, restructuring, shakeout [➥ CHANGE; 372]

shakiness 1 *n* **tremor**, shaking, trembling, shake, jerkiness, unsteadiness [➥ DESCRIBING BODY MOVEMENTS; 288] *Opposite*: control 2 *n* **wobbliness**, instability, flimsiness, fragility, insubstantiality [➥ WEAKNESS; 241] *Opposite*: sturdiness 3 *n* **uncertainty**, precariousness, instability, unreliability, weakness, fragility, tenuousness [➥ UNCERTAIN; 175] *Opposite*: reliability

shaking *n* **vibration**, jolting, juddering, rocking, rattling, shuddering, wobbling, bumping, quivering [➥ DESCRIBING BODY MOVEMENTS; 288]

shaky 1 *adj* **trembling**, shaking, quivering, quaking, shuddering, shivering [➥ ILL AND SICK; 740] *Opposite*: composed 2 *adj* **wobbly**, unstable, unsteady, insecure, rickety, jiggly, precarious [➥ DANGEROUS; 236] *Opposite*: steady 3 *adj* **unsupported**, unsound, questionable, dubious, doubtful, uncertain, unreliable [➥ UNCERTAIN; 175] *Opposite*: dependable

shale *type of* **stone** [➥ STONES, ROCKS, AND BOULDERS; 1057]

shallow 1 *adj* **low**, thin, light, narrow, surface [➥ DEPTH: SHALLOW; 1202] *Opposite*: deep 2 *adj* **superficial**, trivial, slight, insubstantial, petty, one-dimensional, silly [➥ THE NATURE OF IDEAS; 771] *Opposite*: profound

shallowly *adv* **superficially**, trivially, frivolously, pettily, triflingly, foolishly [➥ THE NATURE OF IDEAS; 771] *Opposite*: deeply

shallowness 1 *n* **superficiality**, pettiness, silliness, triviality, frivolousness [➥ AFFECTATION, SELF-SATISFACTION, AND SNOBBISHNESS; 507] 2 *n* **lowness**, thinness, narrowness [➥ DEPTH: SHALLOW; 1202]

shalwar-kameez *type of* **dress** [➥ GARMENTS AND OUTFITS; 865]

sham 1 *n* **pretense**, deception, charade, con, fraud, act [➥ DECEPTION AND LIES; 660] 2 *n* **impostor**, charlatan, con, fake, fraud, cheat [➥ PEOPLE WHO DECEIVE; 661] 3 *n* [➥ FURNISHING AND HOUSEHOLD LINENS; 860] 4 *adj* **fake**, mock, bogus, imitation, pretended, pretend [➥ FALSE AND UNREAL; 173] *Opposite*: bona fide 5 *v* **pretend**, fake, put it on, act, play, imitate, simulate [➥ PRETEND AND MIMIC; 60] *Opposite*: real

shaman *n* [➥ RELIGIOUS PEOPLE; 778]

shamanism *n* [➥ RELIGIOUS PEOPLE; 778]

shamble *v* **shuffle**, amble, waddle, drag your feet, walk [➥ MOVE SLOWLY; 314] *Opposite*: stride

shambles 1 *n* **fiasco**, disaster, failure, mess, botch, hash (*informal*) [➥ DISASTERS; 252] *Opposite*: success 2 *n* **chaos**, muddle, tip, clutter, dump, mess [➥ DISORDER AND CHAOS; 245]

shambling *adj* **awkward**, ungainly, clumsy, uncoordinated, lumbering, doddering [➥ DESCRIBING BODY MOVEMENTS; 288] *Opposite*: graceful

shame 1 *n* **disgrace**, embarrassment, dishonor, humiliation, mortification, indignity, ignominy, infamy [➥ EMBARRASSMENT AND HUMILIATION; 542] *Opposite*: pride 2 *v* **embarrass**, discredit, disgrace, humiliate, mortify, dishonor, degrade, make uncomfortable, bring into disrepute, bring shame on, defame [➥ UPSET, DISTRESS, AND HUMILIATE; 567] *Opposite*: honor

shamefaced *adj* **ashamed**, embarrassed, abashed, sheepish, hangdog, awkward, humiliated, guilty, mortified [➥ EMBARRASSMENT AND HUMILIATION; 542] *Opposite*: proud

shameful *adj* **disgraceful**, reprehensible, dishonorable, discreditable, shocking, appalling, scandalous [➥ DISGUSTING AND REPULSIVE; 230] *Opposite*: honorable

shameless *adj* **brazen**, barefaced, unabashed, blatant, unashamed, bold-faced [➥ BAD MANNERS AND SOCIAL SKILLS; 521] *Opposite*: ashamed

shamelessness *n* **lack of remorse**, brazenness, hardheartedness, boldness, impudence, impenitence [➥ BAD MANNERS AND SOCIAL SKILLS; 521] *Opposite*: repentance

shampoo *n* [➥ PERSONAL HYGIENE; 491]

shanghai *v* [➥ CAUSE OR COMPEL TO ACT; 271]

Shangri-la *n* [➥ NONEXISTENT PLACES; 1066]

shank 1 *n* **stem**, shaft, trunk, rod, bar, pole [➥ STICKS, POLES, AND WEDGES; 1254] 2 *part of* **horse** [➥ HORSES; 985]

shanty *n* [➥ UNDESIRABLE ACCOMMODATIONS; 856]

shanty town *n* [➥ HUMAN SETTLEMENTS; 1070]

shape 1 *n* **form**, figure, outline, silhouette, profile, contour, build [➥ SHAPE; 1216] 2 *n* **character**, nature, form, identity, structure, appearance [➥ STATE; 1208] 3 *v* **influence**, affect, model, mold, whittle, manipulate, smooth, sculpt, form [➥ CHANGE; 372] 4 *v* **sway**, determine, cause [➥ CHANGE; 372]

shape

◆ *types of angular shapes*
box, cross, cube, diamond, dodecahedron, dogleg, lozenge, oblong, parallelogram, pentagon, polygon, pyramid, quadrangle, quadrilateral, rectangle, rhomboid, rhombus, square, star, tetragon, tetrahedron, trapezium, trapezoid, triangle

◆ *types of rounded shapes*
arc, arch, ball, bend, bow, bulb, circle, circlet, coil, cone, crescent, curl, curve, cylinder, dome, figure eight, globe, heart, hemisphere, helix, hoop, horseshoe, kidney, loop, orb, oval, ring, round, semicircle, sphere, spheroid, spiral, teardrop

shapeless *adj* **baggy**, loose-fitting, formless, ill-defined, amorphous, fluid [➥ SHAPELESSNESS; 1219] *Opposite*: defined

shapelessness *n* **amorphousness**, formlessness, bagginess, fluidity [➡ SHAPELESSNESS; 1219] *Opposite*: symmetry

shapely *adj* **well-formed**, attractive, well-rounded, well-proportioned, pleasing, regular, curvaceous, statuesque [➡ BUILD; 477]

shape up 1 *v* **develop**, progress, improve, come along, come together, fall into place, advance [➡ GET BETTER; 375] 2 *v* **improve**, pull yourself together, get it together, reform, mend your ways, turn over a new leaf, pull your socks up (*informal*) [➡ GET BETTER; 375]

shard *n* **sliver**, splinter, spike, shaving, chip, piece, fragment, potsherd [➡ SMALL PIECES; 129]

share 1 *v* **split**, go halves, divide, divide up, divvy (*informal*), carve up (*informal*) [➡ SEPARATE AND DIVIDE; 401] 2 *v* **distribute**, allocate, assign, apportion, allot, give out, parcel out, dole out (*informal*) [➡ DISPENSE, RATION, AND DISTRIBUTE; 434] 3 *v* **communicate**, let somebody in on, impart, reveal, disclose [➡ INFORM, ANNOUNCE, AND ISSUE; 611] 4 *n* **part**, portion, segment, cut, stake, bit, piece [➡ AMOUNTS AND QUANTITIES; 112] *Opposite*: whole

shared *adj* **common**, communal, joint, mutual, collective, cooperative, combined [➡ BELONGING OR RELATING TO PEOPLE; 943]

shareholder *n* [➡ PEOPLE INVOLVED IN FINANCE; 804]

share out *v* **divide up**, give out, parcel out, distribute, allot, split, allocate, divide, dole out (*informal*), carve up (*informal*) [➡ DISPENSE, RATION, AND DISTRIBUTE; 434]

shareware *type of* **software** [➡ COMPUTERS AND COMPUTING; 1127]

shark 1 *type of* **ocean fish** [➡ OCEAN FISH; 1009] 2 *n* (*informal*) [➡ SUPERFICIAL OR INSINCERE PEOPLE; 951]

sharp 1 *adj* **pointed**, razor-sharp, tapered, pointy, jagged, prickly, spiky [➡ PHYSICAL TEXTURE; 1222] *Opposite*: blunt 2 *adj* **quick**, intelligent, razor-sharp, incisive, astute, clever, quick-witted, sharp-witted, on the ball (*informal*) [➡ POSITIVE INTELLECTUAL CHARACTERISTICS; 524] *Opposite*: dull 3 *adj* **abrupt**, sudden, quick, brusque, urgent [➡ HAPPENING QUICKLY; 104] *Opposite*: gentle 4 *adj* **shrill**, piercing, loud, high-pitched, strident [➡ LOUD, HIGH, OR UNPLEASANT SOUNDS; 1266] *Opposite*: soft 5 *adj* **harsh**, severe, snappy, sarcastic, snappish, angry, critical, caustic, biting, accusatory (*formal*) [➡ BAD-TEMPERED AND HUMORLESS; 626] *Opposite*: gentle 6 *adj* **severe**, acute, strong, hard, intense, piercing [➡ PHYSICALLY UNPLEASANT; 226] *Opposite*: mild 7 *adj* **sour**, tangy, acid, acrid, pungent, tart, bitter [➡ TASTE; 703] *Opposite*: sweet 8 *adj* **clear**, well-defined, definite, clear-cut, distinct, precise, in focus [➡ CONCISE AND CLEAR; 202] *Opposite*: imprecise 9 *adv* **exactly**, precisely, on the dot, promptly, punctually [➡ PROMPTNESS: ON TIME; 99]

shar-pei *type of* **small dog** [➡ DOGS; 980]

sharpen 1 *v* **hone**, whet, grind, file, strop [➡ REPAIR AND MEND; 376] *Opposite*: blunt 2 *v* **improve**, hone, perfect, brush up, refine, polish [➡ IMPROVE SOMETHING; 374] *Opposite*: worsen

sharp-eyed 1 *adj* **observant**, watchful, alert, vigilant, attentive, perceptive, sharp-sighted, wide-awake (*informal*), on the ball (*informal*) [➡ POSITIVE INTELLECTUAL CHARACTERISTICS; 524] *Opposite*: unobservant 2 *adj* **eagle-eyed**, with good eyesight, with good vision, with eyes like a hawk, hawk-eyed, sharp-sighted [➡ SEE; 699] *Opposite*: nearsighted

sharply 1 *adv* **abruptly**, suddenly, all at once, hard, tight [➡ HAPPENING QUICKLY; 104] *Opposite*: gradually 2 *adv* **harshly**, severely, cuttingly, unkindly, snappishly, tersely, tartly, caustically, crossly, angrily [➡ BAD-TEMPERED AND HUMORLESS; 626] *Opposite*: gently 3 *adv* **alarmingly**, steeply, greatly, dramatically, suddenly, abruptly, precipitously, out of control [➡ HAPPENING QUICKLY; 104] *Opposite*: gradually 4 *adv* **briskly**, abruptly, suddenly, smartly, swiftly, quickly [➡ HAPPENING QUICKLY; 104] *Opposite*: slowly 5 *adv* **extremely**, clearly, acutely, distinctly, deeply, strongly, intensely [➡ STRENGTH; 201] *Opposite*: subtly 6 *adv* **clearly**, distinctly, strikingly, obviously, eye-catchingly, in sharp contrast [➡ CONCISE AND CLEAR; 202] *Opposite*: hazily

sharpness 1 *n* **acuity**, perceptiveness, intelligence, quickness, keenness, alertness, astuteness, perspicacity, quick-wittedness [➡ POSITIVE INTELLECTUAL CHARACTERISTICS; 524] *Opposite*: slowness 2 *n* **harshness**, severity, unkindness, snappishness, terseness, tartness, crossness, anger [➡ BAD-TEMPERED AND HUMORLESS; 626] *Opposite*: gentleness 3 *n* **clarity**, definition, distinctness, contrast, intensity [➡ CONCISE AND CLEAR; 202] *Opposite*: haziness 4 *n* **acidity**, sourness, bitterness, tanginess, pungency, zing (*informal*), zest, bite [➡ TASTE; 703] *Opposite*: sweetness

sharp-sighted 1 *adj* **eagle-eyed**, with good eyesight, with good vision, with eyes like a hawk, hawk-eyed, sharp-eyed [➡ SEE; 699] *Opposite*: nearsighted 2 *adj* **observant**, watchful, alert, vigilant, attentive, perceptive, sharp-eyed, wide-awake (*informal*), on the ball (*informal*) [➡ POSITIVE INTELLECTUAL CHARACTERISTICS; 524] *Opposite*: unobservant

sharp-tasting *adj* [➡ TASTE; 703]

sharp-tongued *adj* **sarcastic**, caustic, harsh, mean, brusque, critical, hurtful, cruel, unsympathetic [➡ RUDE AND HOSTILE; 625] *Opposite*: gentle

sharp-witted *adj* **quick**, sharp, quick-witted, quick-thinking, acute, bright, intelligent, smart, clever, quick on the uptake (*informal*), on the ball (*informal*) [➡ POSITIVE INTELLECTUAL CHARACTERISTICS; 524]

shatter 1 *v* **smash**, break, smash to smithereens, splinter, destroy, blow apart, fragment, explode, ruin [➡ TEAR, BREAK, AND CUT; 360] 2 *v* **destroy**, wreck, crush, blast, demolish [➡ DESTRUCTION AND DEMOLITION; 359] *Opposite*: build up

shattered 1 *adj* **devastated**, crushed, traumatized, horrified, suffering [➡ SADNESS, DISTRESS, AND DESPAIR; 539] 2 *adj* (*UK*) **tired**, exhausted, all in, spent, prostrate, worn out, wiped out (*slang*), beat (*slang*) [➡ TIRED, ASLEEP, AND UNCONSCIOUS; 738] *Opposite*: lively

shattering *adj* **devastating**, crushing, shocking, earth-shattering, cataclysmic, catastrophic [➡ EMOTIONALLY UNPLEASANT AND UPSETTING; 227] *Opposite*: wonderful

shatterproof *adj* **indestructible**, unbreakable, non-breaking, resistant, strengthened, toughened, reinforced, durable, safety [➡ DURABLE; 1210]

shave *v* **cut off**, shear, cut, trim, clip [➡ EXTRACT AND SEVER; 341]

shaved *adj* [➡ FACIAL HAIR; 489]

shaven *adj* [➡ FACIAL HAIR; 489]

shaving *n* **chip**, splinter, flake, shred, sliver [➡ SMALL PIECES; 129] *Opposite*: chunk

shaving brush *type of* **cosmetic tool** [➡ HAND TOOLS; 1119]

shaving cream *n* [➡ PERSONAL HYGIENE; 491]

shavings *n* [➡ REMAINDER AND REMAINDERS; 125]

shawl *n* **wrap**, stole, scarf, rebozo, cloak [➡ ACCESSORIES, MILLINERY, AND LINGERIE; 867]

sheaf *n* **bundle**, cluster, clump, wad, stack, pile, bunch [➡ AMOUNTS OF SOLID OR SEMISOLID; 115]

shear *v* **cut off**, shave, clip, trim, crop, cut [➡ EXTRACT AND SEVER; 341]

shears *type of* **cutting tool** [➡ CUTTING TOOLS; 1120]

shearwater *type of* **sea bird** [➡ SEA BIRDS; 1002]

sheath 1 *n* **cover**, case, casing, covering, scabbard, holster [➡ COVERS AND COATINGS; 1246] 2 *type of* **dress** [➡ GARMENTS AND OUTFITS; 865]

sheathe 1 *v* **put away**, replace, retract, stash (*informal*) [➡ POSITION SOMETHING: BETWEEN, BESIDE, OR INSIDE SOMETHING; 326] *Opposite:* take out 2 *v* **envelop**, swathe, cloak, wrap, drape, cover, shroud, swaddle, sheath, enclose [➡ DECORATE, ADORN, AND APPLY COATINGS; 405]

sheathing *n* **casing**, covering, outer layer, jacket, shield, cover, shell [➡ COVERS AND COATINGS; 1246]

shebeen *type of* **bar or club** [➡ HOTELS, RESTAURANTS, AND CLUBS; 1082]

shed 1 *v* **radiate**, emit, disperse, cast, project [➡ EMIT AND EMANATE; 361] 2 *v* **cast off**, slough off, get rid of, molt, lose [➡ GET RID OF SOMETHING; 451] 3 *type of* **outbuilding** [➡ ANCILLARY BUILDINGS; 1080] 4 *type of* **storage space** [➡ STORES AND STORAGE BUILDINGS; 1088]

shed light on *v* **clarify**, explain, illuminate, elucidate, clear up, resolve [➡ EXPLAIN AND CLARIFY; 610]

shedload (*UK*) *n* [➡ MANY, MUCH, LARGE AMOUNT; 117]

shed tears *v* [➡ CRYING; 650]

sheen *n* **shine**, polish, luster, gloss, gleam, patina [➡ VISUAL TEXTURE; 1221]

sheep 1 *n* **ewe**, ram, lamb [➡ FARM ANIMALS; 982] 2 *n* **conformist**, follower, traditionalist, lemming, yes man, copycat (*informal*) [➡ LAZY OR UNSUCCESSFUL PEOPLE; 948] *Opposite:* individualist

sheepdog *type of* **large dog** [➡ DOGS; 980]

sheepish *adj* **ashamed**, shamefaced, embarrassed, hangdog, guilty, awkward, uncomfortable [➡ EMBARRASSMENT AND HUMILIATION; 542] *Opposite:* unashamed

sheepishness *n* **shame**, embarrassment, guilt, awkwardness, self-consciousness, humiliation [➡ EMBARRASSMENT AND HUMILIATION; 542]

sheepskin *type of* **leather** [➡ FABRICS; 1132]

sheer 1 *adj* **pure**, complete, absolute, utter, unalloyed, total [➡ ABSOLUTE AND ABSOLUTELY; 133] 2 *adj* **steep**, vertical, perpendicular, precipitous, abrupt, sharp [➡ ORIENTATION AND ALIGNMENT; 1223] *Opposite:* gentle 3 *adj* **fine**, transparent, translucent, thin, diaphanous, filmy, gossamer, gauzy, see through [➡ VISUAL TEXTURE; 1221] *Opposite:* thick 4 *adv* **ver-**

tically, straight up, plumb, precipitously, steeply [➡ ORIENTATION AND ALIGNMENT; 1223]

sheerness *n* **fineness**, thinness, translucence, transparence, gauziness, filminess [➡ VISUAL TEXTURE; 1221] *Opposite:* thickness

sheet 1 *n* **piece**, page, leaf, folio, slip, pane [➡ AMOUNTS OF SOLID OR SEMISOLID; 115] 2 *n* **expanse**, mass, area, layer [➡ COVERS AND COATINGS; 1246] 3 *part of* **sailing vessel** [➡ PARTS OF A SHIP OR BOAT; 1151]

sheet down (*UK*) *v* **pour**, rain heavily, rain cats and dogs (*informal*) [➡ CLOUDY AND RAINY WEATHER; 1052]

sheeting down (*UK*) *adj* [➡ CLOUDY AND RAINY WEATHER; 1052]

sheet lightning *n* [➡ WINDY AND STORMY WEATHER; 1053]

sheik *n* **leader**, ruler, chief, chieftain, head [➡ IMPORTANT OR FAMOUS PEOPLE; 893]

shekel *type of* **currency** [➡ CURRENCIES; 798]

shelf 1 *n* **ledge**, sill, projection, bookshelf, mantelpiece, mantelshelf [➡ SUPPORTS AND BASES; 1255] 2 *n* **layer**, ridge, step, ledge, rock shelf [➡ GEOLOGIC FEATURES; 1056]

shell 1 *n* **case**, casing, covering, shield, crust, defense, skin, armor, capsule, pod, cartridge [➡ COVERS AND COATINGS; 1246] 2 *n* **husk**, skeleton, carcass, remains [➡ REMAINDER AND REMAINDERS; 125] 3 *n* **bomb**, explosive, missile, mortar, projectile, cartridge, bullet [➡ PROJECTILES; 1159] 4 *v* **bombard**, shoot at, fire at, open fire on, shoot down, bomb [➡ DESTRUCTION AND DEMOLITION; 359]

shellfish *n* **prawn**, shrimp, lobster, crab, scallop, oyster, mussel, cockle, whelk, clam [➡ SEAFOOD; 1190]

shelling *n* [➡ WARFARE AND WAR; 830]

shell out (*informal*) *v* **pay out**, pay up, pay, spend, give, cough up (*informal*), fork out (*informal*) [➡ GIVE MONEY; 433]

shell pink *type of* **pink** [➡ COLORS; 1224]

shelter 1 *n* **protection**, cover, refuge, retreat, haven, sanctuary, asylum, safe haven [➡ SAFE BUILDINGS OR PLACES; 1093] 2 *n* **housing**, accommodations, living quarters, lodging, somewhere to stay, somewhere to live, a roof over your head, accommodation (*UK*) [➡ ACCOMMODATIONS; 855] 3 *v* **protect**, shield, cover, defend, harbor, take in, give refuge to [➡ PREVENT CONTACT OR ATTACK; 419] 4 *v* **take shelter**, take refuge, take cover, hide [➡ AVOID OR ESCAPE CONTACT; 418]

sheltered 1 *adj* **protected**, privileged, comfortable, shielded, cozy, cushy (*informal*), wrapped in cotton wool (*UK*) [➡ SAFE AND SAFETY; 191] *Opposite:* harsh 2 *adj* **secluded**, protected, shielded, isolated, insulated, shaded [➡ SAFE AND SAFETY; 191] *Opposite:* exposed

shelve *v* **put on hold**, put on ice, defer, abandon, cancel, drop, table, postpone, set aside [➡ DELAY ACTION OR OCCURRENCE; 278]

shemozzle (*dated informal*) *n* [➡ CHAOS AND UPROAR; 51]

shenanigans (*informal*) 1 *n* **mischief**, trickery, trouble, monkeyshines, to-do (*informal*), monkey business (*informal*) [➡ CHAOS AND UPROAR; 51] 2 *n* **mischief**, playfulness, joking around, pranks, tricks, tomfoolery (*informal*), high jinks (*informal*), messing about (*UK*), larking about (*UK*) [➡ JOKES AND TEASING; 674]

shepherd *v* **marshal**, drive, guide, steer, pilot, propel, direct [➡ ACCOMPANY AND FOLLOW; 337]

sherd *see* **shard**

sheriff *n* [➡ PEOPLE IN LAW COURTS; 820]

sheriff's officer *n* [➡ PEOPLE IN LAW COURTS; 820]

Shetland pony *type of* **horse** [➡ HORSES; 985]

shiatsu *type of* **complementary therapy** [➡ REMEDIES, TREATMENTS, AND OPERATIONS; 731]

shield 1 *n* **protection**, armor, defense, safeguard, buffer [➡ COVERS AND COATINGS; 1246] 2 *v* **protect**, guard, defend, shelter, screen, safeguard [➡ PREVENT CONTACT OR ATTACK; 419] *Opposite:* expose

See Compare and Contrast at **safeguard**.

shielded *adj* **protected**, safeguarded, isolated, defended, sheltered, spared [➡ SAFE AND SAFETY; 191] *Opposite:* exposed

shift 1 *v* **move**, budge, vary, transfer, change, alter, swing, modify [➡ POSITION SOMETHING; 325] 2 *v* (*UK informal*) **remove**, get rid of, loosen, lift, clean, erase [➡ REMOVE SOMETHING; 338] 3 *n* **move**, swing, modification, alteration, change, transference [➡ CHANGE; 372] 4 *n* **stint**, spell, scheduled time, period, turn, hitch, watch [➡ PERIODS OF TIME; 90] 5 *type of* **dress** [➡ GARMENTS AND OUTFITS; 865]

See Compare and Contrast at **change**.

shiftiness *n* [➡ DECEITFUL; 513]

shifting *adj* **unstable**, ever-changing, fluctuating, fluid, flowing, kaleidoscopic [➡ FINITENESS, VARIABILITY, AND TRANSIENCE; 96] *Opposite:* fixed

shiftless *adj* **lazy**, suspicious, dubious, idle, dishonest, good-for-nothing, untrustworthy, indolent, deceitful, slothful, devious, inefficient, workshy (*UK*) [➡ LIFELESS, LAZY, AND UNENTHUSIASTIC; 506] *Opposite:* industrious

shift the blame *v* [➡ ACCUSE, BLAME, AND CRITICIZE; 641]

shifty *adj* **suspicious**, suspect, dubious, dishonest, untrustworthy, deceitful, devious [➡ DECEITFUL; 513] *Opposite:* trustworthy

shih tzu *type of* **small dog** [➡ DOGS; 980]

shillelagh *type of* **club** [➡ BLUNT INSTRUMENTS AND WHIPS; 1158]

shilling *type of* **currency** [➡ CURRENCIES; 798]

shilly-shallier *n* [➡ LAZY OR UNSUCCESSFUL PEOPLE; 948]

shilly-shally 1 *v* **waver**, dilly-dally, dither, hesitate, vacillate, hang back, falter, hem and haw, um and ah (*UK*) [➡ HESITATE; 272] *Opposite:* decide 2 *v* **waste time**, hang around, dawdle, delay, dally, mess around (*informal*) [➡ MOVE SLOWLY; 314] *Opposite:* forge ahead

shilly-shallying *n* [➡ LIFELESS, LAZY, AND UNENTHUSIASTIC; 506]

shimmer *v* **sparkle**, glisten, shine, glitter, gleam, flicker, twinkle [➡ LIGHT EMISSION; 368]

shimmering *adj* **iridescent**, sparkling, shining, gle-aming, glistening, glittering, flickering [➡ DESCRIBING LIGHT; 1228]

shimmery *adj* [➡ VISUAL TEXTURE; 1221]

shimmy *v* [➡ MOVE FAST; 313]

shin *part of* **leg or foot** [➡ PARTS OF THE BODY: LEG AND FOOT; 694]

shinbone *type of* **bone** [➡ THE BONES AND JOINTS; 719]

shindig (*informal*) *n* **party**, bash, jamboree, get-together (*informal*) [➡ PARTIES, DANCES, AND CELEBRATIONS; 37]

shine 1 *v* **glow**, gleam, glimmer, sparkle, glitter, shimmer, glisten, twinkle, flicker, flash [➡ LIGHT EMISSION; 368] 2 *v* **excel**, be good at, stand out, have a gift for, be skilled at, do well [➡ SUCCEED AND WIN; 79] *Opposite:* bomb (*informal*) 3 *v* **polish**, burnish, wax, buff, buff up, put a shine on [➡ CLEAN AND POLISH; 403] 4 *n* **sheen**, polish, luster, gloss, gleam, patina, sparkle, twinkle [➡ VISUAL TEXTURE; 1221]

shingle *n* [➡ BUILDING MATERIALS; 1077]

shininess *n* [➡ VISUAL TEXTURE; 1221]

shining *adj* **outstanding**, excellent, admirable, brilliant, superb, exceptional, magnificent, marvelous, wonderful, splendid [➡ EXTRAORDINARY: AMAZING; 204] *Opposite:* poor

shining example *n* [➡ PERFECT EXAMPLES AND EMBODIMENTS; 67]

shinty *type of* **ball game** [➡ HOBBIES, GAMES, AND SPORTS; 875]

shiny *adj* **glossy**, gleaming, sparkly, glittery, polished, shimmering, glistening, burnished, reflective [➡ VISUAL TEXTURE; 1221] *Opposite:* dull

ship 1 *n* **vessel**, craft, boat [➡ SHIPS AND BOATS; 1150] 2 *v* **send**, transport, distribute, dispatch, convey, consign, express [➡ DISPATCH AND SEND; 333]

ship

◆ *types of historical vessels*
clipper, flagship, galleon, galley, Indiaman, longboat, longship, man-of-war, tall ship, windjammer

◆ *types of military vessels*
aircraft carrier, battle cruiser, battleship, cruiser, cutter, destroyer, frigate, gunboat, minesweeper, PT boat, submarine, warship

◆ *types of motor vessels*
barge, cabin cruiser, canal boat, coaster, container ship, cutter, dredger, factory ship, ferry, ferryboat, freighter, houseboat, hovercraft, hydrofoil, ice-breaker, launch, lifeboat, lighter, lightship, motor-boat, powerboat, speedboat, steamboat, steamer, tanker, trawler, tug, tugboat

◆ *types of sailing vessels*
bark, brig, brigantine, catamaran, catboat, dhow, felucca, junk, ketch, sailboat, schooner, sloop, smack, trimaran, yacht

◆ *types of small vessels*
canoe, dinghy, dory, dugout, gondola, kayak, life raft, pirogue, punt, raft, rowboat, sampan, scull, skiff

◆ *parts of a sailing vessel*
boom, bowsprit, fore-and-aft sail, gaff, jib, mainsail, mainstay, mast, mizzen, pennant, sheet, shroud, spanker, spinnaker, topsail

◆ *parts of a ship or boat*
bilge, bow, bridge, cabin, capstan, crow's nest, deck, engine room, fo'c's'le, galley, gunwale, helm, hold, hull, keel, oarlock, outboard motor, outrigger, poop, prow, rudder, stateroom, stern, superstructure, tiller

shipment *n* **consignment**, delivery, batch, load, cargo, freight [➡ TRANSPORTATION, TRANSPORTERS, AND CARGOS; 322]

shipping *n* **delivery**, transportation, distribution, carriage, freight, shipment, conveyance, transport (*UK*) [➡ TRANSPORTATION, TRANSPORTERS, AND CARGOS; 322]

shipping canal *n* [➡ WATERWAYS AND SEAWAYS; 1108]

shipping lane *n* [➡ WATERWAYS AND SEAWAYS; 1108]

shipshape *adj* **in order**, neat, tidy, organized, spick-and-span, in apple-pie order [➡ ORDER AND ORGANIZATION; 206] *Opposite*: untidy

shipyard *type of* **industrial site** [➡ INDUSTRIAL BUILDINGS; 1087]

shire (*UK*) *n* [➡ COUNTRIES AND REGIONS; 1067]

shire horse *type of* **horse** [➡ HORSES; 985]

shirk *v* **evade**, avoid, dodge, duck, get out of, wriggle out of, shun [➡ NOT DO AND REFUSE TO DO; 274] *Opposite*: accept

shirker *n* **lazy person**, slacker, lazybones (*informal*), idler, loafer, malingerer, clock-watcher, slouch (*informal*) [➡ LAZY OR UNSUCCESSFUL PEOPLE; 948] *Opposite*: worker

shirt *type of* **top** [➡ GARMENTS AND OUTFITS; 865]

shirtdress *type of* **dress** [➡ GARMENTS AND OUTFITS; 865]

shish kebab *n* [➡ PREPARED DISHES; 1170]

shiver 1 *v* **shake**, tremble, quiver, quake, shudder [➡ PHYSICAL REACTIONS; 316] 2 *n* **quiver**, shudder, tremor, tremble, quake (*informal*), frisson [➡ PHYSICAL REACTIONS; 316]

shoal *n* **sandbar**, sandbank, ridge, shallows [➡ THE SEAS, OCEANS, AND SHORES; 1041]

shock 1 *n* **distress**, numbness, devastation, disbelief, astonishment, amazement [➡ SURPRISE, SHOCK, AND AMAZEMENT; 545] 2 *n* **surprise**, jolt, blow, bombshell, kick in the teeth, bolt from the blue, upset, fright [➡ SUDDEN EVENTS; 52] 3 *v* **stun**, alarm, surprise, frighten, astonish, astound, take aback, amaze, stagger, take the wind out of your sails, flabbergast (*informal*) [➡ FRIGHTEN AND SHOCK; 568] *Opposite*: calm 4 *v* **scandalize**, outrage, appall, offend, horrify, provoke [➡ UPSET, DISTRESS, AND HUMILIATE; 567] 5 *v* **traumatize**, upset, devastate, shake up, alarm, disturb [➡ UPSET, DISTRESS, AND HUMILIATE; 567] *Opposite*: reassure

shockability *n* [➡ NEGATIVE INTELLECTUAL CHARACTERISTICS; 525]

shock absorber *n* [➡ PARTS OF MACHINES AND TOOLS; 1118]

shocked 1 *adj* **surprised**, stunned, dazed, upset, shaken, traumatized, taken aback [➡ SURPRISE, SHOCK, AND AMAZEMENT; 545] *Opposite*: indifferent 2 *adj* **scandalized**, outraged, appalled, offended [➡ SURPRISE, SHOCK, AND AMAZEMENT; 545] *Opposite*: indifferent

shocking *adj* **appalling**, dreadful, scandalous, outrageous, awful, ghastly, horrible, disgusting, deplorable, wicked [➡ UNACCEPTABLE AND UNFORGIVABLE; 225]

shockingly 1 *adv* **outrageously**, astonishingly, disgracefully, unpardonably, appallingly, amazingly [➡ UNACCEPTABLE AND UNFORGIVABLE; 225] *Opposite*: understandably 2 *adv* **startlingly**, horrifically, distressingly, upsettingly, disturbingly, grotesquely, gruesomely [➡ EMOTIONALLY UNPLEASANT AND UPSETTING; 227] *Opposite*: tastefully 3 *adv* **atrociously**, lamentably, appallingly, frightfully, dreadfully, unspeakably [➡ TO A GREAT EXTENT; 132]

shocking pink *type of* **pink** [➡ COLORS; 1224]

shock wave 1 *n* **repercussion**, reaction, shock, effect [➡ RESULTS AND OUTCOMES; 83] 2 *n* **tremor**, shudder, shock, trembling, agitation, start [➡ SUDDEN EVENTS; 52]

shoddily 1 *adv* **carelessly**, poorly, badly, sloppily (*informal*), cheaply [➡ BAD AND BADLY; 223] *Opposite*: carefully 2 *adv* **inconsiderately**, meanly, badly, unkindly, disgracefully [➡ SELFISH AND UNKIND; 505] *Opposite*: considerately

shoddy 1 *adj* **careless**, slapdash, sloppy, low, inferior, cheap, substandard, poor, trashy, lousy (*informal*) [➡ BAD AND BADLY; 223] *Opposite*: fine 2 *adj* **inconsiderate**, mean, unkind, dishonest, rotten, disgraceful, lousy (*informal*) [➡ SELFISH AND UNKIND; 505] *Opposite*: considerate

shoe *type of* **shoe** [➡ FOOTWEAR; 871]

shoelace *n* **cord**, lace, bootlace, tie, fastener [➡ FASTENERS, LINKS, AND NETWORKS; 1247]

shoo away *v* **chase off**, drive away, frighten away, scare off [➡ EJECT AND EXCLUDE; 340] *Opposite*: invite

shoot 1 *v* **fire**, open fire, fire off, fire at, bombard, snipe, discharge (*formal*), let off (*UK*) [➡ USE TOOLS AND MACHINERY; 468] 2 *v* **gun down** (*informal*), kill, injure, wound, maim, shoot down, blow away (*slang*), waste (*slang*) [➡ KILL; 923] 3 *v* **spurt**, squirt, burst, jet, gush, force [➡ LIQUID EMISSION; 370] 4 *v* (*informal*) **dart**, dash, run, race, speed, spurt, zoom, whiz, zip (*informal*) [➡ MOVE FAST; 313] 5 *v* **film**, photograph, take, snap, capture [➡ RECORD SOMETHING; 371] 6 *v* **aim**, point, direct, cast, score, net [➡ MOVE SOMETHING THROUGH THE AIR; 334] 7 *v* **start to grow**, produce buds, develop, appear, sprout [➡ GROW AND CULTIVATE; 351] 8 *n* **new growth**, branch, leaf bud, outgrowth, stem, bud [➡ PARTS OF TREES AND PLANTS; 1026]

shoot down 1 *v* **bring down**, kill, slaughter, destroy, murder, fell, gun down (*informal*) [➡ KILL; 923] 2 *v* **attack**, tear to shreds, pick holes in, pillory, criticize, pan, trash (*informal*), rubbish (*UK*) [➡ ACCUSE, BLAME, AND CRITICIZE; 641]

shooter (*informal*) *n* [➡ WEAPONS FOR SHOOTING; 1156]

shooting 1 *n* **gunfire**, shelling, bombardment, fire, firing [➡ AGGRESSIVE EVENTS; 39] 2 *n* **killing**, murder, assassination, execution, slaying, homicide [➡ CAUSES OF DEATH; 921]

shooting star *type of* **heavenly body** [➡ HEAVENLY BODIES; 1061]

shoot the breeze (*slang*) *v* **chat**, gossip, pass the time of day, gas (*informal*), natter (*informal*), yap (*informal*), schmooze (*slang*), chew the fat (*slang*), rap (*slang*) [➡ TWO-WAY COMMUNICATION; 607]

shoot up *v* **appear**, soar, rocket, spring up, mushroom, rise, increase, develop, grow, go sky-high, go through the roof, skyrocket (*informal*) [➡ CHANGE OF SIZE: BIGGER; 392] *Opposite*: plummet

shop 1 *n* **store**, outlet, emporium, showroom [➡ RETAIL

OUTLETS; 1083] **2** *n* **spree**, shopping spree, shopping expedition, walk round the shops (*UK*), binge, retail therapy (*humorous*) [➡ HOBBIES, GAMES, AND SPORTS; 875] **3** *n* **workshop**, plant, factory, garage, yard, works [➡ PLACE OF EMPLOYMENT; 832] **4** *v* **go shopping**, buy groceries, go window-shopping, go on a spree, do the marketing, window-shop, go to the shops (*UK*) [➡ PURCHASE; 422]

shop assistant (*UK*) *n* [➡ SELLERS; 442]

shoplift *v* **steal**, rob, pilfer, filch (*informal*), thieve, knock off (*slang*), pocket [➡ STEAL AND ROB; 426]

shoplifting *n* **stealing**, theft, thieving, pilfering, larceny [➡ CRIMES; 817]

shopper *n* **customer**, consumer, buyer, purchaser, bargain hunter [➡ PURCHASER; 424]

shopping *n* **errands**, spending, clothes shopping, grocery shopping, supermarket run, bargain hunting, shop (*UK*), weekly shop (*UK*) [➡ HOBBIES, GAMES, AND SPORTS; 875]

shopping arcade *n* [➡ RETAIL OUTLETS; 1083]

shopping bag *type of* **bag** [➡ CONTAINERS, RECEPTACLES, AND PACKAGING; 1245]

shopping center *n* [➡ RETAIL OUTLETS; 1083]

shopping complex *n* [➡ RETAIL OUTLETS; 1083]

shopping mall *n* **shopping center**, arcade, arcade, mall, strip mall, shopping plaza, outlet mall, shopping complex, shopping precinct (*UK*), pedestrian precinct (*UK*) [➡ RETAIL OUTLETS; 1083]

shore *n* **coast**, beach, seashore, coastline, seaboard, oceanfront, shoreline, seaside [➡ THE SEAS, OCEANS, AND SHORES; 1041]

shoreline *n* **beach**, shore, seashore, water's edge, coastline, oceanfront [➡ THE SEAS, OCEANS, AND SHORES; 1041]

shore up *v* **prop up**, support, hold up, buttress, bolster, reinforce [➡ IMPROVE STRENGTH AND DURABILITY; 378]

shorn of *adj* **deprived of**, stripped of, minus, less, lacking [➡ LACK OF POSSESSION; 445]

short **1** *adj* **small**, little, petite, tiny, diminutive, squat, undersized, stunted [➡ LENGTH: SHORT; 1198] *Opposite*: tall **2** *adj* **brief**, quick, rapid, fleeting, passing [➡ HAPPENING QUICKLY; 104] *Opposite*: lengthy **3** *adj* **concise**, succinct, condensed, brief, to the point, terse [➡ CONCISE AND CLEAR; 202] *Opposite*: long **4** *adj* **curt**, brusque, snappy, abrupt, unfriendly, terse, brisk, sharp [➡ BAD-TEMPERED AND HUMORLESS; 626] *Opposite*: friendly **5** *adv* **midstream**, abruptly, suddenly, sharply [➡ HAPPENING QUICKLY; 104] *Opposite*: gradually

shortage *n* **lack**, scarcity, deficiency, dearth, famine, absence, unavailability [➡ TOO FEW, TOO LITTLE; 122] *Opposite*: excess

See Compare and Contrast at **lack**.

short and sweet *adj* [➡ FINITENESS, VARIABILITY, AND TRANSIENCE; 96]

short break *n* **break**, rest, weekend away, midweek break, a few days away, vacation, holiday (*UK*), weekend break (*UK*) [➡ PERIODS OF REST; 91]

shortcoming *n* **inadequacy**, failing, fault, deficiency, limitation, weakness, defect, flaw [➡ FAULTS, FLAWS, AND WEAKNESSES; 251] *Opposite*: virtue

short course *n* **crash course**, intensive course, introductory course, refresher course [➡ CLASSES, COURSEWORK, AND EXAMINATIONS; 842]

shortcrust pastry (*UK*) *n* [➡ BREAD, FLOUR, AND BREAD PRODUCTS; 1179]

short-eared owl *type of* **owl** [➡ OWLS; 1001]

shorten *v* **cut down**, cut, cut back, curtail, abbreviate, abridge, condense, contract, truncate, reduce, compress, telescope, take up, diminish [➡ CHANGE OF SIZE: SMALLER; 393] *Opposite*: lengthen

shortening *n* **fat**, lard, margarine, butter, suet [➡ FATS AND OILS; 1173]

shortfall *n* **deficit**, loss, underperformance, gap, lack, shortage [➡ TOO FEW, TOO LITTLE; 122] *Opposite*: excess

short form *n* **abbreviation**, shortening, contraction, acronym, ellipsis [➡ ASPECTS OF LANGUAGE; 682]

short-handed *adj* **short-staffed**, understaffed, short [➡ TOO FEW, TOO LITTLE; 122]

short-list *v* **select**, choose, pick out, cream off, narrow down, sift [➡ MAKE DECISIONS AND CHOICES; 752]

short-lived *adj* **brief**, fleeting, transitory, passing, short, ephemeral, short-term, momentary, transient [➡ FINITENESS, VARIABILITY, AND TRANSIENCE; 96] *Opposite*: long-lasting

See Compare and Contrast at **temporary**.

shortly **1** *adv* **soon**, before long, in a while, in a minute, in a moment, in a bit, just, right away, presently (*formal or literary*) [➡ FUTURE; 86] *Opposite*: later **2** *adv* **curtly**, brusquely, abruptly, briskly, tersely, sharply, gruffly, rudely, discourteously [➡ BAD-TEMPERED AND HUMORLESS; 626] *Opposite*: pleasantly

shortness **1** *n* **smallness**, tininess, squatness, dumpiness [➡ LENGTH: SHORT; 1198] *Opposite*: tallness **2** *n* **quickness**, rapidity, speed, transience [➡ FINITENESS, VARIABILITY, AND TRANSIENCE; 96] *Opposite*: length **3** *n* **briefness**, brevity, terseness, conciseness, concision, succinctness [➡ CONCISE AND CLEAR; 202] *Opposite*: length **4** *n* **curtness**, brusqueness, abruptness, briskness, terseness, sharpness, gruffness, rudeness, discourtesy [➡ BAD-TEMPERED AND HUMORLESS; 626] *Opposite*: pleasantness

short of *prep* **apart from**, other than, without, bar [➡ NOT; 137] *Opposite*: including

short of money *adj* [➡ POVERTY AND POOR; 892]

short-order cook *type of* **person who works in restaurants** [➡ DOMESTIC AND KITCHEN WORKERS; 850]

short-range *adj* [➡ CLOSENESS; 159]

shorts *type of* **pants** [➡ GARMENTS AND OUTFITS; 865]

short-sighted **1** *adj* **ill-considered**, thoughtless, unthinking, imprudent, ill-advised, ill-judged, unwise, rash, hasty, short-term, short-range, limited, restricted [➡ THE NATURE OF IDEAS; 771] *Opposite*: farsighted **2** *adj* (*UK*) **nearsighted**, myopic [➡ SEE; 699] *Opposite*: farsighted

move, elbow, ram, jolt [➡ PUSH, PULL, AND SLIDE; 335] *Opposite*:
pull **2** *v* **put**, throw, toss, slap, sling, fling, chuck (*informal*)
[➡ POSITION SOMETHING; 325] **3** *n* **thrust**, push, heave, jolt [➡ PUSH, PULL, ⋯; 335]

⋯ **spade**, scoop, trowel, tool [➡ SPOONS, SCOOPS, AND ⋯
⋯ **scoop**, move, dig, spoon, heap, ladle [➡ USE ⋯

⋯ [➡ LEAVE AND GO AWAY; 8]

⋯ exhibit, expose, disclose,
⋯ade, show off, flaunt, flash,
⋯oody's nose, put on view [➡ CAUSE ⋯
⋯ **2** *v* **stand out**, stick out, show up,
⋯tch the eye [➡ APPEAR AND EMERGE; 3]
⋯e, guide, direct, point, steer [➡ ACCOMPANY ⋯
prove, illustrate, demonstrate, confirm,
⋯lish [➡ MEAN SOMETHING; 61] *Opposite*: disprove
⋯te, illustrate, explain, teach, point out, indi-
⋯ out [➡ EXPLAIN AND CLARIFY; 610] **6** *n* **demonstration**,
⋯ay, expression, illustration, appearance, spectacle
[➡ PERFORMANCES AND SHOWS; 42] **7** *n* **performance**, musical, cabaret,
play, film, movie, program, TV show, radio show, act,
entertainment, showing, presentation, viewing, scre-
ening [➡ PERFORMANCES AND SHOWS; 42] **8** *n* **fair**, exhibition, trade
show, agricultural display, county show (*UK*) [➡ SALES AND ⋯

show a clean pair of heels (*UK*) *v* [➡ RUN AWAY AND AVOID; 10]

show appreciation *v* [➡ PRAISE AND ENCOURAGE; 647]

show biz (*informal*) *n* [➡ ENTERTAINMENT; 872]

showboat (*informal*) *v* [➡ ROAST; 616]

show business *n* **the stage**, theater, the boards, film,
movies, television, show biz (*informal*) [➡ THE PERFORMING ARTS; 904]

showcase 1 *n* **glass case**, cabinet, display case, display
cabinet, vitrine [➡ FURNITURE; 858] **2** *n* **platform**, vehicle, setting,
stage [➡ ADVERTISING AND PUBLICITY; 604]

showdown *n* **confrontation**, head-to-head, face-off, row,
fight, argument, quarrel, conflict, shootout (*informal*)
[➡ ARGUMENTS; 47]

shower 1 *n* **wash**, dip, rinse, spray [➡ CLEAN AND POLISH; 403]
2 *n* **cascade**, burst, deluge, hail, spray, sprinkling, flood,
splatter [➡ MANY, MUCH, LARGE AMOUNT; 117] **3** *n* **cloudburst**, downpour, storm, rainstorm, flurry, drizzle, rainfall [➡ CLOUDY AND
RAINY WEATHER; 1052] **4** *type of* **plumbing fixtures** [➡ FIXTURES; 859]
5 *v* **wash**, clean up, freshen up, rinse [➡ CLEAN AND POLISH; 403]
6 *v* **rain**, rain down, pour, pour down, sprinkle, fall, drop,
spill, spit [➡ CLOUDY AND RAINY WEATHER; 1052] **7** *v* **overwhelm**, inundate, flood, deluge, bombard, cover [➡ GIVE TOO MUCH AND OVER-
BURDEN; 437]

showery *adj* **rainy**, wet, changeable, damp, spitting,
drizzly [➡ CLOUDY AND RAINY WEATHER; 1052] *Opposite*: dry

showground *n* **arena**, ring, enclosure, field, ground,
fairground [➡ URBAN OUTDOOR SPACES; 1072]

show in *v* [➡ ACCOMPANY AND FOLLOW; 337]

showiness 1 *n* **impressiveness**, attractiveness, magnificence, drama, splendor [➤ BEAUTY AND ATTRACTIVENESS; 189] *Opposite*: modesty **2** *n* **ostentation**, flashiness, show, gaudiness, garishness, tastelessness, show, gaudiglitz, jazziness, brassiness, pretension [➤ IN POOR TASTE AND OVERSENTIMENTAL; 229] *Opposite*: discretion

showing *n* **presentation**, performance, viewing, screening, display, show [➤ PERFORMANCES AND SHOWS; 42]

showing off *n* **bravado**, boastfulness, boasting, bragging, posturing, bluster, swagger, exhibitionism [➤ BOAST; 616]

show jumping *n* [➤ HOBBIES, GAMES, AND SPORTS; 875]

show off **1** *v* **boast**, brag, shoot your mouth off, sing your own praises, pose, swagger, blow your own horn, swank (*slang*), fly your own kite (*UK*) [➤ BOAST; 616] **2** *v* **display**, flaunt, parade, flourish, flash (*informal*) [➤ CAUSE TO APPEAR; 5] *Opposite*: hide

show-off (*informal*) *n* **boaster**, braggart, bragger, exhibitionist, know-it-all (*informal*), bighead (*informal*) [➤ SELF-IMPORTANT AND SELF-SEEKING PEOPLE; 949]

show of hands *n* [➤ GESTURES AND GESTICULATION; 653]

show out *v* [➤ ACCOMPANY A... ...W; 337]

showpiece *n* **centerpiece**, pride... tion, pièce de résistance, masterpiece ... EMBODIMENTS; 67]

showroom *n* **shop**, outlet, store [➤ RETAIL OUTLETS; 1083]

show the way *v* [➤ ACCOMPANY AND FOLLOW; 337]

show to the door *v* [➤ ACCOMPANY AND FOLLOW; 337]

show up **1** *v* (*informal*) **come**, turn up, arrive, put in an appearance, appear, show your face, roll up, attend, crop up (*informal*) [➤ ARRIVE; 12] **2** *v* **highlight**, emphasize, point up, bring to light, reveal, disclose, expose, indicate [➤ CAUSE TO APPEAR; 5] *Opposite*: hide **3** *v* **stand out**, stick out, show, catch your eye, come to light, emerge [➤ APPEAR AND EMERGE; 3] **4** *v* **embarrass**, humiliate, put somebody to shame, mortify, shame, make a fool of, score off [➤ UPSET, DISTRESS, AND HUMILIATE; 567]

showy **1** *adj* **impressive**, attractive, eye-catching, splendid, magnificent, spectacular, dramatic [➤ BEAUTY AND ATTRACTIVENESS; 189] *Opposite*: modest **2** *adj* **ostentatious**, flashy, gaudy, garish, tasteless, brash, vulgar, glitzy, pretentious, jazzy (*slang*) [➤ IN POOR TASTE AND OVERSENTIMENTAL; 229] *Opposite*: restrained

show your face *v* **turn up**, appear, put in an appearance, come, arrive, roll up, attend, emerge, surface, show up (*informal*) [➤ ARRIVE; 12] *Opposite*: hide

shred **1** *n* **scrap**, strip, bit, piece, sliver, tatter, shaving, paring, crumb, fragment [➤ SMALL PIECES; 129] *Opposite*: whole **2** *v* **slice**, cut up, tear up, rip up, grate, mince, chop, destroy, grind [➤ TEAR, BREAK, AND CUT; 360]

shrew *type of* **rodent** [➤ RODENTS; 989]

shrewd *adj* **astute**, sharp, smart, perceptive, discerning, insightful, wise, clever, intelligent, cunning, crafty, sharp-witted, canny, sensible, accurate, judicious, on the ball (*informal*) [➤ POSITIVE INTELLECTUAL CHARACTERISTICS; 524] *Opposite*: naive

shrewdness ... ceptiveness, di... cleverness, inte... niness, accuracy... ACTERISTICS; 524] Oppo...

shrewish *adj* [➤ DIF...

shrewishness *n* [➤...

shriek *n* **screech**, sc... [➤ SOUNDS MADE BY PEOPLE; 1262] ...

shrill *adj* **piercing**, high-... harsh, sharp, jarring [➤ L... *Opposite*: low

shrillness *n* [➤ LOUD, HIGH, OR UN...

shrilly *adv* **piercingly**, strident... sharply, jarringly [➤ LOUD, HIGH, OR ...site: soothingly

shrimp *type of* **crustacean** [➤ AQUA...

shrine **1** *n* **memorial**, monument, ... tabernacle, reliquary, stupa [➤ RELIG... **place of worship** [➤ RELIGIOUS BUILDINGS; 108...

shrink **1** *v* **contra**... shrivel, wither... site: ... waste ...way, disappear [➤ C... away, pull back... fall, drop, decrease... withdraw, shrin... [➤ CHANGE OF S... *Opposite*: stand yo... ...ck, reco... psychoanalyst, the... around shrink back, ... [➤ PEOPLE WHO WORK IN MEDIC... **4** *n* [➤... counselor, a... (sl...

See Compare and Con...

shrinkage *n* **reduction**... fall, drop, disappearance ... growth

shrink back *v* **recoil**, crin... flinch, draw back, withdraw... pull back, back off, fall back... *Opposite*: advance

shrink from *v* **recoil from**, bal... turn away from, spurn, reject, e... DO; 274] *Opposite*: welcome

shrivel *v* **shrink**, wither, dry up, co... away, telescope, shorten [➤ CHANGE OF SIZ... expand

shriveled *adj* [➤ DRY; 1242]

See Compare and Contrast at **dry**.

shrivel up *v* [➤ CHANGE OF SHAPE; 385]

shroud **1** *n* **covering**, cover, blanket, laye... (*literary*) [➤ COVERS AND COATINGS; 1246] **2** *part of* ... VEHICLES; 1063] **3** *part of* **sailing vessel** [➤ PARTS ...

shrouded in mystery *adj* [➤ SECRET AND U...

shrub *n* **bush**, plant, tree, flowering shrub [➡BUSHES AND SHRUBS; 1027]

---

shrub

◆ *types of shrubs or bushs*

azalea, bramble, brier, broom, camellia, elder, forsythia, gardenia, gorse, hawthorn, heather, hydrangea, laurel, lavender, lilac, magnolia, privet, pussy willow, rhododendron, rose, sagebrush, witch hazel

---

shrubbery 1 *n* **bushes**, undergrowth, border, herbaceous border, hedging [➡BUSHES AND SHRUBS; 1027] **2** *part of* **garden** [➡GARDENS; 1074]

shrug *n* [➡GESTURES AND GESTICULATION; 653]

shrug off *v* **dismiss**, pooh-pooh, ignore, treat lightly, make light of, pay no heed to, disregard, reject [➡NOT PAY ATTENTION; 764]

shrunken *adj* **wasted**, emaciated, dried up, withered, shriveled, contracted [➡CHANGE OF SIZE: SMALLER; 393] *Opposite:* bloated

shudder 1 *v* **shake**, tremble, shiver, wince, quake, judder, quiver, jolt, wobble, vibrate, convulse [➡PHYSICAL REACTIONS; 316] **2** *n* **tremble**, shake, shiver, tremor, judder, jolt, wince, convulsion, agitation, quake (*informal*) [➡PHYSICAL REACTIONS; 316]

shuffle 1 *v* **scuffle**, hobble, shamble, lumber, slouch, waddle, trundle [➡WALK UNSTEADILY; 315] **2** *v* **mix up**, jumble up, muddle up, rearrange, reorder, transpose [➡COMBINE AND MIX; 400]

shun *v* **avoid**, turn away from, spurn, reject, eschew, ignore, shirk, recoil from, balk at, shrink from [➡REFUSING OR REJECTING RELATIONS; 975] *Opposite:* court

shunt 1 *v* **push**, shove, move, shift, propel, force, thrust, jolt [➡PUSH, PULL, AND SLIDE; 335] **2** *n* **shove**, thrust, jolt, push, diversion, bypass [➡PUSH, PULL, AND SLIDE; 335]

shush 1 *interj* [➡UNFAVORABLE NONVERBAL RESPONSES; 654] **2** *v* (*informal*) **silence**, shut up, hush, quiet, quiet down, pipe down (*informal*) [➡WITHHOLD INFORMATION; 687]

shut 1 *v* **close**, close up, push to, fasten, secure, bolt, lock, lock up, shut up, slam to, snap to [➡FASTEN, LINK, AND JOIN; 408] *Opposite:* open **2** *v* **close down**, close, close up shop, shut down, go out of business, go bankrupt, go into liquidation, go to the wall, fold, fail, collapse, go under, liquidate, wind up, go bust (*informal*) [➡FAIL OR BE UNSUCCESSFUL; 75] *Opposite:* start up

shut down *v* [➡STOP ACTING; 264]

shutdown *n* **closure**, cessation, stoppage, halt, end, blackout [➡WORK-RELATED ACTIVITIES; 834]

shuteye (*informal*) *n* [➡SLEEP AND DREAM; 723]

shut in 1 *v* **confine**, cage, restrain, imprison, lock in, close in, enclose, shut up [➡CAPTIVITY AND LOSS OF FREEDOM; 248] *Opposite:* let loose **2** *adj* **captive**, imprisoned, locked in, confined, caged, restrained, closed in, shut up [➡CAPTIVITY AND LOSS OF FREEDOM; 248] *Opposite:* free

shut off 1 *v* **switch off**, turn off, close off, close down, shut down, stop, cut out, block, impede [➡CAUSE TO STOP; 266]

Opposite: turn on **2** *v* **isolate**, cut off, separate, seclude, set apart, sequester (*formal*) [➡SEPARATE AND DIVIDE; 401]

shut out *v* **lock out**, keep out, exclude, keep off, debar, keep at arm's length [➡EJECT AND EXCLUDE; 340] *Opposite:* let in

shutter *part of* **camera** [➡PHOTOGRAPHY AND PHOTOGRAPHIC EQUIPMENT; 1122]

shuttle 1 *v* **travel**, go, ferry, transport, transfer, carry, take [➡TRAVEL: WAYS OF TRAVELING; 320] **2** *type of* **public service vehicle** [➡VEHICLES; 1145]

shuttlecock *type of* **sports equipment** [➡SPORTS EQUIPMENT; 879]

shut up 1 *v* (*informal*) **be quiet**, fall silent, clam up (*informal*), quiet down, pipe down (*informal*) [➡WITHHOLD INFORMATION; 687] **2** *v* **confine**, imprison, cage, shut in, lock in, close in, enclose, restrain [➡CAPTIVITY AND LOSS OF FREEDOM; 248] *Opposite:* let loose **3** *v* (*informal*) **silence**, hush, gag, muzzle, cut off, stifle [➡AVOID, PREVENT, LIMIT, AND CONTROL; 277] **4** *v* **close**, close up, lock, lock up, secure, fasten, bolt [➡FASTEN, LINK, AND JOIN, 408] *Opposite:* open up

shut up shop 1 *v* **stop**, call it a day, turn in, close, shut, pack in (*informal*) [➡STOP ACTING; 264] *Opposite:* start up **2** *v* **close**, shut, close down, shut down, go out of business, go bankrupt, go to the wall, go into liquidation, collapse, fail, go under, go bust (*informal*) [➡FAIL OR BE UNSUCCESSFUL; 75] *Opposite:* start up

shy 1 *adj* **introverted**, retiring, withdrawn, timid, bashful, diffident, inhibited, reticent, reserved, quiet, coy [➡RETICENT AND UNFORTHCOMING; 631] *Opposite:* outgoing **2** *adj* **cautious**, wary, nervous, afraid, fearful, reluctant [➡INSECURITY AND LOSS OF COMPOSURE; 544] *Opposite:* confident

shy away *v* **retreat**, shrink, recoil, flinch, back off, back away, draw back, cringe, cower [➡PHYSICAL REACTIONS; 316]

shyly 1 *adv* **timidly**, bashfully, reticently, reservedly, diffidently, quietly, warily, coyly [➡RETICENT AND UNFORTHCOMING; 631] *Opposite:* boldly **2** *adv* **cautiously**, warily, nervously, fearfully, reluctantly [➡INSECURITY AND LOSS OF COMPOSURE; 544] *Opposite:* confidently

shyness *n* **introversion**, timidity, bashfulness, inhibition, reticence, reserve, diffidence, quietness, coyness, caution, wariness, nervousness [➡RETICENT AND UNFORTHCOMING; 631] *Opposite:* boldness

Siamese cat *type of* **cat** [➡FELINES; 983]

sibling *type of* **same-generation relative** [➡SAME-GENERATION RELATIVES; 957]

sibyl *n* [➡PEOPLE WITH SUPERNATURAL POWERS; 788]

sick 1 *adj* **ill**, unwell, bad, under the weather, out of sorts, pale, ailing (*dated*) [➡ILL AND SICK; 740] *Opposite:* well **2** *adj* **nauseous**, queasy, bilious, dizzy, green around the gills (*informal*) [➡ILL AND SICK; 740] **3** *adj* (*informal*) **tasteless**, in bad taste, gruesome, bizarre, sickening, revolting, vile, nauseating [➡IN POOR TASTE AND OVERSENTIMENTAL; 229] **4** *adj* **bored**, up to here, sick and tired, sick to death, fed up (*informal*), had it (*informal*), sick to the back teeth (*UK*) [➡SADNESS, DISTRESS, AND DESPAIR; 539]

sick and tired *adj* **sick**, up to here, sick to death, bored, fed up (*informal*), sick to the back teeth (*UK*) [➡SADNESS, DISTRESS, AND DESPAIR; 539]

sickbay *n* **infirmary**, sanatorium, sickroom, hospital [➡ HOSPITALS AND CLINICS; 826]

sicken *v* **nauseate**, turn your stomach, repel, disgust, appall, make sick, shock, revolt, repulse [➡ UPSET, DISTRESS, AND HUMILIATE; 567]

sickened *adj* [➡ SADNESS, DISTRESS, AND DESPAIR; 539]

sickening *adj* **disgusting**, nauseating, stomach-turning, shocking, appalling, revolting, repulsive, repellent, terrible, horrible, vile, stomach-churning (*UK*) [➡ DISGUSTING AND REPULSIVE; 230] *Opposite*: appealing

sickle *type of* **cutting tool** [➡ CUTTING TOOLS; 1120]

sickly **1** *adj* **unhealthy**, weak, ill, unwell, pale, wan, ailing (*dated*) [➡ UNFIT AND WEAK; 739] *Opposite*: healthy **2** *adj* **cloying**, overpowering, disgusting, suffocating, nauseating, sickening [➡ DISGUSTING AND REPULSIVE; 230] *Opposite*: appealing **3** *adj* **saccharine**, sentimental, cloying, sickly-sweet, mawkish, sugary, soppy (*informal*) [➡ IN POOR TASTE AND OVERSENTIMENTAL; 229] *Opposite*: tough

sickly-sweet *adj* **saccharine**, cloying, mawkish, soppy (*informal*), sentimental, nauseating, sickening [➡ IN POOR TASTE AND OVERSENTIMENTAL; 229]

sickness **1** *n* **illness**, disease, virus, condition, bad health, ill health, infection, bug (*informal*) [➡ SICKNESS; 729] *Opposite*: health **2** *n* **nausea**, vomiting, queasiness, biliousness, throwing up (*informal*) [➡ DISORDERS OF THE DIGESTIVE SYSTEM; 713]

sick to death *adj* [➡ SADNESS, DISTRESS, AND DESPAIR; 539]

sick to the back teeth (*UK*) *adj* [➡ SADNESS, DISTRESS, AND DESPAIR; 539]

side **1** *n* **surface**, face, elevation, wall, plane [➡ EXTREMITIES OF PHYSICAL OBJECTS; 1250] **2** *n* **part**, area, region, section, segment, zone, quarter [➡ AREA AND RANGE; 111] **3** *n* **edge**, boundary, flank, bank, periphery, margin, fringe, border [➡ EXTREMITIES OF PHYSICAL OBJECTS; 1250] **4** *n* **aspect**, facet, feature, quality, characteristic, trait [➡ QUALITIES AND CHARACTERISTICS; 1191] **5** *n* **team**, squad, line-up, group, gang, camp [➡ GROUPS WITH A COMMON INTEREST; 938] **6** *type of* **cut** [➡ TYPES AND CUTS OF MEAT; 1177]

sideboard *type of* **cabinet** [➡ FURNITURE; 858]

sideburns *n* [➡ FACIAL HAIR; 489]

side by side *adj* [➡ CLOSENESS; 159]

side dish *part of* **meal** [➡ MEALS AND PARTS OF MEALS; 1169]

side effect *n* **unexpected result**, secondary effect, byproduct, consequence, result, knock-on effect (*UK*) [➡ RESULTS AND OUTCOMES; 83]

sidekick (*informal*) *n* **assistant**, helper, associate, subordinate, partner, colleague [➡ COLLEAGUES AND EQUALS; 967] *Opposite*: boss

sideline **1** *n* **hobby**, pastime, offshoot, secondary activity, second job, spinoff, byproduct, second string to your bow (*UK*) [➡ LEISURE AND RECREATION; 874] *Opposite*: career **2** *v* **put aside**, shelve, put off, put on the back burner, suspend, slow pedal (*UK*) [➡ NOT PAY ATTENTION; 764] *Opposite*: promote **3** *v* **relegate**, demote, exclude, downgrade, lay off, dismiss [➡ REVOKE STATUS; 459] *Opposite*: promote

sidelong *adj* **sideways**, oblique, slanting, indirect, askew, aslant [➡ DIRECTION OF MOTION; 345] *Opposite*: direct

side mirror *type of* **external feature** [➡ EXTERNAL PARTS OF A VEHICLE; 1147]

sidereal *adj* [➡ THE SUPERNATURAL; 787]

sidesplitting *adj* **hilarious**, riotous, uproarious, rollicking, funny, comic, comical, hysterical (*informal*), rib-tickling (*informal*) [➡ FUNNY AND AMUSING; 216] *Opposite*: dull

See Compare and Contrast at **funny**.

sidestep *v* **avoid**, evade, dodge, duck, bypass, skirt [➡ NOT PAY ATTENTION; 764]

side street *n* **alley**, back street, lane, side road [➡ ROADS; 1106]

sidetrack *v* **distract**, deflect, divert, change the subject, get off the point, lose the thread [➡ CONFUSE AND BEWILDER; 571]

sidetracked *adj* [➡ PENSIVENESS AND INTEREST; 538]

side view *n* **cross section**, profile, section, side, aspect [➡ DRAWINGS, CHARTS, AND TABLES; 594]

sidewalk *n* **path**, footway, walkway, footpath, pavement (*UK*) [➡ PATHWAYS; 1110]

sideways **1** *adj* **oblique**, slanting, indirect, sidelong, slanted, sideward [➡ DIRECTION OF MOTION; 345] *Opposite*: straight **2** *adv* **to one side**, to the left, to the right, askew, askance, aslant [➡ DIRECTION OF MOTION; 345] *Opposite*: straight

sidewinder *type of* **poisonous snake** [➡ SNAKES; 995]

side with *v* **back**, support, take somebody's side, be in somebody's camp, take somebody's part, be on somebody's side [➡ APPROVE AND CONFIRM; 646] *Opposite*: oppose

sidle *v* **edge**, creep, slither, snake, inch, slink [➡ MOVE SLOWLY; 314]

siege **1** *n* **blockade**, cordon, barrier, barricade, obstruction, restriction [➡ AGGRESSIVE EVENTS; 39] **2** *type of* **flock** [➡ GROUPS OF BIRDS; 1007]

siemens *type of* **SI unit** [➡ SIZE AND DIMENSIONS; 1192]

siesta *n* **rest**, nap, sleep, catnap, snooze (*informal*), forty winks (*informal*) [➡ SLEEP AND DREAM; 723]

sieve *type of* **utensil** [➡ TABLEWARE, FLATWARE, AND KITCHENWARE; 861]

sievert *type of* **SI unit** [➡ SIZE AND DIMENSIONS; 1192]

sift **1** *v* **sieve**, filter, separate, put through a sieve, strain [➡ SEPARATE AND DIVIDE; 401] **2** *v* **sort through**, go through, go through with a fine-tooth comb, examine, select, scrutinize [➡ SEEK POSSESSION AND SEARCH; 456]

sigh **1** *v* **exhale**, heave a sigh, moan, groan, breathe [➡ SOUND EMISSION BY PEOPLE; 363] *Opposite*: inhale **2** *v* **yearn**, long, hanker, pine, want, desire [➡ DESIRE AND WANT; 579] *Opposite*: dislike **3** *n* **exhalation**, moan, groan, complaint, lament [➡ SOUNDS MADE BY PEOPLE; 1262]

sight **1** *n* **view**, spectacle, prospect, picture, scene, vista, vision, display [➡ VIEWS AND OUTLOOKS; 1073] **2** *n* **vision**, eyesight, ability to see [➡ SEE; 699] **3** *v* **notice**, catch sight of, spot, see, glimpse, observe, view, espy (*literary*) [➡ SEE; 699] *Opposite*: miss

sighted *adj* **seeing**, keen-sighted, partially sighted, near-sighted, farsighted, eagle-eyed, long-sighted (*UK*), short-sighted (*UK*) [➡ SEE; 699] *Opposite*: blind

sightless *adj* [➡ SEE; 699]

sightlessness *n* [➡ SEE; 699]

sights *n* **tourist attractions**, places of interest, highlights, wonders, marvels [➡ TRAVEL: SIGHTSEEING AND TOURISM; 321]

sightsee *v* [➡ TRAVEL: WAYS OF TRAVELING; 320]

sightseeing *n* **tourism**, visiting the attractions, going to places of interest, seeing the sights, exploration [➡ TRAVEL: SIGHTSEEING AND TOURISM; 321]

sightseer *n* **tourist**, visitor, day tripper, vacationer, holidaymaker (*UK*) [➡ TRAVEL: TRAVELERS AND WALKERS; 319] *Opposite*: resident

sign 1 *n* **symbol**, mark, emblem, insignia, logo, badge [➡ SYMBOLS, SIGNS, AND NUMBERS; 596] 2 *n* **signal**, indication, symptom, warning, clue, hint [➡ INDICATIONS, SIGNS, AND WARNINGS; 68] 3 *n* **notice**, poster, road sign, placard, billboard, hoarding (*UK*) [➡ SIGNPOSTS, SIGNALS, AND BILLBOARDS; 595] 4 *n* **trace**, track, trail, footprint, mark, scent [➡ REPRESENTATIONS AND GENERAL EXAMPLES; 65] 5 *n* **omen**, warning, portent, premonition, indication, prediction [➡ FATE, DESTINY, AND ASTROLOGY; 782] 6 *v* **autograph**, sign your name, initial, authorize, endorse [➡ NAME AND DESCRIBE; 665] 7 *v* **make signs**, signal, gesture, motion, indicate, gesticulate [➡ GESTURES AND GESTICULATION; 653] 8 *v* **employ**, contract, hire, engage, take on, retain, sign up [➡ CONFER STATUS; 458] *Opposite*: dismiss

signal 1 *n* **sign**, indication, gesture, indicator, motion, warning sign, hint, pointer [➡ GESTURES AND GESTICULATION; 653] 2 *v* **communicate**, indicate, suggest, intimate, hint, imply [➡ SUGGEST, HINT, AND COMMENT; 612] 3 *v* **gesture**, gesticulate, motion, sign, beckon, wave, nod [➡ GESTURES AND GESTICULATION; 653] 4 *v* **indicate**, mark, herald, portend, announce, usher in [➡ MEAN SOMETHING; 611]

signally *adv* **completely**, notably, totally, absolutely, one hundred percent, unmistakably, conspicuously, obviously [➡ ABSOLUTE AND ABSOLUTELY; 133]

signatory *n* **party**, participant, guarantor, countersigner, the undersigned, cosigner [➡ PEOPLE INVOLVED IN FINANCE; 804]

signature 1 *n* **name**, autograph, cross, mark, initials, John Hancock (*informal*), moniker (*slang*) [➡ SYMBOLS, SIGNS, AND NUMBERS; 596] 2 *adj* [➡ REPRESENTATIVE; 66]

signboard (*UK*) *n* **sign**, signpost, notice, road sign, billboard, hoarding (*UK*) [➡ SIGNPOSTS, SIGNALS, AND BILLBOARDS; 595]

significance 1 *n* **meaning**, implication, import, worth, connotation, consequence (*formal*) [➡ MEANING; 690] 2 *n* **importance**, impact, substance, weight, magnitude, consequence (*formal*), moment (*formal*) [➡ IMPORTANCE AND SIGNIFICANCE; 192] *Opposite*: meaninglessness

significant 1 *adj* **important**, major, noteworthy, momentous, substantial, weighty [➡ IMPORTANT; 194] *Opposite*: insignificant 2 *adj* **meaningful**, knowing, meaning, suggestive, expressive, pointed [➡ INTERESTING AND MEANINGFUL; 190] *Opposite*: blank 3 *adj* **considerable**, large, major, big, sizable, hefty, substantial [➡ LARGE; 1193] *Opposite*: paltry

significantly 1 *adv* **considerably**, appreciably, drastically, notably, radically, extensively, substantially, a lot [➡ TO A GREAT EXTENT; 132] 2 *adv* **meaningfully**, knowingly, suggestively, pointedly, expressively [➡ INTERESTING AND MEANINGFUL; 190] *Opposite*: innocently

significant other *n* **partner**, lover, spouse, other half, better half, cohabitee, domestic partner, spousal equivalent [➡ SEXUAL AND ROMANTIC RELATIONSHIPS; 964]

signification *n* **meaning**, sense, gist, significance, denotation, connotation [➡ MEANING; 690]

signify *v* **mean**, indicate, show, imply, suggest, be a sign of, denote, connote [➡ MEAN SOMETHING; 61]

signing 1 *n* **ratification**, validation, adoption, passing, authorization, formal acceptance [➡ PERMIT AND ALLOW; 669] *Opposite*: rejection 2 *n* **new employee**, new player, new arrival, recruit, acquisition [➡ WORKERS; 836]

sign on *v* **enlist**, sign up, enroll, put your name down for, register, join [➡ PARTICIPATE; 292]

signpost 1 *n* **signboard**, sign, notice, marker, road sign, finger post (*UK*) [➡ SIGNPOSTS, SIGNALS, AND BILLBOARDS; 595] 2 *n* **indication**, suggestion, pointer, marker, sign, signal [➡ INDICATIONS, SIGNS, AND WARNINGS; 68] 3 *v* **flag**, mark, indicate, label, designate, point out [➡ CLAIM, INSIST, AND EMPHASIZE; 614] *Opposite*: conceal

sign up 1 *v* **recruit**, employ, sign, take somebody on, contract, hire [➡ CONFER STATUS; 458] *Opposite*: fire 2 *v* **enlist**, join, enroll, become a member, put your name down, register, sign on, draft [➡ PARTICIPATE; 292] *Opposite*: quit

silage *n* **fodder**, feed, grass, forage [➡ ANIMAL FEED; 1168]

silence 1 *n* **quietness**, quiet, hush, stillness, peace, calm [➡ ABSENCE OF SOUND; 1257] *Opposite*: noise 2 *n* **muteness**, taciturnity, reticence, reserve, uncommunicativeness, dumbness [➡ RETICENT AND UNFORTHCOMING; 631] *Opposite*: chatter 3 *v* **make quiet**, hush, muzzle, quiet, shut up (*informal*), shush (*informal*) [➡ AVOID, PREVENT, LIMIT, AND CONTROL; 277] 4 *v* **stop**, put an end to, gag, stifle, suppress, quash, smother, curb [➡ CAUSE TO STOP; 266] *Opposite*: encourage

silent 1 *adj* **still**, hushed, soundless, noiseless, quiet, inaudible [➡ ABSENCE OF SOUND; 1257] *Opposite*: noisy 2 *adj* **unspoken**, unvoiced, voiceless, tacit, wordless, understood [➡ SECRET AND UNKNOWN; 179] *Opposite*: spoken 3 *adj* **mute**, tongue-tied, uncommunicative, taciturn, reticent, reserved, quiet [➡ RETICENT AND UNFORTHCOMING; 631] *Opposite*: talkative

Compare and Contrast: *silent, quiet, reticent, taciturn, uncommunicative*

CORE MEANING: not speaking or not saying much

silent not speaking or communicating at any particular time, especially through choice, or not inclined to speak much; *quiet* not inclined to speak much, often because of shyness; *reticent* unwilling to communicate very much, talk freely, or reveal all the facts; *taciturn* habitually reserved in speech and manner; *uncommunicative* not willing to say much, especially not to reveal information, or tending not to say much.

silently *adv* **noiselessly**, without a sound, soundlessly, wordlessly, mutely, inaudibly [➡ ABSENCE OF SOUND; 1257] *Opposite*: noisily

silhouette *n* **outline**, shape, shadow, profile, line, figure [➡ SHAPE; 1216]

silicate *type of* **mineral** [➡ MINERALS; 1277]

silk *type of* **fabric from animals** [➡ FABRICS; 1132]

silken *adj* **smooth**, soft, silky, silky-smooth, glossy, shiny, sleek [➡ PHYSICAL TEXTURE; 1222] *Opposite*: coarse

silkiness *n* [➡ PHYSICAL TEXTURE; 1222]

silkworm *type of* **stage of insect development** [➡ INSECT STAGES; 1020]

silky 1 *adj* **glossy**, smooth, soft, silken, silky-smooth, shiny, sleek [➡ PHYSICAL TEXTURE; 1222] *Opposite*: rough 2 *adj* **smooth**, honeyed, mellifluous, sweet, unctuous, refined [➡ SOFT, LOW, OR PLEASANT SOUNDS; 1265] *Opposite*: harsh

silky-smooth *adj* [➡ PHYSICAL TEXTURE; 1222]

sill *n* **ledge**, shelf, ridge, projection, windowsill [➡ WINDOWS; 1100]

silliness 1 *n* **stupidity**, ridiculousness, childishness, madness, idiocy, absurdity, inanity, folly [➡ BIZARRE AND PECULIAR; 257] *Opposite*: sense 2 *n* **triviality**, meaninglessness, mindlessness, puerility, inanity, senselessness, pointlessness [➡ UNIMPORTANT AND UNNECESSARY; 238] *Opposite*: importance

silly 1 *adj* **stupid**, ridiculous, impractical, childish, asinine, juvenile [➡ BIZARRE AND PECULIAR; 257] *Opposite*: sensible 2 *adj* **trivial**, meaningless, mindless, puerile, senseless, pointless, inane [➡ UNIMPORTANT AND UNNECESSARY; 238] *Opposite*: important

silo *type of* **storage space** [➡ STORES AND STORAGE BUILDINGS; 1088]

silt *n* **deposit**, mud, sediment, sludge, residue [➡ EROSION PRODUCTS AND SOIL; 1058]

Silurian *type of* **period** [➡ EPOCHS AND ERAS; 89]

silver 1 *type of* **metal** [➡ METALS; 1276] 2 *type of* **white** [➡ COLORS; 1224]

silver birch *type of* **deciduous tree** [➡ DECIDUOUS TREES; 1028]

silver gray *type of* **gray** [➡ COLORS; 1224]

silver jubilee *n* [➡ CEREMONIES AND ANNIVERSARIES; 38]

silver-plated *adj* [➡ METALS; 1276]

silver-tongued *adj* **eloquent**, smooth-talking, grandiloquent, fluent, flattering, persuasive [➡ ELOQUENT, TALKATIVE, AND LONG-WINDED; 632] *Opposite*: tongue-tied

silverware *n* [➡ TABLEWARE, FLATWARE, AND KITCHENWARE; 861]

silvery *adj* **silver**, gray, hoary, shiny [➡ DESCRIBING COLORS; 1226]

similar *adj* **alike**, like, comparable, parallel, analogous, related, akin [➡ SIMILARITY; 148] *Opposite*: dissimilar

similarity *n* **resemblance**, comparison, likeness, parallel, correspondence, connection, match, relationship [➡ SIMILARITY; 148] *Opposite*: difference

similarly 1 *adv* **likewise**, also, in the same way, correspondingly, equally, by the same token [➡ ALSO; 138] *Opposite*: on the contrary 2 *adv* **alike**, in the same way, comparably, analogously, relatedly [➡ SIMILARITY; 148] *Opposite*: differently

simile *n* [➡ FIGURES OF SPEECH; 673]

similitude (*formal*) *n* **similarity**, resemblance, likeness, sameness, semblance, identicalness [➡ SIMILARITY; 148] *Opposite*: difference

simmer 1 *v* **boil**, bubble, cook [➡ COOKING AND FOOD PREPARATION; 353] 2 *v* **seethe**, rumble, bubble, boil, fester, smoulder [➡ FROTH AND EFFERVESCE; 389]

simmer down *v* **cool down**, calm down, settle down, regain your self-control, compose yourself, back off, cool off (*informal*), cool it (*slang*), chill out (*slang*) [➡ CHANGE OF MOOD AND COMPOSURE; 580] *Opposite*: blow your top (*informal*)

simoom *type of* **wind** [➡ WINDY AND STORMY WEATHER; 1053]

simper 1 *v* **smirk**, grimace, sneer, look smug, look coy, grin, smile [➡ FACIAL EXPRESSIONS AND BLUSHING; 651] *Opposite*: frown 2 *n* **grimace**, smirk, sneer, smug look, coy look [➡ FACIAL EXPRESSIONS AND BLUSHING; 651] *Opposite*: frown

simple 1 *adj* **easy**, straightforward, uncomplicated, trouble-free, effortless, undemanding [➡ EASE AND SIMPLICITY; 200] *Opposite*: difficult 2 *adj* **plain**, minimal, unadorned, unfussy, down-to-earth, clean, clear-cut, regular, unpretentious, austere [➡ PLAIN; 232] *Opposite*: fancy 3 *adj* **humble**, modest, unassuming, unpretentious, meek, artless [➡ NATURALNESS; 497] *Opposite*: pretentious 4 *adj* **guileless**, ingenuous, naive, unsophisticated, green, unworldly [➡ LEVELS OF EDUCATION AND SOPHISTICATION; 894] *Opposite*: sophisticated

See Compare and Contrast at **easy**.

simple-minded 1 *adj* **naive**, childlike, unsophisticated, artless, guileless, ingenuous, innocent, candid [➡ LEVELS OF EDUCATION AND SOPHISTICATION; 894] *Opposite*: sophisticated 2 *adj* **simplistic**, crude, basic, one-dimensional, unsophisticated [➡ THE NATURE OF IDEAS; 771] *Opposite*: subtle

simplicity 1 *n* **ease**, straightforwardness, effortlessness, easiness, uncomplicatedness [➡ EASE AND SIMPLICITY; 200] *Opposite*: difficulty 2 *n* **plainness**, minimalism, unfussiness, cleanness, lack of adornment, austerity [➡ PLAIN; 232] 3 *n* **humility**, modesty, unpretentiousness, meekness, unassumingness [➡ NATURALNESS; 497] *Opposite*: pride 4 *n* **guilelessness**, naiveté, ingenuousness, lack of sophistication, artlessness, candor, innocence [➡ LEVELS OF EDUCATION AND SOPHISTICATION; 894] *Opposite*: sophistication

simplified *adj* **cut down**, basic, easy, abridged, shortened [➡ EASE AND SIMPLICITY; 200] *Opposite*: complex

simplify *v* **make simpler**, make easier, make straightforward, abridge, shorten, streamline, reduce to the bare bones [➡ CHANGE; 372] *Opposite*: complicate

simplistic *adj* **naive**, unsophisticated, crude, basic, one-dimensional, simple-minded [➡ THE NATURE OF IDEAS; 771] *Opposite*: sophisticated

simply 1 *adv* **just**, only, merely, purely, basically, solely [➡ ABSOLUTE AND ABSOLUTELY; 133] **2** *adv* **plainly**, minimally, cleanly, austerely, unpretentiously [➡ PLAIN; 232] *Opposite*: elaborately **3** *adv* **modestly**, humbly, unassumingly, meekly, unpretentiously, artlessly [➡ NATURALNESS; 497] *Opposite*: proudly **4** *adv* **easily**, straightforwardly, in basic terms, in simple terms, in words of one syllable, crudely [➡ EASE AND SIMPLICITY; 200] *Opposite*: elaborately **5** *adv* **naively**, guilelessly, ingenuously, candidly, innocently, naturally [➡ LEVELS OF EDUCATION AND SOPHISTICATION; 894] *Opposite*: knowingly **6** *adv* **frankly**, absolutely, obviously, undeniably, unquestionably, easily [➡ CERTAIN; 174]

simulate 1 *v* **replicate**, reproduce, imitate, suggest, copy, create, conjure up, mock up [➡ PRETEND AND MIMIC; 60] **2** *v* **fake**, pretend, feign, put on, sham, act out [➡ PRETEND AND MIMIC; 60] **3** *v* **mimic**, ape, copy, imitate, parrot, take off (*informal*) [➡ PRETEND AND MIMIC; 60]

simulated 1 *adj* **virtual**, cyber-, computer-generated [➡ FALSE AND UNREAL; 173] **2** *adj* **fake**, imitation, pretend, counterfeit, sham, fabricated [➡ FALSE AND UNREAL; 173] *Opposite*: genuine

simulation *n* **imitation**, reproduction, replication, recreation, mock-up, model [➡ FALSE AND UNREAL; 173]

simulator *n* **simulant**, emulator, trainer [➡ COMPUTERS AND COMPUTING; 1127]

simulcast *v* [➡ TELEVISION AND RADIO; 606]

simultaneity *n* [➡ CONCURRENT AND CONTEMPORANEOUS; 164]

simultaneous *adj* **concurrent**, immediate, instantaneous, real-time, synchronized, coinciding, coincident [➡ CONCURRENT AND CONTEMPORANEOUS; 164] *Opposite*: separate

sin 1 *n* **crime**, misdemeanor, transgression, misdeed, wrongdoing, lapse [➡ MORALLY BAD OR IMPROPER; 775] *Opposite*: good deed **2** *n* **wickedness**, iniquity, depravity, immorality, debauchery, evil, turpitude (*formal*) [➡ RELIGIOUS CONCEPTS; 776] *Opposite*: goodness **3** *v* **transgress**, do wrong, commit a crime, err, lapse, be led astray, succumb to temptation [➡ RELIGIONS AND RELIGIOUS PRACTICES; 777]

since 1 *conj* **as**, because, given that, seeing as, in view of the fact that, while [➡ CAUSATION; 168] **2** *adv* **meanwhile**, in the meantime, subsequently, later, then [➡ AFTER, LAST, AND FOLLOWING; 165]

sincere 1 *adj* **honest**, open, frank, natural, straight, unaffected, candid [➡ NATURALNESS; 497] *Opposite*: disingenuous **2** *adj* **heartfelt**, genuine, truthful, earnest, serious, authentic [➡ HONEST AND RELIABLE; 502] *Opposite*: insincere

sincerely 1 *adv* **honestly**, openly, frankly, naturally, unaffectedly, candidly [➡ NATURALNESS; 497] *Opposite*: disingenuously **2** *adv* **genuinely**, truthfully, earnestly, seriously, authentically, really, truly [➡ HONEST AND RELIABLE; 502] *Opposite*: insincerely

sincerity *n* **genuineness**, honesty, earnestness, naturalness, unaffectedness, authenticity, candor [➡ HONEST AND OPEN; 630] *Opposite*: insincerity

since time began *adv* [➡ PERMANENCE: WITHOUT END; 94]

since time immemorial *adv* **since time began**, always, for all time, for as long as anyone can remember, for donkey's years (*UK*) [➡ PERMANENCE: WITHOUT END; 94]

sinecure *n* **easy ride**, plum job, soft option, cushy job, plum (*informal*), cushy number (*UK*) [➡ EASY WORK; 299]

sine qua non *n* **prerequisite**, essential condition, precondition, requirement, necessity, must, must-have [➡ MOST IMPORTANT THING; 197]

sinew 1 *n* (*literary*) **strength**, vigor, muscularity, brawn, power, stamina [➡ MUSCLES AND MUSCULATURE; 479] *Opposite*: frailty **2** *type of* **muscle or tendon** [➡ THE MUSCLES; 718]

sinewy *adj* **wiry**, lean, strong, muscly, brawny, powerful [➡ BUILD; 477] *Opposite*: frail

sinfonia *type of* **musical form** [➡ MUSIC, SONGS, AND SINGING; 907]

sinfonietta *type of* **band** [➡ MUSICIANS AND SINGERS; 908]

sinful *adj* **wicked**, bad, evil, corrupt, errant, sinning, aberrant, immoral, iniquitous [➡ RELIGIOUS CONCEPTS; 776] *Opposite*: virtuous

sinfulness *n* [➡ RELIGIOUS CONCEPTS; 776]

sing 1 *v* **croon**, chant, hum, warble, carol, intone (*formal*) [➡ MUSIC, SONGS, AND SINGING; 907] **2** *v* **resonate**, buzz, hum, purr, vibrate, reverberate [➡ EMIT CONTINUOUS SOUNDS; 366] **3** *v* (*slang*) **confess**, talk, own up, implicate, give the game away, let on, blow somebody's cover, let the cat out of the bag, spill the beans (*informal*), come clean (*informal*), grass (*slang*) [➡ BETRAY CONFIDENCES AND GOSSIP; 618]

singe *v* **scorch**, burn, char, sear [➡ FIRE, FLAMMABILITY, AND BURNING; 1165]

singed *adj* [➡ FIRE, FLAMMABILITY, AND BURNING; 1165]

singer 1 *n* **vocalist**, songster, lead singer, soloist [➡ MUSICIANS AND SINGERS; 908] **2** *type of* **entertainer** [➡ WORKERS IN ENTERTAINMENT AND MEDIA; 873]

singing 1 *n* **vocals**, songs, vocal music, chanting, warbling, crooning [➡ MUSIC, SONGS, AND SINGING; 907] **2** *adj* **vocal**, choral, melodic, whistling, humming, ringing [➡ MUSICAL TERMS; 912] *Opposite*: instrumental

single 1 *adj* **solitary**, on its own, lone, sole, solo, only [➡ SOLITARINESS; 941] **2** *adj* **particular**, distinct, separate, specific, definite [➡ UNRELATEDNESS AND SEPARATENESS; 146] *Opposite*: general **3** *adj* **unmarried**, unattached, lone, free [➡ MARITAL STATUS; 890] *Opposite*: attached **4** *n* **record**, song, track, release [➡ RECORDINGS AND PLAYERS; 911]

single bed *type of* **bed** [➡ FURNITURE; 858]

single-breasted jacket *type of* **jacket** [➡ GARMENTS AND OUTFITS; 865]

single-handed 1 *adj* **unassisted**, unaided, lone, solo, unaccompanied [➡ ACTING INDEPENDENTLY; 284] *Opposite*: assisted **2** *adv* **by yourself**, on your own, alone, without help, without assistance, solo, single-handedly [➡ ACTING INDEPENDENTLY; 284]

single-lens reflex *type of* **photographic equipment** [➡ PHOTOGRAPHY AND PHOTOGRAPHIC EQUIPMENT; 1122]

single-minded *adj* **focused**, dedicated, steadfast, resolute, dogged, driven, persistent, tenacious, obsessed, unswerving, unwavering [➡ STRENGTH OF WILL; 501] *Opposite*: unfocused

single-mindedness *n* **sense of purpose**, concentration, application, attention, focus, vision, dedication, determination, drive, perseverance [➡ STRENGTH OF WILL; 501] *Opposite*: aimlessness

single out *v* **pick out**, choose, select, identify, pull out, pluck out, pick on, set apart, differentiate, distinguish, isolate [➡ MAKE DECISIONS AND CHOICES; 752]

single parent *type of* **older relative** [➡ OLDER GENERATION RELATIVES; 959]

single party rule *n* [➡ STYLES AND SYSTEMS OF GOVERNMENT; 806]

singleton *type of* **offspring** [➡ YOUNGER GENERATION RELATIVES; 958]

singly *adv* **individually**, alone, one by one, one at a time, piecemeal, separately [➡ UNRELATEDNESS AND SEPARATENESS; 146] *Opposite*: together

sing out *v* **call out**, pipe up, speak up, speak out, shout, yell, let everybody know [➡ UTTER AND PRONOUNCE; 608]

sing the praises of *v* **eulogize**, acclaim, praise, lionize, extol, rave [➡ PRAISE AND ENCOURAGE; 647] *Opposite*: criticize

singular *adj* **remarkable**, extraordinary, particular, outstanding, curious, odd, unusual [➡ EXTRAORDINARY: UNCOMMON; 205]

singularity *n* **distinctiveness**, individuality, originality, uniqueness, peculiarity [➡ EXTRAORDINARY: UNCOMMON; 205]

sing your own praises *v* **blow your own horn**, fly your own kite, swagger, try to make an impression, brag, boast [➡ BOAST; 616]

sinister *adj* **menacing**, ominous, threatening, evil, disturbing, creepy (*informal*), baleful [➡ DANGEROUS; 236]

sink 1 *v* **go under**, go down, go under the surface, be submerged, go downwards, descend, drop [➡ GO DOWNWARD; 307] *Opposite*: float 2 *v* **fall**, descend, drop, decline, go down, lapse, worsen, deteriorate [➡ GET WORSE; 381] *Opposite*: rise 3 *v* **dig**, drill, mine, bore [➡ BUILD; 352] 4 *n* **basin**, bowl, hand basin, washbasin [➡ FIXTURES; 859]

sink in *v* **go in**, enter, penetrate, diffuse, permeate, be absorbed [➡ MOVE PAST, INTO, OR THROUGH SOMETHING; 331]

sink without trace *v* [➡ DISAPPEAR; 4]

sinless *adj* [➡ RELIGIOUS CONCEPTS; 776]

sinner *n* [➡ RELIGIOUS CONCEPTS; 776]

sinuous *adj* **lithe**, supple, twisting, winding, graceful, flowing [➡ DESCRIBING BODY MOVEMENTS; 288]

sip 1 *v* **taste**, drink, swallow, sup [➡ DRINK; 711] 2 *n* **drink**, swallow, taste, drop, mouthful, nip [➡ DRINK; 711]

siphon *v* **draw off**, tap, drain off [➡ EMPTY AND UNLOAD; 407]

siren *n* **alarm**, alert, warning, alarm bell, danger signal, distress signal [➡ SIGNALING; 1140]

sirloin *type of* **steak** [➡ TYPES AND CUTS OF MEAT; 1177]

sirocco *type of* **wind** [➡ WINDY AND STORMY WEATHER; 1053]

sisal *type of* **fiber** [➡ PLANT MATERIALS; 1133]

sister 1 *type of* **same-generation relative** [➡ SAME-GENERATION RELATIVES; 957] 2 *n* **nun**, holy sister, religious, vestal (*literary*) [➡ RELIGIOUS PEOPLE; 778] 3 *n* **friend**, supporter, ally, associate

[➡ FRIENDS AND GUESTS; 963] 4 *adj* **fellow**, parallel, associated, corresponding, equivalent, related [➡ RELATED; 142]

sisterhood *n* [➡ GROUPS WITH A COMMON INTEREST; 938]

sister-in-law *type of* **in-law** [➡ RELATIVES BY MARRIAGE; 960]

sit 1 *v* **be seated**, sit down, take a seat, take the weight off your feet, park yourself, take a pew [➡ ASSUME A POSITION; 317] *Opposite*: stand 2 *v* **assemble**, meet, convene, be in session [➡ GET CLOSER TOGETHER; 310] *Opposite*: disperse 3 *v* **be placed**, be positioned, lie, rest, be on top of, be situated [➡ EXIST IN A PLACE; 19]

sitar *type of* **stringed instrument** [➡ MUSICAL INSTRUMENTS; 910]

sit around *v* **kill time**, do nothing, lounge around, hang around, hang out (*informal*) [➡ LACK OF ACTIVITY OR MOTION; 342]

sitcom (*informal*) *type of* **broadcast** [➡ TELEVISION AND RADIO; 606]

sit down *v* **be seated**, take a seat, take the weight off your feet, park yourself, take a pew [➡ ASSUME A POSITION; 317] *Opposite*: stand up

sit-down (*informal*) *n* **rest**, break, breather (*informal*), respite [➡ PERIODS OF REST; 91]

site 1 *n* **place**, location, spot, position [➡ PLACE; 1065] 2 *v* **put**, position, place, situate, locate, establish, set [➡ POSITION SOMETHING; 325]

sit-in *n* **protest**, demonstration, rally, march, vigil, demo (*informal*) [➡ MEETINGS AND ASSEMBLIES; 43]

sit on your heels *v* [➡ LACK OF ACTIVITY OR MOTION; 342]

sitting *n* **session**, meeting, hearing [➡ MEETINGS AND ASSEMBLIES; 43]

sitting room *type of* **room in the home** [➡ TYPES OF ROOMS; 1097]

situate *v* **place**, set, put, locate, position, station, site, establish [➡ POSITION SOMETHING; 325]

situated (*formal*) *adj* **located**, positioned, set, placed, sited, found [➡ GENERAL LOCATIONS; 158]

situation 1 *n* **state of affairs**, circumstances, state, condition, status quo [➡ SITUATIONS; 71] 2 *n* **location**, position, site, place, setting, spot [➡ PLACE; 1065]

sitz bath *type of* **plumbing fixtures** [➡ FIXTURES; 859]

SI unit *n* [➡ SIZE AND DIMENSIONS; 1192]

sixth sense *n* **intuition**, feeling, hunch, ESP [➡ THE SUPERNATURAL; 787]

sizable *adj* **substantial**, generous, good-sized, ample, large, considerable, comfortable, spacious [➡ LARGE; 1193]

size *n* **dimension**, mass, bulk, amount, extent, volume, range, magnitude [➡ SIZE AND DIMENSIONS; 1192]

sizeable *see* **sizable**

size up *v* **assess**, look somebody up and down, take stock of, evaluate, appraise [➡ ASSESS QUALITY; 755]

sizzle 1 *v* **crackle**, hiss, sputter, spit [➡ EMIT CONTINUOUS SOUNDS; 366] 2 *type of* **continuous sound** [➡ CONTINUOUS SOUNDS; 1258]

sizzling (*informal*) *adj* **boiling**, red-hot, baking, stifling, steamy, blistering, sweltering, blazing, scorching

(*informal*), roasting (*informal*) [➡ TEMPERATURE: HOT; 1229] *Opposite*: freezing

ska *type of* **dance music** [➡ MUSIC, SONGS, AND SINGING; 907]

skate *type of* **flatfish** [➡ OCEAN FISH; 1009]

skateboarding *type of* **extreme sport** [➡ HOBBIES, GAMES, AND SPORTS; 875]

skean *type of* **sword or knife** [➡ SWORDS AND KNIVES; 1157]

skedaddle (*slang*) *v* [➡ RUN AWAY AND AVOID; 10]

skein 1 *n* **hank**, ball, bundle, length, coil, reel [➡ AMOUNTS OF SOLID OR SEMISOLID; 115] 2 *type of* **flock** [➡ GROUPS OF BIRDS; 1007]

skeletal *adj* **thin**, emaciated, skinny, gaunt, wasted, undernourished [➡ BUILD; 477] *Opposite*: obese

skeleton 1 *n* **frame**, bones, carcass [➡ THE BONES AND JOINTS; 719] 2 *n* **plan**, outline, framework, sketch, bare bones (*informal*) [➡ REPRESENTATIONS AND GENERAL EXAMPLES; 65] 3 *adj* **minimum**, basic, essential, minimal [➡ FUNDAMENTAL; 195] *Opposite*: full

skeptic *n* **cynic**, disbeliever, doubter, doubting Thomas, questioner [➡ UNCERTAINTY; 559] *Opposite*: believer

skeptical *adj* **cynical**, disbelieving, doubtful, doubting, unconvinced, incredulous, uncertain, distrustful, dubious, suspicious, questioning [➡ UNCERTAINTY; 559] *Opposite*: convinced

See Compare and Contrast at **doubtful**.

skepticism *n* **cynicism**, disbelief, doubt, incredulity, uncertainty, suspicion, distrust [➡ UNCERTAINTY; 559] *Opposite*: conviction

sketch 1 *n* **draft**, plan, drawing, rough copy, rough, rough draft, first attempt, outline [➡ DRAWINGS, CHARTS, AND TABLES; 594] 2 *v* **draw**, outline, draft, delineate, block in, rough out [➡ CREATE IMAGES; 356]

sketchbook *n* [➡ WRITING AND DRAWING IMPLEMENTS, AND MEDIA; 601]

sketchiness *n* [➡ VAGUENESS; 243]

sketchpad *n* [➡ WRITING AND DRAWING IMPLEMENTS, AND MEDIA; 601]

sketchy *adj* **vague**, unclear, hazy, imprecise, woolly, rough, superficial [➡ VAGUENESS; 243] *Opposite*: detailed

skew 1 *v* **tilt**, slant, twist, angle, slope, tip [➡ MOVE SOMETHING INTO A NEW POSITION OR OVERTURN; 330] *Opposite*: straighten 2 *v* **distort**, bias, slant, twist, spin, weight, color [➡ FALSIFY AND CHEAT; 176]

skewbald *adj* [➡ DESCRIBING PATTERNS; 1227]

skewed 1 *adj* **tilted**, slanted, twisted, crooked, askew, lopsided, cockeyed, at an angle, off-center, out of true [➡ ORIENTATION AND ALIGNMENT; 1223] *Opposite*: straight 2 *adj* **distorted**, biased, slanted, prejudiced, partial, colored, one-sided [➡ INCORRECT AND ERRONEOUS; 222] *Opposite*: objective

skewer 1 *n* **spit**, brochette, spike, spear, needle, pin, point, rod, stick [➡ STICKS, POLES, AND WEDGES; 1254] 2 *v* **impale**, spear, spike, pierce, stab, bayonet, run through (*literary*) [➡ STAB; 416]

skid *v* **slip**, slide, slew, slither, spin out [➡ CHANGE DIRECTION OF MOTION; 344]

skiff *type of* **small vessel** [➡ SHIPS AND BOATS; 1150]

skiing *type of* **winter sport** [➡ HOBBIES, GAMES, AND SPORTS; 875]

ski jump *type of* **winter sport** [➡ HOBBIES, GAMES, AND SPORTS; 875]

skill *n* **ability**, talent, cleverness, dexterity, expertise, proficiency, skillfulness, handiness, knack, aptitude, competence, flair [➡ SKILLS, TALENTS, AND ABILITIES; 526]

See Compare and Contrast at **ability**.

skilled *adj* **accomplished**, expert, capable, able, trained, skillful, experienced, practiced, proficient, competent, consummate [➡ TALENTED AND SKILLFUL; 527] *Opposite*: untrained

skillet *n* [➡ TABLEWARE, FLATWARE, AND KITCHENWARE; 861]

skillful *adj* **clever**, adroit, dexterous, skilled, expert, practiced, adept, competent, proficient [➡ TALENTED AND SKILLFUL; 527] *Opposite*: incompetent

skillfulness *n* [➡ SKILLS, TALENTS, AND ABILITIES; 526]

skim 1 *v* **glide**, fly, float, soar [➡ MOVE FAST; 313] 2 *v* **scan**, speed-read, browse, glance at, flick through [➡ READ; 758] *Opposite*: peruse

skim off *v* **cull**, cream off, hive off, handpick, choose, select, opt for, cherry-pick, go for (*informal*), plump for (*UK*) [➡ MAKE DECISIONS AND CHOICES; 752]

skimp *v* **stint**, withhold, hold back on, be sparing with, pinch, spare [➡ FORGO AND DENY ONESELF; 449] *Opposite*: lavish

skimpy *adj* **meager**, insufficient, scanty, inadequate, sparse, scant [➡ TOO FEW, TOO LITTLE; 122] *Opposite*: generous

skin 1 *n* **hide**, pelt, fur, coat [➡ THE SKIN; 720] 2 *n* **casing**, covering, membrane, crust, coating, rind, peel, film [➡ COVERS AND COATINGS; 1246] 3 *part of* **fruit** [➡ FRUIT AND VEGETABLES; 1176] 4 *v* **peel**, pare, excoriate, desquamate [➡ COOKING AND FOOD PREPARATION; 353] 5 *v* **graze**, scrape, flay, scuff [➡ WOUND A PERSON OR ANIMAL; 383]

skin-and-bone *adj* [➡ BUILD; 477]

skin and bones *adj* [➡ BUILD; 477]

skincare product *n* [➡ PERSONAL HYGIENE; 491]

skin color *n* [➡ COMPLEXION; 480]

skin-deep *adj* **superficial**, on the surface, on the outside, shallow, artificial, external [➡ UNIMPORTANT AND UNNECESSARY; 238]

skinflint *n* **miser**, niggard, pinchpenny, cheapskate (*informal*), penny pincher (*informal*), scrooge (*informal*) [➡ FINANCIALLY MEAN PEOPLE; 952]

skink *type of* **reptile** [➡ REPTILES; 994]

skinniness *n* **gauntness**, scrawniness, thinness, boniness, leanness, emaciation [➡ BUILD; 477] *Opposite*: plumpness

skinny *adj* **thin**, lean, undernourished, emaciated, scrawny, skeletal, scraggy [➡ BUILD; 477] *Opposite*: fat

See Compare and Contrast at **thin**.

skintight *adj* [➡ DESCRIBING CLOTHES; 869]

skin tone *n* **skin color**, complexion, skin, facial appearance, natural coloring [➡ COMPLEXION; 480]

skip 1 *v* **hop**, bounce, prance, gambol, caper, frisk [➡ BOUNCE, UNDULATE, AND VIBRATE; 308] **2** *v* **omit**, leave out, miss, pass over, miss out (*UK*) [➡ NOT PAY ATTENTION; 764] **3** *v* (*informal*) **avoid**, miss, cut (*informal*) [➡ RUN AWAY AND AVOID; 10] *Opposite:* attend

skiplane *type of* **civil aircraft** [➡ AIRCRAFT; 1148]

skipper (*informal*) *n* **captain**, boss, chief, head, person in charge [➡ BOSSES AND MANAGEMENT; 965]

skirmish 1 *n* **battle**, fight, engagement, scuffle, clash, conflict, brawl, encounter, tussle [➡ AGGRESSIVE EVENTS; 39] **2** *v* **clash**, fight, scuffle, tussle, scrap [➡ COMPETE, CONTEND, AND COMBAT; 303]

See Compare and Contrast at **fight.**

skirt 1 *v* **border**, edge, adjoin, abut, neighbor, hug, line [➡ EXIST IN CLOSE PROXIMITY; 21] **2** *v* **go around**, avoid, evade, bypass, edge past, circle [➡ MOVE PAST, INTO, OR THROUGH SOMETHING; 331] **3** *v* **skim over**, pass over, avoid, evade, bypass, duck [➡ NOT PAY ATTENTION; 764] *Opposite:* tackle

skirt

◆ *types of skirts*
dirndl, hobble skirt, kilt, maxi skirt, miniskirt, pencil skirt, sarong, tutu, wraparound

skit *n* **parody**, satire, spoof, sketch, burlesque, sendup (*informal*) [➡ JOKES AND TEASING; 674]

skittish 1 *adj* **wary**, jumpy, edgy, nervous, uneasy, panicky, flappable [➡ INSECURITY AND LOSS OF COMPOSURE; 544] **2** *adj* **playful**, lively, frisky, excited, restless, animated [➡ POSITIVE IMPATIENCE, ENTHUSIASM, AND ALERTNESS; 537]

skua *type of* **sea bird** [➡ SEA BIRDS; 1002]

skulduggery (*humorous*) *n* **trickery**, tricks, dishonesty, cheating, mischief, monkey business (*informal*), shenanigans (*informal*) [➡ BAD BEHAVIOR OR ACTIONS; 254] *Opposite:* honesty

skulk 1 *v* **lurk**, loiter, creep, prowl, lie in wait [➡ LACK OF ACTIVITY OR MOTION; 342] **2** *type of* **herd** [➡ GROUPS OF ANIMALS; 993]

skull 1 *n* (*informal*) **mind**, brain, head, noggin, pate (*archaic or humorous*) [➡ PARTS OF THE BODY: HEAD; 692] **2** *type of* **bone** [➡ THE BONES AND JOINTS; 719]

skullcap *type of* **headgear** [➡ ACCESSORIES, MILLINERY, AND LINGERIE; 867]

skunk *type of* **small mammal** [➡ SMALL MAMMALS; 990]

sky *n* **heaven**, blue, atmosphere, firmament (*literary*) [➡ THE EARTH'S ATMOSPHERE; 1040]

sky blue *type of* **blue** [➡ COLORS; 1224]

skydive *v* [➡ HOBBIES, GAMES, AND SPORTS; 875]

sky-high *adj* **excessive**, very high, elevated, exorbitant, over-the-top (*informal*) [➡ EXPENSIVE AND OVERPRICED; 247]

skyjack *v* **hijack**, seize, take over, take control of, capture, commandeer [➡ STEAL AND ROB; 426]

skylark *type of* **songbird** [➡ SONGBIRDS; 1003]

skylight *type of* **window** [➡ WINDOWS; 1100]

skyline *n* **horizon**, distant, prospect, vista [➡ VIEWS AND OUTLOOKS; 1073]

skyrocket (*informal*) *v* **rise steeply**, hit the roof, go through the ceiling, climb sharply, shoot up, increase rapidly [➡ CHANGE OF SIZE: BIGGER; 392] *Opposite:* plummet

skyscraper *n* **multistory building**, tower, high-rise, high-rise building [➡ RESIDENTIAL BUILDINGS; 1078]

skysurfing *type of* **extreme sport** [➡ HOBBIES, GAMES, AND SPORTS; 875]

skyward 1 *adv* **heavenward**, upward, up, above, aloft, into the sky, into the clouds [➡ DIRECTION OF MOTION; 345] **2** *adj* **upward**, heavenward, aloft [➡ DIRECTION OF MOTION; 345]

slab *n* **lump**, chunk, block, hunk, piece, portion, wedge [➡ LARGE PIECES; 130]

slack 1 *adj* **loose**, limp, relaxed, baggy, floppy, drooping, sagging [➡ SHAPELESSNESS; 1219] *Opposite:* taut **2** *adj* **careless**, inattentive, idle, inefficient, unprofessional, lazy, inactive, negligent, remiss, sloppy, slovenly, workshy (*UK*) [➡ LIFELESS, LAZY, AND UNENTHUSIASTIC; 506] *Opposite:* diligent **3** *adj* **slow-moving**, slow, dull, quiet, sluggish [➡ BORING AND UNINTERESTING; 234] *Opposite:* brisk

slacken *v* **loosen**, relax, release, slacken off [➡ CHANGE OF INTENSITY: LESS; 395] *Opposite:* tighten

slacker *n* **idler**, lazybones (*informal*), loafer, shirker, freeloader (*informal*) [➡ LAZY OR UNSUCCESSFUL PEOPLE; 948]

slackly *adv* **loosely**, limply, floppily, droopily [➡ MALLEABLE AND ELASTIC; 1212] *Opposite:* tightly

slackness 1 *n* **looseness**, limpness, bagginess, floppiness, droopiness [➡ SHAPELESSNESS; 1219] *Opposite:* tautness **2** *n* **carelessness**, negligence, laxity, inattention, laziness, sloppiness (*informal*) [➡ LIFELESS, LAZY, AND UNENTHUSIASTIC; 506] *Opposite:* meticulousness

slacks *type of* **pants** [➡ GARMENTS AND OUTFITS; 865]

slag *n* [➡ UNPLEASANT, DIRTY, AND TOXIC SUBSTANCES; 1268]

slake *v* **quench**, satisfy, satiate, sate, extinguish [➡ CAUSE TO STOP; 266] *Opposite:* exacerbate

slalom *type of* **winter sport** [➡ HOBBIES, GAMES, AND SPORTS; 875]

slam 1 *v* (*informal*) **criticize**, berate, disparage, deride, pan (*informal*), roast (*informal*), slate (*UK*) [➡ ACCUSE, BLAME, AND CRITICIZE; 641] *Opposite:* praise **2** *type of* **impact sound** [➡ IMPACT SOUNDS; 1260]

slam-dunk 1 *n* [➡ SPORTS TERMS; 877] **2** *n* (*informal*) [➡ AMAZING THINGS; 211]

slam into *v* [➡ CONTACT: IMPACT; 413]

slammer (*slang*) *n* [➡ BUILDINGS FOR CONFINING PEOPLE; 1094]

slander 1 *n* **defamation**, character assassination, disparagement, vilification, calumny (*formal*) [➡ INSULTS, ABUSE, AND SWEARING; 658] **2** *n* **slur**, smear, slight, insult, calumny

(*formal*) [➡ INSULTS, ABUSE, AND SWEARING; 658] **3** *v* insult, malign, slur, smear, disparage, vilify, slight, defame [➡ INSULTS, ABUSE, AND SWEARING; 658] *Opposite*: compliment

See Compare and Contrast at **malign**.

slanderer *n* [➡ PEOPLE WHO DECEIVE; 661]

slanderous *adj* libelous, defamatory, insulting, malicious, disparaging [➡ INSULTS, ABUSE, AND SWEARING; 658]

slang *n* jargon, vernacular, colloquial speech, dialect, argot [➡ THE SPOKEN WORD; 671]

See Compare and Contrast at **language**.

slanging match (*UK*) *n* argument, fight, shouting match, spat, quarrel, row [➡ ARGUMENTS; 47]

slant **1** *v* incline, lean, skew, slope, tilt, list [➡ MOVE SOMETHING: INTO A NEW POSITION OR OVERTURN; 330] **2** *n* angle, incline, diagonal, pitch, gradient, slope [➡ ORIENTATION AND ALIGNMENT; 1223] **3** *n* viewpoint, angle, attitude, point of view, perspective [➡ POINTS OF VIEW; 767]

slanted *adj* biased, prejudiced, one-sided, partial, unfair, distorted, imbalanced, skewed, colored [➡ THE NATURE OF IDEAS; 771] *Opposite*: balanced

slanting *adj* angled, at an angle, sloping, on a slope, oblique, diagonal, inclined, aslant, leaning, sideways [➡ ORIENTATION AND ALIGNMENT; 1223] *Opposite*: level

slantways *adv* diagonally, crossways, crosswise, at an angle, obliquely, transversely, aslant, askew, on the slant, slantwise [➡ ORIENTATION AND ALIGNMENT; 1223] *Opposite*: straight

slantwise *adv* diagonally, crosswise, crossways, at an angle, obliquely, transversely, aslant, askew, on the slant [➡ ORIENTATION AND ALIGNMENT; 1223] *Opposite*: straight

slap **1** *n* smack, blow, spank, cuff, clout, whack [➡ PHYSICAL ATTACK AND PUNISHMENT; 415] **2** *v* hit, smack, spank, cuff, swipe, clout, whack [➡ PHYSICAL ATTACK AND PUNISHMENT; 415]

slapdash *adj* sloppy (*informal*), messy, clumsy, careless, hasty, hurried, haphazard, shoddy [➡ INCAUTIOUS AND CARELESS; 283] *Opposite*: meticulous

slaphappy *adj* slapdash, careless, haphazard, hit-or-miss, irresponsible, casual, chaotic, hasty [➡ INCAUTIOUS AND CARELESS; 283] *Opposite*: meticulous

slapstick *n* farce, clowning, burlesque, comedy, humor, knockabout (*UK*) [➡ JOKES AND TEASING; 674]

slash **1** *v* cut, hack, slice, gash, slit, rip, lacerate [➡ TEAR, BREAK, AND CUT; 360] **2** *v* reduce, cut, lower, drop, decrease [➡ CHANGE OF SIZE: SMALLER; 393] *Opposite*: increase **3** *n* laceration, gash, slit, tear, rip, cut [➡ HOLES, GAPS, AND FORKS; 1252]

slat *n* plank, board, lath [➡ BUILDING MATERIALS; 1077]

slate **1** *n* [➡ BUILDING MATERIALS; 1077] **2** *type of* gray [➡ COLORS; 1224] **3** *type of* stone [➡ STONES, ROCKS, AND BOULDERS; 1057]

slate blue *type of* blue [➡ COLORS; 1224]

slatternly *adj* [➡ BADLY GROOMED; 483]

slaughter **1** *v* (*slang*) defeat, thrash, overwhelm, rout, crush, trounce, beat, hammer (*informal*) [➡ BEAT AND DEFEAT; 80] **2** *v* kill, murder, massacre, butcher, slay (*formal or literary*) [➡ KILL; 923] **3** *n* killing, murder, massacre, carnage, butchery [➡ CAUSES OF DEATH; 921]

See Compare and Contrast at **kill**.

slaughterhouse *type of* industrial site [➡ INDUSTRIAL BUILDINGS; 1087]

slave ant *type of* ant [➡ ANTS; 1014]

slave-making ant *type of* ant [➡ ANTS; 1014]

slaver *v* drool, slobber, dribble, salivate [➡ EXCRETION AND EXCRETA; 722]

slay (*formal or literary*) *v* kill, murder, assassinate, massacre, eliminate, slaughter, butcher, exterminate [➡ KILL; 923]

See Compare and Contrast at **kill**.

slayer (*formal or literary*) *n* killer, butcher, homicide, murderer, cause of death, executioner, parricide, exterminator, assassin, slaughterer, contract killer, eradicator, demolisher, destroyer [➡ PEOPLE WHO KILL; 924]

slaying *n* [➡ CAUSES OF DEATH; 921]

sleaze *n* corruption, dishonesty, malpractice, scandal, foul play, sharp practice, shenanigans (*informal*), skulduggery (*humorous*) [➡ MORALLY BAD OR IMPROPER; 775] *Opposite*: probity

sleaziness *n* [➡ MORALLY BAD OR IMPROPER; 775]

sleazy **1** *adj* seedy, sordid, squalid, grubby, grotty [➡ DISGUSTING AND REPULSIVE; 230] **2** *adj* corrupt, immoral, dishonest, shady, slimy, untrustworthy, crooked (*informal*) [➡ MORALLY BAD OR IMPROPER; 775] *Opposite*: honest

sled *type of* leisure vehicle [➡ VEHICLES; 1145]

sleek *adj* smooth, shiny, glossy, silky, lustrous [➡ PHYSICAL TEXTURE; 1222]

sleep **1** *n* slumber, nap, doze, siesta, catnap, snooze (*informal*), forty winks (*informal*) [➡ SLEEP AND DREAM; 723] **2** *v* be asleep, slumber, be dead to the world, nap, doze, catnap, have a siesta, take a nap, have forty winks (*informal*), snooze (*informal*), have a lie-down (*UK*) [➡ SLEEP AND DREAM; 723]

sleeper *part of* train [➡ RAILROADS; 1107]

sleepers *type of* sleepwear [➡ GARMENTS AND OUTFITS; 865]

sleepily *adv* drowsily, dozily, woozily, wearily, blearily, groggily [➡ TIRED, ASLEEP, AND UNCONSCIOUS; 738] *Opposite*: alertly

sleep in *v* oversleep, sleep late, stay in bed, snooze on, ignore the alarm, sleep too long [➡ SLEEP AND DREAM; 723]

sleepiness *n* drowsiness, tiredness, lethargy, somnolence, lassitude, torpor [➡ TIRED, ASLEEP, AND UNCONSCIOUS; 738] *Opposite*: alertness

sleeping car *part of* train [➡ RAILROADS; 1107]

sleeping policeman (*UK*) *n* [➡ TRAVEL: TRAFFIC PROBLEMS AND TRAFFIC MANAGEMENT; 323]

sleeping quarters *type of* **room in the home** [➡ TYPES OF ROOMS; 1097]

sleepless 1 *adj* **wakeful**, restless, disturbed, unsleeping, awake [➡ WIDE AWAKE AND CONSCIOUS; 735] 2 *adj* **alert**, active, vigilant, attentive, ready, lively [➡ POSITIVE IMPATIENCE, ENTHUSIASM, AND ALERTNESS; 537]

sleeplessness 1 *n* **insomnia**, wakefulness, restlessness [➡ WIDE AWAKE AND CONSCIOUS; 735] 2 *n* **alertness**, vigilance, readiness, liveliness [➡ POSITIVE IMPATIENCE, ENTHUSIASM, AND ALERTNESS; 537]

sleepwear *n* [➡ GARMENTS AND OUTFITS; 865]

sleepwear

◆ *types of sleepwear*
bathrobe, housecoat, negligee, nightcap, nightclothes, nightgown, nightie, nightshirt, nightwear, pajamas, peignoir, sleepers

sleepy 1 *adj* **drowsy**, tired, lethargic, heavy-eyed, sluggish, somnolent [➡ TIRED, ASLEEP, AND UNCONSCIOUS; 738] *Opposite*: alert 2 *adj* **quiet**, dull, slow, inactive, peaceful, boring [➡ BORING AND UNINTERESTING; 234] *Opposite*: lively

sleet *n* **slush**, snow, frozen rain [➡ COLD WEATHER; 1051]

sleeve 1 *n* **cover**, jacket, protective cover, envelope, dust jacket, outer cover, sheath, wrapper [➡ CONTAINERS, RECEPTACLES, AND PACKAGING; 1245] 2 *part of* **garment** [➡ PARTS OF A GARMENT; 870]

sleigh *type of* **leisure vehicle** [➡ VEHICLES; 1145]

sleight of hand *n* **dexterity**, skill, adroitness, cunning, trickery, surreptitiousness [➡ SKILLS, TALENTS, AND ABILITIES; 526]

slender 1 *adj* **slim**, slight, lean, trim, willowy [➡ BUILD; 477] *Opposite*: fat 2 *adj* **small**, slim, meager, slight, little [➡ SMALL; 1195] *Opposite*: considerable

See Compare and Contrast at **thin**.

slenderness *n* **thinness**, slimness, skinniness, fineness, narrowness [➡ BUILD; 477] *Opposite*: stoutness

sleuth 1 *v* **investigate**, look for clues, spy, look into things, check things out, conduct an inquiry, snoop (*informal*) [➡ EXAMINE AND ASSESS; 753] 2 *v* **track**, tail, follow, pursue, stalk, shadow, dog, hunt down, track down [➡ ACCOMPANY AND FOLLOW; 337] 3 *n* (*informal*) **detective**, Sherlock Holmes, investigator, private eye (*informal*), gumshoe (*dated informal*) [➡ THE POLICE, ARREST, AND PRETRIAL PROCEEDINGS; 818]

slew *see* **slue**

slice 1 *n* **piece**, sliver, wedge, portion, segment, serving [➡ AMOUNTS OF SOLID OR SEMISOLID; 115] 2 *n* **share**, cut, portion, part, percentage [➡ AMOUNTS OF SOLID OR SEMISOLID; 115] 3 *v* **cut**, share, carve, divide, cut up [➡ TEAR, BREAK, AND CUT; 360]

slick 1 *adj* **slippery**, smooth, glossy, shiny, glassy, slimy, greasy [➡ PHYSICAL TEXTURE; 1222] 2 *adj* **glib**, superficial, untrustworthy, shallow, facile [➡ LACK OF COMMITMENT AND UNRELIABILITY; 509] 3 *adj* **polished**, professional, efficient, glossy, smooth [➡ ORDER AND ORGANIZATION; 206] *Opposite*: shoddy

slicker *type of* **overcoat** [➡ GARMENTS AND OUTFITS; 865]

slide 1 *v* **glide**, slither, slip, skim, skate, skid [➡ PUSH, PULL,

AND SLIDE; 335] 2 *v* **go down**, fall, decrease, diminish, drop [➡ CHANGE OF INTENSITY: LESS; 395] *Opposite*: rise

sliding doors *n* [➡ DOORS AND ACCESS POINTS; 1101]

slight 1 *adj* **small**, minor, unimportant, trivial, insignificant, slender, slim [➡ FEW, LITTLE, SMALL AMOUNT; 120] *Opposite*: considerable 2 *adj* **slim**, delicate, thin, feeble, slender [➡ BUILD; 477] *Opposite*: stocky 3 *n* **snub**, insult, slur, smear, rebuff, affront [➡ MALICIOUS ACTIONS OR BEHAVIOR; 296] 4 *v* **insult**, offend, snub, scorn, affront [➡ INSULTS, ABUSE, AND SWEARING; 658]

slightly *adv* **somewhat**, to some extent, a little, a touch, a tad (*informal*), marginally, faintly, vaguely [➡ TO A CERTAIN EXTENT; 136] *Opposite*: considerably

slim 1 *adj* **thin**, trim, slender, slight, lean, wiry, svelte [➡ BUILD; 477] *Opposite*: fat 2 *adj* **faint**, slender, remote, poor, slight, unlikely [➡ IMPOSSIBLE AND IMPROBABLE; 178] *Opposite*: considerable 3 *v* **diet**, go on a diet, lose weight, watch your weight, reduce [➡ EAT AND NOT EAT; 710]

See Compare and Contrast at **thin**.

slim down *v* **reduce**, streamline, rationalize, cut, scale back, cut back [➡ CHANGE OF SIZE: SMALLER; 393] *Opposite*: expand

slime *n* **paste**, mucus, glop (*informal*), goop (*informal*), goo (*informal*), gunk (*informal*) [➡ UNPLEASANT, DIRTY, AND TOXIC SUBSTANCES; 1268]

sliminess *n* [➡ PHYSICAL TEXTURE; 1222]

slimming *adj* **low-fat**, lite, light, diet, low-calorie, healthy [➡ FOOD; 1167] *Opposite*: fattening

slimness 1 *n* **narrowness**, fineness, slightness, thinness, flatness, shallowness [➡ WIDTH: NARROW AND THIN; 1200] *Opposite*: bulkiness 2 *n* **slenderness**, leanness, svelteness, trimness, thinness, fineness, elegance [➡ BUILD; 477] *Opposite*: plumpness

slimy 1 *adj* **greasy**, oily, slippery, slick [➡ PHYSICAL TEXTURE; 1222] 2 *adj* **smarmy**, oily, groveling, sycophantic, unctuous, ingratiating, creepy (*informal*) [➡ INGRATIATING; 638]

sling 1 *v* **throw**, toss, lob, fling, hurl, chuck (*informal*) [➡ MOVE SOMETHING: THROUGH THE AIR; 334] 2 *v* **hang**, suspend, dangle, drape, hook up [➡ MOVE SOMETHING: ON THE SPOT; 336]

slingback *type of* **shoe** [➡ FOOTWEAR; 871]

slink *v* **creep**, sneak, tiptoe, steal, skulk [➡ MOVE SLOWLY; 314]

slip 1 *v* **trip**, fall, lose your balance, lose your footing, tumble, stumble [➡ GO DOWNWARD; 307] 2 *v* **slide**, glide, slither, skid, skate [➡ PUSH, PULL, AND SLIDE; 335] 3 *v* **sneak**, steal, creep, flit, slink [➡ PROCEED AND GO; 305] 4 *n* **blunder**, mistake, error, omission, gaffe, slip-up (*informal*) [➡ MISTAKES; 250] 5 *type of* **lower body underwear** [➡ ACCESSORIES, MILLINERY, AND LINGERIE; 867]

See Compare and Contrast at **mistake**.

slip back *v* **revert**, relapse, lapse, slide back, return, slip [➡ GO BACKWARD; 309]

slipcase *n* [➡ CONTAINERS, RECEPTACLES, AND PACKAGING; 1245]

slipcover *n* [➡ FURNISHING AND HOUSEHOLD LINENS; 860]

slip of the tongue *n* [➡ MISTAKES; 250]

slipper *type of* **shoe** [➡ FOOTWEAR; 871]

slipperiness *n* [➡ DECEITFUL; 513]

slippery 1 *adj* **greasy**, oily, slick, icy, slimy, glassy, smooth [➡ PHYSICAL TEXTURE; 1222] *Opposite*: dry 2 *adj* **sneaky**, shifty, crafty, devious, dishonest, untrustworthy [➡ DECEITFUL; 513] *Opposite*: trustworthy

slippery customer *n* [➡ PEOPLE WHO DECEIVE; 661]

slipshod *adj* **careless**, shoddy, slapdash, sloppy, slack [➡ INCAUTIOUS AND CARELESS; 283] *Opposite*: thorough

slip up (*informal*) *v* **make a mistake**, go wrong, get it wrong, blunder, trip up, goof (*informal*), foul up (*informal*), err, mess up (*informal*) [➡ MESS UP AND MAKE MISTAKES; 472]

slip-up (*informal*) *n* **blunder**, slip, mistake, error, omission, gaffe [➡ MISTAKES; 250]

slit 1 *v* **cut**, slash, gash, slice, nick [➡ TEAR, BREAK, AND CUT; 360] 2 *n* **opening**, cut, slash, gash, slot, hole, gap [➡ HOLES, GAPS, AND FORKS; 1252]

See Compare and Contrast at **tear**.

slither *v* **slide**, glide, slink, slip, skid [➡ PROCEED AND GO; 305]

sliver *n* **slice**, shaving, splinter, flake, shard [➡ SMALL PIECES; 129]

slobber *v* **drool**, dribble, salivate, slaver [➡ EXCRETION AND EXCRETA; 722]

slog 1 *v* **plod**, trudge, tramp, trek, hike, trail, schlep (*informal*) [➡ MOVE SLOWLY; 314] 2 *v* **work**, labor, toil, grind, struggle [➡ HARD WORK OR EFFORT; 298] 3 *n* **trek**, hike, tramp, trail, marathon, schlep (*informal*) [➡ PROCEED AND GO; 305] 4 *n* **drag**, effort, strain, grind, struggle [➡ HARD WORK OR EFFORT; 298]

slogan *n* **motto**, saying, jingle, catch phrase, watchword, refrain, mantra [➡ THE SPOKEN WORD; 671]

sloop *type of* **sailing vessel** [➡ SHIPS AND BOATS; 1150]

slop *v* **spill**, slosh, splatter, splash, swill, wash [➡ SPREAD AND SCATTER; 332]

slope 1 *n* **gradient**, grade, incline, hill, rise, angle, slant, drop, ramp [➡ ORIENTATION AND ALIGNMENT; 1223] 2 *v* **incline**, slant, tilt, lean, rise, fall, drop, angle [➡ MOVE SOMETHING INTO A NEW POSITION OR OVERTURN; 330]

sloping *adj* [➡ ORIENTATION AND ALIGNMENT; 1223]

sloppiness 1 *n* (*informal*) **slackness**, shoddiness, carelessness, negligence, laxity, laziness, inaccuracy, ineptness, incompetence, amateurishness [➡ LIFELESS, LAZY, AND UNENTHUSIASTIC; 506] *Opposite*: meticulousness 2 *n* **messiness**, untidiness, disorder, chaos, slovenliness [➡ DISORDER AND CHAOS; 245] *Opposite*: tidiness 3 *n* (*informal*) **slushiness**, sentimentality, sentiment, schmaltz (*informal*), soppiness (*informal*) [➡ IN POOR TASTE AND OVERSENTIMENTAL; 229]

sloppy 1 *adj* (*informal*) **slack**, shoddy, careless, poor, slipshod, casual, slapdash, inept, incompetent, amateurish, lax, negligent, lazy, inaccurate [➡ INCAUTIOUS AND CARELESS; 283] *Opposite*: meticulous 2 *adj* **messy**, untidy, disordered, chaotic, slovenly [➡ DISORDER AND CHAOS; 245] *Opposite*: tidy 3 *adj* (*informal*) **soppy**, slushy, sentimental,

romantic, corny, gushing, mushy, syrupy, mawkish, tacky, schmaltzy (*informal*) [➡ IN POOR TASTE AND OVERSENTIMENTAL; 229]

slops *n* [➡ UNPLEASANT, DIRTY, AND TOXIC SUBSTANCES; 1268]

slosh *v* **spill**, slop, splatter, splash, swill, wash [➡ SPREAD AND SCATTER; 332]

slot 1 *n* **slit**, hole, opening, niche, space, aperture [➡ HOLES, GAPS, AND FORKS; 1252] 2 *n* **time**, window, opening, space, period, gap [➡ PAUSES AND PHASES; 56] 3 *v* **position**, locate, fit, insert, slip, slide, drop in, lower [➡ POSITION SOMETHING: BETWEEN, BESIDE, OR INSIDE SOMETHING; 326]

sloth 1 *n* **laziness**, idleness, indolence, apathy, sluggishness, languor, lethargy [➡ LIFELESS, LAZY, AND UNENTHUSIASTIC; 506] *Opposite*: liveliness 2 *type of* **small mammal** [➡ SMALL MAMMALS; 990]

slothful *adj* **lazy**, idle, sluggish, inactive, indolent, apathetic, languid, lethargic [➡ LIFELESS, LAZY, AND UNENTHUSIASTIC; 506] *Opposite*: energetic

slothfulness *n* **laziness**, indolence, idleness, sluggishness, languor, lethargy [➡ LIFELESS, LAZY, AND UNENTHUSIASTIC; 506] *Opposite*: liveliness

slot in *v* **fit in**, squeeze in, accommodate, accept, see, schedule [➡ ARRANGE AND CREATE ORDER; 357]

slouch 1 *v* **slump**, droop, stoop, sprawl, lounge, sag, hunch [➡ ASSUME A POSITION; 317] 2 *n* (*informal*) **idler**, loafer, slacker, shirker, freeloader (*informal*), lazybones (*informal*) [➡ LAZY OR UNSUCCESSFUL PEOPLE; 948]

slovenliness *n* [➡ BADLY GROOMED; 483]

slovenly *adj* **careless**, disheveled, untidy, messy, unkempt, sloppy [➡ BADLY GROOMED; 483]

slow 1 *adj* **sluggish**, unhurried, measured, deliberate, dawdling, leisurely, relaxed, gentle, gradual [➡ MOVING SLOWLY; 105] *Opposite*: fast 2 *adj* **time-consuming**, drawn-out, protracted, lengthy, lingering, gradual, long-winded, laborious, painful [➡ HAPPENING SLOWLY; 106] *Opposite*: quick 3 *v* **slow down**, decelerate, brake, reduce, slacken [➡ CHANGE OF SPEED: LESS; 397]

slow as molasses *adj* [➡ HAPPENING SLOWLY; 106]

slow but sure *adj* [➡ HAPPENING SLOWLY; 106]

slow cook *v* [➡ COOKING AND FOOD PREPARATION; 353]

slow down 1 *v* **decelerate**, slow up, slow, brake, reduce speed [➡ CHANGE OF SPEED: LESS; 397] *Opposite*: speed up 2 *v* **hold up**, hold back, delay, slow, retard, hinder, set back, impede [➡ DELAY ACTION OR OCCURRENCE; 278] *Opposite*: speed up

slow-going *adj* [➡ HAPPENING SLOWLY; 106]

slow handclap (*UK*) *n* [➡ APPLAUSE; 652]

slow lane (*UK*) *n* [➡ ROADS; 1106]

slowly *adv* **gradually**, unhurriedly, bit by bit, little by little, at a snail's pace, leisurely, sluggishly, deliberately, gently [➡ HAPPENING SLOWLY; 106] *Opposite*: quickly

slowly but surely *adv* [➡ HAPPENING SLOWLY; 106]

slow-moving *adj* [➡ MOVING SLOWLY; 105]

slowness *n* **leisureliness**, sluggishness, deliberateness, gradualness [➡SPEED; 102] *Opposite:* fastness

slow-paced *adj* [➡HAPPENING SLOWLY; 106]

slow up 1 *v* **hold up**, hold back, delay, slow, retard, hinder, set back, impede [➡DELAY ACTION OR OCCURRENCE; 278] *Opposite:* speed up **2** *v* **decelerate**, slow down, slow, brake, reduce speed [➡CHANGE OF SPEED: LESS; 397]

slow-witted (*UK*) *adj* [➡NEGATIVE INTELLECTUAL CHARACTERISTICS; 525]

slowworm *type of* **reptile** [➡REPTILES; 994]

sludge *n* **mud**, slush, mire, muck, slop, slurry [➡UNPLEASANT, DIRTY, AND TOXIC SUBSTANCES; 1268]

sludgy *adj* [➡FLUID AND NONSOLID; 1213]

slue *v* **veer**, swing, slide, skid, swerve, slither [➡CHANGE DIRECTION OF MOTION; 344]

slug 1 *n* **bullet**, shot, shell, cartridge, pellet, ball, projectile, round [➡PROJECTILES; 1159] **2** *n* (*informal*) **shot**, gulp, swallow, mouthful, glassful, drink, hit, swig (*informal*) [➡DRINK; 711] *Opposite:* sip **3** *type of* **land invertebrate** [➡LAND INVERTEBRATES; 1021] **4** *n* **blow**, hit, thump, punch, whack, clout, belt (*informal*), wallop (*informal*) [➡PHYSICAL ATTACK AND PUNISHMENT; 415] **5** *v* (*informal*) **swallow**, gulp, down, drink, swill, swig (*informal*), knock back (*informal*), quaff (*literary or humorous*) [➡DRINK; 711] *Opposite:* sip **6** *v* **hit**, thump, strike, punch, whack, clout, belt (*informal*), wallop (*informal*) [➡PHYSICAL ATTACK AND PUNISHMENT; 415]

sluggish *adj* **inactive**, lethargic, slow, listless, slothful, lazy [➡LIFELESS, LAZY, AND UNENTHUSIASTIC; 506] *Opposite:* energetic

sluggishness *n* **lethargy**, slowness, listlessness, sloth, laziness [➡LIFELESS, LAZY, AND UNENTHUSIASTIC; 506] *Opposite:* alertness

sluice 1 *n* **channel**, conduit, race, drain, gutter, stream [➡WATERCOURSES; 1111] **2** *v* **clean**, flush, rinse, hose, wash, flood [➡CLEAN AND POLISH; 403]

sluicegate *n* [➡BARRIERS; 1113]

slum *n* **shanty town**, favela, colonia [➡UNDESIRABLE ACCOMMODATIONS; 856]

slumber 1 *v* **sleep**, drowse, doze, be dead to the world, catnap, snooze (*informal*) [➡SLEEP AND DREAM; 723] **2** *n* **sleep**, doze, nap, catnap, siesta, rest, snooze (*informal*), forty winks (*informal*) [➡SLEEP AND DREAM; 723] **3** *n* **rest**, inactivity, inertia, torpor, laziness, stagnation [➡PERIODS OF REST; 91]

slumbering *adj* [➡TIRED, ASLEEP, AND UNCONSCIOUS; 738]

slump 1 *v* **collapse**, fall, sink, tumble, lurch [➡ASSUME A POSITION; 317] **2** *v* **slouch**, bend, hunch, droop, sprawl, sag [➡TAKE UP A NEW POSITION; 312] **3** *v* **decrease**, decline, collapse, crash, plummet, drop, plunge, fall, nose-dive [➡FAIL OR BE UNSUCCESSFUL; 75] *Opposite:* rise **4** *n* **recession**, crash, collapse, decline, plummet, drop, depression, plunge, fall, nosedive [➡MARKET FORCES; 803] *Opposite:* rise **5** *type of* **economic condition** [➡FINANCE AND ECONOMICS; 796]

slumped *adj* [➡ORIENTATION AND ALIGNMENT; 1223]

slur 1 *v* **speak**, run together, blend, overlap, overrun, elide [➡CHATTER AND BABBLE; 617] **2** *v* **demean**, smear, insult, slight, besmirch, denigrate [➡ACCUSE, BLAME, AND CRITICIZE; 641] **3** *n* **smear**, disgrace, insult, slight, stain, affront [➡INSULTS, ABUSE, AND SWEARING; 658]

slurp 1 *v* **gulp**, suck, drink, swallow, down, swig (*informal*), knock back (*informal*) [➡DRINK; 711] **2** *n* **smack**, suck, gulp [➡SOUNDS MADE BY PEOPLE; 1262] **3** *n* **mouthful**, swallow, drink, sip, gulp, taste, swig (*informal*) [➡DRINK; 711]

slurred *adj* **indistinct**, inaudible, unclear, garbled, incoherent [➡INARTICULATE, RAMBLING, AND AWKWARD; 633] *Opposite:* distinct

slurry *n* [➡UNPLEASANT, DIRTY, AND TOXIC SUBSTANCES; 1268]

slush *n* **sludge**, mud, mire, muck, slurry [➡UNPLEASANT, DIRTY, AND TOXIC SUBSTANCES; 1268]

slushy 1 *adj* **snowy**, icy, wet, mushy, sloppy, sludgy [➡WET; 1240] *Opposite:* dry **2** *adj* **sentimental**, mushy, corny, syrupy, mawkish, tacky, soppy, gushing, schmaltzy (*informal*) [➡IN POOR TASTE AND OVERSENTIMENTAL; 229] *Opposite:* unsentimental

sly 1 *adj* **crafty**, cunning, clever, knowing, artful, shrewd, ingenious, astute, skillful, nifty (*informal*) [➡TALENTED AND SKILLFUL; 527] **2** *adj* **evasive**, wily, devious, furtive, underhand, tricky, deceitful, surreptitious, sneaky, dishonest [➡DECEITFUL; 513] *Opposite:* honest

slyness 1 *n* **craftiness**, cunning, skill, artfulness, cleverness, shrewdness, ingenuity, astuteness [➡SKILLS, TALENTS, AND ABILITIES; 526] *Opposite:* clumsiness **2** *n* **sneakiness**, evasiveness, furtiveness, dishonesty, underhandedness, deviousness, deceit, deceitfulness, shiftiness [➡DECEITFUL; 513] *Opposite:* openness

smack 1 *v* **hit**, clout, slap, cuff, spank, whack, wham [➡PHYSICAL ATTACK AND PUNISHMENT; 415] **2** *v* **suggest**, imply, hint at, look like, sound like, be reminiscent of, remind of [➡SEEM TO BE SOMETHING; 58] **3** *n* **slap**, blow, clout, cuff, spank, whack [➡PHYSICAL ATTACK AND PUNISHMENT; 415] **4** *n* **taste**, tang, bite, flavor, savor [➡TASTE; 703] **5** *type of* **sailing vessel** [➡SHIPS AND BOATS; 1150]

smacker (*informal*) *n* [➡PHYSICAL CONTACT AS COMMUNICATION; 655]

smack of *v* [➡SEEM TO BE SOMETHING; 58]

small 1 *adj* **little**, minute, tiny, diminutive, miniature, petite, undersized [➡SMALL; 1195] *Opposite:* big **2** *adj* **unimportant**, trivial, slight, lesser, minor, insignificant, trifling [➡UNIMPORTANT AND UNNECESSARY; 238] *Opposite:* major

small amount *n* [➡FEW, LITTLE, SMALL AMOUNT; 120]

small arms *n* **weapons**, guns, firearms, side arms, pistols, handguns, rifles, weaponry, arms, firepower [➡WEAPONS; 1154]

small beer (*informal*) *n* [➡UNIMPORTANT AND UNNECESSARY; 238]

small-boned *adj* [➡BUILD; 477]

smallholding (*UK*) *n* **farm**, croft, plot, allotment (*UK*) [➡AGRICULTURE AND FARMING; 1075]

small intestine *part of* **digestive tract** [➡THE DIGESTIVE TRACT; 709]

smallness *n* **tininess**, littleness, minuteness, compactness [➡SMALL; 1195] *Opposite:* largeness

small potatoes (*informal*) *n* [➡UNIMPORTANT AND UNNECESSARY; 238]

small-scale 1 *adj* **limited**, modest, moderate, minor, unimportant, minimal [➡ UNIMPORTANT AND UNNECESSARY; 238] *Opposite*: large-scale **2** *adj* **little**, small, miniature, minuscule, tiny, reduced [➡ SMALL; 1195] *Opposite*: large-scale

small screen (*informal*) *n* **television**, tube (*informal*), TV (*informal*), boob tube (*informal*), telly (*UK*), box (*UK slang*) [➡ TELEVISION AND RADIO; 606]

small talk *n* **chat**, conversation, pleasantries, gossip, chatter, chitchat (*informal*) [➡ INFORMAL COMMUNICATION; 45]

small-time (*informal*) *adj* **petty**, unimportant, local, minor, insignificant [➡ UNIMPORTANT AND UNNECESSARY; 238] *Opposite*: major

smarminess *n* [➡ INGRATIATING; 638]

smarmy *adj* **sycophantic**, oily, groveling, slimy, creepy (*informal*), unctuous, ingratiating [➡ INGRATIATING; 638]

smart 1 *adj* **clever**, intelligent, bright, sharp, quick, brainy (*informal*) [➡ POSITIVE INTELLECTUAL CHARACTERISTICS; 524] *Opposite*: stupid **2** *adj* **insolent**, rude, facetious, disrespectful, sarcastic, clever, impertinent (*formal*) [➡ RUDE AND HOSTILE; 625] **3** *adj* **elegant**, tidy, stylish, chic, well-dressed, well groomed, neat, dapper, dashing, well-turned-out (*UK*) [➡ WELL-GROOMED; 482] *Opposite*: shabby **4** *adj* **fashionable**, chic, glamorous, stylish, voguish, glitzy, elegant, trendy (*informal*), ritzy (*informal*), swanky (*informal*), hip (*slang*) [➡ EXPENSIVE AND LUXURIOUS; 218] **5** *adj* **lively**, brisk, vigorous, energetic, quick, rapid, speedy [➡ MOVING QUICKLY; 103] **6** *v* **sting**, burn, hurt, chafe, tingle, prickle [➡ PAIN AND OTHER PHYSICAL SENSATIONS; 733]

See Compare and Contrast at **intelligent**.

smart aleck (*informal*) *n* **wise guy** (*informal*), know-it-all (*informal*), smarty pants (*informal*), wag (*informal*), wiseacre (*informal*) [➡ SELF-IMPORTANT AND SELF-SEEKING PEOPLE; 949]

smart-alecky (*informal*) *adj* [➡ POMPOUS, LOUD, AND OVER-CONFIDENT; 635]

smart bomb *type of* **explosive weapon** [➡ EXPLOSIVES; 1155]

smart card *n* [➡ E-COMMERCE; 1129]

smarten 1 *v* **spruce up**, clean up, revamp, do up, redecorate, neaten, improve, jazz up, doll up (*informal*), tidy up (*UK*) [➡ IMPROVE APPEARANCE; 379] *Opposite*: let go **2** *v* **speed up**, accelerate, quicken, increase, pick up [➡ CHANGE OF SPEED: MORE; 396] *Opposite*: slow

smarten up 1 *v* **spruce up**, clean up, revamp, do up, redecorate, tidy up, improve, jazz up, doll up (*informal*) [➡ IMPROVE APPEARANCE; 379] *Opposite*: let go **2** *v* **brighten up**, liven up, cheer up, enliven, energize, stimulate, boost, pep up (*informal*), get your act together (*informal*) [➡ IMPROVE SOMETHING; 374] *Opposite*: stagnate

smartly 1 *adv* **intelligently**, cleverly, ably, knowledgeably, stupidly [➡ POSITIVE INTELLECTUAL CHARACTERISTICS; 524] **2** *adv* **vigorously**, briskly, energetically, quickly, rapidly, speedily [➡ MOVING QUICKLY; 103] **3** *adv* **stylishly**, nattily, neatly, tidily, elegantly [➡ WELL-GROOMED; 482] *Opposite*: untidily

smartly dressed *adj* [➡ WELL-GROOMED; 482]

smartness *n* **neatness**, tidiness, elegance, stylishness, chicness [➡ WELL-GROOMED; 482] *Opposite*: untidiness

smarts (*informal*) *n* [➡ GARMENTS AND OUTFITS; 865]

smarty pants (*informal*) *n* **know-it-all** (*informal*), smart aleck (*informal*), wise guy (*informal*), wiseacre (*informal*), wag (*informal*) [➡ SELF-IMPORTANT AND SELF-SEEKING PEOPLE; 949]

smash 1 *v* **shatter**, break, demolish, destroy, crush [➡ DESTRUCTION AND DEMOLITION; 359] *Opposite*: repair **2** *n* **crash**, bang, crunch [➡ IMPACT SOUNDS; 1260] **3** *n* **blow**, chop, punch, kick, volley, slam, slam-dunk [➡ SPORTS TERMS; 877] **4** *n* **accident**, crash, collision, wreck, fender-bender (*informal*), pileup (*informal*) [➡ TRAFFIC ACCIDENTS; 255]

smash hit *n* [➡ SUCCESS; 82]

smashing (*UK*) *interj* [➡ COMPLIMENTS; 657]

smash into *v* [➡ CONTACT: IMPACT; 413]

smash to smithereens *v* [➡ DESTRUCTION AND DEMOLITION; 359]

smash up *v* **wreck**, damage, ruin, trash (*informal*), total (*slang*), write off (*UK*) [➡ DESTRUCTION AND DEMOLITION; 359]

smashup *n* **crash**, collision, accident, wreck, pileup (*informal*), fender-bender (*informal*) [➡ TRAFFIC ACCIDENTS; 255]

smattering *n* **bit**, modicum, dash, iota, little, smidgen (*informal*) [➡ FEW, LITTLE, SMALL AMOUNT; 120] *Opposite*: lot

smear 1 *v* **spread**, coat, daub, cover, wipe, rub [➡ DECORATE, ADORN, AND APPLY COATINGS; 405] **2** *v* **sully**, discredit, disgrace, besmirch, tarnish, bring into disrepute, ruin, slander, denigrate, slur, badmouth (*slang*) [➡ INSULTS, ABUSE, AND SWEARING; 658] *Opposite*: praise **3** *n* **mark**, smudge, blotch, stain, splotch, blot, splodge (*UK*) [➡ FAULTS, FLAWS, AND WEAKNESSES; 251] **4** *n* **slur**, insult, slight, affront, slander, libel [➡ INSULTS, ABUSE, AND SWEARING; 658]

smear campaign *n* **mudslinging**, whispering campaign, muckraking, defamation, slander, libel, vilification, talk, rumor, gossip [➡ GOSSIP; 678]

smell 1 *v* **stink**, reek [➡ SMELL EMISSION; 369] **2** *v* **sniff**, sense, get a whiff of, suspect, taste, feel [➡ SMELL AND SMELLING; 705] **3** *n* **odor**, aroma, scent, perfume, whiff, fragrance, bouquet, stink, stench, reek [➡ SMELL AND SMELLING; 705]

Compare and Contrast: *smell, odor, aroma, bouquet, scent, perfume, fragrance, stink, stench, reek*

CORE MEANING: the way something smells

smell a neutral, pleasant, or unpleasant quality detected by the nerves of the nose; *odor* a neutral or unpleasant smell; *aroma* a distinctive pleasant smell, especially one related to cooking or food; *bouquet* a characteristic pleasant smell, usually associated with fine wines; *scent* a pleasant, sweet smell, for example, the smell of flowers, or the characteristic smell given off by a particular animal; *perfume* a sweet, pleasant, and heady smell, especially the smell of flowers or plants; *fragrance* a sweet pleasant smell, especially a delicate or subtle one; *stink* a strong unpleasant smell; *stench* a strong unpleasant smell, especially one associated with burning or decay; *reek* a strong unpleasant smell.

smelliness *n* [➡ SMELL AND SMELLING; 705]

smelly *adj* **stinking**, reeking, foul, malodorous, putrid, fetid [➡ SMELL AND SMELLING; 705] *Opposite*: fragrant

smelt 1 *v* **melt**, melt down [➡ SOFTEN, LIQUEFY, AND DAMPEN; 388] 2 *v* **found**, cast, produce, manufacture [➡ MANUFACTURE; 349]

smidge (*informal*) *see* **smidgen**

smidgen (*informal*) *n* **dash**, drop, bit, splash, morsel, soupçon, taste, hint [➡ FEW, LITTLE, SMALL AMOUNT; 120]

smile 1 *v* **grin**, beam, smirk, leer, sneer [➡ FACIAL EXPRESSIONS AND BLUSHING; 651] *Opposite:* frown 2 *n* **beam**, grin, smirk, leer [➡ FACIAL EXPRESSIONS AND BLUSHING; 651] *Opposite:* frown

smiley 1 *adj* **smiling**, happy, cheery, sunny, cheerful [➡ FACIAL EXPRESSIONS AND BLUSHING; 651] *Opposite:* miserable 2 *n* **emoticon**, smiley face, symbol, sign-off [➡ COMPUTERS AND COMPUTING; 1127]

smiling *adj* [➡ FACIAL EXPRESSIONS AND BLUSHING; 651]

smirk 1 *n* **grin**, leer, sneer, simper [➡ FACIAL EXPRESSIONS AND BLUSHING; 651] 2 *v* **sneer**, leer, grin, simper [➡ FACIAL EXPRESSIONS AND BLUSHING; 651]

smite (*literary*) *v* **hit**, strike, beat, punch, thrash, thump, cuff, smack, slug [➡ PHYSICAL ATTACK AND PUNISHMENT; 415]

smithereens (*informal*) *n* **pieces**, bits, fragments, shards [➡ SMALL PIECES; 129]

smithy *type of* **factory** [➡ INDUSTRIAL BUILDINGS; 1087]

smitten (*humorous or archaic or literary*) *adj* **in love**, besotted, enamored, head over heels in love, infatuated, taken, lovesick, hooked (*slang*) [➡ APPRECIATION AND GRATITUDE; 535] *Opposite:* indifferent

smock *type of* **top** [➡ GARMENTS AND OUTFITS; 865]

smocking *type of* **handicraft** [➡ CRAFTS AND CARVING; 355]

smog *n* **pollution**, smoke, fog, haze [➡ CLOUDY AND RAINY WEATHER; 1052]

smogginess *n* [➡ CLOUDY AND RAINY WEATHER; 1052]

smoggy *adj* [➡ CLOUDY AND RAINY WEATHER; 1052]

smoke 1 *n* **fumes**, smog, poisonous gas, firedamp, chokedamp, biogas [➡ PRODUCTS OF FIRE; 1166] 2 *v* **burn**, be on fire, smolder [➡ FIRE, FLAMMABILITY, AND BURNING; 1165]

smoke alarm *n* **device**, smoke detector, fire alarm, sensor [➡ HOUSEHOLD APPLIANCES; 1117]

smoke and mirrors *n* [➡ DECEPTION AND LIES; 660]

smoke bomb *type of* **explosive weapon** [➡ EXPLOSIVES; 1155]

smoked *adj* [➡ STATE OF PREPARED FOOD; 1171]

smoke detector *n* **smoke alarm**, fire alarm, sensor [➡ HOUSEHOLD APPLIANCES; 1117]

smoke out 1 *v* **drive out**, force out, turn out, eject, expel [➡ EJECT AND EXCLUDE; 340] *Opposite:* bring in 2 *v* **bring to light**, reveal, expose, unearth, discover, disclose [➡ CAUSE TO APPEAR; 5] *Opposite:* conceal

smoker 1 *n* **cigarette smoker**, pipe smoker, cigar smoker, chain-smoker, heavy smoker, light smoker [➡ DEVOTEES AND ADDICTED PEOPLE; 556] 2 *n* **smoking compartment**, smoking car, smoking carriage (*UK*) [➡ RAILROADS; 1107]

smoke screen 1 *n* **cover-up**, cover, camouflage, screen,

mask, blind, decoy, diversion, red herring [➡ DECEPTION AND LIES; 660] 2 *n* **cloud of smoke**, wall of smoke, smoke [➡ PRODUCTS OF FIRE; 1166]

smokestack *part of* **building** [➡ PARTS OF A BUILDING; 1095]

smoking car *part of* **train** [➡ RAILROADS; 1107]

smoking compartment *part of* **train** [➡ RAILROADS; 1107]

smoking jacket *type of* **jacket** [➡ GARMENTS AND OUTFITS; 865]

smoky *adj* **misty**, murky, cloudy, foggy, hazy, opaque, gray, smoke-filled [➡ VISUAL TEXTURE; 1221] *Opposite:* clear

smolder 1 *v* **burn**, smoke, glow [➡ FIRE, FLAMMABILITY, AND BURNING; 1165] 2 *v* **fume**, seethe, glower, burn, boil, be angry, bristle [➡ GIVING VENT TO EMOTIONS; 679] 3 *v* **lurk**, fester, rumble, linger, persist, endure, grow, increase [➡ CONTINUE TO EXIST; 17]

smoldering *adj* [➡ FIRE, FLAMMABILITY, AND BURNING; 1165]

smooch (*informal*) 1 *v* **kiss**, cuddle, hug, hold each other close, caress, embrace, neck, canoodle (*informal*) [➡ PHYSICAL CONTACT AS COMMUNICATION; 655] 2 *n* **cuddle**, kiss, hug, caress, embrace [➡ PHYSICAL CONTACT AS COMMUNICATION; 655]

smooth 1 *adj* **flat**, even, level, horizontal, plane [➡ PHYSICAL TEXTURE; 1222] *Opposite:* uneven 2 *adj* **easy**, flowing, effortless, efficient [➡ EASE AND SIMPLICITY; 200] 3 *adj* **charming**, suave, persuasive, glib, silver-tongued, slick [➡ ELOQUENT, TALKATIVE, AND LONG-WINDED; 632] *Opposite:* gauche 4 *adj* **soft**, silky, downy, velvety, shiny, glossy [➡ PHYSICAL TEXTURE; 1222] *Opposite:* rough 5 *v* **flatten**, smooth out, level, iron, press [➡ CHANGE OF SHAPE; 385] *Opposite:* crumple

smooth down *v* **flatten**, iron out, paste down, smooth out, even out, uncrease, level, tidy, adjust, arrange [➡ CHANGE OF SHAPE; 385] *Opposite:* scrunch

smoothie 1 *n* (*informal*) **charmer**, smooth talker, smooth character, fast talker, poser (*informal*) [➡ SUPERFICIAL OR INSINCERE PEOPLE; 951] 2 *n* **drink**, fruit juice, milk shake, yogurt drink [➡ DRINKS; 1187]

smoothly *adv* **easily**, effortlessly, efficiently, well, slickly [➡ EASE AND SIMPLICITY; 200] *Opposite:* awkwardly

smooth muscle *type of* **muscle or tendon** [➡ THE MUSCLES; 718]

smoothness 1 *n* **flatness**, evenness, levelness [➡ PHYSICAL TEXTURE; 1222] *Opposite:* unevenness 2 *n* **softness**, silkiness, velvetiness, sleekness [➡ PHYSICAL TEXTURE; 1222] *Opposite:* roughness 3 *n* **ease**, effortlessness, efficiency [➡ EASE AND SIMPLICITY; 200] *Opposite:* awkwardness 4 *n* **charm**, suaveness, persuasiveness, glibness, slickness [➡ ELOQUENT, TALKATIVE, AND LONG-WINDED; 632] *Opposite:* gaucheness

smooth out 1 *v* **flatten**, iron out, paste down, smooth down, even out, uncrease, level, tidy, adjust, arrange [➡ CHANGE OF SHAPE; 385] *Opposite:* crease 2 *v* **ease**, calm, defuse, soothe, smooth over, iron out, sort out, resolve, clear up [➡ CORRECT AND PUT RIGHT; 377] *Opposite:* stir up

smooth over *v* **ease**, calm, defuse, soothe, smooth out, iron out, sort out, resolve, clear up [➡ CORRECT AND PUT RIGHT; 377] *Opposite:* stir up

smooth-shaven *adj* [➡ FACIAL HAIR; 489]

smooth talk *n* **flattery**, nonsense, rubbish, garbage,

sweet talk (*informal*), soft soap (*informal*), blarney (*informal*), guff (*informal*), claptrap (*informal*) [➡MEANINGLESS SPEECH OR WRITING; 676] *Opposite*: sincerity

smooth-tongued *adj* **smooth-talking**, silver-tongued, eloquent, persuasive, convincing, hard to resist, fast-talking [➡ELOQUENT, TALKATIVE, AND LONG-WINDED; 632]

smoothy *see* **smoothie**

smother 1 *v* **suffocate**, stifle, choke, asphyxiate [➡KILL; 923] 2 *v* **overwhelm**, overpower, oppress, suffocate, stifle, restrict [➡GIVE TOO MUCH AND OVERBURDEN; 437] 3 *v* **suppress**, repress, stifle, hold back, restrain, conceal, hide, check [➡WITHHOLD INFORMATION; 687] *Opposite*: express

SMS *n* [➡TELECOMMUNICATIONS; 1130]

smudge 1 *n* **blotch**, smear, stain, mark, blemish, splotch [➡FAULTS, FLAWS, AND WEAKNESSES; 251] 2 *v* **smear**, blur, distort, blot, smirch [➡DECORATE, ADORN, AND APPLY COATINGS; 405]

smudged *adj* [➡DIRTY, 1235]

smug *adj* **self-satisfied**, superior, self-righteous, arrogant, conceited, full of yourself, haughty, complacent, self-assured [➡AFFECTATION, SELF-SATISFACTION, AND SNOBBISHNESS; 507] *Opposite*: humble

smuggle *v* **handle contraband**, traffic, run, sneak in, bring in, rustle [➡STEAL AND ROB; 426]

smuggler *n* [➡CRIMINALS; 821]

smug look *n* [➡FACIAL EXPRESSIONS AND BLUSHING; 651]

smugness *n* **complacency**, arrogance, self-satisfaction, conceit, self-righteousness, haughtiness, self-assuredness, self-sufficiency [➡AFFECTATION, SELF-SATISFACTION, AND SNOBBISHNESS; 507] *Opposite*: humility

smut 1 *n* **soot**, smudge, ash, grime, dirt, dust, filth, speck, muck (*informal*) [➡PRODUCTS OF FIRE; 1166] 2 *n* **obscenity**, dirt, filth, pornography, erotica [➡MORALLY BAD OR IMPROPER, 775]

smuttiness (*informal*) *n* [➡MORALLY BAD OR IMPROPER; 775]

smutty 1 *adj* **sooty**, smudged, grimy, dirty, grubby, soiled, dusty, filthy, black, mucky (*informal*) [➡DIRTY; 1235] *Opposite*: pristine 2 *adj* (*informal*) **obscene**, dirty, pornographic, filthy, explicit, blue (*informal*), naughty (*humorous*), mucky (*UK*) [➡MORALLY BAD OR IMPROPER; 775] 3 *adj* (*informal*) **crude**, foul-mouthed, indelicate, tasteless, loutish, boorish, gross, obscene [➡BAD MANNERS AND SOCIAL SKILLS; 521]

snack *type of* **meal** [➡MEALS AND PARTS OF MEALS; 1169]

snack bar *type of* **eating place** [➡HOTELS, RESTAURANTS, AND CLUBS; 1082]

snafu (*informal*) *n* [➡PROBLEMS; 256]

snag 1 *n* **problem**, hitch, difficulty, obstacle, hurdle, holdup, catch (*informal*) [➡PROBLEMS; 256] 2 *v* **catch**, rip, tear [➡TEAR, BREAK, AND CUT; 360]

snail *type of* **land invertebrate** [➡LAND INVERTEBRATES; 1021]

snail mail (*informal*) *n* **postal service**, surface mail, airmail, mail, post (*UK*) [➡LETTERS AND WRITTEN MESSAGES; 584]

snail-paced *adj* [➡HAPPENING SLOWLY; 106]

snake 1 *n* **sea snake**, water snake, serpent (*literary*) [➡SNAKES; 995] 2 *v* **wind**, bend, twist, meander, turn [➡PROCEED AND GO; 305]

snake

◆ *types of nonpoisonous snakes*
anaconda, blacksnake, boa, boa constrictor, garter snake, grass snake, king snake, python, rat snake, water snake, whip snake

◆ *types of poisonous snakes*
adder, asp, cobra, copperhead, coral snake, diamondback, fer-de-lance, horned viper, mamba, pit viper, puff adder, rattler, rattlesnake, ringhals, sea snake, sidewinder, taipan, viper, water moccasin

snake in the grass *n* [➡INTERFERING PEOPLE AND TATTLETALES; 950]

snake oil *n* [➡DECEPTION AND LIES; 660]

snakeskin *type of* **fabric from animals** [➡FABRICS; 1132]

snaky *adj* **winding**, twisting, meandering, zigzagged, coiling, windy (*UK*), bendy (*UK*) [➡DIRECTION OF MOTION; 345] *Opposite*: straight

snap 1 *v* **break**, crack, shatter, give way, come apart [➡TEAR, BREAK, AND CUT; 360] 2 *v* **retort**, bark, shout, yell, speak sharply, jump down someone's throat [➡GIVING VENT TO EMOTIONS; 679] 3 *v* **bite**, nip, bite at [➡EAT AND NOT EAT; 710] 4 *n* **child's play**, nothing, piece of cake (*informal*), breeze (*informal*), walk in the park (*informal*), cinch (*informal*), gift (*informal*) [➡EASY WORK; 299] 5 *n* **fastening**, fastener, stud, press stud (*UK*), popper (*UK*), press fastener (*UK*) [➡FASTENERS, LINKS, AND NETWORKS; 1247] 6 *adj* **sudden**, spur-of-the-moment, impulsive, spontaneous, instant, quick [➡HAPPENING QUICKLY; 104] *Opposite*: considered

snapdragon *type of* **perennial flower** [➡FLOWERS; 1032]

snapper *type of* **tropical fish** [➡OCEAN FISH; 1009]

snappiness *n* [➡BAD-TEMPERED AND HUMORLESS; 626]

snapping point *n* [➡DECISIVE MOMENTS; 44]

snappish *adj* **irritable**, snappy, bad-tempered, short-tempered, sharp, ill-humored, curt, brusque, tetchy (*informal*), snippy (*informal*) [➡BAD-TEMPERED AND HUMORLESS; 626] *Opposite*: good-natured

snappishness *n* [➡BAD-TEMPERED AND HUMORLESS; 626]

snappy 1 *adj* (*informal*) **stylish**, chic, fashionable, smart, elegant, trendy (*informal*), snazzy (*informal*), classy (*informal*) [➡WELL-GROOMED; 482] *Opposite*: dowdy 2 *adj* (*informal*) **lively**, brisk, interesting, stimulating, to the point, relevant, pertinent, tight [➡INTERESTING AND MEANINGFUL; 190] *Opposite*: dull 3 *adj* **irritable**, bad-tempered, short-tempered, sharp, ill-humored, curt, brusque, impatient, abrupt, terse, tetchy (*informal*), snippy (*informal*) [➡BAD-TEMPERED AND HUMORLESS; 626] *Opposite*: good-natured 4 *adj* **hasty**, quick, fast, speedy, rapid, swift [➡HAPPENING QUICKLY; 104] *Opposite*: slow

snapshot 1 *n* **photo**, photograph, picture, snap, Polaroid, portrait, print, shot [➡PHOTOGRAPHY AND PHOTOGRAPHIC EQUIPMENT; 1122] 2 *n* **view**, glimpse, outline, idea, thumbnail sketch, record, description [➡RECORDS; 585]

snap up *v* **grab**, seize, pounce on, take up [➡ GET; 420]

snare 1 *n* **trap**, noose, gin, lasso [➡ CAPTIVITY AND LOSS OF FREEDOM; 248] 2 *v* **catch**, trap, capture, ensnare, entrap [➡ CAPTIVITY AND LOSS OF FREEDOM; 248]

snare drum *type of* **percussion instrument** [➡ MUSICAL INSTRUMENTS; 910]

snarl 1 *v* **growl**, roar, bellow [➡ SOUND EMISSION BY ANIMALS OR BIRDS; 364] 2 *v* **speak angrily**, bark, growl, snap, rasp, grumble [➡ SOUND EMISSION BY PEOPLE; 363] 3 *type of* **animal sound** [➡ SOUNDS MADE BY ANIMALS; 1261]

snarl up (*UK*) *v* **jam up**, back up, grind to a halt, come to a standstill, reach gridlock, get held up, get blocked up, get tangled up [➡ FAIL OR CEASE TO FUNCTION; 470] *Opposite*: free up

snarl-up (*UK*) *n* **blockage**, holdup, jam, traffic jam, logjam, tangle, gridlock [➡ PROBLEMS; 256]

snatch 1 *v* **grab**, grasp, seize, take [➡ CONTACT: HOLD; 411] 2 *v* **steal**, run off with, filch (*informal*) [➡ STEAL AND ROB; 426] 3 *v* (*informal*) **kidnap**, abduct, seize, shanghai, capture, hijack, take prisoner, take hostage [➡ CAPTIVITY AND LOSS OF FREEDOM; 248] *Opposite*: release

snazziness (*informal*) *n* [➡ WELL-GROOMED; 482]

snazzy (*informal*) *adj* **flashy**, bright, colorful, loud, ostentatious, flamboyant, fashionable [➡ WELL-GROOMED; 482] *Opposite*: drab

sneak 1 *v* **slip**, steal, creep, slink, tiptoe [➡ MOVE SLOWLY; 314] 2 *v* (*UK*) **tell tales**, inform, tell, snitch (*slang*) [➡ BETRAY CONFIDENCES AND GOSSIP; 618] 3 *n* (*UK*) **informer**, telltale, tattletale (*informal*), snitch (*slang*) [➡ INTERFERING PEOPLE AND TATTLETALES; 950]

sneak a look *v* [➡ LOOKING AND LOOKS; 700]

sneaker *type of* **shoe** [➡ FOOTWEAR; 871]

sneakiness *n* **slyness**, furtiveness, stealth, deviousness, cunning, underhandedness, guile, wiles, artfulness, shiftiness, unfairness [➡ DECEITFUL; 513] *Opposite*: openness

sneaking *adj* **niggling**, uneasy, nagging, uncomfortable, worrying [➡ IRRITATING; 228]

sneak preview *n* **advance showing**, premiere, preview, screening, advance screening, viewing [➡ PERFORMANCES AND SHOWS; 42]

sneak thief *n* **pickpocket**, shoplifter, burglar, thief, robber [➡ CRIMINALS; 821]

sneak up on 1 *v* **creep up on**, steal up on, come up on, come up behind, surprise, take by surprise, catch unawares, approach unnoticed [➡ ACCOMPANY AND FOLLOW; 337] 2 *v* **catch napping**, catch unawares, take by surprise, surprise, creep up on, steal up on, catch out (*informal*) [➡ SURPRISE AND IMPRESS; 574]

sneaky *adj* **sly**, devious, shifty, underhand, mean, tricky, duplicitous, guileful [➡ DECEITFUL; 513] *Opposite*: honest

sneer *v* **scorn**, scoff, turn your nose up at, mock, deride, laugh at, snicker, jeer, smirk, disparage, snigger [➡ PROTEST AND EXPRESS DISAPPROVAL; 642]

sneering *adj* **scornful**, contemptuous, disdainful, sar-

castic, arrogant, condescending, derisive, mocking, disparaging, critical [➡ MOCKING AND DISMISSIVE; 636] *Opposite*: admiring

sneeze 1 *n* **sniff**, sniffle, snuffle, splutter, snort, snivel [➡ BREATHE AND NOT BREATHE; 716] 2 *v* **sniffle**, sniff, snuffle, splutter, snort, snivel [➡ BREATHE AND NOT BREATHE; 716]

snicker 1 *v* **laugh**, smirk, mock, deride, sneer, jeer, snigger [➡ LAUGHTER; 649] 2 *v* (*UK*) **whinny**, neigh, snort, snuffle, bray [➡ SOUND EMISSION BY PEOPLE; 363] 3 *n* **laugh**, sneer, jeer, snort, snigger [➡ LAUGHTER; 649] 4 *n* (*UK*) **neigh**, whinny, snort, snuffle, bray [➡ SOUNDS MADE BY PEOPLE; 1262]

snickering *n* [➡ LAUGHTER; 649]

snide *adj* **sarcastic**, mean, unpleasant, malicious, spiteful, unkind, hurtful, cutting, nasty (*informal*) [➡ RUDE AND HOSTILE; 625] *Opposite*: pleasant

sniff 1 *v* **snuffle**, breathe, inhale [➡ BREATHE AND NOT BREATHE; 716] *Opposite*: exhale 2 *v* **smell**, scent, get a whiff of, catch the scent of [➡ SMELL AND SMELLING; 705] 3 *n* **breath**, snort, snuffle, lungful, inhalation [➡ BREATHE AND NOT BREATHE; 716]

sniff at *v* **turn your nose up at**, sneer at, hold in contempt, look down on, scorn, disdain, refuse, reject, turn down [➡ FORGO AND DENY ONESELF; 449] *Opposite*: accept

sniffle 1 *v* **sniff**, snuffle, snivel, snort, splutter [➡ BREATHE AND NOT BREATHE; 716] 2 *v* **whimper**, snivel, cry, weep, sob, whine, blubber (*informal*) [➡ CRYING; 650] 3 *n* **snuffle**, sniff, snivel, snort, splutter [➡ SOUNDS MADE BY PEOPLE; 1262]

sniff out (*informal*) *v* **discover**, find, unearth, track down, detect, bring to light, reveal, expose, nose out [➡ FIND; 463]

sniffy (*informal*) *adj* **contemptuous**, haughty, disdainful, scornful, superior, proud, arrogant, supercilious, snooty (*informal*), stuck-up (*informal*) [➡ AFFECTATION, SELF-SATISFACTION, AND SNOBBISHNESS; 507] *Opposite*: humble

snifter (*informal*) *n* **drink**, nightcap, tot, splash, nip, dram, tipple (*informal*), shot (*informal*), jigger (*informal*), wee dram (*UK*) [➡ DRINKS; 1187]

snigger 1 *v* **snicker**, laugh, smirk, mock, deride, sneer [➡ LAUGHTER; 649] 2 *n* **snicker**, laugh, sneer, snort [➡ LAUGHTER; 649]

sniggering *n* [➡ LAUGHTER; 649]

snip *v* **cut**, shear, slice, nick, trim, clip [➡ TEAR, BREAK, AND CUT; 360]

snipe *type of* **freshwater bird** [➡ FRESHWATER BIRDS; 1000]

sniper *n* **gunman**, marksman, assassin, rifleman, shooter [➡ PEOPLE WHO KILL; 924]

snippet *n* **extract**, piece, bit, scrap [➡ SMALL PIECES; 129]

snippy (*informal*) *adj* **irritable**, snappy, grumpy, crabby, sharp, short, out of sorts, curt, abrupt, blunt, grouchy (*informal*) [➡ BAD-TEMPERED AND HUMORLESS; 626] *Opposite*: good-tempered

snitch (*slang*) 1 *v* **pilfer**, steal, rob, take, swipe (*informal*), filch (*informal*), lift (*informal*), rip off (*informal*), knock off (*slang*), cop (*slang*), purloin (*formal or humorous*) [➡ STEAL AND ROB; 426] 2 *v* **talk**, tell, tell tales, inform on, let the cat out of the bag, squeal, blab (*informal*), spill the beans (*informal*), tattle (*slang*), stool (*slang*) [➞ BETRAY CONFIDENCES AND GOSSIP; 618] **3** *n* **informer**, telltale, tattler, tattletale, mole, betrayer, tipster, blabbermouth (*informal*), plant (*informal*), stool pigeon (*slang*), stoolie (*slang*), squealer (*slang*), sneak (*UK*) [➞ INTERFERING PEOPLE AND TATTLETALES; 950]

snivel *v* **sob**, sniff, cry, weep, whimper, moan, sniffle, boohoo, blubber (*informal*) [➞ CRYING; 650]

snob *n* **social climber**, name-dropper, elitist [➞ SUPERFICIAL OR INSINCERE PEOPLE; 951]

snobbery *n* **arrogance**, superciliousness, condescension, snobbishness, pretentiousness, conceit, pomposity, affectedness, snootiness (*informal*) [➞ AFFECTATION, SELF-SATISFACTION, AND SNOBBISHNESS; 507] *Opposite*: humility

snobbish *adj* **high and mighty**, superior, arrogant, conceited, condescending, supercilious, patronizing, pretentious, snobby (*informal*), snooty (*informal*), stuck-up (*informal*) [➞ AFFECTATION, SELF-SATISFACTION, AND SNOBBISHNESS; 507] *Opposite*: humble

snobbishness *n* **snobbery**, condescension, superciliousness, pretentiousness, haughtiness, arrogance, disdain, pomposity, affectedness, snootiness (*informal*) [➞ AFFECTATION, SELF-SATISFACTION, AND SNOBBISHNESS; 507] *Opposite*: humility

snobby (*informal*) *adj* **high and mighty**, superior, snobbish, arrogant, conceited, condescending, supercilious, pretentious, stuck-up (*informal*), snooty (*informal*) [➞ AFFECTATION, SELF-SATISFACTION, AND SNOBBISHNESS; 507] *Opposite*: humble

snooker **1** *v* (*informal*) **thwart**, stymie, obstruct, hinder, stop, frustrate, foil, dash, circumvent [➞ MAKE IMPOSSIBLE; 276] *Opposite*: assist **2** *type of* **target ball game** [➞ HOBBIES, GAMES, AND SPORTS; 875]

snoop (*informal*) **1** *v* **spy**, poke around, watch, sneak, pry, interfere, meddle, poke your nose in, nose around (*informal*) [➞ LOOKING AND LOOKS; 700] *Opposite*: mind your own business **2** *n* **spy**, sneak, meddler, intruder, eavesdropper [➞ INTERFERING PEOPLE AND TATTLETALES; 950]

snootily (*informal*) *adv* **snobbishly**, condescendingly, superciliously, patronizingly, pretentiously, haughtily, arrogantly, disdainfully, pompously, affectedly [➞ AFFECTATION, SELF-SATISFACTION, AND SNOBBISHNESS; 507] *Opposite*: humbly

snootiness (*informal*) **1** *n* **snobbishness**, snobbery, condescension, superciliousness, pretentiousness, haughtiness, arrogance, disdain, pomposity, affectedness [➞ AFFECTATION, SELF-SATISFACTION, AND SNOBBISHNESS; 507] *Opposite*: humility **2** *n* **exclusivity**, exclusiveness, selectness, poshness (*informal*) [➞ EXPENSIVE AND LUXURIOUS; 218]

snooty (*informal*) *adj* **high and mighty**, condescending, patronizing, supercilious, snobbish, superior, pretentious, stuck-up (*informal*), snobby (*informal*) [➞ AFFECTATION, SELF-SATISFACTION, AND SNOBBISHNESS; 507] *Opposite*: humble

snooze (*informal*) **1** *v* **doze**, sleep, doze off, nap, nod off, catnap [➞ SLEEP AND DREAM; 723] *Opposite*: wake up **2** *n* **sleep**, doze, nap, catnap, siesta, forty winks (*informal*) [➞ SLEEP AND DREAM; 723]

snore *v* **snort**, breathe heavily, snuffle, wheeze [➞ BREATHE AND NOT BREATHE; 716]

snorkel *v* **swim**, dive, scuba dive [➞ HOBBIES, GAMES, AND SPORTS; 875]

snorkeler *n* [➞ PEOPLE IN SPORTS AND LEISURE; 876]

snort *v* **grunt**, exhale, breathe out, inhale, draw in, breathe in, sniff, expire [➞ BREATHE AND NOT BREATHE; 716]

snout *n* **nose**, muzzle, proboscis, schnozzle (*slang*) [➞ THE NOSE; 704]

snow *n* **sleet**, snowflake, slush, hail, ice, snowfall, snowstorm, blizzard, flurry [➞ COLD WEATHER; 1051]

snowball *v* **increase**, mount, soar, balloon, swell, grow quickly, escalate, magnify, expand, multiply, burgeon (*literary*) [➞ CHANGE OF SIZE: BIGGER; 392] *Opposite*: decrease

snowboarding **1** *type of* **winter sport** [➞ HOBBIES, GAMES, AND SPORTS; 875] **2** *type of* **extreme sport** [➞ HOBBIES, GAMES, AND SPORTS; 875]

snowbound *adj* **snowed in**, cut off, isolated, shut in, blockaded, snowed up (*UK*) [➞ COLD WEATHER; 1051]

snowdrop *type of* **flower grown from bulbs** [➞ FLOWERS FROM BULBS; 1030]

snowfall *n* **snowstorm**, snow, flurry, blizzard, whiteout [➞ COLD WEATHER; 1051]

snow flurry *n* [➞ COLD WEATHER; 1051]

snow job (*slang*) *n* [➞ DECEPTION AND LIES; 660]

snowmobile *type of* **leisure vehicle** [➞ VEHICLES; 1145]

snow pea *type of* **pulse** [➞ PEAS AND BEANS; 1189]

snowplow *type of* **commercial or industrial vehicle** [➞ VEHICLES; 1145]

snowshoe *type of* **shoe** [➞ FOOTWEAR; 871]

snowsquall *n* [➞ COLD WEATHER; 1051]

snowstorm *n* **blizzard**, hail, snowfall, flurry, snow flurry, whiteout, sleet [➞ COLD WEATHER; 1051]

snow under **1** *v* **defeat**, beat, overcome, crush, rout, trounce, thrash, cream (*slang*) [➞ BEAT AND DEFEAT; 80] **2** *v* **inundate**, swamp, bury, overwhelm, overload, drown, flood, deluge, submerge, engulf, bog down (*informal*) [➞ GIVE TOO MUCH AND OVERBURDEN; 437]

snow white *type of* **white** [➞ COLORS; 1224]

snowy *adj* **snow-white**, hoary, white [➞ DESCRIBING COLORS; 1226]

snowy owl *type of* **owl** [➞ OWLS; 1001]

snub **1** *v* **ignore**, coldshoulder, slight, look right through, cut, rebuff, rebuke, shame, humiliate, give the brushoff, ostracize [➞ REFUSING OR REJECTING RELATIONS; 975] *Opposite*: acknowledge **2** *n* **rebuff**, slight, rejection, rebuke, insult, humiliation, brushoff (*informal*) [➞ MALICIOUS ACTIONS OR BEHAVIOR; 296]

snub-nosed *adj* **button-nosed**, pug-nosed, retroussé [➞ FACIAL CHARACTERISTICS; 481]

snuff **1** *v* **extinguish**, put out, douse, snuff out, blow out, smother, quench [➞ CAUSE TO STOP; 266] *Opposite*: light **2** *v* (*informal*) **destroy**, kill, eliminate, abolish, eradicate, annihilate [➞ KILL; 923] *Opposite*: save

snuffle **1** *v* **sniff**, sniffle, snort, snivel, splutter, breathe

noisily, inhale, exhale, pant [➡ BREATHE AND NOT BREATHE; 716]
2 *n* **snort**, sniff, sniffle, snivel, splutter, breath, inhalation, exhalation, pant [➡ BREATHE AND NOT BREATHE; 716]

snug 1 *adj* **cozy**, warm, comfortable, homely, inviting, homey, sheltered, comfy (*informal*) [➡ PHYSICALLY PLEASANT; 186] *Opposite*: uncomfortable **2** *adj* **close**, well-fitting, neat, close-fitting, tight, secure [➡ DESCRIBING CLOTHES; 869] *Opposite*: loose

snuggle *v* **nestle**, nuzzle, cuddle, burrow, huddle, snug [➡ GET CLOSER TOGETHER; 310]

so *adv* **consequently**, as a result, therefore, subsequently, accordingly, thus (*formal*), hence (*formal*) [➡ CAUSATION; 168]

soak 1 *v* **immerse**, steep, marinate, infuse, saturate, bathe, penetrate, pervade [➡ SOFTEN, LIQUEFY, AND DAMPEN; 388] **2** *v* **drench**, douse, saturate, wet, drown, sop [➡ SOFTEN, LIQUEFY, AND DAMPEN; 388] *Opposite*: dry out

soaked *adj* **wet through**, saturated, sodden, waterlogged, drenched, dripping, dripping wet, sopping, sopping wet, soaking, soaking wet, wringing wet [➡ WET; 1240] *Opposite*: dry

soaked to the skin *adj* [➡ WET; 1240]

soaking *adj* **drenched**, soaked, soaking wet, sopping wet, sopping, saturated, sodden, wet through, soaked to the skin, like a drowned rat, wringing, wringing wet, waterlogged [➡ WET; 1240] *Opposite*: dry

See Compare and Contrast at **wet.**

soaking wet *adj* [➡ WET; 1240]

so-and-so (*informal*) *n* **whatchamacallit**, thingamajig (*informal*), thingummy (*informal*), thingamabob (*informal*), whatshisname (*informal*), whatshername (*informal*) [➡ NAME AND DESCRIBE; 665]

soap 1 *n* **cleanser**, detergent, shampoo, soap powder, lather, bubbles, soapsuds, suds, washing powder (*UK*) [➡ CLEANING AGENTS; 863] **2** *n* (*informal*) **serial**, soap opera, series, program [➡ TELEVISION AND RADIO; 606] **3** *v* **cleanse**, lather, wash, wash down, shampoo, sanitize, sterilize, disinfect [➡ CLEAN AND POLISH; 403]

soap opera *n* **serial**, soap, series [➡ TELEVISION AND RADIO; 606]

soap powder *n* **detergent**, soap, soapsuds, cleanser, suds, washing powder (*UK*) [➡ CLEANING AGENTS; 863]

soapstone *type of* **stone** [➡ STONES, ROCKS, AND BOULDERS; 1057]

soapsuds *n* **foam**, lather, suds, froth, bubbles [➡ FOAM; 1273]

soapy *adj* [➡ PHYSICAL TEXTURE; 1222]

soar 1 *v* **fly**, ascend, climb, wheel, circle, rise, mount [➡ GO UPWARD; 306] *Opposite*: plummet **2** *v* **rise**, rocket, climb, mount, increase, go through the roof, go sky-high, escalate, shoot up, skyrocket (*informal*), arise (*archaic or literary*) [➡ CHANGE OF INTENSITY: MORE; 394] *Opposite*: decrease

soaring *adj* **rising**, mounting, climbing, spiraling, increasing, elevated, high, sky-high [➡ CHANGE OF INTENSITY: MORE; 394] *Opposite*: plummeting

sob *v* **moan**, cry, weep, snivel, sniffle, sniff, snuffle, shed tears, howl, bawl (*informal*), blubber (*informal*) [➡ CRYING; 650]

sobbing *n* **crying**, weeping, howling, tears, sniveling, bawling (*informal*) [➡ CRYING; 650]

sober 1 *adj* **abstemious**, clear-headed, temperate, teetotal, moderate, restrained [➡ SELF-DENIAL; 882] **2** *adj* **serious**, somber, solemn, thoughtful, calm, grave, unexcited, unruffled, subdued, restrained, severe, sedate, staid [➡ CONFIDENCE AND COMPOSURE; 499] *Opposite*: frivolous **3** *adj* **dull**, somber, drab, dreary, staid, plain, subdued [➡ DESCRIBING COLORS; 1226] *Opposite*: bright

soberly 1 *adv* **seriously**, solemnly, somberly, gravely, calmly, severely, thoughtfully, pensively, sadly [➡ BAD-TEMPERED AND HUMORLESS; 626] *Opposite*: frivolously **2** *adv* **dully**, drably, plainly, simply, severely, seriously, ascetically, somberly, quietly, moderately [➡ BORING AND UNINTERESTING; 234] *Opposite*: brightly **3** *adv* **rationally**, judiciously, level-headedly, clear-headedly, lucidly, sensibly, cautiously, coherently, rigorously, strictly [➡ POSITIVE INTELLECTUAL CHARACTERISTICS; 524] *Opposite*: fancifully

soberness 1 *n* **seriousness**, solemnity, somberness, gravity, glumness, mournfulness, dolefulness, thoughtfulness, pensiveness, sadness [➡ BAD-TEMPERED AND HUMORLESS; 626] *Opposite*: frivolity **2** *n* **dullness**, drabness, somberness, plainness, simplicity, severity, seriousness, asceticism, moderation, sobriety [➡ BORING AND UNINTERESTING; 234] *Opposite*: brightness **3** *n* **rationality**, judiciousness, level-headedness, clear-headedness, lucidity, sense, rigor, caution, coherence, strictness [➡ POSITIVE INTELLECTUAL CHARACTERISTICS; 524]

sobriety 1 *n* **abstemiousness**, abstinence, temperance, moderation, soberness, clear-headedness [➡ SELF-DENIAL; 882] **2** *n* **seriousness**, somberness, solemnity, thoughtfulness, calm, gravity, sedateness, staidness [➡ CONFIDENCE AND COMPOSURE; 499] *Opposite*: flippancy

sobriquet *n* **nickname**, pet name, term of endearment, alias, assumed name, name, label, tag, epithet, code name, handle (*slang*), moniker (*slang*), appellation (*formal*) [➡ NAME AND DESCRIBE; 665]

sob story (*informal*) *n* **tale of woe**, hard-luck story, sorry tale, sad story [➡ THE ORAL TRADITION; 677]

so-called *adj* **supposed**, alleged, ostensible, purported, self-styled, professed, pretended [➡ FALSE AND UNREAL; 173]

soccer *type of* **ball game** [➡ HOBBIES, GAMES, AND SPORTS; 875]

soccer player *n* [➡ PEOPLE IN SPORTS AND LEISURE; 876]

sociability 1 *n* **gregariousness**, companionability, conviviality, hospitality [➡ FRIENDLINESS AND SOCIABILITY; 494] **2** *n* **friendliness**, pleasantness, amiability, affability, geniality, cordiality, openness, civility [➡ FRIENDLINESS AND SOCIABILITY; 494]

sociable 1 *adj* **gregarious**, companionable, convivial, good company, hospitable [➡ FRIENDLINESS AND SOCIABILITY; 494] *Opposite*: retiring **2** *adj* **friendly**, outgoing, amiable, warm, affable, genial, cordial, jovial [➡ FRIENDLINESS AND SOCIABILITY; 494] *Opposite*: unsociable

social 1 *adj* **communal**, community, common, societal, public, shared, collective, group [➡ BELONGING OR RELATING TO PEOPLE; 943] **2** *n* **party**, gathering, get-together (*informal*) [➡ PARTIES, DANCES, AND CELEBRATIONS; 37]

social call n [➡ INFORMAL COMMUNICATION; 45]

social circle n [➡ FRIENDS AND ACQUAINTANCES; 936]

social class n [➡ STATUS; 888]

social climber n hanger-on, sycophant, toady, snob, socialite, bootlicker (informal) [➡ SUPERFICIAL OR INSINCERE PEOPLE; 951]

social conscience n [➡ MORALLY GOOD; 774]

social democracy n [➡ STYLES AND SYSTEMS OF GOVERNMENT; 806]

social democrat n [➡ PHILOSOPHICAL AND POLITICAL THINKERS; 781]

social event n [➡ PARTIES, DANCES, AND CELEBRATIONS; 37]

socialism n collectivism, social democracy, public ownership, communism, communalism, classless society [➡ STYLES AND SYSTEMS OF GOVERNMENT; 806]

socialist n collectivist, social democrat, communist, communalist [➡ PHILOSOPHICAL AND POLITICAL THINKERS; 781]

socialist realism type of 20th-century art movement [➡ ARTISTIC MOVEMENTS AND STYLES; 899]

socialite n trendsetter, social climber, one of the beautiful people, one of the glitterati, member of café society, one of the in-crowd (informal), jetsetter (informal) [➡ IMPORTANT OR FAMOUS PEOPLE; 893]

socialize v meet people, go out, get out, mix, mingle, entertain, hang out (informal), party (informal) [➡ ESTABLISHING RELATIONSHIPS WITH OTHERS; 974]

socially 1 adv communally, publicly, within society, generally, collectively [➡ BELONGING OR RELATING TO PEOPLE; 943] 2 adv in public, in a social context, with other people, in a crowd [➡ ACTING WITH OTHERS; 285] 3 adv as a friend, outside of work, informally, on a social basis [➡ RELATIONSHIP TO ANOTHER; 973]

social responsibility n [➡ MORALLY GOOD; 774]

social standing n [➡ STATUS; 888]

societal adj social, group, shared, general, common, communal, collective, public [➡ BELONGING OR RELATING TO PEOPLE; 943]

society 1 n civilization, culture, humanity, the social order, the world [➡ GROUPS IN SOCIETY; 940] 2 n people, the public, the general public, the populace, the population [➡ GROUPS IN SOCIETY; 940] 3 n association, union, group, guild, league, organization, club, institute, circle [➡ CLUBS AND SOCIETIES; 939] 4 n high society, the upper classes, polite society, the upper crust (informal) [➡ CLASS STATUS; 889]

sock 1 type of lower body underwear [➡ ACCESSORIES, MILLINERY, AND LINGERIE; 867] 2 n (informal) hit, punch, thump, whack, thwack, smack, wallop (informal) [➡ PHYSICAL ATTACK AND PUNISHMENT; 415] 3 v (informal) hit, punch, thump, whack, thwack, smack, strike, wallop (informal) [➡ PHYSICAL ATTACK AND PUNISHMENT; 415]

socket 1 n hole, opening, hollow [➡ FASTENERS, LINKS, AND NETWORKS; 1247] 2 n outlet, plug (informal), power point (UK) [➡ FIXTURES; 859]

socket wrench type of general tool [➡ HAND TOOLS; 1119]

sod n turf, clod, grass, earth [➡ EROSION PRODUCTS AND SOIL; 1058]

soda bread type of bread [➡ BREAD, FLOUR, AND BREAD PRODUCTS; 1179]

sodden adj saturated, soaking, soaked, soaking wet, sopping wet, sopping, wet, wet through, drenched, wringing wet, wringing [➡ WET; 1240] Opposite: dry

See Compare and Contrast at **wet**.

sofa n settee, couch, chaise longue, day bed, futon, lounger [➡ FURNITURE; 858]

sofa bed type of bed [➡ FURNITURE; 858]

so far adv up to now, thus far, hitherto, until now, to date [➡ PAST; 84]

soffit part of building [➡ PARTS OF A BUILDING; 1095]

soft 1 adj yielding, squashy, spongy, supple, pliable, elastic, malleable, flexible, bendable, ductile, limp [➡ MALLEABLE AND ELASTIC; 1212] Opposite: hard 2 adj smooth, silky, supple, velvety [➡ PHYSICAL TEXTURE; 1222] Opposite: rough 3 adj low, mellifluous, melodious, faint, muted, quiet [➡ SOFT, LOW, OR PLEASANT SOUNDS; 1265] Opposite: loud 4 adj gentle, flowing, delicate, subtle, understated, muted [➡ PHYSICALLY PLEASANT; 186] Opposite: harsh 5 adj dim, diffused, mellow, subtle, gentle [➡ DESCRIBING LIGHT; 1228] Opposite: bright 6 adj lenient, lax, easy, forgiving, overindulgent, indulgent, easygoing, undemanding [➡ GENEROSITY AND KINDNESS; 495] Opposite: strict 7 adj tender, sensitive, gentle, kind, sympathetic, soft-hearted, pleasant, sentimental [➡ GENEROSITY AND KINDNESS; 495] Opposite: hardhearted 8 adj wet, spineless, weak, soppy (informal), pathetic (informal), drippy (slang) [➡ COWARDICE AND WEAKNESS OF WILL; 508]

softball type of ball game [➡ HOBBIES, GAMES, AND SPORTS; 875]

soft-boiled adj soft-hearted, soft, sympathetic, sentimental, indulgent, lenient [➡ GENEROSITY AND KINDNESS; 495] Opposite: hard-boiled (informal)

soften 1 v unstiffen, relax, make softer, make pliable [➡ SOFTEN, LIQUEFY, AND DAMPEN; 388] Opposite: harden 2 v alleviate, lessen, reduce, diminish, mitigate, allay [➡ CHANGE OF INTENSITY: LESS; 395] Opposite: exacerbate 3 v moderate, relax, temper, tone down, assuage, allay, mollify [➡ CHANGE OF INTENSITY: LESS; 395]

soft furnishings n upholstery, curtains, rugs, drapes, cushions, fabrics, throws [➡ FURNISHING AND HOUSEHOLD LINENS; 860]

soft-hearted adj sympathetic, kind, caring, warm, good-natured, considerate, affectionate, loving, soft [➡ GENEROSITY AND KINDNESS; 495] Opposite: hardhearted

soft-heartedness n [➡ GENEROSITY AND KINDNESS; 495]

softie see **softy**

softly 1 adv tenderly, delicately, gently, kindly, sympathetically, sensitively, quietly [➡ GENEROSITY AND KINDNESS; 495] Opposite: severely 2 adv quietly, gently, mellifluously, melodiously, faintly [➡ SOFT, LOW, OR PLEASANT SOUNDS; 1265] Opposite: harshly 3 adv dimly, gently, faintly, lightly, subtly [➡ DESCRIBING LIGHT; 1228] Opposite: brightly

softly lit adj [➡ DESCRIBING LIGHT; 1228]

softly-softly (UK) adj cautious, discreet, tentative, vigilant, mindful, cagey (*informal*) [➡ CAUTIOUS AND CAREFUL; 282] *Opposite*: heavy-handed

softness 1 *n* **gentleness**, smoothness, quietness, faintness [➡ PEACEFULNESS AND GENTLENESS; 214] *Opposite*: harshness 2 *n* **pliability**, suppleness, flexibility, elasticity, malleability [➡ MALLEABLE AND ELASTIC; 1212]

soft on *adj* [➡ APPRECIATION AND GRATITUDE; 535]

soft option *n* [➡ EASY WORK; 299]

soft palate *part of* **mouth** [➡ THE MOUTH; 702]

soft-pedal (*informal*) *v* **play down**, downplay, make light of, underplay, minimize, make little of [➡ CHANGE OF INTENSITY: LESS; 395] *Opposite*: emphasize

soft sell (*informal*) *n* **persuasion**, persuasiveness, subtlety, sweet-talking (*informal*), soft-soaping (*informal*) [➡ INGRATIATING; 638]

soft-soap (*informal*) *v* **flatter**, play up to, lay it on thick, sweet-talk (*informal*), butter up (*informal*), suck up to (*informal*), lay it on with a trowel (*informal*) [➡ FLATTER AND FAWN; 621]

soft-spoken *adj* **quiet**, gentle, calm, tranquil, serene [➡ RETICENT AND UNFORTHCOMING; 631] *Opposite*: loud

soft spot *n* **weakness**, partiality, affection, weak spot, liking, fondness, penchant, inclination, preference, fancy, predilection (*formal*) [➡ APPRECIATION AND GRATITUDE; 535]

soft touch *n* **easy prey**, easy target, easy mark, pushover (*informal*), sucker (*informal*), softy (*informal*) [➡ VICTIMS OF DECEIT; 662]

software *n* [➡ COMPUTERS AND COMPUTING; 1127]

software design *n* [➡ COMPUTERS AND COMPUTING; 1127]

software development *n* [➡ COMPUTERS AND COMPUTING; 1127]

softy (*informal*) *n* **soft touch**, easy target, easy prey, sucker (*informal*) [➡ VICTIMS OF DECEIT; 662]

sogginess *n* [➡ MOIST; 1241]

soggy *adj* **damp**, wet, moist, mushy, squelchy, sodden, waterlogged [➡ MOIST; 1241] *Opposite*: dry

soi-disant (*literary*) *adj* **self-styled**, so-called, self-proclaimed, self-confessed, self-appointed, professed [➡ FALSE AND UNREAL; 173]

soigné *adj* **well-groomed**, neat, elegant, chic, stylish, well turned-out (*UK*) [➡ WELL-GROOMED; 482] *Opposite*: dowdy

soil 1 *n* **earth**, dirt, topsoil, mud, dust, loam [➡ EROSION PRODUCTS AND SOIL; 1058] 2 *n* **territory**, land, country, ground [➡ COUNTRIES AND REGIONS; 1067] 3 *v* **dirty**, get dirty, foul, muddy, stain, sully (*literary*) [➡ DIRTY AND CONTAMINATE; 404] *Opposite*: cleanse

soiled *adj* **dirty**, grubby, muddy, stained, filthy, mucky (*informal*) [➡ DIRTY; 1235] *Opposite*: clean

See Compare and Contrast at **dirty**.

soil science *type of* **earth science** [➡ EARTH SCIENCES; 1059]

soiree *n* **party**, celebration, dinner party, evening, gath-

ering, event, cocktail party, function, evening party, get-together (*informal*), drinks party (*UK*) [➡ PARTIES, DANCES, AND CELEBRATIONS; 37]

soirée *see* **soiree**

sojourn (*literary*) 1 *n* **visit**, stay, stop, stopover [➡ TRAVEL: JOURNEYS AND TRIPS; 318] 2 *v* **stay**, stop, remain, dwell (*literary*), abide (*archaic*) [➡ INHABIT; 20]

sol *type of* **currency** [➡ CURRENCIES; 798]

solace *n* **comfort**, consolation, support, relief, help, succor (*literary*) [➡ KIND ACTIONS OR BEHAVIOR; 295] *Opposite*: aggravation

solar cell *part of* **spacecraft** [➡ SPACE VEHICLES; 1063]

solar heating *n* [➡ HEATING, REFRIGERATION, AND VENTILATION; 1142]

solarium *n* **conservatory**, sun parlor, suntrap, greenhouse, sun lounge (*UK*) [➡ BUILDINGS FOR PUBLIC ENTERTAINMENT; 1084]

solar plexus *part of* **torso** [➡ PARTS OF THE BODY: TORSO; 693]

solar system *n* [➡ THE SOLAR SYSTEM AND ASTRONOMY; 1060]

solder *v* **join**, fuse, weld, bond, connect, repair [➡ USE TOOLS AND MACHINERY; 468]

soldering iron *type of* **general tool** [➡ HAND TOOLS; 1119]

soldier 1 *n* **fighter**, combatant, warrior, regular, legionnaire, GI [➡ MILITARY PERSONNEL; 828] 2 *n* **private**, sapper, gunner, corporal, sergeant, trooper, guardsman [➡ MILITARY PERSONNEL; 828] 3 *n* **worker**, supporter, campaigner, crusader, workhorse [➡ WORKERS; 836]

soldier ant *type of* **ant** [➡ ANTS; 1014]

soldier of fortune *n* **mercenary**, adventurer, hired gun (*slang*) [➡ PEOPLE WHO KILL; 924] *Opposite*: regular

soldier on *v* **persevere**, continue, carry on, keep on, keep going, persist [➡ CONTINUE AN ACTION; 262] *Opposite*: give up

sold on *adj* [➡ APPRECIATION AND GRATITUDE; 535]

sole 1 *adj* **only**, solitary, single, individual, singular, lone, one and only [➡ EXTRAORDINARY: UNCOMMON; 205] 2 *adj* **exclusive**, private, unique, special, individual [➡ UNRELATEDNESS AND SEPARATENESS; 146] 3 *part of* **leg or foot** [➡ PARTS OF THE BODY: LEG AND FOOT; 694] 4 *type of* **flatfish** [➡ OCEAN FISH; 1009]

solecism *n* **error**, mistake, blunder, slip, gaffe, faux pas (*literary*), blooper (*informal humorous*) [➡ MISTAKES; 250]

solely *adv* **exclusively**, only, merely, just, uniquely, specially [➡ MAINLY AND PRIMARILY; 140]

solemn 1 *adj* **somber**, grave, serious, sober, sad, glum, lugubrious, humorless [➡ BAD-TEMPERED AND HUMORLESS; 626] *Opposite*: cheerful 2 *adj* **earnest**, sincere, serious, firm, grave, intense [➡ PENSIVENESS AND INTEREST; 538] *Opposite*: flippant 3 *adj* **formal**, official, ceremonial, ritual, sacred, holy [➡ RELIGIOUS CONCEPTS; 776]

solemnity *n* **somberness**, gravity, seriousness, soberness, sadness, glumness [➡ BAD-TEMPERED AND HUMORLESS; 626]

solemnize *v* **celebrate**, honor, make official, formalize, sanctify, observe [➡ RELIGIONS AND RELIGIOUS PRACTICES; 777]

solenoid *part of* **engine** [➡ PARTS OF AN ENGINE; 1144]

solicit 1 *v* **ask for**, beg, seek, petition for, plead for, request, crave [➡REQUEST AND DEMAND; 663] *Opposite*: grant 2 *v* **ask**, petition, lobby, plead with, implore (*formal*), importune (*formal*), beseech (*literary*) [➡REQUEST AND DEMAND; 663]

solicitor (*UK*) *n* **lawyer**, advocate, legal representative, attorney [➡PEOPLE IN LAW COURTS; 820]

solicitous *adj* **considerate**, caring, attentive, concerned, kind [➡GENEROSITY AND KINDNESS; 495] *Opposite*: uncaring

solicitousness *n* **concern**, attentiveness, consideration, care, kindness, solicitude [➡GENEROSITY AND KINDNESS; 495]

solicitude 1 *n* **concern**, attentiveness, consideration, care, kindness, solicitousness [➡GENEROSITY AND KINDNESS; 495] *Opposite*: negligence 2 *n* **anxiety**, concern, worry, unease, apprehension, apprehensiveness [➡FEELINGS ABOUT THE FUTURE; 533] *Opposite*: serenity

solid 1 *adj* **hard**, rock-hard, rock-solid, concrete, firm, unyielding, frozen, dense, compact, compacted [➡RIGID AND HARD; 1211] *Opposite*: soft 2 *adj* **dense**, unbroken, continuous, closed, blocked, scaled [➡DENSITY AND CONSISTENCY; 1207] *Opposite*: hollow 3 *adj* **pure**, genuine, unadulterated, one hundred percent, unmixed, real [➡TRUE AND REAL; 171] 4 *adj* **sturdy**, strong, secure, fixed, firm, safe, stable, sound, substantial, robust, rugged [➡STRENGTH; 2011] *Opposite*: weak 5 *adj* **reliable**, dependable, sound, trustworthy, level-headed [➡HONEST AND RELIABLE; 502] *Opposite*: unreliable 6 *adj* **unanimous**, universal, widespread, popular, general, total, consistent [➡HARMONY; 155] *Opposite*: patchy 7 *n* **object**, thing, artifact, item, entity, article [➡SOLIDS; 1274] 8 *n* **figure**, pyramid, tetrahedron, sphere, icosahedron, dodecahedron, cube [➡ANGULAR SHAPE; 1217]

solidarity *n* **unity**, harmony, cohesion, commonality, camaraderie, team spirit, esprit de corps, unanimity [➡HARMONY; 155] *Opposite*: discord

solidify *v* **harden**, coagulate, congeal, set, get hard, freeze, go hard (*UK*) [➡HARDEN, CONGEAL, AND DRY; 387] *Opposite*: dissolve

solidity *n* **hardness**, firmness, solidness, sturdiness, strength, toughness [➡DENSITY AND CONSISTENCY; 1207] *Opposite*: softness

solidly 1 *adv* **firmly**, sturdily, stably, steadily, soundly, dependably [➡STRENGTH; 201] *Opposite*: weakly 2 *adv* **unanimously**, universally, totally, consistently, one hundred percent, to the hilt, all the way [➡WHOLENESS AND COMPLETENESS; 198] *Opposite*: sporadically

solidness *n* **hardness**, firmness, sturdiness, solidity, strength, toughness [➡DENSITY AND CONSISTENCY; 1207]

soliloquy *n* **monologue**, speech, declamation, oration, dramatic monologue [➡THE ORAL TRADITION; 677]

solipsism *n* [➡PSYCHOLOGY AND THE MIND; 769]

solipsistic *adj* [➡PSYCHOLOGY AND THE MIND; 769]

solitaire *n* **single stone**, gemstone, jewel, diamond, precious stone, sparkler (*informal*) [➡JEWELRY; 866]

solitariness *n* [➡SOLITARINESS; 941]

solitary 1 *adj* **private**, unsociable, unsocial, self-con-

tained, self-sufficient, independent, lonely, retiring, friendless, introverted [➡UNFRIENDLINESS AND UNSOCIABILITY; 504] *Opposite*: sociable 2 *adj* **lone**, single, sole, individual, solo, unaccompanied [➡SOLITARINESS; 941] *Opposite*: accompanied 3 *adj* **isolated**, desolate, out-of-the-way, secluded, unfrequented, remote [➡DISTANCE; 160]

solitary confinement *n* **isolation**, imprisonment, confinement, detention, custody, solitary, incarceration (*formal*) [➡CAPTIVITY AND LOSS OF FREEDOM; 248]

solitude *n* **loneliness**, privacy, isolation, seclusion, separateness, aloneness [➡SOLITARINESS; 941]

solo 1 *adj* **single**, unaccompanied, lone [➡SOLITARINESS; 941] 2 *adv* **alone**, on your own, singly, by yourself [➡ACTING INDEPENDENTLY; 284]

soloist *n* **artist**, artiste, musician, singer, vocalist, star, virtuoso [➡MUSICIANS AND SINGERS; 908] *Opposite*: accompanist

solon (*literary*) *n* **statesman**, adviser, mentor, elder statesman, sage (*literary*) [➡TALENTED OR INTELLIGENT PEOPLE; 528]

so long (*informal*) *interj* **goodbye**, adieu, ciao (*informal*), see you later (*informal*), bye (*informal*), bye-bye (*informal*), farewell (*literary*) [➡GREETINGS, FAREWELLS, AND SALUTATIONS; 659]

so long as *conj* [➡CAUSATION; 168]

solstice *n* [➡TIMES OF YEAR; 88]

solubility *n* **dissolvability**, deliquescence [➡DENSITY AND CONSISTENCY; 1207] *Opposite*: insolubility

soluble 1 *adj* **solvable**, answerable, fathomable, resolvable, decipherable, doable [➡EASE AND SIMPLICITY; 200] *Opposite*: insoluble 2 *adj* **dissolvable**, deliquescent [➡DENSITY AND CONSISTENCY; 1207] *Opposite*: insoluble

solution 1 *n* **answer**, key, explanation, resolution, way out, result [➡SOLUTIONS; 215] *Opposite*: problem 2 *n* **mix**, mixture, liquid, blend, cocktail [➡LIQUIDS; 1269]

solvable *adj* **soluble**, resolvable, fathomable, answerable, decipherable, doable [➡EASE AND SIMPLICITY; 200] *Opposite*: insoluble

solve *v* **resolve**, crack, answer, explain, get to the bottom of, unravel, decipher, work out, disentangle, unscramble, elucidate [➡SOLVE AND INTERPRET; 760]

solvency *n* **creditworthiness**, affluence, wealth, soundness, comfort [➡WEALTH AND WEALTHY; 891]

solvent 1 *adj* **in the black**, in credit, in the chips, in the money, in clover, flush (*informal*), in funds (*UK*) [➡WEALTH AND WEALTHY; 891] *Opposite*: insolvent 2 *n* [➡LIQUIDS; 1269]

som *type of* **currency** [➡CURRENCIES; 798]

soma *n* [➡BODY; 691]

somber 1 *adj* **dark**, dull, gloomy, drab, dingy [➡SADNESS, DISTRESS, AND DESPAIR; 539] *Opposite*: bright 2 *adj* **muted**, subdued, drab, dull, dark [➡DESCRIBING COLORS; 1226] *Opposite*: light 3 *adj* **melancholy**, lugubrious, sad, depressed, dismal, serious, solemn, sepulchral, funereal [➡EMOTIONALLY UNPLEASANT AND UPSETTING; 227] *Opposite*: cheerful

somberness *n* [➡SADNESS, DISTRESS, AND DESPAIR; 539]

sombrero *type of* **hat** [➡ ACCESSORIES, MILLINERY, AND LINGERIE; 867]

some 1 *adv* **approximately**, about, around, roughly, more or less, nearly, round about, or so [➡ APPROXIMATELY; 135] *Opposite*: exactly **2** *adj* **a number of**, a little, a few, several, various, a quantity of [➡ AMOUNTS AND QUANTITIES; 112] *Opposite*: all **3** *adj* **certain**, particular, selected, specific [➡ AMOUNTS AND QUANTITIES; 112]

somebody 1 *pron* **some person**, someone [➡ PERSON; 931] *Opposite*: nobody **2** *n* **celebrity**, someone, name, superstar, bigwig (*informal*), big shot (*informal*), big cheese (*slang*) [➡ IMPORTANT OR FAMOUS PEOPLE; 893] *Opposite*: nobody

someday *adv* **one day**, sooner or later, sometime, soon, in the future, one of these days [➡ FUTURE; 86] *Opposite*: never

somehow *adv* **one way or another**, someway, by hook or by crook, come what may, come hell or high water [➡ WAYS OF DOING THINGS; 294]

someone 1 *pron* **somebody**, some person [➡ PERSON; 931] *Opposite*: no one **2** *n* **celebrity**, somebody, big name, star, superstar, name, big shot (*informal*) [➡ IMPORTANT OR FAMOUS PEOPLE; 893] *Opposite*: nobody

someplace (*informal*) *adv* **somewhere**, wherever, anywhere, anyplace (*informal*) [➡ GENERAL LOCATIONS; 158]

somersault 1 *n* **tumble**, forward roll, flip-flop, cartwheel, flip [➡ FIDGET AND FROLIC; 311] **2** *v* **turn over**, tumble, flip over, cartwheel, flip [➡ FIDGET AND FROLIC; 311]

something *adv* **a little**, somewhat, to some degree, rather, approximately, roughly, a bit (*informal*) [➡ TO A CERTAIN EXTENT; 136] *Opposite*: exactly

something else entirely *n* [➡ DIFFERENCE; 149]

sometime 1 *adv* **at some point**, someday, at some time, in the future, one day, one of these days [➡ FUTURE; 86] *Opposite*: never **2** *adj* (*formal*) **former**, onetime, previous, earlier, ex (*informal*), erstwhile (*formal*) [➡ PAST; 84] *Opposite*: current

some time ago *adv* [➡ PAST; 84]

sometimes *adv* **occasionally**, now and then, every now and then, every so often, now and again, from time to time, at times, on occasion [➡ NEVER AND INFREQUENCY; 97] *Opposite*: always

someway *adv* **somehow**, one way or another, in some way, by some means, by hook or by crook, come what may, come hell or high water [➡ WAYS OF DOING THINGS; 294]

somewhat *adv* **rather**, fairly, slightly, to some extent, to a certain extent, to some degree, to a certain degree, a bit (*informal*) [➡ TO A CERTAIN EXTENT; 136]

somewhere *adv* **wherever**, anywhere, anyplace (*informal*), someplace (*informal*) [➡ GENERAL LOCATIONS; 158]

sommelier *type of* **person who works in restaurants** [➡ DOMESTIC AND KITCHEN WORKERS; 850]

somnolence *n* [➡ SLEEP AND DREAM; 723]

somnolent *adj* **sleepy**, drowsy, dozy, half asleep, half awake, lethargic, torpid [➡ TIRED, ASLEEP, AND UNCONSCIOUS; 738]

son 1 *n* **child**, lad, boy, kid (*informal*) [➡ CHILD OR YOUTH; 945] **2** *type of* **younger relative** [➡ YOUNGER GENERATION RELATIVES; 958]

sonata *type of* **musical form** [➡ MUSIC, SONGS, AND SINGING; 907]

son et lumière *n* **entertainment**, spectacle, light show, tableau, spectacular [➡ ENTERTAINMENT; 872]

song 1 *n* **tune**, melody, air, refrain, jingle, ditty, nursery rhyme, chorus, solo, carol, hymn, chant, ballad, folk song, piece, number, composition [➡ MUSIC, SONGS, AND SINGING; 907] **2** *n* **birdsong**, call, warble, warbling, cry, chirrup, coo, cooing, mating song, mating call [➡ SOUNDS MADE BY BIRDS; 1263]

songbook *n* **anthology**, collection, hymnbook, book, hymnal, psalter [➡ BOOKS AND BOOKLETS; 590]

songsmith *n* [➡ MUSICIANS AND SINGERS; 908]

songster *n* **singer**, vocalist, lead singer, soloist, chanteuse, diva [➡ MUSICIANS AND SINGERS; 908]

songwriter *n* **composer**, lyricist, songsmith, poet, librettist, writer, artist [➡ MUSICIANS AND SINGERS; 908]

sonic *adj* **auditory**, aural, audible, sound [➡ ACOUSTICS; 1138]

sonic boom *n* **boom**, shock wave, noise, rumble, roar, echo, vibration [➡ CONTINUOUS SOUNDS; 1258]

son-in-law *type of* **in-law** [➡ RELATIVES BY MARRIAGE; 960]

sonnet *n* **poem**, verse, rhyme, Petrarchan sonnet, Shakespearian sonnet [➡ POETRY AND VERSE; 915]

sonny (*informal*) *n* **lad**, young man, my boy, my lad, sonny boy (*informal*), boyo (*informal*), kid (*informal*), kiddo (*informal*) [➡ CHILD OR YOUTH; 945]

sonny boy (*informal*) *see* **sonny**

sonority *n* **resonance**, fullness, roundness, richness, reverberation, vibration [➡ SOUNDS; 1256] *Opposite*: reediness

sonorous *adj* **loud**, deep, resonant, echoing, booming, resounding, plangent [➡ LOUD, HIGH, OR UNPLEASANT SOUNDS; 1266] *Opposite*: thin

soon *adv* **almost immediately**, quickly, rapidly, shortly, before long, in next to no time, in a little while, momentarily, presently (*formal or literary*) [➡ FUTURE; 86]

sooner 1 *adv* **earlier**, faster, more quickly, more rapidly, nearer, closer [➡ PROMPTNESS: EARLY; 98] *Opposite*: later **2** *adv* **rather**, more readily, more willingly, preferably, as soon [➡ THE WILL AND WILLINGNESS; 563]

sooner or later *adv* **eventually**, one day, someday, in time, in due course, sometime [➡ FUTURE; 86] *Opposite*: never

soon-to-be *adj* [➡ FUTURE; 86]

soot *n* **dust**, powder, grime, ashes, dirt, coal, smoke, smut, ash, clinker [➡ PRODUCTS OF FIRE; 1166]

soothe 1 *v* **calm**, pacify, quiet, appease, mollify, lull, relax [➡ SOOTHE AND CALM; 573] *Opposite*: excite **2** *v* **ease**, relieve, alleviate, reduce, palliate, lessen [➡ CORRECT AND PUT RIGHT; 377] *Opposite*: aggravate

soothing *adj* **calming**, comforting, restful, gentle, peaceful, relaxing [➡ CALMING; 188] *Opposite*: irritating

soothsayer *n* **fortune-teller**, oracle, seer, astrologer, clairvoyant, mystic [➡ PEOPLE WITH SUPERNATURAL POWERS; 788]

sooty *adj* **dirty**, grimy, black, filthy, dusty, smutty, smoky, mucky (*informal*), grungy (*informal*) [➡DIRTY; 1235] *Opposite*: clean

sop *n* **concession**, offering, bribe, pacifier, gesture [➡GIFTS; 438]

sophism *n* [➡DECEPTION AND LIES; 660]

sophist *n* [➡PEOPLE WHO DECEIVE; 661]

sophistic *adj* [➡FALSE AND UNREAL; 173]

sophisticate 1 *v* **educate**, school, mold, acculturate, tutor [➡INSTRUCT AND TEACH; 609] 2 *n* **socialite**, trendsetter, connoisseur, aesthete, cognoscente, jetsetter (*informal*), trendy (*informal*) [➡LEVELS OF EDUCATION AND SOPHISTICATION; 894] *Opposite*: hoi polloi

sophisticated 1 *adj* **urbane**, cultured, chic, erudite, refined, stylish, classy (*informal*) [➡LEVELS OF EDUCATION AND SOPHISTICATION; 894] *Opposite*: gauche 2 *adj* **clever**, advanced, high-level, complex, erudite, high-tech, state-of-the-art, cutting-edge, leading-edge, modern [➡POSITIVELY COMPLEX OR COMPLICATED; 217] *Opposite*: crude

sophistication 1 *n* **complexity**, erudition, difficulty, intricacy, cleverness (*UK*) [➡POSITIVELY COMPLEX OR COMPLICATED; 217] *Opposite*: crudeness 2 *n* **refinement**, style, chic, urbanity, elegance, classiness (*informal*) [➡LEVELS OF EDUCATION AND SOPHISTICATION; 894] *Opposite*: naiveté

sophistry *n* **casuistry**, fallaciousness, illogicality, sophism, dishonesty, fraudulence [➡DECEPTION AND LIES; 660] *Opposite*: logic

soporific 1 *adj* **sleep-inducing**, calming, tranquilizing, narcotic, hypnotic (*informal*) [➡TIRED, ASLEEP, AND UNCONSCIOUS; 738] 2 *adj* **tedious**, boring, interminable, turgid, endless, monotonous, dull [➡BORING AND UNINTERESTING; 234] *Opposite*: stimulating

sopping *adj* **drenched**, soaked, dripping, sodden, saturated, sopping wet, waterlogged, wringing wet, soaking, wet [➡WET; 1240] *Opposite*: dry

*See Compare and Contrast at **wet**.*

sopping wet *adj* [➡WET; 1240]

soppy 1 *adj* **soaked**, wet, sopping wet, sopping, dripping, drenched, waterlogged, saturated, sodden, wringing wet, soaking, dripping wet [➡WET; 1240] *Opposite*: dry 2 *adj* (*UK informal*) **sentimental**, mawkish, soft, slushy, corny, mushy, wet, schmaltzy (*informal*) [➡IN POOR TASTE AND OVERSENTIMENTAL; 229] *Opposite*: unsentimental

soprano 1 *n* **singer**, vocalist, soloist, chanteuse, diva [➡MUSICIANS AND SINGERS; 908] 2 *type of* **musical register** [➡MUSICAL TERMS; 912] 3 *adj* **high**, high-pitched, shrill, piercing, soaring [➡MUSICAL TERMS; 912] *Opposite*: bass

sop up *v* **soak up**, mop up, sponge, absorb, wipe, take in [➡GET RID OF SOMETHING; 451]

sorbet *n* **fruit ice**, ice, sherbet, dessert, sweet (*UK*), pudding (*UK*), water ice (*UK*) [➡CAKES, COOKIES, AND DESSERTS; 1181]

sorcerer *n* **wizard**, magician, enchanter, magus, witch, necromancer (*literary*) [➡PEOPLE WITH SUPERNATURAL POWERS; 788]

sorceress *n* **witch**, enchantress, sibyl, magician, necromancer (*literary*) [➡PEOPLE WITH SUPERNATURAL POWERS; 788]

sorcery *n* **witchcraft**, wizardry, magic, black magic, enchantment, witchery, bewitchment, conjuring, necromancy (*literary*) [➡THE SUPERNATURAL; 787]

sordid 1 *adj* **base**, disreputable, sleazy, repugnant, disgusting, despicable, ignoble, wretched, degenerate, decadent, nasty (*informal*) [➡MORALLY BAD OR IMPROPER; 775] *Opposite*: uplifting 2 *adj* **squalid**, distasteful, disgusting, low, dirty, grimy, grubby, foul, filthy, rundown, grungy (*informal*) [➡DISGUSTING AND REPULSIVE; 230] *Opposite*: pleasant

sordidness 1 *n* **baseness**, sleaze, unpleasantness, repugnance, wretchedness, nastiness, decadence [➡MORALLY BAD OR IMPROPER; 775] *Opposite*: pleasantness 2 *n* **squalor**, grime, filth, squalidness, grubbiness, filthiness, foulness [➡DISGUSTING AND REPULSIVE; 230] *Opposite*: cleanliness

sore 1 *adj* **painful**, tender, uncomfortable, stinging, aching, raw [➡PAIN AND OTHER PHYSICAL SENSATIONS; 733] *Opposite*: comfortable 2 *adj* **annoying**, sensitive, embarrassing, controversial, difficult, awkward, contentious [➡EMOTIONALLY UNPLEASANT AND UPSETTING; 227] *Opposite*: uncontroversial 3 *adj* (*informal*) **angry**, cross, mad, annoyed, upset, resentful, bitter, offended [➡IRRITATION AND ANGER; 541] *Opposite*: pleased 4 *n* **wound**, abscess, lesion, eruption, blister, boil, spot, infection [➡CONDITIONS AFFECTING THE SKIN; 721]

sorely (*formal*) *adv* **deeply**, truly, greatly, very much, really, profoundly [➡TO A GREAT EXTENT; 132] *Opposite*: not at all

soreness *n* **tenderness**, pain, discomfort, distress, agony, ache, aching, hurt, redness [➡PAIN AND OTHER PHYSICAL SENSATIONS; 733]

sorghum *type of* **cereal** [➡CEREAL FOODS; 1178]

sorority *n* [➡GROUPS WITH A COMMON INTEREST; 938]

sorrel 1 *type of* **salad vegetable** [➡FRUIT AND VEGETABLES; 1176] 2 *type of* **brown** [➡COLORS; 1224]

sorrow 1 *n* **grief**, mourning, sadness, distress, sorrowfulness, unhappiness, disappointment, regret [➡SADNESS, DISTRESS, AND DESPAIR; 539] *Opposite*: joy 2 *v* (*literary*) **grieve**, mourn, wail, lament, weep, cry [➡BE CONCERNED AND CARE; 581] *Opposite*: rejoice (*literary*)

sorrowful 1 *adj* **sad**, mournful, grief-stricken, distressed, unhappy, regretful, sorrowing, troubled [➡SADNESS, DISTRESS, AND DESPAIR; 539] *Opposite*: joyful 2 *adj* **tragic**, sad, solemn, unhappy, distressing, troubling [➡EMOTIONALLY UNPLEASANT AND UPSETTING; 227] *Opposite*: happy

sorrowfulness *n* [➡SADNESS, DISTRESS, AND DESPAIR; 539]

sorrowing *adj* **sad**, mournful, grief-stricken, distressed, unhappy, regretful, sorrowful, troubled [➡SADNESS, DISTRESS, AND DESPAIR; 539] *Opposite*: joyful

sorry 1 *adj* **apologetic**, regretful, remorseful, repentant, sad, unhappy [➡EMBARRASSMENT AND HUMILIATION; 542] *Opposite*: glad 2 *adj* **pitiful**, miserable, wretched, forlorn, pathetic, poor [➡BAD AND BADLY; 223] *Opposite*: fine

sort 1 *n* **category**, kind, class, type, genus, species, variety, nature, ilk, order [➡VARIETIES, TYPES, AND KINDS; 145] 2 *n* (*informal*) **personality type**, person, character, type, individual, soul [➡PERSON; 931] 3 *v* **arrange**, classify, rank, place, sort out, separate, categorize, group, assort, organize, order [➡ ARRANGE AND CREATE ORDER; 357] *Opposite:* mix up

See Compare and Contrast at **type**.

sortie 1 *n* **attack**, maneuver, foray, incursion, inroad, raid [➡ AGGRESSIVE EVENTS; 39] *Opposite:* retreat **2** *n* (*humorous*) **excursion**, trip, outing, journey, jaunt, trek [➡ TRAVEL: JOURNEYS AND TRIPS; 318]

sort of (*informal*) *adv* [➡ TO A CERTAIN EXTENT; 136]

sort out 1 *v* **resolve**, deal with, solve, iron out, fix, settle, see to, work out [➡ CARRY OUT AN ACTION; 269] **2** *v* **put in order**, arrange, file, disentangle, tidy up, order, organize [➡ ARRANGE AND CREATE ORDER; 357] *Opposite:* mix up **3** *v* **separate**, distinguish, segregate, sort, divide [➡ SEPARATE AND DIVIDE; 401]

SOS *n* **distress signal**, cry for help, call for help, alarm, flare, alert, signal [➡ SIGNPOSTS, SIGNALS, AND BILLBOARDS; 595]

so-so (*informal*) *adj* **average**, fair, mediocre, unremarkable, indifferent, passable, all right, run-of-the-mill, medium, middling, ordinary, okay (*informal*) [➡ ACCEPTABLE AND PASSABLE; 219] *Opposite:* exceptional

sotto voce 1 *adv* **quietly**, softly, inaudibly, gently, faintly, indistinctly, in a murmur [➡ SOFT, LOW, OR PLEASANT SOUNDS; 1265] *Opposite:* loudly **2** *adj* **soft**, quiet, gentle, inaudible, hushed, whispered, muted, low, murmured [➡ SOFT, LOW, OR PLEASANT SOUNDS; 1265] *Opposite:* loud **3** *type of* **musical term** [➡ MUSIC, SONGS, AND SINGING; 907]

soufflé *type of* **dessert** [➡ CAKES, COOKIES, AND DESSERTS; 1181]

sought-after *adj* **desirable**, coveted, in demand, exclusive, fashionable, popular, preferred, trendy (*informal*) [➡ POPULAR AND WANTED; 220] *Opposite:* unpopular

souk *n* **bazaar**, market, marketplace, flea market, emporium [➡ URBAN OUTDOOR SPACES; 1072]

soul 1 *n* **spirit**, consciousness, psyche, will, essence, being [➡ RELIGIOUS CONCEPTS; 776] **2** *n* **depth**, personality, atmosphere, emotion, passion, ambiance, feeling, humanity, compassion, empathy [➡ APPEARANCE AND ATMOSPHERE; 1237] **3** *n* **individual**, person, anyone, someone, example, human being [➡ PERSON; 931] **4** *n* **soul music**, gospel, R & B, rhythm and blues, blues, funk [➡ MUSIC, SONGS, AND SINGING; 907]

soul-destroying *adj* **demoralizing**, depressing, disheartening, unfulfilling, boring, tedious, unsatisfying, monotonous [➡ EMOTIONALLY UNPLEASANT AND UPSETTING; 227] *Opposite:* satisfying

soulful *adj* **expressive**, affecting, sad, moving, poignant, touching, mournful, emotional [➡ EMOTIONALLY PLEASANT; 187] *Opposite:* emotionless

soulfulness *n* **expressiveness**, sadness, poignancy, emotion, mournfulness, feeling [➡ SADNESS, DISTRESS, AND DESPAIR; 539]

soulless *adj* **bleak**, utilitarian, characterless, inexpressive, insensitive, unfeeling, faceless, gray [➡ BORING AND UNINTERESTING; 234] *Opposite:* soulful

soul mate *n* **friend**, mate, boon companion, confidant, confidante, partner, companion, crony, bosom buddy, pal (*informal*), chum (*informal*), buddy (*informal*), bosom friend (*UK*) [➡ FRIENDS AND GUESTS; 963]

soul music *n* [➡ MUSIC, SONGS, AND SINGING; 907]

soul-searching *n* **thought**, consideration, contemplation, introspection, assessment, judgment, examination, deliberation (*formal*) [➡ THINK AND REFLECT; 743]

sound 1 *n* **noise**, resonance, hum, echo, thud, reverberation, crash, jingle, swish, clatter, vibration, crunch, tinkle, jangle, clank, splash [➡ SOUNDS; 1256] *Opposite:* silence **2** *n* **strait**, channel, inlet, fjord [➡ THE SEAS, OCEANS, AND SHORES; 1041] **3** *v* **seem**, appear, look [➡ SEEM TO BE SOMETHING; 58] **4** *v* **announce**, ring out, declare, signal, express, call, advertise, broadcast, proclaim [➡ INFORM, ANNOUNCE, AND ISSUE; 611] **5** *v* **go off**, ring out, explode, ring, wail, clang [➡ EMIT CONTINUOUS SOUNDS; 366] **6** *adj* **complete**, comprehensive, wide-ranging, all-encompassing, thorough, rigorous, encyclopedic [➡ WHOLENESS AND COMPLETENESS; 198] *Opposite:* superficial **7** *adj* **sensible**, good, firm, unassailable, reliable, watertight, valid, secure [➡ SAFE AND SAFETY; 191] *Opposite:* unsound **8** *adj* **whole**, healthy, unblemished, perfect, normal, fit, sturdy, intact, undamaged [➡ SAFE AND SOUND; 737] *Opposite:* infirm **9** *adj* **thorough**, firm, rigorous, good, hard, severe, thoroughgoing [➡ WHOLENESS AND COMPLETENESS; 198] *Opposite:* half-hearted

---

sound

◆ *types of animal sounds*
baa, bark, bay, bleat, bray, caterwaul, croak, growl, grunt, howl, meow, mew, moo, neigh, oink, purr, roar, snarl, squeak, squeal, whinny, woof, yap, yelp

◆ *types of bird sounds*
caw, cheep, chirp, chirrup, cluck, cock-a-doodle-doo, coo, hoot, peep, quack, screak, screech, squawk, trill, tweet, twitter, warble

◆ *types of human sounds*
babble, bawl, bellow, boo, catcall, chatter, chortle, chuckle, cry, gasp, giggle, groan, grunt, holler (*informal*), howl, hum, moan, murmur, mutter, peep, screak, scream, screech, shout, shriek, sigh, slurp, snicker, sniffle, splutter, squeal, titter, wail, wheeze, whimper, whine, whisper, whistle, whoop, yell

◆ *types of continuous sounds*
beep, bleep, boom, burble, buzz, chug, crackle, creak, drone, gurgle, hiss, honk, hoot, hum, purl (*literary*), purr, rasp, rattle, roar, rumble, rustle, sizzle, sonic boom, swish, swoosh, throb, thunder, whir, whiz, whoosh

◆ *types of impact sounds*
bang, beat, bong, bonk (*informal*), bump, clang, clank, clap, clash, clatter, click, clip-clop, clop, clunk, crack, crash, patter, pitter-patter, plop, plunk, pop, rat-a-tat-tat, rattle, slam, smash, splash, splat, squelch, squish, tap, thud, thump, thwack, tick, ticktock, wham

◆ *types of ringing sounds*
chime, chink, clink, ding, ding-a-ling, ding-dong, honk, hoot, jangle, jingle, knell, peal, ping, ring, ting, tinkle, toll, tootle (*informal*)

See Compare and Contrast at **valid**.

sound asleep *adj* **sleeping**, slumbering, out, fast asleep, dead to the world, sleeping like a baby, sleeping like a log [➡ TIRED, ASLEEP, AND UNCONSCIOUS; 738] *Opposite:* awake

sound bite *n* **comment**, announcement, statement, declaration, response, remark, observation, quote [➡ INFORM, ANNOUNCE, AND ISSUE; 611]

sound card *type of* **hardware** [➡ COMPUTERS AND COMPUTING; 1127]

sound effect *n* **sound**, recording, effect, special effect [➡ SOUNDS; 1256]

sounding board *n* **confidant**, confidante, close friend, best friend, intimate, friend, best mate (*UK*) [➡ FRIENDS AND GUESTS; 963]

soundings *n* **investigations**, inquiries, research, surveys, market research, polls [➡ ASK PEOPLE QUESTIONS; 666]

soundless *adj* **silent**, noiseless, still, quiet, mute, speechless [➡ ABSENCE OF SOUND; 1257] *Opposite*: noisy

soundlessness *n* [➡ ABSENCE OF SOUND; 1257]

soundly 1 *adv* **thoroughly**, roundly, severely, firmly, decisively, completely [➡ WHOLENESS AND COMPLETENESS; 198] 2 *adv* **deeply**, well, like a log, peacefully, fast [➡ TO A GREAT EXTENT; 132] *Opposite*: fitfully

soundness 1 *n* **reliability**, unassailability, security, accuracy, dependability, trustworthiness, safety [➡ SAFE AND SAFETY; 191] *Opposite*: unreliability 2 *n* **completeness**, comprehensiveness, thoroughness, depth, range, breadth [➡ WHOLENESS AND COMPLETENESS; 198] *Opposite*: superficiality 3 *n* **wholeness**, completeness, health, healthiness, fitness, intactness, sturdiness, robustness, strength [➡ FIT AND STRONG; 736] *Opposite*: infirmity

sound off (*informal*) *v* **hold forth**, go on, have your say, speak up, speak out, rant and rave, fulminate, rage, mouth off (*informal*) [➡ GIVING VENT TO EMOTIONS; 679]

sound out *v* **investigate**, test, explore, survey, look into, probe, feel out, check out [➡ EXAMINE AND ASSESS; 753]

soundproof 1 *adj* **impenetrable**, insulated, lined, padded, sealed, protected [➡ ACOUSTICS; 1138] 2 *v* **insulate**, line, seal, pad, protect, mask [➡ DECORATE, ADORN, AND APPLY COATINGS; 405]

soundproofing *n* [➡ ACOUSTICS; 1138]

sound quality *n* [➡ QUALITY OF SOUNDS; 1264]

sound system 1 *n* **hi-fi**, stereo, stereo system, audio system, boom box, CD player, record player, cassette recorder, tape deck, cassette deck [➡ RECORDINGS AND PLAYERS; 911] 2 *type of* **audio equipment** [➡ AUDIO EQUIPMENT; 1139]

soundtrack 1 *n* **recording**, music, dialogue, sound, sound effects, background music, incidental music [➡ RECORDINGS AND PLAYERS; 911] 2 *n* **music**, album, LP, tape, CD, DVD [➡ RECORDINGS AND PLAYERS; 911]

soup *n* [➡ PREPARED DISHES; 1170]

soup

◆ *types of soups*
bisque, borscht, bouillabaisse, bouillon, broth, chowder, cock-a-leekie, consommé, gazpacho, gumbo, julienne, minestrone, mulligatawny, pea soup, potage, Scotch broth, vichyssoise

soupçon *n* **hint**, touch, speck, morsel, modicum, dash, drop, bit, trace, splash, tad (*informal*), smidgen (*informal*) [➡ FEW, LITTLE, SMALL AMOUNT; 120] *Opposite*: surfeit

soup ladle *type of* **utensil** [➡ TABLEWARE, FLATWARE, AND KITCHENWARE; 861]

soupspoon *type of* **flatware** [➡ TABLEWARE, FLATWARE, AND KITCHENWARE; 861]

soup up (*informal*) *v* **boost**, enhance, tune up, modify, upgrade, beef up (*informal*), tweak (*informal*) [➡ IMPROVE STRENGTH AND DURABILITY; 378]

sour 1 *adj* **acid**, tart, bitter, acerbic, vinegary, dry, tangy, acrid [➡ TASTE; 703] *Opposite*: sweet 2 *adj* **bad**, rancid, off, curdled, fetid, rank (*literary*) [➡ DECAYING OR INFESTED; 1236] *Opposite*: fresh 3 *adj* **bitter**, disagreeable, unpleasant, bad-tempered, resentful, hostile, unfriendly [➡ BAD-TEMPERED AND HUMORLESS; 626] *Opposite*: agreeable 4 *v* **curdle**, go sour, ferment, turn, go bad, go off (*UK*) [➡ GET WORSE; 381] 5 *v* **taint**, ruin, harm, spoil, embitter, damage [➡ WORSEN SOMETHING; 380] *Opposite*: improve

source 1 *n* **basis**, foundation, starting place, cause, font, spring, birthplace, cradle, home [➡ BEGINNINGS; 53] 2 *n* **informant**, spokesperson, informer, supplier, stool pigeon (*slang*), snitch (*slang*), rat (*slang*), stoolie (*slang*), squealer (*slang*) [➡ INTERFERING PEOPLE AND TATTLETALES; 950] 3 *n* **resource**, supply, fund, mine, well [➡ COLLECTIONS AND MIXTURES OF THINGS; 1244] 4 *n* **natural spring**, upwelling, fount, fountain [➡ RIVERS, LAKES, AND STREAMS; 1042] 5 *v* **obtain**, find, track down, trace, track, locate [➡ FIND; 463]

See Compare and Contrast at **origin**.

sourdough *type of* **bread** [➡ BREAD, FLOUR, AND BREAD PRODUCTS; 1179]

sour grapes *n* **resentment**, jealousy, bitterness, ill feeling, envy, ill will, scorn [➡ ANTAGONISM; 552]

sourly 1 *adv* **tartly**, bitterly, drily, acridly, acidly, sharply [➡ TASTE; 703] *Opposite*: sweetly 2 *adv* **disagreeably**, unpleasantly, bitterly, resentfully, spitefully, nastily [➡ BAD-TEMPERED AND HUMORLESS; 626] *Opposite*: agreeably

sourness 1 *n* **acidity**, tartness, tang, acridness, dryness [➡ TASTE; 703] *Opposite*: sweetness 2 *n* **bitterness**, resentment, acrimony, unpleasantness, hostility, unfriendliness, spite [➡ ANTAGONISM; 552] *Opposite*: pleasantness

sourpuss (*informal*) *n* **complainer**, grumbler, whiner, grouch (*informal*), moaner (*informal*), grump (*informal*) [➡ GRUMPY AND NEGATIVE PEOPLE; 953]

sousaphone *type of* **brass instrument** [➡ MUSICAL INSTRUMENTS; 910]

sous-chef *type of* **person who works in restaurants** [➡ DOMESTIC AND KITCHEN WORKERS; 850]

souse 1 *v* **pickle**, marinade, soak, steep, preserve, infuse [➡ COOKING AND FOOD PREPARATION; 353] 2 *v* **soak**, steep, douse, saturate, immerse, plunge, bathe, drench, dunk, submerge, sink [➡ SOFTEN, LIQUEFY, AND DAMPEN; 388]

soused (*slang*) *adj* [➡ UNDER THE INFLUENCE OF DRUGS OR ALCOHOL; 741]

southeaster *type of* **wind** [➡ WINDY AND STORMY WEATHER; 1053]

southwester *type of* **wind** [➡ WINDY AND STORMY WEATHER; 1053]

souvenir *n* **memento**, reminder, keepsake, knickknack, remembrance, relic, token [➡ ORNAMENTS AND DECORATIONS; 1248]

sou'wester *type of* **hat** [➡ ACCESSORIES, MILLINERY, AND LINGERIE; 867]

sovereign 1 *n* **monarch**, ruler, potentate, king, queen, emperor, empress, sultan, rajah [➡ RULERS AND ARISTOCRACY; 823] 2 *adj* **independent**, autonomous, self-governing, free, self-determining [➡ STYLES AND SYSTEMS OF GOVERNMENT; 806] 3 *adj* **supreme**, dominant, ascendant, predominant, absolute [➡ MOST IMPORTANT AND MAIN; 193] 4 *adj* **outstanding**, superior, supreme, excellent, matchless, peerless [➡ SUPERIORITY; 152]

sovereign state *n* [➡ STYLES AND SYSTEMS OF GOVERNMENT; 806]

sovereignty 1 *n* **dominion**, control, rule, power, authority, dominance [➡ ROYALNESS; 825] 2 *n* **independence**, autonomy, self-government, freedom, self-determination [➡ RELATIONSHIP TO ANOTHER; 973]

sow 1 *v* **spread**, propagate, disseminate, scatter, strew, fling, seed, plant [➡ SPREAD AND SCATTER; 332] 2 *type of* **female animal** [➡ MALE OR FEMALE ANIMALS; 978]

soybean *type of* **pulse** [➡ PEAS AND BEANS; 1189]

soy sauce *type of* **seasonings, sauces, and dips** [➡ SEASONINGS AND SAUCES; 1174]

sozzled (*informal*) *adj* [➡ UNDER THE INFLUENCE OF DRUGS OR ALCOHOL; 741]

spa 1 *n* **health resort**, thalassotherapy center, sanatorium, health spa, fat farm (*informal*), health farm (*UK*) [➡ BUILDINGS FOR PUBLIC ENTERTAINMENT; 1084] 2 *n* **plunge pool**, Turkish bath, sauna, hot tub, bath (*UK*), whirlpool bath (*UK*) [➡ FIXTURES; 859]

space 1 *n* **solar system**, galaxy, outer space, deep space, universe, cosmos [➡ THE SOLAR SYSTEM AND ASTRONOMY; 1060] 2 *n* (*informal*) **leeway**, freedom, autonomy, liberty, latitude, room, scope, opportunity, breathing space, room for maneuver, elbowroom [➡ FREEDOM AND LIBERTY; 208] 3 *n* **interval**, time, period, pause, window, break, gap [➡ PAUSES AND PHASES; 56] 4 *n* **area**, place, seat, bay, plot, gap [➡ PLACE; 1065] 5 *v* **spread out**, move apart, space out, set apart [➡ POSITION SOMETHING; 325]

space-age *adj* **hi-tech**, automated, up-to-the-minute, state-of-the-art, new, modern, ultramodern, futuristic [➡ DESCRIBING TECHNOLOGY; 1160]

space bar *type of* **hardware** [➡ COMPUTERS AND COMPUTING; 1127]

space cadet (*slang*) *n* **dreamer**, idealist, daydreamer, fantasist [➡ LAZY OR UNSUCCESSFUL PEOPLE; 948]

space capsule *n* **spacecraft**, spaceship, rocket, capsule, vehicle, pod, cabin [➡ SPACE VEHICLES; 1063]

spacecraft *n* **rocket**, rocket ship, ship, space capsule, space rocket, space shuttle, space station, spacelab, spaceship [➡ SPACE VEHICLES; 1063]

---

spacecraft

◆ *types of spacecraft*
biosatellite, lander, launch vehicle, lunar module, multistage rocket, orbital space station, orbiter, rocket, rocket ship, rover, satellite, space capsule, spacelab, space probe, space rocket, space shuttle, space station

◆ *parts of a spacecraft*
booster rocket, bus, cabin, command module, drogue parachute, footpad, grain, life-support system, nose cone, plasma engine, pod, retropack, rocket engine, shroud, solar cell, stage, thruster

spaced-out (*slang*) *adj* **dreamy**, lightheaded, inattentive, dazed, woozy, confused [➡ CONFUSION, ANXIETY, AND WORRY; 540] *Opposite*: alert

spaceflight *n* **flight**, rocket flight, shuttle flight, space travel, orbiting [➡ SPACE TRAVEL AND EXPLORATION; 1062]

space heater *type of* **heating appliance** [➡ HEATING, REFRIGERATION, AND VENTILATION; 1142]

space heating *n* [➡ HEATING, REFRIGERATION, AND VENTILATION; 1142]

spacelab *type of* **spacecraft** [➡ SPACE VEHICLES; 1063]

spaceman *n* [➡ SPACE TRAVEL AND EXPLORATION; 1062]

space mission *n* [➡ SPACE TRAVEL AND EXPLORATION; 1062]

space pilot *n* [➡ SPACE TRAVEL AND EXPLORATION; 1062]

space platform *see* **space station**

space probe *n* **rover**, lander, spacecraft, satellite, probe, vehicle, explorer, pod, spaceship [➡ SPACE VEHICLES; 1063]

spacer *n* **insertion**, insert, piece, part, bar [➡ PARTS OF MACHINES AND TOOLS; 1118]

space rocket *type of* **spacecraft** [➡ SPACE VEHICLES; 1063]

spaceship 1 *n* **space capsule**, space shuttle, lunar module, ship, capsule, spacecraft, space rocket, rocket ship, mother ship [➡ SPACE VEHICLES; 1063] 2 *n* **flying saucer**, alien craft, UFO, unidentified flying object [➡ SCIENCE FICTION; 1064]

space shuttle *n* **space capsule**, launch vehicle, spacecraft, vehicle, spaceship, rocket, shuttle, transport [➡ SPACE VEHICLES; 1063]

space station *n* **spacecraft**, space platform, orbital space station, spacelab, satellite, spaceship, ship, base, artificial satellite [➡ SPACE VEHICLES; 1063]

space travel *n* [➡ SPACE TRAVEL AND EXPLORATION; 1062]

space traveler *n* [➡ SPACE TRAVEL AND EXPLORATION; 1062]

spacewalk *n* **excursion**, extravehicular activity, EVA, moonwalk, mission, task [➡ SPACE TRAVEL AND EXPLORATION; 1062]

spacewoman *n* [➡ SPACE TRAVEL AND EXPLORATION; 1062]

spacing 1 *n* **space**, arrangement, layout, spaces, gaps, design, typography, graphics, positioning [➡ PLACE; 1065] 2 *n* **arranging**, positioning, placing, ordering, spacing out, spreading out [➡ MOVE SOMETHING TO ANOTHER LOCATION; 324]

spacious *adj* **roomy**, airy, large, open, expansive, commodious, capacious, voluminous [➡LARGE; 1193] *Opposite:* cramped

spaciousness *n* [➡SIZE AND DIMENSIONS; 1192]

spacy (*slang*) *adj* **dazed**, woozy, dreamy, confused, out of it, lightheaded, inattentive, stoned (*informal*), spaced-out (*slang*), trippy (*slang*) [➡CONFUSION, ANXIETY, AND WORRY; 540] *Opposite:* alert

spade 1 *n* **garden spade**, shovel, scoop, snow shovel [➡SPOONS, SCOOPS, AND SHOVELS; 1121] 2 *type of* **general tool** [➡HAND TOOLS; 1119] 3 *v* **dig**, shovel, scoop, excavate, fill in, pile up, heap up, dig out, dig in [➡USE TOOLS AND MACHINERY; 468]

spadework *n* **groundwork**, research, drudgery, preliminaries, preparatory work, legwork (*informal*) [➡WORK IN GENERAL; 297]

spaghetti *type of* **pasta** [➡PASTA; 1180]

spaghetti western *n* [➡FILM; 901]

spam 1 *n* **junk mail**, unsolicited mail, garbage, mail, direct mail, junk (*informal*) [➡LETTERS AND WRITTEN MESSAGES; 584] 2 *v* **e-mail**, post, block, send, distribute, clog, copy, duplicate [➡THE INTERNET; 1128]

span 1 *n* **distance**, width, length, extent, area [➡WIDTH: WIDE; 1199] 2 *n* **time**, duration, period, limit [➡PERIODS OF TIME; 90] 3 *v* **cross**, cover, reach over, extend over, bridge, traverse [➡EXIST IN CLOSE PROXIMITY; 21]

spandex *type of* **synthetic fabric** [➡FABRICS; 1132]

spangle 1 *n* **sequin**, bead, bauble, star [➡ORNAMENTS AND DECORATIONS; 1248] 2 *v* **sprinkle**, stud, pepper, dot, spot, dot with, speckle [➡DECORATE, ADORN, AND APPLY COATINGS; 405] 3 *v* **sparkle**, glitter, shine, glisten, twinkle, wink [➡LIGHT EMISSION; 368]

spaniel *type of* **small dog** [➡DOGS; 980]

Spanish guitar *type of* **stringed instrument** [➡MUSICAL INSTRUMENTS; 910]

spank *v* **whack**, smack, slap, hit, strike, paddle, thrash, tan (*informal*), give somebody a hiding (*informal*) [➡PHYSICAL ATTACK AND PUNISHMENT; 415]

spanker *part of* **sailing vessel** [➡SHIPS AND BOATS; 1150]

spanking 1 *n* **smacking**, smack, slap, thrashing, beating, hiding (*informal*) [➡PHYSICAL ATTACK AND PUNISHMENT; 415] 2 *adj* **remarkable**, excellent, outstanding, wonderful, marvelous, exceptional, whopping, magnificent [➡EXTRAORDINARY: AMAZING; 204] *Opposite:* ordinary 3 *adj* **vigorous**, brisk, rapid, fast, lively, energetic [➡MOVING QUICKLY; 103] *Opposite:* weak

spanking new *adj* **pristine**, brand-new, new, unused, fresh, mint [➡NEW, MODERN; 166] *Opposite:* old

spar 1 *n* **pole**, arm, boom, mast, rod [➡STICKS, POLES, AND WEDGES; 1254] 2 *v* **scuffle**, fight, box, exchange blows, scrap, brawl [➡COMPETE, CONTEND, AND COMBAT; 303] 3 *v* **argue**, fence, dispute, squabble, bicker, wrangle [➡ARGUE AND FIGHT; 643] *Opposite:* agree

spare 1 *v* **afford**, do without, get by without, manage without, give up, release [➡FORGO AND DENY ONESELF; 449] *Opposite:* need 2 *v* **show mercy to**, free, release, save, pardon, forgive [➡FREEDOM AND LIBERTY; 208] *Opposite:* condemn 3 *adj* **replacement**, extra, auxiliary, standby, additional, emergency, unused

[➡MORE AND EXCESS; 124] *Opposite:* main 4 *adj* **sparse**, thin, mean, insubstantial, frugal, stark [➡TOO FEW, TOO LITTLE; 122] *Opposite:* abundant

spare part *n* **reserve**, extra, standby, part, replacement, spare, backup, new part [➡PARTS OF MACHINES AND TOOLS; 1118]

sparerib *type of* **cut** [➡TYPES AND CUTS OF MEAT; 1177]

spare room *type of* **room in the home** [➡TYPES OF ROOMS; 1097]

spare time *n* **free time**, leisure time, time off, downtime [➡PERIODS OF REST; 91]

sparing 1 *adj* **frugal**, parsimonious, economical, careful, thrifty, cautious, scant, mean [➡GRASPING AND FINANCIALLY MEAN; 519] *Opposite:* generous 2 *adj* **sparse**, limited, meager, restricted, insufficient, scanty [➡TOO FEW, TOO LITTLE; 122] *Opposite:* plentiful

spark 1 *n* **flash**, flicker, sparkle, arc, glint, fire [➡PRODUCTS OF FIRE; 1166] 2 *n* **stimulus**, catalyst, incentive, spur, trigger, inspiration [➡BEGINNINGS; 53] 3 *v* **sparkle**, flicker, glimmer, glint, glow, flash [➡LIGHT EMISSION; 368] 4 *v* **generate**, produce, inspire, initiate, set off, create, incite, kindle, trigger, ignite [➡CAUSE TO START; 265]

sparkle 1 *v* **fizzle**, bubble, fizz, ferment, effervesce, froth [➡FROTH AND EFFERVESCE; 389] 2 *v* **shine**, glitter, glisten, flash, flicker, twinkle, glint, spark, shimmer [➡LIGHT EMISSION; 368] 3 *v* **excel**, scintillate, shine, come into your own, come to life, stand out [➡SUCCEED AND WIN; 79] 4 *n* **life**, vivacity, energy, enthusiasm, gusto, go (*informal*), oomph (*informal*), brio (*literary*) [➡ENERGY AND ENTHUSIASM; 496] *Opposite:* apathy 5 *n* **effervescence**, carbonation, bubbles, aeration, gassiness, fizz [➡FOAM; 1273]

sparkler (*informal*) 1 *n* **gem**, diamond, gemstone, jewel, precious stone, rock (*informal*) [➡PRECIOUS STONES; 1278] 2 *type of* **firework** [➡EXPLOSIVES; 1155]

sparkling 1 *adj* **glittering**, glistening, twinkling, sparkly, iridescent, spangled, glittery, shimmering, shiny, flashing [➡VISUAL TEXTURE; 1221] *Opposite:* dull 2 *adj* **vivacious**, witty, brilliant, scintillating, vibrant, animated, lively, dynamic, full of life, entertaining [➡EMOTIONALLY PLEASANT; 187] *Opposite:* dull 3 *adj* **fizzy**, effervescent, carbonated, bubbly, aerated, bubbling, fizzing, gaseous, gassy (*informal*) [➡DRINKS; 1187] *Opposite:* still

sparkly *adj* **glittering**, glistening, twinkling, sparkling, iridescent, spangled, glittery, shimmering, shiny, flashing [➡VISUAL TEXTURE; 1221] *Opposite:* dull

spark off *v* **generate**, produce, inspire, initiate, set off, create, incite, kindle, trigger [➡CAUSE TO START; 265]

spark plug *part of* **engine** [➡PARTS OF AN ENGINE; 1144]

sparky *adj* **lively**, spirited, enthusiastic, bubbly, feisty (*informal*), zippy (*informal*), spunky (*informal*) [➡ENERGY AND ENTHUSIASM; 496] *Opposite:* lifeless

sparring partner *n* **opponent**, adversary, sworn enemy, counterpart, opposite number, foe (*formal*) [➡ENEMIES AND TORMENTORS; 969]

sparrow *type of* **common bird** [➡BIRDS; 997]

sparrow hawk *type of* **bird of prey** [➡BIRDS OF PREY; 998]

sparse *adj* **thin**, spare, scant, light, scarce, bare, meager, scrubby [➡ TOO FEW, TOO LITTLE; 122] *Opposite*: dense

sparseness *n* **thinness**, scarceness, scarcity, meagerness, bareness, scantiness [➡ TOO FEW, TOO LITTLE; 122]

spartan *adj* **frugal**, simple, basic, meager, bare, severe, plain, austere [➡ PLAIN; 232] *Opposite*: luxurious

spasm *n* **shudder**, contraction, seizure, ripple, paroxysm, twinge, tremor [➡ PHYSICAL REACTIONS; 316]

spasmodic *adj* **fitful**, irregular, intermittent, occasional, sporadic, discontinuous [➡ NEVER AND INFREQUENCY; 97] *Opposite*: continuous

spat *n* **quarrel**, fight, row, argument, tiff, squabble [➡ ARGUMENTS; 47]

spate *n* **flood**, rash, epidemic, wave, sequence, series, outbreak, welter, flurry, run [➡ CHAIN OF EVENTS; 162]

spatial *adj* **three-dimensional**, 3-D, longitudinal, latitudinal, altitudinal, four-dimensional, 4-D [➡ GENERAL LOCATIONS; 158]

spatter 1 *v* **shower**, spray, sprinkle, scatter, splash, disperse [➡ SPREAD AND SCATTER; 332] 2 *v* **spray**, splatter, shower, mark, splash, cover, emit [➡ DECORATE, ADORN, AND APPLY COATINGS; 405]

spatula *type of* **utensil** [➡ TABLEWARE, FLATWARE, AND KITCHENWARE; 861]

spawn 1 *n* **roe**, fish eggs, eggs, seed, frogspawn (*UK*) [➡ EGGS, SPERM, AND SPAWN; 727] 2 *n* **brood**, issue, offspring, progeny, young [➡ YOUNGER GENERATION RELATIVES; 958] 3 *v* **lay**, deposit, produce [➡ REPRODUCTION AND HEREDITY; 725] 4 *v* **reproduce**, give birth, procreate, breed, hatch, germinate [➡ REPRODUCTION AND HEREDITY; 725] 5 *v* **create**, generate, produce, initiate, set off [➡ ENGENDER; 350]

spay *v* **neuter**, sterilize, castrate, operate on, geld, make sterile, emasculate (*formal or literary*) [➡ STERILIZE; 726]

speak 1 *v* **chatter**, talk, verbalize, articulate, chat, natter (*informal*), yak (*informal*) [➡ CHATTER AND BABBLE; 617] *Opposite*: shut up (*informal*) 2 *v* **say**, tell, express, state, voice, declare, communicate [➡ UTTER AND PRONOUNCE; 608] 3 *v* **be fluent in**, converse in, speak a language [➡ UTTER AND PRONOUNCE; 608] 4 *v* **address**, lecture, preach, give a talk, give a lecture, talk [➡ INSTRUCT AND TEACH; 609]

speakeasy (*slang*) *type of* **bar or club** [➡ HOTELS, RESTAURANTS, AND CLUBS; 1082]

speaker 1 *n* **utterer**, chatterer, reciter, talker [➡ SPEAKERS AND ORATORS; 603] 2 *n* **orator**, lecturer, narrator, spokesman, spokeswoman, spokesperson [➡ WORKERS IN ENTERTAINMENT AND MEDIA; 873] 3 *part of* **audio equipment** [➡ AUDIO EQUIPMENT; 1139]

speak for *v* **speak on behalf of**, represent, act on behalf of, stand for, argue for, appear for, speak up for, answer for [➡ APPROVE AND CONFIRM; 646]

speak ill of *v* [➡ ACCUSE, BLAME, AND CRITICIZE; 641]

speaking *n* **speech**, language, communication, discourse, talking, dialogue, spoken language, spoken communication, oral communication, verbal communication [➡ COMMUNICATION; 602]

speak out 1 *v* **talk loudly**, raise your voice, exclaim, shout, speak up [➡ UTTER AND PRONOUNCE; 608] *Opposite*: mutter

2 *v* **be frank**, speak your mind, say your piece, have your say, speak up, protest [➡ PROTEST AND EXPRESS DISAPPROVAL; 642] *Opposite*: equivocate

speak sharply *v* [➡ ACCUSE, BLAME, AND CRITICIZE; 641]

speak to 1 *v* **get in touch with**, contact, approach, talk to, address, talk with [➡ INITIATE AND ESTABLISH COMMUNICATION; 680] 2 *v* (*formal*) **discuss**, consider, go into, deal with, address, mention, examine [➡ ATTEMPT AN ACTION; 261] 3 *v* **reprimand**, discipline, reprove, talk to, have a word with, scold, lecture, talk with, tell off (*informal*) [➡ PROTEST AND EXPRESS DISAPPROVAL; 642]

speak up 1 *v* **be frank**, speak your mind, say your piece, have your say, protest, speak out [➡ PROTEST AND EXPRESS DISAPPROVAL; 642] *Opposite*: equivocate 2 *v* **speak out**, exclaim, talk loudly, raise your voice, shout [➡ UTTER AND PRONOUNCE; 608] *Opposite*: mutter

speak up for *v* **support**, back, argue for, defend, approve, advocate, champion [➡ APPROVE AND CONFIRM; 646] *Opposite*: attack

speak well of *v* [➡ APPROVE AND CONFIRM; 646]

speak your mind *v* **be frank**, not beat around the bush, speak up, speak out, make yourself heard, sound off, share your feelings, spit it out (*informal*) [➡ PROTEST AND EXPRESS DISAPPROVAL; 642] *Opposite*: equivocate

spear 1 *n* **lance**, spike, javelin, assegai, harpoon, gaff [➡ PROJECTILES; 1159] 2 *v* **impale**, spike, stab, pierce, gouge, stick, run through (*literary*) [➡ STAB; 416]

spearhead 1 *n* **driving force**, forefront, head, lead, leader, leading light, commander [➡ IMPORTANT OR FAMOUS PEOPLE; 893] 2 *v* **lead**, front, head, organize, direct, command [➡ BE IN CHARGE; 270]

spearmint *type of* **herb** [➡ HERBS AND SPICES; 1175]

special 1 *adj* **superior**, distinct, different, exceptional, distinctive, singular, unusual, extraordinary, out of the ordinary, unique [➡ SUPERIORITY; 152] *Opposite*: ordinary 2 *adj* **individual**, specific, particular, distinct, one, separate, unique [➡ EXTRAORDINARY: UNCOMMON; 205] *Opposite*: general

special consideration *n* **dispensation**, concession, allowance, indulgence, preference [➡ PERMIT AND ALLOW; 669]

special delivery *n* **express**, courier, premium rate, overnight delivery, registered mail, registered post (*UK*) [➡ LETTERS AND WRITTEN MESSAGES; 584]

special education *n* **special needs education**, remedial education, compensatory education, literacy tuition (*UK*) [➡ TEACHING; 839]

special effects *n* **effects**, FX, computer graphics, lighting, morphing, camerawork, pyrotechnics, post-production [➡ TELEVISION AND RADIO; 606]

special interest group *n* [➡ GROUPS WITH A COMMON INTEREST; 938]

specialism *n* **specialization**, narrowing down, detail, in-depth study, concentration, narrowness, expert knowledge [➡ SUBJECT AREAS; 768]

specialist *n* **authority**, expert, maven, consultant, doyen, whiz (*informal*) [➡ TALENTED OR INTELLIGENT PEOPLE; 528]

specialization 1 *n* **specialism**, narrowing down, concentration, focusing in, gaining expertise, gaining in-depth knowledge, specialty, knowledge, expert knowledge, special study [➡ SUBJECT AREAS; 768] **2** *n* **adaptation**, change, mutation, selection, evolution, transmutation [➡ CHANGE; 372]

specialize *v* **concentrate**, focus, dedicate yourself to, major in [➡ STUDYING; 844]

specialized *adj* **particular**, dedicated, focused, specific, expert [➡ EXTRAORDINARY: UNCOMMON; 205] *Opposite:* generalized

specially 1 *adv* **particularly**, in particular, especially, specifically, expressly [➡ EXTRAORDINARY: AMAZING; 204] *Opposite:* generally **2** *adv* **personally**, individually, to order [➡ ACTING INDEPENDENTLY; 284]

specially made *adj* **custom-built**, custom-made, made to measure, made to order, tailor-made, bespoke (*UK*) [➡ EXTRAORDINARY: UNCOMMON; 205] *Opposite:* off-the-shelf

special needs education *n* [➡ TEACHING; 839]

special occasion *n* [➡ PARTIES, DANCES, AND CELEBRATIONS; 37]

specialty *n* **area of expertise**, subject, sphere, forte, area, field, line, domain, specialism [➡ SUBJECT AREAS; 768]

species *n* **class**, type, kind, sort, genus, variety, order, group [➡ VARIETIES, TYPES, AND KINDS; 145]

See Compare and Contrast at **type**.

specific 1 *adj* **exact**, precise, detailed, explicit, definite, unambiguous [➡ EXACT; 203] *Opposite:* vague **2** *adj* **particular**, peculiar, exclusive, special, restricted, limited [➡ UNRELATEDNESS AND SEPARATENESS; 146] *Opposite:* general **3** *adj* **distinctive**, particular, express, identifiable, certain, given [➡ EXTRAORDINARY: UNCOMMON; 205] *Opposite:* indefinite **4** *n* **detail**, particular, aspect, feature, fact, point [➡ BASIC DETAILS; 688] *Opposite:* generality

specification *n* **requirement**, condition, plan, order, arrangement, measurement, design, pattern, description [➡ BASIC DETAILS, 688]

specifics *n* [➡ BASIC DETAILS; 688]

specified 1 *adj* **stated**, quantified, definite, spelled out, detailed, itemized, identified, indicated, listed [➡ EXACT; 203] *Opposite:* unstated **2** *adj* **stipulated**, required, postulated, restricted, insisted on, agreed [➡ NECESSARY AND ESSENTIAL; 196] *Opposite:* optional

specify 1 *v* **state**, identify, spell out, detail, give, indicate, list, enumerate, itemize [➡ UTTER AND PRONOUNCE; 608] *Opposite:* suggest **2** *v* **stipulate**, agree, lay down, postulate, require, insist on [➡ CLAIM, INSIST, AND EMPHASIZE; 614]

specimen *n* [➡ REPRESENTATIONS AND GENERAL EXAMPLES; 65]

specious *adj* **false**, hollow, erroneous, baseless, inaccurate, unfounded, fallacious, phony, sham, bogus, incorrect, untrue, unsound, wrong, spurious, misleading, deceptive [➡ FALSE AND UNREAL; 173] *Opposite:* valid

speciousness *n* **falsity**, hollowness, inaccuracy, falseness, deceptiveness, erroneousness, spuriousness, phoniness, bogusness [➡ FALSE AND UNREAL; 173] *Opposite:* validity

speck 1 *n* **dot**, fleck, spot, dab, blob [➡ SMALL PIECES; 129] **2** *n* **particle**, fragment, crumb, iota, scrap, smidgen (*informal*) [➡ SMALL PIECES; 129] **3** *v* **dot**, fleck, spot, speckle, stipple, spatter, dust, dapple [➡ DECORATE, ADORN, AND APPLY COATINGS; 405]

specked *adj* [➡ DESCRIBING PATTERNS; 1227]

speckle 1 *n* **fleck**, mark, speck, spot, dot [➡ SMALL PIECES; 129] **2** *v* **mark**, fleck, dust, stipple, dot, spatter, speck, spot, dapple [➡ DECORATE, ADORN, AND APPLY COATINGS; 405]

speckled *adj* **spotted**, freckled, dotted, stippled, dappled, spattered, specked [➡ DESCRIBING PATTERNS; 1227]

specs (*informal*) *n* **spectacles**, glasses, goggles [➡ GLASSES AND SPECTACLES; 1125]

spectacle 1 *n* **sight**, scene, vision, marvel, phenomenon, wonder [➡ AMAZING THINGS; 211] **2** *n* **display**, show, demonstration, exhibition, event, pageant, parade, performance [➡ PERFORMANCES AND SHOWS; 42]

spectacles *n* **glasses**, goggles, specs (*informal*) [➡ GLASSES AND SPECTACLES; 1125]

spectacular 1 *adj* **stunning**, impressive, amazing, fantastic, fabulous, magnificent, brilliant, dramatic, dazzling, breathtaking, astonishing, marvelous, wonderful, exciting, incredible, extravagant [➡ EXTRAORDINARY: AMAZING; 204] *Opposite:* humdrum **2** *adj* **remarkable**, huge, great, enormous, mighty, outstanding, almighty (*informal*) [➡ LARGE; 1193] *Opposite:* unimpressive **3** *n* **show**, display, performance, extravaganza, special, gala, pageant [➡ PERFORMANCES AND SHOWS; 42]

spectacularly *adv* **enormously**, hugely, outstandingly, fabulously, stunningly, amazingly, dramatically, marvelously, astonishingly, wonderfully [➡ EXTRAORDINARY: AMAZING; 204] *Opposite:* mildly

spectate *v* **watch**, look on, observe, take in, look, watch from a distance, witness, view [➡ LOOKING AND LOOKS; 700] *Opposite:* participate

spectator *n* **viewer**, watcher, observer, onlooker, bystander, witness, eyewitness [➡ ONLOOKERS AND SPECTATORS; 701] *Opposite:* participant

specter 1 *n* **ghost**, apparition, phantom, spirit, spook, wraith, vision [➡ THE SUPERNATURAL; 787] **2** *n* **threat**, menace, shadow, danger, possibility, worry, anticipation, Sword of Damocles [➡ DANGER; 235]

spectral *adj* **ghostly**, phantom, ethereal, supernatural, ghostlike, shadowlike, shadowy, unearthly [➡ THE SUPERNATURAL; 787] *Opposite:* real

spectrum *n* **range**, band, field, gamut, variety, continuum, scale [➡ DEGREE AND EXTENT; 110]

speculate 1 *v* **wonder**, guess, conjecture, hypothesize, reason, suppose, surmise [➡ GUESS; 754] *Opposite:* know **2** *v* **consider**, contemplate, reflect on, ponder, deliberate, cogitate (*formal*) [➡ THINK AND REFLECT; 743] *Opposite:* decide **3** *v* **gamble**, take risks, hazard, risk, venture, take a chance [➡ GAMBLE AND TAKE RISKS; 466]

speculation *n* **conjecture**, rumor, opinion, gossip, assumption, theory, guesswork, supposition, hearsay [➡ GOSSIP; 678] *Opposite:* fact

speculative 1 *adj* **tentative**, approximate, rough, exploratory, provisional [➟UNCERTAIN; 175] *Opposite*: definite **2** *adj* **hypothetical**, notional, theoretical, academic, abstract, projected [➟UNCERTAIN; 175] *Opposite*: proven **3** *adj* **dangerous**, risky, unpredictable, uncertain, dicey (*informal*) [➟DANGEROUS; 236] *Opposite*: safe

speculator *n* **risk-taker**, investor, entrepreneur, opportunist, adventurer, fortune hunter, wheeler-dealer (*informal*) [➟PEOPLE INVOLVED IN FINANCE; 804]

speculum *type of* **medical instrument** [➟HAND TOOLS; 1119]

speech 1 *n* **language**, talking, verbal communication, dialogue, words, communication, discourse, speaking, spoken language, oral communication, spoken communication [➟THE SPOKEN WORD; 671] **2** *n* **tongue**, idiom, dialect, vernacular, native tongue [➟COMMUNICATION; 602] **3** *n* **lecture**, oration, sermon, talk, homily, discourse, address [➟ONE-WAY COMMUNICATION; 49]

speech disorder *n* [➟ASPECTS OF LANGUAGE; 682]

speechify (*informal*) *v* **pontificate**, lecture, pronounce, preach, hold forth, spout [➟INSTRUCT AND TEACH; 609]

speech impediment *n* [➟ASPECTS OF LANGUAGE; 682]

speechless *adj* **astonished**, astounded, amazed, dumbstruck, wordless, thunderstruck, flabbergasted (*informal*) [➟SURPRISE, SHOCK, AND AMAZEMENT; 545]

speechlessness *n* [➟SURPRISE, SHOCK, AND AMAZEMENT; 545]

speechmaker *n* **speaker**, orator, raconteur, preacher, lecturer, communicator [➟SPEAKERS AND ORATORS; 603]

speed 1 *n* **pace**, rate, velocity, momentum, tempo [➟SPEED; 102] **2** *n* **haste**, hurry, swiftness, speediness, hustle, rapidity, quickness, promptness [➟SPEED; 102] *Opposite*: slowness **3** *v* **race**, fly, zoom, break the speed limit, drive too fast, hurry, hustle, run, burn rubber, rush, zip (*informal*) [➟MOVE FAST; 313] *Opposite*: crawl

speedboat *type of* **motor vessel** [➟SHIPS AND BOATS; 1150]

speed camera *type of* **photographic equipment** [➟PHOTOGRAPHY AND PHOTOGRAPHIC EQUIPMENT; 1122]

speed garage *type of* **dance music** [➟MUSIC, SONGS, AND SINGING; 907]

speed humps *n* [➟TRAVEL: TRAFFIC PROBLEMS AND TRAFFIC MANAGEMENT; 323]

speedily *adv* **quickly**, promptly, soon, hastily, hurriedly, rapidly, swiftly, fast, without delay, against the clock, immediately, with alacrity [➟MOVING QUICKLY; 103] *Opposite*: slowly

speediness 1 *n* **quickness**, promptness, hastiness, rapidity, speed, pace, haste, hustle [➟SPEED; 102] *Opposite*: slowness **2** *n* **fastness**, swiftness, nimbleness, rapidness, fleetness (*literary*) [➟SPEED; 102] *Opposite*: sluggishness

speeding *adj* **fast-moving**, hurtling, flying, moving, fast, rapid, speedy [➟MOVING QUICKLY; 103] *Opposite*: slow

speed limit *n* **maximum speed**, top speed, permitted speed, limit, restriction [➟SPEED; 102]

speedometer 1 *n* **clock**, gauge, recorder [➟INTERNAL PARTS OF A VEHICLE; 1146] **2** *type of* **measuring device** [➟MEASURING DEVICES; 1123]

speed-read *v* **skim**, scan, read [➟READ; 758]

speed skating *type of* **winter sport** [➟HOBBIES, GAMES, AND SPORTS; 875]

speed trap *n* **radar trap**, police trap, traffic control [➟TRAVEL: TRAFFIC PROBLEMS AND TRAFFIC MANAGEMENT; 323]

speed up *v* **accelerate**, get faster, get moving, get going, hurry up, expedite, get a move on (*informal*) [➟CHANGE OF SPEED: MORE; 396] *Opposite*: slow down

speedway 1 *n* **track**, course, circuit, racecourse [➟URBAN OUTDOOR SPACES; 1072] **2** *type of* **highway** [➟ROADS; 1106]

speedy 1 *adj* **quick**, immediate, prompt, early, fast, swift, rapid, hasty, hurried, breakneck [➟MOVING QUICKLY; 103] *Opposite*: slow **2** *adj* **fast-moving**, speeding, fast, swift, nimble, rapid, fleet (*literary*) [➟MOVING QUICKLY; 103] *Opposite*: slow

speleologist *n* [➟PEOPLE IN SPORTS AND LEISURE; 876]

spell 1 *v* **signify**, mean, bring, predict, imply, presage, suggest, indicate, denote, bring about, lead to, result in, end in, connote, add up to [➟MEAN SOMETHING; 61] **2** *n* **incantation**, curse, enchantment, hex, evil eye, invocation [➟THE SUPERNATURAL; 787] **3** *n* **influence**, fascination, thrall, glamour, enchantment, charm, bewitchment [➟THE SUPERNATURAL; 787] **4** *n* (*informal*) **bout**, interlude, stretch, session, time period, time, stretch of time, period, turn [➟SHORT PERIODS OF TIME; 93]

spellbind *v* [➟APPEAL TO AND AROUSE INTEREST; 575]

spellbinding *adj* **mesmerizing**, enthralling, entrancing, fascinating, captivating, absorbing, engrossing, gripping, hypnotic (*informal*), riveting (*informal*) [➟INTERESTING AND MEANINGFUL; 190] *Opposite*: boring

spellbound *adj* **enthralled**, fascinated, awestruck, rapt, captivated, mesmerized [➟PENSIVENESS AND INTEREST; 538] *Opposite*: distracted

spell-check *v* **check**, check over, check through, correct, proofread [➟EXAMINE AND ASSESS; 753]

spell checker *type of* **software** [➟COMPUTERS AND COMPUTING; 1127]

spell out *v* **make obvious**, explain in simple terms, make clear, explain, interpret, explicate, clarify, elucidate [➟EXPLAIN AND CLARIFY; 610] *Opposite*: obfuscate

spelunker *n* [➟PEOPLE IN SPORTS AND LEISURE; 876]

spend 1 *v* **pay**, expend, pay out, splurge, lay out [➟GIVE MONEY; 433] **2** *v* **devote**, apply, employ, fill, occupy, pass, use [➟GIVE AND PROVIDE; 430] **3** *v* **use**, use up, waste, fritter, squander, consume, finish, exhaust, throw away, run through [➟USE UP AND WASTE; 474] *Opposite*: save

spending *n* **expenditure**, expenses, costs, payments, outlay, disbursements, outgoings (*UK*) [➟EXPENDITURE; 423] *Opposite*: earnings

spending money *n* **cash**, money, ready cash, pin money, pocket money, allowance, mad money (*informal*) [➟MONEY; 797] *Opposite*: savings

spendthrift 1 *n* **wastrel**, squanderer, waster, prodigal, profligate [➤PLEASURE-SEEKERS AND HEDONISTS; 886] *Opposite*: miser 2 *adj* **wasteful**, extravagant, improvident, prodigal, reckless, profligate [➤PLEASURE-SEEKING AND EXCESS; 885] *Opposite*: miserly

spent 1 *adj* **consumed**, used up, expended, paid, paid out, disbursed [➤ABSENT AND UNAVAILABLE; 7] *Opposite*: saved 2 *adj* **exhausted**, tired, washed-out, worn-out, bushed (*informal*) [➤TIRED, ASLEEP, AND UNCONSCIOUS; 738] *Opposite*: fresh 3 *adj* **finished**, over, done, completed, over and done with, at an end [➤ABSENT AND UNAVAILABLE; 7] *Opposite*: new

sperm 1 *n* **semen**, seed, ejaculate, spermatozoa [➤EGGS, SPERM, AND SPAWN; 727] 2 *n* **cell**, gamete, spermatozoon [➤EGGS, SPERM, AND SPAWN; 727]

spermatozoon *n* **sperm**, cell, gamete [➤EGGS, SPERM, AND SPAWN; 727]

sperm whale *type of* **whale** [➤WHALES; 991]

spew 1 *v* **disgorge**, discharge, vomit, send out, churn out, spew out, eject, emit [➤LIQUID EMISSION; 370] 2 *v* **pour out**, pour forth, gush, flow, stream, spill [➤LIQUID EMISSION; 370] *Opposite*: dribble 3 *n* **vomit**, puke (*slang*) [➤VOMIT AND BELCH; 712]

sphere 1 *n* **ball**, globe, orb, bubble [➤ROUNDED SHAPE; 1218] 2 *n* **area**, specialty, subject, field, area of interest, forte, department, realm [➤SUBJECT AREAS; 768] 3 *n* **sphere of influence**, compass, scope, range, domain, province, circle [➤SUBJECT AREAS; 768]

sphere of activity *n* [➤SUBJECT AREAS; 768]

sphere of influence *n* [➤SUBJECT AREAS; 768]

spherical *adj* **sphere-shaped**, globular, rotund, circular, round, orbicular (*formal*) [➤ROUNDED SHAPE; 1218]

sphericalness *n* [➤ROUNDED SHAPE; 1218]

spheroid *type of* **rounded shape** [➤ROUNDED SHAPE; 1218]

sphincter *type of* **muscle or tendon** [➤THE MUSCLES; 718]

sphinx *type of* **mythological creature** [➤MYTHICAL CREATURES; 1036]

sphinxlike *adj* **enigmatic**, mysterious, cryptic, bemusing, baffling, impenetrable, inscrutable [➤DIFFICULTY AND COMPLEXITY; 242] *Opposite*: transparent

spice 1 *n* [➤HERBS AND SPICES; 1175] 2 *n* **interest**, excitement, a little something, zest, seasoning, flavor, color, zing (*informal*), pizzazz (*informal*) [➤INTERESTING AND MEANINGFUL; 190] *Opposite*: blandness 3 *v* **season**, flavor, enhance, lace [➤COOKING AND FOOD PREPARATION; 353] 4 *v* **enliven**, liven up, lace, add zest to, add a little something to, season, pep up (*informal*), jazz up (*informal*), ginger up (*UK*) [➤IMPROVE SOMETHING; 374] *Opposite*: tone down

spice

♦ *types of spices*
allspice, aniseed, black pepper, caraway seed, cardamom, cayenne pepper, chili, cinnamon, clove, coriander, cumin, fenugreek, ginger, ginseng, mace, mustard, nutmeg, paprika, pepper, peppercorn, saffron, turmeric, white pepper

spiced *adj* [➤TASTE; 703]

spicey *adj* [➤TASTE; 703]

spick-and-span 1 *adj* **tidy**, clean, neat, immaculate, spotless, neat and tidy, perfect [➤ORDER AND ORGANIZATION; 206] *Opposite*: untidy 2 *adj* **in perfect condition**, immaculate, as new, in tiptop condition, in mint condition, perfect, mint [➤CLEAN AND HYGIENIC; 1233] *Opposite*: used

spicy *adj* **hot**, spiced, curried, piquant, peppery, fiery, zesty [➤TASTE; 703] *Opposite*: mild

spider *type of* **arachnid** [➤ARACHNIDS; 1018]

spider monkey *type of* **primate** [➤PRIMATES; 988]

spider plant *type of* **foliage plant** [➤FOLIAGE PLANTS; 1035]

spidery 1 *adj* **thin**, spindly, angular, squiggly, jerky, irregular [➤WIDTH: NARROW AND THIN; 1200] *Opposite*: bold 2 *adj* **gangling**, spindly, lanky, skinny, thin, ungainly [➤BUILD; 477] *Opposite*: plump

spiel (*informal*) 1 *n* **patter**, speech, lecture, talk, waffle (*informal*), guff (*informal*), pitch (*informal*) [➤MEANINGLESS SPEECH OR WRITING; 676] 2 *v* **prattle**, pitch, go on, hold forth, jabber, waffle (*informal*), burble (*informal*) [➤CHATTER AND BABBLE; 617]

spigot 1 *n* **faucet**, tap, spout, standpipe, valve [➤FIXTURES; 859] 2 *n* **stopper**, plug, bung, cork, peg [➤PARTS OF MACHINES AND TOOLS; 1118]

spike 1 *n* **point**, barb, spear, thorn, spine, prickle [➤ANGULAR SHAPE; 1217] 2 *v* (*informal*) **thwart**, confound, frustrate, dash, quash, scotch, mess up (*informal*) [➤MAKE IMPOSSIBLE; 276] *Opposite*: foster 3 *v* **spear**, impale, pierce, skewer, run through (*literary*) [➤STAB; 416]

spiked *adj* **spiky**, sharp, pointed, hobnailed, jagged, spiny [➤PHYSICAL TEXTURE; 1222] *Opposite*: smooth

spikes *type of* **sports equipment** [➤SPORTS EQUIPMENT; 879]

spikiness *n* [➤PHYSICAL TEXTURE; 1222]

spiky *adj* **prickly**, thorny, sharp, bristly, spiny, pointed [➤PHYSICAL TEXTURE; 1222] *Opposite*: smooth

spill 1 *v* **slop**, drip, leak, trickle, dribble, spill out, fall, drop, tip out, spatter [➤LIQUID EMISSION; 370] *Opposite*: absorb 2 *n* (*informal*) **tumble**, fall, roll, trip, stumble [➤DISASTERS; 252] 3 *n* **leak**, spillage, escape, discharge, overflow, overspill, slick [➤EMIT AND EMANATE; 361]

spillage 1 *n* **spilling**, spill, discharge, emission, leak, leakage, overflow, release [➤EMIT AND EMANATE; 361] 2 *n* **wastage**, waste, loss, spill, slick, puddle [➤MORE AND EXCESS; 124]

spill over 1 *v* **overflow**, brim over, leak out, run over, spill out, pour out, overspill [➤LIQUID EMISSION; 370] 2 *v* **spread**, extend, overflow, advance, creep, radiate, sprawl [➤TAKE UP A NEW POSITION; 312]

spill the beans (*informal*) *v* **let the cat out of the bag**, give the game away, tell, let on, blow somebody's cover, confess [➤BETRAY CONFIDENCES AND GOSSIP; 618] *Opposite*: keep secret

spin 1 *v* **turn**, revolve, rotate, gyrate, whirl, swirl, twist, twirl [➤MOVE SOMETHING: ON THE SPOT; 336] 2 *n* (*slang*) **point of view**, viewpoint, slant, angle, bias, perspective, complexion [➤POINTS OF VIEW; 767] 3 *n* **gyration**, rotation, turn, whirl, swirl,

twist, twirl, revolution [➡MOVE SOMETHING: ON THE SPOT; 336] **4** *n* **drive**, outing, run, trip, jaunt, turn [➡TRAVEL: JOURNEYS AND TRIPS; 318]

spinach *type of* **vegetable** [➡FRUIT AND VEGETABLES; 1176]

spinal *adj* **back**, backbone, vertebral [➡THE BONES AND JOINTS; 719]

spinal column *n* **spine**, back, backbone, vertebrae, vertebral column [➡THE BONES AND JOINTS; 719]

spin a yarn (*informal*) *v* [➡DECEPTION AND LIES; 660]

spindle **1** *n* **rod**, bar, shaft, axle, pole [➡STICKS, POLES, AND WEDGES; 1254] **2** *n* **leg**, baluster, support, pole, vertical, upright, shaft [➡STICKS, POLES, AND WEDGES; 1254]

spindly *adj* **skinny**, gangly, lanky, thin, frail, gangling [➡BUILD; 477] *Opposite:* sturdy

spin doctor (*slang*) *n* **publicist**, PR expert, propagandist, marketing expert, representative, public relations expert, commentator, adviser, spokesperson [➡POLITICAL OFFICES AND POLITICIANS; 808]

spin doctoring (*slang*) *n* [➡GOVERNMENT POLICIES; 810]

spin-drier *see* **spin-dryer**

spindrift *n* **spray**, sea spray, foam, mist, vapor, haze, moisture [➡THE SEAS, OCEANS, AND SHORES; 1041]

spin-dryer *type of* **appliance** [➡HOUSEHOLD APPLIANCES; 1117]

spine *n* **spinal column**, vertebral column, backbone, back, vertebrae [➡THE BONES AND JOINTS; 719]

spine-chilling *adj* **bloodcurdling**, chilling, terrifying, petrifying, frightening, spine-tingling, macabre, scary (*informal*) [➡FRIGHTENING; 231] *Opposite:* comforting

spineless *adj* **gutless**, cowardly, weak, timid, spiritless, weak-willed, faint-hearted, craven, pathetic (*informal*) [➡COWARDICE AND WEAKNESS OF WILL; 508] *Opposite:* strong-willed

See Compare and Contrast at **cowardly**.

spinelessness *n* **weakness**, gutlessness, cowardice, feebleness, faint-heartedness, fear, fearfulness, ineffectiveness, uselessness [➡COWARDICE AND WEAKNESS OF WILL; 508] *Opposite:* determination

spinet *type of* **keyboard** [➡MUSICAL INSTRUMENTS; 910]

spine-tingling *adj* **hair-raising**, thrilling, frightening, gripping, exciting, chilling, spine-chilling, bloodcurdling, macabre, scary (*informal*) [➡FRIGHTENING; 231] *Opposite:* soothing

spinifex *type of* **grass** [➡GRASS; 1031]

spinnaker *part of* **sailing vessel** [➡PARTS OF A SHIP OR BOAT; 1151]

spinner *n* **rotator**, whirler, whirligig, turner, gyrator [➡DEVICES; 1115]

spinney (*UK*) *n* **wood**, thicket, copse, grove, coppice [➡WOODS, FORESTS, AND JUNGLES; 1047]

spinoff **1** *v* **derive**, result, develop, grow, follow on, produce, trigger [➡CAUSE TO HAPPEN; 31] **2** *n* **byproduct**, deriva-tive, offshoot, extra, bonus, incidental, supplement, sequel, follow-on, follow-up [➡RESULTS AND OUTCOMES; 83]

spin out *v* **drag out**, prolong, keep going, draw out, eke out, extend, lengthen [➡CAUSE TO CONTINUE; 267] *Opposite:* cut

spinster *n* [➡MARITAL STATUS; 890]

spiny *adj* **barbed**, prickly, spiky, bristly, thorny, scratchy, sharp, jaggy (*informal*) [➡PHYSICAL TEXTURE; 1222] *Opposite:* smooth

spiral **1** *v* **escalate**, increase, get worse, run away, rise, mushroom, climb, shoot up, rocket [➡GET WORSE; 381] *Opposite:* plummet **2** *v* **fly**, rise, ascend, descend, soar, eddy, swirl, curl, twist [➡GO UPWARD; 306] **3** *type of* **rounded shape** [➡ROUNDED SHAPE; 1218]

spire *n* **tip**, spike, pinnacle, point, top, peak, summit [➡PARTS OF RELIGIOUS BUILDINGS; 1086] *Opposite:* base

spirillum *type of* **microorganism** [➡MICROORGANISMS, FUNGI, AND ALGAE; 1023]

spirit **1** *n* **will**, strength, courage, character, strength of mind, fortitude, moral fiber, determination, heart, mettle, chutzpah (*informal*), guts (*slang*) [➡STRENGTH OF WILL; 501] **2** *n* **soul**, inner self, life force, chi, essence, life [➡RELIGIOUS CONCEPTS; 776] *Opposite:* body **3** *n* **disposition**, temperament, attitude, nature, temper, personality, character, outlook [➡TEMPERAMENT AND BEHAVIOR; 492] **4** *n* **feeling**, attitude, mood, tendency, atmosphere, air [➡FEELINGS; 531] **5** *n* **ghost**, soul, ghoul, phantom, apparition, specter, spook [➡THE SUPERNATURAL; 787] **6** *v* **remove**, take away, whisk off, steal, abduct, kidnap [➡TAKE SOMETHING AWAY; 425]

spirited *adj* **forceful**, determined, strong-willed, vigorous, energetic, lively, animated, ardent, high-spirited, feisty (*informal*) [➡ENERGY AND ENTHUSIASM; 496] *Opposite:* lackluster

spiritedness *n* [➡ENERGY AND ENTHUSIASM; 496]

spiritless *adj* **spineless**, gutless, cowardly, sad, dejected, downcast, downhearted, depressed, dispirited, apathetic, pathetic (*informal*) [➡COWARDICE AND WEAKNESS OF WILL; 508] *Opposite:* energetic

spiritlessly *adv* [➡WITHOUT ENTHUSIASM; 287]

spirits *n* **emotional state**, frame of mind, state of mind, mental state, feelings, mood [➡FEELINGS; 531]

spiritual **1** *adj* **religious**, holy, sacred, divine, heavenly, saintly, mystical [➡RELIGIOUS CONCEPTS; 776] *Opposite:* secular **2** *adj* **mental**, emotional, psychological, temperamental, internal [➡PSYCHOLOGY AND THE MIND; 769] *Opposite:* physical **3** *type of* **pop and vocal music** [➡MUSIC, SONGS, AND SINGING; 907]

spiritual enlightenment *n* [➡RELIGIOUS CONCEPTS; 776]

spiritual guide *n* [➡RELIGIOUS PEOPLE; 778]

spiritualist *n* **medium**, clairvoyant, seer, psychic, mystic, shaman, diviner [➡PEOPLE WITH SUPERNATURAL POWERS; 788]

spirituality *n* **holiness**, sanctity, religiousness, otherworldliness, unworldliness, piety, devoutness, mysticism [➡RELIGIOUS CONCEPTS; 776]

spiritual leader *n* [➡RELIGIOUS PEOPLE; 778]

spirit world *n* [➡THE SUPERNATURAL; 787]

spirochete *type of* **microorganism** [➡ MICROORGANISMS, FUNGI, AND ALGAE; 1023]

spit 1 *v* **expectorate**, splutter, hawk, expel [➡ EXCRETION AND EXCRETA; 722] *Opposite:* swallow 2 *v* **sputter**, sizzle, pop, spatter, spurt, splatter [➡ EMIT CONTINUOUS SOUNDS; 366] 3 *v* **utter**, splutter, hiss, mutter, say, express [➡ UTTER AND PRONOUNCE; 608] 4 *v* **rain**, shower, drizzle, sprinkle, mizzle [➡ CLOUDY AND RAINY WEATHER; 1052] 5 *v* **impale**, skewer, spear, spike, run through (*literary*) [➡ TEAR, BREAK, AND CUT; 360] 6 *n* **saliva**, spittle, sputum, dribble [➡ EXCRETION AND EXCRETA; 722] 7 *n* **skewer**, rotisserie, brochette, rod, broach [➡ TABLEWARE, FLATWARE, AND KITCHENWARE; 861]

spit and polish (*informal*) *n* **meticulousness**, tidiness, cleanliness, orderliness, neatness, smartness, care [➡ CLEAN AND POLISH; 403]

spite *n* **malice**, ill will, ill feeling, vindictiveness, meanness, nastiness, unkindness, spitefulness, malevolence, viciousness [➡ ANTAGONISM; 552] *Opposite:* goodwill

spiteful *adj* **malicious**, vindictive, mean, nasty, vicious, malevolent, unpleasant, unkind, hurtful, horrid [➡ SELFISH AND UNKIND; 505] *Opposite:* kind

spitefulness *n* **malice**, ill will, ill feeling, vindictiveness, meanness, nastiness, unkindness, spite, malevolence, viciousness [➡ ANTAGONISM; 552] *Opposite:* goodwill

spitting distance (*informal*) *n* [➡ CLOSENESS; 159]

spitting image (*informal*) *n* **double**, twin, clone, image, spit, doppelgänger, dead ringer (*informal*), chip off the old block (*informal*) [➡ COPIES AND REPLICAS; 151] *Opposite:* opposite

spittle *n* **saliva**, spit, sputum, dribble [➡ EXCRETION AND EXCRETA; 722]

spit up *v* [➡ VOMIT AND BELCH; 712]

splash 1 *v* **wallow**, wade, plop, flap, flop, stamp, jump [➡ FIDGET AND FROLIC; 311] *Opposite:* glide 2 *v* **splatter**, get water on, wet, dash, spray, spatter [➡ SPREAD AND SCATTER; 332] *Opposite:* dab 3 *v* **plop**, slop, spatter, spray, slap, smack, splat [➡ SPREAD AND SCATTER; 332] 4 *type of* **impact sound** [➡ IMPACT SOUNDS; 1260]

splashguard *type of* **external feature** [➡ EXTERNAL PARTS OF A VEHICLE; 1147]

splash out *v* [➡ GIVE MONEY; 433]

splashy 1 *adj* **gaudy**, garish, bright, bold, colorful, multicolored [➡ DESCRIBING COLORS; 1226] *Opposite:* drab 2 *adj* (*informal*) **showy**, ostentatious, flamboyant, flashy, bold, sensational [➡ IN POOR TASTE AND OVERSENTIMENTAL; 229] *Opposite:* restrained

splat *n* **smack**, splash, plop, slop, slap [➡ IMPACT SOUNDS; 1260]

splatter *v* **splash**, spatter, bespatter, dash, spray, wet [➡ SPREAD AND SCATTER; 332]

splay 1 *v* **spread**, spread out, spread wide, open, open out, open up, expand, separate, widen, divide [➡ CHANGE OF SIZE: BIGGER; 392] *Opposite:* close up 2 *v* **turn out**, turn outward, twist, bend, distort [➡ CHANGE OF SHAPE; 385] 3 *adj* **outspread**, splayed, splayed-out, spread, spread-out, open, separated [➡ ORIENTATION AND ALIGNMENT; 1223] 4 *n* **slope**, bevel, slant, angle, incline [➡ ORIENTATION AND ALIGNMENT; 1223]

spleen 1 *n* **ill temper**, anger, irritation, annoyance, grumpiness, temper, pique, malice, malevolence, spite [➡ IRRITATION AND ANGER; 541] *Opposite:* contentment 2 *part of* **digestive tract** [➡ THE DIGESTIVE TRACT; 709]

splendid 1 *adj* **magnificent**, grand, superb, impressive, fine, glorious [➡ ADMIRABLE AND COMMENDABLE; 185] *Opposite:* unimpressive 2 *adj* **excellent**, wonderful, fabulous, marvelous, super (*informal*), great (*informal*) [➡ EXTRAORDINARY: AMAZING; 204]

splendiferous (*humorous*) *adj* **magnificent**, splendid, superlative, wonderful, superb, excellent, outstanding, marvelous, glorious [➡ EXTRAORDINARY: AMAZING; 204] *Opposite:* abysmal

splendiferousness (*humorous*) *n* **magnificence**, splendidness, superlativeness, wonderfulness, superbness, excellence, marvelousness, glory [➡ EXTRAORDINARY: AMAZING; 204] *Opposite:* inadequacy

splendor 1 *n* **magnificence**, glory, grandeur, brilliance, finery, impressiveness, majesty, splendidness, luxury, excellence [➡ EXTRAORDINARY: AMAZING; 204] *Opposite:* drabness 2 *n* **wonder**, marvel, miracle, glory, triumph, sensation, sight, spectacle [➡ AMAZING THINGS; 211]

splenetic *adj* **bad-tempered**, spiteful, irritable, peevish, waspish, fractious [➡ NEGATIVITY OF OUTLOOK; 514] *Opposite:* good-tempered

splenetically *adv* **bad-temperedly**, spitefully, irritably, peevishly, waspishly, fractiously [➡ NEGATIVITY OF OUTLOOK; 514] *Opposite:* good-temperedly

splice 1 *v* **join**, intertwine, interweave, merge, fix together, unite, link, tie together, join together [➡ FASTEN, LINK, AND JOIN; 408] *Opposite:* split 2 *v* (*slang*) **marry**, join in matrimony, join together, wed, unite, hitch (*slang*) [➡ ESTABLISHING RELATIONSHIPS WITH OTHERS; 974] *Opposite:* divorce 3 *n* **seam**, join, connection, link, joint [➡ EXTREMITIES OF PHYSICAL OBJECTS; 1250]

spline 1 *n* **key**, tooth, blade, fin, projection [➡ PARTS OF MACHINES AND TOOLS; 1118] 2 *n* **connecting strip**, connector, connection, joining strip, link [➡ FASTENERS, LINKS, AND NETWORKS; 1247]

splint *v* **immobilize**, strap, bind, bandage, secure, support [➡ FASTEN, LINK, AND JOIN; 408]

splinter 1 *n* **fragment**, particle, piece, shard, sliver, chip [➡ SMALL PIECES; 129] 2 *v* **fall apart**, crack, disintegrate, come apart, break up, fragment, shatter [➡ TEAR, BREAK, AND CUT; 360] *Opposite:* mend

splintered *adj* [➡ IN BAD REPAIR; 1234]

splinter group *n* **faction**, sect, offshoot, subset, minority, branch [➡ GROUPS WITH A COMMON INTEREST; 938]

split 1 *v* **divide**, rip, tear, crack, come apart, break, rend, cleave, separate [➡ TEAR, BREAK, AND CUT; 360] *Opposite:* join 2 *v* (*slang*) **go**, leave, depart, head off, make yourself scarce (*informal*), blow (*slang*) [➡ LEAVE AND GO AWAY; 8] *Opposite:* stay 3 *n* **tear**, hole, rip, crack, fissure, opening, division, rift, rent, break [➡ HOLES, GAPS, AND FORKS; 1252] 4 *n* **difference**, breach, breakup, divergence, rift [➡ DISHARMONY; 156] *Opposite:* reconciliation 5 *n* **splitting**, ripping, tearing, cracking, rupture, separation [➡ TEAR, BREAK, AND CUT; 360] 6 *n* **crack**, division, rift, rent, break [➡ DISHARMONY; 156]

split hairs *v* **quibble**, equivocate, be pedantic, argue, mince matters, nitpick, cavil [➡ PROTEST AND EXPRESS DISAPPROVAL; 642]

split-level 1 *adj* **two-tier**, twin-tier, twin-level, two-level [➡ ORIENTATION AND ALIGNMENT; 1223] **2** *type of* **apartment** [➡ RESIDENTIAL BUILDINGS; 1078]

split second *n* **instant**, moment, flash, the twinkling of an eye, second, minute, twinkling, jiffy (*informal*) [➡ SHORT PERIODS OF TIME; 93]

split-second *adj* **instant**, instantaneous, immediate, prompt, high-speed, lightning [➡ HAPPENING QUICKLY; 104] *Opposite*: tardy

splitting *adj* **excruciating**, unbearable, piercing, intense, severe, terrible, awful, dreadful, frightful [➡ PHYSICALLY UNPLEASANT; 226] *Opposite*: slight

split up *v* **part**, break up, split, go your separate ways, end things, separate [➡ REFUSING OR REJECTING RELATIONS; 975]

split-up *n* **breakup**, separation, dissolution, ending, divorce, annulment [➡ ENDS AND DEPARTURES; 54] *Opposite*: marriage

splodge (*UK*) 1 *n* **spot**, stain, mark, blot, blotch, daub, blemish, splotch [➡ FAULTS, FLAWS, AND WEAKNESSES; 251] **2** *v* **mark**, stain, spot, blemish, blot, blotch, daub, splotch [➡ DECORATE, ADORN, AND APPLY COATINGS; 405]

splotch 1 *n* **spot**, stain, mark, blot, blotch, daub, blemish, splodge (*UK*) [➡ FAULTS, FLAWS, AND WEAKNESSES; 251] **2** *v* **mark**, stain, spot, blemish, blot, blotch, daub, splodge (*UK*) [➡ DECORATE, ADORN, AND APPLY COATINGS; 405]

splurge 1 *v* (*informal*) **indulge**, binge, wallow, spoil, treat, luxuriate [➡ OVERDO SOMETHING; 290] **2** *v* **spend**, fritter, waste, squander, run through, shell out, splash out, lay out, blow (*slang*) [➡ GIVE MONEY; 433] *Opposite*: save **3** *n* (*informal*) **bout**, spree, binge, orgy, session, bender (*slang*) [➡ EVENTS AND OCCURRENCES; 35] **4** *n* (*informal*) **display**, exhibition, show, parade, demonstration, spectacle [➡ PERFORMANCES AND SHOWS; 42]

splutter 1 *v* **choke**, gasp, cough, spit, stutter [➡ BREATHE AND NOT BREATHE; 716] **2** *type of* **human sound** [➡ SOUNDS MADE BY PEOPLE; 1262]

spoil 1 *v* **ruin**, blemish, blot, blight, impair, mess up (*informal*) [➡ WORSEN SOMETHING; 380] *Opposite*: improve **2** *v* **indulge**, pander to, be soft on, pamper, cosset, make a fuss of, treat, make a fuss over, make much of [➡ TAKE CARE OF AND SPOIL; 300] *Opposite*: neglect **3** *v* **decay**, go rotten, rot, go bad, putrefy, decompose, go off (*UK*) [➡ GO BAD AND CORRODE; 390]

spoilage 1 *n* **decay**, rot, decomposition, degeneration, putrefaction, damage [➡ WORSEN SOMETHING; 380] **2** *n* **waste**, wastage, loss, leakage, spillage, damage [➡ NUISANCES; 253]

spoiled 1 *adj* **ruined**, damaged, decayed, rotted, rotten, tainted, wasted, sour, rancid [➡ DECAYING OR INFESTED; 1236] *Opposite*: fresh **2** *adj* **overindulged**, ruined, willful, precocious, brattish, self-centered [➡ DIFFICULT TO PLEASE; 515] *Opposite*: neglected

spoiled brat *n* [➡ MISCHIEVOUS OR BADLY BEHAVED CHILD; 946]

spoiler *part of* **external structure** [➡ EXTERNAL PARTS OF A VEHICLE; 1147]

spoiling for a fight *adj* [➡ AGGRESSIVE AND BELLIGERENT; 518]

spoils 1 *n* **plunder**, loot, booty, haul, pickings, swag (*slang*) [➡ PROCEEDS OF CRIME; 427] **2** *n* **reward**, prize, gain, profit, earnings, winnings [➡ REWARDS AND AWARDS; 439]

spoilsport *n* **killjoy**, stuffed shirt, dog in the manger, curmudgeon, wet blanket (*informal*) [➡ GRUMPY AND NEGATIVE PEOPLE; 953]

spoke 1 *n* **rod**, bar, rib, strut, shaft, spar, stay, spindle [➡ STICKS, POLES, AND WEDGES; 1254] **2** *n* **rung**, step, foothold, strut, bar, rod [➡ STICKS, POLES, AND WEDGES; 1254] **3** *part of* **bike** [➡ BIKES, CARS, AND CARRIAGES; 1149]

spoken *adj* **verbal**, vocal, oral, articulated, vocalized, pronounced, enunciated [➡ THE SPOKEN WORD; 671] *Opposite*: written

See Compare and Contrast at **verbal**.

spoken for *adj* **reserved**, kept back, taken, booked, earmarked, set aside [➡ ABSENT AND UNAVAILABLE; 7] *Opposite*: available

spokesperson *n* **representative**, speaker, voice, spokesman, spokeswoman, proxy, envoy [➡ REPRESENTATIVES AND PATRONS; 968]

sponge 1 *type of* **aquatic invertebrate** [➡ AQUATIC INVERTEBRATES; 1022] **2** *n* (*informal*) **parasite**, hanger-on, idler, user, sponger (*informal*), scrounger (*informal*), freeloader (*informal*), cadger (*informal*) [➡ LAZY OR UNSUCCESSFUL PEOPLE; 948] **3** *v* **clean**, wipe, wash, rub, mop, swab [➡ CLEAN AND POLISH; 403]

sponge cake *type of* **cake** [➡ CAKES, COOKIES, AND DESSERTS; 1181]

sponger (*informal*) *n* **parasite**, hanger-on, idler, user, scrounger (*informal*), freeloader (*informal*), cadger (*informal*) [➡ LAZY OR UNSUCCESSFUL PEOPLE; 948] *Opposite*: donor

sponginess *n* [➡ PHYSICAL TEXTURE; 1222]

spongy 1 *adj* **soft**, springy, malleable, elastic, flexible, cushioned [➡ MALLEABLE AND ELASTIC; 1212] *Opposite*: firm **2** *adj* **absorbent**, porous, osmotic, permeable, penetrable, absorptive [➡ DENSITY AND CONSISTENCY; 1207] *Opposite*: impermeable **3** *adj* **soggy**, squishy, moist, sodden, waterlogged, boggy [➡ WET; 1240] *Opposite*: dry

sponsor 1 *n* **backer**, guarantor, patron, promoter, champion, benefactor, supporter, underwriter, angel [➡ REPRESENTATIVES AND PATRONS; 968] **2** *v* **back**, support, pay for, subsidize, fund, underwrite [➡ GIVE MONEY; 433]

See Compare and Contrast at **backer**.

sponsorship *n* **backing**, support, protection, patronage, funding, aid, finance [➡ BUSINESS ACTIVITIES AND PHENOMENA; 794]

spontaneity *n* **impulsiveness**, naturalness, artlessness, extemporaneity, freedom, impulse [➡ NATURALNESS; 497] *Opposite*: constraint

spontaneous *adj* **impulsive**, unprompted, spur-of-the-moment, natural, artless, unstructured, unplanned, extemporaneous, free, instinctive, unrehearsed, unconstrained [➡ AUTOMATIC AND INSTINCTIVE; 280] *Opposite*: planned

spoof 1 *n* **parody**, satire, skit, burlesque, caricature,

sendup (*informal*), takeoff (*informal*) [➡ JOKES AND TEASING; 674] **2** *n* **hoax**, prank, deception, trick, bluff [➡ DECEPTION AND LIES; 660] **3** *v* **deceive**, fool, trick, bluff, hoax, pull somebody's leg (*informal*) [➡ DECEPTION AND LIES; 660] **4** *v* **satirize**, send up (*informal*), burlesque, parody, caricature, take off (*informal*) [➡ JOKES AND TEASING; 674]

spook **1** *n* (*informal*) **ghost**, wraith, phantom, specter, apparition, spirit, vision [➡ THE SUPERNATURAL; 787] **2** *n* **spy**, mole, double agent, sleuth (*informal*), snoop (*informal*), snooper (*informal*) [➡ INTERFERING PEOPLE AND TATTLETALES; 950] **3** *v* **startle**, surprise, shock, alarm, agitate, disturb, frighten [➡ FRIGHTEN AND SHOCK; 568] *Opposite*: soothe

spookiness (*informal*) *n* [➡ FRIGHTENING; 231]

spooky **1** *adj* (*informal*) **frightening**, ghostly, unnerving, mysterious, eerie, uncanny, disturbing, scary (*informal*) [➡ FRIGHTENING; 231] *Opposite*: reassuring **2** *adj* **strange**, amazing, odd, unnerving, extraordinary, unusual, bizarre [➡ BIZARRE AND PECULIAR; 257] *Opposite*: normal

spool **1** *n* **reel**, coil, pin, bobbin [➡ CONTAINERS, RECEPTACLES, AND PACKAGING; 1245] **2** *v* **wind**, reel, coil, roll [➡ POSITION SOMETHING: AROUND SOMETHING; 327]

spoon **1** *v* **serve**, ladle, spoon over, spoon out, serve up, dollop (*informal*) [➡ COOKING AND FOOD PREPARATION; 353] **2** *type of* **flatware** [➡ TABLEWARE, FLATWARE, AND KITCHENWARE; 861]

spoonbill *type of* **freshwater bird** [➡ FRESHWATER BIRDS; 1000]

spoon bread *type of* **bread** [➡ BREAD, FLOUR, AND BREAD PRODUCTS; 1179]

spoonerism **1** *n* **slip of the tongue**, mistake, error, Freudian slip, tongue twister, gaffe [➡ MISTAKES; 260] **2** *type of* **wordplay** [➡ JOKES AND TEASING; 674]

spoon-feed **1** *v* **feed**, nourish, take care of, look after, care for, nurture [➡ TAKE CARE OF AND SPOIL; 300] *Opposite*: neglect **2** *v* **coddle**, overindulge, wait on hand and foot, do everything for, run around after, spoil, ruin, mollycoddle, wrap in cotton wool (*UK*) [➡ TAKE CARE OF AND SPOIL; 300] *Opposite*: neglect

spoonful *n* **spoon**, portion, serving, teaspoonful, dessertspoonful, tablespoonful, dollop (*informal*) [➡ AMOUNTS AND QUANTITIES; 112]

spoor **1** *n* **trail**, track, paw prints, hoof marks, footmarks, footprints [➡ EVIDENCE AND PROOF; 69] **2** *v* **track**, stalk, follow, trail, hunt, pursue, tail [➡ ACCOMPANY AND FOLLOW; 337]

sporadic *adj* **irregular**, intermittent, infrequent, periodic, erratic, patchy, random [➡ FINITENESS, VARIABILITY, AND TRANSIENCE; 96] *Opposite*: regular

See Compare and Contrast at **periodic**.

spore *n* **reproductive structure**, dormant bacterium, bacterium, microorganism [➡ PARTS OF TREES AND PLANTS; 1026]

sporran *n* **pouch**, purse, bag [➡ CONTAINERS, RECEPTACLES, AND PACKAGING; 1245]

sport **1** *n* **diversion**, game, amusement, hobby, pastime, entertainment [➡ HOBBIES, GAMES, AND SPORTS; 875] *Opposite*: work **2** *type of* **broadcast** [➡ TELEVISION AND RADIO; 606] **3** *n* (*formal*) **joking**, clowning, teasing, fooling around, fooling about, larking, horseplay, playing the fool, high jinks (*informal*) [➡ JOKES AND TEASING; 674] **4** *v* (*informal*) **wear**, don, display, exhibit, show off, model [➡ DRESS, WEAR, AND UNDRESS; 868]

sport

◆ *types of ball games*
Australian Rules, baseball, basketball, cricket, field hockey, football, hurling, lacrosse, netball, rounders, rugby, Rugby League, Rugby Union, shinty, soccer, softball

◆ *types of combat sports*
aikido, boxing, fencing, judo, karate, kendo, kickboxing, kung fu, sumo, tae kwon do, wrestling

◆ *types of court games*
badminton, jai alai, rackets, squash, table tennis, tennis, volleyball

◆ *types of extreme sports*
barefoot waterskiing, basejumping, bungee jumping, in-line skating, mountain biking, skateboarding, skysurfing, snowboarding, sport climbing, street luge, stunt bicycling, wakeboarding

◆ *types of sports equipment*
ball, bat, bowl, club, discus, football, glove, helmet, hockey stick, javelin, lacrosse stick, mitt, pad, pigskin, puck, racket, shot, shuttlecock, spikes, tee, wicket

◆ *types of target ball games*
billiards, boules, bowling, croquet, golf, lawn bowling, pool, snooker

◆ *types of track and field*
cross-country, decathlon, discus, hammer throw, heptathlon, high jump, javelin, long jump, marathon, modern pentathlon, pole vault, relay race, shot put, sprint, steeplechase, triathlon, triple jump

◆ *types of winter sports*
alpine skiing, biathlon, bobsled, cross-country skiing, curling, downhill, figure skating, hockey, ice dancing, langlauf, Nordic skiing, skiing, ski jump, slalom, snowboarding, speed skating, toboggan, XC skiing

sport climbing *type of* **extreme sport** [➡ HOBBIES, GAMES, AND SPORTS; 875]

sporting *adj* **fair**, honorable, generous, decent, honest, evenhanded [➡ MORALLY GOOD; 774] *Opposite*: dishonest

sporting chance *n* **fair chance**, good chance, decent chance, fair shot, reasonable chance, sporting shot, even chance [➡ POSSIBLE AND PROBABLE; 177]

sporting event *n* [➡ NON-AGGRESSIVE/SPORTING EVENTS; 40]

sports **1** *adj* **sporting**, games, athletic [➡ HOBBIES, GAMES, AND SPORTS; 875] **2** *adj* **casual**, informal, leisure, outdoor, leisurewear [➡ DESCRIBING CLOTHES; 869]

sports activities *n* [➡ LEISURE AND RECREATION; 874]

sports car *type of* **car** [➡ BIKES, CARS, AND CARRIAGES; 1149]

sportscast *n* **sports broadcast**, sports update, sports program, televised sports event, televised match, televised tournament, televised final [➡ TELEVISION AND RADIO; 606]

sportscaster *n* **sports broadcaster**, sports presenter, sports commentator, sports reporter, sports correspondent, sports journalist [➡ WORKERS IN ENTERTAINMENT AND MEDIA; 873]

sports event *n* [➡ NON-AGGRESSIVE/SPORTING EVENTS; 40]

sports field *n* [➡ URBAN OUTDOOR SPACES; 1072]

sports grounds *n* **stadium**, arena, bowl, field, ground, track, pitch (*UK*) [➡ URBAN OUTDOOR SPACES; 1072]

sports hall *n* [➡ BUILDINGS FOR PUBLIC ENTERTAINMENT; 1084]

sports jacket *type of* **jacket** [➡ GARMENTS AND OUTFITS; 865]

sportsperson *n* **competitor**, player, contestant, athlete [➡ PEOPLE IN SPORTS AND LEISURE; 876]

sports stadium *n* [➡ BUILDINGS FOR PUBLIC ENTERTAINMENT; 1084]

sportswear *n* [➡ GARMENTS AND OUTFITS; 865]

---

sportswear

◆ *types of sportswear*
bathing suit, bathing trunks, beachwear, bikini, jogging suit, leotard, sweat suit, sweatpants, swimming trunks, swimsuit, swimwear, trunks, two-piece, wet suit

---

sport utility vehicle *type of* **car** [➡ BIKES, CARS, AND CARRIAGES; 1149]

sporty 1 *adj* **athletic**, active, good at sport, fit, muscular, energetic [➡ HOBBIES, GAMES, AND SPORTS; 875] *Opposite:* lazy 2 *adj* **flashy**, stylish, jaunty, natty, snazzy (*informal*), nifty (*informal*), jazzy (*slang*) [➡ DESCRIBING CLOTHES; 869] *Opposite:* formal

spot 1 *n* **mark**, blemish, stain, smudge, speck, dot [➡ FAULTS, FLAWS, AND WEAKNESSES; 251] 2 *n* (*informal*) **predicament**, mess, difficulty, awkward situation, quandary, plight [➡ DIFFICULT SITUATIONS; 72] 3 *n* **bit**, touch, dash, soupçon, tad (*informal*), smidgen (*informal*) [➡ FEW, LITTLE, SMALL AMOUNT; 120] 4 *n* **place**, location, site, setting, corner, situation, position, point [➡ PLACE; 1065] 5 *n* **advertisement**, ad, commercial, promotion, plug (*informal*) [➡ ADVERTISING AND PUBLICITY; 604] 6 *n* (*UK*) **pimple**, pustule, boil, blackhead, whitehead, blocked pore, zit (*slang*) [➡ CONDITIONS AFFECTING THE SKIN; 721] 7 *v* **notice**, spy, recognize, catch a glimpse of, catch sight of, see, perceive, discern, identify [➡ SEE; 699] *Opposite:* miss 8 *v* **stain**, dirty, blemish, smudge, speck, sully (*literary*) [➡ DIRTY AND CONTAMINATE; 404] *Opposite:* clean

spot check *n* **inspection**, check, search, examination, visit, inquiry [➡ EXAMINE AND ASSESS; 753]

spot-check *v* **inspect**, check, search, examine, double-check, monitor [➡ EXAMINE AND ASSESS; 753]

spotless 1 *adj* **immaculate**, spick and span, clean, clean as a new pin, pristine, gleaming, squeaky-clean [➡ CLEAN AND HYGIENIC; 1233] *Opposite:* dirty 2 *adj* **unblemished**, flawless, perfect, faultless, impeccable, untarnished, wholesome, innocent, stainless, irreproachable [➡ MORALLY GOOD; 774] *Opposite:* flawed

spotlessly *adv* **immaculately**, impeccably, perfectly, flawlessly, faultlessly, absolutely [➡ ABSOLUTE AND ABSOLUTELY; 133]

spotlessly clean *adj* [➡ CLEAN AND HYGIENIC; 1233]

spotlessness 1 *n* **cleanliness**, cleanness, pristineness, immaculateness, neatness, freshness, hygiene [➡ CLEAN AND

HYGIENIC; 1233] *Opposite:* dirtiness 2 *n* **flawlessness**, wholesomeness, innocence, stainlessness, irreproachability, perfection [➡ MORALLY GOOD; 774] *Opposite:* imperfection

spotlight 1 *n* **attention**, limelight, fuss, focus, interest, public eye [➡ ATTENTION AND ATTENTIVENESS; 763] *Opposite:* anonymity 2 *type of* **light** [➡ LIGHT; 1164] 3 *v* **highlight**, point up, draw attention to, underline, focus on, underscore, illuminate [➡ CLAIM, INSIST, AND EMPHASIZE; 614] *Opposite:* obscure

spotted *adj* **dotted**, marked, speckled, dappled, mottled, stippled, specked, flecked, patterned [➡ DESCRIBING PATTERNS; 1227] *Opposite:* plain

spotty 1 *adj* **mottled**, patterned, blotchy, spotted, dotted, marked, speckled, dappled, stippled, specked, flecked [➡ DESCRIBING PATTERNS; 1227] 2 *adj* (*UK*) **blemished**, pockmarked, pimpled, covered with spots, pimply, blotchy [➡ COMPLEXION; 480] *Opposite:* unblemished

spousal equivalent *n* **cohabitee**, partner, domestic partner, significant other [➡ SEXUAL AND ROMANTIC RELATIONSHIPS; 964]

spouse *n* **other half**, wife, husband, next of kin, partner, significant other [➡ RELATIVES BY MARRIAGE; 960]

spout 1 *v* **spew out**, shoot out, discharge, spurt, emit, gush, issue, send forth (*archaic or literary*) [➡ LIQUID EMISSION; 370] *Opposite:* retain 2 *v* **talk**, utter, pontificate, ramble on, sermonize [➡ CHATTER AND BABBLE; 617] 3 *n* **jet**, fountain, stream, column, spurt, spray, geyser [➡ AMOUNTS OF LIQUID; 114] 4 *n* **tube**, pipe, nozzle, outlet, spray, rose [➡ FIXTURES; 859]

sprain *v* **twist**, pull, injure, strain, crick, wrench, turn, rick (*UK*) [➡ BECOME SICK, TREAT, AND RECOVER; 728]

sprat *type of* **ocean fish** [➡ OCEAN FISH; 1009]

sprawl 1 *v* **slump**, spread out, collapse, lounge, loll, slouch, lie [➡ ASSUME A POSITION; 317] *Opposite:* curl up 2 *v* **spread out**, cover, extend over, stretch over, trail, ramble, straggle [➡ EXIST IN A PLACE; 19] *Opposite:* shrink 3 *n* **stretch**, mass, extension, spread, straggle, trail [➡ AREA AND RANGE; 111]

sprawled *adj* [➡ ORIENTATION AND ALIGNMENT; 1223]

sprawling *adj* **extensive**, rambling, expansive, straggling, straggly, spreading [➡ WIDTH: WIDE; 1199] *Opposite:* contained

spray 1 *n* **gush**, squirt, mist, jet, fountain, shower [➡ AMOUNTS OF LIQUID; 114] 2 *n* **atomizer**, aerosol, spray can, pump dispenser, sprayer, can [➡ CONTAINERS, RECEPTACLES, AND PACKAGING; 1245] 3 *n* **sprig**, bouquet, stem, posy, bunch, nosegay, buttonhole (*UK*) [➡ COLLECTIONS AND MIXTURES OF THINGS; 1244] 4 *v* **scatter**, squirt, send out, spew, spurt, gush [➡ SPREAD AND SCATTER; 332] 5 *v* **cover**, drench, squirt, mist, dose, apply [➡ DECORATE, ADORN, AND APPLY COATINGS; 405]

spray can *n* **aerosol**, atomizer, spray, pump dispenser, sprayer, can [➡ CONTAINERS, RECEPTACLES, AND PACKAGING; 1245]

spray gun *n* **spray**, atomizer, airbrush, sprayer, diffuser [➡ CONTAINERS, RECEPTACLES, AND PACKAGING; 1245]

spread 1 *v* **increase**, extend, multiply, reach, stretch, broaden, widen, swell, proliferate, expand, mushroom [➡ CHANGE OF SIZE: BIGGER; 392] *Opposite:* shrink 2 *v* **open out**, unfold, place, lay out, put out, smooth out, unfurl, unroll [➡ SPREAD AND SCATTER; 332] *Opposite:* furl 3 *v* **apply**, put on, smear, daub, butter, paste [➡ DECORATE, ADORN, AND APPLY COATINGS;

405] *Opposite*: remove   **4** *v* **disperse**, distribute, share out, allot, divide, give out, scatter, strew [➡ DISPENSE, RATION, AND DISTRIBUTE; 434] **5** *v* **broadcast**, disseminate, circulate, publish, propagate, promulgate (*formal*) [➡ INFORM, ANNOUNCE, AND ISSUE; 611] **6** *v* **last**, continue, go on, carry on, persist [➡ CONTINUE TO EXIST; 17] **7** *n* **range**, extent, increase, coverage, span, sweep, compass, expanse, distribution, allotment, division, diffusion [➡ AREA AND RANGE; 111] **8** *n* **variety**, range, selection, array, assortment, choice [➡ COLLECTIONS AND MIXTURES OF THINGS; 1244] **9** *n* **ranch**, estate, farm, plantation, station, holding [➡ AGRICULTURE AND FARMING; 1075] **10** *n* (*informal*) **feast**, banquet, binge, meal, supper, blowout (*slang*) [➡ MEALS AND PARTS OF MEALS; 1169]

spread abroad (*UK*) *v* [➡ INFORM, ANNOUNCE, AND ISSUE; 611]

spread around *v* [➡ INFORM, ANNOUNCE, AND ISSUE; 611]

spread-eagled *adj* **sprawled**, sprawling, prone, prostrate, face down, lying down [➡ ORIENTATION AND ALIGNMENT; 1223] *Opposite*: erect

spread out **1** *v* **move apart**, divide up, split up [➡ SEPARATE AND DIVIDE; 401] *Opposite*: amass **2** *v* **extend**, cover, spread, go as far as, stretch [➡ EXIST IN A PLACE; 19] **3** *v* **share out**, share, divide up, split up [➡ DISPENSE, RATION, AND DISTRIBUTE; 434]

spread rumors *v* [➡ GOSSIP; 678]

spreadsheet **1** *n* **worksheet**, database, table [➡ DRAWINGS, CHARTS, AND TABLES; 594] **2** *type of* **software** [➡ COMPUTERS AND COMPUTING; 1127]

spread the word *v* [➡ INFORM, ANNOUNCE, AND ISSUE; 611]

spread your wings *v* [➡ PREPARE FOR ACTION; 289]

spree **1** *n* **binge**, extravaganza, fling, orgy, splurge (*informal*), bender (*slang*) [➡ EVENTS AND OCCURRENCES; 35] **2** *n* **jaunt**, outing, trip, excursion, break, day out, away day (*UK*) [➡ TRAVEL: JOURNEYS AND TRIPS; 318]

sprig *n* **spray**, twig, stem, branch, twiglet, shoot [➡ PARTS OF TREES AND PLANTS; 1026]

sprightliness *n* [➡ FIT AND STRONG; 736]

sprightly *adj* **energetic**, active, spry, lively, agile, nimble, vigorous, full of beans (*informal*) [➡ FIT AND STRONG; 736] *Opposite*: lethargic

spring **1** *v* **jump**, leap, bounce, pounce, launch yourself, bound, skip [➡ BOUNCE, UNDULATE, AND VIBRATE; 308] **2** *n* **coil**, spiral, helix, mainspring, hairspring [➡ PARTS OF MACHINES AND TOOLS; 1118] **3** *n* **springtime**, season, seedtime, springtide (*literary*) [➡ TIMES OF YEAR; 88] **4** *n* **elasticity**, springiness, bounce, give, flexibility, movement [➡ MALLEABLE AND ELASTIC; 1212] *Opposite*: rigidity **5** *n* **leap**, bound, jump, bounce, vault [➡ BOUNCE, UNDULATE, AND VIBRATE; 308] **6** *n* **source**, upwelling, fount, fountain, water source [➡ BEGINNINGS; 53]

spring back *v* **ricochet**, recoil, shrink [➡ GO BACKWARD; 309]

springboard *n* **catalyst**, facilitator, spur, trigger, launch pad, foundation [➡ BEGINNINGS; 53] *Opposite*: brake

springbok *type of* **deer or antelope** [➡ DEER AND ANTELOPES; 981]

spring-clean *v* **scour**, scrub, wash down, dust down, clean out, spruce up, blitz (*informal*) [➡ CLEAN AND POLISH; 403] *Opposite*: dirty

spring-cleaning *n* [➡ CLEAN AND POLISH; 403]

springiness *n* [➡ MALLEABLE AND ELASTIC; 1212]

springtide (*literary*) *n* [➡ TIMES OF YEAR; 88]

springtime *n* **season**, spring, seedtime, springtide (*literary*) [➡ TIMES OF YEAR; 88]

spring up *v* **appear**, emerge, pop up, come into existence, mushroom, develop, burst forth, arrive, arise, crop up (*informal*) [➡ SUDDENLY COME INTO EXISTENCE; 21] *Opposite*: disappear

springy *adj* **bouncy**, elastic, supple, pliable, soft, yielding [➡ MALLEABLE AND ELASTIC; 1212] *Opposite*: unyielding

sprinkle **1** *v* **shake over**, dust, scatter, cover [➡ DECORATE, ADORN, AND APPLY COATINGS; 405] **2** *v* **intersperse**, pepper, strew, scatter, litter [➡ SPREAD AND SCATTER; 332] **3** *v* **rain**, drizzle, shower [➡ CLOUDY AND RAINY WEATHER; 1052] **4** *n* **sprinkling**, shake, dusting, scattering, scatter, peppering, dash, smidgen (*informal*) [➡ FEW, LITTLE, SMALL AMOUNT; 120]

sprinkler **1** *n* **sprayer**, irrigator, waterer, spray, hose [➡ FIXTURES; 859] **2** *n* **nozzle**, rose, showerhead, spray, diffuser, filter [➡ FIXTURES; 859]

sprinkling *n* **scattering**, dash, shake, pinch, bit, touch, smattering, sprinkle, smidgen (*informal*) [➡ FEW, LITTLE, SMALL AMOUNT; 120] *Opposite*: heap

sprint **1** *n* **dash**, burst, race, run, cycle race [➡ NON-AGGRESSIVE/SPORTING EVENTS; 40] *Opposite*: marathon **2** *type of* **track and field** [➡ HOBBIES, GAMES, AND SPORTS; 875] **3** *v* **hurry**, run, dash, race, gallop, tear [➡ MOVE FAST; 313] *Opposite*: dawdle

sprinter *n* **runner**, athlete, sportsperson, racer, cyclist, competitor [➡ PEOPLE IN SPORTS AND LEISURE; 876]

sprite *n* **fairy**, nymph, elf, dryad, leprechaun, brownie [➡ MYTHICAL BEINGS; 789]

sprocket *n* **tooth**, cog, notch, projection, sprocket wheel [➡ PARTS OF MACHINES AND TOOLS; 1118]

sprocket wheel *n* [➡ PARTS OF MACHINES AND TOOLS; 1118]

sprout **1** *v* **grow**, shoot, develop, bud, spring, germinate, push up, vegetate, burgeon (*literary*) [➡ GROW AND CULTIVATE; 351] *Opposite*: wither **2** *v* **spring up**, spring, emerge, appear, pop up, grow, bud, develop [➡ APPEAR AND EMERGE; 3] **3** *n* **shoot**, bud, leaf, young branch, new growth [➡ PARTS OF TREES AND PLANTS; 1026]

spruce **1** *type of* **evergreen tree** [➡ EVERGREEN AND CONIFEROUS TREES; 1029] **2** *adj* **smart**, neat, dapper, trim, elegant, well-groomed, natty [➡ WELL-GROOMED; 482] *Opposite*: scruffy

spruce up *v* **smarten**, smarten up, tidy, neaten, improve, put in order, clean up [➡ IMPROVE APPEARANCE; 379] *Opposite*: mess up (*informal*)

spry *adj* **sprightly**, lively, active, agile, energetic, alert, nimble, supple, quick, brisk [➡ FIT AND STRONG; 736] *Opposite*: slow

spryness *n* [➡ FIT AND STRONG; 736]

spud (*informal*) *n* **potato**, tater (*informal*), murphy (*dated informal*) [➡ FRUIT AND VEGETABLES; 1176]

spume (*literary*) *n* **foam**, surf, spray, froth, bubbles [➡ FOAM; 1273]

spunk (*informal*) *n* **pluck**, spirit, toughness, determination, nerve, courage, bravery, boldness, guts (*slang*) [➡ COURAGE; 498] *Opposite*: cowardice

spunky (*informal*) *adj* **plucky**, spirited, tough, determined, energetic, courageous, brave, bold, lively, gutsy (*informal*) [➡ COURAGE; 498] *Opposite*: cowardly

spun-out (*UK*) *adj* [➡ HAPPENING SLOWLY; 106]

spur 1 *n* **incentive**, stimulus, incitement, provocation, motive, fillip, goad, impulse, inducement, catalyst [➡ CAUSATION; 168] *Opposite*: disincentive 2 *n* **branch**, limb, shoot, offshoot, outgrowth [➡ SUBDIVISIONS AND OFFSHOOTS; 1253] 3 *n* **spike**, point, barb, spine [➡ ANGULAR SHAPE; 1217] 4 *n* **ridge**, mountainside, projection, edge, saddle, outcrop [➡ MOUNTAINS AND HILLS; 1044] 5 *part of* **flower** [➡ FLOWERS; 1032] 6 *v* **urge**, encourage, incite, prompt, stimulate, goad, impel, drive, prod, provoke, spur on [➡ CAUSE OR COMPEL TO ACT; 271] *Opposite*: discourage 7 *v* (*literary*) **hurry up**, hasten, speed up, speed, rush, drive on, press forward [➡ CHANGE OF SPEED: MORE; 396] *Opposite*: delay

See Compare and Contrast at **motive**.

spurious *adj* **false**, bogus, fake, forged, counterfeit, imitation, specious, inauthentic, phony, sham [➡ FALSE AND UNREAL; 173] *Opposite*: genuine

spurn *v* **reject**, snub, slight, rebuff, repulse, scorn, despise, disdain, look down on, hold in contempt [➡ REFUSING OR REJECTING RELATIONS; 975] *Opposite*: accept

spur-of-the-moment *adj* **spontaneous**, impulsive, unplanned, impromptu, unpremeditated [➡ AUTOMATIC AND INSTINCTIVE; 280] *Opposite*: planned

spurt 1 *n* **jet**, spray, squirt, gush, spout, emission [➡ AMOUNTS OF LIQUID; 114] *Opposite*: trickle 2 *n* **increase**, burst, surge, rush, swell, wave [➡ MORE AND EXCESS; 124] 3 *v* **gush**, spray, burst, jet, erupt, squirt, surge, shoot, rush, spout, emit, issue [➡ LIQUID EMISSION; 370] *Opposite*: trickle

spur to action *v* [➡ CAUSE OR COMPEL TO ACT; 271]

sputter 1 *v* **pop**, splutter, spit, sizzle, crackle [➡ EMIT CONTINUOUS SOUNDS; 366] 2 *v* **splutter**, gasp, spit, stammer, snort [➡ BREATHE AND NOT BREATHE; 716]

sputum *n* **mucus**, phlegm, saliva, spit, spittle [➡ EXCRETION AND EXCRETA; 722]

spy 1 *n* **secret agent**, undercover agent, double agent, mole, infiltrator, plant [➡ INTERFERING PEOPLE AND TATTLETALES; 950] 2 *v* **work undercover**, pry, reconnoiter, snoop (*informal*), nose around (*informal*) [➡ EXAMINE AND ASSESS; 753] 3 *v* **watch**, eavesdrop, listen in, observe, scrutinize [➡ LOOKING AND LOOKS; 700] 4 *v* **spot**, glimpse, notice, observe, see, discern, espy (*literary*), behold (*archaic or literary*) [➡ SEE; 699] 5 *v* **discover**, search out, detect, find out, observe, notice [➡ LEARN AND DISCOVER; 762] *Opposite*: overlook 6 *v* **investigate**, poke around, explore, search, research, examine [➡ LOOKING AND LOOKS; 700]

spyglass *type of* **optical instrument** [➡ OPTICAL INSTRUMENTS; 1124]

spyhole *n* **peephole**, slot, chink, opening, window, hole [➡ HOLES, GAPS, AND FORKS; 1252]

spying *n* **undercover work**, intelligence work, espionage, eavesdropping, infiltration, snooping (*informal*) [➡ EXAMINE AND ASSESS; 753]

spy out *v* **discover**, uncover, seek out, sniff out, nose out, find [➡ FIND; 463] *Opposite*: overlook

spyware *n* [➡ THE INTERNET; 1128]

squab *type of* **young bird** [➡ YOUNG BIRDS; 1004]

squabble 1 *n* **quarrel**, row, tiff, dispute, argument, fight, disagreement, spat [➡ ARGUMENTS; 47] *Opposite*: reconciliation 2 *v* **argue**, bicker, quarrel, disagree, have words, row, fight, wrangle [➡ ARGUE AND FIGHT; 643] *Opposite*: make up

squad *n* **group**, team, crew, company, gang, troop, bevy, squadron, set, force, posse (*informal*) [➡ GROUPS OF PEOPLE; 935]

squad car *n* **police car**, patrol car, prowl car, cruiser, panda car (*UK*) [➡ VEHICLES; 1145]

squadron *n* **regiment**, troop, team, squad, company, unit, group [➡ MILITARY PERSONNEL; 828]

squalid 1 *adj* **filthy**, dirty, foul, nasty, fetid, unclean, neglected, grimy, grubby [➡ DIRTY; 1235] *Opposite*: clean 2 *adj* **seedy**, repulsive, sordid, sleazy, low, immoral, dishonest, disreputable [➡ MORALLY BAD OR IMPROPER; 775] *Opposite*: charming

See Compare and Contrast at **dirty**.

squalidness *n* [➡ DIRTY; 1235]

squall *n* **storm**, gust of wind, windstorm, gust, shower, tempest (*literary*) [➡ WINDY AND STORMY WEATHER; 1053]

squally *adj* **stormy**, gusty, blustery, wild, inclement [➡ WINDY AND STORMY WEATHER; 1053] *Opposite*: fine

squalor 1 *n* **filth**, dirt, dirtiness, foulness, grime, uncleanliness, shabbiness, uncleanness [➡ DIRTY; 1235] *Opposite*: cleanliness 2 *n* **nastiness**, sordidness, unpleasantness, degradation, immorality, sleaziness, seediness, meanness [➡ MORALLY BAD OR IMPROPER; 775] *Opposite*: charm

squander *v* **waste**, spend, throw away, fritter away, dissipate, misuse, lavish, consume [➡ USE UP AND WASTE; 474] *Opposite*: save

square 1 *n* **four-sided figure**, quadrangle, tetragon, rectangle, parallelogram [➡ ANGULAR SHAPE; 1217] 2 *n* **plaza**, open area, marketplace, place, parade, piazza [➡ URBAN OUTDOOR SPACES; 1072] 3 *n* (*slang dated*) **fogy**, reactionary, diehard, stick-in-the-mud (*informal*), fuddy-duddy (*informal*), stuffed shirt (*informal*) [➡ UNCOOPERATIVE OR REBELLIOUS PEOPLE; 566] 4 *adj* **four-sided**, right-angled, rectangular, quadrangular, tetragonal [➡ ANGULAR SHAPE; 1217] 5 *adj* **fair**, honest, genuine, just, straight, upright, ethical [➡ MORALLY GOOD; 774] *Opposite*: dishonest 6 *adj* (*slang dated*) **intransigent**, reactionary, conservative, traditionalist, dyed-in-the-wool, fogyish, conformist, stick-in-the-mud (*informal*) [➡ UNADVENTUROUS AND DULL; 517] 7 *v* **shape**, form, file down, sharpen, even up, square off [➡ CHANGE OF SHAPE; 385] 8 *v* **adjust**, align, realign, set straight, straighten, even up, level [➡ ARRANGE AND CREATE ORDER; 357] *Opposite*: unbalance 9 *v* **pay off**, settle, clear, pay, balance, discharge (*formal*) [➡ GIVE MONEY; 433] 10 *v* **agree**, harmonize, accord, fit, tally, concur, check [➡ TWO-WAY COMMUNICATION; 607] *Opposite*: conflict 11 *adv* **at right angles**, directly, straight [➡ ORIENTATION AND ALIGNMENT; 1223] 12 *adv* (*informal*)

fairly, honestly, openly, straightforwardly, straight, justly [➡ MORALLY GOOD; 774]

square dance *type of* **dance** [➡ DANCE; 903]

squarely *adv* **directly**, exactly, evenly, head-on, straight [➡ EXACT; 203] *Opposite*: indirectly

square meal *n* **nourishment**, hot meal, proper meal, food, sustenance [➡ MEALS AND PARTS OF MEALS; 1169] *Opposite*: snack

square up 1 *v* **settle up**, even up, settle your debts, settle the bill, pay up, be quits (*informal*), cough up (*informal*) [➡ GIVE MONEY; 433] 2 *v* **work out**, turn out fine, sort itself out, be arranged, be organized, be set out, sort out, arrange, organize [➡ ARRANGE AND CREATE ORDER; 357] *Opposite*: go wrong 3 *v* **face up to**, confront, look something in the eye, tackle, take on, deal with, get to grips with [➡ COMPETE, CONTEND, AND COMBAT; 303] *Opposite*: evade 4 *v* **put up your fists**, make a stand, put up a fight, stand your ground, take up the gauntlet, take up the challenge [➡ ASSUME A POSITION; 317] *Opposite*: run away

squash 1 *v* **crush**, flatten, compress, pulp, mash, pound, squeeze, press [➡ CHANGE OF SHAPE; 385] *Opposite*: reshape 2 *v* **cram**, squeeze, wedge, force, jam, pack, crowd, ram [➡ FILL; 406] *Opposite*: coax 3 *v* **overcome**, stop, conquer, suppress, quash, quell, annihilate (*informal*) [➡ BEAT AND DEFEAT; 80] *Opposite*: encourage 4 *n* **squeeze**, crush, congestion, crowd, jam [➡ FILL; 1239] 5 *type of* **court game** [➡ HOBBIES, GAMES, AND SPORTS; 875] 6 *type of* **vegetable** [➡ FRUIT AND VEGETABLES; 1176] 7 *n* (*UK*) [➡ DRINKS; 1187]

squashy *adj* **soft**, yielding, spongy, springy, mushy, pliable, pulpy [➡ MALLEABLE AND ELASTIC; 1212] *Opposite*: firm

squat 1 *v* **crouch**, sit on your heels, hunker down, bend [➡ ASSUME A POSITION; 317] *Opposite*: stand 2 *adj* **short**, thickset, thick, stubby, stocky, pudgy (*informal*) [➡ BUILD; 477] *Opposite*: tall

squatness *n* [➡ BUILD; 477]

squatter *n* **unlawful tenant**, unlawful resident, resident, trespasser [➡ INHABITANTS; 857]

squawk 1 *v* **screech**, call, cry, squeal, shriek, scream [➡ SOUND EMISSION BY ANIMALS OR BIRDS; 364] 2 *v* (*informal*) **complain**, protest, whine, wail, grumble, moan (*informal*) [➡ COMPLAIN AND NAG; 686] 3 *n* **harsh call**, cry, screech, shriek, squeal, scream [➡ SOUNDS MADE BY BIRDS; 1263] 4 *n* (*informal*) **protest**, complaint, whine, wail, grumble, moan (*informal*) [➡ CRITICISMS AND ANGRY OUTBURSTS; 50]

squeak 1 *v* **squeal**, whine, yelp, shrill, pipe, peep, screech [➡ SOUND EMISSION BY ANIMALS OR BIRDS; 364] 2 *type of* **animal sound** [➡ SOUNDS MADE BY ANIMALS; 1261]

squeak through (*informal*) *v* **scrape through**, scrape by, manage, achieve, do [➡ SUCCEED AND WIN; 79]

squeaky *adj* **high-pitched**, shrill, whiny, noisy, creaky, rusty [➡ LOUD, HIGH, OR UNPLEASANT SOUNDS; 1266]

squeaky-clean 1 *adj* **virtuous**, righteous, pure, honorable, unimpeachable, unassailable, untouchable, impeccable, flawless, perfect [➡ MORALLY GOOD; 774] *Opposite*: corrupt 2 *adj* **clean**, clean as a new pin, spotless, dirt-free, pristine, immaculate [➡ CLEAN AND HYGIENIC; 1233]

squeal 1 *n* **screech**, yelp, shriek, yell, cry, howl, wail,

scream, squeak [➡ SOUNDS MADE BY PEOPLE; 1262] 2 *type of* **animal sound** [➡ SOUNDS MADE BY ANIMALS; 1261] 3 *v* **yell**, cry, shriek, yelp, howl, wail, scream, squawk, screech, squeak [➡ SOUND EMISSION BY ANIMALS OR BIRDS; 364] 4 *v* (*slang*) **inform**, betray, denounce, tell on, tattle, blow the whistle on, snitch (*slang*), sneak on (*UK*) [➡ BETRAY CONFIDENCES AND GOSSIP; 618]

squealer (*slang*) *n* **informant**, informer, snake in the grass, grass (*slang*), nark (*slang*), snitch (*slang*), snout (*slang*), stool pigeon (*slang*), sneak (*UK*) [➡ INTERFERING PEOPLE AND TATTLETALES; 950]

squeal on (*slang*) *v* [➡ BETRAY CONFIDENCES AND GOSSIP; 618]

squeamish 1 *adj* **nauseous**, queasy, sick, woozy [➡ ILL AND SICK; 740] 2 *adj* **delicate**, easily upset, easily offended, prudish, puritanical, prim, strait-laced [➡ EXCESSIVE SENSITIVITY; 511] *Opposite*: strong 3 *adj* **fastidious**, particular, scrupulous, fussy, uncompromising [➡ DIFFICULT TO PLEASE; 515] *Opposite*: easygoing

squeamishness 1 *n* **queasiness**, nauseousness, sickness, qualmishness, seediness (*informal*) [➡ ILL AND SICK; 740] 2 *n* **delicacy**, prudishness, prudery, shockability, puritanism, primness [➡ EXCESSIVE SENSITIVITY; 511] *Opposite*: toughness

squeeze 1 *v* **press**, squash, compress, constrict, pinch, mold [➡ CONTACT: EXERT PRESSURE; 414] 2 *v* **grip**, hold on, grasp, hug, clutch, clasp [➡ CONTACT: HOLD; 411] *Opposite*: release 3 *v* **hug**, embrace, cuddle, enfold, clasp, clutch, hold, press [➡ CONTACT: EXERT PRESSURE; 414] *Opposite*: release 4 *v* **crush**, squash, cram, crowd, jam, pack, stuff, wedge, force, ram [➡ FILL; 406] *Opposite*: coax 5 *v* **find time for**, make time for, make room for, fit in, slot in [➡ CARRY OUT AN ACTION; 269] 6 *v* **extract**, wring, expel, drive out, mangle [➡ CHANGE OF SHAPE; 385] 7 *v* **put pressure on**, harass, oppress, lean on (*informal*), hassle (*informal*), pressurize (*UK*) [➡ CAUSE OR COMPEL TO ACT; 271]

squeeze out *v* **exclude**, express, force out, freeze out, ostracize, gouge out, shut out, press out [➡ REFUSING OR REJECTING RELATIONS; 975]

squelch 1 *v* **squish**, splash, splish-splash, suck, gurgle, splosh (*UK*) [➡ EMIT SOUNDS THROUGH IMPACT AND ABRASION; 365] 2 *v* **crush**, squash, flatten, trample, squish, tread on, stamp on [➡ CHANGE OF SHAPE; 385] 3 *v* (*slang*) **suppress**, silence, scotch, squash, quash, crush, stifle, check, repress [➡ MAKE IMPOSSIBLE; 276] *Opposite*: broadcast 4 *n* **splash**, squish, splish-splash, suck, gurgle, splosh (*UK*) [➡ IMPACT SOUNDS; 1260] 5 *n* (*slang*) [➡ CRITICISMS AND ANGRY OUTBURSTS; 50]

squelchy *adj* **soggy**, squishy, wet, watery, damp, squashy, squidgy (*UK*) [➡ WET; 1240] *Opposite*: dry

squib *type of* **firework** [➡ EXPLOSIVES; 1155]

squid *type of* **aquatic invertebrate** [➡ AQUATIC INVERTEBRATES; 1022]

squidgy (*UK*) 1 *adj* **soggy**, squelchy, slimy, mushy, marshy, wet, damp, moist, gooey, sloppy [➡ WET; 1240] *Opposite*: dry 2 *adj* **squashy**, spongy, springy, pliable, soft, yielding [➡ MALLEABLE AND ELASTIC; 1212] *Opposite*: firm

squiggle *n* **scribble**, wavy line, doodle, ornamentation, flourish, scrawl, curlicue, mark [➡ WRITING; 583]

squiggly *adj* **wavy**, curvy, wobbly, bumpy, scribbly, meandering, snaky [➡ ROUNDED SHAPE; 1218] *Opposite*: straight

squillion (*UK*) *n* [➡ MANY, MUCH, LARGE AMOUNT; 117]

squint 1 *v* **narrow your eyes**, peer, peek, look, glance [➡LOOKING AND LOOKS; 700] **2** *n* **peep**, peer, quick look, glance, glimpse, peek [➡LOOKING AND LOOKS; 700] **3** *adj* (*informal*) **crooked**, lopsided, cross-eyed, off balance, uneven, tilted, askew [➡ORIENTATION AND ALIGNMENT; 1223] *Opposite*: straight **4** *adv* (*informal*) **lopsidedly**, askew, crookedly, unevenly [➡ORIENTATION AND ALIGNMENT; 1223] *Opposite*: straight

squire 1 *n* **landowner**, lord, landlord, owner, proprietor, landholder, laird (*UK*) [➡RICH PEOPLE; 895] *Opposite*: tenant **2** *n* **attendant**, retainer, steward, man, servant, page [➡DOMESTIC AND KITCHEN WORKERS; 850]

squirm 1 *v* **wriggle**, writhe, twist, turn, fidget, struggle [➡FIDGET AND FROLIC; 311] **2** *v* **feel shame**, feel embarrassment, feel remorse, feel guilty, feel awkward, feel humiliated [➡CHANGE OF MOOD AND COMPOSURE; 580]

squirmy *adj* [➡INSECURITY AND LOSS OF COMPOSURE; 544]

squirrel 1 *type of* **rodent** [➡RODENTS; 989] **2** *n* (*UK informal*) **hoarder**, collector, accumulator, saver, magpie (*informal*), pack rat (*informal*) [➡PEOPLE WHO COLLECT THINGS; 454] **3** *v* **hoard**, collect, accumulate, store, put aside, save, salt away, squirrel away, stockpile, stash (*informal*) [➡STORE AND KEEP; 453] *Opposite*: throw out

squirrel away *v* [➡STORE AND KEEP; 453]

squirt 1 *v* **spurt**, shoot, jet, gush, spray, spew, spout, squeeze [➡LIQUID EMISSION; 370] **2** *n* **spurt**, jet, fountain, stream, spray, squeeze, shot (*informal*) [➡AMOUNTS OF LIQUID; 114]

squirt gun *type of* **toy** [➡TOYS; 880]

squish 1 *v* **squeeze**, crush, squash, squelch, pinch [➡CHANGE OF SHAPE; 385] **2** *v* **splash**, squelch, splish-splash, suck, gurgle, splosh (*UK*) [➡EMIT SOUNDS THROUGH IMPACT AND ABRASION; 365] **3** *n* **squelch**, splash, splish-splash, suck, gurgle, splosh (*UK*) [➡IMPACT SOUNDS; 1260]

squishy *adj* **squelchy**, soggy, soft, mushy, spongy, slimy, wet, damp, moist, gooey, marshy, sloppy, squidgy (*UK*) [➡WET; 1240] *Opposite*: firm

stab 1 *v* **knife**, wound, pierce, cut, spear, stick, gouge, gore, run through (*literary*) [➡STAB; 416] **2** *n* **pang**, twinge, ache, pain, prick, feeling, sensation [➡PAIN AND OTHER PHYSICAL SENSATIONS; 733] **3** *n* (*informal*) **attempt**, go, try, shot, guess, crack (*informal*) [➡ATTEMPT AN ACTION; 261]

stabbing 1 *n* **knife attack**, assault, wounding, attack [➡AGGRESSIVE EVENTS; 39] **2** *adj* **sharp**, acute, piercing, shooting, intense, severe [➡PHYSICALLY UNPLEASANT; 226]

stability *n* **constancy**, steadiness, firmness, solidity, permanence, immovability, strength [➡PERMANENCE: WITHOUT CHANGE; 95] *Opposite*: instability

stabilization *n* **steadying**, steadiness, maintenance, balance, equilibrium, evening out, calming [➡PROGRESS AND ADVANCEMENT; 213] *Opposite*: change

stabilize *v* **become stable**, even out, become constant, calm, calm down, soothe, alleviate, steady [➡IMPROVE SOMETHING; 374] *Opposite*: change

stab in the back (*informal*) 1 *v* **betray**, let down, be disloyal to, sell out, wound, attack [➡BETRAY CONFIDENCES AND GOSSIP; 618] **2** *n* **betrayal**, wound, attack, act of disloyalty, act of treachery [➡MALICIOUS ACTIONS OR BEHAVIOR; 296]

stable 1 *adj* **steady**, unchanging, even, constant, firm, unwavering, sure, established, secure, committed, longstanding [➡PERMANENCE: WITHOUT CHANGE; 95] *Opposite*: changeable **2** *adj* **secure**, fixed, firm, permanent, rigid, durable, sure, fast [➡DURABLE; 1210] *Opposite*: unstable **3** *adj* **calm**, steady, even, settled, level-headed, collected [➡COOL AND CALM; 536] *Opposite*: erratic **4** *n* **stall**, shed, stabling [➡ANIMAL OR BIRD ACCOMMODATIONS; 1079] **5** *n* **team**, gang, string, group, lineup, set [➡GROUPS OF PEOPLE; 935]

staccato 1 *adj* **clipped**, disjointed, disconnected, faltering, monosyllabic [➡INARTICULATE, RAMBLING, AND AWKWARD; 633] **2** *type of* **musical term** [➡MUSICAL TERMS; 912]

stack 1 *n* **pile**, heap, mass, mound, mountain, load [➡MANY, MUCH, LARGE AMOUNT; 117] **2** *n* **chimney**, smokestack, flue [➡ROOFS, ROOF PARTS, AND CEILINGS; 1103] **3** *v* **pile**, load, heap, mound, amass, assemble [➡MOVE SOMETHING: INTO A NEW POSITION OR OVERTURN; 330]

stacked *adj* **loaded**, weighted, set, slanted, fixed, arranged [➡FULL; 1239]

stacks (*informal*) *n* **lots**, masses, piles (*informal*), tons (*informal*), loads (*informal*), heaps (*informal*) [➡MANY, MUCH, LARGE AMOUNT; 117]

stack up 1 *v* **measure up**, stand up, compare, line up, stand comparison [➡ASSESS QUALITY; 755] **2** *v* **add up**, come to, accumulate, make, total, amount to, make a total of [➡AMOUNT TO AND EQUAL; 70]

stadium *n* **sports grounds**, arena, ground, field, ring, bowl, pitch (*UK*) [➡URBAN OUTDOOR SPACES; 1072]

staff 1 *n* **employees**, personnel, workers, work force, team, body, force, human resources, organization [➡THE WORK FORCE; 837] **2** *n* **rod**, cane, pole, wand, stick, baton [➡STICKS, POLES, AND WEDGES; 1254] **3** *v* **operate**, run, work, control, supervise, man [➡BE IN CHARGE; 270]

stag *type of* **male animal** [➡MALE OR FEMALE ANIMALS; 978]

stag beetle *type of* **beetle** [➡BEETLES AND WEEVILS; 1016]

stage 1 *n* **phase**, period, step, point, leg, juncture, time [➡PERIODS OF TIME; 90] **2** *n* **platform**, rostrum, stand, scaffold, podium, dais [➡STAGES, PLATFORMS, AND RAISED AREAS; 1098] **3** *n* **theater**, arena, playhouse, the boards [➡IN THE THEATER; 906] **4** *part of* **spacecraft** [➡SPACE VEHICLES; 1063] **5** *v* **put on**, perform, present, show, play, act, do [➡CAUSE TO HAPPEN; 31]

stagecoach *n* **carriage**, horse-drawn carriage, cart [➡BIKES, CARS, AND CARRIAGES; 1149]

stage door *n* **back door**, side door, entrance, way in, exit, way out [➡IN THE THEATER; 906]

stage fright *n* **first-night nerves**, fear, panic, nerves (*informal*) [➡FEELINGS ABOUT THE FUTURE; 533]

stage-manage *v* **engineer**, contrive, manipulate, devise, set up, control, direct, maneuver [➡CAUSE TO HAPPEN; 31]

stage name *n* **pseudonym**, alias, assumed name, professional name [➡NAME AND DESCRIBE; 665]

stage whisper *n* **aside**, mutter, murmur [➡IN THE THEATER; 906] *Opposite*: shout

stagey *see* **stagy**

stagflation 1 *n* **slump**, recession, downturn, stagnation, inflation, standstill [➡ MARKET FORCES; 803] *Opposite*: growth 2 *type of* **economic condition** [➡ FINANCE AND ECONOMICS; 796]

stagger 1 *v* **reel**, lurch, sway, totter, wobble, teeter, stumble, walk unsteadily [➡ WALK UNSTEADILY; 315] 2 *v* **astound**, amaze, shock, stun, surprise, astonish, confound, shake, take by surprise [➡ SURPRISE AND IMPRESS; 574] 3 *v* **alternate**, vary, zigzag, rotate, space out, spread out, step [➡ ARRANGE AND CREATE ORDER; 357] *Opposite*: overlap

staggered 1 *adj* **stunned**, shocked, astounded, taken aback, surprised, nonplussed, amazed, flabbergasted (*informal*) [➡ SURPRISE, SHOCK, AND AMAZEMENT; 545] *Opposite*: unaffected 2 *adj* **alternated**, spread out, spaced out, zigzagged [➡ ORIENTATION AND ALIGNMENT; 1223]

staggering *adj* **astounding**, amazing, confounding, overwhelming, stunning, shocking, surprising, incredible, astonishing, unbelievable, hard to believe [➡ EXTRAORDINARY: AMAZING; 204]

staging *n* **performance**, dramatization, production, enactment, presentation [➡ PERFORMANCES AND SHOWS; 42]

staging post (*UK*) *n* **stopover**, halt, stop, break, halfway house, port of call [➡ TRANSPORTATION, TRANSPORTERS, AND CARGOS; 322]

stagnant 1 *adj* **still**, motionless, stationary, standing, immobile, quiet [➡ LACK OF ACTIVITY OR MOTION; 342] *Opposite*: moving 2 *adj* **sluggish**, inactive, inert, torpid, dull, dormant, moribund, heavy [➡ BORING AND UNINTERESTING; 234] *Opposite*: active

stagnate 1 *v* **stand still**, come to a halt, grind to a halt, be idle, languish, idle, decline [➡ GET WORSE; 381] *Opposite*: progress 2 *v* **fester**, rot, deteriorate, decay, go rancid, go stale, go bad, go off (*UK*) [➡ GO BAD AND CORRODE; 390] 3 *v* **vegetate**, be inactive, idle, be idle, sit around, do nothing [➡ LACK OF ACTIVITY OR MOTION; 342]

stagnation *n* **inactivity**, inaction, inertia, torpor, sluggishness, immobility, lack of progress, unproductivity [➡ LACK OF ACTIVITY OR MOTION; 342] *Opposite*: movement

stagy *adj* **theatrical**, dramatic, histrionic, exaggerated, artificial, melodramatic, studied, affected [➡ AFFECTATION, SELF-SATISFACTION, AND SNOBBISHNESS; 507] *Opposite*: unaffected

staid *adj* **sedate**, serious, grave, sober, dull, calm, settled, demure, stolid, solid, unadventurous, somber, steady [➡ UNADVENTUROUS AND DULL; 517] *Opposite*: exciting

staidness *n* [➡ UNADVENTUROUS AND DULL; 517]

stain 1 *n* **mark**, blemish, spot, blot, imperfection, discoloration, tarnish [➡ FAULTS, FLAWS, AND WEAKNESSES; 251] 2 *n* **tint**, dye, color, tinge, pigment, colorwash [➡ DYES AND COLORANTS; 1270] 3 *n* **stigma**, slur, disgrace, dishonor, blemish, reproach, contamination, shame, infamy [➡ NUISANCES; 253] 4 *v* **blemish**, tarnish, soil, discolor, mark, tinge, dirty, blot, spot, dye [➡ DIRTY AND CONTAMINATE; 404] 5 *v* **disgrace**, sully, taint, debase, dishonor, pollute, contaminate, corrupt, deprave, defile (*formal*) [➡ MISUSE AND ABUSE; 471] *Opposite*: honor

stained *adj* **discolored**, marked, blemished, tainted, tarnished, damaged [➡ DIRTY; 1235]

stained glass *type of* **glass** [➡ GLASS; 1136]

stainless steel *type of* **metal** [➡ METALS; 1276]

stair 1 *n* **step**, tread, rung [➡ SUPPORTS AND BASES; 1255] 2 *n* **staircase**, stairway, flight of steps, set of steps, flight of stairs, stairs [➡ STAIRS AND STORIES; 1102]

staircase *n* [➡ STAIRS AND STORIES; 1102]

stairs *n* **staircase**, stair, stairway, flight of steps, set of steps, flight of stairs [➡ STAIRS AND STORIES; 1102]

stairway *n* [➡ STAIRS AND STORIES; 1102]

stairwell 1 *n* **hall**, entrance hall, vestibule, shaft [➡ STAIRS AND STORIES; 1102] 2 *part of* **building** [➡ PARTS OF A BUILDING; 1095]

stake 1 *n* **bet**, wager, ante, risk, venture, hazard, pledge, chance [➡ GAMBLE AND TAKE RISKS; 466] 2 *n* **post**, pale, pole, palisade, picket, stick, rod [➡ STICKS, POLES, AND WEDGES; 1254] 3 *n* **investment**, claim, share, involvement, concern, interest [➡ FUNDS, PAYMENTS, AND CHARGES; 800] 4 *n* **prize**, winnings, purse, stakes [➡ GAMBLE AND TAKE RISKS; 466] 5 *v* **risk**, gamble, bet, venture, hazard, wager [➡ GAMBLE AND TAKE RISKS; 466]

stakeholder *n* **investor**, shareholder, backer, sponsor, participant, patron, interested party [➡ PEOPLE INVOLVED IN FINANCE; 804]

stake out 1 *v* (*informal*) **spy on**, watch, keep under surveillance, keep watch on, keep an eye on, keep under watch [➡ LOOKING AND LOOKS; 700] 2 *v* **mark out**, demarcate, delimit, measure out, fence off, chalk out (*UK*) [➡ SEPARATE AND DIVIDE; 401] 3 *v* **establish**, clarify, define, limit, restrict, delimit, describe [➡ NAME AND DESCRIBE; 665]

stakeout (*informal*) *n* **close watch**, watch, observation, investigation, examination, surveillance, supervision, vigil, guard [➡ LOOKING AND LOOKS; 700]

stake race *n* [➡ NON-AGGRESSIVE/SPORTING EVENTS; 40]

stakes 1 *n* **risk**, risk factor, danger, element of danger [➡ GAMBLE AND TAKE RISKS; 466] 2 *n* **reward**, prize, recompense, incentive, winnings [➡ GAMBLE AND TAKE RISKS; 466]

stale 1 *adj* **decayed**, sour, old, musty, hard, fusty, out-of-date, past its expiration date, flat, past its best, gone off (*UK*) [➡ DECAYING OR INFESTED; 1236] *Opposite*: fresh 2 *adj* **hackneyed**, worn-out, tired, overused, boring, clichéd, unoriginal, insipid, vapid, humdrum, pedestrian, ho-hum (*informal*) [➡ BORING AND UNINTERESTING; 234] *Opposite*: original

stalemate *n* **impasse**, deadlock, standoff, logjam, standstill [➡ DIFFICULT SITUATIONS; 72]

staleness *n* **mustiness**, moldiness, decay, flatness, sourness, fustiness [➡ DECAYING OR INFESTED; 1236] *Opposite*: freshness

stalk 1 *n* **stem**, shoot, twig, branch, trunk [➡ STICKS, POLES, AND WEDGES; 1254] 2 *v* **follow**, trail, track, pursue, shadow, hunt, haunt, tail, hound, lurk, prowl, menace, chase [➡ ACCOMPANY AND FOLLOW; 337]

See Compare and Contrast at **follow.**

stalker *n* **prowler**, pursuer, shadow, tracker, follower, Peeping Tom, lurker [➡ CRIMINALS; 821]

stall 1 *n* **booth**, stand, arcade, shop, kiosk, boutique [➡ ANCILLARY BUILDINGS; 1080] 2 *n* **compartment**, pen, coop, shed, cubicle, box, box stall, loosebox (*UK*) [➡ ALCOVES, CUBICLES, AND

COMPARTMENTS; 1096] **3** *type of* **pen or cage** [➥ANIMAL OR BIRD ACCOM-MODATIONS; 1079] **4** *type of* **seating** [➥FURNITURE; 858] **5** *v* **stop**, cut out, freeze, pause, halt, come to a standstill, peter out, shut down [➥FAIL OR CEASE TO FUNCTION; 470] *Opposite*: keep going **6** *v* **delay**, put off, defer, postpone, suspend, shelve, hold over, arrest, impede, check [➥DELAY ACTION OR OCCURRENCE; 278] *Opposite*: advance **7** *v* **play for time**, prevaricate, equivocate, hedge, hesitate, dither, delay, put off, temporize [➥SHIRK AND DELAY; 273]

stallion *type of* **male animal** [➥MALE OR FEMALE ANIMALS; 978]

stalwart **1** *adj* **resolute**, vigorous, determined, committed, unfaltering, steadfast, unwavering, staunch, firm, unshakable [➥HARD-WORKING AND COMMITTED; 500] *Opposite*: uncommitted **2** *adj* **strong**, muscular, athletic, brawny, sturdy, robust, rugged, hefty, well-built, burly, powerfully built, strapping (*informal*) [➥BUILD; 477] *Opposite*: feeble **3** *adj* **brave**, courageous, daring, fearless, bold, valiant, audacious, stouthearted, indomitable, intrepid (*literary or humorous*) [➥COURAGE; 498] *Opposite*: cowardly **4** *n* [➥PEOPLE WHO ARE APPROVED OF; 955]

stalwartly *adv* **dependably**, loyally, faithfully, steadfastly, unfalteringly, unwaveringly, staunchly, constantly, dedicatedly, reliably, firmly, unshakably [➥HARD-WORKING AND COMMITTED; 500] *Opposite*: unreliably

stamen *part of* **flower** [➥FLOWERS; 1032]

stamina *n* **staying power**, endurance, energy, resilience, resistance, determination, doggedness, vigor, strength, fortitude, sturdiness, grit, hardiness, perseverance [➥STRENGTH OF WILL; 501] *Opposite*: frailty

stammer **1** *v* **stumble**, stutter, falter, hesitate, pause, splutter, hem and haw, mumble, hum and haw (*UK*) [➥CHATTER AND BABBLE; 617] **2** *n* **stutter**, hesitant speech, speech impediment [➥INARTICULATE, RAMBLING, AND AWKWARD; 633]

stamp **1** *n* **mark**, imprint, mold, cast, hallmark, earmark, print, impression, endorsement, seal, signature, identification, trademark, label, brand [➥SYMBOLS, SIGNS, AND NUMBERS; 596] **2** *n* **character**, kind, make, sort, type, quality, form, variety, characteristic [➥VARIETIES, TYPES, AND KINDS; 145] **3** *v* **imprint**, engrave, inscribe, fix, impress, mark, earmark, hallmark, brand, print, seal [➥CREATE IMAGES; 356] **4** *v* **trample**, stomp, crush, squash, plod, trudge, pound, beat [➥CONTACT: EXERT PRESSURE; 414]

stampede **1** *n* **rush**, mad dash, flight, rout, pandemonium, retreat, panic, charge [➥CHAOS AND UPROAR; 51] **2** *v* **rush**, hurry, run, dash, sprint, take flight, flee, scatter, charge [➥MOVE FAST; 313]

stamping ground (*informal*) *n* **patch**, haunt, place, home, territory, familiar territory, hangout (*informal*) [➥PLACE; 1065]

stamp out *v* **eradicate**, banish, destroy, remove, eliminate, extinguish, abolish, put an end to, get rid of, crush, put down, suppress, wipe out (*informal*), squelch (*slang*) [➥GET RID OF SOMETHING; 451] *Opposite*: cultivate

stance **1** *n* **attitude**, position, stand, standpoint, view, viewpoint, point of view, opinion, perspective, outlook [➥POINTS OF VIEW; 767] **2** *n* **posture**, deportment, bearing, attitude, carriage (*formal*) [➥TEMPERAMENT AND BEHAVIOR; 492]

stanch *see* **staunch**

stanchion *n* [➥SUPPORTS AND BASES; 1255]

stand **1** *v* **erect**, mount, hoist, put up, stick up, rear, raise, set upright [➥POSITION SOMETHING; 325] **2** *v* **rise**, get up, stand up, get to your feet, be on your feet, arise (*archaic or literary*) [➥ASSUME A POSITION; 317] *Opposite*: sit **3** *v* **place**, situate, position, set, put, locate, rest, deposit, park (*slang*) [➥POSITION SOMETHING; 325] **4** *v* **tolerate**, endure, put up with, abide, bear, withstand, stand for, stomach, cope with, sustain, survive, take, suffer, brook (*formal*) [➥TOLERATE AND ENDURE; 766] **5** *v* **remain**, halt, stop, continue, exist, pause, stay, remain motionless, remain standing, endure, survive, last, hold, prevail, persist [➥CONTINUE TO EXIST; 17] **6** *n* **stop**, standstill, stay, rest, halt [➥LACK OF ACTIVITY OR MOTION; 342] **7** *n* **attitude**, opinion, stance, position, viewpoint, standpoint, point of view, view, outlook, policy [➥POINTS OF VIEW; 767] **8** *n* **rack**, frame, support, holder, shelf, bracket [➥SUPPORTS AND BASES; 1255] **9** *n* **platform**, rostrum, stage, place, post, position, dais, podium [➥SUPPORTS AND BASES; 1255] **10** *n* **stall**, counter, booth, kiosk, tent [➥ANCILLARY BUILDINGS; 1080]

standard **1** *n* **criterion**, benchmark, touchstone, paradigm, yardstick, model, pattern, measure, requirement, guideline, specification [➥PERFECT EXAMPLES AND EMBODIMENTS; 67] **2** *n* **norm**, average, mean, par, level, degree, rank [➥SCORES AND EVALUATIONS; 598] **3** *n* **flag**, banner, ensign, pennant, colors, streamer, emblem, jack [➥SYMBOLS, SIGNS, AND NUMBERS; 596] **4** *adj* **normal**, typical, average, usual, ordinary, set, customary, orthodox, prevailing, accepted, traditional, basic, everyday, universal, regular, stock [➥ORDINARINESS; 244] *Opposite*: unusual

standard-bearer *n* **leader**, ringleader, prime mover, spearhead, director, chief, commander, captain [➥IMPORTANT OR FAMOUS PEOPLE; 893]

standardize *v* **regulate**, homogenize, normalize, even out, regiment, stereotype, order, systematize [➥ARRANGE AND CREATE ORDER; 357]

standard-length *adj* [➥MEDIUM; 1196]

standard of living *n* **level of comfort**, means, level of affluence, wealth, lifestyle, way of life [➥LIFESTYLE; 881]

standards *n* **principles**, values, morals, ethics, ideals, canon [➥MORAL CONCEPTS; 773]

standard-size *adj* [➥MEDIUM; 1196]

stand by *v* **support**, stick by, back, stick up for, side with, defend, uphold, be there for, maintain, back up [➥APPROVE AND CONFIRM; 646] *Opposite*: abandon

standby **1** *n* **fallback**, reserve, replacement, resource, stand-in, deputy, cover, understudy [➥COLLEAGUES AND EQUALS; 967] **2** *n* **backup**, substitute, replacement, spare, reserve [➥SUBSTITUTES AND STAND-INS; 399] **3** *adj* **reserve**, fallback, replacement, stand-in, deputy, understudy, backup, spare, emergency [➥MORE AND EXCESS; 124] *Opposite*: main **4** *adj* **unreserved**, last-minute, late, for immediate use [➥PROMPTNESS: LATE; 100] *Opposite*: reserved

stand down *v* **resign**, step down, quit, bow out, give up, call it a day [➥STOP ACTING; 264]

stand firm *v* **persevere**, stand your ground, hold on, hold out, dig in your heels, persist [➥CONTINUE AN ACTION; 262] *Opposite*: yield

stand for **1** *v* **mean**, signify, represent, denote, symbolize, indicate, emblematize (*formal*) [➡ MEAN SOMETHING; 61] **2** *v* **advocate**, promote, support, champion, endorse, sponsor, back, be in favor of [➡ APPROVE AND CONFIRM; 646] **3** *v* **put up with**, tolerate, abide, withstand, stand, accept, bear, endure, stomach, suffer, take, brook (*formal*) [➡ TOLERATE AND ENDURE; 766]

stand in *v* **fill in**, substitute, deputize, take somebody's place, do somebody's work, cover, temp, understudy, double, alternate [➡ REPRESENT SOMETHING OR SOMEBODY; 59]

stand-in *n* **replacement**, understudy, deputy, substitute, reserve, double, lieutenant, standby [➡ SUBSTITUTES AND STAND-INS, 399]

stand in for *v* **take the place of**, deputize for, substitute for, cover for, do the work of, understudy [➡ REPRESENT SOMETHING OR SOMEBODY; 59]

standing **1** *n* **rank**, status, position, reputation, station, eminence, footing, place, ranking, order, grade, repute (*formal*) [➡ STATUS; 888] **2** *n* **duration**, existence, continuance, age, tenure, term, life, length, extent [➡ PERIODS OF TIME; 90] **3** *adj* **established**, settled, fixed, immovable, durable, lasting, permanent [➡ PERMANENCE WITHOUT END; 94] *Opposite*: temporary **4** *adj* **stand-up**, vertical, upright, upended, perpendicular, erect [➡ ORIENTATION AND ALIGNMENT; 1223] *Opposite*: horizontal

standing order *n* **rule**, order, instruction, protocol, procedure, guideline [➡ WAYS OF DOING THINGS; 294]

standing ovation *n* [➡ APPLAUSE; 652]

standing stone *n* **obelisk**, menhir, dolmen, megalith, column, stone circle [➡ ANCIENT MANMADE STRUCTURES; 1089]

standoff **1** *n* **stalemate**, impasse, deadlock, logjam, standstill [➡ DIFFICULT SITUATIONS; 72] **2** *n* **tie**, draw, dead heat, photo finish [➡ RESULTS AND OUTCOMES; 83]

standoffish *adj* **distant**, aloof, superior, unapproachable, cold, unfriendly, reticent, unforthcoming, reserved, unsociable, supercilious, detached, snobbish, withdrawn, remote, snooty (*informal*) [➡ UNFRIENDLINESS AND UNSOCIABILITY; 504] *Opposite*: affable

standoffishness *n* [➡ UNFRIENDLINESS AND UNSOCIABILITY; 504]

stand out **1** *v* **be obvious**, be prominent, show up, be conspicuous, stick out, be clear, be noticeable, be notable [➡ APPEAR AND EMERGE; 3] **2** *v* **project**, jut, protrude, jut out, stick out, poke out, overhang [➡ ARRIVE; 12]

standpipe *n* **water pipe**, faucet, emergency pipe, water supply, hydrant, fire hydrant, fireplug, tap (*UK*) [➡ WATERCOURSES; 1111]

standpoint *n* **point of view**, position, stance, angle, viewpoint, perspective, opinion, outlook, view [➡ POINTS OF VIEW; 767]

standstill *n* **halt**, stop, stoppage, cessation, end, dead end, full stop (*UK*) [➡ LACK OF ACTIVITY OR MOTION; 342]

stand the pace *v* [➡ TOLERATE AND ENDURE; 766]

stand up **1** *v* **rise**, stand, get to your feet, get up, arise (*archaic or literary*) [➡ ASSUME A POSITION; 317] *Opposite*: sit down **2** *v* **endure**, last, survive, continue, hold out [➡ CONTINUE TO EXIST; 17]

standup **1** *adj* **solo**, one-man, one-woman, improvised,

off-the-cuff, impromptu, ad-lib [➡ ACTING INDEPENDENTLY; 284] *Opposite*: rehearsed **2** *adj* (*informal*) **trustworthy**, honest, loyal, dependable, reliable, faithful, responsible [➡ HONEST AND RELIABLE; 502] *Opposite*: unreliable **3** *adj* **erect**, upright, standing, upstanding, vertical [➡ ORIENTATION AND ALIGNMENT; 1223] *Opposite*: flat **4** *adj* (*UK*) **intense**, fierce, furious, blazing, violent, noisy, aggressive [➡ EMOTIONALLY UNPLEASANT AND UPSETTING; 227] *Opposite*: mild

standup comedian *type of* **entertainer** [➡ WORKERS IN ENTERTAINMENT AND MEDIA; 873]

stand up to *v* **face**, brave, take on, meet head-on, confront, challenge, resist, defy [➡ ACCUSE, BLAME, AND CRITICIZE; 641] *Opposite*: avoid

stand your ground *v* **stand firm**, persist, persevere, reserve, hold out, hold on, dig in your heels [➡ CONTINUE AN ACTION; 262] *Opposite*: give in

stanza *n* **verse**, section, stave, couplet, triplet, canto [➡ POETRY AND VERSE; 915]

stapes *part of* **ear** [➡ THE EAR; 706]

staphylococcus *type of* **microorganism** [➡ MICROORGANISMS, FUNGI, AND ALGAE; 1023]

staple **1** *n* **clip**, fastener, nail, tack, pin [➡ FASTENERS, LINKS, AND NETWORKS; 1247] **2** *v* **fasten**, affix, clip, attach, secure, fix, nail, pin, tack [➡ FASTEN, LINK, AND JOIN; 408] **3** *adj* **main**, chief, principal, essential, primary, indispensable, basic, fundamental, core, key, prime, vital [➡ FUNDAMENTAL; 195] *Opposite*: minor

star **1** *n* [➡ THE SOLAR SYSTEM AND ASTRONOMY; 1060] **2** *type of* **angular shape** [➡ ANGULAR SHAPE; 1217] **3** *n* **celebrity**, superstar, personality, icon [➡ IMPORTANT OR FAMOUS PEOPLE; 893] **4** *v* **feature**, showcase, head the cast, top the bill, play the lead, take the lead [➡ PARTICIPATE; 292] **5** *v* **do well**, excel, shine, succeed, stand out, steal the show [➡ SUCCEED AND WIN; 79]

star

◆ *types of stars or star systems*
binary star, black hole, brown dwarf, dark star, dwarf star, galaxy, giant star, nebula, nova, pulsar, quasar, red giant, sun, supernova, white dwarf

star attraction *n* [➡ AMAZING THINGS; 211]

star billing *n* **top billing**, star status, top of the bill, main attraction, big name, star turn (*UK*) [➡ THE PERFORMING ARTS; 904]

starboard *adj* **right-hand**, right, right-side [➡ GENERAL LOCATIONS; 158] *Opposite*: port

starch *type of* **nutrient** [➡ FOOD COMPONENTS; 1188]

starched *adj* [➡ LEVELS OF FORMALITY; 522]

starchiness *n* [➡ LEVELS OF FORMALITY; 522]

starchy *adj* **stiff**, solemn, prudish, prim, austere, stuffy, staid [➡ LEVELS OF FORMALITY; 522] *Opposite*: relaxed

star-crossed *adj* **ill-fated**, unlucky, ill-starred, doomed, unfortunate [➡ BAD LUCK AND UNLUCKY; 784] *Opposite*: lucky

stardom *n* **fame**, celebrity, prominence, renown, glory, recognition, eminence [➡ KNOWN AND FAMOUS; 181] *Opposite*: anonymity

stardust *n* **romance**, dreaminess, sentiment, emotion, feeling, fantasy [➡ NONEXISTENT THINGS; 23]

stare 1 *v* **gaze**, gape, look intently, ogle, glare, glower, watch, gawk (*informal*), rubberneck (*informal*) [➡ LOOKING AND LOOKS; 700] *Opposite*: ignore 2 *n* **intent look**, gaze, gape, glare, glower [➡ FACIAL EXPRESSIONS AND BLUSHING; 651]

See Compare and Contrast at **gaze.**

stare down *v* [➡ LOOKING AND LOOKS; 700]

stare into space *v* [➡ LOOKING AND LOOKS; 700]

stare out (*UK*) *v* **outstare**, stare at, look at, gaze at, stare down [➡ LOOKING AND LOOKS; 700]

starfish *type of* **aquatic invertebrate** [➡ AQUATIC INVERTEBRATES; 1022]

star in *v* **play the lead in**, feature in, act in, play in, head the cast, top the bill [➡ PARTICIPATE; 292]

stark 1 *adj* **bleak**, bare, barren, desolate, austere, severe, harsh [➡ PLAIN; 232] *Opposite*: opulent 2 *adj* **plain**, unambiguous, simple, blunt, unadulterated, unadorned, unembellished, blatant, glaring [➡ HONEST AND OPEN; 630] *Opposite*: ambiguous 3 *adj* **complete**, utter, absolute, sheer, downright, pure, out-and-out, total [➡ ABSOLUTE AND ABSOLUTELY; 133] *Opposite*: partial 4 *adv* **completely**, utterly, entirely, wholly, fully, absolutely, altogether [➡ ABSOLUTE AND ABSOLUTELY; 133] *Opposite*: partially

stark-naked *adj* [➡ DRESS, WEAR, AND UNDRESS; 868]

starkness 1 *n* **austerity**, bleakness, harshness, severity, sparseness, asceticism, abstemiousness, simplicity, bareness [➡ PLAIN; 232] *Opposite*: opulence 2 *n* **unambiguity**, blatancy, harshness, bluntness, frankness, baldness, plainness, outspokenness [➡ HONEST AND OPEN; 630] *Opposite*: ambiguity

starlet *n* **actor**, rising young star, new talent, star of tomorrow, star in the making, minor actor, unknown, ingénue, wannabe (*informal*) [➡ PERFORMERS; 905]

starlight *n* **glow**, gleam, sheen, twinkle, sparkle, glint, glitter, flicker, moonlight, light [➡ LIGHT; 1164]

starling *type of* **common bird** [➡ BIRDS; 997]

starlit *adj* **starry**, bright, glowing, gleaming, twinkling, sparkling, glinting, glittering, flickering, moonlit [➡ DESCRIBING LIGHT; 1228] *Opposite*: dark

starry *adj* **glittery**, shiny, bright, sparkly, brilliant, shining, sparkling, twinkling, lustrous, spangled [➡ DESCRIBING LIGHT; 1228] *Opposite*: dull

starry-eyed *adj* **dreamy**, optimistic, idealistic, head-in-the-clouds, happy [➡ PLEASURE, EXCITEMENT, AND ELATION; 534] *Opposite*: cynical

starship *n* **spaceship**, space shuttle, space station, flying saucer [➡ SCIENCE FICTION; 1064]

star sign *n* **sign of the zodiac**, birth sign, sun sign, sign,

astrological sign, house, constellation [➡ FATE, DESTINY, AND ASTROLOGY; 782]

star-spangled *adj* [➡ DESCRIBING PATTERNS; 1227]

star-studded *adj* **star-spangled**, all-star, celebrity, big-name, glittering, glamorous, glitzy [➡ THE PERFORMING ARTS; 904] *Opposite*: unknown

star system *n* **constellation**, galaxy, Milky Way, solar system [➡ THE SOLAR SYSTEM AND ASTRONOMY; 1060]

start 1 *v* **create**, found, begin, establish, set up, initiate, institute, launch, pioneer, inaugurate, father [➡ INSTITUTE AND INAUGURATE; 348] 2 *v* **begin**, commence, start off, get going, set off, open, get under way, switch on, fire up, kick off (*informal*) [➡ START AN ACTION; 260] *Opposite*: finish 3 *v* **set out**, leave, set off, depart, get going, be on your way, be off, start off, take off, start out [➡ LEAVE AND GO AWAY; 8] *Opposite*: arrive 4 *v* **jump**, recoil, flinch, shrink, twitch, jerk [➡ PHYSICAL REACTIONS; 316] 5 *n* **beginning**, birth, foundation, onset, dawn, opening, outset, initiation, inception (*formal*), commencement (*formal*) [➡ BEGINNINGS; 53] 6 *n* **twitch**, jump, jerk, flinch, jolt [➡ PHYSICAL REACTIONS; 316] 7 *n* **shock**, fright, surprise, turn [➡ SURPRISE, SHOCK, AND AMAZEMENT; 545] 8 *n* **lead**, advantage, edge, boon, gain, head start, plus (*informal*) [➡ ADVANTAGES; 212]

start afresh *v* [➡ RECOMMENCE AND RESUME; 268]

start again *v* [➡ RECOMMENCE AND RESUME; 268]

start anew *v* [➡ RECOMMENCE AND RESUME; 268]

starter 1 *n* **hors d'oeuvre**, first course, entrée, appetizer, meze, tapas, antipasto [➡ MEALS AND PARTS OF MEALS; 1169] 2 *part of* **engine** [➡ PARTS OF AN ENGINE; 1144]

starter home *type of* **house** [➡ RESIDENTIAL BUILDINGS; 1078]

starting point 1 *n* **basis**, base, foundation, point of departure, beginning, start, origin, square one, kickoff (*informal*) [➡ BEGINNINGS; 53] 2 *n* **starting line**, starting block, starting grid, starting post, starting gate [➡ SPORTS TERMS; 877] *Opposite*: finishing line

startle *v* **surprise**, disconcert, shock, alarm, frighten, amaze, astound, scare, astonish, disturb, disquiet (*archaic or literary*) [➡ SURPRISE AND IMPRESS; 574]

startled *adj* **surprised**, disconcerted, alarmed, astonished, amazed, frightened, shocked, stunned, scared [➡ SURPRISE, SHOCK, AND AMAZEMENT; 545]

startling *adj* **surprising**, astonishing, amazing, astounding, staggering, shocking, upsetting, disquieting [➡ EXTRAORDINARY: AMAZING; 204] *Opposite*: comforting

start off 1 *v* **begin**, commence, get going, start out, start, make a start, set in motion, kick off (*informal*) [➡ START AN ACTION; 260] *Opposite*: finish 2 *v* **set off**, start out, be off, get going, start, take off, be on your way [➡ LEAVE AND GO AWAY; 8] *Opposite*: arrive

start on 1 *v* (*informal*) **scold**, harass, pester, nag, annoy, tell off (*informal*) [➡ ACCUSE, BLAME, AND CRITICIZE; 641] 2 *v* **begin**, tackle, deal with, embark on, get going on, get underway, make a start on, attack [➡ START AN ACTION; 260] *Opposite*: finish

start out 1 *v* **start off**, start, begin, set off, get going, set out, take off, be on your way, be off, set forth (*literary*) [➡ LEAVE AND GO AWAY; 8] *Opposite*: arrive 2 *v* **intend**, mean, plan, propose, expect, undertake [➡ START AN ACTION; 260]

start over v [➡ RECOMMENCE AND RESUME; 268]

start the ball rolling v [➡ CAUSE TO START; 265]

start up 1 v **switch on**, turn on, fire up, power up, ignite, activate, get going, wind up (*informal*) [➡ USE TOOLS AND MACHINERY; 468] *Opposite*: turn off 2 v **set up**, open, begin, launch, create, initiate, inaugurate, bring into being, install, introduce [➡ INSTITUTE AND INAUGURATE; 348] *Opposite*: close down 3 v **pipe up**, resound, be heard, begin, start, commence [➡ INTERRUPT AND BUTT IN; 619] *Opposite*: quiet down 4 v **leap up**, jump up, stand up, get up, rise, stir, start, arise (*archaic or literary*) [➡ GO UPWARD; 306] *Opposite*: sit down

startup 1 n [➡ BEGINNINGS; 53] 2 n [➡ BUSINESS ENTERPRISES AND RELATED BODIES; 792]

start up again v [➡ HAPPEN AGAIN; 28]

star turn n **main attraction**, star attraction, big name, top of the bill, top act, headliner [➡ PERFORMERS; 905]

starvation n **hunger**, malnourishment, undernourishment, famishment, famine, food shortage [➡ EAT AND NOT EAT; 710]

starve v **have nothing to eat**, go hungry, famish, be malnourished, go short of food, waste away, be hungry, waste with hunger [➡ EAT AND NOT EAT; 710] *Opposite*: eat

starved 1 adj (*informal*) **ravenous**, hungry, famished, starving (*informal*) [➡ EAT AND NOT EAT; 710] *Opposite*: replete 2 adj **deprived**, bereft, devoid, lacking, without [➡ LACK OF POSSESSION; 445]

starved of adj [➡ LACK OF POSSESSION; 445]

starving (*informal*) adj **ravenous**, hungry, famished, starved (*informal*) [➡ EAT AND NOT EAT; 710] *Opposite*: replete

stash 1 n **supply**, hideaway, hoard, mass, pile, stockpile, stack, reserve, heap, store [➡ MANY, MUCH, LARGE AMOUNT; 117] 2 v (*informal*) **hide**, hoard, put away, put by, stockpile, salt away, secrete, squirrel, store [➡ STORE AND KEEP; 453]

stash away v [➡ STORE AND KEEP; 453]

stasis n **stability**, motionlessness, status quo, continuity, inertia, stillness, immobility, lack of change, balance, equilibrium [➡ LACK OF ACTIVITY OR MOTION; 342] *Opposite*: change

state 1 n **condition**, situation, position, status, circumstances, shape [➡ STATE; 1208] 2 n (*informal*) **confusion**, turmoil, disarray, disorder, chaos, mess [➡ DIFFICULT SITUATIONS; 72] 3 n **federation**, kingdom, nation, land, territory, country [➡ COUNTRIES AND REGIONS; 1067] 4 n **grandeur**, ceremony, pomp, splendor, glory, dignity, majesty, magnificence [➡ ROYALNESS; 825] 5 adj **public**, government, municipal, state-run, state-owned, national [➡ GOVERNMENT AND POLITICS; 805] 6 adj **formal**, official, stately, imperial, royal, majestic, ceremonial [➡ ROYALNESS; 825] 7 v **utter**, affirm, declare, assert, express, maintain, say, testify, avow (*formal*), aver (*formal*) [➡ INFORM, ANNOUNCE, AND ISSUE; 611]

statecraft n **government**, management, governance, administration, direction, control, statesmanship, diplomacy [➡ GOVERNMENT AND POLITICS; 805]

stateless adj **homeless**, nationless, displaced, refugee, outlawed, exiled, deported, asylum-seeking, expatriate [➡ NOMADIC AND ROOTLESS LIFESTYLES; 884]

state line n **border**, border line, frontier, boundary [➡ GEOGRAPHIC BORDERS AND BOUNDARIES; 1069]

stateliness n **grandeur**, pomp, glory, dignity, majesty, splendor, formality, magnificence [➡ EXPENSIVE AND LUXURIOUS; 218]

stately adj **grand**, splendid, dignified, imperial, majestic, noble, regal, gracious, distinguished, imposing, august (*formal*) [➡ EXPENSIVE AND LUXURIOUS; 218] *Opposite*: modest

statement 1 n **declaration**, announcement, report, account, speech, proclamation, assertion, testimony, testimonial, avowal (*formal*) [➡ INFORM, ANNOUNCE, AND ISSUE; 611] 2 n **record**, account, report, receipt, invoice [➡ RECORDS; 585]

state of affairs n **situation**, set of circumstances, condition, setup, position, state of play, setting, picture [➡ SITUATIONS; 71]

state of emergency n [➡ DIFFICULT SITUATIONS; 72]

state of grace n [➡ PLEASANT SITUATIONS; 74]

state of mind n **mood**, temper, attitude, feelings, spirits, disposition, mentality [➡ PSYCHOLOGY AND THE MIND; 769]

state of play n [➡ SITUATIONS; 71]

state-of-the-art adj **advanced**, high-tech, up-to-the-minute, up-to-date, contemporary, modern, ultramodern [➡ DESCRIBING TECHNOLOGY; 1160] *Opposite*: antiquated

state of things n [➡ SITUATIONS; 71]

state of undress n [➡ DRESS, WEAR, AND UNDRESS; 868]

state-owned adj **public**, public-sector, state, state-run, nationalized, government, publicly owned, national, municipal [➡ BELONGING OR RELATING TO PEOPLE; 943] *Opposite*: private

stateroom 1 n **first-class compartment**, first-class cabin, sleeping compartment, berth, sleeper [➡ TYPES OF ROOMS; 1097] 2 part of **ship or boat** [➡ PARTS OF A SHIP OR BOAT; 1151]

state school (*informal*) n **reformatory**, juvenile institution, penal institution, prison, reform school [➡ BUILDINGS FOR CONFINING PEOPLE; 1094]

state secret n **confidential matter**, affair of state, top-secret matter, confidential information, classified material [➡ SECRETS AND MYSTERIES; 180]

static 1 adj **still**, motionless, stationary, inert, standing, stagnant, immobile, inactive, fixed, unmoving [➡ LACK OF ACTIVITY OR MOTION; 342] *Opposite*: moving 2 adj **unchanging**, constant, invariable, unvarying [➡ PERMANENCE: WITHOUT CHANGE; 95] *Opposite*: dynamic

station 1 n **rank**, class, status, position, level, standing [➡ STATUS; 888] 2 n **position**, place, post, location, situation [➡ PLACE; 1065] 3 v **post**, base, position, place, situate, locate [➡ POSITION SOMETHING; 325]

stationary adj **motionless**, still, immobile, inactive, fixed, at a stop, at a standstill, at a halt, standing, unmoving, static, inert [➡ LACK OF ACTIVITY OR MOTION; 342] *Opposite*: moving

stationery n **writing materials**, writing implements, pen and paper, writing paper, notepaper, notebook, notepad, envelopes, pencils [➡ WRITING AND DRAWING IMPLEMENTS, AND MEDIA; 601]

station wagon *type of* **car** [➡BIKES, CARS, AND CARRIAGES; 1149]

statistic *n* **number**, figure, digit, piece of data, measurement, indicator, fact, value [➡MATH; 597]

statistics *n* **figures**, data, numbers, information [➡BASIC DETAILS; 688]

statoscope *type of* **measuring device** [➡MEASURING DEVICES; 1123]

statuary *n* **sculptures**, statues, figures, monuments, busts, effigies, statuettes, figurines, heads, bronzes [➡SCULPTURE; 902]

statue *n* **figurine**, figure, sculpture, statuette, effigy, bust, head, bronze, image, model, icon [➡SCULPTURE; 902]

statuesque *adj* **stately**, elegant, graceful, majestic, dignified, poised, grand, well-proportioned [➡BUILD; 477] *Opposite*: ungainly

statuette *n* **figurine**, sculpture, statue, figure, model, bust, head, bronze, carving [➡SCULPTURE; 902]

stature 1 *n* **build**, height, physique, figure, tallness, size [➡BUILD; 477] 2 *n* **standing**, importance, prominence, status, rank, reputation, distinction, eminence [➡STATUS; 888]

status 1 *n* **rank**, position, standing, grade, station [➡STATUS; 888] 2 *n* **eminence**, prestige, prominence, importance, significance, reputation, repute (*formal*) [➡IMPORTANCE AND SIGNIFICANCE; 192] 3 *n* **category**, condition, class, type, stage, level [➡VARIETIES, TYPES, AND KINDS; 145]

status quo *n* **current situation**, existing state of affairs, present circumstances, how things stand [➡SITUATIONS; 71]

status symbol *n* **asset**, must-have, prize possession [➡POSSESSIONS; 461]

statute *n* **decree**, act, ruling, edict, order, law, bill [➡THE LAW AND LEGAL AUTHORITY; 814]

statute book *n* **body of law**, record, legislation, legal code, law book [➡THE LAW AND LEGAL AUTHORITY; 814]

statute law *n* **written law**, law, constitution, legislation, acts of Congress [➡THE LAW AND LEGAL AUTHORITY; 814]

statutory *adj* **constitutional**, legislative, legal [➡LEGAL AND LEGITIMATE; 815]

staunch 1 *v* **stop**, stem, halt, hold back, curb, curtail, hinder, restrict, lessen, decrease, slow, cut off, check, reduce [➡CAUSE TO STOP; 266] 2 *adj* **loyal**, faithful, steadfast, reliable, dependable, constant, firm, devoted, unfaltering, unwavering, resolute, committed, stalwart [➡HARD-WORKING AND COMMITTED; 500] *Opposite*: wavering

stave 1 *n* **plank**, slat, board, lath, band, strip, piece, wood [➡BUILDING MATERIALS; 1077] 2 *n* **bar**, rung, tread, step, crosspiece, crossbar, foothold [➡SUPPORTS AND BASES; 1255] 3 *n* **stanza**, verse, section, couplet, triplet, canto [➡POETRY AND VERSE; 915]

stave in *v* [➡CHANGE OF SHAPE; 385]

stave off *v* **fend off**, keep at bay, hold off, delay, deflect, hinder, avoid, repel, hold back, ward off [➡DELAY ACTION OR OCCURRENCE; 278]

stay 1 *v* **remain**, wait, continue, keep on, hang around [➡CONTINUE TO EXIST; 17] *Opposite*: go 2 *v* **reside**, live, inhabit, settle, dwell (*literary*), lodge (*dated*) [➡INHABIT; 20] 3 *v* **stop**, halt, delay, defer, put off, postpone, adjourn [➡DELAY ACTION OR OCCURRENCE; 278] 4 *n* **visit**, break, stopover, vacation, sojourn (*literary*), holiday (*UK*) [➡PERIODS OF REST; 91] 5 *n* **halt**, stop, delay, deferment, adjournment, postponement [➡PAUSES AND PHASES; 56]

stayer *n* [➡PEOPLE WHO ARE APPROVED OF; 955]

staying power *n* **stamina**, endurance, determination, doggedness, vigor, energy, resilience, resistance, strength, fortitude, grit [➡STRENGTH OF WILL; 501] *Opposite*: frailty

stay on *v* **remain**, stay, stay put, stay behind, stay out, wait, linger, settle, settle down [➡CONTINUE AN ACTION; 262] *Opposite*: leave

stay out *v* **stay on**, keep out, be out, stay behind, stay put, stay, remain, make a night of it [➡CONTINUE AN ACTION; 262]

stay put *v* **remain**, stay, stay still, tarry, hang on, wait, sit tight (*informal*), abide (*archaic*) [➡LACK OF ACTIVITY OR MOTION; 342] *Opposite*: move

stay still *v* [➡LACK OF ACTIVITY OR MOTION; 342]

stay the course *v* [➡TOLERATE AND ENDURE; 766]

stay up *v* **burn the candle at both ends**, stay up till all hours, burn the midnight oil, maintain a vigil, make a night of it, stop up (*UK*) [➡CONTINUE AN ACTION; 262]

steadfast 1 *adj* **unwavering**, unfaltering, resolute, committed, dedicated, unswerving, persistent, firm [➡HARD-WORKING AND COMMITTED; 500] *Opposite*: wavering 2 *adj* **loyal**, trusty, dependable, faithful, trustworthy, devoted, stalwart, reliable, constant [➡HONEST AND RELIABLE; 502] *Opposite*: inconstant (*literary*)

steadfastness 1 *n* **resoluteness**, commitment, dedication, persistence, determination [➡HARD-WORKING AND COMMITTED; 500] *Opposite*: wavering 2 *n* **loyalty**, faithfulness, trustworthiness, devotion, dependability [➡HONEST AND RELIABLE; 502] *Opposite*: disloyalty

steadily *adv* **progressively**, gradually, increasingly, little by little, bit by bit, inch by inch [➡HAPPENING SLOWLY; 106] *Opposite*: suddenly

steadiness 1 *n* **control**, stability, firmness, balance, equilibrium [➡HARMONY; 155] *Opposite*: unsteadiness 2 *n* **calmness**, composure, serenity, reliability, dependability, self-possession, control, equanimity (*formal*) [➡CONFIDENCE AND COMPOSURE; 499] *Opposite*: excitability

steady 1 *adj* **stable**, firm, fixed, solid, sturdy, sound, secure, balanced [➡SAFE AND SAFETY; 191] *Opposite*: rickety 2 *adj* **continual**, constant, perpetual, never-ending, ceaseless, relentless, unbroken, continuous, unremitting [➡PERMANENCE: WITHOUT END; 94] *Opposite*: intermittent 3 *adj* **even**, regular, uniform, unchanging, unvarying, constant [➡PERMANENCE: WITHOUT CHANGE; 95] *Opposite*: irregular 4 *adj* **calm**, cool, collected, composed, unruffled, unexcitable [➡CONFIDENCE AND COMPOSURE; 499] *Opposite*: excitable 5 *v* **stabilize**, secure, fix, support, strengthen [➡IMPROVE STRENGTH AND DURABILITY; 378] *Opposite*: undermine

steak *type of* **cut** [➡TYPES AND CUTS OF MEAT; 1177]

steakhouse *type of* **eating place** [➡HOTELS, RESTAURANTS, AND CLUBS; 1082]

steak knife *type of* **flatware** [➡TABLEWARE, FLATWARE, AND KITCHENWARE; 861]

steak pie (*UK*) *n* [➡PREPARED DISHES; 1170]

steal 1 *v* pilfer, misappropriate, appropriate, embezzle, pocket, thieve, rob, take, filch (*informal*), lift (*informal*), purloin (*formal or humorous*) [➡STEAL AND ROB; 426] *Opposite*: return 2 *v* creep, sneak, slip, slink, tiptoe, slope [➡MOVE SLOWLY; 314] 3 *n* (*informal*) bargain, good deal, good buy, giveaway (*informal*) [➡ECONOMICAL AND RESOURCEFUL; 207] *Opposite*: rip-off (*informal*)

Compare and Contrast: *steal, pinch, nick, filch, purloin, pilfer, embezzle, misappropriate*

CORE MEANING: the taking of property unlawfully

steal to take something that belongs to somebody else, illegally or without the owner's permission; *pinch* (*informal*) to steal something; *nick* (*slang*) to steal something; *filch* (*informal*) to steal something furtively and opportunistically, usually a small item or something of little value; *purloin* (*formal*) to steal something, sometimes used humorously or euphemistically; *pilfer* to steal small items of little value, especially habitually; *embezzle* to take for personal use money or property that has been given on trust by others, without their knowledge; *misappropriate* to take something, especially money, dishonestly or in order to use it for an improper or illegal purpose.

steal a look *v* [➡LOOKING AND LOOKS; 700]

steal away *v* [➡RUN AWAY AND AVOID; 10]

stealing *n* theft, robbery, burglary, larceny, thieving, pilfering, shoplifting, pocketing, embezzlement, appropriation [➡CRIMES; 817]

stealth *n* furtiveness, surreptitiousness, sneakiness, slyness, craftiness, secrecy, covertness [➡SECRET AND UNKNOWN; 179] *Opposite*: openness

stealth bomber *type of* **military aircraft** [➡AIRCRAFT; 1148]

stealthy *adj* furtive, surreptitious, sly, silent, cautious, sneaky, crafty, secret, covert, clandestine, quiet [➡SECRET AND UNKNOWN; 179] *Opposite*: blatant

See Compare and Contrast at **secret**.

steam *n* vapor, condensation, haze, mist, fog [➡GASES; 1275]

steamboat *type of* **motor vessel** [➡SHIPS AND BOATS; 1150]

steam engine 1 *part of* **train** [➡RAILROADS; 1107] 2 *type of* **rail vehicle** [➡RAILROADS; 1107]

steamer *type of* **motor vessel** [➡SHIPS AND BOATS; 1150]

steamroller 1 *v* compress, bulldoze, flatten, crush, squash, trample, demolish, roll over, drive over, steamroll [➡CHANGE OF SHAPE; 385] 2 *v* crush, squash, demolish, destroy, overwhelm, dismiss, smash [➡DENY AND REJECT; 644] 3 *v* force, compel, coerce, bludgeon, bully, intimidate, drive [➡CAUSE OR COMPEL TO ACT; 271] 4 *type of* **commercial or industrial vehicle** [➡VEHICLES; 1145]

steam up *v* mist up, fog up, cloud, cloud over, mist over [➡SOFTEN, LIQUEFY, AND DAMPEN; 388]

steamy 1 *adj* humid, muggy, damp, sticky, hot and sticky, clammy, stifling, moist [➡HOT WEATHER; 1050] 2 *adj* misted up, misty, fogged up, foggy, steamed up, cloudy, clouded [➡VISUAL TEXTURE; 1221] *Opposite*: clear

steed (*literary*) *n* horse, pony, mount, charger [➡HORSES; 985]

steel 1 *type of* **metal** [➡METALS; 1276] 2 *v* **strengthen**, toughen, harden, fortify, brace [➡PREPARE FOR ACTION; 289]

steel band *type of* **band** [➡MUSICIANS AND SINGERS; 908]

steel blue *type of* **blue** [➡COLORS; 1224]

steel drum *type of* **percussion instrument** [➡MUSICAL INSTRUMENTS; 910]

steel gray *type of* **gray** [➡COLORS; 1224]

steel guitar *type of* **stringed instrument** [➡MUSICAL INSTRUMENTS; 910]

steelworks *type of* **factory** [➡INDUSTRIAL BUILDINGS; 1087]

steely 1 *adj* hard, strong, tough, sturdy, rugged [➡STRENGTH; 201] *Opposite*: soft 2 *adj* determined, resolute, unyielding, unbending, rigid, firm, unwavering [➡STRENGTH OF WILL; 501] *Opposite*: irresolute

steel yourself *v* **brace yourself**, harden your heart, pluck up your courage, prepare yourself, compose yourself, get ready [➡PREPARE FOR ACTION; 289]

steep 1 *adj* sheer, vertical, sharp, precipitous, abrupt, sudden [➡ORIENTATION AND ALIGNMENT; 1223] *Opposite*: gentle 2 *adj* (*informal*) unreasonable, extreme, excessive, expensive, dear, exorbitant, extortionate [➡EXPENSIVE AND OVERPRICED; 247] *Opposite*: reasonable 3 *v* soak, immerse, drench, submerge, suffuse, saturate, marinate, stand [➡SOFTEN, LIQUEFY, AND DAMPEN; 388] 4 *v* imbue, permeate, infuse [➡FILL; 406]

steeped *adj* [➡WET; 1240]

steeple *n* tower, spire, turret, bell tower, belfry, campanile [➡PARTS OF RELIGIOUS BUILDINGS; 1086]

steeplechase 1 *n* point-to-point, horserace, stake race [➡NON-AGGRESSIVE/SPORTING EVENTS; 40] 2 *n* hurdles, footrace, flat race, track race, track event [➡NON-AGGRESSIVE/SPORTING EVENTS; 40] 3 *type of* **track and field** [➡HOBBIES, GAMES, AND SPORTS; 875]

steeplechaser *n* [➡PEOPLE IN SPORTS AND LEISURE; 876]

steeply *adv* sharply, precipitously, abruptly, suddenly [➡ORIENTATION AND ALIGNMENT; 1223] *Opposite*: gently

steepness *n* sharpness, abruptness, gradient, sheerness [➡ORIENTATION AND ALIGNMENT; 1223] *Opposite*: gentleness

steer 1 *v* control, drive, pilot, navigate, maneuver [➡TRAVEL: WAYS OF TRAVELING; 320] 2 *v* direct, guide, point, conduct, lead [➡ACCOMPANY AND FOLLOW; 337] 3 *type of* **male animal** [➡MALE OR FEMALE ANIMALS; 978]

See Compare and Contrast at **guide**.

steerage *n* third class, bottom deck, tourist class, lower deck [➡TRANSPORTATION, TRANSPORTERS, AND CARGOS; 322]

steering committee *n* **steering group**, board, panel, team, commission, council, committee [➞ GROUPS WITH A COMMON INTEREST; 938]

steering wheel *type of* **controls** [➞ INTERNAL PARTS OF A VEHICLE; 1146]

stegosaur *type of* **dinosaur** [➞ DINOSAURS; 996]

stein *n* [➞ CONTAINERS, RECEPTACLES, AND PACKAGING; 1245]

stellar 1 *adj* **astral**, astronomical, astrophysical, solar, planetary, cosmological [➞ THE SOLAR SYSTEM AND ASTRONOMY; 1060] *Opposite*: earthly 2 *adj* **all-star**, star-studded, star-spangled, starry, celebrity, big-name, glittering, glamorous, glitzy [➞ THE PERFORMING ARTS; 904] *Opposite*: unknown

stem 1 *n* **stalk**, shoot, trunk, twig, branch [➞ STICKS, POLES, AND WEDGES; 1254] 2 *v* **stop**, staunch, halt, curtail, restrict, slow, lessen, decrease, cut off, curb, hinder, hold back, stanch, reduce, check [➞ AVOID, PREVENT, LIMIT, AND CONTROL; 277] *Opposite*: accelerate

stem from *v* **arise from**, originate from, come from, derive from, develop from, spring from, be a result of, be caused by [➞ CAUSATION; 168]

stench *n* **stink**, reek, disgusting odor, unpleasant smell [➞ SMELL AND SMELLING; 705] *Opposite*: perfume

See Compare and Contrast at **smell**.

stencil 1 *n* **template**, cutout, guide, plate, pattern, model, shape, outline [➞ ARTWORKS; 898] 2 *n* **pattern**, design, lettering, motif, border, frieze, decoration, ornament [➞ ORNAMENTS AND DECORATIONS; 1248] 3 *v* **apply**, paint, work, draw, trace [➞ CREATE IMAGES; 356] 4 *v* **decorate**, adorn, paint, ornament [➞ DECORATE, ADORN, AND APPLY COATINGS; 405]

stentor *type of* **microorganism** [➞ MICROORGANISMS, FUNGI, AND ALGAE; 1023]

stentorian *adj* **loud**, powerful, booming, thunderous, deafening, earsplitting, roaring [➞ LOUD, HIGH, OR UNPLEASANT SOUNDS; 1266] *Opposite*: quiet

step 1 *n* **pace**, footstep, stride [➞ PROCEED AND GO; 305] 2 *n* **stair**, rung, tread [➞ STAIRS AND STORIES; 1102] 3 *n* **move**, movement, action, measure [➞ ACTIONS OR UNDERTAKINGS; 259] 4 *n* **stage**, phase, period [➞ PAUSES AND PHASES; 56] 5 *v* **walk**, tread, march, pace, move, stride [➞ PROCEED AND GO; 305]

step aerobics *n* **leisure**, exercise, workout, training, gymnastics, aerobics [➞ HOBBIES, GAMES, AND SPORTS; 875]

stepbrother *type of* **same-generation relative** [➞ SAME-GENERATION RELATIVES; 957]

step by step *adv* **gradually**, bit by bit, little by little, piece by piece, a bit at a time, a step at a time, inch by inch, stage by stage, slowly but surely, progressively [➞ HAPPENING SLOWLY; 106] *Opposite*: all at once

stepchild *type of* **younger relative** [➞ YOUNGER GENERATION RELATIVES; 958]

step dancing *type of* **dance** [➞ DANCE; 903]

stepdaughter *type of* **younger relative** [➞ YOUNGER GENERATION RELATIVES; 958]

step down 1 *v* **stand down**, resign, retire, bow out, withdraw, quit, call it a day, give up, go, stand aside [➞ STOP ACTING; 264] *Opposite*: stay on 2 *v* **decrease**, reduce, lower, lessen, restrict, drop, phase out, tail off, whittle down, shorten [➞ CHANGE OF INTENSITY: LESS; 395] *Opposite*: step up

stepfather *type of* **older relative** [➞ OLDER GENERATION RELATIVES; 959]

step in *v* **intervene**, intercede, interpose, interrupt, get involved, mediate [➞ INTERRUPT AND BUTT IN; 619]

stepladder *n* **ladder**, portable ladder, folding ladder, stairs, steps (*UK*) [➞ SUPPORTS AND BASES; 1255]

stepmother *type of* **older relative** [➞ OLDER GENERATION RELATIVES; 959]

step on it (*slang*) *v* **drive fast**, hit the gas, put your foot down, accelerate, hurry, floor it (*slang*) [➞ CHANGE OF SPEED: MORE; 396]

step on the gas (*slang*) *v* [➞ CHANGE OF SPEED: MORE; 396]

step out 1 *v* **go out**, step outside, leave, absent yourself, pop out (*informal*), nip out (*UK*) [➞ LEAVE AND GO AWAY; 8] *Opposite*: stay put 2 *v* **march**, tear along, rush, stride, dash, zoom, speed up, jog, stomp, leg it (*informal*), hightail it (*slang*) [➞ MOVE FAST; 313] *Opposite*: crawl

stepparent *type of* **older relative** [➞ OLDER GENERATION RELATIVES; 959]

steppe *n* **prairie**, grassland, plain, savanna, pampas [➞ DESERTS, PLAINS, AND MOORLAND; 1045]

stepping stone 1 *n* **stone**, boulder, rock, foothold, bridge [➞ SUPPORTS AND BASES; 1255] 2 *n* **stage**, step, means of access, stage of progress, stage of advancement, springboard, contact, way in [➞ ADVANTAGES; 212]

steppingstone *see* **stepping stone**

stepsister *type of* **same-generation relative** [➞ SAME-GENERATION RELATIVES; 957]

stepson *type of* **younger relative** [➞ YOUNGER GENERATION RELATIVES; 958]

step up *v* **increase**, intensify, improve, maximize, accelerate, boost [➞ CHANGE OF INTENSITY: MORE; 394] *Opposite*: lower

stereo 1 *n* [➞ ACOUSTICS; 1138] 2 *type of* **audio equipment** [➞ AUDIO EQUIPMENT; 1139]

stereophonic *adj* **stereo**, audio, binaural, hi-fi, high-fidelity [➞ ACOUSTICS; 1138]

stereo system *type of* **audio equipment** [➞ AUDIO EQUIPMENT; 1139]

stereotype *v* **typecast**, label, pigeonhole, categorize, cast, fix [➞ NAME AND DESCRIBE; 665]

stereotypical *adj* **conventional**, orthodox, formulaic, banal, hackneyed, clichéd, trite [➞ SAMENESS; 150] *Opposite*: original

sterile 1 *adj* **germ-free**, disinfected, antiseptic, sterilized, spotlessly clean, hygienic, sanitary [➞ CLEAN AND HYGIENIC; 1233] *Opposite*: dirty 2 *adj* **barren**, childless, unfruitful, fruitless, unproductive, infertile, bare [➞ REPRODUCTION AND HEREDITY; 725]

sterility 1 *n* **barrenness**, unfruitfulness, unproductiveness, desolation, bareness [➡ REDUNDANT AND USELESS; 240] *Opposite*: fruitfulness 2 *n* **infertility**, barrenness, childlessness, subfertility, unproductiveness, impotence [➡ REPRODUCTION AND HEREDITY; 725] *Opposite*: fertility 3 *n* **cleanness**, antisepsis, disinfection, decontamination, purity [➡ CLEAN AND HYGIENIC; 1233] *Opposite*: contamination 4 *n* **dullness**, uncreativeness, unimaginativeness, lack of imagination, lack of creativity, banality [➡ BORING AND UNINTERESTING; 234] *Opposite*: imaginativeness

sterilization 1 *n* **purification**, cleansing, disinfection, fumigation, decontamination, pasteurization [➡ CLEAN AND POLISH; 403] 2 *n* **neutering**, vasectomy, hysterectomy, castration, gelding, spaying [➡ STERILIZE; 726]

sterilize 1 *v* **disinfect**, bleach, make germ-free, fumigate, sanitize, purify, clean thoroughly [➡ CLEAN AND POLISH; 403] 2 *v* **neuter**, spay, geld, castrate [➡ STERILIZE; 726]

sterilized *adj* [➡ CLEAN AND HYGIENIC; 1233]

sterilizer *n* **disinfectant**, germicide, antiseptic, bactericide, sanitizer, purifier, cleaning agent [➡ CLEANING AGENTS; 863]

sterling 1 *adj* **genuine**, authentic, true, pure, real [➡ TRUE AND REAL; 171] *Opposite*: spurious 2 *adj* **excellent**, exceptional, matchless, incomparable, worthy, first-rate [➡ GOOD, WELL, BETTER; 183] *Opposite*: mediocre

stern 1 *adj* **strict**, harsh, severe, austere, unsympathetic, unyielding, uncompromising, hardhearted, firm [➡ DIFFICULT TO PLEASE; 515] *Opposite*: easygoing 2 *adj* **grim**, forbidding, formidable, dour, serious, grave, somber, unsmiling, humorless [➡ BAD-TEMPERED AND HUMORLESS; 626] *Opposite*: cheerful 3 *part of* **ship or boat** [➡ PARTS OF A SHIP OR BOAT; 1151]

sternness 1 *n* **severity**, strictness, harshness, firmness, austerity [➡ DIFFICULT TO PLEASE; 515] *Opposite*: leniency 2 *n* **grimness**, seriousness, somberness, gravity, humorlessness [➡ BAD-TEMPERED AND HUMORLESS; 626] *Opposite*: cheerfulness

sternum *type of* **bone** [➡ THE BONES AND JOINTS; 719]

stet *v* **let it stand**, restore, retain, undo, ignore, undelete, override [➡ FOREIGN WORDS AND PHRASES; 672] *Opposite*: delete

stethoscope *type of* **medical instrument** [➡ HAND TOOLS; 1119]

stew 1 *type of* **cooked dish** [➡ PREPARED DISHES; 1170] 2 *n* (*informal*) **difficult situation**, state (*informal*), flap (*informal*), tizzy (*informal*), lather (*informal*), fix (*informal*) [➡ DIFFICULT SITUATIONS; 72] 3 *v* **simmer**, boil slowly, braise, casserole, parboil, poach, cook slowly [➡ COOKING AND FOOD PREPARATION; 353] 4 *v* **be upset**, be troubled, be agitated, worry, trouble, fret, fuss [➡ GIVING VENT TO EMOTIONS; 679]

stewed 1 *adj* [➡ STATE OF PREPARED FOOD; 1171] 2 *adj* (*slang*) **drunk**, inebriated, intoxicated, plastered (*informal*), smashed (*informal*), under the influence (*informal*) [➡ UNDER THE INFLUENCE OF DRUGS OR ALCOHOL; 741]

stick 1 *n* **twig**, cane, baton, rod, staff, switch, pole, branch [➡ STICKS, POLES, AND WEDGES; 1254] 2 *v* **spear**, stab, penetrate, pierce, spike, gore, run through (*literary*) [➡ STAB; 416] 3 *v* **attach**, glue, fix, fasten, join, fuse, gum, paste, affix, weld, bond [➡ FASTEN, LINK, AND JOIN; 408] *Opposite*: detach 4 *v* (*informal*) **put**, lay, place, set, deposit, plonk, plunk [➡ POSITION SOMETHING; 325] 5 *v* (*informal*) **push**, put, thrust, shove, poke [➡ POSITION SOMETHING; 325] *Opposite*: withdraw

stick around (*informal*) 1 *v* **linger**, wait, stay, remain, hang around, hang out (*informal*) [➡ EXIST IN A PLACE; 19] *Opposite*: leave 2 *v* **stay with**, hang around, hang around with, remain with, be associated with, hang out with (*informal*) [➡ ESTABLISHING RELATIONSHIPS WITH OTHERS; 974] *Opposite*: leave

stick at *v* **persist at**, continue with, persist, persevere with, see through, stay with, continue, stick with, persevere [➡ CONTINUE AN ACTION; 262] *Opposite*: give up

stick by *v* **remain loyal to**, stay loyal to, remain faithful to, support, adhere to, stand by, be there for [➡ TAKE CARE OF AND SPOIL; 300] *Opposite*: let down

sticker *n* **label**, sign, marker, decal, bumper sticker, transfer, sticky label (*UK*) [➡ SYMBOLS, SIGNS, AND NUMBERS; 596]

stickiness *n* **tackiness**, gluiness, gumminess, adhesiveness, pastiness [➡ PHYSICAL TEXTURE; 1222]

sticking plaster (*UK*) *n* **bandage**, dressing, pad, lint, adhesive bandage, adhesive, plaster (*UK*), corn plaster (*UK*) [➡ COVERS AND COATINGS; 1246]

sticking point *n* **stumbling block**, bone of contention, impasse, obstacle, deadlock [➡ PROBLEMS; 256]

stick-in-the-mud (*informal*) *n* **reactionary**, diehard, fogy, fuddy-duddy (*informal*), stuffed shirt (*informal*) [➡ UNCOOPERATIVE OR REBELLIOUS PEOPLE; 566]

stick it out *v* [➡ TOLERATE AND ENDURE; 766]

stickleback *type of* **freshwater fish** [➡ FRESHWATER FISH; 1010]

stickler *n* **pedant**, nitpicker, perfectionist, martinet, hard taskmaster, strict disciplinarian [➡ GRUMPY AND NEGATIVE PEOPLE; 953]

stick out 1 *v* **extend**, poke out, jut out, push out, thrust out, hold out [➡ CAUSE TO APPEAR; 5] 2 *v* **put up with**, endure, bear, weather, see through, withstand, bear with, persevere, persist [➡ TOLERATE AND ENDURE; 766] *Opposite*: give up

stick out like a sore thumb *v* [➡ APPEAR AND EMERGE; 3]

sticks (*informal*) *n* [➡ REMOTE PLACES; 1046]

stick to 1 *v* **adhere**, cling, follow, cling to, hold, keep to [➡ CONTINUE AN ACTION; 262] 2 *v* **follow**, obey, abide by, stand by, remain faithful to [➡ OBEY AND ABIDE BY; 301] *Opposite*: abandon

stick together *v* **stay close**, remain unified, remain loyal, remain friendly, concur, cooperate, cohere (*formal*) [➡ ESTABLISHING RELATIONSHIPS WITH OTHERS; 974] *Opposite*: split up

stick up 1 *v* **protrude**, point up, point upward, stand up, bristle, stand on end [➡ GO UPWARD; 306] 2 *v* **point up**, cock, prick up, make vertical, raise up, raise [➡ GO UPWARD; 306] 3 *v* (*informal*) **rob**, hold up, mug, steal from, pull a gun on, attack [➡ STEAL AND ROB; 426]

stickup (*informal*) *n* **armed robbery**, robbery, mugging, attack, assault, burglary, holdup [➡ CRIMES; 817]

stick up for *v* **support**, defend, stand up for, stand by, argue for, insist [➡ APPROVE AND CONFIRM; 646]

stick with 1 *v* **persist with**, continue with, persevere with, see through, stay with, stick out [➡ CONTINUE AN ACTION; 262] *Opposite*: give up 2 *v* **stay loyal to**, remain loyal to, remain faithful to, stay close to, stay with, stick by [➡ ESTABLISHING RELATIONSHIPS WITH OTHERS; 974] *Opposite:* abandon

sticky 1 *adj* **tacky**, gluey, gummy, adhesive, pasty [➡ PHYSICAL TEXTURE; 1222] **2** *adj* (*informal*) **difficult**, tricky, delicate, awkward, sensitive, complicated [➡ DIFFICULTY AND COMPLEXITY; 242] **3** *adj* **muggy**, humid, close, clammy, sultry, oppressive, steamy, hot [➡ HOT WEATHER; 1050] *Opposite:* dry

stick your nose in *v* [➡ INTERRUPT AND BUTT IN; 619]

stick your oar in (*UK*) *v* [➡ INTERRUPT AND BUTT IN; 619]

sticky situation *n* [➡ DIFFICULT SITUATIONS; 72]

sticky wicket (*informal*) *n* **tricky situation**, awkward situation, difficult situation, difficult problem, embarrassing problem, embarrassing situation, predicament, plight, fix (*informal*), hole (*informal*) [➡ DIFFICULT SITUATIONS; 72]

stiff 1 *adj* **rigid**, firm, inflexible, unbending, unbendable, taut, hard, solid, unyielding [➡ RIGID AND HARD; 1211] *Opposite:* limp **2** *adj* **aching**, painful, arthritic, tender, sore [➡ INJURED; 742] **3** *adj* **severe**, harsh, drastic, stringent, excessive, extreme, steep (*informal*) [➡ ABSOLUTE AND ABSOLUTELY; 133] *Opposite:* lenient **4** *adj* **demanding**, exacting, arduous, testing, tough, laborious, rigorous, difficult, taxing [➡ PHYSICALLY UNPLEASANT; 226] *Opposite:* easy **5** *adj* **strong**, vigorous, powerful, robust, intense [➡ STRENGTH; 201] *Opposite:* weak **6** *adj* **formal**, stuffy, standoffish, aloof, pompous, stilted, wooden [➡ LEVELS OF FORMALITY; 522] *Opposite:* relaxed **7** *n* (*slang*) **person**, soul, individual, body (*informal*), guy (*informal*), bod (*slang*) [➡ PERSON; 931] **8** *n* (*slang*) **dead body**, body, corpse, cadaver, carcass, goner (*slang*) [➡ DEAD PERSON; 926]

stiffen 1 *v* **harden**, thicken, solidify, congeal, become rigid [➡ HARDEN, CONGEAL, AND DRY; 387] *Opposite:* soften **2** *v* **strengthen**, make stronger, reinforce, toughen, brace [➡ IMPROVE STRENGTH AND DURABILITY; 378] *Opposite:* weaken

stiffly *adv* **rigidly**, firmly, inflexibly, unbendingly, tautly, straight, bolt upright [➡ RIGID AND HARD; 1211]

stiff-necked *adj* **obstinate**, arrogant, stubborn, proud, haughty, refractory, aloof, unyielding, unbending [➡ REBELLIOUSNESS AND DISOBEDIENCE; 565] *Opposite:* yielding

stiffness 1 *n* **rigidity**, firmness, inflexibility, tautness, hardness, solidity [➡ RIGID AND HARD; 1211] *Opposite:* limpness **2** *n* **difficulty**, arduousness, laboriousness, rigorousness, toughness, painfulness [➡ PHYSICALLY UNPLEASANT; 226] *Opposite:* ease **3** *n* **severity**, harshness, stringency, excessiveness, extremity, steepness (*informal*) [➡ TOO MUCH; 119] *Opposite:* leniency **4** *n* **strength**, vigor, power, robustness, intensity [➡ STRENGTH; 201] *Opposite:* weakness **5** *n* **formality**, stuffiness, standoffishness, aloofness, pomposity, woodenness [➡ LEVELS OF FORMALITY; 522] *Opposite:* informality

stifle 1 *v* **smother**, asphyxiate, throttle, suffocate, choke, strangle [➡ KILL; 923] **2** *v* **suppress**, repress, restrain, curb, hold back, keep in check, check [➡ WITHHOLD INFORMATION; 687] *Opposite:* let out

stifling 1 *adj* **hot**, boiling, airless, muggy, close, stuffy, roasting (*informal*) [➡ HOT WEATHER; 1050] *Opposite:* cool **2** *adj* **oppressive**, repressive, overpowering, restrictive, inhibiting, domineering [➡ EMOTIONALLY UNPLEASANT AND UPSETTING; 227] *Opposite:* liberating

stigma 1 *n* **shame**, disgrace, dishonor, humiliation [➡ NUISANCES; 253] **2** *part of* **flower** [➡ FLOWERS; 1032]

stigmatize *v* **brand**, slur, defame, mark out, pillory, denounce [➡ INSULTS, ABUSE, AND SWEARING; 658]

stile *n* **step**, steps, rung, rungs, fence, access [➡ STAIRS AND STORIES; 1102]

stiletto *type of* **sword or knife** [➡ SWORDS AND KNIVES; 1157]

stiletto heel *type of* **shoe** [➡ FOOTWEAR; 871]

still 1 *adj* **motionless**, immobile, unmoving, at rest, at a standstill, at a halt, tranquil, silent, stagnant, static, quiet, stationary [➡ LACK OF ACTIVITY OR MOTION; 342] *Opposite:* moving **2** *adj* **flat**, nonsparkling, nonfizzy [➡ DRINKS; 1187] **3** *v* **calm**, allay, dispel, banish, quiet, subdue, calm down [➡ CHANGE OF INTENSITY: LESS; 395] *Opposite:* stir up **4** *adv* **even now**, in spite of everything, even so, nevertheless, nonetheless, be that as it may, however, yet, even, notwithstanding (*formal*) [➡ ALTHOUGH, NEVERTHELESS, AND DESPITE; 169]

stillborn 1 *adj* **born dead**, dead at birth, miscarried, aborted, dead, deceased (*formal*) [➡ DEAD AND DYING; 925] **2** *adj* **ineffectual**, useless, ineffective, unsuccessful, abortive, fruitless [➡ REDUNDANT AND USELESS; 240] *Opposite:* successful

still life *n* [➡ ARTWORKS; 898]

stillness *n* **motionlessness**, immobility, silence, quietness, tranquillity, calm [➡ LACK OF ACTIVITY OR MOTION; 342] *Opposite:* movement

stilt 1 *n* **post**, column, support, pillar, pole, prop [➡ STICKS, POLES, AND WEDGES; 1254] **2** *type of* **toy** [➡ TOYS; 880]

stilted *adj* **affected**, stiff, wooden, mannered, unnatural, pretentious, artificial, pompous, bombastic [➡ INARTICULATE, RAMBLING, AND AWKWARD; 633] *Opposite:* natural

stiltedness *n* [➡ INARTICULATE, RAMBLING, AND AWKWARD; 633]

Stilton *type of* **hard cheese** [➡ DAIRY PRODUCTS AND CHEESES; 1183]

stimulant 1 *n* **stimulating substance**, tonic, pick-me-up (*informal*), upper (*slang*), pep pill (*dated*) [➡ REMEDIES, TREATMENTS, AND OPERATIONS; 731] *Opposite:* sedative **2** *adj* **stimulating**, tonic, restorative, intoxicant, energizing, intoxicating (*formal*) [➡ REMEDIES, TREATMENTS, AND OPERATIONS; 731] *Opposite:* sedative

stimulate 1 *v* **rouse**, arouse, kindle, excite, inspire, motivate, encourage, fuel, incite, fire up [➡ ENCOURAGE; 576] *Opposite:* dampen **2** *v* **quicken**, accelerate, increase, invigorate, promote, speed, speed up, intensify [➡ CHANGE OF INTENSITY: MORE; 394] *Opposite:* slow down

stimulating 1 *adj* **inspiring**, encouraging, motivating, interesting, thought-provoking, exciting [➡ INTERESTING AND MEANINGFUL; 190] *Opposite:* boring **2** *adj* **invigorating**, refreshing, energizing, rousing [➡ PHYSICALLY PLEASANT; 186] *Opposite:* relaxing

stimulation *n* **inspiration**, motivation, encouragement, stimulus, incentive, spur, prompt [➡ CAUSATION; 168]

stimulus *n* **incentive**, spur, inducement, impetus, provocation, motivation, incitement [➡ CAUSATION; 168]

sting 1 *v* **smart**, prick, tingle, throb, hurt [➡ PAIN AND OTHER PHYSICAL SENSATIONS; 733] **2** *n* (*slang*) **swindle**, hoax, fraud, racket, con, rip-off (*informal*), scam (*slang*), confidence trick (*UK*) [➡ DECEPTION AND LIES; 660]

stingily *adv* **grudgingly**, ungenerously, parsimoniously, tightfistedly, meanly [➡ GRASPING AND FINANCIALLY MEAN; 519] *Opposite*: generously

stinginess *n* **miserliness**, ungenerousness, parsimony, meanness, tightfistedness [➡ GRASPING AND FINANCIALLY MEAN; 519] *Opposite*: generosity

stinging *adj* **hurtful**, cutting, harsh, hard, cruel, callous, vicious [➡ RUDE AND HOSTILE; 625]

stinging nettle *type of* **weed** [➡ WEEDS AND THISTLES; 1034]

stingy *adj* **ungenerous**, miserly, parsimonious, sparing, grudging, tightfisted, mean, penny-pinching (*informal*) [➡ GRASPING AND FINANCIALLY MEAN; 519] *Opposite*: generous

stink 1 *v* **smell horrible**, reek, smell [➡ SMELL EMISSION; 369] 2 *n* **stench**, smell, horrible smell, unpleasant odor, reek [➡ SMELL AND SMELLING; 705] *Opposite*: perfume 3 *n* (*informal*) **fuss**, scandal, uproar, rumpus, commotion, brouhaha [➡ CHAOS AND UPROAR; 51]

See Compare and Contrast at **smell***.*

stinker *n* **problem**, nightmare, shocker (*informal*), horror (*informal*) [➡ NUISANCES; 253] *Opposite*: delight

stinkhorn *type of* **fungus** [➡ MICROORGANISMS, FUNGI, AND ALGAE; 1023]

stinking *adj* **foul-smelling**, reeking, smelly, stinky, rotten, putrid, malodorous, fetid, foul (*informal*), rank (*literary*) [➡ SMELL AND SMELLING; 705]

stink up *v* **make smelly**, permeate, pervade, overpower, fill with a smell, make stinky [➡ SMELL EMISSION; 369] *Opposite*: deodorize

stinky 1 *adj* **smelly**, stinking, foul-smelling, putrid, rotten, malodorous, fetid, reeking, foul (*informal*), rank (*literary*) [➡ SMELL AND SMELLING; 705] *Opposite*: fragrant 2 *adj* **nasty**, unfair, dishonest, devious, mean-spirited, unpleasant, malicious [➡ SELFISH AND UNKIND; 505] *Opposite*: pleasant

stint *n* **spell**, stretch, time, shift, period, turn [➡ SHORT PERIODS OF TIME; 93]

stint on *v* **be sparing with**, be mean with, be parsimonious with, be frugal with, ration, skimp on [➡ FORGO AND DENY ONESELF; 449]

stipend *n* **allowance**, salary, payment, pay, wage, reward, scholarship, fellowship [➡ INCOME; 460]

See Compare and Contrast at **wage***.*

stipendiary 1 *adj* **paid**, salaried, earning, remunerated, breadwinning, wage-earning [➡ TYPES OF WORK; 835] 2 *n* **earner**, wage earner, breadwinner, payee, employee, recipient [➡ WORKERS; 836]

stipple *v* **dab**, paint, dot, speckle, fleck, mottle, draw [➡ DECORATE, ADORN, AND APPLY COATINGS; 405]

stippled *adj* **mottled**, dappled, speckled, spotted, flecked, dotted [➡ DESCRIBING PATTERNS; 1227]

stipulate *v* **specify**, lay down, instruct, order, require, demand, insist on [➡ CLAIM, INSIST, AND EMPHASIZE; 614]

stipulation *n* **condition**, requirement, proviso, demand, specification, prerequisite, provision, clause [➡ NECESSARY AND ESSENTIAL; 196]

stir 1 *v* **mix**, blend, swirl, fold, whip, whisk, beat [➡ COOKING AND FOOD PREPARATION; 353] 2 *v* **awaken**, arouse, revive, call to mind, bring back, stir up [➡ REMIND; 747] 3 *v* **rouse**, wake up, move, budge, shift, get up, get going [➡ WAKE AND REGAIN CONSCIOUSNESS; 724] 4 *v* **agitate**, cause feeling, disturb, trouble, upset [➡ UPSET, DISTRESS, AND HUMILIATE; 567] 5 *v* **motivate**, incite, provoke, excite, inspire, stimulate, fire up, stir up [➡ APPEAL TO AND AROUSE INTEREST; 575] 6 *n* **commotion**, disturbance, fuss, uproar, hue and cry, hullabaloo, hubbub, to-do (*informal*) [➡ CHAOS AND UPROAR; 51]

stir-crazy (*informal or humorous*) *adj* **mentally unsettled**, restless, frantic, distraught, agitated, fidgety, jumpy, antsy (*informal*) [➡ CONFUSION, ANXIETY, AND WORRY; 540]

stir-fried *adj* [➡ STATE OF PREPARED FOOD; 1171]

stir-fry 1 *v* **fry**, pan-fry, sauté [➡ COOKING AND FOOD PREPARATION; 353] 2 *type of* **cooked dish** [➡ PREPARED DISHES; 1170]

stirred up *adj* [➡ POSITIVE IMPATIENCE, ENTHUSIASM, AND ALERTNESS; 537]

stirring *adj* **rousing**, inspiring, moving, emotive, exciting, thrilling, magnificent [➡ EMOTIONALLY PLEASANT; 187] *Opposite*: uninspiring

stirrup 1 *n* **foot support**, strap, loop, ring [➡ FASTENERS, LINKS, AND NETWORKS; 1247] 2 *part of* **ear** [➡ THE EAR; 706]

stir up *v* **awaken**, reawaken, bring back, kindle, inflame, inspire, provoke, incite, instigate, agitate [➡ REMIND; 747] *Opposite*: calm

stitch 1 *v* **sew**, sew up, stitch up, darn, baste, tack [➡ CRAFTS AND CARVING; 355] 2 *v* **suture**, sew up, close [➡ FASTEN, LINK, AND JOIN; 400]

stitching *n* **sewing**, stitches, seam, needlework, embroidery, edging, edge, hemming [➡ CRAFTS AND CARVING; 355]

stoat *type of* **small mammal** [➡ SMALL MAMMALS; 990]

stock 1 *n* **supply**, stockpile, hoard, reserve, accumulation, collection, store, stash (*informal*) [➡ STORES AND STORAGE BUILDINGS; 1088] 2 *n* **livestock**, farm animals, domestic animals, cattle, sheep, pigs, horses [➡ FARM ANIMALS; 982] 3 *type of* **annual flower** [➡ FLOWERS; 1032] 4 *adj* **standard**, typical, routine, run-of-the-mill, ordinary, normal [➡ ORDINARINESS; 244] 5 *v* **keep**, have a supply of, have available, carry, supply, sell, deal in, provide [➡ STORE AND KEEP; 453]

stockade 1 *n* **barrier**, fence, enclosure, palisade, paling [➡ BARRIERS; 1113] 2 *n* **enclosure**, fort, pen, fenced area, enclosed area, corral, yard [➡ FORTRESSES AND FORTIFICATIONS; 1090]

stockbroker *n* **securities broker**, broker, investment analyst, financial adviser, investment banker, trader [➡ PEOPLE INVOLVED IN FINANCE; 804]

stock car *n* **racing car**, dragster, hot rod (*slang*) [➡ BIKES, CARS, AND CARRIAGES; 1149]

stock cube (*UK*) *n* **concentrate**, vegetable extract, meat extract, dried food, broth, seasoning, flavoring, bouillon cube [➡ SEASONINGS AND SAUCES; 1174]

stock exchange *n* **stock market**, trading, bourse, exchange, money market, market [➡ACCOUNTING, BANKING, AND BUDGETING; 799]

stockholder *n* **shareholder**, bondholder, owner, stakeholder, investor [➡PEOPLE INVOLVED IN FINANCE; 804]

stockiness *n* [➡BUILD; 477]

stocking filler (*UK*) *n* **stocking stuffer**, Christmas present, Christmas gift, small present, small gift, extra [➡GIFTS; 438]

stockings *n* **leg coverings**, nylons, hose, pantyhose, leggings, thigh-highs, knee-highs, tights [➡ACCESSORIES, MILLINERY, AND LINGERIE; 867]

stocking stuffer *n* **Christmas present**, Christmas gift, small present, small gift, trinket, token, stocking filler (*UK*) [➡GIFTS; 438]

stock-in-trade 1 *n* **basic resource**, staple, commodity [➡BUSINESS PRODUCTS; 795] 2 *n* **goods**, equipment, stock, merchandise, wares, range [➡BUSINESS PRODUCTS; 795]

stockist (*UK*) *n* **seller**, shop, store, wholesaler, retailer, dealer, vendor [➡SELLERS; 442]

stock market *n* **financial market**, stock exchange, exchange, market, bourse, money market [➡ACCOUNTING, BANKING, AND BUDGETING; 799]

stock phrase *n* [➡FIGURES OF SPEECH; 673]

stockpile 1 *n* **supply**, hoard, accumulation, store, stock, stash (*informal*) [➡STORES AND STORAGE BUILDINGS; 1088] 2 *v* **build up stocks**, stock up on, store up, store, squirrel away, hoard, amass, salt away, accumulate, collect [➡STORE AND KEEP; 453]

See Compare and Contrast at **collect**.

stockroom *n* **storeroom**, storehouse, store, warehouse [➡STORES AND STORAGE BUILDINGS; 1088]

stocks 1 *n* **instrument of punishment**, punishment device, framework, pillory, ducking stool, cucking stool [➡ANCIENT MANMADE STRUCTURES; 1089] 2 *n* **shares**, bonds, dividends [➡FUNDS, PAYMENTS, AND CHARGES; 800]

stock-still *adv* **motionless**, completely still, absolutely still, immobile, without moving, unmoving, stationary [➡LACK OF ACTIVITY OR MOTION; 342] *Opposite:* moving

stocktaking 1 *n* **evaluation**, assessment, appraisal, reassessment, reappraisal, taking stock [➡EXAMINE AND ASSESS; 753] 2 *n* **inventory**, listing, itemizing, counting, checking, examination, valuing [➡BUSINESS ACTIVITIES AND PHENOMENA; 794]

stock up *v* **stockpile**, hoard, save up, collect, lay in, store up, accumulate, amass, gather, squirrel away [➡STORE AND KEEP; 453]

stock up on *v* [➡STORE AND KEEP; 453]

stocky *adj* **thickset**, sturdy, solid, stout, squat, burly, hefty, chunky (*informal*) [➡BUILD; 477] *Opposite:* slight

stockyard *n* **yard**, enclosure, farmyard, farm, enclosed yard, pen [➡THE COUNTRYSIDE AND OUTDOOR SPACES; 1071]

stodgy (*informal*) 1 *adj* **heavy**, filling, starchy, indigestible, hard to digest [➡FOOD; 1167] *Opposite:* light 2 *adj*

dull, turgid, uninteresting, unexciting, stuffy, boring, tedious, dreary, stilted [➡BORING AND UNINTERESTING; 234] *Opposite:* lively

stoic 1 *n* **impassive person**, patient person, fatalist, ascetic, unfeeling person [➡PHILOSOPHICAL AND POLITICAL THINKERS; 781] 2 *adj* **enduring**, tolerant, patient, indifferent, apathetic, resigned, passive, stoical [➡STRENGTH OF WILL; 501] *Opposite:* excitable

See Compare and Contrast at **impassive**.

stoical *see* **stoic**

stoicism *n* **impassiveness**, endurance, patience, indifference, fortitude, resignation [➡STRENGTH OF WILL; 501] *Opposite:* excitability

stoke *v* **put fuel on**, stoke up, add fuel to, fuel [➡FIRE, FLAMMABILITY, AND BURNING; 1165]

stoke up 1 *v* **stoke**, put fuel on, add fuel to [➡FIRE, FLAMMABILITY, AND BURNING; 1165] 2 *v* **strengthen**, intensify, stir up, stoke, fuel, encourage, add to [➡CHANGE OF INTENSITY: MORE; 394]

STOL *type of* **civil aircraft** [➡AIRCRAFT; 1148]

stole *n* **garment**, shawl, wrap, scarf, pashmina, tippet, boa [➡ACCESSORIES, MILLINERY, AND LINGERIE; 867]

stolid *adj* **impassive**, unresponsive, dull, emotionless, insensitive, indifferent, slow-witted [➡NEGATIVE INTELLECTUAL CHARACTERISTICS; 525] *Opposite:* emotional

See Compare and Contrast at **impassive**.

stomach *part of* **digestive tract** [➡THE DIGESTIVE TRACT; 709]

stomachache *n* **stomach pain**, colic, indigestion, cramp, stitch, heartburn, upset stomach, bellyache (*informal*), tummy ache (*informal*), tummy pain (*informal*) [➡DISORDERS OF THE DIGESTIVE SYSTEM; 713]

stomach-churning *adj* **sickening**, nauseating, disgusting, revolting, repulsive, stomach-turning, repellent, vile, foul (*informal*), gross (*slang*) [➡DISGUSTING AND REPULSIVE; 230] *Opposite:* appealing

stomach pain *n* [➡DISORDERS OF THE DIGESTIVE SYSTEM; 713]

stomach pump (*informal*) *n* **suction pump**, suction device, aspirator, siphon, syringe, drain [➡REMEDIES, TREATMENTS, AND OPERATIONS; 731]

stomach-turning *adj* **sickening**, nauseating, stomach-churning, revolting, disgusting, repulsive, repellent, vile, foul (*informal*), gross (*slang*) [➡DISGUSTING AND REPULSIVE; 230] *Opposite:* appealing

stomp *v* **tread heavily**, stamp, tramp, clump, plod, trudge, clomp [➡PROCEED AND GO; 305]

stomping ground *n* [➡PLACE; 1065]

stone 1 *n* [➡STONES, ROCKS, AND BOULDERS; 1057] 2 *part of* **fruit** [➡FRUIT AND VEGETABLES; 1176]

lean forward, crouch, crouch down [➡ASSUME A POSITION; 317] *Opposite*: straighten up **2** *v* **lower yourself**, condescend, deign, debase yourself, patronize [➡CHANGE OF MOOD AND COMPOSURE; 580] **3** *see* **stoup**

...ned *adj* [➡BUILD; 477]

... *adj* [➡BUILD; 477]

...continue, end, bring to an end, bring to a ...s to a standstill, bring to a halt [➡CAUSE TO STOP; ...te: begin **2** *v* **prevent**, impede, hinder, prohibit, ..., bar, ban [➡MAKE IMPOSSIBLE; 276] *Opposite*: permit ...d, finish, come to an end, be over, break off, cease, ...r out [➡CEASE TO EXIST; 22] *Opposite*: begin **4** *v* **pause**, inter...pt, break off, stop off, take a break, adjourn, halt, rest [➡STOP ACTING; 264] **5** *v* **block**, block up, block off, obstruct, plug, plug up, stop up [➡FILL; 406] **6** *n* **halt**, break, rest, stopover, stay, sojourn (*literary*) [➡PERIODS OF REST; 91]

stop by *v* **drop in**, call by, call, visit, stop off, come by, pop in (*informal*), call in (*UK*) [➡ARRIVE; 12]

stopcock *n* **valve**, faucet, cock, spigot, stopper, switch, tap [➡PARTS OF MACHINES AND TOOLS; 1118]

stop dead *v* [➡FAIL OR CEASE TO FUNCTION; 470]

stopgap *n* **temporary solution**, substitute, makeshift, expedient, temporary measure, contrivance [➡SOLUTIONS; 215]

stoplight *type of* **external feature** [➡EXTERNAL PARTS OF A VEHICLE; 1147]

stop off *v* **call**, stop by, stop, drop in, visit, call in (*UK*) [➡ARRIVE; 12]

stopover *n* **break in your journey**, stop, halt, pause, stopoff, layover [➡PERIODS OF REST; 91]

stoppage **1** *n* **strike**, work stoppage, wildcat strike, walkout, slowdown, industrial action (*UK*), work to rule (*UK*), go-slow (*UK*) [➡WORK-RELATED ACTIVITIES; 834] **2** *n* **blockage**, obstruction, obstacle, barrier [➡PROBLEMS; 256]

stoppage time (*UK*) *n* **injury time**, timeout, overtime, extension, additional playing time, extra time (*UK*) [➡SPORTS TERMS; 877]

stopped **1** *adj* **stationary**, still, at a standstill, immobile, motionless, not moving [➡LACK OF ACTIVITY OR MOTION; 342] *Opposite*: moving **2** *adj* **clogged**, blocked, congested, backed up, stopped up, bunged, closed [➡FULL; 1239] *Opposite*: open **3** *adj* **not working**, out of order, out of commission, worn-out, crashed, given up the ghost (*informal*) [➡IN BAD REPAIR; 1234] *Opposite*: working

stopper *n* **plug**, bung, cork, top, lid, closure, cover [➡COVERS AND COATINGS; 1246]

stop press (*UK*) *n* **late news**, recent news, last-minute news, news flash, postscript, addendum [➡NEWSPAPERS AND MAGAZINES; 605]

stop up *v* **plug**, plug up, block, block up, block off, bung [➡FILL; 406]

stopwatch *type of* **clock** [➡CLOCKS AND TIMERS; 1126]

stop working *v* **break down**, break, fail, seize up [➡FAIL OR CEASE TO FUNCTION; 470] *Opposite*: function

---

...EAT AND DEFEAT; 80] **4** *v* **rage**, fume, bluster [➡GIVING VENT TO EMOTIONS; ...nce, march [➡MOVE FAST; 313] ...nd, confined, isolated, cut off, ...ined [➡CAPTIVITY AND LOSS OF FREEDOM;

[➡CLOUDY AND RAINY WEATHER; 1052] ...erald, harbinger, danger ...NS, SIGNS, AND WARNINGS; 68] ...ously, gustily, wildly ... calmly

...T SITUATIONS; 72] ...lusteriness [➡WINDY ...ess **2** *n* **tem-** ...iness, passion, *Opposite*: pla- ...vdered

..., short way, ...rt walk, spit- [➡CLOSENESS; 159]

...ng, tough, ...ruct, avoid, refuse, [➡...CCURRENCE; 278] *Opposite*: ...d back, stall [➡SHIRK AND ...channel.

[➡POTTERY; 1135]

..., worn, distressed, washed-out, ..., pale [➡DESCRIBING CLOTHES; 869]

...nry, brickwork, walls [➡BUILDING MATERIALS;

...ype of **marine alga** [➡MICROORGANISMS, FUNGI, AND

...*adj* **rocky**, flinty, pebbly, rock-strewn, shingly, ...gravelly, rough [➡PHYSICAL TEXTURE; 1222] **2** *adj* **pitiless**, ...ting, unsympathetic, unyielding, flinty, com-...sionless, unfriendly, cruel, hard, cold [➡SELFISH AND UNKIND; ...5] *Opposite*: compassionate

stony-faced *adj* **expressionless**, unemotional, unfriendly, blank, cold, grave [➡FACIAL EXPRESSIONS AND BLUSHING; 651] *Opposite*: smiling

stony-hearted *adj* **hardhearted**, unfeeling, pitiless, unsympathetic, hard, cruel [➡SELFISH AND UNKIND; 505] *Opposite*: soft-hearted

stooge *n* **straight partner**, comic actor, comedian, butt, foil, straight man, feed, entertainer [➡WORKERS IN ENTERTAINMENT AND MEDIA; 873]

stool *n* **seat**, chair, footrest, bench, couch, pew [➡FURNITURE; 858]

stoolie (*slang*) *n* [➡INTERFERING PEOPLE AND TATTLETALES; 950]

stool pigeon (*slang*) *n* [➡INTERFERING PEOPLE AND TATTLETALES; 950]

stoop **1** *v* **bend down**, bend forward, bend over, bend,

storage 1 *n* **storing**, stowage, stowing, packing, loading, putting away, tidying away [➡ STORE AND KEEP; 453] **2** *n* **storage space**, storage capacity, storage area, stowage, room, space, accommodation [➡ STORES AND STORAGE BUILDINGS; 1088]

storage

◆ *types of storage spaces*
arms depot, arsenal, attic, barn, basement, bunker, cellar, depository, depot, dump, elevator, garage, garbage dump, gasometer, grain elevator, granary, hangar, hayloft, hold, landfill, larder, loft, luggage compartment, magazine, morgue, mortuary, pantry, shed, silo, strongroom, treasury, warehouse, water tower, weapon store, woodshed

storage bin *type of* **container** [➡ CONTAINERS, RECEPTACLES, AND PACKAGING; 1245]

storage tank *type of* **container** [➡ CONTAINERS, RECEPTACLES, AND PACKAGING; 1245]

store 1 *v* **put away**, stow, keep, deposit, put in storage, warehouse, stockpile [➡ STORE AND KEEP; 453] **2** *n* **supply**, stockpile, hoard, accumulation, collection, mass, pile, stock [➡ COLLECTIONS AND MIXTURES OF THINGS; 1244] **3** *n* **shop**, outlet, emporium, showroom [➡ RETAIL OUTLETS; 1083] **4** *n* **warehouse**, depository, depot, stockroom, repository, storeroom [➡ STORES AND STORAGE BUILDINGS; 1088]

store

◆ *types of food outlets*
bakery, bodega, butcher's, candy store, deli, delicatessen, drive-through, farmers' market, grocer's, grocery store, refreshment stand, supermarket, takeout

◆ *types of retail outlets*
bazaar, beauty parlor, big-box store, bookstore, boutique, chain store, convenience store, corner store, covered market, department store, dime store, dispensary, druggist, drugstore, duty-free, filling station, flea market, garden center, gas station, general store, hair salon, hardware store, hypermarket, kiosk, mall, mart, mom-and-pop store, newsstand, nursery, pharmacy, post office, salesroom, service station, supercenter, superstore, thrift shop, warehouse

storehouse *n* [➡ STORES AND STORAGE BUILDINGS; 1088]

storekeeper *n* **retailer**, seller, salesperson, merchant, trader, shopkeeper (*UK*) [➡ SELLERS; 442]

storeroom *n* [➡ STORES AND STORAGE BUILDINGS; 1088]

stores *n* **supplies**, provisions, equipment, goods, food, rations, vittles (*archaic or humorous*) [➡ POSSESSIONS; 461]

store up *v* **amass**, hoard, save, accumulate, stockpile, squirrel away, collect, salt away [➡ STORE AND KEEP; 453]

stork *type of* **freshwater bird** [➡ FRESHWATER BIRDS; 1000]

storm 1 *n* **tempest**, squall, gale, hurricane, tornado, rainstorm, snowstorm, blizzard, thunderstorm, typhoon, cyclone, downpour [➡ WINDY AND STORMY WEATHER; 1053] **2** *n* **outburst**, outbreak, explosion, eruption, wave, flare-up (*informal*) [➡ SUDDEN EVENTS; 52] **3** *v* **capture**, carry, take by storm, take,

overmaster (*literary*) [➡
rant and rave, thunder,
5 *v* **stamp**, stomp, stalk, flo

stormbound *adj* **housebou
snowed in, snowbound, deta
248]

storm cloud 1 *type of* **cloud
2** *n* **sign of violence**, omen, h
signal, gathering storm [➡ INDICATIO

stormily *adv* **windily**, tempest
[➡ WINDY AND STORMY WEATHER; 1053] *Opposite*

storm in *v* [➡ ARRIVE; 12]

storm in a teacup (*UK*) *n* [➡ DIFFICU

storminess 1 *n* **wildness**, windiness, t
AND STORMY WEATHER; 1053] *Opposite:* calmr
pestuousness, violence, turbulence, fie
frenzy [➡ EMOTIONALLY UNPLEASANT AND UPSETTING; 227
cidity

storm out *v* [➡ LEAVE AND GO AWAY; 8]

storm petrel *type of* **sea bird** [➡ SEA BIRDS; 1002]

stormproof *adj* **storm-resistant**, protected, stro
waterproof, windproof [➡ IN GOOD REPAIR; 1232]

storm sewer *n* **storm drain**, drain, gutter, o
drainage system [➡ WATERCOURSES; 1111]

storm-tossed *adj* **choppy**, stormy, rough, batt
wild, weather-beaten [➡ WINDY AND STORMY WEATHER; 1053] *Oppo
calm

stormy 1 *adj* **squally**, rainy, thundery, blustery, wind
wild, tempestuous [➡ WINDY AND STORMY WEATHER; 1053] *Opposite*
calm **2** *adj* **tempestuous**, violent, turbulent, unsettled
volatile, fiery, passionate, vehement, frenzied [➡ EMOTIONALLY
UNPLEASANT AND UPSETTING; 227] *Opposite:* placid

story 1 *n* **floor**, level, section, division, landing, tier, layer [➡ STAIRS AND STORIES; 1102] **2** *n* **tale**, narrative, account, legend, chronicle, anecdote, fairy tale, yarn (*informal*) [➡ THE ORAL TRADITION; 677] **3** *n* **account**, report, version, statement, description [➡ BASIC DETAILS; 688] **4** *n* (*informal*) **lie**, untruth, falsehood, baldfaced lie, fib (*informal*), whopper (*informal*) [➡ DECEPTION AND LIES; 660] **5** *n* **article**, piece, feature, report, item, scoop [➡ NEWSPAPERS AND MAGAZINES; 605]

story book *n* [➡ BOOKS AND BOOKLETS; 590]

storybook *adj* **fairy-tale**, fictional, make-believe, mythical, fanciful, imaginary [➡ FALSE AND UNREAL; 173] *Opposite:* real

storyland *n* [➡ NONEXISTENT PLACES; 1066]

story line *n* **plot**, narrative, story, theme, scenario, subplot [➡ THE ORAL TRADITION; 677]

storyteller 1 *n* **narrator**, teller of tales, teller, relater, raconteur, minstrel, bard (*literary or humorous*) [➡ SPEAKERS AND ORATORS; 603] **2** *n* (*informal*) **liar**, prevaricator, deceiver, fabricator, fibber (*informal*) [➡ PEOPLE WHO DECEIVE; 661]

stoup *n* **basin**, vessel, bowl, receptacle, chalice, font [➡ RELIGIOUS OBJECTS; 779]

stout 1 *adj* **thickset**, heavy, solid, plump, chubby, corpulent, fat, fleshy, overweight, hefty, portly, round [➡ BUILD; 477] *Opposite:* slender **2** *adj* **brave**, firm, stalwart, determined, resolute, plucky, bold, valiant, courageous, heroic, doughty (*archaic*) [➡ COURAGE; 498] *Opposite:* faint-hearted **3** *adj* **sturdy**, strong, solid, substantial, tough, well-built, well-made, robust, heavy-duty [➡ STRENGTH; 201] *Opposite:* flimsy

stouthearted *adj* **courageous**, brave, resolute, bold, valiant, heroic, dauntless (*literary*) [➡ COURAGE; 498] *Opposite:* cowardly

stoutheartedness *n* [➡ COURAGE; 498]

stoutness 1 *n* **fatness**, heaviness, solidity, plumpness, chubbiness, fleshiness, squatness [➡ BUILD; 477] *Opposite:* slenderness **2** *n* **bravery**, firmness, stalwartness, determination, resoluteness, doughtiness, stoutheartedness, pluckiness, boldness, fearlessness [➡ COURAGE; 498] **3** *n* **sturdiness**, solidity, strength, heftiness, toughness [➡ STRENGTH; 201] *Opposite:* flimsiness

stove 1 *type of* **appliance** [➡ HOUSEHOLD APPLIANCES; 1117]

stovepipe hat *type of* **hat** [➡ ACCESSORIES, MILLINERY, AND LINGERIE; 867]

stow *v* **put away**, put, pack, store, deposit, put in storage, tidy away (*UK*) [➡ STORE AND KEEP; 453]

stowage *n* **stowing**, storage, packing, loading, putting away, tidying away [➡ STORE AND KEEP; 453]

stowaway *n* **runaway**, escapee, escaper, fugitive, refugee, fare-dodger (*UK*) [➡ RUNAWAYS AND ABSENTEES; 9]

straddle 1 *v* **be astride**, bestride, sit astride, stand astride [➡ EXIST IN CLOSE PROXIMITY; 21] **2** *v* **span**, include, overlap, link, connect, be on both sides of [➡ CREATING CONNECTIONS; 144]

strafe 1 *v* **bombard**, attack, fire at, shell, blitz, pepper, barrage, cannonade [➡ WARFARE AND WAR; 830] **2** *n* **aerial attack**, bombardment, air attack, blitz, shelling, barrage, cannonade, bombing, attack [➡ WARFARE AND WAR; 830]

straggle 1 *v* **stray**, ramble, maunder, meander, rove, drift, wander [➡ AIMLESS AND ERRANT MOTION; 343] *Opposite:* keep up **2** *v* **lag**, lag behind, trail, trail behind, fall behind, drop behind, drop back [➡ MOVE SLOWLY; 314] **3** *v* **spread untidily**, spread out, sprawl, extend, spread [➡ EXIST IN A PLACE; 19]

straggler *n* **dawdler**, laggard, loiterer, lingerer, slowpoke (*informal*), foot-dragger (*informal*) [➡ LAZY OR UNSUCCESSFUL PEOPLE; 948] *Opposite:* leader

straggly *adj* **untidy**, unkempt, messy, disheveled, tousled, scruffy, sprawling, higgledy-piggledy [➡ DESCRIBING HAIR; 486] *Opposite:* tidy

straight 1 *adj* **candid**, frank, direct, open, honest, truthful, forthright, blunt, straight-talking, up-front (*informal*) [➡ HONEST AND OPEN; 630] *Opposite:* devious **2** *adj* **level**, upright, horizontal, vertical, perpendicular, erect, even, in line [➡ ORIENTATION AND ALIGNMENT; 1223] *Opposite:* askew **3** *adj* **honest**, straightforward, fair, law-abiding, aboveboard, respectable, upright, trustworthy [➡ HONEST AND RELIABLE; 502] *Opposite:* dishonest **4** *adj* **consecutive**, successive, uninterrupted, in a row, running [➡ AFTER, LAST, AND FOLLOWING; 165] **5** *adj* **undiluted**, neat, plain, unmixed, unadulterated, pure, as it comes [➡ RAW AND NATURAL; 1214] *Opposite:* diluted **6** *adj* **tidy**, neat, in order, orderly, organized, arranged, sorted out, ship-

shape [➡ ORDER AND ORGANIZATION; 206] *Opposite:* untidy **7** *adj* (*slang*) **conventional**, traditional, conservative, orthodox, square (*slang dated*) [➡ UNADVENTUROUS AND DULL; 517] *Opposite:* unconventional **8** *adv* **as the crow flies**, in a straight line, directly, from A to B, by the shortest possible route [➡ DIRECTION OF MOTION; 345] *Opposite:* indirectly **9** *adv* **directly**, without delay, immediately, at once, instantly, without stopping, right away, straightaway [➡ PRESENT; 85] *Opposite:* later

straightaway *adv* **immediately**, at once, without delay, right away, promptly, directly, straight, without further ado, now, without hesitation, straight off (*informal*) [➡ PRESENT; 85] *Opposite:* later

straighten 1 *v* **make straight**, straighten out, unbend, uncurl, flatten, smooth down [➡ CHANGE OF SHAPE; 385] *Opposite:* bend **2** *v* **make level**, level, set straight, straighten up, adjust, align [➡ ARRANGE AND CREATE ORDER; 357] **3** *v* **tidy**, tidy up, order, arrange, organize [➡ ARRANGE AND CREATE ORDER; 357]

straighten out 1 *v* **make straight**, straighten, unbend, uncurl, flatten, smooth down [➡ CHANGE OF SHAPE; 385] *Opposite:* bend **2** *v* **put right**, sort out, set right, settle, rectify, correct [➡ CORRECT AND PUT RIGHT; 377] *Opposite:* confuse

straighten up *v* **align**, justify, straighten, level, make flush, adjust [➡ ARRANGE AND CREATE ORDER; 357]

straight-faced *adj* **deadpan**, poker-faced, expressionless, blank, serious, impassive, solemn, grave, unsmiling, stony-faced [➡ FACIAL EXPRESSIONS AND BLUSHING; 651] *Opposite:* smiling

straightforward 1 *adj* **frank**, forthright, candid, direct, honest, open, straight, sincere, up-front (*informal*) [➡ HONEST AND OPEN; 630] *Opposite:* devious **2** *adj* **easy**, simple, facile, uncomplicated, clear-cut, basic, undemanding [➡ EASE AND SIMPLICITY; 200] *Opposite:* complicated

See Compare and Contrast at **easy**.

straightforwardness 1 *n* **frankness**, candor, honesty, truthfulness, openness, sincerity, forthrightness, directness [➡ HONEST AND OPEN; 630] *Opposite:* deviousness **2** *n* **ease**, facility, simplicity, clarity, easiness [➡ EASE AND SIMPLICITY; 200] *Opposite:* difficulty

straight man *type of* **entertainer** [➡ WORKERS IN ENTERTAINMENT AND MEDIA; 873]

straight off (*informal*) *adv* **at once**, right away, straightaway, immediately, without delay, then and there, directly, promptly [➡ PRESENT; 85] *Opposite:* later

straight out *adv* **unhesitatingly**, without hesitation, directly, straight, without beating around the bush, getting straight to the point, straight from the shoulder [➡ HONEST AND OPEN; 630]

straight-out (*informal*) **1** *adj* **blunt**, unrestrained, direct, frank, honest, straightforward [➡ HONEST AND OPEN; 630] *Opposite:* restrained **2** *adj* **total**, complete, utter, out-and-out, thorough, consummate [➡ ABSOLUTE AND ABSOLUTELY; 133]

straight-talking *adj* **blunt**, direct, frank, candid, forthright, up-front (*informal*), plain-spoken (*UK*) [➡ HONEST AND OPEN; 630] *Opposite:* evasive

straight-thinking *adj* [➡ POSITIVE INTELLECTUAL CHARACTERISTICS; 524]

straightway *adv* [➡ PRESENT; 85]

strain 1 *v* **make a great effort**, try hard, struggle, labor, strive, exert yourself, endeavor (*formal*) [➡ HARD WORK OR EFFORT; 298] 2 *v* **damage**, injure, hurt, pull, sprain, twist, stretch, crick, wrench [➡ WOUND A PERSON OR ANIMAL; 383] 3 *v* **drain**, sieve, filter, sift, separate [➡ SEPARATE AND DIVIDE; 401] 4 *v* **tax**, overburden, overload, burden, overtax [➡ GIVE TOO MUCH AND OVERBURDEN; 437] 5 *n* **nervous tension**, tension, stress, worry, anxiety, pressure, trauma, burden [➡ CONFUSION, ANXIETY, AND WORRY; 540] 6 *n* **exertion**, effort, tension, struggle, force, wrench [➡ HARD WORK OR EFFORT; 298] 7 *n* **injury**, sprain, wrench, crick [➡ PAIN AND OTHER PHYSICAL SENSATIONS; 733] 8 *n* **breed**, species, type, form, sort, variety, kind, subspecies [➡ VARIETIES, TYPES, AND KINDS; 145]

strained 1 *adj* **stressed**, tense, worried, nervous, anxious, edgy, overwrought [➡ CONFUSION, ANXIETY, AND WORRY; 540] *Opposite*: calm 2 *adj* **tense**, forced, artificial, awkward, labored, false, unnatural [➡ EMOTIONALLY UNPLEASANT AND UPSETTING; 227] *Opposite*: natural

strainer *type of* **utensil** [➡ TABLEWARE, FLATWARE, AND KITCHENWARE; 861]

straining at the leash *adj* **raring to go**, eager, enthusiastic, impatient, keen, zealous, champing at the bit [➡ POSITIVE IMPATIENCE, ENTHUSIASM, AND ALERTNESS; 537] *Opposite*: indifferent

strait *n* **passage**, channel, canal, sound [➡ THE SEAS, OCEANS, AND SHORES; 1041]

straitened *adj* **impoverished**, severe, distressed, difficult, pinched, reduced [➡ EMOTIONALLY UNPLEASANT AND UPSETTING; 227] *Opposite*: comfortable

straitjacket *n* **restriction**, limitation, restraint, shackles, constraint, repression [➡ CAPTIVITY AND LOSS OF FREEDOM; 248] *Opposite*: freedom

strait-laced *adj* **prudish**, puritanical, prim, moralistic, strict, severe, narrow-minded, proper, goody-goody (*informal*) [➡ UNADVENTUROUS AND DULL; 517] *Opposite*: broadminded

strait-lacedness *n* [➡ UNADVENTUROUS AND DULL; 517]

strand 1 *n* **thread**, filament, fiber, string, wire [➡ AMOUNTS OF SOLID OR SEMISOLID; 115] 2 *n* **lock**, tress, wisp, curl [➡ AMOUNTS OF SOLID OR SEMISOLID; 115] 3 *n* **element**, component, constituent, aspect, feature, part, thread [➡ PHYSICAL OBJECTS; 1243] 4 *v* **cut off**, maroon, trap, leave high and dry, abandon, leave [➡ REFUSING OR REJECTING RELATIONS; 975] *Opposite*: rescue

strange 1 *adj* **odd**, bizarre, outlandish, eccentric, weird, weird and wonderful, extraordinary, out of the ordinary, peculiar, abnormal, unexpected [➡ BIZARRE AND PECULIAR; 257] *Opposite*: normal 2 *adj* **unfamiliar**, foreign, alien, unknown, mysterious, different, exotic, new, novel [➡ EXTRAORDINARY: UNCOMMON; 205] *Opposite*: familiar 3 *adj* **inexplicable**, surprising, funny, astonishing, perplexing, incomprehensible, puzzling, enigmatic, unexpected, remarkable [➡ BIZARRE AND PECULIAR; 257] *Opposite*: unsurprising

strangely 1 *adv* **oddly**, bizarrely, outlandishly, eccentrically, weirdly, extraordinarily, peculiarly, abnormally [➡ BIZARRE AND PECULIAR; 257] *Opposite*: normally 2 *adv*

inexplicably, surprisingly, funnily, astonishingly, perplexingly, incomprehensibly, puzzlingly, enigmatically, unexpectedly, remarkably [➡ EXTRAORDINARY: AMAZING; 204] *Opposite*: unsurprisingly

strangeness *n* **weirdness**, peculiarity, eccentricity, abnormality, incongruity, oddity, bizarreness, oddness, outlandishness, crankiness (*informal*) [➡ BIZARRE AND PECULIAR; 257] *Opposite*: normality

stranger *n* **foreigner**, alien, outsider, visitor, guest, new arrival [➡ STRANGERS; 972]

strangle 1 *v* **choke**, strangulate, throttle, garrote, asphyxiate, smother, suffocate, crush [➡ KILL; 923] 2 *v* **stifle**, repress, suppress, inhibit, smother [➡ WITHHOLD INFORMATION; 687] *Opposite*: express

stranglehold 1 *n* **power**, dominion, control, sway, domination, monopoly [➡ CAPTIVITY AND LOSS OF FREEDOM; 248] 2 *n* **strong hold**, throttlehold, iron grip, vicelike grip, grip, lock, headlock, clinch, clamp [➡ CAPTIVITY AND LOSS OF FREEDOM; 248]

strangulate *v* **strangle**, throttle, choke, smother, asphyxiate, suffocate, crush [➡ KILL; 923]

strangulation *n* **strangling**, throttling, choking, smothering, asphyxiation, suffocation, crushing [➡ CAUSES OF DEATH; 921]

strap 1 *n* **band**, fastening, belt, strip, leash, tie [➡ FASTENERS, LINKS, AND NETWORKS; 1247] 2 *part of* **garment** [➡ PARTS OF A GARMENT; 870] 3 *v* **fasten**, belt, secure, lash, buckle, tie, bind [➡ FASTEN, LINK, AND JOIN; 408]

straphanger (*informal*) *n* **passenger**, commuter, traveler, rider [➡ TRAVEL: TRAVELERS AND WALKERS; 319]

strapline (*UK*) *n* **subheading**, subhead, heading, head, title, byline [➡ NEWSPAPERS AND MAGAZINES; 605]

strapped (*informal*) *adj* **needy**, wanting, short of money, impecunious, impoverished, poor, short, strapped for cash (*informal*), broke (*informal*) [➡ POVERTY AND POOR; 892] *Opposite*: flush (*informal*)

strapped for cash (*informal*) *adj* [➡ POVERTY AND POOR; 892]

strapping (*informal*) *adj* **robust**, broad-shouldered, burly, well-built, sturdy, brawny, stalwart, muscular, beefy [➡ BUILD; 477] *Opposite*: delicate

strass *n* [➡ ORNAMENTS AND DECORATIONS; 1248]

stratagem *n* **trick**, ruse, ploy, wile, subterfuge, feint, dodge, device, scheme, plot, tactic, maneuver [➡ WAYS OF DOING THINGS; 294]

strategic *adj* **planned**, tactical, calculated, deliberate, premeditated, considered, intentional [➡ INTENTIONAL AND DELIBERATE; 279] *Opposite*: unplanned

strategist *n* **tactician**, planner, policymaker, plotter, schemer [➡ POLITICAL OFFICES AND POLITICIANS; 808]

strategy *n* **plan**, scheme, policy, approach, tactic, line of attack, stratagem [➡ WAYS OF DOING THINGS; 294]

strathspey *type of* **dance** [➡ DANCE; 903]

stratigraphy *type of* **earth science** [➡ EARTH SCIENCES; 1059]

stratocumulus *type of* **cloud** [➡ CLOUDY AND RAINY WEATHER; 1052]

stratosphere n [➡ THE EARTH'S ATMOSPHERE; 1040]

stratum (formal) n **layer**, band, level, division, section, branch, echelon, vein [➡ COVERS AND COATINGS; 1246]

stratus type of **cloud** [➡ CLOUDY AND RAINY WEATHER; 1052]

straw 1 n **grass**, hay, stubble, chaff [➡ ANIMAL FEED; 1168] 2 type of **fiber** [➡ PLANT MATERIALS; 1133]

strawberry type of **fruit** [➡ FRUIT AND VEGETABLES; 1176]

straw-hat adj **summer**, seasonal, temporary, traveling, summer stock [➡ FINITENESS, VARIABILITY, AND TRANSIENCE; 96]

straw poll n **poll**, opinion poll, show of hands, referendum, questionnaire, consultation, survey [➡ ELECTIONS AND VOTING; 807]

stray 1 v **wander away**, wander off, go astray, get lost, drift, lose your way [➡ AIMLESS AND ERRANT MOTION; 343] 2 adj **lost**, wandering, abandoned, homeless, vagrant [➡ AIMLESS AND ERRANT MOTION; 343]

streak 1 n **line**, band, strip, stripe, vein, smudge, splash, flash [➡ PATTERNS; 1225] 2 n **run**, stretch, roll [➡ PERIODS OF TIME; 90] 3 n **element**, side, trait, characteristic, quality, aspect, trace [➡ TEMPERAMENT AND BEHAVIOR; 492] 4 v **mark**, stripe, stain, line, fleck, daub, smudge [➡ DECORATE, ADORN, AND APPLY COATINGS; 405] 5 v **move fast**, fly, flash, zoom, whiz, rush, dart, speed, sprint, shoot (informal), zip (informal) [➡ MOVE FAST; 313]

streaky adj **stripy**, striped, striated, banded, lined, barred [➡ DESCRIBING PATTERNS; 1227]

stream 1 n **watercourse**, river, torrent, rivulet, tributary, creek, crick, brook (literary), beck (UK) [➡ RIVERS, LAKES, AND STREAMS; 1042] 2 n **jet**, spurt, torrent, cascade [➡ AMOUNTS OF LIQUID; 114] 3 n **flood**, torrent, barrage, onslaught [➡ SUDDEN EVENTS; 52] 4 v **flow**, pour out, flood, gush, spill, run, issue, course [➡ LIQUID EMISSION; 370]

streamer n **flag**, banner, bunting, ribbon, decoration [➡ ORNAMENTS AND DECORATIONS; 1248]

streamline v **rationalize**, modernize, update, reorganize, restructure, simplify [➡ ARRANGE AND CREATE ORDER; 357]

streamlined 1 adj **sleek**, smooth, slick, aerodynamic [➡ ROUNDED SHAPE; 1218] 2 adj **efficient**, rationalized, modernized, updated, reorganized, restructured, simplified, well-run [➡ ECONOMICAL AND RESOURCEFUL; 207] Opposite: cumbersome

street type of **secondary road** [➡ ROADS; 1106]

streetcar type of **rail vehicle** [➡ RAILROADS; 1107]

streetcar line type of **railroad** [➡ RAILROADS; 1107]

street credibility n **coolness**, credibility, sophistication, fashionableness, trendiness (informal), hipness (slang) [➡ LEVELS OF EDUCATION AND SOPHISTICATION; 894]

street entertainer type of **entertainer** [➡ WORKERS IN ENTERTAINMENT AND MEDIA; 873]

streetlamp type of **light** [➡ LIGHT; 1164]

streetlight type of **light** [➡ LIGHT; 1164]

street luge type of **extreme sport** [➡ HOBBIES, GAMES, AND SPORTS; 875]

street musician type of **entertainer** [➡ WORKERS IN ENTERTAINMENT AND MEDIA; 873]

street party n [➡ PARTIES, DANCES, AND CELEBRATIONS; 37]

street performer type of **entertainer** [➡ WORKERS IN ENTERTAINMENT AND MEDIA; 873]

street trader (UK) n [➡ SELLERS; 442]

streetwise (informal) adj **astute**, quick-witted, sharp-witted, smart, sharp, experienced, shrewd, hardened, tough, on the ball (informal) [➡ POSITIVE INTELLECTUAL CHARACTERISTICS; 524] Opposite: inexperienced

strength 1 n **power**, force, might, potency, muscle, vigor [➡ STRENGTH; 201] Opposite: weakness 2 n **strong point**, strong suit, forte, asset, métier, gift [➡ SKILLS, TALENTS, AND ABILITIES; 526] Opposite: weakness 3 n **intensity**, concentration, dilution, depth, potency, power [➡ STRENGTH; 201]

strengthen v **make stronger**, reinforce, fortify, brace, toughen, build up [➡ IMPROVE STRENGTH AND DURABILITY; 378] Opposite: weaken

strength of character n [➡ STRENGTH OF WILL; 501]

strength of mind n **resolve**, determination, strength, fortitude, willpower, moral fiber, heart, courage, grit, firmness [➡ STRENGTH OF WILL; 501] Opposite: weakness

strength of will n [➡ STRENGTH OF WILL; 501]

strenuous 1 adj **taxing**, tiring, arduous, exhausting, demanding, backbreaking, laborious, tough, hard [➡ PHYSICALLY UNPLEASANT; 226] Opposite: light 2 adj **active**, energetic, determined, spirited, tireless, persistent, vigorous, dogged [➡ STRENGTH OF WILL; 501] Opposite: half-hearted

See Compare and Contrast at **hard**.

streptococcus type of **microorganism** [➡ MICROORGANISMS, FUNGI, AND ALGAE; 1023]

stress 1 n **strain**, anxiety, worry, tension, trauma, pressure, hassle (informal) [➡ CONFUSION, ANXIETY, AND WORRY; 540] 2 n **emphasis**, importance, weight, accent, urgency [➡ MOST IMPORTANT THING; 197] 3 v **emphasize**, lay emphasis on, underline, underscore, accentuate, point up, highlight [➡ CLAIM, INSIST, AND EMPHASIZE; 614]

See Compare and Contrast at **worry**.

stressed adj **harassed**, worried, strained, tense, anxious, jittery, stressed out (informal), hassled (informal), frazzled (informal) [➡ CONFUSION, ANXIETY, AND WORRY; 540] Opposite: relaxed

stressed out (informal) adj **harassed**, worried, strained, stressed, tense, anxious, jittery, hassled (informal), frazzled (informal) [➡ CONFUSION, ANXIETY, AND WORRY; 540] Opposite: relaxed

stress-free adj [➡ EMOTIONALLY PLEASANT; 187]

stressful adj **demanding**, taxing, worrying, traumatic, tense, nerve-racking, hectic [➡ EMOTIONALLY UNPLEASANT AND UPSETTING; 227] Opposite: relaxing

stress out (informal) v **worry**, bother, get to, harass,

perturb, hassle (*informal*) [➡ UPSET, DISTRESS, AND HUMILIATE; 567]
Opposite: relax

stretch 1 *v* **extend**, elongate, enlarge, widen, broaden, distend, draw out [➡ CHANGE OF SIZE: BIGGER; 392] *Opposite:* shrink 2 *v* **spread out**, extend, unfold, spread, unroll [➡ EXIST IN A PLACE; 19] 3 *v* **be elastic**, give, expand, yield [➡ CHANGE OF SIZE: BIGGER; 392] 4 *n* **give**, bounce, spring, elasticity [➡ MALLEABLE AND ELASTIC; 1212] *Opposite:* rigidity 5 *n* **section**, expanse, bit, area, sweep, tract [➡ AREA AND RANGE; 111] 6 *n* **spell**, period, stint, time, run, term [➡ PERIODS OF TIME; 90]

stretchable *adj* [➡ MALLEABLE AND ELASTIC; 1212]

stretch a point 1 *v* **make allowances**, bend the rules, turn a blind eye, make an exception [➡ NOT PAY ATTENTION; 764] 2 *v* **exaggerate**, overstate, inflate, amplify, embroider, embellish [➡ CLAIM, INSIST, AND EMPHASIZE; 614] *Opposite:* understate

stretched 1 *adj* **extended**, outstretched, elongated, expanded, lengthened, outspread [➡ LENGTH: LONG; 1197] *Opposite:* contracted 2 *adj* **strained**, overextended, pushed, fraught, busy, hard-pressed, stressed, under pressure, struggling [➡ IN TROUBLE AND DISADVANTAGED; 73] *Opposite:* relaxed

stretch out *v* **recline**, lie back, bask, lounge, sprawl, repose [➡ ASSUME A POSITION; 317]

stretch the truth *v* [➡ DECEPTION AND LIES; 660]

stretchy *adj* **elastic**, flexible, springy, pliable [➡ MALLEABLE AND ELASTIC; 1212] *Opposite:* rigid

strew 1 *v* **scatter**, throw, disperse, distribute, spread, cast [➡ SPREAD AND SCATTER; 332] *Opposite:* gather 2 *v* **litter**, cover, fill, sprinkle, dot, clutter, pepper [➡ DECORATE, ADORN, AND APPLY COATINGS; 405]

striated muscle *type of* **muscle or tendon** [➡ THE MUSCLES; 718]

striation *n* **pattern**, marking, corrugation, incision, ridge, groove [➡ PATTERNS; 1225]

stricken 1 *adj* **troubled**, tormented, wracked, disturbed, traumatized, distracted [➡ CONFUSION, ANXIETY, AND WORRY; 540] 2 *adj* **laid low**, afflicted, suffering, affected, wracked, infected [➡ ILL AND SICK; 740] *Opposite:* well 3 *adj* **injured**, damaged, wounded, hurt, struck [➡ INJURED; 742]

strict 1 *adj* **severe**, firm, stern, harsh, stringent, austere, authoritarian, exacting, rigorous [➡ DIFFICULT TO PLEASE; 515] *Opposite:* lenient 2 *adj* **exact**, precise, accurate, narrow, meticulous, close, true, faithful [➡ EXACT; 203] *Opposite:* inaccurate

strictness 1 *n* **severity**, firmness, sternness, harshness, stringency, austerity, rigorousness [➡ DIFFICULT TO PLEASE; 515] *Opposite:* leniency 2 *n* **exactitude**, precision, accuracy, narrowness, meticulousness, closeness, faithfulness [➡ EXACT; 203] *Opposite:* inaccuracy

stricture (*formal*) 1 *n* **criticism**, attack, rebuke, telling off, censure, dressing-down [➡ CRITICISMS AND ANGRY OUTBURSTS; 50] 2 *n* **restriction**, restraint, limit, constraint, limitation, boundary [➡ CAPTIVITY AND LOSS OF FREEDOM; 248]

stride 1 *v* **step**, walk, pace, tread, march, tramp, stomp, step out [➡ MOVE FAST; 313] 2 *n* **pace**, step, tread, gait, walk [➡ PROCEED AND GO; 305] 3 *n* **advance**, progress, development, improvement, headway [➡ PROGRESS AND ADVANCEMENT; 213]

strident 1 *adj* **loud**, harsh, grating, shrill, raucous, piercing, discordant [➡ LOUD, HIGH, OR UNPLEASANT SOUNDS; 1266] *Opposite:* soft 2 *adj* **vociferous**, forceful, persuasive, clamorous, baying, vocal, noisy [➡ POMPOUS, LOUD, AND OVERCONFIDENT; 635] *Opposite:* gentle

strife *n* **trouble**, conflict, discord, contention, fighting, dissension, friction, rivalry [➡ DISHARMONY; 156] *Opposite:* harmony

strike 1 *v* **hit**, beat, smack, thump, clout, punch, sock (*informal*), belt (*informal*), wallop (*informal*), clobber (*informal*) [➡ PHYSICAL ATTACK AND PUNISHMENT; 415] 2 *v* **collide with**, hit, crash into, smash into, bump into, run into, come into contact with [➡ CONTACT: IMPACT; 413] *Opposite:* miss 3 *v* **occur to**, come to mind, dawn on, hit, come to, register, cross your mind [➡ APPEAR AND EMERGE; 3] 4 *v* **attack**, launch an attack, fall on, set on, hit, assail, assault, raid [➡ DESTRUCTION AND DEMOLITION; 359] 5 *v* **take industrial action**, stop work, walk out, down tools (*UK*) [➡ WORK-RELATED ACTIVITIES; 834] 6 *v* **discover**, hit upon, light on, stumble across, chance upon, happen upon, uncover, unearth, turn up [➡ FIND; 463] 7 *v* **reach**, arrive at, attain, achieve, arrange, effect (*formal*) [➡ INSTITUTE AND INAUGURATE; 348] 8 *n* **raid**, attack, assault, foray, air strike, incursion [➡ AGGRESSIVE EVENTS; 39] 9 *n* **slowdown**, walkout, work stoppage, industrial action (*UK*), work-to-rule (*UK*), go-slow (*UK*) [➡ WORK-RELATED ACTIVITIES; 834]

strike back *v* [➡ VENGEANCE AND REVENGE; 685]

strike down 1 *v* **knock down**, floor, fell, bring down, knock out, lay out (*informal*), KO (*informal*) [➡ PHYSICAL ATTACK AND PUNISHMENT; 415] 2 *v* **afflict**, lay low, infect, affect, make ill [➡ BECOME SICK, TREAT, AND RECOVER; 728] 3 *v* **kill**, bring down, murder, assassinate, slaughter, wipe out (*slang*), slay (*formal or literary*) [➡ KILL; 923]

strike it rich *v* **hit the jackpot**, come into money, make your fortune, laugh all the way to the bank, rake it in (*informal*), make a pile (*informal*), make a bundle (*slang*), clean up (*slang*) [➡ GET MONEY OR REWARD; 421]

strike off *v* **delete**, cross off, remove, withdraw [➡ DELETE AND ERASE; 339] *Opposite:* include

strike out 1 *v* (*informal*) **fail**, fall short, miss the boat, mismanage, bomb (*informal*), flop (*informal*) [➡ FAIL OR BE UNSUCCESSFUL; 75] 2 *v* **set out**, leave, depart, go, move off, start out, head off, set forth (*literary*) [➡ LEAVE AND GO AWAY; 8] *Opposite:* arrive 3 *v* **attack**, lash out, set on, assail [➡ PHYSICAL ATTACK AND PUNISHMENT; 415] 4 *v* **cross out**, delete, score out, strike through, cancel, erase, remove [➡ DELETE AND ERASE; 339]

striker 1 *n* **picket**, picketer, demonstrator, protester [➡ WORKERS; 836] 2 *n* **soccer player**, forward, attacker, winger [➡ PEOPLE IN SPORTS AND LEISURE; 876]

strike up *v* **start**, begin, commence, initiate, make a start [➡ CAUSE TO START; 265] *Opposite:* stop

strike up a friendship *v* [➡ ESTABLISHING RELATIONSHIPS WITH OTHERS; 974]

strike while the iron's hot *v* **take the opportunity**, grab the chance, make the most of it, make hay while the sun shines (*informal*) [➡ START AN ACTION; 260]

striking 1 *adj* **conspicuous**, noticeable, marked, remarkable, salient, outstanding, prominent, unusual, arresting, out of the ordinary [➡ EXTRAORDINARY: AMAZING; 204] *Opposite:*

inconspicuous 2 *adj* **good-looking**, handsome, attractive, eye-catching, beautiful, stunning [→ PEOPLE'S PHYSICAL APPEARANCE; 475]

striking distance *n* **stone's throw**, short distance, a hairsbreadth, hop, skip, and jump, spitting distance (*informal*) [→ CLOSENESS; 159]

string 1 *n* **cord**, thread, filament, twine, rope [→ FASTENERS, LINKS, AND NETWORKS; 1247] **2** *n* **sequence**, series, run, chain, succession, row, line [→ COLLECTIONS AND MIXTURES OF THINGS; 1244] **3** *type of* **lower body underwear** [→ ACCESSORIES, MILLINERY, AND LINGERIE; 867]

string along (*informal*) **1** *v* **deceive**, mislead, lead on, lead down the garden path, send on a wild-goose chase, give the runaround (*informal*) [→ DECEPTION AND LIES; 660] **2** *v* **tag along**, hang around, go along, go along for the ride, join in, take part, stick around (*informal*) [→ ACCOMPANY AND FOLLOW; 337] **3** *v* **agree**, go along with, be of one mind, concur, approve, support [→ AGREE; 645] *Opposite*: disagree

string band *type of* **band** [→ MUSICIANS AND SINGERS; 908]

string bean *type of* **pulse** [→ PEAS AND BEANS; 1189]

stringency *n* **severity**, strictness, rigor, harshness, inflexibility, rigidity, toughness [→ EMOTIONALLY UNPLEASANT AND UPSETTING; 227] *Opposite*: flexibility

stringent *adj* **severe**, strict, rigorous, stern, harsh, tough, inflexible, rigid [→ EMOTIONALLY UNPLEASANT AND UPSETTING; 227] *Opposite*: lax

stringer *n* **journalist**, reporter, correspondent, columnist, writer [→ WORKERS IN ENTERTAINMENT AND MEDIA; 873]

string quartet *type of* **band** [→ MUSICIANS AND SINGERS; 908]

stringy *adj* **tough**, chewy, sinewy, gristly, fibrous [→ STATE OF PREPARED FOOD; 1171] *Opposite*: tender

strip 1 *v* **undress**, strip off, doff, shed, peel off, disrobe (*formal*) [→ DRESS, WEAR, AND UNDRESS; 868] *Opposite*: dress **2** *v* **deprive**, take away, divest, deny, rid [→ TAKE SOMETHING AWAY; 425] *Opposite*: furnish (*formal*) **3** *n* **band**, sliver, shred, ribbon, slip, bit, stripe, belt [→ AREA AND RANGE; 111]

stripe *n* **band of color**, strip, band, line, streak, bar [→ PATTERNS; 1225]

striped *adj* [→ DESCRIBING PATTERNS; 1227]

striplight *type of* **light** [→ LIGHT; 1164]

strip off *v* [→ DRESS, WEAR, AND UNDRESS; 868]

stripped *adj* **bare**, exposed, unprotected, uncovered, unvarnished, unpainted [→ LESS; 126] *Opposite*: coated

stripped-down *adj* **lean**, spare, sparse, minimalist, utilitarian, Spartan, functional, basic [→ LESS; 126]

stripped of *adj* [→ LACK OF POSSESSION; 445]

stripy (*UK*) *adj* [→ DESCRIBING PATTERNS; 1227]

strive *v* **struggle**, go all out, do your best, do your utmost, make every effort, try hard, attempt, try, do all you can, pull out all the stops, endeavor (*formal*) [→ HARD WORK OR EFFORT; 298]

See Compare and Contrast at **try**.

stroganoff *type of* **food presentation** [→ COOKING AND FOOD PREPARATION; 353]

stroke 1 *n* **hit**, blow, knock, rap, lash, thump, whack [→ CONTACT: IMPACT; 413] **2** *n* **rub**, caress, fondle, pat [→ CONTACT: TOUCH; 412] **3** *v* **caress**, fondle, pat, rub [→ CONTACT: TOUCH; 412]

stroke of luck *n* [→ LUCK; 783]

stroll 1 *v* **walk**, amble, saunter, ramble, go for a constitutional, wander, promenade (*formal*) [→ MOVE SLOWLY; 314] **2** *n* **saunter**, walk, amble, turn, wander, meander, ramble, constitutional, promenade (*formal*) [→ PROCEED AND GO; 305]

stroller *n* **buggy**, baby carriage, baby buggy, pushchair (*UK*) [→ BIKES, CARS, AND CARRIAGES; 1149]

strong 1 *adj* **powerful**, burly, brawny, muscular, sturdy, well-built, tough, beefy, stalwart, strapping (*informal*) [→ BUILD; 477] *Opposite*: weak **2** *adj* **robust**, sturdy, stout, solid, durable, resilient, tough, heavy-duty, hard-wearing [→ DURABLE; 1210] *Opposite*: fragile **3** *adj* **intense**, concentrated, pungent, piquant, spicy, hot, sharp, biting [→ TASTE; 703] *Opposite*: insipid **4** *adj* **glaring**, dazzling, bright, stark, brilliant, intense [→ DESCRIBING LIGHT; 1228] *Opposite*: dim **5** *adj* **convincing**, sound, clear, clear-cut, persuasive, compelling, effective, formidable [→ STRENGTH; 201] *Opposite*: weak **6** *adj* **fervent**, great, intense, deep, deep-seated, fierce, powerful, potent, passionate, ardent [→ STRENGTH; 201] *Opposite*: weak **7** *adj* **keen**, staunch, dedicated, firm, fanatical, zealous, eager [→ ENERGY AND ENTHUSIASM; 496] *Opposite*: indifferent

strong-arm (*informal*) **1** *adj* **coercive**, forcible, violent, physical, forceful, bullying, aggressive [→ FRIGHTENING; 231] *Opposite*: peaceable **2** *v* **coerce**, compel, force, frighten, bully, threaten [→ CAUSE OR COMPEL TO ACT; 271]

strongbox *n* **safe-deposit box**, cash box, safe, coffer, vault [→ CONTAINERS, RECEPTACLES, AND PACKAGING; 1245]

stronghold *n* **fortress**, refuge, bastion, citadel, sanctuary, fort, castle, fastness (*archaic or literary*) [→ FORTRESSES AND FORTIFICATIONS; 1090]

strong-minded 1 *adj* **determined**, dogged, persevering, persistent, resolute, unyielding, single-minded, tenacious, unwavering, strong-willed, indomitable, firm, uncompromising [→ STRENGTH OF WILL; 501] *Opposite*: weak-willed **2** *adj* **confident**, clear-thinking, certain, intelligent, decisive, independent [→ POSITIVE INTELLECTUAL CHARACTERISTICS; 524]

strong-mindedness 1 *n* **determination**, doggedness, perseverance, persistence, resoluteness, unyieldingness, single-mindedness, tenacity, indomitability, firmness [→ STRENGTH OF WILL; 501] *Opposite*: vacillation **2** *n* **confidence**, strength, strength of character, character, clarity, certainty, intelligence, decisiveness, independence [→ POSITIVE INTELLECTUAL CHARACTERISTICS; 524] *Opposite*: weakness

strong point *n* **strength**, strong suit, forte, asset, métier [→ SKILLS, TALENTS, AND ABILITIES; 526] *Opposite*: weakness

strongroom *type of* **storage space** [→ STORES AND STORAGE BUILDINGS; 1088]

strong suit *n* **forte**, strength, strong point, métier, asset [→ SKILLS, TALENTS, AND ABILITIES; 526] *Opposite*: weakness

strong-willed *adj* **resolute**, determined, strong-minded, iron-willed, unbending, inflexible, uncompromising, forceful, decisive [➡ STRENGTH OF WILL; 501] *Opposite*: weak

strophe *n* [➡ ASPECTS OF LANGUAGE; 682]

structural 1 *adj* **physical**, mechanical, organizational, operational [➡ BUILDING AND ARCHITECTURE; 1076] 2 *adj* **basic**, important, essential, fundamental, underlying [➡ IMPORTANT; 194]

structure 1 *n* **construction**, assembly, building, edifice, erection (*formal*) [➡ BUILDING AND ARCHITECTURE; 1076] 2 *n* **arrangement**, organization, construction, configuration, makeup, constitution, formation, composition [➡ QUALITIES AND CHARACTERISTICS; 1191] 3 *v* **arrange**, construct, configure, put together, make up, shape, form, organize, build up, constitute (*formal*) [➡ ARRANGE AND CREATE ORDER; 357]

structured 1 *adj* **organized**, planned, controlled, designed, arranged, tight, well-thought-out, regulated, systematized, coordinated [➡ ORDER AND ORGANIZATION; 206] *Opposite*: unstructured 2 *adj* **defined**, coordinated, well-defined, designed, formal, fitted, shaped [➡ DESCRIBING CLOTHES; 869] *Opposite*: amorphous

strudel *type of* **cake** [➡ CAKES, COOKIES, AND DESSERTS; 1181]

struggle 1 *v* **writhe**, wriggle, thrash, resist, fight back, fight, kick, thrash about (*UK*) [➡ FIDGET AND FROLIC; 311] 2 *v* **fight**, grapple, tussle, wrestle, brawl, scuffle, battle [➡ COMPETE, CONTEND, AND COMBAT; 303] 3 *v* **strive**, try, strain, fight, labor, work hard, toil [➡ HARD WORK OR EFFORT; 298] 4 *n* **tussle**, fight, brawl, scuffle, skirmish, melee, battle, scrap (*informal*), free-for-all (*informal*) [➡ AGGRESSIVE EVENTS; 39] 5 *n* **effort**, exertion, labor, toil, work [➡ HARD WORK OR EFFORT; 298]

struggle on *v* [➡ TOLERATE AND ENDURE; 766]

struggle through *v* [➡ TOLERATE AND ENDURE; 766]

strum *v* **play**, thrum, improvise, jam, twang, noodle (*slang*) [➡ MUSIC, SONGS, AND SINGING; 907]

strung out (*informal*) *adj* **overwrought**, tense, tired, nervous, irritable, fractious, worked up (*informal*) [➡ CONFUSION, ANXIETY, AND WORRY; 540] *Opposite*: relaxed

strut 1 *v* **swagger**, march, parade, prance, walk, sashay (*humorous*) [➡ MOVE FAST; 313] 2 *n* **support**, rod, brace, crosspiece, girder, bar, beam [➡ BUILDING MATERIALS; 1077]

stub 1 *n* **stump**, end, remains, remnant, counterfoil [➡ JUNK AND USELESS OBJECTS; 1249] 2 *v* **hit**, bump, bang, knock, bash (*informal*) [➡ CONTACT: IMPACT; 413]

stubble 1 *n* **whiskers**, five o'clock shadow, growth, beard, mustache [➡ FACIAL HAIR; 489] 2 *n* **stalks**, stems, debris, refuse, leavings, straw, rubbish (*UK*) [➡ JUNK AND USELESS OBJECTS; 1249]

stubbly *adj* [➡ FACIAL HAIR; 489]

stubborn 1 *adj* **obstinate**, immovable, inflexible, willful, mulish, obdurate, pigheaded, intractable (*formal*) [➡ UNWILLINGNESS AND STUBBORNNESS; 564] *Opposite*: flexible 2 *adj* **persistent**, dogged, tenacious, persevering, determined, stalwart [➡ STRENGTH OF WILL; 501] *Opposite*: half-hearted

stubbornness 1 *n* **obstinacy**, inflexibility, obduracy, pigheadedness, mulishness, willfulness, intractability (*formal*) [➡ UNWILLINGNESS AND STUBBORNNESS; 564] *Opposite*: flexi-

bility 2 *n* **persistence**, tenacity, perseverance, doggedness, stalwartness, determination [➡ STRENGTH OF WILL; 501]

stubby *adj* **short**, broad, thick, stumpy, squat, stout [➡ BUILD; 477] *Opposite*: slender

stub out *v* **extinguish**, put out, snuff [➡ CAUSE TO STOP; 266]

stucco *n* [➡ BUILDING MATERIALS; 1077]

stuccowork *n* [➡ BUILDING MATERIALS; 1077]

stuck 1 *adj* **wedged**, fixed, trapped, caught, jammed, immovable, held [➡ LACK OF ACTIVITY OR MOTION; 342] *Opposite*: loose 2 *adj* **baffled**, mystified, puzzled, without an answer, at a complete loss, stumped [➡ CONFUSION, ANXIETY, AND WORRY; 540]

stuck on (*informal*) *adj* [➡ APPRECIATION AND GRATITUDE; 535]

stuck-up (*informal*) *adj* **snobbish**, arrogant, conceited, superior, self-important, condescending, haughty, snooty [➡ AFFECTATION, SELF-SATISFACTION, AND SNOBBISHNESS; 507] *Opposite*: unassuming

stud 1 *n* **knob**, boss, rivet, nail, screw, protrusion, button, bump [➡ FASTENERS, LINKS, AND NETWORKS; 1247] 2 *type of* **jewelry** [➡ JEWELRY; 866] 3 *v* **dot**, pepper, sprinkle, scatter, speckle, cover [➡ DECORATE, ADORN, AND APPLY COATINGS; 405] 4 *v* **boss**, emboss, fit with studs, decorate, fasten, rivet, secure [➡ FASTEN, LINK, AND JOIN; 408]

student *n* **scholar**, pupil, schoolboy, schoolgirl, school-child, undergraduate, apprentice, learner [➡ STUDENTS AND PUPILS; 841]

student loan *n* **loan**, bank loan, government loan, educational loan, subsidized loan [➡ FUNDS, PAYMENTS, AND CHARGES; 800]

studied *adj* **deliberate**, intentional, calculated, considered, premeditated, planned, willful [➡ INTENTIONAL AND DELIBERATE; 279] *Opposite*: spontaneous

studio 1 *n* **workplace**, workshop, workroom, atelier, pottery, workspace [➡ PLACE OF EMPLOYMENT; 832] 2 *n* **academy**, conservatory, dance school, ballet school, dance academy [➡ EDUCATIONAL INSTITUTIONS; 813] 3 *type of* **apartment** [➡ RESIDENTIAL BUILDINGS; 1078]

studio couch *type of* **bed** [➡ FURNITURE; 858]

studious 1 *adj* **thoughtful**, serious, reflective, bookish, scholarly, academic, intellectual, erudite, brainy (*informal*) [➡ LEVELS OF EDUCATION AND SOPHISTICATION; 894] *Opposite*: frivolous 2 *adj* **diligent**, painstaking, careful, assiduous, industrious, meticulous, hard-working, earnest, purposeful, determined [➡ HARD-WORKING AND COMMITTED; 500] *Opposite*: careless

studiously 1 *adv* **thoughtfully**, seriously, reflectively, deeply, intensely, profoundly [➡ ENTHUSIASTIC AND INQUISITIVE; 628] *Opposite*: frivolously 2 *adv* **diligently**, painstakingly, carefully, assiduously, industriously, meticulously, earnestly, purposefully, determinedly [➡ HARD-WORKING AND COMMITTED; 500] *Opposite*: carelessly

studiousness 1 *n* **thoughtfulness**, application, seriousness, concentration, focus [➡ POSITIVE INTELLECTUAL CHARACTERISTICS; 524] *Opposite*: inattention 2 *n* **diligence**, care, assiduousness, industry, meticulousness, conscientiousness [➡ HARD-WORKING AND COMMITTED; 500] *Opposite*: carelessness

study 1 *v* **learn**, take in, review, grind, read, bone up (*informal*), cram (*informal*), hit the books (*informal*), revise (*UK*) [➡ STUDYING; 844] *Opposite*: forget 2 *v* **investigate**, research, experiment, examine, consider, scrutinize, analyze, look into, explore, probe, delve into [➡ EXAMINE AND ASSESS; 753] 3 *n* **learning**, education, training, schoolwork, lessons, homework, scholarship, revision (*UK*) [➡ CLASSES, COURSEWORK, AND EXAMINATIONS; 842] 4 *n* **report**, findings, conclusions, research paper, analysis, paper, feedback [➡ ANALYTICAL NONFICTION WRITING; 592] 5 *n* **investigation**, survey, experiment, review, inquiry, research, analysis, examination, search, scrutiny, consideration [➡ EXAMINE AND ASSESS; 753] 6 *type of* **room in the home** [➡ TYPES OF ROOMS; 1097]

study leave *n* [➡ PERIODS OF REST; 91]

stuff 1 *v* **fill**, pack, cram, ram, jam, stow, load, squeeze [➡ FILL; 406] 2 *n* **material**, substance, matter, raw material [➡ SUBSTANCES; 1267] 3 *n* **things**, objects, paraphernalia, articles, mess, packages, gear, bits and pieces (*informal*), junk (*informal*) [➡ PHYSICAL OBJECTS; 1243] 4 *n* **possessions**, belongings, things, kit, tackle, personal effects, property, equipment, gear (*informal*), effects (*formal*) [➡ POSSESSIONS; 461]

stuff and nonsense (*UK*) *n* [➡ MEANINGLESS SPEECH OR WRITING; 676]

stuffed 1 *adj* **filled**, lined, packed, jammed, crammed, bursting, jam-packed (*informal*) [➡ FULL; 1239] 2 *adj* (*informal*) **full**, fit to burst, replete, sated, satiated, bloated, satisfied [➡ EAT AND NOT EAT; 710] *Opposite*: hungry

stuffed shirt (*informal*) *n* **fogy**, old fogy, killjoy, spoilsport, fuddy-duddy (*informal*), stick-in-the-mud (*informal*), wet blanket (*informal*) [➡ SELF-IMPORTANT AND SELF-SEEKING PEOPLE; 949]

stuffiness 1 *n* **airlessness**, staleness, closeness, mugginess, fug [➡ HOT WEATHER; 1050] *Opposite*: freshness 2 *n* **formality**, conventionality, staidness, standoffishness, pomposity, aloofness, strictness [➡ UNADVENTUROUS AND DULL; 517] *Opposite*: informality

stuffing *n* [➡ CENTRAL PARTS OF PHYSICAL OBJECTS; 1251]

stuffy 1 *adj* **airless**, stale, smelly, hot, warm, dry, smoky, suffocating, fusty, unventilated, stifling [➡ HOT WEATHER; 1050] *Opposite*: fresh 2 *adj* **strait-laced**, old-fashioned, conventional, formal, pompous, strict, dry, narrow, smug, supercilious, stodgy [➡ UNADVENTUROUS AND DULL; 517] *Opposite*: informal 3 *adj* **congested**, blocked up, rheumy, stopped up, clogged up [➡ FULL; 1239] *Opposite*: clear

stultify 1 *v* **bore**, dull, numb, deaden, put off, put to sleep [➡ BORE AND FAIL TO INTEREST; 570] *Opposite*: stimulate 2 *v* **make a fool of**, belittle, ridicule, humiliate, set up (*informal*) [➡ JOKES AND TEASING; 674] 3 *v* **cancel out**, block, render useless, preempt, vitiate, cripple, hamstring, negate (*formal*), queer somebody's pitch (*UK*) [➡ MAKE IMPOSSIBLE; 276] *Opposite*: advance

stultifying *adj* [➡ PHYSICALLY UNPLEASANT; 226]

stumble 1 *v* **trip**, trip up, lose your footing, lose your balance, falter, fall, sprawl, lurch, topple [➡ GO DOWNWARD; 307] 2 *v* **stagger**, lurch, sway, blunder, roll, totter, teeter, reel, flounder, hobble, pitch [➡ WALK UNSTEADILY; 315] 3 *v* **hesitate**, stop and start, hem and haw, falter, stammer, stutter, blunder, pause, waver [➡ HESITATE; 272] 4 *v* **come across**, find, discover, happen on, chance on, turn up, hit on, fall upon, blunder across [➡ FIND; 463] 5 *n* **blunder**, trip, stagger, false step, mishap, upset, accident, misstep, spill, fall [➡ DISASTERS; 252] 6 *n* **mistake**, hesitation, slip, blunder, slip-up (*informal*), bungle (*informal*) [➡ MISTAKES; 250]

See Compare and Contrast at **hesitate**.

stumble across *v* [➡ FIND; 463]

stumble on *v* [➡ FIND; 463]

stumble upon *v* [➡ FIND; 463]

stumbling block *n* **obstacle**, problem, difficulty, sticking point, obstruction, barrier, snag, hindrance, impediment, hurdle [➡ PROBLEMS; 256] *Opposite*: aid

stump 1 *n* **base**, stub, butt, end, remains, remnant, nubbin [➡ JUNK AND USELESS OBJECTS; 1249] 2 *v* **baffle**, puzzle, perplex, mystify, nonplus, bewilder, confound, confuse, dumbfound, stymie, flummox (*informal*), bamboozle (*informal*) [➡ CONFUSE AND BEWILDER; 571] *Opposite*: enlighten

stumped *adj* [➡ CONFUSION, ANXIETY, AND WORRY; 540]

stumpy *adj* **squat**, stubby, short, thickset, broad, stocky, diminutive [➡ BUILD; 477] *Opposite*: lanky

stun 1 *v* **shock**, upset, dumbfound, daze, amaze, astonish, astound, stagger, confound, bewilder, flabbergast, startle [➡ CONFUSE AND BEWILDER; 571] 2 *v* **knock out**, paralyse, numb, daze, put out of action, stupefy, lay out (*informal*) [➡ BECOME SICK, TREAT, AND RECOVER; 728] *Opposite*: bring around

stung *adj* [➡ SADNESS, DISTRESS, AND DESPAIR; 539]

stunned *adj* [➡ SURPRISE, SHOCK, AND AMAZEMENT; 545]

stunner (*informal*) *n* **star**, smash, sensation, hit, triumph, knockout (*informal*), wow (*informal*), blockbuster (*informal*), lulu (*slang*), doozy (*slang*), humdinger (*slang*) [➡ AMAZING THINGS; 211]

stunning *adj* **spectacular**, striking, fabulous, splendid, superb, magnificent, gorgeous, exquisite, impressive [➡ EXTRAORDINARY: AMAZING; 204] *Opposite*: unimpressive

stunningly *adv* **spectacularly**, strikingly, fabulously, splendidly, superbly, magnificently, gorgeously, exquisitely, impressively, astoundingly, astonishingly [➡ EXTRAORDINARY: AMAZING; 204] *Opposite*: unimpressively

stunt 1 *v* **inhibit**, restrict, arrest, hold back, impede, slow up, slow down, check, curtail, curb, cramp [➡ DELAY ACTION OR OCCURRENCE; 278] *Opposite*: assist 2 *n* **feat**, exploit, act, deed, show, tour de force, trick, number [➡ ACTIONS OR UNDERTAKINGS; 259]

stunt bicycling *type of* **extreme sport** [➡ HOBBIES, GAMES, AND SPORTS; 875]

stunted *adj* **underdeveloped**, undersized, small, short, little, diminutive [➡ LENGTH: SHORT; 1198]

stupefaction 1 *n* (*literary*) **amazement**, astonishment, wonder, surprise, awe, wonderment [➡ SURPRISE, SHOCK, AND AMAZEMENT; 545] 2 *n* **confusion**, befuddlement, bemusement, perplexity, bewilderment, wooziness, doziness [➡ CONFUSION, ANXIETY, AND WORRY; 540]

stupefied 1 *adj* **confused**, fuddled, punch-drunk, stunned, befuddled, bemused, muddled, dazed, staggered

[➡CONFUSION, ANXIETY, AND WORRY; 540] *Opposite:* clear-headed **2** *adj* **amazed**, astonished, astounded, stunned, dazed, confounded, shocked, baffled, mystified, surprised [➡SURPRISE, SHOCK, AND AMAZEMENT; 545]

stupefy 1 *v* **amaze**, astonish, astound, surprise, stagger, overwhelm, shock, flabbergast, nonplus [➡SURPRISE AND IMPRESS; 574] **2** *v* **confuse**, befuddle, bewilder, stun, perplex, bemuse, daze, dumbfound, stagger [➡CONFUSE AND BEWILDER; 571] *Opposite:* enlighten

stupendous 1 *adj* **astonishing**, astounding, amazing, surprising, stunning, awesome, breathtaking, remarkable [➡EXTRAORDINARY: AMAZING; 204] *Opposite:* unremarkable **2** *adj* **fantastic**, wonderful, out of this world, marvelous, great, fabulous, splendid, terrific (*informal*) [➡EXTRAORDINARY: AMAZING; 204] *Opposite:* awful **3** *adj* **huge**, vast, large, colossal, enormous, gigantic, considerable, mammoth, prodigious, tremendous [➡LARGE; 1193] *Opposite:* tiny

stupendously *adv* **tremendously**, impressively, amazingly, exceptionally, remarkably, strikingly, spectacularly, terrifically, extremely, astoundingly, massively (*informal*) [➡TO A GREAT EXTENT; 132] *Opposite:* slightly

stupid 1 *adj* **unintelligent**, dull, brainless, obtuse, witless [➡NEGATIVE INTELLECTUAL CHARACTERISTICS; 525] *Opposite:* intelligent **2** *adj* **unwise**, senseless, ill-advised, imprudent, injudicious, thoughtless, rash, irresponsible, reckless, heedless [➡THE NATURE OF IDEAS; 771] *Opposite:* wise **3** *adj* **foolish**, fatuous, inane, nonsensical, silly, futile, ludicrous, ridiculous, laughable, senseless, absurd, asinine [➡BIZARRE AND PECULIAR; 257] *Opposite:* sensible

stupidity *n* **foolishness**, foolhardiness, silliness, inanity, folly, futility, senselessness, absurdity [➡NEGATIVE INTELLECTUAL CHARACTERISTICS; 525] *Opposite:* sense

stupidly *adv* **foolishly**, unwisely, naively, unthinkingly, inanely, senselessly, nonsensically [➡NEGATIVE INTELLECTUAL CHARACTERISTICS; 525] *Opposite:* sensibly

stupor 1 *n* **torpor**, lethargy, inertness, limpness, blankness, vacancy, apathy, inertia [➡PAIN AND OTHER PHYSICAL SENSATIONS; 733] *Opposite:* activeness **2** *n* **daze**, dream, trance, shock, numbness, paralysis, stupefaction (*literary*) [➡SURPRISE, SHOCK, AND AMAZEMENT; 545] *Opposite:* consciousness

sturdiness *n* **strength**, solidity, durability, toughness, hardiness, robustness, vigor [➡DURABLE; 1210] *Opposite:* weakness

sturdy 1 *adj* **well-made**, durable, robust, tough, strong, solid, secure, substantial, rugged, hard-wearing [➡DURABLE; 1210] *Opposite:* rickety **2** *adj* **well-built**, strong, robust, powerful, muscular, brawny, mighty, burly, strapping (*informal*) [➡BUILD; 477] *Opposite:* frail **3** *adj* **resolute**, decisive, determined, strenuous, enthusiastic, energetic, forceful, steadfast [➡STRENGTH OF WILL; 501] *Opposite:* feeble

sturgeon *type of* **ocean fish** [➡OCEAN FISH; 1009]

stutter 1 *v* **stammer**, trip over your tongue, falter, stumble, hesitate, mumble, sputter, splutter [➡CHATTER AND BABBLE; 617] *Opposite:* enunciate **2** *n* **stammer**, speech disorder, impediment, impairment, speech impediment [➡INARTICULATE, RAMBLING, AND AWKWARD; 633]

sty 1 *n* **cyst**, swelling, lump, boil, sore, spot [➡CONDITIONS

AFFECTING THE SKIN; 721] **2** *type of* **pen or cage** [➡ANIMAL OR BIRD ACCOMMODATIONS; 1079]

style 1 *n* **method**, approach, way, manner, fashion, technique, mode [➡WAYS OF DOING THINGS; 294] **2** *n* **flair**, panache, chic, bravura, stylishness, smartness, good taste, elegance, grace, polish, class, charm [➡WELL-GROOMED; 482] *Opposite:* gracelessness **3** *n* **design**, type, sort, form, variety, quality, character, kind, pattern, mold [➡VARIETIES, TYPES, AND KINDS; 145] **4** *n* **luxury**, luxuriousness, extravagance, lavishness, opulence, grandeur, elegance, comfort, wealth [➡EXPENSIVE AND LUXURIOUS; 218] **5** *part of* **flower** [➡FLOWERS; 1032] **6** *v* (*formal*) **name**, call, nickname, label, term, dub, entitle [➡NAME AND DESCRIBE; 665] **7** *v* **fashion**, design, shape, cut, adapt, tailor [➡CHANGE OF SHAPE; 385]

styling gel *n* [➡PERSONAL HYGIENE; 491]

styling spray *n* [➡PERSONAL HYGIENE; 491]

stylish *adj* **fashionable**, sophisticated, chic, modish, smart, elegant, tasteful, voguish, polished, trendy (*informal*), classy (*informal*) [➡WELL-GROOMED; 482] *Opposite:* unfashionable

stylishness *n* **style**, flair, chic, panache, smartness, good taste, elegance, grace [➡WELL-GROOMED; 482] *Opposite:* dowdiness

stylistic *adj* **formal**, technical, literary, musical, artistic, aesthetic [➡ARTISTIC MOVEMENTS AND STYLES; 899] *Opposite:* spontaneous

stylize *v* **formalize**, abstract, schematize, systematize, outline, reduce, portray, render (*formal*) [➡CREATE IMAGES; 356]

stylized *adj* **conventional**, artificial, formalized, formal, unnatural, flat, schematic [➡FALSE AND UNREAL; 173] *Opposite:* natural

stylus *part of* **audio equipment** [➡AUDIO EQUIPMENT; 1139]

stymie 1 *v* **hinder**, prevent, block, thwart, confound, frustrate, upset, stump, mystify, baffle [➡MAKE IMPOSSIBLE; 276] *Opposite:* enable **2** *n* **impasse**, dead end, stalemate, standstill, deadlock, standoff [➡PROBLEMS; 256] *Opposite:* breakthrough

stymied *adj* [➡CONFUSION, ANXIETY, AND WORRY; 540]

suave *adj* **urbane**, smooth, polished, polite, sophisticated, formal, impeccable, gracious, charming, mannerly [➡LEVELS OF EDUCATION AND SOPHISTICATION; 894] *Opposite:* awkward

sub (*informal*) *v* [➡CHANGE ONE THING FOR ANOTHER; 398]

subcategory *n* **subsection**, subclass, subgroup, subdivision [➡VARIETIES, TYPES, AND KINDS; 145]

subcompact *type of* **car** [➡BIKES, CARS, AND CARRIAGES; 1149]

subconscious *adj* **unconscious**, intuitive, hidden, unintentional, involuntary, subliminal [➡AUTOMATIC AND INSTINCTIVE; 280] *Opposite:* deliberate

subcontract *v* **delegate**, farm out, contract out, commission, mandate, authorize [➡BUSINESS ACTIVITIES AND PHENOMENA; 794]

subcultural *adj* **cultural**, social, ethnic, religious, sociological, socioanthropological, sociocultural, anthropological [➡ BELONGING OR RELATING TO PEOPLE; 943]

subculture *n* subgroup, culture, grouping, group, subdivision, division [➡ GROUPS IN SOCIETY; 940]

subcutaneous *adj* hypodermic, hypodermal, intravenous, internal, dermatological, dermal, medical [➡ THE SKIN; 720]

subdirectory 1 *n* division, subdivision, directory, file, storage space [➡ SUBDIVISIONS AND OFFSHOOTS; 1253] 2 *type of* computer feature [➡ COMPUTERS AND COMPUTING; 1127]

subdivide *v* divide, section, segment, split, cut, partition, divide up, split up, cut up [➡ SEPARATE AND DIVIDE; 401] *Opposite*: unify

subdivision 1 *n* section, part, division, sector, tract, development, portion, slice, unit [➡ AREA AND RANGE; 111] 2 *n* division, sectioning, segmenting, separation, splitting up, partitioning [➡ SEPARATE AND DIVIDE; 401] *Opposite*: unification

subdue 1 *v* restrain, suppress, hold back, control, discipline, tame, check [➡ AVOID, PREVENT, LIMIT, AND CONTROL; 271] 2 *v* pacify, calm, calm down, soothe, mollify, placate, reduce, soften, moderate [➡ SOOTHE AND CALM; 573] 3 *v* subjugate, conquer, vanquish, defeat, overpower, overcome, crush, quell, overwhelm [➡ BEAT AND DEFEAT; 80]

subdued 1 *adj* gentle, low, restrained, muted, subtle, soft, hushed, quiet [➡ DESCRIBING LIGHT; 1228] *Opposite*: loud 2 *adj* passive, cowed, submissive, quiet, unresponsive, restrained, serious, downcast [➡ LIFELESS, LAZY, AND UNENTHUSIASTIC; 506] *Opposite*: uplifted

subeditor (*UK*) *n* assistant editor, editorial assistant, assistant, deputy editor, deputy, second in command, copy editor, editor, proofreader, checker [➡ WORKERS IN ENTERTAINMENT AND MEDIA; 873]

subgroup *n* subcategory, subsection, subclass, subdivision, smaller group, minor group [➡ VARIETIES, TYPES, AND KINDS; 145]

subhuman *adj* bestial, animal, inhuman, inhumane, wicked, less than human [➡ BEASTLY AND BRUTISH; 510]

subject 1 *n* topic, theme, focus, subject matter, area under discussion, question, issue, matter, business, substance, text [➡ SUBJECT AREAS; 768] 2 *n* specialty, field, study, discipline, area [➡ SUBJECT AREAS; 768] 3 *n* subordinate, vassal, liege, dependent, citizen [➡ SUBORDINATES AND ASSISTANTS; 966] *Opposite*: sovereign 4 *type of* grammatical term [➡ ASPECTS OF LANGUAGE; 682]

Compare and Contrast: *subject*, *topic*, *subject matter*, *matter*, *theme*, *burden*

CORE MEANING: what is under discussion

subject a matter that is under discussion or investigation; *topic* a matter dealt with in a text or discussion; *subject matter* the material dealt with in a movie, discussion, or other medium; *matter* the material that is dealt with in speech or writing, as opposed to its presentation; *theme* a distinct, recurring, and unifying idea in music, literature, art, or film; *burden* (*literary*) the main argument or recurrent theme in music or literature.

---

subjection *n* domination, subjugation, overpowering, enslavement, oppression [➡ FAILURE; 77]

subjective 1 *adj* slanted, biased, prejudiced, skewed, one-sided [➡ THE NATURE OF IDEAS; 771] *Opposite*: objective 2 *adj* individual, particular, idiosyncratic, independent, personal [➡ BELONGING OR RELATING TO INDIVIDUALS; 944] *Opposite*: general

subjectively *adv* personally, individually, one-sidedly, instinctively, intuitively, emotionally [➡ THE NATURE OF IDEAS; 771] *Opposite*: objectively

subjectivity *n* bias, prejudice, partisanship, partiality [➡ THE NATURE OF IDEAS; 771] *Opposite*: objectivity

subject matter *n* topic, theme, subject, focus, question, issue, matter, business, substance, text [➡ SUBJECT AREAS; 768]

See Compare and Contrast at **subject**.

---

subject to 1 *v* cause to experience, cause to undergo, expose to, put through, make susceptible, make liable, make prone [➡ CAUSE OR COMPEL TO ACT; 271] 2 *adj* conditional on, dependent on, depending on, bound by, answerable to [➡ RECIPROCITY AND INTERDEPENDENCE; 147] *Opposite*: unrelated

subjugate *v* conquer, vanquish, subdue, defeat, overpower, overcome, crush, suppress, quell, overwhelm [➡ BEAT AND DEFEAT; 80] *Opposite*: liberate

subjunctive *type of* grammatical term [➡ ASPECTS OF LANGUAGE; 682]

sublease *v* [➡ LEND, LEASE, AND BORROW; 428]

sublet *v* [➡ LEND, LEASE, AND BORROW; 428]

sublimate *v* channel, redirect, transfer, direct, reroute [➡ NOT PAY ATTENTION; 764]

sublimation *n* redirection, transferal, direction, rerouting, division [➡ PSYCHOLOGY AND THE MIND; 769]

sublime 1 *adj* inspiring, inspirational, uplifting, awe-inspiring, moving, transcendent, magnificent, heavenly, beautiful, exalted (*formal*) [➡ EMOTIONALLY PLEASANT; 187] *Opposite*: ridiculous 2 *adj* (*informal*) excellent, superb, splendid, marvelous, wonderful, great, terrific [➡ EXTRAORDINARY: UNCOMMON; 205]

subliminal *adj* subconscious, unconscious, hidden, concealed, unintentional [➡ PSYCHOLOGY AND THE MIND; 769] *Opposite*: conscious

submachine gun *type of* gun [➡ WEAPONS FOR SHOOTING; 1156]

submarine *type of* military vessel [➡ SHIPS AND BOATS; 1150]

submerge 1 *v* plunge, immerse, dip, sink, duck, lower [➡ MOVE SOMETHING: DOWNWARD; 329] 2 *v* suppress, conceal, hide, stifle [➡ WITHHOLD INFORMATION; 687] *Opposite*: reveal

submerged *adj* underwater, flooded, inundated, waterlogged, sunken [➡ WET; 1240]

submicroscopic *adj* [➡ SMALL; 1195]

submission 1 *n* obedience, compliance, capitulation, surrender, acquiescence, deference, assent [➡ THE WILL AND WILLINGNESS; 563] *Opposite*: resistance 2 *n* proposal, suggestion, plan, tender, offer, idea [➡ SUGGEST, HINT, AND COMMENT; 612]

submissive *adj* **obedient**, passive, compliant, acquiescent, subservient, docile, meek, dutiful, tractable, deferential, accommodating [➡ THE WILL AND WILLINGNESS; 563] *Opposite*: assertive

submit 1 *v* **present**, propose, tender, offer, suggest [➡ SUGGEST, HINT, AND COMMENT; 612] *Opposite*: withdraw 2 *v* **give in**, yield, agree to, acquiesce, resign yourself to, defer to, bow to, surrender, capitulate [➡ FORGET, FORGIVE, AND ACCEPT; 748] *Opposite*: resist

See Compare and Contrast at **yield**.

subnormal *adj* **substandard**, second-rate, poor, inferior, below average, deficient, insufficient [➡ INFERIORITY; 153] *Opposite*: superior

subordinate 1 *adj* **secondary**, lesser, subsidiary, inferior, lower, outranked, subservient, minor [➡ RELATIONSHIP TO ANOTHER; 973] *Opposite*: main 2 *n* **assistant**, junior, underling, minion, aide, dependent, attendant [➡ SUBORDINATES AND ASSISTANTS; 966] *Opposite*: boss

subordination *n* **relegation**, demotion, reduction, subservience [➡ INFERIORITY; 153]

suborn *v* **incite**, bribe, induce, entice, corrupt, pay off (*informal*) [➡ CAUSE OR COMPEL TO ACT; 271]

subpoena 1 *n* **summons**, order, call [➡ TRIAL, PUNISHMENT, AND LEGAL OUTCOMES; 819] 2 *v* **summon**, compel, require, order, command [➡ TRIAL, PUNISHMENT, AND LEGAL OUTCOMES; 819]

subscribe 1 *v* **donate to**, give to, pledge, promise, contribute, pitch in, kick in (*informal*), chip in (*informal*) [➡ GIVE MONEY; 433] 2 *v* **agree with**, approve of, support, condone, hold with, advocate, endorse, assent, go along with [➡ AGREE; 645] *Opposite*: disagree

subscription *n* **payment**, donation, contribution [➡ EXPENDITURE; 423]

subsequent *adj* **following**, succeeding, ensuing, successive, consequent, later [➡ AFTER, LAST, AND FOLLOWING; 165] *Opposite*: preceding

subservient *adj* **obedient**, compliant, acquiescent, docile, deferential, passive, meek, servile, submissive [➡ THE WILL AND WILLINGNESS; 563] *Opposite*: assertive

subset *n* **subsection**, subdivision, subgroup, subcategory, subclass [➡ VARIETIES, TYPES, AND KINDS; 145]

subside 1 *v* **diminish**, lessen, decrease, dwindle, wane, recede, quieten down, settle down, moderate, abate (*formal or literary*) [➡ CHANGE OF INTENSITY: LESS; 395] *Opposite*: build up 2 *v* **collapse**, cave in, fall down, drop, sink, slip, settle, descend, sag [➡ GO DOWNWARD; 307] *Opposite*: rise

subsidence *n* **subsiding**, sinking, settling, dropping, collapsing, falling, descending, sagging [➡ EROSION AND WEATHERING; 1055]

subsidiary 1 *adj* **subordinate**, lesser, secondary, junior, lower, minor [➡ INFERIORITY; 153] *Opposite*: major 2 *adj* **supplementary**, auxiliary, ancillary, additional, contributory, secondary, extra [➡ MORE AND EXCESS; 124] *Opposite*: main 3 *n* **company**, firm, holding, business, affiliate, division, branch [➡ BUSINESS ENTERPRISES AND RELATED BODIES; 792]

subsidize *v* **finance**, fund, sponsor, back, support, promote, endow, stake, underwrite, bankroll (*informal*) [➡ GIVE MONEY; 433]

subsidy *n* **funding**, financial backing, grant, support, aid, appropriation, backing, sponsorship, subsidization, subvention (*formal*) [➡ EXPENDITURE; 423]

subsist *v* **exist**, survive, live, make ends meet, keep going, eke out a living, keep your head above water [➡ CONTINUE TO EXIST; 17]

subsistence *n* **survival**, existence, maintenance, sustenance [➡ PERMANENCE: WITHOUT END; 94]

subspecies *n* **category**, strain, genus, sort, class [➡ VARIETIES, TYPES, AND KINDS; 145]

substance 1 *n* **material**, matter, stuff, ingredient, body, constituent, element [➡ SUBSTANCES; 1267] 2 *n* **core**, essence, import, gist, nub, basis, crux, theme, soul [➡ MOST IMPORTANT THING; 197] 3 *n* **affluence**, property, money, means, wealth, riches [➡ WEALTH AND WEALTHY; 891] *Opposite*: poverty

substandard *adj* **inferior**, second-rate, poor, subnormal, below average, deficient, insufficient [➡ INFERIORITY; 153] *Opposite*: superior

substantial *adj* **considerable**, large, extensive, significant, important, generous, ample, sizable, plentiful, big, abundant [➡ LARGE; 1193] *Opposite*: small

substantially *adv* **considerably**, significantly, noticeably, markedly, greatly, substantively, extensively [➡ TO A GREAT EXTENT; 132] *Opposite*: insignificantly

substantiate *v* **validate**, authenticate, verify, corroborate, prove, confirm, demonstrate, bear out, support [➡ APPROVE AND CONFIRM; 646] *Opposite*: disprove

substantiated *adj* [➡ TRUE AND REAL; 171]

substantiation *n* **corroboration**, confirmation, validation, authentication, support, evidence, demonstration, verification, proof [➡ EVIDENCE AND PROOF; 69]

substantive 1 *adj* **practical**, applicable, functional, utilitarian [➡ USEFULNESS; 199] *Opposite*: impractical 2 *adj* **essential**, fundamental, basic, central, elementary, principal, primary [➡ IMPORTANT; 194] 3 *adj* **independent**, autonomous, separate, individual [➡ FREEDOM AND LIBERTY; 208] 4 *adj* **substantial**, decent, considerable, respectable, significant, sizable, plentiful, big, large, abundant [➡ LARGE; 1193] 5 *type of* **word class** [➡ ASPECTS OF LANGUAGE; 682]

substantively 1 *adv* **practically**, functionally, applicably [➡ USEFULNESS; 199] 2 *adv* **essentially**, fundamentally, basically, centrally, elementarily, principally, primarily [➡ IMPORTANT; 194] 3 *adv* **independently**, autonomously, individually, separately [➡ ACTING INDEPENDENTLY; 284] 4 *adv* **substantially**, considerably, significantly, noticeably, markedly, greatly, extensively [➡ TO A GREAT EXTENT; 132] *Opposite*: insignificantly

substitute 1 *v* **replace with**, exchange, use instead, switch, swap (*informal*) [➡ CHANGE ONE THING FOR ANOTHER; 398] 2 *v* **stand in for**, fill in for, take the place of, relieve, deputize for, replace [➡ REPRESENT SOMETHING OR SOMEBODY; 59] 3 *n* **alternative**, alternate, replacement, stand-in, locum, surrogate, proxy, deputy, reserve [➡ SUBSTITUTES AND STAND-INS; 399]

substitution *n* **replacement**, switch, exchange, changeover, change, swap (*informal*) [➡CHANGE ONE THING FOR ANOTHER; 398]

substratum *n* [➡COVERS AND COATINGS; 1246]

subsume *v* **include**, incorporate, count, list, consider [➡CREATING CONNECTIONS; 144]

subterfuge *n* **trick**, ploy, ruse, stratagem, maneuver, dodge, deception, machination, duplicity, con, artifice (*formal*) [➡DECEPTION AND LIES; 660]

subterranean 1 *adj* **underground**, deep, below ground, buried, hidden, concealed [➡IMPERCEPTIBLE; 26] 2 *adj* **secret**, clandestine, underground, covert, arcane, hidden, surreptitious [➡SECRET AND UNKNOWN; 179] *Opposite*: open

subtext *n* **implication**, hidden agenda, suggestion, connotation, intimation, insinuation, hint [➡MEANING; 690]

subtitle *n* **caption**, legend, surtitle, supertitle [➡FILM; 901]

subtle 1 *adj* **slight**, faint, fine, thin, imperceptible, negligible [➡IMPERCEPTIBLE; 26] *Opposite*: obvious 2 *adj* **understated**, delicate, indirect, elusive, refined, restrained [➡POSITIVELY COMPLEX OR COMPLICATED; 217] *Opposite*: blatant 3 *adj* **intelligent**, experienced, sensitive, shrewd, perceptive, clever [➡POSITIVE INTELLECTUAL CHARACTERISTICS; 524] *Opposite*: obtuse 4 *adj* **cunning**, sly, crafty, devious, tricky, artful [➡DECEITFUL; 513]

subtleness 1 *n* **delicacy**, subtlety, refinement, intricacy, elusiveness, restraint [➡POSITIVELY COMPLEX OR COMPLICATED; 217] 2 *n* **intelligence**, experience, sensitivity, shrewdness, perceptiveness, cleverness [➡POSITIVE INTELLECTUAL CHARACTERISTICS; 524] 3 *n* **cunning**, deviousness, slyness, craftiness, trickiness, artfulness [➡DECEITFUL; 513]

subtlety 1 *n* **delicacy**, subtleness, refinement, intricacy, elusiveness, restraint [➡POSITIVELY COMPLEX OR COMPLICATED; 217] 2 *n* **detail**, nicety, fine point, nuance [➡FEW, LITTLE, SMALL AMOUNT; 120] 3 *n* **sensitivity**, delicacy, tact, discernment, finesse [➡GOOD MANNERS AND SOCIAL SKILLS; 520]

subtly 1 *adv* **faintly**, delicately, finely, thinly, slightly, imperceptibly, negligibly [➡TO A CERTAIN EXTENT; 136] *Opposite*: obviously 2 *adv* **intelligently**, sensitively, shrewdly, perceptively, cleverly [➡POSITIVE INTELLECTUAL CHARACTERISTICS; 524] 3 *adv* **cunningly**, slyly, ingeniously, deviously, craftily, trickily, artfully [➡DECEITFUL; 513]

subtract *v* **take away**, take from, take off, deduct, withdraw, detract [➡REMOVE SOMETHING; 338] *Opposite*: add

subtraction *n* **deduction**, removal, withdrawal, debit, deletion, detraction [➡MATH; 597]

suburb *n* **conurbation**, district, bedroom community, environs, development, area, exurbia, greenbelt, outskirts, edge city (*informal*), burb (*slang*), commuter belt (*UK*) [➡HUMAN SETTLEMENTS; 1070] *Opposite*: downtown

suburban *adj* **outlying**, peripheral, out-of-town, outer, residential [➡HUMAN SETTLEMENTS; 1070] *Opposite*: central

suburbia *n* **suburbs**, conurbation, greenbelt, environs, exurbia, outskirts, commuter belt (*UK*) [➡HUMAN SETTLEMENTS; 1070] *Opposite*: downtown

subvention (*formal*) 1 *n* **grant**, subsidy, payment, donation, endowment, allocation [➡FUNDS, PAYMENTS, AND CHARGES; 800] 2 *n* **aid**, support, backing, sponsorship, funding, assistance [➡FUNDS, PAYMENTS, AND CHARGES; 800]

subversion *n* **rebellion**, sedition, treason, mutiny, insurrection, sabotage, agitation, destabilization [➡UNWILLINGNESS AND STUBBORNNESS; 564] *Opposite*: compliance

subversive 1 *adj* **dissident**, rebellious, revolutionary, insubordinate, seditious, insurrectionary, destabilizing, treasonous, traitorous [➡REBELLIOUSNESS AND DISOBEDIENCE; 565] *Opposite*: law-abiding 2 *n* **traitor**, collaborator, mutineer, revolutionary, insubordinate, rebel, quisling (*dated*) [➡UNCOOPERATIVE OR REBELLIOUS PEOPLE; 566] *Opposite*: patriot

subvert *v* **undermine**, overthrow, destabilize, sabotage, disrupt, bring down, topple [➡AVOID, PREVENT, LIMIT, AND CONTROL; 277] *Opposite*: support

subway 1 *type of* **railroad** [➡RAILROADS; 1107] 2 *n* (*UK*) **underpass**, tunnel, passageway [➡BRIDGES, TUNNELS, CROSSINGS, AND JUNCTIONS; 1112]

subzero *adj* **freezing**, bitter, icy, ice-cold, glacial, polar, arctic (*informal*) [➡COLD WEATHER; 1051] *Opposite*: tropical

succeed 1 *v* **do well**, get ahead, prosper, be successful, thrive, flourish, get to the top, climb the ladder, make good, make it (*informal*) [➡SUCCEED AND WIN; 79] *Opposite*: fail 2 *v* **achieve**, accomplish, hit the target, turn out well, be successful, win, triumph, go well, work, bear fruit, come off (*informal*) [➡SUCCEED AND WIN; 79] *Opposite*: fail 3 *v* **follow**, come after, replace, supersede, supplant [➡HAPPEN; 27] *Opposite*: precede

succeeding *adj* **following**, subsequent, ensuing, next, successive, later, consequent, future, impending [➡AFTER, LAST, AND FOLLOWING; 165] *Opposite*: preceding

success 1 *n* **achievement**, accomplishment, victory, triumph, feat, realization, attainment [➡SUCCESS; 82] *Opposite*: failure 2 *n* **hit**, winner, sensation, star, triumph, success story [➡SUCCESS; 82] *Opposite*: failure

successful 1 *adj* **fruitful**, positive, effective, efficacious (*formal*) [➡SUCCESSFUL AND PROMISING; 81] *Opposite*: unsuccessful 2 *adj* **popular**, prosperous, up-and-coming, well-off, wealthy, rich [➡WEALTH AND WEALTHY; 891] 3 *adj* **flourishing**, thriving, booming, profitable, lucrative, productive [➡SUCCESSFUL AND PROMISING; 81] *Opposite*: ailing

successfully 1 *adv* **positively**, effectively, efficaciously, fruitfully, magnificently, well [➡SUCCESSFUL AND PROMISING; 81] *Opposite*: unsuccessfully 2 *adv* **productively**, fruitfully, profitably, lucratively, well [➡SUCCESSFUL AND PROMISING; 81] *Opposite*: badly

successfulness *n* **success**, utility, worth, effectiveness, value, merit [➡SUCCESS; 82] *Opposite*: uselessness

succession *n* **series**, sequence, chain, run, string, train, progression [➡CHAIN OF EVENTS; 162] *Opposite*: individual

successive *adj* **consecutive**, succeeding, following, sequential, uninterrupted, continual, continuous, straight, in a row [➡AFTER, LAST, AND FOLLOWING; 165] *Opposite*: single

successor *n* **heir**, inheritor, replacement, beneficiary [➡SUBORDINATES AND ASSISTANTS; 966] *Opposite*: predecessor

success story *n* **success**, winner, sensation, hit, triumph, fairy tale [➡SUCCESS; 82]

succinct *adj* **concise**, pithy, brief, to the point, laconic, neat, crisp [➡ SUCCINCT AND TO THE POINT; 640] *Opposite*: long-winded

succinctness *n* concision, pithiness, conciseness, brevity, briefness, economy, terseness, shortness, clarity, crispness, neatness [➡ SUCCINCT AND TO THE POINT; 640] *Opposite*: long-windedness

succor (*literary*) **1** *n* help, relief, aid, support, assistance, rescue, comfort [➡ KIND ACTIONS OR BEHAVIOR; 295] **2** *n* benefactor, support, rescuer, provider, helpmate, help [➡ SUBORDINATES AND ASSISTANTS; 966] *Opposite*: enemy **3** *v* assist, support, rescue, relieve, aid, comfort, help [➡ TAKE CARE OF AND SPOIL; 300] *Opposite*: abandon

succulence *n* juiciness, lusciousness, tenderness, moistness, tastiness, deliciousness, lushness [➡ TASTE; 703] *Opposite*: dryness

succulent *adj* juicy, moist, tender, luscious, delicious, tasty, mouthwatering [➡ TASTE; 703] *Opposite*: dry

succumb **1** *v* give way, yield, give in, submit, surrender, capitulate, accede [➡ FAIL OR BE UNSUCCESSFUL; 75] *Opposite*: withstand **2** *v* die, pass away, expire, depart, perish (*literary*) [➡ DIE; 922]

See Compare and Contrast at **yield**.

such as *adv* for example, like, namely, viz [➡ EXPRESSIONS INTRODUCING EXAMPLES; 64]

suck **1** *v* draw, pull on, lap, slurp, drink, imbibe (*formal or humorous*) [➡ DRINK; 711] **2** *v* extract, draw, pull, force, take out, withdraw [➡ GET; 420] **3** *v* pull, draw, force, sweep, bear, carry [➡ MOVE SOMETHING TO ANOTHER LOCATION; 324] **4** *n* slurp, draw, pull, drink, taste, mouthful [➡ DRINK; 711]

suck dry *v* [➡ USE UP AND WASTE; 474]

sucker **1** *n* (*informal*) gull, dupe, pushover (*informal*), chump (*informal*), fall guy (*slang*) [➡ VICTIMS OF DECEIT; 662] **2** *n type of* confectionery on a stick [➡ CONFECTIONERY; 1182] **3** *n* (*slang*) thing, contraption, critter, so-and-so (*informal*), blighter (*UK*) [➡ PHYSICAL OBJECTS; 1243] **4** *v* (*informal*) trick, con, fool, gull, dupe, take in, deceive, cheat, swindle, bamboozle (*informal*), hoodwink (*slang*) [➡ DECEPTION AND LIES; 660]

suck in **1** *v* breathe in, inhale, draw in, take in, pull in, gasp [➡ BREATHE AND NOT BREATHE; 716] **2** *v* involve, implicate, entangle, embroil, draw in, drag in, pull in [➡ CAUSE OR COMPEL TO ACT; 271] *Opposite*: exclude

suck the life out of *v* [➡ USE UP AND WASTE; 474]

suck up **1** *v* absorb, soak up, take up, sop up [➡ GET; 420] *Opposite*: exude **2** *v* (*informal*) ingratiate yourself, flatter, grovel, toady, crawl (*informal*), butter up (*informal*) [➡ FLATTER AND FAWN; 621]

sucrose *type of* nutrient [➡ FOOD COMPONENTS; 1188]

suction *n* force, pressure, pull, draw, drag [➡ ENERGY; 1161]

sudden *adj* unexpected, abrupt, rapid, swift, hasty, impulsive, quick, speedy, precipitous [➡ HAPPENING QUICKLY; 104] *Opposite*: gradual

suddenness *n* unexpectedness, quickness, abruptness, rapidity, swiftness, speed, precipitousness [➡ SPEED; 102]

suds *n* lather, bubbles, foam, froth, spume (*literary*) [➡ FOAM; 1273]

sudsy *adj* [➡ PHYSICAL TEXTURE; 1222]

sue **1** *v* (*formal*) petition, beg, plead, appeal, implore (*formal*) [➡ REQUEST AND DEMAND; 663] **2** *v* litigate, prosecute, indict, file a suit, charge [➡ TRIAL, PUNISHMENT, AND LEGAL OUTCOMES; 819]

suede *type of* leather [➡ FABRICS; 1132]

suet *type of* cooking fat and oil [➡ FATS AND OILS; 1173]

suffer **1** *v* feel pain, hurt, agonize, ache, smart, grieve, writhe [➡ PAIN AND OTHER PHYSICAL SENSATIONS; 733] **2** *v* undergo, experience, bear, endure, go through, live through, feel [➡ EXPERIENCE AND ENCOUNTER; 582] **3** *v* tolerate, endure, bear, put up with, stand, stomach [➡ TOLERATE AND ENDURE; 766] **4** *v* deteriorate, fall off, be impaired, drop off (*informal*) [➡ GET WORSE; 381]

sufferance **1** *n* tolerance, toleration, acquiescence, allowance, permission, leniency [➡ NEUTRALITY AND INDIFFERENCE; 553] *Opposite*: prohibition **2** *n* endurance, stamina, staying power, stoicism, fortitude [➡ STRENGTH OF WILL; 501]

sufferer *n* invalid, victim, patient, case, martyr, casualty [➡ UNFIT AND WEAK; 739]

suffering **1** *n* pain, distress, agony, torment, affliction [➡ PAIN AND OTHER PHYSICAL SENSATIONS; 733] **2** *n* sorrow, grief, misery, woe, anguish [➡ SADNESS, DISTRESS, AND DESPAIR; 539]

suffice (*formal*) *v* be sufficient, do, serve, suit [➡ ENOUGH AND SUFFICIENT; 131]

sufficiency *n* modicum, right amount, adequacy, abundance, plenty [➡ ENOUGH AND SUFFICIENT; 131] *Opposite*: insufficiency

sufficient *adj* adequate, enough, satisfactory, necessary, appropriate, ample, plenty, abundant [➡ ENOUGH AND SUFFICIENT; 131] *Opposite*: inadequate

suffix *type of* grammatical term [➡ ASPECTS OF LANGUAGE; 682]

suffocate *v* smother, choke, stifle, throttle, asphyxiate, gag, quash, snuff out [➡ KILL; 923]

suffocation *n* [➡ CAUSES OF DEATH; 921]

suffrage *n* [➡ ELECTIONS AND VOTING; 807]

suffuse *v* spread through, pervade, fill, saturate, flood, permeate, imbue, steep, cover, diffuse [➡ FILL; 406]

sugar **1** *type of* nutrient [➡ FOOD COMPONENTS; 1188] **2** *n* (*informal*) honey, sweetheart, darling, dearest, precious, sweetie (*informal*), love (*informal*), baby (*slang*), pet [➡ ENDEARMENTS; 656] **3** *v* sweeten, dress up, disguise, titivate, improve, make over [➡ IMPROVE APPEARANCE; 379]

sugar beet *type of* root vegetable [➡ FRUIT AND VEGETABLES; 1176]

sugar cane *type of* grass [➡ GRASS; 1031]

sugary **1** *adj* sweet, syrupy, sickly, sugared, sweetened [➡ TASTE; 703] *Opposite*: bitter **2** *adj* sentimental, mawkish, gushy, mushy, syrupy, sickly, saccharine, soppy (*informal*), gooey (*informal*) [➡ IN POOR TASTE AND OVERSENTIMENTAL; 229] *Opposite*: dry

suggest **1** *v* propose, put forward, advise, recommend, advocate, submit [➡ SUGGEST, HINT, AND COMMENT; 612] *Opposite*: veto

2 *v* **remind**, bring to mind, call to mind, evoke, conjure up, be redolent of, smack of [➡ REMIND; 747] **3** *v* **imply**, insinuate, intimate, indicate, hint, allude [➡ SUGGEST, HINT, AND COMMENT; 612] *Opposite*: state

See Compare and Contrast at **recommend**.

suggestibility *n* **susceptibility**, openness, vulnerability, credulousness, credulity, gullibility, malleability [➡ NEGATIVE INTELLECTUAL CHARACTERISTICS; 525] *Opposite*: strong-mindedness

suggestible *adj* **susceptible**, impressionable, gullible, credulous, malleable [➡ NEGATIVE INTELLECTUAL CHARACTERISTICS; 525] *Opposite*: strong-minded

suggestion **1** *n* **proposal**, proposition, submission, recommendation, idea, offer, plan, prompting, advice, counsel (*formal or literary*) [➡ ADVICE; 689] *Opposite*: order **2** *n* **evocation**, air, aura, hint, trace, tinge, sign, shade, touch, taste [➡ APPEARANCE AND ATMOSPHERE; 1237] **3** *n* **implication**, hint, insinuation, intimation, indication, innuendo [➡ SUGGEST, HINT, AND COMMENT; 612] *Opposite*: statement

suggestive **1** *adj* **evocative**, redolent, reminiscent, indicative, expressive, recalling, allusive [➡ REPRESENTATIVE; 66] **2** *adj* **improper**, indelicate, indecent, lewd, risqué, off-color (*informal*) [➡ MORALLY BAD OR IMPROPER; 775]

suicidal **1** *adj* (*informal*) **desperate**, cheerless, hopeless, unhappy, miserable, morbid, forlorn [➡ SADNESS, DISTRESS, AND DESPAIR; 539] **2** *adj* **dangerous**, treacherous, perilous, reckless, madcap [➡ DANGEROUS; 236] *Opposite*: sensible

suicide **1** *n* **death**, self-destruction, self-immolation [➡ CAUSES OF DEATH; 921] **2** *n* **recklessness**, rashness, perversity, irresponsibility, madness [➡ LACK OF COMMITMENT AND UNRELIABILITY; 509]

suit **1** *n* **costume**, ensemble, dress suit, trouser suit, uniform, outfit, garb, getup (*informal*) [➡ CLOTHES AND ACCESSORIES; 864] **2** *n* (*slang*) [➡ BUSINESS PEOPLE; 793] **3** *v* **go with**, match, fit, be fitting, agree with, conform to, befit, harmonize [➡ APPROPRIATE, SUITABLE, AND ADVISABLE; 184] *Opposite*: clash **4** *v* **flatter**, become, show up, enhance [➡ DRESS, WEAR, AND UNDRESS; 868]

suit

◆ *types of suits*
all-in-one, black tie, boiler suit, business suit, catsuit, dress suit, jumpsuit, overalls, pantsuit, pinstripe suit, trouser suit, white tie, zoot suit

suitability *n* **appropriateness**, aptness, fittingness, fitness, correctness, rightness [➡ APPROPRIATE, SUITABLE, AND ADVISABLE; 184] *Opposite*: unsuitability

suitable *adj* **appropriate**, apposite, fit, apt, right, proper, seemly, meet (*archaic*) [➡ APPROPRIATE, SUITABLE, AND ADVISABLE; 184] *Opposite*: inappropriate

suitcase *n* **case**, luggage, baggage, bag, valise, overnight case, grip, portmanteau [➡ CONTAINERS, RECEPTACLES, AND PACKAGING; 1245]

suite **1** *n* **set**, collection, group, complement [➡ COLLECTIONS AND MIXTURES OF THINGS; 1244] **2** *type of* **musical form** [➡ MUSIC, SONGS, AND SINGING; 907]

suited *adj* **right**, matched, well-matched, appropriate,

apposite, apt, fit, befitting, suitable [➡ APPROPRIATE, SUITABLE, AND ADVISABLE; 184] *Opposite*: wrong

suit of armor *n* [➡ GARMENTS AND OUTFITS; 865]

suitor (*formal*) *n* [➡ SEXUAL AND ROMANTIC RELATIONSHIPS; 964]

sulfur *type of* **mineral** [➡ MINERALS; 1277]

sulfurous *adj* **acrid**, reeking, stinking, foul, bitter, harsh [➡ SMELL AND SMELLING; 705]

sulk **1** *v* **mope**, be in a mood, feel sorry for yourself, be in a huff, pout, grumble, fret, be in a funk (*informal*) [➡ GIVING VENT TO EMOTIONS; 679] *Opposite*: rejoice (*literary*) **2** *n* **bad temper**, mood, temper, huff, bad mood, funk (*informal*) [➡ IRRITATION AND ANGER; 541]

sulkiness *n* **moodiness**, resentfulness, temper, bad temper, moroseness, sullenness, huffiness, bad mood, crankiness (*informal*) [➡ IRRITATION AND ANGER; 541] *Opposite*: joviality

sulky *adj* **morose**, angry, resentful, sullen, unsociable, bad-tempered, uncooperative, cross, petulant, brooding, in a mood, in a huff, grouchy (*informal*), in a funk (*informal*) [➡ IRRITATION AND ANGER; 541] *Opposite*: jovial

sullen **1** *adj* **surly**, morose, hostile, bad-tempered, dour, brooding, glowering, angry, grim, gloomy, ill-humored [➡ BAD-TEMPERED AND HUMORLESS; 626] *Opposite*: friendly **2** *adj* (*literary*) **leaden**, cloudy, dull, gray, brooding, gloomy, dark, somber, overcast, glowering [➡ WINDY AND STORMY WEATHER; 1053] *Opposite*: bright

sullenly *adv* **morosely**, hostilely, bad-temperedly, grimly, angrily, dourly, gloomily, resentfully, crossly, sourly, grumpily [➡ BAD-TEMPERED AND HUMORLESS; 626] *Opposite*: cheerfully

sullenness *n* **surliness**, hostility, bad temper, moodiness, moroseness, glumness, grumpiness, petulance, resentment, grouchiness (*informal*) [➡ BAD-TEMPERED AND HUMORLESS; 626] *Opposite*: friendliness

sullied **1** *adj* **tainted**, dishonoured, discredited, corrupt, disgraced, defiled (*formal*) [➡ MORALLY BAD OR IMPROPER; 775] **2** *adj* (*literary*) **polluted**, contaminated, dirty, soiled, foul, adulterated, stained [➡ DIRTY; 1235]

sully **1** *v* **tarnish**, taint, smear, denigrate, spoil, vilify, discredit, corrupt, disgrace, defame, dishonor, defile (*formal*) [➡ PROTEST AND EXPRESS DISAPPROVAL; 642] *Opposite*: praise **2** *v* (*literary*) **pollute**, contaminate, dirty, soil, foul, stain, adulterate, befoul (*archaic or literary*) [➡ DIRTY AND CONTAMINATE; 404] *Opposite*: clean

sultan *n* [➡ RULERS AND ARISTOCRACY; 823]

sultriness *n* [➡ HOT WEATHER; 1050]

sultry *adj* **hot**, humid, muggy, stifling, oppressive, close, sticky, airless, sweltering, baking, boiling, scorching (*informal*), roasting (*informal*) [➡ HOT WEATHER; 1050] *Opposite*: fresh

sum **1** *n* **calculation**, addition, computation, summation [➡ MATH; 597] **2** *n* **figure**, amount, quantity, entirety, totality, summation [➡ ALL; 128]

sumac *type of* **deciduous tree** [➡ DECIDUOUS TREES; 1028]

summarily *adv* **instantly**, immediately, instantaneously, abruptly, suddenly, swiftly, rapidly, without delay, at once, straightaway, right away, precipitously [➡HAPPENING QUICKLY; 104] *Opposite:* eventually

summarize *v* **sum up**, précis, abridge, recap, go over, run through, condense, encapsulate, digest, synopsize, review, recapitulate (*formal*) [➡EXPLAIN AND CLARIFY; 610] *Opposite:* elaborate

summary 1 *n* **précis**, synopsis, digest, sum-up, outline, rundown, abstract, extraction, abridgment, résumé, summation, brief, condensation, review [➡SUMMARIES, OUTLINES, AND EXCERPTS; 588] *Opposite:* exposition 2 *adj* **swift**, rapid, instant, immediate, instantaneous, hasty, sudden, precipitate, rushed, abrupt, peremptory [➡HAPPENING QUICKLY; 104] *Opposite:* considered 3 *adj* **short**, brief, concise, abridged, succinct, condensed, terse [➡CONCISE AND CLEAR; 202]

summation 1 *n* **summary**, summing up, synopsis, outline, précis, rundown, abstract, digest, brief, résumé, condensation, sum-up [➡SUMMARIES, OUTLINES, AND EXCERPTS; 588] 2 *n* **sum total**, total, sum, final total, grand total, aggregate, final amount, whole, tally [➡ALL; 128] 3 *n* **addition**, calculation, computation, sum [➡ASSESS QUANTITY; 757]

summer 1 *n* **summertime**, dog days, midsummer, solstice [➡TIMES OF YEAR; 88] *Opposite:* winter 2 *n* **warm weather**, sun, sunshine, warmth, heat, summertime [➡TIMES OF YEAR; 88] 3 *n* **prime**, best time, summertime, best years, golden age, halcyon days (*literary*) [➡PLEASANT SITUATIONS; 74]

summer clothes *n* [➡GARMENTS AND OUTFITS; 865]

summerhouse *n* **gazebo**, pagoda, hut, shed, shelter [➡ANCILLARY BUILDINGS; 1080]

summer solstice *n* [➡TIMES OF YEAR; 88]

summertime *n* **summer**, dog days, midsummer, solstice, season [➡TIMES OF YEAR; 88]

summery *adj* **warm**, balmy, sunny, hot [➡HOT WEATHER; 1050] *Opposite:* wintry

summit 1 *n* **peak**, top, pinnacle, apex, acme, zenith, brow, crown, hilltop, tip, crest [➡EXTREMITIES OF PHYSICAL OBJECTS; 1250] *Opposite:* base 2 *n* **conference**, meeting, summit meeting, talks [➡MEETINGS AND ASSEMBLIES; 43]

summit meeting *n* [➡MEETINGS AND ASSEMBLIES; 43]

summon 1 *v* **call**, send for, call for, call upon, beckon, subpoena, bid (*archaic*) [➡CAUSE OR COMPEL TO ACT; 271] *Opposite:* dismiss 2 *v* **convene**, call together, get together, gather, assemble [➡INITIATE AND ESTABLISH COMMUNICATION; 680] *Opposite:* dismiss 3 *v* **muster**, rouse, find, activate, rally, mobilize [➡CAUSE OR COMPEL TO ACT; 271]

summons *n* **order**, writ, directive, command, subpoena [➡TRIAL, PUNISHMENT, AND LEGAL OUTCOMES; 819]

sumo *type of* **combat sport** [➡HOBBIES, GAMES, AND SPORTS; 875]

sumptuous *adj* **costly**, lavish, splendid, opulent, spectacular, superb, magnificent, grand, elaborate, luxurious, extravagant, plush (*informal*) [➡EXPENSIVE AND LUXURIOUS; 218] *Opposite:* meager

sumptuousness *n* **luxuriousness**, luxury, lavishness, splendor, opulence, magnificence, grandness, extravagance [➡EXPENSIVE AND LUXURIOUS; 218]

sum total *n* **whole**, totality, entirety, aggregate, summation, sum, grand total [➡ALL; 128]

sum up *v* **summarize**, recap, synopsize, encapsulate, abridge, condense, review, recapitulate (*formal*) [➡EXPLAIN AND CLARIFY; 610] *Opposite:* elaborate

sun *type of* **star or star system** [➡HEAVENLY BODIES; 1061]

sunbaked *adj* **hardened**, dried, sun-dried, heated, cracked, baked [➡DRY; 1242]

sunbathe *v* **sun yourself**, bask, tan, catch some rays (*slang*) [➡LEISURE AND RECREATION; 874]

sunbeam *n* **ray**, beam, shaft, sunlight, sunshine [➡LIGHT; 1164]

sunblock *n* [➡PERSONAL HYGIENE; 491]

sunburn *n* [➡CONDITIONS AFFECTING THE SKIN; 721]

sunburned *adj* [➡CONDITIONS AFFECTING THE SKIN; 721]

sundae *type of* **dessert** [➡CAKES, COOKIES, AND DESSERTS; 1181]

Sunday best *n* **finery**, formal wear, best clothes, best bib and tucker (*informal*) [➡GARMENTS AND OUTFITS; 865]

sun deck *n* [➡STAGES, PLATFORMS, AND RAISED AREAS; 1098]

sunder (*literary*) *v* **separate**, divide, split, sever, cut, break, cleave [➡TEAR, BREAK, AND CUT; 360]

sundial *type of* **clock** [➡CLOCKS AND TIMERS; 1126]

sundown *n* **sunset**, nightfall, twilight, dusk, evening, night, eventide (*literary*) [➡TIMES OF DAY; 87] *Opposite:* sunrise

sundress *type of* **dress** [➡GARMENTS AND OUTFITS; 865]

sun-dried *adj* **dried**, preserved, dried up, dehydrated, jerked, desiccated [➡STATE OF PREPARED FOOD; 1171] *Opposite:* fresh

sundries *n* **miscellany**, hodgepodge, miscellanea, assortment, odds and ends, variety, mixture [➡COLLECTIONS AND MIXTURES OF THINGS; 1244]

sundry *adj* **various**, miscellaneous, assorted, varied, different, diverse, heterogeneous, several, manifold, motley, multifarious, divers (*literary*) [➡DIFFERENCE; 149] *Opposite:* uniform

sunflower *type of* **annual flower** [➡FLOWERS; 1032]

sunflower oil *type of* **cooking fat and oil** [➡FATS AND OILS; 1173]

sunglasses *type of* **glasses** [➡GLASSES AND SPECTACLES; 1125]

sunhat *type of* **hat** [➡ACCESSORIES, MILLINERY, AND LINGERIE; 867]

sunk 1 *adj* **ruined**, dashed, in trouble, defeated, destroyed, done for (*informal*) [➡UNSUCCESSFUL AND UNPROMISING; 76] *Opposite:* successful 2 *adj* **depressed**, downcast, downhearted, dejected, in the dumps, despondent, feeling low [➡SADNESS, DISTRESS, AND DESPAIR; 539] *Opposite:* happy

sunken 1 *adj* **submerged**, underwater, immersed [➡GENERAL LOCATIONS; 158] 2 *adj* **hollow**, gaunt, deep-set, cadaverous, pinched, drawn [➡FACIAL CHARACTERISTICS; 481] 3 *adj* **recessed**, lower, settled, dipped, depressed [➡ORIENTATION AND ALIGNMENT; 1223] *Opposite:* raised

sunlamp *type of* **light** [➡LIGHT; 1164]

sunless *adj* **dark**, cloudy, overcast, murky, gloomy, gray, shady, bleak, dim [➡ CLOUDY AND RAINY WEATHER; 1052] *Opposite*: sunny

sunlight *n* **sunshine**, daylight, light, rays, sunbeams [➡ LIGHT; 1164]

sunlit *adj* **sunny**, bright, light, sundrenched, bathed in light [➡ DESCRIBING LIGHT; 1228] *Opposite*: dark

sun lotion *n* [➡ PERSONAL HYGIENE; 491]

sunnily *adv* **cheerfully**, cheerily, happily, genially, gaily, brightly, affably, smilingly, lightheartedly [➡ CHEERFULNESS OF OUTLOOK; 503] *Opposite*: gloomily

sunny 1 *adj* **sunlit**, bright, luminous, brilliant, unclouded, fine, sunshiny, clear, fair, light [➡ HOT WEATHER; 1050] *Opposite*: dark 2 *adj* **cheerful**, cheery, bright, positive, optimistic, happy, smiling, beaming, genial, cordial, jolly, affable, warm, lighthearted, good-natured, bright and breezy (*UK*) [➡ CHEERFULNESS OF OUTLOOK; 503] *Opposite*: gloomy

sunrise *n* **dawn**, daybreak, break of day, first light, sunup, daylight, morning, crack of dawn [➡ TIMES OF DAY; 87] *Opposite*: sunset

sunroof *part of* **external structure** [➡ EXTERNAL PARTS OF A VEHICLE; 1147]

sunroom *type of* **room in the home** [➡ TYPES OF ROOMS; 1097]

sunscreen *n* **suntan lotion**, sunblock, sun cream (*UK*) [➡ PERSONAL HYGIENE; 491]

sunset *n* **sundown**, dusk, evening, night, nightfall, twilight, the end of the day, day's end [➡ TIMES OF DAY; 87] *Opposite*: sunrise

sunshade *n* **parasol**, umbrella, garden umbrella, beach umbrella, awning [➡ COVERS AND COATINGS; 1246]

sunshine *n* **sunlight**, light, rays, sunbeams, brightness, glare, daylight [➡ LIGHT; 1164]

sunshiny *adj* [➡ HOT WEATHER; 1050]

suntan *n* [➡ CONDITIONS AFFECTING THE SKIN; 721]

suntan lotion *n* **sunscreen**, sunblock, tanning lotion, suntan oil, sun protection, tanning oil, sun lotion, suntan cream (*UK*), sun cream (*UK*) [➡ PERSONAL HYGIENE; 491]

suntanned *adj* **brown**, tanned, bronzed, sunburned [➡ COMPLEXION; 480] *Opposite*: pale

suntan oil *n* [➡ PERSONAL HYGIENE; 491]

sunup *n* **dawn**, sunrise, daybreak, break of day, morning, daylight, first light, crack of dawn [➡ TIMES OF DAY; 87] *Opposite*: nightfall

sup 1 *v* **spoon**, sip, drink, partake of, lap, suck, swallow [➡ DRINK; 711] *Opposite*: gulp 2 *n* **mouthful**, sip, swallow, drink, draft, nip, drop, taste [➡ DRINK; 711] *Opposite*: gulp

super 1 *adj* (*informal*) **wonderful**, fantastic, great, marvelous, fabulous, tremendous, excellent, splendid, superb, brilliant, outstanding, terrific (*informal*), ace (*informal*) [➡ EXTRAORDINARY: AMAZING; 204] *Opposite*: awful 2 *adj* **superior**, better, enhanced, improved, outstanding, high-quality, best quality, first class, high-class, topnotch [➡ SUPERIORITY; 152] *Opposite*: inferior

superabundant *adj* **overabundant**, in excess, excessive, extra, abounding, profuse, surplus [➡ TOO MUCH; 119] *Opposite*: insufficient

superannuated 1 *adj* **retired**, pensioned off, discharged, elderly, aged, old [➡ OLD AGE; 919] *Opposite*: working 2 *adj* **worn out**, worn, unusable, used up, useless, dilapidated, old, aged, decrepit [➡ OLD, OLD-FASHIONED; 167] *Opposite*: new 3 *adj* **out-of-date**, antiquated, out of fashion, outmoded, passé, old, obsolete [➡ OLD, OLD-FASHIONED; 167] *Opposite*: fashionable

superb *adj* **excellent**, outstanding, wonderful, splendid, fabulous, fantastic, marvelous, magnificent, superlative, tremendous, brilliant, inspired, first-class, first-rate, terrific (*informal*) [➡ EXTRAORDINARY: AMAZING; 204] *Opposite*: abysmal

superbug *n* **supergerm**, germ, microorganism, pathogen, bug (*informal*) [➡ MICROORGANISMS, FUNGI, AND ALGAE; 1023]

supercenter *type of* **retail outlet** [➡ RETAIL OUTLETS; 1083]

supercharge 1 *v* **boost**, modify, charge, power up, amplify, soup up (*informal*) [➡ IMPROVE STRENGTH AND DURABILITY; 378] *Opposite*: downgrade 2 *v* **charge**, overdo, load, overload, hype, color [➡ OVERDO SOMETHING; 290] *Opposite*: understate

supercilious *adj* **arrogant**, contemptuous, disdainful, pompous, superior, scornful, condescending, haughty, patronizing, snobbish, stuck-up (*informal*), snooty (*informal*) [➡ AFFECTATION, SELF-SATISFACTION, AND SNOBBISHNESS; 507] *Opposite*: humble

superciliousness *n* **arrogance**, contemptuousness, contempt, condescension, haughtiness, disdain, pomposity, scorn, snobbishness, snootiness (*informal*) [➡ AFFECTATION, SELF-SATISFACTION, AND SNOBBISHNESS; 507] *Opposite*: humility

supercomputer *type of* **computer** [➡ COMPUTERS AND COMPUTING; 1127]

supercool (*informal*) *adj* **cool**, modern, contemporary, fashionable, trendy (*informal*), funky (*informal*), wicked (*slang*), hip (*slang*) [➡ NEW, MODERN; 166] *Opposite*: passé

super-duper (*informal*) *adj* **excellent**, colossal, impressive, pleasing, wonderful, fantastic, fabulous, tremendous, splendid, marvelous, super (*informal*), wicked (*informal*), great (*informal*), terrific (*informal*) [➡ EXTRAORDINARY: AMAZING; 204] *Opposite*: inferior

superego *n* **conscience**, integrity, scruples, sense of propriety, sense of judgment, sense of right and wrong, morality [➡ PSYCHOLOGY AND THE MIND; 769]

superficial 1 *adj* **surface**, shallow, external, exterior, on the surface, outward, skin-deep, outer [➡ FALSE AND UNREAL; 173] *Opposite*: deep 2 *adj* **insincere**, shallow, artificial, phony, apparent, seeming, posturing, feigning, glib [➡ AFFECTATION, SELF-SATISFACTION, AND SNOBBISHNESS; 507] *Opposite*: sincere 3 *adj* **cursory**, sketchy, rapid, hasty, quick, casual [➡ HAPPENING QUICKLY; 104] *Opposite*: thorough 4 *adj* **shallow**, trivial, trifling, unimportant, paltry, frivolous, insignificant, meaningless, lightweight, inconsequential, passing, light, hollow, trite [➡ UNIMPORTANT AND UNNECESSARY; 238] *Opposite*: profound

superficiality *n* **shallowness**, triviality, frivolity, levity, paltriness, insignificance, hollowness, triteness [➡ BORING AND UNINTERESTING; 234] *Opposite*: profundity

superficially 1 *adv* **apparently**, seemingly, supposedly, outwardly, ostensibly, externally, to all appearances, on the face of it, at first glance [➡FALSE AND UNREAL; 173] *Opposite*: wholly 2 *adv* **cursorily**, sketchily, rapidly, hastily, casually, quickly, lightly [➡HAPPENING QUICKLY; 104] *Opposite*: thoroughly

superfine 1 *adj* **delicate**, fine, light, sheer, fragile, flimsy, wispy, thin, translucent [➡FRAGILE; 1209] *Opposite*: coarse 2 *adj* **superior**, first-class, first-rate, high-quality, best, excellent [➡SUPERIORITY; 152] *Opposite*: inferior

superfluity 1 *n* **luxury**, extra, frill, trifle, indulgence [➡AMAZING THINGS; 211] *Opposite*: necessity 2 *n* **oversupply**, excess, overabundance, surfeit, surplus, plethora, glut, flood [➡TOO MUCH; 119] *Opposite*: insufficiency

superfluous *adj* **extra**, surplus, redundant, unnecessary, unessential, excessive, unneeded, needless, gratuitous, spare [➡TOO MUCH; 119] *Opposite*: basic

superglue *n* [➡ADHESIVES; 1271]

superhero *n* **champion**, crusader, rescuer, fighter, protector, hero [➡PEOPLE WHO ARE APPROVED OF; 955]

superhighway 1 *n* [➡THE INTERNET; 1128] 2 *type of* **highway** [➡ROADS; 1106]

superhuman *adj* **phenomenal**, prodigious, staggering, heroic, exceptional, formidable, herculean, extraordinary, godlike, omnipotent, supreme [➡EXTRAORDINARY: AMAZING; 204] *Opposite*: normal

superimpose *v* **place over**, overlay, lay over, apply to, cover [➡POSITION SOMETHING: BETWEEN, BESIDE, OR INSIDE SOMETHING; 326]

superintend *v* **supervise**, manage, oversee, administer, control, run, be in charge of, direct, watch, mind [➡BE IN CHARGE; 270] *Opposite*: ignore

superintendent *n* **manager**, supervisor, administrator, officer, controller, overseer, inspector, examiner, director, head, chief, leader [➡BOSSES AND MANAGEMENT; 965] *Opposite*: underling

superior 1 *adj* **better**, better-quality, advanced, improved, enhanced, a cut above, finer [➡SUPERIORITY; 152] *Opposite*: inferior 2 *adj* **larger**, greater, bigger, higher, more, grander, loftier, longer [➡SUPERIORITY; 152] *Opposite*: smaller 3 *adj* **excellent**, high-class, top-quality, exclusive, first-class, best quality, untouchable, choice, exceptional, outstanding, expert, fine, notable, nonpareil [➡EXTRAORDINARY: AMAZING; 204] *Opposite*: second-rate 4 *adj* **higher**, upper, over, above [➡RELATIVE LOCATION; 161] *Opposite*: lower 5 *adj* **condescending**, arrogant, disdainful, supercilious, aloof, aristocratic, pompous, self-important, haughty, patronizing, imperious, high and mighty, snobbish, stuck-up (*informal*), snooty (*informal*) [➡AFFECTATION, SELF-SATISFACTION, AND SNOBBISHNESS; 507] *Opposite*: humble 6 *n* **boss**, manager, chief, elder, better, director, supervisor, leader, senior, commander, higher-up (*informal*) [➡BOSSES AND MANAGEMENT; 965] *Opposite*: inferior

superiority 1 *n* **advantage**, dominance, lead, preeminence, power, control, authority, supremacy, ascendancy, predominance, upper hand [➡SUPERIORITY; 152] *Opposite*: inferiority 2 *n* **condescension**, arrogance, haughtiness, disdain, aloofness, pomposity, self-importance, super-

ciliousness, snobbishness, snootiness (*informal*) [➡AFFECTATION, SELF-SATISFACTION, AND SNOBBISHNESS; 507] *Opposite*: humility

superiority complex *n* **superiority**, inflated ego, self-importance, disdain, superciliousness, haughtiness [➡PSYCHOLOGY AND THE MIND; 769] *Opposite*: inferiority complex

superlative *adj* **excellent**, unmatched, unbeatable, untouchable, best, matchless, outstanding, exceptional, incomparable, without equal, unparalleled, beyond compare, top, consummate, unrivaled, supreme, unique, peerless [➡EXTRAORDINARY: AMAZING; 204] *Opposite*: unremarkable

supermarket *type of* **food outlet** [➡RETAIL OUTLETS; 1083]

supermax prison *n* [➡BUILDINGS FOR CONFINING PEOPLE; 1094]

supernatural *adj* **paranormal**, mystic, mystical, ghostly, ghostlike, uncanny, weird, bizarre, eerie, magic, unnatural, preternatural, psychic, unearthly [➡THE SUPERNATURAL; 787] *Opposite*: natural

supernova *type of* **star or star system** [➡HEAVENLY BODIES; 1061]

supernumerary 1 *adj* **extra**, excessive, superfluous, spare, surplus, unrequired [➡MORE AND EXCESS; 124] *Opposite*: necessary 2 *adj* **substitute**, extra, auxiliary, ancillary, additional, temporary, standby [➡MORE AND EXCESS; 124] *Opposite*: permanent

superpower *n* **world power**, giant, power bloc, global force, global influence [➡TERRITORIES AND GROUPS OF NATIONS; 1068]

supersaver *n* **discount**, special offer, concession [➡TRANSPORTATION, TRANSPORTERS, AND CARGOS; 322]

supersede *v* **succeed**, take over, overtake, supplant, replace, surpass, displace [➡CHANGE ONE THING FOR ANOTHER; 398] *Opposite*: precede

superstar *n* **star**, megastar, celebrity, icon, luminary, big name, idol [➡IMPORTANT OR FAMOUS PEOPLE; 893] *Opposite*: nobody

superstition *n* **fallacy**, false notion, delusion, misconception, fantasy, falsehood, falsity, irrational belief [➡THE SUPERNATURAL; 787]

superstitious *adj* **credulous**, gullible, illogical, irrational, delusory, illusory [➡NEGATIVE INTELLECTUAL CHARACTERISTICS; 525] *Opposite*: rational

superstore *type of* **retail outlet** [➡RETAIL OUTLETS; 1083]

superstructure 1 *n* **structure**, construction, elevation, frame, framework [➡QUALITIES AND CHARACTERISTICS; 1191] *Opposite*: foundation 2 *n* **idea**, concept, system, structure, argument, theory, deduction, model, elaboration [➡IDEAS AND THOUGHTS; 770] *Opposite*: premise 3 *part of* **ship or boat** [➡PARTS OF A SHIP OR BOAT; 1151]

supertitle *n* **surtitle**, caption, legend [➡FILM; 901] *Opposite*: subtitle

supervene (*formal*) 1 *v* **interrupt**, charge in, butt in, appear, turn up, crop up (*informal*), impinge (*formal*) [➡HAPPEN; 27] 2 *v* **ensue**, follow, supersede, succeed, pursue, follow on, chase after [➡HAPPEN; 27]

supervise *v* **oversee**, manage, administer, control, run, direct, take charge of, handle, superintend, observe, organize, watch, preside over, regulate, conduct [➡BE IN CHARGE; 270] *Opposite*: neglect

supervision 1 *n* **management**, direction, administration, regulation, command, control, observation, organization, guidance [➡BUSINESS ACTIVITIES AND PHENOMENA; 794] *Opposite*: neglect 2 *n* **care**, custody, guardianship, protection, charge, guidance [➡EXAMINE AND ASSESS; 753]

supervision order (*UK*) *n* **charge**, order, authorization, mandate, appointment, nomination [➡SOCIAL WELFARE; 812]

supervisor *n* **manager**, administrator, superintendent, controller, overseer, director, boss, superior, head, chief [➡BOSSES AND MANAGEMENT; 965] *Opposite*: underling

supervisory *adj* **managerial**, administrative, superintendent, managing, controlling, directorial, guiding, regulatory, conducting [➡EXAMINE AND ASSESS; 753] *Opposite*: subordinate

supine 1 *adj* **flat**, horizontal, flat on one's back, prostrate, prone, recumbent (*literary*) [➡ORIENTATION AND ALIGNMENT; 1223] *Opposite*: standing 2 *adj* **lethargic**, passive, inactive, apathetic, listless, enervated, inert [➡TIRED, ASLEEP, AND UNCONSCIOUS; 738] *Opposite*: vigorous

supper *type of* **meal** [➡MEALS AND PARTS OF MEALS; 1169]

suppertime *n* [➡TIMES OF DAY; 87]

supplant *v* **oust**, displace, succeed, replace, unseat, supersede, usurp, depose [➡CHANGE ONE THING FOR ANOTHER; 398] *Opposite*: install

supple 1 *adj* **lithe**, agile, mobile, double-jointed, sinuous, limber, flexible, elastic, coordinated, graceful [➡AGILITY OF THE BODY; 476] *Opposite*: stiff 2 *adj* **flexible**, elastic, plastic, pliant, pliable, malleable, bendable [➡MALLEABLE AND ELASTIC; 1212] *Opposite*: rigid

supplement 1 *n* **addition**, extra, complement, enhancement, increase, increment, add-on, appendage, adjunct, extension, insertion [➡MORE AND EXCESS; 124] *Opposite*: deduction 2 *n* **section**, insert, appendix, attachment, rider, postscript, addendum, annex, codicil (*formal*) [➡PARTS OF BOOKS AND DOCUMENTS; 593] 3 *v* **add**, complement, accompany, enhance, improve, increase, fill out, append, insert, extend, augment (*formal*) [➡CHANGE OF SIZE: BIGGER; 392] *Opposite*: deduct

supplemental *adj* **additional**, extra, added, supplementary, complementary, incremental, add-on, auxiliary, ancillary, accompanying, top-up (*UK*) [➡MORE AND EXCESS; 124] *Opposite*: deducted

supplementary *adj* **extra**, additional, added, add-on, supplemental, accompanying, complementary, auxiliary, ancillary, top-up (*UK*) [➡MORE AND EXCESS; 124] *Opposite*: deducted

suppleness *n* **litheness**, agility, mobility, flexibility, limberness, elasticity, sinuousness, double-jointedness, coordination, grace [➡AGILITY OF THE BODY; 476] *Opposite*: stiffness

suppliant (*formal*) 1 *adj* **prayerful**, petitionary, begging, pleading, supplicant (*formal*), supplicatory (*formal*) [➡REQUEST AND DEMAND; 663] *Opposite*: beneficent 2 *n* **petitioner**, applicant, aspirant, suitor, beggar, appellant, mendicant,

supplicant (*formal*) [➡PEOPLE WHO MAKE REQUESTS; 664] *Opposite*: benefactor

supplicant (*formal*) *n* **petitioner**, applicant, suitor, aspirant, beggar, appellant, mendicant, suppliant (*formal*) [➡PEOPLE WHO MAKE REQUESTS; 664] *Opposite*: donor

supplicate (*formal*) *v* **appeal**, petition, request, beg, entreat, plead, pray, solicit, implore (*formal*), sue (*formal*), beseech (*literary*) [➡REQUEST AND DEMAND; 663] *Opposite*: grant

supplication (*formal*) *n* **appeal**, request, entreaty, petition, plea, prayer, application, solicitation, suit (*formal*) [➡REQUEST AND DEMAND; 663] *Opposite*: concession

supplicatory (*formal*) *adj* [➡REQUEST AND DEMAND; 663]

supplier *n* **provider**, trader, seller, dealer, contractor, merchant, purveyor (*formal*) [➡SELLERS; 442] *Opposite*: consumer

supplies *n* **provisions**, materials, goods, food, stores, purchases, articles, equipment, deliveries, necessities, stock [➡PHYSICAL OBJECTS; 1243]

supply 1 *v* **provide**, give, make available, sell, bring, deliver, contribute, equip, distribute, deal, trade, outfit, stock, present, furnish (*formal*) [➡EQUIP AND SUPPLY; 435] *Opposite*: receive 2 *n* **amount**, quantity, fund, reserve, stock, hoard, resource, source, stream, allocation, store, provision [➡AMOUNTS AND QUANTITIES; 112] *Opposite*: dearth

supply teacher (*UK*) *n* [➡EDUCATORS; 840]

support 1 *v* **hold up**, reinforce, prop up, maintain, shore up, keep up, buoy, buttress, brace, stay, sustain [➡IMPROVE STRENGTH AND DURABILITY; 378] *Opposite*: weaken 2 *v* **sustain**, provide for, keep, take care of, look after, care for, fend for, maintain, subsidize, underwrite [➡TAKE CARE OF AND SPOIL; 300] *Opposite*: neglect 3 *v* **help**, encourage, back up, aid, be there for, assist, sponsor, comfort, carry, strengthen, succor (*literary*) [➡HELP; 293] *Opposite*: abandon 4 *v* **champion**, back, follow, espouse, be in favor of, adopt, cheer on, favor, defend, uphold, stand up for, advocate, speak up for [➡APPROVE AND CONFIRM; 646] *Opposite*: oppose 5 *v* **corroborate**, confirm, verify, bear witness, prove, bear out, strengthen, authenticate, substantiate, uphold, bolster, endorse, make good, establish, vouch for, warrant, ratify, validate [➡APPROVE AND CONFIRM; 646] *Opposite*: deny 6 *v* (*literary*) **bear**, hold, carry, sustain, take, stand, tolerate [➡TOLERATE AND ENDURE; 766] 7 *n* **prop**, foundation, scaffold, brace, stanchion, buttress, reinforcement, base, pillar, column, joist, bracket, underpinning [➡SUPPORTS AND BASES; 1255] 8 *n* **sustenance**, provision, care, funding, funds, backing, financial assistance, maintenance, upkeep, livelihood [➡FUNDS, PAYMENTS, AND CHARGES; 800] *Opposite*: abandonment 9 *n* **assistance**, encouragement, backing, help, aid, sponsorship, defense, finance, patronage, boost, furtherance, promotion [➡KIND ACTIONS OR BEHAVIOR; 295] 10 *n* **corroboration**, confirmation, verification, authentication, substantiation, endorsement, proof, validation, warrant, ratification [➡EVIDENCE AND PROOF; 69] *Opposite*: denial

supportable (*literary*) *adj* **tolerable**, bearable, acceptable, manageable, sustainable, maintainable, viable, workable, justifiable, defensible [➡ACCEPTABLE AND PASSABLE; 219] *Opposite*: insupportable

supporter *n* **follower**, fan, enthusiast, devotee, ally, backer, adherent, sponsor, advocate, exponent, helper, defender, champion, patron, benefactor, guardian [➡ SUPPORTERS, PROTECTORS, AND COMPATRIOTS; 970] *Opposite*: detractor

support group *n* **encounter group**, forum, self-help group, therapy group, circle, group [➡ GROUPS WITH A COMMON INTEREST; 938]

support hose *n* **stockings**, nylons, pantyhose, tights, legwear, hosiery [➡ ACCESSORIES, MILLINERY, AND LINGERIE; 867]

supporting *adj* **secondary**, backup, subsidiary, supportive, auxiliary, ancillary, associate, assistant, accompanying, supplementary [➡ MORE AND EXCESS; 124] *Opposite*: primary

supportive *adj* **helpful**, caring, sympathetic, compassionate, reassuring, understanding, encouraging, kind, loyal, empathetic [➡ GENEROSITY AND KINDNESS; 495] *Opposite*: unhelpful

support system *n* **friends**, network, helpers, group, support, family, contacts [➡ GROUPS WITH A COMMON INTEREST; 938]

suppose 1 *v* **presume**, assume, understand, believe, expect, reason, infer, think, consider, guess, reckon [➡ GUESS; 754] 2 *v* **imagine**, pretend, consider, theorize, hypothesize, postulate, predicate (*formal*), posit (*formal*) [➡ DEVELOP THEORIES AND REASON; 744]

supposed 1 *adj* **hypothetical**, theoretical, imaginary, fictional, made-up, invented [➡ FALSE AND UNREAL; 173] *Opposite*: actual 2 *adj* **thought**, believed, assumed, alleged, understood, rumored, said, held [➡ UNCERTAIN; 175] *Opposite*: known

supposedly *adv* **allegedly**, evidently, apparently, theoretically, hypothetically, by all accounts, so they say, so it is said, it would seem, purportedly (*formal*) [➡ UNCERTAIN; 175] *Opposite*: actually

supposing *conj* **assuming**, suppose, let's say, let's assume, say, if, imagine, what if [➡ SUGGEST, HINT, AND COMMENT; 612]

supposition 1 *n* **belief**, guess, idea, theory, possibility, hypothesis, assumption, deduction, conclusion, presumption, opinion, surmise, thesis [➡ GUESS; 754] *Opposite*: fact 2 *n* **guesswork**, inference, hypothesis, speculation, conjecture [➡ DREAM, IMAGINE, AND FANTASIZE; 749] *Opposite*: knowledge

suppress 1 *v* **hold back**, repress, stifle, restrain, contain, curb, stem, smother, keep in check, control, cover up, hide, conceal, keep inside, bottle up, check, block out [➡ NOT PAY ATTENTION; 764] *Opposite*: express 2 *v* **overpower**, overwhelm, overturn, conquer, defeat, destroy, subdue, quash, quell, crush, put down, clamp down on, control, dominate, squash, overcome, snuff out [➡ BEAT AND DEFEAT; 80] *Opposite*: submit 3 *v* **muffle**, withhold, censor, smother, quash, stifle, kill, sit on, put the lid on, cover up, bury, silence, hush up (*informal*), squelch (*slang*) [➡ WITHHOLD INFORMATION; 687] *Opposite*: publicize

suppression 1 *n* **repression**, containment, control, restraint, inhibition [➡ CAPTIVITY AND LOSS OF FREEDOM; 248] *Opposite*: expression 2 *n* **conquest**, defeat, destruction, overthrow, clampdown, overpowering, dominance, snuffing out (*informal*) [➡ BEAT AND DEFEAT; 80] 3 *n* **withholding**, cover-up, concealment, censorship, veil of secrecy, wraps, conspiracy of silence, squashing, silencing [➡ WITHHOLD INFORMATION; 687] *Opposite*: revelation

suppurate *v* **discharge pus**, fester, weep, ooze, seep, exude [➡ EXCRETION AND EXCRETA; 722]

supranational *adj* **multinational**, international, cosmopolitan, worldwide, universal, global, supernational [➡ COUNTRIES AND REGIONS; 1067] *Opposite*: local

supremacist *n* **chauvinist**, racist, xenophobe, bigot, sexist [➡ PHILOSOPHICAL AND POLITICAL THINKERS; 781]

supremacy 1 *n* **preeminence**, ascendancy, primacy, superiority, domination, incomparability, dominance [➡ SUPERIORITY; 152] *Opposite*: inferiority 2 *n* **reign**, sovereignty, rule, authority, power, hegemony, control, omnipotence [➡ REALMS AND RULES; 824]

supreme 1 *adj* **highest**, best, ultimate, superlative, utmost, absolute, extreme, top, great, greatest, matchless, untouchable, unbeatable, unmatched, nonpareil, consummate, incomparable [➡ SUPERIORITY; 152] *Opposite*: worst 2 *adj* **sovereign**, dominant, uppermost, first, highest, chief, topmost [➡ MOST IMPORTANT AND MAIN; 193]

supremely *adv* **extremely**, completely, enormously, absolutely, superlatively, tremendously, utterly, totally, really, particularly, very [➡ TO A GREAT EXTENT; 132]

supremo (*informal*) *n* **leader**, head, chief, authority, expert, guru [➡ BOSSES AND MANAGEMENT; 965]

surcharge 1 *v* **charge extra**, charge again, charge more, tack on, levy again, add, tax again [➡ FUNDS, PAYMENTS, AND CHARGES; 800] 2 *n* **extra charge**, supplement, extra, price, hidden extra, extra payment, additional charge, addition, padding [➡ FUNDS, PAYMENTS, AND CHARGES; 800]

sure 1 *adj* **unquestionable**, undisputable, certain, definite, guaranteed, assured, inevitable, indubitable, bound to be, unerring, conclusive, infallible, accurate, sure-fire (*informal*) [➡ CERTAIN; 174] *Opposite*: uncertain 2 *adj* **certain**, in no doubt, convinced, positive, confident, clear in your mind, persuaded [➡ CERTAINTY; 561] *Opposite*: uncertain 3 *adj* **dependable**, reliable, effective, trustworthy, trusty, loyal, solid, constant, firm, true, steady [➡ HONEST AND RELIABLE; 502] *Opposite*: unreliable 4 *adv* (*informal*) **really**, certainly, surely, definitely, positively, absolutely, for certain, clearly, indeed, for sure (*informal*) [➡ ABSOLUTE AND ABSOLUTELY; 133] *Opposite*: doubtfully 5 *adv* (*informal*) **of course**, absolutely, yes, certainly, by all means, yes indeed, surely, positively, all right, OK (*informal*), you bet (*informal*), sure thing (*informal*) [➡ EXPRESSIONS OF AGREEMENT; 648]

sure bet *n* [➡ CERTAIN; 174]

sure enough *adv* [➡ EXPRESSIONS OF AGREEMENT; 648]

sure-fire (*informal*) *adj* **guaranteed**, dependable, safe, assured, foolproof, never-failing, sure, certain [➡ CERTAIN; 174] *Opposite*: doubtful

sure-footed 1 *adj* **agile**, skilled, skillful, confident, nimble, adroit [➡ TALENTED AND SKILLFUL; 527] *Opposite*: clumsy 2 *adj* **confident**, competent, unerring, capable, infallible, certain [➡ CERTAINTY; 561]

surely 1 *adv* **confidently**, assuredly, with conviction, with confidence, with assurance [➡ CONFIDENCE AND COMPOSURE; 499] *Opposite*: insecurely 2 *adv* **certainly**, definitely, of course,

without doubt, unquestionably, indisputably, incontestably, indeed, absolutely, clearly, for sure (*informal*), indubitably (*formal*) [➡CERTAIN; 174] *Opposite*: doubtfully

sureness *n* **certainty**, certitude, confidence, assurance, firm belief [➡CERTAINTY; 561] *Opposite*: uncertainty

sure of yourself *adj* **confident**, self-confident, assured, self-assured, poised, secure [➡CONFIDENCE AND COMPOSURE; 499] *Opposite*: insecure

sure thing (*informal*) **1** *n* **certainty**, safe bet, odds-on chance, winner, cinch (*informal*), piece of cake (*informal*) [➡CERTAIN; 174] **2** *adv* **yes**, certainly, of course, surely, absolutely, all right, yes indeed, by all means, for sure (*informal*), OK (*informal*), you bet (*informal*), sure (*informal*) [➡EXPRESSIONS OF AGREEMENT; 648]

surety *n* **security**, indemnity, guarantee, warranty, bond, deposit, collateral, down payment [➡INSURANCE; 801]

surf **1** *n* **waves**, breakers, rollers, whitecaps, spray, sea [➡THE SEAS, OCEANS, AND SHORES; 1041] **2** *v* [➡THE INTERNET; 1128]

surface **1** *n* **outside**, top, exterior, façade, side, shell, plane, face [➡EXTREMITIES OF PHYSICAL OBJECTS; 1250] *Opposite*: inside **2** *adj* **superficial**, shallow, external, exterior, outward, apparent, seeming [➡FALSE AND UNREAL; 173] *Opposite*: inner **3** *v* **rise**, float up, come up, go up, emerge, ascend, break the surface, appear [➡GO UPWARD; 306] *Opposite*: sink **4** *v* **appear**, reappear, turn up, show up, pop up [➡APPEAR AND EMERGE; 3] **5** *v* **become known**, come to light, come out, come out in the open, emerge, get out [➡APPEAR AND EMERGE; 3] **6** *v* **coat**, cover, skim, overlay, resurface [➡DECORATE, ADORN, AND APPLY COATINGS; 405]

surface mail *n* **overland mail**, regular mail, first-class mail, registered mail, special delivery, snail mail (*informal*), second-class mail (*UK*) [➡LETTERS AND WRITTEN MESSAGES; 584] *Opposite*: airmail

surfeit *n* **excess**, surplus, glut, flood, oversupply, overabundance, plethora, profusion [➡TOO MUCH; 119] *Opposite*: deficit

surf 'n' turf *type of* **cooked dish** [➡PREPARED DISHES; 1170]

surge **1** *v* **rush**, rush forward, flow, pour, gush, course, heave, pitch, swell, rise, well up, flood, stream, spill over, spill out [➡MOVE FAST; 313] **2** *n* **flow**, outpouring, gush, rush, heave, pitch, swell, upwelling, flood, stream, spill, wave [➡SUDDEN EVENTS; 52]

surgeon *n* **doctor**, physician, medical practitioner, specialist, neurosurgeon, plastic surgeon [➡PEOPLE WHO WORK IN MEDICINE; 848]

surgical **1** *adj* **medical**, clinical, operating, invasive [➡REMEDIES, TREATMENTS, AND OPERATIONS; 731] **2** *adj* **precise**, exact, accurate, definite, meticulous, punctilious [➡EXACT; 203] *Opposite*: imprecise

surliness *n* [➡BAD MANNERS AND SOCIAL SKILLS; 521]

surly *adj* **gruff**, brusque, abrupt, short, curt, churlish, rude, impolite, discourteous, disagreeable, bad-tempered, truculent, grumpy, short-tempered, irritable, sullen, boorish, unfriendly, crabby, unhelpful, grouchy (*informal*), tetchy (*informal*) [➡BAD TEMPERED AND HUMORLESS; 626] *Opposite*: friendly

surmise **1** *v* **guess**, deduce, infer, construe, gather, work out, conclude, assume, presume, suppose, conjecture, imagine, suspect, postulate, hypothesize, theorize, speculate [➡GUESS; 754] *Opposite*: know **2** *n* **guesswork**, deduction, inference, conclusion, assumption, presumption, supposition, conjecture, suspicion, postulation, hypothesis, theory, speculation [➡GUESS; 754] *Opposite*: knowledge

surmount **1** *v* **overcome**, prevail, conquer, triumph, get through, vanquish, defeat, transcend [➡BEAT AND DEFEAT; 80] *Opposite*: fail **2** *v* (*formal*) **scale**, climb, top, clear, ascend, mount [➡GO UPWARD; 306]

surmountable *adj* **manageable**, conquerable, resolvable, controllable, winnable, attainable, possible, soluble, doable [➡POSSIBLE AND PROBABLE; 177] *Opposite*: intractable

surname *n* **last name**, family name, cognomen [➡NAME AND DESCRIBE; 665] *Opposite*: first name

surpass *v* **exceed**, better, outdo, outshine, improve on, go beyond, outstrip, do better than, go one better than, top, transcend, beat [➡BEAT AND DEFEAT; 80] *Opposite*: follow

surpassing (*literary*) *adj* **outstanding**, superior, exceptional, greater, better [➡EXTRAORDINARY: AMAZING; 204]

surplice *type of* **top** [➡GARMENTS AND OUTFITS; 865]

surplus **1** *n* **excess**, extra, spare, leftovers, remainder, superfluity, overage, surfeit, oversupply, overflow, plethora, glut [➡TOO MUCH; 119] *Opposite*: shortfall **2** *adj* **extra**, excess, spare, remaining, additional, over, superfluous, not needed, excessive, unnecessary, redundant, residual, leftover [➡MORE AND EXCESS; 124] *Opposite*: essential

surplus to requirements *adj* [➡MORE AND EXCESS; 124]

surprise **1** *v* **startle**, alarm, astonish, astound, amaze, stagger, stun, shock, take the wind out of your sails, take aback, bowl over, take by surprise, render speechless, daze, dumbfound, flabbergast (*informal*) [➡SURPRISE AND IMPRESS; 574] **2** *v* **catch unawares**, catch napping, take by surprise, burst in on, intrude on, come upon, interrupt, disturb, disrupt [➡ARRIVE; 12] **3** *n* **shock**, revelation, bolt from the blue, disclosure, bombshell (*informal*), shocker (*informal*) [➡SUDDEN EVENTS; 52] **4** *n* **astonishment**, amazement, wonder, disbelief, shock [➡SURPRISE, SHOCK, AND AMAZEMENT; 545]

surprised *adj* **astonished**, astounded, amazed, taken aback, staggered, stunned, shocked, bowled over, startled, stupefied, flabbergasted (*informal*) [➡SURPRISE, SHOCK, AND AMAZEMENT; 545]

surprising *adj* **astonishing**, astounding, amazing, shocking, startling, unexpected, unanticipated, unforeseen, unpredicted, extraordinary, remarkable, overwhelming [➡EXTRAORDINARY: AMAZING; 204] *Opposite*: expected

surprisingly **1** *adv* **astonishingly**, astoundingly, amazingly, unexpectedly, unpredictably, shockingly, startlingly, remarkably [➡EXTRAORDINARY: AMAZING; 204] **2** *adv* **to my surprise**, to my amazement, out of the blue, without warning, without prior notice [➡EXPRESSIONS OF SURPRISE AND PLEASURE; 546]

surreal *adj* **strange**, weird, odd, unreal, dreamlike, fantastic, bizarre [➡BIZARRE AND PECULIAR; 257] *Opposite*: ordinary

surrealism *type of* **20th-century art movement** [➡ARTISTIC MOVEMENTS AND STYLES; 899]

surrender 1 *v* **give in**, give up, admit defeat, lay down your arms, submit, yield, capitulate, throw in the towel (*informal*) [➡ FAIL OR BE UNSUCCESSFUL; 75] *Opposite*: hold out 2 *v* **relinquish**, give up, hand over, part with, forfeit, abandon, concede, renounce, waive, cede (*formal*) [➡ FORGO AND DENY ONESELF; 449] *Opposite*: retain 3 *n* **admission of defeat**, submission, laying down of arms, capitulation, renunciation [➡ FAILURE; 77]

See Compare and Contrast at **yield**.

surreptitious *adj* **furtive**, secret, sneaky, sly, covert, clandestine, stealthy, secretive, underhand, hush-hush (*informal*) [➡ SECRET AND UNKNOWN; 179] *Opposite*: open

See Compare and Contrast at **secret**.

surreptitiousness *n* **secrecy**, covertness, discretion, concealment, stealth, sneakiness, furtiveness, cunning, slyness, craftiness [➡ SECRET AND UNKNOWN; 179] *Opposite*: openness

surrogacy *n* **substitution**, proxy, standing in, surrogateship, replacement [➡ CHANGE ONE THING FOR ANOTHER; 398]

surrogate *n* **substitute**, replacement, proxy, stand-in, deputy, alternate, backup, understudy [➡ SUBSTITUTES AND STAND-INS; 399]

surround 1 *v* **enclose**, encircle, encase, enfold, envelop, border, contain, bound, circumscribe, encompass, ring, girdle (*literary*) [➡ EXIST IN CLOSE PROXIMITY; 21] 2 *v* **besiege**, lay siege to, encircle, hem in [➡ EXIST IN CLOSE PROXIMITY; 21] 3 *n* **border**, mount, edge, edging, frame, setting, rim, mantle (*literary*) [➡ EXTREMITIES OF PHYSICAL OBJECTS; 1250]

surrounding *adj* **nearby**, close, adjacent, neighboring, immediate, adjoining, near, proximate, contiguous (*formal*) [➡ CLOSENESS; 159] *Opposite*: distant

surroundings *n* **environs**, surrounds, setting, environment, background, backdrop, milieu, context, situation, habitat [➡ PLACE; 1065]

surtax *n* **surcharge**, tax, levy, extra, supplement [➡ TAX AND TAXATION; 802] *Opposite*: relief

surtitle *n* **supertitle**, translation, dialogue, caption, title, dialog, text [➡ FILM; 901] *Opposite*: subtitle

surveillance *n* **observation**, investigation, scrutiny, reconnaissance, shadowing, following, stakeout (*informal*), tailing (*informal*) [➡ LOOKING AND LOOKS; 700]

survey 1 *n* **inspection**, examination, investigation, review, inquiry, study, canvass, probe [➡ EXAMINE AND ASSESS; 753] 2 *n* **analysis**, appraisal, scrutiny, evaluation, assessment, consideration [➡ EXAMINE AND ASSESS; 753] 3 *v* **examine**, study, inspect, assess, analyze, appraise, evaluate, look over, consider, scan, review [➡ EXAMINE AND ASSESS; 753] 4 *v* **look at**, consider, regard, think about, look over [➡ LOOKING AND LOOKS; 700] 5 *v* **plot**, chart, map out, measure, graph, gauge, fathom, plumb [➡ ASSESS QUANTITY; 757] *Opposite*: sketch

surveyor *n* **inspector**, assessor, examiner, reviewer, evaluator, chartered surveyor (*UK*) [➡ SURVEYORS, EXAMINERS, AND JUDGES; 853]

survival *n* **existence**, endurance, being, subsistence, persistence, continued existence [➡ PERMANENCE: WITHOUT END; 94] *Opposite*: death

survive 1 *v* **live**, live on, endure, carry on, go on, persist, continue, last, subsist, stay alive [➡ CONTINUE TO EXIST; 17] *Opposite*: perish (*literary*) 2 *v* **outlive**, outlast, live through [➡ CONTINUE TO EXIST; 17] *Opposite*: die

surviving *adj* **living**, alive, enduring, persisting, remaining, ongoing, extant, current, existing, lasting [➡ PRESENT AND AVAILABLE; 11] *Opposite*: gone

survivor *n* **fighter**, stayer, sticker, toughie (*informal*) [➡ PEOPLE WHO ARE APPROVED OF; 955]

susceptibility 1 *n* **vulnerability**, defenselessness, weakness, exposure, predisposition, proneness, liability [➡ WEAKNESS; 241] *Opposite*: imperviousness 2 *n* **sensitivity**, receptiveness, openness, touchiness, impressionableness, responsiveness, sensibility, impressionability [➡ EXCESSIVE SENSITIVITY; 511] *Opposite*: hardness

susceptible 1 *adj* **vulnerable**, at risk, liable, prone, disposed, inclined, subject, predisposed [➡ IN DANGER; 237] *Opposite*: invulnerable 2 *adj* **sensitive**, receptive, open, impressionable, swayable, amenable, suggestible [➡ NEGATIVE INTELLECTUAL CHARACTERISTICS; 525] *Opposite*: impervious

sushi *n* [➡ PREPARED DISHES; 1170]

sushi bar *type of* **eating place** [➡ HOTELS, RESTAURANTS, AND CLUBS; 1082]

suspect 1 *v* **think**, believe, suppose, imagine, guess, deduce, infer, presume, assume, speculate [➡ GUESS; 754] 2 *v* **doubt**, distrust, mistrust, have doubts, disbelieve, be suspicious, be wary, question [➡ QUESTION THINGS; 751] *Opposite*: trust 3 *n* **accused**, defendant, respondent [➡ TRIAL, PUNISHMENT, AND LEGAL OUTCOMES; 819] 4 *adj* **suspicious**, doubtful, dubious, unsure, questionable, odd, shady, uncertain [➡ UNCERTAIN; 175] *Opposite*: trustworthy

suspend 1 *v* **hang**, hang up, dangle, swing, string up, overhang, append [➡ MOVE SOMETHING: ON THE SPOT; 336] 2 *v* **interrupt**, check, break off, adjourn, hold, stop, quit, halt [➡ CAUSE TO STOP; 266] *Opposite*: resume 3 *v* **postpone**, put on hold, defer, table, delay, stay, shelve, put on ice, put back, put off, push back [➡ DELAY ACTION OR OCCURRENCE; 278] *Opposite*: bring forward

suspended 1 *adj* **hanging**, floating, hovering, dangling, strung up, in the air, overhanging, pendent (*formal or literary*) [➡ ORIENTATION AND ALIGNMENT; 1223] 2 *adj* **postponed**, put off, deferred, adjourned, held over, on hold, on ice, on the back burner, up in the air [➡ NOT HAPPENING; 34] *Opposite*: advanced 3 *adj* **barred**, banned, proscribed, excluded [➡ REFUSE PERMISSION AND NOT ALLOW; 670]

suspended sentence *n* **deferred sentence**, deferment, sentence, punishment, judgment, penalty, ruling [➡ TRIAL, PUNISHMENT, AND LEGAL OUTCOMES; 819]

suspenders *type of* **accessory** [➡ ACCESSORIES, MILLINERY, AND LINGERIE; 867]

suspense 1 *n* **uncertainty**, unsureness, doubt, insecurity, confusion, doubtfulness, indecision [➡ UNCERTAINTY; 559] *Opposite*: knowledge 2 *n* **anticipation**, expectation, expectancy, excitement, tension, thrill [➡ FEELINGS ABOUT THE FUTURE; 533] *Opposite*: flatness 3 *n* **anxiety**, apprehension, tension, fear, nervousness, trepidation, edginess, uneasiness [➡ FEELINGS ABOUT THE FUTURE; 533] *Opposite*: calm

suspenseful *adj* [➡ INTERESTING AND MEANINGFUL; 190]

suspension *n* **interruption**, holdup, check, postponement, delay, deferment, deferral, pause [➡ DELAY ACTION OR OCCURRENCE; 278] *Opposite*: resumption

suspension bridge *type of* **bridge** [➡ BRIDGES, TUNNELS, CROSSINGS, AND JUNCTIONS; 1112]

suspicion 1 *n* **mistrust**, apprehension, distrust, disbelief, wariness, skepticism [➡ UNCERTAINTY; 559] *Opposite*: trust 2 *n* **doubt**, question, inkling, misgiving, feeling, notion, thought, idea, hunch [➡ FEELINGS; 531] *Opposite*: certainty 3 *n* **hint**, suggestion, trace, touch, tinge, soupçon, smidgen (*informal*) [➡ FEW, LITTLE, SMALL AMOUNT; 120]

suspicious 1 *adj* **suspect**, dubious, shady, shifty, untrustworthy, questionable, unreliable [➡ UNCERTAIN; 175] *Opposite*: trustworthy 2 *adj* **doubtful**, distrustful, mistrustful, apprehensive, wary, guarded, chary, skeptical, dubious, leery [➡ UNCERTAINTY; 559] *Opposite*: sure

sustain 1 *v* **withstand**, bear, tolerate, endure, weather, put up with, brook, stand [➡ TOLERATE AND ENDURE; 766] *Opposite*: buckle 2 *v* **experience**, undergo, suffer, incur, contract, meet with, encounter [➡ EXPERIENCE AND ENCOUNTER; 582] 3 *v* **maintain**, continue, carry on, keep up, keep going, uphold, prolong, protract [➡ CAUSE TO CONTINUE; 267] *Opposite*: quit 4 *v* **nourish**, keep going, feed, nurture [➡ TAKE CARE OF AND SPOIL; 300] *Opposite*: deplete 5 *v* **support**, hold up, prop up, keep up, maintain, take [➡ AGREE; 645]

sustainability *n* [➡ PERMANENCE: WITHOUT END; 94]

sustainable 1 *adj* **maintainable**, bearable, justifiable, workable, defensible, viable, supportable (*literary*) [➡ PERMANENCE: WITHOUT END; 94] 2 *adj* **ecological**, environmental, green, natural, balanced, organic [➡ ECONOMICAL AND RESOURCEFUL; 207] *Opposite*: unsustainable

sustained *adj* **continued**, constant, continual, continuous, nonstop, unrelenting, unremitting, persistent, unceasing, prolonged, chronic, lasting, perpetual, unbroken, uninterrupted, never-ending, endless [➡ PERMANENCE: WITHOUT END; 94] *Opposite*: temporary

sustenance *n* **nourishment**, food, nutrition, provisions, rations, victuals, edibles, fuel, wherewithal [➡ FOOD; 1167] *Opposite*: deprivation

susurrate *v* **rustle**, whisper, murmur, breathe [➡ EMIT CONTINUOUS SOUNDS; 366]

suture 1 *n* **seam**, join, junction, joint, closure, seal [➡ FASTENERS, LINKS, AND NETWORKS; 1247] 2 *v* **sew**, sew up, stitch, stitch up, close, seal [➡ FASTEN, LINK, AND JOIN; 408] *Opposite*: cut

SUV *type of* **car** [➡ BIKES, CARS, AND CARRIAGES; 1149]

suzerain *n* **superpower**, colonial power, ruling nation [➡ RULERS AND ARISTOCRACY; 823]

svelte *adj* **lithe**, graceful, slender, willowy, sylphlike, slim, lissome [➡ BUILD; 477] *Opposite*: stocky

svelteness *n* [➡ BUILD; 477]

Svengali *n* **manipulator**, controller, guru, charmer, guide, manager, influence [➡ BOSSES AND MANAGEMENT; 965]

swab 1 *n* **gauze**, lint, cloth, wipe, pad, wad [➡ COVERS AND COATINGS; 1246] 2 *v* **wipe**, clean, cleanse, moisten, wash, sponge, dab, mop, wash out [➡ CLEAN AND POLISH; 403]

swaddle *v* **wrap**, bandage, wrap up, swathe, envelop, enfold, shroud [➡ DECORATE, ADORN, AND APPLY COATINGS; 405] *Opposite*: unwrap

swag 1 *n* **curtain**, drape, hanging, drapery [➡ FURNISHING AND HOUSEHOLD LINENS; 860] 2 *n* (*slang*) **loot**, booty, plunder, spoils, haul, contraband [➡ PROCEEDS OF CRIME; 427] 3 *n* **festoon**, garland, chain [➡ ORNAMENTS AND DECORATIONS; 1248]

swagger 1 *v* **strut**, parade, flounce, prance, sweep, sway, show off, saunter, sashay (*humorous*) [➡ PROCEED AND GO; 305] *Opposite*: creep 2 *n* **boastfulness**, arrogance, bluster, conceit, boasting, bragging, showing-off [➡ BOAST; 616] *Opposite*: timidity

swaggering 1 *adj* **self-important**, self-satisfied, strutting, smug, arrogant, conceited, hubristic [➡ AFFECTATION, SELF-SATISFACTION, AND SNOBBISHNESS; 507] *Opposite*: self-effacing 2 *adj* **boastful**, boasting, blustering, bragging, vaunting, bombastic [➡ POMPOUS, LOUD, AND OVERCONFIDENT; 635] *Opposite*: modest

swags *n* [➡ FURNISHING AND HOUSEHOLD LINENS; 860]

swain (*literary*) *n* **admirer**, boyfriend, young man, lover, suitor (*formal*), beau (*dated*) [➡ SEXUAL AND ROMANTIC RELATIONSHIPS; 964]

swallow 1 *v* **ingest**, consume, take in, down, eat, drink, imbibe (*formal or humorous*) [➡ EAT AND NOT EAT; 710] *Opposite*: vomit 2 *v* **gulp**, sip, gulp down, gobble up, gobble up, swill, swig (*informal*), guzzle (*informal*), scarf (*slang*), scarf down (*slang*) [➡ DRINK; 711] *Opposite*: regurgitate 3 *v* **destroy**, engulf, swallow up, take over, gobble up, consume, absorb [➡ CAUSE TO DISAPPEAR; 6] 4 *v* **suppress**, repress, choke back, hold back, hide, conceal, withhold [➡ WITHHOLD INFORMATION; 687] *Opposite*: express 5 *v* **retract**, take back, back down, recant, eat your words [➡ APOLOGIZE AND RETRACT; 683] 6 *v* (*informal*) **believe**, accept, fall for, credit, buy (*informal*), allow (*formal*) [➡ FORGET, FORGIVE, AND ACCEPT; 748] *Opposite*: reject 7 *n* **gulp**, sip, nip, mouthful, swig (*informal*) [➡ DRINK; 711] 8 *type of* **common bird** [➡ BIRDS; 997]

swallowtail *type of* **butterfly** [➡ MOTHS AND BUTTERFLIES; 1015]

swami *n* [➡ RELIGIOUS PEOPLE; 778]

swamp 1 *n* **wetland**, marsh, bog, mire, fen, quagmire, slough, bayou, everglade [➡ WETLANDS; 1043] 2 *v* **overwhelm**, snow under, overload, inundate, flood, drown, submerge, engulf, besiege, bog down (*informal*) [➡ GIVE TOO MUCH AND OVERBURDEN; 437] 3 *v* **flood**, inundate, deluge, engulf, drown, drench, sink [➡ FILL; 406] *Opposite*: drain

swampland *n* **swamps**, marshes, marshland, bog, everglade, wetland, bayou [➡ WETLANDS; 1043]

swampy *adj* **marshy**, boggy, muddy, slushy, squelchy, wet [➡ WET; 1240] *Opposite*: dry

swan *type of* **freshwater bird** [➡ FRESHWATER BIRDS; 1000]

swank 1 *v* (*slang*) **show off**, boast, brag, strut, swagger, parade [➡ BOAST; 616] 2 *adj* (*informal*) **upmarket**, glamorous, smart, high-class, swanky (*informal*), posh (*informal*), ritzy (*informal*), classy (*informal*) [➡ EXPENSIVE AND LUXURIOUS; 218] *Opposite*: downmarket

swanky (*informal*) *adj* **upmarket**, glamorous, high-class, stylish, elegant, swank (*informal*), posh (*informal*), ritzy (*informal*), classy (*informal*) [➡ EXPENSIVE AND LUXURIOUS; 218] *Opposite*: downmarket

swan song *n* **farewell**, final act, last act, curtain, finale, valediction (*formal*), leave-taking (*literary*) [➡ ENDS AND DEPARTURES; 54] *Opposite*: debut

swap (*informal*) **1** *v* **exchange**, trade, barter, do a deal, change, transact, negotiate, give and take, dicker (*informal*) [➡ EXCHANGE AND INTERCHANGE; 448] **2** *n* **changeover**, substitution, exchange, switch, interchange, change [➡ EXCHANGE AND INTERCHANGE; 448]

swap over (*UK*) *v* **switch**, interchange, change over, change around, change places, exchange [➡ CHANGE ONE THING FOR ANOTHER; 398]

sward *n* **turf**, grass, grassland, green, lawn, meadow [➡ THE COUNTRYSIDE AND OUTDOOR SPACES; 1071]

swarm **1** *n* **group**, cloud, flight [➡ MANY, MUCH, LARGE AMOUNT; 117] **2** *n* **horde**, crowd, throng, flock, bevy, multitude, pack, mass, mob, drove, herd [➡ GROUPS OF PEOPLE; 935] **3** *v* **group**, hover, circle, fly, rise, migrate [➡ GET CLOSER TOGETHER; 310] **4** *v* **teem**, be overrun, bristle, be alive with, be full, be packed, abound, surge [➡ PROSPER AND ABOUND; 16] **5** *v* **crowd**, throng, mass, flock, pile, flood [➡ GET CLOSER TOGETHER; 310]

swarming *adj* **crawling**, teeming, brimming, overrun, crowded, swamped, flooded, packed [➡ FULL; 1239] *Opposite*: empty

swarthy *adj* **dark**, weather-beaten, dark-complexioned, leathery, tanned, tawny, olive-skinned [➡ COMPLEXION; 480] *Opposite*: pale

swashbuckler **1** *n* **adventurer**, daredevil, swash, buccaneer, pirate, swaggerer, fortune hunter [➡ PLEASURE-SEEKERS AND HEDONISTS; 886] **2** *n* **action movie**, period film, action film, adventure movie, actioner (*informal*), pirate film (*UK*) [➡ FILM; 901]

swashbuckling **1** *adj* **daring**, adventurous, heroic, exciting, cavalier, rumbustious [➡ COURAGE; 498] *Opposite*: timid **2** *adj* **strutting**, swaggering, boasting, blustery, blustering, posturing [➡ POMPOUS, LOUD, AND OVERCONFIDENT; 635] *Opposite*: modest

swat *v* **swipe**, slap, hit, smack, thwack, whack, knock, strike, punch, zap (*informal*), belt (*informal*), bash (*informal*), clobber (*informal*), wallop (*informal*), deck (*informal*) [➡ PHYSICAL ATTACK AND PUNISHMENT; 415]

swatch *n* **sample**, batch, strip, snip, piece, tester, length [➡ REPRESENTATIONS AND GENERAL EXAMPLES; 65]

swathe **1** *v* **wrap**, cover, bandage, bind, entwine, sheathe [➡ DECORATE, ADORN, AND APPLY COATINGS; 405] *Opposite*: unwrap **2** *v* **enfold**, envelop, drape, cloak, shroud, surround, swaddle [➡ DECORATE, ADORN, AND APPLY COATINGS; 405] *Opposite*: expose **3** *n* **strip**, ribbon, band, wrapping, bandage, binding [➡ FASTENERS, LINKS, AND NETWORKS; 1247]

sway **1** *v* **swing**, waver, oscillate, move to and fro, rock, wave, fluctuate, vacillate, shift, vary [➡ BOUNCE, UNDULATE, AND VIBRATE; 308] **2** *v* **bend**, lean, veer, slant, tilt, tip over, reel, totter, wobble, stagger, rock [➡ MOVE SOMETHING: ON THE SPOT; 336] **3** *v* **influence**, bias, affect, control, persuade, convince, manipulate, win over, move, prompt, motivate [➡ ENCOURAGE;

4 *n* **power**, influence, control, authority, command, mastery, rule, dominance, grip [➡ RELATIONSHIP TO ANOTHER; 973] *Opposite*: subjection

swear **1** *v* **vow**, pledge, promise, give your word, attest, aver, guarantee, undertake [➡ PROMISE AND ASSURE; 684] **2** *v* **curse**, blaspheme, damn, utter profanities, cuss (*informal*), execrate (*literary or formal*) [➡ INSULTS, ABUSE, AND SWEARING; 658] *Opposite*: bless **3** *v* **affirm**, assert, declare, claim, maintain, insist, avow (*formal*) [➡ CLAIM, INSIST, AND EMPHASIZE; 614]

swear an oath *v* [➡ PROMISE AND ASSURE; 684]

swear by *v* **trust**, rely on, depend on, have faith in, put your faith in, count on, believe in [➡ LIKE, LOVE, VALUE, AND ENJOY; 578] *Opposite*: doubt

swear in *v* **inaugurate**, install, initiate, induct, administer an oath to, invest (*formal*) [➡ CONFER STATUS; 458] *Opposite*: discharge

swear off *v* **give up**, renounce, abstain from, desist from, stop, come off, eschew [➡ FORGO AND DENY ONESELF; 449]

swear-word *n* **expletive**, four-letter word, curse, bad language, profanity, obscenity, oath, cuss-word (*informal*) [➡ INSULTS, ABUSE, AND SWEARING; 658]

sweat **1** *v* (*informal*) **worry**, fret, panic, be anxious, be concerned, be agitated, be on pins and needles, be afraid, dread [➡ BE CONCERNED AND CARE; 581] *Opposite*: relax **2** *v* **perspire**, swelter, wilt, drip [➡ EXCRETION AND EXCRETA; 722]

sweat blood *v* [➡ HARD WORK OR EFFORT; 298]

sweater *type of* **sweater** [➡ GARMENTS AND OUTFITS; 865]

sweat out *v* **wait out**, see through, endure, see out, stick out, see through to the bitter end, sit out [➡ TOLERATE AND ENDURE; 766] *Opposite*: give up on

sweatpants *type of* **sportswear** [➡ GARMENTS AND OUTFITS; 865]

sweatshirt *type of* **top** [➡ GARMENTS AND OUTFITS; 865]

sweatshop **1** *n* **factory**, shop, workshop, place of work, works, plant [➡ PLACE OF EMPLOYMENT; 832] **2** *type of* **factory** [➡ INDUSTRIAL BUILDINGS; 1087]

sweat suit *type of* **sportswear** [➡ GARMENTS AND OUTFITS; 865]

sweaty **1** *adj* **perspiring**, covered with sweat, clammy, damp, sticky, moist, drenched, dripping, soaked, wet [➡ WET; 1240] *Opposite*: dry **2** *adj* **hot**, boiling, warm, sticky, sultry, humid [➡ HOT WEATHER; 1050] *Opposite*: cool

sweep **1** *v* **brush**, clean up, tidy up, clear away, brush off, brush away, clear, remove, clear up, sweep up, clean [➡ CLEAN AND POLISH; 403] **2** *v* **speed**, zoom, race, fly, dash, whiz, dart, rush, hurry, zip (*informal*) [➡ MOVE FAST; 313] *Opposite*: creep **3** *v* **carry**, move, seize, grab, take [➡ GET; 420] **4** *v* **arc**, arch, bend, bow, curve, swoop, swing, swish [➡ CHANGE DIRECTION OF MOTION; 344] **5** *n* **arc**, arch, bend, bow, swing, stroke, swish, swoop, curve [➡ ROUNDED SHAPE; 1218] **6** *n* **scope**, range, extent, stretch, span, distance [➡ DEGREE AND EXTENT; 110]

sweep aside *v* **dismiss**, ignore, brush aside, have done with, reject [➡ NOT PAY ATTENTION; 764] *Opposite*: consider

sweep away **1** *v* **bowl over**, astonish, carry away, astound, overwhelm, amaze, impress, stagger, dumbfound, flabbergast (*informal*) [➡ SURPRISE AND IMPRESS; 574]

2 *v* **brush**, sweep up, clean up, clear up, remove, sweep, clear, brush away, clean, whisk, gather, tidy up [➡CLEAN AND POLISH; 403]

sweeping 1 *adj* **far-reaching**, comprehensive, all-encompassing, extensive, across-the-board, wide, widespread, broad, wide-ranging, full, wholesale, inclusive [➡WHOLENESS AND COMPLETENESS; 198] *Opposite*: restricted **2** *adj* **indiscriminate**, generalized, general, broad, blanket, unselective [➡VAGUENESS; 243] *Opposite*: specific

sweeps (*informal*) *n* [➡GAMBLE AND TAKE RISKS; 466]

sweep somebody off his/her feet *v* **attract**, enchant, charm, allure, beguile, fascinate, bewitch, dazzle, carry away, bowl over [➡SURPRISE AND IMPRESS; 574] *Opposite*: turn off (*informal*)

sweepstakes *n* **lottery**, draw, raffle, game of chance, prize draw, sweeps (*informal*) [➡GAMBLE AND TAKE RISKS; 466]

sweep under the carpet *v* [➡NOT PAY ATTENTION; 764]

sweep up *v* **brush**, tidy up, clean, pick up, clean up, clear up, remove, sweep, clear, scoop up, brush away, clear away [➡CLEAN AND POLISH; 403]

sweet 1 *adj* **sugary**, syrupy, saccharine, sweetened, honeyed [➡TASTE; 703] *Opposite*: bitter **2** *adj* **fresh**, pure, wholesome [➡CLEAN AND HYGIENIC; 1233] *Opposite*: foul **3** *adj* **sweet-smelling**, fragrant, perfumed, scented, odorous [➡SMELL AND SMELLING; 705] *Opposite*: smelly **4** *adj* **melodious**, melodic, harmonious, musical, tuneful, dulcet, easy on the ear, pleasant, mellifluous [➡SOFT, LOW, OR PLEASANT SOUNDS; 1265] *Opposite*: harsh **5** *adj* **satisfying**, gratifying, enjoyable, rewarding, pleasing, agreeable, pleasurable [➡EMOTIONALLY PLEASANT; 187] *Opposite*: unrewarding **6** *adj* **kind**, thoughtful, considerate, pleasant, amiable, friendly, caring, gentle, good-natured, soft-hearted, agreeable, sweet-tempered, accommodating, obliging, sympathetic [➡GENEROSITY AND KINDNESS; 495] **7** *adj* **lovable**, charming, engaging, appealing, attractive, delightful, adorable, cute [➡BEAUTY AND ATTRACTIVENESS; 189] *Opposite*: unappealing

sweet corn *type of* **vegetable** [➡FRUIT AND VEGETABLES; 1176]

sweeten 1 *v* **make sweeter**, add sugar to, sugar-coat, candy-coat, sugar, honey, crystallize [➡COOKING AND FOOD PREPARATION; 353] **2** *v* **enhance**, improve, better, intensify, heighten, augment (*formal*) [➡IMPROVE SOMETHING; 374] **3** *v* **pacify**, mollify, appease, soothe, soften up [➡SOOTHE AND CALM; 573] *Opposite*: aggravate

sweetener 1 *n* **sweet substance**, sugar, saccharine, aspartame, honey, molasses, corn syrup, maple syrup, syrup, treacle (*UK*) [➡ADDITIVES; 1172] **2** *n* (*informal*) **bribe**, inducement, carrot [➡BRIBES; 440]

sweetening *n* **sweet substance**, sweetener, sugar, saccharine, aspartame, honey, molasses, corn syrup, maple syrup, syrup, treacle (*UK*) [➡ADDITIVES; 1172]

sweetheart *n* **darling**, dear, dearest, beloved, precious, sweetie (*informal*), sweetie pie (*informal*), sugar (*informal*), love (*informal*), honey (*informal*), babe (*slang*), pet [➡ENDEARMENTS; 656]

sweetie (*informal*) *see* **sweetie pie**

sweetie pie (*informal*) *n* **sweetheart**, dear, darling, sweetie (*informal*), honey (*informal*), pet [➡ENDEARMENTS; 656]

sweetly 1 *adv* **pleasantly**, kindly, thoughtfully, considerately, amiably [➡GENEROSITY AND KINDNESS; 495] *Opposite*: unkindly **2** *adv* **harmoniously**, beautifully, melodiously, melodically, musically, tunefully, pleasantly, pleasingly, agreeably [➡SOFT, LOW, OR PLEASANT SOUNDS; 1265] *Opposite*: harshly

sweetmeat (*archaic*) *type of* **confectionery** [➡CONFECTIONERY; 1182]

sweetness 1 *n* **sugariness**, syrupiness, saccharinity [➡TASTE; 703] *Opposite*: sourness **2** *n* **melodiousness**, harmony, pleasantness, mellifluousness [➡SOFT, LOW, OR PLEASANT SOUNDS; 1265] *Opposite*: harshness **3** *n* **freshness**, pureness, purity, wholesomeness [➡CLEAN AND HYGIENIC; 1233] **4** *n* **charm**, cuteness, appeal, attractiveness, delightfulness, adorability [➡BEAUTY AND ATTRACTIVENESS; 189] **5** *n* **kindness**, thoughtfulness, consideration, pleasantness, amiability, friendliness, agreeableness [➡GENEROSITY AND KINDNESS; 495] *Opposite*: unkindness

sweetness and light *n* **pleasantness**, harmony, peace, friendliness, concord, amiability [➡HARMONY; 155] *Opposite*: unpleasantness

sweet nothings *n* **romantic words**, romantic phrases, loving words, endearments, pillow talk, honeyed words [➡ENDEARMENTS; 656]

sweet pea *type of* **annual flower** [➡FLOWERS; 1032]

sweet pepper *type of* **salad vegetable** [➡FRUIT AND VEGETABLES; 1176]

sweet potato *type of* **root vegetable** [➡FRUIT AND VEGETABLES; 1176]

sweet-smelling *adj* **aromatic**, perfumed, fragrant, sweet-scented, fresh [➡SMELL AND SMELLING; 705] *Opposite*: smelly

sweet talk (*informal*) *n* **flattery**, smooth talk, cajolery, blarney (*informal*), soft soap (*informal*), blandishment (*formal*) [➡INGRATIATING; 638]

sweet-talk (*informal*) *v* **charm**, flatter, smooth-talk, persuade, cajole, coax, butter up (*informal*), blandish (*archaic*) [➡FLATTER AND FAWN; 621]

sweet-tempered *adj* [➡CHEERFULNESS OF OUTLOOK; 503]

sweet tooth *n* **craving**, taste, fondness, liking, relish, weakness, chocolate addiction, sugar craving [➡TASTE; 703]

sweet william *type of* **perennial flower** [➡FLOWERS; 1032]

swell 1 *v* **puff up**, puff out, swell up, bulge, bloat, distend, engorge, inflate, balloon [➡CHANGE OF SIZE: BIGGER; 392] *Opposite*: deflate **2** *v* **increase**, grow, enlarge, inflate, expand, mushroom, proliferate [➡CHANGE OF SIZE: BIGGER; 392] *Opposite*: decrease **3** *v* **add to**, increase, enhance, improve, expand, amplify, enlarge, supplement, heighten, intensify, raise, augment (*formal*) [➡CHANGE OF SIZE: BIGGER; 392] *Opposite*: diminish **4** *n* **wave**, undulation, billow, breaker, surge, roller [➡THE SEAS, OCEANS, AND SHORES; 1041] **5** *n* (*dated informal*) **fop**, fashion plate, clotheshorse (*informal*), dude (*slang*), dandy (*dated*), beau (*archaic*), coxcomb (*archaic*) [➡MALE PERSON; 934] **6** *adj* (*dated informal*) **really nice**, fantastic, wonderful, marvelous, fabulous, tremendous, good, excellent, great (*informal*), super (*informal*), terrific (*informal*), brilliant (*informal*) [➡EXTRAORDINARY: AMAZING; 204] *Opposite*: awful

swelled head *n* [➡SELF-IMPORTANT AND SELF-SEEKING PEOPLE; 949]

swellheaded (*informal*) *adj* **conceited**, full of yourself, vain, self-important, puffed up, self-satisfied, cocky (*informal*), too big for your boots (*informal*), stuck-up (*informal*), swollen-headed (*UK*) [➡POMPOUS, LOUD, AND OVER-CONFIDENT; 635] *Opposite*: modest

swelling *n* **bulge**, bump, puffiness, inflammation, distension, enlargement, engorgement, growth, blister, bunion, boil, abscess, protuberance [➡ILL AND SICK; 740]

swelter *v* **feel hot**, sweat, perspire, overheat, burn, boil (*informal*), roast (*informal*), bake (*informal*) [➡CHANGE OF TEMPERATURE; 386] *Opposite*: shiver

sweltering *adj* **boiling**, baking, burning up, red-hot, blistering, oppressive, scorching (*informal*), sizzling (*informal*), roasting (*informal*) [➡HOT WEATHER; 1050] *Opposite*: freezing

swerve *v* **veer**, veer off, turn sharply, swing over, change direction, diverge, deviate [➡CHANGE DIRECTION OF MOTION; 344]

swift 1 *adj* **quick**, speedy, fast, rapid, prompt, sudden [➡MOVING QUICKLY; 103] 2 *type of* **common bird** [➡BIRDS; 997]

swiftly *adv* **quickly**, speedily, fast, summarily, rapidly, on the double, promptly, suddenly, in the blink of an eye, like greased lightning, like a shot, expeditiously, precipitously, instantly, immediately, in a flash [➡MOVING QUICKLY; 103] *Opposite*: slowly

swiftness *n* **rapidity**, quickness, fastness, pace, speed, speediness, velocity, dispatch, alacrity, precipitousness, expeditiousness, fleetness (*literary*) [➡SPEED; 102] *Opposite*: slowness

swig (*informal*) 1 *v* **drink**, swill, toss off, take a drop, guzzle (*informal*), imbibe (*formal or humorous*), quaff (*literary or humorous*) [➡DRINK; 711] 2 *n* **mouthful**, nip, draft, drink [➡DRINK; 711]

swill 1 *v* **rinse**, sluice, wash out, wash down, swab, clean, wash [➡CLEAN AND POLISH; 403] 2 *v* **gulp down**, swig (*informal*), guzzle (*informal*), knock back (*informal*), quaff (*literary or humorous*) [➡DRINK; 711] 3 *n* **pig food**, slops, mash, scraps, pigswill (*UK*) [➡ANIMAL FEED; 1168]

swim 1 *v* **bathe**, go for a dip, go swimming [➡HOBBIES, GAMES, AND SPORTS; 875] 2 *v* **spin**, whirl, reel, sway [➡MOVE SOMETHING: ON THE SPOT; 336]

swimmingly *adv* **successfully**, well, smoothly, easily, like a house on fire, satisfactorily, like clockwork, effortlessly [➡GOOD, WELL, BETTER; 183] *Opposite*: laboriously

swimming pool *n* **pool**, plunge pool, lido (*UK*), swimming baths (*UK dated*) [➡BUILDINGS FOR PUBLIC ENTERTAINMENT; 1084]

swimming trunks *type of* **sportswear** [➡GARMENTS AND OUTFITS; 865]

swimsuit *type of* **sportswear** [➡GARMENTS AND OUTFITS; 865]

swimwear *type of* **sportswear** [➡GARMENTS AND OUTFITS; 865]

swindle 1 *v* **cheat**, con, dupe, trick, double-cross, deceive, defraud, fiddle (*informal*), rip off (*informal*), fleece (*informal*), do out of (*informal*), bilk (*informal*), scam (*slang*) [➡STEAL AND ROB; 426] 2 *n* **fraud**, hoax, embezzlement, con, confidence game, racket, rip-off (*informal*), grift (*informal*), scam (*slang*) [➡DECEPTION AND LIES; 660]

swindler *n* **cheat**, trickster, charlatan, fraud, embezzler, faker, shark (*informal*), bilker (*informal*), grifter (*informal*), con artist (*slang*), con man (*slang*) [➡PEOPLE WHO DECEIVE; 661]

swine *n* **hog**, boar, pig [➡FARM ANIMALS; 982]

swing 1 *v* **dangle**, hang, hang down, be suspended, sway, suspend, droop, depend (*archaic*) [➡MOVE SOMETHING: ON THE SPOT; 336] 2 *v* **swerve**, veer, reel, pivot, rotate, turn [➡CHANGE DIRECTION OF MOTION; 344] 3 *v* **rock**, fluctuate, move back and forth, sway, move backward and forward, roll, turn around, spin around, move to and fro, oscillate, shift, alter, change, vacillate, alternate, swivel around, whirl around [➡BOUNCE, UNDULATE, AND VIBRATE; 308] 4 *v* (*informal*) **manage**, succeed in, accomplish, arrange, bring off, pull off (*informal*) [➡CARRY OUT AN ACTION; 269] 5 *n* **swipe**, smack, slap, thump, blow, strike, punch [➡PHYSICAL ATTACK AND PUNISHMENT; 415] 6 *type of* **jazz music** [➡MUSIC, SONGS, AND SINGING; 907]

swing around *v* **turn around**, spin around, whirl around, twirl around, wheel around [➡CHANGE DIRECTION OF MOTION; 344]

swing at *v* **hit**, hit out at, lash out, strike, thump, smack, slap, swipe, punch [➡PHYSICAL ATTACK AND PUNISHMENT; 415]

swing bridge *type of* **bridge** [➡BRIDGES, TUNNELS, CROSSINGS, AND JUNCTIONS; 1112]

swing by *v* [➡ARRIVE; 12]

swingeing (*UK*) *adj* **severe**, harmful, punishing, harsh, draconian, stringent [➡PHYSICALLY UNPLEASANT; 226] *Opposite*: mild

swipe 1 *v* **hit**, swing at, lash out, hit out at, strike, slap, smack, thump, whack, punch, bash (*informal*) [➡PHYSICAL ATTACK AND PUNISHMENT; 415] 2 *v* (*informal*) **steal**, pilfer, make off with, walk off with, run off with, snatch, take, filch (*informal*), lift (*informal*), cop (*slang*) [➡STEAL AND ROB; 426] 3 *n* **blow**, hit, swing, slap, smack, thump, punch, bash (*informal*) [➡PHYSICAL ATTACK AND PUNISHMENT; 415] 4 *n* (*informal*) **critical remark**, cutting remark, dig, putdown (*informal*) [➡CRITICISMS AND ANGRY OUTBURSTS; 50] *Opposite*: compliment

swipe card *n* **plastic card**, magnetic card, smart card, key card, credit card, bank card, debit card [➡ACCOUNTING, BANKING, AND BUDGETING; 799]

swirl 1 *v* **whirl**, twirl, spin, eddy, churn [➡MOVE SOMETHING: ON THE SPOT; 336] 2 *n* **twirl**, whirl, spin, eddy [➡MOVE SOMETHING: ON THE SPOT; 336]

swish 1 *v* **hiss**, whoosh, whistle, whisper, rustle [➡EMIT CONTINUOUS SOUNDS; 366] 2 *n* **rustle**, hiss, whoosh, whisper, whistle [➡CONTINUOUS SOUNDS; 1258]

Swiss *type of* **hard cheese** [➡DAIRY PRODUCTS AND CHEESES; 1183]

Swiss chard *type of* **vegetable** [➡FRUIT AND VEGETABLES; 1176]

switch 1 *n* **control**, lever, button, knob, key, regulator [➡PARTS OF MACHINES AND TOOLS; 1118] 2 *n* **change**, shift, adjustment, difference, modification, alteration [➡CHANGE; 372] 3 *n* **exchange**, substitution, changeover, replacement, trade, swap (*informal*) [➡EXCHANGE AND INTERCHANGE; 448] 4 *n* **whip**, lash, crop, cat-o'-nine-tails [➡BLUNT INSTRUMENTS AND WHIPS; 1158]

switchback *n* **bend**, twist, zigzag, hairpin, turn, corner [➡ROADS; 1106]

switchblade *type of* **knife** [➡CUTTING TOOLS; 1120]

switchboard *type of* **telecommunications equipment** [➡ TELE-COMMUNICATIONS; 1130]

switch off 1 *v* **shut down**, stop, deactivate, disconnect, cut, turn off, kill (*informal*) [➡ CAUSE TO STOP; 266] *Opposite*: switch on 2 *v* (*informal*) **relax**, unwind, stop worrying, stop paying attention, chill out (*slang*) [➡ CHANGE OF MOOD AND COMPOSURE; 580]

switch on *v* **turn on**, start, start up, activate, connect, begin, commence [➡ CAUSE TO START; 265] *Opposite*: switch off

swivel *v* **spin**, rotate, revolve, pivot, turn around, twist, twirl, wheel [➡ MOVE SOMETHING: ON THE SPOT; 336]

swivel around *v* [➡ MOVE SOMETHING: ON THE SPOT; 336]

swivel chair *type of* **seating** [➡ FURNITURE; 858]

swizz (*UK*) *n* [➡ NUISANCES; 253]

swollen *adj* **distended**, inflamed, engorged, puffy, puffed-up, enlarged, inflated, bloated, blown up [➡ CHANGE OF SIZE: BIGGER; 392]

swollen head (*UK*) *n* **swelled head**, conceit, self-conceit, pride, self-satisfaction, vanity, arrogance, self-importance [➡ AFFECTATION, SELF-SATISFACTION, AND SNOBBISHNESS; 507] *Opposite*: modesty

swollen-headed (*UK*) *adj* **conceited**, full of yourself, vain, self-important, puffed up, self-satisfied, swell-headed, cocky (*informal*), too big for your boots (*informal*), stuck-up (*informal*) [➡ POMPOUS, LOUD, AND OVER-CONFIDENT; 635] *Opposite*: modest

swoon 1 *v* **pass out**, faint, black out, lose consciousness, faint away, collapse, keel over (*informal*) [➡ TIRED, ASLEEP, AND UNCONSCIOUS; 738] 2 *n* **faint**, blackout, loss of consciousness, unconsciousness [➡ ILL AND SICK; 740]

swoop *v* **pounce**, jump, leap, dive, fly down, lunge, plunge [➡ GO DOWNWARD; 307]

swoosh 1 *n* **rustle**, swish, rush, swirl, whiz, whirl [➡ CONTINUOUS SOUNDS; 1258] 2 *v* **rustle**, swish, rush, swirl, whiz, whirl [➡ MOVE FAST; 313]

sword *n* [➡ SWORDS AND KNIVES; 1157]

sword

◆ *types of swords or knives*
battleax, bayonet, bowie knife, broadsword, claymore, cutlass, dagger, dirk, foil, machete, poleax, rapier, saber, scimitar, skean, stiletto, swordstick, tomahawk

sword fighter *n* [➡ PEOPLE IN SPORTS AND LEISURE; 876]

sword fighting *n* [➡ HOBBIES, GAMES, AND SPORTS; 875]

swordfish *type of* **tropical fish** [➡ OCEAN FISH; 1009]

sword grass *type of* **grass** [➡ GRASS; 1031]

swordplay *n* **sword fighting**, fencing, dueling, foil fencing, combat [➡ NON-AGGRESSIVE/SPORTING EVENTS; 40]

swordstick *type of* **sword or knife** [➡ SWORDS AND KNIVES; 1157]

sworn *adj* **confirmed**, affirmed, avowed (*formal*) [➡ CERTAINTY; 561]

sworn enemy *n* [➡ ENEMIES AND TORMENTORS; 969]

sybarite *n* **voluptuary**, sensualist, hedonist, epicurean, pleasure-lover [➡ PLEASURE-SEEKERS AND HEDONISTS; 886] *Opposite*: Spartan

sybaritic *adj* [➡ PLEASURE-SEEKING AND EXCESS; 885]

sycamore *type of* **deciduous tree** [➡ DECIDUOUS TREES; 1028]

sycophancy *n* **servility**, obsequiousness, flattery, fawning, toadying, sucking up (*informal*), brownnosing (*slang*) [➡ INGRATIATING; 638]

sycophant *n* **toady**, flatterer, minion, yes man, boot-licker (*informal*) [➡ SUPERFICIAL OR INSINCERE PEOPLE; 951]

sycophantic *adj* **ingratiating**, flattering, kowtowing, obsequious, apple-polishing (*slang*) [➡ INGRATIATING; 638]

syllable *n* [➡ ASPECTS OF LANGUAGE; 682]

syllabub *type of* **dessert** [➡ CAKES, COOKIES, AND DESSERTS; 1181]

syllabus *n* **course outline**, curriculum, program, program of study, prospectus [➡ LISTS AND SCHEDULES; 587]

syllaweb *n* [➡ THE INTERNET; 1128]

sylph *n* **nymph**, sprite, fairy, dryad, naiad [➡ MYTHICAL BEINGS; 789]

sylphlike *adj* **slender**, willowy, lithe, slim, graceful, svelte, slight [➡ BUILD; 477] *Opposite*: hefty

symbiosis *n* **cooperation**, interdependence, relationship, association, synergy, interaction [➡ RECIPROCITY AND INTERDEPENDENCE; 147] *Opposite*: independence

symbiotic *adj* **mutually beneficial**, interdependent, synergetic, cooperative, reciprocal, mutual, related, associated [➡ RECIPROCITY AND INTERDEPENDENCE; 147] *Opposite*: independent

symbol 1 *n* **sign**, representation, character, figure, mark, icon, pictogram [➡ SYMBOLS, SIGNS, AND NUMBERS; 596] 2 *n* **emblem**, image, badge, logo [➡ SYMBOLS, SIGNS, AND NUMBERS; 596]

symbolic *adj* **representative**, figurative, emblematic, representational [➡ REPRESENTATIVE; 66]

symbolism 1 *n* **imagery**, allegory, representation [➡ REPRESENTATIONS AND GENERAL EXAMPLES; 65] 2 *type of* **pre-20th-century art movement** [➡ ARTISTIC MOVEMENTS AND STYLES; 899]

symbolize *v* **represent**, be a symbol of, be a sign of, signify, stand for, denote, indicate, mean, imply, suggest, embody, epitomize [➡ REPRESENT SOMETHING OR SOMEBODY; 59]

symmetrical *adj* **balanced**, even, equal, proportioned, regular [➡ EQUALITY; 154] *Opposite*: asymmetrical

symmetry *n* **regularity**, balance, equilibrium, evenness, proportion [➡ EQUALITY; 154] *Opposite*: asymmetry

sympathetic 1 *adj* **understanding**, concerned, kind, kindly, compassionate, caring, considerate, sensitive, kindhearted, supportive, benevolent [➡ GENEROSITY AND KINDNESS; 495] *Opposite*: unfeeling 2 *adj* **approving**, in agreement, in accord, supportive, well-disposed, in favor [➡ HARMONY; 155] *Opposite*: against 3 *adj* **agreeable**, congenial, likable, friendly, amiable, affable, genial, pleasant [➡ FRIENDLINESS AND SOCIABILITY; 494] *Opposite*: disagreeable

sympathize *v* **empathize**, feel sorry for, commiserate, express sympathy, understand, identify, feel for, be supportive, pity [➡ BE CONCERNED AND CARE; 581]

sympathizer *n* **partisan**, backer, follower, adherent, well-wisher, champion, supporter [➡ SUPPORTERS, PROTECTORS, AND COMPATRIOTS; 970] *Opposite*: opponent

sympathy 1 *n* **understanding**, compassion, kindness, consideration, empathy, fellow feeling [➡ COMPASSION AND FORGIVENESS; 551] *Opposite*: incomprehension **2** *n* **pity**, commiseration, condolences [➡ COMPASSION AND FORGIVENESS; 551] **3** *n* **approval**, agreement, support, backing [➡ HARMONY; 155]

symphonic *adj* **musical**, orchestral, instrumental, classical, philharmonic, ensemble [➡ MUSICAL TERMS; 912]

symphony *type of* **musical form** [➡ MUSIC, SONGS, AND SINGING; 907]

symphony orchestra *type of* **band** [➡ MUSICIANS AND SINGERS; 908]

symposium *n* **conference**, seminar, meeting, convention [➡ MEETINGS AND ASSEMBLIES; 43]

symptom *n* **indication**, sign, warning sign, indicator [➡ INDICATIONS, SIGNS, AND WARNINGS; 68]

symptomatic *adj* **indicative**, suggestive, characteristic [➡ REPRESENTATIVE; 66]

synagogue *type of* **place of worship** [➡ RELIGIOUS BUILDINGS; 1085]

synchronicity *n* [➡ CONCURRENT AND CONTEMPORANEOUS; 164]

synchronism *n* [➡ CONCURRENT AND CONTEMPORANEOUS; 164]

synchronize *v* **harmonize**, coordinate, orchestrate, bring into line, match [➡ ARRANGE AND CREATE ORDER; 357]

synchronized *adj* **coordinated**, harmonized, corresponding, matched, in time, in step, in line [➡ CONCURRENT AND CONTEMPORANEOUS; 164]

synchronous *adj* [➡ CONCURRENT AND CONTEMPORANEOUS; 164]

syncopate *v* **modify**, play, shift, swing, stress, accent [➡ CHANGE; 372]

syncopation *n* **shift of accent**, modification, accent, stress, rhythm [➡ MUSICAL TERMS; 912]

syndicate *n* **association**, collective, consortium, organization, group [➡ GROUPS WITH A COMMON INTEREST; 938]

syndrome *n* **condition**, disease, pattern, set of symptoms, disorder [➡ SICKNESS; 729]

synecdoche *type of* **figure of speech** [➡ FIGURES OF SPEECH; 673]

synergetic *adj* [➡ RECIPROCITY AND INTERDEPENDENCE; 147]

synergy *n* **working together**, interaction, cooperation, combined effect, collaboration, concerted effort [➡ RECIPROCITY AND INTERDEPENDENCE; 147]

synonym *n* **alternative word**, alternative expression, other word, substitute, replacement [➡ ASPECTS OF LANGUAGE; 682]

synonymous *adj* **identical**, the same, one and the same, equal, tantamount [➡ SAMENESS; 150] *Opposite*: different

synopsis *n* **outline**, rundown, précis, summing up, summary, summation, abridgment, abstract [➡ SUMMARIES, OUTLINES, AND EXCERPTS; 588]

syntax *n* **grammar**, sentence structure, language rules, composition, word order, arrangement [➡ ASPECTS OF LANGUAGE; 682]

synthesis 1 *n* **mixture**, amalgamation, combination, blend, fusion [➡ COLLECTIONS AND MIXTURES OF THINGS; 1244] *Opposite*: separation **2** *n* **production**, creation, making, manufacture [➡ CREATION; 346]

synthesize 1 *v* **manufacture**, create, make, produce [➡ MANUFACTURE; 349] **2** *v* **fuse**, blend, combine, amalgamate, integrate, join [➡ COMBINE AND MIX; 400] *Opposite*: separate

synthesizer *type of* **keyboard** [➡ MUSICAL INSTRUMENTS; 910]

synthetic 1 *adj* **artificial**, fake, mock, imitation, faux [➡ FALSE AND UNREAL; 173] *Opposite*: real **2** *adj* **insincere**, sham, bogus, put on, phony [➡ AFFECTATION, SELF-SATISFACTION, AND SNOBBISHNESS; 507] *Opposite*: genuine

syringe *type of* **medical instrument** [➡ HAND TOOLS; 1119]

syrup *n* **maple syrup**, corn syrup, molasses, sauce, golden syrup (*UK*), treacle (*UK*) [➡ SUGAR AND PRESERVES; 1184]

syrupy *adj* **sugary**, thick, sweet, treacly (*UK*) [➡ TASTE; 703]

system 1 *n* **scheme**, arrangement, classification, structure, organism, organization, coordination [➡ ORDER AND ORGANIZATION; 206] **2** *n* **method**, technique, procedure, routine, approach, practice [➡ WAYS OF DOING THINGS; 294] **3** *n* **orderliness**, regularity, method, logic [➡ ORDER AND ORGANIZATION; 206] *Opposite*: disorder

systematic *adj* **methodical**, orderly, organized, efficient, logical, regular [➡ ORDER AND ORGANIZATION; 206] *Opposite*: disorganized

systematization *n* [➡ ARRANGE AND CREATE ORDER; 357]

systematize *v* **arrange**, order, regulate, sort, classify, standardize, put in order, organize [➡ ARRANGE AND CREATE ORDER; 357]

systemic *adj* **universal**, complete, general [➡ ALL; 128]

systemize *v* [➡ ARRANGE AND CREATE ORDER; 357]

system of government *n* [➡ STYLES AND SYSTEMS OF GOVERNMENT; 806]

systems analyst *n* [➡ COMPUTERS AND COMPUTING; 1127]

T

tab 1 *n* **flap**, label, ticket, stub, strip, tag (*UK*) [➡ NAME AND DESCRIBE; 665] **2** *n* (*informal*) **bill**, check, account, running total [➡ RECEIPTS AND INVOICES; 591]

tabard *type of* **top** [➡ GARMENTS AND OUTFITS; 865]

tabasco *type of* **seasonings, sauces, and dips** [➡ SEASONINGS AND SAUCES; 1174]

tabby *type of* **cat** [➡ FELINES; 983]

tabby cat *see* **tabby**

tabernacle 1 *n* **chest**, cabinet, container, case, box, coffer [➡ CONTAINERS, RECEPTACLES, AND PACKAGING; 1245] **2** *type of* **church** [➡ RELIGIOUS BUILDINGS; 1085]

tabla *type of* **percussion instrument** [➡ MUSICAL INSTRUMENTS; 910]

table 1 *n* **bench**, board, desk, counter, stand, stall, slab, tabletop [➡ FURNITURE; 858] **2** *n* **food**, fare, diet, provision, menu, board [➡ FOOD, 1167] **3** *n* **chart**, graph, diagram, spreadsheet, record, register, index, list, catalog, schedule [➡ DRAWINGS, CHARTS, AND TABLES; 594] **4** *v* **postpone**, shelve, defer, put on the back burner, put on ice, hold over, put off [➡ DELAY ACTION OR OCCURRENCE; 278] *Opposite:* bring forward **5** *v* (*UK*) **propose**, put forward, submit, suggest, enter, move [➡ SUGGEST, HINT, AND COMMENT; 612] *Opposite:* withdraw

table

◆ *types of tables*
bedside table, card table, coffee table, console, davenport, desk, dining table, dressing table, end table, escritoire, gateleg table, night table, occasional table, Pembroke table, roll-top desk, tea table, trestle table, vanity table, worktable, writing desk

tableau *n* **display**, picture, montage, scene, representation, image, description [➡ REPRESENTATIONS AND GENERAL EXAMPLES; 65]

tablecloth *n* **cover**, cloth, covering [➡ FURNISHING AND HOUSEHOLD LINENS; 860]

table knife *type of* **knife** [➡ CUTTING TOOLS; 1120]

table lamp *n* [➡ LIGHTING; 862]

tableland *n* **plain**, flatland, prairie, plateau, upland, mesa [➡ DESERTS, PLAINS, AND MOORLAND; 1045] *Opposite:* lowland

table linen *n* [➡ FURNISHING AND HOUSEHOLD LINENS; 860]

table mat *n* **place mat**, coaster, mat, pad, trivet [➡ TABLEWARE, FLATWARE, AND KITCHENWARE; 861]

tablespoon *type of* **flatware** [➡ TABLEWARE, FLATWARE, AND KITCHENWARE; 861]

tablespoonful *n* [➡ AMOUNTS AND QUANTITIES; 112]

tablet 1 *n* **pill**, capsule, lozenge [➡ REMEDIES, TREATMENTS, AND OPERATIONS; 731] **2** *n* **slab**, block, bar, cake, lump [➡ AMOUNTS OF SOLID OR SEMISOLID; 115]

tablet computer *type of* **computer** [➡ COMPUTERS AND COMPUTING; 1127]

table tennis *type of* **court game** [➡ HOBBIES, GAMES, AND SPORTS; 875]

tableware *n* **crockery**, plates, dishes, dinner service, tea service, flatware, glassware, glasses, bowls [➡ TABLEWARE, FLATWARE, AND KITCHENWARE; 861]

tabloid 1 *n* (*UK*) **paper**, newspaper, rag (*informal*), red-top (*informal*) [➡ NEWSPAPERS AND MAGAZINES; 605] **2** *adj* **sensationalist**, shocking, lurid, scandalous, yellow, florid [➡ NEWSPAPERS AND MAGAZINES; 605]

taboo 1 *adj* **offensive**, unmentionable, unthinkable, distasteful, off-limits, out of bounds [➡ MORALLY BAD OR IMPROPER; 775] **2** *adj* **forbidden**, banned, prohibited, barred, proscribed, outlawed [➡ REFUSE PERMISSION AND NOT ALLOW; 670] *Opposite:* acceptable **3** *n* **ban**, prohibition, bar, restriction, interdict, proscription (*formal*) [➡ REFUSE PERMISSION AND NOT ALLOW; 670] **4** *v* **forbid**, ban, prohibit, bar, proscribe, outlaw [➡ REFUSE PERMISSION AND NOT ALLOW; 670] *Opposite:* allow

tabor *type of* **percussion instrument** [➡ MUSICAL INSTRUMENTS; 910]

tabular *adj* **flat**, level, smooth, even, horizontal, plane [➡ ORIENTATION AND ALIGNMENT; 1223]

tabulate *v* **tabularize**, chart, arrange, organize, present, set out, formulate, lay out [➡ ARRANGE AND CREATE ORDER; 357]

tabulation *n* **tabularization**, arrangement, organization, presentation, formulation, layout [➡ DRAWINGS, CHARTS, AND TABLES; 594]

tachometer *type of* **measuring device** [➡ MEASURING DEVICES; 1123]

tacit *adj* **unspoken**, implicit, inferred, implied, understood, unstated, silent, wordless [➡ KNOWN AND FAMOUS; 181] *Opposite:* explicit

taciturn *adj* **reserved**, uncommunicative, reticent, silent, quiet, introverted, shy, distant, aloof [➡ RETICENT AND UNFORTHCOMING; 631] *Opposite:* garrulous

See Compare and Contrast at **silent**.

taciturnity *n* **reserve**, uncommunicativeness, reticence, silence, quietness, introversion, shyness, distance, aloofness [➡ RETICENT AND UNFORTHCOMING; 631] *Opposite:* garrulousness

tack 1 *n* **nail**, pin, screw, staple, clip, fastener [➡ FASTENERS, LINKS, AND NETWORKS; 1247] **2** *n* **approach**, tactic, line, method, policy, scheme, ploy [➡ WAYS OF DOING THINGS; 294] **3** *n* **direction**, path, bearing, course, way, line, route [➡ DIRECTION OF MOTION; 345] **4** *v* **pin**, nail, fasten, attach, affix, fix, staple, clip [➡ FASTEN, LINK, AND JOIN; 408] *Opposite:* unfasten **5** *v* **append**, add on, tag on, stick on, attach, throw in [➡ FASTEN, LINK, AND JOIN; 408] *Opposite:* remove

tackiness (*informal*) *n* **tastelessness**, bad taste, vulgarity, cheapness, nastiness, tawdriness, crudeness, crudity, showiness, ostentation [➡ IN POOR TASTE AND OVERSENTIMENTAL; 229] *Opposite:* taste

tackle **1** *n* **challenge**, attack, block, confrontation, throw, grab, hold [➡ NON-AGGRESSIVE/SPORTING EVENTS; 40] **2** *n* **equipment**, apparatus, kit, outfit, tools, trappings, implements, rigging, gear (*informal*) [➡ DEVICES; 1115] **3** *v* **undertake**, begin, embark upon, attempt, engage in, deal with, attack [➡ ATTEMPT AN ACTION; 261] **4** *v* **confront**, challenge, face, speak to, collar, bend somebody's ear [➡ INITIATE AND ESTABLISH COMMUNICATION; 680] **5** *v* **block**, stop, throw, seize, grab, bring down, halt, attack, grasp, wrestle [➡ PHYSICAL ATTACK AND PUNISHMENT; 415]

tacky **1** *adj* (*informal*) **tasteless**, in bad taste, vulgar, cheap, nasty, tawdry, low, crude, showy, ostentatious [➡ IN POOR TASTE AND OVERSENTIMENTAL; 229] *Opposite:* tasteful **2** *adj* **sticky**, messy, gluey, gummy, adhesive, wet, viscous, waxy [➡ PHYSICAL TEXTURE; 1222] *Opposite:* dry

tacos *type of* **cooked dish** [➡ PREPARED DISHES; 1170]

tact *n* **diplomacy**, discretion, sensitivity, delicacy, thoughtfulness, consideration, perception, insight, discernment, skill, dexterity, subtlety, judgment, care, politeness [➡ GOOD MANNERS AND SOCIAL SKILLS; 520] *Opposite:* tactlessness

tactful *adj* **diplomatic**, discreet, sensitive, delicate, thoughtful, considerate, perceptive, insightful, discerning, skillful, dexterous, subtle, judicious, careful, polite, kind [➡ GOOD MANNERS AND SOCIAL SKILLS; 520] *Opposite:* tactless

tactfulness *n* [➡ GOOD MANNERS AND SOCIAL SKILLS; 520]

tactic *n* **method**, approach, course, ploy, policy, scheme, way, line, tack, device, trick, maneuver [➡ WAYS OF DOING THINGS; 294]

tactical *adj* **strategic**, planned, premeditated, preemptive, psychological, considered, calculated, deliberate, intentional, purposeful, defensive [➡ INTENTIONAL AND DELIBERATE; 279] *Opposite:* accidental

tactician *n* **strategist**, negotiator, planner, schemer, diplomat, spin doctor (*slang*) [➡ POLITICAL OFFICES AND POLITICIANS; 808]

tactics *n* **strategy**, planning, campaign, maneuvers, devices, diplomacy, policy, procedure, scheme [➡ WAYS OF DOING THINGS; 294]

tactile **1** *adj* **tangible**, palpable, perceptible, physical, concrete, solid [➡ PERCEPTIBLE; 25] *Opposite:* intangible **2** *adj* **demonstrative**, physical, affectionate, touchy-feely (*informal*) [➡ HONEST AND OPEN; 630] *Opposite:* reserved

tactless *adj* **insensitive**, undiplomatic, indiscreet, indelicate, thoughtless, inconsiderate, unfeeling, injudicious, careless, impolite, unthinking, rude, unkind, clumsy, gauche, crass [➡ BAD MANNERS AND SOCIAL SKILLS; 521] *Opposite:* tactful

tactlessness *n* **insensitivity**, indiscretion, indelicacy, thoughtlessness, inconsiderateness, injudiciousness, carelessness, impoliteness, rudeness, unkindness, clum-

siness, gaucheness, crassness [➡ BAD MANNERS AND SOCIAL SKILLS; 521] *Opposite:* tact

tad (*informal*) *n* **bit**, little, touch, mite, dash, soupçon, smidgen (*informal*) [➡ FEW, LITTLE, SMALL AMOUNT; 120] *Opposite:* lot

tae kwon do *type of* **combat sport** [➡ HOBBIES, GAMES, AND SPORTS; 875]

taffeta *type of* **fabric from animals** [➡ FABRICS; 1132]

taffy *type of* **confectionery** [➡ CONFECTIONERY; 1182]

tag **1** *n* **label**, ticket, tab, docket, identifier, code, chip, device [➡ NAME AND DESCRIBE; 665] **2** *v* **mark**, label, ticket, docket, identify [➡ NAME AND DESCRIBE; 665] **3** *v* **append**, tack on, add on, attach, stick on, throw in [➡ FASTEN, LINK, AND JOIN; 408] *Opposite:* remove

tag along *v* **link up**, join in, follow, accompany, go with, come with, associate with [➡ ACCOMPANY AND FOLLOW; 337]

tagine *type of* **cooked dish** [➡ PREPARED DISHES; 1170]

tagliatelle *type of* **pasta** [➡ PASTA; 1180]

tahini *type of* **seasonings, sauces, and dips** [➡ SEASONINGS AND SAUCES; 1174]

tai chi *type of* **complementary therapy** [➡ REMEDIES, TREATMENTS, AND OPERATIONS; 731]

tail **1** *part of* **bird** [➡ PARTS OF A BIRD; 1006] **2** *part of* **fish** [➡ PARTS OF A FISH; 1011] **3** *part of* **aircraft** [➡ AIRCRAFT; 1148] **4** *n* (*informal*) **follower**, shadow, stalker, pursuer, tracker [➡ ENEMIES AND TORMENTORS; 969] **5** *v* (*informal*) **follow**, trail, track, shadow, stalk, pursue, go after, chase [➡ ACCOMPANY AND FOLLOW; 337]

See Compare and Contrast at **follow**.

tailback (*UK*) *n* **traffic jam**, line, gridlock, logjam, queue (*UK*) [➡ TRAVEL: TRAFFIC PROBLEMS AND TRAFFIC MANAGEMENT; 323]

tailboard *see* **tailgate**

tailcoat *type of* **jacket** [➡ GARMENTS AND OUTFITS; 865]

tail end *n* **end**, close, ending, conclusion, finish, remainder, residue, remnant [➡ ENDS AND DEPARTURES; 54] *Opposite:* start

tailgate **1** *v* **dog**, hound, be hard on the heels of, follow, pursue, tail [➡ ACCOMPANY AND FOLLOW; 337] **2** *part of* **external structure** [➡ EXTERNAL PARTS OF A VEHICLE; 1147]

taillight *type of* **external feature** [➡ EXTERNAL PARTS OF A VEHICLE; 1147]

tail off *v* **fade**, peter out, dwindle, decrease, fall away, wane, drop, tail away [➡ DISAPPEAR; 4] *Opposite:* increase

tailor **1** *v* **make**, make to measure, cut, fashion, mold, style, shape [➡ CREATION; 346] **2** *v* **adapt**, customize, custombuild, modify, fit, alter, convert, personalize, design, style [➡ CHANGE; 372]

tailored **1** *adj* **custom-made**, made-to-order, made-to-measure, tailor-made, handmade, designer, couture, personalized, bespoke (*UK*) [➡ DESCRIBING CLOTHES; 869] *Opposite:* off-the-rack **2** *adj* **fitted**, shaped, well-cut, figure-hugging, close-fitting, trim, formal [➡ DESCRIBING CLOTHES; 869] *Opposite:* casual **3** *adj* **adapted**, customized, custom-built, modified, altered, converted, personalized, designed, styled [➡ CHANGE; 372]

tailor-made 1 *adj* **perfect**, ideal, right, suitable, appropriate [➡ CORRECT AND FAULTLESS; 182] *Opposite:* wrong 2 *adj* **made-to-measure**, made-to-order, custom-made, tailored, handmade, designer, couture, personalized, bespoke (*UK*) [➡ DESCRIBING CLOTHES; 869] *Opposite:* off-the-rack

tailpiece *n* **end**, end piece, finale, finial, coda, postscript, appendix [➡ EXTREMITIES OF PHYSICAL OBJECTS; 1250]

tailplane *part of* **aircraft** [➡ AIRCRAFT; 1148]

tail rotor *part of* **aircraft** [➡ AIRCRAFT; 1148]

tails *type of* **jacket** [➡ GARMENTS AND OUTFITS; 865]

tailspin 1 *n* **nosedive**, dive, spin, spiral, descent, fall, plunge [➡ GO DOWNWARD; 307] 2 *n* (*informal*) **panic**, flap, turmoil, flat spin, whirl, tizzy (*informal*) [➡ DIFFICULT SITUATIONS; 72]

taint 1 *v* **contaminate**, pollute, stain, spoil, infect, soil, dirty, foul, ruin, corrupt, poison, blemish, defile (*formal*) [➡ DIRTY AND CONTAMINATE; 404] *Opposite:* enhance 2 *n* **stain**, blemish, blot, defect, fault, flaw, smear, spot, stigma, disgrace [➡ FAULTS, FLAWS, AND WEAKNESSES; 251]

tainted *adj* **contaminated**, polluted, stained, spoiled, soiled, infected, dirtied, fouled, ruined, corrupted, poisoned, blemished, defiled (*formal*) [➡ DIRTY; 1235] *Opposite:* pure

taipan *type of* **poisonous snake** [➡ SNAKES; 995]

taka *type of* **currency** [➡ CURRENCIES; 798]

take 1 *v* **remove**, appropriate, acquire, grab, seize, procure, steal, rob, pocket, pilfer, filch (*informal*), purloin (*formal or humorous*) [➡ STEAL AND ROB; 426] *Opposite:* give 2 *v* **grasp**, grab, seize, catch, catch on to, catch hold of, grab hold of, receive [➡ CONTACT: HOLD; 411] *Opposite:* drop 3 *v* **carry**, transfer, fetch, bring, transport, convey, haul, ferry, cart [➡ MOVE SOMETHING TO ANOTHER LOCATION; 324] 4 *v* **conquer**, capture, win, seize, secure, overcome, occupy, gain, appropriate, hijack, take over, annex [➡ BEAT AND DEFEAT; 80] *Opposite:* lose 5 *v* **choose**, select, procure, receive, buy, purchase, pay for, hire, rent, lease, reserve, book, engage [➡ PURCHASE; 422] 6 *v* **accompany**, bring, escort, guide, lead, usher, conduct, convey, show [➡ ACCOMPANY AND FOLLOW; 337] 7 *v* **undertake**, adopt, accept, take on, assume, shoulder [➡ CARRY OUT AN ACTION; 269] *Opposite:* refuse 8 *v* **bear**, stand, endure, tolerate, suffer, accept, withstand, abide, brook, swallow, undergo [➡ TOLERATE AND ENDURE; 766] *Opposite:* reject 9 *v* **support**, hold up, hold, bear, manage [➡ TOLERATE AND ENDURE; 766] 10 *v* **contain**, hold, accept, accommodate, house, support, hold up [➡ HOLD AND CONTAIN; 455] 11 *v* **study**, learn, read, do, take up [➡ STUDYING; 844] *Opposite:* teach 12 *v* **consider**, look at, discuss, examine, think about, ponder [➡ PAY ATTENTION; 765] 13 *v* **require**, need, demand, use, accept, expend, call on, consume, swallow [➡ NEED AND REQUIRE; 464] *Opposite:* reject 14 *v* **derive**, draw, experience, feel, extract, obtain, get [➡ UNDERSTAND AND GRASP; 759] 15 *v* **presume**, assume, believe, consider, perceive, hold, regard, understand, interpret, deduce, deem (*formal*) [➡ UNDERSTAND AND GRASP; 759] 16 *v* **succeed**, work, stick, root [➡ FUNCTION SUCCESSFULLY; 469] *Opposite:* fail 17 *v* **subtract**, deduct, take away, take off, remove, eliminate [➡ REMOVE SOMETHING; 338] *Opposite:* add 18 *n* **receipts**, takings, earnings, income, revenue, gross, proceeds, profits, returns, yield [➡ INCOME; 460] *Opposite:* expenditure 19 *n* **shot**, sequence,

scene [➡ FILM; 901] 20 *n* **impression**, interpretation, opinion, view, point of view, angle [➡ POINTS OF VIEW; 767]

take aback *v* **surprise**, stun, shock, nonplus, bowl over, disconcert, startle [➡ SURPRISE AND IMPRESS; 574]

take a back seat *v* **hold back**, restrain yourself, rein back, stay out of it [➡ AVOID, PREVENT, LIMIT, AND CONTROL; 277]

take a break *v* **rest**, relax, take time out, come up for air, pause, put your feet up, take a rest, ease off, stop, break off, take a breather (*informal*), take five (*informal*) [➡ LACK OF ACTIVITY OR MOTION; 342] *Opposite:* press on

take a breather (*informal*) *v* **rest**, relax, take a break, take time out, come up for air, pause, put your feet up, take a rest, ease off, stop, break off, take five (*informal*) [➡ LACK OF ACTIVITY OR MOTION; 342] *Opposite:* press on

take account of *v* **allow for**, take into consideration, bear in mind, make allowances for, keep in mind, take on board, consider, think about [➡ PAY ATTENTION; 765] *Opposite:* ignore

take a chance *v* **gamble**, venture, risk it, chance it, stick your neck out, play with fire, ask for trouble, ask for it, skate on thin ice, be on dangerous ground [➡ GAMBLE AND TAKE RISKS; 466] *Opposite:* play safe

take action *v* **act**, do something, take the plunge, take the bull by the horns, take steps, make a start, proceed, start, go for it (*slang*), get stuck in (*UK*) [➡ CARRY OUT AN ACTION; 269]

take a deep breath *v* [➡ PREPARE FOR ACTION; 289]

take a dim view of *v* **disapprove of**, not think much of, frown on, object to, dislike, deplore [➡ DISLIKE AND HATE; 577] *Opposite:* approve

take advantage of somebody *v* **exploit**, use, mistreat, abuse, take for a ride, manipulate, rip off (*informal*) [➡ MISUSE AND ABUSE; 471]

take advantage of something *v* **make the most of**, cash in on, profit from, exploit, make use of, manipulate, capitalize on [➡ MAKE GOOD USE OF SOMETHING; 473]

take a fancy to *v* **like**, approve of, take a liking to, be fond of, love, take a shine to (*informal*), be keen on (*UK*) [➡ LIKE, LOVE, VALUE, AND ENJOY; 578] *Opposite:* dislike

take after *v* **resemble**, act like, imitate, look like, bear a resemblance to, be like [➡ SEEM TO BE SOMETHING; 58] *Opposite:* differ

take a gamble *v* **gamble**, venture, risk it, chance it, stick your neck out, play with fire, ask for trouble, ask for it, skate on thin ice, be on dangerous ground [➡ GAMBLE AND TAKE RISKS; 466] *Opposite:* play safe

take a liking to *v* [➡ LIKE, LOVE, VALUE, AND ENJOY; 578]

take a look at *v* [➡ LOOKING AND LOOKS; 700]

take amiss *v* **take the wrong way**, take exception, take umbrage, take offense, be put out, get the wrong end of the stick, get the wrong impression, misconstrue, get the wrong idea, misunderstand, misinterpret [➡ MISUNDERSTAND AND FAIL TO GRASP; 761] *Opposite:* understand

take a nap *v* [➡ SLEEP AND DREAM; 723]

take an oath v **promise**, swear, pledge, vow, give your word [➡ PROMISE AND ASSURE; 684]

take apart 1 v **dismantle**, take to pieces, break up, pull apart, undo, strip down, disassemble, take to bits (*UK*) [➡ UNFASTEN AND UNDO; 409] *Opposite*: assemble 2 v (*informal*) **criticize**, censure, condemn, lash, pan (*informal*) [➡ ACCUSE, BLAME, AND CRITICIZE; 641]

take a rain check (*informal*) v [➡ SHIRK AND DELAY; 273]

take a rest v [➡ LACK OF ACTIVITY OR MOTION; 342]

take a shine to (*informal*) v [➡ LIKE, LOVE, VALUE, AND ENJOY; 578]

take a shot at v [➡ ATTEMPT AN ACTION; 261]

take as read v **accept**, believe, take at face value, take for granted, assume, presume [➡ FORGET, FORGIVE, AND ACCEPT; 748] *Opposite*: challenge

take a stab at (*informal*) v [➡ ATTEMPT AN ACTION; 261]

take at face value v **believe**, accept, take as read, take for granted, rely on, not read the small print, swallow (*informal*) [➡ FORGET, FORGIVE, AND ACCEPT; 748] *Opposite*: question

take a turn for the worse v **go from bad to worse**, deteriorate, decline, slip, relapse, go downhill [➡ GET WORSE; 381] *Opposite*: improve

take away 1 v **remove**, cart off, carry off, carry away, take off, withdraw [➡ REMOVE SOMETHING; 338] *Opposite*: bring 2 v **subtract**, deduct, take, take off [➡ REMOVE SOMETHING; 338] *Opposite*: add

take back 1 v **withdraw**, retract, recant, renounce, disclaim, revoke, disavow, recall, backpedal, backtrack, apologize, eat humble pie, eat your words (*informal*), eat crow (*informal*) [➡ APOLOGIZE AND RETRACT; 683] *Opposite*: stick to 2 v **regain**, recapture, retake, recover, retrieve, restore, repossess [➡ REGAIN POSSESSION; 429] *Opposite*: give back 3 v **return**, exchange, refund, redeem, trade in, swap (*informal*) [➡ EXCHANGE AND INTERCHANGE; 448] *Opposite*: keep 4 v **reinstate**, reaccept, bring back, welcome back, have back, reassume [➡ ACCEPT POSSESSION; 450] 5 v **remind**, transport, jog your memory, put you in mind of, make you think of, ring a bell (*informal*) [➡ REMIND; 747]

take by storm 1 v **capture**, overwhelm, storm, seize, conquer, overrun, win, attack [➡ CAPTIVITY AND LOSS OF FREEDOM; 248] 2 v **captivate**, bowl over, impress, charm, enthrall, knock out (*informal*) [➡ SURPRISE AND IMPRESS; 574]

take by surprise v **surprise**, burst in on, catch napping, take unawares, catch unawares, ambush, catch on the hop, startle, creep up on [➡ SURPRISE AND IMPRESS; 574]

take care 1 v **be careful**, pay attention, look out, watch out, watch your step, go easy (*informal*), mind out (*UK*) [➡ PAY ATTENTION; 765] 2 v **make sure**, ensure, make certain, confirm, check, assure yourself, ascertain (*formal*) [➡ PREDICT AND ANTICIPATE; 750]

take care of 1 v **look after**, care for, nurse, tend, support, watch over [➡ TAKE CARE OF AND SPOIL; 300] *Opposite*: neglect 2 v **deal with**, see to, handle, manage, do, undertake, look after, sort out [➡ BE IN CHARGE; 270]

take charge v **take control**, take over, assume respon- sibility, hold the fort, take the reins, take up the baton,

step in, come to power [➡ BE IN CHARGE; 270] *Opposite*: step down

take control v **take charge**, take over, assume respon- sibility, hold the fort, take the reins, take up the baton, step in, come to power [➡ BE IN CHARGE; 270] *Opposite*: step down

take cover v **hide**, take shelter, shelter, take refuge, conceal yourself, vanish, disappear [➡ RUN AWAY AND AVOID; 10] *Opposite*: emerge

take down 1 v **note**, jot down, write down, make a note of, record, minute, transcribe [➡ RECORD SOMETHING; 371] 2 v **dismantle**, demolish, knock down, pull down, take apart, take to pieces, take to bits [➡ UNFASTEN AND UNDO; 409] *Opposite*: put up 3 v **humiliate**, humble, deflate, embarrass, mortify, abash, crush [➡ UPSET, DISTRESS, AND HUMILIATE; 567] *Oppo- site*: puff up

take effect v **come into force**, come into operation, come into effect, start up, start, begin, commence, succeed, happen [➡ HAPPEN; 27]

take exception v **take offense**, take umbrage, be put out, object, disapprove, take a dim view, protest, come out against [➡ DISLIKE AND HATE; 577] *Opposite*: welcome

take five (*informal*) v **take a break**, take time out, take a rest, rest, relax, put your feet up, come up for air, ease off, break off, stop, pause, take a breather (*informal*) [➡ LACK OF ACTIVITY OR MOTION; 342] *Opposite*: keep on

take flight v **run away**, run off, flee, take off, decamp, scatter, abscond, make yourself scarce (*informal*), ske- daddle (*slang*), vamoose (*slang*) [➡ RUN AWAY AND AVOID; 10] *Oppo- site*: stay put

take for a ride v **cheat**, deceive, swindle, trick, con, dupe, fool, mislead, defraud, hoodwink, lead somebody down the garden path, have [➡ DECEPTION AND LIES; 660]

take for granted 1 v **assume**, presume, take as read, expect, count on, presuppose [➡ PREDICT AND ANTICIPATE; 750] 2 v **undervalue**, underrate, hold cheap, hold in contempt, disregard [➡ DISLIKE AND HATE; 577] *Opposite*: appreciate

take form v [➡ GRADUALLY COME INTO EXISTENCE; 1]

take great delight in v [➡ LIKE, LOVE, VALUE, AND ENJOY; 578]

take heart v **cheer up**, perk up, brighten up, take comfort, snap out of it, buck up (*informal*) [➡ CHANGE OF MOOD AND COMPOSURE; 580] *Opposite*: lose heart

take heed v [➡ PAY ATTENTION; 765]

take home v **make**, be paid, net, earn, get, clear (*informal*), pull down (*slang*) [➡ GET MONEY OR REWARD; 421]

take-home pay n **net income**, after-tax income, net salary, net wages, net pay, net income after deductions, pay envelope, pay packet (*UK*) [➡ INCOME; 460]

take in 1 v **absorb**, understand, comprehend, grasp, assimilate, learn, discern, realize, accept, take on board, remember [➡ UNDERSTAND AND GRASP; 759] *Opposite*: ignore 2 v **include**, contain, comprise, encompass, cover, enclose, embrace [➡ POSSESS; 444] *Opposite*: exclude 3 v **deceive**, dupe, fool, mislead, trick, swindle, defraud, cheat, con, hood- wink, take for a ride, lead down the garden path, have [➡ DECEPTION AND LIES; 660] 4 v **let in**, receive, admit, entertain, accommodate, welcome [➡ ACCEPT POSSESSION; 450] *Opposite*: bar **5** *v* **reduce**, alter, shrink, shorten, draw in, narrow, gather [➡ CHANGE OF SIZE: SMALLER; 393] *Opposite*: let out

take in hand *v* **deal with**, cope with, tackle, get to grips with, take on, take control of, take charge of [➡ BE IN CHARGE; 270]

take into consideration *v* **allow for**, take into account, bear in mind, make allowances for, keep in mind, take on board, consider, think about [➡ PAY ATTENTION; 765] *Opposite*: ignore

take into custody *v* **arrest**, detain, imprison, confine, hold, pick up (*informal*), pull in (*slang*) [➡ THE POLICE, ARREST, AND PRETRIAL PROCEEDINGS; 818] *Opposite*: release

take in your stride *v* **deal with**, cope with, accept, take on board, manage, handle, shrug off, swallow [➡ FORGET, FORGIVE, AND ACCEPT; 748]

take issue with *v* **disagree**, differ, beg to differ, oppose, challenge, be at odds with somebody, take somebody up on (*UK*) [➡ PROTEST AND EXPRESS DISAPPROVAL; 642] *Opposite*: agree

See Compare and Contrast at **disagree**.

take it easy 1 *v* **relax**, unwind, put your feet up, laze around, lounge around, loaf, take a break, take a breather (*informal*), take five (*informal*), hang loose (*informal*), chill out (*slang*) [➡ LACK OF ACTIVITY OR MOTION; 342] **2** *v* **calm down**, relax, simmer down, keep your shirt on, lighten up (*informal*), chill out (*slang*) [➡ CHANGE OF MOOD AND COMPOSURE; 580] *Opposite*: explode

take leave *v* [➡ LEAVE AND GO AWAY; 8]

take legal action *v* **go to court**, sue, press charges, prosecute, litigate, file a suit, bring a claim [➡ TRIAL, PUNISHMENT, AND LEGAL OUTCOMES; 819]

taken *adj* **occupied**, in use, engaged, spoken for, busy, reserved, booked [➡ ABSENT AND UNAVAILABLE; 7] *Opposite*: free

taken aback *adj* **stunned**, shocked, dumbfounded, speechless, bowled over, astonished, astounded, amazed, surprised, dazed, bemused, stupefied [➡ SURPRISE, SHOCK, AND AMAZEMENT; 545]

take no heed of *v* [➡ NOT PAY ATTENTION; 764]

take no notice of *v* **ignore**, disregard, pay no attention, pay no heed, close your eyes, pass by, brush aside, be oblivious, forget [➡ NOT PAY ATTENTION; 764]

take note *v* [➡ PAY ATTENTION; 765]

take notice *v* [➡ PAY ATTENTION; 765]

taken with *adj* [➡ APPRECIATION AND GRATITUDE; 535]

take off 1 *v* **launch**, depart, leave, lift off, fly off, take to the air, ascend [➡ GO UPWARD; 306] **2** *v* **remove**, discard, strip off, slip out of, peel off, doff, divest yourself of (*formal or humorous*) [➡ DRESS, WEAR, AND UNDRESS; 868] *Opposite*: put on **3** *v* **deduct**, subtract, take away, take, remove, eliminate [➡ REMOVE SOMETHING; 338] *Opposite*: add **4** *v* (*informal*) **succeed**, flourish, bloom, boom, prosper, thrive, catch on (*informal*) [➡ SUCCEED AND WIN; 79] *Opposite*: flop (*informal*) **5** *v* (*informal*) **leave**, go, depart, disappear, set out, strike out, set off, scoot (*informal*), skedaddle (*slang*) [➡ LEAVE AND GO

AWAY; 8] *Opposite*: stay **6** *v* (*informal*) **parody**, imitate, mimic, impersonate, satirize, caricature, copy, send up (*informal*) [➡ PRETEND AND MIMIC; 60] **7** *v* **cancel**, suspend, discontinue, abolish, do away with, scrub (*informal*) [➡ CAUSE TO STOP; 266] *Opposite*: reinstate

See Compare and Contrast at **imitate**.

takeoff 1 *n* **departure**, ascent, launch, lift off, start, beginning [➡ BEGINNINGS; 53] *Opposite*: touchdown **2** *n* (*informal*) **imitation**, impersonation, impression, parody, skit, caricature, burlesque, copy, simulation, sendup (*informal*) [➡ REPRESENTATIONS AND GENERAL EXAMPLES; 65]

take offense *v* **take exception**, take umbrage, take amiss, take the wrong way, be put out, go off in a huff, smart, mind, object [➡ DISLIKE AND HATE; 577]

take on 1 *v* **undertake**, assume, deal with, accept, adopt, tackle, handle, shoulder, take [➡ CARRY OUT AN ACTION; 269] *Opposite*: refuse **2** *v* **employ**, hire, engage, sign, bring on board, recruit, appoint, enlist, retain [➡ CONFER STATUS; 458] *Opposite*: fire **3** *v* **adopt**, acquire, gain, display, show, exhibit [➡ GET; 420] *Opposite*: lose **4** *v* **face**, confront, oppose, fight, vie with, stand up to, brave [➡ ACCUSE, BLAME, AND CRITICIZE; 641]

take on board 1 *v* **understand**, grasp, comprehend, realize, absorb, assimilate [➡ UNDERSTAND AND GRASP; 759] *Opposite*: deny **2** *v* (*UK*) **accept**, include, accommodate, implement, allow for, take into account, take into consideration, bear in mind, acknowledge, swallow (*informal*) [➡ FORGET, FORGIVE, AND ACCEPT; 748] *Opposite*: reject

take out 1 *v* **ask out**, invite out, accompany, treat, take, entertain, date [➡ ESTABLISHING RELATIONSHIPS WITH OTHERS; 974] **2** *v* **arrange**, organize, set up, obtain, acquire, get [➡ GET; 420] *Opposite*: cancel **3** *v* **vent**, direct, aim, express, relieve [➡ GIVING VENT TO EMOTIONS; 679] **4** *v* (*slang*) **destroy**, kill, blast, neutralize, get rid of, take care of, shoot, bomb, gun down (*informal*), wipe out (*slang*) [➡ KILL; 923] **5** *v* **remove**, extract, pull out, bring out, fish out, cut out, filter out [➡ EXTRACT AND SEVER; 341] *Opposite*: insert

takeout 1 *adj* **ready-made**, precooked, prepared, carryout, to go, takeaway (*UK*) [➡ STATE OF PREPARED FOOD; 1171] **2** *n* **carryout**, fast food, ready meal, ready-made meal (*UK*), takeaway (*UK*) [➡ MEALS AND PARTS OF MEALS; 1169] **3** *type of* **food outlet** [➡ RETAIL OUTLETS; 1083]

take over 1 *v* **take possession of**, annex, capture, hijack, seize, occupy, appropriate, take, conquer, secure, gain, overcome [➡ TAKE SOMETHING AWAY; 425] *Opposite*: cede (*formal*) **2** *v* **take control**, take charge, take the reins, step in, assume responsibility, take up the baton, come to power, hold the fort [➡ BE IN CHARGE; 270] *Opposite*: step down

takeover *n* **coup**, overthrow, seizure, appropriation, occupation, annexation, coup d'état, buyout, purchase [➡ SUDDEN EVENTS; 52]

take part *v* **join in**, participate, play, play a part, cooperate, have a hand in, opt in [➡ PARTICIPATE; 292] *Opposite*: opt out (*informal*)

take place *v* **happen**, occur, have effect, go on, come about, transpire, come off (*informal*), come to pass (*archaic or literary*) [➡ HAPPEN; 27]

take pleasure in *v* **delight in**, enjoy, be taken with, love, take great delight in, adore, like [➡ LIKE, LOVE, VALUE, AND ENJOY; 578] *Opposite*: hate

take possession of *v* **take over**, take control of, sequester, impound, occupy, appropriate, annex, seize, commandeer, hijack, capture [➡ TAKE SOMETHING AWAY; 425] *Opposite*: abandon

take precedence *v* **have priority**, outweigh, come first, come before, predominate, lead, have the advantage [➡ MOST IMPORTANT AND MAIN; 193]

take prisoner *v* **capture**, take captive, take hostage, seize, imprison, kidnap, snatch (*informal*) [➡ CAPTIVITY AND LOSS OF FREEDOM; 248] *Opposite*: release

taker *n* **customer**, client, patron, purchaser, buyer, player, participant, user [➡ PURCHASER; 424]

take root *v* **set in**, develop, start, grow, settle in, bed in, take hold [➡ GRADUALLY COME INTO EXISTENCE; 1]

take shape *v* **form**, develop, crystallize, take form, shape up, solidify, come together, gel (*informal*) [➡ GRADUALLY COME INTO EXISTENCE; 1] *Opposite*: dissolve

take steps *v* **make a start**, proceed, start, take action, do something, act, take the plunge, take the bull by the horns, go for it (*slang*), get stuck in (*UK*) [➡ CARRY OUT AN ACTION; 269]

take stock *v* **reflect**, sum up, think over, count your blessings, contemplate, examine, consider, assess, weigh up (*UK*) [➡ EXAMINE AND ASSESS; 753]

take the blame *v* **take responsibility**, face the music, own up, take the rap (*slang*), get it in the neck (*UK informal*) [➡ ADMIT AND CONFESS; 615] *Opposite*: get away with

take the bull by the horns *v* **take the plunge**, bite the bullet, take the initiative, jump in, plunge in, dive in, show your mettle, face the music, go for it (*slang*), grasp the nettle (*UK*) [➡ START AN ACTION; 260] *Opposite*: hold back

take the edge off *v* **dampen**, blunt, dilute, relieve, mitigate, tone down, lessen, alleviate, reduce, defuse, detract from [➡ CHANGE OF INTENSITY: LESS; 395] *Opposite*: heighten

take the floor *v* [➡ BE IN CHARGE; 270]

take the lead *v* **blaze a trail**, set a trend, originate, break new ground, break through, show the way, take the initiative, get ahead, forge ahead [➡ SUCCEED AND WIN; 79] *Opposite*: fall behind

take the mickey (*UK informal*) *v* **tease**, make fun of, laugh at, bait, kid, goad, provoke, pull somebody's leg (*informal*) [➡ JOKES AND TEASING; 674]

take the place of *v* **replace**, succeed, displace, supersede, take over from, substitute, relieve, fill in, cover for, deputize, stand in [➡ REPRESENT SOMETHING OR SOMEBODY; 59]

take the plunge *v* **dive in**, jump in, throw caution to the wind, take the bull by the horns, bite the bullet, plunge in, commit, go for it (*slang*) [➡ START AN ACTION; 260] *Opposite*: hold back

take the rap (*slang*) *v* **take the blame**, take responsibility, face the music, own up, get it in the neck (*UK informal*) [➡ ADMIT AND CONFESS; 615] *Opposite*: get off

take the rough with the smooth *v* **take the bad with the good**, make the best of things, look on the bright side, keep your chin up, go with the flow, keep smiling, grin and bear it (*informal*), make the best of a bad job (*UK*) [➡ TOLERATE AND ENDURE; 766]

take the wrong way *v* [➡ MISUNDERSTAND AND FAIL TO GRASP; 761]

take to 1 *v* **warm to**, take a fancy to, take a liking to, fall for, befriend, take a shine to (*informal*), hit it off (*informal*), get on with (*UK*) [➡ LIKE, LOVE, VALUE, AND ENJOY; 578] *Opposite*: dislike 2 *v* **begin**, start, commence, take up, go in for [➡ START AN ACTION; 260] *Opposite*: stop

take to court *v* **prosecute**, sue, take legal action, press charges, file a suit, bring a claim [➡ TRIAL, PUNISHMENT, AND LEGAL OUTCOMES; 819]

take to flight *v* [➡ RUN AWAY AND AVOID; 10]

take to pieces *v* **take apart**, dismantle, disassemble, strip down, break up, pull apart, undo, take to bits (*UK*) [➡ UNFASTEN AND UNDO; 409] *Opposite*: put together

take to task *v* **reprimand**, scold, rebuke, reprove, criticize, tell off (*informal*), give a talking-to (*informal*), slap on the wrist (*informal*), rap on/over the knuckles (*informal*), haul over the coals (*UK*) [➡ ACCUSE, BLAME, AND CRITICIZE; 641] *Opposite*: praise

take to your heels *v* **run away**, run off, flee, run, fly, take flight, beat it (*slang*), skedaddle (*slang*), vamoose (*slang*), show a clean pair of heels (*UK*) [➡ RUN AWAY AND AVOID; 10] *Opposite*: stay put

take umbrage *v* [➡ CHANGE OF MOOD AND COMPOSURE; 580]

take unawares *v* **surprise**, catch on the hop, catch out, catch off guard, take by surprise, startle, wrong-foot, burst in on, creep up on [➡ SURPRISE AND IMPRESS; 574]

take under advisement *v* **consider**, weigh up, mull over, reflect, ponder, ruminate [➡ THINK AND REFLECT; 743]

take up 1 *v* **start**, go in for, adopt, engage in, assume, begin, take to, commence, accept [➡ START AN ACTION; 260] *Opposite*: give up 2 *v* **continue**, resume, go on, pick up, carry on, restart, recommence (*formal*) [➡ RECOMMENCE AND RESUME; 268] *Opposite*: leave off 3 *v* **raise**, lift, pick up, gather up, hoist, winch, elevate [➡ MOVE SOMETHING: UPWARD; 328] *Opposite*: put down 4 *v* **shorten**, raise, lift, pin up, gather up, hem [➡ CHANGE OF SIZE: SMALLER; 393] *Opposite*: let down 5 *v* **occupy**, fill, cover, absorb, consume, monopolize, use up [➡ USE UP AND WASTE; 474]

take-up *n* **acceptance**, reception, use, participation, response [➡ ACCEPT POSSESSION; 450]

take up the baton *v* **take control**, take charge, take over, take the reins, step in, come to power, hold the fort [➡ BE IN CHARGE; 270] *Opposite*: step down

take up the gauntlet *v* **accept a challenge**, take on, confront, stand up to [➡ COMPETE, CONTEND, AND COMBAT; 303]

taking *adj* **captivating**, attractive, enchanting, pleasing, winning, charming, delightful, compelling, fascinating, intriguing [➡ BEAUTY AND ATTRACTIVENESS; 189] *Opposite*: unattractive

taking place *v* [➡ HAPPENING AND IN PROGRESS; 32]

takings *n* **earnings**, income, proceeds, profits, receipts, returns, revenue, gross, take, yield [➡INCOME; 460] *Opposite*: expenditure

tala *type of* **currency** [➡CURRENCIES; 798]

tale 1 *n* **account**, fiction, romance, anecdote, legend, saga, relation, fable, parable, narrative, story, yarn (*informal*) [➡THE ORAL TRADITION; 677] **2** *n* **lie**, untruth, rumor, falsehood, story, fabrication, gossip, fib (*informal*) [➡DECEPTION AND LIES; 660] *Opposite*: truth

Taleggio *type of* **soft cheese** [➡DAIRY PRODUCTS AND CHEESES; 1183]

talent *n* **aptitude**, flair, gift, bent, capacity, faculty, ability, knack, endowment, genius, skill [➡SKILLS, TALENTS, AND ABILITIES; 526]

Compare and Contrast: *talent, gift, aptitude, flair, bent, knack, genius*

CORE MEANING: the natural ability to do something well

talent a natural ability to do something well that can be developed by training; *gift* a natural ability, especially an artistic ability, or a social skill; *aptitude* a natural ability to do or learn something, especially one that is not yet fully developed; *flair* a natural ability to do something well, especially creative or artistic ability; *bent* a natural ability, inclination, or liking for something; *knack* an intuitive ability to do something well, especially one that might not be developed by training; *genius* exceptional intellectual or creative ability.

See Compare and Contrast at **ability**.

talented *adj* **gifted**, able, brilliant, artistic, endowed, capable, clever [➡TALENTED AND SKILLFUL; 527]

talentless *adj* [➡UNSKILLED; 529]

taleteller *n* **informer**, turncoat, tattletale, snitch (*slang*), stool pigeon (*slang*), stooge (*slang*), rat (*slang*), squealer (*slang*) [➡INTERFERING PEOPLE AND TATTLETALES; 950]

talisman *n* **stone**, jewel, amulet, charm, trinket, object, mascot [➡LUCKY CHARMS; 785]

talk 1 *v* **communicate**, speak, chat, gossip, chatter, express, utter, gab (*informal*), yak (*informal*), natter (*informal*) [➡TWO-WAY COMMUNICATION; 607] **2** *v* **converse**, debate, compare notes, have a discussion, discuss, negotiate, confer, reason, deliberate, consult, parley, have a word (*UK*) [➡TWO-WAY COMMUNICATION; 607] **3** *n* **gossip**, conversation, rumor, chatter, speculation, whispers [➡GOSSIP; 678] **4** *v* **confess**, betray, turn over, inform, crack, tell, break, give up, rat (*informal*), sing (*slang*), squeal (*slang*) [➡BETRAY CONFIDENCES AND GOSSIP; 618] **5** *n* **conversation**, exchange, dialogue, tête-à-tête, heart-to-heart, discourse, chat, gossip, chatter, chitchat (*informal*), gab (*informal*), yak (*informal*) [➡INFORMAL COMMUNICATION; 45] **6** *n* **lecture**, speech, address, discourse, oration, sermon [➡ONE-WAY COMMUNICATION; 49] **7** *n* **language**, words, vocabulary, jargon, speech, dialect, slang [➡THE SPOKEN WORD; 671]

talk a mile a minute *v* [➡CHATTER AND BABBLE; 617]

talkative *adj* **chatty**, garrulous, voluble, fluent, glib, gossipy, verbose, loquacious (*formal*) [➡ELOQUENT, TALKATIVE, AND LONG-WINDED; 632] *Opposite*: reticent

---

Compare and Contrast: *talkative, chatty, gossipy, garrulous, loquacious*

CORE MEANING: talking a lot

talkative willing to talk readily and at length; *chatty* talking freely about unimportant things in a friendly way; *gossipy* talking with relish about other people and their lives, often unkindly or maliciously; *garrulous* excessively or pointlessly talkative; *loquacious* (*formal*) tending to talk a great deal.

---

talkativeness *n* **chattiness**, verbosity, garrulousness, volubility, fluency, glibness, wordiness, loquaciousness (*formal*), loquacity (*formal*) [➡ELOQUENT, TALKATIVE, AND LONG-WINDED; 632] *Opposite*: reticence

talk back *v* **argue**, answer back, defy, retort, quibble, come back, sass (*informal*), be cheeky (*UK*) [➡REPLY AND ANSWER; 668]

talker *n* **communicator**, conversationalist, speaker, gossip, chatterer, orator, public speaker, raconteur, chatterbox (*informal*), gabber (*informal*), schmoozer (*slang*) [➡SPEAKERS AND ORATORS; 603]

talk gibberish *v* [➡CHATTER AND BABBLE; 617]

talkie (*dated*) *n* **feature**, film, movie, picture, newsreel, motion picture, flick (*informal*) [➡FILM; 901] *Opposite*: silent movie

talking 1 *n* **speaking**, conversation, chat, chatting, gossip, chatter, chitchat (*informal*), yak (*informal*), gabbing (*informal*), schmooze (*slang*) [➡INFORMAL COMMUNICATION; 45] **2** *n* **debate**, words, discussion, negotiation, conference, deliberation, consultation, exchange, dialogue [➡COMMUNICATION; 602]

talking point *n* **topic of conversation**, debating point, issue, question, hot topic, controversial subject, subject of debate [➡SUBJECT AREAS; 768]

talking-to (*informal*) *n* **dressing-down**, reprimand, lecture, tongue-lashing, scolding, telling-off (*informal*), bawling out (*informal*) [➡CRITICISMS AND ANGRY OUTBURSTS; 50]

talk into *v* **persuade**, coax, induce, convince, move, prevail on, cajole, talk over, twist somebody's arm (*informal*) [➡CAUSE OR COMPEL TO ACT; 271] *Opposite*: talk out of

talk nineteen to the dozen (*UK*) *v* [➡CHATTER AND BABBLE; 617]

talk out of *v* **dissuade**, sway, discourage, deter, advise against, turn against, change somebody's mind, put off (*UK*) [➡AVOID, PREVENT, LIMIT, AND CONTROL; 277] *Opposite*: talk into

talk over *v* **discuss**, negotiate, debate, review, go into, deliberate [➡TWO-WAY COMMUNICATION; 607]

talks *n* **negotiations**, discussions, summit, dialogue, conference, discussion, panel, parley [➡NEGOTIATION AND DEBATE; 46]

talk show *type of* **broadcast** [➡TELEVISION AND RADIO; 606]

talk ten to the dozen *v* [➡CHATTER AND BABBLE; 617]

talk the hind legs off a donkey (*UK*) *v* [➡ CHATTER AND BABBLE; 617]

talk turkey (*informal*) *v* open up, put your cards on the table, get down to brass tacks, get to the point, get to the nitty-gritty, tell the truth, get down to business, not beat around the bush, not pull any punches [➡ INFORM, ANNOUNCE, AND ISSUE; 611] *Opposite*: equivocate

talky *n* [➡ FILM; 901]

tall 1 *adj* high, big, giant, lofty, lanky, elevated, soaring, towering, monumental, colossal, large [➡ HEIGHT: HIGH; 1203] *Opposite*: short 2 *adj* difficult, hard, complicated, demanding, trying, substantial [➡ DIFFICULTY AND COMPLEXITY; 242] *Opposite*: easy 3 *adj* incredible, unbelievable, unlikely, far-fetched, exaggerated, untrue [➡ FALSE AND UNREAL; 173] *Opposite*: likely

tallness *n* height, loftiness, size, lankiness, stature, elevation [➡ HEIGHT: HIGH; 1203] *Opposite*: shortness

tall ship *type of* historical vessel [➡ SHIPS AND BOATS; 1150]

tall story *see* **tall tale**

tall tale *n* cock-and-bull story, unlikely story, tale, tall story, fairy tale, lie, untruth, yarn (*informal*), fib (*informal*), fairy story (*UK*) [➡ DECEPTION AND LIES; 660]

tally 1 *v* match, correspond, agree, check, equate, square, coincide, accord, fit, harmonize [➡ EQUALITY; 154] *Opposite*: clash 2 *v* compute, count, reckon, score, total, register, record, note, calculate, mark [➡ ASSESS QUANTITY; 757] 3 *n* score, count, total, reckoning, calculation, record, register, note, account, mark [➡ SCORES AND EVALUATIONS; 598]

talon *n* claw, nail, fingernail, hook, spur, pincer [➡ PARTS OF A BIRD; 1006]

talus *type of* bone [➡ THE BONES AND JOINTS; 719]

tamale *type of* cooked dish [➡ PREPARED DISHES; 1170]

tambourine *type of* percussion instrument [➡ MUSICAL INSTRUMENTS; 910]

tame 1 *adj* domestic, domesticated, broken, trained, disciplined, pacified, cultivated, friendly, approachable [➡ SAFE AND SAFETY; 191] *Opposite*: wild 2 *adj* docile, meek, compliant, subdued, unresisting, submissive, obedient, gentle, peaceful [➡ THE WILL AND WILLINGNESS; 563] *Opposite*: rebellious 3 *adj* bland, dull, insipid, boring, unexciting, flat, uninspired, tedious [➡ BORING AND UNINTERESTING; 234] *Opposite*: exciting 4 *v* domesticate, break in, train, discipline, pacify, cultivate, reclaim [➡ INSTRUCT AND TEACH; 609] 5 *v* repress, suppress, overcome, subjugate, subdue, conquer, humble, curb, control, moderate [➡ AVOID, PREVENT, LIMIT, AND CONTROL; 277]

tamely 1 *adv* docilely, meekly, compliantly, submissively, obediently, gently, peacefully [➡ THE WILL AND WILLINGNESS; 563] *Opposite*: rebelliously 2 *adv* blandly, dully, insipidly, boringly, unexcitingly, flatly, tediously, languidly [➡ BORING AND UNINTERESTING; 234] *Opposite*: excitingly

tameness 1 *n* docility, meekness, compliance, submissiveness, obedience, gentleness, peacefulness, acceptance [➡ THE WILL AND WILLINGNESS; 563] *Opposite*: rebelliousness 2 *n* blandness, dullness, insipidness, flatness, tedium [➡ BORING AND UNINTERESTING; 234] *Opposite*: excitement

tam-o'-shanter *type of* headgear [➡ ACCESSORIES, MILLINERY, AND LINGERIE; 867]

tamp *v* fill, pack, stuff, cram, compress, push, force [➡ FILL; 406]

tamper 1 *v* interfere, meddle, monkey with, fool with, tinker, alter, damage, fiddle (*informal*), mess around (*informal*) [➡ WORSEN SOMETHING; 380] 2 *v* corrupt, rig, influence, manipulate, bribe, fix (*informal*) [➡ FALSIFY AND CHEAT; 176]

tampon *n* plug, pad, wad, swab, compress, dressing, bung [➡ REMEDIES, TREATMENTS, AND OPERATIONS; 731]

tan 1 *n* suntan, sunburn, color, bronze, brownness [➡ COMPLEXION; 480] 2 *type of* brown [➡ COLORS; 1224] 3 *v* bronze, brown, toast, burn, go brown (*UK*) [➡ CHANGE OF COLOR; 391] 4 *v* treat, preserve, process, dye, wash [➡ CLEAN AND POLISH; 403] 5 *adj* bronzed, sunburned, dark, suntanned, tanned, brown [➡ COMPLEXION; 480]

tanager *type of* common bird [➡ BIRDS; 997]

tandem bicycle *type of* bike [➡ BIKES, CARS, AND CARRIAGES; 1149]

tandoor *n* [➡ TABLEWARE, FLATWARE, AND KITCHENWARE; 861]

tang *n* trace, hint, smack, suggestion, flavor, aftertaste, savor, smell, whiff, odor [➡ FEW, LITTLE, SMALL AMOUNT; 120]

tangent *n* line, curve, angle, refraction, curvature [➡ ORIENTATION AND ALIGNMENT; 1223]

tangential *adj* peripheral, lateral, oblique, divergent, indirect, loose, vague [➡ VAGUENESS; 243] *Opposite*: central

tangerine 1 *type of* citrus fruit [➡ FRUIT AND VEGETABLES; 1176] 2 *type of* orange [➡ COLORS; 1224]

tangibility 1 *n* palpability, perceptibility, physicality, reality, solidity, concreteness, corporeality, presence, visibility [➡ PERCEPTIBLE; 25] *Opposite*: intangibility 2 *n* actuality, reality, clarity, plainness, obviousness [➡ TRUE AND REAL; 171] *Opposite*: intangibility

tangible 1 *adj* palpable, touchable, perceptible, concrete, physical, noticeable, real, solid, definite, substantial, material, corporeal, visible [➡ PERCEPTIBLE; 25] *Opposite*: intangible 2 *adj* actual, substantial, real, certain, evident, definite, plain, clear, demonstrable, quantifiable, obvious, hard, solid [➡ TRUE AND REAL; 171] *Opposite*: intangible

tanginess *n* [➡ TASTE; 703]

tangle 1 *v* knot, twist, snarl, interweave, intertwine, entangle, entwine, jumble, mat, tousle, wind [➡ COMBINE AND MIX; 400] *Opposite*: untangle 2 *v* snag, catch, snarl, snare, hook [➡ FASTEN, LINK, AND JOIN; 408] *Opposite*: undo 3 *v* trap, catch, ensnare, entangle, enmesh, mix up, confuse [➡ CAPTIVITY AND LOSS OF FREEDOM; 248] *Opposite*: release 4 *v* come up against, confront, mess with, square up, oppose, face [➡ INTERRUPT AND BUTT IN; 619] *Opposite*: avoid 5 *n* mass, jumble, knot, mesh, web, twist, welter [➡ COLLECTIONS AND MIXTURES OF THINGS; 1244] 6 *n* mess, jam, difficulty, mix-up, complication, maze, jumble, disorder [➡ DISORDER AND CHAOS; 245] 7 *type of* marine alga [➡ MICROORGANISMS, FUNGI, AND ALGAE; 1023]

tangled 1 *adj* knotted, twisted, snarled, interwoven, intertwined, entangled, entwined, jumbled, matted, tousled, scrambled [➡ IN BAD REPAIR; 1234] *Opposite*: straight 2 *adj* complicated, confused, knotty, complex, messy, intricate, disordered, mixed-up (*informal*) [➡ DIFFICULTY AND COMPLEXITY; 242] *Opposite*: straightforward

tango *type of* **dance** [➡ DANCE; 903]

tangy *adj* **pungent**, sharp, strong, piquant, tasty, spicy, flavorful [➡ TASTE; 703] *Opposite*: bland

tank 1 *n* **cistern**, boiler, reservoir, container, chamber, vat [➡ CONTAINERS, RECEPTACLES, AND PACKAGING; 1245] **2** *type of* **plumbing fixtures** [➡ FIXTURES; 859] **3** *type of* **military vehicle** [➡ VEHICLES; 1145]

tankard *n* **mug**, beer mug, jug, stein, toby jug, cup [➡ TABLEWARE, FLATWARE, AND KITCHENWARE; 861]

tanked-up (*slang*) *adj* [➡ UNDER THE INFLUENCE OF DRUGS OR ALCOHOL; 741]

tank engine *part of* **train** [➡ RAILROADS; 1107]

tanker 1 *n* **transporter**, freighter, truck, lorry (*UK*) [➡ VEHICLES; 1145] **2** *type of* **motor vessel** [➡ SHIPS AND BOATS; 1150]

tank top *type of* **top** [➡ GARMENTS AND OUTFITS; 865]

tanned *adj* **brown**, bronzed, suntanned, dark, sunburned, tan [➡ COMPLEXION; 480] *Opposite*: pale

tannery *type of* **industrial site** [➡ INDUSTRIAL BUILDINGS; 1087]

tantalize *v* **tease**, entice, torment, torture, tempt, provoke, frustrate [➡ APPEAL TO AND AROUSE INTEREST; 575] *Opposite*: turn off (*informal*)

tantalizing *adj* **teasing**, enticing, tormenting, tempting, provocative, provoking, frustrating, alluring, exciting [➡ INTERESTING AND MEANINGFUL; 190] *Opposite*: boring

tantamount *adj* **equal**, equivalent, the same as, synonymous, as good as, identical, indistinguishable, close [➡ SAMENESS; 150] *Opposite*: different

tantrum *n* **outburst**, fit of temper, fit, frenzy, fret, pet, sulk, rage, paroxysm [➡ CRITICISMS AND ANGRY OUTBURSTS; 50]

tap 1 *n* **blow**, rap, knock, bang, beat, hit, pat [➡ CONTACT: IMPACT; 413] **2** *type of* **impact sound** [➡ IMPACT SOUNDS; 1260] **3** *n* **stopper**, plug, bung, cork [➡ COVERS AND COATINGS; 1246] **4** *n* **spigot**, stopcock, valve, spout, faucet [➡ FIXTURES; 859] **5** *v* **rap**, knock, bang, beat, strike, hit, pat, drum [➡ CONTACT: IMPACT; 413] **6** *v* **appoint**, select, nominate, commission, recruit, employ, detail [➡ CONFER STATUS; 458] *Opposite*: pass over **7** *v* **draw off**, draw out, extract, run off, release, collect [➡ GET; 420] *Opposite*: block up **8** *v* **bug**, listen in on, record, monitor, intercept, eavesdrop on, overhear [➡ LISTEN AND LISTENERS; 708] **9** *v* (*informal*) **use**, utilize, draw on, draw off, exploit, mine, take advantage of, milk (*informal*) [➡ MAKE GOOD USE OF SOMETHING; 473]

tapas *part of* **meal** [➡ MEALS AND PARTS OF MEALS; 1169]

tap dance *type of* **dance** [➡ DANCE; 903]

tape 1 *n* **ribbon**, strip, string, tie, band, binding [➡ FASTENERS, LINKS, AND NETWORKS; 1247] **2** *n* **adhesive tape**, duct tape, masking tape, friction tape, packing tape, parcel tape (*UK*), sticky tape (*UK*), insulating tape (*UK*) [➡ FASTENERS, LINKS, AND NETWORKS; 1247] **3** *n* **cassette**, cassette tape, video, video tape, videocassette, audiotape, audiocassette, cartridge, magnetic tape, recording, tape recording, copy [➡ RECORDINGS AND PLAYERS; 911] **4** *n* **tape measure**, measuring tape, measure, tapeline [➡ MEASURING DEVICES; 1123] **5** *v* **record**, tape-record, copy, save, videotape, video (*UK*) [➡ RECORD SOMETHING; 371] **6** *v* **stick**, fasten, attach, secure, bind, fix [➡ FASTEN, LINK, AND JOIN; 408]

tape deck *type of* **audio equipment** [➡ AUDIO EQUIPMENT; 1139]

tape measure *n* **tape**, measuring tape, measure, rule, ruler, tapeline, steel rule (*UK*) [➡ MEASURING DEVICES; 1123]

tape player *type of* **audio equipment** [➡ AUDIO EQUIPMENT; 1139]

taper 1 *v* **narrow**, come to a point, thin down, dwindle, elongate, attenuate, shape [➡ CHANGE OF SIZE: SMALLER; 393] *Opposite*: widen **2** *v* **reduce**, phase out, taper off, tail off, diminish, decrease, lessen, shrink, peter out, contract [➡ CHANGE OF INTENSITY: LESS; 395] *Opposite*: increase **3** *n* **candle**, torch, light, flame [➡ LIGHTING; 862] **4** *n* **narrowing**, point, thinning down, dwindling, elongation [➡ CHANGE OF SIZE: SMALLER; 393]

tape-record *v* **tape**, record, copy, save, video, videotape [➡ RECORD SOMETHING; 371]

tape recorder *type of* **audio equipment** [➡ AUDIO EQUIPMENT; 1139]

tapered 1 *adj* **tapering**, narrowing, pointed, elongated, shaped, conical, thinning, thin, dwindling, attenuated [➡ ANGULAR SHAPE; 1217] *Opposite*: flared **2** *adj* **gradually reduced**, phased out, tailed off, diminished, decreased, lessened, petered out [➡ CHANGE OF SIZE: SMALLER; 393]

tapering *adj* **tapered**, narrowing, pointed, elongated, shaped, conical, thinning, thin, dwindling, attenuating [➡ ANGULAR SHAPE; 1217] *Opposite*: widening

tapestry 1 *n* **wall hanging**, drapery, arras [➡ FURNISHING AND HOUSEHOLD LINENS; 860] **2** *type of* **handicraft** [➡ CRAFTS AND CARVING; 355]

tapeworm *type of* **parasitic insect** [➡ PARASITES; 1017]

tappet *part of* **engine** [➡ PARTS OF AN ENGINE; 1144]

taps *n* [➡ TIMES OF DAY; 87]

tar *n* **asphalt**, tarmac, pitch, blacktop, macadam [➡ BUILDING MATERIALS; 1077]

taramasalata *type of* **seasonings, sauces, and dips** [➡ SEASONINGS AND SAUCES; 1174]

tarantula *type of* **arachnid** [➡ ARACHNIDS; 1018]

tardiness *n* **lateness**, delay, belatedness, unpunctuality [➡ PROMPTNESS: LATE; 100] *Opposite*: punctuality

tardy *adj* **late**, delayed, overdue, belated, unpunctual [➡ PROMPTNESS: LATE; 100] *Opposite*: punctual

target 1 *n* **board**, mark, bull's eye, bull, goal [➡ SYMBOLS, SIGNS, AND NUMBERS; 596] **2** *n* **aim**, goal, objective, object, focus, end, intention [➡ INTENTIONS AND PURPOSES; 772] **3** *n* **butt**, focus, object, recipient, foil, scapegoat, victim [➡ PERSON; 931] **4** *v* **aim at**, aim for, focus on, home in on, seek out, go after, pursue, go for (*informal*) [➡ PAY ATTENTION; 765] **5** *v* **direct**, aim, point, level, train, steer [➡ POSITION SOMETHING; 325]

tariff 1 *n* **tax**, duty, due, excise, levy, toll, import tax, export tax [➡ TAX AND TAXATION; 802] **2** *n* **price**, price list, rate, charge, cost, fare, bill, menu, bill of fare [➡ FUNDS, PAYMENTS, AND CHARGES; 800]

Tarmac *n* **tar**, asphalt, pitch, macadam, blacktop [➡ BUILDING MATERIALS; 1077]

tarn *n* **lake**, pool, pond, lagoon, water, mere (*archaic or literary*), loch (*UK*) [➡ RIVERS, LAKES, AND STREAMS; 1042]

tarnish 1 *v* **dull**, discolor, stain, smear, smudge, blot, blemish, taint, dirty, blacken, mark, oxidize, corrode, rust [➥DIRTY AND CONTAMINATE; 404] *Opposite*: clean 2 *v* **sully**, damage, stain, taint, blot, harm, destroy, blacken, blemish, spoil, ruin [➥WORSEN SOMETHING; 380] *Opposite*: enhance

tarnished 1 *adj* **dull**, discolored, stained, smeared, smudged, blotted, blemished, tainted, dirty, blackened, marked, oxidized, corroded, rusty [➥IN BAD REPAIR; 1234] *Opposite*: shiny 2 *adj* **sullied**, damaged, stained, tainted, blotted, harmed, destroyed, blackened, blemished, spoiled, ruined [➥MORALLY BAD OR IMPROPER; 775] *Opposite*: enhanced

tarp (*informal*) *n* [➥COVERS AND COATINGS; 1246]

tarpaulin 1 *n* **canvas**, cover, sheet, sheeting, tarp (*informal*) [➥COVERS AND COATINGS; 1246] 2 *type of* **fabric from plants** [➥FABRICS; 1132]

tarragon *type of* **herb** [➥HERBS AND SPICES; 1175]

tarry 1 *v* **remain**, stay, stay put, visit, sojourn (*literary*) [➥CONTINUE TO EXIST; 17] 2 *v* **linger**, loiter, dawdle, hang around, hesitate, delay, wait [➥SHIRK AND DELAY; 273]

tarsal *type of* **bone** [➥THE BONES AND JOINTS; 719]

tart 1 *adj* **sharp**, acid, acidic, sour, bitter [➥TASTE; 703] *Opposite*: sweet 2 *adj* **acerbic**, biting, sharp, sour, acid, bitter, critical, cutting, unkind, unpleasant, sarcastic, disapproving, cruel [➥BAD-TEMPERED AND HUMORLESS; 626] *Opposite*: kind 3 *n* **pie**, tartlet, pastry, quiche, flan [➥CAKES, COOKIES, AND DESSERTS; 1181]

tartan *n* **pattern**, plaid, check [➥PATTERNS; 1225]

tartar *n* **plaque**, deposit, residue, coating, scale, film, calculus [➥COVERS AND COATINGS; 1246]

tartare sauce *see* **tartar sauce**

tartar sauce *type of* **seasonings, sauces, and dips** [➥SEASONINGS AND SAUCES; 1174]

tartly *adv* **acerbically**, bitingly, sharply, sourly, acidly, bitterly, critically, cuttingly, unkindly, unpleasantly, sarcastically, disapprovingly, cruelly [➥BAD-TEMPERED AND HUMORLESS; 626] *Opposite*: kindly

tartness 1 *n* **sharpness**, acidity, sourness, bitterness [➥TASTE; 703] *Opposite*: sweetness 2 *n* **acerbity**, sharpness, sourness, acidity, bitterness, unkindness, unpleasantness, sarcasm, disapproval, cruelty [➥BAD-TEMPERED AND HUMORLESS; 626] *Opposite*: kindness

tarty *adj* [➥MORALLY BAD OR IMPROPER; 775]

task *n* **job**, chore, duty, mission, commission, assignment, undertaking, errand, charge, brief [➥WORK IN GENERAL; 297]

See Compare and Contrast at **job**.

task force *n* **team**, unit, squad, detail, crew, cadre, group, hit squad (*slang*), working party (*UK*) [➥GROUPS WITH A COMMON INTEREST; 938]

Tasmanian devil *type of* **marsupial** [➥MARSUPIALS; 992]

tassel *n* **bobble**, tuft, fringe, braid, edging, trimming [➥ORNAMENTS AND DECORATIONS; 1248]

taste 1 *n* **sense of taste**, palate, discrimination, sensitivity, perception, taste buds [➥THE SENSES; 696] 2 *n* **flavor**, tang, savor, hint, smack, aftertaste [➥TASTE; 703] 3 *n* **try**, sample, test, bite, nibble, drink, sip, bit, taster (*UK*) [➥REPRESENTATIONS AND GENERAL EXAMPLES; 65] 4 *n* **liking**, preference, leaning, penchant, fondness, predilection (*formal*) [➥LIKE, LOVE, VALUE, AND ENJOY; 578] *Opposite*: dislike 5 *n* **discrimination**, discernment, judgment, tastefulness, good taste, sophistication, refinement, style, class (*informal*) [➥LEVELS OF EDUCATION AND SOPHISTICATION; 894] 6 *v* **discern**, pick up, recognize, get, feel, notice, savor [➥USING THE SENSES; 697] 7 *v* **sample**, try, test, eat, bite, nibble, drink, sip [➥DRINK; 711] *Opposite*: devour 8 *v* **experience**, sample, preview, get a taste of, get a hint of, be exposed to [➥EXPERIENCE AND ENCOUNTER; 582]

taste bud *part of* **mouth** [➥THE MOUTH; 702]

tasteful *adj* **discerning**, discriminating, sophisticated, refined, stylish, aesthetic, attractive, elegant, chic, beautiful, classy (*informal*) [➥LEVELS OF EDUCATION AND SOPHISTICATION; 894] *Opposite*: tasteless

tastefulness *n* **discernment**, discrimination, judgment, taste, sophistication, refinement, style, good taste, aestheticism, attractiveness, elegance, chic, beauty, class (*informal*) [➥LEVELS OF EDUCATION AND SOPHISTICATION; 894] *Opposite*: tastelessness

tasteless 1 *adj* **bland**, flavorless, flat, insipid, weak, unsavory, dull [➥TASTE; 703] *Opposite*: tasty 2 *adj* **in bad taste**, in poor taste, cheap, flashy, loud, garish, vulgar, offensive, crude, distasteful, tactless, indelicate [➥IN POOR TASTE AND OVERSENTIMENTAL; 229] *Opposite*: tasteful 3 *adj* **vulgar**, crude, foul-mouthed, boorish, gross, obscene [➥BAD MANNERS AND SOCIAL SKILLS; 521]

tastelessness 1 *n* **blandness**, flavorlessness, flatness, insipidness, weakness, dullness, unsavoriness [➥TASTE; 703] *Opposite*: tastiness 2 *n* **bad taste**, poor taste, cheapness, flashiness, loudness, garishness, vulgarity, offensiveness, crudeness, distastefulness, tactlessness, indelicacy [➥IN POOR TASTE AND OVERSENTIMENTAL; 229] *Opposite*: tastefulness

taster 1 *n* **analyst**, sampler, buyer, specialist, connoisseur, blender [➥SURVEYORS, EXAMINERS, AND JUDGES; 853] 2 *n* (*UK*) **preview**, foretaste, sample, excerpt, appetizer [➥INDICATIONS, SIGNS, AND WARNINGS; 68]

tastiness *n* **deliciousness**, flavor, yumminess, juiciness, succulence, scrumptiousness (*informal*) [➥TASTE; 703] *Opposite*: tastelessness

tasty *adj* **delicious**, flavorsome, mouthwatering, appetizing, yummy, juicy, succulent, scrumptious (*informal*) [➥TASTE; 703] *Opposite*: tasteless

tatami *n* [➥FURNISHING AND HOUSEHOLD LINENS; 860]

tater (*informal*) *n* **potato**, spud (*informal*), murphy (*dated informal*) [➥FRUIT AND VEGETABLES; 1176]

tattered *adj* **torn**, ragged, tatty, dilapidated, frayed, threadbare, scruffy, shabby, unkempt [➥IN BAD REPAIR; 1234] *Opposite*: smart

tatters *n* **rags**, shreds, bits, pieces, strips, ruins [➥JUNK AND USELESS OBJECTS; 1249]

tattiness *n* **shabbiness**, scruffiness, raggedness, dilapidation, untidiness, seediness, disrepair [➥IN BAD REPAIR; 1234] *Opposite*: smartness

tatting *type of* **handicraft** [➡ CRAFTS AND CARVING; 355]

tattle 1 *v* **gossip**, tittle-tattle, prattle, chat, chatter, talk, dish the dirt (*informal*), snitch (*slang*), sneak (*UK*) [➡ BETRAY CONFIDENCES AND GOSSIP; 618] *Opposite:* keep secret (*informal*) **2** *n* **gossip**, tattler, telltale, informer, informant, talebearer, tattletale (*informal*), snitch (*slang*), rat (*slang*), stool pigeon (*slang*), squealer (*slang*), sneak (*UK*) [➡ INTERFERING PEOPLE AND TATTLETALES; 950] **3** *n* **tittle-tattle**, gossip, prattle, chat, chatter, hearsay [➡ GOSSIP; 678] *Opposite:* fact

tattler *n* **gossip**, tattle, telltale, informer, informant, talebearer, tattletale (*informal*), snitch (*slang*), rat (*slang*), stool pigeon (*slang*), squealer (*slang*), sneak (*UK*) [➡ INTERFERING PEOPLE AND TATTLETALES; 950]

tattletale *n* **talebearer**, telltale, tattler, informer, snitch (*slang*), rat (*slang*), squealer (*slang*) [➡ INTERFERING PEOPLE AND TATTLETALES; 950]

tattoo 1 *n* **design**, pattern, picture, decoration, mark [➡ DRAWINGS, CHARTS, AND TABLES; 594] **2** *n* **signal**, summons, call, recall, order, command [➡ SIGNALING; 1140] **3** *n* **parade**, display, tournament, show, pageant, cavalcade, march-past [➡ PERFORMANCES AND SHOWS; 42]

tatty *adj* **shabby**, worn, scruffy, dog-eared, down-at-heel, run-down, ragged, frayed, dilapidated, seedy [➡ IN BAD REPAIR; 1234] *Opposite:* smart

taunt 1 *v* **mock**, tease, jeer, sneer, goad, insult, criticize, ridicule, deride, provoke [➡ JOKES AND TEASING; 674] *Opposite:* compliment **2** *n* **insult**, gibe, sneer, affront, criticism, verbal abuse, derision [➡ INSULTS, ABUSE, AND SWEARING; 658] *Opposite:* compliment

taunting *adj* **mocking**, provocative, provoking, teasing, spiteful, hurtful, derisive, jeering [➡ MOCKING AND DISMISSIVE; 636] *Opposite:* kind

tauon *type of* **elementary particle** [➡ ELEMENTARY PARTICLES; 1279]

taupe *type of* **gray** [➡ COLORS; 1224]

Taurus 1 *type of* **astrological sign** [➡ FATE, DESTINY, AND ASTROLOGY; 782] **2** *type of* **constellation** [➡ HEAVENLY BODIES; 1061]

taut 1 *adj* **tight**, stretched, rigid, stiff, tense, extended, strained, firm, inflexible, hard [➡ RIGID AND HARD; 1211] *Opposite:* slack **2** *adj* **tense**, worried, anxious, stressed, nervous, wired, edgy, on edge, strung out [➡ CONFUSION, ANXIETY, AND WORRY; 540] *Opposite:* calm

tauten *v* **tighten**, stretch, stiffen, pull tight, tense, extend, strain, firm up, constrict, squeeze, contract [➡ CHANGE OF SIZE: SMALLER; 393] *Opposite:* slacken

tautness *n* **tightness**, tension, pull, stretch, rigidity, stiffness, firmness, strain, inflexibility, hardness [➡ RIGID AND HARD; 1211] *Opposite:* slackness

tautological *adj* **repetitious**, repetitive, inelegant, reiterative, redundant, superfluous, unneeded, unnecessary, uncalled-for [➡ UNIMPORTANT AND UNNECESSARY; 238]

tautology *n* **repetition**, reiteration, duplication, redundancy, superfluity [➡ UNIMPORTANT AND UNNECESSARY; 238]

tavern *n* **bar**, inn, watering hole (*informal*), roadhouse (*dated*), pub (*UK*) [➡ HOTELS, RESTAURANTS, AND CLUBS; 1082]

tawdriness *n* **cheapness**, gaudiness, flashiness, showiness, tastelessness, crudeness, flamboyance [➡ IN POOR TASTE AND OVERSENTIMENTAL; 229] *Opposite:* tastefulness

tawdry *adj* **cheap**, gaudy, flashy, showy, tasteless, crude, flamboyant [➡ IN POOR TASTE AND OVERSENTIMENTAL; 229] *Opposite:* tasteful

tawny *type of* **brown** [➡ COLORS; 1224]

tawny owl *type of* **owl** [➡ OWLS; 1001]

tax 1 *n* **duty**, levy, toll, excise, tariff [➡ TAX AND TAXATION; 802] **2** *v* **strain**, overtax, overstretch, stretch, overload, burden, challenge, ask too much of, drain, exhaust, test [➡ GIVE TOO MUCH AND OVERBURDEN; 437] *Opposite:* relieve **3** *v* **charge**, hit, burden, cream off, deduct [➡ TAX AND TAXATION; 802] *Opposite:* exempt **4** *v* **accuse**, reproach, blame, confront, present, charge [➡ ACCUSE, BLAME, AND CRITICIZE; 641]

taxable *adj* **chargeable**, assessable, dutiable, rateable, payable [➡ TAX AND TAXATION; 802] *Opposite:* tax-exempt

taxation 1 *n* **fiscal policy**, tax policy, tax system, revenue system, taxes, assessment [➡ TAX AND TAXATION; 802] **2** *n* **duty**, levy, toll, dues, excise, taxes, monies (*formal*) [➡ TAX AND TAXATION; 802]

tax-exempt *adj* **exempt from taxation**, exempt, untaxed, tax-free, duty-free, toll-free, non-VAT (*UK*) [➡ TAX AND TAXATION; 802] *Opposite:* taxable

tax-free *adj* [➡ TAX AND TAXATION; 802]

taxi *type of* **commercial or industrial vehicle** [➡ VEHICLES; 1145]

taxicab 1 *n* [➡ BIKES, CARS, AND CARRIAGES; 1149] **2** *type of* **commercial or industrial vehicle** [➡ VEHICLES; 1145]

taxing *adj* **demanding**, tough, difficult, strenuous, challenging, wearing, tiring, exhausting, draining [➡ DIFFICULTY AND COMPLEXITY; 242] *Opposite:* effortless

taxonomy *n* **classification**, nomenclature, taxonomic system, catalog, categorization, grouping, arrangement, organization [➡ NAME AND DESCRIBE; 665]

taxpayer *n* [➡ TAX AND TAXATION; 802]

tax policy *n* [➡ TAX AND TAXATION; 802]

tax system *n* [➡ TAX AND TAXATION; 802]

T-bone steak *type of* **steak** [➡ TYPES AND CUTS OF MEAT; 1177]

tchotchke *n* [➡ ORNAMENTS AND DECORATIONS; 1248]

tea 1 *n* **drink**, infusion, tisane, brew, decoction [➡ DRINKS; 1187] **2** *type of* **meal** [➡ MEALS AND PARTS OF MEALS; 1169]

tea break (*UK*) *n* **break**, coffee break, rest, refreshment break, breather (*informal*), elevenses (*UK*) [➡ PERIODS OF REST; 91]

tea caddy *type of* **container** [➡ CONTAINERS, RECEPTACLES, AND PACKAGING; 1245]

teach 1 *v* **impart**, communicate, show, explain, clarify, instill, give a grounding in, equip with, inculcate with [➡ INSTRUCT AND TEACH; 609] *Opposite:* learn **2** *v* **educate**, tutor, lecture, instruct, coach, train, school, drill, edify [➡ INSTRUCT AND TEACH; 609] *Opposite:* learn

Compare and Contrast: *teach, educate, train, instruct, coach, tutor, school, drill*

CORE MEANING: to impart knowledge or skill in something

teach to impart knowledge or skill to somebody by instruction or example; **educate** to increase the knowledge or develop the abilities of somebody by formal teaching or training, especially in a school or college context; **train** to teach the skills necessary for a particular task or job by means of instruction, observation, and practice; **instruct** to teach somebody a subject, methodology, or skill, not necessarily in a school or college context; **coach** to give special tuition to one person or a small group of people, especially in preparation for an exam, or to teach sports, artistic, or life skills; **tutor** to give somebody individual tuition in a particular subject or skill; **school** to train somebody in a particular skill or area of expertise in a thorough and detailed way; **drill** to teach something by means of repeated exercises and practice.

teacher *n* **educator**, tutor, instructor, coach, trainer, lecturer, professor, governess, schoolteacher [➡EDUCATORS; 840] *Opposite*: student

teacher's pet *n* [➡STUDENTS AND PUPILS; 841]

teaching 1 *n* **education**, lessons, instruction, coaching, training, schooling [➡TEACHING; 839] *Opposite*: learning 2 *n* **philosophy**, ideas, principles, beliefs, thinking, credo, doctrine [➡IDEAS AND THOUGHTS; 770]

teaching body *n* [➡EDUCATORS; 840]

teaching staff *n* [➡EDUCATORS; 840]

teak *type of* **deciduous tree** [➡DECIDUOUS TREES; 1028]

teal *type of* **freshwater bird** [➡FRESHWATER BIRDS; 1000]

team 1 *n* **side**, squad, players, lineup, crew, club [➡GROUPS WITH A COMMON INTEREST; 938] 2 *n* **group**, band, crew, gang, panel, party, unit, squad [➡GROUPS OF PEOPLE; 935]

teammate *n* **colleague**, co-player, partner, captain, fellow player [➡COLLEAGUES AND EQUALS; 967]

team player *n* [➡PEOPLE WHO ARE APPROVED OF; 955]

teamster 1 *n* **trucker**, truck driver, hauler, driver, lorry driver (*UK*) [➡DRIVERS; 1153] 2 *n* **driver**, carter, charioteer, handler, trainer [➡DRIVERS; 1153]

team up *v* **join forces**, collaborate, cooperate, work together, get together, come together, unite [➡ESTABLISHING RELATIONSHIPS WITH OTHERS; 974] *Opposite*: split up

teamwork *n* **cooperation**, collaboration, joint effort, solidarity, communication, coordination [➡RECIPROCITY AND INTERDEPENDENCE; 147]

teapot *n* [➡TABLEWARE, FLATWARE, AND KITCHENWARE; 861]

tear 1 *v* **rip**, slash, gash, scratch, slit, shred, rend, split, destroy [➡TEAR, BREAK, AND CUT; 360] *Opposite*: join 2 *v* **snatch**, rip, grab, wrench, pluck, force, pull, remove [➡EXTRACT AND SEVER; 341] *Opposite*: coax 3 *v* **dash**, rush, hurry, rip, streak, charge, speed, pelt, run, zip (*informal*) [➡MOVE FAST; 313] *Opposite*: saunter 4 *v* **sprain**, rip, pull, injure, damage, hurt, wrench [➡WOUND A PERSON OR ANIMAL; 383] 5 *n* **slit**, rip, split, slash, gash, hole, rent, scratch [➡HOLES, GAPS, AND FORKS; 1252] *Opposite*:

join 6 *n* **binge**, spree, orgy, rampage, splurge (*informal*), bender (*slang*), blast (*slang*) [➡EVENTS AND OCCURRENCES; 35] 7 *n* **teardrop**, drop, droplet, drip, bead, blob, spot [➡EXCRETION AND EXCRETA; 722]

Compare and Contrast: *tear, rend, rip, split*

CORE MEANING: to pull apart forcibly

tear to pull something apart, either by accident or on purpose, leaving jagged edges; **rend** to pull something apart violently; **rip** to tear something with a sudden rough splitting action, accompanied by a distinctive noise, especially accidentally; **split** to divide something into two parts with a single movement, usually by force.

tear apart 1 *v* **destroy**, fragment, wreck, separate, dismantle, demolish, break [➡TEAR, BREAK, AND CUT; 360] *Opposite*: reunite 2 *v* **distress**, disturb, devastate, pain, hurt, upset, trouble [➡UPSET, DISTRESS, AND HUMILIATE; 567] *Opposite*: reassure

tear a strip off (*UK*) *v* [➡ACCUSE, BLAME, AND CRITICIZE; 641]

tear away *v* **drag away**, pull away, haul away, depart, leave, be off, make tracks (*informal*) [➡LEAVE AND GO AWAY; 8] *Opposite*: linger

tearaway (*UK*) *n* **delinquent**, troublemaker, hoodlum, hooligan (*informal*), rascal (*humorous*) [➡MISCHIEVOUS OR BADLY BEHAVED CHILD; 946]

tear down *v* **demolish**, rip down, pull down, destroy, remove, break up, flatten, dismantle, raze to the ground [➡DESTRUCTION AND DEMOLITION; 359] *Opposite*: construct

teardrop 1 *n* **tear**, drop, droplet, drip, bead, blob, spot [➡AMOUNT OF LIQUID; 114] 2 *type of* **rounded shape** [➡ROUNDED SHAPE; 1218]

tearful 1 *adj* **in tears**, crying, weeping, sobbing, howling, wailing, rueful, sniveling, bawling (*informal*), weepy (*informal*) [➡CRYING; 650] 2 *adj* **sad**, emotional, unhappy, mournful, melancholy, sorrowful, upsetting [➡EMOTIONALLY UNPLEASANT AND UPSETTING; 227] *Opposite*: cheerful

tear gas *type of* **gas** [➡GASES; 1275]

tear gland *n* [➡THE EYE; 698]

tear into *v* **lay into**, attack, go for, round on, set on, fly into, criticize, pitch into (*informal*) [➡ACCUSE, BLAME, AND CRITICIZE; 641] *Opposite*: praise

tearjerker (*informal*) *n* **sentimental story**, drama, tragedy, sad story, weepie (*informal*), sob story (*informal*) [➡FILM; 901] *Opposite*: comedy

tear limb from limb *v* [➡WOUND A PERSON OR ANIMAL; 383]

tearoom *type of* **eating place** [➡HOTELS, RESTAURANTS, AND CLUBS; 1082]

tear to pieces *v* [➡ACCUSE, BLAME, AND CRITICIZE; 641]

tear to shreds *v* [➡ACCUSE, BLAME, AND CRITICIZE; 641]

tear up *v* **rip up**, shred, destroy, rip to pieces, rip to shreds, trash (*informal*) [➡DESTRUCTION AND DEMOLITION; 359]

teary *adj* [➡CRYING; 650]

teary-eyed *adj* [➡CRYING; 650]

tease 1 *v* **torment**, harass, pester, bother, annoy, provoke, badger, irritate, goad, bait [➡ ANGER AND ANNOY; 569] *Opposite*: pet 2 *v* **joke**, laugh, mock, kid, taunt, laugh at, make fun of, rib (*informal*), pull somebody's leg (*informal*), mess around (*informal*), josh (*informal*), rag (*dated*) [➡ JOKES AND TEASING; 674] 3 *v* **tantalize**, arouse, lead somebody on, encourage, excite, manipulate [➡ APPEAL TO AND AROUSE INTEREST; 575] *Opposite*: satisfy 4 *v* **brush**, comb, style, coif (*formal*), backcomb (*UK*) [➡ CHANGE OF SHAPE; 385] 5 *n* **joker**, clown, mocker, teaser, tormentor, josher (*informal*) [➡ JOKERS AND TEASES; 675]

teased *adj* [➡ DESCRIBING HAIR; 486]

teaser 1 *n* **tease**, joker, clown, mocker, josher (*informal*) [➡ JOKERS AND TEASES; 675] 2 *n* **puzzle**, puzzler, brainteaser, tough one, mystery, conundrum, riddle [➡ SECRETS AND MYSTERIES; 180]

tea service *n* **tea set**, cups and saucers, china, porcelain, crockery [➡ TABLEWARE, FLATWARE, AND KITCHENWARE; 861]

tea set *see* **tea service**

teasing 1 *adj* **playful**, mocking, tongue-in-cheek, mischievous, jokey, bantering, joshing (*informal*) [➡ JOKES AND TEASING; 674] *Opposite*: serious 2 *adj* **provocative**, coy, flirtatious, suggestive, tempting, tantalizing, enigmatic, coquettish (*literary*) [➡ FLIRTATIOUS; 639] *Opposite*: straightforward 3 *n* **playfulness**, banter, repartee, raillery, ribbing (*informal*) [➡ JOKES AND TEASING; 674] *Opposite*: seriousness

teaspoon *type of* **flatware** [➡ TABLEWARE, FLATWARE, AND KITCHENWARE; 861]

teaspoonful *n* [➡ AMOUNTS AND QUANTITIES; 112]

tea table *type of* **table** [➡ FURNITURE; 858]

teatime *n* [➡ TIMES OF DAY; 871]

tea towel (*UK*) *n* [➡ TABLEWARE, FLATWARE, AND KITCHENWARE; 861]

tea urn *n* [➡ TABLEWARE, FLATWARE, AND KITCHENWARE; 861]

tech (*informal*) *n* [➡ EDUCATIONAL INSTITUTIONS; 813]

technical 1 *adj* **technological**, scientific, industrial, mechanical [➡ DESCRIBING TECHNOLOGY; 1160] 2 *adj* **practical**, mechanical, procedural, methodological, methodical [➡ POSITIVE INTELLECTUAL CHARACTERISTICS; 524] 3 *adj* **nominal**, official, strict, narrow, literal, pedantic [➡ EXACT; 203] *Opposite*: loose 4 *adj* **specialized**, precise, official, professional, specialist, expert [➡ EXACT; 203] *Opposite*: general

technical college *n* [➡ EDUCATIONAL INSTITUTIONS; 813]

technicalities *n* [➡ BASIC DETAILS; 688]

technicality *n* **detail**, small point, trifle [➡ UNIMPORTANT AND UNNECESSARY; 238]

technician *n* **specialist**, expert, operator, mechanic, engineer, skilled worker [➡ WORKERS; 836]

technique *n* **method**, system, practice, modus operandi, procedure, skill [➡ WAYS OF DOING THINGS; 294]

techno *type of* **dance music** [➡ MUSIC, SONGS, AND SINGING; 907]

technobabble *n* [➡ MEANINGLESS SPEECH OR WRITING; 676]

technocrat *n* [➡ POLITICAL OFFICES AND POLITICIANS; 808]

technological *adj* **technical**, scientific, industrial, high-tech [➡ DESCRIBING TECHNOLOGY; 1160]

technologist *n* **scientist**, engineer, technician, maven [➡ WORKERS; 836]

technology 1 *n* **equipment**, machinery, tools [➡ MACHINERY; 1114] 2 *n* **skill**, knowledge, expertise, know-how (*informal*) [➡ SKILLS, TALENTS, AND ABILITIES; 526]

technophobia *type of* **phobia** [➡ FEARS AND PHOBIAS; 554]

teddy 1 *type of* **upper body underwear** [➡ ACCESSORIES, MILLINERY, AND LINGERIE; 867] 2 *see* **teddy bear**

teddy bear *type of* **toy** [➡ TOYS; 880]

teddy boy *n* [➡ DEVOTEES AND ADDICTED PEOPLE; 556]

tedious *adj* **boring**, dull, dreary, monotonous, mind-numbing, tiresome, wearisome, wearying, uninteresting, deadly (*informal*) [➡ BORING AND UNINTERESTING; 234] *Opposite*: interesting

See Compare and Contrast at **boring**.

tediousness *n* **tedium**, boredom, dullness, dreariness, monotony, tiresomeness, deadliness (*informal*) [➡ BORING AND UNINTERESTING; 234] *Opposite*: excitement

tedium *see* **tediousness**

tee 1 *type of* **sports equipment** [➡ SPORTS EQUIPMENT; 879] 2 (*informal*) *type of* **top** [➡ GARMENTS AND OUTFITS; 865]

teed off (*informal*) *adj* **angry**, annoyed, irritated, furious, fuming, peeved (*informal*), fed up (*informal*), ticked off (*informal*) [➡ IRRITATION AND ANGER; 541] *Opposite*: calm

teem 1 *v* **swarm**, crowd, abound, be full, be stuffed, be loaded, be crammed [➡ PROSPER AND ABOUND; 16] 2 *v* **pour**, pelt, stream, rain, rain cats and dogs (*informal*) [➡ CLOUDY AND RAINY WEATHER; 1052] *Opposite*: drizzle

teeming *adj* **swarming**, packed, crowded, crawling, seething, jam-packed (*informal*), heaving (*UK*) [➡ FULL; 1239] *Opposite*: empty

teen (*informal*) 1 *adj* **teenage**, adolescent, youth, young, juvenile [➡ BABYHOOD, CHILDHOOD, AND ADOLESCENCE; 917] 2 *n* **teenager**, adolescent, young person, youth, youngster, young adult, juvenile, minor [➡ CHILD OR YOUTH; 945]

teenage *adj* **adolescent**, young, youth, juvenile, teen (*informal*) [➡ BABYHOOD, CHILDHOOD, AND ADOLESCENCE; 917]

teenager *n* **adolescent**, young person, youth, youngster, young adult, juvenile, minor, teen (*informal*) [➡ CHILD OR YOUTH; 945]

See Compare and Contrast at **youth**.

teens *n* **adolescence**, youth, young adulthood [➡ BABYHOOD, CHILDHOOD, AND ADOLESCENCE; 917]

teensy (*informal*) *adj* [➡ SMALL; 1195]

teensy-weensy (*informal*) *adj* [➡ SMALL; 1195]

teeny (*informal*) *adj* **tiny**, small, little, minute, wee, minuscule, microscopic, miniature, teensy (*informal*),

teeny-weeny (*informal*), **teensy-weensy** (*informal*) [➡ SMALL; 1195] *Opposite*: enormous

teeny-weeny (*informal*) *adj* [➡ SMALL; 1195]

tee off *v* **drive off**, start, begin, commence, initiate, kick off (*informal*) [➡ START AN ACTION; 260]

tee shirt *see* **T-shirt**

teeter *v* **totter**, stagger, wobble, shake, dodder, waver, hover, reel, rock, sway, lurch, weave [➡ WALK UNSTEADILY; 315]

teething troubles (*UK*) *n* **problems**, glitches, difficulties, snags, hitches, complications [➡ PROBLEMS; 256]

teetotal *adj* **dry**, nondrinking, abstemious, abstinent, sober, on the wagon [➡ SELF-DENIAL; 882]

teetotaler *n* [➡ ASCETIC PEOPLE; 883]

teetotalism *n* [➡ SELF-DENIAL; 882]

telecast *v* [➡ TELEVISION AND RADIO; 606]

telecaster *n* **broadcaster**, announcer, commentator, newscaster, anchor, presenter (*UK*) [➡ WORKERS IN ENTERTAINMENT AND MEDIA; 873]

telecommunications *n* [➡ TELECOMMUNICATIONS; 1130]

telecommunications

◆ *types of telecommunications equipment*
answering machine, antenna, beeper (*informal*), bug, cable, cellphone, cellular phone, e-mail, fax, intercom, landline, mast, modem, netphone, pager, payphone, phone, phonecard, receiver, satellite, satellite dish, switchboard, telephone, telex, transmitter, videophone, voice mail, walkie-talkie, WAP, wiretap

telecommuting *n* **working from home**, freelancing, outworking (*UK*) [➡ TYPES OF WORK; 835]

telegram *n* **wire**, cable, message, telegraph, telex, cablegram [➡ LETTERS AND WRITTEN MESSAGES; 584]

telegraph *v* **send by wire**, send a message, cable, wire, transmit, telex [➡ DISPATCH AND SEND; 333]

telegraphic *adj* **concise**, abbreviated, condensed, truncated, succinct, compressed, elliptical, brief, pithy, curt [➡ SUCCINCT AND TO THE POINT; 640] *Opposite*: verbose

telekinetic *adj* [➡ THE SUPERNATURAL; 787]

telemarketing *n* **telephone selling**, marketing, sales, telesales (*UK*) [➡ BUSINESS ACTIVITIES AND PHENOMENA; 794]

telepathic *adj* **clairvoyant**, psychic, telekinetic, extrasensory, subconscious, parapsychological, intuitive [➡ THE SUPERNATURAL; 787]

telepathist *n* [➡ PEOPLE WITH SUPERNATURAL POWERS; 788]

telepathy *n* **thought transference**, ESP, extrasensory perception, mind-reading, sixth sense, intuition [➡ THE SUPERNATURAL; 787]

telephone 1 *v* **phone**, call, give somebody a call, buzz (*informal*), ring (*UK*) [➡ TELEPHONE, PAGE, AND TEXT; 681] 2 *type of* **telecommunications equipment** [➡ TELECOMMUNICATIONS; 1130]

telephone call *n* **call**, phone call, buzz (*informal*), ring (*UK*), tinkle (*UK*) [➡ TELEPHONE COMMUNICATION; 48]

telephonist *n* [➡ OFFICE WORKERS; 847]

telephoto lens *part of* **camera** [➡ PHOTOGRAPHY AND PHOTOGRAPHIC EQUIPMENT; 1122]

telesales (*UK*) *n* **telemarketing**, telephone sales, marketing, sales [➡ BUSINESS ACTIVITIES AND PHENOMENA; 794]

telescope *type of* **optical instrument** [➡ OPTICAL INSTRUMENTS; 1124]

telescopic 1 *adj* **magnifying**, enlarging, telephoto, zoom [➡ CHANGE OF SIZE: BIGGER; 392] 2 *adj* **collapsible**, retractable, foldaway, foldup, compactible [➡ CHANGE OF SHAPE; 385]

telestich *type of* **wordplay** [➡ JOKES AND TEASING; 674]

telethon *n* **fundraiser**, charity appeal, broadcast appeal, solicitation, benefit [➡ TELEVISION AND RADIO; 606]

televise *v* **broadcast**, emit, relay, put out, put on, show, telecast, simulcast, air [➡ TELEVISION AND RADIO; 606]

television *n* **TV** (*informal*), small screen (*informal*), tube (*informal*), boob tube (*informal*), telly (*UK*), box (*UK slang*) [➡ HOUSEHOLD APPLIANCES; 1117]

teleworker (*UK*) *n* **telecommuter**, freelancer, homeworker (*UK*), outworker (*UK*) [➡ WORKERS; 836]

teleworking (*UK*) *n* **telecommuting**, freelancing, homeworking (*UK*), outworking (*UK*) [➡ TYPES OF WORK; 835]

telex *type of* **telecommunications equipment** [➡ TELECOMMUNICATIONS; 1130]

tell 1 *v* **relate**, narrate, recount, describe, report, impart [➡ RECITE, REPEAT, AND NARRATE; 620] 2 *v* **inform**, let know, say, advise, notify, put in the picture, enlighten, acquaint with [➡ INFORM, ANNOUNCE, AND ISSUE; 611] 3 *v* **express**, say, voice, communicate, state, articulate, speak, convey [➡ UTTER AND PRONOUNCE; 608] 4 *v* **instruct**, order, direct, command, charge, ask, request [➡ REQUEST AND DEMAND; 663] 5 *v* **distinguish**, recognize, differentiate, identify, discriminate, know, judge [➡ LEARN AND DISCOVER; 762] *Opposite*: confuse 6 *v* **divulge**, disclose, expose, reveal, inform, tell on, tattle, gossip, blab (*informal*), spill the beans (*informal*), let the cat out of the bag (*informal*), snitch (*slang*), sneak (*UK*) [➡ BETRAY CONFIDENCES AND GOSSIP; 618]

tell against *v* **count against**, go against, work against, weigh against [➡ DELAY ACTION OR OCCURRENCE; 278]

tell apart *v* **distinguish**, differentiate, tell one from another, identify, tell the difference between, discriminate [➡ MAKE DECISIONS AND CHOICES; 752]

teller *n* **cashier**, banker, bank clerk [➡ PEOPLE INVOLVED IN FINANCE; 804]

telling 1 *adj* **revealing**, informative, significant, telltale, indicative, illuminating [➡ INTERESTING AND MEANINGFUL; 190] *Opposite*: uninformative 2 *adj* **effective**, expressive, important, significant, influential, powerful, forceful, impressive, decisive, potent [➡ STRENGTH; 201] *Opposite*: ineffective

telling-off (*informal*) *n* **reprimand**, scolding, dressing-down, lecture, tongue-lashing, talking-to (*informal*), bawling-out (*informal*) [➡ CRITICISMS AND ANGRY OUTBURSTS; 50]

tell it how it is (*informal*) v [➡ ADMIT AND CONFESS; 615]

tell lies v [➡ DECEPTION AND LIES; 660]

tell off (*informal*) v **reprimand**, scold, rebuke, rake over the coals, take to task, reproach, give a talking-to (*UK*), haul over the coals (*UK*) [➡ ACCUSE, BLAME, AND CRITICIZE; 641] *Opposite*: commend

tell on v [➡ BETRAY CONFIDENCES AND GOSSIP; 618]

tell stories v **tell lies**, lie, tell untruths, prevaricate, fabricate, fib (*informal*), spin a yarn (*informal*) [➡ DECEPTION AND LIES; 660]

telltale adj **revealing**, informative, betraying, significant, divulging, telling, indicative, illuminating [➡ INTERESTING AND MEANINGFUL; 190] *Opposite*: uninformative

tell tales v [➡ BETRAY CONFIDENCES AND GOSSIP; 618]

telltale sign n [➡ EVIDENCE AND PROOF; 69]

tell the truth v **be honest**, give your word, be straight with, be open, be truthful, speak the truth, stick to the facts, give the true story [➡ ADMIT AND CONFESS; 615]

tell untruths v [➡ DECEPTION AND LIES; 660]

temerity n **nerve**, audacity, gall, boldness, impudence, impertinence, cheek (*informal*), chutzpah (*informal*) [➡ BAD MANNERS AND SOCIAL SKILLS; 521] *Opposite*: reticence

temp 1 n **temporary worker**, office temporary, fill-in, stand-in, temporary secretary [➡ OFFICE WORKERS; 847] 2 v **do temporary work**, fill in, stand in [➡ WORK-RELATED ACTIVITIES; 834]

temper 1 n **disposition**, temperament, state of mind, frame of mind, humor, mood, spirit, nature, character, attitude (*informal*) [➡ TEMPERAMENT AND BEHAVIOR; 492] 2 n **anger**, rage, bad mood, bad humor, mood, sulk, tantrum, fit of pique [➡ IRRITATION AND ANGER; 541] 3 v **moderate**, mitigate, alleviate, soften, lighten, assuage, lessen, tone down, soothe, calm, palliate [➡ CHANGE OF INTENSITY: LESS; 395] *Opposite*: intensify

temperament n **nature**, character, personality, disposition, temper, spirit, outlook, makeup, humor [➡ TEMPERAMENT AND BEHAVIOR; 492]

temperamental adj **unpredictable**, erratic, unreliable, undependable, up and down, volatile, changeable, variable [➡ LACK OF COMMITMENT AND UNRELIABILITY; 509] *Opposite*: consistent

temperance 1 n **teetotalism**, sobriety, abstinence, abstemiousness, soberness [➡ SELF-DENIAL; 882] *Opposite*: intemperance 2 n **self-control**, restraint, self-restraint, moderation, self-denial, self-discipline [➡ STRENGTH OF WILL; 501] *Opposite*: indulgence

temperate 1 adj **restrained**, self-controlled, controlled, moderate, reasonable, mild, measured, reserved, muted [➡ CONFIDENCE AND COMPOSURE; 499] *Opposite*: intemperate 2 adj **moderate**, mild, clement, pleasant, comfortable [➡ COLD WEATHER; 1051] *Opposite*: extreme

temperately adv **mildly**, moderately, quietly, with restraint, calmly, smoothly, equably [➡ CONFIDENCE AND COMPOSURE; 499] *Opposite*: intemperately

temperateness n [➡ CONFIDENCE AND COMPOSURE; 499]

temperature n [➡ TEMPERATURE: HOT; 1229]

tempered adj **hardened**, toughened, hard, annealed, strengthened [➡ RIGID AND HARD; 1211]

tempest 1 n (*literary*) **storm**, gale, thunderstorm, hurricane, cyclone, rainstorm, snowstorm, blizzard, whirlwind, high winds [➡ WINDY AND STORMY WEATHER; 1053] *Opposite*: calm 2 n **uproar**, commotion, tumult, upheaval, disturbance, riot, brouhaha [➡ CHAOS AND UPROAR; 51]

tempestuous 1 adj **emotional**, stormy, passionate, turbulent, uncontrolled, violent, hysterical, intense, wild, changeable [➡ EMOTIONALLY UNPLEASANT AND UPSETTING; 227] *Opposite*: relaxed 2 adj **stormy**, rough, turbulent, intemperate, inclement, windy, blustery [➡ WINDY AND STORMY WEATHER; 1053] *Opposite*: calm

tempestuously adv **emotionally**, passionately, turbulently, wildly, furiously, stormily, violently, hysterically, intensely, changeably [➡ EMOTIONALLY UNPLEASANT AND UPSETTING; 227] *Opposite*: calmly

tempestuousness n **violence**, passion, turbulence, fury, storminess, wildness, intensity, changeability, drama [➡ EMOTIONALLY UNPLEASANT AND UPSETTING; 227] *Opposite*: calm

template n **pattern**, master, stencil, model, prototype, original, outline, shape [➡ PATTERNS; 1225]

temple 1 *type of* **place of worship** [➡ RELIGIOUS BUILDINGS; 1085] 2 *type of* **church** [➡ RELIGIOUS BUILDINGS; 1085] 3 *part of* **face** [➡ PARTS OF THE BODY: HEAD; 692]

tempo n **beat**, speed, pulse, rhythm, measure, time, pace [➡ MUSICAL TERMS; 912]

temporal 1 adj **chronological**, time-based, sequential, progressive, historical [➡ CHAIN OF EVENTS; 162] *Opposite*: spatial 2 adj **worldly**, earthly, secular, lay, profane, mundane, terrestrial, mortal [➡ RELIGIOUS CONCEPTS; 776] *Opposite*: spiritual

temporariness n [➡ FINITENESS, VARIABILITY, AND TRANSIENCE; 96]

temporary adj **provisional**, transitory, short-term, short-lived, fleeting, passing, ephemeral, transient, acting, interim, pro tem, evanescent (*literary*) [➡ FINITENESS, VARIABILITY, AND TRANSIENCE; 96] *Opposite*: permanent

Compare and Contrast: *temporary, fleeting, passing, transitory, ephemeral, evanescent, short-lived*

CORE MEANING: lasting only a short time

temporary lasting or designed to last for a short time; *fleeting* very brief or rapid; *passing* superficial and not long-lasting; *transitory* existing only for a short time; *ephemeral* lasting for a short time and leaving no permanent trace; *evanescent* (*literary*) disappearing after a short time and soon forgotten; *short-lived* lasting only for a short time.

temporize v **delay**, defer, procrastinate, take your time, hesitate, tarry, put off [➡ HESITATE; 272] *Opposite*: set to

tempt 1 v **lure**, allure, entice, attract, excite, arouse, seduce, make your mouth water, tantalize, turn on (*informal*) [➡ APPEAL TO AND AROUSE INTEREST; 575] *Opposite*: repel 2 v **invite**, attract, appeal, draw, move [➡ APPEAL TO AND AROUSE INTEREST; 575] *Opposite*: put off

temptation 1 n **lure**, enticement, attraction, offer, invitation, inducement, pull (*informal*), turn-on (*informal*)

[➡ APPRECIATION AND GRATITUDE; 535] **2** *n* **desire**, craving, urge, impulse, compulsion, appetite, wish, longing [➡ DESIRE AND WANT; 579] *Opposite:* repulsion **3** *n* **persuasion**, coaxing, inducement, enticement, invitation, attraction [➡ DESIRE AND WANT; 579] *Opposite:* repulsion

tempted *adj* **of a mind to**, attracted, interested, curious, drawn, desirous (*formal*) [➡ DESIRE AND WANT; 579] *Opposite:* uninterested

tempting *adj* **alluring**, enticing, attractive, appealing, inviting, seductive, mouthwatering, tantalizing, irresistible, persuasive [➡ INTERESTING AND MEANINGFUL; 190] *Opposite:* unappealing

tempura *type of* **cooked dish** [➡ PREPARED DISHES; 1170]

tenable *adj* **reasonable**, acceptable, defensible, plausible, rational, sound, justifiable [➡ POSSIBLE AND PROBABLE; 177] *Opposite:* untenable

tenacious *adj* **stubborn**, obstinate, resolute, firm, persistent, insistent, dogged, determined, steadfast, inflexible [➡ STRENGTH OF WILL; 501] *Opposite:* irresolute

tenaciousness *n* [➡ STRENGTH OF WILL; 501]

tenacity *n* **stubbornness**, obstinacy, resolve, firmness, persistence, insistence, doggedness, determination, steadfastness, tenaciousness [➡ UNWILLINGNESS AND STUBBORNNESS; 564] *Opposite:* irresolution

tenancy *n* **occupancy**, rental, contract, lease, tenure, occupation [➡ ACCOMMODATIONS; 855] *Opposite:* ownership

tenant *n* **renter**, occupier, occupant, resident, lodger, boarder, paying guest, leaseholder, lessee [➡ INHABITANTS; 857] *Opposite:* landlord

ten a penny (*UK*) *adj* **commonplace**, ordinary, run-of-the-mill, common, a dime a dozen [➡ ORDINARINESS; 244] *Opposite:* rare

tench *type of* **freshwater fish** [➡ FRESHWATER FISH; 1010]

tend **1** *v* **have a habit of**, have a tendency to, incline, lean toward, be disposed, be likely to, be apt to, be wont to [➡ LIKE, LOVE, VALUE, AND ENJOY; 578] **2** *v* **incline**, veer, lean, bend, verge [➡ CHANGE DIRECTION OF MOTION; 344] **3** *v* **look after**, care for, take care of, cultivate, attend to, minister to [➡ TAKE CARE OF AND SPOIL; 300] *Opposite:* neglect **4** *v* **be in charge of**, manage, keep an eye on, watch over, watch, supervise, mind [➡ BE IN CHARGE; 270]

tendency **1** *n* **propensity**, bent, leaning, inclination, predisposition, penchant, affinity [➡ TEMPERAMENT AND BEHAVIOR; 492] **2** *n* **trend**, drift, movement, bias, current, shift [➡ DIRECTION OF MOTION; 345]

tendentious *adj* **provocative**, opinionated, biased, partisan, subjective, argumentative, prejudiced, one-sided, questionable, doubtful, partial [➡ THE NATURE OF IDEAS; 771] *Opposite:* impartial

tender **1** *adj* **sensitive**, delicate, sore, raw, painful, inflamed, bruised, aching [➡ PAIN AND OTHER PHYSICAL SENSATIONS; 733] **2** *adj* **loving**, caring, affectionate, fond, kind, kindhearted, gentle, warm, compassionate [➡ GENEROSITY AND KINDNESS; 495] *Opposite:* rough **3** *adj* **young**, youthful, immature, inexperienced, impressionable, green, unsophisticated [➡ UNSKILLED; 529] *Opposite:* seasoned **4** *n* **proposal**, proposition,

bid, offer, submission, estimate [➡ REQUEST AND DEMAND; 663] **5** *v* **offer**, proffer, present, give, hand in, put forward, suggest, submit, propose [➡ SUGGEST, HINT, AND COMMENT; 612] *Opposite:* withdraw

tenderfoot (*informal*) *n* **novice**, recruit, raw recruit, newcomer, beginner, tyro, greenhorn, neophyte, rookie (*informal*) [➡ UNSKILLED PEOPLE; 530] *Opposite:* old hand

tenderhearted *adj* **soft-hearted**, compassionate, sympathetic, kind, soft, tender, benevolent, sensitive, indulgent, gentle [➡ GENEROSITY AND KINDNESS; 495] *Opposite:* hardhearted

tenderheartedness *n* **soft-heartedness**, compassion, sympathy, tenderness, kindness, benevolence, sensitivity, gentleness, indulgence, softness [➡ GENEROSITY AND KINDNESS; 495] *Opposite:* hardheartedness

tenderize *v* **beat**, smash, hit, soak, steep, marinate [➡ COOKING AND FOOD PREPARATION; 353]

tenderloin *type of* **steak** [➡ TYPES AND CUTS OF MEAT; 1177]

tenderly *adv* **sympathetically**, lovingly, caringly, affectionately, fondly, kindly, kindheartedly, gently, warmly, compassionately [➡ GENEROSITY AND KINDNESS; 495] *Opposite:* unkindly

tenderness **1** *n* **sensitivity**, soreness, rawness, painfulness, inflammation, ache, bruising [➡ PAIN AND OTHER PHYSICAL SENSATIONS; 733] **2** *n* **sympathy**, gentleness, kindness, kindheartedness, fondness, love, caring, affection, warmth, compassion, softness [➡ GENEROSITY AND KINDNESS; 495] *Opposite:* unkindness

tendon *type of* **muscle or tendon** [➡ THE MUSCLES; 718]

tendril **1** *n* **stem**, vine, shoot, frond, branch [➡ PARTS OF TREES AND PLANTS; 1026] **2** *n* (*literary*) **twist**, coil, wisp, lock, curl, ringlet, strand [➡ HAIR; 484]

tenebrous (*literary*) *adj* [➡ DESCRIBING LIGHT; 1228]

tenement *n* **apartment building**, apartment house, high-rise, housing project, apartment block (*UK*), block of flats (*UK*) [➡ RESIDENTIAL BUILDINGS; 1078]

tenet *n* **principle**, theory, idea, assumption, belief, doctrine, dogma, precept (*formal*) [➡ IDEAS AND THOUGHTS; 770]

ten-gallon hat *type of* **hat** [➡ ACCESSORIES, MILLINERY, AND LINGERIE; 867]

tenge *type of* **currency** [➡ CURRENCIES; 798]

tenner (*informal*) *n* [➡ CURRENCIES; 798]

tennis *type of* **court game** [➡ HOBBIES, GAMES, AND SPORTS; 875]

tenor **1** *n* **mood**, tone, gist, drift, meaning, sense, theme, intention, tendency, purpose, nature [➡ MEANING; 690] **2** *type of* **musical register** [➡ MUSICAL TERMS; 912]

tense **1** *adj* **anxious**, nervous, stressed, worried, edgy, jumpy, overwrought, on edge, apprehensive, jittery, antsy (*informal*), uptight (*informal*), twitchy (*informal*) [➡ CONFUSION, ANXIETY, AND WORRY; 540] *Opposite:* relaxed **2** *adj* **taut**, tight, rigid, stiff, strained, tensed [➡ RIGID AND HARD; 1211] *Opposite:* loose

tensile *adj* **ductile**, stretchy, stretchable, workable, malleable, flexible [➡ MALLEABLE AND ELASTIC; 1212] *Opposite:* rigid

tension 1 *n* **worry**, nervousness, anxiety, stress, strain, pressure, apprehension [➡ FEELINGS ABOUT THE FUTURE; 533] *Opposite*: relaxation 2 *n* **tautness**, tightness, stiffness, strain, pressure, pull [➡ RIGID AND HARD; 1211] *Opposite*: relaxation 3 *n* **conflict**, ill feeling, friction, hostility, mistrust, unease, strain, stress [➡ DISHARMONY; 156] *Opposite*: ease

ten-speed *type of* **bike** [➡ BIKES, CARS, AND CARRIAGES; 1149]

tent *n* **shelter**, marquee, bivouac, camp, pavilion, big top [➡ RESIDENTIAL BUILDINGS; 1078]

tentacle *n* **limb**, organ, appendage, feeler, antenna, member, arm [➡ PARTS OF THE BODY: ARM AND HAND; 695]

tentative 1 *adj* **hesitant**, cautious, faltering, unsure, timid, shy, uncertain [➡ INSECURITY AND LOSS OF COMPOSURE; 544] *Opposite*: sure 2 *adj* **provisional**, exploratory, speculative, unconfirmed, indefinite, unsettled, not final, rough, open to consideration [➡ UNCERTAIN; 175] *Opposite*: definite

tentatively *adv* **hesitantly**, cautiously, falteringly, uncertainly, timidly, shyly [➡ INSECURITY AND LOSS OF COMPOSURE; 544] *Opposite*: boldly

tenuous *adj* **weak**, shaky, unsubstantiated, questionable, feeble, vague, unconvincing, half-hearted [➡ VAGUENESS; 243] *Opposite*: convincing

tenuousness *n* [➡ VAGUENESS; 243]

tenure 1 *n* **tenancy**, freehold, occupancy, occupation, lease, contract [➡ ACCOMMODATIONS; 855] *Opposite*: ownership 2 *n* (*formal*) **term**, duration, span, period, time, stretch, stint [➡ PERIODS OF TIME; 90]

tepal *part of* **flower** [➡ FLOWERS; 1032]

tepid 1 *adj* **lukewarm**, blood hot, warmish, warm, barely warm, hand hot (*UK*) [➡ TEMPERATURE: MEDIUM; 1230] *Opposite*: icy 2 *adj* **unenthusiastic**, half-hearted, lukewarm, indifferent, apathetic, moderate, lackadaisical [➡ NEUTRALITY AND INDIFFERENCE; 553] *Opposite*: enthusiastic

tercentenary *n* **300th anniversary**, anniversary, commemoration, celebration, festival, 300th year [➡ CEREMONIES AND ANNIVERSARIES; 38]

tercentennial *see* **tercentenary**

teriyaki *type of* **cooked dish** [➡ PREPARED DISHES; 1170]

term 1 *n* **word**, expression, phrase, name, idiom [➡ ASPECTS OF LANGUAGE; 682] 2 *n* (*formal*) **period**, time, stretch, tenure, span, duration, stint [➡ PERIODS OF TIME; 90] 3 *v* **call**, name, label, dub, designate, characterize [➡ NAME AND DESCRIBE; 665]

terminal 1 *adj* **fatal**, incurable, deadly, mortal, lethal, life-threatening [➡ DEADLY; 928] *Opposite*: curable 2 *n* **work-station**, computer, monitor, visual display unit (*UK*), VDU (*UK*) [➡ COMPUTERS AND COMPUTING; 1127] 3 *n* **station**, airport, rail terminal, passenger terminal, terminus, depot [➡ PUBLIC BUILDINGS AND MEETING PLACES; 1081]

See Compare and Contrast at **deadly.**

terminally *adv* **fatally**, incurably, mortally, lethally, critically [➡ CRITICALLY AND SERIOUSLY; 134]

terminal moraine *n* [➡ EROSION PRODUCTS AND SOIL; 1058]

terminate 1 *v* **end**, finish, come to an end, conclude, stop, cease, expire, lapse [➡ CAUSE TO STOP; 266] *Opposite*: start 2 *v* **dismiss**, let go, lay off, fire (*informal*), sack (*informal*), ax (*informal*) [➡ REVOKE STATUS; 459] *Opposite*: hire

termination (*formal*) *n* **end**, finish, close, expiry, conclusion, closure, dissolution, cessation [➡ ENDS AND DEPARTURES; 54] *Opposite*: start

terminology *n* **terms**, language, expressions, vocabulary, jargon, lexicon, lexis, lingo (*informal*) [➡ ASPECTS OF LANGUAGE; 682]

terminus *n* **last stop**, station, end of the line, depot, garage, terminal [➡ PUBLIC BUILDINGS AND MEETING PLACES; 1081]

term of endearment *n* [➡ ENDEARMENTS; 656]

term paper *n* [➡ CLASSES, COURSEWORK, AND EXAMINATIONS; 842]

terms 1 *n* **conditions**, stipulations, provisos, provisions, requisites [➡ NECESSARY AND ESSENTIAL; 196] 2 *n* **footing**, rapport, relations, relationship, standing, position [➡ RELATIONSHIP TO ANOTHER; 973] 3 *n* **language**, expressions, vocabulary, terminology, jargon, nomenclature, lexis [➡ ASPECTS OF LANGUAGE; 682]

tern *type of* **sea bird** [➡ SEA BIRDS; 1002]

terrace *n* **walkway**, patio, porch, veranda, promenade [➡ URBAN OUTDOOR SPACES; 1072]

terraced 1 *adj* **adjoining**, attached, joined [➡ BUILDING AND ARCHITECTURE; 1076] *Opposite*: detached 2 *adj* **in terraces**, stepped, ridged, tiered, split-level, on different levels [➡ MOUNTAINS AND HILLS; 1044]

terra cotta *type of* **pottery** [➡ POTTERY; 1135]

terra firma *n* [➡ THE SEAS, OCEANS, AND SHORES; 1041]

terrain *n* **land**, topography, territory, ground, landscape, environment [➡ THE COUNTRYSIDE AND OUTDOOR SPACES; 1071]

terrapin *type of* **reptile** [➡ REPTILES; 994]

terrazzo *n* [➡ BUILDING MATERIALS; 1077]

terrestrial 1 *adj* **earthly**, worldly, global, telluric [➡ THE EARTH; 1039] *Opposite*: extraterrestrial 2 *adj* **land-dwelling**, surface-dwelling, land, earthbound [➡ THE EARTH; 1039]

terrible 1 *adj* **extreme**, severe, serious, grave, intense, excessive [➡ BAD AND BADLY; 223] *Opposite*: mild 2 *adj* **awful**, dreadful, rotten, appalling, poor, abysmal [➡ BAD AND BADLY; 223] *Opposite*: wonderful 3 *adj* **horrible**, horrifying, horrific, horrendous, frightful, shocking, terrifying [➡ EMOTIONALLY UNPLEASANT AND UPSETTING; 227] *Opposite*: pleasant

terribly 1 *adv* **awfully**, appallingly, offensively, intolerably, horribly, dreadfully [➡ BAD AND BADLY; 223] *Opposite*: pleasantly 2 *adv* **very**, extremely, tremendously, exceedingly, incredibly, inordinately, enormously [➡ TO A GREAT EXTENT; 132] *Opposite*: slightly

terrier *type of* **small dog** [➡ DOGS; 980]

terrific 1 *adj* (*informal*) **wonderful**, marvelous, excellent, remarkable, superb, great, tremendous, super (*informal*) [➡ EXTRAORDINARY: UNCOMMON; 205] *Opposite*: awful 2 *adj* **enormous**, great, huge, massive, tremendous, awesome, extreme, excessive [➡ LARGE; 1193] *Opposite*: insignificant

terrifically *adv* **very**, extremely, tremendously, exceedingly, incredibly, excessively, greatly [➡ TO A GREAT EXTENT; 132] *Opposite:* slightly

terrified *adj* **frightened**, horrified, scared, scared stiff, petrified, shocked, alarmed [➡ FEAR AND PANIC; 543] *Opposite:* unafraid

terrify *v* **frighten**, horrify, scare, petrify, shock, alarm, panic [➡ FRIGHTEN AND SHOCK; 568] *Opposite:* comfort

terrifying *adj* **frightening**, petrifying, chilling, startling, alarming, disturbing, distressing, worrying, horrifying, shocking, dreadful, terrible, dangerous, scary (*informal*) [➡ FRIGHTENING; 231] *Opposite:* reassuring

territorial **1** *adj* **regional**, local, land, provincial, national, international, state [➡ COUNTRIES AND REGIONS; 1067] **2** *adj* **defensive**, protective, possessive, assertive, jealous [➡ ENVY AND JEALOUSY; 548]

territorial army (*UK*) *n* [➡ THE ARMED FORCES; 827]

territory **1** *n* **land**, terrain, ground, area, region, zone, place, space [➡ PLACE; 1065] **2** *n* **country**, land, state, province, region, domain, area, zone, district [➡ TERRITORIES AND GROUPS OF NATIONS; 1068] **3** *n* **field**, subject, specialty, area, terrain, sphere, arena, zone, compass [➡ SUBJECT AREAS; 768] **4** *n* **patch**, beat, domain, pitch, property, home, range, land, ground [➡ GEOGRAPHIC BORDERS AND BOUNDARIES; 1069]

terror **1** *n* **fear**, horror, dread, fright, alarm, trepidation, shock, panic [➡ FEAR AND PANIC; 543] *Opposite:* security **2** *n* (*informal*) **nuisance**, troublemaker, imp, pest (*informal*), ruffian (*dated*) [➡ MISCHIEVOUS OR BADLY BEHAVED CHILD; 946]

terrorism *n* **violence**, intimidation, radicalism, extremism, bombing, kidnapping, assassination, sabotage [➡ CRIMES; 817]

terrorist *n* **guerrilla**, radical, extremist, fanatic, bomber, kidnapper, assassin, saboteur [➡ CRIMINALS; 821]

terrorization *n* [➡ MALICIOUS ACTIONS OR BEHAVIOR; 296]

terrorize *v* **terrify**, frighten, scare, threaten, intimidate, bully, coerce [➡ FRIGHTEN AND SHOCK; 568] *Opposite:* reassure

terrorized *adj* [➡ FEAR AND PANIC; 543]

terror-stricken *adj* **terrified**, petrified, scared to death, scared stiff, frightened out of your wits, panic-stricken, horror-struck, terrorized, afraid, alarmed, horrified [➡ FEAR AND PANIC; 543] *Opposite:* calm

terry *type of* **fabric from plants** [➡ FABRICS; 1132]

terry cloth *type of* **fabric from plants** [➡ FABRICS; 1132]

terse **1** *adj* **abrupt**, curt, short, brusque, clipped, snappy, snappish [➡ BAD-TEMPERED AND HUMORLESS; 626] *Opposite:* expansive **2** *adj* **concise**, brief, succinct, pithy, short and sweet [➡ SUCCINCT AND TO THE POINT; 640] *Opposite:* wordy

terseness **1** *n* **abruptness**, curtness, shortness, brusqueness, snappishness [➡ BAD-TEMPERED AND HUMORLESS; 626] *Opposite:* expansiveness **2** *n* **concision**, brevity, succinctness, pithiness, economy [➡ SUCCINCT AND TO THE POINT; 640] *Opposite:* verbosity

Tertiary *type of* **period** [➡ EPOCHS AND ERAS; 89]

tesla *type of* **SI unit** [➡ SIZE AND DIMENSIONS; 1192]

test **1** *n* **examination**, exam, quiz, trial, assessment, check, experiment, investigation, analysis, assay, scan [➡ EXAMINE AND ASSESS; 753] **2** *n* **trial run**, trial, test drive, run-through, practice, review, tryout [➡ PREPARATORY EVENTS; 57] **3** *n* **proof**, evidence, sign, criterion, yardstick, acid test, litmus test [➡ INDICATIONS, SIGNS, AND WARNINGS; 68] **4** *n* **trial**, ordeal, hardship, tribulation, torment, difficulty [➡ NUISANCES; 253] **5** *v* **try**, try out, put to the test, examine, quiz, assess, check, put something through its paces, experiment with, investigate, analyze, scan [➡ EXAMINE AND ASSESS; 753]

testament *n* **evidence**, witness, testimony, proof, demonstration, verification, authentication, indication [➡ EVIDENCE AND PROOF; 69]

test drive *n* **trial run**, trial, drive, run, spin, test, tryout [➡ PREPARATORY EVENTS; 57]

test-drive *v* **try out**, try, take for a spin, put something through its paces, drive, test [➡ USE TOOLS AND MACHINERY; 468]

tested *adj* **verified**, tried, confirmed, established, experienced, seasoned [➡ OLD, OLD-FASHIONED; 167] *Opposite:* untried

tester *n* **sample**, trial size, free sample, free gift [➡ REPRESENTATIONS AND GENERAL EXAMPLES; 65]

testify **1** *v* **give evidence**, bear witness, appear, swear, state, attest, affirm [➡ CLAIM, INSIST, AND EMPHASIZE; 614] **2** *v* (*formal*) **prove**, show, confirm, bear out, indicate, demonstrate, bear witness, attest [➡ APPROVE AND CONFIRM; 646] *Opposite:* disprove

testily (*informal*) *adv* **irritably**, grumpily, impatiently, touchily, crabbily, temperamentally, snappily, petulantly, peevishly, cantankerously, bad-temperedly, crossly, tetchily (*informal*), grouchily (*informal*), crankily (*informal*) [➡ BAD-TEMPERED AND HUMORLESS; 626]

testimonial **1** *n* **recommendation**, reference, endorsement, confirmation, statement, declaration [➡ LETTERS AND WRITTEN MESSAGES; 584] **2** *n* **tribute**, honor, reward, celebration, acknowledgment, recognition, monument [➡ NAME AND DESCRIBE; 665]

testimony **1** *n* **evidence**, statement, declaration, deposition, affidavit [➡ OFFICIAL DOCUMENTS; 586] **2** *n* **testament**, evidence, witness, proof, demonstration, verification, authentication, indication [➡ EVIDENCE AND PROOF; 69]

testiness (*informal*) *n* **irritability**, grumpiness, impatience, touchiness, crabbiness, crossness, temper, snappiness, petulance, peevishness, cantankerousness, bad temper, tetchiness (*informal*), grouchiness (*informal*), crankiness (*informal*) [➡ BAD-TEMPERED AND HUMORLESS; 626]

testing *adj* **challenging**, difficult, taxing, tough, trying, hard [➡ DIFFICULTY AND COMPLEXITY; 242] *Opposite:* easy

test match (*UK*) *n* **international**, match, game, cricket match, rugby match, test (*UK*) [➡ NON-AGGRESSIVE/SPORTING EVENTS; 40]

test run *n* [➡ PREPARATORY EVENTS; 57]

testy (*informal*) *adj* **irritable**, grumpy, impatient, touchy, crabby, temperamental, snappy, petulant, peevish, cantankerous, bad-tempered, cross, tetchy (*informal*), grouchy (*informal*), crotchety (*informal*), cranky (*informal*) [➡ BAD-TEMPERED AND HUMORLESS; 626] *Opposite:* even-tempered

tetchily (*informal*) *adv* **irritably**, grumpily, impatiently, touchily, crabbily, crossly, temperamentally, snappily, petulantly, peevishly, cantankerously, bad-temperedly, testily (*informal*), grouchily (*informal*), crankily (*informal*) [➡ BAD-TEMPERED AND HUMORLESS; 626]

tetchiness (*informal*) *n* **irritability**, grumpiness, impatience, touchiness, crabbiness, crossness, temper, snappiness, petulance, peevishness, cantankerousness, bad temper, testiness (*informal*), grouchiness (*informal*), crankiness (*informal*) [➡ BAD-TEMPERED AND HUMORLESS; 626]

tetchy (*informal*) *see* **testy**

tête-à-tête *n* [➡ INFORMAL COMMUNICATION; 45]

tether 1 *n* **rope**, chain, lead, rein, tie, fetter, truss, leash [➡ FASTENERS, LINKS, AND NETWORKS; 1247] 2 *v* **tie up**, tie, hitch, fasten, secure, rope, chain, bind, truss [➡ FASTEN, LINK, AND JOIN, 400] *Opposite*: release

tetragon *type of* **angular shape** [➡ ANGULAR SHAPE; 1217]

tetrahedron *type of* **angular shape** [➡ ANGULAR SHAPE; 1217]

text 1 *n* **manuscript**, transcript, typescript, writing, script, copy, edition, version [➡ WRITING; 583] 2 *n* **passage**, piece, article, extract, content, wording [➡ WRITING; 583] 3 *n* **textbook**, schoolbook, reader, primer, manual, workbook, set book (*UK*), course book (*UK*) [➡ BOOKS AND BOOKLETS; 590] 4 *v* [➡ TELEPHONE, PAGE, AND TEXT; 681]

textbook 1 *n* **text**, schoolbook, reader, primer, manual, workbook, course book (*UK*), set book (*UK*) [➡ BOOKS AND BOOKLETS; 590] 2 *adj* **model**, classic, typical, prime, definitive, exemplary, stock, paradigmatic [➡ REPRESENTATIVE; 66] *Opposite*: atypical

textile *n* **fabric**, cloth, material, piece goods, yard goods, knit, weave [➡ TEXTILES AND THREADS; 1131]

text message 1 *n* [➡ TELEPHONE COMMUNICATION; 48] 2 *v* [➡ TELEPHONE, PAGE, AND TEXT; 681]

textual *adj* **written**, word-based, documented, documentary, stylistic, recorded, literal, verbatim [➡ WRITING; 583]

texture *n* **feel**, touch, surface, consistency, quality, grain, roughness, smoothness, coarseness, fineness [➡ TEXTURE; 1220]

textured *adj* **surfaced**, raised, rough, coarse, bumpy [➡ PHYSICAL TEXTURE; 1222] *Opposite*: smooth

TGV *n* [➡ RAILROADS; 1107]

thank *v* **express thanks**, show gratitude, express gratitude, show appreciation, be grateful, acknowledge, recognize [➡ PRAISE AND ENCOURAGE; 647]

thankful 1 *adj* **grateful**, appreciative, gratified, obliged, beholden [➡ APPRECIATION AND GRATITUDE; 535] *Opposite*: ungrateful 2 *adj* **pleased**, glad, relieved, happy, satisfied, content [➡ PLEASURE, EXCITEMENT, AND ELATION; 534] *Opposite*: dissatisfied

thankfully 1 *adv* (*informal*) **luckily**, happily, mercifully, fortunately, as luck would have it [➡ LUCK; 783] 2 *adv* **gratefully**, appreciatively, with gratitude, with thanks [➡ APPRECIATION AND GRATITUDE; 535] *Opposite*: ungratefully

thankfulness *n* **gratitude**, thanks, appreciation, appre-

ciativeness, recognition, acknowledgment [➡ APPRECIATION AND GRATITUDE; 535] *Opposite*: ingratitude

thank goodness *interj* [➡ EXPRESSIONS OF AGREEMENT; 648]

thank heavens *interj* [➡ EXPRESSIONS OF AGREEMENT; 648]

thankless *adj* **unappreciated**, unrewarding, unacknowledged, taken for granted, difficult, trying [➡ EMOTIONALLY UNPLEASANT AND UPSETTING; 227] *Opposite*: rewarding

thanks *n* **gratitude**, appreciation, thankfulness, appreciativeness, recognition, obligation, acknowledgment [➡ APPRECIATION AND GRATITUDE; 535] *Opposite*: ingratitude

thanks a lot *interj* [➡ EXPRESSIONS OF AGREEMENT; 648]

thanks to *prep* **because of**, on account of, due to, owing to, as a result of, through [➡ CAUSATION; 168]

thank you *interj* [➡ EXPRESSIONS OF AGREEMENT; 648]

thatch 1 *n* **roofing**, roof, straw, rushes, reeds, hay, covering [➡ BUILDING MATERIALS; 1077] 2 *n* **thick hair**, hair, shock, mop, tresses, mass, pelt, mane (*literary or informal*), locks (*literary*) [➡ HAIR; 484]

thaw *v* **melt**, defrost, soften, liquefy, warm up [➡ SOFTEN, LIQUEFY, AND DAMPEN; 388] *Opposite*: freeze

theater 1 *n* **playhouse**, auditorium, moviehouse, lecture theater, hall, cinema (*UK*) [➡ BUILDINGS FOR PUBLIC ENTERTAINMENT; 1084] 2 *n* **drama**, plays, dramatic art, the stage, acting, show business, thespianism, dramaturgy, dramatics, role-playing [➡ FICTION AND DRAMA; 913] 3 *n* **sphere**, focus, realm, scene, site, field, area, place [➡ PLACE; 1065]

theater company *n* [➡ PERFORMERS; 905]

theatergoer *n* **playgoer**, drama-lover, spectator [➡ IN THE THEATER; 906]

theater group *n* [➡ PERFORMERS; 905]

theatrical 1 *adj* **dramatic**, acting, stage, dramaturgical [➡ THE PERFORMING ARTS; 904] 2 *adj* **melodramatic**, dramatic, histrionic, exaggerated, affected, artificial, mannered, pretentious, emotional, ostentatious, showy, flamboyant, stagy, hammy (*informal*), over-the-top (*informal*) [➡ AFFECTATION, SELF-SATISFACTION, AND SNOBBISHNESS; 507] *Opposite*: restrained

the back of beyond (*UK*) *n* [➡ REMOTE PLACES; 1046]

the boards *n* [➡ IN THE THEATER; 906]

theft *n* **robbery**, stealing, burglary, shoplifting, holdup, mugging, larceny, embezzlement, pilfering, thievery [➡ CRIMES; 817]

the here and now *n* [➡ PRESENT; 85]

theism *n* **faith**, belief, religion, piety [➡ RELIGIOUS CONCEPTS; 776] *Opposite*: atheism

theme 1 *n* **subject**, topic, idea, subject matter, matter, argument, premise, thesis [➡ SUBJECT AREAS; 768] 2 *n* **melody**, music, refrain, leitmotif, theme tune, theme song, signature tune [➡ MUSIC, SONGS, AND SINGING; 907]

See Compare and Contrast at **subject**.

theme park *n* [➡ URBAN OUTDOOR SPACES; 1072]

theme song n [➡ MUSIC, SONGS, AND SINGING; 907]

theme tune n [➡ MUSIC, SONGS, AND SINGING; 907]

then 1 adv **at that time**, at that moment, at that point, at that juncture, then and there, formerly, before [➡ PAST; 84] Opposite: now 2 adv **next**, afterward, subsequently, later, and, after that, thenceforth, thenceforward [➡ AFTER, LAST, AND FOLLOWING; 165] 3 adv **in that case**, so, therefore [➡ CAUSATION; 168] 4 adv **on the other hand**, but then, then again, but then again, nonetheless, nevertheless [➡ EXPRESSIONS INTRODUCING EXTRA INFORMATION; 139] 5 adv **and**, in addition, too, also, besides [➡ EXPRESSIONS INTRODUCING EXTRA INFORMATION; 139]

thence (formal or literary) 1 adv **on**, onward, forward, thereafter, then, thenceforward, thenceforth [➡ CAUSATION; 168] 2 adv **therefore**, so, then, thus (formal) [➡ CAUSATION; 168] 3 adv **thereafter**, thenceforth, then, from then on, from that time on, subsequently, afterward [➡ AFTER, LAST, AND FOLLOWING; 165] Opposite: hitherto

thenceforth adv **from then on**, from that time on, thereafter, subsequently, then, afterward, thence (formal or literary) [➡ AFTER, LAST, AND FOLLOWING; 165] Opposite: hitherto

thenceforward adv **then**, on, onward, forward, thereafter, thenceforth, subsequently, from then on, from that time on, afterward, thence (formal or literary) [➡ AFTER, LAST, AND FOLLOWING; 165] Opposite: hitherto

the Net (informal) n [➡ THE INTERNET; 1128]

theodolite type of **measuring device** [➡ MEASURING DEVICES; 1123]

theological adj **religious**, scriptural, doctrinal, dogmatic, spiritual, mystical [➡ RELIGIOUS CONCEPTS; 776]

theological college n [➡ EDUCATIONAL INSTITUTIONS; 813]

theology n **divinity**, religion, religious studies, doctrine, dogmatics, spirituality, mysticism [➡ RELIGIOUS CONCEPTS; 776]

theorem n **proposition**, formula, deduction, statement, proposal, hypothesis [➡ MATH; 597]

theoretical adj **theoretic**, hypothetical, academic, notional, imaginary, conjectural, speculative, abstract [➡ FALSE AND UNREAL; 173] Opposite: concrete

theorist n **philosopher**, thinker, theoretician, theorizer, academic, planner [➡ PHILOSOPHICAL AND POLITICAL THINKERS; 781]

theorize v **hypothesize**, conjecture, imagine, conceive, put forward, speculate, posit (formal) [➡ DEVELOP THEORIES AND REASON; 744]

theory 1 n **philosophy**, model, concept, system, scheme, idea, notion, principle, belief, rule, technique [➡ WAYS OF DOING THINGS; 294] 2 n **hypothesis**, premise, presumption, conjecture, supposition, speculation, assumption, guess [➡ IDEAS AND THOUGHTS; 770]

therapeutic 1 adj **healing**, relaxing, calming, satisfying, helpful, salutary, beneficial, tonic [➡ CALMING; 188] Opposite: stressful 2 adj **curative**, remedial, corrective, restorative, medicinal, beneficial [➡ REMEDIES, TREATMENTS, AND OPERATIONS; 731] Opposite: preventive

therapist n **psychoanalyst**, psychotherapist, analyst, psychiatrist, counselor [➡ PEOPLE WHO WORK IN MEDICINE; 848]

therapy n **treatment**, rehabilitation, healing, help, remedy, cure [➡ REMEDIES, TREATMENTS, AND OPERATIONS; 731]

thereabout see **thereabouts**

thereabouts adv **around there**, around then, near there, in that area, or so [➡ APPROXIMATELY; 135]

thereafter adv **after that**, from that time on, afterward, subsequently, then, next, from then on, later [➡ AFTER, LAST, AND FOLLOWING; 165] Opposite: previously

the real McCoy (informal) n **the real thing**, the genuine article, the very thing [➡ TRUE AND REAL; 171]

the real thing n [➡ TRUE AND REAL; 171]

thereby adv **so**, in that way, by this means, in so doing, in this manner, thus (formal) [➡ WAYS OF DOING THINGS; 294]

therefore adv **consequently**, so, and so, then, as a result, for that reason, thus (formal), hence (formal) [➡ CAUSATION; 168]

there or thereabouts (informal) adv **about**, approximately, roughly, more or less, near enough [➡ APPROXIMATELY; 135] Opposite: exactly

thereupon (formal) adv **immediately**, directly, consequently, subsequently, accordingly, forthwith, straightaway, instantly, thus (formal) [➡ AFTER, LAST, AND FOLLOWING; 165]

thermal 1 adj **warm**, hot, tepid, volcanic [➡ TEMPERATURE: HOT; 1229] Opposite: cool 2 n **warm air**, current, updraft [➡ WINDY AND STORMY WEATHER; 1053]

Thermidor type of **food presentation** [➡ COOKING AND FOOD PREPARATION; 353]

thermometer type of **measuring device** [➡ MEASURING DEVICES; 1123]

thermos n [➡ CONTAINERS, RECEPTACLES, AND PACKAGING; 1245]

thermosphere n [➡ THE EARTH'S ATMOSPHERE; 1040]

thermostat n **regulator**, control, device, bimetallic strip, sensor [➡ PARTS OF MACHINES AND TOOLS; 1118]

thesaurus n **dictionary**, vocabulary list, word list, lexicon, glossary [➡ LISTS AND SCHEDULES; 587]

these days n [➡ PRESENT; 85]

thesis 1 n **proposition**, theory, notion, hypothesis, idea, opinion, view, proposal, argument [➡ IDEAS AND THOUGHTS; 770] Opposite: antithesis 2 n **dissertation**, paper, essay, composition, treatise [➡ ANALYTICAL NONFICTION WRITING; 592]

thespian 1 n **actor**, actress, player, artiste, personality, entertainer [➡ PERFORMERS; 905] 2 adj (literary) **theatrical**, dramatic, melodramatic, histrionic, stagy [➡ THE PERFORMING ARTS; 904]

thew (archaic) n [➡ THE MUSCLES; 718]

the Web (informal) n [➡ THE INTERNET; 1128]

the whole n [➡ ALL; 128]

the whole ball of wax (informal) n [➡ ALL; 128]

the whole enchilada (slang) n [➡ ALL; 128]

the whole kit and caboodle (*informal*) *n* [➡ALL; 128]

the whole lot *n* [➡ALL; 128]

the whole shebang (*informal*) *n* [➡ALL; 128]

the worse for wear 1 *adj* dilapidated, tatty, shabby, battered, decrepit, worn, scruffy, run-down, beat-up (*informal*) [➡IN BAD REPAIR; 1234] *Opposite*: pristine 2 *adj* **unwell**, tired, pale, peaked, sickly, wan, drawn, peaky (*UK*) [➡UNFIT AND WEAK; 739] *Opposite*: well

thick 1 *adj* **deep**, broad, fat, wide, chunky, bulky, substantial, swollen [➡WIDTH: WIDE; 1199] *Opposite*: thin 2 *adj* **dense**, profuse, bushy, impenetrable, copious, abundant, heavy, generous, concentrated [➡DENSITY AND CONSISTENCY; 1207] *Opposite*: thin 3 *adj* **viscous**, syrupy, gooey, glutinous, heavy, stodgy, stiff, gelatinous, coagulated, clotted [➡PHYSICAL TEXTURE; 1222] *Opposite*: runny 4 *adj* **filled**, full, covered, crowded, teeming, bursting, overflowing, packed [➡FULL; 1239] *Opposite*: empty 5 *adj* **indistinct**, slurred, muffled, hoarse, gruff, throaty [➡LOUD, HIGH, OR UNPLEASANT SOUNDS; 1266] *Opposite*: clear 6 *adj* **pronounced**, impenetrable, distinct, extreme, marked, broad [➡DIFFICULTY AND COMPLEXITY; 242] *Opposite*: slight

thick as thieves *adj* [➡RELATIONSHIP TO ANOTHER; 973]

thicken *v* **congeal**, stiffen, set, solidify, clot, coagulate, condense [➡HARDEN, CONGEAL, AND DRY; 387] *Opposite*: thin

thicket *n* **copse**, coppice, grove, covert, undergrowth, brush, wood [➡WOODS, FORESTS, AND JUNGLES; 1047] *Opposite*: clearing

thickly 1 *adv* **densely**, heavily, profusely, abundantly, copiously, generously [➡MANY, MUCH, LARGE AMOUNT; 117] *Opposite*: thinly 2 *adv* **throatily**, in a slurred voice, indistinctly, hoarsely, gruffly [➡LOUD, HIGH, OR UNPLEASANT SOUNDS; 1266] *Opposite*: clearly

thickness 1 *n* **width**, breadth, depth, wideness, chunkiness, fatness [➡WIDTH: WIDE; 1199] *Opposite*: thinness 2 *n* **viscosity**, stiffness, body, texture, stodginess [➡DENSITY AND CONSISTENCY; 1207] *Opposite*: fluidity

thickset *adj* **stocky**, heavy, hefty, bulky, solid, husky, chunky (*informal*), strapping (*informal*) [➡BUILD; 477] *Opposite*: slight

thick-skinned 1 *adj* **unsympathetic**, insensitive, callous, unfeeling, tactless, obtuse [➡BAD MANNERS AND SOCIAL SKILLS; 521] *Opposite*: sensitive 2 *adj* **impervious**, unconcerned, unmoved, tough, hardened, hard-boiled (*informal*) [➡NEUTRALITY AND INDIFFERENCE; 553] *Opposite*: thin-skinned

thief *n* **robber**, burglar, shoplifter, pickpocket, bandit, crook (*informal*) [➡CRIMINALS; 821]

thieve *v* **steal**, rob, shoplift, raid, burgle, pilfer, filch (*informal*) [➡STEAL AND ROB; 426] *Opposite*: return

thieving *n* [➡CRIMES; 817]

thigh *part of* **leg or foot** [➡PARTS OF THE BODY; LEG AND FOOT; 694]

thighbone *type of* **bone** [➡THE BONES AND JOINTS; 719]

thigh-highs *type of* **lower body underwear** [➡ACCESSORIES, MILLINERY, AND LINGERIE; 867]

thimble *n* **cover**, cap, protector [➡COVERS AND COATINGS; 1246]

thimbleful *n* [➡FEW, LITTLE, SMALL AMOUNT; 120]

thin 1 *adj* **narrow**, fine, slim, threadlike, slender, delicate, shallow, wafer-thin [➡WIDTH: NARROW AND THIN; 1200] *Opposite*: thick 2 *adj* **skinny**, slim, slender, bony, lean, emaciated, skeletal, slight, scraggy, scrawny [➡BUILD; 477] *Opposite*: fat 3 *adj* **watery**, weak, dilute, diluted, runny, insipid [➡FLUID AND NONSOLID; 1213] *Opposite*: thick 4 *adj* **sheer**, gauzy, diaphanous, light, fine, lightweight [➡VISUAL TEXTURE; 1221] *Opposite*: thick 5 *adj* **reedy**, high, tinny, shrill, squeaky, cracked [➡LOUD, HIGH, OR UNPLEASANT SOUNDS; 1266] *Opposite*: resonant 6 *v* **water down**, dilute, thin out, weaken, disperse, rarefy [➡CHANGE OF INTENSITY: LESS; 395] *Opposite*: condense

Compare and Contrast: *thin, lean, slim, slender, emaciated, scraggy, scrawny, skinny*

CORE MEANING: without much flesh, the opposite of fat

thin having little body fat; *lean* muscular and fit-looking, without excess fat; *slim* pleasingly thin and well-proportioned; *slender* gracefully and attractively thin; *emaciated* unhealthily thin, usually because of illness or starvation; *scraggy* or *scrawny* unpleasantly or unhealthily thin and bony; *skinny* extremely thin.

thing 1 *n* (*informal*) **obsession**, fixation, mania, craze, preoccupation, fascination [➡FADS, FETISHES, AND IDOLATRY; 555] 2 *n* **object**, article, item, entity, gadget, device, mechanism, machine, contraption, thingamajig (*informal*) [➡PHYSICAL OBJECTS; 1243] 3 *n* **detail**, point, idea, issue, feature, factor [➡SUBJECT AREAS; 768] 4 *n* **occurrence**, event, incident, phenomenon, matter, affair, business [➡EVENTS AND OCCURRENCES; 35]

thingamabob (*informal*) *n* **thing**, whatsit (*informal*), thingamajig (*informal*), thingummy (*informal*), thingy (*informal*), doodad (*informal*), gizmo (*informal*), doohickey (*informal*), widget (*humorous*) [➡PHYSICAL OBJECTS; 1243]

thingamajig (*informal*) *n* [➡PHYSICAL OBJECTS; 1243]

things *n* **belongings**, clothes, possessions, equipment, stuff, kit, gear (*informal*), effects (*formal*) [➡POSSESSIONS; 461]

thingumabob (*informal*) *n* [➡PHYSICAL OBJECTS; 1243]

thingumajig (*informal*) *n* [➡PHYSICAL OBJECTS; 1243]

thingummy (*informal*) *n* [➡PHYSICAL OBJECTS; 1243]

thingy (*informal*) *n* **thing**, thingummy (*informal*), whatsit (*informal*), thingamabob (*informal*), thingamajig (*informal*), thingumajig (*informal*), doodad (*informal*), gizmo (*informal*), doohickey (*informal*), widget (*humorous*) [➡PHYSICAL OBJECTS; 1243]

think 1 *v* **reason**, contemplate, reflect, ponder, deliberate, consider, meditate, mull over, ruminate, cogitate (*formal*), weigh up (*UK*) [➡DEVELOP THEORIES AND REASON; 744] *Opposite*: act 2 *v* **believe**, feel, consider, judge, agree, suppose, assume, imagine, sense, deem (*formal*) [➡HAVE AN OPINION OF SOMETHING; 756] *Opposite*: doubt

think a lot of *v* [➡LIKE, LOVE, VALUE, AND ENJOY; 578]

think badly of *v* [➡DISLIKE AND HATE; 577]

thinker *n* **philosopher**, theorist, intellectual, academic, scholar, sage (*literary*) [➡PHILOSOPHICAL AND POLITICAL THINKERS; 781] *Opposite*: doer

think highly of *v* [➡LIKE, LOVE, VALUE, AND ENJOY; 578]

thinking 1 *adj* **rational**, thoughtful, intelligent, discerning, intellectual, sophisticated [➡ POSITIVE INTELLECTUAL CHARACTERISTICS; 524] *Opposite*: unthinking **2** *n* **thoughts**, philosophy, idea, theory, accepted wisdom, opinion, view, assessment, belief [➡ IDEAS AND THOUGHTS; 770]

think little of *v* [➡ DISLIKE AND HATE; 577]

think over *v* **reflect**, deliberate, ponder, chew over, contemplate, mull over, consider, chew on, weigh up (*UK*) [➡ THINK AND REFLECT; 743] *Opposite*: forget

think tank *n* **committee**, body, advisory board, group pf experts, commission, panel [➡ GROUPS WITH A COMMON INTEREST; 938]

think the world of *v* **have a high regard for**, think highly of, like, have a high opinion of, look up to, admire [➡ LIKE, LOVE, VALUE, AND ENJOY; 578]

think through *v* **consider**, contemplate, ponder, mull over, weigh up (*UK*) [➡ THINK AND REFLECT; 743]

think twice *v* **think carefully**, be careful, be wary, take heed, consider, step back, weigh up (*UK*) [➡ THINK AND REFLECT; 743]

think up *v* **invent**, devise, come up with, create, dream up, mastermind, plan, cook up (*informal*) [➡ DEVELOP THEORIES AND REASON; 744]

thinly *adv* **finely**, lightly, delicately, sparsely, sparingly [➡ TO A CERTAIN EXTENT; 136] *Opposite*: thickly

thinner *n* **solvent**, diluent, diluter, stripper, cleaner, turpentine [➡ LIQUIDS; 1269]

thinness 1 *n* **narrowness**, fineness, slenderness, slimness, shallowness, delicacy [➡ WIDTH: NARROW AND THIN; 1200] *Opposite*: thickness **2** *n* **skinniness**, emaciation, leanness, boniness, lankiness, slimness, slenderness, slightness [➡ BUILD; 477] *Opposite*: fatness

thin on the ground *adj* [➡ TOO FEW, TOO LITTLE; 122]

thin on top *adj* [➡ BALDNESS AND BALDING; 487]

thin-skinned *adj* **sensitive**, hypersensitive, easily upset, emotional, touchy, prickly (*informal*), tetchy (*informal*) [➡ EXCESSIVE SENSITIVITY; 511] *Opposite*: thick-skinned

third *n* [➡ MEASURABLE PORTIONS; 127]

third party *n* **intermediary**, go-between, arbitrator [➡ ADVISERS, JUDGES, AND ARBITERS; 971]

third-rate *adj* **poor quality**, inferior, mediocre, poor, shoddy, substandard [➡ INFERIORITY; 153] *Opposite*: first-class

thirst 1 *n* **dehydration**, dryness, thirstiness, thirsting [➡ ILL AND SICK; 740] **2** *n* **craving**, desire, longing, hunger, eagerness, yearning, appetite [➡ DESIRE AND WANT; 579] *Opposite*: apathy **3** *v* **desire**, crave, want, ache, pine [➡ DESIRE AND WANT; 579]

thirst-quencher *n* [➡ DRINKS; 1187]

thirsty 1 *adj* **dehydrated**, dry, parched, thirsting, gasping (*UK*) [➡ DRINK; 711] **2** *adj* **desiring**, craving, eager, keen, hungry, yearning, longing, voracious, avid, desirous (*formal*) [➡ DESIRE AND WANT; 579] *Opposite*: apathetic

this day and age *n* [➡ PRESENT; 85]

this instant *adv* [➡ PRESENT; 85]

thistle *type of* **weed** [➡ WEEDS AND THISTLES; 1034]

Thomson's gazelle *type of* **deer or antelope** [➡ DEER AND ANTELOPES; 981]

thong 1 *n* **string**, cord, band, strap, belt, tie [➡ FASTENERS, LINKS, AND NETWORKS; 1247] **2** *type of* **shoe** [➡ FOOTWEAR; 871] **3** *type of* **lower body underwear** [➡ ACCESSORIES, MILLINERY, AND LINGERIE; 867]

thorax 1 *part of* **torso** [➡ PARTS OF THE BODY: TORSO; 693] **2** *part of* **insect** [➡ PARTS OF AN INSECT; 1019]

thorn *n* **prickle**, barb, spike, spine, point, bristle [➡ PARTS OF TREES AND PLANTS; 1026]

thorn in somebody's flesh *n* [➡ NUISANCES; 253]

thorn in somebody's side *n* [➡ NUISANCES; 253]

thorny 1 *adj* **prickly**, barbed, spiky, spiny, pointed, bristly [➡ PHYSICAL TEXTURE; 1222] **2** *adj* **tricky**, problematic, awkward, controversial, knotty, tough, hard, difficult [➡ DIFFICULTY AND COMPLEXITY; 242] *Opposite*: uncontroversial

thorough 1 *adj* **methodical**, careful, systematic, painstaking, meticulous, scrupulous, punctilious, assiduous [➡ POSITIVE INTELLECTUAL CHARACTERISTICS; 524] *Opposite*: careless **2** *adj* **full**, detailed, systematic, exhaustive, in-depth, comprehensive, thoroughgoing [➡ WHOLENESS AND COMPLETENESS; 198] *Opposite*: careless **3** *adj* **absolute**, complete, total, out-and-out, utter, thoroughgoing, straight-out (*informal*) [➡ ABSOLUTE AND ABSOLUTELY; 133] *Opposite*: partial

See Compare and Contrast at **careful**.

thoroughbred 1 *adj* **pedigree**, purebred, pure [➡ CLASS STATUS; 889] **2** *type of* **horse** [➡ HORSES; 985]

thoroughfare *n* **main road**, through street, street, road, way, access road, through road (*UK*) [➡ ROADS; 1106]

thoroughgoing 1 *adj* **full**, detailed, systematic, exhaustive, in-depth, comprehensive, thorough, methodical, careful, painstaking, meticulous, scrupulous [➡ WHOLENESS AND COMPLETENESS; 198] *Opposite*: careless **2** *adj* **complete**, thorough, absolute, total, out-and-out, utter [➡ ABSOLUTE AND ABSOLUTELY; 133] *Opposite*: partial

thoroughly 1 *adv* **methodically**, carefully, systematically, painstakingly, meticulously, scrupulously, in detail, comprehensively, exhaustively, fully [➡ WHOLENESS AND COMPLETENESS; 198] *Opposite*: carelessly **2** *adv* **completely**, absolutely, totally, utterly, from top to bottom [➡ ABSOLUTE AND ABSOLUTELY; 133] *Opposite*: partially

thoroughness *n* **care**, attention to detail, meticulousness, scrupulousness, diligence, carefulness [➡ POSITIVE INTELLECTUAL CHARACTERISTICS; 524] *Opposite*: carelessness

though 1 *conj* **although**, while, even if, even though, despite the fact that [➡ ALTHOUGH, NEVERTHELESS, AND DESPITE; 169] **2** *adv* **however**, and yet, yet, nevertheless, nonetheless, still, all the same [➡ ALTHOUGH, NEVERTHELESS, AND DESPITE; 169]

thought 1 *n* **consideration**, contemplation, thinking, attention, reflection, meditation, deliberation (*formal*) [➡ IDEAS AND THOUGHTS; 770] **2** *n* **idea**, notion, brain wave, inspiration, concept, belief, theory, opinion, plan, conception [➡ IDEAS AND THOUGHTS; 770] **3** *n* **ideas**, philosophy, thinking, notions, accepted wisdom, planning, concept, design [➡ IDEAS AND THOUGHTS; 770]

thoughtful 1 *adj* **considerate**, kind, caring, unselfish, selfless, attentive, sympathetic, solicitous, helpful, kind-hearted [➡ GENEROSITY AND KINDNESS; 495] *Opposite*: thoughtless 2 *adj* **pensive**, meditative, contemplative, brooding, reflective, deep in thought, absorbed, introspective, wistful [➡ PENSIVENESS AND INTEREST; 538] 3 *adj* **careful**, meticulous, painstaking, thorough, deep, accurate, precise [➡ POSITIVE INTELLECTUAL CHARACTERISTICS; 524] *Opposite*: superficial

thoughtfulness 1 *n* **consideration**, kindness, care, unselfishness, selflessness, attentiveness, attention, sympathy, solicitude, kindheartedness [➡ GENEROSITY AND KINDNESS; 495] *Opposite*: thoughtlessness 2 *n* **pensiveness**, meditation, contemplation, reflection, thought, introspection, wistfulness [➡ ATTENTION AND ATTENTIVENESS; 763] 3 *n* **care**, attention to detail, attention, thought, carefulness, meticulousness, thoroughness, accuracy, precision [➡ POSITIVE INTELLECTUAL CHARACTERISTICS; 524] *Opposite*: superficiality

thoughtless 1 *adj* **inconsiderate**, unkind, uncaring, selfish, insensitive, tactless, rude, impolite [➡ SELFISH AND UNKIND; 505] *Opposite*: thoughtful 2 *adj* **careless**, heedless, reckless, negligent, unthinking, inattentive, foolish, stupid, absent-minded [➡ INCAUTIOUS AND CARELESS; 283] *Opposite*: prudent

thoughtlessness 1 *n* **inconsideration**, unkindness, selfishness, insensitivity, tactlessness, rudeness, impoliteness [➡ SELFISH AND UNKIND; 505] *Opposite*: thoughtfulness 2 *n* **carelessness**, heedlessness, recklessness, negligence, inattention, inattentiveness, foolishness, stupidity, absent-mindedness [➡ LACK OF COMMITMENT AND UNRELIABILITY; 509] *Opposite*: prudence

thought processes *n* [➡ PSYCHOLOGY AND THE MIND; 769]

thought-provoking *adj* **stimulating**, challenging, provocative, interesting, inspiring [➡ INTERESTING AND MEANINGFUL; 190] *Opposite*: dull

thoughts *n* **opinion**, view, point of view, feelings, judgment, belief [➡ POINTS OF VIEW; 767]

thought transference *n* [➡ THE SUPERNATURAL; 787]

thought up *adj* [➡ FALSE AND UNREAL; 173]

Thousand Island dressing *type of* **seasonings, sauces, and dips** [➡ SEASONINGS AND SAUCES; 1174]

thrash 1 *v* **beat**, whip, give a hiding, spank, smack, batter, lash, flog, flay [➡ PHYSICAL ATTACK AND PUNISHMENT; 415] 2 *v* **defeat**, beat, trounce, whip, paste, hammer (*informal*), walk over (*informal*), slaughter (*slang*), cream (*slang*) [➡ BEAT AND DEFEAT; 80] *Opposite*: lose 3 *v* **toss**, writhe, flail, squirm, roll, wriggle, wiggle, toss and turn [➡ FIDGET AND FROLIC; 311]

See Compare and Contrast at **defeat**.

thrash about *v* [➡ FIDGET AND FROLIC; 311]

thrashing 1 *n* **beating**, whipping, spanking, battering, lashing, flogging, flaying, hiding (*informal*) [➡ PHYSICAL ATTACK AND PUNISHMENT; 415] 2 *n* **defeat**, rout, downfall, conquest, beating, trouncing, hammering (*informal*), whipping (*informal*), pasting (*informal*) [➡ BEAT AND DEFEAT; 80] *Opposite*: victory

thrash metal *type of* **rock music** [➡ MUSIC, SONGS, AND SINGING; 907]

thrash out (*UK*) *v* **hash out**, hammer out, resolve, solve, discuss, debate, go into, look into, settle, arrive at [➡ TWO-WAY COMMUNICATION; 607]

thread 1 *n* **cotton**, cord, yarn, strand, fiber, filament, line [➡ TEXTILES AND THREADS; 1131] 2 *n* **idea**, drift, gist, sequence, story line, theme, plot, train of thought [➡ IDEAS AND THOUGHTS; 770] 3 *v* **string**, wind, loop, lace, pass through, pass into, ease [➡ FASTEN, LINK, AND JOIN; 408] 4 *v* **make your way**, pick your way, edge through, squeeze through, negotiate, ease [➡ PROCEED AND GO; 305]

threadbare 1 *adj* **worn**, worn-out, shabby, ragged, thin, frayed, tatty, scruffy, tattered [➡ IN BAD REPAIR; 1234] *Opposite*: new 2 *adj* **well-worn**, trite, hackneyed, clichéd, banal, stale, boring, ineffective, corny [➡ BORING AND UNINTERESTING; 234] *Opposite*: original

threat 1 *n* **warning**, menace, intimidation [➡ ADVICE; 689] 2 *n* **danger**, risk, hazard, menace, peril [➡ DANGER; 235] *Opposite*: promise

threaten 1 *v* **intimidate**, bully, menace, warn, terrorize, pressure, frighten, pressurize (*UK*) [➡ UPSET, DISTRESS, AND HUMILIATE; 567] *Opposite*: reassure 2 *v* **endanger**, jeopardize, menace, compromise, cloud, imperil (*formal*) [➡ PUT AT RISK; 384] *Opposite*: guard 3 *v* **loom**, lurk, hover, portend, creep up, impend (*literary*) [➡ ABOUT TO HAPPEN; 33]

threatened *adj* **endangered**, at risk, in peril, vulnerable, dying out, disappearing [➡ IN DANGER; 237] *Opposite*: safe

threatening 1 *adj* **intimidating**, bullying, menacing, hostile, aggressive, frightening, nasty [➡ RUDE AND HOSTILE; 625] *Opposite*: reassuring 2 *adj* **ominous**, menacing, foreboding, inauspicious, sinister, dark, portentous [➡ DANGEROUS; 236] *Opposite*: reassuring

three-dimensional 1 *adj* **three-D**, solid, deep [➡ ORIENTATION AND ALIGNMENT; 1223] *Opposite*: two-dimensional 2 *adj* **believable**, realistic, convincing, lifelike, true-to-life, real, credible, vivid [➡ TRUE AND REAL; 171] *Opposite*: two-dimensional

three sheets to the wind (*informal*) *adj* [➡ UNDER THE INFLUENCE OF DRUGS OR ALCOHOL; 741]

threesome *n* [➡ GROUPS OF PEOPLE; 935]

three-wheeler 1 *type of* **car** [➡ BIKES, CARS, AND CARRIAGES; 1149] 2 *type of* **bike** [➡ BIKES, CARS, AND CARRIAGES; 1149]

thresh *v* **winnow**, flail, separate, beat, rub [➡ SEPARATE AND DIVIDE; 401]

threshold 1 *n* **doorway**, door, doorstep, entrance, entry [➡ DOORS AND ACCESS POINTS; 1101] 2 *n* **starting point**, verge, brink, edge, dawn, beginning, onset, inception (*formal*) [➡ BEGINNINGS; 53] *Opposite*: end 3 *n* **level**, limit, maximum, ceiling, outside, divide, line, base, tolerance [➡ MAJORITY AND MAXIMUM; 141]

thrift 1 *n* **frugality**, economy, carefulness, caution, prudence, parsimony [➡ ECONOMICAL AND RESOURCEFUL; 207] *Opposite*: extravagance 2 *n* [➡ ACCOUNTING, BANKING, AND BUDGETING; 799]

thrift shop *type of* **retail outlet** [➡ RETAIL OUTLETS; 1083]

thrifty *adj* **frugal**, economical, careful, cautious, prudent, sparing, parsimonious [➡ ECONOMICAL AND RESOURCEFUL; 207] *Opposite*: extravagant

thrill 1 *v* **excite**, electrify, exhilarate, delight, inspire, stimulate, stir, rouse, elate, overjoy, grip [➡ PLEASE AND AMUSE; 572] *Opposite*: bore 2 *n* **adventure**, delight, joy, pleasure, quiver, tremble, kick (*informal*), buzz (*informal*) [➡ AMAZING THINGS; 211] *Opposite*: bore

thrilled *adj* **excited**, electrified, exhilarated, ecstatic, elated, delighted, overjoyed, pleased, tickled, on cloud nine (*informal*), over the moon (*UK informal*) [➡ PLEASURE, EXCITEMENT, AND ELATION; 534] *Opposite*: disappointed

thrilled to pieces (*informal*) *adj* [➡ PLEASURE, EXCITEMENT, AND ELATION; 534]

thriller *n* **whodunit**, murder mystery, crime novel, detective story, page-turner, adventure movie, actioner (*informal*) [➡ FILM; 901]

thrilling *adj* **exciting**, electrifying, exhilarating, delightful, inspiring, stimulating, stirring, rousing, gripping, awe-inspiring, awesome, spine-tingling, breathtaking [➡ EMOTIONALLY PLEASANT; 187] *Opposite*: boring

thrive 1 *v* **grow well**, be healthy, flourish, bloom, blossom [➡ PROSPER AND ABOUND; 16] *Opposite*: deteriorate 2 *v* **flourish**, prosper, boom, bloom, blossom, succeed, increase [➡ SUCCEED AND WIN; 79] *Opposite*: fail

thriving *adj* **flourishing**, prosperous, booming, blooming, blossoming, successful [➡ SUCCESSFUL AND PROMISING; 81] *Opposite*: failing

throat 1 *part of* **digestive tract** [➡ THE DIGESTIVE TRACT; 709] 2 *part of* **respiratory system** [➡ RESPIRATORY ORGANS; 715]

throaty *adj* **husky**, hoarse, croaky, gruff, guttural, deep, low, thick, harsh [➡ LOUD, HIGH, OR UNPLEASANT SOUNDS; 1266] *Opposite*: piping

throb 1 *v* **pound**, thump, pulsate, pulse, thud, beat, vibrate, ache [➡ PHYSICAL REACTIONS; 316] 2 *n* **pounding**, thump, pulsation, pulse, rhythm, thud, beat, vibration, ache, pain [➡ PAIN AND OTHER PHYSICAL SENSATIONS; 733] 3 *type of* **continuous sound** [➡ CONTINUOUS SOUNDS; 1258]

thrombosis *n* **coagulation**, clotting, blockage, occlusion [➡ THE BLOOD AND CIRCULATION; 717]

throne 1 *n* **seat**, chair, cathedra [➡ SUPPORTS AND BASES; 1255] 2 *n* **power**, authority, sovereignty, command, rule, dominion [➡ REALMS AND RULES; 824]

throng 1 *n* **multitude**, mass, crowd, horde, swarm, mob, host [➡ GROUPS OF PEOPLE; 935] *Opposite*: few 2 *v* **crowd**, pack, jam, cram, inundate, swamp, flood, flock, fill [➡ GET CLOSER TOGETHER; 310] *Opposite*: disperse

throng together *v* [➡ GET CLOSER TOGETHER; 310]

throttle 1 *v* **regulate**, control, adjust, correct, check, curb [➡ AVOID, PREVENT, LIMIT, AND CONTROL; 277] 2 *v* **strangle**, choke, garrote, strangulate, suffocate, stifle, smother, asphyxiate [➡ KILL; 923] 3 *v* **silence**, gag, muzzle, stifle, subdue, check, curb, restrain, repress, suppress, hold back, inhibit, shut up (*informal*) [➡ WITHHOLD INFORMATION; 687]

through 1 *prep* **across**, past, throughout, within, around, about, beyond, amid, amidst, among, amongst [➡ RELATIVE LOCATION; 161] 2 *prep* **during**, throughout, during the course

of, in [➡ CONCURRENT AND CONTEMPORANEOUS; 164] 3 *prep* **via**, out of, by way of, by means of [➡ CAUSATION; 168] 4 *prep* **because of**, owing to, due to, as a result of [➡ CAUSATION; 168]

through and through *adv* **completely**, totally, entirely, utterly, at heart, to the core [➡ ABSOLUTE AND ABSOLUTELY; 133] *Opposite*: partially

throughout *prep* **through**, during, all over, during the course of, in [➡ CONCURRENT AND CONTEMPORANEOUS; 164]

throughput *n* **amount**, quantity, data, material, output, input [➡ AMOUNTS AND QUANTITIES; 112]

through road (*UK*) *n* [➡ ROADS; 1106]

through street *n* [➡ ROADS; 1106]

throughway *type of* **highway** [➡ ROADS; 1106]

throw 1 *v* **fling**, toss, hurl, pitch, lob, propel, cast, bowl, chuck (*informal*), heave (*informal*) [➡ MOVE SOMETHING: THROUGH THE AIR; 334] *Opposite*: catch 2 *v* **drop**, leave, put, cast, toss, fling [➡ POSITION SOMETHING; 325] 3 *v* **project**, cast, direct, send out, beam, shine, emit [➡ LIGHT EMISSION; 368] 4 *v* (*informal*) **confuse**, puzzle, bewilder, perplex, baffle, nonplus, disconcert, surprise, catch somebody off balance, catch somebody unawares, bamboozle (*informal*), flummox (*informal*) [➡ CONFUSE AND BEWILDER; 571] 5 *v* **move**, flick, switch, connect, disconnect, put on, put off [➡ CAUSE TO START; 265] 6 *v* **organize**, arrange, host, give, hold, have [➡ CAUSE TO HAPPEN; 31] 7 *n* **toss**, lob, heave, pitch, fling, shy, chuck (*informal*) [➡ MOVE SOMETHING: THROUGH THE AIR; 334] 8 *n* **rug**, cover, blanket, shawl, coverlet, slip cover, loose cover (*UK*) [➡ FURNISHING AND HOUSEHOLD LINENS; 860]

Compare and Contrast: *throw, chuck, fling, heave, hurl, toss, cast*

CORE MEANING: to send something through the air

throw to cause something to go through the air using a physical movement; ***chuck*** (*informal*) to throw something in a reckless or aimless way; ***fling*** to throw something fast using a lot of force; ***heave*** (*informal*) to throw something large or heavy with effort in a particular direction; ***hurl*** to throw something with great force; ***toss*** to throw something small or light in a casual or careless way; ***cast*** to throw something to a particular place or into a particular thing, or to throw a fishing line or net.

---

throw a fit (*informal*) *v* [➡ GIVING VENT TO EMOTIONS; 679]

throw a monkey wrench in the works (*informal*) *v* [➡ MAKE IMPOSSIBLE; 276]

throw a tantrum *v* [➡ GIVING VENT TO EMOTIONS; 679]

throw away 1 *v* **discard**, throw out, get rid of, dispose of, dump, scrap, jettison, reject, ditch (*informal*), chuck (*informal*), bin (*UK*) [➡ GET RID OF SOMETHING; 451] *Opposite*: keep 2 *v* **waste**, squander, fritter away, ruin, spoil, blow (*slang*) [➡ USE UP AND WASTE; 474] *Opposite*: make the most of

throwaway 1 *adj* **off-the-cuff**, casual, offhand, passing, spontaneous, incidental [➡ AUTOMATIC AND INSTINCTIVE; 280] *Opposite*: intended 2 *adj* **disposable**, paper, plastic [➡ FINITENESS, VARIABILITY, AND TRANSIENCE; 96] 3 *adj* **wasteful**, profligate, extravagant, careless, improvident, uneconomical [➡ WASTEFUL AND UNECONOMICAL; 246] *Opposite*: frugal

throwback *n* **reversion**, regression, resemblance, relic, retrogression, recession, return [➡ PAST; 84]

throw caution to the wind *v* [➡ CHANGE OF MOOD AND COMPOSURE; 580]

throw cushion *n* [➡ FURNISHING AND HOUSEHOLD LINENS; 860]

throw in 1 *v* **add**, drop in, include, mention, refer to, contribute [➡ SUGGEST, HINT, AND COMMENT; 612] 2 *v* **include**, add, give, add on, give away, tack on (*UK*) [➡ GIVE AND PROVIDE; 430]

throw in the sponge (*informal*) *v* [➡ FAIL OR BE UNSUCCESSFUL; 75]

throw in the towel (*informal*) *v* **give in**, surrender, give up, admit defeat, concede, throw in your hand (*informal*) [➡ FAIL OR BE UNSUCCESSFUL; 75] *Opposite*: stand firm

throw light on *v* [➡ EXPLAIN AND CLARIFY; 610]

thrown off balance *adj* [➡ INSECURITY AND LOSS OF COMPOSURE; 544]

throw off 1 *v* **shake off**, shed, shrug off, get rid of, discard, drop [➡ GET RID OF SOMETHING; 451] *Opposite*: keep 2 *v* **elude**, evade, escape, give somebody the slip, shake off, lose [➡ AVOID OR ESCAPE CONTACT; 418]

throw out 1 *v* **discard**, throw away, get rid of, dispose of, dump, scrap, jettison, reject, ditch (*informal*), chuck (*informal*), bin (*UK*) [➡ GET RID OF SOMETHING; 451] *Opposite*: keep 2 *v* **expel**, eject, show the door, dismiss, kick out (*informal*), chuck out (*informal*), fire (*informal*) [➡ EJECT AND EXCLUDE; 340] *Opposite*: welcome 3 *v* **dismiss**, reject, disallow, turn down, refuse, kick out (*informal*) [➡ DENY AND REJECT; 644] *Opposite*: pass

throw pillow *n* [➡ FURNISHING AND HOUSEHOLD LINENS; 860]

throw somebody a curve ball (*slang*) *v* [➡ SURPRISE AND IMPRESS; 574]

throw up 1 *v* (*informal*) **abandon**, give up, relinquish, resign, throw away, drop [➡ FORGO AND DENY ONESELF; 449] *Opposite*: keep 2 *v* **cause**, create, produce, bring to light, pose, turn up, reveal, unearth [➡ CAUSE TO APPEAR; 5] *Opposite*: conceal 3 *v* (*informal*) **vomit**, be sick, gag, retch, spew, heave (*informal*), puke (*slang*), hurl (*slang*) [➡ VOMIT AND BELCH; 712]

throw yourself into *v* **engross yourself in**, immerse yourself in, bury yourself in, devote yourself to, commit to, pitch into (*informal*) [➡ PARTICIPATE; 292]

thrum *v* **strum**, pluck, twang, play, brush, tap, drum [➡ EMIT CONTINUOUS SOUNDS; 366]

thrush 1 *type of* **songbird** [➡ SONGBIRDS; 1003] 2 *type of* **common bird** [➡ BIRDS; 997]

thrust 1 *v* **push**, shove, force, propel, prod, plunge, drive, insert [➡ PUSH, PULL, AND SLIDE; 335] 2 *v* **stretch**, extend, stretch out, reach, reach out, jut, stab [➡ MOVE SOMETHING TO ANOTHER LOCATION; 324] 3 *n* **shove**, push, prod, lunge, drive, plunge, insertion, stab [➡ PUSH, PULL, AND SLIDE; 335] 4 *n* **attack**, assault, offensive, push, drive, onslaught [➡ SUDDEN EVENTS; 52] 5 *n* **point**, gist, meaning, focus, direction, aim, purpose [➡ MEANING; 690] 6 *n* **power**, force, propulsion, momentum, impetus, drive [➡ ENERGY; 1161]

thruster *part of* **spacecraft** [➡ SPACE VEHICLES; 1063]

thruway *type of* **highway** [➡ ROADS; 1106]

thud *type of* **impact sound** [➡ IMPACT SOUNDS; 1260]

thug *n* **brute**, criminal, mugger, hoodlum, gangster, goon, hooligan (*informal*), heavy (*slang*), hood (*slang*), ruffian (*dated*) [➡ VILLAINS AND THUGS; 947]

thumb 1 *part of* **arm or hand** [➡ PARTS OF THE BODY: ARM AND HAND; 695] 2 *v* **flick through**, flip through, leaf through, skim, browse through, scan, glance at, look at, turn over, skip through [➡ LOOKING AND LOOKS; 700] *Opposite*: pore over

thumb a lift *v* [➡ TRAVEL: WAYS OF TRAVELING; 320]

thumbnail *part of* **arm or hand** [➡ PARTS OF THE BODY: ARM AND HAND; 695]

thumbs down (*informal*) *n* **disapproval**, rejection, denial, no, veto, rebuff, negation, red light (*informal*) [➡ REFUSE PERMISSION AND NOT ALLOW; 670] *Opposite*: thumbs up (*informal*)

thumbs up (*informal*) *n* **approval**, acceptance, agreement, endorsement, ratification, green light, yes, okay (*informal*) [➡ PERMIT AND ALLOW; 669] *Opposite*: thumbs down (*informal*)

thump 1 *v* **punch**, hit, whack, pummel [➡ PHYSICAL ATTACK AND PUNISHMENT; 415] 2 *type of* **impact sound** [➡ IMPACT SOUNDS; 1260]

thumping (*informal*) 1 *adj* **large**, huge, enormous, impressive [➡ LARGE; 1193] 2 *adv* **very**, exceptionally, extremely, inordinately, really [➡ TO A GREAT EXTENT; 132]

thunder 1 *n* **din**, boom, rumble, roar, clap, crack, rumbling [➡ CONTINUOUS SOUNDS; 1258] 2 *v* **boom**, roar, resound, rumble, clap, crack [➡ EMIT CONTINUOUS SOUNDS; 366] 3 *v* **shout**, bellow, boom, roar, yell, bark [➡ SOUND EMISSION BY PEOPLE; 363] *Opposite*: whisper

thunderbolt 1 *n* **thunderclap**, clap of thunder, thunder, crash of thunder [➡ WINDY AND STORMY WEATHER; 1053] 2 *n* **shock**, bolt from the blue, eye opener, kick in the face, surprise [➡ SUDDEN EVENTS; 52]

thunderclap *see* **thunderbolt**

thundercloud *type of* **cloud** [➡ CLOUDY AND RAINY WEATHER; 1052]

thunderhead *type of* **cloud** [➡ CLOUDY AND RAINY WEATHER; 1052]

thunderous *adj* **deafening**, loud, roaring, booming, crashing, rolling [➡ LOUD, HIGH, OR UNPLEASANT SOUNDS; 1266]

thunderstorm *n* **storm**, downpour, deluge, rainstorm, cloudburst, tempest (*literary*) [➡ WINDY AND STORMY WEATHER; 1053]

thunderstruck *adj* **incredulous**, amazed, taken aback, stunned, shocked, astonished, astounded, bowled over, staggered, dumbfounded, flabbergasted (*informal*) [➡ SURPRISE, SHOCK, AND AMAZEMENT; 545]

thundery *adj* [➡ WINDY AND STORMY WEATHER; 1053]

thus (*formal*) 1 *adv* **therefore**, consequently, as a result, so, accordingly, as a consequence, hence (*formal*), in consequence (*formal*) [➡ RESULTS AND OUTCOMES; 83] 2 *adv* **like this**, in this way, in this manner, as follows, like so, in this fashion, along these lines [➡ WAYS OF DOING THINGS; 294]

thus far *adv* **up till now**, up to now, yet, so far, hitherto, to date, up until now [➡ PAST; 84]

thwack 1 *n* **smack**, clap, knock, rap, whack, sock

(*informal*), wallop (*informal*) [➟ PHYSICAL ATTACK AND PUNISHMENT; 415] **2** *type of* **impact sound** [➟ IMPACT SOUNDS; 1260] **3** *v* **hit**, strike, whack, smack, slap, wallop (*informal*) [➟ PHYSICAL ATTACK AND PUNISHMENT; 415]

thwart *v* **frustrate**, spoil, prevent, foil, ruin, put a stop to, stop, impede, hinder, obstruct [➟ MAKE IMPOSSIBLE; 276]

thylacine *type of* **marsupial** [➟ MARSUPIALS; 992]

thyme *type of* **herb** [➟ HERBS AND SPICES; 1175]

tiara *type of* **jewelry** [➟ JEWELRY; 866]

tibia *type of* **bone** [➟ THE BONES AND JOINTS; 719]

tic *n* **twitch**, spasm, convulsion, fit, paroxysm [➟ PHYSICAL REACTIONS; 316]

tick **1** *type of* **impact sound** [➟ IMPACT SOUNDS; 1260] **2** *type of* **parasitic insect** [➟ PARASITES; 1017]

ticked off (*informal*) *adj* [➟ IRRITATION AND ANGER; 541]

ticket **1** *n* **permit**, travel document, voucher, receipt, coupon [➟ OFFICIAL DOCUMENTS; 586] **2** *n* **label**, tag, tab, marker, sticker, docket [➟ NAME AND DESCRIBE; 665]

ticking *type of* **fabric from plants** [➟ FABRICS; 1132]

tickle **1** *v* **prickle**, irritate, scratch, itch [➟ PAIN AND OTHER PHYSICAL SENSATIONS; 733] **2** *v* **amuse**, entertain, delight, please, make somebody laugh [➟ PLEASE AND AMUSE; 572]

tickled *adj* [➟ PLEASURE, EXCITEMENT, AND ELATION; 534]

tickled pink (*informal*) *adj* **delighted**, thrilled, overjoyed, pleased, thrilled to pieces (*informal*), over the moon (*UK informal*) [➟ PLEASURE, EXCITEMENT, AND ELATION; 534] *Opposite*: horrified

tickle pink (*UK*) *v* [➟ PLEASE AND AMUSE; 572]

tickler *n* **reminder**, prompt, follow-up, chaser [➟ MEMORY; 745]

ticklish *adj* **tricky**, delicate, thorny, awkward, problematic, difficult, hard, sensitive [➟ DIFFICULTY AND COMPLEXITY; 242] *Opposite*: straightforward

tickly *adj* **prickly**, itchy, irritating, scratchy [➟ PHYSICAL TEXTURE; 1222]

tick off (*informal*) *v* **annoy**, irritate, bother, get on your nerves, bug (*informal*) [➟ ANGER AND ANNOY; 569]

ticktock *type of* **impact sound** [➟ IMPACT SOUNDS; 1260]

tidal *adj* [➟ THE SEAS, OCEANS, AND SHORES; 1041]

tidal wave **1** *n* **tsunami**, bore, eagre [➟ THE SEAS, OCEANS, AND SHORES; 1041] **2** *n* **surge**, wave, swell, deluge [➟ SUDDEN EVENTS; 52]

tidbit **1** *n* **morsel**, taste, bite, delicacy, goody, treat, dainty, bonne bouche (*UK*) [➟ MEALS AND PARTS OF MEALS; 1169] **2** *n* **gossip**, news, scandal, latest, scrap, snippet (*UK*) [➟ GOSSIP; 678]

tiddly (*informal*) *adj* **minute**, small, teeny (*informal*), weeny (*informal*), teeny-weeny (*informal*), teensy (*informal*), teensy-weensy (*informal*), titchy (*UK informal*) [➟ SMALL; 1195]

tiddlywink *type of* **game piece** [➟ GAME PIECES; 878]

tide *n* **current**, flow, surge, wave, drift, stream [➟ THE SEAS, OCEANS, AND SHORES; 1041]

tidily *adv* **neatly**, in an orderly way, methodically, well-orderedly, meticulously, trimly, precisely [➟ ORDER AND ORGANIZATION; 206] *Opposite*: untidily

tidiness *n* **neatness**, trimness, orderliness, well-orderedness, order, regulation, organization, arrangement [➟ ORDER AND ORGANIZATION; 206]

tidings (*literary*) *n* **news**, notification, intelligence, information, word, reports, communication, lowdown (*informal*) [➟ BASIC DETAILS; 688]

tidy **1** *adj* **neat**, orderly, shipshape, in order, organized, spick and span, uncluttered [➟ ORDER AND ORGANIZATION; 206] *Opposite*: untidy **2** *adj* **smart**, immaculate, well-groomed, dapper, spruce, trim, neat, well-turned-out (*UK*) [➟ WELL-GROOMED; 482] *Opposite*: untidy **3** *adj* **large**, fair, considerable, sizable, reasonable, ample [➟ LARGE; 1193] *Opposite*: small **4** *v* **neaten**, tidy up, clear up, straighten, arrange, organize [➟ ARRANGE AND CREATE ORDER; 357]

tidy sum (*informal*) *n* [➟ LARGE AMOUNTS OF MONEY; 118]

tidy up *v* **tidy**, clear up, neaten, straighten, arrange, organize, sort out, make spick and span, spruce up [➟ ARRANGE AND CREATE ORDER; 357] *Opposite*: mess up (*informal*)

tie **1** *v* **bind**, fasten, secure, attach, lash, knot, strap, fix, join, bring together [➟ FASTEN, LINK, AND JOIN; 408] *Opposite*: untie **2** *v* **be equal**, draw, finish equal, finish even, be neck and neck (*informal*) [➟ EQUALITY; 154] **3** *n* **bond**, link, connection, relation, join [➟ CONNECTIONS; 143] **4** *type of* **accessory** [➟ ACCESSORIES, MILLINERY, AND LINGERIE; 867] **5** *n* **draw**, dead heat, equal finish, stalemate [➟ SPORTS TERMS; 877]

tie-break *n* [➟ SPORTS TERMS; 877]

tiebreaker *n* **deciding game**, tie-break, decider [➟ SPORTS TERMS; 877]

tie clasp *type of* **jewelry** [➟ JEWELRY; 866]

tied up *adj* **unavailable**, engaged, occupied, busy, otherwise engaged [➟ ABSENT AND UNAVAILABLE; 7] *Opposite*: available

tie in *v* **connect**, associate, relate, link, join, coordinate, affiliate [➟ CREATING CONNECTIONS; 144] *Opposite*: disconnect

tie-in *n* **link**, relationship, connection, linkup, association, affiliation, tie-up [➟ CONNECTIONS; 143]

tie in knots *v* **confuse**, muddle, mix up, baffle, bewilder, perplex, puzzle [➟ CONFUSE AND BEWILDER; 571]

tier *n* **row**, level, layer, stage, rank, step, story [➟ STAIRS AND STORIES; 1102]

tie tack *type of* **jewelry** [➟ JEWELRY; 866]

tie the knot (*informal*) *v* **get married**, marry, wed, walk down the aisle, get hitched (*informal*) [➟ ESTABLISHING RELATIONSHIPS WITH OTHERS; 974]

tie up **1** *v* **lash**, truss, fasten, lace, tie, bind, fix together, join [➟ FASTEN, LINK, AND JOIN; 408] **2** *v* **complete**, clinch, finalize, resolve, end, finish off, wrap up (*informal*) [➟ COMPLETE AN ACTION; 263]

tie-up **1** *n* **link**, connection, linkup, association, relationship, affiliation, tie-in [➟ CONNECTIONS; 143] **2** *n* **delay**, holdup, stoppage, obstruction, hitch, snafu (*informal*) [➡ PROBLEMS; 256]

tiff *n* **quarrel**, argument, row, falling-out, squabble, disagreement, spat, dispute [➡ ARGUMENTS; 47]

tiger *type of* **cat** [➡ FELINES; 983]

tiger moth *type of* **moth** [➡ MOTHS AND BUTTERFLIES; 1015]

tiger swallowtail *type of* **butterfly** [➡ MOTHS AND BUTTERFLIES; 1015]

tight 1 *adj* (*slang*) [➡ UNDER THE INFLUENCE OF DRUGS OR ALCOHOL; 7411 2 *adj* **taut**, stretched, tense, firm, stiff, rigid, constricted [➡ RIGID AND HARD; 1211] *Opposite*: loose 3 *adj* **close-fitting**, body-hugging, skintight, snug, fitted [➡ DESCRIBING CLOTHES; 869] *Opposite*: baggy 4 *adj* **firm**, fixed, strong, unyielding, tough [➡ STRENGTH; 201] *Opposite*: weak 5 *adj* **strict**, stringent, harsh, firm, tough, severe, stern [➡ ORDER AND ORGANIZATION; 206] *Opposite*: lax 6 *adj* **mean**, stingy, miserly, tightfisted, parsimonious, niggardly [➡ GRASPING AND FINANCIALLY MEAN; 519] *Opposite*: generous 7 *adj* **difficult**, problematic, awkward, tricky, tough, troublesome, sticky (*informal*) [➡ DIFFICULTY AND COMPLEXITY; 242] *Opposite*: easy

tight corner *n* [➡ DIFFICULT SITUATIONS; 72]

tighten *v* **make tighter**, tauten, constrict, stiffen, squeeze, tighten up, tense [➡ CONTACT: EXERT PRESSURE; 414] *Opposite*: loosen

tighten your belt *v* **cut back**, economize, retrench, pull in your horns, draw in your horns (*UK*) [➡ FORGO AND DENY ONESELF; 449]

tightfisted *adj* **mean**, stingy, tight, grasping, miserly, parsimonious, niggardly [➡ GRASPING AND FINANCIALLY MEAN; 519] *Opposite*: generous

tightfistedness *n* **scrimping**, meanness, stinginess, tightness, miserliness, parsimony, niggardliness [➡ GRASPING AND FINANCIALLY MEAN; 519] *Opposite*: generosity

tightfitting *adj* **tight**, close-fitting, snug, figure-hugging, skintight, fitted [➡ DESCRIBING CLOTHES; 869] *Opposite*: baggy

tightknit *adj* **closely connected**, integrated, united, interwoven, intertwined [➡ CLOSENESS; 159]

tight-lipped *adj* **silent**, uncommunicative, reticent, withdrawn, taciturn, reserved, quiet, mute, unforthcoming [➡ RETICENT AND UNFORTHCOMING; 631] *Opposite*: loquacious

tightly 1 *adv* **firmly**, strongly, forcefully, closely, securely [➡ STRENGTH; 201] *Opposite*: loosely 2 *adv* **closely**, compactly, snugly, cozily [➡ CLOSENESS; 159] *Opposite*: loosely

tightness *n* **tension**, tautness, stiffness, rigidity [➡ RIGID AND HARD; 1211] *Opposite*: looseness

tight situation *n* [➡ DIFFICULT SITUATIONS; 72]

tight spot *n* **tight corner**, difficult position, tricky situation, predicament, quandary, fix (*informal*), scrape (*informal*) [➡ DIFFICULT SITUATIONS; 72]

tigress *type of* **female animal** [➡ MALE OR FEMALE ANIMALS; 978]

tilapia *type of* **freshwater fish** [➡ FRESHWATER FISH; 1010]

tilde *type of* **diacritic** [➡ ASPECTS OF LANGUAGE; 682]

tile *n* [➡ BUILDING MATERIALS; 1077]

till 1 *n* **cash register**, cash box, box, drawer, tray [➡ CONTAINERS, RECEPTACLES, AND PACKAGING; 1245] 2 *v* **plow**, dig, cultivate, turn over, rake, hoe, prepare [➡ USE TOOLS AND MACHINERY; 468]

tiller *part of* **ship or boat** [➡ PARTS OF A SHIP OR BOAT; 1151]

tilt 1 *v* **tip**, slope, slant, lean, list, angle, roll, incline, bend [➡ TAKE UP A NEW POSITION; 312] *Opposite*: straighten up 2 *n* **slope**, slant, angle, gradient, incline, list [➡ ORIENTATION AND ALIGNMENT; 1223]

tilt back *v* [➡ TAKE UP A NEW POSITION; 312]

tilted *adj* **slanted**, slanting, sloping, sloped, lopsided, skewed, crooked, angled, leaning, listing [➡ ORIENTATION AND ALIGNMENT; 1223] *Opposite*: flat

tilting *adj* [➡ ORIENTATION AND ALIGNMENT; 1223]

timber 1 *n* **trees**, woods, timberland, woodland [➡ WOODS, FORESTS, AND JUNGLES; 1047] 2 *n* (*UK*) **lumber**, wood, logs, planks [➡ BUILDING MATERIALS; 1077]

timbre *n* **tone**, pitch, resonance, sound, quality, tenor, lowness, highness [➡ QUALITY OF SOUNDS; 1264]

time 1 *n* **period**, while, spell, stretch, stint, interval, phase, stage [➡ PERIODS OF TIME; 90] 2 *n* **occasion**, instance, moment, point, instant, minute, hour, point in time, moment in time [➡ SHORT PERIODS OF TIME; 93] 3 *n* **era**, age, epoch, period, season, generation [➡ EPOCHS AND ERAS; 89] 4 *n* **tempo**, measure, rhythm, beat, speed, pace [➡ MUSICAL TERMS; 912] 5 *v* **count**, measure, clock, calculate, record [➡ ASSESS QUANTITY; 757] 6 *v* **schedule**, program, timetable, plan, arrange, organize, book, set up [➡ CAUSE TO HAPPEN; 31]

time

◆ *types of time periods*
calendar month, fortnight, leap year, lunar month, month, quarter, semester, trimester, week, weekend, year

time after time *adv* **again and again**, time and again, time and time again, over and over again, over and over, repeatedly [➡ AGAIN; 109] *Opposite*: rarely

time ahead *n* [➡ FUTURE; 86]

time and again *adv* **time after time**, again and again, time and time again, over and over again, over and over, repeatedly [➡ AGAIN; 109] *Opposite*: rarely

time and time again *see* **time and again**

time bomb 1 *n* **tinderbox**, volcano, accident waiting to happen, flashpoint [➡ PROBLEMS; 256] 2 *type of* **explosive weapon** [➡ EXPLOSIVES; 1155]

time-consuming *adj* **laborious**, slow, inefficient, long, onerous, arduous, timewasting [➡ BORING AND UNINTERESTING; 234] *Opposite*: timesaving

time-honored *adj* **traditional**, customary, habitual, age-old, respected, long-standing, historic, ancient, usual, conventional [➡ OLD, OLD-FASHIONED; 167] *Opposite*: recent

time immemorial *n* [➡ PERMANENCE: WITHOUT END; 94]

time lag *n* **lapse**, interlude, gap, interval, pause, delay [➡ PAUSES AND PHASES; 56]

timeless *adj* **eternal**, ageless, enduring, undying, everlasting, unending, abiding, endless, changeless, unchanging, immutable [➡ PERMANENCE: WITHOUT END; 94] *Opposite*: ephemeral

timelessness *n* **agelessness**, endurance, endlessness, changelessness, immutability, constancy, invariability, persistence [➡ PERMANENCE: WITHOUT END; 94] *Opposite*: ephemeralness

timely *adj* **opportune**, well-timed, appropriate, apt, judicious, sensible, suitable [➡ APPROPRIATE, SUITABLE, AND ADVISABLE; 184] *Opposite*: untimely

time off *n* **leisure**, free time, spare time, leave, time out, vacation, holiday (*UK*) [➡ PERIODS OF REST; 91]

time out *n* **rest**, breathing space, respite, break, leave, time off [➡ PERIODS OF REST; 91]

timepiece *n* **chronometer**, timer, clock [➡ CLOCKS AND TIMERS; 1126]

timer *n* [➡ CLOCKS AND TIMERS; 1126]

timesaving *adj* **quick**, streamlined, efficient, effective, improved, better [➡ ECONOMICAL AND RESOURCEFUL; 207] *Opposite*: time-consuming

timescale *n* **timetable**, schedule, time, period, span, program [➡ PERIODS OF TIME; 90]

timeserver *n* **opportunist**, weathercock, waverer, equivocator, vacillator, turncoat, don't know (*informal*) [➡ LAZY OR UNSUCCESSFUL PEOPLE; 948] *Opposite*: stalwart

times gone by *n* [➡ PAST; 84]

timeshare *type of* **house** [➡ RESIDENTIAL BUILDINGS; 1078]

times of yore *n* [➡ PAST; 84]

timespan *n* **duration**, period, extent, length, span, stretch [➡ PERIODS OF TIME; 90]

times past *n* [➡ PAST; 84]

timetable **1** *n* **schedule**, agenda, plan, program, calendar, diary, rota (*UK*) [➡ LISTS AND SCHEDULES; 587] **2** *v* (*UK*) **schedule**, arrange, plan, organize, program, book, set up, time [➡ PREPARE FOR ACTION; 289]

time to come *n* [➡ FUTURE; 86]

timewaster *n* [➡ LAZY OR UNSUCCESSFUL PEOPLE; 948]

time without end *n* [➡ PERMANENCE: WITHOUT END; 94]

timeworn **1** *adj* **shabby**, tattered, threadbare, worn, well-worn, worn-out, tatty, frayed, used [➡ IN BAD REPAIR; 1234] *Opposite*: brand-new **2** *adj* **hackneyed**, overworked, stale, trite, stock, cliché-ridden, unoriginal, clichéd, well-worn, corny, banal, old hat (*informal*) [➡ BORING AND UNINTERESTING; 234] *Opposite*: original

time zone *n* [➡ TIMES OF DAY; 87]

time zone

◆ *types of time zones*
Alaska, Atlantic, Central, Eastern, Hawaii-Aleutian, Mountain, Pacific, Samoa, Yukon

timid *adj* **nervous**, shy, fearful, timorous, diffident, coy, bashful, reticent, retiring, faint-hearted, cowardly, frightened, tentative, apprehensive, hesitant [➡ RETICENT AND UNFORTHCOMING; 631] *Opposite*: bold

timidity *n* **nervousness**, shyness, fearfulness, timorousness, diffidence, coyness, bashfulness, reticence, faint-heartedness, cowardice, tentativeness, apprehension, apprehensiveness, hesitancy [➡ RETICENT AND UNFORTHCOMING; 631] *Opposite*: boldness

timing *n* **judgment**, effectiveness, control, mastery, technique, skill [➡ SKILLS, TALENTS, AND ABILITIES; 526]

timorous *adj* **nervous**, fearful, timid, frightened, scared, afraid, shy, apprehensive, bashful, diffident, coy, retiring, reticent, cowardly, faint-hearted, hesitant [➡ RETICENT AND UNFORTHCOMING; 631] *Opposite*: brave

timorousness *n* **nervousness**, fearfulness, timidity, shyness, fear, apprehensiveness, apprehension, bashfulness, diffidence, coyness, hesitancy, cowardice, faint-heartedness, reticence [➡ RETICENT AND UNFORTHCOMING; 631] *Opposite*: bravery

timothy *type of* **grass** [➡ GRASS; 1031]

timpani *type of* **percussion instrument** [➡ MUSICAL INSTRUMENTS; 910]

tin **1** *type of* **metal** [➡ METALS; 1276] **2** *n* **box**, container, caddy, cake tin, cookie tin, biscuit tin (*UK*) [➡ CONTAINERS, RECEPTACLES, AND PACKAGING; 1245] **3** *n* (*UK*) **can**, tin can, canister, container, cylinder [➡ CONTAINERS, RECEPTACLES, AND PACKAGING; 1245]

tincture **2** *n* **solution**, essence, distillate, extract, distillation, mixture [➡ LIQUIDS; 1269] **2** *n* **tinge**, tint, hint, nuance, tone, cast, shade, color, coloring, coloration [➡ FEW, LITTLE, SMALL AMOUNT; 120]

tinder *n* **kindling**, firewood, brushwood, sticks, twigs [➡ ENERGY SOURCES; 1162]

tinderbox *n* **flashpoint**, crucible, volcano, no-go area, accident waiting to happen, time bomb [➡ PROBLEMS; 256]

ting **1** *n* *type of* **ringing sound** [➡ RINGING AND HOOTING SOUNDS; 1259] **2** *v* **ding**, ting-a-ling, ring, ping, tinkle, jingle, trill [➡ EMIT RINGING AND HOOTING SOUNDS; 367] *Opposite*: thud

ting-a-ling *v* [➡ EMIT RINGING AND HOOTING SOUNDS; 367]

tinge **1** *n* **hint**, touch, dash, drop, trace, bit, shade, suggestion, tint, nuance, element [➡ FEW, LITTLE, SMALL AMOUNT; 120] **2** *v* **tint**, color, stain, shade, mix, combine, mingle [➡ CHANGE OF COLOR; 391]

tingle **1** *v* **prickle**, sting, itch, tickle, prick, burn [➡ PAIN AND OTHER PHYSICAL SENSATIONS; 733] **2** *n* **sting**, prickle, itch, tickle, prick, burn, pins and needles, irritation [➡ PAIN AND OTHER PHYSICAL SENSATIONS; 733]

tingling *adj* **prickly**, itchy, scratchy, burning, stinging, tickling [➡ PAIN AND OTHER PHYSICAL SENSATIONS; 733]

tininess *n* [➡ SMALL; 1195]

tinker **1** *v* **fiddle**, tamper, interfere, fool around, play, monkey around, toy, mess around (*informal*) [➡ WORSEN SOMETHING; 380] **2** *v* **mend**, repair, fix, put right [➡ REPAIR AND MEND; 376]

tinkle 1 *v* **ring**, jingle, clink, chink, ding, ping, chime [➡EMIT RINGING AND HOOTING SOUNDS; 367] **2** *n* **jingle**, ring, clink, chink, ding, ping, chime [➡RINGING AND HOOTING SOUNDS; 1259] **3** *type of* **ringing sound** [➡CONTINUOUS SOUNDS; 1258]

tinned (*UK*) *adj* [➡STATE OF PREPARED FOOD; 1171]

tinny 1 *adj* **thin**, high, metallic, shrill, ringing, harsh, reedy [➡LOUD, HIGH, OR UNPLEASANT SOUNDS; 1266] *Opposite*: resonant **2** *adj* **shoddy**, cheap, worthless, inferior, poor, tacky (*informal*) [➡IN POOR TASTE AND OVERSENTIMENTAL; 229]

tinsel 1 *n* **metallic thread**, glitter, streamer, spangle, decoration, chain, banner [➡ORNAMENTS AND DECORATIONS; 1248] **2** *n* **showiness**, glitz, flashiness, pretentiousness, glitter, dazzle, splendor, glamour, glitziness [➡IN POOR TASTE AND OVERSENTIMENTAL; 229]

tint 1 *n* **shade**, color, hue, touch, trace, tone, tinge, hint, dash, drop [➡DESCRIBING COLORS; 1226] **2** *n* **rinse**, dye, colorant, streak, highlight, lowlight [➡DYES AND COLORANTS; 1270] **3** *v* **dye**, color, shade, streak, rinse, highlight, lowlight [➡CHANGE OF COLOR; 391]

tinted *adj* [➡DESCRIBING COLORS; 1226]

tiny *adj* **minute**, miniature, minuscule, small, little, petite, infinitesimal, diminutive, microscopic, insignificant, teeny (*informal*) [➡SMALL; 1195] *Opposite*: enormous

tip 1 *v* **tilt**, slope, slant, lean, list, angle, roll, incline, bend [➡TAKE UP A NEW POSITION; 312] *Opposite*: straighten **2** *v* **knock over**, pour, empty, spill, knock, overturn, upend, upset, tip over, turn turtle, capsize, tip up (*UK*) [➡MOVE SOMETHING INTO A NEW POSITION OR OVERTURN; 330] **3** *v* **give**, slip, reward, pay, bribe [➡GIVE MONEY; 433] **4** *n* **slope**, slant, angle, gradient, incline, tilt, lean, list, roll, bend [➡ORIENTATION AND ALIGNMENT; 1223] **5** *n* **gratuity**, gift, reward, bonus, extra, bribe [➡GIFTS; 438] **6** *n* **warning**, clue, pointer, prompt, hint, forewarning, nod, tip-off (*informal*) [➡ADVICE; 689] **7** *n* **hint**, suggestion, idea, pointer [➡ADVICE; 689] **8** *n* (*UK*) **garbage dump**, landfill, civic amenity point (*UK*), rubbish dump (*UK*) [➡URBAN OUTDOOR SPACES; 1072]

tip off *v* **warn**, inform, advise, forewarn, tell [➡ADVISE AND WARN; 613]

tip-off (*informal*) *n* **warning**, clue, hint, pointer, prompt, tip, forewarning, nod [➡ADVICE; 689]

tippet *type of* **headgear** [➡ACCESSORIES, MILLINERY, AND LINGERIE; 867]

tipple (*informal*) *n* [➡DRINKS; 1187]

tipster *n* **adviser**, consultant, analyst, informant, informer, speculator [➡PEOPLE INVOLVED IN FINANCE; 804]

tipsy *adj* [➡UNDER THE INFLUENCE OF DRUGS OR ALCOHOL; 741]

tiptoe *v* **creep**, sneak, steal, skulk, glide, slink, tread [➡MOVE SLOWLY; 314] *Opposite*: stamp

tiptop (*informal*) *adj* **first-rate**, excellent, superb, first-class, superlative, best, topnotch (*informal*) [➡SUPERIORITY; 152] *Opposite*: dreadful

tirade *n* **outburst**, rant, diatribe, harangue, lecture, invective (*formal*) [➡CRITICISMS AND ANGRY OUTBURSTS; 50]

tiramisu *type of* **dessert** [➡CAKES, COOKIES, AND DESSERTS; 1181]

tire 1 *v* **exhaust**, wear out, drain, fatigue, enervate, weary [➡TIRED, ASLEEP, AND UNCONSCIOUS; 738] **2** *type of* **external feature** [➡EXTERNAL PARTS OF A VEHICLE; 1147] **3** *part of* **bike** [➡BIKES, CARS, AND CARRIAGES; 1149]

tired 1 *adj* **weary**, sleepy, drowsy, fatigued, exhausted, worn-out, drained, tired out, spent, bushed (*informal*), dog-tired (*informal*), done in (*informal*), beat (*slang*), wiped out (*slang*), all in (*UK*), shattered (*UK*) [➡TIRED, ASLEEP, AND UNCONSCIOUS; 738] *Opposite*: energetic **2** *adj* **bored**, weary, sick, jaded, dissatisfied, fed up (*informal*) [➡SADNESS, DISTRESS, AND DESPAIR; 539] **3** *adj* **overused**, trite, hackneyed, clichéd, old, worn-out, jaded, stale, corny [➡BORING AND UNINTERESTING; 234] *Opposite*: fresh

tiredly *adv* **wearily**, sleepily, drowsily, blearily, groggily, woozily [➡TIRED, ASLEEP, AND UNCONSCIOUS; 738] *Opposite*: energetically

tiredness *n* **weariness**, sleepiness, fatigue, drowsiness, exhaustion, grogginess, wooziness [➡TIRED, ASLEEP, AND UNCONSCIOUS; 738] *Opposite*: energy

tired out *adj* **exhausted**, worn-out, spent, weary, dog-tired (*informal*), bushed (*informal*), done in (*informal*), beat (*slang*), wiped out (*slang*), beat (*slang*), shattered (*UK*), all in (*UK*) [➡TIRED, ASLEEP, AND UNCONSCIOUS; 738] *Opposite*: energetic

tireless *adj* **untiring**, diligent, determined, unstinting, assiduous, indefatigable, industrious, vigorous, unflagging [➡ENERGY AND ENTHUSIASM; 496] *Opposite*: weary

tirelessness *n* **diligence**, determination, assiduousness, indefatigability, industriousness, vigor [➡ENERGY AND ENTHUSIASM; 496] *Opposite*: weariness

tiresome *adj* **annoying**, irritating, tedious, wearisome, dull, boring, exasperating, irksome [➡IRRITATING; 228]

tiring *adj* **exhausting**, strenuous, arduous, wearing, demanding, laborious [➡PHYSICALLY UNPLEASANT; 226]

tisane *n* [➡DRINKS; 1187]

tissue 1 *n* **soft tissue**, fleshy tissue, flesh, matter, material, skin, muscle, nerve [➡THE SKIN; 720] **2** *n* **web**, net, network, mass, series, chain [➡FASTENERS, LINKS, AND NETWORKS; 1247]

tissue of lies *n* [➡DECEPTION AND LIES; 660]

titan *n* **giant**, superman, superwoman, genius [➡PEOPLE WHO ARE APPROVED OF; 955] *Opposite*: nobody

titanic *adj* **colossal**, monumental, immense, gigantic, massive, enormous, huge, giant [➡LARGE; 1193] *Opposite*: insignificant

titanium *type of* **metal** [➡METALS; 1276]

titanosaur *type of* **dinosaur** [➡DINOSAURS; 996]

tit for tat *n* **retaliation**, revenge, reprisal, vengeance, retribution, an eye for an eye, a tooth for a tooth, a taste of your own medicine, a game at which two can play, blow for blow (*UK*) [➡VENGEANCE AND REVENGE; 685]

tit-for-tat *adj* [➡VENGEANCE AND REVENGE; 685]

tithe *n* **church tax**, tax, duty, contribution, portion, charity [➡RELIGIONS AND RELIGIOUS PRACTICES; 777]

titian *type of* **orange** [➡COLORS; 1224]

titillate *v* [➡ APPEAL TO AND AROUSE INTEREST; 575]

titillating *adj* [➡ INTERESTING AND MEANINGFUL; 190]

titivate *v* **do up**, dress up, adorn, decorate, beautify [➡ IMPROVE APPEARANCE; 379]

titivation *n* **adornment**, embellishment, beautification, prettification, enhancement, sprucing up, ornamentation, trimming, gilding [➡ IMPROVE APPEARANCE; 379]

title 1 *n* **name**, heading, label, designation [➡ NAME AND DESCRIBE; 665] 2 *n* **championship**, trophy, cup, award [➡ NON-AGGRESSIVE/SPORTING EVENTS; 40] 3 *n* **ownership**, entitlement, deed, right, claim [➡ POSSESS; 444] 4 *v* **call**, name, label, designate, refer to, identify [➡ NAME AND DESCRIBE; 665]

titled *adj* **noble**, aristocratic, patrician, blue-blooded, upper-class, well-bred, highborn (*literary*) [➡ CLASS STATUS; 889]

title deed *n* **title**, deed, document, proof of ownership, ownership, legal paper [➡ OFFICIAL DOCUMENTS; 586]

titleholder 1 *n* **champion**, winner, reigning champion, cupholder [➡ PEOPLE IN SPORTS AND LEISURE; 876] 2 *n* **owner**, proprietor, possessor, vendor, holder, landlord [➡ OWNERS; 446]

title page *n* **front page**, title, opening page, frontispiece [➡ PARTS OF BOOKS AND DOCUMENTS; 593]

titmouse *type of* **songbird** [➡ SONGBIRDS; 1003]

titter *type of* **human sound** [➡ SOUNDS MADE BY PEOPLE; 1262]

tittle *n* [➡ SMALL PIECES; 129]

tittle-tattle 1 *n* **gossip**, scandal, rumor, hearsay, tale, word of mouth, idle talk, word, report, talk, chitchat (*informal*) [➡ GOSSIP; 678] 2 *v* **gossip**, chatter, prattle, yak (*informal*), blather (*informal*) [➡ BETRAY CONFIDENCES AND GOSSIP; 618]

titular *adj* **nominal**, in name only, supposed, ostensible, so-called [➡ FALSE AND UNREAL; 173] *Opposite:* actual

tizzy (*informal*) *n* **panic**, dither, flap (*informal*), lather (*informal*), state (*informal*) [➡ INSECURITY AND LOSS OF COMPOSURE; 544]

T-junction *n* **junction**, intersection, fork, road junction [➡ BRIDGES, TUNNELS, CROSSINGS, AND JUNCTIONS; 1112]

TNT *type of* **explosive material** [➡ EXPLOSIVES; 1155]

toad *type of* **amphibian** [➡ AMPHIBIANS; 1008]

toadstool *type of* **fungus** [➡ MICROORGANISMS, FUNGI, AND ALGAE; 1023]

toady 1 *n* **flatterer**, sycophant, groveler [➡ SUPERFICIAL OR INSINCERE PEOPLE; 951] 2 *v* **grovel**, fawn, flatter, kowtow, crawl (*informal*) [➡ FLATTER AND FAWN; 621]

toadying 1 *n* **obsequiousness**, sycophancy, servility, flattery, fawning, groveling, bowing and scraping, crawling (*informal*) [➡ INGRATIATING; 638] 2 *adj* **obsequious**, sycophantic, servile, flattering, fawning, smarmy, groveling [➡ INGRATIATING; 638]

to all intents and purposes *adv* **practically**, in practice, virtually, as good as, pretty much (*informal*), pretty well (*informal*) [➡ TO A CERTAIN EXTENT; 136]

to and fro *adv* **back and forth**, backward and forward, up and down, hither and thither, here and there, hither and yon (*UK*) [➡ DIRECTION OF MOTION; 345]

toast 1 *n* **toasted bread**, grilled bread, browned bread, heated bread, bread [➡ BREAD, FLOUR, AND BREAD PRODUCTS; 1179] 2 *n* **salute**, tribute, pledge, health [➡ GREETINGS, FAREWELLS, AND SALUTATIONS; 659] 3 *n* **darling**, favorite, delight, sweetheart [➡ PEOPLE WHO ARE APPROVED OF; 955] 4 *v* **grill**, brown, crisp, heat, cook, color [➡ COOKING AND FOOD PREPARATION; 353] 5 *v* **warm**, warm up, heat, heat up, roast, bake, cook [➡ COOKING AND FOOD PREPARATION; 353] *Opposite:* freeze 6 *v* **drink to**, pledge, salute, drink the health of [➡ PRAISE AND ENCOURAGE; 647]

toaster *type of* **appliance** [➡ HOUSEHOLD APPLIANCES; 1117]

toasty *adj* **warm**, snug, cozy, pleasant [➡ HOT WEATHER; 1050] *Opposite:* chilly

to be brief *adv* [➡ SUMMARIZING EXPRESSIONS; 622]

to be fair *adv* [➡ EXPRESSIONS OF OPINION; 623]

to be frank *adv* [➡ EXPRESSIONS OF OPINION; 623]

to be honest *adv* [➡ EXPRESSIONS OF OPINION; 623]

to blame *adj* **responsible**, guilty, culpable, at fault, liable [➡ MORALLY BAD OR IMPROPER; 775] *Opposite:* innocent

toboggan 1 *n* **sled**, sleigh, bobsled, luge, sledge (*UK*), bobsleigh (*UK*) [➡ VEHICLES; 1145] 2 *type of* **winter sport** [➡ HOBBIES, GAMES, AND SPORTS; 875] 3 *v* **sled**, sleigh, luge, sledge (*UK*) [➡ TRAVEL: WAYS OF TRAVELING; 320] 4 *v* **slip**, slide, hurtle, tumble [➡ GO DOWNWARD; 307]

to boot *adv* [➡ EXPRESSIONS INTRODUCING EXTRA INFORMATION; 139]

to cap it all (*UK*) *adv* **on top of everything else**, to make matters worse, to top it all off, in addition, additionally [➡ EXPRESSIONS INTRODUCING EXTRA INFORMATION; 139]

tocsin *n* **alarm**, warning, bell, siren, signal [➡ SIGNALING; 1140]

to cut a long story short *adv* **in short**, in a word, in a nutshell, to put it briefly, in brief, to come to the point [➡ SUMMARIZING EXPRESSIONS; 622]

to date *adv* **up to the present time**, so far, up to now, as yet, thus far, up till now (*UK*) [➡ PAST; 84]

today *adv* **nowadays**, these days, currently, now, at the moment, at present [➡ PRESENT; 85]

toddle 1 *v* **totter**, patter, pad, waddle [➡ WALK UNSTEADILY; 315] 2 *v* (*informal*) **walk**, stroll, amble [➡ MOVE SLOWLY; 314]

toddler *n* **child**, baby, tot (*informal*), kid (*informal*) [➡ CHILD OR YOUTH; 945]

to die for *adj* [➡ POPULAR AND WANTED; 220]

to-do (*informal*) *n* **fuss**, commotion, bother, scene [➡ CHAOS AND UPROAR; 51]

toe *part of* **leg or foot** [➡ PARTS OF THE BODY: LEG AND FOOT; 694]

toe-curling (*informal*) *adj* [➡ EMOTIONALLY UNPLEASANT AND UPSETTING; 227]

toehold *n* **start**, advantage, starting point, jumping-off place, beginning, entry, way in [➡ BEGINNINGS; 53]

toenail *part of* **leg or foot** [➡ PARTS OF THE BODY: LEG AND FOOT; 694]

toe the line *v* [➡ OBEY AND ABIDE BY; 301]

to excess *adv* **in large amounts**, excessively, too much, profligately, lavishly, wastefully, extravagantly [➡TOO MUCH; 119] *Opposite*: in moderation

toffee *type of* **confectionery** [➡CONFECTIONERY; 1182]

tofu *type of* **cooked dish** [➡PREPARED DISHES; 1170]

together 1 *adv* **jointly**, as one, mutually, in concert, collectively [➡ACTING WITH OTHERS; 285] *Opposite*: alone 2 *adv* **simultaneously**, at once, at the same time, concurrently, all together, in sync (*informal*) [➡CONCURRENT AND CONTEMPORANEOUS; 164] *Opposite*: separately 3 *adj* (*informal*) **composed**, calm, collected, organized, cool, unruffled, self-possessed, with-it (*informal*), laid-back (*informal*) [➡COOL AND CALM; 536] *Opposite*: flustered

togetherness *n* **closeness**, intimacy, devotedness, friendship, inseparability, inseparableness, attachment [➡RELATIONSHIP TO ANOTHER, 973] *Opposite*: estrangement

together with *prep* **as well as**, accompanied by, with, alongside, in addition to, beside, plus (*informal*) [➡ALSO; 138]

toggle 1 *n* **fastener**, peg, button, buckle, clasp, catch, fastening, closure [➡FASTENERS, LINKS, AND NETWORKS; 1247] 2 *n* **switch**, key, command, button, lever [➡PARTS OF MACHINES AND TOOLS; 1118] 3 *v* **change**, change over, switch, move, transfer, move on, swap (*informal*) [➡COMPUTERS AND COMPUTING; 1127]

togs (*informal*) *n* **clothes**, outfit, dress, clothing, kit, rig out (*informal*), getup (*informal*), gear (*informal*), attire (*formal*) [➡CLOTHES AND ACCESSORIES, 864]

to hand *adv* [➡PRESENT AND AVAILABLE; 11]

toil 1 *n* **work**, labor, drudgery, slog, hard work, sweat (*informal*), gruntwork (*informal*), donkeywork (*informal*), grind (*informal*) [➡HARD WORK OR EFFORT; 298] *Opposite*: relaxation 2 *v* **labor**, strive, work, slog, slave, knuckle down (*informal*), beaver (*informal*), plug away (*informal*), sweat (*informal*), keep your head down (*UK*) [➡HARD WORK OR EFFORT; 298] *Opposite*: laze around

See Compare and Contrast at **work**.

toiler *n* [➡WORKERS; 836]

toilet 1 *n* **lavatory**, chamber pot, urinal, latrine, commode, privy (*informal*) [➡FIXTURES; 859] 2 *n* (*formal*) **washing**, dressing, grooming, bathing, getting dressed, preparations, getting ready, ablutions (*formal or humorous*), toilette (*literary*) [➡PERSONAL HYGIENE; 491] 3 *n* **W.C.**, restroom, washroom, lavatory, powder room, water closet, bathroom, john (*informal*), ladies (*UK*), gents (*UK*), public convenience (*UK*) [➡TYPES OF ROOMS; 1097]

toiletry *n* **soap**, shampoo, conditioner, shaving cream, toothpaste, floss, mouthwash, deodorant, volumizer, beauty product, skincare product, cosmetic product, shower gel (*UK*) [➡PERSONAL HYGIENE; 491]

toilette (*literary*) *n* **dressing**, grooming, bathing, getting dressed, preparations, getting ready, washing, toilet (*formal*), ablutions (*formal or humorous*) [➡PERSONAL HYGIENE; 491]

toilet water *n* **cologne**, eau de cologne, eau de toilette, scent, aftershave, perfume [➡PERSONAL HYGIENE; 491]

toilsome *adj* (*literary*) [➡EMOTIONALLY UNPLEASANT AND UPSETTING; 227]

toing and froing *n* [➡FIDGET AND FROLIC; 311]

token 1 *n* **voucher**, coupon, slip, coin [➡RECEIPTS AND INVOICES; 591] 2 *n* **mark**, demonstration, sign, symbol, indication, gesture, proof [➡REPRESENTATIONS AND GENERAL EXAMPLES; 65] 3 *n* **keepsake**, remembrance, souvenir, reminder, memento [➡ORNAMENTS AND DECORATIONS; 1248] 4 *adj* **symbolic**, nominal, perfunctory, empty [➡REPRESENTATIVE; 66]

tolar *type of* **currency** [➡CURRENCIES; 798]

tolerable 1 *adj* **bearable**, acceptable, endurable, supportable (*literary*) [➡ACCEPTABLE AND PASSABLE; 219] *Opposite*: unbearable 2 *adj* **reasonable**, average, passable, fair, adequate, all right, satisfactory, not bad, pretty good, okay (*informal*) [➡ACCEPTABLE AND PASSABLE; 219] *Opposite*: intolerable

tolerance *n* **broad-mindedness**, acceptance, open-mindedness, lenience, charity, patience, forbearance (*formal*) [➡POSITIVE INTELLECTUAL CHARACTERISTICS; 524] *Opposite*: intolerance

tolerant *adj* **accepting**, easygoing, lenient, broad-minded, open-minded, liberal, understanding, charitable, forbearing (*formal*) [➡POSITIVE INTELLECTUAL CHARACTERISTICS; 524] *Opposite*: intolerant

tolerate *v* **stand**, bear, abide, put up with, endure, accept, stomach, stand for, allow [➡TOLERATE AND ENDURE; 766] *Opposite*: forbid

toleration *n* **allowance**, acceptance, open-mindedness, broad-mindedness, liberality, understanding, consideration [➡POSITIVE INTELLECTUAL CHARACTERISTICS; 524] *Opposite*: prejudice

toll 1 *n* **fee**, tax, levy, payment, duty, excise, charge [➡EXPENDITURE; 423] 2 *n* **peal**, ring, ding-dong, clang, ding-a-ling [➡RINGING AND HOOTING SOUNDS; 1259] 3 *v* **ring**, peal, ding, ding-dong [➡EMIT RINGING AND HOOTING SOUNDS; 367]

tollbooth *n* **barrier**, gate, kiosk, booth, ticket office [➡DOORS AND ACCESS POINTS; 1101]

toll-free *adj* **free**, complimentary, gratis, costless, cost-free (*UK*) [➡GIFTS; 438]

tollgate *n* **barrier**, gate, entrance, exit [➡DOORS AND ACCESS POINTS; 1101]

toll road *type of* **highway** [➡ROADS; 1106]

tom *type of* **male animal** [➡MALE OR FEMALE ANIMALS; 978]

tomahawk *type of* **sword or knife** [➡SWORDS AND KNIVES; 1157]

tomato *type of* **salad vegetable** [➡FRUIT AND VEGETABLES; 1176]

tomb *n* **burial chamber**, catacomb, grave, burial place, crypt, vault, last resting place, sepulcher, ossuary (*formal*) [➡BURIAL PLACES AND ACCESSORIES; 930]

tombola (*UK*) *n* **lottery**, draw, raffle, game of chance [➡GAMBLE AND TAKE RISKS; 466]

tomboyish *adj* **boyish**, unladylike, mannish, boisterous, unruly [➡GENDER IDENTITY AND SEXUALITY; 932]

tombstone *n* **headstone**, gravestone, monument [➡MONUMENTS; 1092]

tomcat *type of* **male animal** [➡ MALE OR FEMALE ANIMALS; 978]

tome *n* **book**, volume, digest, work [➡ BOOKS AND BOOKLETS; 590]

tomfoolery (*informal*) *n* **silliness**, horseplay, mischief, clowning, fooling around, playing around, joking, pranks, monkeyshines, monkey business (*informal*), high jinks (*informal*), shenanigans (*informal*) [➡ JOKES AND TEASING; 674] *Opposite*: sensibleness

Tommy gun (*informal*) *type of* **gun** [➡ WEAPONS FOR SHOOTING; 1156]

tom-tom *type of* **percussion instrument** [➡ MUSICAL INSTRUMENTS; 910]

to my amazement *adv* [➡ EXPRESSIONS OF SURPRISE AND PLEASURE; 546]

to my mind *adv* [➡ EXPRESSIONS OF OPINION; 623]

to my surprise *adv* [➡ EXPRESSIONS OF SURPRISE AND PLEASURE; 546]

ton (*informal*) **1** *n* **mass**, mountain, lot, ocean, stack (*informal*), heap (*informal*) [➡ MANY, MUCH, LARGE AMOUNT; 117] **2** *type of* **nonmetric unit** [➡ SIZE AND DIMENSIONS; 1192]

tonality *n* **tone**, timbre, pitch, sound, sound quality [➡ QUALITY OF SOUNDS; 1264]

tone **1** *n* **quality**, manner, character, attitude, tendency, nature, air [➡ APPEARANCE AND ATMOSPHERE; 1237] **2** *n* **sound**, pitch, quality, timbre [➡ QUALITY OF SOUNDS; 1264] **3** *n* **character**, atmosphere, feel, ambiance [➡ APPEARANCE AND ATMOSPHERE; 1237] **4** *n* **color**, hue, tint, tinge, shade [➡ DESCRIBING COLORS; 1226]

tone arm *part of* **audio equipment** [➡ AUDIO EQUIPMENT; 1139]

tone down *v* **dilute**, moderate, soften, restrain, modulate, diminish, weaken, reduce [➡ CHANGE OF INTENSITY: LESS; 395] *Opposite*: intensify

toneless *adj* **colorless**, expressionless, monotonous, neutral, monochrome, dull [➡ BORING AND UNINTERESTING; 234] *Opposite*: vibrant

tone poem *type of* **musical form** [➡ MUSIC, SONGS, AND SINGING; 907]

toner **1** *n* **cleanser**, cleansing milk, skin preparation, astringent, cosmetic [➡ PERSONAL HYGIENE; 491] **2** *n* **ink**, liquid ink, powdered ink [➡ PRINTING; 600]

tone up *v* **firm up**, strengthen, get in shape, exercise [➡ IMPROVE APPEARANCE; 379]

tongs *type of* **general tool** [➡ HAND TOOLS; 1119]

tongue **1** *n* **language**, patois, dialect, speech, idiom [➡ THE SPOKEN WORD; 671] **2** *part of* **mouth** [➡ THE MOUTH; 702]

See Compare and Contrast at **language**.

tongue-in-cheek *adj* **lighthearted**, ironic, insincere, flippant, whimsical, joking, funny, sardonic, humorous [➡ MOCKING AND DISMISSIVE; 636] *Opposite*: serious

tongue-lashing *n* [➡ CRITICISMS AND ANGRY OUTBURSTS; 50]

tongue-tied *adj* **speechless**, shy, awkward, silent, inarticulate, embarrassed, timid [➡ RETICENT AND UNFORTHCOMING; 631] *Opposite*: talkative

tongue twister *n* [➡ FIGURES OF SPEECH; 673]

tonic *n* **boost**, fillip, stimulant, shot in the arm, livener, energizer, refresher, pick-me-up (*informal*) [➡ TREATS; 210]

tonnage *n* **weight**, heaviness, capacity, size [➡ WEIGHT: HEAVY; 1205]

tonne *type of* **metric unit** [➡ SIZE AND DIMENSIONS; 1192]

tons **1** *adv* **a lot**, a great deal, lots, loads (*informal*) [➡ MANY, MUCH, LARGE AMOUNT; 117] **2** *n* (*informal*) **lots**, plenty, oodles (*informal*), loads (*informal*), piles (*informal*) [➡ MANY, MUCH, LARGE AMOUNT; 117]

tonsils *part of* **mouth** [➡ THE MOUTH; 702]

tonsured *adj* [➡ BALDNESS AND BALDING; 487]

tony (*informal*) *adj* **elegant**, expensive, stylish, fashionable, posh (*informal*), well-heeled (*informal*) [➡ EXPENSIVE AND LUXURIOUS; 218]

too **1** *adv* **also**, as well, in addition, besides, moreover, else, to boot [➡ ALSO; 138] **2** *adv* **excessively**, overly, extremely, exceedingly, overmuch [➡ TOO MUCH; 119] *Opposite*: insufficiently

too few *adj* [➡ TOO FEW, TOO LITTLE; 122]

tool *n* **instrument**, implement, device, means, utensil, apparatus, contrivance, gizmo (*informal*) [➡ DEVICES; 1115]

tool

◆ *types of carpentry tools*
awl, bradawl, drill, hammer, jigsaw, mallet, plane, sander, saw, vise

◆ *types of cosmetic tools*
comb, emery board, hairbrush, nailbrush, nail clippers, nail file, nail scissors, razor, shaving brush, tweezers

◆ *types of general tools*
bellows, blowtorch, crowbar, file, grease gun, jack, jimmy, lathe, machine tool, pincers, pliers, plumb line, plunger, poker, pump, punch, rasp, screwdriver, socket wrench, soldering iron, spade, tongs, trowel, wrench

◆ *types of medical instruments*
forceps, lancet, probe, scalpel, speculum, stethoscope, syringe

too little *adj* [➡ TOO FEW, TOO LITTLE; 122]

too much *adj* [➡ TOO MUCH; 119]

tooth **1** *n* **fang**, tusk, chopper (*slang*) [➡ THE MOUTH; 702] **2** *n* **indentation**, projection, tine, cog, prong [➡ PARTS OF MACHINES AND TOOLS; 1118]

tooth

◆ *types of teeth*
baby tooth, bucktooth (*informal*), canine, chopper, cuspid, denture, eyetooth, fang, incisor, milk tooth, molar, premolar, wisdom tooth

toothless *adj* **powerless**, useless, impotent, ineffective, ineffectual, incapable [➡ WEAKNESS; 241] *Opposite*: effective

toothpaste *n* [➡ PERSONAL HYGIENE; 491]

toothsome *adj* **delicious**, palatable, tasty, appetizing, mouthwatering, scrumptious (*informal*) [➡ TASTE; 703] *Opposite*: unappetizing

tootle (*informal*) **1** *v* **drive slowly**, go slowly, meander, wend your way, crawl, creep, pootle (*UK*) [➡ MOVE SLOWLY; 314] *Opposite*: dash **2** *v* **hoot**, sound, honk, beep, sound the horn [➡ EMIT RINGING AND HOOTING SOUNDS; 367] **3** *n* **honk**, beep, hoot [➡ RINGING AND HOOTING SOUNDS; 1259] **4** *n* **drive**, meander, crawl, pootle (*UK*) [➡ TRAVEL: JOURNEYS AND TRIPS; 318] *Opposite*: dash

top 1 *n* **pinnacle**, summit, peak, apex, crown, crest, acme, zenith [➡ EXTREMITIES OF PHYSICAL OBJECTS; 1250] *Opposite*: bottom **2** *n* **cork**, lid, cap, cover, stopper [➡ COVERS AND COATINGS; 1246] **3** *n* [➡ GARMENTS AND OUTFITS; 865] **4** *adj* **highest**, topmost, maximum, uppermost [➡ RELATIVE LOCATION; 161] *Opposite*: bottom **5** *adj* **best**, first, chief, principal, important, leading, eminent [➡ SUPERIORITY; 152] **6** *v* **outdo**, surpass, better, improve on, cap, crown, exceed, excel, beat [➡ BEAT AND DEFEAT; 80]

---

top

◆ *types of sweaters*
cardigan, crew neck, jersey, mock turtle, pullover, sweater, turtleneck, twin set, V neck

◆ *types of tops*
basque, blouse, bodice, body warmer, bolero, bustier, gilet, halter, jerkin, polo shirt, shirt, smock, surplice, sweatshirt, T-shirt, tabard, tank top, tee, tube top, tunic, vest, vestment

---

topaz *type of* **gemstone** [➡ PRECIOUS STONES; 1278]

top brass (*informal*) *n* [➡ IMPORTANT OR FAMOUS PEOPLE; 893]

top-class *adj* **best**, world-class, first-class, first-rate, topflight, premier, premium, unrivaled, outstanding, exceptional, topnotch (*informal*) [➡ SUPERIORITY; 152]

topcoat *type of* **overcoat** [➡ GARMENTS AND OUTFITS; 865]

top dog (*informal*) *n* [➡ IMPORTANT OR FAMOUS PEOPLE; 893]

top drawer 1 *n* **cream**, crème de la crème, elite, pick, best [➡ SUPERIORITY; 152] **2** *n* **aristocracy**, nobility, high society, gentry, upper class, upper crust (*informal*) [➡ CLASS STATUS; 889]

top-drawer 1 *adj* **topflight**, best, first-rate, first-class, premium, premier, topnotch (*informal*) [➡ SUPERIORITY; 152] **2** *adj* **upper class**, high class, noble, titled, aristocratic [➡ CLASS STATUS; 889]

topee *type of* **headgear** [➡ ACCESSORIES, MILLINERY, AND LINGERIE; 867]

topflight *adj* **top-drawer**, best, first-rate, first-class, premium, premier, top-class, topnotch (*informal*) [➡ SUPERIORITY; 152]

top gun (*informal*) *n* [➡ IMPORTANT OR FAMOUS PEOPLE; 893]

top hat *type of* **hat** [➡ ACCESSORIES, MILLINERY, AND LINGERIE; 867]

top-heavy *adj* **unbalanced**, unstable, uneven, disproportionate, lopsided [➡ ORIENTATION AND ALIGNMENT; 1223]

topic *n* **theme**, subject, matter, issue, subject matter, focus [➡ SUBJECT AREAS; 768]

See Compare and Contrast at **subject**.

---

topical *adj* **up-to-date**, interesting, current, newsworthy, contemporary, relevant [➡ PRESENT; 85]

topicality *n* **interest**, relevance, newsworthiness, current interest, contemporaneity, contemporaneousness [➡ PRESENT; 85]

topknot *type of* **hairstyle** [➡ HAIRSTYLES AND HAIRPIECES; 488]

top-level *adj* **highest**, most senior, most important, most powerful [➡ MOST IMPORTANT AND MAIN; 193]

topmost *adj* **highest**, uppermost, top, peak [➡ SUPERIORITY; 152]

top name *n* [➡ IMPORTANT OR FAMOUS PEOPLE; 893]

topnotch (*informal*) *adj* **top-class**, first-rate, superior, first-class, excellent, top-quality, superlative, exclusive, premium, best, top, premier [➡ SUPERIORITY; 152] *Opposite*: inferior

top-of-the-range *adj* **best**, most expensive, exclusive, premium, premier, excellent [➡ SUPERIORITY; 152] *Opposite*: basic

topographical *adj* **geographic**, structural, natural, landscape, environmental [➡ THE EARTH; 1039]

topography *n* **features**, landscape, geography, structure, countryside [➡ THE COUNTRYSIDE AND OUTDOOR SPACES; 1071]

topper *type of* **hat** [➡ ACCESSORIES, MILLINERY, AND LINGERIE; 867]

topping *n* **top layer**, coating, glaze, garnish, frosting, icing, covering, decoration [➡ COVERS AND COATINGS; 1246] *Opposite*: filling

topple 1 *v* **fall over**, tip over, collapse, fall, tumble, knock down, upset, knock over [➡ GO DOWNWARD; 307] **2** *v* **bring down**, overthrow, depose, oust, remove, unseat [➡ REVOKE STATUS; 459]

top-quality *adj* **choice**, select, fine, rare [➡ SUPERIORITY; 152]

top-ranking *adj* **high-ranking**, senior, important, powerful, high-level [➡ IMPORTANT; 194]

top-rated *adj* **popular**, well-liked, top, top ten, number one, favorite [➡ POPULAR AND WANTED; 220] *Opposite*: unpopular

top round *type of* **cut** [➡ TYPES AND CUTS OF MEAT; 1177]

tops (*informal*) *adv* **at most**, as a maximum, at the most, max (*slang*) [➡ MAJORITY AND MAXIMUM; 141]

topsail *part of* **sailing vessel** [➡ SHIPS AND BOATS; 1150]

top-secret *adj* **undercover**, covert, secret, clandestine, restricted, privileged, classified, confidential, hush-hush (*informal*) [➡ SECRET AND UNKNOWN; 179]

topsoil *n* **soil**, earth, loam, dirt, peat [➡ EROSION PRODUCTS AND SOIL; 1058]

topspin *n* **forward spin**, spin, momentum, force, impetus, energy [➡ SPORTS TERMS; 877]

topsy-turvy *adj* **confused**, disordered, chaotic, in disarray, upside down, in a mess, mixed up, disorganized, all over the place (*informal*) [➡ DISORDER AND CHAOS; 245] *Opposite*: orderly

top up 1 *v* **refill**, replenish, refuel, freshen [➡ FILL; 406]

2 *v* **make up**, augment, complete, chip in (*informal*) [➡FILL; 406]

top-up (*UK*) **1** *n* **refill**, fill-up, replenishment, extra serving, extra measure, more [➡DRINK; 711] **2** *n* **add-on**, addition, extra, supplement, increase, increment [➡MORE AND EXCESS; 124]

to put it briefly *adv* [➡SUMMARIZING EXPRESSIONS; 622]

toque *type of* **hat** [➡ACCESSORIES, MILLINERY, AND LINGERIE; 867]

tor *n* **peak**, crag, outcrop, rock face [➡MOUNTAINS AND HILLS; 1044]

torch (*slang*) *v* **burn down**, set on fire, put a match to, set fire to, incinerate, set light to (*UK*) [➡FIRE, FLAMMABILITY, AND BURNING; 1165]

torchlight *n* **beam**, light, illumination, lamplight [➡DESCRIBING LIGHT; 1228]

torment **1** *v* **annoy**, tease, plague, persecute, taunt, pester, bother, harass, trouble, torture [➡UPSET, DISTRESS, AND HUMILIATE; 567] *Opposite:* comfort **2** *n* **anguish**, suffering, agony, distress, pain, torture, stress [➡SADNESS, DISTRESS, AND DESPAIR; 539] *Opposite:* pleasure **3** *n* **nuisance**, bane, plague, annoyance, irritation, pest (*informal*), pain in the neck (*informal*) [➡NUISANCES; 253] *Opposite:* delight

tormented *adj* **anguished**, tortured, distressed, grief-stricken, plagued, persecuted, haunted [➡SADNESS, DISTRESS, AND DESPAIR; 539]

tormenter *see* **tormentor**

tormenting *adj* [➡EMOTIONALLY UNPLEASANT AND UPSETTING; 227]

tormentor *n* **oppressor**, tyrant, persecutor, bully, teaser [➡ENEMIES AND TORMENTORS; 969]

torn **1** *adj* **ripped**, frayed, ragged, tattered, shabby, shredded, in rags, in tatters, in shreds [➡IN BAD REPAIR; 1234] **2** *adj* **undecided**, of two minds, uncertain, in a quandary, in a dilemma, unable to decide, dithering, wavering [➡UNCERTAINTY; 559] *Opposite:* decided

tornado *n* **hurricane**, whirlwind, cyclone, storm, windstorm, twister (*informal*) [➡WINDY AND STORMY WEATHER; 1053]

torpedo **1** *v* (*informal*) **ruin**, destroy, wreck, spoil, thwart, sink, scupper [➡MAKE IMPOSSIBLE; 276] **2** *type of* **explosive weapon** [➡EXPLOSIVES; 1155] **3** *type of* **firework** [➡EXPLOSIVES; 1155]

torpid *adj* **lazy**, languorous, listless, sluggish, apathetic, sleepy, dreamy, slow, unhurried, indolent, stagnant, lethargic [➡LIFELESS, LAZY, AND UNENTHUSIASTIC; 506] *Opposite:* energetic

torpor *n* **inactivity**, inertia, indolence, languor, lethargy, listlessness, apathy [➡LIFELESS, LAZY, AND UNENTHUSIASTIC; 506] *Opposite:* excitement

torque **1** *n* **rotating force**, rotation, twisting, turning, turning force, spin, force [➡ENERGY GENERAL; 1161] **2** *type of* **necklace** [➡JEWELRY; 866]

torrent **1** *n* **rush**, flood, flow, deluge, gush, stream, surge, downpour, rainstorm, cloudburst, driving rain, soaker, shower, inundation (*formal*) [➡CLOUDY AND RAINY WEATHER; 1052] *Opposite:* trickle **2** *n* **outburst**, flood, flow, tide, stream, deluge, outpouring [➡SUDDEN EVENTS; 52]

torrential *adj* **heavy**, pouring, driving, lashing, drenching, severe [➡CLOUDY AND RAINY WEATHER; 1052] *Opposite:* light

torrid *adj* **hot**, stifling, sweltering, boiling, burning, baking, scorching (*informal*), sizzling (*informal*) [➡HOT WEATHER; 1050] *Opposite:* cool

torridness *n* [➡HOT WEATHER; 1050]

torsion *n* **twisting**, turning, turning force, rotation, spin, force [➡ENERGY; 1161]

torso *n* [➡PARTS OF THE BODY: TORSO; 693]

torso

◆ *parts of a torso*
abdomen, armpit, back, backside (*informal*), belly, bellybutton (*informal*), bosom, bottom, breast, bust, buttock, chest, groin, haunch, hip, midriff, navel, neck, nipple, rib cage, rump, shoulder, solar plexus, thorax, waist, waistline

tort *n* **wrongful act**, unlawful act, illegal act, offense, misdemeanor, wrongdoing, misdeed [➡CRIMES; 817]

torte *type of* **cake** [➡CAKES, COOKIES, AND DESSERTS; 1181]

tortellini *type of* **pasta** [➡PASTA; 1180]

tortilla *type of* **bread** [➡BREAD, FLOUR, AND BREAD PRODUCTS; 1179]

tortoise *type of* **reptile** [➡REPTILES; 994]

tortoiseshell **1** *type of* **cat** [➡FELINES; 983] **2** *type of* **butterfly** [➡MOTHS AND BUTTERFLIES; 1015]

tortuous **1** *adj* **twisting**, winding, convoluted, circuitous, indirect, roundabout, meandering [➡DIRECTION OF MOTION; 345] *Opposite:* direct **2** *adj* **complex**, complicated, intricate, difficult, involved, byzantine, labyrinthine [➡DIFFICULTY AND COMPLEXITY; 242] *Opposite:* simple **3** *adj* **devious**, deceitful, crafty, sly, artful, dishonest, false [➡DECEITFUL; 513] *Opposite:* straightforward

torture **1** *v* **torment**, afflict, persecute, brutalize, punish, mistreat [➡UPSET, DISTRESS, AND HUMILIATE; 567] **2** *n* **agony**, torment, anguish, pain, suffering, distress, cruelty [➡SADNESS, DISTRESS, AND DESPAIR; 539]

torturer *n* **intimidator**, bully, pesterer, harasser, teaser, tormentor, persecutor, oppressor [➡ENEMIES AND TORMENTORS; 969]

toss **1** *v* **throw**, pitch, fling, lob, hurl, let fly, flip, chuck (*informal*) [➡MOVE SOMETHING: THROUGH THE AIR; 334] **2** *v* **mix**, stir, blend, mix up [➡COMBINE AND MIX; 400] **3** *n* **lob**, throw, pitch, heave, fling, shy, chuck (*informal*) [➡MOVE SOMETHING: THROUGH THE AIR; 334]

See Compare and Contrast at **throw**.

toss and turn *v* [➡FIDGET AND FROLIC; 311]

toss off *v* [➡DRINK; 711]

toss-up *n* **even chance**, chance, risk, fifty-fifty, luck of the draw, hit or miss [➡CHANCE, COINCIDENCE, AND ACCIDENT; 786]

to sum up *adv* [➡SUMMARIZING EXPRESSIONS; 622]

tot **1** *n* **dram**, finger, thimbleful, snifter (*informal*) [➡DRINK;

711] **2** *n* (*informal*) **toddler**, child, baby, small child, kid (*informal*) [➡ CHILD OR YOUTH; 945]

total **1** *n* **sum**, whole, entirety, full amount, totality [➡ ALL; 128] **2** *adj* **entire**, whole, full, complete, aggregate [➡ WHOLENESS AND COMPLETENESS; 198] *Opposite*: partial **3** *adj* **complete**, absolute, unmitigated, unreserved, out-and-out, full-blown, utter [➡ ABSOLUTE AND ABSOLUTELY; 133] **4** *v* **add up**, count up, tot up, calculate, sum, compute, totalize [➡ ASSESS QUANTITY; 757] **5** *v* **amount to**, add up to, come to, equal, make [➡ AMOUNT TO AND EQUAL; 70] **6** *v* (*slang*) **wreck**, destroy, smash, ruin, write off (*UK*) [➡ DESTRUCTION AND DEMOLITION; 359]

totalitarian *adj* **authoritarian**, tyrannous, one-party, oppressive, autocratic, despotic, tyrannical, dictatorial [➡ STYLES AND SYSTEMS OF GOVERNMENT; 806] *Opposite*: democratic

totalitarianism *n* **despotism**, absolutism, tyranny, autocracy, authoritarianism, dictatorship [➡ STYLES AND SYSTEMS OF GOVERNMENT; 806]

totality *n* **entirety**, whole, total, sum, full amount [➡ ALL; 128] *Opposite*: part

totally *adv* **completely**, entirely, absolutely, wholly, fully, thoroughly, utterly, perfectly [➡ ABSOLUTE AND ABSOLUTELY; 133] *Opposite*: partly

tote (*informal*) **1** *v* **carry**, cart, lug, haul, heave, drag, transport [➡ MOVE SOMETHING TO ANOTHER LOCATION; 324] **2** *v* **bear**, carry, hold, wield, brandish [➡ CONTACT: HOLD; 411]

tote bag *type of* **bag** [➡ CONTAINERS, RECEPTACLES, AND PACKAGING; 1245]

to tell the truth *adv* [➡ EXPRESSIONS OF OPINION; 623]

totem **1** *n* **ritual object**, sacred symbol, icon, charm, talisman, amulet [➡ LUCKY CHARMS; 785] **2** *n* **symbol**, representation, emblem, image, icon [➡ REPRESENTATIONS AND GENERAL EXAMPLES; 65]

totemic *adj* **symbolic**, emblematic, iconic, representative [➡ REPRESENTATIVE; 66]

to the fore *adv* [➡ RELATIVE LOCATION; 161]

to the left *adv* [➡ RELATIVE LOCATION; 161]

to the letter *adv* **exactly**, precisely, literally, word for word, accurately, strictly [➡ EXACT; 203]

to the point *adj* **relevant**, apt, apposite, pertinent, germane [➡ FUNDAMENTAL; 195] *Opposite*: irrelevant

to the rear *adv* [➡ GENERAL LOCATIONS; 158]

to the right *adv* [➡ RELATIVE LOCATION; 161]

totter *v* **walk unsteadily**, stagger, wobble, teeter, stumble, reel, flounder, falter [➡ WALK UNSTEADILY; 315]

tot up *v* **add up**, total, count up, add together, calculate, compute [➡ ASSESS QUANTITY; 757]

touch **1** *n* **pat**, tap, stroke, fondle, feel, pressure [➡ CONTACT: TOUCH; 412] **2** *n* **trace**, bit, dash, drop, hint, soupçon, little, tad (*informal*) [➡ FEW, LITTLE, SMALL AMOUNT; 120] **3** *n* **style**, facility, gift, knack, ability, talent, flair [➡ SKILLS, TALENTS, AND ABILITIES; 526] **4** *v* **handle**, feel, finger, tap, stroke, contact, pat, fondle, caress [➡ CONTACT: TOUCH; 412] **5** *v* **converge**, meet, come into contact, join, contact, link [➡ CREATING CONNECTIONS; 144] *Opposite*: separate **6** *v* **move**, affect, upset, stir, touch a chord, impress [➡ SURPRISE AND IMPRESS; 574] **7** *v* **match**, come close to,

meet, rival, equal, compete with [➡ COMPETE, CONTEND, AND COMBAT; 303]

touch-and-go *adj* **uncertain**, unpredictable, doubtful, unknown, risky, in the balance, shaky, dicey (*informal*) [➡ UNCERTAIN; 175] *Opposite*: certain

touchdown **1** *n* **landing**, descent, arrival [➡ ARRIVAL; 13] **2** *n* **score**, try, point [➡ SPORTS TERMS; 877]

touched **1** *adj* **affected**, moved, warmed, heartened, impressed, gladdened, gratified [➡ PLEASURE, EXCITEMENT, AND ELATION; 534] *Opposite*: unmoved **2** *adj* (*literary*) **tinged**, tinted, shaded, marked, streaked, spattered [➡ DECORATE, ADORN, AND APPLY COATINGS; 405]

touchiness *n* **irritability**, impatience, grumpiness, cantankerousness, moodiness, crossness, bad temper, petulance, sulkiness, huffiness, sensitivity, tetchiness (*informal*), crankiness (*informal*) [➡ EXCESSIVE SENSITIVITY; 511] *Opposite*: composure

touching *adj* **moving**, poignant, stirring, tender, pitiful, emotive, sad, heartbreaking, heartrending, affecting [➡ EMOTIONALLY PLEASANT; 187]

See Compare and Contrast at **moving**.

touch on *v* **deal with**, refer to, mention, treat, allude to, talk about, go into, discuss, touch upon, be concerned with [➡ SUGGEST, HINT, AND COMMENT; 612]

touch screen *type of* **hardware** [➡ COMPUTERS AND COMPUTING; 1127]

touchstone *n* **criterion**, standard, benchmark, yardstick, hallmark [➡ SCORES AND EVALUATIONS; 598]

touch up *v* **retouch**, restore, freshen, freshen up, refurbish, repaint, smarten up, improve [➡ DECORATE, ADORN, AND APPLY COATINGS; 405]

touchy **1** *adj* **sensitive**, quick-tempered, impatient, petulant, cantankerous, grumpy, moody, sulky, huffy, prickly (*informal*), tetchy (*informal*), cranky (*informal*) [➡ EXCESSIVE SENSITIVITY; 511] *Opposite*: even-tempered **2** *adj* **delicate**, sensitive, tricky, awkward, ticklish, precarious [➡ DIFFICULTY AND COMPLEXITY; 242]

touchy-feely (*informal*) *adj* **demonstrative**, expressive, effusive, unreserved, emotional, gushing, unrestrained, sentimental [➡ FRIENDLINESS AND SOCIABILITY; 494] *Opposite*: undemonstrative

tough **1** *adj* **threatening**, rough, hard, harsh, dangerous, hard-hitting [➡ DANGEROUS; 236] *Opposite*: pleasant **2** *adj* **durable**, strong, sturdy, robust, hardy, resilient, independent [➡ STRENGTH; 201] *Opposite*: weak **3** *adj* **difficult**, hard, demanding, exacting, arduous, strenuous, daunting, taxing, challenging, tricky, testing [➡ DIFFICULTY AND COMPLEXITY; 242] *Opposite*: easy **4** *adj* **severe**, strict, rigid, inflexible, stern, harsh, stringent, firm, uncompromising, unbending, hardheaded [➡ DIFFICULT TO PLEASE; 515] *Opposite*: lenient **5** *adj* **hard**, chewy, stringy, stiff, leathery, gristly [➡ STATE OF PREPARED FOOD; 1171] *Opposite*: tender

See Compare and Contrast at **hard**.

tough as old boots (*UK*) *adj* [➡ STATE OF PREPARED FOOD; 1171]

toughen v **strengthen**, harden, build up, reinforce, fortify, shore up, firm up, beef up (*informal*) [➠ IMPROVE STRENGTH AND DURABILITY; 378] *Opposite*: weaken

toughened adj **hardened**, reinforced, strengthened, fortified, unbreakable, galvanized, tempered [➠ DURABLE; 1210]

tough it out (*informal*) v [➠ TOLERATE AND ENDURE; 766]

tough-minded adj **realistic**, determined, tough, single-minded, resilient, strong, unsentimental, gutsy (*informal*) [➠ STRENGTH OF WILL; 501] *Opposite*: weak-willed

toughness 1 n **durability**, hardiness, robustness, roughness, stoutness, stiffness, sturdiness, strength, resilience [➠ STRENGTH; 201] *Opposite*: flimsiness 2 n **hardness**, chewiness, stringiness, stiffness [➠ PHYSICAL TEXTURE; 1222] *Opposite*: tenderness 3 n **roughness**, harshness, hardness, danger [➠ PHYSICALLY UNPLEASANT; 226] *Opposite*: pleasantness 4 n **difficulty**, arduousness, strenuousness, challenge, trickiness [➠ DIFFICULTY AND COMPLEXITY; 242] *Opposite*: ease 5 n **severity**, strictness, rigidity, inflexibility, firmness, sternness [➠ DIFFICULT TO PLEASE; 515] *Opposite*: leniency

toupee n **wig**, hairpiece, hair extension [➠ HAIRSTYLES AND HAIRPIECES; 488]

tour 1 n **trip**, excursion, expedition, outing, journey, visit, circuit [➠ TRAVEL: JOURNEYS AND TRIPS; 318] 2 v **sightsee**, explore, visit, travel around, go around [➠ TRAVEL: WAYS OF TRAVELING; 320]

tour guide n [➠ TRAVEL: SIGHTSEEING AND TOURISM; 321]

touring company n [➠ PERFORMERS; 905]

tourism n **travel**, travel industry, leisure industry, service sector, holiday business (*UK*) [➠ TRAVEL: SIGHTSEEING AND TOURISM; 321]

tourist n **traveler**, sightseer, visitor, vacationer, day tripper, holidaymaker (*UK*) [➠ TRAVEL: TRAVELERS AND WALKERS; 319]

tourist attractions n [➠ TRAVEL: SIGHTSEEING AND TOURISM; 321]

tourist center n [➠ TRAVEL: SIGHTSEEING AND TOURISM; 321]

tourist class n [➠ TRAVEL: SIGHTSEEING AND TOURISM; 321]

tourist spot n [➠ TRAVEL: SIGHTSEEING AND TOURISM; 321]

touristy adj **crowded**, busy, much-frequented, popular, overvisited, spoiled [➠ POPULAR AND WANTED; 220] *Opposite*: quiet

tourmaline type of **gemstone** [➠ PRECIOUS STONES; 1278]

tournament n **contest**, competition, event, tourney, game, playoffs, match [➠ NON-AGGRESSIVE/SPORTING EVENTS; 40]

tourney n [➠ NON-AGGRESSIVE/SPORTING EVENTS; 40]

tourniquet n **band**, strap, bandage [➠ FASTENERS, LINKS, AND NETWORKS; 1247]

tousle v **tangle**, ruffle, rumple, dishevel, disorder, disarrange, mess up (*informal*) [➠ CREATE DISORDER AND CAUSE CHAOS; 358] *Opposite*: tidy

tousled adj **disheveled**, messy, tangled, ruffled, windswept, rumpled, disarranged [➠ DESCRIBING HAIR; 486] *Opposite*: tidy

tout 1 v **advertise**, hype, flaunt, push, publicize, peddle, puff, ballyhoo, lay it on thick, plug (*informal*) [➠ SELL; 441] *Opposite*: understate 2 n **seller**, hawker, peddler, vendor [➠ SELLERS; 442]

tow v **pull**, drag, draw, haul, lug, tug [➠ PUSH, PULL, AND SLIDE; 335]

See Compare and Contrast at **pull**.

toward 1 prep **in the direction of**, to, near, just before [➠ DIRECTION OF MOTION; 345] 2 prep **regarding**, concerning, for, about, on, with regard to, with respect to, on the subject of, in relation to [➠ EXPRESSIONS OF REFERENCE; 63]

towel 1 n **cloth**, bath towel, hand towel, guest towel, dishtowel, tea towel (*UK*), bath sheet (*UK*) [➠ FURNISHING AND HOUSEHOLD LINENS; 860] 2 v **dry**, rub down, rub, wipe, dab, blot [➠ CLEAN AND POLISH; 403]

towel rail type of **plumbing fixtures** [➠ FIXTURES; 859]

tower 1 v **loom**, overlook, be head and shoulders above, soar, rise [➠ EXIST IN A PLACE; 19] 2 v **surpass**, exceed, excel, top, transcend, outstrip, outdo, outclass [➠ BEAT AND DEFEAT; 80]

tower block (*UK*) n [➠ RESIDENTIAL BUILDINGS; 1078]

towering adj **high**, tall, soaring, lofty, immense, gigantic [➠ HEIGHT: HIGH; 1203] *Opposite*: short

tower of strength (*informal*) n **rock**, mainstay, anchor, helper, advocate, support, pillar [➠ PEOPLE WHO ARE APPROVED OF; 955]

tow-headed adj [➠ HAIR COLOR; 485]

town n **municipality**, city, settlement, township, metropolis, new town (*UK*), garden city (*UK*) [➠ HUMAN SETTLEMENTS; 1070]

See Compare and Contrast at **city**.

town center n [➠ HUMAN SETTLEMENTS; 1070]

town house type of **house** [➠ RESIDENTIAL BUILDINGS; 1078]

townie (*informal*) n **town dweller**, city dweller, urbanite, city slicker [➠ INHABITANTS; 857]

townsfolk n **townspeople**, populace, residents, inhabitants [➠ INHABITANTS; 857]

township n **small town**, urban area, settlement, town, hamlet, community, parish, village, municipality [➠ HUMAN SETTLEMENTS; 1070]

townspeople n **townsfolk**, populace, residents, inhabitants [➠ INHABITANTS; 857]

town square n [➠ URBAN OUTDOOR SPACES; 1072]

towpath n **path**, footpath, canal path, track, pathway, bridleway (*UK*) [➠ PATHWAYS; 1110]

towrope n **towline**, rope, line, cable, cord [➠ FASTENERS, LINKS, AND NETWORKS; 1247]

tow truck type of **commercial or industrial vehicle** [➠ VEHICLES; 1145]

toxic adj **poisonous**, deadly, lethal, noxious, contaminated [➠ DANGEROUS; 236] *Opposite*: harmless

toxicity *n* **poisonousness**, venomousness, deadliness, noxiousness, harmfulness, injuriousness [➡ DANGER; 235] *Opposite*: harmlessness

toxic waste *n* [➡ UNPLEASANT, DIRTY, AND TOXIC SUBSTANCES; 1268]

toxin *n* **poison**, pollutant, contaminant, venom [➡ UNPLEASANT, DIRTY, AND TOXIC SUBSTANCES; 1268]

toy *n* [➡ TOYS; 880]

---

toy

◆ *types of toys*
beach ball, building blocks, doll, dollhouse, dolly (*informal*), hand puppet, jack-in-the-box, jigsaw, kaleidoscope, kite, marble, playhouse, popgun, puppet, rag doll, rocking horse, squirt gun, stilt, teddy bear, yo-yo

---

toy with 1 *v* **flirt with**, tease, philander [➡ APPEAL TO AND AROUSE INTEREST; 575] 2 *v* **think about**, consider, ponder, contemplate, entertain, speculate, play around with [➡ THINK AND REFLECT; 743] *Opposite*: dismiss 3 *v* **play with**, fiddle with, fidget with, handle, finger [➡ CONTACT: TOUCH; 412]

trace 1 *v* **draw**, outline, copy, mark out, sketch, map out [➡ CREATE IMAGES; 356] 2 *v* **find**, locate, discover, hunt down, track down, pin down, track, follow, trail [➡ FIND; 463] 3 *n* **sign**, indication, evidence, remnant, residue, mark, vestige [➡ EVIDENCE AND PROOF; 69] 4 *n* **suggestion**, hint, dash, drop, touch, bit, tinge, smattering, smidgen (*informal*) [➡ FEW, LITTLE, SMALL AMOUNT; 120]

traceable *adj* [➡ PERCEPTIBLE; 25]

tracery *n* **decoration**, pattern, design, interlacing, ornamentation, motif [➡ ORNAMENTS AND DECORATIONS; 1248]

trachea *part of* **respiratory system** [➡ RESPIRATORY ORGANS; 715]

tracheal *adj* [➡ RESPIRATORY ORGANS; 715]

tracheotomy *type of* **medical procedure** [➡ REMEDIES, TREATMENTS, AND OPERATIONS; 731]

track 1 *n* **path**, pathway, road, way, trail, roadway, footpath, trajectory [➡ PATHWAYS; 1110] 2 *n* **trail**, footprints, footsteps, path, trace, marks, paw marks, hoof marks, imprints, spoor [➡ EVIDENCE AND PROOF; 69] 3 *type of* **secondary road** [➡ ROADS; 1106] 4 *v* **follow**, hunt down, chase, pursue, stalk, trace, trail [➡ ACCOMPANY AND FOLLOW; 337]

trackball *type of* **hardware** [➡ COMPUTERS AND COMPUTING; 1127]

track down *v* **find**, hunt down, catch, capture, discover, unearth, locate, trace [➡ FIND; 463]

tracker *n* **trailer**, follower, chaser, hunter, shadow, tail, pursuer, private investigator, private detective, bounty hunter, private eye (*informal*) [➡ ENEMIES AND TORMENTORS; 969]

tract 1 *n* **area**, territory, zone, region, expanse, swathe, band, strip [➡ AREA AND RANGE; 111] 2 *n* **pamphlet**, article, treatise, leaflet [➡ BOOKS AND BOOKLETS; 590]

tractability 1 *n* **docility**, controllability, manageability, obedience, manipulability, submissiveness, compliance, amenableness [➡ THE WILL AND WILLINGNESS; 563] *Opposite*: intractability 2 *n* **malleability**, pliability, workability, ductility,

elasticity, plasticity, flexibility, pliancy, bendiness (*UK*) [➡ MALLEABLE AND ELASTIC; 1212] *Opposite*: intractability

tractable 1 *adj* **docile**, controllable, manageable, obedient, manipulable, submissive, amenable, biddable, compliant, pliant, yielding, easily swayed, impressionable, suggestible [➡ THE WILL AND WILLINGNESS; 563] *Opposite*: intractable 2 *adj* **malleable**, pliable, workable, ductile, elastic, plastic, flexible, bendable, pliant [➡ MALLEABLE AND ELASTIC; 1212] *Opposite*: intractable

traction 1 *n* **adhesive friction**, grip, purchase, adhesion [➡ ENERGY; 1161] 2 *n* **power**, tractive force, pull, tow, tug [➡ ENERGY; 1161]

tractor *type of* **commercial or industrial vehicle** [➡ VEHICLES; 1145]

trade 1 *n* **commerce**, business, industry, market, dealings, transactions [➡ BUSINESS ENTERPRISES AND RELATED BODIES; 792] 2 *n* **occupation**, job, employment, line of work, profession, craft, vocation, skill [➡ PROFESSIONS; 845] 3 *n* **customers**, public, patrons, custom, clientele [➡ PURCHASER; 424] 4 *v* **deal**, buy and sell, do business, operate, traffic, import, export, merchandize, transact [➡ SELL; 441] 5 *v* **exchange**, barter, negotiate, swap (*informal*), dicker (*informal*) [➡ EXCHANGE AND INTERCHANGE; 448]

trade event *n* [➡ SALES AND SHOWS; 443]

trade fair *n* **exhibition**, exposition, fair, display, show [➡ SALES AND SHOWS; 443]

trade in *v* **exchange**, redeem, give in part payment, barter, swap (*informal*) [➡ EXCHANGE AND INTERCHANGE; 448]

trade-in *n* **part exchange**, exchange, deal, transaction, swap (*informal*) [➡ EXCHANGE AND INTERCHANGE; 448]

trademark 1 *n* **symbol**, logo, emblem, brand [➡ SYMBOLS, SIGNS, AND NUMBERS; 596] 2 *n* **characteristic**, feature, trait, attribute, facet, quality, hallmark [➡ PERSONAL ECCENTRICITIES; 493] 3 *adj* [➡ REPRESENTATIVE; 66]

trade name *n* **brand name**, brand, trademark, name, registered trademark, label, product name [➡ NAME AND DESCRIBE; 665]

tradeoff *n* **compromise**, adjustment, interchange, transaction, balance, quid pro quo [➡ EXCHANGE AND INTERCHANGE; 448]

trader *n* **dealer**, buyer, seller, broker, agent, merchant [➡ SELLERS; 442]

trade school 1 *n* [➡ EDUCATIONAL INSTITUTIONS; 813] 2 *type of* **school** [➡ EDUCATIONAL INSTITUTIONS; 813]

trade show *n* [➡ SALES AND SHOWS; 443]

tradesperson (*UK*) *n* [➡ BUSINESS PEOPLE; 793]

trade union *n* [➡ BUSINESS ENTERPRISES AND RELATED BODIES; 792]

trade wind *type of* **wind** [➡ WINDY AND STORMY WEATHER; 1053]

tradition *n* **custom**, institution, ritual, habit, convention, belief, folklore, practice [➡ WAYS OF DOING THINGS; 294] *Opposite*: innovation

See Compare and Contrast at **habit**.

traditional *adj* **usual**, conventional, customary, established, fixed, long-established, time-honored, habitual, accepted, old-fashioned [➡ OLD, OLD-FASHIONED; 167] *Opposite*: progressive

traditionalism *n* **conventionalism**, conservatism, conformity, orthodoxy, fundamentalism [➡ PHILOSOPHIES AND BELIEFS; 780] *Opposite*: progressivism

traditionalist 1 *n* **conservative**, purist, fundamentalist, conformist [➡ PHILOSOPHICAL AND POLITICAL THINKERS; 781] *Opposite*: progressive 2 *adj* **traditional**, conservative, purist, orthodox, conventional, old-school, fundamentalist, traditionalistic [➡ UNADVENTUROUS AND DULL; 517] *Opposite*: progressive

traditionalistic *see* **traditionalist**

traditionally *adv* **usually**, conventionally, customarily, habitually, by tradition [➡ USUALLY; 108] *Opposite*: occasionally

traduce *v* **criticize**, disparage, malign, run down, defame, denigrate, vilify [➡ ACCUSE, BLAME, AND CRITICIZE; 641] *Opposite*: praise

traffic 1 *n* **road traffic**, traffic flow, circulation, stream of traffic, rush-hour traffic, commuter traffic [➡ VEHICLES; 1145] 2 *n* **transportation**, movement, passage, to-ing and fro-ing, travel, transport, transfer [➡ TRAVEL: SIGHTSEEING AND TOURISM; 321] 3 *n* **trade**, business, commerce, dealings, transactions, negotiations [➡ EXCHANGE AND INTERCHANGE; 448] 4 *v* **have dealings**, deal in, trade, trade in, transfer, do business, operate, handle, market, buy and sell [➡ EXCHANGE AND INTERCHANGE; 448] 5 *v* **smuggle**, run, handle [➡ BUSINESS ACTIVITIES AND PHENOMENA; 794]

traffic calming (*UK*) *n* [➡ TRAVEL: TRAFFIC PROBLEMS AND TRAFFIC MANAGEMENT; 323]

traffic circle *n* [➡ BRIDGES, TUNNELS, CROSSINGS, AND JUNCTIONS; 1112]

traffic-free *adj* [➡ PATHWAYS; 1110]

traffic island *n* [➡ BRIDGES, TUNNELS, CROSSINGS, AND JUNCTIONS; 1112]

traffic jam *n* **bottleneck**, gridlock, tie-up, holdup, tailback (*UK*) [➡ TRAVEL: TRAFFIC PROBLEMS AND TRAFFIC MANAGEMENT; 323]

traffic junction *n* [➡ BRIDGES, TUNNELS, CROSSINGS, AND JUNCTIONS; 1112]

traffic lane *n* [➡ ROADS; 1106]

traffic light *type of* **light** [➡ LIGHT; 1164]

tragedian *n* [➡ WRITERS AND STYLES; 914]

tragedy *n* **disaster**, calamity, catastrophe, misfortune, heartbreak [➡ DISASTERS; 252] *Opposite*: joy

tragic *adj* **sad**, disastrous, catastrophic, heartbreaking, heartrending, awful, terrible, dreadful, appalling, unfortunate, wretched [➡ EMOTIONALLY UNPLEASANT AND UPSETTING; 227] *Opposite*: joyous

tragicomic *adj* **bittersweet**, poignant, affecting, moving [➡ EMOTIONALLY UNPLEASANT AND UPSETTING; 227]

trail 1 *v* **follow**, track, tail, shadow, trace, stalk, pursue, chase [➡ ACCOMPANY AND FOLLOW; 337] 2 *v* **tug**, drag, pull, draw, tow, haul [➡ PUSH, PULL, AND SLIDE; 335] *Opposite*: push 3 *v* **drop back**, lag behind, fall behind, straggle, follow on, lag, linger behind, dawdle, hang back [➡ MOVE SLOWLY; 314] *Opposite*: lead 4 *n* **path**, track, way, road, footpath, route, trajectory [➡ PATHWAYS; 1110] 5 *n* **track**, footprints, footsteps, paw marks, paw

prints, hoof marks, trace, imprints, marks [➡ EVIDENCE AND PROOF; 69]

See Compare and Contrast at **follow**.

trail away *v* **fade**, disappear, grow faint, die away, diminish, tail off, tail away [➡ DISAPPEAR; 4] *Opposite*: intensify

trail bike *type of* **bike** [➡ BIKES, CARS, AND CARRIAGES; 1149]

trailblazer *n* **pioneer**, leader, innovator, entrepreneur, architect, creator, originator, initiator, catalyst, torchbearer [➡ DESIGNERS, CREATORS, AND INSTIGATORS; 347]

trailer *n* **clip**, preview, ad, promo (*informal*) [➡ ADVERTISING AND PUBLICITY; 604]

train 1 *type of* **rail vehicle** [➡ RAILROADS; 1107] 2 *n* **procession**, file, convoy, line [➡ GROUPS OF PEOPLE; 935] 3 *n* **sequence**, chain, succession, string, series, progression [➡ CHAIN OF EVENTS; 162] 4 *v* **teach**, coach, educate, instruct, tutor, school, prepare, guide [➡ INSTRUCT AND TEACH; 609] 5 *v* **exercise**, work out, stay fit, stay in shape [➡ HOBBIES, GAMES, AND SPORTS; 875] 6 *v* **aim**, direct, focus, line up, point [➡ PREPARE FOR ACTION; 289]

See Compare and Contrast at **teach**.

trained *adj* **skilled**, qualified, proficient, accomplished, competent, expert [➡ TALENTED AND SKILLFUL; 527]

trainee *n* **apprentice**, learner, novice, beginner [➡ UNSKILLED PEOPLE; 530] *Opposite*: trainer

trainer *n* **coach**, teacher, guide, instructor, mentor [➡ EDUCATORS; 840]

training 1 *n* **tuition**, education, schooling, teaching, guidance, preparation, instruction [➡ TEACHING; 839] 2 *n* **exercise**, working out, physical activity, drill [➡ HOBBIES, GAMES, AND SPORTS; 875]

training college (*UK*) *n* [➡ EDUCATIONAL INSTITUTIONS; 813]

train of thought *n* [➡ IDEAS AND THOUGHTS; 770]

traipse *v* **walk**, roam, rove, wander, ramble, tramp, schlep (*informal*) [➡ PROCEED AND GO; 305]

trait *n* **mannerism**, peculiarity, attribute, characteristic, feature, quality [➡ QUALITIES AND CHARACTERISTICS; 1191]

traitor *n* **conspirator**, collaborator, turncoat, defector, deserter, spy, double agent, quisling (*dated*) [➡ PEOPLE WHO DECEIVE; 661] *Opposite*: loyalist

traitorous *adj* **disloyal**, faithless, duplicitous, deceitful, treacherous, perfidious (*formal*) [➡ LACK OF COMMITMENT AND UNRELIABILITY; 509]

trajectory *n* **route**, course, flight, path, line, arc, trail, trace, track, curve [➡ DIRECTION OF MOTION; 345]

trammel 1 *n* **restriction**, limitation, hindrance, curb, constraint, impediment, handicap [➡ CAPTIVITY AND LOSS OF FREEDOM; 248] 2 *v* **confine**, limit, restrain, restrict, hinder, hamper [➡ AVOID, PREVENT, LIMIT, AND CONTROL; 277] 3 *v* **ensnare**, snare, catch, net, entangle, trap [➡ CAPTIVITY AND LOSS OF FREEDOM; 248]

tramontana *type of* **wind** [➡ WINDY AND STORMY WEATHER; 1053]

tramp 1 *n* **vagrant**, homeless person, beggar, vagabond, hobo [➡ POOR PEOPLE; 896] **2** *n* **traipse**, march, trek, hike, trudge, walk, plod, trail, slog, roam, ramble, schlep (*informal*) [➡ PROCEED AND GO; 305] **3** *v* **trudge**, trek, hike, traipse, march, plod, walk, trail, slog, roam, ramble, schlep (*informal*) [➡ PROCEED AND GO; 305]

trample *v* **crush**, flatten, walk on, stamp on, step on, tread on, walk over, squash [➡ CHANGE OF SHAPE; 385]

trance 1 *n* **dream**, daze, spell, stupor, reverie, daydream, sleep, abstraction [➡ DREAM, IMAGINE, AND FANTASIZE; 749] *Opposite:* alertness **2** *type of* **dance music** [➡ MUSIC, SONGS, AND SINGING; 907]

tranquil 1 *adj* **calm**, serene, peaceful, still, relaxing, restful, soothing, quiet [➡ PEACEFULNESS AND GENTLENESS; 214] *Opposite:* noisy **2** *adj* **composed**, calm, cool, unruffled, unperturbed, self-possessed, unflustered, relaxed, unworried, placid, serene, laid-back (*informal*) [➡ COOL AND CALM; 536] *Opposite:* agitated

tranquility *see* **tranquillity**

tranquilize *v* **sedate**, calm, put out, put under, knock out, anesthetize [➡ REMEDIES, TREATMENTS, AND OPERATIONS; 731]

tranquilizing *adj* [➡ CALMING; 188]

tranquillity 1 *n* **composure**, calmness, coolness, self-possession, serenity, peace of mind, level-headedness, equanimity (*formal*) [➡ CONFIDENCE AND COMPOSURE; 499] *Opposite:* panic **2** *n* **calm**, serenity, stillness, peacefulness, hush, quietness, calmness, peace and quiet [➡ PEACEFULNESS AND GENTLENESS; 214] *Opposite:* turmoil

tranquilly *adv* **serenely**, calmly, quietly, coolly, unperturbedly, unworriedly [➡ COOL AND CALM; 536] *Opposite:* anxiously

transact *v* **carry out**, conduct, manage, handle, perform, do, execute, conclude, take care of, deal with, implement, discharge (*formal*) [➡ CARRY OUT AN ACTION; 269]

transaction *n* **deal**, business, contract, matter, operation, business deal [➡ PURCHASE; 422]

transatlantic *adj* **transoceanic**, intercontinental, long-haul [➡ DISTANCE; 160]

transcend *v* **rise above**, go beyond, exceed, go above, excel, surpass, outdo [➡ BEAT AND DEFEAT; 80]

transcendence 1 *n* **divine existence**, otherworldliness, state of grace, perfection, wholeness [➡ RELIGIOUS CONCEPTS; 776] *Opposite:* mundaneness **2** *n* **superiority**, greatness, excellence, preeminence, loftiness, supremacy [➡ SUPERIORITY; 152] *Opposite:* inferiority

transcendent 1 *adj* **superior**, excellent, supreme, great, unequalled, unmatched [➡ SUPERIORITY; 152] *Opposite:* inferior **2** *adj* **divine**, perfect, heavenly, supernatural, otherworldly, unlimited, unconfined [➡ RELIGIOUS CONCEPTS; 776] **3** *adj* **mystical**, awe-inspiring, uplifting, inspirational, inspiring, moving, sublime, transcendental [➡ EMOTIONALLY PLEASANT; 187]

transcendental 1 *adj* **mystical**, awe-inspiring, uplifting, inspirational, inspiring, moving, sublime, transcendent [➡ EMOTIONALLY PLEASANT; 187] **2** *adj* **divine**, perfect, heavenly, supernatural, otherworldly, unlimited, unconfined, spiritual [➡ RELIGIOUS CONCEPTS; 776]

transcontinental *adj* **pancontinental**, coast-to-coast, continent-wide [➡ GEOGRAPHIC BORDERS AND BOUNDARIES; 1069]

transcribe *v* **copy out**, write out, copy, set down, write down, record [➡ RECORD SOMETHING; 371]

transcript *n* **record**, transcription, copy, text [➡ RECORDS; 585]

transcription *n* **record**, transcript, copy, text [➡ RECORDS; 585]

transect *v* **divide**, bisect, cut, split, cut across [➡ SEPARATE AND DIVIDE; 401]

transept *n* [➡ PARTS OF RELIGIOUS BUILDINGS; 1086]

transfer 1 *v* **move**, transport, relocate, remove, shift, convey, reassign [➡ MOVE SOMETHING TO ANOTHER LOCATION; 324] **2** *v* **transmit**, convey, hand on, hand over, turn over, assign, sign over, pass on [➡ DISPATCH AND SEND; 333] **3** *n* **transmission**, handover, assignment, allocation, transference, transferal [➡ EXCHANGE AND INTERCHANGE; 448] **4** *n* **relocation**, removal, move, resettlement, displacement [➡ MOVE SOMETHING TO ANOTHER LOCATION; 324]

transferal *n* [➡ EXCHANGE AND INTERCHANGE; 448]

transference *n* **transfer**, transferal, conversion, devolution, conveyance, transmission [➡ EXCHANGE AND INTERCHANGE; 448]

transfiguration *n* **metamorphosis**, transformation, makeover, change, conversion, transmutation, alteration [➡ CHANGE; 372]

transfigure *v* **change**, metamorphose, transform, convert, transmute, alter [➡ CHANGE; 372]

transfix 1 *v* **fascinate**, mesmerize, engross, spellbind, hypnotize, grip, hold, root to the spot, rivet (*informal*) [➡ APPEAL TO AND AROUSE INTEREST; 575] **2** *v* **stab**, spike, gore, run through, pierce [➡ STAB; 416]

transfixed *adj* [➡ PENSIVENESS AND INTEREST; 538]

transform *v* **alter**, convert, make over, transmute, renovate, change [➡ CHANGE; 372]

See Compare and Contrast at **change**.

transformation *n* **alteration**, conversion, revolution, renovation, makeover, change [➡ CHANGE; 372]

transfusion *type of* **medical procedure** [➡ REMEDIES, TREATMENTS, AND OPERATIONS; 731]

transgress *v* **misbehave**, disobey, go astray, lapse, sin, contravene, break the rules, do wrong, violate the law [➡ DISOBEY; 302] *Opposite:* behave

transgression *n* **wrongdoing**, misbehavior, disobedience, lapse, sin, contravention, misdemeanor, indiscretion, offense, crime [➡ BAD BEHAVIOR OR ACTIONS; 254]

transgressor *n* **wrongdoer**, lawbreaker, sinner, offender, criminal, evildoer, malefactor (*formal*) [➡ CRIMINALS; 821]

transience *n* **briefness**, brevity, impermanence, transitoriness, shortness, fleetingness, ephemerality, evanescence [➡FINITENESS, VARIABILITY, AND TRANSIENCE; 96] *Opposite*: permanence

transient *adj* **fleeting**, brief, passing, transitory, temporary, momentary, short-lived, ephemeral, evanescent [➡FINITENESS, VARIABILITY, AND TRANSIENCE; 96] *Opposite*: permanent

transistor *type of* **audio equipment** [➡AUDIO EQUIPMENT; 1139]

transit *n* **transportation**, transfer, transport, travel, shipment, passage, journey [➡TRANSPORTATION, TRANSPORTERS, AND CARGOS; 322]

transition *n* **changeover**, shift, change, alteration, move, switch, evolution, conversion [➡CHANGE; 372]

transitional *adj* **intermediate**, in-between, interim, provisional, temporary, impermanent, makeshift [➡FINITENESS, VARIABILITY, AND TRANSIENCE; 96] *Opposite*: permanent

transitive *type of* **grammatical term** [➡ASPECTS OF LANGUAGE; 682]

transitory *adj* **fleeting**, passing, brief, temporary, momentary, short-lived, ephemeral, evanescent, transient [➡FINITENESS, VARIABILITY, AND TRANSIENCE; 96] *Opposite*: permanent

See Compare and Contrast at **temporary**.

translate 1 *v* **interpret**, decode, decipher, explain, render (*formal*) [➡SOLVE AND INTERPRET; 760] **2** *v* **convert**, transform, transmute, turn, change [➡CHANGE; 372]

translation *n* **conversion**, paraphrase, version, rendition, interpretation [➡SUMMARIES, OUTLINES, AND EXCERPTS; 588]

translator *n* **interpreter**, decoder, decipherer, converter [➡PEOPLE WHO WORK WITH LANGUAGE AND CODE; 854]

transliterate *v* **transcribe**, convert, translate, transmute, transform, render (*formal*) [➡CHANGE; 372]

transliteration *n* **transcription**, conversion, translation, transformation, rendering, transmutation [➡CHANGE; 372]

translucence 1 *n* **semitransparency**, sheerness, filminess, limpidity, transparency, translucency, pellucidity (*literary*) [➡VISUAL TEXTURE; 1221] *Opposite*: opacity **2** *n* **glow**, luminosity, brightness, luminescence, luminousness, lucidity, translucency [➡DESCRIBING LIGHT; 1228] *Opposite*: dullness

translucency *n* [➡VISUAL TEXTURE; 1221]

translucent 1 *adj* **transparent**, semitransparent, see-through, lucid, clear, lucent [➡VISUAL TEXTURE; 1221] *Opposite*: opaque **2** *adj* **glowing**, luminous, radiant, shining, lustrous, gleaming [➡DESCRIBING LIGHT; 1228] *Opposite*: dull

transmigrate *v* **wander**, migrate, travel, shift, drift, move [➡TRAVEL: WAYS OF TRAVELING; 320] *Opposite*: settle

transmigration *n* **migration**, wandering, traveling, movement, shifting, drifting [➡SELF-PROPULSION; 304]

transmissible *adj* **communicable**, infectious, contagious, catching [➡SICKNESS; 729]

transmission 1 *n* **show**, broadcast, program [➡TELEVISION AND RADIO; 606] **2** *n* **spread**, communication, diffusion, conduction [➡DISPENSE, RATION, AND DISTRIBUTE; 434]

transmit 1 *v* **put on the air**, send out, put out, broadcast [➡EMIT AND EMANATE; 361] **2** *v* **convey**, hand on, spread, communicate, diffuse, conduct, pass on, transfer [➡DISPENSE, RATION, AND DISTRIBUTE; 434]

transmittable *adj* **communicable**, infectious, catching, contagious [➡SICKNESS; 729]

transmittal *n* [➡EXCHANGE AND INTERCHANGE; 448]

transmittance *n* **transmission**, diffusion, conduction, transfer, transferal, transference, spread [➡EXCHANGE AND INTERCHANGE; 448]

transmitter *type of* **telecommunications equipment** [➡TELECOMMUNICATIONS; 1130]

transmogrification *n* [➡CHANGE; 372]

transmogrify *v* [➡CHANGE; 372]

transmutation *n* **transfiguration**, transmogrification, change, transformation, alteration, metamorphosis, mutation, conversion [➡CHANGE; 372]

transmute *v* **transfigure**, transmogrify, transform, alter, change, turn, convert, metamorphose [➡CHANGE; 372]

See Compare and Contrast at **change**.

transnational 1 *adj* **international**, multinational, transcontinental, intercontinental, global, worldwide, large-scale [➡GEOGRAPHIC BORDERS AND BOUNDARIES; 1069] **2** *n* **multinational**, conglomerate, corporation [➡BUSINESS ENTERPRISES AND RELATED BODIES; 792]

transom *type of* **window** [➡WINDOWS; 1100]

transparency 1 *n* **slide**, photograph, photo, shot [➡PHOTOGRAPHY AND PHOTOGRAPHIC EQUIPMENT; 1122] *Opposite*: print **2** *n* **clearness**, limpidity, translucence, filminess, sheerness, pellucidity (*literary*) [➡VISUAL TEXTURE; 1221] *Opposite*: opacity **3** *n* **clarity**, plainness, obviousness, directness, unambiguousness, unmistakability, intelligibility, comprehensibility, simplicity, lucidity, openness, candidness [➡CONCISE AND CLEAR; 202] *Opposite*: ambiguousness

transparent 1 *adj* **see-through**, clear, translucent, crystal clear [➡VISUAL TEXTURE; 1221] *Opposite*: opaque **2** *adj* **obvious**, clear, apparent, plain, evident, visible, patent, blatant, understandable [➡CONCISE AND CLEAR; 202] *Opposite*: unclear

transpire *v* **happen**, occur, take place, come about, go on, go down (*slang*), come to pass (*archaic or literary*) [➡HAPPEN; 27]

transplant *v* **remove**, relocate, move, transfer, shift, resettle, uproot, displace [➡MOVE SOMETHING TO ANOTHER LOCATION; 324]

transplantation *n* **relocation**, movement, transfer, replacement, uprooting, removal, displacement [➡MOVE SOMETHING TO ANOTHER LOCATION; 324]

transport 1 *v* **convey**, move, bring, carry, transfer, ship [➡DISPATCH AND SEND; 333] **2** *n* **conveyance**, carriage, transportation, transference, passage [➡TRANSPORTATION, TRANSPORTERS, AND CARGOS; 322] **3** *n* **vehicle**, transportation, conveyance, means of transport [➡VEHICLES; 1145] **4** *type of* **military aircraft** [➡AIRCRAFT; 1148]

transportable *adj* **mobile**, portable, movable, travel, transferable, lightweight [➡ TRANSPORTATION, TRANSPORTERS, AND CARGOS; 322]

transportation *n* **transport**, conveyance, carriage, transference, passage [➡ TRANSPORTATION, TRANSPORTERS, AND CARGOS; 322]

transported *adj* [➡ PLEASURE, EXCITEMENT, AND ELATION; 534]

transporter **1** *n* **carrier**, hauler, courier, shipper, delivery service [➡ TRANSPORTATION, TRANSPORTERS, AND CARGOS; 322] **2** *type of* **commercial or industrial vehicle** [➡ VEHICLES; 1145]

transposal *n* [➡ EXCHANGE AND INTERCHANGE; 448]

transpose **1** *v* **invert**, switch, reverse, exchange, swap (*informal*) [➡ EXCHANGE AND INTERCHANGE; 448] **2** *v* **move**, transfer, rearrange, alter, reorder, move around [➡ MOVE SOMETHING TO ANOTHER LOCATION; 324]

transposition **1** *n* **reversal**, inversion, switch, exchange, substitution, swap (*informal*) [➡ EXCHANGE AND INTERCHANGE; 448] **2** *n* **rearrangement**, reordering, recasting, relocation, shuffle [➡ MOVE SOMETHING TO ANOTHER LOCATION; 324]

transubstantiation (*formal*) *n* **conversion**, transformation, metamorphosis, mutation, alteration, change [➡ CHANGE; 372]

transverse *adj* **crosswise**, at right angles, sloping, oblique, slanting, crossways, diagonal, corner to corner [➡ ORIENTATION AND ALIGNMENT; 1223]

trap **1** *n* **ruse**, trick, snare, deception, con, ploy, setup (*informal*) [➡ DECEPTION AND LIES; 660] **2** *n* **mouth**, kisser (*slang*), puss (*slang*), gob (*UK slang*) [➡ THE MOUTH; 702] **3** *type of* **wagon or carriage** [➡ BIKES, CARS, AND CARRIAGES; 1149] **4** *v* **catch**, ensnare, entrap, ambush, corner, shut in, fence in, lock in, confine, block [➡ CAPTIVITY AND LOSS OF FREEDOM; 248] *Opposite*: release **5** *v* **trick**, deceive, dupe, con, ensnare, take in, set up (*informal*) [➡ DECEPTION AND LIES; 660]

trap door *n* **hatch**, flap, small door, entrance, doorway, access [➡ DOORS AND ACCESS POINTS; 1101]

trapdoor spider *type of* **arachnid** [➡ ARACHNIDS; 1018]

trapeze artist *type of* **entertainer** [➡ WORKERS IN ENTERTAINMENT AND MEDIA; 873]

trapezium *type of* **angular shape** [➡ ANGULAR SHAPE; 1217]

trapezoid *type of* **angular shape** [➡ ANGULAR SHAPE; 1217]

trapezoidal *adj* [➡ ANGULAR SHAPE; 1217]

trapped **1** *adj* **shut in**, locked in, stuck, surrounded, hemmed in, cut off, imprisoned, entombed, ensnared, confined [➡ CAPTIVITY AND LOSS OF FREEDOM; 248] *Opposite*: released **2** *adj* **stuck**, caught, jammed, stuck fast, wedged, fixed [➡ LACK OF ACTIVITY OR MOTION; 342] *Opposite*: free

trappings *n* **accessories**, accouterments, paraphernalia, trimmings, frills, symbols [➡ PHYSICAL OBJECTS; 1243]

trash **1** *n* **nonsense**, drivel, gibberish, double talk, rubbish, hogwash (*informal*), hot air (*informal*), bunkum (*informal*), malarkey (*informal*), bunk (*slang*) [➡ MEANINGLESS SPEECH OR WRITING; 676] **2** *n* **garbage**, waste, refuse, litter, debris, scrap, rubbish, junk (*informal*) [➡ JUNK AND USELESS OBJECTS; 1249] **3** *v* (*informal*) **wreck**, destroy, ruin, damage, smash, spoil,

demolish, ravage, vandalize [➡ DESTRUCTION AND DEMOLITION; 359] **4** *v* (*informal*) **condemn**, criticize, censure, pan (*informal*), knock (*slang*), slate (*UK*), rubbish (*UK*) [➡ ACCUSE, BLAME, AND CRITICIZE; 641] *Opposite*: praise

trash can *n* [➡ CONTAINERS, RECEPTACLES, AND PACKAGING; 1245]

trashy *adj* **cheap**, worthless, tasteless, shabby, poor quality, shoddy, rubbishy, tacky (*informal*), crummy (*informal*) [➡ IN BAD REPAIR; 1234] *Opposite*: quality

trattoria *type of* **eating place** [➡ HOTELS, RESTAURANTS, AND CLUBS; 1082]

trauma *n* **shock**, upset, disturbance, ordeal, suffering, strain, distress, damage, pain [➡ DIFFICULT SITUATIONS; 72]

traumatic *adj* **shocking**, disturbing, upsetting, distressing, harrowing, stressful, painful [➡ EMOTIONALLY UNPLEASANT AND UPSETTING; 227]

traumatize **1** *v* **shock**, upset, distress, devastate, disturb, stress, torment [➡ UPSET, DISTRESS, AND HUMILIATE; 567] **2** *v* **injure**, hurt, wound, fracture, break, cut, lacerate, gash [➡ WOUND A PERSON OR ANIMAL; 383]

traumatized *adj* **disturbed**, shocked, upset, troubled, distressed, in shock, devastated [➡ SADNESS, DISTRESS, AND DESPAIR; 539] *Opposite*: unaffected

travail *n* **hard work**, toil, effort, exertion, labor, struggle [➡ HARD WORK OR EFFORT; 298]

travel **1** *v* **journey**, tour, take a trip, voyage, trek, go, pass through, move, cover [➡ TRAVEL: WAYS OF TRAVELING; 320] **2** *adj* **portable**, lightweight, foldaway, collapsible, transportable, mobile [➡ SMALL; 1195]

travel bug *n* [➡ TRAVEL: SIGHTSEEING AND TOURISM; 321]

travel case *type of* **baggage** [➡ CONTAINERS, RECEPTACLES, AND PACKAGING; 1245]

traveler **1** *n* **tourist**, vacationer, passenger, sightseer, visitor, journeyer, holidaymaker (*UK*) [➡ TRAVEL: TRAVELERS AND WALKERS; 319] **2** *n* **itinerant**, traveling worker, nomad, rover, wanderer, New Age traveler [➡ NOMADIC AND ROOTLESS LIFESTYLES; 884]

travel guide *n* [➡ TRAVEL: SIGHTSEEING AND TOURISM; 321]

travelog *see* **travelogue**

travelogue *n* **travel piece**, talk, lecture, travel program [➡ TELEVISION AND RADIO; 606]

travels *n* **voyage**, journey, trip, exploration, trekking, touring [➡ TRAVEL: JOURNEYS AND TRIPS; 318]

travel-sick *adj* **queasy**, nauseous, unwell, ill, seasick, carsick, airsick [➡ ILL AND SICK; 740]

traverse *v* **cross**, pass through, negotiate, navigate, go across, go over, crisscross [➡ MOVE PAST, INTO, OR THROUGH SOMETHING; 331]

travesty *n* **charade**, caricature, sham, parody, pretense, mockery, farce [➡ DECEPTION AND LIES; 660]

trawl **1** *v* **fish**, catch fish, go fishing [➡ HOBBIES, GAMES, AND SPORTS; 875] **2** *v* (*UK*) **hunt**, search, rummage around, sift, look through, scan, check [➡ SEEK POSSESSION AND SEARCH; 456]

3 *n* (*UK*) **search**, investigation, hunt, rummage, scan, look [➡ SEEK POSSESSION AND SEARCH; 456]

trawler *type of* **motor vessel** [➡ SHIPS AND BOATS; 1150]

tray **1** *n* **salver**, platter, serving dish, plate, oven tray, baking tray (*UK*) [➡ TABLEWARE, FLATWARE, AND KITCHENWARE; 861] **2** *n* **receptacle**, container, in-box, out-box, in-tray (*UK*), out-tray (*UK*) [➡ CONTAINERS, RECEPTACLES, AND PACKAGING; 1245]

treacherous **1** *adj* **unfaithful**, traitorous, disloyal, deceitful, false, double-crossing, underhand, two-faced, untrustworthy, shifty, duplicitous, perfidious (*formal*) [➡ LACK OF COMMITMENT AND UNRELIABILITY; 509] *Opposite*: loyal **2** *adj* **dangerous**, hazardous, precarious, unsafe, perilous, risky, unstable, unsound [➡ DANGEROUS; 236] *Opposite*: safe

treacherousness *n* [➡ LACK OF COMMITMENT AND UNRELIABILITY; 509]

treachery *n* **deceit**, treason, deceitfulness, sedition, disloyalty, duplicity, betrayal, perfidy (*formal*) [➡ LACK OF COMMITMENT AND UNRELIABILITY; 509] *Opposite*: loyalty

treacle (*UK*) *n* [➡ SUGAR AND PRESERVES; 1184]

treacly **1** *adj* **sentimental**, mawkish, romanticized, romantic, slushy, corny, sappy, cheesy, hokey, cloying, syrupy, soppy (*informal*) [➡ IN POOR TASTE AND OVERSENTIMENTAL; 229] **2** *adj* (*UK*) **sticky**, glutinous, gooey, gluey, syrupy, gummy, cloying, tacky, glue-like [➡ PHYSICAL TEXTURE; 1222]

tread **1** *v* **trample**, crush, squash, flatten, stomp, press [➡ CHANGE OF SHAPE; 385] **2** *v* **walk**, step, stride, tramp, pace, plod [➡ PROCEED AND GO; 305] **3** *n* **step**, footstep, footfall, tramp, stamp, plod [➡ IMPACT SOUNDS; 1260]

treadle *n* **foot pedal**, lever, control [➡ PARTS OF MACHINES AND TOOLS; 1118]

treadmill *n* **daily grind**, routine, drudgery, toil, slog, grindstone [➡ HARD WORK OR EFFORT; 298]

treason *n* **sedition**, treachery, disloyalty, subversion, betrayal, duplicity, high treason [➡ MORALLY BAD OR IMPROPER; 775] *Opposite*: allegiance

treasonable *adj* **traitorous**, treacherous, subversive, disloyal, rebellious, seditious, mutinous [➡ MORALLY BAD OR IMPROPER; 775]

treasure **1** *n* **wealth**, riches, money, valuables, cache, hoard, booty, plunder [➡ FINANCIAL ASSETS; 462] **2** *n* **star**, paragon, pearl, prize, gem (*informal*), peach (*informal*) [➡ AMAZING THINGS; 211] **3** *v* **cherish**, value, prize, adore, hold dear, appreciate [➡ LIKE, LOVE, VALUE, AND ENJOY; 578] *Opposite*: neglect

treasured *adj* **dear**, precious, loved, cherished, beloved, valued, adored, prized [➡ POPULAR AND WANTED; 220]

treasurer *n* **banker**, bursar, bookkeeper, accountant, financial officer [➡ PEOPLE INVOLVED IN FINANCE; 804]

treasury *type of* **storage space** [➡ STORES AND STORAGE BUILDINGS; 1088]

treat **1** *v* **regard**, behave toward, consider, act toward, think of, deal with, handle [➡ CARRY OUT AN ACTION; 269] **2** *v* **care for**, take care of, doctor, cure, nurse, heal, minister to, remedy [➡ TAKE CARE OF AND SPOIL; 300] **3** *v* **pay for**, pick up the check, pick up the tab, pay the bill, give [➡ GIVE MONEY; 433] **4** *v* **indulge**, spoil, pamper, make a fuss of [➡ TAKE CARE OF AND SPOIL; 300] **5** *v* **deal with**, go into, discuss, handle, touch on, talk about, talk over, talk of, consider, take up, be concerned with [➡ BE ABOUT SOMETHING; 62] **6** *n* **luxury**, extravagance, indulgence, delight, pleasure [➡ TREATS; 210] *Opposite*: necessity

treatise *n* **dissertation**, discourse, essay, thesis, paper, exposition, article, piece, tract [➡ ANALYTICAL NONFICTION WRITING; 592]

treat like royalty *v* [➡ TAKE CARE OF AND SPOIL; 300]

treatment **1** *n* **cure**, healing, care, therapy, medicine, medication, remedy [➡ REMEDIES, TREATMENTS, AND OPERATIONS; 731] **2** *n* **handling**, behavior, conduct, dealing, management, usage [➡ WAYS OF DOING THINGS; 294]

treaty *n* **agreement**, accord, contract, pact, truce, settlement [➡ OFFICIAL DOCUMENTS; 586]

treble **1** *adj* **triple**, three times, thrice, threefold [➡ APPORTIONMENT; 113] **2** *adj* **high-pitched**, high, shrill, piping [➡ LOUD, HIGH, OR UNPLEASANT SOUNDS; 1266] **3** *v* **increase**, triple, increase threefold, increase by three, multiply, swell [➡ CHANGE OF INTENSITY: MORE; 394]

tree **1** *n* **sapling**, bush, shrub [➡ PLANTS AND TREES; 1024] **2** *n* **diagram**, tree diagram, family tree, hierarchy, pyramid, graphic [➡ DRAWINGS, CHARTS, AND TABLES; 594]

tree frog *type of* **amphibian** [➡ AMPHIBIANS; 1008]

treetop *n* **crown**, canopy, foliage [➡ PARTS OF TREES AND PLANTS; 1026]

trek **1** *v* **hike**, walk, ramble, march, tramp, trudge, trail, slog, wander, journey, travel, schlep (*informal*) [➡ TRAVEL: WAYS OF TRAVELING; 320] **2** *n* **walk**, hike, ramble, journey, march, tramp, slog, trudge, trail, wander [➡ TRAVEL: JOURNEYS AND TRIPS; 318]

trekker *n* [➡ TRAVEL: TRAVELERS AND WALKERS; 319]

trekking *n* [➡ HOBBIES, GAMES, AND SPORTS; 875]

trellis *n* **lattice**, grille, fence, fencing, frame, framework [➡ BARRIERS; 1113]

tremble **1** *v* **shiver**, shake, shudder, quiver, judder, quaver, quake (*informal*) [➡ PHYSICAL REACTIONS; 316] **2** *n* **shake**, shiver, shudder, quake, quiver, tremor, vibration, wobble, judder, quaver [➡ PHYSICAL REACTIONS; 316]

trembling **1** *n* **shaking**, vibrating, quivering, shuddering, wobbling, quaking [➡ DESCRIBING BODY MOVEMENTS; 288] **2** *adj* **unsteady**, vibrating, quivering, shuddering, quaking, wobbly, shaky, rocky, juddering [➡ DESCRIBING BODY MOVEMENTS; 288] *Opposite*: still **3** *adj* **timorous**, tremulous, nervous, terrified, fearful, apprehensive [➡ FEAR AND PANIC; 543] *Opposite*: confident

tremblingly *adv* **fearfully**, nervously, apprehensively, timorously, tremulously, hesitantly [➡ FEAR AND PANIC; 543] *Opposite*: confidently

tremendous **1** *adj* **great**, incredible, fabulous, terrific, marvelous, wonderful, fantastic, remarkable, awesome, magnificent, sensational, out of this world, superb, super (*informal*) [➡ EXTRAORDINARY: AMAZING; 204] *Opposite*: awful **2** *adj* **huge**, great, enormous, vast, immense, monstrous, awe-inspiring, terrific, colossal, massive, impressive, humongous (*informal*) [➡ LARGE; 1193] *Opposite*: tiny

tremendously *adv* **very**, extremely, greatly, enormously, vastly, immensely, terrifically, remarkably, exceptionally, extraordinarily, exceedingly, impressively, massively (*informal*) [➡ TO A GREAT EXTENT; 132] *Opposite*: slightly

tremor 1 *n* **shake**, tremble, vibration, quiver, shiver, shudder, judder, quaver [➡ PHYSICAL REACTIONS; 316] 2 *n* **earthquake**, shock, quake (*informal*) [➡ VOLCANOES AND EARTHQUAKES; 1054]

tremulous 1 *adj* **unsteady**, quivering, trembling, quavering, shaky, wobbly [➡ DESCRIBING BODY MOVEMENTS; 288] *Opposite*: steady 2 *adj* **timid**, timorous, trembling, shy, fearful, bashful, shrinking, nervous [➡ FEAR AND PANIC; 543] *Opposite*: confident

trench *n* **ditch**, channel, drain, dugout, trough, gutter, furrow [➡ WATERCOURSES; 1111]

trenchancy *n* **incisiveness**, forcefulness, acerbity, brutality, directness, outspokenness [➡ RUDE AND HOSTILE; 625] *Opposite*: gentleness

trenchant *adj* **incisive**, cutting, sharp, biting, acerbic, severe, scathing, forceful, direct, forthright, caustic, penetrating [➡ RUDE AND HOSTILE; 625] *Opposite*: mild

trench coat *type of* **overcoat** [➡ GARMENTS AND OUTFITS; 865]

trend 1 *n* **tendency**, drift, leaning, inclination, movement, development [➡ DIRECTION OF MOTION; 345] 2 *n* **fashion**, style, look, craze, vogue, fad, thing (*informal*) [➡ FADS, FETISHES, AND IDOLATRY; 555]

trendsetter *n* **innovator**, pacesetter, modernizer, leader, leading light, guru [➡ DESIGNERS, CREATORS, AND INSTIGATORS; 347] *Opposite*: imitator

trendsetting *adj* **influential**, innovative, cutting-edge, leading, new, inventive [➡ EXTRAORDINARY: AMAZING; 204] *Opposite*: conventional

trendy (*informal*) *adj* **fashionable**, in, up-to-the-minute, cool, stylish, chic, all the rage, popular, up-to-date, hip (*slang*) [➡ NEW, MODERN; 166] *Opposite*: unfashionable

trepidation *n* **fear**, anxiety, unease, nervousness, apprehension, consternation, foreboding, concern, misgivings, disquiet [➡ FEELINGS ABOUT THE FUTURE; 533] *Opposite*: equanimity (*formal*)

trespass *v* **intrude**, infringe, encroach, invade, interlope [➡ ARRIVE; 12]

trespasser *n* **intruder**, squatter, interloper, snooper (*informal*) [➡ CRIMINALS; 821] *Opposite*: guest

tress *n* **lock**, strand, curl, tuft, wisp [➡ HAIR; 484]

tresses *n* **locks** (*literary*), hair, curls, ringlets [➡ HAIR; 484]

trestle *n* **support**, bracket, stand, frame, framework, base [➡ SUPPORTS AND BASES; 1255]

trestle table *type of* **table** [➡ FURNITURE; 858]

trews *type of* **pants** [➡ GARMENTS AND OUTFITS; 865]

triad *n* **trio**, threesome, triangle, troika, triumvirate, triplet [➡ GROUPS OF PEOPLE; 935]

trial 1 *n* **test**, examination, experiment, tryout, audition, assessment [➡ PREPARATORY EVENTS; 57] 2 *n* **hearing**, court case, court-martial, prosecution, legal proceedings, legal action [➡ TRIAL, PUNISHMENT, AND LEGAL OUTCOMES; 819] 3 *n* **ordeal**, hardship, suffering, trouble, misery, distress, burden, worry, difficulty, anxiety, tribulation, pain [➡ NUISANCES; 253] 4 *adj* **experimental**, probationary, pilot, provisional, test, sample [➡ EXAMINE AND ASSESS; 753]

trial lawyer *n* [➡ PEOPLE IN LAW COURTS; 820]

trial run *n* [➡ PREPARATORY EVENTS; 57]

trial size *adj* [➡ SMALL; 1195]

triangle 1 *type of* **angular shape** [➡ ANGULAR SHAPE; 1217] 2 *type of* **percussion instrument** [➡ MUSICAL INSTRUMENTS; 910] 3 *n* **threesome**, trio, three-way relationship, triad, trinity, triplet [➡ GROUPS OF PEOPLE; 935]

triangular *adj* **three-sided**, trilateral, three-cornered, wedge-shaped, deltoid [➡ ANGULAR SHAPE; 1217]

Triangulum *type of* **constellation** [➡ HEAVENLY BODIES; 1061]

Triangulum Australe *type of* **constellation** [➡ HEAVENLY BODIES; 1061]

Triassic *type of* **period** [➡ EPOCHS AND ERAS; 89]

triathlon *type of* **track and field** [➡ HOBBIES, GAMES, AND SPORTS; 875]

tribal *adj* **ethnic**, family, ancestral, familial, group [➡ THE FAMILY; 956]

tribe 1 *n* **people**, ethnic group, community, society, population [➡ GROUPS OF PEOPLE; 935] 2 *n* (*informal*) **family**, clan, kinfolk, people (*informal*) [➡ THE FAMILY; 956]

tribulation *n* **misfortune**, trial, suffering, ordeal, distress, difficulty, trouble, problem, hardship, misery, pain [➡ NUISANCES; 253]

tribunal 1 *n* **court**, court of law, law court [➡ TRIAL, PUNISHMENT, AND LEGAL OUTCOMES; 819] 2 *n* **board**, panel, committee, body [➡ BUSINESS ENTERPRISES AND RELATED BODIES; 792]

tributary *n* **branch**, arm, offshoot, river, stream, bayou [➡ RIVERS, LAKES, AND STREAMS; 1042]

tribute 1 *n* **compliment**, mark of respect, honor, praise, acknowledgment, esteem, accolade, homage [➡ PRAISE AND ENCOURAGE; 647] 2 *n* **tax**, duty, excise, toll, payment, fee, levy [➡ TAX AND TAXATION; 802]

trice *n* **instant**, flash, moment, twinkling, no time, blink of an eye, jiffy (*informal*) [➡ SHORT PERIODS OF TIME; 93]

triceps *type of* **muscle or tendon** [➡ THE MUSCLES; 718]

triceratops *type of* **dinosaur** [➡ DINOSAURS; 996]

trick 1 *n* **deception**, ploy, ruse, hoax, dodge, swindle, trap, scam (*slang*) [➡ DECEPTION AND LIES; 660] 2 *n* **joke**, prank, stunt, caper [➡ JOKES AND TEASING; 674] 3 *n* **knack**, technique, skill, secret [➡ WAYS OF DOING THINGS; 294] 4 *n* **habit**, mannerism, trait, characteristic, way, quirk [➡ PERSONAL ECCENTRICITIES; 493] 5 *v* **deceive**, cheat, mislead, trap, fool, dupe, hoodwink, con [➡ DECEPTION AND LIES; 660] 6 *adj* **fake**, false, artificial, bogus, hoax, pretend [➡ FALSE AND UNREAL; 173] *Opposite*: real

trickery 1 *n* **deception**, deceit, fraud, scam (*slang*), sting (*slang*) [➡ DECEPTION AND LIES; 660] 2 *n* **dishonesty**, deception, deceit, fraudulence, chicanery, hocus-pocus [➡ DECEPTION AND LIES; 660]

trickily *adv* **craftily**, sneakily, guilefully, cunningly, slyly, deviously, cleverly [➡DECEITFUL; 513] *Opposite*: straightforwardly

trickiness 1 *n* **difficulty**, complication, delicacy, awkwardness, intricacy, complexity [➡DIFFICULTY AND COMPLEXITY; 242] *Opposite*: simplicity 2 *n* **craftiness**, slipperiness, deviousness, slyness, duplicity, deceitfulness, wiliness, sneakiness, cleverness, cunning [➡DECEITFUL; 513] *Opposite*: honesty

trickle 1 *v* **drip**, drop, seep, dribble, ooze, filter [➡LIQUID EMISSION; 370] *Opposite*: flood 2 *n* **dribble**, drop, drip [➡AMOUNTS OF LIQUID; 114] *Opposite*: flood

trickster *n* **cheat**, swindler, charlatan, fraud, slippery customer, con artist (*slang*) [➡PEOPLE WHO DECEIVE; 661]

tricky 1 *adj* **complicated**, delicate, awkward, thorny, problematic, complex, difficult, risky [➡DIFFICULTY AND COMPLEXITY; 242] *Opposite*: simple 2 *adj* **devious**, sly, deceitful, crafty, cunning, scheming, wily, artful, slippery [➡DECEITFUL; 513] *Opposite*: straight

tricky situation *n* [➡DIFFICULT SITUATIONS; 72]

tricycle *type of* **bike** [➡BIKES, CARS, AND CARRIAGES; 1149]

tried and tested *adj* [➡KNOWN AND FAMOUS; 181]

trier 1 *n* **tester**, experimenter, taster, volunteer, guinea pig, user [➡WORKERS; 836] 2 *n* **sticker**, fighter, striver, struggler, stayer, go-getter (*informal*) [➡PEOPLE WHO ARE APPROVED OF; 955] *Opposite*: defeatist

trifle 1 *n* **nothing**, frippery, triviality [➡UNIMPORTANT AND UNNECESSARY; 238] 2 *n* **smidgen**, bit, little, drop, touch, tad (*informal*) [➡FEW, LITTLE, SMALL AMOUNT; 120]

trifling *adj* **trivial**, petty, small, tiny, silly, slight, unimportant, negligible, inconsequential, minor, marginal, frivolous, insignificant [➡UNIMPORTANT AND UNNECESSARY; 238] *Opposite*: significant

trigger *v* **activate**, set off, cause, generate, start, prompt, elicit, produce, initiate, spark [➡CAUSE TO START; 265] *Opposite*: halt

trigger-happy (*informal*) *adj* **rash**, violent, dangerous, wild, unpredictable [➡AGGRESSIVE AND BELLIGERENT; 518]

trigger off *v* **activate**, set off, cause, generate, start, prompt, elicit, produce, initiate, spark off [➡CAUSE TO START; 265] *Opposite*: halt

trigonometry *n* [➡MATH; 597]

trilateral *adj* [➡ANGULAR SHAPE; 1217]

trilby *type of* **hat** [➡ACCESSORIES, MILLINERY, AND LINGERIE; 867]

trill 1 *v* **warble**, quaver, shrill, tweet, vibrate [➡SOUND EMISSION BY ANIMALS OR BIRDS; 364] 2 *type of* **bird sound** [➡SOUNDS MADE BY BIRDS; 1263]

trillion (*informal*) *n* **lots**, heaps (*informal*), tons (*informal*), loads (*informal*), stacks (*informal*) [➡MANY, MUCH, LARGE AMOUNT; 117]

trilogy *n* **series**, sequence, set, cycle, trio [➡BOOKS AND BOOKLETS; 590]

trim 1 *v* **clip**, cut, shear, pare, prune, shave, lop off

[➡EXTRACT AND SEVER; 341] *Opposite*: lengthen 2 *v* **cut back**, prune, decrease, lower, shave, lop off, edit, truncate, reduce [➡CHANGE OF SIZE: SMALLER; 393] *Opposite*: augment (*formal*) 3 *v* **decorate**, adorn, embroider, embellish, edge, border, deck (*literary*) [➡DECORATE, ADORN, AND APPLY COATINGS; 405] 4 *adj* **tidy**, orderly, smart, spruce, dapper, spick and span, neat, natty [➡ORDER AND ORGANIZATION; 206] *Opposite*: messy 5 *adj* **slim**, fit, shapely, sleek, slender, lean, neat, in shape [➡BUILD; 477] *Opposite*: bulky 6 *n* **decoration**, adornment, frill, edge, border [➡ORNAMENTS AND DECORATIONS; 1248]

trimaran *type of* **sailing vessel** [➡SHIPS AND BOATS; 1150]

trimester *type of* **time period** [➡TIMES OF YEAR; 88]

trimly *adv* **neatly**, sleekly, compactly, tidily [➡ORDER AND ORGANIZATION; 206]

trimming *n* **decoration**, adornment, frill, garnish, extra, edge, border [➡ORNAMENTS AND DECORATIONS; 1248]

trimmings 1 *n* **side dishes**, extras, accompaniments, fixings (*informal*) [➡PREPARED DISHES; 1170] 2 *n* **extras**, accompaniments, add-ons, accessories, embellishments, bells and whistles (*slang*), appurtenances (*formal*), bits and pieces (*UK informal*) [➡ORNAMENTS AND DECORATIONS; 1248] 3 *n* **clippings**, parings, bits, pieces, nail clippings, nail parings [➡REMAINDER AND REMAINDERS; 125]

trimness *n* **neatness**, compactness, tidiness, sleekness, thinness, leanness, slenderness [➡SMALL; 1195]

trinity *n* **threesome**, trio, triad, troika, triplet [➡GROUPS OF PEOPLE; 935]

trinket *n* **ornament**, charm, knickknack, bauble, gewgaw [➡ORNAMENTS AND DECORATIONS; 1248]

trio 1 *n* **threesome**, triad, troika, trinity, triangle, triplet [➡GROUPS OF PEOPLE; 935] 2 *type of* **band** [➡MUSICIANS AND SINGERS; 908]

trip 1 *n* **journey**, tour, excursion, expedition, outing, voyage, jaunt, spree, visit [➡TRAVEL: JOURNEYS AND TRIPS; 318] 2 *n* **slip**, stumble, tumble, fall [➡GO DOWNWARD; 307] 3 *v* **stumble**, trip up, slip, tumble, falter, fall, lose your footing [➡GO DOWNWARD; 307] 4 *v* **skip**, hop, prance, caper, dance [➡FIDGET AND FROLIC; 311]

tripartite *adj* **three-way**, three-party, multilateral, triple [➡APPORTIONMENT; 113]

tripe (*informal*) *n* **rubbish**, nonsense, garbage, drivel, trash, rot (*informal*), claptrap (*informal*), twaddle (*informal*) [➡MEANINGLESS SPEECH OR WRITING; 676] *Opposite*: fact

trip hop *type of* **electronic music** [➡MUSIC, SONGS, AND SINGING; 907]

triple 1 *adj* **tripartite**, three-way, three-layered, triple-decker [➡APPORTIONMENT; 113] *Opposite*: single 2 *adj* **treble**, threefold, multiple [➡APPORTIONMENT; 113] *Opposite*: single 3 *v* **treble**, triplicate, multiply by three, increase, boost, augment (*formal*) [➡CHANGE OF SIZE: BIGGER; 392] *Opposite*: reduce

triple bottom line *n* [➡ACCOUNTING, BANKING, AND BUDGETING; 799]

triple jump *type of* **track and field** [➡HOBBIES, GAMES, AND SPORTS; 875]

triplet 1 *n* **trio**, triad, threesome, troika [➡GROUPS OF PEOPLE; 935] 2 *type of* **offspring** [➡YOUNGER GENERATION RELATIVES; 958]

tripod *type of* **photographic equipment** [➡ PHOTOGRAPHY AND PHOTO-GRAPHIC EQUIPMENT; 1122]

trip up 1 *v* **stumble**, trip, slip, tumble, fall, lose your footing [➡ GO DOWNWARD; 307] 2 *v* **trap**, trick, confuse, disconcert, unsettle, wrong-foot, catch out (*informal*) [➡ CONFUSE AND BEWILDER; 571]

trite *adj* **commonplace**, stale, tired, pedestrian, worn, hackneyed, clichéd, banal, unoriginal, stock, corny, hokey (*informal*) [➡ ORDINARINESS; 244] *Opposite:* original

triteness *n* **dullness**, tiredness, staleness, corniness, banality, unoriginality [➡ ORDINARINESS; 244] *Opposite:* originality

triumph 1 *n* **victory**, achievement, conquest, accomplishment, coup, feat, success [➡ SUCCESS; 82] *Opposite:* failure 2 *n* **rejoicing**, pride, elation, delight, satisfaction, jubilation, exultation, glee, joy [➡ PLEASURE, EXCITEMENT, AND ELATION; 534] *Opposite:* sorrow 3 *v* **succeed**, prevail, win, overcome, be victorious, win out, carry the day, win through (*UK*) [➡ SUCCEED AND WIN; 79] *Opposite:* lose

triumphal *adj* **ceremonial**, commemorative, victory, heroic, celebratory, great, grand [➡ SUCCESSFUL AND PROMISING; 81]

triumphant 1 *adj* **winning**, victorious, glorious, dominant, proud, conquering [➡ SUCCESSFUL AND PROMISING; 81] 2 *adj* **exultant**, celebratory, jubilant, elated, delighted, gleeful [➡ PLEASURE, EXCITEMENT, AND ELATION; 534] *Opposite:* sorrowful

triumphantly *adv* **exultantly**, jubilantly, elatedly, delightedly, gleefully [➡ SUCCESSFUL AND PROMISING; 81] *Opposite:* sorrowfully

triumph over *v* **overcome**, defeat, beat, prevail over, get the better of, humiliate, vanquish, conquer [➡ BEAT AND DEFEAT; 80]

See Compare and Contrast at **defeat**.

triumvirate *n* **trio**, threesome, triad, troika, triplet, triangle [➡ GROUPS WITH A COMMON INTEREST; 938]

trivet *n* **stand**, support, rest, tripod [➡ SUPPORTS AND BASES; 1255]

trivia *n* **minutiae**, trivialities, froth, nonsense, trifles, small beer (*informal*), small potatoes (*informal*) [➡ UNIMPORTANT AND UNNECESSARY; 238] *Opposite:* essentials

trivial *adj* **unimportant**, small, inconsequential, slight, trifling, petty, marginal, frivolous, negligible, minor, insignificant [➡ UNIMPORTANT AND UNNECESSARY; 238] *Opposite:* crucial

triviality 1 *n* **unimportance**, inconsequence, worthlessness, insignificance, pettiness, inconsequentiality, frivolity [➡ UNIMPORTANT AND UNNECESSARY; 238] *Opposite:* importance 2 *n* **trifle**, nothing, frippery [➡ UNIMPORTANT AND UNNECESSARY; 238]

trivialize *v* **play down**, belittle, underestimate, make light of, tone down [➡ UNDERDO SOMETHING; 291] *Opposite:* highlight

trivialness *n* [➡ ORDINARINESS; 244]

troika 1 *n* **trio**, triumvirate, threesome, triad, triplet, triangle [➡ GROUPS OF PEOPLE; 935] 2 *type of* **wagon or carriage** [➡ BIKES, CARS, AND CARRIAGES; 1149]

troll 1 *v* **fish**, angle, trail, spin, lure [➡ SEEK POSSESSION AND SEARCH; 456] 2 *v* **amble**, wander, saunter, drift, walk, stroll [➡ MOVE SLOWLY; 314] 3 *n* **giant**, ogre, hobgoblin, goblin, monster [➡ MYTHICAL BEINGS; 789]

trolley *n* [➡ BIKES, CARS, AND CARRIAGES; 1149]

trombone *type of* **brass instrument** [➡ MUSICAL INSTRUMENTS; 910]

troop 1 *n* **crowd**, horde, throng, multitude, herd, flock, drove, company, pack, group [➡ GROUPS OF PEOPLE; 935] 2 *type of* **herd** [➡ GROUPS OF ANIMALS; 993] 3 *v* **move**, gather, rally, come together, get together, congregate [➡ GET CLOSER TOGETHER; 310] 4 *v* **march**, parade, stream, trudge, traipse, file [➡ PROCEED AND GO; 305]

trooper *n* [➡ PEOPLE WHO ARE APPROVED OF; 955]

troops *n* [➡ THE ARMED FORCES; 827]

trophy *n* **cup**, award, medal, crown, title, plaque, plate, shield, prize [➡ REWARDS AND AWARDS; 439]

tropical *adj* **hot**, steamy, humid, sultry, stifling [➡ HOT WEATHER; 1050] *Opposite:* temperate

tropical forest *n* [➡ WOODS, FORESTS, AND JUNGLES; 1047]

tropical storm *n* [➡ WINDY AND STORMY WEATHER; 1053]

troposphere *n* [➡ THE EARTH'S ATMOSPHERE; 1040]

trot *v* **jog**, run, hurry, scurry, scamper [➡ MOVE FAST; 313] *Opposite:* saunter

Trotskyism *n* [➡ PHILOSOPHIES AND BELIEFS; 780]

trotter *type of* **horse** [➡ HORSES; 985]

troubadour *n* **minstrel**, musician, poet, wandering minstrel, bard (*literary or humorous*) [➡ MUSICIANS AND SINGERS; 908]

trouble 1 *n* **worry**, concern, distress, anxiety, care, misfortune, suffering, woe [➡ CONFUSION, ANXIETY, AND WORRY; 540] 2 *n* **problem**, difficulty, dilemma, nuisance, snag, danger, hitch, fault, trial, tribulation, mess, hassle (*informal*) [➡ PROBLEMS; 256] *Opposite:* ease 3 *n* **complaint**, ailment, disease, illness, malady, upset, disorder, condition [➡ SICKNESS; 729] *Opposite:* good health 4 *n* **effort**, bother, inconvenience, work, thought, attention, care [➡ HARD WORK OR EFFORT; 298] 5 *n* **strife**, unrest, disorder, disturbance, discontent, disruption, turmoil, conflict, discord, bother [➡ DISHARMONY; 156] *Opposite:* accord 6 *v* **concern**, worry, distress, agitate, bother, harass, perturb, vex, upset, disturb, hassle (*informal*), bug (*informal*) [➡ UPSET, DISTRESS, AND HUMILIATE; 567] 7 *v* **bother**, put out, inconvenience, disturb, burden, weigh down, interrupt [➡ UPSET, DISTRESS, AND HUMILIATE; 567] 8 *v* **make an effort**, take pains, exert yourself, bother [➡ ATTEMPT AN ACTION; 261] *Opposite:* hang back

See Compare and Contrast at **bother**.

troubled 1 *adj* **anxious**, concerned, bothered, worried, disturbed, distressed, uneasy, upset, unsettled [➡ CONFUSION, ANXIETY, AND WORRY; 540] *Opposite:* calm 2 *adj* **problematic**, tricky, awkward, difficult [➡ DIFFICULTY AND COMPLEXITY; 242] *Opposite:* easy

trouble-free *adj* **easy**, simple, painless, straightforward, uncomplicated [➡ EASE AND SIMPLICITY; 200] *Opposite:* troublesome

troublemaker *n* **mischief-maker**, menace, agitator,

firebrand, rabble-rouser, pest (*informal*), scalawag (*dated informal*) [➡ UNCOOPERATIVE OR REBELLIOUS PEOPLE; 566]

troubleshooter 1 *n* **technician**, engineer, mechanic, problem solver, expert, genius, whiz (*informal*) [➡ TALENTED OR INTELLIGENT PEOPLE; 528] 2 *n* **mediator**, consultant, ombudsman, adviser, problem solver, counselor [➡ ADVISERS, JUDGES, AND ARBITERS; 971]

troublesome 1 *adj* **disorderly**, rowdy, unruly, uncooperative, undisciplined, disruptive, unmanageable, badly behaved, difficult, naughty [➡ REBELLIOUSNESS AND DISOBEDIENCE; 565] *Opposite*: well-behaved 2 *adj* **worrying**, upsetting, bothersome, wearisome, difficult, hard, niggling, problematic, taxing, trying [➡ IRRITATING; 228] *Opposite*: trouble-free

troubling *adj* [➡ EMOTIONALLY UNPLEASANT AND UPSETTING; 227]

trough 1 *n* **manger**, crib, rack, holder [➡ CONTAINERS, RECEPTACLES, AND PACKAGING; 1245] 2 *n* **channel**, furrow, trench, gutter, ditch, drain [➡ HOLES, GAPS, AND FORKS; 1252] 3 *n* **depression**, low, low pressure area [➡ WINDY AND STORMY WEATHER; 1053] *Opposite*: ridge

trounce *v* **beat**, thrash, rout, crush, overwhelm, defeat, hammer (*informal*), slaughter (*slang*), cream (*slang*), stuff (*UK*) [➡ BEAT AND DEFEAT; 80]

See Compare and Contrast at **defeat**.

trounced *adj* [➡ BEATEN AND DEFEATED; 78]

trouncing *n* **routing**, thrashing, crushing, drubbing, beating, pasting (*informal*), hiding (*informal*), hammering (*informal*) [➡ BEAT AND DEFEAT; 80]

troupe *n* **company**, cast, band, ensemble, group [➡ GROUPS OF PEOPLE; 935]

trousseau *n* **bridal goods**, hope chest, bottom drawer (*UK*) [➡ FURNISHING AND HOUSEHOLD LINENS; 860]

trout *type of* **freshwater fish** [➡ FRESHWATER FISH; 1010]

trowel *type of* **general tool** [➡ HAND TOOLS; 1119]

truancy *n* **absence**, nonattendance, absenteeism, malingering [➡ ABSENT AND UNAVAILABLE; 7] *Opposite*: attendance

truant 1 *n* **absentee**, malingerer, shirker [➡ RUNAWAYS AND ABSENTEES; 9] 2 *v* **shirk**, malinger, play hooky (*informal*), go AWOL (*UK*) [➡ RUN AWAY AND AVOID; 10]

truce *n* **ceasefire**, armistice, treaty, peace, respite, break, lull [➡ PEACEFULNESS AND GENTLENESS; 214]

truck *type of* **commercial or industrial vehicle** [➡ VEHICLES; 1145]

truck driver *n* [➡ DRIVERS; 1153]

trucker *n* [➡ DRIVERS; 1153]

truck farm *n* [➡ AGRICULTURE AND FARMING; 1075]

truckload *n* [➡ MANY, MUCH, LARGE AMOUNT; 117]

truck stop *type of* **eating place** [➡ HOTELS, RESTAURANTS, AND CLUBS; 1082]

truculence *n* **defiance**, belligerence, sullenness, insolence, impertinence, cussedness (*informal*) [➡ AGGRESSIVE AND BELLIGERENT; 518] *Opposite*: enthusiasm

truculent *adj* **hostile**, belligerent, defiant, quarrelsome, argumentative, aggressive, fractious, confrontational, obstreperous, sullen, surly, insolent, cussed (*informal*) [➡ AGGRESSIVE AND BELLIGERENT; 518] *Opposite*: easygoing

trudge 1 *v* **tramp**, traipse, slog, plod, trek, hike, march, lumber, trail, schlep (*informal*) [➡ MOVE SLOWLY; 314] 2 *n* **slog**, trek, hike, march, haul, trail [➡ PROCEED AND GO; 305]

true 1 *adj* **factual**, accurate, right, correct, proper, real, exact [➡ EXACT; 203] *Opposite*: false 2 *adj* **real**, genuine, actual, valid, authentic, veritable, bona fide, rightful [➡ TRUE AND REAL; 171] *Opposite*: fake 3 *adj* **faithful**, dedicated, constant, loyal, sincere, firm, staunch, confirmed, dutiful, devoted [➡ HONEST AND RELIABLE; 502] *Opposite*: unfaithful

true-blue 1 *adj* **loyal**, incorruptible, faithful, honest, staunch, orthodox [➡ HONEST AND RELIABLE; 502] *Opposite*: disloyal 2 *adj* (*UK*) **right-wing**, traditional, conservative, diehard, old-school [➡ STYLES AND SYSTEMS OF GOVERNMENT; 806]

true-life *adj* **genuine**, realistic, real-life, real, true, factual [➡ TRUE AND REAL; 171]

true to life *adj* **realistic**, convincing, accurate, authentic, lifelike [➡ TRUE AND REAL; 171] *Opposite*: unrealistic

truffle 1 *type of* **confectionery** [➡ CONFECTIONERY; 1182] 2 *type of* **fungus** [➡ MICROORGANISMS, FUNGI, AND ALGAE; 1023]

truism *n* **axiom**, cliché, maxim, platitude, saying [➡ FIGURES OF SPEECH; 673]

truly 1 *adv* **sincerely**, faithfully, honestly, in all honesty, genuinely, really [➡ TRUE AND REAL; 171] *Opposite*: insincerely 2 *adv* **very**, greatly, really, indeed, exceptionally, enormously, extremely [➡ TO A GREAT EXTENT; 132] 3 *adv* **really**, in fact, beyond doubt, actually, indeed, in reality [➡ TRUE AND REAL; 171]

trump *v* **outdo**, go one better, call somebody's bluff, undermine, outmaneuver, catch somebody napping, outplay, steal a march on somebody (*UK*) [➡ BEAT AND DEFEAT; 80]

trumped-up *adj* **false**, fake, invented, made-up, fabricated, falsified, phony [➡ FALSE AND UNREAL; 173] *Opposite*: genuine

trumpet *type of* **brass instrument** [➡ MUSICAL INSTRUMENTS; 910]

truncate *v* **shorten**, abbreviate, trim, cut, prune, pare [➡ CHANGE OF SIZE: SMALLER; 393] *Opposite*: lengthen

truncated *adj* [➡ UNFINISHEDNESS; 239]

truncheon *type of* **club** [➡ BLUNT INSTRUMENTS AND WHIPS; 1158]

trundle 1 *v* **roll**, roll along, rattle, labor, wheel, push, lumber, drive [➡ PUSH, PULL, AND SLIDE; 335] 2 *v* **traipse**, trail, saunter, lumber, wander, toddle (*informal*) [➡ MOVE SLOWLY; 314]

trundle bed *type of* **bed** [➡ FURNITURE; 858]

trunk 1 *n* **stem**, bole, stalk [➡ PARTS OF TREES AND PLANTS; 1026] 2 *part of* **external structure** [➡ EXTERNAL PARTS OF A VEHICLE; 1147] 3 *n* [➡ PARTS OF THE BODY: TORSO; 693] 4 *type of* **container** [➡ CONTAINERS, RECEPTACLES, AND PACKAGING; 1245]

trunk route *type of* **highway** [➡ ROADS; 1106]

trunks *n* **swimming trunks**, bathing trunks, shorts [➡ GARMENTS AND OUTFITS; 865]

go, stab (*informal*), crack (*informal*), shot (*informal*) [➡ATTEMPT AN ACTION; 261]

Compare and Contrast: *try, attempt, endeavor, strive*

CORE MEANING: to make an effort to do something

try to make an effort or an attempt to do or achieve something; *attempt* to make an effort to do something, especially without much expectation of success; *endeavor* to make a serious and sincere effort to do or achieve something; *strive* to make persistent efforts to achieve something.

---

 adj **annoying**, tiresome, irritating, wearisome, ing, demanding, vexing, exasperating, taxing, [➡EMOTIONALLY UNPLEASANT AND UPSETTING; 227] *Opposite*:

 v **test**, sample, check out, experiment with, praise, evaluate, audition, rehearse [➡EXAMINE AND ASSESS; 753]

tryout n **practice**, run through, trial, rehearsal, preparation, dry run, dummy run (*UK*) [➡PREPARATORY EVENTS; 57]

tryst n **assignation**, rendezvous, meeting, date, encounter, tête-à-tête [➡MEETINGS AND ASSEMBLIES; 43]

try your hand v **experiment**, try out, take a shot, make an attempt, take a stab (*informal*), take a crack (*informal*) [➡ATTEMPT AN ACTION; 261]

tsar n [➡RULERS AND ARISTOCRACY; 823]

tsarina n [➡RULERS AND ARISTOCRACY; 823]

tsarism n [➡STYLES AND SYSTEMS OF GOVERNMENT; 806]

tsaritsa n [➡RULERS AND ARISTOCRACY; 823]

tsetse fly *typo of* **flying insect** [➡FLYING INSECTS; 1013]

T-shirt *type of* **top** [➡GARMENTS AND OUTFITS; 865]

tsunami n [➡THE SEAS, OCEANS, AND SHORES; 1041]

tub 1 n **container**, carton, pot, drum, barrel, cask, butt [➡CONTAINERS, RECEPTACLES, AND PACKAGING; 1245] **2** n **hot tub**, plunge bath, bathtub, bath (*UK*), hip bath (*UK*) [➡FIXTURES; 859]

tuba *type of* **brass instrument** [➡MUSICAL INSTRUMENTS; 910]

tubbiness (*informal*) n [➡BUILD; 477]

tubby (*informal*) adj **plump**, chubby, portly, overweight, heavy, flabby (*informal*), pudgy (*informal*), podgy (*UK*) [➡BUILD; 477] *Opposite*: skinny

tube 1 n **pipe**, cylinder, hose, conduit, duct, spout [➡WATERCOURSES; 1111] **2** n (*informal*) [➡TELEVISION AND RADIO; 606]

tuber n **storage organ**, rhizome, root, underground stem [➡PARTS OF TREES AND PLANTS; 1026]

tube top *type of* **top** [➡GARMENTS AND OUTFITS; 865]

tubing n **tubes**, pipes, plumbing [➡WATERCOURSES; 1111]

tubular adj **tube-shaped**, cylindrical, tube-like, hollow [➡ROUNDED SHAPE; 1218]

tubular bells *type of* **percussion instrument** [➡MUSICAL INSTRUMENTS; 910]

 , unquestioning, believ- [➡NEGATIVE INTELLECTUAL CHARACTERISTICS; 525]
 Opposite: suspicious

trustworthiness n **honesty**, dependability, reliability, fidelity, constancy, responsibility, credibility [➡HONEST AND RELIABLE; 502] *Opposite*: dishonesty

trustworthy adj **dependable**, reliable, responsible, truthful, honest, constant, honorable, upright, faithful, trusty [➡HONEST AND RELIABLE; 502] *Opposite*: corrupt

trusty adj **faithful**, dependable, reliable, constant, loyal, predictable, trustworthy [➡HONEST AND RELIABLE; 502] *Opposite*: unreliable

truth 1 n **fact**, certainty, reality, actuality, veracity, verity (*formal*) [➡TRUE AND REAL; 171] *Opposite*: untruth **2** n **honesty**, integrity, fidelity, sincerity [➡HONEST AND RELIABLE; 502]

truthful 1 adj **honest**, straight, frank, open, straightforward, ingenuous, candid [➡HONEST AND RELIABLE; 502] *Opposite*: dishonest **2** adj **correct**, true, reliable, accurate, exact, literal, factual, faithful, proper, right [➡EXACT; 203] *Opposite*: false

truthfully adv **honestly**, candidly, frankly, openly, straightforwardly, straight, truly [➡HONEST AND RELIABLE; 502] *Opposite*: dishonestly

truthfulness 1 n **honesty**, truth, candor, frankness, openness, straightforwardness, directness [➡HONEST AND RELIABLE; 502] *Opposite*: dishonesty **2** n **accuracy**, reliability, correctness, exactitude, faithfulness, truth [➡EXACT; 203] *Opposite*: inaccuracy

try 1 v **attempt**, strive, aim, seek, undertake, make an effort, struggle, give it a try, take a crack at (*informal*), have a go (*informal*), endeavor (*formal*) [➡ATTEMPT AN ACTION; 261] **2** v **test**, sample, taste, appraise, evaluate, experiment with, check out [➡EXAMINE AND ASSESS; 753] **3** v **strain**, vex, tax, exasperate, annoy, irritate, frustrate [➡ANGER AND ANNOY; 569] *Opposite*: soothe **4** v **judge**, put on trial, hear, take to court [➡TRIAL, PUNISHMENT, AND LEGAL OUTCOMES; 819] **5** n **attempt**, effort,

tuck 1 *v* **insert**, put, push, slip, place, stick (*informal*), pop (*informal*) [➡ POSITION SOMETHING; 325] *Opposite*: remove 2 *v* **pleat**, fold, dart, gather, pucker, ruche [➡ CHANGE OF SHAPE; 385] 3 *n* **pleat**, fold, dart, gather, pucker, ruche [➡ CHANGE OF SHAPE; 385] 4 *n* **food**, nosh (*informal*), grub (*informal*), tucker (*UK informal*) [➡ FOOD; 1167]

tucker (*UK informal*) *n* **food**, nosh (*informal*), grub (*informal*), chow (*slang*), tuck (*UK*) [➡ FOOD; 1167]

Tudor *type of* **pre-20th-century architecture** [➡ BUILDING AND ARCHITECTURE; 1076]

tuff *type of* **stone** [➡ STONES, ROCKS, AND BOULDERS; 1057]

tuft *n* **clump**, tussock, cluster, bunch, truss, tassel [➡ AMOUNTS OF SOLID OR SEMISOLID; 115]

tufted titmouse *type of* **common bird** [➡ BIRDS; 997]

tug 1 *v* **pull**, tow, haul, heave, jerk, yank, wrench [➡ PUSH, PULL, AND SLIDE; 335] *Opposite*: push 2 *n* **yank**, heave, pull, jerk, haul, wrench [➡ PUSH, PULL, AND SLIDE; 335] *Opposite*: push 3 *see* **tugboat**

See Compare and Contrast at **pull.**

tugboat *type of* **motor vessel** [➡ SHIPS AND BOATS; 1150]

tughrik *type of* **currency** [➡ CURRENCIES; 798]

tug of war *n* **tussle**, power struggle, struggle, battle, wrangle, scrimmage [➡ AGGRESSIVE EVENTS; 39] *Opposite*: agreement

tuition *n* **instruction**, teaching, schooling, training, education, guidance, coaching [➡ TEACHING; 839]

tulip *type of* **flower grown from bulbs** [➡ FLOWERS FROM BULBS; 1030]

tulip tree *type of* **deciduous tree** [➡ DECIDUOUS TREES; 1028]

tulle *type of* **synthetic fabric** [➡ FABRICS; 1132]

tumble 1 *v* **fall over**, fall down, stumble, trip up, topple, lurch [➡ GO DOWNWARD; 307] *Opposite*: stand up 2 *v* **plummet**, drop, nose-dive, plunge, dive, fall [➡ CHANGE OF INTENSITY: LESS; 395] *Opposite*: rise

tumbledown *adj* **ramshackle**, rickety, run-down, derelict, dilapidated, ruined, crumbling [➡ IN BAD REPAIR; 1234]

tumble dryer *type of* **appliance** [➡ HOUSEHOLD APPLIANCES; 1117]

tumbler 1 *n* **glass**, tall glass, whiskey glass, highball glass, beaker [➡ TABLEWARE, FLATWARE, AND KITCHENWARE; 861] 2 *n* **acrobat**, gymnast, aerialist, trapeze artist, entertainer [➡ PEOPLE IN SPORTS AND LEISURE; 876]

tumbleweed *type of* **weed** [➡ WEEDS AND THISTLES; 1034]

tumbril *type of* **wagon or carriage** [➡ BIKES, CARS, AND CARRIAGES; 1149]

tummy (*informal*) *n* **stomach**, abdomen, paunch, pot, gut, belly (*informal*) [➡ THE DIGESTIVE TRACT; 709]

tummy ache (*informal*) *n* [➡ DISORDERS OF THE DIGESTIVE SYSTEM; 713]

tummy pain (*informal*) *n* [➡ DISORDERS OF THE DIGESTIVE SYSTEM; 713]

tumor *n* gr[...]cancer, polyp[...]

tumult *n* **upro**[...]labaloo, din, turm[...]turbulence, mayhe[...]site: peace

tumultuous 1 *adj* **turb**[...] [➡ DISORDER AND CHAOS; 245] 2 *adj* [...]boisterous, rowdy, wild, jo[...]OR UNPLEASANT SOUNDS; 1266]

tumulus *n* [➡ BURIAL PLACES AND ACCESS[...]

tuna *type of* **tropical fish** [➡ OCEAN FISH; [...]

tundra *n* [➡ DESERTS, PLAINS, AND MOORLAND; 104[...]

tune 1 *n* **melody**, song, air, jing[...] [➡ MUSIC, SONGS, AND SINGING; 907] 2 *v* **adjus**[...]alter, modify, regulate, pitch, tweak (*in[...]*)[...]PUT RIGHT; 377]

tuneful *adj* **melodic**, melodious, harmo[...]us, [...]pleasant, sweet [➡ SOFT, LOW, OR PLEASANT SOUNDS; [...]65] *Op*[...]discordant

tunefulness *n* [➡ SOFT, LOW, OR PLEASANT SOUNDS; 1265]

tuneless *adj* **unmusical**, droning, monotone, aton[...]monotonous, discordant [➡ LOUD, HIGH, OR UNPLEASANT SOUNDS; 126[...]*Opposite*: tuneful

tuner *type of* **audio equipment** [➡ AUDIO EQUIPMENT; 1139]

tune-up *n* **service**, overhaul, fine-tune, check, maintenance, once-over (*informal*) [➡ EXAMINE AND ASSESS; 753]

tungsten *type of* **metal** [➡ METALS; 1276]

tunic *type of* **top** [➡ GARMENTS AND OUTFITS; 865]

tunnel 1 *n* **channel**, passageway, subway, shaft, underpass [➡ BRIDGES, TUNNELS, CROSSINGS, AND JUNCTIONS; 1112] *Opposite*: bridge 2 *n* **burrow**, hole, warren, earth, sett, den, lair [➡ ANIMAL OR BIRD ACCOMMODATIONS; 1079] 3 *v* **excavate**, burrow, dig, mine, channel, sap [➡ USE TOOLS AND MACHINERY; 468]

turban *type of* **headgear** [➡ ACCESSORIES, MILLINERY, AND LINGERIE; 867]

turbid 1 *adj* **muddy**, cloudy, opaque, dirty, murky, thick [➡ DENSITY AND CONSISTENCY; 1207] *Opposite*: clear 2 *adj* **confused**, muddled, disorganized, scrambled, chaotic, unclear [➡ DISORDER AND CHAOS; 245] *Opposite*: clear

turbine *n* [➡ ENGINES AND HYDRAULICS; 1143]

turbofan *part of* **aircraft** [➡ AIRCRAFT; 1148]

turbojet *part of* **aircraft** [➡ AIRCRAFT; 1148]

turboprop *part of* **aircraft** [➡ AIRCRAFT; 1148]

turbot *type of* **flatfish** [➡ OCEAN FISH; 1009]

turbulence *n* **commotion**, confusion, turmoil, disorder, unrest, instability, hurly-burly, uproar, tumult, furor, chaos, havoc, mayhem (*informal*) [➡ CHAOS AND UPROAR; 51] *Opposite*: calm

turbulent 1 *adj* **confused**, unstable, chaotic, tumultuous, in turmoil, disorderly [➡ DISORDER AND CHAOS; 245] *Opposite*: orderly 2 *adj* **stormy**, tempestuous, raging, choppy, blustery, wild, windy, unsettled [➡ WINDY AND STORMY WEATHER; 1053] *Opposite*: settled **3** *adj* **violent**, rowdy, unruly, riotous, quarrelsome, restless [➡ REBELLIOUSNESS AND DISOBEDIENCE; 565] *Opposite*: peaceful

tureen *n* **bowl**, serving dish, dish, casserole [➡ TABLEWARE, FLATWARE, AND KITCHENWARE; 861]

turf 1 *n* **lawn**, grass, pasture, meadow, verdure, grazing [➡ THE COUNTRYSIDE AND OUTDOOR SPACES; 1071] **2** *n* (*informal*) **area of expertise**, sphere of influence, field, territory, orbit, ambit [➡ SUBJECT AREAS; 768] **3** *n* (*informal*) **territory**, patch, beat, home turf, neighborhood, haunt, neck of the woods [➡ PLACE; 1065]

turgid *adj* **pompous**, boring, dull, hard going, stilted, pretentious, affected, solemn, self-important, ponderous, stuffy [➡ BORING AND UNINTERESTING; 234] *Opposite*: amusing

turkey 1 *type of* **fowl** [➡ FOOD BIRDS; 999] **2** *type of* **meat** [➡ TYPES AND CUTS OF MEAT; 1177] **3** *n* (*slang*) **failure**, flop, fiasco, washout (*informal*), dud (*informal*), lemon (*informal*) [➡ FAILURE; 77] *Opposite*: success

Turkish coffee *type of* **coffee** [➡ DRINKS; 1187]

turmeric *type of* **spice** [➡ HERBS AND SPICES; 1175]

turmoil *n* **chaos**, disorder, confusion, uproar, tumult, commotion, havoc, turbulence, unrest, upheaval, instability, mayhem (*informal*) [➡ CHAOS AND UPROAR; 51] *Opposite*: order

turn 1 *v* **twist**, revolve, rotate, go around, spin, roll, twirl, gyrate, circle [➡ MOVE SOMETHING: ON THE SPOT; 336] **2** *v* **bend**, change direction, bear, veer, meander, curve [➡ CHANGE DIRECTION OF MOTION; 344] **3** *v* **direct**, aim, point, focus, set, set sights on, concentrate [➡ POSITION SOMETHING; 325] **4** *v* **go**, become, alter, convert, transform, metamorphose, change [➡ CHANGE; 372] **5** *v* **curdle**, go sour, sour, spoil, go bad, go off (*UK*) [➡ GO BAD AND CORRODE; 390] **6** *n* **go**, try, chance, opportunity, shot (*informal*), crack (*informal*) [➡ ACTIONS OR UNDERTAKINGS; 259] **7** *n* **rotation**, revolution, twist, spin, twirl, roll, circle [➡ MOVE SOMETHING: ON THE SPOT; 336] **8** *n* **bend**, corner, junction, fork, curve [➡ ROUNDED SHAPE; 1218] **9** *n* **errand**, favor, good turn, service, good deed [➡ KIND ACTIONS OR BEHAVIOR; 295] **10** *n* **ride**, spin, jaunt, trip, outing, excursion, drive [➡ TRAVEL: JOURNEYS AND TRIPS; 318] **11** *n* **fit**, seizure, attack, funny turn, spasm, bout [➡ PAIN AND OTHER PHYSICAL SENSATIONS; 733] **12** *n* **fright**, scare, shock, start, jolt, surprise [➡ SUDDEN EVENTS; 52] **13** *n* **performance**, act, skit, sketch, recitation, party piece (*UK*) [➡ PERFORMANCES AND SHOWS; 42]

turn a blind eye to *v* **overlook**, ignore, take no notice of, disregard, excuse, let pass, let ride, condone [➡ NOT PAY ATTENTION; 764] *Opposite*: condemn

turnabout *n* **reversal**, sea change, U-turn, change, shift [➡ DECISIVE MOMENTS; 44]

turn against *v* **turn on**, reject, rebuff, spurn, exclude, coldshoulder [➡ REFUSING OR REJECTING RELATIONS; 975]

turn around 1 *v* **complete**, finish, accomplish, process [➡ COMPLETE AN ACTION; 263] **2** *v* **improve**, boost, increase, bump up (*informal*) [➡ IMPROVE SOMETHING; 374]

turnaround 1 *n* **reversal**, U-turn, improvement, change, shift, about-face, about-turn (*UK*) [➡ DECISIVE MOMENTS; 44] **2** *n* **dispatch**, processing, completion [➡ ENDS AND DEPARTURES; 54]

turn away *v* **dismiss**, reject, repel, *rebuff*, refuse, spur... [➡ REFUSING OR REJECTING RELATIONS; 975] *Opposite*: welcome

turn away from *v* **reject**, give up, abandon, abjure, relinquish, forswear (*archaic or literary*) [➡ FORGO AND DENY ONESELF; 449] *Opposite*: take up

turn back 1 *v* **go back**, retrace your steps, return [➡ GO BACKWARD; 309] *Opposite*: continue **2** *v* **fold back**, fold down, fold over, turn down, turn over [➡ CHANGE OF SHAPE; 385]

turncoat *n* **traitor**, deserter, defector, collaborator, double agent, spy [➡ PEOPLE WHO DECEIVE; 661]

turn down 1 *v* **refuse**, decline, reject, disallow, veto, rebuff [➡ FORGO AND DENY ONESELF; 449] *Opposite*: accept **2** *v* **lessen**, lower, decrease, reduce, muffle, mute [➡ CHANGE OF INTENSITY: LESS; 395] *Opposite*: turn up

turned-out *adj* **groomed**, dressed, presented, clad, got up (*informal*) [➡ DRESS, WEAR, AND UNDRESS; 868]

turn in 1 *v* (*informal*) **go to bed**, go to sleep, hit the sack (*informal*), hit the hay (*informal*) [➡ SLEEP AND DREAM; 723] *Opposite*: rise **2** *v* **inform on**, blow the whistle on, betray, report, turn over, hand over, snitch on (*slang*) [➡ BETRAY CONFIDENCES AND GOSSIP; 618] **3** *v* **hand in**, hand over, give in, remit, submit, give back, deliver, surrender [➡ PROFFER AND HAND OVER; 431]

turning 1 *n* **joinery**, carpentry, woodworking, carvin... cabinetmaking [➡ CRAFTS AND CARVING; 355] **2** *n* (*UK*) **juncti...** exit, minor road, ramp, off-ramp, turn, turnoff [➡ B... TUNNELS, CROSSINGS, AND JUNCTIONS; 1112] *Opposite*: entrance

turning point *n* **crossroads**, defining moment, deci... moment, crisis, watershed, milestone [➡ DECISIVE MOMENT...

turnip *type of* **root vegetable** [➡ FRUIT AND VEGETABLES; 1176

turn off 1 *v* **switch off**, deactivate, shut down ... stop, turn out [➡ CAUSE TO STOP; 266] *Opposite*: ... n **2** *v* (*informal*) **disgust**, irritate, bore, deter, disple... pel discourage [➡ BORE AND FAIL TO INTEREST; 570] *Opposit*...tract **3** *v* **relax**, unwind, switch off, wind down, ta...t easy [➡ CHANGE OF MOOD AND COMPOSURE; 580] *Opposite*: gear u...

turnoff *n* **turn**, exit, junction, minor road, tu...ng (*UK*) [➡ BRIDGES, TUNNELS, CROSSINGS, AND JUNCTIONS; 1112]

turn of phrase *n* **way with words**, way of p...ng things, way of speaking, style, manner, choice of ...ds [➡ ASPECTS OF LANGUAGE; 682]

turn on 1 *v* **switch on**, start, activate, g...going, set in motion, trigger, initiate, put on [➡ CAUSE TO S...RT; 265] *Opposite*: turn off **2** *v* **depend on**, rest on, hinge on, ...enter on, hang on [➡ RECIPROCITY AND INTERDEPENDENCE; 147] **3** *v* **atta...k**, go for, round on, lay into, set upon, fall on [➡ PHYSICAL A...TACK AND PUNISHMENT; 415] *Opposite*: defend **4** *v* (*informal*) **arouse**, excite, interest, enthuse, stimulate, please [➡ APPEAL TO AND AROUSE INTEREST; 575] *Opposite*: turn off

turn out 1 *v* **produce**, make, manufacture, churn out, assemble, fabricate [➡ MANUFACTURE; 349] **2** *v* **end up**, work out, come out, transpire, result, come about, finish up, happen, become, come to pass (*archaic or literary*) [➡ HAPPEN; 27] **3** *v* **evict**, throw out, empty, eject, expel, force out, get rid of, send away, kick out (*informal*), chuck out (*informal*), turf out (*UK slang*) [➡ EJECT AND EXCLUDE; 340] *Opposite*: welcome **4** *v* **turn off**, switch off, deactivate, shut

own, disable, stop [➡ CAUSE TO STOP; 266] *Opposite*: turn on
5 *v* **attend**, turn up, show up, appear, put in an appearance, come [➡ ARRIVE; 12]

turnout *n* **crowd**, audience, attendance, gathering [➡ AUDIENCES AND ATTENDEES; 937]

turn over 1 *v* **capsize**, flip over, overturn, upturn, turn turtle, keel over [➡ MOVE SOMETHING: INTO A NEW POSITION OR OVERTURN; 330] 2 *v* **mull over**, think about, go over, consider, reflect on, brood over [➡ THINK AND REFLECT; 743] 3 *v* **hand over**, hand in, give in, remit, submit, deliver [➡ PROFFER AND HAND OVER; 431] *Opposite*: hold onto

turnover 1 *n* **incomings**, income, gross revenue, business, revenue, takings [➡ ACCOUNTING, BANKING, AND BUDGETING; 799] *Opposite*: costs 2 *n* **throughput**, sales, trade, business, buying and selling [➡ BUSINESS PRODUCTS; 795] 3 *n* **staff renewal rate**, hiring and firing rate, staff resignation rate, staff resignations, staff turnover [➡ EXCHANGE AND INTERCHANGE; 448] 4 *type of* **cake** [➡ CAKES, COOKIES, AND DESSERTS; 1181]

turnpike *type of* **highway** [➡ ROADS; 1106]

turnstile *n* **gate**, barrier, entrance, park entrance, issing gate (*UK*) [➡ DOORS AND ACCESS POINTS; 1101]

rntable *part of* **audio equipment** [➡ AUDIO EQUIPMENT; 1139]

n the corner *v* **get better**, start to improve, look up, in the turn, be out of danger, be on the up (*informal*) [➡ BETTER; 375]

tto *v* **consult**, refer to, fall back on, resort to, rely ok to, ask for help [➡ INITIATE AND ESTABLISH COMMUNICATION; 680]

turtle *v* **capsize**, flip over, turn over, overturn, up keel over [➡ MOVE SOMETHING: INTO A NEW POSITION OR OVERTURN; 330]

turn 1 *v* **find**, uncover, unearth, dig up, discover, reve [➡ FIND; 463] *Opposite*: conceal 2 *v* **increase**, amplify, inten, boost, step up, raise [➡ CHANGE OF INTENSITY: MORE; 394] *Oppo*: turn down 3 *v* **come to light**, surface, appear, reap, materialize, crop up (*informal*) [➡ APPEAR AND EMERGE; 3] *Oppo*: disappear 4 *v* **arrive**, appear, attend, put in an appeare, come, show up (*informal*) [➡ ARRIVE; 12]

turn y back on *v* **ignore**, abandon, leave behind, put beh you, forsake, disregard, snub, desert [➡ NOT PAY ATTENTION; 7] *Opposite*: take care of

turn you nose up at *v* **scorn**, disdain, sneer at, sniff at, rej, turn down, refuse [➡ FORGO AND DENY ONESELF; 449] *Opposite*: ac pt

turn your stomach *v* **sicken**, disgust, repel, revolt, nauseate, make you heave (*informal*), turn off (*informal*) [➡ UPSET, DISTRESS, AND HUMILIATE; 567] *Opposite*: attract

turpitude (*formal*) *n* **immorality**, wickedness, depravity, baseness, improbity [➡ MORALLY BAD OR IMPROPER; 775]

turquoise 1 *type of* **gemstone** [➡ PRECIOUS STONES; 1278] 2 *type of blue* [➡ COLORS; 1224]

turret *n* **tower**, battlement, steeple, bartizan [➡ TOWERS; 1099]

turtle *type of* **reptile** [➡ REPTILES; 994]

turtleneck *type of* **sweater** [➡ GARMENTS AND OUTFITS; 865]

Tuscana *type of* **constellation** [➡ HEAVENLY BODIES; 1061]

tussle 1 *v* **fight**, brawl, scuffle, clash, struggle, scrap (*informal*) [➡ COMPETE, CONTEND, AND COMBAT; 303] 2 *n* **brawl**, fight, struggle, scuffle, clash, mêlée, dustup (*slang*), scrap (*informal*) [➡ AGGRESSIVE EVENTS; 39]

tussock moth *type of* **moth** [➡ MOTHS AND BUTTERFLIES; 1015]

tut *v* [➡ UNFAVORABLE NONVERBAL RESPONSES; 654]

tutelage *n* **instruction**, guidance, teaching, coaching, expert hand [➡ TEACHING; 839]

tutor 1 *n* **teacher**, instructor, professor, lecturer, trainer, coach, don (*UK*) [➡ EDUCATORS; 840] 2 *v* **teach**, educate, instruct, school, coach, train, lecture [➡ INSTRUCT AND TEACH; 609]

See Compare and Contrast at **teach**.

tutorial *n* **class**, lesson, seminar, lecture, discussion group [➡ CLASSES, COURSEWORK, AND EXAMINATIONS; 842]

tutu *type of* **skirt** [➡ GARMENTS AND OUTFITS; 865]

tux (*informal*) *type of* **jacket** [➡ GARMENTS AND OUTFITS; 865]

tuxedo *type of* **jacket** [➡ GARMENTS AND OUTFITS; 865]

TV (*informal*) *n* **television**, tube, small screen (*informal*), boob tube (*informal*), telly (*UK*), box (*UK slang*) [➡ TELEVISION AND RADIO; 606]

TV dinner *type of* **meal** [➡ MEALS AND PARTS OF MEALS; 1169]

TV set *n* [➡ TELEVISION AND RADIO; 606]

twaddle (*informal*) *n* **nonsense**, balderdash, rubbish, drivel, garbage, claptrap (*informal*), tripe (*informal*), baloney (*informal*) [➡ MEANINGLESS SPEECH OR WRITING; 676] *Opposite*: sense

twang 1 *n* **accent**, drawl, intonation, inflection, resonance [➡ THE SPOKEN WORD; 671] 2 *v* **reverberate**, vibrate, ping, plunk [➡ MUSIC, SONGS, AND SINGING; 907]

tweak 1 *v* **pinch**, nip, jerk, twist, tug, pull, yank [➡ CONTACT: TOUCH; 412] 2 *v* (*informal*) **fine-tune**, correct, adjust, modify, regulate [➡ CHANGE; 372] 3 *n* **nip**, pinch, twist, jerk, tug, pull, yank [➡ CONTACT: TOUCH; 412]

twee (*UK*) *adj* **cutesy**, dainty, sweet, chocolate-box, quaint [➡ BEAUTY AND ATTRACTIVENESS; 189]

tweed *type of* **fabric from animals** [➡ FABRICS; 1132]

tweedy *adj* **casual**, informal, sporty, horsy, outdoor [➡ DESCRIBING CLOTHES; 869]

tweet *v* **chirp**, peep, chirrup, twitter, cheep [➡ SOUND EMISSION BY ANIMALS OR BIRDS; 364]

tweezers *type of* **cosmetic tool** [➡ HAND TOOLS; 1119]

twelve-tone *type of* **classical music** [➡ MUSIC, SONGS, AND SINGING; 907]

twenty-four-hour-a-day *adj* [➡ PERMANENCE: WITHOUT END; 94]

twenty-four/seven *adv* **around the clock**, all the time, constantly, always [➡ PERMANENCE: WITHOUT END; 94]

twice *adv* **two times**, double, twofold [➡ APPORTIONMENT; 113]

twiddle *v* **fidget**, fiddle, play, toy, handle, wiggle [➡ MOVE SOMETHING: ON THE SPOT; 336]

twiddle your thumbs *v* [➡ LACK OF ACTIVITY OR MOTION; 342]

twig *n* **branch**, shoot, stem, stick [➡ PARTS OF TREES AND PLANTS; 1026]

twilight *n* **dusk**, nightfall, evening, sunset, sundown, half-light [➡ TIMES OF DAY; 87] *Opposite*: dawn

twilit *adj* **dusky**, shady, shadowy, moonlit, crepuscular (*literary*), tenebrous (*literary*) [➡ DESCRIBING LIGHT; 1228] *Opposite*: sunlit

twill *type of* **fabric from animals** [➡ FABRICS; 1132]

twin 1 *n* **double**, doppelgänger, clone, identical twin, Siamese twin, mirror image, look-alike (*informal*) [➡ COPIES AND REPLICAS; 151] 2 *type of* **offspring** [➡ YOUNGER GENERATION RELATIVES; 958] 3 *adj* **identical**, matching, alike, indistinguishable, like [➡ SAMENESS; 150] *Opposite*: different 4 *adj* **dual**, double, twofold, paired [➡ APPORTIONMENT; 113] *Opposite*: single 5 *v* **pair**, link, join, match, associate, connect, relate [➡ CREATING CONNECTIONS; 144]

twin bed *type of* **bed** [➡ FURNITURE; 858]

twine 1 *n* **string**, thread, cord, yarn [➡ FASTENERS, LINKS, AND NETWORKS; 1247] 2 *v* **coil**, twist, wind, loop, snake, twirl, weave, curl, bend, wrap around [➡ POSITION SOMETHING: AROUND SOMETHING; 327]

twinge *n* **pang**, pain, stitch, ache, wrench, cramp, stab, spasm, charley horse (*informal*) [➡ PAIN AND OTHER PHYSICAL SENSATIONS; 733]

twinkle 1 *v* **shine**, sparkle, glimmer, gleam, flicker, glow, glitter [➡ LIGHT EMISSION; 368] 2 *n* **sparkle**, shine, gleam, glimmer, flicker, glow, glitter [➡ LIGHT; 1164]

twinkling *n* **flash**, second, moment, split second, instant, blink [➡ SHORT PERIODS OF TIME; 93]

twin-lens reflex *type of* **photographic equipment** [➡ PHOTOGRAPHY AND PHOTOGRAPHIC EQUIPMENT; 1122]

twin set *type of* **sweater** [➡ GARMENTS AND OUTFITS; 865]

twirl 1 *v* **wind**, coil, twist, curl, bend, loop, snake, weave, twine [➡ POSITION SOMETHING: AROUND SOMETHING; 327] 2 *v* **spin**, rotate, whirl, turn, revolve, pirouette [➡ MOVE SOMETHING: ON THE SPOT; 336] 3 *n* **coil**, spiral, twist, loop [➡ ROUNDED SHAPE; 1218] 4 *n* **whirl**, spin, revolution, rotation, turn, pirouette [➡ MOVE SOMETHING: ON THE SPOT; 336]

twist 1 *v* **wind**, coil, curl, bend, twirl, entwine, interweave, weave, loop, snake [➡ POSITION SOMETHING: AROUND SOMETHING; 327] 2 *v* **rotate**, turn, screw, unscrew, wind, wring [➡ MOVE SOMETHING: ON THE SPOT; 336] 3 *v* **sprain**, pull, hurt, injure, turn, wrench [➡ WOUND A PERSON OR ANIMAL; 383] 4 *v* **distort**, misrepresent, alter, manipulate, warp, change [➡ FALSIFY AND CHEAT; 176] *Opposite*: clarify 5 *v* **meander**, snake, wind, curve, bend, twist and turn, zigzag, loop [➡ CHANGE DIRECTION OF MOTION; 344] 6 *v* **contort**, screw up, grimace, crumple, writhe [➡ CHANGE OF SHAPE; 385] 7 *n* **rotation**, screw, wind, turn [➡ MOVE SOMETHING: ON THE SPOT; 336] 8 *n* **spiral**, coil, kink, curl, bend, curve, turn [➡ ROUNDED SHAPE; 1218] 9 *n* **development**, change, turn, incident, event, variation, surprise [➡ DECISIVE MOMENTS; 44]

twist and turn *v* [➡ CHANGE DIRECTION OF MOTION; 344]

twisted 1 *adj* **warped**, perverse, sick, perverted, abnormal [➡ ECCENTRICITY AND IRRATIONALITY; 562] *Opposite*: wholesome 2 *adj* **misshapen**, distorted, warped, bent, deformed, out of

shape, awry [➡ ORIENTATION AND ALIGNMENT; 1223] *Opposite*: straight

twister (*informal*) *n* [➡ WINDY AND STORMY WEATHER; 1053]

twisting *adj* **winding**, meandering, twisty, windy, snaking, bendy (*UK*) [➡ DIRECTION OF MOTION; 345]

twist of fate *n* [➡ DECISIVE MOMENTS; 44]

twist somebody's arm *v* **compel**, force, pressure, coerce, persuade, bring pressure upon, convince, press, pressurize (*UK*) [➡ CAUSE OR COMPEL TO ACT; 271]

twisty *adj* **winding**, tortuous, meandering, snaking, twisting, bendy (*UK*) [➡ DIRECTION OF MOTION; 345] *Opposite*: straight

twitch 1 *v* **jerk**, jolt, shudder, yank, convulse, tremble, contract [➡ PHYSICAL REACTIONS; 316] 2 *n* **tic**, spasm, jerk, jolt, convulsion, shudder, tremor, contraction [➡ PHYSICAL REACTIONS; 316]

twitchily *adv* **nervously**, anxiously, uneasily, edgily, agitatedly, restlessly, jumpily [➡ INSECURITY AND LOSS OF COMPOSURE; 544]

twitchiness *n* **jitteriness**, jumpiness, restlessness, uneasiness, nervousness, agitation [➡ INSECURITY AND LOSS OF COMPOSURE; 544]

twitchy *adj* **nervous**, fidgety, on edge, agitated, jumpy, edgy, uneasy, jittery, restless, antsy (*informal*) [➡ CONFUSION, ANXIETY, AND WORRY; 540] *Opposite*: still

twitter *type of* **bird sound** [➡ SOUNDS MADE BY BIRDS; 1263]

two a penny (*UK*) *adj* [➡ ORDINARINESS; 244]

two-dimensional 1 *adj* **flat**, flattened, plane, smooth, level, surface [➡ ORIENTATION AND ALIGNMENT; 1223] *Opposite*: three-dimensional 2 *adj* **superficial**, shallow, oversimplified, formulaic, cardboard, weak [➡ BORING AND UNINTERESTING; 234] *Opposite*: complex

two-faced *adj* **hypocritical**, false, insincere, deceitful, double dealing, disingenuous, duplicitous, treacherous [➡ DECEITFUL; 513] *Opposite*: genuine

two-facedness *n* [➡ DECEITFUL; 513]

twofold *adj* **double**, dual, twin [➡ APPORTIONMENT; 113]

two-piece *type of* **sportswear** [➡ GARMENTS AND OUTFITS; 865]

twosome *n* **pair**, duo, couple, two of a kind [➡ GROUPS OF PEOPLE; 935]

two step *type of* **dance music** [➡ MUSIC, SONGS, AND SINGING; 907]

two-time 1 *v* **be unfaithful**, cheat, deceive, step out (*informal*), cuckold (*archaic*) [➡ DECEPTION AND LIES; 660] 2 *v* **betray**, mislead, deceive, double-cross, take in, swindle, trick, stab in the back (*informal*) [➡ DECEPTION AND LIES; 660]

two-tone *adj* **striped**, two-color, light-and-dark, two-hued, two-toned, stripy [➡ DESCRIBING COLORS; 1226] *Opposite*: solid-color

two-way *adj* **reciprocal**, cooperative, shared, mutual, collaborative, give-and-take (*informal*) [➡ RECIPROCITY AND INTERDEPENDENCE; 147]

two-wheeler *type of* **bike** [➡ BIKES, CARS, AND CARRIAGES; 1149]

tycoon _n_ **magnate**, mogul, business person, industrialist [➡BUSINESS PEOPLE; 793]

tyke _n_ **child**, imp, urchin, monkey (_informal_), scamp (_informal_), rascal (_humorous_), rugrat (_informal humorous_), tearaway (_UK_) [➡MISCHIEVOUS OR BADLY BEHAVED CHILD; 946]

tympanic membrane _part of_ **ear** [➡THE EAR; 706]

tympanum _part of_ **ear** [➡THE EAR; 706]

type **1** _n_ (_informal_) **character**, individual, person, sort [➡PERSON; 931] **2** _n_ **kind**, sort, category, form, nature, brand, style, variety, manner, mode, class [➡VARIETIES, TYPES, AND KINDS; 145] **3** _n_ **font**, typeface, lettering, print, style, typography [➡PRINTING; 600] **4** _v_ **key**, input, enter, key in [➡RECORD SOMETHING; 371]

Compare and Contrast: _type_, _kind_, **sort**, _category_, _class_, _species_, _genre_

CORE MEANING: a group having a common quality or qualities

type a group of individuals or items with strongly marked and readily defined similarities; _kind_ a group of individuals or items connected by shared characteristics; _sort_ a general word used in the same way as _kind_; _category_ a set of things that are classified together because of common characteristics; _class_ used in the same way as _category_; _species_ a specific group of animals, plants, insects, or other organisms, used in formal taxonomic classification; _genre_ a particular style of painting, writing, dance, or other art form.

Type A _adj_ **dynamic**, driven, go-getting (_informal_), ambitious, energetic, efficient, influential, high-powered, hard-driving [➡TALENTED AND SKILLFUL; 527]

typecast _v_ **stereotype**, pigeonhole, categorize, limit, restrict, label [➡NAME AND DESCRIBE; 665]

typeface _n_ **script**, type, font, lettering, print, typography, style [➡PRINTING; 600]

typescript _n_ [➡PRINTING; 600]

typesetter _n_ [➡PRINTING; 600]

typesetting _n_ [➡PRINTING; 600]

typhoon _n_ **storm**, cyclone, tornado, hurricane, tropical storm [➡WINDY AND STORMY WEATHER; 1053]

typical **1** _adj_ **characteristic**, archetypal, distinctive, representative, emblematic, classic [➡REPRESENTATIVE; 66] _Opposite_: uncharacteristic **2** _adj_ **usual**, normal, standard, mainstream, average, conventional, regular, predictable [➡ORDINARINESS; 244] _Opposite_: unusual

typically **1** _adv_ **characteristically**, classically, naturally, stereotypically, archetypally [➡REPRESENTATIVE; 66] _Opposite_: uncharacteristically **2** _adv_ **normally**, usually, on average, in general, by and large, more often than not, as a rule, habitually, predictably [➡USUALLY; 108] _Opposite_: unusually

typify _v_ **characterize**, epitomize, symbolize, exemplify, personify, illustrate, demonstrate, represent [➡REPRESENT SOMETHING OR SOMEBODY; 59]

typo (_informal_) _n_ **misprint**, typographical error, keyboarding error, error, mistake [➡PRINTING; 600] _Opposite_: correction

typography **1** _n_ **design**, typesetting, formatting, layout, composition [➡PRINTING; 600] **2** _n_ **print style**, font, type, lettering, script [➡PRINTING; 600]

tyrannical _adj_ **oppressive**, dictatorial, autocratic, despotic, authoritarian, totalitarian, cruel, harsh, domineering, overbearing [➡BOSSY AND OVERBEARING; 516]

tyrannize _v_ **oppress**, dictate, bully, domineer, intimidate, terrorize, torment, browbeat, persecute [➡UPSET, DISTRESS, AND HUMILIATE; 567]

tyrannosaur _type of_ **dinosaur** [➡DINOSAURS; 996]

tyrannous _adj_ [➡BOSSY AND OVERBEARING; 516]

tyranny _n_ **oppression**, dictatorship, autocracy, domination, despotism, totalitarianism, cruelty, oppressiveness, bullying [➡MALICIOUS ACTIONS OR BEHAVIOR; 296]

tyrant _n_ **oppressor**, dictator, bully, autocrat, despot, tormentor, persecutor, martinet [➡VILLAINS AND THUGS; 947]

tyro _n_ **novice**, beginner, learner, newcomer, trainee, apprentice, neophyte, greenhorn [➡UNSKILLED PEOPLE; 530] _Opposite_: veteran

---

See Compare and Contrast at **beginner**.

U

ubiquitous *adj* **omnipresent**, universal, pervasive, global, abundant, permeating [➡ PRESENT AND AVAILABLE; 11]

ubiquitousness *n* [➡ PRESENT AND AVAILABLE; 11]

ubiquity *n* [➡ PRESENT AND AVAILABLE; 11]

UFO *n* **flying saucer**, spaceship, spacecraft [➡ SCIENCE FICTION; 1064]

ugliness 1 *n* **unattractiveness**, unsightliness, hideousness, repulsiveness [➡ UGLINESS AND UNATTRACTIVENESS; 233] *Opposite*: attractiveness **2** *n* **violence**, hostility, cruelty, viciousness, malice, spitefulness, evil [➡ MALICIOUS ACTIONS OR BEHAVIOR; 296] *Opposite*: friendliness **3** *n* **unpleasantness**, dreadfulness, horridness, obnoxiousness, foulness, disagreeableness [➡ EMOTIONALLY UNPLEASANT AND UPSETTING; 227]

ugly 1 *adj* **unattractive**, hideous, unsightly, revolting, repulsive [➡ UGLINESS AND UNATTRACTIVENESS; 233] *Opposite*: attractive **2** *adj* **unpleasant**, horrible, dreadful, horrid, obnoxious, foul, disagreeable [➡ EMOTIONALLY UNPLEASANT AND UPSETTING; 227] *Opposite*: nice **3** *adj* **nasty**, threatening, dangerous, intimidating, menacing, hostile, aggressive, bad-tempered, sour, violent [➡ RUDE AND HOSTILE; 625] *Opposite*: friendly

ukulele *type of* **stringed instrument** [➡ MUSICAL INSTRUMENTS; 910]

ulcer *n* **boil**, abscess, pustule, carbuncle, sore [➡ DISORDERS OF THE DIGESTIVE SYSTEM; 713]

ulna *type of* **bone** [➡ THE BONES AND JOINTS; 719]

ulterior *adj* **hidden**, concealed, secret, underhand, unknown, mysterious, clandestine, underlying [➡ SECRET AND UNKNOWN; 179] *Opposite*: transparent

ulterior motive *n* **hidden agenda**, arrière-pensée (*formal*), mental reservation [➡ CAUSATION; 168]

ultimate 1 *adj* **final**, last, eventual, decisive, definitive, vital, crucial, critical [➡ IMPORTANT; 194] *Opposite*: first **2** *adj* **fundamental**, basic, essential, supreme, extreme, greatest, best [➡ FUNDAMENTAL; 195] *Opposite*: superficial

ultimately *adv* **in the end**, eventually, in due course, finally, at last, in the long run, at the end of the day [➡ AFTER, LAST, AND FOLLOWING; 165] *Opposite*: initially

ultimatum *n* **challenge**, demand, requirement, petition, stipulation, proposition, proviso, last word [➡ REQUEST AND DEMAND; 663]

ultra *adj* **extreme**, radical, revolutionary, excessive, extremist, over-the-top (*informal*), outré [➡ TOO MUCH; 119] *Opposite*: mainstream

ultralight *type of* **civil aircraft** [➡ AIRCRAFT; 1148]

ultramarine *type of* **blue** [➡ COLORS; 1224]

ultramodern *adj* **avant-garde**, progressive, modernistic, radical, futuristic, forward-looking, ahead of its time, high-tech [➡ NEW, MODERN; 166] *Opposite*: old-fashioned

ultrasound scan *type of* **medical procedure** [➡ REMEDIES, TREATMENTS, AND OPERATIONS; 731]

umber *type of* **brown** [➡ COLORS; 1224]

umbilicus *n* [➡ REPRODUCTION AND HEREDITY; 725]

umbrage *n* **offense**, exception, resentment, affront, slight, annoyance, aggravation, irritation, exasperation [➡ FEELINGS ABOUT THE PAST; 532]

umbrella 1 *n* **parasol**, sunshade, canopy [➡ COVERS AND COATINGS; 1246] **2** *n* **aegis**, auspices, authority, protection, support, sponsorship, backing, patronage, supervision [➡ RESPONSIBILITY; 170]

umlaut *type of* **diacritic** [➡ ASPECTS OF LANGUAGE; 682]

umpire 1 *n* **referee**, adjudicator, arbitrator, arbiter, mediator, moderator, official [➡ PEOPLE IN SPORTS AND LEISURE; 876] **2** *v* **adjudicate**, referee, arbitrate, judge, mediate, officiate, supervise [➡ ASSESS QUALITY; 755]

umpteen (*informal*) *adj* **countless**, numerous, innumerable, millions of, myriad, lots of, scads of (*informal*), tons of (*informal*), loads of (*informal*) [➡ MANY, MUCH, LARGE AMOUNT; 117]

unabashed *adj* **unashamed**, unembarrassed, shameless, bold, brazen, forward, blatant, brash, forthright [➡ COOL AND CALM; 536] *Opposite*: abashed

unabated *adj* **persistent**, undiminished, relentless, unrelieved, unrelenting, unrestricted, unceasing, unchanged, constant [➡ PERMANENCE: WITHOUT END; 94] *Opposite*: reduced

unable *adj* **powerless**, incapable, impotent, inept, incompetent [➡ UNSKILLED; 529] *Opposite*: able

unabridged *adj* **full-length**, complete, whole, entire, uncut, unexpurgated, unedited [➡ WHOLENESS AND COMPLETENESS; 198] *Opposite*: abridged

unacceptable *adj* **intolerable**, insupportable, undesirable, objectionable, deplorable, offensive, improper, obnoxious, distasteful [➡ UNACCEPTABLE AND UNFORGIVABLE; 225] *Opposite*: acceptable

unaccommodating *adj* **unhelpful**, awkward, uncooperative, difficult, disobliging, troublesome [➡ UNWILLINGNESS AND STUBBORNNESS; 564] *Opposite*: helpful

unaccompanied *adj* **alone**, by yourself, on your own, lone, solitary, solo, single-handed [➡ ACTING INDEPENDENTLY; 284]

unaccomplished 1 *adj* **unfinished**, incomplete, uncompleted, unexecuted, unfulfilled, unconsummated, undone, unresolved [➡ UNFINISHEDNESS; 239] *Opposite*: accomplished **2** *adj* **unskillful**, amateurish, unpolished, inexpert, untalented, talentless, inept, undeveloped [➡ UNSKILLED; 529] *Opposite*: accomplished

unaccountable *adj* **inexplicable**, puzzling, strange, unfathomable, baffling, peculiar, unexplainable, incomprehensible, extraordinary [➠ BIZARRE AND PECULIAR; 257] *Opposite*: explicable

unaccounted-for *adj* **missing**, lost, absent, gone, disappeared, vanished [➠ ABSENT AND UNAVAILABLE; 7]

unaccustomed 1 *adj* **unused**, not used, inexperienced, unfamiliar, unacquainted [➠ UNSKILLED; 529] *Opposite*: accustomed 2 *adj* **unfamiliar**, unusual, different, new, strange, alien, untried, uncommon [➠ DIFFERENCE; 149] *Opposite*: accustomed

unachievable *adj* **unattainable**, impracticable, impossible, unfeasible, inaccessible [➠ IMPOSSIBLE AND IMPROBABLE; 178] *Opposite*: achievable

unacquainted *adj* **ignorant**, unaccustomed, unaware, uninformed, unknowledgeable [➠ IGNORANCE; 557] *Opposite*: knowledgeable

unadorned *adj* **plain**, bare, austere, simple, unembellished, bald [➠ PLAIN; 232] *Opposite*: ornate

unadulterated *adj* **pure**, untouched, untainted, complete, unmodified, unsullied, unalloyed, undiluted, neat [➠ RAW AND NATURAL; 1214] *Opposite*: tainted

unadventurous *adj* **cautious**, conservative, careful, timid, shy, hesitant, stay-at-home [➠ UNADVENTUROUS AND DULL; 517] *Opposite*: daredevil

unaffected 1 *adj* **unchanged**, unaltered, unmoved, impervious, impassive, untouched [➠ NEUTRALITY AND INDIFFERENCE; 553] *Opposite*: different 2 *adj* **genuine**, natural, unpretentious, sincere, modest, artless, guileless [➠ NATURALNESS; 497] *Opposite*: pretentious

unaffectedly *adv* **genuinely**, modestly, naturally, unpretentiously, sincerely, simply, ingenuously, artlessly, guilelessly [➠ NATURALNESS; 497] *Opposite*: pretentiously

unaffectedness *n* **genuineness**, modesty, naturalness, unpretentiousness, sincerity, simplicity, ingenuousness, guilelessness, artlessness [➠ NATURALNESS; 497] *Opposite*: pretentiousness

unaffordable *adj* [➠ EXPENSIVE AND OVERPRICED; 247]

unafraid *adj* **fearless**, bold, confident, brave, courageous, undaunted, stouthearted [➠ COOL AND CALM; 536] *Opposite*: afraid

unaided *adv* **unassisted**, independently, by yourself, of your own accord, on your own, single-handedly, solo [➠ ACTING INDEPENDENTLY; 284] *Opposite*: jointly

unalike *adj* [➠ DIFFERENCE; 149]

unalleviated *adj* **constant**, unrelieved, unremitting, unmitigated, inexorable, unbearable [➠ PERMANENCE: WITHOUT END; 94] *Opposite*: intermittent

unalloyed *adj* **pure**, sheer, absolute, total, utter, complete, unadulterated, undiminished, undiluted [➠ WHOLENESS AND COMPLETENESS; 198] *Opposite*: partial

unalterable *adj* **unchangeable**, fixed, irreversible, final, set, permanent [➠ PERMANENCE: WITHOUT CHANGE; 95] *Opposite*: impermanent

unambiguous *adj* **unmistakable**, clear-cut, explicit,

definite, decided, unequivocal, instantly recognizable, clear [➠ CONCISE AND CLEAR; 202] *Opposite*: vague

unambiguously *adv* **unmistakably**, decidedly, definitely, explicitly, clearly, unequivocally, recognizably [➠ CONCISE AND CLEAR; 202] *Opposite*: vaguely

unambitious *adj* **unaspiring**, unenterprising, unassertive, lazy, passive, apathetic [➠ LIFELESS, LAZY, AND UNENTHUSIASTIC; 506] *Opposite*: ambitious

unanimity *n* [➠ HARMONY; 155]

unanimous *adj* **common**, agreed, undisputed, undivided, united [➠ HARMONY; 155] *Opposite*: undecided

unannounced *adj* **unexpected**, impromptu, spontaneous, surprise [➠ UNPLANNED AND UNEXPECTED; 281] *Opposite*: arranged

unanswerable *adj* **unfathomable**, insoluble, unresolvable, unsolvable, inexplicable, incomprehensible, insuperable [➠ DIFFICULTY AND COMPLEXITY; 242]

unanticipated *adj* **surprising**, unexpected, unlooked-for, unforeseen, unsuspected, unimagined [➠ SECRET AND UNKNOWN; 179] *Opposite*: expected

unapologetic *adj* **impenitent**, unrepentant, unreformed, unremorseful, unregretful [➠ COOL AND CALM; 536] *Opposite*: penitent

unappealing *adj* **unattractive**, unpleasant, disagreeable, uninviting, unlikable, unappetizing, ugly [➠ UGLINESS AND UNATTRACTIVENESS; 233] *Opposite*: appealing

unappetizing *adj* **unattractive**, unpleasant, unenticing, uninviting, unpalatable, unsavory [➠ UGLINESS AND UNATTRACTIVENESS; 233] *Opposite*: appetizing

unappreciated *adj* [➠ UNPOPULAR AND UNWANTED; 258]

unapprised *adj* [➠ IGNORANCE; 557]

unapproachability *n* [➠ UNFRIENDLINESS AND UNSOCIABILITY; 504]

unapproachable *adj* **distant**, unfriendly, aloof, cold, standoffish, remote, withdrawn, unsociable [➠ UNFRIENDLINESS AND UNSOCIABILITY; 504] *Opposite*: approachable

unarguable *adj* **beyond doubt**, incontestable, incontrovertible, indisputable, beyond question, unquestionable [➠ CERTAIN; 174] *Opposite*: arguable

unarmed *adj* **unprotected**, defenseless, exposed, vulnerable, weaponless [➠ IN DANGER; 237] *Opposite*: armed

unashamed *adj* **unembarrassed**, unapologetic, blatant, brazen, barefaced, insolent, bold, shameless, flagrant, immodest, unabashed [➠ COOL AND CALM; 536] *Opposite*: ashamed

unashamedly *adv* **unapologetically**, flagrantly, blatantly, brazenly, boldly, defiantly, shamelessly, insolently, immodestly, openly [➠ COOL AND CALM; 536] *Opposite*: ashamedly

unasked 1 *adj* **unsolicited**, uninvited, unsought, unexpected, uncanvassed, undreamed-of, unimaginable [➠ UNPOPULAR AND UNWANTED; 258] *Opposite*: expected 2 *adj* **uninvited**, unwelcome, excluded, unexpected, left out, unbidden, unsummoned [➠ UNPOPULAR AND UNWANTED; 258]

unasked-for *adj* [➠ UNPOPULAR AND UNWANTED; 258]

unassailable 1 *adj* **incontrovertible**, unquestionable, impregnable, irrefutable, indisputable, undeniable, incontestable, conclusive, sound, watertight [➡CERTAIN; 174] *Opposite*: tenuous 2 *adj* **invincible**, unbeatable, impregnable, indomitable, invulnerable [➡STRENGTH; 201] *Opposite*: vulnerable

unassertive *adj* [➡COWARDICE AND WEAKNESS OF WILL; 508]

unassisted *adj* **unaided**, single-handed, solo, lone [➡ACTING INDEPENDENTLY; 284] *Opposite*: assisted

unassuming *adj* **modest**, humble, self-effacing, unassertive, meek, inconspicuous, ordinary, unpretentious, down-to-earth [➡NATURALNESS; 497] *Opposite*: arrogant

unassumingness *n* [➡NATURALNESS; 497]

unattached *adj* **free**, uncommitted, single, unmarried, separated [➡MARITAL STATUS; 890] *Opposite*: attached

unattainable *adj* **unachievable**, impossible, unfeasible, inaccessible, unreachable [➡IMPOSSIBLE AND IMPROBABLE; 178] *Opposite*: attainable

unattractive *adj* **unappealing**, ugly, nasty, unpleasant, distasteful, repellent, uninviting, unsightly [➡UGLINESS AND UNATTRACTIVENESS; 233] *Opposite*: attractive

unattractiveness *n* **ugliness**, unpleasantness, unsightliness, distastefulness, repulsiveness, nastiness [➡UGLINESS AND UNATTRACTIVENESS; 233] *Opposite*: attractiveness

unauthorized *adj* **illegal**, unlawful, unofficial, unsanctioned, unlicensed, unapproved, unconstitutional, illicit [➡ILLEGAL; 816] *Opposite*: legitimate

unavailability *n* **unobtainability**, inaccessibility, unattainability, unreachability, absence, unapproachability [➡ABSENT AND UNAVAILABLE; 7] *Opposite*: availability

unavailable 1 *adj* **unobtainable**, inaccessible, unattainable, unreachable, absent, unapproachable [➡ABSENT AND UNAVAILABLE; 7] *Opposite*: available 2 *adj* **engaged**, busy, occupied, unobtainable [➡ABSENT AND UNAVAILABLE; 7] *Opposite*: available

unavailing *adj* **vain**, unsuccessful, futile, failed, ineffective, fruitless, abortive, pointless [➡REDUNDANT AND USELESS; 240] *Opposite*: successful

unavoidability *n* **inevitability**, inescapability, certainty, necessity, obligation, requirement, inexorability (*formal*) [➡CERTAIN; 174]

unavoidable *adj* **inevitable**, inescapable, obvious, manifest, obligatory, necessary, mandatory, compulsory, required, inexorable (*formal*) [➡CERTAIN; 174] *Opposite*: avoidable

unavoidably *adv* **inevitably**, inescapably, manifestly, necessarily, compulsorily [➡NECESSARY AND ESSENTIAL; 196]

unaware *adj* **ignorant**, uninformed, oblivious, unconscious, unmindful, heedless, unacquainted, naive, innocent [➡IGNORANCE; 557] *Opposite*: conscious

unawares *adv* **by surprise**, off guard, unexpectedly [➡UNPLANNED AND UNEXPECTED; 281]

unbalance *v* **disturb**, unhinge, derange, distort, destabilize, confuse [➡CONFUSE AND BEWILDER; 571] *Opposite*: stabilize

unbalanced 1 *adj* **unstable**, disturbed, unhinged, deranged [➡PSYCHOLOGY AND THE MIND; 769] *Opposite*: well-balanced 2 *adj* **uneven**, lopsided, unequal, crooked, top-heavy [➡ORIENTATION AND ALIGNMENT; 1223] *Opposite*: even 3 *adj* **biased**, one-sided, inequitable, prejudiced, unfair, misleading, partial [➡THE NATURE OF IDEAS; 771] *Opposite*: impartial

unbearable *adj* **intolerable**, agonizing, excruciating, awful, insufferable, horrendous, insupportable, unendurable [➡EMOTIONALLY UNPLEASANT AND UPSETTING; 227] *Opposite*: tolerable

unbeatable *adj* **invincible**, supreme, unassailable, unconquerable, peerless, matchless, indomitable [➡STRENGTH; 201] *Opposite*: vulnerable

unbeaten *adj* **undefeated**, unsurpassed, successful, triumphant, victorious, unbowed, winning, champion, number one (*informal*), the best, top-ranking [➡SUCCESSFUL AND PROMISING; 81]

unbecoming *adj* **improper**, inappropriate, incorrect, unsuitable, unflattering, unfitting, indelicate, indecorous [➡INAPPROPRIATE AND UNSUITABLE; 224] *Opposite*: fitting

unbecomingness *n* [➡INAPPROPRIATE AND UNSUITABLE; 224]

unbelief *n* **nonbelief**, skepticism, incredulity, agnosticism, atheism [➡RELIGIOUS CONCEPTS; 776] *Opposite*: faith

unbelievable 1 *adj* **incredible**, amazing, extraordinary, astonishing, great, enormous, mind-boggling [➡EXTRAORDINARY; AMAZING; 204] *Opposite*: ordinary 2 *adj* **implausible**, incredible, far-fetched, fantastic, unlikely, fanciful, preposterous, improbable, unreal [➡IMPOSSIBLE AND IMPROBABLE; 178] *Opposite*: plausible

unbelievably *adv* **extraordinarily**, incredibly, extremely, very, exceptionally, amazingly, astonishingly [➡TO A GREAT EXTENT; 132] *Opposite*: unremarkably

unbeliever *n* **nonbeliever**, skeptic, atheist, agnostic, freethinker, doubter [➡RELIGIOUS CONCEPTS; 776] *Opposite*: believer

unbelieving *adj* **incredulous**, skeptical, doubting, suspicious, questioning [➡UNCERTAINTY; 559] *Opposite*: credulous

unbend *v* **straighten**, release, free, relax, loosen, flatten [➡CHANGE OF SHAPE; 385] *Opposite*: bend

unbending *adj* **inflexible**, fixed, rigid, adamant, obdurate, dogmatic, doctrinaire, formal, pitiless [➡UNWILLINGNESS AND STUBBORNNESS; 564] *Opposite*: flexible

unbiased *adj* **impartial**, balanced, dispassionate, neutral, unprejudiced, fair, evenhanded, disinterested, fair-minded, detached, equitable (*formal*) [➡THE NATURE OF IDEAS; 771] *Opposite*: partial

unbind *v* **untie**, release, free, undo, liberate, unfetter, unchain, set free [➡UNFASTEN AND UNDO; 409] *Opposite*: bind

unblemished *adj* **flawless**, perfect, untarnished, pure, blameless, clear, immaculate [➡MORALLY GOOD; 774] *Opposite*: flawed

unblinking *adj* [➡FACIAL EXPRESSIONS AND BLUSHING; 651]

unblock v **clear**, unclog, free, clear out, clean out, free up (informal) [➡ EMPTY AND UNLOAD; 407] Opposite: block

unbolt v **unfasten**, unlock, open, unscrew, release, unhook, undo [➡ UNFASTEN AND UNDO; 409] Opposite: lock

unbothered adj [➡ COOL AND CALM; 536]

unbounded adj **limitless**, unrestrained, abundant, boundless, uncontrolled, absolute, infinite, immeasurable [➡ FREEDOM AND LIBERTY; 208] Opposite: limited

unbowed adj **undefeated**, defiant, stubborn, determined, relentless, unyielding, resolved [➡ UNWILLINGNESS AND STUBBORNNESS; 564] Opposite: defeated

unbreakable adj **indestructible**, strong, permanent, indissoluble, firm, hard, resilient, shatterproof [➡ DURABLE; 1210] Opposite: fragile

unbridled adj **unrestrained**, uncontrolled, uninhibited, unconcealed, unchecked, intemperate, rampant [➡ FREEDOM AND LIBERTY; 208] Opposite: contained

unbroken adj **continuous**, constant, uninterrupted, steady, complete, endless, perpetual [➡ PERMANENCE: WITHOUT END; 94] Opposite: intermittent

unbuckle v [➡ UNFASTEN AND UNDO; 409]

unburden (formal) v **relieve**, divest, free, release, let go, confess [➡ ADMIT AND CONFESS; 615] Opposite: brood

unbutton v **undo**, open, unfasten [➡ UNFASTEN AND UNDO; 409] Opposite: fasten

uncalled-for adj **unjustified**, unwarranted, undeserved, unprovoked, gratuitous, indefensible, unnecessary, needless, inexcusable, unforgivable, rude, unjustifiable, undue, wanton, unfair [➡ UNIMPORTANT AND UNNECESSARY; 238] Opposite: justifiable

uncanniness n [➡ BIZARRE AND PECULIAR; 257]

uncanny adj **eerie**, weird, strange, mysterious, creepy (informal), supernatural [➡ BIZARRE AND PECULIAR; 257]

uncap v [➡ UNFASTEN AND UNDO; 409]

uncared-for adj **neglected**, unloved, untended, unkempt, unattended, dilapidated, disheveled, forgotten, abandoned [➡ IN BAD REPAIR; 1234] Opposite: cherished

uncaring adj **hardhearted**, unfeeling, heartless, indifferent, cold, callous, selfish, insensible [➡ NEUTRALITY AND INDIFFERENCE; 553] Opposite: caring

unceasing adj **constant**, continuous, interminable, never-ending, perpetual, unending, nonstop, endless [➡ PERMANENCE: WITHOUT END; 94] Opposite: sporadic

unceremonious adj **abrupt**, hasty, rushed, terse, rude, brusque, curt, callous [➡ INCAUTIOUS AND CARELESS; 283] Opposite: gracious

uncertain 1 adj **unsure**, vague, doubtful, hesitant, undecided, indecisive, tentative, in doubt, dubious [➡ UNCERTAINTY; 559] Opposite: sure 2 adj **indeterminate**, inexact, undefined, indefinite, ambiguous, unclear, tentative, unreliable, changeable [➡ UNCERTAIN; 175] Opposite: exact

See Compare and Contrast at **doubtful**.

uncertainly adv **hesitantly**, indecisively, tentatively, nervously, anxiously, apprehensively, timidly, doubtfully [➡ UNCERTAINTY; 559] Opposite: confidently

uncertainness n [➡ UNCERTAIN; 175]

uncertainty n **doubt**, indecision, hesitation, vagueness, ambiguity, insecurity [➡ UNCERTAINTY; 559] Opposite: confidence

unchain v **release**, unlock, unfetter, unshackle, liberate, free [➡ FREEDOM AND LIBERTY; 208] Opposite: chain

unchangeable adj **fixed**, unalterable, unvarying, constant, unchanged, consistent, inflexible, unmovable [➡ PERMANENCE: WITHOUT CHANGE; 95] Opposite: changeable

unchanged adj **unaffected**, unmoved, untouched, unbothered [➡ PERMANENCE: WITHOUT CHANGE; 95] Opposite: affected

unchanging adj **static**, fixed, invariable, unchangeable, rigid, inflexible, set, ageless [➡ PERMANENCE: WITHOUT CHANGE; 95] Opposite: flexible

uncharacteristic adj **unusual**, atypical, abnormal, out of character, unexpected, aberrant, strange [➡ BIZARRE AND PECULIAR; 257] Opposite: typical

uncharitable adj **mean**, unkind, hurtful, spiteful, cruel, mean-spirited, harsh, unmerciful, heartless [➡ SELFISH AND UNKIND; 505] Opposite: generous

uncharted adj **unexplored**, new, unfamiliar, unmapped, unknown, alien, strange, uncultivated [➡ SECRET AND UNKNOWN; 179] Opposite: familiar

unchaste adj [➡ MORALLY BAD OR IMPROPER; 775]

unchasteness n [➡ MORALLY BAD OR IMPROPER; 775]

unchecked adj **unimpeded**, unrestrained, unhindered, unrestricted, unconstrained, unbridled, abandoned, free [➡ FREEDOM AND LIBERTY; 208] Opposite: restricted

uncivil adj **rude**, discourteous, impolite, insulting, bad-mannered, unfriendly [➡ BAD MANNERS AND SOCIAL SKILLS; 521] Opposite: courteous

uncivilized 1 adj **primitive**, barbaric, uncultured, unsophisticated, crude [➡ LEVELS OF EDUCATION AND SOPHISTICATION; 894] Opposite: civilized 2 adj **remote**, distant, far-off, isolated, unreachable, uninhabitable [➡ LEVELS OF EDUCATION AND SOPHISTICATION; 894] Opposite: reachable 3 adj **coarse**, impolite, discourteous, unrefined, vulgar, uncouth, uncultured, rude [➡ BAD MANNERS AND SOCIAL SKILLS; 521] Opposite: polite

unclasp v **unfasten**, undo, open, unbuckle, untie, unpin, unlock [➡ UNFASTEN AND UNDO; 409] Opposite: fasten

unclassified 1 adj **random**, unsystematic, disorganized, unorganized, uncategorized, confused, haphazard, higgledy-piggledy, unarranged, disordered [➡ DISORDER AND CHAOS; 245] Opposite: organized 2 adj **open**, public, released, unconcealed, accessible, public domain [➡ KNOWN AND FAMOUS; 181] Opposite: secret

uncle type of **older relative** [➡ OLDER GENERATION RELATIVES; 959]

unclean 1 adj **impure**, dirty, contaminated, polluted, infected, tainted, unhygienic, grimy, filthy, squalid, unsanitary, soiled [➡ DIRTY; 1235] Opposite: clean 2 adj

unchaste, sinful, impure, unworthy, immoral [➡ MORALLY BAD OR IMPROPER; 775] *Opposite*: chaste

See Compare and Contrast at **dirty**.

uncleanliness *n* [➡ DIRTY; 1235]

uncleanness 1 *n* dirtiness, filthiness, impurity, griminess, squalor, unsanitariness [➡ DIRTY; 1235] *Opposite*: cleanness   2 *n* unchasteness, sinfulness, impurity, unworthiness, immorality [➡ MORALLY BAD OR IMPROPER; 775] *Opposite*: chasteness

unclear 1 *adj* indistinct, hazy, indeterminate, blurred, indistinguishable, vague, imprecise, ambiguous [➡ VAGUENESS; 243] *Opposite*: clear   2 *adj* uncertain, doubtful, undecided, unsure, in doubt, vague [➡ UNCERTAIN; 175] *Opposite*: definite

unclearly *adv* indistinctly, vaguely, imprecisely, ambiguously, indecisively, indistinguishably, indeterminately [➡ VAGUENESS; 243] *Opposite*: precisely

unclearness *n* [➡ VAGUENESS; 243]

unclench *v* relax, release, open, untighten, let go, slacken, loosen [➡ PHYSICAL REACTIONS; 316] *Opposite*: tighten

unclog *v* unblock, clear, free, release, clean out, sluice [➡ EMPTY AND UNLOAD; 407] *Opposite*: block

unclothe *v* undress, strip, unrobe, uncover, disrobe (*formal*) [➡ DRESS, WEAR, AND UNDRESS; 868] *Opposite*: dress

unclothed *adj* bare, naked, uncovered, undressed, nude, stripped [➡ DRESS, WEAR, AND UNDRESS; 868] *Opposite*: dressed

See Compare and Contrast at **naked**.

uncoil *v* unravel, unwind, undo, untwist, release, straighten, straighten out [➡ UNFASTEN AND UNDO; 409] *Opposite*: twist

uncomfortable 1 *adj* painful, tight, rough, scratchy, itchy, bumpy, prickly, sore [➡ PAIN AND OTHER PHYSICAL SENSATIONS; 733] *Opposite*: comfortable   2 *adj* embarrassing, awkward, difficult, tricky, unpleasant, unnerving, distressing [➡ EMOTIONALLY UNPLEASANT AND UPSETTING; 227] *Opposite*: enjoyable   3 *adj* uneasy, awkward, ill at ease, embarrassed, tense, self-conscious, on edge, discomfited (*formal*) [➡ INSECURITY AND LOSS OF COMPOSURE; 544] *Opposite*: relaxed

uncommitted *adj* casual, uninterested, indifferent, unattached, free, apathetic [➡ NEUTRALITY AND INDIFFERENCE; 553] *Opposite*: committed

uncommon *adj* rare, unusual, infrequent, scarce, special, exceptional, singular, surprising [➡ EXTRAORDINARY; UNCOMMON; 205] *Opposite*: common

uncommunicative *adj* reserved, reticent, taciturn, silent, withdrawn, unforthcoming, tight-lipped [➡ RETICENT AND UNFORTHCOMING; 631] *Opposite*: talkative

See Compare and Contrast at **silent**.

uncommunicativeness *n* [➡ RETICENT AND UNFORTHCOMING; 631]

uncomplaining *adj* accepting, tolerant, long-suffering, patient, accommodating, forgiving [➡ CHEERFULNESS OF OUTLOOK; 503] *Opposite*: intolerant

uncompleted *adj* [➡ UNFINISHEDNESS; 239]

uncomplicated *adj* simple, straightforward, unfussy, basic, unsophisticated, easy, down-to-earth [➡ EASE AND SIMPLICITY; 200] *Opposite*: complex

See Compare and Contrast at **easy**.

uncomplicatedness *n* [➡ EASE AND SIMPLICITY; 200]

uncomplimentary *adj* disparaging, derogatory, unflattering, negative, rude, damning, pejorative (*formal*) [➡ RUDE AND HOSTILE; 625] *Opposite*: complimentary

uncompromising *adj* inflexible, rigid, adamant, unbending, obdurate, stubborn, categorical, hard-nosed (*informal*) [➡ UNWILLINGNESS AND STUBBORNNESS; 564] *Opposite*: flexible

unconcealed *adj* obvious, open, evident, apparent, blatant, unrestrained [➡ PERCEPTIBLE; 25] *Opposite*: hidden

unconcern *n* indifference, apathy, disregard, nonchalance, disinterest, detachment [➡ NEUTRALITY AND INDIFFERENCE; 553] *Opposite*: anxiety

unconcerned *adj* indifferent, unworried, nonchalant, undaunted, undisturbed, blasé, apathetic, carefree, blithe (*literary*) [➡ NEUTRALITY AND INDIFFERENCE; 553] *Opposite*: anxious

unconditional *adj* unqualified, total, categorical, absolute, unrestricted, unreserved [➡ WHOLENESS AND COMPLETENESS; 198] *Opposite*: qualified

unconditioned *adj* unrestricted, limitless, undefined, unlimited, open-ended, with no strings [➡ FREEDOM AND LIBERTY; 208] *Opposite*: restricted

unconfident *adj* insecure, unsure, nervous, apprehensive, self-doubting, uncertain, anxious [➡ INSECURITY AND LOSS OF COMPOSURE; 544] *Opposite*: self-assured

unconfined *adj* free, liberated, released, loose, at large, free-range, unconstrained [➡ FREEDOM AND LIBERTY; 208] *Opposite*: restricted

unconfirmed *adj* unverified, unsubstantiated, unproven, unofficial, unendorsed, unsupported, unsupervised, invalid, uncorroborated [➡ UNCERTAIN; 175] *Opposite*: verified

unconformity *n* originality, uniqueness, unconventionality, eccentricity, abnormality, individualism, rebelliousness, freethinking [➡ UNRELATEDNESS AND SEPARATENESS; 146] *Opposite*: conformity

uncongenial *adj* disagreeable, unfriendly, unwelcoming, unpleasant, inhospitable, cool, incompatible [➡ UNFRIENDLINESS AND UNSOCIABILITY; 504] *Opposite*: friendly

unconnected *adj* separate, unrelated, independent, distinct, isolated, disparate [➡ UNRELATEDNESS AND SEPARATENESS; 146] *Opposite*: linked

unconquerable *adj* unbeatable, unassailable, unattainable, insurmountable, indomitable, undefeated, impregnable, invincible [➡ STRENGTH; 201] *Opposite*: vulnerable

unconquered *adj* [➡ SUCCESSFUL AND PROMISING; 81]

unconscionable 1 *adj* **unacceptable**, shocking, horrifying, immoral, reprehensible, inconceivable, outrageous, unthinkable, appalling [➡ UNACCEPTABLE AND UNFORGIVABLE; 225] *Opposite*: acceptable 2 *adj* **unreasonable**, beyond the pale, irrational, ridiculous, illogical, extreme, over-the-top (*informal*) [➡ BIZARRE AND PECULIAR; 257] *Opposite*: reasonable

unconscious 1 *adj* **comatose**, insentient, insensible, out cold, cataleptic, down for the count, lifeless, knocked out [➡ TIRED, ASLEEP, AND UNCONSCIOUS; 738] *Opposite*: awake 2 *adj* **unaware**, oblivious, ignorant, unwitting, insensible, uninformed [➡ IGNORANCE; 557] *Opposite*: aware 3 *adj* **unintentional**, automatic, mechanical, instinctive, involuntary, reflex, intuitive [➡ AUTOMATIC AND INSTINCTIVE; 280] *Opposite*: deliberate 4 *n* id, superego, ego, self, psyche, mind [➡ PSYCHOLOGY AND THE MIND; 769]

unconsciously *adv* **unintentionally**, automatically, mechanically, instinctively, involuntarily, reflexively, intuitively [➡ AUTOMATIC AND INSTINCTIVE; 280] *Opposite*: deliberately

unconsciousness *n* **oblivion**, sleep, nothingness, insentience, catalepsy, coma, blackout, swoon [➡ TIRED, ASLEEP, AND UNCONSCIOUS; 738] *Opposite*: consciousness

unconsecrated *adj* [➡ RELIGIOUS CONCEPTS; 776]

unconsidered *adj* **hasty**, unthinking, impulsive, reactive, imprudent, rash, immediate, knee-jerk (*informal*) [➡ INCAUTIOUS AND CARELESS; 283] *Opposite*: considered

unconstitutional *adj* **illegal**, unauthorized, unlawful, undemocratic, unofficial, illegitimate [➡ ILLEGAL; 816] *Opposite*: lawful

unconstrained *adj* **unimpeded**, free, unrestrained, unrestricted, unhindered, untrammeled, unconfined [➡ FREEDOM AND LIBERTY; 208] *Opposite*: restricted

unconstructive *adj* **unhelpful**, negative, unenthusiastic, uncooperative, ineffectual [➡ REDUNDANT AND USELESS; 240] *Opposite*: constructive

uncontaminated *adj* **pure**, clean, unadulterated, antiseptic, sterilized, unpolluted, germ-free, untainted, uncorrupted, undamaged [➡ CLEAN AND HYGIENIC; 1233] *Opposite*: contaminated

uncontrollable 1 *adj* **irrepressible**, uncontainable, overpowering, wild, overwhelming, strong, intense, abandoned, hysterical, frenzied, violent [➡ STRENGTH; 201] 2 *adj* **unruly**, disobedient, out of control, unmanageable, disorderly, wild, badly-behaved [➡ REBELLIOUSNESS AND DISOBEDIENCE; 565] *Opposite*: well-behaved

uncontrollably *adv* **irrepressibly**, overpoweringly, hysterically, nonstop, wildly, frenziedly, violently, overwhelmingly, strongly, intensely [➡ STRENGTH; 201] *Opposite*: calmly

uncontrolled *adj* **unrestrained**, abandoned, wild, hysterical, uninhibited, frenzied [➡ DISORDER AND CHAOS; 245] *Opposite*: restrained

uncontroversial *adj* **undisputed**, uncontentious, uncontended, unquestionable, indisputable, unde-batable, definitive, authoritative, accepted, self-evident [➡ CERTAIN; 174] *Opposite*: controversial

unconventional *adj* **eccentric**, unusual, alternative, avant-garde, strange, original, progressive, exceptional, irregular, odd, quirky [➡ EXTRAORDINARY: UNCOMMON; 205] *Opposite*: conventional

unconventionality *n* **eccentricity**, originality, nonconformity, oddness, quirkiness, unusualness, irregularity, strangeness [➡ EXTRAORDINARY: UNCOMMON; 205] *Opposite*: conventionality

unconvinced *adj* **skeptical**, incredulous, disbelieving, unimpressed, unmoved, dubious, unsure, uncertain [➡ UNCERTAINTY; 559] *Opposite*: convinced

unconvincing *adj* **unpersuasive**, unimpressive, weak, feeble, unsuccessful, vain, implausible [➡ UNCERTAIN; 175] *Opposite*: persuasive

uncooked *adj* **raw**, rare, fresh, unprepared [➡ STATE OF PREPARED FOOD; 1171] *Opposite*: cooked

uncool (*slang*) *adj* **old-fashioned**, conservative, straitlaced, unrelaxed, uptight (*informal*), unhip (*informal*), straight (*slang*) [➡ UNADVENTUROUS AND DULL; 517] *Opposite*: trendy (*informal*)

uncooperative *adj* **unhelpful**, disobliging, awkward, obstinate, contrary, stubborn, truculent, difficult, perverse [➡ UNWILLINGNESS AND STUBBORNNESS; 564] *Opposite*: amenable

uncoordinated *adj* **clumsy**, ungainly, awkward, ungraceful, inept, all thumbs, all fingers and thumbs (*UK*) [➡ AGILITY OF THE BODY; 476] *Opposite*: graceful

uncork 1 *v* **open**, break open, unplug, break into, pop open, pry open, prize open [➡ UNFASTEN AND UNDO; 409] *Opposite*: plug 2 *v* **unleash**, release, give vent to, pour out, set free, express [➡ GIVING VENT TO EMOTIONS; 679] *Opposite*: hold in

uncorrupted *adj* **unadulterated**, unspoiled, uncontaminated, chaste, pure, innocent, virtuous, untouched, unaffected [➡ MORALLY GOOD; 774] *Opposite*: corrupted

uncountable *adj* [➡ MANY, MUCH, LARGE AMOUNT; 117]

uncounted *adj* **innumerable**, countless, numerous, myriad, incalculable [➡ MANY, MUCH, LARGE AMOUNT; 117] *Opposite*: few

uncouple *v* **undo**, disengage, separate, detach, unyoke, unfasten, disjoin [➡ UNFASTEN AND UNDO; 409] *Opposite*: join

uncouth *adj* **rude**, uncivilized, bad-mannered, ill-mannered, foul-mouthed, coarse, vulgar, improper, impolite, crude [➡ BAD MANNERS AND SOCIAL SKILLS; 521] *Opposite*: polite

uncouthness *n* **rudeness**, vulgarity, bad manners, crudeness, coarseness, impropriety [➡ BAD MANNERS AND SOCIAL SKILLS; 521] *Opposite*: politeness

uncover *v* **expose**, discover, reveal, unearth, find out, come across, bare, find, disclose [➡ FIND; 463] *Opposite*: conceal

uncovered *adj* **exposed**, bare, open, naked, revealed, discovered, disclosed [➡ PERCEPTIBLE; 25] *Opposite*: concealed

uncovering *n* **exposure**, discovery, disclosure, revelation [➡ FIND; 463] *Opposite*: concealment

uncritical *adj* **indiscriminating**, accepting, credulous, naive, gullible, trusting, unsuspecting, impressionable [➡ NEGATIVE INTELLECTUAL CHARACTERISTICS; 525] *Opposite*: discriminating

unction 1 *n* **balm**, ointment, salve, oil, lotion, cream, unguent [➡ LOTIONS, PASTES, AND GELS; 1272] 2 *n* **earnestness**, fervor, zeal, passion, enthusiasm, faith, ardor [➡ POSITIVE IMPATIENCE, ENTHUSIASM, AND ALERTNESS; 537]

unctuous 1 *adj* **ingratiating**, sycophantic, slimy, smarmy, obsequious, groveling, smug, phony, creepy (*informal*), oily [➡ INGRATIATING; 638] *Opposite*: arrogant 2 *adj* **oily**, greasy, fatty, slippery, slimy, well-coated [➡ PHYSICAL TEXTURE; 1222]

unctuousness *n* [➡ INGRATIATING; 638]

uncultivated 1 *adj* **unrefined**, unsophisticated, coarse, uncultured, unpolished, uncivilized [➡ LEVELS OF EDUCATION AND SOPHISTICATION; 894] *Opposite*: refined 2 *adj* **fallow**, untilled, unplanted, unfarmed [➡ REDUNDANT AND USELESS; 240] *Opposite*: cultivated

uncultured *adj* **unrefined**, philistine, boorish, unsophisticated, uncultivated, uncivilized, uncouth, coarse [➡ LEVELS OF EDUCATION AND SOPHISTICATION; 894] *Opposite*: refined

uncurl *v* **straighten**, straighten out, uncoil, flatten, unwind [➡ CHANGE OF SHAPE; 385] *Opposite*: curl

uncut *adj* **unabridged**, complete, full-length, unedited, uncensored, unexpurgated [➡ WHOLENESS AND COMPLETENESS; 198] *Opposite*: abridged

undamaged *adj* **unspoiled**, untouched, unharmed, unhurt, intact, safe, pure, uncontaminated [➡ IN GOOD REPAIR; 1232] *Opposite*: spoiled

undaunted *adj* **fearless**, unconcerned, unworried, carefree, undisturbed, impervious, unafraid, undeterred [➡ COOL AND CALM; 536] *Opposite*: scared

undeceive *v* **inform**, tell, notify, enlighten, disabuse, put in the picture, apprise (*formal*) [➡ INFORM, ANNOUNCE, AND ISSUE; 611] *Opposite*: deceive

undecided 1 *adj* **of two minds**, in doubt, dithering, vacillating, uncertain, irresolute, hesitant, indecisive, unsure [➡ UNCERTAINTY; 559] *Opposite*: decided 2 *adj* **in doubt**, unresolved, open, unclear, vague, ambivalent, doubtful, ambiguous, uncertain [➡ UNCERTAIN; 175] *Opposite*: certain

undecipherable *adj* **illegible**, unreadable, inexplicable, mysterious, unfathomable, unexplained [➡ SECRET AND UNKNOWN; 179] *Opposite*: legible

undecorated *adj* **plain**, simple, unornamented, austere, spartan, bare, understated [➡ PLAIN; 232] *Opposite*: ornate

undefeatable *adj* [➡ SUCCESSFUL AND PROMISING; 81]

undefeated *adj* **unbeaten**, reigning, unvanquished, unconquered, unsubdued, unbowed [➡ SUCCESSFUL AND PROMISING; 81] *Opposite*: defeated

undefended *adj* **unguarded**, unprotected, unfortified, unpatrolled, deserted, defenseless, exposed, vulnerable [➡ IN DANGER; 237] *Opposite*: defended

undefiled *adj* **unsullied**, pure, unpolluted, unblemished, unstained, unsoiled, clean, clear, whole, spotless [➡ MORALLY GOOD; 774] *Opposite*: defiled (*formal*)

undefined *adj* **indeterminate**, vague, approximate, open-ended, indefinite, undecided, unclear [➡ VAGUENESS; 243] *Opposite*: defined

undemanding *adj* **easy**, straightforward, light, simple, unchallenging, cushy (*informal*) [➡ EASE AND SIMPLICITY; 200] *Opposite*: demanding

undemocratic *adj* **inequitable**, unfair, autocratic, high-handed, dictatorial, unconstitutional, unjust [➡ STYLES AND SYSTEMS OF GOVERNMENT; 806] *Opposite*: democratic

undemonstrative *adj* **unemotional**, restrained, phlegmatic, stoical, impassive, apathetic, reticent [➡ RETICENT AND UNFORTHCOMING; 631] *Opposite*: demonstrative

undemonstratively *adv* **unemotionally**, restrainedly, phlegmatically, stoically, impassively, apathetically, reticently [➡ RETICENT AND UNFORTHCOMING; 631] *Opposite*: demonstratively

undemonstrativeness *n* **restraint**, passivity, apathy, reticence, phlegm, stoicism, impassiveness [➡ RETICENT AND UNFORTHCOMING; 631]

undeniable *adj* **irrefutable**, indisputable, incontestable, incontrovertible, unquestionable, patent, indubitable, definite [➡ CERTAIN; 174] *Opposite*: questionable

undependability *n* **unreliability**, untrustworthiness, unpredictability, capriciousness, fickleness [➡ LACK OF COMMITMENT AND UNRELIABILITY; 509] *Opposite*: dependability

undependable *adj* **unreliable**, unpredictable, variable, erratic, fickle, capricious, untrustworthy [➡ LACK OF COMMITMENT AND UNRELIABILITY; 509] *Opposite*: dependable

under 1 *prep* **beneath**, below, in, underneath [➡ RELATIVE LOCATION; 161] *Opposite*: above 2 *prep* **below**, less than [➡ LESS; 126] *Opposite*: over

underachieve *v* **disappoint**, flounder, drift, drop out, underperform [➡ UNDERDO SOMETHING; 291] *Opposite*: excel

under a cloud *adj* [➡ IN TROUBLE AND DISADVANTAGED; 73]

under a curse *adj* [➡ IN TROUBLE AND DISADVANTAGED; 73]

underage *adj* **juvenile**, immature, youthful, young, callow [➡ BABYHOOD, CHILDHOOD, AND ADOLESCENCE; 917]

under arrest *adj* **detained**, held, in custody, imprisoned, jailed, apprehended, seized [➡ CAPTIVITY AND LOSS OF FREEDOM; 248] *Opposite*: released

under attack *adj* **embattled**, besieged, beleaguered, beset, battered, under fire [➡ IN TROUBLE AND DISADVANTAGED; 73]

undercarriage *part of* **aircraft** [➡ AIRCRAFT; 1148]

underclass *n* [➡ CLASS STATUS; 889]

underclothes *n* **underwear**, underclothing, underthings, undies (*informal*) [➡ ACCESSORIES, MILLINERY, AND LINGERIE; 867]

underclothing *see* **underclothes**

undercoat *n* [➡ COVERS AND COATINGS; 1246]

undercook *v* **underdo**, parboil, half-bake, prebake, precook [➡ COOKING AND FOOD PREPARATION; 353] *Opposite*: overcook

undercooked *adj* [➡ STATE OF PREPARED FOOD; 1171]

undercover *adj* **secret**, hidden, covert, disguised, clandestine, buried, concealed, obscured [➡ SECRET AND UNKNOWN; 179] *Opposite*: open

undercurrent **1** *n* **current**, tide, undertow, pull, stream, flow [➡ RIVERS, LAKES, AND STREAMS; 1042] **2** *n* **feeling**, hint, undertow, suggestion, connotation, trace, tinge, nuance [➡ MEANING; 690]

undercut *v* **undermine**, destabilize, detract, weaken, damage, demean, belittle [➡ WORSEN SOMETHING; 380] *Opposite*: strengthen

underdeveloped *adj* **immature**, small, undersized, weak, unused, unfledged, infantile [➡ SMALL; 1195]

underdo *v* **undercook**, parboil, half-bake, prebake, precook [➡ COOKING AND FOOD PREPARATION; 353] *Opposite*: overdo

underdog *n* **loser**, small fry, runner up, second best, little guy [➡ LAZY OR UNSUCCESSFUL PEOPLE; 948]

underdone *adj* **rare**, bloody, pink, undercooked [➡ STATE OF PREPARED FOOD; 1171] *Opposite*: overdone

under duress *adv* [➡ WITHOUT ENTHUSIASM; 287]

underemphasize *v* **play down**, understate, underplay, minimize, underrate, undervalue [➡ UNDERDO SOMETHING; 291] *Opposite*: overemphasize

underestimate *v* **undervalue**, underrate, misjudge, miscalculate [➡ UNDERDO SOMETHING; 291] *Opposite*: overestimate

underestimated *adj* [➡ UNPOPULAR AND UNWANTED; 258]

underfed *adj* **malnourished**, starving, frail, weak, undernourished, hungry, thin, famished [➡ BUILD; 477] *Opposite*: well-fed

under fire *adj* **targeted**, beleaguered, embattled, besieged, beset, battered [➡ IN TROUBLE AND DISADVANTAGED; 73]

undergarments *n* [➡ ACCESSORIES, MILLINERY, AND LINGERIE; 867]

undergo *v* **experience**, feel, suffer, endure, undertake, go through, submit to [➡ EXPERIENCE AND ENCOUNTER; 582] *Opposite*: avoid

undergraduate *n* [➡ STUDENTS AND PUPILS; 841]

underground **1** *adj* **subterranean**, below ground, covered, buried, deep, hidden [➡ IMPERCEPTIBLE; 26] **2** *adj* **subversive**, secretive, dissident, alternative, covert, concealed [➡ SECRET AND UNKNOWN; 179] *Opposite*: open

undergrowth *n* **bushes**, scrub, brushwood, vegetation, understory [➡ VEGETATION; 1025]

underhand **1** *adj* **deceitful**, dishonest, sneaky, mean, sly, low, secretive, secret, crafty, underhanded, below the belt [➡ DECEITFUL; 513] *Opposite*: open **2** *adv* **deceitfully**, dishonestly, sneakily, slyly, craftily, secretively, meanly [➡ DECEITFUL; 513] *Opposite*: openly

underhanded *see* **underhand**

underhandedly *adv* **deceitfully**, dishonestly, sneakily, slyly, secretively, craftily, meanly [➡ DECEITFUL; 513] *Opposite*: openly

underlie *v* **lie beneath**, lie behind, motivate, cause, inspire, trigger, bring about [➡ CAUSE TO HAPPEN; 31]

underline *v* **underscore**, emphasize, highlight, feature, stress, point out, accentuate [➡ CLAIM, INSIST, AND EMPHASIZE; 614] *Opposite*: ignore

underling *n* **minion**, inferior, subject, junior, subordinate, assistant [➡ SUBORDINATES AND ASSISTANTS; 966] *Opposite*: superior

underlying *adj* **fundamental**, original, causal, primary, basic, core, essential, principal, main [➡ FUNDAMENTAL; 195]

undermine *v* **weaken**, dent, chip away at, challenge, destabilize, demoralize, undercut, damage, emasculate (*formal*) [➡ WORSEN SOMETHING; 380] *Opposite*: bolster

underneath **1** *prep* **under**, beneath, below [➡ RELATIVE LOCATION; 161] *Opposite*: on top of **2** *n* **base**, bottom, underside, footing, foundation, substructure [➡ SUPPORTS AND BASES; 1255] *Opposite*: top

under negotiation *adj* **under discussion**, on the agenda, on the table, under debate [➡ HAPPENING AND IN PROGRESS; 32]

under no circumstances *adv* **by no means**, on no account, not at all, in no way, never [➡ NOT; 137]

undernourished *adj* **malnourished**, underfed, starved, hungry, famished [➡ BUILD; 477] *Opposite*: well-fed

undernourishment *n* **malnutrition**, starvation, hunger, famine [➡ DISORDERS OF THE DIGESTIVE SYSTEM; 713]

underpants *type of* **lower body underwear** [➡ ACCESSORIES, MILLINERY, AND LINGERIE; 867]

underpass *n* [➡ BRIDGES, TUNNELS, CROSSINGS, AND JUNCTIONS; 1112]

underperform *v* **fail**, underachieve, disappoint, flounder, drift [➡ UNDERDO SOMETHING; 291] *Opposite*: excel

underpin **1** *v* **shore up**, prop up, reinforce, support, buttress, fortify, underprop, jack up, strengthen, hold up [➡ IMPROVE STRENGTH AND DURABILITY; 378] *Opposite*: undermine **2** *v* **support**, lie beneath, underlie, give support to, bolster, fortify [➡ CHANGE OF INTENSITY: MORE; 394] *Opposite*: weaken

underpinning *n* **foundation**, reinforcement, groundwork, keystone, bedrock, footing, substructure [➡ SUPPORTS AND BASES; 1255]

underplay *v* **make light of**, minimize, understate, play down, talk down, dismiss, underemphasize [➡ UNDERDO SOMETHING; 291] *Opposite*: overplay

under pressure *adj* **stressed**, under duress, harried, on the spot, beleaguered, harassed, hassled (*informal*) [➡ IN TROUBLE AND DISADVANTAGED; 73] *Opposite*: unstressed

underprice *v* **cheapen**, undersell, underrepresent, understate [➡ UNDERDO SOMETHING; 291] *Opposite*: overprice

underprivileged *adj* **disadvantaged**, deprived, poor, needy, neglected, unfortunate, hard up (*informal*) [➡ POVERTY AND POOR; 892] *Opposite*: well-off

underprop *v* **underpin**, shore up, prop up, jack up, reinforce, support, buttress, fortify, hold up [➡ IMPROVE STRENGTH AND DURABILITY; 378] *Opposite*: undermine

under protest *adv* [➡ WITHOUT ENTHUSIASM; 287]

underrate *v* **undervalue**, underestimate, think little of, devalue, misjudge, play down [➡UNDERDO SOMETHING; 291] *Opposite*: overrate

underrated *adj* **undervalued**, underestimated, unappreciated, unrecognized, misunderstood, belittled [➡UNPOPULAR AND UNWANTED; 258] *Opposite*: overrated

underrepresent *v* **understate**, undersell, lessen, play down, make light of, diminish [➡UNDERDO SOMETHING; 291] *Opposite*: overemphasize

underscore *v* **underline**, highlight, emphasize, accentuate, call attention to, draw attention to, stress, feature, point out [➡CLAIM, INSIST, AND EMPHASIZE; 614] *Opposite*: ignore

undersea *adj* **submarine**, underwater, bathyal, bathypelagic [➡THE SEAS, OCEANS, AND SHORES; 1041]

undersell *v* **understate**, play down, make light of, denigrate, cheapen, underrepresent, underprice [➡UNDERDO SOMETHING; 291] *Opposite*: oversell

undershirt *type of* **upper body underwear** [➡ACCESSORIES, MILLINERY, AND LINGERIE; 867]

undershrub *n* **subshrub**, bush, plant [➡BUSHES AND SHRUBS; 1027]

underside *n* **base**, bottom, underneath, basement, foundation, footing [➡SUPPORTS AND BASES; 1255]

undersize *adj* [➡SMALL; 1196]

undersized *adj* **puny**, underdeveloped, small, short, stunted, feeble, measly (*informal*) [➡SMALL; 1195]

underskirt *type of* **lower body underwear** [➡ACCESSORIES, MILLINERY, AND LINGERIE; 867]

understand 1 *v* **comprehend**, appreciate, know, recognize, realize, be aware of, be familiar with, be au fait with, apprehend, fathom, grasp, take in, figure out, work out, see, be with somebody, absorb, get it (*informal*), get the picture (*informal*), cotton on (*informal*), cognize (*formal*) [➡UNDERSTAND AND GRASP; 759] 2 *v* **sympathize**, empathize, identify, appreciate [➡BE CONCERNED AND CARE; 581]

understandable *adj* **comprehensible**, clear, logical, reasonable, fathomable, plausible [➡CONCISE AND CLEAR; 202] *Opposite*: incomprehensible

understanding 1 *n* **agreement**, arrangement, deal, contract, settlement, accord, pact, bond, harmony [➡HARMONY; 155] 2 *adj* **sympathetic**, empathetic, considerate, thoughtful, kind, accepting, indulgent, appreciative, supportive, tolerant, aware [➡GENEROSITY AND KINDNESS; 495] *Opposite*: unsympathetic 3 *n* **sympathy**, empathy, identification, consideration, kindness, compassion, indulgence, tolerance, support [➡COMPASSION AND FORGIVENESS; 551] *Opposite*: indifference 4 *n* **grasp**, perception, intellect, mind, wit, intelligence, cleverness, ability, sense, insight, knowledge, comprehension, awareness, appreciation, discernment, conception [➡POSITIVE INTELLECTUAL CHARACTERISTICS; 524] *Opposite*: ignorance 5 *n* **interpretation**, construction, personal feeling, estimation, perception, belief, opinion [➡POINTS OF VIEW; 767]

understate *v* **play down**, minimize, devalue, belittle, make little of [➡UNDERDO SOMETHING; 291] *Opposite*: exaggerate

understated *adj* **modest**, inconspicuous, discreet, unfussy, minimalist, simple, low-key, unassuming, unobtrusive, unpretentious, restrained [➡ACCEPTABLE AND PASSABLE; 219] *Opposite*: exaggerated

understatement *n* **irony**, dryness, sarcasm, underestimation [➡JOKES AND TEASING; 674] *Opposite*: exaggeration

understood *adj* **unspoken**, tacit, silent, unstated, unwritten, implicit, assumed, agreed, implied [➡KNOWN AND FAMOUS; 181] *Opposite*: explicit

understory *n* **forest floor**, bushes, underwood, brush, scrub, undergrowth [➡VEGETATION; 1025]

understrength 1 *adj* **understaffed**, short-handed, short-staffed, short, down, below par, reduced [➡TOO FEW, TOO LITTLE; 122] 2 *adj* **dilute**, weak, thin, diluted, watered down, watery [➡WEAKNESS; 241]

understudy *n* **substitute**, cover, standby, stand-in, replacement, double, deputy [➡SUBSTITUTES AND STAND-INS; 399]

undertake *v* **take on**, assume, start, commence, embark on, carry out, agree to, accept, take upon yourself [➡ATTEMPT AN ACTION; 261] *Opposite*: relinquish

undertaker *n* **funeral director**, mortician, embalmer [➡BURIAL AND PREPARATION FOR BURIAL; 929]

undertaker's (*UK*) *n* [➡BURIAL AND PREPARATION FOR BURIAL; 929]

undertaking *n* **responsibility**, task, job, enterprise, commission, mission, duty, activity [➡ACTIONS OR UNDERTAKINGS; 259]

under-the-counter *adj* **illegal**, unofficial, illicit, wrongful, on the side, criminal [➡ILLEGAL; 816] *Opposite*: aboveboard

under-the-table *adj* **underhand**, unofficial, secret, surreptitious, sneaky, on the side, furtive, clandestine, unreported, undisclosed, hush-hush (*informal*) [➡SECRET AND UNKNOWN; 179] *Opposite*: aboveboard

under the weather *adj* **ill**, unwell, sick, run-down [➡ILL AND SICK; 740] *Opposite*: well

under the wire *adj* [➡PROMPTNESS: LATE; 100]

underthings *n* **underwear**, underclothes, underclothing, undies (*informal*) [➡ACCESSORIES, MILLINERY, AND LINGERIE; 867]

undertone *n* **hint**, suggestion, trace, tinge, undercurrent, air, feeling, connotation, nuance [➡MEANING; 690] *Opposite*: overtone

undertow *n* **current**, undercurrent, tide, pull, stream, flow [➡THE SEAS, OCEANS, AND SHORES; 1041]

undervalue *v* **underrate**, underestimate, play down, devalue, belittle [➡UNDERDO SOMETHING; 291] *Opposite*: overrate

undervalued *adj* [➡UNPOPULAR AND UNWANTED; 258]

underwater 1 *adj* **submerged**, sunken, flooded, subaquatic, subsurface, immersed, inundated [➡WET; 1240] *Opposite*: dry 2 *adj* **undersea**, submarine, sunken, submerged, marine [➡GENERAL LOCATIONS; 158]

underway *adj* **happening**, in progress, ongoing, on the go, proceeding, in motion [➡HAPPENING AND IN PROGRESS; 32]

underwear *n* **underclothes**, underclothing, underthings, undies (*informal*) [➡ACCESSORIES, MILLINERY, AND LINGERIE; 867]

underwear

◆ *types of lower body underwear*
bloomers (*dated*), boxer shorts, briefs, corset, crinoline, drawers, foundation garment, garter, girdle, G-string, jockstrap, knee-highs, legwarmer, long johns, nylons, panties, pantyhose, petticoat, slip, sock, stockings, string, support hose, thigh-highs, thong, underpants, underskirt

◆ *types of upper body underwear*
basque, body stocking, body suit, bra, camisole, chemise, teddy, undershirt, union suit

underweight *adj* **skinny**, skin-and-bone, scrawny, half-starved, underfed, malnourished, emaciated [➡ BUILD; 477] *Opposite*: overweight

underwing *type of* **moth** [➡ MOTHS AND BUTTERFLIES; 1015]

underwired *adj* [➡ DESCRIBING CLOTHES; 869]

underworld 1 *n* **gangland**, criminal world, netherworld (*formal*) [➡ CRIMINALS; 821] **2** *adj* **criminal**, gangland, illicit, illegal, unlawful, felonious [➡ ILLEGAL; 816] *Opposite*: legal

under wraps (*informal*) *adj* **hidden**, secret, confidential, private, buried, covert, concealed, obscured [➡ SECRET AND UNKNOWN; 179] *Opposite*: open

underwrite *v* **guarantee**, countersign, back, endorse, fund, finance, support, subsidize, bankroll (*informal*) [➡ BUSINESS ACTIVITIES AND PHENOMENA; 794]

underwriter 1 *n* **sponsor**, backer, supporter, guarantor, financier, benefactor, bankroller (*informal*) [➡ REPRESENTATIVES AND PATRONS; 968] **2** *n* [➡ PEOPLE INVOLVED IN FINANCE; 804]

undeserved *adj* **unwarranted**, unmerited, unearned, unfair, unjustifiable, unjustified [➡ UNPOPULAR AND UNWANTED; 258] *Opposite*: deserved

undesirable *adj* **unwanted**, unwelcome, uninvited, objectionable, disagreeable, adverse, detrimental, unattractive, disadvantageous [➡ UNPOPULAR AND UNWANTED; 258] *Opposite*: desirable

undetectable *adj* **untraceable**, indiscernible, unnoticeable, imperceptible, invisible, inaudible, faint [➡ IMPERCEPTIBLE; 26] *Opposite*: obvious

undetected *adj* [➡ SECRET AND UNKNOWN; 179]

undetermined 1 *adj* **hesitating**, undecided, irresolute, unsettled, vacillating, sitting on the fence, uncertain, wavering, hesitant, unsure, faltering [➡ UNCERTAINTY; 559] *Opposite*: decided **2** *adj* **unresolved**, indeterminate, indefinite, undecided, incalculable, uncertain, undefined, unsettled, unspecified [➡ UNCERTAIN; 175] *Opposite*: definite **3** *adj* **unknown**, undiscovered, unidentified, unheard of, unfamiliar, unspecified [➡ SECRET AND UNKNOWN; 179] *Opposite*: known

undeterred *adj* [➡ COOL AND CALM; 536]

undeveloped *adj* **immature**, young, embryonic, unripe, emergent, new, untrained [➡ NEW, MODERN; 166] *Opposite*: mature

undeviating *adj* **unswerving**, firm, solid, absolute, total,

unshakable, loyal, undying, unequivocal [➡ HARD-WORKING AND COMMITTED; 500] *Opposite*: shaky

undies (*informal*) *n* **underwear**, underclothes, underclothing, underthings [➡ ACCESSORIES, MILLINERY, AND LINGERIE; 867]

undifferentiated *adj* [➡ SAMENESS; 150]

undignified *adj* **unseemly**, unbecoming, indecorous, improper, humiliating, degrading, shameful, inappropriate [➡ INAPPROPRIATE AND UNSUITABLE; 224] *Opposite*: dignified

undiluted *adj* **straight**, neat, unadulterated, unmixed, full-strength, pure [➡ RAW AND NATURAL; 1214] *Opposite*: diluted

undiplomatic *adj* **tactless**, crass, thoughtless, indiscreet, inconsiderate, blunt, unthinking, unsubtle, insensitive, indelicate [➡ BAD MANNERS AND SOCIAL SKILLS; 521] *Opposite*: diplomatic

undirected *adj* **purposeless**, aimless, objectiveless, directionless, pointless, wandering [➡ DIRECTION OF MOTION; 345] *Opposite*: purposeful

undiscerning *adj* [➡ NEGATIVE INTELLECTUAL CHARACTERISTICS; 525]

undisciplined *adj* **unmanageable**, out of control, wild, unruly, disobedient, disorderly, disruptive, riotous [➡ REBELLIOUSNESS AND DISOBEDIENCE; 565] *Opposite*: well-behaved

undisclosed *adj* **secret**, unnamed, hidden, unrevealed, unidentified, private, anonymous, nameless [➡ SECRET AND UNKNOWN; 179] *Opposite*: known

undiscovered *adj* [➡ SECRET AND UNKNOWN; 179]

undisguised *adj* **unconcealed**, unchallenged, open, uncontested, overt, accepted, obvious, recognized, evident, plain, blatant [➡ PERCEPTIBLE; 25] *Opposite*: concealed

undisposed *adj* **unwilling**, loath, reluctant, unprepared, hesitant, wary, uninclined [➡ UNWILLINGNESS AND STUBBORNNESS; 564] *Opposite*: disposed

undisputed *adj* **acknowledged**, undoubted, certain, undeniable, unquestionable, definite [➡ CERTAIN; 174] *Opposite*: questionable

undistinctive *adj* [➡ ORDINARINESS; 244]

undistinguished *adj* **ordinary**, everyday, run-of-the-mill, commonplace, nothing special, unremarkable, unexceptional, mediocre, indifferent [➡ ORDINARINESS; 244] *Opposite*: unusual

undistorted *adj* **factual**, truthful, exact, accurate, unembroidered, unvarnished, matter-of-fact, plain, faithful, unembellished [➡ TRUE AND REAL; 171] *Opposite*: inaccurate

undisturbed 1 *adj* **uninterrupted**, in peace, unbroken, unobstructed [➡ WHOLENESS AND COMPLETENESS; 198] *Opposite*: interrupted **2** *adj* **untouched**, intact, whole, flawless, undamaged, in situ, unmoved [➡ IN GOOD REPAIR; 1232] *Opposite*: damaged **3** *adj* **peaceful**, serene, composed, at peace, at ease, unflustered, unworried [➡ COOL AND CALM; 536] *Opposite*: anxious

undivided *adj* **complete**, entire, whole, total, full, exclusive, unbroken [➡ WHOLENESS AND COMPLETENESS; 198] *Opposite*: partial

undo 1 *v* **unfasten**, untie, unbutton, loosen, disengage, unwrap, open, unknot, unravel [➡ ABOLISH AND ANNUL; 452] *Oppo-*

site: fasten **2** *v* **cancel out**, cancel, nullify, invalidate, render null and void, reverse, work against, negate (*formal*) [➡ MAKE IMPOSSIBLE; 276]

undoing *n* **downfall**, ruin, ruination, collapse, destruction, humiliation, shame, defeat [➡ FAILURE; 77] *Opposite*: making

undone **1** *adj* **uncompleted**, unfinished, incomplete, half-done, unconcluded, half-finished [➡ UNFINISHEDNESS; 239] *Opposite*: done **2** *adj* **unfastened**, open, gaping, unzipped, unbuttoned, unlocked, untied [➡ UNFASTEN AND UNDO; 409] **3** *adj* **ruined**, in trouble, lost, in deep water, destroyed, done for (*informal*) [➡ IN TROUBLE AND DISADVANTAGED; 73] *Opposite*: fine

undoubted *adj* **certain**, sure, absolute, definite, indubitable, undisputed, unquestionable, indisputable [➡ CERTAIN; 174] *Opposite*: doubtful

undreamed-of *adj* **unexpected**, unhoped-for, unimaginable, unanticipated, unlooked-for, surprising [➡ EXTRAORDINARY: AMAZING; 204] *Opposite*: anticipated

undress *v* **strip off**, strip, unclothe, uncloak, bare, disrobe (*formal*) [➡ DRESS, WEAR, AND UNDRESS; 868] *Opposite*: dress

undressed *adj* **naked**, bare, nude, stripped, with nothing on, unclothed, in the buff (*informal*), in your birthday suit (*slang humorous*) [➡ DRESS, WEAR, AND UNDRESS; 868] *Opposite*: dressed

See Compare and Contrast at **naked**.

undue *adj* **unwarranted**, excessive, unnecessary, unjustified, unjustifiable, gratuitous, uncalled-for [➡ UNIMPORTANT AND UNNECESSARY; 238] *Opposite*: justified

undulant *see* **undulating**

undulate *v* **roll**, ripple, rise and fall, swell, heave, surge [➡ BOUNCE, UNDULATE, AND VIBRATE; 308]

undulating *adj* **rolling**, rising and falling, swelling, heaving, surging, rippling, undulant (*formal*) [➡ ROUNDED SHAPE; 1218]

undulation *n* **wave**, ripple, furrow, crinkle, wrinkle, fold [➡ BOUNCE, UNDULATE, AND VIBRATE; 308]

unduly *adv* **excessively**, overly, disproportionately, unjustifiably, undeservedly, improperly [➡ TO A GREAT EXTENT; 132] *Opposite*: justifiably

undying *adj* **unending**, never-ending, endless, perpetual, eternal, everlasting, abiding, enduring, constant, ceaseless [➡ PERMANENCE: WITHOUT END; 94] *Opposite*: inconstant

unearned *adj* **undeserved**, unwarranted, unmerited, unjustified, uncalled-for, inappropriate [➡ INCORRECT AND ERRONEOUS; 222]

unearth **1** *v* **disclose**, uncover, discover, find, expose, reveal, bring to light, come across, happen upon [➡ FIND; 463] *Opposite*: cover up **2** *v* **dig up**, exhume, disinter, excavate, extract [➡ CAUSE TO APPEAR; 5] *Opposite*: bury

unearthly **1** *adj* **unreasonable**, inappropriate, outrageous, ridiculous, absurd [➡ UNACCEPTABLE AND UNFORGIVABLE; 225] *Opposite*: acceptable **2** *adj* **eerie**, weird, bizarre, strange, macabre, ghostly, mysterious, supernatural, unnatural, creepy (*informal*) [➡ BIZARRE AND PECULIAR; 257] *Opposite*: normal

unease *n* **anxiety**, nervousness, restlessness, awkwardness, uneasiness, disquiet, discomfort, agitation, apprehension, worry [➡ FEELINGS ABOUT THE FUTURE; 533] *Opposite*: calm

See Compare and Contrast at **worry**.

uneasiness *n* **anxiety**, nervousness, restlessness, awkwardness, unease, disquiet, discomfort, agitation, apprehension, worry [➡ FEELINGS ABOUT THE FUTURE; 533] *Opposite*: calmness

uneasy *adj* **anxious**, nervous, troubled, uncomfortable, ill at ease, perturbed, edgy, on edge, apprehensive, tense [➡ CONFUSION, ANXIETY, AND WORRY; 540] *Opposite*: calm

uneconomic **1** *adj* **unprofitable**, unviable, profitless, lossmaking (*UK*) [➡ UNSUCCESSFUL AND UNPROMISING; 76] *Opposite*: profitable **2** *adj* **inefficient**, wasteful, uneconomical, improvident, extravagant, profligate [➡ WASTEFUL AND UNECONOMICAL; 246] *Opposite*: efficient

uneconomical *adj* **inefficient**, wasteful, extravagant, uneconomic, profligate, improvident [➡ WASTEFUL AND UNECONOMICAL; 246] *Opposite*: efficient

unedited *adj* **complete**, unabridged, unexpurgated, uncut, full-length, whole, unrevised, full [➡ WHOLENESS AND COMPLETENESS; 198] *Opposite*: edited

uneducated *adj* **unschooled**, untaught, ignorant, illiterate, uninformed, untutored, unqualified [➡ LEVELS OF EDUCATION AND SOPHISTICATION; 894] *Opposite*: educated

unembarrassed *adj* [➡ COOL AND CALM; 536]

unembellished **1** *adj* **unadorned**, plain, without ornamentation, simple, straightforward [➡ PLAIN; 232] *Opposite*: fancy **2** *adj* **factual**, unembroidered, undistorted, truthful, straightforward, unvarnished, exact, accurate, literal, faithful [➡ TRUE AND REAL; 171] *Opposite*: fictional

unembroidered *adj* **factual**, unembellished, undistorted, truthful, unvarnished, exact, straightforward, accurate, literal, matter-of-fact [➡ TRUE AND REAL; 171] *Opposite*: florid

unemotional *adj* **impassive**, dispassionate, undemonstrative, unresponsive, detached, inexpressive, poker-faced, composed, objective, cold [➡ NEUTRALITY AND INDIFFERENCE; 553] *Opposite*: emotional

unemployed *adj* **jobless**, out of work, out of a job, laid off, on unemployment, idle, not working, made redundant (*UK*), receiving benefit (*UK*), unwaged (*UK*) [➡ EMPLOYMENT STATUS; 831] *Opposite*: employed

unemployment *n* **joblessness**, job loss, idleness, redundancy (*UK*) [➡ WORK-RELATED ACTIVITIES; 834] *Opposite*: employment

unending *adj* **endless**, never-ending, eternal, everlasting, interminable, unrelenting, continuous, incessant, relentless, unremitting [➡ PERMANENCE: WITHOUT END; 94] *Opposite*: finite

unendurable *adj* **insufferable**, unbearable, intolerable, insupportable, excruciating, agonizing, painful [➡ EMOTIONALLY UNPLEASANT AND UPSETTING; 227] *Opposite*: bearable

unenlightened **1** *adj* **superstitious**, prejudiced, ignorant, uncivilized, benighted, unaware [➡ IGNORANCE; 557] *Oppo-*

site: rational **2** *adj* **ignorant**, benighted, uneducated, uninformed, unsophisticated, uncivilized [➡ LEVELS OF EDUCATION AND SOPHISTICATION; 894] *Opposite*: informed

unenthusiastic *adj* **apathetic**, indifferent, unresponsive, lukewarm, half-hearted, subdued, cool, unimpressed, unexcited, uninterested [➡ NEUTRALITY AND INDIFFERENCE; 553] *Opposite*: enthusiastic

unenticing *adj* [➡ UGLINESS AND UNATTRACTIVENESS; 233]

unenviable *adj* **undesirable**, disagreeable, unpleasant, uninviting, objectionable, unpopular, unwelcome, unattractive, unappealing, distasteful [➡ UNPOPULAR AND UNWANTED; 258] *Opposite*: enviable

unequal **1** *adj* **uneven**, unbalanced, lopsided, asymmetrical, disproportionate, disparate, irregular, dissimilar [➡ DIFFERENCE; 149] *Opposite*: equal **2** *adj* **unfair**, inequitable, one-sided, mismatched, unbalanced [➡ MORALLY BAD OR IMPROPER; 775] *Opposite*: fair **3** *adj* **unsatisfactory**, unfit, unable, incapable, inadequate, wanting [➡ UNSKILLED; 529]

unequaled *adj* **unrivaled**, unique, unmatched, unchallenged, superior, unparalleled, matchless, incomparable, unsurpassed [➡ SUPERIORITY; 152] *Opposite*: ordinary

unequally **1** *adv* **unevenly**, lopsidedly, inequitably, asymmetrically, irregularly, disproportionately [➡ DIFFERENCE; 149] *Opposite*: evenly **2** *adv* **unfairly**, inequitably, one-sidedly, unjustly [➡ MORALLY BAD OR IMPROPER; 775] *Opposite*: fairly

unequivocal *adj* **clear**, plain, unambiguous, unmistakable, explicit, indisputable, undeniable, obvious, definite [➡ CONCISE AND CLEAR; 202]

unerring *adj* **certain**, sure, absolute, positive, definite, unmistaken, correct, infallible, faultless [➡ CORRECT AND FAULTLESS; 182] *Opposite*: faulty

unessential *adj* **dispensable**, superfluous, unnecessary, replaceable, expendable, nonessential [➡ UNIMPORTANT AND UNNECESSARY; 238] *Opposite*: essential

unethical *adj* **unprincipled**, immoral, wrong, bad, unscrupulous, dishonorable, disreputable, corrupt, depraved [➡ MORALLY BAD OR IMPROPER; 775] *Opposite*: ethical

uneven **1** *adj* **rough**, jagged, bumpy, patchy, irregular, potholed, rutted [➡ PHYSICAL TEXTURE; 1222] *Opposite*: level **2** *adj* **unequal**, unbalanced, lopsided, asymmetrical, disproportionate, irregular, unsymmetrical, top-heavy [➡ DIFFERENCE; 149] *Opposite*: equal **3** *adj* **mismatched**, one-sided, unfair, unbalanced, disproportionate [➡ DISHARMONY; 156] *Opposite*: fair

unevenly *adv* **unequally**, asymmetrically, irregularly, unsymmetrically, disproportionately [➡ DIFFERENCE; 149] *Opposite*: equally

unevenness **1** *n* **roughness**, jaggedness, bumpiness, patchiness [➡ PHYSICAL TEXTURE; 1222] *Opposite*: evenness **2** *n* **inequality**, disproportion, irregularity, one-sidedness, disparity, asymmetry [➡ DISHARMONY; 156] *Opposite*: equality

uneventful *adj* **boring**, monotonous, ordinary, humdrum, dull, run of the mill, everyday, nothing to write home about, unexciting [➡ BORING AND UNINTERESTING; 234] *Opposite*: exciting

unexceptionable *adj* **inoffensive**, unobjectionable, faultless, irreproachable, acceptable, beyond reproach, satisfactory [➡ ACCEPTABLE AND PASSABLE; 219] *Opposite*: exceptionable (*formal*)

unexceptional *adj* **undistinguished**, nondescript, anonymous, modest, indifferent, unremarkable, inconspicuous, run-of-the-mill, typical, normal [➡ ORDINARINESS; 244] *Opposite*: extraordinary

unexcited *adj* **calm**, restrained, subdued, unresponsive, impassive, unimpressed, unenthusiastic, indifferent, tepid, lukewarm [➡ NEUTRALITY AND INDIFFERENCE; 553] *Opposite*: excited

unexciting *adj* **dull**, boring, tedious, monotonous, humdrum, dreary, insipid, uninteresting, tame, lackluster [➡ BORING AND UNINTERESTING; 234] *Opposite*: exciting

unexpected *adj* **unforeseen**, unanticipated, unpredicted, surprising, startling, astonishing, sudden, out of the blue [➡ UNPLANNED AND UNEXPECTED; 281] *Opposite*: expected

unexplainable *adj* [➡ BIZARRE AND PECULIAR; 257]

unexplained *adj* **mysterious**, unsolved, inexplicable, impenetrable, arcane, secret, baffling [➡ SECRET AND UNKNOWN; 179] *Opposite*: apparent

unexplored *adj* [➡ SECRET AND UNKNOWN; 179]

unexpressed *adj* **unstated**, unspoken, unsaid, unknown [➡ SECRET AND UNKNOWN; 179] *Opposite*: articulated

unexpurgated *adj* [➡ WHOLENESS AND COMPLETENESS; 198]

unfading *adj* [➡ PERMANENCE: WITHOUT END; 94]

unfailing *adj* **reliable**, certain, dependable, trustworthy, constant, consistent, abiding, lasting, unshakable, enduring [➡ PERMANENCE: WITHOUT END; 94] *Opposite*: erratic

unfair **1** *adj* **unjust**, inequitable, iniquitous, unwarranted, unmerited, undue, unreasonable, excessive, wrong, undeserved [➡ MORALLY BAD OR IMPROPER; 775] *Opposite*: fair **2** *adj* **unethical**, dishonest, dishonorable, deceitful, underhand, unscrupulous, devious, fraudulent, false, crooked (*informal*) [➡ DECEITFUL; 513] *Opposite*: honest **3** *adj* **partial**, one-sided, biased, prejudicial, discriminating, bigoted [➡ MORALLY BAD OR IMPROPER; 775] *Opposite*: fair

unfairness **1** *n* **injustice**, wrongness, wrong, iniquitousness, unreasonableness, inequitableness, inequity, excess, inequality [➡ MORALLY BAD OR IMPROPER; 775] *Opposite*: fairness **2** *n* **unethicalness**, unethicality, dishonesty, dishonorableness, deceitfulness, fraudulence, falseness, underhandedness, crookedness [➡ DECEITFUL; 513] *Opposite*: honesty **3** *n* **partiality**, one-sidedness, bias, prejudice, discrimination, inequity, favoritism, bigotry [➡ PREJUDICE; 550] *Opposite*: fairness

unfaithful *adj* **disloyal**, false, untrue, adulterous, two-timing (*informal*), treacherous, traitorous, faithless, double-crossing [➡ DECEITFUL; 513] *Opposite*: faithful

unfaithfulness *n* **disloyalty**, infidelity, falseness, adultery, treachery, betrayal, deceitfulness, faithlessness [➡ BAD BEHAVIOR OR ACTIONS; 254] *Opposite*: faithfulness

unfaltering *adj* **untiring**, indefatigable, tireless, unflagging, persistent, tenacious, resolute, determined, constant, steadfast, dogged [➡ HARD-WORKING AND COMMITTED; 500] *Opposite*: faltering

unfamiliar 1 *adj* **unknown**, new, untried, strange, alien, different, unusual, foreign, exotic [➡ SECRET AND UNKNOWN; 179] *Opposite*: familiar 2 *adj* **unacquainted**, unaccustomed, unaware, unversed, unskilled, inexperienced, ignorant, unused [➡ UNSKILLED; 529] *Opposite*: familiar

unfamiliarity 1 *n* **newness**, strangeness, unusualness, foreignness, exoticism, exoticness [➡ SECRET AND UNKNOWN; 179] *Opposite*: familiarity 2 *n* **unaccustomedness**, unacquaintedness, inexperience, ignorance, unawareness [➡ IGNORANCE; 557] *Opposite*: familiarity

unfashionable *adj* **out-of-date**, outmoded, dated, old-fashioned, behind the times, obsolete, defunct, passé, outdated [➡ OLD, OLD-FASHIONED; 167] *Opposite*: trendy (*informal*)

unfasten *v* **undo**, unhook, unlock, disengage, detach, untie, unbutton, release, uncouple, unbolt [➡ UNFASTEN AND UNDO; 409] *Opposite*: fasten

unfastened *adj* **undone**, loosened, untied, unbuttoned, unzipped, unlaced, open, unsecured, loose, unattached, unhooked, unstuck [➡ UNFASTEN AND UNDO; 409] *Opposite*: fastened

unfathomability *n* [➡ DIFFICULTY AND COMPLEXITY; 242]

unfathomable 1 *adj* **deep**, profound, bottomless, unsounded, unplumbed, immeasurable, vast [➡ DEPTH: DEEP; 1201] *Opposite*: shallow 2 *adj* **incomprehensible**, impenetrable, inscrutable, unknowable, indecipherable, arcane, enigmatic, mysterious, inexplicable [➡ DIFFICULTY AND COMPLEXITY; 242] *Opposite*: straightforward

unfathomableness *n* [➡ DIFFICULTY AND COMPLEXITY; 242]

unfavorable 1 *adj* **disapproving**, negative, uncomplimentary, opposed, hostile, critical, harsh, disparaging [➡ ACCUSATORY AND DISAPPROVING; 634] *Opposite*: approving 2 *adj* **harmful**, adverse, bad, detrimental, disadvantageous, damaging [➡ BAD AND BADLY; 223] *Opposite*: beneficial

unfeasibility *n* [➡ IMPOSSIBLE AND IMPROBABLE; 178]

unfeasible *adj* **impracticable**, impractical, unworkable, unachievable, out of the question, impossible, unrealistic, unattainable [➡ IMPOSSIBLE AND IMPROBABLE; 178] *Opposite*: feasible

unfeeling *adj* **unsympathetic**, hardhearted, callous, cruel, heartless, pitiless, cold, insensitive, uncaring, inhuman [➡ SELFISH AND UNKIND; 505] *Opposite*: sympathetic

unfeigned *adj* [➡ TRUE AND REAL; 171]

unfetter *v* **release**, liberate, free, unchain, unshackle, unbind, untie, set free, let loose [➡ FREEDOM AND LIBERTY; 208] *Opposite*: fetter

unfettered *adj* **freed**, unencumbered, unconstrained, unregulated, autonomous, unrestrained, unrestricted, unbound, unchained [➡ FREEDOM AND LIBERTY; 208] *Opposite*: constrained

unfilled *adj* **empty**, vacant, void, unoccupied, untaken [➡ EMPTY; 1238] *Opposite*: full

unfinished *adj* **incomplete**, uncompleted, fragmentary,

partial, ongoing, in progress [➡ UNFINISHEDNESS; 239] *Opposite*: finished

unfinished business *n* [➡ UNCERTAINTY; 559]

unfit 1 *adj* **unsuitable**, inappropriate, unsuited, inapt, unacceptable [➡ INAPPROPRIATE AND UNSUITABLE; 224] *Opposite*: suitable 2 *adj* **unqualified**, incompetent, inept, useless, incapable, inadequate, ineligible, inexpert, hopeless, untrained [➡ UNSKILLED; 529] *Opposite*: competent 3 *adj* **out of shape**, out of condition, unhealthy, weak, puny, frail, flabby (*informal*), ailing (*dated*) [➡ UNFIT AND WEAK; 739] *Opposite*: fit

unfitted *adj* **unsuited**, unequipped, unprepared, unsuitable, unqualified, incompatible [➡ INAPPROPRIATE AND UNSUITABLE; 224] *Opposite*: fitted

unfitting *adj* **unsuitable**, inappropriate, unbecoming, out of place, unseemly, unacceptable, improper, unfortunate, incorrect [➡ INAPPROPRIATE AND UNSUITABLE; 224] *Opposite*: fitting

unfix *v* **detach**, loosen, disengage, separate, undo, free [➡ UNFASTEN AND UNDO; 409] *Opposite*: attach

unfixed *adj* [➡ IN BAD REPAIR; 1234]

unflagging *adj* **untiring**, indefatigable, tireless, unfaltering, persistent, tenacious, resolute, determined, steadfast, constant, loyal [➡ HARD-WORKING AND COMMITTED; 500] *Opposite*: weak

unflappability *n* **calmness**, coolness, patience, composure, control, imperturbability, phlegm [➡ CONFIDENCE AND COMPOSURE; 499] *Opposite*: excitability

unflappable *adj* **composed**, calm, unflustered, collected, imperturbable, unexcitable, level-headed, cool as a cucumber, cool, serene, self-possessed [➡ CONFIDENCE AND COMPOSURE; 499] *Opposite*: anxious

unflattering 1 *adj* **unbecoming**, unattractive, unappealing, ugly [➡ UGLINESS AND UNATTRACTIVENESS; 233] *Opposite*: becoming 2 *adj* **critical**, uncomplimentary, faultfinding, unfavorable [➡ ACCUSATORY AND DISAPPROVING; 634] *Opposite*: complimentary

unfledged *adj* **inexperienced**, naive, innocent, fresh, immature, ignorant [➡ IGNORANCE; 557] *Opposite*: experienced

unflinching *adj* **unwavering**, constant, steady, undaunted, persistent, resolute, dogged, steadfast, staunch, fearless [➡ HARD-WORKING AND COMMITTED; 500] *Opposite*: wavering

unflustered *adj* **composed**, calm, unflappable, collected, imperturbable, unruffled, level-headed, cool, in control, serene [➡ COOL AND CALM; 536] *Opposite*: agitated

unfocused 1 *adj* **blurred**, unclear, fuzzy, indistinct, bleary, out-of-focus [➡ VISUAL TEXTURE; 1221] *Opposite*: clear 2 *adj* **ill-defined**, nonspecific, imprecise, woolly, vague [➡ VAGUENESS; 243] *Opposite*: focused

unfold 1 *v* **open out**, open up, unfurl, spread out, display, unroll, unwrap [➡ CAUSE TO APPEAR; 5] *Opposite*: fold up 2 *v* **explain**, clarify, make known, disclose, reveal, describe [➡ EXPLAIN AND CLARIFY; 610] *Opposite*: conceal 3 *v* **develop**, evolve, grow, progress, advance, expand [➡ GRADUALLY COME INTO EXISTENCE; 1] *Opposite*: deteriorate

unforced *adj* **voluntary**, natural, spontaneous, unwitting, unprompted, effortless, artless, genuine [➡ THE WILL AND WILLINGNESS; 563] *Opposite*: forced

unforeseeable *adj* **unexpected**, unanticipated, undreamed-of, unpredictable, surprise [➡ SECRET AND UNKNOWN; 179] *Opposite*: predictable

unforeseen *adj* **unexpected**, unanticipated, unpredicted, surprising, startling, astonishing, sudden [➡ UNPLANNED AND UNEXPECTED; 281] *Opposite*: expected

unforgettable *adj* **memorable**, remarkable, treasured, cherished, haunting, extraordinary, impressive, notable, exceptional [➡ EXTRAORDINARY: AMAZING; 204] *Opposite*: unremarkable

unforgettably *adv* **memorably**, remarkably, hauntingly, notably, exceptionally, extraordinarily [➡ INTERESTING AND MEANINGFUL; 190] *Opposite*: unremarkably

unforgivable *adj* **unpardonable**, inexcusable, indefensible, unjustifiable, intolerable, deplorable, reprehensible, beyond the pale [➡ UNACCEPTABLE AND UNFORGIVABLE; 225] *Opposite*: understandable

unforgiving 1 *adj* **intolerant**, merciless, pitiless, remorseless, vindictive, ruthless, callous, unmoved [➡ SELFISH AND UNKIND; 505] *Opposite*: tolerant 2 *adj* **demanding**, exacting, taxing, challenging, hard, difficult [➡ PHYSICALLY UNPLEASANT; 226] *Opposite*: easy

unformed 1 *adj* **shapeless**, formless, indistinct, imprecise, amorphous, embryonic [➡ SHAPELESSNESS; 1219] *Opposite*: distinct 2 *adj* **undeveloped**, immature, green, callow, underdeveloped, inexperienced [➡ IGNORANCE; 557] *Opposite*: mature

unformulated *adj* **vague**, indistinct, unclear, hazy, nebulous, imprecise [➡ THE NATURE OF IDEAS; 771] *Opposite*: clear

unforthcoming *adj* **uncommunicative**, reticent, taciturn, standoffish, distant, terse, laconic [➡ RETICENT AND UNFORTHCOMING; 631] *Opposite*: voluble

unfortified *adj* [➡ RAW AND NATURAL; 1214]

unfortunate 1 *adj* **unlucky**, luckless, unsuccessful, unhappy, ill-fated, ill-starred [➡ BAD LUCK AND UNLUCKY; 784] *Opposite*: lucky 2 *adj* **disastrous**, calamitous, doomed, hopeless, fateful, ruinous [➡ EMOTIONALLY UNPLEASANT AND UPSETTING; 227] *Opposite*: fortunate 3 *adj* **inappropriate**, inopportune, ill-timed, tactless, untimely, ill-advised, regrettable, awkward [➡ INAPPROPRIATE AND UNSUITABLE; 224] *Opposite*: timely 4 *n* **wretch**, underdog, loser, lame duck, weakling [➡ LAZY OR UNSUCCESSFUL PEOPLE; 948]

unfortunately 1 *adv* **unluckily**, unhappily, regrettably, sadly, alas [➡ EXPRESSIONS OF REGRET; 547] *Opposite*: fortunately 2 *adv* **inappropriately**, inopportunely, tactlessly, ill-advisedly, regrettably, awkwardly [➡ INAPPROPRIATE AND UNSUITABLE; 224] *Opposite*: appropriately

unfounded *adj* **groundless**, unsupported, baseless, unsubstantiated, speculative, tenuous, unproven [➡ FALSE AND UNREAL; 173] *Opposite*: proven

unfreeze *v* **relax**, rescind, repeal, release, liberate, undo [➡ FREEDOM AND LIBERTY; 208] *Opposite*: freeze

unfrequented *adj* **lonely**, neglected, isolated, quiet,

desolate, lone, solitary [➡ UNPOPULAR AND UNWANTED; 258] *Opposite*: busy

unfriendliness *n* **aloofness**, surliness, coldness, coolness, frostiness, unsociability, inhospitality, hostility, antagonism, animosity [➡ UNFRIENDLINESS AND UNSOCIABILITY; 504] *Opposite*: friendliness

unfriendly 1 *adj* **aloof**, distant, surly, cold, frosty, cool, unsociable, inhospitable, hostile, antagonistic [➡ UNFRIENDLINESS AND UNSOCIABILITY; 504] *Opposite*: friendly 2 *adj* **unfavorable**, ill-disposed, inimical, hostile, inauspicious, unpromising [➡ RUDE AND HOSTILE; 625] *Opposite*: well-disposed

unfruitful 1 *adj* **unsuccessful**, unprofitable, unproductive, unrewarding, fruitless, vain [➡ REDUNDANT AND USELESS; 240] *Opposite*: profitable 2 *adj* **infertile**, sterile, barren, bare, fruitless, childless [➡ REPRODUCTION AND HEREDITY; 725] *Opposite*: fertile

unfunny *adj* [➡ BIZARRE AND PECULIAR; 257]

unfurl *v* **open out**, open up, unfold, spread out, expand, develop [➡ CAUSE TO APPEAR; 5] *Opposite*: fold up

unfurnished *adj* **bare**, empty, unequipped, unfitted [➡ EMPTY; 1238] *Opposite*: furnished

unfussy *adj* **understated**, simple, uncomplicated, modest, plain, economical, austere [➡ PLAIN; 232] *Opposite*: fussy

ungainliness 1 *n* **gracelessness**, awkwardness, clumsiness, inelegance, gaucheness, maladroitness (*formal*) [➡ AGILITY OF THE BODY; 476] *Opposite*: gracefulness 2 *n* **awkwardness**, unwieldiness, cumbersomeness, heaviness, clumsiness, inconvenience, bulkiness [➡ WEIGHT: HEAVY; 1205] *Opposite*: convenience

ungainly 1 *adj* **graceless**, awkward, clumsy, inelegant, ungraceful, uncoordinated, maladroit, gauche, shambling [➡ AGILITY OF THE BODY; 476] *Opposite*: graceful 2 *adj* **awkward**, unwieldy, cumbersome, inconvenient, heavy, clumsy, bulky, unmanageable [➡ WEIGHT: HEAVY; 1205] *Opposite*: convenient

ungallant *adj* [➡ BAD MANNERS AND SOCIAL SKILLS; 521]

ungenerous 1 *adj* **stingy**, miserly, tightfisted, parsimonious, grudging, niggardly, mean, penny-pinching (*informal*), measly (*informal*) [➡ GRASPING AND FINANCIALLY MEAN; 519] *Opposite*: generous 2 *adj* **mean-spirited**, nasty, mean, unkind, cruel, callous, uncaring, heartless, selfish, ignoble [➡ SELFISH AND UNKIND; 505] *Opposite*: kind

ungentlemanly *adj* [➡ BAD MANNERS AND SOCIAL SKILLS; 521]

unglamorous *adj* [➡ UGLINESS AND UNATTRACTIVENESS; 233]

unglued 1 *adj* **separated**, detached, parted, disconnected, divided, disjointed [➡ UNFASTEN AND UNDO; 409] *Opposite*: whole 2 *adj* (*informal*) **upset**, angry, disconcerted, hysterical, unnerved, uncontrolled [➡ INSECURITY AND LOSS OF COMPOSURE; 544] *Opposite*: calm

ungodliness *n* [➡ RELIGIOUS CONCEPTS; 776]

ungodly 1 *adj* **impious**, irreligious, irreverent, blasphemous, disrespectful, profane (*formal*) [➡ RELIGIOUS CONCEPTS; 776] *Opposite*: pious 2 *adj* **wicked**, sinful, immoral, corrupt, depraved, vile [➡ MORALLY BAD OR IMPROPER; 775] *Opposite*: virtuous 3 *adj* (*informal*) **unreasonable**, unearthly, late, unsocial, ridiculous, absurd [➡BIZARRE AND PECULIAR; 257] *Opposite*: reasonable

ungovernable *adj* **uncontrollable**, out of control, unmanageable, unruly, anarchic, undisciplined, headstrong, unrestrained, wild, intractable (*formal*) [➡REBELLIOUSNESS AND DISOBEDIENCE; 565] *Opposite*: controllable

ungraceful 1 *adj* **clumsy**, ungainly, graceless, uncoordinated, lumbering, awkward, inelegant, gauche, maladroit, gawky (*informal*) [➡AGILITY OF THE BODY; 476] *Opposite*: elegant 2 *adj* **rude**, impolite, discourteous, gruff, brusque, ill-bred, churlish [➡BAD MANNERS AND SOCIAL SKILLS; 521] *Opposite*: polite

ungracious *adj* **ill-mannered**, discourteous, rude, impolite, bad-mannered, uncivil, disrespectful, insolent, churlish, brusque [➡BAD MANNERS AND SOCIAL SKILLS; 521] *Opposite*: gracious

ungraciousness *n* [➡BAD MANNERS AND SOCIAL SKILLS; 521]

ungrateful 1 *adj* **unappreciative**, thankless, churlish, unmindful, ungracious [➡BAD MANNERS AND SOCIAL SKILLS; 521] *Opposite*: grateful 2 *adj* **unpleasant**, unrewarding, thankless, unsatisfying [➡EMOTIONALLY UNPLEASANT AND UPSETTING; 227] *Opposite*: rewarding

ungratefully *adv* **unappreciatively**, churlishly, thanklessly, ungraciously [➡BAD MANNERS AND SOCIAL SKILLS; 521] *Opposite*: gratefully

ungratefulness *n* **unappreciativeness**, ingratitude, churlishness, thanklessness, ungraciousness [➡BAD MANNERS AND SOCIAL SKILLS; 521] *Opposite*: gratitude

unguarded 1 *adj* **unwary**, careless, indiscreet, thoughtless, imprudent, rash, unthinking, reckless [➡INCAUTIOUS AND CARELESS; 283] *Opposite*: guarded 2 *adj* **unprotected**, undefended, unshielded, unfortified, defenseless, exposed, vulnerable, weak [➡IN DANGER; 237] *Opposite*: guarded

unguent *n* **ointment**, salve, balm, lotion, oil, liniment, cream [➡LOTIONS, PASTES, AND GELS; 1272]

unhampered *adj* **unrestricted**, unimpeded, unhindered, unconstrained, free [➡FREEDOM AND LIBERTY; 208] *Opposite*: restricted

unhappily 1 *adv* **sadly**, miserably, discontentedly, despondently, dejectedly, gloomily, forlornly, sorrowfully, glumly, mournfully [➡SADNESS, DISTRESS, AND DESPAIR; 539] *Opposite*: happily 2 *adv* **unfortunately**, unluckily, regrettably, alas, sadly [➡EXPRESSIONS OF REGRET; 547] *Opposite*: luckily

unhappiness *n* **sadness**, sorrow, grief, misery, discontent, despondency, gloom, melancholy, depression, despair [➡SADNESS, DISTRESS, AND DESPAIR; 539] *Opposite*: happiness

unhappy 1 *adj* **sad**, miserable, discontented, despondent, dejected, gloomy, forlorn, sorrowful, melancholic, depressed, down [➡SADNESS, DISTRESS, AND DESPAIR; 539] *Opposite*: happy 2 *adj* **unfortunate**, ill-fated, hopeless, doomed, fateful, calamitous [➡BAD LUCK AND UNLUCKY; 784] *Opposite*: fortunate 3 *adj* **inappropriate**, ill-chosen, infelicitous, tactless, unfortunate, unsuitable [➡INAPPROPRIATE AND UNSUITABLE; 224] *Opposite*: well-chosen 4 *adj* **displeased**, annoyed, upset, angry, disappointed, put out [➡IRRITATION AND ANGER; 541] *Opposite*: pleased

unharmed *adj* **uninjured**, unhurt, unscathed, undam-

aged, unscratched, without a scratch, safe and sound, in one piece, untouched, intact [➡SAFE AND SOUND; 737] *Opposite*: harmed

unharmonious *adj* [➡DISHARMONY; 156]

unhazardous *adj* [➡SAFE AND SAFETY; 191]

unhealthy 1 *adj* **harmful**, detrimental, injurious, damaging, unwholesome, insanitary, noxious, unhygienic, insalubrious (*formal*) [➡DANGEROUS; 236] *Opposite*: healthy 2 *adj* **sick**, unfit, out of condition, out of shape, sickly, anemic, pallid, frail, weak, ill, unwell [➡UNFIT AND WEAK; 739] *Opposite*: well 3 *adj* **corrupt**, unwholesome, morbid, unnatural, ghoulish, insalubrious (*formal*) [➡MORALLY BAD OR IMPROPER; 775] *Opposite*: wholesome

unheard *adj* **unheeded**, disregarded, ignored, overlooked, unnoticed, unremarked [➡IMPERCEPTIBLE; 26]

unheard-of 1 *adj* **unknown**, unfamiliar, new, obscure, undiscovered, unsung [➡SECRET AND UNKNOWN; 179] *Opposite*: well-known 2 *adj* **unprecedented**, exceptional, extraordinary, novel, unusual, original, unimaginable, undreamed-of, rare [➡EXTRAORDINARY: UNCOMMON; 205] *Opposite*: ordinary 3 *adj* **offensive**, rude, disgusting, repulsive, shocking, repugnant, outrageous [➡DISGUSTING AND REPULSIVE; 230] *Opposite*: inoffensive

unhelpful 1 *adj* **uncooperative**, contrary, awkward, unaccommodating, obstructive, unsupportive, disobliging [➡UNWILLINGNESS AND STUBBORNNESS; 564] *Opposite*: helpful 2 *adj* **useless**, unconstructive, impractical, unnecessary, negative, adverse, of no use [➡REDUNDANT AND USELESS; 240] *Opposite*: useful

unhelpfulness 1 *n* **uncooperativeness**, unsupportiveness, contrariness, impractically [➡UNWILLINGNESS AND STUBBORNNESS; 564] *Opposite*: helpfulness 2 *n* **uselessness**, negativity, pointlessness, needlessness, worthlessness [➡REDUNDANT AND USELESS; 240] *Opposite*: usefulness

unhesitating *adj* **prompt**, unreserved, wholehearted, confident, forthright, rapid, swift, certain, unwavering [➡CONFIDENCE AND COMPOSURE; 499] *Opposite*: tentative

unhidden *adj* [➡KNOWN AND FAMOUS; 181]

unhindered *adj* **unimpeded**, unconstrained, unrestricted, unobstructed, unchecked, unopposed [➡FREEDOM AND LIBERTY; 208]

unhinge *v* **unbalance**, derange, madden, drive insane, disturb, confuse, send over the edge [➡UPSET, DISTRESS, AND HUMILIATE; 567]

unhinged *adj* **unbalanced**, deranged, disturbed, irrational [➡ECCENTRICITY AND IRRATIONALITY; 562] *Opposite*: sane

unhip (*informal*) *adj* [➡OLD, OLD-FASHIONED; 167]

unhitch *v* **unfasten**, untie, undo, uncouple, detach, release [➡UNFASTEN AND UNDO; 409] *Opposite*: fasten

unholy 1 *adj* **unconsecrated**, unhallowed, unblessed, profane, secular [➡RELIGIOUS CONCEPTS; 776] *Opposite*: consecrated 2 *adj* **ungodly**, blasphemous, secular, immoral, evil [➡MORALLY BAD OR IMPROPER; 775] *Opposite*: holy 3 *adj* **outrageous**, ungodly, disgraceful, scandalous, shocking, atrocious [➡DISGUSTING AND REPULSIVE; 230]

unhook v **undo**, release, uncouple, detach, disengage, free [➠UNFASTEN AND UNDO; 409] *Opposite*: hook

unhoped-for adj **unexpected**, unanticipated, surprising, undreamed-of, unforeseen, unimaginable [➠EXTRAORDINARY: UNCOMMON; 205] *Opposite*: expected

unhopeful adj **doubtful**, despondent, gloomy, dejected, pessimistic, downbeat, discouraged, downhearted, negative, uncertain [➠SADNESS, DISTRESS, AND DESPAIR; 539] *Opposite*: hopeful

unhurried adj **slow**, easygoing, dawdling, calm, deliberate, measured, thorough, painstaking, precise, leisurely, methodical [➠CAUTIOUS AND CAREFUL; 282] *Opposite*: hurried

unhurt adj **uninjured**, unharmed, undamaged, unscathed, safe, safe and sound, without a scratch, unscratched, unscarred [➠SAFE AND SOUND; 737] *Opposite*: hurt

unhygienic adj **insanitary**, unclean, polluted, unhealthy, foul, dirty [➠DIRTY; 1235] *Opposite*: hygienic

unicorn type of **mythological creature** [➠MYTHICAL CREATURES; 1036]

unicycle type of **bike** [➠BIKES, CARS, AND CARRIAGES; 1149]

unidentified adj **nameless**, anonymous, faceless, unnamed, unknown, undisclosed, unrevealed, mysterious [➠SECRET AND UNKNOWN; 179] *Opposite*: known

unidentified flying object see **UFO**

unification n **amalgamation**, union, merger, alliance, association, confederation, integration, confederacy, fusion [➠SOCIAL, POLITICAL, AND ECONOMIC CHANGE; 373] *Opposite*: split

unified adj **united**, combined, amalgamated, incorporated, integrated, joined, fused, cohesive [➠RELATED; 142] *Opposite*: disjointed

uniform 1 n **livery**, dress, costume, garb, attire (*formal*), outfit, regalia [➠GARMENTS AND OUTFITS; 865] **2** adj **unchanging**, unvarying, even, unbroken, undeviating, constant [➠PHYSICAL TEXTURE; 1222] *Opposite*: uneven **3** adj **consistent**, standardized, homogeneous, harmonized, regular, monotonous [➠PERMANENCE: WITHOUT CHANGE; 95] *Opposite*: inconsistent **4** adj **identical**, like, alike, similar, equal, equivalent, same [➠SAMENESS; 150] *Opposite*: different

uniformity n **consistency**, regularity, standardization, homogeneousness, homogeneity, evenness, equality, equivalence, sameness [➠SAMENESS; 150] *Opposite*: inconsistency

unify v **unite**, join, amalgamate, merge, combine, coalesce, fuse, bring together [➠CREATING CONNECTIONS; 144] *Opposite*: separate

unilateral adj **one-sided**, independent, autonomous, autarchic, individual [➠ACTING INDEPENDENTLY; 284] *Opposite*: joint

unimaginable adj **inconceivable**, unbelievable, incredible, unthinkable, indescribable, beyond belief, mindboggling, undreamed-of [➠IMPOSSIBLE AND IMPROBABLE; 178] *Opposite*: conceivable

unimaginative adj **dull**, boring, insipid, bland, uninspired, unoriginal, derivative, lackluster, unexciting,

mundane, ordinary, routine [➠BORING AND UNINTERESTING; 234] *Opposite*: imaginative

unimaginativeness n **dullness**, insipidness, blandness, unoriginality, mundaneness, ordinariness [➠BORING AND UNINTERESTING; 234] *Opposite*: imaginativeness

unimpaired adj **undamaged**, unaffected, unhindered, perfect, operational, working [➠WHOLENESS AND COMPLETENESS; 198] *Opposite*: impaired

unimpassioned adj **unemotional**, cool, detached, sober, calm, dispassionate [➠BORING AND UNINTERESTING; 234] *Opposite*: impassioned

unimpeachable adj **faultless**, flawless, impeccable, irreproachable, blameless, unassailable, spotless, perfect [➠MORALLY GOOD; 774] *Opposite*: blameworthy

unimpeded adj **without hindrance**, unhindered, unhampered, unchecked, unconstrained, unobstructed, unrestrained, unrestricted [➠FREEDOM AND LIBERTY; 208] *Opposite*: hindered

unimportance n **insignificance**, inconsequentiality, irrelevance, slightness, triviality, pettiness [➠UNIMPORTANT AND UNNECESSARY; 238] *Opposite*: importance

unimportant adj **inconsequential**, slight, insignificant, trivial, trifling, petty, minor, irrelevant, immaterial, negligible, of no great concern, no great shakes (*informal*) [➠UNIMPORTANT AND UNNECESSARY; 238] *Opposite*: important

unimposing adj [➠ORDINARINESS; 244]

unimpressed adj **unenthusiastic**, uninspired, unconvinced, unmoved, indifferent, apathetic, uninterested, blasé [➠NEUTRALITY AND INDIFFERENCE; 553] *Opposite*: enthusiastic

unimpressive adj **uninspiring**, indifferent, mediocre, unimposing, insignificant, average, insipid, ordinary, nothing special [➠ORDINARINESS; 244] *Opposite*: impressive

unimproved adj **unchanged**, unaltered, unrestored, authentic, original, unworked, virgin [➠UNFINISHEDNESS; 239] *Opposite*: improved

unincorporated adj **independent**, separate, distinct, stand-alone, autonomous, self-governing [➠UNRELATEDNESS AND SEPARATENESS; 146] *Opposite*: incorporated

unindustrialized adj **undeveloped**, farming, agricultural, rural [➠THE COUNTRYSIDE AND OUTDOOR SPACES; 1071] *Opposite*: industrialized

uninformative adj **unhelpful**, vague, uncommunicative, unproductive, useless [➠VAGUENESS; 243] *Opposite*: informative

uninformed adj **ignorant**, uneducated, unapprised, unaware, unacquainted, unfamiliar, in the dark [➠IGNORANCE; 557] *Opposite*: informed

uninhabitable adj **derelict**, dilapidated, ramshackle, tumbledown, run-down, ruined [➠IN BAD REPAIR; 1234] *Opposite*: habitable

uninhabited adj **unoccupied**, unpopulated, deserted, abandoned, unpeopled, vacant, desolate, empty, forsaken, isolated [➠EMPTY; 1238] *Opposite*: inhabited

uninhibited 1 adj **unrestrained**, outgoing, unconstrained, candid, open, natural, unreserved, spontaneous, frank, overt [➡ HONEST AND OPEN; 630] *Opposite*: shy **2** *adj* **wanton**, abandoned, dissolute, licentious, immodest, immoral [➡ MORALLY BAD OR IMPROPER; 775] *Opposite*: restrained

uninhibitedly *adv* overtly, candidly, openly, naturally, frankly, unreservedly, spontaneously [➡ HONEST AND OPEN; 630] *Opposite*: shyly

uninitiated *adj* **inexperienced**, unskilled, unversed, unqualified, untrained, inexpert, green [➡ UNSKILLED; 529] *Opposite*: experienced

uninjured *adj* **unhurt**, unharmed, undamaged, intact, safe, safe and sound, unscathed [➡ SAFE AND SOUND; 737] *Opposite*: hurt

uninspired *adj* **bland**, insipid, boring, dull, unimaginative, unoriginal, featureless, characterless [➡ ORDINARINESS; 244] *Opposite*: inspired

uninspiring *adj* **dull**, lackluster, lifeless, boring, tame, bland, uneventful, undistinguished [➡ BORING AND UNINTERESTING; 234] *Opposite*: inspiring

uninstructed *adj* **untaught**, unschooled, uneducated, uninformed, untutored, ignorant, unversed, in the dark [➡ IGNORANCE; 557] *Opposite*: educated

unintelligence *n* [➡ NEGATIVE INTELLECTUAL CHARACTERISTICS; 525]

unintelligent *adj* **stupid**, foolish, silly, inane [➡ NEGATIVE INTELLECTUAL CHARACTERISTICS; 525] *Opposite*: clever

unintelligibility *n* [➡ DIFFICULTY AND COMPLEXITY; 242]

unintelligible *adj* **incomprehensible**, inarticulate, incoherent, garbled, jumbled, indecipherable, meaningless, inaudible, indistinct [➡ DIFFICULTY AND COMPLEXITY; 242] *Opposite*: intelligible

unintended *see* **unintentional**

unintentional *adj* **accidental**, inadvertent, unintended, unplanned, chance, involuntary, unpremeditated [➡ UNPLANNED AND UNEXPECTED; 281] *Opposite*: intentional

uninterested *adj* **indifferent**, apathetic, blasé, impassive, unconcerned, unresponsive, dispassionate, aloof, remote, casual, distant [➡ NEUTRALITY AND INDIFFERENCE; 553] *Opposite*: concerned

uninteresting *adj* **boring**, dull, unexciting, tedious, monotonous, dreary, dry, arid, insipid, characterless [➡ BORING AND UNINTERESTING; 234] *Opposite*: interesting

See Compare and Contrast at **boring**.

uninterrupted *adj* **continuous**, continual, nonstop, incessant, never-ending, endless, constant, unremitting, ceaseless, unbroken [➡ PERMANENCE: WITHOUT END; 94] *Opposite*: sporadic

uninvited *adj* **unwelcome**, unwanted, undesirable, unsought, unsolicited, unasked-for [➡ UNPOPULAR AND UNWANTED; 258] *Opposite*: welcome

uninviting *adj* **unappealing**, unattractive, bleak, unpalatable, disgusting, nasty, unpleasant, repellent, unenticing, distasteful [➡ UGLINESS AND UNATTRACTIVENESS; 233] *Opposite*: attractive

uninvolved **1** *adj* **detached**, removed, aloof, unconcerned, indifferent, impassive, disinterested, distant [➡ NEUTRALITY AND INDIFFERENCE; 553] *Opposite*: involved **2** *adj* **uncomplicated**, straightforward, easy, simple, plain [➡ EASE AND SIMPLICITY; 200] *Opposite*: convoluted **3** *adj* **single**, footloose and fancy free, unmarried, unattached, free, solo [➡ MARITAL STATUS; 890] *Opposite*: attached (*informal*)

union **1** *n* **amalgamation**, combination, blending, coming together, joining together, unification, merger [➡ CONNECTIONS; 143] *Opposite*: separation **2** *n* **coalition**, alliance, association, confederacy, confederation, federation, league, society, guild, club [➡ CLUBS AND SOCIETIES; 939] **3** *n* **agreement**, harmony, accord, unity, unison, concord [➡ HARMONY; 155] *Opposite*: discord **4** *n* **marriage**, matrimony, wedlock, bond, wedding, tie [➡ MARRIED STATE; 961] *Opposite*: divorce

union suit *type of* **upper body underwear** [➡ ACCESSORIES, MILLINERY, AND LINGERIE; 867]

unique *adj* **sole**, single, exclusive, exceptional, inimitable, distinctive, matchless, irreplaceable, rare, one-off (*UK*) [➡ EXTRAORDINARY: UNCOMMON; 205] *Opposite*: common

uniqueness *n* **individuality**, exclusivity, exceptionality, inimitability, distinctiveness, matchlessness, rareness [➡ EXTRAORDINARY: UNCOMMON; 205] *Opposite*: commonness

unison *n* **agreement**, harmony, accord, unity, union, unanimity [➡ HARMONY; 155] *Opposite*: discord

unit **1** *n* **component**, element, part, piece, item, thing, entity, division, building block, constituent [➡ PHYSICAL OBJECTS; 1243] **2** *n* **corps**, detachment, group, company, troop, organization, section [➡ GROUPS OF PEOPLE; 935]

unite **1** *v* **join**, fuse, mix, bond, come together, bring together, connect, amalgamate, merge, blend, combine, unify [➡ COMBINE AND MIX; 400] *Opposite*: separate **2** *v* **marry**, wed, hitch, bond, tie, yoke, join in matrimony, join in wedlock [➡ ESTABLISHING RELATIONSHIPS WITH OTHERS; 974]

united *adj* **joint**, combined, amalgamated, unified, cohesive, integrated, aggregate [➡ RELATED; 142] *Opposite*: separated

unitize **1** *v* **bring together**, unite, combine, centralize, condense, focus [➡ COMBINE AND MIX; 400] *Opposite*: separate **2** *v* **separate**, take apart, break up, divide up, disassemble, split up [➡ SEPARATE AND DIVIDE; 401] *Opposite*: join

unity *n* **agreement**, harmony, accord, unison, union, concord, unanimity [➡ HARMONY; 155] *Opposite*: disarray

universal *adj* **worldwide**, widespread, general, common, collective, total, entire, complete, unanimous, comprehensive [➡ WHOLENESS AND COMPLETENESS; 198] *Opposite*: local

See Compare and Contrast at **widespread**.

universalism *n* **breadth**, amplitude, diversity, gamut, spectrum [➡ WHOLENESS AND COMPLETENESS; 198]

universe *n* **cosmos**, world, creation, life, space, earth [➡ THE SOLAR SYSTEM AND ASTRONOMY; 1060]

university *n* **institution of higher education**, college, academia, academy, school, academe (*formal*) [➡ EDUCATIONAL INSTITUTIONS; 813]

unjam *v* [➡ UNFASTEN AND UNDO; 409]

unjust *adj* **unfair**, undue, undeserved, unmerited, unwarranted, unreasonable, partial, biased, prejudiced, discriminatory [➡ MORALLY BAD OR IMPROPER; 775] *Opposite*: just

unjustifiable *adj* **indefensible**, unwarrantable, inexcusable, unforgivable, unpardonable, uncalled-for, untenable, beyond the pale [➡ UNACCEPTABLE AND UNFORGIVABLE; 225] *Opposite*: justifiable

unjustified *adj* **unfounded**, baseless, unfair, unwarranted, unpardonable, groundless, inexcusable [➡ UNACCEPTABLE AND UNFORGIVABLE; 225] *Opposite*: justified

unjustly *adv* **unfairly**, unreasonably, partially, one-sidedly, discriminatorily, prejudicially, irrationally [➡ MORALLY BAD OR IMPROPER; 775] *Opposite*: fairly

unkempt *adj* **disheveled**, untidy, rumpled, tousled, messy, scruffy [➡ DESCRIBING HAIR; 486] *Opposite*: tidy

unkind *adj* **nasty**, mean, cruel, callous, heartless, harsh [➡ SELFISH AND UNKIND; 505] *Opposite*: kind

unkindness *n* **nastiness**, meanness, cruelty, callousness, heartlessness, harshness [➡ SELFISH AND UNKIND; 505] *Opposite*: kindness

unknot *v* **untie**, undo, unpick, disentangle, unstitch, unlace, disengage [➡ UNFASTEN AND UNDO; 409] *Opposite*: knot

unknowable *adj* **incomprehensible**, enigmatic, mysterious, indecipherable, arcane, inexplicable, impenetrable, inscrutable [➡ SECRET AND UNKNOWN; 179] *Opposite*: comprehensible

unknowing **1** *adj* **unwitting**, ingenuous, naive, innocent, ignorant, unaware [➡ IGNORANCE; 557] *Opposite*: knowing **2** *adj* **unintentional**, accidental, inadvertent, unintended, unplanned, unforeseen [➡ UNPLANNED AND UNEXPECTED; 281] *Opposite*: deliberate

unknowingly *adv* **naively**, innocently, mistakenly, unwittingly, accidentally, unintentionally, unsuspectingly, inadvertently [➡ UNPLANNED AND UNEXPECTED; 281] *Opposite*: deliberately

unknowledgeable *adj* [➡ IGNORANCE; 557]

unknown **1** *adj* **unidentified**, indefinite, mysterious, strange, unfamiliar, unheard of, nameless, anonymous, new, unspecified, undetermined [➡ SECRET AND UNKNOWN; 179] *Opposite*: known **2** *adj* **unfamiliar**, strange, foreign, alien, undiscovered, new, virgin [➡ NEW, MODERN; 166] *Opposite*: familiar **3** *n* **nonentity**, nobody, newcomer, beginner, stranger, mystery [➡ STRANGERS; 972] *Opposite*: celebrity

unlabored *adj* **effortless**, easy, painless, trouble-free, carefree, smooth, natural, casual [➡ EASE AND SIMPLICITY; 200] *Opposite*: labored

unlace *v* **undo**, unfasten, unthread, unknot, untie, loosen [➡ UNFASTEN AND UNDO; 409] *Opposite*: lace

unladylike *adj* [➡ BAD MANNERS AND SOCIAL SKILLS; 521]

unlatch *v* **open**, undo, unfasten, unlock, unbolt [➡ UNFASTEN AND UNDO; 409] *Opposite*: latch

unlawful *adj* **illegal**, illicit, against the law, illegitimate, criminal, dishonest, unauthorized, prohibited, improper [➡ ILLEGAL; 816] *Opposite*: lawful

Compare and Contrast: *unlawful, illegal, illicit, wrongful*

CORE MEANING: not in accordance with laws or rules

unlawful not permitted by the law or by the rules of an organization or religion, or not recognized as valid by those laws or rules; *illegal* contravening a specific written statute, rule, or law, especially a criminal law; *illicit* not permitted by the law, suggesting especially that something is considered morally wrong or unacceptable; *wrongful* (often used in civil lawsuits) unjust, unfair, or against conscience, or not done according to the law.

unlawful act *n* [➡ CRIMES; 817]

unlawful activity *n* [➡ CRIMES; 817]

unlawfulness *n* [➡ ILLEGAL; 816]

unlearned *adj* **uneducated**, illiterate, unschooled, unlettered, untutored, untaught, untrained [➡ LEVELS OF EDUCATION AND SOPHISTICATION; 894] *Opposite*: educated

unleash *v* **set free**, give a free rein to, allow to run free, allow to run riot, uncheck, unbridle, let loose, release [➡ FREEDOM AND LIBERTY; 208] *Opposite*: control

unless *prep* **if not**, if, except, save, but for, without, lest [➡ NOT; 137]

unlettered *adj* **uneducated**, illiterate, unschooled, untaught, untutored, unlearned [➡ LEVELS OF EDUCATION AND SOPHISTICATION; 894] *Opposite*: educated

unlicensed *adj* **uninhibited**, unrestricted, unrestrained, abandoned, immoral, unconstrained, carefree [➡ FREEDOM AND LIBERTY; 208] *Opposite*: inhibited

unlikable *adj* [➡ UNPOPULAR AND UNWANTED; 258]

unlike *adj* **different**, dissimilar, nothing like, distinct, contrasting, disparate [➡ DIFFERENCE; 149] *Opposite*: like

unlikelihood *n* **improbability**, doubtfulness, implausibility, dubiousness, questionability, incongruousness [➡ IMPOSSIBLE AND IMPROBABLE; 178] *Opposite*: likelihood

unlikeliness *n* [➡ IMPOSSIBLE AND IMPROBABLE; 178]

unlikely **1** *adj* **improbable**, doubtful, dubious, questionable [➡ IMPOSSIBLE AND IMPROBABLE; 178] *Opposite*: likely **2** *adj* **implausible**, dubious, doubtful, suspect, incongruous, unbelievable [➡ UNCERTAIN; 175] *Opposite*: credible

unlimited *adj* **limitless**, infinite, unrestricted, unrestrained, boundless, unconstrained, on tap, indefinite, ad lib, ad nauseam, bottomless [➡ FREEDOM AND LIBERTY; 208] *Opposite*: limited

unlisted *adj* **private**, unpublished, confidential, unpublicized, secret, ex-directory (*UK*) [➡ SECRET AND UNKNOWN; 179] *Opposite*: listed

unlit *adj* **dark**, darkened, dim, pitch-black, murky, gloomy [➡ DESCRIBING LIGHT; 1228] *Opposite*: bright

unload *v* **unpack**, drop off, drop, deliver, take down, discharge, unburden [➡ EMPTY AND UNLOAD; 407] *Opposite*: load

unlock **1** *v* **undo**, release, unchain, open, unbolt, disengage, unfasten [➡ UNFASTEN AND UNDO; 409] *Opposite*: lock

2 *v* **solve**, reveal, answer, expose, get to the bottom of, unravel, work out, explain, crack (*informal*) [➡ SOLVE AND INTERPRET; 760]

unlooked-for *adj* **unexpected**, undreamed-of, unanticipated, uninvited, unsolicited, spontaneous, unprompted [➡ EXTRAORDINARY: UNCOMMON; 205] *Opposite*: expected

unloose *v* **set free**, release, let out, unleash, let off the leash, loose [➡ FREEDOM AND LIBERTY; 208] *Opposite*: tie up

unloved *adj* [➡ UNPOPULAR AND UNWANTED; 258]

unlovely *adj* **unattractive**, objectionable, obnoxious, nasty, ugly [➡ UGLINESS AND UNATTRACTIVENESS; 233] *Opposite*: attractive

unluckiness *n* **bad luck**, misfortune, ill luck, mishap [➡ BAD LUCK AND UNLUCKY; 784] *Opposite*: luck

unlucky **1** *adj* **unsuccessful**, wretched, hapless, unfortunate, tragic, luckless [➡ BAD LUCK AND UNLUCKY; 784] *Opposite*: lucky **2** *adj* **inauspicious**, fateful, ill-fated, doomed, star-crossed, ill-starred, ill omened, ominous, baleful [➡ FATE, DESTINY, AND ASTROLOGY; 782] *Opposite*: fortunate

unmake **1** *v* **undo**, take apart, reverse, deconstruct, dismantle, reorganize [➡ DESTRUCTION AND DEMOLITION; 359] *Opposite*: put back **2** *v* **demote**, fire, sack, replace, expel, vote out, impeach [➡ REVOKE STATUS; 459]

unmanageable *adj* **uncontrollable**, unruly, riotous, out of control, out of hand, wild, impossible, insurmountable [➡ DISORDER AND CHAOS; 245] *Opposite*: manageable

unmanliness *n* **weakness**, cowardliness, timidity, fearfulness, apprehension, shyness [➡ COWARDICE AND WEAKNESS OF WILL; 508] *Opposite*: manliness

unmanly *adj* **weak**, cowardly, timid, fearful, apprehensive, cringing [➡ COWARDICE AND WEAKNESS OF WILL; 508] *Opposite*: manly

unmannered **1** *adj* **rude**, boorish, impolite, crude, coarse, loutish [➡ BAD MANNERS AND SOCIAL SKILLS; 521] *Opposite*: well-mannered **2** *adj* **unaffected**, easy, natural, genuine, simple, sincere, unpretentious [➡ NATURALNESS; 497] *Opposite*: affected

unmannerly *adj* **rude**, impolite, ill-mannered, bad-mannered, disrespectful, insolent, brusque, uncivil [➡ BAD MANNERS AND SOCIAL SKILLS; 521] *Opposite*: polite

unmapped *adj* [➡ SECRET AND UNKNOWN; 179]

unmarked *adj* **spotless**, unblemished, pristine, immaculate, perfect, without a scratch, intact, undamaged [➡ CLEAN AND HYGIENIC; 1233] *Opposite*: marked

unmarried *adj* **single**, unattached, bachelor, spinster, free [➡ MARITAL STATUS; 890] *Opposite*: married

unmask *v* **expose**, blow the whistle on, reveal, unveil, debunk, uncover, make public, bare, make known, lay bare [➡ CAUSE TO APPEAR; 5] *Opposite*: conceal

unmatched *adj* **supreme**, matchless, unrivaled, consummate, unparalleled, unsurpassed, unequaled, beyond compare, incomparable, unique [➡ SUPERIORITY; 152]

unmeant *adj* **unintended**, accidental, inadvertent, unplanned, unintentional [➡ UNPLANNED AND UNEXPECTED; 281] *Opposite*: deliberate

unmelodic *adj* [➡ LOUD, HIGH, OR UNPLEASANT SOUNDS; 1266]

unmelodious *adj* [➡ LOUD, HIGH, OR UNPLEASANT SOUNDS; 1266]

unmemorable *adj* [➡ ORDINARINESS; 244]

unmentionable **1** *adj* **taboo**, offensive, prohibited, forbidden, restricted, proscribed, out of bounds, off-limits [➡ UNACCEPTABLE AND UNFORGIVABLE; 225] *Opposite*: respectable **2** *n* **taboo**, no-go area, anathema, no-no (*informal*) [➡ NUISANCES; 253]

unmerciful **1** *adj* **cruel**, severe, harsh, hard, unsparing, unforgiving, unkind, merciless, punitive [➡ SELFISH AND UNKIND; 505] *Opposite*: merciful **2** *adj* **excessive**, unrelenting, extreme, remorseless, unremitting, constant, merciless [➡ EMOTIONALLY UNPLEASANT AND UPSETTING; 227]

unmerited *adj* **undeserved**, unwarranted, unjustified, unearned, unjust, unfair [➡ MORALLY BAD OR IMPROPER; 775] *Opposite*: fair

unmindful *adj* **unaware**, oblivious, unconscious, careless, heedless, forgetful, neglectful [➡ NEUTRALITY AND INDIFFERENCE; 553] *Opposite*: mindful

unmistakable *adj* **obvious**, definite, distinctive, unambiguous, unique, evident, inimitable, particular [➡ CONCISE AND CLEAR; 202] *Opposite*: ambiguous

unmistakably *adv* **obviously**, clearly, distinctly, unambiguously, definitely, unquestionably [➡ PERCEPTIBLE; 25] *Opposite*: ambiguously

unmitigated *adj* **sheer**, pure, absolute, unadulterated, unalloyed, utter, complete, total [➡ ABSOLUTE AND ABSOLUTELY; 133]

unmodified *adj* **original**, unchanged, basic, untouched [➡ PERMANENCE: WITHOUT CHANGE; 95] *Opposite*: modified

unmotivated *adj* **apathetic**, unenthusiastic, indifferent, shiftless, uninterested, lazy [➡ LIFELESS, LAZY, AND UNENTHUSIASTIC; 506] *Opposite*: keen

unmovable *adj* **inflexible**, rigid, stubborn, obstinate, obdurate, unbending, unwavering, adamant, unyielding, unrelenting, firm [➡ UNWILLINGNESS AND STUBBORNNESS; 564] *Opposite*: flexible

unmoved *adj* **indifferent**, unaffected, cold, unresponsive, insensitive, unyielding, impassive, unfeeling, oblivious, firm, adamant [➡ NEUTRALITY AND INDIFFERENCE; 553] *Opposite*: touched

See Compare and Contrast at **impassive**.

unmoving *adj* **still**, motionless, inactive, lifeless, inert, frozen [➡ LACK OF ACTIVITY OR MOTION; 342] *Opposite*: moving

unmusical *adj* **unmelodic**, dissonant, discordant, jarring, harsh, cacophonous, inharmonious [➡ LOUD, HIGH, OR UNPLEASANT SOUNDS; 1266] *Opposite*: musical

unnamed *adj* **unidentified**, anonymous, unspecified, nameless, unknown, undisclosed [➡ SECRET AND UNKNOWN; 179] *Opposite*: named

unnatural **1** *adj* **abnormal**, aberrant, atypical, unusual, perverted, deviant, anomalous [➡ BIZARRE AND PECULIAR; 257] *Opposite*: normal **2** *adj* **unusual**, abnormal, strange, odd, peculiar, atypical, irregular, uncommon, surprising

[➡ BIZARRE AND PECULIAR; 257] *Opposite*: typical **3** *adj* **supernatural**, weird, bizarre, paranormal, uncanny, inexplicable, eerie, strange, extraordinary [➡ BIZARRE AND PECULIAR; 257] *Opposite*: ordinary **4** *adj* **artificial**, contrived, affected, insincere, pretend, feigned, false, manufactured, put-on, pretentious [➡ FALSE AND UNREAL; 173] *Opposite*: natural

unnaturally 1 *adv* **abnormally**, unusually, extraordinarily, inexplicably, oddly, strangely, uncharacteristically [➡ BIZARRE AND PECULIAR; 257] *Opposite*: normally **2** *adv* **artificially**, insincerely, stiffly, affectedly, falsely, pretentiously [➡ FALSE AND UNREAL; 173] *Opposite*: naturally

unnaturalness *n* **strangeness**, oddness, weirdness, abnormality, irregularity, bizarreness [➡ BIZARRE AND PECULIAR; 257] *Opposite*: normality

unnecessary *adj* **needless**, pointless, redundant, superfluous, gratuitous, unwarranted, uncalled-for, excessive, avoidable, preventable [➡ UNIMPORTANT AND UNNECESSARY; 238] *Opposite*: necessary

unneeded *adj* **extra**, superfluous, unnecessary, surplus, unwanted [➡ UNIMPORTANT AND UNNECESSARY; 238] *Opposite*: necessary

unnerve *v* **alarm**, frighten, scare, upset, nonplus, surprise, demoralize, discourage, worry, set back [➡ UPSET, DISTRESS, AND HUMILIATE; 567] *Opposite*: calm

unnerved *adj* **frightened**, scared, alarmed, unsettled, anxious, panic-stricken, panicky, intimidated, demoralized, upset [➡ FEAR AND PANIC; 543] *Opposite*: calm

unnerving *adj* **frightening**, unsettling, demoralizing, intimidating, upsetting, alarming, scary (*informal*), discomforting (*formal*) [➡ EMOTIONALLY UNPLEASANT AND UPSETTING; 227] *Opposite*: comforting

unnoticeable *adj* **invisible**, imperceptible, unremarkable, inconspicuous, hidden, camouflaged, unobtrusive, discreet [➡ IMPERCEPTIBLE; 26] *Opposite*: conspicuous

unnoticed *adj* **unobserved**, overlooked, ignored, unseen, disregarded, undetected [➡ SECRET AND UNKNOWN; 179]

unnumbered 1 *adj* **numberless**, numerous, myriad, countless, many, untold [➡ MANY, MUCH, LARGE AMOUNT; 117] *Opposite*: few **2** *adj* **unidentified**, unmarked, untagged [➡ NAME AND DESCRIBE; 665]

unobjectionable *adj* **inoffensive**, agreeable, pleasant, innocuous, harmless [➡ ACCEPTABLE AND PASSABLE; 219] *Opposite*: unpleasant

unobservant *adj* **inattentive**, unperceptive, incurious, negligent, careless [➡ NEGATIVE INTELLECTUAL CHARACTERISTICS; 525] *Opposite*: observant

unobserved *adj* **unnoticed**, ignored, overlooked, unseen, disregarded, undetected [➡ SECRET AND UNKNOWN; 179] *Opposite*: evident

unobstructed *adj* **clear**, free, unhindered, passable, open, unbarred [➡ FREEDOM AND LIBERTY; 208] *Opposite*: barred

unobtainable *adj* **unavailable**, unattainable, inaccessible, out of stock [➡ ABSENT AND UNAVAILABLE; 7] *Opposite*: available

unobtrusive *adj* **inconspicuous**, unremarkable, modest, bland, discreet, understated, unassuming, self-effacing,

shy, low-profile [➡ RETICENT AND UNFORTHCOMING; 631] *Opposite*: conspicuous

unoccupied 1 *adj* **inactive**, idle, at loose ends (*informal*), out of work, unemployed [➡ LACK OF ACTIVITY OR MOTION; 342] *Opposite*: busy **2** *adj* **vacant**, untenanted, empty, disused, unused, uninhabited, unlived in, unpopulated, deserted, unfilled [➡ EMPTY; 1238] *Opposite*: occupied

See Compare and Contrast at **vacant**.

unoffending *adj* [➡ ACCEPTABLE AND PASSABLE; 219]

unofficial *adj* **unauthorized**, unsanctioned, informal, unendorsed, private, off-the-record [➡ ILLEGAL; 816] *Opposite*: official

unopposed *adj* **unchallenged**, unobstructed, unrestricted, unhampered, unimpeded, unrestrained [➡ FREEDOM AND LIBERTY; 208] *Opposite*: challenged

unorganized 1 *adj* **chaotic**, disorganized, muddled, messy, disorderly [➡ DISORDER AND CHAOS; 245] *Opposite*: well-organized **2** *adj* **careless**, disorganized, unprepared, sloppy, slapdash, messy [➡ INCAUTIOUS AND CARELESS; 283] *Opposite*: methodical

unoriginal *adj* **derivative**, copied, imitative, clichéd, banal, trite, hackneyed, uninspired, commonplace, corny, plagiarized [➡ SIMILARITY; 148] *Opposite*: original

unoriginality *n* **derivativeness**, triteness, staleness, imitativeness, banality, uninventiveness, unimaginativeness [➡ SIMILARITY; 148] *Opposite*: originality

unorthodox *adj* **unconventional**, nonconformist, untraditional, unusual, eccentric, heretical, anarchic, revolutionary [➡ EXTRAORDINARY: UNCOMMON; 205] *Opposite*: orthodox

unpack *v* **unload**, take out, empty, undo, empty out, discharge [➡ EMPTY AND UNLOAD; 407] *Opposite*: pack up

unpaid 1 *adj* **unsettled**, outstanding, overdue, due, owing, in arrears [➡ OWE AND DESERVE; 465] *Opposite*: paid **2** *adj* **voluntary**, amateur, honorary, free [➡ EMPLOYMENT STATUS; 831] *Opposite*: paid

unpalatable 1 *adj* **inedible**, indigestible, disgusting, revolting, foul-tasting, unpleasant, nasty, bad [➡ TASTE; 703] *Opposite*: tasty **2** *adj* **unacceptable**, unpleasant, painful, disagreeable, harsh, distasteful [➡ UNACCEPTABLE AND UNFORGIVABLE; 225] *Opposite*: acceptable

unparalleled *adj* **unmatched**, supreme, matchless, beyond compare, unequaled, incomparable, consummate [➡ SUPERIORITY; 152] *Opposite*: mediocre

unpardonable *adj* **unforgivable**, indefensible, inexcusable, deplorable, reprehensible, intolerable, awful [➡ UNACCEPTABLE AND UNFORGIVABLE; 225] *Opposite*: understandable

unpeg *v* **undo**, unfasten, untie, detach, release, uncouple [➡ UNFASTEN AND UNDO; 409] *Opposite*: fasten

unperceptive *adj* **undiscerning**, unobservant, insensitive, obtuse, indiscriminating, inattentive [➡ NEGATIVE INTELLECTUAL CHARACTERISTICS; 525] *Opposite*: perceptive

unperturbed *adj* **calm**, at peace, tranquil, collected, composed, cool, at ease, untroubled, unruffled, unworried [➡ COOL AND CALM; 536] *Opposite*: anxious

unpick *v* **unravel**, untangle, untie, undo, disentangle, unstitch [➡ UNFASTEN AND UNDO; 409]

unpin *v* [➡ UNFASTEN AND UNDO; 409]

unpitying *adj* [➡ SELFISH AND UNKIND; 505]

unplanned 1 *adj* **unintended**, accidental, unintentional, unexpected, inadvertent, unforeseen [➡ UNPLANNED AND UNEXPECTED; 281] *Opposite*: planned 2 *adj* **spontaneous**, impromptu, ad hoc, unprepared, spur-of-the-moment, impulsive, unscheduled, out of the blue [➡ HAPPENING QUICKLY; 104] *Opposite*: planned

unpleasant 1 *adj* **disagreeable**, nasty, unlikable, horrible, horrid, distasteful, objectionable, obnoxious, repulsive, foul, bad [➡ DISGUSTING AND REPULSIVE; 230] *Opposite*: pleasant 2 *adj* **unfriendly**, disagreeable, hostile, cold, unkind, spiteful, nasty [➡ SELFISH AND UNKIND; 505] *Opposite*: friendly

unpleasantly 1 *adv* **disagreeably**, nastily, horribly, distastefully, objectionably, obnoxiously, repulsively, unattractively [➡ DISGUSTING AND REPULSIVE; 230] *Opposite*: pleasantly 2 *adv* **nastily**, hostilely, coldly, unkindly, offensively, spitefully [➡ SELFISH AND UNKIND; 505] *Opposite*: nicely

unpleasantness 1 *n* **disagreeableness**, unlikableness, nastiness, horribleness, horridness, distastefulness, objectionableness, obnoxiousness, repulsiveness, foulness, badness [➡ DISGUSTING AND REPULSIVE; 230] *Opposite*: pleasantness 2 *n* **ill feeling**, trouble, fuss, bother, upset, scandal [➡ DISHARMONY; 156] *Opposite*: harmony 3 *n* **unfriendliness**, spitefulness, nastiness, unkindness, offensiveness, hostility, coldness [➡ SELFISH AND UNKIND; 505] *Opposite*: friendliness 4 *n* **disagreement**, conflict, argument, quarrel, dispute, difference of opinion [➡ ARGUMENTS; 47] *Opposite*: agreement

unplug 1 *v* **unblock**, clear, free, clean, release, open up [➡ EMPTY AND UNLOAD; 407] 2 *v* **undo**, switch off, disconnect, take out, remove, disengage [➡ CAUSE TO STOP; 266] *Opposite*: plug in

unplumbed *adj* **unsounded**, mysterious, unfathomable, enigmatic, unexplored, unknowable, incomprehensible [➡ SECRET AND UNKNOWN; 179] *Opposite*: known

unpolluted *adj* **clean**, pure, uncontaminated, untainted, fresh, clear, sterilized [➡ CLEAN AND HYGIENIC; 1233] *Opposite*: contaminated

unpopular *adj* **disliked**, hated, out of favor, shunned, detested, ostracized [➡ UNPOPULAR AND UNWANTED; 258] *Opposite*: popular

unpopulated *adj* **abandoned**, deserted, depopulated, uninhabited, empty, desolate, unoccupied [➡ EMPTY; 1238] *Opposite*: overcrowded

unpracticed *adj* **inexperienced**, unrehearsed, unschooled, untrained, unfamiliar, green [➡ UNSKILLED; 529] *Opposite*: practiced

unprecedented *adj* **unparalleled**, extraordinary, record, first-time, unique, exceptional, unmatched [➡ EXTRAORDINARY: UNCOMMON; 205] *Opposite*: ordinary

unpredictability *n* **randomness**, impulsiveness, volatility, fickleness, changeableness, changeability, irregularity, capriciousness, instability [➡ FINITENESS, VARIABILITY, AND TRANSIENCE; 96] *Opposite*: predictability

unpredictable *adj* **random**, erratic, changeable, impulsive, volatile, fickle, irregular, capricious, variable, arbitrary, unstable [➡ FINITENESS, VARIABILITY, AND TRANSIENCE; 96] *Opposite*: predictable

unpredicted *adj* **surprising**, unexpected, shock, astonishing, unforeseen, sudden [➡ EXTRAORDINARY: AMAZING; 204] *Opposite*: predicted

unprejudiced *adj* **fair**, neutral, tolerant, unbiased, evenhanded, impartial, balanced, objective, rational, open-minded [➡ POSITIVE INTELLECTUAL CHARACTERISTICS; 524] *Opposite*: biased

unpremeditated *adj* **unplanned**, unintended, impulsive, spur-of-the-moment, sudden, accidental, chance, inadvertent [➡ UNPLANNED AND UNEXPECTED; 281] *Opposite*: premeditated

unprepared 1 *adj* **unready**, unsuspecting, ill-equipped, unqualified, untrained, cold, unwary [➡ UNSKILLED; 529] *Opposite*: prepared 2 *adj* **improvised**, unrehearsed, ad hoc, impromptu, spontaneous, spur-of-the-moment, ad lib, ad libitum, off-the-cuff [➡ HAPPENING QUICKLY; 104] *Opposite*: rehearsed

unprepossessing *adj* **ugly**, unattractive, plain, unpleasant, uninviting, ill-favored, homely [➡ PEOPLE'S PHYSICAL APPEARANCE; 475] *Opposite*: attractive

unpretentious *adj* **modest**, unassuming, unaffected, natural, self-effacing, humble, plain, without airs, down-to-earth, simple [➡ NATURALNESS; 497] *Opposite*: pretentious

unpretentiousness *n* **modesty**, humility, humbleness, simplicity, artlessness, ingenuousness, unaffectedness, naturalness [➡ NATURALNESS; 497] *Opposite*: grandiosity

unprincipled *adj* **dishonest**, corrupt, amoral, immoral, devious, cheating, deceitful, wrong, unethical, dishonorable [➡ MORALLY BAD OR IMPROPER; 775] *Opposite*: honest

unprintable *adj* **rude**, foul, offensive, shocking, coarse, vulgar, crass, obscene, scandalous, libelous [➡ MORALLY BAD OR IMPROPER; 775] *Opposite*: inoffensive

unproblematic *adj* **easy**, smooth, straightforward, trouble-free, simple, uncomplicated [➡ EASE AND SIMPLICITY; 200] *Opposite*: tricky

unprocessed *adj* **natural**, whole, unrefined, untreated, crude, organic, macrobiotic [➡ RAW AND NATURAL; 1214]

unproductive 1 *adj* **fruitless**, infertile, barren, sterile, blocked, uncreative [➡ REDUNDANT AND USELESS; 240] *Opposite*: fertile 2 *adj* **idle**, lazy, slow, wasteful, inefficient, ineffective, useless [➡ WASTEFUL AND UNECONOMICAL; 246] *Opposite*: productive

unproductiveness 1 *n* **fruitlessness**, unfruitfulness, barrenness, sterility, infertility, uncreativeness [➡ REDUNDANT AND USELESS; 240] *Opposite*: fertility 2 *n* **idleness**, laziness, slowness, inefficiency, wastefulness, ineffectiveness, uselessness [➡ WASTEFUL AND UNECONOMICAL; 246] *Opposite*: productiveness

unprofessed *adj* [➡ SECRET AND UNKNOWN; 179]

unprofessional 1 *adj* **unethical**, unprincipled, immoral, dishonorable, wrong, improper [➡ MORALLY BAD OR IMPROPER; 775] *Opposite*: ethical 2 *adj* **amateurish**, amateur, slack, inexpert, shoddy, incompetent, slapdash, sloppy (*informal*) [➡UNSKILLED; 529] *Opposite*: expert

unprofitable 1 *adj* **unsuccessful**, running at a loss, nonpaying, insolvent, nonprofit, unbeneficial, lossmaking (*UK*) [➡UNSUCCESSFUL AND UNPROMISING; 76] *Opposite*: profitable **2** *adj* **unhelpful**, useless, pointless, futile, fruitless, wasteful, vain [➡REDUNDANT AND USELESS; 240] *Opposite*: helpful

unpromising *adj* **gloomy**, bleak, discouraging, doubtful, off-putting, unhopeful, dubious [➡UNSUCCESSFUL AND UNPROMISING; 76] *Opposite*: encouraging

unprompted *adj* **spontaneous**, unforced, impulsive, willing, voluntary [➡THE WILL AND WILLINGNESS; 563] *Opposite*: forced

unpronounceable *adj* **unsayable**, difficult, impossible, inarticulate [➡THE SPOKEN WORD; 671]

unpronounced *adj* **silent**, mute, unvoiced, unspoken, unsaid, unarticulated [➡IMPERCEPTIBLE; 26] *Opposite*: voiced

unpropitious *adj* [➡INAPPROPRIATE AND UNSUITABLE; 224]

unprotected *adj* **defenseless**, undefended, open to attack, insecure, vulnerable, unguarded, isolated, exposed, unshielded, at risk [➡IN DANGER; 237] *Opposite*: secure

unproven *adj* **unverified**, unconfirmed, untried, untested, undocumented [➡UNCERTAIN; 175] *Opposite*: proven

unprovoked *adj* **gratuitous**, wanton, senseless, motiveless, uncalled-for, meaningless, malicious [➡REDUNDANT AND USELESS; 240] *Opposite*: provoked

unpunctual *adj* [➡PROMPTNESS: LATE; 100]

unpunctuality *n* [➡PROMPTNESS: LATE; 100]

unqualified 1 *adj* **untrained**, unprofessional, ill-equipped, inexpert, untaught, unskilled, incompetent [➡UNSKILLED; 529] *Opposite*: trained **2** *adj* **definite**, unreserved, absolute, complete, utter, outright, categorical, out-and-out, total [➡ABSOLUTE AND ABSOLUTELY; 133] *Opposite*: qualified

unquantifiable *adj* **immeasurable**, uncountable, unidentifiable, indefinable, indeterminate, unspecifiable, countless, incalculable [➡SECRET AND UNKNOWN; 179] *Opposite*: quantifiable

unquenchable *adj* [➡PERMANENCE: WITHOUT END; 94]

unquestionable *adj* **indisputable**, incontestable, absolute, undeniable, categorical, conclusive, without doubt, indubitable, incontrovertible [➡CERTAIN; 174] *Opposite*: arguable

unquestioned *adj* **undisputed**, accepted, unchallenged, automatic, logical, obvious [➡CERTAIN; 174] *Opposite*: questionable

unquestioning *adj* **unthinking**, wholehearted, obedient, absolute, automatic, unhesitating [➡AUTOMATIC AND INSTINCTIVE; 280] *Opposite*: reluctant

unquiet 1 *adj* **noisy**, turbulent, loud, rowdy, boisterous, uproarious, rackety (*dated*) [➡LOUD, HIGH, OR UNPLEASANT SOUNDS; 1266] *Opposite*: quiet **2** *adj* **anxious**, unsettled, restless, agitated, fidgety, turbulent, jumpy [➡CONFUSION, ANXIETY, AND WORRY; 540] *Opposite*: calm **3** *n* **noise**, noisiness, loudness,

rowdiness, boisterousness, uproariousness [➡LOUD, HIGH, OR UNPLEASANT SOUNDS; 1266] *Opposite*: quietness **4** *n* **anxiety**, concern, agitation, restlessness, disquiet, turbulence, fidgetiness [➡CONFUSION, ANXIETY, AND WORRY; 540] *Opposite*: calmness

unravel 1 *v* **undo**, untie, unknot, loosen, disentangle, untangle, unpick, unstitch, work loose, come undone [➡UNFASTEN AND UNDO; 409] *Opposite*: tie **2** *v* **solve**, clear up, resolve, sort out, get to the bottom of, work out [➡SOLVE AND INTERPRET; 760] **3** *v* **fail**, go wrong, fall apart, collapse, crumble, break down, fall to pieces [➡FAIL OR BE UNSUCCESSFUL; 75] *Opposite*: come together

unreachable *adj* [➡ABSENT AND UNAVAILABLE; 7]

unreadable 1 *adj* **illegible**, incomprehensible, indecipherable, scrawled, scribbled, untidy [➡DIFFICULTY AND COMPLEXITY; 242] *Opposite*: legible **2** *adj* **impenetrable**, dense, tedious, turgid, boring, difficult, heavy [➡BORING AND UNINTERESTING; 234] *Opposite*: readable **3** *adj* **blank**, expressionless, impassive, poker-faced, inscrutable [➡FACIAL EXPRESSIONS AND BLUSHING; 651]

unreal 1 *adj* **imaginary**, dreamlike, illusory, fantastic, weird, incredible, out of this world (*informal*) [➡BIZARRE AND PECULIAR; 257] *Opposite*: real **2** *adj* **false**, artificial, imitation, fake, pretend, faux, replica, mock, reproduction, unnatural [➡FALSE AND UNREAL; 173] *Opposite*: genuine

unrealistic *adj* **impractical**, idealistic, impracticable, improbable, unlikely, unworkable, naive [➡IMPOSSIBLE AND IMPROBABLE; 178] *Opposite*: practical

unreality 1 *n* **illusoriness**, strangeness, incongruity, oddness, weirdness, fantasy, abnormality [➡FALSE AND UNREAL; 173] *Opposite*: reality **2** *n* **fantasy**, delusion, fancy, self-delusion, illusion, fiction [➡DREAM, IMAGINE, AND FANTASIZE; 749] *Opposite*: reality

unreasonable 1 *adj* **irrational**, perverse, arbitrary, unreasoning, awkward, bad-tempered, difficult [➡DIFFICULT TO PLEASE; 515] *Opposite*: rational **2** *adj* **excessive**, exorbitant, immoderate, extravagant, extreme, unwarranted, unnecessary, unprovoked, uncalled-for, imbalanced, out of all proportion, unjust, unfair [➡MORALLY BAD OR IMPROPER; 775] *Opposite*: reasonable

unreasonableness 1 *n* **irrationality**, arbitrariness, awkwardness, perverseness, difficultness [➡DIFFICULT TO PLEASE; 515] *Opposite*: rationality **2** *n* **excessiveness**, injustice, exorbitantness, extravagance, unfairness, immoderation (*formal*), immoderateness (*formal*) [➡MORALLY BAD OR IMPROPER; 775] *Opposite*: reasonableness

unreasonably 1 *adv* **irrationally**, arbitrarily, unreasoningly, awkwardly, perversely [➡DIFFICULT TO PLEASE; 515] *Opposite*: rationally **2** *adv* **excessively**, unjustly, unduly, unfairly, immoderately (*formal*) [➡TO A GREAT EXTENT; 132] *Opposite*: reasonably

unreceptive *adj* **disinclined**, ill-disposed, unwilling, unteachable, defensive, intolerant, adamant, impervious, rigid [➡NEGATIVE INTELLECTUAL CHARACTERISTICS; 525] *Opposite*: receptive

unreceptiveness *n* [➡NEGATIVE INTELLECTUAL CHARACTERISTICS; 525]

unreconstructed 1 *adj* **old-fashioned**, unchanging, unrepentant, dyed-in-the-wool, traditional, unreformed, inveterate, diehard, unapologetic [➡ UNADVENTUROUS AND DULL; 517] **2** *adj* **unrestored**, untransformed, unaltered, unchanged, unvaried [➡ PERMANENCE: WITHOUT CHANGE; 95]

unrefined 1 *adj* **unprocessed**, untreated, raw, crude, untouched, whole, organic, natural, coarse [➡ RAW AND NATURAL; 1214] *Opposite*: refined **2** *adj* **vulgar**, unsophisticated, uncultured, crude, coarse, uncivilized, rough, loutish [➡ LEVELS OF EDUCATION AND SOPHISTICATION; 894] *Opposite*: sophisticated

unreformed *adj* **unapologetic**, unrepentant, dyed-in-the-wool, inveterate, diehard, traditional, unreconstructed [➡ UNADVENTUROUS AND DULL; 517] *Opposite*: reformed

unrehearsed *adj* **unprepared**, impromptu, off-the-cuff, spontaneous, impulsive, cold, improvised, unplanned, ad lib, ad libitum, spur-of-the-moment [➡ HAPPENING QUICKLY; 104] *Opposite*: prepared

unrelated 1 *adj* **unconnected**, separate, distinct, dissimilar, disparate, discrete, isolated [➡ UNRELATEDNESS AND SEPARATENESS; 146] *Opposite*: linked **2** *adj* **irrelevant**, beside the point, extraneous, unconnected, impertinent (*formal*) [➡ UNIMPORTANT AND UNNECESSARY; 238] *Opposite*: relevant

unrelenting *adj* **remorseless**, relentless, insistent, merciless, pitiless, pounding, unremitting, implacable, indefatigable, unyielding, persistent, unmovable, inexorable [➡ PERMANENCE: WITHOUT END; 94] *Opposite*: yielding

unreliability 1 *n* **undependability**, untrustworthiness, unpredictability, changeableness, irregularity, capriciousness, fickleness [➡ LACK OF COMMITMENT AND UNRELIABILITY; 509] *Opposite*: dependability **2** *n* **inaccuracy**, fallibility, untrustworthiness, flimsiness, dubiousness, erroneousness [➡ INCORRECT AND ERRONEOUS; 222] *Opposite*: reliability

unreliable 1 *adj* **undependable**, fly-by-night, variable, unpredictable, changeable, erratic, fickle, capricious, untrustworthy [➡ LACK OF COMMITMENT AND UNRELIABILITY; 509] *Opposite*: dependable **2** *adj* **inaccurate**, fallacious, flimsy, threadbare, untrue, falsified, anecdotal, erroneous, doubtful, untrustworthy [➡ INCORRECT AND ERRONEOUS; 222] *Opposite*: reliable

unreliableness *n* [➡ LACK OF COMMITMENT AND UNRELIABILITY; 509]

unrelieved *adj* **constant**, unbroken, chronic, unmitigated, unalleviated, unremitting, unrelenting, continuous, incessant [➡ PERMANENCE: WITHOUT END; 94] *Opposite*: intermittent

unremarkable *adj* **ordinary**, everyday, commonplace, average, typical, discreet, inconspicuous, unexceptional, routine, normal [➡ ORDINARINESS; 244] *Opposite*: remarkable

unremitting *adj* **constant**, incessant, continuous, chronic, unrelenting, unrelieved, assiduous, unalleviated, interminable, relentless, endless [➡ PERMANENCE: WITHOUT END; 94] *Opposite*: intermittent

unremorseful *adj* **unrepentant**, unapologetic, impenitent, unashamed, shameless, unabashed [➡ COOL AND CALM; 536] *Opposite*: apologetic

unrepentant *adj* **impenitent**, unapologetic, unashamed, shameless, unremorseful, unabashed [➡ COOL AND CALM; 536] *Opposite*: remorseful

unrequired *adj* [➡ UNPOPULAR AND UNWANTED; 258]

unreserved 1 *adj* **unqualified**, total, complete, utter, absolute, wholehearted, unconditional [➡ WHOLENESS AND COMPLETENESS; 198] *Opposite*: qualified **2** *adj* **open**, demonstrative, candid, frank, extrovert, extroverted, uninhibited, outgoing, talkative, chatty, outspoken [➡ HONEST AND OPEN; 630] *Opposite*: reserved

unresisting *adj* [➡ THE WILL AND WILLINGNESS; 563]

unresolved *adj* **unsettled**, unanswered, uncertain, vague, up in the air, unsolved, fluid, in doubt, unclear [➡ UNCERTAIN; 175] *Opposite*: settled

unresponsive *adj* **unfeeling**, insensitive, indifferent, impassive, uncaring, cold, unsympathetic, poker-faced, expressionless, unemotional [➡ NEUTRALITY AND INDIFFERENCE; 553] *Opposite*: responsive

unresponsiveness *n* **unfeelingness**, insensitivity, indifference, impassiveness, coldness, unconcern [➡ NEUTRALITY AND INDIFFERENCE; 553] *Opposite*: responsiveness

unrest 1 *n* **discontent**, turbulence, strife, conflict, disturbance, fighting, turmoil, disorder, instability, trouble [➡ CHAOS AND UPROAR; 51] *Opposite*: calm **2** *n* **anxiousness**, anxiety, disquiet, worry, uneasiness, unease, apprehension, restlessness, nervousness, agitation, fear [➡ FEELINGS ABOUT THE FUTURE; 533] *Opposite*: peace

unrestrained *adj* **uncontrolled**, wild, unrestricted, abandoned, uninhibited, unreserved, unrepressed [➡ FREEDOM AND LIBERTY; 208] *Opposite*: restrained

unrestricted *adj* **open**, unobstructed, unhindered, unlimited, unhampered, at liberty, free, limitless [➡ FREEDOM AND LIBERTY; 208] *Opposite*: restricted

unrevealed *adj* **secret**, hidden, unknown, mysterious, clandestine, private, undisclosed, concealed, unidentified [➡ SECRET AND UNKNOWN; 179] *Opposite*: known

unrewarding *adj* **thankless**, fruitless, unfulfilling, unsatisfactory, difficult [➡ EMOTIONALLY UNPLEASANT AND UPSETTING; 227] *Opposite*: satisfying

unrighteous 1 *adj* **sinful**, wicked, evil, irreligious, unholy, bad, impure [➡ MORALLY BAD OR IMPROPER; 775] *Opposite*: righteous **2** *adj* **unjust**, unfair, ill-deserved, unkind, wrong, mean [➡ MORALLY BAD OR IMPROPER; 775] *Opposite*: just

unripe *adj* **immature**, green, young, fresh, undeveloped [➡ NEW, MODERN; 166] *Opposite*: ripe

unrivaled *adj* **unequaled**, unchallenged, unsurpassed, unbeatable, unparalleled, extraordinary, unmatched, incomparable, matchless, unique, singular [➡ EXTRAORDINARY: UNCOMMON; 205] *Opposite*: ordinary

unroll *v* **open**, unfurl, stretch out, spread out, unfold, undo, open out [➡ CAUSE TO APPEAR; 5] *Opposite*: roll up

unruffled *adj* **calm**, tranquil, unmoved, in control, at ease, relaxed, unflustered, composed, cool, unperturbed [➡ COOL AND CALM; 536] *Opposite*: flustered

unruliness *n* **boisterousness**, disruptiveness, disorderliness, rowdiness, recalcitrance, obstreperousness, willfulness, waywardness, disobedience, wildness, intractability (*formal*) [➡ REBELLIOUSNESS AND DISOBEDIENCE; 565] *Opposite*: orderliness

unruly *adj* **boisterous**, disruptive, disorderly, rowdy, disobedient, wild, uncontrollable, unmanageable, recalcitrant, obstreperous, willful, wayward, intractable (*formal*) [➡ REBELLIOUSNESS AND DISOBEDIENCE; 565] *Opposite*: orderly

Compare and Contrast: *unruly, intractable, recalcitrant, obstreperous, willful, wild, wayward*

CORE MEANING: not submitting to control

unruly boisterous, disruptive, and difficult to control or discipline; *intractable* (*formal*) strong-willed and rebellious, refusing to be controlled or to submit to discipline; *recalcitrant* obstinate and defiant in refusing to submit to discipline or control; *obstreperous* noisy, difficult to control, and uncooperative; *willful* stubbornly disregarding the opinions or advice of others; *wild* showing a general lack of control or restraint; *wayward* disobedient and uncontrollable.

unrushed *adj* **unhurried**, slow, leisurely, calm, gentle, relaxed, laid-back (*informal*) [➡ MOVING SLOWLY; 105] *Opposite*: hurried

unsafe *adj* **dangerous**, insecure, hazardous, risky, perilous, precarious, treacherous [➡ DANGEROUS; 236] *Opposite*: secure

unsaid *adj* **tacit**, unspoken, implicit, silent, unstated, unarticulated, unexpressed [➡ SECRET AND UNKNOWN; 179] *Opposite*: spoken

unsalaried *adj* [➡ EMPLOYMENT STATUS; 831]

unsalvageable *adj* [➡ IN BAD REPAIR; 1234]

unsanitariness *n* [➡ DIRTY; 1235]

unsanitary *adj* [➡ DIRTY; 1235]

unsatisfactory *adj* **inadequate**, unacceptable, substandard, disappointing, insufficient, poor [➡ UNACCEPTABLE AND UNFORGIVABLE; 225] *Opposite*: acceptable

unsatisfied *adj* **displeased**, discontented, unhappy, unfulfilled, disgruntled, disappointed, unconvinced [➡ SADNESS, DISTRESS, AND DESPAIR; 539] *Opposite*: pleased

unsatisfying *adj* [➡ UNACCEPTABLE AND UNFORGIVABLE; 225]

unsavoriness *n* [➡ MORALLY BAD OR IMPROPER; 775]

unsavory 1 *adj* **unpleasant**, disagreeable, revolting, disgusting, nasty, grubby, seedy, sleazy, repellent, unwelcome, distasteful [➡ DISGUSTING AND REPULSIVE; 230] *Opposite*: pleasant 2 *adj* **immoral**, unpleasant, villainous, shady, unacceptable, suspect, dishonest, untrustworthy, disreputable [➡ MORALLY BAD OR IMPROPER; 775] *Opposite*: wholesome

unscathed *adj* **unharmed**, intact, unhurt, untouched, safe, safe and sound, without a scratch, unmarked [➡ SAFE AND SOUND; 737] *Opposite*: injured

unschooled *adj* **uneducated**, untaught, untutored, untrained, illiterate [➡ LEVELS OF EDUCATION AND SOPHISTICATION; 894] *Opposite*: educated

unscientific *adj* **intuitive**, instinctive, irrational, unempirical, seat-of-the-pants (*informal*), half-baked (*informal*) [➡ THE NATURE OF IDEAS; 771] *Opposite*: systematic

unscramble *v* **decode**, sort out, decipher, work out,

make out, decrypt, crack [➡ SOLVE AND INTERPRET; 760] *Opposite*: encode

unscrew *v* **take off**, remove, detach, loosen, undo [➡ UNFASTEN AND UNDO; 409] *Opposite*: tighten

unscripted *adj* **unplanned**, unexpected, impromptu, impulsive, unscheduled, off-the-cuff, ad lib, ad libitum [➡ UNPLANNED AND UNEXPECTED; 281]

unscrupulous *adj* **dishonest**, unprincipled, corrupt, immoral, deceitful, devious, ruthless, crooked (*informal*) [➡ MORALLY BAD OR IMPROPER; 775] *Opposite*: honest

unscrupulously *adv* **dishonestly**, immorally, corruptly, deceitfully, deviously, ruthlessly, crookedly (*informal*) [➡ MORALLY BAD OR IMPROPER; 775] *Opposite*: honestly

unscrupulousness *n* **dishonesty**, corruptness, crookedness, immorality, deviousness, ruthlessness, deceit [➡ MORALLY BAD OR IMPROPER; 775] *Opposite*: honesty

unseal *v* **open**, uncap, unstop, break open, unscrew [➡ UNFASTEN AND UNDO; 409] *Opposite*: seal

unseasonable 1 *adj* **unusual**, abnormal, unexpected, odd, strange, uncommon [➡ EXTRAORDINARY: UNCOMMON; 205] *Opposite*: seasonable 2 *adj* **untimely**, inopportune, ill-timed, inconvenient, unwelcome, obtrusive, unexpected [➡ PROMPTNESS: BADLY TIMED; 101] *Opposite*: seasonable

unseasoned *adj* [➡ STATE OF PREPARED FOOD; 1171]

unseat *v* **depose**, oust, overthrow, dethrone, remove [➡ REVOKE STATUS; 459] *Opposite*: enthrone (*formal*)

unseemliness *n* **impropriety**, tastelessness, uncouthness, loutishness, rudeness, indecorousness, inappropriateness [➡ INAPPROPRIATE AND UNSUITABLE; 224] *Opposite*: propriety

unseemly *adj* **inappropriate**, rude, uncouth, improper, indecorous, unsuitable, unbecoming, tasteless [➡ INAPPROPRIATE AND UNSUITABLE; 224] *Opposite*: proper

unseen *adj* **hidden**, unnoticed, unobserved, invisible, concealed, undetected [➡ IMPERCEPTIBLE; 26] *Opposite*: noticeable

unselective *adj* **indiscriminating**, undiscerning, blanket, haphazard, random, indiscriminate [➡ DISORDER AND CHAOS; 245] *Opposite*: discerning

unselfish *adj* **selfless**, generous, noble, magnanimous, liberal, kind, thoughtful, considerate, altruistic [➡ GENEROSITY AND KINDNESS; 495] *Opposite*: selfish

unselfishness *n* **selflessness**, generosity, magnanimity, kindness, consideration, thoughtfulness, altruism [➡ GENEROSITY AND KINDNESS; 495] *Opposite*: selfishness

unsentimental *adj* **unemotional**, impassive, unfeeling, hard-bitten, tough, cynical, hard-boiled (*informal*) [➡ NEUTRALITY AND INDIFFERENCE; 553] *Opposite*: sentimental

unsettle *v* **worry**, disturb, upset, disconcert, unnerve, perturb, bother, fluster, disquiet (*archaic or literary*) [➡ UPSET, DISTRESS, AND HUMILIATE; 567] *Opposite*: soothe

unsettled 1 *adj* **anxious**, worried, disturbed, upset, disconcerted, ill at ease, uneasy, troubled, uncomfortable, tense, flustered [➡ CONFUSION, ANXIETY, AND WORRY; 540] *Opposite*: at

ease 2 *adj* **changeable**, variable, unpredictable, uncertain, changing [➡ FINITENESS, VARIABILITY, AND TRANSIENCE; 96] *Opposite:* settled **3** *adj* **undecided**, unresolved, undetermined, open-ended, arguable, debatable, moot [➡ UNCERTAIN; 175] *Opposite:* decided

unsettling *adj* **upsetting**, worrying, disturbing, disconcerting, disquieting, troubling [➡ EMOTIONALLY UNPLEASANT AND UPSETTING; 227] *Opposite:* soothing

unshackle *v* **release**, unchain, let loose, set free, liberate, unleash [➡ FREEDOM AND LIBERTY; 208] *Opposite:* chain

unshakable *adj* **steadfast**, resolute, constant, unwavering, entrenched, staunch, immovable, unflinching, sure, firm, unswerving [➡ CERTAINTY; 561] *Opposite:* wavering

unshaped *adj* **unformed**, formless, shapeless, amorphous, indistinct, unstructured [➡ SHAPELESSNESS; 1219] *Opposite:* shaped

unshaven *adj* [➡ FACIAL HAIR; 489]

unsheathe *v* **draw**, pull, remove, extract, rake out, uncover [➡ REMOVE SOMETHING; 338]

unshorn *adj* [➡ DESCRIBING HAIR; 486]

unsightliness *n* **ugliness**, hideousness, horridness, unpleasantness, nastiness, unattractiveness [➡ UGLINESS AND UNATTRACTIVENESS; 233] *Opposite:* attractiveness

unsightly *adj* **unattractive**, ugly, hideous, unpleasant, unprepossessing, nasty, horrid, unappealing [➡ UGLINESS AND UNATTRACTIVENESS; 233] *Opposite:* attractive

unskilled *adj* **inexpert**, amateurish, untrained, uneducated, unqualified, inexperienced, unskillful [➡ UNSKILLED; 529] *Opposite:* trained

unskilled worker *n* [➡ WORKERS; 836]

unskillful *adj* **inept**, unskilled, untrained, untalented, incompetent, awkward, amateurish, clumsy, ham-fisted (*informal*), ham-handed (*informal*), gawky (*informal*) [➡ UNSKILLED; 529] *Opposite:* skillful

unskillfulness *n* [➡ UNSKILLED; 529]

unsmiling *adj* **stern**, severe, serious, dour, grim-faced, disapproving [➡ BAD-TEMPERED AND HUMORLESS; 626] *Opposite:* cordial

unsnag *v* **disentangle**, clear, free, untangle, release [➡ UNFASTEN AND UNDO; 409] *Opposite:* snag

unsnarl *v* **disentangle**, clear, free, untangle, unblock [➡ UNFASTEN AND UNDO; 409] *Opposite:* tangle

unsociable *adj* **unfriendly**, antisocial, aloof, shy, standoffish, distant, hostile, cold [➡ UNFRIENDLINESS AND UNSOCIABILITY; 504] *Opposite:* friendly

unsoiled *adj* [➡ CLEAN AND HYGIENIC; 1233]

unsolicited *adj* **unwelcome**, unwanted, uninvited, unsought, spontaneous, voluntary, uncalled-for [➡ UNPOPULAR AND UNWANTED; 258] *Opposite:* requested

unsolvable *adj* **impenetrable**, unknowable, impossible, unfathomable, insoluble [➡ DIFFICULTY AND COMPLEXITY; 242] *Opposite:* soluble

unsolved *adj* **unexplained**, unresolved, mysterious, baffling [➡ DIFFICULTY AND COMPLEXITY; 242] *Opposite:* resolved

unsophisticated 1 *adj* **unworldly**, naive, inexperienced, ingenuous, simple, artless, innocent, childlike, natural [➡ NATURALNESS; 497] *Opposite:* sophisticated **2** *adj* **crude**, simple, unrefined, basic, primitive, straightforward [➡ ORDINARINESS; 244] *Opposite:* advanced

unsophisticatedly *adv* **naively**, artlessly, ingenuously, innocently, naturally, simply, plainly [➡ NATURALNESS; 497]

unsought *adj* **unsolicited**, spontaneous, uninvited, uncalled-for, unwanted, unlooked-for [➡ UNPOPULAR AND UNWANTED; 258]

unsound 1 *adj* **ill**, frail, unwell, unhealthy, sick [➡ UNFIT AND WEAK; 739] *Opposite:* well **2** *adj* **unsafe**, unstable, rickety, in poor condition, ramshackle, unsteady, shaky, wobbly [➡ DANGEROUS; 236] *Opposite:* secure **3** *adj* **illogical**, specious, flawed, fallacious, erroneous, faulty, unreliable [➡ THE NATURE OF IDEAS; 771] *Opposite:* logical

unsound reasoning *n* [➡ NEGATIVE INTELLECTUAL CHARACTERISTICS; 525]

unsparing 1 *adj* **merciless**, harsh, cruel, unforgiving, severe, hard, unkind, excessive, unrelenting [➡ SELFISH AND UNKIND; 505] *Opposite:* merciful **2** *adj* **generous**, munificent, openhanded, liberal, charitable, unstinting, bountiful (*literary*) [➡ GENEROSITY AND KINDNESS; 495] *Opposite:* sparing

unspeakable 1 *adj* **awful**, disgusting, appalling, foul, revolting, horrifying, terrifying, terrible, horrendous [➡ DISGUSTING AND REPULSIVE; 230] **2** *adj* **indescribable**, inexpressible, unutterable, undefinable, ineffable (*formal*) [➡ EXTRAORDINARY: AMAZING; 204]

unspeakably 1 *adv* **indescribably**, inexpressibly, unutterably, undefinably, unbelievably, ineffably (*formal*) [➡ TO A GREAT EXTENT; 132] **2** *adv* **terribly**, awfully, disgustingly, appallingly, horribly, horrendously, dreadfully [➡ DISGUSTING AND REPULSIVE; 230]

unspeaking *adj* **silent**, mute, wordless, still, speechless, dumbstruck [➡ COMMUNICATIVE STYLE; 624] *Opposite:* verbose

unspecified *adj* **unnamed**, indefinite, vague, indeterminate, undetermined, unstipulated [➡ VAGUENESS; 243] *Opposite:* specific

unspectacular *adj* [➡ ORDINARINESS; 244]

unspiritual *adj* **earthly**, worldly, mundane, irreligious [➡ RELIGIOUS CONCEPTS; 776] *Opposite:* spiritual

unspoiled 1 *adj* **pristine**, pure, perfect, untouched, unharmed, unblemished, undamaged, intact, well-preserved, unchanged [➡ IN GOOD REPAIR; 1232] *Opposite:* marred **2** *adj* **uncorrupted**, natural, innocent, pure, wholesome, artless [➡ NATURALNESS; 497] *Opposite:* spoiled

unspoilt *see* **unspoiled**

unspoken *adj* **tacit**, understood, silent, implicit, undeclared, assumed, unsaid, unexpressed [➡ SECRET AND UNKNOWN; 179] *Opposite:* explicit

unsporting *adj* **dishonest**, unfair, dishonorable, disreputable, mean-spirited [➡ DECEITFUL; 513] *Opposite:* sporting

unsportsmanlike *adj* **dirty**, dishonest, nasty, foul, unethical, bad [➡ DECEITFUL; 513] *Opposite:* exemplary

unspotted 1 *adj* **unstained**, clean, spotless, unblemished, pristine, stainless, immaculate [➡ CLEAN AND HYGIENIC; 1233] *Opposite:* spotted 2 *adj* **pure**, moral, unblemished, faultless, righteous, good [➡ MORALLY GOOD; 774] *Opposite:* impure 3 *adj* **unobserved**, unseen, unnoticed, unperceived, undiscovered, invisible [➡ IMPERCEPTIBLE; 26] *Opposite:* seen

unstable 1 *adj* **unbalanced**, uneven, unhinged, wobbly, rickety, unsound, unsteady, insecure [➡ DANGEROUS; 236] *Opposite:* steady 2 *adj* **volatile**, unpredictable, unsteady, erratic, variable, changeable [➡ FINITENESS, VARIABILITY, AND TRANSIENCE; 96] *Opposite:* stable

unstated *adj* **unspecified**, unspoken, tacit, understood, implicit, assumed, unsaid, unexpressed [➡ THE NATURE OF IDEAS; 771] *Opposite:* specified

unsteadily 1 *adv* **wobblingly**, tremblingly, tremulously, waveringly, unstably, shakily, unevenly, precariously, treacherously, totteringly [➡ DANGEROUS; 236] *Opposite:* securely 2 *adv* **changeably**, erratically, variably, unreliably, irregularly, inconstantly, waveringly [➡ FINITENESS, VARIABILITY, AND TRANSIENCE; 96] *Opposite:* constantly

unsteadiness 1 *n* **tremulousness**, instability, shakiness, unevenness, precariousness, treacherousness, wobbliness [➡ DANGER; 235] *Opposite:* stability 2 *n* **changeability**, erraticism, variability, unreliability, irregularity, inconstancy [➡ FINITENESS, VARIABILITY, AND TRANSIENCE; 96] *Opposite:* constancy

unsteady 1 *adj* **wobbly**, shaky, unstable, uneven, rickety, trembling, tremulous, wavering, vacillating, precarious, treacherous, tottering [➡ DANGEROUS; 236] *Opposite:* stable 2 *adj* **changeable**, erratic, variable, unreliable, irregular, inconstant, wavering [➡ FINITENESS, VARIABILITY, AND TRANSIENCE; 96] *Opposite:* constant

unstick *v* **release**, pry, free, take off, take down, take apart, prize [➡ UNFASTEN AND UNDO; 409] *Opposite:* stick

unstinting *adj* **generous**, charitable, openhanded, liberal, unsparing, magnanimous, bountiful (*literary*) [➡ GENEROSITY AND KINDNESS; 495] *Opposite:* stingy

unstipulated *adj* **unspecified**, unstated, unmentioned, understood, undeclared [➡ VAGUENESS; 243] *Opposite:* specified

unstop *v* **unblock**, free, clear, unplug, open up, release [➡ UNFASTEN AND UNDO; 409] *Opposite:* stop

unstoppable *adj* **irresistible**, overwhelming, overpowering, persistent, unrelenting, persisting, persevering, relentless, inevitable, inescapable, inexorable (*formal*) [➡ PERMANENCE: WITHOUT END; 94] *Opposite:* avoidable

unstrained *adj* **cloudy**, milky, opaque, murky [➡ VISUAL TEXTURE; 1221] *Opposite:* clear

unstrap *v* **undo**, remove, unbuckle, unshackle, unleash, free [➡ UNFASTEN AND UNDO; 409] *Opposite:* tie up

unstressed *adj* **relaxed**, carefree, at ease, cool, calm, tranquil, serene, laid-back (*informal*) [➡ COOL AND CALM; 536] *Opposite:* stressed

unstructured *adj* **formless**, shapeless, amorphous, free [➡ SHAPELESSNESS; 1219] *Opposite:* structured

unstudied *adj* **unaffected**, natural, genuine, sincere, relaxed, open [➡ NATURALNESS; 497] *Opposite:* affected

unsubstantiated *adj* **unconfirmed**, unproven, unsupported, uncorroborated [➡ UNCERTAIN; 175] *Opposite:* proven

unsubtle *adj* [➡ PERCEPTIBLE; 25]

unsuccessful *adj* **ineffective**, failed, vain, unproductive, abortive, futile, fruitless, disastrous [➡ UNSUCCESSFUL AND UNPROMISING; 76] *Opposite:* successful

unsuitability *n* **inappropriateness**, inaptness, unbecomingness, incongruity, incompatibility, unacceptability, improperness, unseemliness [➡ INAPPROPRIATE AND UNSUITABLE; 224] *Opposite:* appropriateness

unsuitable *adj* **inappropriate**, unbecoming, unfitting, inapt, unbefitting, incongruous, incompatible, out of place, improper, unacceptable, unseemly [➡ INAPPROPRIATE AND UNSUITABLE; 224] *Opposite:* appropriate

unsullied *adj* **pure**, clean, unblemished, faultless, untarnished, immaculate [➡ CLEAN AND HYGIENIC; 1233] *Opposite:* tarnished

unsung *adj* **unacknowledged**, silent, unrecognized, anonymous, backroom, nameless, unrewarded [➡ SECRET AND UNKNOWN; 179] *Opposite:* renowned

unsupported *adj* **uncorroborated**, unconfirmed, unsubstantiated, unverified, unfounded, unproven [➡ UNCERTAIN; 175] *Opposite:* supported

unsure 1 *adj* **uncertain**, doubtful, unconvinced, dubious, suspicious, undecided, skeptical [➡ UNCERTAINTY; 559] *Opposite:* certain 2 *adj* **unconfident**, hesitant, shy, insecure, irresolute, uncertain [➡ INSECURITY AND LOSS OF COMPOSURE; 544] *Opposite:* confident

See Compare and Contrast at **doubtful.**

unsurpassed *adj* **unrivaled**, unmatched, supreme, incomparable, unequaled, unparalleled, matchless, consummate [➡ SUPERIORITY; 152] *Opposite:* ordinary

unsurprising *adj* **predictable**, foreseeable, expected, anticipated, foreseen [➡ BORING AND UNINTERESTING; 234] *Opposite:* surprising

unsurprisingly *adv* **of course**, naturally, obviously, expectedly, predictably [➡ Words and Phrases Emphasizing the Truth of a Matter; 172] *Opposite:* surprisingly

unsuspected *adj* **unanticipated**, unpredicted, unknown, unimagined, surprise, hidden [➡ SECRET AND UNKNOWN; 179] *Opposite:* known

unsuspecting *adj* **unwary**, gullible, credulous, innocent, unsuspicious, naive [➡ NEGATIVE INTELLECTUAL CHARACTERISTICS; 525] *Opposite:* wary

unsustainable *adj* **unjustifiable**, unmaintainable, unverifiable, untenable, indefensible, unmanageable, unsanctionable [➡ UNACCEPTABLE AND UNFORGIVABLE; 225] *Opposite:* sustainable

unswerving *adj* **unwavering**, staunch, reliable, trusty, solid, constant, steadfast, unshakable [➡ STRENGTH OF WILL; 501] *Opposite:* wavering

unsymmetrical *adj* **asymmetrical**, uneven, irregular, lopsided [➥ ORIENTATION AND ALIGNMENT; 1223] *Opposite*: symmetrical

unsympathetic *adj* **unfeeling**, uncaring, insensitive, cold, indifferent, heartless, hard, cruel, unconcerned [➥ SELFISH AND UNKIND; 505] *Opposite*: caring

unsystematic *adj* **haphazard**, random, chaotic, disorganized, disorderly, muddled, slapdash, unmethodical [➥ DISORDER AND CHAOS; 245] *Opposite*: organized

untainted *adj* **unpolluted**, undamaged, unblemished, unspoiled, pure, uncorrupted [➥ CLEAN AND HYGIENIC; 1233] *Opposite*: tainted

untaken *adj* **available**, unclaimed, unoccupied, free, spare [➥ PRESENT AND AVAILABLE; 11] *Opposite*: taken

untalented *adj* [➥ UNSKILLED; 529]

untangle *v* **unravel**, disentangle, untie, unpick, straighten out [➥ UNFASTEN AND UNDO; 409] *Opposite*: tangle

untapped *adj* **unused**, unexploited, untouched, available, intact [➥ PRESENT AND AVAILABLE; 11] *Opposite*: used

untarnished *adj* **unblemished**, clean, spotless, shining, unsullied, faultless, immaculate [➥ CLEAN AND HYGIENIC; 1233] *Opposite*: blemished

untaught *adj* **untutored**, uneducated, untrained, natural, born, instinctive, innate, inherent [➥ AUTOMATIC AND INSTINCTIVE; 280] *Opposite*: trained

untenable *adj* **indefensible**, unsustainable, weak, unsound, shaky, invalid, flawed [➥ IMPOSSIBLE AND IMPROBABLE; 178] *Opposite*: watertight

untested **1** *adj* **untried**, unproven, inexperienced, inexpert, new, raw [➥ NEW, MODERN; 166] *Opposite*: experienced **2** *adj* **experimental**, untried, unapproved, unverified, unproven, uncertified, unconfirmed, unproved [➥ UNCERTAIN; 175] *Opposite*: safe

untether *v* **release**, untie, unstrap, unchain, free, unleash [➥ UNFASTEN AND UNDO; 409] *Opposite*: tie up

unthinkable **1** *adj* **absurd**, ridiculous, unlikely, impossible, improbable, extraordinary [➥ IMPOSSIBLE AND IMPROBABLE; 178] *Opposite*: likely **2** *adj* **unimaginable**, impossible, fantastic, unbelievable, incredible, inconceivable [➥ BIZARRE AND PECULIAR; 257] *Opposite*: conceivable

unthinking **1** *adj* **careless**, thoughtless, tactless, undiplomatic, inconsiderate, indiscreet, blunt [➥ INCAUTIOUS AND CARELESS; 283] *Opposite*: thoughtful **2** *adj* **instinctive**, automatic, mechanical, intuitive, impulsive [➥ AUTOMATIC AND INSTINCTIVE; 280] *Opposite*: calculated

unthinkingness *n* [➥ NEGATIVE INTELLECTUAL CHARACTERISTICS; 525]

unthreatened *adj* **secure**, safe, safe and sound, protected, impregnable [➥ SAFE AND SAFETY; 191] *Opposite*: threatened

untidily *adv* **messily**, shabbily, scruffily, sloppily [➥ DISORDER AND CHAOS; 245] *Opposite*: neatly

untidiness *n* **mess**, disorder, muddle, disarray, jumble, clutter, chaos [➥ DISORDER AND CHAOS; 245] *Opposite*: order

untidy **1** *adj* **messy**, in a mess, disorderly, muddled, jumbled, cluttered, chaotic, in a state (*informal*) [➥ DISORDER

AND CHAOS; 245] *Opposite*: neat **2** *adj* **unkempt**, ragged, shabby, scruffy, bedraggled, disheveled, rumpled [➥ BADLY GROOMED; 483] *Opposite*: smart

untie **1** *v* **unknot**, unfasten, loosen, undo, unravel, unpick, disentangle, untangle [➥ UNFASTEN AND UNDO; 409] *Opposite*: fasten **2** *v* **release**, free, set free, unleash, let loose [➥ FREEDOM AND LIBERTY; 208] *Opposite*: tie up

until *prep* **up until**, while waiting for, pending, till, up to [➥ FUTURE; 86]

until further notice *adv* [➥ FUTURE; 86]

until now *adv* **up till now**, so far, thus far, as yet, up to now, hitherto, to date [➥ PAST; 84]

until recently *adv* [➥ PAST; 84]

until the end of time *adv* [➥ PERMANENCE: WITHOUT END; 94]

untimely **1** *adj* **ill-timed**, inconvenient, inappropriate, unfortunate, inopportune, unseasonable [➥ PROMPTNESS: BADLY TIMED; 101] *Opposite*: timely **2** *adj* **premature**, early, precocious, advance [➥ PROMPTNESS: EARLY; 98] *Opposite*: late

untiring *adj* **tireless**, determined, dogged, indefatigable, constant, steady, persistent, patient [➥ STRENGTH OF WILL; 501] *Opposite*: faltering

untold **1** *adj* **indescribable**, inexpressible, indefinable, ineffable (*formal*) [➥ EXTRAORDINARY: UNCOMMON; 205] **2** *adj* **uncountable**, countless, innumerable, myriad, numberless, incalculable, unnumbered [➥ MANY, MUCH, LARGE AMOUNT; 117] *Opposite*: few

untouchable *adj* **unattainable**, matchless, superlative, superior, unrivaled, unchallenged, unbeatable, unparalleled, unassailable [➥ EXTRAORDINARY: AMAZING; 204] *Opposite*: ordinary

untouched **1** *adj* **unhurt**, intact, unharmed, undamaged, safe and sound, unscathed, uninjured [➥ SAFE AND SOUND; 737] *Opposite*: injured **2** *adj* **unaffected**, indifferent, unmoved, unimpressed, unconcerned [➥ NEUTRALITY AND INDIFFERENCE; 553] *Opposite*: affected

untoward **1** *adj* **annoying**, unpleasant, inconvenient, troublesome, awkward, problematic, unfortunate [➥ IRRITATING; 228] *Opposite*: pleasant **2** *adj* **inappropriate**, unfitting, unseemly, improper, unbecoming, indecent [➥ INAPPROPRIATE AND UNSUITABLE; 224] *Opposite*: appropriate

untraceable *adj* [➥ IMPERCEPTIBLE; 26]

untrained *adj* **untaught**, inexpert, untutored, unqualified, inexperienced, amateur [➥ IGNORANCE; 557] *Opposite*: trained

untrammeled *adj* **unrestricted**, free, unhindered, unimpeded, liberated, unrestrained [➥ FREEDOM AND LIBERTY; 208] *Opposite*: restrained

untreated *adj* **unprocessed**, unrefined, natural, raw, crude, basic [➥ RAW AND NATURAL; 1214] *Opposite*: treated

untried *adj* **untested**, inexperienced, unproven, new, novel, experimental [➥ NEW, MODERN; 166] *Opposite*: tested

untroubled *adj* **peaceful**, calm, tranquil, undisturbed, unflustered, serene, unruffled, unworried, placid [➥ COOL AND CALM; 536] *Opposite*: troubled

untrue 1 *adj* **false**, incorrect, wrong, fallacious, untruthful, fictitious, fictional, imaginary [➡ FALSE AND UNREAL; 173] *Opposite*: true 2 *adj* **cheating**, unfaithful, disloyal, treacherous, two-faced, faithless, deceitful, untrustworthy [➡ DECEITFUL; 513] *Opposite*: faithful

untrustworthiness *n* **unreliability**, undependability, dishonesty, deceitfulness, disloyalty, treachery, deviousness [➡ DECEITFUL; 513] *Opposite*: dependability

untrustworthy *adj* **unreliable**, undependable, dishonest, deceitful, disloyal, treacherous, devious [➡ DECEITFUL; 513] *Opposite*: dependable

untruth *n* **lie**, falsehood, fiction, fabrication, deceit, tale, story (*informal*), fib (*informal*) [➡ DECEPTION AND LIES; 660] *Opposite*: truth

See Compare and Contrast at **lie**.

untruthful *adj* **lying**, mendacious, dishonest, deceitful, false, deceptive, misleading, fabricated, fictitious, fibbing (*informal*) [➡ DECEITFUL; 513] *Opposite*: truthful

untruthfulness *n* **dishonesty**, deceit, lies, falsehood, fabrication, mendacity, deception [➡ DECEPTION AND LIES; 660] *Opposite*: truthfulness

untutored *adj* **untaught**, uneducated, untrained, unschooled, unqualified, inexperienced, illiterate [➡ UNSKILLED; 529] *Opposite*: educated

unusable *adj* **useless**, out of commission, unworkable, inoperative, broken [➡ IN BAD REPAIR; 1234] *Opposite*: usable

unused 1 *adj* **new**, brand-new, fresh, pristine [➡ NEW, MODERN; 166] *Opposite*: used 2 *adj* **idle**, vacant, unemployed, unexploited, fallow [➡ LACK OF ACTIVITY OR MOTION; 342] 3 *adj* **unaccustomed**, unfamiliar, unacquainted, inexperienced [➡ UNSKILLED; 529] *Opposite*: familiar

unusual 1 *adj* **uncommon**, rare, infrequent, scarce, unfamiliar, few and far between (*informal*) [➡ EXTRAORDINARY: UNCOMMON; 205] *Opposite*: common 2 *adj* **strange**, odd, curious, extraordinary, abnormal, remarkable, bizarre, atypical [➡ BIZARRE AND PECULIAR; 257] *Opposite*: ordinary

unusualness *n* [➡ EXTRAORDINARY: UNCOMMON; 205]

unutterable *adj* **unspeakable**, indescribable, inexpressible, indefinable, ineffable (*formal*) [➡ UNACCEPTABLE AND UNFORGIVABLE; 225]

unvalued *adj* [➡ UNPOPULAR AND UNWANTED; 258]

unvanquished *adj* [➡ SUCCESSFUL AND PROMISING; 81]

unvaried *adj* [➡ PERMANENCE: WITHOUT CHANGE; 95]

unvarnished *adj* **plain**, straight, honest, unembellished, literal, exact, unadulterated, naked, unembroidered, unadorned, simple, straightforward [➡ TRUE AND REAL; 171] *Opposite*: embellished

unvarying *adj* **unwavering**, constant, unchanging, consistent, inflexible, regular, habitual, stable, steady [➡ PERMANENCE: WITHOUT CHANGE; 95] *Opposite*: varying

unveil 1 *v* **uncover**, unwrap, bare, expose [➡ CAUSE TO APPEAR; 5] *Opposite*: cover 2 *v* **reveal**, expose, make public, divulge,

show, disclose, uncover [➡ INFORM, ANNOUNCE, AND ISSUE; 611] *Opposite*: conceal

unveiling 1 *n* **opening**, launch, presentation, inauguration, debut, entrance [➡ CEREMONIES AND ANNIVERSARIES; 38] *Opposite*: closure 2 *n* **revelation**, disclosure, exposure, uncovering, release, announcement [➡ INFORM, ANNOUNCE, AND ISSUE; 611] *Opposite*: cover-up

unventilated *adj* **airless**, stuffy, unaired, close, stale [➡ PHYSICALLY UNPLEASANT; 226] *Opposite*: airy

unverified *adj* **unconfirmed**, unsupported, unsubstantiated, uncorroborated, unproven, unendorsed [➡ UNCERTAIN; 175] *Opposite*: verified

unversed *adj* [➡ IGNORANCE; 557]

unviability *n* [➡ IMPOSSIBLE AND IMPROBABLE; 178]

unviable *adj* [➡ IMPOSSIBLE AND IMPROBABLE; 178]

unvoiced *adj* **unspoken**, silent, secret, hidden, mute, tacit, unexpressed [➡ SECRET AND UNKNOWN; 179] *Opposite*: spoken

unwaged (*UK*) *adj* **unemployed**, jobless, on welfare, out of work, redundant (*UK*) [➡ EMPLOYMENT STATUS; 831] *Opposite*: employed

unwanted 1 *adj* **surplus**, superfluous, unnecessary, discarded, redundant, useless [➡ MORE AND EXCESS; 124] *Opposite*: necessary 2 *adj* **unwelcome**, unsolicited, annoying, undesirable, uninvited [➡ UNPOPULAR AND UNWANTED; 258] *Opposite*: welcome

unwariness *n* **incautiousness**, unguardedness, rashness, carelessness, gullibility, credulity, naiveté, imprudence [➡ NEGATIVE INTELLECTUAL CHARACTERISTICS; 525] *Opposite*: wariness

unwarrantable *adj* **uncalled-for**, indefensible, unjustifiable, unforgivable, inexcusable, unpardonable, deplorable [➡ UNACCEPTABLE AND UNFORGIVABLE; 225]

unwarranted *adj* **unjustified**, undeserved, unnecessary, gratuitous, needless, uncalled-for, unprovoked, superfluous [➡ UNIMPORTANT AND UNNECESSARY; 238] *Opposite*: justified

unwary *adj* **imprudent**, unguarded, rash, careless, unsuspecting, innocent, gullible, credulous, reckless, naive, trusting, incautious [➡ INCAUTIOUS AND CARELESS; 283] *Opposite*: wary

unwashed *adj* **dirty**, grubby, grimy, sordid, squalid [➡ DIRTY; 1235] *Opposite*: clean

unwavering *adj* **firm**, staunch, solid, steadfast, untiring, dogged, resolute, steady, unswerving [➡ STRENGTH OF WILL; 501] *Opposite*: irresolute

unwearied *adj* **unflagging**, tireless, indefatigable, uncomplaining, unceasing, long-suffering, persistent [➡ STRENGTH OF WILL; 501]

unwelcome *adj* **unwanted**, undesirable, annoying, unsolicited, uninvited [➡ UNPOPULAR AND UNWANTED; 258] *Opposite*: welcome

unwelcoming *adj* **hostile**, unfriendly, standoffish, unreceptive, inhospitable, cold, frosty [➡ UNFRIENDLINESS AND UNSOCIABILITY; 504] *Opposite*: friendly

unwell *adj* **ill**, sick, under the weather, out of sorts, indisposed (*formal*), ailing (*dated*) [➡ ILL AND SICK; 740] *Opposite*: well

unwholesome *adj* **unpleasant**, distasteful, objectionable, nasty, disagreeable, noxious, harmful, insalubrious (*formal*) [➡ DISGUSTING AND REPULSIVE; 230] *Opposite*: pleasant

unwholesomeness 1 *n* **foulness**, insalubriousness, noxiousness, unhealthiness, harmfulness [➡ DISGUSTING AND REPULSIVE; 230] *Opposite*: wholesomeness 2 *n* **coarseness**, indecency, vulgarity, foulness, profanity, obscenity, immorality [➡ MORALLY BAD OR IMPROPER; 775] *Opposite*: wholesomeness

unwieldiness *n* [➡ LARGE; 1193]

unwieldy *adj* **awkward**, heavy, bulky, cumbersome, clumsy, ungainly, unmanageable [➡ LARGE; 1193] *Opposite*: manageable

unwilling *adj* **reluctant**, disinclined, grudging, loath, unenthusiastic, hesitant, averse (*formal*), indisposed (*formal*) [➡ UNWILLINGNESS AND STUBBORNNESS; 564] *Opposite*: willing

---

Compare and Contrast: *unwilling, reluctant, disinclined, averse, hesitant, loath*

CORE MEANING: lacking the desire to do something

unwilling not prepared to do something; *reluctant* showing no enthusiasm for doing something and only doing it if forced; *disinclined* showing a lack of enthusiasm for something rather than a strong objection to it; *averse* (*formal*) strongly opposed to or disliking something; *hesitant* not eager to do something because of uncertainty or lack of confidence; *loath* having reservations about doing something.

---

unwillingness *n* **reluctance**, disinclination, refusal, indisposition, opposition, aversion (*formal*) [➡ UNWILLINGNESS AND STUBBORNNESS; 564] *Opposite*: willingness

unwind 1 *v* **undo**, loosen, unravel, untwist, disentangle, uncoil [➡ UNFASTEN AND UNDO; 409] *Opposite*: wind 2 *v* **relax**, wind down, slow down, calm down, chill out (*slang*) [➡ CHANGE OF MOOD AND COMPOSURE; 580] *Opposite*: work up

unwise *adj* **foolish**, imprudent, rash, ill-advised, injudicious, reckless, hasty, irresponsible, stupid, risky [➡ INCAUTIOUS AND CARELESS; 283] *Opposite*: prudent

unwisely *adv* **foolishly**, rashly, ill-advisedly, injudiciously, recklessly, hastily, irresponsibly, stupidly, riskily, imprudently (*formal*) [➡ INCAUTIOUS AND CARELESS; 283] *Opposite*: prudently

unwitting 1 *adj* **unaware**, unsuspecting, ignorant, innocent, unconscious, unknowing [➡ IGNORANCE; 557] *Opposite*: knowing 2 *adj* **accidental**, involuntary, unintentional, coincidental, inadvertent, chance [➡ UNPLANNED AND UNEXPECTED; 281] *Opposite*: deliberate

unwonted *adj* **unusual**, atypical, uncharacteristic, singular, unexpected, uncommon [➡ EXTRAORDINARY: AMAZING; 204] *Opposite*: customary

unworkable *adj* **impracticable**, unusable, unfeasible, ineffectual, impractical [➡ REDUNDANT AND USELESS; 240] *Opposite*: viable

unworldliness *n* **innocence**, naiveté, simplicity, ingenuousness, callowness, greenness, artlessness, unsophisticatedness, inexperience [➡ LEVELS OF EDUCATION AND SOPHISTICATION; 894] *Opposite*: worldliness

unworldly *adj* **inexperienced**, callow, green, ingenuous, artless, unsophisticated, naive, innocent [➡ LEVELS OF EDUCATION AND SOPHISTICATION; 894] *Opposite*: experienced

unworried *adj* **calm**, untroubled, at ease, unruffled, unflustered, tranquil, unconcerned, unperturbed, relaxed [➡ COOL AND CALM; 536] *Opposite*: perturbed

unworthiness 1 *n* **worthlessness**, contemptibility, pitifulness, unfitness [➡ REDUNDANT AND USELESS; 240] 2 *n* **shamefulness**, dishonor, discredit, shame, disgrace, disrepute [➡ MORALLY BAD OR IMPROPER; 775]

unworthy 1 *adj* **undeserving**, worthless, contemptible, pitiful, unfit [➡ REDUNDANT AND USELESS; 240] *Opposite*: deserving 2 *adj* **shameful**, degrading, dishonorable, disgraceful, disreputable [➡ MORALLY BAD OR IMPROPER; 775] *Opposite*: reputable

unwrap *v* **undo**, unpack, remove, open, tear open [➡ UNFASTEN AND UNDO; 409] *Opposite*: wrap

unwritten 1 *adj* **spoken**, oral, unrecorded, vocal, unprinted [➡ COMMUNICATIVE STYLE; 624] *Opposite*: written 2 *adj* **understood**, accepted, traditional, tacit, known [➡ KNOWN AND FAMOUS; 181]

unyielding 1 *adj* **firm**, unbending, obstinate, steadfast, obdurate, immovable, tough, uncompromising, adamant, staunch, stubborn [➡ STRENGTH OF WILL; 501] *Opposite*: acquiescent 2 *adj* **inflexible**, rigid, stiff, unbending, solid, durable [➡ RIGID AND HARD; 1211] *Opposite*: flexible

unyoke *v* **untie**, separate, disjoin, unhook, loose, untether, unstrap [➡ UNFASTEN AND UNDO; 409] *Opposite*: join

unzip 1 *v* **undo**, unfasten, open, disengage, free [➡ UNFASTEN AND UNDO; 409] 2 *v* **open**, expand, access, decompress [➡ COMPUTERS AND COMPUTING; 1127] *Opposite*: compress

up 1 *adj* **awake**, out of bed, up and about, active, up and around, up and doing [➡ WIDE AWAKE AND CONSCIOUS; 735] *Opposite*: asleep 2 *adj* **happy**, positive, optimistic, hopeful, cheerful, cheery, upbeat (*informal*) [➡ PLEASURE, EXCITEMENT, AND ELATION; 534] *Opposite*: down 3 *adj* **winning**, in the lead, ahead, leading [➡ SUCCESSFUL AND PROMISING; 81] *Opposite*: behind

up and about *adj* **awake**, up, out of bed, active, up and doing, up and around [➡ WIDE AWAKE AND CONSCIOUS; 735] *Opposite*: asleep

up and around *see* up and about

up-and-coming *adj* **emerging**, rising, budding, promising, talented [➡ FUTURE; 86] *Opposite*: over-the-hill

up-and-down 1 *adj* **moody**, temperamental, changeable, tempestuous, turbulent, highly-strung [➡ EXCESSIVE SENSITIVITY; 511] *Opposite*: equable 2 *adj* **rising and falling**, bobbing, bouncing [➡ DIRECTION OF MOTION; 345]

up and running *adj* [➡ HAPPENING AND IN PROGRESS; 32]

upbeat (*informal*) *adj* **optimistic**, cheerful, positive, buoyant, bubbly, up, happy, cheery [➡ PLEASURE, EXCITEMENT, AND ELATION; 534] *Opposite*: downbeat

upbraid *v* **scold**, reproach, chastise, reprimand, rebuke, censure, tell off (*informal*), tear a strip off (*UK*) [➡ACCUSE, BLAME, AND CRITICIZE; 641] *Opposite*: praise

upbringing *n* **education**, childhood, background, rearing, nurture, past [➡BABYHOOD, CHILDHOOD, AND ADOLESCENCE; 917]

upchuck (*informal*) *v* [➡VOMIT AND BELCH; 712]

upcoming *adj* **future**, imminent, forthcoming, impending, approaching, coming [➡ABOUT TO HAPPEN; 33] *Opposite*: past

update 1 *v* **inform**, bring up-to-date, keep informed, keep posted, fill in, apprise (*formal*) [➡INFORM, ANNOUNCE, AND ISSUE; 611] 2 *v* **modernize**, revise, renew, bring up-to-date, renovate [➡IMPROVE SOMETHING; 374]

upend *v* **turn over**, tip over, upset, topple, flip over, overturn, turn turtle, tip up (*UK*) [➡MOVE SOMETHING: INTO A NEW POSITION OR OVERTURN; 330] *Opposite*: right

upended *adj* [➡ORIENTATION AND ALIGNMENT; 1223]

up for grabs (*informal*) *adj* **available**, free, going begging, for the taking [➡PRESENT AND AVAILABLE; 11] *Opposite*: unavailable

up-front (*informal*) *adj* **straightforward**, honest, frank, plain-spoken, open, forthright, candid, direct, blunt [➡HONEST AND OPEN; 630] *Opposite*: coy

upgrade 1 *v* **promote**, advance, elevate, raise, move up, progress, exalt [➡CONFER STATUS; 458] *Opposite*: demote 2 *v* **improve**, update, renew, modernize, renovate, enhance, transform, convert, develop, reconstruct, advance [➡IMPROVE SOMETHING; 374] *Opposite*: downgrade 3 *n* **promotion**, advancement, elevation, exaltation [➡CONFER STATUS; 458] *Opposite*: demotion 4 *n* **improvement**, upgrading, renovation, modernization, enhancement, transformation, conversion, development, reconstruction [➡PROGRESS AND ADVANCEMENT; 213]

upgrading 1 *n* **promotion**, advancement, step up, advance, progression, progress, elevation [➡CONFER STATUS; 458] *Opposite*: demotion 2 *n* **improvement**, renovation, modernization, transformation, enhancement, conversion, development, reconstruction [➡PROGRESS AND ADVANCEMENT; 213]

upheaval *n* **disturbance**, turmoil, disorder, confusion, cataclysm, commotion, disruption, mayhem (*informal*) [➡CHAOS AND UPROAR; 51] *Opposite*: peace

upheave *v* **lift up**, raise, thrust up, elevate, lift [➡MOVE SOMETHING: UPWARD; 328] *Opposite*: drop

uphill 1 *adj* **climbing**, ascending, rising, mounting [➡ORIENTATION AND ALIGNMENT; 1223] *Opposite*: downhill 2 *adj* **difficult**, hard, arduous, demanding, tough, trying, taxing [➡PHYSICALLY UNPLEASANT; 226] *Opposite*: easy

uphill battle *n* [➡HARD WORK OR EFFORT; 298]

uphold *v* **support**, sustain, maintain, defend, endorse, advocate, espouse, encourage [➡APPROVE AND CONFIRM; 646]

upholster *v* **cover**, pad, stuff, fill, decorate, furnish (*formal*) [➡DECORATE, ADORN, AND APPLY COATINGS; 405]

upholstery *n* **fabric**, furnishings, covers, furniture, material, padding, stuffing [➡FURNISHING AND HOUSEHOLD LINENS; 860]

up in arms *adj* **angry**, indignant, offended, resentful,

exasperated, furious, enraged, incensed, infuriated [➡IRRITATION AND ANGER; 541] *Opposite*: unconcerned

up in the air *adj* **uncertain**, undecided, vague, in the balance, unsettled [➡VAGUENESS; 243] *Opposite*: decided

upkeep *n* **maintenance**, repairs, keep, conservation, preservation, running [➡PERMANENCE: WITHOUT END; 94]

upland *n* **moorland**, high ground, highland, plateau, tableland [➡DESERTS, PLAINS, AND MOORLAND; 1045] *Opposite*: lowland

uplift 1 *v* **elevate**, raise, hoist, lift [➡MOVE SOMETHING: UPWARD; 328] *Opposite*: drop 2 *v* **inspire**, enrich, improve, move, hearten, raise, stir [➡ENCOURAGE; 576] *Opposite*: depress

uplifted *adj* [➡PLEASURE, EXCITEMENT, AND ELATION; 534]

uplifting *adj* **inspiring**, elevating, improving, enriching, heartening, moving, inspirational, stirring [➡EMOTIONALLY PLEASANT; 187] *Opposite*: depressing

uplighter (*UK*) *n* **floor lamp**, standard lamp, spotlight, spot, table lamp, bedside lamp, desk lamp, lamp [➡LIGHTING; 862]

upmarket *adj* **expensive**, high-class, smart, chic, exclusive, glamorous, upscale, classy (*informal*), swanky (*informal*) [➡EXPENSIVE AND LUXURIOUS; 218] *Opposite*: downmarket

up on *adj* [➡KNOWLEDGE AND WISDOM; 558]

upper *adj* **higher**, greater, better, superior [➡SUPERIORITY; 152] *Opposite*: lower

upper atmosphere *n* [➡THE EARTH'S ATMOSPHERE; 1040]

upper circle *n* **gallery**, loggia, balcony, circle, dress circle [➡IN THE THEATER; 906]

upper class *n* **aristocracy**, nobility, noblesse, gentry, elite, upper crust (*informal*) [➡CLASS STATUS; 889] *Opposite*: lower class

upper-class *adj* **aristocratic**, noble, blue-blooded, highborn (*literary*) [➡CLASS STATUS; 889] *Opposite*: lower-class

upper crust (*informal*) *n* **upper class**, aristocracy, nobility, gentry, noblesse, elite [➡CLASS STATUS; 889] *Opposite*: proletariat

uppercut *n* **blow**, punch, hit, haymaker (*slang*) [➡PHYSICAL ATTACK AND PUNISHMENT; 415]

upper hand *n* **advantage**, initiative, ascendancy, edge, control, superiority, dominance [➡SOURCE OF HAPPINESS, PLEASURE, OR IMPROVEMENT; 209] *Opposite*: disadvantage

uppermost 1 *adj* **highest**, top, topmost, upmost [➡RELATIVE LOCATION; 161] *Opposite*: bottom 2 *adj* **primary**, main, principal, chief, greatest, dominant [➡MOST IMPORTANT AND MAIN; 193] *Opposite*: last

uppity (*informal*) *adj* **presumptuous**, pretentious, snobbish, haughty, bumptious, superior, arrogant [➡AFFECTATION, SELF-SATISFACTION, AND SNOBBISHNESS; 507] *Opposite*: humble

uprate (*UK*) *v* **increase**, raise, upgrade, up, adjust, enhance, improve, augment (*formal*) [➡IMPROVE SOMETHING; 374] *Opposite*: decrease

upright 1 *adj* **standing**, straight, vertical, erect [➡ORIENTATION AND ALIGNMENT; 1223] *Opposite*: horizontal 2 *adj* **righteous**, moral, honorable, decent, honest, respectable, conscientious, upstanding, principled [➤ MORALLY GOOD; 774] *Opposite*: immoral

uprightness *n* **righteousness**, morality, honorableness, decency, honesty, respectability, honor, worthiness [➤ MORALLY GOOD; 774] *Opposite*: immorality

upright piano *type of* **keyboard** [➤ MUSICAL INSTRUMENTS; 910]

uprising *n* **rebellion**, revolution, revolt, rising, unrest, mutiny, disturbance, civil disobedience, insurrection [➤ AGGRESSIVE EVENTS; 39]

uproar *n* **disturbance**, noise, chaos, pandemonium, upheaval, tumult, din, racket, hue and cry, hullabaloo, turbulence, hubbub [➤ CHAOS AND UPROAR; 51] *Opposite*: quiet

uproarious *adj* **hilarious**, funny, riotous, raucous, boisterous, hysterical (*informal*) [➤ FUNNY AND AMUSING; 216]

uproariousness *n* [➤ FUNNY AND AMUSING; 216]

uproot 1 *v* **pull up**, deracinate, dig up, rip up [➤ EXTRACT AND SEVER; 341] *Opposite*: plant 2 *v* **displace**, evacuate, move on, relocate [➤ MOVE SOMETHING TO ANOTHER LOCATION; 324] *Opposite*: settle

uprush *n* **rush**, surge, updraft, draft, blast, current [➤ SUDDEN EVENTS; 52]

ups and downs *n* [➤ EVENTS AND OCCURRENCES; 35]

upscale *adj* **upmarket**, smart, exclusive, expensive, high-class, glamorous, chic, prestigious, posh (*informal*), swanky (*informal*), classy (*informal*), ritzy (*informal*) [➤ EXPENSIVE AND LUXURIOUS; 218] *Opposite*: downmarket

upset 1 *v* **spill**, knock over, tip over, overturn, upend [➤ MOVE SOMETHING: INTO A NEW POSITION OR OVERTURN; 330] *Opposite*: right 2 *v* **disturb**, disrupt, reorder, reverse, mix up, disorganize, spoil, unbalance, change [➤ CREATE DISORDER AND CAUSE CHAOS; 358] *Opposite*: order 3 *v* **distress**, hurt, disturb, sadden, trouble, wound, offend, disappoint, disconcert, displease, grieve [➤ UPSET, DISTRESS, AND HUMILIATE; 567] *Opposite*: please 4 *n* **defeat**, disappointment, affront, letdown, shock, setback, distress [➤ SADNESS, DISTRESS, AND DESPAIR; 539] 5 *n* **surprise**, shock, confusion, disarray, disruption, disturbance, turmoil, commotion, shake-up [➤ CHAOS AND UPROAR; 51] 6 *adj* **sad**, disturbed, unhappy, hurt, disappointed, saddened, dismayed, wounded, offended, distressed, troubled, distraught [➤ SADNESS, DISTRESS, AND DESPAIR; 539] *Opposite*: composed

upset stomach *n* **indigestion**, stomachache, heartburn, bellyache (*informal*), tummy ache (*informal*) [➤ DISORDERS OF THE DIGESTIVE SYSTEM; 713]

upsetting *adj* **distressing**, disturbing, hurtful, offensive, disappointing, disconcerting, displeasing, shocking, harrowing [➤ EMOTIONALLY UNPLEASANT AND UPSETTING; 227] *Opposite*: pleasing

upshift *v* **gear up**, change gear, change up (*UK*) [➤ USE TOOLS AND MACHINERY; 468]

upshot *n* **result**, outcome, consequence, effect, end, end result, conclusion [➤ RESULTS AND OUTCOMES; 83]

upside *n* **advantage**, benefit, plus (*informal*), positive (*informal*) [➤ SOURCE OF HAPPINESS, PLEASURE, OR IMPROVEMENT; 209] *Opposite*: disadvantage

upside down *adv* [➤ ORIENTATION AND ALIGNMENT; 1223]

upside-down 1 *adj* **upturned**, wrong way up, wrong side up, overturned, on its head, inverted, reversed [➤ ORIENTATION AND ALIGNMENT; 1223] *Opposite*: upright 2 *adj* **in a mess**, messy, untidy, topsy-turvy, in disorder, in disarray, chaotic, disorganized [➤ DISORDER AND CHAOS; 245] *Opposite*: orderly

upstage *v* **outdo**, outmaneuver, put somebody's nose out of joint, outshine, surpass, put in the shade, leave standing, go one better than [➤ BEAT AND DEFEAT; 80]

upstanding *adj* **honorable**, virtuous, honest, decent, respectable, trustworthy, good, moral [➤ MORALLY GOOD; 774] *Opposite*: degenerate

upstart *n* **nobody**, unknown, parvenu, arriviste, nonentity, newcomer, social climber, nouveau riche [➤ SELF-IMPORTANT AND SELF-SEEKING PEOPLE; 949] *Opposite*: grandee

upstretched *adj* **raised**, upraised, upturned, outstretched, extended, upthrust [➤ ORIENTATION AND ALIGNMENT; 1223] *Opposite*: hanging down

upsurge *n* **increase**, rise, surge, gain, expansion, improvement [➤ CHANGE OF INTENSITY: MORE; 394] *Opposite*: decrease

upswing 1 *n* **increase**, improvement, upturn, pickup (*informal*), turnaround, upsurge [➤ CHANGE OF INTENSITY: MORE; 394] *Opposite*: downswing 2 *type of* **economic condition** [➤ FINANCE AND ECONOMICS; 796]

uptake 1 *n* **acceptance**, approval, interest, commitment, agreement, application, endorsement, curiosity [➤ APPROVE AND CONFIRM; 646] *Opposite*: refusal 2 *n* **understanding**, comprehension, perception, appreciation, apprehension, realization [➤ UNDERSTAND AND GRASP; 759] *Opposite*: incomprehension

up-tempo *adj* **exciting**, lively, fast, frenetic, upbeat (*informal*), rapid [➤ HAPPENING QUICKLY; 104] *Opposite*: dull

up the creek (*informal*) *adj* **in trouble**, in dire straits, in difficulty, in a predicament, in hot water (*informal*), in a fix (*informal*) [➤ IN TROUBLE AND DISADVANTAGED; 73]

up the creek without a paddle (*informal*) *adj* [➤ IN TROUBLE AND DISADVANTAGED; 73]

uptight (*informal*) *adj* **tense**, bothered, anxious, neurotic, edgy, uneasy, worked up (*informal*) [➤ CONFUSION, ANXIETY, AND WORRY; 540] *Opposite*: calm

up till now *adv* **so far**, thus far, hitherto, until now, to date, up to now, as yet [➤ PAST; 84]

up-to-date 1 *adj* **informed**, in touch, conversant, in the know, au fait [➤ KNOWLEDGE AND WISDOM; 558] 2 *adj* **current**, latest, new, brand-new, modern, innovative, up-to-the-minute, fresh, state-of-the-art, newfangled, novel, contemporary, advanced [➤ DESCRIBING TECHNOLOGY; 1160] *Opposite*: old-fashioned 3 *adj* **fashionable**, upscale, cool, chic, trendy (*informal*), à la mode (*dated*), with-it (*dated informal*) [➤ NEW, MODERN; 166] *Opposite*: passé

up to now *adv* **until now**, so far, thus far, hitherto, to date, up till now, as yet [➤ PAST; 84]

up to scratch (*informal*) *adj* [➤ ACCEPTABLE AND PASSABLE; 219]

up to speed *adj* **in control**, on top of things, au fait, at home, informed [➤ KNOWLEDGE AND WISDOM; 558] *Opposite*: ignorant

up to standard *adj* [➡ ACCEPTABLE AND PASSABLE; 219]

up-to-the-minute *adj* **latest**, current, contemporary, state-of-the-art, contemporaneous, modern, up-to-date [➡ NEW, MODERN; 166] *Opposite*: out-of-date

up to the present moment *adv* [➡ PAST; 84]

up to the present time *adv* [➡ PAST; 84]

up to your ears *adj* **busy**, snowed under, swamped, flooded, rushed off your feet, inundated [➡ IN TROUBLE AND DISADVANTAGED; 73] *Opposite*: idle

upturn **1** *v* **overturn**, capsize, tip over, upset, turn turtle, turn over, upend [➡ MOVE SOMETHING: INTO A NEW POSITION OR OVERTURN; 330] *Opposite*: right **2** *n* **improvement**, recovery, revival, growth, expansion, rise, increase, upsurge [➡ PROGRESS AND ADVANCEMENT; 213] *Opposite*: slump **3** *type of* **economic condition** [➡ FINANCE AND ECONOMICS; 796]

upturned *adj* [➡ ORIENTATION AND ALIGNMENT; 1223]

up until now *adv* [➡ PAST; 84]

upward **1** *adv* **up**, uphill, in the air, aloft, higher, skyward [➡ DIRECTION OF MOTION; 345] *Opposite*: downward **2** *adj* **ascendant**, mounting, skyward, uphill, ascending, rising [➡ ORIENTATION AND ALIGNMENT; 1223] *Opposite*: downward **3** *adj* **rising**, improving, increasing, growing, expanding, surging [➡ DIRECTION OF MOTION; 345] *Opposite*: downward

upwardly mobile *adj* [➡ CLASS STATUS; 889]

upwelling *n* **upsurge**, surge, burst, outburst, outpouring, gush, emergence, flood, swell, spring [➡ SUDDEN EVENTS; 52]

upwind *adj* **windward**, exposed, open, bare, windy [➡ GENERAL LOCATIONS; 158] *Opposite*: leeward

up with *adj* **abreast**, up-to-date, familiar, conversant, au fait, au courant [➡ KNOWLEDGE AND WISDOM; 558]

uranium *type of* **metal** [➡ METALS; 1276]

Uranus *type of* **planet** [➡ HEAVENLY BODIES; 1061]

urban **1** *adj* **city**, town, built-up, municipal, inner-city, metropolitan, borough [➡ HUMAN SETTLEMENTS; 1070] *Opposite*: rural **2** *type of* **pop and vocal music** [➡ MUSIC, SONGS, AND SINGING; 907]

urbane *adj* **sophisticated**, refined, courteous, suave, polished, stylish, smooth, genteel, elegant, cultured [➡ GOOD MANNERS AND SOCIAL SKILLS; 520] *Opposite*: unsophisticated

urbanite *n* **metropolitan**, cosmopolitan, citizen, resident, townie (*informal*) [➡ INHABITANTS; 857] *Opposite*: rustic

urbanity *n* **sophistication**, refinement, courteousness, courtesy, suaveness, polish, genteelness, gentility, culture, civility [➡ GOOD MANNERS AND SOCIAL SKILLS; 520] *Opposite*: uncouthness

urbanization *n* **development**, suburbanization, expansion, sprawl, spread, growth [➡ HUMAN SETTLEMENTS; 1070]

urban myth *n* **myth**, folk tale, tale, tall story, tall tale, fable, legend, story (*informal*) [➡ THE ORAL TRADITION; 677]

urban sprawl *n* **urbanization**, development, suburbia, sprawl, expansion, overspill, built environment, gated community, ribbon development (*UK*) [➡ HUMAN SETTLEMENTS; 1070]

urchin *n* **imp**, tyke, brat, hooligan (*informal*), kid (*informal*), ragamuffin (*dated*), rascal (*humorous*), tearaway (*UK*) [➡ CHILD OR YOUTH; 945]

urge **1** *v* **advise**, commend, admonish, prevail on, insist, press, counsel (*formal or literary*) [➡ ADVISE AND WARN; 613] *Opposite*: dissuade **2** *v* **advocate**, beg, recommend, advise, plead, exhort, appeal, implore (*formal*), beseech (*literary*) [➡ REQUEST AND DEMAND; 663] *Opposite*: encourage **3** *v* **encourage**, drive, push, force, impel, incite, goad, egg on, compel [➡ CAUSE OR COMPEL TO ACT; 271] *Opposite*: discourage **4** *n* **need**, wish, impulse, desire, inclination, longing, itch, compulsion, craving, yearning [➡ DESIRE AND WANT; 579] *Opposite*: disinclination

urgency **1** *n* **need**, exigency, importance, necessity, hurry, rush, pressure [➡ IMPORTANCE AND SIGNIFICANCE; 192] *Opposite*: unimportance **2** *n* **earnestness**, insistence, perseverance, firmness, resolve, determination, resolution [➡ POSITIVE IMPATIENCE, ENTHUSIASM, AND ALERTNESS; 537] *Opposite*: vacillation

urgent **1** *adj* **earnest**, insistent, persuasive, pleading, demanding, importunate (*formal*), beseeching (*literary*) [➡ ENTHUSIASTIC AND INQUISITIVE; 628] *Opposite*: half-hearted **2** *adj* **vital**, crucial, pressing, imperative, burning, critical, serious, important, exigent (*formal*) [➡ IMPORTANT; 194] *Opposite*: trivial

urgently *adv* **immediately**, straightaway, instantly, at once, directly, right away, now [➡ PRESENT; 85] *Opposite*: whenever

urinate *v* [➡ EXCRETION AND EXCRETA; 722]

urine *n* [➡ EXCRETION AND EXCRETA; 722]

URL *n* [➡ THE INTERNET; 1128]

urn *n* **vase**, container, vessel, pot, jug, pitcher [➡ CONTAINERS, RECEPTACLES, AND PACKAGING; 1245]

Ursa Major *type of* **constellation** [➡ HEAVENLY BODIES; 1061]

Ursa Minor *type of* **constellation** [➡ HEAVENLY BODIES; 1061]

usable *adj* **functional**, practical, serviceable, working, functioning, operational, operating, in working order [➡ IN GOOD REPAIR; 1232] *Opposite*: unusable

usage **1** *n* **treatment**, handling, control, management, running, use, manipulation [➡ USE; 467] **2** *n* **practice**, procedure, custom, norm, tradition, habit [➡ WAYS OF DOING THINGS; 294]

use **1** *v* **employ**, make use of, utilize, exercise, bring into play, apply, exploit, draw on [➡ USE; 467] *Opposite*: forgo **2** *v* **consume**, expend, spend, exhaust, use up, deplete, exploit, get through, wear out, waste [➡ USE UP AND WASTE; 474] *Opposite*: conserve **3** *v* **manipulate**, exploit, take advantage of, mistreat, abuse [➡ MISUSE AND ABUSE; 471] **4** *v* **behave**, handle, treat, manipulate, manage, operate, work [➡ USE TOOLS AND MACHINERY; 468] **5** *v* **benefit**, make use of, enjoy, avail yourself of, tap, source, luxuriate, take pleasure in [➡ MAKE GOOD USE OF SOMETHING; 473] **6** *n* **expenditure**, consumption, wear and tear, wastage, depletion, exhaustion [➡ USE UP AND WASTE; 474] *Opposite*: saving **7** *n* **treatment**, handling, manipulation, exploitation, management, operation [➡ USE; 467] **8** *n* **employment**, application, utilization, exploitation, consumption, exercise [➤ USE; 467] *Opposite*: disuse **9** *n* **purpose**, function, application, service, role, utility [➤ INTENTIONS AND PURPOSES; 772] **10** *n* **usefulness**, help, assistance, benefit, aid, worth, advantage, value [➤ USEFULNESS; 199] *Opposite*: harm **11** *n* (*literary or archaic*) **usage**, custom, habit, practice, routine, procedure [➤ WAYS OF DOING THINGS; 294]

Compare and Contrast: *use, employ, make use of, utilize*

CORE MEANING: to put something to use

use to put something into action or service; *employ* to make use of something such as a tool or a resource in a particular way; *make use of* to use what is readily available, especially in a sensible or economical way; *utilize* to find a practical or unintended use for something.

---

used **1** *adj* **secondhand**, castoff, hand-me-down, recycled [➤ OLD, OLD-FASHIONED; 167] *Opposite*: new **2** *adj* **expended**, old, worn, worn out, consumed, run down, exhausted, depleted, spent, finished [➤ IN BAD REPAIR; 1234] *Opposite*: remaining

used to **1** *adj* **accustomed**, hardened, inured, schooled, conditioned, in the habit of [➤ KNOWLEDGE AND WISDOM; 558] *Opposite*: unaccustomed **2** *adj* **familiar**, at home, au fait, at ease, easy, comfortable, accustomed [➤ KNOWLEDGE AND WISDOM; 558] *Opposite*: unfamiliar

used up *adj* [➤ ABSENT AND UNAVAILABLE; 7]

useful **1** *adj* **practical**, helpful, serviceable, of use, constructive, positive, handy, effective, informative, functional, nifty (*informal*) [➤ USEFULNESS; 199] *Opposite*: useless **2** *adj* **convenient**, valuable, beneficial, advantageous, expedient, suitable, worthwhile [➤ GOOD, WELL, BETTER; 183] *Opposite*: disadvantageous

usefulness **1** *n* **practicality**, helpfulness, worth, utility, convenience, expediency, efficacy, effectiveness, handiness, niftiness (*informal*) [➤ USEFULNESS; 199] *Opposite*: uselessness **2** *n* **valuableness**, convenience, advantageousness, expediency, suitability, worthwhileness [➤ GOOD, WELL, BETTER; 183]

useless **1** *adj* **unusable**, impractical, unserviceable, inoperable, unworkable, inadequate, of no use, hopeless [➤ REDUNDANT AND USELESS; 240] *Opposite*: useful **2** *adj* **unsuccessful**, futile, ineffectual, unavailing, worthless, ineffective [➤ UNSUCCESSFUL AND UNPROMISING; 76] *Opposite*: successful **3** *adj* (*informal*) **inept**, hopeless, incompetent, inefficient, ineffectual, ineffective, pathetic (*informal*) [➤ UNSKILLED; 529] *Opposite*: effective

uselessness **1** *n* **impracticality**, unusableness, unserviceableness, inoperability, unworkability, inadequacy, hopelessness [➤ REDUNDANT AND USELESS; 240] *Opposite*: usefulness **2** *n* **unsuccessfulness**, pointlessness, futility, ineffectualness, ineffectiveness, worthlessness [➤ UNSUCCESSFUL AND UNPROMISING; 76] *Opposite*: successfulness **3** *n* (*informal*) **ineptness**, hopelessness, pointlessness, futility, ineffectiveness, incompetence, inefficiency, ineffectualness [➤ UNSKILLED; 529] *Opposite*: effectiveness

user *n* **operator**, worker, employer, manipulator, handler, manager [➤ USE; 467]

user-friendliness *n* **accessibility**, manageability, easi-

ness, handiness, manipulability, convenience, availability [➤ USEFULNESS; 199] *Opposite*: inaccessibility

user-friendly *adj* **accessible**, comprehensible, intelligible, manipulable, manageable, easy [➤ USEFULNESS; 199] *Opposite*: inaccessible

use up *v* **expend**, consume, exhaust, wear out, deplete, exploit, go through, get through [➤ USE UP AND WASTE; 474] *Opposite*: conserve

usher **1** *n* **attendant**, escort, guide, leader, conductor, marshal, helper [➤ SUBORDINATES AND ASSISTANTS; 966] **2** *v* **escort**, conduct, guide, steer, pilot, help, lead, accompany, marshal, shepherd [➤ ACCOMPANY AND FOLLOW; 337]

See Compare and Contrast at **guide**.

---

usher in *v* **herald**, introduce, lead to, announce, signal, bring in, open up, inaugurate, launch [➤ CAUSE TO HAPPEN; 31] *Opposite*: see out

usual **1** *adj* **normal**, typical, common, standard, natural, traditional [➤ ORDINARINESS; 244] *Opposite*: exceptional **2** *adj* **habitual**, routine, everyday, familiar, predictable, regular, customary, wonted (*literary*) [➤ ORDINARINESS; 244] *Opposite*: irregular

---

Compare and Contrast: *usual, customary, habitual, routine, wonted*

CORE MEANING: often done, used, bought, or consumed

usual normal, common, or typical; *customary* conforming to regular or typical practice; *habitual* done so often or repeatedly that the behavior or practice has become ingrained; *routine* normal, regular, and usual in every way, even predictable, repetitive, and monotonous; *wonted* (*formal*) usual or typical.

---

usually *adv* **normally**, typically, customarily, generally, by and large, commonly, habitually, ordinarily, as a rule, frequently, mostly, regularly [➤ USUALLY; 108] *Opposite*: exceptionally

usurer *n* [➤ CRIMINALS; 821]

usurious *adj* [➤ ILLEGAL; 816]

usurp *v* **seize**, appropriate, take over, assume, commandeer, grab, take, arrogate (*formal*) [➤ TAKE SOMETHING AWAY; 425] *Opposite*: surrender

usury *n* **moneylending**, overcharging, extortion, daylight robbery (*informal*), highway robbery (*informal*) [➤ CRIMES; 817]

utensil *n* **tool**, instrument, implement, appliance, device, gadget [➤ DEVICES; 1115]

---

utensil

◆ *types of utensils*
beater, bottle opener, can opener, corkscrew, drainer, grater, grinder, juice extractor, liquidizer, mill, mortar, nutcracker, opener, peeler, pestle, reamer, sieve, soup ladle, spatula, strainer, whisk

---

utilitarian *adj* **practical**, useful, serviceable, no-frills (*informal*), functional, down-to-earth, effective [➡USE-FULNESS; 199] *Opposite*: useless

utility 1 *n* **usefulness**, practicality, efficiency, handiness, helpfulness, efficacy, effectiveness, functionality, niftiness (*informal*) [➡USEFULNESS; 199] *Opposite*: uselessness 2 *n* **convenience**, service, benefit, worth, advantage, value [➡SOURCE OF HAPPINESS, PLEASURE, OR IMPROVEMENT; 209] *Opposite*: worthlessness

utility room *type of* **room in the home** [➡TYPES OF ROOMS; 1097]

utilization *n* **use**, application, employment, deployment, operation, consumption, exploitation [➡USE; 467]

utilize *v* **use**, apply, employ, operate, develop, exploit, consume, make use of, make the most of [➡USE; 467] *Opposite*: forgo

See Compare and Contrast at **use**.

utmost 1 *adj* **greatest**, highest, extreme, chief, supreme, maximum, paramount, ultimate [➡SUPERIORITY; 152] *Opposite*: least 2 *adj* **farthest**, extreme, most distant, farthermost, remotest, outside, uttermost [➡DISTANCE; 160]

utopia *n* **ideal**, paradise, never-never land, heaven, Shangri-la, dreamland, seventh heaven [➡NONEXISTENT PLACES; 1066]

utopian 1 *adj* **ideal**, perfect, ultimate, best, model, supreme [➡ADMIRABLE AND COMMENDABLE; 185] 2 *adj* **idealistic**, naive, impracticable, impractical, unworkable, unrealistic, quixotic, romantic [➡PHILOSOPHIES AND BELIEFS; 780] *Opposite*: pragmatic 3 *n* **idealist**, romantic, visionary, dreamer, purist, Don Quixote, reformer [➡PHILOSOPHICAL AND POLITICAL THINKERS; 781] *Opposite*: pragmatist

utter 1 *v* **say**, pronounce, express, state, voice, speak, articulate, emit [➡UTTER AND PRONOUNCE; 608] 2 *adj* **absolute**, total, complete, sheer, downright, unreserved, unqualified, thorough, out-and-out [➡ABSOLUTE AND ABSOLUTELY; 133] *Opposite*: partial

utterance 1 *n* **word**, sound, note, noise, exclamation [➡THE SPOKEN WORD; 671] *Opposite*: silence 2 *n* **statement**, speech, remark, declaration, announcement, communication, thesis, expression [➡COMMUNICATION; 602]

U-turn 1 *n* **turn**, rotation, revolution, about-face, volteface, about-turn (*UK*) [➡CHANGE DIRECTION OF MOTION; 344] 2 *n* **change**, reversal, volte face, about-face, climb-down (*UK*), about-turn (*UK*) [➡DECISIVE MOMENTS; 44]

uvula *part of* **mouth** [➡THE MOUTH; 702]

V

vacancy *n* **job**, post, position, opening, opportunity [➡ JOB; 833]

vacant 1 *adj* **empty**, available, unoccupied, not in use, unfilled, untaken, void, unused, free, clear [➡ PRESENT AND AVAILABLE; 11] *Opposite*: occupied **2** *adj* **blank**, empty, expressionless, indifferent, vacuous, inane, uncomprehending [➡ FACIAL EXPRESSIONS AND BLUSHING; 651] *Opposite*: alert

Compare and Contrast: *vacant, unoccupied, empty, void*

CORE MEANING: lacking contents or occupants

vacant without occupants or contents, often temporarily; *unoccupied* not lived in by anybody, or currently without occupants; *empty* not containing or holding anything, or without occupants; *void* having no contents, or having no incumbent, occupant, or holder.

vacate 1 *v* **leave**, relinquish, check out, give up, depart, quit, evacuate [➡ LEAVE AND GO AWAY; 8] *Opposite*: occupy **2** *v* **empty**, evacuate, clear out, free, divest, eject, remove [➡ EMPTY AND UNLOAD; 407] *Opposite*: fill

vacation *n* **holiday**, break, trip, rest, retreat, leave, escape [➡ PERIODS OF REST; 91]

vacationer *n* **vacationist**, traveler, holidaymaker (*UK*) [➡ TRAVEL: TRAVELERS AND WALKERS; 319]

vacation industry *n* [➡ TRAVEL: SIGHTSEEING AND TOURISM; 321]

vacationland *n* [➡ TRAVEL: SIGHTSEEING AND TOURISM; 321]

vaccinate *v* **inoculate**, immunize, protect [➡ BECOME SICK, TREAT, AND RECOVER; 728] *Opposite*: expose

vaccination 1 *n* **inoculation**, injection, immunization, shot (*informal*) [➡ HEALING; 730] **2** *type of* **medical procedure** [➡ REMEDIES, TREATMENTS, AND OPERATIONS; 731]

vaccine *n* **inoculation**, injection, serum, preparation, shot (*informal*) [➡ HEALING; 730]

vacillate *v* **waver**, hesitate, dither, think twice, equivocate, sit on the fence, shilly-shally, chop and change (*UK*) [➡ HESITATE; 272] *Opposite*: decide

See Compare and Contrast at **hesitate**.

vacillating *adj* **irresolute**, indecisive, of two minds, hesitant, dithering, fickle, wavering, equivocal, ambivalent [➡ UNCERTAINTY; 559] *Opposite*: resolute

vacillation *n* **indecisiveness**, irresoluteness, indecision, irresolution, hesitancy, uncertainty, equivocation, ambivalence [➡ UNCERTAINTY; 559] *Opposite*: resolution

vacuity (*formal*) *n* **emptiness**, space, void, nothingness, vacuum, blankness, vacantness [➡ HOLES, GAPS, AND FORKS; 1252]

vacuous 1 *adj* **stupid**, unintelligent, inane, vacant [➡ NEGATIVE INTELLECTUAL CHARACTERISTICS; 525] *Opposite*: bright **2** *adj* **empty**, blank, vacant, void, hollow, unfilled [➡ EMPTY; 1238] *Opposite*: full

vacuously *adv* **stupidly**, unintelligently, blankly, inanely, dimly, vacantly [➡ NEGATIVE INTELLECTUAL CHARACTERISTICS; 525] *Opposite*: brightly

vacuousness *n* [➡ NEGATIVE INTELLECTUAL CHARACTERISTICS; 525]

vacuum *n* **void**, space, emptiness, nothingness, blankness, vacuity (*formal*) [➡ HOLES, GAPS, AND FORKS; 1252]

vade mecum *n* [➡ TRAVEL: SIGHTSEEING AND TOURISM; 321]

vagabond *n* **vagrant**, tramp, beggar, drifter, wanderer, traveler, gypsy, nomad, hobo [➡ POOR PEOPLE; 896] *Opposite*: resident

vagaries *n* [➡ EVENTS AND OCCURRENCES; 35]

vagary *n* **whim**, fancy, notion, mood, quirk, whimsy, caprice [➡ CHANCE EVENTS; 36] *Opposite*: choice

vagrancy *n* **homelessness**, penury, destitution, rootlessness, begging, pennilessness, panhandling [➡ POVERTY AND POOR; 892] *Opposite*: residence

vagrant 1 *n* **vagabond**, tramp, beggar, drifter, hobo, street person, wanderer, nomad [➡ POOR PEOPLE; 896] *Opposite*: resident **2** *adj* **nomadic**, itinerant, wandering, roaming, roving, traveling [➡ NOMADIC AND ROOTLESS LIFESTYLES; 884] *Opposite*: settled

vague 1 *adj* **indistinct**, unclear, indistinguishable, hazy, fuzzy, formless, blurred [➡ VAGUENESS; 243] *Opposite*: clear **2** *adj* **unclear**, imprecise, indefinite, ambiguous, equivocal, nebulous, elusive, inexplicit, indefinable [➡ VAGUENESS; 243] *Opposite*: definite **3** *adj* **absent-minded**, abstracted, distracted, distant, unclear, dreamy, pensive, scatterbrained [➡ NEGATIVE INTELLECTUAL CHARACTERISTICS; 525] *Opposite*: alert

vaguely 1 *adv* **unclearly**, imprecisely, indefinitely, ambiguously, nebulously, elusively, indefinably, loosely [➡ VAGUENESS; 243] *Opposite*: definitely **2** *adv* **indistinctly**, unclearly, dimly, hazily, fuzzily, formlessly, imprecisely [➡ VAGUENESS; 243] *Opposite*: clearly

vagueness 1 *n* **nebulousness**, imprecision, indistinctness, ambiguity, elusiveness [➡ VAGUENESS; 243] *Opposite*: precision **2** *n* **abstraction**, absent-mindedness, pensiveness, dreaminess [➡ NEGATIVE INTELLECTUAL CHARACTERISTICS; 525] *Opposite*: attentiveness **3** *n* **haziness**, fuzziness, formlessness, imprecision, blurredness, indistinctness [➡ VAGUENESS; 243] *Opposite*: clarity

vain 1 *adj* **otiose**, unsuccessful, hopeless, unproductive, futile, useless, abortive, worthless, ineffective [➡ UNSUCCESSFUL AND UNPROMISING; 76] *Opposite*: successful **2** *adj* **empty**, hollow, idle, pointless, futile [➡ REDUNDANT AND USELESS; 240] *Opposite*: reliable **3** *adj* **proud**, conceited, narcissistic, vainglorious, arrogant, self-important, bigheaded (*informal*) [➡ POMPOUS, LOUD, AND OVERCONFIDENT; 635] *Opposite*: humble

Compare and Contrast: *vain, empty, hollow, idle*

CORE MEANING: without substance or unlikely to be carried though

vain failing to have or unlikely to have the intended or desired result; *empty* lacking substance, sincerity, or truthfulness; *hollow* not sincere or genuine; *idle* unlikely to be carried out or impossible to put into effect.

See Compare and Contrast at **proud**.

vainglorious (*literary*) *adj* **proud**, boastful, self-important, conceited, puffed up, pompous, arrogant, bigheaded (*informal*) [➡ POMPOUS, LOUD, AND OVERCONFIDENT; 635]

vainly *adv* **unsuccessfully**, ineffectively, in vain, unproductively, hopelessly, futilely, uselessly, worthlessly [➡ UNSUCCESSFUL AND UNPROMISING; 76] *Opposite*: successfully

valance *n* [➡ FURNISHING AND HOUSEHOLD LINENS; 860]

vale (*literary*) *n* **valley**, dale, gorge, dell (*literary*) [➡ GEOLOGIC FEATURES; 1056] *Opposite*: hill

valediction (*formal*) *n* **farewell**, goodbye, sendoff, adieu, leave-taking (*literary*) [➡ GREETINGS, FAREWELLS, AND SALUTATIONS; 659]

valedictory (*formal*) **1** *n* **farewell**, goodbye, parting, leave-taking (*literary*) [➡ ENDS AND DEPARTURES; 54] *Opposite*: welcome **2** *adj* **parting**, farewell, goodbye, final, last [➡ AFTER, LAST, AND FOLLOWING; 165] *Opposite*: welcoming

valentine *n* [➡ SEXUAL AND ROMANTIC RELATIONSHIPS; 964]

valet **1** *v* **clean**, clean out, vacuum, tidy, polish [➡ CLEAN AND POLISH; 403] **2** *type of* **servant** [➡ DOMESTIC AND KITCHEN WORKERS; 850]

valetudinarian **1** *n* **convalescent**, patient, invalid, valetudinary [➡ UNFIT AND WEAK; 739] **2** *n* **hypochondriac**, neurotic, valetudinary [➡ GRUMPY AND NEGATIVE PEOPLE; 953] **3** *adj* **sickly**, feeble, unhealthy, frail, weak, valetudinary [➡ UNFIT AND WEAK; 739] *Opposite*: healthy

valiant *adj* **brave**, courageous, heroic, fearless, noble, bold, gallant (*literary*), intrepid (*literary or humorous*) [➡ COURAGE; 498] *Opposite*: cowardly

valiantness *n* [➡ COURAGE; 498]

valid **1** *adj* **reasonable**, sound, rational, justifiable, legitimate, well-founded, defensible, bona fide [➡ TRUE AND REAL; 171] *Opposite*: unjustifiable **2** *adj* **lawful**, legal, binding, effective, in force [➡ LEGAL AND LEGITIMATE; 815] *Opposite*: illegal **3** *adj* **usable**, acceptable, authorized, endorsed, official, unexpired [➡ USEFULNESS; 199] *Opposite*: unusable **4** *adj* **convincing**, compelling, sound, persuasive, rational, cogent, logical [➡ THE NATURE OF IDEAS; 771] *Opposite*: unconvincing

Compare and Contrast: *valid, cogent, convincing, reasonable, sound*

CORE MEANING: worthy of acceptance or credence

valid having a solid foundation or justification; *cogent* forceful and convincing to the intellect and reason; *convincing* likely to overcome doubts and win the support of those who hear it; *reasonable* acceptable and according to common sense; *sound* based on good sense and acceptable reasoning and worthy of approval.

validate **1** *v* **prove**, substantiate, confirm, authenticate, corroborate, bear out, endorse, justify, support [➡ APPROVE AND CONFIRM; 646] *Opposite*: disprove **2** *v* **authorize**, certify, endorse, ratify, legalize [➡ PERMIT AND ALLOW; 669] *Opposite*: invalidate

validation **1** *n* **authentication**, proof, endorsement, confirmation, corroboration, justification, substantiation, support [➡ EVIDENCE AND PROOF; 69] **2** *n* **authorization**, endorsement, ratification, certification, legalization [➡ PERMIT AND ALLOW; 669] *Opposite*: invalidation

validity **1** *n* **cogency**, rationality, legitimacy, soundness, strength, force, weight, power, authority [➡ THE NATURE OF IDEAS; 771] *Opposite*: weakness **2** *n* **legality**, authority, legitimacy, authenticity, lawfulness [➡ TRUE AND REAL; 171]

valise *type of* **baggage** [➡ CONTAINERS, RECEPTACLES, AND PACKAGING; 1245]

valley *n* **gorge**, dale, basin, vale (*literary*), dell (*literary*) [➡ GEOLOGIC FEATURES; 1056] *Opposite*: hill

valor *n* **courage**, bravery, heroism, fearlessness, boldness, gallantry, pluck, spirit, lionheartedness [➡ COURAGE; 498] *Opposite*: cowardice

valorous *adj* **noble**, brave, courageous, heroic, fearless, bold, valiant, lionhearted, plucky, gallant (*literary*), intrepid (*literary or humorous*) [➡ COURAGE; 498] *Opposite*: cowardly

valuable **1** *adj* **costly**, expensive, priceless, dear, important, precious [➡ EXPENSIVE AND LUXURIOUS; 218] *Opposite*: inexpensive **2** *adj* **invaluable**, valued, helpful, important, useful, constructive, beneficial, indispensable, effective, worthwhile, advantageous [➡ USEFULNESS; 199] *Opposite*: worthless **3** *adj* **valued**, appreciated, respected, treasured, dear, cherished, prized, loved, esteemed [➡ POPULAR AND WANTED; 220]

valuate *v* [➡ ASSESS QUALITY; 755]

valuation *n* **estimate**, assessment, evaluation, appraisal, survey, judgment, estimation [➡ SCORES AND EVALUATIONS; 598]

value **1** *n* **worth**, price, cost, rate, charge [➡ EXPENDITURE; 423] **2** *n* **benefit**, importance, worth, significance, usefulness, use, merit, help, profit, consequence (*formal*) [➡ USEFULNESS; 199] *Opposite*: insignificance **3** *v* **prize**, appreciate, respect, esteem, treasure, cherish, set store by, regard highly [➡ LIKE, LOVE, VALUE, AND ENJOY; 578] *Opposite*: scorn **4** *v* **rate**, assess, estimate, evaluate, appraise, price, survey [➡ ASSESS QUALITY; 755]

valued *adj* **appreciated**, respected, esteemed, treasured, cherished, dear, loved, prized [➡ POPULAR AND WANTED; 220]

valueless adj **inconsequential**, worthless, insignificant, paltry, miserable, useless [➡ REDUNDANT AND USELESS; 240] Opposite: valuable

values n **principles**, standards, morals, ethics, ideals, beliefs, tenets (formal) [➡ MORAL CONCEPTS; 773]

valve 1 n **regulator**, controller, stopcock, tap, faucet, spigot [➡ PARTS OF MACHINES AND TOOLS; 1118] 2 part of **engine** [➡ PARTS OF AN ENGINE; 1144]

vamoose (slang) v [➡ LEAVE AND GO AWAY; 8]

vampire 1 n **parasite**, hanger-on, predator, sponge, freeloader (informal), sponger (informal), scrounger (informal) [➡ LAZY OR UNSUCCESSFUL PEOPLE; 948] 2 type of **mythological creature** [➡ MYTHICAL CREATURES; 1036]

vampire bat type of **flying mammal** [➡ FLYING MAMMALS; 984]

vamp up v **repair**, rework, revamp, do up, modernize, refurbish, renovate [➡ IMPROVE APPEARANCE; 379]

van 1 n **forefront**, front, lead, head, vanguard, pole position, cutting edge [➡ MOST IMPORTANT THING; 197] 2 type of **car** [➡ BIKES, CARS, AND CARRIAGES; 1149] 3 type of **commercial or industrial vehicle** [➡ VEHICLES; 1145]

vandal n **criminal**, trespasser, delinquent, thug, hooligan (informal), miscreant (literary), ruffian (dated) [➡ VILLAINS AND THUGS; 947]

vandalism n **damage**, destruction, defacement, wreckage, sabotage, harm [➡ BAD BEHAVIOR OR ACTIONS; 254]

vandalize v **destroy**, damage, deface, wreck, break, smash up, sabotage, spoil [➡ WORSEN APPEARANCE; 382]

vane n **blade**, slat, fin, plate, strip, sheet [➡ EXTREMITIES OF PHYSICAL OBJECTS; 1250]

vang n [➡ FASTENERS, LINKS, AND NETWORKS; 1247]

vanguard 1 n **front line**, front, advance guard [➡ THE ARMED FORCES; 827] Opposite: rearguard 2 n **forefront**, front, lead, head, cutting edge, van, precursor, forerunner [➡ MOST IMPORTANT THING; 197]

vanilla adj **plain**, ordinary, boring, unexciting, bland, insipid, dull [➡ BORING AND UNINTERESTING; 234] Opposite: interesting

vanish 1 v **disappear**, evaporate, go missing, fade away, peter out, go [➡ DISAPPEAR; 4] Opposite: appear 2 v **become extinct**, die out, disappear, cease to exist, be exterminated, be wiped out (slang) [➡ CEASE TO EXIST; 22]

vanished adj **disappeared**, missing, died out, gone, extinct, wiped out (informal) [➡ ABSENT AND UNAVAILABLE; 7] Opposite: present

vanity 1 n **pride**, narcissism, self-importance, conceit, arrogance, egotism, airs, bigheadedness (informal) [➡ POMPOUS, LOUD, AND OVERCONFIDENT; 635] Opposite: humility 2 n **futility**, emptiness, uselessness, pointlessness, worthlessness, ineffectuality, insignificance, ineffectiveness, hollowness, unreality [➡ REDUNDANT AND USELESS; 240] Opposite: value 3 type of **plumbing fixtures** [➡ FIXTURES; 859]

vanity case type of **baggage** [➡ CONTAINERS, RECEPTACLES, AND PACKAGING; 1245]

vanity table type of **table** [➡ FURNITURE; 858]

vanquish v **defeat**, conquer, subjugate, crush, subdue, overcome, rout, overpower, triumph over, annihilate (informal) [➡ BEAT AND DEFEAT; 80] Opposite: surrender

See Compare and Contrast at **defeat**.

vanquished adj [➡ BEATEN AND DEFEATED; 78]

vantage point 1 n **viewpoint**, viewing platform, belvedere, lookout, crow's nest [➡ TOWERS; 1099] 2 n **standpoint**, viewpoint, angle, point of view, perspective, position [➡ POINTS OF VIEW; 767]

vapid 1 adj **lifeless**, uninteresting, unexciting, vacuous, tame, uninspiring, flat, dull [➡ BORING AND UNINTERESTING; 234] Opposite: lively 2 adj **flavorless**, insipid, tasteless, weak, tame, bland, watery [➡ TASTE; 703] Opposite: tasty

vapidity n [➡ ORDINARINESS; 244]

vapidness n [➡ ORDINARINESS; 244]

vapor 1 n **gas**, air, ether [➡ GASES; 1275] 2 n **smoke**, fumes, cloud, fog, haze, particles, suspension, miasma, steam, mist, water vapor [➡ GASES; 1275] 3 n **aerosol**, spray, mist [➡ GASES; 1275]

vaporize 1 v **evaporate**, turn to vapor, boil away, boil, heat [➡ FROTH AND EFFERVESCE; 389] Opposite: condense 2 v **vanish**, disappear, evaporate, fade away, go away, dispel, drive away [➡ DISAPPEAR; 4] 3 v **destroy**, annihilate, burn, incinerate, decimate, obliterate, burn away [➡ DESTRUCTION AND DEMOLITION; 369] Opposite: preserve

vaporizer n **nebulizer**, atomizer, aerosol, spray, inhaler, spray can, steamer [➡ CONTAINERS, RECEPTACLES, AND PACKAGING; 1245]

vaporous 1 adj **gaseous**, smoky, misty, steamy, foggy, cloudy, clouded, hazy, murky [➡ FLUID AND NONSOLID; 1213] 2 adj **volatile**, unstable, unpredictable, explosive, flammable [➡ FIRE, FLAMMABILITY, AND BURNING; 1165] Opposite: stable 3 adj **insubstantial**, ephemeral, impermanent, evanescent, nebulous, wraithlike, ethereal, unsubstantial [➡ FINITENESS, VARIABILITY, AND TRANSIENCE; 96] Opposite: solid 4 adj **fanciful**, ridiculous, implausible, fantastic, unreal, insubstantial [➡ BIZARRE AND PECULIAR; 257] Opposite: real 5 adj **murky**, hazy, cloudy, obscure, dim, clouded [➡ VAGUENESS; 243] Opposite: clear

variability 1 n **erraticism**, inconsistency, capriciousness, changeability, unpredictability [➡ UNCERTAIN; 175] Opposite: predictability 2 n **unevenness**, patchiness, irregularity, inconsistency [➡ FINITENESS, VARIABILITY, AND TRANSIENCE; 96] Opposite: consistency 3 n **flexibility**, adaptability, alterability, fickleness, inconstancy, mutability [➡ FINITENESS, VARIABILITY, AND TRANSIENCE; 96] Opposite: fixedness

variable 1 adj **varying**, changing, fluctuating, changeable, erratic, unpredictable, capricious, wavering [➡ UNCERTAIN; 175] Opposite: constant 2 adj **uneven**, patchy, up-and-down, irregular, inconsistent [➡ FINITENESS, VARIABILITY, AND TRANSIENCE; 96] Opposite: consistent 3 adj **mutable**, adjustable, flexible, capricious, inconstant, fickle, adaptable, movable, alterable [➡ FINITENESS, VARIABILITY, AND TRANSIENCE; 96] Opposite: fixed

variableness n [➡ FINITENESS, VARIABILITY, AND TRANSIENCE; 96]

variance 1 n **divergence**, disparity, difference, discrepancy, inconsistency, variation [➡ DIFFERENCE; 149] Opposite: consistency 2 n **alteration**, modification, adjustment, change [➡CHANGE; 372] **3** *n* **conflict**, clash, dissent, dispute, difference of opinion, disagreement [➡DISHARMONY; 156] *Opposite:* agreement

variant 1 *adj* **irregular**, different, optional, modified, abnormal, alternative [➡DIFFERENCE; 149] **2** *n* **variation**, alternate, alternative, deviation, modification, departure, option [➡DIFFERENCE; 149]

variation 1 *n* **difference**, disparity, dissimilarity, distinction, discrepancy, deviation [➡DIFFERENCE; 149] *Opposite:* similarity **2** *n* **variant**, adaptation, reworking, departure, alteration, deviation, modification, change [➡CHANGE; 372]

varicolored *adj* [➡DESCRIBING COLORS; 1226]

varied *adj* **heterogeneous**, diverse, wide-ranging, mixed, different, various, assorted, miscellaneous, sundry [➡DIFFERENCE; 149] *Opposite:* homogeneous

variegated *adj* **spotted**, pied, dappled, speckled, flecked, patchy, mottled, multicolored [➡DESCRIBING PATTERNS; 1227] *Opposite:* uniform

variety 1 *n* **collection**, diversity, assortment, selection, multiplicity, range, mixture, array [➡COLLECTIONS AND MIXTURES OF THINGS; 1244] **2** *n* **diversity**, change, variability, variation [➡CHANGE; 372] **3** *n* **type**, kind, form, sort, category, strain, class, make, brand [➡VARIETIES, TYPES, AND KINDS; 145]

variety meats *n* [➡TYPES AND CUTS OF MEAT; 1177]

variety show *n* **show**, revue, cabaret, entertainment, performance, spectacular, floor show [➡THE PERFORMING ARTS; 904]

various 1 *adj* **a variety of**, a range of, an assortment of, a mixture of, different, a choice of, diverse, assorted [➡DIFFERENCE; 149] *Opposite:* same **2** *adj* **numerous**, many, a number of, several, countless, innumerable [➡MANY, MUCH, LARGE AMOUNT; 117] *Opposite:* few

varnish 1 *n* **lacquer**, paint, finish, glaze, polish, shiny surface, patina, gloss, resin [➡COVERS AND COATINGS; 1246] **2** *v* **paint**, glaze, finish, polish, lacquer, stain [➡DECORATE, ADORN, AND APPLY COATINGS; 405]

vary 1 *v* **change**, alter, fluctuate, adjust, adapt, modify [➡CHANGE; 372] *Opposite:* standardize **2** *v* **diverge**, differ, be different, contrast, fluctuate, disagree [➡DIFFERENCE; 149] *Opposite:* conform

See Compare and Contrast at **change**.

varying *adj* [➡DIFFERENCE; 149]

vascular *adj* [➡THE BLOOD AND CIRCULATION; 717]

vase *n* **rose bowl**, urn, jug, pot, container, bud vase [➡CONTAINERS, RECEPTACLES, AND PACKAGING; 1245]

vasectomize *v* [➡STERILIZE; 726]

vasectomy 1 *n* [➡STERILIZE; 726] **2** *type of* **medical procedure** [➡REMEDIES, TREATMENTS, AND OPERATIONS; 731]

vassal *n* [➡SUBORDINATES AND ASSISTANTS; 966]

vast *adj* **massive**, huge, enormous, gigantic, immense, cosmic, infinite, titanic, immeasurable, measureless, incalculable, limitless [➡LARGE; 1193] *Opposite:* small

vastly *adv* **much**, greatly, infinitely, immensely, immeasurably, hugely, enormously, very, extremely, massively (*informal*) [➡TO A GREAT EXTENT; 132] *Opposite:* slightly

vastness *n* **massiveness**, incalculability, limitlessness, immensity, hugeness, enormity [➡LARGE; 1193]

vat *n* **container**, cask, barrel, tank, drum, tub, bin, silo [➡CONTAINERS, RECEPTACLES, AND PACKAGING; 1245]

VAT *n* [➡TAX AND TAXATION; 802]

vatic *adj* [➡THE SUPERNATURAL; 787]

vatu *type of* **currency** [➡CURRENCIES; 798]

vaudeville *n* **show**, entertainment, variety show, burlesque, revue, floor show, cabaret, music hall (*UK*) [➡THE PERFORMING ARTS; 904]

vault 1 *n* **arch**, dome, cupola [➡ROOFS, ROOF PARTS, AND CEILINGS; 1103] **2** *n* **crypt**, cellar, undercroft, burial chamber, tomb, catacomb, mausoleum, ossuary (*formal*) [➡PARTS OF RELIGIOUS BUILDINGS; 1086] **3** *type of* **room in public buildings** [➡TYPES OF ROOMS; 1097] **4** *n* **strongroom**, treasury, treasure house [➡TYPES OF ROOMS; 1097] **5** *v* **jump**, leap, spring, hurdle, bound [➡BOUNCE, UNDULATE, AND VIBRATE; 308]

vaulted *adj* **curved**, domed, arched [➡ROUNDED SHAPE; 1218]

vaunt *v* **puff**, boast, brag, show off, hype, flaunt, exult in, promote, push, make much of, crow [➡BOAST; 616] *Opposite:* play down

vaunted *adj* **hyped**, praised, promoted, advertised, flaunted, made much of, publicized, overhyped (*informal*) [➡POPULAR AND WANTED; 220] *Opposite:* downplayed

VCR *type of* **video equipment** [➡PHOTOGRAPHY AND PHOTOGRAPHIC EQUIPMENT; 1122]

VDT *type of* **hardware** [➡COMPUTERS AND COMPUTING; 1127]

veal *type of* **meat** [➡TYPES AND CUTS OF MEAT; 1177]

vector *n* **course**, trajectory, path, flight path, route, direction [➡DIRECTION OF MOTION; 345]

veer *v* **change course**, turn, swing, swerve, bend, change direction, deviate, go around [➡CHANGE DIRECTION OF MOTION; 344]

vegan *n* **fruitarian**, vegetarian, veggie (*informal*) [➡EATERS, GOURMETS, AND DIETARY CHOICES; 714]

vegetable 1 *n* [➡FRUIT AND VEGETABLES; 1176] **2** *adj* **plant**, herbal, vegetal [➡VEGETATION; 1025]

vegetable

◆ *types of root vegetables*
beet, bok choy, carrot, cassava, mangel-wurzel, new potato, parsnip, potato, rutabaga, sugar beet, sweet potato, turnip, yam

◆ *types of vegetables*
artichoke, asparagus, brassica, broccoli, Brussels sprout, cabbage, cauliflower, collard greens, eggplant, fennel, garlic, greens, kale, leek, marrow squash, okra, onion, pumpkin, spinach, squash, sweet corn, Swiss chard, zucchini

vegetable garden *type of* **garden** [➡GARDENS; 1074]

veneer

vegetable oil *type of* **cooking fat and oil** [➡ FATS AND OILS; 1173]

vegetable plot *type of* **garden** [➡ GARDENS; 1074]

vegetarian 1 *n* fruitarian, vegan, lactovegetarian, veggie (*informal*) [➡ EATERS, GOURMETS, AND DIETARY CHOICES; 714] 2 *adj* fruit-arian, vegan, lactovegetarian, veggie (*informal*) [➡ EATERS, GOURMETS, AND DIETARY CHOICES; 714]

vegetate *v* sit around, stagnate, twiddle your thumbs, kill time, loaf, veg out (*informal*), veg (*informal*) [➡ LACK OF ACTIVITY OR MOTION; 342]

vegetation *n* plants, plant life, flora, ground cover, bedding, undergrowth, foliage, shrubbery [➡ VEGETATION; 1025]

veggie (*informal*) *n* lactovegetarian, fruitarian, vegetarian, vegan [➡ EATERS, GOURMETS, AND DIETARY CHOICES; 714]

veg out (*informal*) *v* [➡ LACK OF ACTIVITY OR MOTION; 342]

vehemence *n* forcefulness, intensity, fervor, passion, violence, strength, vigor, enthusiasm [➡ ENERGY AND ENTHUSIASM; 496] *Opposite*: indifference

vehement *adj* fervent, passionate, heated, violent, intense, vigorous [➡ ENTHUSIASTIC AND INQUISITIVE; 628] *Opposite*: apathetic

vehemently *adv* fervently, fervidly, passionately, hotly, heatedly, strongly, violently, intensely, vigorously [➡ ENTHUSIASTIC AND INQUISITIVE; 628] *Opposite*: impassively

vehicle 1 *n* [➡ TRANSPORTATION, TRANSPORTERS, AND CARGOS; 322] 2 *n* medium, means of expression, channel, means, mouthpiece, instrument, agent, conduit, tool, intermediary [➡ WAYS OF DOING THINGS; 294]

vehicle

◆ *types of commercial or industrial vehicles*
bulldozer, cab, combino, combine harvester, digger, dump truck, earthmover, hearse, pickup, semitrailer, snowplow, steamroller, tanker, taxi, taxicab, tow truck, tractor, transporter, truck, van, wrecker, yellow cab

◆ *types of leisure vehicles*
bobsled, camper, chair lift, dogsled, dune buggy, go-cart, land yacht, luge, mobile home, motor home, RV, sled, sleigh, snowmobile, toboggan

◆ *types of military vehicles*
amphibian, armored car, jeep, tank

◆ *types of public service vehicles*
ambulance, bus, firetruck, garbage truck, jitney, minibus, police car, prowl car, shuttle, squad car

◆ *types of controls*
accelerator, brake, choke, clutch, gearshift, horn, pedal, rev counter, speedometer, steering wheel, wheel

◆ *types of internal features*
back seat, booster seat, cab, car seat, child seat, dashboard, driver's seat, glove compartment, headrest, passenger seat, rearview mirror, seat belt

◆ *types of external features*
blinker, brake light, bumper, exhaust pipe, fog light, headlight, hubcap, kick-start, license plate, luggage rack, mud flap, mudguard, muffler, parking light, plate, side mirror, splashguard, stoplight, taillight, tire, wheel, windshield wiper

◆ *parts of an external structure*
airfoil, axle, bodywork, chassis, coachwork, fender, fin, grille, hood, hull, spoiler, sunroof, tailgate, trunk, windshield

veil 1 *n* mask, blanket, shroud, covering, curtain, pall, cloak [➡ COVERS AND COATINGS; 1246] 2 *v* cover, conceal, hide, mask, cloak, shroud, envelop, obscure [➡ CAUSE TO DISAPPEAR; 6] *Opposite*: reveal 3 *type of* accessory [➡ ACCESSORIES, MILLINERY, AND LINGERIE; 867]

veiled 1 *adj* indirect, oblique, obscure, covert, roundabout, implied, disguised [➡ SECRET AND UNKNOWN; 179] *Opposite*: overt 2 *adj* masked, cloaked, shrouded, covered, hooded [➡ DRESS, WEAR, AND UNDRESS; 868] *Opposite*: uncovered

vein 1 *n* layer, seam, lode, stratum, deposit [➡ COVERS AND COATINGS; 1246] 2 *n* mood, frame of mind, manner, strain, attitude, disposition, tone, hint, trace [➡ APPEARANCE AND ATMOSPHERE; 1237] 3 *n* streak, strip, stripe, line [➡ FEW, LITTLE, SMALL AMOUNT; 120] 4 *type of* blood vessel [➡ THE BLOOD AND CIRCULATION; 717]

veined *adj* patterned, marbled, lined, streaked [➡ DESCRIBING PATTERNS; 1227]

Vela *type of* **constellation** [➡ HEAVENLY BODIES; 1061]

veld *n* grassland, savanna, prairie, plain [➡ DESERTS, PLAINS, AND MOORLAND; 1045]

veldt *see* **veld**

velociraptor *type of* **dinosaur** [➡ DINOSAURS; 996]

velocity *n* speed, rate, rapidity, swiftness, pace, haste, quickness [➡ SPEED; 102]

velour *type of* **fabric from plants** [➡ FABRICS; 1132]

velvet *type of* **fabric from plants** [➡ FABRICS; 1132]

velvetiness *n* [➡ PHYSICAL TEXTURE; 1222]

velvety *adj* soft, smooth, silky, downy, furry [➡ PHYSICAL TEXTURE; 1222] *Opposite*: rough

venal 1 *adj* corruptible, mercenary, bribable, bent, unprincipled [➡ MORALLY BAD OR IMPROPER; 775] *Opposite*: honest 2 *adj* corrupt, degenerate, decadent, lawless, amoral, crooked (*informal*) [➡ MORALLY BAD OR IMPROPER; 775] *Opposite*: aboveboard

venality *n* [➡ MORALLY BAD OR IMPROPER; 775]

vend *v* sell, trade, deal in, hawk, supply [➡ SELL; 441]

vendetta 1 *n* feud, blood feud, quarrel, dispute, grudge [➡ ARGUMENTS; 47] 2 *n* campaign, crusade, war, battle, hate campaign [➡ BAD BEHAVIOR OR ACTIONS; 254]

vending machine *n* slot machine, dispenser, coin-operated machine [➡ MACHINES AND MACHINE PARTS; 1116]

vendor *n* seller, retailer, dealer, supplier, merchant, hawker [➡ SELLERS; 442]

veneer 1 *n* covering, facing, finish, surface, layer, coating [➡ COVERS AND COATINGS; 1246] 2 *n* appearance, semblance, pretense, guise, show, mask, façade [➡ FALSE AND UNREAL; 173]

3 v **cover**, finish, conceal, plate [➡ DECORATE, ADORN, AND APPLY COATINGS; 405]

venerable adj **respected**, esteemed, honored, revered, admired, august (formal) [➡ POPULAR AND WANTED; 220] Opposite: disreputable

venerate v **revere**, worship, adore, idolize, esteem, honor, respect, look up to, admire [➡ LIKE, LOVE, VALUE, AND ENJOY; 578] Opposite: disrespect

venerated adj [➡ POPULAR AND WANTED; 220]

veneration n **worship**, adoration, reverence, honor, respect, admiration, regard [➡ LOVE, RESPECT, AND GOODWILL; 549] Opposite: disdain

See Compare and Contrast at **regard**.

venetian blind n [➡ FURNISHING AND HOUSEHOLD LINENS; 860]

Venetian glass type of **glass** [➡ GLASS; 1136]

vengeance n **revenge**, retribution, reprisal, retaliation, punishment [➡ VENGEANCE AND REVENGE; 685]

vengeful adj **vindictive**, implacable, unforgiving, revengeful, resentful, rancorous [➡ IRRITATION AND ANGER; 541] Opposite: merciful

venial adj **forgivable**, excusable, pardonable, understandable, minor, mild, allowable [➡ ACCEPTABLE AND PASSABLE; 219] Opposite: unforgivable

venison type of **meat** [➡ TYPES AND CUTS OF MEAT; 1177]

venom 1 n **poison**, toxin, bane [➡ UNPLEASANT, DIRTY, AND TOXIC SUBSTANCES; 1268] Opposite: antidote 2 n **malice**, spite, rancor, spleen, acrimony, hatred, bitterness, virulence, vituperation, malevolence [➡ ANTAGONISM; 552] Opposite: affection

venomous 1 adj **poisonous**, deadly, toxic, noxious, lethal [➡ DEADLY; 928] Opposite: harmless 2 adj **malicious**, spiteful, virulent, bitter, rancorous, vituperative, malevolent, cruel, full of spleen, dripping venom, full of gall [➡ RUDE AND HOSTILE; 625]

venomously adv **spitefully**, maliciously, rancorously, malevolently, vituperatively, cruelly, bitterly [➡ RUDE AND HOSTILE; 625]

vent 1 n **opening**, outlet, aperture, escape, exhaust, chimney, flue, hole, gap [➡ HOLES, GAPS, AND FORKS; 1252] 2 v **express**, give vent to, find expression for, voice, expel, emit, utter, declare [➡ INFORM, ANNOUNCE, AND ISSUE; 611] Opposite: suppress

ventilate 1 v **air**, aerate, air out, freshen [➡ CLEAN AND POLISH; 403] 2 v **publicize**, make public, make known, air, express, discuss, examine [➡ INFORM, ANNOUNCE, AND ISSUE; 611]

ventilation n **air circulation**, airing, aeration [➡ HEATING, REFRIGERATION, AND VENTILATION; 1142]

ventilation system n [➡ HEATING, REFRIGERATION, AND VENTILATION; 1142]

ventilator 1 n **fan**, vent, opening, flue, aperture, duct, air duct [➡ HEATING, REFRIGERATION, AND VENTILATION; 1142] 2 n **life support machine**, respirator, breathing apparatus, iron lung [➡ BREATHE AND NOT BREATHE; 716]

ventriloquist type of **entertainer** [➡ WORKERS IN ENTERTAINMENT AND MEDIA; 873]

venture 1 n **business enterprise**, undertaking, scheme, project, endeavor, gamble, risk, speculation [➡ BUSINESS ENTERPRISES AND RELATED BODIES; 792] 2 n **undertaking**, course, endeavor, project, mission, enterprise [➡ ACTIONS OR UNDERTAKINGS; 259] 3 v **hazard**, dare, undertake, brave, try, take on, risk, embark on [➡ ATTEMPT AN ACTION; 261] 4 v **offer**, put forward, volunteer, express, say, submit [➡ SUGGEST, HINT, AND COMMENT; 612] 5 v **presume**, dare, be so bold, take the liberty, have the audacity, have the nerve, have the cheek [➡ SUGGEST, HINT, AND COMMENT; 612]

venture capitalist n [➡ PEOPLE INVOLVED IN FINANCE; 804]

venture forth v [➡ LEAVE AND GO AWAY; 8]

venturesome (formal) 1 adj **daring**, adventurous, enterprising, bold, brave, audacious, intrepid (literary or humorous) [➡ COURAGE; 498] Opposite: cautious 2 adj **hazardous**, chancy, dangerous, dicey (informal), risky, perilous [➡ DANGEROUS; 236] Opposite: safe

venue n **site**, place, location, scene, setting, spot [➡ PLACE; 1065]

venule type of **blood vessel** [➡ THE BLOOD AND CIRCULATION; 717]

Venus type of **planet** [➡ HEAVENLY BODIES; 1061]

veracious adj **honest**, truthful, genuine, principled, dependable, ethical, reliable [➡ HONEST AND RELIABLE; 502] Opposite: dishonest

veracity 1 n **truth**, accuracy, reliability, genuineness, authenticity, legitimacy, exactness, validity [➡ TRUE AND REAL; 171] Opposite: falsity 2 n **truthfulness**, honesty, integrity, uprightness, reliability, candor [➡ HONEST AND RELIABLE; 502] Opposite: dishonesty

veranda 1 n **terrace**, balcony, loggia, gallery, portico, porch [➡ STAGES, PLATFORMS, AND RAISED AREAS; 1098] 2 part of **building** [➡ PARTS OF A BUILDING; 1095]

verb type of **word class** [➡ ASPECTS OF LANGUAGE; 682]

verbal adj **spoken**, oral, vocal, unwritten, voiced, speaking, uttered, stated [➡ THE SPOKEN WORD; 671] Opposite: unspoken

Compare and Contrast: verbal, spoken, oral

CORE MEANING: expressed in words

verbal using words, especially spoken words, rather than pictures or physical action; **spoken** expressed with the voice; **oral** expressed in spoken form rather than in writing.

verbal abuse n [➡ INSULTS, ABUSE, AND SWEARING; 658]

verbal assault n [➡ INSULTS, ABUSE, AND SWEARING; 658]

verbal communication n [➡ COMMUNICATION; 602]

verbalization n **articulation**, expression, speech, voicing [➡ THE SPOKEN WORD; 671]

verbalize v **express**, articulate, voice, put into words, speak [➡ UTTER AND PRONOUNCE; 608]

verbatim 1 adj **exact**, word for word, precise, literal, letter-perfect, strict, word-perfect (UK) [➡ EXACT; 203] Oppo-

...oint 1 *n* point of view, view, perspective, stand-...position, stance, opinion [➡POINTS OF VIEW; 767] ...tage point, viewing platform, belvedere, lookout, ...nest [➡STAGES, PLATFORMS, AND RAISED AREAS; 1098]

...night watch, watch, wake [➡BURIAL AND PREPARATION FOR ...9]

...ance *n* watchfulness, attentiveness, observance, ...caution, alertness, awareness [➡POSITIVE IMPATIENCE, ENTHU-...AND ALERTNESS; 537] *Opposite*: slackness

...lant *adj* watchful, alert, attentive, on your guard, ...y, cautious, observant, heedful, on the alert, aware ...SITIVE IMPATIENCE, ENTHUSIASM, AND ALERTNESS; 537] *Opposite*: slack

...ee Compare and Contrast at cautious.

...gnette 1 *n* design, decoration, illustration, fron-...spiece, picture, print [➡ORNAMENTS AND DECORATIONS; 1248] ...*n* essay, article, piece, monograph [➡ANALYTICAL NONFICTION ...RITING; 592] 3 *n* picture, painting, drawing, photograph, ...rint, illustration [➡DRAWINGS, CHARTS, AND TABLES; 594] 4 *n* scene, ...xtract, clip, fragment, snippet, snatch [➡SUMMARIES, OUTLINES, AND EXCERPTS; 588]

vigor 1 *n* vitality, strength, energy, robustness, power, potency, verve, exuberance, dynamism, heartiness, drive, vim (*informal*), brio (*literary*) [➡POSITIVE IMPATIENCE, ENTHU-SIASM, AND ALERTNESS; 537] *Opposite*: lethargy 2 *n* intensity, strength, force, ferocity, violence, forcefulness, gusto, spirit, punch [➡ENERGY AND ENTHUSIASM; 496] *Opposite*: feebleness 3 *n* potency, life, robustness, stamina, staying power, strength [➡STRENGTH OF WILL; 501] *Opposite*: weakness

vigorous *adj* robust, active, strong, energetic, dynamic, vital, hearty, forceful, exuberant, spirited [➡ENERGY AND ENTHU-SIASM; 496] *Opposite*: feeble

vile 1 *adj* evil, wicked, shameful, depraved, base, degraded, low, abominable [➡MORALLY BAD OR IMPROPER; 775] *Oppo-site*: good 2 *adj* unpleasant, horrid, horrible, repulsive, nasty, foul, repellent, terrible [➡DISGUSTING AND REPULSIVE; 230] *Opposite*: pleasant 3 *adj* disgusting, loathsome, revolting, dreadful, awful, abominable, hateful, despicable, con-temptible, abhorrent (*formal*) [➡UNACCEPTABLE AND UNFORGIVABLE; 225] *Opposite*: admirable

See Compare and Contrast at mean.

vileness 1 *n* evil, depravity, wickedness, lowness, deg-radation, baseness, abomination, contemptibility, despicability, turpitude (*formal*) [➡MORALLY BAD OR IMPROPER; 775] *Opposite*: goodness 2 *n* unpleasantness, dreadfulness, awfulness, horridness, horribleness, terribleness, loath-someness, nastiness, repulsiveness, repellence, foulness [➡DISGUSTING AND REPULSIVE; 230] *Opposite*: pleasantness

vilification *n* maliciousness, abuse, disparagement, criticism, backbiting, denigration, slander, libel, def-amation, abasement (*literary*) [➡CRITICISMS AND ANGRY OUTBURSTS; 50] *Opposite*: acclaim

vilified *adj* [➡UNPOPULAR AND UNWANTED; 258]

vilify *v* malign, abuse, denigrate, belittle, disparage, libel, slander, criticize, pillory, run down [➡ACCUSE, BLAME, AND CRITICIZE; 641] *Opposite*: compliment

See Compare and Contrast at malign.

villa *type of* house [➡RESIDENTIAL BUILDINGS; 1078]

village *n* hamlet, rural community, settlement [➡HUMAN SETTLEMENTS; 1070]

villager *n* country dweller, rustic, country cousin (*dated*) [➡INHABITANTS; 857]

village square *n* [➡URBAN OUTDOOR SPACES; 1072]

villain *n* scoundrel, rogue, desperado, heavy, baddie (*informal*), nasty (*informal*) [➡VILLAINS AND THUGS; 947] *Opposite*: hero

villainous 1 *adj* wicked, criminal, heinous, depraved, iniquitous, base, evil, infamous, bad, maleficent, debased [➡MORALLY BAD OR IMPROPER; 775] *Opposite*: good 2 *adj* unpleasant, undesirable, obnoxious, offensive, unreliable, vile, hateful, disgusting, detestable, loathsome [➡DISGUSTING AND REPULSIVE; 230] *Opposite*: pleasant

villainy *n* wickedness, wrongdoing, evil, foul play, badness, treachery, crime [➡MORALLY BAD OR IMPROPER; 775] *Oppo-site*: goodness

vim (*informal*) *n* vitality, energy, vigor, exuberance, verve, zest, dash, spirit, enthusiasm, punch, panache [➡POSITIVE IMPATIENCE, ENTHUSIASM, AND ALERTNESS; 537] *Opposite*: leth-argy

vindicate 1 *v* justify, maintain, claim, support, defend, assert, prove, uphold [➡APPROVE AND CONFIRM; 646] 2 *v* clear, exonerate, absolve, acquit, exculpate (*formal*) [➡FORGET, FORGIVE, AND ACCEPT; 748] *Opposite*: implicate

vindication 1 *n* exoneration, absolution, acquittal, exculpation (*formal*) [➡FORGET, FORGIVE, AND ACCEPT; 748] *Opposite*: implication 2 *n* justification, evidence, proof, assertion [➡EVIDENCE AND PROOF; 69]

vindictive 1 *adj* spiteful, malicious, mean, cruel, hurtful, nasty, unkind, malevolent [➡SELFISH AND UNKIND; 505] *Opposite*: kind 2 *adj* vengeful, unforgiving, revengeful, rancorous, implacable, resentful, bitter, ruthless, mer-ciless, pitiless [➡IRRITATION AND ANGER; 541] *Opposite*: forgiving

vindictively *adv* spitefully, maliciously, hurtfully, cruelly, nastily, unkindly, meanly, malevolently [➡SELFISH AND UNKIND; 505] *Opposite*: kindly

vindictiveness *n* spite, malice, cruelty, nastiness, unkindness, meanness, maliciousness, malevolence [➡ANTAGONISM; 552] *Opposite*: kindness

vine *n* climber, creeper, liana [➡CLIMBERS; 1033]

vinegar *type of* seasonings, sauces, and dips [➡SEASONINGS AND SAUCES; 1174]

vinegary 1 *adj* sour, astringent, acidic, acid, tart, sharp, acrid, acerbic [➡TASTE; 703] *Opposite*: sweet 2 *adj* irritable, sour, bitter, embittered, unpleasant, resentful, acerbic, tart [➡IRRITATION AND ANGER; 541] *Opposite*: pleasant

vino (*informal*) *n* [➡DRINKS; 1187]

vintage 1 *n* era, time, age, epoch, period [➡EPOCHS AND ERAS; 89] 2 *adj* classic, typical, traditional, essential, prime, pure, first-class, archetypal, first-rate [➡SUPERIORITY; 152] *Oppo-*

---

site: imprecise 2 *adv* word for word, exactly, precisely, to the letter, literally, accurately, faithfully [➡EXACT; 203] *Oppo-site*: approximately

verbiage *n* verbosity, gobbledygook (*informal*), cir-cumlocution, redundancy, pleonasm, nonsense, waffle (*informal*) [➡MEANINGLESS SPEECH OR WRITING; 676]

verbose *adj* wordy, prolix, long-winded, talkative, bom-bastic, effusive, pompous, garrulous, pretentious, loqua-cious, rambling [➡INARTICULATE, RAMBLING, AND AWKWARD; 633] *Opposite*: taciturn

See Compare and Contrast at wordy.

verboseness *n* [➡MEANINGLESS SPEECH OR WRITING; 676]

verbosity *n* long-windedness, verboseness, garrulity, wordiness, prolixity, turgidity, loquaciousness (*formal*) [➡MEANINGLESS SPEECH OR WRITING; 676] *Opposite*: succinctness

verdant *adj* green, lush, luxuriant, fertile, leafy, grassy [➡VEGETATION; 1025]

verdict *n* decision, judgment, finding, result, outcome, ruling, decree, conclusion [➡TRIAL, PUNISHMENT, AND LEGAL OUTCOMES; 819]

verdigris *n* patina, tarnish, corrosion, greenness, col-oration, rust [➡COVERS AND COATINGS; 1246]

verdure *n* greenery, lushness, vegetation, flora, plant life, plants [➡VEGETATION; 1025]

verge 1 *n* edge, border, threshold, approach, limit, brink, margin, boundary [➡EXTREMITIES OF PHYSICAL OBJECTS; 1250] 2 *v* be near to, approach, border on, come close to, near, be close to, be similar to [➡EXIST IN CLOSE PROXIMITY; 21]

verge on *see* verge

verging on *adj* almost, bordering on, close to, tan-tamount to [➡SIMILARITY; 148]

verifiable *adj* demonstrable, provable, confirmable, cer-tifiable, showable, supportable (*literary*) [➡CERTAIN; 174] *Oppo-site*: moot

verification *n* confirmation, corroboration, proof, sub-stantiation, authentication, certification [➡EVIDENCE AND PROOF; 69] *Opposite*: contradiction

verified *adj* confirmed, proved, shown, tested, sub-stantiated, corroborated, certified [➡CERTAIN; 174] *Opposite*: unconfirmed

verify *v* confirm, bear out, prove, authenticate, validate, substantiate, corroborate, make sure, attest [➡APPROVE AND CONFIRM; 646] *Opposite*: disprove

verisimilitude (*formal*) *n* truth, credibility, authen-ticity, reliability, plausibility, likelihood [➡TRUE AND REAL; 171] *Opposite*: falsity

veritable *adj* absolute, real, genuine, out-and-out, authentic, actual, proper, true [➡TRUE AND REAL; 171] *Opposite*: false

verity (*formal*) *n* truth, fact, principle, reality, sincerity, factualness [➡TRUE AND REAL; 171]

vermicelli *type of* pasta [➡PASTA; 1180]

vermilion *type of* red [➡COLORS; 1224]

vermin *n* [➡LAZY OR UNSUCCESSFUL PEOPLE; 948]

verminous *adj* infested, pest-ridden, louse-ridden, rat-infested, crawling, alive [➡DECAYING OR INFESTED; 1236]

vernacular *n* dialect, language, patois, argot, colloquial speech, lingua franca, lingo (*informal*) [➡THE SPOKEN WORD; 671]

verruca *n* [➡CONDITIONS AFFECTING THE SKIN; 721]

versatile 1 *adj* adaptable, flexible, resourceful, mul-titalented, all-around, all-round (*UK*) [➡TALENTED AND SKILLFUL; 527] *Opposite*: limited 2 *adj* multipurpose, adaptable, handy, useful, nifty (*informal*) [➡USEFULNESS; 199] *Opposite*: inflexible

versatility *n* adaptability, flexibility, resourcefulness, usefulness, changeability [➡USEFULNESS; 199] *Opposite*: inflex-ibility

verse 1 *n* poetry, rhyme, blank verse, free verse, dog-gerel [➡POETRY AND VERSE; 915] *Opposite*: prose 2 *n* stanza, canto, section, unit [➡POETRY AND VERSE; 915]

versed *adj* experienced, competent, conversant, pro-ficient, knowledgeable, familiar, skilled [➡KNOWLEDGE AND WISDOM; 558] *Opposite*: inexperienced

versed in *adj* [➡KNOWLEDGE AND WISDOM; 558]

versifier *n* [➡WRITERS AND STYLES; 914]

version 1 *n* account, description, report, side, story [➡POINTS OF VIEW; 767] 2 *n* form, type, variety, kind, sort, style [➡VARIETIES, TYPES, AND KINDS; 145] 3 *n* adaptation, edition, trans-lation, rendering [➡SUMMARIES, OUTLINES, AND EXCERPTS; 588]

versus 1 *prep* against, contra, in competition with [➡OPPOS-ITE; 157] 2 *prep* as opposed to, contrasted with, set against, against, as against [➡FOREIGN WORDS AND PHRASES; 672]

vertebra *type of* bone [➡THE BONES AND JOINTS; 719]

vertebral *adj* [➡THE BONES AND JOINTS; 719]

vertebral column *n* [➡THE BONES AND JOINTS; 719]

vertebrate *n* animal, mammal, bird, reptile, amphibian, fish [➡LIVING THINGS AND LIVING; 976] *Opposite*: invertebrate

vertex *n* apex, summit, height, pinnacle, apogee, acme, zenith, peak, top [➡EXTREMITIES OF PHYSICAL OBJECTS; 1250] *Opposite*: base

vertical *adj* perpendicular, upright, erect, straight up, straight down, plumb [➡ORIENTATION AND ALIGNMENT; 1223] *Opposite*: horizontal

vertiginous *adj* high, dizzying, tall, lofty, exposed, open [➡HEIGHT: HIGH; 1203]

vertigo *n* dizziness, giddiness, unsteadiness, faintness, lightheadedness [➡ILL AND SICK; 740]

verve *n* vitality, energy, dynamism, vigor, dash, spirit, life, animation, enthusiasm, get-up-and-go (*informal*), vim [➡POSITIVE IMPATIENCE, ENTHUSIASM, AND ALERTNESS; 537] *Opposite*: lethargy

very 1 *adv* extremely, incredibly, awfully, exceptionally, exceedingly, especially, dreadfully, extraordinarily, enormously, fantastically, vastly [➡TO A GREAT EXTENT; 132] 2 *adj*

actual, self-same, same, identical, exact, precise, right, appropriate [➡ SAMENESS; 150]

vessel 1 *n* **container**, pot, bowl, jug, pitcher, receptacle, ewer, basin, bottle [➡ CONTAINERS, RECEPTACLES, AND PACKAGING; 1245] 2 *n* **boat**, ship, craft [➡ SHIPS AND BOATS; 1150]

vest 1 *v* **devolve**, consign, entrust, assign, lodge, confer (*formal*), bestow (*formal*) [➡ GIVE AND PROVIDE; 430] 2 *type of* **top** [➡ GARMENTS AND OUTFITS; 865]

vestal (*literary*) *n* [➡ RELIGIOUS PEOPLE; 778]

vested interest 1 *n* **special interest**, interest, concern, stake, investment, agenda [➡ ATTENTION AND ATTENTIVENESS; 763] 2 *n* **stakeholder**, supporter, shareholder [➡ BUSINESS PEOPLE; 793]

vestibule 1 *n* **entrance hall**, foyer, lobby, antechamber, atrium, hallway, porch, reception area [➡ DOORS AND ACCESS POINTS; 1101] 2 *part of* **building** [➡ PARTS OF A BUILDING; 1095] 3 *part of ear* [➡ THE EAR; 706]

vestige *n* **trace**, sign, mark, indication, hint, suggestion, remnant, evidence [➡ SMALL PIECES; 129]

vestigial 1 *adj* **residual**, remaining, imperceptible, token [➡ IMPERCEPTIBLE; 26] 2 *adj* **nonfunctioning**, functionless, stunted, degenerate, atrophic, shrunken, undeveloped, useless [➡ REDUNDANT AND USELESS; 240] *Opposite*: functional

vestment 1 *n* **robe**, garment, dress, habit, uniform, apparel [➡ CLOTHES AND ACCESSORIES; 864] 2 *n* **surplice**, chasuble, cope, vesture [➡ GARMENTS AND OUTFITS; 865]

vet *v* **examine**, check, scrutinize, inspect, assess, investigate, evaluate, look over, give the once-over (*informal*) [➡ EXAMINE AND ASSESS; 753]

veteran 1 *n* **expert**, old hand, past master, trouper, old-timer [➡ TALENTED OR INTELLIGENT PEOPLE; 528] *Opposite*: novice

veto 1 *n* **rejection**, refusal, bar, disallowance, prevention, quashing, proscription (*formal*) [➡ REFUSE PERMISSION AND NOT ALLOW; 670] *Opposite*: approval 2 *n* **prohibition**, ban, sanction, embargo, order, notice, censure [➡ REFUSE PERMISSION AND NOT ALLOW; 670] 3 *v* **release** 2 *v* **reject**, turn down, bar, disallow, refuse, dissent, disapprove [➡ REFUSE PERMISSION AND NOT ALLOW; 670] *Opposite*: approve 4 *v* **prohibit**, ban, forbid, outlaw, proscribe, censure, disallow [➡ REFUSE PERMISSION AND NOT ALLOW; 670] *Opposite*: sanction

vex 1 *v* **annoy**, upset, displease, irk, irritate, anger, exasperate, incense, aggravate (*informal*), rile (*informal*), bug (*informal*) [➡ ANGER AND ANNOY; 569] *Opposite*: pacify 2 *v* **agitate**, distress, trouble, bother, torment, worry, upset [➡ UPSET, DISTRESS, AND HUMILIATE; 567] *Opposite*: placate 3 *v* **confound**, confuse, perplex, puzzle, tease, mix up, muddle [➡ CONFUSE AND BEWILDER; 571] *Opposite*: enlighten

See Compare and Contrast at **annoy**.

vexation *n* **annoyance**, upset, displeasure, bother, irritation, exasperation, anger [➡ IRRITATION AND ANGER; 541] *Opposite*: satisfaction

vexatious *adj* **annoying**, upsetting, irritating, troublesome, bothersome, exasperating, distressing, irksome, aggravating (*informal*) [➡ IRRITATING; 228] *Opposite*: placatory

vexed 1 *adj* **irritated**, provoked, annoyed, upset, angry, displeased, cross, exasperated, irked, aggravated

(*informal*) [➡ IRRITATION AND ANGER; 541] *Opposite*: calm 2 *adj* **debated**, controversial, contentious, fractious, problematic, troublesome, tricky, awkward, difficult [➡ DIFFICULTY AND COMPLEXITY; 242] *Opposite*: uncomplicated

vexing *adj* **annoying**, puzzling, frustrating, worrying, worrisome, disturbing, troublesome, difficult [➡ IRRITATING; 228] *Opposite*: easy

via *prep* **by way of**, through, by [➡ DIRECTION OF MOTION; 345]

viability *n* **practicability**, feasibility, practicality, capability, sustainability, possibility [➡ POSSIBLE AND PROBABLE; 177] *Opposite*: impracticality

viable *adj* **practicable**, worthwhile, feasible, practical, sustainable, workable, possible, doable [➡ POSSIBLE AND PROBABLE; 177] *Opposite*: impossible

viaduct *type of* **bridge** [➡ BRIDGES, TUNNELS, CROSSINGS, AND JUNCTIONS; 1112]

vial *n* **ampoule**, vessel, container, flask, bottle, phial [➡ CONTAINERS, RECEPTACLES, AND PACKAGING; 1245]

vibe (*slang*) *n* **feeling**, atmosphere, ambiance, feel, sense, air [➡ APPEARANCE AND ATMOSPHERE; 1237]

vibrancy *n* **vitality**, vivacity, animation, enthusiasm, effervescence, liveliness, joie de vivre [➡ POSITIVE IMPATIENCE, ENTHUSIASM, AND ALERTNESS; 537] *Opposite*: lethargy

vibrant 1 *adj* **pulsating**, energetic, vibrating, effervescent, alive, bubbly, lively, exciting [➡ EMOTIONALLY PLEASANT; 187] *Opposite*: listless 2 *adj* **bright**, dazzling, vivid, brilliant, flamboyant, colorful, luminous, radiant, garish, lurid [➡ DESCRIBING COLORS; 1226] *Opposite*: dull

vibrantly *adv* **brightly**, dazzlingly, vividly, brilliantly, flamboyantly, colorfully, luminously, garishly, luridly [➡ DESCRIBING COLORS; 1226] *Opposite*: dully

vibraphone *type of* **percussion instrument** [➡ MUSICAL INSTRUMENTS; 910]

vibrate *v* **shake**, quiver, tremble, shudder, judder, beat, pulsate, oscillate [➡ BOUNCE, UNDULATE, AND VIBRATE; 308]

vibration *n* **shaking**, quivering, trembling, shuddering, juddering, pulsation, tremor [➡ PHYSICAL REACTIONS; 316] *Opposite*: stillness

vicar *n* [➡ RELIGIOUS PEOPLE; 778]

vicarage *n* **rectory**, manse, church house, residence [➡ RELIGIOUS BUILDINGS; 1085]

vicarious 1 *adj* **displaced**, secondhand, indirect, remote, removed, distanced, relayed, mediated [➡ DISTANCE; 160] *Opposite*: direct 2 *adj* **empathetic**, sympathetic, assumed, imagined, adopted [➡ RELATED; 142] 3 *adj* **delegated**, surrogate, substitute, proxy, deputized, passed on [➡ RELATED; 142]

vice 1 *n* **depravity**, iniquity, evil, wickedness, immorality, corruption, badness, sin [➡ MORALLY BAD OR IMPROPER; 775] *Opposite*: goodness 2 *n* **defect**, failing, flaw, imperfection, fault, weakness, foible, shortcoming [➡ FAULTS, FLAWS, AND WEAKNESSES; 251] *Opposite*: strength

vice squad *n* [➡ THE POLICE, ARREST, AND PRETRIAL PROCEEDINGS; 818]

vichyssoise *type of* **soup** [➡ SOUPS; 1186]

---

vicinal 1 *adj* **neighboring**, adjacent, nearby, close, proximate, local [➡ CLOSENESS; 159] *Opposite*: distant 2 *adj* **local**, district, municipal, regional, provincial, parochial, borough, neighborhood [➡ HUMAN SETTLEMENTS; 1070] *Opposite*: international

vicinity *n* **neighborhood**, environs, locality, district, area, locale, purlieu [➡ PLACE; 1065]

vicious 1 *adj* **ferocious**, savage, wild, brutish, fierce, inhuman, violent, sadistic [➡ MORALLY BAD OR IMPROPER; 775] *Opposite*: gentle 2 *adj* **spiteful**, malicious, mean, rancorous, backbiting, venomous, nasty, cruel, brutal, hurtful [➡ RUDE AND HOSTILE; 625] *Opposite*: kind

vicious circle *n* **Catch-22**, no-win situation, impasse, stalemate [➡ DIFFICULT SITUATIONS; 72]

viciously 1 *adv* **ferociously**, fiercely, savagely, wildly, brutishly, inhumanly, violently, sadistically, cruelly [➡ MORALLY BAD OR IMPROPER; 775] *Opposite*: gently 2 *adv* **maliciously**, spitefully, meanly, hurtfully, rancorously, venomously, brutally, nastily, cruelly [➡ RUDE AND HOSTILE; 625] *Opposite*: kindly

viciousness 1 *n* **ferociousness**, savagery, wildness, brutishness, ferocity, fierceness, violence, sadism, inhumanity [➡ MALICIOUS ACTIONS OR BEHAVIOR; 296] *Opposite*: gentleness 2 *n* **maliciousness**, meanness, spitefulness, rancorousness, venomousness, hurtfulness, cruelty, brutality, unkindness, nastiness, malice [➡ SELFISH AND UNKIND; 505] *Opposite*: kindness

vicissitudes *n* **changes**, variations, vagaries, ups and downs, fluctuations, deviations [➡ CHANGE; 372]

victim 1 *n* **fatality**, casualty, sufferer, injured party [➡ DEAD PERSON; 926] 2 *n* **dupe**, butt, target, object, prey, quarry [➡ VICTIMS OF DECEIT; 662]

victimization *n* **persecution**, discrimination, oppression, ill-treatment, harassment, abuse [➡ MALICIOUS ACTIONS OR BEHAVIOR; 296] *Opposite*: favoritism

victimize *v* **persecute**, discriminate against, harass, oppress, pick on, ill-treat, abuse, have it in for [➡ WOUND A PERSON OR ANIMAL; 383] *Opposite*: favor

victor *n* **winner**, champion, conqueror, medalist, prize-winner, champ (*informal*) [➡ TALENTED OR INTELLIGENT PEOPLE; 528] *Opposite*: loser

Victorian *type of* **pre-20th-century architecture** [➡ BUILDING AND ARCHITECTURE; 1076]

victorious *adj* **winning**, triumphant, champion, prize-winning, successful, conquering [➡ SUCCESSFUL AND PROMISING; 81] *Opposite*: losing

victory *n* **conquest**, triumph, win, success [➡ SUCCESS; 82] *Opposite*: defeat

victuals *n* **food**, provisions, supplies, foodstuffs, food and drink, eats (*slang*), comestibles (*formal*), provender (*literary or humorous*) [➡ FOOD; 1167]

vicuna *type of* **fabric from animals** [➡ FABRICS; 1132]

video *v* **videotape**, record, tape, film, capture [➡ RECORD SOMETHING; 371]

◆ *types of video equipment*
camcorder, DVD, palmcorder, videocassette, videocassette re video recorder, videotape, videotap

video camera *type of* **video equipment** PHOTOGRAPHIC EQUIPMENT; 1122]

videocassette *type of* **video equipment** [➡ PHOTOGRAPHIC EQUIPMENT; 1122]

videocassette recorder *type of* **video equip** TOGRAPHY AND PHOTOGRAPHIC EQUIPMENT; 1122]

videoconferencing *n* [➡ TELECOMMUNICATIONS; 1130]

videodisk *type of* **video equipment** [➡ PHOTOGRAPHY AND GRAPHIC EQUIPMENT; 1122]

video display terminal *n* **screen**, monitor, inter terminal, viewer, display [➡ COMPUTERS AND COMPUTING; 1127]

videolink *n* [➡ TELECOMMUNICATIONS; 1130]

videophone *type of* **telecommunications equipment** [➡ TELECOMMUNICATIONS; 1130]

video recorder *type of* **video equipment** [➡ PHOTOGRAPHY AND PHOTOGRAPHIC EQUIPMENT; 1122]

videotape 1 *v* **record**, video, tape, film, capture [➡ RECORD SOMETHING; 371] 2 *type of* **video equipment** [➡ PHOTOGRAPHY AND PHOTOGRAPHIC EQUIPMENT; 1122]

videotape recorder *type of* **video equipment** [➡ PHOTOGRAPHY AND PHOTOGRAPHIC EQUIPMENT; 1122]

vie *v* **compete**, contend, contest, strive, fight, rival, oppose, struggle [➡ COMPETE, CONTEND, AND COMBAT; 303] *Opposite*: collaborate

view 1 *n* **sight**, vision, observation, examination, scrutiny, analysis, inspection [➡ SEE; 699] 2 *n* **scene**, picture, spectacle, prospect, vista, aspect, outlook, landscape, panorama [➡ VIEWS AND OUTLOOKS; 1073] 3 *n* **opinion**, interpretation, assessment, understanding [➡ POINTS OF VIEW; 767] 4 *v* **consider**, regard, think of, perceive, look on, assess, deem (*formal*) [➡ HAVE AN OPINION OF SOMETHING; 756] 5 *v* **inspect**, examine, look over, look at, observe, scrutinize, check over, survey [➡ EXAMINE AND ASSESS; 753] 6 *v* **look at**, see, regard, observe, notice, watch, behold (*archaic or literary*) [➡ LOOKING AND LOOKS; 700]

viewable 1 *adj* **available**, on view, on display, accessible [➡ PRESENT AND AVAILABLE; 11] 2 *adj* **fit**, presentable, acceptable, all right, appropriate, decent, suitable [➡ ACCEPTABLE AND PASSABLE; 219] *Opposite*: inappropriate

viewer *n* **watcher**, spectator, onlooker, ogler, observer, eyewitness, witness [➡ ONLOOKERS AND SPECTATORS; 701]

viewfinder *part of* **camera** [➡ PHOTOGRAPHY AND PHOTOGRAPHIC EQUIPMENT; 1122]

viewing 1 *n* **watching**, inspecting, seeing, observing, looking [➡ LOOKING AND LOOKS; 700] 2 *n* **programming**, broadcasts, programs, broadcasting, showing, screening, presentation, transmission [➡ TELEVISION AND RADIO; 606]

viewing platform *n* [➡ STAGES, PLATFORMS, AND RAISED AREAS; 1098]

site: atypical **3** *adj* **out-of-date**, dated, antique, old, out-moded, antiquated, old-fashioned [➡ OLD, OLD-FASHIONED; 167] *Opposite*: new

vinyl **1** *n* **LPs**, records, discs, singles, albums [➡ RECORDINGS AND PLAYERS; 911] **2** *type of* **plastic** [➡ PLASTICS; 1134]

viol *type of* **stringed instrument** [➡ MUSICAL INSTRUMENTS; 910]

viola *type of* **stringed instrument** [➡ MUSICAL INSTRUMENTS; 910]

viola da gamba *type of* **stringed instrument** [➡ MUSICAL INSTRUMENTS; 910]

violate **1** *v* **disregard**, infringe, defy, breach, disobey, flout, break, contravene [➡ DISOBEY; 302] *Opposite*: obey **2** *v* **defile**, desecrate, spoil, destroy, ruin, abuse, despoil, damage, harm [➡ DESTRUCTION AND DEMOLITION; 359] *Opposite*: respect **3** *v* **disrupt**, disturb, interrupt, encroach upon, intrude upon, break up [➡ INTERRUPT AND BUTT IN; 619] *Opposite*: respect

violation **1** *n* **infringement**, breach, contravention, defiance, disobedience [➡ BAD BEHAVIOR OR ACTIONS; 254] *Opposite*: obedience **2** *n* **defilement**, desecration, destruction, ruin, abuse, damage, harm [➡ DESTRUCTION AND DEMOLITION; 359] *Opposite*: respect **3** *n* **disruption**, intrusion, encroachment, disturbance, interruption [➡ BAD MANNERS AND SOCIAL SKILLS; 521] *Opposite*: respect

violence **1** *n* **physical force**, pugnaciousness, pugnacity, aggression, fighting, savagery, brutality, cruelty, sadism, bloodshed, carnage [➡ MALICIOUS ACTIONS OR BEHAVIOR; 296] *Opposite*: peacefulness **2** *n* **ferocity**, strength, force, fierceness, viciousness, vehemence, forcefulness, passion, might, intensity, power [➡ STRENGTH; 201] *Opposite*: gentleness

violent **1** *adj* **pugnacious**, aggressive, brutal, cruel, sadistic, vicious [➡ MORALLY BAD OR IMPROPER; 775] *Opposite*: peaceful **2** *adj* **fierce**, ferocious, vehement, vicious, forceful, passionate, intense, powerful, furious, strong [➡ STRENGTH; 201] *Opposite*: gentle

violently **1** *adv* **pugnaciously**, aggressively, brutally, cruelly, sadistically, viciously [➡ MORALLY BAD OR IMPROPER; 775] *Opposite*: peacefully **2** *adv* **fiercely**, ferociously, vehemently, viciously, forcefully, passionately, intensely, hard, powerfully, strongly [➡ STRENGTH; 201] *Opposite*: gently

violet **1** *type of* **perennial flower** [➡ FLOWERS; 1032] **2** *type of* **purple** [➡ COLORS; 1224]

violin *type of* **stringed instrument** [➡ MUSICAL INSTRUMENTS; 910]

violoncello (*formal*) *type of* **stringed instrument** [➡ MUSICAL INSTRUMENTS; 910]

VIP *n* **dignitary**, name, luminary, star, celebrity, public figure, big shot (*informal*), bigwig (*informal*) [➡ IMPORTANT OR FAMOUS PEOPLE; 893]

viper *type of* **poisonous snake** [➡ SNAKES; 995]

viperish *adj* **malicious**, spiteful, nasty, unkind, malevolent, unpleasant [➡ SELFISH AND UNKIND; 505] *Opposite*: kind

viral *adj* [➡ MICROORGANISMS, FUNGI, AND ALGAE; 1023]

vireo *type of* **common bird** [➡ BIRDS; 997]

Virginia creeper *type of* **climber** [➡ CLIMBERS; 1033]

Virgo **1** *type of* **astrological sign** [➡ FATE, DESTINY, AND ASTROLOGY;

782] **2** *type of* **constellation** [➡ HEAVENLY BODIES; 1061] **3** *type of* **constellation** [➡ HEAVENLY BODIES; 1061]

viridian *type of* **green** [➡ COLORS; 1224]

virtual **1** *adj* **near**, practical, effective, fundamental, essential, implicit [➡ APPROXIMATELY; 135] *Opposite*: actual **2** *adj* **computer-generated**, simulated, cybernetic [➡ COMPUTERS AND COMPUTING; 1127]

virtually **1** *adv* **almost**, nearly, near, nigh on to, close to, next to [➡ TO A CERTAIN EXTENT; 136] **2** *adv* **in effect**, effectively, essentially, fundamentally, to all intents and purposes, practically [➡ SUMMARIZING EXPRESSIONS; 622]

virtual reality *n* **simulated reality**, computer simulation, simulation, VR, cyberspace, computer modeling, computer graphics [➡ COMPUTERS AND COMPUTING; 1127]

virtue **1** *n* **asset**, feature, quality, advantage, benefit, plus, pro [➡ SOURCE OF HAPPINESS, PLEASURE, OR IMPROVEMENT; 209] *Opposite*: disadvantage **2** *n* **goodness**, righteousness, integrity, honesty, morality, uprightness [➡ MORALLY GOOD; 774] *Opposite*: wickedness

virtuosity *n* **skill**, technique, brilliance, flair, talent, ability, expertise [➡ SKILLS, TALENTS, AND ABILITIES; 526]

virtuoso **1** *n* **musician**, bravura player, artist, maestro [➡ MUSICIANS AND SINGERS; 908] **2** *n* **wunderkind**, genius, prodigy, ace (*informal*), wizard (*informal*), maven [➡ TALENTED OR INTELLIGENT PEOPLE; 528]

virtuous *adj* **good**, righteous, worthy, honorable, moral, upright, honest [➡ MORALLY GOOD; 774] *Opposite*: bad

virtuousness *n* [➡ MORALLY GOOD; 774]

virulent **1** *adj* **infectious**, contagious, poisonous, lethal, strong, dangerous, active, powerful, potent [➡ STRENGTH; 201] *Opposite*: weak **2** *adj* **malicious**, bitter, vituperative, venomous, fierce, harsh, spiteful, hostile [➡ RUDE AND HOSTILE; 625] *Opposite*: kind

virus **1** *n* **illness**, infection, sickness, disease [➡ ILLNESSES AND DISORDERS; 732] **2** *n* **computer program**, Trojan horse, worm [➡ COMPUTERS AND COMPUTING; 1127] **3** *type of* **microorganism** [➡ MICROORGANISMS, FUNGI, AND ALGAE; 1023]

visa *n* **endorsement**, pass, entry permit, documents, papers [➡ OFFICIAL DOCUMENTS; 586]

visage **1** *n* (*literary*) **face**, expression, countenance, features, mug (*slang*) [➡ PARTS OF THE BODY: HEAD; 692] **2** *n* **look**, appearance, aspect, form, mien (*formal*) [➡ APPEARANCE AND ATMOSPHERE; 1237]

vis-à-vis **1** *prep* **regarding**, in relation to, in respect of, re, with reference to, concerning, about, with regard to, apropos (*formal*) [➡ FOREIGN WORDS AND PHRASES; 672] **2** *prep* **versus**, compared with, contrasted with, in comparison with, opposite to, face to face with [➡ FOREIGN WORDS AND PHRASES; 672]

viscera *n* **internal organs**, intestines, entrails, guts, bowels, innards (*informal*), insides (*informal*) [➡ THE DIGESTIVE TRACT; 709]

visceral *adj* **instinctual**, instinctive, intuitive, gut, primitive, animal, primeval [➡ AUTOMATIC AND INSTINCTIVE; 280] *Opposite*: reasoned

viscid *adj* **thick**, sticky, gooey, gluey, gummy, viscous, tacky, treacly (*UK*) [➡ PHYSICAL TEXTURE; 1222] *Opposite*: runny

viscose *type of* **synthetic fabric** [➡ FABRICS; 1132]

viscosity *n* **viscidness**, thickness, stickiness, gluiness, gooeyness, tackiness, gumminess [➡ DENSITY AND CONSISTENCY; 1207] *Opposite*: fluidity

viscount *type of* **aristocrat** [➡ RULERS AND ARISTOCRACY; 823]

viscountess *type of* **aristocrat** [➡ RULERS AND ARISTOCRACY; 823]

viscous *adj* **viscid**, thick, sticky, glutinous, gelatinous, gluey, tacky, gooey, gummy, treacly (*UK*) [➡ PHYSICAL TEXTURE; 1222] *Opposite*: runny

vise *type of* **carpentry tool** [➡ HAND TOOLS; 1119]

visibility 1 *n* **discernibility**, perceptibility, conspicuousness, distinguishability, prominence, reflectiveness, reflectivity, brightness, luminosity [➡ PERCEPTIBLE; 25] *Opposite*: invisibility 2 *n* **prominence**, familiarity, profile, image, high profile [➡ KNOWN AND FAMOUS; 181]

visible *adj* **noticeable**, observable, perceptible, evident, in evidence, discernible, detectable, obvious [➡ PERCEPTIBLE; 25] *Opposite*: invisible

vision 1 *n* **revelation**, prophecy, dream, hallucination, apparition [➡ DREAM, IMAGINE, AND FANTASIZE; 749] 2 *n* **concept**, mental picture, idea, image, visualization [➡ IDEAS AND THOUGHTS; 770] 3 *n* **foresight**, imagination, forethought, prescience, farsightedness [➡ PREDICT AND ANTICIPATE; 750] 4 *n* **eyesight**, sight, ability to see [➡ SEE; 699]

visionary 1 *adj* **inventive**, creative, farsighted, prescient, original, prophetic, imaginative [➡ POSITIVE INTELLECTUAL CHARACTERISTICS; 524] *Opposite*: short-sighted 2 *adj* **unrealistic**, impracticable, quixotic, fanciful, unworkable, idealistic, unrealizable [➡ IMPOSSIBLE AND IMPROBABLE; 178] *Opposite*: practicable 3 *n* **prophet**, dreamer, thinker, seer [➡ TALENTED OR INTELLIGENT PEOPLE; 528]

vision-impaired *adj* [➡ SEE; 699]

visit 1 *v* **go to**, stay in, stay at, stop with, stop at, stay, holiday at (*UK*) [➡ TRAVEL: WAYS OF TRAVELING; 320] 2 *v* **call on**, drop in on, go to see, pay a visit, pop in (*informal*), call in on (*UK*) [➡ INITIATE AND ESTABLISH COMMUNICATION; 680] 3 *n* **social call**, official visit, call, duty call [➡ ARRIVAL; 13] 4 *n* **stay**, stopover, break, trip, outing, vacation, holiday (*UK*) [➡ TRAVEL: JOURNEYS AND TRIPS; 318]

visitation 1 *n* **visit**, examination, inspection, check, checkup [➡ EXAMINE AND ASSESS; 753] 2 *n* **punishment**, curse, calamity, blight, catastrophe, disaster [➡ DISASTERS; 252]

visitor *n* **caller**, guest, tourist, sightseer [➡ TRAVEL: TRAVELERS AND WALKERS; 319]

visitor center *n* **tourist center**, information office, information center, inquiry office (*UK*), information point (*UK*), help point (*UK*) [➡ TRAVEL: SIGHTSEEING AND TOURISM; 321]

visor *n* **screen**, blind, eyeshade [➡ COVERS AND COATINGS; 1246]

vista *n* **view**, panorama, outlook, scene, landscape, seascape [➡ VIEWS AND OUTLOOKS; 1073]

visual 1 *adj* **graphic**, pictorial, filmic, painterly, photographic, graphical [➡ ARTISTIC MOVEMENTS AND STYLES; 899] 2 *adj* **optical**, chromatic, ophthalmic, ocular [➡ SEE; 699] 3 *adj* **concrete**, visible, discernible, observable, evident [➡ PERCEPTIBLE; 25] 4 *n* **graphic**, visual aid, illustration, picture, photograph, chart, graph [➡ DRAWINGS, CHARTS, AND TABLES; 594]

visual aid *n* **model**, film, video, chart, illustration, diagram, image, visual [➡ DRAWINGS, CHARTS, AND TABLES; 594]

visual art *n* [➡ THE PICTORIAL ARTS; 897]

visualization 1 *n* **imagining**, conjuring up, picturing, conception [➡ DREAM, IMAGINE, AND FANTASIZE; 749] 2 *n* **mental image**, mental picture, vision, hallucination, image, picture [➡ NONEXISTENT THINGS; 23] 3 *n* **positive thinking**, therapy, cognitive therapy, meditation, image creation [➡ PSYCHOLOGY AND THE MIND; 769]

visualize *v* **imagine**, envisage, picture, see in your mind's eye, dream of, think about, envision [➡ DREAM, IMAGINE, AND FANTASIZE; 749]

vital 1 *adj* **important**, crucial, fundamental, imperative, essential, critical, central, necessary [➡ IMPORTANT; 194] *Opposite*: unimportant 2 *adj* **energetic**, vigorous, vivacious, dynamic, vibrant, bubbly, spirited, animated, lively [➡ ENERGY AND ENTHUSIASM; 496] *Opposite*: lifeless

See Compare and Contrast at **necessary**.

vitality *n* **liveliness**, energy, vivacity, life, animation, vigor, buoyance, verve, joie de vivre, strength, get-up-and-go (*informal*) [➡ ENERGY AND ENTHUSIASM; 496] *Opposite*: lethargy

vitalize *v* **animate**, energize, buoy up, bolster, hearten, enliven, embolden, invigorate [➡ IMPROVE STRENGTH AND DURABILITY; 378] *Opposite*: deaden

vitally *adv* **extremely**, indispensably, enormously, absolutely, really, very, crucially, critically, fundamentally, essentially [➡ TO A GREAT EXTENT; 132]

vitamin *type of* **nutrient** [➡ FOOD COMPONENTS; 1188]

vitreous *adj* **enamel**, vitric, vitriform, glasslike, glassy, clear, transparent, translucent, vitrified, fused, crystal [➡ VISUAL TEXTURE; 1221]

vitreous humor *part of* **eye** [➡ THE EYE; 698]

vitriol *n* **hatred**, bitterness, venom, spleen, sarcasm, contempt, scorn, cruelty, maliciousness, viciousness, bile (*literary*) [➡ ANTAGONISM; 552] *Opposite*: love

vitriolic *adj* **spiteful**, venomous, hurtful, acerbic, bitter, cruel, rancorous, malicious, hateful, sarcastic, vicious, caustic [➡ RUDE AND HOSTILE; 625] *Opposite*: kind

vittles (*archaic*) *n* [➡ FOOD; 1167]

vituperate *v* [➡ ACCUSE, BLAME, AND CRITICIZE; 641]

vituperation 1 *n* **outburst**, attack, criticism, censuring, condemnation, dressing down, reprimand [➡ CRITICISMS AND ANGRY OUTBURSTS; 50] 2 *n* **abuse**, venom, vitriol, savaging, mauling, criticism, censure, reproach [➡ ANTAGONISM; 552]

vituperative *adj* **insulting**, abusive, offensive, malicious, slanderous, scathing, critical, censorious [➡ ACCUSATORY AND DISAPPROVING; 634]

vivacious *adj* **vibrant**, lively, bubbly, cheerful, spirited, full of life, energetic, effervescent, animated, chirpy (*informal*) [➡ ENERGY AND ENTHUSIASM; 496] *Opposite*: languid

vivaciousness *n* [➡ ENERGY AND ENTHUSIASM; 496]

vivacity *n* high-spiritedness, liveliness, animation, verve, vivaciousness, exuberance, cheerfulness, energy, life, sparkle, vitality, chirpiness (*informal*) [➡ ENERGY AND ENTHUSIASM; 496] *Opposite*: lethargy

viva voce *adj* [➡ CLASSES, COURSEWORK, AND EXAMINATIONS; 842]

vivid 1 *adj* intense, rich, gaudy, bright, glowing, vibrant, colorful, brilliant, flamboyant [➡ DESCRIBING COLORS; 1226] *Opposite*: dull 2 *adj* striking, powerful, strong, clear, intense, graphic [➡ STRENGTH; 201] *Opposite*: understated 3 *adj* active, lively, creative, ingenious, original, inventive [➡ INTERESTING AND MEANINGFUL; 190] *Opposite*: prosaic 4 *adj* fresh, distinct, clear, crystal clear, lucid, plain [➡ CONCISE AND CLEAR; 202] *Opposite*: vague

vividly 1 *adv* intensely, richly, gaudily, brightly, vibrantly, brilliantly, colorfully [➡ DESCRIBING COLORS; 1226] *Opposite*: dully 2 *adv* strikingly, powerfully, strongly, clearly, intensely, graphically [➡ STRENGTH; 201] 3 *adv* distinctly, clearly, lucidly, freshly, plainly, keenly, acutely [➡ CONCISE AND CLEAR; 202] *Opposite*: vaguely

vividness 1 *n* richness, gaudiness, colorfulness, brightness, vibrancy, brilliance, intensity, radiance [➡ DESCRIBING COLORS; 1226] *Opposite*: dullness 2 *n* freshness, distinctness, clarity, lucidity, clearness, plainness [➡ CONCISE AND CLEAR; 202] *Opposite*: vagueness 3 *n* power, strength, clarity, intensity [➡ STRENGTH; 201] 4 *n* liveliness, creativity, ingeniousness, flamboyance, intensity, richness, originality, inventiveness [➡ INTERESTING AND MEANINGFUL; 190] *Opposite*: prosaicness

vixen *type of* female animal [➡ MALE OR FEMALE ANIMALS; 978]

viz. *adv* [➡ EXPRESSIONS INTRODUCING EXAMPLES; 64]

vocabulary 1 *n* language, words, terms, expressions, terminology, lexis, jargon [➡ ASPECTS OF LANGUAGE; 682] 2 *n* dictionary, glossary, lexicon, word list [➡ LISTS AND SCHEDULES; 587]

See Compare and Contrast at **language**.

vocal 1 *adj* uttered, verbal, voiced, spoken, unwritten, speaking, singing, choral, oral [➡ THE SPOKEN WORD; 671] *Opposite*: silent 2 *adj* outspoken, frank, insistent, vociferous, voluble, forceful, strident, raucous, noisy, loud, forthright [➡ HONEST AND OPEN; 630] *Opposite*: quiet

vocal cords *part of* respiratory system [➡ RESPIRATORY ORGANS; 715]

vocalist *n* singer, lead vocalist, backing vocalist, lead singer, songster, backup singer, backup vocalist, backing singer (*UK*) [➡ MUSICIANS AND SINGERS; 908]

vocalize *v* express, voice, articulate, give voice to, put into words, state, enunciate, spell out, talk about, put forward, utter, intone, chant [➡ UTTER AND PRONOUNCE; 608]

vocally *adv* outspokenly, frankly, insistently, vociferously, volubly, forcefully, raucously, noisily, stridently, loudly [➡ HONEST AND OPEN; 630] *Opposite*: quietly

vocals *n* lyrics, words, singing, chorus [➡ MUSIC, SONGS, AND SINGING; 907]

vocation 1 *n* career, profession, job, occupation, work, calling, trade, craft, art [➡ PROFESSIONS; 845] 2 *n* aptitude, inclination, talent, bent, urge, natural ability [➡ SKILLS, TALENTS, AND ABILITIES; 526]

vocational *adj* occupational, professional, job-related, career, work, employment [➡ EMPLOYMENT STATUS; 831]

vocational school *type of* school [➡ EDUCATIONAL INSTITUTIONS; 813]

vocative *n type of* grammatical term [➡ ASPECTS OF LANGUAGE; 682]

vociferate *v* [➡ PROTEST AND EXPRESS DISAPPROVAL; 642]

vociferous *adj* clamorous, vocal, loud, voluble, raucous, strident, noisy, enthusiastic [➡ HONEST AND OPEN; 630] *Opposite*: quiet

vogue *n* fashion, trend, craze, rage, mode, fad, style [➡ FADS, FETISHES, AND IDOLATRY; 555]

voguish 1 *adj* fashionable, elegant, chic, stylish, modish, classy (*informal*), à la mode (*dated*) [➡ NEW, MODERN; 166] *Opposite*: unfashionable 2 *adj* passing, in vogue, in, up-to-the-minute, popular, now, all the rage, faddish, trendy (*informal*), happening (*informal*), hip (*slang*) [➡ POPULAR AND WANTED; 220] *Opposite*: unpopular

voice 1 *n* speech, singing, vocal sound, power of speech [➡ COMMUNICATION; 602] 2 *n* opinion, say, right of speech, expression, declaration [➡ POINTS OF VIEW; 767] 3 *v* express, assert, declare, proclaim, opine (*formal*) [➡ CLAIM, INSIST, AND EMPHASIZE; 614] 4 *v* pronounce, articulate, utter, intone [➡ UTTER AND PRONOUNCE; 608]

voice box *part of* respiratory system [➡ RESPIRATORY ORGANS; 715]

voiced *adj* stated, enunciated, spoken, uttered, expressed, articulated, pronounced [➡ THE SPOKEN WORD; 671]

voiceless 1 *adj* silent, unspeaking, mute, taciturn, wordless, uncommunicative [➡ RETICENT AND UNFORTHCOMING; 631] *Opposite*: speaking 2 *adj* unrepresented, disenfranchised, invisible, ignored, forgotten, abandoned, overlooked, disadvantaged [➡ CLASS STATUS; 889] *Opposite*: represented

voice mail *type of* telecommunications equipment [➡ TELECOMMUNICATIONS; 1130]

voiceover *n* narration, commentary, narrative [➡ TELEVISION AND RADIO; 606]

void 1 *adj* annulled, canceled, invalid, null and void, negated (*formal*) [➡ REDUNDANT AND USELESS; 240] *Opposite*: valid 2 *n* empty space, emptiness, vacuum, hollowness, abyss, space, nothingness, cavity, hole [➡ HOLES, GAPS, AND FORKS; 1252] 3 *v* cancel, annul, render null and void, vacate, reject, throw out, empty [➡ ABOLISH AND ANNUL; 452]

See Compare and Contrast at **vacant**.

voilà *interj* [➡ FOREIGN WORDS AND PHRASES; 672]

voile *type of* fabric from plants [➡ FABRICS; 1132]

Volans *type of* constellation [➡ HEAVENLY BODIES; 1061]

volatile 1 *adj* unpredictable, explosive, hot-blooded, impulsive, fickle, capricious, hot-tempered [➡ EXCESSIVE SENSITIVITY; 511] *Opposite*: placid 2 *adj* precarious, dangerous, hazardous, unstable, explosive, changeable [➡ DANGEROUS; 236] *Opposite*: stable

volatility *n* **instability**, unpredictability, precariousness, hot-bloodedness, explosiveness, impulsiveness, capriciousness [➡ EXCESSIVE SENSITIVITY; 511] *Opposite*: stability

volcanic *adj* [➡ VOLCANOES AND EARTHQUAKES; 1054]

volcanic activity *n* [➡ VOLCANOES AND EARTHQUAKES; 1054]

volcano *n* [➡ VOLCANOES AND EARTHQUAKES; 1054]

vole *type of* **rodent** [➡ RODENTS; 989]

volition *n* **wish**, will, decision, choice, desire, preference, option [➡ THE WILL AND WILLINGNESS; 563] *Opposite*: coercion

volley 1 *n* **torrent**, shower, stream, cascade, barrage, hail, broadside [➡ SUDDEN EVENTS; 52] 2 *v* **lob**, hit, strike, kick [➡ MOVE SOMETHING: THROUGH THE AIR; 334]

volleyball *type of* **court game** [➡ HOBBIES, GAMES, AND SPORTS; 875]

volt *type of* **SI unit** [➡ SIZE AND DIMENSIONS; 1192]

volte-face *n* **U-turn**, reversal, change of direction, about-face, change of heart, turn, turnabout, turnaround, about-turn (*UK*) [➡ DECISIVE MOMENTS; 44]

voluble *adj* **vociferous**, fluent, articulate, verbose, talkative, garrulous [➡ ELOQUENT, TALKATIVE, AND LONG-WINDED; 632] *Opposite*: taciturn

volume 1 *n* **quantity**, amount, degree, size, level, number [➡ AMOUNTS AND QUANTITIES; 112] 2 *n* **capacity**, size, dimensions, measurements, bulk [➡ SIZE AND DIMENSIONS; 1192] 3 *n* **book**, tome, work [➡ BOOKS AND BOOKLETS; 590] 4 *n* **part**, section, edition [➡ BOOKS AND BOOKLETS; 590]

voluminous *adj* **big**, huge, large, capacious, roomy, ample, baggy [➡ LARGE; 1193] *Opposite*: small

voluminousness *n* [➡ LARGE; 1193]

voluntarily *adv* **willingly**, of your own accord, happily, gladly, freely [➡ THE WILL AND WILLINGNESS; 563] *Opposite*: reluctantly

voluntary 1 *adj* **unpaid**, charitable, volunteer [➡ EMPLOYMENT STATUS; 831] *Opposite*: professional 2 *adj* **intended**, intentional, controlled, deliberate, chosen, with intent [➡ INTENTIONAL AND DELIBERATE; 279] *Opposite*: involuntary

volunteer 1 *n* **helper**, candy striper, unpaid worker [➡ WORKERS; 836] 2 *v* **offer**, come forward, agree, step up, undertake [➡ AGREE; 645] 3 *v* **give**, offer, tell, advise, inform, notify, acquaint [➡ INFORM, ANNOUNCE, AND ISSUE; 611]

voluptuary *n* [➡ PLEASURE-SEEKERS AND HEDONISTS; 886]

voluptuous *adj* [➡ BUILD; 477]

vomit 1 *v* **be sick**, be nauseous, be nauseated, gag, retch, spew, throw up (*informal*), heave (*informal*), barf (*informal*), puke (*slang*), hurl (*slang*) [➡ VOMIT AND BELCH; 712] 2 *v* **expel**, spew out, spew forth, eject, ejaculate, send out, throw out, emit, send forth (*archaic or literary*) [➡ LIQUID EMISSION; 370] 3 *n* **sick**, vomitus, barf (*informal*), puke (*slang*), bile (*literary*) [➡ VOMIT AND BELCH; 712]

vomitus *n* [➡ VOMIT AND BELCH; 712]

voodoo *n* [➡ THE SUPERNATURAL; 787]

voracious *adj* **insatiable**, avid, hungry, ravenous, gluttonous, greedy, rapacious [➡ EAT AND NOT EAT; 710] *Opposite*: sated

voraciousness *n* **greed**, greediness, gluttony, hunger, rapaciousness, avidity [➡ EAT AND NOT EAT; 710]

vortex 1 *n* **whirlpool**, whirlwind, waterspout, tornado, cyclone, maelstrom, twister (*informal*) [➡ WINDY AND STORMY WEATHER; 1053] 2 *n* **quagmire**, morass, maelstrom, turbulence, whirlwind, blizzard, storm, flood, tidal wave [➡ DIFFICULT SITUATIONS; 72]

vorticism *type of* **20th-century art movement** [➡ ARTISTIC MOVEMENTS AND STYLES; 899]

votary *n* [➡ DEVOTEES AND ADDICTED PEOPLE; 556]

vote 1 *n* **ballot**, election, secret ballot, show of hands, poll, division (*UK*) [➡ ELECTIONS AND VOTING; 807] 2 *v* **choose**, cast your vote, elect, opt for, support, back, return [➡ MAKE DECISIONS AND CHOICES; 752]

voter *n* **elector**, constituent, supporter, backer [➡ ELECTIONS AND VOTING; 807]

votive 1 *adj* **ritual**, prayerful, supplicatory (*formal*), precatory (*formal*) [➡ REQUEST AND DEMAND; 663] 2 *adj* **promised**, pledged, vowed, contractual, agreed [➡ RELIGIOUS CONCEPTS; 776]

voucher *n* **coupon**, ticket, receipt, check, chit (*dated*) [➡ RECEIPTS AND INVOICES; 591]

vouch for *v* **speak for**, support, guarantee, back up, stand up for, endorse, certify [➡ APPROVE AND CONFIRM; 646]

vouchsafe 1 *v* **give**, grant, offer, bestow (*formal*) [➡ GIVE AND PROVIDE; 430] 2 *v* (*formal*) **promise**, agree, allow, permit, consent, approve [➡ PROMISE AND ASSURE; 684]

vow 1 *n* **promise**, oath, pledge, guarantee, declaration, undertaking [➡ PROMISE AND ASSURE; 684] 2 *v* **swear**, promise, guarantee, undertake, declare, assert, pledge [➡ PROMISE AND ASSURE; 684]

voyage 1 *n* **journey**, trip, expedition, passage, crossing, cruise, flight, tour [➡ TRAVEL: JOURNEYS AND TRIPS; 318] 2 *v* **journey**, sail, cruise, travel [➡ TRAVEL: WAYS OF TRAVELING; 320]

voyager *n* **traveler**, explorer, adventurer, tourist, vacationer [➡ TRAVEL: TRAVELERS AND WALKERS; 319]

voyeur *n* **ghoul**, observer, onlooker, spy, watcher, viewer, busybody (*informal*), rubberneck (*informal*) [➡ INTERFERING PEOPLE AND TATTLETALES; 950]

voyeurism *n* **prurience**, ghoulishness, nosiness (*informal*), rubbernecking (*informal*) [➡ LOOKING AND LOOKS; 700]

voyeuristic *adj* **prurient**, morbid, ghoulish, nosy, unhealthy [➡ NOSY AND INTERFERING; 512]

VR *n* [➡ COMPUTERS AND COMPUTING; 1127]

VTOL *type of* **military aircraft** [➡ AIRCRAFT; 1148]

vulgar 1 *adj* **rude**, offensive, crude, bad, earthy, improper, coarse, blue (*informal*), naughty (*humorous*) [➡ MORALLY BAD OR IMPROPER; 775] *Opposite*: decent 2 *adj* **tasteless**, brash, common, kitsch, ostentatious, outlandish [➡ IN POOR TASTE AND OVERSENTIMENTAL; 229] *Opposite*: tasteful 3 *adj* **bad-mannered**, uncouth, discourteous, unrefined, rude, ill-mannered, rough, loutish, boorish [➡ BAD MANNERS AND SOCIAL SKILLS; 521] *Opposite*: polite

vulgarian *n* [➡ LEVELS OF EDUCATION AND SOPHISTICATION; 894]

vulgarism 1 *n* **obscenity**, swear word, four-letter word, expletive, rude word, bad word, vulgarity, profanity, oath [➡ INSULTS, ABUSE, AND SWEARING; 658] **2** *n* **colloquialism**, popular expression, idiom, common term [➡ FIGURES OF SPEECH; 673]

vulgarity 1 *n* **rudeness**, offensiveness, crudeness, crudity, earthiness, impropriety [➡ MORALLY BAD OR IMPROPER; 775] *Opposite*: decency **2** *n* **bad manners**, uncouthness, rudeness, loutishness, boorishness [➡ BAD MANNERS AND SOCIAL SKILLS; 521] *Opposite*: politeness **3** *n* **tastelessness**, brashness, ostentatiousness, commonness, kitsch [➡ IN POOR TASTE AND OVER-SENTIMENTAL; 229] *Opposite*: tastefulness **4** *n* **swear word**, bad

language, four-letter word, rude word, expletive, vulgarism, oath [➡ INSULTS, ABUSE, AND SWEARING; 658]

vulgar language *n* **swear word**, bad language, four-letter word, rude word, vulgarity, expletive, vulgarism [➡ INSULTS, ABUSE, AND SWEARING; 658]

vulnerability *n* **susceptibility**, weakness, defenselessness, helplessness, exposure, liability [➡ DANGER; 235] *Opposite*: invincibility

vulnerable *adj* **susceptible**, weak, defenseless, helpless, exposed, in danger, at risk [➡ IN DANGER; 237] *Opposite*: invincible

vulpine *adj* [➡ BEASTLY AND BRUTISH; 510]

vulture *type of* **scavenger** [➡ BIRDS; 997]

vulturine *adj* **opportunistic**, exploitative, greedy, avaricious, grasping [➡ BEASTLY AND BRUTISH; 510]

W

wackiness (*informal*) *n* **zaniness**, silliness, wildness, eccentricity, oddness, strangeness, craziness (*informal*) [➡ BIZARRE AND PECULIAR; 257] *Opposite:* conventionality

wacky (*informal*) *adj* **silly**, zany, madcap, way out, off the wall, crazy (*informal*), wild (*informal*) [➡ BIZARRE AND PECULIAR; 257] *Opposite:* conventional

wad 1 *n* (*informal*) [➡ LARGE AMOUNTS OF MONEY; 118] 2 *n* **bundle**, roll, sheaf, stack, pile [➡ AMOUNTS OF SOLID OR SEMISOLID; 115] 3 *n* **lump**, mass, cushion, clump, chunk [➡ LARGE PIECES; 130] 4 *n* **twist**, chew, portion, gob (*slang*) [➡ MANY, MUCH, LARGE AMOUNT; 117] 5 *v* **plug**, lag, stuff, fill, pad [➡ FILL; 406] 6 *v* **compress**, scrunch, squeeze, compact, screw, crumple [➡ CHANGE OF SHAPE; 385]

wadding *n* **padding**, lining, insulation, lagging, filling, stuffing [➡ CENTRAL PARTS OF PHYSICAL OBJECTS; 1251]

waddle *v* **toddle**, sway, shuffle, wobble [➡ WALK UNSTEADILY; 315]

wade *v* **paddle**, stride, walk, splash [➡ PROCEED AND GO; 305]

wader *type of* **sea bird** [➡ SEA BIRDS; 1002]

waders *type of* **boot** [➡ FOOTWEAR; 871]

wade through *v* **plow through**, struggle through, battle through, tackle, deal with, buckle down and do (*informal*), plug away (*informal*) [➡ CONTINUE AN ACTION; 262]

wafer-thin *adj* **thin**, paper-thin, slim [➡ WIDTH: NARROW AND THIN; 1200]

waffle 1 *v* (*informal*) **equivocate**, prevaricate, vacillate, beat around the bush, dither, waver, shilly-shally [➡ HESITATE; 272] 2 *n* (*informal*) **nonsense**, rubbish, drivel, balderdash, guff (*informal*), blather (*informal*), hooey (*informal*), gobbledygook (*informal*), flimflam (*slang*) [➡ MEANINGLESS SPEECH OR WRITING; 676] 3 *type of* **pancake** [➡ CAKES, COOKIES, AND DESSERTS; 1181]

waft 1 *v* **drift**, float, glide, sail, fan, blow [➡ MOVE SLOWLY; 314] 2 *n* **puff**, breath, gust, breeze, draft [➡ AMOUNTS OF GAS; 116]

wag 1 *v* **wave to and fro**, move from side to side, flap, wiggle, waggle, shake, twitch [➡ MOVE SOMETHING: ON THE SPOT; 336] 2 *n* (*informal*) **wit**, humorist, comedian, comic, joker, satirist [➡ JOKERS AND TEASES; 675] 3 *n* **wiggle**, waggle, shake, twitch, wave [➡ MOVE SOMETHING: ON THE SPOT; 336]

wage 1 *n* **salary**, pay, earnings, income, take-home pay, remuneration, fee, honorarium, stipend, emolument (*formal*) [➡ INCOME; 460] 2 *v* **carry on**, conduct, pursue, engage in, fight, instigate [➡ CARRY OUT AN ACTION; 269]

Compare and Contrast: *wage, salary, pay, fee, remuneration, emolument, honorarium, stipend*

CORE MEANING: money given for work done

wage a fixed regular payment made on an hourly, weekly, or daily basis, especially to manual workers; *salary* a fixed regular annual sum, usually paid on a monthly basis, especially to clerical or professional workers; *pay* a wage or salary; *fee* a payment made to a professional person by a client; *remuneration* payment for work, goods, or services; *emolument* (*formal*) any payment for work; *honorarium* money given in exchange for services for which there is normally no fixed charge; *stipend* a regular payment or allowance for living expenses, especially one made to a member of the clergy or a student.

waged (*UK*) *adj* [➡ EMPLOYMENT STATUS; 831]

wage earner *n* **breadwinner**, provider, earner, worker, supporter, wage slave (*informal*) [➡ WORKERS; 836]

wage packet (*UK*) *n* **wage**, salary, wages, earnings, income, pay packet (*UK*) [➡ INCOME; 460]

wager 1 *n* **bet**, gamble, stake, ante [➡ GAMBLE AND TAKE RISKS; 466] 2 *v* **bet**, gamble, stake, risk, venture, lay a wager [➡ GAMBLE AND TAKE RISKS; 466]

wages *n* **salary**, pay, earnings, income, take-home pay, remuneration, gross, net [➡ INCOME; 460]

wage war on *v* **oppose**, combat, resist, fight, do battle, battle [➡ COMPETE, CONTEND, AND COMBAT; 303]

waggish (*informal*) *adj* **humorous**, witty, mischievous, droll, jocular, facetious, amusing [➡ GOOD-TEMPERED AND HUMOROUS; 627]

waggishness (*informal*) *n* **humorousness**, wit, mischievousness, mischief, drollness, jocularity, facetiousness [➡ GOOD-TEMPERED AND HUMOROUS; 627]

waggle *v* **wiggle**, wag, shake, wave to and fro, move from side to side, jiggle, joggle, flap [➡ MOVE SOMETHING: ON THE SPOT; 336]

wagon 1 *n* [➡ BIKES, CARS, AND CARRIAGES; 1149] 2 *part of* **train** [➡ RAILROADS; 1107]

---

wagon

◆ *types of wagons or carriages*
barouche, brougham, buggy, cart, chariot, coach, Conestoga wagon, covered wagon, dray, landau, landaulet, phaeton, prairie schooner, stagecoach, trap, troika, tumbril

---

wagtail *type of* **songbird** [➡ SONGBIRDS; 1003]

waif *n* **stray**, soul, urchin, orphan, ragamuffin (*dated*) [➡ CHILD OR YOUTH; 945]

waiflike *adj* [➡ BUILD; 477]

wail 1 *v* **howl**, moan, weep, yowl, keen, scream, cry, screech [➡ SOUND EMISSION BY PEOPLE; 363] 2 *v* **complain**, fuss, raise a ruckus, kick up a storm, whine [➡ COMPLAIN AND NAG; 686] 3 *n* **howl**, moan, yowl, scream, cry, screech, yelp, whine [➡ SOUNDS MADE BY PEOPLE; 1262] 4 *n* **complaint**, protest, whine, fuss, scream, howling [➡ COMPLAIN AND NAG; 686]

wainscot 1 *n* **paneling**, wainscoting, cladding, lining [➡ BUILDING MATERIALS; 1077] 2 *type of* **general fixtures** [➡ FIXTURES; 859]

waist *part of* **torso** [➡ PARTS OF THE BODY: TORSO; 693]

waistband *part of* **garment** [➡ PARTS OF A GARMENT; 870]

waistline *n* **waist**, middle, midriff [➡ PARTS OF THE BODY: TORSO; 693]

wait 1 *v* **stay**, remain, hang around, linger, stop, kill time, pass the time [➡ CONTINUE TO EXIST; 17] 2 *v* **delay**, pause, hold your fire, postpone, hang on, put off, hold your horses (*informal*) [➡ SHIRK AND DELAY; 273] *Opposite*: begin 3 *v* **expect**, anticipate, await, wait on [➡ PREDICT AND ANTICIPATE; 750] 4 *n* **delay**, pause, interval, postponement, gap, time lag [➡ PERIODS OF TIME; 90]

waiter *n* **server**, attendant, maître d'hôtel, maître d', waitperson, headwaiter, waitron (*slang*) [➡ DOMESTIC AND KITCHEN WORKERS; 850]

waiting area *n* **concourse**, foyer, meeting point, waiting room, reception [➡ PUBLIC BUILDINGS AND MEETING PLACES; 1081]

waiting room *type of* **room in public buildings** [➡ TYPES OF ROOMS; 1097]

wait on 1 *v* **care for**, serve, mother, nurse, take care of, minister to [➡ TAKE CARE OF AND SPOIL; 300] 2 *v* (*informal*) **expect**, anticipate, await, wait for [➡ PREDICT AND ANTICIPATE; 750]

waitron (*slang*) *type of* **person who works in restaurants** [➡ DOMESTIC AND KITCHEN WORKERS; 850]

waive *v* **surrender**, give up, relinquish, put aside, ignore, abandon, renounce [➡ FORGO AND DENY ONESELF; 449] *Opposite*: retain

waiver 1 *n* **disclaimer**, relinquishment, renunciation, abdication, abandonment, sacrifice, loss [➡ FORGO AND DENY ONESELF; 449] 2 *n* **contract**, agreement, bond [➡ OFFICIAL DOCUMENTS; 586]

wake 1 *v* **wake up**, awaken, stir, come around, come to, get up, rouse, waken [➡ WAKE AND REGAIN CONSCIOUSNESS; 724] 2 *v* **arouse**, stir, awaken, rouse, kindle, challenge [➡ APPEAL TO AND AROUSE INTEREST; 575] *Opposite*: stifle

wakeboarding *type of* **extreme sport** [➡ HOBBIES, GAMES, AND SPORTS; 875]

wakeful 1 *adj* **restless**, disturbed, sleepless, unable to sleep, insomniac, tossing and turning, awake, restive [➡ WIDE AWAKE AND CONSCIOUS; 735] *Opposite*: drowsy 2 *adj* **alert**, vigilant, on guard, attentive, aware, on the lookout, watchful [➡ POSITIVE IMPATIENCE, ENTHUSIASM, AND ALERTNESS; 537] *Opposite*: inattentive

wakefulness 1 *n* **restlessness**, sleeplessness, insomnia, tossing and turning, restiveness [➡ WIDE AWAKE AND CONSCIOUS; 735] *Opposite*: drowsiness 2 *n* **alertness**, vigilance, attentiveness, awareness, watchfulness [➡ POSITIVE IMPATIENCE, ENTHUSIASM, AND ALERTNESS; 537] *Opposite*: inattentiveness

waken 1 *v* **awaken**, wake up, wake, arouse, get up [➡ WAKE AND REGAIN CONSCIOUSNESS; 724] 2 *v* **arouse**, stir, awaken, kindle, rouse, challenge [➡ APPEAL TO AND AROUSE INTEREST; 575] *Opposite*: suppress

wakening *n* [➡ WAKE AND REGAIN CONSCIOUSNESS; 724]

wake up 1 *v* **wake**, awaken, stir, come around, come to, get up, rouse [➡ WAKE AND REGAIN CONSCIOUSNESS; 724] 2 *v* **liven up**, come to life, come alive, revive, animate, galvanize, perk up, get going [➡ CHANGE OF MOOD AND COMPOSURE; 580]

waking *n* [➡ WAKE AND REGAIN CONSCIOUSNESS; 724]

walk 1 *v* **go on foot**, stroll, amble, saunter, march, hike, stride, toddle, promenade (*formal*), perambulate (*formal*) [➡ PROCEED AND GO; 305] 2 *n* **stroll**, saunter, march, amble, promenade (*formal*) [➡ PROCEED AND GO; 305] 3 *n* **gait**, pace, tread, stride, way of walking [➡ TEMPERAMENT AND BEHAVIOR; 492]

walkabout (*informal*) *n* **walk**, stroll, saunter, amble, tour, wander, trip [➡ TRAVEL: JOURNEYS AND TRIPS; 318]

walk a tightrope *v* **tread dangerously**, invite trouble, ask for trouble, ask for it, skate on thin ice, take a chance, walk a thin line [➡ GAMBLE AND TAKE RISKS; 466]

walk away 1 *v* **abandon**, leave, withdraw, abdicate, back down from, run away [➡ RUN AWAY AND AVOID; 10] 2 *v* **win**, triumph, sail through, succeed, walk it (*informal*), romp (*informal*), ace (*slang*) [➡ SUCCEED AND WIN; 79]

walkaway (*informal*) *n* **cinch** (*informal*), piece of cake (*informal*), breeze (*informal*), pushover (*informal*), walkover (*informal*) [➡ EASY WORK; 299] *Opposite*: challenge

walk down the aisle *v* **get married**, marry, tie the knot (*informal*), get hitched (*informal*), get spliced (*slang*), wed (*formal or literary*) [➡ ESTABLISHING RELATIONSHIPS WITH OTHERS; 974]

walker *n* **hiker**, rambler, mall walker, stroller [➡ TRAVEL: TRAVELERS AND WALKERS; 319]

walkie-talkie *type of* **telecommunications equipment** [➡ TELECOMMUNICATIONS; 1130]

walking *adj* **outdoor**, hiking, rambling, cross-country, heavy-duty, tough, hard-wearing [➡ DESCRIBING CLOTHES; 869]

walking boot *type of* **boot** [➡ FOOTWEAR; 871]

walking stick *n* **cane**, stick, bamboo, staff [➡ STICKS, POLES, AND WEDGES; 1254]

walk in on *v* **barge in**, march in, interrupt, intrude, butt in, blunder in [➡ ARRIVE; 12]

walk in the park (*informal*) *n* [➡ EASY WORK; 299]

walk off *v* **turn your back**, walk away, leave, go, quit, abandon ship, desert, walk out [➡ LEAVE AND GO AWAY; 8] *Opposite*: remain

walk off with *v* **steal**, embezzle, pocket, appropriate, take, shoplift, filch (*informal*), lift (*informal*), swipe (*informal*), knock off (*slang*), cop (*slang*), purloin (*formal or humorous*) [➡ STEAL AND ROB; 426]

walk-on *n* **bit part**, cameo, minor part, minor role, nonspeaking part [➡ PERFORMERS; 905]

walk out **1** *v* **leave**, storm out, go off in a huff, flounce out, take yourself off (*informal*) [➡ LEAVE AND GO AWAY; 8] **2** *v* **go on strike**, take industrial action, stop work, down tools (*UK*) [➡ WORK-RELATED ACTIVITIES; 834]

walkout *n* **strike**, stoppage, protest, industrial action (*UK*) [➡ WORK-RELATED ACTIVITIES; 834]

walk out on (*informal*) *v* **leave**, abandon, leave in the lurch, go, desert, ditch (*informal*), throw over (*informal*), dump (*informal*) [➡ REFUSING OR REJECTING RELATIONS; 975]

walk over (*informal*) *v* **defeat**, beat, overpower, trounce, thrash, annihilate (*informal*), cream (*slang*) [➡ BEAT AND DEFEAT; 80]

walkover (*informal*) *n* **easy victory**, child's play, runaway, runaway victory, pushover (*informal*), cakewalk (*informal*), cinch (*informal*), piece of cake (*informal*) [➡ EASY WORK; 299] *Opposite:* challenge

walk through *v* **rehearse**, practice, run through [➡ PREPARE FOR ACTION; 289]

walk-up *type of* **house** [➡ RESIDENTIAL BUILDINGS; 1078]

walkway **1** *n* **path**, footpath, pathway, sidewalk, alley, causeway, catwalk, boardwalk, pavement (*UK*) [➡ PATHWAYS; 1110] **2** *n* **aisle**, corridor, passage, passageway [➡ PATHWAYS; 1110] **3** *type of* **bridge** [➡ BRIDGES, TUNNELS, CROSSINGS, AND JUNCTIONS; 1112]

wall **1** *n* **partition**, divider, screen, panel, bulkhead [➡ WALLS AND PARTITIONS; 1104] **2** *part of* **building** [➡ PARTS OF A BUILDING; 1095]

wallaby *type of* **marsupial** [➡ MARSUPIALS; 992]

wallet *n* **folder**, file, case, holder [➡ CONTAINERS, RECEPTACLES, AND PACKAGING; 1245]

wall flower *type of* **perennial flower** [➡ FLOWERS; 1032]

wallop (*informal*) **1** *v* **thump**, smack, thwack, strike, hit, punch, whack, bang, bump, crack, bash (*informal*), biff (*informal*) [➡ PHYSICAL ATTACK AND PUNISHMENT; 415] **2** *v* **defeat**, beat, shut out, trounce, whip, destroy, cream (*slang*) [➡ BEAT AND DEFEAT; 80] **3** *n* **blow**, thump, bash, smack, thwack, punch, whack, bang, bump, crack, hit, biff (*informal*) [➡ CONTACT: IMPACT; 413] **4** *n* **fizz**, punch, clout, pizazz (*informal*), buzz (*informal*), bang (*informal*) [➡ TREATS; 210]

walloping (*informal*) **1** *n* **beating**, thrashing, hiding (*informal*) [➡ PHYSICAL ATTACK AND PUNISHMENT; 415] **2** *n* **defeat**, drubbing, hiding (*informal*) [➡ BEAT AND DEFEAT; 80] **3** *adj* **huge**, enormous, gigantic, stupendous, massive, mammoth, whopping (*informal*) [➡ LARGE; 1193] **4** *adv* **extremely**, very, tremendously, inordinately, stupendously, breathtakingly, outrageously, massively (*informal*) [➡ TO A GREAT EXTENT; 132]

wallow *v* **flounder**, stumble, lurch, stagger, welter, reel [➡ AIMLESS AND ERRANT MOTION; 343]

wallow in *v* **enjoy**, bask in, revel in, relish, make the most of, take pleasure in, luxuriate in, glory in, exult in, roll about in, immerse yourself in, indulge in, delight in [➡ LIKE, LOVE, VALUE, AND ENJOY; 578]

wallpaper **1** *n* **wall covering**, paper, lining paper (*UK*) [➡ COVERS AND COATINGS; 1246] **2** *type of* **computer feature** [➡ COMPUTERS AND COMPUTING; 1127]

wall-to-wall (*informal*) *adj* **omnipresent**, all-pervasive, nonstop, ceaseless, never-ending, unending, endless, continuous [➡ PRESENT AND AVAILABLE; 11]

walnut **1** *type of* **nut** [➡ NUTS; 1185] **2** *type of* **brown** [➡ COLORS; 1224]

walrus *type of* **marine mammal** [➡ MARINE MAMMALS; 987]

walrus mustache *n* [➡ FACIAL HAIR; 489]

waltz **1** *type of* **dance** [➡ DANCE; 903] **2** *type of* **musical form** [➡ MUSIC, SONGS, AND SINGING; 907] **3** *n* (*informal*) **snap**, cinch (*informal*), piece of cake (*informal*), breeze (*informal*), pushover (*informal*), walkaway (*informal*), walkover (*informal*) [➡ EASY WORK; 299] **4** *v* **walk**, stroll, swan, breeze, saunter [➡ PROCEED AND GO; 305] **5** *v* **romp**, sail, steam, whizz, cruise, zap (*informal*), zip (*informal*) [➡ MOVE FAST; 313]

wan **1** *adj* **pallid**, ashen, ashy, drawn, washed-out, white, gray, waxen, pale [➡ COMPLEXION; 480] **2** *adj* **listless**, feeble, weak, down, depressed, low [➡ UNFIT AND WEAK; 739] *Opposite:* strong

wand *n* **baton**, stick, rod, pointer [➡ STICKS, POLES, AND WEDGES; 1254]

wander **1** *v* **stroll**, meander, walk, ramble, roam, amble, mosey (*informal*), mooch (*slang*) [➡ MOVE SLOWLY; 314] **2** *v* **drift**, stray, digress, lose the point, lose the thread, lose concentration, go off on a tangent, deviate [➡ NOT PAY ATTENTION; 764] **3** *n* **walk**, stroll, ramble, mosey (*informal*), mooch (*slang*) [➡ PROCEED AND GO; 305]

wander away *v* [➡ LEAVE AND GO AWAY; 8]

wanderer *n* **nomad**, vagrant, itinerant, traveler, rover, rambler, drifter, rolling stone, tramp, hobo [➡ TRAVEL: TRAVELERS AND WALKERS; 319]

wandering *adj* **itinerant**, nomadic, peripatetic, traveling, drifting, rootless, roving [➡ AIMLESS AND ERRANT MOTION; 343] *Opposite:* settled

wanderlust *n* **desire to travel**, itchy feet, travel bug [➡ DESIRE AND WANT; 579]

wander off *v* [➡ LEAVE AND GO AWAY; 8]

wane *v* **diminish**, decrease, decline, get smaller, fade, disappear, vanish [➡ DISAPPEAR; 4] *Opposite:* wax (*literary*)

wangle (*informal*) *v* **engineer**, contrive, obtain, get (*informal*), fix (*informal*), swing (*informal*), finagle (*informal*) [➡ OBTAIN POSSESSION BY PERSUASION; 457]

waning *adj* **fading**, declining, weakening, diminishing, disappearing, vanishing [➡ CEASE TO EXIST; 22] *Opposite:* increasing

wannabe (*informal*) **1** *n* **hopeful**, aspirant, imitator, clone, camp follower, fellow traveler, copycat (*informal*), would-be (*informal*) [➡ SUPPORTERS, PROTECTORS, AND COMPATRIOTS; 970] **2** *adj* **aspiring**, aspirational, would-be, hopeful, budding, potential, embryonic [➡ POSITIVE IMPATIENCE, ENTHUSIASM, AND ALERTNESS; 537]

wanness *n* [➡ COMPLEXION; 480]

want 1 *v* **desire**, wish for, long for, crave, covet, yearn for, hanker after, be after, be looking for, hope for, aspire [➡ DESIRE AND WANT; 579] 2 *v* **need**, require, lack, be short of, miss [➡ NEED AND REQUIRE; 464] 3 *n* **lack**, absence, shortage, scarcity, dearth, deficiency [➡ NONEXISTENCE; 24] 4 *n* **poverty**, famine, hunger, need, neediness [➡ POVERTY AND POOR; 892]

Compare and Contrast: *want, desire, wish, long for, yearn, covet, crave*

CORE MEANING: to seek to have, do, or achieve something

want to feel a need or desire for something; *desire* to want something very strongly; *wish* to have a strong, sometimes unrealistic, desire to have or to do something; *long for* to have a strong desire for somebody or something, especially something difficult to achieve; *yearn* to want something very much, especially with a feeling of sadness when it seems unlikely that it can ever be obtained; *covet* to have a strong desire to possess something that belongs to somebody else, or (*formal*) to want something very much; *crave* to want something very much, especially when this desire is physical.

See Compare and Contrast at **lack**.

want ad (*informal*) *n* [➡ ADVERTISING AND PUBLICITY; 604]

wanted *adj* **required**, sought, sought after, hunted, desired, needed [➡ POPULAR AND WANTED; 220]

wanting 1 *adj* **deficient**, inadequate, imperfect, not good enough, not up to standard, defective, below par, not up to scratch (*informal*) [➡ INAPPROPRIATE AND UNSUITABLE; 224] *Opposite:* adequate 2 *prep* **without**, lacking, in need of, short of, minus, sans (*literary or humorous*) [➡ LACK OF POSSESSION; 445]

wanton 1 *adj* **gratuitous**, motiveless, meaningless, reckless, needless, unjustifiable, willful, uncalled-for, unprovoked [➡ UNIMPORTANT AND UNNECESSARY; 238] *Opposite:* justifiable 2 *adj* **immoral**, immodest, abandoned, licentious, lustful, impious, dissipated, dissolute, shameless [➡ MORALLY BAD OR IMPROPER; 775] *Opposite:* restrained 3 *adj* **malevolent**, malicious, cruel, vicious, nasty, maleficent [➡ SELFISH AND UNKIND; 505] *Opposite:* benign 4 *adj* **excessive**, extravagant, unrestrained, heedless, unreasonable [➡ TOO MUCH; 119] *Opposite:* restrained

wantonness *n* **depravity**, debauchery, immorality, shamelessness, impiety, dissipation, dissoluteness, licentiousness (*formal*) [➡ MORALLY BAD OR IMPROPER; 775] *Opposite:* restraint

wants *n* **needs**, requirements, desires, requests, wishes [➡ DESIRE AND WANT; 579]

WAP 1 *n* [➡ THE INTERNET; 1128] 2 *type of* **telecommunications equipment** [➡ TELECOMMUNICATIONS; 1130]

wapiti *type of* **deer or antelope** [➡ DEER AND ANTELOPES; 981]

war 1 *n* **conflict**, warfare, hostilities, fighting, confrontation, combat, action [➡ WARFARE AND WAR; 830] *Opposite:* peace 2 *n* **campaign**, battle, struggle, crusade [➡ AGGRESSIVE EVENTS; 39] 3 *n* **competition**, rivalry, feud, battle, struggle [➡ DISHARMONY; 156]

See Compare and Contrast at **fight**.

warble 1 *v* **sing**, trill, pipe up, chirrup, sing out [➡ SOUND EMISSION BY ANIMALS OR BIRDS; 364] 2 *type of* **bird sound** [➡ SOUNDS MADE BY BIRDS; 1263]

warbler *type of* **songbird** [➡ SONGBIRDS; 1003]

war cry *n* **battle cry**, rallying call, call to arms [➡ SOUNDS MADE BY PEOPLE; 1262]

ward *type of* **room in public buildings** [➡ TYPES OF ROOMS; 1097]

warden *n* **custodian**, curator, keeper, steward, superintendent, supervisor, guardian [➡ PEOPLE WHO GUARD AND PROTECT; 846]

warder (*UK*) 1 *n* **prison officer**, warden, jailer, custodian, guard, turnkey (*archaic*) [➡ PEOPLE WHO GUARD AND PROTECT; 846] 2 *n* **guard**, custodian, keeper, monitor, sentry, sentinel [➡ PEOPLE WHO GUARD AND PROTECT; 846]

ward off *v* **defend against**, protect against, deflect, hold off, keep at bay, fend off, fight off, discourage [➡ AVOID OR ESCAPE CONTACT; 418]

wardrobe 1 *n* **clothes**, clothing, apparel, gear (*informal*), attire (*formal*) [➡ CLOTHES AND ACCESSORIES; 864] 2 *type of* **cabinet** [➡ FURNITURE; 858]

warehouse 1 *type of* **retail outlet** [➡ RETAIL OUTLETS; 1083] 2 *type of* **storage space** [➡ STORES AND STORAGE BUILDINGS; 1088]

wares *n* **goods**, merchandise, produce, products, commodities, stuff [➡ BUSINESS PRODUCTS; 795]

warfare 1 *n* **fighting**, conflict, combat, war [➡ WARFARE AND WAR; 830] 2 *n* **rivalry**, feud, competition, contest, struggle [➡ DISHARMONY; 156]

warhead *type of* **explosive weapon** [➡ EXPLOSIVES; 1155]

warhorse 1 *n* **campaigner**, warrior, stalwart, old hand, master, veteran [➡ TALENTED OR INTELLIGENT PEOPLE; 528] 2 *type of* **horse** [➡ HORSES; 985]

wariness *n* **caution**, suspicion, care, circumspection, guardedness, caginess (*informal*) [➡ FEELINGS ABOUT THE FUTURE; 533] *Opposite:* recklessness

warlike 1 *adj* **belligerent**, aggressive, bellicose, confrontational, hostile, pugnacious [➡ AGGRESSIVE AND BELLIGERENT; 518] *Opposite:* friendly 2 *adj* **martial**, military, militaristic, warring, war [➡ MILITARY; 829]

warlock *n* **sorcerer**, wizard, enchanter, witch, necromancer (*literary*) [➡ PEOPLE WITH SUPERNATURAL POWERS; 788]

warlord *n* **military leader**, general, chieftain, guerrilla leader, commander [➡ MILITARY PERSONNEL; 828]

warm 1 *adj* **temperate**, tepid, balmy, hot, lukewarm [➡ HOT WEATHER; 1050] *Opposite:* cool 2 *adj* **kind**, kindly, warm-hearted, kindhearted, friendly, cordial, convivial, genial, hospitable, welcoming, congenial, amiable, affectionate, loving, tender [➡ FRIENDLINESS AND SOCIABILITY; 494] *Opposite:* unfriendly 3 *adj* **cozy**, inviting, restful, cheerful, cheery, snug, welcoming [➡ PHYSICALLY PLEASANT; 186] *Opposite:* unwelcoming 4 *adj* **sincere**, heartfelt, deep, earnest, wholehearted [➡ HONEST AND RELIABLE; 502] 5 *adj* **lively**, passionate, ardent, fiery, enthusiastic, zealous [➡ APPRECIATION AND GRATITUDE; 535] *Opposite:* cool 6 *v* **take to**, become fond of, take a liking to, take a fancy to, get along with, take a shine to (*informal*), hit it off (*informal*), get on with (*UK*) [➡ LIKE, LOVE,

VALUE, AND ENJOY; 578] *Opposite*: cool off **7** v **heat**, heat up, reheat, warm up, melt, thaw, thaw out [➡ CHANGE OF TEMPERATURE; 386] *Opposite*: cool **8** v **become enthusiastic about**, get going on, get fired up about, get excited, become enthused, get stirred up [➡ CHANGE OF MOOD AND COMPOSURE; 580] **9** n **warmth**, warmness, heat [➡ TEMPERATURE: MEDIUM; 1230] *Opposite*: cold

warm-blooded *adj* **passionate**, impetuous, enthusiastic, ardent, emotional, excitable, spirited [➡ ENERGY AND ENTHUSIASM; 496] *Opposite*: cold-blooded

war memorial *n* [➡ MONUMENTS; 1092]

warm front *n* [➡ HOT WEATHER; 1050]

warm-hearted *adj* **kindly**, tender, kind, sympathetic, affectionate, loving, compassionate, kindhearted [➡ GENEROSITY AND KINDNESS; 495] *Opposite*: cold-hearted

warm-heartedness *n* **tenderness**, kindness, sympathy, affection, love, compassion, kindheartedness [➡ GENEROSITY AND KINDNESS; 495] *Opposite*: cold-heartedness

warmly **1** *adv* **lovingly**, tenderly, kindly, sincerely, affectionately [➡ GENEROSITY AND KINDNESS; 495] **2** *adv* **cordially**, genially, in a friendly way, amiably [➡ FRIENDLINESS AND SOCIABILITY; 494] **3** *adv* **ardently**, enthusiastically, favorably, passionately, eagerly, with enthusiasm, with eagerness, with fervor [➡ ENTHUSIASTIC AND INQUISITIVE; 628] *Opposite*: apathetically

warmness **1** *n* **warmth**, heat, hotness [➡ TEMPERATURE: MEDIUM; 1230] *Opposite*: coldness **2** *n* **balminess**, temperateness, high temperature [➡ HOT WEATHER; 1050] *Opposite*: coldness **3** *n* **warm-heartedness**, kindheartedness, kindness, friendliness, affection, cordiality, tenderness [➡ GENEROSITY AND KINDNESS; 495] *Opposite*: cold-heartedness **4** *n* **eagerness**, passion, enthusiasm, ardor, fervor [➡ POSITIVE IMPATIENCE, ENTHUSIASM, AND ALERTNESS; 537] *Opposite*: apathy

warmonger *n* **hawk**, belligerent, jingo, jingoist, aggressor, saber-rattler [➡ UNCOOPERATIVE OR REBELLIOUS PEOPLE; 566] *Opposite*: peacemaker

warmongering *n* **saber rattling**, belligerence, aggression, jingoism, hawkishness [➡ REBELLIOUSNESS AND DISOBEDIENCE; 565] *Opposite*: peacemaking

warmth **1** *n* **warmness**, heat, hotness [➡ HOT WEATHER; 1050] *Opposite*: cold **2** *n* **balminess**, temperateness, warmness [➡ TEMPERATURE: MEDIUM; 1230] *Opposite*: coldness **3** *n* **friendliness**, cordiality, warm-heartedness, kindheartedness, warmness, affection, tenderness, love, kindness [➡ FRIENDLINESS AND SOCIABILITY; 494] *Opposite*: cold-heartedness **4** *n* **enthusiasm**, eagerness, earnestness, ardor, fervor, warmness, passion [➡ POSITIVE IMPATIENCE, ENTHUSIASM, AND ALERTNESS; 537] *Opposite*: apathy

warm through (*UK*) v [➡ MEAL PREPARATION; 354]

warm to v [➡ LIKE, LOVE, VALUE, AND ENJOY; 578]

warm up **1** v **warm**, heat, heat up, reheat, warm over, melt, thaw, thaw out, warm through (*UK*) [➡ CHANGE OF TEMPERATURE; 386] *Opposite*: cool off **2** v **limber up**, loosen up, get loose, stretch [➡ PREPARE FOR ACTION; 289] *Opposite*: cool off

warm-up *n* **exercises**, limbering up, loosening up, preparation [➡ PREPARATORY EVENTS; 57]

warm weather *n* [➡ HOT WEATHER; 1050]

warn **1** v **caution**, advise, inform, notify, tell, tip off, counsel (*formal or literary*) [➡ ADVISE AND WARN; 613] **2** v **alert**,

forewarn, advise, tell, notify, give notice [➡ ADVISE AND WARN; 613]

warning **1** *n* **notice**, caution, caveat, word of warning, heads-up, advice, admonition, forewarning, counsel (*formal or literary*) [➡ ADVICE; 689] **2** *n* **threat**, indication, portent, wakeup call, forewarning, sign, omen [➡ INDICATIONS, SIGNS, AND WARNINGS; 68] **3** *adj* **cautionary**, threatening, cautioning [➡ ADVISE AND WARN; 613]

warn off v **deter**, discourage, dissuade, put off, scare off, frighten off [➡ ADVISE AND WARN; 613]

war of words *n* **argument**, row, slinging match, disagreement, fight, slanging match (*UK*) [➡ ARGUMENTS; 47]

warp **1** v **distort**, twist, deform, bend, buckle, go out of shape [➡ CHANGE OF SHAPE; 385] *Opposite*: straighten **2** v **change**, pervert, damage, distort, misrepresent, confuse, bend, twist [➡ FALSIFY AND CHEAT; 176] **3** *n* **twist**, bend, distortion, deviation, alteration, change [➡ CHANGE OF SHAPE; 385]

warped **1** *adj* **misshapen**, distorted, deformed, twisted, bent, out of shape [➡ IN BAD REPAIR; 1234] **2** *adj* **changed**, damaged, distorted, misrepresented, confused, bent, perverted, twisted [➡ BIZARRE AND PECULIAR; 257] **3** *adj* **partial**, biased, one-sided, prejudiced, skewed [➡ INCORRECT AND ERRONEOUS; 222] *Opposite*: impartial

warrant **1** *n* **authorization**, license, permit, authority, certification [➡ OFFICIAL DOCUMENTS; 586] **2** v **merit**, deserve, necessitate, call for, demand, justify [➡ NEED AND REQUIRE; 464] **3** v **guarantee**, affirm, certify, secure, assure, insure [➡ PROMISE AND ASSURE; 684]

warranty *n* **guarantee**, contract, pledge, assurance [➡ OFFICIAL DOCUMENTS; 586]

war-ravaged *adj* [➡ IN BAD REPAIR; 1234]

warren **1** *n* **hole**, earth, habitat, burrow, lair, den [➡ ANIMAL OR BIRD ACCOMMODATIONS; 1079] **2** *n* **maze**, labyrinth, catacomb [➡ DISORDER AND CHAOS; 245]

warring *adj* **belligerent**, combatant, fighting, sparring, opposing, contending, aggressive [➡ AGGRESSIVE AND BELLIGERENT; 518] *Opposite*: friendly

warrior *n* **soldier**, fighter, combatant, trooper [➡ MILITARY PERSONNEL; 828]

war-scarred *adj* [➡ IN BAD REPAIR; 1234]

warship *type of* **military vessel** [➡ SHIPS AND BOATS; 1150]

wart *n* **lump**, growth, verruca [➡ CONDITIONS AFFECTING THE SKIN; 721]

wart hog *type of* **large mammal** [➡ LARGE MAMMALS; 986]

war-torn *adj* **war-ravaged**, frontline, battle-weary, war-scarred, battle-scarred, battle-damaged, bomb-damaged, devastated, disrupted [➡ IN BAD REPAIR; 1234] *Opposite*: peaceful

warts and all *adv* [➡ ALL; 128]

wary *adj* **watchful**, cautious, suspicious, distrustful, mistrustful, chary, guarded, circumspect, careful [➡ CAUTIOUS AND CAREFUL; 282] *Opposite*: careless

See Compare and Contrast at **cautious**.

wasabi *type of* **seasonings, sauces, and dips** [➡ SEASONINGS AND SAUCES; 1174]

wash **1** *v* **clean**, bathe, rinse, sponge down, wash down, cleanse, sluice, swab, shampoo, launder [➡ CLEAN AND POLISH; 403] **2** *v* **erode**, wash away, carry away, bear away, sweep away [➡ DELETE AND ERASE; 339] **3** *v* **bathe**, bath, clean up, wash up [➡ CLEAN AND POLISH; 403] **4** *v* **flow over**, splash, lap, swish, pound, slap, lave (*archaic*) [➡ TAKE UP A NEW POSITION; 312] **5** *n* **stain**, tint, rinse, suffusion, coloring [➡ DYES AND COLORANTS; 1270] **6** *n* **shower**, shampoo, sponge, rinse, wash-down, launder, swab, bath [➡ CLEAN AND POLISH; 403] **7** *n* **washing**, layer, film, coat, overlay, coating [➡ COVERS AND COATINGS; 1246]

washable *adj* **easy-care**, colorfast, preshrunk, launderable, unfading, wash-and-wear, permanent-press, noniron (*UK*) [➡ DESCRIBING CLOTHES; 869]

wash-and-wear *adj* [➡ DESCRIBING CLOTHES; 869]

washbasin *n* **hand basin**, basin, bowl, sink, washbowl [➡ FIXTURES; 859]

washbowl *n* **washbasin**, basin, sink, hand basin [➡ FIXTURES; 859]

wash down *v* **clean**, rinse, sluice, sponge down, hose down, wash [➡ CLEAN AND POLISH; 403]

washed-out **1** *adj* **exhausted**, tired out, used up, drained, all in, done in (*informal*), wasted (*slang*), beat (*slang*) [➡ TIRED, ASLEEP, AND UNCONSCIOUS; 738] *Opposite*: energetic **2** *adj* **wan**, gray, pallid, ashen, ashy, drawn, white, pale [➡ COMPLEXION; 480]

washed-up (*informal*) *adj* **unsuccessful**, finished, defeated, through, failed, has been, manqué, done for (*informal*) [➡ UNSUCCESSFUL AND UNPROMISING; 76] *Opposite*: successful

washer *n* **seal**, gasket, liner, ring, lining [➡ FASTENERS, LINKS, AND NETWORKS; 1247]

wash-hand basin *type of* **plumbing fixtures** [➡ FIXTURES; 859]

washing **1** *n* **laundry**, dirty linen, dirty clothes [➡ CLOTHES AND ACCESSORIES; 864] **2** *n* **wash**, weekly wash, clothes wash [➡ CLOTHES AND ACCESSORIES; 864] **3** *n* **coat**, coating, film, layer, overlay, wash [➡ COVERS AND COATINGS; 1246]

washing machine *type of* **appliance** [➡ HOUSEHOLD APPLIANCES; 1117]

wash out *v* **wash**, rinse, flush, swill, hose [➡ CLEAN AND POLISH; 403]

washout (*informal*) *n* **failure**, dead loss, disaster, disappointment, bomb (*informal*), flop (*informal*) [➡ FAILURE; 77] *Opposite*: success

wash over *v* **flow over**, engulf, sweep over, overwhelm, come over, swamp, overflow [➡ HAPPEN TO SOMEBODY; 30]

washroom *n* **restroom**, bathroom, toilet, lavatory, powder room, men's room, ladies' room, gents (*UK*), ladies (*UK*) [➡ TYPES OF ROOMS; 1097]

wash your hands of *v* **disown**, abandon, refuse to have anything to do with, absolve yourself, ignore, reject [➡ NOT PAY ATTENTION; 764]

wasp *type of* **flying insect** [➡ FLYING INSECTS; 1013]

waspish **1** *adj* **irritable**, touchy, irascible, cantankerous, peevish, waspy, tetchy (*informal*) [➡ IRRITATION AND ANGER; 541] *Opposite*: affable **2** *adj* **malignant**, spiteful, malicious, nasty, vindictive, venomous, waspy [➡ RUDE AND HOSTILE; 625] *Opposite*: friendly

waspishness **1** *n* **irritability**, touchiness, irascibility, cantankerousness, peevishness, bad temper, tetchiness (*informal*) [➡ IRRITATION AND ANGER; 541] *Opposite*: affability **2** *n* **spitefulness**, spite, malice, maliciousness, nastiness, vindictiveness, venomousness, venom [➡ RUDE AND HOSTILE; 625] *Opposite*: friendliness

waspy **1** *see* **waspish** **2** *see* **waspish**

wastage *n* **waste**, surplus, excess, leftovers [➡ REMAINDER AND REMAINDERS; 125]

waste **1** *v* **squander**, fritter away, misuse, dissipate, throw away, blow (*slang*) [➡ USE UP AND WASTE; 474] *Opposite*: save **2** *v* **ravage**, devastate, ruin, spoil, despoil, destroy [➡ DESTRUCTION AND DEMOLITION; 359] **3** *v* (*slang*) **kill**, murder, assassinate, execute, dispatch, bump off (*slang*) [➡ KILL; 923] **4** *v* **atrophy**, wither, become emaciated, waste away, weaken [➡ GET WORSE; 381] *Opposite*: strengthen **5** *n* **litter**, garbage, trash, gray water, rubbish (*UK*) [➡ JUNK AND USELESS OBJECTS; 1249] **6** *adj* **excess**, surplus, unwanted, discarded, remaining, spare, leftover, unused [➡ MORE AND EXCESS; 124] **7** *adj* **uncultivated**, barren, bare, fallow [➡ EMPTY; 1238] *Opposite*: cultivated

waste away *v* **wither**, waste, atrophy, become emaciated, weaken [➡ GET WORSE; 381] *Opposite*: strengthen

wastebasket *n* [➡ CONTAINERS, RECEPTACLES, AND PACKAGING; 1245]

waste bin (*UK*) *n* [➡ CONTAINERS, RECEPTACLES, AND PACKAGING; 1245]

wasted **1** *adj* (*slang*) **exhausted**, tired, worn out, shattered, tired out, washed out, done in (*informal*) [➡ TIRED, ASLEEP, AND UNCONSCIOUS; 738] *Opposite*: fresh **2** *adj* **missed**, misused, lost, unexploited, unused, squandered [➡ WASTEFUL AND UNECONOMICAL; 246] **3** *adj* **ravaged**, withered, shrunken, atrophied, emaciated, thin, cadaverous [➡ BUILD; 477] *Opposite*: healthy **4** *adj* **futile**, fruitless, unproductive, worthless, useless, pointless, needless [➡ UNIMPORTANT AND UNNECESSARY; 238] *Opposite*: worthwhile

wasteful *adj* **extravagant**, careless, uneconomical, profligate, lavish, inefficient, spendthrift, improvident [➡ WASTEFUL AND UNECONOMICAL; 246] *Opposite*: frugal

wastefulness *n* **extravagance**, carelessness, profligacy, improvidence, lavishness, squandering [➡ WASTEFUL AND UNECONOMICAL; 246] *Opposite*: frugality

wasteland *n* **wilds**, wilderness, desert, badlands [➡ DESERTS, PLAINS, AND MOORLAND; 1045]

wastepaper basket *n* [➡ CONTAINERS, RECEPTACLES, AND PACKAGING; 1245]

wastepaper bin (*UK*) *n* [➡ CONTAINERS, RECEPTACLES, AND PACKAGING; 1245]

waste pipe *n* [➡ WATERCOURSES; 1111]

waste product *n* [➡ UNPLEASANT, DIRTY, AND TOXIC SUBSTANCES; 1268]

waster *n* [➡ LAZY OR UNSUCCESSFUL PEOPLE; 948]

wastes n wilds, wilderness, wastelands [➡DESERTS, PLAINS, AND MOORLAND; 1045]

wasting away adj [➡UNFIT AND WEAK; 739]

wastrel n [➡LAZY OR UNSUCCESSFUL PEOPLE; 948]

watch 1 type of clock [➡CLOCKS AND TIMERS; 1126] **2** n guard, lookout, sentry, sentinel, watchdog [➡PEOPLE WHO GUARD AND PROTECT; 846] **3** (literary) type of flock [➡GROUPS OF BIRDS; 1007] **4** v observe, look at, stare at, gaze at, survey, view, examine, scrutinize, inspect [➡LOOKING AND LOOKS; 700] Opposite: ignore **5** v pay attention to, beware, mind, be cautious about, consider, keep an eye on, attend to [➡PAY ATTENTION; 765] **6** v spy on, stalk, keep under observation, keep an eye on, keep under surveillance [➡ACCOMPANY AND FOLLOW; 337] **7** v look after, keep an eye on, mind, guard, watch over, take care of [➡TAKE CARE OF AND SPOIL; 300] Opposite: neglect

watchdog n ombudsman, supervisory body, regulator, overseer [➡BUSINESS ENTERPRISES AND RELATED BODIES; 792]

watcher n observer, onlooker, spectator, viewer, witness [➡ONLOOKERS AND SPECTATORS; 701]

watchful adj observant, attentive, alert, vigilant, on the alert, on the lookout [➡POSITIVE IMPATIENCE, ENTHUSIASM, AND ALERTNESS; 537] Opposite: inattentive

watchfulness n alertness, attention, vigilance, caution, care [➡POSITIVE INTELLECTUAL CHARACTERISTICS; 524] Opposite: inattentiveness

watchman n night watchman, guard, security guard, custodian, caretaker [➡PEOPLE WHO GUARD AND PROTECT; 846]

watch out 1 v be careful, look out, be alert, be wary, take care, be cautious, take heed, be watchful, pay attention, mind out (UK) [➡PAY ATTENTION; 765] **2** v look out, look, wait, watch, be on the lookout, keep your eyes open, be vigilant, keep a sharp lookout [➡LOOKING AND LOOKS; 700]

watch over v supervise, look after, keep an eye on, guard, mind, watch [➡TAKE CARE OF AND SPOIL; 300] Opposite: neglect

watchtower n lookout tower, lookout post, observation tower, crow's nest [➡TOWERS; 1099]

watchword n motto, slogan, maxim, byword, catch phrase, saying [➡THE SPOKEN WORD; 671]

watch your step v be careful, take care, watch out, look out, pay attention, be cautious, mind your Ps and Qs, mind out (UK) [➡PAY ATTENTION; 765]

watch your weight v be on a diet, diet, slim, watch what you eat, cut down, count calories, cut back, watch your waistline, reduce [➡EAT AND NOT EAT; 710]

water 1 n liquid, rainwater, seawater, mineral water, tap water, bath water, H_2O [➡LIQUIDS; 1269] **2** v soak, spray, irrigate, drench, sprinkle, hose, hose down, wet, dampen [➡SOFTEN, LIQUEFY, AND DAMPEN; 388] **3** v fill with tears, stream, run, fill up, well [➡LIQUID EMISSION; 370]

waterbed type of bed [➡FURNITURE; 858]

water beetle type of beetle [➡BEETLES AND WEEVILS; 1016]

water bird n waterfowl, freshwater bird, duck [➡FRESHWATER BIRDS; 1000]

waterborne 1 adj aquatic, floating, marine, riverine [➡THE SEAS, OCEANS, AND SHORES; 1041] **2** adj transmissible, contagious, catching [➡SICKNESS; 729]

watercolorist n [➡ARTISTS; 900]

watercourse 1 n ditch, conduit, drain, culvert [➡WATERCOURSES; 1111] **2** n waterway, channel, stream, river, rivulet, canal, brook (literary) [➡RIVERS, LAKES, AND STREAMS; 1042]

watercress type of salad vegetable [➡FRUIT AND VEGETABLES; 1176]

water down 1 v dilute, thin down, weaken, attenuate [➡CHANGE OF INTENSITY: LESS; 395] Opposite: thicken **2** v soften, reduce, moderate, mitigate, regulate, tone down, temper [➡CHANGE OF INTENSITY: LESS; 395] Opposite: beef up (informal)

watered-down 1 adj diluted, dilute, thin, weak, insipid, bland, watery, wishy-washy (informal) [➡WEAKNESS; 241] Opposite: concentrated **2** adj moderated, weakened, vapid, qualified, toned-down, diluted [➡WEAKNESS; 241] Opposite: unqualified

waterfall n cascade, cataract, falls, weir, force (UK) [➡RIVERS, LAKES, AND STREAMS; 1042]

water feature part of garden [➡GARDENS; 1074]

water flea type of crustacean [➡AQUATIC INVERTEBRATES; 1022]

waterfowl 1 n water bird, freshwater bird, duck [➡FRESHWATER BIRDS; 1000] **2** type of fowl [➡FOOD BIRDS; 999]

waterfront n harbor, lakefront, oceanfront, seafront, water's edge, riverside [➡THE SEAS, OCEANS, AND SHORES; 1041]

water garden type of garden [➡GARDENS; 1074]

water hole n oasis, pool, pond, water source, spring, watering hole, wallow [➡RIVERS, LAKES, AND STREAMS; 1042]

watering hole n oasis, pool, pond, water hole, wallow, water source, spring [➡RIVERS, LAKES, AND STREAMS; 1042]

waterless adj dry, arid, parched, dehydrated [➡DRY; 1242]

waterlessness n [➡DRY; 1242]

water line 1 n load line, Plimsoll line, Plimsoll mark, watermark [➡SYMBOLS, SIGNS, AND NUMBERS; 596] **2** n tideline, tidemark, watermark, high watermark, floodmark [➡THE SEAS, OCEANS, AND SHORES; 1041]

waterlogged adj sodden, sopping, drenched, wet, soaking, saturated, soaked [➡WET; 1240] Opposite: dry

watermark 1 n mark, imprint, logo, emblem [➡DRAWINGS, CHARTS, AND TABLES; 594] **2** n water line, load line, Plimsoll line, Plimsoll mark [➡SYMBOLS, SIGNS, AND NUMBERS; 596] **3** n tideline, tidemark, water line, high watermark, floodmark [➡THE SEAS, OCEANS, AND SHORES; 1041]

watermelon type of fruit [➡FRUIT AND VEGETABLES; 1176]

water mill type of factory [➡INDUSTRIAL BUILDINGS; 1087]

water moccasin type of poisonous snake [➡SNAKES; 995]

water pipe n [➡WATERCOURSES; 1111]

waterproof adj water-resistant, rainproof, watertight, impermeable [➡IN GOOD REPAIR; 1232] Opposite: permeable

waterproofed *adj* [➡ IN GOOD REPAIR; 1232]

waterproof jacket *type of* **jacket** [➡ GARMENTS AND OUTFITS; 865]

water-resistant *adj* [➡ IN GOOD REPAIR; 1232]

watershed *n* **turning point**, defining moment, breaking point, seminal moment, crisis, crunch [➡ DECISIVE MOMENTS; 44]

waterside 1 *n* **riverbank**, shore, bank, water's edge, waterfront, oceanfront, seaside, seafront, beach, sea shore, shoreline, lakeside, riverside, quayside, lakefront [➡ THE SEAS, OCEANS, AND SHORES; 1041] 2 *adj* **waterfront**, beachfront, seaside, lakeside, riverside, littoral [➡ THE SEAS, OCEANS, AND SHORES; 1041]

water snake *type of* **nonpoisonous snake** [➡ SNAKES; 995]

water spider *type of* **arachnid** [➡ ARACHNIDS; 1018]

watertight 1 *adj* **sealed**, waterproof, impermeable, rainproof [➡ IN GOOD REPAIR; 1232] *Opposite*: permeable 2 *adj* **incontrovertible**, unassailable, sound, firm, irrefutable, indisputable [➡ CERTAIN; 174] *Opposite*: weak

water tower *type of* **storage space** [➡ STORES AND STORAGE BUILDINGS; 1088]

waterway *n* **watercourse**, canal, river, channel, stream, shipping canal [➡ RIVERS, LAKES, AND STREAMS; 1042]

waterworks *n* **tears**, crying, weeping, sobbing, blubbering (*informal*) [➡ CRYING; 650]

watery 1 *adj* **watered-down**, thin, weak, runny, dilute, diluted [➡ FLUID AND NONSOLID; 1213] *Opposite*: thick 2 *adj* **wet**, soggy, squelchy, boggy, moist, waterlogged [➡ WET; 1240] *Opposite*: dry 3 *adj* **feeble**, weak, faint, wan, hazy, dim, pale [➡ WEAKNESS; 241] *Opposite*: forceful 4 *adj* **bland**, tasteless, insipid, weak, diluted, dilute, watered-down [➡ TASTE; 703] *Opposite*: strong

watt *type of* **SI unit** [➡ SIZE AND DIMENSIONS; 1192]

wave 1 *v* **gesticulate**, gesture, signal, beckon [➡ GESTURES AND GESTICULATION; 653] 2 *v* **brandish**, flourish, wield, wag, shake, flail [➡ MOVE SOMETHING: ON THE SPOT; 336] 3 *v* **flutter**, flap, sway, undulate, move to and fro [➡ BOUNCE, UNDULATE, AND VIBRATE; 308] 4 *n* **breaker**, roller, dumper, ripple, surge, surf, swell [➡ THE SEAS, OCEANS, AND SHORES; 1041] 5 *n* **upsurge**, groundswell, tendency, trend, movement, surge, flood, swell [➡ SUDDEN EVENTS; 52] 6 *n* **gesture**, signal, sign [➡ GESTURES AND GESTICULATION; 653] 7 *n* **rash**, spate, outbreak, epidemic, series, flood, eruption [➡ SUDDEN EVENTS; 52] 8 *n* **current**, surge, impulse, oscillation, undulation [➡ ENERGY; 1161] 9 *n* **curl**, kink, undulation, ringlet [➡ ROUNDED SHAPE; 1218]

waver 1 *v* **dither**, hesitate, be indecisive, be irresolute, vacillate, falter, shilly-shally, whiffle, whaffle, hem and haw [➡ HESITATE; 272] 2 *v* **tremble**, shake, flutter, flicker, shudder, quiver [➡ PHYSICAL REACTIONS; 316]

See Compare and Contrast at **hesitate**.

wavering 1 *n* **fluctuation**, vacillation, indecisiveness, irresolution, uncertainty, indecision, hesitation, hesitancy [➡ UNCERTAINTY; 559] *Opposite*: resolution 2 *adj* **indecisive**, uncertain, undecided, vacillating, uncommitted, irresolute, of two minds [➡ UNCERTAINTY; 559] *Opposite*: decisive 3 *adj* **flickering**, shaky, trembling, quivering, unsteady, shaking, wobbling [➡ DESCRIBING BODY MOVEMENTS; 288]

waveringly *adv* **indecisively**, uncertainly, irresolutely, vacillatingly, hesitantly, ditheringly, undecidedly [➡ UNCERTAINTY; 559] *Opposite*: decisively

waviness *n* **curliness**, twistiness, crinkliness, unevenness, undulation, corrugation, sinuosity [➡ ROUNDED SHAPE; 1218]

wavy *adj* **curly**, curvy, crimped, undulating [➡ ROUNDED SHAPE; 1218] *Opposite*: straight

wax 1 *n* **beeswax**, candlewax, tallow [➡ SOLIDS; 1274] 2 *v* (*literary*) **expand**, increase, enlarge, get bigger, grow, swell [➡ CHANGE OF SIZE: BIGGER; 392] *Opposite*: wane 3 *v* (*literary*) **become**, turn, grow, start to be [➡ GRADUALLY COME INTO EXISTENCE; 1] 4 *v* **polish**, shine, buff, put a shine on, buff up [➡ CLEAN AND POLISH; 403]

waxen *adj* **pale**, pallid, ashen, ashy, wan, white, washed-out, gray, pasty, sickly, colorless [➡ COMPLEXION; 480]

waxiness *n* **greasiness**, fattiness, slipperiness, shininess, slickness [➡ PHYSICAL TEXTURE; 1222]

waxwork *n* **figure**, manikin, model, effigy, replica, representation [➡ SCULPTURE; 902]

way 1 *n* **method**, means, technique, mode, system, approach, manner, line of attack, tactic, fashion, style [➡ WAYS OF DOING THINGS; 294] 2 *n* **custom**, style, practice, tradition, discipline [➡ WAYS OF DOING THINGS; 294] 3 *n* **route**, road, direction, path [➡ ROADS; 1106] 4 *n* **street**, avenue, lane, path, pathway, track [➡ ROADS; 1106]

wayfarer (*literary*) *n* **traveler**, wanderer, walker, rover, roamer, journeyer, voyager [➡ TRAVEL: TRAVELERS AND WALKERS; 319]

waylay *v* **accost**, intercept, surprise, ambush, lie in wait for, approach, stop, nail, bushwhack (*informal*), buttonhole (*informal*) [➡ INITIATE AND ESTABLISH COMMUNICATION; 680]

way of life *n* **lifestyle**, customs, habits, traditions [➡ LIFESTYLE; 881]

way of thinking *n* **ideas**, beliefs, opinion, philosophy, position, mindset, point of view, viewpoint [➡ POINTS OF VIEW; 767]

way-out 1 *adj* (*informal*) **unusual**, peculiar, odd, strange, weird, eccentric, unconventional, avant-garde, far-out (*slang*) [➡ BIZARRE AND PECULIAR; 257] *Opposite*: conventional 2 *adj* (*dated informal*) **excellent**, wonderful, terrific, fantastic, super (*informal*), great (*informal*) [➡ EXTRAORDINARY: AMAZING; 204]

ways *n* **habits**, conduct, customs, behavior, traditions [➡ TEMPERAMENT AND BEHAVIOR; 492]

ways and means *n* **methods**, approaches, means, devices, systems, procedures [➡ WAYS OF DOING THINGS; 294]

wayside *n* **roadside**, curb, edge, shoulder, hard shoulder (*UK*), verge (*UK*) [➡ PATHWAYS; 1110]

way to go (*informal*) *interj* [➡ COMPLIMENTS; 657]

wayward *adj* **willful**, naughty, unruly, errant, disobedient, badly behaved, strong-willed, rebellious, insubordinate, defiant, contrary, ornery (*informal*) [➡ REBELLIOUSNESS AND DISOBEDIENCE; 565] *Opposite*: well-behaved

See Compare and Contrast at **unruly**.

waywardness *n* **willfulness**, naughtiness, disobedience, unruliness, rebelliousness, defiance, contrariness [➡ REBELLIOUSNESS AND DISOBEDIENCE; 565] *Opposite*: obedience

weak 1 *adj* **feeble**, frail, infirm, debilitated, puny, scrawny, enervated, decrepit (*archaic or humorous*) [➡ BUILD; 477] *Opposite*: robust 2 *adj* **tired**, faint, anemic, exhausted, drained, enervated, limp, floppy, shaky [➡ UNFIT AND WEAK; 739] *Opposite*: strong 3 *adj* **delicate**, insubstantial, flimsy, wispy, fragile [➡ FRAGILE; 1209] *Opposite*: sturdy 4 *adj* **vulnerable**, defenseless, helpless, unprotected, unguarded, exposed [➡ IN DANGER; 237] *Opposite*: invulnerable 5 *adj* **powerless**, ineffectual, toothless, inadequate, feeble, ineffective [➡ WEAKNESS; 241] *Opposite*: powerful 6 *adj* **cowardly**, spineless, faint-hearted, timid, weak-willed, irresolute, easily led, corruptible, vacillating [➡ COWARDICE AND WEAKNESS OF WILL; 508] *Opposite*: bold 7 *adj* **faint**, feeble, low, dim, soft, imperceptible [➡ IMPERCEPTIBLE; 26] *Opposite*: strong 8 *adj* **watery**, diluted, insipid, bland, tasteless, flavorless, watered-down, dilute [➡ FLUID AND NONSOLID; 1213] *Opposite*: strong 9 *adj* **unconvincing**, half-hearted, ineffectual, feeble, implausible, flimsy, uncertain [➡ UNCERTAIN; 175] *Opposite*: convincing

> **Compare and Contrast:** *weak, feeble, frail, infirm, debilitated, decrepit, enervated*
>
> CORE MEANING: lacking physical strength or energy
>
> ***weak*** not physically fit or mentally strong; ***feeble*** lacking physical or mental strength or health; ***frail*** in a physically weak state as a result of illness or advanced years; ***infirm*** lacking strength as a result of long illness or advanced years; ***debilitated*** with strength and energy temporarily diminished as a result of illness or physical exertion; ***decrepit*** (*archaic or humorous*) made weak by advanced years; ***enervated*** made weak and tired by physical or mental exertion.

weaken 1 *v* **grow weaker**, deteriorate, fail, decline, wane, fade, flag, dwindle, wear off, subside, reduce, lessen, diminish, fall off, abate (*formal or literary*) [➡ DISAPPEAR; 4] *Opposite*: strengthen 2 *v* **give in**, cave in, give way, yield, vacillate, hesitate, falter, waver [➡ FORGET, FORGIVE, AND ACCEPT; 748] *Opposite*: stand firm 3 *v* **damage**, destabilize, detract from, shake, undermine [➡ CHANGE OF INTENSITY: LESS; 395] *Opposite*: bolster 4 *v* **dilute**, water down, thin, adulterate [➡ CHANGE OF INTENSITY: LESS; 395] *Opposite*: strengthen 5 *v* **enfeeble**, exhaust, enervate, debilitate, sap, impair [➡ WOUND A PERSON OR ANIMAL; 383] *Opposite*: fortify

weakened *adj* **debilitated**, enfeebled, deteriorated, declining, faded, sapped [➡ WEAKNESS; 241]

weakening *n* **deterioration**, decline, damage, destabilization, undermining, decay [➡ CHANGE OF INTENSITY: LESS; 395] *Opposite*: strengthening

weak-kneed *adj* **spineless**, cowardly, weak, feeble, submissive, weak-willed, cowed, pusillanimous [➡ COWARDICE AND WEAKNESS OF WILL; 508] *Opposite*: courageous

weakly *adv* **feebly**, faintly, dimly, softly, inadequately, half-heartedly, uncertainly, insipidly, blandly, indecisively, unconvincingly, ineffectually [➡ WEAKNESS; 241] *Opposite*: strongly

weakness 1 *n* **flaw**, fault, Achilles' heel, weak spot, weak point, failing, limitation, disadvantage, drawback, difficulty, chink in somebody's armor [➡ FAULTS, FLAWS, AND WEAKNESSES; 251] *Opposite*: strength 2 *n* **frailty**, feebleness, flimsiness, fragility, debility, infirmity [➡ UNFIT AND WEAK; 739] *Opposite*: robustness 3 *n* **powerlessness**, vulnerability, defenselessness, helplessness, impotence [➡ WEAKNESS; 241] *Opposite*: strength 4 *n* **fondness**, liking, taste, soft spot, penchant, partiality, appetite, predilection (*formal*) [➡ LIKE, LOVE, VALUE, AND ENJOY; 578] *Opposite*: dislike 5 *n* **faintness**, softness, dimness, paleness, feebleness [➡ IMPERCEPTIBLE; 26] *Opposite*: strength

weak point *n* **weakness**, Achilles heel, failing, fault, weak spot, limitation, drawback, flaw, chink in somebody's armor [➡ FAULTS, FLAWS, AND WEAKNESSES; 251] *Opposite*: strong point

weak spot *n* **weakness**, Achilles heel, failing, fault, weak point, chink in somebody's armor, flaw, drawback, limitation [➡ FAULTS, FLAWS, AND WEAKNESSES; 251]

weak-willed *adj* **irresolute**, spineless, vacillating, easily led, spiritless, weak, biddable, lily-livered (*dated*) [➡ COWARDICE AND WEAKNESS OF WILL; 508] *Opposite*: resolute

weal *see* **wheal**

wealth 1 *n* **riches**, prosperity, affluence, means, assets, capital, mammon, possessions, material goods, worldly goods, funds, treasure, fortune, resources, holdings [➡ FINANCIAL ASSETS; 462] *Opposite*: poverty 2 *n* **large quantity**, abundance, cornucopia, variety, choice, store, multiplicity, profusion, multitude, plethora, array [➡ MANY, MUCH, LARGE AMOUNT; 117] *Opposite*: dearth

wealthy *adj* **rich**, well-off, well-to-do, affluent, prosperous, moneyed, well-heeled (*informal*), rolling in it (*informal*), flush (*informal*), loaded (*slang*) [➡ WEALTH AND WEALTHY; 891] *Opposite*: poor

weapon 1 *n* **armament**, firearm, missile, gun [➡ WEAPONS; 1154] 2 *n* **defense**, deterrent, big stick [➡ WEAPONS; 1154]

weaponry *n* **arms**, armaments, arsenal, weapons, ordnance, munitions [➡ WEAPONS; 1154]

weapon store *n* **arsenal**, armory, storeroom, store, cache, stockpile, munitions store, stash (*informal*) [➡ STORES AND STORAGE BUILDINGS; 1088]

wear 1 *v* **be dressed in**, dress in, show off, have on, put on, sport (*informal*) [➡ DRESS, WEAR, AND UNDRESS; 868] 2 *v* **display**, bear, carry, hold, show [➡ CAUSE TO APPEAR; 5] 3 *v* **rub**, fray, scuff, grind, wear out, wear through, wear down, wear away, erode [➡ DELETE AND ERASE; 339] 4 *n* **deterioration**, wear and tear, friction, abrasion, scuffing, attrition, erosion, corrosion [➡ IN BAD REPAIR; 1234] 5 *n* **dress**, clothing, clothes, garments, uniform, costume, apparel, garb, attire (*formal*) [➡ CLOTHES AND ACCESSORIES; 864]

wear and tear *n* **deterioration**, wear, attrition, abrasion, erosion, corrosion, wearing away [➡ IN BAD REPAIR; 1234]

wear away *v* **erode**, wear down, wear out, eat at, eat away at [➡ DELETE AND ERASE; 339]

wear down *v* **overcome**, weaken, erode, wear away, wear out, eat away, break down [➡ DELETE AND ERASE; 339]

wearily *adv* **resignedly**, jadedly, with a sigh, despairingly, unenthusiastically, tiredly [➤ WITHOUT ENTHUSIASM; 287] *Opposite*: energetically

weariness *n* **tiredness**, exhaustion, fatigue, lethargy, inertia, apathy, disillusionment, lassitude [➤ LIFELESS, LAZY, AND UNENTHUSIASTIC; 506] *Opposite*: energy

wearing *adj* **tiring**, exhausting, trying, tiresome, wearisome, irksome, taxing, draining [➤ EMOTIONALLY UNPLEASANT AND UPSETTING; 227] *Opposite*: refreshing

wearisome *adj* **tiresome**, boring, tedious, trying, thankless, frustrating, wearying, uninteresting, dreary [➤ EMOTIONALLY UNPLEASANT AND UPSETTING; 227] *Opposite*: stimulating

wear off *v* **weaken**, fade, lessen, diminish, disappear, subside, wane, abate (*formal or literary*) [➤ CHANGE OF INTENSITY: LESS; 395] *Opposite*: increase

wear out **1** *v* **exhaust**, tire out, fatigue, sap, drain, wear down [➤ TIRED, ASLEEP, AND UNCONSCIOUS; 738] *Opposite*: invigorate **2** *v* **use up**, run down, fray, deplete, trash (*informal*) [➤ USE UP AND WASTE; 474] *Opposite*: renovate

weary **1** *adj* **tired**, tired out, exhausted, worn out, fatigued, drained, sleepy, somnolent, drowsy, all in, done in (*informal*), wiped out (*slang*), beat (*slang*), shattered (*UK*) [➤ TIRED, ASLEEP, AND UNCONSCIOUS; 738] *Opposite*: fresh **2** *adj* **disillusioned**, disenchanted, jaded, worn down, fed up (*informal*) [➤ LIFELESS, LAZY, AND UNENTHUSIASTIC; 506] **3** *v* **drain**, sap, exhaust, tire, lose patience [➤ TIRED, ASLEEP, AND UNCONSCIOUS; 738]

wearying *adj* **tiresome**, wearisome, tiring, exhausting, wearing, taxing, trying, draining, arduous [➤ PHYSICALLY UNPLEASANT; 226]

wear yourself out *v* **tire yourself out**, exhaust yourself, run yourself into the ground, overdo it, burn the candle at both ends [➤ OVERDO SOMETHING; 290]

weasel *type of* **small mammal** [➤ SMALL MAMMALS; 990]

weasel word (*informal*) *n* [➤ FIGURES OF SPEECH; 673]

weather **1** *n* **climate**, meteorological conditions, climatic conditions, elements [➤ WEATHER AND CLIMATE; 1049] **2** *v* **endure**, withstand, sit out, ride out, last out, stick out, survive, live through, get through, come through [➤ TOLERATE AND ENDURE; 766] *Opposite*: succumb **3** *v* **erode**, corrode, season, toughen, harden, coarsen, wear away, wear down [➤ WORSEN APPEARANCE; 382]

weather-beaten *adj* **worn**, battered, windswept, weathered, gnarled, wrinkled, craggy, eroded, lined [➤ IN BAD REPAIR; 1234]

weather-bound *adj* **delayed**, held up, fogbound, snowbound, postponed, icebound, stormbound [➤ WINDY AND STORMY WEATHER; 1053]

weathercock *n* **weather vane**, wind indicator, wind gauge, anemometer, windsock [➤ MEASURING DEVICES; 1123]

weathered *adj* **worn**, battered, windswept, weatherbeaten, gnarled, wrinkled, craggy, eroded [➤ IN BAD REPAIR; 1234]

weatherproof *adj* **watertight**, waterproof, rainproof, stormproof, windproof, galeproof, impermeable [➤ IN GOOD REPAIR; 1232]

weather vane *n* **wind indicator**, wind gauge, weathercock, anemometer, windsock [➤ MEASURING DEVICES; 1123]

weave **1** *v* **interlace**, lace, intertwine, plait, knit, entwine, merge, unite, interweave [➤ CRAFTS AND CARVING; 355] *Opposite*: unpick **2** *v* **invent**, create, compose, construct, fabricate, contrive, put together, concoct, make up, spin, tell [➤ CREATION; 346] **3** *v* **zigzag**, stagger, wind, twist, crisscross, snake, meander, lurch, careen [➤ CHANGE DIRECTION OF MOTION; 344] **4** *n* **pile**, texture, nap [➤ TEXTURE; 1220]

weaverbird *type of* **songbird** [➤ SONGBIRDS; 1003]

weaving *type of* **handicraft** [➤ CRAFTS AND CARVING; 355]

web **1** *n* **network**, mesh, net, tissue, grid, matrix, lattice [➤ FASTENERS, LINKS, AND NETWORKS; 1247] **2** *part of* **bird** [➤ PARTS OF A BIRD; 1006]

webbing *n* **lattice**, trellis, netting, network, strap work [➤ FASTENERS, LINKS, AND NETWORKS; 1247]

Web bug *n* [➤ THE INTERNET; 1128]

Webcam *n* [➤ THE INTERNET; 1128]

Webcast *n* [➤ THE INTERNET; 1128]

Web conferencing *n* [➤ THE INTERNET; 1128]

Web-enable *v* [➤ THE INTERNET; 1128]

weber *type of* **SI unit** [➤ SIZE AND DIMENSIONS; 1192]

Web folio *n* [➤ THE INTERNET; 1128]

Webhead (*slang*) *n* [➤ THE INTERNET; 1128]

Webisode *n* [➤ THE INTERNET; 1128]

Webliography *n* [➤ THE INTERNET; 1128]

Weblish *n* [➤ THE INTERNET; 1128]

Web log *n* [➤ THE INTERNET; 1128]

Weblogger *n* [➤ THE INTERNET; 1128]

Webmaster *n* [➤ THE INTERNET; 1128]

Web page *n* [➤ THE INTERNET; 1128]

Webphone *n* [➤ THE INTERNET; 1128]

Web ring *n* [➤ THE INTERNET; 1128]

Web site *n* [➤ THE INTERNET; 1128]

Webstorefront *n* [➤ THE INTERNET; 1128]

Webzine *n* [➤ THE INTERNET; 1128]

wed **1** *v* (*formal or literary*) **marry**, take in marriage, espouse (*archaic*) [➤ ESTABLISHING RELATIONSHIPS WITH OTHERS; 974] *Opposite*: divorce **2** *v* **get married**, walk down the aisle, say "I do", get hitched (*informal*), tie the knot (*informal*) [➤ ESTABLISHING RELATIONSHIPS WITH OTHERS; 974] *Opposite*: split up **3** *v* **join in matrimony**, marry, join in wedlock, unite [➤ ESTABLISHING RELATIONSHIPS WITH OTHERS; 974] **4** *v* **unite**, join, link, marry, merge, fuse, ally, yoke [➤ FASTEN, LINK, AND JOIN; 408] *Opposite*: separate

wedded **1** *adj* **marital**, conjugal, married, matrimonial, connubial (*literary*) [➤ MARRIED STATE; 961] **2** *adj* **committed**, devoted, linked, connected, attached, married [➡ RELATED; 142] *Opposite*: unattached

wedding *n* **marriage**, wedding ceremony, marriage ceremony, nuptials (*formal*) [➡ CEREMONIES AND ANNIVERSARIES; 38]

wedding cake *type of* **cake** [➡ CAKES, COOKIES, AND DESSERTS; 1181]

wedding ceremony *n* [➡ CEREMONIES AND ANNIVERSARIES; 38]

wedding dress *type of* **dress** [➡ GARMENTS AND OUTFITS; 865]

wedge **1** *n* **segment**, block, chock, sliver, hunk, piece, slice [➡ AMOUNTS OF SOLID OR SEMISOLID; 115] **2** *v* **lodge**, hold, fix, jam, block, chock [➡ POSITION SOMETHING: BETWEEN, BESIDE, OR INSIDE SOMETHING; 326] *Opposite*: dislodge **3** *v* **cram**, pack, jam, ram, stuff, push, thrust, force, squeeze [➡ POSITION SOMETHING: BETWEEN, BESIDE, OR INSIDE SOMETHING; 326] **4** *type of* **flock** [➡ GROUPS OF BIRDS; 1007]

wedge heel *type of* **shoe** [➡ FOOTWEAR; 871]

wedge-shaped *adj* [➡ ANGULAR SHAPE; 1217]

wedlock *n* **matrimony**, marriage, married state [➡ MARRIED STATE; 961]

wee *adj* **small**, minute, petite, little, tiny, diminutive, miniature [➡ SMALL; 1195] *Opposite*: big

weed **1** *v* **hoe**, tidy, pick over, clear [➡ EXTRACT AND SEVER; 341] **2** *n* [➡ VEGETATION; 1025]

weed

◆ *types of weeds*
bindweed, burdock, chickweed, dandelion, dock, goldenrod, jimsonweed, nettle, poison ivy, poison oak, ragweed, stinging nettle, thistle, tumbleweed

weed out *v* **remove**, extract, discard, get rid of, eliminate, reject, set aside [➡ EXTRACT AND SEVER; 341] *Opposite*: select

weeds (*archaic or literary*) *n* [➡ CLOTHES AND ACCESSORIES; 864]

weedy *adj* **weak**, puny, thin, scraggy, feeble, frail [➡ UNFIT AND WEAK; 739] *Opposite*: strong

week *type of* **time period** [➡ TIMES OF YEAR; 88]

weekend **1** *n type of* **time period** [➡ TIMES OF YEAR; 88] **2** *v* **stay**, vacation, take a break, visit, holiday (*UK*) [➡ TRAVEL: WAYS OF TRAVELING; 320]

weekend bag *type of* **baggage** [➡ CONTAINERS, RECEPTACLES, AND PACKAGING; 1245]

weekender *n* **tourist**, vacationer, visitor, sightseer, holidaymaker (*UK*) [➡ TRAVEL: TRAVELERS AND WALKERS; 319]

weekly *adv* [➡ TIMES OF YEAR; 88]

weensy (*informal*) *adj* [➡ SMALL; 1195]

weeny (*informal*) *adj* **tiny**, little, small, wee, minute, weensy (*informal*), teeny (*informal*), teensy (*informal*), teeny-weeny (*informal*), teensy-weensy (*informal*) [➡ SMALL; 1195] *Opposite*: huge

weep **1** *v* **cry**, sob, wail, snivel, boohoo, shed tears, blubber (*informal*), bawl (*informal*) [➡ CRYING; 650] **2** *v* **leak**, suppurate, seep, exude, ooze, discharge, drip [➡ LIQUID EMISSION; 370]

weeper (*informal*) *see* **weepie**

weepie (*informal*) *n* **movie**, film, melodrama, tearjerker (*informal*) [➡ FILM; 901]

weepy **1** *adj* (*informal*) **tearful**, emotional, sad, miserable, sensitive, maudlin, mawkish [➡ SADNESS, DISTRESS, AND DESPAIR; 539] **2** *adj* **oversentimental**, slushy, mushy, syrupy, over-emotional, mawkish [➡ IN POOR TASTE AND OVERSENTIMENTAL; 229]

weevil *type of* **beetle** [➡ BEETLES AND WEEVILS; 1016]

weigh *v* **consider**, ponder, think about, evaluate, meditate on, reflect on, mull over, chew over, assess, think over, contemplate, deliberate, weigh up (*UK*) [➡ THINK AND REFLECT; 743]

weigh against *v* **count against**, tell against, militate against, countervail [➡ AVOID, PREVENT, LIMIT, AND CONTROL; 277]

weigh down **1** *v* **worry**, depress, get down, trouble, burden, afflict [➡ UPSET, DISTRESS, AND HUMILIATE; 567] *Opposite*: hearten **2** *v* **burden**, load down, overload, charge, encumber [➡ GIVE TOO MUCH AND OVERBURDEN; 437]

weighed down *adj* **oppressed**, burdened, worried, troubled, overloaded, fraught, beset, beleaguered, plagued [➡ SADNESS, DISTRESS, AND DESPAIR; 539] *Opposite*: untroubled

weighing machine (*UK*) *type of* **measuring device** [➡ MEASURING DEVICES; 1123]

weighing scale (*UK*) *type of* **measuring device** [➡ MEASURING DEVICES; 1123]

weigh into (*informal*) *v* [➡ PHYSICAL ATTACK AND PUNISHMENT; 415]

weight **1** *n* **heaviness**, mass, bulk, heft, weightiness [➡ WEIGHT: HEAVY; 1205] **2** *n* **burden**, load, encumbrance [➡ PROBLEMS; 256] **3** *n* **influence**, power, substance, significance, import, importance, authority, clout (*informal*), consequence (*formal*) [➡ IMPORTANCE AND SIGNIFICANCE; 192]

weighted *adj* **biased**, prejudiced, slanted, subjective, one-sided, partisan [➡ THE NATURE OF IDEAS; 771] *Opposite*: impartial

weightiness **1** *n* **weight**, heaviness, mass, bulk, heft [➡ WEIGHT: HEAVY; 1205] **2** *n* **gravity**, seriousness, importance, heaviness, import, significance, consequence (*formal*) [➡ IMPORTANCE AND SIGNIFICANCE; 192]

weighting *n* **allowance**, premium, increment [➡ WORK-RELATED ACTIVITIES; 834]

weightless *adj* **light**, feathery, insubstantial, ethereal, airy, floaty [➡ WEIGHT: LIGHT; 1206] *Opposite*: heavy

weightlessness *n* [➡ WEIGHT: LIGHT; 1206]

weighty **1** *adj* **heavy**, big, substantial, hefty, bulky, cumbersome [➡ WEIGHT: HEAVY; 1205] *Opposite*: insubstantial **2** *adj* **important**, serious, grave, solemn, momentous, influential, significant [➡ IMPORTANT; 194] *Opposite*: frivolous

weigh up (*UK*) *v* **assess**, evaluate, consider, examine, size up, balance, ponder, think about, take stock of, contemplate, deliberate, reflect on, chew over, mull over [➡ EXAMINE AND ASSESS; 753]

weir *n* **dam**, barrage, dike, barrier, wall, levee [➡ RIVERS, LAKES, AND STREAMS; 1042]

weird *adj* **strange**, odd, bizarre, peculiar, uncanny, eerie, creepy (*informal*), unusual, curious, improbable [➤ BIZARRE AND PECULIAR; 257] *Opposite*: normal

weird and wonderful *adj* [➤ EXTRAORDINARY: AMAZING; 204]

weirdness *n* **strangeness**, oddness, eeriness, eccentricity, improbability, creepiness (*informal*) [➤ BIZARRE AND PECULIAR; 257] *Opposite*: normality

welcome 1 *adj* **at home**, comfortable, at ease, relaxed, comfy (*informal*) [➤ COOL AND CALM; 536] *Opposite*: unwelcome **2** *adj* **longed-for**, long-awaited, timely, opportune, heaven-sent [➤ POPULAR AND WANTED; 220] *Opposite*: untimely **3** *adj* **appreciated**, pleasurable, delightful, pleasing, pleasant, acceptable [➤ ACCEPTABLE AND PASSABLE; 219] *Opposite*: unwelcome **4** *n* **greeting**, reception, salutation, salute, hospitality, red carpet treatment [➤ GREETINGS, FAREWELLS, AND SALUTATIONS; 659] *Opposite*: farewell **5** *v* **greet**, receive, hail, meet, salute, cheer, applaud [➤ INITIATE AND ESTABLISH COMMUNICATION; 680] *Opposite*: snub **6** *v* **accept**, appreciate, approve, jump at, be grateful for, embrace, applaud [➤ ACCEPT POSSESSION; 450] *Opposite*: reject

welcoming *adj* **friendly**, warm, hospitable, convivial, openhearted [➤ EMOTIONALLY PLEASANT; 187] *Opposite*: unwelcoming

weld 1 *v* **fuse**, join, repair, solder, link, connect, bond [➤ FASTEN, LINK, AND JOIN; 408] *Opposite*: separate **2** *n* **repair**, join, link, joint, bond, seal, seam [➤ FASTENERS, LINKS, AND NETWORKS; 1247]

welfare 1 *n* **well-being**, interests, happiness, good, safety, health, prosperity [➤ SAFE AND SAFETY; 191] *Opposite*: harm **2** *n* **benefits**, aid, assistance [➤ SOCIAL WELFARE; 812]

well 1 *n* **shaft**, bore, borehole, pit [➤ HOLES, GAPS, AND FORKS; 1252] **2** *n* **spring**, fountain, artesian well, source, water supply, fountainhead, wellspring, fount (*literary*) [➤ RIVERS, LAKES, AND STREAMS; 1042] **3** *v* **spring up**, brim, surge, rise, gush, flood [➤ LIQUID EMISSION; 370] *Opposite*: subside **4** *v* **grow**, rise, swell, intensify, increase, grow stronger [➤ CHANGE OF INTENSITY, MORE; 394] *Opposite*: subside **5** *adv* **pleasingly**, splendidly, perfectly, pleasantly, nicely, desirably [➤ GOOD, WELL, BETTER; 183] *Opposite*: badly **6** *adv* **properly**, ethically, acceptably, correctly, suitably, agreeably [➤ CORRECT AND FAULTLESS; 182] *Opposite*: improperly **7** *adv* **competently**, ably, skillfully, capably, satisfactorily, expertly [➤ GOOD, WELL, BETTER; 183] *Opposite*: badly **8** *adv* **justly**, appropriately, fairly, fittingly, justifiably [➤ GOOD, WELL, BETTER; 183] *Opposite*: unfairly **9** *adv* **comfortably**, easily, agreeably [➤ EMOTIONALLY PLEASANT; 187] *Opposite*: uncomfortably **10** *adv* **favorably**, highly, admiringly, kindly, positively, fondly, benevolently [➤ GOOD, WELL, BETTER; 183] *Opposite*: unfavorably **11** *adv* **thoroughly**, fully, carefully, completely, meticulously [➤ WHOLENESS AND COMPLETENESS; 198] *Opposite*: partially **12** *adv* **clearly**, precisely, in detail, distinctly, perfectly, efficiently, effectively [➤ CONCISE AND CLEAR; 202] *Opposite*: poorly **13** *adv* **familiarly**, intimately, closely, personally, deeply [➤ WHOLENESS AND COMPLETENESS; 198] *Opposite*: slightly **14** *adv* **good-naturedly**, good-humoredly, cheerfully, jovially, genially, jestingly (*literary*) [➤ GOOD-TEMPERED AND HUMOROUS; 627] **15** *adv* **anyway**, anyhow, in any case, to cut a long story short, now then, so [➤ SUMMARIZING EXPRESSIONS; 622] **16** *adj* **healthy**, glowing, fit, fighting fit, in good health, able-bodied, sound, in good form, thriving, fine (*informal*) [➤ FIT AND STRONG; 736] *Opposite*: unwell **17** *adj* **satisfactory**, all right, good, lucky, fortunate, fine (*informal*), okay (*informal*) [➤ GOOD, WELL, BETTER; 183] *Opposite*: unsatisfactory

well-acquainted *adj* [➤ RELATIONSHIP TO ANOTHER; 973]

well-adjusted *adj* **stable**, normal, level-headed, well-balanced, sane, steady, secure [➤ CONFIDENCE AND COMPOSURE; 499] *Opposite*: maladjusted

well-advised *adj* **sensible**, prudent, wise, judicious, shrewd, astute [➤ THE NATURE OF IDEAS; 771] *Opposite*: ill-advised

well-appointed *adj* **well-equipped**, well-resourced, fully furnished, well-furnished, luxurious [➤ EXPENSIVE AND LUXURIOUS; 218]

well-argued *adj* **clear**, clearly stated, cogent, sensible, lucid, rational, logical [➤ CONCISE AND CLEAR; 202] *Opposite*: illogical

well-balanced 1 *adj* **harmonious**, balanced, well-proportioned, proportionate, coordinated [➤ HARMONY; 155] *Opposite*: unbalanced **2** *adj* **sensible**, rational, stable, judicious, well-adjusted, level-headed, steady [➤ POSITIVE INTELLECTUAL CHARACTERISTICS; 524] *Opposite*: unstable

well-behaved *adj* **good**, obedient, dutiful, well-mannered, polite, biddable [➤ GOOD MANNERS AND SOCIAL SKILLS; 520] *Opposite*: disobedient

well-being *n* **happiness**, comfort, security, good, welfare, safety, health, good fortune [➤ PLEASANT SITUATIONS; 74]

well-beloved 1 *adj* **loved**, cherished, desired, beloved, adored, treasured [➤ POPULAR AND WANTED; 220] *Opposite*: hated **2** *adj* **respected**, honored, venerated, revered, esteemed [➤ POPULAR AND WANTED; 220] *Opposite*: disgraced

wellborn *adj* **aristocratic**, blue-blooded, noble, patrician, highborn (*literary*), genteel (*dated*) [➤ CLASS STATUS; 889] *Opposite*: lowly

well-bred *adj* **polite**, well mannered, mannerly, courteous, refined [➤ GOOD MANNERS AND SOCIAL SKILLS; 520] *Opposite*: common

well-built *adj* **sturdy**, strong, muscular, muscly, burly, solid, powerful [➤ BUILD; 477] *Opposite*: puny

well-chosen *adj* **choice**, appropriate, apposite, apt, relevant, pertinent, suitable [➤ APPROPRIATE, SUITABLE, AND ADVISABLE; 184] *Opposite*: inappropriate

well-defined *adj* **distinct**, sharp, definite, clear, precise, exact [➤ CONCISE AND CLEAR; 202] *Opposite*: vague

well-designed 1 *adj* **elegant**, stylish, well-made, chic, classy (*informal*) [➤ BEAUTY AND ATTRACTIVENESS; 189] **2** *adj* **handy**, ingenious, clever, useful, neat, nifty (*informal*) [➤ USEFULNESS; 199]

well-developed 1 *adj* **well-built**, strong, toned, finely honed, muscular, powerful, strapping (*informal*) [➤ BUILD; 477] *Opposite*: puny **2** *adj* **sophisticated**, well-rounded, strong, mature, acute, keen, sharp [➤ STRENGTH; 201] *Opposite*: underdeveloped

well-disposed *adj* **approving**, friendly, kindly, sympathetic, benevolent, supportive [➤ APPRECIATION AND GRATITUDE; 535] *Opposite*: hostile

well done *interj* **bravo**, congratulations, hurrah, good for you, hooray, good job, way to go (*informal*), good on you (*UK*) [➤ COMPLIMENTS; 657]

well-dressed *adj* **smart**, chic, stylish, elegant, dapper, spruce, neat, well-groomed, well-presented, well turned-out (*UK*) [➥ WELL-GROOMED; 482] *Opposite*: scruffy

well-educated *adj* **cultured**, erudite, knowledgeable, well-read, learned [➥ LEVELS OF EDUCATION AND SOPHISTICATION; 894] *Opposite*: ignorant

well-endowed 1 *adj* **affluent**, wealthy, well-to-do, rich, moneyed, prosperous, well-off, well-heeled (*informal*), well-fixed (*informal*), loaded (*slang*) [➥ WEALTH AND WEALTHY; 891] *Opposite*: poor 2 *adj* **gifted**, skilled, talented, able, skillful, accomplished [➥ TALENTED AND SKILLFUL; 527]

well-equipped *adj* **well-appointed**, well-resourced, well-furnished, luxurious, lavish [➥ EXPENSIVE AND LUXURIOUS; 218] *Opposite*: Spartan

well-established *adj* **firm**, deep-rooted, unshakable, fixed, ingrained, entrenched [➥ PERMANENCE: WITHOUT END; 94] *Opposite*: shaky

well-expressed *adj* **eloquent**, persuasive, fluent, expressive, articulate, telling [➥ ELOQUENT, TALKATIVE, AND LONG-WINDED; 632] *Opposite*: inarticulate

well-fed 1 *adj* **healthy**, well-nourished, thriving, flourishing [➥ EAT AND NOT EAT; 710] 2 *adj* **overweight**, fat, obese, bulky, stout, portly, matronly [➥ BUILD; 477] *Opposite*: thin

well-fixed (*informal*) *adj* **well-to-do**, wealthy, prosperous, well-off, moneyed, well-endowed, rich, well-heeled (*informal*), loaded (*slang*) [➥ WEALTH AND WEALTHY; 891] *Opposite*: poor

well-founded *adj* **logical**, understandable, justifiable, substantiated, sound, rational, well-grounded [➥ THE NATURE OF IDEAS; 771] *Opposite*: illogical

well-groomed *adj* **well-turned-out**, well-dressed, smart, dapper, spruce, neat, well-presented [➥ WELL-GROOMED; 482] *Opposite*: unkempt

well-grounded 1 *adj* **knowledgeable**, well-informed, au fait, conversant, well-acquainted, in the know [➥ KNOWLEDGE AND WISDOM; 558] *Opposite*: ignorant 2 *adj* **well-founded**, logical, understandable, justifiable, substantiated, sound, rational [➥ THE NATURE OF IDEAS; 771] *Opposite*: illogical

well-heeled (*informal*) *adj* **wealthy**, well-off, comfortable, rich, affluent, well-to-do, moneyed, prosperous, well-fixed (*informal*), loaded (*slang*) [➥ WEALTH AND WEALTHY; 891] *Opposite*: poor

well-informed *adj* **knowledgeable**, informed, in the know, up-to-date, educated, well-read [➥ KNOWLEDGE AND WISDOM; 558] *Opposite*: uneducated

wellington *see* **wellington boot**

well-intentioned *adj* **well-meant**, well-meaning, kindly, goodhearted, benevolent, benign [➥ GENEROSITY AND KINDNESS; 495] *Opposite*: malicious

well-kept 1 *adj* **neat**, tidy, well-maintained, orderly, ordered, spick-and-span [➥ ORDER AND ORGANIZATION; 206] *Opposite*: untidy 2 *adj* **preserved**, safe, cherished, treasured, confidential, hidden [➥ SECRET AND UNKNOWN; 179]

well-known *adj* **famous**, renowned, eminent, familiar, recognized, celebrated, distinguished, illustrious, notorious, infamous [➥ KNOWN AND FAMOUS; 181] *Opposite*: unknown

well-mannered *adj* **polite**, mannerly, decent, decorous, courteous, refined, well-bred [➥ GOOD MANNERS AND SOCIAL SKILLS; 520] *Opposite*: impolite

well-matched *adj* **compatible**, suited, complementary, well-suited, suitable, like-minded [➥ HARMONY; 155] *Opposite*: incompatible

well-meaning *adj* **well-intentioned**, kind, kindly, goodhearted, benevolent, benign, kindhearted [➥ GENEROSITY AND KINDNESS; 495] *Opposite*: malicious

well-meant *adj* **well-intentioned**, kind, kindly, kindhearted, goodhearted, benevolent, benign [➥ GENEROSITY AND KINDNESS; 495] *Opposite*: malicious

well-nigh *adv* **nearly**, almost, nigh on to, practically, just about, virtually [➥ TO A CERTAIN EXTENT; 136] *Opposite*: totally

well-off 1 *adj* **wealthy**, rich, comfortable, affluent, prosperous, well-to-do, moneyed, well-heeled (*informal*), loaded (*slang*) [➥ WEALTH AND WEALTHY; 891] *Opposite*: poor 2 *adj* **lucky**, fortunate, in luck, privileged, blessed, favored [➥ LUCK; 783] *Opposite*: unfortunate

well-oiled *adj* **efficient**, smooth-running, well-organized, effective, well-ordered, disciplined [➥ ORDER AND ORGANIZATION; 206] *Opposite*: inefficient

well-ordered *adj* **tidy**, regimented, disciplined, efficient, well-organized, ordered, effective, regular, neat [➥ ORDER AND ORGANIZATION; 206] *Opposite*: inefficient

well-organized *adj* **efficient**, disciplined, well-ordered, regimented, ordered, effective [➥ ORDER AND ORGANIZATION; 206] *Opposite*: inefficient

well-paid *adj* **lucrative**, profitable, productive, rewarding, remunerative, gainful [➥ ECONOMICAL AND RESOURCEFUL; 207]

well-presented *adj* [➥ WELL-GROOMED; 482]

well-preserved *adj* **youthful**, fresh-looking, young-looking, girlish, boyish, young [➥ PEOPLE'S PHYSICAL APPEARANCE; 475] *Opposite*: wizened

well-read *adj* **knowledgeable**, educated, cultured, erudite, well-educated, well-informed, well-versed [➥ LEVELS OF EDUCATION AND SOPHISTICATION; 894] *Opposite*: uninformed

well-regarded *adj* [➥ POPULAR AND WANTED; 220]

well-respected *adj* [➥ POPULAR AND WANTED; 220]

well-rounded 1 *adj* **experienced**, seasoned, accomplished, well-versed, mature [➥ LEVELS OF EDUCATION AND SOPHISTICATION; 894] *Opposite*: inexperienced 2 *adj* **comprehensive**, varied, wide, balanced, broad, extensive [➥ WHOLENESS AND COMPLETENESS; 198] *Opposite*: narrow 3 *adj* **shapely**, pleasing, well-formed, attractive, curvaceous, comely (*archaic or literary*) [➥ BUILD; 477] *Opposite*: unattractive

well-spoken *adj* **articulate**, eloquent, refined, fluent, coherent, clear [➥ ELOQUENT, TALKATIVE, AND LONG-WINDED; 632] *Opposite*: inarticulate

well-suited *adj* **compatible**, well-matched, complementary, of a kind, suited, suitable, like-minded [➥ HARMONY; 155] *Opposite*: incompatible

well-thought-of *adj* **respected**, esteemed, highly

regarded, reputable, admired, revered [➞POPULAR AND WANTED; 220] *Opposite*: despised

well-thought-out *adj* **well-planned**, well-organized, ingenious, elegant, neat, considered, clever (*UK*) [➞THE NATURE OF IDEAS; 771] *Opposite*: disorganized

well-timed *adj* **timely**, opportune, propitious, felicitous, appropriate, convenient [➞APPROPRIATE, SUITABLE, AND ADVISABLE; 184] *Opposite*: untimely

well-to-do *adj* **wealthy**, rich, well-off, affluent, prosperous, comfortable, moneyed, well-heeled (*informal*), well-fixed (*informal*), loaded (*slang*) [➞WEALTH AND WEALTHY; 891] *Opposite*: poor

well-tried *adj* **tried and tested**, established, well-founded, tried and true, acknowledged, well-known [➞KNOWN AND FAMOUS; 181] *Opposite*: untried

well-turned **1** *adj* **shapely**, graceful, elegant, well-formed, pretty, comely (*archaic or literary*) [➞BEAUTY AND ATTRACTIVENESS; 189] *Opposite*: inelegant **2** *adj* **eloquent**, well-crafted, well-expressed, articulate, witty [➞ELOQUENT, TALKATIVE, AND LONG-WINDED; 632] *Opposite*: clumsy

well-turned-out *adj* **neat**, smart, spruce, dapper, well-dressed, stylish, chic, well-groomed, well-presented [➞WELL-GROOMED; 482] *Opposite*: unkempt

well under way *adj* [➞HAPPENING AND IN PROGRESS; 32]

well up *v* **surge**, gush forth, spring up, spill over, emanate, flow, issue, swell, arise (*archaic or literary*) [➞LIQUID EMISSION; 370] *Opposite*: subside

well-versed *adj* **knowledgeable**, familiar, experienced, informed, well-read, well-informed [➞KNOWLEDGE AND WISDOM; 558] *Opposite*: ignorant

well-wisher *n* **supporter**, sympathizer, friend, guardian angel (*informal*) [➞SUPPORTERS, PROTECTORS, AND COMPATRIOTS; 970] *Opposite*: detractor

well-worn **1** *adj* **worn**, worn out, ragged, threadbare, frayed, shabby, tattered [➞IN BAD REPAIR; 1234] *Opposite*: brand-new **2** *adj* **hackneyed**, timeworn, unoriginal, banal, over-worked, clichéd, stale, trite, corny [➞BORING AND UNINTERESTING; 234] *Opposite*: original

welt *n* **wheal**, swelling, ridge, wound, mark, stripe, bump [➞CONDITIONS AFFECTING THE SKIN; 721]

welter **1** *n* **flurry**, jumble, mass, confusion, muddle [➞DISORDER AND CHAOS; 245] **2** *v* **wallow**, roll, pitch and toss [➞MOVE SOMETHING: ON THE SPOT; 336]

wend *v* **proceed**, go, travel, move, journey, progress [➞PROCEED AND GO; 305] *Opposite*: stay put

werewolf *type of* **mythological creature** [➞MYTHICAL CREATURES; 1036]

westerly *type of* **wind** [➞WINDY AND STORMY WEATHER; 1053]

western *n* **cowboy movie**, spaghetti western, horse opera [➞FILM; 901]

wet **1** *adj* **damp**, soaked, soaking, drenched, sodden, soggy, sopping, dripping, moist, dank, humid, watery, wet through [➞WET; 1240] *Opposite*: dry **2** *adj* **rainy**, showery, drizzly, damp, misty, foggy, raining, pouring, drizzling

[➞CLOUDY AND RAINY WEATHER; 1052] *Opposite*: dry **3** *n* **wet weather**, rain, drizzle, damp, dampness [➞CLOUDY AND RAINY WEATHER; 1052] *Opposite*: dry **4** *n* **moisture**, wetness, liquid, damp, dampness, water [➞WET; 1240] *Opposite*: dry **5** *v* **make wet**, dampen, moisten, soak, saturate, drench, douse, spray, splash, sprinkle [➞SOFTEN, LIQUEFY, AND DAMPEN; 388] *Opposite*: dry

Compare and Contrast: *wet*, *damp*, *moist*, *dank*, *humid*, *sodden*, *saturated*, *soaking*, *sopping*

CORE MEANING: not dry

wet a general word used to cover everything from paint that is not yet quite dry to something that is completely covered in water; *damp* slightly wet, especially undesirably so; *moist* slightly wet, usually desirably so; *dank* describes a place that is unpleasantly damp and cold and that usually also has a bad smell; *humid* describes air that has a high water content, often also suggesting accompanying heat; *sodden* extremely wet and heavy with retained moisture; *saturated* suggests that moisture has penetrated something and soaked it thoroughly; *soaking* an informal word meaning extremely and undesirably wet; *sopping* an informal word emphasizing that something is extremely and undesirably wet.

wet behind the ears *adj* [➞UNSKILLED; 529]

wet blanket (*informal*) *n* **spoilsport**, killjoy, party pooper (*informal*), stick-in-the-mud (*informal*), stuffed shirt (*informal*) [➞GRUMPY AND NEGATIVE PEOPLE; 953]

wether *type of* **male animal** [➞MALE OR FEMALE ANIMALS; 978]

wetland *n* **marsh**, swamp, fen, bog, marshes, fens, fenland, marshland, peat bog, wetlands [➞WETLANDS; 1043] *Opposite*: desert

wetness *n* **dampness**, damp, humidity, condensation, moisture, liquid, water [➞WET; 1240] *Opposite*: dryness

wet suit *type of* **sportswear** [➞GARMENTS AND OUTFITS; 865]

wet weather *n* [➞CLOUDY AND RAINY WEATHER; 1052]

whack **1** *v* **hit**, thump, slap, strike, clout, thwack, smack, wallop (*informal*), belt (*informal*) [➞PHYSICAL ATTACK AND PUNISHMENT; 415] **2** *n* **thump**, blow, slap, thwack, clout, smack, wallop (*informal*) [➞PHYSICAL ATTACK AND PUNISHMENT; 415]

whale *type of* **marine mammal** [➞MARINE MAMMALS; 987]

whale

◆ *types of whales*
blue whale, gray whale, humpback whale, killer whale, minke whale, narwhal, pilot whale, right whale, sperm whale, white whale

wham (*informal*) *type of* **impact sound** [➞IMPACT SOUNDS; 1260]

whammy (*informal*) *n* [➞PROBLEMS; 256]

wharf *n* **quay**, quayside, jetty, pier, dock, dockside, waterfront, landing stage [➞WATERWAYS AND SEAWAYS; 1108]

whatchamacallit *n* **whatnot**, thingamabob, thingumajig (*informal*), thingy (*informal*), thingummy (*informal*), thingumabob (*informal*), thingamajig (*in-*

formal), whatsit (*informal*), doodad (*informal*), doohickey (*informal*) [➡ PHYSICAL OBJECTS; 1243]

whatever 1 *pron* **anything**, everything, all, no matter what, whatsoever [➡ ALL; 128] 2 *adv* **at all**, whatsoever, of any kind [➡ ALL; 128]

what is more *adv* [➡ EXPRESSIONS INTRODUCING EXTRA INFORMATION; 139]

whatnot *type of* **cabinet** [➡ FURNITURE; 858]

whatsit (*informal*) *n* [➡ PHYSICAL OBJECTS; 1243]

what's more *adv* **besides**, moreover, in addition, also, furthermore, plus (*informal*) [➡ EXPRESSIONS INTRODUCING EXTRA INFORMATION; 139]

whatsoever *adj* **at all**, whatever, of any kind [➡ ALL; 128]

wheal *n* **swelling**, welt, wound, mark, contusion [➡ CONDITIONS AFFECTING THE SKIN; 721]

wheat *type of* **cereal** [➡ CEREAL FOODS; 1178]

wheatmeal *type of* **flour** [➡ BREAD, FLOUR, AND BREAD PRODUCTS; 1179]

wheedle 1 *v* **coax**, cajole, inveigle, charm, persuade, talk [➡ CAUSE OR COMPEL TO ACT; 271] *Opposite*: bully 2 *v* **coax out**, get out, draw out, obtain, extract, finagle (*informal*), winkle out (*UK*) [➡ OBTAIN POSSESSION BY PERSUASION; 457]

wheel 1 *type of* **controls** [➡ INTERNAL PARTS OF A VEHICLE; 1146] 2 *type of* **external feature** [➡ EXTERNAL PARTS OF A VEHICLE; 1147] 3 *part of* **bike** [➡ BIKES, CARS, AND CARRIAGES; 1149] 4 *v* **roll**, trundle, maneuver, move [➡ MOVE SOMETHING: ON THE SPOT; 336] 5 *v* **turn**, veer, swing, circle, swivel, rotate [➡ CHANGE DIRECTION OF MOTION; 344]

wheel around *v* **swivel around**, swing around, turn around, spin around, turn full circle, veer (*UK*) [➡ CHANGE DIRECTION OF MOTION; 344]

wheel clamp *n* **Denver boot**, clamp, lock, immobilizer [➡ FASTENERS, LINKS, AND NETWORKS; 1247]

wheel-clamp (*UK*) *v* **clamp**, immobilize, secure, lock [➡ FASTEN, LINK, AND JOIN; 408]

wheeler-dealer (*informal*) *n* **fixer**, negotiator, dealer, trader [➡ BUSINESS PEOPLE; 793]

wheelie bin (*UK*) *n* [➡ CONTAINERS, RECEPTACLES, AND PACKAGING; 1245]

wheeze 1 *v* **breathe heavily**, gasp, rasp, pant, rattle, cough, whistle, puff [➡ BREATHE AND NOT BREATHE; 716] 2 *v* **speak hoarsely**, whisper, hiss, rasp, pant, gasp [➡ SOUND EMISSION BY PEOPLE; 363] 3 *n* **rattle**, rasp, gasp, whistle [➡ SOUNDS MADE BY PEOPLE; 1262]

wheeziness *n* **breathlessness**, hoarseness, gasping, puffing, panting, huskiness, breathiness, chestiness, frog in the throat [➡ BREATHE AND NOT BREATHE; 716]

wheezy *adj* **breathless**, hoarse, short of breath, out of breath, husky, breathy, rasping, puffing, panting, gasping, chesty (*UK*) [➡ BREATHE AND NOT BREATHE; 716]

whelk *type of* **aquatic invertebrate** [➡ AQUATIC INVERTEBRATES; 1022]

whelp 1 *n* **cub**, pup, puppy, baby, offspring, runt [➡ YOUNG ANIMALS; 977] 2 *v* **give birth**, bear young, pup, cub, litter [➡ REPRODUCTION AND HEREDITY; 725]

when all's said and done *adv* **all things considered**, basically, all in all, altogether, at the end of the day, the long and short of it [➡ SUMMARIZING EXPRESSIONS; 622]

whenever *conj* **every time**, each time, each and every time, on every occasion, when, whensoever [➡ CONCURRENT AND CONTEMPORANEOUS; 164]

whereabouts *n* **location**, situation, position, site, place, locus [➡ PLACE; 1065]

whereas *conj* **while**, where, but, however, although, though [➡ ALTHOUGH, NEVERTHELESS, AND DESPITE; 169]

whereupon (*formal*) *conj* **at which point**, at which, as a result of which, so, and so [➡ AFTER, LAST, AND FOLLOWING; 165]

wherewithal *n* **means**, ability, resources, money, finances, funds, assets [➡ POSSESSIONS; 461]

whet 1 *v* **sharpen**, hone, grind, file [➡ CLEAN AND POLISH; 403] *Opposite*: blunt 2 *v* **stimulate**, arouse, augment, rouse, kindle, increase, awaken [➡ CHANGE OF INTENSITY: MORE; 394] *Opposite*: quell

whiff 1 *n* **smell**, aroma, scent, odor, reek [➡ SMELL AND SMELLING; 705] 2 *n* **trace**, vestige, sign, hint, soupçon, suggestion, whisper [➡ FEW, LITTLE, SMALL AMOUNT; 120]

while 1 *conj* **as**, at the same time as, even as, during which [➡ CONCURRENT AND CONTEMPORANEOUS; 164] 2 *conj* **even though**, though, although, despite the fact, whereas [➡ ALTHOUGH, NEVERTHELESS, AND DESPITE; 169] 3 *conj* **but**, however, in contrast, whereas [➡ ALTHOUGH, NEVERTHELESS, AND DESPITE; 169] 4 *n* **time**, period, interval, little, bit [➡ PERIODS OF TIME; 90]

while away *v* **pass**, spend, idle, fritter away, kill [➡ USE UP AND WASTE; 474]

whim *n* **impulse**, urge, notion, quirk, caprice, fancy [➡ IDEAS AND THOUGHTS; 770]

whimper 1 *v* **cry**, whine, sob, snivel, moan, grumble, gripe (*informal*) [➡ CRYING; 650] 2 *type of* **human sound** [➡ SOUNDS MADE BY PEOPLE; 1262]

whimsical 1 *adj* **fanciful**, quirky, unusual, imaginative, original, creative, impulsive [➡ EXTRAORDINARY: UNCOMMON; 205] *Opposite*: practical 2 *adj* **amusing**, playful, humorous, witty, quaint, old-fashioned, off-the-wall, quirky [➡ FUNNY AND AMUSING; 216] *Opposite*: serious 3 *adj* **erratic**, unpredictable, random, impulsive, capricious, flighty, fickle, wayward [➡ LACK OF COMMITMENT AND UNRELIABILITY; 509] *Opposite*: dependable

whimsicality 1 *n* **fancifulness**, quirkiness, imaginativeness, originality, creativity, impulsiveness [➡ EXTRAORDINARY: AMAZING; 204] *Opposite*: practicality 2 *n* **playfulness**, humorousness, whimsy, wit, quaintness, quirkiness [➡ PERSONAL ECCENTRICITIES; 493] *Opposite*: seriousness 3 *n* **unpredictability**, impulsiveness, randomness, capriciousness, flightiness, fickleness, waywardness [➡ LACK OF COMMITMENT AND UNRELIABILITY; 509] *Opposite*: dependability

whimsically 1 *adv* **fancifully**, quirkily, imaginatively, creatively, impulsively, originally, unusually [➡ EXTRAORDINARY: UNCOMMON; 205] *Opposite*: practically 2 *adv* **playfully**, amusingly, humorously, wittily, quaintly, endearingly, quirkily [➡ FUNNY AND AMUSING; 216] *Opposite*: seriously 3 *adv* **unpredictably**, erratically, randomly, impulsively, capriciously, flightily, waywardly [➡ LACK OF COMMITMENT AND UNRELIABILITY; 509] *Opposite*: dependably

whimsy 1 *n* quaintness, oddity, oddness, eccentricity, quirkiness, humorousness, whimsicality [➡ PERSONAL ECCENTRICITIES; 493] *Opposite*: seriousness 2 *n* fancy, flight of fancy, whim, caprice, fantasy, notion, quirk [➡ IDEAS AND THOUGHTS; 770]

whine 1 *v* whimper, cry, moan, wail, bleat, plead [➡ SOUND EMISSION BY PEOPLE; 363] 2 *v* wail, moan, howl, drone, hum, screech, squeal, scream [➡ SOUND EMISSION BY ANIMALS OR BIRDS; 364] 3 *v* grumble, complain, gripe (*informal*), moan (*informal*), bellyache (*informal*), kvetch (*informal*), grouse (*informal*) [➡ COMPLAIN AND NAG; 686] *Opposite*: accept 4 *n* complaint, wail, whimper, cry, moan (*informal*) [➡ COMPLAIN AND NAG; 686] 5 *type of* human sound [➡ SOUNDS MADE BY PEOPLE; 1262]

See Compare and Contrast at **complain.**

whiner *n* grumbler, complainer, moaner (*informal*), grouch (*informal*) [➡ GRUMPY AND NEGATIVE PEOPLE; 953]

whinny 1 *v* neigh, whicker, nicker [➡ SOUND EMISSION BY ANIMALS OR BIRDS; 364] 2 *type of* animal sound [➡ SOUNDS MADE BY ANIMALS; 1261]

whiny *adj* [➡ BAD-TEMPERED AND HUMORLESS; 626]

whip 1 *v* flog, thrash, beat, lash, flagellate, belt (*informal*) [➡ WHIP AND CLUB; 417] 2 *v* whisk, beat, cream, aerate, stir [➡ COOKING AND FOOD PREPARATION; 353] 3 *n* lash, crop, cat-o'-nine-tails, switch [➡ BLUNT INSTRUMENTS AND WHIPS; 1158]

whiplash *n* blow, stroke, lash, hit, impact [➡ CONTACT: IMPACT; 413]

whippersnapper (*dated*) *n* [➡ MISCHIEVOUS OR BADLY BEHAVED CHILD; 946]

whippet *type of* small dog [➡ DOGS; 980]

whipping (*informal*) *n* [➡ BEAT AND DEFEAT; 80]

whipping boy *n* [➡ SUBORDINATES AND ASSISTANTS; 960]

whip snake *type of* nonpoisonous snake [➡ SNAKES; 995]

whip up 1 *v* stir up, drum up, incite, provoke, arouse [➡ CAUSE TO HAPPEN; 31] *Opposite*: pacify 2 *v* (*informal*) rattle off, prepare, concoct, cook, produce, throw together (*informal*), rustle up (*informal*) [➡ MEAL PREPARATION; 354]

whir 1 *v* hum, purr, buzz, whine, drone [➡ EMIT CONTINUOUS SOUNDS; 366] 2 *type of* continuous sound [➡ CONTINUOUS SOUNDS; 1258]

whirl 1 *v* spin, twirl, reel, rotate, turn, swivel [➡ MOVE SOMETHING: ON THE SPOT; 336] 2 *n* rotation, spin, twirl, turn, twizzle, flick [➡ MOVE SOMETHING: ON THE SPOT; 336] 3 *n* flurry, bustle, hustle, commotion, tumult [➡ DISORDER AND CHAOS; 245]

whirlpool 1 *n* eddy, vortex, swirl, current, waterspout [➡ THE SEAS, OCEANS, AND SHORES; 1041] 2 *type of* plumbing fixtures [➡ FIXTURES; 859]

whirlwind 1 *n* tornado, hurricane, cyclone, waterspout, vortex, dust devil, twister (*informal*) [➡ WINDY AND STORMY WEATHER; 1053] 2 *adj* rapid, short-lived, tumultuous, brief, swift, hasty, lightning [➡ HAPPENING QUICKLY; 104] *Opposite*: leisurely

whisk 1 *type of* utensil [➡ TABLEWARE, FLATWARE, AND KITCHENWARE; 861] 2 *v* beat, whip, cream, aerate, stir [➡ COOKING AND FOOD PREPARATION; 353] 3 *v* take, bundle, bustle, hustle, whip, zip (*informal*) [➡ MOVE FAST; 313] *Opposite*: drag

whisker *n* hairsbreadth, fraction, inch, millimeter [➡ FEW, LITTLE, SMALL AMOUNT; 120]

whiskers *n* facial hair, sideburns, mustache, muttonchops, stubble, growth, beard, goatee [➡ FACIAL HAIR; 489]

whiskery *adj* [➡ FACIAL HAIR; 489]

whisper 1 *v* murmur, sigh, mutter, breathe, utter, hiss, mouth [➡ SOUND EMISSION BY PEOPLE; 363] *Opposite*: shout 2 *n* rumor, word, gossip, tale, hint [➡ GOSSIP; 678] 3 *type of* human sound [➡ SOUNDS MADE BY PEOPLE; 1262]

whispered *adj* [➡ SOFT, LOW, OR PLEASANT SOUNDS; 1265]

whistle 1 *v* screech, shrill, shriek, hoot [➡ EMIT RINGING AND HOOTING SOUNDS; 367] 2 *n* shriek, signal, screech, hoot [➡ SOUNDS MADE BY PEOPLE; 1262]

whistle-blower *n* informer, mole, telltale, tattletale (*informal*), snitch (*slang*), stool pigeon (*slang*) [➡ INTERFERING PEOPLE AND TATTLETALES; 950]

whistle-stop *adj* barnstorming, whirlwind, lightning, rapid, speedy [➡ HAPPENING QUICKLY; 104] *Opposite*: relaxed

whit (*dated*) *n* iota, bit, jot, grain, speck, fig [➡ SMALL PIECES; 129]

white 1 *adj* snowy, silver, silvery, bleached, gray, graying, hoary [➡ HAIR COLOR; 485] *Opposite*: black 2 *adj* pale, pallid, ashen, wan, washed-out, anemic, waxen, drawn, pasty, gray [➡ COMPLEXION; 480] *Opposite*: flushed 3 *adj* frosty, snowy, hoary, icy, frozen, freezing [➡ COLD WEATHER; 1051] 4 *type of* color [➡ COLORS; 1224]

white

◆ *types of white*
cream, eggshell, ivory, magnolia, off-white, oyster, pearl, platinum, silver, snow white

white ant *type of* ant [➡ ANTS; 1014]

white as a sheet *adj* [➡ COMPLEXION; 480]

whitebait *type of* ocean fish [➡ OCEAN FISH; 1009]

white blood cell *n* [➡ THE BLOOD AND CIRCULATION; 717]

white bread *type of* bread [➡ BREAD, FLOUR, AND BREAD PRODUCTS; 1179]

white-bread (*informal*) *adj* bland, dull, conventional, boring, routine, uninteresting, prosaic, vanilla (*slang*) [➡ BORING AND UNINTERESTING; 234] *Opposite*: extraordinary

whitecap *n* crest, surf, breaker, wave, white horses (*UK*) [➡ THE SEAS, OCEANS, AND SHORES; 1041]

white-collar *adj* professional, managerial, management, salaried, office, executive, administrative [➡ TYPES OF WORK; 835] *Opposite*: blue-collar

white-collar worker *n* [➡ WORKERS; 836]

white corpuscle *n* [➡ THE BLOOD AND CIRCULATION; 717]

white dwarf *type of* star or star system [➡ HEAVENLY BODIES; 1061]

whitefly *type of* flying insect [➡ FLYING INSECTS; 1013]

whitehead *n* [➡ CONDITIONS AFFECTING THE SKIN; 721]

white-hot 1 *adj* **incandescent**, glowing, white, luminescent, hot, molten [➡ TEMPERATURE: HOT; 1229] *Opposite*: ice-cold 2 *adj* **intense**, fevered, frenetic, frenzied, excited [➡ PLEASURE, EXCITEMENT, AND ELATION; 534] *Opposite*: lethargic

white knight *n* [➡ BUSINESS PEOPLE; 793]

white-knuckle *adj* **exhilarating**, frightening, terrifying, exciting, roller-coaster, adrenaline-charged, nerve-racking [➡ FRIGHTENING; 231] *Opposite*: safe

white lie *n* [➡ DECEPTION AND LIES; 660]

See Compare and Contrast at lie.

white lightning *n* [➡ DRINKS; 1187]

whiten *v* **blanch**, whitewash, bleach, fade, pale [➡ CHANGE OF COLOR; 391] *Opposite*: darken

whiteness *n* **paleness**, milkiness, lightness, pallor, wanness, sallowness, pastiness, anemia [➡ COMPLEXION; 480] *Opposite*: ruddiness

whiteout *n* **blizzard**, snowstorm, storm, snowfall, snowsquall [➡ WINDY AND STORMY WEATHER; 1053]

white pepper *type of* **spice** [➡ HERBS AND SPICES; 1175]

white-tailed deer *type of* **deer or antelope** [➡ DEER AND ANTELOPES; 981]

white tie *type of* **suit** [➡ GARMENTS AND OUTFITS; 865]

whitewash 1 *n* **distemper**, lime, whitening, paint [➡ DYES AND COLORANTS; 1270] 2 *n* **cover-up**, deception, conspiracy, plot, concealment, misrepresentation [➡ DECEPTION AND LIES; 660] *Opposite*: exposure 3 *n* (*informal*) **defeat**, rout, one-horse race, trouncing, beating, setback, shutout, wipeout (*informal*) [➡ BEAT AND DEFEAT; 80] *Opposite*: triumph 4 *v* **paint**, decorate, distemper, cover, smear, daub [➡ DECORATE, ADORN, AND APPLY COATINGS; 405] 5 *v* **misrepresent**, cover up, conceal, explain away, gloss over, sweep under the carpet, suppress [➡ CAUSE TO DISAPPEAR; 6] *Opposite*: expose 6 *v* **trounce**, defeat, beat, shut out, rout, outclass, crush, cream (*slang*), see off (*UK*) [➡ BEAT AND DEFEAT; 80] *Opposite*: succumb

white water 1 *n* **rapids**, torrents, foam, spray, current [➡ THE SEAS, OCEANS, AND SHORES; 1041] 2 *n* **shallows**, shoals, sandbanks, sandbar [➡ THE SEAS, OCEANS, AND SHORES; 1041]

white whale *type of* **whale** [➡ WHALES; 991]

whiting *type of* **ocean fish** [➡ OCEAN FISH; 1009]

whittle *v* **carve**, shape, fashion, shave, sculpt, cut [➡ CRAFTS AND CARVING; 355]

whittle away *v* **eat into**, erode, eat away at, reduce, consume, corrode [➡ USE UP AND WASTE; 474] *Opposite*: build up

whittle down *v* **cut down**, trim, pare down, reduce, diminish, lessen [➡ CHANGE OF SIZE: SMALLER; 393] *Opposite*: increase

whiz 1 *v* **whir**, hum, hiss, buzz, rattle, whoosh [➡ EMIT CONTINUOUS SOUNDS; 366] 2 *v* **dash**, go, pop (*informal*), zip (*informal*), zap (*informal*), shoot (*informal*) [➡ MOVE FAST; 313] *Opposite*: dawdle 3 *n* **whirring**, humming, hissing, buzzing, rattling, whoosh [➡ CONTINUOUS SOUNDS; 1258] 4 *n* (*informal*) **expert**, prodigy, genius, whiz kid (*informal*), wizard (*informal*) [➡ TALENTED OR INTELLIGENT PEOPLE; 528]

whiz kid (*informal*) *n* **prodigy**, expert, genius, wizard (*informal*), whiz (*informal*) [➡ TALENTED OR INTELLIGENT PEOPLE; 528]

whizz *v* [➡ MOVE FAST; 313]

whodunit *n* **mystery**, thriller, cliffhanger [➡ FICTION AND DRAMA; 913]

whole 1 *adj* **entire**, complete, full, in one piece, total, unabridged, uncut [➡ WHOLENESS AND COMPLETENESS; 198] *Opposite*: partial 2 *adj* **intact**, in one piece, unbroken, undivided, undented, unspoiled [➡ IN GOOD REPAIR; 1232] *Opposite*: broken 3 *adj* **unimpaired**, healthy, sound, fit, well, sturdy [➡ SAFE AND SOUND; 737] *Opposite*: unhealthy 4 *adj* **healed**, cured, healthy, restored, rehabilitated, mended [➡ FIT AND STRONG; 736] *Opposite*: ill 5 *n* **sum total**, aggregate, total, unit, entity, ensemble [➡ MEASURABLE PORTIONS; 127] 6 *n* **entirety**, totality, unity, everything, all [➡ ALL; 128] *Opposite*: part

wholehearted *adj* **enthusiastic**, passionate, unreserved, total, unstinting, unequivocal, hundred percent, unswerving, committed [➡ POSITIVE IMPATIENCE, ENTHUSIASM, AND ALERTNESS; 537] *Opposite*: grudging

whole lot *n* [➡ ALL; 128]

wholeness *n* **completeness**, entirety, totality, unity, fullness, comprehensiveness [➡ WHOLENESS AND COMPLETENESS; 198]

wholesale 1 *adj* **extensive**, comprehensive, across-the-board, indiscriminate, blanket, general [➡ WHOLENESS AND COMPLETENESS; 198] *Opposite*: partial 2 *adv* **indiscriminately**, extensively, comprehensively, generally, broadly, universally [➡ WHOLENESS AND COMPLETENESS; 198] *Opposite*: partially

wholesaler *n* **trader**, retailer, supplier, dealer, vendor, broker, merchant, importer, exporter [➡ SALES AND SHOWS; 443]

wholesome 1 *adj* **healthy**, healthful, nutritious, good, nourishing, hearty, health-giving [➡ FOOD; 1167] *Opposite*: unwholesome 2 *adj* **decent**, moral, clean, honest, clean-living, open-faced, upright [➡ MORALLY GOOD; 774] *Opposite*: unwholesome 3 *adj* **sensible**, open, honest, commonsensical, practical, helpful [➡ POSITIVE INTELLECTUAL CHARACTERISTICS; 524] *Opposite*: unhelpful 4 *adj* **fit**, healthy, clean-cut, ruddy, blooming, hale and hearty, fresh-faced [➡ COMPLEXION; 480] *Opposite*: unhealthy

wholesomeness 1 *n* **freshness**, healthiness, healthfulness, naturalness, goodness, nutritiousness, purity [➡ FOOD; 1167] *Opposite*: unwholesomeness 2 *n* **morality**, uprightness, decency, integrity, virtuousness, righteousness, respectability, virtue [➡ MORALLY GOOD; 774] *Opposite*: immorality 3 *n* **common sense**, sense, practicality, good sense, openness, helpfulness [➡ POSITIVE INTELLECTUAL CHARACTERISTICS; 524] *Opposite*: impracticality 4 *n* **healthiness**, fitness, glow, ruddiness, haleness [➡ COMPLEXION; 480] *Opposite*: unwholesomeness

whole-wheat *type of* **flour** [➡ BREAD, FLOUR, AND BREAD PRODUCTS; 1179]

wholly 1 *adv* **completely**, entirely, totally, altogether, utterly, in every respect [➡ WHOLENESS AND COMPLETENESS; 198] *Opposite*: partially 2 *adv* **solely**, exclusively, only, just, absolutely, entirely [➡ ABSOLUTE AND ABSOLUTELY; 133] *Opposite*: generally

whoop 1 *v* **cry out**, shout, scream, howl, hoot, yell, roar, holler (*informal*) [➡ GIVING VENT TO EMOTIONS; 679] 2 *n* **shout**, cry, howl, scream, hoot, yell, roar, holler (*informal*) [➡SOUNDS MADE BY PEOPLE; 1262]

whoosh 1 *n* **rushing**, hiss, swish, whistle, roar, whisper, rustle [➡CONTINUOUS SOUNDS; 1258] **2** *n* **dash**, zoom, rush, spurt, surge, burst, spate [➡SUDDEN EVENTS; 52] **3** *v* **rush**, zoom, burst, whistle, whiz, shoot (*informal*), zap (*informal*), zip (*informal*) [➡MOVE FAST; 313] *Opposite*: dawdle **4** *v* **zoom**, whistle, swish, hiss, roar, whisper, rustle [➡EMIT CONTINUOUS SOUNDS; 366]

whopper (*informal*) **1** *n* **monster**, giant, elephant, Goliath, leviathan, mammoth, whale (*informal*) [➡BIG THINGS; 1194] **2** *n* **lie**, untruth, tale, fabrication, falsehood, fib (*informal*), story (*informal*) [➡DECEPTION AND LIES; 660] *Opposite*: truth

whopping (*informal*) **1** *n* **thrashing**, defeat, drubbing, pasting (*informal*), licking (*informal*), hammering (*informal*) [➡BEAT AND DEFEAT; 80] **2** *adj* **enormous**, gigantic, monstrous, huge, big, massive, mammoth [➡LARGE; 1193] *Opposite*: tiny

whorl *n* **spiral**, coil, curl, twist, swirl, vortex [➡ROUNDED SHAPE; 1218]

whortleberry *type of* **berry** [➡FRUIT AND VEGETABLES; 1176]

whys and wherefores *n* **reasons**, ins and outs, details, the full picture, motives, explanations [➡BASIC DETAILS; 688]

wicked **1** *adj* **evil**, bad, wrong, depraved, immoral, iniquitous, sinful, impious, heinous, nefarious, fiendish [➡MORALLY BAD OR IMPROPER; 775] *Opposite*: good **2** *adj* (*informal*) **distressing**, dreadful, awful, atrocious, severe, appalling, terrible [➡EMOTIONALLY UNPLEASANT AND UPSETTING; 227] *Opposite*: excellent **3** *adj* **mischievous**, naughty, roguish, impish, teasing, cheeky (*informal*) [➡JOKES AND TEASING; 674] *Opposite*: respectful **4** *adj* **mean**, cutting, acerbic, sharp, malicious, sarcastic [➡RUDE AND HOSTILE; 625] *Opposite*: gentle **5** *adj* (*slang*) **good**, great, terrific, fabulous, fantastic, impressive, cool (*slang*), fab (*dated informal*) [➡EXTRAORDINARY: AMAZING; 204] *Opposite*: unimpressive

wickedly **1** *adv* **mischievously**, impishly, roguishly, teasingly, naughtily [➡JOKES AND TEASING; 674] *Opposite*: respectfully **2** *adv* **meanly**, acerbically, sharply, maliciously, sarcastically, hurtfully [➡RUDE AND HOSTILE; 625] *Opposite*: gently

wickedness **1** *n* **evil**, badness, iniquity, sin, impiety, malice, evilness [➡MORALLY BAD OR IMPROPER; 775] *Opposite*: goodness **2** *n* **impishness**, cheekiness, naughtiness, mischievousness [➡JOKES AND TEASING; 674]

wicker *n* **cane**, rattan, wickerwork, bamboo [➡PLANT MATERIALS; 1133]

wicket **1** *n* **gate**, door, opening, aperture, entrance, exit [➡DOORS AND ACCESS POINTS; 1101] **2** *type of* **sports equipment** [➡SPORTS EQUIPMENT; 879]

wide **1** *adj* **broad**, ample, large, thick, spacious, expansive, open [➡WIDTH: WIDE; 1199] *Opposite*: narrow **2** *adj* **extensive**, varied, widespread, inclusive, eclectic, catholic, comprehensive, wide-ranging [➡WHOLENESS AND COMPLETENESS; 198] *Opposite*: narrow **3** *adj* **baggy**, roomy, loose, loose-fitting, capacious, comfortable [➡DESCRIBING CLOTHES; 869] *Opposite*: tight **4** *adv* **off course**, off target, off the mark, wide of the mark, out [➡INCORRECT AND ERRONEOUS; 222]

wide-awake (*informal*) *adj* **fully awake**, alert, bright-eyed and bushy-tailed, perky, watchful, vigilant, on the ball (*informal*) [➡POSITIVE IMPATIENCE, ENTHUSIASM, AND ALERTNESS; 537] *Opposite*: asleep

wide-eyed **1** *adj* **amazed**, astonished, open-mouthed, dumbfounded, flabbergasted (*informal*) [➡SURPRISE, SHOCK, AND AMAZEMENT; 545] *Opposite*: impassive **2** *adj* **naive**, innocent, inexperienced, green, credulous, gullible [➡NEGATIVE INTELLECTUAL CHARACTERISTICS; 525] *Opposite*: knowing

widely *adv* **extensively**, broadly, generally, far and wide, commonly, usually [➡GENERAL LOCATIONS; 158] *Opposite*: narrowly

widen *v* **broaden**, extend, expand, enlarge, make wider, amplify [➡CHANGE OF SIZE: BIGGER; 392] *Opposite*: narrow

wide of the mark *adj* [➡INCORRECT AND ERRONEOUS; 222]

wide-open **1** *adj* **open wide**, gaping, yawning, cavernous, agape (*literary*) [➡WIDTH: WIDE; 1199] **2** *adj* **unpredictable**, undecided, anybody's guess, unsettled, in the balance, indeterminate, up in the air, up for grabs (*informal*) [➡UNCERTAIN; 175] *Opposite*: settled **3** *adj* **vulnerable**, unprotected, exposed, unguarded, at risk, in danger, defenseless [➡IN DANGER; 237] *Opposite*: protected

wide-ranging *adj* **extensive**, widespread, comprehensive, across-the-board, inclusive, thorough, sweeping, all-embracing [➡WHOLENESS AND COMPLETENESS; 198] *Opposite*: narrow

widespread *adj* **extensive**, prevalent, general, common, rife, pervasive, epidemic [➡PRESENT AND AVAILABLE; 11] *Opposite*: limited

Compare and Contrast: *widespread, prevalent, rife, epidemic, universal*

CORE MEANING: occurring over a wide area

widespread existing or happening in many places, or affecting many people; *prevalent* occurring commonly or widely as a dominant feature; *rife* full of or severely affected by something undesirable that occurs frequently or in great numbers over a wide area, especially when it appears to be uncontrollable; *epidemic* spreading more quickly and more extensively than expected; *universal* affecting the whole world or everyone in the world.

widget (*humorous*) *n* [➡PHYSICAL OBJECTS; 1243]

widow *n* [➡MARITAL STATUS; 890]

widowed *adj* [➡MARITAL STATUS; 890]

widower *n* [➡MARITAL STATUS; 890]

width *n* **breadth**, thickness, girth, size, measurement [➡WIDTH: WIDE; 1199]

wield **1** *v* **exercise**, exert, use, have, employ, apply [➡USE; 467] **2** *v* **brandish**, manipulate, handle, ply, carry, wave around, sport (*informal*) [➡MOVE SOMETHING: ON THE SPOT; 336] *Opposite*: conceal

wiener *type of* **processed meat** [➡TYPES AND CUTS OF MEAT; 1177]

wienerwurst *type of* **processed meat** [➡TYPES AND CUTS OF MEAT; 1177]

wife *n* **spouse**, partner, mate, consort [➡ RELATIVES BY MARRIAGE; 960]

wife-to-be *n* [➡ RELATIVES BY MARRIAGE; 960]

wig *n* **toupee**, hairpiece, periwig, extension, rug (*informal*) [➡ HAIRSTYLES AND HAIRPIECES; 488]

wiggle 1 *v* **wriggle**, waggle, twist, jiggle, squirm, worm [➡ MOVE SOMETHING: ON THE SPOT; 336]   2 *n* **jiggle**, shake, wriggle, twist, waggle [➡ MOVE SOMETHING: ON THE SPOT; 336]

wiggly *adj* **undulating**, wavy, curved, curvy, curving, meandering, sinuous [➡ ANGULAR SHAPE; 1217] *Opposite*: straight

wigwam *n* **tepee**, tent, yurt, hut, lodge, dwelling (*formal*) [➡ RESIDENTIAL BUILDINGS; 1078]

wild 1 *adj* **untamed**, undomesticated, uncultivated, natural, feral [➡ DANGEROUS; 236] *Opposite*: tame   2 *adj* (*informal*) **outrageous**, madcap, foolish, unconventional, irrational, reckless, crazy (*informal*) [➡ ECCENTRICITY AND IRRATIONALITY; 562] *Opposite*: sensible   3 *adj* **rough**, desolate, barren, remote, uninhabited, bare, harsh [➡ PHYSICALLY UNPLEASANT; 226] *Opposite*: gentle   4 *adj* **enthusiastic**, eager, mad, excited, thrilled, crazy (*informal*) [➡ PLEASURE, EXCITEMENT, AND ELATION; 534] *Opposite*: unenthusiastic   5 *adj* **rowdy**, undisciplined, riotous, unruly, rough, unmanageable, uncontrollable, disorderly [➡ REBELLIOUSNESS AND DISOBEDIENCE; 565] *Opposite*: orderly   6 *adj* **stormy**, blustery, squally, tempestuous, windswept, turbulent, rough [➡ WINDY AND STORMY WEATHER; 1053] *Opposite*: calm   7 *adj* **overwhelmed**, overcome, overpowered, devastated, destroyed [➡ IN BAD REPAIR; 1234]   8 *adj* **untidy**, disheveled, unkempt, tousled, messy, scruffy [➡ BADLY GROOMED; 483] *Opposite*: tidy

See Compare and Contrast at **unruly**.

wild boar *type of* **meat** [➡ TYPES AND CUTS OF MEAT; 1177]

wildcat *type of* **cat** [➡ FELINES; 983]

wilderness *n* **wilds**, rough country, wasteland, desert, outback [➡ DESERTS, PLAINS, AND MOORLAND; 1045]

wildfowl *type of* **fowl** [➡ FOOD BIRDS; 999]

wildlife *n* **flora and fauna**, nature, natural world, environment, biota [➡ LIVING THINGS AND LIVING; 976]

wildlife park *n* [➡ THE COUNTRYSIDE AND OUTDOOR SPACES; 1071]

wildlife refuge *n* [➡ THE COUNTRYSIDE AND OUTDOOR SPACES; 1071]

wildlife sanctuary *n* [➡ THE COUNTRYSIDE AND OUTDOOR SPACES; 1071]

wildness 1 *n* **rowdiness**, lack of control, lack of discipline, unruliness, roughness, violence [➡ REBELLIOUSNESS AND DISOBEDIENCE; 565] *Opposite*: orderliness   2 *n* (*informal*) **recklessness**, madness, foolishness, passion, waywardness, zaniness, craziness (*informal*) [➡ ECCENTRICITY AND IRRATIONALITY; 562]   3 *n* **roughness**, remoteness, desolation, barrenness, harshness [➡ PHYSICALLY UNPLEASANT; 226]

wilds *n* [➡ THE COUNTRYSIDE AND OUTDOOR SPACES; 1071]

wiles *n* **tricks**, trickery, guile, deceit, artifice (*formal*) [➡ DECEPTION AND LIES; 660]

wiliness *n* **cunning**, wiles, craftiness, guile, craft, slyness, deviousness, sneakiness, shrewdness, astute-

ness, scheming, cleverness [➡ DECEITFUL; 513] *Opposite*: ingenuousness

will 1 *n* **mind**, brain, consciousness, thoughts, thought processes, self-determination [➡ PSYCHOLOGY AND THE MIND; 769]   2 *n* **determination**, resolve, willpower, motivation, spirit, strength of character, self-control, backbone, drive, guts (*slang*) [➡ STRENGTH OF WILL; 501]   3 *n* **desire**, inclination, wish, longing, determination, ambition [➡ DESIRE AND WANT; 579]   4 *n* (*formal*) **bidding**, command, dictate, wish, desire, instructions [➡ DESIRE AND WANT; 579]   5 *v* **want**, wish, yearn, desire, long, pray, hope against hope [➡ DESIRE AND WANT; 579]

willful 1 *adj* **deliberate**, determined, intentional, conscious, malicious, purposive, malevolent, malign, maleficent [➡ INTENTIONAL AND DELIBERATE; 279] *Opposite*: unwitting   2 *adj* **stubborn**, obstinate, headstrong, perverse, obstreperous, awkward, self-willed, unruly, difficult [➡ UNWILLINGNESS AND STUBBORNNESS; 564] *Opposite*: compliant

willfulness 1 *n* **premeditation**, consciousness, deliberateness, maliciousness, purposiveness, malevolence, malice [➡ ANTAGONISM; 552]   2 *n* **stubbornness**, obstinacy, perverseness, perversity, obstreperousness, awkwardness, unruliness [➡ UNWILLINGNESS AND STUBBORNNESS; 564] *Opposite*: compliance

willies (*informal*) *n* **shakes**, goose bumps, jitters (*informal*), creeps (*informal*), shivers (*informal*), butterflies (*informal*), heebie-jeebies (*slang*) [➡ FEAR AND PANIC; 543]

willing 1 *adj* **eager**, keen, enthusiastic, game, helpful, cooperative, alacritous [➡ POSITIVE IMPATIENCE, ENTHUSIASM, AND ALERTNESS; 537] *Opposite*: reluctant   2 *adj* **prepared**, ready, set, agreeable, disposed, happy, inclined [➡ THE WILL AND WILLINGNESS; 563] *Opposite*: unwilling

willingly 1 *adv* **freely**, readily, gladly, happily, cheerfully, voluntarily, of your own accord, without a fight [➡ THE WILL AND WILLINGNESS; 563] *Opposite*: unwillingly   2 *adv* **eagerly**, enthusiastically, keenly, cooperatively, readily, happily, gamely, with a will [➡ WITH ENTHUSIASM; 286] *Opposite*: reluctantly

willingness 1 *n* **readiness**, inclination, will, preparedness, disposition [➡ THE WILL AND WILLINGNESS; 563] *Opposite*: unwillingness   2 *n* **enthusiasm**, alacrity, motivation, eagerness, keenness, cooperation, commitment [➡ POSITIVE IMPATIENCE, ENTHUSIASM, AND ALERTNESS; 537] *Opposite*: reluctance

willing to please *adj* [➡ THE WILL AND WILLINGNESS; 563]

will-o'-the-wisp *n* [➡ NONEXISTENT THINGS; 23]

willow *type of* **deciduous tree** [➡ DECIDUOUS TREES; 1028]

willowy 1 *adj* **graceful**, slim, elegant, lissom, svelte, lithe [➡ BUILD; 477] *Opposite*: stocky   2 *adj* **flexible**, bendable, malleable, springy, supple [➡ MALLEABLE AND ELASTIC; 1212] *Opposite*: stiff

willpower *n* **determination**, resolve, resolution, iron will, strength of will, strength of mind, self-control, self-discipline [➡ STRENGTH OF WILL; 501] *Opposite*: weakness

willy-nilly 1 *adv* **regardless**, anyway, in any case, like it or not, unceremoniously [➡ UNPLANNED AND UNEXPECTED; 281]   2 *adj* **haphazard**, random, unsystematic, arbitrary, unselective [➡ DISORDER AND CHAOS; 245] *Opposite*: methodical

wilt *v* **droop**, shrivel, wither, fade, wane, sag [➡CEASE TO EXIST; 22] *Opposite:* flourish

wilted *adj* [➡IN BAD REPAIR; 1234]

wily *adj* **crafty**, cunning, guileful, sly, devious, sneaky, shrewd, astute, scheming, clever [➡DECEITFUL; 513] *Opposite:* ingenuous

win 1 *v* **come first**, succeed, triumph, be victorious, be successful, prevail [➡SUCCEED AND WIN; 79] *Opposite:* lose **2** *v* **gain**, earn, secure, attain, collect, accomplish, acquire, obtain, achieve [➡GET; 420] *Opposite:* lose **3** *n* **victory**, success, triumph, landslide, conquest [➡SUCCESS; 82] *Opposite:* defeat

wince 1 *n* **grimace**, scowl, flinch, gasp, cringe, shudder [➡FACIAL EXPRESSIONS AND BLUSHING; 651] *Opposite:* smile **2** *n* **cringe**, recoil, flinch, jump, start [➡PHYSICAL REACTIONS; 316] **3** *v* **grimace**, scowl, shudder, flinch, gasp, blench [➡FACIAL EXPRESSIONS AND BLUSHING; 651] *Opposite:* smile **4** *v* **recoil**, flinch, jump, cringe, shrink, start, shy, blench [➡PHYSICAL REACTIONS; 316]

See Compare and Contrast at **recoil**.

winch 1 *n* **hoist**, windlass, pulley, crane, capstan, crank, block and tackle [➡MACHINES AND MACHINE PARTS; 1116] **2** *v* **raise**, hoist, lift, lift up, pull, haul, wind [➡MOVE SOMETHING: UPWARD; 328]

wind 1 *n* **current of air**, breeze, gale, squall, gust, airstream [➡WINDY AND STORMY WEATHER; 1053] **2** *v* **coil**, twist, encircle, roll, wrap around, curl, twine [➡POSITION SOMETHING: AROUND SOMETHING; 327] *Opposite:* unwind **3** *v* **snake**, meander, bend, curve, twist, twist and turn [➡CHANGE DIRECTION OF MOTION; 344]

wind

◆ *types of winds*
antitrade, bise, chinook, cyclone, foehn, harmattan, hurricane, khamsin, levanter, mistral, monsoon, northeaster, northwester, Santa Ana, simoom, sirocco, southeaster, southwester, tornado, trade wind, tramontana, typhoon, westerly

windbreak *n* **shelter**, panel, barrier, screen, fence, wall, hedge, hedgerow, windscreen [➡BARRIERS; 1113]

windbreaker *type of* **jacket** [➡GARMENTS AND OUTFITS; 865]

wind down *v* **relax**, unwind, rest, loosen up, hang loose (*informal*), chill out (*slang*) [➡CHANGE OF MOOD AND COMPOSURE; 580]

winded *adj* **breathless**, out of breath, short of breath, panting, gasping, puffing [➡INJURED; 742]

windfall *n* **bonus**, handout, bonanza, payout, dividend, win [➡TREATS; 210]

wind gauge *type of* **measuring device** [➡MEASURING DEVICES; 1123]

winding *adj* **zigzagging**, snaky, snaking, twisting, curving, windy, meandering [➡ROUNDED SHAPE; 1218] *Opposite:* straight

windjammer *type of* **historical vessel** [➡SHIPS AND BOATS; 1150]

windlass *n* **winch**, hoist, crane, capstan, pulley, lifter, crank [➡MACHINES AND MACHINE PARTS; 1116]

window 1 *n* **pane**, windowpane, glass, glazing [➡WINDOWS; 1100] **2** *part of* **building** [➡PARTS OF A BUILDING; 1095] **3** *n* **opportunity**, period, chance, slot, window of opportunity [➡SHORT PERIODS OF TIME; 93] **4** *n* **gap**, space, opening, hole [➡HOLES, GAPS, AND FORKS; 1252] **5** *n* **dialogue box**, box, frame, display, interface, graphic [➡COMPUTERS AND COMPUTING; 1127]

window

◆ *types of windows*
bay window, casement, dormer window, fanlight, French window, lancet window, picture window, porthole, rose window, sash window, skylight, transom

◆ *parts of a window*
ledge, pane, sill, window ledge, windowpane, windowsill

window box *part of* **garden** [➡GARDENS; 1074]

window ledge *part of* **window** [➡WINDOWS; 1100]

windowpane *n* **pane**, window, glass, glazing [➡WINDOWS; 1100]

windowsill *n* **ledge**, window ledge, sill, shelf [➡WINDOWS; 1100]

windpipe *part of* **respiratory system** [➡RESPIRATORY ORGANS; 715]

windscreen *n* **windbreak**, screen, shelter, barrier [➡BARRIERS; 1113]

windshield *part of* **external structure** [➡EXTERNAL PARTS OF A VEHICLE; 1147]

windshield wiper *type of* **external feature** [➡EXTERNAL PARTS OF A VEHICLE; 1147]

windsock *type of* **measuring device** [➡MEASURING DEVICES; 1123]

Windsor chair *type of* **seating** [➡FURNITURE; 858]

windstorm *n* **storm**, wind, gale, hurricane, cyclone, tornado, whirlwind, dust devil, twister (*informal*) [➡WINDY AND STORMY WEATHER; 1053]

windswept *adj* **desolate**, windy, barren, inhospitable, exposed, bleak, unsheltered, bare [➡EMPTY; 1238] *Opposite:* sheltered

wind up 1 *v* **end**, conclude, bring to an end, complete, finish, close, shut down, wrap up (*informal*) [➡COMPLETE AN ACTION; 263] *Opposite:* start off **2** *v* (*UK informal*) **infuriate**, enrage, madden, annoy, irritate, put your back up [➡ANGER AND ANNOY; 569] *Opposite:* amuse **3** *v* **prepare**, get ready, take aim, pitch [➡PREPARE FOR ACTION; 289] **4** *v* (*UK*) **liquidate**, close down, close, shut down, terminate (*formal*) [➡BUSINESS ACTIVITIES AND PHENOMENA; 794]

windup *adj* **clockwork**, mechanical, spring-operated, manual [➡MACHINERY; 1114]

windy 1 *adj* **blustery**, breezy, stormy, gusty, squally, bracing, turbulent, blowy (*informal*) [➡WINDY AND STORMY WEATHER; 1053] *Opposite:* still **2** *adj* (*informal*) **wordy**, voluble, verbose, pompous, bombastic, boastful [➡POMPOUS, LOUD, AND OVERCONFIDENT; 635] *Opposite:* meek

wine *type of* **red** [➡COLORS; 1224]

winery *n* **vineyard**, wine producer, wine grower, estate, chateau, vinery [➡INDUSTRIAL BUILDINGS; 1087]

wine waiter *type of* **person who works in restaurants** [➡ DOMESTIC AND KITCHEN WORKERS; 850]

wing 1 *part of* **bird** [➡ PARTS OF BIRDS; 1006] 2 *part of* **insect** [➡ PARTS OF AN INSECT; 1019] 3 *part of* **aircraft** [➡ AIRCRAFT; 1148] 4 *type of* **cut** [➡ TYPES AND CUTS OF MEAT; 1177] 5 *n* **annex**, extension, part, arm, section [➡ PARTS OF A BUILDING; 1095] 6 *n* **division**, subdivision, arm, section, department, branch [➡ SUBDIVISIONS AND OFFSHOOTS; 1253] 7 *v* **fly**, head, speed, race, whiz, dash, hurry [➡ MOVE FAST; 313] 8 *v* **injure**, wound, hurt, maim, shoot, damage [➡ WOUND A PERSON OR ANIMAL; 383]

wing chair *type of* **seating** [➡ FURNITURE; 858]

wingtip 1 *part of* **bird** [➡ PART OF A BIRD; 1006] 2 *type of* **shoe** [➡ FOOTWEAR; 871]

wink *v* **flash**, twinkle, sparkle, glitter, glint, shine [➡ LIGHT EMISSION; 368]

winkle *type of* **aquatic invertebrate** [➡ AQUATIC INVERTEBRATES; 1022]

winkle out (*UK*) *v* **extract**, worm, draw out, prize, wheedle, coax [➡ OBTAIN POSSESSION BY PERSUASION; 457]

winner 1 *n* **victor**, champion, conqueror, leader, frontrunner (*informal*), champ (*informal*) [➡ IMPORTANT OR FAMOUS PEOPLE; 893] *Opposite*: loser 2 *n* **success**, hit, sensation, triumph, sure thing (*informal*) [➡ SUCCESS; 82] *Opposite*: failure

winning 1 *adj* **charming**, captivating, endearing, persuasive, engaging, disarming, appealing, prepossessing, attractive [➡ BEAUTY AND ATTRACTIVENESS; 189] *Opposite*: unprepossessing 2 *adj* **successful**, triumphant, victorious, best, champion, star [➡ SUCCESSFUL AND PROMISING; 81]

winningly *adv* **charmingly**, captivatingly, endearingly, persuasively, disarmingly, winsomely, convincingly, believably, credibly [➡ BEAUTY AND ATTRACTIVENESS; 189]

winnings *n* **prize money**, prize, money, earnings, receipts, takings, kitty, jackpot, loot (*informal*) [➡ INCOME; 460]

winnow *v* **examine**, go through, sort through, pick over, inspect, sort [➡ EXAMINE AND ASSESS; 753]

win over *v* **convince**, persuade, convert, win around, bring around, gain somebody's support, get somebody on your side, charm [➡ ENCOURAGE; 576]

winsome *adj* **charming**, fetching, sweet, lovely, attractive, engaging, endearing, appealing, pleasant [➡ BEAUTY AND ATTRACTIVENESS; 189]

winter 1 *n* **wintertime**, midwinter, depth of winter [➡ TIMES OF YEAR; 88] *Opposite*: summer 2 *n* **end**, twilight, close, closing, ending, conclusion, decline [➡ ENDS AND DEPARTURES; 54]

winter solstice *n* [➡ TIMES OF YEAR; 88]

wintertime *n* [➡ TIMES OF YEAR; 88]

wintriness *n* **chilliness**, coldness, bitterness, iciness, bleakness, frostiness [➡ COLD WEATHER; 1051] *Opposite*: warmth

wintry *adj* **chilly**, cold, bracing, freezing, nippy, bitter, icy, bleak, frosty [➡ COLD WEATHER; 1051] *Opposite*: summery

wipe 1 *v* **rub**, polish, mop, swab, clean, dry [➡ CLEAN AND POLISH; 403] 2 *v* **smear**, spread, rub, distribute, streak, apply, sponge, dab [➡ DECORATE, ADORN, AND APPLY COATINGS; 405] 3 *v* **erase**,

remove, delete, obliterate, destroy, record over [➡ DELETE AND ERASE; 339]

wiped out (*slang*) *adj* **exhausted**, tired, worn-out, all in, drained, wiped, bushed (*informal*), done for (*informal*), dead (*informal*), beat (*slang*), shattered (*UK*) [➡ TIRED, ASLEEP, AND UNCONSCIOUS; 738] *Opposite*: full of beans (*informal*)

wipe out 1 *v* (*informal*) **annihilate**, destroy, eradicate, obliterate, exterminate, eliminate, remove [➡ DESTRUCTION AND DEMOLITION; 359] *Opposite*: protect 2 *v* (*slang*) **kill**, murder, assassinate, take out, do in (*informal*), do away with (*informal*), finish off (*informal*) [➡ KILL; 923]

wipe the floor with (*informal*) *v* **defeat**, beat hollow, thrash, trounce, outclass, crush, walk over (*informal*), annihilate (*informal*), slaughter (*slang*), cream (*slang*) [➡ BEAT AND DEFEAT; 80]

wipe the slate clean (*informal*) *v* **make a fresh start**, start over, start afresh, forgive and forget, bury the hatchet, let bygones be bygones, turn over a new leaf [➡ FORGET, FORGIVE, AND ACCEPT; 748]

wire 1 *n* **cable**, lead, line, filament, cord, flex (*UK*) [➡ ELECTRONICS AND ELECTRICS; 1137] 2 *v* **connect**, hook up, install, equip [➡ FASTEN, LINK, AND JOIN; 408]

wired 1 *adj* **strengthened**, supported, reinforced, held together, bound, underwired [➡ DESCRIBING CLOTHES; 869] 2 *adj* (*informal*) **online**, on the Net, on the Web, connected, equipped, kitted out (*UK*) [➡ COMPUTERS AND COMPUTING; 1127] 3 *adj* (*slang*) **bugged**, tapped, wired up, under surveillance, miked (*informal*), miked up (*informal*) [➡ ACOUSTICS; 1138] 4 *adj* (*slang*) **nervous**, on edge, edgy, taut, tense, restless, manic (*informal*), hyper (*informal*), strung out (*informal*) [➡ CONFUSION, ANXIETY, AND WORRY; 540]

wireless (*dated*) *type of* **audio equipment** [➡ AUDIO EQUIPMENT; 1139]

wiretap 1 *v* **tap**, bug, monitor, listen in on, eavesdrop, spy [➡ LISTEN AND LISTENERS; 708] 2 *n* **tap**, monitor, bug (*informal*) [➡ TELECOMMUNICATIONS; 1130]

wiriness 1 *n* **leanness**, slimness, thinness, muscularity, sinewiness, strength, toughness [➡ MUSCLES AND MUSCULATURE; 479] *Opposite*: fatness 2 *n* **coarseness**, stiffness, bristliness, roughness, scratchiness, toughness [➡ PHYSICAL TEXTURE; 1222] *Opposite*: softness

wiry 1 *adj* **lean**, slim, thin, muscular, sinewy, strong, tough [➡ MUSCLES AND MUSCULATURE; 479] *Opposite*: fat 2 *adj* **coarse**, stiff, bristly, rough, scratchy, tough, thick [➡ PHYSICAL TEXTURE; 1222] *Opposite*: soft

wisdom *n* **understanding**, sense, knowledge, insight, perception, astuteness, acumen, intelligence, prudence, sagacity [➡ KNOWLEDGE AND WISDOM; 558] *Opposite*: foolishness

See Compare and Contrast at **knowledge**.

wisdom tooth *type of* **tooth** [➡ THE MOUTH; 702]

wise 1 *adj* **astute**, intelligent, clever, prudent, sensible, judicious, sagacious, sage (*literary*) [➡ POSITIVE INTELLECTUAL CHARACTERISTICS; 524] *Opposite*: foolish 2 *adj* **knowledgeable**, learned, informed, erudite, aware, clued-in, in the know, au fait [➡ KNOWLEDGE AND WISDOM; 558] *Opposite*: ignorant 3 *adj*

shrewd, cunning, crafty, devious, wily, sly, artful [➞ POSITIVE INTELLECTUAL CHARACTERISTICS; 524]

wiseacre (*informal*) *n* [➞ SELF-IMPORTANT AND SELF-SEEKING PEOPLE; 949]

wisecrack (*informal*) **1** *n* **witticism**, quip, riposte, gibe, retort, joke, gag, one-liner, epigram, bon mot, jest (*literary*) [➞ JOKES AND TEASING; 674] **2** *v* **joke**, quip, jest (*literary*), gibe, retort, gag [➞ JOKES AND TEASING; 674]

wisecracker (*informal*) *n* [➞ JOKERS AND TEASES; 675]

wise guy (*informal*) *n* [➞ SELF-IMPORTANT AND SELF-SEEKING PEOPLE; 949]

wish 1 *v* **want**, desire, crave, require, covet, need [➞ DESIRE AND WANT; 579] **2** *v* **demand**, ask, request, ask for, bid, command [➞ REQUEST AND DEMAND; 663] **3** *n* **desire**, aspiration, hope, yearning, longing, craving, fancy, inclination [➞ DESIRE AND WANT; 579] *Opposite*: disinclination **4** *n* **request**, demand, bidding, command, requirement [➞ REQUEST AND DEMAND; 663]

See Compare and Contrast at **want**.

wishbone *part of* **bird** [➞ PARTS OF A BIRD; 1006]

wished-for *adj* [➞ POPULAR AND WANTED; 220]

wishful thinking *n* **delusion**, fantasy, self delusion, self-deception, idealism [➞ NONEXISTENT THINGS; 23] *Opposite*: reality

wishlist *n* [➞ LISTS AND SCHEDULES; 587]

wishy-washy (*informal*) **1** *adj* **indecisive**, irresolute, weak, feeble, spineless, spiritless, ineffectual, ineffective, pathetic (*informal*), namby-pamby (*informal*) [➞ COWARDICE AND WEAKNESS OF WILL; 508] *Opposite*: decisive **2** *adj* **watery**, insipid, bland, tasteless, weak, watered-down, flavorless [➞ TASTE; 703] *Opposite*: strong

wisp 1 *n* **strand**, scrap, tendril, thread, lock, curl, tuft [➞ SMALL PIECES; 129] **2** *type of* **flock** [➞ GROUPS OF BIRDS; 1007]

wispy *adj* **flimsy**, fine, thin, light, slight, delicate [➞ FRAGILE; 1209] *Opposite*: substantial

wisteria *type of* **climber** [➞ CLIMBERS; 1033]

wistful *adj* **pensive**, melancholy, thoughtful, reflective, contemplative, regretful, sad, longing [➞ PENSIVENESS AND INTEREST; 538] *Opposite*: satisfied

wistfulness *n* **melancholy**, pensiveness, reminiscence, nostalgia, dreaminess, absent-mindedness [➞ FEELINGS ABOUT THE PAST; 532] *Opposite*: contentment

wit 1 *n* **wittiness**, jocularity, facetiousness, fun, humor, waggishness (*informal*) [➞ JOKES AND TEASING; 674] *Opposite*: seriousness **2** *n* **intelligence**, smartness, cleverness, intellect, keenness, incisiveness, sharpness [➞ DESCRIBING SOMEBODY'S INTELLECT; 523] *Opposite*: stupidity **3** *n* **wag** (*informal*), comedian, humorist, comic, joker, satirist, clown [➞ JOKERS AND TEASES; 675]

witch *n* **enchantress**, sorceress, magician, occultist, necromancer (*literary*) [➞ PEOPLE WITH SUPERNATURAL POWERS; 788]

witchcraft *n* [➞ THE SUPERNATURAL; 787]

witch doctor *n* **shaman**, healer, soothsayer, medium, druid, magician [➞ PEOPLE WITH SUPERNATURAL POWERS; 788]

witchery *n* [➞ THE SUPERNATURAL; 787]

witch hazel *type of* **shrub or bush** [➞ BUSHES AND SHRUBS; 1027]

with 1 *prep* **together with**, along with, in conjunction with, beside, alongside, next to [➞ RELATIVE LOCATION; 161] *Opposite*: without **2** *prep* **in addition to**, plus, including, as well as, and [➞ ALSO; 138] *Opposite*: without

with alacrity *adv* [➞ HAPPENING QUICKLY; 104]

with bated breath *adv* **expectantly**, in anticipation, on the edge of your seat, anxiously, hopefully, eagerly, on edge [➞ APPRECIATION AND GRATITUDE; 535]

with care *adv* [➞ CAUTIOUS AND CAREFUL; 282]

with child (*archaic or literary*) *adj* [➞ REPRODUCTION AND HEREDITY; 725]

withdraw 1 *v* **remove**, take out, extract, pull out, draw, take away [➞ REMOVE SOMETHING; 338] *Opposite*: insert **2** *v* **retract**, renounce, disavow, revoke, take back, unsay [➞ APOLOGIZE AND RETRACT; 683] *Opposite*: confirm **3** *v* **leave**, depart, retire, pull out, retreat, go away [➞ LEAVE AND GO AWAY; 8] *Opposite*: remain

withdrawal 1 *n* **removal**, extraction, drawing, taking out, taking away [➞ REMOVE SOMETHING; 338] *Opposite*: insertion **2** *n* **retreat**, departure, leaving, abandonment, retirement, secession [➞ ENDS AND DEPARTURES; 54] *Opposite*: arrival **3** *n* **retraction**, renunciation, revocation, disclaimer, abjuration, disavowal (*formal*) [➞ APOLOGIZE AND RETRACT; 683] *Opposite*: confirmation **4** *n* **alienation**, depression, isolation, detachment [➞ SOLITARINESS; 941]

withdraw from the world *v* [➞ RUN AWAY AND AVOID; 10]

withdrawn *adj* **reserved**, inhibited, solitary, introverted, introvert, quiet, thoughtful [➞ RETICENT AND UNFORTHCOMING; 631] *Opposite*: outgoing

with ease *adv* **easily**, effortlessly, confidently, efficiently, smoothly [➞ EASE AND SIMPLICITY; 200]

with enthusiasm *adv* [➞ WITH ENTHUSIASM; 286]

wither 1 *v* **shrivel**, wilt, dry up, shrink, droop, fade [➞ HARDEN, CONGEAL, AND DRY; 387] *Opposite*: bloom **2** *v* **weaken**, waste away, decline, fade, wane, wilt [➞ CEASE TO EXIST; 22] *Opposite*: strengthen **3** *v* **crush**, mortify, humiliate, abash, put down, discomfit (*formal*) [➞ UPSET, DISTRESS, AND HUMILIATE; 567]

withered *adj* [➞ DECAYING OR INFESTED; 1236]

withering *adj* **contemptuous**, scornful, sarcastic, sneering, arrogant, crushing, dismissive, disdainful [➞ MOCKING AND DISMISSIVE; 636] *Opposite*: complimentary

withers *part of* **horse** [➞ HORSES; 985]

with fervor *adv* [➞ WITH ENTHUSIASM; 286]

with good cheer *adv* [➞ WITH ENTHUSIASM; 286]

with gusto *adv* [➞ WITH ENTHUSIASM; 286]

withheld *adj* [➞ ABSENT AND UNAVAILABLE; 7]

with hindsight *adv* **in retrospect**, retrospectively, looking back, from experience [➞ SUMMARIZING EXPRESSIONS; 622]

withhold *v* **hold back**, keep back, refuse, deny, suppress, reserve [➞ STORE AND KEEP; 453] *Opposite*: give

withhold information *v* [➡WITHHOLD INFORMATION; 687]

within *adv* **inside**, in, indoors, in the interior [➡GENERAL LOCATIONS; 158] *Opposite*: outside

within an ace of *prep* **within reach of**, a hairsbreadth from, a stone's throw from, on the verge of [➡CLOSENESS; 159]

within grasp *adj* [➡CLOSENESS; 159]

within reach *adj* **within your grasp**, reachable, accessible, at hand, at your fingertips, attainable [➡CLOSENESS; 159]

within reach of *prep* [➡CLOSENESS; 159]

within spitting distance (*informal*) *adj* [➡CLOSENESS; 159]

within walking distance *adj* [➡CLOSENESS; 159]

within your rights *adj* **justified**, correct, right, vindicable, vindicated, innocent [➡MORALLY GOOD; 774] *Opposite*: unjustified

with it (*informal*) *adj* [➡POSITIVE INTELLECTUAL CHARACTERISTICS; 524]

with-it (*dated informal*) *adj* **cool**, fashionable, up-to-date, modern, modish, trendy (*informal*), happening (*informal*), hip (*slang*) [➡NEW, MODERN; 166]

with no holds barred *adv* [➡WITH ENTHUSIASM; 286]

with one heart *adv* [➡ACTING WITH OTHERS; 285]

with one voice *adv* **unanimously**, simultaneously, as one, all together, in unison, with one heart [➡ACTING WITH OTHERS; 285]

without *prep* **devoid of**, lacking, minus, in default of, sans (*literary or humorous*) [➡LESS; 126] *Opposite*: with

without a doubt *adv* **undoubtedly**, without doubt, without question, certainly, no doubt, doubtless, beyond doubt, definitely, unquestionably, indubitably (*formal*) [➡CERTAIN; 174] *Opposite*: possibly

without a second thought *adv* **without hesitation**, unhesitatingly, straightaway, without question, readily, confidently, surely [➡HAPPENING QUICKLY; 104] *Opposite*: hesitantly

without a shadow of a doubt *adv* [➡CERTAIN; 174]

without a sound *adv* [➡ABSENCE OF SOUND; 1257]

without demur *adv* [➡HAPPENING QUICKLY; 104]

without due care and attention *adv* [➡INCAUTIOUS AND CARELESS; 283]

without due consideration *adv* [➡INCAUTIOUS AND CARELESS; 283]

without end *adv* [➡PERMANENCE: WITHOUT END; 94]

without equal *adj* [➡EXTRAORDINARY: UNCOMMON; 205]

without fail *adv* **for certain**, reliably, like clockwork, unfailingly, dependably, religiously [➡CERTAIN; 174]

without fear *adv* [➡COURAGE; 498]

without foundation *adj* [➡FALSE AND UNREAL; 173]

without further ado *adv* **immediately**, at once, straight-

away, forthwith, on the double, without delay, right away, straightway [➡HAPPENING QUICKLY; 104]

without help *adv* [➡ACTING INDEPENDENTLY; 284]

without hesitation *adv* [➡HAPPENING QUICKLY; 104]

without precedent *adj* **unprecedented**, unheard-of, unique, unparalleled, groundbreaking, original [➡EXTRAORDINARY: UNCOMMON; 205] *Opposite*: unoriginal

without question *adv* [➡CERTAIN; 174]

with passion *adv* [➡WITH ENTHUSIASM; 286]

with reason *adv* **rightly**, with good cause, justifiably, justly, properly, correctly [➡CORRECT AND FAULTLESS; 182] *Opposite*: unjustifiably

with reference to *prep* **regarding**, with regard to, in regard to, as regards, relating to, pertaining to, in connection with, concerning, about, vis-à-vis, re, respecting, apropos (*formal*) [➡EXPRESSIONS OF REFERENCE; 63]

with regard to *prep* **regarding**, as regards, with reference to, relating to, pertaining to, in connection with, concerning, about, vis-à-vis, in regard to, re, respecting, apropos (*formal*) [➡EXPRESSIONS OF REFERENCE; 63]

with respect to *prep* **regarding**, respecting, with regard to, in regard to, relating to, as regards, pertaining to, about, concerning, in connection with, re, vis-à-vis, apropos (*formal*) [➡EXPRESSIONS OF REFERENCE; 63]

withstand *v* **endure**, survive, resist, bear, weather, tolerate [➡CONTINUE TO EXIST; 17]

with your back to the wall *adj* **in trouble**, in difficulties, in a tight corner, in a tight spot, in dire straits, between a rock and a hard place, in hot water (*informal*), in a jam (*informal*), in a fix (*informal*), up the creek (*informal*), up the creek without a paddle (*informal*) [➡IN TROUBLE AND DISADVANTAGED; 73]

witless *adj* **foolish**, stupid, mindless, unintelligent, silly, clueless (*informal*) [➡NEGATIVE INTELLECTUAL CHARACTERISTICS; 525] *Opposite*: sensible

witlessness *n* [➡NEGATIVE INTELLECTUAL CHARACTERISTICS; 525]

witness **1** *n* **observer**, spectator, bystander, onlooker, watcher, eyewitness [➡ONLOOKERS AND SPECTATORS; 701] **2** *v* **see**, observe, view, perceive, watch, behold (*archaic or literary*) [➡SEE; 699] **3** *v* **countersign**, endorse, sign, attest, authenticate, corroborate, certify, notarize [➡NAME AND DESCRIBE; 665]

wits *n* **reason**, shrewdness, acumen, faculties, mind, intelligence, brains, intellect, common sense, understanding [➡DESCRIBING SOMEBODY'S INTELLECT; 523]

witticism *n* **quip**, joke, riposte, gibe, one-liner, retort, gag, bon mot, wisecrack (*informal*), jest (*literary*) [➡JOKES AND TEASING; 674]

wittiness *n* **cleverness**, sharpness, keenness, comedy, sense of humor, drollness, humor, funniness [➡POSITIVE INTELLECTUAL CHARACTERISTICS; 524] *Opposite*: dullness

wittingly *adv* **knowingly**, consciously, purposely, on purpose, intentionally, deliberately [➡INTENTIONAL AND DELIBERATE; 279] *Opposite*: unwittingly

witty *adj* **amusing**, droll, humorous, funny, entertaining, clever, sharp, inventive [➡ FUNNY AND AMUSING; 216] *Opposite:* dull

See Compare and Contrast at **funny**.

wiz (*informal*) *n* **expert**, prodigy, genius, wizard (*informal*), ace (*informal*), whiz (*informal*), whiz kid (*informal*), dab hand (*informal*) [➡ TALENTED OR INTELLIGENT PEOPLE; 528]

wizard 1 *n* **sorcerer**, warlock, magician, shaman, witch doctor, conjurer [➡ PEOPLE WITH SUPERNATURAL POWERS; 788] 2 *n* (*informal*) **expert**, prodigy, genius, virtuoso, ace (*informal*), whiz (*informal*), whiz kid (*informal*), wiz (*informal*) [➡ TALENTED OR INTELLIGENT PEOPLE; 528]

wizardry 1 *n* **sorcery**, magic, divination, shamanism, spells, witchcraft [➡ THE SUPERNATURAL; 787] 2 *n* **skill**, expertise, genius, brilliance, accomplishment, know-how (*informal*) [➡ SKILLS, TALENTS, AND ABILITIES; 526]

wizened *adj* **wrinkled**, lined, shriveled, wrinkly, withered, crinkly [➡ FACIAL CHARACTERISTICS; 481] *Opposite:* smooth

wobble 1 *v* **shake**, vibrate, tremble, bob, quiver, sway [➡ PHYSICAL REACTIONS; 316] 2 *v* **quaver**, wave, shake, vary, oscillate, fluctuate [➡ MOVE SOMETHING: ON THE SPOT; 336] 3 *v* **dither**, waver, vacillate, shilly-shally, hesitate, dilly-dally, falter [➡ HESITATE; 272]

wobbliness 1 *n* **shakiness**, unsteadiness, instability, ricketiness, rockiness [➡ WEAKNESS; 241] *Opposite:* steadiness 2 *n* (*informal*) **weakness**, unsteadiness, shakiness, trembling, reeling, vertigo [➡ DESCRIBING BODY MOVEMENTS; 288] *Opposite:* steadiness

wobbly 1 *adj* **shaky**, unsteady, unstable, rickety, rocky [➡ WEAKNESS; 241] *Opposite:* steady 2 *adj* (*informal*) **weak**, shaky, trembling, woozy, dizzy, unsteady, faint, unwell [➡ UNFIT AND WEAK; 739] *Opposite:* fit

woe 1 *n* **grief**, distress, anguish, affliction, sadness, despair, misery, wretchedness [➡ SADNESS, DISTRESS, AND DESPAIR; 539] *Opposite:* happiness 2 *n* **affliction**, misfortune, calamity, disaster, trouble, trial [➡ DISASTERS; 252] *Opposite:* joy

woebegone *adj* **miserable**, anguished, despairing, sad, wretched, distressed, sorrowful [➡ SADNESS, DISTRESS, AND DESPAIR; 539] *Opposite:* cheerful

woeful 1 *adj* **unhappy**, doleful, sad, sorrowful, mournful, miserable [➡ SADNESS, DISTRESS, AND DESPAIR; 539] *Opposite:* cheerful 2 *adj* **distressing**, traumatic, harrowing, tragic, unpleasant, depressing, upsetting [➡ EMOTIONALLY UNPLEASANT AND UPSETTING; 227] 3 *adj* **pathetic**, pitiful, regrettable, bad, inadequate, deplorable [➡ BAD AND BADLY; 223] *Opposite:* wonderful

wok *n* **pan**, frying pan, skillet [➡ TABLEWARE, FLATWARE, AND KITCHENWARE; 861]

wolf 1 *type of* **canine** [➡ CANINES; 979] 2 *n* (*informal*) **Casanova**, Don Juan, Romeo, womanizer, Lothario (*literary*), philanderer (*dated*) [➡ PLEASURE-SEEKERS AND HEDONISTS; 886] 3 *v* **gobble**, bolt, gulp down, devour, gorge, guzzle (*informal*), put away (*informal*), scarf (*informal*), scarf down (*informal*), scoff (*informal*) [➡ EAT AND NOT EAT; 710] *Opposite:* nibble

wolfhound *type of* **large dog** [➡ DOGS; 980]

wolf spider *type of* **arachnid** [➡ ARACHNIDS; 1018]

wolverine *type of* **small mammal** [➡ SMALL MAMMALS; 990]

woman *n* **female**, lady, matron [➡ FEMALE PERSON; 933] *Opposite:* man

womanhood 1 *n* **adulthood**, maturity, independence [➡ ADULTHOOD; 918] *Opposite:* mankind 2 *n* **women**, womankind, females, womenfolk [➡ FEMALE PERSON; 933] *Opposite:* manhood

womanizer *n* [➡ PLEASURE-SEEKERS AND HEDONISTS; 886]

womankind *n* **women**, womanhood, females, womenfolk [➡ FEMALE PERSON; 933] *Opposite:* mankind

womanlike *adj* [➡ GENDER IDENTITY AND SEXUALITY; 932]

womanliness *n* [➡ GENDER IDENTITY AND SEXUALITY; 932]

womanly *adj* **female**, feminine [➡ GENDER IDENTITY AND SEXUALITY; 932] *Opposite:* manly

wombat *type of* **marsupial** [➡ MARSUPIALS; 992]

won *type of* **currency** [➡ CURRENCIES; 798]

wonder 1 *n* **surprise**, astonishment, awe, amazement, admiration, incredulity [➡ SURPRISE, SHOCK, AND AMAZEMENT; 545] 2 *n* **miracle**, phenomenon, marvel, sensation, curiosity, spectacle [➡ AMAZING THINGS; 211] 3 *v* **speculate**, doubt, question, conjecture, ponder, deliberate [➡ QUESTION THINGS; 751] 4 *v* **marvel**, admire, gaze at, be amazed [➡ PRAISE AND ENCOURAGE; 647]

wonderful 1 *adj* **magnificent**, superb, amazing, astonishing, fantastic, breathtaking, marvelous [➡ EXTRAORDINARY: AMAZING; 204] *Opposite:* awful 2 *adj* **delightful**, pleasing, great, brilliant, perfect, ideal [➡ EXTRAORDINARY: AMAZING; 204]

wonderland *n* **utopia**, paradise, heaven, never-never land, nirvana, seventh heaven, fairyland [➡ NONEXISTENT PLACES; 1066]

wonderment *n* **amazement**, astonishment, awe, surprise, bewilderment, admiration, stupefaction (*literary*) [➡ SURPRISE, SHOCK, AND AMAZEMENT; 545]

wondrous (*literary*) *adj* **wonderful**, astounding, incredible, astonishing, marvelous, extraordinary, miraculous, phenomenal, amazing [➡ EXTRAORDINARY: AMAZING; 204] *Opposite:* mediocre

wont (*formal*) 1 *adj* **accustomed**, used, in the habit of, inclined, liable, habituated (*formal*) [➡ THE WILL AND WILLINGNESS; 563] *Opposite:* unaccustomed 2 *n* **habit**, custom, tendency, preference, practice, predilection (*formal*) [➡ WAYS OF DOING THINGS; 294]

See Compare and Contrast at **habit**.

wonted (*literary*) *adj* **usual**, typical, customary, preferred, chosen, of choice, habitual [➡ ORDINARINESS; 244] *Opposite:* unaccustomed

See Compare and Contrast at **usual**.

woo (*literary*) *v* **court**, persuade, encourage, entice, pursue, flatter [➡ ESTABLISHING RELATIONSHIPS WITH OTHERS; 974] *Opposite:* discourage

wood 1 *n* **lumber**, firewood, logs, planks, kindling, timber

(*UK*) [➡ BUILDING MATERIALS; 1077] **2** *n* **forest**, woodland, copse, covert, coppice, thicket [➡ WOODS, FORESTS, AND JUNGLES; 1047]

woodbine *type of* **climber** [➡ CLIMBERS; 1033]

woodcarving **1** *n* **carving**, sculpture, woodworking, art, craft [➡ CRAFTS AND CARVING; 355] **2** *n* **sculpture**, figure, embellishment, adornment, feature, design, pattern [➡ SCULPTURE; 902]

woodchuck *type of* **rodent** [➡ RODENTS; 989]

woodcock *type of* **fowl** [➡ FOOD BIRDS; 999]

woodcut **1** *n* **block**, carving, design, matrix [➡ ARTWORKS; 898] **2** *n* **print**, engraving, picture, illustration, portrait, diagram, map [➡ ARTWORKS; 898]

wooded *adj* **forested**, woody, timbered, arboreal, sylvan (*literary*) [➡ VEGETATION; 1025]

wooden **1** *adj* **wood**, woody, ligneous, timber [➡ RIGID AND HARD; 1211] **2** *adj* **stilted**, inexpressive, stiff, emotionless, deadpan, impassive [➡ FACIAL EXPRESSIONS AND BLUSHING; 651] *Opposite*: expressive **3** *adj* **dull**, toneless, flat [➡ UNINTERESTED AND DETACHED; 629] *Opposite*: resonant

woodenly **1** *adv* **awkwardly**, clumsily, gracelessly, stiffly, uncomfortably, inelegantly [➡ AGILITY OF THE BODY; 476] *Opposite*: gracefully **2** *adv* **inexpressively**, stiltedly, ineptly, unconvincingly, mechanically [➡ INARTICULATE, RAMBLING, AND AWKWARD; 633] *Opposite*: expressively **3** *adv* **dully**, tonelessly, flatly [➡ UNINTERESTED AND DETACHED; 629] *Opposite*: resonantly

woodenness **1** *n* **awkwardness**, clumsiness, gracelessness, stiffness, discomfort, inelegance [➡ AGILITY OF THE BODY; 476] *Opposite*: gracefulness **2** *n* **inexpressiveness**, stiltedness, ineptness, unconvincingness, mechanicalness, artificiality [➡ INARTICULATE, RAMBLING, AND AWKWARD; 633] *Opposite*: expressivity **3** *n* **dullness**, tonelessness, flatness [➡ UNINTERESTED AND DETACHED; 629] *Opposite*: resonance

woodland *n* **forest**, wood, woods, timberland [➡ WOODS, FORESTS, AND JUNGLES; 1047]

woodlark *type of* **songbird** [➡ SONGBIRDS; 1003]

wood louse *type of* **land invertebrate** [➡ LAND INVERTEBRATES; 1021]

wood nymph *n* [➡ MYTHICAL BEINGS; 789]

woodpecker *type of* **common bird** [➡ BIRDS; 997]

woods *n* **wood**, forest, woodland, copse, covert, coppice, thicket [➡ WOODS, FORESTS, AND JUNGLES; 1047]

woodshed *n* **shed**, outbuilding, outhouse, garden shed, lean-to, hut, potting shed (*UK*) [➡ STORES AND STORAGE BUILDINGS; 1088]

woodwork *n* **fixtures**, doors, window frames, paneling, skirting, wainscot, skirting boards (*UK*) [➡ FIXTURES; 859]

woodworking *n* **carpentry**, joinery, cabinetmaking, turning [➡ CRAFTS AND CARVING; 355]

woodworking

◆ *types of woodworking*
cabinetmaking, carpentry, carving, joinery, marquetry, woodcarving

woodworm *type of* **stage of insect development** [➡ INSECT STAGES; 1020]

woody *adj* **forested**, wooded, timbered, woodland, arboreal, sylvan (*literary*) [➡ VEGETATION; 1025]

woof **1** *v* **bark**, yap, yelp [➡ SOUND EMISSION BY ANIMALS OR BIRDS; 364] **2** *n* **bark**, yap, yelp [➡ SOUNDS MADE BY ANIMALS; 1261]

wool *type of* **fabric from animals** [➡ FABRICS; 1132]

woolen *adj* **knitted**, woven, wool, woolly, crocheted, spun [➡ PHYSICAL TEXTURE; 1222]

woolens *n* **clothing**, sweaters, jumpers, cardigans [➡ GARMENTS AND OUTFITS; 865]

woolgather *v* **daydream**, dream, be miles away, fantasize, be lost in thought, stare into space [➡ DREAM, IMAGINE, AND FANTASIZE; 749]

woolgatherer *n* [➡ LAZY OR UNSUCCESSFUL PEOPLE; 948]

woolgathering *n* [➡ DREAM, IMAGINE, AND FANTASIZE; 749]

wooliness *n* **confusion** [➡ VAGUENESS; 243]

woollen *see* **woolen**

woollens *see* **woolens**

woolly **1** *adj* **woolen**, knitted, woven, wool, crocheted [➡ PHYSICAL TEXTURE; 1222] **2** *adj* **vague**, confused, unfocused, unclear, ill-defined, woolly-headed, woolly-minded [➡ VAGUENESS; 243] *Opposite*: clear

woolly-headed *adj* [➡ NEGATIVE INTELLECTUAL CHARACTERISTICS; 525]

woolly-minded *adj* [➡ NEGATIVE INTELLECTUAL CHARACTERISTICS; 525]

wooziness *n* [➡ ILL AND SICK; 740]

woozy *adj* **dizzy**, faint, lightheaded, unsteady, nauseous [➡ ILL AND SICK; 740] *Opposite*: clear-headed

Worcestershire sauce *type of* **seasonings, sauces, and dips** [➡ SEASONINGS AND SAUCES; 1174]

word **1** *n* **term**, expression, name [➡ ASPECTS OF LANGUAGE; 682] **2** *n* **chat**, conversation, talk, discussion, announcement, comment, declaration, statement [➡ INFORMAL COMMUNICATION; 45] **3** *n* **information**, news, communication, info (*informal*), skinny (*slang*), tidings (*literary*) [➡ BASIC DETAILS; 688] **4** *n* **rumor**, report, whisper, gossip, tittle-tattle, hearsay, buzz (*informal*) [➡ GOSSIP; 678] **5** *n* **promise**, assurance, guarantee, oath, pledge, declaration, undertaking, assertion [➡ PROMISE AND ASSURE; 684] **6** *n* **command**, order, authorization, say-so (*informal*), go-ahead (*informal*), okay (*informal*) [➡ REQUEST AND DEMAND; 663] **7** *n* **password**, code word, magic word, keyword [➡ COMMUNICATION; 602] **8** *type of* **computer feature** [➡ COMPUTERS AND COMPUTING; 1127] **9** *v* **express**, phrase, couch, utter, articulate, verbalize, formulate [➡ UTTER AND PRONOUNCE; 608]

word for word *adv* **verbatim**, in the same words, faithfully, exactly, precisely, accurately, to the letter, literally [➡ EXACT; 203] *Opposite*: loosely

word-for-word *adj* **verbatim**, faithful, exact, precise, accurate, strict, literal [➡ EXACT; 203] *Opposite*: loose

wordiness *n* **long-windedness**, verbosity, prolixity, loquaciousness (*formal*) [➡ MEANINGLESS SPEECH OR WRITING; 676] *Opposite*: conciseness

wording *n* **phrasing**, words, language, phraseology, diction, expression [➡ASPECTS OF LANGUAGE; 682]

wordless *adj* **silent**, mute, nonverbal, mimed, gestured, telepathic [➡ABSENCE OF SOUND; 1257]

word list *n* **vocabulary**, glossary, dictionary, thesaurus, lexicon [➡LISTS AND SCHEDULES; 587]

word of honor *n* [➡PROMISE AND ASSURE; 684]

word-perfect **1** *adj* **correct**, accurate, exact, precise, literal [➡EXACT; 203] **2** *adj* (*UK*) **verbatim**, word for word, perfect, impeccable, consummate, prepared, letter-perfect [➡EXACT; 203] *Opposite*: unprepared

wordplay *n* **punning**, puns, repartee, wit, banter, badinage [➡JOKES AND TEASING; 674]

wordplay

◆ *types of wordplay*
acrostic, anagram, logogram, malapropism, palindrome, pun, spoonerism, telestich

word processor *type of* **software** [➡COMPUTERS AND COMPUTING; 1127]

words **1** *n* **argument**, disagreement, difference of opinion, dispute, confrontation, falling out [➡ARGUMENTS; 47] **2** *n* **lyrics**, verses, chorus, libretto, text [➡MUSIC, SONGS, AND SINGING; 907]

wordy *adj* **verbose**, long-winded, rambling, loquacious, prolix, diffuse [➡ELOQUENT, TALKATIVE, AND LONG-WINDED; 632] *Opposite*: concise

Compare and Contrast: *wordy, verbose, long-winded, rambling, prolix, diffuse*

CORE MEANING: too long or not concisely expressed

wordy using an excessive number of words in writing or speech; *verbose* expressed in language that is wordy and not precise; *long-winded* tediously wordy in speech or writing; *rambling* excessively long with many changes of subject, making it difficult to follow; *prolix* tiresomely wordy; *diffuse* lacking organization and conciseness.

work **1** *n* **labor**, employment, job, vocation, occupation [➡JOB; 833] **2** *n* **effort**, exertion, labor, toil, slog, drudgery, grind (*informal*) [➡HARD WORK OR EFFORT; 298] **3** *n* **composition**, design, creation, opus, masterpiece, piece, product, production, handiwork, oeuvre (*formal*) [➡ARTWORKS; 898] **4** *v* **toil**, labor, slog, drudge [➡WORK-RELATED ACTIVITIES; 834] **5** *v* **perform**, bring about, produce, effect (*formal*) [➡CARRY OUT AN ACTION; 269] **6** *v* **succeed**, be successful, work out, thrive [➡SUCCEED AND WIN; 79] **7** *v* **operate**, control, drive, run, function [➡FUNCTION SUCCESSFULLY; 469]

Compare and Contrast: *work, labor, toil, drudgery*

CORE MEANING: sustained effort required to do or produce something

work the physical or mental effort required to do or achieve something. It can be used of animals and machines as well as people; *labor* strenuous work, usually physical; *toil* tiring, often tedious, physical work, usually over a long period; *drudgery* work that is strenuous and unrewarding, especially work that continues over a long period.

workable *adj* **practical**, practicable, feasible, doable [➡POSSIBLE AND PROBABLE; 177] *Opposite*: impracticable

workaday *adj* **everyday**, ordinary, plain, homespun, commonplace, mundane, routine [➡ORDINARINESS; 244] *Opposite*: extraordinary

work against *v* **counteract**, cancel out, oppose, run counter to, interfere with, negate (*formal*) [➡MAKE IMPOSSIBLE; 276] *Opposite*: support

workaholic *n* **overachiever**, type A, workhorse (*informal*) [➡WORKERS; 836]

workbench *n* **bench**, worktop, work surface, worktable [➡FIXTURES; 859]

workbook *n* **exercise book**, schoolbook, notebook, notepad, book, legal pad, scratchpad, jotter (*UK*) [➡WRITING AND DRAWING IMPLEMENTS, AND MEDIA; 601]

work day and night *v* [➡HARD WORK OR EFFORT; 298]

worked up (*informal*) *adj* **agitated**, upset, excited, worried, hot and bothered, in a state (*informal*) [➡CONFUSION, ANXIETY, AND WORRY; 540] *Opposite*: calm

worker *n* **employee**, member of staff, hand, operative, wage earner [➡WORKERS; 836]

worker ant *type of* **ant** [➡ANTS; 1014]

work flat out *v* [➡HARD WORK OR EFFORT; 298]

work force *n* **personnel**, staff, employees, workers, human resources, labor force [➡THE WORK FORCE; 837]

work hard *v* [➡HARD WORK OR EFFORT; 298]

workhorse **1** *n* (*informal*) **hard worker**, good worker, rock, mainstay, pillar, doer, toiler, slogger [➡WORKERS; 836] **2** *type of* **horse** [➡HORSES; 985]

working **1** *adj* **operational**, functioning, effective, running [➡HAPPENING AND IN PROGRESS; 32] **2** *adj* **employed**, occupied, at work, salaried, in work (*UK*), waged (*UK*) [➡EMPLOYMENT STATUS; 831]

working class *n* **manual workers**, hoi polloi, the masses, proletariat, wage-earners [➡CLASS STATUS; 889]

working-class *adj* [➡CLASS STATUS; 889]

working example *n* [➡REPRESENTATIONS AND GENERAL EXAMPLES; 65]

working from home *adj* [➡EMPLOYMENT STATUS; 831]

working group *n* **task force**, team, ad hoc group, committee, unit, working party (*UK*) [➡WORKERS; 836]

working out *n* **exercising**, physical exercise, exercise, training, physical training, gymnastics, aerobics [➡HOBBIES, GAMES, AND SPORTS; 875]

working party (*UK*) *n* **task force**, team, ad hoc group, working group, committee, unit [➡WORKERS; 836]

workings *n* **mechanism**, machinery, works, moving parts [➡CENTRAL PARTS OF PHYSICAL OBJECTS; 1251]

work like a dog *v* [➡HARD WORK OR EFFORT, 298]

workload *n* **amount of work**, assignment, job, load, capacity, capability [➡WORK IN GENERAL; 297]

workmate *n* **colleague**, coworker, fellow worker [➡ COL-LEAGUES AND EQUALS; 967]

work of art 1 *n* **objet d'art**, creation, painting, sculpture, picture, piece, masterpiece, opus, magnum opus, oeuvre (*formal*) [➡ ARTWORKS; 898] 2 *n* **masterpiece**, beauty, tour de force, pièce de résistance, work of genius [➡ AMAZING THINGS; 211] *Opposite:* disaster (*informal*)

work on 1 *v* **develop**, hone, build up, work up, perfect, improve, practice [➡ IMPROVE SOMETHING; 374] 2 *v* **influence**, sway, persuade, pressure, pressurize (*UK*) [➡ CAUSE OR COMPEL TO ACT; 271]

work out 1 *v* **exercise**, train, drill [➡ HOBBIES, GAMES, AND SPORTS; 875] 2 *v* **solve**, figure out, crack, decipher, resolve, puzzle out, deduce, infer, conclude [➡ SOLVE AND INTERPRET; 760] 3 *v* **understand**, comprehend, make sense of, fathom, conceive [➡ UNDERSTAND AND GRASP; 759] 4 *v* **plan**, devise, outline, sketch, arrange, set up, develop [➡ DEVELOP THEORIES AND REASON; 744]

See Compare and Contrast at **deduce**.

workout 1 *n* **exercise session**, exercises, training, aerobics, calisthenics, weightlifting [➡ HOBBIES, GAMES, AND SPORTS; 875] 2 *n* **test**, road test, trial, run [➡ PREPARATORY EVENTS; 57]

work overtime *v* [➡ HARD WORK OR EFFORT; 298]

workplace *n* **place of work**, workshop, workstation, work, office, factory, shop floor, factory floor, workroom [➡ PLACE OF EMPLOYMENT; 832]

workroom *n* **room**, workshop, study, office, studio, workplace [➡ PLACE OF EMPLOYMENT; 832]

works 1 *n* **factory**, plant, installation, industrial unit, manufacturing plant, shop floor (*UK*) [➡ INDUSTRIAL BUILDINGS; 1087] 2 *n* (*informal*) **everything**, the whole thing, the lot, all of it, the whole kit and caboodle (*informal*) [➡ PHYSICAL OBJECTS; 1243] 3 *n* **mechanism**, workings, machinery, moving parts [➡ CENTRAL PARTS OF PHYSICAL OBJECTS; 1251]

worksheet 1 *n* **homework sheet**, questionnaire, test, quiz, question sheet [➡ LISTS AND SCHEDULES; 587] 2 *n* **schedule**, job sheet, log, record [➡ RECORDS; 585]

workshop *type of* **factory** [➡ INDUSTRIAL BUILDINGS; 1087]

workshy (*UK*) *adj* **lazy**, idle, indolent, slothful, apathetic, shirking [➡ LIFELESS, LAZY, AND UNENTHUSIASTIC; 506]

workspace *n* **working area**, workstation, workplace, booth, cubicle, desk, office [➡ PLACE OF EMPLOYMENT; 832]

workstation 1 *n* **workplace**, workspace, computer terminal [➡ PLACE OF EMPLOYMENT; 832] 2 *type of* **computer** [➡ COMPUTERS AND COMPUTING; 1127]

work surface *n* **surface**, worktop, workbench, workspace, work unit, countertop, table top, counter [➡ FIXTURES; 859]

worktable *type of* **table** [➡ FURNITURE; 858]

worktop *n* **counter**, bench, work surface [➡ FIXTURES; 859]

work to rule (*UK*) *v* **go slow**, take industrial action, slow down [➡ WORK-RELATED ACTIVITIES; 834]

work-to-rule (*UK*) *n* **slowdown**, rule-book slowdown, industrial action (*UK*), go-slow (*UK*) [➡ WORK-RELATED ACTIVITIES; 834]

work up 1 *v* **develop**, work on, hone, improve, refine, cultivate [➡ IMPROVE SOMETHING; 374] 2 *v* **agitate**, upset, disturb, provoke, irritate, nettle (*informal*), stress out (*informal*) [➡ ANGER AND ANNOY; 569] *Opposite:* calm

workup *n* **diagnosis**, examination, checkup, medical [➡ EXAMINE AND ASSESS; 753]

work up a sweat *v* [➡ HARD WORK OR EFFORT; 298]

world 1 *n* **Earth**, planet, globe [➡ THE EARTH; 1039] 2 *n* **biosphere**, ecosphere, creation, all God's creatures, flora and fauna, natural world [➡ NATURE AND THE ENVIRONMENT; 1038] 3 *n* **humankind**, humanity, the human race [➡ GROUPS IN SOCIETY; 940] 4 *n* **domain**, realm, sphere, circle, area [➡ SUBJECT AREAS; 768]

world-beater *n* **champion**, superstar, one in a million, star, classic, number one (*informal*), one-off (*UK*) [➡ AMAZING THINGS; 211]

world-class *adj* **first-rate**, first-class, superlative, outstanding, topnotch (*informal*) [➡ SUPERIORITY; 152]

world-famous *adj* **famous**, renowned, popular, acclaimed, notorious, well-loved, celebrated [➡ KNOWN AND FAMOUS; 181] *Opposite:* unknown

worldliness 1 *n* **materialism**, consumerism, acquisitiveness, greed, secularism [➡ MORALLY BAD OR IMPROPER; 775] 2 *n* **experience**, knowledge, sophistication, worldly wisdom [➡ KNOWLEDGE AND WISDOM; 558]

worldly *adj* **experienced**, sophisticated, mature, knowing, worldly wise [➡ KNOWLEDGE AND WISDOM; 558] *Opposite:* naive

worldly goods *n* **possessions**, belongings, assets, property [➡ POSSESSIONS; 461]

worldly-wise *adj* **sophisticated**, experienced, mature, knowing, worldly [➡ KNOWLEDGE AND WISDOM; 558] *Opposite:* naive

world-shattering *adj* [➡ EXTRAORDINARY: AMAZING; 204]

world-weariness *n* **discontent**, melancholy, boredom, ennui [➡ SADNESS, DISTRESS, AND DESPAIR; 539]

world-weary *adj* **jaded**, discontented, bored, melancholic [➡ SADNESS, DISTRESS, AND DESPAIR; 539]

worldwide *adj* **universal**, international, all-inclusive, wide-reaching, global [➡ GENERAL LOCATIONS; 158] *Opposite:* local

World Wide Web *n* [➡ THE INTERNET; 1128]

worm 1 *type of* **land invertebrate** [➡ LAND INVERTEBRATES; 1021] 2 *type of* **software** [➡ COMPUTERS AND COMPUTING; 1127]

worm-eaten 1 *adj* **wormy**, worm-infested, holey, rotten, decaying, putrid, flyblown, maggoty, putrescent [➡ DECAYING OR INFESTED; 1236] 2 *adj* **dilapidated**, ramshackle, tumbledown, rickety [➡ IN BAD REPAIR; 1234]

worm-infested *adj* [➡ DECAYING OR INFESTED; 1236]

worm out *v* **elicit**, find out, coax out, ferret out, inveigle, sniff out (*informal*) [➡ SEEK POSSESSION AND SEARCH; 456]

wormy *adj* [➡ DECAYING OR INFESTED; 1236]

worn adj **damaged**, shabby, tatty, dog-eared, dilapidated, tattered, worn out, threadbare [➡ IN BAD REPAIR; 1234]

worn down adj **overcome**, weakened, browbeaten, downtrodden, oppressed [➡ SADNESS, DISTRESS, AND DESPAIR; 539]

worn out 1 adj **exhausted**, tired, done in (informal), done for (informal), wiped out (informal), dog-tired (informal), beat (slang) [➡ TIRED, ASLEEP, AND UNCONSCIOUS; 738] **2** adj **tatty**, tattered, shabby, dilapidated, battered, the worse for wear, threadbare, beat up (informal) [➡ IN BAD REPAIR; 1234]

worn to shreds adj [➡ IN BAD REPAIR; 1234]

worried adj **concerned**, anxious, apprehensive, nervous, bothered, troubled, vexed, upset, agitated [➡ CONFUSION, ANXIETY, AND WORRY; 540] Opposite: unconcerned

worried sick adj [➡ CONFUSION, ANXIETY, AND WORRY; 540]

worrier n **pessimist**, neurotic, fidget, worrywart (informal), fussbudget (informal) [➡ GRUMPY AND NEGATIVE PEOPLE; 953]

worrisome adj **troublesome**, worrying, annoying, irritating, bothersome [➡ IRRITATING; 228]

worry 1 v **be anxious**, fret, be troubled, be concerned, be bothered, agonize, lose sleep, stew, fuss [➡ BE CONCERNED AND CARE; 581] **2** v **annoy**, pester, bother, trouble, disturb, irk, bug (informal) [➡ ANGER AND ANNOY; 569] **3** v **touch**, pick, interfere with, claw at, tear at, fiddle with [➡ CONTACT: TOUCH; 412] **4** n **anxiety**, unease, uneasiness, disquiet, discomfort, apprehension, nervousness, stress, angst, care [➡ FEELINGS ABOUT THE FUTURE; 533]

Compare and Contrast: *worry, unease, care, anxiety, angst, stress*

CORE MEANING: a troubled mind

worry a troubled state of mind resulting from concern about current or potential difficulties; **unease** a feeling of anxiousness or lack of satisfaction with a situation; **care** a state of troubled anxiety; **anxiety** nervous apprehension about a future event or a general fear of possible misfortune; **angst** nonspecific chronic anxiety about the human condition or the state of the world; **stress** the worry and nervous apprehension related to a particular situation or event, for example, a job or the process of moving house.

See Compare and Contrast at **bother.**

worrying adj **perturbing**, disturbing, upsetting, disquieting, nerve-racking, distressing, tormenting [➡ EMOTIONALLY UNPLEASANT AND UPSETTING; 227] Opposite: reassuring

worrywart (informal) n [➡ GRUMPY AND NEGATIVE PEOPLE; 953]

worse adj **not as good as**, inferior, of inferior quality, poorer, of poorer quality, shoddier [➡ BAD AND BADLY; 223] Opposite: better

worsen 1 v **get worse**, deteriorate, degenerate, go downhill, degrade [➡ GET WORSE; 381] Opposite: improve **2** v **make something worse**, exacerbate, aggravate, impair, inflame [➡ WORSEN SOMETHING; 380] Opposite: improve

worsening n **deterioration**, aggravation, degeneration, decline [➡ WORSEN SOMETHING; 380] Opposite: improvement

worship 1 v **adore**, love, revere, adulate, deify, pray to, venerate [➡ RELIGIONS AND RELIGIOUS PRACTICES; 777] **2** n **adoration**, love, reverence, respect, devotion, adulation, veneration [➡ LOVE, RESPECT, AND GOODWILL; 549]

worshiper n **celebrant**, participant, member of congregation, believer, convert [➡ RELIGIOUS PEOPLE; 778]

worshipful adj **reverential**, respectful, reverent, deferential, adoring [➡ APPRECIATION AND GRATITUDE; 535]

worst adj **nastiest**, vilest, poorest, wickedest, foulest [➡ BAD AND BADLY; 223] Opposite: best

worsted type of **fabric from animals** [➡ FABRICS; 1132]

worth 1 n **value**, price, cost, rate [➡ FUNDS, PAYMENTS, AND CHARGES; 800] **2** n **merit**, appeal, significance, attraction, importance, value, meaning [➡ IMPORTANCE AND SIGNIFICANCE; 192] **3** n **wealth**, means, assets, value, substance [➡ POSSESSIONS; 461]

worthiness 1 n **merit**, value, worth, praiseworthiness [➡ SOURCE OF HAPPINESS, PLEASURE, OR IMPROVEMENT; 209] **2** n **dullness**, earnestness, boringness, routineness [➡ BORING AND UNINTERESTING; 234]

worthless 1 adj **valueless**, of no value, of little worth, insignificant, useless, without value, no use [➡ REDUNDANT AND USELESS; 240] Opposite: valuable **2** adj **empty**, hollow, meaningless, futile, pointless [➡ REDUNDANT AND USELESS; 240]

worthlessness n **insignificance**, unimportance, irrelevance, triviality [➡ REDUNDANT AND USELESS; 240] Opposite: value

worth mentioning adj [➡ INTERESTING AND MEANINGFUL; 190]

worthwhile adj **valuable**, useful, meaningful, sensible, advisable, worthy [➡ USEFULNESS; 199] Opposite: worthless

worthy 1 adj **commendable**, praiseworthy, laudable, admirable, valuable, worthwhile, creditable [➡ ADMIRABLE AND COMMENDABLE; 185] **2** adj **well-intentioned**, well-meaning, earnest, pedestrian, dull, routine [➡ BORING AND UNINTERESTING; 234]

worthy of note adj [➡ INTERESTING AND MEANINGFUL; 190]

would-be adj **hopeful**, aspiring, prospective, budding, potential, embryonic, possible, wannabe (informal) [➡ POSSIBLE AND PROBABLE; 177]

wound 1 n **injury**, lesion, cut, gash, sore, abrasion, laceration [➡ PAIN AND OTHER PHYSICAL SENSATIONS; 733] **2** v **injure**, hurt, harm, damage, mutilate, maim, lacerate [➡ WOUND A PERSON OR ANIMAL; 383] **3** v **offend**, upset, hurt, injure, distress [➡ UPSET, DISTRESS, AND HUMILIATE; 567]

See Compare and Contrast at **harm.**

wounded 1 adj **injured**, hurt, suffering [➡ INJURED; 742] **2** adj **offended**, hurt, upset, distressed, aggrieved, stung, anguished, pained [➡ SADNESS, DISTRESS, AND DESPAIR; 539]

wounding adj **hurtful**, cutting, acerbic, sharp [➡ RUDE AND HOSTILE; 625] Opposite: kind

wound up (informal) adj **stressed**, annoyed, upset, tense, infuriated, exasperated, irritated, stressed out (informal) [➡ IRRITATION AND ANGER; 541] Opposite: relaxed

wow (*informal*) *n* **winner**, smash, triumph, sensation, knockout (*informal*) [➡ AMAZING THINGS; 211] *Opposite:* flop (*informal*)

wraith *n* **ghost**, phantom, apparition, spirit, specter, shade (*literary*) [➡ THE SUPERNATURAL; 787]

wraithlike *adj* [➡ BUILD; 477]

wrangle 1 *v* **argue**, dispute, quarrel, bicker, squabble, fight, battle, disagree [➡ ARGUE AND FIGHT; 643] **2** *n* **dispute**, argument, quarrel, squabble, disagreement, altercation, tussle, spat, row [➡ ARGUMENTS; 47]

wrangler *n* **ranch hand**, farm hand, cowboy, cowgirl, cowpoke (*informal*) [➡ FARMERS, GARDENERS, AND MANUAL WORKERS; 849]

wrap 1 *v* **enfold**, drape, swathe, cover, envelop, bind, enclose [➡ POSITION SOMETHING: AROUND SOMETHING; 327] **2** *v* **wrap up**, gift wrap, package [➡ DECORATE, ADORN, AND APPLY COATINGS; 405] *Opposite:* unwrap **3** *n* **shawl**, cloak, stole, cape [➡ ACCESSORIES, MILLINERY, AND LINGERIE; 867] **4** *n* **wrapping**, packaging, casing, covering [➡ COVERS AND COATINGS; 1246]

wraparound *type of* **skirt** [➡ GARMENTS AND OUTFITS; 865]

wrap in cotton wool (*UK*) *v* [➡ TAKE CARE OF AND SPOIL; 300]

wrapped up in *adj* **engrossed**, absorbed, preoccupied, obsessed, fascinated, gripped, hooked (*slang*) [➡ PENSIVENESS AND INTEREST; 538]

wrapper *n* **covering**, wrapping, wrap, cover, packaging, package [➡ COVERS AND COATINGS; 1246]

wrapping *n* **packaging**, covering, casing, wrap, cover [➡ COVERS AND COATINGS; 1246]

wrap up 1 *v* **wrap**, gift wrap, parcel, package [➡ DECORATE, ADORN, AND APPLY COATINGS; 405] *Opposite:* unwrap **2** *v* (*informal*) **conclude**, complete, finish, finish off, end, bring to a close [➡ COMPLETE AN ACTION; 263] *Opposite:* begin **3** *v* **dress warmly**, muffle up, bundle up (*informal*) [➡ DRESS, WEAR, AND UNDRESS; 868]

wrap-up *n* [➡ ENDS AND DEPARTURES; 54]

wrath *n* **anger**, rage, fury, madness, ire (*formal*) [➡ IRRITATION AND ANGER; 541]

See Compare and Contrast at **anger**.

wrathful *adj* **furious**, angry, irate, enraged, fuming, steaming (*informal*) [➡ IRRITATION AND ANGER; 541]

wreak *v* **cause**, do, inflict, create, bring about [➡ CAUSE TO HAPPEN; 31]

wreath *n* **garland**, circlet, headdress, laurel [➡ ORNAMENTS AND DECORATIONS; 1248]

wreathe 1 *v* **adorn**, cover, garland, swathe, festoon [➡ DECORATE, ADORN, AND APPLY COATINGS; 405] **2** *v* **twist**, writhe, coil, wind [➡ POSITION SOMETHING: AROUND SOMETHING; 327]

wreck 1 *v* **destroy**, ruin, demolish, break, shatter, smash, spoil, reduce to rubble [➡ DESTRUCTION AND DEMOLITION; 359] **2** *n* **ruin**, remains, wreckage, shell, hulk, shipwreck [➡ JUNK AND USELESS OBJECTS; 1249] **3** *n* **crash**, collision, accident, smashup, fender bender (*informal*) [➡ TRAFFIC ACCIDENTS; 255]

wreckage *n* **ruins**, remains, debris, wreck, rubble, shards [➡ JUNK AND USELESS OBJECTS; 1249]

wrecked 1 *adj* (*informal*) **exhausted**, worn-out, bushed (*informal*), done in (*informal*) [➡ TIRED, ASLEEP, AND UNCONSCIOUS; 738] **2** *adj* **broken**, smashed, damaged, ruined, cracked, destroyed, totaled (*informal*) [➡ IN BAD REPAIR; 1234]

wrecker *type of* **commercial or industrial vehicle** [➡ VEHICLES; 1145]

wren *type of* **common bird** [➡ BIRDS; 997]

wrench 1 *v* **strain**, injure, hurt, pull, sprain, twist, stretch, crick, damage [➡ WOUND A PERSON OR ANIMAL; 383] **2** *v* **pull**, tug, haul, heave, jerk, yank [➡ PUSH, PULL, AND SLIDE; 335] **3** *n* **injury**, sprain, strain, crick [➡ PAIN AND OTHER PHYSICAL SENSATIONS; 733] **4** *n* **pull**, tug, haul, heave, jerk, yank [➡ PUSH, PULL, AND SLIDE; 335] **5** *type of* **general tool** [➡ HAND TOOLS; 1119]

wrest 1 *v* **gain**, take, seize, grasp [➡ GET; 420] **2** *v* **grab**, snatch, tug, pull [➡ CONTACT: HOLD; 411]

wrestle *v* **struggle**, fight, grapple, tussle, brawl [➡ COMPETE, CONTEND, AND COMBAT; 303]

wrestler *n* [➡ PEOPLE IN SPORTS AND LEISURE; 876]

wrestling *type of* **combat sport** [➡ HOBBIES, GAMES, AND SPORTS; 875]

wretch 1 *n* **unfortunate**, victim, languisher, sufferer, poor thing [➡ LAZY OR UNSUCCESSFUL PEOPLE; 948] **2** *n* (*formal*) **scoundrel**, rascal, rogue, villain, blackguard, cad (*dated*), rotter (*dated informal*) [➡ VILLAINS AND THUGS; 947] **3** *n* (*humorous*) **rogue**, rascal, imp, scalawag (*dated informal*) [➡ MISCHIEVOUS OR BADLY BEHAVED CHILD; 946]

wretched 1 *adj* **miserable**, desolate, heartbroken, pitiful, dejected, abject [➡ SADNESS, DISTRESS, AND DESPAIR; 539] *Opposite:* happy **2** *adj* **worthless**, base, despicable, inadequate, inferior, shameful, vile [➡ UNACCEPTABLE AND UNFORGIVABLE; 225] *Opposite:* noble

wretchedly 1 *adv* **miserably**, desolately, pitifully, dejectedly, piteously [➡ SADNESS, DISTRESS, AND DESPAIR; 539] *Opposite:* happily **2** *adv* **dreadfully**, terribly, shamefully, hopelessly, woefully, extremely [➡ TO A GREAT EXTENT; 132]

wretchedness *n* **misery**, woe, unhappiness, dejection, desolation [➡ SADNESS, DISTRESS, AND DESPAIR; 539] *Opposite:* happiness

wriggle *v* **wiggle**, writhe, turn, squirm, twist, fidget [➡ FIDGET AND FROLIC; 311]

wriggle out of *v* [➡ NOT DO AND REFUSE TO DO; 274]

wring *v* **squeeze**, twist, mangle, press, compress [➡ CONTACT: EXERT PRESSURE; 414]

wringing *adj* [➡ WET; 1240]

wringing wet *adj* [➡ WET; 1240]

wrinkle 1 *n* **crease**, crinkle, line, fold, furrow [➡ CHANGE OF SHAPE; 385] **2** *v* **screw**, crumple, crinkle, crease, fold, rumple [➡ CHANGE OF SHAPE; 385] *Opposite:* smooth

wrinkled 1 *adj* **crumpled**, creased, crinkly, rucked, rumpled [➡ IN BAD REPAIR; 1234] *Opposite:* smooth **2** *adj* **wrinkly**, wizened, weathered, lined, furrowed, craggy [➡ FACIAL CHARACTERISTICS; 481] *Opposite:* smooth

wrinkly *adj* **lined**, creased, furrowed, wrinkled, wizened, weathered [➡ FACIAL CHARACTERISTICS; 481] *Opposite:* smooth

damage, insult, injustice, offense [➡ MORALLY BAD OR IMPROPER; 775]
5 *v* **insult**, injure, wound, harm, ill-treat, abuse, sin against, offend, trespass (*archaic*) [➡ MISUSE AND ABUSE; 471]

wrongdoer *n* **criminal**, offender, sinner, reprobate, outlaw, evildoer, transgressor, malefactor (*formal*) [➡ CRIMINALS; 821]

wrongdoing *n* **bad behavior**, unlawful activity, crime, ffense, misconduct [➡ CRIMES; 817]

ng-foot *v* **catch out**, surprise, take unawares, take rprise, trip up, outmaneuver, throw (*informal*) [➡ SUR-
IMPRESS; 574]

gful *adj* **illegal**, unlawful, unfair, unjust, criminal, cked, evil [➡ ILLEGAL; 816] *Opposite*: rightful

See Compare and Contrast at **unlawful**.

wrongful act *n* [➡ CRIMES; 817]

wrongfully 1 *adv* **unlawfully**, illegally, wrongly, improperly [➡ ILLEGAL; 816] **2** *adv* **unfairly**, unjustly, inequitably [➡ MORALLY BAD OR IMPROPER; 775]

wrong-headed 1 *adj* **unreasonable**, obstinate, stubborn, perverse [➡ NEGATIVE INTELLECTUAL CHARACTERISTICS; 525] **2** *adj* **irrational**, unreasoning, unthinking, ill-considered, ill-conceived, misguided, mistaken [➡ THE NATURE OF IDEAS; 771]

wrong-headedness *n* [➡ NEGATIVE INTELLECTUAL CHARACTERISTICS; 525]

wrongly 1 *adv* **incorrectly**, mistakenly, erroneously, imperfectly, faultily, accidentally, by mistake [➡ INCORRECT AND ERRONEOUS; 222] *Opposite*: correctly **2** *adv* **immorally**, wickedly, dishonestly, illegally, sinfully, criminally, unlawfully [➡ MORALLY BAD OR IMPROPER; 775] *Opposite*: rightly **3** *adv* **unsuitably**, improperly, inappropriately, incorrectly [➡ INAPPROPRIATE AND UNSUITABLE; 224] *Opposite*: suitably

wrong side up *adj* [➡ ORIENTATION AND ALIGNMENT; 1223]

wrong way up *adj* [➡ ORIENTATION AND ALIGNMENT; 1223]

wrought-up *adj* **tense**, nervous, agitated, excited, on edge, edgy, jumpy, worked up (*informal*), twitchy (*informal*) [➡ CONFUSION, ANXIETY, AND WORRY; 540]

wry *adj* **ironic**, cynical, sardonic, dry, droll [➡ MOCKING AND DISMISSIVE; 636]

wryness *n* **humor**, irony, satire, dryness, drollness [➡ JOKES AND TEASING; 674]

wunderkind *n* [➡ TALENTED OR INTELLIGENT PEOPLE; 528]

695]

set
CCEPT; 748]
(*informal*),

nt, poet, journalist,
14]

, piece, review, critique [➡ ANA-

urm, wriggle, twist, struggle, thrash, thrash
(UK) [➡ FIDGET AND FROLIC; 311]

writing 1 *n* **script**, symbols, inscription, marks, characters, letters, lettering [➡ WRITING; 583] **2** *n* **text**, literature, prose, journalism, copy [➡ FICTION AND DRAMA; 913]

writing board *n* [➡ WRITING AND DRAWING IMPLEMENTS, AND MEDIA; 601]

writing desk *type of* **table** [➡ FURNITURE; 858]

writing pad *n* [➡ WRITING AND DRAWING IMPLEMENTS, AND MEDIA; 601]

writing paper *n* [➡ WRITING AND DRAWING IMPLEMENTS, AND MEDIA; 601]

written *adj* **on paper**, printed, in black and white, in print [➡ WRITING; 583]

written off (*informal*) *adj* [➡ IN BAD REPAIR; 1234]

wrong 1 *adj* **incorrect**, mistaken, erroneous, off beam, wide of the mark [➡ INCORRECT AND ERRONEOUS; 222] *Opposite*: right **2** *adj* **immoral**, wicked, dishonest, illegal, sinful, iniquitous, criminal, unethical [➡ MORALLY BAD OR IMPROPER; 775] *Opposite*: right **3** *adj* **amiss**, not right, unsuitable, improper, inappropriate, incorrect [➡ INAPPROPRIATE AND UNSUITABLE; 224] *Opposite*: suitable **4** *n* **sin**, crime, injury, harm,

XYZ

XC skiing *type of* **winter sport** [➡ HOBBIES, GAMES, AND SPORTS; 875]

xenophobia *n* **chauvinism**, racial intolerance, dislike of foreigners, nationalism, prejudice, racism [➡ PREJUDICE; 550] *Opposite*: tolerance

xenophobic *adj* **chauvinistic**, intolerant, nationalistic, prejudiced, racist [➡ NEGATIVE INTELLECTUAL CHARACTERISTICS; 525] *Opposite*: tolerant

xenopus *type of* **amphibian** [➡ AMPHIBIANS; 1008]

X-ray *type of* **medical procedure** [➡ REMEDIES, TREATMENTS, AND OPERATIONS; 731]

xylophone *type of* **percussion instrument** [➡ MUSICAL INSTRUMENTS; 910]

yacht *type of* **sailing vessel** [➡ SHIPS AND BOATS; 1150]

yak (*informal*) **1** *v* **chatter**, chat, talk, gossip, natter (*informal*), gab (*informal*), shoot the breeze (*slang*), chew the fat (*slang*), rap (*slang*), schmooze (*slang*) [➡ TWO-WAY COMMUNICATION; 607] **2** *n* **chat**, heart-to-heart, talk, gossip, gab (*informal*), rap (*slang*), schmooze (*slang*) [➡ INFORMAL COMMUNICATION; 45]

yakitori *type of* **cooked dish** [➡ PREPARED DISHES; 1170]

yam *type of* **root vegetable** [➡ FRUIT AND VEGETABLES; 1176]

yammer (*informal*) **1** *v* **chatter**, chat, talk, gossip, blab (*informal*), burble (*informal*), yap (*informal*) [➡ GOSSIP; 678] **2** *n* **chatter**, chat, talk, gossip, blab (*informal*), yap (*informal*) [➡ INFORMAL COMMUNICATION; 45]

yank **1** *v* **pull**, tug, jerk, wrench, snatch, heave, haul [➡ PUSH, PULL, AND SLIDE; 335] **2** *n* **tug**, pull, jerk, wrench, heave [➡ PUSH, PULL, AND SLIDE; 335]

See Compare and Contrast at **pull**.

yank somebody's chain (*informal*) *v* [➡ JOKES AND TEASING; 674]

yap **1** *v* **bark**, yelp, bay, woof [➡ SOUND EMISSION BY ANIMALS OR BIRDS; 364] **2** *v* (*informal*) **chatter**, chat, talk, gossip, yammer (*informal*), blab (*informal*) [➡ GOSSIP; 678] **3** *n* **yelp**, bark, woof, baying [➡ SOUNDS MADE BY ANIMALS; 1261] **4** *n* (*informal*) **chatter**, chat, talk, gossip, yammer (*informal*), blab (*informal*), burble (*informal*) [➡ INFORMAL COMMUNICATION; 45]

yard **1** *n* **plot**, patch, grass, lawn [➡ GARDENS; 1074] **2** *n* **patio**, courtyard, terrace, back yard [➡ URBAN OUTDOOR SPACES; 1072] **3** *n* **enclosure**, work area, storage area [➡ URBAN OUTDOOR SPACES; 1072] **4** *type of* **nonmetric unit** [➡ SIZE AND DIMENSIONS; 1192]

yard sale *n* [➡ SALES AND SHOWS; 443]

yardstick *n* **measure**, index, gauge, benchmark, standard, touchstone [➡ SCORES AND EVALUATIONS; 598]

yarmulke *type of* **headgear** [➡ ACC... 867]

yarn **1** *n* **thread**, fiber, wool [➡ T... **2** *n* (*informal*) **story**, tale, tall story, ta... story, fish story, anecdote, joke [➡ THE ORA...

yashmak *type of* **headgear** [➡ ACCESSORIES, MI... 867]

yaw *v* [➡ TAKE UP A NEW POSITION; 312]

yawn **1** *v* **stretch**, stretch yourself, rub your ey... nod, drowse [➡ SLEEP AND DREAM; 723] **2** *v* **gape**, split, f... gap, crack [➡ SEPARATE AND DIVIDE; 401] *Opposite*: close up **3** ... nonevent, waste of time, mind-numbing experience,... (*informal*) [➡ NUISANCES; 253] *Opposite*: laugh

yawning *adj* **deep**, cavernous, gaping, wide, open, va... [➡ WIDTH: WIDE; 1199] *Opposite*: narrow

yea (*archaic*) *interj* [➡ EXPRESSIONS OF AGREEMENT; 648]

yeah (*informal*) *interj* [➡ EXPRESSIONS OF AGREEMENT; 648]

year *type of* **time period** [➡ TIMES OF YEAR; 88]

yearbook *n* **annual**, annual report, almanac [➡ RECORDS; 585]

yearling *type of* **young animal** [➡ YOUNG ANIMALS; 977]

yearly **1** *adj* **annual**, twelve-monthly, year on year (*UK*) [➡ TIMES OF YEAR; 88] **2** *adv* **annually**, every year, once a year [➡ TIMES OF YEAR; 88]

yearn *v* **desire**, long, crave, ache, hanker, want, covet, hunger, thirst [➡ DESIRE AND WANT; 579]

See Compare and Contrast at **want**.

yearning *n* **desire**, longing, yen, hunger, thirst, ache, craving, nostalgia, urge, hankering [➡ DESIRE AND WANT; 579]

yearningly *adv* **longingly**, wistfully, unrequitedly, achingly, nostalgically, desirously (*formal*) [➡ POSITIVE IMPATIENCE, ENTHUSIASM, AND ALERTNESS; 537]

year-round *adj* **constant**, continual, continuous, perennial [➡ PERMANENCE: WITHOUT END; 94]

years *n* **an age**, an inordinate length of time, eons, ages (*informal*), centuries (*informal*), a month of Sundays (*informal*) [➡ LONG PERIODS OF TIME; 92]

years to come *n* [➡ FUTURE; 86]

yeast *type of* **fungus** [➡ MICROORGANISMS, FUNGI, AND ALGAE; 1023]

yell **1** *v* **shout**, scream, shriek, roar, bellow, bawl, screech, howl, holler (*informal*) [➡ SOUND EMISSION BY PEOPLE; 363] **2** *n* **shriek**, shout, scream, roar, bellow, screech, howl, holler (*informal*) [➡ SOUNDS MADE BY PEOPLE; 1262]

yell at *v* **scold**, shout at, rebuke, lash, chew out (*informal*), tell off (*informal*), bawl out (*informal*), tear off a strip (*UK*) [➞ACCUSE, BLAME, AND CRITICIZE; 641]

yellow *type of* **color** [➞COLORS; 1224]

yellow

◆ *types of yellow*
canary yellow, chrome yellow, citrine, citron, flaxen, gold, lemon, lemon yellow, mustard, saffron

yellow cab *type of* **commercial or industrial vehicle** [➞VEHICLES; 1145]

yellowed *adj* [➞IN BAD REPAIR; 1234]

yellowhammer *type of* **songbird** [➞SONGBIRDS; 1003]

yelp 1 *v* **bark**, yap, cry, squeal, squeak [➞SOUND EMISSION BY ANIMALS OR BIRDS; 364] 2 *n* **yap**, bark, cry, squeal, squeak [➞SOUNDS MADE BY ANIMALS; 1261]

yen 1 *n* **urge**, desire, wish, longing, yearning, craving, hankering [➞DESIRE AND WANT; 579] 2 *type of* **currency** [➞CURRENCIES; 798]

yep (*informal*) *interj* [➞EXPRESSIONS OF AGREEMENT; 648]

yes 1 *adv* **affirmative**, sure, certainly, absolutely, of course, indeed, naturally, surely, sure thing (*informal*) [➞EXPRESSIONS OF AGREEMENT; 648] *Opposite*: no 2 *n* **affirmative**, positive response, nod, aye, thumbs up (*informal*), okay (*informal*) [➞AGREE; 645] *Opposite*: no

yes indeed *adv* [➞EXPRESSIONS OF AGREEMENT; 648]

yesterday *n* [➞PAST; 84]

yesteryear *n* **past**, long ago, former times, days gone by, olden days [➞PAST; 84] *Opposite*: today

yet 1 *adv* **up to now**, so far, thus far, hitherto, until now [➞PAST; 84] 2 *adv* **however**, nevertheless, nonetheless, still, in spite of that, but [➞ALTHOUGH, NEVERTHELESS, AND DESPITE; 169]

yet again *adv* **once more**, again, once again, over again [➞AGAIN; 109]

yeti *n* [➞MYTHICAL BEINGS; 789]

yet to be *adv* [➞FUTURE; 86]

yet to come *adj* [➞FUTURE; 86]

yew *type of* **evergreen tree** [➞EVERGREEN AND CONIFEROUS TREES; 1029]

yield 1 *v* **produce**, bear, generate, bring in, return, bring forth [➞ENGENDER; 350] 2 *v* **give way**, submit, acquiesce, capitulate, accede, defer, surrender, succumb, give in [➞FAIL OR BE UNSUCCESSFUL; 75] *Opposite*: resist 3 *v* **give up**, concede, grant, relinquish, resign, surrender [➞GIVE AND PROVIDE; 430] *Opposite*: keep 4 *n* **harvest**, crop, produce, vintage [➞AMOUNTS AND QUANTITIES; 112] 5 *n* **profit**, earnings, income, revenue, return [➞INCOME; 460]

Compare and Contrast: *yield, capitulate, submit, succumb, surrender*

CORE MEANING: to give way

yield to give way to something such as force, pressure, entreaty, or persuasion; *capitulate* to cease to resist a superior force, especially one that seems invincible, sometimes without having offered strong opposition; *submit* to accept somebody else's authority or will, especially reluctantly or under pressure; *succumb* to give in to something due to weakness or the failure to offer effective opposition; *surrender* to give way to the power of another person and stop offering resistance, usually after active opposition.

yielding 1 *adj* **soft**, elastic, springy, squashy, resilient [➞MALLEABLE AND ELASTIC; 1212] *Opposite*: firm 2 *adj* **compliant**, acquiescent, docile, accommodating, tractable, malleable [➞THE WILL AND WILLINGNESS; 563] *Opposite*: stubborn

yodel *type of* **world music** [➞MUSIC, SONGS, AND SINGING; 907]

yoga *type of* **complementary therapy** [➞REMEDIES, TREATMENTS, AND OPERATIONS; 731]

yogurt *n* [➞DAIRY PRODUCTS AND CHEESES; 1183]

yoke *n* **repression**, oppression, burden, bondage, encumbrance, drag, load, annoyance [➞NUISANCES; 253]

yonder *adv* [➞GENERAL LOCATIONS; 158]

Yorkshire terrier *type of* **small dog** [➞DOGS; 980]

young 1 *adj* **youthful**, little, juvenile, adolescent, immature, childish, babyish, infantile [➞BABYHOOD, CHILDHOOD, AND ADOLESCENCE; 917] *Opposite*: old 2 *adj* **new**, early, undeveloped, fledgling, beginning, fresh [➞NEW, MODERN; 166] *Opposite*: established 3 *n* **offspring**, children, babies, litter, brood, issue, progeny [➞YOUNGER GENERATION RELATIVES; 958]

young

◆ *types of young animals*
bullock, calf, colt, cub, fawn, foal, heifer, joey, kid, kitten, lamb, leveret, piglet, pup, puppy, whelp, yearling

◆ *types of young birds*
chick, cygnet, duckling, eaglet, eyas, fledgling, gosling, nestling, owlet, pullet, squab

young child *n* [➞CHILD OR YOUTH; 945]

younger generation *n* **young people**, youth, teenagers, adolescents, youngsters, kids (*informal*) [➞CHILD OR YOUTH; 945]

young lady *n* [➞FEMALE PERSON; 933]

young-looking *adj* [➞PEOPLE'S PHYSICAL APPEARANCE; 475]

young man *n* [➞MALE PERSON; 934]

young offenders' institution (*UK*) *n* [➞BUILDINGS FOR CONFINING PEOPLE; 1094]

young people *n* [➞CHILD OR YOUTH; 945]

young person *n* **teenager**, adolescent, youngster, juvenile, child, minor, teen (*informal*), kid (*informal*) [➡CHILD OR YOUTH; 945] *Opposite*: adult

youngster *n* **child**, young person, teenager, youth, adolescent, minor, kid (*informal*), teen (*informal*) [➡CHILD OR YOUTH; 945] *Opposite*: adult

See Compare and Contrast at **youth**.

young'un (*informal*) *n* [➡CHILD OR YOUTH; 945]

you said it! *interj* [➡EXPRESSIONS OF AGREEMENT; 648]

youth 1 *n* **childhood**, adolescence, formative years, infancy, early life, early stages, minority [➡BABYHOOD, CHILD-HOOD, AND ADOLESCENCE; 917]   2 *n* **child**, teenager, youngster, minor, young person, kid (*informal*) [➡CHILD OR YOUTH; 945]

Compare and Contrast: *youth, child, kid, teenager, youngster*

CORE MEANING: somebody who is young

youth a man or boy who is in his teens or early twenties; *child* a young person between birth and the onset of puberty; *kid* (*informal*) a child or young person; *teenager* somebody between the ages of thirteen and nineteen; *youngster* somebody who is young, or (*humorous*) somebody younger than others mentioned or present.

youth custody centre (*UK*) *n* [➡BUILDINGS FOR CONFINING PEOPLE; 1094]

youthful 1 *adj* **young**, childlike, childish, boyish, girlish, young at heart, young-looking [➡PEOPLE'S PHYSICAL APPEARANCE; 475] *Opposite*: old   2 *adj* **vigorous**, energetic, lively, enthusiastic, active, sprightly [➡ENERGY AND ENTHUSIASM; 496] *Opposite*: sluggish

youthfulness 1 *n* **youth**, freshness, newness, childishness, first flush of youth, boyish charm [➡PEOPLE'S PHYSICAL APPEARANCE; 475] *Opposite*: age   2 *n* **enthusiasm**, energy, radiance, vigor, liveliness, vivacity, bloom [➡ENERGY AND ENTHUSIASM; 496] *Opposite*: sluggishness

youth hostel *type of* **hotel** [➡HOTELS, RESTAURANTS, AND CLUBS; 1082]

yowl *v* **howl**, squall, squeal, wail, caterwaul [➡SOUND EMISSION BY ANIMALS OR BIRDS; 364]

yo-yo *type of* **toy** [➡TOYS; 880]

yuan *type of* **currency** [➡CURRENCIES; 798]

yucca *type of* **foliage plant** [➡FOLIAGE PLANTS; 1035]

yucky (*informal*) *adj* **nasty**, revolting, horrid, unpleasant, disgusting, repugnant [➡DISGUSTING AND REPULSIVE; 230] *Opposite*: yummy

Yukon *type of* **time zone** [➡TIMES OF DAY; 87]

yumminess *n* [➡TASTE; 703]

yummy *adj* **delicious**, tasty, mouthwatering, delectable, luscious, scrumptious (*informal*) [➡TASTE; 703] *Opposite*: yucky (*informal*)

yurt *n* [➡RESIDENTIAL BUILDINGS; 1078]

zabaglione *type of* **dessert** [➡CAKES, COOKIES, AND DESSERTS; 1181]

zany *adj* **unconventional**, madcap, crazy (*informal*), wacky (*informal*) [➡BIZARRE AND PECULIAR; 257]

zap (*informal*) 1 *v* **destroy**, kill, annihilate, exterminate, delete, obliterate [➡DESTRUCTION AND DEMOLITION; 359]   2 *v* **change channels**, switch channels, flick through, cruise, surf [➡TELEVISION AND RADIO; 606]   3 *v* **whiz**, zoom, tear, rip, shoot, dash, zip (*informal*) [➡MOVE FAST; 313] *Opposite*: dawdle

zappy (*informal*) *adj* **lively**, forceful, striking, eye-catching, energetic [➡INTERESTING AND MEANINGFUL; 190]

zeal *n* **enthusiasm**, passion, fanaticism, fervor, ardor, keenness, eagerness, vehemence, intensity [➡POSITIVE IMPA-TIENCE, ENTHUSIASM, AND ALERTNESS; 537] *Opposite*: apathy

zealot *n* **extremist**, fanatic, bigot, evangelist, dogmatist, enthusiast [➡DEVOTEES AND ADDICTED PEOPLE; 556] *Opposite*: moderate

zealotry *n* [➡FADS, FETISHES, AND IDOLATRY; 555]

zealous *adj* **enthusiastic**, keen, passionate, fervent, ardent, fanatical, obsessive, eager, extreme, vehement, intense [➡ENERGY AND ENTHUSIASM; 496] *Opposite*: apathetic

zebra crossing (*UK*) *n* [➡BRIDGES, TUNNELS, CROSSINGS, AND JUNCTIONS; 1112]

zenith *n* **peak**, summit, pinnacle, top, acme, high point, apex [➡EXTREMITIES OF PHYSICAL OBJECTS; 1250] *Opposite*: nadir

zeppelin *n* **airship**, dirigible, blimp, aircraft, balloon [➡AIRCRAFT; 1148]

zero *n* **nothing**, nil, naught, zip (*informal*), zilch (*informal*), zippo (*informal*) [➡NONE; 123]

zero tolerance *n* [➡REFUSE PERMISSION AND NOT ALLOW; 670]

zest 1 *n* **enthusiasm**, keenness, gusto, relish, appetite, passion [➡POSITIVE IMPATIENCE, ENTHUSIASM, AND ALERTNESS; 537] *Opposite*: apathy   2 *n* **taste**, tang, piquancy, bite, spice [➡TASTE; 703]

zestful *adj* **enthusiastic**, keen, passionate, dynamic, energetic [➡ENERGY AND ENTHUSIASM; 496] *Opposite*: apathetic

zesty *adj* [➡TASTE; 703]

zeugma *type of* **figure of speech** [➡FIGURES OF SPEECH; 673]

zigzag *v* **wind**, meander, crisscross, weave, snake, twist and turn, corkscrew [➡CHANGE DIRECTION OF MOTION; 344]

zilch (*informal*) *n* **nothing**, zero, nil, naught, zip (*informal*), zippo (*informal*) [➡NONE; 123]

zillion (*informal*) *n* **million**, billion, truckload, mountain, gazillion (*slang*), squillion (*UK*), shedload (*UK*) [➡MANY, MUCH, LARGE AMOUNT; 117]

zinc *type of* **metal** [➡METALS; 1276]

zing (*informal*) *n* **vitality**, dynamism, energy, punch, vigor [➡POSITIVE IMPATIENCE, ENTHUSIASM, AND ALERTNESS; 537] *Opposite*: lifelessness

zip 1 *n* (*informal*) **energy**, vigor, vitality, dynamism, punch, go (*informal*), pep (*informal*), spunk (*informal*) [➡POSITIVE IMPATIENCE, ENTHUSIASM, AND ALERTNESS; 537] *Opposite*: apathy   2 *n* (*informal*) **nothing**, nil, zero, zilch (*informal*), zippo (*informal*) [➡NONE; 123]   3 *v* **compact**, compress [➡COMPUTERS AND

COMPUTING; 1127]   **4** *v* (*informal*) **go fast**, whiz, zoom, rocket, whoosh, go like a bullet [➡MOVE FAST; 313] *Opposite*: dawdle

zipper *part of* **garment** [➡PARTS OF A GARMENT; 870]

zit (*slang*) *n* **pimple**, spot, boil [➡CONDITIONS AFFECTING THE SKIN; 721]

zither *type of* **stringed instrument** [➡MUSICAL INSTRUMENTS; 910]

zloty *type of* **currency** [➡CURRENCIES; 798]

zodiac *n* **astrologer's chart**, astrological diagram, astrological calendar [➡FATE, DESTINY, AND ASTROLOGY; 782]

zodiacal *adj* **astrological**, horoscopic, celestial [➡FATE, DESTINY, AND ASTROLOGY; 782]

zombie (*informal*) *n* **automaton**, robot, machine, sleepwalker (*informal*) [➡LAZY OR UNSUCCESSFUL PEOPLE; 948]

zonal *adj* **regional**, territorial, area, district, zone-specific, region-specific [➡COUNTRIES AND REGIONS; 1067]

zone *n* **area**, region, district, sector, neighborhood, precinct [➡PLACE; 1065]

zoo *n* **zoological gardens**, menagerie, safari park, wildlife refuge, game reserve, children's zoo, park reserve, petting zoo, city farm (*UK*), wildlife park (*UK*) [➡URBAN OUTDOOR SPACES; 1072]

zoological *adj* [➡BIOLOGICAL SCIENCES; 1037]

zoological gardens *n* [➡URBAN OUTDOOR SPACES; 1072]

zoology *type of* **bioscience** [➡BIOLOGICAL SCIENCES; 1037]

zoom **1** *v* **go fast**, whiz, whoosh, rocket, go like a bullet, zip (*informal*) [➡MOVE FAST; 313] *Opposite*: dawdle **2** *v* **increase**, shoot up, rise, rocket, take off, skyrocket (*informal*) [➡GO UPWARD; 306] *Opposite*: plummet

zoom in *v* **home in**, pinpoint, focus, narrow down, concentrate, zero in [➡FIND; 463]

zoom lens *part of* **camera** [➡PHOTOGRAPHY AND PHOTOGRAPHIC EQUIPMENT; 1122]

zoophobia *type of* **phobia** [➡FEARS AND PHOBIAS; 554]

zoot suit *type of* **suit** [➡GARMENTS AND OUTFITS; 865]

zori *type of* **shoe** [➡FOOTWEAR; 871]

zucchini *type of* **vegetable** [➡FRUIT AND VEGETABLES; 1176]

zygomatic bone *type of* **bone** [➡THE BONES AND JOINTS; 719]

THEMATIC
SECTION

The Way Things Are or Seem to Be

Becoming, Appearing, and Disappearing

1 Gradually Come into Existence

Great oaks from little acorns grow. **Proverb**

(*v*) appear, arise, become, come, come into being, come out of, crystallize, derive, descend, develop, emanate, emerge, ensue, evolve, flow, form, gel (*informal*), grow up, issue, jell, make, materialize, originate, prove, rise, *take form*, take root, take shape, unfold, wax (*literary*)

2 Suddenly Come into Existence

The one and only basis of the moral life must be spontaneity, that is, the immediate, the unreflective. **Jean-Paul Sartre**

(*v*) break out, burst out, come on, come up, crop up (*informal*), dawn, erupt, flare up, kick in (*informal*), spring up

3 Appear and Emerge

At a given moment I open my eyes and exist. And before that, during all eternity, what was there? Nothing. **Ugo Betti**

(*v*) appear, break, come into sight, come out, come to light, emerge, fall into place, get around, glare, leak out, leap out at, loom, make inroads, materialize, obtrude, occur, rear its head, *rematerialize, resurface*, riot, rise up, show, show up, sprout, stand out, *stick out like a sore thumb*, strike, surface, turn up

4 Disappear

In the night reason disappears, only the lives of things remaining. **Antoine de Saint-Exupéry**

(*v*) clear, decline, decrease, disappear, dry up, dwindle, ebb, evaporate, fade, fade away, fail, *fall away*, fizzle, give out, go away, melt, *melt away*, peter out, run out, *sink without trace*, tail off, trail away, vanish, vaporize, wane, weaken

5 Cause to Appear

For words, like Nature, half reveal/And half conceal the Soul within. **Alfred Tennyson**

(*v*) bare, bring out, bring to light, call attention to, conjure, conjure up, demonstrate, dig up, disinter (*formal*), display, disport (*archaic or humorous*), draw, dredge up, evidence, evince, exhibit, expose, feature, flash (*informal*), flaunt, invoke, lay bare, manifest, mine, model, open up, parade, present, preview, register, render (*formal*), reveal, revive, set off, set out, show, show off, show up, smoke out, stick out, throw up, unearth, unfold, unfurl, unmask, unroll, unveil, wear

6 Cause to Disappear

There is a theory which states that if ever anyone discovers exactly what the Universe is for and why it is here, it will instantly disappear. **Douglas Adams**

(*v*) blanket, block off, blot out, blur, bury, camouflage, cloak, cloister, closet, cloud, conceal, cover, cover up, disguise, drown, eclipse, encase, encode, enshroud, extinguish, heel in, hide, mask, mist over, obscure, paper over, plant (*informal*), screen, secrete, shade, shadow, swallow, veil, whitewash

See also REMOVE SOMETHING (338), TAKE SOMETHING AWAY (425)

7 Absent and Unavailable

It's when the thing itself is missing that you have to supply the word. **Henri de Montherlant**

(*adj*) absent, absent without leave, away, AWOL, busy, discontinued, engaged, forgotten, gone, irrecoverable, lacking, *long-gone*, long-lost (*humorous*), lost, mislaid, misplaced, missing, occupied, *omitted*, on loan, on the run, out, *out of stock*, reserved, spent, spoken for, taken, tied up, unaccounted-for, unavailable, unobtainable, *unreachable, used up*, vanished, *withheld*

(*n*) absence, exception, exile, nonattendance, no-show, omission, scarceness, scarcity, truancy, unavailability

See also NONEXISTENCE (24)

8 Leave and Go Away

Absence makes the heart grow fonder,/Isle of Beauty, Fare thee well! **Thomas Haynes Bayly**

(*v*) absent yourself, check out, clear out, *cut your losses*, depart, emigrate, *excuse yourself*, exit, *flounce out*, get off, get out, go, go away, go off, *go off in a huff*, head off, *hit the road*, hole up (*slang*), leave, make tracks (*informal*), *make yourself scarce* (*informal*), move on, move out, *pull away*, pull out, push off, put forth (*formal*), quit, retire, run along, sally, separate, set forth (*literary*), set off, set out, *set sail, shove off* (*informal*), split (*slang*), start, start off, start out, step out, *storm out*, strike out, *take leave*, take off (*informal*), tear away, vacate, *vamoose* (*slang*), *venture forth*, walk off, walk out, *wander away, wander off*, withdraw

9 Runaways and Absentees

I fled Him, down the labyrinthine ways/Of my own mind; and in the mist of tears. **Francis Thompson**

(*n*) absconder, absentee, deserter, escapee, fugitive, outlaw, runaway, stowaway, truant

10 Run Away and Avoid

Stop the World, I Want to Get Off **Anthony Newley**

(*v*) abandon, *abandon ship*, abscond, bail out, beat a hasty retreat, beat it (*slang*), bolt, break out, *buzz off* (*informal*), cut loose (*informal*), decamp, defect, desert, elope, escape, evacuate, flee, fly, fly the coop (*informal*), forsake, get away, *go AWOL*, go missing, *go underground*, hide, *hightail it* (*slang*), *jump ship*, leg it (*informal*), light out (*informal*), *make a break for it*, *make a dash for it*, *make a run for it*, *make a sharp exit*, make off, play hooky (*informal*), *play truant*, run away, *run for it*, run off, scat (*informal*), scoot (*informal*), scram (*informal*), *send your apologies*, *show a clean pair of heels* (*UK*), *skedaddle* (*slang*), skip (*informal*), *steal away*, take cover, take flight, *take to flight*, take to your heels, truant, walk away, *withdraw from the world*

11 Present and Available

Sometime they'll give a war and nobody will come.
Carl Sandburg

(*adj*) attached, at the ready, available, *bookable*, down, endemic, epidemic, ever-present, existent (*formal*), for sale, forthcoming, going, *going begging*, immanent (*formal*), *in attendance*, included, *in evidence*, *in existence*, in hand, *in situ*, listed, obtainable, omnipresent, on board, on hand, on sale, on stand-by, on tap, on the market, open, out, participatory, pervasive, popular, present, prevailing, prevalent, *procurable*, reachable, *reservable*, rife, surviving, ubiquitous, untaken, untapped, up for grabs (*informal*), vacant, viewable, wall-to-wall (*informal*), widespread

(*adv*) aboard (*informal*), about, around, *in the area*, *to hand*

(*n*) attendance, availability, currency, pervasiveness, presence, prevalence, *ubiquitousness*, *ubiquity*

12 Arrive

The hero appears only when the tiger is dead. **Burmese proverb**

(*v*) appear, arrive, attend, barge in, *blunder in*, book in (*UK*), *breeze in*, burst in on, butt in, call in (*UK*), check in, close in, come, come along, come around, come back, come forward, descend, draw near, drop in, enter, gain access, gatecrash, get in, get to, go in, go into, *heave into view* (*literary*), hit (*slang*), invade, make, poke, *pop by* (*UK*), pop in (*informal*), *pop round* (*informal*), present, put in an appearance, queue-jump (*UK*), raid, reach, *reemerge*, reenter, report, return, revisit, roll in, roll up, set foot in, show up (*informal*), show your face, stand out, stop by, stop off, *storm in*, surprise, *swing by*, trespass, turn out, turn up, walk in on

13 Arrival

The story of my life is about back entrances and side doors and secret elevators and other ways of getting in and out of places so that people won't bother you. **Greta Garbo**

(*n*) appearance, arrival, call, coming, debarkation, disembarkation, entrance, entry, homecoming, immigration, incursion (*formal*), infestation, infiltration, inflow, influx, infringement, landfall, landing, penetration, reentry, return, touchdown, visit

14 Arrive by Transport

When a train pulls into a great city I am reminded of the closing moments of an overture. **Graham Greene**

(*v*) alight, berth, come in, debark, disembark, dock, land, pull up

Being and Not Being

15 Exist

There are two senses, and two only, of the word "exist": one exists as a thing or else one exists as a consciousness.
Maurice Merleau-Ponty

(*v*) be, be alive, exist, live

16 Prosper and Abound

Earth's crammed with heaven,/And every common bush afire with God. **Elizabeth Barrett Browning**

(*v*) abound, be alive with, bloom (*literary*), blossom, blossom out, boom, bristle, burgeon (*literary*), flourish, flower, overflow with, predominate, prevail (*formal*), proliferate, prosper, seethe, swarm, teem, thrive

17 Continue to Exist

We always find something, eh, Didi, to give us the impression that we exist? **Samuel Beckett**

(*v*) abide (*archaic*), bear up, come through, continue, cope, endure, exist, extend, fare, fend for yourself, get along, get by, get over, get through, hold, hold up, keep, last, last out, lie, live on, make do, make ends meet, manage, outlast, outlive, outride, outstay, overwinter, persist, remain, run, scrape by, see out, set in, smolder, spread, stand, stand up, stay, subsist, survive, tarry, wait, withstand

18 Exist with Others

Until knowledge is understood in human and political terms as something to be won to the service of coexistence and community, not of particular races, nations, or religions, the future augurs badly. **Edward W. Said**

(*v*) coexist, cohabit, colonize, concur, co-occur

19 Exist in a Place

There is only one home to the life of a tortoise; there is only one shell to the soul of man. **Wole Soyinka**

(*v*) be, be there, cling, come, come from, extend, frequent, haunt, hover, jut, lie, lie around (*informal*), look out, overhang, overlook, patronize (*formal*), perch, project, protrude, remain, reside, roost, run through, sit, sprawl, spread out, stick around (*informal*), straggle, stretch, tower

20 Inhabit

I believe that if God had wanted us to share our homes with insects, He would not have made them so unattractive.
Dave Barry

(*v*) abide (*archaic*), board, dwell (*literary*), encamp, inhabit, live, lodge, occupy, people, populate, reside, settle, sojourn (*literary*), stay

21 Exist in Close Proximity

Do not love your neighbor as yourself. If you are on good terms with yourself it is an impertinence; if on bad, an injury.
George Bernard Shaw

(*v*) abut, adjoin, be adjoining, beleaguer, besiege, border, border on, bound, box in, circle, communicate, dominate, edge, encircle, enclose, enfold, engulf, envelop, face, flank, frame, hedge, mold, *neighbor*, overlap, *overlie*, ring, skirt, span, straddle, surround, verge

See also POSITION SOMETHING: AROUND SOMETHING (327)

22 Cease to Exist

Fish die belly-upward and rise to the surface; it is their way of falling. **André Gide**

(*adj*) declining, diminishing, dwindling, dying, fading, falling, flagging, waning

(*v*) be no more, *cease to exist*, collapse, decay, *dematerialize*, *die a death* (*UK*), die away, die off, die out, diminish, disappear, disintegrate, dissolve, end, expire, fade, falter, flag, gutter, implode, languish, lapse, pass away, stop, vanish, wilt, wither

See also CAUSES OF DEATH (921), DEAD AND DYING (925)

23 Nonexistent Things

A robust sense of reality is very necessary in framing a correct analysis of propositions about unicorns, golden mountains, round squares, and other such pseudo-objects. **Bertrand Russell**

(*n*) castles in Spain, castles in the air, castles in the sky, chimera, concoction, delusion, dream, fancy, fantasy, *fata morgana* (*literary*), figment, *figment of the imagination*, flight of fancy, hallucination, illusion, mirage, myth, optical illusion, phantasmagoria, pipe dream, pretense, stardust, visualization, *will-o'-the-wisp*, wishful thinking

See also FALSE AND UNREAL (173), DREAM, IMAGINE, AND FANTASIZE (749), MYTHICAL BEINGS (789), MYTHICAL CREATURES (1036), NONEXISTENT PLACES (1066)

24 Nonexistence

What's past, and what's to come is strew'd with husks/And formless ruin of oblivion. **William Shakespeare**

(*n*) nonexistence, nothingness, oblivion, want

See also ABSENT AND UNAVAILABLE (7)

25 Perceptible

In a dark time, the eye begins to see. **Theodore Roethke**

(*adj*) apparent, attention-grabbing, audible, broad, clear, conspicuous, cut-and-dried, demonstrable, detectable, discernible, distinct, distinguishable, exposed, glaring, identifiable, *in plain sight*, manifest, marked, measurable, naked, noticeable, observable, obtrusive, obvious, *on display*, *on show*, *on view*, outright, outward, overt, palpable, patent, *perceivable*, perceptible, physical, plain, prominent, pronounced, *protruding*, protrusive, proud (*UK*), tactile, tangible, *traceable*, unconcealed, uncovered, undisguised, *unsubtle*, visible, visual

(*adv*) aloud, conspicuously, demonstrably, distinctly, evidently, externally, glaringly, in broad daylight, *in full view*, *in sight*, in the open, manifestly, on the surface, out loud, plainly, prominently, publicly, unmistakably

(*n*) audibility, blatancy, conspicuousness, *distinctness*, *distinguishability*, nakedness, obviousness, *overtness*, *palpability*, *perceptibility*, plainness, tangibility, visibility

See also THE SENSES (696)

26 Imperceptible

We never knows wot's hidden in each other's hearts; and if we had glass winders there, we'd need keep the shutters up.
Charles Dickens

(*adj*) *cloaked*, concealed, delicate, discreet, disembodied, disguised, fine, hidden, ignored, impalpable (*formal*), imperceptible, inappreciable, inarticulate, inaudible, inconspicuous, indiscernible, indistinct, indistinguishable, insensible, intangible, invisible, latent, light, masked, obscure, *out of focus*, out of sight, *out of view*, quiet, recessive, *secreted*, shadowy, subterranean, subtle, underground, undetectable, unheard, unnoticeable, unpronounced, unseen, unspotted, *untraceable*, vestigial, weak

(*adv*) delicately, *indistinguishably*, intangibly, invisibly, lightly, obscurely

(*n*) *impalpability* (*formal*), *imperceptibility*, inarticulacy, inaudibility, *inconspicuousness*, *indiscernibility*, indistinctness, intangibility, invisibility, latency, weakness

See also THE SENSES (696), ABSENCE OF SOUND (1257)

Happen

27 Happen

But the universe exists, things must happen in it, all equally improbable, and man is one of these things.
Jacques Lucien Monod

(*v*) arise, be, come, come about, come to pass (*archaic or literary*), elapse, ensue, follow, go by, go down (*slang*), go on, happen, intervene, occur, pan out (*informal*), pass, result, run, succeed, supervene (*formal*), take effect, take place, transpire, turn out

28 Happen Again

Anything that, in happening, causes itself to happen, happens again. **Douglas Adams**

(*v*) reappear, recur, *start up again*

See also AGAIN (109)

29 Repetition

Experience isn't interesting till it begins to repeat itself—in fact, till it does that, it hardly is experience. **Elizabeth Bowen**

(*n*) *action replay*, comeback, encore, reappearance, rebirth, *recommencement*, recrudescence, recurrence, rediscovery, *reemergence*, reinstatement, reiteration, *rekindling*, renaissance, *reoccurrence*, repeat, repetition, *repetitiousness*, *repetitiveness*, replay, replication, reprise, resumption, resurgence, resurrection, resuscitation

See also AGAIN (109), RECOMMENCE AND RESUME (268)

30 Happen to Somebody

Every man meets his Waterloo at last. **Wendell Phillips**

(*v*) attack, become of, befall (*archaic or literary*), beset, come over, curse, descend, grip, hit, wash over

See also EXPERIENCE AND ENCOUNTER (582)

31 Cause to Happen

We have no other notion of cause and effect, but that of certain objects, which have always conjoin'd together, and which in all past instances have always been found inseparable.
David Hume

(*v*) *actualize*, arrange, beget, bring, bring about, bring forward, *bring to fruition*, *bring to pass*, call, call forth, cause, connive, contrive, determine, dictate, effect (*formal*), elicit, engineer, ensure, entail, excite, ferment, fix, foment, forward, *give rise to*, have, hold, ignite, incur, induce, inflict, instigate, jump-start, kindle, lead, lead to, leave, make, make for, make happen, mean, motivate, occasion, organize, plan, plot, prearrange, precipitate, predestine, predetermine, present, program, promote, prompt, provoke, push through, put on, raise, rekindle, restart, result, see, see to it, sensitize, spinoff, stage, stage-manage, throw, time, underlie, usher in, whip up, wreak

32 Happening and In Progress

Going to trial with a lawyer who considers your life-style a Crime in Progress is not a happy prospect. **Hunter S. Thompson**

(*adj*) active, afoot, astir, developmental, effective, functional, *going on*, in commission, in force, in full swing, in hand, *in progress*, *in the wind* (*UK*), *in the works*, on the go, on the move, *on track*, operating, operational, operative, progressive, rolling, *taking place*, under negotiation, underway, *up and running*, *well under way*, working

(*adv*) in flagrante delicto, in the throes of, midstream, midway, on, progressively

33 About to Happen

You can only predict things after they've happened.
Eugène Ionesco

(*adj*) awakening, bordering on, developing, imminent, impending, in for, *in store*, in the air, in the offing, in the pipeline, *in the stars*, looming, oncoming, onrushing, *on the agenda*, *on the horizon*, on the point of, on the verge of, on the way, pendent (*formal or literary*), pending, poised, primed, upcoming

(*adv*) *about to happen*, in store

(*v*) await, be on course, brew, impend (*formal*), loom, threaten

See also FUTURE (86)

34 Not Happening

Sometimes virtual crimes lie dormant, and operas are stored away in a maestro's head, only to await the creative influence of genius to inspire their opening bars.
Joaquim Maria Machado de Assis

(*adj*) *canceled*, in abeyance, in limbo, *on hold*, *on ice*, *on the back burner*, *postponed*, suspended

Events and Occurrences

35 Events and Occurrences

You put up with the bloody and botched events in the hope of the one occasion when it becomes beautiful. **Peter Brook**

(*n*) activity, adventure, binge, business, caper, chain reaction, circumstance (*formal*), comings and goings, development, episode, escapade, event, experience, fact, goings-on (*informal*), happening, incident, merry-go-round, occasion, occurrence, phenomenon, proceedings, splurge (*informal*), spree, tear, thing, *ups and downs*, *vagaries*

See also CHAIN OF EVENTS (162)

36 Chance Events

Not only does God play dice. He does not tell us where they fall. **Stephen Hawking**

(*n*) *chance meeting*, chance occurrence, coincidence, contingency, encounter, eventuality (*formal*), fluke (*informal*), freak, *happenchance*, happenstance, quirk, vagary

See also LUCK (783)

37 Parties, Dances, and Celebrations

If an earthquake were to engulf England to-morrow, the English would manage to meet and dine somewhere among the rubbish, just to celebrate the event. **Douglas Jerrold**

(*adj*) celebratory, festive

(*n*) banquet, bash, benefit, bop (*informal*), carnival, carousal (*literary*), carousing (*literary*), celebration, *cocktail party*, dance, *drinks party* (*UK*), feast, festival, festivities, festivity, fete, fiesta, function, gala, *garden party*, hoedown, holiday, hop (*dated informal*), jamboree, jollification, levee, masque, merrymaking, *orgy*, pageant, pageantry, parade, party, prom, rave, reception, revel, revelry, *revels*, saturnalia, shindig (*informal*), social, *social event*, soiree, *special occasion*, *street party*

38 Ceremonies and Anniversaries

The punctuation of anniversaries is. . .like the closing of doors, one after another between you and what you want to hold on to. **Anne Morrow Lindbergh**

(*adj*) bridal, ceremonial, commemorative, nuptial, processional, ritual, ritualistic

(*n*) anniversary, betrothal (*formal*), bicentennial, celebration, centenary (*UK*), centennial, ceremonial, ceremony, commemoration, commemorative, graduation, inauguration, induction, jubilee, marriage, memory, nuptials (*formal*), observance, rite, ritual, *silver jubilee*, tercentenary, unveiling, wedding, *wedding ceremony*

39 Aggressive Events

Detested sport,/That owes its pleasures to another's pain.
William Cowper

(*n*) action, affray, aggression, air raid, air strike, assault, battle, beating, bloodbath, bombardment, brawl, broil (*archaic*), combat, conflict, confrontation, counterattack, coup, coup d'état, dogfight, duel, encounter, fight, fighting, *fist fight*, foray, fray, gunfight, *holocaust*, hostilities,

insurrection, inva-
riot, se, onslaught, ouster,
age, resistance, revolt, revo-
bbinal), scrape (informal),
ting, siege, skirmish,
g of war, tussle, upris-

rting Events

Ralph Ellison

mpetition, contest,
final, fixture (UK),
n, playoff, point-to-
inal, quiz, race,
rting event, sports
wordplay, tackle,
rney

s, and a lion to

/), champion,
ist, entrant,
t, nominee,

the moment of waking
moment after death.

), adieu, annulment,
breakup, cessation,
down, closing stages,
usion, coup de grâce,
n, curfew, cutoff, dead-
knell, death warrant,
(formal), denouement, dis-
tion, destination, dis-
discontinuation, divorce,
dissolution, escape, evap-
radication, expiry, extinction, fare-
on, finalization, finish, flight,
going, goodbye, halt, invali-
n the coffin, last resort, last
y), neutralization, occlusion,
pullout, retirement, retreat,
tion, split-up, swan song, tail
al), turnaround, valedictory
wal, wrap-up

EMENT (927)

e Stages

n and death save to enjoy the interval.

apotheosis, flowering, golden age,
prime

TIME (90), PERIODS OF REST (91)

44 Decisive Moments

The good things in history are usually of very short duration, but afterwards have a decisive influence over what happens over long periods of time. **Hannah Arendt**

(n) about-face, boiling point, breaking point, cave-in, change of heart, cliffhanger, climax, climbdown, crisis, crisis point, crossroads, crunch, defining moment, eye opener, flashpoint, highlight, high point, high spot (UK), knife-edge, landmark, milestone, *point of no return*, red-letter day, revelation, reversal, reversion, *seminal moment, snapping point*, turnabout, turnaround, turning point, twist, *twist of fate*, U-turn, volte-face, watershed

45 Informal Communication

It usually takes more than three weeks to prepare a good impromptu speech. **Mark Twain**

(n) chat, chatter, chitchat (informal), confab (informal), conversation, dialogue (formal), discourse, discussion, exchange, gab (informal), gabbing (informal), gossip, heart-to-heart, *nattering* (informal), *one-on-one*, palaver, pleasantries, schmooze (slang), small talk, *social call*, talk, talking, *tête-à-tête*, word, yak (informal), yammer (informal), yap (informal)

See also TWO-WAY COMMUNICATION (607), MEANINGLESS SPEECH OR GOSSIP (618)

46 Negotiation and Debate

It's a well-known proposition that you know who's going to win a negotiation: it's he who pauses the longest. **Robert Holmes à Court**

(n) airing, arbitration, consultation, debate, delib-eration, dialogue, head-to-head, intercession, inter-vention, mediation, negotiation, negotiations, parley, peacekeeping, peacemaking, talks

(v) liaise, parley

Arguments

uarrels of lovers are the renewal of love. **Terence**

ercation, argument, brush, clash, collision, con-frontation, controversy, crossfire, dialectic, dif-*ifference of opinion*, disagreement, disputation ispute, face-off, falling-out, feud, fight, go-*informal*), incident, infighting, mis-g, *power struggle*, quarrel, rhubarb, rift, *nformal*), rupture, set-to (informal), shou-howdown, slanging match (UK), spat, npleasantness, vendetta, war of words,

UPROAR (51), ARGUE AND FIGHT (643)

Communication

e the most historic phone call ever
ronauts on the moon **Richard Nixon**

normal), call, *phone call*, ring, telephone call,
essage

See also TELEPHONE, PAGE, AND TEXT (681), TELECOMMUNICATIONS (1130)

49 One-Way Communication

A professor is one who talks in someone else's sleep.
W. H. Auden

(*n*) address, aside, declaration, discourse, disquisition (*formal*), excursion (*formal*), exposition, homily, ice-breaker, improvisation, interjection, lecture, monologue, narration, oration, *panegyric, passing comment*, patter, pep talk (*informal*), peroration (*formal*), pleasantry, presentation, regurgitation, rendering, rendition, report, speech, talk

50 Criticisms and Angry Outbursts

The secret of our tragedy is/that our screams are louder than our voices/and our swords taller than ourselves. **Nizar Qabbani**

(*n*) accusation, admonishment, admonition, attack, broadside, castigation (*formal*), chastisement (*formal*), condemnation, contention, contumely (*archaic or literary*), criticism, denigration, denunciation, deprecation, diatribe, disparagement, earful (*informal*), explosion, flak (*informal*), going-over (*informal*), harangue, imputation, indictment, intimidation, invective (*formal*), *jeremiad* (*formal*), lecture, mauling, moralizing, mouthful, objection, obloquy (*formal or literary*), outcry, paroxysm, *Parthian shot*, parting shot, philippic, polemic, public disgrace, putdown (*informal*), rant, rap, rebuke, recrimination, remonstrance, reprimand, reproach, reproof, saber rattling, scold, squawk (*informal*), *squelch* (*slang*), stricture (*formal*), swipe (*informal*), talking-to (*informal*), tantrum, telling-off (*informal*), tirade, *tongue-lashing*, vilification, vituperation

See also ACCUSE, BLAME, AND CRITICIZE (641)

51 Chaos and Uproar

There is nothing stable in the world; uproar's your only music.
John Keats

(*n*) ado, anarchy, ballyhoo, bedlam, bloodletting, brouhaha, bustle, cacophony, clamor, commotion, din, disturbance, *donnybrook*, ferment, *foofaraw*, fracas, free-for-all (*informal*), furor, fuss, high jinks (*informal*), histrionics, hoo-hah (*slang*), hubbub, hue and cry, hullabaloo, hurly-burly, hustle and bustle, lawlessness, melodrama, outcry, palaver (*UK*), pandemonium, racket, rambunctiousness, rampage, raucousness, rough-and-tumble, roughhouse (*informal*), rout, row, rowdiness, ruckus, ruction, ructions, rumpus, scene, scrimmage, scrum (*UK*), sensation, *shemozzle* (*dated informal*), shenanigans (*informal*), stampede, stink (*informal*), stir, tempest, to-do (*informal*), tumult, turbulence, turmoil, unrest, upheaval, uproar, upset

See also ARGUMENTS (47)

52 Sudden Events

ACCIDENT, *n. An inevitable occurrence due to the action of immutable natural laws.* **Ambrose Bierce**

(*n*) ambush, attack, barrage, blackout, blast, blitz (*informal*), bolt from the blue, bombardment, bombshell (*informal*), boom, brainstorm, burst, cannonade, detonation, epidemic, eruption, explosion, flare-up (*informal*), flurry, fright, gallop, gust, hail, heart attack (*informal*), implosion, jailbreak, jolt, onrush, outbreak, outburst, outpouring, raid, rain, rash, rush, sally, salvo, scramble, shock, shock wave, stor... prise, takeover, thrust, thunderbo... turn, uprush, upwelling, volley, ...

53 Beginnings

With the possible exception of the arrival, ... somewhere. **Peter Fleming**

(*n*) accession, activation, ad...ing ground authorship, awakening, bap...(*formal*), co... beginning, birth, birthplace...ion, creati... bridgehead, brink, catalyst, ...out, deriva... mencement (*formal*), conce...ablishment, ge... crucible, curtain raiser, ...e... embryo, emergence, ...tainhead, ...goad, head, ... (*literary*), forefront, fou...al, ...ion, ...nception ... germ, germination, get-g...ion, ...nception, inst... ignition, impulsion, in..., initiation, intr... incitement, induction, o... (*informal*), intr... instigation, institutio...al), launch, laun... jump-start, kickoff (...ftoff, materializat... lead-in, leading edg...ivity, onset, opener ization, *naissance*, ...ivity, onset, opener opening, orientatio... origin, origination, port, planning, p...of departure, prelimi... preparation, prep...duction, principle, pr... prompting, pr...venance, *push-start* ... reintroductio..., reissue, repository sp... (*UK*), seed, source, spark, ...f, thresho...

54 Ends and Departures

We sometimes congratulate ourselves at ... from a troubled dream; it may be so the ... **Nathaniel Hawthorne**

(*n*) abolition, abrogation (*forma... autumn, breakaway, breakout, ... clampdown, cleanup, close, clos... closure, coda, completion, conc... crack-up (*informal*), culminatio... line, death, deathblow, death... decay, demerger (*UK*), demis... departing, departure, dese... appearance, disconnection, ... engagement, disintegration... elopement, end, ending, e... oration, exit, exodus, *expirat*... well, *final curtain*, finale, ... freeze, fruition, getaway, ... dation, *last leg, last nail* ... straw, leave-taking (*litera*... parting, passing, perfectio... secession, sendoff, separ... end, termination (*form*... (*formal*), winter, withdr...

See also DEATH AND BEREA...

55 Intermedia...

There is no cure for bir... **George Santayana**

(*n*) acme, *apogee*, ... high, low, low poin...

See also PERIODS OF...

56   Pauses and Phases

It is not enough/to be pause, to be hole/to be void, to be silent.
Edward Kamau Brathwaite

(*n*) break, breakoff, breathing space, ceasefire, deferral, gap, grace period, hiatus, installment, interception, interim, interlude, intermission, interregnum, interruption, interval (*UK*), juncture, lag, lap, lapse, layover, leg, letup (*informal*), lull, meantime, moratorium, pause, phase, pit stop, plateau, respite, slot, space, stay, step, time lag

See also PERIODS OF TIME (90), PERIODS OF REST (91), LACK OF ACTIVITY OR MOTION (342)

57   Preparatory Events

When we mean to build,/We first survey the plot, then draw the model. **William Shakespeare**

(*n*) audition, casting, dress rehearsal, drill, dry run, dummy run, field test, fire drill, fire practice, knock-up (*UK*), practice, *practice session*, probation, rehearsal, road test, run-through, test, test drive, *test run*, trial, *trial run*, tryout, warm-up, workout

See also PREPARE FOR ACTION (289)

Seeming, Appearing to Be, and Representing

58   Seem to Be Something

All that we see or seem/Is but a dream within a dream.
Edgar Allan Poe

(*v*) appear, approach, be close to, come across, feel like, look, reek, resemble, seem, smack, *smack of*, sound, take after

59   Represent Something or Somebody

How can we be sure that we are not impostors? **Jacques Lacan**

(*v*) act, *act for*, *act on behalf of*, be a symbol of, betoken (*literary*), capture, characterize, depict, deputize, embody, epitomize, exemplify, herald, illustrate, immortalize, mime, mirror, objectify, *personate*, personify, portray, present, reflect, represent, stand in, stand in for, substitute, symbolize, take the place of, typify

60   Pretend and Mimic

Those who do not want to imitate anything, produce nothing.
Salvador Dalí

(*v*) act, affect, ape, assume, copy, emulate, fake, feign, imitate, impersonate, let on, look like, masquerade, mime, mimic, mirror, mock, parody, parrot, pass for, personify, play, play-act (*informal*), pose, pretend, pretend to be, put on, put on an act, reflect, role-play, sham, simulate, take off (*informal*)

See also JOKES AND TEASING (674)

61   Mean Something

The use...of words is to be sensible marks of ideas, and the ideas they stand for are their proper and immediate signification. **John Locke**

(*v*) add up, augur, be a sign of, bespeak, bode, connote, convey, count, denote, foreshadow, hang together, imply, indicate, make a statement, make sense, mark, matter, mean, portend, presage, prognosticate, promise, refer, show, signal, signify, spell, stand for

See also MEANING (690)

62   Be About Something

Any general statement is like a check drawn on a bank. Its value depends on what is there to meet it. **Ezra Pound**

(*v*) appertain (*formal*), apply, be anchored in, center, concern, cover, have to do with, involve, pertain to, refer, regard, treat

63   Expressions of Reference

A spade is never so merely a spade as the word/Spade would imply. **Christopher Fry**

(*adj*) abovementioned, aforementioned (*formal*), said

(*conj*) as far as, seeing, *seeing as*, *seeing that*

(*prep*) about, according to, apropos (*formal*), as per, as regards, as to, concerning, considering, due to, on the subject of, re, regarding, relating to, relative to, respecting, toward, with reference to, with regard to, with respect to

64   Expressions Introducing Examples

A precedent embalms a principle. **William Scott**

(*adv*) *for a start*, *for example*, *for instance*, namely, such as, *viz.*

65   Representations and General Examples

Modern art can only be born where signs become symbols.
Wassily Kandinsky

(*n*) adaptation, casting, characterization, copy, core, counterfeit, cross section, decoy, demo (*informal*), depiction, draft, dummy, effigy, emulation, example, *exemplification*, expression, fabrication, *graven image*, guise, guy (*UK*), illustration, image, imagery, imitation, imitator, impersonation, impression, imprint, incarnation, instance, likeness, macrocosm, manifestation, mannequin, microcosm, misrepresentation, mock-up, model, parody, pattern, *personation*, personification, piece, plug, portrait, portrayal, precedent, proxy, redolence, reflection, rendering, representation, sample, sampler, sampling, scarecrow, sign, skeleton, *specimen*, swatch, symbolism, tableau, takeoff (*informal*), taste, tester, token, totem, *working example*

66   Representative

Imaginative consciousness represents a certain type of thought; a thought which is constituted in and by its object.
Jean-Paul Sartre

(*adj*) archetypal, archetypical, characteristic, classic, classical, diagrammatic, emblematic, emblematical, exemplary (*formal*), expressive, figurative, honorary, illustrative, incarnate, indicative, *metaphoric*, metaphorical, model, *prototypical*, quintessential, redolent, representational, representative, *signature*, suggestive, symbolic, symptomatic, textbook, token, totemic, *trademark*, typical

(*adv*) by way of, typically

67 Perfect Examples and Embodiments

So excellent a king, that was to this/Hyperion to a satyr.
William Shakespeare

(*n*) archetype, baseline, bastion, beacon (*literary*), benchmark, byword, case, *case in point*, classic, crystallization, distillation, embodiment, epitome, example, exemplar (*literary*), gold standard, guide, ideal, index, litmus test, model, mold, norm, original, paradigm, paragon, picture, prototype, queen, quintessence, role model, *shining example*, showpiece, standard

68 Indications, Signs, and Warnings

Signatures of all things I am here to read,/seaspawn and seawrack, the nearing tide, that rusty/boot. Snot-green, bluesilver, rust: colored signs. **James Joyce**

(*n*) appetizer, augury, auspice, cue, forerunner, foretaste, harbinger, herald (*literary*), idea, indication, lead, mark, marker, omen, portent, prognostication, reminder, sign, signpost, storm cloud, symptom, taster (*UK*), test, warning

69 Evidence and Proof

What is now proved was once, only imagin'd. **William Blake**

(*n*) a case in point, acid test, authority, confirmation, demonstration, evidence, facts, fingerprint, footprint, giveaway, lead, proof, *proof of identity*, *proof of ownership*, *proof positive*, scent, spoor, substantiation, support, *telltale sign*, testament, testimony, trace, track, trail, validation, verification, vindication

70 Amount to and Equal

Enough is equal to a feast. **Henry Fielding**

(*v*) account for, add up to, amount to, average, boil down to (*informal*), come down to, come to, consist, constitute, equal, make, make up, number, *run to*, stack up, total

Situations and Outcomes

71 Situations

In some situations the right answer is the best answer, the wrong answer is the second best answer, and no answer is the worst answer. **Scott McNealy**

(*n*) affair, backdrop, background, *best-case scenario*, canvas, case, circumstance, climate, conditions, context, environment, forum, *how the land lies*, *how things stand*, landscape, lay of the land (*informal*), *present circumstances*, scenario, *set of circumstances*, situation, state of affairs, *state of play*, *state of things*, status quo

72 Difficult Situations

Comin' in on a Wing and a Prayer **Harold Adamson**

(*n*) adversity, bind, Catch-22, crucible, crucifixion, deadlock, disfavor, disgrace, dishonor, disrepute, distress, emergency, entanglement, firing line, fix (*informal*), flashpoint, front line, *hard times*, *harsh conditions*, hell, *hornet's nest*, hot water (*informal*), hurry, imbroglio, impasse, indignity, jam (*informal*), kettle of fish, mess, minefield, nadir, *no-win situation*, obloquy (*formal or literary*), ordeal, pass, pickle (*informal*), plight, predicament, pressure, quagmire, quandary, rock bottom, ruin, ruination, scrape (*informal*), spot (*informal*), stalemate, standoff, state (*informal*), *state of emergency*, stew (*informal*), *sticky situation*, sticky wicket (*informal*), *storm in a teacup* (*UK*), tailspin (*informal*), *tight corner*, *tight situation*, tight spot, trauma, *tricky situation*, vicious circle, vortex

See also PROBLEMS (256), UNCERTAINTY (559)

73 In Trouble and Disadvantaged

Like a dull actor now/I have forgot my part and I am out,/Even to a full disgrace. **William Shakespeare**

(*adj*) abused, aggrieved, at a disadvantage, *between a rock and a hard place*, disregarded, done for (*informal*), doomed, down, hamstrung, harassed, *hard-pressed*, high and dry, *in a bind*, in a fix (*informal*), in a hurry, in a jam (*informal*), *in a predicament*, in a rush, *in a tight corner*, *in a tight spot*, *in bad odor*, *in deep trouble*, *in deep water*, *in difficulty*, in dire straits, *in disgrace*, in extremis, in hot water, *in serious trouble*, in the doghouse (*informal*), *in the lurch*, in the soup (*informal*), in trouble, losing, lost, mistreated, misunderstood, neglected, on the horns of a dilemma, on the spot, *oppressed*, *ostracized*, *ousted*, *out of favor*, *overburdened*, *overlooked*, *overstretched*, *overworked*, *persecuted*, poor, pressed, *pressed for time*, pushed (*informal*), put-upon, stretched, *under a cloud*, *under a curse*, under attack, under fire, under pressure, undone, up the creek (*informal*), *up the creek without a paddle* (*informal*), up to your ears, with your back to the wall

See also BEATEN AND DEFEATED (78), IN DANGER (237)

74 Pleasant Situations

Bliss was it in that dawn to be alive,/But to be young was very heaven! **William Wordsworth**

(*adj*) in the ascendant, *in the lap of luxury*, in the lead

(*n*) *bed of roses*, clover, domesticity, ease, *easy street*, *glory days*, good life, halcyon days (*literary*), *heaven on earth*, heyday, high life, *honeymoon period*, idyll, lap of luxury, *life of ease*, *life of Riley*, nirvana, pinnacle, salad days (*dated*), seventh heaven, *state of grace*, summer, well-being

See also SUCCESSFUL AND PROMISING (81)

75 Fail or Be Unsuccessful

My reputation grew with every failure. **George Bernard Shaw**

(*v*) backfire, bite the dust (*informal*), bomb (*informal*), cease trading, collapse, come down (*UK*), come to grief, *come to naught* (*archaic or literary*), come to nothing, *cut no ice*, draw the short straw, fail, fall by the wayside, fall down, fall flat, fall short, fall through, flop (*informal*), flunk (*informal*), fold, founder, free-fall, get a raw deal, go bankrupt, *go belly up, go down the drain, go down the tube* (*informal*), *go into liquidation, go off the rails*, go over like a lead balloon (*slang*), *go to seed*, go to the wall, go to waste, go under, go up in smoke, go wrong, knuckle under, leave much to be desired, lose, lose out (*informal*), miscarry (*formal*), misfire, nose-dive, sell out, shut, shut up shop, slump, strike out (*informal*), succumb, surrender, *throw in the sponge* (*informal*), throw in the towel (*informal*), unravel, yield

76   Unsuccessful and Unpromising

Many go out for wool, and come home shorn themselves. **Miguel de Cervantes**

(*adj*) abortive, ailing, botched, disastrous, failed, failing, fruitless, frustrated, inauspicious, manqué, sunk, uneconomic, unprofitable, unpromising, unsuccessful, useless, vain, washed-up (*informal*)

(*adv*) in vain, vainly

(*n*) uselessness

77   Failure

Failure is inevitable. Success is elusive. **Steven Spielberg**

(*n*) also-ran, anticlimax, bathos, belly flop, breakdown, capitulation, collapse, comedown (*informal*), crash, decline, descent, disaster (*informal*), downfall, dud (*informal*), failure, fiasco, flop (*informal*), free fall, lemon (*informal*), letdown, loss, malfunction, meltdown (*informal*), nonstarter (*informal*), rout, ruin, ruination, subjection, surrender, turkey (*slang*), undoing, washout (*informal*)

78   Beaten and Defeated

A man is not finished when he is defeated. He is finished when he quits. **Richard Nixon**

(*adj*) beaten, conquered, defeated, finished, *overpowered*, overwhelmed, *trounced, vanquished*

See also IN TROUBLE AND DISADVANTAGED (73)

79   Succeed and Win

It is not enough to succeed. Others must fail. **Gore Vidal**

(*v*) ace (*slang*), achieve, arrive, attain, bear fruit, be a success, blossom, bring home the bacon (*UK informal*), burgeon (*literary*), carry off, catch on (*informal*), come first, come off (*informal*), come out on top, compare, compete, *cut it* (*informal*), *cut the mustard* (*informal*), excel, forge ahead, fulfill, gain ground, get ahead, get away with, get in, get somewhere, *go well, hit the big time* (*slang*), hit the jackpot, land on your feet, lead, live up to, make, make a name for yourself, make a splash, make good, make headway, make inroads, make it (*informal*), make out, make progress, make the grade, make your mark, manage, max (*slang*), pass, *pass with flying colors*, pay off, prevail, prosper, pull off (*informal*), qualify, rise to (*informal*), romp (*informal*), sail through, shine, sparkle, squeak through (*informal*), star, succeed, take off (*informal*), take the lead, thrive, triumph, walk away, win, work

80   Beat and Defeat

As always, victory finds a hundred fathers, but defeat is an orphan. **Galeazzo Ciano**

(*n*) annihilation, beating, conquest, defeat, drubbing, hammering (*informal*), licking (*informal*), pasting (*informal*), pounding, pulverization (*informal*), rout, suppression, thrashing, trouncing, walloping (*informal*), whipping (*informal*), whitewash (*informal*), whopping (*informal*)

(*v*) annihilate (*informal*), beat, beggar, best, better (*formal*), blow away (*slang*), break, break down, bring down, cap, conquer, cream (*slang*), crush, defeat, demolish (*informal*), destroy, down, drub, eclipse, finish (*informal*), get the better of, go one better, hammer (*informal*), improve on, knock out, leapfrog, leave behind, lick (*informal*), make mincemeat of, master, outclass, outdistance, outdo, outface, outflank, outfox, outgrow, outjockey, outmaneuver, outnumber, outpace, outperform, outride, outrun, outshine, outsmart, outstrip, outwit, overcome, overhaul, overpower, overshadow, overtake, overthrow, overwhelm, pulverize (*informal*), put in the shade, quash, rise above, rival, rout, run rings around, see off (*UK*), seize, slaughter (*slang*), snow under, squash, storm, subdue, subjugate, suppress, surmount, surpass, take, thrash, top, tower, transcend, triumph over, trounce, trump, upstage, vanquish, walk over (*informal*), wallop (*informal*), whitewash, wipe the floor with (*informal*)

81   Successful and Promising

Success is counted sweetest/By those who ne'er succeed. **Emily Dickinson**

(*adj*) alive, auspicious, bestselling, blockbusting, blooming, blossoming, boom, booming, budding, burgeoning, flourishing, fruitful, going, *going strong*, mobile, moneymaking, *on a roll* (*informal*), prizewinning, prolific, promising, *propitious, prospering*, prosperous, rampant, rank, renascent, resurgent, roaring, rosy, runaway (*informal*), successful, thriving, triumphal, triumphant, unbeaten, *unconquered, undefeatable*, undefeated, *unvanquished*, up, victorious, winning

(*adv*) famously, in front, on the move, on the up and up (*informal*), on top, promisingly, rampantly, successfully, triumphantly

See also PLEASANT SITUATIONS (74)

82   Success

Eighty percent of success is showing up. **Woody Allen**

(*n*) accomplishment, achievement, attainment, blockbuster (*informal*), checkmate, conquest, coup, fruitfulness, fulfillment, glory, good name, headway, hit, landslide, laurels, lifework, mobility, *propitiousness*, realization, rise, runaway success, *runaway victory*, sellout, *smash hit*, success, successfulness, success story, triumph, victory, win, winner

83   Results and Outcomes

Our greatest glory is not in never falling, but in rising every time we fall. **Confucius**

(*adv*) as a result, duly, in consequence (*formal*), in the event, thus (*formal*)

(*n*) aftereffect, aftermath, *aftershock*, avail, backlash, brunt, byproduct, child, close call, comeuppance (*informal*), consequence, corollary, dead heat, derivative, draw, effect, end, end product, end result, fallout, fate, finding, follow-on, fruit, hangover, impact, impression, judgment, just deserts, just reward, knock-on effect (*UK*), narrow escape, narrow squeak, near miss, offshoot,

outcome, outgrowth, penalty, price, product, punishment, ramification, ravages, reflex, repercussion, result, reverberations, scar, sequel, shock wave, side effect, spinoff, standoff, upshot

See also AFTER, LAST, AND FOLLOWING (165)

Concepts and Ideas

Time, Duration, and Speed

84 Past

The past is never dead, it is not even past. **William Faulkner**

(*adj*) all over, ancient, *ancient history*, antebellum, antediluvian, bygone, defunct, erstwhile, ex, former, in retrospect, lapsed, long-ago, old, onetime, outgoing, over, over and done with, past, prehistoric, primitive, retroactive, retrospective, sometime (*formal*)

(*adv*) ago, at one time, formerly, freshly, *heretofore* (*formal*), historically, hitherto, in retrospect, *in the past*, late, lately, latterly, of late, once, *once upon a time*, originally, recently, retrospectively, so far, *some time ago*, then, thus far, to date, until now, *until recently*, up till now, up to now, *up to the present moment*, up to the present time, up until now, yet

(*n*) antecedents, antiquity, *bygone days*, days gone by, *former times*, history, *long ago*, past, *past history*, prehistory, run-up, throwback, *times gone by*, *times of yore*, *times past*, *yesterday*, yesteryear

See also BEFORE, FIRST, AND PRECEDING (163), OLD, OLD-FASHIONED (167)

85 Present

PRESENT, *n. That part of eternity dividing the domain of disappointment from the realm of hope.* **Ambrose Bierce**

(*adj*) contemporary, current, existing, extant, firsthand, latter-day, modern-day, present, present-day, topical

(*adv*) already, at once, at present, at the moment, at the present time, at this moment, *at this point*, *at this point in time*, at this time, for now, for the meantime, for the time being, forthwith, here, in-between, *in this day and age*, just, just now, meanwhile, newly, now, nowadays, presently, *right now*, straight, straightaway, straight off (*informal*), *straightway*, *this instant*, today, urgently

(*n*) actuality, present, present day, *the here and now*, *these days*, *this day and age*, topicality

86 Future

Time present and time past/Are both perhaps present in time future,/And time future contained in time past. **T. S. Eliot**

(*adj*) advanced, anticipated, approaching, at hand, awaited, coming, coming up, designate, due, elect, embryonic, emergent, foreseeable, forthcoming, future, intended, in the making, long-range, nascent, primordial, projected, prospective, ready, *soon-to-be*, up-and-coming, *yet to come*

(*adv*) ahead, anon (*archaic or literary*), awhile (*literary*), before long, by and by (*literary*), hence (*formal*), henceforth, *henceforward* (*formal*), hereafter (*formal*), *in a bit*, in a jiffy (*informal*), *in a little while*, *in a minute*, *in a second*, *in a short time*, *in a trice*, in a while, in due course, *in future*, *in half a shake* (UK), *in the fullness of time*, *in the future*, in the long run, *in the near future*, in the short term, in time, later, momentarily, *one of these days*, shortly, someday, sometime, soon, sooner or later, *until further notice*, *yet to be*

(*n*) future, *imminence*, lead time, outlook, *posterity*, *time ahead*, *time to come*, *years to come*

(*prep*) about to, ahead of, close to, on the threshold of, pending, until

See also ABOUT TO HAPPEN (33)

87 Times of Day

And wisely tell what hour o' the day/The clock does strike, by algebra. **Samuel Butler**

(*adj*) a.m., circadian, daily, diurnal, late, nightly, nocturnal, *off-peak*, per diem, p.m., *quotidian* (*formal*)

(*n*) afternoon, bedtime, break of day, cockcrow (*archaic or literary*), crack of dawn, darkness, dawn, day, daybreak, daylight, daytime, dinnertime, dusk, even (*literary*), evening, *eventide* (*literary*), first light, hour, lights out, *lunchtime*, mealtime, midday, midnight, morning, night, nightfall, nighttime, noon, noonday (*literary*), reveille, roll call, sundown, sunrise, sunset, sunup, *suppertime*, taps, *teatime*, time zone, twilight

types of time zones Alaska, Atlantic, Central, Eastern, Hawaii-Aleutian, Mountain, Pacific, Samoa, Yukon

See also CLOCKS AND TIMERS (1126)

88 Times of Year

Four seasons fill the measure of the year;/There are four seasons in the mind of man. **John Keats**

(*adj*) annual, autumnal, biannual, biennial, monthly, quarterly, seasonal, yearly

(*adv*) biweekly, *fortnightly*, per annum, *weekly*, yearly

(*n*) autumn (UK), birthday, date, day, *dog days*, Eastertide (*literary*), *Eastertime*, equinox, eve, fall, midsummer, midwinter, season, *solstice*, spring, *springtide* (*literary*), springtime, summer, *summer solstice*, summertime, winter, *winter solstice*, *wintertime*

types of time periods calendar month, fortnight, leap year, lunar month, month, quarter, semester, trimester, week, weekend, year

89 Epochs and Eras

History is a clock that people use to tell their political and cultural time of day. **John Henrik Clarke**

(*n*) age, century, date, decade, epoch, era, generation, geologic division, lifetime, millennium, period, time, vintage

types of eons (from oldest to most recent) pre-Archean, Archean, Proterozoic, Phanerozoic

types of eras (from oldest to most recent) Paleozoic, Mesozoic, Cenozoic

types of periods (from oldest to most recent) Cambrian, Ordovician, Silurian, Devonian, Carboniferous, Permian, Triassic, Jurassic, Cretaceous, Tertiary, Quaternary

types of epochs (from oldest to most recent) Paleocene, Eocene, Oligocene, Miocene, Pliocene, Pleistocene, Holocene

90 Periods of Time

Art is long, life short; judgment difficult, opportunity transient.
Johann Wolfgang von Goethe

(*n*) chapter, duration, extension, hour, length, period, run, session, shift, span, stage, standing, streak, stretch, tenure (*formal*), term (*formal*), time, timescale, timespan, wait, while

See also INTERMEDIATE STAGES (55), PAUSES AND PHASES (56), CHAIN OF EVENTS (162)

91 Periods of Rest

It is well to lie fallow for a while. **Martin Farquhar Tupper**

(*n*) break, breather (*informal*), coffee break, *day off*, downtime, free time, furlough, holiday, leave, leave of absence, *leisure time*, *lunch break*, pause, playtime, *public holiday* (*UK*), recess, *refreshment break*, repose, respite, rest, retirement, sabbatical, short break, sit-down (*informal*), slumber, spare time, stay, stop, stopover, *study leave*, tea break (*UK*), time off, time out, vacation

See also INTERMEDIATE STAGES (55), PAUSES AND PHASES (56), LACK OF ACTIVITY OR MOTION (342)

92 Long Periods of Time

Hold Infinity in the palm of your hand/And Eternity in an hour.
William Blake

(*n*) *aeons*, ages (*informal*), eon, eternity, lifetime (*informal*), years

93 Short Periods of Time

Thought is only a flash between two long nights, but this flash is everything. **Jules Henri Poincaré**

(*n*) bit, *blink of an eye*, bout, dose (*informal*), flash, instant, *jiff* (*informal*), jiffy (*informal*), minute, moment, nanosecond, point, second, spell (*informal*), split second, stint, time, trice, twinkling, window

94 Permanence: Without End

History never stops. It progresses ceaselessly day and night. Trying to stop it is like trying to stop Geography.
Augusto Monterroso

(*adj*) abiding, ageless, all-weather, *around-the-clock*, boundless, ceaseless, chronic, classic, constant, continual, continuing, continuous, customary, deathless, endless, enduring, eternal, evergreen, everlasting, full-time, habitual, haunting, immemorial, immortal, imperishable (*literary*), incessant, indelible, indestructible, indissoluble, ineradicable, *inextinguishable*, infinite, ingrained, insistent, interminable, lasting, lifelong, limitless, lingering, long-lasting, long-lived, long-standing, long-term, never-ending, nonstop, ongoing, per-

ennial, permanent, perpetual, persistent, prolonged, protracted, relentless, remaining, remorseless, rooted, round-the-clock, standing, steady, sustainable, sustained, timeless, *twenty-four-hour-a-day*, unabated, unalleviated, unbroken, unceasing, undying, unending, *unfading*, unfailing, uninterrupted, *unquenchable*, unrelenting, unrelieved, unremitting, unstoppable, well-established, year-round

(*adv*) ad infinitum, ad nauseam, all along, all the time, always, around the clock, at every turn, consistently, constantly, day after day, *day in day out*, ever, evermore (*literary*), forever, forevermore (*literary*), for life, *immortally*, imperishably (*literary*), indefinitely, indelibly, *in perpetuity*, on, *since time began*, since time immemorial, twenty-four/seven, *until the end of time*, *without end*

(*n*) ceaselessness, continuance, continuation, continuousness, *continuum*, endurance, *immortality*, imperishability (*literary*), *infinitude*, infinity, *limitlessness*, longevity, maintenance, permanence, perpetuation, perpetuity, persistence, preservation, prolongation, protraction, relentlessness, subsistence, survival, *sustainability*, *time immemorial*, timelessness, *time without end*, upkeep

95 Permanence: Without Change

Who can speak of eternity without a solecism, or think thereof without an ecstasy? Time we may comprehend, 'tis but five days elder than ourselves. **Thomas Browne**

(*adj*) changeless, consistent, constant, even, fixed, flat, immutable, in a rut, incorruptible, invariable, irretrievable, irreversible, irrevocable, nonnegotiable, same, stable, static, steady, unalterable, unchangeable, unchanged, unchanging, uniform, unmodified, unreconstructed, *unvaried*, unvarying

(*adv*) consistently, irrevocably

(*n*) changelessness, consistency, constancy, continuity, fixedness, *immutability*, *invariability*, stability

96 Finiteness, Variability, and Transience

All finite things reveal infinitude. **Theodore Roethke**

(*adj*) acting, alternate, changeable, changing, checkered, closed, discontinuous, disposable, ephemeral, episodic, erratic, evanescent, expendable, finite, fitful, fleeting, floating, fluctuating, fluid, freakish, here today and gone tomorrow, impermanent, inconsistent, inconstant, interim, intermittent, irregular, movable, mutable, patchy, periodic, protean, provisional, provisory, quick, reversible, seasonal, shifting, *short and sweet*, short-lived, short-term, sporadic, straw-hat, temporary, throwaway, transient, transitional, transitory, unpredictable, unsettled, unstable, unsteady, vaporous, variable

(*adv*) alternately, off and on, quickly, unsteadily

(*n*) brevity, changeability, discontinuity, ephemeralness, *evanescence*, fluctuation, fluidity, impermanence, *inconstancy*, *mutability*, patchiness, shortness, *temporariness*, transience, unpredictability, unsteadiness, variability, *variableness*

97   Never and Infrequency

You may as well expect pears from an elm. **Miguel de Cervantes**

(*adj*) casual, episodic, few and far between (*informal*), infrequent, occasional, *once-in-a-lifetime*, rare, scattered, spasmodic

(*adv*) at times, *every now and again*, every now and then, *every so often*, from time to time, *hardly ever*, never, now and again, now and then, on and off, *once in a blue moon* (*informal*), once in a while, rarely, seldom, sometimes

(*n*) exceptionality, infrequency

98   Promptness: Early

Three o'clock is always too late or too early for anything you want to do. **Jean-Paul Sartre**

(*adj*) early, premature, untimely

(*adv*) ahead, *ahead of schedule*, ahead of time, beforehand, early, *in plenty of time*, in time, sooner

99   Promptness: On Time

The only way to be sure of catching a train is to miss the one before it. **G. K. Chesterton**

(*adj*) on time, prompt, punctual

(*adv*) at the appointed time, *in good time*, *in the nick of time*, on the dot, on time, sharp

(*n*) promptness, punctuality

100   Promptness: Late

I've been on a calendar, but never on time. **Marilyn Monroe**

(*adj*) behind, behindhand, behind schedule, belated, delayed, *down to the wire*, eleventh-hour, last-minute, late, overdue, standby, tardy, *under the wire*, *unpunctual*

(*adv*) late

(*n*) *belatedness*, *eleventh hour*, last minute, lateness, tardiness, *unpunctuality*

101   Promptness: Badly Timed

Vain favor! coming, like most other favors long deferred and often wished for, too late! **Charlotte Brontë**

(*adj*) badly timed, ill-timed, inexpedient, inopportune, *mistimed*, *out of sync*, unseasonable, untimely

(*adv*) inconveniently, inopportunely

102   Speed

Or like a poet woo the moon,/Riding an armchair for my steed,/And with a flashing pen harpoon/Terrific metaphors of speed. **Roy Campbell**

(*n*) abruptness, acceleration, alacrity, briskness, celerity (*literary*), differential, fastness, *fleetness* (*literary*), haste, *momentariness*, pace, *precipitateness*, *precipitousness*, promptness, quickness, rapidity, *rapidness*, rate, readiness, rush, slowness, speed, speediness, speed limit, suddenness, swiftness, velocity

See also CHANGE OF SPEED: MORE (396), CHANGE OF SPEED: LESS (397)

103   Moving Quickly

Celerity is never more admir'd/Than by the negligent. **William Shakespeare**

(*adj*) accelerated, agile, brisk, fast, gushing, hasty, *hurtling*, nippy (*UK*), plunging, precipitate, quick, rapid, rattling, smart, spanking, speeding, speedy, swift

(*adv*) agilely, at a rate of knots (*UK*), cleanly, fast, *full speed ahead*, *full steam ahead*, hotfoot, in a flash, in a hurry, *like a bat out of hell* (*informal*), *like the wind*, on the double, quickly, smartly, speedily, swiftly

See also MOVE FAST (313)

104   Happening Quickly

The dawn speeds a man on his journey, and speeds him too in his work. **Heslod**

(*adj*) abrupt, *alacritous*, breakneck, brief, cursory, expeditious, express, extemporaneous, extempore, extraordinaire, fast, flying, fugitive, furious, headlong, hurried, immediate, instant, instantaneous, lightning, machine-gun, meteoric, momentary, overnight, passing, precipitate, prompt, quick, quick-fire, *rapid-fire*, ready, rushed, sharp, short, snap, snappy, split-second, sudden, summary, superficial, unplanned, unprepared, unrehearsed, up-tempo, whirlwind, whistle-stop

(*adv*) all at once, all of a sudden, apace, *ASAP*, at speed, directly (*formal*), double-quick (*informal*), extempore, furiously, hastily, headlong, hurriedly, immediately, in a flash, in a rush, *in haste*, in less than no time, *in next to no time*, in no time, *in one fell swoop*, instantly, *in the blink of an eye*, *in the twinkling of an eye*, *in two shakes of a lamb's tail*, lickety-split (*informal*), *like a bolt from the blue*, like greased lightning, momentarily, now, on the spot, out of the blue, outright, overnight, pdq (*informal*), pell-mell, posthaste, pronto (*informal*), *quick as a flash*, quickly, readily, responsively, right away, sharply, short, summarily, superficially, *with alacrity*, without a second thought, *without demur*, without further ado, *without hesitation*

(*interj*) chop-chop (*informal*)

105   Moving Slowly

How slow the Wind—/how slow the sea—/how late their feathers be! **Emily Dickinson**

(*adj*) dawdling, dilatory, leaden, leisurely, measured, plodding, poky (*informal*), slow, *slow-moving*, unrushed

See also MOVE SLOWLY (314)

106   Happening Slowly

To live is to be slowly born. **Antoine de Saint-Exupéry**

(*adj*) draggy (*informal*), drawn-out, extended, gradual, lengthy, lingering, long, long-drawn-out, marathon, organic, retarded, slow, *slow as molasses*, *slow but sure*, *slow-going*, *slow-paced*, *snail-paced*, *spun-out* (*UK*)

(*adv*) at your leisure, at your own pace, bit by bit, by degrees, day by day, little by little, piecemeal, slowly, *slowly but surely*, steadily, step by step

107 Frequent and Often

Man is frequently overwhelmed by the immense and alien power of the universe. **Wilson Harris**

(*adj*) congenital, constant, cyclical, frequent, monthly, periodic, recurrent, recurring, regular, repeated, rhythmic

(*adv*) daily, monthly, much, nightly, often, regularly, repetitively

(*n*) frequency, incidence, occurrence, rhythm

108 Usually

It's deadly commonplace, but, after all, the commonplaces are the great poetic truths. **Robert Louis Stevenson**

(*adv*) as a rule, averagely, broadly, by and large, characteristically, commonly, customarily, generally, generically, habitually, historically, in general, *in most cases*, mainly, more often than not, mostly, normally, on the whole, ordinarily, overall, popularly, routinely, traditionally, typically, usually

109 Again

Once more unto the breach, dear friends, once more. **William Shakespeare**

(*adv*) afresh, again, again and again, *all over again*, anew, *de novo*, newly, *once again*, *once more*, *over again*, *over and over*, *over and over again*, time after time, time and again, yet again

See also HAPPEN AGAIN (28), REPETITION (29), RECOMMENCE AND RESUME (268)

Quantity, Portion, Extent, and Degree

110 Degree and Extent

Measure what is measurable, and make measurable what is not so. **Galileo**

(*n*) ambit, breadth, degree, dilution, extent, gamut, gradation, grasp, layer, level, magnitude, margin, measure, orbit, parameter, perspective, portion, proportion, radius, rate, reach, room, scope, spectrum, sweep

111 Area and Range

The wonder is, not that the field of the stars is so vast, but that man has measured it. **Anatole France**

(*n*) area, band, column, corridor, cross section, elbowroom, file, line, mileage, module, panel, parcel, part, patch, piece, plot, queue (*UK*), range, row, scale, section, sector, segment, side, sprawl, spread, stretch, strip, subdivision, tract

112 Amounts and Quantities

I must have a prodigious quantity of mind; it takes me as much as a week, sometimes, to make it up. **Mark Twain**

(*adj*) any, certain, selected, several, some

(*n*) allocation, amount, buildup, burden, complement, count, *dessertspoonful*, diet, dosage, dose, element, figure, finger, fix (*humorous*), fund, helping, lot, number, pair, part, portion, quantity, ration, serving, share, spoonful, supply, *tablespoonful*, *teaspoonful*, throughput, volume, yield

113 Apportionment

All who joy would win/Must share it,—Happiness was born a twin. **Lord Byron**

(*adj*) bipartite, double, dual, *duple*, per capita, *per head*, *per person*, treble, tripartite, triple, twin, twofold

(*adv*) apiece, double, percent, piecemeal, twice

(*prep*) per

114 Amounts of Liquid

You don't water a camel with a spoon. **Proverb**

(*n*) bead, dab, dash, dewdrop, dot, drip, drop, droplet, gush, jet, puddle, spout, spray, spurt, squirt, stream, teardrop, trickle

See also DRINK (711)

115 Amounts of Solid or Semisolid

When the aggregate amount of solid matter transported by rivers...shall be reduced to arithmetical computation, the result will appear most astonishing. **Charles Lyell**

(*n*) bar, belt, blob, brick, briquette, cake, chew, chuck, clod, clot, clove, coagulation, *cob*, daub, divot, dollop (*informal*), fist, fistful, glob (*informal*), globule, gob (*slang*), *gobbet*, hank, ingot, length, lump, nugget, part, piece, *plateful*, plug, ream, ribbon, ruck, sheaf, sheet, skein, slice, strand, tablet, tuft, wad, wedge

116 Amounts of Gas

It was a giant column that soon took the shape of a supramundane mushroom. Referring to the explosion of an atomic bomb. **William L. Laurence**

(*n*) billow, breath, pall, plume, puff, waft

117 Many, Much, Large Amount

My bounty is as boundless as the sea,/My love as deep; the more I give to thee,/The more I have, for both are infinite. **William Shakespeare**

(*adj*) abounding, abundant, *aplenty*, appreciable, bounteous (*literary*), bountiful (*literary*), bumper, copious, countless, galore, generous, goodly, great, handsome, incalculable, incredible (*informal*), inexhaustible, innumerable, large, lavish, liberal, manifold, many, much, multiple, *multitudinous*, myriad, numberless, numerous, opulent, plenteous (*literary*), plentiful, princely, profuse, prolific, rich, umpteen (*informal*), *uncountable*, uncounted, unnumbered, untold, various

(*adv*) a great deal, a lot, appreciably, hand over fist, handsomely, in abundance, in bulk, in force, in strength, *in throngs*, much, thickly, tons

(*n*) abundance, accretion, acres (*informal*), avalanche, bank, battalion, bounty (*literary*), buckets (*informal*), *busload*, cornucopia, deluge, dozens (*informal*), droves, flood, flood tide, gallons (*UK*), *gazillion* (*slang*), heap, heaps (*informal*), *hordes*, horn of plenty, host, inundation (*formal*), *large amount*, lavishness, loads (*informal*), lots, maximum, millions, mine, mound, mountain, multiplicity, multitude, myriad, *numerousness*, oodles (*informal*), pile, plenty, plurality, pots (*informal*), predominance, preponderance (*formal*), profusion, raft (*informal*), scads (*informal*), scores, *shedload* (*UK*), shower, *squillion* (*UK*), stack, stacks (*informal*), stash, swarm, ton (*informal*), tons (*informal*), trillion (*informal*), *truckload*, wad, wealth, zillion (*informal*)

(*pron*) a lot, no end of (*informal*)

118 Large Amounts of Money

Where large sums of money are concerned, it is advisable to trust nobody. **Agatha Christie**

(*n*) an arm and a leg (*informal*), *boodle* (*slang*), bundle (*slang*), fortune, mint (*informal*), pile (*informal*), *tidy sum* (*informal*), *wad* (*informal*)

119 Too Much

'Tis not the drinking that is to be blamed, but the excess. **Edward Dyer**

(*adj*) astronomical (*informal*), *de trop*, excessive, inordinate, inundated, larger-than-life, lavish, *OTT* (*informal*), *overabundant*, overblown, overmuch, over-the-top (*informal*), superabundant, superfluous, *too much*, ultra, wanton

(*adv*) disproportionately, overly, overmuch, to excess, too

(*n*) excess, excessiveness, *exorbitance*, glut, inundation (*formal*), lavishness, overabundance, overcrowding, overkill, overload, overmuch, overspill, oversupply, plethora, stiffness, superfluity, surfeit, surplus

120 Few, Little, Small Amount

There are no intrinsic reasons for the scarcity of capital. **John Maynard Keynes**

(*adj*) endangered, few, least, marginal, minimal, minor, *not many*, *not much*, one or two, piddling (*informal*), slight

(*n*) *a drop in the bucket*, *a drop in the ocean* (*UK*), bagatelle (*formal*), billionth, element, flavor, flicker, glimpse, handful, hint, iota, jot, minimum, mite (*dated*), modicum, note, nuance, ounce, particle, pin (*dated informal*), pinch, scattering, scent, scintilla, semblance, shade, shadow, *small amount*, smattering, smidgen (*informal*), soupçon, spot, sprinkle, sprinkling, subtlety, suspicion, tad (*informal*), tang, *thimbleful*, tincture, tinge, touch, trace, trifle, vein, whiff, whisker

(*pron*) a few, *hardly any*, little

121 Small Amounts of Money

Lack of money is the root of all evil. **George Bernard Shaw**

(*n*) chicken feed (*informal*), peanuts (*informal*), pin money, pittance, pocket money

122 Too Few, Too Little

Just one being is lacking, and the whole world is empty of people. **Alphonse de Lamartine**

(*adj*) bare, inadequate, in short supply, insufficient, lacking in, low, meager, mean, measly (*informal*), mere, miserable, niggardly, paltry, scant, scanty, scarce, short-handed, short-staffed, skimpy, spare, sparing, sparse, *thin on the ground*, *too few*, *too little*, understrength

(*n*) austerity, dearth, deficiency, deficit, dispossession, drought, inadequacy, insufficiency, lack, loss, mea-

gerness, nonexistence, *paltriness*, paucity, poverty, rareness, rarity, *scantiness*, *scantness*, scarceness, scarcity, shortage, shortfall, sparseness

123 None

None but himself can be his parallel. **Lewis Theobald**

(*adj*) no

(*n*) cipher, *goose egg* (*slang*), naught, nil, nix (*dated slang*), zero, zilch (*informal*), zip (*informal*)

(*pron*) nobody, none, no one, nothing

124 More and Excess

To seek the beauteous eye of heaven to garnish,/Is wasteful and ridiculous excess. **William Shakespeare**

(*adj*) accompanying, added, additional, add-on, another, auxiliary, emergency, excess, extra, further, last, more, new, other, residual, spare, standby, subsidiary, supernumerary, supplemental, supplementary, supporting, surplus, *surplus to requirements*, unwanted, waste

(*adv*) else, extra

(*n*) *added extras*, addition, add-on, alloy, *appurtenance* (*formal*), backlog, backup, bonus, *extra*, frill, frills, inclusion, makeweight, overflow, permeation, proliferation, *reinforcements*, replenishment, spillage, spurt, supplement, top-up (*UK*)

(*prep*) above, in excess of, over

125 Remainder and Remainders

The poem is not made up of these letters that I plant like nails, but of the white that remains on the paper. **Paul Claudel**

(*n*) ashes, balance, carryover, clippings, deposition, dinosaur, dregs (*literary*), end, fossil, leavings, lees, leftover, leftovers, legacy, oddments, odds and ends, *odds and sods* (*UK*), ort, parings, peelings, relic, remainder, *remainders*, remains, remnant, *remnants*, residue, rest, ruin, scraps, *shavings*, shell, trimmings, wastage

See also JUNK AND USELESS OBJECTS (1249), UNPLEASANT, DIRTY, AND TOXIC SUBSTANCES (1268)

126 Less

Less is more. **Ludwig Mies van der Rohe**

(*adj*) expurgated, fewer, less, net, stripped, stripped-down

(*n*) abatement, cutback, dip, drop, falloff, minus, relaxation

(*prep*) below, less, under, without

127 Measurable Portions

I have measured out my life with coffee spoons. **T. S. Eliot**

(*n*) cut (*informal*), fourth, fraction, golden mean, *half*, mean, percent, percentage, *percentile*, proportion, quarter, *quartile*, quota, quotient, ratio, *third*, whole

128 All

All is for the best in the best of all possible worlds. **Voltaire**

(*adj*) across-the-board, aggregate (*formal*), all-or-nothing, any, at large, each, every, gross, *hundred percent*, systemic, whatsoever

(*adv*) all told, altogether, bag and baggage, en bloc, en

masse, globally, in all, *in its entirety*, *in total*, lock, stock, and barrel, *warts and all*, whatever

(*n*) all-comers (*UK*), caboodle (*informal*), everybody, everyone, everything, *grand total*, sum, summation, sum total, *the whole ball of wax* (*informal*), *the whole enchilada* (*slang*), *the whole kit and caboodle* (*informal*), *the whole, the whole lot, the whole shebang* (*informal*), total, totality, whole, *whole lot*

(*pron*) all, all and sundry, each, one and all, whatever

See also WHOLENESS AND COMPLETENESS (198)

129 Small Pieces

It is a small thing that is taken to measure a big thing.
African (Ashanti) proverb

(*n*) atom, bit, bite, chip, chipping, chippings (*UK*), crumb, *elementary particle*, filing, flake, fleck, fraction, fragment, grain, granule, molecule, morsel, mote, nibble, nip, particle, scale, scrap, shard, shaving, shred, sliver, smithereens (*informal*), snippet, speck, speckle, splinter, *tittle*, vestige, whit (*dated*), wisp

130 Large Pieces

There is always something larger than what is large. **Anaxagoras**
(*n*) block, chunk, hunk, slab, wad

131 Enough and Sufficient

The greatest thing in the world is to know how to be self-sufficient. **Michel de Montaigne**

(*adj*) adequate, ample, enough, moderate, modest, plenty (*informal*), satisfying, sufficient

(*adv*) amply, plenty (*informal*)

(*n*) adequacy, quorum, sufficiency

(*v*) suffice (*formal*)

132 To a Great Extent

What we think and feel and are is to a great extent determined by the state of our ductless glands and our viscera.
Aldous Huxley

(*adv*) acutely, altogether, astronomically (*informal*), awfully, big time (*slang*), bitterly, by far, considerably, crushingly, dearly, deeply, desperately, devoutly (*formal*), dreadfully, eminently, enormously, especially, ever so, excessively, extensively, extra, extraordinarily, extremely, fairly, famously, far, far and away, fearfully (*informal*), fiendishly, fiercely, frightfully, gigantically, greatly, grossly, heartily, heavily, highly, hopelessly, horribly, hugely, immeasurably, immensely, implicitly, impossibly, *in a big way*, incalculably, incredibly (*informal*), indescribably, inestimably, infinitely, *inordinately*, intensely, madly, massively (*informal*), measurably, mightily, monstrously, monumentally, mortally, most, notoriously, overpoweringly, overwhelmingly, particularly, peculiarly, powerfully, prodigiously, profoundly, rather, real (*informal*), really, richly, right, rotten (*informal*), savagely, seriously (*informal*), shockingly, significantly, sorely (*formal*), soundly, stupendously, substantially, substantively, supremely, terribly, terrifically, thumping (*informal*), tremendously, truly, unbelievably, unduly, unreasonably, unspeakably, vastly, very, vitally, walloping (*informal*), wretchedly

133 Absolute and Absolutely

To die for a religion is easier than to live it absolutely.
Jorge Luis Borges

(*adj*) abject, absolute, arrant, blank, complete, consummate, definitive, drastic, entire, flat, great, mortal, out-and-out, outright, pure, rank, sheer, stark, stiff, straight-out (*informal*), thorough, thoroughgoing, total, unmitigated, unqualified, utter

(*adv*) decidedly, definitively, diametrically, directly, downright, dramatically, exclusively, just, outright, plumb (*informal*), purely, quite, radically, roundly, signally, simply, spotlessly, stark, stone-cold (*informal*), sure (*informal*), thoroughly, through and through, totally, wholly

134 Critically and Seriously

Everything must be taken seriously, nothing tragically.
Adolphe Thiers

(*adv*) badly, critically, dangerously, deadly, deathly, fatally, gravely, grievously, lethally, mortally, seriously, terminally

135 Approximately

None of us can estimate what we do when we do it from instinct. **Luigi Pirandello**

(*adj*) approximate, ballpark (*informal*), broad, crude, inexact, pushing, rough, virtual

(*adv*) about, *give or take*, going on for (*UK*), *in the region of*, just about, more or less, *near enough*, not quite, *of the order of* (*UK*), *on the order of*, or so, roughly, *roughly speaking*, say, some, thereabouts, there or thereabouts (*informal*)

(*prep*) around, circa, round about

See also VAGUENESS (243)

136 To a Certain Extent

Partial nuclear disarmament...is...like talking about partial circumcision. **Robin Williams**

(*adj*) comparative, relative

(*adv*) a bit (*informal*), almost, any, as good as, barely, by a hairsbreadth, close on (*UK*), close to, fairly, fractionally, halfway, hardly, ill, imperceptibly, in moderation, in part, just, kind of (*informal*), little, marginally, merely, mildly, minimally, moderately, modestly, narrowly, near, nearly, negligibly, only, partially, partly, partway, practically, pretty, quite, rather, reasonably, remotely, scarcely, slightly, something, somewhat, *sort of* (*informal*), subtly, thinly, to all intents and purposes, virtually, well-nigh

137 Not

Outside the huge negations pass/Like whirlwinds writing on the grass. **George Barker**

(*adj*) exclusive of

(*adv*) by no means, even less, negatively, never, no, on no account, on the contrary, under no circumstances

(*prep*) apart from, aside from, bar, barring, but, except, *except for*, excepting (*formal*), excluding, minus, not counting, notwithstanding (*formal*), sans (*literary or humorous*), save, save for, short of, unless

138   Also

Every spark adds to the fire. **Proverb**

(*adj*) either, plus

(*adv*) also, as well, besides, equally, similarly, too

(*conj*) and, and/or, as well as

(*prep*) along with, among, apart from, aside from, coupled with, cum (*informal*), in addition to, including, in conjunction with, in cooperation with, over and above, plus, together with, with

139   Expressions Introducing Extra Information

I knew one that when he wrote a letter, he would put that which was most material in the postscript, as if it had been a by-matter. **Francis Bacon**

(*adv*) additionally, alternatively, besides, by the way, furthermore, in addition, in any case, in any event, incidentally, *into the bargain*, moreover, nay (*archaic or literary*), secondly, then, *to boot*, to cap it all (*UK*), what is more

140   Mainly and Primarily

Be careful still of the main chance. **John Dryden**

(*adv*) above all, chiefly, especially, essentially, even more, first and foremost, in essence, in particular, largely, mostly, *most of all*, particularly, predominantly, preponderantly, primarily, principally, purely, solely

See also MOST IMPORTANT AND MAIN (193)

141   Majority and Maximum

Fools are in a terrible, overwhelming majority, all the wide world over. **Henrik Ibsen**

(*adv*) max (*slang*), tops (*informal*)

(*n*) bottom line, bulk, ceiling, greatest, limit, lion's share, majority, mass, maximum, plurality, threshold

(*pron*) most

Relatedness and Connection

142   Related

It is the attainment of a new kind of relationship with others and with himself which ultimately heals the patient.
Anthony Storr

(*adj*) *affiliated*, aligned, allied, amalgamated, assistant, associate, associated, attendant, built-in, caught up, causative, cognate, coincidental, concomitant, confederate, connected, contextual, cumulative, imitative, in-built (*UK*), incidental, incorporated, indivisible, instrumental, integral, integrated, interactive, involved, joined, kindred, linked, piggyback, related, sister, unified, united, vicarious, wedded

(*adv*) accompanied by

(*prep*) after, by

143   Connections

The word connects the visible trace with the invisible thing...like a frail emergency bridge flung over an abyss.
Italo Calvino

(*n*) adhesion, affiliation, alignment, allegiance, alliance, amalgamation, attribution, axis, bond, bonding, bridge, causality, coincidence (*formal*), common denominator, communion, comparison, concomitance, confluence, conjunction, connection, consolidation, convergence, correlation, correspondence, coupling, crossover, hierarchy, interplay, intersection, involvement, juxtaposition, kinship, ladder, liaison, ligature (*formal*), link, linkage, linkup, membership, nexus, order, overlap, participation, partisanship, pecking order, rapport, *relatedness*, relationship, relativity, tie, tie-in, tie-up, union

See also FASTEN, LINK, AND JOIN (408)

144   Creating Connections

A hidden connection is stronger than an obvious one. **Heraclitus**

(*v*) affiliate, ascribe (*formal*), associate, blame, bracket, bring together, compare, confederate, connect, correlate, correspond, equate, federate, identify, impute, interact, interconnect, interrelate, intersect, involve, join, liken, link, meet, overlap, pair, relate, reunify, reunite, straddle, subsume, tie in, touch, twin, unify

See also COMBINE AND MIX (400)

145   Varieties, Types, and Kinds

Variety is the soul of pleasure. **Aphra Behn**

(*n*) bracket, brand, breed, category, class, classification, description, division, family, form, genre, genus, grade, grouping, hue, ilk, isotope, kind, make, manner, mode, model, mold, nature, notch, pigeonhole, quality, rubric, sort, species, stamp, status, strain, style, subcategory, subgroup, subset, subspecies, type, variety, version

146   Unrelatedness and Separateness

I never found the companion that was so companionable as solitude. **Henry David Thoreau**

(*adj*) breakaway, detachable, detached, discrete, divisible, exclusive, foreign, freestanding, heterogeneous, individual, isolated, lone, removable, separable, separate, single, sole, specific, unconnected, unincorporated, unrelated

(*adv*) aside, distinctively, in isolation, separately, severally, singly

(*n*) disjointedness, distinctiveness, individualism, individuality, otherness, separateness, unconformity

See also SAMENESS (150), EXTRAORDINARY: UNCOMMON (205)

147   Reciprocity and Interdependence

Action and counteraction...in the natural and in the political world...draws out the harmony of the universe. **Edmund Burke**

(*adj*) conditional, contingent, dependent, ensemble, inseparable, interdependent, interracial, modular, multilateral, mutual, reciprocal, subject to, symbiotic, *synergetic*, two-way

(*adv*) communally, inextricably

(*n*) arrangement, collaboration, complicity, cooperation,

dependence, give-and-take (*informal*), reciprocation, reciprocity, reliance, symbiosis, synergy, teamwork

(*v*) accompany, depend, depend on, hang on, hinge on, live off, rely, rest on, ride, turn on

See also ACTING WITH OTHERS (285)

148 Similarity

As lyke as one pease is to another. **John Lyly**

(*adj*) akin, alike, analogous, close, comparable, derivative, like, mimetic, *not unlike*, *of a kind*, parallel, reminiscent, resembling, similar, unoriginal, verging on

(*adv*) likewise, similarly

(*n*) affinity, *alikeness*, analogue, community, likeness, parallel, resemblance, similarity, similitude (*formal*), unoriginality

(*prep*) after, close to, like, near

149 Difference

There is more difference within the sexes than between them. **Ivy Compton-Burnett**

(*adj*) aberrant, alternate, alternative, assorted, catholic, clashing, composite, contrasting, deviant, different, disparate, disproportionate, dissimilar, distinct, distinguishable, divergent, divers (*literary*), diverse, eclectic, else, incommensurate, loose, miscellaneous, mixed, motley, multicultural, multifarious, multiracial, *nothing like*, pluralistic, poles apart, portmanteau (*UK*), ragtag, sundry, unaccustomed, *unalike*, unequal, uneven, unlike, variant, varied, various, *varying*

(*adv*) differently, diversely, else, in lieu, *in sharp contrast*, instead, rather, unequally, unevenly

(*n*) aberration, a whole new ball game (*slang*), contrast, *crosscurrent*, deviance, deviation, dichotomy, difference, differentiation, digression, disagreement, discrepancy, discrimination, disparity, disproportion, dissimilarity, distinction, divergence, dualism, duality, eclecticism, gap, *heterogeneity*, imbalance, inconsistency, inequality, irregularity, *multifariousness*, nonconformity, *odd one out*, particularity, pluralism, *something else entirely*, variance, variant, variation

(*prep*) far from, instead of

(*v*) contrast, differ, disagree, *run counter to*, set apart, vary

See also OPPOSITE (157)

150 Sameness

The man who views the world at 50 the same as he did at 20 has wasted 30 years of his life. **Muhammad Ali**

(*adj*) duplicate, equal, exchangeable, homogeneous, identical, indistinguishable, interchangeable, *like two peas in a pod*, matching, no different, one and the same, same, selfsame, stereotypical, synonymous, tantamount, twin, *undifferentiated*, uniform, very

(*n*) duplication, homogeneity, homogeneousness, *identicalness*, monotony, oneness, reduplication, regularity, sameness, uniformity

See also UNRELATEDNESS AND SEPARATENESS (146)

151 Copies and Replicas

Man, as he is, is not a genuine article. He is an imitation of something, and a very bad imitation. **Peter Ouspensky**

(*n*) backup, carbon copy, chip off the old block (*informal*), clone, copy, dead ringer (*informal*), doppelgänger, double, dummy, duplicate, duplication, facsimile, knock-off (*informal*), look-alike (*informal*), mirror image, reflection, replica, reprint, reproduction, rubbing, spitting image (*informal*), twin

See also COPY AND DUPLICATE (402)

152 Superiority

Sometimes I feel so unutterably superior to the people surrounding me that I marvel at my ability to live among them. **Kenneth Williams**

(*adj*) a cut above, choice, chosen, crack, exalted (*formal*), finest, foremost, greater, highest, high-grade, in charge, lofty, noble, peak, peerless, picked, preferential, premier, premium, prime, red-carpet, select, sovereign, special, super, superfine, superior, supreme, tiptop (*informal*), top, top-class, top-drawer, topflight, topmost, topnotch (*informal*), top-of-the-range, top-quality, transcendent, unequaled, unmatched, unparalleled, unsurpassed, upper, utmost, vintage, world-class

(*n*) ascendancy, cream, crème de la crème, edge, flower, precedence, predominance, preeminence, seniority, superiority, supremacy, top drawer, transcendence

See also EXTRAORDINARY: AMAZING (204)

153 Inferiority

No one can make you feel inferior without your consent. **Eleanor Roosevelt**

(*adj*) ancillary, buck, inferior, junior, lesser, lower, minor, secondary, second best, second class, second-rate, subnormal, subsidiary, substandard, third-rate

(*adv*) below

(*n*) inferiority, subordination

See also ORDINARINESS (244)

154 Equality

EQUALITY. . .*is the thing. It is the only true and central premise from which constructive ideas can radiate freely and be operated without prejudice.* **Mervyn Peake**

(*adj*) commensurate (*formal*), democratic, egalitarian, equal, equitable (*formal*), equivalent, even, evenhanded, fair, level, nondiscriminatory, *on a par*, on a par with, proportional, proportionate, quits (*informal*), symmetrical

(*adv*) equally, evenhandedly, fairly, fifty-fifty, neck and neck (*informal*)

(*n*) analogy, equal, equality, equity, equivalence, equivalent, evenhandedness, fairness, level pegging (*UK*), match, offset, parallel, parity, rival, symmetry

(*prep*) as good as

(*v*) balance out, come up to, draw, equal, equalize, even out, fit, match, rival, tally, tie

See also MORALLY GOOD (774)

155   Harmony

I have cherished the ideal of a democratic and free society in which all persons live together in harmony and with equal opportunities. **Nelson Mandela**

(*adj*) *at one with*, cohesive, compatible, complementary, compliant, congruent (*formal*), consistent, consonant with (*formal*), corresponding, harmonious, harmonized, harmonizing, in keeping, integrated, *in tune*, like-minded, matching, *of one mind*, on the same wavelength, solid, sympathetic, unanimous, well-balanced, well-matched, well-suited

(*adv*) *in agreement*, *in harmony*, in line, in step, *in sync* (*informal*), in time

(*n*) accord, accordance, agreement, armistice, balance, bargain, coexistence, cohesion, complement, compliance, conciliation, concord, concurrence, conformity, congeniality, consensus, détente, *entente*, equilibrium, harmony, oneness, peace, peace agreement, rapprochement, reconciliation, reunion, solidarity, steadiness, sweetness and light, sympathy, *unanimity*, understanding, union, unison, unity

(*prep*) according to, in line with

(*v*) accord, agree, be compatible, be consistent with, belong, chime in, coexist, cohere (*formal*), coincide, complement, compromise, conform, fulfill, harmonize, match, mix

156   Disharmony

Out of the tension of duality life always produces a "third" that seems somehow incommensurable or paradoxical.
Carl Gustav Jung

(*adj*) adverse, at loggerheads, at odds, at variance, conflicting, contradictory, contrary, differing, discordant, disharmonious, divisive, factional, factious, ill-assorted, incompatible, inconsistent, inharmonious, *in opposition*, irreconcilable, mismatched, schismatic, uneven, *unharmonious*

(*n*) agitation, bone of contention, breach, contradiction, discord, disharmony, dissension, dissent, dissonance, disunity, divergence, division, divisiveness, faction, friction, incompatibility, misalliance, mismatch, quibble, schism, split, strife, tension, trouble, unevenness, unpleasantness, variance, war, warfare

(*v*) be at odds, be at variance, belie, clash, conflict, contradict, fall foul of

See also DISORDER AND CHAOS (245)

157   Opposite

The comic is the perception of the opposite; humor is the feeling of it. **Umberto Eco**

(*adj*) antithetical (*formal*), converse, inverse, obverse, opposed, opposing, opposite, reverse

(*adv*) conversely, on the other hand

(*n*) antithesis, *antonym*, contrary, converse, inverse, inversion, negation, obverse, opposite, pole, reverse

(*prep*) against, counter to, versus

See also DIFFERENCE (149)

158   General Locations

My center is giving way, my right is retreating; situation excellent. I shall attack. **Ferdinand Foch**

(*adj*) aerial, airborne, alfresco, all-around, all-round (*UK*), dotted, extensive, far-flung, flying, general, indoor, in-flight, inland, inside, interior, inward, leeward, left-hand, midair, national, nationwide, open-air, outboard, outdoor, outside, right-hand, scattered, situated (*formal*), spatial, starboard, sunken, underwater, upwind, worldwide

(*adv*) alfresco, all over the place (*informal*), aloft, anyplace (*informal*), anywhere, around, downstairs, everywhere, far and wide, herewith, high and low, in, *in back*, indoors, in front, inside, *in the background*, in the midst of, *in the rear*, midway, out, outdoors, out-of-doors, outside, overhead, someplace (*informal*), somewhere, *to the rear*, widely, within, *yonder*

See also PLACE (1065)

159   Closeness

Once the realization is accepted that even between the closest human beings infinite distances continue to exist, a wonderful living side by side can grow up. **Rainer Maria Rilke**

(*adj*) abutting, adjacent, adjoining, bonded, bordering, close, close at hand, close by, close-run, connected, contiguous (*formal*), *cross-border*, *face-to-face*, hand-to-hand, handy, head-to-head, hereabout, immediate, local, near, nearby, neighboring, next-door, nigh, *proximate*, *short-range*, *side by side*, surrounding, tightknit, vicinal, *within grasp*, within reach, *within spitting distance* (*informal*), *within walking distance*

(*adv*) around, at hand, cheek by jowl, cheek-to-cheek, closely, face to face, handily, head-to-head, immediately, *in close proximity*, *in easy reach*, *in the vicinity*, locally, near, nearby, next door, point blank, *round here* (*UK*), *shoulder to shoulder*, tightly

(*n*) closeness, contiguity (*formal*), earshot, handiness, hearing, nearness, propinquity (*formal*), proximity, *spitting distance* (*informal*), stone's throw, striking distance

(*prep*) against, along, alongside, around, at the side of, near, within an ace of, *within reach of*

160   Distance

Man is slightly nearer to the atom than the stars. From his central position he can survey the grandest works of Nature with the astronomer, or the minutest works with the physicist.
Arthur Eddington

(*adj*) distant, extreme, far, *far away*, faraway, far-flung, far-off, *farthermost*, farthest, foreign, furthermost, furthest, inaccessible, isolated, lonely, lonesome, *off the beaten path*, off the beaten track (*informal*), opposite, outermost, outlying, outmost, out-of-the-way, private, remote, solitary, transatlantic, utmost, vicarious

(*adv*) afar (*literary*), apart, far, far afield, *far off*, in the distance

(*n*) distance, inaccessibility, isolation, miles (*informal*), remoteness

161 Relative Location

That white horse you see in the park could be a zebra synchronized with the railings. **Ann Jellicoe**

(*adj*) bottom, bottommost, built-in, equidistant, fitted, frontal, halfway, hind, hindmost (*literary*), in-between, inside, intermediary, intermediate, *intertwined*, *interwoven*, lowermost, mid, middle, nearside (*UK*), nether (*formal*), peripheral, rearmost, rearward, superior, top, uppermost

(*adv*) abreast, ahead, astern, at the rear, behind, below, beneath, halfway, *to the fore*, *to the left*, *to the right*

(*prep*) aboard, above, after, amid, among, around, astride, atop (*literary*), before, behind, beneath, beside, between, beyond, by, facing, in, in between, in front of, inside, on, on top of, opposite, outside, over, round, through, under, underneath, with

162 Chain of Events

The hour of their crime does not strike simultaneously for all nations. This explains the permanence of history. **E. M. Cioran**

(*adj*) chronological, sequential, temporal

(*n*) chain, chronology, cycle, kaleidoscope, progression, sequence, *sequence of events*, series, *series of events*, spate, succession, train

See also EVENTS AND OCCURRENCES (35), PERIODS OF TIME (90)

163 Before, First, and Preceding

The original is unfaithful to the translation. **Jorge Luis Borges**

(*adj*) *anterior* (*formal*), earlier, earliest, early, eldest, fast, first, foregoing, inaugural, initial, introductory, last, maiden, original, past, preceding, predetermined, preexisting, preliminary, preparatory, prescribed, preset, previous, primary, prior

(*adv*) as yet, at first, at the outset, at the start, before, before now, earlier, first, firstly, in advance

(*n*) *antecedence*, antecedent, precursor, predecessor, progenitor

(*prep*) ahead of, before, by, prior to

(*v*) *antecede*, antedate, anticipate, forego (*formal*), precede, predate, preexist, preface, prefigure, prefix

See also PAST (84)

164 Concurrent and Contemporaneous

Contemporary man has rationalized the myths, but he has not been able to destroy them. **Octavio Paz**

(*adj*) coexistent, coextensive, concomitant, concurrent, contemporaneous, simultaneous, synchronized, *synchronous*

(*adv*) all at once, all together, at once, at one fell swoop, at one go (*UK*), at that moment, at the same time, *contemporarily*, together

(*conj*) as, immediately, whenever, while

(*n*) coexistence, concurrence, contemporaneity, contemporaries, *simultaneity*, *synchronicity*, *synchronism*

(*prep*) amid, during, *in the course of*, pending, through, throughout

165 After, Last, and Following

For all at last return to the sea—to Oceanus, the ocean river, like the ever-flowing stream of time, the beginning and the end. **Rachel Carson**

(*adj*) back-to-back, closing, concluding, consecutive, consequent, consequential, dying, ensuing, eventual, final, following, follow-on, last, last-ditch, latter, *next to last*, penultimate, posterior (*formal*), resultant, resulting, second, secondary, sequential, serial, straight, subsequent, succeeding, successive, valedictory (*formal*)

(*adv*) after, after that, afterward, at last, at length, at long last, eventually, finally, in a row, in order, *in sequence*, *in succession*, in the end, just, just now, late, latterly, next, once, one after another, one after the other, one by one, on end, on the trot (*UK*), running, sequentially, since, then, thence (*formal or literary*), thenceforth, thenceforward, thereafter, thereupon (*formal*), ultimately

(*conj*) after, as soon as, whereupon (*formal*)

(*n*) follow-up, sequel

(*prep*) after, as of (*formal*)

See also RESULTS AND OUTCOMES (83)

166 New, Modern

Fashion is made to become unfashionable. **Coco Chanel**

(*adj*) ageless, ahead of its time, avant-garde, brand-new, cool (*informal*), cutting-edge, fashionable, fresh, funky (*informal*), futuristic, happening (*informal*), hip (*slang*), in, incoming, innovative, latest, modern, modernistic, modish, new, newborn, newfangled, pioneering, pop (*informal*), reborn, recent, spanking new, supercool (*informal*), trendy (*informal*), ultramodern, undeveloped, unknown, unripe, untested, untried, unused, up-to-date, up-to-the-minute, voguish, with-it (*dated informal*), young

(*n*) cutting edge, *hipness* (*slang*), innovation, modernism, modernity

167 Old, Old-Fashioned

For an idea ever to be fashionable is ominous, since it must afterwards be always old-fashioned. **George Santayana**

(*adj*) age-old, anachronistic, ancient, antediluvian (*informal*), antiquated, antique, archaic, atavistic, behind the times, *centuries old*, dated, folk, hand-me-down, historic, historical, hoary, institutionalized, long-established, matured, medieval, obsolescent, obsolete, old, olden (*archaic or literary*), old-fashioned, old hat (*informal*), old-style, old-time, old-world, out, outdated, outmoded, out-of-date, *out of fashion*, outworn, passé, poky (*informal*), prehistoric, primal, primeval, primitive, primordial, retro, roman, secondhand, senior, superannuated, tested, time-honored, traditional, unfashionable, *unhip* (*informal*), used, vintage

(*n*) anachronism, maturity, obsolescence, *outmodedness*, primitiveness, ripeness

See also PAST (84), IN BAD REPAIR (1234)

168   Causation

The final cause of the World at large, we allege to be the consciousness of its own freedom on the part of Spirit, and ipso facto, the reality of that freedom. **G. W. F. Hegel**

(*adj*) causal, contributory, extenuating

(*adv*) accordingly, consequently, hence (*formal*), ipso facto, so, then, thence (*formal or literary*), therefore

(*conj*) and, as, as long as, because, forasmuch as (*formal*), given that, inasmuch as, in order to, insofar as, insomuch as, in that, provided that, providing, since, *so long as*

(*n*) agency, agent, causation, cause, enticement, excuse, explanation, factor, grounds, hidden agenda, impetus, impulse, incentive, inspiration, mitigation, motivation, motivator, motive, occasion, pretext, push, reason, spur, stimulation, stimulus, ulterior motive

(*prep*) as a result of, because of, given, in the light of, in the name of, in view of, on account of, on the strength of, owing to, thanks to, through

(*v*) be caused by, come from, stem from

169   Although, Nevertheless, and Despite

I have always found that the man whose second thoughts are good is worth watching. **J. M. Barrie**

(*adv*) after all, all the same, anyhow, anyway, aside, at least, be that as it may, but then again, come what may, even so, however, in any case, irrespective, just the same, leastways (*informal*), leastwise (*informal*), nevertheless, no matter what, nonetheless, notwithstanding (*formal*), otherwise, regardless, still, though, yet

(*conj*) albeit, although, even if, though, whereas, while

(*prep*) despite, for all, in spite of, in the face of, irrespective of, regardless of

170   Responsibility

Alas, after a certain age every man is responsible for his face. **Albert Camus**

(*adj*) accountable, answerable, bound, duty-bound, liable, litigable, responsible

(*n*) accountability, aegis, *answerability*, auspices, buck (*informal*), care, charge, control, custody, debt, duty, fault, incumbency (*formal*), liability, mantle (*formal*), obligation, onus, responsibility, trust, umbrella

See also MORALLY BAD OR IMPROPER (775)

Truth, Reality, Certainty, and Possibility

171   True and Real

The life of an honest man must be a perpetual infidelity. **Charles Pierre Péguy**

(*adj*) actual, authentic, autobiographical, biographical, bona fide, canonical, card-carrying, *certifiable*, concrete, convincing, credible, de facto, devout (*formal*), earnest, effective, empirical, *fact-based*, factional, factual, faithful, full-fledged, genuine, heartfelt, hearty, kosher (*informal*), legit (*slang*), legitimate, lifelike, literal,

material, matter-of-fact, native, natural, naturalistic, nonfiction, objective, practical, pure, real, realistic, real-life, real-world, self-confessed, solid, sterling, *substantiated*, tangible, three-dimensional, true, true-life, true to life, undistorted, unembellished, unembroidered, *unfeigned*, unvarnished, valid, veritable

(*adv*) by nature, convincingly, effectively, factually, honestly, in earnest, in effect, in fact, in reality, literally, naturally, physically, truly

(*n*) absolute, actuality, authenticity, believability, credence, credibility, fact, fact of life, *fait accompli*, faithfulness, genuineness, justice, legitimacy, reality, *real life*, realness, real world, the real McCoy (*informal*), *the real thing*, truth, validity, veracity, verisimilitude (*formal*), verity (*formal*)

172   Words and Phrases Emphasizing the Truth of a Matter

If the truth were self-evident, eloquence would be unnecessary. **Cicero**

(*adv*) actually, as a matter of fact, from the horse's mouth, if truth be told, in actual fact, indeed, in fact, in point of fact, *in truth*, really, unsurprisingly

173   False and Unreal

If there were a verb meaning "to believe falsely", it would not have any significant first person, present indicative. **Ludwig Wittgenstein**

(*adj*) abstract, academic, allegorical, *all in the mind*, apocryphal, artificial, assumed, bogus, canned, cardboard, chimerical, contrived, copied, counterfeit, *counterfeited*, deceptive, delusive, distorted, diversionary, dreamlike, dummy, ersatz, fabled, fabricated, factitious, fairy-tale, fake, *faked*, fallacious, false, falsified, *fantastical*, faux, feigned, fictional, fictitious, forged, fraudulent, hollow, hypothetical, illusive, illusory, imaginary, imagined, imitation, inauthentic, incorporeal (*formal*), invalid, invented, invisible, legendary, literary, loaded, made-up, magic, magical, make-believe, man-made, mendacious, meretricious, misleading, mock, mythical, mythological, nominal, nonexistent, notional, perverted, phony, plastic, pretend, *pretended*, propagandist, *pseudo*, purported, put-on, quasi, reproduction, sham, simulated, so-called, soi-disant (*literary*), *sophistic*, specious, spurious, storybook, stylized, superficial, supposed, surface, synthetic, tall, theoretical, *thought up*, titular, trick, trumped-up, unfounded, unnatural, unreal, untrue, *without foundation*

(*adv*) deceitfully, falsely, hollowly, in name only, nominally, superficially, unnaturally

(*n*) deceptiveness, *fallaciousness*, fiction, hollowness, *illusoriness*, *imaginariness*, magic, *phoniness*, simulation, speciousness, unreality, veneer

See also NONEXISTENT THINGS (23), AFFECTATION, SELF-SATISFACTION, AND SNOBBISHNESS (507), DECEITFUL (513), DECEPTION AND LIES (660)

174   Certain

Science has proof without any certainty. **Ashley Montagu**

(*adj*) absolute, agreed, airtight, arranged, assured, axiomatic, bound, carried, categorical, certain, clear, conclusive, decided, definite, demonstrable, evident, final, foregone, guaranteed, inalienable (*formal*), incontestable, incontrovertible, indisputable, indubitable, ineluctable (*literary*), inescapable, inevitable, inexorable (*formal*), infallible, in the bag (*informal*), irrefutable, positive, preordained, provable, proven, resounding, self-evident, settled, sure, sure-fire (*informal*), unarguable, unassailable, unavoidable, uncontroversial, undeniable, undisputed, undoubted, unquestionable, unquestioned, verifiable, verified, watertight

(*adv*) admittedly, *beyond a doubt*, *beyond a shadow of a doubt*, *beyond doubt*, *beyond question*, certainly, clearly, definitely, doubtless, easily, finally, for sure (*informal*), hands down, indeed, inevitably, inexorably (*formal*), infallibly, no doubt, of course, positively, rightly (*informal*), simply, surely, without a doubt, *without a shadow of a doubt*, without fail, *without question*

(*n*) authentication, certainty, cinch (*informal*), definiteness, finality, *indisputability*, inevitability, inexorability (*formal*), inexorableness (*formal*), infallibility, predictability, predictableness, *safe bet*, *sure bet*, sure thing (*informal*), unavoidability

See also CERTAINTY (561)

175   Uncertain

When nothing is sure, everything is possible. **Margaret Drabble**

(*adj*) alleged, anecdotal, apparent, arguable, assumed, baseless, borderline, circumstantial, conjectural, contentious, controversial, debatable, disputable, doubtful, dubious, flimsy, iffy (*informal*), incalculable, inconclusive, indecisive, indefinite, indeterminable, indeterminate, in doubt, *in question*, moot, negotiable, notional, *open to question*, ostensible, *ostensive*, professed, putative, questionable, reputed, rumored, seeming, shaky, speculative, supposed, suspect, suspicious, tentative, touch-and-go, uncertain, unclear, unconfirmed, unconvincing, undecided, undetermined, unlikely, unproven, unresolved, unsettled, unsubstantiated, unsupported, untested, unverified, variable, weak, wide-open

(*adv*) abstractly, apparently, at first sight, evidently, flimsily, incalculably, *indeterminately*, notionally, reportedly, seemingly, supposedly

(*conj*) in case, lest

(*n*) disequilibrium, dubiety (*formal*), dubiousness, fragility, if, indecisiveness, *indeterminacy*, shakiness, *uncertainness*, variability

See also UNCERTAINTY (559)

176   Falsify and Cheat

A man is to be cheated into passion, but to be reasoned into truth. **John Dryden**

(*v*) cheat, cook the books (*slang*), counterfeit, crib (*informal*), fake, falsify, fiddle (*informal*), fix (*informal*), forge, frame (*slang*), fudge (*informal*), juggle, maneuver, massage, misrepresent, pervert, rig, skew, tamper, twist, warp

See also COPY AND DUPLICATE (402), DECEPTION AND LIES (660)

177   Possible and Probable

Probable impossibilities are to be preferred to improbable possibilities. **Aristotle**

(*adj*) achievable, attainable, believable, calculable, conceivable, credible, discretionary, doable, earthly, expected, feasible, foreseeable, hopeful, imaginable, *in the cards* (*informal*), in the running, likely, logical, operable, optional, plausible, possible, potential, practicable, predictable, presumptive (*formal*), probable, realizable, surmountable, tenable, viable, workable, would-be

(*adv*) arguably, credibly, debatably, hopefully, humanly, ideally, in principle, in theory, maybe, *most likely*, *most probably*, odds-on (*informal*), on paper, perchance (*archaic or literary*), perhaps, possibly, presumably

(*n*) chance, danger, feasibility, hope, likelihood, occasion, off chance, plausibility, possibility, practicability, probability, prospect, risk, room, scope, sporting chance, viability

178   Impossible and Improbable

How next to impossible is the exercise of virtue! It requires a constant watchfulness, constant guard. **William Golding**

(*adj*) doubtful, fairy-tale, fanciful, fantastic, far-fetched, *highly unlikely*, implausible, impossible, impracticable, impractical, improbable, inconceivable, incredible, inoperable, out, out of the question, outside, remote, slim, unachievable, unattainable, unbelievable, unfeasible, unimaginable, unlikely, unrealistic, untenable, unthinkable, *unviable*, visionary

(*adv*) incredibly, indefensibly

(*n*) doubtfulness, hopelessness, implausibility, impossibility, impracticability, impracticality, improbability, inaccessibility, long shot, *unfeasibility*, unlikelihood, *unlikeliness*, *unviability*

179   Secret and Unknown

I know that's a secret, for it's whispered everywhere. **William Congreve**

(*adj*) alien, anonymous, arcane, backroom, between ourselves, buried, censored, clandestine, classified, cloak-and-dagger, closet, concealed, confidential, covert, cryptic, deep, enigmatic, faceless, furtive, hidden, hole-and-corner (*UK*), hush-hush (*informal*), imponderable, indefinite, informal, inmost, inner, innermost, inside, intimate, invisible, inward, latent, *little-known*, mystery, nameless, obscure, off the record, outside, pent-up, private, privileged, quiet, recondite, repressed, restricted, secluded, secret, sensitive, *sequestered* (*formal*), shadowy, *shrouded in mystery*, silent, stealthy, subterranean, surreptitious, top-secret, ulterior, unanticipated, uncharted, undecipherable, undercover, underground, under-the-table, under wraps (*informal*), *undetected*, undetermined, undisclosed, *undiscovered*, unexplained, *unexplored*, unexpressed, unfamiliar, unforeseeable, unheard-of, unidentified, unknowable, unknown, unlisted, *unmapped*, unnamed, unnoticed, unobserved, unplumbed, *unprofessed*, unquantifiable, unrevealed, unsaid, unspoken, unsung, unsuspected, unvoiced, veiled, well-kept

(*adv*) abstrusely, anonymously, backstage, behind closed doors, behind the scenes, behind your back, confidentially, implicitly, in camera, incognito, in confidence, informally, *in secrecy*, in secret, inwardly, on the sly, privately, secretly

(*n*) anonymity, concealment, covertness, furtiveness, mystery, mystique, obscurity, privacy, seclusion, secrecy, stealth, surreptitiousness, unfamiliarity

180   Secrets and Mysteries

I cannot forecast to you the action of Russia. It is a riddle wrapped in a mystery inside an enigma. **Winston Churchill**

(*n*) closed book, confidence, conundrum, enigma, imponderable, mystery, paradox, poser, problem, puzzle, puzzler, riddle, secret, state secret, teaser

See also DIFFICULTY AND COMPLEXITY (242)

181   Known and Famous

For famous men have the whole earth as their memorial. **Pericles**

(*adj*) acknowledged, all-star, avowed (*formal*), celebrated, eminent, established, fabled, famed, familiar, famous, given, grand, great, high-profile, ill-disguised, illustrious, immortal, implicit, implied, important, infamous, institutional, *in the limelight*, in the open, *in the public domain*, known, legendary, noted, notorious (*archaic*), out, *out in the open*, preeminent, prestigious, professed, prominent, proverbial, public, putative, recognizable, recognized, renowned, tacit, *tried and tested*, unclassified, understood, *unhidden*, unwritten, well-known, well-tried, world famous

(*n*) celebrity, fame, high profile, infamy, limelight, name, notoriety, popularity, prominence, renown, stardom, visibility

See also IMPORTANT OR FAMOUS PEOPLE (893)

Positive Qualities of Things

182   Correct and Faultless

I know I'm not clever but I'm always right. **J. M. Barrie**

(*adj*) correct, explicable, faultless, flawless, impeccable, infallible, legitimate, right, tailor-made, unerring

(*adv*) according to plan, A-OK (*informal*), beautifully, correctly, flawlessly, legitimately, nicely, right, rightly, well, with reason

(*n*) faultlessness, flawlessness, infallibility, legitimacy, perfection, rectitude (*formal*), rightness

See also EXACT (203), MORALLY GOOD (774)

183   Good, Well, Better

It is better to die on your feet than to live on your knees. **Dolores Ibárruri**

(*adj*) *above average*, best, better, blue-chip, dandy (*informal dated*), enhanced, favorable, fine, golden, good, *Grade A*, grand, *high-quality*, ideal, improved, just right, maximal, optimal, optimum, peachy (*informal*), perfect, preferable, redeeming, reformed, regenerative, ringside, seamless, sterling, useful, well

(*adv*) finely, perfectly, swimmingly, well

(*n*) *impeccability*, *ne plus ultra*, optimum, quality, usefulness

184   Appropriate, Suitable, and Advisable

The thing to remember is that each time of life has its appropriate rewards, whereas when you're dead it's hard to find the light switch. **Woody Allen**

(*adj*) accredited, advisable, applicable, apposite, appropriate, approved, apropos (*formal*), apt, becoming, befitting, convenient, cut out for, decent, due, eligible, expedient, favorable, felicitous, fit, fitting, *hunky-dory* (*informal*), in accordance, kosher (*informal*), *meet* (*archaic*), opportune, pertinent, proper, qualified, right, savory, seasonable, seemly, suitable, suited, timely, well-chosen, well-timed

(*adv*) accordingly, adequately, aptly, correctly, expediently, *in good taste*, properly, right

(*n*) advisability, amenity, *appositeness*, appropriateness, conventionality, correctness, desirability, eligibility, expediency, felicity, fitness, fittingness, *opportuneness*, pertinence, rightness, rip, *seemliness*, suitability

(*v*) befit, behoove (*formal*), suit

185   Admirable and Commendable

Always do right. This will gratify some people, and astonish the rest. **Mark Twain**

(*adj*) admirable, commendable, creditable, deserving, estimable, exemplary, golden, laudable, meritorious, number one (*informal*), plum (*informal*), plus, praiseworthy, pukka, reputable, respectable, splendid, utopian, worthy

186   Physically Pleasant

A thing of beauty is a joy for ever:/Its loveliness increases; it will never/Pass into nothingness. **John Keats**

(*adj*) bracing, brisk, comfortable, comfy (*informal*), cozy, easy, energizing, erotic, *exhilarating*, invigorating, livable, painkilling, palliative, *paradisiac*, refreshing, *rejuvenating*, revitalizing, sensual, sexy, snug, soft, stimulating, warm

187   Emotionally Pleasant

Wrapt in a pleasing fit of melancholy. **John Milton**

(*adj*) action-packed, agreeable, atmospheric, blessed, blissful, bustling, calmative, cathartic, cheering, comforting, conducive, cozy, delicious, delightful, disarming, divine (*informal or humorous*), easy, elegiac (*formal*), emotional, emotive, encouraging, endearing, enjoyable, entertaining, eventful, exciting, familiar, feel-good, flattering, fulfilling, fun (*informal*), good, grateful (*archaic or literary*), gratifying, heady, heartwarming, heavenly, hopeful, intoxicating, joyful, lovely, lyric, lyrical, melting, nice, pacific, pacifist, pleasant, pleasing, pleasurable, poetic, proud, quiet, recreational, relaxed, rewarding, rose-colored, rose-tinted, rosy, rousing, satisfying, soulful, sparkling, stirring, *stress-free*, sublime, sweet, thrilling, touching, transcendent, transcendental, uplifting, vibrant, welcoming

(*adv*) agreeably, divinely (*informal*), enchantingly, endearingly, entertainingly, headily, quietly, well

(*n*) deliciousness, *delightfulness*, hopefulness, pleasantness

188   Calming

Music that gentlier on the spirit lies,/Than tir'd eyelids upon tir'd eyes. **Alfred Tennyson**

(*adj*) anodyne (*literary*), calming, conciliatory, consolatory, emollient, escapist, halcyon (*literary*), heartening, idyllic, mitigating, palliative, placatory, propitiatory, reassuring, relaxing, restful, restorative, sedative, soothing, therapeutic, *tranquilizing*

189   Beauty and Attractiveness

Only stay quiet while my mind remembers/The beauty of fire from the beauty of embers. **John Masefield**

(*adj*) adorable, appealing, arresting, attractive, beauteous (*literary*), beautiful, becoming, beguiling, *bewitching*, captivating, charming, darling, decorative, delectable, delicate, diamanté, enchanting, engaging, enticing, exquisite, eye-catching, flattering, frilly, gorgeous, graceful, idyllic, lovable, lovely, nice, nifty, ornamental, *picture-perfect*, picture-postcard, picturesque, *pleasing to the eye*, quaint, resplendent, scenic, showy, sweet, taking, twee (*UK*), well-designed, well-turned, winning, winsome

(*adv*) attractively, beautifully, delectably, delicately, enticingly, exquisitely, picturesquely, winningly

(*n*) appeal, attraction, attractiveness, beauty, character, charm, cuteness, delicacy, desirability, dreaminess, exquisiteness, glamour, glitter, gorgeousness, gracefulness, lure, magic, magnificence, *picturesqueness*, quaintness, showiness, sweetness

See also PEOPLE'S PHYSICAL APPEARANCE (475)

190   Interesting and Meaningful

It is more important that a proposition be interesting than that it be true. **A. N. Whitehead**

(*adj*) absorbing, *adrenaline-charged*, *adrenaline-fueled*, alluring, appetizing, catchy, challenging, charged, charismatic, colorful, compelling, compulsive, cultural, deep, didactic, edifying, educational, electric, electrifying, engrossing, enlightening, enthralling, entrancing, evocative, fascinating, gripping, hypnotic (*informal*), *hypnotizing*, illuminating, infectious, informative, ingenious, inspirational, inspiring, instructive, interesting, intriguing, inviting, irresistible, juicy (*informal*), magnetic, meaningful, meaty, mesmeric, mesmerizing, motivating, newsworthy, newsy, *of interest*, piquant, pregnant, provocative, revealing, riveting (*informal*), scintillating, significant, snappy (*informal*), spellbinding, stimulating, *suspenseful*, tantalizing, telling, telltale, tempting, thought-provoking, *titillating*, vivid, *worth mentioning*, *worthy of note*, zappy (*informal*)

(*adv*) expressively, refreshingly, revealingly, significantly, unforgettably

(*n*) allure, charisma, magnetism, pull (*informal*), *razzledazzle*, razzmatazz, spice, vividness

191   Safe and Safety

It's often safer to be in chains than to be free. **Franz Kafka**

(*adj*) airworthy, bulletproof (*informal*), childproof, covered, custodial, fail-safe, firm, foolproof, fortified, *goofproof* (*informal*), guarded, harmless, immune, innocent, innocuous, inoffensive, *in safe hands*, invulnerable, *nonfatal*, *nonhazardous*, nontoxic, onside, *out of harm's way*, precautionary, preservative, protected, protective, repellent, *risk-free*, roadworthy, rock-solid, safe, *safe as houses* (*UK*), secure, sheltered, shielded, sound, steady, tame, *unhazardous*, unthreatened

(*adv*) inoffensively, onside, safely, securely

(*n*) airworthiness, asylum, bulwark, *Chinese walls* (*UK*), defense, *firewall*, firmness, harmlessness, immunity, indemnity, *invulnerability*, protection, protectiveness, roadworthiness, safeguard, safekeeping, safety, safety net, safety valve, sanctuary, security, self-defense, soundness, welfare

192   Importance and Significance

I find no hint throughout the universe/Of good or ill, of blessing or of curse;/I find alone Necessity Supreme. **James Thomson**

(*n*) accentuation, bearing, centrality, consequence (*formal*), consideration, emphasis, gravitas, gravity, greatness, hold, *imperativeness*, import, importance, interest, invaluableness, magnitude, meaning, meaningfulness, merit, moment (*formal*), *momentousness*, notability, pregnancy, preponderance (*formal*), primacy, purport (*formal*), relevance, seriousness, significance, status, urgency, weight, weightiness, worth

193   Most Important and Main

It has long been an axiom of mine that the little things are infinitely the most important. **Arthur Conan Doyle**

(*adj*) *all-important*, ascendant, chief, core, deciding, determining, dominant, first, flagship, landmark, lead, leading, magic, main, major, master, number one, overarching, overriding, paramount, predominant, preponderant, prevailing, primary, prime, principal, quantum, ruling, salient, sovereign, supreme, top-level, uppermost

(*v*) bulk large, come first, outweigh, take precedence

See also MAINLY AND PRIMARILY (140)

194   Important

The essential thing in life is not conquering but fighting well. **Pierre de Coubertin**

(*adj*) acute, at issue, big, burning, cardinal, central, consequential, critical, crucial, decisive, definite, earthshaking, earthshattering, elevated, epoch-making, exigent (*formal*), fatal, fateful, front-page, fundamental, grave, great, heavy (*slang*), high, historic, immediate, important, instant, key, keynote, large-scale, life-and-death, major, material, meaningful, momentous, monumental, notable, noteworthy, of note, ponderable, portentous, pressing, relevant, resonant, seminal, serious, significant, structural, substantive, top-ranking, ultimate, urgent, vital, weighty

(*adv*) decisively, importantly, materially, portentously, substantively

195   Fundamental

The core reductive mistake is. . .the idea of a single fundamental explanation. **Mary Midgley**

(*adj*) alpha, basic, bread-and-butter, constituent, elemental, essential, first, focal, formative, fundamental, germane, integral, intrinsic, meat-and-potatoes, pivotal, primary, radical, skeleton, staple, to the point, ultimate, underlying (adv) at heart, at the heart of, center stage, fundamentally

196   Necessary and Essential

We have to believe in free will. We've got no choice.
Isaac Bashevis Singer

(adj) binding, compulsory, *de rigueur*, essential, imperative, incumbent (*formal*), indispensable, mandatory, necessary, *necessitous* (*formal*), *needed*, needful (*formal or archaic*), obligatory, of the essence, required, requisite (*formal*), specified

(adv) if need be, indispensably, of necessity, perforce (*literary*), unavoidably

(n) condition, demand, disclaimer, exigency (*formal*), if, necessity, precondition, prerequisite, provision, proviso, qualification, requirement, reservation, stipulation, terms

197   Most Important Thing

Winning isn't everything. It's the only thing. **Vince Lombardi**

(n) accent, bedrock, big deal (*informal*), bottom line, bread and butter, centerpiece, core, crux, determinant, essence, essentials, flagship, imperative, keynote, keystone, lifeblood, linchpin, mainspring, mainstay, marrow (*literary*), meat, must, necessitude, necessity, need, nub, pith, priority, sine qua non, stress, substance, van, vanguard

See also NEED AND REQUIRE (464)

198   Wholeness and Completeness

Now a whole is that which has a beginning, a middle, and an end. **Aristotle**

(adj) absolute, all-around, all-embracing, all in (*UK*), all-inclusive, all-out, all-round (*UK*), blanket, blow-by-blow, broad, broad-brush, broadly-based, catchall, coast-to-coast, complete, completed, comprehensive, concluded, convincing, cut-and-dried, detailed, done, *done and dusted* (*UK*), encyclopedic, entire, exhaustive, far-reaching, finished, full, full-blown, full-frontal (*informal*), full-length, full-scale, general, generalized, global, holistic, implicit, inclusive, in-depth, intact, integral, intimate, mass, overall, perfect, plenary (*formal*), radical, sound, sweeping, thorough, thoroughgoing, total, unabridged, unalloyed, unconditional, uncut, undisturbed, undivided, unedited, *unexpurgated*, unimpaired, universal, unreserved, well-rounded, whole, wholesale, wide, wide-ranging

(adv) all (*informal*), back to front (*UK*), completely, extensively, fully, globally, in depth, in detail, in full, inside out, intimately, perfectly, solidly, soundly, thoroughly, well, wholesale, wholly

(n) broadness, completeness, comprehensiveness, entirety, fullness, soundness, universalism, wholeness

See also ALL (128)

199   Usefulness

Have nothing in your houses that you do not know to be useful, or believe to be beautiful. **William Morris**

(adj) accessible, adaptable, adjustable, advantageous, all-purpose, applied, approachable, beneficent, beneficial, character-building, clever (*UK*), convenient, convertible, effective, effectual (*formal*), efficacious (*formal*), elastic, expedient, exploitable, fecund, fertile, functional, gainful, good, handy, helpful, invaluable, manageable, multipurpose, nifty (*informal*), *of use*, practical, productive, profitable, redeemable, remedial, salutary, sensible, serviceable, substantive, useful, user-friendly, utilitarian, valid, valuable, versatile, well-designed, worthwhile

(adv) accessibly, constructively, conveniently, effectively, expediently, handily, ideally, substantively

(n) accessibility, adaptability, approachability, convenience, effectiveness, efficacy, expediency, fertility, handiness, helpfulness, *niftiness* (*informal*), practicality, productiveness, profitability, richness, service, use, usefulness, user-friendliness, utility, value, versatility

200   Ease and Simplicity

Everything should be made as simple as possible, but not simpler. **Albert Einstein**

(adj) accessible, austere, bare, basic, black-and-white, classic, cushy (*informal*), downhill, easy, effortless, elementary, fathomable, *hassle-free* (*informal*), introductory, *laborsaving*, light, minimalist, open-and-shut, painless, *plain sailing*, quiet, rudimentary, simple, simplified, smooth, soluble, solvable, straightforward, trouble-free, uncomplicated, undemanding, uninvolved, unlabored, unproblematic

(adv) accessibly, easily, readily, simply, smoothly, with ease

(n) ease, effortlessness, fluency, fluidity, minimalism, neatness, simplicity, smoothness, straightforwardness, *uncomplicatedness*

201   Strength

I count life just a stuff/To try the soul's strength on. **Robert Browning**

(adj) acute, aggressive, *all-consuming*, all-powerful, almighty, armored, armor-plated, at an advantage, authoritative, blazing, buoyant, burning, clear, commanding, compelling, concentrated, concerted, deep, deep-rooted, defensible, defensive, driving, emphatic, exquisite, ferocious, fierce, fiery, flaming, forceful, forcible, fortified, *hard-hitting*, hard-wearing, hardy, heavy-duty, impregnable, influential, intense, intensive, intoxicating (*formal*), invincible, inviolable, inviolate, irresistible, keen, masterful, mighty, omnipotent, overpowering, overwhelming, penetrating, penetrative, plenipotentiary, potent, powerful, profound, proof, *puissant* (*literary*), rabid, raging, raw, resistant, rich, rugged, sacrosanct, serviceable, solid, steely, stiff, stout, strong, telling, tight, tough, unassailable, unbeatable, unconquerable, uncontrollable, violent, virulent, vivid, well-developed

(adv) authoritatively, ferociously, fiercely, firmly, forcibly, headily, heavily, irresistibly, keenly, powerfully, sharply, solidly, tightly, uncontrollably, violently, vividly

(n) aggressiveness, authoritativeness, authority, command, defenses, depth, dominance, domination, dominion, Draconian, ferociousness, ferocity, fierceness, force, forcefulness, grip, hardiness, hegemony, influence, intensity, invincibility, keenness, leverage, mastery, might, muscle, omnipotence, potency, power, profoundness, profundity, rawness, richness, ruggedness, stiffness, stoutness, strength, toughness, violence, vividness

See also STRENGTH OF WILL (501), FIT AND STRONG (736), DURABLE (1210)

202 Concise and Clear

As clear and as manifest as the nose in a man's face.
Robert Burton

(*adj*) clear, clear-cut, comprehensible, concrete, crystal clear, decipherable, defined, explicit, fine, graphic, in focus, intelligible, knowable, legible, limpid, lucid, nice, *plain as a pikestaff* (*UK*), prima facie, readable, self-explanatory, sharp, short, summary, transparent, unambiguous, understandable, unequivocal, unmistakable, vivid, well-argued, well-defined

(*adv*) finely, lucidly, nicely, sharply, unambiguously, vividly, well

(*n*) clarity, clearness, lucidity, lucidness, nicety, sharpness, shortness, transparency, vividness

203 Exact

Ramp up my genius, be not retrograde;/But boldly nominate a spade a spade. **Ben Jonson**

(*adj*) accurate, certain, close, correct, definite, delicate, direct, exact, explicit, express, fingertip, letter-perfect, literal, mathematical, minute, particular, perfect, photographic, precise, rigorous, scientific, sensitive, specific, specified, strict, surgical, technical, true, truthful, verbatim, word-for-word, word-perfect

(*adv*) closely, delicately, exactly, just, on the button (*informal*), *on the nail*, on the nose (*informal*), pat, plumb (*informal*), squarely, to the letter, verbatim, word for word

(*n*) accuracy, attention to detail, clockwork, correctness, definition, delicacy, exactitude, exactness, *preciseness*, precision, rigorousness, strictness, truthfulness

See also CORRECT AND FAULTLESS (182)

204 Extraordinary: Amazing

I have had a dream, past the wit of man to say what dream it was. **William Shakespeare**

(*adj*) A1 (*informal*), acclaimed, ace (*informal*), *all-singing, all-dancing*, all-time, amazing, ambitious, astonishing, astounding, awe-inspiring, awesome, blinding (*informal*), breathtaking, brilliant (*informal*), consummate, cool (*slang*), dazzling, definitive, dreamy, elite, epic, especial, excellent, exceptional, exquisite, extraordinaire, extraordinary, fabulous, fairy-tale, fantastic, far-out (*slang*), fearsome, first-class, first-rate, flamboyant, formidable, glittering, glorious, golden, grand, grandiose, great, groundbreaking, *huge* (*informal*), humbling, impressive, incomparable, incredible, indescribable, ineffable (*formal*), inexpressible, inimitable, inspired, leonine, magic, magical, magisterial, magnificent, majestic, marvelous, matchless, memorable, mind-blowing (*informal*), miraculous, out of this world (*informal*), outstanding, phenomenal (*informal*), powerful, prodigious, redoubtable, remarkable, sensational (*informal*), shining, spanking, spectacular, splendid, splendiferous (*humorous*), staggering, startling, striking, stunning, stupendous, super (*informal*), superb, super-

duper (*informal*), superhuman, superior, superlative, surpassing (*literary*), surprising, swell (*dated informal*), tremendous, trendsetting, unbelievable, undreamed-of, unforgettable, unpredicted, unspeakable, untouchable, unwonted, way-out (*dated informal*), *weird and wonderful*, wicked (*slang*), wonderful, wondrous (*literary*), world-shattering

(*adv*) awesomely, brilliantly, devastatingly, exceedingly, exquisitely, formidably, grandly, greatly, outstandingly, powerfully, prodigiously, specially, spectacularly, strangely, stunningly, surprisingly

(*n*) excellence, fineness, flamboyance, grandeur, grandiosity, grandness, greatness, impressiveness, majesty, originality, pomp, prodigiousness, *remarkability*, *remarkableness*, splendiferousness (*humorous*), splendor, whimsicality

See also SUPERIORITY (152)

205 Extraordinary: Uncommon

When you can do the common things of life in an uncommon way you'll command the attention of the world.
George Washington Carver

(*adj*) all-round (*UK*), alternative, banner, bravura, custom-built, customized, custom-made, different, distinctive, distinguishing, exotic, experimental, extraordinary, foreign, fresh, fringe, iconoclastic, idealized, idiosyncratic, imposing, individual, irreplaceable, made-to-measure, made-to-order, millennial, *never-to-be-repeated*, new, nonpareil, nonstandard, novel, one, one and only, one of a kind, one-off (*UK*), original, out of the ordinary, out-of-the-way, particular, peculiar, phenomenal, proud, rare, rarefied, recherché, revolutionary, rip-roaring (*informal*), rollicking, scarce, sensational, singular, sole, special, specialized, specially made, specific, strange, sublime (*informal*), terrific (*informal*), uncommon, unconventional, unheard-of, unhoped-for, unique, unlooked-for, unorthodox, unprecedented, unrivaled, unseasonable, untold, unusual, whimsical, *without equal*, without precedent

(*adv*) extraordinarily, whimsically

(*n*) curiosity, freshness, memorability, newness, novelty, one-off (*UK*), peculiarity, rareness, rarity, singularity, unconventionality, uniqueness, *unusualness*

See also UNRELATEDNESS AND SEPARATENESS (146)

206 Order and Organization

How could things have been as they are, were there not an original, inherent principle or order somewhere? **David Hume**

(*adj*) alphabetical, clean, controlled, disciplined, geared up, geometric, hierarchical, methodological, neat, on an even keel, ordered, orderly, organized, prim, procedural, regimental, regimented, regular, regulatory, ripe, set, shipshape, slick, spick-and-span, straight, structured, systematic, tidy, tight, trim, well-kept, well-oiled, well-ordered, well-organized

(*adv*) like clockwork, neatly, regularly, tidily, trimly

(*n*) coherence, compactness, discipline, neatness, normality, order, orderliness, organization, primness, scheme, system, tidiness

207   Economical and Resourceful

Heaven has its seasons; Earth has its resources; Man has his government. This means that man is capable of forming a trinity with the other two. **Xunzi**

(*adj*) biodegradable, conservative, cost-effective, eco-friendly, economic, economical, efficient, environmental, lucrative, productive, profitable, profitmaking, provident, *recyclable*, recycled, reusable, rich, self-supporting, *self-sustaining*, streamlined, sustainable, thrifty, timesaving, well-paid

(*n*) bargain, *cost-effectiveness*, economy, keenness (*UK*), profitability, steal (*informal*), thrift

See also CHEAP AND INEXPENSIVE (221), MAKE GOOD USE OF SOME-THING (473)

208   Freedom and Liberty

Freedom is always and exclusively the freedom for the one who thinks differently. **Rosa Luxemburg**

(*adj*) abandoned, at large, at leisure, at liberty, classless, elective, *emancipated*, excused, exempt, free, free-range, freewheeling, immune, independent, in the clear, loose, on the loose, redemptive, substantive, unbounded, unbridled, unchecked, unconditioned, unconfined, unconstrained, unfettered, unhampered, unhindered, unimpeded, unlicensed, unlimited, unobstructed, unopposed, unrestrained, unrestricted, untrammeled

(*adv*) freely, independently, scot-free

(*n*) abandon, breadth, carte blanche, catharsis, deliverance (*formal*), delivery, demobilization, discharge, dispensation, elbowroom, emancipation, empowerment, exemption, exoneration, freedom, freeing, free will, immunity, impunity, independence, latitude, leeway, legroom, liberation, liberty, license, *manumission* (*formal*), prerogative, privilege, redemption, release, relief, remittance, rescue, salvation, space (*informal*)

(*v*) clear, decontrol, deliver (*literary*), demobilize, deregulate, discharge, dislodge, emancipate, excuse, free, let go, let loose, let out, liberate, ransom, redeem, release, rescue, save, set free, spare, unchain, unfetter, unfreeze, unleash, unloose, unshackle, untie

209   Source of Happiness, Pleasure, or Improvement

Happiness: a good bank account, a good cook, a good digestion. **Jean-Jacques Rousseau**

(*n*) advantage, asset, backing, beauty, benediction, benefit, blessing, boon, break (*informal*), *catbird seat* (*informal*), change for the better, encouragement, favor, favorite, gain, godsend, golden opportunity, good, good thing, good word, initiative, interest, jump-start, kick-start (*informal*), kudos, lead, manna, merit, mileage (*informal*), pick, *pick of the bunch*, *pick of the litter*, *pièce de résistance*, plus (*informal*), plus point (*UK*), pole position, *redeeming feature*, *redeeming quality*, saving grace, upper hand, upside, utility, virtue, worthiness

210   Treats

The great consolation in life is to say what one thinks. **Voltaire**

(*n*) amends, bait, balm, bonanza, boost, comfort, comforter, compensation, consolation, crutch, draw, extravagance, feast, festivity, fillip, gas (*slang*), glory, gold mine,

high (*informal*), honor, joy, kick (*informal*), lift, magnet, mercy, pick-me-up (*informal*), pride and joy, privilege, shot in the arm, tonic, treat, wallop (*informal*), windfall

211   Amazing Things

I wonder if we could contrive…some magnificent myth that would in itself carry conviction to our whole community. **Plato**

(*n*) beaut (*informal*), buzz (*informal*), *corker* (*dated informal*), *dilly* (*slang*), *doozy* (*slang*), dream, gem (*informal*), goody, *humdinger* (*slang*), *icing on the cake*, indulgence, *jewel in the crown* (*UK*), *jim-dandy* (*informal*), knockout (*informal*), luxury, marvel, miracle, nonessential, peach (*informal*), pearl, phenomenon, plum (*informal*), portent (*formal*), sensation, *slam-dunk* (*informal*), spectacle, splendor, *star attraction*, stunner (*informal*), superfluity, thrill, treasure, wonder, work of art, world-beater, wow (*informal*)

212   Advantages

Success is man's god. **Aeschylus**

(*n*) beachhead, bestseller, foothold, footing, gateway, head start, let-out (*UK*), moneymaker, record, start, stepping stone

213   Progress and Advancement

We have stopped believing in progress. What progress that is! **Jorge Luis Borges**

(*n*) advance, advancement, betterment (*formal*), breakthrough, cultivation, development, enhancement, evolution, fast track, growth, improvement, incubation, lucky break, maturation, movement, opening, opportunity, progress, progression, rally, recovery, reform, reformation, regeneration, stabilization, stride, upgrade, upgrading, upturn

214   Peacefulness and Gentleness

That sweet, deep sleep, so close to tranquil death. **Virgil**

(*adj*) bloodless, gentle, nonviolent, pacific, peaceable, peaceful, quiet, relaxed, serene, tranquil

(*adv*) peaceably, peacefully, quietly

(*n*) gentleness, law and order, mildness, nonaggression, nonviolence, order, peace, *peace and quiet*, peacefulness, *peace of mind*, peacetime, quietness, *restfulness*, serenity, softness, tranquillity, truce

215   Solutions

What destroys one man preserves another. **Corneille**

(*n*) answer, antidote, compromise, cure-all, fallback, fix (*informal*), key, *lifesaver* (*informal*), nostrum, panacea, recourse, remedy, resolution, resort, result, settlement, solution, stopgap

216   Funny and Amusing

Everything is funny, as long as it's happening to somebody else. **Will Rogers**

(*adj*) amusing, comic, comical, droll, farcical, foolish, funny, hilarious, humorous, hysterical (*informal*), light, lighthearted, madcap, priceless (*informal*), *rib-tickling* (*informal*), rich (*informal*), sidesplitting, uproarious, whimsical, witty (*adv*) drolly, funnily, hysterically (*informal*), riotously, whimsically

(*n*) a bundle of laughs, comicality, *comicalness*, *drollness*, funniness, hilariousness, hoot (*slang*), humor, riot (*informal*), *uproariousness*

See also BIZARRE AND PECULIAR (257)

217 Positively Complex or Complicated

An object the sum of its complications, seen/And unseen. This is everybody's world. **Wallace Stevens**

(*adj*) advanced, challenging, complex, compound, cosmopolitan, elaborate, esoteric, fancy, flowery, high-level, irreducible, many-sided, multifaceted, multilateral, multipartite, sophisticated, subtle

(*n*) sophistication, subtleness, subtlety

218 Expensive and Luxurious

Every tooth in a man's head is more valuable than a diamond. **Miguel de Cervantes**

(*adj*) baronial, costly, deluxe, exclusive, executive, expensive, fancy, gracious, high-class, lush, luxuriant, luxurious, opulent, ornate, palatial, plush (*informal*), posh (*informal*), precious, priceless, rich, *ritzy* (*informal*), royal, select, sensuous, smart, stately, sumptuous, swank (*informal*), swanky (*informal*), tony (*informal*), upmarket, upscale, valuable, well-appointed, well-equipped

(*adv*) elaborately, expensively, graciously, ornately, richly

(*n*) exclusiveness, lushness, luxuriance, luxuriousness, luxury, opulence, *ornateness*, preciousness, richness, snootiness (*informal*), stateliness, style, sumptuousness

See also EXPENSIVE AND OVERPRICED (247)

219 Acceptable and Passable

Only the mediocre are always at their best. **Jean Giraudoux**

(*adj*) acceptable, adequate, admissible, allowable, all right, bearable, decent, defensible, endurable, excusable, fair, fair enough, *fair to middling*, fine (*informal*), forgivable, good enough, in order, justifiable, justified, livable, middle, middling, normal, not bad, okay (*informal*), orthodox, palatable, passable, potable, presentable, reasonable, regular, respectable, satisfactory, so-so (*informal*), supportable (*literary*), tolerable, understated, unexceptionable, unobjectionable, *unoffending*, *up to scratch* (*informal*), *up to standard*, venial, viewable, welcome

(*adv*) acceptably, all right, averagely, defensibly, normally, passably

(*n*) acceptability, adequacy, admissibility

(*v*) measure up, pass muster

220 Popular and Wanted

All wars are popular for the first thirty days. **Arthur Schlesinger, Jr.**

(*adj*) admired, adored, *all the rage*, beloved, cherished, coveted, dear, desirable, desired, enviable, esteemed, favorite, handpicked, *in demand*, *longed-for*, looked-for, loved, marketable, *much-admired*, much-loved, pet, popular, precious, preferred, prized, recognized, respected, revered, reverend (*formal*), sought-after, to

die for, top-rated, touristy, treasured, valuable, valued, vaunted, venerable, *venerated*, voguish, wanted, welcome, well-beloved, *well-regarded*, *well-respected*, well-thought-of, *wished-for*

See also LIKE, LOVE, VALUE, AND ENJOY (578)

221 Cheap and Inexpensive

If we cannot be free, at least we can be cheap! **Frank Zappa**

(*adj*) affordable, bargain, bargain-basement, budget, cheap, *cheapo* (*informal*), competitive, cut-rate, dirt-cheap (*informal*), discounted, economy, giveaway (*informal*), inexpensive, keen (*UK*), knockdown, reasonable, reduced

(*adv*) cheaply, dirt-cheap (*informal*), on a shoestring, on the cheap (*informal*)

See also ECONOMICAL AND RESOURCEFUL (207)

Negative Qualities of Things

222 Incorrect and Erroneous

No amount of experimentation can ever prove me right; a single experiment can prove me wrong. **Albert Einstein**

(*adj*) amiss, at fault, awry, erroneous, false, faulty, inaccurate, incorrect, in the wrong, mistaken, off beam, skewed, unearned, unreliable, warped, *wide of the mark*, wrong

(*adv*) amiss, falsely, faultily, wide, wrongly

(*n*) falseness, inaccuracy, incorrectness, invalidity, unreliability

See also MORALLY BAD OR IMPROPER (775)

223 Bad and Badly

I never resist temptation because I have found that things that are bad for me never tempt me. **George Bernard Shaw**

(*adj*) abysmal, aggravated, appalling, atrocious, awful, bad, catastrophic, confounded (*informal*), deplorable, despicable, disappointing, execrable (*formal*), fearful (*informal*), frightful, grievous, ill, irrecoverable, irremediable, irreparable, lamentable, lousy (*informal*), negative, painful, pitiable, pitiful, rotten (*informal*), seedy, shoddy, sorry, terrible, unfavorable, woeful, worse, worst

(*adv*) atrociously, awfully, badly, deplorably, ill, mindlessly, negatively, rottenly (*informal*), shoddily, terribly

(*n*) seediness

224 Inappropriate and Unsuitable

A puritan's a person who pours righteous indignation into the wrong things. **G. K. Chesterton**

(*adj*) *below average*, *below standard*, deficient, *displeasing*, improper (*formal*), inapplicable, inapposite, inappropriate, *inapt*, incorrect, indecent, inexpedient (*formal*), infra dig (*informal*), irregular, laughable, misplaced, pathetic (*informal*), unbecoming, undignified, unfit, unfitted, unfitting, unfortunate, unhappy, *unpropitious*, unseemly, unsuitable, untoward, wanting, wrong (*adv*) deficiently, improperly (*formal*), unfortunately, wrongly

(*n*) inapplicability, inappositeness (*formal*), inappropriateness, *inaptness*, incorrectness, indecency, insufficiency, *unbecomingness*, unseemliness, unsuitability

225   Unacceptable and Unforgivable

Laws can be unjust because they are contrary to the divine good...in no way is it permissible to observe them.
Thomas Aquinas

(*adj*) beyond the pale, contemptible, cursed (*informal*), dire, discreditable, disgraceful, exceptionable (*formal*), forbidden, improper, indefensible, inexcusable, inglorious, monstrous, *not on* (*UK*), outrageous, outré, paltry, punishable, reprehensible, repugnant, scabby (*slang*), shocking, unacceptable, unconscionable, unearthly, unforgivable, unjustifiable, unjustified, unmentionable, unpalatable, unpardonable, unsatisfactory, *unsatisfying*, unsustainable, unutterable, unwarrantable, vile, wretched

(*adv*) improperly, indefensibly, shockingly

(*n*) contemptibility

226   Physically Unpleasant

I'm sure if everyone knew how physically cruel dancing really is, nobody would watch. **Margot Fonteyn**

(*adj*) airless, arduous, backbreaking, bumpy, claustrophobic, coercive, debilitating, difficult, draining, energetic, enervating, excruciating, exhausting, exigent (*formal*), *fatiguing*, forcible, gory, grinding, harsh, heavy, high-pressure, hostile, *incapacitating*, incommodious (*formal*), inhospitable, murderous (*informal*), operose (*formal*), punishing, *racking*, rough, rugged, savage, searing, sharp, splitting, stabbing, stiff, strenuous, *stultifying*, swingeing (*UK*), tiring, unforgiving, unventilated, uphill, wearying, wild

(*adv*) grindingly, roughly

(*n*) harshness, roughness, ruggedness, stiffness, toughness, wildness

See also PAIN AND OTHER PHYSICAL SENSATIONS (733)

227   Emotionally Unpleasant and Upsetting

The superior man is satisfied and composed; the mean man is always full of distress. **Confucius**

(*adj*) accursed (*archaic or literary*), affecting, affective, agonizing, alarmist, appalling, bathetic, bittersweet, calamitous, cheerless, cloying, cruel, crushing, crying, dark, deathly, degrading, demoralizing, deplorable, depressing, depressive, desolate, detestable, devastating, disagreeable, discomfiting (*formal*), disconcerting, discouraging, disheartening, dismal, dispiriting, disquieting, distressing, disturbing, embarrassing, excruciating, forbidding, foul (*informal*), funereal, grievous, grim, gritty, grueling, harrowing, heartbreaking, heartrending, hopeless, horrendous, horrible, horrifying, humbling, humiliating, hurtful, ignominious, impossible, intolerable, invidious, jarring, joyless, lachrymose (*literary*), lamentable (*literary*), messy, miserable, mortifying, moving, nameless, nerve-racking, numbing, off-putting, oppressive, opprobrious, painful, pathetic, personal, *perturbing*, piteous, pitiable, pitiful, regret-

table, rotten (*informal*), sad, *saddening*, sensitive, sepulchral, severe, shattering, somber, sore, sorrowful, soul-destroying, standup (*UK*), stifling, stormy, strained, straitened, stressful, stringent, tearful, tempestuous, terrible, thankless, *toe-curling* (*informal*), *toilsome*, tormenting, tragic, tragicomic, traumatic, *troubling*, trying, ugly, unbearable, uncomfortable, unendurable, unfortunate, ungrateful, unmerciful, unnerving, unrewarding, unsettling, upsetting, wearing, wearisome, wicked (*informal*), woeful, worrying

(*adv*) grievously, grimly, horribly, horridly, shockingly, tempestuously

(*n*) cheerlessness, dreariness, grimness, messiness, severity, storminess, stringency, tempestuousness, ugliness

228   Irritating

Being misunderstood by someone is vexation. Being misunderstood by everyone is tragedy. **Liu Shahe**

(*adj*) aggravating, annoying, bothersome, burdensome, cursed, disruptive, distracting, exasperating, frustrating, galling, grating, inconvenient, infuriating, insufferable, insupportable, irksome, irritating, maddening, nagging, niggling, pesky (*informal*), pestilent (*literary or humorous*), provoking, sneaking, tiresome, troublesome, untoward, vexatious, vexing, worrisome

229   In Poor Taste and Oversentimental

The aristocratic pleasure of displeasing is not the only delight that bad taste can yield. One can love a certain kind of vulgarity for its own sake. **Aldous Huxley**

(*adj*) baroque, bathetic, bold, brash (*UK*), cheap, cheesy (*informal*), chintzy, chocolate-box, cutesy, extravagant, flashy, florid, fussy, garish, gaudy, glitzy, gooey (*informal*), icky (*informal*), in bad taste, inelegant, *in poor taste*, kiss-and-tell (*informal*), kitsch, kitschy, loud, lurid, maudlin, mawkish, meretricious (*formal*), misty-eyed, mushy, ostentatious, oversentimental, overstated, pompous, punk (*informal*), purple, raffish, saccharine, schmaltzy (*informal*), sensational, sensationalist, sentimental, showy, sick (*informal*), sickly, sickly-sweet, sloppy (*informal*), slushy, soppy (*UK informal*), splashy (*informal*), sugary, tacky (*informal*), tasteless, tawdry, tinny, treacly, vulgar, weepy

(*n*) bad taste, cheapness, flashiness, fussiness, garishness, gaudiness, glitziness, goo (*informal*), inelegance, kitsch, luridness, mawkishness, mush, obscenity, ostentation, *ostentatiousness*, pompousness, schmaltz (*informal*), schmaltziness (*informal*), sensationalism, sentiment, sentimentality, showiness, sloppiness (*informal*), tackiness (*informal*), tastelessness, tawdriness, tinsel, vulgarity

230   Disgusting and Repulsive

Something nasty in the woodshed. **Stella Gibbons**

(*adj*) abhorrent (*formal*), abominable, atrocious, disgusting, dislikable, distasteful, dreadful, evil, foul, ghastly, gory, gross (*slang*), hateful, horrid, horrific, horrifying, icky (*informal*), loathsome, nasty, nauseating, nauseous, noisome, noxious, objectionable, obnoxious, obscene, odious, offensive, off-putting, rebarbative (*formal*), *repellant*, repellent, repugnant, repulsive, revolting, *revulsive*, sanguinary (*formal*), seamy, shameful, sickening, sickly, sleazy, sordid, stomach-churning, stomach-turning, unheard-of, unholy, unpleasant, unsavory, unspeakable, unwholesome, vile, villainous, yucky (*informal*)

(*adv*) appallingly, atrociously, foully, unpleasantly, unspeakably

(*n*) atrociousness, distastefulness, dreadfulness, fearfulness (*informal*), frightfulness, *grossness*, horridness, *obnoxiousness*, repulsiveness, rottenness (*informal*), sordidness, unpleasantness, unwholesomeness, vileness

231 Frightening

It is a terrible thing for a man to find out suddenly that all his life he has been speaking nothing but the truth. **Oscar Wilde**

(*adj*) alarming, baleful, bloodcurdling, bullyboy, chilling, creepy (*informal*), daunting, fearful, fearsome, formidable, frightening, ghastly, ghoulish, Gothic, grim, grisly, gruesome, hair-raising, haunted, horrid, intimidating, macabre, menacing, morbid, nail-biting, nightmare, nightmarish, petrifying, scary (*informal*), spinechilling, spine-tingling, spooky (*informal*), strong-arm (*informal*), terrifying, white-knuckle

(*adv*) fearfully, formidably, grimly

(*n*) creepiness (*informal*), fearfulness, grimness, grisliness, gruesomeness, horridness, scariness, *spookiness* (*informal*)

232 Plain

An honest tale speeds best being plainly told.
William Shakespeare

(*adj*) austere, bare, bleak, drab, featureless, homely, homespun, low-key, mere, no-frills (*informal*), nondescript, plain, severe, simple, spartan, stark, unadorned, undecorated, unembellished, unfussy

(*adv*) plainly, simply

(*n*) austerity, bareness, bleakness, severity, simplicity, starkness

See also ORDINARINESS (244)

233 Ugliness and Unattractiveness

A good heart will help you to a bonny face, my lad...and a bad one will turn the bonniest into something worse than ugly.
Emily Brontë

(*adj*) distorted, grim, grotesque, hideous, monstrous, ugly, unappealing, unappetizing, unattractive, *unenticing*, unflattering, *unglamorous*, uninviting, unlovely, unsightly

(*n*) blot on the landscape, grimness, hideousness, monstrosity, ugliness, unattractiveness, unsightliness

See also PEOPLE'S PHYSICAL APPEARANCE (475)

234 Boring and Uninteresting

A universe in which everything is known would be static and dull, as boring as the heaven of some weak-minded theologians. **Carl Sagan**

(*adj*) anodyne (*literary*), antiseptic, arid, banal, bland, boring, characterless, clichéd, *cliché-ridden*, colorless, commonplace, corny, dead, deadly (*informal*), drab, dragging, draggy (*informal*), dreary, dry, dull, facile, flat, formulaic, fusty, hackneyed, humdrum, humorless, impersonal, indistinctive, insipid, institutional, jejune,

lackluster, leaden, lifeless, menial, mindless, mindnumbing, monochromatic, monochrome, monotonous, mundane, ordinary, overused, platitudinous, ponderous, predictable, prosaic, repetitious, repetitive, routine, slack, sleepy, soporific, soulless, stagnant, stale, stodgy (*informal*), tame, tedious, threadbare, time-consuming, timeworn, tired, toneless, turgid, two-dimensional, uneventful, unexciting, unimaginative, unimpassioned, uninspiring, uninteresting, unreadable, unsurprising, vanilla, vapid, well-worn, white-bread (*informal*), worthy

(*adv*) drably, drearily, dully, heavily, insipidly, ponderously, soberly, tamely

(*n*) blandness, boredom, characterlessness, drabness, dreariness, dullness, flatness, insipidness, monotony, mundaneness, ordinariness, platitude, *ponderousness*, predictability, predictableness, prosaicness, sameness, soberness, sterility, superficiality, tameness, tediousness, unimaginativeness, worthiness

See also UNADVENTUROUS AND DULL (517), BORE AND FAIL TO INTEREST (570)

235 Danger

Diseases of the soul are more dangerous and more numerous than those of the body. **Cicero**

(*n*) danger, *dangerousness*, defenselessness, destructiveness, fatality, firetrap, hazard, *hazardousness*, *insidiousness*, instability, jeopardy, menace, nakedness, *noxiousness*, peril, *perilousness*, perniciousness, powder keg, *precariousness*, rapaciousness, *recipe for disaster*, risk, *risk factor*, riskiness, rockiness, severity, specter, threat, toxicity, unsteadiness, vulnerability

See also PUT AT RISK (384)

236 Dangerous

A desperate disease requires a dangerous remedy. **Guy Fawkes**

(*adj*) adverse, bad, bleak, brooding, cancerous, carcinogenic, cataclysmic, chancy, costly, crippling, critical, damaging, dangerous, daring, dark, deadly, deleterious, desperate, destructive, detrimental, devastating, dicey (*informal*), disadvantageous, explosive, extreme, fatal, feral, ferocious, forbidding, foreboding, grave, hairy (*informal*), harmful, hazardous, iffy (*informal*), ill, inimical, injurious, insecure, insidious, internecine, leaky (*informal*), lethal, major, malign, maneating, *mephitic* (*formal*), nasty, noxious, ominous, parlous (*archaic or humorous*), perilous, pernicious, pestilent, precarious, prejudicial, rapacious, risky, rocky, ruinous, savage, serious, severe, shaky, sinister, speculative, suicidal, threatening, tough, toxic, treacherous, unhealthy, unsafe, unsound, unstable, unsteady, venturesome (*formal*), volatile, wild

(*adv*) adversely, dangerously, disadvantageously, ferociously, ill, unsteadily

See also DEADLY (928)

237 In Danger

Look back, and smile at perils past. **Sir Walter Scott**

(*adj*) at risk, at stake, defenseless, disappearing, *imperiled* (*formal*), *in danger*, in jeopardy, in peril, on the rocks (*informal*), open, *open to attack*, protected, susceptible, threatened, unarmed, undefended, unguarded, unprotected, vulnerable, weak, wide-open

(*adv*) at risk

See also IN TROUBLE AND DISADVANTAGED (73)

238 Unimportant and Unnecessary

To a mind of sufficient intellectual power, the whole of mathematics would appear trivial, as trivial as the statement that a four-footed animal is an animal. **Bertrand Russell**

(*adj*) avoidable, beside the point, cosmetic, derisory, expendable, extraneous, fiddling, footling (*informal*), frivolous, frothy, idle, immaterial, inconsequential, inconsiderable, inessential, insignificant, irrelevant, lightweight, little, marginal, meaningless, mild, negligible, neither here nor there, niggling, nonessential, nugatory, null, of no account, of no consequence, *of no importance*, peripheral, pettifogging, petty, piffling (*informal*), preventable, silly, skin-deep, small, small-scale, small-time (*informal*), superficial, tautological, trifling, trivial, uncalled-for, undue, unessential, unimportant, unnecessary, unneeded, unrelated, unwarranted, wanton, wasted

(*adv*) frivolously, inappreciably, peripherally

(*n*) anonymity, frivolity, frothiness, *immateriality*, *immaterialness*, inconsequence, inconsequentiality, indifference, insignificance, irrelevance, meaninglessness, pettiness, silliness, *small beer* (*informal*), *small potatoes* (*informal*), tautology, technicality, trifle, trivia, triviality, unimportance

See also REDUNDANT AND USELESS (240)

239 Unfinishedness

Think nothing done while aught remains to do. **Samuel Rogers**

(*adj*) bitty (*UK*), crude, fragmentary, fragmented, incomplete, limited, partial, patchy, piecemeal, scrappy, *truncated*, unaccomplished, *uncompleted*, undone, unfinished, unimproved

(*n*) crudeness, patchiness

240 Redundant and Useless

'Tis not necessary to light a candle to the sun. **Algernon Sidney**

(*adj*) absurd, bootless, dead, dispensable, dud (*informal*), empty, extraneous, fallow, *functionless*, futile, *garbagy*, *good-for-nothing*, gratuitous, groundless, idle, ineffective, invalid, meaningless, mindless, motiveless, needless, *no good*, *no great shakes*, *no use*, *of no use*, *of no value*, otiose, outmoded, pointless, puny, purposeless, redundant, senseless, stillborn, unavailing, unconstructive, uncultivated, unfruitful, unhelpful, unproductive, unprofitable, unprovoked, unworkable, unworthy, useless, vain, valueless, vestigial, void, worthless

(*adv*) gratuitously, idly, *purposelessly*, redundantly

(*n*) absurdness, aimlessness, defectiveness, emptiness, fruitlessness, futility, gratuitousness, ineffectiveness, invalidity, *mindlessness*, needlessness, pointlessness, *purposelessness*, senselessness, sterility, unhelpfulness, unproductiveness, unworthiness, uselessness, vanity, worthlessness

See also UNIMPORTANT AND UNNECESSARY (238)

241 Weakness

Never support two weaknesses at the same time. **Thornton Wilder**

(*adj*) anemic, delicate, feeble, flimsy, fragile, frail, indefensible, insubstantial, poor, powerless, sensitive, toothless, understrength, watered-down, watery, weak, weakened, wobbly

(*adv*) feebly, flimsily, poorly, weakly

(*n*) delicacy, delicateness, faintness, feebleness, flimsiness, insubstantiality, powerlessness, shakiness, susceptibility, weakness, wobbliness

See also COWARDICE AND WEAKNESS OF WILL (508), UNFIT AND WEAK (739)

242 Difficulty and Complexity

It is as easy to count atomies as to resolve the propositions of a lover. **William Shakespeare**

(*adj*) abstruse, awkward, *bemusing*, bewildering, bureaucratic, busy, byzantine, complex, complicated, confusing, convoluted, delicate, demanding, dense, difficult, elaborate, exacting, extreme, fathomless, fiendish, formidable, grandiose, hard, *hard to follow*, heavy, *heavy-going*, *horny*, illegible, impenetrable, inaccessible, incomprehensible, indecipherable, indescribable, indigestible, inextricable, insoluble, insuperable, insurmountable, intractable, intricate, involved, knotty, labored, *labor-intensive*, laborious, labyrinthine, mind-boggling (*informal*), nasty (*informal*), no joke, obscure, onerous, opaque, ornate, painful, perplexing, persnickety (*informal*), problematic, puzzling, rigorous, rocky, sphinxlike, sticky (*informal*), tall, tangled, taxing, testing, thick, thorny, ticklish, tight, tortuous, touchy, tough, tricky, troubled, unanswerable, unfathomable, unintelligible, unreadable, unsolvable, unsolved, vexed

(*adv*) formidably, hard, indescribably, obscurely, problematically

(*n*) abstruseness, acuteness, arduousness, complexity, denseness, depth, difficulty, *elaborateness*, grandiosity, impenetrability, inaccessibility, *incomprehensibility*, insolubility, *insuperability*, intractability, intricacy, laboriousness, *obtuseness*, *onerousness*, opacity, profundity, rigor, rigorousness, toughness, trickiness, *unfathomability*, *unfathomableness*, *unintelligibility*

See also SECRETS AND MYSTERIES (180)

243 Vagueness

It is easy to be certain. One has only to be sufficiently vague. **C. S. Peirce**

(*adj*) ambiguous, blurred, blurry, cloudy, dim, distant, double-edged, elusive, ethereal, euphemistic, foggy, fuzzy, general, ghostlike, ghostly, hazy, ill-defined, imprecise, impressionistic, inchoate (*formal*), incipient, indefinable, indefinite, indeterminable, indeterminate, indistinct, indistinguishable, inexplicit, intangible, misty, muzzy, nebulous, nonspecific, open-ended, sketchy, sweeping, tangential, tenuous, unclear, undefined, unfocused, uninformative, unspecified, unstipulated, up in the air, vague, vaporous, woolly

(*adv*) dimly, distantly, hazily, unclearly, vaguely

(*n*) ambiguity, ambiguousness, blur, carelessness, cloudiness, dimness, elusiveness, fuzziness, haziness, *impreciseness*, imprecision, incoherence, indistinctness, inexactness, intangibility, mistiness, *nebulousness*, obliqueness, obscurity, penumbra, roughness, *sketchiness*, *tenuousness*, *unclearness*, vagueness, wooliness

See also APPROXIMATELY (135)

244 Ordinariness

Some men are born mediocre, some men achieve mediocrity, and some men have mediocrity thrust upon them. **Joseph Heller**

(*adj*) accepted, accustomed, a dime a dozen, anonymous, average, below par, cheap, common, commonplace, conventional, customary, day-to-day, *downhome* (*informal*), downmarket, downscale, everyday, familiar, forgettable, formulaic, *garden-variety*, general, generic, habitual, indifferent, low-grade, mainstream, majority, mass-produced, mediocre, medium, middlebrow (*informal*), middle-of-the-road, middling, moderate, modest, natural, *nothing special*, *nothing to write home about*, off-the-shelf, one-dimensional, ordinary, overrated, pedestrian, primitive, prosaic, proverbial, ritual, routine, run-of-the-mill, standard, stock, ten a penny (*UK*), trite, *two a penny* (*UK*), typical, *undistinctive*, undistinguished, unexceptional, *unimposing*, unimpressive, uninspired, *unmemorable*, unremarkable, unsophisticated, *unspectacular*, usual, wonted (*literary*), workaday

(*n*) banality, commonness, conformity, mediocrity, ordinariness, plainness, poorness, primitiveness, *routineness*, triteness, *trivialness*, *vapidity*, *vapidness*

See also INFERIORITY (153), PLAIN (232)

245 Disorder and Chaos

Things fall apart; the center cannot hold;/Mere anarchy is loosed upon the world. **W. B. Yeats**

(*adj*) all over the place (*informal*), anarchic, chaotic, cluttered, confused, desultory, disarranged, disordered, disorderly, disorganized, frantic, frenetic, frenzied, haphazard, haywire (*informal*), hectic, helter-skelter, higgledy-piggledy, hit-or-miss, *in a jumble*, in disarray, indiscriminate, jumbled, knockabout, lawless, mad, messy, muddled, rampant, random, riotous, rough, scattershot, scrappy, self-contradictory, sloppy, topsy-turvy, tumultuous, turbid, turbulent, unclassified, uncontrolled, unmanageable, unorganized, unselective, unsystematic, untidy, upside-down, willy-nilly

(*adv*) at random, desultorily, frenziedly, helter-skelter, madly, pell-mell, riotously, untidily

(*n*) chaos, clutter, confusion, derangement, disarray, dislocation, disorder, disorderliness, distraction, farce, frenzy, furiousness, *haphazardness*, havoc, *huggermugger*, hurry, jumble, jungle, labyrinth, litter, maelstrom, mayhem (*informal*), maze, mess, messiness, misrule, morass, muddle, randomness, *riotousness*, roughness, shambles, sloppiness, tangle, untidiness, warren, welter, whirl

See also DISHARMONY (156)

246 Wasteful and Uneconomical

Men deal with life as children with their play,/Who first misuse, then cast their toys away. **William Cowper**

(*adj*) empty, extravagant, inefficient, misspent, profligate, throwaway, uneconomic, uneconomical, unproductive, wasted, wasteful

(*n*) extravagance, inefficiency, profligacy, unproductiveness, wastefulness

See also USE UP AND WASTE (474)

247 Expensive and Overpriced

Computers are big, expensive, fast, dumb adding-machine-typewriters. **Robert Townsend**

(*adj*) costly, dear, exorbitant, expensive, extortionate, high, horrendous (*informal*), overpriced, pricey (*informal*), prohibitive, sky-high, steep (*informal*), *unaffordable*

See also EXPENSIVE AND LUXURIOUS (218)

248 Captivity and Loss of Freedom

Caged birds accept each other but flight is what they long for. **Tennessee Williams**

(*adj*) bounded, caged, captive, confined, constrained, constricted, contained, custodial, detained, encased, enclosed, enforced, forced, *hemmed in*, imprisoned, *incarcerated* (*formal*), *in prison*, inside (*informal*), involuntary, *jailed*, localized, *locked up*, occupied, on a tight rein, repressed, repressive, restricted, restrictive, shut in, stormbound, trapped, under arrest

(*n*) bondage, captivity, capture, compulsion, confinement, constraint, constriction, control, curb, custody, detention, duress, entrapment, imprisonment, incarceration, in custody, internment, prison, repression, restraint, restriction, ring-fence (*UK*), roundup, seizure, servitude, snare, solitary confinement, straitjacket, stranglehold, stricture (*formal*), suppression, trammel

(*v*) cage, capture, catch, confine, constrict, enmesh, enslave, ensnare, entangle, fetter, foul, gag, handcuff, hem in, *hold captive*, hold in, *hold prisoner*, immure (*literary*), keep down, kidnap, localize, lock away, lock up, manacle, occupy, oppress, pen, pen up, pin, pin down, pinion, quarantine, repress, restrain, seize, shackle, shut in, shut up, snare, snatch (*informal*), take by storm, take prisoner, tangle, trammel, trap

See also THE POLICE, ARREST, AND PRETRIAL PROCEEDINGS (818), BUILDINGS FOR CONFINING PEOPLE (1094)

249 Captives and Prisoners

It is not the world that confines you, you yourself are the World, which holds you so fast a prisoner with yourself in yourself. **Angelus Silesius**

(*n*) captive, con (*slang*), convict, detainee, hostage, inmate, internee, jailbird (*slang*), prisoner

See also CRIMINALS (821)

250 Mistakes

To conduct great matters and never commit a fault is above the force of human nature. **Plutarch**

(*n*) anomaly, blooper (*informal humorous*), *blooper* (*informal humorous*), blunder, bobble (*informal*), boner (*informal*), boo-boo (*informal*), botch (*informal*), confusion, error, fallacy, false impression, fault, faux pas (*literary*), foul-up (*informal*), freak, fumble, gaffe, goof (*informal*), howler (*slang*) inaccuracy, inadvertence, lapse, mess-up (*informal*), miscalculation, miscarriage (*formal*), misconception, mishit, misjudgment, misprint, miss, misspelling, misstep, mistake, mix-up, omission, oversight, own goal (*UK*), slip, *slip of the tongue*, slip-up (*informal*), solecism, spoonerism, stumble

See also MESS UP AND MAKE MISTAKES (472), MISUNDERSTAND AND FAIL TO GRASP (761)

251   Faults, Flaws, and Weaknesses

The deficits in the eyelashes are not apparent to the eye. **Tamil proverb**

(*n*) abnormality, Achilles heel, apology (*humorous*), awfulness, bad habit, blemish, blight, blind spot, blip, blot, blotch, blur, bug (*informal*), chink in somebody's armor, chip, crack, damage, debility, defect, deficiency, demerit, disadvantage, failing, fault, flaw, frailty, *handicap*, hole, impairment, imperfection, inadequacy, inferiority, limitation, loophole, malformation, mark, minus, pip, scuff, shortcoming, smear, smudge, splodge (*UK*), splotch, spot, stain, taint, vice, weakness, weak point, weak spot

252   Disasters

When disasters come at the same time, they compete with each other. **Naguib Mahfouz**

(*n*) accident, blow, body blow, bomb (*informal*), calamity, cataclysm, catastrophe, cave-in, crisis, debacle, destroyer, disaster, doom, *double whammy* (*slang*), drama, killer, misadventure, misfortune, mishap, *natural disaster*, nonevent, nosedive, pity, shambles, spill (*informal*), stumble, tragedy, visitation, woe

253   Nuisances

Roses have thorns, and silver fountains mud;/Clouds and eclipses stain both moon and sun. **William Shakespeare**

(*n*) abomination, affliction, anathema, bane, bind, bother, bummer (*slang*), burden, cancer, canker, chill, chore, cost, curse, disappointment, disservice, disturbance, downer (*informal*), downside, *drag* (*informal*), drawback, encumbrance, excrescence, expense, eyesore, forfeit, grievance, hassle (*informal*), headache (*informal*), ill, imposition, inconvenience, irritant, irritation, let (*formal*), loss, menace (*informal*), mischief, nuisance, pain (*informal*), *pain in the neck* (*informal*), peeve (*informal*), pest (*informal*), plague, provocation, rigmarole, scandal, scourge, spoilage, stain, stigma, stinker, *swizz* (*UK*), test, *thorn in somebody's flesh*, *thorn in somebody's side*, torment, trial, tribulation, unmentionable, yawn, yoke

254   Bad Behavior or Actions

For every inch that is not fool is rogue. **John Dryden**

(*n*) breach, carrying-on (*informal*), conspiracy, contravention, defacement, delinquency, dereliction, desecration, encroachment, enormity, indiscretion, infamy, interference, intrusion, irregularity, irresponsibility, misbehavior, mischief, misconduct, misdeed, misdemeanor, monkey business (*informal*), outrage, rabble-rousing, roguery, roguishness, rottenness (*informal*), sabotage, skulduggery (*humorous*), transgression, unfaithfulness, vandalism, vendetta, violation

255   Traffic Accidents

The crash of the whole solar and stellar systems could only kill you once. **Thomas Carlyle**

(*n*) accident, blowout (*slang*), collision, crack-up (*informal*), crash, *fender-bender* (*informal*), pileup (*informal*), *rear-ender* (*informal*), smash, smashup, wreck

See also PROBLEMS (256), TRAVEL: TRAFFIC PROBLEMS AND TRAFFIC MANAGEMENT (323)

256   Problems

The best way to solve any problem is to remove its cause. **Martin Luther King, Jr.**

(*n*) airlock, albatross, bar, barrier, *bete noire* (*literary*), blockage, bogey, brake, bugaboo, bugbear, but (*informal*), catch (*informal*), complication, con, congestion, damper, dead end, deathtrap (*informal*), delay, demon, dent (*informal*), deterrence, detriment, difficulty, dilemma, discouragement, disincentive, disruption, fly in the ointment, football, frustration, fuss, glitch, gremlin (*informal*), handful (*informal*), hiccup (*informal*), hindrance, hitch, holdup, hot potato, hurdle, impediment, interference, iron curtain, jinx, kick in the teeth, knock (*informal*), liability, matter, millstone, no-no (*informal*), objection, obstacle, obstruction, pitfall, prevention, problem, relapse, retardation, reversal, reverse, setback, snafu (*informal*), snag, snarl-up (*UK*), sticking point, stoppage, stumbling block, stymie, teething troubles (*UK*), tie-up, time bomb, tinderbox, trouble, weight, *whammy* (*informal*)

See also DIFFICULT SITUATIONS (72), TRAFFIC ACCIDENTS (255), TRAVEL: TRAFFIC PROBLEMS AND TRAFFIC MANAGEMENT (323)

257   Bizarre and Peculiar

They were a tense and peculiar family, the Oedipuses, weren't they? **Max Beerbohm**

(*adj*) abnormal, absurd, anomalous, atypical, baffling, bizarre, blown-up, cockeyed (*informal*), crackbrained, cranky (*UK informal*), cuckoo (*informal*), cult, curious, dotty, eccentric, eerie, exaggerated, fishy (*informal*), freaky, funny, gonzo (*slang*), grotesque, *idiotic, incongruent*, incongruous, inexplicable, inflated, inhuman, insane, ironic, irrational, kinky (*informal*), ludicrous, mysterious, mystifying, nonsensical, odd, *oddball* (*informal*), offbeat, off-center, off-the-wall (*informal*), *otherworldly, out in left field*, outlandish, *out to lunch* (*slang*), paradoxical, peculiar, phantasmagoric, preposterous, quaint, queer (*dated*), ridiculous, risible, senseless, silly, spooky, strange, stupid, surreal, unaccountable, uncanny, uncharacteristic, unconscionable, unearthly, *unexplainable, unfunny*, ungodly (*informal*), unnatural, unreal, unthinkable, unusual, vaporous, wacky (*informal*), warped, way-out (*informal*), weird, zany

(*adv*) absurdly, eerily, funnily, improbably, paradoxically, peculiarly, strangely, unnaturally

(*n*) absurdity, absurdness, *bizarreness*, crankiness (*UK informal*), curiousness, *eeriness, incongruence*, incongruity, *incongruousness*, irony, irrationality, ludicrousness, mysteriousness, oddity, oddness, *otherworldliness, outlandishness*, peculiarity, preposterousness, quaintness, queerness (*dated*), ridiculousness, risibility, senselessness, silliness, strangeness, *uncanniness*, unnaturalness, wackiness (*informal*), weirdness

See also FUNNY AND AMUSING (216)

258 Unpopular and Unwanted

My definition of a free society is a society where it is safe to be unpopular. **Adlai Stevenson**

(*adj*) abandoned, castoff, despised, *detested*, discarded, disgraced, disregarded, hated, *loathed*, *reviled*, *ridiculed*, scorned, *unappreciated*, unasked, *unasked-for*, *under-estimated*, underrated, *undervalued*, undeserved, undesirable, unenviable, unfrequented, uninvited, *unlikable*, *unloved*, unpopular, *unrequired*, unsolicited, unsought, *unvalued*, unwanted, unwelcome, *vilified*

See also DISLIKE AND HATE (577)

Move and Function

Action: Start, Continue, and Finish

259 Actions or Undertakings

Great actions are not always true sons/Of great and mighty resolutions. **Samuel Butler**

(*n*) act, action, affairs, contribution, deed, departure, doings (*informal*), endeavor, enterprise, exploit, feat, flier (*informal*), handiwork, maneuver, move, movements, performance, precaution, project, step, stunt, turn, undertaking, venture

260 Start an Action

The origin of action—its efficient, not its final cause—is choice, and that of choice is desire and reasoning with a view to an end. **Aristotle**

(*v*) act on, approach, attack, begin, bestir yourself (*formal*), *blaze a trail*, break into, break new ground, buckle down (*informal*), buck up (*informal dated*), commence, *cut your teeth on*, embark on, enter on, enter upon, get cracking (*informal*), get down to, get down to business, *get down to it*, get going, get on (*UK*), *get stuck in* (*UK*), *get to work*, get under way, initiate, jump in, kick off (*informal*), lapse into, launch, launch into, launch out (*UK*), lead off, lead the way, lead up to, make a start, move into, open, pioneer, set about, set off, set out, set to, start, start off, start on, start out, *strike while the iron's hot*, take the bull by the horns, take the plunge, take to, take up, tee off

261 Attempt an Action

Accustom yourself continually to make many acts of love, for they enkindle and melt the soul. **Saint Teresa of Ávila**

(*n*) attempt, bid, effort, endeavor, go, potshot, shot, shot in the dark, stab (*informal*), try

(*v*) address, aim, assay (*literary*), attempt, bid, bother, dare, do, endeavor (*formal*), essay (*formal*), field-test, *give a shot* (*informal*), *give it a try*, go after, go for (*informal*), *go for it* (*slang*), grapple with, grasp the nettle (*UK*), *have a crack* (*informal*), *have a go* (*informal*), *have a shot*, *have a stab* (*informal*), make a stab at (*informal*), mean well, presume, seek, seek to, set out, speak to (*formal*), tackle, *take a shot at*, *take a stab at* (*informal*), trouble, try, try your hand, undertake, venture

262 Continue an Action

There must be a beginning of any great matter, but the continuing unto the end until it be thoroughly finished yields the true glory. **Francis Drake**

(*v*) beaver (*informal*), brazen out, carry on, chug (*informal*), continue, drag out, get on, go on, hang on, hold your own, keep, keep at, *keep at it*, keep going, keep on, keep up, persevere, persist, pick up, plow on, plow through, plug (*informal*), *plug away* (*informal*), *press ahead*, press on, run on, see through, soldier on, stand firm, stand your ground, stay on, stay out, stay up, stick at, stick to, stick with, wade through

263 Complete an Action

Time is a traitor, millimeter by millimeter it betrays/the hope of uniting discontinuity,/of securing the incomplete. **Antonio Martínez-Sarrión**

(*v*) be through with , *bring to completion*, close, come in, complete, conclude, consummate, crown, end up, finalize, finish, finish off, follow through, fulfill, get done, go the distance, make, mop up (*informal*), perfect, seal, sew up, tie up, turn around, wind up, wrap up (*informal*)

264 Stop Acting

But it stopped short—never to go again—/When the old man died. Referring to a clock. **Henry Clay Work**

(*v*) adjourn (*informal*), break, break off, call it a day, *call it quits* (*informal*), cease, chill (*slang*), chuck (*informal*), close, close down, come to a close, come to a halt, come to an end, come to a standstill, come to rest, come up for air, culminate, desist, drop, drop out, freeze, give up, give up on, knock off (*informal*), lay off (*informal*), leave off, pack in (*informal*), pack up, pause, put your feet up, quit, refrain, *shut down*, shut up shop, stand down, step down, stop

265 Cause to Start

Liberty does not consist in mere declarations of the rights of man. It consists in the translation of those declarations into definite action. **Woodrow Wilson**

(*v*) activate, actuate (*formal*), awaken, begin, bring in, bring on, christen (*informal*), crank up, detonate, galvanize, get going, inaugurate, jump-start, kick-start, *phase in*, set in motion, *set in train* (*UK*), set off, *set rolling*, *set the ball rolling*, spark, spark off, *start the ball rolling*, strike up, switch on, throw, trigger, trigger off, turn on

See also INSTITUTE AND INAUGURATE (348)

266 Cause to Stop

Life in itself is short enough, but the physicians with their art, know to their amusement, how to make it still shorter. **Petrarch**

(*v*) abandon, abort, arrest (*formal*), blow out, break, bring to a close, *bring to a halt*, bring to an end, *bring to a standstill*, call a halt, call off, cancel, close down, cut, cut off, cut short, deactivate, destroy, disable, discontinue, dissolve, end, extinguish, freeze, halt, hush, immobilize, inactivate, intercept, interrupt, kill off, mothball, nip in the bud (*informal*), nix (*slang*), *phase out*, pull the plug, put an end to, put a stop to, put down, put out, *put the lid on*, quell, quench, raise, run down, satisfy, shut off, silence, slake, snuff, staunch, stop, stub out, suspend, switch off, take off, terminate, turn off, turn out, unplug

See also MAKE IMPOSSIBLE (276)

267 Cause to Continue

To preserve a man alive in the midst of so many chances and hostilities, is as great a miracle as to create him. **Jeremy Taylor**

(*v*) buoy, continue, draw out, eke out, extend, further, keep the ball rolling, maintain, nurse, nurture, perpetuate, prolong, protract, spin out, sustain

268 Recommence and Resume

The chain of memory is resurrection. **Charles Olson**

(*v*) reactivate, reawaken, recommence, reconvene, redo, rehash, renew, repeat, replay, reprise, resit (*UK*), restart, resume, retake, *start afresh, start again, start anew, start over,* take up

See also REPETITION (29), AGAIN (109)

269 Carry Out an Action

The greatest pleasure I know, is to do a good action by stealth, and to have it found out by accident. **Charles Lamb**

(*n*) accomplishment, enforcement, execution, implementation, manipulation, performance, perpetration, pursuance (*formal*), running

(*v*) accomplish, acquit yourself (*formal*), act, attend to, behave, blitz (*informal*), bring off, carry out, come to grips with, commit, conduct yourself, dare, deal with, dispose of (*formal*), do, enforce, execute, field, fit in, get into your stride, give, go about, handle, implement, juggle, make short work of, manage, manipulate, operate, perform, perpetrate, ply, practice, process, pursue, put into action, put into effect, put into operation, put into practice, realize, respond, run through, see to, sort out, squeeze, swing (*informal*), take, take action, take on, take steps, transact, treat, wage, work

270 Be In Charge

You don't lead by pointing a finger and telling people some place to go. You lead by going to that place and making a case. **Ken Kesey**

(*v*) administer, administrate, be in charge of, captain, chair, conduct, control, direct, edit, govern, head, hold sway, hold the fort, manage, monopolize, officiate, overlook, overrule, oversee, pace, possess, preside, reign, rule, rule the roost, run, spearhead, staff, superintend, supervise, take care of, take charge, take control, take in hand, take over, *take the floor,* take up the baton, tend

271 Cause or Compel to Act

The people may be made to follow a course of action, but they may not be made to understand it. **Confucius**

(*v*) abet, bind, blackmail, bludgeon, boss, boss around, bribe, buffalo (*informal*), bulldoze (*informal*), buy off, cajole, call in, chivvy, coax, coerce, command, compel, constrain, detail, dominate, dragoon, drive, egg, egg on, enforce, enjoin (*formal*), exhort, force, get, goad, impel, incite, induce, influence, instruct, inveigle, involve, jockey, lean on (*informal*), let in for (*informal*), make, manipulate, motivate, move, obligate, oblige, order

around, persuade, press, press-gang, pressure, pressurize (*UK*), prevail on, *prevail upon,* prod, prompt, push, *push into, put pressure on, put the arm on* (*informal*), put up to, railroad (*informal*), require, *rope in,* rouse, seduce, *shanghai,* spur, *spur to action,* squeeze, steamroller, strong-arm (*informal*), subject to, suborn, suck in, summon, talk into, twist somebody's arm, urge, wheedle, work on

See also APPEAL TO AND AROUSE INTEREST (575), ENCOURAGE (576)

272 Hesitate

Thus conscience does make cowards of us all;/And thus the native hue of resolution/Is sicklied o'er with the pale cast of thought. **William Shakespeare**

(*v*) balk, blench, buck, dither, dry up (*informal*), falter, flounder, *hem and haw,* hesitate, *hum and haw* (*UK*), lose the thread, oscillate, pause, pussyfoot (*informal*), shilly-shally, stumble, temporize, vacillate, waffle (*informal*), waver, wobble

See also DELAY ACTION OR OCCURRENCE (278)

273 Shirk and Delay

Delay is the deadliest form of denial. **Cyril Northcote Parkinson**

(*v*) bide your time, dally, dilly-dally, drag your feet, fudge (*informal*), *hang fire,* hedge, hesitate, hold off, hold on, leave, procrastinate, stall, stonewall (*informal*), *take a rain check* (*informal*), tarry, wait

See also DELAY ACTION OR OCCURRENCE (278)

274 Not Do and Refuse to Do

No task is a long one but the task on which one dare not start. It becomes a nightmare. **Charles Baudelaire**

(*v*) abstain, back out, beg off, *beg off,* bow out, *bow out,* capitulate, chicken out (*slang*), dig in your heels, duck, duck out, eschew, *fight shy of, fink out* (*slang*), forbear (*formal*), get around, get out of, jib (*UK*), leapfrog, malinger, neglect, omit, opt out (*informal*), rebel, renege, resist, scratch, shirk, shrink from, *wriggle out of*

275 Make Possible

There is radiance in the darkness...all you need do is to cultivate the courage to look. **Obafemi Awolowo**

(*v*) assure, choreograph, cultivate, ease, emcee (*informal*), enable, encourage, expedite (*formal*), facilitate, fast-track, favor, foster

276 Make Impossible

I am the spirit that always denies. **Johann Wolfgang von Goethe**

(*v*) bar, block, blockade, cancel out, combat, count against, counter, counteract, damp, dash, derail, disarm, discourage, embargo, exclude, foil, foreclose (*formal*), forestall, frustrate, gag, inhibit, keep from, muzzle, *paralyze,* preclude (*formal*), prevent, *put a spanner in the works* (*UK*), put a spoke in somebody's wheel (*UK*), put a wrench in the works, put off, rain off (*UK*), rule out, sabotage, scotch, scupper, scuttle, snooker (*informal*), spike (*informal*), squelch (*slang*), stop, stultify, stymie, *throw a monkey wrench in the works* (*informal*), thwart, torpedo (*informal*), undo, work against

See also CAUSE TO STOP (266)

277 Avoid, Prevent, Limit, and Control

A speculator is a man who observes the future, and acts before it occurs. **Bernard Mannes Baruch**

(*adj*) deterrent, obstructionist, preemptive, preventive

(*n*) avoidance, check, curtailment, delimitation (*formal*), deterrent, nonproliferation, obstructionism, preclusion (*formal*), preemption, prevention, preventive

(*v*) avert, avoid, boycott, bridle, check, circumscribe (*formal*), clamp down, constrain, contain, control, cramp, crimp, curb, curtail, dam, debilitate, encumber, get in the way, hamper, help, hinder, hold back, hold in, impede, inhibit, interfere, keep, keep back, keep down, keep in check, keep the lid on, keep under control, limit, manage, micromanage, moderate, obstruct, obviate, organize, peg, police, preempt, regiment, regulate, *rein back*, rein in, restrain, restrict, ring-fence (*UK*), save, shackle, shut up (*informal*), silence, stem, subdue, subvert, take a back seat, talk out of, tame, throttle, trammel, weigh against

278 Delay Action or Occurrence

Delay always breeds danger. **Miguel de Cervantes**

(*n*) adjournment, dawdling, deferment, delay, *dilly-dally-ing*, postponement, procrastination, *rain check* (*informal*), rearrangement, rescheduling, suspension

(*v*) adjourn, carry over, dawdle, defer, delay, detain, hold over, hold up, mothball, postpone, put back, put off, put on hold, put on ice, put on the back burner, rain out, rearrange, reschedule, retard, set back, shelve, slow down, slow up, stall, stave off, stay, stonewall (*informal*), stunt, suspend, table, tell against

See also HESITATE (272), SHIRK AND DELAY (273)

279 Intentional and Deliberate

We know what a person thinks not when he tells us what he thinks, but by his actions. **Isaac Dashevis Singer**

(*adj*) appointed, blatant, calculated, conscious, controlled, deliberate, face-saving, flagrant, gross, intended, intentional, knowing, meant, planned, prearranged, premeditated, programmed, rehearsed, scheduled, self-imposed, strategic, studied, tactical, voluntary, willful

(*adv*) advisedly, by design, calculatingly, consciously, decisively, deliberately, designedly, expressly, in cold blood, nakedly, on purpose, purposely, wittingly

280 Automatic and Instinctive

Mistrust first impulses; they are nearly always good. **Charles Maurice de Talleyrand**

(*adj*) automatic, instinctive, involuntary, knee-jerk (*informal*), mechanical, mechanistic, perfunctory, physical, reflexive, spontaneous, spur-of-the-moment, subconscious, throwaway, unconscious, unquestioning, untaught, unthinking, visceral

(*adv*) by itself, instinctively, of its own accord, on the spur of the moment, unconsciously

281 Unplanned and Unexpected

Improvisation is the touchstone of wit. **Molière**

(*adj*) ad hoc, ad-lib, arbitrary, impromptu, improvised, inadvertent, indirect, offhand, off-the-cuff, un-

announced, unexpected, unforeseen, unintentional, unknowing, unmeant, unplanned, unpremeditated, unscripted, unwitting

(*adv*) accidentally, by accident, by mistake, capriciously, indirectly, offhandedly, *on a whim*, *on impulse*, unawares, unknowingly, willy-nilly

See also CHANCE, COINCIDENCE, AND ACCIDENT (786)

282 Cautious and Careful

Some craven scruple/Of thinking too precisely on th' event. **William Shakespeare**

(*adj*) careful, cautious, deliberate, measured, methodical, softly-softly (*UK*), unhurried, wary

(*adv*) deliberately, gingerly, impulsively, meticulously, minutely, narrowly, *with care*

283 Incautious and Careless

To lose one parent, Mr. Worthing, may be regarded as a misfortune; to lose both looks like carelessness. **Oscar Wilde**

(*adj*) brash, careless, desperate, improvident, imprudent, impulsive, inattentive, incautious, indiscreet, loose (*dated*), perfunctory, precipitate, precipitous, rash, reckless, remiss, slapdash, slaphappy, slipshod, sloppy (*informal*), thoughtless, unceremonious, unconsidered, unguarded, unorganized, unthinking, unwary, unwise

(*adv*) carelessly, headily, lightly, loosely (*dated*), mindlessly, no holds barred, unwisely, *without due care and attention*, *without due consideration*

284 Acting Independently

Deliberation is the work of many men. Action, of one alone. **Charles De Gaulle**

(*adj*) lone, single-handed, standup, unaccompanied, unassisted, unilateral

(*adv*) all by yourself, alone, by yourself, independently, individually, in person, in the flesh, in your own right, on your own, separately, single-handed, solo, specially, substantively, unaided, *without help*

See also SOLITARINESS (941)

285 Acting with Others

Every sin is the result of a collaboration. **Stephen Crane**

(*adj*) assisted, bilateral, bipartisan, collaborative, combined, concerted, joint

(*adv*) all together, as one, collectively, cooperatively, in chorus, in concert, in step, in tandem, *in unison*, socially, together, *with one heart*, with one voice

See also RECIPROCITY AND INTERDEPENDENCE (147)

286 With Enthusiasm

Man is only truly great when he acts from the passions. **Benjamin Disraeli**

(*adv*) actively, avidly, busily, eagerly, energetically, enthusiastically, *feistily* (*informal*), friskily, greedily, happily, heartily, hungrily, perkily, purposefully, readily, willingly, *with enthusiasm*, *with fervor*, *with good cheer*, *with gusto*, *with no holds barred*, *with passion*

See also THE WILL AND WILLINGNESS (563)

287 Without Enthusiasm

If you want to know where the apathy is, you're probably sitting on it. **Florynce R. Kennedy**

(*adv*) contrarily, dourly (*UK*), forcibly, half-heartedly, inflexibly, involuntarily, obdurately, reluctantly, resignedly, *spiritlessly*, *under duress*, *under protest*, wearily

See also NEUTRALITY AND INDIFFERENCE (553), UNWILLINGNESS AND STUBBORNNESS (564), UNINTERESTED AND DETACHED (629)

288 Describing Body Movements

A dance is a measured pace, as a verse is a measured speech. **Francis Bacon**

(*adj*) blundering, bumbling (*informal*), clumsy, convulsive, dainty, doddering, halting, jerky, jumpy, neat, nifty, quick, quivering, shambling, sinuous, trembling, tremulous, wavering

(*adv*) neatly

(*n*) jerkiness, jumpiness, neatness, shakiness, shaking, trembling, wobbliness (*informal*)

See also AGILITY OF THE BODY (476)

289 Prepare for Action

A cause is like champagne and high heels—one must be prepared to suffer for it. **Arnold Bennett**

(*v*) bite the bullet, brace yourself, gear up, get ready, gird your loins, grit your teeth, intend, lead up to, limber up, line up, loosen up, *make preparations*, mean, *pave the way*, pluck up courage, practice, prepare, *prepare the ground*, *prepare the way*, prepare yourself, *preplan*, prime, propose, psych, purport (*formal*), ready, *ready yourself*, rehearse, schedule, scheme, *spread your wings*, steel, steel yourself, *take a deep breath*, timetable (*UK*), train, walk through, warm up, wind up

See also PREPARATORY EVENTS (57)

290 Overdo Something

A man's reach should exceed his grasp,/Or what's a heaven for? **Robert Browning**

(*v*) binge, *bite off more than you can chew*, burn out (*informal*), double-book (*UK*), dramatize, exceed, *get carried away*, gild the lily, go beyond, go over the top, *go too far*, ham, *ham it up*, make a point of, overact, overcompensate, overdo, *overdo it*, overdo things, *overdramatize*, overeat, *over-egg the pudding* (*UK*), overestimate, overextend, overindulge, overreach, overreact, oversimplify, overstay, overstep, overstretch, overuse, overvalue, play to the gallery, rush, splurge (*informal*), supercharge, wear yourself out

291 Underdo Something

Anything worth doing is worth doing poorly at first. **Robert Downey, Jr.**

(*v*) *cut corners*, go easy on (*informal*), make light of, minimize, play down, trivialize, underachieve, underemphasize, underestimate, underperform, underplay, underprice, underrate, underrepresent, undersell, understate, undervalue

292 Participate

A life is not important except in the impact it has on other lives. **Jackie Robinson**

(*v*) appear, contribute, dabble, encroach, enlist, enroll, enter, enter into, feature, figure, get in on the act (*informal*), get involved, go in for (*UK*), have a hand in, integrate, intercede, interpose, intervene, join, join in, join up, matriculate, observe, partake, participate, play, *play a part*, register, sign on, sign up, star, star in, take part, throw yourself into

293 Help

Everybody wants to do something to help, but nobody wants to be the first. **Pearl Bailey**

(*v*) abet, accommodate, aid, aid and abet, assist, bail out, collaborate, cooperate, *give a hand*, help, help out, lend a hand, make yourself useful, *pitch in*, pull together, *rally round*, serve, support

See also KIND ACTIONS OR BEHAVIOR (295), TAKE CARE OF AND SPOIL (300)

294 Ways of Doing Things

Suit the action to the word, the word to the action; with this special observance, that you o'erstep not the modesty of nature. **William Shakespeare**

(*adv*) by dint of, by means of, how, like so, somehow, someway, thereby, thus (*formal*)

(*n*) algorithm, alternative, apparatus, approach, arrangement, avenue, bureaucracy, channel, choreography, code, *code of behavior*, code of conduct, code of practice, conduct, contrivance, convention, course, course of action, criterion, custom, design, device, doctrine, expedient, fashion, form, formality, formula, framework, gambit, game plan, gimmick, going, golden rule, ground rule, *guidelines*, *guiding principle*, habit, improvisation, institution, instrument, intrigue, law, line of attack, machine, machinery, maneuver, manner, means, mechanics, mechanism, medium, method, methodology, *modus*, modus operandi, modus vivendi, mores, movement, operation, organ (*formal*), outlet, plan, plot, ploy, policy, practice, *praxis* (*formal*), principle, procedure, process, program, protocol, recipe, red tape (*informal*), regime, regimen, regulation, rite, ritual, route, routine, rubric, *rules and regulations*, scheme, setup, standing order, stratagem, strategy, style, system, tack, tactic, tactics, technique, theory, tradition, treatment, trick, usage, use (*literary or archaic*), vehicle, way, ways and means, wont (*formal*)

295 Kind Actions or Behavior

Evil has encircled man from all sides, so man has devised good in all courses of action. **Naguib Mahfouz**

(*n*) aid, assist, assistance, attention, backup, benevolence, charity, concession, facilitation, favor, gesture, good deed, good offices, good turn, hand, help, helping hand, indulgence, lifeline, ministration (*formal*), philanthropy, relief, service, solace, succor (*literary*), support, turn

See also HELP (293), TAKE CARE OF AND SPOIL (300)

quivering, recoil, seizure, shiver, shudder, spasm, start, tic, tremble, tremor, twitch, vibration, wince

(v) convulse, cower, cringe, dodder, flinch, jerk, jump, kick, lock, palpitate, pound, pulsate, pulse, quail, quake, quaver, quiver, shake, shiver, shrink, shrink back, shudder, shy away, start, throb, tremble, twitch, unclench, waver, wince, wobble

317   Assume a Position

Squat like a toad, close at the ear of Eve. **John Milton**

(v) bend, bestride, crouch, curl up, duck, grovel, huddle, hunch, hunker, hunker down, kneel, lean, lie, lie back, lie down, loll, mount, plop down, plump, *plump down*, plunk down, poise, pose, recline, remount, rise, sit, sit down, slouch, slump, sprawl, square up, squat, stand, stand up, stoop, stretch out

318   Travel: Journeys and Trips

A journey is a person in itself, no two are alike. **John Steinbeck**

(n) airing, aviation, *away day* (UK), circuit, crossing, cruise, day out, day trip, detour, emigration, excursion, expedition, exploration, flight, *hajj*, hike, hop (*informal*), jaunt, journey, junket, long haul (*informal*), march, migration, odyssey, outing, passage, peregrination (*literary*), pilgrimage, ride, round trip, run, safari, sojourn (*literary*), sortie (*humorous*), spin, spree, tootle (*informal*), tour, travels, trek, trip, turn, visit, voyage, walkabout (*informal*)

See also VEHICLES (1145)

319   Travel: Travelers and Walkers

I took my mind a walk/or my mind took me a walk—/whichever was the truth of it. **Norman McCaig**

(n) adventurer, arrival, backpacker, *bicoastal*, biker, day tripper, deck hand, explorer, fare, globetrotter, *hajji*, *hitchhiker*, holidaymaker (UK), jaywalker, *jetsetter* (*informal*), mariner, *New Age traveler*, NY-LON, passenger, pathfinder, pedestrian, pilgrim, rambler, ranger, roamer, rover, sailor, sightseer, straphanger (*informal*), tourist, traveler, *trekker*, vacationer, visitor, voyager, walker, wanderer, wayfarer (*literary*), weekender

See also PEOPLE IN SPORTS AND LEISURE (876)

320   Travel: Ways of Traveling

No other form of transport in the rest of my life has ever come up to the bliss of my pram. **Osbert Lancaster**

(adj) mounted, onboard, on the road

(adv) en route, on foot, on the move, on tour

(v) *backpack*, board, bus, circumnavigate, commute, cover, cox, coxswain, cruise, drive, embark, explore, gallivant (*informal*), get on, globetrot, go, go around, guide, hitch, hitchhike, immigrate, island-hop, journey, migrate, motor (*formal*), navigate, orbit, paddle, pass through, pedal, pilot, ride, row, sail, scull, shuttle, *sightsee*, steer, *thumb a lift*, toboggan, tour, transmigrate, travel, trek, visit, voyage, weekend

See also COMMUNICATION NETWORKS (1105)

321   Travel: Sightseeing and Tourism

Tourism is the march of stupidity. **Don DeLillo**

(n) courier (UK), guide, sights, sightseeing, *tour guide*, tourism, *tourist attractions*, *tourist center*, *tourist class*, *tourist spot*, traffic, *travel bug*, *travel guide*, *vacation industry*, *vacationland*, *vade mecum*, visitor center

322   Transportation, Transporters, and Cargos

Rowing home to haven in sunny Palestine,/With a cargo of ivory,/. . .Sandalwood, cedarwood, and sweet white wine.
John Masefield

(adj) mobile, movable, oceangoing, seafaring, seagoing, transportable

(n) cargo, carriage, carrier, consignment, conveyance, delivery, freight, load, payload, *ridership*, shipment, shipping, staging post (UK), steerage, supersaver, transit, transport, transportation, transporter, *vehicle*

See also COMMUNICATION NETWORKS (1105)

323   Travel: Traffic Problems and Traffic Management

Rush hour: that hour when traffic is almost at a standstill.
J. C. Morton

(n) backup, *bicycle lane*, bike lane, bottleneck, *bus lane*, chicanes, cycle lane (UK), cycle track (UK), gridlock, *high-occupancy vehicle lane*, HOV lane, jam, logjam, queue (UK), *raised crossing*, rumble strip, *sleeping policeman* (UK), *speed humps*, speed trap, tailback (UK), *traffic calming* (UK), traffic jam

See also PROBLEMS (256), TRAFFIC ACCIDENTS (255)

324   Move Something to Another Location

A poem is energy transferred from where the poet got it. . .by way of the poem itself to, all the way over to, the reader.
Charles Olson

(n) conduction, deployment, dislocation, dispersal, dispersion, displacement, distribution, move, placement, redeployment, redirection, relocation, repatriation, repositioning, resettlement, spacing, transfer, transplantation, transposition

(v) bear, bring, bring back, budge, canalize (*formal*), carry, cart, channel, deliver, displace, disturb, ferry, funnel, hustle, move, offload, put aside, put back, rehouse, relocate, reposition, resettle, run, suck, take, thrust, tote (*informal*), transfer, transplant, transpose, uproot

325   Position Something

(v) arrange, balance, center, change around, deploy, deposit, direct, dispose (*formal*), ensconce (*archaic or literary*), hang, hang out, hang up, install, lay out, leave, line up, load, locate, move, park (*slang*), pile, pile up, place, plant, plonk, plop (*informal*), plunk, point, pop (*informal*), position, put, rack, redeploy, replace, seat, set, shift, shove, site, situate, space, stand, station, stick (*informal*), target, throw, tuck, turn

326   Position Something: Between, Beside, or Inside Something

(*v*) embed, implant, incorporate, inject, insert, inset, intercalate, intercut, interlace, interlard, interleave, interlink, interlock, intermesh, interpolate, intertwine, interweave, juxtapose, sandwich, sheathe, slot, superimpose, wedge

327   Position Something: Around Something

(*v*) coil, curl, furl, loop, spool, twine, twirl, twist, wind, wrap, wreathe

See also EXIST IN CLOSE PROXIMITY (21)

328   Move Something: Upward

(*v*) elevate, grub, heft, hoist, jack up, level, lift, pick up, raise, send up, take up, upheave, uplift, winch

See also GO UPWARD (306)

329   Move Something: Downward

(*v*) depress, down, drop, dunk, immerse, lay, lay down, let down, lower, plunge, put down, set down, submerge

See also GO DOWNWARD (307)

330   Move Something: Into a New Position or Overturn

(*v*) aim, angle, bowl over, bring down, capsize, cock, fell, flatten, flip, flip over, invert, keel, keel over (*informal*), knock down, knock over, lean, mow down, orient, orientate, overturn, rest, retract, skew, slant, slope, stack, tip, turn over, turn turtle, upend, upset, upturn

331   Move Past, Into, or Through Something

(*v*) breach, break into, break through, crisscross, cross, drive, entrench, ford, get ahead of, get through, infest, infiltrate, instill, leapfrog, negotiate, overshoot, pass, pass by, penetrate, percolate, permeate, pervade, push in, run through (*literary*), sink in, skirt, traverse

332   Spread and Scatter

Money is like muck, not good except it be spread. **Francis Bacon**

(*v*) broadcast, diffract, disperse, dissipate, distribute, pepper, punctuate, rake, scatter, slop, slosh, sow, spatter, splash, splatter, spray, spread, sprinkle, strew

333   Dispatch and Send

Sir, more than kisses, letters mingle souls. **John Donne**

(*v*) address, airdrop, airlift, airmail, catapult, consign, convey, dispatch, e-mail, fax, forward, launch, mail, misdirect, post (*UK*), redirect, refer, remit, return, route, second (*UK*), send, send off, send on (*UK*), ship, telegraph, transfer, transport

334   Move Something: Through the Air

It is a mathematical fact that the casting of this pebble from my hand alters the center of gravity of the universe.
Thomas Carlyle

(*n*) lob, pass, throw, toss

(*v*) blast off, blow, blow away, bowl, cast, chuck (*informal*), dash (*formal*), flick, fling, flirt, heave (*informal*), hurl, launch, let fly, lob, pass, pelt, pitch, pitchfork, project, propel, punt, send, shoot, sling, throw, toss, volley

335   Push, Pull, and Slide

The man who pulls the plow gets the plunder in politics.
Huey Long

(*n*) pull, putt, shove, shunt, thrust, tug, wrench, yank

(*v*) caddie, drag, draw, drive, ease, haul, heave, hydroplane, impel (*formal*), jerk, lug, pole, pull, pump, push, putt, roll, shove, shunt, slide, slip, thrust, tow, trail, trundle, tug, wrench, yank

336   Move Something: On the Spot

Midnight shakes the memory/As a madman shakes a dead geranium. **T. S. Eliot**

(*n*) flap, gyration, jerk, jolt, judder, rev, revolution, rotation, shake, spin, swirl, turn, twirl, twist, wag, whirl, wiggle

(*v*) agitate, bat, brandish, crank, dandle, fan, flail, flourish, flutter, go around, gyrate, jar, jerk, jiggle, joggle, jolt, judder, lash, nod, pirouette, pivot, reel, revolve, rewind, rock, roll, rotate, screw, shake, sling, spin, suspend, sway, swim, swing, swirl, swivel, *swivel around*, turn, twiddle, twirl, twist, wag, waggle, wave, welter, wheel, whirl, wield, wiggle, wobble

337   Accompany and Follow

She is so conjunctive to my life and soul/That, as the star moves not but in his sphere,/I could not but by her.
William Shakespeare

(*v*) accompany, catch up, chase, come along, conduct, creep up on, direct, dog, drive, escort, follow, frogmarch, gain on, give chase (*formal*), go around with (*informal*), guide, head, herd, hound, hunt, keep up, lead, lock on, partner, pick up, pursue, run after, see, see off, see out, send, shadow, shepherd, show, *show in, show out, show the way, show to the door*, sleuth, sneak up on, spoor, stalk, steer, string along (*informal*), tag along, tail (*informal*), tailgate, take, track, trail, usher, watch

338   Remove Something

Do not remove a fly from your friend's forehead with a hatchet.
Proverb

(*n*) abstraction, deduction, deletion, disposal, elimination, erasure, excision, expression, extraction, extrication, loss, purge, removal, withdrawal

(*v*) carry off, cart off, deduct, denude, express, extricate, lop, pluck, remove, shift (*UK informal*), subtract, take, take away, take off, unsheathe, withdraw

See also CAUSE TO DISAPPEAR (6), TAKE SOMETHING AWAY (425), GET RID OF SOMETHING (451)

339 Delete and Erase

Every sentence...that appears in the public press is perused and revised and deleted in the interests of advertisers and bondholders. **John Dos Passos**

(*v*) burn, cross out, cut, delete, edit out, efface, erase, expunge, remove, rub out, strike off, strike out, wash, wear, wear away, wear down, wipe

340 Eject and Exclude

It is an old maxim of mine that when you have excluded the impossible, whatever remains, however improbable, must be the truth. **Arthur Conan Doyle**

(*n*) banishment, deportation, evacuation, eviction, exclusion, expulsion, extradition, segregation

(*v*) banish, boot out (*informal*), count out, deport, draw off, eject, evacuate, evict, exile, expel, extradite, fire (*informal*), force out, keep off, kick out (*informal*), omit, oust, repatriate, segregate, send packing (*informal*), shoo away, shut out, smoke out, throw out, turn out

See also REVOKE STATUS (459)

341 Extract and Sever

Time will not be ours for ever,/He, at length, our good will sever. **Ben Jonson**

(*v*) abstract, amputate, aspirate, crop, cut off, cut out, deadhead, excise, extract, fish out (*informal*), gouge, gouge out, lop, mow, pare, pluck, prune, pull, pull out, quarry, sever, shave, shear, take out, tear, trim, uproot, weed, weed out

342 Lack of Activity or Motion

Nothing in progression can rest on its original plan. We may as well think of rocking a grown man in the cradle of an infant. **Edmund Burke**

(*adj*) aground, at rest, beached, becalmed, dead, dormant, frozen, idle, immobile, impacted, inactive, inert, jammed, motionless, poised, quiescent, *run aground*, stagnant, static, stationary, still, stopped, stuck, trapped, unmoving, unoccupied, unused

(*adv*) aboard, at a standstill, stock-still

(*n*) gridlock, idleness, immobility, inaction, inactivity, inertia, logjam, motionlessness, quiescence, repose, stagnation, stand, standstill, stasis, stillness

(*v*) bask, *flop about* (*UK*), *flop around*, fool around, footle (*informal*), freewheel, goldbrick (*informal*), hang (*informal*), hang around, *hang loose* (*informal*), hang on, hang out (*informal*), holiday (*UK*), idle, kill time, knock around (*informal*), laze, lie around (*informal*), lie in wait, loaf, *loaf around*, loiter, *loll around*, lollop (*UK*), *lollygag* (*dated*), lounge, *lounge around*, lurk, mess around (*informal*), mooch (*slang*), putter, relax, repose (*formal*), rest, *rest up*, sit around, *sit on your heels*, skulk, stagnate, stay put, *stay still*, take a break, take a breather (*informal*), *take a rest*, take five (*informal*), take it easy, *twiddle your thumbs*, vegetate, *veg out* (*informal*)

See also PAUSES AND PHASES (56), PERIODS OF REST (91)

343 Aimless and Errant Motion

Wandering between two worlds, one dead,/The other powerless to be born. **Matthew Arnold**

(*adj*) adrift, lost, off course, stray, wandering

(*adv*) adrift, astray

(*v*) blunder, careen, get lost, go adrift, go astray, lose your bearings, lose your way, lurch, meander, puddle (*UK*), roam, rove, straggle, stray, wallow

344 Change Direction of Motion

Digressions, incontestably, are...the life, the soul of reading; take them out of this book for instance, you might as well take the book along with them. **Laurence Sterne**

(*n*) about-face, deflection, deviation, diffraction, refraction, ricochet, U-turn

(*v*) avert, boomerang, *change course*, change direction, deflect, depart, deviate, divert, *do a U-turn*, dogleg, *double back*, glance off, head off, jackknife, meander, radiate, rebound, refract, ricochet, skid, slue, sweep, swerve, swing, swing around, tend, turn, twist, *twist and turn*, veer, weave, wheel, wheel around, wind, zigzag

345 Direction of Motion

Truly there is a tide in the affairs of men; but there is no gulfstream setting forever in one direction. **James Russell Lowell**

(*adj*) *anticlockwise* (*UK*), ascendant (*literary*), *back-and-forth*, backward, ballistic, circuitous, *clockwise*, *counterclockwise*, descendent, devious, direct, directional, downward, forward, gyratory, inbound, incoming, indirect, ingoing, inward, left-handed, one-way, onward, *outbound*, outgoing, *outward-bound*, pitching, receding, recessive, retrograde, retrogressive, revolving, right-handed, *rightward*, rotary, serpentine, sidelong, sideways, skyward, snaky, tortuous, twisting, twisty, undirected, up-and-down, upward

(*adv*) ashore, aside, astern, *as the crow flies*, asunder (*formal*), back, back and forth, backward, backward and forward, by way of, circuitously, direct, directly, *downriver*, *downward*, due, earthward, forth (*formal*), forward, frontward, headfirst, headlong, head-on, head over heels, heavenward, hither and thither, *hither and yon* (*UK*), home, indirectly, inland, inshore, inward, landward, onward, outward, rearward, round, *seaward*, sideways, skyward, straight, to and fro, upward

(*n*) course, direction, heading, orbit, path, tack, tendency, trajectory, trend, vector

(*prep*) down, toward, via

Creation, Production, and Emission

346 Creation

We live at a time when man believes himself fabulously capable of creation, but he does not know what to create. **José Ortega y Gasset**

(*n*) authorship, casting, construction, creation, discovery, erection, fabrication, formation, formulation, generation, invention, making, manufacture, manufacturing, output, production, reconstitution, reconstruction, recreation, redevelopment, synthesis

(*v*) breed, bring forth, bring to life, build, cast, cobble together, construct, create, design, determine, fashion, form, improvise, invent, knock together (*informal*), make, make up, map out, pose, produce, put together, re-create, *redesign*, reestablish, remake, remix, rig up, tailor, weave, write

347 Designers, Creators, and Instigators

Every animal leaves traces of what it was; man alone leaves traces of what he created. **Jacob Bronowski**

(*n*) architect, author, creator, designer, developer, discoverer, executor, facilitator, father, founder, generator, *graphic designer*, initiator, instigator, inventor, maker, manufacturer, originator, pioneer, planner, producer, propagator, trailblazer, trendsetter

348 Institute and Inaugurate

In analyzing history do not be too profound, for often the causes are quite superficial. **Ralph Waldo Emerson**

(*v*) base, bring into being, carve out, coin, compose, conceive, constitute (*formal*), create, curate, devise, erect, establish, form, formulate, found, generate, ground, inaugurate, institute, introduce, launch, mastermind, mount, orchestrate, originate, predicate (*formal*), *redevise*, reintroduce, restore, roll out, set up, start, start up, strike

See also CAUSE TO START (265)

349 Manufacture

Nothing should be made by man's labor which is not worth making or which must be made by labor degrading to the makers. **William Morris**

(*v*) cast, churn out, craft, create, develop, fabricate, forge, knock off (*informal*), make, manufacture, mass-produce, mechanize, mint, mold, prefabricate, smelt, synthesize, turn out

350 Engender

Eminence engenders enemies. **C. L. R. James**

(*v*) bear, breed, bring forth, engender, hatch, have, spawn, yield

351 Grow and Cultivate

I have a garden of my own,/But so with roses overgrown,/And lilies, that you would it guess/To be a little wilderness. **Andrew Marvell**

(*n*) cultivation, fertilization, pollination, propagation

(*v*) afforest, bloom, blossom, bud, come into bud, come into flower, crop, cultivate, farm, fertilize, flower, fruit, garden, germinate, grow, mulch, pick, plant, pollinate, propagate, rear, repot, seed, shoot, sprout

352 Build

When we build let us think that we build for ever. **John Ruskin**

(*v*) assemble, build, construct, erect, jerrybuild, make, piece together, pitch, put together, put up, raise,

reassemble, rebuild, reconstitute, reconstruct, redevelop, rig, set up, sink

353 Cooking and Food Preparation

Cookery...a form of pandering which corresponds to medicine. **Plato**

(*n*) cookery, cooking, heating

(*v*) barbecue, baste, beat, boil, braise, brew, broil, brown, caramelize, casserole, *chargrill*, cook, cream, cure, deseed, fillet, flavor, flour, frizzle, fry, garnish, grate, griddle, grill, gut, hash, heat, homogenize, liquidize, make, marinate, microwave, overcook, overdo, *pan-fry*, *parboil*, pare, pasteurize, peel, pickle, poach, pot, *prebake*, precook, preheat, purée, *recook*, *refry*, reheat, roast, sauté, scald, season, simmer, skin, *slow cook*, souse, spice, spoon, stew, stir, stir-fry, sweeten, tenderize, toast, undercook, underdo, whip, whisk

types of food presentations à la grecque, à la king, à la mode, Alfredo, au gratin, cacciatore, carbonara, chasseur, en brochette, en croûte, en papillote, florentine, julienne, lyonnaise, marinière, meunière, mornay, Newburg, ripieno, stroganoff, Thermidor

See also STATE OF PREPARED FOOD (1171)

354 Meal Preparation

The vulgar boil, the learned roast an egg. **Alexander Pope**

(*v*) concoct, cook up, fix (*informal*), prepare, rustle up (*informal*), scare up (*informal*), *warm through* (*UK*), whip up (*informal*)

355 Crafts and Carving

That lyf so short, the craft so long to lerne,/Th' assay so hard, so sharp the conquerynge. **Geoffrey Chaucer**

(*n*) handicraft, handwork, *needlecraft*, sampler, turning, woodworking

(*v*) baste, braid, carve, darn, embroider, hem, hew, model, run up, sculpt, sew, stitch, weave, whittle

types of handicrafts appliqué, basketry, crochet, dressmaking, embroidery, knitting, lacemaking, macramé, needlepoint, needlework, sewing, smocking, stitching, tapestry, tatting, weaving

types of woodworking cabinetmaking, carpentry, carving, joinery, marquetry, woodcarving

See also HOBBIES, GAMES, AND SPORTS (875)

356 Create Images

The painting is finished when it has blotted out the idea. **Georges Braque**

(*v*) brand, chalk, doodle, draft, draw, draw up, emboss, engrave, etch, hatch, inscribe, map, monogram, outline, photograph, postmark, print, scan, scribble, sketch, stamp, stencil, stylize, trace, write

357 Arrange and Create Order

Oh! Blessed rage for order, pale Ramon/The maker's rage to order words of the sea. **Wallace Stevens**

(*n*) cataloguing, categorization, codification, collation, compilation, coordination, counterbalance, graduation, orchestration, prioritization, rationalization, realignment, rearrangement, regimentation, reorganization, reshuffle, restructuring, *systematization*

(*v*) align, array (*formal*), assort, average out, blitz (*informal*), bring into line, bring together, catalog, categorize, choreograph, class, classify, clear, clear up, codify, collate, comb, compose, configure, coordinate, counterbalance, disentangle, even out, even up, filter, fix up, format, grade, graduate, group, harmonize, homogenize, justify, line up, marshal, neaten, orchestrate, order, organize, pack, plan, prioritize, program, pull together, put away, rationalize, readjust, realign, reallocate, rearrange, regiment, regroup, regularize, regulate (*formal*), rejigger (*informal*), reorder, reorganize, reshuffle, restructure, rig, schematize, slot in, sort, sort out, square, square up, stagger, standardize, straighten, straighten up, streamline, structure, synchronize, systematize, *systemize*, tabulate, tidy, tidy up

See also IMPROVE SOMETHING (374)

358 Create Disorder and Cause Chaos

Where eldest Night/And Chaos, ancestors of Nature, hold/Eternal anarchy, amidst the noise/Of endless wars, and by confusion stand. **John Milton**

(*v*) clutter, *clutter up*, complicate, confuse, derange, disarrange, dislocate, disorganize, disrupt, disturb, garble, jumble, mess up (*informal*), muddle, muddle up, obfuscate, obscure, riffle, scramble, tousle, upset

See also WORSEN SOMETHING (380), MESS UP AND MAKE MISTAKES (472)

359 Destruction and Demolition

The body politic, like the human body, begins to die from the moment of its birth, and bears in itself the causes of its destruction. **Jean-Jacques Rousseau**

(*n*) demolition, depredation, despoilment, destruction, devastation, harm, mutilation, obliteration, pulverization, violation

(*v*) annihilate, blast, blow up, bombard, bulldoze, burst, chew up, consume, damage, decimate, deforest, degrade, demolish, destroy, devastate, dynamite, explode, extinguish, go off, knock down, *lay waste*, level, mutilate, nuke (*slang*), obliterate, pull apart, pull down, pulverize, rack, ravage, raze, *raze to the ground*, *reduce to ashes*, *reduce to rubble*, ruin, sack, shatter, shell, smash, *smash to smithereens*, smash up, strike, tear down, tear up, total (*slang*), trash (*informal*), unmake, vaporize, violate, waste, wipe out (*informal*), wreck, write off (*UK*), zap (*informal*)

See also WORSEN SOMETHING (380), CONTACT: IMPACT (413), FIRE, FLAMMABILITY, AND BURNING (1165)

360 Tear, Break, and Cut

Smashing things, tearing them up, using the tongs as a sword— these represent the...weapons of the child's primary sadism. **Melanie Klein**

(*n*) breakage, breakup, dissection, fragmentation, split

(*v*) ax, bisect, bore, break, break up, bust (*informal*), carve, chip, chop, chop up, cleave, clip, come apart, crack, crumble, cut, cut down, cut up, dash (*formal*), dice, dig, dint, dissect, drill, fall apart, fall to pieces, flake, fracture, fragment, fray, gash, give, grind, grind down, hack, hew, incise, indent, lacerate, lance, mince,

nick, nip, open up, perforate, pierce, pound, prick, pull to pieces, punch, puncture, razor, rend, riddle, rip, *rip apart*, *rip open*, *rip to pieces*, *rip to shreds*, rip up, rupture, scale, scarify, score, scrape, shatter, shred, slash, slice, slit, snag, snap, snip, spit, splinter, split, sunder (*literary*), tear, tear apart

361 Emit and Emanate

Women are not the moon. Emit your own light. **Bai Fengxi**

(*n*) discharge, emission, hemorrhage, leak, leakage, outflow, secretion, seepage, spill, spillage

(*v*) debouch, emanate (*formal*), emit, escape, exude, froth, give off, give out, go out, issue, let out, ooze, produce, pump out, radiate, send, send forth (*archaic or literary*), shed, transmit

362 Sound Emission

Be not afeard. The isle is full of noises,/Sounds, and sweet airs, that give delight, and hurt not. **William Shakespeare**

(*v*) *make a racket*, resound, reverberate, ring

See also SOUNDS (1256)

363 Sound Emission by People

A human being...is a whispering in the steam pipes on a cold night. **Christopher Darlington Morley**

(*n*) screech

(*v*) bawl, bray, clamor, croak, croon, cry, exclaim, groan, gurgle, holler (*informal*), keen, moan, screak, scream, shout, sigh, snarl, snicker (*UK*), thunder, wail, wheeze, whine, whisper, yell

See also SOUNDS MADE BY PEOPLE (1262)

364 Sound Emission by Animals or Birds

The forms take shape in the dark air:/Puss-purr of leopard, footfall of padding bear. **T. S. Eliot**

(*v*) bark, bay, bray, caterwaul, caw, cheep, cluck, croak, crow, growl, grunt, hoot, howl, meow, mew, peep, purr, screak, screech, snarl, squawk, squeak, squeal, trill, tweet, warble, whine, whinny, woof, yap, yelp, yowl

See also SOUNDS MADE BY ANIMALS (1261), SOUNDS MADE BY BIRDS (1263)

365 Emit Sounds Through Impact and Abrasion

(*v*) beat, clack, clang, clash, clatter, click, clink, clonk, clump, crackle, crash, creak, drum, grind, groan, jangle, jingle, patter, plunk, pop, rasp, rattle, squelch, squish

366 Emit Continuous Sounds

(*v*) beep, blare, blare out, blast (*informal*), blast out, boom, burble, buzz, drone, echo, gargle, gurgle, hiss, hum, purl (*literary*), purr, rumble, sing, sizzle, sound, spit, sputter, susurrate, swish, thrum, thunder, whir, whiz, whoosh

367 Emit Ringing and Hooting Sounds

(*v*) chime, ding, honk, hoot, knell, *parp* (*UK*), peal, ping, quaver, resonate, ring, ring out, ting, *ting-a-ling*, tinkle, toll, tootle (*informal*), whistle

368 Light Emission

Be thou the rainbow to the storms of life!/The evening beam that smiles the clouds away,/And tints to-morrow with prophetic ray! **Lord Byron**

(*v*) beam, blink, burn, flash, flicker, floodlight, *fluoresce*, glance, glare, gleam, glimmer, glint, glisten, glitter, illuminate, *illumine* (*formal*), incandesce, indicate (*UK*), irradiate, light up, *luminesce*, scintillate, shimmer, shine, spangle, spark, sparkle, throw, twinkle, wink

See also LIGHT (1164)

369 Smell Emission

Precious odors—most fragrant when they are incensed or crushed. **Francis Bacon**

(*v*) reek, smell, stink, stink up

See also SMELL AND SMELLING (705)

370 Liquid Emission

Spilled water is not picked up again. **African (Bemba) proverb**

(*v*) discharge, disgorge, dribble, drip, drop, exude, filter, gush, hemorrhage, leach, leak, ooze, percolate, pour, secrete, seep, shoot, spew, spill, spill over, spout, spurt, squirt, stream, trickle, vomit, water, weep, well, well up

371 Record Something

What is not recorded is not remembered. **Benazir Bhutto**

(*v*) annotate, catalog, chart, chronicle, compile, document, enter, fictionalize, file, fill in, fill out, film, ghostwrite, input, inscribe, itemize, jot down, key, keyboard, key in, list, log, make a note of, make out, matriculate, minute, note, *note down*, pen, pencil, plot, prerecord, punctuate, put down, put in writing, record, register, rough out, scrawl, scribble, set down, shoot, take down, tape, tape-record, transcribe, type, video, videotape, write, write down

See also COPY AND DUPLICATE (402), WRITING (583)

Change and Transformation

372 Change

All conservatism is based upon the idea that if you leave things alone you leave them as they are. But you do not. If you leave a thing alone you leave it to a torrent of change. **G. K. Chesterton**

(*adj*) changed, conditioned, edited, modified, qualified, reconstructed, tailored

(*n*) acclimatization, accommodation, adaptation, adjustment, alchemy, alteration, alternation, amendment, assimilation, biorhythm, calibration, change, conditioning, conversion, crossover, departure, diversification, diversion, dynamics, ebb and flow, *expurgation*, flux, graduation, habituation (*formal*), inurement, inversion, metamorphosis, modification, modulation, move, mutation, normalization, orientation, permutation, readjustment, reconstitution, redraft, regulation, revocation, revolution, rewrite, sea change, shakeout, shake-up, shift, specialization, switch, transfiguration, transformation, transition, transliteration, *transmogrification*, transmutation, transubstantiation (*formal*), variance, variation, variety, vicissitudes

(*v*) acclimate, acclimatize, accommodate, act on, adapt, adjust, affect, age, alter, alternate, change, change around, color, condition, convert, customize, develop, distort, diversify, doctor, ebb and flow, elaborate, fiddle, fit, flavor, fluctuate, gear to, get used to, get your bearings, go, grow up, impinge (*formal*), individualize, inflect, influence, level off, level out, make a difference, mature, metamorphose, militate, modify, modulate, mold, morph, mutate, naturalize, objectify, personalize, range, react, readjust, recast, reconstitute, re-form, *reformat*, *reinvent*, reset, reshape, revolutionize, ripen, set, settle in, shake up, shape, simplify, syncopate, tailor, transfigure, transform, translate, transliterate, *transmogrify*, transmute, turn, tweak (*informal*), vary

373 Social, Political, and Economic Change

Revolution is…as natural as natural selection, as devastating as natural selection, and as horrible. **William Golding**

(*n*) *denationalization*, depopulation, gentrification, industrialization, perestroika, politicization, *regionalization*, unification

(*v*) *denationalize*, depoliticize, disestablish, gentrify, industrialize, nationalize, politicize, *regionalize*

See also GOVERNMENT AND POLITICS (805), STYLES AND SYSTEMS OF GOVERNMENT (806)

374 Improve Something

Let a king recall that to improve his realm is better than to increase his territory. **Desiderius Erasmus**

(*n*) amelioration, correction, enrichment, fine-tuning, modernization, *palliation*, rectification, redemption, refinement, refining, rejuvenation, renewal, renovation, revision, revitalization, revival

(*v*) add, advance, ameliorate (*formal*), become, benefit, better (*formal*), boost, brighten, bring alive, brush up, change for the better, civilize, correct, defuse, enhance, enliven, enrich, grace, heal, help, hone, humanize, improve, innovate, liven, liven up, make better, mellow, modernize, normalize, optimize, *palliate*, pep up (*informal*), perfect, polish, polish up, polish up on, profit, raise, refine, reform, regenerate, rehabilitate, remodel, renew, sharpen, smarten up, spice, stabilize, sweeten, turn around, update, upgrade, uprate (*UK*), work on, work up

See also ARRANGE AND CREATE ORDER (357)

375 Get Better

If I had my way I'd make health catching instead of disease. **Robert G. Ingersoll**

(*v*) bounce back, buck up, come alive, come along, improve, look up, make progress, mend, outgrow, pick up (*informal*), progress, pull through, rally, revive, shape up, turn the corner

376   Repair and Mend

Many men on the point of an edifying death would be furious if they were suddenly restored to life. **Cesare Pavese**

(*n*) care, mend, mending, overhaul, refit, refurbishment, repair, restoration, service

(*v*) cobble, debug, fix, fix up, heel, knit, maintain, mend, overhaul, patch, patch up, piece, put back together, rebuild, recondition, refit, refurbish, renew, renovate, repair, restore, rewire, service, sew up, sharpen, tinker

377   Correct and Put Right

As if religion was intended/For nothing else but to be mended. **Samuel Butler**

(*v*) amend, calibrate, compensate, correct, ease, edit, emend, *expurgate*, fine-tune, iron out, make up, mend, neutralize, offset, put right, rationalize, reconcile, rectify, redraft, redress, remedy, revise, reword, rework, rewrite, right, set right, settle, smooth out, smooth over, soothe, straighten out, tune

378   Improve Strength and Durability

He is a man of brick. As if he was born as a baby literally of clay and decades of exposure have baked him to the color and hardness of brick. **John Updike**

(*n*) consolidation, fortification, rearmament, reinforcement

(*v*) barricade, beef up (*informal*), boost, boost up, breathe new life into, buffer, buttress, cement, confirm (*formal*), consolidate, empower, energize, feed, firm up, fortify, *give a new lease on life*, harden, hold up, invigorate, nourish, pad, prop, prop up, reanimate, rearm, recharge, refresh, reincarnate, reinforce, rejuvenate, resurrect, resuscitate, revitalize, revive, revivify, shore up, soup up (*informal*), steady, stiffen, strengthen, supercharge, support, toughen, underpin, underprop, vitalize

379   Improve Appearance

It is proportion that beautifies everything, this whole Universe consists of it, and Musicke is measured by it. **Orlando Gibbons**

(*n*) adornment, beautification, decoration, face-lift, makeover, ornamentation, revamp, titivation

(*v*) beautify, coiffure (*formal*), decorate, embellish, glamorize, *glam up* (*slang*), *gussy up* (*informal*), jazz up (*informal*), landscape, manicure, preen, prettify, *pretty up*, primp, retouch, revamp, smarten, smarten up, spruce up, sugar, titivate, tone up, vamp up

See also DECORATE, ADORN, AND APPLY COATINGS (405)

380   Worsen Something

For sweetest things turn sourest by their deeds:/Lilies that fester smell far worse than weeds. **William Shakespeare**

(*adj*) degenerative, deteriorating, regressive, retrograde, retrogressive

(*n*) debasement, decay, degeneration, destabilization, deterioration, impoverishment, regression, retrogression, reversion, spoilage, worsening

(*v*) aggravate, break down, cast a shadow over, cheapen, chip away at, debase, defile (*formal*), deprave, desecrate, destabilize, detract, eat into, exacerbate, fan the flames, hurt, impair, infect, inflame, pervert, puncture, put a damper on, *rain on somebody's parade* (*informal*), reduce,

sour, spoil, tamper, tarnish, tinker, undercut, undermine, worsen

See also CREATE DISORDER AND CAUSE CHAOS (358), DESTRUCTION AND DEMOLITION (359)

381   Get Worse

Everything is perfect coming from the hands of the Creator; everything degenerates in the hands of man. **Jean-Jacques Rousseau**

(*v*) atrophy, backslide, degenerate, descend, deteriorate, droop, fester, *get worse*, go down, go downhill, go from bad to worse, go to pot (*informal*), go to rack and ruin (*informal*), go to the dogs (*informal*), languish, lapse, lapse into, pall, pine, regress, relapse, retrogress, revert, sink, sour, spiral, stagnate, suffer, take a turn for the worse, waste, waste away, worsen

382   Worsen Appearance

What deep wounds ever closed without a scar? **Lord Byron**

(*v*) abrade, blast, blemish, blight, blot, bruise, chafe, chip, deface, dent, litter, mar, roughen, ruffle, scar, scrape, scratch, scuff, vandalize, weather

See also FIRE, FLAMMABILITY, AND BURNING (1165)

383   Wound a Person or Animal

Would you hurt a man keenest, strike at his self-love. **Lew Wallace**

(*n*) disfigurement, dismemberment

(*v*) abuse, batter, brutalize, dehumanize, disembowel, disfigure, dismember, enfeeble, *eviscerate*, excoriate, graze, harm, hurt, ill-treat, ill-use, incapacitate, injure, *interfere with* (*UK*), knife, knock out, maim, maltreat, misuse, overcome, pull, rick (*UK*), rough up (*informal*), rub, skin, strain, tear, *tear limb from limb*, traumatize, twist, victimize, weaken, wing, wound, wrench

See also PHYSICAL ATTACK AND PUNISHMENT (415), STAB (416), INJURED (742), KILL (623)

384   Put at Risk

Those who mill around at the crossroads of history do so at their own peril. **David L. Boren**

(*v*) endanger, expose, impend (*literary*), imperil (*formal*), jeopardize, menace, put at risk, put in danger, risk, threaten

See also DANGER (235)

385   Change of Shape

Spirits when they please/Can either sex assume, or both.../Not tied or manacled with joint or limb,/Nor founded on the brittle strength of bones,/Like cumbrous flesh. **John Milton**

(*adj*) collapsible, folding, inflatable, pop-up, retractable, telescopic

(*n*) crease, crinkle, deformation, distortion, fold, pleat, pucker, ruck, tuck, warp, wrinkle

(*v*) arch, backcomb (*UK*), bend, blur, bow, buckle, bulge, cave in, collapse, contort, crease, crimp, crinkle, crumple, crush, curve, deform, distort, double, double up, flatten, flex, flop, fluff, fold, fold up, frizz, frizzle, furrow, gather, hammer out, indent, iron, kilt (*UK*), level, macerate, mangle, mash, open out, open up, perm, pleat, powder, press, pucker, pulp, purse, ridge, riffle, roll up, ruck, rumple, sag, screw, scrunch, *shrivel up*, smooth, smooth down, smooth out, splay, square, squash, squeeze, squelch, squish, *stave in*, steamroller, straighten, straighten out, style, tease, trample, tread, tuck, turn back, twist, unbend, uncurl, wad, warp, wrinkle

386 Change of Temperature

As Freezing persons, recollect the Snow/First—Chill—then Stupor—then the letting go. **Emily Dickinson**

(*v*) bake (*informal*), boil over, chill, cool, cool down, cool off, freeze, ice, refrigerate, swelter, warm, warm up

387 Harden, Congeal, and Dry

Beauty halts and freezes the melting flux of nature. **Camille Paglia**

(*n*) coagulation, fossilization, icing, *ossification*, *petrification*

(*v*) anneal, bake, calcify, clot, coagulate, coarsen, concentrate, congeal, curdle, dehydrate, desiccate, dry, dry out, dry up, firm, fossilize, freeze, freeze up, gel, go hard (*UK*), harden, ice, ice over, ice up, jell, jellify, jelly, mummify, ossify, parch, petrify, set, solidify, stiffen, thicken, wither

388 Soften, Liquefy, and Dampen

For pity melts the mind to love. **John Dryden**

(*v*) bathe, damp, dampen, defrost, deice, *deliquesce*, deluge, dip, dissolve, douse, drench, drown, film over, humidify, infuse, irrigate, liquefy, macerate, melt, moisten, moisturize, render, saturate, smelt, soak, soften, souse, steam up, steep, thaw, water, wet

389 Froth and Effervesce

What is fame? an empty bubble;/Gold? a transient, shining trouble. **James Grainger**

(*v*) bubble, effervesce, fizz, fizzle, foam, froth, lather, seethe, simmer, sparkle, vaporize

390 Go Bad and Corrode

When I die I want to decompose in a barrel of porter and have it served in all the pubs in Dublin. **J. P. Donleavy**

(*n*) corrosion, decomposition, *oxidation*, oxidization, rot, rust

(*v*) corrode, curdle (*informal*), decay, decompose, degrade, gangrene, go bad, *go moldy*, go off (*UK*), *go rancid*, *go rotten*, *go sour*, *go stale*, molder, oxidize, putrefy, rot, rust, spoil, stagnate, turn

391 Change of Color

'Tis the last rose of summer/Left blooming alone;/All her lovely companions/Are faded and gone. **Thomas Moore**

(*v*) blacken, blanch, bleach, blench, brighten, burn, color, darken, discolor, dye, flush, pale, peroxide, redden, rouge (*dated*), shade, tan, tinge, tint, whiten

392 Change of Size: Bigger

The mind, once expanded to the dimensions of larger ideas, never returns to its original size. **Oliver Wendell Holmes**

(*adj*) accumulative, burgeoning, distended, flaring, growing, swollen, telescopic

(*n*) accretion, accrual, accumulation, aggrandizement, amplification, appreciation, dilation, distension, enlargement, expansion, explosion, extension, groundswell, growth, magnification, maximization

(*v*) accrue, aggrandize, average up, balloon, billow, bloat, blow up, boost up, broaden, build up, bulk up (*informal*), bump up (*informal*), climb, complement, develop, dilate, distend, elongate, engorge, enlarge, expand, extend, fatten, fatten up, fill out, flesh out, gain, get bigger, get longer, go through the roof, grow, increase, inflate, lengthen, let down, let out, magnify, make up, maximize, multiply, mushroom, open out, outgrow, outspread, pad, plump up, puff out, puff up, pump up, put on, quadruple, raise, rocket (*informal*), shoot up, skyrocket (*informal*), snowball, splay, spread, stretch, supplement, swell, triple, wax (*literary*), widen

393 Change of Size: Smaller

Learning which does not advance each day will daily decrease. **Chinese proverb**

(*adj*) abbreviated, abridged, condensed, decreasing, edited, shrunken, tapered

(*n*) constriction, contraction, cut, decrease, dent (*informal*), depletion, detraction, fall, miniaturization, narrowing, reduction, remission, shrinkage, taper

(*v*) abbreviate, abridge, abstract, average down, cap, chop down, compact, compress, condense, contract, cut, cut back, cut down, decrease, deflate, dent, erode, fall, fall off, flex, get less, get smaller, get thinner, halve, let down (*UK*), macerate, miniaturize, narrow, narrow down, pare down, prune, shorten, shrink, shrivel, slash, slim down, take in, take up, taper, tauten, trim, truncate, whittle down

394 Change of Intensity: More

The intensity of an idea depends upon the somatic excitation with which it is connected. **Wilhelm Reich**

(*adj*) escalating, mounting, rising, soaring

(*n*) aggravation, augmentation, climb, crescendo, escalation, increase, increment, intensification, leap, multiplication, raise, rise, upsurge, upswing

(*v*) amplify, augment (*formal*), bolster, deepen, double, eke out, enlarge, escalate, exalt (*formal*), fan, fortify, fuel, *go sky-high*, heighten, inflate, intensify, jack up, leap, mount, ramify, ratchet, redouble, scale up, soar, step up, stimulate, stoke up, treble, turn up, underpin, well, whet

395 Change of Intensity: Less

Moderation is a fatal thing. **Oscar Wilde**

(*n*) alleviation, attenuation, de-escalation, depreciation, dilution, diminution, dive, mitigation, qualification, sag, weakening

(*v*) abate (*formal or literary*), allay, alleviate, assuage, attenuate, blunt, cool, cushion, damp down, dampen, deaden, deepen, de-escalate, depreciate, devalue, die down, dilute, dim, diminish, dive, douse, downplay, dull, eat away, fade, grow less, lessen, let up, liberalize, lighten, lower, minimize, mitigate, moderate, modify, modulate, muffle, pale, pipe down, qualify, quell, quiet, quiet down, recede, reduce, relax, relieve, remit, sap, satiate, scale down, slacken, slide, soften, soft-pedal (*informal*), step down, still, subside, take the edge off, taper, temper, thin, tone down, tumble, turn down, water down, weaken, wear off

396   Change of Speed: More

In my time, the follies of the town crept slowly among us, but now they travel faster than a stagecoach. **Oliver Goldsmith**

(*n*) acceleration

(*v*) accelerate, get a move on (*informal*), get moving, hurry, hurry up, open up (*informal*), pick up, *pick up speed*, *pick up the pace*, quicken, rev, smarten, speed up, spur (*literary*), step on it (*slang*), *step on the gas* (*slang*)

See also SPEED (102)

397   Change of Speed: Less

Ah! the clock is always slow;/It is later than you think. **Robert W. Service**

(*n*) deceleration

(*v*) brake, decelerate, *reduce speed*, slow, slow down, slow up

See also SPEED (102)

398   Change One Thing for Another

Love, in the form in which it exists in society, is nothing but the exchange of two fantasies. **Nicolas Chamfort**

(*n*) changeover, conversion, substitution, surrogacy

(*v*) alternate, change over, commute, convert, depute, fill in, override, relieve, reverse, rotate, *sub* (*informal*), substitute, supersede, supplant, swap over (*UK*)

See also EXCHANGE AND INTERCHANGE (448)

399   Substitutes and Stand-Ins

A vacuum is a hell of a lot better than some of the stuff that nature replaces it with. **Tennessee Williams**

(*n*) alter ego, alternate, fill-in, replacement, reserve, standby, stand-in, substitute, surrogate, understudy

400   Combine and Mix

Mix a little foolishness with your serious plans: it's lovely to be silly at the right moment. **Horace**

(*n*) absorption, agglutination, assimilation, coalescence, conflation, cross-fertilization, desegregation, graft, hybrid, incorporation, injection, insertion, integration

(*v*) agglutinate, aggregate, amalgamate, assemble, assimilate, blend, bring together, build in, call together, centralize, churn, coalesce, cohere (*formal*), collect, combine, commingle (*literary*), compose, conflate, confuse, consolidate, convene, crossbreed, desegregate, embroil, emulsify, federate, fit in, focus, fuse, gather, heap, heap up, herd, *hybridize*, include, incorporate, integrate, intermingle, intermix, intersperse, lace, lump, *lump together*, marshal, mat, meld, merge, mingle, mix,

mix up, pool, ravel, shake, shake up, shuffle, synthesize, tangle, toss, unite, unitize

See also CREATING CONNECTIONS (144)

401   Separate and Divide

True Love in this differs from gold and clay,/That to divide is not to take away. **Percy Bysshe Shelley**

(*n*) bisection, demarcation, detachment, diaspora, disconnection, dissociation, division, filtration, fission, insulation, marginalization, partition, polarity, polarization, segmentation, separation, severance, subdivision

(*v*) bifurcate, branch, branch off, branch out, break away, break down, break off, break open, break up, come between, *compartmentalize*, cordon off, decentralize, delimit (*formal*), demarcate, disassociate, disband, disjoint, *dissever* (*formal*), dissociate, distinguish, diverge, divide, divorce, *divvy up* (*informal*), fan out, filter, gape, graduate, halve, hive off, insulate, isolate, marginalize, part, partition, polarize, quarter, ramify, riddle, scatter, screen, secede, seclude, section, segment, separate, separate off, separate out, sequester (*formal*), sever, share, shut off, sift, sort out, spread out, stake out, strain, subdivide, thresh, transect, unitize, yawn

See also UNFASTEN AND UNDO (409)

402   Copy and Duplicate

All art is but imitation of nature. **Seneca the Elder**

(*v*) back up, clone, copy, duplicate, photocopy, plagiarize, reduplicate, replicate, reprint, reproduce

See also COPIES AND REPLICAS (151), FALSIFY AND CHEAT (176), RECORD SOMETHING (371)

403   Clean and Polish

What separates two people most profoundly is a different sense and degree of cleanliness. **Friedrich Wilhelm Nietzsche**

(*n*) ablutions (*formal or humorous*), bath, cleaning, cleansing, desalination, detoxification, distillation, fumigation, going-over (*informal*), irradiation, pasteurization, purification, refining, rinse, scrub, shower, spit and polish (*informal*), *spring-cleaning*, sterilization, wash

(*v*) aerate, air, bathe, brush, buff, burnish, clarify, clean, cleanse, clean up, decontaminate, deodorize, desalinate, descale, detoxify, disinfect, distill, dry-clean, dust, finish, flush, freshen, freshen up, fumigate, gargle, grind, groom, hone, hose, hose down, launder, moisturize, mop, mop up, polish, polish up, purge, purify, refine, rub, rub down, sand, sandpaper, sanitize, scald, scour, scrub, shine, shower, sluice, soap, sponge, spring-clean, sterilize, swab, sweep, sweep away, sweep up, swill, tan, towel, valet, ventilate, wash, wash down, wash out, wax, whet, wipe

See also CLEAN AND HYGIENIC (1233)

404   Dirty and Contaminate

Reactors breed plutonium/bloodcells pay their dues/radiation keeps leaking & seeping/and I've got the Chernobyl Three Mile Island Blues. **Jayne Cortez**

(*n*) adulteration, contamination, infection, pollution

(*v*) adulterate, *begrime* (*literary*), *besmear*, *bespatter*, contaminate, dirty, foul, infect, mark, poison, pollute, run through, soil, spot, stain, sully (*literary*), taint, tarnish

See also DIRTY (1235)

405　Decorate, Adorn, and Apply Coatings

PAINTING, *n. The art of protecting flat surfaces from the weather and exposing them to the critic.* **Ambrose Bierce**

(*adj*) beaded, beady, bedecked (*literary*), coated, cosmetic, crusted, decorated, encrusted, festooned, nonstick, paved, touched (*literary*)

(*v*) adorn, airbrush, anoint, apply, array (*literary*), bandage, bedeck (*literary*), blazon, blob, braid, cake, cap, carpet (*literary*), caulk, coat, cover, dab, daub, deck (*literary*), decorate, drape, dress, dress up, dust, emblazon, enamel, festoon, giftwrap, *gild, gird* (*literary*), glaze, grace, grease, grout, ice, insulate, lag, laminate, line, lubricate, *mottle*, oil, ornament, overlay, pack, package, paint, paper over, parcel, parcel up (*UK*), pave, perfume, personalize, plaster, plate, redecorate, repaint, *repaper*, resurface, rustproof, scent, sheathe, smear, smudge, soundproof, spangle, spatter, speck, speckle, splodge (*UK*), splotch, spray, spread, sprinkle, stencil, stipple, streak, strew, stud, surface, swaddle, swathe, touch up, trim, upholster, varnish, veneer, whitewash, wipe, wrap, wrap up, wreathe

See also IMPROVE APPEARANCE (379), ORNAMENTS AND DECORATIONS (1248)

406　Fill

One of the few remaining freedoms we have is the blank page. No one can prescribe how we should fill it. **James Kelman**

(*v*) absorb, block up, choke, clog, clog up, congest, cram, crowd, fill, fill in, fill up, imbue, impregnate, infuse, jam, *jam-pack* (*informal*), load, load up, overflow, pack, *pad out*, permeate, plug, ram, refill, refuel, reload, replenish, restock, squash, squeeze, steep, stop, stop up, stuff, suffuse, swamp, tamp, top up, wad

See also FULL (1239)

407　Empty and Unload

It is not good to unpack in an open place. **Tamil proverb**

(*v*) clean out, clear, clear out, decant, deflate, depopulate, empty, free up, gut, hollow, overspill, pour, scrape out, siphon, unblock, unclog, unload, unpack, unplug, vacate

See also EMPTY (1238)

408　Fasten, Link, and Join

If two lives join, there is oft a scar./They are one and one, with a shadowy third;/One near one is too far. **Robert Browning**

(*adj*) articulated, barred, clip-on, closed, joined, mounted, sealed

(*n*) connection, implantation, installation, occlusion, reconnection

(*v*) add, affix, anchor, append, attach, belt, belt up, bind, bolt, bond, bridge, buckle, bundle up, button, catch, cauterize, cement, chain, chock, cinch, clamp, clip, close, close up, conjoin (*formal*), connect, converge, couple, dovetail, engage, entwine, fasten, fix, glue, graft, gum, harness, hitch, hold, hook, hook up, join, knit, knot,

lace, lash, lock, lodge, mesh, moor, mount, nail, paste, peg, pin, plait, plug in, reconnect, *recouple*, rivet, rope, screw, seal, secure, shut, shut up, splice, splint, staple, stick, stitch, strap, stud, suture, tack, tag, tangle, tape, tether, thread, tie, tie up, truss, wed, weld, wheel-clamp (*UK*), wire

See also CONNECTIONS (143), FASTENERS, LINKS, AND NETWORKS (1247)

409　Unfasten and Undo

Unaccommodated man is no more but such a poor, bare, forked animal as thou art. Off, off, you lendings! Come; unbutton here. **William Shakespeare**

(*adj*) disconnected, open, undone, unfastened, unglued

(*v*) cut off, detach, disassemble, disconnect, disengage, disjoint, dislocate, *dismantle*, disunite, divide, free up (*informal*), jimmy, loosen, open, prize, *prize open*, pry, *pry open*, set free, take apart, take down, take to pieces, unbind, unbolt, *unbuckle*, unbutton, *uncap*, unclasp, uncoil, uncork, uncouple, unfasten, unfix, unhitch, unhook, *unjam*, unknot, unlace, unlatch, unlock, unpeg, unpick, *unpin*, unravel, unscrew, unseal, unsnag, unsnarl, unstick, unstop, unstrap, untangle, untether, untie, unwind, unwrap, unyoke, unzip

See also SEPARATE AND DIVIDE (401), FASTENERS, LINKS, AND NETWORKS (1247)

410　Bar and Obstruct Access

I'll put a spoke among your wheels. **Francis Beaumont**

(*v*) bar, batten, block off, board up, enclose, fence, lock, obstruct, occlude, picket, seal off, secure

Contact and Impact

411　Contact: Hold

I have embraced the summer dawn. **Arthur Rimbaud**

(*n*) clinch, *clutch*, grasp, grip, hold, lunge, purchase

(*v*) adhere, capture, catch, catch hold of, clasp, cleave (*literary*), cling, clutch, cradle, gather up, get ahold of, grab, grab hold of, grapple, grasp, grip, hang on, hold, hold close, hold on, hold onto, lunge, reach, seize, snatch, squeeze, take, tote (*informal*), wrest

See also PHYSICAL CONTACT AS COMMUNICATION (655)

412　Contact: Touch

Whatever you touch and believe in...today, is going to be—like the reality of yesterday—an illusion tomorrow. **Luigi Pirandello**

(*n*) brush, dig, jab, jerk, nip, nudge, pat, peck, poke, prod, stroke, touch, tweak

(*v*) brush, *brush against*, caress, claw, come into contact with, dig, dig into, fiddle, fidget, finger, fondle, graze, grope (*informal*), handle, jab, kiss, mess around (*informal*), monkey with, nip, nudge, nuzzle, pat, paw, peck, pet, poke, prod, scrabble, scratch, stroke, touch, toy with, tweak, worry

413   Contact: Impact

When he goes hunting/he aims at a bird and/brings a landscape down. **Norman McCaig**

(*n*) bash (*informal*), beat, blow, bump, hit, impact, stroke, tap, wallop (*informal*), whiplash

(*v*) bang, bang into, barge, barge into, batter, beat, bonk (*informal*), buffet, bump, bump into, butt, *career into*, catch, collide, crack, crash, elbow, hit, jog, jostle, kick, knock, lash, lob, plow into, pound, ram, rear-end, run into, run over, *slam into, smash into*, strike, stub, tap

See also DESTRUCTION AND DEMOLITION (359), IMPACT SOUNDS (1260)

414   Contact: Exert Pressure

The force of mind is only as great as its expression; its depth only as deep as its power to expand and lose itself. **G. W. F. Hegel**

(*n*) massage

(*v*) bear down on, clench, constrict, force, grit, jam, knead, massage, pack, pat, pinch, press, pull, rub, rub down, squeeze, stamp, tighten, wring

415   Physical Attack and Punishment

I'm all for bringing back the birch, but only between consenting adults. **Gore Vidal**

(*n*) assault, bang, bash (*informal*), battering, buffeting, clout, flagellation, hammering, head-butt, hiding (*informal*), knock, lash, *pummeling*, punch, rap, slap, slug, smack, sock (*informal*), spanking, swing, swipe, thrashing, thwack, uppercut, walloping (*informal*), whack

(*v*) assail, assault, attack, bash (*informal*), baste, beat up (*informal*), belabor (*literary or humorous*), belt (*informal*), biff (*informal*), bite, bop (*informal*), box, cane, clobber (*informal*), clock (*slang*), clout, cuff, deck (*informal*), exchange blows, flail, give a beating (*UK*), go for, hammer (*informal*), head-butt, hit, hit out, kick, kick in, knock around (*informal*), KO (*informal*), lash, lash out, lay about (*UK*), lay into, light into (*informal*), manhandle, maul, mob, molest, mug, overrun, pounce, pummel, punch, *put the boot in* (*UK*), rap, sally, savage, set on, set upon, slap, slug, smack, smite (*literary*), sock (*informal*), spank, strike, strike down, strike out, swat, swing at, swipe, tackle, thrash, thump, thwack, turn on, wallop (*informal*), *weigh into* (*informal*), whack

See also WOUND A PERSON OR ANIMAL (383)

416   Stab

We are more sensible of one little touch of a surgeon's lancet than of twenty wounds with a sword in the heat of fight. **Michel de Montaigne**

(*v*) bayonet, gore, impale, skewer, spear, spike, stab, stick, transfix

See also WOUND A PERSON OR ANIMAL (383), KILL (923)

417   Whip and Club

A whipping never hurts so much as the thought that you are being whipped. **Edgar Watson Howe**

(*v*) birch, bludgeon, club, cosh, cudgel, flagellate, flay, flog, whip

See also KILL (923), BLUNT INSTRUMENTS AND WHIPS (1158)

418   Avoid or Escape Contact

The apostles of the martial virtues...tend not to die fighting when the time comes. History is full of ignominious getaways by the great and famous. **George Orwell**

(*v*) avoid, break free, bypass, dodge, elude, escape, fend off, get away from, give a wide berth, give somebody the slip, head off, hold off, keep at bay, keep away, nestle, outrun, parry, repel, repulse, shake off, shelter, throw off, ward off

419   Prevent Contact or Attack

The ultimate result of shielding men from the effects of folly, is to fill the world with fools. **Herbert Spencer**

(*n*) conservation, preservation, safeguarding

(*v*) cover, cushion, defend, deflect, fight off, fortify, guard, harbor, keep from, pillow, protect, resist, safeguard, shelter, shield

Obtaining, Losing, and Exchanging Possession

420   Get

The knowledge of the world is only to be acquired in the world, and not in a closet. **Lord Chesterfield**

(*v*) accede, accumulate, acquire, amass, attract, bag, benefit from, capture, catch, clock up, collar (*slang*), come by, cull, derive, develop, distill, draw, drum up, enlist, fetch, field, find, gain, garner, gather, get, get hold of, *glean*, harvest, have, help yourself, land, lay in, net (*informal*), notch (*slang*), obtain, pluck, pot, procure, purchase, reach, reap, retake, round up, *run to ground*, run up, scare up (*informal*), scoop, scrape together, scratch together, screw up, scrounge (*informal*), secure, seize, snap up, suck, suck up, sweep, take on, take out, tap, win, wrest

421   Get Money or Reward

Not all that tempts your wand'ring eyes/And heedless hearts, is lawful prize;/Nor all that glisters, gold. **Thomas Gray**

(*v*) bring, bring home the bacon (*informal*), bring in, chalk up, claim, clean up (*slang*), clear (*informal*), come into, debit, earn, fetch, gross, inherit, make, net, profit, rack up (*informal*), *rake it in* (*informal*), reap, score, strike it rich, take home

422   Purchase

When I want a peerage, I shall buy one like an honest man. **Lord Northcliffe**

(*n*) acquisition, buy, mail order, order, purchase, transaction

(*v*) afford, barter, book, buy, buy out, charter, import, order, purchase, shop, take

See also GIVE MONEY (433)

423 Expenditure

Superfluous wealth can buy superfluities only.
Henry David Thoreau

(*n*) admission, asking price, bill, charge, concession (*UK*), cost, costs, damage (*informal*), disbursement, expenditure, expense, expenses, fare, investment, outflow, outgo, outgoings (*UK*), outlay, overhead, overheads (*UK*), payout, postage, prepayment, price, rate, spending, subscription, subsidy, toll, value

See also MONEY (797), FUNDS, PAYMENTS, AND CHARGES (800)

424 Purchaser

In a consumer society there are inevitably two kinds of slaves: the prisoners of addiction and the prisoners of envy. **Ivan Illich**

(*n*) buyer, consumer, customer, patron, payer, procurer, purchaser, shopper, taker, trade

See also SELLERS (442)

425 Take Something Away

Property is organized robbery. **George Bernard Shaw**

(*n*) annexation, apprehension, appropriation, arrogation (*formal*), commandeering, confiscation, seizure, sequestration

(*v*) annex, appropriate, arrogate (*formal*), bankrupt, capture, clean out (*informal*), commandeer, confiscate, deprive, dispossess (*archaic or formal*), divest, dock, *do out of* (*informal*), embargo, expropriate, extract, freeload (*informal*), gouge, grab, hijack, hog (*informal*), impound, impoverish, leap at, requisition, rip, rob, seize, sequester, sequestrate (*UK*), spirit, strip, take over, take possession of, usurp

See also REMOVE SOMETHING (338), CAUSE TO DISAPPEAR (6)

426 Steal and Rob

A man who will steal for me will steal from me.
Theodore Roosevelt

(*v*) abduct, borrow, break in, burglarize, burgle, *carjack*, con, defraud, despoil, embezzle, extort, fiddle (*informal*), filch (*informal*), fleece (*informal*), hijack (*informal*), hold up, joyride, knock off (*slang*), launder, lift (*informal*), loot, make off with, maraud, misappropriate, mooch (*slang*), nab, nip, overcharge, *peculate* (*formal*), pilfer, pillage, plunder, poach, pocket, purloin (*formal or humorous*), *purse-snatch*, raid, ram-raid (*UK*), ransack, rip off (*informal*), rob, shoplift, skyjack, smuggle, snatch, snitch (*slang*), steal, stick up (*informal*), swindle, swipe (*informal*), take, thieve, walk off with

See also CRIMES (817), CRIMINALS (821)

427 Proceeds of Crime

Stolen sweets are always sweeter,/Stolen kisses much completer. **Leigh Hunt**

(*n*) booty, *contraband*, hush money (*informal*), *ill-gotten gains*, loot, pickings, pillage, plunder, ransom, spoils, swag (*slang*)

428 Lend, Lease, and Borrow

Your borrowers of books—those mutilators of collections, spoilers of the symmetry of shelves, and creators of odd volumes. **Charles Lamb**

(*v*) borrow, hire, hire out, lease, lend, let, loan, rent, rent out, reserve, *sublease*, *sublet*

429 Regain Possession

Yet beauty, though injurious, hath strange power,/After offense returning, to regain/Love once possessed. **John Milton**

(*n*) reclamation, recovery, recuperation, repossession, restitution, retrieval

(*v*) call in, claw back, get back, recapture, reclaim, recoup, recover, recuperate, regain, repossess, retrieve, salvage, take back

430 Give and Provide

The manner of giving is worth more than the gift. **Corneille**

(*v*) accord, afford (*formal*), ascribe (*formal*), attach, bestow (*formal*), come up with, commend, commit, contribute, dedicate, deliver, devolve, devote, donate, entrust, fulfill, give, give back, give over to, give up, grant, lend, make up, provide, raffle, reciprocate, return, spend, throw in, trust, vest, vouchsafe, yield

431 Proffer and Hand Over

Liberality lies less in giving liberally than in the timeliness of the gift. **Jean de La Bruyère**

(*v*) extend, give in (*UK*), give over to (*literary*), give up, hand, hand in, hand over, hold out, lay before, present, proffer, turn in, turn over

432 Bequeath and Bequests

Behold, I do not give lectures or a little charity,/When I give I give myself. **Walt Whitman**

(*n*) bequest, birthright, endowment, heirloom, heritage, inheritance, legacy

(*v*) bequeath, hand down, *hand on*, leave, *pass down*

433 Give Money

The man who leaves money to charity in his will is only giving away what no longer belongs to him. **Voltaire**

(*v*) amortize, bank, bankroll (*informal*), capitalize, chip in (*informal*), cough up (*informal*), defray, deposit, dissipate, expend (*formal*), finance, *fork out* (*informal*), *fork over* (*informal*), *fork up* (*informal*), fund, indemnify, invest, liquidate, outlay, pay, pay back, pay off, put back, put in, put into (*UK*), put up, redress, refund, reimburse, remit, remunerate, settle, settle up, shell out (*informal*), spend, *splash out*, splurge, sponsor, square, square up, subscribe, subsidize, tip, treat

See also PURCHASE (422)

434 Dispense, Ration, and Distribute

There is only a certain sized cake to be divided up, and if a lot of people want a larger slice they can only take it from others.
Stafford Cripps

(*n*) administration, allocation, allotment, assignment, carve-up, delegation, diffusion, distribution, division,

issue, penetration, provision, redistribution, remit (*UK*), transmission

(*v*) administer, allocate, allot, allow, apportion, assign, budget, carve up (*informal*), consign, contract out, deal, deal out, delegate, diffuse, disburse, dish out (*informal*), dispense, distribute, divide, divvy (*informal*), dole out (*informal*), dot, drop off (*informal*), earmark, export, farm out, give, give away, give out, halve, *hand around*, hand out, *hand round* (*UK*), issue, make available, mete out, offer, parcel out, pass, pass out, piece out (*UK*), portion, ration, ration out, redistribute, serve, share, share out, spread, spread out, transmit

435 Equip and Supply

Once we are destined to live out our lives in the prison of our mind, our one duty is to furnish it well. **Peter Ustinov**

(*v*) arm, cater, deliver, equip, feed into, fill, fit, fit out, fit up, furnish (*formal*), install, kit out (*UK*), lay on, ⟨re⟩fit, pipe, ply, provide, rearm, render (*formal*), rig out ⟨⟩al), supply

436 ⟨Rew⟩ard

⟨i⟩ce is's own⟨⟩

(*v*) a⟨⟩d. **Quentin Crisp**
⟨c⟩ompens⟨⟩ compe⟨⟩ate, confer (*formal*), endow, rec-
see als⟨⟩em, repay, reward

437 ⟨⟩ AWARDS (439)

The only ⟨⟩
Herbert Bee⟨⟩
(*v*) bog do⟨⟩h and Overburden
dump on, ⟨⟩
date, lavish, ov⟨⟩being lionized was Daniel.
overstress, saturate⟨⟩
with, saturate⟨⟩
swamp, tax, we⟨⟩den, cloy, deluge,
⟨⟩impose, inun-
⟨⟩overstrain,
438 Gifts ⟨⟩n, saddle
If one receives a plum ⟨⟩thing, fr⟨⟩
Vietnamese proverb ⟨⟩e, toll-free ⟨⟩
(*adj*) at no cost, c⟨⟩ation, dowry,
of charge, gratis, ⟨⟩ benefit, gift,
(*n*) alms, conc⟨⟩dout, hon-
favor, freebie ⟨⟩esent, pre-
giveaway (in⟨⟩ tuffer, tip
orarium, lar⟨⟩
sentation, s⟨⟩

439 ⟨⟩
He who ⟨⟩e prize
⟨⟩ of trut⟨⟩tion,
(*n*) dis-
⟨⟩cor⟨⟩rk,
⟨⟩tiss,

---

440 Bribes

Richer than doing nothing for a bribe,⟨⟩ unpaid-for silk. **William Shakespeare**

(*n*) baksheesh, bribe, carrot, in⟨⟩ payoff (*informal*), payola (*informal*)

441 Sell

Money demands that you sell, not you⟨⟩ stupidity, but your talent to their reaso⟨⟩

(*v*) bill, bring out, cash in, deal, ⟨⟩ hustle (*slang*), invoice, knock dow⟨⟩ market, merchandise, outsell, p⟨⟩ (*formal*), push (*slang*), put on th⟨⟩ tout, trade, vend

442 Sellers

Every one lives by selling something. ⟨⟩

(*n*) hawker, *huckster*, merchant, ⟨⟩ veyor (*formal*), pusher (*slang*), re⟨⟩ *sales manager*, salesperson, *sales*⟨⟩ representative, seller, *shop assista*⟨⟩ storekeeper, *street trader* (*UK*), s⟨⟩ vendor

See also PURCHASER (424)

443 Sales and Shows

Pile it high, sell it cheap. **Jack Cohen**

(*n*) auction, *car boot sale* (*UK*), ⟨⟩ garage sale, jumble sale (*UK*), p⟨⟩ sale, sale, show, *trade event*, tr⟨⟩ wholesaler, *yard sale*

444 Possess

The metaphor is probably the most fe⟨⟩ man. **José Ortega y Gasset**

(*n*) claim, entitlement, occupa⟨⟩ ⟨po⟩ssion, title

445 ⟨⟩boast, comprise, consist, ⟨⟩
⟨po⟩ss, enjoy, have, h⟨⟩
The great curse of our modern society⟨⟩
of money as the fact that the lack of n⟨⟩
to a squalid and incomplete existence.
(*adj*) bereft, deficient, deprived⟨⟩
handed, intestate, needful (*formal*)⟨⟩
starved of, stripped of
(*prep*) failing, minus, wanting

446 Owners

When I buy pictures/. . .I look at that of which⟨⟩ myself as the imaginary possessor. **Marianne**⟨⟩

(*n*) bearer, beneficiary, freeholder, hold⟨⟩ landholder, landlady, landlord, landown⟨⟩ mistress, owner, possessor, property owne⟨⟩ recipient, titleholder

---

447 ⟨⟩
There ⟨⟩
than ⟨⟩
(*v*) f⟨⟩
miss ⟨⟩
See a⟨⟩

448 ⟨⟩
It is b⟨⟩
(*n*) ⟨⟩
chan⟨⟩
swap⟨⟩
fer, *tr*⟨⟩
trans⟨⟩
(*v*) ⟨⟩
hock ⟨⟩
(*infor*⟨⟩
See a⟨⟩

449 ⟨⟩
Easy ⟨⟩
do fo⟨⟩
(*n*) a⟨⟩
ance, ⟨⟩
(*v*) a⟨⟩
decli⟨⟩
forgo⟨⟩
go w⟨⟩
relin⟨⟩
spare⟨⟩
tighte⟨⟩
nose ⟨⟩
See ⟨⟩
PEOPL⟨⟩

450 ⟨⟩
Words⟨⟩
mone⟨⟩
(*n*) a⟨⟩
(*v*) a⟨⟩
for, s⟨⟩

45⟨⟩
You⟨⟩
glad⟨⟩
(*v*) ⟨⟩
as⟨⟩
(*i*⟨⟩
de⟨⟩
w⟨⟩
c⟨⟩
b⟨⟩
⟨⟩

Lose and Forfeit

...are occasions when it is undoubtedly better to incur loss ...o make gain. **Plautus**

...rfeit, let slip, lose, lose track of, mislay, misplace, ...ut, miss the boat, molt

...lso GET RID OF SOMETHING (451)

Exchange and Interchange

...est not to swap horses in mid-stream. **Abraham Lincoln**

...ross-fertilization, deal, exchange, handover, inter-
...e, quid pro quo, redemption, referral, rotation,
...(*informal*), switch, trade-in, tradeoff, traffic, trans-
...ansferal, transference, *transmittal*, transmittance,
...osal, transposition, turnover

...hange, change around, cross-fertilize, exchange,
...(*slang*), interchange, redeem, replace, rotate, swap
...mal), take back, trade, trade in, traffic, transpose

...lso CHANGE ONE THING FOR ANOTHER (398)

Forgo and Deny Oneself

...or nuns to talk about giving up things. That's what they ...a living. **Garrison Keillor**

...bdication, abjuration, abnegation (*formal*), avoid-
...rrenunciation, sacrifice, waiver

...dicate, abjure (*literary*), abnegate (*formal*), cut out,
...e, deny, disown, do without, economize, forfeit,
...forsake, forswear (*archaic or literary*), give up,
...ithout, keep off, kick (*informal*), miss, *pass up*,
...quish, renounce, sacrifice, scrimp, skimp, sniff at,
...stint on, surrender, swear off, throw up (*informal*),
...en your belt, turn away from, turn down, turn your
...up at, waive

...lso DENY AND REJECT (644), SELF-DENIAL (882), ASCETIC
...E (883)

Accept Possession

...are the tokens current and ...ys are for values. **Franci...**

...ion, take-up

...cceptance, recoi..., ...ume, bear, embrace, receive, settle
...ccept, adopt, ... back, take in, welcome
...houlder, take

Get Rid of Something

*...ve got the brain of a four-year-old boy, and I bet he ...
...to get rid of it.* **Groucho Marx**

...abandon, act out, banish, bin (UK), bo...
...e, cast away, cast off, cast out (for...
...formal), chuck out (*informal*), clean up ...
...molish (*informal*), deselect, discard, ...
...th, dispose of, dump, eject, elimina...
...e, get free of, get rid of, jettison, ju...
...hind, lose, offload, *palm off*, purge, r...
...p up, stamp out, throw away, throw off, ...

...ee also REMOVE SOMETHING (338), LOSE AND FORFEIT (4...

452   Abolish and Annul

We all know that books burn—yet...no force can abolish memory. **Franklin D. Roosevelt**

(*v*) abolish, abrogate (*formal*), annul, cancel, do away with, invalidate, nullify, override, overrule, overturn, quash, repeal, rescind, reverse, revoke, scrap, scratch, scrub (*informal*), undo, void

453   Store and Keep

To expect a man to retain everything that he has ever read is like expecting him to carry about in his body everything that he has ever eaten. **Arthur Schopenhauer**

(*n*) keeping, retention, storage, stowage

(*v*) bank, cache, carry, cling, collect, compile, conserve, heap up, hive, hoard, hold back, hold down (*informal*), hold onto, keep, keep back, lock away, preserve, put aside, put away, put by, reserve, retain, salt away, save, set apart, set aside, squirrel, *squirrel away*, stash (*informal*), *stash away*, stock, stockpile, stock up, *stock up on*, store, store up, stow, withhold

See also STORES AND STORAGE BUILDINGS (1088)

454   People Who Collect Thi...

*I am a sort of collector of religions...
that I find I can believe in them...*

(*n*) accumulator, bea...
magpie (*informal*), ...omprehend (*formal*),
...house, seat, take

455   ...on and Search

The va... a kingdom. **John Milton**
Zhua...

(*v*) ...comb, delve (*archaic*), dredge,
...rret out, fish, forage, frisk,
...rope, grub, hunt, forage, hunt down,
...nose around (*informal*), poke,
...rest, rake, ransack, rifle, root,
...fer, scavenge, scour, scout, scout
...fu...search through, seek, seek out,
...n out

...forage, hunt, pursuit, quest,

...ssion by Persuasion

...ds. **F. Scott Fitzgerald**
...icit, finagle (*informal*),
...raise, scrounge (*informal*), fish
...winkle out (UK),

...embarrass the superior, and
...orge Bernard Shaw
...investment (*formal*), nom-
...promotion, reelection, res-

(v) appoint, assign, beatify, canonize, commission, contract, co-opt, decorate, designate, dignify, elect, elevate, enthrone (*formal*), hire, inaugurate, induct, install, instate, invest (*formal*), make, name, nominate, *ordain*, place, promote, reelect, reinstate, sign, sign up, swear in, take on, tap, upgrade

459 Revoke Status

Modern heretics are not burned at the stake. They are relegated to backwaters or pressured to resign. **Art Kleiner**

(n) demotion, deposition, disenfranchisement, dismissal, relegation, sack (*informal*), sacking (*informal*)

(v) ax (*informal*), blacklist, can (*slang*), cashier, decommission, defrock, demote, depose, dethrone, discharge, disenfranchise, disinherit, dismiss, displace, downgrade, expel, *give notice*, *give somebody their cards* (*UK*), *give the boot* (*informal*), *give the heave ho* (*informal*), *give the sack* (*informal*), idle, lay off, *make redundant* (*UK*), *reduce to the ranks*, relegate, relieve, sack (*informal*), send down (*UK*), sideline, terminate, topple, unmake, unseat

See also EJECT AND EXCLUDE (340)

460 Income

There are few sorrows, however poignant, in which a good income is of no avail. **Logan Pearsall Smith**

(n) allowance, annuity, bread and butter, bursary, commission, earnings, emolument (*formal or humorous*), exhibition (*UK*), fee, gain, gate, *gross revenue*, harvest, income, jackpot, livelihood, living, means, *net income*, pay, payback, paycheck, pay envelope, payment, payoff (*informal*), payout, proceeds, profit, purse, remuneration, return, returns, revenue, royalty, salary, stipend, take, take-home pay, takings, wage, wage packet (*UK*), wages, winnings, yield

See also FINANCIAL ASSETS (462), MONEY (797)

461 Possessions

Why grab possessions like thieves, or divide them like socialists, when you can ignore them like wise men?
Natalie Clifford Barney

(n) asset, baggage, bags, belongings, bits and pieces (*informal*), chattels, effects (*formal*), freehold, gear (*informal*), goods, *goods and chattels*, holding, kit, paraphernalia, *personal belongings*, personal effects, *personal possessions*, *personal property*, possessions, property, real estate, realty, status symbol, stores, stuff, things, wherewithal, worldly goods, worth

462 Financial Assets

And, as their wealth increaseth, so enclose/Infinite riches in a little room. **Christopher Marlowe**

(n) assets, bullion, capital, coffers, estate, finances, fortune, gold, *liquid assets*, liquidity, mammon, money, reserves, resources, riches, savings, treasure, wealth

See also INCOME (460), MONEY (797)

463 Find

What the superior man seeks is in himself. What the mean man seeks is in others. **Confucius**

(n) acquisition, detection, discovery, find, procurement, uncovering

(v) catch, chance on, come across, come upon, dig out, dig up (*informal*), discover, excavate, ferret out, find, find out, *happen on*, *happen upon*, home in, localize, locate, look up, pin down, pinpoint, root out, search out, sniff out (*informal*), source, spy out, strike, stumble, *stumble across*, *stumble on*, *stumble upon*, trace, track down, turn up, uncover, unearth, zoom in

464 Need and Require

It is necessary to assume something which is necessary of itself, and has no cause of its necessity outside itself...is rather the cause of necessity in other things. **Thomas Aquinas**

(v) demand, have, *have need of*, involve, lack, must, necessitate, need, require, should, take, want, warrant

See also MOST IMPORTANT THING (197)

465 Owe and Deserve

I owe a duty, where I cannot love. **Aphra Behn**

(adj) due, in line for, outstanding, owed, owing, payable, unpaid

(n) amortization, arrears, debt, default, *gearing* (*UK*), *leverage*

(v) default, deserve, earn, fall behind, merit, owe

466 Gamble and Take Risks

Life is a gamble, at terrible odds—if it was a bet, you wouldn't take it. **Tom Stoppard**

(n) ante, bet, cardsharping, chance, gamble, gambling, lottery, odds, punt (*UK*), raffle, stake, stakes, *sweeps* (*informal*), sweepstakes, tombola (*UK*), wager

(v) bet, challenge, chance, *cut it close*, dare, dice, dice with death, gamble, hazard, *lay a wager*, lay bets, outbid, *put money on*, risk, run a risk, speculate, stake, take a chance, take a gamble, wager, walk a tightrope

Using and Functioning

467 Use

O, it is excellent/To have a giant's strength! But it is tyrannous/To use it like a giant. **William Shakespeare**

(n) appliance, application, deployment, exercise (*formal*), exploitation, handling, manipulation, operating, operation, usage, use, user, utilization

(v) apply, control, deploy, draw on, employ, exercise, exert, handle, harness, make use of, manipulate, ply, *put to use*, resort to, run, use, utilize, wield

468 Use Tools and Machinery

If you are an anvil, bear the strokes; if you become a hammer, strike. **Lebanese proverb**

(v) dig, drive, file, fire, fire up, fuel, hammer, hoe, log in, log off, log on, log out, man, open up, pitchfork, plow, rake, rasp, saw, scoop, scythe, shoot, shovel, solder, spade, start up, test-drive, till, tunnel, upshift, use

469   Function Successfully

Get on with it, keep moving, keep in/. . .keep it moving as fast as you/can. **Charles Olson**

(*v*) act, function, go, idle, operate, serve, take, work

470   Fail or Cease to Function

Honorable errors do not count as failures in science, but as seeds for progress. **Stephen Jay Gould**

(*v*) act up, break, break down, conk out (*informal*), crack, crack up (*informal*), crash, die, fail, give out, *go awry*, *go dead*, *go haywire* (*informal*), *go on the blink* (*informal*), *grind to a halt*, jam, labor, malfunction, play up (*UK*), seize up, snarl up (*UK*), stall, *stop dead*, stop working

471   Misuse and Abuse

The greater the power, the more dangerous the abuse. **Edmund Burke**

(*n*) abuse, exploitation, malpractice, manipulation, misapplication, mismanagement, misrule, misuse, monopolization, perversion

(*v*) abuse, corrupt, exploit, *meddle with*, mess around (*informal*), misapply, misdirect, *misemploy*, mishandle, mismanage, misspend, mistreat, misuse, pollute, prey on, profiteer, stain, take advantage of somebody, use, wrong

472   Mess Up and Make Mistakes

Great men too make mistakes, and many among them do it so often that one is almost tempted to call them little men. **Georg Christoph Lichtenberg**

(*v*) blunder, botch, *botch up*, bungle (*informal*), butcher (*informal*), err, *flub* (*slang*), fluff (*informal*), *fluff up*, *foul up* (*informal*), fumble, goof (*informal*), go wrong, make a dog's breakfast/dinner of (*UK*), make a hash of (*informal*), make a mess of, *make a mistake*, *make a pig's ear of* (*UK*), mess up (*informal*), mishandle, mishit, mistime, muck up (*informal*), muff, slip up (*informal*)

See also MISTAKES (250), CREATE DISORDER AND CAUSE CHAOS (358)

473   Make Good Use of Something

The ass will carry his load, but not a double load; ride not a free horse to death. **Miguel de Cervantes**

(*v*) avail yourself, capitalize on, cash in on, develop, exploit, get the most out of, make the most of, maximize, milk (*informal*), put to good use, recycle, reprocess, reuse, take advantage of something, tap (*informal*), use

See also ECONOMICAL AND RESOURCEFUL (207)

474   Use Up and Waste

Time waste differs from material waste in that there can be no salvage. **Henry Ford**

(*n*) consumption, overuse, use

(*v*) bleed (*informal*), bleed dry (*informal*), blow (*slang*), burn, consume, deplete, dispose of (*formal*), drain, eat into, eat up, exhaust, expend, finish, finish off, fritter away, gamble away, get through, gobble (*informal humorous*), go through, guzzle (*informal*), idle away, lose, run through, sell out, spend, squander, *suck dry*, *suck the life out of*, take up, throw away, use, use up, waste, wear out, while away, whittle away

See also WASTEFUL AND UNECONOMICAL (246)

People and their Way of Life

Qualities and Characteristics

475 People's Physical Appearance

A man who looks a part has the soul of that part.
Guy de Maupassant

(*adj*) attractive, beautiful, bonny, boyish, cherubic, comely (*archaic or literary*), cute, dishy (*informal*), fair, fetching, *gamine*, girlish, good-looking, handsome, hunky (*informal*), ill-favored, nice-looking, photogenic, plain, prepossessing (*formal*), pretty, ravishing, striking, unprepossessing, well-preserved, *young-looking*, youthful

(*n*) attractiveness, comeliness (*archaic or literary*), girlishness, good looks, loveliness, prettiness, youthfulness

See also BEAUTY AND ATTRACTIVENESS (189), UGLINESS AND UNATTRACTIVENESS (233)

476 Agility of the Body

I have the body of a man half my age. Unfortunately, he's in terrible shape. **George Foreman**

(*adj*) acrobatic, *all fingers and thumbs* (UK), *all thumbs*, athletic, awkward, *butterfingered* (*informal*), double-jointed, elephantine, feline, gawky (*informal*), graceful, graceless, gymnastic, heavy-handed, inelegant, light, light-footed, limber, lissom, lithe, lithesome (*archaic or literary*), loose-limbed, lumbering, lumpy, mincing, nimble, supple, uncoordinated, ungainly, ungraceful

(*adv*) awkwardly, lightly, woodenly

(*n*) agility, athleticism, awkwardness, clumsiness, *gaucherie*, gawkiness (*informal*), gracelessness, heavy-handedness, inelegance, lightness, *litheness*, nimbleness, suppleness, ungainliness, woodenness

See also DESCRIBING BODY MOVEMENTS (288)

477 Build

Of physiology from top to toe I sing. **Walt Whitman**

(*adj*) angular, bandy-legged, *barrel-chested*, birdlike, bony, bowlegged, burly, butch, buxom (*humorous*), cadaverous, chubby, chunky (*informal*), corpulent, curvaceous, elfin, emaciated, fat, fleshy, full, gangling, gangly, gaunt, gross, heavyset, hefty, husky, lanky, large, lean, *leggy*, lissom, matronly, obese, overweight, paunchy, pear-shaped, petite, pigeon-breasted, plump, podgy (UK), portly, *potbellied*, pudgy (*informal*), puny, rangy, *rawboned*, reedy, rotund, round-shouldered, scraggy, scrawny, sexy, shapely, sinewy, skeletal, *skin-and-bone, skin and bones*, skinny, slender, slight, slim, *small-boned*, spidery, spindly, squat, stalwart, statuesque, stocky, *stooped, stooping*, stout, strapping (*informal*), strong, stubby, stumpy, sturdy, svelte, sylphlike, thickset, thin, trim, tubby (*informal*), underfed, undernourished, underweight, *voluptuous*, *waiflike*, wasted, weak, well-built, well-developed, well-fed, well-rounded, willowy, *wraithlike*

(*n*) angularity, *boniness*, *brawniness*, burliness, chubbiness, *chunkiness* (*informal*), corpulence, *dumpiness*, emaciation, fatness, fleshiness, fullness, gauntness, *lankiness*, obesity, plumpness, *podginess* (UK), portliness, *pudginess* (*informal*), *ranginess*, rotundity, *rotundness*, roundness, ruggedness, scragginess, scrawniness, skinniness, slenderness, slimness, *squatness*, stature, *stockiness*, stoutness, *svelteness*, thinness, tubbiness (*informal*)

See also BODY (691), HEIGHT: HIGH (1203), HEIGHT: LOW (1204), WEIGHT: HEAVY (1205), WEIGHT: LIGHT (1206), SHAPE (1216)

478 Extra Weight

I have tried to remove weight, sometimes from people, sometimes from heavenly bodies, sometimes from cities.
Italo Calvino

(*n*) *beer belly* (*slang*), *beer gut* (*slang*), flab, *love handles* (*informal*), paunch, pot (*informal*), *potbelly*

479 Muscles and Musculature

The brain has muscles for thinking as the legs have muscles for walking. **Julien Offroy de La Mettrie**

(*adj*) beefy, brawny, bullish, bullnecked, flabby (*informal*), meaty, *muscly*, muscular, powerful, wiry

(*n*) beefiness, brawn, flabbiness (*informal*), *muscularity*, sinew (*literary*), wiriness

See also THE MUSCLES (718)

480 Complexion

His complexion was the sort you find in those who suffer from piles...but there's nothing anyone can do about that: the Petersburg climate is to blame. **Nikolay Gogol**

(*adj*) acned, ashen, bloodless, blotchy, blowzy, bronzed, brown, cadaverous (*literary*), chalky, clear, deathlike, florid, flushed, freckled, *freckly*, ghastly (*literary*), glowing, *olive-skinned*, pale, pallid, pasty, pasty-faced, *pimpled*, pimply, pink, red-faced, rosy, rubicund (*literary*), ruddy, rugged, sallow, spotty (UK), suntanned, swarthy, tan, tanned, wan, washed-out, waxen, white, *white as a sheet*, wholesome

(*n*) coloring, complexion, freckle, pallor, *pastiness*, redness, rosiness, ruddiness, ruggedness, *sallowness*, *skin color*, skin tone, tan, *wanness*, whiteness, wholesomeness

See also THE SKIN (720)

481 Facial Characteristics

My face looks like a wedding cake left out in the rain.
W. H. Auden

(*adj*) baby-faced, beady (*informal*), *button-nosed*, chiseled, craggy, dimpled, fresh-faced, haggard, lined, lived-in, owlish, *owl-like*, pinched, popeyed, *pug-nosed*, snub-nosed, sunken, wizened, wrinkled, wrinkly

(*n*) crease, crow's foot, dimple, feature, lineament (*literary*)

See also FACIAL HAIR (489), PARTS OF THE BODY: HEAD (692)

482 Well-groomed

A man who's active and incisive/can yet keep nail-care much in mind. **Alexander Pushkin**

(*adj*) chic, clean-cut, dandified, *dandyish* (*dated*), dapper, dashing, debonair, elegant, fashion-conscious, foppish, glamorous, natty, presentable, rakish, sartorial, smart, *smartly dressed*, snappy (*informal*), snazzy (*informal*), soigné, spruce, stylish, tidy, well-dressed, well-groomed, *well-presented*, well-turned-out

(*adv*) fashionably, gracefully, smartly

(*n*) chic, daintiness, dress sense, elegance, glamour, glitz, glitziness, grace, smartness, *snazziness* (*informal*), style, stylishness

See also DRESS, WEAR, AND UNDRESS (868), DESCRIBING CLOTHES (869)

483 Badly Groomed

The elect, the elected...they come here bright as dimes,/and die dishevelled and soft. **Robert Lowell**

(*adj*) bedraggled, blowzy, disheveled, dowdy, frowzy, *frumpy*, raddled, ragged, raggedy, ragtag, ratty (*informal*), scraggly, scruffy, shabby, *slatternly*, slovenly, untidy, wild

(*adv*) dowdily, raggedly, rattily (*informal*)

(*n*) dowdiness, *frumpiness*, raggedness, shabbiness, *slovenliness*

See also DRESS, WEAR, AND UNDRESS (868), DESCRIBING CLOTHES (869)

484 Hair

When a woman isn't beautiful, people always say, "You have lovely eyes, you have lovely hair." **Anton Chekhov**

(*n*) curl, fuzz, hair, hairiness, *hirsuteness*, lock, mane (*literary or informal*), ringlet, ringlets, shagginess, tendril (*literary*), thatch, tress, tresses

485 Hair Color

Only God, my dear,/Could love you for yourself alone/And not your yellow hair. **W. B. Yeats**

(*adj*) blond, brunette, carroty, *chestnut-haired*, dark, fair, fair-haired, flaxen, *golden-haired*, hoary, redheaded, *tow-headed*, white

486 Describing Hair

'Tis the voice of the lobster; I heard him declare,/"You have baked me too brown, I must sugar my hair." **Lewis Carroll**

(*adj*) *backcombed* (*UK*), bouffant, bushy, clipped, close-cropped, *crimped*, cropped, flyaway, *frizzed*, frizzy, fuzzy, hairy, hirsute, lank, *relaxed*, shaggy, straggly, *teased*, tousled, unkempt, *unshorn*

487 Baldness and Balding

According to the doctors, I'm only suffering from a light form of premature baldness. **Federico Fellini**

(*adj*) bald, *bald as a coot*, baldheaded, balding, hairless, *thin on top*, tonsured

(*n*) baldness

488 Hairstyles and Hairpieces

Very hard for a man with a wig to keep order. **Evelyn Waugh**

(*n*) coiffure (*formal*), haircut, hairdo (*informal*), hairdressing, *hairpiece*, hairstyle, periwig, rug (*informal*), toupee, wig

types of hairstyles Afro, bangs, beehive, big hair (*informal*), bob, bouffant, braids, bun, buzz cut, chignon, cornrow, cowlick, crew cut, crop, dreadlocks, flat top, French twist, mohawk, mullet, pageboy, pigtail, plait, pompadour, ponytail, ringlet, topknot

489 Facial Hair

Old men and comets have been reverenced for the same reason; their long beards, and pretenses to foretell events.
Jonathan Swift

(*adj*) bearded, *beardless*, *bewhiskered*, clean-shaven, *shaved*, *shaven*, smooth-shaven, *stubbly*, unshaven, *whiskery*

(*n*) beard, bristle, *facial hair*, five o'clock shadow, *goatee*, *handlebar mustache*, mustache, *muttonchops*, *pencil mustache*, sideburns, stubble, *walrus mustache*, whiskers

See also FACIAL CHARACTERISTICS (481)

490 Makeup and Beauty Products

You can now see the Female Eunuch the world over...Wherever you see nail varnish, lipstick, brassieres, and high heels, the Eunuch has set up her camp. **Germaine Greer**

(*n*) blusher (*UK*), cleanser, *eye pencil*, face pack, facial, *greasepaint*, *makeup remover*, moisturizer, mouthwash, mudpack

types of cosmetics beauty product, blush, concealer, eyeliner, eye shadow, face powder, foundation, greasepaint, kohl, lip pencil, lipstick, makeup, maquillage, mascara, nail polish, powder, rouge (*dated*)

491 Personal Hygiene

Every Englishman's home is his hospital, particularly the bathroom. **Oliver St. John Gogarty**

(*n*) *aftershave*, attar, *body mist*, *body spray*, *breath freshener*, cologne, deodorant, eau de cologne, *eau de toilette*, fragrance, loofa, patchouli, pedicure, perfume, *personal hygiene*, scent, *shampoo*, *shaving cream*, *skincare product*, *styling gel*, *styling spray*, *sunblock*, *sun lotion*, sunscreen, suntan lotion, *suntan oil*, toilet (*formal*), toiletry, toilette (*literary*), toilet water, toner, *toothpaste*

492 Temperament and Behavior

He who lacks temperament must look for ornament. **Karl Kraus**

(*n*) affectation, animus, antics, attitude, bearing, bedside manner, behavior, carriage (*formal*), character, comportment (*formal*), conduct, delivery, demeanor, deportment, disposition, eccentricity, gait, habit, heart, identity, instinct, makeup, manner, manners, mien (*formal*), nature, person (*formal*), persona, personality, poise, pose, position, posture, predisposition, presence, propensity, public image, spirit, stance, streak, temper, temperament, tendency, walk, ways

493 Personal Eccentricities

Cultivate only the habits that you are willing should master you. **Elbert Hubbard**

(*n*) distinction, eccentricity, foible, idiosyncrasy, oddity, particularity, quirk, trademark, trick, whimsicality, whimsy

494 Friendliness and Sociability

Society is no comfort/To one not sociable. **William Shakespeare**

(*adj*) accessible, affable, affectionate, agreeable, amiable, approachable, brotherly, charitable, chummy (*informal*), close, companionable, comradely, congenial, convivial, cordial, demonstrative, easygoing, extrovert, fraternal, friendly, genial, good-natured, gregarious, hospitable, likable, loving, matey (*UK*), open, outgoing, peaceable, peaceful, *peace-loving*, personable, pleasant, receptive, responsive, sociable, sympathetic, touchy-feely (*informal*), warm

(*adv*) familiarly, peaceably, receptively, warmly

(*n*) affability, amiability, approachability, bonhomie, companionability, conviviality, cordiality, extroversion, familiarity, fraternity, friendliness, geniality, *good-naturedness*, gregariousness, hospitality, *matiness* (*UK*), neighborliness, pleasantness, receptiveness, receptivity, responsiveness, sociability, warmth

495 Generosity and Kindness

I must be cruel only to be kind. **William Shakespeare**

(*adj*) altruistic, attentive, beneficent, benevolent, benign, big-hearted, bounteous (*literary*), bountiful (*literary*), careful, caring, charitable, compassionate, considerate, consoling, devoted, fatherly, fond, forgiving, freehanded, generous, gentle, goodhearted, humane, indulgent, kind, kindhearted, kindly, large-hearted, lenient, long-suffering, magnanimous, maternal, merciful, mild, motherly, munificent, nice, openhanded, openhearted, philanthropic, pitying, public-spirited, remissive, selfless, self-sacrificing, sensitive, soft, soft-boiled, soft-hearted, solicitous, supportive, sweet, sympathetic, tender, tenderhearted, thoughtful, understanding, unselfish, unsparing, unstinting, warm-hearted, well-intentioned, well-meaning, well-meant

(*adv*) devotedly, generously, kindly, maternally, mildly, softly, sweetly, tenderly, warmly

(*n*) altruism, beneficence, benignity, consideration, fatherliness, forbearance (*formal*), generosity, gentleness, helpfulness, humanity, kindheartedness, kindliness, kindness, largesse, laxity, lenience, leniency, magnanimity, mellowness, *mercifulness*, munificence, openhandedness, openheartedness, selflessness, self-sac-

rifice, sensitivity, *soft-heartedness*, solicitousness, solicitude, sweetness, tenderheartedness, tenderness, thoughtfulness, unselfishness, warm-heartedness, warmness

496 Energy and Enthusiasm

Nothing is so contagious as enthusiasm...It is the genius of sincerity and truth accomplishes no victories without it.
Bulwer Lytton

(*adj*) abuzz, active, alive, boisterous, bouncy, devoted, dynamic, ebullient, effervescent, energetic, exuberant, fanatic, fanatical, feisty (*informal*), frisky, frolicsome, full of beans (*informal*), full of life, go-getting (*informal*), gung ho (*informal*), hands-on, hearty, high-spirited, irrepressible, keen, kittenish, lively, mettlesome, motivated, overenthusiastic, peppy (*informal*), perky, playful, proactive, rambunctious, sassy, self-motivated, sparky, spirited, strong, tireless, vigorous, vital, vivacious, warm-blooded, youthful, zealous, zestful

(*adv*) keenly, overtime

(*n*) activeness, alertness, animation, boisterousness, bounciness, brio (*literary*), dash, dedication, devotion, drive, dynamism, ebullience, effervescence, élan (*literary*), energy, expansiveness, *feistiness* (*informal*), friskiness, get-up-and-go (*informal*), go, heartiness, jazz (*slang*), keenness, life, liveliness, oomph, pep (*informal*), perkiness, pizzazz (*informal*), playfulness, punch, punchiness, sap, sassiness, sparkle, *spiritedness*, tirelessness, vehemence, vigor, vitality, *vivaciousness*, vivacity, youthfulness

See also POSITIVE IMPATIENCE, ENTHUSIASM, AND ALERTNESS (537), ENTHUSIASTIC AND INQUISITIVE (628)

497 Naturalness

First feelings are always the most natural. **Louis XIV**

(*adj*) artless, folksy, guileless, just-folks (*informal*), modest, naive, natural, self-effacing, simple, sincere, unaffected, unassuming, unmannered, unpretentious, unsophisticated, unspoiled, unstudied

(*adv*) naturally, simply, sincerely, unaffectedly, unsophisticatedly

(*n*) artlessness, *guilelessness*, ingenuousness, naiveté, naturalness, simplicity, spontaneity, unaffectedness, *unassumingness*, unpretentiousness

See also HONEST AND OPEN (630)

498 Courage

Real nobility is based on scorn, courage, and profound indifference. **Albert Camus**

(*adj*) adventuresome, adventurous, audacious, bold, brave, courageous, daredevil, daring, dashing (*dated*), dauntless (*literary*), doughty (*archaic*), fearless, gallant (*literary*), game, gritty, gutsy (*informal*), heroic, intrepid, lionhearted, manful, nervy (*informal*), plucky, scrappy (*informal*), spunky (*informal*), stalwart, stout, stouthearted, swashbuckling, valiant, valorous, venturesome (*formal*)

(*adv*) boldly, daringly, dashingly, gamely, *without fear*

(*n*) audaciousness, audacity, backbone, boldness, bravery, bravura, daring, *dauntlessness* (*literary*), derring-do (*dated*), fearlessness, fiber, fortitude, gallantry (*literary*), grit, gumption (*informal*), guts (*slang*), heart, heroics, heroism, *intrepidity*, *lionheartedness*, manhood, mettle, nerve, pluck, pluckiness, prowess, spunk (*informal*), *stouteheartedness*, stoutness, *valiantness*, valor

499 Confidence and Composure

Confidence and hope do more good than physic. **Galen**

(*adj*) assertive, assured, balanced, bold, *bold as brass* (*UK*), can-do (*informal*), confident, controlled, crisp, dignified, equable, even-tempered, imperturbable, level-headed, mellow, patient, poised, presidential, secure, sedate, self-assertive, self-assured, self-confident, self-possessed, sober, steady, sure of yourself, temperate, unflappable, unhesitating, well-adjusted

(*adv*) boldly, equably, levelly, patiently, presidentially, surely, temperately

(*n*) *amour-propre* (*formal*), aplomb, assertiveness, assurance, authoritativeness, boldness, chutzpah (*informal*), confidence, dignity, discretion, flair, *imperturbability*, level-headedness, panache, patience, phlegm, poise, presence of mind, pride, restraint, sang-froid, security, sedateness, self-assurance, *self-assuredness*, self-confidence, self-possession, self-regard, self-respect, self-worth, sobriety, steadiness, *temperateness*, tranquillity, unflappability

See also COOL AND CALM (536), SOOTHE AND CALM (573)

500 Hard-Working and Committed

I have nothing to offer but blood, toil, tears, and sweat. **Winston Churchill**

(*adj*) ambitious, aspirational, assiduous, businesslike, busy, careerist, committed, conscientious, constant, dedicated, devoted, diligent, driven, dutiful, efficient, faithful, *hard-working*, idealistic, industrious, meticulous, organized, painstaking, precise, punctilious, scrupulous, sedulous (*literary*), *self-starting*, stalwart, staunch, steadfast, studious, undeviating, unfaltering, unflagging, unflinching

(*adv*) ambitiously, dedicatedly, devotedly, faithfully, microscopically, stalwartly, studiously

(*n*) application, assiduity, assiduousness, careerism, carefulness, commitment, constancy, diligence, efficiency, endurance, fastidiousness, firmness, idealism, industriousness, industry (*formal or literary*), insistence, meticulousness, punctiliousness, purposefulness, scrupulousness, *sedulity* (*literary*), *sedulousness* (*literary*), steadfastness, studiousness

See also HARD WORK OR EFFORT (298), STRENGTH OF WILL (501)

501 Strength of Will

There is no such thing as a great talent without great willpower. **Honoré de Balzac**

(*adj*) determined, forbearing (*formal*), indefatigable, indomitable, insistent, iron, patient, persevering, persistent, pertinacious, pressing, resilient, resolute, resolved, *self-controlled*, *self-disciplined*, single-minded, steely, stoic, strenuous, strong-minded, strong-willed, stubborn, sturdy, tenacious, tough-minded, unswerving, untiring, unwavering, unwearied, unyielding

(*n*) determination, discipline, endurance, *indomitability*, patience, perseverance, persistence, resilience, resoluteness, resolution, resolve, self-control, self-discipline,

self-restraint, single-mindedness, spirit, stamina, staying power, stoicism, *strength of character*, strength of mind, *strength of will*, strong-mindedness, stubbornness, sufferance, temperance, *tenaciousness*, vigor, will, willpower

See also STRENGTH (201), HARD-WORKING AND COMMITTED (500)

502 Honest and Reliable

An honest God's the noblest work of man. **Samuel Butler**

(*adj*) above reproach, above suspicion, authoritative, confidential, conscientious, dependable, fast, genuine, high-minded, incorruptible, just, loyal, on the level (*informal*), orderly, real, reliable, religious, responsible, safe, scrupulous, sincere, solid, standup (*informal*), steadfast, straight, sure, true, true-blue, trustworthy, trusty, truthful, veracious, warm

(*adv*) religiously, seriously, sincerely, truthfully

(*n*) conscientiousness, dependability, faithfulness, frankness, honesty, *incorruptibility*, loyalty, reliability, scrupulousness, seriousness, steadfastness, trustworthiness, truth, truthfulness, veracity

See also HONEST AND OPEN (630), MORALLY GOOD (774)

503 Cheerfulness of Outlook

An optimist, in the atomic age, thinks the future is uncertain. **Russell M. Crouse**

(*adj*) blithe (*literary*), breezy, bright, *bright-eyed and bushy-tailed*, bubbly, constructive, freewheeling, frivolous, fun-loving, giggly, happy-go-lucky, jolly, jovial, optimistic, pert, positive, puckish, risible (*formal*), sunny, *sweet-tempered*, uncomplaining

(*adv*) frivolously, pertly, positively, sunnily

(*n*) *blitheness* (*literary*), breeziness, *bubbliness*, buoyancy, *chirpiness* (*informal*), exuberance, frivolity, humor, joviality, optimism, pertness, risibility (*formal*), *sense of humor*

See also ENTHUSIASTIC AND INQUISITIVE (628)

504 Unfriendliness and Unsociability

A little disdain is not amiss; a little scorn is alluring. **William Congreve**

(*adj*) aloof, antisocial, chilly, clannish, cliquey, closed, cold, compassionless, cozy, elitist, frigid, frosty, icy, inhospitable, misanthropic, remote, solitary, standoffish, unapproachable, uncongenial, unfriendly, unsociable, unwelcoming

(*n*) aloofness, austerity, dourness, frigidity, frostiness, iciness, misanthropy, mischievousness (*formal*), remoteness, reservation, *standoffishness*, *unapproachability*, unfriendliness

See also BAD MANNERS AND SOCIAL SKILLS (521), RUDE AND HOSTILE (625)

505 Selfish and Unkind

The cruelty of most people is lack of imagination, their brutality is ignorance. **Kurt Tucholsky**

(*adj*) antisocial, bloodsucking, brutal, brutish, callous, charmless, cold-blooded, cold-hearted, cruel, cutthroat, egocentric, egoistic, *egoistical*, *egotistic*, *egotistical*, flinty, ghoulish, hard, *hard as nails*, hard-bitten, hard-boiled (*informal*), hardened, hardhearted, *hard-nosed* (*informal*), harsh, heartless, inconsiderate, inhuman, insensate (*literary*), insensitive, intolerant, judgmental, loveless, malicious, malignant, mean, *mean-minded*, mean-spirited, merciless, mischievous (*formal*), nasty, obdurate, parasitic, petty, piggish, pitiless, possessive, predatory, relentless, remorseless, ruthless, sanguinary (*formal*), savage, self-absorbed, self-centered, self-indulgent, self-interested, selfish, self-obsessed, self-regarding, self-seeking, self-serving, shabby, shoddy, spiteful, stinky, stony, stony-hearted, thoughtless, uncharitable, unfeeling, unforgiving, ungenerous, unkind, unmerciful, *unpitying*, unpleasant, unsparing, unsympathetic, vindictive, viperish, wanton

(*adv*) brutishly, cruelly, insensitively, intolerantly, malignantly, malignly, meanly, nastily, savagely, shoddily, unpleasantly, vindictively

(*n*) brutishness, callousness, *egocentricity*, *egocentrism*, egoism, egotism, hardheartedness, harshness, heartlessness, *inconsiderateness*, inhumanity, insensitivity, malice, *maliciousness*, malignancy, *mean-mindedness*, meanness, *mean-spiritedness*, mercilessness, pettiness, pitilessness, possessiveness, relentlessness, ruthlessness, self-absorption, self-centeredness, self-indulgence, self-interest, selfishness, self-love, self-regard, thoughtlessness, unkindness, unpleasantness, viciousness

See also BEASTLY AND BRUTISH (510)

506   Lifeless, Lazy, and Unenthusiastic

I make no secret of the fact that I would rather lie on a sofa than sweep beneath it. **Shirley Conran**

(*adj*) bone idle, idle, inactive, inanimate, indolent, inert, lazy, passive, shiftless, slack, slothful, sluggish, subdued, torpid, unambitious, unmotivated, weary, workshy (*UK*)

(*adv*) idly, lazily

(*n*) inactivity, indolence, laziness, passiveness, passivity, *shilly-shallying*, slackness, sloppiness (*informal*), sloth, slothfulness, sluggishness, torpor, weariness

507   Affectation, Self-Satisfaction, and Snobbishness

It is impossible, in our condition of society, not to be sometimes a Snob. **William Makepeace Thackeray**

(*adj*) affected, chichi, dramatic, genteel, goody-goody (*informal*), gracious, *hammy* (*informal*), haughty, hifalutin (*informal*), high and mighty, highfalutin (*informal*), histrionic, hoity-toity (*informal*), holier-than-thou (*informal*), la-di-da (*informal*), mannered, melodramatic, narcissistic, pious, plummy (*UK*), pompous, pontifical, portentous, precious, pretentious, proud, sanctimonious, self-righteous, self-satisfied, smug, sniffy (*informal*), snobbish, snobby (*informal*), snooty (*informal*), stagy, stuck-up (*informal*), supercilious, superficial, superior, swaggering, synthetic, theatrical, uppity (*informal*)

(*adv*) dramatically, haughtily, portentously, preciously, proudly, snootily (*informal*)

(*n*) affectation, affectedness, artificiality, conceit, conceitedness, dramatics, haughtiness, hauteur, narcissism, piety, piousness, pomposity, pompousness, *portentousness*, posturing, preciousness, pretension, sanctimoniousness, self-conceit, self-congratulation, self-righteousness, self-satisfaction, shallowness, smugness,

snobbery, snobbishness, snootiness (*informal*), superciliousness, superiority, swollen head (*UK*)

See also FALSE AND UNREAL (173)

508   Cowardice and Weakness of Will

None but a coward dares to boast that he has never known fear. **Ferdinand Foch**

(*adj*) chicken (*informal*), chinless, cowardly, craven, emasculated, faint-hearted, fallible, gutless, helpless, lily-livered (*dated*), namby-pamby (*informal insult*), pusillanimous, soft, spineless, spiritless, *unassertive*, unmanly, weak, weak-kneed, weak-willed, wishy-washy (*informal*)

(*n*) cowardice, *cowardliness*, cravenness (*literary*), *faintheartedness*, feebleness, *gutlessness*, helplessness, pusillanimity, spinelessness, unmanliness

See also WEAKNESS (241)

509   Lack of Commitment and Unreliability

I am a feather for each wind that blows. **William Shakespeare**

(*adj*) aimless, capricious, cavalier, delinquent (*formal*), disloyal, ditsy (*informal*), dizzy (*informal*), faithless, feckless, fey, fickle, flighty, fly-by-night, giddy (*dated*), heady, impetuous, impish, irresponsible, mercurial, neglectful, negligent, quicksilver, roving, slick, temperamental, traitorous, treacherous, undependable, unreliable, whimsical

(*adv*) faithlessly, giddily (*dated*), whimsically

(*n*) capriciousness, casualness, changeability, disloyalty, faithlessness, fecklessness, fickleness, flightiness, giddiness (*dated*), hastiness, impetuosity, impetuousness, impishness, impulsiveness, looseness (*dated*), rashness, recklessness, suicide, thoughtlessness, *treacherousness*, treachery, undependability, unreliability, *unreliableness*, whimsicality

510   Beastly and Brutish

A belief in a supernatural source of evil is not necessary; men alone are quite capable of every wickedness. **Joseph Conrad**

(*adj*) bitchy (*slang*), brutish, *hoggish*, *hoglike*, inhuman, inhumane, piggish, piggy, porcine, reptilian, subhuman, *vulpine*, vulturine

See also SELFISH AND UNKIND (505), PLEASURE-SEEKERS AND HEDONISTS (886)

511   Excessive Sensitivity

Some people are so sensitive they feel snubbed if an epidemic overlooks them. **Frank McKinney Hubbard**

(*adj*) demure, excitable, explosive, high-strung, hot, hot-blooded, hotheaded, hot-tempered, hyper (*informal*), hypersensitive, overemotional, oversensitive, overstrung, overwrought, passionate, prickly (*informal*), prim, prudish, quick-tempered, reactive, sensitive, squeamish, thin-skinned, touchy, up-and-down, volatile

(*adv*) demurely, hotly

(*n*) excitability, *hotheadedness*, *hypersensitivity*, *oversensitivity*, primness, prudery, squeamishness, susceptibility, touchiness, volatility

See also BAD-TEMPERED AND HUMORLESS (626)

512 Nosy and Interfering

The people who are regarded as moral luminaries are those who forego ordinary pleasures themselves and find compensation in interfering with the pleasures of others.
Bertrand Russell

(*adj*) inquiring, inquisitive, interfering, intrusive, invasive, meddlesome, meddling, nosy (*informal*), obtrusive, prying, rubbernecked (*informal*), voyeuristic

(*n*) indiscretion, inquisitiveness, intrusiveness, meddling, *nosiness* (*informal*)

513 Deceitful

Force and fraud are in war the two cardinal virtues.
Thomas Hobbes

(*adj*) artful, byzantine, calculating, captious, cheating, conniving, crafty, crooked (*informal*), cunning, deceitful, deceiving, designing, devious, dishonest, disingenuous, double-dealing, double-faced, duplicitous, foxy, guileful, hypocritical, inconstant (*literary*), insincere, lying, Machiavellian, manipulative, mendacious, perfidious (*formal*), phony, roguish, scheming, shifty, slippery, sly, sneaky, subtle, tortuous, tricky, two-faced, underhand, unfair, unfaithful, unsporting, unsportsmanlike, untrue, untrustworthy, untruthful, wily

(*adv*) crookedly (*informal*), deviously, mendaciously, subtly, trickily, underhand, underhandedly

(*n*) artfulness, craft, craftiness, crookedness, cunning, deceitfulness, deviousness, disingenuousness, *duplicitousness*, furtiveness, guile, hypocrisy, insincerity, mendacity, *perfidiousness* (*formal*), perfidy (*formal*), roguery, roguishness, *shiftiness*, *slipperiness*, slyness, sneakiness, subtleness, trickiness, *two-facedness*, unfairness, untrustworthiness, wiliness

See also FALSE AND UNREAL (173), DECEPTION AND LIES (660), MORALLY BAD OR IMPROPER (775)

514 Negativity of Outlook

The pessimist is the man who believes things couldn't possibly be worse, to which the optimist replies "Oh yes they could."
Vladimir Bukovsky

(*adj*) casehardened, curmudgeonly, cynical, defeatist, humorless, *ill-humored*, jaded, jaundiced, mirthless, negative, pessimistic, serious, splenetic

(*adv*) negatively, splenetically

See also GRUMPY AND NEGATIVE PEOPLE (953)

515 Difficult to Please

A cat loves fish, but hates to get his fur wet. **Anonymous**

(*adj*) argumentative, blimpish (*UK*), cantankerous, captious, choosy (*informal*), demanding, disputatious (*formal*), disputative (*formal*), faddy (*UK*), fastidious, faultfinding, finicky, fussy, *hard to please*, hypercritical, moody, nice, nitpicking, ornery (*informal*), overcritical, particular, persnickety (*informal*), picky, quarrelsome, rigid, *shrewish*, spoiled, squeamish, stern, strict, tough, unreasonable

(*adv*) moodily, unreasonably

(*n*) *argumentativeness*, *cantankerousness*, *choosiness* (*informal*), crotchetiness (*informal*), disputatiousness (*formal*), faddiness (*UK*), faddishness, fussiness, hairsplitting, *huffiness*, importunity (*formal*), moodiness, nit-

picking, particularity, perfectionism, *persnicketiness* (*informal*), pickiness, rigidity, rigor, *shrewishness*, sternness, strictness, toughness, unreasonableness

516 Bossy and Overbearing

Where a system of oppression has become institutionalized it is unnecessary for individuals to be oppressive.
Florynce R. Kennedy

(*adj*) authoritarian, autocratic, bossy, competitive, despotic, dictatorial, dominant, domineering, heavy-handed, high-handed, imperative (*formal*), imperious, importunate (*formal*), magisterial, megalomaniac, monopolistic, officious, overbearing, overconfident, overweening, pushing, pushy (*informal*), self-opinionated, tyrannical, *tyrannous*

(*adv*) bossily, imperiously

(*n*) bossiness, brass (*informal*), heavy-handedness, high-handedness, imperiousness, megalomania, *officiousness*, *overbearingness*, overconfidence, pushiness

See also POMPOUS, LOUD, AND OVERCONFIDENT (635)

517 Unadventurous and Dull

The most awful thing about power is not that it corrupts absolutely but that it makes people so utterly boring, so predictable. **Chinua Achebe**

(*adj*) conformist, conservative, conventional, dyed-in-the-wool, hidebound, obscurantist, sedate, square (*slang dated*), staid, straight (*slang*), strait-laced, stuffy, traditionalist, unadventurous, uncool (*slang*), unreconstructed, unreformed

(*n*) sedateness, *staidness*, *strait-lacedness*, stuffiness

See also BORING AND UNINTERESTING (234)

518 Aggressive and Belligerent

The great questions of our day cannot be solved by speeches and majority votes. . .but by iron and blood.
Prince Otto von Bismarck

(*adj*) adversarial, aggressive, bellicose, belligerent, *brattish*, bratty, confrontational, contentious, disagreeable, fierce, fighting, hawkish, homicidal, hostile, ill-natured, ill-tempered, invasive, irascible, martial, militant, militarist, militaristic, offensive, on the warpath (*informal*), poisonous, pugnacious, sadistic, scrappy (*informal*), *spoiling for a fight*, trigger-happy (*informal*), truculent, warlike, warring

(*adv*) fiercely, poisonously

(*n*) aggressiveness, *bellicosity*, belligerence, bitchiness (*slang*), destructiveness, *irascibility*, militancy, militarism, pugnacity, truculence

See also RUDE AND HOSTILE (625)

519 Grasping and Financially Mean

Everybody wants to do something to help, but nobody wants to be the first. **Pearl Bailey**

(*adj*) accumulative, acquisitive, cheap, cheeseparing, chintzy, close, close-fisted (*informal*), economical, frugal, gluttonous, grasping, greedy, illiberal (*formal*), insatiable, materialistic, mean (*UK*), mercenary, miserly, *moneygrubbing*, niggardly, parsimonious, penny-pinching (*informal*), *penny-wise*, penurious (*literary*), pinchpenny, rapacious, ravening, ravenous, sparing, stingy, tight, tightfisted, ungenerous

(*adv*) greedily, meanly (*UK*), stingily

(*n*) acquisitiveness, cheapness, cheeseparing, economy, frugality, *graspingness*, greed, greediness, insatiability, materialism, meanness (*UK*), miserliness, *niggardliness*, parsimoniousness, parsimony, rapaciousness, seaman, stinginess, tightfistedness

See also FINANCIALLY MEAN PEOPLE (952)

520   Good Manners and Social Skills

Friends and good manners will carry you where money won't go. **Margaret Walker**

(*adj*) chivalrous, civil, civilized, courteous, courtly, decent, decorous, delicate, demure, diplomatic, discreet, domesticated, fastidious, gallant, genteel, gentlemanly, good, *good-mannered*, graceful, gracious, mannerly, mild-mannered, nice, polished, polite, politically correct, proper, proud, punctilious, refined, respectful, tactful, urbane, well-behaved, well-bred, well-mannered

(*adv*) civilly, decently, delicately, demurely, graciously, nicely, politely

(*n*) attentiveness, chivalry, civility, class, classiness (*informal*), courteousness, courtesy, decency, *decorousness*, decorum, delicacy, *demureness*, dignity, diplomacy, etiquette, fastidiousness, finesse, gallantry, *genteelness*, gentility, good manners, gracefulness, graciousness, honor, manners, moderation, modesty, polish, politeness, *politesse*, political correctness, propriety, punctiliousness, refinement, subtlety, tact, *tactfulness*, urbanity

521   Bad Manners and Social Skills

I don't mind if you don't like my manners. I don't like 'em myself. They're pretty bad. I grieve over 'em on long winter evenings. **Humphrey Bogart**

(*adj*) badly behaved, bad-mannered, boorish, caddish, cheeky (*informal*), childish, churlish, coarse, crass, crude, discourteous, disrespectful, foul-mouthed, gauche, graceless, gross, ill-bred, ill-mannered, immature, impertinent (*formal*), impolite, impudent, indecorous, indelicate, indiscreet, infantile, insolent, loutish, low-minded, obscene, picaresque, politically incorrect, presumptuous, rascally (*humorous*), roguish, rough, rough-hewn, rude, sassy, saucy, shameless, smutty (*informal*), tactless, tasteless, thick-skinned, uncivil, uncivilized, uncouth, undiplomatic, *ungallant, ungentlemanly*, ungraceful, ungracious, ungrateful, *unladylike*, unmannered, unmannerly, vulgar

(*adv*) badly, brazenly, *churlishly*, coarsely, immaturely, impertinently (*formal*), insolently, ungratefully

(*n*) abrasiveness, attitude (*informal*), audacity, back talk, bad manners, boorishness, cattiness, cheekiness (*informal*), childishness, *churlishness*, chutzpah (*informal*), coarseness, cold-bloodedness, cold-heartedness, coolness, crassness, crudeness, crudity, discourteousness, discourtesy, effrontery, face (*informal*), front (*UK*), gall, gaucheness, gracelessness, immaturity, impertinence, impoliteness, impropriety, impudence, incivility, *indecorousness*, indecorum, indelicacy, *indelicateness*, ingratitude, insolence, lip (*slang*), loutishness, mouth (*informal*), nerve, offensiveness, presumption, presumptuousness, roughness, rudeness, sass (*informal*),

sassiness, sauce (*informal*), shamelessness, *surliness*, tactlessness, temerity, uncouthness, *ungraciousness*, ungratefulness, violation, vulgarity

See also UNFRIENDLINESS AND UNSOCIABILITY (504), RUDE AND HOSTILE (625)

522   Levels of Formality

It is not everyone who has the right to be plainly dressed. **Napoleon I**

(*adj*) ceremonious, chatty, formal, humble, informal, intimate, majestic, prim, prissy, *starched*, starchy, stiff

(*adv*) abjectly, formally, humbly, informally, intimately

(*n*) abjection, formality, informality, intimacy, primness, prissiness, *starchiness*, stiffness

523   Describing Somebody's Intellect

The more intelligence one has the more people one finds original. Commonplace people see no difference between men. **Blaise Pascal**

(*n*) brain, brainpower, brains, intellect, intelligence, intelligence quotient, judgment, mind, reason, sense, wit, wits

See also THE NATURE OF IDEAS (771)

524   Positive Intellectual Characteristics

Sublime moments, heroic acts, are rather the deeds of an exalted intelligence than of the will. **Pío Baroja**

(*adj*) able, acute, agile, astute, brainy (*informal*), bright, broad-minded, canny, clear-headed, clear-sighted, *clear-thinking*, clever, compos mentis, creative, cunning, cute, dexterous, discerning, discriminating, disinterested, down-to-earth, eagle-eyed, enlightened, enterprising, exact, exquisite, fair-minded, fiendish, focused, forward-thinking, freethinking, hardheaded, imaginative, incisive, insightful, intellectual, intelligent, intuitive, inventive, judicious, keen, lambent, liberal, liberated, logical, mature, nonjudgmental, observant, open-minded, penetrating, penetrative, perceptive, percipient, permissive, perspicacious, *perspicuous*, pervious, philosophic, philosophical, piercing, politic, practical, pragmatic, progressive, provident, prudent, prudential, quick, *quick off the mark*, quick on the uptake (*informal*), *quick-thinking*, quick-witted, rational, ready, realistic, reasonable, receptive, resourceful, right-minded, *right-thinking*, sane, selective, sensible, sensitive, sentient, serious-minded, sharp, sharp-eyed, sharp-sighted, sharp-witted, shrewd, smart, *straight-thinking*, streetwise (*informal*), strong-minded, subtle, technical, thinking, thorough, thoughtful, tolerant, unprejudiced, visionary, well-balanced, wholesome, wise, *with it* (*informal*)

(*adv*) cleverly, liberally, maturely, permissively, piercingly, practically, reasonably, sensibly, smartly, soberly, subtly

(*n*) acuity, acuteness, astuteness, brilliance, broad-mindedness, canniness, carefulness, caution, cautiousness, cleverness, common sense, creativeness, creativity, cuteness, detachment, dexterity, discernment, discrimination, disinterestedness, enterprise, farsightedness, foresight, genius, good judgment, good sense, gravity, gumption (*informal*), head, horse sense (*informal*), imagination, imaginativeness, *incisiveness*, ingenuity, initiative, inquisitiveness, insight, insight-fulness, inspiration, intuitiveness, invention, invent-iveness, judiciousness, keenness, liberalism, maturity, *moxie* (*slang*), nous, open-mindedness, penetration, per-ceptiveness, percipience, permissiveness, perspicacity, *perspicuity*, practicality, pragmatism, progressiveness, providence, provision, prudence, quickness, quick-witt-edness, rationality, realism, reasonableness, recep-tiveness, resourcefulness, rigor, sanity, selectivity, sensibleness, sharpness, shrewdness, soberness, strong-mindedness, studiousness, subtleness, thoroughness, thoughtfulness, tolerance, toleration, understanding, watchfulness, wholesomeness, wittiness

See also KNOWLEDGE AND WISDOM (558), LEVELS OF EDUCATION AND SOPHISTICATION (894)

525 Negative Intellectual Characteristics

No one ever went broke underestimating the intelligence of the American people. **H. L. Mencken**

(*adj*) absent-minded, asinine, babyish, benighted, bigoted, birdbrained (*informal*), blinkered, bovine (*literary*), brainless, chauvinistic, childish, childlike, class-conscious, closed, closed-minded, credulous, daffy (*informal*), deluded, dewy-eyed, doctrinaire, dogmatic, *dopey*, dotty, dozy (*UK*), dull, *dull-witted*, empty-headed, exploitable, extreme, fatuous, feeble-minded (*archaic*), foolhardy, foolish, forgetful, gullible, *homophobic*, hys-terical, idealistic, illiberal, *imperceptive*, impractical, impressionable, indecisive, indiscriminate, ineffectual, ingenuous, insular, jejune, jingoistic, juvenile, light-minded, myopic, naive, narrow-minded, *obsessional*, obsessive, obtuse, opinionated, overactive, parochial, partisan, pedantic, petty, *petty-minded*, *picayune* (*informal*), *pointy-headed* (*slang*), prejudiced, puerile, quixotic, racist, reactionary, romantic, scatterbrained, sectarian, *slow-witted* (*UK*), stolid, stupid, suggestible, superstitious, susceptible, trusting, uncritical, *undis-cerning*, unintelligent, unobservant, unperceptive, unre-ceptive, unsuspecting, vacuous, vague, wide-eyed, witless, *woolly-headed*, *woolly-minded*, wrong-headed, xenophobic

(*adv*) ambitiously, dully, fatuously, hysterically, indeci-sively, ingenuously, stupidly, vacuously

(*n*) absent-mindedness, blindness, blinkeredness, *cal-lowness*, *closed-mindedness*, credulity, dogmatism, facetiousness, fallibility, fatuity (*formal*), fatuousness, feeble-mindedness, folly, foolhardiness, foolishness, for-getfulness, gullibility, idealism, *idiocy*, immaturity, *impressionability*, *impressionableness*, imprudence, inad-vertence, inanity, indiscretion, ineffectuality, *inef-fectualness*, insularity, madness, myopia, narrow-mindedness, parochialism, pedantry, *pettifoggery*, petti-ness, *petty-mindedness*, puerility, *shockability*, short-sightedness, stupidity, suggestibility, trustfulness, *unin-telligence*, unreceptiveness, *unsound reasoning*, *unthin-kingness*, unwariness, *vacuousness*, vagueness, *witlessness*, *wrong-headedness*

See also PREJUDICE (550), IGNORANCE (557)

526 Skills, Talents, and Abilities

Talent develops in quiet places, character in the full current of human life. **Johann Wolfgang von Goethe**

(*n*) ability, accomplishment, acrobatics, acumen, adept-ness, adroitness, aptitude, art, artistry, attainment, bent, caliber, capability, capacity, clout (*informal*), com-petence, control, coordination, craft, craftsmanship, cunning, deftness, dexterity, *dexterousness*, ear, endow-ment, expertness, eye, facility, faculty, finesse, flair, forte, gift, handiness, handiwork, instinct, knack, know-how (*informal*), *legerdemain*, makings, mastery, merit, *natural ability*, *natural gift*, potential, power, pre-cociousness, precocity, professionalism, proficiency, promise, prowess, qualification, skill, *skillfulness*, sleight of hand, slyness, strength, strong point, strong suit, talent, technology, timing, touch, virtuosity, voca-tion, wizardry

527 Talented and Skillful

If a man has talent and cannot use it, he has failed...If he has a talent and learns somehow to use the whole of it, he has...won a satisfaction and a triumph few men ever know. **Thomas Wolfe**

(*adj*) able, accomplished, adept, adroit, all-around, apt, born, brilliant, capable, clever, competent, consummate, deft, dexterous, equal to, expert, finished, gifted, good, handy, high-powered, ingenious, magisterial, masterful, masterly, *multitalented*, polished, practiced, precocious, proficient, promising, seasoned, skilled, skillful, sly, sure-footed, talented, trained, Type A, versatile, well-endowed

(*adv*) ably, brilliantly, capably, ingeniously

528 Talented or Intelligent People

Whom the gods wish to destroy they first call promising. **Cyril Connolly**

(*n*) ace, achiever, authority, *boy wonder*, brain (*informal*), *brainbox* (*UK*), buff, connoisseur, demon (*informal*), expert, genius, guru, highbrow, maestro, magician, marvel, master, mastermind, maven, mind, mistress, old hand, phenomenon, polymath, powerhouse (*informal*), pro, prodigy, professional, pundit, sage (*literary*), savant, scholar, solon (*literary*), specialist, troubleshooter, veteran, victor, virtuoso, visionary, war-horse, whiz (*informal*), whiz kid (*informal*), wiz (*informal*), wizard (*informal*), *wunderkind*

See also PEOPLE WHO ARE APPROVED OF (955)

529 Unskilled

To be conscious that you are ignorant is a great step to knowledge. **Benjamin Disraeli**

(*adj*) amateur, amateurish, bungling (*informal*), callow, fledgling, ham-handed (*informal*), hopeless, illiterate, impotent, inadequate, incapable, incompetent, inept, inexperienced, inexpert, lay, maladroit, new, raw, rusty, *talentless*, tender, unable, unaccomplished, unaccus-tomed, unequal, unfamiliar, unfit, uninitiated, unprac-ticed, unprepared, unprofessional, unqualified, unskilled, unskillful, *untalented*, untutored, unused, useless (*informal*), *wet behind the ears*

(*n*) amateurishness, disorganization, *ham-handedness* (*informal*), hopelessness, impotence, inability, incapacity, incompetence, ineptitude, ineptness, inexperience, maladroitness (*formal*), rawness, *unskillfulness*, uselessness (*informal*)

530 Unskilled People

Man arrives as a novice at each age of his life. **Nicolas Chamfort**

(*n*) amateur, apprentice, beginner, bungler (*informal*), cub, dilettante, fledgling, greenhorn, junior, laity, learner, neophyte, newcomer, novice, pledge, *raw recruit*, recruit, rookie (*informal*), tenderfoot (*informal*), trainee, tyro

Emotions and States of Mind

531 Feelings

Few people realize that they are looking at the world of their own thoughts and the world of their own feelings. **Wallace Stevens**

(*n*) emotion, feeling, gut feeling, gut reaction, hunch, instinct, intuition, mood, morale, notion, sense, sensibility, sentiment, spirit, spirits, suspicion

532 Feelings About the Past

The urban man is an uprooted tree, he can put out leaves, flowers and grow fruit but what a nostalgia his leaf, flower, and fruit will always have for mother earth. **Juan Ramón Jiménez**

(*n*) bitterness, compunction, contrition, guilt, guiltiness, guilty conscience, nostalgia, qualm, regret, remorse, repentance, resignation, romance, self-reproach, umbrage, wistfulness

533 Feelings About the Future

The future is like heaven—everyone exalts it but no one wants to go there now. **James Baldwin**

(*n*) ambition, anticipation, apprehension, aspiration, bleakness, bullishness (*informal*), butterflies (*informal*), compulsion, defeatism, expectancy, expectation, fatalism, fearfulness, foreboding, foreknowledge, gloom, gloominess, hope, hopefulness, hopelessness, impatience, misgiving, negativity, nerves (*informal*), nerviness, nervousness, optimism, pessimism, premonition, presentiment, qualm, second thoughts, solicitude, stage fright, suspense, tension, trepidation, unease, uneasiness, unrest, wariness, worry

See also DESIRE AND WANT (579), PREDICT AND ANTICIPATE (750)

534 Pleasure, Excitement, and Elation

Fine pictures, fine statues, beautiful music; pleasure for the senses, and let the devil take the soul! **Benito Pérez Galdós**

(*adj*) aflame, agape (*literary*), *all of a flutter*, amused, *aroused*, buoyant, *carried away*, cheerful, cheery, chipper (*informal*), chirpy (*informal*), cock-a-hoop, content, contented, delighted, delirious, ecstatic, elated, *enraptured* (*formal*), *enthused*, euphoric, excited, exhilarated, expectant, exultant, fired up, glad, *gladdened*, gleeful, *gloating*, *gratified*, happy, honored, infected, *in good spirits*, *in high spirits*, *in raptures*, *in seventh heaven*, jaunty, joyful, joyous, jubilant, light, lighthearted, manic (*informal*), merry, mirthful, on cloud nine (*informal*), on fire, overexcited, overjoyed, over the

moon (*UK*), pleased, proud, radiant, rapt, rapturous, satiated, satisfied, starry-eyed, thankful, thrilled, *thrilled to pieces* (*informal*), *tickled*, tickled pink (*informal*), touched, *transported*, triumphant, up, upbeat (*informal*), *uplifted*, white-hot, wild

(*adv*) aflutter, blissfully, buoyantly, cheerfully, excitedly, expectantly, gaily, happily, mirthfully, proudly

(*n*) afterglow, arousal, bliss, brightness, cheer, cheerfulness, cheeriness, cloud nine, delectation (*formal*), delight, delirium, ecstasy, elation, enchantment, enjoyment, euphoria, exaltation (*formal*), exhilaration, exultation, fascination, felicity, fervor, festiveness, gaiety, gladness, glee, *gleefulness*, *good humor*, gratification, gusto, happiness, high spirits, jauntiness, joie de vivre, jollity, joy, joyfulness, joyousness, jubilation, merriment, overexcitement, pleasure, radiance, rapture, relish, rhapsody, romance, satisfaction, triumph

See also PLEASE AND AMUSE (572)

535 Appreciation and Gratitude

I want to thank you for stopping the applause. It is impossible for me to look humble for any period of time. **Henry Kissinger**

(*adj*) admiring, adoring, amorous, appreciative, besotted, *bewitched*, broody, captivated, charmed, crazy (*informal*), doting, dotty (*informal*), enamored, enchanted, enthusiastic, fervent, *fervid*, fond of, fulfilled, grateful, *head over heels in love*, hung up (*informal*), inclined, indebted, infatuated, *in favor*, in love, into, keen on (*UK*), lovesick, *love-struck*, mad, *obligated*, obliged, partial to, rabid, romantic, smitten (*humorous or archaic or literary*), *soft on*, *sold on*, *stuck on* (*informal*), *taken with*, thankful, warm, well-disposed, worshipful

(*adv*) devotedly, gratefully, head over heels, rabidly, thankfully, with bated breath

(*n*) appreciation, contentment, devotion, druthers (*informal*), gratefulness, gratitude, indebtedness, liking, penchant, predilection (*formal*), pride, proclivity, recognition, satisfaction, soft spot, temptation, thankfulness, thanks

536 Cool and Calm

Calmness is great advantage; he that lets another chafe may warm him at his fire, mark all his wand'rings and enjoy his frets, as cunning fencers suffer heat to tire. **George Herbert**

(*adj*) accustomed, adamant, all set, at ease, at home, at peace, at rest, bullish (*informal*), calm, carefree, chilled (*slang*), *chilled out* (*slang*), collected, comfortable, comforted, composed, convinced, cool, fatalistic, fluent, fluid, fortified, free-and-easy, *heartened*, hopeful, laid-back (*informal*), lucid, philosophic, philosophical, phlegmatic, placid, ready, *ready and waiting*, *ready for action*, *ready for anything*, *reassured*, relieved, sanguine, serene, stable, together (*informal*), tranquil, unabashed, unafraid, unapologetic, unashamed, *unbothered*, undaunted, *undeterred*, undisturbed, *unembarrassed*, unflustered, unperturbed, unremorseful, unrepentant, unruffled, unstressed, untroubled, unworried, welcome

(*adv*) bullishly (*informal*), comfortably, coolly, fluently, hopefully, tranquilly, unashamedly

(*n*) calm, calmness, carefreeness, complacency, composure, confidence, coolness, courage, credit, equanimity, faith, fulfillment, lucidity, lucidness, placidity, reassurance, *sanguineness*, *sanguinity*, serenity

See also CONFIDENCE AND COMPOSURE (499), SOOTHE AND CALM (573)

537 Positive Impatience, Enthusiasm, and Alertness

One's prime is elusive…be on the alert to recognize your prime at whatever time of your life it may occur. You must then live it to the full. **Muriel Spark**

(*adj*) agog, alert, alive, animated, anxious, ardent, born-again, desirous (*formal*), desperate, edgy, fevered, feverish, hungry, impatient, inspired, *in suspense*, itching, *like a cat on a hot tin roof*, mindful, on the alert, on the ball (*informal*), on your mettle, passionate, prepared, purposeful, restive, restless, skittish, sleepless, *stirred up*, straining at the leash, vigilant, wakeful, wannabe (*informal*), watchful, wholehearted, wide-awake (*informal*), willing

(*adv*) breathlessly, *desirously* (*formal*), edgily, like a shot, like mad, passionately, yearningly

(*n*) ambition, buoyancy, drive, eagerness, *edginess*, enthusiasm, excitement, fever, fire, go (*informal*), heat, immersion, *itchy feet*, *mindfulness*, passion, preparedness, purpose, restiveness, restlessness, sleeplessness, unction, urgency, verve, vibrancy, vigilance, vigor, vim (*informal*), wakefulness, warmness, warmth, willingness, zeal, zest, zing (*informal*), zip (*informal*)

See also ENERGY AND ENTHUSIASM (496)

538 Pensiveness and Interest

Philosophy, as we use the word, is a fight against the fascination which forms of expression exert upon us. **Ludwig Wittgenstein**

(*adj*) absorbed, *all ears* (*informal*), attentive, *beguiled*, captive, caught up, contemplative, curious, daydreaming, deep in thought, engrossed, enthralled, *entranced*, fascinated, fixated, gripped, heedful, hooked (*slang*), immersed, intent, interested, introspective, knee-deep, lost, lost in thought, meditative, *mesmerized*, musing, nostalgic, obsessed, pensive, rapt, reflective, *riveted* (*informal*), ruminant, ruminative, *sidetracked*, solemn, spellbound, thoughtful, *transfixed*, wistful, wrapped up in

(*adv*) broodingly, fixatedly, gravely, intently

See also APPEAL TO AND AROUSE INTEREST (575), ATTENTION AND ATTENTIVENESS (763)

539 Sadness, Distress, and Despair

My only hope lies in my despair. **Racine**

(*adj*) afflicted, affronted, aggrieved, agonized, angst-ridden, anguished, bad, beleaguered, beside yourself, besieged, bleak, blue (*informal*), broken, brokenhearted, broody, bruised, burdened, careworn, choked up (*informal*), *close to tears*, crestfallen, crying, cut up (*informal*), deflated, dejected, demoralized, depressed, desolate, despairing, desperate, despondent, devastated, disappointed, disconsolate, discontented, discouraged, disenchanted, disgusted, disheartened, disillusioned, dismayed, dispirited, distressed, doleful, doom-laden (*UK*), down, downcast, downhearted, down in the dumps, *down in the mouth* (*informal*), downtrodden, dreary, fed

up (*informal*), forlorn, gloomy, glum, grief-stricken, harassed, harried, heartbroken, heavy-hearted (*literary*), heavy-laden (*literary*), homesick, hopeless, horrified, hurried, hurt, hurting, *in a funk* (*informal*), in a huff (*informal*), *in a mood*, in a tizzy (*informal*), inconsolable, in despair, in distress, in low spirits, insulted, in the doldrums, in the dumps, in turmoil, lachrymose (*literary*), lousy (*informal*), low, lugubrious, malcontent, melancholic, melancholy, miserable, morbid, morose, mournful, offended, overwhelmed, pained, plaintive, poignant, pressured, prostrate, regretful, rotten (*informal*), sad, *saddened*, saturnine, self-pitying, shattered, sick, sick and tired, *sickened*, *sick to death*, *sick to the back teeth* (*UK*), somber, sorrowful, sorrowing, *stung*, suicidal (*informal*), sunk, tired, tormented, traumatized, unhappy, unhopeful, unsatisfied, upset, weepy (*informal*), weighed down, woebegone, woeful, world-weary, worn down, wounded, wretched

(*adv*) abjectly, bleakly, broodily, desolately, desperately, forlornly, gloomily, hopelessly, miserably, sadly, unhappily, wretchedly

(*n*) abjection, agony, angst, anguish, blackness, blues (*informal*), broodiness, consternation, dejection, demoralization, depression, desolation, despair, desperation, despondency, disappointment, discontent, discontentment, discouragement, disenchantment, disillusionment, dismay, distress, doldrums, dolefulness, glumness, grief, heartache, heartbreak, *homesickness*, hurt, joylessness, lugubriousness, malaise, martyrdom, melancholy, misery, *moroseness*, mournfulness, pain, pall, pathos, poignance, poignancy, purgatory, regret, sadness, self-pity, *somberness*, sorrow, *sorrowfulness*, soulfulness, suffering, torment, torture, unhappiness, upset, woe, world-weariness, wretchedness

See also UPSET, DISTRESS, AND HUMILIATE (567)

540 Confusion, Anxiety, and Worry

Confusion is a word we have invented for an order which is not understood. **Henry Miller**

(*adj*) addled, addlepated (*archaic*), agitated, alarmed, anxious, apprehensive, at sea, baffled, *bamboozled* (*informal*), bedazzled (*literary*), befuddled, bemused, beset, bewildered, bogged down (*informal*), bothered, browbeaten, clouded, concerned, confounded, confused, dazed, desperate, disconcerted, distracted, distraught, disturbed, excited, fearful, flummoxed (*informal*), flustered, frantic, fraught, fretful, *fuddled*, grave, *hassled* (*informal*), haunted, het up, hot and bothered, hung up (*informal*), *in a flap* (*informal*), *in a frenzy*, *in a lather* (*informal*), *in high dudgeon*, jittery, jumpy, keyed up (*informal*), lost, *mired*, mixed-up (*informal*), moonstruck (*informal humorous*), muddled, muddleheaded, mystified, nervous, nonplussed, on edge, on tenterhooks, perplexed, perturbed, preoccupied, punch-drunk (*informal*), punchy, puzzled, senile, *shaken*, spaced-out (*slang*), spacy (*slang*), stir-crazy (*informal or humorous*), strained, stressed, stressed out (*informal*), stricken, strung out (*informal*), stuck, *stumped*, stupefied, *stymied*, taut, tense, troubled, twitchy, uneasy, unquiet, unsettled, uptight (*informal*), wired (*slang*), worked up (*informal*), worried, *worried sick*, wrought-up

(*n*) agitation, anxiety, *anxiousness*, bafflement, befuddlement, *bemusement*, bewilderment, blankness, care, concern, confusion, daze, desperation, disorientation, distraction, fear, fogginess, fretfulness, fuddle, *jitteriness*, jitters (*informal*), jumpiness, mystification, niggle, perplexity, perturbation, preoccupation, puzzlement, strain, stress, stupefaction, trouble, unquiet

See also CONFUSE AND BEWILDER (571)

541   Irritation and Anger

Anger is a momentary madness, so control your passion or it will control you. **Horace**

(*adj*) aggravated (*informal*), angry, annoyed, antagonistic, antipathetic, *antsy* (*informal*), *apoplectic*, bad-tempered, beside yourself, bitter, *choleric* (*literary*), combative, crabbed, crabby, cranky (*informal*), crazed, cross, crotchety (*informal*), disgruntled, displeased, dissatisfied, embittered, enraged, exasperated, fractious, frustrated, fuming, furious, grizzly (*UK*), grumpy, hopping mad (*informal*), hot under the collar (*informal*), ill-disposed, impatient, *in a bad mood*, incensed, indignant, infuriated, inimical, irate, *ireful* (*literary*), irked, irritable, irritated, liverish, livid, mad, maddened, miffed (*informal*), *nettled* (*informal*), out of sorts, outraged, overheated, peeved (*informal*), peevish, pettish, petulant, piqued, provoked, *repelled*, repulsed, resentful, revolted, *riled* (*informal*), seething, short-tempered, sore (*informal*), sulky, teed off (*informal*), *ticked off* (*informal*), unhappy, up in arms, vengeful, vexed, vindictive, vinegary, waspish, wound up (*informal*), wrathful

(*adv*) furiously, indignantly, lividly

(*n*) anger, annoyance, aversion (*formal*), bad mood, bad temper, *bad-temperedness*, bile (*literary*), blackness, *choler* (*literary or archaic*), crabbiness, crankiness (*informal*), detestation, disapproval, displeasure, dissatisfaction, exasperation, *excoriation* (*formal*), frustration, furiousness, fury, grumpiness, huff, ill humor, impatience, indignation, ire (*formal*), irritability, irritation, mood, offense, opprobriousness, opprobrium, outrage, passion, peevishness, persecution, pet, petulance, pique, provocation, rage, reprehension, spleen, sulk, sulkiness, temper, vexation, waspishness, wrath

See also ANGER AND ANNOY (569)

542   Embarrassment and Humiliation

Speak the truth and shame the Devil. **François Rabelais**

(*adj*) abashed, apologetic, ashamed, *chagrined*, conscience-stricken, contrite, deprecatory, embarrassed, guilt-ridden, guilty, hangdog, humbled, humiliated, mortified, penitent, penitential, red-faced, regretful, remorseful, repentant, rueful, shamefaced, sheepish, sorry

(*n*) abasement (*literary*), chagrin, confusion, debasement, degradation, discomfiture (*formal*), discomfort, discomposure, embarrassment, humiliation, ignominy, mortification, opprobriousness, opprobrium, self-abasement, shame, sheepishness

543   Fear and Panic

He who has been bitten by a snake fears a piece of string. **Persian proverb**

(*adj*) afraid, cowed, frightened, hunted, *hysteric*, hysterical, *in a panic*, intimidated, *panicked*, panicky, panic-stricken, petrified, phobic, scared, *scared rigid* (*UK*), *scared stiff*, *scared to death*, terrified, *terrorized*, terror-stricken, trembling, tremulous, unnerved

(*adv*) fearfully, hysterically, tremblingly

(*n*) alarm, awe, chill, dread, fear, fright, heebie-jeebies (*slang*), horror, hysterics, lather (*informal*), panic, scare, terror, willies (*informal*)

See also FEARS AND PHOBIAS (554), FRIGHTEN AND SHOCK (568)

544   Insecurity and Loss of Composure

Life is our reaction to the basic insecurity which constitutes its substance. **José Ortega y Gasset**

(*adj*) *all at sea*, *aquiver*, awkward, cagey (*informal*), chary, circumspect, *daunted*, defensive, *discomfited* (*formal*), disoriented, *disquieted* (*archaic or literary*), downbeat, fidgety, hesitant, hyper (*informal*), hyperactive, ill at ease, insecure, jealous, mistrustful, paranoid, queasy, self-conscious, shy, skittish, *squirmy*, tentative, *thrown off balance*, uncomfortable, unconfident, unglued (*informal*), unsure

(*adv*) awkwardly, cagily (*informal*), defensively, insecurely, shyly, tentatively, twitchily

(*n*) apprehensiveness, awkwardness, caginess (*informal*), chariness, circumspection, disquiet, excitement, fidgetiness, flutter, frenzy, hesitancy, hysteria, insecurity, jealousy, *self-consciousness*, *self-contempt*, *self-disgust*, *self-dislike*, self-doubt, self-hatred, *self-loathing*, tizzy (*informal*), twitchiness

545   Surprise, Shock, and Amazement

Between ourselves the best thing of all is a combination of the surprising and the beautiful. **Ludwig van Beethoven**

(*adj*) aghast, amazed, appalled, astonished, astounded, awestruck, bowled over, dumbfounded, *dumbstruck*, electrified, flabbergasted (*informal*), horrified, horror-struck, *impressed*, *in a daze*, *in a state of shock*, in awe of, incredulous, in disbelief, *in shock*, knocked out (*informal*), open-mouthed, *overawed*, overwhelmed, *scandalized*, shocked, speechless, staggered, startled, *stunned*, stupefied, surprised, taken aback, thunderstruck, wide-eyed

(*n*) amazement, astonishment, awe, incomprehension, incredulity, shock, *speechlessness*, start, stupefaction (*literary*), stupor, surprise, wonder, wonderment

See also SURPRISE AND IMPRESS (574)

546   Expressions of Surprise and Pleasure

Perhaps one has to be very old before one learns how to be amused rather than shocked. **Pearl Buck**

(*adv*) fortunately, paradoxically, surprisingly, *to my amazement*, *to my surprise*

(*interj*) gee (*informal*), *gee whiz* (*informal*), golly (*dated informal*), goodness gracious, goody (*informal*), gosh (*informal*), heavens (*informal*), heavens to Betsy (*informal*), *hey presto* (*informal*), ho hum (*informal*), hooray, hurrah, jeepers (*dated informal*), *my*, *my goodness*, *my word* (*dated*), *oh my* (*informal*)

547   Expressions of Regret

But with the morning cool repentance came. **Sir Walter Scott**

(*adv*) alas, sadly, unfortunately, unhappily

(*interj*) commiserations

548 Envy and Jealousy

Envy will merit as its shade pursue,/But like a shadow proves the substance true. **Alexander Pope**

(*adj*) covetous, envious, *green-eyed*, *green with envy*, jealous, possessive, proprietary, proprietorial, territorial

(*n*) avidity, *enviousness*, envy, jealousy, possessiveness, protectiveness

549 Love, Respect, and Goodwill

Be warm, but pure: be amorous, but be chaste. **Lord Byron**

(*n*) admiration, adoration, adulation, affection, affinity, ardor, attachment, crush (*informal*), deference, devotion, esteem, fondness, goodwill, homage, honor, love, obeisance, regard, respect, respectfulness, reverence, veneration, worship

550 Prejudice

Prejudice is planted in childhood, learnt like table manners and cadences of speech, nurtured through fictions like Uncle Tom's Cabin *and* Gone With the Wind. **Beryl Bainbridge**

(*n*) bias, chauvinism, cronyism, discrimination, elitism, exclusiveness, favoritism, flag-waving, intolerance, jingoism, nepotism, partisanship, preconception, prejudice, racism, *sexism*, unfairness, xenophobia

See also NEGATIVE INTELLECTUAL CHARACTERISTICS (525)

551 Compassion and Forgiveness

It is the enemy who can truly teach us to practice the virtues of compassion and tolerance. **Dalai Lama**

(*n*) commiseration, compassion, condolence, empathy, feeling, fellow feeling, forgiveness, heart, identification, mercy, pardon, pity, sympathy, understanding

552 Antagonism

Antagonism is a form of struggle within a contradiction, but not the universal form. **Mao Zedong**

(*n*) acrimony, animosity, animus, antagonism, antipathy, bad blood, bad feeling, *censoriousness*, censure, chill, chilliness, condescension, contempt, disapprobation (*formal*), disrespect, enmity, grudge, *hard feelings*, hostility, ill feeling, ill will, lese majesty, rancor, rancorousness, *reproachfulness*, *resentfulness*, resentment, scorn, scornfulness, sour grapes, sourness, spite, spitefulness, venom, vindictiveness, vitriol, vituperation, willfulness

See also RUDE AND HOSTILE (625)

553 Neutrality and Indifference

It is not the neutrals or the lukewarm who make history. **Adolf Hitler**

(*adj*) absent, abstracted, alienated, apathetic, blasé, blithe, bored, *bored rigid*, *bored stiff*, *bored to death*, *bored to tears*, businesslike, careless, casual, catatonic, chill, clinical, complacent, damp, deaf, detached, disaffected, dispassionate, distracted, distrait (*literary*), dreamy, dry-eyed, emotionless, faraway, half-hearted, hands-off, heedless, impartial, impassive, impervious, in a world of your own, incurious, independent, indifferent, insensitive, *insouciant*, inured to, lackadaisical, lax,

lukewarm, *miles away*, negligent (*literary*), neutral, nonaligned, nonchalant, noninterventionist, nonpartisan, numb, objective, off-guard, passionless, robotic, tepid, thick-skinned, unaffected, uncaring, uncommitted, unconcerned, unemotional, unenthusiastic, unexcited, unimpressed, uninterested, uninvolved, unmindful, unmoved, unresponsive, unsentimental, untouched

(*adv*) absently, blithely, carelessly, casually, damply, dreamily, independently, neutrally, numbly

(*n*) apathy, casualness, coldness, demotivation, detachment, disaffection, disinterest, dispassion, disregard, ennui, glibness, heedlessness, impartiality, *impassiveness*, *impassivity*, imperviousness, independence, indifference, insouciance, laissez-faire, laxity, neutrality, nonalignment, nonchalance, nonintervention, numbness, objectivity, sufferance, unconcern, unresponsiveness

See also WITHOUT ENTHUSIASM (287), UNWILLINGNESS AND STUBBORNNESS (564), UNINTERESTED AND DETACHED (629)

554 Fears and Phobias

The taxonomy of fear has long been a subject of interest to psychiatrists, who have delighted in compiling lists of phobias and calling them by Greek names. **Anthony Stevens**

(*adj*) phobic

(*n*) paranoia, phobia

(*v*) dread, fear, have a horror of

types of phobias acrophobia (fear of high places), agoraphobia (fear of public or open spaces), ailurophobia (fear of cats), arachnophobia (fear of spiders), claustrophobia (fear of confined or enclosed spaces), hydrophobia (fear of water), necrophobia (fear of death or dead bodies), nyctophobia (fear of night or darkness), photophobia (fear of light or lighted spaces), pyrophobia (fear of fire), technophobia (fear of new technology or computerization), zoophobia (fear of animals)

See also FEAR AND PANIC (543)

555 Fads, Fetishes, and Idolatry

Fashions, after all, are only induced epidemics. **George Bernard Shaw**

(*n*) addiction, bandwagon, canonization, craze, cult, enthusiasm, extremism, fad, fanaticism, fashion, fetish, fixation, habit, hero worship, hobbyhorse, icon, idée fixe, idolatry, idolization, infatuation, mania, obsession, *obsessiveness*, overenthusiasm, *pyromania*, *religious fervor*, *religious zeal*, thing (*informal*), trend, vogue, *zealotry*

556 Devotees and Addicted People

One week he's in polka dots, the next week he's in stripes./'Cos he's a dedicated follower of fashion. **Ray Davies**

(*n*) acolyte, addict, adherent, admirer, advocate, aficionada, aficionado, *bibliophile*, *book lover*, booster, campaigner, canvasser, champion, crusader, defender, devotee, enthusiast, exponent, fan, fanatic, freak (*informal*), gladiator, groupie (*informal*), hanger-on, *hero-worshiper*, idealist, idolater, loyalist, maniac, monarchist, nut (*informal*), partisan, patriot, pyromaniac, reader, rocker (*informal*), royalist, smoker, *teddy boy*, *votary*, zealot

557 Ignorance

Ignorance is the mother of devotion. **Jeremy Taylor**

(*adj*) clueless (*informal*), ignorant, insensible, insensitive, oblivious, unacquainted, *unapprised*, unaware, unconscious, unenlightened, unfledged, unformed, uninformed, uninstructed, unknowing, *unknowledgeable*, untrained, *unversed*, unwitting

(*n*) amnesia, *cluelessness* (*informal*), ignorance, oblivion, unfamiliarity

See also NEGATIVE INTELLECTUAL CHARACTERISTICS (525), UNCERTAINTY (559)

558 Knowledge and Wisdom

A study of history shows that civilizations that abandon the quest for knowledge are doomed to disintegration. **Bernard Lovell**

(*adj*) abreast, academic, accustomed to, *all-knowing, all-seeing*, at home, *au courant, au fait*, aware, bookish, clued-in, cognizant (*formal*), conscious, conversant, enlightened, experienced, familiar, informed, in the know, *in the picture*, knowing, knowledgeable, learned, numerate, omniscient, on top of, primed, privy, sagacious, sage (*literary*), sapient, *up on*, up-to-date, up to speed, up with, used to, versed, *versed in*, well-grounded, well-informed, well-versed, wise, worldly, worldly-wise

(*adv*) by heart, by rote, like the back of your hand

(*n*) acquaintance, acquaintanceship, awakening, awareness, cognizance (*formal*), command, comprehension, consciousness, conversance, enlightenment, erudition, experience, expertise, exposure, familiarity, familiarization, grasp, ken, knowledge, learning, literacy, numeracy, omniscience, recognition, sagacity, *sapience*, savoir-faire, savvy (*informal*), scholarship, science, wisdom, worldliness

(*v*) be acquainted with, be aware of, discern, *have down pat, have knowledge of, have off pat* (*UK*), know, know back to front (*UK*), know backward and forward, recognize

See also POSITIVE INTELLECTUAL CHARACTERISTICS (524), CERTAINTY (561)

559 Uncertainty

Negative Capability, that is, when a man is capable of being in uncertainties, mysteries, doubts, without any irritable reaching after fact and reason. **John Keats**

(*adj*) agnostic, ambivalent, *at a complete loss*, at a loss, clingy, disbelieving, distrustful, doubtful, doubting, dubious, faltering, *in a cleft stick* (*UK*), *in a dilemma, in a quandary*, irresolute, leery, on the fence, pendulous, skeptical, suspicious, torn, unbelieving, uncertain, unconvinced, undecided, undetermined, unsure, vacillating, wavering

(*adv*) askance, doubtfully, dubiously, falteringly, uncertainly, waveringly

(*n*) agnosticism, ambivalence, cynicism, disbelief, distrust, dithering, doubt, doubter, doubtfulness, dubiousness, hesitation, inaction, *incertitude*, indecision, indecisiveness, *irresoluteness*, irresolution, mistrust, query, question, question mark, reservations, scruple, skeptic, skepticism, suspense, suspicion, uncertainty, *unfinished business*, vacillation, wavering

(*v*) disbelieve, doubt, expect

See also DIFFICULT SITUATIONS (72), UNCERTAIN (175), IGNORANCE (557)

560 Expressions of Uncertainty

Doubt is a necessary precondition to meaningful action. **Donald Barthelme**

(*adv*) apparently, by all accounts, *on the face of it, rumor has it that*, seemingly

561 Certainty

Faith is a risk and a gamble. Absolute certainty can never be faith. **Adam Clayton Powell, Jr.**

(*adj*) certain, confident, convinced, decided, decisive, definite, firm, *in no doubt*, peremptory, *persuaded*, positive, sure, sure-footed, sworn, unshakable

(*adv*) certainly, firmly

(*n*) authority, belief, certainty, certitude, conviction, decision, decisiveness, sureness, trust

(*v*) believe, lean on, put your faith in, trust

See also CERTAIN (174), KNOWLEDGE AND WISDOM (558)

562 Eccentricity and Irrationality

The irregular side of nature, the discontinuous and erratic side—these have been puzzles to science, or worse, monstrosities. **James Gleick**

(*adj*) *around the bend* (*slang*), batty (*informal*), berserk, cracked (*informal*), crazy (*informal*), demented (*informal*), *deranged, dippy* (*UK*), disturbed, *nuts* (*slang*), pathological, possessed, potty (*UK informal*), queer (*dated*), quirky, raving, twisted, unhinged, wild (*informal*)

(*n*) character, craziness (*informal*), derangement, insanity, quirkiness, wildness (*informal*)

563 The Will and Willingness

Will power is the only tensile strength of one's own disposition. One cannot increase it by a single ounce. **Cesare Pavese**

(*adj*) accepting, accommodating, acquiescent, agreeable, amenable, apt to, biddable, complaisant, compliant, controllable, cooperative, disposed, docile, flexible, forthcoming, game, glad, helpful, liable, likely, malleable, meek, minded (*formal*), obedient, obliging, pliable, pliant, predisposed (*formal*), prone, raring, ready, resigned, submissive, subservient, tame, tractable, unforced, unprompted, *unresisting*, willing, *willing to please*, wont (*formal*), yielding

(*adv*) by choice, cheerfully, compliantly, cooperatively, flexibly, helpfully, of your own accord, sooner, tamely, voluntarily, willingly

(*n*) adherence, amenability, compliance, conformism, *cooperativeness*, docility, malleability, meekness, obedience, observance, pliability, pliancy, readiness, submission, tameness, tractability, volition, willingness

See also WITH ENTHUSIASM (286)

564 Unwillingness and Stubbornness

He who is reluctant to recognize me opposes me. **Frantz Fanon**

(*adj*) anti (*informal*), averse (*formal*), bullheaded (*informal*), cast-iron, confirmed, contrary, cussed (*informal*), diehard, difficult, disinclined, dogged, dour (*UK*), grudging, hard-core, hardline, headstrong, immovable, implacable, incorrigible, incurable, indisposed (*formal*), inexorable, inflexible, intractable (*formal*), intransigent, inveterate, iron-clad, *iron-willed*, irredeemable, loath, mulish, obdurate, obstinate, opposed to, opposing, perverse, pigheaded, rebellious, reluctant, seditious, self-willed, set, stubborn, unaccommodating, unbending, unbowed, uncompromising, uncooperative, undisposed, unhelpful, unmovable, unwilling, willful

(*n*) bullheadedness (*informal*), contrariness, cussedness (*informal*), disinclination, doggedness, dourness (*UK*), hesitation, implacability (*formal*), indisposition, inflexibility, intractability (*formal*), intransigence, mulishness, obduracy, *obdurateness*, obstinacy, opposition, perverseness, perversity, pigheadedness, rebelliousness, reluctance, sedition, *seditiousness*, self-will, stubbornness, subversion, tenacity, unhelpfulness, unwillingness, willfulness

(*prep*) against

See also WITHOUT ENTHUSIASM (287), NEUTRALITY AND INDIFFERENCE (553)

565 Rebelliousness and Disobedience

Acts of disobedience are the postal service of disbelief. **Muhyid-Din Abu Zakariyya ibn Sharaf al-Nawawi**

(*adj*) anarchic, anarchistic, awkward (*UK*), bad, *begrudging*, blocking, challenging, contumacious (*formal*), defiant, disobedient, disobliging, disorderly, dissident, extremist, *fogyish*, incendiary, insubordinate, insurgent, mischievous, mutinous, naughty, noncompliant, nonconformist, obstreperous, obstructive, perverse, problem, rabble-rousing, radical, raucous, rebellious, recalcitrant, refractory, resistant, revolutionary, riotous, rowdy, stiff-necked, subversive, troublesome, turbulent, uncontrollable, undisciplined, ungovernable, unruly, wayward, wild

(*n*) defiance, disobedience, disruptiveness, dissidence, freedom, indiscipline, insubordination, mischievousness, naughtiness, noncompliance, nonconformity, noncooperation, *obstreperousness*, *obstructiveness*, perverseness, rebelliousness, recalcitrance, resistance, unruliness, warmongering, waywardness, wildness

566 Uncooperative or Rebellious People

What is a rebel? A man who says no: but whose refusal does not imply a renunciation. **Albert Camus**

(*n*) abolitionist, activist, agitator, apostate, attacker, bourgeois, combatant, conservative, counter-revolutionary, defector, demagogue, demonstrator, diehard, dissenter, dissident, firebrand, *fogy*, free spirit, freethinker, fuddy-duddy (*informal*), guerrilla, heckler, hothead, iconoclast, incendiary (*formal*), insurgent, intransigent (*formal*), *irredentist*, malcontent, marcher, militant, mischief-maker, mutineer, nationalist, nonconformist, obscurantist, picket, protester, rabble-rouser, radical, reactionary, rebel, revolutionary, ring-leader, rioter, *saber-rattler*, saboteur, separatist, square (*slang dated*), stick-in-the-mud (*informal*), subversive, troublemaker, warmonger

567 Upset, Distress, and Humiliate

When you have a great cause to fight for, the moment of greatest humiliation is the moment when the spirit is proudest. **Christabel Pankhurst**

(*v*) abase (*literary*), affect, afflict, aggrieve (*formal*), ail (*archaic or literary*), appall, beleaguer, belittle, beset (*formal*), bother, bring down a peg, bring down to earth, bring into disrepute, bring shame on, brutalize, burn up (*informal*), cast down, cause offense, chasten, chill, concern, crush, debase, deflate, degrade, demean, demoralize, demotivate, depress, derange, deter, devastate, devour (*literary*), disaffect, disappoint, discourage, *disenchant*, disgrace, dishearten, dishonor, disillusion, dismay, dispirit, disquiet (*archaic or literary*), distress, disturb, eat (*slang*), emasculate (*formal*), embarrass, embitter, fail, flurry, gnaw, grieve, grind down, gross out (*slang*), horrify, humble, humiliate, hurt, incommode (*formal*), let down, mortify, nauseate, offend, oppress, overcome, overpower, overtake, pain, persecute, perturb, pierce, plague, preoccupy, prey on, psych, put off, rack, rattle, *reduce to tears*, repel, revolt, ruffle, sadden, scar, scourge, send over the edge, shake, shame, shock, show up, sicken, stir, stress out (*informal*), take down, tear apart, threaten, torment, torture, traumatize, trouble, turn your stomach, tyrannize, unhinge, unnerve, unsettle, upset, vex, weigh down, wither, wound

See also SADNESS, DISTRESS, AND DESPAIR (539)

568 Frighten and Shock

You can discover what your enemy fears most by observing the means he uses to frighten you. **Eric Hoffer**

(*v*) alarm, bully, cow, daunt, disgust, frighten, horrify, intimidate, menace, overawe, panic, petrify, *root to the spot*, scandalize, scare, scare off, scarify (*informal*), shake up, shock, spook, terrify, terrorize

See also FEAR AND PANIC (543)

569 Anger and Annoy

Anger is one of the sinews of the soul. **Thomas Fuller**

(*v*) aggravate (*informal*), anger, annoy, antagonize, bedevil, bother, bug (*informal*), chafe, cross, disgruntle, displease, dissatisfy, disturb, drive up the wall (*informal*), enrage, exasperate, frustrate, gall, get at, get on your nerves, get to, grate, gravel (*informal*), harass, harry, hassle (*informal*), haunt, incense, inconvenience, inflame, infuriate, irk, irritate, jar, madden, make somebody's blood boil, make somebody's hackles rise, miff (*informal*), molest, nag, needle (*informal*), nettle (*informal*), niggle, outrage, peeve (*informal*), pester, pique, plague, provoke, put out, put somebody's back up (*informal*), rankle, rile (*informal*), rub the wrong way, tease, tick off (*informal*), try, vex, wind up (*UK informal*), work up, worry

See also IRRITATION AND ANGER (541)

570 Bore and Fail to Interest

I have ten commandments. The first nine are, thou shalt not bore. The tenth is, thou shalt have right of final cut. **Billy Wilder**

(*v*) bore, *bore rigid, bore stiff, bore to death, bore to tears,* disincline, stultify, turn off (*informal*)

See also BORING AND UNINTERESTING (234)

571 Confuse and Bewilder

By the glare of false science betray'd,/That leads to bewilder, and dazzles to blind. **James Beattie**

(*v*) *abash*, addle, agitate, baffle, bamboozle (*informal*), bedazzle, befuddle, bemuse, bewilder, boggle (*informal*), buffalo (*informal*), confound, confuse, daze, dazzle, defeat, *discombobulate* (*informal*), discomfit (*formal*), disconcert, disorient, distract, *drive insane, drive mad* (*informal*), *drive nuts* (*informal*), *drive round the bend* (*UK*), dumbfound, elude, faze, flabbergast (*informal*), floor, flummox (*informal*), fluster, fog, fox, fuddle, gravel (*informal*), mess up (*informal*), muddle, mystify, nonplus, perplex, poleax, put off (*UK*), puzzle, *render speechless,* sidetrack, stump, stun, stupefy, throw (*informal*), tie in knots, trip up, unbalance, vex

See also CONFUSION, ANXIETY, AND WORRY (540)

572 Please and Amuse

The beautiful is that which pleases universally without a concept. **Immanuel Kant**

(*v*) amuse, cheer up, content, crack up (*informal*), delight, disarm, distract, divert, elate, entertain, gladden, gratify, oblige, please, regale, satisfy, thrill, tickle, *tickle pink* (*UK*)

See also PLEASURE, EXCITEMENT, AND ELATION (534)

573 Soothe and Calm

Isn't everyone consoled when faced with a trouble or fact he does not understand, by a word? **Luigi Pirandello**

(*v*) appease, bring around, calm, comfort, console, desensitize, inure, lull, mollify, pacify, placate, propitiate, reassure, salve, satisfy, soothe, subdue, sweeten

See also CONFIDENCE AND COMPOSURE (499), COOL AND CALM (536)

574 Surprise and Impress

Stars open among the lilies./Are you not blinded by such expressionless sirens?/This is the silence of astounded souls. **Sylvia Plath**

(*v*) amaze, astonish, astound, blow away (*slang*), bowl over, catch napping, catch out (*informal*), catch unawares, dazzle, enrapture (*formal*), entrance, exhilarate, impress, *knock down with a feather,* knock out, knock over (*informal*), *knock somebody's socks off,* rock (*informal*), sneak up on, stagger, startle, stupefy, surprise, sweep away, sweep somebody off his/her feet, take aback, take by storm, take by surprise, take unawares, *throw somebody a curve ball* (*slang*), touch, wrong-foot

See also SURPRISE, SHOCK, AND AMAZEMENT (545)

575 Appeal to and Arouse Interest

You do not get a man's most effective criticism until you provoke him. **Henry David Thoreau**

(*v*) absorb, amuse, appeal, arouse, arrest (*formal*), attract, bait, beguile, bewitch, *bewitch,* captivate, capture your imagination, charm, divert, draw, draw in, eat up, electrify, enchant, engage, engross, enthrall, enthuse, entice, excite, fascinate, grab (*informal*), grip, hypnotize, infect, inspire, interest, intrigue, invite, involve, lead on, lure, magnetize, mesmerize, obsess, occupy, overexcite, pack in, pique, prejudice, pull, pull in, ravish, reach, rivet (*informal*), rouse, scintillate, *spellbind,* stir, tantalize, tease, tempt, *titillate,* toy with, transfix, turn on (*informal*), wake, waken

See also CAUSE OR COMPEL TO ACT (271), PENSIVENESS AND INTEREST (538)

576 Encourage

In this country it is good to kill an admiral from time to time, to encourage the others. **Voltaire**

(*v*) animate, brighten up, build up, buoy up, dispose, embolden, encourage, fire, fire up, fortify, give a boost, give a lift, hearten, lift, perk up, persuade, predispose (*formal*), *raise the spirits,* raise your spirits, stimulate, sway, uplift, win over

See also CAUSE OR COMPEL TO ACT (271)

577 Dislike and Hate

We have just enough religion to make us hate, but not enough to make us love one another. **Jonathan Swift**

(*n*) abhorrence, abomination (*literary*), allergy (*informal*), disdain, disfavor, disgust, dislike, distaste, hate, hatred, loathing, nausea (*literary*), odium, repugnance, repulsion, revulsion

(*v*) abhor (*formal*), abominate (*formal*), bear a grudge, begrudge, despise, detest, disapprove, disdain, dislike, frown on, grudge, hate, have it in for, *hold in contempt,* loathe, look down on, resent, take a dim view of, take exception, take for granted, take offense, *think badly of, think little of*

See also UNPOPULAR AND UNWANTED (258)

578 Like, Love, Value, and Enjoy

They that love beyond the world cannot be separated by it. **William Penn**

(*n*) appreciation, approval, inclination, keenness (*UK*), leaning, orientation, partiality, pleasure (*formal or literary*), preference, taste, weakness

(*prep*) all for, for, in favor of

(*v*) admire, adore, appreciate, bank on, bask, be attracted, be crazy about (*informal*), be partial to, be sure of, canonize, care for, cherish, count on, deify, delight, depend on, enjoy, enshrine, esteem, fall for, *fetishize,* follow, glory in, go for (*informal*), go in for, *have a crush on* (*informal*), *have a high opinion of, have a high regard for, have a soft spot for, have a weakness for, hero-worship, hold dear,* hold in high regard, *hold in the highest regard,* honor, idealize, idolize, incline, lap up, latch onto (*informal*), lean, like, look up to, love, luxuriate, please, prefer, pride yourself on, privilege, prize, put a premium on, *regard highly,* relish, respect, revel, revere, romance, romanticize, savor, set store by, swear by, take a fancy to, *take a liking to*, *take a shine to* (*informal*), *take great delight in*, take pleasure in, take to, tend, *think a lot of*, *think highly of*, think the world of, treasure, value, venerate, wallow in, warm, *warm to*

See also POPULAR AND WANTED (220)

579 Desire and Want

The desire of the moth for the star. **James Joyce**

(*adj*) aspiring, avid, bent, *chomping at the bit*, dependent, dying to, eager, gasping (*UK*), hungry (*informal*), intent, lustful, tempted, thirsty

(*n*) aching (*formal*), appetite, craving, dependence, desire, *desirousness* (*formal*), dream, hankering, hope, hunger, impulse, impulsion, itch, longing, lust, passion, temptation, thirst, urge, wanderlust, wants, will, wish, yearning, yen

(*prep*) after

(*v*) ache (*formal*), aspire, be after, be burning to, be spoiling for, cling, covet, crave, desire, envy, feel like, hanker, *hanker after*, *have a yen for*, have your eye on, hope, hunger, *hunger after*, itch, languish, long for, lust, miss, pine, pray, sigh, thirst, want, will, wish, yearn

See also FEELINGS ABOUT THE FUTURE (533)

580 Change of Mood and Composure

Before the cherry orchard was sold everybody was worried and upset, but as soon as it was all settled finally and once for all, everybody calmed down, and felt quite cheerful. **Anton Chekhov**

(*v*) *acclimatize yourself*, *accustom yourself*, adapt, attune, be carried away, brighten, buck up (*informal*), calm down, chill out (*slang*), compose yourself, cool down, cool off (*informal*), demean yourself, despair, ease up, get a grip (*informal*), give up, give up on, groove (*slang*), habituate, immerse, let your hair down, let yourself go, lighten, lighten up (*informal*), light up, loosen up, lose heart, lose your nerve, lower yourself, make a fool of yourself, make an exhibition of yourself, mellow, *nerve yourself*, pull yourself together (*informal*), regret, relax, rise to the bait, rue, settle, settle down, settle in, simmer down, squirm, stoop, switch off (*informal*), take heart, take it easy, *take umbrage*, *throw caution to the wind*, turn off, unwind, wake up, warm, wind down

581 Be Concerned and Care

Nothing is more fatal to Health, *than an* over Care *of it.* **Benjamin Franklin**

(*v*) be a bundle of nerves (*informal*), be bothered, be concerned, care, eat your heart out (*informal*), empathize, feel for, feel sorry for, fret, fuss, identify with, mind, pity, sorrow (*literary*), sweat (*informal*), sympathize, understand, worry

582 Experience and Encounter

History is the record of an encounter between character and circumstance. **Donald Creighton**

(*v*) bump into, come into contact with, come up against, contend with, encounter, experience, *fall prey to*, *fall victim to*, go through, have, *have a brush with*, incur,

know, labor under, live through, meet, plumb, run into, run the gauntlet, suffer, sustain, taste, undergo

See also HAPPEN TO SOMEBODY (30)

The Written Word

583 Writing

A good book is a piece of writing that implies that things don't exist, a kind of absence, or death…it is futile to look outside the book for a realm that is located beyond the words. **Orhan Pamuk**

(*adj*) annotated, printed, scrawled, scribbled, textual, written

(*adv*) in print

(*n*) calligraphy, copy, dictation, document, graffiti, hand, handwriting, lettering, printing, scrawl, scribble, script, squiggle, text, writing

See also RECORD SOMETHING (371)

584 Letters and Written Messages

When an actor has money he doesn't send letters, he sends telegrams. **Anton Chekhov**

(*n*) aerogram, aide-mémoire (*formal*), billet-doux (*literary*), *cablegram*, card, communiqué, dispatch, epistle (*formal*), fax, inscription, letter, letter card (*UK*), mail, mailbag, memo, memorandum, message, missive, note, notelet (*UK*), postcard, reference, resignation, snail mail (*informal*), spam, special delivery, surface mail, telegram, testimonial

585 Records

The critic is the historian who records the order of creation. **Margaret Fuller**

(*n*) almanac, annals, archive, books, chronicle, diary, docket, dossier, entry, file, journal, ledger, library, log, logbook, memoir, minutes, proceedings, readout, record, scorecard, scoresheet, snapshot, statement, transcript, transcription, worksheet, yearbook

586 Official Documents

Remove the document—and you remove the man. **Mikhail Bulgakov**

(*n*) accord, affidavit, agreement, bill, blueprint, card, certificate, certification, charter, concord, contract, convention, covenant, credentials, deed, documentation, edict, form, guarantee, ID, identification, identity card, indenture, insurance policy, license, manifesto, pass, passport, patent, permit, policy, scroll, testimony, ticket, title deed, treaty, visa, waiver, warrant, warranty

587 Lists and Schedules

Hungry Joe collected lists of fatal diseases and arranged them in alphabetical order so that he could put his finger without delay on any one he wanted to worry about. **Joseph Heller**

(*n*) agenda, bibliography, calendar, catalog, checklist, chronology, diary (*UK*), dictionary, glossary, index, inventory, lexicon, list, listing, listings, mailing list, menu, organizer, personal organizer, planner, program, register, registration, roll call, roster, rota (*UK*), schedule, syllabus, thesaurus, timetable, vocabulary, *wishlist*, word list, worksheet

588   Summaries, Outlines, and Excerpts

Good things, when short, are twice as good. **Baltasar Gracián**

(*n*) abridgment, abstract, aide-mémoire (*formal*), article, blurb (*slang*), brief, citation, clause, clip, clipping, condensation, *curriculum vitae*, CV, digest, excerpt, extract, generality, generalization, itinerary, listing, outline, overview, paraphrase, précis, profile, quotation, quote, recap, recapitulation (*formal*), refresher, résumé, rough copy, roundup, rundown, run-through, summary, summation, synopsis, translation, version, vignette

589   Manuals and Instructions

The most important thing about Spaceship Earth—an instruction book didn't come with it. **R. Buckminster Fuller**

(*n*) check, fact sheet, guide, guidebook, handbook, information sheet, introduction, manual, primer, prospectus, rubric, rulebook

590   Books and Booklets

The good of a book lies in being read. **Umberto Eco**

(*n*) album, atlas, book, booklet, brochure, casebook, codex, digest, edition, encyclopedia, lexicon, limited edition, literature, manuscript, memoirs, monograph, *palimpsest*, pamphlet, paperback, phrase book, picture book, publication, songbook, *story book*, text, textbook, tome, tract, trilogy, volume

See also FICTION AND DRAMA (913)

591   Receipts and Invoices

We are all gratified by advancing the frontiers of scientific knowledge, but the only thing that ever gets invoiced is the product. **Richard J. Mahoney**

(*n*) account, bill, check, chit (*dated*), coupon, docket, invoice, paystub, postmark, *proof of posting, proof of purchase*, receipt, tab (*informal*), token, voucher

592   Analytic Nonfiction Writing

It requires a very unusual mind to undertake the analysis of the obvious. **A. N. Whitehead**

(*n*) article, biography, commentary, critique, dissertation, essay, memoir, paper, piece of writing, study, thesis, treatise, vignette, write-up

See also NEWSPAPERS AND MAGAZINES (605)

593   Parts of Books and Documents

A page of history is worth a volume of logic. **Oliver Wendell Holmes, Jr.**

(*n*) addendum, annotation, appendix, caption, chapter, coda, codicil (*formal*), cross-reference, dateline, enclosure, epilogue, episode, flyleaf, footer, footnote, foreword, frontispiece, gloss, header, heading, insert, insertion, inset, introduction, leaf, notation, note, passage, postscript, preamble, preface, pullout, rider, rubric, scene, supplement, title page

594   Drawings, Charts, and Tables

Just as the painters seek to imitate objects exactly. . .geometricians and astronomers delineate on a flat plane solid objects, such as octahedrons and cubes and all spherical bodies, like the stars, the heavens, and the earth. **Nicephorus Gregoras**

(*n*) artwork, chart, design, diagram, drawing, figure, floor plan, graph, ground plan, illustration, *illustrations*, layout, *lithograph*, map, piechart, protraction, rough, schema, scheme, scribble, side view, sketch, spreadsheet, table, tabulation, tattoo, tree, vignette, visual, visual aid, watermark

See also THE PICTORIAL ARTS (897)

595   Signposts, Signals, and Billboards

I think that I shall never see/A billboard lovely as a tree. **Ogden Nash**

(*n*) alert, banner, beacon, billboard, buoy, cairn, hoarding (*UK*), mayday, milepost, milestone, nameplate, notice, noticeboard (*UK*), placard, plaque, poster, road sign, scoreboard, sign, signboard (*UK*), signpost, SOS

596   Symbols, Signs, and Numbers

Numbers constitute the only universal language. **Nathanael West**

(*n*) ABCs, alphabet, ampersand, arrow, asterisk, badge, brand, chevron, cipher, coat of arms, code, colors, combination, crest, cross, decimal, device, digit, emblem, *emoticon*, ensign, figure, flag, *glyph*, gonfalon, hallmark, hieroglyph, imprint, insignia, letter, logo, *mimeograph*, notation, number, numeral, patch, pennant, pennon, pictograph, rune, sign, signature, stamp, standard, sticker, symbol, target, trademark, water line, watermark

types of alphabets Arabic, Braille, cuneiform, Cyrillic, Greek, Hebrew, hieroglyphics, hiragana, ideogram, kanji, katakana, phonetic alphabet, pictogram, Roman alphabet, runic

597   Math

(*adj*) *arithmetical*, binary, digital, mathematical, mean, numerical, quantitative

(*n*) algebra, *arithmetic*, *arithmetic mean*, average, calculation, *calculus*, coefficient, computation, equation, *geometry*, integer, mathematics, median, reckoning, statistic, subtraction, sum, theorem, *trigonometry*

598   Scores and Evaluations

Read not to contradict and confute, nor to believe and take for granted, nor to find talk and discourse, but to weigh and consider. **Francis Bacon**

(*n*) appraisal, calibration, count, estimate, evaluation, grade, mark, par, quotation, quote, rating, reappraisal, reassessment, record, re-count, result, score, standard, tally, touchstone, valuation, yardstick

599   Written Conventions

All styles are good except the tiresome sort. **Voltaire**

(*adv*) e.g., et al., etc., idem, i.e., inter alia (*formal*), *N.B.*, passim (*formal*), P.S., *P.T.O.*

600 Printing

I, according to my copy, have done set it in imprint, to the intent that noble men may see and learn the noble acts of chivalry. **William Caxton**

(*adj*) bold, boldface, italic, lightface, roman

(*n*) font, printing, toner, type, typeface, *typescript, typesetter, typesetting,* typo (*informal*), typography

601 Writing and Drawing Implements and Media

(*n*) blackboard, blotter, *chalkboard,* easel, *gouache,* jotter (*UK*), notepad, notepaper, pad, page, *papyrus,* parchment, pastel, *pen,* rubber stamp, *scratchpad, scribbler, scribbling pad,* seal, *sketchbook, sketchpad,* stationery, workbook, *writing board, writing pad, writing paper*

types of pens ballpoint, felt-tipped pen, fountain pen, highlighter, marker, quill, rollerball

Communication and Interaction

602 Communication

The present century, in proclaiming the advent of a new age of communication and information...forgot to deal with the great problem of talk, which is how to find someone to listen. **Theodore Zeldin**

(*n*) chemistry, communication, communications, contact, correspondence, dealings, fraternization, interaction, intercourse, *nonverbal communication,* oratory, self-expression, speaking, speech, talking, utterance, *verbal communication,* voice, word

603 Speakers and Orators

The arrow belongs not to the archer when it has once left the bow; the word no longer belongs to the speaker when it has once passed his lips. **Heinrich Heine**

(*n*) conversationalist, debater, interlocutor, orator, polemicist, propagandist, proselytizer, raconteur, rhetorician, schmoozer (*slang*), speaker, speechmaker, storyteller, talker

604 Advertising and Publicity

Advertising may be described as the science of arresting human intelligence long enough to get money from it. **Stephen Leacock**

(*adj*) promotional

(*n*) ad, advertisement, advertising, bill, buildup, *bulk mail,* circular, commercial, direct mail, flier, flysheet, handbill, handout, hype, infomercial, junk mail, leaflet, mailer, mailshot (*UK*), marketing, media, personal, personal ad (*UK*), plug (*informal*), poster, press release, preview, promo (*informal*), promotion, propaganda, publicity, public relations, road show, showcase, spot, trailer, *want ad* (*informal*)

(*v*) advertise, bill, hype, plug (*informal*), promote, sell

605 Newspapers and Magazines

A good newspaper is never nearly good enough but a lousy newspaper is a joy forever. **Garrison Keillor**

(*adj*) journalistic, tabloid

(*n*) broadsheet, bulletin, byline, circulation, column, comic, comics, coverage, editorial, exposé, exposure, feature, gazette, *glossy magazine* (*UK*), headline, issue, journal, journalism, leading article (*UK*), *mag* (*informal*), magazine, masthead, monthly, newsletter, newspaper, newsprint, newssheet (*UK*), organ (*formal*), paper, paragraph, periodical, photojournalism, quarterly, rag (*informal*), reportage, review, scoop (*informal*), stop press (*UK*), story, strapline (*UK*), tabloid (*UK*)

See also ANALYTIC NONFICTION WRITING (592), WORKERS IN ENTERTAINMENT AND MEDIA (873)

606 Television and Radio

Why should people go out and pay money to see bad movies when they can stay at home and see bad television for nothing? **Samuel Goldwyn**

(*adj*) on-screen, on the air

(*n*) airplay, airwaves, boob tube (*informal*), box (*slang*), broadcast, bulletin, CB, channel, flash, footage, newsroom, photo opportunity, program, reception, rerun, satellite, *satellite television, shortwave radio,* small screen (*informal*), special effects, transmission, *tube* (*informal*), TV (*informal*), *TV set,* viewing, voiceover

(*v*) broadcast, rerun, screen, *simulcast, telecast,* televise, zap (*informal*)

types of broadcasts call-in, commercial, concert, current affairs, distance learning, docudrama, documentary, drama, game show, infomercial, infotainment, makeover program, miniseries, news, newscast, news flash, newsreel, play, reality show, sitcom (*informal*), soap (*informal*), soap opera, sport, sportscast, talk show, telethon, travelogue

See also WORKERS IN ENTERTAINMENT AND MEDIA (873)

607 Two-way Communication

Online conversation is...talking by writing. **John Coate**

(*v*) argue, bandy, chat, chew the fat (*slang*), chitchat (*informal*), communicate, compare notes, confer, converse, cross-fertilize, debate, discourse (*formal*), discuss, hammer out, intercommunicate, jaw (*slang*), *make small talk,* mediate, natter (*informal*), negotiate, rap (*slang*), schmooze (*slang*), shoot the breeze (*slang*), square, talk, talk over, thrash out (*UK*), yak (*informal*)

See also INFORMAL COMMUNICATION (45)

608 Utter and Pronounce

I always start too soon and arrive too late and eventually come back in the middle—stuttering. **Jean-Luc Godard**

(*v*) ad-lib, articulate, aspirate, call, call out, chorus, ejaculate (*literary*), enunciate, express, extemporize, externalize, formulate, hold forth, improvise, intone, mouth, observe, orate (*formal*), phrase, pontificate, print, pronounce, put into words, rap out, say, sing out, speak, speak out, speak up, specify, spit, tell, utter, verbalize, vocalize, voice, word

609   Instruct and Teach

It is the supreme art of the teacher to awaken joy in creative expression and knowledge. **Albert Einstein**

(*v*) address, brainwash, break in, coach, convert, convince, declaim, discipline, domesticate, drill, drum into, edify, educate, equip, *expatiate*, familiarize, force-feed, groom, ground, imprint, inculcate, indoctrinate, induct, infuse, ingrain, initiate, instill, instruct, introduce, lecture, orate, *perorate* (*formal*), potty-train (*informal*), preach, prepare, prime, proselytize, reeducate, rehabilitate, school, sermonize, sophisticate, speak, speechify (*informal*), tame, teach, train, tutor

See also TEACHING (839), EDUCATORS (840)

610   Explain and Clarify

Never explain: your friends don't need it and your enemies won't believe it. **Victor Grayson**

(*adj*) descriptive, explanatory, interpretative, interpretive

(*n*) account, alibi (*informal*), amplification, clarification, delineation (*formal*), demystification, elaboration, elucidation, explanation, *explication*, formulation, illumination, interpretation, justification, plea, popularization, rationale, rationalization

(*v*) account for, amplify, be blunt, bring home, call a spade a spade, clarify, clear up, *cut to the chase* (*informal*), demonstrate, demystify, describe, detail, develop, dilate, elaborate, elucidate, encapsulate, enlighten, enunciate, expand upon, explain, explicate, expound, fill in, generalize, get across, *get to the point*, *give a rough idea*, give instructions, go into detail, illuminate, interpret, irradiate, justify, lay it on the line (*informal*), lay out, make clear, nail down, not mince words, outline, popularize, précis, put across, rationalize, recap, recapitulate (*formal*), run by, run over, set forth (*formal*), set out, shed light on, show, spell out, summarize, sum up, *throw light on*, unfold

611   Inform, Announce, and Issue

A drama critic is a person who surprises the playwright by informing him what he meant. **Wilson Mizner**

(*n*) affirmation, announcement, declassification, disinterment (*formal*), dissemination, enunciation, leak, notification, popularization, proclamation, promulgation (*formal*), pronouncement, propagation, protestation, publishing, release, revelation, sound bite, statement, unveiling

(*v*) acquaint, advertise, advise, air, announce, *apprise* (*formal*), brief, bring up-to-date, broadcast, bugle, circulate, communicate, declare, declassify, disabuse, disclose, disseminate, editorialize, get over, give out, go around, herald, impart, inform, introduce, issue, let in on, let into (*UK*), let know, make known, make public, notify, pass on, point out, popularize, post, present, proclaim, promulgate (*formal*), pronounce, propagate, publicize, publish, put about, put forth (*formal*), put forward, put out, reissue, relay, release, remind, sensitize, share, sound, spread, *spread abroad* (*UK*), *spread around*, *spread the word*, state, talk turkey (*informal*), tell, undeceive, unveil, update, vent, ventilate, volunteer

612   Suggest, Hint, and Comment

Had I been present at the Creation, I would have given some useful hints for the better ordering of the universe. **Alfonso X**

(*conj*) supposing

(*n*) allusion, comment, commentary, evocation, hint, inference, innuendo, insinuation, intimation, mention, motion, mover, observation, offer, overtone, proposal, proposition, reference, remark, rumbling (*informal*), submission, suggestion

(*v*) adduce (*formal*), allude, bid, bring forward, bring up, broach, comment, commentate, drag in, drag up, enter, float, hazard, hint, imply, infer, insinuate, intimate, make out, mention, moot, note, offer, pick up on (*informal*), pitch, present (*formal*), propose, propound, put forward, put in, raise, rake up (*informal*), refer, remark, signal, submit, suggest, table (*UK*), tender, throw in, touch on, venture

613   Advise and Warn

Advice is seldom welcome; and those who want it the most always like it the least. **Lord Chesterfield**

(*adj*) admonitory, advisory, cautionary, dissuasive, premonitory, warning

(*v*) advise, alert, caution, counsel, dissuade, forearm, forewarn, preach, prescribe, recommend, tip off, urge, warn, warn off

See also ADVICE (689)

614   Claim, Insist, and Emphasize

For what is passes so swiftly and irrevocably into what was, no human claim can be of the least significance. **Joyce Carol Oates**

(*n*) allegation, assertion, claim, exaggeration, iteration, overstatement, overstress, reaffirmation, reassertion, reinforcement, representation

(*v*) accent, accentuate, affirm, allege, argue, assert, aver (*formal*), avow (*formal*), belabor, blow up (*informal*), claim, contend, din, embroider, emphasize, exaggerate, highlight, impress, insist, labor, *labor the point*, lay it on thick, *lay it on with a trowel* (*informal*), maintain, make a big thing of, make a mountain out of a molehill, opine (*formal*), overemphasize, overpitch, overplay, overrate, oversell, overstate, overstress, play up, plead, point out, point up, protest, purport, put your foot down, ram home, reaffirm, reason, reassert, reinforce, signpost, specify, spotlight, stipulate, stress, stretch a point, swear, testify, underline, underscore, voice

615   Admit and Confess

It is not the criminal things which are hardest to confess, but the ridiculous and shameful. **Jean-Jacques Rousseau**

(*n*) admission, avowal (*formal*), confession, disclosure, self-incrimination

(*v*) acknowledge, admit, allow (*formal*), come clean (*informal*), come out with, confess, *disburden* (*archaic*), *fess up* (*slang*), get it off your chest, let on, make a clean breast of things, own (*formal*), own up, profess, take the blame, take the rap (*slang*), *tell it how it is* (*informal*), tell the truth, unburden (*formal*)

616   Boast

I'm so fast I could hit you before God gets the news.
Muhammad Ali

(*n*) aggrandizement (*formal*), boast, boasting, *braggadocio*, bragging, bravado, embellishment, grandiloquence, grandiosity, rhetoric, self-aggrandizement, self-flattery, self-glorification, self-promotion, showing off, swagger

(*v*) aggrandize (*formal*), blow your own horn, boast, brag, crow, embellish, glamorize, gloat, grandstand, lay it on, *mouth off* (*informal*), name-drop, roister, *showboat* (*informal*), show off, sing your own praises, swank (*slang*), vaunt

See also POMPOUS, LOUD, AND OVERCONFIDENT (635)

617   Chatter and Babble

The arts babblative and scribblative. **Robert Southey**

(*v*) babble (*UK*), beat around the bush, blabber, blather (*informal*), *blither* (*informal*), bumble, burble (*informal*), chatter, digress, diverge, *drone on*, footle (*informal*), gab (*informal*), gabble, gibber, go on, gush, jabber, mispronounce, mumble, murmur, mutter, patter, prate, prattle, ramble, ramble on, rattle on, slur, speak, spiel (*informal*), spout, stammer, stutter, *talk a mile a minute*, *talk gibberish*, *talk nineteen to the dozen* (*UK*), *talk ten to the dozen*, *talk the hind legs off a donkey* (*UK*)

See also MEANINGLESS SPEECH OR WRITING (676)

618   Betray Confidences and Gossip

I delight in sinning and hate to compose a mask for gossip.
Sulpicia

(*v*) betray, blab (*informal*), blow somebody's cover, blow the whistle, blurt, burst out, confide, *dish the dirt* (*informal*), divulge, expose, give away, give up, gossip, inform, leak, let drop, let out, let slip, let the cat out of the bag, pour out, put your foot in it (*informal*), put your foot in your mouth (*informal*), rat on (*informal*), reveal, say, sing (*slang*), sneak (*UK*), snitch (*slang*), spill the beans (*informal*), squeal (*slang*), *squeal on* (*slang*), stab in the back (*informal*), talk, tattle, tell, *tell on*, *tell tales*, tittle-tattle, turn in

See also GOSSIP (678), INTERFERING PEOPLE AND TATTLETALES (950)

619   Interrupt and Butt In

Writing is a way of talking without being interrupted.
Jules Renard

(*v*) barge in, break in, burst in on, butt in, chime in, chip in (*informal*), contribute, cut in, cut off, get a word in edgewise, *horn in* (*informal*), impose, infringe, interfere, interject, interpolate, interpose, interrupt, intrude, meddle, muscle in (*informal*), obtrude, pipe up, put in, put your oar in (*UK*), start up, step in, *stick your nose in*, *stick your oar in* (*UK*), tangle, violate

620   Recite, Repeat, and Narrate

It's better to be quotable than to be honest. **Tom Stoppard**

(*v*) cite (*formal*), dictate, echo, iterate, misquote, narrate, paraphrase, quote, rattle off, read, read out, recite, recount, *reecho*, reel off, regurgitate, reiterate, relate, repeat, rephrase, report, restate, retell, tell

621   Flatter and Fawn

Be advised that all flatterers live at the expense of those who listen to them. **Jean de La Fontaine**

(*v*) abase yourself (*literary*), *blandish* (*archaic*), butter up (*informal*), court, crawl (*informal*), fawn, flatter, genuflect, grovel, kowtow, make points with, play up to, soft-soap (*informal*), suck up (*informal*), sweet-talk (*informal*), toady

See also INGRATIATING (638), PRAISE AND ENCOURAGE (647)

622   Summarizing Expressions

An aphorism is something which spares the writer an essay by way of commentary, but in consequence is deeply shocking to the reader. **Peter Altenberg**

(*adv*) all in all, all things considered, altogether, as it were (*formal*), at any rate, at least, at the end of the day, essentially, finally, generally speaking, in a nutshell, in brief, *in other words*, in short, *in sum*, *in summary*, in the main, lastly, on balance, *to be brief*, to cut a long story short, *to put it briefly*, *to sum up*, virtually, well, when all's said and done, with hindsight

623   Expressions of Opinion

A man's opinion on tramcars matters; his opinion on Botticelli matters; his opinion on all things does not matter.
G. K. Chesterton

(*adv*) *as far as I'm concerned*, between ourselves, *between you and me*, between you, me, and the bedpost, if you ask me, in all fairness, in all honesty, in all likelihood, in all probability, in my book, *in my opinion*, *in my view*, personally, *to be fair*, *to be frank*, *to be honest*, to my mind, to tell the truth

624   Communicative Style

Proper words in proper places, make the true definition of a style. **Jonathan Swift**

(*adj*) colloquial, conversational, idiomatic, unspeaking, unwritten

625   Rude and Hostile

The right people are rude. They can afford to be.
Somerset Maugham

(*adj*) abrasive, abusive, acerbic, acid, acrid, acrimonious, astringent, audacious, austere, backhanded, barbed, biting, bitter, brutish, catty, caustic, cool, corrosive, cutting, destructive, forbidding, glacial, head-on, impenitent, mordant, offensive, piquant, pointed, provocative, rancorous, rude, scurrilous, sharp-tongued, smart, snide, stinging, threatening, trenchant, ugly, uncomplimentary, unfriendly, venomous, vicious, virulent, vitriolic, waspish, wicked, wounding

(*adv*) abrasively, acidly, bitchily (*slang*), bitingly, bitterly, blackly, cheekily (*informal*), condescendingly, cuttingly, derisively, disputatiously (*formal*), frigidly, frostily, ghoulishly, head-on, offensively, pointedly, venomously, viciously, wickedly

(*n*) acerbity, astringency, trenchancy, waspishness

See also UNFRIENDLINESS AND UNSOCIALBILITY (504), AGGRESSIVE AND BELLIGERENT (518), BAD MANNERS AND SOCIAL SKILLS (521), ANTAGONISM (552)

626 Bad-Tempered and Humorless

The sort of eye that can open an oyster at sixty paces.
P. G. Wodehouse

(*adj*) abrupt, brisk, brusque, churlish, crusty, curt, earnest, grim, grouchy (*informal*), gruff, huffy, po-faced (*UK*), querulous, sharp, short, snappish, snappy, snippy (*informal*), solemn, sour, stern, sullen, surly, tart, terse, testy (*informal*), unsmiling, *whiny*

(*adv*) blackly, crossly, darkly, dourly, earnestly, ghoulishly, grimly, grouchily (*informal*), heavily, huffily, sharply, shortly, soberly, sourly, sullenly, tartly, testily (*informal*), tetchily (*informal*)

(*n*) abruptness, asperity (*formal*), briskness, earnestness, grimness, grouchiness (*informal*), gruffness, querulousness, sharpness, shortness, *snappiness, snappishness*, soberness, solemnity, sternness, sullenness, tartness, terseness, testiness (*informal*), tetchiness (*informal*)

See also ESCESSIVE SENSITIVITY (511)

627 Good-Tempered and Humorous

Good humor is the seasoning of truth. **Johann Heinrich Pestalozzi**

(*adj*) airy, arch, avuncular, good-humored, good-tempered, hearty, jesting (*literary*), *jocose* (*literary*), jocular, jocund (*literary*), jokey, joking, lighthearted, playful, waggish (*informal*)

(*adv*) airily, archly, blithely (*literary*), breezily, brightly, convivially, drily, good-temperedly, heartily, humorously, jokily, joyfully, lightheartedly, well

(*n*) airiness, archness, jocularity, *jocundity* (*literary*), *jokiness*, levity, playfulness, waggishness (*informal*)

628 Enthusiastic and Inquisitive

Only connect the prose and the passion, and both will be exalted. **E. M. Forster**

(*adj*) appreciative, emphatic, gushing, gutsy (*informal*), heated, impassioned, inquiring, inquisitorial, interrogative, questioning, quizzical, rhapsodic, searching, urgent, vehement

(*adv*) effusively, emotionally, expansively, gushingly, highly, studiously, vehemently, warmly

See also ENERGY AND ENTHUSIASM (496), CHEERFULNESS OF OUTLOOK (503)

629 Uninterested and Detached

Perfect behavior is born of complete indifference.
Cesare Pavese

(*adj*) casual, clever, crisp, distant, glib, impersonal, inexpressive, offhand, wooden

(*adv*) casually, coolly, dispassionately, distantly, dully, flatly, impassively, offhandedly, woodenly

(*n*) blankness, brusqueness, distance, *offhandness*, woodenness

See also WITHOUT ENTHUSIASM (287), NEUTRALITY AND INDIFFERENCE (553)

630 Honest and Open

He that resolves to deal with none but honest men must leave off dealing. **Thomas Fuller**

(*adj*) bald, barefaced, bluff, blunt, candid, direct, explicit, expressive, forthright, frank, free, heart-to-heart, honest, ingenuous, matter-of-fact, no-nonsense, open, outspoken, plain, *plain-speaking*, plain-spoken, polemic, serious, stark, straight, straightforward, straight-out (*informal*), straight-talking, tactile, uninhibited, unreserved, upfront (*informal*), vocal, vociferous

(*adv*) avowedly (*formal*), baldly, bluntly, demonstratively, directly, explicitly, face to face, flatly, from the bottom of your heart, honestly, ingenuously, openly, outright, plainly, point-blank, straight out, uninhibitedly, vocally

(*n*) baldness, bluffness, bluntness, candidness, candor, directness, forthrightness, freedom, *matter-of-factness*, openness, outspokenness, plainness, *plain-spokenness*, sincerity, starkness, straightforwardness

See also NATURALNESS (497), HONEST AND RELIABLE (502)

631 Reticent and Unforthcoming

The cruellest lies are often told in silence.
Robert Louis Stevenson

(*adj*) allusive, backward, bashful, blushing, buttoned-down (*informal*), camera-shy, close, close-lipped, close-mouthed, coy, diffident, equivocal, evasive, guarded, humble, impersonal, indirect, inhibited, inquisitive, inscrutable, introvert, introverted, mealy-mouthed, meek, modest, monosyllabic, mum (*informal*), mysterious, noncommittal, private, reserved, restrained, reticent, retiring, secretive, self-critical, self-deprecating, shy, silent, soft-spoken, taciturn, tight-lipped, timid, timorous, tongue-tied, uncommunicative, undemonstrative, unforthcoming, unobtrusive, voiceless, withdrawn

(*adv*) darkly, guardedly, humbly, indirectly, modestly, shyly, undemonstratively

(*n*) bashfulness, diffidence, evasiveness, humbleness, humility, inhibition, inscrutability, meekness, reticence, *secretiveness*, self-deprecation, shyness, silence, taciturnity, timidity, timorousness, *uncommunicativeness*, undemonstrativeness

632 Eloquent, Talkative, and Long-winded

Revolutions are always verbose. **Leon Trotsky**

(*adj*) articulate, chatty, communicative, conversational, declamatory, demagogic, descriptive, discursive, effusive, eloquent, emotional, expansive, fluent, gabby (*informal*), garrulous, gaseous (*informal*), gassy (*informal*), glib, inflammatory, long-winded, loquacious, oratorical, persuasive, poetic, pungent, silver-tongued, smooth, smooth-tongued, talkative, voluble, well-expressed, well-spoken, well-turned, wordy

(*adv*) chattily, commandingly, evocatively, expansively, feelingly

(*n*) articulacy, articulateness, chattiness, discursiveness, eloquence, expressivity, garrulousness, *gift of gab* (*informal*), glibness, long-windedness, *loquaciousness* (*formal*), lyricism, oratory, persuasion, persuasiveness, poeticality, pungency, smoothness, talkativeness

633   Inarticulate, Rambling, and Awkward

If I reprehend any thing in this world, it is the use of my oracular tongue, and a nice derangement of epitaphs!
Richard Brinsley Sheridan

(*adj*) circuitous, circumlocutory, diffuse, disjointed, disquisitional (*formal*), elliptical, forced, garbled, *gibbering*, inarticulate, incoherent, mumbled, oblique, *prattling*, prolix, rambling, roundabout, slurred, staccato, stilted, verbose

(*adv*) at length (*formal*), circuitously, diffusely, *gibberingly*, in a roundabout way, woodenly

(*n*) circularity, circumlocution, inarticulacy, *inarticulateness*, *prolixity*, stammer, *stiltedness*, stutter, woodenness

634   Accusatory and Disapproving

Go out and speak for the inarticulate and the submerged.
Lord Beaverbrook

(*adj*) accusatorial (*formal*), *accusatory* (*formal*), accusing, admonitory, carping, *castigatory* (*formal*), censorious, condemnatory, critical, damning, defamatory, deprecating, deprecatory, depreciatory, derogatory, disapproving, disparaging, moralistic, moralizing, opprobrious, pejorative (*formal*), querulous, reprehensive, reproachful, reproving, scalding, sententious, unfavorable, unflattering, vituperative

635   Pompous, Loud, and Overconfident

The louder he talked of his honor, the faster we counted our spoons. **Ralph Waldo Emerson**

(*adj*) arrogant, assuming, bald-faced, bigheaded (*informal*), boastful, boasting, bold-faced, bombastic, bragging, brash, brassy, brazen, bumptious, cocksure, cocky (*informal*), conceited, condescending, flatulent, forward, full of yourself, grandiloquent, grandiose, high-flown, high-sounding, immodest, in-your-face (*slang*), lofty, loud, loudmouthed (*informal*), *magniloquent*, *mouthy* (*informal*), orotund (*formal*), overblown, peremptory, perky, protrusive, puffed-up, rhetorical, rumbustious, *self-admiring*, *self-aggrandizing*, self-important, self-opinionated, *smart-alecky* (*informal*), strident, swaggering, swashbuckling, swellheaded (*informal*), swollen-headed (*UK*), vain, vainglorious (*literary*), windy (*informal*)

(*adv*) brashly, disruptively, grandly, immodestly, loftily, loudly, *orotundly* (*formal*), peremptorily, perkily

(*n*) boastfulness, brashness, brazenness, bumptiousness, *cockiness*, *cocksureness*, flatulence, forwardness, immodesty, loftiness, *magniloquence*, *mouthiness* (*informal*), *orotundity* (*formal*), perkiness, puffiness, self-importance, vanity

See also BOSSY AND OVERBEARING (516), BOAST (616)

636   Mocking and Dismissive

Mock on, Mock on, Voltaire, Rousseau:/Mock on, Mock on: 'tis all in vain! **William Blake**

(*adj*) belittling, contemptuous, cynical, derisive, disdainful, dismissive, dry, facetious, flip (*informal*), flippant, ironic, irreverent, jeering, mocking, patronizing, sarcastic, sardonic, satirical, scathing, scoffing, scornful, sneering, taunting, tongue-in-cheek, withering, wry

(*n*) contemptuousness, dryness, flippancy, irony, irreverence, sarcasm, *sardonicism*, satire

637   Expressing Respect and Approval

Self-respect—the secure feeling that no one, as yet, is suspicious. **H. L. Mencken**

(*adj*) abject, affirmative, *approbatory*, approving, complimentary, deferential, favorable, glowing, laudatory, reverent, reverential

(*adv*) appreciatively, approvingly, cap in hand

(*prep*) pro

See also APPROVE AND CONFIRM (646)

638   Ingratiating

Good intentions can be evil,/Both hands can be full of grease./You know that sometimes Satan comes as a man of peace. **Bob Dylan**

(*adj*) adulatory, fawning, flattering, fulsome, honeyed, ingratiating, obsequious, servile, slimy, smarmy, sycophantic, toadying, unctuous

(*n*) blandishment, *cajolery*, flattery, jive (*slang*), obsequiousness, *servility*, *smarminess*, soft sell (*informal*), sweet talk (*informal*), sycophancy, toadying, *unctuousness*

See also FLATTER AND FAWN (621)

639   Flirtatious

Merely innocent flirtation,/Not quite adultery, but adulteration.
Lord Byron

(*adj*) coquettish (*literary*), coy, *flirtatious*, kittenish, teasing

640   Succinct and To The Point

I strive to be brief, and I become obscure. **Horace**

(*adj*) brief, clipped, concise, laconic, pithy, punchy, succinct, telegraphic, terse

(*n*) brevity, conciseness, concision, curtness, *laconicism*, pithiness, succinctness, terseness

641   Accuse, Blame, and Criticize

The worst libel is the truth. **Proverb**

(*v*) accuse, admonish, *anathematize*, assail, attack, bash (*informal*), bawl out (*informal*), beard, berate, besmirch, bitch (*slang*), blame, blast (*informal*), call down, castigate (*formal*), challenge, charge, chasten, chastise, chew out (*informal*), chide (*literary*), come down on, *come down on like a ton of bricks* (*informal*), condemn, conflict, confront, corner, criticize, crucify, denigrate, denounce, depreciate, dis (*slang*), disparage, dress down, excoriate (*formal*), fault, *find fault with*, finger (*slang*), flay, gang up on, hammer (*informal*), harangue, haul over the coals, heckle, *hold accountable*, *hold responsible*, *hurl abuse*, *hurl insults*, implicate, impute, incriminate, judge, knock (*slang*), lambaste, lash, lash out, lay into (*informal*), lecture, maul, moralize, nag, pan (*informal*), pass the buck (*informal*), penalize, pick holes in, pillory, *point the finger*, pull to pieces, pull up (*UK*), punish, put down (*informal*), *rake over the coals*, rap on/over the knuckles (*informal*), *read the riot act*, rebuke, *reprehend*, reprimand, reproach, reprove, run down, savage, scapegoat, scold, set against, *shift the blame*, shoot down, shout at, slam (*informal*), slur, *speak ill of*, *speak sharply*, stand up to, start on (*informal*), take apart (*informal*), take on, take to task, tax, *tear a strip off* (*UK*), tear into, *tear to pieces*, *tear to shreds*, tell off (*informal*), traduce, trash (*informal*), upbraid, vilify, *vituperate*, yell at

See also CRITICISMS AND ANGRY OUTBURSTS (50)

642　Protest and Express Disapproval

I disapprove of what you say, but I will defend to the death your right to say it. **Voltaire**

(*v*) agitate, be against, blacken, bluster, censure, condemn, decry, demonstrate, demur, denounce, denunciate (*formal*), deplore, deprecate, deride, disagree, disapprove (*formal*), disrespect, dissent, diverge, disapprove (*formal*), expostulate, fight, fight back, fulminate, hit out, inveigh, kick up a fuss, *kick up a rumpus* (*UK*), *kick up a storm*, make waves, object, oppose, pass judgment, picket, pour scorn on, protest, quibble, rail, *raise a fuss*, *raise a ruckus*, raise objections, remonstrate, revolt, riot, rise, rise up, rock the boat (*informal*), say your piece, scoff, scorn, sneer, speak out, speak to, speak up, speak your mind, split hairs, sully, take issue with, *vociferate*

See also UNFAVORABLE NONVERBAL RESPONSES (654)

643　Argue and Fight

The daughter of debate, that eke discord doth sow. **Elizabeth I**

(*v*) altercate, argue, bandy words with, bicker, cavil, clash, cross swords, dicker (*informal*), differ, disagree, dispute, fall out, haggle, joust, lock horns, quarrel, row, spar, squabble, wrangle

See also ARGUMENTS (47)

644　Deny and Reject

We have been taught to hate or deny our differences rather than to welcome them. **Nancy Kline**

(*n*) contradiction, denial, disavowal (*formal*), disclaimer, negation, rebuff, rebuttal, refusal, refutation, rejection, renunciation, repudiation

(*v*) abjure, beg to differ, challenge, contest, contradict, counter, debunk, deny, disavow, disclaim, disprove, explode, forswear (*archaic or literary*), gainsay (*formal*), give the lie to, *naysay*, negate (*formal*), pass by, pooh-pooh, rebut, refuse, refute, reject, renounce, repudiate, scorn, steamroller, throw out

See also FORGO AND DENY ONESELF (449)

645　Agree

He is indeed one of the very greatest masters of painting...And I may add that in this opinion Mr. Whistler himself entirely concurs. **Oscar Wilde**

(*n*) acceptance, accession, acknowledgment, acquiescence, assent, espousal, green light, yes

(*v*) accede, accept, acquiesce, agree, assent, concur, consent, defer, deign, fall in with, grant, say yes, see eye to eye, string along (*informal*), subscribe, sustain, volunteer

646　Approve and Confirm

Let age approve of youth, and death complete the same! **Robert Browning**

(*n*) accreditation, adoption, advocacy, approval, blessing, commendation, enactment, endorsement, formalization, nomination, okay (*informal*), passage, promotion, proselytization, ratification, recommendation, sanction, uptake

(*v*) accept, accredit, advocate, affirm, answer for, approve, attest, authenticate, back up, bear out, bless, carry, certify, champion, check, cinch (*dated informal*), clinch, come down in favor of, conclude, confirm, corroborate, credit, defend, enact, endorse, espouse, excuse, explain, favor, formalize, get behind, go with, hail, hold with, make certain, make sure, notarize, okay (*informal*), pass, plead, promote, prove, push, ratify, recommend, rubber-stamp, second, side with, speak for, speak up for, *speak well of*, stand by, stand for, stick up for, substantiate, support, testify (*formal*), uphold, validate, verify, vindicate, vouch for

See also EXPRESSING RESPECT AND APPROVAL (637)

647　Praise and Encourage

Flow gently, sweet Afton, among thy green braes;/Flow gently, I'll sing thee a song in thy praise. **Robert Burns**

(*n*) acclaim, acclamation, applause, approbation, compliment, credit, deification, *encomium* (*formal*), eulogy, exaltation (*formal*), glorification, plaudit, praise, puff, respects, tribute

(*v*) acclaim, adulate, applaud, celebrate, cheer, cheer on, commend, compliment, congratulate, credit, eat up (*informal*), emblazon (*literary*), encourage, enthuse, eulogize, exalt (*formal*), extol (*formal or literary*), fete, glorify, hymn, laud, lionize, magnify (*formal*), mark, marvel, *panegyrize* (*archaic*), *pay homage to*, *pay tribute*, plump for, praise, *praise to the skies*, put on a pedestal, rave, recognize, rhapsodize, root, *root for*, *show appreciation*, sing the praises of, thank, toast, wonder

See also FLATTER AND FAWN (621), APPLAUSE (652)

648　Expressions of Agreement

When you say that you agree to a thing in principle you mean that you have not the slightest intention of carrying it out in practice. **Prince Otto von Bismarck**

(*adv*) all right (*UK*), by all means, by hook or by crook, for sure, naturally, of course, *OK* (*informal*), *okeydokey* (*informal*), sure (*informal*), *sure enough*, sure thing (*informal*), yes, *yes indeed*

(*interj*) all right, amen (*informal*), aye, fair enough (*informal*), no problem (*informal*), okay (*informal*), roger (*informal*), *thanks a lot*, *thank goodness*, *thank heavens*, *thank you*, yea (*archaic*), yeah (*informal*), yep (*informal*), *you said it!*

649　Laughter

Laughter is as ridiculous as it is deceptive. **Paul Verlaine**

(*n*) belly laugh, chortle, chuckle, giggle, guffaw, hysterics (*informal*), laugh, laughter, mirth, *mirthfulness*, snicker, *snickering*, snigger, *sniggering*

(*v*) cackle, chortle, chuckle, giggle, guffaw, *have hysterics* (*informal*), kill yourself laughing, laugh, *laugh your head off, roll in the aisles, scream with laughter*, snicker, snigger

650 Crying

It's not whether you really cry. It's whether the audience thinks you are crying. **Ingrid Bergman**

(*adj*) *in floods* (*UK*), *in floods of tears* (*UK*), *in tears*, misty-eyed, tearful, *teary, teary-eyed*

(*n*) *blubbering* (*informal*), sobbing, waterworks

(*v*) bawl (*informal*), blubber (*informal*), burst into tears, cry, cry your eyes out, *shed tears*, sniffle, snivel, sob, weep, whimper

651 Facial Expressions and Blushing

A smile that snapped back after using, like a stretched rubber band. **Sinclair Lewis**

(*adj*) beaming, beatific (*literary*), blank, bug-eyed (*informal*), deadpan, dour, drawn, expressionless, glassy, glazed, glowering, *goggle-eyed, grim-faced, grinning*, impassive, mobile, penetrating, poker-faced, round-eyed, smiley, *smiling*, stony-faced, straight-faced, *unblinking*, unreadable, vacant, wooden

(*n*) beam, *black look, dirty look*, expression, face, *facial expression*, frown, glare, grimace, grin, leer, *long face*, rictus, scowl, simper, smile, smirk, *smug look*, stare, wince

(*v*) beam, blush, color, frown, glare, glow, glower, gnash, *go pale, go red, go white*, grimace, grin, keep a straight face, *knit your brow*, leer, look daggers, pout, *pull a face, purse your lips*, scowl, simper, smile, smirk, wince

652 Applause

Applause is a receipt, not a note of demand. **Artur Schnabel**

(*n*) acclamation, applause, clapping, hand, ovation, *round of applause, slow handclap* (*UK*), *standing ovation*

(*v*) applaud, clap

See also PRAISE AND ENCOURAGE (647)

653 Gestures and Gesticulation

All the dancer's gestures are signs of things, and the dance...signifies and displays something over and above the pleasure of the senses. **Saint Augustine of Hippo**

(*n*) body language, bow, *bowing and scraping*, curtsy, flourish, genuflection, gesticulation, gesture, kowtow, mannerism, motion, nod, obeisance (*formal*), pat on the back (*informal*), prostration, salute, *show of hands*, *shrug*, signal, wave

(*v*) acknowledge, beckon, bob, bow, *bow and scrape*, cue, curtsy, genuflect, gesticulate, gesture, greet, hail, indicate, kowtow, motion, nod to, prostrate yourself, salaam, salute, sign, signal, wave

654 Unfavorable Nonverbal Responses

Her very frowns are fairer far,/Than smiles of other maidens are. **Samuel Taylor Coleridge**

(*interj*) hush, *shush*

(*n*) boo, *Bronx cheer* (*informal*), heckling, *hiss, raspberry* (*slang*)

(*v*) boo, catcall, hiss, howl down, *tut*

See also PROTEST AND EXPRESS DISAPPROVAL (642)

655 Physical Contact as Communication

You cannot shake hands with a clenched fist. **Indira Gandhi**

(*n*) bear hug, caress, cuddle, embrace, handshake, hug, kiss, *osculation* (*formal or humorous*), peck (*informal*), *smacker* (*informal*), smooch (*informal*)

(*v*) canoodle (*informal*), chuck, cuddle, dandle, embrace, *French kiss*, hug, kiss, make out (*informal*), neck (*informal*), osculate (*formal or humorous*), peck (*informal*), smooch (*informal*)

See also CONTACT: HOLD (411)

656 Endearments

Come live with me, and be my love,/And we will some new pleasures prove. **John Donne**

(*n*) babe (*slang*), baby (*slang*), darling, dear, dearest, endearment, honey (*informal*), *honeybun* (*informal*), *honeybunch* (*informal*), *honey-pie* (*informal*), *kiddo* (*informal*), love, pet, sugar (*informal*), sweetheart, sweetie pie (*informal*), sweet nothings, *term of endearment*

657 Compliments

(*interj*) *bravo*, congratulations, *good on you* (*UK*), *smashing* (*UK*), *way to go* (*informal*), well done (*UK*)

658 Insults, Abuse, and Swearing

One does not insult the river god while crossing the river. **Proverb**

(*adj*) dysphemistic, insulting, libelous, slanderous

(*n*) abuse, affront, aspersion, backbiting, bad language, belittlement, blasphemy, brickbat, calumny (*formal*), character assassination, curse, defamation, denigration, detraction (*formal*), dirty word, dysphemism, *execration* (*literary or formal*), expletive, four-letter word, imprecation (*formal*), insult, jeer, jeering, jibe, libel, name-calling, oath, obscenity, offense, profanity, slander, slur, smear, swear-word, taunt, *verbal abuse, verbal assault*, vulgarism, vulgarity, vulgar language

(*v*) abuse, affront, attack somebody's dignity, badmouth (*slang*), blaspheme, call names, condescend, curse, cuss (*informal*), defame, denigrate, dis (*slang*), discredit, *execrate* (*literary or formal*), humble, imprecate (*formal*), insult, jeer, jeer at, libel, malign, patronize, revile, slander, slight, smear, stigmatize, swear

659 Greetings, Farewells, and Salutations

Faithless is he that says farewell when the road darkens. **J. R. R. Tolkien**

(*interj*) adieu, adios (*informal*), *auf Wiedersehen, au revoir, bon voyage*, bye (*informal*), cheers (*UK*), ciao (*informal*), *good afternoon*, goodbye, *good day, good luck, good morning*, good night, *hasta la vista* (*informal*), hello, hi (*informal*), howdy (*informal*), night (*informal*), sayonara, *see you* (*informal*), *see you later* (*informal*), so long (*informal*)

(*n*) acknowledgment, condolences, farewell (*literary*), felicitations (*formal*), greeting, reception, salaam, salutation, *salutations* (*formal*), toast, valediction (*formal*), welcome

660   Deception and Lies

Cunning and deceit will every time serve a man better than force. **Niccolò Machiavelli**

(*n*) act, artifice (*formal*), *barefaced lie*, bluff, booby trap, brinkmanship, cabal, cant, charade, charlatanism, cheating, *cock-and-bull story*, con, con game (*informal*), deceit, deception, dirty tricks, dishonesty, disinformation, dissimulation (*formal*), distortion, doublecross, double-dealing, *doublespeak*, double talk, duplicity, fabrication, fairy story (*UK*), fairy tale, fake, falsehood, falseness, falsification, falsity, feint, fib (*informal*), *fibbing* (*informal*), fiction, *figleaf*, fix (*informal*), *flimflam* (*slang*), frame-up (*slang*), fraud, fraudulence, gold brick, *half-truth*, hoax, humbug, illusion, imposture (*formal*), intrigue, invention, lese majesty, lie, lying, machination, mannerism, masquerade, *mendaciousness*, misinformation, mockery, noose, obfuscation, perjury, pose, pretense, prevarication, *primrose path* (*literary*), propaganda, put-on (*informal*), quackery, red herring, rip-off (*informal*), romance, ruse, scam (*slang*), setup (*informal*), *shaggy-dog story*, sham, *smoke and mirrors*, smoke screen, *snake oil*, *snow job* (*slang*), *sophism*, sophistry, spoof, sting (*slang*), story (*informal*), subterfuge, swindle, tale, tall tale, *tissue of lies*, trap, travesty, trick, trickery, untruth, untruthfulness, *white lie*, whitewash, whopper (*informal*), wiles

(*v*) bamboozle (*informal*), bear false witness, bilk (*informal*), bluff, con (*informal*), deceive, decoy, delude, dissemble, do (*informal*), double-cross, dupe, entrap, fabricate, fib (*informal*), flirt, fob off, fool, fox, hoax, hoodwink, inflate, kid (*informal*), lead astray, *lead down the garden path*, lie, make a fool of, *make a monkey of* (*informal*), misinform, mislead, overreach, pass off, perjure, play games with, prevaricate, pull a fast one (*slang*), pull the wool over somebody's eyes, scam (*slang*), set up (*informal*), *spin a yarn* (*informal*), spoof, *stretch the truth*, string along (*informal*), sucker (*informal*), take for a ride, take in, *tell lies*, tell stories, *tell untruths*, trap, trick, two-time

See also FALSE AND UNREAL (173), FALSIFY AND CHEAT (176), DECEITFUL (513)

661   People who Deceive

He led a double life. Did that make him a liar? He did not feel a liar. He was a man of two truths. **Iris Murdoch**

(*n*) cardsharp, charlatan, cheat, collaborator, con artist (*slang*), con man (*slang*), conniver, conspirator, deceiver, *dissembler* (*formal*), double-crosser, double-dealer, faker, *fast talker*, fibber (*informal*), flatterer, fraud, fraudster (*UK*), hoaxer, *hustler*, hypocrite, impostor, *intriguer*, liar, manipulator, mountebank (*literary*), *perjurer*, phony, plant (*informal*), plotter, *prevaricator*, profiteer, quack, scammer (*slang*), schemer, serpent, sham, *slanderer*, *slippery customer*, *sophist*, storyteller (*informal*), swindler, traitor, trickster, turncoat

See also SUPERFICIAL OR INSINCERE PEOPLE (951)

662   Victims of Deceit

The intellect is always fooled by the heart.
François La Rochefoucauld

(*n*) dupe, fall guy (*slang*), monkey (*informal*), pigeon (*informal*), pushover (*informal*), soft touch, softy (*informal*), sucker (*informal*), victim

663   Request and Demand

Ask no one's view but your own. **Persius**

(*adj*) beseeching (*literary*), imploring (*formal*), pleading, suppliant (*formal*), *supplicatory* (*formal*), votive

(*n*) appeal, application, behest (*literary*), bid, bidding, call, charge, claim, clamor, command, commission, decree, demand, dictate, diktat, directive, entreaty, entry, fiat, importunity (*formal*), instruction, invitation, invite (*informal*), invocation, mandate, order, ordinance, petition, plea, prayer, prescript (*formal*), request, requisition, supplication (*formal*), tender, ultimatum, wish, word

(*v*) adjure, appeal, apply, ask, ask for, bay for, beg, beseech (*literary*), bid (*archaic*), call, call down, call for, call on, call out for, call upon, claim, clamor, command, crave (*archaic*), cry out, decree, demand, desire (*formal*), dictate, direct (*formal*), entreat, exact, expect, implore (*formal*), insist, invite, invoke, lay claim to, lay down, lay down the law, lobby, mandate, ordain (*formal*), order, petition, plead, pray, prescribe, press, press for, provide, *push for*, request, requisition, seek, solicit, sue (*formal*), supplicate (*formal*), tell, urge, wish

664   People who Make Requests

Not everybody can be a leader, but everybody can be an intermediary. **Theodore Zeldin**

(*n*) claimant, petitioner, suppliant (*formal*), supplicant (*formal*)

665   Name and Describe

The act of naming is the great and solemn consolation of mankind. **Elias Canetti**

(*adj*) a.k.a., alias, code-named, entitled, named, née, self-styled, unnumbered

(*n*) alias, appellation (*formal*), assumed name, autograph, *bar code*, brand, brand name, Christian name, *cognomen* (*formal*), definition, delineation, description, designation, epithet, family name, first name, forename, given name, handle (*slang*), honor, identification, inscription, John Hancock (*informal*), label, last name, marque, *matronymic*, *middle name*, misnomer, mnemonic, moniker (*slang*), name, naming, nickname, *nom de guerre*, nom de plume, nomenclature, *paternal name*, *patronymic*, pen name, pet name, *praenomen*, *price tag*, pseudonym, second name (*UK*), so-and-so (*informal*), sobriquet, stage name, surname, tab, tag, taxonomy, testimonial, ticket, title, trade name

(*v*) anthropomorphize, asterisk, backdate, brand, call, characterize, christen, couch, define, delineate, describe, designate, docket, dub, entitle, enumerate, flag, humanize, identify, inscribe, invoke, label, mark out, name, nickname, paint, particularize, pick out, picture, pigeonhole, preview, profile, rename, sign, stake out, stereotype, style (*formal*), tag, term, title, typecast, witness

666 Ask People Questions

The world is but a school of inquiry. **Michel de Montaigne**

(*n*) catechism, debriefing, inquiry, inquisition, interrogation, opinion poll, query, question, questionnaire, soundings

(*v*) ballot, consult, cross-examine, debrief, enquire, *give the third degree* (*informal*), grill (*informal*), inquire, interrogate, interview, make inquiries, poll, pose, pry, pump, query, question, quiz

See also QUESTION THINGS (751)

667 Questioners

The historian is…the skilled detective who asks questions, locates and follows clues. **John Clive**

(*n*) canvasser, inquisitor, interrogator, interviewer, questioner, question master (*UK*)

668 Reply and Answer

Today we no longer seek…Our thinking is a thought in retreat or in reply. **Maurice Merleau-Ponty**

(*n*) acknowledgment, answer, comeback, feedback, reaction, rejoinder (*formal*), reply, response, retort, riposte, R.S.V.P.

(*v*) acknowledge, answer, answer back, come back, greet, react, rejoin (*formal*), reply, respond, retort, riposte, R.S.V.P., talk back

669 Permit and Allow

Finding language that will allow people to act together while cherishing each other's individuality is probably the…truly revolutionary function of writers. **Gloria Steinem**

(*adj*) entitled, laissez-faire, lax, licensed, permissible, permitted

(*n*) access, admission, admittance, all clear, authorization, clearance, confirmation, consent, empowerment, entrance, fiat, franchise, go-ahead (*informal*), leave (*formal*), mandate, permission, power, sanction, say-so (*informal*), signing, special consideration, thumbs up (*informal*), validation

(*v*) admit, agree, allow, approve, authorize, concur, condescend, consent, decriminalize, empower, entitle, franchise, *give leave* (*formal*), give permission, *give the go-ahead*, invest, leave, let, let in, let into, let pass, let through, license, permit, qualify, sanction, validate

670 Refuse Permission and Not Allow

Forbidden fruit tastes the sweetest. **Proverb**

(*adj*) banned, barred, disallowed, disqualified, inadmissible, ineligible, not allowed, off-limits, out, out of bounds, proscribed, *proscriptive* (*formal*), suspended, taboo

(*n*) blackout, circumscription (*formal*), denial, disbarment, disqualification, exclusion, interdict, negative, no, prohibition, proscription (*formal*), red light (*informal*), renunciation, sanction, taboo, thumbs down (*informal*), veto, *zero tolerance*

(*v*) ban, bar, confine, crack down (*informal*), criminalize, debar, deny, disallow, disbar, disqualify, estop (*archaic*), forbid, ground, interdict, keep out, outlaw, prohibit, proscribe, taboo, veto

671 The Spoken Word

And the whole earth was of one language, and of one speech. **Bible**

(*adj*) articulated, broad, oral, spoken, unpronounceable, verbal, vocal, voiced

(*n*) accent, argot, articulation, aside, cadence, catch phrase, catchword, effusion, expression, intonation, language, lilt, mispronunciation, modulation, monologue, parlance, patois, pidgin, pronunciation, rhetoric, slang, slogan, speech, talk, tongue, twang, utterance, verbalization, vernacular, watchword

See also ASPECTS OF LANGUAGE (682)

672 Foreign Words and Phrases

Hebrew and Arabic,/which are like stones on the tongue and sand on the throat,/have softened for tourists like oil. **Yehuda Amichai**

(*adj*) pro bono, pro tem

(*adv*) de facto, entre nous (*formal*), et cetera, per contra, per se (*formal*), prima facie, *pro rata*, pro tem

(*interj*) *voilà*

(*n*) je ne sais quoi, pro forma

(*prep*) *contra*, in memoriam, versus, vis-à-vis

(*v*) stet

673 Figures of Speech

Through metaphor to reconcile/the people and the stones./Compose. (No ideas but in things.) Invent! **William Carlos Williams**

(*n*) aphorism, axiom, buzzword (*informal*), byword, cliché, colloquialism, epigram, euphemism, figure of speech, formula, generality, idiom, maxim, motto, parenthesis, platitude, proverb, refrain, saw, saying, set phrase, *stock phrase, tongue twister*, truism, vulgarism, *weasel word* (*informal*)

types of figures of speech alliteration, antonomasia, assonance, chiasmus, hendiadys, hypallage, hyperbaton, hyperbole, litotes, meiosis, metaphor, metonymy, oxymoron, personification, prosopopeia, simile, synecdoche, zeugma

674 Jokes and Teasing

Forgive, O Lord, my little jokes on Thee/And I'll forgive Thy great big one on me. **Robert Frost**

(*adj*) facetious, *punning*, teasing, wicked

(*adv*) *at somebody's expense, in jest*, wickedly

(*n*) antics, badinage, banter, barb, boisterousness, bon mot, brainteaser, buffoonery, burlesque, *canard* (*literary*), caricature, chaff, chestnut (*informal*), clowning, crack (*informal*), derision, dig, facetiousness, fencing, *fun and games*, funny (*informal*), gag (*informal*), gibe, humor, in-joke, jape (*archaic or literary*), jest (*literary*), jesting (*literary*), joke, joking, *joshing* (*informal*), knockabout, lampoon, lark, laugh (*informal*), laughingstock, mimicry, mockery, one-liner, parody, pastiche, practical joke, prank, *private joke*, quip, raillery, repartee, *ribbing* (*informal*), ridicule, *running joke*, satire, sendup (*informal*), shenanigans (*informal*), skit, slapstick, spoof, sport (*formal*), teasing, tomfoolery (*informal*), trick, understatement, wickedness, wisecrack (*informal*), wit, witticism, wordplay, wryness (*v*) bait, banter, burlesque, chaff, clown, *clown around*, crack a joke, gibe, *goof around* (*informal*), goof off (*informal*), *have a joke with*, *have a lark* (*UK*), *have a laugh*, jape (*archaic or literary*), jest (*literary*), jibe, joke, josh (*informal*), kid, lampoon, lark around, laugh at, laugh out of court, make fun of, mess around (*informal*), mimic, mock, monkey around, parody, pick on, play, poke fun at, pull somebody's leg (*informal*), quip, rag (*dated*), razz (*informal*), rib (*informal*), ride (*informal*), ridicule, satirize, send up (*informal*), spoof, stultify, take the mickey (*UK informal*), taunt, tease, wisecrack (*informal*), *yank somebody's chain* (*informal*)

types of wordplay acrostic, anagram, logogram, malapropism, palindrome, pun, spoonerism, telestich

See also PRETEND AND MIMIC (60), ENTERTAINMENT (872)

675   Jokers and Teases

He who endeavors to ridicule other people, especially in things of a serious nature, becomes himself a jest. **Giovanni Boccaccio**

(*n*) *clown* (*informal*), cutup (*informal*), humorist, jester, joker, *josher* (*informal*), kidder, mimic, mocker, parrot, prankster, *punster*, rascal (*humorous*), scream (*informal*), tease, teaser, wag (*informal*), *wisecracker* (*informal*), wit

See also WORKERS IN ENTERTAINMENT AND MEDIA (873)

676   Meaningless Speech or Writing

Whenever a poet or preacher, chief or wizard spouts gibberish, the human race spends centuries deciphering the message. **Umberto Eco**

(*n*) balderdash, baloney (*informal*), bilge (*informal*), blarney (*informal*), blather (*informal*), bombast, bunk (*slang*), bunkum (*informal*), cant, chicanery, claptrap (*informal*), crud (*informal*), doggerel, double talk, drivel, footle (*informal*), froth, fudge (*informal*), gabble, garbage, gas (*slang*), gibberish, gobbledygook (*informal*), guff (*informal*), hogwash (*informal*), hokum (*informal*), hooey (*informal*), *hoopla* (*informal*), hot air (*informal*), humbug, jargon, jazz (*slang*), legalese, *malarkey* (*informal*), moonshine, mumbo jumbo (*informal*), nonsense, oratory, padding, piffle (*informal*), *pleonasm*, poppycock (*dated informal*), prattle, rigmarole, rot (*informal*), rubbish, smooth talk, spiel (*informal*), *stuff and nonsense* (*UK*), *technobabble*, trash, tripe (*informal*), twaddle (*informal*), verbiage, *verboseness*, verbosity, waffle (*informal*), wordiness

See also INFORMAL COMMUNICATION (45), CHATTER AND BABBLE (617)

677   The Oral Tradition

Old man history tells us that it's better to be a little more noisy. A silent era cannot be a little more noisy. **Liu Binyan**

(*n*) adage, allegory, anecdote, dictum (*formal*), fable, fairy story (*UK*), folklore, *folk story*, folk tale, legend, lore, myth, mythology, narration, narrative, narrator, *oral tradition*, parable, plot, rumor, saga, sob story (*informal*), soliloquy, story, story line, tale, urban myth, yarn (*informal*)

678   Gossip

History a distillation of rumor. **Thomas Carlyle**

(*adv*) secondhand

(*n*) buzz (*informal*), dirt, gossip, grapevine, hearsay,

muckraking, mudslinging, *rumormongering*, scandal, *scandalmongering*, scuttlebutt (*slang*), smear campaign, speculation, talk, tattle, tidbit, tittle-tattle, whisper, word

(*v*) gas (*informal*), purvey, rumor, *spread rumors*, yammer (*informal*), yap (*informal*)

See also INFORMAL COMMUNICATION (45), BETRAY CONFIDENCES AND GOSSIP (618), INTERFERING PEOPLE AND TATTLETALES (950)

679   Giving Vent to Emotions

Where can you scream? It's a serious question: where can you go in society and scream? **R. D. Laing**

(*v*) be angry, bellow, *blow a fuse* (*informal*), *blow a gasket* (*informal*), blow up (*informal*), blow your top (*informal*), boil, *boil with rage*, break down, *break down and cry*, bridle, bristle, *burst out crying*, choke, cluck, commiserate, cry out, erupt, explode, exult, flip (*slang*), flip your lid (*slang*), fly into a rage, fly off the handle (*informal*), foam at the mouth, fume, get angry, *get in a lather* (*informal*), *get in a state*, get on your high horse, *get stirred up*, gnash your teeth, *go ballistic* (*slang*), go bananas (*informal*), go berserk, go nuts (*slang*), go off the deep end, *go on the rampage*, go postal (*informal*), go to pieces, go wild, grieve, *have a conniption* (*informal*), *have a fit* (*informal*), *have kittens* (*informal*), hit the roof, lament, let fly, *let off steam*, lose control, lose it (*informal*), lose your cool (*informal*), lose your patience, lose your temper, make a scene, mourn, open up, panic, rage, rampage, rant, rant and rave, rave, rejoice (*literary*), run amok, run riot, see red (*informal*), seethe, smolder, snap, sound off (*informal*), stew, storm, sulk, take out, *throw a fit* (*informal*), *throw a tantrum*, uncork, whoop

680   Initiate and Establish Communication

The word, even the most contradictory word, preserves contact—it is silence which isolates. **Thomas Mann**

(*v*) accost, ambush, approach, *ask out*, be in contact with, break the ice, buttonhole (*informal*), call, call by, call on, call out, come over (*UK*), commune, contact, correspond, court, drop a line, encounter, face, get at, hear from, hook up (*informal*), look up, make contact, *make overtures*, make yourself known, reach, rendezvous, see, send for, speak to, summon, tackle, turn to, visit, waylay, welcome, write

See also ESTABLISHING RELATIONSHIPS WITH OTHERS (974)

681   Telephone, Page, and Text

You cannot settle the problems of Europe by long-distance telephone calls and telegrams. **Ernest Bevin**

(*v*) bleep (*UK*), call, call in, call up, dial, get hold of, get in touch with, *give a call*, *give a ring* (*UK*), *give a tinkle*, hang up, hold, page, phone, *phone up* (*UK*), ring, ring off (*UK*), ring up (*UK*), telephone, *text*, *text message*

See also TELEPHONE COMMUNICATION (48), TELECOMMUNICATIONS (1130)

682   Aspects of Language

I master the language of others. Mine does what it wants with me. **Karl Kraus**

(*adj*) alliterative, bilingual, grammatical, informal,

lexical, linguistic, multilingual, phrasal, polysyllabic, rhetorical, *semantic*

(*n*) abbreviation, accentuation, acronym, alliteration, assonance, brogue, burr, *coinage*, *collocation*, contraction, *diacritic*, dialect, diction, drawl, *elision*, ellipsis, elocution, enunciation, *etymology*, grammar, idiolect, idiom, jargon, language, *lexis*, lingo (*informal*), *lingua franca*, linguistics, *locution*, monosyllable, neologism, nomenclature, *oxymoron*, paragraph, password, patois, patter, phrase, phraseology, phrasing, polysyllable, *punctuation*, *Received Pronunciation*, regionalism, rhetoric, R.P., *semantics*, *sentence structure*, short form, *speech disorder*, *speech impediment*, *strophe*, *syllable*, synonym, syntax, term, terminology, terms, turn of phrase, vocabulary, word, wording

types of diacritics accent, acute, apostrophe, cedilla, circumflex, dieresis, grave, háček, krouźek, ogonek, tilde, umlaut

types of grammatical terms ablative, accusative, adjunct, affix, apposition, attributive, clause, combining form, conditional, conjugation, dative, diphthong, genitive, indicative, infinitive, inflection, intransitive, modal, nominative, object, participle, plural, predicate, prefix, prenominal, preterit, sentence, subject, subjunctive, suffix, transitive, vocative

types of punctuation marks asterisk, backslash, bracket, colon, comma, dash, exclamation mark, hyphen, parenthesis, semicolon

types of word classes adjective, adverb, article, collective noun, common noun, conjunction, definite article, determiner, indefinite article, interjection, modifier, noun, particle, phrasal verb, preposition, pronoun, proper noun, qualifier, quantifier, substantive, verb

See also THE SPOKEN WORD (671)

683   Apologize and Retract

Apologies only account for that which they do not alter.
Benjamin Disraeli

(*n*) apology, appeasement, atonement, attestation, *expiation*, olive branch, peace offering, penance, penitence, placation, propitiation (*formal*), recantation, retraction, withdrawal

(*v*) apologize, atone (*formal*), back down, back off, backpedal, backtrack, beg forgiveness, climb down, conciliate, countermand, crawl, eat crow (*informal*), *eat humble pie*, eat your words (*informal*), expiate, go back on, lift, make amends, *make reparations*, recall, recant, regret (*formal*), repent, retract, say you're sorry, swallow, take back, withdraw

684   Promise and Assure

Promises are the uniquely human way of ordering the future, making it predictable and reliable. **Hannah Arendt**

(*n*) assurance, binder, bond, commitment, compact, guarantee, oath, obligation, pact, pledge, promise, resolution, vow, word, *word of honor*

(*v*) assure, commit, give your word, guarantee, keep your word, pledge, promise, swear, *swear an oath*, take an oath, vouchsafe (*formal*), vow, warrant

685   Vengeance and Revenge

A man that studieth revenge keeps his own wounds green.
Francis Bacon

(*adj*) punitive, recriminatory, retaliatory, retributive, *revengeful*, *tit-for-tat*

(*n*) payback (*informal*), reprisal, retaliation, retribution, revenge, *settling of scores*, tit for tat, vengeance

(*v*) answer for, avenge, get back at, get even, get your own back (*UK*), pay back, retaliate, revenge, *strike back*

686   Complain and Nag

Who complains without cause, let a cause be made for him.
Welsh proverb

(*n*) beef (*slang*), bellyache (*informal*), carping, complaint, faultfinding, grievance, gripe (*informal*), grouch (*informal*), grouse (*informal*), grumble, moan (*informal*), niggle, protest, quarrel, wail, whine

(*v*) badger, beef (*slang*), bellyache (*informal*), bemoan, bewail (*formal*), bitch (*slang*), bleat, browbeat, carp, carry on, complain, croak (*informal*), deplore, dog, find fault, gripe (*informal*), groan (*informal*), grouch (*informal*), grouse (*informal*), grumble, harp on, hector, huff, importune (*formal*), kvetch (*informal*), make a fuss, moan (*informal*), murmur, mutter, nag, niggle, nitpick, persecute, ply, squawk (*informal*), wail, whine

687   Withhold Information

The most difficult secret for a man to keep is his own opinion of himself. **Marcel Pagnol**

(*n*) censorship, cover-up, equivocation, evasion, suppression

(*v*) bottle up, bowdlerize, button up (*informal*), censor, choke back, clam up (*informal*), conceal, cover up, dissemble (*formal*), dissimulate, draw a veil over, equivocate, evade, gulp back, hide, hold out on, hush up (*informal*), internalize, keep, keep a secret, keep back, keep from, keep in, keep in the dark, keep mum (*informal*), *keep quiet*, keep secret, *keep to yourself*, keep under wraps, *keep under your hat*, parry, play your cards close to your chest, repress, sanitize, shush (*informal*), shut up (*informal*), smother, stifle, strangle, submerge, suppress, swallow, throttle, *withhold information*

688   Basic Details

All my novels are an accumulation of detail. I'm a bit of a bower-bird. **Patrick White**

(*n*) *411* (*slang*), ABCs, advice, baseline, basics, brass tacks, brief, *building blocks*, bulletin, content, data, *datum*, details, dynamics, elements, fact, facts, *fine points*, *first principles*, flesh, fundamentals, *generalities*, info (*informal*), information, input, ins and outs, intelligence, intricacies, knowledge, lowdown (*informal*), material, minutiae, news, nicety, nitty-gritty (*informal*), nuts and bolts (*informal*), particulars, rudiments, specific, specification, *specifics*, statistics, story, *technicalities*, tidings (*literary*), whys and wherefores, word

689   Advice

One gives nothing so freely as advice. **François La Rochefoucauld**

(*n*) advice, caution, caveat, clue, counsel (*formal or literary*), directions, discouragement, dissuasion, exhortation (*formal*), forewarning, guidance, guideline, hint, home truth, invitation, notice, pointer, recommendation, suggestion, threat, tip, tip-off (*informal*), warning

See also ADVISE AND WARN (613)

690   Meaning

The least of things with a meaning is worth more in life than the greatest of things without it. **Carl Gustav Jung**

(*n*) association, connotation, denotation, drift, effect, gist, implication, lesson, meaning, message, moral, point, resonance, sense, significance, signification, subtext, tenor, thrust, undercurrent, undertone

See also MEAN SOMETHING (61)

The Human Body and Bodily Functions

691   Body

If anything is sacred the human body is sacred. **Walt Whitman**

(*n*) bod (*slang*), body, build, flesh, organ, person, physique, *soma*

See also BUILD (477), SHAPE (1216)

692   Parts of the Body: Head

Uneasy lies the head that wears a crown. **William Shakespeare**

(*n*) countenance, face, head, *maxilla*, mug (*slang*), noddle (*dated informal*), noggin (*dated informal*), *noodle* (*slang*), nut (*informal*), pate (*archaic or humorous*), physiognomy, puss (*slang*), skull (*informal*), visage (*literary*)

parts of a face brow, cheek, cheekbone, chin, chops (*informal*), eye, eyebrow, hairline, jaw, jawline, jowl, lips, mandible, mouth, nose, temple

See also FACIAL CHARACTERISTICS (481)

693   Parts of the Body: Torso

DIAPHRAGM, *n. A muscular partition separating disorders of the chest from disorders of the bowels.* **Ambrose Bierce**

(*n*) appendage, extremity, limb, member, *torso*, *trunk*

parts of a torso abdomen, armpit, back, backside (*informal*), belly, bellybutton (*informal*), bosom, bottom, breast, bust, buttock, chest, groin, haunch, hip, midriff, navel, neck, nipple, rib cage, rump, shoulder, solar plexus, thorax, waist, waistline

694   Parts of the Body: Leg and Foot

You cannot make a man by standing a sheep on its hind legs. But by standing a flock of sheep in that position you can make a crowd of men. **Max Beerbohm**

(*n*) foot, foreleg, *hindleg*, leg, *peg* (*informal*), *pins* (*informal*)

parts of a leg or foot ankle, big toe, calf, haunch, heel, instep, knee, lap, little toe, shin, sole, thigh, toe, toenail

695   Parts of the Body: Arm and Hand

An arm/Rose up from out the bosom of the lake,/Clothed in white samite, mystic, wonderful. **Alfred Tennyson**

(*n*) arm, claw, mitt (*slang*), nipper, paw (*informal*), tentacle

parts of an arm or hand ball, cuticle, elbow, finger, fingernail, fingerprint, fingertip, fist, forearm, forefinger, funny bone (*informal*), hand, hangnail, heel, index finger, knuckle, little finger, middle finger, palm, pinkie (*informal*), ring finger, thumb, thumbnail, wrist

696   The Senses

But perhaps it is this distrust of our senses that prevents us from feeling comfortable in the universe. **Italo Calvino**

(*n*) ear, faculty, feeling, perception, sensation, sense, *sense of smell*, *sense of taste*, *senses*, taste

See also PERCEPTIBLE (25), IMPERCEPTIBLE (26)

697   Using the Senses

The five senses are as spies. Each one of them has been entrusted with making one of the arts, so the eye has been entrusted with the world of colors, hearing with the world of voices, and so on. **Muhammad**

(*v*) detect, feel, sense, taste

698   The Eye

Explore thyself. Herein are demanded the eye and the nerve. **Henry David Thoreau**

(*n*) *eyebrow, eyelash, eyelid, orbit, tear gland*

parts of an eye aqueous humor, cone, conjunctiva, cornea, eyeball, iris, lens, macula, optic nerve, pupil, retina, rod, vitreous humor

699   See

We should not ask ourselves if we perceive the world truly; on the contrary: the world is that which we perceive. **Maurice Merleau-Ponty**

(*adj*) bleary, blind, bloodshot, *farsighted*, hawk-eyed, keen-sighted, myopic, nearsighted, ocular, *ophthalmic*, optical, *partially sighted*, photosensitive, sharp-eyed, sharp-sighted, short-sighted (*UK*), sighted, *sightless*, *vision-impaired*, visual

(*n*) blindness, eyesight, *farsightedness*, line of sight, myopia, *nearsightedness*, observation, regard (*formal*), short-sightedness (*UK*), sight, *sightlessness*, view, vision

(*v*) behold (*archaic or literary*), catch a glimpse of, catch sight of, *descry* (*literary*), espy (*literary*), glimpse, notice, observe, perceive, see, set eyes on, sight, spot, spy, witness

See also READ (758)

700   Looking and Looks

Look round this universe...The whole presents nothing but the idea of blind nature, impregnated by a great vivifying principle. **David Hume**

(*n*) contemplation, eyeful (*informal*), gander (*informal*), gaze, glance, glimpse, lookover (*informal*), look-see (*informal*), oversight, peek, peep, recce (*slang*), reconnaissance, reconnoiter, riffle, *rubbernecking* (*informal*), scan, squint, stakeout (*informal*), surveillance, viewing, voyeurism

(*v*) blink, browse, cast an eye over, contemplate, discern, distinguish, examine, eye, eyeball (*informal*), *eye up* (*UK*), follow, gape, gawk (*informal*), gaze, glance, goggle, *have a look at*, *have a look-see*, invigilate, keep an eye on, leaf through, look, look back, make out, observe, ogle, overlook, peek, peep, peer, read, recce (*slang*), regard, riffle, rubberneck (*informal*), scan, scout, see, *sneak a look*, snoop (*informal*), spectate, spy, squint, stake out (*informal*), stare, *stare down*, *stare into space*, stare out (*UK*), *steal a look*, survey, *take a look at*, thumb, view, watch, watch out

701 Onlookers and Spectators

All in all the creative act is not performed by the artist alone; the spectator brings the work in contact with the external world by deciphering and interpreting its inner qualifications and thus adds his contribution to the creative act. **Marcel Duchamp**

(*n*) bystander, eyewitness, invigilator, looker, observer, onlooker, spectator, viewer, watcher, witness

702 The Mouth

A portrait is a picture in which there is something wrong with the mouth. **Eugene Speicher**

(*n*) *maw*, mouth, trap

parts of a mouth adenoids, denture, gum, lip, palate, roof, soft palate, taste bud, tongue, tonsils, tooth, uvula

types of teeth baby tooth, bucktooth (*informal*), canine, chopper, cuspid, denture, eyetooth, fang, incisor, milk tooth, molar, premolar, wisdom tooth

703 Taste

I hate a man who swallows it, affecting not to know what he is eating. I suspect his taste in higher matters. **Charles Lamb**

(*adj*) acid, acidic, acrid, appetizing, bitter, bland, brackish, briny, cloying, delectable, delicious, *delish* (*slang*), flavorful, flavorless, *flavorsome*, foul-tasting, fresh, fruity, full-bodied, hot, insipid, juicy, lemony, limy, lipsmacking, luscious, mature, mellow, mild, mouthwatering, palatable, peppery, piquant, pungent, rancid, rich, saccharine, saline, salty, savorless, savory, scrumptious (*informal*), sharp, *sharp-tasting*, sour, *spiced*, *spicey*, spicy, strong, succulent, sugary, sweet, syrupy, tangy, tart, tasteless, tasty, toothsome, unpalatable, vapid, vinegary, watery, wishy-washy (*informal*), yummy, *zesty*

(*adv*) acridly, delectably, sourly

(*n*) acidity, *aftertaste*, bite, bitterness, blandness, deliciousness, flavor, *flavorlessness*, freshness, hotness, insipidness, juiciness, lusciousness, mellowness, *pepperiness*, piquancy, pungency, rancidness, savor, savorlessness, *scrumptiousness* (*informal*), sharpness, smack, sourness, succulence, sweetness, sweet tooth, *tanginess*, tartness, taste, tastelessness, tastiness, *yumminess*, zest

704 The Nose

Any nose/May ravage with impunity a rose. **Robert Browning**

(*adj*) *nasal*

(*n*) nose, *nostril*, schnozzle (*slang*), snout

705 Smell and Smelling

No matter how well you clean a goat it will still smell like a goat. **Philippine proverb**

(*adj*) aromatic, *cheesy*, foul-smelling, foxy, fragranced, fragrant, funky (*slang*), heady, malodorous, musky, *odoriferous*, odorless, odorous (*literary*), perfumed, rank (*literary*), redolent, ripe (*informal*), scented, smelly, stinking, stinky, sulfurous, sweet, sweet-smelling

(*n*) aroma, BO (*informal*), *body odor*, bouquet, fragrance, fume, funk (*slang*), musk, odor, perfume, *rankness*, redolence (*literary*), reek, scent, smell, *smelliness*, stench, stink, whiff

(*v*) scent, smell, sniff

See also SMELL EMISSION (369)

706 The Ear

A knavish speech sleeps in a foolish ear. **William Shakespeare**

(*n*) ear, *earlobe*, lobe, outer ear

parts of an ear anvil, auricle, cochlea, eardrum, hammer, incus, internal ear, malleus, middle ear, stapes, stirrup, tympanic membrane, tympanum, vestibule

707 Hear

There is no worse lie than a truth misunderstood by those who hear it. **William James**

(*adj*) audio, auditory, aural, deaf, *hearing-impaired*

(*v*) catch, hear, receive

708 Listen and Listeners

But I did not remove my glasses, for I had not asked for her company in the first place, and there is a limit to what one can listen to with the naked eye. **Muriel Spark**

(*n*) auditor (*formal*), eavesdropper, listener

(*v*) bug, eavesdrop, hear, *hearken* (*archaic*), lend an ear, listen, listen in, overhear, tap, wiretap

709 The Digestive Tract

The abdomen is the reason why man does not easily take himself for a god. **Friedrich Wilhelm Nietzsche**

(*adj*) abdominal, gastric, gastrointestinal, intestinal, *peptic*

(*n*) *alimentary canal*, bowels, digestive tract, guts, innards (*informal*), insides (*informal*), tummy (*informal*), viscera

parts of a digestive tract anus, appendix, bile duct, bladder, bowel, cecum, colon, duodenum, esophagus, gallbladder, gullet, gut, intestine, kidney, large intestine, liver, pancreas, rectum, small intestine, spleen, stomach, throat

710 Eat and Not Eat

Appetite comes with eating. **François Rabelais**

(*adj*) digestive, famished, full, full up, hungry, malnourished, peckish (*informal*), replete, sated, satiated, starved (*informal*), starving (*informal*), stuffed (*informal*), voracious, well-fed

(*n*) appetite, consumption, digestion, famine, fast, *gourmandise*, *gourmandising*, hunger, intake, mastication, metabolism, ravenousness, rumination, starvation, voraciousness

(*v*) bite, bolt, champ, chew, chew up, chomp (*informal*), chow down (*informal*), chug (*slang*), consume, crunch, demolish, devour, diet, digest, dine, down, eat, *famish*, fast, feast, feed, finish up, gobble, gobble down, gobble up, gorge, graze, guzzle (*informal*), have, ingest, lose weight, masticate, metabolize, munch, nibble, nosh (*informal*), nourish, partake, peck, pig out (*informal*), polish off, put away (*informal*), raven (*literary*), reduce, ruminate, sate, satiate, scarf (*informal*), scarf down (*informal*), scoff (*informal*), slim, snap, starve, swallow, watch your weight, wolf

See also FOOD (1167)

711   Drink

Drinking when we are not thirsty and making love all year round, madam; that is all there is to distinguish us from other animals. **Pierre-Augustin Caron de Beaumarchais**

(*adj*) dry, gasping (*UK*), parched (*informal*), thirsty

(*n*) draft (*dated*), drink, *glassful*, gulp, mouthful, sip, slug (*informal*), slurp, suck, sup, swallow, swig (*informal*), top-up (*UK*), tot

(*v*) *chugalug* (*informal*), drink, gulp, gulp down, imbibe (*formal or humorous*), knock back (*informal*), lap, lap up, put back, quaff (*literary or humorous*), quench, sip, slug (*informal*), slurp, suck, sup, swallow, swig (*informal*), swill, taste, *toss off*

See also AMOUNTS OF LIQUID (114)

712   Vomit and Belch

There's not a sea the passenger e'er pukes in,/Turns up more dangerous breakers than the Euxine. **Lord Byron**

(*n*) *barf* (*informal*), belch, *burp*, puke (*slang*), regurgitation, spew, vomit, *vomitus*

(*v*) barf (*Informal*), belch, bring up, *burp*, gag, *hiccup*, hurl (*slang*), puke (*slang*), regurgitate, retch, *spit up*, throw up (*informal*), *upchuck* (*informal*), vomit

713   Disorders of the Digestive System

An indigestion is an excellent common-place for two people that never met before. **William Hazlitt**

(*n*) *acid stomach*, bellyache (*informal*), colic, dyspepsia, heartburn, indigestion, *malnourishment*, malnutrition, sickness, stomachache, *stomach pain*, *tummy ache* (*informal*), *tummy pain* (*informal*), ulcer, undernourishment, upset stomach

714   Eaters, Gourmets, and Dietary Choices

Tell me what you eat and I will tell you what you are. **Anthelme Brillat-Savarin**

(*adj*) carnivorous, vegetarian

(*n*) carnivore, dieter, diner, eater, epicure, foodie (*informal*), food lover (*UK*), gastronome, gourmet, vegan, vegetarian, veggie (*informal*)

See also PLEASURE-SEEKERS AND HEDONISTS (886)

715   Respiratory Organs

Cough. A convulsion of the lungs, vellicated by some sharp serosity. **Samuel Johnson**

(*adj*) bronchial, *pleural*, pulmonary, *tracheal*

parts of a respiratory system air sac, airway, alveolus, bronchial tube, bronchiole, bronchus, larynx, lung, pharynx, throat, trachea, vocal cords, voice box, windpipe

716   Breathe and Not Breathe

No life that breathes with human breath/Has ever truly long'd for death. **Alfred Tennyson**

(*adj*) breathless, breathy, gasping, out of breath, puffed (*UK*), *puffed out* (*UK*), puffing, respiratory, *rheumy*, wheezy

(*n*) asphyxia, breath, breathing, breathlessness, gasp, inhalation, mouth-to-mouth, puffing, respiration, respirator, *rheum*, sneeze, sniff, snuffle, ventilator, wheeziness

(*v*) breathe, exhale, huff, *hyperventilate*, inhale, pant, puff, respire, sneeze, sniff, sniffle, snore, snort, snuffle, splutter, sputter, suck in, wheeze

717   The Blood and Circulation

Nothing like blood, sir, in hosses, dawgs, and men. **William Makepeace Thackeray**

(*adj*) *cardiac*, cardiovascular, intravenous, *vascular*

(*n*) *anemia*, bleed, bleeding, blood, bloodstream, *blood vessel*, lifeblood (*literary*), nosebleed, *plasma*, *red corpuscle*, thrombosis, *white blood cell*, *white corpuscle*

(*v*) bleed

types of blood vessels aorta, artery, capillary, jugular vein, vein, venule

718   The Muscles

The human body. . .indeed is like a ship; its bones being the stiff standing-rigging, and the sinews the small running ropes, that manage all the motions. **Herman Melville**

(*n*) *brawn*, muscle, *thew* (*archaic*)

types of muscles or tendons abdominals, Achilles tendon, biceps, diaphragm, hamstring, pectoral, quadriceps, sinew, smooth muscle, sphincter, striated muscle, tendon, triceps

See also MUSCLES AND MUSCULATURE (479)

719   The Bones and Joints

Parents are the bones on which children sharpen their teeth. **Peter Ustinov**

(*adj*) arthritic, pelvic, rheumatic, spinal, *vertebral*

(*n*) arthritis, back, *bone*, carcass, *cartilage*, frame, gristle, *repetitive strain injury*, RSI, skeleton

types of bones anklebone, backbone, breastbone, carpal, cheekbone, clavicle, coccyx, collarbone, cranium, femur, fibula, humerus, ilium, jawbone, kneecap, long bone, mandible, maxilla, metacarpal, metatarsal, patella, pelvis, pubis, radius, rib, sacrum, shinbone, shoulder blade, skull, spinal column, spine, sternum, talus, tarsal, thighbone, tibia, ulna, vertebra, vertebral column, zygomatic bone

720 The Skin

Skin is like wax paper that holds everything in without dripping.
Art Linkletter

(*adj*) *dermal*, *dermatological*, subcutaneous

(*n*) *dermis*, epidermis, flesh, follicle, fur, hair, *integument*, pelt, skin, tissue

See also COMPLEXION (480)

721 Conditions Affecting the Skin

Style, like sheer silk, too often hides eczema. **Albert Camus**

(*adj*) calloused, pocked, pockmarked, prickly, purulent, scabrous, scarred, *sunburned*

(*n*) abrasion, abscess, *acne*, bedsore, birthmark, bite, blackhead, blister, *blood blister*, boil, bruise, bump, bunion, burn, callus, carbuncle, cellulite, chilblain, dandruff, *edema*, *furuncle*, *goose bumps*, *graze*, *heat rash*, hives, itchiness, *melanoma*, *naevus* (*UK*), *nevus*, pimple, pockmark, *pressure sore*, prickle, prickling, *prickly heat*, pustule, rash, rawness, redness, rubbing, scar, scurf, sore, spot (*UK*), sty, *sunburn*, *suntan*, *verruca*, wart, welt, wheal, *whitehead*, zit (*slang*)

722 Excretion and Excreta

In fantasy the excreta are transformed into dangerous weapons.
Melanie Klein

(*adj*) cathartic, *excretory*, purgative (*formal*)

(*n*) body fluid, catarrh, defecation, droppings, *excrement*, *excreta*, *excretion*, *feces*, lymph, manure, mucus, perspiration, phlegm, pus, saliva, spit, spittle, sputum, tear, *urine*

(*v*) blister, defecate (*formal*), dribble, drool, eliminate, *excrete*, perspire, salivate, slaver, slobber, spit, suppurate, sweat, *urinate*

See also UNPLEASANT, DIRTY, AND TOXIC SUBSTANCES (1268)

723 Sleep and Dream

He used to sleep like a glass of water/held up in the hand of a very young girl. **Rita Dove**

(*n*) catnap, doss (*UK*), doze, forty winks (*informal*), insomnia, nap, nightmare, *shuteye* (*informal*), siesta, sleep, slumber, snooze (*informal*), *somnolence*

(*v*) *catch some z's* (*informal*), catnap, conk out (*informal*), doze, doze off, drop off (*informal*), drowse, fall asleep, flake out (*slang*), go to bed, go to sleep, *have forty winks* (*informal*), hibernate, hit the hay (*informal*), nap, nod off, oversleep, retire, sleep, sleep in, slumber, snooze (*informal*), *take a nap*, turn in (*informal*), yawn

See also TIRED, ASLEEP, AND UNCONSCIOUS (738)

724 Wake and Regain Consciousness

Was it a vision, or a waking dream?/Fled is that music:—Do I wake or sleep? **John Keats**

(*n*) *wakening*, *waking*

(*v*) awaken, bring around, bring to, come around, come to, come to life, *regain consciousness*, stir, wake, waken, wake up

See also WIDE AWAKE AND CONSCIOUS (735)

725 Reproduction and Heredity

Every baby born into the world is a finer one than the last.
Charles Dickens

(*adj*) antenatal (*UK*), asexual, barren, birth, congenital, developmental, expectant, expecting, fecund (*formal*), genetic, *gravid*, *heavy with child* (*archaic or literary*), hereditary, heritable, inborn, inbred, in-built, infertile, inherent, innate, instinctive, *in the family way* (*dated informal*), *perinatal*, postnatal, *postpartum*, pregnant, prenatal, *procreative*, reproductive, *sexual*, sterile, unfruitful, *with child* (*archaic or literary*)

(*n*) *artificial insemination*, *autogamy*, barrenness, birth, childbearing, childbirth, chromosome, confinement (*dated*), fecundity, fertilization, gene, gestation, *gravidity*, *gravidness*, infertility, *insemination*, labor, *miscarriage*, motherhood, *ovary*, *parturition* (*formal*), pregnancy, *procreation*, reproduction, RNA, self-fertilization, *sexual maturity*, sterility, *umbilicus*

(*v*) calve, engender (*formal*), father, fertilize, foal, incubate, *inseminate*, interbreed, mate, *procreate*, proliferate, pup, reproduce, spawn, whelp

726 Sterilize

Vasectomy means not ever having to say you're sorry. **Larry Adler**

(*n*) *castration*, *hysterectomy*, sterilization, *vasectomy*

(*v*) castrate, geld, neuter, spay, sterilize, *vasectomize*

727 Eggs, Sperm, and Spawn

A hen is only an egg's way of making another egg. **Samuel Butler**

(*n*) egg, frogspawn (*UK*), *ova*, *ovule*, *ovum*, *reproductive cell*, *semen*, spawn, sperm, spermatozoon

728 Become Sick, Treat, and Recover

A person often falls very ill in order to become someone else and then returns to health much disappointed. **Elias Canetti**

(*v*) ail (*archaic or literary*), black out, catch, come down with, contract, convalesce, cure, faint, get, get better, go down with (*informal*), go under, have, immunize, inject, inoculate, keel over (*informal*), lose consciousness, pass out, quarantine, rebound, recover, recuperate, remedy, resurrect, resuscitate, revive, sedate, shake off, sprain, strike down, stun, vaccinate

See also ILL AND SICK (740)

729 Sickness

No man needs curing of his individual sickness; his universal malady is what he should look to. **Djuna Barnes**

(*adj*) allergic, cancerous, *carcinomatous*, catching, communicable, contagious, gangrenous, incurable, infectious, infective, inoperable, malignant, pathological, septic, transmissible, transmittable, waterborne

(*n*) complaint, condition, disease, disorder, epidemic, malady, malaise, malignancy, pandemic, pestilence (*archaic*), plague, sickness, syndrome, trouble

730 Healing

Earth hath no sorrow that heaven cannot heal. **Thomas Moore**

(*adj*) better, convalescent, curable, curative, healing, on the mend, operable, recuperative

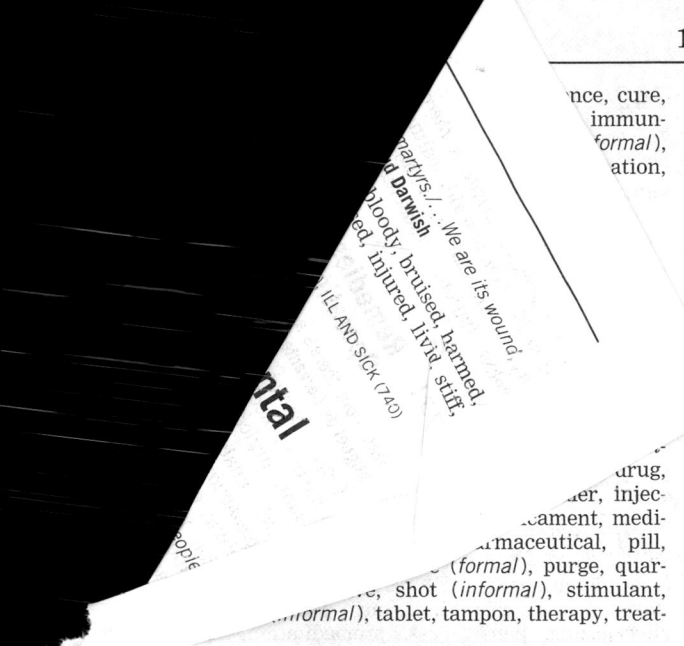

stupor, suffering, tenderness, throb, tingle, turn, twinge, wound, wrench

(*v*) ache, bite, boil (*informal*), broil, burn, crick, hurt, irritate, itch, numb, prickle, smart, sting, suffer, tickle, tingle

See also PHYSICALLY UNPLEASANT (226)

734 Physical States

To animate, in the precise sense of the word: to give life to.
Federico García Lorca

(*n*) constitution, fitness, health, healthiness

735 Wide Awake and Conscious

Music, Beauty, are within us. . .great works are those that awaken our spirit. **Louis-Ferdinand Céline**

(*adj*) astir, awake, aware, conscious, fresh, invigorated, *refreshed*, *reinvigorated*, *rejuvenated*, *revitalized*, *revived*, sensible (*formal*), sleepless, up, up and about, wakeful

(*n*) awareness, *sentience*, sleeplessness, wakefulness

See also WAKE AND REGAIN CONSCIOUSNESS (724)

736 Fit and Strong

Nutritional research, like a modern star of Bethlehem, brings hope that sickness need not be a part of life. **Adelle Davis**

(*adj*) able-bodied, alive and kicking (*informal*), buff (*informal*), *fighting fit*, fit, full-blooded, hale, *hale and hearty*, healthy, *in fine fettle*, in good condition, in good form, in good health, in good shape, in peak condition, in shape, in the pink (*dated*), in your prime, lusty, mobile, on top form, red-blooded, rested, robust, sprightly, spry, well, whole

(*n*) good health, robustness, soundness, *sprightliness*, *spryness*

See also STRENGTH (201)

737 Safe and Sound

The only way to be absolutely safe is never to try anything for the first time. **Henri Frédéric Amiel**

(*adj*) alive and well, all right, right, safe, safe and sound, sound, unharmed, unhurt, uninjured, unscathed, untouched, whole

738 Tired, Asleep, and Unconscious

A drowsy numbness pains/My sense. **John Keats**

(*adj*) all in, anesthetized, asleep, beat (*slang*), bleary-eyed, burned-out, bushed (*informal*), *cataleptic*, catatonic (*informal*), comatose, conked-out (*informal*), dead, deadened, dead to the world, dog-tired (*informal*), done for (*informal*), *done in* (*informal*), dormant, dozy, drained, droopy, drowsy, *enervated*, exhausted, *fast asleep*, fatigued, footsore, frazzled (*informal*), fried (*slang*), groggy, had it (*informal*), insensate, insensible, insentient, jaded, knocked out, languid, *languishing*, languorous, lethargic, lifeless, listless, logy, out, *out cold*, out for the count (*informal*), pooped (*informal*), *ready to drop*, run-down, semiconscious, senseless, shattered (*UK*), sleepy, *slumbering*, somnolent, soporific, sound asleep, spent, supine, tired, tired out, unconscious, washed-out, wasted (*slang*), weary, wiped out (*slang*), worn out, wrecked (*informal*)

(*v*) anesthetize, put to sleep, put under, tranquilize

types of complementary therapies   acupressure, acupuncture, Alexander technique, Ayurvedic medicine, Bach flower remedy, chiropractic, color therapy, cranial osteopathy, flotation, herbal medicine, homeopathy, hydrotherapy, hypnotherapy, iridology, kinesiology, massage, music therapy, naturopathy, neurolinguistic programming, osteopathy, Pilates, reflexology, reiki, shiatsu, tai chi, yoga

types of medical procedures   amniocentesis, amputation, anesthesia, angioplasty, appendectomy, biopsy, booster, bypass, CAT scan, Cesarean section, checkup, chemotherapy, diagnosis, dialysis, endoscopy, facelift, graft, hysterectomy, immunization, keyhole surgery, laparoscopy, manipulation, mastectomy, operation, physical therapy, plastic surgery, radiotherapy, resuscitation, sedation, tracheotomy, transfusion, ultrasound scan, vaccination, vasectomy, X-ray

732 Illnesses and Disorders

Most of those evils we poor mortals know/From doctors and imagination flow. **Charles Churchill**

(*n*) affliction, ailment, allergy, back pain, blackout, cancer, cold, collapse, cyst, disability, disablement, fever, fit, *flu*, gall, ganglion, gangrene, growth, heart attack (*informal*), infection, influenza, lesion, polyp, *sarcoma*, *sciatica*, tumor, virus

733 Pain and Other Physical Sensations

Remember that pain has this most excellent quality: if prolonged it cannot be severe, and if severe it cannot be prolonged. **Seneca the Younger**

(*adj*) aching, achy, burning, *dyspeptic*, ingrowing, *in pain*, itchy, numb, numbing, painful, paroxysmal, psychedelic, raw, sore, tender, tingling, uncomfortable

(*n*) ache, aching, backache, contraction, convulsion, cramp, crick, discomfort, flush, fog, headache, hurt, injury, irritation, itch, lumbago, numbness, pain, pang, paroxysm, pins and needles, soreness, stab, strain,

(*adv*) blearily, dozily, groggily, lethargically, lifelessly, sleepily, tiredly

(*n*) analgesia, *catalepsy*, coma, doziness, droopiness, drowsiness, *enervation*, exhaustion, fatigue, fugue, grogginess, languor, lassitude, lethargy, lifelessness, *listlessness*, loss of consciousness, prostration, sleepiness, tiredness, unconsciousness

(*v*) enervate, exhaust, swoon, tire, wear out, weary

See also SLEEP AND DREAM (723)

739   Unfit and Weak

Minds like bodies, will often fall into a pimpled, ill-conditioned state from mere excess of comfort. **Charles Dickens**

(*adj*) at death's door, bedridden, cadaverous (*formal or literary*), crummy (*informal*), debilitated, decrepit (*archaic or humorous*), dizzy, doddery, feeble, fragile, frail, funny, in bad shape, incapable, incapacitated, *in poor condition*, invalid, *out of condition, out of shape*, peaked, run-down, sickly, the worse for wear, unfit, unhealthy, unsound, valetudinarian, wan, *wasting away*, weak, weedy, wobbly (*informal*)

(*n*) decrepitude, dizziness, fragility, frailty, invalid, martyr, sufferer, valetudinarian, weakness

See also WEAKNESS (241)

740   Ill and Sick

To preserve one's health by too strict a regime is in itself a tedious malady. **François La Rochefoucauld**

(*adj*) ailing (*dated*), airsick, bilious, bloated, burning, burning up, carsick, delirious, diseased, *disease-ridden*, faint, febrile, ghastly (*informal*), giddy, *green around the gills* (*informal*), ill, indisposed (*formal*), infected, infirm, inflamed, *in poor health*, laid up, lightheaded, *motion sick*, muzzy, *nauseated*, nauseous, off-color (*UK*), out of sorts, puffy, queasy, queer (*dated*), rabid, rotten (*informal*), seasick, seedy (*informal*), shaky, sick, squeamish, stricken, travel-sick, under the weather, unwell, woozy

(*adv*) dizzily, feebly, giddily, muzzily, queasily

(*n*) airsickness, burnout, dehydration, delirium, faintness, giddiness, hotness, ill health, illness, indisposition, infirmity, inflammation, morbidity, nausea, puffiness, queasiness, roughness (*informal*), seediness (*informal*), squeamishness, swelling, swoon, thirst, vertigo, *wooziness*

See also BECOME SICK, TREAT, AND RECOVER (728), INJURED (742)

741   Under the Influence of Drugs or Alcohol

I've a head like a concertina, I've a tongue like a buttonstick,/I've a mouth like an old potato, and I'm more than a little sick. **Rudyard Kipling**

(*adj*) addicted, blitzed (*informal*), bombed (*slang*), drunk, happy (*informal*), inebriated, intoxicated, liquored up (*informal*), out of it, plastered (*informal*), sedated, soused (*slang*), sozzled (*informal*), stewed (*slang*), tanked-up (*slang*), three sheets to the wind (*informal*), tight (*slang*), tipsy

(*n*) dependence, inebriation, intoxication

742   Injured

This land absorbs the skins of [...] but a wound that fights. **Mahmou[...]**

(*adj*) battered, black-and-blue, [...] hors de combat, ill-treated, ill-u[...] stricken, winded, wounded

See also WOUND A PERSON OR ANIMAL (383[...])

The Mind and Me[...] Processes

743   Think and Reflect

Thinking is the most unhealthy thing in the world, and p[...] die of it just as they die of any other disease. **Oscar Wilde**

(*n*) cogitation (*formal*), contemplation, deliberatic[...] (*formal*), heart-searching, introspection, meditation, navel-gazing, pensiveness, premeditation, reflection, rumination, soul-searching

(*v*) agonize, brainstorm, brood, *chew on*, chew over, *chew the cud*, cogitate (*formal*), concentrate, consider, contemplate, deliberate, dwell on, entertain, flirt with, go back over, harbor, *intellectualize*, meditate, mope, mull, mull over, muse, *perpend* (*archaic*), ponder, puzzle, rack your brains, reflect, ruminate, see, speculate, take under advisement, think over, think through, think twice, toy with, turn over, weigh

See also ATTENTION AND ATTENTIVENESS (763)

744   Develop Theories and Reason

Nothing is so practical as a good theory. **Kurt Levin**

(*v*) abstract, assume, collude, conceive, conspire, cook up (*informal*), count, deduce, do, hatch, have, hold, hypothesize, imagine, machinate, philosophize, piece out, piece together, posit (*formal*), postulate, reason, reckon, sense, suppose, theorize, think, think up, work out

See also ATTENTION AND ATTENTIVENESS (763), IDEAS AND THOUGHTS (770)

745   Memory

It has memory's ear/that can hear without/having to hear. **Marianne Moore**

(*n*) flashback, hindsight, memory, recall, recollection, remembrance, reminiscence, retention, retrospect, rote, tickler

746   Remember

Memory believes before knowing remembers. Believes longer than recollects, longer than knowing even wonders. **William Faulkner**

(*v*) bear in mind, celebrate, commemorate, commit to memory, keep count, keep in mind, keep track of, look back, make a note of, make a point of, memorize, recall, recapture, recollect, rediscover, relive, remember, reminisce, retain

747   Remind

When you sleep you remind me of the dead. **Siegfried Sassoon**

(*v*) bring back, bring to mind, call to mind, conjure up, evoke, hark back, remind, ring a bell (*informal*), stir, stir up, suggest, take back

748   Forget, Forgive, and Accept

If there's anyone listening to whom I owe money, I'm prepared to forget it if you are. **Errol Flynn**

(*n*) acceptance, exculpation (*formal*), exoneration, vindication

(*v*) absolve, admit defeat, bow to, bury the hatchet, buy (*informal*), cave in, cede (*formal*), come around, come to terms with, concede, condone, exculpate (*formal*), excuse, exempt, exonerate, face, face the music, face up to, fall for, forget, forgive, get over, give in, go along with, lap up, laugh off, leave behind, *let bygones be bygones*, let off, live down, make up, miss, overlook, pardon, purge (*formal*), put behind you, relent, resign yourself, set aside, submit, swallow (*informal*), take as read, take at face value, take in your stride, take on board (*UK*), vindicate, weaken, wipe the slate clean (*informal*), write off (*informal*)

749   Dream, Imagine, and Fantasize

The power of dreams...is tied to the multiformity of animals: with their disappearance one may soon expect the dreams to dry up as well. **Elias Canetti**

(*n*) daydream, daydreaming, imagination, make-believe, reverie, romanticism, supposition, trance, unreality, vision, visualization, *woolgathering*

(*v*) conceive, concoct, contemplate, daydream, dream, dream up, fancy, fantasize, hallucinate, have in mind, imagine, invent, make believe, make up, moon (*literary or humorous*), picture, pretend, romance, romanticize, see, see in your mind's eye, sentimentalize, visualize, woolgather

See also NONEXISTENT THINGS (23)

750   Predict and Anticipate

My doctor has advised me to cut back on predictions. **Conor Cruise O'Brien**

(*adj*) predicted, predictive, premonitory, prophetic

(*n*) divination, ESP, forecast, foresight, forethought, oracle, prediction, prescience, prognosis, prognostication, projection, prophecy, vision

(*v*) anticipate, await, bargain for, bargain on, bet (*informal*), conspire, contemplate, design, envisage (*formal*), envision, expect, forecast, foresee, forestall (*archaic*), foretell (*literary*), guess, lick your lips, look ahead, look forward to, predict, prejudge, presume, presuppose, prognosticate, project, prophesy, reckon on (*informal*), reckon with, scent, second-guess, take care, take for granted, trust, wait, wait on (*informal*)

See also FEELINGS ABOUT THE FUTURE (533)

751   Question Things

I am too much of a skeptic to deny the possibility of anything. **T. H. Huxley**

(*v*) call into question, canvass, daresay, debate, discredit, dispute, distrust, impugn (*formal*), inquire into, look into, mistrust, query, question, suspect, wonder

See also ASK PEOPLE QUESTIONS (666)

752   Make Decisions and Choices

He had decided to live for ever or die in the attempt. **Joseph Heller**

(*n*) alternative, bet, choice, decision, discretion, option, resolution, rethink, ruling

(*v*) agree, appoint (*formal*), arrive, burn your bridges, change direction, change your mind, cherry-pick, choose, choose up, come down on the side of, come to a decision, conclude, cream off, decide, designate, determine, diagnose, dispose, elect, fall back on, firm up, go for (*informal*), have second thoughts, make up your mind, mean business, mean it, opt, pick, *pick and choose*, pick out, plump for (*UK*), predetermine, prioritize, render (*formal*), resolve, rethink, select, set, settle on, short-list, single out, skim off, tell apart, vote

753   Examine and Assess

The examined life has always been pretty well confined to a privileged class. **Edgar Z. Friedenberg**

(*adj*) diagnostic, estimated, exploratory, investigative, probing, retrospective, supervisory, trial

(*n*) analysis, anatomy, audit, breakdown, check, comparison, criticism, crosscheck, dialectic, dissection, double check, estimate, estimation, examination, experiment, experimentation, exploration, going-over (*informal*), inquiry, inspection, investigation, once-over (*informal*), perusal, postmortem, probe, reading, reconsideration, reexamination, research, reevaluation, review, road test, screening, scrutiny, spot check, spying, stocktaking, study, supervision, survey, test, tune-up, visitation, workup

(*v*) analyze, appraise, assay, assess, audit, audition, balance, break down, check, check out, check over, check up on, compare, consult, contrast, control, criticize, critique, crosscheck, deconstruct, delve, differentiate, dig into, discriminate, dissect, distinguish, double-check, do your homework (*informal*), examine, experiment, explore, gauge, give the once-over (*informal*), go into, go over, go through, inspect, investigate, judge, look, look over, monitor, parse, peruse, pore over, probe, reappraise, reassess, reconnoiter, reconsider, reexamine, refer, referee, research, revalue, revert, review, revisit, road-test, sample, scan, screen, scrutinize, see about, set against, sleuth, sound out, spellcheck, spot-check, spy, study, survey, take stock, test, try, try out, vet, view, weigh up (*UK*), winnow

754   Guess

What I have learned I no longer know. The little that I do know, I guessed. **Nicolas Chamfort**

(*n*) *ballpark figure* (*informal*), conjecture, educated guess, guess, guesstimate (*informal*), guesswork, supposition, surmise

(v) conjecture, guess, guesstimate (*informal*), speculate, suppose, surmise, suspect

755   Assess Quality

The quality of moral behavior varies in inverse ratio to the number of human beings involved. **Aldous Huxley**

(v) adjudge, adjudicate, arbitrate, evaluate, examine, judge, mark, overestimate, peg, price, rank, rate, size up, stack up, umpire, *valuate*, value

756   Have an Opinion of Something

The English think of an opinion as something which a decent person, if he has the misfortune to have one, does all he can to hide. **Margaret Halsey**

(v) believe, consider, deduce, deem (*formal*), feel, figure, judge, reckon, regard, think, view

757   Assess Quantity

Size determines an object, but scale determines art. **Robert Smithson**

(adj) calculable, countable, measurable, quantifiable, quantitative, reckonable

(n) addition, approximation, summation

(v) add, add up, assess, balance, calculate, compute, count, count up, enumerate, estimate, fathom, judge, measure, miscount, quantify, quote, re-count, score, survey, tally, time, total, tot up

758   Read

The simpler the alphabet, the easier it is to read. **Joan Miró**

(v) dip into, flick through, flip through, proofread, read, reread, run through, skim, speed-read

See also SEE (699)

759   Understand and Grasp

The apprehension that one is someone else is all that one needs to believe that the world has changed from top to bottom. **Orhan Pamuk**

(n) appreciation, conception, grip, realization, uptake

(v) absorb, accept, appreciate, catch on (*informal*), click (*informal*), comprehend, construe, cotton on (*informal*), dawn, digest, discern, divine, fathom, figure out, follow, gather, get (*informal*), get it, get the drift, get the hang of, get the message (*informal*), get the picture (*informal*), *get to grips with*, *get up to speed*, grasp, intuit, keep abreast, keep up, master, penetrate, perceive, pick up, plumb, realize, recognize, see, see into, see through, sense, take, take in, take on board, understand, work out

760   Solve and Interpret

Interpretation is the revenge of the intellectual upon art. **Susan Sontag**

(v) answer, break, crack (*informal*), decipher, decode, extrapolate, infer, interpret, make out, make sense of, penetrate, puzzle out, read, *read between the lines*, resolve, solve, translate, unlock, unravel, unscramble, work out

761   Misunderstand and Fail to Grasp

Is an intelligent human being likely to be much more than a large-scale manufacturer of misunderstanding? **Philip Roth**

(n) cross-purposes, delusion, misapprehension, misconstruction, misinterpretation, misjudgment, misunderstanding

(v) *get hold of the wrong end of the stick*, get it wrong, get the wrong end of the stick, get the wrong idea, *get the wrong impression*, misapprehend, miscalculate, *miscomprehend*, misconceive, misconstrue, mishear, misinterpret, misjudge, *misperceive*, misread, miss, miss the point, mistake, misunderstand, mix up, take amiss, *take the wrong way*

See also MISTAKES (250)

762   Learn and Discover

The man of reflection discovers Truth; but the one who enjoys it and makes use of its heavenly gifts is the man of action. **Benito Pérez Galdós**

(v) accustom, acquire, ascertain, assimilate, become aware of, determine, discover, establish, familiarize yourself, find out, *get wind of*, hear, hit on, hit upon, internalize, learn, note, orient, orientate, see, spy, tell

763   Attention and Attentiveness

It's easy to get people's attention, what counts is getting their interest. **A. Philip Randolph**

(n) absorption, attention, attentiveness, *beguilement*, care, concentration, curiosity, focus, heed, intentness, interest, involvement, mind, spotlight, thoughtfulness, vested interest

See also PENSIVENESS AND INTEREST (538), THINK AND REFLECT (743), DEVELOP THEORIES AND REASON (744)

764   Not Pay Attention

My thoughts ran a wool-gathering; and I did like the countryman who looked for his ass while he was mounted on his back. **Miguel de Cervantes**

(n) abstractedness, abstraction, avoidance, circumvention, cop-out (*slang*), dreaminess, evasion, inattention, inattentiveness, neglect, negligence

(v) avoid, blank out, block out, blot out, blow off (*slang*), circumvent, close your eyes to, cop out (*slang*), cut out, discount, dismiss, disregard, distance, dodge, evade, exclude, fight back, forget, gloss over, ignore, leave alone, leave in peace, leave out, let alone, let be, let pass, let ride, mind your own business, miss out (*UK*), neglect, overlook, pardon, pass by, pass over, *pay no attention*, *pay no heed*, put aside, rule out, shrug off, sideline, sidestep, skip, skirt, stretch a point, sublimate, suppress, sweep aside, *sweep under the carpet*, *take no heed of*, take no notice of, turn a blind eye to, turn your back on, wander, wash your hands of

765   Pay Attention

The quality of your attention determines the quality of other people's thinking. **Nancy Kline**

(v) allow for, apply yourself, attend, beware, consider, engage, *give heed*, hark (*literary or humorous*), heed, listen up (*slang*), look out, mind, *pay attention*, *pay heed*, play safe, respect, take, take account of, take care, *take heed*, take into consideration, *take note*, *take notice*, target, watch, watch out, watch your step

766　Tolerate and Endure

We tolerate shapes in human beings that would horrify us if we saw them in a horse. **William Ralph Inge**

(*v*) abide, accept, bear, bear the brunt, bear with, brave, brave out, brook (*literary*), come out of, countenance (*formal*), endure, get it in the neck (*informal*), grin and bear it (*informal*), hack (*informal*), have, hear of, hold on, hold out, hold your own, keep your chin up, keep your cool, live with, look on the bright side, lump (*informal*), make allowances, make the best of a bad job (*UK*), make the best of things, put on a brave front, put up with, resist, ride out, stand, stand for, *stand the pace*, *stay the course*, *stick it out*, stick out, *struggle on*, *struggle through*, suffer, support (*literary*), sustain, sweat out, take, take the rough with the smooth, tolerate, *tough it out* (*informal*), weather

767　Points of View

The worth of a man is certain only if he is prepared to sacrifice his own life for his convictions. **Henning von Tresckow**

(*n*) angle, argument, aspect, assessment, attitude, belief, *belief system*, contention, conviction, diagnosis, estimation, feeling, frame of reference, gloss, judgment, line, mentality, mind, mindset, opinion, orthodoxy, outlook, perception, perspective, persuasion, point, point of view, politics, position, premise, presumption, presupposition, pretense, reckoning, remonstrance, say, school of thought, sense, slant, spin (*slang*), stance, stand, standpoint, take, thoughts, understanding, vantage point, version, view, viewpoint, voice, way of thinking

768　Subject Areas

There is no such thing on earth as an uninteresting subject; the only thing that can exist is an uninterested person. **G. K. Chesterton**

(*n*) area, *area of expertise*, *bailiwick*, branch, *burden* (*literary*), business, concern, consideration, department (*informal*), field, issue, jurisdiction, leitmotif, line, matter, motif, point, preserve, province, question, realm, respect, specialism, specialization, specialty, sphere, *sphere of activity*, *sphere of influence*, subject, subject matter, talking point, territory, theme, thing, topic, turf (*informal*), world

769　Psychology and the Mind

Psychology has a long past, but only a short history. **Hermann Ebbinghaus**

(*adj*) behavioral, cognitive, compulsive, maladjusted, mental, mixed-up (*informal*), neurological, neurotic, primeval, psychic, psychological, psychosomatic, *solipsistic*, spiritual, subliminal, unbalanced

(*n*) analysis, autosuggestion, being, cognition, complex (*informal*), counseling, daemon, ego, frame of mind, *guilt complex*, hang-up (*informal*), inferiority complex, influence, introversion, I.Q., *lateral thinking*, maladjustment, marbles (*slang*), *nervous breakdown*, *nervous tension*, neurosis (*dated*), psyche, *psychiatry*, *psychoanalysis*, psychology, *psychosis*, *psychotherapy*, reason, self, self-esteem, self-help, self-image, self-preservation, *solipsism*, state of mind, sublimation, superego, superiority

complex, *thought processes*, unconscious, visualization, will

770　Ideas and Thoughts

Ideas do not show themselves productive with those who suggest them. . .but with those persevering workers who feel them strongly and put all their faith and love in their efficacy. **Santiago Ramón y Cajal**

(*n*) abstraction, afterthought, *arrière-pensée* (*formal*), assumption, brainchild, brainstorm (*informal*), caprice, case, concept, conception, conclusion, consideration, construct, construction, deduction, dictate, dogma, ethic, feeling, *fixed idea*, hypothesis, idea, illusion, image, impression, inference, initiative, inkling, inspiration, ism (*informal*), logic, maxim, *mental image*, *mental picture*, musing, notion, precept (*formal*), premeditation, premise, principle, *ratiocination* (*formal*), reasoning, rhyme or reason, superstructure, teaching, tenet, theory, thesis, thinking, thought, thread, *train of thought*, vision, whim, whimsy

See also DEVELOP THEORIES AND REASON (744)

771　The Nature of Ideas

Many ideas grow better when transplanted into another mind than in the one where they sprang up. **Oliver Wendell Holmes, Jr.**

(*adj*) abstract, analytic, backward-looking, biased, careful, cerebral, clinical, cogent, coherent, commonsense, *commonsensical*, considered, crackpot (*informal*), critical, deductive, deep, deep-seated, deliberative (*formal*), farsighted, forward-looking, gut, half-baked (*informal*), heuristic, highbrow, idle, ill-advised, ill-conceived, ill-considered, ill-founded, ill-judged, illogical, impolitic, inadvisable, inane, incoherent, injudicious, intuitive, just, knee-jerk (*informal*), lowbrow, misbegotten, misconceived, misguided, modern, muddleheaded, neat, one-sided, oriented, partial, political, preconceived, prescriptive, profound, pure, rational, reasoned, retrospective, revisionist, sane, sensitive, serious, shallow, short-sighted, simple-minded, simplistic, slanted, stupid, subjective, tendentious, unbalanced, unbiased, unformulated, unscientific, unsound, unstated, valid, weighted, well-advised, well-founded, well-grounded, well-thought-out, wrong-headed

(*adv*) comprehensibly, ill-advisedly, intuitively, neatly, shallowly, subjectively

(*n*) cogency, illogicality, *inaneness*, inanity, injudiciousness, neatness, one-sidedness, partiality, prejudice, prescriptiveness, profoundness, profundity, sanity, subjectivity, validity

See also DESCRIBING SOMEBODY'S INTELLECT (523)

772　Intentions and Purposes

Intention is the measure for rendering actions true, so that where intention is sound action is sound, and where it is corrupt then action is corrupt. **Muhyid-Din Abu Zakariyya ibn Sharaf al-Nawawi**

(*n*) aim, butt, calculation, casuistry, design, destination, destiny, direction, end, function, goal, idea, intent (*formal*), intention, object, objective, point, predetermination, purport (*formal*), purpose, raison d'être, reason, scheme, sense, target, use

(*prep*) for

Philosophies, Beliefs, and Morality

773 Moral Concepts

Morality which is based on ideas, or on an ideal, is an unmitigated evil. **D. H. Lawrence**

(*n*) conscience, ethics, ethos, high ground, ideal, morality, morals, standards, values

774 Morally Good

Man's goodness is a flame that can be hidden but never extinguished. **Nelson Mandela**

(*adj*) aboveboard, *above criticism*, angelic, balanced, blameless, characterful, chaste, civilizing, clean, decent, ethical, good, gracious, guiltless, harmless, honest, honorable, humanitarian, humanizing, innocent, in the right, irreproachable, just, law-abiding, moral, noble, principled, pure (*literary*), refining, right, *right and proper*, righteous, sporting, spotless, square, squeaky-clean, unblemished, uncorrupted, undefiled, unimpeachable, unspotted, upright, upstanding, virtuous, wholesome, within your rights

(*adv*) decently, deservedly, *irreproachably*, justly, purely, square (*informal*)

(*n*) character, chasteness, chastity, citizenship, clemency, decency, devotion (*formal*), dignity, good faith, goodness, grace, *guiltlessness*, harmlessness, honesty, honor, innocence, integrity, *irreproachability*, justice, morality, nobility, nobleness, piety, piousness, probity, propriety, purity, rectitude, respectability, right, righteousness, *social conscience*, *social responsibility*, spotlessness, uprightness, virtue, *virtuousness*, wholesomeness

See also EQUALITY (154), CORRECT AND FAULTLESS (182), HONEST AND RELIABLE (502), LEGAL AND LEGITIMATE (815)

775 Morally Bad or Improper

A bad cause will ever be supported by bad means and bad men. **Thomas Paine**

(*adj*) abusive, *adulterous*, amoral, avaricious, bad, barbaric, barbarous, base, bawdy, bestial, blameworthy, bloodthirsty, brutal, carnal (*formal*), cat-and-mouse, corrupt, criminal, culpable, dastardly, debauched, defiled (*formal*), degenerate, delinquent, depraved, dirty, discriminatory, dishonorable, disreputable, disrespectable, dubious, earthy, errant, evil, exploitative, extracurricular (*informal*), extramarital, fast, fiendish, filthy, fleshly, foul, greedy, grubby, guilty, heinous, heretical, ignoble, ill, immoral, impious, improper, indecent, indefensible, inequitable, infamous, iniquitous, in the wrong, *lascivious*, lecherous, lewd, libidinous, licentious, light-fingered, louche, *maleficent*, malevolent, nasty (*informal*), nefarious, notorious, obscene, off-color (*informal*), oppressive, overindulgent, pernicious, perverted, profane (*formal*), profligate, promiscuous, prurient, racy, raffish, rakish, rascally, *raunchy* (*informal*), responsible, ribald, risqué, salacious,

scandalous, shady, sleazy, smutty (*informal*), sordid, squalid, suggestive, sullied, taboo, tarnished, *tarty*, to blame, treasonable, *unchaste*, unclean, unequal, unethical, unfair, ungodly, unhealthy, unholy, uninhibited, unjust, unmerited, unprincipled, unprintable, unprofessional, unreasonable, unrighteous, unsavory, unscrupulous, unworthy, venal, vicious, vile, villainous, violent, vulgar, wanton, wicked, wrong

(*adv*) contemptibly, discreditably, fiendishly, grossly, improperly, oppressively, *profanely* (*formal*), unequally, unjustly, unscrupulously, viciously, violently, wrongfully, wrongly

(*n*) *adultery*, amorality, arrogance, avarice, avariciousness, badness, barbarism, barbarity, baseness, bestiality, bigotry, blame, bloodthirstiness, *carnality* (*formal*), coercion, corruption, corruptness, covetousness, crime, culpability, cupidity (*formal*), debauchery, decadence, degeneracy, delinquency (*formal*), depravity, despotism, evil, evilness, excess, excesses, filth, filthiness, foulness, foul play, gluttony, greed, greediness, grubbiness, guilt, guiltiness, heresy, immorality, impiety, impiousness, *improbity*, indecency, inequity (*formal*), infection, infidelity, iniquity, injustice, *lewdness*, *licentiousness* (*formal*), *maleficence*, malevolence, *malfeasance*, *nefariousness*, obscenity, opportunism, opportunistic, overindulgence, peccadillo, perniciousness, pride, *profanation* (*formal*), *prurience*, ribaldry, shadiness, sin, sleaze, *sleaziness*, smut, *smuttiness* (*informal*), sordidness, squalor, treason, turpitude (*formal*), *unchasteness*, uncleanness, unfairness, unreasonableness, *unsavoriness*, unscrupulousness, unwholesomeness, unworthiness, *venality*, vice, vileness, villainy, vulgarity, wantonness, wickedness, worldliness, wrong

See also RESPONSIBILITY (170), INCORRECT AND ERRONEOUS (222), DECEITFUL (513), ILLEGAL (816)

776 Religious Concepts

Things divine are believed in/But by those who themselves are so. **Friedrich Hölderlin**

(*adj*) baptismal, biblical, blasphemous, blessed, celestial, cherubic, clerical, consecrated, devout, divine, fleshly, *godless*, godlike, godly (*formal*), hallowed, heavenly, holy, irreligious, mortal, pious, *precatory* (*formal*), religious, revered, sacred, sacrilegious, sacrosanct, saintly, sanctified, secular, sinful, *sinless*, solemn, spiritual, temporal, theological, transcendent, transcendental, *unconsecrated*, ungodly, unholy, unspiritual, votive

(*n*) *act of contrition*, afterlife, afterworld, angel, apocalypse, *archangel*, *archbishopric*, Armageddon, *bishopric*, blasphemer, blasphemy, bull, catechism, cherub, consecration, credo, *Day of Judgment*, deity, devoutness, *divine intervention*, doomsday, *eternal life*, *evil spirit*, faith, *fire and brimstone*, *fundamentalism*, god, goddess, *godlessness*, godliness, grace, heaven, hell, *heretic*, holiness, *holy day*, *holy of holies*, *holy rites*, inferno, *Judgment Day*, karma, libation, *limbo*, monotheism, netherworld (*formal*), *next world*, nirvana, paradise, perdition, polytheism, *profaner*, *promised land*, reincarnation, religiousness, *sacredness*, sacrilege, saintliness, *saint's day*, *sanctification*, sanctity, *seraph*, sin, *sinfulness*, *sinner*, soul, spirit, *spiritual enlightenment*, spirituality, theism, theology, transcendence, unbelief, unbeliever, *ungodliness*

777   Religions and Religious Practices

The mystical and the ethical. . .There is no holiness and therefore no living religion without both elements. **Paul Tillich**

(*adj*) devotional, ecclesiastical, evangelical, interdenominational, pontifical, reverend, sacerdotal, sectarian

(*n*) absolution, adoration, beatification, blessing, canonization, *catechesis*, catechism, christening, creed, devotions, dirge, excommunication, incantation, litany, liturgy, mantra, ordination, praise, prayer, psalm, purdah, religion, requiem, sacrament, sermon, service, tithe

(*v*) adore, baptize, bless, *catechize*, christen, consecrate, defile (*formal*), *evangelize*, excommunicate, hallow, praise, pray, sanctify, sin, solemnize, worship

See also INSTITUTIONS (790)

778   Religious People

Religions, which condemn the pleasures of sense, drive men to seek the pleasures of power. **Bertrand Russell**

(*n*) *abbot*, apostle, *archbishop*, *army chaplain*, believer, *bishop*, chaplain, churchgoer, clergy, *clergyman*, *clergywoman*, cleric, communicant, congregation, cult, curate, *druid*, ecclesiastic, *evangelist*, father, *friar*, *fundamentalist*, guru, *Holy Father*, holy man, holy sister, laity, lama, maharishi, martyr, minister, missionary, monk, *nun*, *padre*, *parish priest*, parson, pastor, patriarch, pontiff, pope, preacher, prelate, *presbyter*, priest, priesthood, primacy, primate, *prison chaplain*, pulpit, rabbi, rector, reverend, *saint*, sect, *shaman*, *shamanism*, sister, *spiritual guide*, *spiritual leader*, swami, vestal (*literary*), *vicar*, worshiper

779   Religious Objects

Holy images. . .perfect our understanding, move our will, refresh our memory of divine things. **Francisco Pacheco**

(*n*) breviary, crèche, cross, idol, missal, *paten*, *prayer book*, psalter, pulpit, reliquary, shrine, stoup

See also PARTS OF RELIGIOUS BUILDINGS (1086)

780   Philosophies and Beliefs

Philosophy is the childhood of the intellect, and a culture that tries to skip it will never grow up. **Thomas Nagel**

(*adj*) atheistic, ideological, *Leninist*, *Maoist*, *Marxist*, metaphysical, nationalistic, nihilistic, patriotic, philosophic, philosophical, relativist (*UK*), utopian

(*n*) ·atheism, communism, culture, empiricism, feminism, ideology, *leftism*, *Leninism*, *Maoism*, *Marxism*, nationalism, nihilism, obscurantism, *pantheism*, patriotism, philosophy, progressivism, radicalism, relativism, revisionism, traditionalism, *Trotskyism*

781   Philosophical and Political Thinkers

The philosophers have only interpreted the world in various ways; the point is to change it. **Karl Marx**

(*n*) agnostic, anarchist, atheist, bolshevik (*informal*), bolshie (*informal dated*), communist, disbeliever, ecologist, empiricist, environmentalist, *existentialist*, extremist, feminist, *leftie* (*informal*), *leftist*, left-winger, missionary, modernizer, moralist, nihilist, nonbeliever, pacifist, philosopher, realist, reformer, reformist, relativist, revisionist, right-winger, *social democrat*, socialist, stoic, supremacist, theorist, thinker, traditionalist, utopian

782   Fate, Destiny, and Astrology

There's a divinity that shapes our ends,/Rough-hew them how we will. **William Shakespeare**

(*adj*) astral, astrological, destined, doomed, fated, meant, predestined, predetermined, providential, unlucky, zodiacal

(*n*) astrologer, astrological sign, *astrologist*, astrology, birth sign, destiny, doom, fate, fortune, kismet, lot, luck, nemesis (*literary*), portion (*literary*), predestination, predetermination, providence, sign, star sign, zodiac

types of astrological signs Aquarius, Aries, Cancer, Capricorn, Gemini, Leo, Libra, Pisces, Sagittarius, Scorpio, Taurus, Virgo

783   Luck

Fortune is for all; judgment is theirs who have won it for themselves. **Aeschylus**

(*adj*) charmed, felicitous, *fluky* (*informal*), fortunate, happy, *in luck*, lucky, merciful, providential, serendipitous, well-off

(*adv*) fortunately, happily, providentially, thankfully (*informal*)

(*n*) fortune, good fortune, lottery, luck, *luck of the draw*, lucky dip (*UK*), potluck, serendipity, *stroke of luck*

See also CHANCE EVENTS (36)

784   Bad Luck and Unlucky

We are all strong enough to bear the misfortunes of others. **François La Rochefoucauld**

(*adj*) accident-prone, accursed (*archaic or literary*), fateful, hapless, ill-fated, ill-omened, ill-starred, jinxed, luckless, star-crossed, unfortunate, unhappy, unlucky

(*n*) bad luck, haplessness, hex, malediction (*formal*), mischance, unluckiness

785   Lucky Charms

It is the customary fate of new truths to begin as heresies and to end as superstitions. **T. H. Huxley**

(*n*) amulet, fetish, *good luck charm*, horseshoe, *juju*, lucky charm, mascot, philter (*literary*), talisman, totem

786   Chance, Coincidence, and Accident

Time/moves about/dressed/in fortune/or misfortune. **Johannes Bobrowski**

(*adj*) accidental, casual, chance, coincidental, fortuitous

(*adv*) by chance, by coincidence, coincidentally

(*n*) accident, chance, toss-up

See also UNPLANNED AND UNEXPECTED (281)

787   The Supernatural

Religion/Has made an honest woman of the supernatural,/And we won't have it kicking over the traces again. **Christopher Fry**

(*adj*) clairvoyant, extrasensory, magic, magical, mystic, mystical, *occult*, *oracular*, *paranormal*, *para-psychological*, prescient, preternatural (*literary*), psychic, psychical, *second-sighted*, *sidereal*, spectral, super-natural, *telekinetic*, telepathic, *vatic*

(*interj*) abracadabra

(*n*) apparition, augury, banshee, *black magic*, clair-voyance, demon, *extrasensory perception*, *fortune telling*, *ghost*, *ghoul*, *ghoulishness*, intuition, magic, phantasm, phantom, poltergeist, precognition, premonition, presage, presence, second sight, shadow, sixth sense, sorcery, specter, spell, spirit, *spirit world*, spook (*informal*), superstition, telepathy, *thought transference*, voodoo, *witchcraft*, *witchery*, wizardry, wraith

788   People with Supernatural Powers

Mystics always hope that science will some day overtake them. **Booth Tarkington**

(*n*) clairvoyant, *faith healer*, fortune-teller, magician, *magus*, mystic, *occultist*, oracle, *parapsychologist*, prog-nosticator, prophet, psychic, seer, *sibyl*, soothsayer, sor-cerer, sorceress, spiritualist, *telepathist*, warlock, witch, witch doctor, wizard

789   Mythical Beings

There is precious little in civilization to appeal to a Yeti. **Edmund Hillary**

(*n*) *Abominable Snowman*, *Bigfoot*, bogey, daemon, dryad, elf, fairy, *fay* (*literary*), genie, *giant*, gnome, goblin, *gremlin* (*informal*), hobgoblin, imp, *incubus*, *jinne*, lep-rechaun, little people, *naiad*, nymph, ogre, pixie, sas-quatch, sprite, sylph, troll, *wood nymph*, *yeti*

See also NONEXISTENT THINGS (23), MYTHICAL CREATURES (1036)

Social Structures and Institutions

790   Institutions

Any institution which does not suppose the people good, and the magistrate corruptible, is evil. **Maximilien Robespierre**

(*n*) agency, authority, body, brotherhood, establishment, federation, fellowship, foundation, guild, infrastructure, institute, institution, polity

See also RELIGIONS AND RELIGIOUS PRACTICES (777)

791   Business

What good is the moon if you cannot buy it or sell it? **Ivan Boesky**

(*adj*) business, commercial, corporate, entrepreneurial, industrial, mercantile

(*n*) big business, business, commerce, direction, indus-try, marketplace

See also PROFESSIONS (845)

792   Business Enterprises and Related Bodies

CORPORATION, *n. An ingenious device for securing individual profit without individual responsibility.* **Ambrose Bierce**

(*n*) business, chain, combine, company, concern, con-cession, conglomerate, consortium, co-op (*informal*), cor-poration, dealership, *dot-com*, *e-business*, enterprise, firm, house, *joint-stock company*, *joint venture*, *keiretsu*, labor union, limited company, multinational, *OEM*, operation, outlet, partnership, *PLC* (*UK*), presidium, *public limited company*, *startup*, subsidiary, trade, *trade union*, transnational, tribunal, venture, watchdog

See also GROUPS WITH A COMMON INTEREST (938)

793   Business People

If you drag an executive away from business, he goes on running on the spot, pawing the ground, talking business. **Jean Baudrillard**

(*n*) adventurer, advertiser, bidder, *black knight*, broker, businessperson, capitalist, *captain of industry*, C.E.O., chair, chairperson, chief executive, C in C, contractor, *COO*, *corporate raider*, *creative* (*informal*), developer, dis-tributor, entrepreneur, *exec* (*informal*), executive, *fat cat* (*slang*), *headhunter*, hotelier, importer, impresario, industrialist, *intrapreneur*, landlady, landlord, *man-aging director* (*UK*), member, merchant, middleman, *president*, *suit* (*slang*), *tradesperson* (*UK*), trustee, tycoon, vested interest, wheeler-dealer (*informal*), *white knight*

794   Business Activities and Phenomena

Commerce is the art of exploiting the need or desire someone has for something. **Edmond de Goncourt**

(*n*) aftercare, asset-stripping, booking, business, buyout, client, clientele, *credit control*, custom, *delayering*, *due diligence*, end user, flotation, *globalization*, import, importation, industrial espionage, *just-in-time*, *kaizen*, *LBO*, *leveraged buyout*, liquidation, management, *man-agement buyout*, *MBO*, merger, monopoly, privatization, procurement, purchase, receivership, *reengineering*, repo (*informal*), *repossession*, reservation, retail, retrenchment, sale, selling, sponsorship, stocktaking, supervision, telemarketing, telesales (*UK*)

(*v*) ax, *demutualize*, *divest*, downsize, go bust (*informal*), go out of business, liquidate, open up, package, privatize, rebadge, *repossess*, retrench, revalue, *right-size*, sub-contract, traffic, underwrite, wind up (*UK*)

795   Business Products

Creation comes before distribution—or there will be nothing to distribute. **Ayn Rand**

(*n*) commodity, goods, merchandise, productivity, ser-vices, stock-in-trade, turnover, wares

796   Finance and Economics

Economics is as much a study in fantasy and aspiration as in hard numbers—maybe more so. **Theodore Roszak**

(*adj*) *accounting*, budgetary, economic, financial, infla-tionary, lossmaking (*UK*), monetary, negotiable, non-negotiable, pecuniary, proprietary, recessionary

types of economic conditions austerity, boom, boom and

bust, deflation, depression, downswing, downturn, hyperinflation, inflation, inflationary spiral, recession, recovery, reflation, slump, stagflation, upswing, upturn

types of economic systems collectivism, command economy, free enterprise economy, free market economy, market economy, mixed economy, new economy, planned economy, private economy, service economy

797 Money

If you borrow $2,000 dollars from a bank and can't pay it back, you have a problem, but if you borrow a million and can't repay, they have a problem. **Anonymous**

(*n*) bread (*dated slang*), cash, change, coin, dough (*slang*), kitty, loot (*informal*), money, nest egg, pool, *ready cash*, *ready money*, spending money

See also EXPENDITURE (423), INCOME (460), FINANCIAL ASSETS (462), FUNDS, PAYMENTS, AND CHARGES (800)

798 Currencies

Finance is the art of passing currency from hand to hand until it finally disappears. **Robert W. Sarnoff**

(*n*) banknote, buck (*informal*), *cent*, *coinage*, currency, *dime*, *fiver*, *nickel*, pound, *quarter*, *tenner* (*informal*)

types of currencies afghani (Afghanistan), baht (Thailand), balboa (Panama), birr (Ethiopia), bolivar (Venezuela), boliviano (Bolivia), cedi (Ghana), CFA franc (Benin, Burkina Faso, Cameroon, Central African Republic, Chad, Rep. of Congo, Côte d'Ivoire, Equatorial Guinea, Gabon, Guinea-Bissau, Mali, Niger, Senegal, Togo), colón (Costa Rica, El Salvador), Congo franc (Dem. Rep. of Congo), córdoba (Nicaragua), dalasi (Gambia), denar (Former Yugoslav Rep. of Macedonia), deutsche mark (Germany), dinar (Algeria, Bahrain, Iraq, Jordan, Kuwait, Libya, Sudan, Tunisia, Yugoslavia), dirham (Morocco, United Arab Emirates), dobra (São Tomé and Príncipe), dollar (Antigua and Barbuda, Australia, Bahamas, Barbados, Belize, Canada, Dominica, Ecuador, Fiji, Grenada, Guyana, Hong Kong, Jamaica, Kiribati, Liberia, Marshall Islands, Micronesia, Namibia, Nauru, New Zealand, Palau, St. Kitts and Nevis, St. Lucia, St. Vincent and the Grenadines, Singapore, Solomon Islands, Taiwan, Trinidad and Tobago, Tuvalu, United States, Zimbabwe), dong (Vietnam), drachma (Greece), dram (Armenia), escudo (Cape Verde, Portugal), euro (Austria, Belgium, Finland, France, Germany, Greece, Ireland, Italy, Luxembourg, Netherlands, Portugal, Spain), forint (Hungary), franc (Belgium, Burundi, Comoros, Djibouti, France, Guinea, Liechtenstein, Luxembourg, Madagascar, Monaco, Rwanda, Switzerland), gourde (Haiti), guarani (Paraguay), guilder (Netherlands, Suriname), hryvnia (Ukraine), kina (Papua New Guinea), kip (Laos), koruna (Czech Republic, Slovakia), krona (Iceland, Sweden), krone (Denmark, Norway), kroon (Estonia), kuna (Croatia), kwacha (Malawi, Zambia), kwanza (Angola), kyat (Myanmar), lari (Georgia), lat (Latvia), lek (Albania), lempira (Honduras), leone (Sierra Leone), leu (Moldova, Romania), lev (Bulgaria), lilangeni (Swaziland), lira (Italy, Malta, Turkey), litas (Lithuania), loti (Lesotho), manat (Azerbaijan, Turkmenistan), marka (Bosnia and Herzegovina), markka (Finland), metical (Mozambique), naira (Nigeria), nakfa (Eritrea), ngultrum (Bhutan), ouguiya (Mauritania), pa'anga (Tonga), pataca (Macau), peseta (Andorra, Spain), peso (Argentina, Chile, Columbia, Cuba, Dominican Republic, Mexico, Philippines, Uruguay), pound (Cyprus, Egypt, Lebanon, Syria, United Kingdom), pula (Botswana), punt (Ireland), quetzal (Guatemala), rand (South Africa), real (Brazil), rial (Iran, Oman, Yemen), riel (Cambodia), ringgit (Malaysia), riyal (Qatar, Saudi Arabia), rubel (Belarus), ruble (Russia, Tajikistan), rufiyaa (Maldives), rupee (India, Mauritius, Nepal, Pakistan, Seychelles, Sri Lanka), rupiah (Indonesia), santim (Latvia), schilling (Austria), shekel (Israel), shilling (Kenya, Somalia, Tanzania, Uganda), sol (Peru), som (Kyrgyzstan, Uzbekistan), taka (Bangladesh), tala (Samoa), tenge (Kazakhstan), tolar (Slovenia), tughrik (Mongolia), vatu (Vanuatu), won (North Korea, South Korea), yen (Japan), yuan (China), zloty (Poland)

799 Accounting, Banking, and Budgeting

Capital accounting in its formally most rational shape...presupposes the battle of man with man. **Max Weber**

(*n*) account, *account holder*, accounts, advance, assessment, ATM, bank account, banking, bankruptcy, *bottom line*, budget, *building society* (*UK*), cashpoint (*UK*), *Chapter 11*, cost-cutting, crash, *credit union*, debit, fund, funding, futures, insolvency, loan, mortgage, nonpayment, *pension fund*, *private banking*, *profit and loss*, *profit margin*, *S&L*, *savings and loan association*, stock exchange, stock market, swipe card, *thrift*, *triple bottom line*, turnover

(*v*) appreciate, bank, crash, mortgage, negotiate, pay in, reflate

800 Funds, Payments, and Charges

Money differs from an automobile, a mistress, or cancer in being equally important to those who have it and those who do not. **J. K. Galbraith**

(*n*) abatement, airfare, alimony, blood money, capitation, damages, deposit, discount, dividend, down payment, *expenses*, fee, finance, going rate, *golden handshake* (*informal*), *golden parachute* (*informal*), installment, maintenance, markdown, markup, nonperformance, pension, petty cash, pledge, premium, rake-off (*informal*), rebate, refund, reimbursement, remittance, rent, rental, reparation, repayment, retainer, saving, scholarship, security, seed capital (*UK*), seed money, settlement, severance, stake, stocks, student loan, subvention (*formal*), support, surcharge, tariff, worth

(*v*) discharge (*formal*), discount, impose, levy, overprice, surcharge

See also EXPENDITURE (423), MONEY (797)

801 Insurance

INSURANCE, *n. An ingenious modern game of chance in which the player is permitted to enjoy the comfortable conviction that he is beating the man who keeps the table.* **Ambrose Bierce**

(*n*) collateral, deposit, insurance, insurance policy, insurer, reinsurance, surety

(*v*) indemnify, insure, reinsure, secure

802 Tax and Taxation

He's spending a year dead for tax reasons. **Douglas Adams**

(*adj*) chargeable, duty-free (*informal*), taxable, tax-exempt, *tax-free*

(*n*) capitation, dues, duty, income tax, levy, *pay-as-you-earn*, PAYE (*UK*), *revenue system*, surtax, tariff, tax, taxation, *taxpayer*, *tax policy*, *tax system*, tribute, *VAT*

(*v*) tax

803 Market Forces

It doesn't take much to derail a market that has gone to the moon. **Stephen S. Roach**

(*n*) deflation, depression, devaluation, downswing, downturn, inflation, recession, reflation, slump, stagflation

804 People Involved in Finance

A baited banker thus desponds. . .They have his soul, who have his bonds. **Jonathan Swift**

(*n*) accountant, *accounts clerk*, *actuary*, analyst, auditor, banker, *bean counter* (*slang*), *bookkeeper*, cashier, *CFO*, dealer, debtor, defaulter, depositor, financier, forecaster, guarantor, investor, lender, liquidator, *market analyst*, moneylender, *number-cruncher* (*slang*), *securities broker*, *shareholder*, signatory, speculator, stakeholder, stockbroker, stockholder, teller, tipster, treasurer, *underwriter*, *venture capitalist*

See also OFFICE WORKERS (847)

805 Government and Politics

Governments need to have both shepherds and butchers. **Voltaire**

(*adj*) governmental, home, interstate, legislative, ministerial, political, state

(*n*) establishment, government, politicking, politics, regime, statecraft

See also SOCIAL, POLITICAL, AND ECONOMIC CHANGE (373)

806 Styles and Systems of Government

The voice of the people is the voice of God. **Kemal Ataturk**

(*adj*) autocratic, autonomous, bicameral, bureaucratic, capitalist, centrist, collectivist, colonial, colonialist, counterrevolutionary, democratic, diplomatic, *expansionist*, federal, feudal, industrialized, internationalist, left-wing, parliamentary, patriarchal, populist, presidential, protectionist, republican, rightist, right-wing, self-governing, sovereign, totalitarian, true-blue (*UK*), undemocratic

(*n*) absolutism, autarchy, authoritarianism, autocracy, autonomy, bureaucracy, centralism, collectivism, colonialism, colonization, decentralization, democracy, devolution, dictatorship, *expansionism*, home rule, imperialism, isolationism, junta, martial law, *meritocracy*, *military government*, *military rule*, monarchism, nationalism, *ochlocracy*, *parliamentary government*, protectionism, protectionist, protectiveness, raison d'état, *realpolitik*, regionalism, republicanism, reunification, self-determination, self-government, self-rule, *single*

party rule, *social democracy*, socialism, *sovereign state*, *system of government*, totalitarianism, *tsarism*

See also SOCIAL, POLITICAL, AND ECONOMIC CHANGE (373)

807 Elections and Voting

The vote is the most powerful instrument ever devised by man for breaking down injustice. **Lyndon Baines Johnson**

(*adj*) elected, elective, electoral

(*n*) abstainer, abstention, ballot, by-election, candidacy, census, election, elector, electorate, enfranchisement, *general election*, plebiscite, poll, polling, polling booth, referendum, *secret ballot*, straw poll, *suffrage*, vote, voter

(*v*) abstain, campaign, canvass, electioneer, enfranchise, naturalize

808 Political Offices and Politicians

The politician is an acrobat. He keeps his balance by saying the opposite of what he does. **Maurice Barrès**

(*n*) administrator, attaché, bureaucrat, chancellor, commissioner, congressperson, consul, democrat, diplomat, *frontbencher* (*UK*), governorship, head of government, head of state, incumbent, mandarin, mandate, *member of parliament*, MP, office holder, parliamentarian, *PM*, politician, premier, premiership, presidency, president, prime minister, republican, senator, spin doctor (*slang*), strategist, tactician, *technocrat*

See also OFFICE WORKERS (847)

809 Legislative Bodies and Legislation

A parliament can do any thing but make a man a woman, and a woman a man. **Earl of Pembroke**

(*n*) administration, assembly, bureau, CIA, constitution, council, diet, embargo, injunction, junta, *legislator*, legislature, parliament, ruling body, senate

810 Government Policies

Our policy is directed not against any country or doctrine but against hunger, poverty, desperation, and chaos. **George Marshall**

(*n*) activism, centralization, diplomacy, party line, platform, *spin doctoring* (*slang*)

811 Administrative Offices

A civil servant doesn't make jokes. **Eugène Ionesco**

(*n*) chamberlain, civil servant, customs, diplomat, embassy, mission, officer, official, officialdom (*informal*), registrar, registration, registry

812 Social Welfare

In place of the conception of the Power-State we are led to that of the Welfare-State. **William Temple**

(*n*) benefit, *public amenities*, *public services*, *public transport*, sanitation, services, supervision order (*UK*), welfare

813   Educational Institutions

Education is a leading out of what is already there in the pupil's soul. **Muriel Spark**

(*n*) *academe* (*formal*), academia, *academic circles*, *academic world*, alma mater, college, conservatory, crèche (*UK*), ivory tower, *medical school*, nursery, playschool, polytechnic, *reform school*, school, *school of dance*, *school of the arts*, seminary, studio, *tech* (*informal*), *technical college*, *theological college*, *training college* (*UK*), university

types of schools academy, boarding school, elementary school, grade school, grammar school, high school, junior high, kindergarten, middle school, nursery school, prep school, preschool, primary school, private school, public school, trade school, vocational school

See also EDUCATION (838)

814   The Law and Legal Authority

The big print giveth and the fine print taketh away.
Fulton J. Sheen

(*n*) act, ban, bylaw, civil liberties, civil rights, criminalization, human rights, judiciary, jurisdiction, law, law and order, legislation, penalization, probate, right, rule, statute, statute book, statute law

815   Legal and Legitimate

When the President does it, that means it is not illegal.
Richard Nixon

(*adj*) allowed, authorized, constitutional, decriminalized, endorsed, judicial, lawful, legal, legalized, legit (*slang*), legitimate, licit, official, rightful, statutory, valid

(*adv*) aboveboard, by rights, legitimately, rightly

(*n*) legality, legitimacy, rightfulness

See also MORALLY GOOD (774)

816   Illegal

People got so used to staying indoors/that curfews were declared illegal. **Can Yücel**

(*adj*) actionable, *against the law*, banned, bigamous, *bookable*, bootleg, chargeable, criminal, *felonious*, illegal, illegitimate, ill-gotten, illicit, indictable, *larcenous*, null, null and void, piratic, prohibited, unauthorized, unconstitutional, under-the-counter, underworld, unlawful, unofficial, *usurious*, wrongful

(*adv*) criminally, wrongfully

(*n*) illegality, *illicitness*, *unlawfulness*

See also MORALLY BAD OR IMPROPER (775)

817   Crimes

How many crimes committed merely because their authors could not endure being wrong! **Albert Camus**

(*n*) abduction, *aggravated burglary*, *armed robbery*, arson, banditry, bigamy, blackmail, breach of the peace, break-in, breaking, *breaking and entering*, bribery, burglary, *carjacking*, *car theft*, corruption, crime, criminality, despoliation, *disorderly conduct*, embezzlement, extortion, felony, fiddle (*informal*), fiddling (*informal*), forgery, fraud, gangland, heist (*slang*), *highway robbery* (*informal*), hijack, holdup, illegality, infraction, infringement, joyriding, larceny, misappropriation, mis-

demeanor, mugging, offense, *organized crime*, *petty larceny*, *pilfering*, plagiarism, *public disturbance*, *public nuisance*, racket, *racketeering*, robbery, *shakedown* (*slang*), shoplifting, stealing, stickup (*informal*), terrorism, theft, *thieving*, tort, *unlawful act*, *unlawful activity*, usury, wrongdoing, *wrongful act*

See also STEAL AND ROB (426)

818   The Police, Arrest, and Pretrial Proceedings

Police and government officials have contempt for innocence; they are, in some way, offended by an innocent man.
Walter Mosley

(*n*) *agent provocateur*, arrest, bust (*slang*), charge, *constable*, constabulary, detective, *drug squad*, *fraud squad*, gumshoe (*dated informal*), investigator, *law enforcement agency*, *law enforcement officer*, *litigant*, marshal, officer, PC (*UK*), police, *police cadet*, *police constable* (*UK*), *police department*, police force, police officer, polygraph, private detective, private eye (*informal*), private investigator, *riot police*, sleuth (*informal*), *vice squad*

(*v*) apprehend, arrest, bust (*slang*), detain, imprison, incarcerate (*formal*), intern, jail, nab (*informal*), pull in (*slang*), put away (*informal*), *put behind bars*, *put in jail*, *put in prison*, take into custody

See also CAPTIVITY AND LOSS OF FREEDOM (248), BUILDINGS FOR CONFINING PEOPLE (1094)

819   Trial, Punishment, and Legal Outcomes

Punishment has passed from being an art of unsupportable sensations to an economy of suspended rights. **Michel Foucault**

(*adj*) disciplinary, penal

(*n*) acquittal, action, adjudication, amnesty, *appellant*, arraignment, assize, assizes (*UK*), award, bail, call, *capital punishment*, case, condemnation, conviction, court, court case, courthouse, court order, criminalization, cross-examination, cross-questioning, decriminalization, defense, deposition, discipline, finding, fine, forfeiture, gag, gag order, hearing, high court, indictment, industrial tribunal (*UK*), *judicial proceedings*, lawsuit, legalization, litigation, miscarriage of justice, mistrial, parole, penalty, plaint, plaintiff, plea, prosecution, recidivism, *release on bail*, remand, reprieve, restraining order, sentence, subpoena, summons, suspect, suspended sentence, trial, tribunal, verdict, writ

(*v*) acquit, adjudge, arraign, bail out, condemn, convict, criminalize, cross-question, discipline, fine, hear, hold, impeach, indict, legalize, legislate, litigate, parole, plea-bargain, prosecute, *release on parole*, remand, reprieve, sentence, subpoena, sue, take legal action, take to court, try

820   People in Law Courts

If there were no bad people there would be no good lawyers.
Charles Dickens

(*n*) accuser, attorney, *attorney at law*, bailiff, barrister (*UK*), *criminal lawyer*, defendant, *district attorney*, JP, judge, juror, jury, justice, *Justice of the Peace*, lawgiver, lawmaker, lawyer, legal eagle (*slang*), magistrate, notary, *prosecuting attorney*, prosecutor, *public defender*, *public prosecutor, Queen's Counsel, respondent, sheriff, sheriff's officer,* solicitor *(UK), trial lawyer*

See also SURVEYORS, EXAMINERS, AND JUDGES (853)

821 Criminals

What man have you ever seen who was content with one crime only? **Juvenal**

(*n*) abductor, accessory, accomplice, arsonist, assassin, *bag-snatcher,* bandit, bigamist, blackmailer, brigand (*literary*), burglar, captor, *carjacker, car thief, cat burglar, cattle thief,* counterfeiter, criminal, criminal world, crook (*informal*), culprit, delinquent, *drug-dealer, drug-runner,* embezzler, felon, forger, gangster, *guilty party, hardened criminal, horse thief, housebreaker,* incendiary, joyrider, *kidnapper, larcenist,* lawbreaker, looter, mafia, *Mafioso,* malefactor (*formal*), mugger, *mule* (*slang*), *netherworld* (*literary*), offender, *Peeping Tom, perp* (*slang*), perpetrator, *petty thief,* pickpocket, pilferer, pillager, plagiarist, poacher, *purse snatcher,* racketeer, raider, ram-raider (*UK*), recidivist, *reoffender, repeat offender,* ring, robber, rustler, *smuggler,* sneak thief, stalker, terrorist, thief, transgressor, trespasser, underworld, *usurer,* wrongdoer

See also CAPTIVES AND PRISONERS (249), STEAL AND ROB (426), VILLAINS AND THUGS (947)

822 Charity and Charitable Institutions

In charity there is no excess. **Francis Bacon**

(*adj*) nonprofit

(*n*) *aid agency, aid organization, charitable foundation, charitable organization, charitable trust,* charity, fundraiser, good cause, orphanage

823 Rulers and Aristocracy

A monarchy is a merchantman which sails well, but will sometimes strike a rock, and go to the bottom; whilst a republic is a raft which would never sink, but then your feet are always in the water. **Fisher Ames**

(*n*) aristocrat, emir, emperor, empress, monarch, noble, nobleman, noblewoman, patrician, peer, peerage (*UK*), peer of the realm (*UK*), Pharaoh, potentate, rajah, rani, regent, *royal family,* royals, royalty, ruler, sovereign, *sultan,* suzerain, *tsar, tsarina, tsaritsa*

types of aristocrats baron, baroness, baronet, count, countess, crown prince, duchess, duke, earl, king, knight, maharajah, maharani, marchioness, marquess, prince, princess, queen, viscount, viscountess

824 Realms and Rules

The king, and his faithful subjects, the lords and commons of this realm, the triple cord, which no man can break. **Edmund Burke**

(*n*) *demesne* (*formal*), duchy, dynasty, kingdom, monarchy, reign, rule, supremacy, throne

825 Royalness

That perfect bliss and sole felicity,/The sweet fruition of an earthly crown. **Christopher Marlowe**

(*adj*) imperial, kingly, queenly, regal, royal, state

(*n*) kingship, sovereignty, state

826 Hospitals and Clinics

There they stand, isolated, majestic, imperious...the asylums which our forefathers built with such immense solidity to express the notions of their day. **Enoch Powell**

(*n*) clinic, hospice, hospital, infirmary, intensive care, intensive care unit, *nursing home, residential care, residential home, rest home,* sanatorium, sanitarium, sickbay

See also PEOPLE WHO WORK IN MEDICINE (848)

827 The Armed Forces

If you don't want to use the army, I should like to borrow it for a while. Yours respectfully, A. Lincoln. **Abraham Lincoln**

(*n*) *airborne army, air force,* airpower, armed forces, *armed services,* army, cavalry, corps, defense force, forces, *ground forces, infantry,* land forces, *merchant navy* (*UK*), military, *military establishment, military unit,* militia, *national guard,* navy, services, *territorial army* (*UK*), *troops,* vanguard

828 Military Personnel

The soldier's body becomes a stock of accessories that are not his property. **Antoine de Saint-Exupéry**

(*n*) adjutant, aide-de-camp, *army cadet, artilleryman, bombardier, brigadier, colonel, combat officer,* commandant, commander, commando, conscript, detachment, detail, *dog of war* (*UK*), *field marshal, fusilier,* GI, gunner, *legionnaire,* line officer, mercenary, *military attaché,* noncombatant, officer, paramilitary, patrol, platoon, rating (*UK*), regiment, regular, reservist, *rifleman,* soldier, squadron, warlord, warrior

See also PROFESSIONS (845)

829 Military

When I was in the military, they gave me a medal for killing two men, and a discharge for loving one. **Leonard Matlovich**

(*adj*) armed, gung ho (*informal*), martial, militarized, military, paramilitary, warlike

830 Warfare and War

What they could do with around here is a good war. **Bertolt Brecht**

(*n*) *airborne operation, air offensive,* armament, *arms reduction, army camp,* battlefield, blitz, *blitzkrieg,* call-up (*UK*), charge, combat zone, conscription, disarmament, draft, engagement, exercises, firing line, operation, rearmament, *saturation bombing, shelling,* strafe, war, warfare

(*v*) battle, blitz, bomb, conscript, draft, fight, outflank, strafe

Work and Leisure: Lifestyles and the Home

831 Employment Status

The test of a vocation is the love of the drudgery it involves.
Logan Pearsall Smith

(*adj*) active, amateur, employed, freelance, honorary, *in work* (*UK*), jobbing, jobless, laid off, nonprofessional, off duty, *on benefit* (*UK*), on call, *on unemployment, on welfare*, part-time, peripatetic, probationary, professional, redundant (*UK*), retired, salaried, self-employed, unemployed, unpaid, *unsalaried*, unwaged (*UK*), vocational, voluntary, *waged* (*UK*), working, *working from home*

832 Place of Employment

Stick close to your desks and never go to sea,//And you all may be Rulers of the Queen's Navee! **W. S. Gilbert**

(*n*) base, branch, cooperative, dealership, head office, headquarters, ministry, nerve center, office, shop, studio, sweatshop, workplace, workroom, workspace, workstation

833 Job

It's a recession when your neighbor loses his job; it's a depression when you lose yours. **Harry S. Truman**

(*n*) appointment, assignment, capacity, commission, duty, employment, engagement, incumbency (*formal*), internship, job, labor, livelihood, part, placement, post, posting, presidency, residency, role, vacancy, work

See also WORK IN GENERAL (297)

834 Work-Related Activities

There is dignity in work only when it is work freely accepted. **Albert Camus**

(*n*) absenteeism, *admin*, administration, appointment, *attrition*, employ, employment, *flextime*, furlough, go-slow (*UK*), *graveyard shift*, incumbency (*formal*), industrial action (*UK*), *joblessness*, job-sharing, layoff, overtime, paperwork, patrol, picket, recruitment, redundancy (*UK*), shutdown, stoppage, strike, unemployment, walkout, weighting, work-to-rule (*UK*)

(*v*) employ, engage, moonlight (*informal*), recruit, resign, retire, serve, strike, temp, walk out, work, work to rule (*UK*)

835 Types of Work

The price one pays for pursuing any profession or calling is an intimate knowledge of its ugly side. **James Baldwin**

(*adj*) administrative, blue-collar, cash-in-hand, clerical, executive, in-service, managerial, manual, occupational, organizational, paid, sedentary, stipendiary, white-collar

(*n*) *casual work, freelancing, homeworking* (*UK*), *manual labor, outworking* (*UK*), *part-time work*, piecework, telecommuting, teleworking (*UK*)

836 Workers

The worker becomes an ever cheaper commodity the more commodities he creates. **Karl Marx**

(*n*) applicant, aspirant, *blue-collar worker*, breadwinner, *casual worker, commuter*, drudge, *factory worker, freelancer*, full-timer, gofer (*informal*), *guest worker*, hack (*informal*), *homeworker* (*UK*), *job-sharer*, laborer, *manual laborer, manual worker, migrant worker, office worker*, operative, operator, *outworker* (*UK*), *paper-pusher* (*informal*), part-timer, *part-time worker*, pencil pusher, peon, performer, *portfolio worker, professional, seasonal worker, semiskilled worker*, signing, soldier, stipendiary, striker, technician, technologist, teleworker (*UK*), *toiler*, trier, *unskilled worker*, volunteer, wage earner, *white-collar worker*, workaholic, worker, workhorse (*informal*), working group, working party (*UK*)

See also BOSSES AND MANAGEMENT (965), SUBORDINATES AND ASSISTANTS (966), COLLEAGUES AND EQUALS (967)

837 The Work Force

The only irreplaceable capital an organization possesses is the knowledge and ability of its people. **Andrew Carnegie**

(*n*) crew, labor, payroll, personnel, staff, work force

838 Education

Education is simply the soul of a society as it passes from one generation to another. **G. K. Chesterton**

(*adj*) academic, collegial, collegiate, extramural, intramural, pedagogical, professorial, scholastic

See also EDUCATIONAL INSTITUTIONS (813)

839 Teaching

Education is an admirable thing, but it is well to remember from time to time that nothing that is worth knowing can be taught. **Oscar Wilde**

(*n*) coaching, development, domestication, edification, education, enrollment, grounding, indoctrination, induction, initiation, instruction, parenting, *pedagogics* (*formal*), pedagogy, potty-training (*informal*), preparation, reeducation, registration, schooling, special education, *special needs education*, teaching, training, tuition, tutelage

See also INSTRUCT AND TEACH (609)

840 Educators

A schoolmaster should have an atmosphere of awe, and walk wonderingly, as if he was amazed at being himself. **Walter Bagehot**

(*n*) academic, coach, demonstrator, don (*UK*), *educationalist*, educator, faculty, governess, handler, *head* (*UK*), *headmaster, headmistress*, head teacher (*UK*), instructor, lecturer, master, mistress (*UK*), pedagogue, professor, provost, rector, *schoolteacher, supply teacher* (*UK*), teacher, *teaching body, teaching staff*, trainer, tutor

See also INSTRUCT AND TEACH (609), PROFESSIONS (845)

841 Students and Pupils

Time is a great teacher, but unfortunately it kills all its pupils.
Hector Berlioz

(*n*) abecedarian, alum (*informal*), alumna, alumnus, cadet, class, classmate, fraternity, *graduate student*, intake, intern, *medical student*, plebe, *postgrad* (*informal*), postgraduate, prefect, pupil, researcher, *schoolboy*, schoolchild, *schoolgirl*, *schoolkid* (*informal*), student, *teacher's pet*, undergraduate

842 Classes, Coursework, and Examinations

Examinations are formidable even to the best prepared, for the greatest fool may ask more than the wisest man can answer.
Charles Colton

(*adj*) extracurricular, intercollegiate, *viva voce*

(*n*) apprenticeship, articles (*UK*), class, commencement (*formal*), course, coursework, crash course, curriculum, discipline, discussion group, divinity, exam, examination, fieldwork, graduation, homework, *humanities*, lesson, matriculation, *medical training*, physical education, *pupillage* (*formal*), *religious education*, *religious instruction*, religious studies, resit (*UK*), retake, *schoolwork*, seminar, session, short course, study, *term paper*, tutorial

843 Qualifications

People at the top of the tree are those without qualifications to detain them at the bottom. **Peter Ustinov**

(*adj*) certified, credentialed, qualified

(*n*) credential, diploma, doctor, doctorate, headship, qualification

844 Studying

You taught me language; and my profit on't/Is, I know how to curse: the red plague rid you/For learning me your language!
William Shakespeare

(*v*) bone up (*informal*), cram (*informal*), learn, read, read up, review, revise (*UK*), specialize, study, take

845 Professions

Writing is the only profession where no one considers you ridiculous if you earn no money. **Jules Renard**

(*n*) avocation (*formal*), calling, career, craft, job, line of work, métier, mission, niche, occupation, profession, trade, vocation

See also BUSINESS (791), MILITARY PERSONNEL (828), EDUCATORS (840), WORKERS IN ENTERTAINMENT AND MEDIA (873)

846 People who Guard and Protect

(*n*) bailiff (*UK*), bodyguard, caretaker (*UK*), concierge, curator, custodian, defender, guard, jailer, *janitor*, keeper, lifeguard, lookout, minder (*UK*), muscle (*slang*), nanny, *night watchman*, porter, ranger, scout, *security guard*, *security officer*, sentinel, sentry, warden, warder (*UK*), watch, watchman

847 Office Workers

(*n*) *clerical worker*, clerk, keyboarder, *office assistant*, receptionist, secretary, *telephonist*, temp

See also PEOPLE INVOLVED IN FINANCE (804), POLITICAL OFFICES AND POLITICIANS (808)

848 People who Work in Medicine

(*n*) analyst, *clinical psychologist*, *clinician*, doctor, druggist, GP, healer, medic (*informal*), *medical practitioner*, naturopath, *neurosurgeon*, nurse, pharmacist, *pharmacologist*, physician, *plastic surgeon*, practitioner, *psychiatrist*, *psychoanalyst*, *psychotherapist*, registrar (*UK*), shrink (*slang*), surgeon, therapist

See also HOSPITALS AND CLINICS (826)

849 Farmers, Gardeners, and Manual Workers

(*n*) cowboy, cultivator, digger, farmer, farm hand, gamekeeper, gardener, machinist, *mechanic*, miner, navvy (*dated*), peasant, rancher, *ranch hand*, reaper, wrangler

850 Domestic and Kitchen Workers

(*n*) barkeeper, char (*UK*), home help (*UK*), *housekeeper*, servant, squire

types of people who work in restaurants barista, bartender, busboy, chef, greeter, headwaiter, maître d', pastry chef, prep cook, short-order cook, sommelier, sous-chef, waiter, waitron (*slang*), wine waiter

types of servants butler, chambermaid, cleaner, cook, factotum, flunky, footman, lackey, maid, maidservant, major-domo, valet

851 Hair Stylists

(*n*) barber, *coiffeur* (*formal*), *coiffeuse* (*formal*), hairdresser, *hair stylist*

852 Messengers and Couriers

(*n*) bearer, courier, dispatch rider, herald, messenger, runner

See also DRIVERS (1153)

853 Surveyors, Examiners, and Judges

(*n*) checker, critic, examiner, inspector, judge, *ombudsman*, sampler, selector, surveyor, taster

See also PEOPLE IN LAW COURTS (820)

854 People who Work with Language and Code

(*n*) decoder, interpreter, *linguist*, polyglot, translator

855 Accommodations

A house is a machine for living in. **Le Corbusier**

(*adj*) domestic, *domiciliary*, home, household

(*n*) abode (*literary*), accommodation (*UK*), accommodations, *bed and board*, billet, domicile (*formal*), dwelling (*formal*), freehold, habitation, home, housing, let (*UK*), *living quarters*, lodging, lodgings (*dated*), pad (*slang dated*), place, *private residence*, quarters, residence, rooms, shelter, tenancy, tenure

See also RESIDENTIAL BUILDINGS (1078)

856 Undesirable Accommodations

Born in a cellar, and living in a garret. Samuel Foote

(*n*) *colonia*, dump (*informal*), *favela*, *fleabag* (*informal*), *flophouse* (*informal*), *ghetto*, hole (*informal*), hovel, lair (*informal*), pigpen, pigsty (*UK*), *shanty*, slum

857 Inhabitants

What's the good of a home, if you are never in it?
George Grossmith

(*n*) boarder, burgher, citizen, city dweller, constituent, denizen, dweller, inhabitant, islander, local, lodger, national, native, occupant, occupier, *paying guest*, people, resident, roomer, squatter, tenant, townie (*informal*), townsfolk, townspeople, urbanite, villager

See also GROUPS IN SOCIETY (940)

858 Furniture

No furniture so charming as books. Sydney Smith

(*n*) arm, armrest, *bed*, bedhead, bedstead, bookshelf, *cabinet*, coat rack, coat tree, footrest, footstool, furnishings, furniture, *hassock*, *hat stand*, *headboard*, lectern, ottoman, pouf (*UK*), *reading desk*, *reading stand*, seat, seating, showcase, table

types of beds bassinet, berth, bunk, bunk bed, cot, couchette, cradle, crib, day bed, divan, double bed, four-poster, futon, hammock, king-size bed, Murphy bed, queen-size bed, single bed, sofa bed, studio couch, trundle bed, twin bed, waterbed

types of cabinets armoire, bookcase, breakfront, bureau, cassone, chest of drawers, china cabinet, closet, cocktail cabinet, commode, credenza, cupboard, display cabinet, display case, dresser, highboy, liquor cabinet, lowboy, press, secretary, sideboard, wardrobe, whatnot

types of seating Adirondack chair, armchair, beach chair, bench, bleachers, Boston rocker, bucket seat, carver, chair, chaise longue, chesterfield, couch, davenport, deck chair, easy chair, highchair, ladder-back, lounger, love seat, pew, recliner, rocking chair, settee, sofa, stall, stool, swivel chair, Windsor chair, wing chair

types of tables bedside table, card table, coffee table, console, davenport, desk, dining table, dressing table, end table, escritoire, gateleg table, night table, occasional table, Pembroke table, roll-top desk, tea table, trestle table, vanity table, worktable, writing desk

859 Fixtures

(*n*) bath, fixtures, tap, woodwork, workbench, work surface, worktop

types of general fixtures baseboard, ceiling rose, dado, fender, fireplace, looking glass, mantel, mantelpiece, mirror, picture molding, radiator, socket, wainscot

types of plumbing fixtures ball cock, basin, bathtub, bidet, drinking fountain, faucet, hand basin, hot tub, nozzle, plumbing, rose, sauna, shower, sink, sitz bath, spa, spigot, spout, sprinkler, tank, toilet, towel rail, tub, vanity, washbasin, washbowl, wash-hand basin, whirlpool

860 Furnishing and Household Linens

(*n*) arras, beanbag, bedding, bed linen, bedspread, carpet, carpeting, cloth, comforter, *continental quilt*, coverlet, curtain, cushion, dishcloth, drapery, dust cloth, duster (*UK*), duvet, eiderdown, *electric blanket*, *fitted carpet*, *floorcovering*, *floor cushion*, hanging, *hearth rug*, *lampshade*, mat, mattress, napkin, pad, *paillasse*, *pallet*, pelmet (*UK*), pillow, pillowcase, *pillow sham*, *pillowslip*, quilt, rug, *sham*, *slipcover*, soft furnishings, swag, *swags*, tablecloth, *table linen*, tapestry, *tatami*, throw, *throw cushion*, *throw pillow*, towel, trousseau, upholstery, *valance*, *venetian blind*

861 Tableware, Flatware, and Kitchenware

(*n*) *baking dish*, *baking sheet*, bowl, carafe, casserole, china, *cocotte*, crockery, cup, decanter, *dinner service*, dish, ewer, filter, flagon, flask, flatware, frying pan, glass, *glassware*, goblet, jug, kettle, *oven dish* (*UK*), *oven tray*, ovenware, pan, pitcher, *place mat*, *place setting*, plate, platter, *pressure cooker*, ramekin, salver, samovar, saucepan, saucer, serving dish, *silverware*, *skillet*, spit, table mat, tableware, *tandoor*, tankard, *teapot*, tea service, *tea towel* (*UK*), *tea urn*, tray, tumbler, tureen, wok

types of flatware butter knife, carving knife, chopstick, dessertspoon, fish knife, fork, knife, pastry fork, pastry slice, serving spoon, soupspoon, spoon, steak knife, tablespoon, teaspoon

types of utensils beater, bottle opener, can opener, corkscrew, drainer, grater, grinder, juice extractor, liquidizer, mill, mortar, nutcracker, opener, peeler, pestle, reamer, sieve, soup ladle, spatula, strainer, whisk

See also HOUSEHOLD APPLIANCES (1117), CONTAINERS, RECEPTACLES, AND PACKAGING (1245)

862 Lighting

(*n*) *bedside lamp*, candelabrum, candle, candlestick, *desk lamp*, *fairy lights* (*UK*), *floor lamp*, sconce, *table lamp*, taper, uplighter (*UK*)

See also LIGHT (1164)

863 Cleaning Agents

(*n*) cleaner, cleanser, detergent, disinfectant, purifier, soap, soap powder, sterilizer

864 Clothes and Accessories

Beware of all enterprises that require new clothes.
Henry David Thoreau

(*n*) apparel, array, attire (*formal*), clothes, clothing, costume, dress, *dress code*, duds (*informal*), ensemble, finery, garb, garment, gear (*informal*), *get-out* (*UK*), getup (*informal*), glad rags (*informal*), guise, habit, kit, laundry, mask, outfit, raiment (*archaic or literary*), rig (*informal*), *rigout* (*UK*), suit, togs (*informal*), vestment, wardrobe, washing, wear, *weeds* (*archaic or literary*)

865 Garments and Outfits

None of the Emperor's clothes had ever had such a success before. "But, Daddy, he's got nothing on!" piped up a small child. **Hans Christian Andersen**

(*n*) apron, armor, *babywear*, battle dress, *best bib and tucker* (*informal*), *best clothes* (*UK*), *best togs* (*informal*), capsule collection, castoffs, casual clothes, casuals, casual wear, ceremonial dress, civilian clothes, civvies, coat, coordinates, *coveralls*, disguise, DJ, *dress uniform*, evening dress, *footwear, formal attire, formal wear,* full dress, *haberdashery, headgear,* layette, leisurewear, livery, *men's clothing,* menswear, mufti, *one-piece, outerwear,* pants, pinafore, *protective clothing, separates, sleepwear, smarts* (*informal*), sportswear, *suit of armor, summer clothes,* Sunday best, *top,* uniform, woolens

types of dresses ball gown, caftan, cheongsam, cocktail dress, evening gown, frock, gown, jumper, kimono, muumuu, robe, sari, shalwar-kameez, sheath, shift, shirtdress, sundress, wedding dress

types of jackets anorak, blazer, blouson, bomber jacket, double-breasted jacket, flak jacket, fleece, jacket, Nehru jacket, reefer, safari jacket, single-breasted jacket, smoking jacket, sports jacket, tailcoat, tails, tux (*informal*), tuxedo, waterproof jacket, windbreaker

types of overcoats cape, cloak, duffle coat, frock coat, greatcoat, overcoat, parka, pea coat, poncho, raincoat, slicker, topcoat, trench coat

types of pants bell-bottom pants, Bermuda shorts, breeches, capri pants, cargo pants, chaps, chinos, clam diggers, cords, culottes, cutoffs, fatigues, harem pants, hip-huggers, hot pants, jeans, jodhpurs, khakis, knickerbockers, lederhosen, leggings, overalls, palazzo pants, pedal pushers, plus fours, shorts, slacks, trews

types of skirts dirndl, hobble skirt, kilt, maxi skirt, miniskirt, pencil skirt, sarong, tutu, wraparound

types of sleepwear bathrobe, housecoat, negligee, nightcap, nightclothes, nightgown, nightie, nightshirt, nightwear, pajamas, peignoir, sleepers

types of sportswear bathing suit, bathing trunks, beachwear, bikini, jogging suit, leotard, sweat suit, sweatpants, swimming trunks, swimsuit, swimwear, trunks, two-piece, wet suit

types of suits all-in-one, black tie, boiler suit, business suit, catsuit, dress suit, jumpsuit, overalls, pantsuit, pinstripe suit, trouser suit, white tie, zoot suit

types of sweaters cardigan, crew neck, jersey, mock turtle, pullover, sweater, turtleneck, twin set, V-neck

types of tops basque, blouse, bodice, body warmer, bolero, bustier, gilet, halter, jerkin, polo shirt, shirt, smock, surplice, sweatshirt, T-shirt, tabard, tank top, tee, tube top, tunic, vest, vestment

866 Jewelry

Kissing your hand may make you feel very very good but a diamond and sapphire bracelet lasts forever. **Anita Loos**

(*n*) coronet, crown, diadem, solitaire

types of jewelry anklet, armlet, badge, bangle, bracelet, brooch, cameo, charm, cuff link, eardrop, earring, necklace, nose ring, nose stud, pin, ring, stud, tiara, tie clasp, tie tack, wristlet

types of necklaces beads, chain, choker, collar, locket, medallion, pendant, torque

See also ORNAMENTS AND DECORATIONS (1248)

867 Accessories, Millinery, and Lingerie

Hats divide generally into three classes: offensive hats, defensive hats, and shrapnel. **Katharine Whitehorn**

(*n*) accessory, hosiery, lingerie, underclothes, *undergarments,* underthings, underwear, undies (*informal*)

types of accessories ascot, bandanna, belt, bootlace, bow tie, corsage, cravat, cummerbund, earmuffs, glove, handkerchief, hat, jewelry, mitt, mitten, muff, muffler, neckerchief, necktie, pashmina, sash, scarf, shawl, stole, suspenders, tie, veil, wrap

types of hats beanie, boater, bonnet, cloche, cowboy hat, deerstalker, derby, fedora, homburg, Panama hat, picture hat, pillbox, porkpie hat, rain hat, sailor hat, sombrero, sou'wester, stovepipe hat, sunhat, ten-gallon hat, top hat, topper, toque, trilby

types of headgear balaclava, bandeau, baseball cap, bearskin, beret, biretta, busby, cap, chaplet, cloth cap, cowl, crash helmet, fez, glengarry, hairband, hardhat, hat, headband, headdress, headscarf, helmet, hood, mantilla, mobcap, skullcap, tam-o'-shanter, tippet, topee, turban, yarmulke, yashmak

types of lower body underwear bloomers (*dated*), boxer shorts, briefs, corset, crinoline, drawers, foundation garment, garter, girdle, G-string, jockstrap, knee-highs, legwarmer, long johns, nylons, panties, pantyhose, petticoat, slip, sock, stockings, string, support hose, thigh-highs, thong, underpants, underskirt

types of upper body underwear basque, body stocking, body suit, bra, camisole, chemise, teddy, undershirt, union suit

868 Dress, Wear, and Undress

Woe to him who doesn't know how to wear his mask, be he king or pope! **Luigi Pirandello**

(*adj*) attired (*formal*), bare, barefoot, clad, decent (*informal*), dressed, garbed, *got up* (*informal*), in the altogether (*informal*), *in the buff* (*informal*), *in the nude,* in the raw (*informal*), liveried, naked, nude, *stark-naked,* turned-out, unclothed, undressed, veiled

(*n*) nakedness, nudity, *state of undress*

(*v*) accessorize, bundle up (*informal*), clothe, disrobe (*formal*), doff, doll up (*informal*), don, dress, garb, get into, have on, put on, rig out (*informal*), sport (*informal*), strip, *strip off,* suit, take off, unclothe, undress, wear, wrap up

See also WELL-GROOMED (482), BADLY GROOMED (483)

869 Describing Clothes

(*adj*) ankle-length, bespoke (*UK*), bias-cut, black-tie, body-hugging, clingy (*informal*), close-fitting, décolleté, designer, *distressed,* dressy, drip-dry, *figure-hugging,* fitted, flared, full-fashioned, full-length, *in vogue, knee-high, knee-length,* knockabout, loose, loose-fitting, low-cut, low-necked, noniron (*UK*), off-the-rack, *permanent-press,* plain-clothes, plunging, preppy (*informal*), *preshrunk,* prêt-à-porter, ready-made, ready-to-wear, revealing, reversible, scanty, *skintight*, snug, sports, sporty, stonewashed, structured, tailored, tailor-made, tight, tightfitting, tweedy, *underwired*, walking, washable, *wash-and-wear*, wide, wired

See also WELL-GROOMED (482), BADLY GROOMED (483)

870   Parts of a Garment

parts of a garment brim, buckle, button, buttonhole, coattail, collar, cuff, décolletage, drawstring, gusset, hem, lace, lapel, leg, lining, neck, neckband, neckline, pocket, sash, sleeve, strap, waistband, zipper

See also FASTENERS, LINKS, AND NETWORKS (1247)

871   Footwear

Can you take your country with you on the soles of your shoes?
Georg Büchner

types of boots boot, bootee, cowboy boot, galoshes, gum boot, hiking boot, jackboot, mukluk, rubber, waders, walking boot

types of shoes ballet shoe, clog, espadrille, flip-flop (*informal*), moccasin, mule, oxford, platform, plimsoll, pump, sandal, shoe, slingback, slipper, sneaker, snowshoe, stiletto heel, thong, wedge heel, wingtip, zori

872   Entertainment

I have noticed that what cats most appreciate in a human being is not the ability to produce food which they take for granted—but his or her entertainment value.
Geoffrey Household

(*n*) carousel, comedy, entertainment, escapism, hilarity, karaoke, nightlife, *party piece*, pleasure, roundabout, *show biz* (*informal*), son et lumière

(*v*) busk (*UK*), entertain, headline, host, introduce

See also PERFORMANCES AND SHOWS (42), JOKES AND TEASING (674), FILM (901), THE PERFORMING ARTS (904)

873   Workers in Entertainment and Media

Journalists say a thing that they know isn't true, in the hope that if they keep on saying it long enough it will be true.
Arnold Bennett

(*n*) anchor, anchorperson, announcer, broadcaster, columnist, commentator, correspondent, critic, editor, emcee (*informal*), entertainer, hack (*informal*), host, hostess, humorist, *illusionist*, imitator, interviewer, journalist, lineup, MC, newscaster, newshawk (*informal*), newshound (*informal*), newsman, newspaperman, newspaperwoman, newswoman, *paparazzo*, presenter (*UK*), press, press officer, proofreader, publisher, quiz master, *radio presenter* (*UK*), reporter, ringmaster, satirist, speaker, sportscaster, stringer, subeditor (*UK*), telecaster

types of entertainers actor, actress, clown, comedian, comic, conjurer, contortionist, costar, dancer, DJ, double act, impressionist, juggler, magician, mime, movie star, musician, rapper, singer, standup comedian, stooge, straight man, street entertainer, street musician, street performer, trapeze artist, ventriloquist

See also NEWSPAPERS AND MAGAZINES (605), TELEVISION AND RADIO (606), JOKERS AND TEASES (675), PROFESSIONS (845)

874   Leisure and Recreation

We are closer to the ants than to the butterflies. Very few people can endure much leisure. **Gerald Brenan**

(*n*) activity, amusement, avocation (*formal*), distraction, diversion, escape, fun, game, hobby, horseplay, interest, leisure, *leisure pursuit*, pastime, play, pursuit, recreation, relaxation, sideline, *sports activities*

(*v*) carouse (*literary*), celebrate, enjoy yourself, fool around, gad (*humorous*), go out, let yourself go, live it up (*slang*), *make merry*, mess around (*informal*), muck around (*informal*), paint the town red (*informal*), party (*informal*), picnic, play, revel, roister, sunbathe

875   Hobbies, Games, and Sports

Serious sport...is war minus the shooting. **George Orwell**

(*adj*) sports, sporty

(*n*) acrobatics, aerobatics, aerobics, *alpinism*, *amateur dramatics* (*UK*), *amateur photographer*, *angling*, *athletics*, ball game, *bingo*, calisthenics, climbing, *combat sports*, crossword, dip, exercise, extreme sport, fishing, gymnastics, *horseback riding*, hunting, isometrics, motocross, *mountain climbing*, *mountaineering*, *orienteering*, pony-trekking (*UK*), PT (*UK*), pugilism, riding, *rock climbing*, sailing, shop, shopping, *show jumping*, sport, step aerobics, *sword fighting*, training, *trekking*, working out, workout

(*v*) bathe, bivouac, camp, conjure, fish, jockey, rollerskate, *scuba dive*, *skydive*, snorkel, swim, train, trawl, work out

types of ball games Australian Rules, baseball, basketball, cricket, field hockey, football, hurling, lacrosse, netball, rounders, rugby, Rugby League, Rugby Union, shinty, soccer, softball

types of combat sports aikido, boxing, fencing, judo, karate, kendo, kickboxing, kung fu, sumo, tae kwon do, wrestling

types of court games badminton, jai alai, rackets, squash, table tennis, tennis, volleyball

types of extreme sports barefoot waterskiing, basejumping, bungee jumping, in-line skating, mountain biking, skateboarding, skysurfing, snowboarding, sport climbing, street luge, stunt bicycling, wakeboarding

types of target ball games billiards, boules, bowling, croquet, golf, lawn bowling, pool, snooker

types of track and field cross-country, decathlon, discus, hammer throw, heptathlon, high jump, javelin, long jump, marathon, modern pentathlon, pole vault, relay race, shot put, sprint, steeplechase, triathlon, triple jump

types of winter sports alpine skiing, biathlon, bobsled, cross-country skiing, curling, downhill, figure skating, hockey, ice dancing, langlauf, Nordic skiing, ski jump, skiing, slalom, snowboarding, speed skating, toboggan, XC skiing

See also CRAFTS AND CARVING (355)

876   People in Sports and Leisure

How vainly men themselves amaze/To win the palm, the oak, or bays. **Andrew Marvell**

(*n*) acrobat, *alpinist*, athlete, *baseball player*, bather, batsman, birdwatcher, body builder, bookworm (*informal*), *boxer*, caddie, camper, *caver*, cheerleader, climber, *cricketer*, diver, *fencer*, fielder, *funambulist*, gambler, *gymnast*, hiker, horseman, horsewoman, hunter, jockey, jogger, jumper, mountaineer, *ornithologist*, player, potholer, pug (*informal*), pugilist, racer, *rock climber*, rocker (*UK*), rower, runner, runner-up, *scuba diver*, *snorkeler*, *soccer player*, *speleologist*, *spelunker*, sportsperson, sprinter, *steeplechaser*, striker, *sword fighter*, titleholder, tumbler, umpire, *wrestler*

See also COMPETITORS (41), COMPETE, CONTEND, AND COMBAT (303), TRAVEL: TRAVELERS AND WALKERS (319)

877   Sports Terms

(*n*) bully-off (*UK*), deuce, goal, goalmouth, header, injury time (*UK*), innings, lap, no ball (*UK*), photo finish, *slam-dunk*, smash, starting point, stoppage time (*UK*), tie, *tie-break*, tiebreaker, topspin, touchdown

878   Game Pieces

types of game pieces checker, chessman, chip, counter, domino, jack, tiddlywink

879   Sports Equipment

types of sports equipment ball, bat, bowl, club, discus, football, glove, helmet, hockey stick, javelin, lacrosse stick, mitt, pad, pigskin, puck, racket, shot, shuttlecock, spikes, tee, wicket

880   Toys

Deceive boys with toys, but men with oaths. **Lysander**

(*n*) *game piece*, plaything, *toy*

types of toys beach ball, building blocks, doll, dollhouse, dolly (*informal*), hand puppet, jack-in-the-box, jigsaw, kaleidoscope, kite, marble, playhouse, popgun, puppet, rag doll, rocking horse, squirt gun, stilt, teddy bear, yo-yo

881   Lifestyle

I've been trying for some time now to develop a lifestyle that doesn't require my presence. **Garry Trudeau**

(*n*) ethnicity, lifestyle, modus vivendi, standard of living, way of life

882   Self-Denial

Self-denial is not a virtue; it is only the effect of prudence on rascality. **George Bernard Shaw**

(*adj*) abstemious, abstinent, ascetic, celibate, clean-living, dry, monastic, *on the wagon*, puritanical, *self-denying*, sober, teetotal

(*n*) abstemiousness, abstinence, asceticism, *celibacy*, puritanism, self-denial, sobriety, *teetotalism*, temperance

See also FORGO AND DENY ONESELF (449)

883   Ascetic People

Throughout history power has been the vice of the ascetic. **Bertrand Russell**

(*n*) abstainer, ascetic, *celibate*, moralist, *puritan*, *tee-totaler*

See also FORGO AND DENY ONESELF (449)

884   Nomadic and Rootless Lifestyles

Over all the world/Men move unhoming, and eternally/Concerned: a swarm of bees who have lost their queen. **Christopher Fry**

(*adj*) dispossessed, drifting, itinerant, migrant, migratory, nomadic, nonresident, roaming, rootless, roving, stateless, vagrant

(*n*) *bird of passage*, drifter, gypsy, hobo, knight, migrant, nomad, runabout, traveler

See also SOLITARINESS (941)

885   Pleasure-Seeking and Excess

Nothing succeeds like excess. **Oscar Wilde**

(*adj*) bohemian, decadent, dissipated, dissolute, epicurean, fancy-free, footloose, hedonistic, immoderate, intemperate, luxurious, *philandering*, *pleasure-loving*, *pleasure-seeking*, prodigal, self-indulgent, spendthrift, *sybaritic*

(*adv*) decadently, intemperately

(*n*) dissipation, dissoluteness, *epicureanism*, hedonism, *immoderateness* (*formal*), immoderation (*formal*), intemperance, license, *prodigality*, self-gratification, self-indulgence

886   Pleasure-Seekers and Hedonists

DEBAUCHEE, *n.* One who has so earnestly pursued pleasure that he has had the misfortune to overtake it. **Ambrose Bierce**

(*n*) aesthete, bohemian, bon vivant, *bon viveur* (*literary*), *carouser* (*literary*), Casanova, *debauchee*, Don Juan, Don Quixote, *drunkard*, extrovert, gadabout (*humorous*), *gigolo*, glutton, gourmand, hedonist, *libertine*, Lothario (*literary*), merrymaker, *party animal* (*informal*), party-goer, philanderer, pig (*informal*), *pleasure-lover*, *pleasure-seeker*, raver (*informal*), reveler, roisterer, Romeo, *roué* (*literary*), *satyr*, *sensualist*, spendthrift, swashbuckler, sybarite, *voluptuary*, wolf (*informal*), *womanizer*

See also BEASTLY AND BRUTISH (510), EATERS, GOURMETS, AND DIETARY CHOICES (714)

887   People Living Away From Home

Soaring falcon, noble Poet, come to my aid...help me to live without roots: ever on the move: my only sustenance your nourishing language. **Juan Goytisolo**

(*n*) colonial, colonist, colonizer, deportee, emigrant, *émigré*, evacuee, exile, expat (*informal*), expatriate, immigrant, migrant, refugee, settler

888   Status

Status is an influence at every level...all part of what I call plutography: depicting the acts of the rich. **Tom Wolfe**

(*n*) background, blood, bloodline, breeding, cachet, chieftainship, citizenship, credit, echelon, importance, place, position, prestige, rank, ranking, reputation, repute (*formal*), *social class*, *social standing*, standing, station, stature, status

889   Class Status

There are two classes in good society in England. The equestrian classes and the neurotic classes.
George Bernard Shaw

(*adj*) aristocratic, august (*formal*), blue-blooded, bourgeois, cut-glass (*UK*), *déclassé, highborn* (*literary*), *high-ranking*, humble, landed, lower-class, lowly, *middle-class*, noble, patrician, pedigree, poor, proletarian, purebred, senior, thoroughbred, titled, top-drawer, upper-class, *upwardly mobile*, voiceless, wellborn, *working-class*

(*n*) aristocracy, caste, *chattering classes* (*UK*), commoner, eminence, gentleman, gentry, grassroots, high society, hoi polloi, *landed gentry*, lower class, lowliness, *lumpenproletariat*, masses, mob (*informal*), nobility, parvenu, peasant, peerage (*UK*), *prole* (*slang*), proletariat, society, top drawer, *underclass*, upper class, upper crust (*informal*), working class

890   Marital Status

Married life requires shared mystery even when all the facts are known. **Richard Ford**

(*adj*) affianced (*formal*), divorced, eligible, engaged, *footloose and fancy free*, marriageable, single, unattached, uninvolved, unmarried, *widowed*

(*n*) bachelor, cohabitation, marriageability, *spinster, widow, widower*

See also MARRIED STATE (961)

891   Wealth and Wealthy

Wealth has never been a sufficient source of honor in itself. It must be advertised, and the normal medium is obtrusively expensive goods. **J. K. Galbraith**

(*adj*) affluent, better-off, *born with a silver spoon in your mouth,* comfortable, developed, fat, *flush* (*informal*), *fortunate,* in clover, *in funds* (*UK*), in the black, *in the chips,* in the money, leisured, loaded (*slang*), moneyed, *nouveau riche,* privileged, propertied, prosperous, rich, rolling in it (*informal*), solvent, successful, wealthy, well-endowed, well-fixed (*informal*), well-heeled (*informal*), well-off, well-to-do

(*n*) affluence, opulence, prosperity, richness, solvency, substance

892   Poverty and Poor

Money is better than poverty, if only for financial reasons.
Woody Allen

(*adj*) badly off, bankrupt, broke (*informal*), cleaned out (*informal*), dependent, depressed, deprived, destitute, disadvantaged, down-and-out, *down-at-heel, flat broke* (*informal*), hard up (*informal*), homeless, impecunious, impoverished, in arrears, in debt, in debt, indigent (*formal*), *in need,* insolvent, in the red, landless, mean (*archaic*), mendicant, needy, *on the breadline* (*UK*), *on the skids* (*slang*), *on the streets,* out of cash, overdrawn, penniless, penurious (*literary*), poor, poverty-stricken, pushed (*informal*), ruined, *short of money,* stone-broke (*informal*), strapped (*informal*), *strapped for cash* (*informal*), underprivileged

(*adv*) from hand to mouth, meanly

(*n*) deprivation, destitution, hardship, *homelessness,*

impecuniousness (*formal*), impoverishment, indigence (*formal*), misery, need, neediness, *pennilessness,* penury, poorness, poverty, privation, vagrancy, want

893   Important or Famous People

A celebrity is a person who works hard all his life to become known, then wears dark glasses to avoid being recognized.
Fred Allen

(*n*) authority figure, baron, big cheese (*slang*), *big enchilada* (*slang*), biggie (*slang*), big name, big shot (*informal*), bigwig (*informal*), captain, *celeb* (*informal*), celebrity, dignitary, doyen, doyenne, *figurehead,* frontrunner (*informal*), *glitterati, grandee,* haut monde, *head honcho* (*slang*), heavyweight (*slang*), hero, heroine, high achiever, high-flier, *honcho* (*slang*), hotshot (*informal*), household name, *kahuna* (*informal*), key player, king, kingpin (*informal*), lead, leader, leading light, legend, luminary, *megastar,* mover, *mover and shaker,* name, notability, notable, number one (*informal*), pacemaker, personage (*formal*), personality, prince, principal, public figure, queen, sheik, socialite, somebody, someone, spearhead, standard-bearer, star, superstar, *top brass* (*informal*), *top dog* (*informal*), *top gun* (*informal*), *top name,* VIP, winner

See also KNOWN AND FAMOUS (181)

894   Levels of Education and Sophistication

Hip is the sophistication of the wise primitive in a giant jungle.
Norman Mailer

(*adj*) art-house (*UK*), citified, classy (*informal*), common, countrified, cracker-barrel, cross-cultural, cultivated, cultured, distinguished, donnish (*UK*), earthy, educated, erudite, folksy, gross, innocent, lettered, literary, literate, philistine, polite, provincial, rough and-ready, scholarly, simple, simple-minded, sophisticated, studious, suave, tasteful, uncivilized, uncultivated, uncultured, uneducated, unenlightened, unlearned, unlettered, unrefined, unschooled, unworldly, well-educated, well-read, well-rounded

(*adv*) simply

(*n*) bookishness, *bumpkin* (*informal*), civilization, *cognoscente,* cognoscenti, *country cousin,* crudity, cultivation, culture, egghead (*informal*), elite, good taste, ingenuousness, innocence, intellectual, intelligentsia, letters, literati (*formal*), philistinism, provincialism, simplicity, sophisticate, sophistication, street credibility, taste, tastefulness, unworldliness, *vulgarian*

See also POSITIVE INTELLECTUAL CHARACTERISTICS (524)

895   Rich People

We may see the small value God has for riches, by the people he gives them to. **Alexander Pope**

(*n*) *beau monde, beautiful people,* billionaire, *café society, fat cat* (*slang*), *high roller* (*slang*), *idle rich,* in-crowd (*informal*), jet set (*informal*), magnate, millionaire, mogul, moneybags (*informal*), moneymaker, multimillionaire, plutocrat, *rich and famous,* squire

896   Poor People

I owe much; I have nothing; the rest I leave to the poor.
François Rabelais

(*n*) beggar, have-not, mendicant (*formal*), *panhandler*, pauper, *poor person*, tramp, vagabond, vagrant

897   The Pictorial Arts

Paint becomes painting when color establishes surface.
Jules Olitski

(*n*) animation, art, *fine art*, *graphic arts*, painting, photography, portraiture, *visual art*

See also DRAWINGS, CHARTS, AND TABLES (594)

898   Artworks

A great work of art bears its meaning on its face. **C. L. R. James**

(*n*) artwork, blowup, canvas, caricature, cartoon, carving, composition, doodle, engraving, etching, fresco, frieze, icon, image, *magnum opus*, masterpiece, masterwork, motif, mural, objet d'art, oeuvre (*formal*), *oil painting*, *old master*, opus, painting, picture, print, remake, stencil, *still life*, woodcut, work, work of art

899   Artistic Movements and Styles

We cannot use Impressionism when we paint a huge street in New York, nor can we use Futurism when we paint a beautiful woman. . .May our brush keep time with our vibrations.
Joan Miró

(*adj*) aesthetic, artistic, artsy-craftsy (*informal*), baroque, cubist, freehand, graphic, photographic, pictographic, pictorial, picturesque, stylistic, visual

types of 20th-century art movements abstract expressionism, art deco, conceptual art, constructivism, cubism, Dada, expressionism, Fauvism, futurism, minimalism, modernism, op art, photorealism, pop art, postmodernism, socialist realism, surrealism, vorticism

types of pre-20th-century art movements art nouveau, Arts and Crafts, Baroque, classicism, impressionism, Mannerism, pointillism, postimpressionism, Pre-Raphaelitism, realism, Renaissance, Romanticism, symbolism

900   Artists

There is no neutral naturalism. The artist, no less than the writer, needs a vocabulary before he can embark on a "copy" of reality. **E. H. Gombrich**

(*n*) artisan, artist, caricaturist, cartoonist, craftsperson, interpreter, *miniaturist*, painter, photographer, *portraitist*, *sculptor*, *watercolorist*

901   Film

A film is a petrified fountain of thought. **Jean Cocteau**

(*n*) actioner (*informal*), *action movie*, *adventure movie*, *animated film*, *animatronics*, biopic, B movie, *B picture*, cartoon, cinema, cinematography, *cowboy movie*, *feature film*, film, flick (*informal*), motion picture, movie, movies, *moving picture*, picture, rushes, screening, screenplay, *screen test*, *spaghetti western*, subtitle, supertitle, surtitle, swashbuckler, take, talkie (*dated*), *talky*, tearjerker (*informal*), thriller, weepie (*informal*), western

See also ENTERTAINMENT (872)

902   Sculpture

You can't make a sculpture, in my opinion, without involving your body. You move and you feel and you breathe and you touch. **Barbara Hepworth**

(*n*) bas-relief, bronze, bust, death mask, figurine, gargoyle, sculpture, statuary, statue, statuette, waxwork, woodcarving

903   Dance

Lighter than a cork I danced on the waves. **Arthur Rimbaud**

(*n*) choreography, pirouette

types of dances ballet, barn dance, belly dance, bop (*informal*), bossa nova, cancan, cha-cha, Charleston, fandango, flamenco, foxtrot, jig, jitterbug, jive, lambada, limbo, lindy hop, line dancing, macarena, mambo, merengue, minuet, morris dancing, polka, quadrille, quickstep, rumba, salsa, samba, square dance, step dancing, strathspey, tango, tap dance, waltz

See also PERFORMANCES AND SHOWS (42)

904   The Performing Arts

Art cannot be described. It proves itself only in its performance.
Gerhard Richter

(*adj*) audiovisual, cinematic, star-studded, stellar, theatrical, thespian (*literary*)

(*n*) acting, costume drama, *dramaturgy*, *performance art*, *performing arts*, repertory, *repertory company*, *repertory theater*, role-playing, show business, star billing, variety show, vaudeville

(*v*) act, act out, costar, enact, feature, headline, perform, recast

See also PERFORMANCES AND SHOWS (42), ENTERTAINMENT (872)

905   Performers

An actor is never so great as when he reminds you of an animal—falling like a cat, lying like a dog, moving like a fox.
François Truffaut

(*n*) actor, actress, cast, company, costar, *dramatis personae*, performer, player, role, starlet, star turn, *theater company*, *theater group*, thespian, *touring company*, walk-on

906   In the Theater

We respond to a drama to that extent to which it corresponds to our dreamlife. **David Mamet**

(*n*) backcloth, backdrop, *bit part*, cameo, *dress circle*, footlights, *front of house*, playgoer, scenery, set, stage, stage door, stage whisper, theatergoer, *the boards*, upper circle

907   Music, Songs, and Singing

One composes because of an interior impulse; music has no other sources of improvisation any longer, apart from our own spirit. **Karlheinz Stockhausen**

(*n*) air, *barbershop*, carol, chant, *chanting*, chorus, descant, ditty, elegy, intonation, jingle, lullaby, lyrics, melody, music, *musical instrument*, orchestration, piece of music, romance, singing, *soul music*, theme, *theme song*, *theme tune*, tune, vocals, words (*v*) chant, intone (*formal*), pipe, pluck, riff, serenade, sing, strum, twang

types of classical music Baroque, chamber music, comic opera, early music, opera, operetta, Romantic, twelvetone

types of dance music acid house, acid jazz, big beat, boogie, broken beat, disco, drum 'n' bass, funk, garage, hardcore, hip hop, house, jungle, ragga, raggamuffin, rap, rave, reggae, rock steady, ska, speed garage, techno, trance, two step

types of electronic music ambient, breakbeat, breaks and beats, chillout, downbeat, dub, electro, electronica, new age, trip hop

types of jazz music bebop, boogie-woogie, cool jazz, Dixieland, honky-tonk, jazz, jazz funk, jazz fusion, jazz rock, jive, modal jazz, New Orleans jazz, ragtime, swing

types of musical forms anthem, aria, bagatelle, ballad, cantata, canticle, capriccio, chorale, coloratura, concerto, étude, fantasia, fugue, hymn, intermezzo, madrigal, mass, nocturne, oratorio, overture, prelude, requiem, rondo, scherzo, sinfonia, sonata, song, suite, symphony, tone poem, waltz

types of pop and vocal music bluegrass, blues, country and western, doowop, easy listening, folk, gangsta rap, gospel, lounge, Motown, new wave, pop, R&B, rap metal, rare soul, rockabilly, soul, spiritual, urban

types of rock music grunge, heavy metal, indie, metal, punk, rock, rock 'n' roll, thrash metal

types of world music afrobeat, bhangra, calypso, flamenco, latin, mento, raga, rai, roots, salsa, yodel

See also PERFORMANCES AND SHOWS (42)

908   Musicians and Singers

A musician, if he's a messenger, is like a child who hasn't been handled too many times by man, hasn't had too many fingerprints across his brain. **Jimi Hendrix**

(*n*) accompanist, artist, artiste, band, *chanteuse*, chorister, composer, consort, diva, folk singer, group, instrumentalist, *lyricist*, minstrel, musician, rapper, rocker (*informal*), *rock musician, rock singer, rock star*, singer, soloist, *songsmith*, songster, songwriter, soprano, troubadour, virtuoso, vocalist

types of bands big band, brass band, chamber orchestra, choir, chorale, chorus, dance band, duo, ensemble, jazz band, mariachi, octet, orchestra, pipe band, pop group, quartet, quintet, septet, sextet, sinfonietta, steel band, string band, string quartet, symphony orchestra, trio

909   Notes and Chords

The heart of the melody can never be put down on paper. **Pablo Casals**

(*n*) chord, fanfare, instrumentation, key, meter, rhythm, riff

910   Musical Instruments

Knowing how to play an instrument is the barest superficiality if one is thinking of becoming a musician. It is the ideas that one utilizes instinctively *that determine the degree of profundity any artist reaches.* **Imamu Amiri Baraka**

types of brass instruments bugle, cornet, euphonium, flugelhorn, French horn, horn, post horn, saxhorn, saxophone, sousaphone, trombone, trumpet, tuba

types of keyboards accordion, baby grand, celesta, clavichord, concertina, grand piano, harpsichord, organ, piano, pianoforte, spinet, synthesizer, upright piano

types of percussion instruments bass drum, bongo drums, castanet, chimes, conga drum, cymbal, drum, gamelan, glockenspiel, gong, kettledrum, maraca, marimba, metallophone, snare drum, steel drum, tabla, tabor, tambourine, timpani, tom-tom, triangle, tubular bells, vibraphone, xylophone

types of stringed instruments balalaika, banjo, bass guitar, bouzouki, cello, double bass, electric guitar, fiddle, guitar, harp, Hawaiian guitar, lute, lyre, mandolin, sitar, Spanish guitar, steel guitar, ukulele, viol, viola, viola da gamba, violin, violoncello, zither

types of wind instruments bagpipes, bassoon, clarinet, crumhorn, didgeridoo, English horn, fife, fipple flute, flute, harmonica, nose flute, oboe, ocarina, panpipes, penny whistle, piccolo, recorder

911   Recordings and Players

People don't understand the sort of fight it takes to record what you want, to record the way you want to record it. **Billie Holiday**

(*n*) album, *audio equipment*, cassette, CD player, compact disc player, hi-fi (*dated*), *LP*, playback, recording, remix, single, sound system, soundtrack, tape, vinyl

See also AUDIO EQUIPMENT (1139)

912   Musical Terms

I tried to resist his overtures, but he plied me with symphonies, quartettes, chamber music, and cantatas. **S. J. Perelman**

(*adj*) choral, funky (*slang*), orchestral, *philharmonic*, rhythmic, singing, symphonic

(*adv*) in concert

(*n*) cadence, cadenza, *libretto, ostinato*, syncopation, tempo, time

types of musical registers alto, baritone, bass, countertenor, falsetto, mezzo-soprano, soprano, tenor

types of musical terms a cappella, adagio, allegro, andante, appassionato, arpeggio, capriccioso, con brio, con moto, crescendo, decrescendo, diminuendo, forte, fortissimo, grave, larghetto, largo, legato, lentissimo, lento, moderato, pianissimo, piano, pizzicato, rubato, sotto voce, staccato

913   Fiction and Drama

A novel is a static thing that one moves through; a play is a dynamic thing that moves past one. **Kenneth Tynan**

(*n*) autobiography, crime novel, *detective novel, detective story*, doggerel, drama, dramatization, epic, *fairy tale*, fiction, fictionalization, *graphic novel*, history, literature, melodrama, mystery, novel, novelette, novella, prequel, prose, romance, romp (*informal*), *science fiction*, script, short story, theater, whodunit, writing

See also BOOKS AND BOOKLETS (590), SCIENCE FICTION (1064)

914   Writers and Styles

An author arrives at a good style when his language performs what is required of it without shyness. **Cyril Connolly**

(*n*) author, *autobiographer*, bard (*literary or humorous*), biographer, diarist, dramatist, exponent, ghostwriter, librettist, literati (*formal*), *memoirist*, novelist, parodist, playwright, poet, *poetaster*, *potboiler*, propagandist, screenwriter, scribe, scriptwriter, *tragedian*, versifier, writer

915 Poetry and Verse

Poetry is the supreme fiction. **Wallace Stevens**

(*n*) *blank verse*, canto, couplet, *free verse*, *limerick*, ode, poem, *poesy* (*archaic or literary*), poetry, quatrain, rhyme, sonnet, stanza, stave, verse

916 The Stages of Life

The four stages of man are infancy, childhood, adolescence, and obsolescence. **Art Linkletter**

(*n*) age, being, existence, life, life cycle, life expectancy, life span, lifetime, mortality

917 Babyhood, Childhood, and Adolescence

I have all that I lost/and I go carrying my childhood/like a favorite flower/that perfumes my hand. **Gabriela Mistral**

(*adj*) adolescent, immature, infantile, juvenile, neonatal, newborn, *preadolescent*, prepubescent, preschool, *pubertal*, pubescent, teen (*informal*), teenage, underage, young

(*n*) adolescence, babyhood, boyhood, childhood, early years, formative years, girlhood, immaturity, infancy, puberty, teens, upbringing, youth

See also CHILD OR YOUTH (945)

918 Adulthood

Adults are obsolete children. **Dr. Seuss**

(*adj*) adult, big, full-fledged, full-grown, grown, grown-up, mature

(*n*) adulthood, majority, manhood, maturity, *prime of life*, womanhood

919 Old Age

Self-parody is the first portent of age. **Larry McMurtry**

(*adj*) aged, elderly, geriatric, old, over-the-hill, superannuated

920 Old People

If I'd known I was gonna live this long, I'd have taken better care of myself. **Eubie Blake**

(*n*) *golden ager*, *old fogy*, *old person*, *old-timer*, pensioner, senior, senior citizen

921 Causes of Death

I feel nothing, apart from a certain difficulty in continuing to exist. **Bernard le Bovier Fontenelle**

(*n*) asphyxiation, assassination, bloodshed, butchery, carnage, crucifixion, decapitation, decimation, execution, extermination, genocide, gore, hanging, *hara-kiri*, homicide, immolation (*formal*), killing, manslaughter, martyrdom, massacre, murder, *parricide*, patricide, pogrom, self-immolation, shooting, slaughter, *slaying*, strangulation, *suffocation*, suicide

See also CEASE TO EXIST (22)

922 Die

He who would teach men to die would at the same time teach them to live. **Michel de Montaigne**

(*v*) bite the dust (*informal*), breathe your last (*literary*), commit hara-kiri, commit suicide, *croak* (*slang*), depart (*formal*), *depart this life* (*formal*), die, die of, drown, end it all, expire (*formal or literary*), *give up the ghost* (*literary*), go, *go to meet your maker*, kick the bucket (*slang*), kill yourself, pass away, perish (*literary*), succumb

923 Kill

The man who murdered his parents, then pleaded for mercy on the grounds that he was an orphan. **Abraham Lincoln**

(*v*) asphyxiate, assassinate, behead, blow away (*slang*), bump off (*slang*), butcher, choke, crucify, cut down (*informal*), decapitate, dispatch, dispose of, do away with (*informal*), do in (*informal*), eliminate, execute, exterminate, finish off (*informal*), *garrote*, guillotine, gun down (*informal*), hang, immolate (*literary*), kill, knock off (*slang*), liquidate, lynch, machine-gun, massacre, mow down, murder, poison, prey on, put to death, shoot, shoot down, slaughter, slay (*formal or literary*), smother, snuff (*informal*), stifle, strangle, strangulate, strike down, suffocate, take out (*slang*), throttle, waste (*slang*), wipe out (*slang*)

See also WOUND A PERSON OR ANIMAL (383), STAB (416), WHIP AND CLUB (417)

924 People who Kill

Kill a man, and you are a murderer. Kill millions of men, and you are a conqueror. Kill everyone, and you are a god. **Jean Rostand**

(*n*) butcher, gunman, *hired gun* (*slang*), hit man (*slang*), hunter, killer, murderer, patricide, poisoner, slayer (*formal or literary*), sniper, soldier of fortune

925 Dead and Dying

If I must die,/I will encounter darkness as a bride,/And hug it in mine arms. **William Shakespeare**

(*adj*) at peace, at rest, dead, *dead as a dodo*, *dead as a doornail*, deceased (*formal*), defunct, departed (*formal or literary*), extinct, gone (*informal*), inanimate, in extremis, late, moribund, *no longer with us*, *passed on*, stillborn, stone-dead

See also CEASE TO EXIST (22)

926 Dead Person

He'd make a lovely corpse. **Charles Dickens**

(*n*) body, cadaver, casualty, corpse, death, death toll, deceased (*formal*), goner (*slang*), martyr, prey, quarry, remains, stiff (*slang*), victim

927 Death and Bereavement

Happiness is beneficial for the body, but it is grief that develops the powers of the mind. **Marcel Proust**

(*adj*) bereaved, bereft, *in mourning*

(*n*) bereavement, death, decease (*formal*), demise (*formal*), end, expiry (*formal or literary*), fatality, *grieving*, loss, mourner, mourning, passing, *rigor mortis*

See also ENDS AND DEPARTURES (54)

928 Deadly

There is no trap so deadly as the trap you set for yourself.
Raymond Chandler

(*adj*) deadly, fatal, life-threatening, mortal, murderous, poisonous, terminal, venomous

See also DANGEROUS (236)

929 Burial and Preparation for Burial

When we attend the funerals of our friends we grieve for them, but when we go to those of other people it is chiefly our own deaths that we mourn for. **Gerald Brenan**

(*adj*) funerary, obituary, posthumous, *post-obit* (*formal*)

(*n*) autopsy, burial, cemetery, cremation, disinterment, epitaph, funeral, *funeral director, funeral home, funeral mass, funeral parlor, funeral rites*, gravedigger, *grave mound*, inquest, interment, monument, *mortician*, mummy, obituary, *pallbearer*, postmortem, *postmortem examination, service for the dead*, undertaker, *undertaker's* (*UK*), vigil

(*v*) bury, disinter, embalm, exhume, inter, lay to rest, mummify

930 Burial Places and Accessories

The grave is either like a ditch from the ditches of Hell, or like a luxuriant garden from the luxuriant gardens of Paradise.
Al-Tirmidhi

(*n*) barrow, burial chamber, burial ground, burial place, casket, catacomb, *charnel house*, churchyard, coffin, *God's Acre* (*archaic*), grave, gravestone, graveyard, headstone, necropolis, ossuary (*formal*), *resting place*, sarcophagus, sepulcher, tomb, *tumulus*

See also MONUMENTS (1092)

People

931 Person

The liberty of the individual must be thus far limited; he must not make himself a nuisance to other people. **John Stuart Mill**

(*n*) bod (*slang*), character, civilian, cookie (*informal*), creature, figure, hominid, *homo sapiens*, human, human being, humanity, humankind, *humanoid*, human race, individual, mankind, *mensch* (*informal*), mortal, party (*formal*), person, persona, sort (*informal*), soul, stiff (*slang*), target, type (*informal*)

(*pron*) anybody, anyone, somebody, someone

932 Gender Identity and Sexuality

There is no essential sexuality. Maleness and femaleness are something we are dressed in. **Naomi Wallace**

(*adj*) *androgynous*, asexual, *epicene*, female, feminine, *genderless*, hermaphrodite, macho, male, manly, masculine, *sexless*, tomboyish, *womanlike*, womanly

(*n*) femininity, gender, *hermaphroditism*, machismo, manliness, masculinity, sex, *sexual category, sexual characteristics, womanliness*

933 Female Person

Man is defined as a human being and woman as a female—whenever she behaves as a human being she is said to imitate the male. **Simone de Beauvoir**

(*n*) damsel (*archaic or literary*), female, *girl*, lady, lass, *mademoiselle*, maiden, matron, woman, womanhood, womankind, *young lady*

934 Male Person

The male ego with few exceptions is elephantine to start with.
Bette Davis

(*n*) beau (*archaic*), boy, cat (*dated slang*), codger (*informal*), dandy (*dated*), dude (*slang*), *fella* (*informal*), fellow, fop, *geezer* (*informal*), gent (*informal*), gentleman, guy (*informal*), *hipster* (*slang*), lad (*informal*), male, man, manhood, mankind (*dated*), swell (*dated informal*), *young man*

935 Groups of People

A crowd is not company, and faces are but a gallery of pictures, and talk but a tinkling cymbal, where there is no love.
Francis Bacon

(*n*) age group, army, band, bunch (*informal*), cadre, cohort, colony, contingent, convoy, corps, couple, crew (*informal*), crowd, crush, double, drove, duet, duo, foursome, gaggle, gang, generation, group, grouping, herd, horde, huddle, knot, legion, lineup, mob, multitude, outfit (*informal*), pack, party, phalanx, pool, press, rabble, school, squad, stable, swarm, team, *threesome*, throng, train, triad, triangle, tribe, trinity, trio, triplet, troika, troop, troupe, twosome, unit

See also THE FAMILY (956)

936 Friends and Acquaintances

The good person is related to his friend as to himself (for his friend is another self). **Aristotle**

(*n*) acquaintanceship, circle, clan (*informal*), clique, company, coterie, entourage, gang, guys (*informal*), in-group, posse (*informal*), retinue, set, *social circle*

See also FRIENDS AND GUESTS (963)

937 Audiences and Attendees

Audiences? No, the plural is impossible. Whether it be in Butte, Montana, or Broadway, it's an audience. The same great hulking monster with four thousand eyes and forty thousand teeth. **John Barrymore**

(*n*) assemblage, attendance, audience, concourse, conference, congregation, gate, turnout

See also MEETINGS AND ASSEMBLIES (43)

938 Groups with a Common Interest

There is apt to be a lunatic fringe among the votaries of any forward movement. **Theodore Roosevelt**

(*n*) advocacy group, alliance, board, brigade, cabal, cadre, camp, cartel, caucus, cell, coalition, collective, commission, committee, confederacy, confederation, crowd, delegation, deputation, enclave, excursion, expedition, faction, fraternity, *ginger group*, group, hit squad (*slang*), interest group, junta, league, lineup, lobby, lobby group (*UK*), membership, minority, movement, panel, party, readership, search party, sect, *self-help group*, side, *sisterhood*, *sorority*, *special interest group*, splinter group, steering committee, support group, support system, syndicate, task force, team, think tank, triumvirate, trust

See also BUSINESS ENTERPRISES AND RELATED BODIES (792)

939 Clubs and Societies

Please accept my resignation. I don't want to belong to any club that will accept me as a member. **Groucho Marx**

(*n*) association, club, interest group, order, organization, society, union

940 Groups in Society

(*n*) citizenry, civilization, community, constituency, country, culture, edifice, folk, folks (*informal*), general public, nation, people, populace, population, public, race, *rank and file*, society, subculture, world

See also INHABITANTS (857)

941 Solitariness

You find in solitude only what you take to it. **Juan Ramón Jiménez**

(*adj*) *all alone*, alone, aloof, cloistered, deserted, forlorn, forsaken, *friendless*, incommunicado, isolated, lone, lonely, lonesome, marooned, monkish, only, on your own, reclusive, single, solitary, solo

(*n*) alienation, aloofness, loneliness, *lonesomeness*, privacy, *reclusiveness*, *solitariness*, solitude, withdrawal

See also ACTING INDEPENDENTLY (284), NOMADIC AND ROOTLESS LIFESTYLES (884)

942 Solitary People and Misfits

But there comes a moment in everybody's life when he must decide whether he'll live among human beings or not—a fool among fools or a fool alone. **Thornton Wilder**

(*n*) anchorite, castaway, eccentric, *eremite* (*literary*), fifth wheel, foundling (*dated*), hermit, individualist, introvert, leper, loner, *lone wolf*, maverick, misfit, oddity, outcast, outsider, *pariah*, recluse, scapegoat

943 Belonging or Relating to People

Individuals pass like shadows; but the commonwealth is fixed and stable. **Edmund Burke**

(*adj*) civil, collective, collegial, common, communal, cooperative, corporate, cultural, ethnic, grassroots, national, nationalized, public, racial, shared, social, societal, state-owned, subcultural

(*adv*) socially

944 Belonging or Relating to Individuals

A man may be in as just possession of truth as of a city, and yet be forced to surrender. **Thomas Browne**

(*adj*) individual, internal, internecine, minority, one-on-one, own, personal, private, proper, proprietary, respective, subjective

(*adv*) firsthand, one-on-one, personally

945 Child or Youth

A child is a guest in the house, to be loved and respected—never possessed, since he belongs to God. **J. D. Salinger**

(*n*) adolescent, babe (*literary or archaic*), *babe in arms*, baby, child, infant, juvenile, kid (*informal*), *kiddie* (*informal*), lad, minor, moppet (*informal*), *neonate*, newborn, orphan, prepubescent, preschooler, *preteen*, *preteenager*, ragamuffin (*dated*), *rug rat* (*informal humorous*), sapling (*literary*), son, sonny (*informal*), teen (*informal*), teenager, toddler, tot (*informal*), urchin, waif, *young child*, younger generation, *young people*, young person, *young'un* (*informal*), youngster, youth

See also BABYHOOD, CHILDHOOD, AND ADOLESCENCE (917)

946 Mischievous or Badly Behaved Child

It was no wonder that people were so horrible when they started life as children. **Kingsley Amis**

(*n*) brat, imp, mischief, monkey (*informal*), pup, puppy, *rapscallion* (*archaic or humorous*), rascal, scalawag (*dated informal*), scamp (*informal*), *spoiled brat*, tearaway (*UK*), terror (*informal*), tyke, *whippersnapper* (*dated*), wretch (*humorous*)

947 Villains and Thugs

One murder makes a villain. Millions a hero. Numbers sanctify. **Charlie Chaplin**

(*n*) *adulterer*, animal, *antihero*, autocrat, baddie (*informal*), *bad guy*, beast, blackguard, boor, bruiser (*informal*), brute, buccaneer, bully, bullyboy, cad (*dated*), desperado, despot, *devil*, dictator, disciplinarian, evildoer, fiend, goon, gorilla (*informal*), *hatchet man* (*slang*), heavy (*slang*), heavyweight, hood (*slang*), hoodlum, hooligan (*informal*), marauder, miscreant (*literary*), mobster (*informal*), monster, oppressor, philistine, pig (*informal*), predator, prowler, rake, rat (*slang*), renegade, reprobate, rogue, rotter (*dated informal*), roughneck (*informal*), ruffian (*dated*), scoundrel, thug, tyrant, vandal, villain, wretch (*formal*)

See also CRIMINALS (821)

948 Lazy or Unsuccessful People

That indolent but agreeable condition of doing nothing. **Pliny the Younger**

(*n*) backslider, *barfly* (*slang*), boob (*informal*), buffoon, *bumbler*, conformist, coward, dawdler, daydreamer, deadbeat (*slang*), defeatist, ditherer, dreamer, fool, *fraidy-cat* (*informal*), freeloader (*informal*), goldbrick (*informal*), idealist, idler, joke, laggard, *lame duck*, latecomer, layabout, lazybones (*informal*), lemming, lightweight, loafer, lollygagger (*dated*), loser, lotus-eater, lout, *malingerer*, minnow, moocher (*informal*), ne'er-do-well, nobody, nonentity, nothing, oaf, parasite, *persona non grata*, plodder, quitter (*informal*), runt, scrounger (*informal*), sellout (*informal*), sheep, *shilly-shallier*, shirker, slacker, slouch (*informal*), space cadet (*slang*), sponge (*informal*), sponger (*informal*), straggler, timeserver, *timewaster*, underdog, unfortunate, vampire, *vermin*, *waster*, *wastrel*, *woolgatherer*, wretch, zombie (*informal*)

949   Self-Important and Self-Seeking People

EGOIST, *n. A person of low taste, more interested in himself than in me.* **Ambrose Bierce**

(*n*) *arriviste*, *attention seeker*, bighead (*informal*), bigmouth (*informal*), blower (*informal*), *blowhard*, *boaster*, braggart, *bragger*, chauvinist, daredevil, egoist, egomaniac, egotist, exhibitionist, *fashionista* (*informal*), *fashion victim*, *jingoist*, know-it-all (*informal*), *loudmouth* (*informal*), megalomaniac, name-dropper, *narcissist*, peacock, roisterer, *self-seeker*, show-off (*informal*), smart aleck (*informal*), smarty pants (*informal*), stuffed shirt (*informal*), *swelled head*, upstart, *wiseacre* (*informal*), *wise guy* (*informal*)

950   Interfering People and Tattletales

No one gossips about other people's secret virtues.
Bertrand Russell

(*n*) accuser, bigmouth (*informal*), blabbermouth (*informal*), busybody (*informal*), chatterbox (*informal*), chatterer, *do-gooder* (*informal*), double agent, gadfly (*dated*), gossip, gossipmonger, infiltrator, informant, informer, interloper, magpie (*informal*), meddler, mole, muckraker, mudslinger, obstructionist, purveyor (*formal*), rumor mill, rumormonger, scandalmonger, secret agent, *snake in the grass*, sneak (*UK*), snitch (*slang*), snoop (*informal*), source, spook, spy, squealer (*slang*), *stoolie* (*slang*), *stool pigeon* (*slang*), taleteller, tattle, tattler, tattletale, voyeur, whistle-blower

See also BETRAY CONFIDENCES AND GOSSIP (618), GOSSIP (678)

951   Superficial or Insincere People

In our way we were both snobs, and no snob welcomes another who has risen with him. **Cecil Beaton**

(*n*) *bootlicker* (*informal*), chameleon, charmer, courtier, *gold digger*, goody-goody (*informal*), *goody two-shoes* (*informal*), lapdog, *leech*, opportunist, poser (*informal*), poseur, pseud (*UK*), *shark* (*informal*), smoothie (*informal*), snob, social climber, sycophant, toady

See also PEOPLE WHO DECEIVE (661)

952   Financially Mean People

Who lendeth nothing is an ugly and wicked creature.
François Rabelais

(*n*) cheapskate (*informal*), miser, niggard, penny pincher (*informal*), pinchpenny, scrooge (*informal*), skinflint

See also GRASPING AND FINANCIALLY MEAN (519)

953   Grumpy and Negative People

Petulance is not sarcasm, and. . .insolence is not invective.
Benjamin Disraeli

(*n*) alarmist, *backbiter*, bigot, *carper*, Cassandra, complainer, crosspatch (*dated informal*), curmudgeon, cynic, detractor, *dog in the manger* (*UK*), faultfinder, fussbudget (*informal*), *gloomy Gus*, grouch (*informal*), grumbler, *hardliner*, *hard taskmaster*, hypochondriac, killjoy, knocker (*UK informal*), martinet, misanthrope, misanthropist, moaner (*informal*), nitpicker, party pooper (*informal*), pedant, perfectionist, pessimist, purist, scaremonger, sourpuss (*informal*), spoilsport,

stickler, valetudinarian, wet blanket (*informal*), whiner, worrier, *worrywart* (*informal*)

See also NEGATIVITY OF OUTLOOK (514)

954   Dirty and Slovenly People

She wears her clothes, as if they were thrown on her with a pitchfork. **Jonathan Swift**

(*n*) dumper, litterbug (*informal*), polluter

955   People who are Approved Of

Today's hero, the urban animal. . .can no longer be exclusively national, or even European, but instead must be. . .fertilized by the contributions of any number of different civilizations.
Juan Goytisolo

(*n*) altruist, *arbiter*, *battler*, careerist, darling, doer, dynamo (*informal*), favorite, go-getter (*informal*), good guy (*informal*), goody (*UK*), *guardian angel* (*informal*), hero, heroine, idol, *knight in shining armor*, liberator, *life and soul of the party*, live wire (*informal*), messiah, optimist, pet, pillar, pragmatist, prince (*informal*), *prodigal son*, protagonist, pussycat (*informal*), rainmaker (*informal*), rationalist, *ray of sunshine*, rock, savior, *self-starter*, *stalwart*, *stayer*, superhero, survivor, *team player*, titan, toast, tower of strength (*informal*), trier, trooper

See also TALENTED OR INTELLIGENT PEOPLE (528)

Relationships with Others

956   The Family

The family is strongest where objective reality is most likely to be misinterpreted. **Don DeLillo**

(*adj*) ancestral, biological, dynastic, familial, family, filial, fraternal, genealogical, hereditary, parental, tribal

(*n*) ancestor, ancestry, blood, *blood relation*, *blood relative*, clan, *close relative*, connections, descendant, descent, dynasty, extraction, family, family circle, *family member*, family tree, family unit, flesh, *flesh and blood*, folks, forebear, genealogy, hearth, home, house, household, kin, kindred, kinsfolk, kinsman (*formal*), kinswoman (*formal*), kith and kin, line, lineage, loved ones, menfolk, *nearest and dearest*, next of kin, *nuclear family*, parentage, pedigree, people (*informal*), relation, relations, relative, tribe (*informal*)

See also GROUPS OF PEOPLE (935)

957   Same-Generation Relatives

Too many cousins ruin the shopkeeper. **Proverb**

types of same-generation relatives brother, cousin, second cousin, senior, sibling, sister, stepbrother, stepsister

958   Younger Generation Relatives

Every generation revolts against its fathers and makes friends with its grandfathers. **Lewis Mumford**

(*n*) brood, *first-born*, heir, issue, offspring, progeny, scion, spawn, young

types of offspring only child, quadruplet, quintuplet, singleton, triplet, twin

types of younger relatives child, daughter, dependent, grandchild, granddaughter, grandson, great-grandchild, great-granddaughter, great-grandson, great-nephew, great-niece, nephew, niece, son, stepchild, stepdaughter, stepson

959 Older Generation Relatives

Parents are sometimes a bit of a disappointment to their children. They don't fulfill the promise of their early years.
Anthony Powell

(*n*) ancestor, *forebear*, *forefather*, forerunner, *materfamilias* (*formal*), matriarch, nanny (*informal*), *paterfamilias*, patriarch, progenitor

types of older relatives adoptive parent, aunt, biological parent, dad (*informal*), father, gramps (*informal*), gran (*informal*), granddad (*informal*), grandfather, grandma (*informal*), grandmother, grandpa (*informal*), grandparent, granny (*informal*), great-aunt, great-grandfather, great-grandmother, great-grandparent, great-uncle, lone parent, ma (*informal*), mama (*informal*), mammy (*informal*), mom, momma (*informal*), mommy (*informal*), mother, nan (*informal*), nana (*informal*), nanna (*informal*), papa (*dated*), parent, poppa (*informal*), single parent, stepfather, stepmother, stepparent, uncle

960 Relatives by Marriage

A husband is what is left of the lover after the nerve has been extracted. **Helen Rowland**

(*n*) betrothed (*formal*), *better half*, bride, *bride and groom*, bridegroom, consort (*formal*), fiancé, fiancée, *groomsman*, *hubby* (*informal*), husband, *husband-to-be*, intended (*dated or humorous*), newlyweds, spouse, wife, *wife-to-be*

types of in-laws brother-in-law, daughter-in-law, father-in-law, mother-in-law, sister-in-law, son-in-law

961 Married State

Every marriage tends to consist of an aristocrat and a peasant. Of a teacher and a learner. **John Updike**

(*adj*) conjugal, connubial (*literary*), marital, married, matrimonial, wedded

(*n*) *arranged marriage*, matrimony, union, wedlock

See also MARITAL STATUS (890)

962 Adoption, Fostering, and Extended Family

I had cherished a profound conviction that her bringing me up by hand, gave her no right to bring me up by jerks.
Charles Dickens

(*n*) caretaker, foster child, *foster father*, *foster mother*, foster parent, *godparent*, guardian, guardianship

963 Friends and Guests

Love is rarer than genius itself. And friendship is rarer than love. **Charles Pierre Péguy**

(*n*) acquaintance, ally, *amigo*, associate, *best friend*, *best mate* (*UK*), blood brother, *boon companion*, *bosom buddy*, *bosom friend* (*UK*), brother, buddy (*informal*), caller, chum (*informal*), *close friend*, cohort, companion, company, comrade, confidant, confidante, crony, friend, guest, house guest, mate (*UK*), pal (*informal*), pen friend

(*UK*), pen pal (*informal*), playfellow (*archaic*), playmate, *schoolmate*, sister, soul mate, sounding board

See also FRIENDS AND ACQUAINTANCES (936)

964 Sexual and Romantic Relationships

A lover without indiscretion is no lover at all. **Thomas Hardy**

(*n*) beau (*dated*), boyfriend, cohabitee, concubine, courtship, dalliance (*literary*), domestic partner, *ex* (*informal*), fling (*informal*), girlfriend, *inamorata* (*literary*), item (*informal*), lady friend (*informal*), man friend (*informal*), matchmaker, mistress, *old flame* (*informal*), *other half*, *paramour* (*literary*), partner, past love, romance, significant other, spousal equivalent, *suitor* (*formal*), swain (*literary*), *valentine*

965 Bosses and Management

The first responsibility of a leader is to define reality.
Max de Pree

(*n*) boss, chief, chieftain, consultant, controller, director, directorate, director-general, directorship, elder, employer, floor manager, governor, head, leader, line manager, management, manager, master, *MD* (*UK*), mistress, number one (*informal*), organizer, overseer, principal, secretary-general, senior, skipper (*informal*), superintendent, superior, supervisor, supremo (*informal*), Svengali

See also WORKERS (836)

966 Subordinates and Assistants

The crow does not roost with the phoenix. **Chinese proverb**

(*n*) acolyte, adjunct, affiliate, aide, amanuensis, assistant, attendant, concierge, deputy, employee, flunky (*informal*), functionary, helper, helpmate, *helpmeet* (*archaic*), inferior, interviewee, lackey, *lieutenant*, *locum*, minion, personal assistant, protégé, puppet, representative, right hand, subject, subordinate, successor, succor (*literary*), underling, usher, *vassal*, *whipping boy*

See also WORKERS (836)

967 Colleagues and Equals

When we ask advice, we are usually looking for an accomplice.
Joseph Louis Lagrange

(*n*) associate, collaborator, colleague, confrère (*formal*), contemporary, counterpart, coworker, fellow, mate, opposite number, partner, partner in crime, peer, peer group, roomie (*informal*), roommate, sidekick (*informal*), standby, teammate, workmate

See also WORKERS (836)

968 Representatives and Patrons

Patron. Commonly a wretch who supports with insolence, and is paid with flattery. **Samuel Johnson**

(*n*) agent, ambassador, angel, backer, benefactor, delegate, donor, emissary, envoy, intermediary, legate, middleman, mouthpiece, negotiator, patron, philanthropist, plenipotentiary, provider, proxy, rep (*informal*), representative, spokesperson, sponsor, underwriter

969   Enemies and Tormentors

There's a snake hidden in the grass. **Virgil**

(*n*) accuser, adversary, aggressor, antagonist, arch-enemy, assailant, avenger, chaser, conqueror, critic, enemy, foe (*formal*), invader, nemesis (*literary*), opponent, opposition, persecutor, pursuer, rival, shadow, sparring partner, *sworn enemy*, tail (*informal*), tormentor, torturer, tracker

970   Supporters, Protectors, and Compatriots

Comrades, leave me here a little, while as yet 'tis early morn:/Leave me here, and when you want me, sound upon the bugle-horn. **Alfred Tennyson**

(*n*) apologist, apostle, best man, bridesmaid, *caregiver*, chaperon, *coauthor*, coconspirator, compatriot, confederate, connections, contact, contributor, correspondent, countryman, countrywoman, cousin, custodian, devotee, disciple, escort, flatmate (*UK*), follower, guardian, outrider, party, preserver, promoter, proponent, proposer, *proselyte*, protector, provider, rescuer, seconder, shadow, supporter, sympathizer, trustee, wannabe (*informal*), well-wisher

971   Advisers, Judges, and Arbiters

A judge is a law student who marks his own examination papers. **H. L. Mencken**

(*n*) adjudicator, adviser, appeaser, arbiter, arbitrator, assessor, conciliator, counselor, evaluator, go between, guidance counselor, guide, informant, mediator, mentor, moderator, monitor, peacekeeper, peacemaker, piggy in the middle (*UK*), ref (*informal*), referee, regulator, reviewer, third party, troubleshooter

972   Strangers

Be not forgetful to entertain strangers: for thereby some have entertained angels unawares. **Bible**

(*n*) alien, foreigner, gatecrasher (*UK*), incomer (*UK*), interloper, intruder, newcomer, nonmember, nonresident, party crasher, passer-by, stranger, unknown

973   Relationship to Another

Hunger is my native place in the land of the passions. Hunger for...a fellowship founded on righteousness, and a righteousness attained in fellowship. **Dag Hammarskjöld**

(*adj*) *acquainted*, adoptive, amicable, attached (*informal*), beholden, bosom (*informal*), close-knit, *codependent*, confidential, conspiratorial, estranged, foster, harmonious, independent, inferior, inseparable, interpersonal, intimate, maternal, monogamous, *pally* (*informal*), paternal, paternalistic, platonic, reliant, right-hand, rival, self-contained, self-reliant, self-sufficient, separate, subordinate, *thick as thieves*, *well-acquainted*

(*adv*) amicably, harmoniously, intimately, socially

(*n*) acquaintance, amity (*formal*), antagonism, association, brotherhood, camaraderie, chumminess (*informal*), closeness, collusion, companionship, company, comradeship, dependency, estrangement, fatherhood, fellowship, fidelity, flirtation, friendship, guidance, independence, intimacy, kinship, leadership, maternity, monogamy, parentage, parenthood, partnership, paternalism, paternity, *peaceful coexistence*, power, relations, rivalry, romance, self-reliance, self-sufficiency, servitude, sovereignty, sway, terms, togetherness

974   Establishing Relationships with Others

Ye gods! annihilate but space and time./And make two lovers happy. **Alexander Pope**

(*v*) align, ally, ask, associate, assort with, be accepted, become acquainted, befriend, bond, circulate (*informal*), click (*informal*), connect, consort with (*formal*), cooperate, court (*dated*), cozy up, curry favor, endear, espouse (*archaic*), fall in with, fraternize, gel (*informal*), *get acquainted*, get along, get hitched (*informal*), *get in good with*, get in with, get married, get on (*UK*), get to know, go in with, go with (*informal*), greet, hang around, hang out (*informal*), hit it off (*informal*), hit on (*slang*), hobnob, ingratiate, insinuate, integrate, jell, join forces, join together, join up (*UK*), latch onto (*informal*), make contacts, make friends, make somebody's acquaintance, marry, meet, merge, mess around (*informal*), mingle, mix, *pay court to* (*dated*), receive, relate, remarry, romance, run around, socialize, splice (*slang*), stick around (*informal*), stick together, stick with, *strike up a friendship*, take out, team up, tie the knot (*informal*), unite, walk down the aisle, wed, woo (*literary*)

See also INITIATE AND ESTABLISH COMMUNICATION (680)

975   Refusing or Rejecting Relations

Learn to reject friendship, or rather the dream of friendship...friendship ought to be a gratuitous joy, like the joys afforded by art. **Simone Weil**

(*v*) alienate, blackball, break up, break with, brush off, cut dead, desert, ditch (*informal*), dump (*informal*), freeze out, *give the brushoff*, *give the bum's rush* (*slang*), give the cold shoulder to, *go separate ways*, jilt, leave, leave be, look through, maroon, orphan, ostracize, rebuff, repulse, send to Coventry (*UK*), separate, shun, snub, split up, spurn, squeeze out, strand, turn against, turn away, walk out on (*informal*)

The World Around Us

Living Things

976 Living Things and Living

The generations of living things pass in a short time, and like runners hand on the torch of life. **Lucretius**

(*adj*) alive, animal, animate, bodily, breathing, *flesh-and-blood*, fleshly, human, live, living, organic, physical, sensual, sentient

(*n*) *amphibian*, animal, *arachnid*, *bat*, beast, being, biped, *bird*, *bird of prey*, brute (*literary*), creature, *deer*, farm animal, fauna, *fish*, *flora and fauna*, fowl, invertebrate, *life form*, *living being*, living thing, mammal, *marsupial*, *organic matter*, organism, pet, *primate*, quadruped, *reptile*, *rodent*, vertebrate, wildlife

977 Young Animals

types of young animals bullock, calf, colt, cub, fawn, foal, heifer, joey, kid, kitten, lamb, leveret, piglet, pup, puppy, whelp, yearling

978 Male or Female Animals

types of female animals bitch, cow, dam, doe, ewe, filly, heifer, hind, jenny, lioness, mare, nanny goat, sow, tigress, vixen

types of male animals billy goat, boar, buck, bull, bullock, colt, hart, jackass, ram, stag, stallion, steer, tom, tomcat, wether

979 Canines

types of canines coyote, dingo, dog, fox, jackal, wolf

980 Dogs

(*adj*) canine, *doggy*

(*n*) canine (*humorous*), cur, dog, hound, mongrel, *mutt* (*slang*), pooch (*informal*), *pye-dog*

types of large dogs Afghan hound, Alsatian, bloodhound, borzoi, boxer, bulldog, collie, dalmatian, Doberman pinscher, German shepherd, Great Dane, greyhound, guide dog, husky, Labrador, mastiff, Newfoundland, Old English sheepdog, Pyrenean mountain dog, retriever, rottweiler, Saint Bernard, setter, sheepdog, wolfhound

types of small dogs affenpinscher, airedale, basenji, basset, beagle, Border terrier, bull terrier, cairn terrier, chihuahua, chow, corgi, dachshund, fox terrier, foxhound, Jack Russell, Pekingese, pomeranian, poodle, pug, Scottie, sealyham, shar-pei, shih tzu, spaniel, terrier, whippet, Yorkshire terrier

981 Deer and Antelopes

types of deer or antelope antelope, caribou, chamois, chevrotain, dik-dik, elk, fallow deer, gazelle, gnu, impala, moose, okapi, reindeer, springbok, Thomson's gazelle, wapiti, white-tailed deer

982 Farm Animals

(*n*) cattle, livestock, stock, swine

types of farm animals ass, cow, donkey, goat, hog, horse, mule, ox, pig, sheep

983 Felines

(*n*) cat, kitty (*informal*), puss (*informal*), pussy (*informal*), pussycat

types of cats Abyssinian, American shorthair, big cat, Birman, bobcat, British shorthair, Burmese cat, calico cat, cheetah, Egyptian mau, jaguar, leopard, lion, lynx, Maine coon, Manx cat, mountain lion, Norwegian forest cat, ocelot, panther, Persian cat, Siamese cat, tabby, tiger, tortoiseshell, wildcat

984 Flying Mammals

types of flying mammals flying fox, flying squirrel, fruit bat, pipistrelle, vampire bat

985 Horses

(*adj*) equestrian, *equine*, horsy

(*n*) horse, mount, steed (*literary*)

parts of a horse croup, fetlock, flank, foreleg, hindquarters, hock, hoof, mane, pastern, shank, withers

types of horses Arabian horse, bronco, broodmare, carthorse, charger, cob, hack, hunter, mustang, pacer, packhorse, pony, racehorse, saddle horse, Shetland pony, shire horse, thoroughbred, trotter, warhorse, workhorse

986 Large Mammals

types of large mammals alpaca, bactrian camel, bear, bison, boar, buffalo, camel, dromedary, elephant, giraffe, hippopotamus, llama, panda, polar bear, rhinoceros, wart hog

987 Marine Mammals

types of marine mammals dolphin, dugong, grampus, manatee, porpoise, seal, sea lion, walrus, whale

988 Primates

types of primates ape, aye-aye, baboon, Barbary ape, bonnet monkey, capuchin, chimp, chimpanzee, colobus, gibbon, gorilla, human, lemur, macaque, mandrill, marmoset, monkey, orangutan, proboscis monkey, rhesus monkey, spider monkey

989   Rodents

types of rodents beaver, capybara, chinchilla, chipmunk, coypu, dormouse, gerbil, gopher, groundhog, guinea pig, hamster, jerboa, lemming, marmot, mole, mouse, muskrat, prairie dog, rat, shrew, squirrel, vole, woodchuck

990   Small Mammals

types of small mammals anteater, armadillo, badger, ferret, hare, hedgehog, hyrax, marten, mink, mongoose, otter, pine marten, polecat, porcupine, rabbit, raccoon, skunk, sloth, stoat, weasel, wolverine

991   Whales

types of whales blue whale, gray whale, humpback whale, killer whale, minke whale, narwhal, pilot whale, right whale, sperm whale, white whale

992   Marsupials

types of marsupials bandicoot, bettong, bilby, kangaroo, koala, opossum, phalanger, potoroo, Tasmanian devil, thylacine, wallaby, wombat

993   Groups of Animals

(*n*) brood, *herd*, litter

types of herds bale (of turtles), band (of gorillas), bevy (of roe deer), colony (of ants/sealions), drove (of sheep), flock (of sheep), gam (of whales), gang (of elk), kennel (of dogs), leash (of foxes), litter (of cubs/kittens), mob (of kangaroos), pack (of wolves), pod (of porpoises/seals/walrus/whales), pride (of lions), rookery (of seals), school (of porpoises/whales), skulk (of foxes), troop (of kangaroos/monkeys)

994   Reptiles

types of reptiles alligator, basilisk, bearded dragon, cayman, chameleon, crocodile, gecko, gila monster, glass snake, goanna, horned lizard, iguana, Komodo dragon, lizard, moloch, monitor lizard, mugger, skink, slowworm, terrapin, tortoise, turtle

995   Snakes

(*n*) *sea serpent*, serpent (*literary*), snake

types of nonpoisonous snakes anaconda, blacksnake, boa, boa constrictor, garter snake, grass snake, king snake, python, rat snake, water snake, whip snake

types of poisonous snakes adder, asp, cobra, copperhead, coral snake, diamondback, fer-de-lance, horned viper, mamba, pit viper, puff adder, rattler, rattlesnake, ringhals, sea snake, sidewinder, taipan, viper, water moccasin

996   Dinosaurs

types of dinosaurs allosaurus, ankylosaur, apatosaur, brachiosaurus, brontosaurus, cotylosaur, dicynodont, diplodocus, hadrosaur, ichthyosaur, iguanodon, megalosaur, mosasaur, oviraptor, pelycosaur, plesiosaur, pteranodon, pterodactyl, pterosaur, stegosaur, titanosaur, triceratops, tyrannosaur, velociraptor

997   Birds

types of common birds blue jay, bluebird, camp robber, cardinal, chickadee, finch, flycatcher, gorsbeak, grackle, hummingbird, mockingbird, mourning dove, nuthatch, pigeon, robin, sparrow, starling, swallow, swift, tanager, thrush, tufted titmouse, vireo, warbler, woodpecker, wren

types of flightless birds dodo, emu, kiwi, ostrich, peacock, penguin

types of pet birds budgerigar, canary, cockatoo, homing pigeon, lovebird, macaw, mynah, parakeet, parrot

types of scavengers buzzard, condor, crow, jackdaw, lammergeier, magpie, marabou, raven, rook, vulture

998   Birds of Prey

types of birds of prey bald eagle, buteo, caracara, eagle, falcon, golden eagle, hawk, kestrel, kite, osprey, owl, peregrine falcon, sea eagle, sparrow hawk

999   Food Birds

types of fowl bantam, broiler, chicken, duck, goose, grouse, guinea fowl, partridge, pheasant, pigeon, quail, turkey, waterfowl, wildfowl, woodcock

1000   Freshwater Birds

(*n*) water bird, waterfowl

types of freshwater birds barnacle goose, bittern, Canada goose, canvasback, coot, crane, duck, egret, flamingo, grebe, heron, ibis, kingfisher, loon, mallard, merganser, moorhen, snipe, spoonbill, stork, swan, teal

1001   Owls

types of owls barn owl, fish owl, hoot owl, little owl, long-eared owl, screech owl, short-eared owl, snowy owl, tawny owl

1002   Sea Birds

types of sea birds albatross, auk, avocet, cormorant, flamingo, fulmar, gannet, guillemot, gull, kittiwake, osprey, oystercatcher, pelican, plover, puffin, seagull, shag, shearwater, skua, storm petrel, tern, wader

1003   Songbirds

types of songbirds bluebird, flycatcher, hedge sparrow, lark, linnet, meadowlark, nightingale, nightjar, oriole, pied wagtail, pipit, skylark, thrush, titmouse, wagtail, warbler, weaverbird, woodlark, yellowhammer

1004   Young Birds

types of young birds chick, cygnet, duckling, eaglet, eyas, fledgling, gosling, nestling, owlet, pullet, squab

1005   Male or Female Birds

types of male birds or female birds capon, cob, cock, cockerel, drake, duck, gander, goose, hen, pen, rooster

1006   Parts of a Bird

parts of a bird beak, bill, breast, carina, cockscomb, comb, crest, crop, down, feather, gizzard, gorge, plumage, plume, quill, ruff, tail, talon, web, wing, wingtip, wishbone

1007   Groups of Birds

types of flocks bevy (of quail/larks), brood (of chickens), cast (of hawks), charm (of finches), clutch (of chickens), colony (of gulls), covey (of partridges), exaltation (of larks) (*literary*), flight (of doves/swallows), gaggle (of geese), herd (of swans), kettle (of hawks), mob (of emus), murmuration (of starlings) (*literary*), muster (of peacocks), nye (of pheasants) (*literary*), rookery (of penguins), siege (of herons), skein (of geese), watch (of nightingales) (*literary*), wedge (of swans in flight), wisp (of snipe)

1008   Amphibians

types of amphibians axolotl, bullfrog, cane toad, frog, horned toad, midwife toad, natterjack toad, newt, salamander, toad, tree frog, xenopus

1009   Ocean Fish

types of flatfish angelfish, brill, flounder, halibut, lemon sole, manta, plaice, pompano, ray, skate, sole, turbot

types of ocean fish anchovy, anglerfish, cod, dogfish, eel, haddock, hake, herring, John Dory, ling, mackerel, monkfish, pilchard, salmon, sardine, sea bream, shark, sprat, sturgeon, whitebait, whiting

types of tropical fish barracuda, flying fish, kingfish, mahimahi, marlin, pomfret, sailfish, sawfish, snapper, swordfish, tuna

1010   Freshwater Fish

types of freshwater fish bass, bream, carp, catfish, crappie, goldfish, grayling, guppy, loach, minnow, mullet, Nile perch, perch, pike, piranha, roach, stickleback, tench, tilapia, trout

1011   Parts of a Fish

parts of a fish air bladder, anal fin, dorsal fin, fin, gill, pectoral fin, pelvic fin, roe, scale, tail

1012   Insects

(*n*) ant, *beetle*, bug, *butterfly*, creepy-crawly (*informal*), *fly*, gnat, insect, moth, pest

1013   Flying Insects

types of flying insects aphid, bee, black fly, bluebottle, bumblebee, cicada, crane fly, deer fly, dragonfly, firefly, fruit fly, gnat, grasshopper, greenfly, hornet, horsefly, locust, mayfly, midge, mosquito, no-see-um, punkie, tsetse fly, wasp, whitefly

1014   Ants

types of ants army ant, carpenter ant, fire ant, flying ant, leafcutter ant, Pharaoh ant, red ant, slave ant, slave-making ant, soldier ant, white ant, worker ant

1015   Moths and Butterflies

types of butterflies cabbage butterfly, emperor butterfly, monarch butterfly, mourning cloak, painted lady, peacock butterfly, red admiral, swallowtail, tiger swallowtail, tortoiseshell

types of moths cinnabar moth, clearwing, clothes moth, death's head moth, emperor moth, goat moth, gypsy moth, hawk moth, luna moth, peppered moth, pyralid, tiger moth, tussock moth, underwing

1016   Beetles and Weevils

types of beetles cockroach, Colorado potato beetle, deathwatch beetle, dung beetle, flea beetle, Japanese beetle, ladybug, rhinoceros beetle, roach (*informal*), scarab, stag beetle, water beetle, weevil

1017   Parasites

(*adj*) parasitic

(*n*) bloodsucker, parasite

types of parasitic insects bedbug, botfly, chigger, chigoe, crab louse, deer tick, flea, gadfly, harvest mite, head louse, horsefly, louse, mite, sand flea, sandfly, tapeworm, tick

1018   Arachnids

types of arachnids black widow, brown recluse, daddy longlegs, funnel-web spider, harvestman, jumping spider, mite, money spider, redback, scorpion, spider, tarantula, trapdoor spider, water spider, wolf spider

1019   Parts of an Insect

parts of an insect abdomen, antenna, feeler, proboscis, thorax, wing

1020   Insect Stages

types of stages of insect development caterpillar, chrysalis, glowworm, grub, imago, larva, maggot, nit, pupa, silkworm, woodworm

1021   Land Invertebrates

types of land invertebrates centipede, earthworm, millipede, mollusk, slug, snail, wood louse, worm

1022   Aquatic Invertebrates

types of aquatic invertebrates abalone, barnacle, bivalve, clam, cockle, conch, coral, crustacean, cuttlefish, jellyfish, limpet, mollusk, mussel, octopus, oyster, Portuguese man-of-war, quahog, scallop, sea anemone, sea urchin, sponge, squid, starfish, whelk, winkle

types of crustaceans crab, crayfish, hermit crab, horseshoe crab, langoustine, lobster, prawn, sand flea, shellfish, shrimp, water flea

See also SEAFOOD (1190)

1023   Microorganisms, Fungi, and Algae

The Microbe is so very small/You cannot make him out at all.
Hilaire Belloc

(*adj*) *amoebic*, bacterial, fungal, *microbial*, *viral*

(*n*) *alga*, bug (*informal*), *fungus*, germ, microbe, microorganism, superbug

types of fungi beefsteak fungus, boletus, bracket fungus, cep, chanterelle, death cap, destroying angel, fairy ring champignon, field mushroom, fly agaric, horn of plenty, inky cap, lichen, mildew, mold, morel, mushroom, orange-peel fungus, oyster mushroom, puffball, stinkhorn, toadstool, truffle, yeast

types of marine algae bladder wrack, brown alga, fucus, green alga, gulfweed, Irish moss, kelp, laminaria, phytoplankton, pond scum, red alga, rockweed, sea lettuce, seaweed, sea wrack, stonewort, tangle

types of microorganisms amoeba, bacteriophage, bacterium, botulinum, candida, ciliate, coccus, E. coli, flagellate, listeria, mycoplasma, protozoan, rhizopod, salmonella, spirillum, spirochete, staphylococcus, stentor, streptococcus, virus

1024 Plants and Trees

Trees are poems that the earth writes upon the sky. **Kahlil Gibran**

(*n*) *conifer*, *deciduous tree*, *evergreen*, plant, sapling, seedling, tree

See also WOODS, FORESTS, AND JUNGLES (1047)

1025 Vegetation

(*adj*) blooming, grassy, leafy, lush, luxuriant, mossy, *scrubby*, vegetable, verdant, wooded, woody

(*n*) brushwood, bushes, flora, *grass*, greenery, greens, lushness, scrub, undergrowth, understory, vegetation, verdure, *weed*

1026 Parts of Trees and Plants

(*n*) *achene*, *berry*, bloom (*literary*), blossom, bole, bough, branch, bud, bulb, bur, canopy, catkin, cutting, *fir cone*, floret, flower, foliage, frond, fruit, gum, husk, latex, leaf, nectar, needle, *nut*, offshoot, pine cone, pod, posy, resin, rhizome, root, rosebud, sap, scion, *seed case*, *seed husk*, *seedpod*, shoot, spore, sprig, sprout, tendril, thorn, treetop, trunk, tuber, twig

1027 Bushes and Shrubs

(*n*) bush, hedge, hedgerow, shrub, shrubbery, undershrub

types of shrubs or bushes azalea, bramble, brier, broom, camellia, elder, forsythia, gardenia, gorse, hawthorn, heather, hydrangea, laurel, lavender, lilac, magnolia, privet, pussy willow, rhododendron, rose, sagebrush, witch hazel

1028 Deciduous Trees

types of deciduous trees acacia, alder, ash, aspen, baobab, beech, birch, chestnut, dogwood, elder, elm, ginkgo, gleditsia, hawthorn, hickory, hornbeam, horse chestnut, Judas tree, laburnum, lime, magnolia, maple, mesquite, mimosa, mulberry, oak, plane tree, poplar, rowan, sassafras, silver birch, sumac, sycamore, teak, tulip tree, willow

1029 Evergreen and Coniferous Trees

types of evergreen trees bay, bo tree, boxwood, bunya, carob, cedar, cola, cypress, eucalyptus, fir, fir tree, gum tree, holly, juniper, kahikatea, kauri, larch, laurel, mahogany, mangrove, monkey puzzle, pine, redwood, sandalwood, sequoia, spruce, yew

1030 Flowers from Bulbs

types of flowers grown from bulbs anemone, bluebell, crocus, cyclamen, daffodil, dahlia, freesia, gladiolus, hyacinth, iris, jonquil, lily, narcissus, snowdrop, tulip

1031 Grass

types of grass bamboo, beach grass, bluegrass, bulrush, couch grass, crabgrass, esparto, fescue, Kentucky bluegrass, lyme grass, marram, meadow fescue, pampas grass, reed, rye grass, spinifex, sugar cane, sword grass, timothy

1032 Flowers

parts of a flower androecium, anther, bract, calyx, carpel, corolla, fall, filament, floret, glume, gynoecium, involucre, lemma, lip, nectary, ovary, ovule, palea, pedicel, peduncle, perianth, petal, pistil, receptacle, sepal, spur, stamen, stigma, style, tepal

types of annual flowers aster, forget-me-not, lobelia, marigold, nasturtium, pansy, petunia, poppy, stock, sunflower, sweet pea

types of perennial flowers African violet, begonia, buttercup, carnation, chrysanthemum, columbine, cowslip, daisy, delphinium, foxglove, fuchsia, geranium, lily of the valley, lotus, lupine, orchid, pelargonium, peony, pink, primrose, rose, snapdragon, sweet william, violet, wallflower

1033 Climbers

(*n*) climber, creeper, vine

types of climbers bougainvillea, bryony, clematis, convolvulus, grapevine, honeysuckle, ivy, jasmine, kudzu, liana, morning glory, passionflower, rattan, sarsaparilla, Virginia creeper, wisteria, woodbine

1034 Weeds and Thistles

types of weeds bindweed, burdock, chickweed, dandelion, dock, goldenrod, jimsonweed, nettle, poison ivy, poison oak, ragweed, stinging nettle, thistle, tumbleweed

1035 Foliage Plants

(*n*) *bonsai*, foliage plant, houseplant, *pot plant* (*UK*), *potted plant*

types of foliage plants aspidistra, coleus, fern, moss, poinsettia, rubber plant, sansevieria, spider plant, yucca

1036 Mythical Creatures

A dragon stranded in shallow water furnishes amusement for the shrimps. **Chinese proverb**

types of mythological creatures centaur, Chimera, dragon, griffin, mermaid, sphinx, unicorn, vampire, werewolf

See also NONEXISTENT THINGS (23), MYTHICAL BEINGS (789)

1037   Biological Sciences

No species. . .possesses a purpose beyond the imperatives created by genetic history. **Edward O. Wilson**

(*adj*) anatomical, bacteriological, biochemical, biological, botanical, ecological, microbiological, natural, physiological, *zoological*

types of biosciences anatomy, bacteriology, biochemistry, biology, biomedicine, biophysics, biotechnology, botany, ecology, genetics, microbiology, molecular biology, physiology, zoology

The Natural Environment and The Forces of Nature

1038   Nature and the Environment

Nature contains the elements, in color and form, of all pictures, as the keyboard contains the notes of all music.
James Abbott McNeill Whistler

(*n*) biosphere, creation, ecosystem, environment, natural world, nature, world

1039   The Earth

The earth is blue like an orange. **Paul Éluard**

(*adj*) earthly, geographic, terrestrial, topographical

(*n*) earth, globe, planet, world

1040   The Earth's Atmosphere

Man has in him the silence of the sea, the noise of the earth and the music of the air. **Rabindranath Tagore**

(*n*) aerospace, air, atmosphere, ether (*literary*), exosphere, firmament (*literary*), heaven, ionosphere, mesosphere, ozonosphere, sky, *stratosphere*, *thermosphere*, troposphere, *upper atmosphere*

1041   The Seas, Oceans, and Shores

The voice of the sea speaks to the soul. **Kate Chopin**

(*adj*) aquatic, coastal, deep-sea, landlocked, littoral, marine, maritime, naval, ocean, oceanic, sea, *tidal*, undersea, waterborne, waterside

(*n*) bay, beach, *beachfront*, *bight*, breaker, briny (*UK*), cape, coast, coastline, cove, creek, delta, dry land, dune, ebb, firth (*UK*), fjord, flood tide, foreshore, groundswell, gulf, harbor, haven (*literary*), headland, inlet, isthmus, lagoon, lakeside, landfall, lido (*UK*), littoral, loch (*UK*), lough (*UK*), marina, mouth, ocean, point, port, promontory, reef, roller, sand, sandbank, sandbar, sea, seaboard, seacoast, seafront, seaport, seashore, seaside, shoal, shore, shoreline, sound, spindrift, strait, surf, swell, *terra firma*, tidal wave, tide, *tsunami*, undertow, waterfront, water line, watermark, waterside, wave, whirlpool, whitecap, white water

1042   Rivers, Lakes, and Streams

You can't step twice into the same river. **Heraclitus**

(*n*) bayou, beck (*UK*), broad (*UK*), brook, burn (*UK*), cascade, cataract, chute, creek, current, eddy, estuary, fall, flow, font (*literary*), fount (*literary*), fountain, foun-

tainhead, geyser, lagoon, lake, loch (*UK*), lough (*UK*), mere (*archaic or literary*), pond, pool, rapids, reservoir, river, *riverbank*, riverside, rivulet, sault, source, stream, tarn, tributary, undercurrent, watercourse, waterfall, water hole, watering hole, waterway, weir, well

1043   Wetlands

My ghost town—/A place of interminable afternoons. . ./Of so many hesitant surrenders to/Enfolding bog. **Michael Longley**

(*n*) bog, *everglade*, fen, fenland, floodplain, marsh, marshland, mire, morass, *mudflat*, quagmire, quicksand, *salt flat*, swamp, swampland, wetland

1044   Mountains and Hills

Mountains are the beginning and the end of all natural scenery. **John Ruskin**

(*adj*) alpine, hilly, mountainous, terraced

(*n*) *alp*, ascent, bluff, butte, cliff, crag, foothill, glacier, grade, gradient, high ground, highland, hill, hillock, hilltop, hummock, incline, knoll, massif, mesa, mound, mountain, mountainside, mountaintop, pass, peak, rise, rock face, scarp, spur, tor

1045   Deserts, Plains, and Moorland

The mesa plain had an appearance of great antiquity, and of incompleteness. . .the country was still waiting to be made into a landscape. **Willa Cather**

(*n*) bush, desert, dust bowl, grassland, *heath*, *heathland* (*UK*), lowland, moonscape, moor, moorland, *pampas*, plain, plateau, prairie, savanna, *scrubland*, *semidesert*, steppe, tableland, *tundra*, upland, veld, wasteland, wastes, wilderness

1046   Remote Places

Space isn't remote at all. It's only an hour's drive away if your car could go straight upward. **Fred Hoyle**

(*n*) back country, backwater, backwoods, *badlands*, boondocks (*informal*), outback, *sticks* (*informal*), *the back of beyond* (*UK*)

1047   Woods, Forests, and Jungles

Are not these woods/More free from peril than the envious court? **William Shakespeare**

(*n*) coppice, copse, covert, forest, grove, jungle, orchard, *rain forest*, spinney (*UK*), thicket, timber, *tropical forest*, wood, woodland, woods

See also PLANTS AND TREES (1024)

1048   The Continents and Islands

It is not easy to shake off the spell of island life. **Joseph Conrad**

(*n*) *archipelago*, atoll, continent, island, isle, landmass, mainland, peninsula

1049   Weather and Climate

The climate and the chemical properties of the Earth now and throughout its history seem always to have been optimal for life. **James Lovelock**

(*adj*) barometric, *climatic*, meteorological

(*n*) climate, *climate change*, *climatology*, clime (*literary*), isobar, isotherm, meteorology, weather

1050 Hot Weather

"Heat, ma'am!" I said; "it was so dreadful here that I found there was nothing left for it but to take off my flesh and sit in my bones." **Sydney Smith**

(*adj*) baking, balmy, blistering, boiling, *boiling hot*, clammy, clear, clement, close, cloudless, fair, fine, fuggy (*UK*), good, hot, mild, muggy, oppressive, scorching (*informal*), searing, steamy, sticky, stifling, stuffy, sultry, summery, sunny, *sunshiny*, sweaty, sweltering, toasty, torrid, tropical, warm

(*n*) *balminess*, clamminess, closeness, fug, heat wave, *Indian summer*, mugginess, stuffiness, *sultriness*, torridness, *warm front*, warmness, warmth, *warm weather*

See also TEMPERATURE: HOT (1229)

1051 Cold Weather

The ways deep and the weather sharp,/The very dead of winter. **T. S. Eliot**

(*adj*) arctic (*informal*), biting, bitter, bleak, chill, chilly, cool, crisp, cutting, freezing, frosted, frosty, frozen, glacial, ice-cold, icy, inclement, keen, miserable, nippy, perishing, piercing, polar, raw, snowbound, subzero, temperate, white, wintry

(*n*) blizzard, chill, chilliness, *cold front*, cold snap, *cold spell*, coolness, frost, frostiness, hoar frost, ice, keenness, rawness, rime, sleet, snow, snowfall, *snow flurry*, *snowsquall*, snowstorm, wintriness

See also TEMPERATURE: COLD (1231)

1052 Cloudy and Rainy Weather

Rain is grace; rain is the sky condescending to the earth; without rain there would be no life. **John Updike**

(*adj*) cloudy, driving, *drizzling*, drizzly, dull, foggy, foul, hazy, leaden, misty, murky, overcast, pouring, rainy, *sheeting down* (*UK*), showery, *smoggy*, sunless, torrential, wet

(*n*) brume (*literary*), cloud, cloudburst, cloudiness, deluge, downpour, *driving rain*, drizzle, dullness, flash flood, flood, fog, fogginess, haze, haziness, *heavy shower*, mist, mistiness, *mizzle*, monsoon, murkiness, *peasouper* (*UK*), precipitation, rain, rainbow, *raindrops*, rainfall, rainstorm, rainwater, *rainy season*, shower, smog, *smogginess*, torrent, wet, *wet weather*

(*v*) *cloud over*, come down in sheets (*informal*), come down in torrents, drizzle, haze, pelt, *pelt down*, pour, pour with rain, rain, rain cats and dogs (*informal*), sheet down (*UK*), shower, spit, sprinkle, teem

types of clouds altocumulus, altostratus, cirrocumulus, cirrus, cumulonimbus, cumulus, funnel cloud, mare's-tail, nimbus, rain cloud, storm cloud, stratocumulus, stratus, thundercloud, thunderhead

1053 Windy and Stormy Weather

Hoist up saile while gale doth last,/Tide and wind stay no man's pleasure. **Robert Southwell**

(*adj*) blowy (*informal*), blustery, breezy, choppy, *gale-force*, gusty, howling, rough, squally, storm-tossed,

stormy, sullen (*literary*), tempestuous, *thundery*, turbulent, weather-bound, wild, windy

(*adv*) stormily

(*n*) boisterousness, breeze, draft, flurry, *forked lightning* (*UK*), *fulguration* (*formal*), gale, gust, headwind, lightning, puff, roughness, *sheet lightning*, squall, storm, storminess, tempest (*literary*), thermal, thunderbolt, thunderstorm, *tropical storm*, trough, *twister* (*informal*), vortex, whirlwind, whiteout, wind, windstorm

(*v*) blow, bluster, gust

types of winds antitrade, bise, chinook, cyclone, foehn, harmattan, hurricane, khamsin, levanter, mistral, monsoon, northeaster, northwester, Santa Ana, simoom, sirocco, southeaster, southwester, tornado, trade wind, tramontana, typhoon, westerly

1054 Volcanoes and Earthquakes

You no more win a war than you can win an earthquake. **Jeannette Rankin**

(*adj*) *seismic*, *volcanic*

(*n*) earthquake, fault line, quake (*informal*), *seismic activity*, *seismic wave*, tremor, *volcanic activity*, *volcano*

1055 Erosion and Weathering

For water continually dropping will wear hard rocks hollow. **Plutarch**

(*n*) attrition, avalanche, erosion, landslide, *mudslide*, subsidence

1056 Geologic Features

It was a miracle of rare device,/A sunny pleasure-dome with caves of ice! **Samuel Taylor Coleridge**

(*n*) bowl, canyon, cave, cavern, cirque, col, *corrie* (*UK*), crater, crevasse, dale, defile, escarpment, floe, gap, *glaciated valley*, glen, gorge, grotto, gulch, gully, hollow, *iceberg*, *icecap*, outcrop, overhang, pothole, precipice, ravine, shelf, vale (*literary*), valley

1057 Stones, Rocks, and Boulders

When the torrent sweeps a man against a boulder, you must expect him to scream, and you need not be surprised if the scream is sometimes a theory. **Robert Louis Stevenson**

(*n*) boulder, cobble, cobblestone, gravel, magma, ore, pebble, rock, sarsen, *stone*

types of stones alabaster, basalt, chalk, conglomerate, flint, gneiss, granite, hornblende, lava, limestone, malachite, marble, pumice, quartzite, sandstone, schist, shale, slate, soapstone, tuff

1058 Erosion Products and Soil

An inch of soil is an inch of gold. **Vietnamese proverb**

(*adj*) alluvial, *sedimentary*

(*n*) clay, dirt, *glacial deposit*, grit, *loam*, moraine, mud, peat, *permafrost*, sand, scree, silt, sod, soil, *terminal moraine*, topsoil

1059   Earth Sciences

types of earth sciences geochemistry, geology, hydrogeology, mineralogy, orology, pedology, petrology, soil science, stratigraphy

Space and the Universe

1060   The Solar System and Astronomy

Astronomy teaches the correct use of the sun and the planets. **Stephen Leacock**

(*adj*) astral, astronomical, celestial, cosmic, extraterrestrial, galactic, intergalactic, interplanetary, interstellar, lunar, planetary, stellar

(*n*) astronomer, astronomy, *constellation*, cosmos, *heavenly body*, *Milky Way*, outer space, *planet*, *solar system*, space, *star*, star system, universe

1061   Heavenly Bodies

In my studies of astronomy and philosophy I hold this opinion about the universe, that the Sun remains fixed in the center of the circle of heavenly bodies, without changing its place. **Galileo**

types of constellations (of the northern hemisphere) Andromeda, Aquila, Aries, Auriga, Boötes, Camelopardalis, Cancer, Canes Venatici, Canis Minor, Cassiopeia, Cepheus, Coma Berenices, Corona Borealis, Cygnus, Delphinus, Draco, Equuleus, Gemini, Hercules, Hydra, Lacerta, Leo, Leo Minor, Lyra, Mynx, Ophiuchus, Orion, Pegasus, Perseus, Pisces, Polaris (Northern Star), Sagitta, Serpens, Taurus, Triangulum, Ursa Major, Ursa Minor, Virgo

types of constellations (of the southern hemisphere) Apus, Aquarius, Aquila, Ara, Canis Major, Capricornus, Carina, Centaurus, Cetus, Chamaeleon, Columba, Corona Australis, Corvus, Crater, Crux, Dorado, Eridanus, Fornax, Grus, Hydra, Hydrus, Indus, Lepus, Libra, Lupus, Monoceros, Musca, Octans, Ophiuchus, Orion, Pavo, Phoenix, Pictor, Piscis Austrinus, Puppis, Pyxis, Sagittarius, Scorpius, Sculptor, Serpens, Sextans, Triangulum Australe, Tuscana, Vela, Virgo, Volans

types of heavenly bodies asteroid, bolide, comet, falling star, fireball, meteor, meteorite, moon, planet, shooting star

types of planets Earth, Jupiter, Mars, Mercury, Neptune, Pluto, Saturn, Uranus, Venus

types of stars or star systems binary star, black hole, brown dwarf, dark star, dwarf star, galaxy, giant star, nebula, nova, pulsar, quasar, red giant, sun, supernova, white dwarf

1062   Space Travel and Exploration

Outer space is no place for a person of breeding. **Lady Violet Bonham-Carter**

(*n*) astronaut, *cosmonaut*, moonshot, spaceflight, *spaceman*, *space mission*, *space pilot*, *space travel*, *space traveler*, spacewalk, *spacewoman*

1063   Space Vehicles

I am a passenger on the spaceship, Earth. **R. Buckminster Fuller**

(*n*) spacecraft, spaceship

parts of a spacecraft booster rocket, bus, cabin, command module, drogue parachute, footpad, grain, life-support system, nose cone, plasma engine, pod, retropack, rocket engine, shroud, solar cell, stage, thruster

types of spacecraft biosatellite, lander, launch vehicle, lunar module, multistage rocket, orbital space station, orbiter, rocket, rocket ship, rover, satellite, space capsule, space probe, space rocket, space shuttle, space station, spacelab

See also VEHICLES (1145)

1064   Science Fiction

Science fiction is the search for a definition of mankind and his status in the universe which will stand in our advanced but confused state of knowledge. **Brian Aldiss**

(*n*) alien, *alien craft*, android, earthling, extraterrestrial, flying saucer, little green man (*humorous*), Martian, spaceship, starship, UFO

See also FICTION AND DRAMA (913)

Places and Human Geography

1065   Place

If time imposes on us its evolution, place also imposes upon us its reality. **Gamal Abdel Nasser**

(*n*) area, center, corner, domain, dominion, element, environment, environs, habitat, hinterland, hood (*slang*), landmark, locale, locality, location, *locus*, matrix, milieu, *neck of the woods*, neighborhood, place, point, position, power base, precinct, premises, property, purlieu, scene, seat, setting, site, situation, space, spacing, spot, stamping ground (*informal*), station, *stomping ground*, surroundings, territory, turf (*informal*), venue, vicinity, whereabouts, zone

See also GENERAL LOCATIONS (158)

1066   Nonexistent Places

The unrest which keeps the never stopping clock of metaphysics going is the thought that the non-existence of the world is just as possible as its existence. **William James**

(*n*) *arcadia*, cloud-cuckoo-land, dreamland, dream world, *El Dorado*, fairyland, *fantasy world*, land of make-believe, *never-never land*, paradise (*informal*), *Shangri-la*, *storyland*, utopia, wonderland

See also NONEXISTENT THINGS (23)

1067   Countries and Regions

If people behaved in the way nations do they would all be put in straitjackets. **Tennessee Williams**

(*adj*) aboriginal, *autochthonous*, domestic, indigenous, intercontinental, intergovernmental, international, local, multinational, native, overseas, regional, supranational, territorial, zonal (*adv*) abroad, nationally, nationwide, overseas

(*n*) *barrio*, canton, center, *city-state*, country, county, dependency, district, emirate, fatherland, heartland, home, homeland, land, motherland, nation, nationality, nation-state, native land, principality, province, provinces, region, republic, sector, *shire* (*UK*), soil, state

1068   Territories and Groups of Nations

Colonies are made to be lost. **Henri de Montherlant**

(*n*) bloc, colony, commonwealth, empire, enclave, power, protectorate, realm, satellite, superpower, territory

1069   Geographic Borders and Boundaries

The love of one's country is a natural thing. But why should love stop at the border? **Pablo Casals**

(*adj*) transcontinental, transnational

(*n*) border, borderland, borderline, boundary, dividing line, division, frontier, front line, state line, territory

1070   Human Settlements

If cities were built by the sound of music, then some edifices would appear to be constructed by grave, solemn tones; others to have danced forth to light, fantastic airs. **Nathaniel Hawthorne**

(*adj*) built-up, city, civic, inner-city, metropolitan, municipal, provincial, residential, suburban, urban, vicinal

(*n*) *bedroom community*, bivouac, borough, *burb* (*slang*), camp, capital, center, city, commune, community, *commuter belt* (*UK*), constituency, conurbation, *edge city* (*informal*), encampment, estate, hamlet, homestead, home town, *housing development*, housing estate, *housing project*, inner city, kibbutz, laager, land, metropolis, municipality, outpost, outskirts, parish, quarter, *residential area*, settlement, *shanty town*, suburb, suburbia, town, *town center*, township, urbanization, urban sprawl, village

1071   The Countryside and Outdoor Spaces

Fortunate too is the man who has come to know the gods of the countryside. **Virgil**

(*adj*) bucolic, countrified, cross-country, greenfield (*UK*), open, pastoral, rural, rustic, unindustrialized

(*n*) barnyard, campground, campsite, clearing, common, country, *countryside*, dell (*literary*), enclosure, estate, farmyard, field, firebreak, fireguard, geography, glade, grass, *greenbelt*, *greenfield site*, ground, grounds, holding, land, landscape, lea (*literary*), meadow, *meadowland*, *millpond*, national park, *nature preserve*, *nature reserve*, *paddock*, parkland, *pasturage*, pasture, *pastureland*, plantation, preserve, reservation, reserve, *safari park*, sanctuary, stockyard, sward, terrain, topography, turf, *wildlife park*, *wildlife refuge*, *wildlife sanctuary*, *wilds*

1072   Urban Outdoor Spaces

The Park throughout is a single work of art, and as such subject to the primary law of every work of art, namely, that it shall be framed upon a single, noble motive. **Frederick Law Olmsted**

(*n*) *adventure playground*, amusement park, arena, ballpark, bazaar, bomb site, *brownfield site*, campus, car-

nival, *carpark* (*UK*), concourse, court, courtyard, fairground, field, forecourt, funfair (*UK*), garden, *goods yard*, ground, industrial estate (*UK*), lido (*UK*), market, marketplace, *market square*, menagerie, park, parking, *parking lot*, piazza, pitch (*UK*), playground, playing field, plaza, quad (*informal*), quadrangle, racecourse, racetrack, raceway, *recreation area*, *recreation ground*, *school yard*, *science park*, scrapheap, *scrapyard* (*UK*), showground, souk, speedway, *sports field*, sports grounds, square, stadium, terrace, *theme park*, tip (*UK*), *town square*, *village square*, yard, zoo, *zoological gardens*

1073   Views and Outlooks

'Tis distance lends enchantment to the view,/And robes the mountain in its azure hue. **Thomas Campbell**

(*n*) horizon, outlook, panorama, perspective, prospect, scene, scenery, sight, skyline, view, vista

1074   Gardens

You may drive out nature with a pitchfork, yet she'll be constantly running back. **Horace**

(*n*) allotment (*UK*), backyard, *botanical garden*, bower, garden, yard

parts of a garden arbor, arboretum, bed, border, container, flowerbed, lawn, patio, pergola, planter, rockery, shrubbery, water feature, window box

types of gardens bog garden, community garden, container garden, cottage garden, cutting garden, flower garden, herb garden, Japanese garden, kitchen garden, knot garden, orchard, raised bed garden, rock garden, rose garden, vegetable garden, vegetable plot, water garden

1075   Agriculture and Farming

Man... must fit his actions into the rhythm of the seasons and the often mysterious requirements of organic life. **E. F. Schumacher**

(*adj*) agrarian, agricultural, *agronomic*, horticultural

(*n*) agribusiness, *agricultural science*, *agricultural show*, agriculture, *agroindustry*, *agronomy*, farm, farming, *farmland*, farmstead, horticulture, *market garden* (*UK*), ranch, smallholding (*UK*), spread, *truck farm*

Buildings and Structures

1076   Building and Architecture

Architecture is inhabited sculpture. **Constantin Brancusi**

(*adj*) *architectural*, purpose-built (*UK*), roofed, structural, terraced

(*n*) architecture, assembly, building, complex, construction, edifice, erection (*formal*), fabric, habitation, structure

types of 20th-century architecture art deco, Bauhaus, brutalist, Federation, minimalist, moderne, modernist, postmodern

types of pre-20th-century architecture art nouveau, Baroque, Byzantine, cinquecento, classical, colonial, Corinthian, Decorated, Doric, Elizabethan, Empire, Georgian, Gothic, Gothic revival, Ionic, Mission, Moorish, neoclassical, Norman, Palladian, perpendicular, Renaissance, rococo, Romanesque, Tudor, Victorian

1077   Building Materials

(*n*) *adobe*, beam, bitumen, board, *breeze block* (*UK*), brick, *bricks and mortar*, brickwork, cantilever, *cement*, *chipboard*, *cinder block*, *clapboard*, *concrete*, cornerstone, *fiberboard*, filler, flagstone, *floorboards*, flooring, *floor tiles*, girder, grout, insulator, joist, lumber, masonry, *mortar*, *parget*, *pargeting*, parquet, *parquetry*, paving, *paving slab*, *paving stone*, pebbledash (*UK*), piping, *plank*, *planking*, *plaster*, *plasterboard*, plasterwork, *plywood*, pointing (*UK*), *putty*, rafter, rib, roofing, roughcast, *sand*, *sealant*, sett, *shingle*, slat, *slate*, stave, stonework, strut, *stucco*, *stuccowork*, tar, Tarmac, *terrazzo*, thatch, *tile*, timber (*UK*), wainscot, wood

1078   Residential Buildings

(*n*) *apartment building*, *apartment house*, barracks, bivouac, block (*UK*), *block of flats* (*UK*), *casern*, condo (*informal*), co-op (*informal*), dorm (*informal*), dormitory, garrison, hall, hall of residence (*UK*), high-rise, house, *pup tent*, skyscraper, tenement, tent, *tower block* (*UK*), wigwam, *yurt*

types of apartments apartment, bed-sitter, condominium, dockominium, duplex, efficiency apartment, garden apartment, loft, penthouse, split-level, studio

types of houses brownstone, bungalow, cabana, cabin, cape, Cape Cod, chalet, chateau, colonial, contemporary, cottage, country house, detached house, Dutch colonial, farmhouse, hacienda, homestead, igloo, lodge, manor, manor house, mansion, mobile home, palace, pied-à-terre, raised ranch, ranch, ranch house, row house, semidetached, shack, starter home, timeshare, town house, villa, walk-up

See also ACCOMMODATIONS (855)

1079   Animal or Bird Accommodations

(*n*) cage, *den*, pen, run

types of den or nests aerie, burrow, drey, earth, form, hole, lair, lodge, nest, sett, tunnel, warren

types of pens or cages apiary, aquarium, aviary, beehive, birdcage, chicken coop, coop, corral, cowshed, doghouse, dovecote, henhouse, hutch, kennel, piggery, pigpen, pound, stable, stall, sty

1080   Ancillary Buildings

(*n*) *ancillary building*, annex, arcade, colonnade, extension, gallery, outbuilding

types of outbuildings barn, booth, carport, conservatory, cowshed, garage, garden shed, gatehouse, gazebo, greenhouse, guardhouse, hothouse, hut, kiosk, lean-to, lodge, orangery, outhouse, pavilion, privy (*informal*), sentry box, shed, stall, stand, summerhouse

1081   Public Buildings and Meeting Places

(*n*) assembly point, center, depot, gathering place, hangout (*informal*), haunt, home, rendezvous, terminal, terminus, waiting area

1082   Hotels, Restaurants, and Clubs

(*n*) bar, club, *hotel*, *restaurant*

types of bars or clubs bodega, casino, country club, joint (*slang*), nightclub, nightspot, roadhouse (*dated*), saloon, shebeen, speakeasy, tavern, wine bar

types of eating places bistro, brasserie, café, cafeteria, canteen, chophouse, coffee bar, coffee shop, commons, cybercafé, diner, drive-in, eatery, gastrodome, greasy spoon, hole-in-the-wall (*informal*), kaiten sushi restaurant, lunch counter, luncheonette, lunchroom, mess, pizzeria, refectory, roadside café, salad bar, snack bar, steakhouse, sushi bar, tearoom, trattoria, truck stop

types of hotels B & B (*informal*), bed and breakfast, boarding house, boutique hotel, capsule hotel, hostel, inn, lodge, motel, pension, rooming house, youth hostel

1083   Retail Outlets

(*n*) arcade, emporium, garage, parlor, petrol station (*UK*), plaza, retailer, *retail outlet*, *retail store*, salon, services, shop, *shopping arcade*, *shopping center*, *shopping complex*, shopping mall, showroom, store

types of food outlets bakery, bodega, butcher's, candy store, deli, delicatessen, drive-through, farmers' market, grocer's, grocery store, refreshment stand, supermarket, takeout

types of retail outlets bazaar, beauty parlor, big-box store, bookstore, boutique, chain store, convenience store, corner store, covered market, department store, dime store, dispensary, druggist, drugstore, duty-free, filling station, flea market, garden center, gas station, general store, hair salon, hardware store, hypermarket, kiosk, mall, mart, mom-and-pop store, newsstand, nursery, pharmacy, post office, salesroom, service station, supercenter, superstore, thrift shop, warehouse

1084   Buildings for Public Entertainment

(*n*) amphitheater, *amusement arcade*, arcade, *assembly hall*, *assembly room*, auditorium, bandstand, baths, *big top*, bowl, bullring, cabaret, casino, *cinema* (*UK*), *circus*, *concert hall*, dive (*informal*), *exhibition hall*, fleapit (*UK*), gym (*informal*), gymnasium, *honky-tonk* (*slang*), *lecture hall*, *lecture room*, *lecture theater*, marquee, multiplex, museum, *music hall*, *opera house*, *planetarium*, playhouse, rink, solarium, spa, *sports hall*, *sports stadium*, swimming pool, theater

1085   Religious Buildings

(*n*) cloister, convent, friary, *hermitage*, *house of God*, house of worship, manse, meetinghouse, monastery, nunnery, parsonage, *place of worship*, priory, rectory, sanctum, vicarage

types of churches abbey, basilica, cathedral, chapel, meeting house, minster, tabernacle, temple

types of places of worship church, gurdwara, mosque, shrine, synagogue, temple

1086   Parts of Religious Buildings

(*n*) altar, *apse*, *chancel*, *chantry*, *clerestory*, cloister, crypt, *nave*, spire, steeple, *transept*, vault

See also RELIGIOUS OBJECTS (779)

1087   Industrial Buildings

(*n*) *cooling tower*, factory, *industrial site*, *industrial unit*, *installation*, plant, works

types of factories assembly plant, brewery, cannery, distillery, forge, foundry, machine shop, maquiladora, mill, mint, pottery, sawmill, smithy, steelworks, sweatshop, water mill, workshop

types of industrial sites business park, coalfield, coalmine, colliery, depot, dock, dockyard, enterprise zone, garage, gasworks, industrial park, industrial zone, lab (*informal*), laboratory, mine, nuclear power plant, nuclear reprocessing plant, office block, oil rig, pit, pithead, power plant, quarry, refinery, rig, shipyard, slaughterhouse, tannery, winery

See also ENERGY STORAGE AND GENERATION (1163)

1088   Stores and Storage Buildings

(*n*) *Aladdin's cave*, armory, *meat locker*, repository, stock, stockpile, stockroom, storage, store, *storehouse*, *storeroom*

types of storage spaces arms depot, arsenal, attic, barn, basement, bunker, cellar, depository, depot, dump, elevator, garage, garbage dump, gasometer, grain elevator, granary, hangar, hayloft, hold, landfill, larder, loft, luggage compartment, magazine, morgue, mortuary, pantry, shed, silo, strongroom, treasury, warehouse, water tower, weapon store, woodshed

See also STORE AND KEEP (453)

1089   Ancient Manmade Structures

(*n*) dolmen, gallows, megalith, monolith, scaffold, standing stone, stocks, *stone circle*

1090   Fortresses and Fortifications

(*n*) bastion, castle, citadel, defenses, earthwork, fastness (*archaic or literary*), fort, fortification, fortress, pillbox, redoubt (*literary*), stockade, stronghold

1091   Parts of Fortresses

(*n*) barbican, battlements, *parapet*, portcullis, rampart

1092   Monuments

(*n*) cairn, cenotaph, mausoleum, memorial, *memorial stone*, monument, obelisk, tombstone, *war memorial*

See also BURIAL PLACES AND ACCESSORIES (930)

1093   Safe Buildings or Places

(*n*) aerie, asylum, bolthole, bunker, haven, hideaway, hideout, hidey-hole (*informal*), hiding place, high ground, hostel, lee, oasis, *place of safety*, refuge, retreat, safe haven, safe house, safe place, sanctuary, sanctum, shelter

1094   Buildings for Confining People

(*n*) borstal (*UK*), cell, *clink* (*dated slang*), *cooler* (*slang*), *correctional facility*, *detention center*, *detention facility*, dungeon, guardhouse, *house of correction*, jail, lockup, *maximum-security prison*, *medium-security prison*, oubliette, *pen* (*slang*), *penal colony*, *penal complex*, *penal institution*, penitentiary, *pokey* (*slang*), prison, *prison cell*,

reformatory, *remand home* (*UK*), *secure unit* (*UK*), *slammer* (*slang*), state school (*informal*), *supermax prison*, *young offenders' institution* (*UK*), *youth custody centre* (*UK*)

See also CAPTIVITY AND LOSS OF FREEDOM (248), THE POLICE, ARREST, AND PRETRIAL PROCEEDINGS (818)

1095   Parts of a Building

parts of a building balcony, buttress, chimney, colonnade, doorway, elevation, elevator, escalator, exterior, façade, fire escape, frame, frontage, gable, guttering, landing, paternoster, porch, roof, smokestack, soffit, stairwell, veranda, vestibule, wall, window, wing

1096   Alcoves, Cubicles, and Compartments

(*n*) alcove, bay, booth, box, cabin, cockpit, compartment, cubbyhole, cubicle, fireplace, fireside, hearth, inglenook, loge, *loggia*, niche, nook, recess, stall

1097   Types of Rooms

(*n*) airlock, chamber, facilities, room

types of rooms in public buildings antechamber, anteroom, ballroom, banqueting hall, boardroom, bunkhouse, cell, classroom, dining hall, dormitory, dressing room, entrance hall, foyer, gallery, games room, hall, lavatory, library, lobby, lounge, meeting room, men's room, office, operating room, powder room, reception room, refectory, restroom, schoolroom, stateroom, vault, waiting room, ward, washroom

types of rooms in the home atelier, attic, bathroom, bedchamber (*archaic or literary*), bedroom, boudoir, closet, day room, den, dining room, drawing room, family room, garret, guestroom, kitchen, kitchenette, laundry room, living room, loft, parlor, playroom, rec room, recreation room, salon, scullery, sitting room, sleeping quarters, spare room, study, sunroom, toilet, utility room

1098   Stages, Platforms, and Raised Areas

(*n*) balcony, catwalk, dais, *lanai*, platform, podium, rostrum, stage, *sun deck*, veranda, *viewing platform*, viewpoint

1099   Towers

(*n*) belfry, *bell tower*, *campanile*, listening post, lookout, *lookout tower*, minaret, *observation tower*, observatory, pylon, rotunda, turret, vantage point, watchtower

1100   Windows

parts of a window ledge, pane, sill, window ledge, windowpane, windowsill

types of windows bay window, casement, dormer window, fanlight, French window, lancet window, picture window, porthole, rose window, sash window, skylight, transom

1101   Doors and Access Points

(*n*) access, aisle, arch, archway, atrium, check-in, corridor, door, doorplate, doorstep, doorway, entrance, entrance hall, entry, exit, foyer, front door, gate, gateway, hallway, ingress (*formal*), lobby, mouth, portal (*literary*), portico, *sliding doors*, threshold, tollbooth, tollgate, trap door, turnstile, vestibule, wicket

1102   Stairs and Stories

(*n*) balcony, basement, *elevator*, *entresol*, escalator, fire escape, floor, gallery, ladder, landing, *lower ground floor*, mezzanine, *mezzanine floor*, paternoster, stair, *staircase*, stairs, *stairway*, stairwell, step, stile, story, tier

1103   Roofs, Roof Parts, and Ceilings

(*n*) *ceiling*, *cornice*, *coving*, cupola, dado, *dado rail*, dome, eaves, flue, funnel, mansard, *roof space*, rooftop, rose, stack, vault

1104   Walls and Partitions

(*n*) bulkhead, divider, partition, purdah, screen, separator, wall

See also BARRIERS (1113)

1105   Communication Networks

Civilization is a movement, not a condition; it is a voyage, not a harbor. **Arnold Toynbee**

(*adj*) arterial, intercity, mainline (*UK*)

(*n*) communications, infrastructure

See also TRAVEL: WAYS OF TRAVELING (320), TRANSPORTATION, TRANSPORTERS, AND CARGOS (322)

1106   Roads

(*n*) *carpool lane*, carriageway (*UK*), circuit, *fast lane*, pavement, ramp (*UK*), road, roadway, route, *slow lane* (*UK*), switchback, thoroughfare, *through road* (*UK*), *through street*, *traffic lane*, way

types of highways artery, avenue, beltway, boulevard, bypass, divided highway, expressway, freeway, highway, interstate, limited-access highway, main road, overpass, parkway, speedway, superhighway, throughway, thruway, toll road, trunk route, turnpike

types of secondary roads access road, access strip, alley, alleyway, backstreet, blind alley, byroad, byway, corniche, cul-de-sac, dead end, dirt track, driveway, esplanade, lane, parade, path, service road, side street, slip road, street, track

1107   Railroads

(*n*) line, main line, railhead, *rail line*, *rail network*, railroad, *railroad station*, *rail route*, *rail terminal*, *rail transportation system*

parts of a train box car, cabin, caboose, car, coach, compartment, dining car, freight car, locomotive, luggage compartment, observation car, Pullman, sleeper, sleeping car, smoker, smoking car, smoking compartment, steam engine, tank engine, wagon

types of railroads cable railroad, monorail, streetcar line, subway, underground

types of rail vehicles cable car, funicular, locomotive, steam engine, streetcar, train

1108   Waterways and Seaways

(*n*) anchorage, berth, breakwater, canal, channel, dock, dockside, dockyard, floodgate, jetty, landing, landing stage, mooring, pier, quay, quayside, sea lane, seaway, *shipping canal*, *shipping lane*, wharf

1109   Airways

(*n*) aerodrome (*UK*), airfield, airport, airspace, airstrip, airway, helideck, helipad, landing field, landing strip, runway

1110   Pathways

(*adj*) pedestrianized, *traffic-free*

(*n*) boardwalk, bridle path, *bridleway* (*UK*), duckboard, footpath, footway, gangway, passage, passageway, path, pathway, pavement (*UK*), *pedestrian precinct* (*UK*), prom (*UK informal*), promenade, ramp, run, sidewalk, towpath, track, trail, walkway, wayside

1111   Watercourses

(*n*) aqueduct, canal, catheter, cesspit, channel, chute, conduit, culvert, dike, ditch, drain, duct, *fosse*, furrow, gutter, guttering, hose, hosepipe, intake, moat, outfall, pipe, pipeline, raceway, *runnel*, sewer, sluice, standpipe, storm sewer, trench, tube, tubing, *waste pipe*, watercourse, *water pipe*

1112   Bridges, Tunnels, Crossings, and Junctions

(*n*) *bridge*, catacomb, catwalk, causeway, *center island*, cloverleaf, corner, crossing, crossroads, *crosswalk*, ford, interchange, intersection, level crossing (*UK*), pedestrian crossing, pelican crossing (*UK*), roundabout (*UK*), subway (*UK*), T-junction, *traffic circle*, *traffic island*, *traffic junction*, tunnel, turning (*UK*), turnoff, *underpass*, *zebra crossing* (*UK*)

types of bridges aqueduct, arch bridge, Bailey bridge, bascule bridge, beam bridge, cable-stayed bridge, cantilever bridge, drawbridge, footbridge, gangplank, overpass, pontoon bridge, suspension bridge, swing bridge, viaduct, walkway

1113   Barriers

(*n*) bank, barrage, barricade, barrier, blockade, bulwark, *central reservation* (*UK*), checkpoint, cordon, dam, dike, embankment, fence, fencing, groin, jump, levee, *median strip*, *paling*, *palisade*, rail, railing, ring-fence (*UK*), roadblock, sea wall, *sluicegate*, stockade, trellis, windbreak, windscreen

See also WALLS AND PARTITIONS (1104)

Technology

1114 Machinery

Technology is the knack of so arranging the world that we don't have to experience it. **Max Frisch**

(*adj*) automated, automatic, bionic, mechanized, push-button, robotic, windup

(*n*) automation, instrumentation, machinery, mechanization, robotics, technology

1115 Devices

(*n*) apparatus, contraption, contrivance, device, equipment, gadget, gizmo (*informal*), hardware, implement, installation, instrument, invention, kit, machine, mechanism, robot, sensor, spinner, tackle, tool, utensil

1116 Machines and Machine Parts

(*n*) automaton, crane, derrick, dispenser, hoist, machine, vending machine, winch, windlass

1117 Household Appliances

types of appliances blender, chiminea, coffeemaker, dishwasher, food processor, garbage disposal, grill, iron, juicer, microwave, microwave oven, minibar, mixer, percolator, potbelly stove, range, rotisserie, smoke alarm, smoke detector, spin dryer, stove, television, toaster, tumble dryer, washing machine

See also TABLEWARE, FLATWARE, AND KITCHENWARE (861), CONTAINERS, RECEPTACLES, AND PACKAGING (1245)

1118 Parts of Machines and Tools

(*n*) adapter, *armature*, attachment, button, circuitry, clock, clockwork, cog, cogwheel, control panel, controls, cutout, damper, detector, dial, dimmer, fulcrum, gasket, *gearwheel*, hand, handle, indicator, *instrument panel*, key, keyboard, knob, lever, machinery, moving parts, needle, *pawl*, pedal, pendulum, pivot, pointer, pulley, ratchet, regulator, safety valve, separator, *shock absorber*, spacer, spare part, spigot, spline, spring, sprocket, *sprocket wheel*, stopcock, switch, thermostat, toggle, tooth, treadle, valve

1119 Hand Tools

(*n*) broom, brush, *mop*

types of carpentry tools awl, bradawl, drill, hammer, jigsaw, mallet, plane, sander, saw, vise

types of cosmetic tools comb, emery board, hairbrush, nailbrush, nail clippers, nail file, nail scissors, razor, shaving brush, tweezers

types of general tools bellows, blowtorch, crowbar, file, grease gun, jack, jimmy, lathe, machine tool, pincers, pliers, plumb line, plunger, poker, pump, punch, rasp, screwdriver, socket wrench, soldering iron, spade, tongs, trowel, wrench

types of medical instruments forceps, lancet, probe, scalpel, speculum, stethoscope, syringe

1120 Cutting Tools

types of cutting tools ax, billhook, chisel, chopper, clippers, cutter, hatchet, hoe, knife, machete, pickax, plow, razor blade, scissors, scythe, shears, sickle

types of knives bread knife, butcher knife, carving knife, clasp knife, cleaver, jackknife, paperknife, penknife, pocketknife, switchblade, table knife

1121 Spoons, Scoops, and Shovels

(*n*) dipper, *ladle*, scoop, shovel, spade

1122 Photography and Photographic Equipment

(*n*) close-up, mug shot, photo, photocopy, photograph, print, scan, shot, snapshot, transparency

parts of a camera autofocus, diaphragm, exposure meter, film, filter, fisheye lens, flash, lens, lens cap, rangefinder, shutter, telephoto lens, viewfinder, zoom lens

types of photographic equipment box camera, camera, darkroom, developer, disc camera, enlarger, microfiche, microfilm, movie camera, pinhole camera, printer, projector, reflex camera, single-lens reflex, speed camera, tripod, twin-lens reflex

types of video equipment camcorder, DVD, palmcorder, VCR, video camera, videocassette, videocassette recorder, videodisk, video recorder, videotape, videotape recorder

1123 Measuring Devices

(*n*) *counter*, gauge, measure, measuring device, meter, weathercock

types of measuring devices altimeter, anemometer, aneroid barometer, balance, barograph, barometer, calipers, clock, compass, dipstick, dividers, dropper, Geiger counter, level, measuring tape, micrometer, odometer, pipette, protractor, quadrant, rule, scale, speedometer, statoscope, tachometer, tape, tape measure, theodolite, thermometer, weather vane, weighing machine, weighing scale, wind gauge, windsock

1124 Optical Instruments

types of optical instruments astronomical telescope, binoculars, electron microscope, laser, magnifying glass, microscope, optometer, periscope, spyglass, telescope

1125 Glasses and Spectacles

(*n*) glasses, goggles, specs (*informal*), spectacles

types of glasses bifocals, dark glasses, eyeglasses (*formal*), monocle, pince-nez, shades (*informal*), sunglasses

1126 Clocks and Timers

(*n*) *chronometer*, clock, *metronome*, timepiece, *timer*

types of clocks alarm, alarm clock, clock radio, cuckoo clock, digital clock, grandfather clock, hourglass, pocket watch, quartz clock, stopwatch, sundial, watch, wristwatch

See also TIMES OF DAY (87)

1127　Computers and Computing

The rise of computers...is forcing machinery to adapt to our idiosyncratic humanity. **Thomas A. Stewart**

(*adj*) electronic, off-line, online, *real-time*, virtual, wired (*informal*)

(*n*) *assembler, computer, computer graphics, computer modeling, computer processing, computer program, computer programmer, computer science, computer scientist, computer technology, crash,* cybernetics, data processing, information processing, information retrieval, information technology, IT, multimedia, programmer, programming, *software, software design, software development, systems analyst,* virtual reality, *VR*

(*v*) access, *crash,* get into, initialize, reboot, toggle, unzip, zip

types of computer features bit, bitmap, buffer, byte, cache, cursor, desktop, directory, emoticon, folder, pixel, platform, smiley, subdirectory, wallpaper, window, word

types of computers adder, calculator, handheld computer, laptop, mainframe, microcomputer, minicomputer, notebook, palmtop, PC, PDA, personal computer, personal digital assistant, personal organizer, supercomputer, tablet computer, workstation

types of hardware accelerator card, accumulator, backspace, bus, CD burner, CD writer, CD-ROM, central processing unit, chip, console, CPU, disk, disk drive, diskette, DVD, firmware, floppy disk, FPU, hard disk, integrated circuit, interface, joystick, keyboard, memory, microchip, microprocessor, modem, monitor, motherboard, mouse, network, numeric keypad, parallel, platform, port, printed circuit, printer, processor, RAM, readout, ROM, scanner, screen, serial, server, simulator, sound card, space bar, terminal, touch screen, trackball, VDT, video display terminal, visual display unit

types of software application, browser, CAD, codec, computer-aided design, cookie, database, emulator, firmware, freeware, GUI, interface, macro, OCR, operating system, OS, patch, program, screensaver, search engine, shareware, simulator, spell checker, spreadsheet, virus, word processor, worm

1128　The Internet

Computer networks have a tremendous capacity...to bring people together by extending the already diverse and complex ties that people have among themselves. **Philip A. Agre**

(*n*) *ASP, bandwidth, bot, browser, bulletin board, chat room, click rate, cookie,* cyberspace, *cyber warfare, DNS, domain, DOS,* e-mail, *encryption, e-zine,* home page, *HTML,* information superhighway, *instant messaging, Internet, ISP,* newsgroup, *portal, robot, router, search engine, service provider, spyware, superhighway, syllaweb, the Net* (*informal*), *the Web* (*informal*), *URL, wap,* Web bug, Webcam, Webcast, *web conferencing* (*UK*), *Web conferencing, web folio* (*UK*), *Web folio, Webhead* (*slang*), *Webisode, Webliography, Weblish, Web log, Weblogger, Webmaster, Web page, Webphone, Web ring, Web site, Webstorefront, Webzine, World Wide Web*

(*v*) *browse, chat, decrypt,* download, encrypt, *flame, hack, ping,* spam, *surf, Web-enable*

1129　E-Commerce

(*adj*) *B2B, B2C, brick-and-mortar, BtoB, clicks-and-mortar, P2P*

(*n*) *access profile, cybermall, cybermarketing, cybermediary, digital cash, digital signature, e-business, e-commerce, electronic cash, electronic signature, e-tailing, infomediary, m-commerce, online banking, payment gateway, point and click agreement, secure electronic transaction, smart card*

1130　Telecommunications

(*n*) bleeper (*UK*), *SMS, telecommunications, video-conferencing, videolink*

types of telecommunications equipment answering machine, antenna, beeper (*informal*), bug (*informal*), cable, cellphone, cellular phone, e-mail, fax, intercom, landline, mast, modem, netphone, pager, payphone, phone, phonecard, receiver, satellite, satellite dish, switchboard, telephone, telex, transmitter, videophone, voice mail, walkie-talkie, WAP, wiretap

See also TELEPHONE, PAGE, AND TEXT (681), TELEPHONE COMMUNICATION (48)

1131　Textiles and Threads

(*n*) catgut, cloth, fabric, fiber, filament, *leather,* material, *natural fiber,* purl, textile, thread, yarn

1132　Fabrics

types of fabrics from animals alpaca, angora, astrakhan, baize, bearskin, brocade, camel hair, cashmere, chenille, crepe de Chine, felt, flannel, fur, gabardine, horsehair, jersey, lambswool, leather, loden, mohair, shahtoosh, silk, snakeskin, taffeta, tweed, twill, vicuna, wool, worsted

types of fabrics from plants burlap, calico, canvas, chambray, cheesecloth, chintz, corduroy, cotton, cretonne, damask, denim, drill, flannelette, gauze, gingham, grosgrain, hessian, lawn, linen, madras, moleskin, muslin, organdy, poplin, sacking, sailcloth, seersucker, tarpaulin, terry, terry cloth, ticking, velour, velvet, voile

types of leather buckskin, calf, calfskin, chamois, hide, kid, morocco, patent leather, pigskin, rawhide, sheepskin, suede

types of synthetic fabrics acrylic, chiffon, crepe, fishnet, fleece, lamé, moquette, nylon, percale, polyester, PVC, rayon, sateen, satin, spandex, tulle, viscose

1133　Plant Materials

types of fibers cane, coconut matting, coir, jute, kapok, matting, raffia, ramie, rattan, seagrass, sisal, straw, wicker

1134　Plastics

types of plastics acetate, celluloid, epoxide, latex, melamine, neoprene, polyethylene, polystyrene, polyurethane, vinyl

1135 Pottery

types of pottery bone china, ceramic, china, delft, earthenware, enamel, faience, Limoges, Meissen, porcelain, Sèvres, stoneware, terra cotta

1136 Glass

types of glass bulletproof glass, crystal, cut glass, ground glass, lead glass, optical glass, plate glass, quartz glass, safety glass, stained glass, Venetian glass

1137 Electronics and Electrics

(*adj*) electrified, electronic

(*n*) anode, control, controller, electrode, electronics, limiter, plug (*informal*), point (*UK*), power line, power point (*UK*), resistor, rheostat, wire

1138 Acoustics

(*adj*) acoustic, *high-fidelity*, mono, *monophonic*, sonic, soundproof, stereophonic, wired (*slang*)

(*n*) acoustics, atmospherics, damper, mono, *soundproofing*, stereo

1139 Audio Equipment

parts of audio equipment audiotape, cartridge, cassette, CD, compact disc, DVD, earphone, earpiece, handset, headphones, headpiece, headset, loudspeaker, microphone, record, speaker, stylus, tone arm, turntable

types of audio equipment amp, amplifier, boom box, cassette recorder, CD player, compact disc player, gramophone (*dated*), hi-fi (*dated*), horn, jukebox, megaphone, PA, personal stereo, phonograph, preamplifier, radio, radio set, record player, sound system, stereo, stereo system, tape deck, tape player, tape recorder, transistor, tuner, wireless (*dated*)

See also RECORDINGS AND PLAYERS (911)

1140 Signaling

(*n*) *alarm, alarm bell, all clear signal*, bell, buzzer, fire alarm, foghorn, Klaxon, red light, reveille, siren, tattoo, tocsin

1141 Navigation

(*adj*) navigational

(*n*) bearing, latitude, longitude, map reading, navigation, navigator, orientation, radar, reference

1142 Heating, Refrigeration, and Ventilation

(*n*) aeration, *air-circulation system*, air conditioning, *air-cooling system*, *air duct*, *air exchange system*, airing, *central heating*, cooler, heating, refrigeration, *solar heating*, *space heating*, ventilation, *ventilation system*, ventilator

types of cooling appliances air conditioner, air cooler, air exchanger, deepfreeze, freezer, fridge, icebox, refrigerator

types of heating appliances boiler, electric fire, furnace, heater, heat pump, immersion heater, oil burner, quartz heater, radiator, space heater, storage heater

1143 Engines and Hydraulics

(*adj*) mechanical, motor, motorized

(*n*) engine, motor, *turbine*

1144 Parts of an Engine

parts of an engine alternator, ball bearing, cam, camshaft, cog, cogwheel, coil, crank, crankshaft, cylinder, distributor, gasket, gear, gearbox, gearing, lever, manifold, oil pan, piston, pump, radiator, seal, shaft, solenoid, spark plug, starter, tappet, valve

1145 Vehicles

The car has become the carapace, the protective and aggressive shell, of urban and suburban man. **Marshall McLuhan**

(*n*) traffic, transport

types of commercial or industrial vehicles bulldozer, cab, combine, combine harvester, digger, dump truck, earthmover, hearse, pickup, semitrailer, snowplow, steamroller, tanker, taxi, taxicab, tow truck, tractor, transporter, truck, van, wrecker, yellow cab

types of leisure vehicles bobsled, camper, chair lift, dogsled, dune buggy, go-cart, land yacht, luge, mobile home, motor home, RV, sled, sleigh, snowmobile, toboggan

types of military vehicles amphibian, armored car, jeep, tank

types of public service vehicles ambulance, bus, firetruck, garbage truck, jitney, minibus, police car, prowl car, shuttle, squad car

See also TRAVEL: JOURNEYS AND TRIPS (318), COMMUNICATION NETWORKS (1105), SPACE VEHICLES (1063)

1146 Internal Parts of a Vehicle

types of controls accelerator, brake, choke, clutch, gearshift, horn, pedal, rev counter, speedometer, steering wheel, wheel

types of internal features back seat, booster seat, cab, car seat, child seat, dashboard, driver's seat, glove compartment, headrest, passenger seat, rearview mirror, seat belt

1147 External Parts of a Vehicle

parts of an external structure airfoil, axle, bodywork, chassis, coachwork, fender, fin, grille, hood, hull, spoiler, sunroof, tailgate, trunk, windshield

types of external features blinker, brake light, bumper, exhaust pipe, fog light, headlight, hubcap, kick-start, license plate, luggage rack, mud flap, mudguard, muffler, parking light, plate, side mirror, splashguard, stoplight, taillight, tire, wheel, windshield wiper

1148 Aircraft

(*n*) aeroplane (*UK*), aircraft, airline, airplane, balloon, plane

parts of an aircraft aileron, air brake, autopilot, cabin, cockpit, ejection seat, fin, flight deck, flight recorder, fuselage, jet engine, joystick, landing gear, nose cone, nose wheel, propeller, rotor, rudder, tail, tailplane, tail rotor, turbofan, turbojet, turboprop, undercarriage, wing

types of civil aircraft airliner, airship, autogiro, biplane, blimp, dirigible, executive jet, glider, hang glider, helicopter, jet, light plane, monoplane, paraglider, seaplane, skiplane, STOL, ultralight, zeppelin

types of military aircraft bomber, convertiplane, fighter, fighter-bomber, helicopter gunship, stealth bomber, transport, VTOL

1149 Bikes, Cars, and Carriages

(*n*) *auto* (*informal*), *automobile*, barrow, beater (*informal*), bicycle, bike (*informal*), car, carriage, *clunker* (*informal*), jalopy (*dated informal*), perambulator (*UK formal*), pram (*UK*), pushcart, pushchair (*UK*), rattletrap (*informal*), *rust bucket* (*informal humorous*), stroller, *taxicab*, *trolley*, *wagon*

parts of a bike brake, chain, crossbar, derailleur, fender, fork, frame, handlebars, pedal, reflector, seat, spoke, tire, wheel

types of bikes boneshaker, dirt bike, exercise bike, moped, motor scooter, mountain bike, racing bike, rickshaw, scooter, scrambler, tandem bicycle, ten-speed, three-wheeler, trail bike, tricycle, two-wheeler, unicycle

types of cars all-terrain vehicle, compact, convertible, coupe, dragster, four-by-four, hatchback, hot rod (*slang*), limo, limousine, minivan, off-roader (*informal*), racing car, roadster (*dated*), runabout, sedan, sport utility vehicle, sports car, station wagon, stock car, subcompact, SUV, three-wheeler, van

types of wagons or carriages barouche, brougham, buggy, cart, chariot, coach, Conestoga wagon, covered wagon, dray, landau, landaulet, phaeton, prairie schooner, stagecoach, trap, troika, tumbril

1150 Ships and Boats

(*n*) boat, craft, ship, vessel

types of historical vessels clipper, flagship, galleon, galley, Indiaman, longboat, longship, man-of-war, tall ship, windjammer

types of military vessels aircraft carrier, battle cruiser, battleship, cruiser, cutter, destroyer, frigate, gunboat, minesweeper, PT boat, submarine, warship

types of motor vessels barge, cabin cruiser, canal boat, coaster, container ship, cutter, dredger, factory ship, ferry, ferryboat, freighter, houseboat, hovercraft, hydrofoil, icebreaker, launch, lifeboat, lighter, lightship, motorboat, powerboat, speedboat, steamboat, steamer, tanker, trawler, tug, tugboat

types of sailing vessels bark, brig, brigantine, catamaran, catboat, dhow, felucca, junk, ketch, sailboat, schooner, sloop, smack, trimaran, yacht

types of small vessels canoe, dinghy, dory, dugout, gondola, kayak, life raft, pirogue, punt, raft, rowboat, sampan, scull, skiff

1151 Parts of a Ship or Boat

(*n*) blade, *boat hook*, oar, paddle, scull

parts of a sailing vessel boom, bowsprit, fore-and-aft sail, gaff, jib, mainsail, mainstay, mast, mizzen, pennant, sheet, shroud, spanker, spinnaker, topsail

parts of a ship or boat bilge, bow, bridge, cabin, capstan, crow's nest, deck, engine room, fo'c's'le, galley, helm, hold, hull, keel, oarlock, outboard motor, out-

rigger, poop, prow, rudder, stateroom, stern, superstructure, tiller

1152 Groups of Vehicles

(*n*) armada, caravan, convoy, fleet, flotilla, motorcade

1153 Drivers

(*n*) *aeronaut*, aviator, chauffeur, driver, motorist, *pilot*, teamster, *truck driver*, *trucker*

See also MESSENGERS AND COURIERS (852)

1154 Weapons

Every gun that is made, every warship launched, every rocket fired signifies, in the final sense, a theft from those who hunger and are not fed, those who are cold and are not clothed.
Dwight D. Eisenhower

(*n*) armaments, arms, artillery, firepower, guns, munitions, ordnance, *projectile*, small arms, weapon, weaponry

1155 Explosives

types of explosive material dynamite, gelignite, gunpowder, napalm, nitroglycerin, plastic explosive, propellant, TNT

types of explosive weapons A-bomb, antiballistic missile, atomic bomb, ballistic missile, bomb, booby trap, cruise missile, depth charge, firebomb, guided missile, hand grenade, hydrogen bomb, mine, missile, Molotov cocktail, nail bomb, neutron bomb, nuclear missile, nuclear warhead, nuclear weapon, pipe bomb, smart bomb, smoke bomb, time bomb, torpedo, warhead

types of fireworks cherry bomb, firecracker, girandole, pinwheel, rocket, Roman candle, sparkler, squib, torpedo

1156 Weapons for Shooting

(*n*) *bow*, firearm, gun, *shooter* (*informal*)

types of bows crossbow, Cupid's bow, longbow

types of guns air pistol, air rifle, antiaircraft gun, automatic, bazooka, blunderbuss, cannon, carbine, flamethrower, handgun, howitzer, machine gun, magnum, mortar, musket, pistol, revolver, rifle, sawed-off shotgun, semiautomatic, shotgun, submachine gun, Tommy gun (*informal*)

1157 Swords and Knives

types of swords or knives battleax, bayonet, bowie knife, broadsword, claymore, cutlass, dagger, dirk, foil, machete, poleax, rapier, saber, scimitar, skean, stiletto, swordstick, tomahawk

1158 Blunt Instruments and Whips

(*n*) birch, cat-o'-nine-tails, club, lash, switch, whip

types of clubs baton, billy club, blackjack, bludgeon, cudgel, mace, nightstick, shillelagh, truncheon

See also WHIP AND CLUB (417)

1159 Projectiles

types of projectiles arrow, arrowhead, assegai, bolt, boomerang, brickbat, buckshot, bullet, cannonball, dart, dumdum bullet, grenade, harpoon, javelin, lance, pellet, plastic bullet, rubber bullet, shell, shot, slug, spear

1160 Describing Technology

(*adj*) cordless, high-tech, *hi-tech*, industrial, pilot, pneumatic, radio-controlled, self-acting, space-age, state-of-the-art, technical, technological, up-to-date

Energy, Fuels, and Foods

1161 Energy

Energy is Eternal Delight. **William Blake**

(*n*) combustion, energy, force, friction, gravitation, gravity, impetus, impulse, magnet, magnetism, momentum, pressure, propulsion, rubbing, suction, thrust, torque, torsion, traction, wave

1162 Energy Sources

(*adj*) atomic, electric, nuclear, radioactive

(*n*) electricity, firewood, fuel, *gasoline*, kerosene, *paraffin oil* (*UK*), *petrol* (*UK*), *petroleum*, radiation, radioactivity, tinder

1163 Energy Storage and Generation

(*n*) *battery*, dynamo, *generator*, reactor

See also INDUSTRIAL BUILDINGS (1087)

1164 Light

(*n*) beam, candlelight, daylight, firelight, flare, flash, glare, glitter, glow, illumination, illuminations, incandescence, irradiation, *light*, lighting, moonbeam, nimbus, radiance, ray, scintillation, starlight, sunbeam, sunlight, sunshine, twinkle

types of lights arc lamp, chandelier, flashlight, floodlight, fluorescent lamp, footlights, headlight, hurricane lamp, lamp, lamppost, lantern, LED, light bulb, neon light, nightlight, penlight, searchlight, spotlight, standard lamp, streetlamp, streetlight, striplight, sunlamp, traffic light

See also LIGHT EMISSION (368), LIGHTING (862), DESCRIBING LIGHT (1228)

1165 Fire, Flammability, and Burning

Look not for fire in Hell, each man brings his own fire. **Yasar Kemal**

(*adj*) ablaze, aflame, alight, blazing, burning, combustible, fireproof, flameproof, flaming, flammable, incendiary, incombustible, in flames, inflammable, nonflammable, on fire, singed, *smoldering*, vaporous

(*n*) beacon, blaze, bonfire, brazier, *brushfire*, burner, conflagration, fire, fireball, flame, *forest fire*, forge, furnace, *incineration*, incinerator, inferno, kiln, pyre, *pyrotechnics*

(*v*) blaze, burn, burn down, burn up, *burst into flames*, *catch fire*, *catch light*, char, cremate, fire up, flame, flare,

frizzle, go up, go up in smoke, gut, ignite, incinerate, kindle, let off (*UK*), light, put a match to, scald, scorch, sear, set alight, set fire to, *set light to* (*UK*), set on fire, singe, smoke, smolder, stoke, stoke up, torch (*slang*)

See also DESTRUCTION AND DEMOLITION (359), WORSEN APPEARANCE (382)

1166 Products of Fire

I am ashes where once I was fire. **Lord Byron**

(*n*) ash, cinders, *clinker*, ember, smoke, smoke screen, smut, soot, spark

1167 Food

Food is the beginning of wisdom. The first condition of putting any thing into your head and heart, is to put something into your stomach. **Ludwig Andreas Feuerbach**

(*adj*) comestible (*formal*), culinary, dietary, digestible, edible, fattening, filling, gastronomic, *halal*, hearty, indigestible, inedible, *kosher*, nourishing, nutritional, nutritious, nutritive, slimming, stodgy (*informal*), wholesome

(*n*) board, bread, chow (*slang*), chuck, comestibles (*formal*), cuisine, diet, eats (*slang*), fare, food, foodstuff, gastronomy, groceries, grub (*informal*), junk food, manna, nosh (*informal*), nourishment, *nutrient*, nutrition, produce, provender (*literary or humorous*), provisions, rations, refreshment, refreshments, sustenance, table, tuck, tucker (*UK informal*), victuals, *vittles* (*archaic*), wholesomeness

See also EAT AND NOT EAT (710)

1168 Animal Feed

Oats. A grain, which in England is generally given to horses, but in Scotland supports the people. **Samuel Johnson**

(*n*) birdseed, carrion, feed, *feedstuff*, fodder, forage, hay, pigswill (*UK*), provender (*archaic*), silage, straw, swill

1169 Meals and Parts of Meals

In my philosophy of food, the perfect meal is the short meal. Naurally, one presupposes in a short meal that the few dishes served will be perfection and served generously. **Elsie De Wolfe**

(*n*) blowout (*slang*), *bonne bouche* (*UK*), carryout, collation, elevenses (*UK*), feast, meal, repast (*literary*), spread (*informal*), square meal

parts of a meal antipasto, aperitif, appetizer, canapé, delicacy, dessert, entrée, hors d'oeuvre, main course, meze, side dish, starter, tapas

types of meals clambake, cookout, banquet, barbecue, breakfast, brunch, buffet, dinner, English breakfast, lunch, picnic, ready-made meal, snack, supper, takeout, tea, tidbit, TV dinner

1170 Prepared Dishes

(*n*) carpaccio, *club sandwich*, *cocktail snacks*, coleslaw, dish, *fast food*, *finger food*, fixings, *hoagie*, mash, *meat pie*, *purée*, *salad*, sandwich, *sashimi*, *shish kebab*, *soup*, *steak pie* (*UK*), *sushi*, trimmings

types of cooked dishes bruschetta, burritos, casserole, cassoulet, ceviche, chop suey, chow mein, couscous, curry, fajitas, falafel, fish cake, fondue, fricassee, frijoles, frittata, goulash, gruel, Irish stew, kedgeree, lasagne, meat loaf, miso, moussaka, nachos, nasi goreng, paella, pilaf, pirozkhi, pizza, quiche, ragout, ratatouille, risotto, sambal, satay, sauerkraut, stew, stir-fry, surf 'n' turf, tacos, tagine, tamale, tempura, teriyaki, tofu, yakitori

1171   State of Prepared Food

(*adj*) *al dente*, *barbecued*, *braised*, *broiled*, *burnt to a crisp*, candied, canned, *charbroiled*, chewy, cooked, *curried*, *fried*, *glacé*, gristly, gutted, instant, jellied, *marinated*, microwaved, mulled, overcooked, overdone, pickled, pink, *poached*, potted, *precooked*, preserved, rare, raw, rubbery, *sautéed*, *smoked*, stewed, *stir-fried*, stringy, sun-dried, takeout, *tinned* (*UK*), tough, *tough as old boots* (*UK*), uncooked, *undercooked*, underdone, *unseasoned*

See also COOKING AND FOOD PREPARATION (353)

1172   Additives

(*n*) additive, flavor, flavoring, preservative, sweetener, sweetening

1173   Fats and Oils

Jack Sprat could eat no fat, His wife could eat no lean.
Nursery rhyme

(*n*) fat, grease, oil

types of cooking fats and oils butter, canola oil, corn oil, dripping, ghee, lard, margarine, olive oil, peanut oil, rape oil, sesame oil, shortening, suet, sunflower oil, vegetable oil

1174   Seasonings and Sauces

In England there are sixty different religions, and only one sauce. **Francesco Caracciolo**

(*n*) arrowroot, aspic, *condiment*, *dip*, garnish, *sauce*, seasoning, stock cube (*UK*)

types of relishes caponata, chow-chow, chutney, cornichon, gherkin, piccalilli, pickled cucumber

types of seasonings, sauces, and dips aioli, applesauce, barbecue sauce, béarnaise, béchamel sauce, chili sauce, coulis, dressing, French dressing, gravy, guacamole, hollandaise, hummus, ketchup, marinade, mayonnaise, mint sauce, raita, ranch dressing, salsa, satay, soy sauce, tabasco, tahini, taramasalata, tartar sauce, Thousand Island dressing, vinegar, wasabi, Worcestershire sauce

1175   Herbs and Spices

Anything green that grew out of the mold/Was an excellent herb to our fathers of old. **Rudyard Kipling**

(*n*) *herb*, *spice*

types of herbs angelica, basil, bay leaf, borage, caraway, chamomile, chervil, chive, cilantro, coriander, dill, fennel, hyssop, lemongrass, lovage, marjoram, mint, oregano, parsley, rosemary, sage, savory, spearmint, tarragon, thyme

types of spices allspice, aniseed, black pepper, caraway seed, cardamom, cayenne pepper, chili, cinnamon, clove, coriander, cumin, fenugreek, ginger, ginseng, mace, mustard, nutmeg, paprika, pepper, peppercorn, saffron, turmeric, white pepper

1176   Fruit and Vegetables

Planthouses force Italian heat/On melon, pepper, peach, and vine/And horticultural conceit/Perfects a Scottish aubergine.
Douglas Dunn

(*n*) *fruit*, *vegetable*

parts of a fruit flesh, juice, kernel, peel, pip, pit, pith, pulp, rind, seed, skin, stone

types of berries bilberry, blackberry, black currant, blueberry, boysenberry, cranberry, currant, elderberry, gooseberry, huckleberry, juniper, loganberry, mulberry, raspberry, red currant, rowan, whortleberry

types of citrus fruit blood orange, citron, clementine, grapefruit, lemon, lime, mandarin, orange, ortanique, pomelo, satsuma, tangerine

types of fruit apple, apricot, avocado, banana, blackcurrant, cherry, citrus, damson, date, fig, grape, guava, kiwi fruit, kumquat, lychee, mango, melon, nectarine, olive, papaya, passion fruit, peach, pear, pineapple, plum, pomegranate, quince, raspberry, redcurrant, strawberry, watermelon

types of processed potatoes chip, croquette, French fries, fries, hash browns, home fries, knish, latke, potato cake, potato chip, potato pancake, rösti

types of root vegetables beet, bok choy, carrot, cassava, mangel-wurzel, new potato, parsnip, potato, rutabaga, sugar beet, sweet potato, turnip, yam

types of salad vegetables alfalfa, arugula, bean sprout, capsicum, celery, cherry tomato, chicory, cress, cucumber, endive, green onion, lettuce, pepper, radicchio, radish, scallion, sorrel, sweet pepper, tomato, watercress

types of vegetables artichoke, asparagus, brassica, broccoli, Brussels sprout, cabbage, cauliflower, collard greens, eggplant, fennel, garlic, greens, kale, leek, marrow squash, okra, onion, pumpkin, spinach, squash, sweet corn, Swiss chard, zucchini

1177   Types and Cuts of Meat

A couple of flitches of bacon are worth fifty thousand Methodist sermons and religious tracts. They are great softeners of temper and promoters of domestic harmony. **William Cobbett**

(*n*) flesh, game, giblets, kebab, meat, *offal*, *variety meats*

types of cuts breast, brisket, chop, chuck, cutlet, drumstick, flank, foreshank, hock, joint, leg, loin, neck, rasher, rib, round, scrag end, shoulder, side, sparerib, steak, top round, wing

types of meats beef, chicken, duck, gammon, goat, goose, grouse, hare, lamb, mutton, partridge, pheasant, pork, rabbit, turkey, veal, venison, wild boar

types of processed meats bacon, beefburger, bologna, bratwurst, bresaola, burger, chorizo, foie gras, frankfurter, ground beef, ground meat, ham, hamburger, jerky, liverwurst, meat loaf, meatball, merguez, mincemeat, mortadella, pancetta, parma ham, pastrami, pâté, patty, pepperoni, rissole, salami, sausage, saveloy, wiener, wienerwurst

types of steaks Chateaubriand, fillet, porterhouse steak, rump, sirloin, T-bone steak, tenderloin

1178 Cereal Foods

Do you know what breakfast cereal is made of? It's made of all those little curly wooden shavings you find in pencil sharpeners! **Roald Dahl**

(*n*) *breakfast cereal*, cereal, grain, *grits*, porridge (*UK*)

types of cereals barley, corn, millet, oat, rice, rye, sorghum, wheat

1179 Bread, Flour, and Bread Products

Bread is the staff of life. **Proverb**

(*n*) *choux pastry*, *Cornish pasty* (*UK*), *filo pastry*, *flaky pastry*, flan, *pasta*, pastry, *pasty* (*UK*), patty, *puff pastry*, *shortcrust pastry* (*UK*)

types of bread baguette, black bread, brioche, brown bread, challah, chapati, ciabatta, corn bread, crouton, flat bread, focaccia, matzo, nan, pita, poppadom, pumpernickel, puri, roti, rye bread, soda bread, sourdough, spoon bread, toast, tortilla, white bread

types of flour cornmeal, cornstarch, meal, plain flour, self-rising flour, wheatmeal, whole-wheat

types of rolls or buns bagel, brioche, bun, croissant, crumpet, English muffin, roll

1180 Pasta

No man is lonely while eating spaghetti. **Robert Morley**

types of pasta cannelloni, capellini, cappelletti, conchiglie, fettuccine, fusilli, linguine, macaroni, penne, ravioli, rigatoni, spaghetti, tagliatelle, tortellini, vermicelli

1181 Cakes, Cookies, and Desserts

Let them eat cake. **Marie-Antoinette**

(*n*) *biscuit, cookie*, jelly, *pancake*, pastry

types of cakes angel food cake, birthday cake, Black Forest cake, brownie, carrot cake, cheesecake, coffeecake, cruller, cupcake, Danish pastry, devil's food cake, doughnut, éclair, flapjack, fruitcake, gateau, gingerbread, jelly roll, key lime pie, macaroon, Madeira cake, madeleine, mince pie, muffin, pain au chocolat, petit four, seedcake, sponge cake, strudel, Swiss roll, torte, turnover, wedding cake

types of desserts baklava, blancmange, bombe, brownies, cake, cassata, clafoutis, cobbler, crème brûlée, crème caramel, crisp, custard, flan, fruit salad, granita, ice cream, junket, meringue, mousse, pannacotta, pavlova, peach Melba, pie, profiteroles, pudding, sorbet, soufflé, sundae, syllabub, tart, tiramisu, zabaglione

types of pancakes battercake, blini, blintz, crepe, flapjack, griddlecake, hotcake, johnnycake, waffle

1182 Confectionery

Do not make a fetish of truffles as the bourgeois do. Truffles are excellent, but they are not sublime. **Anonymous**

(*n*) *confectionery*, goody, *sweetie* (*UK informal*)

types of confectionery bonbon, bubble gum, butterscotch, candy, caramel, chewing gum, chocolate, fondant, fudge, goody, gum, gumdrop, hard candy, humbug, jawbreaker, jellybean, licorice, marshmallow, marzipan, nougat, peppermint, praline, rock candy, sweetmeat (*archaic*), taffy, toffee, truffle

types of confectionery on a stick candy apple, cotton candy, lollipop, sucker

1183 Dairy Products and Cheeses

(*n*) *cheese, cream, crème fraiche, curd, milk, quark, yogurt*

types of hard cheeses cheddar, Edam, Emmenthaler, Gouda, Gruyère, Monterey Jack, Parmesan, pecorino, Provolone, Stilton, Swiss

types of soft cheeses blue cheese, Brie, Camembert, chèvre, cottage cheese, cream cheese, feta, Gorgonzola, mascarpone, mozzarella, ricotta, Roquefort, Taleggio

1184 Sugar and Preserves

(*n*) *confectioners' sugar, corn syrup*, frosting, *golden syrup* (*UK*), *maple syrup*, molasses, *preserve*, syrup, *treacle* (*UK*)

types of preserves compote, conserve, honey, jam, jelly, lekvar, lemon curd, marmalade, mincemeat, peanut butter

1185 Nuts

Here we come gathering nuts in May/...On a cold and frosty morning. **Nursery rhyme**

types of nuts acorn, almond, Brazil nut, cashew, chestnut, cob, cobnut, coconut, cola nut, groundnut, hazelnut, hickory nut, horse chestnut, macadamia nut, peanut, pecan, pine nut, pistachio, walnut

1186 Soups

I live on good soup, not fine words. **Molière**

types of soups bisque, borscht, bouillabaisse, bouillon, broth, chowder, cock-a-leekie, consommé, gazpacho, gumbo, julienne, minestrone, mulligatawny, pea soup, potage, Scotch broth, vichyssoise

1187 Drinks

There are two reasons for drinking; one is, when you are thirsty, to cure it; the other, when you are not thirsty, to prevent it. **Thomas Love Peacock**

(*adj*) alcoholic, nonalcoholic, sparkling, still

(*n*) *aperitif*, beverage (*formal*), brew (*informal*), *chaser, coffee, cordial, digestif, dram*, drink, elixir, *frappe, frappé, fruit juice*, homebrew, hooch (*slang*), *hot toddy, lemonade*, libation (*humorous*), *liqueur*, liquor, *milkshake*, moonshine (*informal*), nightcap, nip, *potation* (*literary*), poteen, potion, shot (*informal*), smoothie, snifter (*informal*), *squash* (*UK*), tea, *thirst-quencher*, tipple (*informal*), *tisane, vino* (*informal*), *white lightning*

types of coffee americano, café au lait, café noir, caffè latte, cappuccino, decaf, espresso, Greek coffee, iced coffee, Irish coffee, latte, mocha, mochaccino, Turkish coffee

1188 Food Components

(*n*) albumen, bran, cholesterol, roughage, *saturated fat, saturated fatty acid*

types of nutrients amino acid, carbohydrate, dextrose, fat, fiber, fructose, glucose, lactose, mineral, protein, salt, starch, sucrose, sugar, vitamin

1189 Peas and Beans

I eat my peas with honey/I've done it all my life,/They do taste kind of funny,/But it keeps them on my knife.
Traditional nonsense rhyme

(*n*) legume, *leguminous plant*, pulse

types of pulses bean, black bean, black-eyed pea, broad bean, butter bean, chickpea, fava bean, French bean, garbanzo, haricot, kidney bean, lentil, lima bean, mung bean, navy bean, pea, petits pois, pinto bean, runner bean, snow pea, soybean, string bean

1190 Seafood

He was a bold man that first ate an oyster. **Jonathan Swift**

(*n*) caviar, *scampi*, shellfish

See also AQUATIC INVERTEBRATES (1022)

Physical Qualities of Objects

1191 Qualities and Characteristics

Things are entirely what they appear to be and behind them...there is nothing. **Jean-Paul Sartre**

(*n*) anatomy, aspect, attribute, characteristic, component, composition, constitution, detail, dimension, element, fabric, facet, feature, fiber, format, formation, framework, hallmark, makeup, organization, physics, quality, side, structure, superstructure, trait

1192 Size and Dimensions

There is a right physical size for every idea. **Henry Moore**

(*n*) acreage, acres, bulk, caliber, capacity, compass, dimension, dimensions, expanse, extent, greatness, mass, measurement, *metric unit*, *nonmetric unit*, *proportions*, scale, *SI unit*, size, *spaciousness*, volume

types of metric units centigram, centiliter, centimeter, decagram, decaliter, decameter, decigram, deciliter, decimeter, gram, hectare, hectogram, hectoliter, hectometer, kilogram, kiloliter, kilometer, liter, meter, microgram, micrometer, milligram, milliliter, millimeter, tonne

types of nonmetric units acre, barrel, bushel, degree Fahrenheit, dram, fluid dram, fluid ounce, foot, gallon, gill, inch, mile, ounce, peck, pint, pound, quart, rod, ton, yard

types of SI units becquerel (radioactivity), coulomb (electric charge), degree Celsius (temperature), farad (capacitance), gray (radiation dose), henry (inductance), hertz (frequency), joule (energy), lumen (luminous flux), lux (illuminance), newton (force), ohm (electric resistance), pascal (pressure), siemens (electric conductance), sievert (radiation effects), tesla (magnetic flux density), volt (electric potential), watt (power), weber (magnetic flux)

1193 Large

Size is not a deterrent to success. I've never seen a small company that didn't want to be a big one. **Louis Gerstner, Jr.**

(*adj*) airy, almighty (*informal*), awkward, big, bulging, bulky, capacious, cavernous, colossal, commodious, considerable, cosmic, *cumbrous* (*archaic or literary*), ele-

phantine, enormous, expansive, extensive, extra-large, fantastic, fat, full-size, galactic (*informal*), gargantuan, giant, *giant-sized*, gigantic, global, good-sized, grand, great, herculean, huge, hulking, humongous (*informal*), immeasurable, immense, inestimable, infinite, jumbo, king-size, large, life-size, mammoth, massive, maxi, measureless, *mega*, mighty, monolithic, monster, monstrous, monumental, mountainous, outsize, oversize, prodigious, queen-size, rambling, roomy, significant, sizable, spacious, spectacular, stupendous, substantial, substantive, terrific, thumping (*informal*), tidy, titanic, tremendous, unwieldy, vast, voluminous, walloping (*informal*), whopping (*informal*)

(*n*) airiness, amplitude, bulkiness, *capaciousness*, *chunkiness*, cumbersomeness, enormity, expansiveness, extensiveness, *immenseness*, immensity, largeness, prodigiousness, roominess, *unwieldiness*, vastness, *voluminousness*

1194 Big Things

(*n*) *behemoth*, biggie (*informal*), colossus, *giant*, hulk, juggernaut (*UK*), leviathan, monster, whopper (*informal*)

1195 Small

The best things come in small packages. **Proverb**

(*adj*) atomic, beady, bite-sized, bitty (*informal*), compact, confined, cramped, diminutive, dinky (*informal*), fractional, incommodious (*formal*), infinitesimal, itsy-bitsy (*informal*), *itty-bitty* (*informal*), little, microscopic, mini (*informal*), miniature, minimal, minimum, minuscule, minute, miserly, neat, nominal, peewee (*informal*), pint-size (*informal*), *pint-sized* (*informal*), pitiful, pocket, pocket-sized, poky (*informal*), pygmy, slender, small, small-scale, *submicroscopic*, teensy (*informal*), teensy-weensy (*informal*), teeny (*informal*), *teeny-weeny* (*informal*), tiddly (*informal*), tiny, travel, *trial size*, underdeveloped, *undersize*, undersized, wee, *weensy* (*informal*), weeny (*informal*)

(*n*) minuteness, smallness, *tininess*, trimness

1196 Medium

(*adj*) *medium-large*, *medium-sized*, *standard-length*, *standard-size*

1197 Length: Long

The only thing I regret about my past life is the length of it. If I had my past life over again I'd make all the same mistakes—only sooner. **Tallulah Bankhead**

(*adj*) elongated, full-length, long, stretched

(*n*) length, *lengthiness*

1198 Length: Short

(*adj*) short, stunted

(*n*) shortness

1199 Width: Wide

A wide screen just makes a bad film twice as bad. **Samuel Goldwyn**

(*adj*) big, broad, gaping, sprawling, thick, wide, wide-open, yawning (*n*) breadth, broadness, diameter, girth, radius, span, thickness, width

1200   Width: Narrow and Thin

(*adj*) fine, narrow, *paper-thin*, spidery, thin, wafer-thin

(*n*) fineness, narrowness, slimness, thinness

1201   Depth: Deep

The gods approve/The depth, and not the tumult, of the soul.
William Wordsworth

(*adj*) bottomless, deep, fathomless, unfathomable

(*n*) deepness, depth, *fathomlessness*, profoundness, profundity

1202   Depth: Shallow

(*adj*) shallow

(*n*) shallowness

1203   Height: High

Never measure the height of a mountain, until you have reached the top. Then you will see how low it was. **Dag Hammarskjöld**

(*adj*) big, elevated, high, high-rise, lofty, multistory, tall, towering, vertiginous

(*n*) altitude, elevation, height, tallness

See also BUILD (477)

1204   Height: Low

(*adj*) low, low lying, low-rise

See also BUILD (477)

1205   Weight: Heavy

The weight of the world/is love./Under the burden/of solitude.
Allen Ginsberg

(*adj*) chunky, clumpy, clunky, cumbersome, heavy, hefty, leaden, massive, ponderous, ungainly, weighty

(*n*) ballast, heaviness, heft, heftiness, makeweight, tonnage, ungainliness, weight, weightiness

See also BUILD (477)

1206   Weight: Light

You often lighten your troubles by telling of them. **Corneille**

(*adj*) buoyant, light, portable, weightless

(*n*) buoyancy, lightness, portability, *weightlessness*

See also BUILD (477)

1207   Density and Consistency

Matter...a convenient formula for describing what happens where it isn't. **Bertrand Russell**

(*adj*) absorbent, *absorptive*, beaten, close, *coagulated*, compact, congealed, dense, impenetrable, impermeable, impervious, *penetrable*, permeable, pervious, porous, retentive, set, solid, soluble, spongy, thick, turbid

(*n*) absorbency, *absorptivity*, compactness, concentration, condensation, consistency, denseness, density, impenetrability, impermeability, imperviousness, *penetrability*, permeability, permeation, per-

viousness, *porosity*, *porousness*, solidity, solidness, solubility, thickness, viscosity

1208   State

(*n*) condition, form, shape, state

1209   Fragile

(*adj*) breakable, brittle, crumbly, ethereal, fine, fragile, frangible, friable, papery, superfine, weak, wispy

(*n*) brittleness, fragility, *friability*

1210   Durable

(*adj*) durable, imperishable, indestructible, rock-solid, rustproof, shatterproof, stable, strong, sturdy, toughened, unbreakable

(*n*) durability, imperishability, *indestructibility*, sturdiness

See also STRENGTH (201)

1211   Rigid and Hard

(*adj*) blown-up, bulletproof, *calcified*, firm, hard, immobile, immovable, inelastic, inflexible, knotted, *ligneous*, *ossified*, petrified, rigid, rock-hard, solid, stiff, taut, tempered, tense, tight, unyielding, wooden

(*adv*) fast, stiffly

(*n*) firmness, hardness, inflexibility, rigidity, rigor, stiffness, tautness, tension, tightness

1212   Malleable and Elastic

(*adj*) bendable, bendy (*UK*), bouncy, droopy, ductile, elastic, elasticized, expandable, flaccid, flexible, floppy, *jellylike*, lax, limp, loose, malleable, mushy, plastic, pliable, pliant, resilient, soft, spongy, springy, squashy, squidgy (*UK*), *stretchable*, stretchy, supple, tensile, tractable, willowy, yielding

(*adv*) flexibly, slackly

(*n*) *bendability*, *bendiness*, bounciness, droopiness, flexibility, floppiness, limpness, malleability, plasticity, pliability, pliancy, resilience, softness, spring, *springiness*, stretch, tractability

1213   Fluid and Nonsolid

The terrible fluidity of self-revelation. **Henry James**

(*adj*) dilute, diluted, fluid, gaseous, gassy, *goopy* (*informal*), *liquefied*, liquescent, liquid, molten, runny, seething, *sludgy*, thin, vaporous, watery, weak

(*n*) gluiness, gooeyness, *gumminess*, *liquescence*, liquidity, *mushiness*, runniness

1214   Raw and Natural

(*adj*) coarse, crude, inorganic, macrobiotic, natural, neat, organic, perishable, raw, rough-hewn, straight, unadulterated, undiluted, *unfortified*, unprocessed, unrefined, untreated

(*adv*) naturally

1215 Not in a Natural State

(*adj*) concentrated, condensed, ground, manufactured, pasteurized, *processed*, *purified*, refined, stoneground

1216 Shape

If a fish is the movement of water embodied, given shape, then cat is a diagram and pattern of subtle air. **Doris Lessing**

(*n*) body, bulk, configuration, contour, cutout, figure, form, mass, morphology, outline, profile, shadow, shape, silhouette

See also BODY (691), BUILD (477)

1217 Angular Shape

(*adj*) *aquiline*, beaked, *deltoid*, equilateral, forked, *hexagonal*, irregular, *octagonal*, peaked, *pentagonal*, pointed, *pointy*, polygonal, rectangular, rectilinear, right-angled, tapered, tapering, *trapezoidal*, triangular, *trilateral*, *wedge-shaped*, wiggly

(*n*) barb, corner, *pointiness*, solid, spike, spur

types of angular shapes box, cross, cube, diamond, dodecahedron, dogleg, lozenge, oblong, parallelogram, pentagon, polygon, pyramid, quadrangle, quadrilateral, rectangle, rhomboid, rhombus, square, star, tetragon, tetrahedron, trapezium, trapezoid, triangle

1218 Rounded Shape

(*adj*) aerodynamic, arched, bandy, *bell-shaped*, bent, blunt, bowed, bulbous, camelback, circular, coiled, concave, convex, curly, curved, curving, curvy, cylindrical, domed, elliptical, flowing, globular, *helical*, *hemispherical*, hollow, hooked, meandering, *orbicular* (*formal*), ovate, *ovoid*, prominent, protuberant, recurvate, rolling, rounded, *semicircular*, spherical, squiggly, streamlined, tubular, undulating, vaulted, wavy, winding

(*n*) bulge, curvature, curviness, halo, hump, kink, knob, knot, knuckle, lump, node, nodule, prominence, protuberance, radius, *rondure* (*archaic*), *sphericalness*, sweep, turn, twirl, twist, wave, waviness, whorl

types of rounded shapes arc, arch, ball, bend, bow, bulb, circle, circlet, coil, cone, crescent, curl, curve, cylinder, dome, figure eight, globe, heart, hemisphere, helix, hoop, horseshoe, kidney, loop, orb, oval, ring, round, semicircle, sphere, spheroid, spiral, teardrop

1219 Shapelessness

Twice or thrice had I loved thee,/Before I knew thy face or name/So in a voice, so in a shapelesse flame,/Angels affect us oft, and worshiped be. **John Donne**

(*adj*) amorphous, baggy, formless, loose, sagging, shapeless, slack, unformed, unshaped, unstructured

(*n*) *amorphousness*, bagginess, *formlessness*, looseness, *misshapenness*, *sagginess*, shapelessness, slackness

1220 Texture

He gave the impression that very many cities had rubbed him smooth. **Graham Greene**

(*n*) feel, finish, nap, pile, roughness, texture, weave

1221 Visual Texture

(*adj*) aglow, clear, clouded, cloudy, crystalline, diaphanous, effervescent, filmy, fizzy, frothy, fuzzy, gauzy, glassy, glazed, gleaming, glossy, gossamer, *grainy*, heavy, iridescent, lacy, limpid, lusterless, matte, metallic, milky, muddy, *opalescent*, opaque, pearly, *pellucid* (*literary*), polished, satiny, see-through, sheer, *shimmery*, shiny, smoky, sparkling, sparkly, steamy, thin, translucent, transparent, unfocused, unstrained, vitreous

(*n*) clearness, cloudiness, frosting, frothiness, fuzziness, glossiness, *graininess*, luster, muddiness, opacity, *opaqueness*, patina, *pellucidity* (*literary*), polish, sheen, sheerness, shine, *shininess*, translucence, *translucency*, transparency

1222 Physical Texture

(*adj*) abrasive, bald, barbed, bobbly (*UK*), bristly, brushed, bubbly, bumpy, caustic, chalky, chunky, coarse, cobbled, corrosive, corrugated, crinkled, crisp, crispy, crunchy, crusty, cuddly, downy, even, fat, fatty, feathery, fibrous, fleecy, floury, fluffy, fluted, furred, furry, gelatinous, gluey, glutinous, gooey, granular, granulated, gravelly, greasy, gritty, gummy, icky (*informal*), jagged, keen (*literary*), knobby, laminated, level, lumpy, mucous, oily, *oleaginous*, peachy, pitted, potholed, powdered, powdery, prickly, ragged, resinous, ribbed, rock-strewn, rocky, rough, rough-hewn, ruched, rugged, rutted, scaly, scratchy, serrated, sharp, silken, silky, *silky-smooth*, sleek, slick, slimy, slippery, smooth, *soapy*, soft, spiked, spiky, spiny, sticky, stony, *sudsy*, tacky, textured, thick, thorny, tickly, treacly (*UK*), unctuous, uneven, uniform, velvety, viscid, viscous, wiry, woolen, woolly

(*adv*) coarsely, evenly, levelly, raggedly, roughly

(*n*) bumpiness, clamminess, coarseness, downiness, evenness, flatness, fleeciness, fluffiness, furriness, fuzziness, greasiness, jaggedness, keenness (*literary*), *oleaginousness*, raggedness, roughness, ruggedness, *silkiness*, *sliminess*, smoothness, *spikiness*, *sponginess*, stickiness, toughness, unevenness, *velvetiness*, waxiness, wiriness

1223 Orientation and Alignment

Where there is matter, there is geometry. **Johannes Kepler**

(*adj*) agape (*literary*), ajar, aslant, asymmetric, awry, beveled, breadthwise, buried, cockeyed, craggy, crooked, *dangling*, deformed, diagonal, diffuse, end on (*UK*), erect, flat, flush, folded, glancing, horizontal, inclined, inside out, landward, lateral, level, linear, lopsided, malformed, misaligned, misshapen, mutant, oblique, off-center, *off the beam*, *on a slope*, *out of kilter*, *out of true*, outspread, outstretched, *overturned*, pendent, pendulous, perpendicular, plumb, precipitous, prone, prostrate, radial, recumbent (*literary*), sheer, skewed, slanting, *sloping*, *slumped*, splay, split-level, *sprawled*, spread-eagled, squint (*informal*), staggered, standing, standup, steep, straight, sunken, supine, suspended, tabular, three-dimensional, tilted, *tilting*, top-heavy, transverse, twisted, two-dimensional, unbalanced, unsymmetrical, *upended*, uphill, upright, upside-down, upstretched, *upturned*, upward, vertical, *wrong side up*, *wrong way up*

(*adv*) across, askew, aslant, *at an angle*, athwart, *at right angles*, back to front (*UK*), backward, bolt upright,

(*n*) abandonment, blankness, clearness, desolation, emptiness

See also EMPTY AND UNLOAD (407)

1239 Full

A full bottle won't shake; a half-empty one will. **Chinese proverb**

(*adj*) alive, awash, blocked, blown-up, brimful, brimming, bulging (*informal*), bursting, bursting at the seams, buzzing, caked, chock-a-block (*informal*), chock-full (*informal*), *choked*, choked up, clogged, *clogged up*, congested, crammed, crowded, dense, *engorged*, fraught, full, full of, *full to bursting*, *full to capacity*, *full to overflowing*, full up, furnished, heaving (*UK*), inhabited, jammed, jam-packed (*informal*), laden, loaded, overcrowded, overflowing, overladen, overloaded, overrun, overstuffed, packed, populous, replete, rife, saturated, seething, stacked, stopped, stuffed, stuffy, swarming, teeming, thick

(*n*) congestion, *engorgement*, repletion, satiety, saturation, squash

See also FILL (406)

1240 Wet

Much water goeth by the mill/That the miller knoweth not of. **John Heywood**

(*adj*) afloat, awash, boggy, drenched, dripping, *dripping wet*, flooded, inundated, marshy, saturated, slushy, soaked, *soaked to the skin*, soaking, *soaking wet*, sodden, sopping, *sopping wet*, soppy, spongy, squelchy, squidgy (*UK*), squishy, *steeped*, submerged, swampy, sweaty, underwater, waterlogged, watery, wet, *wringing*, *wringing wet*

(*n*) immersion, saturation, wet, wetness

1241 Moist

I see a lily on thy brow,/With anguish moist and fever dew. **John Keats**

(*adj*) beaded, clammy, damp, dank, dewy, humid, moist, soggy

(*n*) condensation, damp, dampness, dankness, dew, humidity, moistness, moisture, *sogginess*

1242 Dry

The fountains are dry and the roses over. **Sylvia Plath**

(*adj*) arid, bone dry, dehydrated, desiccated, dried, dry, *dry as a bone*, parched, scorched, *sere* (*literary*), *shriveled*, sunbaked, waterless

(*n*) aridity, aridness, desiccation, dryness, *waterlessness*

Physical Objects

1243 Physical Objects

An object in possession seldom retains the same charm that it had in pursuit. **Pliny the Younger**

(*n*) accompaniment, accouterment, adjunct, amenity, antiquity, appendage, article, artifact, constituent, *doodad* (*informal*), *doofer* (*slang*), doohickey (*informal*), entity, facility, gadget, ingredient, item, jazz (*slang*), makings, materials, member, object, product, strand, stuff, sucker (*slang*), supplies, thing, thingamabob (*informal*), *thingamajig* (*informal*), *thingumabob* (*informal*), *thingumajig* (*informal*), *thingummy* (*informal*), thingy (*informal*), trappings, unit, whatchamacallit, *whatsit* (*informal*), *widget* (*humorous*), works (*informal*)

1244 Collections and Mixtures of Things

The true University of these days is a collection of books. **Thomas Carlyle**

(*n*) accumulation, *admixture*, agglomeration, aggregate (*formal*), aggregation, alloy, amalgam, amalgamation, anthology, armory, arrangement, array, arsenal, assemblage, assortment, bale, bank, batch, battery, bits and pieces (*informal*), blend, body, bouquet, brew, bunch, bundle, cache, catalog, categorization, choice, classification, clump, cluster, cocktail, collage, collection, combination, compendium, compilation, composite, compound, concoction, conglomeration, constellation, crop, diversity, emulsion, ensemble, farrago, fusion, galaxy, *grab bag*, group, hoard, hodgepodge, infusion, inventory, kaleidoscope, litany, lot, marriage, medley, melange (*literary or formal*), meld, *melding*, melee, melting pot, memorabilia, merger, *miscellanea*, miscellany, mishmash, mix, mixed bag, mixture, montage, mosaic, multimedia, nosegay, omnibus, pack, package, panoply, patchwork, portfolio (*formal*), posy, potpourri, procession, ragbag (*informal*), range, repertoire, repertory, reserve, reserves, resource, selection, sequence, set, source, spray, spread, store, string, suite, sundries, synthesis, tangle, variety

1245 Containers, Receptacles, and Packaging

I might give my life for my friend, but he had better not ask me to do up a parcel. **Logan Pearsall Smith**

(*n*) aerosol, ampoule, atomizer, bag, basin (*UK*), basket, bath, beaker, bedpan, billfold, bin, binder, birdbath, bobbin, bottle, bucket, *bud vase*, bunker, butt, *caldron*, canister, capsule, carousel, cassette, cauldron, chalice (*literary*), *chamber pot*, cistern, coffer, *container*, cool bag (*UK*), cool box (*UK*), cradle, crucible, demijohn, dragnet, dustbin (*UK*), dustpan, file, *firkin*, flowerpot, garbage can, hayrack, *hip flask*, in-box, inkwell, in-tray (*UK*), letterbox (*UK*), magnum, mailbox, *maildrop*, mailer, manger, mold, money box, package, packaging, packet, *pail*, parcel, phial, piggy bank, pillar box (*UK*), planter, pocket, portfolio, postbox (*UK*), propagator, *rain barrel*, receptacle, reel, *rehoboam*, roll, sac, sachet, sack, saddlebag, safe, scabbard, *septic tank*, sleeve, *slipcase*, spool, spray, spray can, spray gun, *stein*, strongbox, tabernacle, tank, *thermos*, till, tin, *trash can*, tray, trough, tub, urn, vaporizer, vase, vat, vessel, vial, wallet, *wastebasket*, waste bin (*UK*), *wastepaper basket*, wastepaper bin (*UK*), wheelie bin (*UK*)

types of baggage attaché case, backpack, briefcase, carryall, carrycase, case, duffel bag, haversack, kit bag, knapsack, luggage, overnight bag, pack, portmanteau, rucksack, suitcase, travel case, valise, vanity case, weekend bag

types of bags clutch purse, fanny pack, handbag, mailbag, nosebag, pocketbook, pouch, purse, reticule, satchel, shopping bag, shoulder bag, sporran, tote bag

types of containers barrel, box, caddy, can, cardboard box, carton, cartridge, case, cask, casket, chest, cover, crate, creel, cylinder, drawer, drum, hamper, holder, jar, jerry can, jewel case, keg, pencil case, pigeonhole, pillbox, pot, storage bin, storage tank, tea caddy, trunk

See also TABLEWARE, FLATWARE, AND KITCHENWARE (861), HOUSE-HOLD APPLIANCES (1117)

1246   Covers and Coatings

Never judge a cover by its book. **Fran Lebowitz**

(*n*) armor, asphalt, awning, bandage, bed, beermat (*UK*), blacktop, blanket, blind, blindfold, buffer, bung, camouflage, canopy, cap, carapace, cardboard, carpet, casing, cladding, cloak (*literary*), cloche, coat, coating, cocoon, compress, cover, covering, crust, dressing, dubbin (*UK*), dust jacket, dustsheet (*UK*), eggshell, enamel, envelope, film, fireguard, fixative, gilt, glaze, gloss, glossiness (*informal*), grate, grating, ground cloth, guard, housing, icing, incrustation, insulation, jacket, lacquer, lagging, layer, leaf, lid, liner, lining, macadam, mantle (*literary*), membrane, mulch, nutshell, parasol, patch, patina, plaster (*UK*), plating, plug, ply, poultice, protective covering, protector, rendering, scab, scale, screen, scurf, seal, seam, shade, sheath, sheathing, sheet, shell, shield, shroud, skin, sticking plaster (*UK*), stopper, stratum (*formal*), *substratum*, sunshade, swab, tap, *tarp* (*informal*), tarpaulin, tartar, thimble, top, topping, umbrella, *undercoat*, varnish, veil, vein, veneer, verdigris, visor, wallpaper, wash, washing, wrap, wrapper, wrapping

1247   Fasteners, Links, and Networks

Our buttons operate in synchronization with ourselves; they form a sort of cheap and comfortable senate, which always votes in favor of our motions. **Joaquim Maria Machado de Assis**

(*n*) belt, binding, bolt, buckle, catch, chain, cinch, clasp, clip, cord, coupling, crisscross, cuff (*slang*), *Denver boot*, dowel, drawstring, fastener, fastening, fetter, *flange*, gag, gossamer, grid, gridiron, grille, guywire, halter, handcuff, *hasp*, hawser, hook, hook and eye, join, joint, junction, juncture (*formal*), key, knot, lace, lanyard, lariat, lasso, latch, lattice, lead, leash, ligature, line, lock, manacle, maze, mesh, nail, net, netting, network, node, noose, *padlock*, *paperclip*, peg, *popper* (*UK*), press stud (*UK*), rein, restraint, rigging, ripcord, rivet, rope, safety belt, shackles, shoelace, snap, socket, spline, staple, stirrup, strap, string, stud, suture, swathe, tack, tape, tether, thong, tissue, toggle, tourniquet, towrope, twine, *vang*, washer, web, webbing, weld, wheel clamp

See also FASTEN, LINK, AND JOIN (408), UNFASTEN AND UNDO (409), PARTS OF A GARMENT (870)

1248   Ornaments and Decorations

Ornament should consist of enrichment of the essential construction of the building. **Augustus Pugin**

(*n*) accessory, *accouterments*, bauble, beading, bobble (*UK*), bunting, button, buttonhole (*UK*), charm, corsage, curio, decor, decoration, *doily*, embellishment, epaulet, festoon, filigree, fixings (*informal*), flourish, frill, fringe, garland, garnish, gather, *gewgaw*, glitter, headpiece, inlay, interior decoration, ironwork, jewel, keepsake,

knickknack, knocker, lei, marquetry, medallion, memento, molding, monogram, oddments, ornament, piping, pom-pom, purl, *refrigerator magnet*, regalia, reminder, rhinestone, ribbon, rose, rosette, scallop, sequin, souvenir, spangle, stencil, *strass*, streamer, swag, tassel, *tchotchke*, tinsel, token, tracery, trim, trimming, trimmings, trinket, vignette, wreath

See also DECORATE, ADORN, AND APPLY COATINGS (405), JEWELRY (866)

1249   Junk and Useless Objects

An Aristotle was but the rubbish of an Adam, and Athens but the rudiments of Paradise. **Robert South**

(*n*) bric-a-brac, castoff, cull, debris, detritus, driftwood, dross, flotsam, *flotsam and jetsam*, *frippery*, garbage, jetsam, jumble (*UK*), junk (*informal*), kitsch, litter, pap, rag, refuse, rubbish, rubble, schlock (*slang*), stub, stubble, stump, tatters, trash, waste, wreck, wreckage

See also REMAINDER AND REMAINDERS (125), UNPLEASANT, DIRTY, AND TOXIC SUBSTANCES (1268)

1250   Extremities of Physical Objects

Think of it, soldiers; from the summit of these pyramids, forty centuries look down upon you. **Napoleon I**

(*adj*) exterior, external, fringe, outer

(*n*) apex, baseline, bed, blade, border, bottom, bounds, brim, brink, brow, butt, cap, circumference, confines, crest, crown, cusp, cutting edge, dead end, edge, edging, end, extreme, extremity, face, facet, flank, flap, flat, floor, foot, fore (*literary*), forefront, frame, fringe, front, head, height, horn, hulk, interface, leaf, ledge, limit, limits, line, lip, lobe, margin, matrix, meridian (*literary*), mold, neck, nib, *nubbin*, *nub end*, obverse, outside, overlap, peak, perimeter, periphery, pinnacle, pit, plating, point, prickle, projection, prong, protrusion, rear, rearguard, reverse, ridge, rim, seam, side, splice, summit, surface, surround, tailpiece, top, vane, verge, vertex, zenith

1251   Central Parts of Physical Objects

I live in peace with men and at war with my innards. **Antonio Machado**

(*adj*) central, inner, internal

(*n*) backbone, bosom (*literary*), bull's eye, center, core, entrails, *epicenter*, filler, filling, flesh, focal point, focus, foreground, guts, hinge, hub, inside, interior, kernel, mecca, middle, midpoint, midst, nucleus, packing, pad, padding, pulp, *stuffing*, wadding, workings, works

1252   Holes, Gaps, and Forks

(*n*) abyss, aperture, armhole, bifurcation, blank, borehole, branch, breach, cavity, chamber, chasm, chink, cleft, crack, cranny, crevice, cut, dent, depression, diggings, ding (*informal*), dint, dip, divide, dugout, eyelet, fissure, flute, fork, fracture, gap, gash, gouge, groove, gulf, gully, hole, hollow, hollowness, impression, imprint, incision, indentation, interstice, interval, keyhole, laceration, lacuna (*literary*), *mail slot*, nick, notch, opening, orifice (*literary*), outlet, peephole, perforation, pinprick, pit, plughole (*UK*), pore, pothole, prick, puncture, rent, rift, rupture, rut, score, scrape, scratch, slash, slit, slot, split, spyhole, tear, trough, vacuity (*formal*), vacuum, vent, void, well, window

1253 Subdivisions and Offshoots

(*n*) arm, branch, department, division, limb, spur, sub-directory, wing

1254 Sticks, Poles, and Wedges

(*n*) baluster, balustrade, banister, bar, baton, beanpole, bollard, boom, broomstick, caber, cane, chock, column, crook, crosier, crutch, drumstick, flagpole, flagstaff, gatepost, goad, guardrail, handrail, maypole, picket, pile, pointer, pole, post, rod, scepter, shank, skewer, spar, spindle, spoke, staff, stake, stalk, stem, stick, stilt, walking stick, wand

1255 Supports and Bases

(*n*) abutment, base, bedrock, bier, brace, bracket, derrick, footing, foundation, gantry, grassroots, hanger, jamb, ledge, leg, mount, pedestal, *pilaster*, pillar, plinth, podium, pontoon, prop, rack, rest, rung, scaffold, scaffolding, shelf, stair, *stanchion*, stand, stave, stepladder, stepping stone, support, throne, trestle, trivet, underneath, underpinning, underside

Sounds

1256 Sounds

When it sounds good, it is good. **Duke Ellington**

(*n*) echo, noise, reverberation, sonority, sound, sound effect

See also SOUND EMISSION (362)

1257 Absence of Sound

All artists dream of a silence which they must enter, as some creatures return to the sea to spawn. **Iris Murdoch**

(*adj*) *dumb*, mute, noiseless, quiet, silent, soundless, wordless

(*adv*) quietly, silently, *without a sound*

(*n*) hush, *noiselessness*, quiet, quietness, silence, *soundlessness*

See also IMPERCEPTIBLE (26)

1258 Continuous Sounds

The most persistent sound which reverberates through men's history is the beating of war drums. **Arthur Koestler**

types of continuous sounds beep, bleep, boom, burble, buzz, chug, crackle, creak, drone, gurgle, hiss, honk, hoot, hum, purl (*literary*), purr, rasp, rattle, roar, rumble, rustle, sizzle, sonic boom, swish, swoosh, throb, thunder, whir, whiz, whoosh

1259 Ringing and Hooting Sounds

types of ringing sounds chime, chink, clink, ding, ding-a-ling, ding-dong, honk, hoot, jangle, jingle, knell, peal, ping, ring, ting, tinkle, toll, tootle (*informal*)

1260 Impact Sounds

(*n*) clink, drumming, drumroll, firing, footfall, footstep, gunfire, gunshot, *paradiddle* (*UK*), percussion (*formal*), report, shot, tread

types of impact sounds bang, beat, bong, bonk (*informal*), bump, clang, clank, clap, clash, clatter, click, clip-clop, clop, clunk, crack, crash, patter, pitter-patter, plop, plunk, pop, rat-a-tat-tat, rattle, slam, smash, splash, splat, squelch, squish, tap, thud, thump, thwack, tick, ticktock, wham

See also CONTACT: IMPACT (413)

1261 Sounds Made by Animals

One dog barks at something and a hundred bark at the sound. **Chinese proverb**

types of animal sounds baa, bark, bay, bleat, bray, caterwaul, croak, growl, grunt, howl, meow, mew, moo, neigh, oink, purr, roar, snarl, squeak, squeal, whinny, woof, yap, yelp

See also SOUND EMISSION BY ANIMALS OR BIRDS (364)

1262 Sounds Made by People

All the live murmur of a summer's day. **Matthew Arnold**

(*n*) battle cry, call, death rattle, distress signal, exclamation, lament, lamentation, war cry

types of human sounds babble, bawl, bellow, boo, catcall, chatter, chortle, chuckle, cry, gasp, giggle, groan, grunt, holler (*informal*), howl, hum, moan, murmur, mutter, peep, screak, scream, screech, shout, shriek, sigh, slurp, snicker, sniffle, splutter, squeal, titter, wail, wheeze, whimper, whine, whisper, whistle, whoop, yell

See also SOUND EMISSION BY PEOPLE (363)

1263 Sounds Made by Birds

A nightingale dies for shame if another bird sings better. **Robert Burton**

(*n*) birdsong, call, cheeping, song

types of bird sounds caw, cheep, chirp, chirrup, cluck, cock-a-doodle-doo, coo, hoot, peep, quack, screak, screech, squawk, trill, tweet, twitter, warble

See also SOUND EMISSION BY ANIMALS OR BIRDS (364)

1264 Quality of Sounds

Heard melodies are sweet, but those unheard/Are sweeter; therefore, ye soft pipes, play on. **John Keats**

(*n*) resonance, *sound quality*, timbre, tonality, tone

1265 Soft, Low, or Pleasant Sounds

(*adj*) *assonant*, bass, clear, deep, dulcet, *easy on the ear*, euphonious, faint, fruity, full, *harmonic*, harmonious, hollow, honeyed, humming, hushed, low, low-pitched, lyric, mellifluous, mellow, melodic, melodious, muffled, *murmured*, musical, muted, plummy, pure, *quavering*, silky, soft, sotto voce, sweet, tuneful, *whispered*

(*adv*) faintly, harmoniously, hollowly, softly, sotto voce, sweetly

(*n*) deepness, *ear candy* (*slang*), euphoniousness, euphony, faintness, *harmoniousness*, *mellifluousness*, mellowness, melodiousness, pureness, sweetness, *tunefulness*

1266 Loud, High, or Unpleasant Sounds

(*adj*) adenoidal, atonal, blaring, booming, brassy, braying, cacophonous, carrying, chesty (*UK*), clamorous, *clanging*, creaky, croaky, deafening, discordant, dissonant, earsplitting, echoing, grating, gravelly, grinding, gruff, guttural, harsh, high, high-pitched, hoarse, husky, inharmonious, jarring, loud, metallic, noisy, off-key, orotund (*formal*), penetrating, piercing, piping, *plangent*, rasping, reedy, resonant, *resonating*, resounding, *reverberant*, reverberating, roaring, rough, sharp, shrill, sonorous, squeaky, stentorian, strident, thick, thin, throaty, thunderous, tinny, treble, tumultuous, tuneless, *unmelodic*, *unmelodious*, unmusical, unquiet

(*adv*) aloud, grindingly, huskily, loudly, off-key, piercingly, shrilly, thickly

(*n*) atonality, discord, edge, gruffness, hoarseness, huskiness, loudness, monotone, *noisiness*, pitch, reediness, roughness, *shrillness*, unquiet

Substances

1267 Substances

Beware that you do not lose the substance by grasping at the shadow. **Aesop**

(*n*) chemical, material, matrix, matter, *metal*, *mineral*, natural resource, *raw material*, reagent, sediment, stuff, substance

1268 Unpleasant, Dirty, and Toxic Substances

(*n*) bilge, cobwebs, crud (*slang*), dinge, dirt, dregs, dung, dust, *effluence*, effluent, fat, fertilizer, filth, fluff, glop (*informal*), goo (*informal*), *gook* (*informal*), goop (*informal*), grime, grounds, grouts (*UK*), grunge (*informal*), *guano*, gunk (*informal*), impurity, mold, muck, ordure (*formal*), poison, pollutant, pollution, scum, *sewage*, *slag*, slime, *slops*, sludge, *slurry*, slush, *toxic waste*, toxin, venom, *waste product*

See also REMAINDER AND REMAINDERS (125), EXCRETION AND EXCRETA (722), JUNK AND USELESS OBJECTS (1249)

1269 Liquids

(*n*) brine, distillate, distillation, essence, fluid, juice, liquid, liquor, oil, salt water, solution, *solvent*, thinner, tincture, water

1270 Dyes and Colorants

(*n*) cochineal, color, colorant, dye, peroxide, pigment, rinse, stain, tint, wash, whitewash

1271 Adhesives

(*n*) adhesive, cement, fixative, glue, gum, paste, *superglue*

1272 Lotions, Pastes, and Gels

(*n*) balm, cream, gel, jelly, liniment, lotion, mush, ointment, paste, pulp, purée, salve, unction, unguent

1273 Foam

(*n*) effervescence, fizz, foam, froth, lather, soapsuds, sparkle, spume (*literary*), suds

1274 Solids

O! that this too too solid flesh would melt,/Thaw, and resolve itself into a dew. **William Shakespeare**

(*n*) concentrate, deposit, powder, rubber, solid, wax

1275 Gases

There can no great smoke arise, but there must be some fire. **John Lyly**

(*n*) *biogas*, fume, *fumes*, gas, miasma, steam, vapor

types of gases acetylene, argon, butane, chlorine, coal gas, greenhouse gas, helium, hydrogen, inert gas, marsh gas, methane, mustard gas, natural gas, neon, nerve gas, nitrogen, nitrous oxide, noble gas, oxygen, poison gas, propellant, tear gas

1276 Metals

(*adj*) gilded, gilt, golden, gold-plated, metallic, plated, *silver-plated*

types of metals aluminum, brass, chromium, copper, gold, iron, lead, magnesium, mercury, molybdenum, nickel, pewter, platinum, radium, silver, stainless steel, steel, tin, titanium, tungsten, uranium, zinc

1277 Minerals

types of minerals arsenic, asbestos, asphalt, bauxite, carbon, clay, coal, coke, feldspar, fluorite, graphite, gypsum, jet, kaolin, lime, mica, pyrite, quartz, silicate, sulfur

1278 Precious Stones

Sweet are the uses of adversity,/Which like the toad, ugly and venomous,/Wears yet a precious jewel in his head. **William Shakespeare**

(*n*) crystal, diamanté, gem, gemstone, jewel, precious stone, *semiprecious stone*, sparkler (*informal*)

types of gemstones agate, amethyst, aquamarine, beryl, bloodstone, carnelian, chalcedony, chrysoprase, diamond, emerald, garnet, jade, lapis lazuli, moonstone, mother-of-pearl, onyx, opal, pearl, ruby, sapphire, sard, topaz, tourmaline, turquoise

1279 Elementary Particles

MASTER *They split the atom by firing particles at it, at 5,500 miles a second./*BOY *Good heavens. And they only split it?* **Will Hay**

types of elementary particles antineutron, antiproton, antiquark, baryon, boson, electron, fermion, hadron, kaon, lepton, meson, muon, neutrino, neutron, photon, pion, positron, proton, quark, tauon